HAYDN'S
DICTIONARY OF DATES

HAYDN'S
DICTIONARY OF DATES

AND

UNIVERSAL INFORMATION

RELATING TO ALL AGES AND NATIONS.

JOSEPH HAYDN

BY THE LATE BENJAMIN VINCENT.

GYAN

Published by

GYAN

Gyan Publishing House
5, Ansari Road
Daryaganj, New Delhi-110002
Phone: 011-47034999, 9811692060
E-mail: books@gyanbooks.com

Distribution Network
gyanbooks.com
India, USA, Canada, UK, Australia

ISBN: 978-81-212-7483-8 (PB)
First Published, 1841

2nd Impression 2024

Printed at: Gyan Press, Delhi.

HAYDN'S DICTIONARY OF DATES
Author: JOSEPH HAYDN, BENJAMIN VINCENT

HAYDN'S

DICTIONARY OF DATES

HAYDN'S

DICTIONARY OF DATES

AND

UNIVERSAL INFORMATION

RELATING TO ALL AGES AND NATIONS.

BY THE LATE BENJAMIN VINCENT.

REVISED AND BROUGHT UP TO DATE BY EMINENT AUTHORITIES.

TWENTY-THIRD EDITION,

CONTAINING THE HISTORY OF THE WORLD TO THE END OF 1903.

NEW YORK

G. P. PUTNAM'S SONS

27 AND 29 WEST 23D ST.

1904.

PREFACE TO THE TWENTY-THIRD EDITION.

THIS well-known and standard work of reference first appeared in 1841, and then consisted of 568 pages of smaller size and larger type than those of later editions. Mr. Joseph Haydn, the compiler, whose name is identified with the title of the book, in 1855 resigned the editorship owing to failing health, and was succeeded by Mr. Benjamin Vincent, who undertook the continuance of the work, and the superintendence of its SEVENTH EDITION while passing through the press. This led eventually to the reconstruction of the book, which has been gradually effected by revision and copious additions. The new features included Chronological Tables at the beginning of the volume, innumerable historical, literary, scientific, topographical facts inserted in the body of the work, and a Dated Biographical Index. To make room for these additions the size of the page has been enlarged, many articles have been condensed or printed in smaller type, and matter of inferior importance expunged.

Numerous excellent year-books record the events and supply statistics of the preceding year, and are, consequently, of the greatest utility, but HAYDN supplies a public want in that it furnishes a systematized record from an early date to the present time of historical, political, ecclesiastical, legal, social, commercial, scientific, literary, artistic, educational and other movements and occurrences—everything, in fact, which comes under the purview of the student, the public man, and the intelligent reader of the daily newspaper. HAYDN is, therefore, not only indispensable to the journalist, to every public and private library, but to *everyone* who desires, either in public or private life, to possess an intelligent acquaintance with the facts and occurrences of the present day and of past events, which so many persons find most difficult to retain in the mind.

We have with much regret to record the death of Mr. Benjamin Vincent, 3rd May, 1899, whose painstaking and conscientious labours have so largely contributed to the reputation which HAYDN'S DICTIONARY OF DATES enjoys.

Our thanks are due to those friends who have pointed out errors and omissions, which, in a work of such scope and magnitude, are almost unavoidable, since much of the information contained in its pages necessarily depends on varying statements often difficult to verify.

The present edition has been enlarged, and contains 197 more pages than the previous issue.

The more important events that have occurred or come under notice during the printing of the Dictionary are included in its ADDENDA, at the end of the volume.

EDITOR.

PREFACE TO THE FIRST EDITION.

THE design of the Author has been to attempt the compression of the greatest body of general information that has ever appeared in a single volume, and to produce a Book of Reference whose extensive usefulness may render its possession material to every individual—in the same manner that a London *Directory* is indispensable, on business affairs, to a London merchant. . . . .

The Compiler persuades himself that the DICTIONARY OF DATES will be received as a useful companion to all Biographical works, relating, as it does, to *things* as those do to *persons*, and affording information not included in the range or design of such publications.

JOSEPH HAYDN.
[Died *Jan.* 18, 1856.]

LONDON, *May*, 1841.

TABLE OF CONTEMPORARY

Great Britain.		France.	Peninsula.			Germany.	Hungary.
England.	Scotland.		Castile and Leon.	Arragon.	Portugal.		
1066. Will. I. 1087. Will. II.	1057. Malc. 3. 1093. Donald 1094. Dunc. 1094. Donald again. 1098. Edgar.	1060. Philip I.	1066. Sancho II. 1072. Alfonso VI.	1065. Sancho. 1094. Peter.	1065. Sancho of Castile. 1072. Alfonso VI. 1093. Henry, *count*.	1056. Hen. 4, *emperor*.	1064. Solom. 1075. Geisa. 1076. Lad. 1. 1098. Coloman.
1100. Hen. I. 1135. Steph. 1154. Hen. 2. 1172. (*Ireld. annexed.*) 1189. Rich. I. 1199. John.	1107. Alex. I. 1124. Dav. I. 1153. Mal. IV. 1165. Will.	1108. Louis VI. 1137. Louis VII. 1180. Philip II.	1109. Urraca and Alfonso VII. 1126. Alfon. VII. 1157. Sancho III. 1158. Alfon. VIII. 1188. Alfon. IX. (Leon.)	1104. Alfonso I. 1134. Ramiro. 1137. Petronella and Raymond. 1163. Alfonso II. 1196. Peter II.	1112. Alfonso, as *count*. 1139. Alfonso I., as *king*. 1185. Sancho I.	1106. Hen. 5. 1125. Loth. 2. 1138. Conr. 3. 1152. Fred. 1. 1190. Hen. 6. 1198. Philip.	1114. Step. 2. 1131. Bela 2. 1141. Geisa 3. 1161. Step. 3. 1173. Bela 3. 1196. Emeric
1216. Hen. 3. 1272. Ed. I. 1282. (*Wales annexed.*)	1214. Alex. 2. 1249. Alex. 3. *Interregnum.* 1292. John Baliol.	1223. Louis VIII. 1226. Louis IX. 1270. Philip III. 1285. Philip IV.	1214. Henry I. 1217. Ferdin. III. (Castile.) 1230. (Leon.) 1252. Alfonso X. 1284. Sancho IV. 1295. Ferdin. IV.	1213. James I. 1276. Peter III. 1285. Alfons. III. 1291. James II.	1212. Alfonso II. 1223. Sancho II. 1248. Alfon. III. 1279. Dionysius or Denis.	1208. Otho 4. 1215. Fred. 2. 1250. Con. 4. 1254. Will. 1257. Rich. 1273. Rodolph. 1292. Adolp. 1298. Alb. 1.	1204. Ladislas II. 1205. Andrew II. 1235. Bela 4. 1270. Ste. 4. 1272. Lad. 3. 1290. And. 3.
1307. Ed. II. 1327. Ed. III. 1377. Rich. 2. 1399. Hen. 4.	1306. Robert (Bruce) I. 1329. Dav. II. 1332. Ed. Bal. 1342. Dav. II. again. 1371. Rob. II. (Stuart) 1390. Rob. 3.	1314. Louis X. 1316. John I. Phil. V. 1321. Chas. IV. 1328. Phil. VI. 1350. John II. 1364. Chas. V. 1380. Chas. VI.	1312. Alfonso XI. 1350. Peter. 1369. Henry. 1379. John I. 1390. Henry II.	1327. Alfonso IV. 1336. Peter IV. 1387. John I. 1395. Martin.	1325. Alfonso IV. 1357. Peter. 1367. Ferdinand. 1383. John I.	1308. Hen. 7. 1314. Lou. 5. 1347. Chas. 4. 1378. Wenceslas. 1400. Rupert.	1301. Charobert. 1342. Louis. 1382. Mary. 1387. Mary & Sigismund.
1413. Hen. 5. 1422. Hen. 6. 1461. Ed. IV. 1483. Ed. V. Rich. 3. 1484. Hen. 7.	1406. Jas. I. 1437. Jas. II. 1460. Jas. III. 1488. Jas. IV.	1422. Chas. VII. 1461. Louis XI. 1483. Chas. VIII. 1498. Louis XII.	1406. John II. 1454. Henry IV. 1474. Isabella.	1410. *Interregnm.* 1412. Ferdinand of Sicily. 1416. Alfonso V. 1458. John II. 1479. Ferdin. II.	1433. Edward. 1438. Alfonso V. 1481. John II. 1495. Emanuel.	1410. Sigismund. 1438. Albert. 1440. Fred. 3. 1493. Max. 1. 1499. *Switz. independ.*	1440. Lad. 4. 1445. Lad. 5. 1458. Matthias. 1490. Lad. 6.
			Spain. 1479. Ferdinand and Isabella.				

EUROPEAN SOVEREIGNS.

Scandinavia.			Poland.	Eastern Empire.	Italy.		
SWEDEN.	NORWAY.	DENMARK.			POPES.	NAPLES AND SICILY.	
1066. Halstan. 1090. Ingo.	1069. Olaf. 1093. Magnus.	1047. Sweyn II. 1076. Harold. 1080. Canute IV. 1086. Olaus IV. 1095. Eric I.	1058. Boleslas. 1082. Ladislas.	1068. Rom. 4 1071. Mich. 7. 1078. Nicep. 3 1081. Alexius	1061. Alex. II. 1073. Greg. VII. 1086. Victor III. 1088. Urban II. 1099. Pascal II.		
1112. Philip. 1118. Ingo II. 1129. Swerker. 1155. Eric I. 1161. Char. VII. 1167. Canute. 1199. Swerk. II.	1103. Sigurd I., and others. 1122. Sigurd I. 1130. Magnus IV. and others. *Civil war and anarchy.* 1186. Swerro.	1105. Eric II. 1137. Eric III. 1147. Sweyn III. Canute V. 1157. Waldemar. 1182. Canute VI.	1102. Boles. 3 1138. Lad. 2. 1145. Boles. 4 1173. Miecislas III. 1178. Casimir II. 1194. Lesk. 5.	1118. John Comnenus. 1143. Manuel Comnenus. 1180. Alex. 2. 1183. Andronicus C. 1185. Isaac 2. 1195. Alex. 3.	1118. Gelas. II. 1119. Calixt. II. 1124. Honor. II. 1130. Innoc. II. 1143. Celest. II. 1144. Lucius II. 1145. Eugen. III. 1153. Anasta. IV. 1154. Adrian IV. 1159. Alex. III. 1181. Lucius III. 1185. Urban III. 1187. Greg. VIII. Clem. III. 1191. Celest. III. 1198. Innoc. III.	1131. Roger Guiscard II. 1154. William I. 1166. William I. 1189. Tancred. 1194. William III. 1197. Fred. II. of Germany.	
1210. Eric II. 1216. John I. 1222. Eric III. 1250. Birger Jarl 1266. Waldemar. 1275. Magnus I. 1290. Birger II.	1202. Hako III. and others. 1207. Hako IV. 1263. Magnus VI. 1280. Eric. 1299. Hako V.	1202. Walde. II. 1241. Eric IV. 1250. Abel. 1252. Christoph. 1259. Eric V.	1200. Miec. 3. 1202. Lad. 3. 1227. Boles. 5. 1279. Lesk. 6. 1289. *Anarch.* 1290. Premislas. 1296. Ladis. 4	1204. Theodo. 1222. John Ducas. 1255. Theo. 2. 1258. John Lascaris. 1259. Mich. 8. 1282. Andronicus II.	1216. Honor. III. 1227. Greg. IX. 1241. Celest. IV. 1243. Innoc. IV. 1254. Alex. IV. 1261. Urban IV. 1265. Clem. IV. 1268-9. *Vacant.* 1271. Gregory X. 1276. Innoc. V. Adrian V. 1276. John XXI. 1277. Nichol. III. 1281. Martin IV. 1285. Honor. IV. 1288. Nich. IV. 1292-3. *Vacant.* 1294. Celest. V. Bonif. VIII.	1250. Conrad. 1254. Conradin. 1258. Manfred. 1266. Charles of Anjou. 1285. Chas. 2.	**Sicily.** 1282. Peter of Arragon. 1285. James. 1295. Fred. 2.
1319. Magn. II. 1350. Eric IV. 1359. Magnus II. 1363. Albert. 1389. Margaret.	1319. *United to Sweden.* 1389. *United to Denmark.*	1320. Christopher II. 1334. *Interregnm.* 1340. Wald. III. 1375. *Interregnm.* 1376. Olaus V. 1387. Margaret.	1300. Winceslas. 1333. Cas. 3. 1370. Louis. 1382. Mary. 1384. Hedw. 1396. Lad. 5.	1332. And. 3. 1341. John 5. 1391. Manuel VI.	1303. Bened. XI. 1305. Clement V. (*Avignon*). 1314-15. *Vacant.* 1316. John XXII. 1334. Bene. XII. 1342. Clem. VI. 1352. Innoc. VI. 1362. Urban V. (*Rome*). 1370. Greg. XI. 1378. Urban VI. 1389. Bonif. IX.	1309. Robt. 1343. Joan & Andrew of Hung. 1349. Louis. 1381. Chas. 3. 1385. Ladislas.	1337. Peter 2. 1342. Louis. 1355. Fred. 3. 1376. Maria & Martin.
1412. Eric XIII. 1440. Christopher III. 1448. Chas. VIII. 1457. Christian I. 1483. John of Denmark.		1448. Christian I. 1481. John.	1434. Lad. 6. 1445. Casi. 4. 1492. Albert	1425. John 6. 1448. Constant. 13. **Turkey.** 1433. Mahomet II. 1481. Bajaz. 2	1404. Innoc. VII. 1406. Greg. XII. 1409. Alex. V. 1410. John XXIII 1417. Martin V. 1431. Eugen. IV. 1447. Nicholas V. 1455. Calix. III. 1458. Pius II. 1464. Paul II. 1471. Sixtus IV. 1484. Inno. VIII. 1492. Alex. VI.	1414. Joan 2. 1435. Alfonso I. 1458. Ferd. 1. 1494. Alfo. 2. 1495. Ferd. 2. 1496. Fred. 2.	1402. Mart. 1. 1409. Mart. 2. (*United to Arragon.*) 1410. Ferd. 1. 1416. Alfo. 1. 1458. John. 1479. Ferd.

EUROPEAN SOVEREIGNS, *continued.*

Scandinavia. Sweden.	Scandinavia. Norway.	Scandinavia. Denmark.	Poland.	Turkish Empire.	Italy. Popes.	Italy. Naples and Sicily.	Italy. Sardinia.†
1520. Christian II. 1523. Gustavus Vasa. 1560. Eric XIV. 1568. John III. 1592. Sigismund	**Russia.*** 1533. Ivan IV. 1584. Feodor I. 1598. Boris.	1513. Christn. II. 1523. Fredrick I. *and Norway.* 1534. Christ. III. 1559. Fred. II. 1588. Christn. IV.	1501. Alex. 1506. Sig. I. 1548. Sig. II. 1573. Henry. 1575. Steph. 1587. Sig. 3.	1512. Selim. 1520. Solyman II. 1566. Sel. 2. 1574. Amurath III. 1595. Mah. 3.	1503. Pius III. Julius II. 1513. Leo X. 1522. Adrian VI. 1523. Clem. VII. 1534. Paul III. 1550. Julius III. 1555. Marcel. II. Paul IV. 1559. Pius IV. 1566. Pius V. 1572. Greg. XIII. 1585. Sixtus V. 1590. Urban VII. Greg. XIV. 1591. Innoc. IX. 1592. Clem. VIII.	1501. *United to Spain.*	
1604. Chas. IX. 1611. Gustavus Adolphus. 1633. Christina. 1654. Chas. X. 1660. Chas. XI. 1697. Chas. XII.	1606. Basil. 1613. Michael (Romanoff). 1645. Alexis. 1676. Feodor. 1682. Ivan V. & Peter I. 1689. Peter I.	1648. Fred. III. 1670. Christn. V. 1699. Fred. IV.	1632. Lad. 7. 1648. John C. 1669. Mich. 1674. John Sobieski. 1697. Fredk. August. 1.	1603. Ach. 1. 1617. Mus. 1. 1618. Osm. 2. 1622. Mustapha, again. 1623. Am. 4. 1640. Ibrah. 1648. Mah. 4. 1687. Sol. 3. 1691. Ach. 2. 1695. Mus. 2.	1605. Leo. XI. Paul V. 1621. Greg. XV. 1623. Urban VIII. 1644. Innocent X. 1655. Alex. VII. 1667. Clem. IX. 1670. Clem. X. 1676. Innoc. XI. 1689. Alex. VIII. 1691. Innoc. XII.		
1719. Ulrica and Frederick I. 1741. Fred. I. 1751. Adolphus Frederick. 1771. Gustav. III. 1792. Gustav. IV.	1725. Cather. I. 1727. Peter II. 1730. Anne. 1740. Ivan VI. 1741. Elizabeth. 1762. Peter III. Cather. II. 1796. Paul I.	1730. Christn. VI. 1746. Fred. V. 1766. Christ. VII. 1784. Prince Fred. *regent.*	1704. Stan. 1. 1709. Fredk. Augustus, *restored.* 1733. Fredk. August. 2. 1764. Stan. 2. 1795. *Partition.*	1703. Ach. 3. 1730. Mah. 5. 1754. Osm. 3. 1757. Mus. 3. 1774. Abdul-Hamid I. or Ach. 4. 1789. Selm. 3.	1700. Clem. XI. 1721. Inno. XIII. 1724. Bene. XIII. 1730. Clem. XII. 1740. Bene. XIV. 1758. Clem. XIII. 1769. Clem. XIV. 1775. Pius VI. 1800. Pius VII.	**Naples and Sicily.** 1713. Chas. 3. *Naples.* Victor-Am. of Savoy, *Sicily.* 1720 *Annexed to Germany.* 1738. Chas. 4. *Naples.* 1759. Fred. 4. *Sicily.*	**Sardinia.†** 1720. Victor-Amadeus. 1730. Charles Emman. 1. 1773. Victor-Amadeus 2. 1796. Charles Emman. 2.
1809. Chas. XIII. 1814. *Norway annexed.* 1818. Chas. XIV. 1844. Oscar I. 1859. Chas. XV. 1872. Oscar II.	1801. Alexand. I. 1828. Nicholas. 1855. Alex. II. 1881. Alex. III. 1894. Nicholas II.	1808. Fred. VI. 1814. *Norway taken away.* 1839. Chris. VIII. 1848. Fred. VII. 1863. Chrisn. IX.	**Greece.** 1832. Otho I. 1863. Geo. I.	1807. Mus. 4. 1808. Mahmud 6. 1839. Abdul Medjid. 1861. Abdul Aziz. 1876. Amurath V. *May* 1876. Abdul-Hamid II. *Aug.*	1823. Leo XII. 1829. Pius VIII. 1831. Greg. XVI. 1846. Pius IX. 1878. Leo XIII. 1903. Pius X.	**Naples.** 1806. Joseph Bonaparte 1808. Joach. Murat. **Naples and Sicily.** 1815. Ferd. 1. 1825. Fran. 1. 1830. Ferd. 2. 1859. Fran. 2. 1860 *Annexed to Italy.*	1802. Victor-Emman. 1. 1805 *Annexed to kingdom of Italy.* 1814. Victor-Emman. 1. 1821. Charles Felix. 1831. Charles Albert. 1849. Victor-Emman. 2.
						Italy. 1861. Victor-Emmanuel. 1878. Humbert. 1900. Victor-Emmanuel III.	

* See Article RUSSIA for preceding Rulers.
† See Article SAVOY.

POPULATION AND GOVERNMENTS OF THE WORLD.

(According to the Almanach de Gotha; see articles Population, *and the countries throughout the book.)*

COUNTRIES—RELIGIONS.		POPULATION.	RULERS.	BIRTH.	ACCESSION.
Anhalt, *E. Population in* Dec.	1900	316,027	Frederick, *duke*	19 Aug. 1856	1904
Argentine Confederation, *R.C.* Dec.	1900	4,794,149	Gen. Roca, *president*	1843	12 Oct. 1898.
Austrian Emp. *R.C.* (after cession 1866) Dec.	1900	45,310,835	Francis-Joseph, *emperor*	18 Aug. 1 30	2 Dec. 1848.
Baden, *R.C.* Dec.	1900	1,866,584	Frederick, *grand-duke*	9 Sept. 1826	5 Sept. 1856.
Bavaria, *R.C.* (after cessions 1866)	1900	6,175,153	Otho, *king*	27 April, 1848	13 June, 1886.
Belgium, *R.C.* Dec.	1900	6,815,054	Leopold II., *king*	9 April, 1835	10 Dec. 1865.
Bolivia, *R.C.*	1897	2,000,000	Gen. José M. Pando, *pres.*	25 Dec. 1849	25 Oct. 1899.
Brazil, *R.C.*	1891	17,000,000	Dr. F. de P. R. Alves		15 Nov. 1902.
Brunswick, *L.*	1900	464,333	Prince Albert of Prussia, *regt.*	8 May, 1837	21 Oct. 1885.
Bulgaria	1900	3,733,189	Ferdinand, *prince*	26 Feb. 1861	7 July, 1887.
Chili, *R.C.* (estimated)	1899	3,110,085	Sen. German Riesco		18 Sept. 1901.
Chinese Empire (estimated), *B.*	1897	303,241,969	Kwang Hsu, *emperor*	15 Aug. 1871	12 Jan. 1875.
Colombia, state, *R.C.*	1895	5,000,000	J. M. Marroquin, *president*	7 Aug. 1827	Jan. 1900.
Costa Rica, *R.C.* (estimated)	1899	310,000	Asencion Esquivel, *pres.*		8 May, 1902.
Denmark & colonies, *L.* (estm.)	1901	2,578,999	Christian IX., *king*	8 April, 1818	15 Nov. 1863.
Egypt, &c., *M.*	1897	9,700,000	Abbas Hilmi, *khedive*	14 July, 1874	7 Jan. 1892.
Equator (Ecuador), *R.C.*	1897	1,270,000	Gen. L. Plaza, *president*		17 Sept. 1901.
France alone, *R.C.*	1896	38,517,975	Emile Loubet, *president*	31 Dec. 1838	18 Feb. 1899.
Germany, *R.C.*, *L.* and *E.* Dec.	1900	56,356,246	William II., *emperor*	27 Jan. 1859	15 June, 1888.
Great Britain and colonies, *P.* (estimated)	1901	394,064,800	Edward VII., *king*	9 Nov. 1841	22 Jan. 1901.
Greece & Ion. Is. *G.C.* (estim.)	1896	2,430,807	George I., *king*	24 Dec. 1845	5 June, 1863.
Guatemala, *R.C.*	1900	1,574,338	Manuel E. Cabrera, *pres.*		2 Oct. 1898.
Hayti (estimated)	1894	1,000,000	Gen. Nord Alexis, *pres.*		1902.
Hesse-Darmstadt, *L.*	1900	1,119,893	Ernest Louis, *grand-duke*	25 Nov. 1868	13 March, 1892.
Holland, not colonies, *C.* Dec.	1900	5,179,138	Wilhelmina, *queen*	31 Aug. 1880	23 Nov. 1890.
Honduras, *R.C.*	1900	587,500	Gen. M. Bonilla, *president*	1849	1 Feb. 1903.
Italy, *R.C.*	1901	32,449,754	Victor Emmanuel, III., *king*	11 Nov. 1869	29 July, 1900.
Japan (estimated)	1899	46,450,911	Mutsuhito, *mikado*	3 Nov. 1852	13 Feb. 1867.
Liberia, *P.*	1897	1,500,000	, *president*		May, 1903.
Liechtenstein, *R.C.*	1891	9,434	John II., *prince*	5 Oct. 1840	12 Nov. 1858.
Lippe, *C.* Dec.	1900	139,238	Alexander, *prince*	16 Jan. 1831	20 March, 1895.
Luxemburg, *R.C.*	1900	236,543	Adolphus, *grand-duke*	21 July, 1817	23 Nov. 1890.
Mecklenburg-Schwerin, *L.* Dec.	1900	607,835	Frederic Francis IV. *gd.-duke*	9 April, 1882	10 April, 1897.
Mecklenburg-Strelitz, *L.*	1900	102,628	Frederic William, *grnd-duke*	17 Oct. 1819	6 Sept. 1860.
Mexico, *R.C.* (estimated)	1900	13,545,462	Porfirio Diaz, *president*		1 Dec. 1884.
Monaco, *R.C.*	1901	15,180	Albert Honoré Charles, *prnce*	13 Nov. 1848	10 Sept. 1889.
Montenegro, *G.C.* (estimated)	1891	200,000	Nicholas I., *prince*	7 Oct. 1841	14 Aug. 1860.
Morocco, *M.*	about	8,000,000	Muley Abdul Aziz, *sultan*		11 June, 1894.
Nicaragua, *R.C.*	1897	310,000	Gen. Zelaya, *president*	1852	June, 1901.
Oldenburg, *P.* (estimated)	1900	399,183	Frederick Augustus, *gd.duke*	16 Nov. 1852	13 June, 1900.
Panama, *R.C.*	1896	311,000			
Papal States *annexed to Italy*	1870				
Paraguay, *R.C.*	1900	635,571	Sen. Escurra, *president*		28 Sept. 1902.
Persia, *M.* (estimated)		7,500,000	Muzaffer-ed-Deen, *shah*	25 March, 1853	1 May, 1896.
Peru, *R.C.* (estimated)	1896	4,559,550	Sen. Manuel Candamo, *pres.*		8 Sept. 1903.
Portugal, *R.C.* Dec.	1900	5,428,800	Carlos, *king*	28 Sept. 1863	19 Oct. 1889.
Prussia, *E.* Dec.	1900	34,468,730	William II., *king*	27 Jan. 1859	15 June, 1888.
Reuss, *L.*	1900	138,993	Henry XXIV., *prince*	20 March, 1878	19 April, 1902.
Roumania	1899	5,912,520	Chs. of Hohenzollern, *king*	20 April, 1839	20 April, 1866.
Russia, *G.C.*, Poland, &c. (est.)	1897	129,211,113	Nicholas II., *czar*	18 May, 1868	1 Nov. 1894.
San Marino, *R.C.* (estimated)	1901	9,535	*Capitani reggenti*		
San Salvador, *R.C.* Jan.	1901	915,512	Sen. Escalon, *president*	24 March, 1857	1 March, 1903.
Saxe-Altenburg, *P.*	1900	194,914	Ernest, *duke*	16 Sept. 1826	3 Aug. 1853.
Saxe-Coburg-Gotha, *L.*	1900	229,550	Charles Edward	19 July, 1884	30 July, 1900.
Saxe-Meiningen, *L.*	1900	250,683	George II., *duke*	2 April, 1826	20 Sept. 1866.
Saxe-Weimar-Eisenach, *L.*	1900	362,873	William Ernest, *grand-duke*	10 June, 1876	5 Jan. 1901.
Saxony, *P.*	1900	4,199,758	George, *king*	8 Aug. 1832	19 June, 1902.
Schaumburg-Lippe, *L.*	1900	43,132	George, *prince*	10 Oct. 1846	8 May, 1893.
Schwartzburg-Rudolstadt, *L.*	1900	93,059	Gonthier, *prince*	21 Aug. 1852	19 Jan. 1890.
Schwartzburg-Sondershaus. *L.*	1900	80,898	Charles, *prince*	7 Aug. 1830	17 July, 1880.
Servia, *G.C.*	1900	2,493,770	Peter I., *king*	1844	15 June, 1903.
Spain, *R.C.* Dec.	1897	18,089,500	Alfonso XIII., *king*	17 May, 1886	17 May, 188
St. Domingo, *R.C.* (estimated)	1887	350,000	A. Woss, *president*		1903.
Sweden, Norway, *L.* (estmtd.)	1900	7,376,321	Oscar II., *king*	21 Jan. 1829	18 Sept. 1872.
Switzerland, *R.C.* and *P.* Dec.	1900	3,313,817	B. Comtesse, *president*		1 Jan. 1904.
Transvaal, C. (estimated)	1895	325,000	Lord Milner, *governor*		21 June, 1902.
Turkish Empire, *M.* (estimtd.)	1897	39,500,000	Abdul-Hamid II., *sultan*	22 Sept. 1842	31 Aug. 1876.
Uruguay, *R.C.* Dec.	1900	930,680	Sen. Batele, *president*		1 March, 1903.
Venezuela, *R.C.*	1891	2,323,527	Gen. Castro, *president*	12 Oct. 1860	28 Oct. 1901.
Würtemberg, *L.*	1900	2,169,434	William II., *king*	25 Feb. 1848	6 Oct. 1891.
United States of N. America, *P.*	1900	76,356,000	Theodore Roosevelt, *pres.*	27 Oct. 1858	14 Sept. 1901.

Predominant Religions.—*R.C.*, Roman Catholic; *G.C.*, Greek Church; *P.*, Protestant; *L.*, Lutheran; *E.*, Evangelical Church—a combination of Calvinists and Lutherans; *C.*, Calvinist or Reformed; *M.*, Mahometan; *B.*, Buddhist.

DICTIONARY OF DATES.

AARGAU (Switzerland), till 1798 included in Berne, was made an independent canton in 1803, and settled as such in 1815. Population 188,000. Augustine Keller (d. 1883), Swiss educationalist, successfully agitated against Jesuit teaching in schools 1840-4; and the expulsion of the Jesuits was decreed in 1847. The capital is Aarau. Population 6,800. Heinrich Zschokke, novelist and historian (d. 1848), lived here.

ABACUS, the tile on the capital of a column. That on the Corinthian column is ascribed to Callimachus, about 540 B.C.—This name is also given to a frame traversed by stiff wires, on which beads are strung, used for calculating by the Greeks, Romans, and Chinese. M. Lalanne published an ABACUS at Paris in 1845, a form of which is used in English infant schools, 1902. In the United States it is called "The Adder."—The multiplication table has been called the Pythagorean abacus.

ABANCAY, a river in Peru, on the banks of which the Spanish marshal Almagro defeated and took prisoner Alvarado, a partisan of Pizarro, 12 July, 1537.

ABATTOIRS, slaughter-houses for cattle. In 1810 Napoleon decreed that five should be erected near Paris, which were opened on 15 Sept. 1818. One was erected at Edinburgh in 1851, and they form part of the London metropolitan cattle-market, opened on 13 June, 1855.

ABBASSIDES (ab'as-sidz). The name of the Arabian dynasty, descendants of Mahomet's uncle, Abbas-Ben-Abdul-Motalleb, born 556, died 652. Merwan II., the last of the Ommiades, was defeated and slain by Abul Abbas in 750, who became caliph. Thirty-seven Abbasside caliphs (including Haroun al Raschid, 786-809) reigned from 750 to 1258. They settled at Bagdad, built by Al-Mansour about 762. Their colour was black; that of the Fatimites being green, and that of the Ommiades white.

ABBAYE, a military prison near St. Germain des Prés, Paris, where 164 prisoners were murdered by infuriated republicans led by Maillard, 2 and 3 Sept. 1792.

ABBEVILLE, fortified port, N. France. Here Henry III. met Louis IX. of France and made peace, renouncing his right to Normandy and other provinces, 20 May, 1259. In 1841 flint implements found here associated with remains of the mammoth and rhinoceros gave rise to the controversy on the antiquity of man. Pop. 19,772.

ABBEYS, monasteries for men or women; see *Monachism* and *Convents*. The first abbey founded in England was at Bangor in 560; in France, at Poitiers, about 360; in Ireland in the fifth century; in Scotland in the sixth century. 110 alien priories were suppressed in England, 2 Henry V. 1414. *Salmon.* The gross disorders in these establishments occasioned their destruction in Britain. After visitations of inquiry, king Henry VIII. commenced the suppression of small monasteries to raise revenues for Wolsey's colleges at Oxford and Ipswich, 7 June, 1525; many small monasteries were suppressed in 1536; and all religious houses were suppressed throughout the realm by parliament, 1539-40:—186 large monasteries (revenue 104,919*l.* 13*s.* 3*d.*), 374 lesser monasteries (revenue 33,479*l.* 13*s.* 7¾*d.*), and 48 houses of the knights hospitallers (revenue 2385*l.* 12*s.* 8*d.*; total, houses, 608; estimated revenue, 140,784*l.* 19*s.* 6¾*d.*) *Tanner.* The Anglo-Norman record society for the publication of the early chartularies and charters of the Norman and English abbeys was founded by the duke of Norfolk and others, 9 June, 1893. Abbeys were suppressed in Austria (by Joseph II.) in 1780, in France in 1790, in Portugal in 1834, in Sardinia in 1855, in Mexico in 1861, in Spain in 1837 and 1868, and in Italy in July, 1866, and April, 1873.

ABBOT (from *Ab*, father), the head of an abbey. In England, mitred abbots were lords of parliament; twenty-seven abbots and two priors thus distinguished, 1329; the number reduced to twenty-five, 1396. *Coke.* The abbots of Reading, Glastonbury, and St. John's, Colchester, were executed as traitors for denying the king's supremacy, probably for not surrendering their abbeys, 1539; see *Glastonbury*.

ABBOT'S RIPTON, see *Railway Accidents*, 1876.

A B C CLUB, a name adopted by certain republican enthusiasts in Paris, professing to relieve the *abaissés*, or depressed. Their insurrection 5 June, 1832, was suppressed with bloodshed, 6 June. These events are described by Victor Hugo in "*Les Misérables*" (1862).

A B C PROCESS, derives its name from a method of purifying sewage by sulphate of alumina, blood, charcoal and clay.

A B C RESTAURANTS, see under *Aërated Waters*.

ABDICATIONS of sovereigns, voluntary or compulsory, have been numerous:—

Sylla, Roman dictator . . . . . . B.C. 79

Diocletian, Roman emperor . . . . . A.D. 305
Stephen II., of Hungary 1131
Albert, the Bear of Brandenburg 1142
Lescov V. of Poland 1200
Uladislaus III. of Poland 1206
John Balliol, of Scotland 1296
Otho (of Bavaria), of Hungary 1309
Eric IX., of Denmark, &c. 1439
Pope Felix V. 1449
Charles V., as emperor of Germany . . 25 Oct. 1555
,, as Charles I. king of Spain 16 Jan. 1556
Christina, of Sweden . . . . . 16 June, 1654
John Casimir, of Poland 1669
James II., of England . . . . fled 11 Dec. 1688
Frederick Augustus II., of Poland 1704
Philip V. of Spain (resumed) 1724
Victor Amadeus, of Sardinia 1730
Charles, of Naples 1759
Stanislaus, of Poland 1795
Charles Emmanuel II., of Sardinia . . . 4 June, 1802
Francis II., of Germany, who became emperor of Austria . . . . 11 Aug. 1804
Charles IV., of Spain, in favour of his son, 19 March; in favour of Bonaparte; see *Spain* . . 1 May, 1808
Joseph Bonaparte, of Naples (for Spain) . 1 June, 1808
Gustavus IV., of Sweden 1809
Louis, of Holland . . . . . . 1 July, 1810
Jerome, of Westphalia . . . . . 20 Oct. 1813
Napoleon I., of France . . . . . 5 April, 1814
Victor Emmanuel of Sardinia . . . 13 March, 1821
Pedro IV., of Portugal . . . . . 2 May, 1826
Charles X., of France . . . . . 2 Aug. 1830
Pedro I., of Brazil . . . . . . 7 April, 1831
Dom Miguel, of Portugal (by leaving it) 26 May, 1834
William I., of Holland . . . . . 8 Oct. 1840
Louis-Philippe, of France . . . . 24 Feb. 1848
Louis Charles, of Bavaria . . . . 21 March, 1848
Ferdinand, of Austria . . . . . 2 Dec. 1848
Charles Albert, of Sardinia . . . 23 March, 1849
Leopold II., of Tuscany . . . . . July, 1859
Bernhard, of Saxe-Meiningen . . . . 20 Sept. 1866
Isabella II., of Spain . . . . . 25 June, 1870
Amadeus, of Spain . . . . . . 11 Feb. 1873
Prince Alexander of Bulgaria (*compulsory*) . 7 Sept. 1886
Milan, King of Servia . . . . . . 6 March, 1889

ABECEDARIANS, followers of Storch, an Anabaptist in the sixteenth century, derived their name from their rejection of all worldly knowledge, even of the alphabet.

ABDUCTION. Carrying off of women in the Middle Ages was regarded rather as gallantry than crime: since the Statute of Merton, 20 Hen. III., many Acts passed, since repealed. The Acts now in force are the Criminal Law Consolidation Act 1861, and the Criminal Law Amendment Act, 1885. It is felony to take away or detain against her will for improper purposes any woman of any age, or to allure or take from her parents or legal guardians a woman under the age of 21. The mere abduction of an unmarried girl under 16 is punishable by two years' imprisonment, and if taken away for the purpose of seduction under the age of 18 the same penalty is incurred. The consent of the girl is no defence. The abduction of a child under 14 is punishable by 14 years' imprisonment as the maximum penalty.

ABELARD, a celebrated teacher of theology and logic, in 1118 fell in love with Héloïse, the niece of Fulbert, a canon of Paris, became her tutor, and seduced her. After a compulsory marriage, he placed her in a convent. Having been cruelly mutilated at the instigation of her relatives, he entered the abbey of St. Denis. Compelled to depart thence, accused of heresy, he built and lectured at the Paraclete, which eventually he made a convent, with Héloïse for the abbess. He died 21 April, 1142, and was buried in the Paraclete, where also Héloïse was laid, 17 May, 1164. Their ashes were removed to the garden of the Muséum Français in 1800, and to Père la Chaise in 1817. Their epistles, &c., were published in 1616.

ABENCERRAGES, a Moorish tribe of Granada, opposed to the Zegris. From 1480 to 1492 they constantly fought. They were exterminated by Boabdil (Abu Abdallah), the last king, who was dethroned by Ferdinand and Isabella in 1492; his dominions were annexed to Castile.

ABENSBERG, Bavaria. The Austrians were here defeated by Napoleon I., 20 April, 1809.

ABEOKUTA, see *Dahomey*.

ABERDEEN (N. Scotland), said to have been founded in the third century after Christ, and erected into a city about 893. Old Aberdeen was made a royal burgh in 1154; the thatched timber-town was burnt by the English in 1336; and soon after New Aberdeen was built. Since building of Union Street in 1800 it has been termed the "Granite City." A statue of the prince consort was inaugurated by the queen 13 Oct. 1863; and one of queen Victoria by the prince of Wales, 20 Sept. 1866. Population, 1901, 153,108.

St Machar's cathedral, 1357-1527, restored 1869.
King's college was founded by bishop William Elphinstone, who had a bull from pope Alexander VI. in 1494.
The *University* was erected in 1500-6. *Marischal college* was founded by George Keith, earl marischal of Scotland, in 1593; rebuilt in 1837. In 1860 the university and colleges were united. By the reform act of 1868, the universities of Aberdeen and Glasgow send one member to parliament. Sir Erasmus Wilson gives 10,000*l.* to endow a chair of pathological anatomy, 1882.
Lord Strathcona, lord rector of the university, gives 25,000*l.* towards the building fund (the public subscribed 30,000*l.*), is presented with the freedom of the city, 9 April, 1902.
Robert Gordon's college, royal charters 1772-1779. In 1881 reorganised.
Aberdeen Journal 1748. The oldest newspaper north of the Forth.
Royal infirmary established 1740, re-built 1840. Lord Mount Stephen gives 25,000*l.*, and endows it with 1000*l.* per ann., April, 1902.
Above 30 persons drowned by overcrowding a boat, April, 1876.
Aberdeen farmers agitate for change in land laws; abatement of rent, &c., Sept. 1881.
Aberdeen market destroyed by fire, 29 April, 1882.
Duthie-park, presented by Miss Duthie, opened by princess Beatrice, 27 Sept. 1883.
The British Association meets here, 14 Sept. 1859; and 9 Sept. 1885.
The marquis of Lorne uncovers a colossal statue of Wallace, 29 June, 1888.
Mr. John Gray Chambers, of Banchory, bequeaths 10,000*l.* to found a professorship of English literature in the university, with other bequests, Nov. 1890.
Bronze statue of the queen, by Mr. Birch, A.R.A., unveiled, 9 Nov. 1893.
Address to czar on his way to Balmoral, 22 Sept. 1896.
Fire at a music-hall (by panic 6 deaths), 30 Sept. 1896.
Miss Jane Cruikshank gives 15,000*l.* for a botanic garden, April, 1898.
Sir George White opens the Gordon Highlanders' Memorial Institute, 23 Aug. 1902.

Malcolm III. having gained a great victory over the Danes in the year 1010, resolved to found a new *Bishopric*, in token of his gratitude for his success, and chose Mortlach in Banffshire, where St. Beanus was consecrated first bishop, 1015. The see, removed to Aberdeen early in the twelfth century, was discontinued at the revolution, 1689, and is now a post-revolution bishopric, instituted in 1721; see *Bishops in Scotland*.

ABERDEEN ACT, introduced by the earl of Aberdeen, and passed, 1845, to enforce the observance of a convention made with Brazil in 1826 to put down the slave trade. Repealed in April, 1869.

ABERDEEN ADMINISTRATION, called the *Coalition Ministry*, as including Whigs, Radicals, and followers of sir R. Peel. Formed in consequence of the resignation of the first Derby administration; sworn in, 28 Dec. 1852; resigned 30 Jan. 1855; succeeded by the *Palmerston* administration, *which see*.

Earl of Aberdeen,* *first lord of the treasury*.
Lord Cranworth, *lord chancellor*.
Earl Granville, *president of the council*.
Duke of Argyll, *lord privy seal*.
Lord John Russell,† *foreign secretary*.
Viscount Palmerston, *home secretary*.
Duke of Newcastle,‡ *colonial* and *war secretary*.
William Ewart Gladstone, *chancellor of exchequer*.
Sir James Graham, *first lord of the admiralty*.
Sir Charles Wood, *president of the India board*.
Edward Cardwell, *president of board of trade*.
Hon. Sidney Herbert, *secretary-at-war*.
Sir William Molesworth, *chief commissioner of works*.
Marquess of Lansdowne (without office).
Viscount Canning, lord Stanley of Alderley, right hon. Edward Strutt, &c.

ABERDEEN PEERAGE CASE. George, earl of Aberdeen, grandson of the premier, succeeded his father, 22 March, 1864. After travelling in a yacht, he became a merchant seaman, and chief mate of the *Hera*; he was drowned 27 Jan. 1870. His brother John's claim to the succession was allowed by the house of lords, 3 May, 1872.

ABER EDW, S. Radnorshire. Near here Llewelyn, the last independent prince of Wales, was surprised and defeated by the lords marchers, 11 Dec. 1282. He escaped, but was betrayed and slain at Builth.

ABERGELE (N. Wales), see *Railway Accidents*, 20 Aug. 1868.

ABERRATION OF LIGHT; the alteration in apparent position of a star produced by the motion of the earth in its orbit during the time that the light is coming from the star to the eye. Discovered by James Bradley (aft. astronomer-royal), through his observation of an apparent motion of γ *Draconis*, a fixed star, 1727.

ABERYSTWYTH (Cardigan Bay). One of the chief watering-places of Wales. There are remains of the castle founded by Gilbert de Strongbow 1109. Below the castle is the University College of Wales, 1872; destroyed by fire 1885, restored 1887 at a cost of £17,900. Pop. 1891, 6,725; 1901, 8013.

ABHORRERS, a name given in 1679 (reign of Charles II.) to the court party in England, the opponents of the Addressers (afterwards *Whigs*), so called from their address to the king praying for the immediate assembly of the parliament, which was delayed on account of its being adverse to the court. The former (afterwards *Tories*) expressed their abhorrence of those who endeavoured to encroach on the royal prerogative, 1680. *Hume*. The commons expelled several members for being Abhorrers, among them sir Francis Withens (whom they sent to the Tower), and prayed his majesty to remove others from places of trust. Oct. 1680.

* Born in 1784; engaged in foreign diplomacy, 1813; became foreign secretary, Jan. 1828; joined the party of sir R. Peel, 1846; died 13 Dec. 1860. His "Life," by his son, 1893.

† Lord John Russell was succeeded as foreign secretary by the earl of Clarendon (Feb. 1853), but continued a member of the cabinet, without office; he afterwards became president of the council, in the room of earl Granville, appointed to the duchy of Lancaster (June, 1854).

‡ In June, 1854, the offices were separated; the duke of Newcastle remained *secretary of war*, and sir George Grey was made *colonial secretary*.

ABINGDON, BERKS. The ancient monastery, rebuilt about 955, was surrendered at the Reformation, 1538. The grammar school was founded in 1563, rebuilt 1870. Population in 1901, 6,480; In 1645, lord Essex and Waller held Abingdon against Charles I. The town was unsuccessfully attacked by sir Stephen Hawkins in 1644, and by prince Rupert in 1645. On these occasions the defenders put every prisoner to death without trial; hence the term "Abingdon law."

ABIOGENESIS, a term applied by prof. Huxley, 1870, to the theory that living matter may be produced from non-living. See *Spontaneous Generation*.

ABJURATION of the pope was enjoined by statute in the reigns of Henry VIII., Elizabeth, and James I., and of certain doctrines of the church of Rome by stat. 25 Charles II. 1673. The oath of abjuration of the house of Stuart was enjoined by stat. 13 & 14 Will. III. 1701; the form was changed in after reigns. By 21 & 22 Vict. c. 48 (1858) one oath for the three oaths of abjuration, allegiance, and supremacy was substituted. See *Oaths*.

ABKASIA, a province of the Caucasus, annexed by Russia, the last prince Michael Shervashiji being deposed: an insurrection against the Russian authorities, 8 Aug. 1866, was quelled with much bloodshed.

ABNEY PARK, see *Cemeteries*.

ABO, a port of Russia, founded prior to 1157, was till 1819 capital of Swedish Finland. It has suffered much by fire, especially in 1775 and 1827; was seized by the Russians in Feb. 1808; ceded to them, 17 Sept. 1809; and rebuilt by them after the great fire in 1827. The university, erected by Gustavus Adolphus and Christina, 1640 *et seq.*, was removed to Helsingfors, 1827. The *peace of Abo*, by which Sweden ceded part of Finland to Russia, was signed, 18 Aug. 1743. Pop. 38,000.

ABOLITIONISTS, the party in the northern part of the United States opposed to slavery. A congress was held, 1774, and legislation attempted by the U.S. congress April 6, 1776. They formed a small society at Boston about 1832; which became the nucleus of a great political party, and ultimately attained its object by the war of 1861-4. See *Slavery in United States*.

ABORIGINES (without origin), a name given to the earliest inhabitants of Italy; now applied to the original inhabitants of any country.—The Aborigines Protection Society was established in 1838; annual meetings are held. Select Committee of the House of Commons report on natives in British colonies, 1837. Kidnapping Act, 1872, also a Protection Act, 1875, applies to Pacific Islands. African Conference of States at Brussels, 1885 and 1889–90, to protect natives and suppress slavery.

ABORTION. Any woman who unlawfully administers to herself any noxious thing, or uses any means whatever to procure a miscarriage, is guilty of felony. Any person aiding her is likewise guilty of felony, 24 & 25 Vict. c. 100, 1861. If the woman dies, or if the child is born alive but does not survive, the offence becomes murder. See *Trials*.

ABOUKIR (Egypt), the ancient Canopus. In the bay Nelson defeated the French fleet, 1 Aug. 1798; see *Nile*. A Turkish army of 15,000 was defeated here by 5000 French under Bonaparte, 25 July, 1799. A British expedition to Egypt under general sir Ralph Abercromby landed here, and

Aboukir surrendered to them after an obstinate and sanguinary conflict with the French, 8 March, 1801; see *Alexandria*.

ABRAHAM, ERA OF, used by Eusebius; so called from the patriarch Abraham, who died 1822 B.C. The era began 1 Oct. 2016 B.C. To reduce this era to the Christian, subtract 2015 years and three months.

ABRAHAM, HEIGHTS OF, near Quebec, Lower Canada. The French were defeated and Montcalm, their commander, killed here by general Wolfe, who fell in the moment of victory, 13 Sept. 1759; see *Quebec*.

ABRAHAMITES, a sect holding the errors of Paulus, was suppressed by Cyriacus, the patriarch of Antioch, early in the ninth century. A deistical sect (followers of John Huss) of this name was banished from Bohemia by Joseph II. in 1783.

ABRANTES (Portugal). By a treaty between France and Portugal, signed here 29 Sept. 1801, the war was closed, and the French army withdrew; a money compensation having been agreed to, and territories in Guiana ceded to France. Pop. 6380.

ABSCONDING DEBTORS ACT, passed 9 Aug. 1870.

ABSENTEE TAX (4*s*. in the pound), levied in Ireland in 1715 on the incomes and pensions of absentees (long complained of), ceased in 1753. A tax of 2*s*. in the pound was proposed in vain by Mr. Flood in 1773, and by Mr. Molyneux in 1783.

ABSOLUTION. Till the 3rd century, the consent of the congregation was necessary to absolution; but soon after the power was reserved to the bishop; and in the 12th century the form "*I absolve thee*" had become general. See *Holy Cross*.

ABSTINENCE. It is mythically said that St. Anthony lived to the age of 105 on twelve ounces of bread and water daily, and James the hermit to the age of 104; that St. Epiphanius lived to 115; Simeon the Stylite to 112.

Cicely de Ridgway, said to have fasted 40 days rather than plead when charged with the murder of her husband John; discharged as miraculously saved, 1347.

Ann Moore, the fasting woman of Tutbury, Staffordshire, said to have lived 20 months without food; her imposture detected by Dr. A. Henderson, Nov. 1808.

A man named Cavanagh at Newry, in Ireland, was reported to have lived two years without meat or drink, Aug. 1840. His imposture was discovered in England, where he was imprisoned as a cheat, Nov. 1841.

Sarah Jacobs, the Welsh fasting girl, aged 13, said by her father to have lived for more than a year without food, after being closely watched for a week, died from exhaustion 17 Dec. 1869. Her parents were sentenced at Carmarthen to imprisonment for fraudulent deception, 13 July, 1870.

Dr. Tanner, at New York, was stated to have fasted 40 days and nights, drinking a little water occasionally; losing 36 lb. from 157½ lb., noon 28 June to noon 7 Aug. 1880.

Mr. Griscom, of Chicago, said to have fasted 36 days, 5 July, 1881.

Louise Lateau, Belgian fanatic, at Bois d'Haine, said to have lived twelve years without food, died, aged 33. Aug. 1883.

[She had remarkable wounds resembling the stigmata on the crucifix.]

Signor Succi, of Rome, said to have fasted 30 days, 1886; fast of 30 days, at Barcelona, 22 Sept.–23 Oct. 1888. Fasted 40 days at Westminster Aquarium, 17 March–26 April, 1890. Fast of 42 days by M. Alexandre Jacques at the same place, 21 June–2 Aug. 1890; again 31 July–19 Sept. (50 days), 1891. Succi fasted 45 days at New York, concluded 20 Dec. 1890; at the Westminster Aquarium he engaged to fast 52 days, but stopped on the 44th day, 29 Jan. 1892.

Signor Merlatti, of Paris, alleged to have fasted 50 days, drinking water; in good health, but greatly emaciated, 15 Dec. 1886.

Auguste Christensen, said to have fasted 35 days, drinking water, 10 Oct.–14 Nov. 1901.

Many other cases of long abstinence have been recorded. See *Fasts, Teetotalers*.

ABSTINENTS, an ascetic sect in Gaul and Spain: about 288.

ABU KLEA, about 120 miles from Khartoum. Here General Sir Herbert Stewart defeated the Mahdi's troops, 17 Jan. 1885. See under *Soudan*.

ABYDOS, a city of Upper Egypt. Here a tablet was discovered dedicated to the memory of his ancestors by Rameses II. (about 1322 B.C.). It was bought for the British Museum, 1837. Another tablet was discovered by Mariette in 1865. Other discoveries 1902-03. Also a town in Asia Minor, celebrated as the place whence (480 B.C.) Xerxes and his great army passed into Europe. See *Hellespont*.

ABYSSINIA, the country of the Habese, N.E. Africa. Its ancient history is very uncertain. The kingdom of the Axumitæ (its chief town Axum) flourished in the 1st and 2nd centuries after Christ. Christianity was introduced about 329 by Frumentius, consecrated Bishop of Abyssinia by St. Athanasius. Between 470 and 480 monasteries were established. In 522 Caleb, king of Abyssinia, at the request of the emperor Justinian, conquered Yemen. The Ethiopians possessed at that time the richest part of Arabia, traded to India, and were in constant communication with Greece. In the 7th century the Mohammedans expelled them from Arabia, and by the conquest of Egypt cut them off from the civilised world. About 960, Judith, a Jewish princess, murdered a great part of the royal family, and reigned forty years. The young king escaped: and the royal house was restored in 1268 in the person of his descendant Icon Amlac. In the middle ages it was said to be ruled by Prester John, or Prete Janni. The Portuguese missions, commenced in the 15th century, after much struggling against opposition, were expelled about 1633. The encroachments of the Gallas and intestine disorders soon after broke up the empire into petty governments. From the visits of James Bruce, 1768-73; Henry Salt, 1809-10; Edward Rüppell, 1834-7; major Harris, 1841; Mansfield Parkyns, 1844-7, much information respecting Abyssinia has been gained. Several expeditions into Abyssinia have been organised by the French government. The brothers Antoine and Arnauld Abbadie visited the country 1837-45. Abyssinia was divided into four provinces. In 1847 Ras Ali was ruler of Amhara; Ras Ubie of Tigré and Samien; and Sahela Selassie of Shoa. Population between 3,000,000 and 4,000,000. The ruler of Abyssinia is termed *Negus*, a title dating from the 13th century.

Treaty of commerce with the king of Shoa concluded by major Harris . . . 16 Nov. 1841

Mr. Plowden (made British consul at Massowah, 1848) concludes treaty with Ras Ali, ruler of Amhara . . . . 2 Nov. 1849

Ras Ali deposed by his son-in-law Theodore, who is crowned, and takes the title of *negus*, or king of kings . . . . . . 11 Feb. 1855

Protestant missionaries received, replacing Roman catholics . . . . ,,

Mr. Plowden (who had joined the party of Theodore) killed by rebels, Feb.; his friend Bell killed soon after, when avenging him; Theodore overcomes the rebels and massacres about 150 prisoners as a sacrifice to their manes . . . 1860
Captain C. D. Cameron appointed to succeed consul Plowden . . . . Nov. 1861
He arrived at Massowah 9 Feb. 1862, goes to Abyssinia, May; received by Theodore, 7 Oct.; is sent away with a letter for the queen, desiring alliance against the Turks; which arrived 12 Feb. 1863
It is decided that this letter is not to be answered; Cameron, ordered by earl Russell to remain at Massowah, returns to Abyssinia . . . June, ,,
Rev. H. Stern, missionary, beaten and imprisoned for alleged intrusion upon Theodore . . Oct. ,,
Cameron, and all British subjects and missionaries, imprisoned for pretended insults, 3 Jan.; report of imprisonment reached London 7 May; prisoners sent to Magdala, and chained like criminals . . . . Nov. 1864
Mr. Hormuzd Rassam, a Chaldee Christian, first assistant British political resident at Aden, sent on mission to Abyssinia; arrives at Massowah, 24 July; lieut. Prideaux and Dr. Blanc appointed to accompany him . . . . . ,,
Mr. Rassam having negotiated without effect for a year, Mr. Gifford Palgrave is appointed by earl Russell to go to Abyssinia, July; but is stopped on the intelligence that Theodore has invited Rassam to come to him . . . . 12 Aug. 1865
Mr. Rassam, lieut. Prideaux, and Dr. Blanc arrive at Matemma from Massowah, 21 Nov. 1865; and are well received by Theodore . . 28 Jan. 1866
Prisoners released, 12 March; all seized and imprisoned . . . . . . about 13 April, ,,
Mr. Flad sent to England by Theodore to obtain British workmen, April; arrives, July; introduced to queen Victoria, and receives from her an autograph letter, dated . . . 4 Oct. ,,
Mr. Flad returned with workmen to Massowah, 29 Oct.; Theodore received the queen's letter about 19 Dec. ,,
Lord Stanley's ultimatum to Theodore, demanding release of the captives in three months (not received), sent . . . . . 16 April, 1867
Mr. Flad received by the king, and made to join his family in prison . . . . . May, ,,
Preparations for war; sir Robert Napier appointed commander of an expedition; pioneer force sails from Bombay . . . . . . 14 Sept. ,,
A formal letter from the British government sent to Theodore (never arrived) . . 9 Sept. ,,
Advanced brigade (3500) sail from Bombay, 7, 8 Oct.; land at Zoulla . . . . 21 Oct. ,,
Napier's proclamation issued in Abyssinia, 26 Oct. ,,
Captives at Magdala reported well . . 11 Nov. ,,
Report that the Gallas have joined the revolt against Theodore . . . . 25 Nov. ,,
The British parliament meets; the queen's speech announces the war, 19 Nov.; 2,000,000*l.* voted, 26, 27 Nov. ,,
Third ultimatum sent by sir R. Napier; intercepted by a rebel chief and given to Mr. Rassam, who suppressed it as likely to endanger the lives of the captives 1868
Arrival of sir R. Napier at Annesley bay . 4 Jan. ,,
The captives relieved of their chains . 29 March, ,,
Sir R. Napier arrives below Magdala . 2 April, ,,
Theodore massacres about 300 native prisoners, 9 April, ,,
Battle of Arogee; Theodore's troops attack the British first brigade; defeated with much slaughter (Good Friday) . . . 10 April, ,,
Theodore requests Mr. Rassam to mediate; lieut. Prideaux, sent to sir R. Napier, returns with a letter; Theodore receives it indignantly, and sends an insulting reply . . . 11 April, ,,
Theodore sends a letter of apology offering a present of cattle; Mr. Rassam understanding this present to have been accepted, tells the king's agents; the European artizans and families sent to the British camp . . . . . 12 April, ,,
Part of the Abyssinian troops mutiny; Magdala bombarded and stormed; Theodore kills himself . . . . 13 April, ,,
["I fail to discover a single point of view from which it is possible to regard his removal with regret."—*Sir R. Napier* . . . . 18 June, 1869]
Magdala burnt to the ground . . . 17 April, 1868
Death of Theodore's queen . . . 10 May, ,,
Henry Dufton of the "Intelligence department" shot by Shosho robbers . . . 28 May, ,,
Immediate return of the troops;—all had embarked, 2 June, ,,
Troops arrive at Plymouth, 21 June; sir R. Napier at Dover . . . . 2 July, ,,
[Cattle said to have been employed in the expedition: 45 elephants, 7417 camels, 12,920 mules and ponies, 7033 bullocks, 827 donkeys. Natives largely employed in the transport service.]
Theodore's son Alamayoú, aged 7, arrives at Plymouth, 14 July; presented to queen Victoria, 16 July, ,,
Pension of 350*l.* to col. Cameron [he died 30 May, 1870]; 5000*l.* given to Mr. Rassam; 2000*l.* to Dr. Blanc; 2000*l.* to lieut. Prideaux; announced 23 Dec. ,,
Prince Alamayoú sailed to India for education (returned to England end of 1871) . . 26 Jan. 1869
Expenses of the war: 5,000,000*l.* voted 18 Dec. 1868; 3,300,000*l.* more voted . . . 4 Mar. ,,
[Total: 8,977,500*l.* Feb. 1880.]
Report of a commission on the expenses of the expedition disclosed much waste, attributed to urgency and divided authority . . . . Aug. 1870
War between Gobazye, king of Amhara and Kassa, king of Tigré; Kassa victor . . . 21 June, 1871
Gobazye beaten and taken prisoner . . 11 July, ,,
Kassa proposes to be crowned emperor and negus of all Abyssinia, 21 Nov.; punishes the Catholic missionaries for partisanship; and forms alliance with Egypt . . . . July, ,,
Kassa crowned at Axum as Johanni II. . 12 Jan. 1872
Said to be ruling tyrannically 1873–4
War with Egypt; the khedive's troops enter Abyssinia; the natives retire, but surprise and defeat the Egyptians at Kherad Iska (a massacre), and at Gonda Gouddi (a desperate fight) . 16 Oct. 1875
Abyssinians defeated in three days' conflict, 17–10 Feb. 1876
Col. Gordon said to be negotiating peace for Egypt, June, 1877
King Johanni totally defeats Menelek, king of Shoa, middle of June, ,,
Menelek submits, permitted to rule;—reported great battle; Menelek said to be killed . 17 Sept. ,,
Col. Gordon concludes peace; Abyssinia to have a port . . . . Oct. 1879
Prince Alamayoú dies at Leeds, 14 Nov., buried at Windsor . . . . ,,
King Johanni receives adm. Hewett from Souakim, and signs a treaty respecting Massowah, &c., about 26 May 1884
Two Abyssinian envoys arrive at Plymouth 19 Aug. ,,
Received by the queen . . . . . 20 Aug. ,,
Start on return . . . . 11 Sept. ,,
Captain Harrison Smith, British agent, well received by king Johanni . . . . . . 19 May, 1886
For disputes with Italy see *Massowah.*
Mr. Portal, and a mission from queen Victoria to mediate between Italy and Abyssinia (see *Massowah*) received by the king, after much delay; without effect . . . . . 10–16 Dec. 1887
The Italians march to Saati to form a camp, announced . . . . 1 Feb. 1888
Abyssinians defeated in a skirmish . . 6 Feb. ,,
Slight beginning of actual hostilities, 4 March; slight firing near Saati, 28 March; the negus, through deficiency in commissariat, &c., sues for peace; two chiefs sent to general San Marzano, 29 March, ,,
The negus refuses the terms and retires . 2 April ,,
The Italian troops return to Italy, 13 April *et seq.* ,,
Rebellion of Menelek, king of Shoa, against king John . . . . Dec. ,,
The negus is stated to have been defeated in his attack on the dervishes, 10 March; and to have been attacked and killed by them 12 March 1889
Mission from Menelek, king of Shoa, with presents, received by king Humbert, 28 Aug.; the treaty between Italy and Abyssinia (2 May) ratified, 2 Oct. ,,

Protectorate of Italy over Abyssinia accepted and announced . . . . 14 Oct. 1889
The Italian National Bank agree to lend Menelek 4,000,000 francs . . . . . . 26 Oct. „
Menelek crowned negus of Abyssinia . 3 Nov. „
Ras Mangascia and other opponents of Menelek defeated . . . . Nov.-Dec. „
Gen. Orero, on behalf of Menelek, marches on Adua, and is warmly received . . 27 Jan. 1890
Submission of Degiac Mangascia, 17 March; he meets count Antonelli at Adowa. . 16 May, „
Count Antonelli visits the negus in relation to the treaty; count leaves, 11 Feb.; the negus writes to king Humbert . . . . . . March, 1891
The chief Debeb defeated and killed by the chiefs Mangascia and Ras Alula . . . 29 Sept. „
King Menelek's present of two tame lions and a decoration received by pres. Carnot at Paris, Dec. „
Mr. Theodore Bent published an account of his explorations of "The Sacred City of the Ethiopians" (Aksum) . . . . . . Nov. 1893
Russian Red Cross expedition starts from Odessa, under gen. Shvedoff, 11 April; well received by Menelek at Entoto, 26 July; letter and presents from the emperor Menelek received by the czar at Kieff . . . . 2 Sept. 1896
Arrival of major Nerazzini to negotiate, 7 Oct.; treaty of peace (independence of Ethiopia, release of prisoners, indemnity to be fixed) signed at Adis Abeba, 26 Oct.; ratified by Italy . 16 Nov. 1896
Commercial treaty with France announced, 2 Feb. 1897
Ras Alula (born about 1845), powerful chief and able general, died . . . . mid Feb. „
M. Lagarde with a French mission cordially received by the emperor at Adis Abeba, 7–29 March „
An Italian expedition under capt. Bottego treacherously attacked by the Abyssinians in the Gabo district, capt. Bottego and 66 men killed, mid March; 2 Italian prisoners released . 22 June „
British mission under Mr. Rennell Rodd (K.C.M.G. 1899) well received at Harar by Ras Makonnen, 2 April; warmly received by Menelek at Adis Abeba, 29 April; treaty signed, 14 May; ratified, 28 July; the party dismissed with honours, and a letter and presents to the queen . 15 May „
Prince Henry of Orleans received by the emperor at Adis Abeba, 12 April; an Italian resident appointed at Adis Abeba . . . . Aug. „
The emperor made K.C.M.G. . . . 25 Oct. „
Lieut. Harrington, British diplomatic agent, splendidly received at Adis Abeba . . 20 April, 1898
Bayade, a French post, burnt by the Danakils; 18 deaths. . . . . 2 Oct. „
Lieut. Harrington (made C.B. 1902) delivers a phonographic message and presents from the queen to Menelek at Adis Abeba . 30 Oct. „
Ras Makunen (ruler of Tigré) is defeated by Ras Mangascia . . . . 11 Jan. 1899
Ras Mangascia and Ras Sebath captured, pay homage to Menelek . . . . . 18 Feb. „
The Marchand mission welcomed at Adis Abeba, mid April „
Capt. Wellby explores the mountain districts of Kambat, Walamo and Gamo (10,500 ft. alt.), lakes Rudolf and Gallop, and discovers two sources of the river Sobat, etc., Jan.-July [died of his wounds in the S. African war, 5 Aug. 1900] „
Capt. Bulatovich crosses the region S. of Kaffa and W. of the Omo, and discovers a chain of mountains, reported . . . . . . Sept. „
Mahdist bands beaten by Ethiopians in Ogaden, 19 March, 1900
Italian frontier, the Mareb-Belesa-Muna line, settled, March 1899; treaty signed . . 10 July „
Successful expedition against the Mad Mullah; see *Somaliland* . . . . . . 17 July, 1901
Major Austin's Anglo-Abyssinian frontier expedition to delimit boundary between lake Rudolf and the Sobat, Oct. *et seq.* 1899, returned, Oct. 1900, left Omdurman Dec., surveyed and mapped country between Nasser and the north of lake Rudolf (45 Sudanese died), reached Mombasa, 6 Sept. „
Mining concessions to the Abyssinian exploration co. refused . . . . Dec. „
The emperor accepts a gift of books from the trustees of the British museum . . Jan. 1902
Boundary of the British Soudan fixed, agreement signed . . . . . about 31 May, 1902
S.W. boundary of Eritrea settled, protocol signed, mid June, „
Ras Makunen, emperor's envoy, visits England, 23 June-July; France, mid July; received by the king, made K.C.M.G., London, 8 Aug.; returns to Zibuti . . . . . . 9 Sept. „
Troops co-operate with British against Mad Mullah; dervishes defeated, 300 killed . . 4 May, 1903
See *Russia*, *Massowah*, 1895–6; *Somaliland*, 1902–3.
Party of exploration of S. Abyssinian frontier, under Mr. A. E. Butler, reached Lake Rudolph, having accomplished its purpose . . 5 May „

ABYSSINIAN ERA is reckoned from the creation, which the Abyssinians place in the 5493rd year B.C., on 29 Aug. old style; their dates consequently exceed ours by 5492 years, 125 days. To reduce Abyssinian time to the Julian year, subtract 5492 years, 125 days.

ACACIANS. 1. Followers of Acacius, bishop of Cæsarea in the fourth century, who held peculiar doctrines respecting the nature of Christ. 2. Partisans of Acacius, patriarch of Constantinople, promoter of the Henoticon (*which see*), 482-4.

ACADEMIES. *Academia*, a shady grove without the walls of Athens, said to have belonged to the hero Academus, was adorned with statues by Cimon, the son of Miltiades, and adapted for gymnastic exercises. Here Plato, 428-389 B.C., first taught philosophy, and his followers took the title of Academics.—Rome had no academies.*—Ptolemy Soter is said to have founded an academy at Alexandria, about 314 B.C. Abderahman I., caliph of Spain, founded academies about A.D. 773. Theodosius the Younger, Charlemagne, and Alfred are also named as founders of academies. Italy is celebrated for its academies; and Jarckius mentions 550, of which 25 were in Milan. In 1874 Girolamo Ponti, of Milan, bequeathed about 35,000*l.* to the academies of science of London, Paris, and Vienna. Many of the following dates are doubtful.

PRINCIPAL ACADEMIES.

American Academy of Sciences, Boston, 1780.
American Acad. of Nat. Science, Philadelphia, 1812.
Amsterdam, of Sciences, 1808.
Ancona, of the *Caliginosi*, 1642.
Basil, 1460.
Berlin; Royal, of Arts, 1696; of Princes, 1703; Architecture, 1799; Sciences, 1800.
Bologna, Ecclesiastical, 1687; Mathematics, 1690; Sciences and Arts, 1712.
Brescia, of the *Erranti*, 1626.
Brest and Toulon, Military, 1682.
British, Historical, Philosophical, Philological, 1902.
Brussels, *Belles Lettres*, 1773.
Budapest, of Sciences, 1825.
Caen, *Belles Lettres*, 1705.
Christiania, 1837.
Copenhagen, of Sciences, 1743.
Cortona, Antiquities, 1726.
Dublin, Arts, 1742; Painting, Sculpture, &c., 1823.
Erfurt, Saxony, Sciences, 1754.
Faenza, the *Philoponi*, 1612.
Florence, *Belles Lettres*, 1272; *Della Crusca* (now united with the *Florentine*, and merged under that name), 1582; *Del Cimento*, 1657 (by cardinal de' Medici); Antiquities, 1807.
Geneva, Medical, 1715.
Genoa, Painting, &c., 1751; Sciences, 1783.
Germany, *Naturæ Curiosi*, now *Leopoldine*, 1662.
Göttingen, 1734-7.
Haarlem, the Sciences, 1760.
Irish Academy, Royal, Dublin, 1782.
Leipzig, of Sciences, 1846.
Lisbon, History, 1720; Sciences, 1779.
London; see *London* and *Societies*. Royal Academy of Fine Arts, 1768; of Music, 1734-43 and 1822.

* Cicero termed his villa "Academia," and here composed his "Academic Questions."

Lyons, Sciences, 1710; Physic and Mathematics added, 1758.
Madrid, the Royal Spanish, 1713; History, 1738; Painting and the Arts, 1753; Mathematics and Natural Science, 1847.
Manheim, Sciences, 1755; Sculpture, 1775.
Mantua, the *Vigilanti*, Sciences, 1704.
Marseilles, *Belles Lettres*, 1726.
Massachusetts, Arts and Sciences, 1780.
Milan, Architecture, 1380; Sciences, 1719.
Munich, Arts and Sciences, 1759; Sciences, 1779.
Naples, *Rossana*, 1540; Mathematics, 1560; Sciences, 1695; *Herculaneum*, 1755.
New York, Literature and Philosophy, 1814.
Nismes, Royal Academy, 1682.
Padua, for Poetry, 1613; Sciences, 1792.
Palermo, Medical, 1645.
Paris, *Sorbonne*, 1253; Painting, 1391; Music, 1543 and 1671; French (by Richelieu), 1635; Fine Arts, 1648; *Inscriptions et Belles Lettres* (by Colbert), 1663; Sciences (by Colbert), 1666; Architecture, 1671; Surgery, 1731; Military, 1751; Natural Philosophy, 1796, see *Institute*.
Parma, the *Innominati*, 1550.
Perousa, *Insensati*, 1561; *Filigirti*, 1574.
Philadelphia, Arts and Sciences, 1749.
Portsmouth, Naval, 1722; enlarged, 1806.
Rome, *Umoristi*, 1611; *Fantastici*, 1625; *Infecondi*, 1653; Painting, 1656; *Arcadi*, 1656; English, 1752; *Lincei*, about 1600; *Nuovi Lincei*, 1847.
Sandhurst, Military, 1822.
St. Petersburg, Sciences, 1725; Military, 1732; the School of Arts, 1764.
Stockholm, of Science, 1741; *Belles Lettres*, 1753; Agriculture, 1781; Royal Swedish, 1786.
Toulon, Military, 1682.
Turin, Sciences, about 1759 (royal, 1783); Fine Arts, 1778.
Turkey, Military School, 1775.
Upsal, Royal Society, Sciences, 1720.
Venice, Medical, &c., 1701.
Verona, Music, 1543; Sciences, 1780.
Vienna, Sculpture and the Arts, 1705; Surgery, 1783; Oriental, 1810; Royal, 1847.
Warsaw, Languages, and History, 1753.
Washington, U.S., 1863; Smithsonian Inst., 1846, Science.
Woolwich, Military, 1741.

ACADEMY, The, now a weekly journal treating of literary, scientific, and artistic topics, was founded by Mr. John Murray, 9 Oct. 1869, as an organ of learning and advanced criticism. In 1896 it was acquired by Mr. J. M. Richards, who put it on more popular lines, and introduced special features, among these its "Suggested Academy of Letters" in 1897, followed by the "Academy Awards" for literary merit, exchanged in 1900 for liberal awards to amateurs for essays and other compositions. A feature of the *Academy* is its weekly art article by "C. L. H.," the Drama by K. E. Chambers, and Science Notes by C. W. Saleeby. Distinguished writers have contributed to its pages. Edited by Dr. Appleton, 1869–1879; C. E. Doble, 1879–1881; J. S. Cotton, 1881–1896; C. L. Hind, 1896–1903, rev. T. Shore, 1903.

ACADIA, see *Nova Scotia*.

ACANTHUS, the foliage forming the volutes of the Corinthian capital, ascribed to Callimachus, about 540 B.C.

ACAPULCO, Mexico. A Spanish galleon, from Acapulco, laden with gold and precious wares (estimated at above 1,000,000*l.* sterling), taken by commodore Anson, who had previously acquired booty in his voyage amounting to 600,000*l.*, June, 1743. He arrived at Spithead in the *Centurion*, having circumnavigated the globe, 15 June, 1744.

ACARNANIA, N. Greece. The people became prominent in the Peloponnesian war, having invited the help of the Athenians against the Ambracians, 432 B.C. The Acarnanians were subdued by the Lacedæmonians in 390; they took part with Macedon against the Romans in 200, by whom they were defeated in 197, and subjugated in 145.

ACCADIANS, a name now given to the primitive inhabitants of Babylon. They are considered to have been the earliest civilisers of Eastern Asia, and the source of the philosophy and arts of the Assyrians and Phœnicians, and hence of Greece. Their libraries are said to have existed seventeen centuries B.C.

ACCENTS were first introduced in the Greek language by Aristophanes of Byzantium, a grammarian and critic who taught at Alexandria about 264 B.C. Accents were first used by the French in the reign of Louis XIII. (about 1610).

ACCESSION, The, *i.e.*, that of the House of Hanover to the throne of Great Britain, in the person of George I., elector of Hanover, son of Sophia, daughter of Elizabeth, daughter of James I. He succeeded, 1 Aug. 1714, by virtue of the act of settlement passed in the reign of William III., 12 June, 1701, which limited the succession to his mother (as a Protestant) in the event of queen Anne dying without issue. Royal declaration bill modifying the terms of the oath, passed the lords, 5 Aug., dropped by the commons, 8 Aug., 1901. See *Roman Catholics* and *Parliament*.

ACCESSORIES to Crimes. The law respecting them consolidated and amended in 1861.

ACCIDENTS, see under *Coal*, *Fires*, *Railways*, &c. For compensation for accidents, see *Campbell's Acts* and *Passengers*. In 1869, it was computed that, in one year, about 192 persons are killed, and 1200 injured, in the streets of London; 231 were killed in 1875; 237 killed, 3185 injured, 1 Jan. 1878—31 Jan. 1879. 163 killed in 1879; 252 in 1881.

Accident Relief Society, London, established 1836.
Society for Preventing Street Accidents and Dangerous Driving, formed in 1879; met at the Mansion House, London, 30 Jan. 1880; wound up, 1 July, 1881.
The Fatal Accidents Inquiry Bill was read 2nd time by the Commons . . . 25 April, 1895

ACCIDENTAL DEATHS IN ENGLAND AND WALES.

1856,	9716	1867,	11,172	1878,	12,108	1888,	11,556
1857,	8930	1868,	11,033	1879,	10,787	1889,	10,513
1858,	8947	1869,	10,725	1880,	10,807	1890,	11,322
1859,	9241	1870,	10,906	1881,	11,404	1891,	11,467
1860,	9225	1871,	11,316	1882,	11,269	1892,	11,265
1861,	9213	1872,	11,435	1883,	11,539	1893,	11,664
1862,	9005	1873,	11,284	1884,	11,549	1895,	11,977
1863,	9952	1874,	11,783	1885,	11,149	1899,	14,964
1864,	10,997	1875,	12,254	1886,	11,003	1900,	14,707
1865,	11,397	1876,	11,681	1887,	11,983	1901,	14,001
1866,	11,262	1877,	11,194				

ACCLIMATISATION of Animals. This has been prosecuted with great vigour since the establishment of the Zoological society of London in 1829, and of the Société d'Acclimatation in Paris. Numbers of European animals have been naturalised in Australia; the camel has been conveyed to Brazil (1859); alpacas are bred at Paris; and ostriches in Italy (1859). On 6 Oct. 1860, the Bois de Boulogne, near Paris, was opened as a zoological garden, containing only acclimatised animals. An acclimatising garden was established at Melbourne, Australia, in Feb. 1861, and efforts made to naturalise English birds, fishes, &c. See *Fish* and *Climate*.

ACCOLADE.—The embrace (*ad collum*) or slight blow on the neck or cheek when a neophyte was received into an order of knighthood. The custom is of great antiquity. Later, as at present, the flat of a sword was laid on the neck of the kneeling candidate. See *Knights*.

ACCOLTELLATORI (gladiators), secret assassins, at Ravenna and other places in Italy, 1874.

ACCORDION, a small free-reed wind-instrument with keys, invented at Vienna by Damian about 1829, and soon after introduced into England.

ACCOUNTANT-GENERAL IN CHANCERY, &c., an office instituted in 1726, and abolished by an act passed 6 Aug. 1872. In 1841, the office of accountant-general of the court of exchequer was abolished, and the duties transferred to the accountant in chancery.

ACCOUNTANTS' INSTITUTE, established at a meeting, 30 July, 1870; the Accountants' Society in 1872. Five societies were incorporated as "The Chartered Institute of Accountants of England and Wales," in 1880.

ACCUSERS. By occult writers, such as Agrippa, accusers are the eighth order of devils, whose chief is called Asteroth, or Spy. In *Revelation*, ch. xii. 10, the devil is called "the accuser of the brethren."—*False accusers* were to be hanged, by 24 Henry VI. 1446; and burnt in the face with an F, by 37 Henry VIII. 1545. *Stow*.

ACEPHALI (Greek *a*, no; *cephalē*, head), a term applied to certain sects who resisted their bishops and met privately, about 450; and also in canon law applied to such bishops, clerks, monks, &c., as claim or enjoy independence of the jurisdiction of the ordinary or metropolitan.

ACETYLENE, a luminous hydrocarbon gas resembling coal gas, discovered by Berthelot. In 1862 Wohler discovered that carbide of calcium treated with water produced lime and acetylene. In 1895 acetylene was cheaply produced on a commercial scale; it has since come into use for general lighting. A committee on acetylene generators reported to parliament, 1902.

ACHÆMENIDŒ, a dynasty of Persian kings of which Cyrus the Great was the founder. It was overthrown by Alexander the Great.

ACHAIA (N. Peloponnesus), Greece, settled by the Achæi, reputed descendants of Achæus, the son of Xuthus. The kingdom was united with Sicyon or subject to the Ætolians until about 284 B.C. The Achæi originally inhabited the neighbourhood of Argos; but when the Heraclidæ drove them thence, they retired among the Ionians, expelled the natives, and seized their thirteen cities, viz. Pellene, Ægira, Ægium, Bura, Tritæa, Leontium, Rhypes, Cerynea, Olenos, Helice, Patræ, Dyme, and Pharæ, forming the ACHÆAN LEAGUE.

Achaia invaded by Epaminondas . . . . B.C. 366
The ACHÆAN LEAGUE revived by four cities about 280, and by others 275, 274
Aratus made prætor 245
The league joined by Corinth (captured 243), Megara, &c. . . . . 242—228
Supported by Athens and Antigonus Doson . . 229
The Achæans defeated at Ladocea, by the Spartans, under Cleomenes III., 226; totally defeat them at Sellasia 221
The Social war begun; battle of Caphyæ in Arcadia; Aratus defeated 220
The Peloponnesus ravaged by the Ætolians . . 219
Peace of Naupactus 217
Aratus poisoned at Ægium 213
Philopœmen, leader of the league, defeats the Spartan tyrant Machanidas 208
Alliance of the league with the Romans . . 198
Philopœmen defeated by Nabis in a naval battle . 194
All the Peloponnesus joins the league . . 191
War with Messene: Philopœmen made prisoner and slain 183
The Achæans overrun Messenia with fire and sword 182
The Romans enter Achaia, and carry off numbers, including Polybius the historian 165
War with Rome, 150; Metellus enters Greece . . . 147
The Achæans defeated by Mummius at Leucopetra, 147; the league dissolved; Corinth taken; Greece subjected to Rome, and named the province of Achaia 146
Achaia made a Latin principality by William of Champlitte . . . . . . A.D. 1205
Obtained by Geoffrey Villehardouin, 1210; by Geoffrey II. 1218
By his brother William, 1246; who conquers the Moors, 1248; makes war with the emperor Michael, 1259; and gains three fortresses . . . 1262
Succeeded by Isabella, 1277; who marries Florenz of Hainault 1291
Their daughter Maud, princess, 1311; thrice married; forcibly married to John de Gravina, and dies in prison 1324
Achaia, a fief of Naples . . . . . 1246—1430
Conquered by the Turks . . . . . about 1540

ACHEEN, capital of a kingdom N.W. of Sumatra, was visited by the Portuguese about 1509. Factories were set up here by the Dutch, 1596; by the English, 1602; by the French, 1621. For the war with the Dutch, see *Sumatra*.

The *Nisero* of Sunderland, with sugar from Sourabaya, stranded on territory of the chief of Pangah, a Malay dependent of Tuku Imam Muda, the rajah of Tenom, subject to the sultan of Acheen, 16 Nov. 1883.
18 British and 6 foreign sailors made prisoners; the captain released to negotiate; efforts to obtain their release, by warlike attacks and proffered ransom, ineffectual; the Dutch storm Tenom, but prisoners carried off, 7 Jan. 1884.
H.M.S. *Pegasus* sent there. The rajah demands free trade, and desires subjection to Great Britain. Earl Granville recommends conciliation to the Dutch government, announced May, 1884. See under *Mansion House*.
Eighteen prisoners released 11 Sept., arrived in the Thames, 26 Oct. 1884.
The natives attacking the Dutch garrison defeated; 160 killed, reported 15 May; another engagement, in which the Dutch lose 19 killed, reported 2 Aug. 1889.
The Dutch repulsed at Benting, near Edi, 14 May, 1890; successful in conflicts about 11–13 June. War continues, reported 1891–4. End of hostilities, reported, 2 April, 1894.
Fresh conflicts reported, 8 Mar.; victory of the Dutch reported 23 July, 1896. See *Holland*, 1896–7.

ACHONRY, SLIGO (N. Ireland), a bishopric founded by St. Finian, who erected the church of Achad, or Achonry, about 520, and conferred it on his disciple Nathy (Dathy, or David), the first bishop. The see, held with Killala since 1612, was united with Tuam in 1834.

ACHROMATIC TELESCOPES, in which colour is got rid of, were invented by John Dollond, and described in *Phil. Trans.* of the Royal Society, London, 1753-8.

ACIDS (now defined as salts of hydrogen) are generally soluble in water, redden organic blues, decompose carbonates, and destroy the properties of alkalies, forming alkaline salts. The number of acids was increased by the Arabs; Geber (8th century) knew nitric acid and sulphuric acid. Theories of the constitution of acids were put forth by Becher (1669), Lemery (1675), and Stahl (1723). After the discovery of oxygen by Priestley, 1 Aug. 1774, Lavoisier (1778) concluded that oxygen was a constituent of all acids; but about 1810 Davy, Gay-Lussac, and others, proved the existence of acids free from oxygen. In 1816 Dulong proposed the binary or hydrogen theory of acids, and in 1837 Liebig applied the theories of Davy and Dulong to explain the constitution of several organic acids. Oxygen acids were termed anhydrides by Gerhardt (died 1856). Many acids have been discovered through the advance of organic chemistry.

ACOLYTES, an inferior order of clergy in the Latin church, unknown to the Greek church for four hundred years after Christ.

ACOUSTICS (from *akouō*, Greek, I hear), the science of sound, so named by Sauveur in the 17th century. The formation of sound in the air by the vibrations of the atmosphere, strings, &c., was explained by Pythagoras about 500 B.C., and by Aristotle, 330 B.C. See *Telephone*, *Microphone*, *Megaphone*.

The speaking trumpet said to have been used by Alexander the Great, 335 B.C.
Galileo's discoveries, about A.D. 1600.
His theorem of the harmonic curve demonstrated by Dr. Brook Taylor, in 1714; further perfected by D'Alembert, Euler, Bernouilli, and La Grange, at various periods of the eighteenth century.
Hooke calculated the vibration of sounds by the striking of the teeth of brass wheels, 1681.
Sauveur determined the number of vibrations belonging to a given note, about 1700.
Velocity of sound said to be 1473 feet in a second, by Gassendi; 1172 feet by Cassini, Römer, and others; 968 feet by Newton; 1090 feet, at the temperature of 32° Fahrenheit, by Tyndall; the velocity increases with the rise of temperature.
Chladni (who raised acoustics to an independent science) published his important discoveries on the figures produced in layers of sand by harmonic chords, &c., in 1787, and since.
Cagniard-Latour invented the *Sirène* (*which see*), 1819.
Savart determined the range of the perception of the human ear to be from 7 to 24,000 vibrations a second, 1830.
Biot, Savart, Wheatstone, Lissajous, Helmholtz, Tyndall, lord Rayleigh, and others in the 19th century have greatly increased our knowledge of acoustics.
Over-tones, harmonics, well investigated by Helmholtz; under-tones by Auerbach, 1878.
Tyndall's experiments off the South Foreland on fog-signals and gun-cotton, demonstrated that the transmission of sound is checked by the non-homogeneity of the air, independently of fog and rain, July, 1873.
The results of Tyndall's experiments showed that the parabolic-muzzle gun with gun-cotton, and that of sir Richard Collinson's gun-cotton rocket, are very effective fog-signals. Fine-grain gunpowder with howitzers is the best sound-producer; pebble powder the worst, 1874-7.
Sound produced by electricity, light, and from radiant heat, see *Telephone* and *Photophone*, 1881.
Mr. A. Stroh exhibits the attraction and repulsion (resembling magnetic) produced by sonorous vibrations in tubes to the Telegraph Engineers, 27 April, 1882.

ACRE, a land measure, formerly of uncertain quantity, and differing in various parts of the country, was reduced to a standard by Edward I., about 1305. In 1824 the standard acre was ordered by statute to contain 4840 square yards.

ACRE, Acca, anciently Ptolemais, in Syria, was taken by the Saracens in 638; by the crusaders under Baldwin I. in 1104; by Saladin in 1187; and again by Richard I. and other crusaders, 12 July, 1191, after a siege of 2 years, with a loss of 6 archbishops, 12 bishops, 40 earls, 500 barons, and 300,000 soldiers. It was then named *St. Jean d'Acre*. It was retaken by the Saracens in 1291, when 60,000 Christians perished, and the nuns, who had mangled their faces, were put to death. Acre was gallantly defended by Djezzar Pacha against Bonaparte, till relieved by sir Sidney Smith, who resisted twelve attempts by the French, between 16 March and 20 May, 1799, when Bonaparte retreated. Acre, as a Turkish pachalic, was seized 27 May, 1832, by Ibrahim Pacha, who had revolted. On 3 Nov. 1840, it was stormed by the allied fleet under sir Robert Stopford, and taken after a bombardment of a few hours, the Egyptians losing upwards of 2000 in killed and wounded, and 3000 prisoners, while the British had but 12 killed and 42 wounded; see *Syria* and *Turkey*.

ACROBAT, from the Greek *akron*, extremity, *baino*, I go, a person who does difficult feats in tumbling, vaulting, trapezing, rope walking, &c. Among the more noted performers during the 19th century were Farioso, Mme. Saqui, Diavolo, Risley, Leotard (the first to do the flying trapeze), Onri, Niblo (the originator of the double somersault from the trapeze), Lulu and C. Elliot, Chantrell, and Matthews families, De la Vanti, and J. W. Cragg and family, still performing. Blondin (Jean François Gravelet), a noted acrobat, crossed the Falls of Niagara in 1859 and 1860 (see *Niagara*) on the tight-rope, and performed similar feats at the Crystal Palace 1861–2; his last performance was at Belfast in 1896. He died 22 Feb. 1897.

ACROPOLIS, the ancient citadel of Athens, built on a rock. Near it stood the temple of Minerva, the Parthenon, *which see*. Other cities had similar fortresses.

ACROSTIC, a poem in which the first or last letters of each line, read downwards, form a word or sentence, is said to have been invented by Porphyrius Optalianus in the 4th century. Double acrostics became very popular in 1867.

ACS or **ACZ** (Hungary). The Hungarians under Görgey were defeated here by the Austrians and Russians, on 2 and 10 July, 1849.

ACT OF SETTLEMENT, &c.; see *Accession*, *Succession*, *Supremacy*, and *Uniformity Acts*.

The Act of Settlement passed in 1662, which secured to various persons the possession of forfeited estates of Irish rebels, was repealed by acclamation by the Parliament summoned by James II. in May, 1689, and much confiscation of the property of Protestants ensued. The act was restored by William III., 1690.

ACTA DIURNA; see *Newspapers*.

ACTA SANCTORUM ("acts of the saints"), a work begun by the Jesuits. The first volume appeared in 1643: the publication was interrupted in 1794, when 54 volumes, bringing the work down to 15 October, had been published. The work was resumed by the Jesuits in 1837, and 6 more volumes had been published in 1867. The writers have been named *Bollandists*, from John Bolland, who published the first two volumes.

ACTINOMETER, an instrument to measure the heating power of the solar rays, invented by sir John F. Herschel, and described by him in 1825. Others have since been invented. See *Sun*.

ACTIUM, a promontory of Acarnania, W. Greece, near which was fought, 2 Sept. 31 B.C., the battle between the fleet of Octavius Cæsar, and that of Marc Antony and Cleopatra, which decided the fate of Antony; 300 of his galleys going over to Cæsar. This victory made Octavius master of the world and the Roman empire is commonly dated 1 Jan. 30 B.C. (the *Actian Era*). The conqueror built Nicopolis (the city of victory), and instituted the Actian games.

ACTON BURNEL, or Shrewsbury. At the parliament held here by Edward I., Oct. 1283, the "statute of merchants" against debtors was enacted.

ACTONIAN PRIZE, see under *Royal Institution*.

ACTRESSES appear to have been unknown to the ancients in the earliest times, men or eunuchs performing the female parts. They appeared under the Roman empire. Mrs. Colman was the first English public actress; she performed the part of *Ianthe* in Davenant's "Siege of Rhodes," in 1656.

ACTS OF THE APOSTLES, supposed to have been written by Luke in continuation of his Gospel. It terminates A.D. 63.

ACTS OF PARLIAMENT, OR STATUTES, see *Parliament* and *Statutes*. The following are among the most celebrated early statutes:—

Provisions of Merton, 1235-6.
Statute of Marlborough, 1267.
,, of Bigamy, 1275-6.
,, of Gloucester, the earliest statute of which any record exists, 6 Edw. I. 1278.
,, of Mortmain, 1279.
Quo Warranto, Oct. 1280.
Statute of Merchants or Acton-Burnel, 1283.
Statutes of Wales, 1284.
,, of Winchester, Oct. 1284.
,, of Westminster, 1275, 1285, 1290.
Statute forbidding the levying of taxes without the consent of parliament, 1297.
,, of Præmunire, 1306.
Statutes first printed in the reign of Richard III., 1483.
Statutes of the Realm, from Magna Charta to George I., printed from the original records and MSS. in 12 vols. folio, under the direction of commissioners appointed in 1801, 1811-28.
The statutes passed during each session were formerly printed annually in 4to and 8vo, now in 8vo only. Abstracts are given in the *Cabinet Lawyer*.
Between 1823 and 1829, 1126 acts were wholly repealed, and 443 repealed in part, chiefly arising out of the consolidation of the laws by Mr. (afterwards sir Robert) Peel; of these acts, 1344 related to the kingdom at large, and 225 to Ireland solely; and in 1856 many obsolete statutes (enacted between 1285 and 1777) were repealed.
By the Statute Law Revision Act of 1861, 770 acts were wholly repealed, and a great many partially. By similar acts since passed, a great number of enactments have been repealed, commencing with the Provisions of Merton, 20 Henry III. (1235-6), and ending 1844.
"Acts of parliament abbreviation bill" introduced by lord Brougham 12 Feb., passed 10 June, 1850.
The Interpretation Act passed, 30 Aug. 1889.
1410 acts (passed between 1689 and 1770) partially or wholly repealed, 1867.
"Chronological Table and Index to the Statutes to the end of 1869," published 1870. Ninth Edition (1235-1883), published 1884.
Publication of the revised edition of the statutes (1325-1878); 18 volumes published, 1870-85.
Report of select committee on acts of parliament, published July, 1875.
New edition of the revised statutes proposed 1888, see *Statutes*.
Short Titles Act passed, 20 May, 1892.
Agitation for improvement in private bills system, 1897.
The greatest number of acts passed in any one year since 1800 was 570, in 1846 (the railway year); 402 were local and personal, 51 private, and 117 public acts. In 1841, only 13 were passed (the lowest number), of which two were private. The average number of the first ten years of the 19th century was 132 public acts. In the ten years ending 1850, the average number of acts, of public interest, was 112.
The number of *public general acts* passed in 1851 was 106; in 1852, 88; in 1853, 137; in 1854, 125; in 1855, 134; in 1856, 120; in 1857, 86; in 1858, 109; in 1859, 101; in 1860, 154; in 1861, 134; in 1862, 114; in 1863, 125; in 1864, 121; in 1865, 127; in 1866, 122; in 1867, 146; in 1868, 130; in 1869, 117; in 1870, 112; in 1871, 117; in 1872, 98; in 1873, 91; in 1874, 96; in 1875, 96; in 1876, 81; in 1877, 69; in 1878, 79; in 1879, 78; in 1880, 19 and 48 (new parliament); 1881, 72; 1882, 82; 1883, 62; 1884, 78; 1885, 80; 1886 (1st sess.), 59; 1887, 73; 1888, 66; 1889, 76; 1890, 72; 1891, 76; 1892, 65; 1893, 73; 1894, 60; 1895, 44; 1896, 59; 1897, 67; 1898, 62; 1899, 51; 1900, 63; 1901, 40; 1902, 42.
Acts in operation: 75 vols. had been replaced by 5 vols., reported; Dec. 1892.

ACTS, in dramatic poetry, first employed by the Romans. *Five* acts are mentioned by Horace (Art of Poetry) as the rule (about 8 B.C.).

ACTUARY, ACTUARIUS, the Roman accountant. The Institute of Actuaries, founded in 1848, publishes its proceedings in the "Assurance Magazine." International congress, London, 16 May, 1898.

ADAM AND EVE, ERA OF, in the English Bible, 4004 B.C.; see *Creation*.

ADAMITES, a Gnostic sect in Africa about 130, who appeared quite naked in their religious assemblies, asserting that if Adam had not sinned there would have been no marriages. Their chief was named Prodicus; they defied the elements, rejected prayer, and said it was not necessary to confess Christ. *Eusebius*. A sect with this name arose at Antwerp in the 12th century, under Tandemus or Tanchelin, whose followers, 3000 soldiers and others, committed many crimes. It became extinct soon after the death of its chief; but another of the same kind, named Turlupins, appeared shortly after in Savoy and Dauphiny. Picard, a Fleming, revived this sect in Bohemia, about 1415; it was suppressed by Ziska, 1420.

ADDA, a river N. Italy, passed by Suwarrow after defeating the French, 27 April, 1799.

ADDINGTON ADMINISTRATION. Mr. Pitt, having engaged to procure Roman Catholic emancipation to promote the union with Ireland, and being unable to do so *as a minister*, resigned 3 Feb. 1801. A new ministry was formed by Mr. Addington, March-July, 1801; after various changes it terminated about 10 May, 1804.

Henry Addington,* *first lord of the treasury and chancellor of the exchequer.*
Lord Eldon, *lord chancellor.*
Duke of Portland, *lord president.*
Earl of Westmoreland, *lord privy seal.*
Lord Pelham, *home secretary.*
Mr. R. B. Jenkinson (lord Hawkesbury, 1803; and earl of Liverpool, 1808), *foreign secretary.*
Lord Hobart, *colonial secretary.*
Earl St. Vincent, *first lord of admiralty.*
Earl of Chatham, *ordnance.*
Charles Yorke, *secretary-at-war.*
Viscount Lewisham, lord Auckland, &c.

ADDISCOMBE COLLEGE, near Croydon, Surrey, purchased by the East India company in 1809, for education of candidates for scientific branches of the Indian army, was closed in 1861; here were educated, Henry Lawrence, Eldred Pottinger, Arthur Cotton, Proby Cautley, Robert Napier, Henry Durand, John Jacob, and others, including F.M. earl Roberts of Candahar and Pretoria.

ADDISON'S DISEASE, a dangerous affection of the renal capsules, described by its discoverer, Dr. Thomas Addison, in 1855.

ADDITIONAL CURATES, the society for their employment in populous places was founded 1837. Income, 1902, 68, 300*l*.

ADDLED PARLIAMENT, see *Parliament*, 1614.

ADDRESSERS, see *Abhorrers*.

* Born 1757; became viscount Sidmouth, Jan. 1805; held various offices afterwards, and died in 1844. His *circular* to the lords-lieutenants, dated 27 March, 1817, directing them to adopt severe measures against the authors of blasphemous and seditious pamphlets, was greatly censured, and not carried into effect.

ADELAIDE, the capital of South Australia, was founded in 1836. Population, 14,000 in 1850; about 30,000 in 1875; 1891, 133,220; 1901, 160,691. It was made a bishopric in 1847. It was visited by the duke of Edinburgh, 1 March, 1869, and by the duke of Cornwall and York (prince of Wales) 8-15 July, 1901. University founded, 1876; 20,000*l.* given by sir Thos. Elder, who died 7 March, 1897; he bequeathed 155,000*l.* for public objects in Adelaide, including 65,000*l.* for the university, 25,000*l.* for a picture gallery, and 25,000*l.* for workmen's homes, ann., 10 March, 1897.

The Queen's Jubilee International Exhibition opened, 21 June, 1887; reported successful, 17 Jan. 1888.
Mr. Martin bequeaths 170,000*l.* to charities, July, 1898.
Adelaide time advanced ½ hr. in accordance with the standard time act, midnight, April 30, 1899.

ADELPHI (Greek for brothers) several streets on the south side of the Strand, London, erected about 1768 by the brothers, John, Robert, James, and William Adam, after whom the streets are named. ADELPHI THEATRE, built 1806, rebuilt 1858; see under *Theatres.*

ADEN. Known to the Romans as Arabia Felix and Attaux, taken by them 24 B.C. Taken by the Turks from the Portuguese, 1538. From 1730 it was governed by an independent sultan. In Dec. 1836 a British ship was wrecked and plundered. The sultan promised compensation, and agreed to cede the place to the English. The sultan's son refusing to fulfil this agreement to captain Haynes, a naval and military force, under captain H. Smith, of the *Volage*, was dispatched to Aden, which captured it, 19 Jan. 1839. It is now a garrison and coal depôt for Indian steamers, &c. *Aden*, steamer, see *Wrecks*, 9 June, 1897. Population in 1901, 41,222.

Protocol fixing the boundaries of the Italian and British influence, signed, 5 May, 1894. See *Somaliland.*
The duke and duchess of Cornwall received here, 5 April, 1901.
British expedition from Aden destroys a Turkish fort erected at Ad Dareja, within the British sphere, after hard fighting, 26, 27 July, 1901. Boundary of Hinterland agreed to, Turkish troops withdrawn, 18 Mar. 1903.
100 men of 1st Hants. regt. and 100 men of 23rd Bombay inf. forming escort into Shaibi, treacherously fired on by Arabs, 10 Sept. 1903.

ADIAPHORISTS (from *adiaphora*, indifferent things), a term applied to Melanchthon and others, who were willing to give up certain things to the Romanists as indifferent, about 1548.

ADIGE, a river in N. Italy, near which the Austrians defeated the French on 26, 30 March, and 5 April, 1799.

ADJUTATORS, see *Agitators.*

ADMINISTRATIONS OF ENGLAND AND OF GREAT BRITAIN. Until the Restoration, 1660, there was not any cabinet approaching to the modern sense. The sovereign was aided by privy councillors, varying in number, the men and offices being frequently changed. The separation of the cabinet from the privy council became greater during the reign of William III. His ministers included both Whigs and Tories, and their dissensions led to much maladministration, civil, military, and naval, and consequent popular discontent; the king was therefore compelled to have a united ministry, at first wholly composed of Whigs. The change was gradually effected, 1694-6. The control of the chief, now termed the "*premier*," began in the reign of Anne. "The era of ministries may most properly be reckoned from the day of the meeting of the parliament after the general election of 1698." *Macaulay.** For a fuller account of each administration, since 1700, see separate articles headed with the name of the PREMIER, *given below in italics.*

HENRY VIII.—Abp. Warham; bps. Fisher and Fox; earl of Surrey, &c. . . . . . A.D. 1509
Cardinal Thomas Wolsey, &c. 1514
Earl of Surrey; Tunstall, bishop of London, &c. . 1523
Sir Thos. More; bps. Tunstall and Gardiner, and Cranmer (afterwards abp. of Canterbury) . . 1529
Abp. Cranmer; lord Cromwell, aft. earl of Essex; Thos. Boleyn, earl of Wiltshire, &c. . . . 1532
Thomas, duke of Norfolk; Henry, earl of Surrey; Thomas, lord Audley; bishop Gardiner; sir Ralph Sadler, &c. 1540
Lord Wriothesley; Thomas, duke of Norfolk; lord Lisle; sir William Petre; sir William Paget, &c. 1544
EDWARD VI. — Lord Wriothesley, now earl of Southampton, lord chancellor (expelled); Edward, earl of Hertford, lord protector, created duke of Somerset; John, lord Russell; Henry, earl of Arundel; Thomas, lord Seymour; sir Wm. Paget; sir Wm. Petre, &c 1547
John Dudley, late lord Lisle and earl of Warwick, created duke of Northumberland; John, earl of Bedford; bishop Goodrich, sir William Cecil, &c. 1551
MARY.—Stephen Gardiner, bp. of Winchester; Edmund Bonner, bp. of London; William, marq. of Winchester; sir Edwd. Hastings, &c. . . 1554
ELIZABETH.—Sir Nicholas Bacon; Edward lord Clinton; sir Robert Dudley, aftds. earl of Leicester; sir William Cecil, aftds. lord Burleigh . 1558
William, lord Burleigh (minister during nearly all the reign); sir N. Bacon, &c. 1572
Lord Burleigh; sir Thomas Bromley; Robert Devereux, earl of Essex (a favourite); earl of Leicester; earl of Lincoln; sir Walter Mildmay; sir Francis Walsingham, &c. 1579
Lord Burleigh; Robert, earl of Essex; sir Christopher Hatton, &c. 1587
Thomas Sackville, lord Buckhurst, afterwards earl of Dorset; sir Thomas Egerton, afterwards lord Ellesmere and viscount Brackley; sir Robert Cecil, &c. 1599
JAMES I.—Thomas, earl of Dorset; Thomas, lord Ellesmere; Charles, earl of Nottingham; Thomas, earl of Suffolk; Edward, earl of Worcester; Robert Cecil, afterwards earl of Salisbury, &c. 1603
Robert Cecil, earl of Salisbury; Thomas, lord Ellesmere; Henry, earl of Northampton; Charles, earl of Nottingham; Thomas, earl of Suffolk, &c. 1609
Henry, earl of Northampton; Thomas, lord Ellesmere; Edward, earl of Worcester; sir Ralph Winwood; Charles, earl of Nottingham; Robert, viscount Rochester, aftds. earl of Somerset, &c. 1612
Thomas, lord Ellesmere; Thomas, earl of Suffolk; Charles, earl of Nottingham; sir George Villiers (a favourite), afterwards viscount Villiers, and successively earl, marquis, and duke of Buckingham 1615
Sir Henry Montagu, afterwards viscount Mandeville and earl of Manchester 1620

* Till 1850 the cabinet council usually consisted of the following twelve members: First lord of the treasury; lord chancellor; lord president of the council; chancellor of the exchequer; lord privy seal; home, foreign, and colonial secretaries; first lord of the admiralty; president of the board of trade; president of the board of control; chancellor of the duchy of Lancaster. In 1850 the number was *fifteen*, and included the secretary-at-war, the postmaster-general, and the chief secretary for Ireland. In the Palmerston-Russell cabinet (*which see*), the president of the poor-law-board replaced the secretary for Ireland. In 1868 the Gladstone cabinet consisted of 15; that of Mr. Disraeli, in Feb. 1874, of 12. The *average duration* of a ministry has been set down at four, five, and six years; but instances have occurred of the duration of a ministry for much longer periods: sir Robert Walpole was minister from 1721 to 1742 (21 years); Mr. Pitt, 1783 to 1801 (18 years); and lord Liverpool, 1812 to 1827 (15 years). Several ministries have not lasted beyond a few months, as the *Coalition Ministry* in 1783, and the "*Talents*" Ministry in 1806. The "*Short-lived*" Administration lasted 10 to 12 Feb. 1746.

Lionel, lord Cranfield, afterwards earl of Middlesex; Edward, earl of Worcester; John, earl of Bristol; John Williams, dean of Westminster; George Villiers, now marquis of Buckingham; sir Edward Conway, &c. 1621

CHARLES I.—Richard, lord Weston, afterwards earl of Portland; sir Thomas Coventry, afterwards lord Coventry; Henry, earl of Manchester (succeeded by James, earl of Marlborough, who, in turn, gave place to Edward, lord, afterwards viscount, Conway); William Laud, bp. of London; sir Albert Morton, &c. . . . 1628

William Laud, now archbishop of Canterbury; Francis, lord Cottington; James, marquis of Hamilton; Edward, earl of Dorset; sir John Coke; sir Francis Windebank, &c. . . . 1635

William Juxon, bishop of London; sir John Finch, afterwards lord Finch; Francis, lord Cottington; Wentworth, earl of Strafford; Algernon, earl of Northumberland; James, marquis of Hamilton; Laud, archbishop of Canterbury; sir Francis Windebank; sir Henry Vane, &c. . . . 1640

[The king beheaded, 30 Jan. 1649.]

COMMONWEALTH. — Oliver Cromwell, protector, named a council, the number not to exceed 21 members, or be less than 13 1653

Richard Cromwell, son of Oliver, succeeded on the death of his father. A council of officers ruled at Wallingford house 1658

CHARLES II.—Sir Edward Hyde, afterwards earl of Clarendon; George Monk, created duke of Albemarle; Edward Montagu, created earl of Sandwich; lord Saye and Sele; earl of Manchester; lord Seymour; sir Robert Long, &c. . . . 1660

George Monk, duke of Albemarle, made first commissioner of the treasury, &c. 1667

"*Cabal*" Ministry; Clifford, Ashley, Buckingham, Arlington, Lauderdale (see *Cabal*) . . . 1670

Thomas, lord Clifford; Anthony, earl of Shaftesbury; Henry, earl of Arlington; Arthur, earl of Anglesey; sir Thomas Osborne, created viscount Latimer; Henry Coventry; sir George Carteret; Edward Seymour, &c. 1672

Thomas, viscount Latimer, afterwards earl of Danby, made lord high treasurer . . . . 26 June, 1673

Arthur, earl of Essex (succeeded by Lawrence Hyde, aft. earl of Rochester); Robert, earl of Sunderland, &c. 1679

[The king nominated a new council on 21 April, consisting of 30 members only, of whom the principal were the great officers of state and great officers of the household.]

Sidney, lord Godolphin; Lawrence, earl of Rochester; Daniel, earl of Nottingham; Robert, earl of Sunderland; sir Thomas Chicheley; George, lord Dartmouth; Henry, earl of Clarendon; earls of Bath and Radnor . . . . ,,

JAMES II.—Lawrence, earl of Rochester; George, marquis of Halifax; sir George Jeffreys, afterwards lord Jeffreys; Henry, earl of Clarendon; sir John Ernley; viscount Preston, &c. . . 1684

The earl of Rochester was displaced, and John, lord Belasyse, made first commissioner of the treasury in his room, 4 Jan.; the earl of Sunderland made president of the council; viscount Preston, secretary of state, &c. 1685

[The king left Whitehall in the night of 11 Dec., and quitting the kingdom, landed at Ambleteuse, in France, Dec. 1688. 1687-8

WILLIAM III. AND MARY.—Charles, viscount Mordaunt; Thomas Osborne, earl of Danby, created marquis of Carmarthen, afterwards duke of Leeds; George, marquis of Halifax; Arthur Herbert, afterwards lord Torrington; earls of Shrewsbury, Nottingham, and Sunderland; earl of Dorset and Middlesex; William, earl (afterwards duke) of Devonshire; lord Godolphin; lord Montagu; lord De la Mere, &c. 1689

Sidney, lord Godolphin; Thomas, earl of Danby; Richard Hampden; Thomas, earl of Pembroke; Henry, viscount Sydney; Daniel, earl of Nottingham, &c. 1690

Sir John Somers became lord Somers in 1697, and lord chancellor; Charles Montagu, afterwards lord Halifax, was made first commissioner of the treasury, 1 May, 1698, succeeded by Ford, earl of Tankerville 1699

ANNE.—Sidney, lord (afterwards earl of) *Godolphin*; Thomas, earl of Pembroke, &c. . . May, 1702

Robert Harley, earl of *Oxford*; sir Simon Harcourt, &c. . . . . 1 June, 1711

Charles, duke of *Shrewsbury*, made lord treasurer three days before the queen's death, &c. 30 July, 1714

GEORGE I.—Charles, earl of *Halifax* (succeeded on his death by the earl of Carlisle), &c. . . . ,,

Robert *Walpole*, first lord of the treasury, and chancellor of the exchequer, &c. 1715

James (afterwards earl) *Stanhope*; William, lord Cowper, &c. 1717

Charles, earl of *Sunderland*, &c. 1718

Robert *Walpole*, afterwards sir Robert Walpole, and earl of Orford, &c. 1721

GEORGE II.—Robert Walpole *continued* . . . 1727

[Sir Robert remained prime minister twenty-one years; numerous changes occurring in the time; see *Walpole*.]

Earl of *Wilmington*; lord Hardwicke, &c. . . 1742

Henry *Pelham*, in the room of earl of Wilmington, deceased . . . . Aug. 1743

"*Broad-bottom*" administration—Henry *Pelham*; lord Hardwicke, &c. . . . . . . Nov. 1744

"*Short-lived*" administration—earl of *Bath*; lords Winchilsea and Granville . . . . 10-12 Feb. 1746

Henry Pelham, &c., again . . . . 12 Feb. 1746

Thos. H. Pelham, duke of *Newcastle*; earl of Holderness, &c. . . . . April, 1754

Duke of *Devonshire*; William Pitt, &c. . . Nov. 1756

Duke of *Newcastle*, and Mr. Pitt, afterwards earl of Chatham, &c. . . . . . . June, 1757

GEORGE III.—Duke of Newcastle, Mr. Pitt's ministry, *continued* 1760

Earl of *Bute*; lord Henley, &c. . . . . May, 1762

George *Grenville*; earls of Halifax and Sandwich, &c. . . . . April, 1763

Marquis of *Rockingham*; earl of Winchilsea, &c. July, 1765

Earl of *Chatham*; duke of Grafton, &c. . Aug. 1766

Duke of *Grafton*; lord North, &c. . . . Dec. 1767

Frederick, lord *North*; earl Gower, &c. . Jan. 1770

[Lord North was minister during the whole of the American war.]

Marquis of *Rockingham*; lord Camden; C. J. Fox; Edmund Burke, &c. . . . . . March, 1782

Earl of *Shelburne* (afterwards marquis of Lansdowne); William Pitt, &c. . . . . July, ,,

"*Coalition Ministry*," duke of *Portland*; lord North; C. J. Fox; Edmund Burke, &c. . . . April, 1783

William *Pitt*; Henry Dundas, &c. . . . Dec. ,,

[During Mr. Pitt's long administration, numerous changes in the ministry took place.]

Henry *Addington*; duke of Portland; lord Eldon, &c. . . . . March *et seq.* 1801

William *Pitt*; lord Eldon; George Canning, &c. May *et seq.* 1804

[Mr. Pitt died 23 Jan. 1806.]

"*All the Talents*"—lord *Grenville*; lord Henry Petty; lord Erskine; C. J. Fox; sir Charles Grey (afterwards earl Grey). . . . . Feb. 1806

[Mr. Fox's death, 13 Sept. 1806, led to numerous changes.]

Duke of *Portland*; lord Eldon, &c.* . . . March, 1807

Spencer *Perceval*; earl of Liverpool; viscount Palmerston, &c. . . . . Nov. and Dec. 1809

REGENCY.—Mr. Spencer *Perceval* (shot by Bellingham, 11 May, 1812), &c. . . . . 5 Feb. 1811

Earl of *Liverpool*; lord Eldon; Mr. Vansittart; lord Melville; viscounts Castlereagh, Palmerston, &c. . . . . May, June, 1812

GEORGE IV.—Earl of *Liverpool*, &c. . . 29 Jan. 1820

[During lord Liverpool's long administration numerous changes occurred.]

George *Canning*; lord Lyndhurst; viscount Goderich; William Huskisson; viscount Palmerston; duke of Clarence, &c. . . . . . April, 1827

[Mr. Canning died 8 August, 1827.]

Viscount *Goderich*; viscount Palmerston; marquis of Lansdowne; W. Huskisson, &c. . . . Aug. ,,

Duke of *Wellington*; Robert Peel; Mr. Huskisson; &c. . . . . Jan. 1828

[The ministry reconstructed on the retirement of the earl of Dudley, lord Palmerston, Mr. Grant, Mr. Huskisson.] . . . . . May and June, ,,

* The duel between lord Castlereagh and Mr. Canning, 22 Sept. 1809, led to the breaking up of this administration.

WILLIAM IV.—Duke of *Wellington*, &c. 26 June, 1830
Earl *Grey*; marquis of Lansdowne; lord Brougham; viscount Althorp; earl of Durham; viscounts Melbourne, Palmerston, and Goderich; sir James Graham; lord John Russell, &c. . . . Nov. ,,
[Earl Grey resigns, owing to a majority against him in the lords, on the Reform Bill, 10 May; but resumes his post, 18 May, 1832.]
Viscount *Melbourne*; &c. . . . . . July, 1834
[Melbourne administration dissolved, Nov. 1834. The duke of Wellington held the seals of office till the return of sir Robert Peel from Italy, Dec. 1834.]
Sir Robert *Peel*; lord Lyndhurst; duke of Wellington; earl of Aberdeen, &c. . Nov. and Dec. ,,
Viscount *Melbourne*, &c. . . . . . April, 1835
VICTORIA.—Viscount *Melbourne*, &c. . 20 June, 1837
Subsequent accessions, F. T. Baring; earl of Clarendon; T. B. Macaulay, &c. Viscount Melbourne resigned, and sir Robert Peel received the queen's commands to form a new administration, 8 May. This command was withdrawn, and lord Melbourne returned to power . . 10 May, 1839
Sir Robert *Peel*; duke of Wellington; lord Lyndhurst; sir James Graham; earl of Aberdeen; lord Stanley, &c. . . . Aug. and Sept. 1841
[Accessions, Sidney Herbert; W. E. Gladstone, &c.]
Lord John *Russell*; viscount Palmerston; earl Grey, &c. . . . . July, 1846
[Accessions: earl Granville; Mr. Fox Maule; earl of Carlisle; sir Thomas Wilde, created lord Truro, &c.]
Lord John Russell and the marquis of Lansdowne on the 24 Feb. announced the resignation of ministers, owing to their defeat on Mr. Locke King's motion respecting the franchise; they informed parliament, that it having been found impossible to construct a coalition ministry, the queen, by the advice of the duke of Wellington, had called upon her late ministers to resume office. Lord Stanley (since earl of Derby), in the interval, had been unable to form a cabinet . 3 March, 1851
Earl of *Derby* (late lord Stanley); lord St. Leonards; Benjamin Disraeli; Spencer H. Walpole; earl of Malmesbury; sir John Pakington; duke of Northumberland, &c. . . . 27 Feb. 1852
Earl of *Aberdeen*; lord John Russell; viscount Palmerston, &c. . . . . . . 28 Dec. ,,
Various changes of offices took place; a fourth secretary of state was appointed, by the separation of the *war* from the *colonial* department; see *Secretaries of State*. The retirement of lord J. Russell, 24 Jan. 1855, and a majority in the commons against ministers of 157 (305 to 148), on Mr. Roebuck's motion respecting the conduct of the war, led to the resignation of lord Aberdeen and his colleagues, 30 Jan.; the cabinet was reconstructed by
Viscount *Palmerston*; lord Cranworth; &c. 7 Feb. 1855
[Secession of sir J. Graham, Mr. Gladstone, and Mr. S. Herbert. Accession of lord John Russell; earl of Clarendon; sir G. Grey; sir G. C. Lewis; sir W. Molesworth, &c., Feb. 24, 1855.]
On the second reading of the Foreign Conspiracy bill, the government (defeated by a vote of censure being passed by a majority of 19, on the motion of Mr. Milner Gibson) resigned immediately . . . . 19 Feb. 1858
Earl of *Derby*; B. Disraeli; Spencer Walpole; lord Stanley; sir F. Thesiger (lord Chelmsford), &c. 26 Feb. ,,
[The Derby administration, in consequence of a vote of want of confidence in it being carried by a majority of 13, 10 June, 1859, resigned the next day. Earl Granville failed to form an administration.]
Viscount *Palmerston*; lord John (since earl) Russell, &c. . . . . 18 June, 1859
[Lord Palmerston died 18 Oct. 1865.]
Earl *Russell*; W. E. Gladstone; earl of Clarendon; &c. . . . . Oct. 1865
[Resigned, in consequence of a minority on the Reform Bill, 19 June, 26 June, 1866.]
Earl of *Derby*, B. Disraeli, lord Stanley, &c.; for changes see *Derby Administrations*. . 6 July, 1866
[Earl of *Derby* resigned through ill-health, Feb. 25, 1868.]
B. *Disraeli* reconstituted the administration 29 Feb. 1868
[Mr. Disraeli resigned in consequence of the elections in November giving a majority of about 114 to the Liberals, 2 Dec. 1868.]
W. E. *Gladstone*; earl of Clarendon; Robert Lowe; John Bright, and others, received seals 9 Dec. 1868
[Lost their majority by the general election, Feb.; resigned, 17 Feb. 1874.]
B. *Disraeli* (earl of Beaconsfield, 16 Aug. 1876), the earl of Derby, the marquis of Salisbury, and others, received seals . . . 21 Feb. 1874
[For changes, see *Disraeli Administrations*.]
[Lost their majority by elections in April; resigned, 22 April, 1880.]
W. E. *Gladstone*; earl Granville, marquis of Hartington, duke of Argyll, sir Wm. Harcourt, John Bright, and others, received seals . 28 April, 1880
[Resigned in consequence of a minority on the Budget Bill (264–252), 9 June, 1885.]
Marquis of *Salisbury*; sir Stafford Northcote (lord Iddesleigh), sir Michael Hicks-Beach, lord Randolph Churchill and others received seals 24 June, 1885
[Resigned in consequence of a minority on the amendment to the address (329–250), 27 Jan. 1886.]
W. E. *Gladstone*; earl Granville, earl Spencer, earl of Rosebery and others . . 2–6 Feb. 1886
[Resigned in consequence of a majority against his Irish Home Rule Bill (343–313) 20 July, 1886.]
Marquis of *Salisbury*; and former colleagues received seals 26 July, 1886; resigns . 12 Aug. 1892
W. E. *Gladstone*; with some of former colleagues, and others, 18 Aug. 1892; resigns . 3 March, 1894
Earl of *Rosebery*, with nearly all Mr. Gladstone's cabinet, 3 March *et seq.*; resigns . 22 June, 1895
Marquis of *Salisbury*; conservatives and unionists, 25–28 June, ,,
Marquis of *Salisbury*; conservatives and unionists, [resigned 11 July, 1902] . . . . . 12 Nov. 1900
A. J. *Balfour*; conservatives and unionists, 12 July, 1902
For details and changes, see separate articles under the Premier's name.

ADMINISTRATIVE REFORM ASSOCIATION derived its origin from an opinion that the disasters which occurred to the army in the Crimea in 1854-5 were attributable to the inefficient and irresponsible management of the various departments of the state. The association was organised in London, 5 May, 1855. A meeting was held in Drury-lane theatre on 13 June, and Mr. Layard's motion on the subject in parliament was negatived 18 June following. The association was reorganised in 1856, Mr. Roebuck, M.P., becoming chairman, but soon became unimportant; see *Civil Service*.

ADMIRAL. The title, derived from the Arabic, emir-al-bahr, "Lord of the sea," which occurs in the *Chanson de Roland*, 11th century, does not appear to have been adopted in England until about 1300. Alfred, Athelstan, Edgar, Harold, and other kings, were commanders of their own fleets. The first French admiral is said to have been appointed 1284. The rank of *admiral of the English seas* was first given to William de Leybourne by Edward I. in 1297. *Spelman; Rymer*. The first LORD HIGH ADMIRAL in England was created by Richard II. in 1385: there had been previously high admirals of *districts*—the north, west, and south. The duties have generally been executed by lords commissioners; see *Admiralty*. A similar dignity existed in *Scotland* from the reign of Robert III. In 1673, Charles II. bestowed it upon his natural son Charles Lennox, afterwards duke of Richmond, then an infant, who resigned the office to the crown in 1703: after the union it was discontinued.—The dignity of lord high admiral of *Ireland* (of brief existence) was conferred upon James Butler by Henry VIII., in May, 1534. The *Admiral of the Fleet* is the highest rank in the Royal Navy, corresponding to that of field-marshal in the army. We have now (Oct. 1903) on the active list 5 admirals of the fleet; senior admiral the hon. sir Henry Keppel, Aug. 1877; sir Fred. W. Richards, Nov. 1898; sir Norvell Salmon, Jan. 1899; Sir Jas. E. Erskine, Oct. 1902; sir Charles F. Hotham, Aug. 1903; the German emperor, *hon.*, Aug. 1889; the king of Portugal, *hon.*, Sept. 1903; 10 admirals, 22 vice-admirals, 41 rear-admirals, 217 captains. The prince of Wales, naval aide-de-camp to the king 21 June, 1887; was made rear-admiral Jan. 1901; vice-admiral 26 June, 1903. Admiral of the fleet, sir Provo Wallis, b. 12 April, 1791, d. 13 Feb. 1892, sir Lewis Tobias Jones, b. 24 Dec., 1797, d. 11 Oct., 1895. Vice-admiral sir Robt. O'Brien Fitzroy, K.C.B., b. 1839, d. 7 May, 1896; sir Alex. Milne, G.C.B., b. 11 Nov. 1806, d. 29 Dec. 1896; sir W. R. Mends, b. 1812, d. 26 June, 1897. Admiral sir W. Hornby, b. 1812 (retired 1892), d. 28 June, 1899; vice-admiral P. H. Colomb, b. 1831, d. 13 Oct. 1899; see *Fog;* the duke of Edinburgh, 1876-1893; d. 30 July, 1900: see *Saxe-Coburg;* sir George Willes, d., aged 77, 18 Feb. 1901; sir George Wellesley, b. 1814, d. 6 April, 1901; sir J. E. Commerell, d., aged 72, 21 May, 1901; sir A. Hoskins, d., aged 73, 21 June, 1901; sir W. H. Stewart, G.C.B., d. 13 Nov. 1901; lord Hood of Avalon, d. 16 Nov., aged 77, 1901; sir G. Elliot, d. 13 Dec., aged 88, 1901; sir Edw. Sotheby, d., aged 88, 6 Jan. 1902; sir Edw. B. Rice, d., aged 83, 30 Oct., 1902; sir J. E. Montgomerie, aged 77, d. 10 Sept. 1902; sir Edw. S. Adeane, d., aged 66, 18 Oct. 1902; Edw. C. T. D'Eyncourt, aged 89, 14 Jan. 1903; Thos. Saumarez, aged 75, d. 22 Jan. 1903; hon. F. A. C. Foley, aged 80, d. 26 July, 1903; R. P. Cator, d. 31 July, 1903; *r.-adm.* A. G. Bogle, d. 15 Aug. 1903; *r.-adm.* hon. Albert Denison S. Denison, aged 68, 2 Sept., 1903; sir Alexander Buller, d., aged 69, 3 Oct. 1903.

ADMIRALTY, COURT OF, a court for the trial of causes relating to maritime affairs, said to have been erected by Edward III., in 1357. It was enacted in the reign of Henry VIII., that criminal causes should be tried by witnesses and a jury, some of the judges at Westminster (or, as now, at the Old Bailey) assisting. The judgeship of the admiralty was constituted in 1514, and was filled by two or more functionaries until the Revolution, when it was restricted to one. *Beatson.* The judge has usually been an eminent doctor of the civil law. In 1844 the criminal jurisdiction of this court was removed, and by 20 & 21 Vict. c. 77 (1857), the judge of the Probate court was to be also judge of the Admiralty court. The judge of the Admiralty court, Dr. Stephen Lushington (appointed in 1838), resigned 1 July, 1867, and was succeeded by sir Robert Phillimore, who retired March, 1883. The jurisdiction of this court was extended in 1861. The very ancient gilt anchor is set up in the Admiralty Court of the Royal Courts of Justice. The ancient silver oar is laid on the Registrar's Table, Oct. 1885. By the acts 1873-5, appeal is now to the Supreme Court of Judicature. See *Supreme Court and Probate Court.*

ADMIRALTY OFFICE dates from 1512, when Henry VIII. appointed commissioners to inspect his ships of war. During the Commonwealth the admiralty affairs were managed by a committee of the parliament; and at the restoration in 1660, James, duke of York, became lord high admiral. In 1662 the admiralty was first put into commission, the great officers of state being the commissioners; see succeeding changes *below.* In 1688-9 the admiralty was put into commission, and the board appears to have assembled at admiral Herbert's lodgings, in Channel-row, Westminster, he being at that time first lord. In 1830, 1832, and 1836 various changes were made in the civil departments, several offices being abolished or consolidated with others. In March, 1861, a royal commission recommended the abolition of the board of admiralty and the appointment of a minister of the navy department. The board was reconstituted 14 Jan. 1869, and 4 May, 1872. The collective action of the board was taken away, and concentrated in the person of the first lord.

The office removed from Somerset House to Whitehall, 1874-5.

New buildings erected by virtue of the Public Offices Site Act passed 24 July, 1882. The designs of Messrs. Leeming & Leeming, of Halifax, selected for approval by parliament, July, 1884.

FIRST LORDS OF THE ADMIRALTY.

1660. JAMES, DUKE OF YORK, *lord high admiral,* 6 June.
1673. KING CHARLES II., 14 June.
,, PRINCE RUPERT, 9 July.
1679. Sir Henry Capel, 14 Feb.
1680. Daniel Finch, esq., 19 Feb.
1681. Daniel, lord Finch, 20 Jan.
1683. Daniel, earl of Nottingham, 17 April.
1684. KING CHARLES II.
1685. KING JAMES II., 17 May. *Office in commission.*
1689. Arthur Herbert, esq., 8 March.
1690. Thomas, earl of Pembroke and Montgomery, 20 Jan.
1692. Charles, lord Cornwallis, 10 March.
1693. Anthony, viscount Falkland, 15 April.
1694. Edward Russel, esq. (aft. earl of Orford), 2 May.
1699. John, earl of Bridgewater, 2 June.
1701. Thomas, earl of Pembroke, 4 April.
1702. GEORGE, PRINCE OF DENMARK, *lord high admiral,* 20 May.
1708. Thomas, earl of Pembroke, *ditto,* 29 Nov. *Office in commission.*
1709. Edward, earl of Orford, 8 Oct.
1710. Sir John Leake, 4 Oct.
1712. Thomas, earl of Strafford, 30 Sept.
1714. Edward, earl of Orford, 14 Oct.
1717. James, earl of Berkeley, 19 March.
1727. George, viscount Torrington, 2 Aug.
1733. Sir Charles Wager, knt., 25 June.
1742. Daniel, earl of Winchilsea, 19 March.
1744. John, duke of Bedford, 27 Dec.
1748. John, earl of Sandwich, 10 Feb.
1751. George, lord Anson, 22 June.
1756. Richard, earl Temple, 19 Nov.
1757. Daniel, earl of Winchilsea, 6 April.
,, George, lord Anson, 2 July.
1762. George M. Dunk, earl of Halifax, 19 June.
1763. George Grenville, esq., 1 Jan.
,, John, earl of Sandwich, 23 April.
,, John, earl of Egmont, 10 Sept.
1766. Sir Charles Saunders, 10 Sept.
,, Sir Edward Hawke, 10 Dec.
1771. John, earl of Sandwich, 12 Jan.
1782. Hon. Augustus Keppel, 1 April.
,, Augustus, viscount Keppel, 18 July.
1783. Richard, viscount Howe, 28 Jan.
1788. John, earl of Chatham, 16 July.
1794. George John, earl Spencer, 20 Dec.
1801. John, earl St. Vincent, 19 Feb.
1804. Henry, viscount Melville, 15 May.
1805. Charles, lord Barham, 2 May.
1806. Hon. Charles Grey, 10 Feb.
1806. Thomas Grenville, esq., 23 Oct.
1807. Henry, lord Mulgrave, 6 April.
1809. Charles Yorke, esq., 10 May.
1812. Robert, viscount Melville, 25 March.
1827. WILLIAM HENRY, DUKE OF CLARENCE, *lord high admiral,* 2 May, resigned 12 Aug. 1828.
1828. Robert, viscount Melville, 19 Sept.
1830. Sir James R. G. Graham, bart., 25 Nov.
1834. George, lord Auckland, 11 June.
,, Thomas Philip, earl de Grey, 23 Dec.
1835. George, lord Auckland, 25 April.
,, Gilbert, earl of Minto, 19 Sept.
1841. Thomas, earl of Haddington, 8 Sept.
1846. Edward, earl of Ellenborough, 13 Jan.
, George, earl of Auckland, 24 July.

1849. Sir Francis Thornhill Baring, 18 Jan.
1852. Algernon, duke of Northumberland, 28 Feb.
1853. Sir James Robert George Graham, 5 Jan.
1855. Sir Charles Wood, bart., 24 Feb.
1858. Sir John Pakington, bart., 26 Feb.
1859. Edward, duke of Somerset, June.
1866. Sir John Pakington, bart., 6 July.
1867. Henry Lowry Corry, 8 March.
1868. Hugh Culling Eardley Childers, 9 Dec.
1871. George Joachim Goschen, 9 March.
1874. George Ward Hunt, 21 Feb.; *died* 29 July, 1877.
1877. Wm. Henry Smith, about 7 Aug.
1880. Thos. Geo. Baring, earl of Northbrook, 28 April.
1885. Lord George Francis Hamilton, 24 June.
1886. George Frederick Samuel Robinson, Marquis of Ripon, about 6 Feb.
,, Lord George Francis Hamilton, 26 July.
1892. John Poyntz, earl Spencer, 18 Aug.
1895. George Joachim Goschen, 25 June.
1900. William Waldegrave Palmer, earl of Selborne, 12 Nov.

ADMIRALTY, Whitehall. "At the south end of Duke-street, Westminster, was seated a large house made use of for the admiralty office, until the business was removed to Greenwich, and thence to Wallingford-house, against Whitehall." It was rebuilt by Ripley about 1726; the screen was erected, to conceal the ugliness of the building, by the brothers Adam, in 1776.—Lord Nelson lay in state in one of the apartments on 8 Jan. 1806; and on the next day was buried at St. Paul's.

Explosion in clerks' room (ascribed to gunpowder in an iron pot); Mr. Swainson much hurt; about 11 A.M. 23 April, 1885.

ADMIRALTY ISLANDS. A group of coral islands to the N.E. of New Guinea, about 2° S. lat. and 147° E. long., discovered by the Dutch 1616, area 878 sq. m., inhabited by a race of savages 800 in number. Together with New Britain annexed by Germany in 1885, and now form part of the Bismarck Archipelago.

ADMIRALTY AND WAR OFFICE ACT, to facilitate improvements in the organisation of these offices, by the retirement of clerks from certain of the civil departments by granting gratuities, was passed 10 Aug. 1878.

"ADMONITION TO THE PARLIAMENT," condemning all religious ceremonies but those commanded by the New Testament, was published by certain Puritans in 1571. Its presumed authors, Field and Wilcox, were imprisoned. A second Admonition by Thomas Cartwright was answered by archbishop Whitgift.

ADORNO AND FREGOSO, two families, of which the doges were frequently members, disturbed Genoa from the 14th to the 16th centuries, the former favouring the emperor, the latter the French king. Their power was annihilated by Andrea Doria about 1528.

ADOWA, battle of, see *Massowah*, 29 Feb., 1 March, 1896.

ADRIAN'S OR HADRIAN'S WALL (to prevent the irruptions of the Scots and Picts into the northern counties of England, then under the Roman government) extended from the Tyne to Solway frith, and was eighty miles long, twelve feet high, and eight feet in thickness, with watch-towers; built 121. It was repaired and strengthened by Severus, 207—210.

ADRIANOPLE, in Turkey, so named after its restorer the emperor Adrian (who died 10 July, 138). Near here Constantine defeated Licinius and gained the empire, 3 July, 323; also, near here the emperor Valens was defeated and slain by the Goths, 9 Aug. 378. Adrianople was taken by the Turks under Amurath in 1361, and was their capital till the capture of Constantinople in 1453. It was taken by the Russians on 20 Aug. 1829; and restored 14 Sept. same year; after the capture of the Turkish army in the Shipka pass it was occupied by the Russians, without resistance, 20 Jan. 1878. Population 1885, 70,886; 1901, *about* 81,000. See *Turkey*.

ADRIATIC. The ceremony of the doge of Venice wedding the Adriatic sea (instituted about 1173), took place annually on Ascension-day. The doge dropped a ring into the sea from his bucentaur, or state barge, being attended by his nobility and foreign ambassadors. The ceremony was first omitted in 1797.

ADULLAM, a cave to which David fled from the persecution of Saul about 1062 B.C. (1 *Sam.* xxii. 1, 2.)

Mr. Horsman, Mr. R. Lowe, earl Grosvenor, lord Elcho, and other liberals who opposed the Franchise Bill in 1866 were termed "Adullamites." During a debate on this bill on 13 March, 1866, Mr. Bright said of Mr. Horsman, that he "had retired into what may be called his political cave of Adullam, to which he invited every one who was in debt, and every one who was discontented," &c. On 19 April, lord Elcho said, "No improper motive has driven us into this cave, where we are a most happy family, daily—I may say, hourly—increasing in number and strength, where we shall remain until we go forth to deliver Israel from oppression." Although their opposition led to the resignation of the Russell ministry, they declined to take office under lord Derby in July, 1866. They did not vote together uniformly in 1867, and (lord Elcho and Mr. Wyld excepted) voted with Mr. Gladstone, for the disestablishment of the Irish church, 1 May, 1868.

ADULTERATION. That of food was prohibited in England in 1267, and punishments for it enacted, 1581, 1604, 1836, 1851, &c. Much attention was drawn to it in 1822, through Mr. Accum's book, called "Death in the Pot," and in 1855 through Dr. Hassall's book, "Food and its Adulterations." By an act for preventing the adulteration of food, passed in 1860, parochial chemical analysts may be appointed. An act to prevent adulteration of seeds passed 16 Aug. 1869, amended 1878. Another to prevent adulteration of food and drugs passed 10 Aug. 1872. Penalties for adulterating liquors were imposed by the new licensing act passed same time. The report of a commission, issued in July, 1874, declared that the public "were cheated rather than poisoned." All the anti-adulteration acts were repealed by the Sale of Food and Drugs Act, passed 11 Aug. 1875; which was amended in 1879; reported very effectual Dec. 1884. Act regulating sale of margarine, 9 Aug., 1899. The report of the select committee appointed in 1894, with suggestions, was issued in July, 1896.

ADULTERY was punished with death by the law of Moses (1490 B.C; *Lev.* xx. 10)—and by Lycurgus (884 B.C.). The early Saxons burnt the adulteress, and erected a gibbet over her ashes, whereon they hanged the adulterer. The ears and nose were cut off under Canute, 1031. Adultery was ordained to be punished capitally by the parliament, May 14, 1650: but there is no record of this law taking effect; and it was repealed at the restoration. In New England the punishment for adultery was made capital to both parties, and several suffered for it, 1662. *Hardie.* Till 1857 the legal redress against the male offender was by civil action for a money compensation; the female being liable to divorce. By 20 & 21 Vict. c. 85 (1857) the "action for criminal conversation" was abolished and the Court for Divorce and Matrimonial Causes established with power to grant divorces for adultery and ill usage; see *Divorce*. An act was passed in 1869 permitting parties to suits for adultery to give evidence.

ADVENT (*adventus*, "the coming"). The season includes four Sundays, previous to Christmas, the first the nearest Sunday to St. Andrew's day (Nov. 30), before or after. Homilies respecting Advent are mentioned prior to 378. Advent Sunday, 1896, 29 Nov.; 1897, 28 Nov.; 1898, 27 Nov.; 1899, 3 Dec.; 1900, 2 Dec.; 1901, 1 Dec.; 1902, 30 Nov.; 1903, 29 Nov.; 1904, 27 Nov.; 1905, 3 Dec.

ADVENTISTS (Seventh-day), an American sect in Massachusetts, U.S.A. A large conference of delegates from 30 States of the Union, and from Europe, met at Michigan, 7 March, 1891. The president Elson reported the building of a college at Lincoln, Nebraska, and that the Pitcairn Islanders had become Adventists.

ADVENTURE BAY, S.E. end of Van Diemen's Land, discovered in 1773 by capt. Furneaux in his first voyage to the Pacific, and named from his ship *Adventure*. It was visited by capt. Cook 1777; by capt. Bligh in 1788 and 1792.

ADVENTURERS, *see* MERCHANTS.

ADVERTISEMENTS IN NEWSPAPERS, as now published, were not general in England till the beginning of the eighteenth century. A penalty of 50*l*. was inflicted on persons advertising a reward with "No questions to be asked" for the return of things stolen, and on the printer, 1754. The *advertisement duty*, (first enacted, 1712,) formerly charged according to the number of lines, was afterwards fixed, in England, at 3*s*. 6*d*., and in Ireland at 2*s*. 6*d*. each advertisement. The duty (further reduced, in England to 1*s*. 6*d*., and in Ireland to 1*s*. each, in 1833) was abolished in 1853.

Early advertisements are found in "*Perfect Occurrences of every Daie*," 26 March to 2 April, 1647, and "*Mercurius Elencticus*" . . . 4 Oct. 1648
H. Sampson's "History of Advertising," published . . . . . Nov. 1874
The whole libretto of Macfarren's Opera, *Robin Hood*, inserted as an advertisement in the *Times* (4½ columns) . . . . . 16 Oct. 1860
A debate in the Portuguese parliament, translated, inserted as advertisement in the *Daily News* (8 columns) . . . . . 3 May, 1877
ADVERTISING VANS, a great nuisance, prohibited . 1853
Advertising Stations (Rating) Act, passed . . 1889
The name of Mr. H. F. Partridge, surgeon-dentist, Dublin, was struck off the registry of the General Medical Council for advertising as contrary to professional rules, June 1886; confirmed by the Court of Appeal, 22 March, 1892.
Posting illustrated advertisements on walls, &c., much censured, Nov. 1892; society formed to check the practice . . . . early April, 1893
Advertisers' exhibition, Niagara-hall, London, opened . . . . . . 22 April, 1899
International exhibition (1st) at the Crystal palace, May, 1900

ADVOCATUS DIABOLI (Devil's Advocate), in the Roman Catholic Church, the functionary appointed to state the objections against a deceased person proposed for canonization. The side for its defence is undertaken by the *Advocatus Dei* (God's Advocate).

ADVOCATE, THE KING'S (always a doctor of the civil law), was empowered to prosecute at his own instance certain crimes about 1597. The LORD ADVOCATE in Scotland is the same as the attorney-general in England, with judicial powers.—It was decided in the parliament of Paris, in 1685, that the king's advocate of France might at the same time be a judge; and in Scotland sir William Oliphant (1612) and sir John Nesbit (1666) were lord advocates and lords of session at the same time. *Beatson*.—The powers were diminished in 1881, when John Blair Balfour was made Lord Advocate; the right hon. J. H. A. Macdonald, 1885-8; Mr. J. P. B. Robertson, 1888-Sept. 1891, succeeded by sir Charles John Pearson, 1891, by Mr. J. B. Balfour, 1892; sir Charles Pearson, Sept. 1895; rt. hon. Andrew Graham Murray, May, 1896; Mr. C. S. Dickson, Oct. 1903; Mr. G. W. T. Omond's work, "The Lord Advocates of Scotland," pub. 1884. Advocates' library in Edinburgh established by sir G. Mackenzie about 1682; in 1709 it obtained the right to a copy of every new book published in Britain. Number of volumes over 350,000 MSS. over 3,000; see *Judge Advocate*.

ADVOWSONS, right of a presentation to a church living. First recorded instance in 448, when a bishop was permitted by the council of Orange to nominate a clerk to a church he had built outside his diocese. Advowsons were allowed in the 6th cent. (123 Novel of Justinian). Patronage has grown as part of the feudal system. The Decretals stated that if with the consent of the bishop any man built a church he acquired the right of patronage. In Thomas à Becket's time presentations were often made against the will of the bishop, and for money payments. Exchange of advowsons is now regulated by various Acts, notably 23 & 24 Vict. c. 124, 1860, 31 & 32 Vict. c. 114, and 33 & 34 Vict. c. 39, 1868-70. See *Benefice*.

ÆDILES. Roman city officers. 1. Two plebeian ædiles were appointed to look after buildings, weights and measures, the supply of provisions, &c., 494 B.C. 2. The *ædiles curules* were appointed 365 B.C. 3. Julius Cæsar appointed *ædiles cereales* for watching over the supply of corn. The ædiles became a kind of police under the emperors.

ÆDUI OR HEDUI, a Celtic people, N.E. France, subjugated by Julius Cæsar, B.C. 52. An insurrection, A.D. 21, was quelled by C. Silius.

ÆGATES ISLES, W. of Sicily: near these the Roman consul, C. Lutatius Catulus, gained a victory over the Carthaginian fleet under Hanno, 10 March, 241 B.C. Peace ensued, the Romans obtaining Sicily and a tribute of 3200 talents.

ÆGINA, a Greek island, a rival of Athens, was humbled by Themistocles, 485 B.C.; and taken and its works destroyed 455. Its inhabitants, expelled, 431, were restored by the Spartans, 404; they renewed war with Athens, 388, and made peace, 387. In 1811, from the temple of Pallas Athene, many statues, dating from 50 years before Phidias, were taken to Munich, one group represents a combat of Greeks and Trojans for the body of Achilles.

ÆGOSPOTAMI, (the Goat-rivers), in the Chersonesus, where Lysander, the Lacedæmonian, defeated the Athenian fleet, 405 B.C., and ended the Peloponnesian war.

A. E. I. O. U. (for "Austriæ est imperare orbi universi," (German, *alle Erde ist Oesterreichs unterthan*,) "Austria is to rule all the world"), was the motto of the weak and unfortunate emperor, Frederick III., 1440—1493.

ÆLFRIC SOCIETY; founded 1842; closed 1856; published "Homilies of Ælfric, archbishop of Canterbury," and other Anglo-Saxon works.

ÆNEID, the great Latin epic poem, relating the adventures of Æneas, written about 24 B.C. by Virgil, who died 22 Sept. 19 B.C., before he had finally corrected the poem. It was first printed in 1469, at Rome.

ÆNIGMA. Samson's riddle (about 1141 B.C.; *Judges* xiv. 12) is the earliest on record. Gale attributes ænigmatical speeches to the Egyptians. The ancient oracles frequently gave responses admitting of perfectly contrary interpretations. In Nero's time, the Romans had recourse to this method of concealing truth. The following epitaph on Fair Rosamond (mistress of our Henry II. about 1173) is a mediæval specimen:—"Hic jacet in tombâ Rosa mundi, non Rosa munda; Non redolet, sed olet, quæ redolere solet."

ÆOLIA, in Asia Minor, was colonised by a principal branch of the Hellenic race about 1124 B.C. The Æolians built several large cities; Mitylene, in Lesbos, was considered the capital.

ÆOLIAN HARP. Its invention is ascribed to Kircher, 1650, who wrote on it, but it was previously known. St. Dunstan is traditionally said to have been its inventor.

ÆOLOPILE, a hollow ball with an orifice in which a tube might be screwed, was used in the 17th century as a boiler for experimental steam-engines; a similar apparatus is described by Vitruvius, first century, A.D. Its invention attributed to Hiero of Alexandria.

ÆQUI, an Italian race, subdued by the Romans and their lands annexed, 471-302 B.C.

AËRATED WATERS. Solution of carbonic acid in water discovered by Priestley. Suggested as a prevention of scurvy. Paper presented to the Admiralty 1773. A bottle of soda-water from the *Royal George*, sunk in 1780, sold by auction Mar. 10, 1903. Apparatus for combining gases with water were patented by Thomson in 1807; F. C. Bakewell in 1832 and 1847; Tylor in 1840, and by others. AËRATED BREAD is made by processes patented by Dr. Dauglish, 1856-7. Aërated Bread Company formed 28 Oct. 1862. A.B.C. Restaurants very successful and extending, 1903.

AERIANS, followers of Aerius, a presbyter, in the 4th century, who held that there was no distinction between a bishop and a presbyter, and that prayers should not be offered for the dead. *Epiphanius.*

AEROLITES, see *Meteors*.

AERONAUTICS AND AEROSTATICS, see *Balloons* and *Flying*. The Aeronautical Society of Great Britain was established by the duke of Argyll and others, 12 Jan. 1866. Annual meetings.

AEROPHORE, an apparatus invented by M. Denayrouze, to enable persons to enter a noxious inflammable atmosphere. It comprises an air-pump, lamp, and flexible tubing. It was tried at Chatham, 12-14 Jan. 1875, and reported successful.

The name *Aerophor* was given to an apparatus, invented by a German engineer, to introduce a very fine water-cloud into textile factories to nullify the injurious effects of the frictional electricity generated by the machinery. In 1890 the apparatus was reported successful in Germany and England.

ÆSCULAPIUS, god of medicine: his worship introduced at Rome, about 291 B.C.

ÆSOP'S FABLES, see *Fables*.

ÆSTHETICISM, an art movement to carry the love of the beautiful into home-life, sprang up during the latter part of the 19th century. It was strongly supported by Mr. Ruskin, sir (d. 1896) Frederick Leighton, Mr. (knt. 1899) Alma-Tadema, Mr. Holman Hunt, Mr. (bart. 1894) P. Burne-Jones, Mr. Gabriel Dante Rossetti and others associated with the Pre-Raphaelite movement (*which see*). The fantastic extravagances of some of the followers of the cult were cleverly hit off by Gilbert and Sullivan in "Patience," produced in 1881, and satirised in *Punch* about that period. The influence of Æstheticism has been felt in the improvement of decorative art in modern houses, and increased artistic refinement.

ÆSTHETICS (from the Greek *aisthesis*, perception), the science of the beautiful (especially in art); a term invented by Baumgarten, a German philosopher, whose work "Æsthetica" was published in 1750.

ÆTHIOPIA, see *Ethiopia*.

"**ÆTHIOPICA**," see *Romances*.

AETIANS, followers of Aëtius, an Arian heretic about 351.

ÆTOLIA, in Greece, a country named after Ætolus of Elis, who is said to have accidentally killed a son of Phoroneus, king of Argos, left the Peloponnesus, and settled here. After the ruin of Athens and Sparta, the Ætolians became the rivals of the Achæans, and were alternately allies and enemies of Rome.

The Ætolians join Sparta against Athens	B.C. 455
The Ætolian league of tribes opposes Macedon	323
Invaded by Antipater during the Lamian war	322
Aid in the expulsion of the Gauls	279
Invade the Peloponnesus, and ravage Messenia (Social War), and defeat the Achæans at Caphyæ	220
Philip V., of Macedon, invades Ætolia, and takes Thermum—Peace of Naupactus concluded	217
Alliance with Rome	211
Deserted by the Romans, the Ætolians make peace with Philip	205
War with Philip, 200; he is defeated at Cynoscephalæ	197
The Ætolians invite the kings of Macedon, Syria, and Sparta, to coalesce against the Romans	193-2
Defeat of the allies near Thermopylæ	191
Conquered by the Romans under Fulvius	189
Leading patriots massacred by the Roman party	167
Ætolia made a province of Rome	146

Seized by Theodorus Angelus, 13th century. Amurath II. in 1432 expelled the Greek governors. It is now part of the kingdom of Greece.

AFFINITY. Marriage within certain degrees of kindred was prohibited in almost every age and country, but has yet taken place to a considerable extent. The Jewish law is given in *Leviticus* xviii. (1490 B.C.) In the English prayer-book the table restricting marriage within certain degrees was set forth by authority, 1563. Prohibited marriages were adjudged to be incestuous and unlawful by the 99th canon, in 1603. All marriages within the forbidden degrees are declared to be absolutely void by 5 & 6 Will. IV. c. 54, 1835; see *Marriage* (*of Wife's Sister*). The prohibited degrees were set forth in 25 Hen. VIII. c. 22, 1533-4. See *Incest*.

AFFIRMATION; see *Quakers*. The affirmation was altered in 1702, 1721, 1837, and in April, 1859.—The indulgence was granted to persons who were formerly Quakers, but who had seceded from that sect, 2 Vict. 1838; and extended to other dissenters by 9 Geo. IV. c. 32 (1828), and 18 & 19 Vict. c. 2 (1855). For Mr. Bradlaugh's case, see *Parliament*, 1880-1, 1883, and *Oaths*.

Affirmation Bill for M.P.'s introduced, 1883; rejected in the commons (292–289) 3–4 May, 1883. Affirmations were substituted for oaths by an act passed 24 Dec. 1888.

AFGHANISTAN (the Greek *Ariana*), a large country in central Asia, successively part of the Persian and Greek empires. Chief cities, Cabul, Herat, Candahar, Ghuznee. The tribes are ruled by sirdars. Population 1903, about 4,000,000.

Early Afghan conquests in India . . . 1200-1290

Conquests of Genghis Khan about 1221, and by Tamerlane 1398

Baber conquered Cabul 1525

On his death Afghanistan divided between Persia and Hindostan.

The Afghans revolt in 1720; invade Persia and take Ispahan; repulsed by Nadir Shah in 1728, who subdues the whole of the country . . . 1738

On his assassination, one of his officers, Ahmed Shah, an Afghan, made Afghanistan independent, and reigned prosperously . . . 1747-73

Timur Shah (son), succeeds, 1773; rules cruelly; dies leaving 23 sons 1793

Zeman becomes ameer, 1793; cripples the power of the sirdars; blinded and dethroned . . . 1800

Mahmud Shah, son, ameer 1800; deposed for his brother, Suja Shah, 1803; Mahmud restored, Futtih Khan the vizier predominant, 1809; Futtih blinded; Mahmud flees from Cabul and becomes ruler at Herat 1816

Impotent rulers at Cabul; Dost Mohammed Khan becomes ameer 1826

He is dethroned by the British, and sent to Calcutta; Suja Shah restored 1838

British occupation of Cabul causes great discontent; insurrection; sir Alexander Burnes and 23 others killed . . . . 2 Nov. 1841

Akbar Khan, son of Dost Mohammed, head of the rebels; invites sir Wm. Macnaghten to meet, and assassinates him and others . . 23 Dec. ,,

The British army retires from Cabul, and is destroyed by the Ghilzais in the Khyber pass; of 3849 soldiers, and about 12,000 camp followers, only Dr. Brydone and four or five natives escaped massacre . . . . . 6-13 Jan. 1842

Sir George Pollock forces the Khyber pass; defeats Akbar Khan at Tezeen; captures Cabul and releases lady Sale and others, 16 Sept.; destroys the great bazaar; retires . . . 12 Oct. ,,

Dost Mohammed becomes ameer . . . . ,,

His treaty of friendship with lord Dalhousie (faithfully kept) . . . . . 30 March, 1855

He dies leaving 16 sons; appointing as his successor Shere Ali, the third son, 9 June; who is much opposed by his brothers, especially by Ufzul, the eldest son (and his son Abdul-Rahman, or Abdur-Rahman), Azim, Ameen, and Shureef; yet is recognized by them . . . Sept. 1863

Unsuccessful insurrection of Ufzul and Azim; Azim flees to British territories, 16 May; Ufzul reconciled to Shere Ali . . . 2 June, 1864

Insurrection of Abdul-Rahman; Ufzul imprisoned Aug. ,,

Shere Ali enters Cabul . . . 14 Nov. ,,

Azim and his confederates defeated at Kujhboz, near Khelat-i-Ghilzye, by Shere Ali (whose gallant son is killed), 6 June; he enters Candahar, 14 June, 1865

Azim joins his nephew Abdul-Rahman; defection of Mahomed Rufeek from Ibrahim (Shere Ali's son) weakly ruling Cabul; it surrenders to Azim . . . . . . 2 March, 1866

Shere Ali rouses himself from his grief; raises an army; some of his treacherous friends return to him; he is defeated at Sheikhabad, and flees to Candahar . . . . . . 10 May, ,,

Ufzul (sensual and easy), and Azim (cruel and tyrannical) rule at Cabul . . . May, *et seq.* ,,

Azim and Abdul-Rahman defeat Shere Ali at Kujhbaz, 17 Jan.; he flees to Candahar: shut out, flees to Herat held by his son, Yakoob . Jan. 1867

His army again defeated and his general and brother, Fyz Mahommed, killed . . 17 Sept. ,,

Ufzul dies; Azim sole ruler at Cabul . . Oct. ,,

He quarrels with Abdul-Rahman; who leaves him, and refuses to help him . . . . March, 1868

Yakoob defeats Azim's troops, and enters Candahar . . . . April, 1868

Azim leaves Cabul, July; his army dissolves by desertion; Shere Ali enters Cabul . 8 Sept. ,,

Sir John Lawrence helps Shere Ali with arms and money; the attempts of Abdul-Rahman repulsed, Nov., Dec. ,,

Shere Ali totally defeats him and Azim (who dies soon after) . . . . Jan. 1869

Shere Ali honourably received at Umballah by the viceroy, the earl of Mayo, and receives a subsidy, 27 March, *et seq.* ,,

The limits of his territories defined, about June, 1870

His son, Yakoob, rebels; captures Herat 6 May, ,,

Feramoz Khan, his father's general, assassinated, June, 1871

Yakoob reconciled to his father through lord Mayo, July; made governor of Herat; soon rebels, Sept. ,,

Uslum, murderer of Feramoz, killed in prison, Oct. ,,

Shere Ali agrees to new boundaries, and receives another British subsidy, Oct.; nominates his youngest son, Abdoola Jan, his successor, to the great dissatisfaction of his older son Yakoob, Dec. 1873

Yakoob Khan, imprisoned by his father about Dec. 1874

Shere Ali refusing to allow a British Resident, the subsidy withheld; he raises an army, and is said to promote disaffection to the British . 1877-8

Death of the heir Abdoola Jan . . . 17 Aug. 1878

Stolietoff, a Russian envoy, favourably received at Cabul, June; a treaty signed; Russia to be the guardian of the Ameer . . . . Aug. ,,

The nawab Gholam Hussein Khan sent as envoy to the ameer with letters from the viceroy (16 and 24 Aug.), 30 Aug.; dismissed with presents; intercourse with the British declined . Sept. ,,

A mission with military escort under sir Neville B. Chamberlain, commander of the Madras army, starts from Peshawur . . . . 21 Sept. ,,

At Ali Musjid, a fort in the Khyber pass, major Cavagnari and an advance party are threatened with attack if they proceed, 22 Sept.; they retire to Peshawur, 23, 24 Sept.; Gholam Hussein sent with an ultimatum (answer required before 20 Nov.) . . . . 28 Oct. ,,

British army formed in three divisions: at Quettah, Peshawur, and Kuram (34,730 natives, 12,740 Europeans) . . . . about 16 Nov. ,,

Dispatch from lord Cranbrook supporting the viceroy . . . . 18 Nov. ,,

No answer received from the ameer; the army advances . . . . 21 Nov. ,,

Ali Musjid shelled and occupied by the British; 21 guns taken; major Birch and lieut. Fitzgerald and about 35 men killed . . . 22 Nov. ,,

The viceroy's proclamation to the Afghans, issued 23 Nov. ,,

Occupation of Dakka and Pisheen, 23 Nov.; of Kuram fort . . . . . . 25 Nov. ,,

Kuddum burnt to punish marauding hillmen, 1 Dec. ,,

Gen. Roberts victorious at Peiwar pass (*which see*) 2 Dec. ,,

Evasive reply of the ameer dated 19 Nov., received 3 Dec. ,,

The British occupy Jellalabad . . . 20 Dec. ,,

Shere Ali flees from Cabul to Balkh, 13 Dec.; Yakoob Khan assumes command; the Russian mission withdraws . . . . . . Dec. ,,

Gen. Roberts proclaims annexation of Kuram district, &c. . . . . . 26 Dec. ,,

He enters the Khoost territory 3 Jan.; defeats the Mangals near Matoon . . . . . 7 Jan. 1879

Candahar abandoned, 6 Jan.; entered by general Stewart unopposed . . . . . 7 Jan. ,,

Wali Mahomed, a relative of Shere Ali, joins the British . . . . Jan. ,,

The Alizais defeated in an attack . . 16 Feb. ,,

Death of Shere Ali, the ameer (announced) 20 Feb. ,,

About 46 of the 10th hussars drowned by current while crossing the Cabul river, 10 p.m. 31 March, ,,

Gen. Gough, with the 10th hussars and others, defeats about 5000 Khugianis near Futtehabad; gallant major Wigram Batty killed . 2 April, ,,

Yakoob Khan, son of the late ameer, arrives at Gandamak to negotiate, 8 May; recognised as ameer . . . . 9 May, 1879
Treaty of peace signed at Gandamak; (the British to occupy Khyber pass, and the Kuram and Pisheen valleys; to have a Resident at Cabul; and to pay an annual subsidy of 60,000*l.* to the ameer), 26 May; ratified 30 May; the British troops retire 8 June, „
Sir Louis Cavagnari and escort honourably received in Cabul . . . . 24 July, „
Thanks of the house of lords voted to the viceroy, officers, and men . . . . . 4 Aug. „
Several regiments of Afghan soldiers arrive in Cabul from Herat; about 13 Aug aided by the populace they besiege the British residents, who after a brave resistance are massacred (including sir L. Cavagnari, Mr. Jenkyns, his secretary, lieut. Hamilton, and Dr. Ambrose Kelly), with about 26 native cavalry and 50 infantry; a few natives escape . . . . 3, 4 Sept. „
Gen. Roberts marches towards Cabul 6 Sept. *et seq.* „
Mutiny at Herat; military and civil governors killed 5 Sept. „
Repulse of an attack on Baker's entrenchments at Shutargardan . . . . . . 19 Sept. „
A British convoy attacked by Mongols, near Shutargardan; 8 sepoys and 15 muleteers killed; mules taken . . . . . . 22 Sept. „
Gen. Baker reaches Kushi 24 Sept.; receives the ameer Yakoob and his son, his general Daoud, and suite . . . . 27 Sept. „
Gen. Roberts arrives at Cabul, 28 Sept.; occupies Dakka . . . . 29 Sept. „
Attack on British camp at Shutargardan repulsed 2 Oct „
Battle of Char-asiab; severe conflict with Afghans before Cabul; captain Young, Dr. Duncan, lieut. Fergusson, and about 70 killed and wounded 6 Oct. „
The enemy decamps; about 98 guns abandoned; pursued by cavalry; small parties only overtaken 8-9 Oct. „
Gen. Roberts visits the abandoned Bala Hissar, 11 Oct.; enters Cabul, 12 Oct.; Jellalabad occupied by Gough . . . . 14 Oct. „
Gen. Roberts' proclamation; heavy fine; martial law; gen. Hills to be military governor, with Gholab Hussein Khan . . . . 14 Oct. „
Great explosions (supposed treacherous) in the Bala Hissar; destruction of much arms and ammunition; capt. Shafto and about 20 others missing 16 Oct. „
Abdication of Yakoob Khan announced 19 Oct. „
5 prisoners (mollahs and others) hanged as murderers of major Cavagnari and others 20-24 Oct. „
Sahib Jan, a freebooter, with a strong force of Taraki Ghilzais, defeated and killed by general Hughes at Shahjui, near Candahar . 24 Oct. „
Proclamation of gen. Roberts announcing British occupation of Cabul, &c. . . . . 30 Oct. „
Junction of columns of generals Macpherson and Bright at Katasang . . . . . 6 Nov. „
163 Afghan mutineers, &c., tried; 87 executed as murderers; 76 released . . . Oct., Nov. „
Combination of tribes under Mohammed Jan Wardak . . . . Dec. „
Continued severe fighting, with heavy loss on both sides . . . . 11-14 Dec. „
Gen. Roberts concentrates his forces in the Sherpur cantonments . . . . . 14 Dec. „
Musa Khan, son of Yakoob, said to be proclaimed ameer . . . . about 17 Dec. „
Gen. Gough at Jugdulluk attacked; retreats into the fort, 16 Dec.; indecisive conflicts 18, 19 Dec. „
The Afghans (25,000) defeated with great loss near Sherpur cantonments, by gens. Roberts and Gough . . . . 23 Dec. „
Cabul left by the enemy, 24 Dec.; the city and Bala Hissar reoccupied by the British 26 Dec. „
The enemy dispersed . . . . . 28 Dec. „
Attack of Afghan chiefs on col. Norman repulsed at Jugdulluk . . . . . . 29 Dec. „
Ghuznee seized and held for Musa Khan as the new ameer, by Mohammed Jan . . about 10 Jan. 1880
Gen. Roberts proclaims an amnesty with few exceptions; the hill tribes generally subdued, about 6 Jan. „
Mohmands and other tribes defeated in an attack near Daka . . . . 15 Jan. 1880
Correspondence with Russia; papers found in Cabul (to be kept secret) . . . . 6 Feb. „
Musa Khan and chiefs at Ghuznee submit 21 March, „
Mohammed Jan defeated and killed, fighting with Hazaris . . . . . . about 3 April, „
A camp at Duwai attacked by Pathans; garrison killed . . . . 16 April, „
Shere Ali, cousin of the late ameer, made wali or governor of Candahar by the British (see *Candahar*) . . . . April, „
Gen. sir Donald Stewart defeats a furious attack of Ghilzais at Ahmad Khel, 19 April; again near Ghuznee . . . . 23 April, „
Col. Jenkins, at Char-asiab, attacked by 4000 Logaris; resists till reinforced by gen. Macpherson; totally defeats them . . 25 April, „
Sir D. Stewart takes chief command at Cabul, 2 May, „
Alleged defeats of Safis and Ghazis near Jellalabad 19, 22 May, „
Gen. Burrows (with about 2400 men) sent from Bombay towards Candahar . . . 1 July, „
The troops of the inefficient wali of Candahar, Shere Ali, revolt and join Ayoob Khan, about 14 July, „
Gen. Burrows at Maiwand, near Kusck-i-Nakhud (*which see*) . . . . . . 17 July, „
Abdul-Rahman, or Abdur-Rahman, born 1845 (see above, 1863 *et seq.*), recognised as ameer at Cabul by the British (previously an exile at Samarcand), and proclaimed . . . . 22 July, „
Ayoob Khan (son of the late ameer, Shere Ali), governor of Herat, marches upon Candahar with about 12,000 men and 20 guns; defeats the attack of gen. Burrows after severe conflicts; heavy loss on both sides; many officers of 66th regiment killed . . . . 27 July, „
Candahar citadel held by British with about 4000 men . . . . 28 July, „
Ayoob encamped at Kokaran . . . . 9 Aug. „
Gen. sir F. Roberts with about 10,000 men, &c., marches from Cabul to relieve Candahar 9 Aug. „
Sir D. Stewart, with all the troops, after an interview with the ameer Abdur-Rahman, withdraws from Cabul . . . . 11 Aug. „
Attack of Pathans (hill tribes) on the post at Kaeh Amadan firmly beaten off by sepoys; 80 Pathans killed . . . . 16 Aug „
Ineffectual sortie from Candahar, under gen. Primrose, against Deh Kwajee village, with heavy loss on both sides; gen. Brooke, col. Newport, majors Vandaleur and French, capt. Cruickshank, lieut. Marsh, and rev. Mr. Gordon, and 180 men killed . . . . 16 Aug. „
Ayoob Khan's army (strengthened by Ghilzais) about 20,000, about 25 Aug.; he retires from Candahar . . . . . . about 30 Aug. „
Gen. Roberts arrives at Candahar, 31 Aug.; declines Ayoob's terms; defeats and disperses his army at Mazra near the Argandab; and captures his camp at Baba Wali Kotal (see *Mazra*) 1 Sept. „
Ayoob Khan arrives in Herat; reported 10 Oct. „
Tranquillity at Cabul, announced . . Nov. „
Shere Ali, wali of Candahar, resigns and retires to India . . . . Dec. „
Alleged expenses of the war, 1878-80, 23,494,480*l.*, of which 5,000,000*l.* paid by British exchequer, Aug. 1881
Russian correspondence with the ameer Shere Ali in 1878, published; explained by Russia as relating to probable war in the east . 9, 10 Feb. „
Thanks of parliament voted to gen. Roberts and the army in both houses . . . . 5 May, „
Prospect of war between Ayoob Khan of Herat and Abdur-Rahman of Cabul . . May, June, „
Conflicts between partisans of the ameer and Ayoob Khan; the latter defeated . . 3 & 11 June „
Ayoob Khan defeats the ameer's army under Gholam-Hyder at Karez-i-atta, 26 July; enters Candahar . . . . 30 July, „
Gholam Hyder holding Kelat i-Ghilzai, 6 Aug.; receives reinforcements from Cabul . 21 Aug. „
Ayoob prepares to march; the ameer's troops at Kelat-i-Ghilzai; rejects Ayoob's proposals, 1-4 Sept.; marches to Candahar . about 8 Sept. „
Ayoob, defeated at Old Candahar chiefly through desertion of his troops, flees to Herat . 22 Sept. „
The ameer enters Candahar . . . . 30 Sept. „

His army under Abdul-Kudus Khan twice defeats Ayoob's adherents, Oct.; again . . . . 2 Oct. 1881
Enters Herat . . . . 4 Oct. „
Ayoob flees to Persia . . . . . . 4 Oct. „
Abdur-Rahman now virtual ruler of all Afghanistan Oct. „
Afzul Khan chosen by the ameer as British resident in Cabul . . . . Feb. 1882
The ameer defeats the Shinwarris about 27 April, 1883
Peace made . . . . . about 21 June, „
Indian government grants subsidy to the ameer: accepted . . . . 21 July, „
Slight insurrection of the Ghilzais under Mollah Mushki Alum, announced . . . 24 Aug. „
The proposal of an Afghan frontier commission accepted by the ameer . . . . Aug. 1884
Gen. Sir Peter Lumsden with staff proceeds, and successful progress reported . . Oct., Dec. „
Penjdeh assured to Afghanistan by Lord Auckland, 1840; Russian advances resisted up to Nov. 1884. The ameer visits Lord Dufferin, the viceroy, at Rawul Pindi 2–12 April, who declares at a grand durbar, England and Afghanistan will stand side by side . . . . 8 April 1885
Sir Peter Lumsden arrives in London . 6 June, „
Difference between England and Russia respecting the Zulfikar Pass . . . . . July, „
Strong Russian garrison at Askabad . . July, „
The Russians relinquish Zulfikar Pass, announced 22 Aug. „
Anglo-Russian Protocol, closing the dispute, signed in London . . . . . . 10 Sept. „
Construction of Quetta Railway begun Sept. 1879; stopped Oct. 1880; resumed April 1884. Lower Bolan Railway joining India opened . 28 Oct. „
Penjdeh given up to Russia, July, 1885, entered 13 Feb. 1886
Joint Commission appointed; First boundary pillar formally erected 12 Nov. 1885; the last, many perils and privations endured . . . . July, „
Joint Commission dissolved . . . . 6 Sept. „
Sir Joseph West Ridgeway, chief, and the Commission warmly received at Cabul . . . 15 Oct. „
Rising against taxation (treasure seized in transit) about 30 Oct.; rebellion said to be repressed Nov. „
The ameer's troops defeated by the Ghilzais, announced 19 April; again at Khelat-i-Ghilzai, announced . . . . 25 April, 1887
Meetings of Afghan Frontier Commission at St. Petersburg; temporarily closed 12 May; resumed 6 July; question settled . . . . 20 July, „
Mutiny of Ghilzais at Herat, suppressed with much bloodshed . . . . 9 June, „
General Gholam reported that he defeated the Ghilzais . . . . 13 & 16 June, „
The ameer proclaims peace, amnesty and remission of taxes for two years, announced . 8 July, „
Taimar Shah, chief of the Herat mutineers, executed at Cabul . . . . . 13 July, „
Great defeat of the rebels at Mashakai, announced 15 July, „
Reported conflicting accounts of victory of Gholam Hyder Khan at Kotaldab . . . 26 July, „
Rebellion said to have collapsed 21 Aug.; several tribes return home . . . . 29 Aug. „
Escape of Ayoob Khan from Teheran, 14 Aug.; enters Afghanistan with a few followers and is driven out . . . . . . early Sept. „
Severe fighting at Mashakai between the ameer's troops and the insurgents . . . 31 Aug. „
Fighting near Mukur; rebel leader, Jalander Khan, captured . . . . 7 Sept. „
Reported fighting with varying success Sept.–Oct. „
Ayoob Khan surrenders at Meshed to the Indian government, announced . . . 9 Nov. „
Southern Afghanistan quiet, announced . 13 Nov. „
Reported conflict between ameer's troops and the insurgents, 60 killed . . . . 15 Nov. „
Amnesty proclamation issued by the ameer 10 Dec. „
Conflict between Afghans and Turcomans, Afghans victorious . . . . 9 May, 1888
Revolt of Ishak Khan, governor of Afghan Turkestan, Aug.; defeated at Tash Kurgan 29 Sept. 1888; at Mazari Sherif 30 Sept.; Ishak Khan a fugitive in Russian territory . . . . „
The ameer narrowly escapes assassination. 26 Dec. „

The ameer's troops under Gholam Hyder defeat the Shinwarris . . . . 3 Feb. 1889
Gholam Hyder Khan, made Governor-General 20 Feb. „
Abdur-Rahman (two years absent) returns to Cabul with strengthened power . . . . . Aug. 1890
Prof. James Darmsteter, during a scientific mission in 1886, collected the "Chants populaires des Afghans," which he published . . . 1888–90
Disputes with the Russians respecting the Pamir frontier . . . . Sept., Oct. 1891
Mr. T. Salter Pyne, engineer-in-chief to the ameer (5½ years), reports great progress in arts and manufactures, many English being employed Feb. 1892
The ameer's encroachments on the Hazaras (checked by the Indian government) lead to frequent conflicts, and insurrection of other tribes, May, June; the ameer unsuccessful. Rebels join the Hazara tribes . . . . July, „
The Indian government proposes to send to the ameer a deputation headed by lord Roberts; he approves, but defers receiving it, about 7 Aug.; the ameer's army about 40,000 reported . Aug. „
The governor of Candahar and his troops repulsed by the Hazaras, reported . . . 22 Aug. „
The ameer's troops capture Kamsin from the rebels, reported 30 Aug.; the war continues with varying results . . . . Sept., Oct. „
The ameer's troops occupy Oruzghan, reported 2 Oct. „
Death of Abdul Kudus Khan, the ameer's general, reported . . . . 25 Oct. „
Amicable despatches from the ameer to the viceroy brought by Mr. Pyne, reported . . 16 March 1893
Boundary disputes with Russia settled by capt. Yates, reported . . . . . . 12 Sept. „
The British mission under sir Henry Mortimer Durand and maj. Elles cordially received at Dakka by gen. Gholam Haidar, 20 Sept.; at Jellalabad, 23 Sept., at Cabul, with much honour, 2 Oct.; cordial interview of three hours with the ameer, 10 Oct.; agreement signed, 12 Nov.; friendly speech of the ameer at a durbah, 13 Nov.; sir Henry Mortimer Durand and his party leave Cabul . . . . . . 15 Nov. „
Mr. (aft. sir) Thomas Salter Pyne in London, reports successful progress, *Times*, 19 Jan.; knighted . . . . March 1894
Frontier warfare, see *India* . . . . 3 Nov. „
The order of the bath presented to the ameer by the British agent . . . . . . 16 Jan. 1895
The Afghan boundary commission complete their work, agreement signed by Mr. Udney and Gholam Haidar Khan, 13 April; ratified by the Ameer July „
The Shahzada Nasrulla Khan, second son of the ameer, arrives in London, 24 May: received by the Prince of Wales and the royal family, 25 May; by the queen at Windsor, 27 May and 2 July; at the Derby, 29 May; visits the ld.-mayor at the Guildhall, 6 June; tour in the provinces, June; farewell to the queen at Windsor, 20 July; he leaves England for Paris, 3 Sept. [returns to Cabul, Feb. 1896] . . . . „
Lieut.-col. Mahomed Akram Khan, British agent in Cabul, and his son killed by a messenger, the murderer killed; reported . . . . 4 Nov. „
The ameer attacks the Kafirs in the Verno valley 20 Dec. „
The Bashgol valley dominated, the chiefs submit; reported . . . . 19 Jan. 1896
The ameer's two sons made K.C.M.G. . April, „
The ameer swears loyalty to the British government at a durbar; reported, 25 Aug. 1897; again 5 Oct. 1897
Army reserve and reforms started; reported, Aug. 1900
Cholera epidemic; government houses closed; 4,500 deaths in Kabul, June–July „
"The life of the Ameer," edited by Mir Munshi, sultan Mahomed Khan, published . . . . „
Death of the ameer, a great ruler and a firm ally of the British; aged 61, 1 Oct. 1901
Habibullah, his son, proclaimed ameer; declares his intention to maintain the boundaries, and remain in alliance with Gt. Britain, 3 Oct. „
Proclamation issued; reducing the taxes and land revenue and raising the pay of the army, reported, 16 Oct. . . . . „
Release of tribal prisoners . . . . . Oct. „

The Hadda Mullah received by the ameer, 29 March 1902
Ameer divorces all his wives except four, forbids his subjects to have more, reported , 10 Feb. 1903
British Commission under Maj McMahon to settle Persia-Afghan frontier dispute, arrives at the Helmand river . . . . 12 Feb. ,,
Col. Yate detained as prisoner for crossing the border . . . . April, ,,

AFRICA, called *Libya* by the Greeks, one of the three parts of the ancient world, and the greatest peninsula of the globe. For its history, see *Egypt*, *Ethiopia*, *Carthage*, *Cyrene*, *Abyssinia*, *Cape*, *Algiers*, *Morocco*, *Ashantee*, *South Africa*, *Guinea*, *&c.* "European 'spheres' of influence extended from under 500,000 square miles in 1875 to about 10,000,000 square miles in 1900." Exports to the United Kingdom, 26,435,000*l.*; imports, 32,288,000*l.* in 1901.

Carthage subdued by the Romans, 146 B.C.; other provinces gained by Pompey, 82.
Revolts subdued by Diocletian, A.D. 296; by Theodosius, 373.
N. Africa conquered by the Vandals under Genseric, 429-35; re-conquered by Belisarius, 533-55.
The Saracens subdue the north of Africa, 637-709.
Portuguese settlements begun, 1450.
Cape of Good Hope discovered by Diaz, 1487.
Vasco de Gama doubles the Cape and explores the coast, 19 Nov. 1497.
English merchants visit Guinea in 1550; and Elizabeth granted a patent to an African company in 1588 (*which see*).
Dutch colony at the Cape founded, 1650.
Capt. Stubbs sailed up the Gambia, 1723.
Bruce commenced his travels in 1768.
Sierra Leone settled by the English, 1787.
Mungo Park made his first voyage to Africa, 22 May, 1795; his second, 30 January, 1804, and never returned (see *Park*).
Africa visited by Salt, 1805 and 1809; Burckhardt, 1812; Campbell, 1813; Hornemann, 1816; Denham and Clapperton, 1822; Laing, 1826; the brothers Lander, 1830.
Expedition to the Niger originated by Mr. Macgregor Laird of Liverpool; he went out with Mr. Lauder and lieut. Wm. Allen and they made a reliable survey of the river; July, *et seq.* 1832.
The great Niger expedition to start a colony in Central Africa (for which parliament voted 60,000*l.*), consisting of the *Albert*, *Wilberforce*, and *Soudan* steamships, commenced the ascent of the Niger, 20 Aug. 1841; when they reached Iddah, fever broke out among the crews, and they were successively obliged to return, the *Albert* having ascended the river to Egga, 320 miles from the sea, 28 Sept. The expedition was relinquished owing to disease, heat, and hardships, and all the vessels had cast anchor at Clarence Cove, Fernando Po, 17 Oct. 1841.
James Richardson explored the great Sahara in 1845-6, and in 1849 (by direction of the Foreign Office) he left England to explore central Africa, accompanied by Drs. Barth and Overweg. Richardson died 4 March, 1851; and Overweg died 27 Sept. 1852.
Dr. Vögel sent out with reinforcements to Dr. Barth, 20 Feb. 1853; in April, 1857, said to have been assassinated.
Dr. Barth returned to England, and received the Royal Geographical Society's medal, 16 May, 1856. His travels were published in 5 vols. in 1858.
Dr. David Livingstone, a missionary traveller, returned to England in Dec. 1856, after an absence of 16 years, during which he traversed a large part of the heart of S. Africa, and walked about 11,000 miles, principally over country hitherto unexplored. His book was published in Nov. 1857. In Feb. 1858, he was appointed British consul for the Portuguese possessions in Africa, and left England shortly after.
Du Chaillu's travels in central Africa, 1856-59, created much controversy, 1861.
Second expedition of Dr. Livingstone, March, 1858.
Captains Speke and Grant announce the discovery of a source of the Nile in Lake Victoria Nyanza, 23 Feb. 1863.
[Capt. Speke was accidentally shot by his own gun while alone near Bath, 15 Sept. 1864.]
Some Dutch ladies unsuccessfully explore the White Nile, and undergo many privations, July, 1863–1864. (One, Miss Tinne, said to have been killed; reported 5 Sept. 1869.)
The "Universities Mission to east central Africa," consisting of Charles F. Mackenzie, bishop of central Africa, and six clergymen and others, started Dec. 1860, and arrived at the Zambesi, in Feb. 1861. All died from privations and disease except two, who returned in 1864. The bishop died 31 Jan. 1862; succeeded by Dr. Tozer.
Du Chaillu starts on a fresh expedition, 6 Aug. 1863; after being robbed, and undergoing many privations, returned to London near the end of 1865. He gave an account of his journey at a meeting of the Royal Geographical Society, 8 Jan. 1866.
Dr. Livingstone returns, 23 July, 1864.
Death of Dr. W. B. Baikie, at Sierra Leone, 30 Nov. 1864. [He was sent as special envoy to the Negro tribes near the Niger by the Foreign Office about 1854. He opened commercial relations with central Africa.]
National African company, 1864.
Mr. (afterwards sir) Samuel Baker discovered a lake, supposed to be another source of the Nile, which he named Lake Albert Nyanza, 14 March, 1864.
Dr. Livingstone appointed British consul for inner Africa, 24 March, 1865.
Narrative of Livingstone's Zambesi expedition 1858–64, published 1866.
Livingstone left Zanzibar to continue his search for the sources of the Nile, March, 1866.

[*See his narrative below.*]

Reports of the murder of Livingstone near Lake Nyassa, in Sept. 1866—March, 1867; doubted, July, 1867.
Expedition of E. D. Young in search of Livingstone, sailed 9 July, 1867, returned and reported to the Royal Geographical Society his conviction that Livingstone was alive, 27 Jan. 1868.
Letter from Dr. Livingstone dated Bembo, 2 Mar. 1867; heard of down to Dec. 1867.
His despatch to lord Clarendon, dated 7 July, 1868; read to the Royal Geographical Society, 8 Nov. 1869.
Letter dated 30 May, 1869, published Dec. 1869.
Uncredited reports of his murder by negroes, Jan.; his probable safety reported by Dr. Kirk, 22 June; said to be at Mozambique, Nov. 1870.
Expedition of sir Samuel Baker to put down slave trade on the Upper Nile (see *Egypt*), Jan. 1870.
Expedition in search of Livingstone under lieut. Dawson, organised by the Royal Geographical Society; started 9 Feb. 1872.
[It returned on hearing that Stanley had found Livingstone.]
Dutch Guinea settlements purchased and transferred (see *Elmina*), 6 April, 1872.
Reports current that Livingstone is alive, May, June, 1872.
Expedition sent in search of Livingstone by Mr. James Gordon Bennett, proprietor of the *New York Herald*, at a cost of about 8,000*l.*:—
Mr. Henry M. Stanley, chief of the expedition, left Zanzibar, and, after much opposition from the native chiefs, accidentally fell in with Livingstone at Ujiji, near Unyanyembe, 10 Nov. 1871, and remained with him till 14 March, 1872, when he brought away his diary and other documents. Mr. Stanley reported that Livingstone had arrived at Ujiji in bad condition, having been robbed and deserted by his attendants.
Much controversy ensued between Mr. Stanley, the members of lieut. Dawson's expedition, Dr. Livingstone, Dr. Kirk, the Royal Geographical Society, and others, Aug.-Oct. 1872.
Letter from Dr. Livingstone, at Ujiji, dated Nov. 1871, to Mr. Bennett (printed in *New York Herald*, 26 July, and reprinted in the *Times* 27 July, 1872). He describes his explorations and his painful journey to Ujiji; his meeting with Mr. Stanley; and he speaks of the Nile springs being about 600 miles south of the most southerly part of Lake Victoria Nyanza; and also of about 700 miles of watershed in central Africa, of which he had explored about 600; and of the convergence of the watershed first into four, and then into two, mighty rivers in the great Nile valley (?) between 10° and 12° south latitude. Second letter (dated Feb. 1872) describes the horrors of the slave trade in eastern Africa, printed in the *Times* 29 July, 1872.

Livingstone's despatches, dated Nov. 1 and 15, 1871, received by the Foreign Office, 1 Aug.; letter dated 1 July, received 2 Oct. 1872.

Mr. Stanley described his discovery of Livingstone to the British Association at Brighton in presence of the ex-emperor and empress of the French, 16 Aug., and received a gold snuff-box from the queen about 30 Aug. 1872.

Livingstone died of dysentery in Ilala, Central Africa; his pupil, Jacob Wainwright, a young negro missionary, present, 1 May, 1873; his remains interred in Westminster Abbey, 18 April; his last journals published, Dec. 1874.

New Expedition, under sir Bartle Frere, to Zanzibar, to suppress the east African slave trade; lieut. Verney Lovett Cameron's offer to aid in the furtherance of Livingstone's expedition was accepted; sailed 20 Nov. 1872, see *Zanzibar*.

Expedition to explore the upper part of the Congo (Mr. Young, of Kelly, to subscribe 2000*l*. Royal Geographical Society to supplement it), proposed Nov. 1872.

Lieut. Verney Cameron, after the finding of Livingstone, continued his explorations, 1872–3.

Leaving Ujiji, 14 May, 1874, he followed Livingstone's route; explored 1200 miles of fertile country; arriving at Portuguese settlements, 4 Nov. 1875.

He was received by Royal Geographical Society, and gave account of his journey, 11 April, 1876.

Expedition of Mr. H. M. Stanley (supported by *Daily Telegraph* and *New York Herald*); he surveyed Lake Victoria Nyanza (230 miles by 180), 1875; well and successful, last letter dated 24 April, 1876.

Stanley reports survey of lake Tanganyika; and states that he left Ujiji and crossed Africa from east to west, and identified the Lualaba with the Congo river, which has an uninterrupted course of over 1400 miles, 24 Aug. 1876—6 Aug. 1877.

Arrives at Cape Town, 21 Oct. 1877; in London, 22 Jan.; published "Through the Dark Continent," May, 1878.

Italian expedition under marchese Antinori, well received by king of Scida; announced 2 Dec. 1876; his death reported, Nov. 1877.

Portuguese government grant 20,000*l*. for expedition into the interior, announced Dec. 1876.

Dr. Güssfeld, a German, after his exploration into S.W. Central Africa, 1873, declared the difficulties insuperable, 1875.

Mr. H. M. Stanley, with an international Belgian expedition, explored the Congo, 1879–80.

R. Geographical Society's successful expedition into Eastern Africa under Mr. A. Keith Johnston leaves England 14 Nov. 1878, starts from Zanzibar about 14 May, 1879; Mr. Johnston dies 28 June, succeeded by Joseph Thomson, who returns to England Aug. 1880.

The Royal Geographical Society grants 2,600*l*. for an expedition to Africa under Joseph Thomson, which starts 13 Dec. 1882; after successful exploration arrives at Zanzibar in June; describes to the R. Geo. Soc. his exceedingly perilous adventures, in beautifully varied country, with vicious escort, among savage tribes of different manners, 3 Nov. 1884. See *Morocco*.

Death of Dr. Moffat, missionary, aged 87, 9 Aug. 1883. See under *Congo*.

Count Teleki's expedition into the Masai country, &c., 23 Jan. 1887—25 Oct. 1888. For Mr. H. M. Stanley's expedition to relieve Emin pasha, see *Soudan*, Jan. 1887–9.

Trade route with 4 stations on the Congo reported to be established by Mr. Stanley (a great work) announced, 14 Aug. 1882.

Expedition of Mr. J. T. Last, supported by the Royal Geographical Society, to S.W. Zanzibar, Sept. 1885.

Italian scientific expedition under count Porro massacred, reported 26 April, 1886.

Dr. Junker reports to the Royal Geographical Society his eventful travels in Central Africa in 1885-6, 9 May, 1887.

Assassination of M. Camille Douls, the explorer, while crossing the Sahara, reported Sept. 1889.

Austro-Hungarian expedition under count Samuel Teleki to relieve Emin pasha arrives near him, but is superseded by Mr. Stanley, 1886—9. See *Kilima-Njaro*.

Mr. H. M. Stanley, in his expedition to relieve Emin pasha (see *Soudan*, 1887) at Wadelai, and during his return march, makes many discoveries, and re-names lake, South Nyanza (which he discovered in 1887), Albert Edward Nyanza, 1889.

Major Casati publishes his book "Ten years in Equatoria —the Return with Emin Pasha," translated by the Hon. Mrs. J. Randolph Clay, March, 1891.

[Gaetani Casati, scholar, born 1838; soldier 1859; left Italy for Africa 24 Dec. 1879; at Khartoum about May, 1880; received by Emin pasha April, 1883; after many perilous adventures with Emin pasha, 1889; received by the khedive at Cairo, 4 May, at Rome 14 July, by the king 17 July, 1890; died, 7 March, 1902.]

For a German exploring expedition, west, see *Cameroons*, 1891.

The German government sends an exploring expedition into S.W. African coast, Damaraland, *which see*.

French expedition into the interior between the Central Soudan and the French Congo under M. Fourneau; starts from Ouassou, 7 March; arrived at the confluence of the Massa Sangha and the Kalle, 15 April; at the Sodi, 1 May; attacked by natives he burns the village; encamped at a village, 10 May; suddenly attacked, fighting began; M. Fourneau wounded, many of his men killed, the rest demoralized and some fled, retreat began under fire from the savages, 11 May; and the party reached Ouassou, 18 May, 1891.

Mr. Joseph Thomson returns from an expedition in British South Africa, having visited the neighbourhood of lakes Nyassa and Bangweolo and made treaties with numerous chiefs, 18 Oct. 1891 [he died 2 Aug. 1895]. See *Anglo-French Agreement* and others.

MM. Monteil and Badaire explore country near lake Tchad, Central Africa, 9 Oct., 1890 *et seq.*, return to Paris, 20 Dec. 1892

Mr. J. Scott's Keltie's "Partition of Africa" published, Feb. 1893.

Death of Mr. W. Cotton Oswell, discoverer of lake Ngami, &c., a companion of Livingstone, aged 75, 1 May, 1893.

Death of sir Theophilus Shepstone at Durban, aged 76 (active in S. Africa. 1835 *et seq.*), 26 June, 1893.

Mr. Selous's "Travels and Adventures in S. E. Africa' (1881 *et seq.*) published, 28 Sept. 1893.

Death of Sir Samuel Baker (see *Egypt*, 1869), aged 72, 30 Dec. 1893.

Death (by accident) of capt. Lovett Cameron, explorer, companion of Burton and others, aged 49, 26 March, 1894.

Sir Edw. Hertslet's work, "The Map of Africa by Treaty," published, 7 Feb. 1895.

Contract signed at Berlin for the establishment of an Anglo-German company to acquire 1,000,000 acres of land in S.W. Africa, 2 May, 1895.

Death of Herr Friedrich Gerhard Rohlfs, eminent explorer, 3 June, 1896.

Death of Dr. J. A. Moloney, African explorer (1892 *et seq.*), aged 38, 5 Oct. 1896.

Death of lieut. Edward D. Young, an explorer, *see above*, 1867, 4 Nov. 1896.

"Through Unknown African Countries," by A. Donaldson Smith. M.D., published 1897.

M. Antoine d'Abbadie, explorer of Abyssinia, &c., 1837–48; died 20 March, 1897.

"Impressions of S. Africa," by Jas. Bryce, published 1897.

M. E. A. Foa, French explorer, with a mission crossed the continent from Zanzibar to the Congo, 1894–97.

"South Africa of To-day," by capt. Francis Younghusband, published 1897.

Capt. Roberto Ivens, eminent explorer, died 28 Jan. 1898.

M. Gentil's 3 years' successful exploration in Central Africa to lake Chad; reported, 21 July, 1898.

Major Marchand's expedition lands at Loango, 23 July, 1896, reaches Loudima, 27 Sept.; defeats the rebels, and arrives at Brazzaville, 8 Nov.; ascends the Congo, and up the M'Bornu to Mehreh, 1 March—12 Sept. 1897; crossed the bush and reaches Fashoda (*which see*) 10 July, 1898; left Fashoda, 11 Dec.; ascended the Sobat river; crossed Abyssinia to Adis-Abeba, 10 March, 1899; reaching Jibuti, mid May, 1899.

Mr. J. Moore's expedition explores the great lakes; prooves Nyasa's greatest depth, 430 fathoms, mid Aug. 1899; scientific collections made at Tanganyika and other places, 20 Sept. *et seq.*; returns to London, July, 1900.

Internat. conference in London agree to protect wild animals from 20° N. to the Zambesi and N. of German S.W. Africa, May—June, 1900.

Major Gibbon's expedition leaves England, May, 1898; explores Marotseland, over 13,000 miles traversed; discovers the source of the Middle Zambesi, and reaches Omdurman, 20 Aug. 1900.

Messrs. E. S. Grogan and A. H. Sharp cross Africa from the Cape to Cairo, Oct. 1898—Feb. 1900.

Major Serpa Pinto, Portuguese African explorer, dies, aged 54, 28 Dec. 1900.

Herr Oscar Neumann and party journey from Zeila to Khartoum, chiefly through new country, some valuable discoveries and collections made, Jan. 1900—June, 1901.

Dr. Emil Holub, eminent (Austrian) explorer, died, 21 Feb. 1902.

Revolution in Wadai, fierce battle, sultan Ahmed succeeded by Mohamed Dudu; reported, 17 March, 1902.

Death of Sheikh Senussi El-Mahdi, a pious Moslem and idealist, aged about 65, at Kanem, Lake Chad; reported, 15 Aug. 1902.

GERMAN EAST AFRICA. Dr. Carl Peters goes to Africa as chief agent for the committee for German colonization, concludes treaties with 10 sultans; the German flag hoisted, Nov.-Dec. 1884.

The German East African Company, mainly founded by Dr. Peters, at Berlin, chartered, 12 Feb. 1886.

Settlements founded in the valley of the Kingani, March, April, 1886.

Treaty with the sultan of Zanzibar comes into force 19 Aug. 1886.

Dr. Peters, with a party of 23 engineers, medical men, &c., leaves Germany as the agent of the German Emin Pasha Relief Society, April, 1887.

The Germans attack Bagamoyo and kill natives, 23 Sept. 1888.

Collapse of the German settlement, attributed to the Arab slave-dealers; reported Oct. 1888.

The East African Bill passed by the Parliament, granting money for the defence of German interests, and the suppression of the slave trade, 30 Jan. 1889.

The Germans defeat the Arabs at Bagamoyo, 6 March, 1889.

Capt., after major, Wissmann, appointed imperial commissioner in East Africa, 21 Feb. (dissension with Dr. Peters), 31 March, 1889.

The German flag hoisted at the consulate; capt. Wissmann assumes the command, 5 April, 1889.

Dr. Peters organizing his Emin Relief Expedition; men and camels engaged, March, April, 1889.

Capt. Wissmann, aided by 200 German sailors, defeats Bushiri, an Arab slave-dealer, with little loss; Bushiri loses 80 killed and 20 prisoners, his camp destroyed, May, 1889.

Capt. Wissmann captures Pangani, 8 July, 1889.

Adm. Freemantle seizes the steamship *Neera*, belonging to the Emin Relief Expedition at Lamu, and takes it to Zanzibar, June; Dr. Peters remonstrates, 29 June; after a trial the ship is released, the owners paying costs, 6 Aug.; Dr. Peters directed by his committee to proceed no farther, 31 Oct. 1889.

Differences between the sultan of Zanzibar and the Germans respecting territory, about 8 Nov. 1889.

Major Wissmann receives Mr. H. M. Stanley, Emin pasha and party at Bagamoyo, 5 Dec. 1889.

After fights, Bushiri captured and hanged, 16 Dec. 1889.

Major Wissmann, after severe fighting, captures Bwana Heri's fortified position near Saadani, 5 Jan. 1890.

Arab tribes come to Bagamoyo and submit, about Jan. 18, 1890.

Bwana Heri holds a considerable force against major Wissmann, reported 16 Feb. 1890.

Emin pasha, after a long illness, occasioned by a fall from a window at Bagamoyo, 5 Dec. 1889, arrives at Zanzibar, 2 March; accepts the offers of major Wissmann, enters the German service, and proceeds with a military expedition to Victoria Nyanza, 31 March *et seq.* 1890.

Major Wissmann occupies Kilwa without resistance, 4 May; also Mikindani, 14 May; letter from Dr. Peters dated Kapte in Kamassia, 16 Jan., stating that he was 340 English miles from Wadelai in good health, received May, 1890.

Many losses by death and desertion; reported 13 May, 1890.

Major Wissmann leaves for Germany, lieut. Schmidt left in command, 26 May, 1890.

German forces: 207 officers, military and naval; 1,200 Soudanese, 380 Zulus, 120 Askaris, a number of Soumalis as police, a medical staff and sanitary officers; a fleet of 4 steamers, besides whale-boats; reported May, 1890.

A letter from Dr. Peters dated Rubaga in Uganda, 2 March, received 28 May; another dated Ukumi in Ussukuma, 13 April, received 20 May, 1890.

The German Parliament votes 4,850,000 marks for East African service, 24 June, 1890.

Mahomed Bin Cassim and three companions were hanged at Bagamoyo, after trial for murder of a German merchant about 8 years previously, 27 June, 1890.

Anglo-German convention, *which see*, signed at Berlin by the Emperor, 1 July, 1890.

Major von Wissmann, ennobled and warmly received in Berlin and other places, June; unwell, enjoined absolute rest, 14 July, 1890.

Dr. Peters and party arrive at Zanzibar about 10 July, telegraphs to his company 18 July, 1890.

[His treaty with the king of Uganda invalid; he is accused of living by raids on the natives.]

Advance of Emin pasha, severe fighting with the Masai in Ugogo, reported 31 July, 1890.

Dr. Carl Peters arrives in Berlin, 25 Aug. 1890.

The German East Africa Company cedes all its territorial rights to the Imperial Government, reported 28 Oct. 1890.

The emperor contributes 3,000 marks towards the building of the steamer *Wissmann*, to be placed on Lake Victoria Nyanza, about 5 Dec. 1890.

The Emin Pasha Relief Committee dissolves itself, 15 Dec. 1890.

Emin Pasha (refractory) recalled to the coast by major von Wissmann, imperial commissary, reported 19 Dec. 1890.

The German Imperial flag hoisted at Bagamoyo, 1 Jan.; Major von Wissmann established there, 26 Jan. 1891.

Baron von Soden appointed governor of German East Africa, Dr. Carl Peters his commissary, Feb., with a peaceful progressive programme, March, 1891.

Major von Wissmann severely punishes the Kishobo tribe for robbery, reported 6 March, 1891.

Returns to Bagamoyo 15 March, recalled for rest, reported 14 April, 1891.

Dr. Peters' "New Light on Dark Africa," published, spring, 1891.

The German expeditionary colonial troops under lieut. von Zelewski attacked by the natives (about 3,000) S. of the Ruaha river, the lieut. and other officers killed, 10 Europeans, and about 300 native members of the expedition massacred near the station Mpwapwa, Kondora; large capture of arms and ammunition, 17 Aug. 1891.

Captain Ruediger, appointed acting-governor of German East Africa, about 1 Oct. 1891.

Movements of Emin pasha about Albert Nyanza, repudiated by the German government, July; resignation of major von Wissmann, Oct. 1891.

Revolt of the Wadigoes against taxation; the Germans under captain Krenzler defeated 12 Dec., defeated again 19 Dec. 1891.

Baron von Soden pursues a peaceful policy in opposition to major von Wissmann, Jan. 1892.

He meets lieut. C. S. Smith and Dr. Peters, joint commissioners for the delimitation of the territories at Wanga, Feb. 1892.

The German parliament votes 2,500,000 marks for German interests in E. Africa and the suppression of the slave trade, 5 March, 1892.

Dr. Kayser sent to E. Africa to examine the state of the colony, May, 1892.

Emin pasha's geographical expedition starts from Kahura, 22 March, with Dr. Stuhlmann; suffers by want of provisions, &c., Dec. 1891; expedition divides, Emin ill, left behind by Dr. Stuhlmann, who goes to the German station on lake Victoria, 15 Feb., reported, May, 1892.

An expedition defeated by the natives in Moshi territory, near Kilima Njaro, baron von Bülow, lieut. Wolfram, and 30 men killed, 10 June, *et seq.*, the station at Kilima Njaro abandoned, reported, 30 June; re-occupied without fighting, 29 July, 1892.

Dr. Stuhlmann at Bagamoyo, 1 Aug. 1892.

Collision of Germans with the Wahehes near Kilossa, lieut. Brüning and 4 soldiers killed, 6 Oct. 1892.

Tranquillity restored, Dec. 1892.

Baron von Soden commended by the government, 2 March, resigns April, 1893.
Explorations of Dr. Oscar Baumann, 1892; discovers Lake Eiassi, etc., near Victoria Nyanza, reported, March, 1893. He died, aged 35, mid Oct. 1899.
Emin pasha murdered near Wadelai, about 20 Oct. 1892; reported, May, 1893.
Sultan Meli's camp stormed on Kilima-Njaro by Freiherr von Schele, 12 Aug. 1893.
Baron von Schele appointed governor of German East Africa, 21 Sept. 1893.
Sultan Meli submits to the Germans, reported, 24 Oct. 1893.
German flag hoisted at Kionga, Portugal objects, July, 1894; but afterwards yields, 10 Sept. 1894.
Successful campaign of baron von Schele against the Wahehe, Kuirenga destroyed, 30 Oct.–Nov. 1894.
Severe famine, through drought and locusts, Nov. to Jan.; relief measures undertaken, reported, Feb. 1895.
Major von Wissmann appointed governor, April, 1895; returns home, June, 1896; succeeded by major-gen. Liebert, Dec., 1896.
Dr. Peters, governor of Lake Tanganyika, &c., charged in the diet at Berlin with great inhumanity to the natives while acting as imperial commissioner, in Africa, 13 March, 1896; judicial inquiry ordered, 16 March; dismissed the service and fined 24 April, 1897, appeal dismissed Nov. 1897.
Two missionaries murdered by natives of Meru in the Kilima-Njaro district, 19 Oct. 1896.
Punitive expedition from Mochi very successful, natives sue for peace, 30 Oct.–6 Nov., reported 3 Feb., 1897.
Friedrich Schröder, agent, sentenced to 5 yrs. imprisonment for cruelty to the natives, 9 Nov. 1896.
Suicide of the sultan of Quawa to avoid capture; end of the Wahehe rising, reported, 7 Sept. 1898.
Agreement *re* the Trans-African telegraph from Cape Town to Cairo, signed at Berlin, 15 March, ratified, 28 Oct. 1899.
Great mortality from famine, plague and leprosy prevalent, reported, 12 Jan. 1900.
General von Liebert, governor, succeeded by count von Götzen Dec. 1900.
Sentence of death on prince Prosper Arenberg for murder of a native commuted to 15 years' imprisonment, reported, 12 March, 1901.
Financial report, 1901, unsatisfactory, issued, Sept. 1902.

GERMAN S.-W. AFRICA, see *Cameroons.*

ITALIAN AFRICA, see *Zanzibar*, 1893, *Somaliland* 1897, and *Massowah.*

PORTUGUESE E. AFRICA, see *Lourenço Marques.*

PORTUGUESE W. AFRICA.—Count Almoster, with a small force, massacred by natives near Humbe, reported 23 December, 1897.
Native attacks on fort Humbe repulsed with loss, reported 3 Feb., 1898.
Revolt suppressed, 4 native chiefs and 13 others arrested at Bailundu, reported, 29 May, 1902; natives repulsed at Bailundu, 13, 14 July, 1902; further successes, 20, 28 Aug.; 6 Sept. 1902.

BRITISH E. AFRICA.—The Imperial British East Africa Company, supported by Mr. Wm. Mackenzie, lord Brassey, gen. Donald Stewart, Mr. Burdett-Coutts, and others, sir Wm. Mackinnon, chairman; charter 3 Sept. 1888; large territories having been conceded to Mr. W. Mackenzie by the sultan of Zanzibar; concession signed, 9 Oct. 1888; confirmed, 1 Sept. 1889.
The sultan of Zanzibar surrenders all control over the British East Africa Company's territory for an annual payment of 26,000 dollars; reported 26 Dec. 1889.
Successful tour of Mr. Mackenzie through the company's territory, April, 1890.
Sir Francis de Winton appointed administrator of the company's territories, May; arrives at Zanzibar and proceeds to Mombasa, the chief station, Lamu, &c., 1890.
All slaves in the territory declared free by Mr. Mackenzie about 4 May; his final departure for Europe, much regretted, 26 May, 1890.
Mr. George S. Mackenzie, administrator of the territory, returns to England, July, 1890.
Anglo-German Convention (*which see*), 1 July, 1890.
Successful progress; army recruited from India; continued peace with the natives, July, 1890.
First general meeting of the company, London; report and statement of accounts read, 25 July, 1890.
Inauguration of the railway between Mombasa and Victoria Nyanza, 26 Aug. 1890.
Resignation of sir Francis de Winton, Feb. 1891.
Mr. George Mackenzie, director of the company, welcomed by the sultan of Zanzibar; the government of Witu assumed by the company; the country quite pacified, March, 1891.
Protocol for the delimitation of the British and Italian spheres of influence in East Africa, signed at Rome 24 March, 1891.
General Mathews, H.M.'s commissioner, arrives at Zanzibar, Sept. 1891.
Proposed withdrawal of representative from Uganda; serious consequences apprehended; great need of a railway from coastline to Victoria Nyanza, Sept. 1891.
Sir Gerald H. Portal appointed commissioner and consul-general in British East Africa, Feb. He and Mr. E. J. L. Berkeley, the administrator, suppress a revolt in Witu, April, 1892.
Witu tranquillised by Mr. Berkeley; the ex-sultan submits, reported, 10 June, 1892.
The company's new courts of justice at Mombasa opened by judge Cracknall, 10 June, 1892.
Treaty of the company with the king of Uganda (*which see*), 1891–92.
Disaffection of the Somalis suppressed with bloodshed, reported 5 Feb. 1893.
Uganda evacuated by the company, 31 March, 1893.
Meeting of the company in London; illness and resignation of sir William Mackinnon, 29 May; he died 22 June, 1893.
Evacuation of Witu by the company, 31 July, 1893; the deposed sultan Fumo Omari resists the British occupation, his stronghold stormed and captured, reported, 13 Aug.; Jongeni stormed by Mr. R. Rodd, Aug.; the Somalis at Kismayu revolt; part of the garrison desert, Mr. Hamilton, superintendent, killed in an attack, 11 Aug.; the mutiny suppressed by lieut. Lewes and count Lovatelli (Italian traveller), 18–23 Aug. 1893.
The rioters and murderers of Mr. Hamilton tried at Mombasa and punished, 30 June, 1894.
"The Rise of our East African Empire," by capt. aft. sir F. D. Lugard, published Nov. 1893.
Annual meeting (see *Uganda*), 31 July, 1894.
Special meeting: resolution adopted for dividing the company's capital into 1*l.* shares; discussion on the claims of the company on the government relative to Uganda, 22 Aug. 1894.
Counter proposals by the government, 14 Nov. 1894.
Commissioner and consul-gen. sir A. H. Hardinge, Jan. 1895.
At a meeting of directors in London, arbitration having been refused, they resolve to accept 250,000*l.* in return for the surrender of their charter, concessions, and assets, with some exceptions, and to request compensation for expenses connected with holding Uganda, 27 March, 1895; adopted 11 April, 1895; 50,000*l.* voted to the company, with 30,000*l.* for administration of territory, 13 June, 1895; a resolution for the winding-up of the company, etc., passed 24 July, confirmed 30 Oct. 1895. [The territory made a Protectorate 1895.]
Famine through drought and locusts, reported, 20 March, 1895.
Expedition of admiral Rawson and sir Wm. Matthews against M'bruck bin Rashed, leaves Mombasa 12 Aug.; his stronghold taken at M'wele, 17 Aug.; his camp burnt 2 Oct. 1895.
Punitive expedition against Hamis Kombo, an ally of Rashed, at Mpwapwa; capt. Lawrence killed in a skirmish near Gazi; Mpwapwa captured, Oct. 1895.
Ali bin Abdullah a powerful Arab, sentenced to 7 yrs. imprisonment and a fine of 5,000 rupees for cruelty to slaves; reported, 29 Feb. 1896.
An expedition sent from Mombasa against the rebel chief M'Baruk Aziz; 15–22 March, he and 1,000 followers surrendered to major von Wissmann in German territory; reported 22 April, 1896.
British judicial system introduced by order in council; 9 July, 1897.
Sir Arthur Hardinge's report on the protectorate published, Jan. 1898; the silver rupee of India ordered to be the standard coin from 1 Jan. 1899; 20 May, 1898.

Punitive expedition under Mr. Jenner against the Ogaden Somalis in Jubaland, June, some fighting, chiefs surrender, 21 Aug. 1898.

Col. Macdonald's successful expedition returns to Mombasa (see *Uganda*), 5 March, 1899.

Famine in several provinces, great mortality, March–Aug. 1899

Mt. Kenya, over 17,000 ft. high, first ascended by Mr. H. J. Mackinder, 12, 13 Sept., 1899.

Mr. Jenner, commissioner, murdered by the Ogaden Somalis in Jubaland, 16 Nov.; the Ogaden sultan taken prisoner and Aff-Madu occupied by the British, 5 Feb. 1901 (see *Somaliland*). Sir Chas. Eliot, commissioner, 1901; Mr. F. J. Jackson appointed dep.-commissioner, Nov. 1901.

BRITISH CENTRAL AFRICA (N. of the Zambesi, *which see*), and a protectorate of the districts around lake Nyasa.—Mr. H. H. Johnston (see *Kilima-Njaro*) appointed commissioner of British Central Africa, the districts N. of the South Africa Company's territories, March, 1891.

He and capt. Cecil Maguire attack the Arab slave-dealers, and release a large number of slaves, Oct., Nov. 1891.

Capt. Maguire with 30 sepoys, releases a number of slaves in a caravan and burns dhows in presence of a large party of enemies, but is killed while swimming to his ship; Dr. Boyce and Mr. M'Ewan are treacherously killed when about to treat for a truce, 15–17 Dec. 1891.

The Arabs surprise Fort Johnston and capture a gun; Mr. H. H. Johnston has only 70 sepoys and two gunboats on the Shiré; reported, April, 1892.

Mr. H. H. Johnston reports the pacification of the district, about 4 April, 1892.

Makanjira, and two other chiefs, slave-dealers, predominant, Jan. 1892.

Commissioner Johnston, reinforced with 2 gunboats, &c., captures Makanjira's positions; releases many slaves, and founds Fort Maguire on Lake Nyasa, reported, 12 Jan.; arrives in England, reports the defeat of Makanjira, general submission of chiefs, by maj. C. A. Edwards at Fort Maguire, and peace made in Nyasaland, 4 June, 1894; returns, May, 1895.

Death of Jumbe, Arab Sultan, on W. coast of lake Nyasa, a friend of the British, July, 1894.

Municipal powers given to Blantyre, the capital; reported, 20 Nov. 1894.

Mr. H. Johnston returns to Zomba from his tour of inspection; 28 July, 1895.

Successful N.W. expedition of Mr. Codrington; treaties with several chiefs; reported, 3 Sept. 1895.

Zarafi slave-trading chief completely defeated by a British expedition under major C. A. Edwards, his town occupied, 28 Oct. 1895, and many slaves released; expedition returns to Zomba, 17 Nov.; North Nyasa Arabs severely defeated after 3 days fighting; 1–3 Dec. 1895.

Mlozi, a slave-raiding chief, tried by native chiefs under commissioner Johnston, condemned and hanged, 4 Dec. 1895.

Commissioner H. H. Johnston made K.C.B., telegraphic communication opened, message to the queen, and her reply sent, 19 Dec. 1895; arrives in London, on leave, 26 June, 1896.

John S. Brabant, H.M. commissioner in Nyasaland, 1895.

Great victories over Mwasi and other slave-dealing chiefs, by lieut. Alston and capt. F. T. Stewart on the west of lake Nyasa; British forts erected; power of the slave-trade completely broken; total of slaves released, 1,184; reported, 25 Jan. 1896.

Lieut. Alston captures Katuri, a cruel Yao chief, releases many slaves, and burns his town, other Yao chiefs submit to the British; reported, 30 Sept. 1896.

Serious attacks on the S.-W. frontier, by the Angoni-Zulus under Chikusi, villages raided and people massacred; Mr. Sharpe, acting-commissioner at Blantyre, sends 3 columns under capts. Stewart, Manning, and lieut. Alston, 12 Oct. [lieut. Alston died of fever, much lamented; reported, 8 May, 1897.]

The rising in S. Nyasaland suppressed, and Chikusi captured, tried and hanged, 21 Oct.; Odete's stronghold carried by assault by Capt. Manning, and Odete exiled, 10 Oct. 1896.

North Charterland exploration company; lieut.-col. R. Gardner Warton successfully occupies Mpseni's country in Central Africa, north of the Zambesi, and establishes friendly relations with this chief; reported, *Times*, 12 Oct. 1896.

"British Central Africa," by sir H. H. Johnston, map, etc., published June, 1897.

Expedition under major Macdonald into the interior organized at Kikuyu, 16 Aug. 1897.

Punitive expedition under capt. W. H. Manning against the Angurus for raids, &c., S.-E. lake Shirwa, Serumba's town and he himself taken, 9, 10 Aug. 1897.

Raids and revolt of the Angoni Zulus, Jan. 1898; repressed by a strong force under col. Manning, about 20 natives killed, and the impi broken up; Mr. Carl Wiese and party relieved, 18 Jan.; successful campaign against Mpseni, he surrenders, 9 Feb. 1898.

Mr. Sharpe's report 1901-2 satisfactory; *Times* 11 Aug., 1902.

THE BRITISH SOUTH AFRICA COMPANY chartered (see *Rhodesia*, 1896–7, and under *Zambesi*, 29 Oct. 1889).

BRITISH SOUTH AFRICAN COLONIES are Cape Colony, Natal, Basutoland, Orange River Colony, and the Transvaal, with a protectorate over part of Bechuanaland, 1900, *et seq.*; high commissioner, Lord Milner, Jan. 1901.

Proposed international peace exhibition in S. Africa, near Johannesburg, in 1904; committee formed, lord Strathcona, sir Robert Herbert, sir Albert Rollit, sir Alfred Jones, sir J. Jejeebhoy, the maharajah of Tagore, and others, *Times*, 13 Aug. 1902.

BRITISH WEST AFRICA. See *Niger Coast, Lagos, etc.*

FRENCH WEST AFRICA, *which see*, and *Senegal*.

French Guinea, Ivory Coast, and Benin constituted separate possessions by decree, 17 March, 1893.

Expedition of M. Maistre and 5 others, July, 1892; after many difficulties arrives near the mouth of the Niger, 26 March, 1893; treaties signed with the Garua and Sarra countries, reported, Nov. 1893; decree issued at Paris for the establishment of a colony, the French Soudan, under a civil governor, M. Grodet, 22 Nov. 1893

Franco-German agreement signed at Berlin as to the Hinterland of the Cameroons, 15 March, 1894.

The king of Bariba, or Borgou, submits to the French, by treaty reported, 16 Dec. 1894.

BRITISH SOUTH-WEST AFRICA COMPANY (see *Damaraland*), Sept. 1892.

AFRICAN ASSOCIATION, for promoting the exploration of central Africa, was formed in June, 1788, principally by sir Joseph Banks; and under its auspices many additions were made to African geography by Ledyard, Park, Burckhardt, Hornemann, &c. It merged into the Royal Geographical Society, July, 1831.

AFRICAN CHURCH. In 1866 Robert Gray, bishop of Capetown (in consequence of a decision of the privy council; see *Church of England*), established synods of the "Church of South Africa."

AFRICAN COMPANY (merchants trading to Africa) arose out of an association in London formed in 1588. A charter was granted to a joint-stock company in 1618; a second company was created in 1631; a third corporation in 1662; another was formed in 1672; remodelled in 1695. In 1821 the company was abolished.

AFRICAN EXPLORATION FUND, founded by Royal Geographical Society, May, 1877.

AFRICAN INSTITUTION, founded in London in 1807, for the abolition of the slave trade, and the civilization of Africa. Many schools have been established with success, particularly at Sierra Leone.

NATIONAL AFRICAN COMPANY incorporated in 1882; chartered, 10 July, 1886, as the Royal Niger Company. See *Niger*.

AFRICAN EXHIBITION, in Pall-Mall, chiefly illustrative of life in Central Africa, especially near lake Tanganyika; arranged by captain Edward C. Hore; opened 18 May, 1893. The exhibition was patronized by the Royal Geographical, Anti-Slavery, and London Missionary societies.

African exhibition at the Crystal Palace; a Somaliland village, with natives and animals, and a loan exhibition, including the collections of Mr. F. C. Selous and Mr. H. M. Stanley, &c.; 18 May *et seq.* 1895.

AFRIKANDER BUND. A confederation of the descendants of the Dutch settlers in South

Africa, formed to extend their influence, became prominent after the Transvaal war in 1881. Title changed to S. African Association, 2 Dec. 1902. See *Boers* and *Transvaal*. A congress of the Bund opened at Burghersdorp, 4 Nov. 1891, for the settlement of the land question. Annual congresses held. Opposition to Mr. Cecil Rhodes voted, 18 March, 1897. See *Cape of Good Hope*, Dec. 1900 and 1903.

AGAPÆ (*agapē*, Greek for love, charity), "feasts of charity," referred to *Jude* 12, and described by Tertullian, of which the first Christians of all ranks as one family partook, as Christ did with his disciples. Disorders creeping in, these feasts were forbidden to be celebrated in churches by the councils of Laodicea (366) and Carthage (390). They are still recognised by the Greek church, and are held in their original form weekly by the Glassites or Sandemanians, and in some degree by the Moravians, Wesleyans, and others.

AGAPEMONE (Greek, "the abode of love"), an establishment at Charlinch, near Bridgwater, Somersetshire, founded in 1845, where Henry James Prince,* and his deluded followers, formerly persons of property, lived in common, professing to devote themselves to innocent recreation and to maintain spiritual marriage. The Agapemone is described by Mr. Hepworth Dixon in his "Spiritual Wives," published in Jan. 1868. Meetings of the sect were held at Hamp, near Bridgwater, Dec., 1872. An "abode" at Spaxton (1849) and at Clapton, about 1895. The latter disused in 1902 through reprobation of the public. See *Impostors*.

AGAR-TOWN, the name given to a district in St. Pancras parish, N. London. It consisted of hovels, erected on the site of the grounds of councillor Agar, after 1841, which, from their filthy and uncivilised condition, were termed by Charles Dickens, in 1851, the English Connemara. The entire district was cleared by the Midland Railway Company.

AGE. Chronologers have divided the time between the creation and the birth of Christ into ages. Hesiod (735 B.C.) described the Golden, Silver, Brazen, Heroic, and Iron Ages; Ovid (43 B.C.—18 A.D.) omits in his enumeration the Heroic Age; see *Dark Ages*.

	B.C.
FIRST AGE (from the Creation to the Deluge)	4004–2349
SECOND AGE (to the coming of Abraham into Canaan)	2348–1922
THIRD AGE (to the Exodus from Egypt)	1921–1491
FOURTH AGE (to the founding of Solomon's Temple)	1490–1014
FIFTH AGE (to the capture of Jerusalem)	1014– 588
SIXTH AGE (to the birth of Christ)	588– 4
SEVENTH AGE (to the present time)	

* Prince was born in 1811, died Jan., 1899; educated for the medical profession and licensed to practise, 1832; gave it up for the church and entered St. David's college, Lampeter, and there commenced ultra-revivalist movements in 1836; and finally claimed to be an incarnation of the Deity, with corresponding authority over his followers. On 22 May, 1850, Thomas Robinson sought to recover the possession of his child from the care of its mother (from whom he had separated); the application was refused by the vice-chancellor, to "save the child from the pollution of the parent's teaching."—On 21 Aug. 1858, Miss Louisa Jane Nottidge died, having transferred her property to Mr. H. J. Prince. Her brother, Mr. Nottidge, by an action, recovered from Prince 5728*l*., as having been fraudulently obtained. Extraordinary disclosures were made during the trial, 25 July, 1860. In the autumn of 1860, the Rev. Mr. Price, after several vain attempts, succeeded in rescuing his wife from the Agapemone. They had both been early supporters of it.

ARCHÆOLOGICAL AGES. The various stages through which man has passed in the process of development and civilization are divided into the *Stone Age*—(*a*) Palæolithic, rough stone cutting tools and weapons; (*b*) Neolithic, polished stone implements—the *Bronze Age* (with an *Age of Copper* in place of, or in addition to, the Age of Bronze), and (*c*) the *Iron Age*, the two last characterised by tools and weapons of such materials. No sharply defined chronological division can be made between these Ages, the Stone Age of one area sometimes co-existing with that of the Bronze or Iron Age of another area of the same period.

AGE. In Greece and Rome twenty-five was full age for both sexes, but a greater age was requisite for the holding certain offices: *e.g.* thirty for tribunes; forty-three for consuls. In England the minority of a male terminates at twenty-one, and of a female in some cases, as that of a queen, at eighteen. In 1547, the majority of Edward VI. was, by the will of his father, fixed at eighteen years; previously to completing which age, his father, Henry VIII., had assumed the reins of government, in 1509.—A *male* of twelve may take the oath of allegiance; at fourteen he may consent to a marriage, or choose a guardian; at seventeen he may be an executor, and at twenty-one he is of age; but according to the Statute of Wills, 7 Will. IV. & 1 Vict. c. 26, 1837, no will made by any person under the age of twenty-one years shall be valid. A *female* at twelve may consent to a marriage, at fourteen she may choose a guardian, and at twenty-one she is of age.

AGED PILGRIMS' FRIEND SOCIETY, founded 1807, provides pensions to Protestants over 60 years of age; asylums, 1826, 1871, 1879, 1884; income 1900, 15,000*l*.

AGINCOURT, OR AZINCOUR (N. France), a village where Henry V. of England, with about 9000 men, defeated about 60,000 French on St. Crispin's day, 25 Oct. 1415. Of the French, there were, according to some accounts, 10,000 killed, including the dukes of Alençon, Brabant, and Bar, the archbishop of Sens, one marshal, thirteen earls, ninety-two barons, and 1500 knights; and 14,000 prisoners, among whom were the dukes of Orleans and Bourbon, and 7000 barons, knights, and gentlemen. The English lost the duke of York, the earl of Suffolk, and about 20 others. St. Rémy asserts with more probability that the English lost 1600 men. Henry V. soon after obtained the kingdom of France.

AGIO, the difference between the real and the nominal value of money.

AGITATORS (or Adjutators), officers appointed by the Parliamentary army in 1647, to take care of its interests: each troop or company had two. The general Cromwell was eventually obliged to repress their seditious power. At a review he seized the ringleaders of a mutiny, shot one instantly, in the presence of his companions and the forces on the ground, and thus restored discipline. *Hume*.—Daniel O'Connell, the *agitator of Ireland*, was born in 1775. He began to agitate at the elections in 1826; was elected for Clare, 5 July, 1828; the election being declared void, he was re-elected 30 July, 1829. After the passing of the Catholic emancipation bill, he agitated in vain for the repeal of the union, 1834 to 1843. He died 15 May, 1847.—Richard Cobden and John Bright were the chief *Anti-corn-law agitators*, 1841-45.—Mr. Bright became a *Reform agitator* in 1866.

AGNADELLO (N. E. Italy). Here Louis XII. of France gained a great victory over the Venetians, some of whose troops were accused of cowardice and treachery; 14 May, 1509. The conflict is also termed the battle of the Rivolta.

AGNOITÆ (from *agnoia*, Greek, *ignorance*). I. A sect founded by Theophronius of Cappadocia about 370: said to have doubted the omniscience of God. II. The followers of Themistius of Alexandria, about 530, who held peculiar views as to the body of Christ, and doubted his divinity.

AGNOSTICS, name given to philosophers who assert that we have no knowledge but what we acquire by means of our senses, about 1876. The word Agnostic was introduced by the late Professor Huxley in 1869. "An Agnostic Apology," by Mr. Leslie Stephen, published 1893.

AGNUS DEI (Lat. "Lamb of God"), the title of a prayer set to music in the Roman Catholic Mass. Also a figure of a lamb bearing a cross impressed on a gold, silver, or wax disc, consecrated by the popes since the 14th cent. The A. D. with the banner of the cross is used as a symbol of Jesus Christ in ecclesiastical art.

AGONISTICI (from *agōn*, Greek, *a conflict*), also termed *circutores*, a branch of the Donatists (*which see*) in the 4th century. They preached with boldness, and incurred severe persecution.

AGRA (N. W. India), founded by Akbar in 1566, was the capital of the Great Mogul; see *Mausoleums*. In 1658 Aurungzebe removed to Delhi.—The fortress of Agra, "the key of Hindostan," in the war with the Mahrattas surrendered to the British forces, under general Lake, 17 Oct. 1803, after one day's siege: 162 pieces of ordnance and 240,000*l*. were captured.—In June, 1857, the city was abandoned to the mutineers by the Europeans, who took refuge in the fort, from which they were rescued by major Montgomery and colonel Greathed. Visit of the prince of Wales, 25 Jan., 1876.—Allahabad was made capital of the N.W. provinces of India, instead of Agra, in 1861. Pop. 1901, 188,300.

AGRAM (formerly Zagrab), a city of Croatia, Hungary, residence of the ban; suffered much by earthquakes, 9–12 Nov. 1880. See *Croatia*.

AGRARIAN LAW (*Agraria lex*), decreed an equal division among the Roman people of all the lands acquired by conquest, limiting the acres which each person should enjoy. It was first proposed by the consul Spurius Cassius, 486 B.C., and occasioned his judicial murder when he went out of office in 485.—An agrarian law was passed by the tribune Licinius Stolo, 376; and for proposing further amendments Tiberius Gracchus in 133, and his brother Cornelius in 121, were murdered. Livius Drusus, a tribune, was murdered for the same cause, 91. Julius Cæsar propitiated the plebeians by passing an agrarian law in 59.—In modern times the term has been misinterpreted to signify a division of the lands of the rich among the poor, frequently proposed by demagogues, such as *Gracchus* Babeuf, editor of the *Tribun du Peuple*, in 1794. In 1796 he conspired against the directory with the view of obtaining a division of property, was condemned, and killed himself, 27 May, 1797. *Agrarian league*, see *Germany*, 1895.

AGRICOLA'S WALL, see *Roman Walls*.

AGRICULTURAL CHILDREN ACT prohibits employment of children under eight years of age, and provides for the education of older children, 5 Aug. 1873.

AGRICULTURAL HALL, Islington, N. London, chiefly for the meetings of the Smithfield Club. The foundation stone was laid by the president, lord Berners, 5 Nov. 1861. The hall has been much used for industrial exhibitions, public meetings, equestrian and pedestrian performances, concerts, &c. The hall was visited by queen Victoria, 5 March, 1891. See *Horses*.

It was opened for an exhibition of dogs, 24 June, 1862; horses and donkeys exhibited, July, 1864, and annually since.
First Smithfield annual cattle show here, 6 Dec. 1862.
A great reform demonstration was made here, 30 July, 1866.
Grand ball to the Belgian visitors, volunteers and garde civique; prince of Wales present, 18 July, 1867.
Excellent horse-shows held here, May, 1868, *et seq.*
Theatrical bull-fights here stopped, on account of cruelty, 28 Mar. 1870.
Workmen's International exhibition opened by the prince of Wales, 16 July, 1870.
National Exhibition of machinery, appliances, manufactures, and produce, opened 29 Sept. 1879.
Exhibition by the building trades, opened 12 April, 1880.
Tournaments (*which see*) held here 21 June, 1880, *et seq.*
International food exhibition, opened 13 Oct. 1880.
Milling exhibition (under direction of National Association of British and Irish Millers), 10–18 May, 1881.
"Arcadia," rural entertainment, July to Sept. 1887, and dairy shows, held annually.
International shoe and leather fair opened, 10 April, 1899; and Salvation Army exhibition, 24 July, 1899.
International tramways and light railways congress and exhibition opened 30 June, 1902.

NATIONAL AGRICULTURAL HALL, W. Kensington; foundation laid by the earl of Zetland 21 July, 1885; main hall 440 feet long, 250 feet wide and 100 feet high; with a minor hall for offices, &c.; the roof consists of iron and glass; designed by the late Mr. Henry E. Coe; present architect Mr. James Edmeston; contractors Messrs. Lucas and others; cost of erection about 131,000*l*.; named OLYMPIA. Opened with horse-racing and other diversions 27 Dec. 1886; horse show opened 14 May, 1887; (another 16 May, 1889); opened by the Paris Hippodrome Company 22 Oct. 1887. See *Irish Exhibition*.

AGRICULTURAL HOLDINGS ACT, passed 13 Aug. 1875, relates to compensations of landlords and tenants, for improvements, &c. Two other important acts: for England 46 & 47 Vict. c. 61, for Scotland, c. 62, were passed 25 Aug. 1883, to begin 1 Jan. 1884. Another act, introduced by Mr. H. Chaplin, 22 Feb., passed 27 June, 1892; another passed, 8 Aug., 1900.

AGRICULTURAL LAND RATING, reduction of rates by half the deficiency being supplied by imperial taxation; the act introduced by Mr. Chaplin, 20 April; passed committee after 22½ hours' sitting, 22 May; royal assent, 20 July, 1896; continuance act passed, 15 Aug., 1901; a similar act for Scotland passed, 14 Aug., 1896.

AGRICULTURE. "Abel was a keeper of sheep, but Cain was a tiller of the ground," *Genesis* iv. 2.

Cato the Censor (died 149 B.C.) and Varro (died 28 B.C.) were eminent Roman writers on agriculture.
Virgil's Georgics, 30 B.C. Agriculture in England improved by the Romans after A.D. 44.
Fitzherbert's "Book of Husbandry," printed 1523.
Tusser's "Five Hundred Points of Husbandry," 1562.
Blythe's "Improver," 1649.
Hartlib's "Legacy," 1650.
Jethro Tull's "Horse-hoeing Husbandry," 1701.
About the end of the 18th century, fallowing was gradually superseded by turnips and green crops.
Board of Agriculture, proposed by Sir John Sinclair, afterwards president, established 1793. Arthur Young

many years secretary. Communications published in 7 vols., 1797—1811.

A parliamentary committee to inquire into agricultural distress appointed early in 1836.

In Aug. 1855, a committee presented a report on the best mode of obtaining accurate Agricultural Statistics. There were, in 1831, 1,055,982 agricultural labourers in Great Britain, and in Ireland, 1,131,715.

Acreage of crops, and number of cattle, sheep, and pigs in Great Britain and Ireland, beginning with 1866, published in the annual "Statistical Abstract," since 1869. See p. 29.

It was reckoned by the Agricultural Committee, that the cultivation of waste lands would yield above 20,000,000*l.* a year. It was calculated in 1854 that there were in England 32,160,000 acres in cultivation, of the annual value of 37,412,000*l.* Since that time, much land has been brought into cultivation; see *Wheat*.

"History of Agriculture and Prices in England (1259-1702)," by Professor James T. Rogers, published, June, 1866-1887.

Sir James Caird, eminent agriculturist and writer, dies 9 Feb. 1892.

National conference on agricultural depression in St. James's hall, London; landowners, tenant-farmers, labourers and delegates from clubs, &c. Mr. James Lowther, chairman; Mr. Henry Chaplin, chief speaker; remedies proposed by resolutions: moderate protection, reduced rents and taxes, bi-metallism and the formation of an agricultural union of all classes, 7, 8 Dec. The earl of Winchilsea appeals to the labourers to support the union, 22 Dec. 1892; not accepted in some counties; a committee to carry out the scheme formed Jan.; first report of the organizing committee issued 10 Jan. 1893.

Meetings in favour of the union, the earl of Winchilsea frequently present: at York, 5 Jan. 1893; Winchester, 14 Jan.; Gloucester, 14 Jan.; Bungay and other places, Jan.; Ipswich, 17 Jan.; Plymouth, 19 Jan.; Lincoln, 20 Jan.; Tunbridge Wells, 25 Jan. 1893.

Meeting of the Central and Associated Chambers of Agriculture, London; the report of the committee for organizing the establishment of the "National Agricultural Union," adopted 14 Feb. 1893.

First meeting of the elected council of the National Agricultural Union, at St. James's hall (the union has 334 branches, and 35 rural councils), the earl of Winchilsea elected president 10 October, 1894 (died 1898); annual congresses, 13 Dec. 1894; 12 Dec. 1895; 3 Dec. 1896; 9 Dec. 1897; 7 Dec., lord Templetown president, 1898.

Mr. R. M. Garnier's History of the English landed interest, published 1892 and 1894.

Royal commission to inquire into agricultural depression appointed, Mr. Shaw Lefevre (chairman); Mr. H. Chaplin, viscount Cobham, lord Vernon, Mr. R. Giffen, Mr. C. Mellor, Mr. Walter Long, and others, Mr. Herbert Lyon, secretary, Sept. 1893. Meeting at Westminster, 14 Sept. 1893; first report presented to parliament 2 April, 1894; interim report, 2 March, 1896; final report, Aug. 1897.

Second annual agricultural congress, opened at St. James's hall, 7 Dec. 1893.

"Cable farm" established at Haverholme, Lincolnshire, by the earl of Winchilsea, for experiments in the growth of flax, &c., the results to be reported in the *Cable*, a newspaper, April, 1894.

AGRICULTURAL SOCIETIES.—The earliest mentioned in the British Isles was the Society of Improvers of Agriculture in Scotland, instituted in 1723. A Dublin Agricultural Society (1749) gave a stimulus to agriculture in Ireland; its origin is attributed to Mr. Prior of Rathdowney, Queen's County, in 1731. The Bath and West of England Society established, 1777; and the Highland Society of Scotland, 1784. County Agricultural Societies are now numerous.

Royal counties show at Windsor, 5 June, 1899.

Opened by the prince of Wales at Reading, 12 June, 1902.

London Board of Agriculture established by act of parliament, 1793.

Francis, duke of Bedford, a great promoter of agriculture, died 2 March, 1802; the duke of Bedford publishes "A Great Agricultural Estate: the story of the origin and administration of Woburn and Thorney," 1897.

Royal Agricultural Society of England established in 1838, by noblemen and gentlemen, the chief landed proprietors in the kingdom, and incorporated by royal charter, 26 March, 1840. It holds two meetings annually, one in London, the other in the country. It awards prizes, and publishes a valuable journal. The Society's permanent Show Yard at Park Royal, near Twyford Abbey, was opened, and the London show held there, 23–27 June, 1903.

1839. Oxford.
1840. Cambridge.
1841. Liverpool.
1842. Bristol.
1843. Derby.
1844. Southampton.
1845. Shrewsbury.
1846. Newcastle.
1847. Northampton.
1848. York.
1849. Norwich.
1850. Exeter.
1851. Windsor.
1852. Lewes.
1853. Gloucester.
1854. Lincoln.
1855. Carlisle.
1856. Chelmsford.
1857. Salisbury.
1858. Chester.
1859. Warwick.
1860. Canterbury.
1861. Leeds.
1862. Battersea.
1863. Worcester.
1864. Newcastle-on-Tyne.
1865. Plymouth.
1866. Bury St. Edmunds.
1867. No meeting.
1868. Leicester.
1869. Manchester.
1870. Oxford.
1871. Wolverhampton.
1872. Cardiff.
1873. Hull.
1874. Bedford.
1875. Taunton.
1876. Birmingham
1877. Liverpool.
1878. Bristol.
1879. London.
1880. Carlisle.
1881. Derby.
1882. Reading.
1883. York.
1884. Shrewsbury
1885. Preston.
1886. Norwich.
1887. Newcastle-on-Tyne.
1888. Nottingham
1889. Windsor.
1890. Plymouth.
1891. Doncaster.
1892. Warwick.
1893. Chester.
1894. Cambridge.
1895. Darlington
1896. Leicester.
1897. Manchester
1898. Birmingham
1899. Maidstone
1900. York
1901. Cardiff
1902. Carlisle (last country meeting)

Jubilee state banquet at St. James's Palace, prince of Wales in the chair, 26 March, 1889.

Institute of Agriculture; South Kensington; courses of lectures given, Oct. 1883.

International Agricultural Exhibition, promoted by the society, and held at Kilburn, London, N.W. Occupied 106 acres. It was opened by the prince of Wales 30 June, visited by the Queen in July, and closed finally, 10 July, 1879.

Royal Agricultural Society of Ireland, instituted 1841.

Farmers' Club, 1843.

"*Chambers of Agriculture*" were established in France in 1851. In Great Britain, the *Central Chamber* was founded 1865; the associated Chambers in 1903 (Sept.) numbered 70, with a membership of about 20,000. A journal commenced early in 1868.

Royal Agricultural College at Cirencester organised, 1842; chartered, 1845.

Agricultural College in Wiltshire; its establishment proposed by the Mercers' Company, London, by the gift of 60,000*l.* Oct. 1888.

Suffolk Agricultural College at Bury St. Edmunds opened 1874. Other colleges opened.

South-Eastern Agricultural College at Wye, near Ashford, opened 1894.

Lady Warwick Hostel, Agricultural college for women, at Reading, opened, Oct. 1898.

British Dairy Farmers' Association.—Inaugurated; first show opened at Agricultural hall, London, 24–28 Oct. 1876.

Royal Agricultural Benevolent Institution.—It relieves farmers and their widows and orphans; founded chiefly by Mr. Mechi, 1860.

The Associated Agriculturists of Great Britain, a limited company, proposed April, 1881.

AGRICULTURAL CHEMISTRY.—Sir Humphry Davy delivered lectures on this subject (afterwards published), at the instance of the Board of Agriculture, in 1812; but it excited little attention till the publication of Liebig's work in 1840, which made a powerful impression. Liebig's "Letters on Agriculture" appeared in 1859. Boussingault's "Economie Rurale" appeared in 1844; his "Agronomie" in 1860-8. He died May, 1887. Great progress made by the experiments of Lawes, Gilbert, Pasteur, and others.

The important experiments of sir John Bennet Lawes and Dr. J. H. Gilbert (knt., Aug. 1893; died 23 Dec., 1901) began at Rothamsted, Herts, in 1843. The jubilee was observed at a meeting of the Royal Agricultural society, 1 March, 1893, the prince of Wales in the chair, when it was determined to set up a granite memorial on the spot where the experiments were carried on. Sir John, by the gift of 100,000*l*., endowed their continuance after his death. The memorial was set up, Mr. Herbert Gardner, M.P., present, 29 July, 1893. Sir John Lawes died, aged 85, 31 Aug., 1900.

AGRICULTURAL GANGS.—In the spring of 1867, most painful exposures were made of the prevalence of much cruelty and immorality in the gang system (in which boys and girls are employed) in several of the eastern and midland counties; and in consequence an act was passed 20 Aug. for regulating these gangs, licensing gang-masters, &c.

A Union of Agricultural Labourers, managed chiefly by Joseph Arch, formerly a labourer, afterwards a Methodist preacher (M.P. 1885) (his autobiography, edited by the countess of Warwick, published 1898), was inaugurated at Leamington, Warwickshire, 29 March, 1872. The movement spread, being countenanced by Auberon Herbert, M.P., and others. The Union met in London, Arch re-elected president, 16, 17 May, 1877; at Bedford, 16 Sept. 1881.

Lock-out of agricultural labourers belonging to the Union (lasted 18 weeks, costing the Union much money), began at Alderton, Suffolk, March, 1872.

Dispute between Lincolnshire farmers and labourers settled, 18–20 May; Suffolk and Norfolk farmers refuse compromise, about 25 May: the Union ceased to support the locked-out labourers, leaving them to emigration, or to seek employment, 27 July, 1872.

The agitation subsided; the labourers were employed, autumn, 1875; agricultural return for Great Britain, 1873; reported steady increase in prosperity, 1875.

The delegates of the National Agricultural Labourers' Union met, 26 Oct. 1875.

Very great agricultural depression through bad seasons, and foreign importations; many landlords remit large part of rents, 1877–9.

Royal Commission of Inquiry appointed 4 July, 1879.

Committee of Council on Agriculture appointed, earl of Rosebery president, about 27 April, 1883.

The Agricultural Returns of Great Britain were issued for the first time by the newly-constituted Agricultural Department, 1883. Second return presented, 27 Oct. 1884, and continued annually.

The Departmental Committee recommend State aid for education, dairy schools, &c., March, 1888.

A new Board of Agriculture was established by Act passed 12 Aug.; Henry Chaplin appointed president and cabinet minister, 5 Sept. The board assumed the duties previously fulfilled by a department of the privy council, 1889. Herbert Gardner, president, Aug. 1892; Walter Long, July, 1895; enlarged powers given. Land Transfer act, 1897; Universities and College Estates act, 1898; Commons act, 1899; Sale of Food and Drugs act, 1899; Improvement of Land act, 1899; Quarterly Journal, No. 1, published 7 Sept. 1894.

In accordance with the Board of Agriculture and Fisheries Act, 1903, the powers of the Board of Trade relating to fisheries were from 1 Oct. 1903 transferred to the Board of Agriculture, which from that date is styled the Board of Agriculture and Fisheries.

International Agricultural Congress, at Paris, 1889; at Vienna, 2 Sept., 1890; The Hague, 7 Sept. 1891; Brussels, 8–16 Sept. 1895; Budapest, 17–20 Sept. 1896; Lausanne, 12–17 Sept. 1898.

Much injury caused by the diamond-back moth, summer, 1891, 1892.

Chaff Cutting Machines (Accidents) act, 1897.

An agricultural education committee, a private association formed with a view of making the present educational system more applicable to country life and pursuits, first meeting, London, sir W. Hart Dyke in the chair, sir Henry Roscoe and others present, 20 Oct., 1899.

Scientific agriculture in the United States, experiment stations established under the act of 1887, 445 annual reports in 1899.

The following table, drawn up by Mr. William Couling, C.E., in 1827, is extracted from the Third Report of the Emigration Committee:—

Countries.	Cultivated.	Wastes capable of improvement.	Unprofitable.	Total.
	ACRES.	ACRES.	ACRES.	ACRES.
England	25,632,000	3,454,000	3,256,400	32,342,400
Wales	3,117,000	530,000	1,105,000	4,752,000
Scotland	5,265,000	5,950,000	8,523,930	19,738,930
Ireland	12,125,280	4,900,000	2,416,664	19,441,944
Brit. Isles	383,690	166,000	569,469	1,119,159
	46,522,970	15,000,000	15,871,463	77,394,433

About that period it was computed that the soil of the United Kingdom was annually cropped in the following proportions:

	ACRES.
Wheat	7,000,000
Barley and rye	1,950,000
Potatoes, oats and beans	6,500,000
Turnips, cabbages, and other vegetables	1,150,000
Clover, rye-grass, &c.	1,750,000
Fallow	2,800,000
Hop-grounds	60,000
Nursery grounds	20,000
Inclosed fruit, flower, kitchen and other gardens	110,000
Pleasure grounds	100,000
Land depastured by cattle	21,000,000
Hedge-rows, copses, and woods	2,000,000
Ways, water, &c.	2,100,000
Cultivated land	46,540,000

CROPS OF GREAT BRITAIN AND IRELAND:—

		Corn Crops. Acres.	*Green Crops.* Acres.	*Grasses, &c.* Acres.
1866.	Great Britain	9,252,784	3,562,434	15,964,553
	Ireland	2,174,033	1,481,525	12,006,191
1870.	Great Britain	9,548,041	3,586,730	16,577,740
	Ireland	2,173,109	1,498,719	....
1876.	Great Britain	9,194,669	3,571,874	18,056,217
	Ireland	1,848,487	1,363,224	....
1883.	Great Britain	8,618,675	3,454,579	19,461,295
	Ireland	1,678,125	1,230,253	....
1887.	Great Britain	8,145,894	3,463,706	20,452,422
	Ireland	1,562,463	1,229,092	....
1889.	Great Britain	8,075,172	3,299,647	15,865,863
	Ireland	1,535,102	1,219,549	....
1890.	Great Britain	8,033,133	3,297,528	16,017,492
	Ireland	1,514,607	1,214,396	....
1893.	Great Britain	7,655,739	3,286,906	16,492,567
	Ireland	1,489,393	1,153,527	......
1896.	Great Britain	7,416,690	3,258,591	16,726,476
	Ireland	1,420,721	1,147,717	.....
1899.	Great Britain	7,406,887	3,149,103	21,488,193
	Ireland	1,371,608	1,102,041	12,693,919
1901.	Great Britain	7,133,708	3,129,198	21,683,636
	Ireland	1,317,590	1,079,429	12,756,399
1902.	United King'm	8,517,000	4,241,000	28,409,000

See also *Breadstuffs*.

AGRIGENTUM (now *Girgenti*), a city of Sicily, built about 582 B.C. It was governed by tyrants from 566 to 470; among these were—Phalaris (see *Brazen Bull*); Alcamanes; Theron who, with his step-father Gelon, defeated the Carthaginians at Himera, 480: and Thrasydæus, his son, expelled in 470; when a republic was established. It was taken by the Carthaginians in 405 B.C., and held, except during short intervals, till gained by the Romans in 262 B.C. From A.D. 825 till 1086 it was held by the Saracens.

AHMEDNUGGUR (W. India), once capital of a state founded by Ahmed Shah, about 1493. After having fallen into the hands of the Moguls and the Mahrattas, 1797, it was taken from the latter by Arthur Wellesley, 12 Aug. 1803, and restored to the British dominions, June, 1817, made a municipality 1855.

AIDE, see *Ayde*.

AID TO THE SICK AND WOUNDED, NATIONAL SOCIETY FOR. On 4 Aug. 1870, soon after the breaking out of the Franco-German war, a meeting was held in London, which established this society under the rules of the Geneva Convention, *which see.*

The Queen, patron; the prince of Wales, president; col. Loyd-Lindsay, chairman of committees; active supporters, duke of Manchester, earl of Shaftesbury, lords Overstone and Bury, sir Harry Verney, general sir John Burgoyne, surgeon-general Longmore, and captain (aft. sir) Douglas Galton. The operations were chiefly directed by capt. Henry Brackenbury, at the seat of war, and by Mr. John Furley and general sir Vincent Eyre.

A fruitless meeting to promote the incorporation of the society. It was then reported that 296,298*l*. had been received; together with stores valued at 45,000*l*. . . . . 1 Aug. 1871

Col. Loyd Lindsay conveyed to Versailles and Paris from the society 40,000*l*., equally divided between the Germans and French (gratefully acknowledged) . . . . . about 11 Oct. 1870

The crown-prince of Prussia wrote to colonel Loyd Lindsay:—"In this, as on other occasions of distress, the help of the English public has been poured out with a liberal and an impartial hand. The gifts which have been offered in a truly Christian spirit have excited a feeling of heartfelt gratitude among those on whose behalf I speak." 2 Nov. 1870

The society afforded much help in the Servian war, July—Sept. 1876, the Russo-Turkish war, 1877–8, and the Boer war, 1899–1902.

The Princess of Wales' branch of the society closed with a surplus of 6,417*l*. June, 1886.

AIR OR ATMOSPHERE. Anaximenes of Miletus (530 B.C.) declared air to be a self-existent deity, and the first cause of everything created. Posidonius (about 79 B.C.) calculated the height of the atmosphere to be 800 stadia. The pressure of air, about 15 lb. to the square inch, was discovered by Galileo, 1564, and demonstrated by Torricelli (who invented the barometer) about A.D. 1643, and was found by Pascal, in 1647, to vary with the height. Halley, Newton, and others, up to the present time have illustrated the agency and influences of this great power by various experiments, and numerous inventions have followed; among others, the AIR-GUN of Guter of Nuremberg about 1656; the AIR-PUMP, invented by Otto von Guericke of Magdeburg about 1650; improved by Robert Boyle in 1657, by Robert Hooke about 1659;* and the AIR-PIPE, invented by Mr. Sutton, a brewer of London, about 1756. The density and elasticity of air were determined by Boyle; and its relation to light and sound by Hooke, Newton, and Derham. The extension of our atmosphere above the surface of the earth, has been long considered as about 45 miles.—Its *composition*,† about 77 parts of nitrogen, 21 of oxygen, and 2 of other matters (such as carbonic acid, watery vapour, a trace of ammonia, &c.) was ascertained by Priestley (who discovered oxygen gas in 1774), Scheele (1775), Lavoisier, and Cavendish; and its laws of refraction were investigated by Dr. Bradley, 1737. The researches of Dr. Schönbein, a German chemist of Basel, between 1840 and 1859, led to his description of two states of the oxygen in the air, which he calls *ozone* and *antozone*. In Aug., 1894, at Oxford, Lord Rayleigh and Professor Ramsay reported to the British Association their discovery of a new gas in air, afterwards termed Argon, *which see.* Dr. Stenhouse's *Air-filters* (in which powdered charcoal is used) were first set up at the Mansion-house, London, in 1854. In 1858, Dr. R. Angus Smith made known a chemical method of ascertaining the amount of organic matter in the air, and published his "Air and Rain" in 1872. See *Oxygen, Nitrogen, Ozone, Atmospheric Railway, Balloons,* and *Pneumatic Despatch.*

The *Aero-steam Engine*, the invention of George Warsop, a mechanic of Nottingham, who, by employing compressed air united with steam, is said to have effected the saving of 47 per cent. of fuel. The plan was reported to the British Association, at Exeter, in Aug. 1869, and was said to act successfully in a tug steamer (for China) in the Thames, 26 March, 1870. Mr. Edward Field, in his new motive power, introduced a small volume of steam into a large volume of heated air, and effected an economy of 12½ to 20 per cent. of steam. The system was exhibited in London, July, 1891.

Col. Beaumont's *air-engine* for propelling railway carriages, tried at Woolwich, reported successful (a little steam is used), 6 Oct. 1880. His system largely employed in various ways by the Paris Compressed Air company, described to the British Association at Newcastle-upon-Tyne, Sept. 1889.

Victor Popp applies compressed air as a motive power to clocks, 1881.

An *air-telegraph*, in which the waves of air in a tube are employed instead of electricity, invented by sig. Guattari, was exhibited in London in 1870. It obtained a gold medal in Naples.

Isaac Wilkinson patented a method of compressing air by a column of water in 1757, and William Mann patented stage pumping by compressed air in 1829. The force of compressed air was employed in boring the Cenis tunnel (see under *Alps*), and in making the Blackwall tunnel, 1891–7.

Tram-cars driven by compressed air on the Mekarski system in N. London, for a time, June, 1883; resumed, after improvements made, for a time, 1885; again for a time, Feb. 1888.

Prof. Dewar gave six well-illustrated lectures on "Air, gaseous and liquid," at the Royal Institution, London, 28 Dec. 1893—9 Jan. 1894. (Some of the air of the room was liquefied in the presence of the audience, and remained so for some time, when enclosed in a vacuum jacket); again, 1 April, 1898.

Prof. Dewar demonstrated by some very remarkable experiments the intimate connection between phosphorescence and photographic action of the electric light on bodies cooled to the temperature of boiling liquid air at the Royal Institution, 18 Jan. 1895.

Liquid air for refrigeration and other purposes largely produced by machinery, invented by Herr Linde; reported, 21 Oct. 1895.

Prof. Dewar's new apparatus for the production of liquid air, exhibited at the Royal Institution, 2 Dec. 1895.

Experiments with hydrogen, reported 27 March, 1896.

M. Paul Giffard, inventor of compressed air and other apparatus, died, abt. 8 April, 1897.

The *Aerograph*, an air brush, an application of compressed air, invented by Mr. C. L. Burdick (1893); used by artists.

Dr. Linde's machine for the liquefaction of air, shown at the Society of Arts, 14 March, 1898.

Argon, a new constituent of air, neon and metargon, discovered by prof. Ramsay and Lord Rayleigh, Jan. 1895.

"Lord Rayleigh and professor Ramsay had discovered four other aërial elements, helium, neon, krypton and xenon, which were identified as constituents of the atmosphere by prof. Ramsay and M. H. Travers, 1895–1900."

Major MacMahon's address at the British Association, 12 Sept. 1901.

Prof. Dewar exhibited air in the solid state and a jet of liquid air rising to about 6 ft., with beautiful effects, before the prince and princess of Wales, 6 June, 1902.

AIR-GUN. A pressure of 500 atmospheres has about half the elastic force of fired gunpowder.

* Sprengel's excellent air-pump, in which water or mercury is employed, was invented in 1863, see *Vacuum*.

† Air, as well as its gaseous components, has been compressed into the liquid state by means of great pressure and intense cold, 1877–8, by Raoul Pictet of Geneva, and Cailletet of Paris, Dec. 1877, Jan. 1878. At the Royal Institution, 5 June, 1885, professor James Dewar exhibited liquid air obtained at the temperature of —192° Cent. In March, 1893, he produced solid air in the form of ice. Several physical properties of liquid air were exhibited, and solid air was produced at the Friday meeting, 19 Jan. 1894.

English patents, for guns shooting shot and bullets, P. Giffard, 1872; A. Pope (H. M. Quackenbush), 1874; G. G. Bussey, 1876; F. Worth, in 1877. Compressed air to project large shot with pieces of ordnance, patented by Bessemer (1867) and others. Capt. Zalinski, of U.S. artillery (1866), made a practical gun for throwing dynamite shells; it was used in the Cuban war (1898).

AIR-SHIPS, see *Balloons*.

AIX-LA-CHAPELLE (Aachen), a Roman city, now in Rhenish Prussia. Several ecclesiastical councils held here (799-1165). Here Charlemagne was born, 742, and died, 814; having built the minster (796-804), and conferred many privileges on the city, in which fifty-five emperors have since been crowned. Its mineral springs in use since 1170. The city was taken by the French in Dec. 1792; retaken by the Austrians, March, 1793; by the French, Sept. 1794; ceded to Prussia, 1814. Population, 1900, 135,235.

First *Treaty of Peace* signed here was between France and Spain, when France yielded Franche Comté, but retained her conquests in the Netherlands, 2 May, 1668.

The second celebrated *treaty* between Great Britain, France, Holland, Germany, Spain, and Genoa. (By it the treaties of Westphalia in 1648, of Nimeguen in 1678 and 1679, of Ryswick in 1697, of Utrecht in 1713, of Baden in 1714, of the Triple Alliance in 1717, of the Quadruple Alliance in 1718, and of Vienna in 1738, were renewed and confirmed.) Signed on the part of England by John, earl of Sandwich, and sir Thomas Robinson, 7 Oct. 1748.

Congress of the sovereigns of Austria, Russia and Prussia, assisted by ministers from England and France, met at Aix-la-Chapelle, and a convention signed, 9 Oct. 1818, which led to the withdrawal of the army of occupation from France.

AIX ROADS, see *Rochefort*.

AIZNADIN or **AJNADIN** (Syria). Here the Mahometans defeated the army of the emperor Heraclius, 13 July, 633. They took Damascus in 634.

AJMERE-MERWARA, area 2,711 square miles, (1897-8) 404,413 acres cultivated, in great measure dependent on irrigation; 1899-1900 a drought cost thousands of lives, pop. 476,330 (1901): ceded in 1818, lies within Rajputana.

AJACCIO, see *Corsica*.

AKERMAN (Bessarabia). After being several times taken, it was ceded to Russia in 1812. Here the celebrated treaty between Russia and Turkey was concluded, 4 Sept. 1826, which secured for the former the navigation of the Black Sea, recognised the Danubian principalities, &c.

AKHALZIKH (Armenia). Near here prince Paskiewitch and the Russians defeated the Turks, 24 Aug., and gained the city, 28 Aug. 1828.

ALABAMA, a Southern state, originally part of Georgia, N. America. The country was first settled by the French, 1702, who built Mobile, 1712; part of it was ceded to Great Britain, 1763. It was gradually acquired by the United States, and was made a state in 1819; commercial metropolis, Mobile. It seceded from the union by an ordinance passed 11 Jan. 1861, was reunited in 1865; and readmitted to congress, 1868.

Murder of about 26 negro miners at the Carbon Hill coal mines, Walker county, by white strikers, 30, 31 Jan.—rioting quelled by troops, 1, 2 Feb. 1891.

Population, 1890, 1,513,017; 1900, 1,828,697.

Conflict with strikers at Pratt's mines, near Birmingham, 6 deaths . . . . . 17 July, 1894

Lynching of negroes 1900-1903, some burnt alive.

False alarm of fire at negro Baptist chapel in Birmingham, 115 killed . . . 19 Sept. 1902

ALABAMA, a steam vessel of 900 tons, with engines of 300 horse-power, constructed by Messrs. Laird at Birkenhead, for the confederate service; launched 15 May, 1862. During the judicial enquiries after her character, she sailed from the Mersey, 28 July, the day before the British government telegraphed to detain her. Under the command of capt. Semmes, she did great damage to the American mercantile shipping, until her destruction by the federal ironclad *Kearsage*, capt. Winslow, off Cherbourg, 19 June, 1864. Several of his crew were saved by Mr. John Lancaster, in his yacht. Admiral Semmes died Sept. 1877.

Discussion between the two governments, respecting claims for damage by the *Alabama* . . 1865

A fruitless convention for their settlement, by a commission signed at London . . 10 Nov. 1868

Another convention, signed by the earl of Clarendon and Mr. Reverdy Johnson, signed 14 Jan.; rejected by the United States senate . 13 April, 1869

Joint commission (*British*, earl de Grey, sir Stafford Northcote and others; *American*, secretary Fisk, general Schenk, and others) to settle fishery disputes, Alabama claims, &c. Announced, 9 Feb., met at Washington, 27 Feb., signed a treaty at Washington . . . . . 8 May, 1871

Commission for Anglo-American claims, met at Washington . . . . . 25 Sept. „

Formal meeting of the arbitration commission at Geneva; (adjourns to 15 June) . 18 Dec. „

The British and American cases presented 20 Dec. Great excitement in England at the introduction of enormous claims for indirect losses into the American case, loss by transfer of trade from American to British ships, increased rates of marine insurance, and losses incident to the prolongation of the war. . . . . Jan. 1872

Correspondence between the governments: British despatch, 3 Feb.; reply, 1 March; continued; counter cases presented at Geneva . 15 April, „

Continued correspondence, draft for a supplementary treaty, by which both nations agree in future to abstain from claims for indirect losses, presented to American senate; approved 25 May, „

The British government object to certain modifications; further correspondence; great excitement in parliament; proposed adjournment of the meeting of the arbitration commission; differences about the mode of procedure; congress adjourns, leaving the affair unsettled . 10 June, „

The Arbitration tribunal, consisting of count Frederic Sclopis for Italy, president, baron Staempfl for Switzerland; vicomte d'Itajuba for Brazil; Mr. G. F. Adams for United States, and sir Alexander E. Cockburn for Great Britain, meet at Geneva; The British government presents a note of the existing differences; the conference adjourns, 15 June, „

Further adjournment, 17 June; the arbitrators voluntarily declare that the indirect claims are invalid, and contrary to international law, 19 June; president Grant consents to their withdrawal . . . . 25 June, „

The British government withdraw their application for adjournment of the conference . 27 June, „

The Arbitration commission records its decision against the indirect claims, and the proposed long adjournment, and adjourns to 15 July . 28 June, „

Final meeting; all the arbitrators agree to award damages for the injuries done by the *Alabama*; four, for those done by the *Florida*; and three for those done by the *Shenandoah*. The judgment not signed by sir A. Cockburn, whose reasons were published; the damages awarded (including interest), about 3,229,166*l.* 13*s.* 4*d.*; those claimed 9,476,166*l.* 13*s.* 4*d.* (Decision based on the admission of a *new ex-post facto* international law, by Great Britain by the treaty of Washington.) 14 Sept. „

The judgment of sir A. Cockburn (a powerful and indignant reply to unjust aspersions, admitting the award for the *Alabama*; opposing the other awards; yet counselling submission to the judg-

50,000*l.* towards it. Mr. H. Hucks Gibbs also contributed largely to the restoration (1889). The nave was opened 21 Oct. 1885. Verulam was built on the site of the capital of Cassivelaunus, taken by Julius Cæsar, 54 B. C. It was retaken after much slaughter by Boadicea or Bunduica, queen of the Iceni, A. D. 61.

First Battle of St. Albans, when the Lancastrians were defeated, their leader, Edmund duke of Somerset slain, and king Henry VI. taken prisoner, by the duke of York and his partisans, 22 or 23 May, 1455.

Second battle, queen Margaret totally defeated the Yorkists under the earl of Warwick, and rescued the king, Shrove Tuesday, 17 Feb. 1461.

St. Albans incorporated by Edward VI. 1553.

Disfranchised for bribery, 17 June, 1852.

St. Albans Murder, see *Trials*, 1880.

Act passed to make arrangements for erecting a bishopric of St. Albans, 29 June 1875. See constituted, 30 April; made a city, 28 Aug. 1877. Population, 1881, 10,931; 1891, 12,895; 1901, 16,019.

St. Albans Raid, see *United States*, Oct. 1864.

BISHOPS.

1877. Thomas Legh Claughton (trans. from Rochester); resigned 21 March, 1890; died 25 July, 1892.

1890. John Wogan Festing; died, 28 Dec. 1902.

1903. Edgar Jacob (trans. from Newcastle-on-Tyne); enthroned, 16 May.

ALBANY or **Albainn**, the ancient name of the Scottish Highlands. Robert Stewart, the brother of King Robert III., was created the first duke of Albany in 1398, and the title has ever since been connected with the crown of Scotland. The young pretender, prince Charles Edward, and his wife took the title of count and countess of Albany. See *York*.

DUKES OF ALBANY.

1398. Robert; regent; 1406; died 3 Sept. 1420.

1420. Murdoch, son; regent; executed for treason by king James I., 1424.

1452. Alexander, brother of king James II.; acted treasonably; exiled; killed accidentally at Paris, 1485.

1514. John, son; regent; went abroad; died at Paris, 1526.

See *York and Albany, dukes*.

1881. Prince Leopold, fourth son of queen Victoria, was created duke of Albany 24 May, 1881; died 28 March, 1884.

1884. Leopold Charles Edward, son, born 19 July; duke of Saxe-Coburg and Gotha, 30 July, 1900.

See under *England*.

ALBANY, capital of the state of New York. The Dutch erected a block-house near here in 1614, and villages soon arose. The town took its name from James, duke of York and Albany, to whom it had been given by his brother, King Charles II., after its cession to Great Britain in 1664. Albany received a charter in 1686; the first general congress met here in 1764, and in 1797 the city became the capital of the state. Centenary celebrated Jan. 6, 1897. Population, 1800, 5349; 1860, 62,367; 1890, 94,923; 1900, 94,151.

ALBERT MEMORIALS. (See *England, Queen*.) The Prince Consort died on 14 Dec. 1861, deeply lamented by the whole civilised world. His remains were transferred to the mausoleum of Frogmore, 18 Dec. 1862. The sarcophagus is composed of the largest known block of granite without flaw. A meeting to organise a method of receiving contributions for a great national memorial was held at the Mansion-house, 14 Jan. 1862; and a large sum was quickly subscribed. 36,000*l.* had been received on 1 March; 50,220*l.* on 11 June, 1862; and parliament voted 50,000*l.*, in addition to the 60,000*l.* received by voluntary contributions, 23 April, 1863.

The nature of the memorial was referred to the queen herself. In a letter to the lord mayor, dated 19 Feb. 1862, sir Charles Grey says, on behalf of her majesty, "It would be more in accordance with her own feelings, and she believes with those of the country in general, that the monument should be directly personal to its object. After giving the subject her maturest consideration, her majesty has come to the conclusion, that nothing would be more appropriate, provided it is on a scale of sufficient grandeur, than an obelisk to be erected in Hyde-park on the site of the Great Exhibition of 1851, or on some spot immediately contiguous to it. Nor would any proposal that could be made be more gratifying to the queen herself personally, for she can never forget that the prince himself had highly approved of the idea of a memorial of this character being raised on the same spot in remembrance of the Great Exhibition." In a second letter the queen expressed her intention of personally contributing towards erecting the memorial, that "it might be recorded in future ages as raised by the queen and people of a grateful country to the memory of its benefactor." Shortly after a committee was appointed to fulfil her majesty's desire. As a suitable block of granite could not be obtained, the proposal for an obelisk was given up.

The queen approved of the design of Mr. Gilbert G. Scott for an Eleanor Cross, with a spire 150 feet high, accompanied by statues, &c., 22 April, 1863; work begun 13 May, 1864.

The sculptors employed were M'Dowell, Foley, Theed, John Bell, and Armistead: material, Sicilian marble. (Jan. 1865.)

The memorial, complete, except the statue, by Foley (delayed through illness), was given up to her majesty privately, 1 July, 1872. The gilt statue by Foley uncovered 9 March, 1876. Having been much damaged by weather, it was restored 1902.

Doyne C. Bell's Descriptive and Illustrated Account of this Monument, published by Mr. John Murray, 1873.

Inscription on the "Memorial Cairn" on a high mountain overlooking Balmoral Palace:—"To the beloved memory of Albert the great and good Prince Consort, erected by his broken-hearted widow, Victoria R 21 Aug. 1862." Upon another dressed slab, a few inches below the above, is this quotation:—"He being made perfect in a short time, fulfilled a long time: for his soul pleased the Lord, therefore hasted he to take him away from among the wicked."—*Wisdom of Solomon*, chap. iv. 13, 14.

A statue of the prince-consort (by Theed) inaugurated at Rosenau, his birth-place, in the presence of the queen and the royal family, 19 Aug. 1865.

"Early Years of the Prince Consort;" edited by the Hon. Chas. Grey; published 6 July, 1867.

Statue by Theed at Balmoral, inaugurated 15 Oct. 1867.

The statue at the Holborn circus, uncovered by the prince of Wales, 9 Jan. 1874.

The Albert Memorial Chapel at Windsor, opened to the public, 1 Dec. 1875.

Life, by Theodore Martin; 5 vols. published, 1875-80.

The Scottish National Memorial to the Prince, Edinburgh, inaugurated by the queen, 17 Aug. 1876.

Statue at Fitzwilliam Museum, Cambridge, uncovered by the prince of Wales, 22 Jan. 1878.

A bronze equestrian statue of the prince set up near Virginia Water in the Great Park, Windsor, by means of the women's offering, see *Jubilee*, 1887-9; uncovered by the queen, 12 May, 1890.

Many other memorials of the prince have been set up throughout the empire.

Royal Albert Hall of Arts and Sciences; The erection of a great building for congresses, concerts, &c., was proposed by the prince-consort at the close of the exhibition of 1851, and an estate at Kensington was purchased; a committee, with the prince of Wales at the head, to erect the building, was appointed 6 July, 1865; circulars soliciting subscriptions were issued April, 1866; and the first stone was laid by the queen, 20 May, 1867.

The building was erected by col. Scott, chiefly after designs by capt. Fowke, and cost about 200,000*l.* The organ, by Willis, is said to be the largest in the world. An experimental concert was given to the workmen 25 Feb., and the hall was opened by the queen 29 March, 1871, when a grand concert was given, and many since.

The hall is said to contain seats for 10,000 persons (orchestra 2,000, oval arena 1,000, balcony 2,300, and gallery 2,000).

50,000*l.* towards it. Mr. H. Hucks Gibbs also contributed largely to the restoration (1889). The nave was opened 21 Oct. 1885. Verulam was built on the site of the capital of Cassivelaunus, taken by Julius Cæsar, 54 B. C. It was retaken after much slaughter by Boadicea or Bunduica, queen of the Iceni, A. D. 61.

First Battle of St. Albans, when the Lancastrians were defeated, their leader, Edmund duke of Somerset slain, and king Henry VI. taken prisoner, by the duke of York and his partisans, 22 or 23 May, 1455.

Second battle, queen Margaret totally defeated the Yorkists under the earl of Warwick, and rescued the king, Shrove Tuesday, 17 Feb. 1461.

St. Albans incorporated by Edward VI. 1553.

Disfranchised for bribery, 17 June, 1852.

St. Albans Murder, see *Trials*, 1880.

Act passed to make arrangements for erecting a bishopric of St. Albans, 29 June 1875. See constituted, 30 April; made a city, 28 Aug. 1877. Population, 1881, 10,931; 1891, 12,895; 1901, 16,019.

St. Albans Raid, see *United States*, Oct. 1864.

BISHOPS.

1877. Thomas Legh Claughton (trans. from Rochester); resigned 21 March, 1890; died 25 July, 1892.

1890. John Wogan Festing; died, 28 Dec. 1902.

1903. Edgar Jacob (trans. from Newcastle-on-Tyne); enthroned, 16 May.

ALBANY OR ALBAINN, the ancient name of the Scottish Highlands. Robert Stewart, the brother of King Robert III., was created the first duke of Albany in 1398, and the title has ever since been connected with the crown of Scotland. The young pretender, prince Charles Edward, and his wife took the title of count and countess of Albany. See *York*.

DUKES OF ALBANY.

1398. Robert; regent; 1406; died 3 Sept. 1420.

1420. Murdoch, son; regent; executed for treason by king James I., 1424.

1452. Alexander, brother of king James II.; acted treasonably; exiled; killed accidentally at Paris, 1485.

1514. John, son; regent; went abroad; died at Paris, 1526.

See *York and Albany, dukes*.

1881. Prince Leopold, fourth son of queen Victoria, was created duke of Albany 24 May, 1881; died 28 March, 1884.

1884. Leopold Charles Edward, son, born 19 July; duke of Saxe-Coburg and Gotha, 30 July, 1900.

See under *England*.

ALBANY, capital of the state of New York. The Dutch erected a block-house near here in 1614, and villages soon arose. The town took its name from James, duke of York and Albany, to whom it had been given by his brother, King Charles II., after its cession to Great Britain in 1664. Albany received a charter in 1686; the first general congress met here in 1764, and in 1797 the city became the capital of the state. Centenary celebrated Jan. 6, 1897. Population, 1800, 5349; 1860, 62,367; 1890, 94,923; 1900, 94,151.

ALBERT MEMORIALS. (See *England, Queen.*) The Prince Consort died on 14 Dec. 1861, deeply lamented by the whole civilised world. His remains were transferred to the mausoleum of Frogmore, 18 Dec. 1862. The sarcophagus is composed of the largest known block of granite without flaw. A meeting to organise a method of receiving contributions for a great national memorial was held at the Mansion-house, 14 Jan. 1862; and a large sum was quickly subscribed. 36,000*l.* had been received on 1 March; 50,220*l.* on 11 June, 1862; and parliament voted 50,000*l.*, in addition to the 60,000*l.* received by voluntary contributions, 23 April, 1863.

The nature of the memorial was referred to the queen herself. In a letter to the lord mayor, dated 19 Feb. 1862, sir Charles Grey says, on behalf of her majesty, "It would be more in accordance with her own feelings, and she believes with those of the country in general, that the monument should be directly personal to its object. After giving the subject her maturest consideration, her majesty has come to the conclusion, that nothing would be more appropriate, provided it is on a scale of sufficient grandeur, than an obelisk to be erected in Hyde-park on the site of the Great Exhibition of 1851, or on some spot immediately contiguous to it. Nor would any proposal that could be made be more gratifying to the queen herself personally, for she can never forget that the prince himself had highly approved of the idea of a memorial of this character being raised on the same spot in remembrance of the Great Exhibition." In a second letter the queen expressed her intention of personally contributing towards erecting the memorial, that "it might be recorded in future ages as raised by the queen and people of a grateful country to the memory of its benefactor." Shortly after a committee was appointed to fulfil her majesty's desire. As a suitable block of granite could not be obtained, the proposal for an obelisk was given up.

The queen approved of the design of Mr. Gilbert G. Scott for an Eleanor Cross, with a spire 150 feet high, accompanied by statues, &c., 22 April, 1863; work begun 13 May, 1864.

The sculptors employed were M'Dowell, Foley, Theed, John Bell, and Armistead: material, Sicilian marble. (Jan. 1865.)

The memorial, complete, except the statue, by Foley (delayed through illness), was given up to her majesty privately, 1 July, 1872. The gilt statue by Foley uncovered 9 March, 1876. Having been much damaged by weather, it was restored 1902.

Doyne C. Bell's Descriptive and Illustrated Account of this Monument, published by Mr. John Murray, 1873.

Inscription on the "Memorial Cairn" on a high mountain overlooking Balmoral Palace:—"To the beloved memory of ALBERT the great and good Prince Consort, erected by his broken-hearted widow, VICTORIA R 21 Aug. 1862." Upon another dressed slab, a few inches below the above, is this quotation:—"He being made perfect in a short time, fulfilled a long time: for his soul pleased the Lord, therefore hasted he to take him away from among the wicked."—*Wisdom of Solomon*, chap. iv. 13, 14.

A statue of the prince-consort (by Theed) inaugurated at Rosenau, his birth-place, in the presence of the queen and the royal family, 19 Aug. 1865.

"Early Years of the Prince Consort;" edited by the Hon. Chas. Grey; published 6 July, 1867.

Statue by Theed at Balmoral, inaugurated 15 Oct. 1867.

The statue at the Holborn circus, uncovered by the prince of Wales, 9 Jan. 1874.

The Albert Memorial Chapel at Windsor, opened to the public, 1 Dec. 1875.

Life, by Theodore Martin; 5 vols. published, 1875-80.

The Scottish National Memorial to the Prince, Edinburgh, inaugurated by the queen, 17 Aug. 1876.

Statue at Fitzwilliam Museum, Cambridge, uncovered by the prince of Wales, 22 Jan. 1878.

A bronze equestrian statue of the prince set up near Virginia Water in the Great Park, Windsor, by means of the women's offering, see *Jubilee*, 1887-9; uncovered by the queen, 12 May, 1890.

Many other memorials of the prince have been set up throughout the empire.

ROYAL ALBERT HALL OF ARTS AND SCIENCES; The erection of a great building for congresses, concerts, &c., was proposed by the prince-consort at the close of the exhibition of 1851, and an estate at Kensington was purchased; a committee, with the prince of Wales at the head, to erect the building, was appointed 6 July, 1865; circulars soliciting subscriptions were issued April, 1866; and the first stone was laid by the queen, 20 May, 1867.

The building was erected by col. Scott, chiefly after designs by capt. Fowke, and cost about 200,000*l.* The organ, by Willis, is said to be the largest in the world. An experimental concert was given to the workmen 25 Feb., and the hall was opened by the queen 29 March, 1871, when a grand concert was given, and many since.

The hall is said to contain seats for 10,000 persons (orchestra 2,000, oval arena 1,000, balcony 2,300, and gallery 2,000).

An International Ice Carnival for the West End Hospital for Paralysis, &c., inaugurated by the duchess of Teck, 14 March, 1889.
State concert for the German emperor and empress, 9 July, 1891.
Great unionist meeting (see *Ireland*), 22 April, 1893.
Grand military and patriotic concert in aid of the troops, &c., in S. Africa, the prince of Wales present, 5 Dec. 1899.
International cookery exhibition opened 19 March, 1902.
Lads' Drill association, lord Neath president, prince and princess of Wales present, 7 June, 1902.
ALBERT BRIDGE, Chelsea, opened 23 Aug. 1873; freed from toll 24 May, 1879.
ALBERT EMBANKMENT, &c., see *Thames*, 1869; *Docks*.
ALBERT INSTITUTE, Windsor, opened by the prince of Wales, 10 Jan. 1880.
ALBERT MEDALS, to be awarded to persons who endanger their lives by saving others from shipwreck, appointed by royal warrant, 7 March, 1866. The first was given to Samuel Popplestone on 14 May, 1866, for saving life on 23 March previous. Two decorations instituted, April, 1867, first and second class; extended, April, 1877, for gallantry in preventing loss of life on land; medals awarded to Pontypridd miners and others for saving men imprisoned in a mine through inundation (see *Coal: Accidents*), April, 1877.
ALBERT MEDAL (Gold), founded in 1862, awarded by the Society of Arts to sir Rowland Hill, 1864; Napoleon III. 1865; Michael Faraday, 1866; Charles Wheatstone and William Fothergill Cooke, 1867; Joseph Whitworth, 1868; Justus Liebig, 1869; Ferdinand de Lesseps, 1870; Henry Cole, C.B., 1871; Henry Bessemer, 1872; Michel Eugène Chevreul, 1873; C. William Siemens, 1874; Michel Chevallier, 1875; sir G. B. Airy, 1876; Jean Baptiste Dumas, 1877; sir Wm. G. Armstrong, 1878; sir William Thomson (lord Kelvin, 1892), 1879; James Prescott Joule, 1880; Aug. Wm. Hofmann, 1881; Louis Pasteur, 1882; sir Joseph D. Hooker, 1883; capt. James Buchanan Eads, 1884; Henry Doulton, 1885; Samuel Cunliffe Lister, 1886; the Queen, 1887 (6 June, presented 8 March, 1888); prof. Hermann Louis Helmholtz, 1888; John Percy, 1889; William Henry Perkin, 1890; sir Frederick Abel, 1891; Thos. Alva Edison, 1892; sir John Bennet Lawes and sir John H. Gilbert, 1893; sir Joseph Lister (lord Lister, 1897), 1894; sir Isaac Lowthian Bell, 1895; David Edward Hughes, 1896; G. T. Symons, 1897; Robert Bunsen, 1898; sir Wm. Crookes, 1899; Henry Wilde, 1900; king Edward VII., 1901; Alexander Graham Bell, 1902.
ALBERT EXHIBITION PALACE, BATTERSEA, opened 6 June, 1885, closed 1888.
Royal Albert Orphan Asylum, Bagshot; founded 1864.

ALBERT NYANZA, see *Victoria Nyanza*.

ALBERT UNIVERSITY, the name proposed for a new teaching university, in and for London, advocated by University college and King's college in 1891. A draft charter was submitted to the privy council and approved in July, 1891. The subject was eventually referred to a royal commission in March following. See *Gresham College* and *London University*.

ALBIGENSES, a name given to various persons who opposed the doctrines and corruptions of the church of Rome, living at Albi, in Languedoc, and at Toulouse in the 12th century. They were persecuted as alleged Manichæans, 1163, and a crusade (proclaimed by pope Innocent III.) against them commenced in 1207. Simon de Montfort commanded 500,000 men, and at Beziers, 1209, he and the pope's legate put friends and foes to the sword, saying, "God will find his own!" * At Minerba he burnt 150 of the Albigenses alive; and at La Vaur he hanged the governor, and beheaded the chief people, drowning the governor's wife, and murdering other women. He defeated Raymond, count of Toulouse, but was himself killed in 1218. Louis VIII. and IX., kings of France, patronised the crusade; count Raymond was subdued, and abdicated in 1229; and the heretics were given up to the Inquisition. They had little in common with the *Waldenses*, *which see*.

* Now contradicted.

ALBION. Britain is said to have been so called by Aristotle (died 322 B.C.). Julius Cæsar and others are said to have given it the name (from *albus*, white) on account of its chalky cliffs.

ALBUERA or ALBUHERA, Estremadura, Spain. Here a battle was fought between the French, commanded by marshal Soult, and the British and Anglo-Spanish army, under marshal, afterwards lord Beresford, 16 May, 1811. The allies obtained a brilliant victory. The French loss exceeded 8000 men previously to their retreat; but the allies lost a large number. The chief brunt of the action fell on the British; colonel Inglis, 22 officers, and more than 400 men, out of 570 who had mounted a hill, fell, out of the 57th regiment alone; the other regiments were scarcely better off, not one-third being left standing; "1500 unwounded men, the remnant of 6000 unconquerable British soldiers, stood triumphant on this fatal hill." *Napier*.

ALBUFERA (Spain, East Central), a lagoon, near which the French marshal Suchet (afterwards duke of Albufera) defeated the Spaniards under Blake, 4 Jan. 1812: this led to his capture of Valencia on 9 Jan.

ALCALA DE HENARES, Spain, the Roman Complutum. At its once famous university founded by cardinal Ximenes, 1510, was printed the Complutensian Polyglot bible, at his expense, 1502–15. Cervantes, the author of "Don Quixote," was born here, 1547.

ALCANTARA, a town on the Tagus, W. Spain. A fine bridge was built here by Trajan 105. The duke of Alva acquired Portugal for Spain by defeating the Portuguese army here, 24 June, 1580. The Spanish military order of knighthood of Alcantara was established in 1156. The sovereign of Spain has been grand master since 1495. Population, 4,000.

ALCAZAR-QUIVER, near Fez, N. W. Africa, where the Moors totally defeated the Portuguese, whose gallant king Sebastian was slain, 4 Aug. 1578. The Portuguese disbelieved his death, and long expected his return; this led to the appearance of five impostors.

ALCHEMY, the forerunner of chemistry; its chief objects being the discovery of the philosopher's stone (which was to effect the transmutation of metals into gold), an alkahest or universal menstruum, and the elixir of life.* The alchemists assert that their founder was Hermes *Trismegistus* (thrice greatest), an ancient Egyptian king.—Pliny says the emperor Caligula was the first who prepared natural arsenic, in order to make gold of it, but left it off, because the charge exceeded the profit.
Zosimus wrote on the subject about 410.
The Arabians cultivated alchemy, and were followed (in the 13th century) by Roger Bacon, Albertus Magnus, Aquinas, Raymond Lullius, Basil Valentine (born 1394), Paracelsus (died 1541), and others.
In 1404 the craft of multiplying gold and silver was made felony by 5 Hen. IV. c. 4, which act was repealed in 1689.

* M. Martin Ziegler, about 1868, patented a method of producing a "vital fluid" by combining nitrogen and carbon in a porous cell containing ammonia, immersed in a vessel filled with molasses. The current was to flow through silk threads attached to the vessel.

A licence for practising alchemy with all kinds of metals and minerals was granted to one Richard Carter, 1475. *Rymer's Fœdera.*

Dr. Price, of Guildford, in 1782 published an account of his experiments and brought specimens of gold to the king, affirming that they were made by means of a red and white powder. Being a fellow of the Royal Society, he was required, under pain of expulsion, to repeat his experiments before Messrs. Kirwan and Wolfe (some say Higgins); but after much equivocation and delay he took poison and died, Aug. 1783.

ALCOHOL. Pure spirit of wine or hydrated alcohol is said to have been obtained by the distillation of fermented liquors by Abucasis in the 12th century; and the dehydration of this liquor to have been partially effected by Raymond Lullius in the 13th century by carbonate of potassium. In 1820, Faraday and Hennell obtained traces of alcohol by passing olefiant gas (bi-carburetted hydrogen) through sulphuric acid; and in 1862 this process was examined and confirmed by Berthelot. Alcohol has been artificially formed from its elements (carbon, hydrogen and oxygen) by chemists; it was solidified by Prof. Dewar at the Royal Institution, 1886; see *Distillation, Spirits, Brandy, Gin, Rum.* About 250 medical men, including the president of the Royal College of Physicians, and many hospital officials, issued a cautionary declaration concerning the use of alcohol in medicine, Dec. 1871. See *Temperance.*

ALCOLEA (Andalusia, S. Spain). Near the bridge a sharp engagement took place between the royalists under general Pavia y Lacy, marquis de Novaliches, and the insurgents under marshal Serrano, 27 Sept. 1868. The former was defeated.

AL-CORAN OR AL-KORAN, see *Koran, Mahometanism,* &c.

ALDERMAN. The Saxon *ealdorman* was next to the king, and frequently a viceroy; but after the settlement of the Danes the title was gradually displaced by that of *earl.* Aldermen in corporations are next in dignity to the mayor. A curious list of aldermen and their wards is assigned to the year 1290. *Loftie.* Aldermen chosen for life, instead of annually, 17 Rich. II. 1394. Aldermen made justices of the peace, 15 Geo. II., 1741. The council of a borough consists of mayor, aldermen, and councillors, Acts, 1835.

The 26 London (City) aldermen are elected by the wards. In 1877 the court of aldermen exercised their ancient right of veto against Sir John Bennett (thrice chosen alderman for the ward of Cheap), and chose Mr. Edgar Breffitt, 23 Oct. 1877.

Aldermen elected by the councillors form part of the County Councils established by the Local Government Act, 1888, and of the London municipal boroughs, created by the London Government Act, 1899.

ALDERNEY (English Channel), with Jersey, &c., was acquired by William the Conqueror, 1066. The "Race" is celebrated for two fatal occurrences; William of Normandy, son of Henry I. of England, and many young nobles (140 youths of the principal families of France and Britain), were overtaken by a storm, and all lost, 25 Nov. 1120. The British man-of-war *Victory,* of 100 guns and 1160 men, was wrecked here, 5 Oct. 1744; the admiral, sir John Balchen, and all his crew perished. Through this strait the French escaped after their defeat at La Hogue by admirals Russell and Rooke, 19 May, 1692. The construction of a breakwater, in order to make Alderney a naval station, was begun in 1852, and after having cost 1,337,100*l.*, was suspended by parliament in 1871. In 1874 the harbour and lands were transferred from the control of the board of trade to that of the admiralty and the war department. See *Wrecks* 30 March, 1899.

ALDERSHOT CAMP, on a moor near Farnham, about 35 miles from London. In April, 1854, the War office, having obtained a grant of 100,000*l.*, purchased 4000 acres of land for a permanent camp for 20,000 men.

Additional land purchased in 1856.

Barracks since erected for 4000 infantry, 1500 cavalry, and several batteries of artillery. Great improvements in military cookery introduced (see *Cookery*) under the superintendence of captain John Grant, 1857.

Visited by the queen, 18, 19 April, 1856.

The troops returned from the Crimea, reviewed by her, 7, 16 July, 1856.

About 15,000 men were stationed here, 1859.

Cost of the camp, said to be 1,291,531*l.* up to Feb. 1860.

An industrial and fine-art exhibition, furnished by officers and men and their wives, opened, 29 June; closed 14 July, 1864.

Camp set up for 40,000 men to execute military manœuvres, Aug., Sept. 1871. Many horses broke away through a fright, 30 Aug. 1871.

Review of 14,000 men by the queen, 5 July, 1872.

Summer manœuvres here, 1874, 1875, 1876, 1877.

Review by the queen, 13 May, 1878; again (all branches of the service represented), 2 July, 1886.

March of a force equipped for war, 17 Aug. 1886.

Review and sham fight, 23 June, 1887.

The queen reviews about 60,000 men, about half volunteers; grand march past, 9 July, 1887.

Sir Evelyn Wood appointed commander, 1889.

Theatre Royal burned down, 8 Feb. 1889.

The queen reviews 11,945 of all ranks, 31 May, 1889.

A sham fight and review, in which about 25,530 troops, regulars and volunteers, were engaged, took place here in the presence of the Emperor William II., the Princess of Wales, the Duke of Cambridge, and others of the royal family, 7 Aug. 1889.

The queen reviews the troops, 16 July, 1891; 27 June, 1892; 17 March, 1893; 12 June, 1894; 13 July, 1895.

Duke of Connaught appointed commander at the camps 9 Oct. 1893; succeeded by sir Redvers H. Buller 9 Oct. 1898; sir A. G. M. Moore, *temporary,* 15 Dec. 1899; sir Redvers Buller resumes command, 1 Oct. (for a speech on 10 Oct. to the Queen's Westminster Volunteers, placed on half-pay, 23 Oct. 1901); sir H. J. T. Hildyard, *temporary,* 25 Oct. 1901; sir J. D. P. French appointed, 15 Sept. 1902.

Queen Victoria reviews on Laffan's plain about 28,000 troops 5,029 horses, and 57 guns, including the Colonial, Indian and African forces, grand march past, 1 July, 1897; again, 12,000 troops, 7 July, 1898; again, over 14,000, 26 June, 1899.

New hospital opened, 13 Aug. 1897.

Manœuvres, 4 deaths from sunstroke, 11 June, 1900.

The king attends a military tattoo, 14 June (indisposed); the queen reviews over 31,000 troops, 16 June, 1902.

Official residence of sir John French burnt down, 15 Jan. 1903.

ALDINE PRESS, that of Aldo Manuzio (Aldus Manutius), at Venice, where were printed many of the first editions of the Greek, Latin, and Italian classics, commencing in 1494 with Musæus.

ALDWYCH, the name given to one of the two streets, now (1903) in the course of construction, which will join the Strand with Holborn. The name is derived from the old Danish settlement of Aldwych that once covered the site, and left the trace of its former existence in the name of Wych-street now demolished.

ALE, BEER, and Wine. Ale is said to have been known as a beverage at least in 404 B.C. Herodotus ascribes the first discovery of the art of brewing barley-wine to Isis, the wife of Osiris, and a beverage of this kind is mentioned by Xenophon, 401 B.C. The Romans and Germans very early learned from the Egyptians the process of preparing a liquor from corn by means of fermentation. *Tacitus.* Alehouses are mentioned in the laws of Ina, king of

Wessex. Booths were set up in England, 728, when laws were passed for their regulation. None but freemen were allowed to keep ale-houses in London, 13 Edw. I. 1285. They were further subjected to regulation by 5 & 6 Edw. VI. c. 25 (1551). By 1 James I. c. 9 (1603), one full quart of the best, and two quarts of small ale were to be sold for one penny. Excise duty on ale and beer was imposed by the parliament in 1643, and continued by Charles II. (1660); repealed, 1 Will. IV. c. 51 (1830); see *Beer*, *Porter*, *Wine*, *Victuallers*. Michael Thomas Bass, the eminent brewer of Burton, died 28 April, 1884, aged 84.

Mr. John Bickerdyke's book on "The Curiosities of Ale and Beer" was published in 1886.

ALEMANNI, or ALL MEN (*i.e.* men of all nations), hence *Allemand*, German. A body of Suevi, who took this name, were attacked by Caracalla, 211. After several repulses, they invaded the empire under Aurelian, who subdued them in three battles, 271. They were again vanquished by Julian, 356, 357; by Jovinus, 368. They were defeated and subjugated by Clovis at Tolbiac (or Zulpich), 496. The Suabians are their descendants.

ALENÇON (N. France) gave title to a count and duke.

1268–82. Peter, made Count by his father king Louis IX.
1293. Charles I. of Valois, made Count by his brother king Philip the Fair.
1325. Charles II. (his son), killed at Crecy.
1346. Charles III. (his son), became a priest.
1361. Peter, his brother.
1404. John (his son), made DUKE in 1414, killed at Agincourt, 1415.
1415. John II. (his son), prisoner in England, 1424–9; intrigued against the French king; died in prison, 1470.
1476. Charles IV. fled after the battle of Pavia in 1525, and died shortly after of chagrin. The duchy was annexed by the crown.

ALEPPO, North Syria, a large town named Berœa by Seleucus Nicator, about 299 B.C. The pachalic of Aleppo is one of the five governments of Syria. It was taken by the Saracens, A.D. 638, who restored its ancient name Haleb or Chaleb; by Saladin, 1193; and sacked by Timour, Nov. 1400. Its depopulation by the plague has been frequent; 60,000 persons were computed to have perished by it in 1797; many in 1827. The cholera raged here in 1832. Aleppo suffered severely from the terrible earthquakes in 1822 and 1830; and has often been the scene of fanatical massacres. On 16 Oct. 1850, the Mahometans attacked the Christians, burning everything. Three churches were destroyed, five others plundered, and thousands of persons slain. The total loss of property amounted to about a million sterling; no interference was attempted by the pacha. Population in 1885, 110,000; 1901, *abt.* 127,149.

ALESSANDRIA, a city of Piedmont, built in 1168 under the name of Cæsar by the Milanese and Cremonese, to defend the Tanaro against the emperor, and afterwards named after pope Alexander III. It has been frequently besieged and taken. The French took it in 1796, but were driven out by Suwarrow, 21 July, 1799. They recovered it after the battle of Marengo, 14 June, 1800, and held it till 1814, when the strong fortifications erected by Napoleon were destroyed. These have been restored since June, 1856.

ALEUTIAN ISLES, in the North Pacific Ocean, discovered by Behring, 1741, visited by Cook, 1778, and settled by Russians, 1785.

"ALEXANDRA CASE," see *Trials*, 1862–64.

ALEXANDRA CLUB, an exclusive club for ladies of position, was established 1884. It has a membership of 850. Premises 12, Grosvenor street, W.

ALEXANDRA PARK, Muswell Hill, London, N. purchased by a company, and named after the princess of Wales, was opened with a flower show, 23 July, 1863. A portion of the Exhibition building of 1862 was erected here. The work proceeded rapidly in 1864, was suspended in 1865, recommenced in 1866, and completed in 1873.

Horse-races first held here . . 30 June, 1 July, 1868
The prospectus of a scheme to organise an institution resembling the South Kensington Museum and the Crystal Palace, by means of a tontine (to cease 30 June, 1886), was issued . 22 July, 1871
The affairs were to be managed by "The Alexandra Palace and Muswell-hill Estate Management Company (limited)." Public lectures on the subject, Aug. 1871; the company's affairs were wound up Feb. 1872
The purchase of the land and buildings for the public proposed by the lord mayor and others July ,,
The palace was opened with a grand concert, &c., 24 May; destroyed by fire . . . . 9 June, 1873
Two women, incautiously viewing the ruins, buried, 25 June; bodies found . . . . 21 Aug. ,,
The new building (386 by 184 feet) opened, 1 May, 1875
94,125 persons said to have entered the park, Whit-Monday . . . . 17 May, ,,
Balfe memorial festival . . . . . 29 July, 1876
The estate taken over by the London Financial Association, creditors of the company . . 1876–7
The palace re-opened . . . . . . 10 May, ,,
Arrival of Nubian hunters, with elephants, rhinoceroses, camels, dromedaries, buffaloes, zebras, ostriches, &c. (imported by Carl Hagenbeck), 7 Sept.–13 Oct. ,,
Opened by new proprietors (Mr. Willing and others) with new attractions . . . 17 May, 1880
107,852 visitors (bank holiday) . . . 2 Aug. ,,
Taken by Jones and Barber . . . Nov. ,,
Put up for sale: unsold . . . . . 11 Feb. 1881
Varied entertainments 1881–2
Act for relieving the London Financial Association from charge of the Palace (withdrawn March *et seq.*) . . . . . . 1883, again 1884
Proposals for purchasing the land for recreation, June, 1883
Put up for sale; no bidders . . . . 20 July, ,,
London Financial Association *v.* Sir John Kelk, Lucas & Co. (contractors), and others (directors, &c.), 400,000*l.* claimed as misappropriated; about 25 days' trial; Vice-Chancellor Bacon dismisses case with costs . . . . . . 8 Mar. 1884
The Palace let to Mr. George Collins Levy, for International Exhibition, announced . 25 July, ,,
Temporary Industrial Exhibition opened 31 March, 1885
Palace closed in 1886; re-opened for the season, 11 April, 1887, Mr. H. W. Hayward, lessee; 54,720 visitors on Whit Monday, 30 May, 1887; reported unsuccessful, Feb. 1888; re-opened with a grand concert (1,000 performers), 12 May; second grand concert. . . . . 9 June, 1888
Celebration of the 23rd anniversary of the organization of the Salvation Army . . . 9 July, ,,
For Professor Baldwin's ascents and descents see under *Balloons* . . . . ,,
The park re-opened for the season; exhibition of nearly 1,000 monkeys, balloons and parachutes, &c., professor Baldwin, Mr. Young, and others, 1 June, 1889
Comic opera by Mr. C. Wibrow . 17 June *et seq.* ,,
French national fête, Gen. Boulanger present, 13 July ,,
Professor Baldwin, after 98 ascents and descents, retires with intention of returning to America, about . . . . 17 July, ,,
The London Financial Association apply for the appointment of a provisional liquidator pending the winding-up of the Alexandra Palace and Park company, Mr. C. L. Nichols appointed . 27 July, ,,

The palace closed . . . . . Sept. 1889
Licenses renewed to Mr. Charles James Hayter, 14 Nov. „
Bill for repealing the protective clauses of the Acts of 1866 and 1877, promoted by the association, withdrawn from the Commons . . April, 1891
Purchase of the palace and grounds proposed to the Middlesex county council by R. D. M. Littler, chairman, Dec. 1891; proposal deferred . May, 1892
Meeting at the Mansion-house; committee to promote the purchase formed (275,000*l.* required), 8 Feb. 1893
The London county council decline to support the scheme . . . . . . March, „
Lease of the palace obtained by Mr. T. J. Hawkins: announced . . . 28 Oct. 1897
The palace re-opened on Good Friday, performance of the *Messiah*, etc. . . 8 April, 1898
"Christian Endeavour Societies," convention opened, over 25,000 present . . 16 July, 1900
The palace and land bought for 150,120*l.* raised by the Middlesex and other county councils, and opened free (except bank holidays and race days) to the public by the duke of Bedford . 18 May, 1901
Statue of queen Victoria unveiled, and an exhibition of the Jubilee and Diamond Jubilee presents opened by the lord mayor . . . . 5 Oct. „
Physical culture classes inaugurated by the princess Louise and the duke of Argyll . . 18 Jan. 1902
"London's welcome to the Colonial troops," 21 June, „
Duke of Connaught inspects the Colonial and Indian troops encamped here, and presents medals . . . . 18 June and 16 July, „
Grand military fêtes, Fiji war dance, &c. 12, 19 July, „
Islington children's coronation fêtes (30,000), 5 Sept.; about 5,500 more (Hornsey) . 9 Sept. „
Great meeting to protest against the Education bill; speeches by sir H. Campbell-Bannerman, Mr. Asquith, and others . . . 1 Nov. „
Exhibition of balloons, airships, and aeronautical appliances, under auspices of the Aeronautical Institute, opened . . . . . 17 Sept. 1903

ALEXANDRIA (Egypt), the walls whereof were six miles in circuit, was founded by Alexander the Great, 332 B.C., who was buried here, 322. It became the residence of the Greek sovereigns of Egypt, the Ptolemies, 323; seventeen councils were held here, A.D. 231-633. Population, with its suburbs, in 1883, 208,775; 1901, 319,766.

Ptolemy Soter erects the Museum, the Serapeum, the Pharos, and other edifices, and begins the library about . . . . B.C. 298
These works completed by his son P. Philadelphus and his grandson P. Euergetes . . . 283–222
Alexandria taken by Julius Cæsar, when a library is burnt 47
Which Antony replaces by one brought from Pergamus 36
The city restored by Adrian . . . . A.D. 122
Massacre of the youth by Caracalla, in revenge for an insult 215
Alexandria supporting the usurper Achilleus is taken by Diocletian after a long siege . . 297
Alexandria disturbed by the feuds between the Athanasians and Arians 321
George of Cappadocia was killed, 362, and Athanasius finally restored 363
50,000 persons perish by an earthquake . . . 365
Paganism suppressed by Theodosius, when a second library is burnt 390
Alexandria captured by Chosroes II. of Persia . 616
And by Amrou, the general of the caliph Omar,* 22 Dec. 640
Recovered by the Greeks; retaken by Amrou. . 644
Cairo founded by the Saracens, which tends to the decay of Alexandria 969

* The statement that Amrou ordered the remains of the library to be burnt is apocryphal. The saying of Omar —"That if the books agreed with the book of God, they were useless: if they disagreed, they were pernicious" —is denied by Mahometans. It is also attributed to Theophilus, archbishop of Alexandria (390), and to cardinal Ximenes (1500).

Alexandria plundered by the Crusaders . . . 1365
The French capture Alexandria . . . July, 1798
Battle of Alexandria or Canopus: the British under gen. sir Ralph Abercromby defeat the French under Menou . . . . . 21 March, 1801
Abercromby dies of his wounds, 28 March; Menou and 10,000 French surrender to Hutchinson, 2 Sept. „
Alexandria taken by the British under Fraser, 20 March; evacuated by them . . 23 Sept. 1807
By the convention of Alexandria, Egypt was guaranteed to Mehemet Ali and his successors (and greatly favoured by them) 1841
Railway to Cairo formed 1851
New port, first stone laid by the khedive 15 May, 1871
Fierce riots against Europeans (see *Egypt*), 11 June, 1882
Panic and great emigration of Europeans . June, „
Bombardment of the forts, conflagration and abandonment of the city (see *Egypt*) . 11–13 July, „
New museum of antiquities, &c., opened by the khedive . . . . . . 17 Oct. 1892
New harbour works by Messrs. Pearson completed June, 1893
First exhibition of national art and industry, opened by the khedive . . . 22 April 1894
Serious assaults on the British and other Europeans . . . . Feb. 1895
New museum and public library opened by the khedive . . . . 26 Sept. „
Bishop Macarius enthroned as R.C. Coptic patriarch, under the title of Cyril II. (see *Copts*) . 21 July, 1899
M. G. Averoff, benefactor, devoted large sums to public and charitable works, dies . 27 July, „
Ptolemaic monuments, discovered during excavations, erected by Dr. Schiess Bey, one to commemorate the queen's jubilee in 1897, and another of the fall of Omdurman and Khartum (2 Sept. 1898) . . . . 7 Sept. „
First sod cut of the new graving dock at Gabbari, 24 Aug. 1900
Riot, due to the murder of an Egyptian police corporal by an Italian . . . . 7 Aug. 1901
Slight epidemics of plague, 45 deaths from May to Nov. 1899; 20 deaths in 1900; 18 deaths up to Sept. „

ALEXANDRIAN CODEX, a MS. of the Septuagint translation of the Bible in Greek, said to have been transcribed by a lady named Thecla, in the 6th century, and to have belonged to the patriarch of Alexandria in 1098. It was presented to Charles I. of England in 1628 by Cyrillus Leucaris, patriarch of Constantinople, and was placed in the British Museum in 1753. It was printed in facsimile, 1786–1821.

ALEXANDRIAN ERA, see *Eras*.

ALEXANDRIAN SCHOOLS OF PHILOSOPHY. The first school arose B.C. 323, soon after the foundation of Alexandria. It flourished under the patronage of the Ptolemies till about 30 B.C. It included Euclid (300), Archimedes (287–212), Apollonius (250), Hipparchus (150), and Hero (150). The second school dates from 30 B.C., and lasted till about 640. Its most eminent members were Ptolemy, the author of the Ptolemaic system (150), Diophantus the arithmetician (200), and Pappus the geometer (350).

ALEXANDRINES, verses of twelve syllables, first written by Alexander of Paris, about 1164, and since called after him. The last line of the Spenserian stanza is an Alexandrine. In Pope's *Essay on Criticism*, this verse is thus happily exemplified:—

> "A needless Alexandrine ends the song,
> That, like a wounded snake, drags its slow length along."

The longest English poem wholly in Alexandrine verse is Drayton's Polyolbion, published 1612–22.

ALEXINATZ, a town in Servia. Severe fighting took place here between the Turks and Servians,

Aug.–Sept. 1876. The town, head-quarters of the Servians, was captured 31 Oct. This led to an armistice and peace. See *Turkey*.

ALFORD (N. Scotland), **BATTLE OF.** General Baillie, with a large body of covenanters, was defeated by the marquis of Montrose, 2 July, 1645.

ALGEBRA: Diophantus, of Alexandria, wrote a work upon Algebra consisting of 13 books, 6 of which are extant, 4th century. It was cultivated in the 9th century by the Arabs, who derived their knowledge from the Hindus and brought it into Spain; and in Italy by Leonardo Bonaccio of Pisa, in 1220. In 1494 Luca Paciolo published the first printed book on Algebra in Europe. Some of the algebraic signs were introduced either by Christophe Rudolph (1522–26) or Michael Stifelius of Nuremberg, 1544, and others by Francis Vieta, in 1590, when algebra came into general use. Jerome Cardan published his "Ars Magna," containing his rule, 1545. Thos. Harriot's important discoveries appeared in his "Artis Analyticæ Praxis," 1631. Descartes applied algebra to geometry about 1637. The binomial theorem of Newton, the basis of the doctrine of fluxions, and the new analysis, 1668. Subsequently Euler, Lagrange, Fourier, Peacock, De Morgan, Sylvester, and Cayley.

ALGERIA, see *Algiers*.

ALGESIRAS, or **OLD GIBRALTAR** (S. Spain). Here the Moors entered Spain in 711, and held it ill taken by Alfonso XI. March, 1344.—Two engagements took place here between the English fleet under sir James Saumarez and the United French and Spanish fleets, 6 and 12 July, 1801. In the first the enemy was victorious; but the British honour was redeemed in the latter conflict, the *San Antonio*, 74 guns, being captured. Two Spanish ships fired on each other by mistake, and took fire; of 2000 men on board, 250 were saved by the English. *Alison.*

ALGIERS, now **ALGERIA**, N.W. Africa; part of the ancient Mauritania, which was conquered by the Romans, 46 B.C.; by the Vandals, A.D. 439; recovered for the empire by Belisarius, 534; and subdued by the Arabs about 690. Population of Algeria in 1866, 2,921,146; 1872, 2,146,225; 1875, 2,448,691; 1886, 3,910,399; 1891, 4,124,732; 1896, 4,429,421; 1901, 4,790,000.

The town Algiers founded by the Arabs near the site of Icosium . . . . about 935
Becoming the seat of the Barbary pirates, captured by Ferdinand of Spain, 1509; retaken by Horuc Barbarossa, and made the capital of a state; governed by a dey, nominally subject to Turkey, 1516. Barbarossa was defeated and slain by the Spaniards 1518
The emperor Charles V. loses a fine fleet and army in an expedition against Algiers 1541
Algiers terrified into pacific measures by Blake, 1655; by Du Quesne 1683-4
For continued piracy, the city successfully bombarded by the British fleet under lord Exmouth, 27 Aug. 1816
A new treaty followed, and Christian slavery was abolished . . . . ,,
Algiers surrendered to a French armament under Bourmont and Duperré, after severe conflicts; the dey deposed, and the barbarian government wholly overthrown . . . . . 5 July, 1830
The Arab chief Abd-el-Kader preaches a holy war, becomes powerful, and attacks the French, at first successfully 1833
He is recognised as emir of Mascara, by treaty with the French 1834
The French ministry announce their intention to retain Algiers permanently . . . . 20 May, ,,
War renewed 1835-6
The French take Mascara . . . . 5 Dec. 1835
Marshal Clausel defeats the Arabs in two battles, and enters Mascara . . . . 8 Dec. 1836
Gen. Damremont killed in taking Constantina, 13 Oct. 1837
Abd-el-Kader, thoroughly defeated, recognises the French supremacy . . . . . . 30 May, ,,
War renewed; French defeated . . . . Dec. 1839
Algeria annexed to France, and the emir declared a rebel . . . . Feb. 1842
He is defeated by Bugeaud at Isly . . . 14 Aug. 1844
500 Arabs in a cave at Khartani refuse to surrender; suffocated by smoke, said to have been ordered by general Pelissier . . . 18 June, 1845
After a long struggle Abd-el-Kader surrenders to Lamoricière . . . . . 23 Dec. 1847*
Fresh revolts, 1849; subdued 1850
An insurrection of the Kabyles subdued by the French, after several sharp engagements . . 1852
Another insurrection suppressed 1857
The government entrusted (for a short time) to prince Napoleon 1858
The Arab tribes attack the French; defeated, 31 Oct. and 6 Nov. 1859
Algiers visited by Napoleon III. . . . . Sept. 1860
Marshal Pelissier, duke of Malakhoff, appointed governor-general of Algeria . . . . Nov. ,,
The emperor promises a constitution securing the rights of the Arabs, saying: "I am as much emperor of the Arabs as of the French." . Feb. 1863
Insurrection of the Arabs, May; submission, June, 1864
Death of marshal Pelissier, 22 May; MacMahon, duke of Magenta, succeeds him . . . 8 Sept. ,,
Fresh revolts; insurgents defeated by Jolivet 2 Oct. ,,
The emperor well received during his visit, 3 May—June, 1865
More rights and privileges promised to the natives. July, ,,
The emperor publishes his letter on the policy of France in Algeria (20 July) . . . Nov. 1865
4000 Arabs defeated by col. Sounis . . 2 Feb. 1869
Resignation of marshal MacMahon . . July, 1870
Algeria proclaimed in a state of siege . 15 Aug. ,,
State of siege raised . . . . . . 24 June, 1871
Gen. Chanzy accused of governing despotically; his resignation not accepted by Marshal MacMahon, July; replaced by Albert Grévy . . . 1878
An insurrection soon quelled . . . . June, 1879
Dispute with Tunis; outrages of the savage tribes, Kroumirs, &c. (see *Tunis*) . . . April, 1881
Arab insurrection, headed by Bou Ameema, June; he is said to be defeated, and a fugitive, 13 July, ,,
Insurrection dreaded; troops sent from France about 26 Aug. ,,
Bou Ameema defeated by the French, 13th July; said to be preparing for a fresh revolt; three French columns advancing against him, Aug.; indecisive skirmishes . . . . . . Aug. ,,
Resignation of the governor, A. Grévy (died 11 July, 1899) . . . . Nov. ,,
M. Tirman appointed . . . . . . Dec. ,,
Topographical expedition attacked, 40 said to be killed . . . . April, 1882
The province Mzab annexed to Algeria, announced Dec. ,,
Submission of insurgents announced . 13 June, 1883
Plague of locusts . . . . . . July, 1888-92
The chamber of deputies, Paris, direct the appointment to inquire respecting Algerian political affairs . . . . 5 March, 1892

* He, with his suite, embarked at Oran, and landed at Toulon on 28 Dec. following. He was removed to the castle of Amboise, near Tours, 2 Nov. 1848, and released from his confinement by Louis Napoleon, 16 Oct. 1852, after swearing on the Koran never to disturb Africa again; he was to reside henceforward at Broussa, in Asia Minor; but in consequence of the earthquake at that place, 28 Feb. 1855, he removed to Constantinople. In July, 1860, Abd-el-Kader held the citadel of Damascus, and there protected many of the Christians whom he had rescued from the massacres then in perpetration by the Turks. He received honours from the English, French, and Sardinian sovereigns. He visited Paris and London in Aug. 1865. He offered to serve in the French army in July, 1870. He died May, 1883, aged 76.

Resignation of M. Louis Tirman (dies July, 1899), ten years governor, March; succeeded by M. Jules Cambon, arrived . . 11 May, 1891
Remains of a church of the 5th or 6th century discovered during excavations at Tigziat, with Pagan relics, reported . . . June, 1894
Forest fires round Bona, with loss of life, 12—19 Sept. „
Irruption of locusts in Oran energetically suppressed in 1896
Collision between a military and passenger train near Adelia station, 7 officers killed . 10 May, „
M. Lépine appointed governor-gen., arrives 31 Oct. 1897
Severe famine, M. Lépine appeals for help, 120,000 francs granted . . . . . 28 Dec. „
Serious riots in connection with the Dreyfus case (see *France*, 1894 and 1898), against the Jews, 2 deaths, and shops, etc., pillaged, 23-24 Jan. 1898; over 78 persons sentenced to various terms of imprisonment, 26 Jan.; order restored, 28 Jan.; 58 Anti-Semites pardoned . . 13 June, 1898
M. Leferrière appointed governor-gen. reported, 27 July, „
Anti-Jewish rioting in Tunis, 12 Nov. 1898; M. Max Regis, anti-Semite mayor, suspended, 12 Dec.; M. Pujade (mayor) and municipality suspended for anti-Semitic agitation, he dies, 5 Feb.; fatal rioting . . . . . 9 Feb. 1899
Anti-Semitic demonstrations by M. Max Regis, some fighting . . . . . 20—22 Sept. „
Military operations in S. Algeria, Insalah occupied by the French, 28 Dec.; natives routed at Inrhar, 19 March, 1900; the oases of Twab, Tidikelt, and Gurara and the district of Igli occupied . . . . 5 April–May, 1900
Further fighting with Berbers near Timmimum, French loss, 17 killed . 28 Aug., 7 Sept. „
Berbers routed at Timmimum, capt. Guisard and 9 others killed . . . . . 18 Feb. 1901
Marguerite, a village, sacked by Arabs, reported, 28 April, „
M. Jounart appointed gov.-gen., 5 Oct. 1900; resigns . . . . May, „
Convention with Morocco, settled in Paris . July, „
M. Paul Revoil, new governor, arrives . 6 Oct. „
M. Max Regis imprisoned for 3 years . 14 Jan. 1902
Expedition against the Tuaregs . . 31 May, „
Morocco frontier question settled . 13 Oct. „
Earthquake shocks at Oran and Oned Marsa, 17 Nov. „
M. Revoil, gov.-gen., resigns . . . . 11 April, 1903
Pres. Loubet well received . . 15 April, „
Organized system of female medical doctors for the Zenanas; dispensary opened at Algiers, other establishments in progress, reported, July, „

ALHAMA, a town of Granada, S. Spain, destroyed by an earthquake, 25 Dec. 1884; 5 churches, 5 convents, and other buildings thrown down; reported deaths above 300.

ALHAMBRA, a Moorish palace and fortress near Granada, S. Spain, founded by Mohammed I. of Granada about 1253. It was surrendered to the Christians about Nov. 1491. The remains have been described in a magnificent work by Owen Jones and Jules Goury, published 1842-5. A fac-simile of a part of this palace in the Crystal Palace at Sydenham, was destroyed by the fire, 30 Dec. 1866. By a fire at the Alhambra, near Granada, the roof of the Sala de la Barca was destroyed; except the court of the Alberca, other courts were uninjured, 15, 16 Sept. 1890.—The Panopticon (*which see*) was opened as a circus, &c., under the name of Alhambra, in March, 1858. The Alhambra Palace Company, incorporated in July 1863, applied for dissolution in Jan. 1865. The Royal Alhambra Theatre was destroyed by fire, 7 Dec. 1882: 2 firemen lost their lives; reopened, 3 Dec. 1883. Noted for the magnificence of its ballets and spectacular performances.

ALI, SECT OF (Shiites, or Fatimites). Ali, born about 598, married Mahomet's daughter Fatima, about 619; became vizier, 614; and caliph, 656. Ali was called by the prophet, "the lion of God, always victorious;" and the Persians follow the interpretation of the Koran according to Ali, while other Mahometans adhere to that of Abubeker and Omar. Ali was assassinated 23 Jan. 661.*

ALIENS or **FOREIGNERS** were banished in 1155, being thought too numerous. In 1343 they were excluded from enjoying ecclesiastical benefices. By 2 Rich. II. st. 1, 1378, they were much relieved. When they were to be tried criminally, the juries were to be half foreigners, if they so desired, 1430. They were restrained from exercising any trade of handicraft by retail, 1483, a prohibition which was relaxed in 1663.

Alien priories (cells and estates belonging to foreign persons) suppressed in England, 1414.
The *Alien Act* passed, Jan. 1793.
Act to register aliens, 1795.
Baron Geramb, a fashionable foreigner, known at court, ordered out of England, 6 April, 1812.
Bill to abolish naturalisation by the holding of stock in the banks of Scotland, June, 1820.
New registration act, 7 George IV. 1826. This last act was repealed and another statute passed, 6 Will. IV. 1836.
The rigour of the alien laws was mitigated by acts passed in 1844 and 1847.
"*Foreigners* have reclaimed our marshes, drained our fens, fished our seas, and built our bridges and harbours." *Smiles*, 1861.
Their status defined by the Naturalisation Act, passed 12 May, 1870. See under *Law*.
The votes of some Hanoverians at the Stepney Parliamentary Election disallowed by the judges, 5 April, 1886.
The prohibition of aliens holding land in the United States of North America adopted by several western states; and also stringent restrictions on the employment of aliens in manufactures, 1885 *et seq*.
A decree respecting aliens and immigrants with restrictions was issued in France, 2 Oct. 1888.
New alien immigration bill, specially against anarchists and incurables, read 2nd time 17 July, 1894; dropped.
Naturalization act amended, naturalizing children of British subjects in the service of the crown abroad, July 6, 1895.
Alien immigration committee met June, 1902; reported 29,793 Russian, Polish, and Roumanian immigrants in 1902; excess of 7,717 over 1901, May, 1903.
Report of royal commission on alien immigration, issued Aug. 11, 1903.
Increase of foreign population of United Kingdom, 135,000 in 1881 to 286,000 in 1901.

ALIWAL, a village N. W. India, the site of a battle, 28 Jan. 1846, between the Sikh army under sirdar Runjoor Singh Majeethea, 19,000 strong, supported by 68 pieces of cannon, and the British under sir Harry Smith, 12,000 men with 32 guns. The contest was obstinate, but ended in the defeat of the Sikhs, who lost nearly 6000 killed or drowned.

ALIZARINE, a crystalline body, the colouring principle of madder discovered in it by Robiquet and Colin in 1831. Schunck showed that all the finest madder colours contained only alizarine combined with alkalies and fatty acids. Graebe and Liebermann obtained anthracene from alizarine in 1868, and alizarine from anthracene in 1869. The crystalline body anthracene was discovered in coal oils by Dumas and Laurent in 1832. See *Madder*.

* The first four successors of Mahomet—Abubeker, Omar, Othman, and Ali, his chief agents in establishing his religion and extirpating unbelievers, and whom on that account he styled the "cutting swords of God"—all died violent deaths; and his family was wholly extirpated within thirty years after his own decease.

ALJUBARROTA, Portugal. Here John I. of Portugal defeated John I. of Castile, and secured his country's independence, 14 Aug. 1385; see *Batalha*.

ALKALIES (from *kali*, the Arabic name for the plant from which an alkaline substance was first procured) are ammonia, potash, soda, and lithia. Black discovered the nature of the difference between caustic and mild alkalies in 1736.

The fixed alkalies, potash and soda, decomposed, and the metals potassium and sodium formed, by Humphry Davy at the Royal Institution, London, 1807.

Dr. Ure invented an alkalimeter, 1816.

The manufacture of alkalies, very extensive in Lancashire and Cheshire, is based on the decomposition of common salt (chloride of sodium), by a process invented by a Frenchman named Nicolas Le Blanc. about 1792; his statue set up in Paris, summer, 1885.

Mr. Losh obtained crystals of soda from brine about 1814. Various modifications of these processes are now in use.

"*Alkali works*" are defined as works for the manufacture of alkali, sulphates of soda, sulphate of potash, and in which muriatic gas is evolved.

Mr. Wm. Gossage's process for condensing muriatic acid gas patented in 1836.

The "ammonia process" of making soda, invented by Dyer and Hemming, in 1838; patents respecting it taken out by Solvay, 1863, 1867, 1872; Gossage, 1854; Schlœsing, 1854, 1858; Young, 1871, 1872; Weldon, 1872, 1873; and by others.

Mr. Walter Weldon received the French Lavoisier medal for his most important improvements in the alkali manufacture, July, 1877. He died of overwork, 20 Sept. 1885, aged 53.

In consequence of the injury to vegetation produced by the alkali works in Lancashire and Cheshire, the Alkali Works act "for the more effectual condensation [of 95 per cent.] of muriatic acid gas" (or hydrochloric acid) was passed, 28 July, 1863. It came into operation 1 Jan. 1864, proved successful; was re-enacted, 1868; and amended, 1874, 1881, and 1892. Mr. James Greenwood's electrolytic process for the direct production of caustic soda and chlorine from common salt reported successful, Jan. 1892. See *Bleaching Chemical Works* and *Union*.

Manufacture of ammonia-soda by the Solvay process by sir J. Brunner and Dr. L. Mond at Northwich, 1873. Patents taken out for making chlorine in conjunction with soda. These alkali works now the largest in the world, 1903.

ALKMAER, see *Bergen*.

ALLAHABAD (N. W. Hindostan), the "holy city" of the Indian Mahometans, situated at the junction of the rivers Jumna and Ganges. The main station of the Grand Trunk road and East Indian railway. Here is the pillar of Asoka, 240 B.C. The province of Allahabad was successively subject to the sovereigns of Delhi and Oude, but in 1801 was partially and in 1803 wholly incorporated with the British possessions. By treaty here, Bengal, &c., was ceded to the English in 1765.—During the Indian mutiny several sepoy regiments rose and massacred their officers, 4 June, 1857; colonel Neil marched promptly from Benares and suppressed the insurrection. In Nov. 1861, lord Canning made this city the capital of the N. W. provinces. Visit of the Prince of Wales, 7 March, 1874. University instituted, 1887. A fair is held Dec.-Jan., visited by about 300,000 persons. Population, 1891, 175,246; 1901, 172,032.

ALLEGORY abounds in the Bible and in Homer: see Jacob's blessing upon his sons, *Genesis* xlix. (1689 B.C.), *Psalm* lxxx., and all the prophets. Spenser's *Faerie Queene* (1590) and Bunyan's *Pilgrim's Progress* (1678) are allegories throughout. The *Spectator* (1711), by Addison, Steele, and others, abounds in allegories. The allegorical interpretation of the scriptures is said to have begun with Origen in the 3rd century; but see *Gal.* iv. 24.

ALLIA (more correctly Alia), Italy, a small river flowing into the Tiber, where Brennus and the Gauls defeated the Romans, 16 July, 390 B.C. The Gauls sacked Rome and committed so much injury that the day was thereafter held to be unlucky (*nefastus*), and no public business was permitted to be done thereon.

ALLIANCE, TREATIES OF, between the high European powers. The following are the principal: see *Coalitions*, *Conventions*, *Treaties*.

ALLIANCE.	
Of Leipsic	9 April, 1631
Of Vienna	27 May, 1657
The Triple	28 Jan. 1668
Of Warsaw	31 March, 1683
The Grand	12 May, 1689
The Hague	4 Jan. 1717
The Quadruple	2 Aug. 1718
Of Vienna	16 March, 1731
Of Versailles	1 May, 1756
Germanic	23 July, 1785
Of Paris	16 May, 1795
Of St. Petersburg	8 April, 1805
Austrian	14 March, 1812
Of Sweden	24 March, ,,
Of Töplitz	9 Sept. 1813
Holy Alliance	26 Sept. 1815
Of England, France, and Turkey	12 Mar. 1854
Of England and France ratified	3 April, ,,
Of Sardinia with the Western Powers (at Turin)	26 Jan. 1855
Of Sweden with the Western Powers	19 Dec. ,,
Of Prussia and Italy	June, 1866
Of France and Russia, confirmed	Aug. 1897
Triple (of Germany, Austria and Italy, which see)	13 March, 1887
England and Japan	30 Jan. 1902

ALLISON ISLAND, in the Pacific, n. of German New Guinea, discovered early in 1887.

ALL NIGHT SITTINGS, see *Parliament*, 1877 and 1881. Have since become of frequent occurrence.

ALL SAINTS' DAY (Nov. 1), or All-Hallows, a festival said to have been begun by pope Boniface IV. about 607, celebrated in the Pantheon at Rome, and established by pope Gregory IV. (about 830) for the commemoration of all those saints and martyrs in whose honour no particular day is assigned. The reformers of the English church, 1549, struck out of their calendar a great number of anniversaries, leaving only those which were connected with popular tradition.

ALL SOULS' COLLEGE, Oxford; see *Oxford*.

ALL SOULS' DAY (2 Nov.), a festival of the Roman Catholic church to commemorate the souls of the faithful, instituted, it is said, at Cluny about 993 or 1000.

"ALL THE TALENTS" ADMINISTRATION, see *Grenville Administrations*.

ALLOBROGES, Gauls, defeated by Q. Fabius Maximus, near the confluence of the Rhone and Saone, 121 B.C.

ALLOTMENTS, see *Land*.

ALMA, a river in the Crimea, near which was fought a great battle on 20 Sept. 1854. (See *Russo-Turkish War* and *Crimea*.) The English, French, and Turkish army (about 57,000 men) moved out of their first encampment in the Crimea on 19 Sept., and bivouacked for the night on the left bank of the Bulganac. The Russians (commanded by prince Menschikoff), mustering 40,000 infantry, had 180 field-pieces on the heights, and on the morning of 20 Sept. were joined by 6000 cavalry from Theodosia (or Kaffa). The English forces, under lord Raglan, consisted of 26,000 men; the French of 24,000, under marshal St. Arnaud. At 12 o'clock the signal to advance was made; the river Alma was crossed, while prince Napoleon took possession of the village under the fire of the Russian batteries, and at 4, after a sanguinary fight, the allies were completely victorious. The enemy, utterly routed, threw away their arms and knapsacks in their flight, having lost about 5000 men, of whom 900 were made prisoners, mostly wounded. The loss of the British was 26 officers and 327 men (chiefly from the 23rd, 7th, and 33rd regiments); that of the French, 3 officers and 233 men killed. Total loss of the allies about 3400.

ALMACK'S ASSEMBLY-ROOMS, King-street, St. James's, London, at first very exclusive, were erected by a Scotchman named Almack or M'Call, and opened 12 Feb. 1765. They have long been termed Willis's rooms from the name of later proprietors; they were offered for sale in April and July, 1890.

ALMANACS (from the Arabic *al manah*, to count; or better, the Coptic *al*, computation, and *men*, memory). The Egyptians computed time by instruments; the Alexandrians had almanacs, and log calendars are ancient. In the British Museum and universities are specimens of early almanacs. Michael Nostradamus, the astrologer, wrote an almanac in the style of Merlin, 1556. *Dufresnoy.* Professor Augustus De Morgan's valuable "*Book of Almanacs*, with an index of reference, by which the almanac may be found for every year," was published in March, 1851.* Among the earlier and more remarkable almanacs were—

John Somer's Calendar, written in Oxford	1380
One in Lambeth Palace, written in	1460
First printed one, published at Buda	1472
"Shepheard's Kalendar" (first printed in England), by Richard Pynson	1497
Tybalt's Prognostications	1533
Almanac Liégeois	1636
Lilly's Ephemeris	1644
Poor Robin's Almanac	1652
British Merlin	1658
Connaissance des Temps (by Picard)	1679
Edinburgh Almanac	1683
Moore's Almanac	1698 or 1713
Lady's Diary	1705
Season on the Seasons	1735
Gentleman's Diary	1741
Nautical Almanac, begun by Dr. Neville Maskelyne (materially improved, 1834)	1767
Annual Register	1758
British Imperial Kalendar	1809
Hone's Every Day Book	1826
British Almanac and Companion	1828
Anniversary Calendar, published by W. Kidd	1832
Chambers' Book of Days	1862-63
The Statesman's Year-book	1864
Whitaker's Almanack	1869
Hazell's Annual	1886
Mr. F. Mayer's International Almanac for 1890, in five languages, published	Dec. 1889

Mr. A. Hall's Almanac, designed April, 1899, calls New Year's Day Jan. 0, the remaining 364 days being divided into 13 months of 28 days each, thus causing any day of any month to fall on the same day of the week. The extra month he proposes to call "Christember."

* *Murphy's Almanack* for 1838 predicted correctly a frost on 7 Jan.; thaw and frost 14th; severe frost 21st, and then thaw. A great sale of the almanac ensued. Afterwards the predictions failed.

The Stationers' company claimed the exclusive right of publishing almanacs in virtue of letters patent from James I., granting the privilege to them and the two Universities; but the monopoly was broken up by a decision of the Court of Common Pleas in 1775. A bill to renew the privilege was lost in 1779.

The *Stamp Duty* on English almanacs first imposed in 1710, was abolished in August, 1834; since when almanacs have become innumerable, being issued by tradesmen with their goods.

Of Moore's (under the management of Henry Andrews, the able computer of the *Nautical Ephemeris*) at one time upwards of 430,000 copies were annually sold. He died in 1820.

Of *Foreign Almanacs*, the principal are the "Almanach de France," first published in 1699, the "Almanach de Gotha," 1764, in 150 pages; in 1895, 1,367, and the "Livre d'Or des Souverains," by H. R. Hiort-Lorenzen, published in Paris, July, 1895.

ALMANZA (S. E. Spain). Here on 25 April (O. S. 14), 1707, the English, Dutch, and Portuguese forces under the earl of Galway, were totally defeated by the French and Spanish commanded by James Fitzjames, duke of Berwick (illegitimate son of James II.). Most of the English were killed or made prisoners, having been abandoned by the Portuguese at the first charge.

ALMEIDA (Portugal), a frontier town, captured by Massena, 27 Aug. 1810. The French entered Spain, leaving a garrison at Almeida, blockaded by the English, 6 April, 1811. Almeida was retaken by Wellington (11 May), and Massena retired from Portugal.

ALMENARA, a village N. E. Spain, where on 28 July, 1710, an English and German army defeated the Spanish army supporting Philip V., the grandson of Louis XIV. of France. Stanhope, the English general, killed the Spanish general, Amezaga, in single conflict; an act almost unexampled in modern warfare.

ALMOHADES, Mahometan partisans, followers of Mohammed ben Abdalla, surnamed El-Mehedi, in Africa, about 1120. They subdued Morocco, 1145; entered Spain and took Seville, Cordova, and Granada, 1146-56; and founded a dynasty and ruled Spain till 1232, and Africa till 1278.

ALMONER, an office anciently allotted to a dignified clergyman who gave the first dish from the royal table to the poor, or an alms in money. By an ancient canon all bishops were required to keep almoners. The grand almoner of France was the highest ecclesiastical dignity in that kingdom before the revolution, 1789. Hereditary grand almoner of England, the marquis of Exeter, 1895. The king's almoner (Right Rev. lord Alwyne Compton, dean of Worcester, 1882, consecrated bishop of Ely, 1886) or the sub-almoner distributes the king's gifts on *Maundy Thursday* (*which see*).

ALMORAVIDES, Mahometan partisans in Africa, rose about 1050; entered Spain by invitation, 1086; were overcome by the Almohades in 1147.

ALMSHOUSES for aged and infirm persons have been erected by many public companies and benevolent individuals, particularly since the abolition of religious houses at the Reformation in the 16th century. A list of them, with useful information, will be found in "Low's Charities of London," 1862; frequently republished.

Armourers' almshouses, Bishopsgate	1551
Cornelius Van Dun founded the Red Lion almshouses, Westminster	1577
Emmanuel College, Westminster, founded by Lady Dacre	1594

Alleyn's almshouses, near City road, founded by E. Alleyn 1620
Whittington's almshouses, founded in 1621, were rebuilt near Highgate-hill by the Mercers' company 1826
The Fishmongers' company founded almshouses in 1618, and rebuilt them on Wandsworth common 1850
Haberdashers' almshouses, Hoxton, founded by Robert Aske 1692
Dame Owen's almshouses, Islington, built in 1613 (in gratitude for her escape from an arrow-shot), were rebuilt by the Brewers' company. See *Owen's college* 1839
Bancroft's almshouses, Mile End, were erected . . 1735
The London almshouses, in commemoration of the passing of the Reform Bill, built at Brixton . 1833
Numerous almshouses since erected for printers, bookbinders, &c.

ALNEY, an island in the Severn, near Gloucester. Here a combat is asserted to have taken place between Edmund Ironside and Canute the Great, in sight of their armies, 1016. The latter was wounded, and proposed a division of the kingdom, the south part falling to Edmund. Edmund was murdered at Oxford shortly after, it is said by Ædric Streon; and Canute obtained possession of the whole kingdom.

ALNWICK (Saxon *Ealnwic*), on the river Alne in Northumberland, was given at the conquest to Ivo de Vesci. It has long belonged to the Percies. Malcolm, king of Scotland, besieged Alnwick, and he and his sons were killed 13 Nov. 1093. It was taken by David I. in 1136, and attempted in July, 1174, by William the Lion, who was defeated and taken prisoner. It was burnt by king John in 1215, and by the Scots in 1448. Since 1854 the castle has been repaired and enlarged with great taste and at unsparing expense.

ALPACA (or Paco), a species of the S. American quadruped, the Llama, the soft hairy wool of which is now largely employed in the fabrication of cloths. It was introduced into this country about 1836, by the earl of Derby. An alpaca factory (covering 11 acres), with a town, park, almshouses, &c., for the workpeople, was erected at Saltaire, near Shipley, Yorkshire, by Mr. (afterwards sir) Titus Salt in 1852. A statue of him at Bradford was unveiled 1 Aug. 1874. He died 29 Dec. 1876. Saltaire visited by the prince and princess of Wales 22 June, 1882.

The Royal Yorkshire Jubilee Exhibition at Saltaire opened by the Princess Beatrice . . 6 May, 1887

ALPHABET, so called from the first two Greek letters *alpha, beta* (Hebrew *aleph beth*). The statements that Cadmus brought the Phœnician letters from Egypt into Greece are legendary. M. de Rougé about 1859 demonstrated the true origin of the alphabet. Dr. Isaac Taylor's learned work, "The Alphabet," was published May, 1883; he died, aged 72, 18 Oct. 1901.

Nearly 200 alphabets are known, of which about 50 are in use, mostly developed from the Phœnician alphabet itself, said to have been derived from the Egyptian hieroglyphic picture writing; the Roman alphabet was based upon the Greek. The alphabets of the different nations contain the following number of letters :—

English	26	Arabic	28
French	25	Persian	32
Italian	22	Turkish	28
Spanish	27	Sanscrit	44
German	26	Chinese radical characters	214
Slavonic	42		
Russian	35	Chinese alphabet said to be invented by bishop Eligius Cosi of Canton (1880)	33
Latin	22		
Greek	24		
Hebrew	22		

ALPHONSINE TABLES, astronomical tables, composed by Spanish and Arab astronomers, and collected in 1253 under the direction of Alphonso X. of Castile, surnamed the Wise, who is said to have expended upwards of 400,000 crowns in completing the work; he himself wrote the preface. The Spanish government ordered the work of Alphonso to be reprinted from the best MSS.; the publication began in 1863.

ALPS, European mountains. Those between France and Italy were passed by Hannibal, 218 B.C.; by the Romans, 154 B.C.; and by Napoleon I. May, 1800. Roads over Mont Cenis and the Simplon, connecting France and Italy, were constructed, by order of Napoleon, between 1801-6; see *Simplon*. The "Alpine Club," which consists of British travellers in the Alps, was founded in 1858, and published its first work, "Peaks, Passes, and Glaciers," 1859; and a journal since. Mr. John Ball, F.R.S., long the able first president, and author of excellent "Guides," died 21 Oct. 1889. See *Jungfrau, Matterhorn*. An International Alpine Congress opened at Salzburg 14 Aug. 1882.

Alpine Clubs.—Austrian founded, 1862; Swiss, 1863; Italian, 1863; German, 1869, united with the Austrian 1874, and numbers some 40,000 members. The Appalachian Mountain Club of Boston is the principal mountaineering Club in the United States.
Mont Cenis or Col de Fréjus Tunnel.—A tunnel, 7½ miles long through Mont Cenis, connecting Savoy and Piedmont, was proposed by M. Medail, and, after long lying dormant, was discussed and plans drawn up in 1848. The execution was prevented by the war of 1849.
The work of excavation was begun by king Victor Emmanuel, 31 Aug. 1857.
The boring was at first effected by ordinary piercing machinery; steam power was employed in 1860; and latterly compressed air.
Engineers—Grattoni, Grandis, and Sommeiller; the boring was completed, 25 Dec. 1870.
The total cost was about 2,600,000*l.* As the Italians had executed the work within the given time, the French government bore the chief expense.
The first experimental trip was made in 40 minutes, 13 Sept., and the tunnel was solemnly inaugurated by the passage of 22 carriages in 20 minutes, 17 Sept. 1871; regular trains pass through, 16 Oct. 1871.
A railway for locomotives over Mont Cenis was constructed upon Mr. Fell's plan in 1867 (see *Railways*), and opened for traffic, 15 June, 1868.
The overland mail first travels through the tunnel to Brindisi, saving 24 hours, 5 Jan. 1872.
St. Gothard Tunnel (part of a railway system to connect the North Sea and the Mediterranean), about 9¼ miles; compressed air employed in boring; begun June, 1872; completed 29 Feb. 1880; through failure in vaulting, May, 1880, opening deferred.
The first complete train, carrying one hundred passengers, passed through the St. Gothard Tunnel in 50 minutes, 1 Nov. 1881; partially opened 1 Jan. 1882; completely opened June, 1882.
Simplon tunnel, convention for its construction by the Italian and Swiss governments, signed 25 Nov. 1895.
275 fatal Alpine accidents, 1891—1900; 136 in 1903.
New Rhætian Railway, begun 1898, opened 27 June, 1903. Scheme of railway to top of Mt. Blanc proposed by M. Vallot, Sept. 1903.

ALRESFORD, battle of, or Cheriton, *which see*.

ALSACE, Elsass, formerly part of the kingdom of Austrasia, afterwards the French departments of the Upper and Lower Rhine. It was incorporated with the German empire in the 10th century. A portion was restored to France, 1648, and the whole, including Strasburg, in 1697. Alsace was re-conquered by the Germans, Aug.-Sept. 1870; and annexed to their empire, May, 1871; by law, 9 June, 1871. The Alsatians were permitted to choose their nationality, before 30 Sept. 1872. Many emigrated into France, with much regret.—ALSACE-LORRAINE was constituted a province of the German empire, having been ceded by France by the treaty of peace concluded 10 May, 1871, see *Belfort*. The province sends 15 members to the German parliament. Administrators, prince Bismarck, 1871; field-marshal Manteuffel, 1 Oct. 1879; prince Hohenlohe, July, 1885; prince Hohenlohe-Langenburg, Oct. 1894. Population of Alsace-Lorraine, 1885, 1,564,355; 1890, 1,603,107; 1900, 1,717,451. See *Germany*, 1887, and *Strasburg*. The emperor William II. visited the province 20 Aug. *et seq.* 1889, and 19 Oct. 1895. The stringent passport regulations greatly relaxed 1 Oct. 1891; the "dictatorship paragraph" repealed 11 May, 1902.

ALSATIA, a name given to the precinct of Whitefriars, London, is described in Scott's "Fortunes of Nigel." Its privilege of sanctuary was abolished in 1697.

ALSEN (Denmark), besieged by the Prussians, and heroically defended, 26 June; taken, 29 June, 1864.

ALTAR. One was built by Noah, 2348 B.C.; 3154 *Hales*; 2481 *Clinton* (*Gen.* viii. 20); others by Abraham, 1921 (*Gen.* xii. 8). Directions for making an altar are given, *Exod.* xx. 24, 1491 B.C. The erection of altars in Greece is mythically assigned to Cecrops. The term "altar" was early applied to the table used in the celebration of the Lord's Supper in Christian churches (*Heb.* xiii. 10). Since the time of Elizabeth there has been much controversy on the subject, and the Puritans in the civil war destroyed many of the ancient stone altars, substituting wooden tables. In Jan. 1845 it was decided in the Arches Court that *stone altars* were not to be erected in English churches.

ALTENKIRCHEN (Prussia). The French, who had defeated the Austrians here, 4 June, 1796, were themselves defeated, and their general, Marceau, killed, 19 Sept. following.

ALTER EGO (*another* or *second I*), a term applied to Spanish viceroys when exercising regal power; used at Naples when the crown prince was appointed vicar-general during an insurrection in July, 1820.

ALTONA (Holstein, N. Germany), acquired by the Danes, 1660, and made a city, 1664. It was occupied first by the German federal troops, 24 Dec. 1863, and then by the Prussians (the federal diet protesting), 12 Feb. 1864.

ALT-RANSTADT (Prussia), where the treaty of peace dictated by Charles XII. of Sweden, to Frederick Augustus of Poland, was signed, 24 Sept. 1706, O.S. Frederick, deposed in 1704, regained the throne of Poland after the defeat of Charles XII., in 1709.

ALUM, a salt, is said to have been first discovered at Roccha, in Syria, about 1300; it was found in Tuscany about 1470; its manufacture was brought to perfection in England by sir T. Challoner, who established large alum works near Whitby in 1608; it was discovered in Ireland in 1757; and in Anglesey in 1790. Alum is used as a mordant in dyeing, to harden tallow, and in the paper manufacture.

Messrs. Peter Spence & Sons produced a colossal crystal of alum weighing over eight tons . April, 1886

ALUMBAGH, a palace with other buildings near Lucknow, Oude, India, taken during the mutiny from the rebels, 23 Sept. 1857, and heroically defended by the British under sir James Outram. He defeated an attack of 30,000 sepoys on 12 Jan. 1858, and of 20,000 on 21 Feb., and was relieved by sir Colin Campbell in March.

ALUMINIUM, a metal, the base of the earth alumina, which is combined with silica in clay, and which was shown to be a distinct earth by Marggraff in 1754, having been previously confounded with lime. It is very light (sp. g. 2·25), malleable, and sonorous; when pure does not rust, and is not acted on by sulphur or any acid except hydrochloric. Oerstedt in 1826 obtained the chloride of aluminium; and in 1827 the metal itself was got from it by F. Wöhler, but was long a scientific curiosity, the process being expensive. The mode of production was afterwards simplified by Bunsen and others, more especially by H. Ste.-Claire Deville, who in 1856 succeeded in procuring considerable quantities of this metal by the aid of the metal sodium. A cheaper me hod was devised by Mr. Webster, of Hollywood, near Birmingham, in 1881. Since 1890 by electrolytic methods, as th t of Messrs. Cowles of Milton, near Stoke-on-Trent, and of Lockport, in New York, the chemical process has been practically superseded. In March, 1856, it was 3*l.* the ounce; in June, 1857, 11*s.* or 12*s.*, and it gradually became much cheaper, at the present time, 1903, it is 1*s.* 3*d.* per lb. The eagles of the French colours have been made of it, and many other ornamental and useful articles. Deville's work, "De l'Aluminium," was published in 1859. An aluminium manufactory was established at Newcastle in 1860, by Messrs. Bell. They obtain the metal from a French mineral, bauxite. Their aluminium bronze, an alloy of copper and aluminium, invented by Dr. John Percy, F.R.S., was made into watch cases, &c., by Messrs. Reid of Newcastle, in 1862. Aluminium bronze, which can be manufactured with a textile strength equal to steel, renders it a useful material for field guns; its endurance and resistance to friction, combined with its lightness, adapt it specially for the bearings of shafts and other kinds of machinery. Its cost of production is, however, high. Combined with tin aluminium is used for optical instruments, and alloyed with silver forms a metal named *Tiers Argent*, from which forks and spoons are manufactured. "Aluminium gold," used for imitation gold jewelry, is an alloy of aluminium with copper. Aluminium entered largely into the construction of the deck of Shamrock III.

A steam launch wholly made of aluminium (alloy), 6 mètres long, 1½ mètres wide, was constructed at Zurich by Messrs. Escher, Wyss & Co., Sept. 1892.

An aluminium yacht, *Vendenesse*, launched on the Seine, 6 Dec. 1893.

The *Jules Davoust*, 33 feet long, weighs 18 cwt., also exhibited on the Seine, Dec. 1893.

An aluminium torpedo-boat, built by Messrs. Yarrow for the French government, successfully tried at Greenwich, 29 Sept. 1894.

The British aluminium company (registered 1894) establish works at Foyers, and utilize the Falls; reported June, 1896; reservoir works completed, Jan. 1898.

AMADIS OF GAUL, a Spanish or Portuguese romance, stated to have been composed about 1370 by Vasco de Lobeira. It was enlarged by De Montalvo, about 1465; and first printed (in Spanish) 1519; in French, 1540-56. Translation by Southey, 1803.

AMALEKITES (descendants of Amalek, grandson of Esau, brother of Jacob) attacked the Israelites, 1491 B.C., when perpetual war was denounced against them. They were subdued by Saul about 1079, by David, 1058 and 1056; and by the Simeonites about 715 B.C.

AMALFI, a city on the gulf of Salerno, Naples, in the 8th century became the seat of a republic, and flourished by its commerce till 1075, when it was taken by Roger Guiscard, and eventually incorporated with Naples. The Pisans, in their sack of the town in 1135, are said to have found a copy of the Pandects of Justinian, and thus to have induced the revival of the study of Roman law in Western Europe; the story is now doubted. Flavio Gioia, a native of Amalfi, is the reputed discoverer of the mariner's compass, about 1302.

AMATI, a family of celebrated violin makers of Cremona, 16th and 17th centuries. Andrea (1540–1600) founded the business, which was carried on by his sons Geronimo and Antonio and his grandson Niccolo. The last-named was the master of both Guarnerio and Stradivario, whose violins are so highly prized.

AMATONGALAND, between Zululand and the Portuguese possessions, South Africa. The territory annexed to the British possession of Zululand, 30 Nov. 1897.

AMAZON, West India mail steam ship, left Southampton on her first voyage, Friday, 2 Jan. 1852, and on Sunday morning, Jan. 4, was destroyed by fire at sea, about 110 miles W.S.W. of Scilly (ascribed to the spontaneous ignition of combustible matter placed near the engine-room). Out of 161 persons on board, 102 persons must have perished by fire or drowning. 21 persons were saved by the life-boat of the ship; 25 more were carried into Brest harbour by a Dutch vessel passing by; and 13 others were picked up in the bay of Biscay, also by a Dutch galliot. Eliot Warburton, a distinguished writer in general literature, was among those lost.

AMAZON (S. America). The longest river in the world. Navigable for large steam vessels 2,500 miles from the sea. Was discovered by Pinzon in 1500, and explored by Francisco Orellana in 1540. Coming from Peru, he sailed down the Amazon to the Atlantic, and observing companies of women in arms on its bank, he called the country Amazonia, and gave the name of Amazon to the river, previously called Marañon. Steam navigation commenced 1850. There is now, 1903, a regular service of ocean-going steamers up the Amazon.

AMAZONS. Three nations of Amazons have been mentioned—the Asiatic, Scythian, and African. They are mythically said to have been the descendants of Scythians inhabiting Cappadocia, where their husbands, having made incursions, were all slain, being surprised in ambuscades by their enemies. Their widows formed a female state, and decreed that matrimony was a shameful servitude. *Quintus Curtius.* They were said to have been conquered by Theseus. The Amazons were constantly employed in wars; and that they might bend the bow with more force, their right breasts were burned off, whence their name from the Greek, *a*, no, *mazos*, breast. Others derive the name from *maza*, the moon, which they are supposed to have worshipped. About 330 B.C. their queen, Thalestris, visited Alexander the Great, whilst he was pursuing his conquests in Asia, with three hundred females in her train. *Herodotus.* For modern amazons, see *Dahomey.*

AMBASSADORS. Accredited agents, and representatives from one court to another, are referred to in early ages. In most countries they have great privileges; and in England, they and their servants are secured against arrest. England has eight *ambassadors* (at Berlin, Constantinople, Madrid, Paris, Rome, St. Petersburg, Vienna, Washington), twenty-six ministers, and about thirty chief consuls, resident at foreign courts, exclusive of inferior agents; the ambassadors and other chief agents from abroad at the court of London in 1865 were 47; in 1868, 43; in 1872, 42; in 1878, 39; in 1889, 43; in 1902, 39.

The Russian ambassador being imprisoned for debt by a lace-merchant, 27 July, 1708, led to the passing the statute of 7 Anne, for the protection of ambassadors, 1708.

Two men, convicted of arresting the servant of an ambassador, were sentenced to be conducted to the house of the ambassador, with a label on their breasts, to ask his pardon, and then one of them to be imprisoned three months, and the other fined, 12 May, 1780.

The first minister from the United States of America to England, John Adams, presented to the king, 1 June, 1785; the first from Great Britain to America was Mr. Hammond, in 1791. Mr. Thos. F. Bayard, first U. S. *ambassador* to London, appointed 1893; died, aged 69, 28 Sept. 1898. Sir Julian Pauncefote (after lord, 1899), British minister, 1889, made *ambassador*, 1893; died, 24 May, 1902.

A Japanese minister received by the queen, 3 March, 1875.

The first accredited ambassador from China, Kus-ta-Jên, landed at Southampton, 21 Jan. 1877.

In the case of Sir H. Macartney, secretary to the Chinese legation *v.* the Vestry of Marylebone, the Queen's Bench decided that the plaintiff was free from parish rates and taxes, 24 Feb. 1890.

AMBER, a semi-mineral substance, probably fossil resin, derived from extinct coniferæ. From its property of becoming highly negatively electric by friction the term electricity is derived; *elektron* being the Greek word for amber. Its use for ornaments is of great antiquity, it is found among the prehistoric remains of the Swiss lake dwellers, and is alluded to in Homer. Theophrastus wrote upon it 300 B C. Amber was much valued as a charm against witchcraft and disease. It is principally found in the northern parts of Europe. "The Tears of the Heliades: Amber as a Gem," by W. A. Buffum, published 1896.

AMBLEF, near Cologne, Germany. Here Charles Martel defeated Chilperic II., and Ragenfroi, mayor of the Neustrians, 716.

AMBOISE (Central France). A conspiracy of the Huguenots against Francis II., Catherine de Medicis, and the Guises, was suppressed at this place in Jan. 1560. On 19 March, 1563, the Pacification of Amboise was published, granting toleration to the Huguenots. The civil war was however soon renewed.

AMBOYNA, chief of the Molucca isles, discovered about 1512 by the Portuguese, but not wholly occupied by them till 1580. It was taken by the Dutch in 1605. The English factors at this settlement were cruelly tortured and put to death, 17 Feb. 1623-4, by the Dutch, on an accusation of a conspiracy to expel them from the island, where the two nations jointly shared in the pepper trade of Java. Cromwell compelled the Dutch to give a sum of money to the descendants of the sufferers. Amboyna was seized by the English, 16 Feb. 1796, but was restored by the treaty of Amiens, in 1802. It was again seized by the British, 17-19 Feb. 1810; and again restored at the peace of May, 1814. *Amboyna wood*, a beautiful coloured wood, yielded by *Pterospernum irdicum.*

AMBROSIAN CHANT, see *Chant*, *Liturgy*, &c.

AMBULANCE ASSOCIATION, see under *John's, St.*

First "ambulance ship" (for small-pox convalescents), *Red Cross*, constructed for Metropolitan Asylums Board, launched at Millwall, 8 Aug. 1883.

AMEN, an ancient Hebrew word meaning *true, faithful, certain*, is used in the Jewish and Christian assemblies, at the conclusion of prayer: see 1 *Cor.* xiv. 16 (A.D. 59). It is translated "*verily*" in the Gospels.

AMENDE HONORABLE, in France, in the 9th century, was a punishment inflicted on traitors and sacrilegious persons: the offender was delivered to the hangman: his shirt was stripped off, a rope put round his neck, and a taper in his hand; he was then led into court, and was obliged to beg pardon of God and the country. Death or banishment sometimes followed. These words also denote a recantation in open court, or in presence of the injured person.

AMERCEMENT, in Law, a fine assessed for an offence done, or pecuniary punishment at the *mercy* of the court: thus differing from a fine directed and fixed by a statute. By Magna Charta, 1215, a freeman cannot be amerced for a small fault, but in proportion to the offence he has committed; the mode was determined by 9 Hen. III., 1225.

AMERICA,* the great Western Continent, is about 9000 miles long, with an area of about 16,500,000 square miles. It is now believed to have been visited by the Norsemen or Vikings in the 10th and 11th centuries; but the modern discovery is due to the sagacity and courage of the Genoese navigator, Christopher Columbus.† "History of the New World called America," by Edw. J. Payne. Vol. 2. 1899. See *Chicago*.

Columbus sailed on his first expedition from Palos in Andalusia on Friday, with vessels supplied by the sovereigns of Spain . . . . . . 3 Aug. 1492
He lands on the island of Guanahani, one of the Bahamas; takes possession of it in the name of Ferdinand and Isabella of Castile, and names it San Salvador . . . Friday, 12 Oct. 1492
He discovers Cuba, 28 Oct.; and Hispaniola (now Hayti), where he builds a fort, La Navidad, 6 Dec. ,,
He returns to Spain. . . . . . 15 March, 1493
He sails from Cadiz on his *second* expedition, 25 Sept.; discovers the Caribbee Isles,—Dominica, 3 Nov.; Guadaloupe, 4 Nov.; Antigua, 10 Nov.; founds Isabella in Hispaniola, the first Christian city in the New World . . . . . Dec. ,,
He discovers Jamaica, 3 May; and Evangelista (now Isle of Pines), 13 June; war with the natives of Hispaniola. 1494
He visits the various isles, and explores their coasts 1495-6
Returns to Spain to meet the charges of his enemies 11 June, 1496
John Cabot (Giovanni Cabotto) a Venetian pilot, said to have settled in Bristol, 1472, and to have sailed thence with his son Sebastian, with letters patent from Henry VII., and to have discovered Labrador on the coast of North America, 24 June, 1497
Columbus sails on his *third* voyage, 30 May; discovers Trinidad, 31 July; lands on Terra Firma, without knowing it to be the new continent, naming it Isla Santa . . . . . . 1 Aug. 1498
Ojeda discovers Surinam, June; and the gulf of Venezuela 1499
Vicente Yañez Pinzon discovers Brazil, *South America*, 26 Jan.; and the river Marañon (the Amazon); Cabral the Portuguese lands in Brazil (see *Brazil*) 3 May, 1500
Gaspar Cortereal discovers Labrador . . . ,,
Columbus is imprisoned in chains at San Domingo by Bobadilla, sent out to investigate into his conduct, May; conveyed to Spain, where he is honourably received . . . . . . 17 Dec. ,,
Columbus sails on his *fourth* voyage, 9 May; discovers various isles on the coast of Honduras, and explores the coast of the isthmus, July, &c.; discovers and names Porto Bello . 2 Nov. 1502
Negro slaves imported into Hispaniola . . 1501-3
Worried by the machinations of his enemies, he returns to Spain, 7 Nov.; his friend, queen Isabella, dies . . . . 20 Nov. 1504
He dies while treated with base ingratitude by the Spanish government . . . . . 20 May, 1506
Solis and Pinzon discover Yucatan . . . ,,
Ojeda founds San Sebastian, the first colony on the mainland 1510
Subjugation of Cuba by Velasquez 1511
The coast of Florida discovered by Ponce de Leon . 1512
Vasco de Balboa crosses the isthmus of Darien, and discovers the South Pacific Ocean. . . . 1513
Mexico discovered by Fernando de Cordova . . 1517
Grijalva penetrates into Yucatan, and names it New Spain 1518
Passage of Magellan's Straits by him 1520
Conquest of Mexico by Fernando Cortes . . 1519-21
Pizarro discovers the coast of Quito . . . 1526
He invades and conquers Peru 1532-5
Cartier, a Frenchman, enters the Gulf of St. Lawrence, and sails up to Montreal . . . 1534-5
Grijalva's expedition, equipped by Cortes, discovers California 1535
Mendoza founds Buenos Ayres, and conquers the adjacent country . . . . ,,
Orellana sails down the Amazon to the sea . . 1540-1
Louisiana conquered by De Soto . . . . ,,
Chili conquered by Valdivia 1541
Rebellion in Peru—tranquillity established by Gasca 1548
Davis's Straits discovered by him 1585
Raleigh establishes the first English settlement—at Roanoke, Virginia . . . . . . ,,
Falkland isles discovered by Davis 1592
De Monts, a Frenchman, settles in Acadia, now Nova Scotia 1604
Jamestown, in Virginia, the first English settlement on the mainland, founded by lord de la Warr . 1607
Quebec founded by the French 1608
Hudson's bay discovered by him 1610
The Dutch build Manhattan, or New Amsterdam (now New York) on the Hudson 1614
Settlement in New England begun by capt. Smith . ,,
New Plymouth built by the English nonconformist exiles 1620
Nova Scotia settled by the Scotch under sir Wm. Alexander 1622
Delaware settled by the Swedes and Dutch . . 1627
Massachusetts, by sir H. Boswell 1628
Maryland, by lord Baltimore 1633

* The name is derived from Amerigo Vespucci, a Florentine merchant, who died in 1512. He accompanied Ojeda in his voyage on the eastern coast in 1498; and described the country in letters sent to his friends in Italy. He is charged with presumptuously inserting "Tierra de Amerigo" in his maps. Irving discusses the question in the Appendix to the Life of Columbus, but comes to no conclusion. Humboldt asserts that the name was given to the continent in the popular works of Waldseemüller, a German geographer, without the knowledge of Vespucci. To America we are indebted, among other things, for maize, the turkey, the potato, Peruvian bark, and tobacco. See *Florence*, 1898.

† Christophoro Columbo was born about 1445 (or between 1435 and 1449); first went to sea about 1460; settled at Lisbon in 1470, where he married Felipa, the daughter of Perestrello, an Italian navigator, whereby he obtained much geographical knowledge. He is said to have laid the plans of his voyage of discovery before the republic of Genoa, in 1485, and other powers, and finally before the court of Spain, where at length the queen Isabella became his patron. After undergoing much ingratitude and cruel persecution from his own followers and the Spanish court, he died on 20 May, 1506, and was buried with much pomp at Valladolid. His remains were transferred, in 1513, to Seville; in 1536 to San Domingo; and in Jan. 1796 to the Havanna, Cuba; to Seville, 19 Jan. 1899. The original inscription on his tomb is said to have been "A Castilla y á Leon Nuevo Mundo dió Colon." "To Castile and Leon Colon gave a New World." Humboldt says beautifully, that the success of Columbus was "*a conquest of reflection.*" It was stated in Nov. 1890, that Columbus' log-book had been fished up from the sea.

Connecticut granted to lords Say and Brooke in 1630; but no English settlement was made here till 1635
Rhode Island settled by Roger Williams and his brethren, driven from Massachusetts . . . ,,
New Jersey settled by the Dutch, 1614, and Swedes, 1627; granted to the duke of York, who sells it to lord Berkeley 1664
New York captured by the English . . . . . ,,
South Carolina settled by the English 1669
Pennsylvania settled by William Penn, the celebrated Quaker 1682
Louisiana settled by the French . . . . . . ,,
The Mississippi explored 1699
The Scotch settlement at Darien (1698-9) abandoned 1700
New Orleans built. 1717
Georgia settled by general Oglethorpe 1732
Kentucky, by colonel Boon 1754
Canada conquered by the English, 1759-60; ceded to Great Britain 1763
American war—declaration of independence by the United States, 1776; recognised by Great Britain 1783
Louisiana ceded to Spain, 1763; transferred to France, 1800; sold to the United States . . . 1803
Florida ceded to Great Britain, 1763; taken by Spain, 1781; to whom it is ceded, 1783; ceded to the United States 1820
Revolution in Mexico—declaration of independence 1821
Revolutions in Spanish America; independence established by Chili, 1810; Paraguay, 1811; Buenos Ayres, and other provinces, 1816; Peru, 1826.
[See *United States*, *Mexico*, and other states, throughout the volume. For the American International Congress, see *United States*, Oct. 1889.]

AMERICA, Central, Republics of, includes Guatemala, San Salvador, Honduras, Nicaragua, and Costa Rica (*which see*). They declared their independence, Sept. 21, 1821, and separated from the Mexican confederation, 21 July, 1823. The states made a treaty of union between themselves, 21 March, 1847. There has been among them since much anarchy and bloodshed, aggravated greatly by the irruption of American filibusters under Kenny and Walker, 1854-5. In Jan. 1863, a war began between Guatemala (afterwards joined by Nicaragua) and San Salvador (afterwards supported by Honduras). The latter were defeated at Santa Rosa, 16 June, and San Salvador was taken, 26 Oct.; the president of San Salvador, Barrios, fled; and Carrera, the dictator of Guatemala, became predominant over the confederacy. Gen. Barrios, president of Guatemala, attempts the union of the five states, himself to be dictator; opposed by all except Honduras, Feb. He is defeated and killed in a prolonged battle at Chalchuapa, 2 April; peace with the states signed 16 April, 1885. The union of the states, under one principal president, was proposed at the Pan-American Congress, 1889-90. Nicaragua, Salvador and Honduras united as a Central American republic, signed, 28 June, 1895. A constitution established, reported, Aug. 1898. The five states formed into the republic of Central America, autonomy to be preserved, by treaty, signed, 15 June, 1897. Each state resumes its absolute sovereignty, reported 30 Nov. 1898. See *Darien* and *Panamá*.

AMERICA, Russian, sold to the United States for about 400,000*l*., March, 1867. See *Alaska*.

AMERICA, South, see *Brazil*, *Argentine*, *Peru*, *Paraguay*, *Uruguay*, *&c*.

"AMERICA," and AMERICA CUP, see *Yacht*.

AMERICAN ASSOCIATION for the Advancement of Science, resembling the British Association, held its first meeting at Philadelphia 20 Sept. 1848, its 28th at Saratoga, 27 Aug. 1879; 29th at Boston, 23-28 Aug. 1880; met at Cincinnati, 17 Aug. 1881; at Montreal, 26 Aug. 1882; at Minneapolis, Minnesota, 15 Aug. 1883; Philadelphia, 4 Sept. 1884; Ann Arbor, 1885; Buffalo, 1886; New York, 1887; Cleveland, 1888; Toronto, Aug. 1889; Indianapolis, 19 Aug. 1890; Washington, 11 Aug. 1891; Rochester, N.Y., 18 Aug. 1892; Madison, Wisconsin, Aug. 1893; Brooklyn, 16 Aug. 1894; Springfield, Mass. 29 Aug. 1895; Detroit, 9 Aug. 1897; Boston, 22 Aug. 1898; Columbus, Ohio, 19 Aug. 1899; New York, 23 June, 1900; Denver, Colorado, 24 Aug. 1901; Pittsburg, 28 June, 1902; Washington, 29 Dec. 1902–3 Jan. 1903.

AMERICAN BASEBALL, a game resembling cricket and rounders, introduced into this country by teams from Philadelphia and Boston in 1875 without success. The American teams (Chicago and All America), after a tour round the world, played a game at Kennington Oval in the presence of the Prince of Wales and many distinguished spectators 12 March, 1889, and since.

AMERICAN BOOTS, see under *Boots*.

AMERICAN CLUB, &c., London, for Anglo-Saxons interested in the Western Hemisphere, established autumn 1887. *American society in London* founded to assist distressed Americans; first dinner, Mr. Bayard, the U.S. ambassador, in the chair, 19 April, 1895.

AMERICAN EXHIBITION of the Arts, Inventions, Manufactures, Products, and Resources of the United States—Earl's Court, West Brompton, and West Kensington. (A private speculation.)
It included works of art, specimens of manufacture, a "Wild West" section, feats of horsemanship by Buffalo Bill (col. the hon. Wm. F. Cody), Red Shirt, a Sioux chief, and other Indians; buffalo hunts, horse catching, &c.
Visited by the prince and princess of Wales 5 May, 1887.
Opened by colonel Russell, the president, lord Ronald Gower, archdeacon Farrar, and others, 9 May.
Visited by the Queen, 11 May.
Closed by a meeting advocating the establishment of an International Court of Arbitration, the marquis of Lorne in the chair, 31 Oct. 1887.

AMERICANISMS: a dictionary of these expressions was compiled by John R. Bartlett, and first published in 1848; 4th edition, 1877. Another by John S. Farmer appeared in 1889.

AMERICANISTS, a name assumed by some persons devoted to the study of the archæology, ethnology, &c., of North and South America, who held their first international congress at Nancy in July, 1875; one at Luxemburg, Sept. 1877; at Brussels, Sept. 1879; at Madrid, 27 Sept. 1881; Copenhagen, 21 Aug. 1883; Turin, 1886; Berlin, 2 Oct. 1888; Paris, 14 Oct. 1890; Huelva, 7 Oct. (the queen-regent of Spain present), 1892; Stockholm, 3 Aug. 1894.

AMERICAN ORGAN, a free-reed keyed wind instrument, resembling the harmonium, with important differences; the principle was discovered about 1835 by a workman employed by Alexandre of Paris. The invention was taken to America, where instruments were made by Mason and Hamlin, of Boston, about 1860.

AMETHYST, the ninth stone upon the breast-plate of the Jewish high priest, 1491 B.C. It is of a rich violet colour. One worth 200 rix-dollars, having been rendered colourless, equalled a diamond in lustre, valued at 18,000 gold crowns. *De Boot.*—Amethysts discovered at Kerry, in Ireland, in 1775.

AMIENS, a city in Picardy (N. France); the cathedral was built in 1220. It was taken by the Spanish, 11 March, and retaken by the French, 25 Sept. 1597. The preliminary articles of the peace between Great Britain, Holland, France, and Spain, were signed in London by lord Hawkesbury and M. Otto, on the part of England and France, 1 Oct. 1801; and the definitive treaty was subscribed at Amiens, on 27 March, 1802, by the marquis of Cornwallis for England, Joseph Bonaparte for France, Azara for Spain, and Schimmelpenninck for Holland. War was declared again in 1803.—After a conflict, in which the French were defeated, 27 Nov. 1870, the German general Von Goeben entered Amiens, 28 Nov. Population in 1901, 90,038.

AMMONIA, the volatile alkali, mainly produced by the decomposition of organic substances. Its name is ascribed to its having been procured from heated camels' dung near the temple of Jupiter Ammon in Libya. The discovery of its being a compound of nitrogen and hydrogen is ascribed to Joseph Priestley in 1774. By the recent labours of chemists both the oxide of the hypothetical metal ammonium, and ammonium amalgam, have been formed; and specimens of each were shown at the Royal Institution in 1856 by Dr. A. W. Hofmann, who has done very much for the chemical history of ammonia.

Ammoniaphone. An apparatus for the improvement of the voice and lungs, by inhaling combinations of ammonia, hydrogen, &c., invented by Dr. Carter Moffat, of Edinburgh, 1883. He asserted that this mixture resembles Italian air. The successful effects of inhaling the gas were shown at St. James's Hall, 6 Nov. 1884.

Ammonite. A new explosive for use in coal mines, said to be safer than those in use, composed of pure ammonium nitrate and nitro-naphthaline. Experiments with this explosive exhibited by sir George Elliot at the works of the Miners' Safety Explosive Company, Stanford-le-Hope, Essex, were considered very satisfactory, 9 July, 1891.

AMMONITES, descended from Ben-Ammi, the son of Lot (1897 B.C.), invaded Canaan and made the Israelites tributaries, but were defeated by Jephthah, 1143 B.C. They again invaded Canaan, intending to put out the right eye of all they subdued; but Saul overthrew them, 1095 B.C. They were afterwards many times vanquished; and Antiochus the Great took Rabbah, their capital, and destroyed the walls, 198 B.C. *Josephus*.

AMNESTY (a general pardon after political disturbances, &c.) was granted by Thrasybulus, the Athenian patriot, after expelling the thirty tyrants, 403 B.C. Acts of amnesty were passed after the civil war in 1651, and after the two rebellions in England in 1715 and 1745.—After his victorious campaign in Italy, Napoleon III. of France granted an amnesty to all political offenders, 17 Aug. 1859. An amnesty, with certain exemptions, was granted to the vanquished southern states of North America by president Johnson, 29 May, 1865. An amnesty for political offences was granted by the emperor of Austria at his coronation as king of Hungary, 8 June, 1867; a rather sweeping amnesty bill was passed in the United States regarding the rebellion, 10 April, 1871. An amnesty association on behalf of the Fenians was active in Britain, Oct. 1873. 2245 French communists pardoned by decree, published 17 Jan. 1879; many others during the year: a general amnesty for political offences passed by the chamber (333-140) 21 June, 1880. An amnesty was granted to the Cretans after the disturbances, by the Sultan of Turkey, Dec. 1889.

AMOAFUL, near Coomassie, West Africa. After a severe conflict, 31 Jan. 1874, the Ashantees were defeated at this place by Sir Garnet Wolseley. Captain Buckle was killed, and about 20 officers and 200 men were wounded. The 42nd Highland Regiment was very energetic.

AMŒBA, see *Protoplasm*.

AMOY, see *China*, 1853-5.

AMPHICTYONIC COUNCIL, asserted traditionally to have been established at Thermopylæ by Amphictyon, for the management of all affairs relative to Greece. This celebrated council, composed of twelve of the wisest and most virtuous men of various cities of Greece, began 1498 [1113, *Clinton*] B.C., and existed 31 B.C. Its immediate office was to attend to the temples and oracles of Delphi. Its calling on the Greek States to punish the Phocians for plundering Delphi caused the Sacred wars, 595-586, and 356-346.

AMPHION, a British frigate, of 38 guns, blown up while riding at anchor in Plymouth Sound, and the whole of her crew then on board, consisting of more than two hundred and fifty persons, officers and men, perished, 22 Sept. 1796.

AMPHIPOLIS, Macedon (N. Greece). A city founded here by the Athenians, 437 B.C.; was seized by Brasidas the Spartan, 424; both he and the Athenian general, Cleon, were killed in a fruitless attempt at the capture of the city by the Athenians, 422.

AMPHITHEATRES, round or oval buildings, said to have been first constructed by Curio, 76 B.C., and by Julius Cæsar 46 B.C. In the Roman amphitheatres, the people witnessed the combats of gladiators with wild beasts, &c. They were generally built of wood, but Statilius Taurus made one of stone, under Augustus Cæsar; see *Coliseum*. The amphitheatre of Vespasian (capable of holding 87,000 persons) was built between A.D. 70 and 80; and is said to have been a fortress in 1312. The amphitheatre at Verona was next in size, and then that of Nismes.

AMPHITRITE, THE SHIP, see *Wrecks*, 30 Aug. 1833.

AMPUTATION, in surgery was greatly aided by the invention of the tourniquet by Morel, a French surgeon, in 1674, and of the flap-method by Lowdham of Exeter in 1679.

AMSTERDAM (Holland). The castle of Amstel was commenced in 1100; the building of the city in 1203. Its commerce was greatly increased by the decay of that of Antwerp after 1609. The exchange was built in 1634; and the noble stadthouse in 1648; the latter cost three millions of guilders, then a large sum. It was built upon 13,659 piles. Amsterdam surrendered to the king of Prussia, when that prince invaded Holland, in favour of the stadtholder, in 1787. The French were admitted without resistance, 18 Jan. 1795. The Dutch government was restored in Dec. 1813. A crystal palace for an industrial exhibition was opened by prince Frederick of the Netherlands, 16 Aug. 1864. The canal, from Amsterdam to the North Sea, was inaugurated by the king, 1 Nov. 1876. A new university was opened, Dec. 1877. International exhibition opened by the king, 1 May, 1883. International Agricultural exhibition opened 26 Aug. 1884. The Grand theatre destroyed by fire 20 Feb. 1890. Population, 1890, 417,539; 1897, 494,189; 1901, 520,800.

Violent rioting through prohibition of eel-baiting on the canal; 35 killed, 90 wounded; 25-26 July, 1886.

Riots of the unemployed; conflicts with the police, about, 17 Jan. 1893.

International exhibition opened by baron van Bellinchave 11 May, 1895.

Queen Wilhelmina "inaugurated," 6 Sept., and Rembrandt exhibition, see *Holland*, Sept. 1898.

Great strike, see *Holland*, April 1903.

AMYL, a chemical alcohol radical (first isolated by professor (afterwards sir) Edward Frankland in 1849; he died 9 Aug. 1899).

AMYLENE, a colourless, very mobile liquid, first procured by M. Balard of Paris in 1844, by distilling fusel oil (potato-spirit) with chloride of zinc. The vapour was employed instead of chloroform first by Dr. Snow in 1856. It has since been tried in many hospitals here and in France. The odour is more unpleasant than chloroform, and more vapour must be used.

ANABAPTISTS, those who baptize at full age, and reject infant baptism; see *Baptists*. The name was first given to Thomas Münzer, Storck, and other fanatics who preached in Saxony in 1521, and excited a rebellion of the lower orders in Germany, which was quelled with bloodshed in 1525. A similar insurrection took place in Westphalia, headed by Matthias, 1533, and, after his assassination, by John Boccold of Leyden, who was crowned "king of Sion" in Münster, 24 June, 1534. Münster was taken in June, 1535; and John was executed 13 Feb. 1536. Several anabaptists were executed in England in 1535, 1538, and 1540. On 6 Jan. 1661, about 80 anabaptists in London appeared in arms, headed by their preacher, Thomas Venner, a wine-cooper. They fought desperately, and killed many of the soldiers brought against them. Their leader and sixteen others were executed, 19 and 21 Jan. *Annals of England*.

ANACHORETS, see *Monachism*.

ANACREONTIC VERSE, of the bacchanalian strain, named after Anacreon of Teos, the Greek lyric poet, whose odes are much prized. He died in his eighty-fifth year, about 478 B.C. His odes (many said to be spurious) have been frequently translated; Thomas Moore's version was published in 1800.

ANADOLIA (Asia Minor), comprises the ancient Lycia, Caria, Lydia, Mysia, Bithynia, Paphlagonia and Phrygia (*which see*).

ANÆSTHETICS, agents for producing total or partial loss of sensibility, see *Opium*, *Chloroform*, *Ether*, *Amylene*, *Kerosolene*, *Nitrous oxide* under *nitric acid*, *Cocaine*, *Ethyl bromide*, *Somnoform*. Intense cold has been also employed in deadening pain.

ANÆSTHESIMETER, an instrument for measuring the quantity of an anæsthetic administered.

ANAGRAMS, formed by the transposition of the letters of a word or sentence (as *army* from *Mary*). Much importance was attached to anagrams by the Jewish Cabalists, the Greek Platonists, and the Puritans. Mr. H. B. Wheatley's work "On Anagrams" was published in 1862. Ingenious examples: the question by Pilate, "*Quid est veritas?*" (what is truth?) the anagram, "*Est vir qui adest*" (the man who is here); from "*Horatio Nelson*," is "*Honor est a Nilo*" (Honour from the Nile).

ANALYSTS, Society of Public, founded by Professor Redwood, Dr. Dupré, and others, 7 Aug. 1874. Dr. Charles Meymott Tidy, an eminent analyst and toxicologist, died 15 March, 1892. See *Adulteration*.

ANAM, see *Annam*.

ANARCHY (Greek *an*, no, *archos*, chief), described *Judges* xvii. 6, "In those days there was no king in Israel, but every man did that which was right in his own eyes," about B.C. 1406. Anarchy frequently prevailed in ancient times. Similar principles, now termed socialism, have been eminently advanced by P. J. Proudhon 1809—65, to whom is ascribed the maxim, "La propriété c'est le vol." See *France*, Oct. 1882. Many Anarchists tried and punished in Austria and other countries, 1883 *et seq.* Anarchists expelled from Switzerland, 1885, but return, and cause much trouble; they held a congress at Ticino Jan. 1891. The modern anarchists declare war against society and all its institutions, and frequently employ dynamite as a destructive agent. An "anarchist album," containing about 500 photographs of anarchists, published by the French government April, 1894. The anarchists term the assassination of M. Carnot an *execution*, 26 June, 1894. Twenty-eight Spanish anarchists arrive in London, 30 July, 1897. Plot against the German emperor frustrated, 9 Italian anarchists arrested with bombs at Alexandria, 13 Oct. 1898. Asdrubal Malavasi, armed, captured in Islington, 14 Oct. An anti-anarchist international conference, *in camera*, adm. Canevaro, president, opened at Rome (sir Philip Currie, sir Godfrey Lushington, and sir Howard Vincent, British delegates), 24 Nov. to 21 Dec. 1898. Tsar abandons his visit to Rome as the result of the socialist and anarchist agitation in Italy, 11 Oct. 1903. See *Dynamite*, *France*, *Spain*, *London*, *Italy*, *Austria*, *Barcelona*, and *Trials*, 1892, 1894.

ANATHEMA, the sentence of excommunication (1 *Cor.* xvi. 22), used by the early churches, 365; see *Excommunication*. Pope Pius IX. propounded a series of anathemas, Feb. 1870.

ANATOMY (Greek, cutting up). The human body was studied by Aristotle about 350 B.C., and became a branch of medical education under Hippocrates, about 420 B.C. Erasistratus and Herophilus first dissected the human form, having been previously confined to animals: it is said that they practised upon the bodies of living criminals, about 300 and 293 B.C. Galen, who died A.D. 193, was a great anatomist. In England, the schools were long supplied with bodies unlawfully exhumed from graves; and until 1832, the bodies of executed murderers were ordered for dissection.* Pope Boniface VIII. forbade the dissection of dead bodies, 1297.—The first anatomical plates, designed by Titian, were employed by Vesalius, about 1538. Leonardo da Vinci, Raphael, and Michael Angelo, studied anatomy. The great discovery of Harvey was made in 1619. William and John Hunter were great anatomists: William died 1783, and John, 1793. Quain's and Wilson's large anatomical plates were published 1842, and Bourgery's great work by Jacob, 1830-55. *Comparative anatomy* has been treated systematically by Cuvier, Owen, Müller, Huxley, Virchow, Schwann, Haeckel, Agassiz, Burmeister, Carpenter, Flower, Thompson, and others. The practice of anatomy greatly aided

* By 32 Hen. VIII. c. 42 (1540), surgeons were granted four bodies of executed malefactors for "*anathomyes*," which privilege was extended in following reigns: but in consequence of the crimes committed by resurrection-men in order to supply the surgical schools (robbing churchyards and even committing murder, see *Burking*), a new statute was passed in 1832, which abated the ignominy of dissection by prohibiting that of executed murderers, and made provision for the wants of surgeons by permitting, under certain regulations, the dissection of persons dying in workhouses, &c. The act also appointed inspectors of anatomy, regulated the schools, and required persons practising anatomy to obtain a licence. It repealed the clauses of the act of 1828, which directed the dissection of the body of an executed murderer.

by the use of the microscope, 1898. See *Röntgen Rays*. Mr. Thos. Cooke, founder of Cooke's school of anatomy, &c., died 8 Feb. 1899.—The anatomy of plants has been studied since 1680; see *Botany*.

ANATOMICAL SOCIETY OF GREAT BRITAIN founded 1887.

ANCHORITES, see *Monachism*.

ANCHORS were invented by the Tuscans. *Pliny*. The second tooth, or fluke, was added by Anacharsis the Scythian (592 B.C.). *Strabo*. Anchors said to have been forged in England A.D. 578. The Admiralty anchor was introduced about 1841. Improved anchors were made by Pering and Rodgers about 1828; by Porter, 1838; by Costell, 1848; by Trotman, 1853; and by several other persons. The anchors of ocean steamships are of enormous size. Acts for the proving and sale of chain cables and anchors were passed in 1864 and 1871.

ANCIENT, see *Britons, Councils, French*.

ANCIENT BUILDINGS: a society for their protection from injudicious restoration, &c., was established in 1877; Lord Houghton, Professor S. Colvin, Thomas Carlyle, and many eminent artists, members. Annual meetings, reports issued.

ANCIENT CONCERTS, or "King's Concerts," London. "The Concert of Antient Music" was established in 1776 by the earls of Sandwich and Exeter, and others. Sir Henry Bishop was sole conductor from 1843 to 1848, when the concerts ceased.

ANCIENT HISTORY commences in the Holy Scriptures 4004 B.C., and in the history of Herodotus about 1687 B.C., and is considered to end with the destruction of the Roman empire in Italy, A.D. 476. Modern history begins with Mahomet (A.D. 622), or with Charlemagne (768).

ANCIENT MONUMENTS in Britain. Acts for their preservation were passed in 1882, 1892, and 1900. An edict for their preservation in the Papal dominions was issued by card. Pacca, in 1820, and has been continued by the Italian government, and similar laws exist in France, Spain, Greece, Sweden and the United States.

ANCONA, an ancient Roman port on the Adriatic. The mole was built by Trajan, 107. After many changes of rulers (Lombards, Saracens, Greeks, and Germans) Ancona was annexed to the papal states in 1532. It was taken by the French, 1797; retaken by the Austrians, 1799; reoccupied by the French, 1801; restored to the pope, 1802. It was occupied by the French in 1832; evacuated in 1838, and after an insurrection was bombarded and captured by the Austrians, 18 June, 1849. The Marches (comprising this city) rebelled against the Papal government in Sept. 1860. Lamoricière, the papal general, fled to Ancona after his defeat at Castelfidardo, but was compelled to surrender himself, the city, and the garrison, on 29 Sept. The king of Sardinia entered soon after. Population of the city in 1881, 31,277; 1901, 56,825.

ANCYRA, now Angora or Engour, a town in ancient Galatia, Asia Minor. Councils were held here, 314, 358, 375. It was taken by the Persians, 616; by the Saracens, 1085; by the crusaders, 1102. Near this city, on 28 July, 1402, Timour or Tamerlane defeated and took prisoner the sultan Bajazet, and is said to have conveyed him to Samarcand in a cage.

ANDALUSIA (S. Spain), a province once part of the ancient Lusitania and Bætica. The name is a corruption of Vandalitia, it having been held by the Vandals from 419 to 429, when it was acquired by the Visigoths. The latter were expelled by the Moors in 711, who established the kingdom of Cordova, and retained it till 1236. Andalusia suffered much by the earthquakes of Dec. 1884.

ANDAMAN ISLANDS, in the Bay of Bengal. The inhabitants are dwarfs, and in the lowest state of barbarism. At Port Blair, on South Island, made a penal settlement for the Sepoy rebels in 1858, the earl of Mayo, viceroy of India, was assassinated by Shere Alee, a convict, 8 Feb. 1872, when going on board the *Glasgow*. Above 200 persons perished on land through a cyclone; see *Wrecks*, 2 Nov. 1891. Chief commissioner col. N. M. T. Horsford, 1892; Col. R. Temple, May, 1894; he reports the success of the system of penal discipline at Port Blair, March, 1899.

ANDERNACH, Rhenish Prussia, once an imperial city. Near here, the emperor Charles I., while attempting to deprive his nephews of their inheritance, was totally defeated by one of them, Louis of Saxony, 8 Oct. 876.

ANDES, CORDILLERA DE LOS, the great mountain system of South America.

Chimborazo, perpetually snowclad, was ascended by Alexander Von Humboldt to the height of 19,286 feet, 23 June 1802; by Boussingault and Hall, 19,695 feet, 16 Dec. 1831; by Edward Whymper, 20,545 feet, 3 Jan.; and 20,489 feet . . . 3 July, 1880

Cotopaxi, volcanic; ascended by Edward Whymper, 19,600 feet . . . . 18 Feb. ,,

He also first ascended Antisana, 19,260 feet, 10 March; and Cayambe, 19,200 feet . 4 April, ,,

[All these mountains are in Ecuador.]

Mr. Whymper's work on the "Great Andes" was published in March, 1892.

Railway across the Andes constructing, autumn, 1893.

Expedition of the R. Geographical Society, headed by Mr. E. A. Fitzgerald; *Aconcagua* 23,080 ft., ascended by Zurbriggen, Swiss guide, 14 Jan., 1897; by Mr. Vines, 13 Feb. 1897.

Sir Martin Conway explores the Bolivian Andes, the Cordillera Real, and ascends the highest peaks (*Aconcagua*) in 5½ days, 1898 and 1900.

ANDORRA, a small republic in the Pyrenees, bearing the title of "the valleys and sovereignties of Andorra," was made independent by Charlemagne about 778, certain rights being reserved to the bishop of Urgel. The feudal sovereignty, which long appertained to the counts of Foix, reverted to the French king, Henry IV., in 1589; but was given up in 1790. On 27 March, 1806, an imperial decree restored the old relations between Andorra and France. The republic is now governed by a council elected for four years; but the magistrates are appointed alternately by the French government and the Spanish bishop of Urgel, to both of whom tribute is paid. The population 1875 about 5,800. Andorra, though neutral, was attacked by the Carlists in Sept. 1874. Disputes between the French government and the bishop, respecting arrests, &c. made by him, March; amicably settled, April, 1884.

ANDRE'S EXECUTION, see *United States*, 1780.

ANDREW, ST., said to have been martyred by crucifixion, 30 Nov. 69, at Patræ, in Achaia. His festival was instituted about 359. The Royal Society's anniversary is kept on St. Andrew's day. The Russian order of St. Andrew was instituted in 1698 by Peter I. For the British order, see *Thistle*.

ANDREW'S, ST. (E. Scotland), made a royal burgh after 1140. Here Robert Bruce held his first parliament in 1309; and here Wishart was burnt by archbishop Beaton, 1545, who himself was murdered here in 1546. The university was founded in 1411 by bishop Wardlaw. The cathedral (built 1159-1318) was destroyed by a mob, excited by a sermon of John Knox, June, 1559.* Sir R. Sibbald's list of the bishops commences with Killach, 872. The see became archiepiscopal in 1470, ceased soon after 1689; was re-instituted in 1844; see *Bishops*. Sir William Taylour Thomson bequeathed 30,000*l.* to the university, announced Oct. 1883. University college of Dundee joined to the university, Jan. 1897. Population, 1891, 6,853; 1901, 7,621.

Mr. David Berry, an Australian colonist, a native of Cupar in Fife, who died Sept. 1889, bequeathed 100,000*l.* to the University, in accordance with the unsigned will of his brother, Dr. Alexander Berry, who died in 1873.
The Marquis of Dufferin was elected lord rector, 1889; address 6 April, 1891.
The marquis of Bute elected lord rector, 24 Nov. 1892; Mr. James Stuart, M.P., 23 Jan. 1899.
Accidental death by poison of Dr. Boyd, "A.K.H.B.," aged 74, 1 March, 1899.
Lord Bute founds a new chair of anatomy with a gift of 20,000*l.*, July, 1900; he died 9 Oct. 1900.
Lord Balfour installed chancellor, 24 Oct. 1901.
Lord Elgin, lord Balfour, and Mr. Andrew Carnegie presented with the freedom, 18 July, 1902.
Mr. A. Carnegie installed lord rector, 22 Oct. 1902.
Chancellor, lord Balfour of Burleigh (1902).
Dr. Charles Wordsworth, bishop 1852, warm advocate for the union of the churches, dies, aged 86, 5 Dec. 1892; succeeded by George H. Wilkinson, retired bishop of Truro, Feb. 1893.

ANDRUSSOV, PEACE OF (30 Jan. 1667), between Russia and Poland, for 13 years.

ANEMOMETER (Greek, *anemos*, the wind), a measurer of the strength and velocity of the wind, was invented by Wolfius, in 1709. The extreme velocity was found by Dr. Lind to be 93 miles per hour. Osler's and Whewell's anemometers were highly approved of in 1844. "Robinson's anemometer is the simplest and best," *Buchan*, 1867.

ANEROID, see *Barometer*.

ANGEL, a gold coin, impressed with an angel, weighing four pennyweights, valued at 6*s.* 8*d.* in the reign of Henry VI., and at 10*s.* in the reign of Elizabeth, 1562. The *Angelot*, a gold coin, value half an angel, was struck at Paris when held by the English, 1431. *Wood.*

ANGELIC KNIGHTS OF ST. GEORGE. This order is said to have been instituted by Constantine, who died 337. The *Angelici* were instituted by the emperor Angelus Comnenus, 1191.—The *Angelicæ*, an order of nuns, founded at Milan by Louisa Torelli, 1534.

ANGERS (W. Central France), the Roman Juliomagus, possessing an amphitheatre; afterwards Andegavum, the capital of Anjou (*which see*). It was frequently besieged, and many councils were held in it between 453 and 1448, relating to ecclesiastical discipline. Population in 1901, 82,966.

ANGERSTEIN GALLERY, see *National Gallery*.

* The marquis of Bute having purchased the land, Oct. 1893, began excavations on the site of the ancient priory, and gradually came upon remains of the prior's house (*Hospitium Vetus*), built about 1140, and monastic buildings, the great hall, refectory, &c.; remains of mutilated statues were also found.

ANGLESEY, called by the Romans Mona (N. Wales), the seat of the Druids, who were massacred in great numbers, when Suetonius Paulinus ravaged the isle, 61. It was conquered by Agricola in 78; occupied by the Normans, 1090; and with the rest of Wales annexed by Edward I. in 1284. He built the fortress of Beaumaris in 1295. The Menai suspension bridge was erected 1818-25, and the Britannia tubular bridge 1849-50.

ANGLICAN CHURCH, see *Church of England* and *Pan Anglican*.

ANGLING. Allusion is made to it in the Bible; *Isaiah* xix. 8; *Amos* iv. 2. Known as a pastime to the Egyptians, Greeks, and Romans.

Oppian wrote his "Halieutics," a Greek epic poem on Fishes and Fishing, about A.D. 198.
In the book on "*Hawkynge and Huntynge*," by Juliana Berners or Barnes, prioress of Sopwell, near St. Albans, "emprinted at Westmestre by Wynkyn de Worde," in 1496, is "*The treatise of fysshyng with an Angle.*"
Izaac Walton's "*Compleat Angler*" was first published in 1653.

ANGLO-AMERICAN ASSOCIATION, to cultivate more cordial relations between Great Britain and the United States, established 25 Jan. 1871; a league formed, 13 July, 1898.

ANGLO-CATHOLIC, a term used to designate the Church of England generally, but applied more especially to the high church section, which claims that the Anglican church is catholic, and favours a doctrine and ritual to some extent approaching that of the Roman church.

ANGLO-CONTINENTAL SOCIETY founded in 1853 to diffuse the principles of the Church of England abroad.

ANGLO-DANISH EXHIBITION, South Kensington, opened by the Princess (and Prince) of Wales, 14 May, 1888. The profits devoted to the rebuilding of the British Home for Incurables.

ANGLO-FRENCH, ETC. Agreements respecting Africa and other British interests.

ANGLO-FRENCH AGREEMENT respecting Africa signed by the Marquis of Salisbury and M. Waddington, French ambassador in London, 5 Aug. 1890. By this agreement the British protectorate over Zanzibar and the French protectorate over Madagascar are recognized, and the delimitation of territories in Africa, subject to the influence of France, was to be settled by two commissioners at Paris. A delimitation convention signed, July 1893. One settling the bend of the Niger signed at Paris, 14 June, 1898; ratified, June, 1899; another, by which France renounces territory within the Nile basin, but holds her right over Wadai; signed 21 March, 1899.
ANGLO-GERMAN AGREEMENT of 1890 determined the boundaries of the British and German proposed territories in East Africa; the protectorate of Zanzibar, Witu, Somaliland or Vitu, was given up to Great Britain; Kilima-Njaro assigned and Heligoland ceded to Germany; signed at Berlin by sir Edward Malet and sir Henry Percy Anderson for England; by gen. von Caprivi and Dr. Krauel for Germany, 1 July; ratified by an act of parliament which received the royal assent, 4 Aug. 1890. Boundary agreement signed at Berlin, 25 July, 1893. Others signed, autumn, 1898; 23 Feb. 1901. See *West African Settlements*, 1893; 16 Oct. 1900. See *China*.
ANGLO-JAPANESE IMPORTANT AGREEMENT; the *status quo* and independence of China and Corea and open-door policy to be maintained; signed, 30 Jan. 1902.
ANGLO-ITALIAN AGREEMENT respecting Africa. Sir Evelyn Baring and gen. sir Francis Grenfell received at Rome by sig. Crispi, 24 Sept. 1890. Meeting of the conference at Naples, lord Dufferin and sig. Crispi present; no result, 4—10 Oct. 1890. Treaty for the delimitation of the British and Italian spheres of

influence in East Africa; signed at Rome, 15 April, 1891; another, delimiting boundaries to the n. of Erythrea, ratified 28 Jan. 1899.

ANGLO-PORTUGUESE AGREEMENT delimiting the territories subject to the influence of Great Britain and Portugal in East Africa; the text of the agreement was settled in London 20 Aug. and published in the *Times*. The free navigation of the Zambezi, and uninterrupted communication between British territories ensured, 26 Aug. 1890. Portugal gives up all claim to Zambezi and Nyasaland. The agreement was annulled, and a *modus vivendi* agreed to, 14 Nov. 1890. A new modified treaty, signed at Lisbon, 11 June, 1891, and afterwards ratified.

ANGLO-RUSSIAN AGREEMENT regarding railway extension in China, signed at St. Petersburg, 28 April, 1899.

ANGLO-FRENCH AGREEMENT for arbitration of disputes, signed 14 Oct. 1903, see *Addenda*.

ANGLO-GERMAN association formed in London, June, 1897.

ANGLO-ISRAELISM is the theory held by many in Britain and the United States that the English race is ethnologically connected with the lost ten tribes of Israel, who were carried into captivity by the Assyrians 721 B.C.

ANGLO-NORMAN RECORD SOCIETY, founded by the duke of Norfolk and others in 1893 for the printing of early ecclesiastical charters.

ANGLO-SAXONS or ANGLES, derive their name from a village near Sleswick, called *Anglen*, whose population (called *Angli* by Tacitus) joined the first Saxon freebooters. East Anglia was a kingdom of the heptarchy, founded by the Angles, one of whose chiefs, Uffa, assumed the title of king, 571; the kingdom ceased in 792. See *Britain*. Cædmon paraphrased part of the Bible in Anglo-Saxon about 680; a translation of the gospels was made by abbot Egbert, of Iona, 721; of Boethius, Orosius, &c., by Alfred, 888. The Anglo-Saxon laws were printed by order of government, in 1840.

A professorship of Anglo-Saxon at Oxford was founded by Dr. Richard Rawlinson in 1795; one at Cambridge by Dr. Joseph Bosworth in 1867.

ANGLO-TURKISH CONVENTION, see *Turkey*, 4 June, 1878.

ANGOLA (S. W. Africa), settled by the Portuguese soon after the discovery, by Diego Cam about 1484. Loando, their capital, was built 1578.

ANGORA, see *Ancyra*.

ANGOULÊME, (the Roman Iculisma,) capital of the province of Angoumois, Central France, W., was a bishopric in 260. Angoulême became an independent country about 856; was united to the French crown in 1308; was held by the English, 1360 to 1372, in the reign of Edward III. The count of Angoulême became king of France as Francis I. in 1515. Population 36,000.

ANGRA PEQUEÑA; the German settlement here, north of the Orange river, South Africa, declared by prince Bismarck to be under the protection of the empire, 24 April, 1884; after alleged vacillating British diplomacy, 1882-3.

ANGRIA'S FORT, see *India*, 1756.

ANGUILLA, Snake Island, West Indies, settled by the British, 1666. Valuable deposits of phosphate of lime were found here in 1859. The island suffered by a famine due to long drought and failure of crops early in 1891. Population 1901, 3,890.

ANHALT, HOUSE OF, in Germany, deduces its origin from Berenthobaldus, who made war upon the Thuringians in the sixth century. In 1606, the principality was divided among the four sons of Joachim Ernest, by the eldest, John-George. Thus began the four branches — Anhalt-Dessau (descended from John-George); Zerbst, extinct, 1793; Plotsgau or Coethen, extinct, 1847; and Bernburg, extinct, 1863; (the last duke died without issue, 22 Aug. 1863.) The princes of Anhalt became dukes in 1809. Anhalt is an hereditary constitutional monarchy (by law 19 Feb. 1872); population in 1871, 203,437; in 1875, 213,565; in 1885, 248,166; 1890, 271,759; 1894, 271,963; 1900, 316,085.

Anhalt joined the North German Confederation, 18 Aug. 1866.

Leopold (born Oct. 1, 1794), became duke of Anhalt-Dessau, 9 Aug. 1817, and of Anhalt-Bernburg, 30 Aug. 1863; died 22 May, 1871.

Frederic, duke of Anhalt; born 29 April, 1831.
Heir: Frederic; born 19 Aug. 1856.

Marriage of prince Aribert to princess Louise, a daughter of prince and princess Christian, 6 July, 1891.

ANHOLT, ISLAND OF, Denmark, was taken possession of by England, 18 May, 1809, in the French war, on account of Danish cruisers injuring British commerce. The Danes made a fruitless attempt to regain it, 27 March, 1811.

ANILINE, an oily alkaline body, discovered in 1826 by Unverdorben among the products of distillation of indigo. From benzole (*which see*) Bechamp, in 1856, obtained it by successive treatment with concentrated nitric acid and reducing agents. The scientific relations of aniline have been carefully examined by several chemists, especially by Dr. A. W. Hofmann. It was long known to yield a series of coloured compounds, but it was not till 1856 that Mr. W. H. Perkin showed how a violet oxidation-product (mauve) could be applied in dyeing. Aniline is now manufactured on a large scale for the commercial production of "Mauve" and "Magenta" (rosaniline) (*which see*), and several other colouring matters, aniline blue, 1861; violet, 1863; "night" green, &c. The patent of Simpson, Maule, and Nicholson, for aniline colours, was annulled by the house of lords, 27 July, 1866. See *Alizarine*. Poisoning from the inhalation of aniline vapours, characterised by the bluish colour of the lips, cheeks and ears of the persons affected, is termed *Anilism*.

ANIMALCULES, Leeuwenhoek's remarkable microscopical discoveries were published in the Philosophical Transactions of the Royal Society, for 1677, in his "Arcana Naturæ," at Leyden, 1696. The great works of Ehrenberg of Berlin on the Infusorial Animalculæ, &c., were issued 1838-57. Pritchard's *Infusoria*, ed. 1861, and Mr. W. Savile Kent's *Manual of Infusoria*, 3 volumes, 1880-2, are valuable. The Rev. W. H. Dallinger, Dr. Drysdale and other distinguished scientists, by their microscopical observations of bacteria and other low forms of life, have greatly increased our knowledge.

ANIMAL MAGNETISM (to cure diseases by *sympathetic affection*) was introduced by father Hehl, a Jesuit, at Vienna, about 1774, and had its believers in France and England about 1788-89. Hehl for a short time associated with Mesmer, but they soon quarrelled.—Mr. Perkins (who died in 1799) invented "Metallic Tractors for collecting, condensing, and applying animal magnetism;" but Drs. Falconer and Haygarth put an end to his pretensions by performing many wonders with a pair of *wooden* tractors. *Brande*. See *Mesmerism*. Animal magnetism disproved by commissions of the

French Academy of Sciences, 1837-8; investigation closed as of a "dead letter," 1840. Remarkable feats were performed by Miss Abbott, "the magnetic lady," at the Alhambra theatre, 14 Nov. *et seq.* 1891.

ANIMALS. Mr. Martin, M.P., as a senator, zealously laboured to repress cruelty, and in 1824 the *Royal Society for the Prevention of Cruelty to Animals* was instituted. Its new house in Jermyn-street, London, was founded 4 May, 1869. It opposed vivisection in 1860, in unison with a French society, and in Oct. 1873, offered premiums for improved trucks for conveying cattle. A jubilee congress of this and similar societies met in London 17 June, 1874. Convictions obtained by the society 1835 to June, 1876, 28,209. Convictions in England and Wales, 7,320, 1896; 8,033, 1901; 40,000*l.* bequeathed by Mr. J. H. Long, Dec. 1902. Annual meetings are held. See *Vivisection*. Mr. Martin's act was passed 1822, and similar acts were passed in 1827, 1835, 1837, 1849, and 1854. Dogs were forbidden to be used for draught in 1839. See *Cattle*.

"*Fellowship of Animals' Friends*," organised about 10 July, 1879; earl of Shaftesbury, president. With similar object Mr. Ruskin founded St. George's Guild. The Dicky Birds Society in the northern counties numbered 8,000 members in 1883.

The Animals' Institute, Knightsbridge, distributed prizes for inventions for the relief of horses and other animals, 28 July, 1890.

A hospital for animals was opened at 75, Kinnerton-st., Wilton place, S.W., April, 1896. See *Brown institution*.

Wild animals in captivity protection act passed, 6 Aug. 1900.

ANIMISM, the name given to the doctrine propounded by George E. Stahl about 1707, that the soul (*anima*) is the proper principle of life, "the vital principle" in opposition to materialism, *which see*. The term *animism* was given by Dr. Edward B. Tylor in 1869, to the belief in the existence of active spiritual beings common alike among civilized and uncivilized peoples. He lectured on animism (terming it a minimum definition of religion) at the Royal institution, March 1895.

ANJOU, a province, W. France, was taken by Henry II. of England from his brother Geoffrey, in 1156; their father Geoffrey Plantagenet, count of Anjou, having married the empress Matilda in 1127. It was taken from king John by Philip of France in 1205; was reconquered by Edward III.; relinquished by him at the peace of Brétigny in 1360, and given by Charles V. to his brother Louis with the title of duke. The university was formed in 1349.

1360. Louis I. duke, invested by the pope with the dominions of Joanna of Naples, 1381; his invading army destroyed by the plague, 1383; he dies, 1384.

1384. Louis II., his son, receives the same grant, but is also unsuccessful.

Louis III., adopted by Joanna; dies 1434.

1434. Regnier or René le bon (a prisoner) declared king of Naples, 1435; his daughter, Margaret, married Henry VI. of England, 1445; he was expelled from Anjou by Louis XI., 1474, and his estates confiscated.

Francis, duke of Alençon, brother to Henry III. of France, became duke of Anjou; at one time he favoured the Protestants, and vainly offered marriage to Elizabeth of England, 1581-82; died 1584.

ANJOU or BEAUGÉ, BATTLE OF, between the English and French; the latter commanded by the dauphin of France, 22 March, 1421. The English were defeated: the duke of Clarence was slain by sir Allan Swinton, a Scotch knight, and 1500 men perished on the field; the earls of Somerset, Dorset, and Huntingdon were taken prisoners. Beaugé was the first battle that turned the tide of success against the English.

ANNAM or ANAM, an empire of Asia, to the east of India, nominally subject to China, formerly comprising Tonquin, Cochin China, part of Cambodia, and various islands in the Chinese Sea; said to have been conquered by the Chinese, 234 B.C., and held by them till A.D. 263. In 1406 they reconquered it, but abandoned it in 1428. After much anarchy, bishop Adran, a French missionary, obtained the friendship of Louis XVI. for his pupil Gia-long, the son of the nominally reigning monarch, and with the aid of a few of his countrymen established Gia-long on the throne, who reigned till his death in 1821, when his son became king. In consequence of the persecution of the Christians, war broke out with the French, who defeated the army of Annam, 10,000 strong, about 22 April, 1859, when 500 were killed. On 3 June, 1862, peace was made; three provinces were ceded to the French, and toleration of the Christians granted. An insurrection in these provinces against the French, begun about 17 Dec. 1862, was suppressed in Feb. 1863. Ambassadors sent from Annam with the view of regaining the ceded provinces arrived at Paris in Sept. 1863, had no success. Cochin China and other provinces were annexed to the French empire by proclamation, 25 June, 1867. Several native Christians were massacred by order of a bonze, July, 1868. Population about 3,000,000, capital Hué. Buddhism, ancestor worship, communal life, and education prevail.

By a treaty concluded 15 March, 1874, at Saigon, the independence of the king of Annam was recognized by France, the ports were opened to commerce, and toleration of the Christian religion was secured.

Tu Duc, emperor, 34 years, resists the French in *Tonquin*, (which see), 1883; dies aged 54, 17 July, 1883; Heiphma succeeds.

The French protectorate recognized by treaty signed at Hué . . . . 25 Aug. "

The King assassinated by enemies of the French, Dec., succeeded by Yoe-Duc . about 14 Dec. "

The prince who promoted massacres of Christians in December and January executed about 26 Mar. 1884

The king dies, succeeded by his brother Kienphuoc (a boy) . . . . . . announced 2 Aug. "

Treacherous attack of the Regent Thu-Hong, with 30,000 men, on General de Courcy with 1,000 men at the French camp at Hué; repulsed with heavy loss, and the Regent captured . . 5-6 July, 1885

French protectorate: Chaul Mong, adopted son of Tu Duc (named Douck Hanh) crowned 19 Sept. "

Reported great massacre of Christians . Oct. "

The king dies; Bun Lañ, his son, 10 years old (called Tham Thai), proclaimed . . . 31 Jan. 1889

ANNAPOLIS, see *Port Royal*.

ANNATES, see *First Fruits*.

ANNO DOMINI, A.D., the year of Our Lord, of Grace, of the Incarnation, of the Circumcision, and of the Crucifixion (Trabeatonis). The Christian era commenced 1 Jan. in the middle of the 4th year of the 194th Olympiad, the 753rd year of the building of Rome, and in 4714 of the Julian period. This era was invented by a monk, Dionysius Exiguus, about 532. It was introduced into Italy in the 6th century, and ordered to be used by bishops by the council of Chelsea, in 816, but was not generally employed for several centuries. Charles III. of Germany was the first who added "in the year of our Lord" to his reign, in 879. It was formerly held that Christ was born 4 B.C. Mr. W. T. Lynn considers that probably Christ was born towards the end of the year 5.

ANNO MUNDI, see *Creation*.

"ANNOYANCE JURIES," of Westminster, chosen from the householders in conformity with 27 Eliz. c. 17 (1585), were abolished in 1861.

ANNUAL REGISTER, a summary of the history of each year (beginning with 1758, and continued to the present time), was commenced by R. & J. Dodsley. (Edmund Burke at first wrote the whole work, but afterwards became only an occasional contributor. *Prior.*) A similar work, "Annuaire des Deux Mondes," began in Paris 1850.

ANNUALS, a name given to richly bound volumes, containing poetry, tales, and essays, by eminent authors, illustrated by engravings, published annually, at first in Germany, and also in London in 1823. The duration of the chief of these publications is here given:

Forget-me-not (Ackerman's)	1823-48
Friendship's Offering	1824-44
Literary Souvenir (first as "the Graces")	1824-34
Amulet	1827-34
Keepsake	1828-56
Hood's Comic Annual	1830-42

ANNUITIES or **PENSIONS**. In 1512, 20*l.* a year were given to a lady of the court for services done; and 6*l.* 13*s.* 4*d.* for the maintenance of a gentleman, 1536. 13*l.* 6*s.* 8*d.* deemed competent to support a gentleman in the study of the law, 1554. An act was passed empowering the government to borrow one million sterling upon an annuity of fourteen *per cent.*, 4-6 Will. & Mary, 1691-3. This mode of borrowing soon afterwards became general among governments. An annuity of 1*l.* 2*s.* 11*d.* *per annum*, accumulating at 10 *per cent.*, compound interest, amounts in 100 years to 20,000*l.* The Government Annuities and Life Assurances Act was passed in 1864, for the benefit of the working classes; since it enables the government to grant deferred annuities for sums payable in small instalments. New system of government annuities came into operation 3 June, 1884. Works on annuities were published by De Witt, 1671; De Moivre, 1724; Simpson, 1742; Tables by Price, 1792; Milne, 1815; Jones, 1843; Farre, 1864; Institute of Actuaries, 1872 and 1882–7.

ANNUITY TAX: a tax levied to provide stipends for ministers in Edinburgh and Montrose, and which caused much disaffection, was abolished in 1860, and other provisions made for the purpose. These, however, proved equally unpalatable, and their abolition was provided for by an act passed 9 Aug. 1870.

ANNUNCIATION OF THE VIRGIN MARY, 25th of March, Lady-day (*which see*), a festival commemorating the tidings brought to Mary by the angel Gabriel (*Luke* i. 26): its origin is referred to the 4th or 5th century. The *religious order* of the Annunciation was instituted in 1232, and the *military order*, in Savoy, by Amadeus, count of Savoy 1360, in memory of Amadeus I., who had bravely defended Rhodes against the Turks, 1355. New statutes, 1869. It is the highest Italian order.

ANOINTING, an ancient ceremony observed at the inauguration of priests, kings, and bishops. Aaron was anointed as high priest, 1491 B.C.; and Saul, as king, 1095 B.C. Alfred the Great is said to have been the first English king anointed, A.D. 871; and Edgar of Scotland, 1098.—The *religious rite* is derived from the epistle of *James* v. 14, about A.D. 60. Some authors assert that in 550, dying persons, and persons in extreme danger of death, were anointed with consecrated oil, and that this was the origin of Extreme Unction (one of the sacraments of the Roman Catholic Church).

ANONYMOUS LETTERS, see *Threatening Letters*.

ANORTHOSCOPE, an optical apparatus, described by Dr. Carpenter in 1868. In it distorted figures lose their distortion when in rapid motion.

"ANTAGONISM," was demonstrated to be a universal principle throughout Nature with beneficial results by Sir W. R. Grove in a discourse at the Royal Institution, London, 20 April 1888.

ANTALCIDAS, PEACE OF. In 387 B.C. Antalcidas the Lacedæmonian made peace with Artaxerxes of Persia, on behalf of Greece, but principally in favour of Sparta, giving up the cities of Ionia to the king.

ANTARCTIC POLE, &c., the opposite to the north or *arctic* pole; see *Southern Continent*.

Antarctic Expedition proposed by the Australian Colonies; a committee of the Royal Society formed, Professor Stokes, president, Lord Rayleigh, Professor Huxley, and others, Nov. 1887.

Baron Oscar Dickson, of Gothenburg, undertook to subscribe 5,000*l.* and procure the remainder of the expense from the Swedish government, if the Australasian colonies should subscribe 5,000*l.*; the project appeared to be in abeyance, Dec. 1891.

Antarctic whaling expedition from Dundee arrived at Port Stanley, Falkland Islands, 11 Dec. 1892.

Mr. C. E. Borchgrevink, a Norwegian explorer, first to land at Cape Adair, on the S. continent, 23 Feb. 1895; a scientific expedition under him, equipped by sir Geo. Newnes, left London in the *Southern Cross* (capt. B. Jensen) for S. Victoria Land, 22 Aug. 1898; reached Cape Adair, 17 Feb. 1899, which they ascend to 3,670 ft., 12 March; valuable collection made at Duke of York island and Geikie land (so named by Mr. Borchgrevink). Mr. N. Hansen died, 5 Oct.; magnetic position of the S. pole fixed at about lat. 73, 20 S. and 146 E.; furthest point S. ever reached 78° 50′, 17 March 1900; they returned to Stewart island, 4 April, 1900.

The De Gerlache expedition in the *Belgica* leaves Antwerp, 16 Aug., 1897; explored the S. Shetlands, 21 Jan. 1898; discovered strait Belgica, land to the east, named Danco Land, 23 Jan.; ice-bound, 23 Feb., continual night, 17 May—21 July; lieut. Danco died, 5 June; Punta Arenas, Patagonia, reached, good scientific results, 28 March, 1899.

British Expedition Fund started by a donation of 25,000*l.* from Ll. W. Longstaff received a treasury grant of 45,000*l.* The *Discovery*, capt. Scott, built at Dundee, inspected by the king and queen at Cowes, Aug. 5, left Port Chalmers Dec. 24, 1901. The *Morning*, relief ship, left London Aug. 2, 1902, found letters from capt. Scott at Cape Crozier, Jan. 18, 1903. Penetrated ice-pack to within 10 miles of the *Discovery*, transferred coal stores, &c., and left the *Discovery* snugly berthed, her men blasting the ice to force a passage, March 2, 1903. Relief ship *Terra Nova* left Portland for Hobart, Tasmania, to be joined there by the *Morning*, from Lyttleton, N. Zealand, Aug. 24.

German expedition. The *Gauss*, capt. Hans Ruser, left Hamburg 11 Aug. 1901, reached Kerguelen Island, 2 Jan. 1902; a magnetic station founded there. Found bottom at 3,950 fathoms, 18° 15′ W. 0° 11′ S.

ANTHEMS were originally antiphons—short pieces of plain-song sung before the psalms. Generally responsive antiphonic music was used in Jewish and early christian worship. Hilary, bishop of Poictiers, and St. Ambrose composed such about the middle of the 4th century. *Lenglet.* The modern anthem, a passage of scripture set to music, was introduced into the Reformed churches in queen Elizabeth's reign, about 1560.

ENGLISH ANTHEM WRITERS: 1520-1625, Tye, Tallis, Byrd, Gibbons; 1650-1720, Humphrey, Blow, Purcell, Croft, Clarke; 1720-1900, Greene, Boyce, Hayes, Battishill, Attwood, Walmisley, Wesley, Goss, Elvey, Sullivan.

ANTHOLOGY, GREEK, a collection of popular epigrams and small poems written by Archilochus, Sappho, Simonides, Meleager, Plato and others, between 680 and 95 B.C. They were collected by Meleager, Philippus, Agathias, and others, especially by Maximus Planudes, a monk in the 14th century A.D., and a MS. collection by Constantine Cephalas was found at Heidelberg by Salmasius in 1606; and published by Brunck 1772-6. Translations have been made by Bland, Merivale, and others.

ANTHRACENE, see *Alizarine.*

ANTHROPOLOGICAL SOCIETY (*anthropos*, Greek for man), for promoting the science of man and mankind, held its first meeting on 24 Feb. 1863; Dr. James Hunt, president, in the chair. The "Anthropological Review" first came out in May, 1863. The Anthropological and Ethnological Societies were amalgamated 17 Jan. 1871, and styled "The Anthropological Institute," Sir John Lubbock, president. The London Anthropological Society established 1873, ceased 1875. An Anthropological congress at Paris was opened 16 Aug. 1878; others since; at Moscow, 13 Aug. 1892. The Anthropometrical Committee reported to the British Association the results of measuring about 53,000 persons in the United Kingdom, Sept. 1883.

Fourth international congress of Criminal Anthropology opened at Geneva, 24 Aug., 1896; 5th, Amsterdam, 9-14 Sept. 1901. See *Torres.*

ANTHROPOMORPHITES, a name given to the Audiani, *which see.*

ANTHROPOPHAGI (eaters of human flesh), see *Cannibals.*

ANTI-AGGRESSION LEAGUE (opposing interference in foreign affairs) formed by Mr. John Morley and others, Feb. 1882.

ANTIBURGHERS, see *Burghers.*

ANTICHRIST (opposed to Christ), 1 *John* ii. 18, termed the "Man of sin," 2 *Thess.* ii. 3; of these passages many interpretations have been given, and many myths were current in the middle ages, respecting the incarnation of the devil, &c. The term is applied to each other by Roman Catholics and Protestants.

ANTI-CORN-LAW LEAGUE (for procuring the repeal of the laws charging duty on the importation of corn), sprung from various metropolitan and provincial associations, was founded at Manchester, 18 Sept. 1838, and supported by Messrs. Charles Villiers, Richard Cobden, John Bright, &c.; John Benjamin Smith, 1st chairman, *d.* 15 Sept. 1879. See *Corn Laws.* and *Protectionists.*

Meetings held in various places . March & April, 1841
Excited meeting at Manchester . . . 18 May, „
A bazaar held at Manchester, at which the League realised 10,000*l.* . . . . . . 2 Feb. 1842
About 600 deputies connected with provincial associations assemble in London . . . Feb.-Aug. „
The League at Manchester proposed to raise 50,000*l.*, to depute lecturers throughout the country, and to print pamphlets . . 20 Oct. „
First meeting at Drury-lane Theatre . . 15 March, 1843
Monthly meetings at Covent-Garden, commenced 28 Sept.; great free-trade meetings at Manchester 14 Nov. 1843, and 22 Jan. 1845
Bazaar at Covent-Garden, 25,000*l.* obtained, 5 May-June, „
Great Manchester meeting, at which the League proposed to raise 250,000*l.* . . . . 23 Dec. „
The Corn Importation Bill having passed, 26 June, the League is formally *dissolved*; Mr. Cobden was rewarded by a national subscription, nearly 80,000*l.* . . . . 2 July, 1846
On the accession of the Derby ministry, a revival of the Anti-Corn-Law League was proposed at Manchester, and a subscription was opened, which produced within half an hour 27,520*l.* (soon proved unnecessary) . . . . 2 Mar. 1852
Death of Richard Cobden, 2 April, 1865; John Bright . . . . 27 Mar. 1889

ANTIETAM CREEK, near Sharpsburg, Maryland, U.S. Here was fought a terrible battle on 17 Sept. 1862, between the Federals under general M'Clellan, and the Confederates under Lee. After his victory at Bull Run or Manassas, 30 Aug. Lee invaded Maryland, and was immediately followed by M'Clellan. On 16 Sept. Lee was joined by Jackson, and at five o'clock next morning the conflict began. About 100,000 men were engaged, and the battle raged till night. The Federals were repeatedly repulsed; but eventually the Confederates retreated and repassed the Potomac on 18 and 19 Sept. Federals' loss was estimated at 12,469; the Confederates, 14,000. A national cemetery here, was dedicated 17 Sept. 1867.

ANTI-GAMBLING LEAGUE, NATIONAL, instituted 1889, to awaken public opinion on the subject of betting and gambling, and suppress these evils. The work of the league is carried on by the dissemination of literature, the organisation of lectures and public meetings, the promotion of amending measures in parliament, and the enforcement of existing laws. President, right hon. the earl of Aberdeen. Offices, 13, Victoria-street, Westminster. See also *Betting-houses.*

ANTIGUA, a West Indian island, discovered by Columbus in Nov. 1493; settled by the English in 1632; made a bishopric, 1842. Population in 1861, 36,412; 1881, 34,964; 1891, 36,699: 1901, 34,953. Governor, sir B. C. C. Pine, 1869; hon. H. T. Irving, 1873; hon. Geo. Berkeley, 1874-80; sir J. H. Glover, 1881; sir Wm. Fred. Haynes Smith, 1895. Antigua is the seat of government of the Leeward Isles, *which see.* Antigua becomes a crown colony, 23 March, 1898.

"**ANTI-JACOBIN** or Weekly Examiner," a satirical paper, opposed to revolutionary principles, published by George Canning and his friends 1797-98; its poetry included the "Needy Knife Grinder.

ANTILLES, or CARIBBEE ISLANDS, an early name of the West Indies (*which see*).

ANTIMONY, a white brittle metal, compounds of which were early known. It was, and is still, used to blacken both men's and women's eyes in the east (2 *Kings* ix. 30, and *Jeremiah* iv. 30). Mixed with lead it forms printing type metal. Basil Valentine wrote on antimony about 1410. *Priestley.* See *Bravo Case* and *Trials*, 1902, *Chapman's Case.*

ANTINOMIANS (from the Greek *anti*, against, and *nomos*, law), a name given by Luther (in 1538) to John Agricola, who is said to have held "that it mattered not how wicked a man was if he had but faith." (Opposed to *Rom.* iii. 28, and v. 1, 2.) He retracted these doctrines in 1540. The Antinomians were condemned by the British parliament, 1648.

ANTIOCH, now ANTAKIEH, Syria, built by Seleucus, 300 B.C. after the battle of Ipsus, 301. acquired the name "Queen of the East." Here the disciples were first called Christians, A.D. 42 (*Acts* xi. 26). Antioch was taken by the Persians, 540; by the Saracens about 638; recovered for the Eastern emperor, 966; lost again in 1086; retaken by the Crusaders in June, 1098, and made capital of a principality, 1099; and held by them till June, 1268, when it was captured by the sultan of Egypt.

It was taken from the Turks in the Syrian war, 1 Aug. 1832, by Ibrahim Pacha, but restored at the peace. Antioch suffered much by an earthquake, and about 1600 persons were killed, 3 April, 1872. A Syrian church still exists at Antioch.—The CÆSAREAN ERA of Antioch, 48 B.C., is much used by the early Christian writers of Antioch and Alexandria; it placed the Creation 5492 years B.C. 31 councils were held at Antioch, 252-1161.

ANTI-PARNELLITES, see under *Parnellites*, 1890.

ANTIPHONS, see *Anthems*.

ANTIPODES. Plato is said to be the first who thought it possible that antipodes existed (about 388 B.C.). Boniface, archbishop of Mentz, legate of pope Zachary, is said to have denounced a bishop as a heretic for maintaining this doctrine, A.D. 741. The antipodes of England lie to the south-east of New Zealand, near Antipodes Island.

ANTI-POPES, rival popes elected at various times, especially by the French and Italian factions, from 1305 to 1439. In the article *Popes*, the Anti-popes are printed in *italics*.

ANTIPYRINE, an artificial alkaloid obtained from coal-tar, discovered in 1883 by Knorr, of Erlangen, is said to be a remedy for sea sickness; a substitute for quinine and a source of aniline colours.

ANTIQUARIES. A college of antiquaries is said to have existed in Ireland 700 B.C. The annual International Congress of Prehistoric Archæology originated at La Spezzia in 1865; meetings have been held since at Paris, Norwich, &c.

A society was founded by archbishop Parker, Camden, Stow, and others in 1572. *Spelman.*

Application was made to Elizabeth for a charter, her death ensued, and her successor, James I., was far from favouring the design.

The "Antiquaries' feast," mentioned by Ashmole, 2 July, 1659.

The Society of Antiquaries revived, 1707; received its charter of incorporation from George II., 2 Nov. 1751; met in Chancery-lane, 1753; apartments in Somerset House (granted 1776;) occupied, 15 Feb. 1781; removed to Burlington House, 1874; first meeting 14 Jan. 1875. Memoirs, entitled "Archæologia," first published in 1770; president, earl Stanhope, elected 1846; died 24 Dec. 1875; Frederic Ouvry, 1875; by the earl of Carnarvon, 1878; Mr. John Evans, 1885; sir Augustus W. Banks, 1893; Viscount Dillon, 1900.

British Archæological Association founded Dec. 1843; jubilee celebrated 31 July—5 Aug. 1893.

Archæological Institute of Great Britain formed by a seceding part of the Association, 1845. Annual meetings held in the provinces by both bodies.

Society of Antiquaries of Edinburgh founded in 1780.

Royal Society of Antiquaries of Ireland founded 1849.

Since 1845 many county archæological societies have been formed in the United Kingdom. The fourth congress of these archæological societies, 20 July, 1892; ninth, 1 Dec. 1897; tenth, London, 6 July, 1898.

The Society of Antiquaries of France (1814) began in 1805 as the Celtic Academy.

"The Antiquary," a magazine, began 1880.

British School of Archæology (first director, F. C. Penrose) opened at Athens Nov. 1886.

The Illustrated Archæologist (quarterly), June, 1893.

ANTISANA, see *Andes*.

ANTISEPTIC SURGERY, see *Germ Theory*.

ANTI-SLAVERY SOCIETY. See under *Slave Trade*.

ANTITOXIN, a substance present or generated in the body, which neutralises the action of poisons introduced or generated there. The serum of the blood of an animal in which the bacillus (*b. diphtheriæ*) of diphtheria has been injected, is used in the treatment of *Diphtheria* (*which see*).

ANTI-TRINITARIANS. Theodotus of Byzantium, at the close of the 2nd century, is supposed to have been the first who advocated the simple humanity of Jesus. See *Arians*, *Socinians*, *Unitarians*.

ANTIUM, maritime city of Latium, now Porto d'Anzio, near Rome, after a long struggle for independence, became a Roman colony, at the end of the great Latin war, 340-338 B.C. It is mentioned by Horace, and was a favourite retreat of the emperors and wealthy Romans, who erected many villas in its vicinity. The treasures deposited in the temple of Fortune here were taken by Octavius Cæsar during his war with Antony, 41 B.C.

ANTI-VACCINATION LEAGUE, see under *Vaccination*.

ANTIVARI, a seaport on the Adriatic, ceded to Montenegro by the Berlin treaty, 13 July, 1878.

ANTONELLI CASE, see *Italy*, 1877–9.

ANTONINUS' WALL, see *Roman Walls*.

ANTWERP (French, Anvers), the principal port of Belgium, is mentioned in history in 517. It was a small republic in the 11th century, and was the first commercial city in Europe till the wars of the 16th and 17th centuries. Population, 1890, 227,225; 1900, 285,600.

Its fine exchange built 1531

Taken after 14 months' siege by the prince of Parma 17 Aug. 1585

Truce of Antwerp (between Spain and United Provinces) for 12 years, concluded . . . 29 Mar. 1609

After Marlborough's victory at Ramillies, Antwerp surrenders at once . . . . 6 June, 1706

The Barrier treaty concluded here . . 16 Nov. 1715

Taken by marshal Saxe . . . . . 9 May, 1746

Occupied by the French 1792-3, 1794-1814

Civil war between the Belgians and the House of Orange. (See *Belgium*.) 1830-31

The Belgian troops, having entered Antwerp, were opposed by the Dutch garrison, who, after a dreadful conflict, being driven into the citadel, cannonaded the town with red-hot balls 27 Oct. 1830

The citadel bombarded by the French, 4 Dec.; surrendered by gen. Chassé . . . 23 Dec. 1832

Exchange burnt; archives, &c., destroyed 2 Aug. 1858

A fine-art fête held . . . . . . 17-20 Aug. 1861

Great Napoleon wharf destroyed by fire; loss 25 lives and about 400,000*l*. . . . 2 Dec. ,,

Great fête at the opening of the port by the abolition of the Scheldt dues . . . . 3 Aug. 1863

Fortifications constructed 1860–70

Statue of Leopold I. uncovered . . . 2 Aug. 1868

Tercentenary of Rubens' birth, celebrated . 18 Aug. 1877

Plantin-Moretus Museum, containing collections of about 300 years, viz.: 12,000 old letters, printing types, portraits, &c., made by the Plantins (descendants of Charles de Tiercelin, seigneur de la Roche du Maine), who were printers to the kings of Spain; opened . . about 20 Aug. ,,

International Exhibition, opened by the king 2 May, 1885; closed . . . . . 5 Oct. 1885

New quays opened by the King . . . 26 July, ,,

Great explosion at M. Corvilain's cartridge factory, behind the docks in the port; large Russian petroleum warehouses take fire, causing great destruction of property, 6 Sept., the shipping only escaped by the direction of the wind; the fire subdued; visit of the king, 13 Sept.; reported deaths, 120; injured, 130 . . . 18 Sept. 1889

Trial of M. Corvilain and his engineer, M. Delauney, for homicide, &c.; M. Corvilain sentenced to 5½ years' penal servitude, and his engineer, M. Delauney, to 1½ years, at Brussels, 14—27 Nov. 1889, and . . . . . . 17 Feb. 1890

Great fire at the African warehouses; loss about 1,000,000 francs . . . . . . 8 May, 1893

International, industrial and fine arts exhibition; area, near the Scheldt, between 200 and 300 acres; main building about 1,300 yards long, erected according to plans of Mr. J. F. Hasse; Belgian industry specially represented; models of old Antwerp and of a settlement in the Congo Free State; the naval models included the ill-fated *Victoria*; opened by the king and queen, 5 May *et seq.*; state visit of the lord mayor of London and others, 3 Aug. *et seq.*; distribution of awards to exhibitors by the king . . . . 2 Oct. 1894
Expulsion of Mr. Sexton, Mr. Ben Tillett, and others, trade unionists . . . . . . Aug. 1896
Compensation to Mr. Ben Tillett referred to arbitration; announced . . . . . 4 March, 1897
Vandyck tercentenary exhibition opened, 12 Aug. 1899
Historical procession through the city 14 Aug. ,,
Shipping dispute, on hours of labour, strike begins, 17 Dec. 1900, some rioting . . 22, 31 Dec. 1900

ANVAR-I-SUHAILI, or the Lights of Canopus, the ancient Persian version of the ancient Fables of Pilpay, Bidpai, or Vishnu Sarma, made by Husain Vaiz, at the order of Nushirvan, king of Persia. The English translation by E. B. Eastwick, published 1854. See *Fables*.

ANZIN COAL MINES, near Valenciennes, N. France: first tapped 24 June, 1734. The company formed is immensely rich: cabinet ministers generally directors. Output, in 1790, 300,000 tons: 1902, over 4,000,000 tons. The new hauling engine, with flat ropes, lifts 15 tons at a time, 1902.

APATITE, mineral phosphate of lime. About 1856 it began to be largely employed as manure. It is abundant in Norway, and in Sombrero, a small West India island.

APOCALYPSE or REVELATION, written by St. John in the isle of Patmos about A.D. 95.*

APOCRYPHA. In the preface to the Apocrypha it is said, "These books are neyther found in the Hebrue nor in the Chalde." *Bible*, 1539. The history of the Apocrypha ends 135 B.C. The books were not in the Jewish canon, were rejected at the council of Laodicea held A.D. 363, but were received as canonical by the Roman Catholic church at the council of Trent on 8 April, 1546. Parts of the Apocrypha were admitted to be read as *lessons* by the church of England, by the 6th article, 1563. Many of these were excluded by the act passed 1871. Revised version completed, Oct., published Nov., 1895.

1 Esdras	from about B.C.	623-445
2 Esdras	,,	* *
Tobit	,,	734-678
Judith	,,	656
Esther	,,	510
Wisdom of Solomon		* *
Ecclesiasticus	B.C.	300 or 180
Baruch		* *
Song of the Three Children		* *
History of Susannah		* *
Bel and the Dragon		* *
Prayer of Manasses	B.C.	676
1 Maccabees	about	323-135
2 Maccabees	from about	187-161

There are also Apocryphal writings in connection with the New Testament, such as gospels, epistles, &c., attributed to Clement, Barnabas, and others. Fragments of a gospel attributed to St. Peter were found in an Egyptian tomb in 1886-7, and printed with a translation in 1892; two leaves of a new gospel in Coptic discovered by Dr. Jacoby at Strasbourg among papyri from Egypt, translated and printed in 1900.

* Some ascribe the authorship to Cerinthus, the heretic, and others to John, the presbyter, of Ephesus. In the first centuries many churches disowned it, and in the 4th century it was excluded from the sacred canon by the council of Laodicea, but was again received by other councils, and confirmed by that of Trent, held in 1545, *et seq.* Its canonical authority is almost universally acknowledged.

APOLLINARISTS, followers of Apollinaris, a reader in the church of Laodicea, who taught (366) that the divinity of Christ was instead of a soul to him; that his flesh was pre-existent to his appearance upon earth, and was sent down from heaven, and conveyed through the Virgin; that there were two sons, one born of God, the other of the Virgin, &c. These opinions were condemned by the council of Constantinople, 381.

APOLLO, the god of the fine arts, medicine, music, poetry, and eloquence, had many temples and statues, particularly in Greece and Italy. See *Delphi*. The statue of Apollo Belvedere, discovered at Antium, in Italy, in 1503, was purchased by pope Julius II., who placed it in the Vatican.

APOLLONICON, an elaborate musical instrument, constructed on the principle of the organ (keys and barrel), was invented by Messrs. Flight and Robson, of St. Martin's lane, Westminster, and exhibited by them first in 1817. *Timbs*.

APOLOGIES FOR CHRISTIANITY were addressed by Justin Martyr to the emperor Antoninus Pius about 139, and to the Roman senate about 164. Other apologies were written by Quadratus, Aristides, and other early fathers of the Church.

APOSTLES (Greek, *apostolos*, one sent forth). Twelve were appointed by Christ, A.D. 31; viz. Simon Peter and Andrew (brothers), James and John (sons of Zebedee), Philip, Nathanael (or Bartholomew), Matthew (or Levi), Thomas, James the Less (son of Alphæus), Simon the Canaanite and Jude or Thaddeus (brothers), and Judas Iscariot. Matthias was elected in the room of Judas Iscariot, A.D. 33 (*Acts* i.); and Paul and Barnabas were appointed by the Holy Spirit, A.D. 45 (*Acts* xiii. 2).

"*The Teaching of the Twelve Apostles*," a small vellum volume in Greek, dated about 1056, discovered by Philotheos Bryennios, metropolitan of Nicomedea, in the library of the Holy Sepulchre monastery at Constantinople in 1873; and published by him in 1875. The composition is ascribed to the first century. The text, with English translation and introduction, was published by R. D. Hitchcock and Francis Brown in 1884; improved edition, spring, 1885.

APOSTLE SPOONS, given as a baptismal present in the 16th and 17th centuries, are named from the figures of the Apostles, which crown the handle. A complete set of 16, same date (10 Henry VIII.), was sold, 1903, for 4,900*l*.

APOSTLES' CREED, erroneously attributed to the apostles, is mentioned as the Roman creed by Rufinus, died about 410. Irenæus, bishop of Lyons, died 202, gives a creed resembling it. Its repetition in public worship was ordained in the Greek church at Antioch, and in the Roman church in the 11th century, whence it passed to the church of England.

APOSTOLICAL, see *Canons* and *Fathers*.

APOSTOLIC BRETHREN, a sect, 13th century, founded by Sagarelli, a weaver of Parma. Its leading tenets were the return to the primitive life of the apostolic age and community of goods. The sect incurred papal censure, and Sagarelli was burned 1300.

APOSTOLIC CONSTITUTIONS, eight books, the *Constitutiones Apostolicæ*, which had much influence on the development of Christian doctrine, dogma, and liturgy, written in 3rd and 4th centuries. *The Apostolic Canons*, 85 ecclesiastical precepts on the priest's office and life, extracted from the scriptures and synodical decrees. The first 50, compiled 5th century, only were recognised by the Roman Church; the 35 canons, put forth 6th century, were received by the Greek Church. Tradition ascribes both the Constitutions and the Canons to Clement of Rome.

APOSTOLICAL SUCCESSION, the doctrine of the uninterrupted transmission of the ministerial authority from Christ, as the fountain of grace, to the Apostles, and from them to the episcopate.

APOSTOLICI, a sect, at the end of the 2nd century, which renounced marriage, wine, flesh, &c. A second sect, founded by Sagarelli about 1261, wandered about, clothed in white, with long beard, dishevelled hair, and bare heads, accompanied by women called spiritual sisters, preaching against the growing corruption of the church of Rome, and predicting its downfall. They renounced baptism, the mass, purgatory, &c., and by their enemies were accused of gross licentiousness. Sagarelli was burnt alive at Parma in 1300, and his followers were dispersed in 1307, and extirpated about 1404.

APOTHECARY (literally, a keeper of a storehouse). On 10 Oct. 1345, Edward III. settled sixpence *per diem* for life on Coursus de Gangeland, *Apothecarius London'*, for taking care of him during his severe illness in Scotland. *Rymer's Fœdera;* see *Pharmacy* and *Medical Council.*

Apothecaries exempted from serving on juries or other civil offices 1712
London Apothecaries' Company separated from the Grocers' and incorporated, 1617; hall built . . 1670
Their practice regulated and their authority extended over all England, by the Apothecaries act, 55 Geo. III. c. 19 (1815), amended by 6 Geo. IV. c. 133, 1825; and by 37 & 38 Vict. c. 34 . . 1874
Women allowed to qualify by act of 1876.
Qualifying examination in medicine, surgery, and midwifery imperative, Medical Act . . . 1886
Botanical Garden at Chelsea left by sir Hans Sloane to the company, Jan. 1753, on condition of their introducing every year fifty new plants, until their number should amount to 2000, Jan. 1755; re-opened by lord Cadogan . 25 July, 1902
The Dublin guild incorporated 1745

APOTHEOSIS, a ceremony of the ancient nations of the world, by which they raised their kings and heroes to the rank of deities. The deifying a deceased emperor was begun at Rome by Augustus, in favour of Julius Cæsar, 13 B.C. *Tillemont.*

APPEAL or **ASSIZE OF BATTLE.** By the old law of England, a man charged with murder might fight with the appellant, thereby to make proof of his guilt or innocence. In 1817, a young maid, Mary Ashford, was believed to have been violated and murdered by Abraham Thornton, who, on trial, was acquitted. In an appeal, he claimed his right by wager of battle, which the court allowed; but the appellant (the brother of the maid) refused the challenge, and the accused was discharged, 16 April, 1818. This law was struck off the statute-book, by 59 Geo. III. c. 46 (1819).

In 1631 lord Rea impeached Mr. David Ramsey of treason and offered battle in proof; a commission was appointed, but the duel was prohibited by king James I.

APPEALS. In the time of Alfred (869-901), appeals lay from courts of justice to the king in council. *Courts of appeal at the Exchequer Chamber*, in error from the judgments of the superior and criminal courts, were regulated by statutes in 1357, 1559, 1830 and 1848. *Appeals* from English tribunals *to the pope* were first introduced about 1151, were long vainly opposed, and were abolished by Henry VIII. 1534; restored by Mary, 1554; again abolished by Elizabeth, 1559. House of Lords sat as court of appeal in 1278. By 14 Edw. III., c. 5, 1340, a prelate, two earls, and two barons formed the court. Protest by House of Commons against appeal to the Lords, 1675, resisted by the peers; hearing of appeals resumed, 1677. The principle that this jurisdiction was a delegation by the crown of its final authority was reaffirmed 1876. See *Privy Council* and *Justices, Lords, Common Pleas.*

Court of appeal abolished by the Judicature Act, 1873; abolition suspended and a provisional court established . . . . . 8 Nov. 1875
The House of Lords was reconstructed as a court of final appeal by the Appellate Jurisdiction Act, passed 11 Aug.; the Act came into force 1 Nov. 1876; it enacts that every appeal shall be brought by petition to the House of Lords, that the matter may be reviewed before the Sovereign in Parliament. The court first sat . . 21 Nov. 1876
The Act was amended by the Appellate Jurisdiction Act 1887, the Appeal Act (*formâ pauperis*) 1893, and the Statute Law Revision Act . . 1894
The members usually attending (1903) are:—The Lord Chancellor, lord Hobhouse, lord Macnaghten, lord Shand, lord Davey, lord James of Hereford, lord Brampton, lord Ashbourne, and lord Robertson.

APPELLATE JURISDICTION, see under *Appeals.*

APPENZELL, a Swiss canton, threw off the supremacy of the abbots of St. Gall early in the 15th century, and became the thirteenth member of the Swiss confederation, 1513.

APPIAN WAY, a Roman road to Capua, made by Appius Claudius Cæcus, while censor, 312-308 B.C.

APPLES. Several kinds are indigenous to England; but those in general use have been brought at various times from the continent. Richard Harris, fruiterer to Henry VIII., is said to have planted a great number of the orchards in Kent, and lord Scudamore, ambassador to France in the reign of Charles I., planted many of those in Herefordshire. Ray reckons 78 varieties of apples in his day (1688). In 1903 there were some 2000 varieties cultivated in Great Britain. The scientific study and classification of apples is entitled Pomology.

APPORTIONMENT ACT (for rents, annuities, dividends, and other periodical payments) passed 1 Aug. 1870.

APPRAISERS. The valuation of goods for another was an early business in England; and so early as 1283, by the statute of merchants, or of Acton Burnel, "it was enacted that if they valued the goods of parties too high, the appraisers should take them at such price as they have limited." In 1845 their annual licence was raised from 10*s.* to 40*s.* A duly licensed auctioneer or house agent may act as appraiser.

APPRENTICES. Those of London were obliged to wear blue cloaks in summer, and blue gowns in winter, in the reign of queen Elizabeth, 1558. Ten pounds was then a great apprentice fee. From twenty to one hundred pounds were given in the reign of James I. *Stow's Survey.* The apprentice tax enacted 43 Geo. III. 1802. The term of seven years, not to expire till the apprentice was 24 years old, required by the statute of Elizabeth (1563), was abolished in 1814. An act for the protection of apprentices, &c., was passed in 1851. The apprentices of London have been at times very riotous; they rose into insurrection against foreigners on *Evil May-day* (*which see*) 1 May, 1517.

Exhibition of apprentices' work at the People's Palace opened by the prince of Wales 10 Dec. 1888.

APPROPRIATION ACT passed annually by a clause prohibits the treasury officials from applying public money to any service other than that to which it has been specially appropriated. The principle was adopted by the commonwealth, and was definitely established in 1665.

APPROPRIATION CLAUSE, of the Irish Tithe Bill of 1835, brought forward by lord John Russell, whereby any surplus revenue that might accrue by the working of the act was to be appropriated for the education of all classes of the people. The principle was adopted by the commons, but rejected by the lords in 1835 and 1836, and was abandoned.

APPROPRIATIONS (property taken from the church), began in the time of William I. The parochial clergy, then commonly Saxons, were impoverished by the bishops and higher clergy (generally Normans) to enrich the monasteries possessed by the conqueror's friends. Where the tithes were so appropriated, the vicar had only such a competency as the bishop or superior thought fit to allow. Pope Alexander IV. complained of this as the bane of religion, the destruction of the church, and a poison that had infected the whole nation. Lay appropriations began after the dissolution of the monasteries, 1536.

APRICOT (*præcox*, early ripe), *Prunus Armeniaca*, from Asia Minor, said to have been first planted in England about 1540, by the gardener of Henry VIII.

APRIL, the fourth month of our year, the second of the ancient Romans.

APTERYX (wingless), a bird, a native of New Zealand, first brought to this country in 1813, and deposited in the collection of the earl of Derby. Fossil specimens of a gigantic species of this bird (named *Dinornis*) were discovered in New Zealand by Mr. Walter Mantell in 1843 and since, and much studied and many papers written on it by Professor Owen.

APULIA, a province in S.E. Italy. The people favoured Hannibal, and were severely punished by the Romans at his retreat, 207 B.C. Apulia was conquered by the Normans, whose leader Guiscard received the title of duke of Apulia from pope Nicholas II. in 1059. After many changes of masters, it was absorbed into the kingdom of Naples, in 1265.

Strike riot, conflict with troops at Candela, 5 deaths, 8 Sept. 1902.

AQUACULTURE, see under *Fisheries*.

AQUARII, a sect said to have been founded by Tatian in the 2nd century, who forebore the use of wine even in the sacrament; during persecution they met secretly at night. For this they were censured by Cyprian (martyred, 258).

AQUARIUM or **AQUAVIVARIUM**, a vessel containing water (marine or fresh) in which animals and plants may co-exist, mutually supporting each other; snails being introduced as *scavengers*. In 1849, Mr. N. B. Ward succeeded in growing seaweeds in artificial sea-water; in 1850, Mr. R. Warington demonstrated the conditions necessary for the growth of animals and plants in jars of water; and in 1853 the glass tanks in the Zoological Gardens, Regent's Park, were set up by Mr. D. Mitchell. In 1854, Mr. Gosse published "The Aquarium." Mr. W. Alford Lloyd, late of Portland-road, London, who by his enterprise in collecting specimens did much to increase the value and interest of aquaria, has been much employed in erecting aquaria. The great aquarium (50 yards long and 12 wide) at the Jardin d'Acclimatation at Paris, was constructed under his direction in 1860. He also constructed the aquarium at Hamburg and others. That at Brighton was inaugurated by prince Arthur, 30 March, and publicly opened by the mayor, 10 Aug. 1872. That at the Crystal Palace was opened, Jan. 1872.

The ROYAL AQUARIUM and SUMMER and WINTER GARDEN SOCIETY was established 1874; the building at Westminster, planned by Mr. Wybrow Robertson and Mr. A. Bedborough, was opened by the duke of Edinburgh, 22 Jan. 1876.

A woman surnamed "Zazel" permitted herself to be safely shot from a cannon (by a spring or other mechanical contrivance); summer of 1877, *et seq.*

Living whales shown here soon died; see *Whale*; Sept., 1877; June, 1878.

The Imperial theatre added, 1879.

Purchased by the Wesleyan Methodists with a portion of their 20th Century Fund. Celebration meeting held 2 Feb. 1903.

AQUATINT, see *Engraving*.

AQUEDUCT, an artificial watercourse. Appius Claudius Cæcus, while censor, advised and constructed the first Roman aqueduct, as well as the *Appian way*, about 312-308 B.C.* There are now some remarkable aqueducts in Europe: that at Lisbon is of great extent and beauty; that at Segovia has 129 arches; and that at Versailles is three miles long, and of immense height, with 242 arches in three stories. The stupendous aqueduct on the Ellesmere canal, in England (1007 feet in length, and 126 feet high) was completed by T. Telford, and opened 26 Dec. 1805. The Lisbon aqueduct was completed in 1738, and the Croton aqueduct, near New York, was constructed between 1837 and 1842. The aqueduct to supply Marseilles with water was commenced in 1830. An aqueduct to supply London with water from the Welsh lakes was proposed by Mr. J. F. Bateman in 1865.

AQUIDABAN, Paraguay. Here the war with Brazil was ended with the defeat and death of president Lopez, 1 March, 1870.

AQUILA, S. Italy. Near here the Arragonese under the condottiere Braccio Forte-Braccio were defeated by the allied Papal, Neapolitan, and Milanese army under Jacob Caldora, 2 June, 1424. Braccio, a wounded prisoner, refused to take food, and died, 5 June.

AQUILEIA (Istria), made a Roman colony about 180 B.C. and fortified A.D. 168. Constantine II. was slain in a battle with Constans, fought at Aquileia towards the close of March, 340. Maximus defeated and slain by Theodosius, near Aquileia, 28 July, 388. Theodosius defeated Eugenius and Arbogastes, the Gaul, near Aquileia, and remained sole emperor, 6 Sept. 394. Eugenius was put to death, and Arbogastes died by his own hand, mortified by his overthrow. St. Ambrose held a synod

* Remains of these and other noble aqueducts, constructed by emperors, still remain, and some supply water to the city.

here in 381. In 452 Aquileia was almost totally destroyed by Attila the Hun, and near it in 489 Theodoric and the Ostrogoths totally defeated Odoacer, the king of Italy. Aquileia was an early patriarchal see.

AQUITAINE, the Roman province Aquitania (S.W. France), conquered by the Romans 28 B.C.; by the Visigoths, A.D. 418; taken from them by Clovis in 507. Henry II. of England obtained it with his wife Eleanor, 1152. It was erected into a principality for Edward the Black Prince in 1362; but was annexed to France in 1370. The title of duke of Aquitaine was taken by the crown of England on the conquest of this duchy by Henry V. in 1418. The province was lost in the reign of Henry VI.

ARABIA (W. Asia). The terms *Petræa* (stony), *Felix* (happy), and *Deserta* are said to have been applied to its divisions by Ptolemy, about A.D. 140. The Arabs claim descent from Ishmael, the eldest son of Abraham, born 1910 B.C. *Gen.* xvi. Arabia was unsuccessfully invaded by Gallus, the Roman governor of Egypt, 24 B.C. The Abyssinians conquered part of Arabia Felix, and retained it 76 years. In A.D. 622, the Arabians under the name of Saracens, followers of Mahomet (born at Mecca, 570), their general and prophet, commenced their course of conquest; see *Mahometanism*. Arabia was conquered by the Ottomans 1518-39. The Arabs greatly favoured literature and the sciences, especially mathematics, astronomy, and chemistry. The Koran was written in Arabic (622-632). The Bible was printed in Arabic in 1671. See *Wahabees*.

The aggression of the Turks on the South Arabs excited jealousy in England, and was checked by the sultan	Nov.	1873
Insurrection in Yemen or Arabia Felix;	5 Jan.-7 Feb.	1882
Egyptian commission for preservation of Arab monuments appointed	Jan.	,,
Revolts in Yemen, announced	17 Mar.	1883
Conflicts reported	Sept.	1884
Several revolts against the Turkish government suppressed	June—Oct.	1891
Rebellion headed by Iman Ahmed Eddin, Jan.; reinforcements sent, successful	May—July,	1892
Iman Ahmed Eddin, killed; the rebellion quelled, and the province Yemen pacified by the Turkish governor, reported	7 Sept.	,,
Insurrection in Yemen; the Turks defeated by the Imam of Sana in three engagements, Nov. 1895; another spreading, Abdullah pasha ordered to take the command	14 June,	1898
Insurgents routed in Shanei, Turkish loss heavy,	30 Nov.	,,
Turkish atrocities, continued fighting	April,	1899
Abdullah pasha forced to retire on Sana	June,	,,
Ibn Rashid, ex-king of Nejd, defeats Mabaroukh, the conqueror of Nejd, with great slaughter, reported	12 April,	1901
Turks attempt to land troops at Koweyt, foiled by the captain of H.M.S. *Perseus*	24 Aug.	,,
Abdullah pasha made vali, Yemen	20 Oct.	1902
Ibn Rashid defeats the Wahabis	Dec.	,,

ARABIAN NIGHTS' ENTERTAINMENTS (or 1001 Tales) were translated into French by Galland, and published in 1704; but their authenticity was not acknowledged till many years after. The best English translation from the Arabic is that of Mr. E. W. Lane, published in 1839, with valuable notes and beautiful illustrations. Sir Richard F. Burton's elaborate translation in 10 vols. was printed at Benares for subscribers 1885-7. Lady Burton's expurgated edition, edited by Mr. Justin H. McCarthy, with scholarly notes and appendices, was published in 1887 *et seq.*; she died 22 March, 1896. He died, aged 69, 20 Oct. 1890. "*The Thousand and One Days*" (inferior to the "Nights"): a translation from the Persian by Petis de la Croix, was published in 1710. Versions are said to have existed in Turkish and other Eastern languages.

ARABIC FIGURES (1, 2, 3, &c.), see *Arithmetic*. ARABIC NEWSPAPER, "*Mar-âtu-'l-Ahwâl*" ("Mirror of Passing Events"), published in London end of 1876.

ARABICI, a sect which sprung up in Arabia, about 207, whose distinguishing tenet was, that the soul dies with the body, and will rise again with it.

ARAGON, part of the Roman Tarraconensis, a kingdom, N.E. Spain, was conquered by the Carthaginians, who were expelled by the Romans about 200 B.C. It became an independent monarchy in A.D. 1035; see *Spain*.

ARAM. Aramæa, from the Hebrew Aram (signifying "high land" as distinguished from Canaan, "low land"), a name given to all the country N.E. of Palestine; which included Syria, Babylonia and Mesopotamia. The people used two dialects, in the west Syriac, in the east Aramaic (improperly termed Chaldee), called Hebrew at the time of Christ.

ARANJUEZ (Central Spain), contains a fine royal palace, at which several important treaties were concluded. On 17 March, 1808, an insurrection broke out here against Charles IV. and his favourite, Godoy, the prince of the peace, who received that title for concluding the treaty of Basle. The former was compelled to abdicate in favour of his son, Ferdinand VII., 19 March.

ARARAT, a mountain in Armenia (about 17,112 feet above the sea-level), on which Noah's ark is supposed to have rested, B.C. 2348, now termed by the Persians, Koh-i-Nuh (Noah's mountain); by the Armenians, Masis; by the Turks, Agri-Dagh.

It was ascended by Dr. Parrot, 27 Sept. 1829; by Major Stuart, 1856, and by others since. Mr. James Bryce, who ascended 11, 12 Sept. 1876, described the summit as a little plain of snow, silent and desolate, with a bright, green sky above; the view stern, green, and monotonous. Ascended by professor Mackoff and M. Popoff, Russians, Aug. 1888; by Mr. H. F. B. Lynch and capt. Lynch, 19 Sept. 1893.

ARAUCANIA, a province in S. America. Its inhabitants maintained almost unceasing war with the Spaniards from 1537 to 1773, when their independence was recognised. They are now nominally subject to Chili.

ARAUSIO (now ORANGE), S. E. France. Through the jealousy of the Roman proconsul Q. Servilius Cæpio, who would not wait for the arrival of the army of the consul C. Manlius, both were defeated here by the Cimbri with much slaughter, 105 B.C.

ARBELA. The third and decisive battle between Alexander the Great and Darius Codomanus decided the fate of Persia, 1 Oct. 331 B.C., on a plain in Assyria, between Arbela and Gaugamela. The army of Darius consisted of 1,000,000 foot and 40,000 horse; the Macedonian army amounted to only 40,000 foot and 7000 horse. *Arrian.* The gold and silver found in the cities of Susa, Persepolis, and Babylon, which fell to Alexander from this victory, amounted to thirty millions sterling; and the jewels and other precious spoil, belonging to Darius, sufficed to load 20,000 mules and 5000 camels. *Plutarch.*

ARBITRATION. Submission to arbitration was authorised and made equivalent in force to the decision of a jury, by 9 & 10 Will. III. (1698).

Further enforced by 3 & 4 Will. IV. c. 42 (1833); see *Ouzel Galley*. The Common Law Procedure Act (1854) authorises the judges of superior courts to order compulsory arbitration; and, by an act passed in 1859, railway companies may settle disputes with each other by arbitration. The Arbitration (Masters and Workmen) Act was passed 6 Aug. 1872. See *Prud'hommes*.

For Arbitration between Nations, see under *Peace*. *United States*, April, 1896; Jan.-May, 1897; Oct. 1903; *Mexico*, 1902; Venezuela, 1903.

Codification of the Arbitration Acts was effected by the Arbitration Act passed 26 Aug. 1889.
Address in favour of arbitration presented by eminent British M.P.s and politicians at Washington, U.S., 1887.
Arbitration Alliance founded in Feb. 1894, to promote international arbitration, first annual meeting in London, 30 May, 1895.

See *London Chamber of Arbitration*.

ARBORICULTURE. See *Trees*.

ARBUTUS. The *Arbutus Andrachne*, oriental strawberry-tree, was brought to England from the Levant about 1724.

ARC DE TRIOMPHE, Paris, begun in 1806 in honour of the Grande Armée, continued in 1823, and completed in 1836. The list of battles, &c. (158), begins with Volmy, 20 Sept. 1792, and the last Ligny, 16 June, 1815. The Arc de Triomphe is 165 feet high, 150 feet broad and 75 feet thick.

ARCADES, or walks arched over. The principal in London are the Burlington-arcade, opened 20 March, 1819; the Lowther-arcade, Strand, opened 1831, closed 1902; between Old Bond-street and Albemarle-street, opened May, 1880; see *Strand*, and *Exeter Change*. The Royal-arcade, Dublin, opened June, 1820, was burnt to the ground, 25 April, 1837. The Great Western-arcade, Birmingham, opened 28 Sept. 1876.

ARCADIA, in the centre of the Peloponnesus, Greece, named after Arcas, a king. The Arcadians regarded their nation as the most ancient of Greece. The early history of Arcadia is fabulous.

Sir Philip Sidney's *Arcadia*, a pastoral romance, was published in 1590, the 8th edition in 1633.
Magna Græcia, in S. Italy, said to have been colonised by Arcadians under Œnotrus, about 1710 B.C.; and under Evander . . . B.C. 1240
Arcas taught his subjects agriculture and to spin wool . . . 1514
Lycæan games instituted, in honour of Pan . . . 1320
Agapenor appears at the head of the Arcadians at the siege of Troy (*Homer*) . . . 1194
The Lacedæmonians invade Arcadia, and are beaten by the women of the country in the absence of their husbands (?) . . . 1102
Aristocrates I. (of Orchomenus) put to death for offering violence to the priestess of Diana . . . 715
Aristocrates II. stoned; a republic founded . . . 681
Supremacy of Sparta (acknowledged 560) abolished by the Thebans; Megalopolis founded by Epaminondas . . . 371
The Arcadians make alliance with Athens, and are defeated by Archidamus . . . 367
Arcadia, having joined the Achæan league, on its suppression is annexed by Rome . . . 146

ARCADIANS, an ultra-conservative French political club, composed of a section of the majority in the chambers, and opposed to liberal measures, even when emanating from the emperor (such as the new press law). It derived its name from Rue de l'Arcade, where its meetings were held: Feb. 1868.

ARCH. It appears in early Egyptian and Assyrian architecture. The oldest arch in Europe is probably in the Cloaca Maxima, at Rome, constructed under the early kings, about 588 B.C. The Chinese bridges, which are very ancient, are of great magnitude, and are built with stone arches similar to those that have been considered a Roman invention.*—The TRIUMPHAL arches of the Romans formed a leading feature in their architecture. The arch of Titus (A.D. 80), that of Trajan (114), and that of Constantine (312), were magnificent. The arches in our parks in London were erected about 1828. The Marble Arch, which formerly stood before Buckingham Palace (whence it was removed to Cumberland-gate, Hyde Park, in 1851) was modelled from the arch of Constantine; see *Hyde Park*.

ARCHÆOPTERYX (ancient bird); the name given to the earliest known remains of a bird, found in the lithographic slate of Solenhofen, by Herman von Meyer and Dr. Häberlein in 1861. Its structure approximated more to that of a reptile than that of modern birds does. It was described by Owen in 1863.

ARCHANGEL (N. Russia), a city, is thus named from a monastery founded here, and dedicated to St. Michael in 1584. The passage to Archangel was discovered by the English navigator Richard Chancellor in 1553, and it was the only seaport of Russia till the formation of the docks at Cronstadt, and foundation of St. Petersburg in 1703. The dreadful fire here, by which the cathedral and upwards of 3000 houses were destroyed, occurred in June, 1793. Increased commercial development under gov. Engelhardt; Alexandrovsk, a new ice-free port, opened by the grand duke Vladimir, 6 July, 1899. Population of the province, 1886, 328,819; 1897, 346,536.

ARCHBISHOP (Greek *archiepiscopos*), a title given in the 4th and 5th centuries to the bishops of chief cities, such as Rome, Alexandria, Antioch, and Constantinople, who presided over the other metropolitans and bishops in the districts attached to those places. The word is first found in the Apology against the Arians by Athanasius, who died 373. Four archbishops of the Eastern church are styled *patriarchs*. *Riddle*.

Before the Saxons came to England, there were three archbishops: London, York, and Caerleon-upon-Usk; but soon after St. Augustin settled the metropolitan see at Canterbury, 602; see *Canterbury*.
York continued archiepiscopal; but London and Caerleon lost the dignity; see *St. David's*.
The bishoprics in *Scotland* were under the jurisdiction of the archbishop of York until the erection of the archiepiscopal sees of St. Andrew's and Glasgow in 1470 and 1491; these last were discontinued at the Revolution; see *Glasgow* and *St. Andrew's*.
The bishop of Brechin was chosen *Primus*, 1886, the title being conferred on one of the bishops by election.
The rank of archbishop was early in *Ireland*; see *Ferns*.
Four archbishops were constituted, Armagh, Cashel, Dublin, and Tuam; (until then the archbishop of Canterbury had jurisdiction over the Irish as well as English bishops, in like manner as the archbishop of York had jurisdiction over those of Scotland), 1151.
Of these four archbishoprics two were reduced to bishoprics (Cashel and Tuam) conformably with the

* The bridge of Chester, whose span is 200 feet, was commenced in 1829. The central arch of London Bridge is 152 feet; and the three cast iron arches of Southwark Bridge, which rest on massive stone piers and abutments are, the two side ones 210 feet each, and the centre 240 feet: thus the centre arch exceeds the admired bridge of Sunderland by four feet in the span, and the long-famed Rialto at Venice, by 167 feet: see *Bridges*.

stat. 3 & 4 Will. IV. by which also the number of sees in Ireland was to be reduced from twenty-two to twelve (see *Bishops, Cashel, Tuam, Pallium, &c.*), 1833.

ARCH-CHAMBERLAIN. The elector of Brandenburg was appointed the hereditary arch-chamberlain of the German empire by the golden bull of Charles IV. in 1356, and in that quality he bore the sceptre before the emperor.

ARCH-CHANCELLORS were appointed under the two first races of the kings of France (418-986), and when their territories were divided, the archbishops of Mentz, Cologne, and Treves became arch-chancellors of Germany, Italy, and Arles.

ARCHDEACON, a name early given to the first or eldest deacon, who attended on the bishop without any power; but since the council of Nice, his function has become a dignity above a priest. The appointment in these countries is referred to the eighth century. There are seventy-five archdeacons in England (1878). The archdeacon's court is the lowest in ecclesiastical polity; an appeal lies from it to the consistorial court, by 24 Henry VIII. (1532).

ARCHERY is ascribed to Apollo, who communicated it to the Cretans.

Ishmael "became an archer" (*Gen.* xxi. 20), B.C. 1892
The Philistine archers overcame Saul (1 *Sam.* xxxi. 3). 1056
David commanded the use of the bow to be taught (2 *Sam.* i. 18) 1055
Archery introduced into England previous to A.D. 440
Harold and his two brothers were killed by arrows shot from the cross-bows of the Norman soldiers at the battle of Hastings 1066
Richard I. revived archery in England in 1190, and was himself killed by an arrow 1199
The victories of Crecy (1346), Poictiers (1356), and Agincourt (1415), were won chiefly by archers.
Four thousand archers of the king surrounded the houses of Parliament ready to shoot; pacified by the king, 21 Richard II. (*Stow.*) 1397
The citizens of London formed into companies of archers in the reign of Edward III.; and into a corporate body by the style of "The Fraternity of St. George," 29 Henry VIII. 1538
Roger Ascham's "*Toxophilus, the School of Shooting,*" published 1571
Scorton Annual Arrow Meetings—a silver arrow shot for; articles agreed to . . . 14 May, 1673
Royal company of archers, instituted by the marquis of Athol, as the king's body guard for Scotland 1676
The *long bow* was six feet long, and the arrow three feet: the usual range from 300 to 500 yards. Robin Hood is said to have shot from 600 to 800 yards. The cross-bow was fixed to a stock, and discharged with a trigger.

See *Artillery Company, Toxophilites, &c.*

ARCHES, COURT OF, the most ancient consistory court, chiefly a court of appeal from inferior jurisdictions within the province of Canterbury; it derives its name from the church of St. Mary-le-Bow (*Sancta Maria de Arcubus*), London, where it was formerly held, and whose top is raised on stone pillars built archwise. *Cowell.* Appeals from this court lie to the judicial committee of the privy council, by statute, 1832. The Dean and Official Principal, Dr. Stephen Lushington, (appointed in 1828) resigned 1 July, 1867; succeeded by sir Robert J. Phillimore, who resigned, 1875. Lord Penzance succeeded him; resigned, 1899; died 9 Dec. 1899; succeeded by sir Arthur Charles.

ARCHIEPISCOPAL COURT, see under *Canterbury*.

ARCHITECTURE (from the Greek *architektōn*, chief artificer). The five great orders are, —the Doric, Ionic, and Corinthian (*Greek*);—the Tuscan and Composite (*Roman*). Gothic began to prevail in the 9th century. See *the Orders* and *Gothic*.

The Pyramids of Egypt, begun . . . . about B.C. 1500
Solomon's Temple, begun 1004
Birs Nimroud, in Assyria . . . . . about 900
The Doric order begins . . . . . . about 650
Doric Temple at Ægina 550
Temple of Jupiter and Cloaca Maxima, at Rome founded 616
Babylon built 600
The Ionic order begins . . . . . about 500-420
The Corinthian order begins 335
Choragic Monument of Lysicrates 335
Architecture flourishes at Athens 480-320
Erechtheum at Athens 450-420
The Parthenon finished 438
The Pantheon, &c., built at Rome . . . . A.D. 13
The Colosseum (or Coliseum) 70
Hadrian builds temples at Rome, &c. 117
Diocletian's palace at Spalatro 284
Basilicas at Rome 330-900
St. Sophia, at Constantinople, begun . . . A.D. 532
Rock-cut temples in India—Caves of Ellora . . 500-800
Canterbury cathedral, founded 602
Mosque of Omar at Jerusalem 637
York Minster (present building) begun . . about 1172
St. Peter's, Rome 1450-1626
St. Paul's, London 1675-1710
R. Cath. Cathedral, Westminster, foundation stone laid, 29 June, 1895; opened Dec. 1903.

EMINENT ARCHITECTS.

	Born. Died.
Vitruvius, about	B.C. 27
William of Wickham	A.D. 1324—1405
Filippo Brunelleschi	1377—1444
Michael Angelo Buonarotti	1474—1564
Jacopo Tatti Sansovino	1479—1570
Galeazzo Alessi	1500—1572
Giacomo Barozzio da Vignola	1507—1573
A. Palladio	1518—1580
Vincenzo Scamozzi	1552—1616
Carlo Maderno	1556—1629
Inigo Jones	1572—1652
Bernini	1598—1680
Christopher Wren	1632—1723
J. Vanbrugh	1670—1726
James Gibbs	1674—1754
Sir Robert Taylor	1714—1788
James Stuart	1713—1788
R. and J. Adam	1728—1794
Sir William Chambers	1726—1796
Sir John Soane	1753—1837
William Wilkins	1778—1839
Augustus W. Pugin	1811—1852
Sir Charles Barry	1795—1860
C. R. Cockerell	1788—1863
Sir Joseph Paxton	1803—1865
Sir Robert Smirke	1780—1867
James Fergusson	1808—1886
Sir Geo. Gilbert Scott	1811—1878
George Edmund Street	1824—1881
E. Barry	1830—1881
John Gibson	1816—1892
C. J. Phipps, theatres: Gaiety, Savoy, Her Majesty's, 1897, &c.	1837—1897
John L. Pearson	1817—1897
Thomas Hayter Lewis	1818—1898
Sir Arthur Blomfield	1829—1899
Sir Thos. N. Deane	1828—1899
William Butterfield	1814—1900
J. M. Brydon	1840—1901

An Architectural Club was formed in 1791. An Architectural Society existed in London in 1806. The ROYAL INSTITUTE OF BRITISH ARCHITECTS was founded in 1834. The Architectural Society, established in 1831, was united to the Institute in 1842. The ARCHITECTURAL ASSOCIATION began about 1846. The ROYAL ARCHITECTURAL MUSEUM, Westminster, opened, 21 July, 1869.

Mr. James Fergusson's "History of Architecture," 4 vols., 1865-76.

ARCHIVISTS, SOCIETY OF. In 1893, Mr. Saxe Wyndham founded a society with this title consisting of autograph and MSS. collectors, &c.

ARCHONS. When royalty was abolished at Athens, in memory of king Codrus, killed in battle, 1044 or 1068 B.C., the executive government was vested in elective magistrates called archons, whose office continued for life. Medon, eldest son of Codrus, was the first archon. The office was limited to ten years, 752 B.C., and to one year 683 B.C.

ARCOLA (Lombardy), the site of battles between the French under Bonaparte, and the Austrians under field-marshal Alvinzi, fought 14-17 Nov. 1796. The Austrians lost 18,000 men in killed, wounded, and prisoners, four flags and eighteen guns. The French lost about 15,000, and became masters of Italy. In one contest Bonaparte, in most imminent danger, was rescued by the impetuosity of his troops.

ARCOT (East Indies). This city (founded 1716) was taken by colonel Clive, 31 Aug. 1751; was retaken, 1758, but again surrendered to colonel Coote, 10 Feb. 1760; besieged and taken by Hyder Ali, when the British under colonel Baillie suffered severe defeat, 31 Oct. 1780. Arcot has been subject to Great Britain since 1801; see *India*.

ARCTIC EXPEDITIONS, see *North West Passage*, and *Franklin's Expedition*.

ARDAGH, an ancient bishopric in Ireland, founded by St. Patrick, who is said to have made his nephew, Mell, the first bishop, 454. This see, held with Kilmore since 1742, was held *in commendam* with Tuam (*which see*). It was united with Kilmore in 1839, and with Elphin in 1841.

ARDAHAN, a town in Turkish Armenia, ceded to Russia by the Berlin treaty, 13 July, 1878.

ARDFERT AND AGHADOE, bishoprics in Ireland long united; the former was called the bishopric of Kerry; Ert presided in the 5th century; William Fuller, appointed in 1663, became bishop of Limerick in 1667, since when Ardfert and Aghadoe have been united to that prelacy. Near the cathedral an anchorite tower, 120 feet high, the loftiest and finest in the kingdom, suddenly fell, 1770.

AREIOPAGUS or **AREOPAGUS**, a Greek tribunal, said to have heard causes in the dark, because the judges should be blind to all but facts, instituted at Athens about 1507 B.C.; also ascribed to Cecrops, 1556. The name is derived from the Greek *Areios pagos*, the hill of Mars, through the tradition that Mars was the first who was tried there for the murder of Halirrhotius, who had violated his daughter Alcippe. The powers of this court were enlarged by Solon, about 594 B.C., and diminished by Pericles, 461 B.C. Paul preached on Mars' hill A.D. 52. (*Acts* xvii.) See *Press*.

AREOMETER or **ARÆOMETER** (from Greek *araios*, thin), an instrument for measuring the density and specific gravity of fluids. Baumé described his areometer in 1768. Others made by Nicholson and Mohr. Also called *Hydrometer*.

AREQUIPA, Peru, founded by Pizarro, 1539; was destroyed by an earthquake, 13 Aug. 1868; surrendered to the Chilians 26 Oct. 1883. The town is 7,850 ft. above the sea. Pop. 37,000. In the neighbourhood is the Harvard University high level Observatory (alt. 16,275 ft.); in 1903 under the charge of Prof. Barley. The Arequipa-Puno section of the Mollendo to Cuzco railway (completed in 1873 at a cost of over 5,000.000*l*.) is 218 miles long, and at its highest level is 14,466 ft. above the sea. Puno, pop. 7,000, is a town on the lake Titicaca; alt. 12,600 ft. Steamers ply 117 miles across this lake to Cuilaya, Bolivia

ARETHUSA, see *Naval Battles*, 1778, and *Chichester*.

AREZZO, near the ancient Arretium or Aretinum, an Etrurian city, which made peace with Rome for 30 years, 308 B.C., was besieged by the Galli Senones, about 283 B.C., who defeated the Roman army Metellus sent to its relief—a disgrace avenged signally by Dolabella. Arezzo was an ancient bishopric: the cathedral founded in 1277. It is renowned as the birthplace of Mæcenas, Petrarch, Vasari, and other eminent men. Michael Angelo was born in the vicinity.

ARGANDAB, a river in Afghanistan. See *Afghanistan*, 1880.

ARGAUM, in the Deccan, India, where sir Arthur Wellesley, on 29th Nov. 1803, thoroughly defeated and subjugated the rajah of Berar and the Mahratta chief Scindiah.

ARGENTARIA, Alsace (now COLMAR, N.E. France), where the Roman emperor Gratian totally defeated the Alemanni, and secured the peace of Gaul, May, 378.

ARGENTINE (or LA PLATA) **CONFEDERATION**, S. America, 14 provinces (Buenos Ayres, one). The city Buenos Ayres is the capital. This country was discovered by the Spaniards in 1515, settled by them in 1553, and formed part of the vice-royalty of Peru till 1778, when it became that of Rio de la Plata. It joined the insurrection in 1811, and became independent in 1816. It was at war with Brazil from 1826 to 1828, for the possession of Uruguay, which became independent as Monte-Video; and at war with France from 1838-40.—Population, in 1869, 1,877,490; 1887, 3,805,000; 1900, 4,794,149. See *Buenos Ayres*.

Buenos Ayres seceded in 1853; reunited . . . 1859
An insurrection in San Juan in Nov. 1860; suppressed in . . . . Jan. 1862
J. Urquiza, elected president, 20 Nov. 1853, was succeeded by Dr. S. Derqui . . . 8 Feb. 1860
Gen. Bartholomew Mitre, elected for six years, assumed the president's office . . . . 12 Oct. 1862
Lopez, president of Paraguay, declared war against Mitre, and invaded the Argentine territories, May. Mitre declared war against Paraguay, 16 April; and made alliance with Brazil and Uruguay . . . . 4 May, 1865
See *Buenos Ayres* for the disputes with that state, and *Brazil* for the war with *Paraguay*.
Col. Dominique F. Sarmiento elected president for six years . . . . 12 Oct. 1868
He suppresses the insurrection of Corrientes, Nov. „
Urquiza murdered . . . . . . 12 April, 1870
Treaty with Brazil . . . . . . Jan., 1873
Defeat of Lopez Jourdan, rebel, announced Dec. „
Dr. N. Avellaneda inaugurated president (for 6 years) 12 Oct. 1874
Insurrection of Mitre at Buenos Ayres, Sept.-Nov. suppressed; he submits . . . . 2 Dec. „
National bank stops; suspension of specie payments by government . . . . 16 May, 1876
End of rebellion; capture of Jourdan; announced 12 Dec. „
Disputes with Buenos Ayres; settled June-July, 1880
General Roca (opposed to supremacy of Buenos Ayres) nominated to become president in October, opposed by Dr. Tejedor . . June-July, „
General Roca becomes president . . . Oct. „
Tranquillity restored: Buenos Ayres to be definitive capital of the Republic . . . . 7 Dec. „
The Buenos Ayres Exhibition, under the patronage of the Government, opened . . 15 Feb. 1882
Dr. M. Juarez Celman, President . . 12 Oct. 1886
Negotiations for a loan fail; a panic on the Buenos Ayres bourse, 7 July; the president and chambers authorize the issue of notes to the amount of 100,000,000 dollars . 8—12 July, 1890
Dissensions in the army; arrest of officers; trials about 22 July,

Insurrection in Buenos Ayres, instigated by the Union Civica, headed by sen. Aleru, Romero, and Del Valle against president Celman and his ministry, charged with corruption; a provisional government proclaimed; the insurgents supported by troops and artillery and many civilians; the government supported by infantry, armed police and part of the navy; the city bombarded; severe fighting in the streets . . . . 26 July, 1890
The president retires, leaving Dr. Pellegrini, vice-president, in command; brief armistice; fighting resumed; the government troops under gen. Roca victorious; surrender of the insurgents, general amnesty (about 1,000 persons killed and much property destroyed) . . . . 28 July, „
Resignation of Dr. Celman demanded, he refuses, 30 July; financial chaos, bourse closed 31 July, „
Boastful manifesto of president Celman, 31 July; he is compelled to resign, 5 Aug.; succeeded by Carlos Pellegrini, 6 Aug.; new ministry, sen. Lopez, gen. Roca, and others; business resumed, great rejoicings . . . . 7—11 Aug. „
Great preparations against a dreaded attempt at a revolution . . . . . about 6 Oct. „
Commission to inquire into reported corruptions in government financial affairs appointed . Nov. „
Financial crisis at Buenos Ayres, several credit houses stop payment; successful intervention of the government . . . . 24 Nov. „
Re-organization of the finances, by a plan proposed by a committee in London (lord Rothschild and others) . . . . about 4 Dec. „
Cordova city flooded by the canal bursting its embankments, about 150 persons drowned, and many houses destroyed . . . . 21 Dec. „
Excitement on account of proposed tax on deposits in private banks . . . . . 15 Jan. 1891
The officers implicated in the late rebellion exiled about 19 Feb. „
A state of siege proclaimed in Buenos Ayres to check conspiracies . . . . . 20 Feb. „
Riots at Cordova; state of siege proclaimed, about 22 Feb. „
Financial panic, 4 March; business suspended by decree, 6—11 March; panic ended; a national loan for 100,000,000 dollars at 6 per cent., well taken up by the public . . 8 March, *et seq.* „
Banks re-opened . . . . . . 13 March, „
Arrival of gen. Mitre, warmly received, 18 March; he joins gen. Roca . . . . 24 March, „
The National and Provincial Banks suspend payment till 1 June by decree . . . 7 April, „
State of siege at Buenos Ayres raised, 17 April; the congress opened by president Pellegrini, with a hopeful message . . . . . 9 May, „
Run on the banks at Buenos Ayres, 2 June; panic abating through the firm conduct of the British residents . . . . . 4 June, „
The "Bank of the Argentine Nation" created by vote of the Senate . . . . 12 Aug. „
Forced paper currency, premium on gold to be 150 per cent. and payment in gold suspended for two years, authorized by the government to support the national bank, 30 Sept.; the scheme rejected by the senate, reported . . . 14 Oct. „
Ministerial crisis . . . . 16—23 Oct. „
Confidence in the ministry voted by the senate and deputies . . . . . . 20 Oct. „
Election riots with loss of life and state of siege at Cordova and Tucuman, reported . 27 Oct. „
Destructive tornado in Santa Fé, 10 persons killed middle Nov. „
The Bank of the Argentine Nation opened . 1 Dec. „
Baron Hirsch reports that the Jewish settlements in the republic are prospering . . . Jan. 1892
Disturbances at Mendoza; assassinations; government intervention . . . . 22—24 Jan. „
Elections for senate and deputies favour the party of Mitre and Roca . . . about 8 Feb. „
Attempt at revolution discovered; a state of siege proclaimed; the radical leaders arrested; military precautions adopted . . . 2, 3 April, „
Dr. Luiz Saenz-Peña elected president, about 12 June, „
State of siege raised . . . . . 7 July, „
The war-vessel, *Rosales*, founders off Uruguay, 9 July, „
Conspiracy of about 30 officers in the army, who confess their guilt when arrested, tried by court-martial . . . . . 22 Sept. *et seq.* 1892
President Dr. Saenz-Peña assumes office 12 Oct. „
Insurrection in the province of Santiago del Estero; the governor and his ministers prisoners, reported 19 Oct.; peace restored about 1 Nov. „
Insurrection in the province of Corrientes, about 24 Oct. 1892; again 25 Dec. 1892; conflicts with varying results; suppressed by gen. Avellaneda, reported . . . . 12 Jan. 1893
Insurrection in Catamarca . . . . March „
New ministry; Dr. Wenceslao Escalante, premier, reported 8 June; resigned 3 July; succeeded by sen. Lucio Lopez . . . 6 July, „
Radical insurrections in different provinces, reported 29 July; continued fighting, 31 July; the radicals enter La Plata; reported 10 Aug. „
New cabinet formed under sen. Manuel Quintana at Buenos Ayres . . . . 13 Aug. „
La Plata held by national troops; radicals expelled . . . . 15 Aug. „
Argentina placed in a state of siege . 17 Aug. „
The rebels enter Corrientes; the authorities retire, reported . . . . . . 21 Aug. „
The rebels defeat col. Acuna near Corrientes, reported . . . . . . 22 Aug. „
Revolt in Tucuman . . . . . 7 Sept. „
Rosario taken by the rebels, Dr. Alem head of the insurgents, 25 Sept.; retaken by the government 1 Oct. „
Rebels in Santa Fé defeated, reported . 28 Sept. „
Colonel Espina concerned in the insurrection, sentenced to 20 years' imprisonment, others exiled; Dr. Alem arrested, 2 Oct., released . 16 Dec. „
Insurrection ended . . . . . 11 Oct. „
State of siege in Buenos Ayres raised . 27 Feb. 1894
General state of financial embarrassment June, „
Extradition of Jabez Balfour, see *Building Societies*, 1893-95 . . . . . . Aug. „
Destructive earthquake in San Juan, with great loss of life . . . . . . 27 Oct. „
Destructive inundation in the province of Menduza, 20 lives lost, reported . . . . 9 Jan. 1895
The ministry resigns through the president's refusal to grant an amnesty to persons concerned in the late revolution . . . . 16 Jan. „
Resignation of pres. Saenz-Peña . . 22 Jan. „
Dr. J. E. Uriburu becomes president . 23 Jan. „
Amnesty bill passed and budget voted . 24 Jan. „
Congress opened, progress reported . 7 May, 1896
Flights of locusts in Buenos Ayres, reported 23 June, 1897
Large financial deficit; national debt, 62,000,000*l.*, July; national loan, 39,000,000 dollars, announced . . . . 10 May, 1898
Gen. Roca elected president, 12 June; forms a ministry . . . . . . 12 Oct. „
Bad administration of justice, inadequate protection of life and property, reported . . Nov. „
Congress opened, large deficit reported, 1 May, 1899
Destructive floods in the Rio Negro valley, early June, „
Meeting in Buenos Ayres, petition (50,000 signatures) for reforms, reduction of duties, &c. 28 June, „
Commission appointed to inquire into administration of justice . . . . . June, „
President Roca visits Brazil, returns to Buenos Ayres . . . . 22 Aug. „
Conversion bills (unpopular) passed . 29 Oct. „
Congress opened, general improvement reported, 1 May, 1900
Bill to check extraordinary expenditure, becomes law . . . . 28 Sept. „
Dr. Campos Salles, Brazilian president, visits Buenos Ayres, 24 Oct.; leaves . . 1 Nov. „
Boundary protocol with Chili signed . 27 Dec. „
Congress opened, deficit 40,000*l.* for 1900, 3 May, 1901
Agitation, with fatal rioting, against the unification of the Argentine debt, 3 July; bill withdrawn, finance minister resigns, 4, 5 July; state of siege ends . . . . . . 30 July, „
Bill imposing obligatory military service adopted by the chamber (56—21) . . . 21 Sept. „
Monument to gen. Urquiza unveiled at Parana, 18 Oct. „

Frontier dispute, relations with Chili strained, Dec.; closed; the question referred to arbitration of Great Britain, reported . . 26 Dec. 1901
Budget, good surplus for 1902; passed, 10 Jan. 1902
Mr. Wm. Barnett brutally murdered at Zuviria, in Cordoba, 26 April; Aug. Grau sentenced to 8 years' imprisonment . . . . . 28 Nov. „
Arbitration treaty and other agreements with Chili (*which see*) signed at Santiago, 28 May; ratified, 28 June and . . . . . 31 July, „
Budget: financial improvement, reported 8 Aug. „
Harbour works at Rosario opened . . 26 Oct. „
General strike. State of siege decreed in Buenos Ayres and Santa Fé . . . . 21–24 Nov. „
See *Chili*, 1898, and *Italy*, 1898

ARGINUSÆ, isles between Lesbos and Asia Minor; near these Conon and the Athenian fleet defeated the Spartan admiral Callicratidas, 406 B.C.

ARGON (from the Greek *a* and *ergon*), a new gas discovered by lord Rayleigh and prof. Ramsay, in their researches on Air, by different methods; remarkable for some of its physical properties and chemical inertness; see *Air*, 1894–5.

The subject was reported to the British Association at Oxford, Aug. 1894; to the Royal Society at the London University, 31 Jan. 1895, and in the Royal Institution, 5 April, 1895; and again . . 17 Jan. 1896
Lord Rayleigh received the Faraday medal of the Chemical Society . . . . . 27 March, 1895
The combination of argon with benzene and other organic compounds by means of the silent electric discharge, reported by M. Berthelot at Paris March, „
The Smithsonian institution, Washington, awarded the first Hodgkins prize of 10,000 dollars to lord Rayleigh and prof. William Ramsay for their discovery of argon . . . . . . Aug. „
The R. S. Davy medal presented to prof. W. Ramsay, 30 Nov.; the Lecomte prize of 50,000 francs awarded to prof. Ramsay and lord Rayleigh by the French Academy of Sciences . . 16 Dec. „

ARGONAUTIC EXPEDITION, dated by Hales 1225, by Clinton 1169, said to have been undertaken by Jason, to avenge the death of his kinsman Phryxus, and to recover the treasures seized by his murderer, Æëtes, king of Colchis. The ship in which Phryxus had sailed to Colchis having been adorned with the figure of a ram, led to the fiction that the journey was to recover the golden fleece. This is the first naval expedition on record. Many kings and heroes accompanied Jason, whose ship was called *Argo*, from its builder.

ARGONAUTS OF ST. NICHOLAS, military knights; an order founded by Charles III. of Naples, 1382.

ARGOS, the most ancient city of Greece, mythically said to have been founded either by Inachus or his son, Phoroneus, received its name from Argus, the fourth of the Inachidæ. The early history is fabulous.

Reign of Triopas; Polycaon seizes part of the kingdom and calls it after his wife, *Messenia* . 1552
Gelanor, last of the Inachidæ, deposed by Danaus, an Egyptian 1475
Feast of the *Flambeaux*, instituted in honour of Hypermnestra, who saved her husband, Lynceus, son of Ægyptus, on his nuptial night, while her forty-nine sisters sacrificed theirs, at the command of their father, Danaus 1425
Lynceus dethrones Danaus 1425
The kingdom divided by the brothers Acrisius and Prœtus . . . . . . 1344 (1313 *Clinton*.)
Perseus, grandson of Acrisius, leaves Argos and founds Mycenæ (*which see*) 1313
The Heraclidæ retake the Peloponnesus, and Temenus seizes Argos 1102
Pheidon's prosperous rule 770–730
War with Sparta: combat of 300 on each side . . 547
The Argives fine Sicyon and Ægina for helping their enemy, Cleomenes of Sparta . . . . . B.C. 514
Sparta becomes superior to Argos . . . 495–490
Themistocles an exile at Argos 471
The Argives destroy Mycenæ and regain their superiority 468
Peloponnesian war—Argos long neutral, joins Athens 420
The aristocratical party makes peace with Sparta, and overthrows the democracy 417
A reaction—alliance with Athens resumed . . . 395
Pyrrhus of Macedon besieging Argos, slain . . 272
Argos governed by tyrants supported by Macedon; freed; joins the Achæan league 229
Subjugated by the Romans 146
Argos taken from the Venetians . . . . A.D. 1686
Taken by the Turks 1716, who held it until . . 1826
United to Greece under king Otho (see *Greece*) 25 Jan. 1833
Excavations of the American School of Archæology under Dr. Charles Waldestein begun Feb. 1892 *et seq.*: ruins of the temple of Hera (or Juno) near Argos (destroyed in the middle ages); remains of cyclopean masonry, sculpture, &c., discovered; reported, 1894.

ARGUIN, battle of, see *Soudan*, 2 July, 1889.

ARGYLE (W. Scotland), bishopric of, founded about 1200, Evaldus being the first bishop; the diocese, previously united with Dunkeld, ended 1688. Argyle and the Isles is a post-revolution bishopric, 1847; see *Bishoprics*.

ARGYLL ROOMS, near Oxford-street, London, opened for musical and other entertainments early in the 19th century; re-erected by Nash, 1818; held by the Philharmonic Society, 1813-30. Here appeared Spohr, 1820; Weber, 3 April, 1826; and Mendelssohn, 25 May, 1829. While held by M. Chabert, the fire-king, the building was burnt down, 5, 6 Feb. 1830. The new building was eventually converted into shops.

The *Argyll Rooms* in Windmill-street obtained a very vile reputation. The *Trocadero* now occupies the site.

ARIAN or **ARYAN** (in Sanskrit signifying noble, warlike), a term applied to the Indo-Germanic nations, including the Greek, Latin, Scandinavian, Keltic, and Teutonic races, the western branch; and the Persian, Armenian, Northern Hindu races, the eastern branch.

ARIANS, followers of Arius* of Alexandria, who preached against the doctrine of the Trinity, about 315, and died in 336. The controversy was taken up by Constantine, who presided at the council of Nice, June to Aug. 325, when the Arians were condemned; but their doctrine long prevailed. It was favoured by Constantius II. 341; and carried into Africa by the Vandals in the 5th century, and into Asia by the Goths. Servetus published his treatise against the Trinity, 1531, and was burnt, 1553. Leggatt, an Arian, was burnt at Smithfield in 1614; see *Athanasian Creed*, *Socinians*, and *Unitarians*.

ARICA, Peru, destroyed by an earthquake, and inundated by waves of the sea, 13 Aug. 1868.

ARIKERA, near Seringapatam. Here lord Cornwallis defeated Tippoo Sahib, 15 May, 1791.

ARISTOTELIAN PHILOSOPHY: the most comprehensive ever devised by man. Aristotle was born at Stageira (hence termed the Stageirite), 384 B.C.; was a pupil of Plato from 364 to 347; became preceptor of Alexander, son of Philip of Macedon, in 342; and died in 322. He divided the

* Arius maintained that the Son of God was a secondary God created by the Father, who raised Him far above all men, and consequently not equal with the Father.

circle of knowledge into metaphysics and logic, physics (including part of the science of mind), and ethics. His philosophy was too much exalted by the schoolmen during the middle ages, and too much depreciated after the Reformation. His works on natural science contain a vast collection of facts and an extraordinary mixture of sound and chimerical opinions. To him is attributed the assertion that nature abhors a vacuum, an opinion now maintained by eminent modern philosophers.

An *Aristotelian Society*, for the systematic study of philosophy, was founded in the spring of 1880; Dr. Shadworth H. Hodgson, president.

M. Barthélemy St. Hilaire's complete translation of Aristotle, 35 vols., published early in 1891.

A papyrus containing the lost treatise of Aristotle on the "Constitution of Athens," discovered in Egypt and conveyed to the British Museum, was published by the trustees, with a preface and notes by Mr. F. G. Kenyon, Jan.; and photographs of the MS. were published March, 1891; prof. J. E. Sandys's elaborate edition, Jan. 1893. The work was hitherto only known by extracts in ancient writers. The MS. was considered genuine by M. Barthélemy St. Hilaire, March, 1891.

A family tomb, discovered at Eretria, in the island of Eubœa, by Dr. Charles Waldstein, early in 1891, was considered by him to be really that of Aristotle and his family.

ARITHMETIC is said to have been introduced from Egypt into Greece by Thales, about 600 B.C. The Chinese used the abacus, or *swanpan*, at an early period. It is asserted that the ancient Hindus adopted a system having ten as a basis.

The oldest treatise upon arithmetic is by Euclid (7th, 8th, and 9th books of his *Elements*), about B.C. 300

The sexagesimal arithmetic of Ptolemy was used A.D. 130

Diophantus, of Alexandria, was the author of thirteen books of arithmetical questions (of which six are now extant) . . . . . about 156

Notation by nine digits and zero (*Arabic figures*), known at least as early as the 6th century in Hindostan—introduced from thence into Arabia, about 900—into Spain, about 980—into France, by Gerbert, soon after—into England, probably in 14th or 15th century.

The date in Caxton's *Mirrour of the World*, Arabic characters, is 1480

Arithmetic of decimals invented 1482

John Sherwood, bishop of Durham's *Ludus Arithmo-Machinæ*, printed at Rome . . . . ,,

First work printed in England on arithmetic (*de Arte Supputandi*) was by Tonstall, bishop of Durham 1522

The theory of decimal fractions perfected by Napier in his *Rhabdologia* 1617

Cocker's Arithmetic appeared in 1677

Nystrom's Tonal system with 16 as a basis, published 1862

Sawyer's "Automatic System," published . . 1878

ARITHMOMETER, see *Calculating Machines*.

ARIZONA, a territory of the United States, originally part of New Mexico, was organised 24 Feb. 1863; capital, Tucson. It was colonised by the Jesuits in the 17th century. Population, 1880, 40,440; 1890, 59,620; 1900, 122,931.

By the bursting of the great dams at Prescott, Seymore and other mining villages were destroyed by the great rush of water and about 70 persons are said to have perished, 22 Feb. 1890.

Yuma nearly destroyed by floods; about 100 lives lost, 1,400 homeless, reported 2 March, 1891.

The town of Jerome burnt down, 11 deaths, 12 Sept. 1898.

ARK. Mount Ararat (*which see*) is venerated from a belief of its being the place on which Noah's Ark rested, after the universal deluge, 2348 B.C.; see *Gen.* vi. vii. Some assert Apamea, in Phrygia, to be the spot; and medals have been struck there with a chest on the waters, and the letters NOE, and two doves; this place is 300 miles west of Ararat. The *Ark of the Covenant*, made by Moses to contain the two tables of the law, 1491 B.C. (*Exod.* xxv.), was placed in Solomon's temple, 1004 B.C. (1 *Kings* viii.). The Babylonian ark, *papakhu*, derived from the *ma*, or ship of the pre-Semitic Sumerians, furnished with a mast, oar and rudder, bears a close parallel to the Israelitish ark. Hibbert lecture 1887, by professor Sayce.

ARKANSAS, originally part of Louisiana, ceded by Spain to France, 1763; and purchased by the United States in 1803, was made a territory, 1819; and a state, 1836; seceded from the union 6 May, 1861; re-admitted, 1868. Several battles were fought in this state in 1862. Capital, Little Rock. Population, 1890, 1,128,179; 1900, 1,311,564.

Cherokee Strip, a reserve, opened to settlers, many arrive; towns planned . . . . . 16 Sept. 1893

Little Rock partially destroyed by a cyclone, 8 deaths . . . . 3 Oct. 1894

Great fire at Hot Springs, 5 lives lost, 28 houses burnt . . . . 22 Feb. 1895

Tornado at Fort Smith city, buildings destroyed by fire, 31 deaths . . . . . 12 Jan. 1898

ARKLOW (in Wicklow), where a battle was fought between the insurgent Irish, amounting to 31,000, and a small regular force of British, which signally defeated them, 10 June, 1798. The town was nearly destroyed by the insurgents in May previous.—Native gold was discovered in Arklow, in Sept. 1795. *Phil. Trans.* vol. 86.

ARLBERG, see under *Tunnels*.

ARLES (Arelatum, from the Celtic *Ar-lait*, near the waters), S. France (said to have been founded 2000 B.C.), a powerful Roman city, was made capital of the kingdom of Provence by Boson in 879 A.D.; and of the kingdom of Arles or Transjurane Burgundy by Rodolph II. in 933. He was succeeded by Conrad I. 937; and by Rodolph III. 993; who in 1032, transmitted his kingdom to the emperor Conrad II. After various changes it was annexed to France in 1486. Many councils (314-1275) were held at Arles; the most celebrated in 314, when British bishops were present.

ARMADA, THE INVINCIBLE, collected and equipped by Philip II. king of Spain, for the subjugation of England. Morant's historical account (accompanying Pine's engravings of the tapestries formerly in the house of lords) was printed 1739.

It consisted of 130 ships (besides caravels), 3165 cannon, 8050 sailors, 2088 galley-slaves, 18,973 soldiers, 1382 volunteers (noblemen, gentlemen, and their attendants), and 150 monks, with Martin Alarco, vicar of the Inquisition,—the whole under the command of the duke of Medina-Sidonia . 1587

The English fleet 80 *vessels* under lord Charles Howard, sir Francis Drake, and sir John Hawkins, ready for sea, and three armies on land. Dec. ,,

The Armada sailed from Lisbon; soon after dispersed by a storm . . . . . 19 May, 1588

Re-collected, entered the Channel off Cornwall, 19 July, ,,

Suffered in a series of engagements (the sharpest on 25 July) . . . . . 21-27 July, ,,

Dispersed by fire-ships sent into the midst, 28 July, ,,

Many vessels sunk or taken by the English, 29 July, ,,

The remainder retreat northward to Spain, suffering much loss by severe storms, Aug. and Sept. ,,

Computed Spanish loss—35 ships; 13,000 men.

The queen attended a most solemn thanksgiving at St. Paul's . . . . 24 Nov. ,,

An annual thanksgiving sermon was endowed by Mr. Chapman, who died 1616; it was preached at St. Mary-le-Bow . . . . 12 Aug. 1877
Tercentenary at Plymouth celebrated with exhibitions, &c., 18 July, 1888; National memorial founded . . . . 19 July, 1888
Fund established at the Mansion House . 3 May, „
Relics exhibited at Drury Lane Theatre 24 Oct. „
"The Spanish Armada," a play at Drury Lane Theatre; first performance . . . 22 Sept. „
A bronze statue of Britannia, set up at Plymouth Hoe as a National Memorial of the defeat of the Armada, was unveiled by the duke of Edinburgh on behalf of the queen . . . 21 Oct. 1890
"The Spanish story of the Armada," by Mr. J. A. Froude, published 1892

ARMAGH, N. Ireland, of which it was the metropolis from the 5th to the 9th century, the seat of the first ecclesiastical dignity in Ireland, said to have been founded by St. Patrick, its first bishop, about 444, and said to have built the first cathedral, 450. Six saints of the Roman calendar have been bishops of this see. Until lately the value was estimated at 15,000*l.* per annum. The see was re-constituted (see *Pallium*) in 1151. *Beatson.* Armagh was ravaged by the Danes on Easter-day, 852, and by O'Neil in 1564. See *Railway Accidents*, 12 June, 1889. Population, 1871, 8,946; 1881, 10,070; 1891, 7,800; 1901, 7,569. Great fire, shops and buildings destroyed, damage 80,000*l*, 25 Jan. 1903. Robert Bent Knox, abp., primate, 1886; died, aged 85, 23 Oct., 1893, succeeded by R. S. Gregg, bp. of Cork, elected, 14 Dec. 1893; died, aged 61, 10 Jan. 1896; William Alexander, bp. of Derry, elected, 25 Feb. 1896. Michael Card. Logue, R.C. abp., 1879.

ARMAGNACS, a political party in France, followers of the duke of Orleans, murdered by the Burgundians, 23 Nov. 1407, derived their name from his father-in-law, the count of Armagnac. About 3500 of this party were massacred at Paris in June, 1418, by their opponents, the followers of the duke of Burgundy.

ARMED NEUTRALITY, the confederacy against England, formed by Russia, Sweden, and Denmark, 1780; ended, 1781; renewed, and a treaty ratified in order to cause their flags to be respected by the belligerent powers, 16 Dec. 1800. The principle that neutral flags protect neutral bottoms being contrary to the maritime system of England, the British cabinet remonstrated, war ensued, and Nelson and Parker destroyed the fleet of Denmark before Copenhagen, 2 April, 1801. This event and the murder of the emperor Paul of Russia led to the dissolution of the Armed Neutrality.

ARMENIA, Asia Minor, after forming part of the Assyrian, Median, and Persian empires, became subject to the Greek kings of Syria, after the defeat of Antiochus the Great, 190 B.C. The Romans established the kingdoms of Armenia Major and Minor, but their influence over them was frequently interrupted by the aggressions of the Parthians. In all their political troubles the Armenians have maintained the profession of Christianity, and their church is governed by patriarchs, not subject to Rome. Since 1715 an Armenian convent has existed at Venice, where books on all subjects are printed in the Armenian language.

City of Artaxarta built . . . . . . B.C. 186
Antiochus Epiphanes invades Armenia . . . 165
Tigranes the Great reigns in Armenia Major . . 95
Becomes King of Syria, and assumes the title of "King of Kings" 83
Defeated by Lucullus, 69; he lays his crown at the feet of Pompey 66
His son, Artavasdes, reigns, 54; he assists Pompey against Julius Cæsar, 48; and the Parthians against Marc Antony
Antony subdues, and sends him loaded with silver chains to Egypt 36
Artaxias, his son, made king by the Parthians . . 34
Deposed by the Romans, who enthrone Tigranes II. 33
Armenia subjected to Parthia . . . . . A.D. 20
Reconquered by Germanicus, grandson of Augustus 15
After many changes Tiridates is made king by the Romans 18
The Parthian conquerors of Armenia are expelled by Trajan 58
Severus makes Volagarses king of part of Armenia . 115
Christianity introduced, between . . . A.D. 100-300 199
Armenia added to the Persian empire 232
Tiridates obtains the throne through Diocletian, 286; is expelled by Narses, 294; restored by Galerius 298
On his death, Armenia becomes subject to Persia, 342; is made neutral by Rome and Persia, 384; who divide it by treaty 443
Armenia conquered and reconquered by the Greek and Persian sovereigns 577-687
And by the Greek emperors and Mahometans 693-1065
The Armenian church reconciled to Rome, about . 1330
Leon VI., last king of Armenia, taken prisoner by the Saracens, 1375; released: he dies at Paris . 1393
Overrun by the Mongols, 1235; by Timour, 1383; by the Turks, 1516; by the Persians, 1534; by the Turks 1583
Shah Abbas, of Persia, surrenders Armenia to the Turks, but transports 22,000 Armenian families into his own states 1604
Armenia overrun by the Russians 1828
Surrender of Erzeroum . . . . . 9 July, 1829
(See *Syria* and *Russo-Turkish Wars* I. and II.)
By the Berlin treaty, Kars, Ardahan, and Batoum were ceded to Russia, with other changes July, 1878
The Turkish government charged with oppression and cruelty, Aug.; doubted by some . Sept. 1889
Moussa Bey, a Kurdish chief, tried at Constantinople for alleged cruelties, 23 Nov.; acquitted (a new trial refused), 2 Dec. *et seq.* 1889; eventually exiled to Medina . . . . . Sept. Oct. 1890
Riotous conflicts between Armenians and Mussulmans at Erzeroum, 9 persons killed, reported 27 June, „
The Armenians in Constantinople attack their patriarch, Achikian, in a church during service, riot suppressed by the military with loss of life, 27 July; many arrested Aug., and punished, Oct.; the patriarch resigns, 31 July; the chief rioter sentenced to death, others to imprisonment 16 Aug. „
The sultan agrees to many reforms in Armenia, reported . . . . 20 Aug. „
Armed band of Armenians on the Turco-Russian frontier dispersed by the Turks and Russians, reported . . . . 2 Nov.
Friendly negotiations with the Porte; loyal address to the sultan, and gracious reply; the patriarch withdraws his resignation . . . . 28 Dec. „
He is received by the sultan, who announces a general amnesty, with great release of prisoners 17 Jan. *et seq.* 1891
The central committee for reforms, issue a proclamation against the Turkish government, about 25 Jan. „
Death of Abp. Chorène Nar Bey Lusignan, a descendant of the house of Lusignan of Cyprus, an eminent preacher and writer, 18 Nov. 1892, succeeded by Mgr. Khrimian, Dec. 1892, anointed supreme patriarch . . . . . . 8 Oct. 1893
Annual meeting of the Anglo-Armenian Association in London . . . . 6 Jan. „
Seventeen Christians, as alleged revolutionists, condemned to death at Angora; appeal, 20 June, 1893; alleged unfair trial, fresh arrests, 26 June; appeal; British intervention; sentences of death confirmed in 5 cases; other cases, various degrees of imprisonment, exile, and hard labour, reported, 28 July, 1893; investigation, some sentences remitted; 170 prisoners released, reported . 10 Sept. 1894
Sanguinary conflict between the Armenians and Turks at Yuzgat, 2 Feb.; foreign intervention reported, 1 March; attempted assassination of the

Armenian patriarch by discontented Armenians, 25 March; he resigns his office . 12 April, 1894
The Armenians impoverished by frequent raids of the Kurds in the districts of Sasun, Bitlis, Mush, &c., are unable to pay the government taxes, and are consequently subjected to great cruelty and oppression, 1892-4 [*Times*, 29, 30 March, 13, 15 April, 1895] . . . . ,,
Markar, an Armenian teacher who had been to report their wrongs at Constantinople, hanged at Bitlis . . . . . 8 Feb. ,,
Ten days' conflict between the Kurds aided by the Turkish troops and the Armenians in the Shadak district; 41 Armenians, who had surrendered on promise of an amnesty, massacred by order end of June, ,,
Massacre of a great number of fugitives on Mount Andoke, 32 villages burnt and the inhabitants killed by the Kurds and Turkish troops 25 Aug. *et seq.* ,,
British remonstrance; investigations ordered by the Sultan, Nov.; a commission of inquiry consisting of delegates of Great Britain, France, and Russia, appointed . . . . Dec. ,,
Mgr. Izmirlian elected patriarch, Dec.; enthroned at Kum-Kapu, 8 Jan.; received by the sultan Jan. 1895
The foreign commission holds its first meeting at Mush . . . . . . Jan. ,,
Protocols of the first 12 sittings, issued . 2 March, ,,
Over 2,500 political prisoners reported . 8 March, ,,
Conflict between Mahometans and Christians at Tokat, 5 persons killed . . . 20 March, ,,
Several ecclesiastical prisoners at Constantinople released and sent to Armenia, reported 15 April–May, ,,
Sir Philip Currie reports to the Porte the cruelty and oppression to the Armenians and the imminent danger, if redress and thorough reforms are not granted; favourable promises given . 19 April, ,,
A commission appointed by the sultan to consider a scheme for reforms in Armenia, first meeting in Constantinople . . . . . 23 April,
Great meeting in St. James's hall, London, respecting the atrocities, the duke of Argyll and the duke of Westminster presiding . . 7 May, ,,
Zeki Pasha, Turkish commander of the troops, concerned in the massacres; recalled . 8 May, ,,
Scheme of Armenian reform drawn up by the British, French, and Russian ambassadors presented to the sultan; terms: appointment of a high commissioner, general amnesty and release of prisoners, political reforms, abolition of torture, &c., about . . . . 11 May ,,
The commissioners visit the scene of the atrocities of Aug. 1894, in the Sasun district, pass through ruined villages and discover two pits in which were buried wholesale the victims of the soldiery, reported . . . . . 13 May, ,,
Great European meeting at Paris on behalf of the Armenians . . . . . 25 May, ,,
The foreign delegates insulted by the Turkish police at Mush, end of May; satisfaction granted by the Porte . . . . . 2 June, ,,
Famine in the Sasun district, June; 2,000*l.* sent from England . . . . . July, ,,
Amnesty to political prisoners, many released July, ,,
Renewed conflicts between the Mahometans and the Armenians, oppression and extortion of Turkish officials, reported . . . 27 Sept. ,,
Terrible massacres of Armenians at Baiburt, 1,000 killed, 13 Oct.; Erzingjan, 1,000, 21 Oct.; Bitlis, 900, 25 Oct.; Diarbekr, 2,500, 25 Oct.; Harpoot, 1,000, 11 Nov.; Sivas, 1,200, 12 Nov.; Marash, 1,000, 18 Nov.; Gurun, 3,000, 10 Nov.; Arabkir, 2,000, 6 Nov.; Cesarea, 1,000, 30 Nov.; and many killed at other places
The sultan's decree approving the Armenian reform scheme promulgated; no results . . 20 Oct. ,,
The reform scheme forwarded to Shakir pasha, high commissioner for Armenia, with instructions for action . . . . . abt. 22 Oct. ,,
The Porte in a circular declares the Armenians to be the aggressors . . . . . 20 Oct. ,,
Turkish troops surrounded at Zeitun surrender to the Armenians . . . . . . 11 Nov. ,,
Estimated loss (10,000,000*l.*) of the Armenians during the late events in Asia Minor; 40,000 deaths, reported . . . . . 25 Nov. 1895
Six judicial inspectors appointed for the Asiatic provinces, and three for the European, announced 26 Nov. ,,
Massacres and atrocities by the Hamidieh cavalry in the province of Van; reported . . 28 Nov. ,,
The U.S. minister demands redress for destruction of missions, &c., at Marash, reported . 5 Dec. ,,
Great distress in six districts, reported . 9 Dec. ,,
The Armenian patriarch reports to the sultan details of the massacres and destructions in the provinces, reported . . . . . 19 Dec. ,,
Total sum, 13,000*l.*, collected in Great Britain remitted by the duke of Westminster . 26 Dec. ,,
[3,000*l.* received from Liverpool, Manchester and Leeds, 11 Feb. 1896.]
Continued barbarities in Sivas, Biredjik, &c., reported . . . . . . 23 Dec. ,,
Summary of massacres from 30 Sept.—30 Nov. given in *Times*. . . . . . 30 Dec. ,,
[Two blue books published, Jan. 1896.]
Massacre at Orfah, 28, 29 Oct; a state of siege for 2 months; final massacre, about 8,000 killed; the cathedral burnt, and about 3,000 men, women and children perished, 126 families utterly wiped out (*Times*, 19 May, 1896) . . . 28, 29 Dec. ,,
Mediation of the consuls at Aleppo accepted, hostilities suspended at Zeitun . . . 3 Jan. 1896
A decree for strengthening the army, issued 4 Jan. ,,
The Board of Control for Reforms declared by the foreign embassies to be inefficient . 18 Jan. ,,
Refugees at Zeitun (14,000) invited to return to their villages under the supervision of the foreign consuls . . . . . . 14 Feb. ,,
The marquis of Salisbury and sir Philip Currie appeal to the Armenian relief committee, London, for help, 22 Feb.; 50,000*l.* distributed by sir Philip Currie, reported . . . 22 June, ,,
Rioting at Adana, 15 Armenians killed . 23 Feb. ,,
The massacre of 15 Armenian families reported from Mush . . . . . . 1 March, ,,
Resolution of the house of commons expressing deep sympathy with the Armenians . 3 March, ,,
180,000*f.* collected in Paris for Armenian sufferers, announced . . . . . 1 April, ,,
Disturbances at Van, reported, 19 June; renewed conflicts, 400 killed; many refugees at the British consulate . . . . . 22 June ,,
Forced resignation of the Mgr. Izmirlian, 4 Aug.; Mgr. Bartolomeos installed as *locum tenens* 11 Aug. ,,
Massacre of Armenians by Kurds and Turks at Egin, vilayet of Kharput, about 2,000 killed, houses pillaged and burnt . . 15-17 Sept. ,,
10 Armenians killed at Angora; outrages in other villages, and 60 Armenians killed . 18-19 Sept. ,,
Slaughter at Kaiserieh, Ghemerek and Kharput, houses pillaged and burnt, reported, 24 Sept.; at Everek and Feiresse . . . . . Oct. ,,
Five Christian governors appointed in various districts, announced . . . . 28 Oct. ,,
Armenian refugees settled in Greece and Bulgaria Nov. ,,
Eniz pasha, vali of Diarbekr, concerned in the late massacres, dismissed . . . . 7 Nov. ,,
Execution of reforms ordered . . . 11 Nov. ,,
Mgr. Malachias Ormanian, bishop of Armash, elected patriarch . . . . . 18 Nov. ,,
"Armenian Cave," see *Liberals*, Dec. 1896.
Sir Philip Currie appeals for 11,000*l.* to the foreign office for destitute Armenians, 30 Dec. 1896; 2,000*l.* sent 28 Jan.; again . . . Feb. 1897
40,000 Armenian emigrants settled in S. Russia, relief sent from Moscow and Astrakhan, many children perish; reported . . . 22 Jan. ,,
Massacre of 100 Armenians, houses sacked at Tokat, 19, 20 March; the embassies demand redress, and send consuls to attend the Turkish commission of inquiry, under Hassan Fehmi pasha, reported, 27 March; 9 Mahometans sentenced to death, commuted to penal servitude for life, 23 Aug.; disturbances in Adana and other provinces, reported . . . . 21 March, ,,
Concessions granted to the Armenians by iradé 30 March, ,,

Fresh petition for the execution of reforms; presented by the patriarch to the porte; reported 6 May, 1897
A commission appointed by the sultan to raise subscriptions for rebuilding schools, churches, &c., destroyed during the disturbances . Oct. ,,
The patriarch receives 1,000*l*T. from the Porte for distressed Armenians, and 10 prisoners released; reported . . . . 19 Oct. ,,
Mr. Waugh, British vice-consul, distributes 1,850*l*. in Diarbekr, in 9 months, ending 31 March, 1898
Fatal conflicts between Turks and Armenians in Van district . . . . . . Sept. ,,
Great distress round Van, many deaths, the Porte prohibits relief . . . . . . Feb. 1899
An iradé granting certain reforms (54 Armenian prisoners pardoned and 24 death sentences commuted to life imprisonment) issued 11 Oct. ,,
Massacre at Spaghank, in Sasun, by Turks and Kurds, villages burnt . . . . 16 July ,,
Ali pasha, governor of Bitlis, dismissed 26 Aug. 1900
Kurdish raids in Mush and Van; terrible distress reported . . . . 20 Oct. ,,
Council of the Patriarchate suspends sittings owing to the Porte's persistent disregard of petitions . . . . Nov. ,,
Kurdish outrages in Mush and Sasun districts, over 100 Armenians killed . . early Sept. 1901
The patriarch resigns as a protest against the Porte, 2 Aug., but resumed his duties on the repeal of oppressive laws by iradé issued . 31 Aug. 1902
State of siege at Mush and Sasun . . 26 Sept. ,,
Earthquake in Van vilayet, Melazgard and other villages totally destroyed, 860 deaths, many cattle and sheep killed . . . 29 April, 1903

See *Turkey*, 1895, 1896 *et seq.*

ARMENIAN ERA, commenced on 9 July, 552; the ecclesiastical year on 11 Aug. To reduce this last to our time, add 551 years and 221 days; and in leap years subtract one day from 1 March to 10 Aug. The Armenians used the old Julian style and months in their correspondence with Europeans.

ARMILLARY SPHERE, an astronomical instrument composed of brass circles disposed in such a manner that the greater and lesser circles of the sphere may be seen in their natural position and motion. It is said to have been invented by Eratosthenes, about 255 B.C.; and was employed by Tycho Brahe and others.

ARMINIANS, or **REMONSTRANTS**, derive their former name from James Arminius (or Harmensen), a Protestant divine of Leyden, Holland (died 19 Oct. 1609); the latter name from his followers having presented a *Remonstrance* to the states-general in 1610. They separated from the Calvinists, objecting to their views respecting predestination, &c. Their doctrines were condemned in 1619, at the synod of Dort (*which see*); they were exiled till 1625. The Calvinists were sometimes styled *Gomarists*, from Gomar, the chief opponent to Arminius. James I. and Charles I. favoured the Arminian doctrine.

ARMORIAL BEARINGS became hereditary in families at the close of the 12th century. They were employed by the crusaders, 1100. The lines to denote colours in arms, by their direction or intersection, were invented by Columbière in 1639. The armorial bearings of the English sovereigns are given under the article *England*. Armorial bearings were taxed in 1798, and again in 1808. The tax produced 64,515*l*. in the year ending 31 March, 1868; 1872, 64,228*l*.; 1876, 83,527*l*.; 1878, 83,104*l*.; 1879, 81,854*l*.; 1881, 79,014*l*.; 1882, 79,196*l*.; 1901-2. 74,703*l*. The tax is now 2*l*. 2*s*.; if not on carriages, it is 1*l*. 1*s*. annually (1903). Sir Bernard Burke's "General Armory," 1883, contains the arms of above 66,000 British families, &c. Sir Roper Lethbridge, in his "Golden Book of India," describes the early armorial bearings of the Indian princes, especially the Rajputs, 1893.

ARMORICA, now Brittany, N. France, was conquered by Julius Cæsar, 56 B.C. Many Gauls are said to have retired there and preserved the Celtic tongue, A.D. 584. A colony of West Britons settled in Armorica in the latter part of the 4th century, hence the modern name Brittany, *which see*.

ARMOUR. That of Goliath is described (about 1063 B.C.) 1 *Sam.* xvii. 5. Skins and padded hides were early used, and brass and iron armour, in plates or scales, followed. The body armour of the Britons was skins of wild beasts, exchanged, after the Roman conquest, for the well-tanned leathern cuirass. *Tacitus.* Hengist is said to have had scale armour, A.D. 449.

The Norman armour formed breeches and jacket . 1066
The hauberk had its hood of the same piece . . 1100
John wore a surtout over a hauberk of rings set edgeways 1199
The heavy cavalry covered with a coat of mail. Some horsemen had vizors and skull-caps, about. 1216
Armour exceedingly splendid, about 1350
Black armour, used not only for battle, but for mourning, Henry V. 1413
Armour of Henry VII. consisted of a cuirass of steel, in the form of a pair of stays, about . . 1500
Armour ceased to reach below the knees, Charles I. 1625
In the reign of Charles II. officers wore no other armour than a large gorget, which is commemorated in the diminutive ornament known at the present day. *Meyrick.*
The Zschille armour sold at Christie, Manson, and Woods, 862 lots, realised 11,257*l*. 11*s*. . 1 Feb. 1897

ARMOUR PLATES, see *Iron*, and *Navy of England*.

ARMS. The club was the first offensive weapon; then followed the mace, battle-axe, pike, spear, javelin, sword and dagger, bows and arrows. Pliny ascribes the invention of the sling to the Phœnicians; see *Cannon, Firearms, Swords, Bayonets, and other articles on the various weapons throughout the volume.*

Committee to enquire into the arms (swords and bayonets) supplied by the War Office to the Admiralty since 1871 appointed (Sir Hussey Vivian chairman) . . . . . 14 Feb. *et seq.* 1887
Report these weapons to be badly designed and manufactured and untrustworthy . 29 March, ,,

ARMS, see *Armorial bearings*, and *Heraldry*.

ARMS BILLS, for the repression of crime and insurrection in Ireland, were passed 1807, 1810, 1823, 1829, and 15 Oct. 1831. The guns registered under the last act at the close of the first year scarcely amounted to 3000, and the number was equally small of all other kinds of arms. The new Arms bill, passed 22 Aug. 1843, has been since renewed, but was not rigidly enforced till 1867. Another Arms bill brought into the Commons, "An act to amend the law relating to the carrying and possession of arms, and for the preservation of public peace in Ireland," to last till 1 June, 1886; Royal Assent, 21 March, 1881. Act renewed till 31 Dec. 1887, 4 June, 1886. See *Ireland*.

Exportation of arms act, royal assent . 6 Aug. 1901

ARMSTRONG GUN, see under *Cannon*.

ARMY. Ninus and Semiramis had armies amounting to nearly two millions of fighting men. *Diodorus.* The first guards and regular troops as a standing army were formed by Saul, 1093 B.C. 1 *Sam.* xiii. 2. The army of Xerxes invading Greece is said to have been 1,700,000 foot and 80,000 horse:

480 B.C. One of the first standing armies of which we have any account, is that of Philip of Macedon. The army which Darius opposed to Alexander the Great (332 B.C.) is set down as between 750,000 and a million. The first standing army which existed as such, in modern times, was maintained in France by Charles VII. in 1445. The chief European nations have had in their service the following armies: Spain, 150,000 men; Great Britain, 310,000; Prussia, 350,000; Turkey, 450,000; Austria, 500,000; Russia, 560,000; and France, 1,000,000. Estimated number in Europe in 1863, 6,000,000 soldiers, 1,000,000 horses, 11,000 guns. The European powers are still increasing their armies. Estimated to consist of 12,000,000 men in Nov. 1888.

January, 1902—	Germany	3,036,000
,, ,,	France	3,500,000
,, ,,	Russia	3,975,500
,, ,,	Great Britain	808,752

ARMY, British, mainly arose in the reign of Charles II. in 1661, in consequence of the extinction of feudal tenures. The first five regiments of British infantry were established between 1633 and 1680. James II. established several regiments of dragoon guards (1685-8). In 1685 the army consisted of 7000 foot and 1700 cavalry. The Militia then consisted of about 130,000 men, horse and foot. *Standing armies* were introduced by Charles I. in 1638; they were declared illegal in England, 31 Car. II. 1679; but one was then gradually forming, which was maintained by William III. 1689, when the Mutiny Act was passed. Grose's "History of the British Army" was published in 1801. See *Regiments*, *Recruiting*, *Militia*, and *Volunteers*.

BRITISH ARMY.

	Men.	Sum voted.
1780, Time of war: troops of the line	110,000	£7,847,000
1800, War	168,082	17,973,000
1810, War: army including foreign troops	300,000	26,748,000
1815, Last year of the war	300,000	39,150,000
1820, Time of peace; war incumbrances	88,100	18,253,000
1830, Peace	89,300	6,991,000
1840, Peace	93,471	6,890,267
1850, Peace	99,118	6,763,488
1852, Peace (except Kaffir war)	101,937	7,018,104
1854, War with Russia	112,977	7,387,000

	Total men.	In India* men.	Sum voted (including ordnance, &c.)
1855-6,† War with Russia.	223,224	29,629	£32,006,603
1856-57, War with Persia.	265,466	26,363	20,811,242
1857-58, Indian Mutiny	175,858	30,197	14,405,850
1858-59	222,874	92,739	13,294,814
1859-60, Chinese War	229,551	91,897	14,915,243
1860-61	228,854	71,528	18,013,896
1861-62	212,773	60,041	16,854,299
1862-63	228,973	83,523	16,264,790
1863-64	220,918	72,676	14,723,976
1864-65	219,450	72,684	14,382,672
1865-66	213,521	71,044	14,569,279
1866-67	203,404	65,827	14,675,540
1867-68, Abyssinian War	204,455	65,292	15,418,582
1868-69	203,157	64,466	15,000,000
1869-70	191,073	63,907	13,565,400
1870-71, Franco-German War	178,000	62,963	13,430,400
1871-72	197,911	62,864	15,521,580
1872-73	196,606	62,957	14,729,700
1873-74	187,928	62,924	14,426,990
1874-75	224,835	62,840	14,591,434
1875-76	225,931	62,850	
1876-77	132,884	62,849	15,281,600
1877-78	133,720	62,652	15,919,492
1879-80	135,625	—	13,019,900
1880-81	131,859	62,588	12,707,000

* Supported by the Indian government.
† Ending March 31.

1899—1902. South African Boer Republics War and China, total cost 165,034,000*l.*

Total home and colonial establishments, 632,649; *cost*, 16,641,300*l.*

Expended by army purchase commission:—

1871-2	£340,000
1872-3	683,500
1873-4	713,974
1874-5	579,115

Regular troops for home service:—

	1853	1875	1902
Cavalry	7,606	12,945	12,900
Artillery	8,710	18,853	31,623
Engineers	1,039	4,074	7,811
Infantry	53,651	63,371	104,141
	71,006	99,243	154,465

	Average strength of the army.	Cost.
1879	191,290	*£16,945,153
1880	188,986	15,025,145
1881	188,798	14,680,762
1882	189,229	15,738,002
1883	181,971	15,133,451
1884	183,004	16,095,326
1885	198,064	18,600,338
1886	203,805	17,027,084
1887	209,574	18,429,272
1888	211,105	18,167,196
1888–9	211,105	16,700,300
1889–90	210,298	17,384,732
1890–1	209,221	17,897,900
1891–2	209,699	17,545,300
1892–3	213,540	17,541,700
1893–4	217,279	17,939,700
1894–5	219,121	17,899,800
1896 (31 Dec.)	220,869	18,459,800
1897 (31 Dec.)	219,283	18,269,800
1898	225,027	23,724,599
1899	238,739	46,817,333
1900	383,037	†95,309,153
1901	414,917	†96,781,539

Volunteers in Great Britain, in 1862, 167,921; in 1872, 172,891; in 1875, 181,080; in 1878, 193,026, (with staff) 245,648; 1879, 206,265; 1880, 206,537; 1881, 208,308; 1882, 207,336; 1883, 206,365; 1884, 215,015; 1885, 224,012; 1886, 226,752; 1887, 228,038; 1890, 221,048; 1893, 227,741; 1898, 230,678; 1899, 229,854; 1900, 277,628; 1902, 277,396.

Militia, 1872, 139,018; 1879, 127,749; 1880, 130,331; 1881,‡ 99,002; 1882,§ 92,094; 1883, 116,642; 1884, 113,787; 1885, 119,356; 1886, 122,428; 1887, 121,411; 1890, 113,163; 1893, 124,692; 1897, 117,773; 1898, 105,531; 1899, 109,551; 1900, 96,232.

Yeomanry, 1872, 15,455; 1879, 12,010; 1880, 11,598; 1881, 10,617; 1882, 11,173; 1883, 11,204; 1884, 11,488; 1885, 11,590; 1886, 11,499; 1887, 11,267; 1890, 10,697; 1893, 10,400; 1897, 10,184; 1898, 10,207; 1899, 10,114; 1900, 10,157; 1901, 11,907; 1902, 17,407.

Recruits of all classes in 1902, 50,753. See *Recruiting*.

Army Reserves, 1 Jan. 1869, 17,948; 1874, 31,046; 1879, 37,512; 1881, 41,796; 1882,‡ 34,636; 1883,§ 26,203; 1885, 47,024; 1887, 52,553; 1888, 55,200; 1892, 68,933; 1893, 76,874; 1897, 78,182; 1898, 82,005; 1899, 24,159; 1900, 5,275; 1902, nominally 80,000, actual number only 2,398.

Men voted, 1901-2, ordinary services, 219,800, war, 230,000; 1902-3, ordinary services, 219,700, war, 200,300; 1903–4, ordinary services, 221,561, temporary (due to war) 14,200.

The Mutiny Act passed annually since 1689; alterations made in this act and in the Articles of War. (*See below*, 1879.) . . . 1855

Army Service Acts: 12 & 13 Vict. c. 37 (21 June, 1847), and 18 Vict. c. 4 . . . 27 Feb. ,,

Officers in the service of the East India Company to have the same rank and precedence as those in the regular army . . . 25 April, ,,

The office of Master-General of the Ordnance abolished, and the civil administration of the Army and Ordnance vested in the hands of lord Panmure, the Minister of War . . . 25 May, ,,

* Extra on account of Russo-Turkish war. † Extra on account of South African war. ‡ Exclusive of Irish. § Exclusive of army pensioners.

Examination of staff officers previous to their appointment ordered . . . . . 9 April, 1857
The army largely recruited for Indian war . . 1857-8
Examination of candidates for the Military Academy, previously confined to pupils from Sandhurst, was thrown open, 1855; the principle of this measure was affirmed by the house of commons by vote . . . . . 26 April, 1858
The East India Company's army was transferred to the Queen 1859
Much dissatisfaction arose in that army in consequence of no bounty being granted; and threatenings of mutiny appeared, which subsided after an arrangement was made granting discharge to those who desired it . . . . ,,
By 22 & 23 Vict. c. 42, provision made for a reserve force, not to exceed 20,000 men, who had been in her majesty's service . . . . . . ,,
Flogging virtually abolished in the army: First class soldiers to be degraded to second class before being liable to it . . . . 9 Nov. ,,
A report of a commission in 1858 causes great sanitary improvements in the army, barracks, &c., under direction of Mr. Sidney Herbert . 1859-60
A commission recommend the establishment of a recruiting department, increase of pensions, &c. 31 Oct. 1866
Flogging restricted to insubordination (with violence) and indecency . . . . March (?) 1867
New Army Enlistment Act (limiting period of enlistment to 12 years, &c.) passed . 20 June, ,,
Increased pay to all soldiers (except to life-guards) from 1 April, 1867; by warrant, dated . 29 June, ,,
Act to form a reserve of men in the militia to join the army in the event of war, passed . 20 Aug. ,,
"War Department Stores" Act passed . 20 Aug. ,,
Sir Hy. Storks appointed controller-in-chief, 1 Jan. 1868
Flogging abolished in time of peace, by an amendment in the Mutiny Act . . . . Mar. ,,
Edward Cardwell, secretary for war . . 9 Dec. ,,
Royal commission on military education appointed, 23 June, 1868; report with recommendations issued about . . . . Oct. 1869
Army Service Corps, to be composed of volunteers commanded by regular officers, established by royal warrant . . . . 12 Nov. ,,
Royal commission on the purchase system, &c., appointed 5 April; report recognises the "over regulation payments" hitherto ignored . Aug. 1870
Regulations under the new "Army Enlistment Act" issued . . . . . . 12 Aug. ,,
2,000,000*l.* voted to increase the army by 20,000 men . . . . 1 Aug. ,,
Deaths in the army reduced from 17 per 1000 to 9½, in consequence of sanitary improvements, &c., (out of 175,460 men, 33,797 under 20, 18,614 under 19); *Lord Northbrook* . . . . . June, 1871
Army Regulation bill (the abolition of the purchase system, &c.) passed in the commons, 289-231, early 4 July; introduced in the lords, 13 July; able speech of the duke of Cambridge in its favour, 14 July; rejected (155-130), 2 a.m., 18 July, ,,
Purchase system abolished by royal warrant (in pursuance of acts 5 & 6 Edw. VI. c. 16, and 49 Geo. III. c. 126) on and after 1 Nov. 1871, 20 July, ,,
Regulation of the Forces Act passed . . 17 Aug. ,,
Autumn Campaign in Hampshire; about 40,000 men engaged; the duke of Cambridge and others umpires; the prince of Wales and prince Arthur engaged; foreign officers present . . . ,,
Manœuvres according to the Prussian system; field days, &c. . . . . . . 8-12 Sept.
Invading force of 24,000, under Staveley and Carey; marching towards London, opposed by sir Hope Grant . . . . 13 Sept. ,,
Series of battles near the Hog's Back, Aldershot; Grant declared victor . . . . . 16-19 Sept. ,,
Battle of Fox's-hill; Carey defeats Staveley, 21 Sept. ,,
[*Reported results:* artillery magnificent; cavalry superb; infantry very good; transport insufficient; greater distribution of responsibility among officers needed.]
Sham fight; Chatham stormed . . . . 24 Oct. ,,
Warrant published, 30 Oct., inaugurating the new system of promotion of officers (partly by seniority and partly by selection) on . . . 1 Nov. ,,
New organisation of the army proposed by Mr. Cardwell: brigade districts, England, 49; Scotland, 8; Ireland 8 = 65 . . . . . Feb. 1872
The duke of Cambridge's favourable report was laid before parliament early in . . March, ,,
Army estimates passed in commons (234-63) 12 Mar.
Review of 14,000 men by the queen at Aldershot, 5 July, ,,
Autumn Manœuvres in Wiltshire: 50,000 men commanded by sir John Mitchell supposed to land at Weymouth, and march towards London, opposed by sir R. Walpole; campaign begins; skirmishes near Blandford . . . . . . 21 Aug. ,,
Sir A. Horsford repulses gen. Brownrigg at Winchampton . . . . 27 Aug. ,,
Prince of Wales arrives at Salisbury . . 3 Sept. ,,
Battle of Wishford, 7 Sept.; battle of the Avon, 10 Sept.; grand march past near Beacon Hill 12 Sept. ,,
The new drill and tactics for the army were published . . . . 23 Nov. ,,
Mr. Cardwell's estimates; proposes increasing pay of soldiers; and establishment of a chief of the staff . . . . 24 Feb. 1873
The Military Intelligence Department established 1 April, ,,
Review of troops at Windsor, before the Shah, 24 June, ,,
Autumn Manœuvres at Dartmoor, Cannock Chase, and at the Curragh, Dublin . . July, Aug. ,,
Royal Commission on compensation to officers for changes; appointed . . . . . 11 Oct. ,,
Report issued (admits cause for compensation; and considers that officers will be satisfied with whatever the nation chooses to decide for them) June, 1874
Change of ministry; Mr. Gathorne Hardy (afterwards Lord Cranbrook), secretary for war 21 Feb. ,,
The victorious troops from Ashantee reviewed by the queen . . . . 30 March, ,,
Summer Manœuvres at Aldershot . . June, ,,
New regulations respecting first applications for commissions; issued . . . . . Sept. ,,
Royal commission on more rapid promotion; gazetted . . . . 10 Nov. ,,
Manœuvres at Aldershot . . . . . July, 1875
Royal warrant respecting regimental exchanges, dated 6 Aug.; issued . . . . 9 Aug. ,,
Scheme completed for mobilisation of the army, announced . . . . Dec. ,,
"*Control*" *Department* divided into "commissariat and transport departments," and "ordnance store departments" . . . . . 11 Dec. ,,
Mobilisation of the army and the reserve; experiment in Surrey reported successful . . July, 1876
New cavalry regulations issued . . . Aug. ,,
Report of commission on promotion issued; recommends compulsory retirement in some cases, and other changes . . . . Aug. ,,
New organisation of artillery proposed about 26 Feb. 1877
Manœuvres on a small scale . . . . July, ,,
Review by the queen at Windsor . . 10 July, ,,
Army promotion and retiring scheme: royal warrant published . . . . . . 28 July, ,,
New army medical warrant issued . . 1 Sept. ,,
About 20,000 recruits in 1877; announced Mar. 1878
Col. F. A. Stanley, war secretary . . 2 April, ,,
Reserves (about 35,000) called out, 2 April; commended; disbanded . . . . . 31 July
The report of the commission on the mutiny acts recommends consolidation of the mutiny acts and the articles of war, and simplification of martial law, &c. . . . . July, ,,
Warrant establishing new warrant officers ("conductors") a grade between commissioned and non-commissioned . . . . 24 Jan. 1879
Army Discipline and Regulation Acts, introduced 27 Feb.; passed . . . . . . 24 July, ,,
[They relate to discipline, enlistment, billeting, court-martials, military law, &c.]
Army Medical Department; changes made by a new warrant issued 2 Dec. 1879; amended Jan. 1880
Mr. Hugh E. Childers, war secretary, 28 April, ,,
New system of Military Examination for officers; introduced . . . . Oct. ,,
Alterations in officers' dress, by orders . Nov. ,,
System of compulsory retirement of officers came into operation . . . . 1 Jan. 1881
Great army reform measures laid before the Commons by Mr. Childers . . . 3 March, ,,

Alterations made in the uniform and organisation of the infantry . . April *et seq.* 1881
New organisation comes into effect . . 1 July, „
Regulation of the Forces and the Army Discipline Act (amending the Acts of 1879) passed 27 Aug. „
See *Flogging*.
Army Act amended . . . . . 28 April, 1882
Reserves called out (for Egypt) . . . 25 July, „
Success of the changes in the army system demonstrated by the Egyptian campaign; within 7 weeks a large well appointed army was conveyed 3000 miles under most unfavourable conditions and achieved the object of the expedition July—Sept. „
Review of the return troops and Indian contingent by the queen in St. James's Park. 18 Nov. „
Queen's thanks published 21 Nov.; she distributes medals, &c., at Windsor . . . . 21 Nov. „
Formation of an Army Telegraph Corps ordered, Feb. 1883
Army Medical Service: system, &c., censured by report of lord Morley's committee . . May, „
Great increase of recruits; above 33,000 in 1883.
Report of committee on colour of uniform recommending change of red to grey, July, 1882: issued 29 March „
Effective strength of the army reported 1 Dec. 1884, 188,216; about 35,000 added . . . April, 1885
Order prohibiting officers and soldiers from publishing military information in the press, &c. 1 April, 1886
Training of boys between 14 and 17; formation of battalions, &c., sanctioned . . . June, „
Committee to inquire into the organization and administration of the manufacturing departments of the army appointed; announced . 23 June, „
Suspension of compulsory retirement of officers, Aug. „
Summary court-martial abolished by statute, 29 April, „
A force of all arms fully equipped as for war marches at Aldershot . . . . . . 17 Aug. „
Royal ordnance commission on military stores appointed (sir J. F. Stephen, sir A. Alison, Dr. Percy and others) about 16 Sept.; first sat, 16 Nov. 1886; they report the system to be bad and inefficient; results bad, guns and weapons faulty; charge of corruption not proved; the commissioners recommend revival of the office of Master of Ordnance with council, &c. May, 1887.
Changes in discipline made; courts-martial to be much discontinued; summary powers given to officers 1 Jan. 1887.
Including the yeomanry, the general total of the army, first class army reserve, and auxiliary forces, 577,740 in 1886; 595,159 . . . in 1887
Reorganization of the War Office, civil and military, announced in the Commons 8 Sept. 1887; new arrangement announced . . . . . Feb. 1888
Royal commission on Naval and Military Administration (*which see*); lord Hartington, chairman, appointed . . . . 7 June, „
Diminution of severity leads to less crime and irregularities; reported . . . . Oct. „
Warrant for removal of undesirable officers . 3 Jan. 1889
[Alterations made after complaints, Jan. 1890]
New arrangements of the military district proposed to be effected in April . . . . . Jan. „
Increased vote 5,004,500*l.* for 152,282 men 12 March, „
Total estimate for 1889–90 17,335,900*l.* . March, „
First report, containing various recommendations with evidence, issued . . . . 20 March, 1890
Military exhibition (*which see*) opened . 7 May, „
The Jubilee offering of the army presented to the queen at Buckingham palace by the duke of Cambridge (see *Jubilee*) . . . 10 May, „
Insubordination of some of the 2nd Battalion Grenadier Guards at Wellington barracks, S.W., 7 July; court martial on 6 of the oldest privates; sentenced to imprisonment with hard labour (1 man to 2 years and dismissal with ignominy; 3 men, 2 years; 2 men, 18 months), 18–21 July, [released, 24 Nov.]. Colonel Maitland superseded. The battalion, under col. Eaton, sent to Bermuda 23 July, „
[Highly commended there, return to England 28 July, 1891.]
Viscount Wolseley, adjutant general (1882, *et seq.*), succeeded by sir Redvers Buller . . 1 Oct. „
The duke of Connaught appointed commander of the southern military district . . Aug. „
Army manœuvres near Petersfield, Hants 10 Sept. 1891
Report of lord Wantage's committee on service in the army (appointed April, 1891), issued Feb., evidence April, much discussed . . May, 1892
See *Barracks*.
Manœuvres (regulars and volunteers) in Surrey, Hants, and Berks; battles, &c., commanders, sir Evelyn Wood and others . 18 July–20 Aug. „
Mr. Henry Campbell-Bannerman appointed secretary for war . . . . . . 18 Aug. „
"The Army Book for the British Empire" first published 1893
Manœuvres, Berks, Hants, and Wilts 29 Aug.–15 Sept. „
New order respecting the employment of troops in civil disorders . . . . . 2 March, 1895
Army estimates, 1895–6, 17,983,100*l.* . 7 March, „
Changes in the war office (*which see*) announced 21 June „
Army manœuvres in Surrey and Hants, under the duke of Connaught and lord Methuen . Aug. „
Army order issued by the duke of Cambridge on retiring from the command-in-chief . 31 Oct. „
Order issued by visct. Wolseley on assuming the chief command . . . . . . 1 Nov. „
New order in council issued defining the duties of the principal officers of the army, the commander-in-chief and others . . . 21 Nov. „
Army net estimates, 1896–7, 18,056,600*l.* 5 March, 1896
Six regiments ordered to South Africa end of April, „
Army manœuvres at Aldershot, &c. . 28 Aug. „
Aggregate military expenditure has advanced from about 25½ millions to 46½ during the last 30 years; reported . . . . 4 Jan. 1897
William Anderson, made K.C.B., Jan. 1897, died, 11 Dec. 1898. See *Cordite*, 1895.
Army: 76 battalions abroad, 65 at home, proposed addition of 2 battalions of Guards, making a total of nine; announced . . . . 4 Feb. „
Army net estimates, 1897–8, 18,340,500*l.* . May, „
Army manœuvres at Aldershot . 16–25 Aug. „
Army net estimates, 1898–9, 19,220,500*l.*, net increase, 880,000*l.*; proposed increase of men, 25,083 (exclusive of India).—*Times* . . 21 Feb. 1898
Army manœuvres on Salisbury plain, July, Aug. Sept. „
Sir Harry Brackenbury appointed director-gen. of ordnance; Col. Bainbridge, chief superintendent of ordnance factories . . . . . Feb. 1899
The army largely recruited for S. African war Oct. *et seq.* „
Reserves called out (for S. Africa) . 7 Oct. 1899-1900
Army net estimates, 1899-1900, 20,978,200*l.*, 21 Feb. 1890, supplementary votes reached a gross grant of 46,817,333*l.* for year ended . . 31 March 1900
Supplementary estimate of 13,000,000*l.*, and 120,000 men, voted for S. African war . . 16 Jan. „
The queen orders the shamrock to be worn on St. Patrick's day in honour of her "brave Irish" 7 March „
Army estimates; 430,000 men provided till Sept. 8 March „
Commissions in the army offered to Australians.—*Times*. . . . . . . 22 March „
"Irish Guards" formed by the queen's orders, in honour of their bravery in S. Africa . 5 April „
Electoral disabilities (military service) act passed Aug. „
Lord Roberts of Kandahar appointed to succeed lord Wolseley . . . . . 30 Sept. „
The hon. St. John Brodrick, secretary for war, 12 Nov. „
Lord Wolseley active in army reforms, such as selection by merit, short service; retires from command-in-chief. . . . . . 30 Nov. „
Total estimates for 1900-1, 91,999,400*l.*; supplementary estimates, 16,000,000*l.*, voted 11 Dec. „
Supplementary war loan (No. 2) passed 15 Dec. „
Army order: war gratuity to troops, issued, 8 Dec. „
Reorganisation of the War office, *which see* Dec. „
Army order for the formation of the new "Royal Garrison regiment" issued . . . 23 Feb. 1901
Army estimate for 1901-2, 87,915,000*l.* issued, 1 March „
Mr. Brodrick's scheme raising the forces from 563,000 to 680,000 men, and dividing them into 6 army corps (to be commanded in peace by the men who would command them in war) proposed 8 March „
Army gross expenditure, 96,242,833*l.* . 31 March „

Reorganisation of the Yeomanry (to be styled "Imperial") by order issued . . 18 April 1901
Committee appointed to consider the reorganisation of the army medical services, Mr. Brodrick (*chairman*); report issued . . . 30 Sept. ,,
Regulations respecting War office administration (more control given to the commander-in-chief) issued . . . . 5 Nov. ,,
Additional drafts of Imperial Yeomanry and militia ordered; 6 battalions volunteer to serve outside the kingdom . . . . 4 Feb. 1902
Army estimates: total, 1901-2, 92,915,000*l.*, 450,000 men; 1902-3, 69,310,000*l.*, 420,000 men; 219,700 men for ordinary service, 200,300 men for war service; soldiers' pay increased; issued 15 Feb. ,,
Spion Kop dispatches issued, on account of controversy relating to the operations in Natal, Jan. 1900.—*Times* . . . . . . 18 April, ,,
Military lands provisional order (No. 1) act, royal assent . . . . 28 April ,,
Military education committee issue their report; Sandhurst system and existing methods condemned; new syllabus drawn up . 7 June ,,
Army order, special gratuity to the troops for service since 31 Dec., 1901; issued . . 9 June ,,
Army estimates: 1902-03, 39,650,000*l.* (28,000,000*l.* to be spent), issued . . . . . 10 June ,,
Major C. W. Studdert and others charged with breach of contract as to the purchase of horses for S. Africa; case closed by a settlement, Dublin. See *Ireland*, 4 Dec. 1902 . 1 July, 1902
Royal commission (lords Elgin, Esher, sir H. W. Norman, adm. sir J. Hopkins, and others) appointed to inquire into the military preparations and conduct of the S. African war up to the occupation of Pretoria . . . . . Sept. ,,
Committee of inquiry into the administration of remount department, reports favourably. *Times*, 10 Oct. ,,
Grenadier guards "ragging" case . about 10 Feb. 1903
Army estimates, 1903-4. 34,500,000*l.*, 235,761 men, 221,561 (ordinary services), issued . 5 March, ,,
War blanket scandal . . . . about 20 May ,,
Royal Commission on South African War issues its report: see *South African War* . 25 Aug. ,,

ARMY (ANNUAL) ACT, see *Mutiny Act*.

ARMY OF OCCUPATION. By treaty, signed 20 Nov. 1815, the allied powers established the boundaries of France, and occupied certain fortresses for three years.—Franco-Prussian War, 1870-1. The departure of the German army of occupation began about 20 Sept. 1871; completed 16 Sept. 1873.

ARNOLDISTS, followers of Arnold of Brescia, who protested against the corruptions of the Papacy, and who was burnt alive by pope Adrian IV. 1155.

AROGEE, Abyssinia. Here sir Robert (afterwards lord) Napier defeated the Abyssinians, who lost about 700 killed and wounded, 10 April, 1868. The British had 20 wounded.

ARPAD DYNASTY, see *Hungary*.

ARPINUM (now Arpino, S. Italy), the birth-place of Cicero, 3 Jan. 106 B.C.; many remains still bear his name.

ARQUEBUS, see *Fire Arms*.

ARQUES (N. France). Near here the league army, commanded by the duc de Mayenne, was defeated by Henry IV. 21 Sept. 1589.

ARRACAN, a province of N.E. India. Arracan, the capital, captured by the Burmese, 1783, was taken from them by general Morrison, 1 April, 1825. The subjugation of the province followed, 1826.

ARRAIGNMENT consists in reading the indictment by the officer of the court, and calling upon the prisoner to say whether he is guilty or not guilty. He must not be in fetters, unless it be made necessary by apprehended violence. Before the question is answered, all legal exceptions or objections are to be stated. If he fails, or refuses to plead, a jury is sworn to determine, if he is mute of malice or by visitation of God, whether he is able to plead and understand the course of his trial, whether he is insane. If the prisoner is found to be insane, so as to be unfit to plead, the court orders his detention during his Majesty's pleasure, otherwise the court directs entry of a plea of not guilty and the clerk proceeds to call and swear the jury. On a plea of guilty, the court proceeds to judgment. A previous conviction must not be mentioned on arraignment. Formerly, persons who refused to plead in cases of felony were pressed to death by weights placed upon the breast. A person standing mute was declared convicted by an act passed 1772; but in 1827, the court was directed to enter a plea of "not guilty" in such cases; see *Mute*.

ARRAS (N. E. France), the country of the ancient Atrebates, the seat of a bishop since 390. Here a treaty was concluded between the king of France and duke of Burgundy, when the latter abandoned his alliance with England, 21 Sept. 1435. Another treaty was concluded by Maximilian of Austria with Louis XI. of France, whereby Burgundy and Artois were given to the dauphin as a marriage portion, 23 Dec. 1482. *Velly*. Arras was held by the Austrians from 1493 till 1640, when it was taken by Louis XIII.

ARRAY. On 23 Dec. 1324, Edward II. directed the bishop of Durham to make "arraier" his men of arms, horse and foot, and cause them to proceed to Portsmouth; thence to proceed to the war in Gascony. *Rymer's Fœdera*. Hallam says that this was the earliest commission of array that he could find, and that the latest was dated 1557. The attempt of Charles I. to revive commissions of array in 1642, founded on a statute of Henry IV., was strenuously opposed as illegal.

ARREARS OF RENT ACT, Ireland, May, 1882; 45 & 46 Vict. c. 47, passed 18 Aug. 1882.

ARREST FOR DEBT. The persons of peers, members of parliament, &c., are protected from arrest; see *Ambassadors*, *Debt*, *Ferrars' Arrest*.

Clergyman performing divine service privileged, 50 Edw. III. 1375
Seamen privileged from debts under 20*l.*, by 30 Geo. III. 1756
Barristers are privileged from arrest while going to, attending upon, and returning from court, on the business of their clients.
By stat. 29 Car. II. no arrest can be made, nor process served, upon a Sunday; this law was extended by Will. III.
Vexatious arrests prevented by act, May, 1733. Prohibited for less than 10*l.* on process, 1779; and for less than 20*l.* . . . . July, 1827
Arrests for less than 10*l.* were prohibited on mesne process in Ireland, in June 1829
Statute abolishing arrest for debt on mesne process, except in cases wherein there is ground to show that the defendant designs to leave the country, 2 Vict. . . . . Aug. 1838
By 7 & 8 Vict. c. 96, the power of imprisonment even upon final process, that is judgment debts, is abolished if the sum does not exceed 20*l.* exclusive of costs, 1844; and by 9 & 10 Vict. c. 95, the judge has no power to punish, except in case of fraud or contempt of court 1846
By the Absconding Debtors' Arrest Act, absconding debtors owing 20*l.* and upwards are liable to arrest 1851
By 32 & 33 Vict. c. 62, and 33 & 34 Vict. c. 76. Arrests of persons on civil process is abolished, except in cases of contempt of court, of fraudulent debtors, or debtors who are about to go

abroad, or absent themselves to avoid proceedings in bankruptcy 1869–70

(See *Debt.*)

ARSACIDÆ, a Parthian dynasty, began with Arsaces about 250 B.C., and ended with Artabanus, killed in battle with Artaxerxes, the founder of the Sassanidæ, A.D. 226.

ARSENIANS, partisans of Arsenius, patriarch of Constantinople, who excommunicated the emperor Michael Palæologus for blinding his colleague the young John Lascaris, 1261, and was deposed 1264.

ARSENIC, a steel-grey coloured brittle mineral, extremely poisonous, known in early times. Brandt, in 1733, made the first accurate experiments on its chemical nature. The heinous crimes committed by its means induced the legislature to enact regulations for its sale, 1851. In 1858 Dr. A. S. Taylor asserted that green paper-hangings and dresses prepared from arsenic are injurious to health.

Much illness and many deaths in Manchester and Liverpool and district due to arsenic (Oct.-Nov.) found in certain kinds of beer, and finally traced back to glucose and invert sugar made from impure sulphuric acid, containing arsenic; enormous quantities of contaminated beer destroyed; see *Times*, 20 Dec. 1900; royal commission (lord Kelvin and others) appointed, Feb. 1901; first report, preventive measures recommended, 24 July, 1901; meeting held to consider the outbreak of arsenical poisoning at Halifax (Dec. 1901), 11 April, 1902.

ARSON, punished with death by the Saxons still remained a capital crime on the consolidation of the laws in 1827 and 1837. By the act of 1861 it is punishable by penal servitude for life and minor degrees of imprisonment. William Anthony was convicted of arson, having set many houses on fire, for the sake of obtaining the reward for giving alarm, 13 Dec. 1871. There were many incendiary fires in Kent, Suffolk, and other counties in 1830; about 14 at Farthinghoe, in S. Northamptonshire, Aug., Sept., 1896, further fires 11 Oct., 14 Jan., 1897.

Convicted of arson in England and Wales in 1887–8, 315; 1888–9, 402.

Wm. Nash was convicted of murder for setting fire to his house at Notting-hill, and causing six deaths, 30 May; sentenced to death (but reprieved) 3, 4 Aug. 1881

Léon Serné sentenced to twenty years' penal servitude for arson, 274 Strand (property over-insured; his two boys burnt) . . . . 21 Jan. 1888

Conspiracy to defraud insurance companies by arson: George Cullmer sentenced to 12 years, — Trew and Mrs. Wheeler to 5 years' penal servitude . . . 16 Feb. 1891

William Parsons sentenced to 20 years' penal servitude for arson near Dorchester . . 18 Feb. ,,

Alfred W. Walsh sentenced to 7 years' penal servitude for setting fire to his house . 29 March, 1895

Elizabeth Ann Rowse sentenced to 4 years' penal servitude for arson at Bath . . . 4 Nov. ,,

Henri and Marie Schaar sentenced to 7 years' penal servitude for arson at Edmonton . . 29 Oct. 1896

George Barber sentenced to 5 years' penal servitude for arson at Pangbourne . . 8 Nov. 1897

Edward Peters, 22, sentenced to 3 years' penal servitude for arson, in London . . 15 Jan. 1898

Arthur Collinson (16) sentenced to 4 years' imprisonment for arson in Lambeth . . 24 Nov. ,,

Charles Price (27) pleaded guilty to setting fire to a shed in the Victoria Docks, sentenced to 5 years' imprisonment . . . 19 Dec. 1901

(See *Fires* and *Trials.*)

ARSOUF (Syria). At a battle here Richard I. of England, commanding the Christian forces, reduced to 30,000, defeated Saladin's army of 300,000 Saracens and other infidels, on 6 Sept. 1191. Ascalon surrendered, and Richard marched towards Jerusalem, 1192.

ART ACT, facilitating the public exhibition of works of art (lent to the president of the privy council), passed April, 1866. See *Arts, Exhibitions*, and *National Portrait Gallery*.

ARTEMISIUM, a promontory in Eubœa, near which indecisive conflicts took place between the Greek and Persian fleets for three days; 480 B.C. The former retired on hearing of the battle of Thermopylæ.

ARTESIAN WELLS (from *Artesia*, now Artois, in France, where they frequently occur) are formed by boring through the upper soil to strata containing water which has percolated from a higher level, and which rises to that level through the boring tube. The fountains in Trafalgar-square and government offices near have been supplied since 1844 by two of these wells (393 feet deep). At Paris the Grenelle well (1798 feet deep), was completed in 1841, after eight years of exertion, by M. Mulot at an expense of about 12,000*l.*; and the well at Passy, which it is said will supply sufficient water for nearly 500,000 persons, was begun in 1855, and completed in 1860 by M. Kind. Messrs. Amos and Easton completed an Artesian well for the Horticultural Society's garden in 1862, which yielded 880,000 gallons of water, at the temperature of 81° Fahr., in twenty-four hours. The well at Kissingen was completed in 1850. Artesian wells are now common. Many London breweries, clubs, printing offices have deep wells; these need lowering from time to time as their number increases. That at the Reform Club is 345 feet in depth. Artesian wells, some 4,000 feet in depth, are much used for irrigation purposes in W. Australia.

ARTHUR, king of Britain, said, mythically, to have lived A.D. 500—532.

The events of his life and the conflicts of the knights of his round table, as sung by the Welsh poets Taliesin, Llywarch Hên, and Aneurin, were incorporated into his Latin history by Geoffrey of Monmouth, about 1115, who died 1154; put into French verse by Geoffrey Gaisnar, and by Wace soon after; and set forth in an English poem called Brut by Layamon, about . 1205

Walter Map by incorporating in his version the legend of the Holy Graal, introduced the religious element about 1171

Sir Thomas Malory's "Morte d'Arthur," printed by Wm. Caxton 1485

Lord Lytton's "King Arthur," published . . . 1848

Tennyson's "Idylls of the King" 1859–69

ARTICHOKES are said to have been introduced from the East into Western Europe in the 15th cent. and to have reached England in the 16th.

ARTICLES OF RELIGION. On 8 June, 1536, after much disputing, the English clergy in convocation published "Articles decreed by the king's highness" Henry VIII., who published in 1539 the "Statute of Six Articles," decreeing the acknowledgment of transubstantiation, communion in one kind, vows of chastity, private masses, celibacy of the clergy, and auricular confession. Offenders were punishable as heretics. In 1551 forty-two were prepared, and published in 1553. These were modified by the convocation, and reduced to THIRTY-NINE in Jan. 1563; and they received the royal authority and the authority of parliament in 1571. The *Lambeth Articles*, of a more Calvinistic character, proposed by archbishop Whitgift, were withdrawn in consequence of the displeasure of queen Elizabeth, 1595. One hundred and four Articles were drawn up for Ireland by archbishop Usher in 1614; but in 1635 the Irish church adopted the English articles. See *Perth Articles*. The 39

Articles were ordered to be removed from the studies at Oxford in Nov. 1871.

ARTICLES OF WAR were decreed in the time of Richard I. and John. Those made by Richard II. in 1385 appear in "Grose's Military Antiquities." The articles of war now in force are based upon an act, passed by William III. in 1689, to regulate the army about to engage in his continental warfare.

ARTIFICERS AND MANUFACTURERS. Their affairs were severely regulated by the statutes of labourers, 1349, 1350, 1360, 1549, and especially of 1562. They were prohibited from leaving England, and those abroad were outlawed, if they did not return within six months after the notice given them. A fine of 100*l*., and imprisonment for three months, were the penalties for seducing them from these realms, by 9 Geo. II. (1736) and other statutes. The law was modified in 1824; see *Artisans, Workmen*, &c.

ARTILLERY, a term including properly all missiles, now restricted to *cannon*. A small piece was contrived by Schwartz, a German cordelier, soon after the invention of gunpowder, in 1330. Artillery was used, it is said, by the Moors of Algesiras, in Spain, in 1343; and according to some historians, at the battle of Crecy, in 1346, when Edward III. had four pieces of cannon. We had artillery at the siege of Calais, 1347. The Venetians employed artillery against the Genoese at sea, 1377. *Voltaire*. Said to have been cast, with mortars for bomb-shells, by Flemish artists, in Sussex, 1543. *Rymer's Fœdera*. Made of brass 1635; improvements by Browne, 1728; see *Cannon, Bombs, Carronades* (under *Carron*), *Mortars, Howitzers, Petard, Rockets, Fire-arms*. "Artillery: its Progress and Present Position," by E. W. Lloyd and A. G. Hadcock, published, Aug. 1894. The *Royal Artillery-regiment* was established in the reign of Anne. See *Archery*.

HONOURABLE ARTILLERY COMPANY of London.—The company incorporated by Henry VIII. for military exercise and better defence of the realm, with special privileges, 25 Aug. 1537. Obtained lease of the Tessell ground, Bishopsgate, from the last prior of the convent of St. Mary, Spittle, for thrice 99 years—afterwards known as the old artillery ground, 3 Jan. 1540. Obtained lease of the "new" artillery ground, Finsbury, their present head-quarters, 1641. In the civil war, 1642-8, the company, as a body, took no part, but most of the officers of the Trained Bands were also members of the company. James, duke of York, afterwards James II., appointed captain-general, 1660. The company ordered to take precedence next after the regular forces, 1 June, 1883. The company numbered 1200 in 1803 and 800 in 1861. Since 1842 the officers have been appointed by the queen. On the decease of the duke of Sussex in 1843, the prince consort became captain-general and colonel. He died 14 Dec. 1861, and the prince of Wales was appointed his successor, 24 Aug. 1863. 350th anniversary celebrated by a grand review, 11 July, 1887.

On the annual general court, officers and others declining to vote 500*l*. for the payment of Col. Borton the adjutant, and other expenses, the prince of Wales, the captain-general, resigns, and the company is disarmed by the War Office 18 Dec. 1888

The drill of the company resumed . . 17 Jan. 1889

Reorganisation as an independent force of 2,000 men by Royal warrant 12 March; promulgated 16 March, „

New regulations issued by the War Office . 28 Jan. 1890

The ancient and Hon. ARTILLERY COMPANY of Massachusetts, U.S.A., which was founded in 1638 by Robert Keayne, who, with some other members of the London company, had emigrated to New England, still maintains friendly relations with the elder company. About 200 members of this corps visited London, 7–23 July; received by the queen at Windsor . . . 8 July, 1896

Delegation of the company pay return visit to the Hon. Artillery Company of Massachusetts, leave London . . . . . 23 Sept. 1903

NATIONAL VOLUNTEER ARTILLERY ASSOCIATION held its first annual meeting for shooting for prizes given by the queen and others: at Shoeburyness, July, 1865. Meetings were held and prizes distributed in July, 1866, and since, generally in August. Owing to the S. African war no meetings were held in 1900, 1901, 1902.

ROYAL ARTILLERY INSTITUTION, established at Woolwich, proposed by lieuts. F. Eardley-Wilmot, and J. H. Lefroy, Feb. 1838; approved June, 1838; building completed Sept. 1840. Proceedings are published.

The alleged great deficiency of artillery in the British army, much discussed Sept. 1870; Artillery brought to the camp at Aldershot, reported to be very fine . . . . Sept. 1870

New organisation of the artillery proposed about 26 Feb. 1877

Great improvement made in field guns, and impulse given to the subject by war in S. Africa, 1899–1903

Gun Committee adopt new type of field gun, 15-pounder, quick firer, with effective shrapnel range of 6,500 yards, and further range of 10,000 yards, said to be the best of its kind, announced, 23 Sept. 1903

ARTISANS' AND LABOURERS' DWELLINGS, Act "to provide better dwellings," passed 31 July, 1868, another Act was passed 29 June, 1875, "to facilitate the improvement of the dwellings of the working classes in large towns;" one for Scotland, 2 Aug. 1875; other acts passed in 1879; amended 1882. See *Peabody* and *Rowton*.

ARTISANS', LABOURERS', AND GENERAL DWELLINGS COMPANY, registered 31 Dec. 1866; purchased estates in various parts of the country. The Shaftesbury estate (*which see*) was formally opened 18 July, 1874

The director (Dr. John Baxter Langley), secretary (Mr. Wm. Swindlehurst), were sentenced to be imprisoned 18 months; and Mr. Edwd. Saffery, estate agent, 12 months, for conspiring to defraud the company of about 24,312*l*.; trial 23-26 Oct. 1877

Royal commission to enquire into the condition of the housing of the working classes, appointed, consisting of sir Charles Dilke, chairman, the prince of Wales, the marquis of Salisbury, archbishop Manning, sir R. A. Cross, Mr. Goschen, Mr. Samuel Morley, and ten others, gazetted 4 March. First met 6 March, 1884. Report issued May, 1885.

Housing of the Poor Act (introduced by the marquis of Salisbury) passed . . 14 Aug. 1885

Sir C. Dilke lays foundation stone of a large block of buildings on charity land in Hoxton 1 July, 1885; and the prince of Wales opened them 1 July, 1886

Two of seven blocks of buildings opened in Seward St., Goswell Rd. by the lord mayor about 10 June, „

Sir Edward Cecil Guinness, afterwards Baron Iveagh, presents 250,000*l*. to trustees for the erection of dwellings for the labouring poor, 200,000*l*. for London and 50,000*l*. for Dublin, announced . . . . 20 Nov. 1889

50,000*l*. to be lent to Dublin in addition by government. Earl Cadogan presents to the trust an acre of land in Chelsea, valued at about 40,000*l*., announced . . . . 21 March, 1890

The important Housing of the Working Classes act passed 18 Aug. 1890; amended . . 1893, 1894

The lord mayor, Stuart Knill, reports valuable work done by the Mansion House council for dwellings of the poor . . . . 28 Jan. 1893

The Working Men's Dwelling bills passed 1893 and 1894

London County Council Artisans' Dwellings, Boundary Estate opened, 1895; 3,445 tenements erected 1902

New model artisans' dwellings, in Shoreditch, opened by lord Rosebery . . . 13 Nov. 1899

Housing of the working classes, act passed . . 1900
Twenty-five associations let dwellings at 3 to 4 per cent. interest on outlay. Total income 625,526*l*., 1902
ARTISANS' INSTITUTE, for promoting general and technical knowledge; near St. Martin's Lane; established by aid of the duke of Bedford, lord Lyttelton, Mr. S. Morley, and others . 14 Oct. 1874

ARTISTS' FUND, was established in 1810 to provide allowances for sick, and annuities for incapacitated, members. *Artists' General Benevolent Institution*, established 1814. *Artists' Orphan Fund*, 1871.

ARTOIS (N. France), a province once held by the Atrebates, conquered by the Franks in the fifth century, given by Charles the Bold, with Flanders, as a dowry to his daughter Judith, on her marriage with Baldwin Bras-de-fer in 863. Louis XV. created his grandson, Charles Philippe, count of Artois, who became king as Charles X., 16 Sept. 1824.

Re-united to the crown by Philip Augustus . . 1180
Formed into a county for his brother Robert, by Louis IX. 1237
Acquired, with Flanders, through marriage, by the duke of Burgundy 1384
Passed, by marriage of Mary of Burgundy to Maximilian, to the house of Austria 1477
Restored to France 1482
Reverted to Austria 1493
Conquered for France 1640
Finally confirmed to it by the treaty of Nimeguen, 10 Aug. 1678

ARTS. In the 8th century, the circle of sciences was composed of seven liberal arts—the *trivium* (grammar, rhetoric, logic), the *quadrivium* (arithmetic, music, geometry, and astronomy). *Harris.* The Royal Society of England (*which see*) obtained its charter, 2 April, 1663.

The *Society of Arts*, to promote the polite arts, commerce, manufactures, and mechanics, originated in the patriotic zeal of Mr. Wm. Shipley, and its first president, lord Folkestone, March, 1754; the prince of Wales (now king Edward VII.), June, 1899; succeeded by his son, now prince of Wales.

FINE ARTS.

First public exhibition by the artists of the British metropolis took place at the rooms of the Society of Arts 1760
Repeated there for several years, till the Royal Academy was founded 1768
Society of British Artists was instituted 21 May, 1823; styled *Royal* by order . . 16 Aug. 1887
Their first exhibition opened 19 April . . . 1824
Pre-Raphaelites (*which see*) became prominent about 1850
Society for the Encouragement of the Fine Arts founded in Dec. 1858
Art Unions began in France and Germany early in the present century.
The first in Britain was established at Edinburgh.
The *Art Union of London*, 112, Strand, was founded (chiefly by the exertions of George Godwin, the architect, long hon. sec.) 14 Feb. 1837; and chartered 1 Dec. 1846. The Art Union indemnity act was passed 3 Aug. 1844. Subscription for 1876, 20,932*l*.; 1877, 15,586*l*. (depression of trade); 1884, 9,634*l*. Annual meetings; 61st, 30 April, 1897
Burlington Fine Arts Club, for exhibition of works of art, &c., founded 1868
A memorial of a convention for promoting universally reproductions of works of art for the benefit of museums of all countries, signed by the prince of Wales, and the crown princes of Prussia, Russia, Denmark, Sweden, Italy, Saxony, and others, was sent to the duke of Marlborough, 12 March, ,,
"The Grosvenor Gallery," Bond Street, W. opened 1 May, 1877
Mr. Hubert Herkomer's new School of Art, Bushey, Herts, opened 26 Nov. 1883; incorporated 1887.
A new Art Union established by the Royal Institute of Painters in Water Colours announced . Sept. 1887
"The New Gallery," Regent St., W., opened 9 May, 1888
"National Association for the Advancement of Art," president sir Frederick Leighton, established 8 June; first meeting (at Liverpool) 3–7 Dec. 1888
Second congress at Edinburgh, president, the Marquis of Lorne . . . . 28 Oct.—2 Nov. 1889
Third Birmingham, president Mr. J. E. Hodson, R.A. 4—8 Nov. 1890
Arts and Crafts Society (Mr. Wm. Morris, Mr. (aft. sir E.) Burne-Jones, Mr. Walter Crane, and others), begun 1888; exhibitions since held.
Arts and Letters, established by sir Edwin Arnold, Mr. D'Oyly Carte, and others . . 7 Nov. 1889
The Home Arts and Industries Association, begun . 1885
The 11th annual exhibition opened in the Albert hall, 21 June, 1895; donation of 1,000 guineas by Mr. G. F. Watts, R.A. . . . . May, 1895
Society of Portrait Painters, founded . . July, 1891
Ninth exhibition of the New English Art Club in the Dudley Gallery, opened . . . 19 Nov. 1892
Sir John Gilbert presents a collection of his own paintings to the art galleries of London, Liverpool, and Manchester 1893
The sale of the art property of the late duchess of Montrose realized close on 54,200*l*. . May, 1895
Mrs. Lyne Stephens' art collection, pictures, sold for 113,557*l*. . . . . . 17 May, ,,
Prof. H. Herkomer, R.A., explains his "New Black and White Art" to the Fine Art society, London . . . . . . 28 Jan. 1896
The Society of Antiquaries' exhibition of English mediæval art, at Burlington House . June, ,,
The National Art training school at S. Kensington ordered to be styled the "Royal College of Art," 4 Sept. ,,
The late Mr. Heckscher's collection of works of art sold for 64,705*l*. 10*s*. . . . 6 May, 1898
Internat. art exhibition, at Knightsbridge, opened, May, 1898; another . . . . . May, 1899
The Forman collection of Egyptian, Greek, and Roman antiquities realised 22,389*l*. . 23 June, ,,
Mr. Constantine Ionides bequeaths his fine art collection to the S. Kensington Museum, July 1900
Mr. C. Gassiot bequeaths his collection of English pictures, value abt. 60,000*l*., to the City art gallery (except 4 for the National Gallery), announced . . . . 29 May 1902
British colonial art exhibition opened in Piccadilly 13 June, ,,

See *British Institution; National Gallery; Royal Academy; Albert Hall; British Museum*, 1899.

ARUNDEL CASTLE (Sussex), built by the Saxons about 800. The duke of Norfolk enjoys the earldom of Arundel, as a feudal honour, by inheritance and possession of the castle, without any other creation. Philip Howard, son of the attainted duke of Norfolk, was made earl of Arundel, by summons, as possessor of this castle, 1580. It was thoroughly repaired by a late duke at a vast expense, but repairs still going on, 1902.

ARUNDEL SOCIETY, for the promotion of the knowledge of art, was established in 1848. It publishes fac-similes and photographs; society dissolved, announced, Sept. 1898.

ARUNDELIAN MARBLES, called also Oxford Marbles; one containing the chronology of ancient history from 1582 to 355 B.C., and said to have been sculptured 264 B.C. They consist of 37 statues, 128 busts, and 250 inscriptions, and were found in the isle of Paros, in the reign of James I., about 1610. They were collected by Mr. W. Petty, purchased by lord Arundel, and given by his grandson Henry Howard, afterwards duke of Norfolk, to the university of Oxford in 1667; and are therefore called also OXFORD MARBLES. The characters of the inscriptions are Greek. A variorum edition of the inscriptions, by Maittaire, appeared in 1732, and a fine one by Chandler in 1763; and translations by Selden, 1628; by Prideaux, 1676; see *Kidd's Tracts;* and *Porson's Treatise*, 1789.

ARUSPICES, see *Haruspices*.

ARYAN, see *Arian*, and *Language*.

AS, a Roman weight and coin: as a weight, it was a pound; as a coin, it had different weights, but the same value. In the reign of Servius, the *as* weighed a pound of brass; in the first Punic war, it weighed two ounces, 264 B.C.; in the second Punic war, one ounce, 218 B.C.; and afterwards half an ounce; its value about three farthings sterling.

ASAPH, St. (N. Wales), a bishopric said to have been founded by Kentigern, bishop of Glasgow. On returning into Scotland about 560, he left St. Asaph his successor, from whom the see is named. It is valued in the king's books at 187*l.* 11*s.* 6*d.* The present cathedral was erected by bishop Redman, 1472-95. By an order in council, 1838, the sees of St. Asaph and Bangor were to have been united on the next vacancy in either, and the bishopric of Manchester created. This order was annulled in 1846. Present income 4,200*l.*; see *Manchester*. The cathedral, restored by sir Gilbert Scott, re-opened 2 Sept., 1875.

BISHOPS OF ST. ASAPH.

1802. Samuel Horsley, died 4 Oct. 1806.
1806. William Cleaver, died 15 May, 1815.
1815. John Luxmoore, died 21 Jan. 1830.
1830. William Carey, died 13 Sept. 1846.
1846. Thomas Vowler Short, resigned Feb. 1870; died 13 April, 1872.
1870. Joshua Hughes, died 21 Jan. 1880.
1889. Alfred George Edwards, elected 2 March.

ASBESTOS, a mineral, which may be split into threads and filaments, and which is endued with the property of remaining unconsumed by fire. Cloth was made of it by the Egyptians (*Herodotus*), and napkins in the time of Pliny, 74; and also paper. The spinning of asbestos known at Venice, about 1500. *Porta.* Asbestos non-inflammable paints tried in, and proposed for use in theatres, &c., 23 Dec. 1881. Asbestos proposed as an insulator for electric wires by M. H. Geoffroy, Paris, Sept. 1882. Exhibition of fire-resisting fabrics, &c., made of asbestos by the United Asbestos Company at St. James's hall, opened 31 May, 1897. Extensively used at present time (1903) for packing, fire-proof garments, boiler and steam-pipe sheathing, millboard, gas fires, and other purposes.

ASCALON (Syria), a city of the Philistines, shared the fate of Phœnicia and Judea. The Egyptian army was defeated here by the crusaders under Godfrey of Bouillon, 12 Aug. 1099. Ascalon was besieged by the latter in 1148, taken in 1153; and again in 1191. Its fortifications were destroyed for fear of the crusaders by the sultan, 1270.

ASCENSION, an island in the Atlantic ocean, 800 miles N. W. of St. Helena, discovered by the Portuguese on Ascension day, 20 May, 1501; and taken possession of by the English, Oct. 1815.

ASCENSION DAY, also called Holy Thursday, when the church celebrates the ascension of our Saviour, the fortieth day after his resurrection from the dead, 14 May, 33; first commemorated, it is said, 68. Ascension day, 1893, 11 May; 1894, 3 May; 1895, 23 May; 1896, 14 May; 1897, 27 May; 1898, 19 May; 1899, 11 May; 1900, 24 May; 16 May, 1601; 8 May, 1902; 21 May, 1903; 12 May, 1904; 1 June, 1905.

Society for the better observance of Ascension Day, formed June, 1869.

ASCHAFFENBURG, on the Maine, Bavaria, S. W. Germany. Here, on 14 July, 1866, the Prussians defeated the German Federal army, captured the town, and took 2000 prisoners.

ASCHAM SOCIETY, formed to promote social intercourse among gentlemen engaged in education, and improve educational methods, &c. 1880. First president, J. A. Froude; honorary members, professors Huxley, Tyndall, Morley, &c., sirs F. Pollock, J. Lubbock, F. Leighton, and other eminent men.

ASCOT RACES, see *Races*.

ASCULUM, now ASCOLI, Apulia, S. Italy. Near it, Pyrrhus of Epirus defeated the Romans, 279 B.C. Asculum, a city of the Piceni, with all their country, was conquered by the consul Sempronius, 268 B.C. Here Andrea, general of the emperor Henry VI., endeavouring to wrest Naples from Tancred, was defeated and slain, A.D. 1190.

ASHANTEES, warlike negroes of West Africa. In 1807 they conquered Fantee, in which the British settlement Cape Coast Castle is situated.

On the death of their king, who had been friendly to the English, hostilities began; the Ashantees defeated about 1,000 British under sir Charles M'Carthy at Accra, and brought away his skull with others as trophies . . . . 21 Jan. 1824
They were totally defeated by col. Purdon, 7 Aug. 1826
Treaty of peace and commerce concluded by Mr. Maclean; the independence of the Fantees recognised . . . . 29 April, 1831
The governor of Cape Coast Castle began war with Ashantees early in 1863; suspended through sickness of our troops . . . . May, 1864
Offended at the British occupation of Elmina, the Ashantees attacked the Fantees, our allies, with varying success . . . . April, 1873
They were severely repulsed, 13 June; Elmina partially bombarded by the British for favouring them . . . . . . 14 June, ,,
Commodore Commerell and his party, sailing up the Prah, attacked and wounded; 4 men killed by people of Chamah, which is bombarded 14 Aug. ,,
Sir Garnet Wolseley (see *Hudson Bay*) appointed governor of the colonies on West Coast of Africa, sails with troops, &c. . . . 12 Sept. ,,
He arrives at Cape Coast Castle, 2 Oct.; addresses an assembly of friendly chiefs, urging them to faithful action and promising rewards (the war to be defensive, if possible) . . . 4 Oct. ,,
Ashantees defeated in a conflict in the bush, at Essaman, near Elmina; villages burnt, 14 Oct.; again at Escabeo, near Dunquah, by col. Festing 27 Oct. ,,
Despatch from sir Garnet Wolseley, declaring native allies worthless, and more British troops needed . . . . 31 Oct ,,
Indecisive conflict at Dunquah; lieut. Eardley Wilmot killed, 3 Nov.; Ashantees' attack on Abrakampra totally defeated; their camp taken; disorderly retreat . . . . 5, 6 Nov. ,,
Col. Wood's indecisive attack at Faisorah 27 Nov. ,,
The Ashantees said to be retreating in disorder, 15 Dec. ,,
Sir Garnet Wolseley marches towards the Prah, 27 Dec. ,,
The King Koffee Kalcalli pretends to accept the terms offered; releases captives; prepares for battle . . . . Jan. 1874
Skirmish at Borborassie; captain Nicol killed, 29 Jan. ,,
Ashantees defeated by sir Garnet Wolseley at Amoaful . . . . . . 31 Jan. ,,
Bocquah captured by sir A. Alison . 1 Feb. ,,
Ashantee attack at Fommanah repulsed 2 Feb. ,,
The king takes command: defeated at Ordahsa, 4 Feb. ,,
Sir Garnet Wolseley enters Coomassie . 4 Feb. ,,
The king not acceding to proposals, his palace and city burnt . . . . . 6 Feb. ,,
Daring ride through Coomassie by capt. Sartorius, 11 Feb. ,,

The British retreat; a treaty of peace (terms: perpetual peace; indemnity of 50,000 oz. of gold; supremacy over Adansi and other tribes renounced; free trade guaranteed; human sacrifices to be prohibited;) signed . . 13 Feb. 1874

The king fearing attack from capt. Glover, sends first instalment of gold (1000 oz.) . 13 Feb. „

Sir Garnet Wolseley enters Cape Coast Castle, 19 Feb.; sails; arrives at Portsmouth 21 March „

The courage, skill, and discipline of the troops and sailors highly commended; expedition cost about 900,000*l.*

The troops reviewed by the Queen at Windsor; sir Garnet Wolseley, commodores Commerell and Hewett, col. Festing, capt. Fremantle, sir A. Alison, and commander Glover thanked by parliament . . . . 30 March, „

The deposed King Koffee Kalcalli, said to be defeated in his attack on his brother, king Mensah . . . . Sept. 1876

The king demands surrender of a fugitive prince by the governor of Cape Coast Castle, 18 Jan.; no result; professes desire of peace . . April, 1881

The king sends the golden axe to the queen, who receives it at Windsor Castle . . . 30 June, „

Deposition of king Mensah, and desire of British protection announced . . . . . 28 June, 1883

Fighting at Coomassie between partizans of king Mensah and the ex-king Koffee Kalcalli 3 and 5 Aug. „

King Bugay requests British intervention Aug. „

Koffee Kalcalli's partizans totally defeated, announced . . . . 31 Aug. „

He and Mensah prisoners . . . . Aug.—Nov. „

Massacre of Koffee's adherents . . . . Dec. „

Death of the king, and Koffee Kalcalli; civil war reported . . . . . . Aug.—Dec. 1884

Troubles in the country; col. sir Francis Scott sent to protect the British settlement; arrives at Abetifi, reported . . . . 21 Nov. 1893

Expedition successful, reported . . . . April, 1894

Prempeh the young king of Coomassie installed 11 June, „

Accused of promoting slave trade, human sacrifices, attacking friendly tribes, and obstructing commerce, all contrary to treaties, British negotiations fruitless . . . . Feb. *et seq.* „

The king protests against a British protectorate April, 1895

The king's envoys not received at the colonial office, summer . . . . „

Ultimatum sent to the king . . . . . Oct. „

Expedition under col. sir Francis Scott, including prince Henry of Battenberg, prince Christian Victor, son of prince Christian, and 30 officers leaves England, 23 Nov. *et seq.*; arrives at Cape Coast Castle . . . . 13 Dec. „

Native kings support the British . Nov.—Dec. „

Bridge over the river Prah completed, reported, 25 Dec. „

The road to Coomassie cleared by the withdrawal of the Ashanti pickets at Essian Kwanta 5 Jan. 1896

Major Ferguson dies of fever at Prahsu . 9 Jan. „

Bekwai and Abodom placed under British protection by treaty signed by the kings at Essian Kwanta . . . . 11 Jan. „

Coomassie occupied unopposed by sir Francis Scott, . 17-18 Jan. „

Grand palaver; John and Albert Ansah envoys, returned from England act as interpreters, the king reminded of his offences, by governor Maxwell, accedes to all the British demands including the payment of 50,000 oz. of gold for the expenses of the expedition; unable to pay, he is arrested with his relatives; (2 war-chiefs, and the kings of Mampon, Ejesu and Ofesu, secured as hostages), John and Albert Ansah arrested for alleged forgery, &c.; 20 Jan., released . 20 May, „

Prince Henry of Battenberg, dies of African fever on board H.M.S. *Blonde* . . . . 20 Jan. „

General native rejoicing at British success, reported . . . . 27 Jan. „

Capt. Donald Stewart appointed British resident with a detachment of troops at Coomassie; 22 Jan. (major C. B. Pigott temporary acting resident). . . . . 28 Jan. „

Special service corps with sir Francis Scott, prince Christian Victor and staff return to Cape Coast Castle; 1 Feb., arrive in London . . 26 Feb. 1896

King Prempeh and prisoners arrive at Cape Coast Castle, embark for Elmina . . . . 4 Feb „

Mr. Maxwell on his tour north of Coomassie, received with great enthusiasm at Insuta, 3 Feb. 1896, treaties concluded with 7 tribes; Mr. (aft. sir) Wm. Maxwell returns to Cape Coast Castle; 25 Feb.; see *Gold Coast* . . . . „

Sir Francis Scott made K.C.B. and other officers promoted . . . . . . 31 March, „

British improvements at Coomassie; reported, May, „

Col. Pigott relieved at Coomassie by capt. Donald Stewart, Nov.; country quiet and trade reviving, reported . . . . 9 Nov. „

Sir Fred. and lady Hodgson arrived at Coomassie, about 25 March; he holds a palaver of kings and chiefs, 28 March, 1900; capt. Armitage's small force sent in quest of the "Golden stool" symbol of royalty is attacked by Ashantees . 31 March 1900

Fort Coomassie closely invested by rebels; 6 April; capt. Middlemist and about 50 men charge through into Coomassie . . . mid. April „

Rebels defeated round Coomassie, 23, 25 April; Capt. Aplix's force arrives after 2 days' hard fighting . . . . 29 April, „

Great suffering, 30 and 40 deaths per day in the fort, April—May; great loss inflicted on the rebels, 2 May; maj. Morris with 230 men arrives, 15 May; the loyal Bekwais after much fighting burn Abodom, 24 May; Hausa quarters destroyed at Coomassie, capts. Maguire and Slater and others killed . . . . 29 May „

Carter and Hall rout the enemy at Bekwai; capt. Wilson and 6 men killed . . . . 6 June, „

Col. Burroughs is repulsed at Kokofu, lieut. Brownlie and 5 men killed . . . 3 July, „

Flight of sir Fred. and lady Hodgson with 600 men under maj. Morris and 1,000 non-combatants (capts. Bishop and Ralph with 115 men left behind), 23 June; they break through the rebels, capturing a stockade, capts. Leggett and Marshall being mortally wounded, and after a hard march and much fighting reach Ekwanta, 26 June; cross the river Ofin, 30 June, and arrive at Accra after great suffering and many deaths, 11 July, „

Relief of Coomassie by col. Willcocks (K.C.M.G. 28 July) after a rapid march with his black troops and severe fighting, 15 July; leaves capt. Eden there in command and returns with the remainder of the sick and starving garrison to Bekwai, 17 July; Morland and Mellis destroy a rebel camp at Kokofu, 30 killed . 22 July, „

Beddoes routs the rebels at Formera . 30 July, „

Coomassie reinforced by Burroughs, camp and stockades destroyed; lieut. Greer and 5 others killed . . . . 7 Aug. „

Opoku defeated, many captured, camp destroyed, Aug. „

Col. Brake destroys Ojesu a fetish town; lieut. Burton and capt. Benson killed . 29, 31 Aug. „

Continued fighting, villages destroyed, 1, 22 Sept. „

Sir J. Willcocks totally defeats about 4,000 rebels at Obassa, 30 Sept.; enemy pursued and completely dispersed, reported . . . . 4 Oct. „

Rebel chief of Odumasi surprised and captured, 14 Nov. „

Major Nathan (aft. sir) governor, receives the kings and chiefs of Ashanti at Coomassie, 14, 15 March, 1901

Mutiny in a native regiment at Coomassie, early April, deserters captured, some shot, 128 surrender, reported . . . . . 21 April, „

Capt. Donald Stewart, chief commissioner, made K.C.M.G. . . . . 9 Nov. 1902

ASHBOURNE'S (Lord) ACT, see *Ireland*, 14 Aug. 1885, and Nov. 1888; new act passed 24 Dec. 1888. Reported very successful, Dec. 1890-1.

ASHBURTON TREATY, concluded at Washington, 9 Aug. 1842, by Alexander lord Ashburton, and John Tyler, president of the United

States: it defined the boundaries of the respective countries between Canada and the state of Maine, settled the extradition of criminals, &c.

ASHDOD, or **Azotus**, seat of the worship of the Phœnician god, Dagon, which fell down before the ark of the Lord, captured by the Philistines from the Israelites, about 1141 B.C. (1 *Sam.* v.) Ashdod was taken by the Egyptians after 29 years' siege, the longest recorded, B.C. 630. *Herodotus.*

ASHDOWN, or **Assendune**, now thought to be Aston, Berks, where Ethelred and his brother Alfred defeated the Danes in 871. At Ashdown, near Saffron-Walden, Essex, Canute defeated Edmund Ironside with great slaughter, 1016.

Tradition says that the day after the battle in 871 Alfred caused his army to carve the figure of a white horse, the standard of Hengist, in the vale. Mr. Thomas Hughes ("Tom Brown"), in his book "The Scouring of the White Horse" (1859), describes the work and festival on 17 and 18 Sept. 1857, a ceremony performed at intervals from time immemorial. Records are found of the "scouring" in 1755, 27 May, 1776, 15 May, 1780, 1785, 1803, 1812 or 1813, 1825, 19, 20 Sept., Sept. 1843.

The scouring was again effected under the direction of Mr. Andrew Dudgeon by order of lady Craven at the cost of 10*l.*; reported Jan. 1893.

ASHMOLEAN MUSEUM (books, manuscripts, coins, &c.), was presented to the university of Oxford by Elias Ashmole, the herald and antiquary, and opened 1682. It included the collections of the Tradescants, to whom he was executor. He died at Lambeth in 1692. Dr. C. D. Fortnum presented his art collections and a sum of money to found the new galleries, about 1888; he died, 6 March, 1899. The *Ashmolean Society*, Oxford (scientific), was established in 1828.

ASHTAROTH, a Phœnician goddess, occasionally worshipped by the Israelites (see *Judges* ii. 13) about 1406 B.C., and even by Solomon, about 984 B.C. (1 *Kings* xi. 5.) Greek, *Astarte.*

ASH-WEDNESDAY, the first day of Lent, which in early times began on the Sunday now called the first in Lent. It is said that pope Felix III., in 487, first added the four days preceding the old Lent Sunday, to raise the number of fasting days to forty; that Gregory the Great (pope, 590) introduced the sprinkling of ashes on the first of the four additional days, and hence the names of *Dies Cinerum*, or Ash-Wednesday. At the Reformation this practice was abolished, "as being a mere shadow, or vain show." Ash-Wednesday, 1893, 15 Feb.; 1894, 7 Feb.; 1895, 27 Feb.; 1896, 19 Feb.; 1897, 3 Mar.; 1898, 23 Feb.; 1899, 15 Feb.; 1900, 28 Feb.; 1901, 20 Feb.; 1902, 12 Feb.; 1903, 25 Feb.; 1904, 17 Feb.; 1905, 8 March.

ASIA, the largest division of the globe; part of it was so called by the Greeks. The area of Asia and its islands is estimated at 17,255,890 square miles. Asia was the first quarter of the world peopled: here the law of God was first promulgated; here many of the greatest monarchies of the earth had their rise; and hence most of the arts and sciences have been derived. Its early history is derived from the Bible and from Herodotus, who relates the wars of Crœsus, Cyrus, and others. The Central Asian Railway from the Caspian to Samarcand constructed by general Annenkoff for Russia, which now possesses very great influence over the country, opened 1888; branch line to Bokhara completed. M. Sven Hedin successfully explores over 12,000 mi. in Central Asia, 1894-1900. See *Population, Jews, China, India, Persia, Turkey, and the other countries.*

Capt. Deasy discovers the source of the Khotan-daria in N. Tibet, summer of 1898; explores the Garkand region and other districts, 5,300 mi., high altitudes, over 15,000 ft. reached, Nov. 1898-Dec. 1899.

The czar grants 42,000 roubles for exploration in Central Asia, Jan. 1899.

M. Sven Hedin explores Lob Nor, discovers new lakes, and makes many ascents, March-Oct. 1900.

ASIA MINOR, now **Anatolia**, comprised the Ionian colonies on the coast, the early seats of Greek civilisation, and the countries Mysia, Phrygia, Lycia, Bithynia, Caria, Lydia, Cappadocia, Galatia, &c., with the cities Troy, Ephesus, Smyrna (*all which see*). From the time of the rise of the Assyrian monarchy, about 2000 B.C., to that of the Turks under Osman, Asia Minor was the battlefield of the conquerors of the world. See *Seven Churches.*

First settlement of the Ionian Greeks - about B.C.	1043
Asia Minor subdued by the Medes . . about	711
Conquered by Cyrus . . . . . about	546
Contest between the Greeks and Persians begins	544
Asia Minor conquered by Alexander	332
Contended for by his successors; separate kingdoms established	321-278
Gradually acquired by the Romans B.C. 188 to A.D.	15
Possessed by the Persians	609
Partially recovered by the emperor Basil. . . .	874
Invaded by Timour	1402
Taken from the Greek emperor, and established as an empire by the Turks under Mahomet I. . . See *Turkey.*	1413

The Asia Minor Exploration Fund established, 1882, by sir Charles Wilson and others, enabled Mr. W. M. Ramsay to continue his researches. Valuable results were reported in 1884 from Lydia and the early home of the Greeks. In Jan. 1890–93, the committee appeal for pecuniary help. See *Hittites.*

Results of Mr. Anderson's explorations, reported, *Times* 27 Aug. 1897.

Railway from Mersina on the coast to Tarsas and Adana, 42 miles, constructing under sir T. Tancred, Aug. 1884; first section opened 4 May, 1886, wholly opened Aug. 1886.

Conflicts between Christians and Mahometans throughout the provinces; Nov. 1892 *et seq.* See *Armenia* and *Turkey*, 1895–96.

Anarchy in N.E. provinces, Moslem crimes unpunished; reported, 13 Jan. 1897.

ASIATIC SOCIETIES. The "Asiatic Society of Bengal," at Calcutta, was established by sir William Jones in 1784, "the bounds of its investigation to be the geographical limits of Asia." The "Royal Asiatic Society," which has several branches in India, was founded in 1823. It established the "Oriental Translation Fund," in 1828, which had published 83 volumes of Eastern literature in 1865. The Fund ceased to exist in 1878. The Fund was revived in a new form mainly by Mr. F. F. Arbuthnot, and volumes since issued, 1896 *et seq.* The "Literary Society of Madras," 1845. The "Asiatic Quarterly Review," London, begun 1886.

ASKESIAN SOCIETY (from the Greek *askēsis*, exercise), instituted in March, 1796, by some young men for discussing philosophical subjects. Its founders were Wm. Allen, Wm. Phillips, Alex. Tilloch, Luke Howard, W. H. Pepys and others. In 1806 it merged into the Geological Society.

ASMONÆANS, the proper name of the family termed Maccabees (*which see*).

ASPERN, Great, a town, and Essling, a village near the Danube and Vienna, where a series of desperate conflicts took place between the Austrian army under the archduke Charles, and the French under Napoleon, Massena, &c., on 21-22 May, 1809, ending in the retreat of Napoleon. The Austrian loss exceeded 20,000 men, and the French 30,000.

Marshal Lannes, mortally wounded 22 May, died 31 May. The bridge of the Danube was destroyed, and Napoleon's retreat endangered; but the success of the Austrians was fruitless to them.

ASPHALT, a solid bituminous substance, probably derived from decayed vegetable matter. It was used as a building material in ancient Babylon. Its application for this purpose was revived by Eirinus, a Greek physician, who discovered beds of it near Neufchatel in 1712. Asphalt stone was found at Seyssel near Geneva in 1802; and after several failures, count Sassenay brought it into use for pavement about 1832. The artificial asphalt obtained from gas-works began to be used as pavement about 1838. Claridge's patent asphalt was laid down in Trafalgar-square, Jan. 1864. Various kinds of asphalt pavement have been since laid on in London.

ASPINWALL, or Colon, see *Panama*.

ASPROMONTE, Naples. Here Garibaldi was defeated, wounded, and taken prisoner 29 Aug. 1862, having injudiciously risen against the French occupation of Rome.

ASSAM (N. E. India) acquired by the British in 1825, and surrendered by the king of Ava in 1826 The tea-plant was discovered here by Mr. Bruce in 1823. A superintendent of the tea-forests was appointed in 1836, the cultivation of the plant having been recommended by lord William Bentinck in 1834. The Assam Tea Company, by whom Chinese labourers and coolies were introduced, was established in 1839. After several years, the plantations suffered severely, it is said through over speculation and neglect of the labourers; as a remedy a labour act was passed at Calcutta, about July, 1867; labour and emigration act passed, 1901. Population, 1901, 6,122,000.

Mr. James Wallace Quinton, chief commissioner, a valuable officer, esteemed by three viceroys, killed at Manipur (*which see*) . . 24 March, 1891
Chief commissioner, William Erskine Ward . . „
Petroleum discovered; large quantities obtained, reported . . . 11 Feb. 1892
Chief commissioner, Sir Henry Cotton . . . 1897
Destructive earthquake; public buildings and crops destroyed, June–July, 1897. See *India*, 12–18 June, 1897
Depression and difficulties in the tea trade, reported, Sept. 1902

ASSASSINATION PLOT to kill William III., formed by some of the Jacobites, simultaneously with one for an insurrection to be aided by French invaders, in 1696. James II. and several noblemen and others were said to be privy to it; including the earl of Ailesbury. About forty ruffians undertook to kill William near Turnham Green, Middlesex, when returning from hunting, 14 Feb. 1696. Information was given to William by Mr. Prendergast, a Roman Catholic, through horror of the crime. The following were executed: —Charnock, King, and Keyes, 18 March; sir John Friend and sir Wm. Parkyns, 3 April; Rookwood, Lowick, and Cranbourne, 29 April, 1696; sir John Fenwick (by attainder), 28 January, 1697. Sir George Barclay, a chief organiser of the plot, escaped to France.

ASSASSINS, or **ASSASSINIANS**, fanatical Mahometans, collected by Hassan-ben-Sabah, and settled in Persia about 1090. They murdered the marquis of Montferrat in 1192, Lewis of Bavaria in 1213, and the khan of Tartary in 1254. They were extirpated in Persia about 1258 and in Syria about 1272. The chief of the corps was named "*Ancient of the Mountain*," and "*Old Man of the Mountain*." They trained up young people to assassinate such persons as their chief had devoted to destruction. *Hénault*. From them came the word *assassin*. See *Mafia*, *Anarchy*, *and Vehmic Tribunals*.

REMARKABLE ASSASSINATIONS AND ATTEMPTS.

See *Rome*, *Emperors*, for many assassinations.

Abdul Aziz, sultan (see *Turkey*, 1881) . 4 June, 1876
Abdurrahman, Ameer of Afghanistan; *attempt* 26 Dec. 1888
Albert I., emperor of Germany, by his nephew John . . . . 1 May, 1308
Albert Edward, prince of Wales, *attempt* by Sipido, aged 15, at Brussels . . . 5 April, 1900
Alexander II. of Russia; *attempts:* by Karakozow at St. Petersburg, 16 April, 1866; by Berezowski at Paris, 6 June, 1867; by Alexander Solovieff, 14 April, 1879; by undermining a railway train, 1 Dec. 1879; by explosion of Winter palace, St. Petersburg, 17 Feb. 1880; killed by explosion of a bomb thrown by a man who is himself killed, St. Petersburg . . . 2 p.m. 13 March, 1881
Alexander III.; *attempts:* 13 March, 1887; May, 1888
Alexander I. of Servia, with his wife Draga, 11 June, 1903
Alfonso XII. of Spain, *attempts:* by J. O. Moncasi, 25 Oct. 1878; by Francisco Otero Gonzalez, 30 Dec. 1879
Amadeus, when king of Spain; *attempt* . 19 July, 1872
Artaxerxes III. of Persia; by Bagoas . about B.C. 338
Aumale, duc d'; *attempt* . . . 13 Sept. 1841
Beaton, David, cardinal; by reformers . 29 May, 1546
Becket, Thomas à, abp. of Canterbury . 29 Dec. 1170
Berri, Charles duc de (father of the comte de Chambord) . . . . . 13 Feb. 1820
Bismarck, prince; *attempt*, by Blind, 7 May, 1866; by Kullmann . . . . 13 July, 1874
Bogoliepoff, M., Russian statesman, by P. Karpovich . . . . . 27 Feb. 1901
Borda Idiarte, president of Uruguay; by Avelino Arredondo . . . . 25 Aug. 1897
Bratiano, premier of Roumania; *attempt*, by J. Pietraro . . . . 14 Dec. 1880
Buckingham, George Villiers, duke of; by John Felton . . . . . 23 Aug. 1628
Burgundy, John the Fearless, duke of; by Orleanists, 10 Sept. 1419
Cæsar, Julius; by Brutus and others 15 March, B.C. 44
Canovas del Castillo, Antonio, premier of Spain; by Michele Angine Golli . . . 8 Aug. 1897
Capo d'Istria, count; Greek statesman . 9 Oct. 1831
Carnot, Marie François Sadi, president of the French republic (see *France*), by Cesare Giovanni Santo . . . . . 24 June, 1894
Cavendish, lord Frederick, chief Secretary for Ireland, and T. H. Burke, under Secretary, in Phœnix Park, Dublin, by 4 men 1882
Crispi, Francesco, premier of Italy; *attempt*, by Paolo Lega . . . . 16 June, 1894
Daniel, prince of Montenegro . . . 13 Aug. 1860
Darboy, Georges, abp. of Paris; by communists, 24 May, 1871
Darius III. of Persia; by Bessus . . July, B.C. 330
Edmund the Elder, of England . . 26 March, 946
Edward the Martyr „ „ . . 18 March, 979
Edward II. „ „ . . 27 Sept. 1327
Edward V. „ „ . . July, 1483
Elizabeth, empress of Austria, by L. Luccheni, 10 Sept. 1898
Estrup, M.; *attempt* 21 Oct. 1885; and by Payitch *alias* Knezevitch . . . . 6 July, 1899
Ferry, Jules, ex-French premier; by Aubertin, 10 Dec. 1887
Francis Joseph of Austria; *attempt*, by Libenyi, 18 Feb. 1853; by Overdank . . . 1882
Frederick William IV. of Prussia: *attempt*, by Sofelage . . . . . 22 May, 1850
Garfield (Gen.), president of the United States (by Charles Jules Guiteau): Washington, 2 July, died . . . . . 19 Sept. 1881
George III. of England, *mad attempts*, by Margaret Nicholson, 2 Aug. 1786; by James Hatfield, 15 May, 1800
George IV. (when regent), *attempt* . . 28 Jan. 1817
George I. of Greece; *attempt*; by Karditzis, 26 Feb. 1898
Guise, Henry duke of; by order of Henry III. of France . . . . . 23 Dec. 1588
Gustavus III. of Sweden; by Ankarström, 16 March, died . . . . . 29 March, 1792
Henry III. of France; by Jacques Clément, 1 Aug. died . . . . . . 2 Aug. 1589

Henry IV. of France; *attempt*, by Jean Châtel, 27 Dec. 1594; killed by Ravaillac . . 14 May, 1610
Heureaux, gen., president of Dominica, see *Hayti*. by Ramon Caceres . . . . . 26 July, 1899
Humbert I., king of Italy, *attempt*, by John Passanti, at Naples, 17th Nov. 1878; *attempt*, by Pietro Acciarito, at Rome, 22 April, 1897; by Gaetano Bresci, at Monza . . . 29 July, 1900
Hussein Avni and other Turkish ministers; by Hassan, a Circassian officer . 15 June, 1876
Isabella II. of Spain; *attempts*, by La Riva, 4 May, 1847; by Merino, 2 Feb. 1852; by Raymond Fuentes . . . . . . 28 May, 1856
James I. of Scotland; by nobles . . 21 Feb. 1437
James III. of Scotland; by nobles . 11 June, 1488
Kotzebue, August, German dramatist, for political motives; by Karl Sand . . 23 March, 1819
Leopold, king of the Belgians; attempt, by Rubino, 15 Nov. 1902.
Lincoln, Abraham, president of United States, N.A.; by Wilkes Booth, 14 April; died . 15 April, 1865
Lorraine, Louis of Guise, cardinal of; by order of Henry III. of France . . 24 Dec. 1588
Louis XV. of France; *attempt*, by Damiens, 5 Jan. 1757
Louis Philippe of France; many *attempts*; by Fieschi, 28 July, 1835; by Alibaud, 25 June, 1836; by Meunier, 27 Dec. 1836; by Darmès, 15 Oct. 1840; by Lecomte, 14 April, 1846; by Henry. 29 July, 1846
Lytton, lord, viceroy of India; *attempt*, by Busa 12 Dec. 1878
Marat; by Charlotte Corday . . . 13 July, 1793
Mayo, Richard, earl of, gov.-gen. of India; by Shere Ali, a convict, in Andaman isles . 8 Feb. 1872
McKinley, William, president of United States, at Buffalo, by Leon Czolgosz, 5 Sept.; died 14 Sept. 1901
Mehemet Ali Pacha, by Albanians . 7 Sept. 1878
Melikoff, gen. Loris; *attempt* (see *Russia*) 4 March, 1880
Michael, prince of Servia . . . 10 June, 1868
Milan IV. of Servia, *attempts*, 23 Oct. 1882; by Payitch *alias* Knezevitch . . 6 July, 1899
Murray, James, earl of, regent of Scotland, 23 Jan. 1570
Muzaffer-ed-Deen, shah of Persia, *attempt*, by Salsou . . . . . . 2 Aug. 1900
Napoleon I.; *attempt*, by infernal machine, 24 Dec. 1800
Napoleon III.; *attempts*, by Pianori, 28 April, 1855; by Bellemarre, 8 Sept. 1855; by Orsini and others . . . . . . 14 Jan. 1858
Nasr-ed-Deen, shah of Persia; by Mollah Reza, a Sayyid . . . . . 1 May, 1896
Obolenski, prince, gov. of Kharkoff, *attempt*, by Katchoor, a peasant . . . 11 Aug. 1902
Orange, William, prince of; by Balthasar Gerard 10 July, 1584
Orleans, Louis Valois, duke of; by Burgundians 23 Nov. 1407
Parma, Ferdinand Charles III., duke of; 26 March, died . . . . . 27 March, 1854
Paul, czar of Russia; by nobles . 24 March, 1801
Pedro II. of Brazil; *attempt*, by Volti . 15 July, 1889
Percival, Spencer, premier; by Bellingham, 11 May, 1812
Philip II. of Macedon; by Pausanias . . B.C. 336
Prim, marshal; 28 Dec. died . . 30 Dec. 1870
Roosevelt, pres. U.S., *attempt* by Weilbrenner, a lunatic . . . . . . 1 Sept. 1903
Rossi, conte Pellegrino, Roman statesman, 15 Nov. 1848
Sibour, M. W. A., abp. of Paris, by Jean Verger, a priest . . . . . . 3 Jan. 1857
Sipiguine, M., Russian statesman, by Bolmascheff . . . . . . 15 April, 1902
Stamboloff, M., ex-premier of Bulgaria, 15 July, died . . . . . . 18 July, 1895
Victoria, queen, *attempts* (?). Edwd. Oxford, 10 June, 1840; John Francis, 30 May, 1842; Bean, 3 July, 1842; Wm. Hamilton, 19 May, 1849; R. Maclean, at Windsor . . . 2 March, 1882
William I. of Prussia and Germany; *attempts*, by Oscar Becker, 14 July, 1861; by Hödel, 11 May, 1878 by Dr. Nobiling . . . 2 June, 1878
William III. of England see *Assassination-plot* . 1695-6
William, prince of Würtemberg; *attempt*, by M. Müller . . . . . . 20 Oct. 1889

ASSAY OF GOLD AND SILVER, originated with the bishop of Salisbury, a royal treasurer in the reign of Henry I. *Du Cange.* But certainly some species of assay was practised as early as the Roman conquest. Assay early established in England was regulated by statutes, 1238, 1700, and 1705. Assay masters appointed at Newcastle, 1701; Sheffield and Birmingham, 1773. The laws respecting assay were amended in 1854 and 1855. The alloy of gold is silver and copper, that of silver is copper. Standard gold is 2 carats of alloy to 22 of fine gold. Standard silver is 18 dwts. of copper to 11 ozs. 2 dwts. of fine silver; see *Goldsmiths' Company* and *Pyx*.

ASSAYE (E. Indies). The British army, under general Arthur Wellesley (afterwards duke of Wellington), entered the Mahratta states on the south; took the fort of Ahmednuggur, 12 Aug.; and defeated Scindiah and the rajah of Berar at Assaye, 23 Sept. 1803. This was Wellesley's first great battle, in which he opposed 40,000 with only 9,600 men. The enemy fled, leaving their artillery, &c.

ASSEMBLY OF (130) DIVINES, held at Westminster, 1 July, 1643, convoked by order of parliament to consider the liturgy, government, and doctrines of the church. Two members were elected for each county. The presbyterian majority adopted the Scottish covenant, and drew up the directory for public worship, a confession, and the catechisms now used by the church of Scotland. The last (1163rd) meeting was on 22 Feb. 1649; see *Church of Scotland*.

ASSENT, see *Royal Assent*.

ASSESSED TAXES. By some the date is referred to Ethelbert, in 991; to Henry VIII. 1522; and to William III. 1689, when a land-tax was imposed; see *Land Tax*. The assessed taxes yielded in 1815 (the last year of the war), exclusively of the land-tax, 6,524,766*l.*, their highest amount. These imposts have varied in their nature and amount, according to the exigencies of the state. They were considerably advanced in 1797 and 1801, *et seq.*, but reduced in 1816, and in subsequent years. An act for the repeal of certain assessed taxes was passed 16 & 17 Vict. c. 90, 20 Aug. 1853, explained and amended by 17 & 18 Vict. c. 1, 17 Feb. 1854.—Acts for the better securing and accounting for the Assessed and Income Taxes, 10 Aug. 1854; see *Taxes*, and *Income Tax*. Changes were made in the assessed taxes, their time of collection, &c., by the Revenue act, passed 24 June, 1869. Licences for servants, dogs, and armorial bearings were also introduced. An act to provide for uniformity in the assessment of rateable property in the metropolis was passed 9 Aug. 1869. The "Court of General Assessment" first met 19 May, 1870. See *House Duty* and *Land (Tax)*.

ASSIENTO, a contract between the king of Spain and other powers, for furnishing the Spanish dominions in America with negro slaves, began with the Flemings. By the treaty of Utrecht, 13 July, 1713, the British government engaged to furnish 4800 negroes annually to Spanish America for thirty years. The contract was renewed in 1748, but given up in 1750; see *Guinea*.

ASSIGNATS, a forced paper currency, ordered by the National Assembly of France to support public credit during the revolution, April, 1790. At one period, eight milliards, or nearly 350 millions of pounds sterling, of this paper were in circulation in France and its dependencies. *Alison.* Assignats were superseded by mandats in 1796.

ASSISTANT MASTERS' ASSOCIATION, founded, 1891, holds annual meetings in London and provinces; at Manchester, 14, 15 Sept. 1900.

ASSIZE OF BATTLE, see *Appeal*.

ASSIZE of BREAD, &c., see *Bread*, and *Wool*.

ASSIZE of JERUSALEM, a valuable code of laws compiled under the direction of Godfrey of Bouillon, king of Jerusalem, in 1100.

ASSIZE COURTS (from *assideo*, *I sit*) are very ancient in England, and in old law books are defined to be an assembly of knights and other substantial men, with the justice, to meet at a certain time and place: regulated by Magna Charta, 1215. The present justices of assize and *Nisi Prius* are derived from the statute of Westminster, 13 Edw. I. 1284. *Coke; Blackstone*. "The king doth will that no lord, or other of the country, shall sit upon the bench with the justices to take assize in their sessions in the counties of England, upon great forfeiture to the king." 20 Rich. II. 1396. *Statutes, Brough Act*. Assizes are general or special; general when the judges go their circuits, and special when a commission is issued to take cognisance of one or more causes.; see *Bloody Assize*.

ASSOCIATIONS, see *British, National Associations, Christian, &c.*

ASSOUAN VILLAGE EXHIBITION, illustrating native village life in Egypt, opened at Earl's Court, May, 1903.

ASSUMPTION, FEAST OF THE, 15 Aug. It is observed by the church of Rome in honour of the Virgin Mary, said to have been taken up to heaven in her corporeal form, body and spirit, on this day, A.D. 45, in her 75th year. The festival was instituted in the 7th century, and enjoined by the council of Mentz, 813.

ASSURANCE, see *Insurance*.

ASSYRIA, originally Assur, an Asiatic country between Mesopotamia and Media, was the seat of the earliest recorded monarchy. Till recently its history was mainly derived from Greek historians, Ctesias, Herodotus, and Diodorus Siculus, Berosus, a Græco-Chaldean priest, and the Holy Scriptures. The discovery by Mr. (aft. sir) Austin Layard of the Ninevite antiquities, now in the British Museum, and the deciphering of many ancient cuneiform inscriptions, by Grotefend, sir H. Rawlinson, and other scholars, have thrown much light upon Assyrian history. The chronologers, Blair, Usher, Hales, and Clinton, differ much in the dates. The results of recent investigations are given in the rev. G. Rawlinson's "Five Great Monarchies of the Ancient World," and in prof. A. Sayce's "Assyria, its Princes, Priests, and People," 1885. Mr. W. Boscawen's article "Assyria" in "Chambers' Encyclopædia," 1888, has been used for much of the following summary.

Nimrod or Belus reigns . . B.C. [2554 *H.* 2235 *C.*] 2245
"Asshur builded Nineveh" (*Gen.* x. 11) about . 2218
Ninus, son of Belus, reigns in Assyria, and names his capital Nineveh . . . . . . [2182 *C.*] 2069
Babylon taken by Ninus, who, having subdued the Armenians, Persians, Bactrians, and all Asia Minor, establishes what is properly the Assyrian monarchy, of which Nineveh was the seat of empire. *Blair* . . . . [2233 *C.*] 2059
Ninyas, an infant, succeeds Ninus . . . 2017
Semiramis, mother of Ninyas, usurps the government, enlarges and embellishes Babylon [2130 *C.*] 2007
She invades Libya, Ethiopia, and India . *Lenglet* 1975
She is put to death by her son Ninyas . . . 1965
Ninyas put to death, and Arius reigns . . . 1927
Reign of Aralius 1897
Belochus, the last king of the race of Ninus . . 1446
He makes his daughter Atossa, surnamed Semiramis II., his associate on the throne . . . 1433
Atossa procures the death of her father, and marries Belatores (or Belaperes) who reigns . . . 1421

* * * *

Sardanapalus, luxurious and effeminate when attacked by Arbaces Satrap of Media, suddenly becomes energetic and warlike, defends himself in Nineveh for two years, and when overcome burns himself in his palace, with his wives and treasures, thus ending the first Assyrian Empire. (Ctesias) 876

[This story and most of what is given above, is now considered mythical.] The following is based upon the records in the ancient Assyrian tablets and the Bible.

Assyria, a province of Babylonia, becomes independent; first king, Bel-kapkapi, under his successors the kingdom is greatly enlarged; Rimmon-nirari I. becomes powerful about . B.C. 1320
His son, Shalmaneser I. founds Calah, and his grandson, Tiglath Adar I. captures Babylon . 1280
His descendant, Tiglath-pileser I. a great conqueror and the real founder of the Assyrian empire 1140
His son, Assur-bel-Kala, a weak prince . . . 1110
The empire falls into decay for nearly two centuries.
The empire revives under Assur-dân II., and is fully restored by his successors, Rimmonnirari II. 911–889 and Assur-natsir-pal 883–858
His son, Shalmaneser II. makes large conquests in W. Asia . . . . 858, *et seq.*
At Karkar he defeats Benhadad, king of Damascus, Ahab, king of Israel, and Irkhuleni, king of Hamath 854
The empire enlarged by his son, Samas-Rimmon II. B.C. 823–810
The Assyrian eponym canon records a solar eclipse, and is thereby the basis of Assyrian chronology . 763
Assur-nirari king; many revolts . . 753, *et seq.*
Pulu, or Pul, usurps the throne and styles himself Tiglath Pileser. He consolidated the empire, reformed the government, quelled revolts and enlarged his dominions by the conquest of Babylon, &c. 745–727
His weak son, Shalmaneser IV. king, 727; died, or was murdered by Sargon the Tartan, who continues the war in Assyria, captures Samaria and replaces the inhabitants by colonists. 2 *Kings* xvii. 720
At the battle of Raphia he checks the advances of Egypt, and captures the rich Hittite capital, Carchemish 717
Merodach-baladan III. raises a revolt against Sargon, who, after a severe campaign, captures Babylon, and is proclaimed king 710
Sargon is killed in his new palace . . . July, 705
His son, Sennacherib, succeeds him.
Babylonia revolts; Merodach-baladan returns, but is defeated at Kisu; Sennacherib conquers Phœnicia, and having been offended by Hezekiah, he ravages Judæa, and besieges Jerusalem, which is saved by the sudden destruction of his army, *Isaiah* xxxvii. 36–38; he is killed by his sons . . . . Dec. 681
His son, Esar-haddon defeats his brothers, and becomes king at Nineveh, and reorganizes the empire . . . . 680, *et seq.*
He invades Judæa, makes Manasseh prisoner.
He invades Egypt and captures Memphis, and after a long campaign, subdues the country and becomes ruler of nearly all the ancient world 675, *et seq.*
Disturbed by a rising in Egypt and conspiracies at home, he makes his son, Assur-bani-pal, king at Nineveh, April, 669, and dies during a campaign, Oct. 667. Assur-bani-pal (Sardanapalus?), weak but ambitious, continues the war in Egypt and captures Thebes, invades Phœnicia and captures Tyre.
He appoints his brother, Samas-sum-yukin, viceroy of Babylon, who heads a great revolt, which lasts five years; Babylon is taken and the rebel prince burns himself in his palace with many of his followers 647
Gradual fall of the empire; new revolts; Egypt becomes independent; Kandanalu, viceroy of Babylon, and his successor, father of Nebuchadnezzar, become independent; Assur-bani-pal succeeded by his son, Assur-etil-ilîyukinni . . 640

Esar-haddon II. (the Sarakos of Ctesias), the last king; the N.E. provinces invaded by a vast confederation under the command of Kazaril (Cyaxares the Mede)
Disruption and anarchy closed by the siege and destruction of Nineveh . . . . about 606
Assyria becomes a Median province.
Assyria subdued by Alexander the Great . . . 332
It subsequently formed part of the kingdoms of Syria, Parthia, and Persia.
It was conquered by the Turks . . . A.D. 1637
Explored by col. Chesney and the Euphrates exploring expedition . . . 1835-37
Layard's Discoveries published (see *Nineveh*) . 1848-53
Mr. George Smith, of British Museum, began to study inscriptions, 1866; (received aid from proprietors of *Daily Telegraph*), and started to explore Assyrian remains, 20 June, 1873; worked in 1873-74; published "Assyrian Discoveries" March, 1875
Started to renew his explorations, Oct. 1875; died at Aleppo . . . . . . 19 Aug. 1876
The explorations resumed by Mr. Hormusd Rassam, see *Nineveh*.
Classes for the study of Assyrian language formed; rev. A. H. Sayce publishes an Assyrian grammar 1875

(See *Nineveh*.)

ASTEROIDS, a name improperly given to the minor planets, see under *Planets*.

ASTLEY'S AMPHITHEATRE, see under *Theatres*.

ASTON RIOTS, see *Birmingham*, 1884.

ASTOR BEQUESTS, see *Libraries*.

ASTORGA (N. W. Spain), the ancient Asturica Augusta, was taken by the French, 22 April, 1810, and treated with great severity.

ASTRAKHAN (S.E. Russia), a province acquired from the Mogul's empire in 1554; visited and settled by Peter the Great in 1722. Collision between two steamers on the Volga, 40 deaths; reported, 16 Sept. 1897. Population, 516,000.

ASTROLABE, an instrument for observing the stars, said to have been employed by Hipparchus about 130 B.C.; and by Ptolemy about 140 A.D. The modern astrolabe was described by Fabricius in 1513. Chaucer's "Treatise on the Astrolabe," published 1872 by the Early English Text Society.

ASTROLOGY was cultivated by the Chaldæans, Egyptians, Hindus, Etruscans, Chinese, Greeks, and Romans. It was much in vogue in Italy and France in the 16th century. It is said that Bede, 673-735, was addicted to it; and Roger Bacon, 1214-1292. Lord Burleigh is said to have calculated the nativity of Elizabeth, and she, and other princes, were dupes of Dee, the astrologer. It is stated that Lilly was consulted by Charles I. respecting his projected escape from Carisbrook castle in 1647. *Ferguson*. Astrological almanacs are still published in London.

Michael Nostradamus, a French physician (1503–1566), cultivated astrology, published almanacs, and in 1555, "Centuries" and "Presages." His oracles, edited by Mr. Chas. A. Ward, appeared in 1892. He was consulted by Catherine de Medici, Henry II. and Charles IX. of France.
The Astrological Society of Great Britain founded 19 Feb. 1879.
"Neptune," an astrologer, fined for practising 29 May, 1886

ASTRONOMER-ROYAL, see *Greenwich*.

ASTRONOMY. The earliest astronomical observations were made at Babylon it is said about 2234 B.C. The study was much advanced in Chaldæa under Nabonassar; was known to the Chinese about 1100 B.C.; some say many centuries before, see *Eclipses, Stars, Planets, Comets, Sun, Moon, Jupiter, Venus, Saturn, Neptune, Mars, Observatories, &c.*

Lunar eclipses observed at Babylon, and recorded by Ptolemy . . . . about B.C. 720
Spherical form of the earth, and the true cause of lunar eclipses, taught by Thales . . about 600
Further discoveries by Pythagoras, who taught the doctrine of celestial motions, and believed in the plurality of habitable worlds; died . about 470
Meton introduces the lunar-solar cycle . . . 433
Treatises of Aristotle "concerning the heavens," and of Autolycus "on the motion of the sphere" (earliest extant works on astronomy) . about 350
Aratus writes a poem on astronomy 281
Archimedes observes solstices, &c. 212
Hipparchus, greatest of Greek astronomers, determines mean motion of sun and moon; discovers precession of equinoxes, &c. 160-125
The precession of the equinoxes confirmed, and the places and distances of the planets discovered, by Ptolemy . . . . A.D. 139-161
Astronomy and geography cultivated by the Arabs about 760; brought into Europe . . about 1200
Alphonsine tables (*which see*) composed . about 1253
Clocks first used in astronomy . . . about 1500
True doctrine of the motions of the planetary bodies revived by Copernicus, founder of modern astronomy; his "Revolution of the Heavenly Bodies" published 1543
Astronomy advanced by Tycho Brahe, who opposed the Ptolemaic system and started one of his own, in which the sun is supposed to move round the earth . . . . about 1582
Galileo constructs a telescope, 1609; and discovers Jupiter's satellites, &c. . . . . 8 Jan. 1610
True laws of the planetary motions announced by Kepler; 1st and 2nd, 1609; 3rd 1618
Various forms of telescopes and other instruments used in astronomy invented 1608-40
Cartesian system published by Des Cartes . . . 1637
The transit of Venus over the sun's disc first observed by Horrocks . . . . 24 Nov. 1639
Huyghens completes the discovery of Saturn's ring 1654
Cassini draws his meridian line, after Dante; see *Bologna* 1655
The aberration of the light of the fixed stars discovered by Horrebow 1659
Gregory invents a reflecting telescope . . . 1663
Discoveries of Picard 1669
Charts of the moon constructed by Scheiner, Langrenus, Hevelius, Riccioli, &c. . . . about 1670
Discoveries of Römer on the velocity of light, and his observation of Jupiter's satellites . . . 1675
Greenwich Observatory founded . . . . . "
Motion of the sun round its own axis proved by Halley 1676
Newton's *Principia* published; and the system, as now taught, demonstrated 1687
Catalogue of the stars made by Flamsteed . . . 1688
Cassini's chart of the full moon executed . . . 1692
Satellites of Saturn, &c., discovered by Cassini . 1701
Halley predicts the return of the comet (of 1758) . 1705
Flamsteed's *Historia Cœlestis* published . . . 1725
Aberration of the light of the stars discovered and explained by Dr. Bradley 1727
John Harrison produces chronometers for determining the longitude, 1735 *et seq.*, and obtains the reward 1764
"Nautical Almanac" first published 1767
Celestial inequalities found by La Grange . . . 1780
Uranus and satellites discovered by Herschel; see *Georgium Sidus* . . . . . 13 March, 1781
Mécanique Céleste, by La Place, published . . 1796
ROYAL ASTRONOMICAL SOCIETY OF LONDON founded, 1820; chartered 1831
Beer and Mädler's map of the moon published . . 1834
Lord Rosse's telescope constructed . . . 1828-45
The planet Neptune (*which see*) discovered, 23 Sept. 1846
Bond photographs the moon (see *Photography, celestial*) 1851
Hansen's table of the moon published at expense of the British government 1857
Trustees of the rev. Richard Sheepshanks present 10,000*l.* stock to Trinity College, Cambridge, for promotion of the study of astronomy, meteorology, and magnetism . . . . 2 Dec. 1858

Spectrum analysis applied in astronomy (see *Spectrum*) 1861
Large photograph of the moon by W. de la Rue . 1863
Royal Astronomical Society removed from Somerset-house to Burlington-house 1874
Two satellites of Mars discovered by prof. Asaph Hall, at Washington, U.S. . . 11, 18 Aug. 1877
Astronomical Congress opened at Paris; arrangements made for photographing charts of the heavens at different observatories 16–26 April, 1887
Met again, Sept. 1889; April, 1891, 1896, and 1900; vol. ii. of the charts begun 1892; the work progressing slowly, reported 1902
Mr. G. F. Chambers' "Handbook of Astronomy," new edition 1889–90
Mr. C. H. F. Peters, of Hamilton college observatory, New York, discovered 48 minor planets and several comets; born in Schleswig, 19 Sept. 1813; died, 19 July, 1890; his son, prof. C. A. F. Peters, of the Königsberg observatory, died . 2 Dec. 1894
British Astronomical association: first meeting 24 Oct. 1890
Mr. (after sir) Wm. Huggins, president, at the meeting of the British Association at Cardiff, describes the results of the application of spectrum analysis and photography to astronomy . 19 Aug. 1891
ASTRONOMICAL SOCIETY OF FRANCE inaugurated 12 Oct. ,,
Mr. Norman Lockyer announces his theory respecting the constitution of the heavenly bodies (see under *Meteors*) . . . . . 17 Nov. ,,
New star in Auriga (see *Milky way*) . . 1 Feb. 1892
Mr. (aft. sir) Norman Lockyer's "Dawn of Astronomy," published . . . . . Feb. 1894
Mr. John Russell Hind born 1823, died 23 Dec. 1895 (see *Planets* and *Comets*).
M. Tisserand, director of the Paris observatory, born 1845, author of "Traité de Mécanique Céleste," died . . . . . 20 Oct. 1896
Prof. Hugo Gylden, director of the Stockholm observatory, died, aged 55 . . . . 9 Nov. ,,
Astronomical Congress (17th) at Budapest, end Sept. 1898
Miss Elizabeth Brown, eminent astronomer (dies 5 March, 1899) bequeaths her observatory at Farther Burton and 1,000*l*. to the British Astronomical Society.
"Atlas of Representative Stellar Spectra," by sir William and lady Huggins, published (see *Royal Institution Actonian Prize*) . . . early 1900
Large projection of Mars discovered 26 May at Harvard observatory, 3-35 a.m. g.m.t. reported 28 May, 1903
Dr. Andrew A. Common, F.R.S., eminent astronomer, died, aged 62 . . . . 2 June, ,,
Enormous sunspot . . . . . . Oct. ,,

ASTROPHYSICS, the science of applying physics and chemistry and other terrestrial sciences to the heavenly bodies by means of spectrum analysis, photography, &c., developed by sir Wm. Huggins from the work of Kirchhoff and Bunsen, 1861 *et seq*.

ASTURIAS (Oviedo, since 1833), N.W. Spain, an ancient principality. Here Pelayo collected the Gothic fugitives, about 713, founded a new kingdom, and by his victories checked Moorish conquest. For his successors, see *Spain*. The heir-apparent of the monarchy has borne the title "prince of Asturias" since 1388, when it was assumed by Henry, son of John I. king of Leon, on his marriage with a descendant of Peter of Castile. In 1808, the junta of Asturias began the organised resistance to the French usurpation.

ASYLUMS, or **PRIVILEGED PLACES**, at first were places of refuge for those who by accident or necessity had done things that rendered them obnoxious to the law. God commanded the Jews to build cities of refuge, 1451 B.C., *Numbers* xxv.—Cadmus is mythically said to have built one at Thebes, and Romulus one at Mount Palatine, 151 B.C.; see *Sanctuaries; Metropolitan District*.

ATALANTA (formerly *Juno*), training-ship, left Bermuda on a trial voyage, under capt. Stirling, 31 Jan. 1880. On board, 15 officers, and 255 petty officers, seamen, marines, and boys; never heard of again. Many merchant vessels were wrecked during a terrific gale, 12-16 Feb. 1880. See *Mansion House Funds*.

ATAVISM (Latin *atavus*, "an ancestor"), the reappearance of an ancestral type in an animal or plant; see also *Heredity*. Dr. Darwin's "Variation under Domestication," pub. 1868. F. Galton's "Natural Inheritance," pub. 1889.

ATCHINOFF INCIDENT, see under *Russia*, 1889.

ATELIERS NATIONAUX (National Workshops), were established by the French provisional government in Feb. 1848. They interfered greatly with private trade, as about 100,000 workmen threw themselves upon the government for labour and payment. The breaking-up of the system led to the fearful conflicts in June following; and the system was abolished in July.

ATHANASIAN CREED. Athanasius, of Alexandria, elected bishop, 326. He firmly opposed the doctrines of Arius (who denied Christ's divinity), was several times exiled; died in 373.

Lumby, in "History of the Creeds' (1874), asserts that this creed, beginning "*Quicunque vult*," was not composed by Athanasius; that it is made up of two distinct parts, and was originally written in Latin and put into its present shape between 813 and 850; not connected with Athanasius's name by any trustworthy authority before 809; set forth first in Gaul, about 870; gradually extended into Italy, Britain, &c.; accepted by the Greek church about 1200.
This creed asserts the procession of the Holy Ghost from the Father and the Son, see *Filioque*.
Dr. Waterland's Critical History of this creed, 1723.
Much agitation against the general use of this creed has arisen in the Church of England among both clergy and laity, 1870-73.
Modifications approved by several bishops were negatived by the lower house in convocation (62-7) early in May, 1872. The vote was rejected by the bishops, and the agitation continued.
In a letter to the earl of Shaftesbury, 22 July, 1872, the archbishops of Canterbury and York expressed their hope of devising a way for rendering the reading of the creed during public worship not compulsory.
Great meeting of laity at St. James's Hall in defence of the creed, 31 Jan. 1873.
Omission of "damnatory clauses" in the creed at services in Westminster abbey revives discussion as to its use, Jan. *et seq.* 1903.

ATHEISM (from the Greek *a*, without, *Theos*, God, see *Psalm* xiv. 1). It was professed by Epicurus, Lucretius, and other philosophers. Spinoza was the defender of a similar doctrine (1632-1677). Lucilio Vanini publicly taught atheism in France, and was condemned to be burnt at Toulouse in 1619. Mathias Knutzen, of Holstein, openly professed atheism, and had upwards of a thousand disciples in Germany about 1674; he travelled to make proselytes, and his followers were called *Conscienciaries*, because they held that there is no other deity than conscience. Atheism prevailed during the French republic, 1794 till 1801; see *Materialism*. Bill to prevent Atheists sitting in Parliament, read, 7 March, 1882; dropped. Mr. Bradlaugh's Oaths bill to relieve Atheists, passed, 24 Dec. 1888. See *Parliament*.

ATHENÆA were great festivals celebrated at Athens in honour of Minerva. One was called Panathenæa, the other Chalcea; they are mythically said to have been instituted by Erechtheus or Orpheus, 1397 or 1495 B.C.; and revived by Theseus, who caused them to be observed by all the Athenians, the first every fifth year, 1234 B.C. *Plutarch.*

ATHENÆUM, a place at Athens, sacred to Minerva, where the poets and philosophers recited their compositions. That of Rome, of great beauty, was erected by the emperor Adrian, 133.—The ATHENÆUM CLUB of London was formed 16 Feb. 1824, for the association of persons of scientific and literary attainments, and artists, also noblemen and gentlemen, patrons of learning, &c., by the earls of Liverpool and Aberdeen, the marquis of Lansdowne, Dr. T. Young, Moore, Davy, Scott, Mackintosh, Faraday, Croker, Chantrey, Lawrence, and seven future premiers. The clubhouse was erected in 1829-30 on the site of the late Carlton palace; it is of Grecian architecture, and the frieze is an exact copy of the Panathenaic procession which formed the frieze of the Parthenon.—The Liverpool Athenæum was opened 1 Jan. 1799.—At Manchester, Bristol, and many other places, buildings under this name, and for a like purpose, have been founded. — The *Athenæum*, a weekly literary and scientific journal in relation to literature, science, and the fine arts, originated by James Silk Buckingham, first appeared in 1828. John Francis, publisher, 1831-82, died 6 April, 1882. Rev. Henry Stebbing, first editor, died 22 Sept. 1883, aged 84. The *Athenæum* became the property of Mr. C. W. Dilke in 1830, and speedily became an influential critical journal; a review of the literature in thirteen countries, appeared, 2 July, 1898. Prof. Almeric Ramsey, an admirable reviewer, born, 31 Jan. 1825, died mid-April, 1899. See *Trials*, 1875.

ATHENRY (Galway). Near here the Irish were totally defeated, and a gallant young chief, Feidlim O'Connor, slain 10 Aug. 1316.

ATHENS, the capital of ancient Attica, and of modern Greece. The first sovereign mentioned is Ogyges, who reigned in Bœotia, and was master of Attica, then called Ionia. Tradition states that in his reign (about 1764 B.C.) a deluge laid waste the country, which so remained till the arrival of the Egyptian Cecrops and a colony, by whom the land was re-peopled, and twelve cities founded, 1556 B.C. The city, said to have been first called Cecropia, was afterwards named Athens in honour of Minerva (Athenē), her worship having been introduced by Erechtheus, 1383 B.C. Athens was ruled by seventeen successive kings (487 years), by thirteen *perpetual* archons (316 years), seven *decennial* archons (70 years), and lastly by *annual* archons (760 years). It attained great power, and no other city has had, in a short space of time, so great a number of illustrious citizens. The ancients called Athens *Astu*, the *city*, by eminence, and one of the eyes of Greece; see *Greece*. The early history is mythical and the dates conjectural.

Population of modern Athens, 1871, 48,107; 1879, 63,374; 1889, 114,355; 1896, 179,755 (with Pireus).

The MS. text of the recovered work of Aristotle on the Constitution of Athens, was published by the British Museum . . . . Jan. 1891

[See *Aristotelian Philosophy.*]

	B.C.
Arrival of Cecrops [1558 *Hales*, 1433 *Clinton*] *Usher*	1556
The Areopagus established	1507
Deucalion arrives in Attica	1502
Reign of Amphictyon . . . [1499 *H.*]	1497
The Panathenæan Games . . . [1481 *H.*]	1495
Erichthonius reigns	1487
Erechtheus teaches husbandry	1383
Eleusinian mysteries introduced by Eumolpus	1356
Erechtheus killed in battle with the Eleusinians	1347
Ægeus invades Attica, and ascends the throne	1283
He throws himself into the sea, and is drowned: hence the name of the Ægean Sea. *Eusebius.*	,,
Theseus, his son, succeeds, and reigns 30 years	1235
He collects his subjects into one city, and names it Athens	1234
Reign of Mnestheus, 1205; of Demophoön	1182
Court of Ephetes established	1179
The Prianepsæ instituted	1178
Melanthus conquers Xuthus in single combat and is chosen king	1128
Reign of Codrus, his son, the last king	1092
In a battle with the Heraclidæ, Codrus is killed: he had resolved to perish; the oracle having declared that the victory should be with the side whose leader was killed	1070
Royalty abolished;—Athens governed by archons, Medon the first . . . (1070 *H.*)	1044
Alcmeon, last *perpetual* archon, dies	753
Cherops, first *decennial* archon	752
Hippomenes deposed for his cruelty	713
Erixias, 7th and last *decennial* archon, dies	684
Creon, first *annual* archon	683
Draco, the 12th annual archon, publishes his laws said "to have been written in blood"	B.C. 621
Solon supersedes them by his excellent code	594
Pisistratus, the "tyrant," seizes the supreme power, 560; flight of Solon, 559. Pisistratus establishes his government, 537; collects a public library, 531; dies	527
First tragedy acted at Athens, on a waggon, by Thespis	535
Hipparchus assassinated by Harmodius and Aristogeiton	514
The law of ostracism established; Hippias and the Pisistratidæ banished	510
Lemnos taken by Miltiades	504
The Persian invaders defeated at Marathon	490
Death of Miltiades	489
Aristides, surnamed the *Just*, banished	483
Athens taken by the Persian Xerxes	480
Burnt to the ground by Mardonius	479
Rebuilt and fortified by Themistocles; Piræus built	478
Themistocles banished	471
Cimon, son of Miltiades, overruns all Thrace	469
Pericles takes part in public affairs, 469; he and Cimon adorn Athens, 464; the latter banished	461
Athens begins to tyrannise over Greece	459
The long wall built	457
Literature, philosophy, and art flourish	448
The first sacred (or social) war; (*which see*)	,,
Tolmidas conducts an expedition into Bœotia, and is defeated and killed near Coronea	447
The thirty years' truce between the Athenians and Lacedæmonians	445
Herodotus said to have read his history in the council at Athens	,,
Pericles obtains the government	444
Pericles subdues Samos	440
Satirical comedies prohibited at Athens	,,
Alliance between Athens and Corcyra, then at war with Corinth, 433; leads to the Peloponnesian war (lasted 27 years); it began	431
A dreadful plague, which had ravaged Ethiopia, Libya, Egypt, and Persia, extends to Athens, and continues for five years	430
Death of Pericles of the plague	429
Disastrous expedition against Sicily; death of the commanders, Demosthenes and Nicias; Athenian fleet destroyed by Gylippus	415-413
Government of the "four hundred"	411
Alcibiades defeats the Lacedæmonians at Cyzicus; (*which see*)	410
Alcibiades, accused of aspiring to sovereign power, banished	407
Athens victorious in a sea fight at Arginusæ	406
Athenian fleet destroyed by Lysander at Ægospotami	405
He besieges Athens by land and sea; its walls are destroyed, and it capitulates, and the Peloponnesian war terminates	404
Rule of the thirty tyrants, who are overthrown by Thrasybulus	403
Socrates (aged 70) put to death	399
The Corinthian war begins	395
Conon rebuilds the long walls, and fortifies the Piræus	393
Plato founds the academy	388
War against Sparta	378
The Lacedæmonian fleet defeated at Naxus by Chabrias	376

General peace 371
Philip, king of Macedon, opposes the Athenians; see *Macedon* 359
Second sacred (or social) war 357-355
First Philippic of Demosthenes 352
Peace with Macedon 346
Battle of Cheronæa (*which see*); the Athenians and Thebans defeated by Philip . . . 7 Aug. 338
Philip assassinated by Pausanias 336
Athens submits to Alexander, who spares the orators 335
Death of Alexander 323
The Lamian war; the Athenians and others rise against Macedon, 323; defeated at Cranon; Demosthenes poisons himself 322
Athens surrenders to Cassander, who governs well, 318; execution of Phocion 317
Demetrius Poliorcetes expels Demetrius Phalereus, and restores the Athenian democracy, 307; the latter takes the chair of philosophy 296
A league between Athens, Sparta, and Egypt . B.C. 277
Athens taken by Antigonus Gonatas, king of Macedon, 268; restored by Aratus 256
The Athenians join the Achæan league . . . 229
They join the Ætolians against Macedon, and send for assistance to Rome 215
A Roman fleet arrives at Athens 211
The Romans proclaim liberty at Athens . . . 196
Subjugation of Greece 144
The Athenians implore assistance against the Romans from Mithridates, king of Pontus, whose general, Archelaus, makes himself master of Athens 88
Athens besieged by Sylla, the Roman general; it is reduced to surrender by famine 86
Cicero studies at Athens, 79; and Horace . . . 42
The Athenians desert Pompey, to follow the interests of Cæsar 47
Athens visited by the apostle Paul . . . A.D. 52
Many temples, &c., erected by Hadrian . . 122-135
Athens taken by Alaric, and spared from slaughter 396
Acquired by Otho de la Roche, and afterwards made a duchy 1205
Subjected by the Turks 1444
By Mahomet II. 1456
By the Venetians 1466
Restored to the Turks 1479
Athens suffered much during the War of Independence, 1821-7. Taken by the Turks (see *Greece*) 17 May, 1827
Becomes the capital of the kingdom of modern Greece, 1833
British School of Archæology, much promoted by Sir C. T. Newton, 1883; (first director, F. C. Penrose), opened . . . . . Nov. 1886
The Parthenon and other buildings injured by earthquake (*which see*) . . . 20 April, *et seq.* 1894
See *Greece*.
The restoration of the ancient stadium in marble by M. Averoff; see *Olympic Games* . . . 1896
Destructive thunderstorm, slight shocks of earthquake, overflow of the Kephisos Ilissos, houses and bridges wrecked, great destruction at the Piræus, serious loss of life; (relief fund opened by the king) . . . . . 26 Nov. ,,
Student riots in Athens, military called out, 27 Jan. 1897; the university held by the students, blockaded by troops, conflicts with the police 29 Jan.; intervention of the professors, revolt ended. . . . . 30 Jan. 1897
Mdme. Syngros presents over quarter million sterling for improvement of the water supply, March, 1899
Government scheme to provide Athens with water from Lake Stymphalus in the Morea, reported, June, ,,
M. G. Averoff, benefactor, bequeaths large sums to public works and charities, dies . 27 July, ,,
The Piræus and part of city flooded . 17 Nov. ,,
A statue of Mr. Gladstone unveiled by the king, 7 July, 1900
Opposition to the translation of the Gospel into modern Greek, published under the queen's direction in 1900; fatal rioting, the metropolitan and the prefect of police resign, 20, 21 Nov; the university held by the students, 24 Nov.; evacuated, quiet restored . . . . . 26 Nov. 1901
French school of archæology: new building opened, fêtes, &c. . . . . . . 2 April, 1902
International Exhibition at Athens opened, 3 June, 1903

ATHLETIC SPORTS were first organised by the Greeks. On the plain of Olympia at the great national festival held every fourth year in honour of Zeus, athletes trained to the highest degree of physical perfection contested in foot, horse and chariot races, wrestling, boxing and kindred sports, receiving for prizes garlands of wild olives, which also conferred various civic honours and privileges. Similar in their character were the Isthmian, Nemean and Pythian games. The consul, M. Fulvius, in 186 B.C., introduced athletic sports in Rome, but these speedily degenerated into gladiatorial contests. Among Old English sports were running, jumping, archery, quarterstaff, singlestick, and throwing the bar, in which pastime Henry VIII. (1509-47) was an adept. The Cotswold games were celebrated in the 16th and 17th centuries, as were also the Cumberland and Westmoreland sports. In more recent times amateur athletic sports may be said to have begun their revival at the great athletic meeting of the civil service sports in 1864, and the university sports from the meeting at Christchurch, Oxford, in 1861, when our king, then prince of Wales, was present. Numerous clubs, such as the London athletic club, the national cyclists' club, the Blackheath harriers, the amateur athletic association, the national football association, the Rugby union, the M.C.C. represent the interests of the various branches of athletic sports, which continue yearly to increase in popularity. See under *various headings*, as *Cricket*, *Football*, &c.

ATHLONE, Roscommon, Ireland, was burnt during the civil war in 1641. After the battle of the Boyne, colonel R. Grace held Athlone for James II. against a besieging army, but was killed when it was taken by assault by Ginckel, 30 June, 1691; see *Aughrim*.

ATHOS. A mountain in Roumelia, termed Monte Santo from its numerous monasteries whose libraries contain many MSS. especially of the old and new testaments, of great antiquity. Professor Lambros is preparing a catalogue, 1889.

By a great fire in the forests, many monasteries and hermitages were destroyed, and about 12 monks or hermits perished, reported about . 2 Aug. 1890
A monastery was burnt about . . 14 June, 1891

ATLANTA, Georgia, population, 1890, 65,533; 1900, 89,872. See *United States*, 1864.

ATLANTIC TELEGRAPH, see *Electric Telegraph*, under *Electricity*.

ATLANTIC UNION formed for the purpose of uniting by ties of personal friendship the various English-speaking peoples; committee: sir Walter Besant (hon. treasurer), died 9 June, 1901; Dr. (after sir) Conan Doyle, lord Coleridge, and many others; Feb. 1900.

ATLAS, see *Charts* and *Mercator*.

ATMOLYSIS, a method of separating the constituent gases of a compound gas (such as atmospheric air) by causing it to pass through a vessel of porous material (such as graphite); first made known in Aug. 1863, by the discoverer, the late professor T. Graham, F.R.S., master of the mint.

ATMOSPHERE, see *Air*.

ATMOSPHERIC RAILWAYS. The idea of producing motion by atmospheric pressure was conceived by Papin, the French engineer, about 1680. Experiments were made on a line of rail, laid down across Wormwood Scrubs, London, between Shepherd's Bush and the Great Western railroad, to test the efficacy of atmospheric tubes, the working of the air-pump, and speed of carriages upon this new principle on railroads in June, 1840, and then tried for a short time on a line between Croydon and London, 1845. Atmospheric pressure was also tried and abandoned, in 1848, on the South Devon line. An atmospheric railway was commenced between Dalkey and Killiney, in the vicinity of Dublin, in Sept. 1843; opened 29 March, 1844; discontinued in 1855. A similar railway was proposed to be laid down in the streets of London by Mr. T. W. Rammell, in 1857. Mr. Rammell's Pneumatic Railway was put in action successfully at the Crystal Palace on 27 Aug. 1864, and following days. An act for a pneumatic railway between the Waterloo railway station and Whitehall was passed in July, 1865. Atmospheric pressure was proposed for a submarine railway from Dover to Calais, in 1869; see *Pneumatic Despatch*.

ATOMIC THEORY, in chemistry, deals with the indivisible particles of all substances. The somewhat incoherent labours of his predecessors (such as Wenzel, in 1777) were reduced by John Dalton to four laws of combining proportion, which have received the name of "Atomic Theory." His "Chemical Philosophy," containing the exposition of his views, appeared in 1808. Dr. C. Daubeny's work on the Atomic Theory was published in 1850. In his standard of *Atomic weights* Dalton takes hydrogen as 1. Berzelius, who commenced his elaborate researches on the subject in 1848, adopts oxygen as 100. The former standard is used in this country, the latter on the continent. The theory is accepted by some, and rejected by other chemists. In 1855 Hinrichs propounded a new hypothetical science, *Atomechanics*, in which *pantogen*, composed of panatoms, is regarded as the primary chemical principle. "A New View of the Origin of Dalton's Atomic Theory," by Sir H. E. Roscoe and Arthur Harden, published April, 1896.

ATOMS. Democritus (about 400 B.C.) held that the only existing things are innumerable indestructible atoms, varying in form, and combined in obedience to mechanical laws, and that the soul consists of free, smooth, round atoms like those of fire; and that nothing happens by chance. His philosophy was adopted by Epicurus (about 306 B.C.), whose doctrines are luminously expounded by Lucretius in his great poem, "*De Rerum Naturâ*" (On the Nature of Things), 57 B.C. The atomic philosophy, in a modified form, was recognised by Gassendi, who died 1655 A.D. Sir Wm. Thomson's discourse "On the Size of Atoms," at the Royal Institution, 2 Feb. 1883, is printed in the "Proceedings," vol. x. See *Times*, 13 June, 1883.

ATREBATES, a Belgic people, subdued by Cæsar, 57 B.C.; see *Artois*.

ATTAINDER, ACTS OF, whereby a person not only forfeited his land, but his blood was attainted, have been numerous. Two witnesses in cases of high treason are necessary where corruption of blood is incurred, unless the party accused shall confess, or stand mute, 7 & 8 Will. III. 1694-5. *Blackstone*. The attainder of lord Wm. Russell, who was beheaded in Lincoln's-inn-fields, 21 July, 1683, was reversed under William, in 1689. The rolls and records of the acts of attainder passed in the reign of James II. were cancelled and publicly burnt, 2 Oct. 1695. Sir John Fenwick was the *last* person executed by act of attainder, 28 Jan. 1697. Amongst the last acts reversed was the attaint of the children of lord Edward Fitzgerald (who was implicated in the rebellion in Ireland of 1798), 1 July, 1819. In 1814 and 1833 the severity of attainders was mitigated. Several attainders reversed about 1827, and one in 1853 (the earl of Perth).

ATTICA, see *Athens*.

ATTILA, surnamed the "*Scourge of God*," and thus distinguished for his conquests and his crimes, having ravaged the eastern empire from 445 to 450, when he made peace with Theodosius. He invaded the western empire, 450, and was defeated by Aëtius at Châlons, 451; he then retired into Pannonia, where he died through the bursting of a blood vessel on his nuptials with Ildico, a beautiful virgin, 453.

ATTORNEY (from *tour*, turn), a person appointed to act for another. An attorney-at-law was a properly qualified law agent practising in the common law courts; persons conducting suits in the courts of chancery being termed solicitors. The number in Edward III.'s reign was under 400 for the whole kingdom. In the 32nd of Henry VI., 1454, a law reduced the practitioners in Norfolk, Norwich, and Suffolk, from eighty to fourteen, and restricted their increase. The number of attorneys practising in the United Kingdom was said to be 13,824 (1872). By the Judicature Act, 1873, which came in force, 1 Nov. 1875, all solicitors, attorneys and proctors are now called "solicitors of the supreme court."

ATTORNEY-GENERAL, the chief law officer of the crown, is appointed by letters patent. He acts for the crown in all proceedings at law and equity affecting the royal prerogative; and prosecutes for the crown in criminal and in revenue cases, and grants fiats for writs of error. His sanction is required before proceedings can be taken under the Public Health Act, Corrupt Practices Act. He may, in his discretion, prosecute for any misdemeanour, and can stay proceedings in any indictment without consent of prosecutor. In his absence his duties are performed by the "solicitor-general." The first attorney-general was William Bonneville, 1277.

1660. Sir Jeffrey Palmer.
1670. Sir Heneage Finch, afterwards earl of Nottingham.
1673. Sir Francis North, knt., afterwards lord Guilford.
1675. Sir William Jones.
1679. Sir Cresvel Levinz, or Levinge, knt.
1681. Sir Robert Sawyer, knt.
1687. Sir Thomas Powis, knt.
1689. Henry Pollexfen, esq.
,, Sir George Treby, knt.
1692. Sir John Summers, knt., afterwards lord Somers.
1693. Edward Ward, esq.
1695. Sir Thomas Trevor, knt., afterwards lord Trevor.
1701. Edward Northey, esq.
1707. Sir Simon Harcourt, knt.
1708. Sir James Montagu, knt.
1710. Sir Simon Harcourt, again; aft. lord Harcourt.
,, Sir Edward Northey, knt.
1718. Nicholas Lechmere, esq., aft. lord Lechmere.
1720. Sir Robert Raymond, aft. lord Raymond.
1724. Sir Philip Yorke, aft. earl of Hardwicke.
1734. Sir John Willes, knt.
1737. Sir Dudley Ryder, knt.
1754. Hon. William Murray, aft. earl of Mansfield.
1756. Sir Robert Henley, knt., aft. earl of Northington.
1757. Sir Charles Pratt, knt., afterwards lord Camden.
1762. Hon. Charles Yorke.
1763. Sir Fletcher Norton, knt., aft. lord Grantley.
1765. Hon. Charles Yorke, again; afterwards lord Morden and lord chancellor; see *Chancellors*.
1766. William de Grey, afterwards lord Walsingham.
1771. Edward Thurlow, esq., afterwards lord Thurlow.
1778. Alex. Wedderburn, aft. lord Loughborough.
1780. James Wallace, esq.
1782. Lloyd Kenyon, esq.
1783. James Wallace, esq.
,, John Lee, esq.
,, Lloyd Kenyon, again; afterwards lord Kenyon.

1784. Sir Richard P. Arden, aft. lord Alvanley.
1788. Sir Archibald Macdonald.
1793. Sir John Scott, afterwards lord Eldon.
1799. Sir J. Mitford, afterwards lord Redesdale.
1801. Sir Edward Law, aft. lord Ellenborough, 14 Feb.
1802. Hon. Spencer Percival (murdered by Bellingham, 11 May, 1812), 15 April.
1806. Sir Arthur Pigott, 12 Feb.
1807. Sir Vicary Gibbs, afterwards chief justice of the common pleas, 7 April.
1812. Sir Thomas Plumer, afterwards first vice-chancellor of England, 26 June.
1813. Sir William Garrow, 4 May.
1817. Sir Samuel Shepherd, 7 May.
1819. Sir Robert Gifford, aft. lord Gifford, 24 July.
1824. Sir John Singleton Copley, afterwards lord Lyndhurst, 9 Jan.
1826. Sir Charles Wetherell, 20 Sept.
1827. Sir James Scarlett, 27 April.
1828. Sir Charles Wetherell, again, 19 Feb.
1829. Sir Jas. Scarlett, again; aft. lord Abinger, 29 June.
1830. Sir Thos. Denman, aft. lord Denman, 26 Nov.
1832. Sir William Horne, 26 Nov.
1834. Sir John Campbell, 1 March.
,, Sir Frederick Pollock, 17 Dec.
1835. Sir John Campbell, again, afterwards lord Campbell (and, 1859, lord chancellor), 30 April.
1841. Sir Thomas Wilde, 3 July.
,, Sir F. Pollock, again; aft. chief baron, 6 Sept.
1844. Sir William W. Follett, 15 April.
1845. Sir Frederick Thesiger, 4 July.
1846. Sir Thomas Wilde, again: afterwards lord Truro, and lord chancellor, 6 July.
,, Sir John Jervis, afterwards chief justice of the common pleas, 13 July.
1850. Sir John Romilly, aft. master of the rolls, 11 July.
1851. Sir Alex. James Edmund Cockburn, 28 March.
1852. Sir Frederick Thesiger, again; afterwards lord Chelmsford, and lord chancellor, 2 March.
1852. Sir Alexander Cockburn, again; aft. chief justice of common pleas and queen's bench, 28 Dec.
1856. Sir Richard Bethell, 15 Nov.
1858. Sir Fitzroy Kelly, 27 Feb., aft. chief baron, 1866; *d.* 1880.
1859. Sir R. Bethell (since lord Westbury, and lord chancellor), 18 June.
1861. Sir William Atherton, 27 July.
1863. Sir Roundell Palmer, aft. lord Selborne, and lord chancellor, 2 Oct.
1866. Sir Hugh M. Cairns, aft. lord Cairns, and lord chancellor, 13 July.
,, Sir John Rolt (made justice of appeal), 28 Oct.
1867. Sir John Karslake, 1 July.
1868. Sir Robert Porrett Collier, 12 Dec.
1871. Sir John Duke Coleridge, aft. lord Coleridge, and lord chief justice, 10 Nov.
1873. Sir Henry James, Nov.
1874. Sir John Karslake, Feb.
,, Sir Richard Baggallay, 22 April.
1875. Sir John Holker, 25 Nov.
1880. Sir Henry James, 13 May.
1885. Sir Richard E. Webster, June.
1886. Sir Charles Russell, about 6 Feb.
,, Sir Richard E. Webster, 26 July.
1892. Sir Charles Russell, 18 Aug.; see *Appeal*, 1894.
1894. Sir John Rigby, 1 May (lord justice of appeal, Oct. 1894).
,, Sir Robert Threshie Reid, 10 Oct.
1895. Sir Richard E. Webster, 9 July.
1900. Sir Robert Bannatyne Finlay, 12 Nov.

ATTRACTION, described by Copernicus, about 1520, as an appetence or appetite which the Creator impressed upon all parts of matter; by Kepler as a corporeal affection tending to union, 1605. In 1687, sir I. Newton published his "Principia," containing his important researches on this subject. See *Gravitation*, *Magnetism*, and *Electricity*.

ATWOOD'S MACHINE, for proving the laws of accelerated motion by the falling of weights, invented by George Atwood; described 1784: he died 11 July, 1807.

AUBAINE, a right of the French kings, which existed from the beginning of the monarchy, whereby they claimed the property of every stranger who died in their country, without having been naturalised, was abolished by the national assembly in 1790-91; re-established by Napoleon in 1804, and finally annulled 14 July, 1819.

AUBEROCHE, Guienne, S. France. The earl of Derby defeated the French, besieging this place, 19 Aug. 1344.

AUCKLAND, capital of North Island (New Zealand), was founded Sept. 1840. The population of the district, in 1857, was estimated at 15,000 Europeans, and 35,000 natives; 1901, 67,226 (city and suburbs). The seat of government was removed to Wellington on Cook's Strait, Dec. 1864. Visit of the duke of Cornwall and York (prince of Wales), 10 July, 1901.

AUCTION, a kind of sale known to the Romans, mentioned by Cicero, Livy, and Petronius Arbiter. The first in Britain was about 1700, by Elisha Yale, a governor of Fort George, now Madras, in the East Indies, who thus sold the goods he had brought home. Auction and sales' tax began, 1779. Various acts of parliament have regulated auctions and imposed duties, in some cases as high as five per cent. By 8 Vict. c. 15 (1845), the duties were repealed, and a charge imposed "on the licence to be taken out by all auctioneers in the United Kingdom, of 10*l*." In 1858 there were 4358 licences granted, producing 43,580*l*.; 90,774*l*. in 1902. The abuses at auctions, termed "knock-outs," caused by combinations of brokers and others, excited much attention in Sept. 1866. An act regulating sales of land by auction was passed 15 July, 1867. Certain sales are now exempt from being conducted by a licensed auctioneer, such as goods and chattels under a distress for rent, and sales under the provisions of the Small Debts' acts for Scotland and Ireland. See the very important *Sale of Goods Act*.

AUDIANI, followers of Audæus of Mesopotamia, who, having been expelled from the Syrian church on account of his severely reproving the vices of the clergy, about 338, formed a sect and became its bishop. He was banished to Scythia, where he is said to have made many converts. His followers celebrated Easter at the time of the Jewish passover, attributed the human figure to the Deity, and had other peculiar tenets.

AUDIOMETER (from *audio*, I hear), an instrument for the measurement of the faculty of hearing; invented by professor Hughes (died 22 Jan. 1900). It consists of a battery of two Leclanché's cells connected with a simple microphone and telephone; described to the Royal Society, 15 May, 1879.

AUDIPHONE, an instrument to assist the partially deaf, invented by Mr. R. G. Rhodes of Chicago, and modified by M. Colladon of Geneva, in 1880. It consists of a thin sheet of hard ebonite rubber or card-board. This should be placed against the teeth, through which and other bones the vibrations are conveyed to the auditory nerve.

AUDIT-OFFICE, Somerset House. Commissioners for auditing the public accounts were appointed in 1785, and many statutes regulating their duties have since been enacted.

AUDLEY'S REBELLION, see *Rebellions*, 1497.

AUERSTÄDT (Prussia). Here on 14 Oct. 1806, the French, under Davoust, signally defeated the Prussians, under Blucher, see *Jena*.

AUGHRIM, near Athlone, in Ireland, where on 12 July, 1691, a battle was fought between the Irish, headed by the French general St. Ruth, and the English under general Ginckel. The former were defeated and lost 7000 men; the latter lost only 600 killed and 960 wounded. St. Ruth was slain. This engagement proved decisively fatal to the interest of James II., and Ginckel was created earl of Athlone.

AUGMENTATION OF POOR LIVINGS' OFFICE, established in 1704. 5597 clerical livings, not exceeding 50*l.* *per annum*, were found by the commissioners under the act of Anne capable of augmentation, by means of the bounty then established.

AUGMENTATIONS COURT, established in 1535 by 27 Hen. VIII. c. 27, in relation to cap. 28 same session, which gave the king the property of all monasteries having 200*l.* a year. The court was abolished by Mary, 1553, and restored by Elizabeth, 1558.

AUGSBURG (Bavaria), originally a colony settled by Augustus, about 12 B.C.; became a free city, and flourished during the middle ages. Here many important diets of the empire have been held. In A.D. 952, a council confirmed the order for the celibacy of the priesthood. Augsburg has suffered much by war, having been frequently taken by siege,—in 788, 1703, 1704, and, last, by the French, 10 Oct. 1805, who restored it to Bavaria in March, 1806. Population, 1890, 75,523; 1900, 89,109.

Augsburg Diet, summoned by the emperor Charles V., to settle the religious disputes of Germany, met 20 June, and separated . . . Nov. 1530
Confession of Augsburg, compiled by Melanchthon, Luther and others, signed by the Protestant princes, presented to the emperor Charles V., and read to the diet . . . . . 25 June, 1530
Interim of Augsburg, a document issued by Charles V.: an attempt to reconcile the Catholics and Protestants: (it was fruitless and was withdrawn) . . . . read 15 May, 1548
"Peace of Religion" signed at Augsburg, 25 Sept. 1555
League of Augsburg, for maintenance of the treaties of Münster, Nimeguen: a treaty between Holland and other powers against France, signed 9 July, 1686

AUGURY. Three augurs, at Rome, with vestals and several orders of the priesthood, were formally constituted by Numa, about 710 B.C. The number increased, and was fifteen at the time of Sylla, 81. The college of augurs was abolished by Theodosius about A.D. 390.

AUGUST, the sixth month of the Roman year (originally called *Sextilis*, or the sixth from March), by a decree of the senate received its present name in honour of Augustus Cæsar, in the year 8 B.C., because in this month he was created consul, had thrice triumphed in Rome, added Egypt to the Roman empire, and made an end of the civil wars. He added one day to the month, making it 31 days. The appearance of shooting stars on the 10th of Aug. was observed in the middle ages, when they were termed "St. Lawrence's tears." Their periodicity was noticed by Mr. Forster early in the present century. See under *France*, 10 *August*, 1792.

AUGUSTAN ERA began 14 Feb. 27 B.C., or 727 years after the foundation of Rome.

AUGUSTIN OR AUSTIN FRIARS, a religious order, which ascribes its origin to St. Augustin, bishop of Hippo, who died 430. They first appeared about the 11th century, and the order was constituted by pope Alexander IV., 1256. The rule requires poverty, humility, and chastity. Martin Luther was an Augustin monk. The Augustins held the doctrine of free grace, and were rivals of the Dominicans. The order appeared in England soon after the conquest, and had 32 houses at the suppression, 1536. One of their churches, at Austin Friars, London, erected 1354, and since the Reformation used by Dutch protestants, was partially destroyed by fire, 22 Nov. 1862. It was restored, and reopened, 1 Oct. 1865. A religious house of the order, dedicated to St. Monica, mother of Augustin, was founded in Hoxton-square, London, 1864. Letters and documents of the Dutch Church of London, 1462–1874, edited by J. H. Hessels; completed, 1897.

AULIC COUNCIL, a sovereign court in Germany, established by the emperor Maximilian I., being one of the two courts, the first called the Imperial Chamber civil and criminal, instituted at Worms, 1495, and afterwards held at Spires and Wetzler, and the other the Aulic council at Vienna, 1506. These courts having concurrent jurisdiction, were instituted for appeals in particular cases from the courts of the Germanic states.

AURAY (N. W. France). Here, on 29 Sept. 1364, the English, under John Chandos, defeated the French and captured their leader Du Guesclin. Charles of Blois, made duke of Brittany by the king of France, was slain, and a peace was made in April, 1365.

AURICULAR CONFESSION. The confession of sin at the ear (Latin, *auris*) of the priest was an early practice. It is incorrectly stated to have been forbidden in the 4th century by Nectarius, archbishop of Constantinople. It was enjoined by the council of Lateran in 1215, and by the council of Trent in 1551. It was one of the six articles of faith enacted by our Henry VIII. in 1539, but was abolished in England at the Reformation. Its revival here has been attempted by the extreme or Ritualistic section of the high church party.

The rev. Alfred Poole, a curate of St. Barnabas, Knightsbridge, was suspended by his bishop from his office for practising auricular confession in June, 1858, and the suspension was confirmed in Jan. 1859. Much excitement was created by a similar attempt by the rev. Temple West at Boyne Hill, in Sept. 1858.
In May, 1873, 483 clergymen of the Church of England presented a petition to convocation for the education, selection, and licensing of duly qualified confessors, in accordance with the provisions of canon law. Strongly disapproved of by the bishops.
Letter from the bishop of London asserting that confession should be to God; that to the minister optional, 21 July, 1873.
Archdeacon Denison (in a letter) declares war against all opposing auricular confession, 22 Aug. 1873.
96 peers send an address against auricular confession to the archbishop of Canterbury about 9 Aug. 1877.
For refusal of confessors to give evidence, see *Ireland* . . . . March, 1887
See *Holy Cross*.

AURIFLAMMA OR ORIFLAMME, the national banner mentioned in French history, belonging to the abbey of St. Denis, and suspended over the tomb of that saint. Louis le Gros was the first king who took this standard from the abbey to battle, 1124. *Hénault*. It appeared for the last time at Agincourt, 25 Oct. 1415. *Tillet*. Others say at Montlhery, 16 July, 1465.

AURORA, FRIGATE, sailed from Britain in 1771, to the East Indies, and was never again heard of.—AURORA, daily papal newspaper, appeared at Rome 1 June, 1880.

AURORÆ BOREALES AND AUSTRALES (Northern and Southern Polar Lights).

though rarely seen in central Europe, are frequent in the arctic and antarctic regions. In March, 1716, an aurora borealis extended from the west of Ireland to the confines of Russia. The whole horizon lat. 57° N. was overspread with continuous haze of a dismal red during a whole night, Nov. 1765.—Mr. Foster, the companion of captain Cook, saw the aurora in lat. 58° S. The aurora is now attributed to the passage of electric light through the rarefied air of the polar regions. In August and September, 1859 (and about 24 Oct. 1870), when brilliant auroræ were very frequent, the electric telegraph wires were seriously affected, and communications interrupted. Auroræ were seen at Rome and Basel, and also in Australia. A magnificent aurora appeared in New York and other states, evening of 13 Feb. 1892. A Danish expedition under lieut. Le Com starts for N. Finland to study the aurora, Dec. 1900.

AUSCULTATION, see *Stethoscope*.

AUSTERLITZ, a town in Moravia, where a battle was fought between the French and the allied Austrian and Russian armies, 2 Dec. 1805. Three emperors commanded: Alexander of Russia, Francis of Austria, and Napoleon of France. The killed and wounded exceeded 30,000 on the side of the allies, who lost forty standards, 150 pieces of cannon, and thousands of prisoners. The decisive victory of the French led to the treaty of Presburg, signed 26 Dec. 1805; see *Presburg*.

AUSTIN FRIARS, see *Augustin Friars*.

AUSTRALASIA, the fifth great division of the world. This name, originally given it by De Brosses, includes Australia, Van Diemen's Land (or Tasmania), New Guinea, New Zealand, New Britain, New Caledonia, &c., mostly discovered within two centuries. Accidental discoveries were made by the Spaniards as early as 1526; but the first accurate knowledge of these southern lands is due to the Dutch, who in 1606 explored a part of the coast of Papua or New Guinea. Torres, a Spaniard, passed through the straits which now bear his name, between that island and Australia, and gave the first correct report of the latter, 1606. The Dutch continued their discoveries. Grant in 1800, and Flinders again (1801-5) completed the survey. *M'Culloch*. Estimated population of the Australasian colonies in 1891, 3,932,000; 1897, 4,410,124; census 1901, 4,544,434. See *Australia*, *Gold*, &c.

Gen. Edwardes having recommended the federal action of all the Australian troops for colonial defence, Mr. D. Gillies, premier of Victoria, communicates his approval to sir H. Parkes, premier of New South Wales, who in his reply considers that the federal council act does not authorize this combined action, and strongly recommends the establishment of an Australian Federation with a governor-general, with a constitution like that of the Dominion of Canada, and desires a meeting of delegates from each colony to consider the matter . . . . . . 30 Oct. 1889

Conference of delegates from all the Australian colonies at Melbourne to consider a scheme of Australasian federation and federal defence; Mr. Duncan Gillies elected chief representative 6 Feb. 1890

Sir H. Parkes' motion for the union of the colonies under one government unanimously adopted 13 Feb. „

Loyal address to the queen voted, and the meeting of a national convention in 1891 agreed to 14 Feb. „

Mr. Goschen's plan for uniform colonial postage (2½d.) accepted by all the colonies, reported May-June, 1890; to begin . . . . 1 Jan. 1891

The federal council meets at Hobart; Victoria, Queensland, and Tasmania represented; an address to the queen respecting trade voted, 20-24 Jan. 1891

National Australasian Federation Convention, chief delegates: New South Wales, sir Henry Parkes; Victoria, hon. James Munro; Queensland, sir Samuel Griffith; South Australia, hon. Thomas Playford; Tasmania, hon. P. O. Fysh; New Zealand, sir George Grey; Western Australia, hon. John Forrest; sir Henry Parkes elected president; sir Samuel Griffith, vice-president; meeting in the legislative chamber, Sydney, 11 a.m. At the evening banquet, principal toast, "One people, one destiny" . . . 2 March, „

The title, the "Commonwealth of Australia," adopted by the convention (26 to 13) 1 April, „

The federal constitution adopted, 9 April, to be accepted by the several colonies and confirmed by the British parliament. The Victoria parliament requires the title to be changed from "Commonwealth" to "Federation" . . . 21 July, „

The Commonwealth bill passed in South Australia, about . . . . . . 1 Nov. 1892

Committee to consider Australasian federation appointed, lord Brassey chairman, Mr. Arnold-Forster, lord Lamington, lord Playfair, lord Reay, sir Charles Tupper, and others, reported autumn, „

The federal council meets at Hobart, 26 Jan.; the commonwealth bill approved; closed, 3 Feb. 1893

The Australasian federation league meets at Melbourne; chairman, sir John Madden, chief justice of Victoria; federation of the states approved, 23 Jan. 1895

A conference of premiers at Hobart, 29 Jan.; resolution adopted; a convention of 10 delegates from each colony proposed; charged to frame a federal constitution to be submitted to the queen after approval by the colonies . . . 30 Jan. „

Australasian federal council opened at Hobart by visc. Gormanston, governor of Tasmania . 31 Jan. „

The Australasian federation enabling act approved 6 Feb., 1895; amendment bill passed at Sydney, reported . . . . . . 27 Nov. 1897

All the Australian governments telegraph their hearty approval to lord Salisbury of the action of his government with regard to the Transvaal (*which see*) and promise support, 12 Jan., 1896; thanks returned; announced . . 14 Jan. 1896

Conference of Australian premiers at Sydney, resolutions for federation, federal defence, restrictions on immigration, &c., adopted, 4, 5, March; the scheme suspended through the opposition of Queensland (*which see*) . . . . . . Oct. „

Australian federal council meets at Hobart, sir John Forrest president 26 Jan. *et seq.* 1897

Conference of premiers at Hobart . . 2-4 Feb. „

Australian federal convention meets at Adelaide, Mr. C. C. Kingston (S. Australia) elected president; delay allowed to Queensland . 22 March „

New constitution adopted; constitutional, finance, and judiciary committees appointed, 31 March; draft constitution bill presented by Mr. Barton, 12 April; carried . . . . . 23 April „

Federal convention meets at Sydney, 2-24 Sept., 1897; final session at Melbourne, 20 Jan.; the federation (commonwealth) bill, adopted, 16 Mar. 1898

Premiers' conferences on federation, in Melbourne, result in agreement . . 28 Jan.-2 Feb. 1899

Address to the queen from all legislatures, except Western Australia, praying for the adoption of the commonwealth bill and the grant of a federal constitution . . . . Sept. „

Federal delegates received by the queen at Windsor, 27 March, 1900

Premiers' conference on proposed amendments to the federation bill at Sydney, 24 Jan. and 19 April „

Blue-book on federation published. See *Times*. 12 May, „

Commonwealth bill introduced into the Commons, 14 May, „

Commonwealth of Australia Constitution Act, uniting the 6 Australasian colonies (New Zealand excepted), royal assent given . . 9 July, „

Commonwealth bill adopted by a *referendum*, in W. Australia, federation completed, end July, „

Lord Hopetoun appointed gov.-gen., 14 July; welcomed at Sydney . . . . . 15 Dec. „

First federal cabinet formed; Mr. Edmund Barton, premier (G.C.M.G. 26 June, 1902) and minister for external affairs; Mr. Deakin, att.-general; sir W. Lyne, home; sir Geo. Turner, treasurer; Mr. Kingston, commerce; Mr. Dickson, defence (knt. 1 Jan., died 10 Jan. 1901); sir John Forrest, defence; Mr. J. Drake, postmaster-gen., 30 Dec–Jan. 1901

Lord Hopetoun installed governor-gen. of the commonwealth at Sydney; message from the queen, expressing her "earnest wish that under Divine Providence the commonwealth may ensure the increased prosperity and well-being of her loyal and beloved subjects in Australia," 1 Jan. ,,

Commonwealth celebrations in Sydney very successful . . . . 1–8 Jan. ,,

Universal mourning on the death of the queen, 22 Jan.; business suspended, memorial service held, 2 Feb. ,,

Elections for the first commonwealth parliament, 29, 30 March ,,

The duke and duchess of Cornwall warmly welcomed at Melbourne . . . . . 6 May, ,,

The first PARLIAMENT consisting of the (king) represented by the governor-general lord Hopetoun, a senate or upper-house, composed of 6 senators from each of the 6 states (elected for 6 years), and a house of representatives (more varied) composed of 75 members, total 111, opened in state by the duke and duchess of Cornwall, in the exhibition building at Melbourne; king's message read amid great rejoicings, over 15,000 present . . . . 9 May, ,,

Sir R. Baker elected president of the senate and Mr. F. W. Holder speaker of the house of representatives; the houses then adjourned, 9 May, ,,

The federal parliament meets, Melbourne, 21 May, ,,

The duke of Cornwall reviews 15,000 sailors and soldiers; presents many commonwealth honours; takes his degree at the university, 10, 11 May; lays a memorial stone, at Ballarat, to those who fell in S. Africa, 13 May; opens the new Alexandra-avenue, 17 May; reviews 4,000 troops at Lytton Plain, Brisbane, and lays the foundation stone for cathedral, 21, 22 May; visits a squatting station, near Cambogga, 24 May; arrives at Sydney, reviews the troops, 27, 28 May; present at a naval review and sham fight, lays the first stone of the Queen Victoria Memorial Pavilion, and is made LL.D. at the university, 30 May; presents S. African war medals, 1 June; visits an industrial exhibition, 3 June; they leave for New Zealand (*which see*), 6 June; welcomed at Hobart, Tasmania, 3 July; lays the stone for a soldiers' memorial, 4 July, and the first stone of the Post Office, 6 July; they arrive at Adelaide, 9 July; stone laid for the Maternity Hospital, reviews troops, 13 July; leave, 15 July; ceremonial progress through Perth, memorial stone to soldiers killed in S. African war laid, 22, 23 July; they leave Fremantle for S. Africa . . . . 26 July, ,,

Sir George Turner's budget, high tariff bill, new duties, partly fixed and partly *ad valorem*, on tea, sugar, alcohol, and tobacco, introduced, 8 Oct. ,,

Immigration restriction bill read, third time, in the house of representatives, 9 Oct.; read second time in the senate . . . . . 15 Nov. ,,

Mr. Reid's motion of want of confidence on the tariff proposals rejected, after 27 hours debate, 39—25, 1 Nov.; midnight sittings on the tariff bill, 33 hours . . . . 27 Nov. ,,

Total revenue for the year, 29,337,064*l.*; expenditure, 30,019,395*l.* . . . . . . 31 Dec. ,,

Loyal and patriotic speech by Mr. Edmund Barton (G.C.M.G. 1902); resolution condemning the baseless charges against Great Britain and her brave army, affirming readiness to give all requisite aid to the mother country, adopted by the Federal house of representatives . . 14 Jan. 1902

Many patriotic demonstrations in Sydney and elsewhere, Jan.; mass meeting at Melbourne, confidence expressed in the imperial government's policy in S. Africa . . . . . . 17 Feb. ,,

Lord Hopetoun's resignation accepted . . May ,,

Conference of state premiers at Melbourne, 15, 16 May ,,

Protracted drought in Australia . . . May 1902

State capitals illuminated to celebrate the king's recovery . . . . 10 July ,,

Lord Hopetoun resigns, mid May; created marquis of Linlithgow, 26 June; sends farewell letters and thanks to the Australian people; leaves Brisbane, 16 July; succeeded by lord Tennyson for 1902–3 . . . . 17 July, ,,

Budget, probable deficit for 1902–03 from the drought, &c., 650,000*l.* . . . . . Aug. ,,

Estimated loss of 40,000,000 sheep and lambs through the drought, reported . . 26 Aug. ,,

Federal parliament agrees to allow the gov.-gen. 5,500*l.* per ann., for the maintenance of the Government Houses in Sydney and Melbourne, reported . . . . 4 Sept. ,,

Day of humiliation and prayer for rain . 7 Sept. ,,

General rainfall reported . . . 10, 11 Sept. ,,

Commonwealth tariff bill passed by the senate, 9 Sept. ,,

Commonwealth revenue, 28,206,469*l.*; expenditure, 29,240,334*l.* . . . . 31 Dec. ,,

Conference of premiers, Sydney . . . 15 April, 1903

Coronation honours distributed . . . 17 April, ,,

Resignation of Mr. Kingston, home minister, succeeded by Sir Wm. Lyne, re-arrangement in ministry . . . . mid-Aug. ,,

Lord Northcote appointed to succeed lord Tennyson in Dec. announced . . . . . mid Aug. ,,

Senate passed the Naval Agreement bill, 20,000*l.* yearly for 10 years to Imperial navy . 25 Aug. ,,

Defeat of Government on an amendment to the Conciliation bill . . . . 9 Sept. ,,

Sir E. Barton announces bill dropped for the session . . . . 10 Sept. ,,

Tumut, N. S. Wales, selected by Committee to consider site for Federal capital of Australia, reported, 20 July; rejected by senate . 15 Oct. ,,

AUSTRALASIAN ASSOCIATION, for the advancement of science, was founded mainly by the exertions of prof. Liversidge, 1886, held its first meeting in Sydney, Aug. 1888; the 2nd at Melbourne, 7 Jan. 1890, president baron von Mueller, hon. sec. prof. W. B. Edwin Spencer; 3rd Christchurch, New Zealand, 15 Jan. 1891; 4th Hobart, 7 Jan. 1892; 5th Adelaide, 25 Sept. 1893; Brisbane, 1894; Sydney, 6 Jan., 1898; Melbourne, 9 Jan. 1900; Hobart, 8 Jan. 1902.

AUSTRALIA (formerly New Holland), the largest island and smallest continent; estimated area about 2,954,417 square miles, including five provinces—New South Wales, Victoria (formerly Port Phillip), South Australia, West Australia (or Swan River), and Queensland (*all which see*). Population, with Tasmania and New Zealand, in 1871, about 1,958,650; 1874, 2,334,210; 1878, 2,705,700; 1882, 2,936,409; 1888, 3,546,725; 1895, 4,323,171; 1901, 4,550,651; of the commonwealth, 3,775,356, Nov. 1901.

Mr. R. H. Major, in 1872, alleged that Australia was known to the French prior to 1531

Alleged discovery by Manoel Godinho de Eredia, a Portuguese 1601

The Dutch also discover Australia . . . March, 1606

The coast surveyed by Dutch navigators; north, by Zeachen, 1618; west, by Edels, 1619; south, by Nuyts, 1627; north, by Tasman 1627

Tasman coasts S. Australia, and Van Diemen's Land 1642-4

Terra Australia (Western Australia) named New Holland by order of the States-General . . 1665

Wm. Dampier explores the W. and N. W. coasts, 1684-90

William Dampier lands in Australia . . Jan. 1686

Explorations of Willis and Carteret . . . 1763-6

Capt. Cook, sir Joseph Banks, and others, land at Botany Bay, and name the country "New South Wales" . . . . 28 April, 1770

Exploration of Furneaux 1773

Governor Arthur Phillip founds Sydney near Port Jackson, with 1030 persons . . . 26 Jan. 1788

[The 82nd anniversary of this event was kept with much festivity, 26 Jan. 1870.]

Great distress in consequence of the loss of the store-ship "Guardian," captain Riou . . . 1790
Voyages of Bligh 1789-92
First church erected . . . . Aug. 1793
Government gazette first printed . . . 1795
Bass's straits discovered by Bass and Flinders . 1798
First brick church built 1802
Colony of Van Diemen's land (now Tasmania) established 1803
Grant, 1800, and Flinders survey the coasts of Australia 1801-5
Insurrection of Irish convicts quelled . . . 1804
Governor Bligh for his tyranny deposed and sent home 1808
Superseded by governor Macquarie . . . 1809
Expeditions into the interior by Wentworth, Lawson, Bloxland, 1813; Oxley, &c. . . 1817-1823
Population, 29,783 (three-fourths convicts) . . 1821
West Australia formed into a province . . . 1829
Legislative council established . . . ,,
Sturt's expeditions into South Australia . . 1828-31
South Australia erected into a province . Aug. 1834
Sir T. Mitchell's expeditions into E. Australia . 1831-6
First Roman Catholic bishop (Polding) arrives, Sept. 1835
Port Phillip (now Victoria) colonised . Nov. ,,
First Church of England bishop of Australia (Broughton) arrives . . . June, 1836
Colony of *South Australia* founded . . Dec. ,,
Eyre's expedition overland from Adelaide to King George's Sound 1836-7
Melbourne founded . . . . Nov. 1837
Capt. Grey explores N. W. Australia . . . 1837-9
Count Strzelecki explored New South Wales and Tasmania, 1838-43; discovered gold-fields in Bathurst, Wellington, &c. (kept secret by sir George Gipps) 1839
Suspension of transportation . . . ,,
Strzelecki explores the Australian Alps; discovers Gipps' land; Eyre explores west Australia . 1840
Great exertions of Mrs. Chisholm; establishment of "Home for Female Emigrants" . . 1841-6
Census—87,200 males; 43,700 females . . 1841
Very numerous insolvencies . . . 1841-2
Incorporation of city of Sydney . . . 1842
Landor and Lefroy explore Western Australia . . 1843
Sturt proceeds from South Australia to the middle of the continent 1845
Census (including Port Phillip)—114,700 males; 74,800 females 1846
Kennedy's 1st expedition 13 Aug. 1847; killed 13 Nov. 1848
Dr. Leichhardt's expedition leaves Moreton bay, Aug. 1844; arrives at Port Essington, 17 Dec. 1845; starts again, not heard of after . ? April, ,,
Great agitation against transportation, which had been revived by earl Grey 1849
Port Phillip erected into a separate province as *Victoria* 1850
Gold discovered by Mr. Hargreaves, &c.* . . . 1851

Census—males, 106,000; females, 81,000 (exclusive of Victoria, 80,000) 1851
Mints established . . . . . March, 1853
Transportation ceased . . . . . ,,
A. C. Gregory, accompanied by Ferdinand von Mueller as botanist (see *Victoria*, Oct., 1896), explored the north and interior . . 1848, 1855-8
Death of archdeacon Cowper (aged 80), after about fifty years' residence . . . July, 1858
Queensland made a province . . . 4 Dec. 1859
J. M'Douall Stuart's expeditions . . . 1858-62
Expedition into the interior under Mr. Landells organised . . . . . Aug. 1860
Robert O'Hara Burke, Wm. John Wills, and others, start from Melbourne . . . 20 Aug. ,,
Burke, Wills, and two others, cross the Australian continent to the gulf of Carpentaria; all perish on their return, except John King, who arrives at Melbourne . . . . . Nov. 1861
Stuart, M'Kinlay, and Landsborough cross Australia from sea to sea 1861-2
Remains of Burke and Wills recovered; public funeral . . . . . 21 Jan. 1863
Strong and general resistance throughout Australia to the reception of British convicts in West Australia . . . . . about June, 1864
Cessation of transportation to Australia in three years announced amid much rejoicing . 26 Jan. 1865
Morgan, a desperate bushranger and murderer, surrounded and shot . . . . April, ,,
Boundary disputes between New South Wales and Victoria, summer 1864; settled amicably 19 April, ,,
Total population of Australia, exclusive of natives, 1,298,667 . . . . . Jan. 1866
Royal Society of New South Wales (originally the Philosophical Society of Australia, founded 1821), established . . . . . May, ,,
Meeting of ministers from the Australian colonies at Melbourne to arrange postal communication with Europe . . . . . March, 1867
Exploration of South Australia; capt. Cadell discovers mouth of the river Roper, and fine pastoral country, lat. 14° S. . . . . Nov. ,,
Despatch from lord Kimberley objecting to the complex tariffs between the Australian colonies, 13 July, 1871
Meeting of delegates from New South Wales, Victoria, South Australia, and Tasmania; they object to imperial interference with their mutual fiscal arrangements . . . . . 27 Sept. ,,
Synod of the church of Australia and Tasmania held at Sydney . . . . 25 Oct. 1872
Mr. Ernest Morrison walks across the continent from the Gulf of Carpentaria to Melbourne in 120 days, starting . . . about 18 Dec. 1882
Completion of the direct railway between Melbourne and Sydney . . . . June, 1883
Gradual formation of a defensive Australian fleet and army . . . . . . ,,
The Intercolonial conference of delegates on proposed annexation of New Guinea, at Sydney, recommended, 6 Dec.; and the formation of an Australasian federal council 7 Dec.; closes 8 Dec. ,,
Canon Barry consecrated bishop of Sydney and metropolitan of Australia . . . 1 Jan. 1884
Mr. Charles Winnicke's exploring party mapped 40,000 miles of unknown country, announced Jan. ,,
Victoria, Tasmania, and Queensland accept the scheme of federation, Aug.; opposed by New South Wales . . . . about 1 Nov. ,,
Lord Derby's dispatch deferring consideration of the federal scheme . . . . 11 Dec. ,,
Several states protest against the German annexations in New Guinea, &c. . . . . Dec. ,,
British flag hoisted on Woodlark and other islands Jan. 1885
The Australian colonies proffer military contingents for the Soudan; thanked by the queen . Feb. ,,

* Gold Discovery.—Mr. Edward Hargreaves went to California in search of gold, and was struck with the similarity between the rocks and strata of California and those of his own district of Conobolas, some thirty miles west of Bathurst. On his return home, he examined the soil, and after one or two months' digging, found a quantity of gold, 12 Feb. 1851. He applied to the colonial government for a reward, which he readily obtained, with an appointment as commissioner of crown lands. The excitement became intense throughout the colony of New South Wales, rapidly spread to that of Victoria and other places; and in the first week of July, 1851, an aboriginal inhabitant, formerly attached to the Wellington mission, and then in the service of Dr. Kerr, of Wallawa, discovered, while tending his sheep, a mass of gold among a heap of quartz. Three blocks of quartz (from two to three hundred weight), found in the Murroo Creek, fifty miles to the north of Bathurst, contained 112 lb. of pure gold, valued at 4000*l.* The "Victoria nugget," a magnificent mass of virgin gold, weighing 340 ounces, was brought to England from the Bendigo diggings; and a piece of pure gold of 106 lb. weight was also found. From the gold fields of Mount Alexander and Ballarat, in the district of Victoria, up to Oct. 1852, there were found 2,532,422 ounces, or 105 tons 10 cwt. of gold; and the gold exported up to the same date represented 3,863,477*l.* sterling. In Nov. 1856, the "James Baines" and "Lightning" brought gold from Melbourne valued at 1,200,000*l.* The "Welcome nugget" weighed 2019¾ ounces; value, 8376*l.* 10*s.* 10*d.*; found at Baker's Hill, Ballarat, 11 June, 1858. Between May, 1851, and May, 1861, gold to the value of 96,000,000*l.* had been brought to England from New South Wales and Victoria. Mr. Hargreaves died about 2 Nov. 1891.

Federal council of Australasia act passed 14 Aug. 1885
Federation of the Australasian Colonies, except New South Wales and New Zealand, completed 9 Dec. 1885. The formal opening of the council took place at Hobart, 25 Jan. 1886. The council met at Hobart on 16-19 Jan. 1888; again 29 Jan.-4 Feb. 1889
Australasian Conference requests the British government to treat with China for restriction of Chinese immigration, but recommends immediate local action 14-16 June, 1888
See *Imperial Defence.*
Mr. Ernest Favenc's "History of Australian Exploration from 1788 to 1888," published ,,
Irish home rule delegates (Mr. Dillon, sir Thomas Esmond, and Mr. Deasy, M.P.'s), coolly received or opposed in Australia, Tasmania and New Zealand . April *et seq.* 1889
The Australian colonies contribute about 31,000*l.* to the dock labourers of London, *see Strikes* Sept.-Dec. ,,
Australian warships launched at Newcastle-on-Tyne; *Pelorus,* 25 Nov. 1889, *Persia* . 5 Feb. 1890
Memorial of Mr. William Bede Dalley, Australian statesman (1831—88), erected in the crypt of St. Paul's, London, unveiled . 17 July, ,,
Formation of the National Association (of Australia), proposed in Melbourne . 3 July, 1891
The earl of Kintore, governor of South Australia, and party, travel overland from Adelaide (26 Feb. *et seq.*) to Brisbane, and thence by boat to Port Darwin in the extreme north, arriving 31 March, after inspecting the town, &c., he commenced his journey south (about 2,125 miles), 9 April, reaching Adelaide 23 May, ,,
The auxiliary squadron visits all the colonies, beginning with Queensland . Aug. *et seq.* ,,
Mr. David Lindsay, commander of the exploring expedition in N. and Central Australia, fitted out by sir Thomas Elder, arrives at Esperance bay, 14 Oct. 1891; members resign; reported 13 Jan., and the expedition is suspended, reported 14 March, 1892
Twelve Australian banks stop payment, see *New South Wales, Queensland,* and *Victoria,* reported 17 May, 1893; conference of colonial premiers at Melbourne; a common action adopted . 27 May, 1893
The Australian Federation conference opened at Sydney . 31 July, ,,
The Horn scientific expedition to Central Australia, May, 1894; returned in Aug., report issued Dec. 1896
Diamond Jubilee celebrations throughout Australia . 20-22 June, *et seq.* 1897
Intense heat, averaging 107° in the shade, in Victoria, S. Australia, and New South Wales, many bush fires raging, 26 Dec., *et seq.*, 1897; loss of life and many townships, &c., destroyed; reported . 13 Jan. 1898
Church congress at Ballarat . mid Nov. ,,
Federal demonstration at Melbourne, on the anniversary of the foundation of Australia, 25 Jan. 1899
Australian naval conference in favour of a naval reserve, &c., at Melbourne . Aug. ,,
Loyal support of the Imperial government in the S. African war; contingents sent; see *Colonies,* Oct.; offers accepted . 16 Dec. 1899—Feb. 1901
Gold output for the year, 16,000,000*l.* . end Dec. ,,

For Federation *see Australasia,* 1889, *et seq.*

GOVERNORS.

Captain Arthur Philip . 1788
Captain Hunter . 1795
Captain Philip G. King . 1800
Captain William Bligh . 1806
Colonel Lachlan Macquarie (able and successful administration) . 1809
General sir Thomas Brisbane . 1821
Sir Richard Bourke . 1831
Sir George Gipps . 1838
Sir Charles Fitzroy, *governor-general* of all the Australian colonies, with a certain jurisdiction over the lieutenant-governors of Van Diemen's Land, Victoria, and South and Western Australia . 1846
Sir William T. Denison . 1854
Sir John Young, of New South Wales only . 1860

See *New South Wales.*

Acts for the government of Australia, 10 Geo. IV. c. 22, 14 May (1829), 6 & 7 Will. IV. c. 68, 13 Aug. (1836), 13 & 14 Vict. c. 59, 5 Aug. (1850). Act for regulating the sale of waste lands in the Australian colonies, 5 & 6 Vict. c. 36, 22 June (1842).

AUSTRASIA, *Œsterreich* (Eastern Kingdom), also called Metz, a French kingdom which lasted from the 6th to the 8th century. It began with the division of the territories of Clovis by his sons, 511, and ended by Carloman becoming a monk and surrendering his power to his brother Pepin, who thus became sole king of France, 747.

AUSTRIA, a Hamburg company's steamship, sailed from Southampton to New York 4 Sept. 1858, with 528 persons on board. On 13 Sept. in lat. 45° N., long. 41° 30′ W., it caught fire through the carelessness of some one in burning some tar to fumigate the steerage. Only 67 persons were saved —upwards of 60 by the *Maurice,* a French barque; the rest by a Norwegian barque. A heartrending account was given in the *Times,* 11 Oct. 1858, by Mr. Charles Brews, an English survivor.

AUSTRIA, *Œsterreich* (Eastern Kingdom), anciently Noricum and part of Pannonia, was annexed to the Roman empire about 33; was overrun by the Huns, Avars, &c., during the 5th and 6th centuries, and taken from them by Charlemagne, 791-796. He divided the government of the country, establishing *margraves* of Eastern Bavaria and Austria. Louis the German, son of Louis le Débonnaire, about 817, subjugated Radbod, margrave of Austria; but in 883 the descendants of the latter raised a civil war in Bavaria against the emperor Charles the Fat, and eventually the margraves of Austria were declared immediate princes of the empire. In 1156 the margraviate was made an hereditary *duchy* by the emperor Frederic I.; and in 1453 it was raised to an *archduchy* by the emperor Frederic III. Rodolph, count of Hapsburg, elected emperor of Germany in 1273, acquired Austria in 1278; and from 1493 to 1804 his descendants were *emperors.* On 11 Aug. 1804, the emperor Francis II. renounced the title of emperor of Rome and king of Germany (popularly termed emperor of Germany), and became hereditary *emperor of Austria.* The condition of Austria is now greatly improving under the enlightened rule of the present emperor. The political constitution of the empire is based upon—1. The pragmatic sanction of Charles VI., 1734, which declares the indivisibility of the empire and rules the order of succession. 2. The pragmatic sanction of Francis II., 1 Aug. 1804, when he became emperor of Austria only. 3. The diploma of Francis Joseph, 20 Oct. 1860, whereby he imparted legislative power to the provincial states and the council of the empire (Reichsrath). 4. The law of 26 Feb. 1861, on the national representation. Self-government was granted to Hungary, 17 Feb. 1867. Each country has its parliament, and a controlling body termed the Delegations, consisting of 120 members, half elected by Austria and half by Hungary, was also established in 1867. The empire was ordered to be named henceforth the Austro-Hungarian monarchy, or Austria-Hungary, by decree, 14 Nov. 1868. On 19 Oct. 1889, the army was ordered to be styled "Imperial and Royal." Population of the empire* in Oct. 1857, 35,018,988; reduced

* The empire is now divided into two parts, separated by the river Leithe. The Cis-Leithan section comprises 14 provincial diets: Galicia, Bohemia, Silesia, Moravia, lower and upper Austria, Styria, the Tyrol and Vorarlberg, Salzburg, Carinthia, Carniola, Trieste, and Istria, Dalmatia, and the Bukovina. The Trans-Leithan section comprises Hungary, Transylvania, Croatia, Slavonia, and the city of Fiume.

to 32,530,000 by the loss of Venetia, &c., in 1866 (about 16,000,000 Slavs of different dialects). Population, Austria and other Cis-Leithan provinces, 20,396,580 (31 Dec. 1869); Hungary and Trans-Leithan provinces, 15,509,455; the empire, in 1880, 37,882,712; in 1890, 41,345,329; 1900, 47,013,835; 1894, revenue (Austria), 52,910,000*l.*; expenditure, 52,740,000*l.*; 1902, revenue, 71,675,00*l.*; expenditure, 71,020,00*l.*

Frederic II., the last male of the house of Bamberg, killed in battle with the Hungarians . 15 June, 1246

Disputed succession: the emperor Frederic II. sequestered the provinces, appointing Otto, count of Eberstein, governor in the name of the emperor; they are seized by Ladislaus, margrave of Moravia, in right of his wife, Frederic's niece, Gertrude: he died childless 1247

Herman, margrave of Baden, marries Gertrude, and holds the provinces till his death . . . 1250

Premislas Ottocar, of Bohemia, acquires the provinces 1254

Compelled to cede Styria to Hungary, he makes war and recovers it, in consequence of a great victory 1260

He inherits Carinthia, 1263; refuses to become emperor of Germany, 1272; and to render homage to Rodolph of Hapsburg, elected emperor . . 1273

War against Ottocar as a rebel: he is compelled to cede Austria, Carinthia, and Styria to Rodolph 1274

The war renewed: Ottocar perishes in the battle of Marchfeld . . . 26 Aug. 1278

The emperor Rodolph establishes the duchy of Austria, &c. . . . 27 Dec. 1282

Albert I. assassinated by his nephew while attempting to enslave the Swiss . . . 1 May, 1308

Successful revolt of the Swiss . . . 1307-9

They totally defeat the Austrians under duke Leopold, at Morgarten . . . 16 Nov. 1315

The Tyrol acquired 1363

The duke Leopold imposes a toll on the Swiss; which they resist with violence: he makes war on them, and is defeated and slain at Sempach July, 1386

Duke Albert V. obtains Bohemia and Hungary, and is elected emperor of Germany . . . 1437

The emperor Frederic III., as head of the house of Hapsburg, creates the archduchy of Austria with sovereign power . . . 6 Jan. 1453

Austria divided between him and his relatives, 1457; war ensues between them till . . . 1463

The Low countries accrue to Austria by the marriage of Maximilian with Mary, the heiress of Burgundy 1477

Also Spain, by the marriage of Philip I. of Austria, with the heiress of Arragon and Castile . . 1496

Bohemia and Hungary united to Austria under Ferdinand I. 1526

Austria harassed by Turkish invasions . . . 1529-45

Charles V., reigning over Germany, Austria, Bohemia, Hungary, Spain, the Netherlands, and their dependencies, abdicates (see *Spain*) . . 1556

The destructive 30 years' war . . . 1618-48

War of Spanish succession . . . 1701-14

Mantua ceded to the emperor . . . 3 Jan. 1708

By treaty of Utrecht he obtains part of the duchy of Milan . . . . 11 April, 1713

By treaty of Rastadt he acquires the Netherlands . 1714

Naples, &c., added to his dominions . 15 Nov. 1715

Further additions on the east (Temeswar, &c.) by the peace of Passarowitz 1718

Naples and Sicily given up to Spain . . . 1735

Death of Charles VI., the last sovereign of the male line of the house of Hapsburg; his daughter, Maria Theresa, becomes queen of Hungary 20 Oct. 1740

Silesian wars 1740-2; 1744-5

Maria Theresa is attacked by Prussia, France, Bavaria, and Saxony; but supported by Great Britain 1741

Francis, duke of Lorraine, who had married Maria Theresa in 1736, elected emperor . . . 1745

Peace of Aix-la-Chapelle: Parma, Milan, &c. ceded to Spain 1748

Seven years' war; Silesia ceded to Prussia . . 1745-63

Galicia, &c., acquired from Poland . . . 1772

War with France (see *Battles*) 1792-7

By the treaty of Campo Formio, the emperor gives up Lombardy (*which see*) and obtains Venice 15 Oct. 1797

Treaty of Luneville (more losses) . . . 1801

Francis II., emperor of Germany, becomes *Francis I. of Austria*: declared hereditary emperor of Austria 11 Aug. 1804

His declaration against France . . . 5 Aug. 1805

Capitulation of his army at Ulm . . 20 Oct. ,,

War: Napoleon enters Vienna . . . 14 Nov. ,,

Austrians and Russians defeated at Austerlitz, 2 Dec. ,,

By treaty of Presburg, Austria loses Venice and the Tyrol . . . . . 1 Jan. 1806

Vienna evacuated by the French . . . 12 Jan. ,,

Dissolution of the Germanic confederation, and formal abdication of the emperor . . . 6 Aug. ,,

The French again take Vienna . . . 13 May, 1809

But restore it at the peace . . . 24 Oct. ,,

Napoleon marries the archduchess Maria Louisa, the daughter of the emperor . . . 1 April, 1810

Congress at Vienna . . . . . 2 Oct. 1814

Treaty of Vienna . . . . . 25 Feb. 1815

Italian provinces restored with additions—Lombardo-Venetian kingdom established, 7 April.]

Francis I. dies; Ferdinand I. succeeds . 2 March, 1835

New treaty of commerce with England . 3 July, 1838

Insurrection at Vienna; flight of Metternich, 13 March, 1848

Insurrection in Italy, see *Milan*, *Venice*, and *Sardinia* . . . . . 18 March, ,,

Another insurrection at Vienna; the emperor flees to Inspruck . . . . 15-17 May, ,,

Archduke John appointed vicar-general of the empire . . . . . 29 May, ,,

A constituent assembly meet at Vienna . 22 July, ,,

Revolution in Hungary, see *Hungary* . 11 Sept. ,,

Insurrection of Vienna; murder of count Latour, 6 Oct. ,,

The emperor abdicates in favour of his nephew, Francis-Joseph . . . . . 2 Dec. ,,

Convention of Olmütz . . . . 29 Nov. 1850

The emperor revokes the constitution of 4 March, 1849 . . . . . 31 Dec. 1851

Trial by jury abolished in the empire . 15 Jan. 1852

Death of prince Schwartzenburg, prime minister, 4 April, ,,

Attempted assassination of the emperor by Libenyi, 18 Feb.; who was executed . . . 28 Feb. 1853

Commercial treaty with Prussia . . . 19 Feb. ,,

Austrians enter Danubian principalities . Aug. 1854

Alliance with England and France relative to eastern question . . . . . 2 Dec. ,,

Great reduction of the army . . . 24 June, 1855

By a concordat the pope acquires great power in the empire . . . . . 18 Aug. ,,

Amnesty for political offenders of 1848-9, 12 July, 1856

Austria remonstrates against the attacks of the free Sardinian press . . . . 10 Feb. 1857

Firm reply of count Cavour . . . 20 Feb. ,,

Austrians quit the Danube principalities . March, ,,

Diplomatic relations between Austria and Sardinia broken off in consequence . . 23-30 March, ,,

Emperor and empress visit Hungary . . May, ,,

Death of marshal Radetzky (aged 92) . . 5 Jan. 1858

Excitement throughout Europe, caused by the address of the emperor Napoleon III. to the Austrian ambassador:—"I regret that our relations with your government are not as good as formerly, but I beg of you to tell the emperor that my personal sentiments for him have not changed" . . . . . 1 Jan. 1859

The emperor of Austria replied in almost the same words . . . . . 4 Jan. ,,

Prince Napoleon Bonaparte marries princess Clotilde of Sardinia . . . . 30 Jan. ,,

Austria prepares for war; enlarges her armies in Italy; and strongly fortifies the banks of the Ticino, the boundary of her Italian provinces, and Sardinia . . . . Feb. & March, ,,

Lord Cowley at Vienna on a "mission of peace," 27 Feb. ,,

Intervention of Russia—proposal for a congress; disputes respecting the admission of Sardinia—Sardinia and France prepare for war, March & April, ,,

Austria demands the disarmament of Sardinia and the dismissal of the volunteers from other states within three days . . . 23 April, 1859
This demand rejected . . . . 26 April, „
The Austrians cross the Ticino . . 26 April, „
The French troops enter Piedmont . . 27 April, „
The French emperor declares war (to expel the Austrians from Italy) . . . . . 3 May, „
Resignation of count Buol, foreign minister; appointment of count Rechberg . 13-18 May, „
The Austrians defeated at Montebello, 20 May; at Palestro, 30-31 May; at Magenta, 4 June; at Malegnano (Marignano) . . . . 8 June, „
Prince Metternich dies, aged 86 (he had been actively engaged in the wars and negotiations of Napoleon I.) . . . . . . 11 June, „
Austrians defeated at Solferino (near the Mincio); the emperors of Austria and France and king of Sardinia present . . . . . 24 June, „
Armistice agreed upon, 6 July; the emperors meet, 11 July; the preliminaries of peace signed at Villa Franca (Lombardy given up to Sardinia, and an Italian confederation proposed to be formed), 12 July, „
Manifesto justifying the peace issued to the army, 12 July; to the people . . . . 15 July, „
Patent issued, granting greatly increased privileges to the Protestants,—announced . . Sept. „
Conference between the envoys of Austria and France at Zurich . . . 8 Aug. to Sept. „
Many national reforms proposed . . . Sept. „
Treaty of Zurich, confirming the preliminaries of Villa Franca, signed . . . . 10 Nov. „
Decrees removing Jewish disabilities, 6, 10 Jan., 18 Feb. 1860
Patent issued for the summoning the great imperial council (Reichsrath), composed of representatives elected by the provincial diets . . 5 March, „
Discovery of great corruptions in the army financial arrangements, a deficiency of about 1,700,000*l.* discovered; general Eynatten commits suicide; 82 persons arrested . . . . . March, „
Austria protests against the annexation of Tuscany, &c., by Sardinia . . . . March, „
Baron Brück, suspected of complicity in the army frauds, dismissed 20 April; commits suicide, 23 April, „
The Reichsrath assembles, 30 May; addressed by the emperor . . . . . . 1 June, „
Liberty of the press further restrained. . July, „
Unsettled state of Hungary (*which see*) . July-Oct. „
Friendly meeting of the emperor and the regent of Prussia at Töplitz . . . . 26 July, „
Free debates in the Reichsrath; strictures on the concordat, the finances, &c.; proposals for separate constitutions for the provinces, Aug. & Sept. „
The Reichsrath adjourned . . . . 29 Sept. „
Diploma conferring on the Reichsrath legislative powers, the control of the finances, &c., a manifesto issued to the populations of the empire (not well received) . . . . . . 20 Oct. „
Meeting of the emperor with the emperor of Russia and prince regent of Prussia at Warsaw: no important result . . . . 20-26 Oct. „
The government professes non-intervention in Italy, but increases the army in Venetia, Oct. & Nov. „
The empress goes to Madeira for health . Nov. „
Sale of Venetia, publicly spoken of, is repudiated in Dec. „
Ministerial crisis: M. Schmerling becomes minister—more political concessions . . . . 13 Dec. „
The proscribed Hungarian, count Teleki, at Dresden, is given up to Austria, which causes general indignation, about 20 Dec.; he is released on parole 31 Dec. „
Amnesty for political offences in Hungary, Croatia, &c., published . . . . . . 7 Jan. 1861
Reactionary policy of the court leads to increased general disaffection . . . Jan. & Feb. „
The statutes of the new constitution for the Austrian monarchy published . . . 26 Feb. „
Civil and political rights granted to Protestants, throughout the empire except in Hungary and Venice . . . . 8 April, „
Meeting of Reichsrath—no deputies present from Hungary, Croatia, Transylvania, Venetia, or Istria 29 April, „

Ministry of marine created . . . . . Jan. 1862
Inundation of the Danube, causing great distress, 4 Feb. „
Increased taxation proposed . . . . March, „
At an imperial council, the emperor present, the principle of ministerial responsibility is resolved on . . . . 26 April, „
Deficiency of 1,400,000*l.* in financial statement—indignation of the Reichsrath . . . . June, „
Amnesty to condemned political offenders in Hungary proclaimed . . . . . 18 Nov. „
Reduction in the army assented to; and a personal liberty law (resembling our habeas corpus act) passed . . . . Dec. „
Insurrection in Russian Poland, Jan.; Austria joins in the intercession of England and France April 1863
Meeting of the German sovereigns (except kings of Prussia, Holland, and Denmark) with the emperor of Austria at Frankfort, by his invitation; the draft of a reform of the federal constitution agreed to . . . . 16-31 Aug. „
Transylvanian deputies accept the constitution, and take seats in the Reichsrath . . 20 Oct. „
Austria joins Prussia in war with Denmark (see *Denmark*) . . . . Jan. 1864
Galicia and Cracow declared to be in a state of siege 29 Feb. „
The Archduke Maximilian becomes emperor of Mexico (see *Mexico*) . . . . April, „
The emperor and the king of Prussia meet at Carlsbad 22 June, „
Resignation of count Rechberg, foreign minister, succeeded by count Mensdorff-Pouilly 27 Oct. „
Peace with Denmark, signed at Vienna . 30 Oct. „
Emperor opens Reichsrath, 14 Nov.; great freedom of debate; the state of siege in Galicia censured Dec. „
Austria supports the confederation in the dispute respecting the duchies . . . . . Dec. „
Apparent reunion between Austria and Prussia, Jan. 1865
Great financial difficulty; proposed reduction in the army by the chambers . . . . Jan. „
Contest between the government and the chambers April, „
Reported failure of Mr. Hutt's mission to Vienna, to promote free trade . . . . June, „
New ministry formed; count Mensdorff as nominal premier; counts Belcredi and Esterhazy as ministers: conciliatory measures towards Hungary, proposed . . . . 27 July, „
Convention of Gastein (see *Gastein*) signed 14 Aug. „
Emperor's rescript suppressing the constitution, with the view of giving autonomy to Hungary (*which see*) . . . . . 20 Sept. „
Rejoicings in Hungary, but dissatisfaction in Austria, Croatia, &c. . . . Nov., Dec. „
Treaty of commerce with Great Britain, signed 16 Dec. „
Amnesty for Italy issued . . . . . 1 Jan. 1866
Warm disputes with Prussia (aggressive), respecting the settlement of Holstein . . . Jan., Mar. „
Preparations for war begin . . . . March, „
The archduke Albrecht made commander of the southern army, 6 May; Benedek of the Northern 12 May, „
War declared by Prussia, 18 June; by Italy (*which see*) . . . . 20 June, „
The Austrians enter Silesia, 18 June; and the Prussians Bohemia . . . . . 23 June „
The Italians defeated by the archduke Albrecht, at Custozza . . . . . . 24 June, „
Prussian victories at Nachod, &c. . . 27-29 June, „
Benedek totally defeated at Königgrätz or Sadowa 3 July, „
(For details of the war see *Prussia* and *Italy*.)
The emperor cedes Venetia to the emperor Napoleon, and requests intervention . . . . 4 July, „
Preliminaries of peace signed at Nikolsburg, 26 July, „
Treaty of peace with Prussia signed at Prague, 23 Aug. „
Treaty of peace with Italy signed at Vienna, ceding Venetia, 3 Oct. The iron crown given up 11 Oct. „
The Quadrilateral and Venice surrendered to the Italians . . . . 11-19 Oct. „
Baron Ferdinand von Beust, late Saxon minister of foreign affairs, made Austrian foreign minister 30 Oct. „
Meeting of the Reichsrath . . . . 19 Nov. „

Commercial treaty with France (to commence 1 Jan. 1867), signed . . . 11 Dec. 1866

Great dissension among the nationalities of the empire . . . Dec. ,,

Extraordinary diet convoked (for 25 Feb.). 3 Jan. 1867

Establishment of autonomy for Hungary announced, mainly the work of Von Beust; resignation of Belcredi, 4 Feb.; Von Beust made president of the council . . . 7 Feb. ,,

Rescript restoring a separate ministry for Hungary, count Andrassy president . . . 17 Feb. ,,

Death of archduke Stephen (palatine of Hungary in 1848) . . . Feb. ,,

Commercial treaty with Italy, signed . 23 April, ,,

Reichsrath opened at Vienna . . . 20 May, ,,

The Czechs (of Bohemia and Moravia), Croats, Slavonians, Serbs, Roumans (of Transylvania), and Russinians (of Galicia), protest against absorption, and demand national legislative powers May & July, ,,

Painful death of the archduchess Matilda through burns . . . 6 June, ,,

The emperor and empress crowned king and queen of Hungary at Buda . . . 8 June, ,,

Von Beust made chancellor of the empire, 23 June, ,,

The sultan visits Vienna . . . 27 July—1 Aug. ,,

The emperors of Austria and France meet at Salzburg 18-23 Aug. ,,

Arrangements for the dividing the financial affairs of Austria and Hungary, signed . . 13 Sept. ,,

Changes (respecting marriage and education) in the concordat, proposed . . . Sept. ,,

28 bishops demand the maintenance of the concordat 28 Sept. ,,

Letter from the emperor to cardinal Rausch, declaring for complete liberty of conscience in opposition to the concordat; the concordat almost annulled by the lower house . . . Oct. ,,

Emperor of Austria and king of Prussia meet at Oos, near Baden-Baden . . . 22 Oct. ,,

Emperor arrives at Paris, 23 Oct.; leaves 5 Nov. ,,

Dualism accepted by the Reichsrath at Vienna Nov. ,,

New Austrian ministry under prince Auersperg constituted . . . 30 Dec. ,,

Civil marriages bill (annulling clerical jurisdiction over them) passed by the upper house, after sharp resistance, 21-23 March; received the emperor's assent . . . 25 May, 1868

German sharp-shooting match, held at Vienna, 26 July, ,,

Von Beust justifies the maintenance of an army of 800,000, 11 Oct.; is made a count . . Dec. ,,

Continued opposition of the clergy to the government Jan. 1869

The frigate *Radetsky* blown up, about 340 lives lost 20 Feb. ,,

The crown prince of Prussia visits Vienna 7 Oct. ,,

The emperor visits the East;—at Jerusalem, 10 Nov.; present at the opening of the Suez canal 17 Nov. 1869

Successful insurrection against the conscription in Dalmatia, Oct.; ceased . . . Nov. ,,

The Reichsrath opened by the emperor at Vienna 13 Dec. ,,

Ministerial crisis, Jan.: the Cis-Leithan ministry resigns; count Potocki, prime minister 4 April, 1870

Neutrality in the Franco-Prussian war announced 18 July, ,,

The concordat with Rome declared to be suspended in consequence of the promulgation of the doctrine of papal infallibility . . 30 July, ,,

The Reichsrath opened by the emperor; no deputies from Bohemia . . . 17 Sept. ,,

Dissension between the federal and national parties 29 Sept., Oct. ,,

The Reichsrath adjourned . . . 22 Nov. ,,

The ministry support Great Britain in opposing the Russian repudiation of the treaty of Paris (see *Russia*) . . . Nov. ,,

Austrian army, 864,869 regulars; 187,527 landwehr (militia) . . . Dec. ,,

The new German empire recognised by the emperor Jan. 1871

Dismissal of Potocki; count Hohenwart, minister Feb. ,,

Meeting of the Reichsrath . . . 20 Feb. ,,

Death of adm. Tegethoff, much lamented 7 April, ,,

First meeting of "Old Catholics" at Vienna, 26 July, 1871

An international exhibition at Vienna in 1873, proposed . . . Sept. ,,

Meeting of emperor with emperor William 6-8 Sept. ,,

Meeting of 17 provincial diets; struggle between the (Slavonian) conservatives and the (German) constitutionalists renewed . . 14 Sept. ,,

Political crisis: dissension between German and Slavonian parties, Oct.; resignation of the Hohenwart ministry . . . 25 Oct. ,,

A ministry formed under baron Kellersperg 4 Nov. ,,

Resignation of count Beust, the arch-chancellor; much excitement . . . 6 Nov. ,,

Count Andrassy (see *Hungary*, 1849 *et seq.*), having opposed von Beust's policy of alliance with France, succeeds him as minister of the imperial household and of foreign affairs; Von Beust to be ambassador at London; Lonyay, premier of Hungarian ministry . . . 13-14 Nov. ,,

New Austrian ministry formed by prince Auersperg . . . about 25 Nov. ,,

The Reichsrath opened by the emperor with speech announcing political and educational reforms 28 Dec. ,,

New constitutional law promulgated, giving the emperor power to order new elections of the chambers . . . 13 March, 1872

Meeting of the emperor with the emperor of Germany and other sovereigns at Berlin 6-12 Sept. ,,

Reform bill passed changing the Reichsrath into a national representative assembly . 10 March, 1873

Great international exhibition at Vienna; opening, 1 May, ,,

Financial crisis through overtrading in 1872; panic in . . . May, ,,

Visits to Vienna; the prince of Wales, 28 April; the czar of Russia, 1 June: the shah of Persia, 30 July; the king of Italy, 17 Sept.; the emperor of Germany . . . 17 Oct. ,,

Elections for the Reichsrath; 228 constitutionalists; 125 federals, 30 Oct.; the Reichsrath opened by the emperor, 5 Nov.; 25th anniversary of the emperor's accession celebrated throughout the empire; amnesty for political offenders . 2 Dec. ,,

The emperor at St. Petersburg . . . 13 Feb. 1874

Encyclical letter from the pope condemning the new ecclesiastical laws, dated . 7 March, ,,

Protest of the Austrian bishops; adoption by both parties of Cavour's cry, "A free church in a free state" . . . April, ,,

The empress at the Isle of Wight . July-Aug. ,,

Ofenheim, railway financier connected with Messrs. Brassey, after long trial for fraud, acquitted at Vienna . . . 27 Feb. 1875

The emperor warmly received at Venice by the king of Italy . . . 5 April, ,,

Inauguration of the new bed of the Danube by the emperor . . . 30 May, ,,

The czar meets the emperor at Eger . 28 June, ,,

Death of the ex-emperor Ferdinand . 29 June, ,,

Koloman de Tisza, president of Hungarian ministry, 20 Oct. ,,

Deficiency in the budget for 1876; revenue about 37,800,000*l.*; expenditure, 40,300,000*l.* . . Nov. ,,

Death of cardinal Rauscher, prince bishop of Vienna . . . 24 Nov. ,,

The czar and the emperor meet at Reichstadt; agree to neutrality in the Servio-Turkish war, 8 July, 1876

New treaty of commerce with Great Britain, signed 5 Dec. ,,

Declaration of neutrality in Russo-Turkish war by Austrian and Hungarian ministers; foreign policy to be for "the interest of the monarchy, to the exclusion of all antipathies and sympathies," M. de Tisza (Hungarian) . 26 June, 1877

Resignation of Austrian ministry, 26 Jan.; withdrawn . . . 5 Feb. 1878

Prince Auersperg announces disagreement with the proposed Russian conditions of peace, 19 Feb. ,,

Death of archduke Francis Charles, the emperor's father . . . 8 March, ,,

The *Sphinx* burnt at sea, near Cape St. Erlie, 500 perish . . . 8 March, ,,

Resignation of ministry; withdawn . 6, 7 July, ,,

Count Andrassy at the Berlin conference 13 June—13 July

Austria to occupy and administer Bosnia and Herzegovina, by treaty of Berlin . . 13 July, 1878

The Austrians enter, and war ensues (see *Bosnia*) 20 July, ,,

Resignation of Auersperg ministry announced to the Reichsrath . . . 22 Oct. ,,

Bosnia occupied (except Novi Bazar) . . Oct. ,,

Baron de Pretis fails to form a ministry . 30 Oct. ,,

New ministry under Dr. Stremayr . 15 Feb. 1879

Silver wedding of the emperor and empress kept, 24 April, ,,

Liberal majority at elections . . . 11 July, ,,

Resignation of count Andrassy, the premier; ministry formed by count Edw. Taaffe, 12 Aug.; baron von Haymerle, foreign minister 22 Aug. ,,

Bismarck's visit to Vienna; warmly received 21-24 Sept. ,,

Reichsrath opened; the Czech deputies attend 8 Oct. ,,

Andrassy formally resigns; succeeded by baron Haymerle as foreign minister and president of the council . . . . 8 Oct. ,,

Opening of all the diets of the empire . 8 June, 1880

Sudden death of baron Haymerle . . 10 Oct. 1881

The king and queen of Italy warmly received at Vienna . . . . 28-31 Oct. ,,

Count Gustav Kalnoky becomes foreign minister, 20 Nov. ,,

Temporary rupture with Roumania respecting the Danube about . . . . . . 27 Dec. ,,

Insurrection in Herzegovina, &c.; several small engagements with Austrians, 16-31 Jan.; insurgents defeated 1882

Provisional government said to have been formed by insurgents . . . . . about 9 Feb. ,,

Alleged defeat of insurgents at Glavalicevo and in other small engagements . . 16 Feb. *et seq.* ,,

Severe conflict at Cettinje; alleged great loss by Austrians; small loss by insurgents . 25 Feb. ,,

Mahometans sympathise with Christian insurgents Feb. ,,

Successful advance of the Austrians; capture of Dragali announced . . . . . 14 March, ,,

Insurgents adopting guerilla warfare about 12 May, ,,

"New German People's party" formed, manifesto published . . . . . about 29 May, ,,

Fall of a railway bridge over the Drave; about 27 soldiers in a train drowned . . . 23 Sept. ,,

Insurrection suppressed, announced . 26 Oct. ,,

Execution of Overdank, a soldier, for attempted assassination of emperor . . . . 20 Dec. ,,

600th anniversary of the establishment of the House of Hapsburg celebrated throughout the empire . . . . 27 Dec. ,,

Slavonic agitation against Germans and the Magyars and taxation, see *Croatia*, Aug.—Sept.; conciliatory policy adopted by the government, Sept. 1883

Marriage of the archduke Rodolph and the princess Stephanie of Belgium, 10 May, 1881; birth of princess . . . . 2 Sept. ,,

Much social disaffection at Vienna; two detective policemen assassinated, Hlubek, Bloch . Jan. 1884

Corporal Hermann Stellmacher, assassin of Bloch, captured, 25 Jan.; a great conspiracy suspected; law decreed by count Taaffe repressing public meetings, the press, trials by jury, &c., 30 Jan.; many arrested or expelled . . Jan. ,,

Another policeman murdered . . . 9 Feb. ,,

Government measures adopted by the chambers 15 Feb. ,,

700 expelled at Vienna . . about 15 March, ,,

The crown prince and princess visit Constantinople 17 April, *et seq.* ,,

Hugo Schenk and Schlossarck executed for murder of several servant girls . . . . 22 April, ,,

Stellmacher executed . . . . . 8 Aug. ,,

Hans Makart, historical painter, died . 3 Oct. ,,

Grand funeral at Vienna . . . . 6 Oct. ,,

For 1885; estimated revenue 504,800,000 fl.; expenditure 519,800,000fl. . . . . Dec. ,,

Heavy bank frauds; suicide of culprits . . Dec. ,,

Prince Adolph Auersperg, statesman, died . 5 Jan. 1885

Dissolution of the Reichsrath, 22 April; meeting of the new Reichsrath . . . . 22 Sept. ,,

Imperial assent given to the reform act of the upper house . . . . 30 April, ,,

Cordial meeting of the emperor and the czar at Kremsier in Moravia . . . . 25-26 Aug. ,,

Political crisis relating to duties on Russian petroleum, end of May, settled . . about 2 June, 1886

Death of Count F. von Beust, great liberal statesman, ex-chancellor . . . . . 24 Oct. ,,

Increased army estimates voted . . 26 Feb. 1887

Treaty of alliance with Germany and Italy signed 13 March ,,

Anarchists sentenced to imprisonment for dynamite plot . . . . 28 March, ,,

Successful military manœuvres in Transylvania Sept. ,,

Panic at the Bourse at Vienna, through article in the *Invalide Russe* (see *Russia*) . 16-17 Dec. ,,

Money granted for war preparations . 19 Dec. ,,

Defensive treaty with Germany against Russian or other aggression, 7 Oct. 1879; first published 3 Feb. 1888

Visit of the German emperor William II., at Vienna 3 Oct. ,,

Changes in the Taaffe ministry . . . Oct. ,,

Fortieth anniversary of the emperor's accession celebrated by charities . . . . 2 Dec. ,,

Suicide of the archduke Rodolph, heir to the throne, 30 Jan.; solemn funeral . . 5 Feb. 1889

Changes in the cabinet, announced . . March, ,,

New army bill as amended by the Hungarian diet adopted by the upper house . . 8 April, ,,

Catholic congress of nobles and clergy met at Vienna . . . . 29 April, ,,

Death of count Alfred Potocki, statesman, aged 72, about . . . . 20 May, ,,

The emperor and his nephew visit Berlin, 12-15 Aug. ,,

Temporary reconciliation of the Czechs and Germans in Bohemia in a conference, by the intervention of the emperor . . . 17-19 Jan. 1890

Formation of the Anglo-Austrian printing and publishing company in Vienna (Lord Mayor Isaacs and others, directors), middle . . Feb. ,,
[Reported unsuccessful, March, 1891.]

Count Julius Andrassy dies in Istria . 18 Feb. ,,

Thirty-two persons out of 62 charged, convicted of criminal practices in Galicia connected with emigration; four months' trial; sentence, 4½ years and other terms of imprisonment 12 March, ,,

Riot of about 1,000 workmen at Biala on the Galician frontier, suppressed by military; 3 men killed and about 14 died of wounds 23 April, ,,

Labour agitation, strikes with rioting in different provinces (*see Vienna*), April, 1890, gradually subsides . . . . May, ,,

The May day demonstration in favour of an eight hours labour day passes off tranquilly at Vienna, &c. . . . . 1 May, ,,

Marriage of the emperor's youngest daughter, archduchess Marie Valérie, to her cousin, the archduke Francis Salvator . . . . 31 July, ,,

Edward von Bauernfeld, poet and dramatist, dies, aged 88 . . . . 10 Aug. ,,

Austrian fleet under archduke Stephen, reviewed by queen Victoria off Cowes, Isle of Wight 11 Aug. ,,

Great loss of life and property through storms and floods . . . . 12-14 Aug. ,,

Cordial meeting of the Austrian and German emperors at Rhonstock in Silesia, 17-20 Sept., at Vienna . . . . 1-8 Oct. ,,

The archduke John of the Tuscan branch, who resigned his dignities and took the name of Johann Orth, Oct. 1889, became captain of a merchant ship, the *St. Margaret*, supposed to have been lost off the coast of S. America Aug., reported . . . . Oct. ,,

The compromise between the Germans and the Czechs in Bohemia not effected, through the opposition of the Young Czechs; *see Bohemia* 30 Nov. ,,

Coal mine explosion at Polish Ostrau; about 50 men perish . . . . 3 Jan. ,,

Dissolution of the Reichsrath; liberal manifesto issued by the government . . . 24 Jan. ,,

The archduke Franz Ferdinand d'Este, heir to the emperor, warmly received at St. Petersburg, Feb.; at Moscow . . . . 14 Feb. ,,

Result of elections: German Liberals, 110; Poles, 57; Young Czechs, 36; Old Czechs, 10; Clericals, 31; Bohemian Conservatives, 18; Miscellaneous, 93; total, 353; reported . . 15 March, 1891

The German Liberals and Poles support count Taaffe's ministry, about . . . . 26 March, ,,

The Reichsrath opened . . . . . 11 April, ,,

New treaty of commerce between Austria-Hungary and Germany, signed at Vienna . . . 3 May, 1891
The triple alliance renewed . . . . 28 June, „
Military manœuvres at Horn, the emperor and the German emperor present . . 3 Sept. *et seq.* „
New commercial treaty with Germany, Italy, Belgium, and Switzerland, adopted by the lower house, 19 Jan., by the senate . . . 25 Jan. 1892
Conference of Austrian bishops at Vienna . March, „
Currency reform bill passed . . . . 27 May, „
By a panic in a church at Vinagora, in Upper Austria, during a gale, 25 persons were crushed to death . . . . 31 Oct. „
The government defeated on a vote for secret service money by union of Germans and Czechs, 2 Dec. „
The new Bourse tax passed, 18 Sept. 1892; comes into operation . . . . . 1 Jan. 1893
Tour of the archduke Franz Ferdinand, the heir-presumptive; starts, 14 Dec. 1892; visits Ceylon, 5 Jan.; Bombay, 17 Jan.; Hyderabad, 24 Jan.; Calcutta, 1 Feb.; Sydney, 16 May; Hong Kong, July; Yokohama . . . . . 2 Aug. „
Meeting of Christian socialists, many eminent persons, at Vienna . . . . . 13 March, „
The Reichsrath prorogued . . . . 26 March, „
Heavy rains and destructive inundations in Bukowina and in Galicia, reported . . 7 June, „
Strike of 5,000 miners at Kladno, reported 12 June, „
Sir Edward Monson, British ambassador, arrives 27 June, „
The Reichsrath reopened; count Taaffe introduces a bill for electoral reform, leading to universal suffrage . . . . . . 10 Oct. „
Ministerial crisis; conference of heads of parties, 4 Nov.; count Taaffe, the premier, succeeded by prince Windischgrätz . . . . 12 Nov. „
Opening of the Reichsrath; statement of prince Windischgrätz . . . . . 23 Nov. „
Dr. Kohn, Dr. Platzau, and H. Pick, mountaineers, perish in attempting the ascent of the Gross Glockner . . . . . . 24–25 Dec. „
The *Omladina* (*which see*), a political society, active in 1893; trial began, 15 Jan. 1894: many sentenced to various terms of imprisonment for treason and other serious offences . . 21 Feb. 1894
Trial of anarchists (14); 8 sentenced to various terms of imprisonment, 6 acquitted . 19–23 Feb. „
Ottokar Dolezal, Franz Dragoum, and Joseph Kriz, members of the *Omladina*, charged with the murder of Mrva, an official at Prague, 23 Dec. 1893; sentenced to ten years' penal servitude, 20 March, „
Meeting of the Austrian and German emperors at Abbazia . . . . 29 March, „
Commercial treaty between Austria-Hungary and Russia, ratified . . . . . 6 July, „
Schmul Bibrovic, a Jewish farmer, and his family (8 persons) murdered, and his house plundered and burnt, at Boschewin . . . 24 Aug. „
Death of the archduke Albrecht; eminent in the army, liberal and popular; born, 1817, son of archduke Charles (see *Aspern*) . 18 Feb. 1895
Death of prince Richard Metternich, diplomatist 1 March, „
26 students tried at Tarnopol, Galicia, for high treason, and conspiring for the independence of Poland, 4 March; all acquitted . 13 March, „
Resignation of count Kalnoky, prudent foreign minister, on account of differences with Hungary respecting the action of the papal nuncio, Mgr. Agliardi, 16 May; succeeded by count Agenor Goluchowski, conservative and clerical, 17 May, „
New electoral reform bill in preparation . May, „
Resignation of the Windischgrätz (coalition) ministry, through the withdrawal of the German liberals . . . . 19 June „
Provisional cabinet: count Kielmansegg premier, 20 June, „
Death of the archduke Ladislaus by an accident while hunting . . . . . . Sept. „
New ministry, count Badeni, premier . 2 Oct. „
Opening of the Reichsrath: count Badeni declares a neutral policy . . . . . 22 Oct. „
Anti-Semitic movement; see *Vienna* . . 1895–96
Financial crisis at Vienna and Budapest in relation to Turkey . . . . 9 Nov. „
Death of count Taaffe, ex-premier, aged 63, 29 Nov. „

The emperor and empress received by queen Victoria at Nice . . . . . . 13 March, 1896
Visit of the German emperor and empress at Vienna; 14 April; grand military review; banquet, the two emperors present . . . . 15 April, „
Death of the archduke Karl Ludwig, heir-presumptive, much lamented . . . 19 May, „
Electoral reform bill passed by the Reichsrath, and adopted by the peers . . . 28 May, „
German progressist party founded . . 29 June, „
Differences between Austria and Hungary settled by compromise at a meeting of the ministers in Vienna . . . . 19 July, „
The archduchess Maria Dorothea niece of the emperor married to the duke of Orleans at Vienna 5 Nov. „
Sir Horace Rumbold, G.C.B., 1897; appointed British minister; 18 Aug., 1896; received by the emperor . . . . 11 Jan. 1897
The Railway labourers' association dissolved by government order . . . . . 21 March, „
The Reichsrath opened by the emperor, harmony of the powers reported . . . 29 March, „
The Badeni cabinet resigns, 2 April; resignation not accepted by the emperor . . . 4 April „
Grand military review by the emperors Francis Joseph and William II. . . . 22 April, „
The emperor arrives at St. Petersburg, received by the czar . . . . . . 27–30 April, „
Impeachment of the ministry; disorderly scenes in the Reichsrath; 6, 7, 24 May; deadlock; the session closed, 2 June; reassembled . 23 Sept. „
Agrarian association founded at Vienna . 29 Aug. „
Duel between count Badeni the premier and Herr Wolf in consequence of insulting language used by the latter, the count wounded . . 25 Sept. „
Renewed disorders in the Reichsrath . 19 Oct. „
Nearly 24 hrs. debate in the Reichsrath on the renewal of the *Ausgleich* with Hungary; 12 hrs. speech by Dr. Lecher; 28–29 Oct.; long sitting, bill read 1st time, amidst great disorder, 5 Nov.; violent scenes, socialists expelled by the police, 24–26 Nov.; Reichsrath prorogued, 27 Nov.; count Badeni resigns, 28 Nov.; baron Gautsch forms a new ministry, 30 Nov.; deadlock, 12 Dec.; the Reichsrath closed by decree 29 Dec. „
Count Kalnoky, born, 29 Dec., 1832, foreign minister from 1881–95; died . . . 13 Feb. 1898
Political agitation, large meetings in Styria and Bohemia . . . . 27 Feb. „
The language ordinances (modified) published 5 March, „
Baron Gautsch resigns, 5 March; new cabinet formed by count Thun . . . 7 March, „
Prince Ferdinand received by the emperor at Vienna . . . . 7 March, „
Increase of the navy determined on, 31 March; 30,000,000*fl.* demanded for fortifications May, „
Bills for the renewal of the *Ausgleich* with Hungary, introduced . . . . 20 April, „
Impeachment of count Badeni carried by a majority of 8 in the Reichsrath, 26 April, 1898; rejected in the lower house, 193-174 . . . 17 Nov. „
Jubilee of the emperor's reign celebrated, exhibition opened (see *Vienna*) . . . 8 May, „
Reichsrath re-assembled (deadlock), 1 June *et seq.*; prorogued . . . . . . 13 June, „
Anti-Semitic outrages, &c. in W. Galicia, houses plundered in 30 villages, troops called out, outbreak spreading, 24-28 June; martial law and other strong measures adopted with good effect, 29 June, „
Assassination of the empress Elizabeth (born 27 Dec. 1837) at Geneva by Luigi Luccheni (aged 25), an Italian anarchist, about 2 p.m., 10 Sept.; deeply lamented, public demonstration of Swiss sympathy, 12 Sept.; lying in state in the Imperial Chapel, Vienna, 16 Sept.; funeral, the emperor of Germany and other royal personages present, 17 Sept.; two anarchists arrested at Lausanne, 15 Sept. „
Luccheni sentenced to life imprisonment, 10 Nov. „
Jubilee amnesty, to army and navy, issued 20 Nov. „
Increasing agrarian revolt against clerical interference in secular affairs; see *Hungary*, 21 Nov. „
Count Thun protests against the expulsion of Austrians from Prussia . . . 29 Nov. „
Celebration of the emperor's jubilee . . 2 Dec.

The Austro-Hungarian *Ausgleich* renewed for 1899 by imperial rescript . . . . . 31 Dec. 1898

Disorderly scenes in the Reichsrath, crisis, 15 Dec. *et seq.* . . . . 17 Jan. 1899

Violent scene in the Reichsrath, 27 Jan. 1899; Reichsrath prorogued . . . . . 1 Feb. ,,

Mass meetings of social democrats in Vienna, 6 Feb.; manifesto against the Germans by the young Czechs, issued . . . . . 11 Feb. ,,

Count Rechberg, diplomatist, born 1806, died 25 Feb. ,,

Conference of R.C. bishops of Vienna, at Austria, on the "emancipation from Rome" movement; repressive measures; 4 societies dissolved in Vienna; reported . . . . . 12 April ,,

Count Karl Hohenwart, ex-premier, federalist, died aged 75 . . . . 26 April ,,

Johann Strauss, "Walzerkönig," popular composer, died, aged 73, 3 June; public funeral at Vienna, 6 June ,,

Chevalier von Blumencorn (ex-soldier, musician, and diplomatist), editor of the *Fremdenblatt*, died, aged 95 . . . . 29 June, ,,

Negotiations respecting the Austro-Hungarian *Ausgleich*, 24 May; a bill passed 2nd reading, 4 July ,,

Agitation against the government increasing, meetings violently suppressed . . . July ,,

Demonstrations against the increased sugar duty in Salzburg and elsewhere . . . 1 Aug. ,,

Count Thun's ministry promulgates the outstanding portions of the *Ausgleich*, and resigns 23 Sept.; count Clary forms a cabinet . . . . 1 Oct. ,,

Prince Ferdinand of Bulgaria received with honours at Vienna . . . . 26-27 Sept. ,,

Jewish meeting at Vienna to protest against the charge of ritual murder revived against their creed . . . . 7 Oct. ,,

Language-ordinances repealed, announced, 17 Oct. ,,

Reichsrath meets, premier states neutral policy, 18 Oct.; stormy scene, sitting closed . 24 Oct. ,,

Fatal Czech riots in Moravia, German and Jewish houses looted, troops called out . 22-24 Oct. ,,

Anti-Semitism and agitation against the use of German as the official language in the army, rioting in Bohemia and Moravia . . Nov. ,,

Disorder in the Reichsrath, provoked by the Czechs and Anti-Semites, 9-10 Nov.; crisis averted by the emperor . . . . 20-21 Nov. ,,

The Austro-Hungarian delegates received by the emperor with a speech from the throne, 1 Dec.; deadlock in the Reichsrath continues . 19 Dec. ,,

Count Clary's cabinet resigns, 21 Dec.; Dr. von Wittek forms a "provisional" ministry, 22 Dec. ,,

The emperor intimates firmly to Dr. Stransky, a Czech leader, that the language of the army must remain German . . . . 13 Jan. 1900

Coalminers' strike, 91,000 men involved, commission of inquiry appointed, reported . 23 Jan. ,,

Nationality conference (Czechs and Germans) on the language question, Dr. von Körber, premier, present, 5 Feb.; closed, sub-committee appointed, 22 March ,,

Reichsrath meets, Dr. von Körber, premier, declares the cabinet to be neutral . . . . 22 Feb. ,,

New language bills for Bohemia and Moravia introduced, noisy scene in the Reichsrath . 8 May ,,

Deadlock continues, session closed by the emperor's order . . . . 9 June ,,

Sir Francis Plunkett appointed ambassador at Vienna . . . . 7 Aug. ,,

Dissolution of the Reichsrath . . . . 7 Sept. ,,

The emperor attends the army manœuvres in Galicia, receives a Polish parliamentary deputation, threatens the suspension of the constitution if obstruction continues . . . . 13 Sept. ,,

The shah of Persia visits the emperor . 20 Sept. ,,

Leopold Hilsner, a Jew (22), sentenced to death for complicity in the murder of a Christian girl, Oct. 1899; sentence quashed May, 1900; 2nd trial at Pisek, Bohemia, for another murder, 25 Oct.; again found guilty and sentenced to death (ritual murder theory rejected) . . . 14 Nov. ,,

Elections, 3 Jan. 1901, defeat of Clericals and Anti-Semites, reported 15 Jan.; the Reichsrath opened 31 Jan. 1901

The emperor's speech from the throne, proposes industrial, economic and social reforms, and earnestly protests against the strife of nationalities . . . . 4 Feb. 1901

Violent scenes in the Reichsrath, 20 Feb.-5 March ,,

Stormy debates in the Reichsrath on the action of the archduke Franz Ferdinand assuming the protectorate over the Catholic schools' association 23-24 April ,,

Pan-Germanic union advocating emancipation from Rome meets in Vienna . . . . 5 May ,,

Canal bill and government railway bill read 3rd time by the Reichsrath . . . . 1 June ,,

The emperor visits Prague . . . 12-18 June ,,

Dr. Lueger and the Anti-Semitic party beaten at the polls in Lower Austria . . . . 2 July ,,

Reichsrath meets, the premier protests against the nationality strife . . . . . 17 Oct. ,,

The emperor interviews the king of Greece and prince George of Crete . . . . 7 Nov. ,,

Manifesto against obstruction issued by the Germans in the Reichsrath . . . 19 Nov. ,,

Anti-Clerical association founded, first meeting held in Vienna . . . . . . 18 Dec. ,,

The Reichsrath meets . . . . 4 Feb. 1902

Archduke Franz Ferdinand visits the czar 7 Feb. ,,

Reichsrath: Pan-Germanic demonstration, 18 March; uproar over the language question, 9 April ,,

Count von Bülow, German imperial chancellor, received by the emperor . . . . 10 April ,,

Conference of Austrian and Hungarian premiers at Budapest on the *Ausgleich* and tariff questions, 21, 22 and 26 May; Vienna, 10 July and 22 Aug. ,,

The triple alliance renewed . . . 28 June ,,

The king of Roumania visits Austria . 2 Aug. ,,

Conference on the *Ausgleich* in Vienna . 22 Aug. ,,

Riots in Agram (see *Croatia*) . . . Sept. ,,

Reichsrath meets, 15 Oct.; deadlock on the *Ausgleich* negotiations . . . . 17 Oct. ,,

Violent scenes between Czechs and Germans, 11, 13 Nov. ,,

Reichsrath meets. Renewal of *Ausgleich* for 10 years agreed to . . . . . 31 Dec. ,,

Floods and loss of life in many parts, reported, 7 Jan. 1903

Act of economic union with Hungary signed 11 Jan. New customs tariff, &c. . . 15, 17 Jan. ,,

Sugar convention ratified . . . . 31 Jan. ,,

Debt conversion bill passed . . . 16 Feb. ,,

Army bills passed . . . . . 20 Feb. ,,

Emperor conferred grand cross of the order of St. Stephen on Dr. von Körber, the Austrian premier . . . . mid-April, ,,

Dispute between Austrian and Hungarian parliaments respecting the sugar allotment system, 29 July, ,,

King Edward VII. visits Marienbad . . 13 Aug. ,,

Visit of the king to Vienna, enthusiastic reception, 31 Aug. ,,

Takes leave of the emperor and makes him hon. field-marshal of British army . . . . 3 Sept. ,,

Lord Milner visits Vienna, received by Austro-Hungarian foreign minister . . . 3 Sept. ,,

Death of count Deym, Austro-Hungarian ambassador to Great Britain, from 8 Oct. 1888 . 3 Sept. ,,

Inter-parliamentary conference at Vienna adopt resolution in favour of a new international congress to consider the disarmament schemes formulated by Russia in 1898 . . . . 9 Sept. ,,

(See *Germany, Hungary, Vienna, &c.*, and *Addenda*.)

MARGRAVES OF AUSTRIA.

Leopold I., 982; Albert I., 1018; Ernest, 1056; Leopold II., 1075; Leopold III., 1096; Albert II., 1136; Leopold IV., 1136; Henry II., 1142 (made a duke, 1156).

DUKES.

1156. Henry II.
1177. Leopold V. He made prisoner Richard I. of England when returning incognito from the crusade, and was compelled to surrender him to the emperor Henry VI.
1194. Frederic I., the catholic.
1198. Leopold VI., the glorious. Killed in battle.
1230. Frederic II., the warlike. Killed in a battle with the Hungarians, 15 June, 1246
Interregnum.
1276. Rodolph I.
1282. Albert I. and his brother Rodolph II. Albert becomes emperor of Germany, 1298.
1308. Frederic I. and Leopold I.

1326. Frederic I.
1330. Albert II. and Otho, his brother.
1339. Albert II.
1358. Rodolph IV.
1365. Albert III. and Leopold II. or III. (killed at Sempach).
1395. William I. and brothers, and their cousin Albert IV.
1411. The same. The provinces divided into the duchies of Austria and Carinthia, and the county of Tyrol.
1411. Albert V., duke of Austria; obtains Bohemia and Moravia; elected king of Hungary and emperor, 1437; dies, 1439; succeeded by his posthumous son,
1439. Ladislaus, who dies childless, 1457.
1457. The emperor Frederic III. and Albert VI.
1493. Maximilian I., son of Frederick III. (*archduke*), emperor; see *Germany*.

EMPERORS.

1804. Francis I. (late Francis II. of *Germany*), styled emperor of Austria only, 11 Aug. 1804; resigned empire of Germany, 6 Aug. 1806; died 2 Mar. 1835.
1835. Ferdinand, his son, 2 March; abdicated in favour of his nephew (his brother Francis-Charles having renounced his rights), 2 Dec. 1848; died 29 June, 1875.
1848. Francis-Joseph (son of Francis-Charles), born 18 Aug. 1830; succeeded, 2 Dec. 1848; married 24 April, 1854, to Elizabeth of Bavaria, assassinated (see *Austria*) 10 Sept. 1898; crowned king of Hungary, 8 June, 1867; their son, the archduke Rodolph, born 21 Aug. 1858; married to princess Stephanie Clotilde of Belgium, 10 May, 1881; died, 30 Jan. 1889 (she married count Elemer Lonyay, 22 March, 1900).
Heir presumptive, brother, archduke Charles Louis, born 30 July, 1833; died 19 May, 1896; his son, archduke Francis Ferdinand d'Este, *born* 18 Dec. 1863; married to countess Sophia Chotek (created princess von Hohenberg, 1 July), 1 July, 1900.

AUTHORS. See *Copyrights*. The Society of Authors established for self-defence, to maintain copyrights, protection, &c., by sir W. Frederick Pollock, cardinal Manning, and others, lord Tennyson, president, met 18 Feb., incorporated May, 1884. In 1884 there were 68 paying members; in 1902, about 1500. Organ of the soc. *The Author*.

It sent a deputation to the celebration of the 50th anniversary of the Société des Gens de Lettres at Paris, 10 Dec. 1887. Annual meetings.

AUTO DA FÉ (Act of faith), the term given to the punishment of a heretic, generally burning alive, inflicted by the Inquisition (*which see*).

AUTOGRAPHS. J. G. Nicholls' "Autographs of Royal and Remarkable Personages in English History," 4to, 1829. "Isographie des Hommes Célèbres," 4 vols., Paris, 1843. Signatures of some Eminent Fellows of the Royal Society (lithographs), 4to, 1851. F. G. Netherclift's "Handbook of Autographs," 1860. "Royal, Historical, Literary, and other Autographs" in the British Museum (photo-lithographs), first publication, Nov., 1895.

AUTOMATON FIGURES (or ANDROIDES), made to imitate living actions, are of early invention. Friar Bacon is said to have made a brazen head which spoke, A.D. 1264. Albertus Magnus spent thirty years in making another. A coach and two horses, with a footman and page, and a lady inside, were made by Camus for Louis XIV. when a child; the horses and figures moved naturally, variously, and perfectly, 1649. Vaucanson, in 1738, made an artificial duck, which performed many functions of a real one—eating, drinking, and quacking; and he also made a flute-player. The writing automaton, exhibited in 1769, was a pentagraph worked by a confederate out of sight. The automaton chess-player, of Maelzel, exhibited the same year, was also worked by a hidden person; so was the "invisible girl," 1800. See *Chess*. Maelzel made a trumpeter about 1809. Early in this century, an automaton was exhibited in London which pronounced several sentences with tolerable distinctness. The "anthropoglossus," an alleged talking-machine, exhibited at St. James's hall, London, July, 1864, was proved to be a gross imposition. The exhibition of the talking-machine of professor Faber of Vienna, in London, began 27 Aug. 1870, at the Palais Royal, Argyll-street, W. Psycho, an automaton card-player, invented by J. N. Maskelyne and John Algernon Clarke, exhibited in London, Jan. 1875. Another Zoë, which played cards, was exhibited by Mr. Maskelyne, 1877. An automaton hare was hunted at Hendon, near London, 9 Sept. 1876.

Automatic machine for producing photographic portraits on metal for 1*d*., exhibited by Messrs. Salter & Co., West Bromwich . . March, 1890
Automatic machines for supplying gas "penny in the slot," sweetmeats, and other articles, trying the weight, &c., much in vogue 1903

AUTOMOBILE CLUB, was founded 1897 for the social intercourse of persons interested in motor locomotion and its development. 2,000 members in 1903. *Ladies' Automobile Club*, instituted 1903, see *Motors*.

AUTONOMISTS, a name assumed by a socialist party in Paris (see *Possibilists*), 1887.

AUTOTYPOGRAPHY, a process of producing a metal plate from drawings, made known by Mr. Wallis, in April, 1863; it resembled *Nature-printing* (*which see*).

AUXERRE DECLARATION, see *France*, May, 1866.

AVA, the capital of the Burmese empire from 1364 to 1740, and from 1822 to 1838. Destroyed by an earthquake in 1839. See *Burmah*.

AVARS, barbarians who ravaged Pannonia, and annoyed the eastern empire in the 6th and 7th centuries, subdued by Charlemagne about 799, after an eight years' war.

AVEBURY, or ABURY (Wiltshire). Here are the remains of the largest so-called Druidical work in this country. They have been surveyed by Aubrey, 1648; Dr. Stukeley, 1720; and sir R. C. Hoare, in 1812, and by others. Much information may be obtained from Stukeley's "Abury" (1743), Hoare's "Ancient Wiltshire" (1812-21), and the rev. A. C. Smith's work (1884). They are considered to have been set up during the "stone age," *i.e.*, when weapons and implements were mainly formed of that material. Sir John Lubbock, now lord Avebury, takes his title from this place, 22 Jan. 1900.

AVEIN, or AVAINE (Luxemburg, Belgium). Here the French and Dutch defeated the Spaniards, 20 May, 1635.

"AVE MARIA!" the salutation of the angel Gabriel to the Virgin (*Luke* i. 28), was made a formula of devotion by pope John XXI. about 1326. In the beginning of the 15th century Vinceutius Ferrerius used it before his discourses. *Bingham*.

AVENIN. The stimulating qualities of this nitrogenous alkaloid in oats were discovered by Mr. Sanson in 1882.

AVENUE THEATRE, Thames Embankment, opened 11 March, 1882.

AVIGNON, a city, S. E. France, ceded by Philip III. to the pope in 1273. The papal seat was removed by Clement V. to Avignon, in 1309. In 1348 Clement VI. purchased the sovereignty from Jane, countess of Provence and queen of Naples. In 1408, the French, wearied of the schism, expelled Benedict XIII., and Avignon ceased to be the seat of the papacy. Here were held nine councils (1080-1457). Avignon was seized and restored several times by the French kings; the last time restored, 1773. It was claimed by the national assembly, 1791, and was confirmed to France by the congress of sovereigns in 1815. In Oct. 1791, horrible massacres took place here. See *Popes*, 1309-94.

AXE, frequently mentioned in the Bible, *Deut.* xix. 5; *Judges*, ix. 48; 1 *Sam.* xiii. 20; *Psalm* lxxiv. 5, etc. See *Tools*.

AXUM, or AUXUME, a town in Abyssinia said to have been the capital of a kingdom whose people were converted to Christianity by Frumentius about 330, and were allies of Justinian, 533.

AYACUCHO (Peru). Here the Peruvians finally achieved their independence by defeating the Spaniards, 9 Dec. 1824.

AYDE, or AIDE, the tax paid by the vassal to the chief lord upon urgent occasions. In France and England an *aide* was due for knighting the king's eldest son. One was demanded by Philip the Fair, 1313. The *aide* due upon the birth of a prince, ordained by the statute of Westminster (Edward I.), 1285, was not to be levied until he was fifteen years of age, for the ease of the subject. The *aide* for the marriage of the king's eldest daughter could not be demanded in this country until her seventh year. In feudal tenures there was an *aide* for ransoming the chief lord; so when our Richard I. was kept a prisoner by the emperor of Germany, an *aide* of 20s., to redeem him, was enforced upon every knight's fee; see *Benevolence*.

AYLESBURY, Buckinghamshire, was reduced by the West Saxons in 571. Incorporated by charter in 1554; absorbed into the county 1889. The ancient parish church was restored by sir G. G. Scott, 1849-67. Visited by the queen 14 May, 1890. Population 1881, 7,795; 1891, 8,674; 1901, 9,244.

AYLESFORD (Kent). Here, it is said, the Britons were victorious over the Saxon invaders, 455, and Horsa was killed.

AYR, capital of Ayrshire, S. W. Scotland: chartered and endowed by William the Lion, 12th century; fortified by Oliver Cromwell.—By a sudden fire at Templeton's carpet works, 29 persons perished, 16 June, 1876. Statue of Burns at Irvine unveiled by Mr. Alfred Austin, poet laureate, 18 July, 1896. Town hall, &c., burnt down, estimated loss, 20,000*l*., 1 July, 1897. Population, 1881, 20,821; 1891, 24,800; 1901, 28,624.

AZINCOUR, see *Agincourt*.

AZOFF, SEA OF, the Palus Mæotis of the ancients, communicates by the strait of Yenikalé (the Bosporus Cimmerius) with the Black Sea, and is entirely surrounded by Russian territory; Taganrog and Kertch being the principal places. An expedition, composed of British, French, and Turkish troops, commanded by sir G. Brown, arrived at Kertch, 24 May, 1855, when the Russians retired, after blowing up the fortifications. On the 25th the allies marched upon Yenikalé, which also offered no resistance. On the same evening the allied fleet entered the Sea of Azoff, and in a few days completed their occupation of it, after capturing a large number of merchant vessels, &c. An immense amount of stores was destroyed by the Russians to prevent their falling into the hands of the allies.

AZOIMIDE, a compound of hydrogen and nitrogen (azote), a very explosive gas, obtained from organic sources, such as benzoyl-glycollic acid and hippuric acid, by prof. Curtius in 1890. It forms salts by combination with metals; it is described in *Nature*, 10 Dec. 1891.

AZORES, or WESTERN ISLES (N. Atlantic), belonging to Portugal, the supposed site of the ancient Atlantis, are said to have been discovered in the 15th century by Vanderberg of Bruges, who was driven on their coasts by the weather. Cabral, sent by the Portuguese court, fell in with St. Mary's in 1432, and in 1457 they were all discovered and named Azores from the number of goshawks found on them. They were given by Alfonso V. to the duchess of Burgundy in 1466, and colonised by Flemings. They were subject to Spain 1580-1640. The isle Terceira, during the usurpation of dom Miguel, declared for donna Maria, 1829, and a government was established at the capital Angra, 1830-33. A volcano at St. George's destroyed the town of Ursulina, May, 1808; and in 1811 a volcano appeared near St. Michael's, in the sea, where the water was eighty fathoms deep; an island then formed gradually disappeared. A destructive earthquake lasting 12 days, happened in St. Michael's, 1591. The telegraphic cable from Lisbon to the Azores was inaugurated by the king and queen at Carcavellos, 27 Aug. 1893.

AZOTE, the name given by French chemists to nitrogen (*which see*).

AZOTUS, see *Ashdod*.

AZRAEL, according to Mohammedan mythology, the "Angel of Death," who "separates men's souls and bodies, and with his assistants either tears them asunder with violence, or draws them apart with gentleness."

AZTECS, the ruling tribe in Mexico at the time of the Spanish invasion (1519). In June, 1853, two pretended Aztec children were exhibited in London. They were considered by professor Owen to be merely South American dwarfs. They were married in London, 1 April, 1867, and exhibited for some time after.

B.

BAAL (Lord), the male deity of the Phœnician nations, frequently worshipped by the Israelites, especially by Ahab, 918 B.C. His priests and votaries were massacred by Jehu, and his temple defiled, 884 B.C.

BAALBEC, HELIOPOLIS (both meaning "City of the Sun"), an ancient city of Syria, of which magnificent ruins remain, visited by Wood (in 1751), and others. Its origin is lost in antiquity. Here Septimius Severus built a temple to the sun, 200. The city was sacked by the Moslems, 748, and by Timour Beg, 1400. Visited by terrible earthquake, 1759. See *Heliopolis*; and *Germany*, 10 Nov. 1898.

BABA WALI. See *Afghanistan*, 1 Sept. 1880; and *Mazra*.

BABBAGE, see *Calculating Machines*.

BABBICOMBE MURDER, see *Trials*, Feb. 1885.

BABEL, TOWER of, built by Noah's posterity, 2247 B.C. (*Genesis*, ch. xi.) The magnificent temple of Belus, asserted to have been originally this tower, is said to have had lofty spires, and many statues of gold, one of them forty feet high. In the upper part of this temple was the tomb of the founder, Belus (the Nimrod of the sacred scriptures), who was deified after death. *Blair*. The Birs Nimroud, the site of a temple dedicated to Nebo and called the "Temple of the Seven Lights" (planets), examined by Rich, Layard, and others, is conjectured by some to be the remains of the tower of Babel.

BABEUF'S CONSPIRACY, see *Agrarian Law*.

BABY-FARMING, see *Infanticide*.

BABYLONIA* (*Babilu* Assyrian, *Babirush* Persian, the Shinar, Babel, and land of the Chaldees of the Old Testament), a vast plain watered by the Tigris and Euphrates, the seat of a great Asiatic empire, traditionally stated to have been founded by Belus, supposed to have been the Nimrod of *Gen.* x. 1, 8. See *Assyria*. According to the earliest existing history the country was divided between two races, the Sumir (Turanian), the probable inventors of cuneiform writing; and the Accad or Akkad (Semitic), which became predominant. See *Accadians*. "The fragmentary Canon of Kings," given by Berosus the Græco-Chaldean priest 268 B.C., had been superseded by the newly-discovered Babylonian canon inscriptions on tablets carefully dated from 2200 to 647 B.C., an unequalled chronological series. Summaries are given by Mr. Boscawen in the articles "Assyria" and "Babylonia" in "Chambers' Encyclopædia," 1901.

Earliest astronomical observations at Babylon, B.C. 2234, [2230, *H.*; 2233, *Cl.*]

Nabonassar governor, 747; His son Nadinu, 734; a revolt, Ukinziru, king, about 732

Babylonia conquered by Pul (Tiglath-Pileser) king of Assyria, 729; becomes independent; Merodach-baladan II. king about 722

Sargon, king of Assyria, captures Babylon; Merodach-baladan returns, but is soon expelled by Sennacherib 705

Babylonia ruled by viceroys, *see Assyria*.

Nabu-abla-utzar (Nabopolassar), general, seizes the power about 640; proclaimed king . . . 625

Succeeded by his son Nebuchadnezzar, very great and powerful, 604; he restores the empire, and rebuilds Babylon.

[His acts are recorded on innumerable tablets and in the Bible; 2 *Kings*, xxiv., xxv.; 2 *Chron.* xxxvi.; *Jer.*, xxxvii.—xxxix.; lii.; *Daniel*, i.—iv.]

He captures Jerusalem, 599; and destroys the city and carries most of the inhabitants captives to Babylon, 588; dies 569

Evil Merodach, 561; Neriglissar, king . . . 551

Labynetus, 556; Nabonadius, a great monarch, 551; Belshazzar king 539

Babylon taken by the Medes and Persians, under Cyrus, and Belshazzar slain. *Daniel* v. . . 538

Babylon revolts, and is taken by Darius . . . 518

Taken by Alexander, 331; he dies here . . . 323

Seleucus Nicator, who died 280 B.C., transfers the seat of government to Seleucia, and Babylon is deserted. Babylonia was conquered by the Parthians about 140 B.C., and became part of the Persian empire. On the overthrow of the Sassanides by the Mahometans 650 A.D., Babylonia became the seat of the califs till 1258. Since 1638 it has been subject to Turkey.

BABYNGTON'S CONSPIRACY, to assassinate queen Elizabeth, and make Mary of Scotland queen, was devised by John Savage, a

* The city of Babylon was at one time the most magnificent in the world. The *Hanging Gardens* are described as having been of a square form, and in terraces one above another until they rose as high as the walls of the city, the ascent being from terrace to terrace by steps. The whole pile was sustained by vast arches raised on other arches; and on the top were flat stones closely cemented together with plaster of bitumen, and that covered with sheets of lead, upon which lay the mould of the garden, where there were large trees, shrubs, and flowers, with various sorts of vegetables. There were five of these gardens, each containing about four English acres, and disposed in the form of an amphitheatre. *Strabo; Diodorus*. Pliny said that in his time it was but a desolate wilderness. Mr. Rich visited the ruins in 1811, and sir R. Ker Porter in 1818. The laborious researches of Mr. (after sir A. H.) Layard, sir H. Rawlinson, M. Botta, and others, and the interesting relics excavated and brought to this country between the years 1849 and 1855, have caused very much attention to be given to the history of Babylon. Many of the inscriptions in the cuneiform or wedge-like character have been translated, principally by col. (after sir Henry) Rawlinson, and published in the Journal of the Royal Asiatic Society. In the spring of 1855 he returned to England, bringing with him many valuable relics, drawings, &c., which are now in the British Museum. He gave discourses on the subject at the Royal Institution, London, in 1851, 1855, and 1865. The rev. A. Sayce lectured on Babylonian literature at the same place in 1877. Important exploration of the ruins of Niffer, near Babylon, at the cost of the Babylonian Exploration Fund of Philadelphia, conducted by Dr. Peters, 1888–94, *et seq.*; an ancient temple of Bel was discovered, with many other relics; reported Dec. 1894. American explorations on the site of N. Babylonia renewed, under Mr. Haynes, in 1893; cities of Nippur, or Niffer, and Mul-lil "Older Bel." in S. Babylonia excavated; reported, *Times* 24 June, 1897. Explorations carried on at Susa, first by Loftus, palaces uncovered by M. Dieulafoy, 1884-86, and by M. de Morgan, Dec. 1897, palace ruins, monuments, etc., discovered, *Times*, 10 Jan. 1900. King Khammurabi's laws abt. B.C. 2200, trans. by Dr. Schiel, *Times*, 14 April, 1903.

soldier of Philip of Spain, and approved by Wm. Gifford and John Ballard, catholic priests. Anthony Babyngton and others joined in the scheme. They were betrayed by Pooley, a spy, and fourteen were executed, 20, 21 Sept. 1586.

BÂBI-ISM, a new sect in Persia, founded in 1843 by Mirza Ali Mahomed, an enthusiast, at Shiraz. He termed himself the "Bâb," or "gate," of knowledge, and, giving a new exposition of the Koran, claimed to be the incarnate Holy Spirit. The destruction of himself and the greater number of his followers was due to Hossein, one of his disciples, who combined political and warlike principles with spiritual dogmas. The sect was tolerated by the shah Mohammed, but nearly exterminated by his successor in 1848-9. The Bâb himself was executed 15 July, 1849. The head of the sect, Beheyah Allah, propounded a doctrine, termed "Bâb el Huk," gate of truth. The persecuted sect has been favoured by Turkey, and been settled latterly at Bagdad. Mr. Edwd. G. Brown's "Narrative" respecting Bâbi-ism, was published in 1892. See *Persia*, 1 May, 1896.

BACCARAT CASE, see *Trials*, June, 1891.

BACCHUS, the name given after the 4th century B.C. to Dionysus (*which see*), the Greek god of wine, poetry, and music.

BACCON or **BACON**, see *Orleans*.

BACH SOCIETY, instituted in London in 1849, for the collection of the works of J. S. Bach, and the promotion of their public performance. The original committee included W. Sterndale Bennett, Sir G. Smart, J. Hullah, C. Potter, and other eminent musicians. The society was dissolved, 21 March, 1870, and the music given up to the Royal Academy of Music.

BACHELORS. The Roman censors frequently imposed fines on unmarried men; and men of full age were obliged to marry. A tax laid upon bachelors in England, twenty-five years of age (varying from 12*l.* 10*s.* for a duke, to 1*s.* for a common person), lasted from 1695 to 1706. Bachelors (Romanist priests excepted) were subjected to an extra tax on their male and female servants in 1785. A *grand ball* given by 84 bachelors at Kensington House; the prince and princess of Wales present, 22 July 1880. The Bachelors' Club, London, founded in 1881, consisted of 950 members in 1903. Members marrying may be elected honorary members by the Committee.

BACILLI (little rods), one of the forms of, and a division of Bacteria. See *Germ Theory*.

BACONIAN PHILOSOPHY, propounded by Francis Bacon, specially in his "Novum Organon," published in 1620. Its principles are Utility and Progress; and its objects the alleviation of the sufferings and promotion of the comforts of mankind. *Macaulay*, 1837.

BACON SOCIETY, established in December, 1885, for the study of the works and life of Francis Bacon, and to investigate claims for his supposed authorship of certain works, including the Shakespearian dramas and poems. A journal is published.

BACTERIA, Schizomycetes, or Bacilli. Established by Cohn (1853) to be small, single-celled fungoid plants. They are found everywhere, and through the researches of Koch, Pasteur, Duguid, Burdon Sanderson, Klein, Fullerton, and others the bacilli of many diseases have been identified. Prof. Molisch, of Prague, reports a lamp illuminated by means of bacteria, March, 1903. See *Germ Theory*.

BACTRIANA, a province in Asia, was subjugated by Cyrus and formed part of the Persian empire, when conquered by Alexander, 330 B.C. About 254 B.C., Theodotus or Diodotus, a Greek, threw off the yoke of the Seleucidæ, and became king. Eucratides I. reigned prosperously about 181 B.C., and Menander about 126 B.C. The Greek kingdom appears to have been broken up by the irruption of the Scythians shortly after.

BADAJOZ (S. W. Spain). An important barrier fortress, surrendered to the French, under Soult, 11 March, 1811; invested by the British, under lord Wellington, on 16 March, 1812, and stormed and taken on 6 April following. The French retreated in haste. A short military insurrection, 5 and 6 Aug. 1883. Population, 1887, 27,279; 1897, 490,551.

BADDESDOWN HILL, or Mount Badon, near Bath, where Bede says the Britons defeated the Saxons, 493; others say 511 or 520, all doubtful.

BADEN (S. W. Germany). The house of Baden is descended from Hermann, regarded as the first margrave (1052), son of Berthold I., duke of Zähringen; but Hermann II. assumed the title, Feb. 1130. From Christopher, who died 1527, proceeded the branches Baden-Baden and Baden-Dourlach, united in 1771. Baden is an hereditary constitutional monarchy by charter, 26 May, 1818; it joined the German empire by treaty, 15 Nov. 1870. Population, 1 Dec. 1871, 1,461,562; Dec. 1875, 1,507,179; 1885, 1,601,255; 1890, 1,656,817; 1900, 1,866,584.

Louis William, margrave of Baden-Baden, a great general, born 1665; sallied out from Vienna and defeated the Turks, 1683; died 1707.

Charles William, margrave of Baden-Dourlach, born 1679, died 1746; succeeded by his son,

Charles Frederic, born 1728; margrave of Baden-Dourlach, 1738; acquired Baden-Baden, 1771, made grand-duke by Napoleon, 1806.

Treaty of Baden:—Landau ceded to France, 7 Sept. 1714

Baden made a *grand-duchy*, with enlarged territories 1806

A representative constitution granted by charter, 18 Aug. 1818

Republican agitation . . . . . . during 1848

Insurrection; joined by the free city Rastatt; the grand-duke flees . . . . May, 1849

The Prussians enter Baden, 15 June; defeat the insurgents commanded by Mierolawski; Rastatt surrenders, 23 July; the grand-duke re-enters Carlsruhe . . . . 18 Aug. ,,

Arrests for political offences . . . . 9 July, 1857

Concordat with the pope signed . . . 28 June, 1859

Greatly opposed by the chambers; annulled by the grand-duke by a manifesto, securing autonomy to the Catholic and Protestant churches; signed 7 April, 1860

Interview at Baden-Baden of the emperor Napoleon III., the prince regent of Prussia, and the German kings and princes . . . . 16 June, ,,

The new ecclesiastical law (adopted by the chambers) promulgated . . . . . . 16 Oct. ,,

Opposition of the archbishop of Friburg and the clerical party 1860-65

Disputes in the German diet; the grand-duke vainly endeavours to obtain a reconciliation; and remains neutral . . . . . . June, 1866

Baden joins the Zollverein (*which see*) . . July, 1867

Meeting of the chambers; liberal measures promised, 24 Sept.; universal suffrage adopted by the second chamber . . . . . . 29 Oct. 1869

Civil marriage made obligatory . . . 17 Nov. ,,

Baden joins Prussia in the war with France, about 20 July, 1870

Gambling houses suppressed; finally closed 31 Oct. 1872

Death of prince William brother of the grand-duke, 27 April, 1897

The grand-duke's jubilee celebrated, internat. art and horticultural exhibition opened at Carlsruhe, 25 April; the German emperor arrives 26 April, 1902

GRAND-DUKES.

1806. Charles Frederic; dies 1811; succeeded by his grandson,
1811. Charles Louis Frederic, who died without issue in 1818; succeeded by his uncle,
1818. Louis William, died without issue in 1830; succeeded by his brother,
1830. Leopold, died in 1852; succeeded by his second son (the first being imbecile),
1852. Frederic (born 9 Sept. 1826), regent 24 April, 1852; declared grand-duke, 5 Sept. 1856; becomes ill, his son appointed regent, 11 Nov. 1881.

Heir: his son Frederic William, born 9 July, 1857.

BADMINTON LIBRARY. A series of 28 vols. by eminent writers relating to sports and pastimes, edited by the duke of Beaufort (a devoted sportsman, born, 1824, died, 30 April, 1899), dedicated to the prince of Wales, published 1885–96.

BAFFIN'S BAY (N. America), discovered by William Baffin, an Englishman, 1616. The extent of this discovery was much doubted, until the expeditions of Ross and Parry proved that Baffin was substantially accurate in his statement. Parry entered Lancaster Sound, and discovered the islands known by his name, in 1818. British flag hoisted at Cumberland Sound, territory annexed by Canadian government, Sept., 1897. See *North-West Passage.*

BAGDAD, in Asiatic Turkey, built by Al Mansour, and made the seat of the Saracen empire, about 762. Taken by the Tartars, and a period put to the Saracen rule, 1258. Often taken by the Persians, and retaken by the Turks, with great slaughter: the latter have held it since 1638. Population, 1885, 100,000; 1901, 145,000. See *Turkey,* Nov. 1899 *et seq.*, for *Baghdad Railway Concession.*

BAGPIPE, an ancient Greek and Roman instrument. On a piece of ancient Grecian sculpture, now in Rome, a bagpiper is represented dressed like a modern highlander. Nero is said to have played upon a bagpipe, 51. Our highland regiments retain their pipers. Patrick Bohan, the celebrated Irish piper, died 9 April, 1884.

BAHAMA ISLES (N. America) were the first points of discovery by Columbus. San Salvador was seen by him on the night of 11 Oct. 1492; he landed next day. New Providence was settled by the English in 1629. They were expelled by the Spaniards, 1641; returned, 1666; again expelled in 1703. The isles were formally ceded to the English in 1783. Population in 1861, 35,287 (see *Cyclones,* Oct. 1866); in 1871, 39,162; in 1881, 43,521; 1892, 48,913; 1901, 53,725. The Bahamas profited by blockade-running during the American civil war, 1862-5. Governors, William Rawson, 1864; sir James Walker, 1868; John Pope Hennessy, 1871; Wm. Robinson, 1874; Thos. F. Callaghan, 1879; Charles Cameron Lees, 5 Oct. 1881; H. A. Blake, Jan. 1884; Sir Ambrose Shea, Oct. 1887; sir W. F. Haynes Smith, Jan. 1895; sir Gilbert T. Carter, Nov. 1897.

Chief Justice Yelverton's sentence of fine and imprisonment against Mr. Moseley, editor, for contempt of court, May, 1892, annulled by the judicial committee of the privy council, 2 Feb. 1893.

Famine in the Bemini islands, destructive storms, many deaths, reported, 26 Dec. 1898.

BAHAR (N. India), a province (conquered by Baber in 1530), with Bengal and Orissa, a princely dominion, became subject to the English East India company in 1765 by the treaty of Allahabad for a quit-rent of about 300,000*l.*

BAIL. By ancient common law, before and since the conquest, all felonies were bailable, till murder was excepted by statute; and by the 3 Edward I. (1275) the power of bailing in treason, and in divers instances of felony, was taken away. Bail was further regulated in later reigns. It is now accepted in all cases, except felony; and where a magistrate refuses bail, it may be granted by a judge. Acts respecting bail passed 1826, 1852, and 1898.

BAILIFF, or SHERIFF, said to be of Saxon origin. London had its *shire-reve* prior to the conquest, and this officer was generally appointed for counties in England in 1079. Hen. Cornehill and Rich. Reynere were appointed bailiffs or sheriffs in London in 1189. *Stow.* Sheriffs were appointed in Dublin under the name of bailiffs, in 1308; and the name was changed to sheriff in 1548. There are still places where the chief magistrate is called bailiff, as the high bailiff of Westminster. *Bum-bailiff* is a corruption of bound-bailiff, every bailiff being obliged to enter into bonds of security for his good behaviour. *Blackstone.*

BAIRAM, or BEIRAM, Mahometan festivals. The Little Bairam, follows the fast of Ramadán (*which see*): the Great Bairam, or feast of sacrifices, takes place 70 days after the shorter one.

BAIRD LECTURES, were founded in 1871 by Mr. James Baird, a wealthy ironmaster and M.P. for Falkirk burghs (1851–57), for the defence of orthodox theology in Scotland.

BAIZE, a species of coarse woollen manufacture, was brought into England by some Flemish or Dutch emigrants who settled at Colchester, in Essex, about 1568.

BAKER AND BAKEHOUSES; see *Bread.*

BAKERIAN LECTURES, Royal society, originated in a bequest of 100*l.* by Henry Baker, F.R.S., the interest of which was to be given to one of the fellows, for a scientific discourse to be delivered annually. Peter Woulfe gave the first lecture in 1765. Latterly it has been the custom to nominate as the lecture a paper written by one of the fellows. Davy, Faraday, Tyndall, and other eminent men, have given the lecture.

BAKU. See under *Petroleum.*

BALAKLAVA, a small town in the Crimea, with a fine harbour, 10 miles S.E. from Sebastopol. After the battle of the Alma, the allies advanced upon this place, 26 Sept. 1854.

Battle of Balaklava:—About 12,000 Russians, commanded by general Liprandi, attacked and took some redoubts in the vicinity, which had been entrusted to about 250 Turks. They next assaulted the English, by whom they were compelled to retire, mainly through the charge of the heavy cavalry, led by brigadier Scarlett, under the orders of lord Lucan. After this, from an unfortunate misconception of lord Raglan's order, lord Lucan ordered lord Cardigan, with the light cavalry, to charge the Russian army, which had reformed on its own ground with its artillery in front. The order was most gallantly obeyed, and great havoc was made on the enemy: but of 670 British horsemen, only 198 returned. (Termed by Tennyson "The Charge of the Six Hundred.") The infantry engaged were termed a "thin red line" . . . . 25 Oct. 1854

[A banquet was given to the survivors at the Alexandra Palace, 25 Oct. 1875.]

[A subscription for the relief of about 20 destitute

out of 100 survivors of the Light Brigade was opened in April, 1890, by the agency of Mr. Herbert and lieut. Wightman, two of their comrades, and supported by the *St. James's Gazette*, rt. hon. E. Stanhope, and sir W. Marriott, lords Tennyson, Wolseley, Hartington, and others, May, 1890; above 4,000*l.* received, 28 July, 1890.]

[Total received, including sums from India and the colonies, 6,753*l.* 1*s.* 4*d.*, 6 April, 1891.]

A sortie from the garrison of Sebastopol led to a desperate engagement here, in which the Russians were vigorously repulsed, with the loss of 2000 men killed and wounded; the allies losing about 600 . . . . 22 March, 1855

The electric telegraph between London and Balaklava completed . . . . . . April, „

A railway between Balaklava and the trenches completed . . . . June, „

BALAMBANGAN, an uninhabited island, N. coast of Borneo, about 50 miles in circumference, conceded to Mr. Francis, Q.C., in 1889.

BALANCE OF POWER, to assure the independency and integrity of states, and control the ambition of sovereigns; a principle said to have been first laid down by the Italian politicians of the 15th century, on the invasion of Charles VIII. of France, 1494. *Robertson.* It was recognised by the treaty of Münster, 24 Oct. 1648. The arrangements for the balance of power in Europe made in 1815, without the consent of the people of the countries concerned, have been nearly all set aside since 1830. See *Powers, European.*

BALAWAT, see *Nineveh.*

BALDACHIN, or **BALDACHINO**, more properly *ciborium* (*which see*), a canopy placed over the altar in some ancient churches; the practice, beginning about 1130, was introduced into England, 1279. The proposal to erect one in St. Barnabas' church, Pimlico, was opposed in the consistory court, Aug. 1873. The trial took place 23, 24 Oct. Dr. Tristram decided against the erection of the baldachin, 15 Dec. 1873.

BALEARIC ISLANDS, in the Mediterranean, called by the Greeks Balearides, and by the Romans Baleares, from the dexterity of the inhabitants at slinging: they include Majorca, Minorca, Iviça, Formentera, Cabrera, Conejera, and other islets. They were conquered by the Romans, 123 B.C.: by the Vandals, about A.D. 426, and formed part of Charlemagne's empire in 799. Conquered by the Moors about 1005, and held by them till about 1286, when they were annexed by Arragon; see *Majorca* and *Minorca.*

BALFOUR ADMINISTRATION.* Lord Salisbury (aged 72) resigned, 11 July, 1902 (died 22 Aug. 1903), and was succeeded by his nephew, Mr. Arthur J. Balfour, without changes in the Cabinet, etc. See *Salisbury*, 4th administration.

Prime Minister, First Lord of the Treasury, and Lord Privy Seal	(12 July, 1902) Mr. Balfour.
Lord High Chancellor	Earl of Halsbury.
Lord President of Council	Duke of Devonshire.
Secretaries:	
Home	Mr. Akers Douglas.
Foreign	Marquis of Lansdowne.
Colonial	Mr. Chamberlain.
War	Mr. Brodrick.
Indian	Lord George Hamilton.
First Lord of the Admiralty	Earl of Selborne.
Chancellor of the Exchequer	Mr. Ritchie.
Lord Chancellor of Ireland	Lord Ashbourne.
Chief Secretary for Ireland	Mr. George Wyndham.
Secretary for Scotland	Lord Balfour of Burleigh.
President of the Board of Trade	Mr. Gerald Balfour.
President of the Local Government Board	Mr. Walter Long.
President of the Board of Agriculture	Mr. Hanbury (died 28 Ap. aged 58). The earl of Onslow succ. 21 May.
President of the Board of Education	Marquis of Londonderry.
Postmaster-General	Mr. Austen Chamberlain.

The above form the Cabinet.

Chancellor Duchy of Lancaster	Sir William Walrond.
First Commissioner of Works	Lord Windsor.
Junior Lords of the Treasury	Mr. Anstruther. Mr. Ailwyn Fellowes. Mr. H. W. Forster.
Financial Secretary to the Treasury	Mr. Hayes Fisher, resigned 8 Ap. 1902. Mr. A. R. D. Elliot succeed.
Parliamentary Secretary to the Treasury	Sir Alexander Acland Hood.
Paymaster-General	Sir S. B. Crossley
Judge-Advocate-General	Sir Francis Jeune.
Civil Lord of the Admiralty	Mr. Pretyman.
Secretary to the Admiralty	Mr. Arnold-Forster.
Under Secretaries:	
Home	Mr. Cochrane.
Foreign	Viscount Cranborne.
Colonial	Duke of Marlborough.
War	Earl of Hardwicke.
Indian	Earl Percy.
Financial Secretary, War Office	Lord Stanley.
Parliamentary Secretaries:	
Board of Trade	Mr. Bonar Law.
Local Government Board	Mr. Grant Lawson.
Board of Education	Sir William Anson.
Attorney-General	Sir Robert Finlay.
Solicitor-General	Sir Edward Carson.
Lord Advocate for Scotland	Mr. Graham Murray.
Solicitor-General for Scotland	Mr. Scott Dickson.
Lord-Lieutenant for Ireland	Earl of Dudley.
Attorney-General for Ireland	Mr. Atkinson.
Solicitor-General for Ireland	Mr. Campbell.

For Reconstructed Cabinet see *Addenda.*

BALFOUR'S ACTS, see *Ireland*, 1890-1.

BALHAM MYSTERY, see *Bravo.*

BALIZE, see *Honduras.*

BALKANS, the ancient Hæmus, a range of mountains extending from the Adriatic to the Euxine. The passage, deemed impracticable, was completed by the Russians under Diebitsch, during the Russian and Turkish war, 26 July, 1829. An armistice was the consequence; and a treaty of peace was signed at Adrianople, 14 Sept. following. The Balkans were crossed by the Russians under Gourko, 13 July, 1877, see *Russo-Turkish War II.* By the treaty of Berlin, 13 July, 1878, the Balkans became the frontiers of the Sultan's European dominions.

The Balkan States are Servia, Bulgaria, and Roumelia (*which see*, also *Macedonia*, 1902–3).

* Arthur James Balfour, born 27 July, 1848; M.P. for Hertford, 1874; private secretary to lord Salisbury, whom he accompanied to the Berlin congress, 1878-80; he led the attack on the *Kilmainham treaty*, 1882; M.P. for E. Manchester and president of the local government board, 1885; secretary for Scotland, 1886; chief-secretary for Ireland, 1887; first lord of the treasury and leader of the Commons, 1895 *et seq.*

BALLADS may be traced in the British history to the Anglo-Saxons. *Turner.* Adhelme, who died 709, is mentioned as the first who introduced ballads into England. "The harp was sent round, and those might sing who could." *Bede.* Alfred sung ballads. *Malmesbury.* Canute composed one. *Turner.* Minstrels were protected by a charter of Edward IV.; but by a statute of Elizabeth they were made punishable among rogues and vagabonds, and sturdy beggars. *Viner.* Fletcher, of Saltoun (died 1716) in a letter to Montrose expressed his opinion that making ballads was more important than law-making. The sea-ballads of Dibdin were very popular in the French war; he died 20 Jan. 1833. Patriotic songs during South African war, 1899–1902. Mr. Rudyard Kipling's "Pay, pay, pay," very popular. Mr. John Boosey's "Ballad Concerts," St. James's Hall, began 1866.

Collections.—Bishop Percy's "Reliques of Ancient English Poetry," 1765 *et seq.* Publications of the Percy Society, 1840–52; of the Ballad Society, 1868 *et seq.*, including the Roxburghe ballads.

Sir Walter Scott's "Minstrelsy of the Scottish Border," 1802 *et seq.*

Professor Child's collection, 8 vols., Boston, U.S.A., 1857–59; his greater work, 1888 *et seq.*

Johnson's Scots Musical Museum, 6 vols. 1787–1803.

Many smaller collections.

New edition of the Roxburghe ballads edited by the rev. J. W. Ebsworth, with much labour and expense, completed, 1897-99.

BALLARAT, an Australian town in Victoria, which arose after the discovery of gold in 1851; see *Australia* and *Melbourne*, 1854. The "Welcome Nugget," largest ever discovered, found at Bakery hill, 1858. Ballarat possesses many handsome buildings and churches, and has Protestant and R. C. bishops. Population 1881, 37,260; 1891, 46,033; 1901, 46,410.

BALLETS began through the meretricious taste of the Italian courts. Bergonzio di Botta gave one of great magnificence at Tortona, 1489, in honour of the marriage of the duke of Milan. One performed at the interview between our Henry VIII. and Francis I. of France in the Field of the Cloth of Gold, at Ardres, 1520. Ballets became popular in France, and Louis XIV. bore a part in one, 1664. Introduced into England with operas early in the 18th century.

BALLINAMUCK, Longford. Here, on 8 Sept. 1798, the Irish rebels and their French auxiliaries were defeated and captured.

BALLISTITE, a nearly smokeless gunpowder, invented and patented by Mr. Alfred Nobel, and assigned by him to a company in 1892, see *Cordite*.

BALLOONS.* A just idea of the principle of the construction of balloons was formed by Albert of Saxony, an Augustine monk in the 14th century, and adopted by a Portuguese Jesuit, Francesco Mendoza, who died at Lyons in 1626. The idea is also attributed to Bartolomeo de Guzmao, who died in 1724. The principles of *aëronautics* include:—1, the power of a balloon to rise in the air; 2, the velocity of its ascent; and 3, the stability of its suspension at any given height. In 1872 Helmholtz thought balloons might be steered, if moving slowly. Fatal accidents to the voyagers have been estimated at 2 or 3 per cent. The Aëronautical Society of Great Britain, founded with the object of fostering and developing aëronautics and aërology, by the duke of Argyll, Mr. James Glaisher, sir Charles Bright, and others, 12 Jan. 1866.

* "Astra Castra; Experiments and Adventures in the Atmosphere; by Hatton Turnor," a copious work, appeared in 1865.

Francis Lana, a Jesuit, proposed to navigate the air by means of a boat raised by four hollow balls made of thin copper, from which the air had been exhausted 1670

Joseph Galien suggested the filling a bag with the fine diffuse air of the upper regions of the atmosphere 1755

Henry Cavendish discovered that hydrogen gas is 10·8 times lighter than common air . . . 1766

And soon after Black, of Edinburgh, filled a bag with hydrogen, which rose to the ceiling of the room 1767

Cavallo filled soap bubbles with hydrogen . . 1782

Joseph Montgolfier made a silken bag ascend with heated air (first *fire balloon*) . . . Nov. ,,

Joseph and Stephen Montgolfier ascend and descend safely by means of a fire balloon at Annonay, for which they received many honours . 5 June, 1783

First ascent in a balloon filled with hydrogen, at Paris, by MM. Robert and Charles . 27 Aug. ,,

Joseph Montgolfier ascends in a balloon inflated with smoke of burnt straw and wool 19 Sept. ,,

First aërial voyage in a fire balloon—Pilâtre de Rozier and the marquis d'Arlandes 21 Nov. ,,

Second ascent of Charles in a hydrogen balloon to the height of 9770 feet . . . 1 Dec. ,,

Mr. Tytler ascended in a Montgolfier balloon at Edinburgh . . . . . 27 Aug. 1784

Ascents become numerous: Andreani, 25 Feb.; Blanchard, 2 March; Guyton de Morveau, the chemist, 25 April and 12 June; Fleurant and Madame Thiblé (the first female aëronaut), 28 June; the duke of Chartres (Philip Egalité) 19 Sept. ,,

The first ascent in England, made by Vincent Lunardi, at Moorfields, London . . 15 Sept. ,,

[Centenary: three balloons ascend at same place, one of them "The Colonel" containing col. Brine and M. L'Hoste, from Finsbury, 15 Sept. 1884.]

Blanchard and Jeffries ascend at Dover; cross the Channel; alight near Calais . . 7 Jan. 1785

[Centenary celebrated at Guines, 25 May, 1885.]

The first ascent in Ireland, from Ranelagh gardens, Dublin . . . . . 19 Jan. ,,

Rozier and Romain killed in their descent near Boulogne; the balloon took fire . . 15 June, ,,

Parachutes constructed and used by Blanchard, Aug. ,,

Garnerin's narrow escape when descending in one in London . . . . . 2 Sept. 1802

Sadler, who made many previous expeditions in England, fell into the sea, near Holyhead, but was taken up . . . . . 9 Oct. 1812

Madame Blanchard ascended from Tivoli at night; the balloon, being surrounded by fireworks, took fire, and she was precipitated to the ground and killed . . . . . . 6 July, 1819

Mr. Charles Green's first ascent (he introduced coal gas in ballooning) . . . 19 July, 1821

Lieut. Harris killed in a balloon descent 25 May, 1824

Sadler, jun., killed, falling from a balloon . . 1825

The great Nassau balloon, which had for some time previously been exhibited to the inhabitants of London in repeated ascents from Vauxhall gardens, started from that place on an experimental voyage, Mr. C. Green, Mr. R. Holland, and Mr. Monck-Mason in the car, and after having been eighteen hours in the air descended at Weilburg, in the duchy of Nassau . . . 7 Nov. 1836

Mr. Cocking ascended from Vauxhall to try his parachute; in its descent from the balloon it collapsed, and he was thrown out and killed, 24 July, 1837

An Italian aëronaut ascended from Copenhagen, in Denmark; his corpse was subsequently found on the sea-shore in a contiguous island, dashed to pieces . . . . . 14 Sept. 1851

J. B. Lassie's model of an "aërial ship," in which the screw was used, was submitted to the academy of sciences at Paris, 1859; and exhibited at Washington, U.S. 1859

Mr. Wise and three others ascended from St. Louis (after travelling 1150 miles they descended in Jefferson county, New York, nearly dead) 23 June, 1859

Nadar's great balloon (largest ever made) when fully inflated contained 215,363 cubic feet of gas; the car, a cottage in wicker work, raised 35 soldiers at Paris; Nadar hoped by means of a screw to steer a balloon in the heavens: his first ascent, with 14 persons, successful . . 4 Oct. 1863

His second ascent; voyagers injured; saved by presence of mind of M. Jules Godard; descend at Nienburg, Hanover . . . 12 Oct. ,,

Nadar and his balloon at the Crystal palace, Sydenham . . . . . Nov. ,,

Society for promoting aërial navigation formed at M. Nadar's, at Paris; president, M. Barral, 15 Jan. 1864

Godard's great Montgolfier or fire balloon ascends, 28 July and 3 Aug. ,,

Ascent of Nadar and others in his great balloon at Brussels . . . . . . 26 Sept. ,,

Mr. Coxwell ascends from Belfast in a new balloon; several persons are injured by the balloon becoming uncontrollable; it escapes . . 3 July, 1865

Ascent of Nadar in his Géant balloon, Paris, June 23, 1866

Mr. Coxwell said to have made 550 successful ascents . . . . . . up to April, 1867

An aërial screw machine (helicopteric) suggested, in Paris, 1863; described by Dr. J. Bell Pettigrew, in London, at the Royal Institution, 22 March, ,,

Mr. Hodsman crossed the Channel from Dublin, and descended at Appleby, Westmoreland 22 April, ,,

A great balloon exhibited at Ashburnham-park, London, escaped, and was captured at Bouldon, Bucks . . . . 25 May, 1869

Charles Green, aëronaut, said to have made about 600 ascents, died aged 84 . . . 27 Mar. 1870

Dupuy de Lôme at Vincennes ascended with his "navigable" balloon, with 13 persons; experiment reported to be successful . . 2 Feb. 1871

Professor Wise proposed to cross the Atlantic from New York to Liverpool in a balloon, 100 feet in diameter, 110 feet perpendicular, with a supplementary balloon 36 feet in diameter; the two giving a lifting power of 15,900 lbs., a carrying power of 9,500 lbs., and disposable ballast 7,500 lbs., July; the balloon was reported inadequate, Sept.; a smaller balloon started (with a life-boat) 9.19 A.M., 6 Oct., and descended during a storm over Connecticut; the men narrowly escaped . . . . . . 7 Oct. 1873

Vincent de Groof, a Belgian (named the "flying man"), constructed a parachute to imitate the flight of a bird; he brought it to London; ascended from Cremorne-gardens, and descended from a height between 300 and 400 feet in Essex, 29 June; at his next attempt, the parachute, either detached by himself or by accident, was disarranged, and he was killed by falling, 9 July, 1874

Under the Government Balloon Committee, Mr. Coxwell ascended at Woolwich to try C. A. Bowdler's apparatus (based on the screw-propeller) for steering balloons; failure reported, 25 July, ,,

[It has been proved that a screw with a vertical axis can raise or depress a balloon, and thereby save gas and ballast.]

M. and Mme. Dufour (see below, 1870), ascend from Calais to cross the channel, 31 Aug.; carried out to sea; the balloon fell into the water and drifted towards Norway; rescued by a smack (the *Grand Charge*); the aëronauts were landed at Grimsby . . . . . . 4 Sept. ,,

Dufour and others ascend from the Crystal-palace, 14 Sept. ,,

Menier's new hot-air balloon fails on trial, 5 Sept. and 16 Oct. ,,

Ascent of capt. Burnaby at the Crystal palace to try his machine for ascertaining the course of the wind above the clouds; reported successful, 10 Nov. ,,

MM. Tissandier, Croce-Spinelli, and Sivel ascend in the "Zenith" from La Villette, near Paris; at 26,160 feet Croce throws out ballast; they ascend rapidly; he and Sivel die through suffocation; Tissandier recovered . . . . . 15 April, 1875

Washington J. Donaldson, eminent aëronaut, perishes in Lake Michigan during a storm, 18 July, ,,

Reported failure of Carrol's directing apparatus at Paris . . . . July, 1878

Frequent ascents in a "captive balloon" . Aug. ,,

Mr. Giffard's great captive balloon, "Paris," burst, 16 or 17 Aug. 1879

Five balloons start from various places near London, competing for a silver medal given by the Balloon Society; the "Owl," Mr. Wright and Commander Cheyne, travelled 48 miles in one hour (no medal awarded) . . . 4 Sept. 1880

International balloon contest at the Crystal palace; England ("Eclipse"), Mr. Wright: France, M. de Fonvielle; both alighted near Portsmouth, 21 Oct. ,,

Giffard and De Lôme's aërial ship said to be successful for direction, speed, &c. . . . . Jan. 1881

Mr. Eugène (who had ascended about 2,000 times) narrowly escapes destruction by a storm at Vienna . . . . 21 Aug. ,,

Mr. Walter Powell, M.P., crossed the Bristol Channel in a balloon and descended at Dingeston, and afterwards went on to Hereford, 3 Nov.; Mr. Walter Powell, M.P., capt. Templer, and Mr. Agg Gardner ascend at Bath in war-office balloon "Saladin"; the balloon descends near Bridport; two fell out; the balloon ascends with Mr. Powell and drifts to sea; not found . . 10 Dec. ,,

Col. (aft. Gen.) Brine and Mr. Simmons' attempt to cross the Channel from Canterbury; they and the balloon picked up half-way . . 4 Mar. 1882

Col. Burnaby crosses the Channel from Dover, and lands near Dieppe . . . . 23 Mar. ,,

Mr. Simmons goes from Maldon, Essex, to Arras (140 miles) 2 h. . . . . . 10 June ,,

Mr. Simmons and sir Claude C. de Crespigny crossed the Channel from Maldon, Essex, to Oudekerk, near Flushing (140 miles in 6 hours) . 1 Aug. 1883

By Mr. Simmons and Mr. Small from Hastings to Cape La Hague (8 hours) . . . 13 Sept. ,,

Electrical balloon constructed by Gaston and Albert Tissandier, successful trial reported 8 Oct. ,,

By M. Lhoste from Boulogne to Ashford, 15 Sept. 1883; again from Boulogne to New Romney, 2 hours . . . . 7 Aug. 1884

Gen. Brine crosses from Hythe to Hervelinghen 15 Aug. ,,

Balloon navigation said to be effected by M. Renard at Meudon, by an electrical machine 9 Aug. ,,

Another trial, result uncertain . . 12 Sept. ,,

Reported success by M. Tissandier . 26 Sept. ,,

By Capt. Renard . . . . . 8 Nov. ,,

M. Lhoste crosses from Cherbourg to Tottenham near London; attained height 3,600 feet, lowest temperature 7° C. . . . . 29–30 July, 1886

Mr Lorraine's attempt to propel and steer a balloon by boat apparatus at Uxbridge, Middlesex, containing three persons, fails . . 24 Aug. ,,

MM. Jovis and Mallet report that they reached the altitude of 7,000 mètres, in an ascent at Paris 13 Aug. 1887

Successful voyage of Mr. Morton from Dover to Loon, near Dunkirk . . . . 13 Oct. ,,

M. Lhoste and M. Mangot ascend at Mondidier near Amiens, 6 Nov.; Mr. Macdonald, master of the steamer *Prince Leopold*, witnessed the falling of the balloon and the drowning of the aëronauts 39 miles S.W. of the Isle of Wight, 13 Nov.; reported . . . . Dec. ,,

Aëronautical Exhibition at Vienna, opened 1 April 1888

Professor Baldwin, at Rockaway, New York, said to have descended safely from a balloon a mile high by means of a parachute in 84 seconds, 9 Aug. 1887. He did the same at Alexandra Park, London, N. 28 July, 1888, and since. After the 10th time the balloon society gave him a gold medal, 1 Sept. 1888; prevented in his attempt to descend from an altitude of two miles; descends from between 6,000 and 7,000 feet, 13 Sept., 16th ascent, 22 Sept.; at Manchester, 24 Sept.; (9,100 feet) 18 Oct.; at Sheffield (42nd descent) 22 Oct.; final descent at Alexandra palace, 5000 feet, the Prince of Wales present . . . . 30 Oct. ,,

The aëronaut, Mr. Joseph Simmons, ascends from Olympia, London, W., and is killed on his descent 27 Aug. 1888

George Higgins, an Englishman, descends from a balloon in a parachute at Lea Bridge Road 27 Oct. ,,

Ascent of Mr. Percival Spencer, without his parachute, at Calcutta 19 March; afterwards with his parachute 1889

Prof. Dale and five others ascend from Gibraltar (2nd ascent there) . . . . . 7 Dec. ,,

Mr. Percival Spencer at Secunderabad, Central India, ascends in his patent asbestos (Montgolfier) balloon, the air being heated by burning methylated spirit inside the balloon; he descended by his parachute . . . . 13 Jan. 1890

Death of Eugène Godard, aged 64, at Brussels, said to have made 2,000 ascents . . . 11 Nov. ,,

Mr. Higgins, aëronaut, killed at Kirkstall, near Leeds, through a parachute descent . . 8 Aug. 1891

Mr. Logan ascends with a parachute at Detroit; falls and is killed . . . . . 29 Aug. ,,

Prince and princess Henry of Prussia, the grand-duke of Hesse and other personages ascend in a balloon at Frankfort . . . . 23 Sept. ,,

Mr. Percival Spencer ascends in a very large balloon at Dover, and lands near Hastings 24 Nov. ,,

Lieut. Mansfield, at Bombay, is killed by falling from his balloon, which burst . . 10 Dec. ,,

Miss Van Tassel, at Dacca, descending with her parachute, falls 16 March, and dies . 18 March, 1892

Capt. Wm. Duncan Dale and three others ascend in balloon at the Crystal palace; the balloon bursts; capt. Dale killed by the fall, 29 June; Mr. Cecil V. Shadbolt dies, 8 July; William Dale (son) and Mr. John Macintosh, much injured, recover July, ,,
[Capt. Dale had made nearly 200 ascents.]

M. Mallet in a balloon left Paris, 23 Oct. and arrived at Wallenrod, in Darmstadt, 360 direct miles, in 36 hours . . . . 25 Oct. ,,

Commandant Renard's new "dirigible" balloon with propelling mechanism, described . 25 Nov. ,,

Capt. Whelan (after 315 ascents) dies after a fall from his balloon near Shrewsbury (23 Aug.) 1 Sept. 1893

M. Charbonnet, his wife, and an assistant, ascend in Piedmont; he is killed by the fall of the balloon, near Turin . . . . . 11 Oct. ,,

Miss Bassett killed by an accident to her parachute 5 Aug. 1895

Balloon accidents near Paris during a storm, 4 aëronauts killed . . . . . 26 July, 1896

Balloon voyage by Mr. Chas. Pollock, from Eastbourne to Domart near Abbeville . 12 Oct. 1897

Mr. S. Spencer and Dr. Berson ascend to 27,500 ft. from the Crystal palace . . . 15 Sept. 1898

Mr. P. Spencer and others experiment with steering apparatus, Earl's Court, 5 Nov.; he and Mr. L. Swinburne ascend from Crystal palace, 11.30 a.m., cross the Channel and arrive at St. Romain, 4.30 p.m., 20 Dec.; again, 29 July and 15 Sept. 1899

Capt. Lorraine, aëronaut, ascends from Christchurch, New Zealand, is carried out to sea and drowned . . . . 1 Nov. ,,

Dr. Danilewsky experiments successfully with his dirigible balloon, reported, Feb.; Mr. Edward Anderson's contrivance for steering, successfully tried from Fulham to Witley . . 3 Sept. 1900

Herr Berson and Dr. Süring reached a height of over 10,800 mètres from Berlin . . 31 July, 1901

Count von Zeppelin ascends in his air-ship at lake Constance, 2 July; again . 17 and 21 Oct. ,,

M. Santos Dumont's steerable balloon successful in Paris, 12, 29 July, 1901; his air-ship was wrecked, but he himself saved, 8 Aug.; he wins the Deutsch prize, 100,000 f. by steering from St. Cloud, round the Eiffel tower and back 30 secs. less than 30 mins., 19 Oct.; his 5th trip at Monaco failed, owing to a rent in the balloon, which fell into the sea, but he was saved by a boat . . . . 14 Feb. 1902

Capt. von Sigsfeld killed trying to escape from a balloon near Antwerp, ... 1 Feb. ,,

M. Severo makes a trial trip in his air-ship at Vaugirard, Paris, the balloon exploded and fell at the height of about 1,200 feet; Severo and his companion Sachet, were instantly killed, 12 May ,,

Miss Edith Brookes, 23, parachutist killed at Sheffield . . . . 20 May, 1902

Mr. Stanley Spencer with his little niece steers the "Mellin" air-ship, Crystal palace . 6 July, ,,

Mr. S. Spencer, in the "Mellin," crossed London, 19 Sept. ,,

Baron von Bradsky and Morin, his assistant, killed by the break-up of his steerable balloon near Pierrefitte . . . . 13 Oct. ,,

Many air-ships building. One by Dr. F. A. Barton for the War Office . . . . . . May, 1903

New method of inflating balloons by means of hot air, heated by the vaporisation of petroleum. Successful trial made by Mr. T. N. Maskelyne, the inventor, at Cold Ash, Newbury, . 10 April, ,,

Spencer airship ascends from the Crystal palace and descends at New Barnet. Attempt to round the dome of St. Paul's unsuccessful . 17 Sept. ,,

MILITARY AND POSTAL APPLICATIONS.

Guyton de Morveau ascended twice during the battle of Fleurus, and gave important information to Jourdain . . . . 21 June, 1794

The use of balloons for postal purposes invented by Mr. G. Shepherd, C.E. 1851

Balloons were used during the battle of Solferino, 24 June, 1859; and by the Federal army near Washington . . . . July, 1861

M. Dufour conveyed the mail bags from Paris to Tours during the siege, 23 Sept. 1870, (he died, 7 March, 1899).

Postal balloons from Metz and Paris . Sept.–Dec. ,,

Postal balloon sent up from Crystal palace, Sydenham (successfully) . . . . . 6 Oct. ,,

M. Gambetta, with his secretary and aëronaut, escaped from Paris in a balloon, and fell in the Forêt d'Epineuse (Somme) 7 Oct.; he arrived at Rouen . . . . 8 Oct. ,,

Sixty-six balloons with 168 persons despatched from Paris and other places (*Gen. Brine*), 23 Sept. 1870–28 Jan. 1871

Military experiments; ascent of *Univers*; very cold weather; valve burst; several hurt; near Vincennes; no deaths . . . . 8 Dec. 1875

Military ascents and balloon equipment for military purposes adopted at Woolwich, announced April, 1879

Captive balloon at the volunteer review, Brighton, 29 March, 1880

Royal Engineers' Balloon Corps arrives at Souakim, 7 March, 1885

Mr. F. A. Gower's experiments at Hythe, June, 1885; ascended and not heard of since . July, ,,

Mr. Eric S. Bruce's mode of electric signalling from balloons reported successful at Albert-palace 20 July, ,,

EQUESTRIAN ASCENTS.

Mr. Green affirmed that he ascended from London, on a horse attached to a balloon . . May, 1828

He did so from Vauxhall gardens with a very diminutive pony . . . . . . July, 1850

Lieut. Gale, an Englishman, made an ascent with a horse from the Hippodrome of Vincennes, near Bordeaux. On descending and detaching the animal from the balloon, the people who held its ropes, from some misconception, prematurely let them go, and the unfortunate aëronaut was rapidly borne in the air before he was quite ready to resume his voyage. (He was discovered next morning dashed to pieces in a field a mile from where the balloon was found) . . 8 Sept. ,,

The ascent of Madame Poitevin from Cremorne gardens, near London, as "Europa on a bull" (a feat she had often performed in France), and several ascents on horses, brought the parties concerned before the police-courts on a charge of cruelty to animals, and put an end to experiments that outraged public feeling . . . . Aug. 1852

M. Poitevin ascended on a horse in the vicinity of Paris, about the time just mentioned; was nearly drowned in the sea, near Malaga, while descending from his balloon (and died soon after) . . . 1858

SCIENTIFIC ASCENTS.

Gay-Lussac and Biot at Paris, 23 Aug.; Gay-Lussac (to the height of 22,977 feet) . . 15 Sept. 1804

Bixio and Barral at Paris (to the height of 19,000 feet. They passed through a cloud 9,000 feet thick) 1850

Mr. Welsh ascends, 17, 26 Aug. 21 Oct., 10 Nov. 1852

Scientific balloon ascents having been recommended by the British Association and funds provided, Mr. James Glaisher (died 7 Feb. 1903) commenced his series of ascents, provided with suitable apparatus, in Mr. Coxwell's great balloon, at Wolverhampton: he reached the height of 5 miles . . . . 17 July, 1862
He ascended to the height of about 7 miles at Wolverhampton; at 5½ miles high he became insensible; Mr. Coxwell lost the use of his hands, but was able to open the valve with his teeth; they thus descended in safety . . 5 Sept. 1862
He ascended at the Crystal palace 18 April, 11, 21 July; at Wolverton, 26 June; at Newcastle, during the meeting of the British Association 31 Aug. 1863
His 16th ascent; surveys London . . 9 Oct. ,,
His 17th ascent at Woolwich; descends at Mr. Brandon's, Suffolk (1st winter ascent this century), 12 Jan. 1864; ascends from Woolwich (24th time) 30 Dec.; 25th ascent, 27 Feb. 1865; other ascents . . 2 Oct., 2 Dec. and in May, 1866
Glaisher's "Travels in the Air" published . Jan. 1871
Mr. Coxwell's ascent at Hornsey, 22 Sept. 1873; he continued his ascents till 1885, and died, aged 81, 5 Jan. 1900
A so-called "navigable balloon," during its ascent near Berlin caught fire and exploded; Dr. Wölfert the inventor and his companion killed 12 June, 1897
See *N.E. & W. Passage*, 1896–7.
Three balloons sent up from La Villette, simultaneous ascents in other countries . 8 June, 1898
Experiments in wireless telegraphy and acoustics, "echoes from the earth" by the rev. J. M. Bacon and the Messrs. Maskelyne at Newbury, 26 July, 1899
The rev. J. M. Bacon and others ascend from Neath, S. Wales, to see the meteors, and narrowly escape destruction . . . . . 15 Nov. ,,
M. Gaston Tissandier made 44 ascents, see 1875, 1883; died, aged 56 . . . . Sept. ,,
Four scientific ascents under Mr. Percival Spencer's direction, London . . . . . 1 May, 1901
Many international scientific ascents in Gt. Britain and on the continent, 8 Nov., 1900; 10 Jan., 7 Mar., 13 June, and 5 Dec., 1901; also 9 Jan., 6 March, 5 May, and in July, Aug., Sept. . . 1902
Lieut. Baudie fell from the car of French naval balloon off Toulon, and was drowned . 9 June, ,,
The rev. J. M. Bacon and Mr. Percival Spencer cross from Douglas, I. of Man, to Dunscore, nr. Dumfries, in 3½ hrs. Experimental signalling, Morse Code, with H.M.S. *Renard* tried successfully . . . . . . 10 Nov. ,,
110 registering and 52 manned balloons sent up by the International Society in . . . . ,,

BALLOON SOCIETIES.

The French Académie d'Aérostation de Météorologique, authorised . . . . . 20 Sept. 1872
BALLOON SOCIETY OF GREAT BRITAIN, was formed 21 July, 1880, by some members of the Aëronautical, Geographical, Astronomical, Chemical, and Meteorological societies, and other scientific bodies, to promote aëronautics and record and utilise observations made during ascents. Silver medals were awarded for ascents . 4 Sept. 1880
German Aëronautical Society founded at Berlin Sept. 1881
International congress on aërostatics met at Strasburg . . . . . . 31 March, 1898
International commission for scientific ballooning met at Berlin . . . . mid. May, 1902
First meeting of the Aero club, Crystal palace, 25 April, 1903

BALLOT (French *ballotte*, a little ball). Secret voting was practised by the ancient Greeks and Romans, and the modern Venetians, and is now employed in France, in the United States of North America, and, since 1872, in Great Britain, and Colonies. See *Scrutin*.

A ballot-box used in the election of aldermen of London 1526
Its use by the company of merchant adventurers, in electing an agent, prohibited by Charles I. 17 Dec. 1637
The ballot-box used by the "Rota," a political club at Miles's coffee-house, Westminster . . . 1659
A tract entitled "The Benefit of the Ballot," said to have been written by Andrew Marvell, was published in the "State Tracts" . . . 1693
Proposed, in a pamphlet, to be used in the election of members of parliament 1705
A bill authorising vote by ballot passed the commons, but rejected by the lords . . . 1710
George Grote introduced into the commons a ballot bill six times 1833-39
The ballot an open question in whig governments, 1835-72
The house of commons rejected the ballot—257 being against, and 189 for it . . 30 June, 1851
Secret voting existed in the chamber of deputies in France from 1840 to 1845. It has been employed since the coup d'état in . . . Dec. ,,
The ballot authorised in the Metropolitan Management Act 1855
The ballot adopted in Victoria, Australia . . 1856
A test-ballot at Manchester; Ernest Jones elected for the city; he died the next day . 22, 23 Jan. 1869
For many years annually proposed by Mr. Henry Berkeley; rejected 12 July, 1867; he died 10 Mar. 1870
Mr. E. Leatham introduced a ballot bill into parliament, March; and Mr. Gladstone spoke in favour of the ballot; bill withdrawn 27 July, ,,
The ballot was employed in electing the London school board in 9 districts . . 29 Nov. ,,
The ballot recommended in the queen's speech, 9 Feb.; a bill for it introduced, passed by the commons; rejected by the lords (97 to 48) . 10 Aug. 1871
Bill to amend the law relating to procedure at parliamentary and municipal elections, including the ballot, read in the commons, 2nd time, 109-51, 15 Feb.; passed the commons, 271-216, 30 May; read second time in the lords (86-56), important amendments carried in committee, making secret voting optional (162-91); read a third time, and passed, 25 June; lords' amendments mostly rejected by the commons; the optional clause given up by the lords, 8 July; royal assent; (to continue in force till 31 Dec. 1880) . . 18 July, 1872
The first election by ballot was at Pontefract, when Mr. H. E. Childers was re-elected . 15 Aug. ,,
Mr. John Leighton makes known his system (invented in 1886) of secret postal ballot—every post-box being used as a ballot box; Mr. James Withers and Mr. John Imray describe voting apparatus; *Society of Arts*, 18 Jan. 1888; another invented by Mr. W. H. Howe to supersede the ballot-box exhibited, London . . . Aug. 1901

BALL'S BLUFF, Virginia, on the banks of the Potomac, North America. On 21 Oct. 1861, by direction of the Federal general C. P. Stone, the heroic col. Baker crossed the river to reconnoitre. He attacked the Confederate camp at Leesburg, and was defeated with great loss. The disaster was attributed to mismanagement, and in Feb. 1862, general Stone was arrested on suspicion of treason.

BALLYNAHINCH (Ireland), where a sanguinary engagement took place between a large body of the insurgent Irish and the British troops, under gen. Nugent, 13 June, 1798. A large part of the town was destroyed, and the royal army suffered very severely.

BALMORAL CASTLE, Deeside, Aberdeenshire; visited by her majesty in 1848, 1849, 1850. The estate was purchased for 31,500*l*. by prince Albert in 1852. A cairn was erected in presence of queen Victoria and the prince Consort to commemorate the purchase, 11 Oct. 1852. The present building, begun 1853, is a castellated mansion, mixed Elizabethan and Scottish style, with a tower at one end flanked by turrets. The whole is of white Crathie granite, designed by the prince Consort to occupy the place of an older building. It is now occupied by H.M. king Edward VII.

The new parish church of Crathie, to the erection and adornment of which the queen, her family, and the gentry liberally contributed, was publicly dedicated in her presence . . 18 June, 1895
Bust of Queen Victoria in Crathie Church unveiled by the King . . . . . . 20 Sept. 1903

BALTIC MERCANTILE AND SHIPPING EXCHANGE, see *Exchange*.

BALTIC SEA,* OSTSEE, or EASTERN SEA, separates Sweden and the Danish isles from Russia, Prussia, and Germany. Declared neutral for commerce by treaty between Russia and Sweden, 1759, and Denmark, 1760. It is often partially frozen, Charles X. of Sweden, with an army, crossed the Belts in 1658, and the Russians passed from Finland to Sweden on the ice in 1809.

A ship canal between the Baltic and the North Seas proposed Jan. 1884; adopted by the Reichstag, 25 Feb. 1886. First stone of opening lock laid by the emperor William I. at Kiel, 3 June, 1887; the dam pierced and the water let in by the emperor William II., who sails on the canal to Rendsburg . . . 6 April, 1891
Completion of the work; see *Kiel*; opened 20 June, 1895
A lofty bridge over the canal near Kiel, opened by the emperor . . . . 3 Dec. 1894

BALTIC EXPEDITIONS.

Against Denmark. See *Armed Neutrality*.—1. Under lord Nelson and admiral Parker, Copenhagen was bombarded, and twenty-eight sail of the Danish fleet taken or destroyed . . . . 2 April, 1801
2. Under admiral Gambier and lord Cathcart, eighteen sail of the line, fifteen frigates, and thirty-one brigs and gunboats surrendered to the British, 26 July, 1807

Against Russia.—1. The British fleet, commanded by sir Charles Napier, sailed from Spithead in presence of the queen, who led it out to sea in her yacht, the Fairy . . . . . . 11 March, 1854
It arrived in Wingo Sound, 15 March; and in the Baltic . . . . 20 March, ,,
The gulf of Finland blockaded . . . 12 April, ,,
10,000 French troops embarked at Calais for the Baltic in English ships of war, in presence of the emperor . . . . 15 July, ,,
Capture of Bomarsund, one of the Aland islands, and surrender of the garrison; see *Bomarsund*, 16 Aug. ,,
English and French fleets begin to return homeward to winter . . . . 15 Oct. ,,
2. Expedition sailed . . . 20 March—4 April, 1855
It consisted of 85 English ships (2098 guns), commanded by admiral R. S. Dundas; 16 French ships (408 guns), under admiral Pernand, joined it, June, ,,
Three vessels silenced the Russian batteries at Hogland island . . . . . 21 July, ,,
The fleet proceeded towards Cronstadt. Many infernal machines † were discovered. Sveaborg was attacked (see *Sveaborg*) . . . . 9 Aug. ,,
Shortly after the fleet returned to England.
THE BALTIC AND BLACK-SEA CANAL, nearly 1,000 miles, to begin at Riga, 875 miles in canalized rivers, 125 miles excavated, ending at Cherson; proposed, Nov. 1897; estimated cost 20,000,000*l*., work to begin spring 1898

BALTIMORE, a maritime city in Maryland, United States, founded in 1729. On 12 Sept. 1814, the British army under col. Ross advanced against this place. He was killed in a skirmish; and the command was assumed by col. Brooke, who attacked and routed the American army, which lost 600 killed and wounded and 300 prisoners. The projected attack on the town was, however, abandoned. *Alison*. See *United States*, 1861. About 70 persons drowned while on an excursion on the Patapsco river, about 23 July, 1883. By a false alarm of fire at a theatre 24 persons were killed, 27 Dec. 1895. See *Roman Catholics* and *Chili*, 1891. Population, 1890, 434,439; 1901, 541,000.

* *Baltic Provinces* of Russia, a kind of provincial federation since 1800, were incorporated with the empire on the death of the governor-general Bagration, 29 Jan. 1876.

† These were cones of galvanised iron, 16 inches in diameter, and 20 inches long. Each contained 9 or 10 lb. of powder, with apparatus for firing by sulphuric acid. Little damage was done by them. They were said to be the invention of the philosopher Jacobi.

BALTIMORE, fishing village, Cork, raised from penury to prosperity by the judicious beneficence of the Baroness Burdett-Coutts, aided by Father Davis, since 1877. She opened an Industrial Fishing School, 17 Aug. 1887. Prosperity reported, Oct. 1888.

BALUCHISTAN, see *Beloochistan*.

BAMBERG (Bavaria), said to have been founded by Saxons, in 804, and endowed with a church by Charlemagne. It was made a bishopric in 1007, and the bishop was a prince of the empire till the treaty of Luneville, 1801, when Bamberg was secularised. It was incorporated with Bavaria in 1803. The noble cathedral, rebuilt in 1110, has been recently repaired. Bamberg was taken and pillaged by the Prussians in 1759.

BAMBOROUGH, or Bamburg, Northumberland, according to the "Saxon Chronicle," was built by king Ida about 547, and named Bebbanburgh. The castle and estate, the property of the Forsters, and forfeited to the crown, through their taking part in the rebellion in 1715, were purchased by Nathaniel lord Crewe, bishop of Durham, and bequeathed by him for various charitable purposes. The valuable library was founded by the trustees in 1778. The books are lent to persons residing within 20 miles of the castle.

BAMPTON LECTURES (Theological), delivered at Oxford annually, began in 1780, with a lecture by James Bandinel, D.D. The lecturer is paid out of the proceeds of an estate bequeathed for the purpose by the rev. John Bampton (died 1751) and the lectures are published. Among the more remarkable lectures were those by White (1784), Heber (1815), Whately (1822), Milman (1827), Hampden (1832), Mansel (1858), Liddon (1866), Hatch (1880), Bigg (1886), Gore (1891).

BANBURY, Oxfordshire, a Saxon town. The castle, erected by Alexander de Blois, bishop of Lincoln, 1125, has been frequently besieged. In 1646 it was taken by the parliamentarians and demolished. At Edgecot or Danesmore, near Banbury, during an insurrection, the army of Edward IV., under the earl of Pembroke, was defeated by queen Margaret and her adherents 26 July, 1469: the earl and his brother were soon after taken prisoners and executed. Banbury cakes were renowned in the time of Ben Jonson, and Banbury Cross was destroyed by the Puritans. Cakes were presented to the queen at Banbury 30 Nov. 1866.

BAND OF GENTLEMEN PENSIONERS, see *Gentlemen-at-Arms*.

BAND OF HOPE, see under *Temperance*, 1855.

BANDA ISLES (ten), Eastern Archipelago, visited by the Portuguese in 1511, who settled on them, 1521, but were expelled by the Dutch about 1600. Rohun island was ceded to the English in 1616. The Bandas were taken by the latter in 1796; restored in 1801; retaken in 1811; and restored in Aug. 1816.

BANDA ORIENTAL (South America), a portion of the viceroyalty of Buenos Ayres, one part of which, in 1828, was incorporated with Brazil, while another part became independent, as the republic of Uruguay.

BANGALORE (S. India) was besieged by the British under lord Cornwallis, 6 March, and taken by storm, 21 March, 1791. Bangalore was restored to Tippoo in 1792, when he destroyed the strong fort, deemed the bulwark of Mysore. Population, 1901, 159,046.

BANGKOK, capital of Siam. Estimated population in 1891, 100,000.

BANGOR (Banchor Iskoed, or Monachorum), Flintshire, the site of an ancient monastery, very populous, if it be true that 1200 monks were slain by Ethelfrid, king of the Angles, for praying for the Welsh in their conflict with him in 607. *Tanner*.

BANGOR (N. Caernarvonshire). The church is dedicated to St. Daniel, who was a bishop, 516. Owen Glendower greatly defaced the cathedral; and the bishop Bulkeley alienated many of the lands, and even sold the bells of the church, 1553. The see is valued in the king's books at 131*l.* 16*s.* 4*d.* An order in council directing that the sees of Bangor and St. Asaph be united on the next vacancy in either, was issued in 1838; but rescinded in 1847. Present income, 4,200*l.* Bangor was incorporated in 1883. North Wales University College opened, 18 Oct. 1884. Population, 1881, 9,005; 1891, 9,892; 1901, 11,770.

BISHOPS OF BANGOR.

1800. Wm. Cleaver, translated to St. Asaph, 1806.
1806. John Randolph, translated to London, 1809.
1809. Henry William Majendie, died 9 July, 1830.
1830. Christopher Bethell, died 19 April, 1859.
1859. James Colquhoun Campbell. Resigned April, 1890.
1890. Daniel Lewis Lloyd, elected 27 May; resigns 29 Nov. 1898, died 4 August, 1899.
1899. Watkin Herbert Williams, elected 3 January.

The cathedral was re-opened after restoration, 11 May, 1880.

BANGORIAN CONTROVERSY was occasioned by Dr. Benjamin Hoadley, bishop of Bangor, preaching a sermon before George I., 31 March, 1717, upon the text, "*My kingdom is not of this world*" (*John*, xviii. 36), in which he demonstrated the spiritual nature of the church and kingdom of Christ. He thereby drew upon himself the indignation of almost all the clergy, who published hundreds of pamphlets.

BANISHMENT, an ancient punishment. By 39 Eliz. c. 4 (1597) dangerous rogues were to be banished out of the realm, and to be liable to death if they returned; see *Transportation*.

BANK. The name is derived from *banco*, a bench, erected in the market-place for the exchange of money. The first was established in Italy, 808, by the Lombard Jews, of whom some settled in Lombard-street, London, where many bankers still reside. The Mint in the Tower of London was anciently the depository for merchants' cash, until Charles I. seized the money as a loan, and in 1640 the traders lodged their money with the goldsmiths in Lombard-street. See *Bank of England*; *Bankers' Books*; *Drafts*; *Savings Banks*.

Egibe's bank at Babylon, mentioned about B.C. 700
[The Bank of England (1890) possesses a Chinese bank note, supposed to be of the 14th century, A.D.]
Barcelona bank (earliest existing bank) founded about . . . 1401
Samuel Lamb, a London banker, recommended the Protector Cromwell to establish a public bank, 1656 and 1658
Francis Child, a goldsmith, established a bank about 1663; he died 4 Oct. 1713
Run on the London bankers (said to be the first) . 1667
Charles II. arbitrarily suspends all payments to bankers out of the exchequer of monies deposited there by them; they lost ultimately 3,321,313*l.* 2 Jan. 1672
Hoare's bank began about . . . 1680
Bank of England established (*see next article*) . . 1694
Wood's bank at Gloucester, the oldest county bank, established . . . 1716
Drummond's bank, Charing-cross, Westminster, was founded by Andrew Drummond, brother of viscount Strathallan, a Jacobite, who was killed at Culloden . . . 16 April, 1746
[Andrew was cleared from the charge of complicity in the insurrection, and private accounts of George II. and George III. were kept at his bank.]
A list of bankers given in the "Royal Kalendar" . 1765
Forgeries of Henry Fauntleroy, banker; executed, 30 Nov. 1824
Act passed permitting establishment of joint-stock banks (*which see*) . . . 1826
Rowland Stephenson, M.P., banker and treasurer of St. Bartholomew's hospital, absconds; defaulter to the amount of 200,000*l.*; 70,000*l.* in exchequer bills; (caused a great depression among bankers) 27 Dec. 1828
Establishment of joint-stock banks . . . 1834
Rogers's bank robbed of nearly 50,000*l.* (bank notes afterwards returned) . . 24 Nov. 1844
Failure of Strahan, Paul, and Bates (securities unlawfully used); private banking much injured, 11 June, 1855
Cheque Bank (*which see*), opened in Pall Mall, 23 July, 1873
Prescott's, Dimsdale's (London) united with Tugwell's (Bath) and Miles's (Bristol) as a company 1 Jan. 1891
A youth named Mackenzie, in the National Provincial Bank of England, robbed of a bag containing 11,000*l.* in bank notes . 16 Feb. 1891
Death of Mr. Bertram Wodehouse Currie, of the firm of Glyn, Mills, Currie & Co. . . 29 Dec. 1896
Charles Deane, cashier, pleads guilty of stealing 3,734*l.* from the bank of Australasia, sentenced to 5 yrs. penal servitude . . 13 Sept. 1899
Parr's bank, Bartholomew-lane, robbed of 60,610*l.* in bank of England notes, 23 Jan. 1899; 40,000*l.* of notes returned by post, 26 Jan.; notes amounting to 19,400*l.* found at the bank, 8 Feb. 1900; Chas. Edw. Goss pleads guilty, sentenced to 7 yrs. penal servitude . . 13 Sept. 1900
The Dumbell bank case (see *Man, Isle of*) . . 1900
Goudie, a clerk in the bank of Liverpool, absconds, his defalcations about 170,000*l.* . 21 Nov. 1901

Banks in 1855.		*Notes allowed to be issued.*
Bank of England	1	£14,000,000
English private banks	196	4,999,444
English joint-stock banks (see *Banks, Joint Stock*)	67	3,418,277
Banks in Scotland	18	3,087,209
Banks in Ireland	8	6,354,494
	290	£31,859,424

Bank of	
Venice formed	1157
Geneva	1345
Barcelona	1401
Genoa	1407
Naples	1539
Amsterdam	1607
Hamburg	1619
Rotterdam	1635
Stockholm	1688
England	1694
Scotland	1695
Copenhagen	1736
Berlin	1765
Caisse d'Escompte, France	1776
Ireland	1783
St. Petersburg	1786
In the East Indies	1787
In North America	1791
France,* founded by Napoleon, aided by count Mollien	1800–3

* Supported by laws passed 14 April, 1803, and 22 April, 1806. The statutes were approved 16 Jan. 1808. In 1810 Napoleon said that its duty was to provide money at all times at 4 per cent. interest; average rate of discount till 1815, 6 per cent.; much variation since; in 1893, 2·50; the lowest in Europe. In 1890 the bank joined with others in supporting Messrs. Baring. See *London*, Nov. 1890.

Italy 1865
Imperial Bank of Germany (formerly of Prussia) 1 Jan. 1876

BANK OF ENGLAND was projected by William Paterson, a Scotch merchant (see *Darien*), to meet the difficulty experienced by William III. in raising the supplies for the war against France. By the influence of Paterson and Michael Godfrey, 40 merchants (aided by Charles Montague) subscribed 500,000*l.* towards the sum of 1,200,000*l.* to be lent to the government at 8 per cent., in consideration of the subscribers being incorporated as a bank. The scheme was violently opposed in parliament, but the bill (a tonnage act), obtained the royal assent 25 April, 1694, and the charter was granted 27 July following, appointing sir John Houblon the first governor, and Michael Godfrey the first deputy-governor. The bank commenced active operations on 1 Jan. 1695, at Grocers' Hall, Poultry,* issuing notes for 20*l.* and upwards, and discounting bills for 4½ to 6 per cent. The charter was renewed in 1697, 1708, 1713, 1716, 1721, 1724, 1746, 1749, 1764, 1781, 1800, 1808, 1816, 1833, 1844. *Lawson.*

Run on the bank: its notes at 20 per cent. discount; capital raised to 2,201,171*l.* 10*s.* . . Nov. 1696
The bank monopoly established by the prohibition of any company exceeding six persons acting as bankers (Scotland not included in the act) . . 1708
Capital raised to 5,559,995*l.* 10*s.* 1710
Bank post bills issued (1st record) . 14 Dec. 1738
Run for gold through rebellion in the North; bank bills paid in silver; the city support the bank, Sept. 1745
Rd. Vaughan hanged for forging notes . 1 May, 1758
10*l.* notes issued 1759
Gordon riots; since then the bank has been protected by the military 1780
5*l.* notes issued 1793
Cash payments suspended, in conformity with an order in council . . . . . 26 Feb. 1797
1*l.* and 2*l.* notes issued . . . . . March, „
Bank restriction act passed . . . . 3 May, „
Voluntary contribution of 200,000*l.* to the government 1798
Loss by Aslett's frauds (see *Exchequer*) 342,697*l.* . 1803
Resignation of Abraham Newland, 50 years cashier, 18 Sept. 1807
Bramah's machine for numbering notes adopted . 1809
The bank issues silver tokens for 3*s.* and 1*s.* 6*d.* 9 July, 1811
Peel's act for the gradual resumption of cash payments . . . . July, 1819
Cash payments for notes to be in bullion at the mint price, 1 May, 1821; in the current coin of the realm, 1 May, 1823
Great commercial panic—many 1*l.* notes (accidentally found in a box) issued with most beneficial effects . . . . Dec. 1825
The act for the establishment of joint-stock banks breaks up the monopoly 1826
By the advice of the government, branch banks opened at Gloucester, 19 July; Manchester, 21 Sept.; Swansea, 23 Oct. . . . . . „
And at Birmingham, 1 Jan.; Liverpool, 2 July; Bristol, 12 July; Leeds, 23 Aug.; Exeter, 17 Dec. 1827
The bank loses 360,000*l.* by Fauntleroy's forgeries, estimated, in 1830
Statements of the bank affairs published quarterly 1833
Peel's bank charter act (7 & 8 Vict. c. 32); renews charter till 1 Aug. 1855, and longer, if the debt due from the public to the bank (11,015,100*l.*), with interest, &c., be not paid after due notice; established the issue department; requires weekly returns to be published; limited the issue of notes to 14,000,000*l.*, &c. . . . . 19 July, 1844
Commercial panic: lord John Russell authorises relaxation of restriction of issuing notes (not acted on); bank discount 8 per cent. Sunday, 24–25 Oct. 1847
Gold bullion in the bank (consequent on discovery of gold in Australia), 21,845,390*l.* . . 10 July, 1852
Branch bank, Burlington-gardens, London, W. opened . . . . 1 Oct. 1856
Committee on the bank acts appointed . 12 May, 1857
Bank discount 9 per cent.; lord Palmerston authorises addition to issue of notes [to the amount of 2,000,000*l.* were issued] . . . . 12 Nov. „
Much alarm through the announcement of the bank solicitor that a quantity of bank paper had been stolen from the makers (forged notes soon appeared) . . . . 16 Aug. 1862
The culprits, soon detected, were tried and convicted (see *Trials*) . . . . . 7–12 Jan. 1863
See *Bills of Exchange*, 1873.
For the Vagliano case, see *Trials*, 2 Nov. 1888.
Branch bank, in Fleet Street, opened . 17 Dec. 1888
The bank authorised (in accordance with the Act of 1844) to increase their issue of notes by 250,000*l.* about . . . . 11 Feb. 1890
The bank, aided by the Bank of France and others, assists Messrs. Baring, and thereby averts a panic . . . . 15 Nov. „
Important changes in the management of the bank, proposed by the chancellor of the exchequer, 4 April, approved by the directors and adopted by the proprietors . . . . . 16 June, 1892
Resignation of Mr. May, chief cashier, on account of grave irregularities; the loss to the bank, 250,000*l.*, covered by reserve; bank dividend 4½ per cent. reported . . . . 15 March, 1894
One-fifth of the metallic reserve to be held in silver bullion, proposed . . . . . . 16 Sept. 1897
Disapproved by the London bankers; at a meeting, 22 Sept. „
Meeting of bankers and representatives of the principal financial institutions of the city, Mr. S. S. Gladstone, chairman, to consider the national war loan, 35,000,000*l.* (5,000,000 to be reserved for issue as Treasury bills); the remainder to be redeemable in 10 years at 2¾ per cent.; price of issue, 98½ per cent. . . . 9 March, 1900

Bank Discount.

1858, 3 per cent. Feb. 1.
1860 (demand for gold in France), 6, Nov. 15.
1861, 7, Jan. 7; 8 (demand for money in France, India, United States, &c.), Feb. 14; 3, Nov. 7.
1862, 2½, Jan.; 3, April; 2½, July; 2, July 24; 3, Oct.—Dec.
1863, *raised* to 4 per cent., Jan. 16; to 5, Jan. 28; *reduced* to 4, Feb.; to 3½ and 3, April; *raised* to 4, May; *raised* to 5, 6, in Nov.; to 7 and 8, and *reduced* to 7 in Dec.
1864, *raised* to 8, Jan. 20; *reduced* to 7, Feb. 12; to 6, Feb. 25; *raised* to 7, April 16; to 8, May 2; to 9, May 5; *reduced* to 8, May 19; to 7, May 26; to 6, June 16; *raised* to 7, July 25; to 8, Aug. 4; to 9, Sept. 5; *reduced* to 8, Nov. 10; to 7, Nov. 24.
1865, *reduced* to 5½, Jan. 12; to 5, Jan. 20; *raised* to 5½, March 2; *reduced* to 4, March 30; *raised* to 4½, May 4; *reduced* to 3½, June 1; to 3, June 15; *raised* to 3½; July 27; to 4, Aug. 3; to 4½, Sept. 28; to 5, Oct. 2, to 6, Oct. 5; to 7, Oct. 7 (*three times in one week*); *reduced* to 6, Nov. 23; *raised* to 7, Dec. 28.
1866, *raised* to 8, Jan. 4; *reduced* to 7, Feb. 22; to 6, March 15; *raised* to 7, May 3; to 8, May 8; to 9, May 11 (*panic*—suspension of Bank Act authorised by government); to 10, May 12; *reduced* to 8, Aug. 16; to 7, Aug. 23; to 6, Aug. 30; to 5, Sept. 6; to 4½, Sept. 27; to 4, Nov. 8; to 3½, Dec. 20.
1867, *reduced* to 3, Feb. 7; to 2½, May 30; to 2, July 25.
1868, *raised* to 2½ per cent. Nov. 19; to 3, Dec. 3.
1869, *raised* to 4, April 1; to 4½, May 6; *reduced* to 4, June 10; to 3½, June 24; to 3, July 15; to 2½, Aug. 19; *raised* to 3, Nov. 4.
1870, *raised* to 3½, July 21; to 4, July 23; to 5 (*Franco-Prussian War*), July 28; to 6, Aug. 4; *reduced* to 5½, Aug. 11; to 4½, Aug. 18; to 4, Aug. 25; to 3½, Sept. 1; to 3, Sept. 15; to 2½, Sept. 29.

* The foundation of the building in Threadneedle-street was laid 1 Aug. 1732, by sir Edward Bellamy, governor, and the bank removed there 5 June, 1734; it was erected by G. Sampson, architect. Great additions have been made from time to time by successive architects: sir Robert Taylor, sir John Soane, and Mr. C. R. Cockerell. It now occupies the site of the church, and nearly all the parish of St. Christopher-le-Stocks. The churchyard is now termed "the garden." Another entrance opened in Princes-street, 1882.

1871, *raised* to 3, March 2; *reduced* to 2½, April 13; to 2½, June 15; to 2, July 13; *raised* to 3, Sept. 21; to 4, Sept. 28; to 5, Oct. 7; *reduced* to 4, Nov. 16; to 3½, Nov. 30; to 3, Dec. 14.

1872, *raised* to 3½, April 4; to 4, April 11; to 5, May 9; *reduced* to 4, May 30; to 3½, June 13; to 3, June 20; *raised* to 3½, July 18; to 4, Sept. 18; to 4½, Sept. 26; to 5, Oct. 2; to 6, Oct. 10; to 7, Nov. 9; *reduced* to 6, Nov. 28; to 5, Dec. 12.

1873, *reduced* to 4½, Jan. 9; to 4, Jan. 23; to 3½, Jan. 30; *raised* to 4, March 26; to 4½, May 7; to 5, May 10; to 6, May 17; to 7, June 4; *reduced* to 6, June 12; to 5, July 10; to 4½, July 17; to 4, July 24; to 3½, July 31; to 3, Aug. 21; *raised* to 4, Sept. 25; to 5 (panic in New York), Sept. 29; to 6, Oct. 14; to 7, Oct. 18; to 8, Nov. 1; to 9, Nov. 7; *reduced* to 8, Nov. 20; to 6, Nov. 27; to 5, Dec. 4; to 4½, Dec. 11.

1874, *reduced* to 4, Jan. 8; to 3½, Jan. 15; *raised* to 4, April 30; *reduced* to 3½, May 28; to 3, June 4; to 2½, June 18; *raised* to 3, July 30; to 4, Aug. 6; *reduced* to 3½, Aug. 20; to 3, Aug. 27; *raised* to 4, Oct. 15; to 5, Nov. 16; to 6, Nov. 30.

1875, *reduced* to 5, Jan. 7; to 4, Jan. 14; to 3, Jan. 27; *raised* to 3½, Feb. 18; to 3, July 8; *reduced* to 2½, July 29; to 2, Aug. 12; *raised* to 2½, Oct. 7; to 3½, Oct. 14; to 4, Oct. 21; *reduced* to 3, Nov. 18; *raised* to 4, Dec. 30.

1876, *raised* to 5, Jan. 6; *reduced* to 4, Jan. 27; to 3½, March 23; to 3, April 6; to 2, April 20.

1877, *raised* to 3, May 3; *reduced* to 2½, July 5; to 2, July 12; *raised* to 3, Aug. 28; to 4, Oct. 4; to 5, Oct. 11; *reduced* to 4, Nov. 29.

1878, *reduced* to 3, Jan. 10; to 2, Jan. 31; *raised* to 3, March 28; *reduced* to 2½, May 30; [*minimum* omitted in bank notices, June]; *raised* to 3, June 27; to 3½, July 4; to 4, Aug. 1; to 5, Aug. 12; to 6, Oct. 14; *reduced* to 5, Nov. 21.

1879, *reduced* to 4, Jan. 16; to 3, Jan. 30; to 2½, March 13; to 2, April 10; *raised* to 3, Nov. 6.

1880, *reduced* to 2½, June 17; *raised* to 3, Dec. 9.

1881, *raised* to 3½, Jan.; *reduced* to 3, Feb. 17; to 2½, April 27; *raised* to 3, Aug. 3; to 4, Aug. 25; to 5, Oct 6.

1882, *raised* to 6, Jan. 30; *reduced* to 5, Feb. 23; to 4, Mar. 9; to 3, Mar. 23; *raised* to 4, Aug. 17; to 5, Sept. 14.

1883, *reduced* to 4, Jan. 25; to 3½, Feb. 15; to 3, March 1; *raised* to 4, May 10; *reduced* to 3½, Sept. 13; to 3, Sept. 27.

1884, *raised* to 3½, Feb. 7; *reduced* to 3, Mar. 13; to 2½ April 3; to 2, June 19; *raised* to 3, Oct. 9; to 4, Oct. 30; to 5, Nov. 6.

1885, *reduced* to 4, Jan. 29; to 3½, March 19; to 3, May 7; to 2½, May 14; to 2, May 28; *raised* to 3, Nov. 12; to 4, Dec. 17.

1886, *reduced* to 3, Jan. 21; to 2, Feb. 18; *raised* to 3, May 6; *reduced* to 2½, June 10; *raised* to 3½, Aug. 26; to 4, Oct. 21; to 5, Dec. 16.

1887, *reduced* to 4, Feb. 3; to 3½, March 10; to 3, March 24; to 2½, April 14; to 2, April 28; *raised* to 3, Aug. 4; to 4, Sept. 1.

1888, *reduced* to 3½, Jan. 12; to 3, Jan. 19; to 2½, Feb. 16; to 2, March 15; *raised* to 3, May 10; *reduced* to 2½, June 7; *raised* to 3, Aug. 9; to 4, Sept. 13; to 5, Oct. 4.

1889, *reduced* to 4, Jan. 10; 3½, Jan. 24; to 3, Jan. 31; to 2½, April 18; *raised* to 3, Aug. 8; to 4, Aug. 29; to 5, Sept. 26; to 6, Dec. 30.

1890, *reduced* to 5, Feb. 20; to 4½, March 6; to 4, March 13; to 3½, April 10; to 3, April 17; *raised* to 4, June 26; to 5, July 31; *reduced* to 4, Aug. 21; *raised* to 5, Sept. 25; to 6, Nov. 7; *reduced* to 5, Dec. 4.

1891, *reduced* to 4, Jan. 8; to 3½, Jan. 22; to 3, Jan. 29; *raised* to 3½, April 16; to 4, May 7; to 5, May 14; *reduced* to 4, June 4; to 3, June 18; to 2½, July 2; *raised* to 3, Sept. 24; to 4, Oct. 29; *reduced* to 3½, Dec. 10.

1892, *reduced* to 3, Jan. 21; to 2½, April 7; to 2, April 28; *raised* to 3, Oct 20.

1893, *reduced* to 2½, Jan. 26; *raised* to 3, May 4; to 3½, May 11; to 4, May 18; *reduced* to 3, June 8; to 2½, June 15; *raised* to 3, Aug. 3; to 4, Aug. 10; to 5, Aug. 24; *reduced* to 4, Sept. 14; to 3½, Sept. 21; to 3, Oct. 5.

1894, *reduced* to 2½, Feb. 1; to 2, Feb. 22.

1895, *unchanged.*

1896, *raised* to 2½, Sept. 10; to 3, Sept. 24; to 4, Oct. 22.

1897, *reduced* to 3½, Jan. 21; to 3, Feb. 4; to 2½, April 8; to 2, May 13; *raised* to 2½, Sept. 23; to 3, Oct. 14.

1898, *raised* to 4, April 7; to 3½, May 26; *reduced* to 3, June 2; 2½, June 30; *raised* to 3, Sept. 22; to 4, Oct. 13.

1899, *reduced* to 3½, Jan. 19; to 3, Feb. 2; *raised* to 3½, July 13; to 4½, Oct. 3; to 5, Oct. 5; to 6, Nov. 30.

1900, *reduced* to 5, Jan. 11; to 4½, Jan. 18; to 4, Jan. 25; to 3½, May 24; to 3, June 14; *raised* to 4, July 19.

1901, *raised* to 5, Jan. 2; *reduced* to 4½, Feb. 7; to 4, Feb. 21; to 3½, June 6; to 3, June 13; *raised* to 4, Oct. 31.

1902, *reduced* to 3½, Jan. 23; to 3, Feb. 6; *raised* to 4, Oct. 2.

1903, *reduced* to 3½, May 21; to 3, June 25; *raised* to 4, Sept. 3.

AVERAGE AMOUNT OF BANK OF ENG. NOTES IN CIRCULATION.

Year	Amount	Year	Amount
1718	£1,829,930	1835	£18,215,220
1778	7,030,680	1840	17,231,000
1790	10,217,000	1845	19,262,327
1800	15,450,000	1850	19,776,814
1810	23,904,000	1855	19,616,627
1815	26,803,520	1857	21,036,430
1820	27,174,000	1859	22,705,780
1830	20,620,000		

DEC. 27, 1856.

Assets—Securities	£29,484,000	£39,589,000
Bullion	10,105,000	
Liabilities		36,329,000
Balance		£3,260,000

Nov. 11, 1857 (*Time of Panic*).

Assets—Securities	£35,480,281	£42,650,789
Bullion	7,170,508	
Liabilities		39,286,433
Balance or rest		£3,364,356

	Assets.—Securities.	Coin and Bullion.	*Liabilities.*	*Balance.*
Sept. 14, 1859	£30,090,179	£17,120,822	£43,503,214	£3,716,787
Aug. 30, 1862	30,106,295	17,678,698	44,453,778	3,331,215
Aug. 9, 1865	31,823,066	14,223,390	42,528,577	3,517,879
Mar. 14, 1866	29,415,059	14,327,618	39,934,150	3,808,527
Sept. 26, ,,	34,418,382	16,929,262	47,039,390	4,108,254
June 19, 1867	31,849,662	21,882,770	50,612,342	3,120,090
March 5, 1868	31,226,793	21,136,192	48,752,291	3,610,694
Dec. 29, 1869	34,040,941	19,196,622	50,134,262	3,103,301
June 2, 1870	32,402,200	20,494,392	49,799,528	3,097,069
Jan. 5, 1871	32,274,967	22,382,934	51,512,339	3,145,562
June 29, ,,	34,100,342	26,609,540	57,594,133	3,115,749
Jan. 3, 1872	36,393,708	25,291,761	58,497,293	3,188,176
July 3, ,,	37,090,281	24,065,094	57,894,811	3,250,564
Jan. 8, 1873	32,138,990	24,051,412	52,772,403	3,417,999
July 9, ,,	33,395,344	22,374,582	52,338,203	3,431,723
Dec. 17, ,,	30,922,266	22,477,563	50,248,577	3,151,252
July 1, 1874	36,596,872	23,929,601	57,315,010	3,211,463
Jan. 6, 1875	33,985,823	22,085,311	52,786,516	3,302,618
June 30, ,,	39,660,166	26,690,116	63,252,111	3,107,171
Jan. 5, 1876	38,398,985	21,215,761	56,362,426	3,252,320
July 5, ,,	32,247,018	30,190,692	60,186,939	3,250,771
Jan. 3, 1877	35,998,482	28,214,165	61,091,620	3,121,027
July 4, ,,	35,865,522	26,948,340	59,682,894	3,130,968

Jan. 2, 1878	34,335,978	24,386,794	55,560,422	3,162,350
June 26, ,,	37,366,472	23,438,504	57,726,813	3,078,163
Jan. 2, 1879	44,286,663	28,088,361	69,062,479	3,312,545
July 2, ,,	34,951,837	35,286,269	67,067,079	3,171,027
Jan. 1, 1880	41,330,212	27,601,562	65,866,659	3,065,115
July 1, ,,	39,398,901	29,319,390	65,634,195	3,084,096
Jan. 5, 1881	39,955,274	24,269,276	61,006,233	3,218,317
June 8, 1881	35,890,517	25,902,159	58,721,068	3,071,608
Jan. 5, 1882	40,438,605	20,249,034	57,505,540	3,182,099
June 28, ,,	37,486,806	24,380,941	58,772,276	3,095,471
Jan. 3, 1883	41,688,522	20,353,791	58,856,634	3,185,679
July 4, ,,	39,827,144	22,266,535	58,939,347	3,154,332
Jan. 2, 1884	41,217,256	21,437,365	59,531,153	3,123,468
July 2, ,,	38,323,187	25,075,683	60,236,310	3,162,560
Jan. 1, 1885	41,663,958	20,695,496	59,243,143	3,116,311
Jan. 6, 1886	41,446,936	19,964,811	58,109,621	3,302,126
Jan. 29, 1887	37,545,742	23,190,671	57,685,104	3,051,309
Jan. 4, 1888	38,133,062	20,164,214	55,175,337	3,121,939

July 4, 1888.—Government debt, 11,015,100*l*. Other securities, 5,184,900*l*. Gold coin and bullion, 20,316,920*l*. Notes issued, 36,516,920*l*. Balance or rest, 3,140,748*l*.

Jan. 2, 1889.—Government debt, 11,015,100*l*. Other securities, 5,184,900*l*. Gold coin and bullion, 18,439,030*l*. Notes issued, 34,639,030*l*. Balance or rest, 3,217,808*l*.

July 3, 1889.—Government debt, 11,015,100*l*. Other securities, 5,184,900*l*. Gold coin and bullion, 22,719,385*l*. Notes issued, 38,919,385*l*. Balance or rest, 3,148,924*l*.

Jan. 1, 1890.—Government debt, 11,015,100*l*. Other securities, 5,184,900*l*. Gold coin and bullion, 17,116,690*l*. Notes issued, 33,316,690*l*. Balance or rest, 3,177,007*l*.

July 2, 1890.—Government debt, 11,015,100*l*. Other securities, 5,434,900*l*. Gold coin and bullion, 20,084,600*l*. Notes issued, 36,534,600*l*. Balance or rest, 3,184,670*l*.

Jan. 7, 1891.—Government debt, 11,015,100*l*. Other securities, 5,434,900*l*. Gold coin and bullion, 23,352,635*l*. Notes issued, 39,802,635*l*. Balance or rest, 3,462,192*l*.

July 1, 1891.—Government debt, 11,015,100*l*. Other securities, 5,434,900*l*. Gold coin and bullion, 27,285,550*l*. Notes issued, 43,735,550*l*. Balance or rest, 3,226,321*l*.

Jan. 6, 1892.—Government debt, 11,015,100*l*. Other securities, 5,434,900*l*. Gold coin and bullion, 21,690,030*l*. Notes issued, 38,140,030*l*. Balance or rest, 3,408,148*l*.

Jan. 4, 1893.—Government debt, 11,015,100*l*. Other securities, 5,434,900*l*. Gold coin and bullion, 23,052,150*l*. Notes issued, 39,502,150*l*. Balance or rest, 3,236,173*l*.

July 5, 1893.—Government debt, 11,015,100*l*. Other securities, 5,434,900*l*. Gold coin and bullion, 27,945,965*l*. Notes issued, 44,395,965*l*. Balance or rest, 3,349,434*l*.

Jan. 3, 1894.—Government debt, 11 015,100*l*. Other securities, 5.434,900*l*. Gold coin and bullion, 22,882,720*l*. Notes issued, 39,332,720*l*. Balance or rest, 3,244,437*l*.

July 4, 1894.—Government debt, 11,015,100*l*. Other securities, 5,784,900*l*. Gold coin and bullion, 36,486,455*l*. Notes issued, 53,286,455*l*. Balance or rest, 3,154,098*l*.

Jan. 2, 1895.—Government debt, 11,015,100*l*. Other securities, 5,784,900*l*. Gold coin and bullion, 30,849,895*l*. Notes issued, 47,649,895*l*. Balance or rest, 3,192,427*l*.

July 3, 1895.—Government debt, 14,481,477*l*. Other securities, 22,512,705*l*. Gold coin and bullion, 37,933,838*l*. Notes issued, 26,309,820*l*. Balance or rest, 3,074,457*l*.

Jan. 1, 1896.—Government debt, 11,015,100*l*. Other securities, 5,784,900*l*. Gold coin and bullion, 42,968,325*l*. Notes issued, 59,768,325*l*. Balance or rest, 3,111,056*l*.

July 1, 1896.—Government debt, 11,015,100*l*. Other securities, 5,784,900*l*. Gold coin and bullion, 46,129,400*l*. Notes issued, 62,929,400*l*. Balance or rest, 3,123,614*l*.

Jan. 6, 1897.—Government debt, 11,015,100*l*. Other securities, 5,784,900*l*. Gold coin and bullion, 32,462,765*l*. Notes issued, 49,262,765*l*. Balance or rest, 3,406,871*l*.

July 7, 1897.—Government debt, 11,015,100*l*. Other securities, 5,784,900*l*. Gold coin and bullion, 34,401,990*l*. Notes issued, 51,201,990*l*. Balance or rest, 3,331,673*l*.

Jan. 5, 1898.—Government debt, 11,015,100*l*. Other securities, 5,784,900*l*. Gold coin and bullion, 29,188,060*l*. Notes issued, 45,988,060*l*. Balance or rest, 3,388,138*l*.

July 6, 1898.—Government debt, 11,015,100*l*. Other securities, 5,784,900*l*. Gold coin and bullion, 34,736,595*l*. Notes issued, 51,536,595*l*. Balance or rest, 3,436,734*l*.

Jan. 4, 1899.—Government debt, 11,015,100*l*. Other securities, 5,784,900*l*. Gold coin and bullion, 28,418,120*l*. Notes issued, 45,218,120*l*. Balance or rest, 3,284,950*l*.

July 5, 1899.—Government debt, 11,015,100*l*. Other securities, 5,784,900*l*. Gold coin and bullion, 30,314,865*l*. Notes issued, 47,114,865*l*. Balance or rest, 3,415,616*l*.

Jan. 3, 1900.—Government debt, 11,015,100*l*. Other securities, 5,784,900*l*. Gold coin and bullion, 30,745,660*l*. Notes issued, 47,545,660*l*. Balance or rest, 3,337,866*l*.

July 4, 1900.—Government debt, 11,015,100*l*. Other securities, 6,759,900*l*. Gold coin and bullion, 30,980,750*l*. Notes issued, 48,755,750*l*. Balance or rest, 3,381,817*l*.

Jan. 9, 1901.—Government debt, 11,015,100*l*. Other securities, 6,759,900*l*. Gold coin and bullion, 27,991,970*l*. Notes issued, 45,766,970*l*. Balance or rest, 3,511,725*l*.

July 3, 1901.—Government debt, 11,015,100*l*. Other securities, 6,759,900*l*. Gold coin and bullion, 35,535,305*l*. Notes issued, 53,310,305*l*. Balance or rest, 3,213,740*l*.

Jan. 1, 1902.—Government debt, 11,015,100*l*. Other securities, 6,759,900*l*. Gold coin and bullion, 30,633,890*l*. Notes issued, 48,408,890*l*. Balance or rest, 3,218,295*l*.

July 9, 1902.—Government debt, 11,015,100*l*. Other securities, 6,759,900*l*. Gold coin and bullion, 35,405,510*l*. Notes issued, 53,180,510*l*. Balance or rest, 3,424,240*l*.

Jan. 7, 1903.—Government debt, 11,015,100*l*. Other securities, 7,159,900*l*. Gold coin and bullion, 28,798,700*l*. Notes issued, 46,973,700*l*. Balance or rest, 3,500,655*l*.

July 2, 1903.—Government debt, 11,015,100*l*. Other securities, 7,159,900*l*. Gold coin and bullion, 35,155,230*l*. Notes issued, 53,330,230*l*. Balance or rest, 3,218,378*l*.

PUBLIC DEBT TO THE BANK OF ENGLAND.

1694	£1,200,000	1716	£4,175,027	1742	£10,700,000	1816	£14,686,000
1708	2,175,027	1721	9,100,000	1746	11,686,000	1844-1903	11,015,100

BANK OF IRELAND. On 9 Dec. 1721, the Irish house of commons rejected a bill for establishing a national bank. Important failures in Irish banks occurred in 1727, 1733, and 1758: this led gradually to the establishment of the Bank of Ireland at St. Mary's abbey, Dublin, 1 June, 1783. The business was removed to the late parliament house, in College-green, in May, 1808. Branch banks of this establishment have been formed in most of the provincial towns in Ireland, all since 1828. Irish Banking Act passed, 21 July, 1845.

BANK OF SAVINGS, see *Savings' Banks*.

BANKERS' BOOKS EVIDENCE ACT, 39 & 40 Vict. c. 48, passed 11 Aug. 1876; repealed by a fresh act 23 May, 1879.

BANKERS' INSTITUTE, meeting to establish it, 29 May, 1878; Sir John Lubbock elected president 11 March, 1879, 1st general meeting 23 May, 1879. (1952 members, May, 1887.) One inaugurated at Dublin, 29 Oct. 1898.

BANKS OF SCOTLAND. The old bank of Scotland was set up in 1695, at Edinburgh, and began 1 Nov., the second institution of the kind in the empire: lending money to the crown was prohibited.

Royal bank of Scotland chartered . . . 8 July, 1727
British Linen company bank 1746
First stone of present bank of Scotland laid 3 June, 1801
Commercial bank 1810
National bank 1825
Union bank 1830
City of Glasgow bank* 1839
Scotch banking act passed . . . 21 July, 1845
Western bank of Scotland and the Glasgow bank stopped, causing much distress . . . Nov. 1857

BANKS, JOINT STOCK. Since the act of 1826, a number of these banks have been established.† In *Ireland* similar banks have been instituted, the first being the Hibernian bank. By the new Companies Act, passed 15 Aug. 1879, unlimited companies may register as limited. The joint-stock banks agreed to support the Bank of England, and to issue monthly balance sheets, May, June, 1891.

Chief London Joint-Stock Banks.	*Founded.*
London and Westminster (*becomes limited*, 1879) .	1834
London Joint-Stock	1836
London and County (*becomes limited*, 1879) . .	,,
Union Bank of London	1839
City Bank . . . (*ditto*, 1880) . .	1855

A full list of joint-stock banks, with their date, capital, &c., is given in *Whitaker's Almanack*.

BANK HOLIDAYS ACT passed 25 May, 1871, chiefly by the instrumentality of sir John Lubbock, now lord Avebury.

BANK HOLIDAYS.—*England and Ireland:* Easter Monday; Monday in Whitsun-week; first Monday in August; 26 December (if a week day). *St. Patrick's Day* legalised as a bank holiday, in Ireland, by Act of 1903.—*Scotland:* New Year's day; Christmas day (if either falls on Sunday, the following Monday to be a bank holiday); Good Friday; first Monday in May and August.

BANKRUPT (signifying either bank or bench broken), a trader declared to be unable to pay his just debts. The laws on the subject (1543, 1571 *et seq.*) were consolidated and amended in 1825, 1849, 1852, 1854, 1861, 1868, 1869, 1883. See *Debtors*.

Lord Chancellor Thurlow refused a bankrupt his certificate, because he had lost five pounds at one time in gaming . . . . . 17 July, 1788
Enacted that members of the house of commons becoming bankrupt, and not paying their debts in full, should vacate their seats 1812
Lord Eldon's Act appointing commissioners . . 1825
New Bankruptcy Court (including a court "of review," 3 judges) erected by 2 Will. IV. c. 56 (Lord Brougham's Act); official assignees appointed, &c. 1831
Bills for reforming bankruptcy law were in vain brought before parliament . . . 1859, 1860
Bill by the lord chancellor Westbury (formerly sir R. Bethell), 24 & 25 Vict. c. 134, passed (1861); great changes made; the court for relief of insolvent debtors abolished, and increased powers given to the commissioners in bankruptcy, &c.; the new orders issued . . . . 12 Oct. 1861
By lord Hatherley's Bankruptcy Act, passed 9 Aug. 1869, a new bankruptcy court was established in place of the commissioners', which sat last time, when above 300 petitions of bankruptcy were received, 31 Dec. 1869. "Paid trustee system," clauses 125, 126, termed "a gentlemanly way of getting rid of debts." The new judge, the hon. James Bacon, sat . . . . 1 Jan. 1870
Justice Giffard, the judge of the Bankruptcy Appeal Court, decided (in the case of the duke of Newcastle) that a peer can be made a bankrupt, Nov. 1869, which decision was affirmed on appeal to the house of lords in the following year; other petitions against peers have been filed. It was decided that bankrupts cannot sit in the house of peers . . . . 10 Feb. 1871

* CITY OF GLASGOW BANK (with unlimited liability); founded 1839, identified with Glasgow; held Free Church Sustentation Fund; stopped for a few days during crisis, Nov. 1857. In 1878 paid dividend 12 per cent. (100*l.* stock, 236*l.*); 1272 shareholders, very many in humble circumstances. The bank stopped 2 Oct. Investigation showed great fraud and false accounts. Estimated loss, 6,783,000*l.* causing much calamity and ruin to many. The directors, J. Stewart, Lewis Potter, R. Salmond, Wm. Taylor, H. Inglis, and J. I. Wright, and the manager, R. S. Stronach, were committed for trial, 30 Oct. Stronach and Potter were convicted of falsifying and fabricating balance sheets (18 months' imprisonment; the others of uttering the same (8 months' imprisonment), 1 Feb. 1879.

The liquidators reported that about 1819 contributors had paid about 4,500,000*l.* (13*s.* 4*d.* in the pound) 1 Dec. 1879; 20*s.* in the pound paid to depositors, 2 March, 1880.

Mr. James N. Fleming was arrested 25 Jan. for embezzlement, and sentenced to 8 months' imprisonment, 3 July, 1882.

Close of the liquidation; 13,644,856*l.* paid, announced Nov. 1882.

The receipts by subscription, &c., for the relief of the sufferers amounted to 380,000*l.*; interest 47,000*l.*, making a total of 427,000*l.*

† THE ROYAL BRITISH BANK was established in 1849, by Mr. John McGregor, M.P., and others, under sir R. Peel's joint-stock banking act, 7 & 8 Vict. c. 113 (1844), as an attempt to introduce the Scotch banking system of cash credits into England. On 3 Sept. 1856, it stopped payment, occasioning much distress and ruin to many small tradesmen and others. In consequence of strong evidence of the existence of fraud in the management of the bank, elicited during the examination before the court of bankruptcy, the government instructed the attorney-general to file *ex-officio* informations against the manager, Mr. H. Innes Cameron, and several of the directors. They were convicted 27 Feb. 1858, after 13 days' trial, and sentenced to various degrees of imprisonment. Attempts to mitigate the punishment failed (May, 1858); but all were released except Cameron and Esdaile, in July, 1858. In April, 1860, dividends had been paid to the amount of 15*s.* in the pound. The attorney-general brought in a bill called the Fraudulent Trustees' Act, 20 & 21 Vict. c. 54, to prevent the recurrence of such transactions.

On 19 April, 1860, a deficiency of 263,000*l.* was discovered in the *Union Bank of London*. Mr. George Pullinger, a cashier, confessed himself guilty of forgery and fraud, and was sentenced to 20 years' imprisonment.

On 18 Feb. 1861, it was discovered that John Durden, a clerk of the *Commercial Bank of London*, had robbed his employers of 67,000*l.*, of which 46,000*l.* might be recovered.

In Dec. 1864, J. W. Terry and Thomas Burch, manager and secretary of the *Unity Bank*, were committed on a charge of conspiracy for fabricating accounts; but were acquitted on their trial.

BANKRUPTCY DISQUALIFICATION ACT disqualifies a peer from sitting or voting in parliament, passed 13 July, 1871

Irish bankruptcy laws consolidated in 1836, and further amended in 1857

Scotch bankruptcy laws consolidated in 1856, and further amended in . . . . ,,

New Bankruptcy Act for Ireland, passed . 6 Aug. 1872

Four Bankruptcy bills introduced by lord chancellor Cairns, and withdrawn . . . . 1876—80

Bankruptcies have diminished through great number of liquidations by arranged compositions; many said to be fraudulent; 3651 of these in 1870; 11,976 in 1879; about 20,000,000*l.* wasted.

New bankruptcy bill brought in by Mr. Chamberlain . . . . . . 8 April, 1881 (dropped)

New Bankruptcy Act passed 25 Aug., 1883, 46 & 47 Vict. c. 52, places bankrupts' assets in charge of board of trade, and makes other important changes. By this act bankrupts are disqualified for election and sitting as members of the house of commons.

The court in Portugal Street closed; business transferred to High Court of Justice, Jan.; new judge first sat . . . . 18 Feb. 1884

Bankruptcy (Discharge and Closure) Act passed . 1887

Sir Albert Rollit's Bankruptcy Act, 1883–90, passed 18 Aug. 1890

Mr. E. T. Hooley, manufacturer, and promoter of companies, became bankrupt, his statements at his public examinations commencing 27 July, respecting monetary transactions with eminent persons emphatically denied by them. 17 Aug., 1898

Case resumed 2 Nov.; he gave about 39,000*l.* in charities in 1897, plate to St. Paul's 1,500*l.*; case adjourned till 14 Nov.; 7 Nov. his public examination closed . . . . . . 18 Nov. ,,

(Mr. Martin Rucker fined 200*l.* with costs, for endeavouring to bribe Mr. Hooley to suppress evidence, 2 Nov. 1898).

NUMBER OF BANKRUPTS IN GREAT BRITAIN.

Year		Number	Year		Number
1700	. . .	38	1881	England & Wales	1005
1725	. . . . .	416	1882	ditto	995
1750	. . . . .	432	1883	ditto	1046
1775	. . . . .	520	1884	ditto	2998
1800	. . . . .	1339	1885	ditto	3965
1810	. . about	2000	1886	ditto	4566
1820	. . . . .	1358	1887	ditto	4681
1825*	. . . . .	2683	1888	ditto	4695
1830	. . . . .	1467	1889	ditto	4415
1840	. . . . .	1308	1890	ditto	3924
1845	England & Wales	1028	1891	ditto	4150
1850	ditto	1298	1892	ditto	4575
1857	ditto	1488	1893	ditto	4805
1860	ditto	1268	1894	ditto	4702
1863	ditto	8470	1895	ditto	4349
1864	ditto	7224	1896	ditto	4109
1867	ditto	8994	1897	ditto	4032
1869	ditto	10,396	1898	ditto	4247
1873	ditto†	915	1899	ditto	4045
1876	ditto	976	1900	ditto	4343
1878	ditto	1084	1901	ditto	4176
1879	ditto	1156	1902	United Kingdom	4749
1880	ditto	995			

Bankrupts in Scotland: 1860, 445; 1876, 482; 1880, 582; 1885, 362; 1890, 339; 1896, 317; 1899, 297; 1900, 341.
In Ireland: 1880, 312; 1885, 216; 1887, 204;

BANNATYNE CLUB, named after George Bannatyne (the publisher), was established in 1823 by sir Walter Scott and others, for printing works illustrative of the history, antiquities, and literature of Scotland, of which about 113 volumes were issued: dissolved, 1860.

* According to a return to parliament made at the close of Feb. 1826, there had become bankrupt *in the four months preceding*, 59 banking-houses, comprising 144 partners; and 20 other banking establishments had been declared insolvent. Every succeeding week continued to add from seventy to a hundred merchants, traders, and manufacturers to the bankrupt list. This was the period of bubble speculation.

† Liquidations under deeds of arrangement nearly as numerous as bankruptcies, 1903. Costs 21 per cent. of the estate.

BANNER CROSS MURDER. See *Trials* 1879.

BANNERET, KNIGHT, a dignity between baron and knight, anciently conferred by the king under the royal standard on the field of battle. Its origin is of uncertain time: Edmondson dates it 736; but it was probably created by Edward I. John Chandos is said to have been made a banneret by the Black Prince and the king of Castile at Najara, 3 April, 1367. The dignity was conferred on John Smith, who rescued the royal standard at Edgehill fight, 23 Oct. 1642. It fell into disuse, but was revived by George III. for sir William Erskine, in 1764, and for admiral Pye and captains Knight, Bickerton, and Vernon, in 1773.

BANNERS were common to all nations. The Jewish tribes had standards or banners—*Num.* ii. (1490 B.C.). See *Cross*, *Auriflamma*, *Standards*, *&c.* The magical banner of the Danes (said to have been a black raven on a red ground) was taken by Alfred when he defeated Hubba, 878.

BANNOCKBURN (Stirlingshire), the site of two battles: (1) between Robert Bruce of Scotland and Edward II. of England, 24 June, 1314. The army of Bruce consisted of 30,000; that of Edward of 100,000 men, of whom 52,000 were archers. The English crossed a rivulet to the attack, and Bruce having dug and covered pits, they fell into them, and were thrown into confusion. The rout was complete: the English king narrowly escaped, and 50,000 were killed or taken prisoners. (2) At Sauchieburn, near here, James III. was defeated and slain on 11 June, 1488, by his rebellious nobles.

BANNS, in the feudal law, were a solemn proclamation of any kind: hence arose the present custom of asking banns, or giving notice before marriage; said to have been introduced into the English church about 1200. The proper time of publishing banns in the church was the subject of much discussion in 1867.

BANQUETING-HOUSE, Whitehall, London, built by Inigo Jones, about 1619. Occupied by the museum of the United Service Institution, 1895.

BANTAM (Java). Here a British factory was established by captain Lancaster, in 1603. The English and Danes were driven from their factories by the Dutch in 1683. Bantam surrendered to the British in 1811, but was restored to the Dutch at the peace in 1814.

BANTINGISM, see *Corpulence*.

BANTRY BAY (S. Ireland), where a French fleet bringing succour to the adherents of James II., attacked the English under admiral Herbert, 1 May, 1689: the latter retired to form in line and were not pursued. A French squadron of seven sail of the line and two frigates, armed *en flûte*, and seventeen transports, anchored here for a few days, without effect, Dec. 1796. MUTINY of the Bantry Bay squadron under admiral Mitchell was in Dec. 1801. In Jan. 1802, twenty-two of the mutineers were tried on board the *Gladiator*, at Portsmouth, when seventeen were condemned to death, of whom eleven were executed; the others were sentenced to receive each 200 lashes. The executions took place on board the *Majestic*, *Centaur*, *Formidable*, *Téméraire*, and *L'Achille*, 8 to 18 Jan. 1802. Mock battle here, 30 June, 1885.

BAPAUME, N. FRANCE, the site of severe indecisive engagements between the French army of the north under Faidherbe, and the Germans under Manteuffel; the French retreated, 2, 3 Jan. 1871.

BAPHOMET, the name of an imaginary idol or symbol having two heads, male and female, surrounded with a crescent moon and serpents, which the knights templars were accused of employing in their mysterious rites. The word is said to be a corrupted form of Mahomet.

BAPTISM, the ordinance of admission into the church, practised by all Christian sects except Quakers. John *the Baptist* baptized Christ, 30. (*Matt.* iii.) Infant baptism is mentioned by Irenæus about 97. In the reign of Constantine, 319 baptisteries were built and baptism was performed by dipping the person all over. In the west sprinkling was adopted. Much controversy has arisen since 1831 (particularly in 1849 and 1850), in the church of England, respecting baptismal regeneration, which the Arches' Court of Canterbury decided to be a doctrine of the church of England. See *Trials*, 1849, and *note*. Demanding fees for baptisms was made unlawful by an act passed 18 July, 1872.

BAPTISTS (see *Anabaptists*). A sect distinguished by their opinions respecting (1) the proper *subjects*, and (2) the proper *mode* of baptism: the former they affirm to be those who are able to make a profession of faith; the latter to be total immersion. There are seven sections of Baptists—Arminian, Calvinistic (or Particular), &c. The first Baptist church formed in London was about 1608. They published their confession of faith in 1643; revised in 1689. Rhode Island, America, was settled by Baptists in 1635.

Baptist Union of the United Kingdom; annual meeting held.
Particular Baptist Fund established 1717
Baptist Missionary Society inaugurated 1792
Baptist College, Regent's Park, founded . . . 1810
Mr. C. H. Spurgeon's great Baptist tabernacle, Newington Butts, opened, 31 March, 1861; burnt down, 1 p.m.; 20 April, 1898; reconstructed at a cost of about 45,000*l*, and re-opened . 19 Sept., 1900
A Baptist Pastors' College near it, founded by Mr. Spurgeon . . . . 14 Oct. 1873
[Mr. Charles Haddon Spurgeon was born 19 June, 1834, and when quite a youth became a powerful preacher, attracting large congregations. He died at Mentone, 31 Jan. 1892. There was a very great concourse at his funeral in Norwood Cemetery, 11 Feb., on which day S. London appeared to be in mourning. His "Autobiography" published, Dec. 1897, 2nd vol. Aug. 1898. His son, Thomas Spurgeon, received as pastor, 12 April, 1894.]
A great tabernacle at Shoreditch (rev. Wm. Cuff), opened . . . . 11 Nov. 1879
In United Kingdom 3,738 chapels; 304,802 baptised members in 1883; 3,842 chapels, 364,779 members, Dec. 1897; 3,961 chapels, 377,747 members, Dec. 1902
Baptist Chapel House, Southampton Row, opened, 28 April, 1903

BAR SUR AUBE, N. E. France. Here the French, under Oudinot and Macdonald, were defeated by the allies, 27 Feb. 1814.

BARBADOES, a West India island, one of the Windward isles, discovered by the Portuguese about 1600, taken possession of by the English 1605, and settled by sir Wm. Courteen, who founded Jamestown, 1625. As many royalists settled here, the island was taken by the parliamentarians in 1652. Population, 1876, 162,042: white, 16,560; coloured, 145,482; 1881, 173,522; 1891, 182,322; 1901, 195,000.

A dreadful hurricane, over 4,000 deaths . 10 Oct. 1780
A large plantation with all its buildings destroyed, by the land removing from its original site to another, and covering everything in its peregrination . . . . 17 Oct. 1784
An inundation, Nov. 1795; and two great fires, May and Dec. 1796
Bishopric established 1824
Awful devastation, with the loss of thousands of lives and of immense property, by a hurricane Aug. 1831
Nearly 17,000 persons died of cholera . . . 1854
Property to the amount of about 300,000*l*. destroyed by a fire at Bridgetown . . . 14 Feb. 1860
Great increase in growth of cotton, 1864-5.
Governor, James Walker 1861
,, Rawson W. Rawson, 1868; retired 1875, died 1899
,, John Pope Hennessy 1875
Proposed confederation of the Windward isles; supported by the governor in a speech, 3 March; opposed by the planters . . . . March, 1876
The coloured population ignorantly expecting advantage from the confederation, rise, plundering and destroying much property and cattle; negroes killed and wounded by police . 21, 22 April, ,,
Great panic among the planters; the governor and clergy said to have acted judiciously; peace restored . . . . 24 April, ,,
The governor exonerated from serious blame July, ,,
Trial of 450 rioters; 82 punished (17 penal servitude; others light sentences) . . 12-21 Oct. ,,
Capt. Geo. C. Strahan appointed governor Nov. ,,
Sir Henry Bulwer, governor 1880
Sir William Robinson, governor 1881
Sir C. C. Lees, governor . . . . Aug. 1885
Sir Walter J. Sendall . . . . . Sept. 1889
Sir James Shaw Hay . . . . . . Feb. 1892
The hon A. J. Pile, speaker in the house of assembly, dies of wounds, inflicted by an unknown assailant . . . . . 2 Sept. 1898
Great hurricane, 112 deaths (see *West Indies*) 10 Sept. ,,
(Home government grants 40,000*l*. to aid the distress).
Reciprocity treaty between U.S.A. and Barbadoes, signed by Gt. Britain . . . 16 June, 1899
Revenue, 185,475*l*.; expenditure, 182,866*l*. . for 1900
Sir Fred. M. Hodgson, appointed governor . Oct. ,,
Much incendiarism of sugar-cane crops . Feb. 1901
Sir Conrad Reeves, eminent chief justice, of negro blood, died, aged 75 . . . . . 8 Jan. 1902
Sugar crisis, cost of production greater than the sale . . . . Feb. ,,
Estimated fall of 2,000,000 tons of volcanic dust in the island from Mt. Souffrière in St. Vincent; *which see* . . . . . . 7-10 May, ,,
Outbreak of smallpox reported . . 2 Aug. ,,
Smallpox riot at Bridgetown . . . 25 Aug. ,,
Epidemic ceases . . . . . . 4 April, 1903

BARBARY, in N. Africa, considered to comprise Algeria, Morocco, Fez, Tunis, and Tripoli, with their dependencies. Piratical states (nominally subject to Turkey) were founded on the coast by Barbarossa about 1518.

BARBERS lived in Greece in the 5th century, and at Rome in the 3rd century B.C. In England, formerly, the business of a surgeon was united to the barber's, and he was denominated a BARBER-SURGEON. A London company was formed in 1308, and incorporated, 1462. This union was partially dissolved in 1540, and wholly so in 1745. "No person using any shaving or barbery in London shall occupy any surgery, letting of blood, or other matter, except only drawing of teeth." 32 Hen. VIII. 1540.

BARBUDA, a small West India isle, a dependant of Antigua, *which see*.

BARCA (N. Africa), the Greek Barce, a colony of Cyrene. It was successively subjugated by the Persians, Egyptians, and Saracens. In 1550 the sultan Solyman combined Barca with the newly conquered pashalik of Tripoli.

BARCELONA (N. E. Spain), an ancient maritime city, said to have been rebuilt by Hamilcar Barca, father of the great Hannibal, about 233 B.C. It was held by the Romans, Goths, Moors, and Franks, and, with the province of which it is the capital, was made an independent country about A.D. 864, and incorporated with Aragon, 1164, the last count becoming king. The city has suffered much by war. The siege by the French in 1694 was relieved by the approach of the English fleet, commanded by admiral Russell; but the city was taken by the earl of Peterborough in 1706. It was bombarded and taken by the duke of Berwick and the French in 1714, and was taken by Napoleon in 1808, and retained till 1814. It revolted against the queen in 1841, and was bombarded and taken in Dec. 1842, by Espartero. Frequent insurrections here; one suppressed Jan. 1874. An exhibition opened by the king, Alfonso XII., 4 March, 1877. Barcelona very prosperous, 1879. Violent riots on account of French treaty, March; Catalonia in a state of siege, 30 March, 1882. Barcelona tranquil, 1 April, 1882. Population, 1887, 272,481; 1897, 509,589.

An international exhibition opened 8 April, by the queen of Spain, in the name of the infant king, who was present, with the duke and duchess of Edinburgh and other royal personages, 20 May; there was also an unexampled naval exhibition representing the fleets of ten powers; closed 9 Dec. 1888. For the disturbances here and in Catalonia, see *Spain*, March *et seq.* 1890, and Feb. 1892.

By the explosion of a bomb thrown into the midst of the audience, at the Liceo theatre, during the performance, 20 persons were killed and many wounded; many anarchists arrested, 7 Nov.; royal decree enlarging the power of arresting suspected persons, 9 Nov.; discoveries at the house of an anarchist club, chemicals, &c., Miguel Nacher (president) and over 200 persons under arrest, 22 Nov. 1893.

An anarchist laboratory discovered in a cave, with 40 bombs and large quantities of explosives, near Vallvidrera, 23 Dec. 1893.

Six men sentenced to death for attempt on the life of marshal Campos and others, and for participation in the outrage at the Liceo theatre, 4 sentenced to hard labour for life, 30 April; 2 executed, 21 May, 1894.

Salvador Franch condemned for the bomb outrage at the Liceo theatre, 11 July; executed, 21 Nov. 1894.

During a religious procession, a bomb was thrown into the crowd, about 15 persons were killed and 50 injured; 48 anarchists arrested; 7 June, 1896.

Thomas Ascheri-Jesatti, actual perpetrator of the crime, and 5 anarchists sentenced to death; executed 4 May, 1897 (20 sentenced to imprisonment; 63 acquitted); F. Callis sentenced to life imprisonment; 1 Dec. 1897

Sewer, in course of construction, falls in, 18 deaths, 11 Dec., 1898.

Anti-budget riots, Jesuit schools and convent attacked, 1–5 June, 1899.

Señ. Salvador Victory, a local politician, assassinated in the Calle Lesna, 18 Jan., 1900.

Strike riots and anti-clerical demonstrations, mid-March; again, April; state of siege proclaimed, 7 May, 1901; quiet restored, 12 May, 1901.

Many strikes and labour troubles, Jan., 1902.

Spinning factory destroyed by an explosion, about 60 deaths, 18 Jan., 1902.

General strike, fatal rioting, state of siege proclaimed, 17 Feb.; some anarchists arrested; quiet restored, 21–24 Feb. 1902.

Labour riots, the police fire on the mob, man killed, several wounded, 7 Sept.; state of siege raised, 8 Oct. 1902.

BARDESANISTS, followers of Bardesanes, of Mesopotamia, who embraced the errors of Valentinus, after refuting them, and added denial of the incarnation, resurrection, &c., about 175.

BARDS. Demodocus is mentioned as a bard by Homer; and we find bards, according to Strabo, among the Romans before the age of Augustus. The *Welsh* bards formed an hereditary order, regulated, it is said, by laws, enacted about 940 and 1078. They lost their privileges at the conquest by Edward I. in 1284. The institution was revived by the Tudor sovereigns; and their Eisteddfods (properly Eisteddfodau), meetings of 4 days, are still frequently held; at Swansea, Aug. 1863; at Llandudno, Aug. 1864; in the vale of Conway, 7 Aug. 1865, at Chester, 4 Sept. 1866; at Carmarthen, 3 Sept. 1867; at Ruthin, 5-7 Aug. 1868; at Rhyl, 8-12 Aug. 1870; at Portmadoc, Aug. 1872; at Mold, Aug. 1873; at various places in 1874-1876; at Carnarvon, 21 Aug. 1877; at Llanrwst, 1-3 Aug.; at Menai Bridge, Aug. 1878; at Conway, 6 Aug. and at other places, 1879. The Cymmrodorion Society held an Eisteddfod at Carnarvon, 23 Aug. 1880. Royal National Eisteddfod at Merthyr-Tydvil, 30 Aug. 1881; at Denbigh, 22 Aug. 1882; at Cardiff, 6 Aug. 1883; Liverpool, 16 Sept. 1884; Aberdare, Aug. 1885; Carnarvon, 14 Sept. 1886; Albert Hall, London, 9 Aug. 1887; Wrexham, 4 Sept. 1888; at Brecon, 27 Aug. 1889; Bangor (the queen of Roumania present), 2 Sept. 1890; Swansea, 18 Aug. 1891; Rhyl, 6 Sept. 1892; Pontypridd, 1 Aug. 1893; Carnarvon (prince and princess of Wales present), 10 July, 1894; Llanelly, 30 July-2 Aug. 1895; Llandudno, 29 June, 1896; Newport, 2-6 Aug. 1897; Festiniog, 19 July, 1898; Cardiff, 18 July, 1899; Liverpool, 18 Sept., 1900; Merthyr Tydvil, 6-9 Aug., 1901; Bangor, 9 Sept., 1902. The Gwyneddigion Society of Bards was founded in 1770. Turlogh O'Carolan, the last of the *Irish* bards, died in 1738. *Chambers.* Evan Davies, termed the Arch-Druid of Wales, an eminent Welsh scholar, aged 89, died at Pontypridd 23 February, 1888. In 1880 the bards determined that the Annual National Eisteddfod should be held alternately in North and South Wales. Above 100 Eisteddfodau are held every year. Clwydfardd, the Arch-Druid, aged nearly 95, died, 30 Oct. 1894. "Eisteddfod Caerlydd" held in the queen's hall, London, 22, 23 Feb., 1899. Arch-Druid, 1903, Hwfa Muo.

BAREBONE'S PARLIAMENT. Cromwell, supreme in the three kingdoms, summoned 122 persons, such as he thought he could manage, who, with six from Scotland and five from Ireland, met, as a parliament, 4 July, 1653. It obtained its appellation from a nickname given to one of its members, a leather-seller, named "Praise-God Barbon." The majority evinced much sense and spirit, proposing to reform abuses, improve the administration of the law, &c. The parliament was suddenly dissolved, 13 Dec. 1653, and Cromwell made lord protector.

BAREILLY, province of Delhi (N. W. India), ceded to the East India company by the ruler of Oude in 1801. A mutiny at Bareilly, the capital, was suppressed in April, 1816. On 7 May, 1858, it was taken from the cruel sepoy rebels.

BARFLEUR (N. France), where William, duke of Normandy, equipped the fleet by which he conquered England, 1066. Near it, William, duke of Normandy, son of Henry I., in his passage from Normandy, was shipwrecked, 25 Nov. 1120, when the prince, his bride, and many others perished. Barfleur was destroyed by the English in the campaign in which they won the battle of Crecy, 1346. The French navy was destroyed near the cape by admiral Russell, after the victory of La Hogue, 19 May, 1692.

BARI (S. Italy), the Barium of Horace, was, in the 9th century, a stronghold of the Saracens, and was captured by the emperor Louis II., a descendant of Charlemagne, in 871. In the 10th century it became subject to the eastern empire, and remained so till it was taken by Robert Guiscard, the Norman, about 1060. A great ecclesiastical council was held here on 1 Oct. 1098, when the *filioque* article of the creed and the procession of the Holy Spirit were the subjects of discussion. Conflicts between the military and populace with bloodshed, 9 Jan. 1894; and 1898.

BARING ISLAND, Arctic Sea, discovered by captain Penny in 1850-1, and so named by him after sir Francis Baring, first lord of the admiralty in 1849.

BARIUM (Greek, *barys*, heavy), a metal found abundantly as carbonate and sulphate. The oxide baryta was first recognised as an earth distinct from lime by Scheele, in 1774; and the metal was first obtained by Humphry Davy, in 1808. *Watts.*

BARK, see *Jesuits' Bark*.

BARLAAMITES, followers of Barlaam, a learned Calabrian monk of the order of St. Basil, who maintained various peculiar tenets, attacked the Greek monks, supported the Latin against the Greek church in a controversy at Constantinople, 1337, and acted as the emperor's envoy in an attempt to reconcile the churches in 1339. Died about 1348.

BARMECIDES, a powerful Persian family, celebrated for virtue and courage, were massacred through the jealousy of the caliph Haroun-al-Raschid, about 802. His visir Giafar was a Barmecide. The phrase Barmecide (or imaginary) feast originated in the story of the barber's sixth brother, in the Arabian Nights' Entertainments.

BARNABITES, an order of monks, established in Milan about 1530, were much engaged in instructing youth, relieving the sick and aged, and converting heretics.

BARNARD'S, SIR JOHN, ACT (7 Geo. II., c. 8), entitled, "an act to prevent the infamous practice of stock-jobbing," was passed in 1734, and repealed in 1860. Sir John Barnard (born 1685, died 1764) was an eminent lord mayor of London. *Barnard Peerage* case, see *Trials*, 30 May, 1892.

BARNARDO HOMES (named National Waifs Association 1899). Dr. T. J. Barnardo, of German extraction, born in Ireland, came to London, and in 1866 began energetically to promote the welfare of homeless children.

His home for boys at Stepney, founded 1870, was followed by one for girls, at Barkingside, Essex, with infirmary, schools, &c.; all were reported successful in 1874.

A Babies' Castle at Hawkhurst, Kent, for 100 infants, opened 9 Aug. 1886.

His disinterestedness and management having been impugned, he gave up the management to trustees, and invited investigation. The arbiters (Canon Miller and Messrs. J. B. Maule and Wm. Graham) in their report, after commenting on the imperfect evidence, commended the charities, and generally exonerated Dr. Barnardo, 15 Oct. 1877.

See *Coffee Palaces* and *East End Juvenile Mission*.

Several legal decisions, requiring Dr. Barnardo to produce children who had been committed to his charge, were pronounced, 1889–91.

Dr. Barnardo's appeal respecting a boy named Gossage to the house of lords was dismissed, 30 July, 1891; again, 25 July, 1892. The boy was not found, May, 1893.

Jubilee testimonial 3,417*l*. 10*s*. 4*d*. to Dr. Barnardo at Exeter-hall by 1,100 subscribers, presented by lord Kinnaird; 26 Nov. 1895.

Mr. E. H. Watts gives a large building at North Elmham, Norfolk, and 9,200*l*., etc., to the homes, Dec., 1901.

The duke of Argyll laid the foundation stones of new buildings at the Girls' Village Home, Barkingside, Essex, 11 July, 1903.

48,057 children admitted to the homes up to 31 Dec. 1902. Children maintained and educated in 1902, 9,785. Boys and girls emigrated to the colonies in 1902, 1053. Total emigrated 1867–1902, 13,184. Over 50 separate institutions are maintained in the United Kingdom and the colonies, including an immigration depot in Ontario, and an industrial farm in Manitoba.

Annual displays of the children at Albert Hall now held.

BARNET, Hertfordshire. Here, at Gladsmore heath, Edward IV. gained a decisive victory over the Lancastrians, on Easter-day, 14 April, 1471, when the earl of Warwick and his brother the marquis of Montacute, or Montague, were killed. A column commemorative of this battle has been erected at the meeting of the St. Albans and Hatfield roads. Is celebrated for its horse fairs.

BARNUM'S SHOW. The great show of Messrs. P. T. Barnum and Mr. J. A. Bailey, conveyed from Brooklyn, New York, arrived at Olympia 1 Nov., opened 11 Nov. 1889, closed Feb. 1890; re-visited England 1898; converted into a limited company, Feb., 1899. See *Olympia*, 1897, *et seq*.

The show included a Roman hippodrome and a triple American circus, a museum of living human curiosities termed "freaks of nature," a double menagerie, Jumbo's skeleton and stuffed skin, performing men and animals of many kinds (17 elephants); Imré Kiralfy's grand spectacle, "Nero; or, the destruction of Rome" (1,200 Roman characters, wild beasts, &c.). A great many simultaneous performances.

The establishment included about 1,200 people and 380 horses.

Visited by the prince of Wales and family, 20 Nov. 1889.

George Stevens, an attendant, accidentally killed by an elephant, 3 Dec. 1889.

The show closed 15 Feb.; Mr. Barnum reported his success, and thanked the British public, 17 Feb. 1890.

[Phineas T. Barnum, born at Bethel, Connecticut, U.S.A., 5 July, 1810, died at Bridgeport, 7 April, 1891. Besides very different occupations, he specially devoted himself to catering for the amusement of the people, by setting up museums, shows and other entertainments; in 1842, he brought out Charles S. Stratton, generally termed Tom Thumb (see *Dwarfs*), and in 1846 he engaged the celebrated vocalist, Jenny Lind, afterwards Mde. Goldschmidt. In 1887, his great menagerie was destroyed by fire, but was speedily renovated. His life, by himself, published 1888, and other works since.]

BARODA. See *India*, 1874—5, 1892, 1896.

BAROMETERS. Torricelli, a Florentine, knowing that water did not rise in a pump through what was supposed to be nature's abhorrence of a vacuum, imitated the action of a pump with mercury, and made the first barometer, about 1643. Pascal's experiments (1646) enhanced the value of the discovery by applying it to the measurement of heights. Wheel barometers were contrived in 1668; pendent barometers in 1695; marine in 1700; and many improvements have been made since. In the *aneroid* barometer (from *a*, no, and *neros*, watery) no liquid is employed; the atmospheric pressure being exerted on a metallic spring. Its invention (attributed to Conté, in 1798, but due to Vidi, who died in April, 1866), excited much attention in 1848–9. Barometers were placed at N.E. coast stations in 1860, by the duke of Northumberland and others.

Mr. James B. Jordan's very delicate glycerine barometer, in which one inch is expanded to nearly eleven inches, was described to the Royal Society 22 Jan., 1880, and was set up during the year at Kew and other places. The publication of two-hourly variations of one at the office begun in the *Times* 25 Oct. 1880.

A new very delicate barometer, invented by Mr. C. O. Bartrum and made by Mr. J. J. Hicks, of Hatton Garden, London, announced Aug. 1894.

Col. H. Watkin's mountain aneroid and others described *Times*, 17 Dec., 1898.

BARON, formerly the only title in our peerage, now the lowest. Its original name in England, *Vavasour*, was changed by the Saxons into *Thane*, and by the Normans into *Baron*. The council of the realm was composed of the greater barons, the lesser barons were merely tenants of the crown. Many barons had undoubtedly assisted in, or been summoned to parliament (in 1205); but the first precept found is of no higher date than the 49 Hen. III. 1265. The first raised to this dignity by patent was John de Beauchamp, created baron of Kidderminster, by Richard II., 1387. The barons took arms against king John, and compelled him to grant the great charter of our liberties, and the charter of our forests, at Runnymede, near Windsor, June, 1215. Charles II. granted a coronet to barons on his restoration, 1660.

BARON AND FEMME, or Femme, terms of Norman-French origin, used in English law signifying husband and wife.

BARONETS, the first in rank among the gentry, and the only knighthood that is hereditary, were instituted by James I., 1611. The rebellion in Ulster gave rise to this order, it having been required of a baronet, on his creation, to pay into the exchequer as much as would maintain "thirty soldiers three years at eightpence a day in the province of Ulster in Ireland." It was further required that a baronet should be a gentleman born, and have a clear estate of 1000*l.* per annum. The first baronet was sir Nicholas Bacon (his descendant, sir H. B. Bacon, is styled *Primus Baronettorum Angliæ*), 22 May, 1611. The baronets of Ireland were created in 1619; the first being sir Francis Blundell.—Baronets of Nova Scotia were created, 1625; sir Robert Gordon the first baronet.—All baronets created since the Irish union in 1801 are of the United Kingdom. Hon. Society of Baronetage formed, 26 Jan., first annual meeting, 22 July, 1898, presents memorial to the government against unauthorised assumption of the title of baronet, June, 1903.—"Complete Baronetage," by C. E. Cokayne, publication commenced 1900.

BARONS' WAR, arose in consequence of the faithlessness of Henry III. and the oppression of his favourites in 1258. The barons, headed by Simon de Montfort, earl of Leicester, and Gilbert de Clare, earl of Gloucester, met at Oxford in 1262, and enacted statutes to which the king objected. In 1263 their disputes were in vain referred to the decision of Louis IX. of France. War broke out, and on 14 May, 1264, the king's party was totally defeated at Lewes; and De Montfort became the virtual ruler of the kingdom. The war was renewed; and at the battle of Evesham, 4 Aug. 1265, De Montfort was slain, and the barons were defeated; but they did not render their final submission till 1268. A history of this war was published by Mr. W. H. Blaauw, in 1844; 2nd ed., 1871.

BARRACKS (from "*Baraque—Hutte que font les soldats en campagne pour se mettre à couvert*") were not numerous in this country until about 1789. A superintendent-general was appointed in 1793, and barracks built in the garrison towns and central points of the empire.—A report on the state of barracks, in 1858, led to their improvement under Mr. Sidney (afterwards lord) Herbert; see *Aldershot*. Mr. E. Stanhope's scheme for increase and improvement of barracks, camps, &c. (to cost about 4,100,000*l.*) submitted to the commons, 27 Feb.; the Barracks Act passed, 25 July, 1890.

BARRAGE. See under *Nile*.

BARRATRY is a general term for the stirring up suits and quarrels among the people. *Maintenance* is an officious intermeddling in a quarrel or suit; by assisting either party with money or otherwise. It is punishable by old statutes (of Richard II., and others), with fine and imprisonment. *Champerty* is an illegal bargain with either plaintiff or defendant to share in the profits of the matter in dispute.

Mr. Bradlaugh's action against Mr. Newdigate for maintenance in the case of *Clarke* v. *Bradlaugh* (see *Parliament*, 1881) was dismissed, 20 Sept. 1881.

BARREL-ORGANS, see *Organs*.

BARRICADES, mounds formed of trees and earth, for military defence. During the wars of the League in France, in 1588, the people made *barricades* by means of chains, casks, &c., and compelled the royal troops to retire. During the war of the Fronde, a barricade was erected in Paris on 27 Aug. 1648. Barricades composed of overturned vehicles, &c., were erected in Paris in the insurrections of 27-30 July, 1830, and 23-26 June, 1848, when sanguinary conflicts took place; and also 2 Dec. 1851.

BARRIER TREATIES. The first, between England and the Netherlands, was signed at the Hague, 29 Oct. 1709, for mutual support; annulled 1712; another treaty was concluded at Utrecht, 29 Jan. 1713. The third, by which the Low Countries were ceded to the emperor Charles VI., was signed by the British, Imperial, and Dutch ministers, 15 Nov. 1715.

BARRISTERS are said to have been first appointed by Edward I., about 1291, but there is earlier mention of professional advocates. They are of various ranks, as king's or queen's counsel, serjeants, &c., *which see*. Students for the bar must keep a certain number of terms at the inns of court, previously to being called; and by the regulations of 1853 must pass a public examination. See *Women*, 1900.

A committee of the bar, formed about 1885 to protect the rights of barristers in relation to the Inns of Court, merged into the general council. At a meeting of the bar in Lincoln's Inn hall, called by the general council, a compromise was arranged. The Inns of Court agreed to give an annual contribution of 600*l.* to the bar, 19 June, 1895.

BARROSA, or Barossa (S. Spain). The British army, commanded by major-general sir Thomas Graham, afterwards lord Lynedoch, totally defeated the French under marshal Victor, 5 March, 1811, the French leaving nearly 3000 dead, six pieces of cannon, and an eagle, the first that the British had taken; the loss of the British was 1169 men killed and wounded.

BARROW ISLAND (Arctic Sea), discovered by Captain Penny in 1850-51, and named by him in honour of John Barrow, Esq., son of sir John.

BARROW-IN-FURNESS (Lancashire), in 1847, was a village with a population of about 330, which, in 1867, had increased to above 17,000, and in 1874 to 35,000, in consequence of the large manufacture of iron from the ore (hæmatite) found there. On 19 Sept. 1867, new docks were opened in the presence of the dukes of Devonshire and Buccleuch (proprietors of the land), Mr. Gladstone, and others. Barrow was made a municipal borough in 1867. Sir James Ramsden, an eminent promoter of the prosperity of the town and its first mayor, died, aged 74, 19 Oct. 1896. Population in 1881, 47,259; 1891, 51,712; 1901, 57,584.

BARROW'S STRAITS (N. Arctic Sea), explored by Edwd. Parry, as far as Melville island, lat. 74° 26′ N., and long. 113° 47′ W. The strait, named after sir John Barrow, was entered on 2 Aug., 1819. The thermometer was 55° below zero of Fahrenheit.

BARROWISTS, a name given to the *Brownists, which see.*

BARROWS, circular or oblong mounds, found in Britain and other countries, were ancient sepulchres. Sir Richard Hoare caused several barrows near Stonehenge to be opened; in them were found Celtic ornaments, such as beads, buckles, and brooches, in amber, wood, and gold: Nov. 1808. 230 barrows were opened and discoveries made, chiefly in Yorkshire, 1866 *et seq.*, under the superintendence of the rev. canon Wm. Greenwell, who published his elaborate work, "British Barrows," in December, 1877.

Barrows at Aldbourne, North Wilts, were opened by canon Greenwell and rev. Walter Money, Sept.-Oct. 1878.

Canon Greenwell gave urns and other results of his explorations to the British museum in 1879.

BARS in music appear in Agricola's "Musica Instrumentalis," 1529; and in Morley's "Practical Music," 1597, for score music. Henry Lawes used them in his "Ayres and Dialogues," 1653.

BARTHOLOMEW, ST., THE APOSTLE, martyred 71. The festival (24 Aug. O.S., 3 Sept. N.S.) is said to have been instituted 1130.

Monastery of St. Bartholomew (of Austin Friars) founded by Rahere, a minstrel of Henry I. . 1102
The *hospital* founded by him . . . . . about 1123
Refounded after the dissolution of monasteries (it then contained 100 beds, with 1 physician and 3 surgeons), 1544; incorporated 1546
William Harvey, physiologist, physician here 1609-43
Earliest record of medical school 1662
Hospital rebuilt by subscription 1729
Medical college founded 1843
New buildings for *Medical School*, museum, &c., opened by the prince of Wales . . 3 Nov. 1879
The Convalescent Home at Swanley, Kent, for which C. T. Kettlewell gave 10,000*l.*, was opened by the prince of Wales . . . . 13 July, 1885
Acquired portion of site of Christ's Hospital. Mansion House committee of inquiry as to enlargement (300,000*l.* required, present income 70,554*l.*), lord Sandhurst and 8 others . . . . Jan. 1903
Bartholomew the Great, St., near Smithfield. The building of the church said to have begun 1102, restored by subscription and re-opened 29 March, 1868; again, 14 March, 1891; further restored; re-opened by the abp. of Canterbury, 5 June, 1893; the Lady Chapel re-opened . 18 May, 1897
Bartholomew Fair. The charter was granted by Henry I., 1133, and was long held in Smithfield, *which see.* The shows were discontinued in 1850, and the fair was proclaimed for the last time in 1855. In 1858 Mr. H. Morley published his "History of Bartholomew Fair," with many illustrations.

The Massacre of St. Bartholomew commenced at Paris on the night of the festival . 24 Aug. 1572

According to Sully, 70,000 Huguenots, or French Protestants, including women and children, were murdered throughout the kingdom by secret orders from Charles IX., at the instigation of his mother, the queen dowager, Catherine de Medicis.

La Popélionère calculates the victims at 20,000; Adriani, De Serres, and De Thou say 30,000; Davila states them at 40,000; and Péréfixe makes the number 100,000. Above 500 persons of rank, and 10,000 of inferior condition, perished in Paris alone, besides those slaughtered in the provinces. Pope Gregory XIII. ordered a *Te Deum* to be performed, with other rejoicings.

BARTHOLOMEW, ST., a West Indian island, held by Sweden. It was colonised by the French in 1648; and has been several times taken and restored by the British. It was ceded to Sweden by France in 1785; captured by the English and restored, 1801; ceded to France, 1877.

BARTHOLOMITES, a religious order expelled from Armenia, settled at Genoa 1307, where is preserved in the Bartholomite church the image which Christ is said to have sent to king Abgarus. The order suppressed by pope Innocent X. 1650.

BARTON AQUEDUCT (near Manchester) was constructed by James Brindley, to carry the Bridgewater canal over the Irwell, at a height of 39 feet above the river; completed in 1761.

BASEBALL, see *American Baseball.*

BASEL (Basle, French Bâle), a rich city in Switzerland. The 18th general council sat here from Dec. 1431 to May, 1443. Many important reforms in the church were proposed, but not carried into effect: among others the union of the Greek and Roman churches. The university was founded in 1460. Treaties of peace between France, Spain, and Prussia were concluded here in 1795. It was made a free imperial city 1392, but joined the Swiss confederation 1501. Pop. 1901, 111,009. Zionist Congress held here 23 August, 1903.

BASHI-BAZOUKS, irregular Turkish troops, employed partially in the Crimean war, 1854-6, and the Russo-Turkish war of 1877-78.

BASIENTELLO (S. Naples). Here the army of Otho II., in an ambuscade, was nearly cut to pieces by the Greeks and Saracens 13 July, 982; the emperor barely escaped.

BASILIANS, an order of monks, which obtained its name from St. Basil (who died 380); was reformed by pope Gregory, in 1569.—A *sect*, founded by Basil, a physician of Bulgaria, which rejected the books of Moses, the eucharist, and baptism, and are said to have had everything in common, 1110. Basil was burnt alive in 1118.

BASILICA, a body of law, in Greek, including the Institutes of Justinian, the Pandects, &c., arranged by order of the emperor Basil the Macedonian, and his son Leo the Philosopher, 875—911. The term *basilica* (palace) was applied to places of worship under the early Christian emperors from their general resemblance to the Roman basilica.

BASILIKON DORON (Royal Gift), precepts on the art of government, composed by James I. of England for his son Henry, and first published at Edinburgh in 1599. The collected works of this monarch were published at London, 1616-20, in one vol. fol.

BASQUE PROVINCES, N. W. Spain (Biscay, Guipuscoa, and Alava). The Basques are considered by some to be descendants of the ancient Iberi, were termed Vascones by the Romans, whom they successfully resisted. They were subdued with great difficulty by the Goths about 580, and were united to Castile in the 13th and 14th centuries. The origin of the Basque language, like its ethnology, is very obscure; it is polysynthetic, and no connection between it and any other language has yet been determined.

BASQUE ROADS (W. France). Fourteen French ships of the line, riding at anchor here, were attacked by lords Gambier and Cochrane (the latter commanding the fireships), and all were destroyed, 11—29 April, 1809. Cochrane accused Gambier of neglecting to support him. At a court-martial, 26 July—4 Aug., lord Gambier was acquitted.

BASSANO (N. Italy). Here the Austrians, under Wurmser, were defeated by the French under Massena, 8 Sept. 1796.

BASSEIN, Bombay; a Mahratta town, taken by the British, 1774, 1780; finally annexed by them, 1818. By treaty here, 31 Dec. 1802, they engaged to support the peishwa's rights.

BASSETERRE-ROADS, St. Christopher's, West Indies. Here the French admiral, the comte de Grasse, was repulsed with loss in three desperate attacks on the British fleet, commanded by sir Thomas Graves, 25, 26 Jan. 1782.

BASSETT, or BASSETTE, or *Pour et Contre*, a game at cards, said to have been invented by a noble Venetian, in the 15th century; introduced into France, 1674.

BASSOON, a wooden double-reed wind instrument, said to have been invented by Afranio, a canon of Ferrara, early in the sixteenth century.

BASSORAH, BUSSORAH, or BASRAH (Asia Minor), a Turkish city, founded by the caliph Omar, about 635. It has been several times taken and retaken by the Persians and Turks.

BASS ROCK, an isle in the Frith of Forth (S. Scotland), was granted to the Lauders, 1316; purchased for a state prison, 1671; taken by the Jacobites, 1690; surrendered, 1694; granted to the Dalrymples, 1706.

BASS'S STRAIT, AUSTRALIA. Mr. Bass, surgeon of the *Reliance*, in an open boat from Port Jackson, in 1796, penetrated as far as Western Port, and affirmed that a strait existed between New South Wales and Van Diemen's Land. Lieutenant Flinders circumnavigated Van Diemen's Land, and named the strait after Mr. Bass, 1798–9.

BASTARD, a child not born in lawful wedlock. An attempt in England, in 1236, to legitimate bastard children by the subsequent marriage of the parents, failed. The barons assembled in the parliament of Merton answered: *Nolumus leges Angliæ mutari* ("We will not have the laws of England changed"). Women concealing their children's birth deemed guilty of murder, 21 James I., 1624. In Scotland bastard children could not dispose of their movable estates by will until 1836. A new act, facilitating the claims of mothers, and making several provisions for proceeding in bastardy cases, was passed 1845. The Bastardy Laws Amendment Act was passed 10 Aug. 1872. See *Russia*, 1891.

BASTARNÆ, a warlike tribe in Podolia and Moldavia, hired by Perseus, king of Macedon, in his wars with Rome, 168 B.C.; driven across the Danube by M. Crassus for their encroachments, 30.

BASTILLE, Paris, a castle built by Charles V., king of France, in 1369, for the defence of Paris against the English; completed in 1383, and afterwards used as a state prison. Henry IV. and his veteran army assailed it in vain in the siege of Paris, during the war (1587—1594). "The man with the iron mask," the most mysterious prisoner known, died here, 19 Nov. 1703; see *Iron Mask*. On 14-15 July, 1789, the Bastille was pulled down by the populace; the governor and other officers were conducted to the Place de Grève; their hands and heads were cut off, and the heads carried on pikes through the streets. A centenary was celebrated 14 July, 1889.

BASUTO LAND, near Orange River, South Africa, including the Transkei territory, was annexed to Cape Colony in 1871. Population in 1875, whites, 469; natives, 127,707: in 1891, 218,324 natives, and 578 Europeans. Resident commissioner, col. sir M. J. Clarke, Jan. 1894; Godfrey Y. Lagden (aft. sir), 1895; Herbert C. Slobey, 1902.

Moiroso, a warlike chief, entrenches himself on a mountain and makes predatory sallies, Feb. *et seq.*; his stronghold captured and himself killed during the fight . . . . . 20 Nov. 1879
The Basutos ordered to give up their arms; many resist; Letsi, Molappo, and others who surrender, attacked by Masupha, Lerothodi, and others, June, July, who make war on the colonist forces . . . . . 13 Sept. 1880
Lerothodi defeated in attack on Mafeteng by col. Carrington . . . . . 21 Sept. ,,
Mafeteng, besieged, relieved by col. Clarke, after a severe conflict . . . . 19 Oct. ,,
Lerothodi's village stormed and his forces dispersed 22 Oct. ,,
Moletsane's stronghold stormed by colonel Clarke 31 Oct. ,,
Mr. Hope, magistrate, and others treacherously murdered by Umhlonhlo, Oct.; who is defeated by Mr. Hawthorn; announced . . 12 Nov. ,,
Umhlonhlo totally defeated by Baker 21 Dec. ,,
Victories of col. Carrington about 10, 14 Jan. 1881
Armistice granted 18–24 Feb. ,,
Hostilities resumed; indecisive; col. Carrington wounded . . . . 26 March, ,,
Basutos severely defeated . . about 16 April, ,,
Peace concluded . . . . . . May, ,,
The chief Masupha submits . . . . Sept. ,,
Again troublesome . . . . . . Oct. 1882
Gen. Gordon appointed to settle difficulties, resigns through disagreement with the Cape government, announced autumn . . . . ,,
Peace restored . . . . Dec. ,,
Self-government granted . . . . . Feb. 1883
Much fighting among chiefs; subsides . . May, ,,
The British agree to resume the government as a crown colony under conditions . . . June, ,,
The Cape parliament assents . . . 27 July, ,,
The Basuto chiefs accept conditions at a great meeting; Masupha stands aloof . announced 8 Dec. ,,
Jonathan defeats Joel with great slaughter, 15-16 Mar. 1884
Battles between Khetisa, Masupha, and Lerothodi, 23 March, ,,
Basuto land reported quiet and prosperous . 1887-90
Masupha (died, July, 1899) refuses to give up his son Moiketsi (for assault and gaol-breaking in the Orange Free State); Lerothodi, the paramount chief, captures Thaba Besigo . 7 Jan. 1898
Moiketsi given up to Lerothodi, 18 Jan.; Masupha surrenders, 31 Jan.; is banished and fined; Moiketsi sentenced to over a year's imprisonment 1 Feb. ,,
Lerothodi and his chiefs pledge loyalty to the queen, sir Godfrey Lagden present . 24 Oct. 1899
Steady progress, country quiet and prosperous, reported . . . . end Dec. 1901
Joel Molapo, a minor chief, sentenced to a year's imprisonment for treason, etc. . 17 July, 1902

BATALHA, Portugal. The monastery here was built by John I., of Portugal, as a token of gratitude for his victory over John I. of Castile, at Aljubarrota, 14 Aug. 1385, securing the independence of his kingdom. The restoration of the monastery began in 1839.

BATAVIA AND BATAVIAN REPUBLIC, see *Holland*.

BATAVIA, the capital of Java, and of all the Dutch settlements in the East Indies, built by that people about 1619. Taken from the French (who had seized it) by sir Samuel Auchmuty, 26 Aug. 1811; restored to the Dutch in 1814. See *Java*.

BATH (Somerset), named "*Aquæ solis*" by the Romans, being remarkable for its hot springs. They built extensive baths, the exact site disputed. Coel, a British king, is said to have given this city a charter, and the Saxon king Edgar was crowned here, 973. See *Population*.

Bath plundered and burnt in the reign of William Rufus, and again in 1137
The abbey church commenced in 1405; finished . 1609
Beau (Richard) Nash, "king of Bath," who promoted fame of the waters, and amusements, died Feb. 1761
Present assembly-rooms built 1771
Pump-room erected 1704; rebuilt 1797
Theatre, Beaufort-square, opened 1805
Bath philosophical society formed 1817
Bath royal literary and scientific institution established 1825
Victoria park opened by princess Victoria . . 1830
Theatre burnt . . . . 18 April, 1862
Restoration of the abbey by Sir G. G. Scott 1863 *et seq.*
British association met here 14 Sept. 1864; and 5 Sept. 1888
Museum destroyed by fire . . . . 20 Jan. 1867
Bath and West of England society centenary celebrated, 4 June; fall of Widcombe bridge, 2 persons killed and many injured . . 6 June, 1877
Remains of Roman baths discovered . 1877, *et seq.*
The art museum, containing pictures, etc. bequeathed by sir Thomas Holburne, opened, June 1893
Much suffering through overflow of the Avon, Nov. 1894
Death of Mrs. Roxburgh, benefactress to the city Nov. 1896
New pump-room opened and the Victoria art gallery founded by the duke of Cambridge . . 18 Oct. 1897
Lord Rosebery unveils memorials to the two Pitts, is presented with the freedom of the city, 27 Oct. 1898
State visit of the lord mayor of London, 10, 11 Sept. 1902
Lord Roberts presented with the freedom, 26 Sept. ,,

BATH AND WELLS, BISHOPRIC OF. The see of Wells, whose cathedral church was built by Ina, king of the West Saxons, in 704, was established in 905, Adelme first bishop. John de Villula, bishop, transferred his seat from Wells to Bath in 1091. *Tanner*. Disputes between the monks of Bath and the canons of Wells about the election of a bishop, were compromised in 1135. Henceforward the bishop was to be styled from both places; the precedency to be given to Bath. The see is valued in the king's books at 531*l.* 1*s.* 3*d.* per annum. Present income, 5000*l.*

Recent Bishops.

1802. Richard Beadon, died . . . 21 April, 1824
1824. George Henry Law, died . . 22 Sept. 1845
1845. Richard Bagot, died . . . 5 May, 1854
1854. Robert John, baron Auckland, resigned 6 Sept. 1869
1869. Lord Arthur Charles Hervey, elected 10 Nov. 1869; died . . . . . 9 June, 1894
1894. George Wyndham Kennion, bp. of Adelaide, elected 4 Sept. 1894.

BATH ADMINISTRATION. Mr. Pelham and his friends having tendered their resignation to king George II., 10 Feb. 1746, the formation of a new ministry was undertaken by William Pulteney, earl of Bath. This expired on 12 Feb., while yet incomplete, and received the name of the "Short-lived" administration. The members of it were: the earl of Bath, *first lord of the treasury;* lord Carlisle, *lord privy seal;* lord Winchilsea, *first lord of the admiralty;* and lord Granville, one of the secretaries of state, with the seals of the other in his pocket, "to be given to whom he might choose." Mr. Pelham and his colleagues returned to power.

BATH, ORDER OF THE, said to be of early origin, but formally constituted 11 Oct., 1399, by Henry IV., two days previous to his coronation in the Tower, when he conferred the order upon forty-six esquires, who had watched the night before, and bathed. After the coronation of Charles II. the order was neglected until 18 May, 1725, when it was revived by George I., who fixed the number of knights at 37.

The prince regent (afterwards George IV.) created classes of knights grand crosses (72), knights commanders (180), with an unlimited number of companions . . . . 2 Jan. 1815
By an order, the existing statutes of this order were annulled; and by new statutes, the order, hitherto exclusively military, was opened to civilians . . . . 25 May, 1847
Dr. Lyon Playfair and other promoters of the Great Exhibition received this honour . . . 1851

CONSTITUTION.		*Military.*	*Civil.*
1st Class.	Knights grand cross,	50	25
2nd Class.	Knights commanders,	100	50
3rd Class.	Companions,	525	200

The order was further enlarged, June, 1861.

BATHOMETER (Greek, *bathus*, deep), an apparatus invented by Dr. C. William Siemens to measure the depth of water without submerging a sounding-line, 1861-76.

Its action depends on the diminution of the effect of gravitation on the surface of the water as compared with its effect on the earth, owing to the mass of water (of less density) which replaces earth (of greater density): which is duly registered.

BATHS were early used in Asia and Greece, and introduced by Agrippa into Rome, where many were constructed by Augustus and his successors. The thermæ of the Romans and gymnasia of the Greeks (of which baths formed merely an appendage) were sumptuous. The marble group of Laocoön was found in 1506 in the baths of Titus, erected about 80, and the Farnese Hercules in those of Caracalla, erected 211.

In LONDON, St. Agnes Le Clere, in Old-street-road, was a spring of great antiquity; baths said to have been formed in 1502.
St. Chad's-well, Gray's-inn-road, derives its name from St. Chad, the fifth bishop of Lichfield, 667.
A bath opened in Bagnio-court, now Bath-street, Newgate-street, London, is said to have been the first bath in England for hot bathing . . . 1679
Old Bath-house, Coldbath-square, in use . . 1697
Peerless (Perilous) Pool, Baldwin-street, City-road, mentioned by Stow (died 1605); enclosed as a bathing place 1743
Turkish sweating baths became popular . . . 1860
The Oriental baths in Victoria-street, Westminster, completed 1862

PUBLIC BATHS AND WASH-HOUSES.

The first established by Mr. Bowie in the neighbourhood of the London docks 1844
The public baths and wash-houses in Liverpool founded (through the instrumentality of Catherine Wilkinson, who in 1832 began to lend her room and appliances to poor people for washing) ,,
Acts passed to encourage the establishment of public baths and wash-houses, "for the health, comfort, and welfare of the inhabitants of populous towns and districts," in England and Ireland . . . 1846

Public baths and wash-houses have since been established throughout the empire.

Baths and Wash-houses Act authorises establishment of cheap swimming baths, &c., 27 May, 1878; amended, 1882. Swimming baths when closed may, by license, be used for music or dancing, 1896 and 1899

Swimming classes for boys and girls provided for by many Board Schools 1903

See *Laundry*.

BATHYBIUS HÆCKELII (Greek, *bathus*, deep; *bios*, life), the name given by Huxley, 1868, to a supposed low form of animal life, a gelatinous substance found on stones at the bottom of the sea, in *Deep Sea Soundings* (*which see*). Described by Hæckel, 1870. Its existence is now doubted by naturalists.

BATHYMETRY, the art of measuring depths in the sea, especially for scientific investigation; see *Deep Sea Soundings*.

BATON, a truncheon borne by generals in the French army, and afterwards by the marshals of other nations. Henry III. of France, before he ascended the throne, was made generalissimo of the army of his brother Charles IX., and received the *bâton* as the mark of the high command, 1569. *Henault*. The baton used by conductors of concerts is said to have been introduced into England by Spohr, in 1820.

BATON ROUGE, Louisiana, United States, was captured by the Federals, 5 Aug. 1862, after a fierce conflict; see *United States*, 1862.

BATOUM, or **BATUM**, a seaport in Lazistan, on the Black Sea. After having repulsed the Russians in the war, 4 May, 1877, the place was ceded to Russia by the treaty of Berlin, 13 July, 1878, to become a free commercial port. The port was closed by Russia on and after 17 July, 1886.

The inhabitants at first resisted, but were persuaded to submit; many emigrating, July–Sept. The Russians entered, 6 Sept. 1878.

Foundation of a new cathedral laid by the czar, 7 Oct. 1888.

Disastrous explosion, great loss of life and property, 25 July, 1901.

BATTERIES along the coasts were constructed by Henry VIII. (who reigned 1509-47). The ten floating batteries with which Gibraltar was attacked, in the siege of that fortress, were invented by D'Arcon, a French engineer. They resisted the heavy shells and 32-pound shot, but ultimately yielded to red-hot shot, 13 Sept. 1782; see *Gibraltar*. Formidable floating batteries are now erected. See *Navy*, *Electricity*.

BATTERING-RAM, *Testudo Arietaria*, with other military implements, are said to have been invented by Artemon, a Lacedæmonian, and employed by Pericles, about 441 B.C. Sir Christopher Wren employed a battering-ram in demolishing the walls of old St. Paul's cathedral, 1675.

BATTERSEA PARK; an act of parliament passed in 1846, empowered her majesty's commissioners of woods to form a royal park in Battersea-fields. Acts to enlarge their powers were passed in 1848, 1851, and 1853. The park and the new bridge connecting it with Chelsea were opened in April, 1858; the bridge freed from toll, 24 May, 1879. Albert Exhibition palace opened here, 6 June, 1885; closed 1888. Battersea returns two M.P.'s by Act passed 25 June, 1885. New Battersea bridge opened by the earl of Rosebery, 21 July, 1890. See *Parks*. A new Polytechnic hall opened by Mr. Balfour, 3 Feb. 1899. Sir C. Dilke opens public baths and washhouses, 20 April, 1901.

Battersea Training College, founded 1840.

BATTLE, TRIAL BY, or WAGER OF, a trial by combat formerly allowed by our laws, where the defendant in an appeal of murder might fight with the appellant, and make proof thereby of his guilt or innocence; see *Appeal*.

BATTLE-ABBEY, Sussex, founded by William I., 1067, on the plain where the battle of Hastings was fought, 14 Oct. 1066. It was dedicated to St. Martin, and given to Benedictine monks, who were to pray for the souls of the slain. The original name of the plain was Hetheland; see *Hastings*. After the battle of Hastings, a list was taken of William's chiefs, amounting to 629, and called the "BATTEL-ROLL;" and among these chiefs the lands and titles of the followers of the defeated Harold were distributed. "The Roll of Battle Abbey," edited by the duchess of Cleveland, was published, with notes, &c., in 1889. The abbey and domain, 6,118 acres, sold to sir Augustus Webster for 200,000*l.*, 26 Nov. 1901; pictures and heirlooms, etc., realized, 16,500*l.*, 8 March, 1902.

BATTLE-AXE, a weapon of the Celts. The Irish were constantly armed with an axe. *Burns*. At the battle of Bannockburn king Robert Bruce clove an English champion down to the chine at one blow with a battle-axe, 1314. The battle-axe guards, or beaufetiers, vulgarly called beef-eaters, and whose arms are a sword and lance, were first raised by Henry VII. in 1485. They were originally attendants upon the king's buffet; see *Yeoman of the Guard*.

BATTLEFIELD, BATTLE OF, see *Shrewsbury*.

BATTLES. Palamedes of Argos is mythically said to have been the first who ranged an army in a regular line of battle, placed sentinels round a camp, and excited the soldier's vigilance by giving him a watchword, and to have been treacherously slain by the Greeks before Troy. See *Naval Battles, British*. The following are the most memorable battles, arranged in chronological order; further details of the greater part are given in separate articles; *n.* signifies *naval*.

The following are the battles described by Professor Creasy in his "Fifteen Decisive Battles of the World":—

		B.C.			A.D.
Marathon		490	Hastings	14 Oct.	1066
Syracuse		413	Orleans	29 April,	1429
Arbela	1 Oct.	331	Spanish Armada	July,	1588
Metaurus		207	Blenheim	13 Aug.	1704
		A.D.	Pultowa	8 July,	1709
Teutoburg		9	Saratoga	17 Oct.	1777
Chalons		451	Valmy	20 Sept.	1792
Tours	10 Oct.	732	Waterloo	18 June,	1815

		B.C.
Abraham defeats kings of Canaan (*Gen.* xiv.)		1913
Joshua subdues five kings of Canaan (*Josh.* x.)		1451
Gideon defeats the Midianites (*Judges* vii.)		1245
Trojan war commenced		1193
Troy taken and destroyed		1184
Jephthah defeats Ammonites		1143
Ethiopians defeated by Asa (2 *Chron.* xiv.)		941
Horatii vanquish Curiatii		669
Halys (*Medes and Lydians stopped by eclipse*)	584 or	585
Thymbra (*Cyrus defeats Crœsus*)		548
Lake Regillus (*Romans defeat Latins*)		499
Marathon (*Greeks defeat Persians*)	28 or 29 Sept.	490
Thermopylæ (*heroism of Leonidas*)	7-9 Aug.	480
Salamis *n.* (*Greeks defeat Persians*)	20 Oct.	,,
Himera (*Gelon defeats Carthaginians*)		,,
Mycale (*Greeks defeat Persians*)	22 Sept.	479
Platæa (*ditto: Pausanias*)	22 Sept.	,,

Eurymedon *n.* (*Greeks defeat Persians: Cimon*) B.C. 469
Tanagra (*Spartans defeat Athenians*) 457
Œnophyta (*Athenians defeat Bœotians*) 456
Coronea (*Bœotians defeat Athenians*) 447
Romans totally defeat Veientes 437
Tanagra (*Athenians defeat Spartans*) 426
Delium (*Bœotians defeat Athenians*) 424
Amphipolis (*Spartans repulse Athenians: Cleon and Brasidas killed*) 422
Mantinea (*Spartans defeat Athenians*) 418
Athenians defeated before Syracuse 413
Cyzicus *n.* (*Alcibiades defeats Spartans*) 410
Arginusæ *n.* (*Conon defeats Spartan fleet*) 406
Ægospotamos *n.* (*Athenian fleet destroyed*) 405
Cunaxa (*Cyrus defeated and killed by Artaxerxes*) 401
Corinthian War 395-387
Haliartus (*Lysander killed*) 395
Cnidus *n.* (*Conon defeats Spartans*) 394
Coronea (*Argesilaus defeats Athenians and allies*) ,,
Allia (*Brennus and the Gauls defeat Romans*) 16 July, 390
Volsci defeated by Camillus 381
Volsci defeat the Romans 379
Naxus (*Chabrias defeats Lacedæmonians*) 376 or 377
Tegyra (*Thebans defeat Spartans*) 375
Leuctra (*Thebans defeat Spartans*) 371
"Tearless Victory" of Archidamus over Argives, &c. 367
Camillus defeats the Gauls ,,
Cynoscephalæ (*Thebans defeat Thessalians*) 364
Mantinea (*Thebans victors: Epaminondas slain*) 362
Tamynæ (*Æschines there*) 358
Crimisus (*Timoleon defeats Carthaginians*) 339
Chæronea (*Philip defeats Athenians, &c.*) Aug. 338
Thebes destroyed by Alexander 335
Granicus (*Alexander defeats Darius*) 22 May, 334
Issus (*ditto*) Oct. 333
Arbela (*ditto*) 1 Oct. 331
Pandosia (*Alexander of Epirus defeated and killed*) 326
Cranon (*Antipater defeats Greeks*) 322
Caudine Forks (*Roman army captured*) 321
Gaza (*Ptolemy defeats Demetrius*) 312
Ecnomus or Himera (*Carthaginians defeat Agathocles*) 310
Fabius defeats the Tuscans ,,
Vadimonian Lake (*Etruscans defeated*) 309
Ipsus (*Seleucus defeats Antigonus, who is slain*) 301
Sentinum (*Romans defeat Samnites*) 295
Gauls defeat Romans at Arretium, 284; defeated by Dolabella 283
Vadimonian Lake (*Etruscans defeated*) ,,
Corus (*Lysimachus defeated and killed*) 281
Pandosia (*Pyrrhus defeats Romans*) 280
Asculum (*ditto*) 279
Beneventum (*Romans defeat Pyrrhus*) 275
First Punic War begins 264
Mylæ *n.* (*Romans defeat Carthaginians*) 260
Xantippus defeats Regulus 255
Panormus (*Asdrubal defeated by Metellus*) 250
Drepanum *n.* (*Carthaginians defeat Romans*) 249
Lilybæum taken by Romans 241
Ægates *n.* (*Romans defeat Carthaginians*) ,,
Ladocea (*Achæans defeated*) 226
Clusium or Pisæ (*Gauls defeated*) 225
Sellasia (*Macedonians defeat Spartans*) 221
Caphyæ (*Achæans defeat Ætolians*) 220
Saguntum (*taken by Hannibal*) 219
Second Punic War. — Ticinus (*Hannibal defeats Romans*) 218
Ticinus and Trebia (*ditto*) ,,
Trasimene (*ditto*) 217
Raphia (*Antiochus defeated by Ptol. Philopater*) ,,
Cannæ (*Victory of Hannibal*) 2 Aug. 216
Munda (*Scipio defeats Hasdrubal*) ,,
Marcellus and Hannibal (*former killed*) 209
Metaurus (*Nero defeats Hasdrubal, who is killed*) 207
Zama (*Scipio defeats Hannibal*) 202
Abydos (*siege of*) 200
Paneas (*Antiochus defeats Egyptians, &c.*) 198
Cynoscephalæ (*Romans defeat Macedonians*) 197
Boii defeated at the Vadimonian lake 191
Thermopylæ (*Greeks defeated*) ,,
Magnesia (*Scipio defeats Antiochus*) 190
Pydna (*Romans defeat Perseus*) 22 June, 168
Eleasa (*Judas Maccabæus killed*) 161
Third Punic War 149
Leucopetra (*Mummius defeats Achæans*) 147
Carthage taken by Publius Scipio 146
Mummius takes Corinth ,,
Allobroges defeated by Q. Fabius Maxim 121

Metellus defeats Jugurtha 109
Arausio (*Cimbri defeat Romans*) 105
Aquæ Sextiæ (Aix; *Marius defeats the Teutones*) 102
Cimbri and Romans (*defeated by Marius*) 101
Chæronea (*Sylla defeats Mithridates' army*) 86
Sacriportus (*Marius defeated by Sylla*) 82
Cabeira (*Lucullus defeats Mithridates*) 71
Petelia (*Spartacus defeated by Crassus*) ,,
Tigranocerta (*Lucullus defeats Tigranes*) 69
Pistoria (*Catiline defeated*) 62
Cæsar defeats Cassivelaunus in Britain 54
Carrhæ (*Crassus defeated by Parthians*) 9 June, 53
Pharsalia (*Cæsar defeats Pompey*) 9 Aug. 48
Zela (*Cæsar defeats Pharnaces; writes, "Veni, vidi, vici"*) 47
Thapsus (*Cæsar defeats Pompey's friends*) 46
Munda (*ditto*) 17 March, 45
Mutina (*Hirtius defeats Antony*) 27 April, 43
Philippi (*Brutus and Cassius defeated*) 42
Mylæ, *n.* (*Agrippa defeats Pompey the Younger*) 36
Actium *n.* (*Octavius defeats Antony*) 2 Sept. 31
Teutoburg (*Varus defeated by Herman*) A.D. 9
Shropshire (*Caractacus taken*) 50
Sunbury (?) (*Romans defeat Boadicea*) 61
Jerusalem taken by Titus 70
Agricola conquers Mona or Anglesea 78
Ardoch (*he defeats Galgacus and Caledonians*) 84
Dacians defeated and Decebalus slain 106
Issus (*Niger slain*) 194
Lyons (*Severus defeats Albinus*) 197
Verona (*emperor Philip defeated and killed*) 249
Decius defeated and slain by Goths 251
Valerian defeated and captured by Sapor 260
Naïssus (*Claudius defeats Goths, many slain*) 269
Chalons (*Aurelian victor over rivals*) 274
Allectus defeated in Britain 296
Constantine def. Maxentius (see *Cross*) 27 Oct. 312
Adrianople (*Constantine defeats Licinius*) 3 July, 323
Aquileia (*Constantine II. slain*) March, 340
Julian defeats Alemanni 356, 357
Thyatira and Nacolea (*Procopius defeated*) 366
Argentaria (*Gratian defeats Alemanni*) May, 378
Adrianople (*Gauls defeat Valens*) 9 Aug. ,,
Aquileia (*Maximus slain*) 28 July, 388
Aquileia (*Eugenius slain*) 6 Sept. 394
Pollentia (*Stilicho defeats Alaric*) 29 Mar. 403
Rome taken by Alaric 24 Aug. 410
Ravenna taken by Aspar 425
Franks defeated by Aëtius 428
Genseric takes Carthage 439
Châlons-sur-Marne (*Attila defeated by Aëtius*) 451
Aylesford (*Britons defeat Saxons; ? Horsa killed*) 455
Crayford, Kent (*Hengist defeats Britons*) 457
Soissons (*Clovis defeats Syagrius and Romans*) 486
Verona (*Theodoric defeats Odoacer*) 27 Sept. 489
Tolbiach or Zulpich (*Clovis defeats Alemanni*) 496
Vouglé (*Clovis defeats Visigoths*) 507
Baddesdown hill (*Britons defeat Saxons*) ? 493, 511
Veseronce (*Gondemar defeats Clodomir*) 524
Victories of Belisarius in Africa, &c. 533-4
Narses defeats Totila, 552; and Teias 553
Heraclius defeats the Persians (*Chosroes*) 622
Beder (*first victory of Mahomet*) 623
Muta (*Mahometans defeat Christians*) 629
Hatfield (Heathfield; *Penda defeats Edwin*) 633
Ajnadin (*Saracens defeat Heraclius*) 13 July, ,,
Yermuk (*Saracens victors*) 23 Aug. 634
Yermuk (*Saracens defeat Heraclius*) Nov. 636
Saracens subdue Syria 636-8
Kadseah (*Arabs defeat Persians*) 638
Saracens take Alexandria 640
Near Oswestry (*Penda defeats Oswald of Northumberland*) 5 Aug. 642
Leeds (*Oswy defeats Penda, who is slain*) 655
Day of the Camel (*Ali victor*) 4 Nov. 656
Saracens defeated by Wamba, in Spain 675
Testri (*Pepin defeats Thierry*) 687
Xeres (*Saracens defeat Roderic*) 19-26 July, 711
Amblef and Vincy (*Chas. Martel def. Neustrians*) 716-17
Tours (*Charles Martel defeats the Saracens*) 10 Oct. 732
Victories of Charlemagne 775-800
Roncesvalles (*death of Roland*) 778
Hengestdown (*Danes defeated by Egbert*) 835
Charmouth (*Ethelwolf defeated by the Danes*) 840
Fontenaille or Fontaneta (*Lothaire defeated by Charles and Louis*) 25 June, 841
Clavijo (*Moors defeated*) 844
Albaida (*Musa and Moors defeated*) 852

Danes defeat king Edmund of East Anglia . . . 870
Assendon or Ashdown (*Danes defeated*) . . . 871
Basing and Merton (*Danes victorious*) . . . ,,
Hafsfiord (*Harold Härfager's final victory*) . . . 872
Wilton (*Danes victorious over Alfred*) . . . ,,
Andernach (*Charles the Bald defeated*) . . 8 Oct. 876
Ethandun (*Alfred defeats Danes*) . . . 878
Farnham (*Danes defeated*) . . . 894
Zamora (*Alfonso defeats Moors*) . . . 901
Bury (*Edward defeats Ethelwald and Danes*) . . . 905
Tettenhall (*Danes defeated*) . . . 6 Aug. 910

Soissons (*king Robert, victor, killed*) . . . 923
Merseburg (*Germans defeat Hungarians*) . . . 934
Brunanburg (*Northmen defeated*) . . . 937
Simancas (*Spaniards defeat Moors*) . . 6 Aug. 939
Nicephorus Phocas defeats Saracens . . . 962
Basientello (*Otho II. defeated by Greeks*) . 13 July, 982

Clontarf (*Danes defeated in Ireland*) . . 23 April, 1014
Zetunium (*Bulgarians defeated*) . . 29 July, ,,
Brentford (*Edmund defeats Danes*) . . . May, 1016
Assingdon, Ashdon (*Canute defeats Edmund*) . . ,,
Sticklestadt (*Olaf defeated by Swedes*) . 29 July, 1030
Civitella (*Normans defeat Leo IX.*) . . . 1053
Dunsinane (*Macbeth defeated*) . . . 1054
Fulford (*Norwegians defeat English*) . 20 Sept. 1066
Stamford Bridge (*Harold defeats Tostig*) . 25 Sept. ,,
Hastings (*William I. defeats Harold*) . . 14 Oct. ,,
Fladenheim (*emperor Henry defeated*) . . . 1080
Crusades commence 1090
Alnwick (*Scots defeated, Malcolm slain*) 13 Nov. 1093
Dorylæum (*Crusaders defeat Turks*) . 1 July, 1097
Ascalon (*Crusaders victorious*) . 12 Aug. 1099
Tinchebray (*Robert of Normandy defeated*) . . 1106
Brenneville (*Henry I. defeated French*) . . Aug. 1119
Fraga (*Moors defeat Spaniards*) . 17 July, 1134
Northallerton, or Battle of the Standard (*David I. and Scots defeated*) . . . 22 Aug. 1138
Ourique (*Portuguese defeat Moors*) . 25 July, 1139
Lincoln (*Stephen defeated*) . . 2 Feb. 1141
Jaen (*Moors defeated by Spaniards*) . . . 1157
Carcano (*Frederic I. defeated by Italians*) 9 Aug. 1160
Alnwick (*William the Lion defeated*) . . 12 July, 1174
Legnano (*Italians defeat emperor*) . 29 May, 1176
Tiberias (*Saladin defeats Crusaders*) 3, 4 July, 1187
Ascoli (*Tancred defeats emperor Henry VI.'s army*) 1190
Acre taken by Crusaders . . 12 July, 1191
Arsouf (*Richard I. defeats Saracens*) . 6 Sept. ,,
Frèteville (*Richard I. defeats Philip II.*). 15 July, 1194
Arcadiopolis (*Bulgarians defeat emperor Isaac*) ,,
Alarcos (*Moors defeat Spaniards*). . 19 July, 1195
Gisors (*Richard I. defeats French*) 20 Sept. 1198
Tolosa (*Moors defeated*). . . 16 July, 1212
Muret (*Albigenses defeated*) . . 12 Sept. 1213
Bouvines (*French defeat Germans*) . 27 July, 1214
Lincoln (*French defeated*) . . 20 May, 1217
Corte Nuova (*Frederick II. defeats Milanese*) 27 Nov. 1237
Taillebourg (*French defeat Henry III.*) 20 July, 1242
Carizmians defeated twice . . . 1247
Fossalta (*Ghibelines defeated*) . . 26 May, 1249
Mansourah (*Louis IX. and Crusaders defeated*). 1250
Largs (*Scots defeat Northmen*) . 3 Oct. 1263
Lewes (*English barons victorious*) . 14 May, 1264
Evesham (*Barons defeated; De Montfort killed*) 4 Aug. 1265
Benevento (*Chas. of Anjou defeats Manfred*) 26 Feb. 1266
Tagliacozzo (*Charles defeats Conradin*) 23 Aug. 1268
Marchfeld (*Austrians defeat Bohemians*). 26 Aug. 1278
Aber Edw (*Llewellyn of Wales defeated*) 11 Dec. 1282
Zagrab (*defeat of Charles Martel*) . . 1292
Dunbar (*Scots defeated*) . . 27 April, 1296
Cambuskenneth (*Wallace defeats English*) 10 Sept. 1297
Gœlheim (*Adolphus of Nassau defeated*) . 2 July, 1298
Falkirk (*Wallace defeated*) . . 22 July, ,,
Courtray (*Flemings defeat count of Artois*) 11 July, 1302
Roslin, Scotland (*Comyn defeats English*) 24 Feb. 1303
Cephisus (*Brienne, duke of Athens defeated*) March, 1311
Bannockburn (*Bruce defeats English*) . 24 June, 1314
Morgarten (*Swiss defeat Austrians*) . 15 Nov. 1315
Athenry (*Irish defeated*) . . 10 Aug. 1316
Foughard or Dundalk (*Ed. Bruce defeated*) 5 Oct. 1318
Boroughbridge (*Edward II. defts. Barons*) 16 Mar. 1322
Mühldorf (*Bavarians defeat Austrians*) . 28 Sept. ,,
Dupplin (*Edward Baliol defeats Mar*) . 11 Aug. 1332
Halidon Hill (*Edward III. defts. Scots*) . 19 July, 1333
Tarifa (*Moors defeated*) . . 28 or 30 Oct. 1340
Auberoche (*earl of Derby defeats French*). 19 Aug. 1344

Crecy (*English defeat French*) . . . 26 Aug. 1346
Durham, Nevil's Cross (*Scots defeated*) 17 Oct. ,,
La Roche Darien (*Charles of Blois defeated*) . . 1347
Poitiers (*English defeat French*) . . 19 Sept. 1356
Cocherel (*Du Guesclin defeats Navarre*) . 16 May, 1364
Auray (*Du Guesclin defeated*). . 29 Sept. ,,
Najara (Navarrete, Logrono) (*Black Prince defeats Henry of Trastamare*) . . . 3 April, 1367
Montiel (*Peter of Castile defeated*) 14 March, 1369
Rosbecque (*French defeat Flemings*) . 27 Nov. 1382
Aljubarrota (*Portuguese defeat Spaniards*) . 14 Aug. 1385
Sempach (*Swiss defeat Austrians*) . . 9 July, 1386
Otterburn (*Chevy Chase; Scots victors*). . 10 Aug. 1388
Näfels (*Swiss defeat Austrians*) . . . ,,
Cossova (*Turks defeat Albanians, and Amurath I. killed*) . . . Sept. 1389
Nicopolis (*Turks defeat Christians*) . . 28 Sept. 1396
Nesbit (*Scots defeated*) . . . 7 May, 1402
Ancyra (*Timour defeats Bajazet*) . . 28 July, ,,
Homeldon Hill (*English defeat Scots*) . 14 Sept. ,,
Shrewsbury (*Percies, &c. defeated*) . 23 July, 1403
Bramham Moor (*Henry IV. defeats rebels*) . 19 Feb. 1408
Tannenberg (*Poles defeat Teuton knights*). 15 July, 1410
Harlaw (*Lord of the Isles defeated*) . . 24 July, 1411
Agincourt (*English defeat French*) . . 25 Oct. 1415
Prague (*Hussites under Ziska victors*) . . 14 July, 1420
Anjou, Beaugé (*English deft. by Scots*) . 22 March, 1421
Crevant (*English deft. French and Scots*) . 11 June, 1423
Aquila (*Arragonese defeated by Italians*) . 2 June, 1424
Verneuil (*English defeat French and Scots*) . 17 Aug. ,,
Herrings (*English defeat French*). . . 12 Feb. 1429
Orleans (*siege relieved*) . . . 29 April, ,,
Patay (*English defeated by Joan of Arc*) . 18 June, ,,
Lippau, or Böhmischbrod (*Hussites deftd.*) 28 May, 1434
Kunobitza (*Hunniades defeats the Turks*) 24 Dec. 1443
St. Jacob (*French defeat Swiss*) . . 26 Aug. 1444
Varna (*Turks defeat Hungarians*) . . 10 Nov. ,,
Cossova (*Turks defeat Hunniades*) . 17 Oct. 1448
Formigni (*English defeated by French*) . 15 April, 1450
Sevenoaks (*Jack Cade defeats Stafford*) . 27 June, ,,
Aibar (*Agramonts defeat Beaumonts*) . . 23 Oct. 1452
Brechin, Scotland (*Huntley defeats Crawford*) 18 May, ,,
Castillon Chatillon, (*French defeat Talbot*) 17 or 23 July, 1453

WAR OF THE ROSES—YORKISTS AND LANCASTRIANS.

St. Albans (*Yorkists victorious*) . . 22 or 23 May, 1455
Bloreheath (*Yorkists victors*) . . 23 Sept. 1459
Northampton (*ditto, Henry VI. taken*) . 10 July, 1460
Wakefield (*Lancastrians victors*). . . 31 Dec. ,,
Mortimer's Cross (*Yorkists victorious*) . . 2 Feb. 1461
St. Albans (*Lancastrians victors*) . . 17 Feb. ,,
Towton (*Yorkists victorious*) . . 29 March, ,,
Hexham (*Yorkists victors*) . . . 15 May, 1464
Edgecote or Banbury (*Yorkists defeated*) 26 July, 1469
Stamford (*Lancastrians defeated*) . . 13 March, 1470
Barnet (*ditto*) . . . 14 April, 1471
Tewkesbury (*ditto*) . . . 4 May, ,,

Belgrade (*Mahomet II. repulsed*) . . 4 Sept. 1456
Montlhery (*Louis XI. and nobles; indec.*) 16 July, 1465
Granson (*Swiss defeat Charles the Bold*) 3 March, 1476
Morat (*ditto*) . . . 22 June, ,,
Nancy (*Charles the Bold killed*) . . 5 Jan. 1477
Bosworth (*Richard III. defeated*) . 22 Aug. 1485
Stoke (*Lambert Simnel taken*) . 16 June, 1487
St. Aubin (*Orleans defeated*) . . 28 July, 1488
Sauchieburn, near Bannockburn (*James III. deftd. by rebels*) . . . ,,
Fornovo (*French defeat Italians*) . . 6 July, 1495
Seminara (*French defeat Spaniards*) . . ,,
Blackheath (*Cornish rebels defeated*) . 22 June, 1497
Seminara (*Gonsalvo defeats French*) . 21 April, 1503
Cerignola (*Gonsalvo defeats French*) . 28 April, ,,
Garigliano (*Gonsalvo defeats French*) . 27 Dec. ,,
Agnadello (*French defeat Venetians*) . 14 May, 1509
Ravenna (*Gaston de Foix, victor, killed*) 11 April, 1512
Novara (*Papal Swiss defeat French*) . 6 June, 1513
Guinegate (Spurs) (*French defeated*) . 16 Aug. ,,
Flodden (*English defeat Scots*) . . 9 Sept. ,,
Marignano (*French defeat Swiss*) . 13-15 Sept. 1515
Bicocca, near Milan (*Lautrec defeated*) 29 April, 1522
Pavia (*Francis I. defeated*). . 24 Feb. 1525
Frankenhausen (*Anabaptists defeated*) . 15 May, ,,
Mohacz (*Turks defeat Hungarians*) . 29 Aug. 1526
Cappel (*Zwinglius slain*) . . 11 Oct. 1531
Lauffen (*Hessians defeat Austrians*) . 13 May, 1534
Assens (*Christian III. defeats Danish rebels*) . . 1535

Battle	Date	Year
Abancay (*Almagro defeated Alvarado*)	12 July,	1537
Solway Moss (*English defeat Scots*)	25 Nov.	1542
Ceresuola (*French defeat Imperialists*)	14 April,	1544
Mühlberg (*Chas. V. defeats Protestants*)	24 April,	1547
Pinkey (*English defeat Scots*)	10 Sept.	,,
Ket's rebellion suppressed by Warwick	Aug.	1549
Marciano (*Florentines defeat French*)	3 Aug.	1554
St. Quentin (*Span. & Eng. deft. French*)	10 Aug.	1557
Calais (*taken*)	7 Jan.	1558
Gravelines *n.* (*Span. & Eng. deft. French*)	13 July,	,,
Dreux, in France (*Huguenots defeated*)	19 Dec.	1562
Carberry Hill (*Mary of Scotland defeated*)	15 June,	1567
St. Denis (*Huguenots defeated*)	10 Nov.	,,
Langside (*Mary of Scotland defeated*)	13 May,	1568
Jarnac (*Huguenots defeated*)	13 March,	1569
Moncontour (*Coligny defeated*)	3 Oct.	,,
Lepanto, *n.* (*Don John defeats Turks*)	7 Oct.	1571
Dormans (*Guise defeats Huguenots*)	10 Oct.	1575
Alcazar-quiver (*Moors defeat Portuguese*)	4 Aug.	1578
Alcantara (*Spaniards defeat Portuguese*)	24 June,	1580
Zutphen (*Dutch & English def. Spaniards*),	22 Sept.	1586
Coutras (*Henry IV. defeats League*)	20 Oct.	1587
Spanish Armada defeated, *n.*	July, Aug.	1588
Arques (*Henry IV. defeats League*)	21 Sept.	1589
Ivry or Yvres (*ditto*)	14 March,	1590
Epernay taken by Henry IV. of France	26 July,	1592
Fontaine Française (*Henry IV. beats Spaniards*)	5 June,	1595
Blackwater (*Tyrone and rebels def. Bangal*),	14 Aug.	1598
Nieuport (*Maurice defeats Austrians*)		1600
Kinsale (*Tyrone reduced by Mountjoy*)		1601
Kirchholm (*Poles defeat Swedes*)		1605
Gibraltar (*Dutch defeat Spaniards*)		1607
Prague (*king of Bohemia defeated*)	8 Nov.	1620
Dessau (*Wallenstein defeats Mansfeld*)	25 April,	1626
Rochelle (*taken*)	28 Oct.	1628
Stuhm (*Gustavus defeats Poles*)		,,
Leipsic or Breitenfeld (*Gustavus def. Tilly*),	7 Sept.	1631
Lech (*Imperialists defeated; Tilly killed*)	5 April,	1632
Lippstadt, Lutzingen, or Lutzen (*Swedes victorious; Gustavus slain*) (N.S.)	16 Nov.	,,
Nordlingen (*Swedes defeated*)	27 Aug.	1634
Arras (*taken by the French*)	10 Aug.	1640
Leipsic (*Swedes defeat Austrians*)	23 Oct.	1642
Rocroy (*French defeat Spaniards*)	May,	1643
Friedburg (*Condé victor*)	Aug.	1644
Nordlingen (*Turenne defeats Austrians*)		1645

CIVIL WAR IN ENGLAND.

Battle	Date	Year
Worcester (*prince Rupert victor*)	23 Sept.	1642
Edgehill fight (*issue doubtful*)	23 Oct.	,,
Bradock-down (*Parliamentarians defeated*)	Jan.	1643
Bramham Moor (*Fairfax defeated*)	29 March,	,,
Stratton (*Royalists victorious*)	16 May,	,,
Chalgrove (*Hampden killed*)	18 June,	,,
Atherton Moor (*Royalists victorious*)	30 June,	,,
Landsdown (*Royalists victorious*)	5 July,	,,
Devizes or Roundway-down (*ditto*)	13 July,	,,
Gainsborough (*Cromwell victor*).	27 July,	,,
Newbury (*fav. to Royalists*)	20 Sept.	,,
Cheriton or Alresford (*ditto*)	29 March,	1644
Cropredy Bridge (*Charles I. victor*)	29 June,	,,
Marston Moor (*prince Rupert defeated*)	2 July,	,,
Tippermuir (*Montrose defeats Covenanters*)	1 Sept.	,,
Newbury (*indecisive*)	27 Oct.	,,
Naseby (*Charles I. totally defeated*)	14 June,	1645
Alford (*Montrose defeats Covenanters*)	2 July,	,,
Kilsyth (*ditto*)	15 Aug.	,,
Philiphaugh (*Covenanters defeat Montrose*)	13 Sept.	,,
Benburb (*O'Neill defeats English*)	5 June,	1646
Dungan-hill (*Irish defeated*)	8 Aug.	1647
Preston (*Cromwell victor*)	17 Aug.	1648
Rathmines (*Irish Royalists defeated*)	2 Aug.	1649
Drogheda (*taken by storm*)	12 Sept.	,,
Corbiesdale (*Montrose defeated*)	27 April,	1650
Dunbar (*Cromwell defeats Scots*)	3 Sept.	,,
Worcester (*Cromwell defeats Charles II.*)	3 Sept.	1651
Galway (*surrendered*)		1652
Daventry (*Lambert defeated by Monk*)	21 April,	1660

Battle	Date	Year
Arras, France (*Turenne defeats Condé*)		1654
Dunkirk (*ditto*)	14 June,	1658
Estremoz (*Don John def. by Schomberg*)	8 June,	1663
St. Gotthard (*Montecuculi defeats Turks*)	1 Aug.	1664
Villa Viciosa (*Portuguese defeat Spaniards*)		1665
Pentland hills (*Covenanters defeated*)	28 Nov.	1666
Candia (*taken by Turks*)	6 Sept.	1669
Choczim (*Sobieski defeats Turks*)	11 Nov.	1673
Seneffe (*French and Dutch, indecisive*)	11 Aug.	1674
Ensisheim (*Turenne defeats Imperialists*)	4 Oct.	,,
Mulhausen (*ditto*)	31 Dec.	,,
Turckheim (*ditto*)	5 Jan.	1675
Salzbach (*Turenne killed*)	27 July,	,,
Drumclog (*Covenanters defeat Claverhouse*)	1 June,	1679
Bothwell Brigg (*Monmouth defeats Covenanters*)	22 June,	,,
Vienna (*Turks defeated by Sobieski*)	12 Sept.	1683
Sedgemoor (*Monmouth defeated*).	6 July,	1685
Mohacz (*Turks defeated*)	12 Aug.	1687
Killiecrankie (*Highlanders def. Mackay*)	27 July,	1689
Newtown-butler (*Jacobites defeated*)	30 July,	,,
Boyne (*William III. defeats James II.*)	1 July,	1690
Fleurus (*Charleroi, Luxembourg victor*)	1 July	,,
Athlone taken by Ginckel	30 June,	1691
Aughrim (*James II.'s cause ruined*)	12 July,	,,
Salenckemen (*Louis of Baden def. Turks*)	19 Aug.	,,
Enghein or Steenkirk (*William III. defeated*)	24 July,	1692
Landen (*William III. defeated*)	19 July,	1693
Marsaglia (Pignerol) (*French victors*)	4 Oct.	,,
Zenta (*prince Eugène defeats Turks*)	11 Sept.	1697
Narva (*Charles XII. defeats Russians*)	30 Nov.	1700
Carpi, Modena (*Allies defeat French*)	9 July,	1701
Chiari (*Austrians defeat French*)	1 Sept.	,,
Clissau (*Charles XII. defeats Poles*)	20 July,	1702
Santa Vittoria (*French victors*)	26 July,	,,
Friedlingen (*French defeat Germans*)	14 Oct.	,,
Pultusk (*Swedes defeat Poles*)	1 May,	1703
Hochstadt (*French defeat Austrians*)	20 Sept.	,,
Donauwerth (*Marlborough victor*)	2 July,	1704
Gibraltar (*taken by Rooke*)	24 July,	,,
Blenheim or Hochstadt (*Marlborough victor*), (O. S.)	2 Aug.	
Tirlemont (*Marlborough successful*)	18 July,	1705
Cassano (*prince Eugène; indecisive*)	16 Aug.	,,
Mittau (*taken by Russians*)	14 Sept.	,,
Ramillies (*Marlborough defeats French*)	23 May,	1706
Turin (*French defeated by Eugène*)	7 Sept.	,,
Kalitsch (*Russians defeat Swedes*)	19 Nov.	,,
Almanza (*French defeat Allies*)	14 (O. S.) or 25 April,	1707
Oudenarde (*Marlborough victor*)	11 July,	1708
Liesna, Lenzo (*Russians defeat Swedes*)	autumn,	,,
Lisle (*taken by the Allies*)	Dec.	,,
Pultowa (*Peter defeats Charles XII.*)	8 July,	1709
Malplaquet (*Marlborough victor*)	11 Sept.	,,
Dobro (*Russians defeat Swedes*)	20 Sept.	,,
Almenara (*Austrians defeat French*)	28 July,	1710
Saragossa (*ditto*)	20 Aug.	,,
Villa Viciosa (*Austrians defeated*)	10 Dec.	,,
Arleux (*Marlborough forces French lines*)	5 Aug.	1711
Bouchain (*taken by Marlborough*)	13 Sept.	,,
Denain (*Villars defeats Allies*)	24 July,	1712
Friburg (*taken by French*)	7 Nov.	1713
Preston (*rebels defeated*)	12, 13 Nov.	1715
Dumblane or Sheriff-Muir (*indecisive*)	13 Nov.	,,
Peterwardein (*Eugène defeats Turks*)	5 Aug.	1716
Belgrade (*ditto*)	16 Aug.	1717
Bitonto (*Spaniards defeat Germans*)	27 May,	1734
Parma (*Austrians and French, indecisive*)	29 June,	,,
Guastalla (*Austrians defeated*)	19 Sept.	,,
Erivan (*Nadir Shah defeats Turks*)	June,	1735
Krotzka (*Turks defeat Austrians*)	22 July,	1739
Molwitz (*Prussians defeat Austrians*)	10 April,	1741
Dettingen (*George II. defeats French*)	16 June,	1743
Fontenoy (*Saxe defeats Cumberland*)	30 April,	1745
Hohenfreiburg (*Prussians defeat Austrians*)	4 June,	,,

SCOTS' REBELLION.

Battle	Date	Year
Gladsmuir near Preston Pans (*rebels defeat Cope*)	21 Sept.	1745
Clifton Moor (*rebels defeated*)	18 Dec.	,,
Falkirk (*rebels defeat Hawley*)	17 Jan.	1746
Culloden (*Cumberland defeats rebels*)	16 April,	,,

Battle	Date	Year
St. Lazaro (*Sardinians defeat French*)	4 June,	,,
Placentia (*Austrians defeat French*)	16 June,	,,
Raucoux (*Saxe defeats Allies*)	11 Oct.	,,
Laffeldt (*Saxe defeats Cumberland*)	2 July,	1747
Exilles (*Sardinians defeat French*)	19 July,	,,
Bergen-op-Zoom (*taken*)	15 Sept.	,,
Fort du Quesne (*Braddock killed*)	9 July,	1755
Calcutta (*taken by Surajah Dowlah*)	20 June,	1756

SEVEN YEARS' WAR, 1756-63.

Battle	Date	Year
Prague (*Frederick defeats Allies*)	6 May,	1757
Kollin (*Frederick defeated*)	18 June,	,,

Norkitten (*Russians defeated*) . . . 13 Aug. 1757
Rosbach (*Frederick defeats French*) . . 5 Nov. ,,
Breslau (*Austrians victors*) . . . 22 Nov. ,,
Lissa (*Frederick defeats Austrians*) . . 5 Dec. ,,
Creveldt (*Ferdinand defeats French*) . 23 June, 1758
Zorndorff (*Frederick defeats Russians*) 25, 26 Aug. ,,
Hochkirchen (*Austrians defeat Prussians*) 14 Oct. ,,
Bergen (*French defeat Allies*) . . . 13 April, 1759
Zullichau (*Russians defeat Prussians*) . 23 July, ,,
Minden (*Ferdinand defeats French*) . 1 Aug. ,,
Cunnersdorf (*Russians defeat Prussians*) 12 Aug. ,,
Wandewash (*Coote defeats Lally*) . . 22 Jan. 1760
Landshut, Silesia (*Prussians defeated*) . 23 June, ,,
Warburg (*Ferdinand defeats French*) . 31 July, ,,
Pfaffendorf (*Frederick defeats Austrians*) . 15 Aug. ,,
Kloster Campen (*English and Germans with French, indecisive*) . . . 15, 16 Oct. ,,
Torgau (*Frederick defeats Austrians*) . . 3 Nov. ,,
Kirchdenkern (*Allies defeat French*) . 15 July, 1761
Schweidnitz (*Frederick II. def. Austrians*) 16 May, 1762
Johannisberg (*French defeat Prussians*) 30 Aug. ,,
Freiberg (*Prussians defeat Austrians*) . 29 Oct. ,,

Plassey (*Clive's victory*) . . . 23 June, 1757
Niagara (*English take Fort*) . . . 24 July, 1759
Quebec (*Wolfe, victor, killed*) . . 13 Sept. ,,
Buxar (*Munro defeats army of Oude*) . 23 Oct. 1764
Choczim (*Russians defeat Turks*) 30 April & 13 July, 1769
Galatz (*Russians defeat Turks*) . . . Nov. ,,
Bender taken by Russians . . . 28 Sept. 1770
Brailow (*Russians defeat Turks*) . 19 June, 1773
Silistria (*taken*) 1774

AMERICAN WAR.

Lexington (*Gage victor, with great loss*) . 19 April, 1775
Bunker's Hill (*Americans repulsed*) . 17 June, ,,
Long Island (*Americans defeated*) . 27 Aug. 1776
White Plains (*Howe defeats Americans*) . 28 Oct. ,,
Rhode Island (*taken by Royalists*) . 8 Dec. ,,
Princeton (*Washington defeats British*) . 3 Jan. 1777
Brandywine (*Howe defeats Washington*) . 11 Sept. ,,
Germanstown (*Burgoyne's victory*) . 3, 4 Oct. ,,
Saratoga (*he is compelled to surrender*) . 7 Oct. ,,
Briar's Creek (*Americans defeated*) . 3 March, 1779
Camden (*Cornwallis defeats Gates*) . 16 Aug. 1780
Arcot (*Hyder defeats British*) . . . 31 Oct. ,,
Guildford (*Cornwallis defeats Gates*) . 15 March, 1781
Camden (*Americans defeated*) . 25 April, ,,
Porto Novo (*Coote defeats Hyder*) . . 1 July, ,,
Eutaw Springs (*Arnold defeats Americans*) . 8 Sept. ,,
York Town (*Cornwallis surrenders*) . 19 Oct. ,,
[Many inferior actions with various success.]
Rodney's victory over De Grasse, *n.* 12 April, 1782
Arnee (*Coote defeats Hyder*) . . 2 June, ,,
Attack on Gibraltar fails . . 13 Sept. ,,
Bednore (*taken by Tippoo Sahib*) . 30 April, 1783
Martinesti (*Austrians defeat Turks*) . 22 Sept. 1789
Ismail (*taken by storm by Suwarrow*) . 22 Dec. 1790
Bangalore (*taken by storm*) . 21 March, 1791
Arikera (*Tippoo defeated*) . . 15 May, ,,
Seringapatam (*ditto*) . . . . 6 Feb. 1792

FRENCH REVOLUTIONARY WAR BEGINS.

Quiévrain (*French repulsed*) . . 28 April, 1792
Valmy (*French defeat Prussians*) . 20 Sept. ,,
Jemappes (*French victorious*) . . 6 Nov. ,,
Neerwinden (*French beaten by Austrians*) 18 March, 1793
St. Amand (*French defeated by English*) . 8 May, ,,
Valenciennes (*ditto*) . 23 May, 26 July, ,,
Lincelles (*Lake defeats French*) . 18 Aug. ,,
Dunkirk (*duke of York defeated*) . 7, 8 Sept. ,,
Quesnoy (*reduced by Austrians*) . 11 Sept. ,,
Pirmasens (*Prussians defeat French*) . 14 Sept. ,,
Wattignies (*French defeat Coburg*) . 14, 15, 16 Oct. ,,
Toulon (*retaken by British*) . . 19 Dec. ,,
Cambray (*French defeated*) . . 24 April, 1794
Troisville, Landrecy (*taken by Allies*) . 30 April, ,,
Tourcoing (*Moreau defeats Allies*) . 18-22 May, ,,
Espierres (*taken by Allies*) . . 22 May, ,,
Howe's naval victory . . . 1 June, ,,
Charleroi or Fleurus (*French defeat Allies*) 26 June, ,,
Misdon (*Vendeans defeated*) . . 28 July, ,,
Bois-le-Duc (*duke of York defeated*) . 14 Sept. ,,
Boxtel (*ditto*) . . . . 17 Sept. ,,
Maciejowice (*Poles defeated*) . . 10 Oct. ,,
Nimeguen (*French victorious*) 28 Oct., (*def.*) 4 May, ,,
Praga (*Warsaw taken by Suwarrow*) . . 4 Nov. ,,
Bridport's victory off l'Orient, *n.* . . 22 June, 1795

Quiberon (*Emigrants defeated*) . . . 21 July, 1795
Mannheim (*taken by Pichegru*) . . 20 Sept. ,,
Loano (*French defeat Austrians*) . . 23, 24 Nov. ,,
Montenotte (*Bonaparte victorious*) . 12 April, 1796
Mondovi (*ditto*) . . . . . 22 April, ,,
Lodi (*ditto*) . . . . . . 10 May, ,,
Altenkirchen (*Austrians defeated*) . . 4 June, ,,
Radstadt (*Moreau defeats Austrians*) . 5 July, ,,
Altenkirchen (*Austrians victors*) . . 16 Sept. ,,
Roveredo (*French defeat Austrians*) . 4 Sept. ,,
Bassano (*ditto*) . . . . . 8 Sept. ,,
Biberach (*ditto*) . . . . . 2 Oct. ,,
Lonato and Castiglione (*ditto*) . . 3-5 Aug. ,,
Neresheim (*Moreau def. archduke Charles*) 10 Aug. ,,
Arcola (*Bonaparte victorious*) . . 14-17 Nov. ,,
Castelnuovo (*ditto*) . . . . 21 Nov. ,,
Rivoli (*ditto*) . . . . . 14, 15 Jan. 1797
Cape St. Vincent, *n.* (*Spaniards defeated*) 14 Feb. ,,
Tagliamento (*Bonaparte def. Austrians*) 16 March, ,,
Camperdown, *n.* (*Duncan defeats Dutch*) 11 Oct. ,,

IRISH REBELLION BEGINS . . . . May, 1798

Kilcullen (*rebels successful*) . . 23 May, ,,
Naas (*rebels defeated*) . . . 24 May, ,,
Tara (*rebels defeated*) . . . 26 May, ,,
Oulart (*rebels successful*) . . 27 May, ,,
Gorey or New Ross (*rebels defeated*) . 4 June, ,,
Antrim (*rebels defeated*) . . . 7 June, ,,
Arklow (*rebels beaten*) . . . 10 June, ,,
Ballynahinch (*Nugent defeats rebels*) 13 June, ,,
Vinegar Hill (*Lake defeats rebels*) . 21 June, ,,
Castlebar (*French auxiliaries defeated*) . 27 Aug. ,,
Pyramids (*Bonaparte def. Mamelukes*) 13, 21 July, ,,
Nile, *n.* (*Nelson defeats French fleet*) . 1 Aug. ,,
Ballinamuck (*French and rebels defeated*) . 8 Sept. ,,
El Arisch (*French defeat Turks*) . . 18 Feb. 1799
Jaffa (*stormed by Bonaparte*) . . 7-10 March, ,,
Stokach (*Austrians defeat French*) . 25 March, ,,
Verona (*Austrians defeat French*) . 28-30 March, ,,
Magnano (*Kray defeats French*) . . 5 April, ,,
Mount Thabor (*Bonaparte defeats Turks*) 16 April, ,,
Cassano (*Suwarrow defeats Moreau*) . 27 April, ,,
Adda (*Suwarrow defeats French*) . . ,, ,,
Seringapatam (*Tippoo killed*) . . 4 May, ,,
Acre (*relieved by sir Sydney Smith*) . 20 May, ,,
Zurich (*French defeated*) . . . 5 June, ,,
Trebia (*Suwarrow defeats French*) . 17-19 June, ,,
Alessandria (*taken from French*) . 21 July, ,,
Aboukir (*Turks defeated by Bonaparte*) 25 July, ,,
Novi (*Suwarrow defeats French*) . . 15 Aug. ,,
Zuyper Sluys (*French defeated*) . . 9 Sept. ,,
Bergen and Alkmaer (*Allies defeated*) 26 Oct. 19 Sept. ,,
Zurich (*Massena defeats Russians*) . 25 Sept. ,,
Heliopolis (*Kleber defeats Turks*) . 20 Mar. 1800
Engen (*Moreau defeats Austrians*) . . 3 May, ,,
Mœskirch (*ditto*) . . . . 5 May, ,,
Biberach (*ditto*) . . . . 9 May, ,,
Montebello (*Austrians defeated*) . . 9 June, ,,
Marengo (*Bonaparte defeats Austrians*) . 14 June, ,,
Hochstadt (*Moreau defeats Austrians*) 19 June, ,,
Hohenlinden (*ditto*) . . . . 3 Dec. ,,
Mincio (*French defeat Austrians*) . 25-27 Dec. ,,
Aboukir (*French defeated*) . . . 8 March, 1801
Alexandria (*Abercrombie's victory*) . 21 March, ,,
Copenhagen (*bombarded by Nelson*) . 2 April, ,,
Ahmednuggur (*Wellesley victorious*) . 12 Aug. 1803
Assaye (*ditto, his first great victory*) . 23 Sept. ,,
Argaum (*Wellesley victor*) . . 29 Nov. ,,
Furruckabad (*Lake defeats Holkar*) . 17 Nov. 1804
Bhurtpore (*taken by Lake*) . . 2 April, 1805
Elchingen (*Ney defeats Austrians*) . 14 Oct. ,,
Ulm surrenders (*Ney defeats Austrians*) 17-20 Oct. ,,
Trafalgar (*Nelson destroys Fren. fleet; killed*) 21 Oct. ,,
Austerlitz (*Napoleon defeats Austrians & Russ.*) 2 Dec. ,,
Buenos Ayres (*taken by Popham*) . . 27 June, 1806
Maida (*Stuart defeats French*) . . 4 July, ,,
Saalfeld (*French defeat Prussians*) . 10 Oct. ,,
Auerstadt } Jena } (*French defeat Prussians*) . 14 Oct. ,,
Halle stormed by French . . . 17 Oct. ,,
Pultusk (*French and Allies, indecisive*) . 26 Dec. ,,
Mohrungen (*French def. Russ. & Pruss.*) . 25 Jan. 1807
Montevideo (*taken*) . . . . 3 Feb. ,,
Eylau (*indecisive*) . . . . 7, 8 Feb. ,,
Ostrolenka (*French defeat Prussians*) . 16 Feb. ,,
Friedland (*French defeat Russians*) . 14 June, ,,
Buenos Ayres (*Whitelock defeated*) . 5 July, ,,
Copenhagen (*bombarded by Cathcart*) . 2-5 Sept. ,,

Medina de Rio Seco (*French defeat Spaniards*) 15 July, 1808
Baylen (*Spaniards defeat French*) . . 20 July, ,,

PENINSULAR CAMPAIGN BEGINS.

Vimiera (*Wellesley defeats Junot*) . . 21 Aug. 1808
Tudela or Ebro (*French defeat Spaniards*) 23 Nov. ,,
Corunna (*Moore defeats French*) . . . 16 Jan. 1809
Abenberg (*Austrians defeated*) . . . 20 April, ,,
Landshut (*ditto*) . . . . . . 21 April, ,,
Eckmühl (*Davoust defeats Austrians*) . 22 April, ,,
Ebersberg (*French defeat Austrians*) . . 4 May, ,,
Oporto (*taken*). . . . . 29 March, 12 May, ,,
Aspern } Essling } (*Napoleon defeated*) . . . 21, 22 May, ,,
Wagram (*Austrians defeated*) . . . 5, 6 July, ,,
Talavera (*Wellesley defeats Victor*) . 27, 28 July, ,,
Silistria (*Turks defeat Russians*) . . 26 Sept. ,,
Ocana (*Mortier defeats Spaniards*) . . 19 Nov. ,,
Busaco (*Wellington repulses Massena*) . 27 Sept. 1810
Barrosa (*Graham defeats Victor*) . . 5 March, 1811
Badajoz (*taken by the French*) . . 11 March, ,,
Fuentes de Onoro (*Wellington defeats Massena*) 3, 5 May, ,,
Albuera (*Beresford defeats Soult*) . . 16 May, ,,
Ximena (*Spaniards defeat French*) . . 10 Sept. ,,
Merida (*Hill defeats French*) . . . 28 Oct. ,,
Albufera (*Suchet defeats Spaniards*) . . 4 Jan. 1812
Ciudad Rodrigo (*stormed by English*) . 19 Jan. ,,
Badajoz (*taken by Wellington*) . . 6 April, ,,
Llerena (*Cotton defeats Soult*) . . 11 April, ,,
Salamanca (*Wellington defts. Marmont*) . 22 July, ,,
Mohilow (*French defeat Russians*) . . 23 July, ,,
Polotzk (*French and Russians*) . . 30, 31 July, ,,
Krasnoy, Smolensko (*French defeat Russians*) 15, 19 Aug. ,,
Moskwa } Borodino } (*ditto*) . . . . . . 7 Sept. ,,
Moscow (*burnt by Russians*) . . . 15 Sept. ,,
Queenstown (*Americans defeated*) . . 13 Oct. ,,
Polotzk (*retaken by Russians*) . . 19, 20 Oct. ,,
Malo-Jaroslawatz (*French victors*) . . 24 Oct. ,,
Witepsk (*French defeated*) . . . 14 Nov. ,,
Krasnoi (*ditto*) . . . . . . 16-18 Nov. ,,
Beresina (*ditto*) . . . . . . 25-29 Nov ,,
French Town (*taken by Americans*) . . 22 Jan. 1813
Kalitsch (*Saxons defeated*) . . . 13 Feb. ,,
Möckern (*Eugène defeats Russians*) . . 5 April, ,,
Castalla (*sir J. Murray defeats Suchet*) . 13 April, ,,
Lutzen (*Napoleon checks Allies*) . . . 2 May, ,,
Bautzen (*Nap. and Allies; indecisive*) . 20 May, ,,
Wurschen (*ditto*) . . . . . 21, 22 May, ,,
Hochkirchen (*French deft. Aust. and Russ.*), 22 May, ,,
Vittoria (*Wellington defts. king Joseph*) . 21 June, ,,
Pyrenees (*Wellington defeats Soult*) 28 July, 2 Aug. ,,
Katzbach (*Blücher defeats Macdonald*) . 26 Aug. ,,
Dresden (*Napoleon checks Allies*) . . 26, 27 Aug. ,,
St. Sebastian (*stormed by Graham*) . . 31 Aug. ,,
Dennewitz (*Ney defeated*) . . . . 6 Sept. ,,
Möckern (*French defeated*) . . . . 16 Oct. ,,
Leipzic (*Napoleon defeated*) . . . 16-18 Oct. ,,
Hanau (*Napoleon defeats Bavarians*) . . 30 Oct. ,,
St. Jean de Luz (*Wellington defts. Soult*) . 10 Nov. ,,
Passage of the Nive, 9 Dec.; several engagements between the Allies and French . 10 to 13 Dec. ,,
St. Dizier, France (*French victors*) . . 26 Jan. 1814
Brienne (*Allies defeated*) . . . . 29 Jan. ,,
La Rothière (*Napoleon defeats Allies*). . 1 Feb. ,,
Bar-sur-Aube (*Allies victors*) . . . 7 Feb. ,,
Mincio (*pr. Eugène defeats Austrians*) . 8 Feb. ,,
Champ Aubert (*French defeat Allies*) . 10-12 Feb. ,,
Montmirail (*ditto*) . . . . . . 11 Feb. ,,
Vauchamp (*ditto*) . . . . . . 14 Feb. ,,
Fontainebleau (*ditto*) . . . . . 17 Feb. ,,
Montereau (*ditto*) . . . . . . 18 Feb. ,,
Orthez (*Wellington defeats Soult*) . . 27 Feb. ,,
Craonne (*French victors*) . . . . 7 March, ,,
Bergen-op-Zoom (*Graham defeated*) . . 8 March, ,,
Laon (*French defeated*) . . . . 9-10 March, ,,
Rheims (*Napoleon defeats St. Priest*) . 13 March, ,,
Tarbes (*Wellington defeats Soult*) . . 20 March, ,,
Fère Champenoise (*French defeated*) . . 25 March, ,,
St. Dizier (*French victors*) . . . 28 March, ,,
Paris, Montmartre, Romainville (*ditto*) 30 March, ,,
Battle of the Barriers, 30 March; (*Marmont evacuates Paris, and the Allies enter it*) 31 March, ,,
Toulouse (*Wellington defeats Soult*) . 10 April, ,,
Tolentino (*Murat defeated*) . . . . 3 May, 1815
Ligny (*Blücher repulsed*). . . . . 16 June, 1815
Quatre Bras (*Ney repulsed*). . . . 16 June, ,,
Waterloo (*Napoleon finally beaten*). . 18 June, ,,

AMERICAN WAR.

Fort George, at Niagara (*taken by Americans*), 27 May, 1813
"Stoney Creek," Upper Canada (*Americans routed*) 6 June, ,,
Chrysler's Farm, Canada . . . . . 11 Nov. ,,
Black-rock, America, opposite Buffalo . 30 Dec. ,,
Longwood (*English defeated*) . . . 4 May, 1814
Chippawa (*British defeated*) . . . 5 July, ,,
Lundy's Lane (*Americans defeated*) . . 25 July, ,,
Fort Erie (*British repulsed*) . . . 15 Aug. ,,
Bladensburg, near Washington (*Americans defeated*) 24 Aug. ,,
Bellair or Moor's Fields (*British repulsed*), 30 Aug. ,,
Baltimore (*British victors*) . . . 12 Sept. ,,
New Orleans (*British repulsed*) . 8, 12, & 13 Jan. 1815

Algiers (*bombarded by Exmouth*). . . 27 Aug. 1816
Chacabuco (*Chilians defeat Spaniards*) . 12 Feb. 1817
Kirkee (*Hastings defeats Pindarrees*) . . 5 Nov. ,,
Mehadpore (*Hislop defeats Holkar*). . 21 Dec. ,,
Valtezza (*Turks defeated*) . . . . 27 May, 1821
Dragaschan (*Ipsilanti defeated*) . . 19 June, ,,
Tripolitza (*stormed by Greeks*) . . 5 Oct. ,,
Thermopylæ (*Greeks defeat Turks*) . . 13 July, 1822
Corinth (*taken*) . . . . . . 16 Sept. ,,
Accra (*Ashantees defeat sir C. Macarthy*) 21 Jan. 1824
Ayacucho (*Peruvians defeat Spaniards*) . 9 Dec. ,,
Bhurtpore (*taken by Combermere*) . . 18 Jan. 1826
Accra (*Ashantees defeated*) . . . . 7 Aug. ,,
Athens (*taken*) . . . . . . 17 May, 1827
Navarino (*Allies destroy Turkish fleet*) . 20 Oct. ,,
Brahilow (*Russians and Turks*) . . 18 June, 1828
Akhalzikh (*ditto*) . . . . . 24 Aug. ,,
Varna (*surrenders to Russians*) . . 11 Oct. ,,
Silistria (*ditto*) . . . . . . 30 June, 1829
Kainly (*Russians defeat Turks*) . . 1 July, ,,
Balkan (*passed by Russians*) . . . 26 July, ,,
Adrianople (*Russians enter*) . . . 20 Aug. ,,
Algiers (*captured by French*) . . . 5 July, 1830
Paris (*Days of July*) . . . 27, 28, 29 July, ,,
Grochow (*Poles defeat Russians*) . . 19, 20 Feb. 1831
Praga (*Poles defeat Russians*) . . . 25 Feb. ,,
Wawz (*Skrzynecki defeats Russians*) . . 31 March, ,,
Seidlice (*Poles defeat Russians*) . . 10 April, ,,
Ostrolenka (*ditto*) . . . . . . 26 May, ,,
Wilna (*Poles and Russians*) . . . 18 June, ,,
Warsaw (*taken by Russians*) . . . 7 Sept. ,,
Homs (*Egyptians defeat Turks*) . . 8 July, 1832
Beylan (*Ibrahim defeats Turks*) . . 29 July, ,,
Konieh (*Egyptians defeat Turks*) . . 21 Dec. ,,
Antwerp citadel taken by Allies . . 23 Dec. ,,
Hernani (*Carlists defeated*) . . . 5 May, 1836
St. Sebastian (*ditto*) . . . . . 1 Oct. ,,
Bilboa (*siege raised; British Legion*) . 24 Dec. ,,
Hernani (*Carlists repulsed*) . . . 16 March, 1837
Irun (*British Legion defeats Carlists*) . 17 May, ,,
Valentia (*Carlists attacked*) . . . 15 July, ,,
Herera (*Don Carlos defeats Buereno*) . 24 Aug. ,,
Constantina (*Algiers; taken by French*) 13 Oct. ,,
St. Eustace (*Canadian rebels defeated*) . 14 Dec. ,,
Pennecerrada (*Carlists defeated*) . . 22 June, 1838
Prescott (*Canadian rebels defeated*) . 17 Nov. ,,
Aden (*taken*) . . . . 19 Jan. 1839
Ghiznee (*taken by Keane*) . . . . 23 July, ,,
Sidon (*taken by Napier*) . . . . 27 Sept. 1840
Beyrout (*Allies defeat Egyptians*) . . 10 Oct. ,,
Afghan War. (See *India*.)
Acre (*stormed by Allies*) . . . . 3 Nov. ,,
Kotriah (*Scinde; English victors*) . . 1 Dec. ,,
Chuen-pe (*English victors*) . . . . 7 Jan. 1841
Canton (*English take Bogue forts*) . . 26 Feb. ,,
Amoy (*taken*) . . . . 27 Aug. ,,
Chin-hae, &c. (*taken*) . . . . 10, 13 Oct. ,,
Candahar (*Afghans defeated*) . . . 10 March, 1842
Ningpo (*Chinese defeated*) . . . 10 March, ,,
Jellalabad (*Khyber Pass forced*) . . 5, 6 April, ,,
Chin-keang (*taken*) . . . . . 21 July, ,,
Ghiznee (*Afghans defeated by Nott*) . . 6 Sept. ,,
Meeanee (*Napier defeats Ameers*) . . 17 Feb. 1843
Hyderabad . . . . 24 March, ,,
Maharajpoor (*Gough defeats Mahrattas*) . 29 Dec. ,,
Isly (*French defeat Abd-el-Kader*) . . 14 Aug. 1844
Moodkee (*Gough defeats Sikhs*). . . 18 Dec. 1845

Ferozeshah (*ditto*) . . . . . . 21, 22 Dec. 1845
Aliwal (*Smith defeats Sikhs*) . . . 28 Jan. 1846
Sobraon (*Gough defeats Sikhs*) . . . 10 Feb. ,,
Palo Alto (*Taylor defeats Mexicans*) . . 8, 9 May, ,,
Montery (*Mexicans def. by Americans*) 21-23 Sept. ,,
Bueno Vista (*Americans defeat Mexicans*) . 22 Feb. 1847
St. Ubes (*Portugal*) . . . . . 9 May, ,,
Ozontero (*Americans defeat Mexicans*) . 19, 20 Aug. ,,
Flensborg (*Danes defeat rebels*) . . 9 April, 1848
Dannawerke (*Prussians defeat Danes*) . 23 April, ,,
Curtatone (*Austrians defeat Italians*) . 29 May, ,,
Custozza (*ditto*) . . . . . . 23 July, ,,
Velencze (*Croats and Hungarians*) . . 29 Sept. ,,
Mooltan (*Sikhs repulsed*) . . . . 7 Nov. ,,
Chilianwallah (*Gough defeats Sikhs*) . . 13 Jan. 1849
Goojerat (*ditto*) . . . . . . 21 Feb. ,,
Gran (*Hungarians victors*) . . . . 27 Feb. ,,
Novara (*Radetzky defeats Sardinians*) . 23 March, ,,
Velletri (*Roman Republicans defeat Neapolitans*) 19 May, ,,
Pered (*Russians defeat Hungarians*) . . 21 June, ,,
Acs (*Hungarians repulsed*) . . . 2 & 10 July, ,,
Waitzen (*taken by Russians*) . . . 17 July, ,,
Schässberg (*Russians defeat Bem*) . . 31 July, ,,
Temeswar (*Haynau defeats Hungarians*) . 10 Aug. ,,
Idstedt (*Danes defeat Holsteiners*) . . 25 July, 1850
Nankin taken by Imperialists . . . 19 July, 1853

RUSSO-TURKISH WAR.

Oltenitza (*Turks repulse Russians*) . . 4 Nov. 1853
Sinope, *n.* (*Turkish fleet destroyed*) . 30 Nov. ,,
Citate (*Turks defeat Russians*) . . . 6 Jan. 1854
Silistria (*ditto*) . . . . . . 13-15 June, ,,
Giurgevo (*ditto*) . . . . . . 7 July, ,,
Bayazid (*Russians defeat Turks*) . 29, 30 July, ,,
Kuruk-Derek (*ditto*) . . . . . 5 Aug. ,,
Alma (*English and French defeat Russians*) 20 Sept. ,,
Balaklava (*ditto*) . . . . . 25 Oct. ,,
Inkermann (*ditto*) . . . . . 5 Nov. ,,
Eupatoria (*Turks defeat Russians*) . . 17 Feb. 1855
Malakhoff tower (*Allies and Russians; indec. night combats*) . . . 22, 23, 24 May, ,,
Capture of the Mamelon, &c. . . . 7 June, ,,
Unsuccessful attempt on Malakhoff tower, and Redan (*Allies and Russians*) 18 June. ,,
Tchernaya or Bridge of Traktir (*Allies def. Russians*) 16 Aug. ,,
Malakhoff taken by the French . . 8 Sept. ,,
Ingour (*Turks defeat Russians*) . . 6 Nov. ,,
Baïdar (*French defeat Russians*) . . 8 Dec. ,,

PERSIAN WAR.

Bushire (*English defeat Persians*) . . 10 Dec. 1856
Kooshab (*ditto*) . . . . . . 8 Feb. 1857
Mohammerah (*ditto*) . . . . . 26 March, ,,

INDIAN MUTINY. (See *India*.)

Conflicts before Delhi. 30, 31 May; 8 June; 4, 9, 18, 23 July, 1857
Victories of General Havelock, near Futtehpore, 11 July, Cawnpore, &c. 12 July to 16 Aug. ,,
Pandoo Nuddee (*victory of Neill*) . . 15 Aug. ,,
Nujuffghur (*death of Nicholson, victor*) . 25 Aug. ,,
Assault and capture of Delhi . . 14-20 Sept. ,,
Conflicts before Lucknow, 25, 26 Sept.; 18, 25 Nov. ,,
Victories of Col. Greathed . 27 Sept; 10 Oct. ,,
Cawnpore (*victory of Campbell*) . . . 6 Dec. ,,
Futteghur (*ditto*) . . . . . 2 Jan. 1858
Calpi (*victory of Inglis*) . . . . 4 Feb. ,,
Alumbagh (*victories of Outram*) 12 Jan. and 21 Feb. ,,
Conflicts at Lucknow (*taken*) . . 14-19 March, ,,
Jhansi (*Rose victorious*) . . . . 4 April, ,,
Kooneh (*ditto*) . . . . . . 11 May, ,,
Gwalior (*ditto*) . . . . . . 17 June, ,,
Bajghur (*Mitchell defeats Tantia Topee*) . 15 Sept. ,,
Dhoodea Khera (*Clyde defeats Beni Mahdo*) 24 Nov. ,,
Gen. Horsford defeats the Begum of Oude and Nana Sahib . . . . . . 10 Feb. 1859

ITALIAN WAR. (See *Italy*.)

Austrians cross the Ticino . . . 27 April, 1859
French troops enter Piedmont . . . May, ,,
Montebello (*Allies victorious*) . . . 20 May, ,,
Palestro (*ditto*) . . . . . 30, 31 May, ,,
Magenta (*ditto*) . . . . . . 4 June, ,,
Malegnano (*ditto*) . . . . . 8 June, ,,
Solferino (*ditto*) . . . . . 24 June, ,,
(Armistice agreed to, 6 July, 1859.)

Taku, at the mouth of the Peiho or Tien-Tsin-ho (*English attack on the Chinese Forts defeated*) . 25 June, 1859
Taku forts taken (see *China*) . . . 21 Aug. 1860
Chang-kia-wan, 18 Sept.; and Pa-li-chiau (*Chinese defeated*) . . . . . . 21 Sept. ,,

---

Castillejo (*Spaniards defeat Moors*) . . 1 Jan. ,,
Tetuan (*ditto*) . . . . . . 4 Feb. ,,
Guad-el-Ras (*ditto*) . . . . 23 March, ,,

Calatifimi (*Garibaldi defeats Neapolitans*) 15 May, 1860
Melazzo (*Garibaldi defeats Neapolitans*) 20, 21 July, ,,
Castel Fidardo (*Sardinians defeat Papal troops*), 18 Sept. ,,
Volturno (*Garibaldi defeats Neapolitans*) . 1 Oct. ,,
Isernia (*Sardinians defeat Neapolitans*) . 17 Oct. ,,
Garigliano (*Sardinians defeat Neapolitans*) 3 Nov. ,,
Sardinians defeat Neapolitan re-actionists 22 Jan. 1861
Gaeta taken by the Sardinians . . . 13 Feb. ,,
Turks defeat Montenegrins . 19 Oct., 21 Nov. ,,
Aspromonte (*Garibaldi and his volunteers captured by Royal Italian Troops*) . . 29 Aug. 1862

Insurrection in New Zealand; English repulsed, 14, 28 March; 27 June; 10, 19 Sept.; 9, 12 Oct. 1860
Maohetia (*Maories defeated*) . . . . 6 Nov. ,,

CIVIL WAR IN UNITED STATES*—WAR IN MEXICO.

Big Bethel (*Federals repulsed*) . . . 10 June, 1861
Booneville (*Lyon defeats Confederates*) . 18 June, ,,
Carthage (*Federal victory*) . . . . 5 July, ,,
Rich Mountain (*ditto*) . . . . . 11 July, ,,
Bull Run or Manassas (*Federal defeat and panic*) 21 July, ,,
Springfield or Wilson's Creek (*Feds. victors*) 10 Aug. ,,
Carnifex ferry (*Rosencrans defeats Floyd, Confederate*) 10 Sept. ,,
Lexington (*taken by Confederates*) . . 20 Sept. ,,
Pavon, South America (*Mitra def. Urquiza*) 17 Sept. ,,
Ball's Bluff (*Federals defeated*) . . 21 Oct. ,,
Mill Springs, Kentucky (*Confederates defeated and their general Zollicoffer killed*) . . 19 Jan. 1862
Roanoke Island, N.C. (*Federals victors*) 7, 8 Feb. ,,
Sugar Creek, Arkansas (*Confederates defeated*) 8 Feb. ,,
Fort Donnelson (*taken by Federals*) . . 16 Feb. ,,
Pea Ridge, Arkansas (*Federals victors*) 6-8 March, ,,
Hampton roads *n.* (*Merrimac repulsed by Monitor*) 9 March, ,,
Pittsburg Landing, or Shiloh (*favourable to Confederates*) . . . . . . 6, 7 April, ,,
Williamsburg (*Federals repulsed*) . . 5 May, ,,
Puebla (*Mexicans defeat French*) . . 5 May, ,,
Richmond (*successful sorties of Confederates*) 14 May, ,,
Orizaba (*Mexicans defeat French*) . . 18 May, ,,
Winchester (*Federals repulsed*) . . 18 May, ,,
Fairoaks (*before Richmond, indecisive*) . 31 May 1 June, ,,
Near Orizaba (*French defeat Mexicans*) . 13 June, ,,
Chickahominy (*severe conflicts before Richmond; Confederates retreat*) . 25 June to 1 July, ,,
Baton Rouge (*taken by Federals*) . . 5 Aug. ,,
Cedar Mountain (*favourable to Confederates*) 9 Aug. ,,
Severe conflicts on the Rappahannock 23-29 Aug. ,,
Bull Run (*defeat of Federals*) . . 29, 30 Aug. ,,
Antietam (*severe; Confederates retreat*) 17 Sept. ,,
Perryville (*Confederates worsted*) . . 8, 9 Oct. ,,
Fredericksburg (*Federals defeated by Lee*) 13 Dec. 1863
Murfreesburgh (*indecisive*) 29 Dec. 1862—3 Jan. ,,
Nashville (*Confederates defeated*) . . 2 Jan. ,,
Chancellorsville (*Confederates victors*) . 2-4 May, ,,
Winchester (*Ewell defeats Federals*) . 14 June, ,,
Gettysburg (*severe but indecisive*) . . 1-3 July, ,,
Chicamauga (*Confederates victorious*) 19-20 Sept. ,,
Chattanooga (*Confederates defeated*) . 23-26 Nov. ,,
Spottsylvania, &c., in the Wilderness, near Chancellorsville (*indecisive*) . . 10-12 May, 1864
Petersburg, near Richmond (*indecisive, but Grant advances*) . . . . . . 15-18 June, ,,
Winchester (*Confederates defeated*) . . 19 Sept. ,,
Cedar Creek (*ditto*) . . . . . 19 Oct. ,,
Franklin (*ditto*) . . . . . . 30 Nov. ,,
Nashville (*Thomas, Federal, defeats Hood*) 14-16 Dec. ,,

---

* There were many smaller conflicts, of which the accounts were very uncertain.

Five Forks (*Lee totally defeated*) . . . 1 April, 1865
Farmville (*Lee finally defeated*) . . . 6 April, ,,

Oeversee (*Danes and Allies*) . . . 6 Feb. 1864
Düppel (*taken by the Prussians*) . . . 18 April, ,,
Alsen (*ditto*) . . . 29 June, ,,
Rendsburg (*ditto*) . . . 21 July, ,,

SOUTH AMERICAN WAR. (See *Brazil.*)

Santayuna (*Allies defeat Paraguayans; Uruguyana taken*) . . . 18 Sept. 1865
Paso de la Patria (*indecisive*) . . . 25 Feb. 1866
Parana (*Allies victors*) . . . 16 April, ,,
Estero Velhaco (*ditto*) . . . 2 May, ,,
Tuyuty (*Allies defeated*) . . . 16, 18 July, ,,
Curupaïti (*ditto*) . . . 17, 19, 22 Sept. ,,
Tuyuty (*Allies victors*) . . . 30 Oct. ,,
Corumba (*taken by Brazilians*) . . . 13 June, 1867

SEVEN WEEKS' WAR (*Austria and Prussia*).

Custozza (*Austrians defeat Italians*) . . . 24 June, 1866
Lissa (*ditto, naval battle*) . . . 20 July, ,,
Prussian victories (as inscribed on shield exhibited at Berlin, 20 Sept. 1866, see *Prussia*).
Liebenau, Türnau, Podoll . . . 26 June, ,,
Nachod, Langensalza (*which see*), Oswiecin, Hühnerwasser . . . 27 June, ,,
Münchengrätz, Soor, Trautenau, Skalitz, 28 June, ,,
Gitschin, Königinhof, Jaromier, Schweinschädel, . . . 29 June, ,,
Koniggrätz or Sadowa . . . 3 July, ,,
Dermbach, 4 July; Hünfeld . . . 5 July, ,,
Waldaschach, Hausen, Hammelburg, Friedericshall, Kissingen . . . 10 July, ,,
Laufach, 13 July; Aschaffenburg . . . 14 July, ,,
Tobitschau, 15 July; Blumenau, 22 July; Hof, . . . 23 July, ,,
Tauber-Bischofsheim, Werbach, Hochhausen, . . . 24 July, ,,
Neubrunn, Helmstadt, Gerchsheim . . . 25 July, ,,
Roszbrunn, Wurzburg, Baireuth . . . 28 July, ,,

Monte Rotondo (*Garibaldians victors*) . . . 27 Oct. 1867
Mentana (*Garibaldi defeated*) . . . 3 Nov. ,,
Arógee or Fahla (*Abyssinians defeated*) . . . 10 April, 1868
Magdala stormed . . . 13 April, ,,
Russians defeat Bokharians and occupy Samarcand, . . . 25 May, ,,
Alcolea (*Spanish royalists defeated*) . . . 27, 28 Sept. ,,
Villeta (*Lopez defeated by Brazilians*), &c. . . . 11 Dec. ,,
Lopez defeated . . . 12, 16, 18, 21 Aug. 1869
Aquidaban (*Lopez defeated and killed*) . . . 1 March, 1870

FRANCO-PRUSSIAN WAR (*which see*).

Saarbrück, taken by the French, and Prussians repulsed . . . 2 Aug. 1870
Wissembourg (*French defeated*) . . . 4 Aug. ,,
Wörth (*ditto*) . . . 6 Aug. ,,
Saarbrück or Forbach (*ditto*) . . . 6 Aug. ,,
Courcelles or Pange (*ditto*) . . . 14 Aug. ,,
Strasburg (*ditto*) . . . 16 Aug. ,,
Vionville or Mars-la-Tour (*ditto*) . . . 16 Aug. ,,
Gravelotte or Rézonville (*ditto*) . . . 18 Aug. ,,
Beaumont (*ditto*) . . . 30 Aug. ,,
Carignan (*ditto*) . . . 31 Aug. ,,
Metz (*ditto*) . . . 31 Aug. ,,
Sedan (*ditto*) . . . 31 Aug., 1 Sept. ,,
Before Paris (*French defeated*) . . . 30 Sept. ,,
Thoury (*Germans surprised and repulsed*) . . . 5 Oct. ,,
St. Rémy (*French defeated*) . . . 6 Oct. ,,
Before Metz (*ditto*) . . . 7 Oct. ,,
Artenay (*ditto*) . . . 10 Oct. ,,
Cherizy (*Germans repulsed*) . . . 10 Oct. ,,
Orleans (*French defeated*) . . . 11 Oct. ,,
Ecouis (*indecisive*) . . . 14 Oct. ,,
Châteaudun (*French defeated*) . . . 18 Oct. ,,
Coulmiers, near Orleans (*Germans defeated*), . . . 9, 10 Nov. ,,
Near Amiens (*French defeated*) . . . 27 Nov. ,,
Villiers, before Paris (*French retreat*) . . . 30 Nov. ,,
. . . 2 Dec. ,,
Before Orleans (*French defeated*) . . . 4 Dec. ,,
Beaugency (*ditto*) . . . 7, 8 Dec. ,,
Nuits (*ditto*) . . . 18 Dec. ,,
Pont à Noyelles (*French claim a victory*) . . . 23 Dec. ,,
Bapaume (*indecisive*) . . . 2, 3 Jan. 1871
Le Mans (*indecisive*) . . . 6 Jan. ,,
Le Mans (*Chanzy def. by pr. Fred. Chas.*), 10-12 Jan. ,,

Belfort (*Bourbaki defeated*) . . . 15-17 Jan. 1871
St. Quentin (*Faidherbe defeated*) . . . 19 Jan. ,,
Paris (*Trochu's grand sortie repulsed*) . . . 19 Jan. ,,

Oroquieta (*Carlists defeated*) . . . 4 May, 1872
Elmina (*Ashantees defeated by British*) . . . 13 June, 1873
Elgueta (*Carlists said to be victorious*) . . . 5, 6 Aug. ,,
Mañeru (*Carlists and Republicans: indecisive*) 6 Oct. ,,
Abrakampra (*Ashantees defeated*) . . . 5, 6 Nov. ,,
Borborassie (*ditto*) . . . 29 Jan. 1874
Amoaful (*ditto*) . . . 31 Jan. ,,
Bocquah (*ditto*) . . . 1 Feb. ,,
Fommanah (*ditto*) . . . 2 Feb. ,,
Ordahsa (*ditto*) . . . 4 Feb. ,,
Before Bilbao (*several days; Carlists retreat; Concha enters Bilbao*) . . . 2 May, ,,
Estella (*sharp conflicts; Carlists retreat; Concha killed*) . . . 25, 27 June, ,,
Irun (*Laserna defeats Carlists*) . . . 10 Nov. ,,
Sorota, Peru (*Pierota and insurgents defeated*) 3 Dec. ,,
Near Tolosa (*Carlists repulse Loma*) . . . 7, 8 Dec. ,,
Khokand (*Russians under Kaufman defeat the Khan's troops, &c.*) . . . 4, 21 Sept. 1875
Abyssinians defeat Egyptians . . . Oct. ,,
Assake (*Khokand chiefs defeated*) . . . 30 Jan. 1876
Servian war begins . . . 1 July, ,,
Saitschar (*severe conflicts; Servians retreat*) 2, 3 July, ,,
Urbitza (*Montenegrins defeat Turks*) . . . 28 July, ,,
TURKISH WARS *with Servia, and Montenegro*, declared . . . 2 July, ,,
Zaicar or Saitschar (*Turks and Servians, indecisive*) . . . 3 July, ,,
Novi Bazar (*Turks said to be victors*) . . . 6 July, ,,
Urbitza (*Montenegrins victors*) . . . 28 July, ,,
Gurgusovatz (*Turks victors*) . . . 5–7 Aug. ,,
Medun (*Montenegrins victors*) . . . 7 or 14 Aug. ,,
Morava valley near Alexinatz (*severe conflicts, favourable to Turks*) . . . 19–27 Aug. ,,
Podgoritza (*Montenegrins victors*) . . . 26 Aug. ,,
Alexinatz (*Turks victors*), 1, 2, 28, 29 Sept., captured . . . 31 Oct. ,,
Peace between Turkey and Servia . . . 1 March, 1877
RUSSO-TURKISH WAR (*which see*), began . 24 April, ,,
Tahir (*Turks defeated*) . . . 16 June, ,,
Nicopolis (*stormed by Russians, severe fights*) . . . 15, 16 July, ,,
Plevna (*Russians defeated*) 19, 20, & 30, 31 July, ,,
Kurukdara or Kizil Tepe (*ditto*) . . . 24, 25 Aug. ,,
Valley of Lom (*ditto*) . . . 22–24 Aug. ,,
Schipka Pass (*dreadful conflicts, Turks under Suleiman repulsed*) . . . 20–27 Aug. ,,
Karahassankoi, &c., on the Lom (*severe; Russians retreat*) . . . 30 Aug. ,,
Lovatz or Luftcha (*taken by Russians*) . . . 3 Sept. ,,
Plevna (*held by Osman Pasha, severe conflicts, Russians defeated*) . . . 11, 12 Sept. ,,
Schipka Pass (*Suleiman defeated*). . . . 17 Sept. ,,
Near Kars (*Russians defeated*) . . . 2–4 Oct. ,,
Aladja Dagh, near Kars (*Turks under Mukhtar totally defeated*) . . . 14, 15 Oct. ,,
Deve-Boyun, Armenia (*Turks under Mukhtar defeated after 9 hours' fighting*) . . . 4 Nov. ,,
Azizi, near Erzeroum (*Russians defeated*) . . . 9 Nov. ,,
Kars taken by storm by Russians . . . 17, 18 Nov. ,,
Elena (*taken by Turks after sharp conflict*) . 4 Dec. ,,
Plevna (*Osman Pasha endeavours to break out; totally defeated; surrenders unconditionally*) . . . 9, 10 Dec. ,,
Senova in the Balkans (*Turks defeated*) 9-10 Jan. 1878
Near Philippopolis (*ditto*) . . . 14, 15 Jan. ,,

AFGHAN WAR (see *Afghanistan*).

Ali Musjid captured by British . . . 22 Nov. 1878
Peiwar Pass (*victory of gen. Roberts*) . . . 2 Dec. ,,
Futtehabad (*victory of gen. Gough*) . . . 2 April, 1879
Char-aseab (*Afghans defeated*) . . . 6 Oct. ,,
Severe fighting near Cabul . . . Dec. 1879–April, 1880
Ahmed Khel (*Stewart defeats Afghans*) 19–23 April, ,,
Kuschki-Nakhud or Maiwand (*Ayoob Khan defeats Burrows*) . . . 27 July, ,,
Mazra or Baba Wali (*Roberts totally defeats Ayoob Khan*) . . . 1 Sept. ,,

ZULU WAR (see *Zululand*).

Isandula (*British surprised and defeated*) . . . 22 Jan. 1879
Rorke's Drift (*successfully defended by British*) 22 Jan. ,,
Ulundi (*Cetewayo totally defeated by lord Chelmsford*) . . . 4 July, ,,

CHILIAN AND PERUVIAN WAR (see *Chili*).

Iquique (*Chilians defeat Peruvians*) . . Nov. 1879
Choukos and Miraflores (*ditto*) . . 17 Jan. 1881

RUSSIAN WAR.

Geok or Denghli Tepé (*Russians and Turkomans, indecisive*) . . 9 Sept. 1879
Geok Tepé (*besieged by Russians, severe conflicts*), 24 Dec. 1880, 4, 9, 10, Jan., taken . 24 Jan. 1881

TRANSVAAL WAR.

Laing's Nek (*British defeated*) . . . 28 Jan. 1881
Ingogo River (*ditto*) . . . 8 Feb. ,,
Majuba Hill (*ditto*) . . . 27 Feb. ,,

WAR IN EGYPT (see *Egypt*).

Bombardment of forts at Alexandria . 11 July, 1882
Tel-el-Mahuta and Masameh (*rebels defeated by British*) . . . . 24, 25 Aug. ,,
Kassasin (*ditto*) . . 28 Aug. and 9 Sept. ,,
Tel-el-Kebir (*ditto—decisive*) . . 13 Sept. ,,

[See *Soudan*.]

Rebels in the Soudan defeated by Hicks 29 April, 1883
El Obeid or Kashgal (*Hicks and his army destroyed*) 3-5 Nov. ,,
Tokar (*Egyptians defeated*) . . . 6 Nov. ,,
Near Teb, Baker with Egyptians was defeated by rebels . . . . 4 Feb. 1884
Teb (*Graham totally defeats rebels*) . . 29 Feb. ,,

For Chinese and French war, see *China* and *Tonquin*.

Abu Klea (*Stewart defeats rebels*) . . 17 Jan. 1885
Gubat (*rebels defeated*) . . . 19 Jan. ,,
Kerkeban (*ditto, gen. Earle killed*) . . 10 Feb. ,,
Hasheen (*rebels defeated*) . . 20 March, ,,
Rebel attack near Souakim repulsed 22 March, ,,
Ak Tapa (*Russians defeat Afghans*) 30 March, ,,
Chalchuapa (*Barrios defeated and killed*) see *America, Central* . . . 2 April, ,,
Fish Creek (*Canadians defeat rebels*) 24 April, ,,
Battleford (*ditto*) . . . 3 May, ,,
Batoche (*ditto*) . . . 9 May, ,,

[See *Bulgaria, Burmah,* and *Soudan*.]

Dagoli near Massowah (*Italians destroyed in heroic attack on Abyssinians*) [See *Abyssinia*] 25-26 Jan. 1887
Jelapla Pass (*Tibetans defeated*) . 24 Sept. 1888
Taskkurgan and Mazari Sherif (*Ishak Khan, rebel, defeated*) . . . 29-30 Sept. ,,
Suakim (*defeat of the Arab Dervishes by gen. Grenfell*) 20 Dec. ,,

Dervishes repulsed, 19, 29, 30 April; 2 June; 4 July 1890
Arguin (*Col. Wodehouse defeats Dervishes*) . 2 July, ,,
Anabi (*Dervishes defeated*) . . 31 July, ,,
Toski (*ditto by gen. Grenfell*) . . 3 Aug. ,,
Witu stormed, see *Zanzibar* . . 27 Oct. ,,
Wounded Knee Creek, see *Indians* . 29 Dec. ,,
Tokar, Soudan (*Osman Digna defeated*) . 19 Feb. 1891
Placilla, Chili (*Balmaceda defeated by congressists*) 28 Aug. ,,

Dogba (Dahomeyans defeated by the French), 17 Sept. 1892

Adowa (*Italians defeated by Abyssinians*), 29 Feb.–1 March, 1896

Ferkeh, Soudan (*Dervishes defeated by gen. Kitchener*) . . . 7 June, ,,
Bida (*Fulahs defeated*); see *Niger* 26, 27 Feb. 1897
Atbara, Soudan (*Dervishes defeated by gen. Kitchener*) 8 April, 1898

Omdurman or Khartum, Soudan (*total defeat of the Khalifa*) . . . 2 Sept. ,,
Om Debrikat, Soudan (*the Khalifa defeated and killed*) [see *Soudan*] . . Nov. 1899

WAR IN KOREA. See *Corea*.

Ping-Yang (*Chinese defeated by Japanese*) 15, 16 Sept. 1894
Yalu river (*Naval—ditto*) . 17 Sept. ,,
Wei-hai-wei (bombardment) 30 Jan.–12 Feb. 1895

GRECO-TURKISH WAR (*which see*).

Analipsis (*Turks defeated*) 16–18 April, 1897
Maluna Pass (*Greeks defeated*) 17–19 April, ,,
Mati (*Greeks defeated*) . 22 April, ,,
Larissa, plain of (*Greeks defeated*) 20–23 April, ,,
Pentepigadia (*Greeks defeated*) 28–29 April, ,,
Phersala (*Greeks defeated*) . . 5 May, ,,
Gribovo (*indecisive*) . . . . 14 May, 1897
Domoko (*indecisive*) . . . . 17 May, ,,

Spanish-American war (*which see*).

SOUTH AFRICAN WAR.

Talana Hill (*Boers defeated*) . . . 20 Oct. 1899
Glencoe or Dundee (*ditto*) . . . 20 Oct. ,,
Elandslaagte (*ditto*) . . . 21 Oct. ,,
Nicholson's Nek (*British defeated*) . . 30 Oct. ,,
Belmont (*Boers defeated*) . . . 23 Nov. ,,
Enslin (Graspan) (*ditto*) . . . 25 Nov. ,,
Modder River (*Methuen forced Cronje to quit his positions*) . . . . 28 Nov. ,,
Stormberg (*British defeated*) . . . 10 Dec. ,,
Magersfontein (*ditto*) . . . 11 Dec. ,,
Colenso (*ditto*) . . . . 15 Dec. ,,
Ladysmith (*Boers defeated*) . . 6 Jan. 1900
Spion Kop (*captured by the British and afterwards evacuated*) . . . 17–24 Jan. ,,
Paardeberg (*Boers defeated*) . 16, 18–27 Feb. ,,
Driefontein (*ditto*) . . . 10 March, ,,
Sanna's Post (*British defeated*) . . 31 March, ,,
Reddersburg (*ditto*) . . . 3, 4 April, ,,
Senekal (*Boers defeated*) . . . 29 May, ,,
Johannesburg (*ditto*) . . . 29 May, ,,

(For minor engagements, see *S. African War*).

(For numerous small conflicts and skirmishes, see *Franco-Prussian War, Herzegovina, Russo-Turkish Wars, Spain, Sumatra, Turkey, United States, Kaffirs, Egypt, Zululand, Basutoland, Chili, Soudan, Tonquin, Salvador, India, Burmah, Manipur, Lagos, Senegal, Dahomey, Mashonaland, Brazil, Corea, Chitral, Cuba, Madagascar, Massowah, Rhodesia,* &c., and for details of important engagements see *separate articles*. Frontier war; see *India*, 1897.)

BATUM, see *Batoum*.

BAUGÉ, see *Anjou*.

BAUTZEN, a town in Saxony, near which desperate battles were fought 20, 21, and 22 May, 1813, between the French, commanded by Napoleon, and the allies under the emperor of Russia and the king of Prussia. The struggle commenced on the 19th, with a contest on the outposts, which cost each army a loss of above 2000 men. On the 20th (at Bautzen) the French were more successful; and on the 21st (at Wurschen) the allies were compelled to retire; but Napoleon obtained no permanent advantage. Duroc was killed at Reichenbach by a cannon-ball, on 22 May.

BAVARIA (part of ancient Noricum and Vindelicia), a kingdom in South Germany, conquered from the Celtic Gauls (Boii) by the Franks between 630 and 660. The country was afterwards governed by dukes subject to the French monarchs. Tasillon II. was deposed by Charlemagne, who established margraves in 788. The margrave Leopold, 895, father of Arnulph the Bad, is styled the first duke. Bavaria made a kingdom from 1 Jan. 1806, was made a constitutional monarchy, 26 May, 1818. It joined the German empire, 22 Nov. 1870. Population, 1 Dec. 1871, 4,863,450; Dec. 1875, 5,022,390; 1885, 5,420,199; 1890, 5,594,982; 1900, 6,200,000. See *Munich*.

Bavaria supports Austria in the contest with Prussia . . . . June, 1866
Made peace with Prussia . . . 22 Aug. ,,
Population (after cessions, 1866), 4,824,421 . Dec. 1867
An international exhibition in a crystal palace opened . . . . 20 July, 1869
The chambers dissolved, as, through a party struggle, no president was elected . . 6 Oct. ,,
Resignation of the ministry, 25 Nov.; only partially accepted by the king . . 9 Dec. ,,
Vote of want of confidence in prince Hohenlohe, the president, 12 Feb.; he resigns . 14 Feb. 1870
The king announces his intention of joining Prussia in the war with France . . about 20 July, ,,

The Bavarian contingent highly distinguishes itself in the war; Otho, duke of Bavaria, killed near Beglie . . . . . 27 Jan. 1871
President of council, and foreign minister, A. de Pfretzschner . . . . . 22 Aug. „
[See *Franco-Prussian War.*]
The king in a letter to the king of Saxony, proposes that the king of Prussia should be made emperor of Germany . . . . . about 5 Dec.
Dr. Döllinger excommunicated for opposing papal infallibility, 18 April; elected rector of the university of Munich . . . . . 20 July, „
Government protests against papal infallibility (see *Germany*) . . . . . 27 Sept. „
"Old Catholic" church opened at Munich, end of Sept. „
The king charges Von Gasser to form an Ultramontane ministry, opposed to German unity, 3 Sept. he fails . . . . . Sept. 1872
Queen dowager, Mary of Prussia, received into the Catholic Church . . . . . 12 Oct. 1874
New Ultramontane party ("popular Catholic") formed . . . . . 6 March, 1877
International exhibition at Munich opened 19 July, 1879
Seventh centenary of foundation of the dynasty (Otto of Wittelsbach made duke by Frederick Barbarossa) . . . . . 25 Aug. 1880
Prince Luitpold proclaimed Regent on account of the king's mental illness . . . . . 10 June, 1886
The king drowns himself in Starnberg Lake; Dr. Gudden drowned in attempting to save him, 13 June, „
The emperor William II. present at the Bavarian military manœuvres near Munich 7 Sept. *et seq.* 1891
An agreement arranged between the emperor and prince regent regarding military judicial procedure, announced . . . . . 24 Nov. 1898

DUKES.

1071. Guelf I., an illustrious warrior.
1101. Guelf II.; son; married the countess Matilda, 1089.
1120. Henry the Black; brother.
1126. Henry the Proud; son. (He competed with Conrad of Hohenstaufen for the empire, failed, and was deprived of Bavaria.)
1138. Leopold, margrave of Austria; *d.* 1142.
1142. Henry of Austria; brother; *d.* 1177.
1154. Henry the Lion (son of Henry the Proud), ancestor of the Brunswick family, restored by the emperor Frederick Barbarossa, but expelled by him 1180; (see *Brunswick*): *d.* 1195.
1180. Otho, count of Wittelsbach, made duke; *d.* 1183.
1183. Louis; son.
1231. Otho II., the Illustrious; son; gained the palatinate; assassinated 1231.
1253. Louis II., the Severe; son; *d.* 1294.
1294. Louis III.; son (without the palatinate) emperor; *d.* 1347.
1347. Stephen I.; son; *d.* 1375.
1375. John; brother; *d.* 1397.
1397. Ernest; brother; *d.* 1438.
1438. Albert I.; son; *d.* 1460.
1460. John II. and Sigismund; sons; resigned to
1465. Albert II.; brother; *d.* 1508.
1508. William I.; son; opposed the reformation, 1522; *d.* 1550.
1550. Albert III.; son; *d.* 1573.
1579. William II.; son; abdicated, 1596; *d.* 1626.
1596. Maximilian the Great; son; the first ELECTOR of Bavaria, 25 Feb. 1623; the palatinate restored, 1648; *d.* 27 Sept. 1651.
1651. Ferdinand-Mary; *d.* 26 May, 1679.
1679. Maximilian Emanuel; son; allies with France, 1702; defeated at Blenheim, 1704; restored to his dominions, 1714; *d.* 26 Feb. 1726.
1726. Charles Albert; son; elected emperor, 1742; defeated, 1744; *d.* 20 Jan. 1745.
1745. Maximilian-Joseph I.; son; as elector; *d.* 30 Dec. 1777; *end of younger line of Wittelsbach.*
1778. Charles Theodore (the *elector palatine* of the Rhine since 1743). The French take Munich; he treats with them, 1796; *d.* 1799.
1799. Maximilian-Joseph II.; elector; territories changed by treaty of Luneville, 1801; enlarged when made king, by treaty of Presburg, Dec. 1805.

KINGS OF BAVARIA.

1806. Maximilian-Joseph I. He deserted Napoleon, and had his enlarged territories confirmed to him, Oct. 1813; grants a constitutional charter, 22 Aug. 1818; *d.* 13 Oct. 1825.
1825. Louis I., 13 Oct.; abdicated 21 March, 1848;* died 29 Feb. 1868.
1848. Maximilian-Joseph II.; son; born 28 Nov. 1811; died 10 March, 1864.
1864. Louis II. (son) amiable and eccentric, great patron of composer Wagner: born 25 Aug. 1845; deposed 10 June; suicide 13 June, 1886.
1886. Otho William (brother of Louis II.); 13 June; born 27 April, 1848 (insane).
Regent (heir) Prince Luitpold, uncle; 10 June, 1886; (born, 22 March, 1821.)

BAVENO, a village of Piedmont, on the Lago Maggiore. At a villa here queen Victoria resided from 28 March to 23 April, 1879.

BAY ISLANDS (the chief, Ruatan), in the bay of Honduras, central America, belonged to Spain till 1821; then to Great Britain, which formed them into a colony in 1852, but ceded them to Honduras, 28 Nov. 1859: see *Honduras.*

BAYEUX TAPESTRY, mythically said to have been wrought by Matilda, queen of William I., or to have been made under the direction of his brother Odo, bishop of Bayeux. It is 19 inches wide, 214 feet long, and is divided into compartments showing the events from the visit of Harold to the Norman court to his death at Hastings; it is now preserved in the public library of Bayeux near Caen. A copy, drawn by C. Stothard, and coloured after the original, was published by the Society of Antiquaries in 1821-3. Reproduced by autotype process by F. R. Fowke, with notes, 1875; new edition 1889.

BAYLEN (S. Spain), where on 20 July, 1808, the French, commanded by generals Dupont and Wedel, were defeated by the Spaniards under Reding, Coupigny, and other generals.

BAYONET, the short dagger fixed at the end of fire-arms, said to have been invented at Bayonne, in France, about 1647, 1670, or 1690. It was used at Killiecrankie in 1689, and at Marsaglia by the French, in 1693, "with great success, against the enemy unprepared for the encounter with so formidable a novelty." The ring-bayonet was adopted by the British, 24 Sept. 1693.
New pattern of bayonets adopted in 1876; asserted to be defective in the Soudan campaign 1884-5.
Strict examination ordered 1885. See under *Arms.*

BAYONNE (S. France), an ancient city. It was held by the English from 1295 till it was taken by Charles VII. The queens of Spain and France met the cruel duke of Alva here, June, 1556, it is supposed to arrange the massacre of St. Bartholomew. Charles IV. of Spain abdicated here in favour of "his friend and ally" the emperor Napoleon, 4 May, and his sons, Ferdinand prince of Asturias, don Carlos, and don Antonio renounced their rights to the Spanish throne, 6 May, 1808. In the neighbourhood of Bayonne was much desperate fighting between the French and British armies, 9-13 Dec. 1813. Bayonne was invested by the British, 14 Jan. 1814; on 14 April, the French

* The abdication of Charles-Louis was mainly caused by his attachment to an intriguing woman, known throughout Europe by the assumed name of Lola Montes, who, in the end, was expelled the kingdom for her interference in state affairs, and afterwards led a wandering life. She delivered lectures in London, in 1859; thence proceeded to the United States; and died at New York, 17 Jan. 1861.

made a sally, and attacked the English with success, but were at length driven back. The loss of the British was considerable, and lieut.-gen. sir John Hope was wounded and taken prisoner.—A Franco-Spanish industrial and fine arts exhibition was opened at Bayonne in July, 1864.

BAYREUTH (N. Germany), a margraviate, held formerly by a branch of the Brandenburg family, was with that of Anspach abdicated by the reigning prince in favour of the king of Prussia, 1790. The archives were brought (in 1783) from Plassenburg to the city of Bayreuth, which was incorporated with Bavaria by Napoleon in 1806. National Theatre erected for the performance of Wagner's works, completed 1875. Opened with grand representation of his Nibelungen trilogy 1876. Wagner buried here, 14 Feb. 1883.

BAZAAR, or covered market, a word of Arabic origin. The magnificent bazaar of Ispahan was excelled by that of Tauris, which has held 30,000 men in order of battle. In London the Soho-square bazaar was opened by Mr. Trotter in 1816 to relieve the relatives of persons killed in the war, offered for sale 1879, closed shortly afterwards. The Queen's bazaar, Oxford-street, a very extensive one, was (with the Diorama) burnt down, and the loss estimated at 50,000*l.*, 27 May, 1829. It was rebuilt, and converted into the Princess's Theatre, opened 30 Sept. 1841. The St. James's bazaar (built by Mr. Crockford) in 1832. The Pantheon, made a bazaar in 1834, closed March 2, 1867; see *Pantheon*. The Corinthian bazaar, Argyll-street, Oxford-street (to replace the bazaar at the Pantheon) opened 30 July, 1867; closed in 1868. The Lowther Arcade, a covered walk from West Strand to St. Martin's Churchyard, built 1830-32. The last public bazaar in London closed 1902.

BAZAINE, Marshal, trial, &c., Dec. 1873 and Aug. 1874. See *Metz* and *France*.

BAZEILLES, a village in the Ardennes, N.E. France. During the dreadful battle of Sedan, 1 Sept. 1870, Bazeilles was burnt by the Bavarians, and atrocious outrages were said to have been committed. Of nearly 2000 inhabitants it was asserted scarcely fifty remained alive, and these indignantly denied having given provocation. Much controversy ensued, and in July, 1871, gen. Von der Tann asserted correctly that the number of deaths had been grossly exaggerated, that there had been much provocation, and denied the alleged cruelties.

BAZOCHE-DES-HAUTES, near Orleans, central France. Here a part of the army of the Loire, under gen. D'Aurelle de Paladines, was defeated after a severe action, by the Germans under the grand-duke of Mecklenburg, 2 Dec. 1870. See *Orleans*.

BEACHY HEAD, a promontory, S. E. Sussex, near which the British and Dutch fleet, commanded by the earl of Torrington, was defeated by a superior French force under admiral Tourville, 30 June, 1690; the allies suffered very severely. The Dutch lost two admirals, 500 men, and several ships—sunk to prevent them from falling into the hands of the enemy; the English lost two ships and 400 men.

BEACONS, see *Lighthouses, Jubilee*, 1887.

BEACONSFIELD Administration, see *Disraeli* and *People's Tribute*.

BEADS were early used in the east for reckoning prayers. St. Augustin mentions them 366. About 1090, Peter the Hermit is said to have made a series of 55 beads. To Dominic de Guzman is ascribed the invention of the Rosary (a series of 15 large and 150 small beads), in honour of the Blessed Virgin, about 1202. Beads soon after were in general use. The Bead-roll was a list of deceased persons, for the repose of whose souls a certain number of prayers was recited. Beads have been found in British barrows.

BEAM and Scales. The apparatus for weighing goods was so called, "as it weighs so much at the king's *beam*." A public beam was set up in London, and all commodities ordered to be weighed by the city officer, called the weigh-master, who was to do justice between buyer and seller, stat. 3 Edw. II. 1309. *Stow*. Beams and scales, with weights and measures, were ordered to be examined by the justices at quarter sessions, 35 Geo. III. 1794; see *Weights and Measures*.

BEANS, Black and White, were used by the ancients in gathering the votes of the people for the election of magistrates. A white bean signified absolution, and a black one condemnation. The precept of Pythagoras to abstain from beans, *abstine a fabis*, has been variously interpreted. "Beans do not favour mental tranquillity." *Cicero*. The finer kinds of beans were brought here with other vegetables, in Henry VIII.'s reign.

BEAR-BAITING, an ancient popular English sport, prohibited by parliament in 1835.

BEARDS.* The Egyptians did not wear beards; the Assyrians did. They have been worn for centuries by the Jews, who were forbidden to mar their beards, 1490 B.C. *Lev.* xix. 27. The Tartars waged a long war with the Persians, declaring them infidels, because they would not cut their beards, after the custom of Tartary. The Greeks wore their beards till the time of Alexander, who ordered the Macedonians to be shaved, lest the beard should give a handle to their enemies, 330 B.C. Beards were worn by the Romans, 390 B.C. The emperor Julian wrote a diatribe (entitled "*Misopogon*") against wearing beards, A.D. 362.—In England, they were not fashionable after the conquest, 1066, until the 13th century, and were discontinued at the Restoration. Peter the Great enjoined the Russians, even of rank, to shave, but was obliged to keep officers on foot to cut off the beard by force. Since 1851 the custom of wearing the beard gradually increased in Great Britain.

BEARER COMPANY, introduced in the British army 1873 for the removal of the wounded from the battle-field and to render first aid. On active service half a company is attached to each army corps.

BÉARN, S. France, the ancient Benecharnum, was held successively by the Romans, Franks, Goths,

* A bearded woman was taken by the Russians at the battle of Pultowa, and presented to the Czar, Peter I., 1724: her beard measured 1½ yard. A woman is said to have been seen at Paris with a bushy beard, and her whole body covered with hair. *Dict. de Trévoux*. The great Margaret, governess of the Netherlands, had a very long stiff beard. In Bavaria, in the time of Wolfius, a virgin had a long black beard. Mdlle. Bois de Chêne, born at Geneva (it was said) in 1834, was exhibited in London, in 1852-3, when, consequently, eighteen years of age; she had a profuse head of hair, a strong black beard, large whiskers, and thick hair on her arms and down from her neck on her back, and masculine features.

and Gascons, and became a hereditary viscounty in 819, under Centule I., son of Loup, duke of Gascony. From his family it passed to the houses—of Gabaret, 1134; of Moncade, 1170; of Foix, 1290; and of Bourbon, 1550. Its annexation to France was decreed by Henry IV., 1594; affirmed by Louis XIII., 1620.

BEARS and BULLS, see *Stocks*.

BEAUGÉ, see *Anjou*.

BEAULIEU, ABBEY OF, (reformed Benedictines) founded by king John, in the New Forest, Hampshire, in 1204, and dedicated to the Blessed Virgin, had the privilege of sanctuary. It afforded an asylum to Margaret, queen of Henry VI., after the defeat of the earl of Warwick at Barnet, 14 April, 1471; and to Perkin Warbeck, Sept. 1497.

BEAUMONT, a village near Sedan, department of Ardennes, N.E. France. Near here a part of the army of marshal MacMahon under De Failly, which, after vainly endeavouring to reach Metz, was retreating before the Germans under the crown prince of Prussia, was surprised, defeated, and driven across the Meuse at Mouzon, 30 Aug. 1870. The French loss included about 7000 prisoners, many guns, and much camp equipage. The victory was chiefly gained by the Bavarians.

BEAUMONT TRUST. Mr. John Thomas Barber Beaumont, artist, financier, founder of the London and County Fire Office (born 1774, died 1840), bequeathed 12,500*l.* to establish an institution for the moral and intellectual improvement of the working classes of east London, which was opened in Beaumont-square, Mile-end.

By the munificence of the Drapers' Company, the Royal Family, the duke of Westminster, and many others, the fund in June, 1886, amounted to 75,000*l.* The trustees proposed the erection of a "People's Palace," to include a public library and reading rooms, technical schools, summer and winter gardens, a concert hall, swimming baths and gymnasia. The queen was patron of the undertaking, which is partly supported by subscription.

The foundation stone of the "Queen's hall" was laid by the prince of Wales 28 June, 1886; opened by the queen (who also laid the foundation of the Technical schools) 14 May, 1887; Mr. John Rogers Jennings, Master of the Drapers' Company, knighted.

The undertaking greatly supported by sir Edmund Currie, and the late Mr. (afterwards sir) Walter Besant.

Exhibition of East London Industries opened in the Queen's hall by Lady Rosebery 24 May, 1887.

Queen's Jubilee; 10,000 girls and 10,000 boys entertained by the Drapers' Company 23, 24 June, 1887.

Educational classes, &c., open 3 Oct. 1887. In Oct. 1888, the institution was reported to be highly successful.

New Technical School opened 5 Oct. 1888.

The palace opened on Sundays for reading and sacred music, 1889. About 3,000 persons attended 2 Oct. 1889.

Industrial and art exhibition opened by the prince and princess of Wales; 6 June, 1896.

BEAUNE-LA-ROLLANDE, a village in the Loiret, France, a chief seat of the Burgundy wine trade, giving its name to one of the best of the Burgundies. Here the French army of the Loire, under general D'Aurelle de Paladines, was defeated by the Germans, under prince Frederick Charles, in an attempt to march in the direction of Fontainebleau to relieve Paris, 28 Nov. 1870. The French loss was reported by the Germans to be 1000 dead, 4000 wounded; above 1700 prisoners. Their own loss was heavy. Pop. 12,000.

BEAUTY SHOW opened at Spa, Belgium, 19 Sept. 1888. Of 350 candidates for the prize of 10,000 francs who sent in their photographs, many were excluded from competition, only 20 ladies were present on the opening day, representing many countries. M. Emile d'Hainault, the director, proposed annual competitions. The first prize awarded to Mdlle. Berthe Soucaret, a creole of Guadeloupe, aged 18, 29 Sept. 1888. Another show at Turin, 26 Jan. 1889; and other places since.

BEAUVAIS (N. France), the ancient Bellovacum, or Cæsaroniagus, formerly capital of Picardy. When besieged by Charles the Bold, duke of Burgundy, with 80,000 men, the women under Jeanne Fourquet or Lainé, also de la Hachette, from her using that weapon, particularly distinguished themselves, and the duke raised the siege, 10 July, 1472. In memory of this the young girls of Beauvais walk in procession on the anniversary of their deliverance, bearing a banner commemorating the tearing down by Jeanne of the standard of the Burgundians.

BECHUANA LAND, South Africa, a large British colony (1885), capital, Vryburg, see *Transvaal*.

The Bechuanas invade Griqualand West, and are repulsed, and part of their territory subdued by British volunteers 1878

Rev. John Mackenzie (an active missionary, died 23 March, 1899) appointed British resident, 13 March; compelled to resign by the Dutch party, replaced by Mr. Cecil Rhodes . . Aug. 1884

Sir Charles Warren made special commissioner Oct. ,,

The Boer filibusters seize and annex the territory of Montsioa, under British protection; compelled to retire . . . . Sept., Oct. ,,

Military expedition against Dutch freebooters Nov. ,,

(Stellaland and Goshen republics) who accept allotments of land, announced, 27 Nov.; this policy of the Cape government strongly disapproved by colony . . . . Dec. ,,

Sir Charles Warren meets president Krüger, 24 Jan. and comes to an agreement . . . . 29 Jan. 1885

Military government established by sir C. Warren, announced . . . . 24 Feb. ,,

Arrest of Mr. Van Niekirk, president of Stellaland republic, and others, on charge of murder of Mr. Honey, an Englishman, in 1883. Announced 24 March, 1885; released about 27 May. Sir C. Warren thanks the volunteers . . . 8 July, ,,

Judge (afterwards sir S.) Shippard nominated administrator; sir C. Warren after great success recalled . . . . Aug. ,,

Bechuanaland proclaimed British territory 8 Oct. ,,

A proposal to annex it to Cape Colony was negatived, autumn, 1888; adopted . . . 11 June, 1895

Sir Sydney Shippard nominated commissioner-administrator . . . . Sept. 1892

Khama and 2 other chiefs received at the Colonial office by Mr. Chamberlain, 11 Sept.; visited Birmingham and other places, Sept., Oct.; received presents from the queen, at Windsor, 20 Nov; left England . . . . 23 Nov. 1895

Difficulties with the S. Africa company settled by Mr. Chamberlain; imperial government granted.

Bechuanaland made a protectorate . . 6 Nov. ,,

Mr. F. J. Newton appointed resident commissioner; announced . . . . 19 Nov. ,,

Montsioa and Ikanning withdrawn from the British S. Africa company and placed under the high commissioner; Mr. Surmon appointed assistant-commissioner; announced . . . . 6 Feb. 1896

Sir Richard E. R. Martin, appointed commandant-gen. of police forces, and deputy-commissioner for S. Africa; announced . . . 12 March, ,,

Distress through the cattle-disease; etc. See *Mansion house* . . . . . April *et seq.* ,,

Native rising through the killing of diseased cattle, at Pokwani; expedition sent under major Peakman; reported . . . . 23 Dec. ,,

Pokwani, Galishwe's stronghold, taken by Mr. Robinson and natives routed, 27 Dec.; many natives captured, rising quelled . . 29 Dec. ,,

Mr. Robinson, a trader, murdered on the Mashowing river; the Batlaros tribe in revolt; reported; 5 Jan.; further raid reported . . 8 Jan. 1897

Rebels totally defeated, 40 killed in the Takoon district; reported . . . . . 16 Jan. 1897
Capt. Wood and a small patrol surprised by rebels in Langeberg; lieut. Hopkins and private Venn killed, rebel loss heavy; reported . 18 Feb. ,,
Gamasep, Lukas Jantje's village, captured and burnt, lieut. Harris killed, 6 April; other kraals burnt by col. Dalgety's column, announced 10 April; further fighting, reported . 30 April, ,,
Toto's stronghold captured by col. Dalgety, 3 privates killed . . . . . 9 May, ,,
Rebels repulsed with loss at Gamasep . 3 June, ,,
Reinforcements sent to Langeberg, 30 June; several skirmishes reported, 25 July; decisive victory over the rebels, at Langeberg 30 July and 1 Aug.; many surrenders . . 2 Aug. ,,
Major Goold-Adams appointed resident-commissioner; reported . . . . 21 Dec. ,,
Ralph Champneys Williams, C.M.G., resident-commissioner . . . . Jan. 1901

(See *S. African War.*)

BECKET'S MURDER.* Thomas Becket, archbishop of Canterbury, was murdered at the altar, 29 Dec. 1170. The king was absolved of guilty knowledge of the crime in 1172, and did penance at the tomb in 1174. The bones of Becket were enshrined in gold and jewels in 1220. They were ordered to be burned in the reign of Henry VIII. 24 April, 1538. A stone coffin, supposed by some persons to contain Becket's bones (?), discovered in a crypt at Canterbury cathedral, Jan. 1888. The Merchant Adventurers were at one time termed "the Brotherhood of St. Thomas à Becket." A Roman catholic church at Canterbury, dedicated to him, was opened by cardinal Manning, 13 April, 1875.

BECKETT-DENISON ART COLLECTION, (including much of the Hamilton Collection) sold for 92,231*l.*, 6 June—15 July, 1885. Mr. Christopher Beckett-Denison, brother of sir Edmund Beckett (since lord Grimthorpe), died suddenly in Ireland, 1884.

BECKFORD, see under *Libraries.*

BED. The ancients slept on skins. Beds were afterwards made of loose rushes, heather, or straw. The Romans are said to have first used feathers. An air-cushion is said to have been used by Heliogabalus, 218-222; *air-beds* were in use in the 16th century. Feather-beds were in use in England in the reign of Henry VIII. The bedsteads of the Egyptians and later Greeks, like modern couches, became common among the Roman upper classes.

The ancient great bed at Ware, Herts, capable of holding twelve persons, is of the 16th cent. Referred to in Shakespeare's *Twelfth Night.*
A bedstead of gold was presented to the queen on 2 Nov. 1859, by the Maharajah of Cashmere.
Air-beds and water-beds have been made since the manufacture of india-rubber cloth by Clark in 1813; and by Macintosh in 1823.
Dr. Arnott's hydrostatic bed invented in 1830.

BED OF JUSTICE, a French court presided over by the king, whose seat was termed a "bed." It controlled the ordinances of the parliament. The last was held by Louis XVI. a Versailles, 19 Nov. 1787, to raise a loan.

* Thomas Becket was born in 1119. His father Gilbert was a London trader, and his mother is stated to have been a convert from Mahometanism. He was educated at Oxford, and made archdeacon by Theobald, archbishop of Canterbury, who introduced him to the king, Henry II. He became chancellor in 1155, but on being elected archbishop of Canterbury in 1162, he resigned the chancellorship, to the great offence of the king. He opposed strenuously the constitutions of Clarendon in 1164, and fled the country; and in 1166, excommunicated all the clergy who agreed to abide by them. He and the king met at Fretville, in Touraine, on 22 July, 1170, and were formally reconciled. On his return he re-commenced his struggle with the king, which led to his tragical death, after which he was canonized.

BEDER (Arabia). Here Mahomet gained his first victory (over the Koreish of Mecca), 623. It was considered to be miraculous.

BEDFORD, a town, N.N.W. of London, renowned for its many free educational establishments, endowed in 1561 by sir Wm. Harpur, a London alderman. Here John Bunyan preached, was imprisoned, and wrote "The Pilgrim's Progress." Population 1881, 19,533; 1891, 28,023; 1901, 35,144.

A statue of Bunyan, the gift of the duke of Bedford, was uncovered here, 10 June, 1874. Bronze gates for the Bunyan church, given by the duke, were inaugurated by him 5 July, 1876. New extensive building of the grammar school opened by the duke of Bedford 29 Oct. 1891.
Statue of John Howard, the philanthropist, by Mr. Alfred Gilbert, in the market-place; unveiled by the duke of Bedford, 28 March, 1894.
Recreation ground presented by the duke, April 1894.
Mr. George Hurst, born 1800, 5 times mayor, died 26 Dec. 1898.
Lieut.-gen. sir John French presented with an address by the mayor, 24 July, received the freedom 10 Oct. 1902.

BEDFORD LEVEL, a portion of the great fen districts in the eastern counties, drained in the early part of the 17th century by the earl of Bedford, aided by the celebrated Dutch engineer, sir Cornelius Vermuyden, amid great opposition; see *Levels.*

BEDLAM, see *Bethlehem.*

BEDOUINS, wandering tribes of Arabs, living on the plunder of travellers, &c. They profess a form of Mahometanism, and are governed by sheikhs. They are said to be descendants of Ishmael, and appear to fulfil the prophecy respecting him, *Gen.* xvi. 12, 1911 B.C.

BEEF-EATERS, see *Battle-axe.*

"**BEEF STEAKS,** the Sublime Society of," was established in 1735 by Rich, an actor at Covent Garden Theatre, in the painting-room of which the members dined upon beef-steaks. The society became fashionable, and long included among its members the prince of Wales, royal dukes, and other eminent persons, who submitted to its somewhat ludicrous regulations. It became extinct in 1867, its last place of meeting being a room in the Lyceum theatre. Its history was published by Brother Arnold in 1871.

BEEHIVE HOUSES, are primitive dwellings of an unknown antiquity found in Scotland and Ireland. They are constructed with undressed stones and without mortar, conical in shape, with a hole at the top of the roof.

BEER. The manufacture of beer and intoxicating liquors of kindred nature is of very high antiquity. A kind of beer was brewed from barley by the Egyptians as early as 3000 B.C. Herodotus ascribes its invention to the goddess Isis, and Xenophon refers to the use of beer in Armenia. Pliny mentions an intoxicating liquor made of corn and water in common use among the peoples of Western Europe, including the Gauls. Mead and cider were chiefly drunk in Britain prior to the Roman invasion. In the 8th cent. ale booths were subject to legal regulations. Beer is manufactured in a primitive manner from millet by native tribes in Africa, and from maize by the

Indians of South America. There are numerous varieties of beer (including ale) consumed in Britain, known as "pale ale," "bitter beer," "mild ale," &c., the most celebrated of the mild ales being those manufactured at Burton-on-Trent. Porter and stout, dark-coloured varieties of beer, are produced chiefly in London and Dublin. "Lager beer," a German beer, which in recent years has come into use in this country, is also manufactured in England and in America. The annual consumption of beer in gallons per head in the various countries of Europe and in the United States and Canada is shown as under:—Belgium, 36·00; United Kingdom, 26·27; Germany, 20·00; United States, 14·14; Denmark, 11·65; Holland, 8·46; Austria-Hungary, 7·10; Norway, 6·36; Switzerland, 5·87; France, 5·21; Sweden, 4·20; Canada, 3·17; Russia, 0·84; Italy, 0·18.—*Chambers*. Condensed beer patented by P. E. Lockwood, 1875. Condensed wort patented by Hermann Mertens, of Margate, in 1853. Beer and ale exported from the United Kingdom: 1876, 484,919 barrels; 1880, 412,192; 1884, 437,241; 1888, 447,940; 1890, 503,221; 1900, 510,843. Excise duty on beer (1893) 6s. 3*d*. per barrel; addition of 6*d*. June, 1894; raised to 1s. April, 1900. Beer, for purposes of taxation, is defined by the inland revenue acts of 1880 and 1885. Adulteration, or addition of anything except finings for clarification, or even the mixing of small beer with strong beer, incurs a fine of 50*l*. and forfeiture of the beer. In the case of a beer-seller conviction of adulteration is registered and may be endorsed on his licence; see *Ale*, *Brewers*, *Porter*, *Victuallers*, *Arsenic*.

BEES. Mount Hybla, on account of its odoriferous flowers, thyme, and abundance of honey, has been poetically called the "empire of bees." Hymettus, in Attica, was also famous for its bees and honey. The economy of bees was admired in the earliest ages; and Eumelus, of Corinth, wrote a poem on bees, 741 B.C. Bees were introduced into Boston, New England, in 1670, and have since spread over the continent. Mandeville's satirical "Fable of the Bees" appeared in 1723. Huber published his observations on bees in 1792. The Apiarian Society had an establishment at Muswell Hill, near London (1860-2). The Ligurian variety of the honey-bee was successfully introduced into England in 1860.

A British Beekeepers' Association founded 16 May (sir John Lubbock became first president); first exhibition, in Crystal palace, 8 Sept. 1874; at other places since.

Spelling bees, of American origin, introduced into London in autumn of 1875; first at Holloway. Geographical, musical, and other bees began early in 1876.

Mr. F. R. Cheshire's "Bees and Beekeeping" published in 1886–8.

Maeterlinck. "Life of the Bee," trans. by A. Sutro. May, 1901.

BEES, ST., Cumberland. A monastery was founded here by St. Bega, 650; a grammar school by abp. Grindal, 1583; a clerical training college by bp. Law, 1817.

BEET-ROOT is extensively grown in England. *Beta vulgaris*, red beet, is used for the table as a salad. Margraff first produced sugar from the *white* beet-root in 1747. M. Achard produced excellent sugar from it in 1799; and the chemists of France, at the instance of Bonaparte, largely extracted sugar from the beet-root in 1800. More than half the sugar consumed in France is now manufactured in that country from beet. It is also largely manufactured in other countries, especially in Germany. A refinery of sugar from beet-root has been erected at the Thames bank, Chelsea. The cultivation of beet-root in England and Ireland much advocated, 1871, and again, in 1884, when great improvements were proposed, especially at Lavenham, Suffolk, by Messrs. Bolton, of Westminster.

BEGGARS were tolerated in ancient times, being often musicians and ballad-singers. In 1388, 1530, 1535, 1547-50 severe laws were passed against them. By 14 Eliz., c. 5, 1572, sturdy beggars were ordered to be "grievously whipped and burnt through the right ear;" punished capitally for the third offence: acts consolidated 1731. By the Vagrant Act (1824), 5 Geo. IV. c. 83, all public beggars are liable to a month's imprisonment. About 30,000 tramps in England and Wales. *Judicial Statistics*, 1865. See *Poor Laws*, *Mendicity Society*, and *Vagrants*. The "BEGGAR'S OPERA," by John Gay, a satire against the government of sir Robert Walpole, was produced at the Lincoln's-inn-fields theatre, 29 Jan. 1727–8, and had a run of 63 nights; see *Gueux*.

BEGUINES, a congregation of nuns first established at Liège, and afterwards at Nivelle, in 1207, some say 1226. The "Grand Beguinage" of Bruges was the most extensive. Some of these nuns imagined that they could become sinless. The council of Vienne condemned this error, and abolished a branch of the order in 1311. They still exist in Germany and Belgium, acting as nurses to the sick and wounded, &c.

BEHEADING, the *Decollatio* of the Romans, introduced into England from Normandy (as a less ignominious mode of putting high criminals to death), by William the Conqueror, 1076, when Waltheof, earl of Huntingdon, Northampton, and Northumberland, was first so executed. Since then this mode of execution became frequent, particularly in the reigns of Henry VIII., Mary, and Elizabeth, when even women of the noblest blood thus perished; the aged countess of Salisbury, 27 May, 1541; lady Jane Grey, 12 Feb. 1554.

BEHISTUN, in Persia. At this place is a rock containing important inscriptions of Darius Hystaspes about 518 B.C., in three languages, in cuneiform (or wedge-shaped) characters, which were deciphered and translated by sir H. Rawlinson in 1844-6, and published in the Journal of the Royal Asiatic Society.

BEHRING'S STRAIT, discovered by captain Vitus Behring, a Danish navigator in the service of Russia. He thus proved that the continents of Asia and America are distant from each other about thirty-nine miles, 1728. He died at Behring's island in 1741. In 1778 captain James Cook surveyed the coasts of both continents. See *United States*, 1889-91.

The czar Alexander I., in 1821, declared the Behring seas closed to foreign fishing; this was at once repudiated by Mr. J. Quincy Adams, secretary of the United States. Alaska was purchased in 1867 from Russia, by the States, who afterwards assumed the Russian claim upon the seas, and seized the British Columbia's sealing vessels. The seizure of the *Black Diamond* sealer by the U.S. revenue cutter *Rush*, 3 July, was declared legal by Mr. Secretary Blaine, U.S., 1 Aug. 1889; while the British government claimed, as heretofore, the right of fishing in waters beyond the territorial limits. The governments agreed to refer the question to arbitration, Feb. 1890. President Harrison proclaimed the Behring sea closed to unlicensed seal fishing, 25 March. A Blue Book was published, 15 Aug., containing the correspondence between the two governments from 1 Sept. 1886, to

2 Aug. 1890. The marquis of Salisbury demanded that, pending arbitration, British sealing vessels should not be molested, adding that if so, they should be protected, 2 Aug. 1890.
Negotiations resumed, arbitration refused by Mr. Blaine . . . . end of Oct. 1890
Correspondence referred to the U.S. congress, 5 Jan. 1891
The owner of the British sealing schooner, *W. P. Sayward* (which was seized and condemned in 1887), supported by the Canadian government, brings the Behring sea difficulty before the U.S. Supreme Court at Washington, 12 Jan., case opens, 27 Jan.; the court decides to hear the appeal on . . . . . . 13 April, 2 Feb. ,,
[The case decided in favour of the United States, 29 Feb. 1892.]
Further correspondence; lord Salisbury consents to the proposal to refer the matter to arbitration, 21 Feb. ,,
Letter from Mr. Blaine to sir Julian Pauncefote, specifying six points for arbitration. 14 April, ,,
A *modus vivendi* respecting the seal fishery agreed on by Great Britain and the United States 15 June, ,,
Catching of seals by British ships prohibited from 24 June, 1891, to 1 May, 1892, *London Gazette*, 24 June, ,,
Sir George Baden-Powell and Dr. G. M. Dawson, commissioners respecting the seal-fishery, arrive at British Columbia, 15 July; interviews with sealers, 16 July; arrive at Ounalaska island, 25 July, ,,
The Behring sea blocked by 3 American and 3 British warships, announced . . . 27 July, ,,
Behring sea commission meets at Washington, 8 Feb.; sign their report . . . 4 March, 1892
The governments agree to refer the question to arbitration; arbiters to be appointed by Italy, France, and Sweden . . . . . Feb. ,,
The arbitration treaty signed at Washington, 29 Feb.; ratified by the senate . . . 29 March, ,,
Mr. Blaine, after requiring the renewal of the *modus vivendi*, accepts the arrangements proposed by lord Salisbury . . . 28 March, ,,
New *modus vivendi* (to last till 31 Oct. 1893) ratified 19 April and 4 May, ,,
A "tribunal" of seven arbitrators appointed to settle the dispute: British, lord Hannen and sir John Thompson; American, Mr. justice Harlan, and senator J. P. Morgan; French, baron Alphonse de Courcel: Italian, marquis Visconti Venosta; one Swedish, M. Gram . July, Aug. ,,
The British steamer *Coquittam*, and 25 sealers belonging to Victoria, British Columbia, seized by the U. S. cutter *Corwin*, 22 June; the Canadian government protests . . . . . . July, ,,
The British schooner *Winifred* seized by the U. S. *Rush* . . . . 20 July, ,,
Several Victoria sealers seized in the N. Pacific by a Russian gunboat, as being in Russian waters; the crews made to sign papers and dismissed, July; Canadian government protests and acts, Sept.; controversy ensues . . . . . Oct. ,,
The seizure of the Canadian schooner *Oscar and Hattie* declared legal at Victoria; appeal 5 Jan. 1893
Russian commission appointed respecting the seized British sealers, about 9 Jan.; agreement settled, reported . . . . . . June, ,,
British agents: hon. C. H. Tupper, sir Charles Russell, attorney-general, and sir Richard Webster. United States agents: Mr. Foster and Mr. Phelps.
The arbitrators meet at Paris, 23 Feb., baron de Courcel chosen president, 23 March; able speeches delivered; arguments closed, 8 July; award delivered, generally favourable to Great Britain (Russian territorial claims set aside; American fisheries limited to three miles from Behring sea islands; three months' close time for seal fishery decreed; claims for injuries on both sides to be settled) . . . . . 15 Aug. ,,
The treaty bill passed by parliament in England, 23 April, 1894; in United States, 7 April; came into operation . . . . 1 May, 1894
Claims of British sealers on United States for seizures to be settled by payment of 425,000 dollars . . . . 6 Sept. ,,
Agreed to, but disallowed by congress . March, 1895
A treaty settling the dispute concluded in Feb.; ratified [473,151 dollars voted by the U.S. senate for payment of British claims 21 April, 1898, paid 16th June, 1898.] . . . . . 3 June, 1896
Dispute renewed; despatch from Mr. Sherman to col. Hay, U.S. ambassador, London, for the suspension of pelagic sealing, 10 May, 1897; negotiations: Gt. Britain declines to join a conference where Russia and Japan are represented . . . . 7 Oct. 1897
Conference between Russia, Japan, and United States, Mr. Foster chairman, at Washington 23 Oct.; convention signed for a temporary suppression of pelagic sealing . . . . 6 Nov. ,,
Canada refuses consent to a year's suspension of pelagic sealing, but agrees to a joint commission ,,
The Canadian and U.S. commissioners report to their governments; awarding 464,000 dollars to Canadian sealers for losses by seizures from U.S. cruisers, 1886–97, 23 Dec. 1897, see *above*, June, 1898
40,000 dollars indemnity received by Canada from Russia . . . . 4 March, ,,
Hague court of arbitration decrees Russia to pay the United States 28,688 dols. and 32,444 dols. with interest from 1892 and 1893 for seizure of U.S. vessels . . . . 29 Nov. 1902

BELFAST, capital of Ulster, N. Ireland. Its castle, supposed to have been built by John de Courcy, was destroyed by the Scots under Edward Bruce, 1315; see *Orange*. Belfast returns four M.P.'s by Act passed 25 June, 1885. Population, 1821, 37,117; 1851, about 100,000; 1881, 208,122; 1891, 255,896; 1901, 348,965.

Belfast granted by James I. to sir Arthur Chichester, lord deputy, 1612: and erected into a corporation 1613
The long bridge (21 arches, 2562 feet long) built . 1682-6
The first edition of the Bible in Ireland, printed here 1704
The castle burnt . . . . 4 April, 1708
The bank built 1787
The mechanics' institute established 1825
The Queen's bridge (5 arches) built on site of the long bridge 1841
Of three colleges established in Ireland in 1845, one inaugurated in Belfast (see *Colleges*) . . Oct. 1849
Victoria Channel opened . . . . ,,
British association met here 1852
Much rioting at Belfast through Mr. Hanna's open-air preaching . . . . . . July–Sept. 1857
"Victoria chambers" burnt down; the loss estimated at 100,000*l*. . . . . . . 1 July, 1859
Exciting religious revivals . . . . . Sept. ,,
Fierce conflicts between Roman Catholics and Protestants on account of the foundation of the O'Connell monument at Dublin—9 lives lost and 150 persons injured . . . . . 10–27 Aug. 1864
Rioting again . . . . 30 April, 1865
Visit of the lord lieutenant, the marquis of Abercorn 2–4 Oct. 1867
Severe rioting; much destruction of property and many persons injured. Civil war raging between Catholics and Protestants, 15–21 Aug. Peace restored . . . . 22 Aug. 1872
British association here (2nd time) . . 19 Aug. 1874
End of strike of linen manufacturers . . 26 Aug. ,,
Riots at W. Belfast between Catholic and Protestant workmen, with loss of life; suppressed by the military and police, 3–13 June; more rioting; the town proclaimed, 21 July; violent conflicts between the mobs and the military and police, 11 killed, many wounded; order restored by additional military . . . . . . 9 Aug. *et seq.* 1886
Renewed rioting suppressed . . . 14, 15 Aug. ,,
Quietness reported 18 Aug.; occasional rioting 1 Sept. *et seq.* ,,
Part of Albert bridge falls with loss of life 15 Sept. ,,
Rioting (2 deaths) 19–20 Sept. 26 Sept. and 29 Sept. ,,
A commission to inquire into the riots began to sit 4 Oct.
Report published; Protestant attacks on the police; weak magisterial action referred to, about 25 Jan. 1887
Renewed rioting; the police compelled to fire; about 50 arrests . . . . 29–30 Jan. ,,
Prince Albert Victor of Wales opens the new Alexandra docks 20 May, and lays the foundation of Albert bridge . . . . . . 22 May, 1889

Victoria channel extension opened for traffic 7 July, 1891
The mayor ordered to be styled "lord" . May, 1892
Meeting of Ulster Convention (*which see*) against Home Rule . . . . 17 June, ,,
See *Ulster*, 1892-3. Fighting between Catholic and Protestant workmen, suppressed . 24 April, 1893
Visit of the duke of Devonshire; banquet 0 Nov. ,,
An art and industrial exhibition opened by the lord mayor . . . . 24 March, 1894
Art and industrial exhibition opened by the marquis and marchioness of Londonderry; pictures sent by the queen and others . 11 April, 1895
Eight servants of the marquis drowned by the upsetting of a boat on Strangford Lough 11 April, ,,
Strike in the shipbuilding trade; begun, 11 Oct; about 3,000 out, closed; an advance conceded to the men . . . . 17 Dec. ,,
New Empire theatre damaged by fire . 27 Dec. ,,
Messrs. R. M. Robb & Co., and Messrs. Walpole Bros.' warehouses destroyed by fire 28 Jan. 1897
Visit of the duke and duchess of York . 8 Sept. ,,
Sharp rioting (Shankhill-road) suppressed by the troops and police, houses looted 6, 7 June, 1898
Foundation-stone of a new city hall laid by lord Cadogan . . . . 18 Oct. ,,
Death of the rev. Dr. Kane, benefactor . 20 Nov. ,,
Statue of the queen (Guildhall) unveiled by the lord-lieut. . . . . . . 24 Nov. ,,
Frequent disturbances at St. Clement's against ritualistic practices . . . Feb.–March, 1899
Anti-ritualistic meeting in the Ulster hall, 29 March, ,,
Riot, attributed to offensive language used at certain open-air meetings, 1 death 21 May ,,
United Irish league demonstration, fighting, 7 p.m. riot act read, troops called out, 5 June; again, police stoned, over 40 arrests . . 6 June ,,
Mr. T. H. Ismay, of the White Star line receives the freedom of the city . . . 20 July ,,
Rioting in connection with the Nationalists 14–15 Aug. ,,
Lady Shaftesbury lays the first stone of the cathedral . . . . 6 Sept. ,,
Mr. Gerald Balfour receives addresses and speaks on the agricultural and technical instruction (Ireland) act . . . . . . 19 Jan. 1900
Sir George White (the defender of Ladysmith) receives the freedom . . . . 12 June ,,
Lord Dufferin opens a new municipal school of art 25 Sept. 1901
Collapse of a spinning mill at Smithfield, 14 deaths, many injured (2,000*l.* relief fund, 28 Jan.) 20 Jan. 1902
Clonard print works burnt down, 1 death, over 20,000*l.* damage . . . . . 2, 3 July ,,
Mr. Wm. Johnston, M.P., died . . . 17 July ,,
British association met here (3rd time) . 10 Sept. ,,
Mr. A. Carnegie gives 15,000*l.* for a library . 3 Nov. ,,
Lord Dudley lays first stone of a technical institute 24 Nov. ,,
F.M. Earl Roberts receives the freedom of the city 8 Sept. ,,
King visits the city . . . . . . 27 July, 1903

BELFORT, or **BEFORT**, a fortified town in Alsace, E. France, was invested by the Germans 3 Nov. 1870; capitulated 16 Feb. 1871; reserved to France when Alsace was ceded 26 Feb.; quitted by the Germans Aug. 1873.

BELGIUM, the southern portion of the Netherlands, and anciently the territory of the Belgæ, who were finally conquered by Julius Cæsar, 51 B.C. Its size is about one-eighth of Great Britain. Its government is a liberal constitutional monarchy, founded in 1831. For previous history, see ***Flanders***, ***Netherlands***, and ***Holland***. The population (31 Dec.) 1862, 4,836,566; 1865, 4,984,451; 1866, 4,829,320; 1870, 5,087,105; 1879, 5,536,146; 1887, 5,974,743; 1890, 6,147,041; 1896, 6,495,886; 1901, 6,693,000

The revolution commences at Brussels 25 Aug. 1830
The provisional government declares Belgium independent (M. Van de Weyer, active) . 4 Oct. ,,
Antwerp taken (except the citadel) . . 23 Dec. ,,
Belgian independence acknowledged by the allied powers . . . . 26 Dec. ,,
Duc de Nemours elected king (his father, the French king, refused his consent) . . 3 Feb. 1831
Surlet de Chokier is elected regent . 24 Feb. ,,
Leopold, prince of Saxe-Coburg, accepted the crown, 12 July; enters Brussels . 19 July, ,,
War with the Netherlands commences . 3 Aug. ,,
France sends 50,000 troops to assist Belgium, and an armistice ensues . . . . . Aug. ,,
Conference of ministers of the five great powers held in London: acceptance of 24 articles of pacification 15 Nov. ,,
Convention between England and France against Holland . . . . 22 Oct. 1832
Antwerp besieged, 30 Nov.; the citadel taken by the French . . . . 23 Dec. ,,
The French army returns to France . . 27 Dec. ,,
Preliminary convention with Holland signed 21 May 1833
Riot at Brussels (see *Brussels*) . . 6 April, 1834
Treaty* between Holland and Belgium signed in London . . . . 19 April, 1839
Clerical education bill passed 1842
Queen of England visits Belgium . . . Aug. 1852
The king and his son visit England . . Oct. ,,
Increase of army to 100,000 men voted . 10 May, 1853
Opposition to religious charities' bill† . June, 1857
A new ministry under M. Charles Rogier 9 Nov. ,,
The chambers dissolved; re-assembled . 10 Dec. ,,
The king proclaims Belgium neutral in the Italian war . . . . May, 1859
Birth of prince Leopold Ferdinand . . 12 June, ,,
Death of M. Potter . . . . . . 22 July, ,,
The king visits England . . . . . June, 1860
Vague rumours of annexation to France produce warm loyal addresses to the king . . 13 June, ,,
The octrois abolished . . . . . 21 July, ,,
Successful military volunteer movement . Aug. ,,
Commercial treaty with France signed . . 1 May, 1861
Continued illness of the king, with occasional amendment . . . . . May, June, 1862
Commercial treaty with Great Britain adopted by the chamber . . . . 22 Aug. ,,
Great distress through decay of trade . Aug. ,,
Fierce dissensions through Roman Catholics, Jan.; 1864
the ministry resigns, but resumes office, 4 Feb.; ,,
dissolution of the chambers, 17 July; the Protestants superior in the election . . . Aug. ,,
Death of Leopold I. . . . . . . 10 Dec. 1865
The new king and queen visit England, 5 July; and Ghent and other Belgian cities . . . July, 1866
National rifle meeting (*tir*) . . . 12-16 Oct. ,,
Mr. Phillips, lord mayor of London, and 1100 English volunteers visit Belgium under col. Loyd Lindsay; other foreigners attend; grand banquet given by the king at Brussels . . . . . 20 Oct. ,,
Opening of the chambers, with a reassuring speech from the king . . . . 13 Nov. ,,
Violent rioting in mining districts (Marchienne-au-Pont) on account of reduction in wages; suppressed by the military . . . . 1-2 Feb. 1867
About 2400 Belgians (of the garde civique and volunteers) visit England; arrive, 10 July; received by lord mayor, 12 July; by prince of Wales at Wimbledon, 13 July; dine at Windsor, 16 July; at a ball at Agricultural hall, 18 July; received by Miss Burdett-Coutts, 19 July; attend the review at Wimbledon, 20 July; leave London 22 July, ,,
New ministry (under M. Frère-Orban); liberal; 3 Jan. 1868
Serious riots in the mining districts; put down by the military; 10 lives lost . . 25-29 March, ,,
Monument to Charlemagne at Liège, inaugurated 26 July, ,,
Intern. congress of workmen at Brussels, 6-13 Nov. ,,
The crown prince Leopold Ferdinand, duke of Brabant, died . . . . 22 Jan. 1869

* This treaty arose out of the conference held in London on the Belgian question; by the decision of which, the treaty of 15 Nov. 1831, was maintained, and the pecuniary compensation of sixty millions of francs offered by Belgium for the territories adjudged to Holland was declared inadmissible.

† At the revolution in 1830, the Roman Catholic clergy lost the administration of the public charities, which they have struggled to recover ever since. In April, 1857, M. Decker, the head of the ministry, brought in a bill for this purpose, but was compelled to withdraw it, and eventually to resign.

Concession of a Luxembourg railway to a French railway company, without the assent of the state, prohibited by the assembly, 13 Feb.; dispute with the French government arranged . . May, 1869

International rifle meeting held at Liége . 19 Sept. ,,

Resignation of Frère-Orban ministry, about 19 June, 1870

M. d'Anethan's ministry announced . 3 July, ,,

Warm gratitude to Great Britain expressed by the king and people . . . . . 8 Aug. ,,

Treaty for the neutrality of Belgium between Great Britain and Prussia, signed 9 Aug.; and France, signed . . . . 11 Aug. ,,

After surrender of Sedan many French soldiers enter Belgium; disarmed and interned . . 1-2 Sept. ,,

Strong opposition to the ministry by M. Barra and others; riots at Brussels . . 22-25 Nov. ,,

Resignation of D'Anethan; M. Malou (a moderate) forms a ministry . . . . . 7 Dec. 1871

The comte de Chambord arrives at Antwerp, 17 Feb.; compelled to quit Belgium through popular demonstrations . . . . 27 Feb. 1872

The French government denounce the treaty of commerce with Belgium . . . 29 March, ,,

Treaty of commerce with France signed . 5 Feb. 1873

The czar at Brussels . . . . 22 May, ,,

M. Van de Weyer, statesman; active during the revolution of 1830; ambassador to England 1831-67; died . . . . . . 23 May, 1874

International conference at Brussels respecting rights of neutrals during war—no results, 27 July-28 Aug. ,,

Notes from the German government, complaining of publications favouring the censured German ecclesiastics, Feb.; respecting the *Duchesne's* proposal to the archbishop of Paris to assassinate Bismarck . . . . 15 April, 1875

Dignified Belgian replies . . March and May, ,,

The court at Liége cannot interfere, May; modification of the criminal law proposed . June, ,,

Much popular opposition to religious processions: riots . . . . May, June, ,,

The king visits England . . . . 29 May, 1876

Catholic successes in the elections; riots against them at Brussels and Antwerp about 16, 17 June, ,,

Statue of Van de Weyer, at Louvain, inaugurated by the king . . . . . . 1 Oct. ,,

International congress respecting hygiene, &c., held at Brussels . . . 27 Sept.–2 Oct. ,,

Catholic minority in elections; the Malou ministry resign, 13, 14 June, M. Frère-Orban forms a liberal ministry . . . . . 20 June, 1878

Gigantic weir for water-distribution at La Gileppe, near Verviers, inaugurated by the king, 28 July, ,,

The king's silver wedding enthusiastically celebrated . . . . . . 22-25 Aug. ,,

Eugene T' Kindt de Rooden Veke, a clerk, convicted of embezzlement of 20,000,000 francs of the Bank of Belgium (149 thefts); the governor Fortamps, of fraudulently repurchasing shares, &c. 3 Dec. ,,

The king sanctions the new law of public instruction . . . . 1 July, 1879

Pastoral of the R. C. hierarchy against the government plan of mixed education (sacraments to be refused to teachers and parents, &c.) published in Germany . . . . Sept. ,,

Archduke Rodolph of Austria betrothed to the princess Stephanie . . . . March, 1880

Permanent international exhibition opened at Brussels . . . . 1 June, ,,

Elections for parliament; severe struggle between liberals and clerical party respecting education; liberals retain moderate majority . . June, ,,

National exhibition at Brussels opened by the king and queen . . . . . . 16 June, ,,

Representative at the Vatican recalled through ecclesiastical disputes; suspension of diplomatic arrangements . . . . . . 28 June, ,,

Jubilee to celebrate national independence 18 July, ,,

Statue of Leopold I. unveiled at Laeken 21 July, ,,

Patriotic fête in the Brussels exhibition 16 Aug. ,,

Trial of Armand and Leon Peltzer, for the murder of Wilhelm Bernays: (an injured husband, a faithless wife and her accomplices) . 27 Nov. 1882

Sentenced to death (commuted) . . 22 Dec. ,,

Dynamite explosion at Ganshorten, near Brussels; 1 death (arrests made) . . . 23 Feb. 1883

Parliamentary reform bill passed by representatives 17 Aug. ,,

Henri Conscience, eminent national Flemish poet and novelist, died, aged 73 . . . 9 Sept. 1883

Death of cardinal Deschamps, abp. of Mechlin, the primate . . . . 29 Sept. ,,

The king and queen warmly received at Amsterdam 18 Oct. *et seq.* ,,

King and queen of Holland warmly received at Brussels . . . . . . 20-22 May, 1884

Elections; majority of clericals through dissension of moderate liberals and reformers, about 10 June; resignation of M. Frère-Orban 11 June, ,,

M. Jules Malou forms a conservative catholic ministry . . . . . . 12, 13 June, ,,

Senate dissolved, June; new senate clerical July, ,,

Great meeting of burgomasters at Brussels to oppose M. Jacobs' new reactionary education bill, 9 Aug., which is accepted by the deputies (80-49), 30 Aug.; by the senate (40-25) . . 10 Sept. ,,

Liberal riots at Brussels and Antwerp . 7 Sept. ,,

Royal assent to the bill . . . . 13 Sept. ,,

Communal elections; great liberal majority 19 Oct. ,,

MM. Malou, Jacobs, and Wœste (catholics) resign, M. Beernaert becomes premier . . . 24 Oct. ,,

Parliament meets . . . . . . 11 Nov. ,,

King Leopold proclaimed sovereign of the new Congo state . . . . 2 May, 1885

Universal exhibition opened at Antwerp by the king 2 May, ,,

Death of Charles Rogier (aged 85), member of the provisional government in 1830, six times minister 27 May, ,,

Riotous strikes in the coal districts between Namur and Liége and collision with the military, many killed and wounded; convents, country houses, factories, &c., pillaged, works stopped about 22-29 March, 1886

Liége quieted by vigorous action; great disorder in Charleroi, Mons, &c. . . . . 27-29 March, ,,

Outrages greatly attributed to the criminal classes; order restored, reported . . . . 7 April ,,

M. Vandersmissen, a clerical member for Brussels, convicted of killing his wife, a scandalous case; 15 years' penal servitude . . . . 2 June, ,,

Increased army expenditure proposed . 8 Feb. 1887

Revival of strikes; arrival of French dynamitards; universal suffrage demanded; the strikes subside about . . . . 31 May, ,,

New Army Bill rejected by the Chamber (69-62) 14 July, ,,

State trials of 27 socialists at Mons, nearly all acquitted, 25 May; the minister of justice was censured for the prosecution . . . May, 1889

Great colliery strike at Charleroi, &c., about 20,000 men out . . . . . . 21 Dec. *et seq.* ,,

Settled by compromise . . . . 13 Jan. 1890

The castle of Laeken, built 1782, 4 miles from Brussels, a royal palace, destroyed by fire; the governess of princess Clementine, Madame de Grandcour, perished. Valuable works of art, furniture, historical documents, &c., lost. 1 Jan. ,,

The king visits England . . . . 10–26 May, ,,

Loan to Congo State, see *Congo* . . . July, ,,

National fête, 25th anniversary of the king's accession; grotesque procession of giants, &c., at Brussels . . . . . . 19 July *et seq.* ,,

Strike of about 10,000 miners at Mons, 22 Aug.; strike over . . . . 1 Sept. ,,

Death of prince Baldwin, aged 21, greatly lamented, 23 Jan.; grand funeral . . . . 29 Jan. 1891

Great political strike of colliers at Mons, Charleroi, and other places, with rioting, about 2 May; state of siege in the Liége district, about 100,000 men out . . . . 7 May, ,,

Strike of the metallurgists in Charleroi district, the progressist party demand the revision of the constitution . . . . . . about 10 May, ,,

Strike abating near Liége, &c. . . 13 May, ,,

End of the coal-miners' strike of 70 days . 9 July, ,,

Coal-mine explosion at Forchies in Hainault; 27 deaths . . . . 19 Sept. ,,

Meeting of the chambers . . . . 10 Nov. ,,

The hon. sir Edmund Monson succeeds lord Vivian as British minister . . . . . Jan. 1892

Death of M. Emile de Laveleye, eminent publicist and writer, aged 69 . . . . 3 Jan. ,,

The commercial treaties with Austria-Hungary and Germany adopted by the chamber, 28 Jan.; by the senate . . . . 1 Feb. ,,

Discussion in the chamber on the revision of the constitution of 1831 . . . . . . 2 Feb. 1892
Elections: clerical majority, June; the new senate and chamber unite to form a constituent assembly to consider the revision of the constitution 12 July *et seq.* ,,
The committee of the chamber meets 3 Oct.; universal suffrage rejected, 2 Nov.; household suffrage adopted . . . . 3 Nov. ,,
Riotous meetings at Ghent and Brussels demanding universal suffrage, quelled by police 7, 8 Nov. ,,
The chambers opened by the king, who advocates revision of the constitution, 8 Nov.; universal suffrage rejected . . . . . 18 Nov. ,,
Referendum: manhood suffrage voted for at Brussels . . . . 26 Feb. 1893
All revision proposals rejected by the chamber, 12 April; consequent large strike of workmen in the Mons district, etc., 13 April *et seq.*; rioting at Brussels, 14 April; the civic guard at Mons fires on the miners, 4 men killed; above 1,000 dockers on strike at Antwerp . . . 17 April, ,,
Manhood suffrage with plural voting for some persons adopted by the chamber (119–14) 18 April; by the senate . . . 27 April, ,,
The strikes end; order restored 18 April *et seq.* ,,
Sir Francis Plunkett appointed British minister May, ,,
The bill for the revision of the constitution ratified by the senate . . . . 2 Sept. ,,
Strike of miners in the centre coal fields and the Charleroi district, reported 28 Sept. closed by compromise . . . . 10 Oct. ,,
Parliament re-assembles to prepare for the new constitution . . . . . . 17 Oct. ,,
The Flemish volksraad (people's council) opposed to predominance of French influence, annual meeting at Brussels . . . . 1 Nov. ,,
New electoral bill passed by the chamber 17 Feb 1894
Resignation of M. Beernaert the premier, and M. Le Jeune, minister of justice. New ministry, M. de Burlet, premier . . . 25 March, ,,
Opening of the chamber . . . . 3 April, ,,
Exhibition opened at Antwerp, *which see* 5 May, ,,
Marriage of the princess Josephine, daughter of the count of Flanders, to prince Charles of Hohenzollern-Sigmaringen at Brussels . 28 May, ,,
The electoral reform bill finally passed by the chamber, 6 June; by the senate . 27 June, ,,
Treaty with Great Britain respecting the Congo, *which see* . . . . . . 12 May, ,,
Parliament dissolved . . . . . 20 Sept. ,,
Parliamentary elections: 104 catholics, 19 liberals, 29 socialists and radicals . . . 21 Oct. ,,
The chambers opened . . . . . 13 Nov. ,,
Annexation of the Congo state proposed by the government . . . . . . 4 Jan. 1895
Mdme. Joniaux after 21 days' trial sentenced to death for poisoning 3 relatives, 3 Feb.; commuted 12 May, ,,
The chamber of representatives adopt the bill for conversion of the 3½ per cent. rente into 3 per cent. stock . . . . . . 13 Feb. ,,
General strike ordered by the labour syndicates against the communal electoral bill . 26 March, ,,
Stopped by the leaders . . . about 30 March, ,,
Rioting at Renaix, collision with the police, one man killed . . . . . 30 March, ,,
The masters yield to men's demands . 31 March, ,,
Labour bureau with large powers established by decree . . . . 30 April, ,,
Great meeting at Antwerp to protest against the government's protective policy . . 20 May, ,,
Re-adjustment of the ministry; M. de Burlet becomes foreign minister . . . 26 May, ,,
Proposed payment of the debt of the Congo state, voted . . . . . . 27, 28 June, ,,
National demonstration against the government education bill (religious instruction made compulsory) at Brussels . . . . 28 July, ,,
Education bill passed by the chamber, 16 Aug.; royal assent . . . . . 17 Sept. ,,
Annexation of the Congo state postponed 5 Sept. ,,
Parliament opened, with an address by M. Beernaert . . . . 12 Nov. ,,
M. Frère-Orban, eminent liberal statesman, born, 1812; died . . . . . . 2 Jan. 1896
Resignation of M. de Burlet, 25 Feb.; succeeded by M. de Smet de Naeyer . . . 26 Feb. 1896
Royal warrant withdrawing the proposal for the annexation of the Congo state, read in the chamber . . . . 19 June ,,
New chamber of deputies: 111 clericals, 12 liberals, 29 socialists; reported . . . 13 July, ,,
Jan Verhas, eminent painter, died, aged 63; 31 Oct. ,,
Gen. Brassine, minister of war, resigns, on his scheme of military reform being rejected, 9 Nov.; chambers opened . . . . . 10 Nov. ,,
Official use of Flemish ordered . . . 5 Feb. 1897
Coal miners' strike, 16,500 men out, round Mons; reported . . . . 30 June, ,,
The Anglo-Belgian commercial treaty (1862) to be annulled in 1898, announced . . 1 Aug. ,,
New chamber of deputies, 112 catholics, etc. June, 1898
Congo fêtes at Antwerp, the king present, 15 Oct. ,,
Georges Rodenbach, novelist and poet, died, aged 44 26 Dec. ,,
M. de Smet de Nayer, premier, opposes uninominal voting and resigns . . . 23 Jan. 1899
M. Vandenpeereboom forms a cabinet . . Jan. ,,
Stormy scene in the chamber, soldiers called in, 29 March, ,,
Explosion in the fortress at Huy, 6 deaths, 7 April, ,,
Rioting in Brussels, agitation against the electoral reform bill, 1 death . . . 28–30 June, ,,
Socialist obstruction in the chamber, sitting suspended, 28, 29 June; conciliation offered by the premier, chamber adjourns . . 30 June, ,,
Agitation for universal suffrage throughout the country . . . . 4 July, ,,
Electoral reform bill rejected by the chamber, 31 July; the cabinet resigns, 1 Aug.; new ministry; M. de Smet de Nayer, premier and finance minister, proposes the adoption of proportional representation; long debate in the chamber, 8 Aug.; motion for considering the revision of the constitution rejected by the deputies (59–31) . . . . . 31 Aug. ,,
Vandyck tercentenary, see *Antwerp* . 12 Aug. ,,
M. Janson's universal suffrage bill rejected (47–16), 7 Dec. ,,
Bill for proportional representation becomes law, Dec. ,,
The king presents his *real estate* to the nation April, 1900
Parliamentary elections: new chamber, 85 clericals, 33 liberals, and 33 radicals . . . May, ,,
Debate in the chamber on the extradition of Sipido from Paris (26 Oct.); see *Wales, prince of*, 1900; large majority for the government carried, 20, 21 Nov. ,,
Prince Louis de Ligne's château de Belœil, near Tournay, with art collections, burnt down, 14 Dec. ,,
Socialist and anarchist meetings held in Liège and Brussels in favour of universal suffrage, 7, 8 April, 1901
Angry scene in the chamber on the proposal for restoring temporal power to the pope . 17 May, ,,
Charleroi glass-workers' strike began, 1 Aug. 1900, closed . . . . 20 May, ,,
Congo State bill passed by the chamber; annexation postponed . . . . . 17 July, ,,
Old-age pensions act comes into operation, 175,000 applications . . . . . early Aug. ,,
Mathilde Ramboux, "Hilda Ram," popular Flemish poetess, died aged 43 . . . early Aug. ,,
Miners' strike in the Liège basin begins, 27 Sept. closed . . . . Oct. ,,
Debate on the prosecution of M. Smeets for using seditious language at a meeting; wild uproar, sitting suspended, many arrests . 30 Jan. 1902
Military reform bill passed the chamber, 24 Jan.; the senate . . . . . . 20 March, ,,
Anti-gambling bill finally passed (Ostend and Spa granted 7,000,000f. as indemnity, 7 May), 22 March, ,,
Socialist agitation for electoral reform at Brussels, Liège, and elsewhere; general strike; fatal rioting, 8–12 April, ,,
Eight rioters killed at Louvain, 18 April; strikes closed, except in the coal district . 22 April, ,,
Revision of the suffrage question, rejected in the chamber; government majority (20), 18 April, ,,
Budget passed, 25 April; session closed, 20 May, ,,
Elections: Catholic majority increased to 24 in the chamber . . . . 25 May, ,,

The king opens an early Flemish art exhibition at Bruges . . . . . . 15 June, 1902
Internat. congress *re* lunacy reforms at Antwerp, 1 Sept. ,,
Death of the queen . . . . . 19 Sept. ,,
Frontier riots between French and Belgian miners 12–14 Oct. ,,
Attempt to assassinate king Leopold by Rubino, an anarchist (sentenced to life imprisonment 10 Feb. 1903) . . . . 15 Nov. ,,
British Baptist Society thanks the king for his support in the Congo . . . . . 6 Jan. 1903
Dynamite outrage in Brussels by Vandermeuben (sentenced to 10 years' imprisonment) . 4 Feb. ,,
International congress of miners at Brussels 1 June, ,,
1901. Revenue, just under 20,000,000*l.*, surplus 130,208*l.*;
1903. Estimated surplus 7,000*l.*

KINGS.

1831. Leopold,* first king of the Belgians; born 16 Dec. 1790; inaugurated 21 July, 1831, at Brussels; married, 9 Aug. 1832, Louise, eldest daughter of Louis Philippe, king of the French (she died 11 Oct. 1850). He died 10 Dec. 1865.

1865. Leopold II., son; born 9 April, 1835; married archduchess Maria Henrietta of Austria, 22 Aug. 1853 (she died 19 Sept. 1902, aged 66).

Daughter. Princess Louise, born 18 Feb. 1858; married duke Philip of Saxony, 4 Feb. 1875.

Heir, brother. Philip, count of Flanders; born 24 March, 1837; married Mary, princess of Hohenzollern-Sigmaringen, 25 April, 1867; *son*, Baldwin, born 3 June, 1869; died 23 Jan. 1891; Albert, born 8 April, 1875; married Elizabeth, duchess of Bavaria, 2 Oct. 1900; *son*, Leopold, born 3 Nov. 1901.

BELGRADE, capital of Servia, a city on the right bank of the Danube. It was taken from the Greek emperor by Solomon, king of Hungary, in 1072; gallantly defended by John Huniades against the Turks, under Mahomet II., July to Sept. 1456, when the latter was defeated, with the loss of 40,000 men. Belgrade was taken by sultan Solyman, Aug. 1521, and retaken by the Imperialists in 1688, from whom it was again taken by the Turks, 1690. It was besieged in May, 1716, by prince Eugene. In that year the Turkish army, 200,000 strong, approached to relieve it, and on 5 Aug. a sanguinary battle was fought at Peterwaradein, in which the Turks lost 20,000 men. Eugene defeated the Turks here, 16 Aug. 1717, and Belgrade surrendered 18 Aug. In 1739 it was ceded to the Turks, after its fine fortifications had been demolished. It was retaken in 1789, and restored at the peace of Reichenbach, in 1790. The Servian insurgents had possession of it, 1806–13. In 1815 it was placed under prince Milosch, subject to Turkey. The fortifications were restored in 1820. On 19 June, 1862, the Turkish pasha was dismissed for firing on the town during a riot. The university was established by private munificence, 1863. The fortress was surrendered by the Turks to the Servians, 18 April, 1867. The independence of Servia proclaimed here, 22 Aug. 1878. Fatal rioting 5 April, 1903. Revolt by officers of the army, king Alexander I. and queen Draga murdered in their palace between 12 and 2 a.m., 10 June, 1903. Ministers, guards and officers loyal to the king, with the two brothers of the queen, also killed. Prince Peter Karageorgevich made king. He swore fealty to the constitution at Belgrade 25 June. The leading assassins promoted in rank July, 1903. Population in 1890, 54,458; 1901, 72,000. See *Servia*.

* Leopold married, in May, 1816, the princess Charlotte of Wales, daughter of the prince regent, afterwards George IV. of England; she died in childbed, 6 Nov. 1817.

BELGRAVIA, a south-western district of the metropolis, built between 1826 and 1852 upon land belonging to the marquis of Westminster, who is also viscount Belgrave.

BELL, BOOK, AND CANDLE: in the Romish ceremony of excommunication (*which see*), the bell is rung, the book is closed, and candle extinguished; the effect being to exclude the excommunicated from the society of the faithful, divine service, and the sacraments. Its origin is ascribed to the 8th century.

BELL ROCK LIGHTHOUSE, nearly in front of the Frith of Tay, one of the finest in Great Britain; it is 115 feet high, is built upon a rock that measures 427 feet in length, and 200 feet in breadth, and is about 12 feet under water.* It was erected in 1806–10. It has two bells for hazy weather.

BELLAIR, North America. The town was attacked by the British forces under sir Peter Parker, who, after an obstinate engagement, was killed, 30 Aug. 1814.

BELLEISLE, an isle on the south coast of Brittany, France, erected into a duchy for marshal Belleisle, in 1742, in reward of his military and diplomatic services, by Louis XV. Belleisle was taken by the British forces under commodore Keppel and general Hodgson, after a desperate resistance, 7 June, 1761, but was restored to France in 1763.

BELLES-LETTRES, or POLITE LEARNING, see *Academies*, and *Literature*.

BELLEVILLE, the red republican stronghold of Paris, defended by seven barricades, was captured by L'Admirault and Vinoy, 27, 28 May, 1871, when the insurrection was suppressed.

BELLEVILLE BOILERS, see *Navy Boilers*.

BELLITE, a Swedish explosive invented by Mr. Carl Lamm in 1885.

BELLMEN, appointed in London to proclaim the hour of the night before public clocks became general, were numerous about 1556. They were to ring a bell at night, and cry, "Take care of your fire and candle, be charitable to the poor, and pray for the dead."

BELLOWS. Anacharsis, the Scythian, is said to have been the inventor of them, about 569 B.C.; and to him is ascribed the invention of tinder, the potter's wheel, anchors for ships, &c. Bellows were not used in the furnaces of the Romans. The great bellows of our foundries must have been early used; see *Blowing Machines*.

BELLS were used among the Jews, Greeks, and Romans. The responses of the Dodonæan oracle were in part conveyed by bells. *Strabo*. The monument of Porsenna was decorated with pinnacles, each surmounted by bells. *Pliny*. Said to have been introduced by Paulinus, bishop of Nola, in Campagna, about 400; and first known in France in 550. The army of Clothaire II., king of France, was frightened from the siege of Sens by the ringing of the bells of St. Stephen's church. The second excerption of our king Egbert commands every

* Upon this rock, it is said, the abbots of Aberbrothock fixed the *Inchcape bell*, so that it was rung by the impulse of the sea, thus warning mariners. It is also said that a Dutchman, who took the apparatus away, was here lost with his ship and crew.

priest, at the proper hours, to sound the bells of his church. Bells were used in churches by order of pope John IX., about 900, *as a defence, by ringing them, against thunder and lightning*. Bells are mythically said to have been cast by Turketul, abbot of England, about 941. The celebrated "Song of the Bell," by Schiller (died 1805), has been frequently translated. The following list is that given by Mr. E. Beckett-Denison (afterwards Lord Grimthorpe) in his discourse on bells at the Royal Institution, 6 March, 1857. The lecture of the Rev. H. R. Haweis, at the same place, 7 Feb., 1879, was well illustrated. See *Imperial Institute*.

	Weight. Tons	Cwt.		Weight. Tons	Cwt.
Moscow, 1736;* broken, 1737	250	?	York, 1845	10	15
Another, 1817	110	?	Bruges, 1680	10	5
Three others	16 to 31		St. Peter's, Rome	8	0
Novgorod	31	0	Oxford, 1680	7	12
Olmütz	17	18	Lucerne, 1636	7	11
Vienna, 1711	17	14	Halberstadt, 1457	7	10
Westminster, 1856,† "Big Ben"	15	8½	Antwerp	7	3
Erfurt, 1497	13	15	Brussels	7	1½
Westminster, 1858,‡ "St. Stephen"	13	10¾	Dantzic, 1453	6	1
Sens	13	?	Lincoln, 1834	5	8
Paris, 1680	12	16	St. Paul's, 1716 §	5	4
Montreal, 1847	12	15	Ghent	4	18
Cologne, 1448	11	3	Boulogne, new	4	18
Breslau, 1507	11	0	Exeter, 1675	4	10
Görlitz	10	17	Old Lincoln, 1610	4	8
			Fourth quarter-bell, Westminster, 1857	4	0
London, 1882 (St. Paul's) Great Paul ‖				about 17½	0
Cologne, 1887 ¶				about 26	13

Baptism of Bells.—They were anointed and baptized in churches, it is said, from the 10th century. *Du Fresnoy.* The bells of the priory of Little Dunmow, in Essex, were baptized by the names of St. Michael, St. John, Virgin Mary, Holy Trinity, &c., in 1501. *Weever.* The great bell of Notre Dame, of Paris, was baptized by the name of duke of Angoulême, 1816. On the continent, in Roman Catholic states, they baptize bells as we do ships, but with religious solemnity. *Ashe.*

Ringing of Bells, in changes of regular peals, is almost peculiar to the English. *Stow.*

"Companie of the Schollers of Chepeside," 1603; "Society of College Youths," 1637; "Society of Cumberlands," 1683; the "Society of Union Scholars," 1713; the "Society of Eastern Scholars," 1733; "London Youths," 1753; "Westminster Youths," 1776.

* The metal has been valued at the lowest estimate, at 66,565*l*. Gold and silver are said to have been thrown in as votive offerings.

† The largest bell in England (named Big Ben, after sir Benjamin Hall, the then chief commissioner of works), cast at Houghton-le-Spring, Durham, by Messrs. Warner, under the superintendence of Mr. E. Beckett-Denison, and the Rev. W. Taylor, at an expense of 3343*l*. 14*s*. 9*d*. The composition was 22 parts copper and 7 tin. The diameter was 9 ft. 5½ in.; the height, 7 ft. 10½ in. The clapper weighed 12 cwt. *Rev. W. Taylor.*

‡ The bell "Big Ben" having been found to be cracked on 24 Oct. 1857, it was broken up and another bell cast with the same metal, in May, 1858, by Messrs. Mears, Whitechapel. It is rather different in shape from its predecessor, "Big Ben," and about 2 tons lighter. Its diameter is 9 ft. 6 in.; the height 7 ft. 10 in. It was struck for the first time, 18 Nov. 1858. The clapper weighs 6 cwt.—half that of the former bell. The note of the bell is E natural; the quarter-bells being G, B, E, F. On 1 Oct. 1859, this bell was also found to be cracked.

§ The clapper of St. Paul's bell weighs 180 lbs.; the diameter of the bell is 10 feet (Mr. Walesby says 6 ft. 9½ in.), and its thickness 10 in. The hour strikes upon this bell, the quarters upon two smaller ones; see *Clocks*.

‖ Height, 8 feet 10 in.; diameter, 9 feet 6¾ in.; note E♭; materials tin and copper; cost about 3000*l*.; cast by Mr. Taylor, at Loughborough; raised to its place 31 May, dedicated 3 June, 1882.

¶ Height 14¼ feet; diameter at the mouth 11½ feet; note C♯ or D; materials chiefly French cannon; cast by Andreas Hamm of Frankenthal; dedicated July, 1887.

Fabian Stedman, about 1650, invented a system known as "Stedman's principle." Benjamin Anable soon after invented "Grandsire Triples."

720 changes can be rung in an hour upon 12 bells; 479,001,600 changes rung upon them, require 75 years, 10 months, and 10 days.

Nell Gwynne left the ringers of the bells of St. Martin's-in-the-fields money for a weekly entertainment, 1687, and many others have done the same.

A central council of Church Bell Ringers, representing many societies, was established at the Inns of Court hotel, London, 10 April, 1890.

Carillons, a collection of bells, arranged in two or three chromatic scales, played by pedals or keyboards, or by machinery. The first set is said to have been made at Alost in Flanders, in 1487, and that country and Holland are renowned for carillons. Matthias van den Gheyn was an eminent maker (1721-85). Excellent carillon machines are now made by Messrs. Gillett, Bland & Co., Croydon. One at Manchester was started 1 Jan. 1879. It plays 35 tunes on 20 bells.

BELOOCHISTAN, the ancient Gedrosia (S. Asia). Khelat, the capital, was taken by the British in the Afghan war, 1839; abandoned, July, 1840; taken and held a short time, Nov. 1840.

The khan was subsidised in 1854, under certain conditions, which were not observed; the arrangement was broken up in 1873; the negotiations of major (after sir Robert) Sandeman in 1875 were successful, and Quettah was occupied by the British in 1877, and has since become a prosperous station. The khan proffered assistance after the defeat of gen. Burrows in July, 1880.

Quettah, with districts of Pishin, Thal Chotiali, and Sibi, annexed to British territories, and placed under a chief commissioner; announced, Nov. 1887.

Col. sir Robert G. Sandeman, the chief commissioner, brave and conciliatory, dies, 29 Jan.; he was succeeded by major-gen. sir James Browne, Feb. 1892; died at Quettah, 13 June, 1896.

The *Zhob Valley* annexed by sir Robert Sandeman at the request of the chiefs (1888); 25 Dec. 1889. The first station was named Fort Sandeman. Good report received, Dec. 1892.

Khan of Khelat, Mir Mahmud Khan, 1893.

Lieut. George J. Home and 6 men killed near Fort Sandeman . . . . 6 June, 1895

Col. Holdich appointed commissioner in settling the frontier between British Beloochistan and Persia; announced . . . . . . Feb. 1896

Lieuts. R. H. M. Yeates and O. L. Downes and 2 men killed by a mad sepoy at Fort Sandeman 28 Oct. ,,

A survey party under capt. J. M. Burn and lieut. Turner attacked at Kej, in Makrah, by Gichkis, native guards killed, camp looted, 13,000 rupees carried off, and Pasni looted; rising among the tribes general . . . . . . 9 Jan. 1898

Enemy (1,500) routed by col. Mayne near Turbat, about 100 men killed . . . . . . 31 Jan. ,,

Mehrab Khan besieged at Turbat by col. Mayne; evacuates the fort . . . . . . 9 Feb. ,,

Lieut.-col. Gaisford murdered by a Ghazi 15 March, ,,

Persian raids frequent; fort in Mekran recaptured by the British . . . . mid. Dec. 1901

Railway from Quettah to Nushki begun . autumn, 1902

Land on the Upper Sinde frontier leased to the Indian government, reported . . 6 August, 1903

BELT CASE, see *Trials*, 1882-4.

BELVEDERE EXPLOSION, see *Gunpowder* (note).

BENARES, in India, a holy city of the Hindoos, abounding in temples. It was ceded by the nabob of Oude, Asoph-ud-Dowlah, to the English in 1775. An insurrection took place here, which had nearly proved fatal to the British interests in Hindostan, 1781. The rajah, Cheyt Sing, was deposed in consequence of it, in 1783. Mr. Cherry, capt. Conway, and others, were assassinated at Benares, by vizier Aly, 14 Jan. 1799. In June, 1857, col. Neil succeeded in suppressing attempts of the native infantry to join the mutiny; see

India. Visit of prince of Wales, 5 Jan. 1876. Pop., 1901, 209,331.

New water-works: foundation laid by prince Albert Victor, Jan. 1890; opposed by the Brahmins as interfering with the sacred waters and temples; serious riots, with destruction of property, suppressed by the military, 16, 17 April, 1891; peace restored by a compromise.

BENBURB, near Armagh (N. Ireland). Here O'Neill totally defeated the English under Monroe, 5 June, 1646. Moore says that it was "the only great victory since the days of Brian Boru, achieved by an Irish chieftain in the cause of Ireland."

BENCOOLEN (Sumatra). The English East India company made a settlement here which preserved to them the pepper trade after the Dutch had dispossessed them of Bantam, 1682. *Anderson.* York fort was erected by the East India company, 1690. In 1693 a dreadful mortality raged here, occasioned by the town being built on a pestilent morass; among others the governor and council perished. The French, under count D'Estaing, destroyed the English settlement, 1760. Bencoolen was reduced to a residency under the government of Bengal, in 1801, and was ceded to the Dutch, in 1824, in exchange for their possessions in Malacca; see *India.*

BENDER, Bessarabia, European Russia. Near it was the asylum of Charles XII. of Sweden, after his defeat at Pultowa by the czar Peter the Great, 8 July, 1709. The peace of Bender was concluded in 1711. Bender was taken by storm, by the Russians, 28 Sept. 1770; was taken by Potemkin in 1789, and again in 1809. It was restored at the peace of Jassy, but retained at the peace of 1812.

BENEDICTINES, an order of monks founded by St. Benedict (lived 480-543), who introduced the monastic life into Western Europe, in 529, when he founded the monastery on Monte Casino in Campania, and eleven others afterwards. His *Regula Monachorum* (rule of the monks) soon became the common rule of western monachism. No religious order has been so remarkable for extent, wealth, and men of note and learning, as the Benedictine. Among its branches the chief were the Cluniacs, founded in 912; the Cistercians, founded in 1098, and reformed by St. Bernard, abbot of Clairvaux, in 1116; and the Carthusians, from the Chartreux (hence Charter-house), founded by Bruno about 1080. The Benedictine order was introduced into England by Augustin, in 596; and William I. built an abbey for it on the plain where the battle of Hastings was fought, 1066; see *Battle-Abbey.* William de Warrenne, earl of Warrenne, built a convent at Lewes, in Sussex, in 1077. Of this order it is reckoned that there have been 40 popes, 200 cardinals, 50 patriarchs, 116 archbishops, 4600 bishops, 4 emperors, 12 empresses, 46 kings, 41 queens, and 3600 saints. Their founder was canonised. *Baronius.* The Benedictines have taken little part in politics, but have produced many valuable literary works. The congregation of St. Maur published the celebrated "l'Art de Vérifier les Dates," in 1750, and edited many ancient authors.

The Benedictines with other orders were expelled from France by decree . . . . 29 March, 1880
The 14th centenary of the birth of St. Benedict was kept at Monte Casino and other places April, ,,

BENEFICE (literally a good deed or favour), or FIEF. Clerical benefices originated in the 12th century, when the priesthood began to imitate the feudal lay system of holding lands for performing certain duties: till then the priests were supported by alms and oblations at mass. Vicarages, rectories, perpetual curacies, and chaplaincies, are termed benefices, in contradistinction to dignities, such as bishoprics, &c. A rector is entitled to all the tithes; a vicar, to a small part or to none.—All benefices that should become vacant in the space of six months, were given by pope Clement VII. to his nephew, in 1534. *Notitia Monastica.* Union of Benefices (Metropolis) Act was passed in 1860; amended, 6 Aug. 1900. An act for the augmentation of poor benefices by the sale of some of those in the presentation of the lord chancellor, was passed in 1863, and an act respecting the sequestration of benefices and their union passed, 1871. See *Patronage.*

The Commission on Ecclesiastical Benefices reported, recommending amendments in sales of advowsons, discontinuance of sale by auction, &c. Nov. 1879
Mr. Lyttelton's Benefices Bill, patronage, discipline, etc., read 2nd time . . . 2 March, 1898
Mr. Balfour's Union of Benefices bill (patronage) and to amend the Pluralities Acts of 1838 and 1885 (no relation to doctrine or ritual); passed 12 Aug. ,,

BENEFIT OF CLERGY, see *Clergy.*

BENEFIT SOCIETIES, see *Friendly Societies.*

BENEVENTUM (now Benevento), an ancient city in South Italy, said to have been founded by Diomedes the Greek, after the fall of Troy. Pyrrhus of Macedon, during his invasion of Italy, was totally defeated near Beneventum, 275 B.C. Near it was erected the triumphal arch of Trajan, A.D. 114. Benevento was formed into a duchy by the Lombards, 571. At a battle fought here, 26 Feb. 1266, Manfred, king of Sicily, was defeated and slain by Charles of Anjou, who thus became virtually master of Italy. The castle was built 1323; the town was nearly destroyed by an earthquake, 1688, when the archbishop, afterwards pope Benedict XIII., was dug out of the ruins alive, and contributed to its subsequent rebuilding, 1703. It was seized by the king of Naples, but restored to the pope on the suppression of the Jesuits, 1773. Talleyrand de Périgord, Bonaparte's arch-chancellor, was made prince of Benevento, 1806. Benevento was taken by the French, 1798, and restored to the pope in 1815.

BENEVOLENCES (Aids, Free Gifts, actually Forced Loans) appear to have been claimed by our Anglo-Saxon sovereigns. Special ones were levied by Edward IV., 1473, by Richard III., 1485 (although a statute forbidding them was enacted in 1484), by Henry VII., 1492; and by James I., in 1613, on occasion of the marriage of the princess Elizabeth with Frederick, the elector palatine, afterwards king of Bohemia. In 1615 Oliver St. John, M.P., was fined 5000*l.*, and chief justice Coke disgraced, for severely censuring such modes of raising money. Benevolences were declared illegal by the bill of rights, Feb. 1689.

BENEVOLENT, or Strangers' Friend Society, established 1785; Loan Society, 1817; Society of Blues, 1824; Society of St. Patrick, 1784.

BENGAL, chief presidency of British India, containing Calcutta, the capital. Its governors were appointed by the sovereigns of Delhi, till 1340, when it became independent. It was added to the Mogul empire by Baber, about 1529; see *India* and *Calcutta.* Population 1881, 66,589,553; 1891, 71,346,987; 1901, 74,713,020.

The English first permitted to trade to Bengal. . 1534
They establish a settlement at Hooghly . about 1652
Factories of the French and Danes set up . . 1660
Bengal made a distinct agency 1864

Mr. William Hedges appointed agent and governor 1681
The English settlement removed to Fort William . 1698
Imperial grant vesting the revenues of Bengal in the company, by which it gained the sovereignty of the country . . . . 12 Aug. 1765
Mr. Warren Hastings governor 1772
India Bill; Bengal made chief presidency; supreme court of judicature established . . 16 June, 1773
Bishop of Calcutta appointed . . . 21 July, 1813
Railway opened . . . . . . 15 Aug. 1854
Awful famine in Orissa (*which see*) . . . 1865-66
Lieut.-governor, hon. Wm. Grey 1867
" Geo. Campbell 1871
Drought; consequent famine (see *India*) . Oct. 1873
Cyclone: Mednapore destroyed; about 2000 perish Oct. 1874
Lieut.-governor, sir Richard Temple . . . "
" " hon. sir Ashley Eden . . . 1877
" " Mr. (aft. sir) Rivers Thompson . March, 1882
" " Sir C. S. Bayley . . April, 1887
" " Sir Chas. A. Elliott . . . 1890
" " Sir Alexander Mackenzie . . 1895
" " Sir John Woodburn . March, 1898
died 20 Nov. 1902
" " Mr. A. H. Leith Fraser . Dec. 1902
Bengal Tenancy Bill passed . . . . 11 March, 1885
Cyclone on the Orissa coast; about 5000 perish 22 Sept. "
For changes in the jury system, see *India*, Nov. 1892 . . . . March, 1893
The indigo crops much injured by floods . Aug. "
Epidemic of murder, arms called in . Sept. 1896
Destructive cyclone at Chittagong, 3 deaths, 24 Oct. 1897
Plague epidemic severe in parts, Feb.-March, 1899; 4,725 deaths week ending . . 17 March, 1900
Tornado over Dacca 416 deaths, crops destroyed 1 May, 1902

BENIN RIVER, see *Oil rivers protectorate*.

BEN NEVIS, a mountain in Inverness-shire, the loftiest in Britain, 4,406 feet above the sea; see *Meteorology*, 1883-4.

BENWELL TOWER, about two miles W. of Newcastle [value above 12,000*l.*], was presented by Mr. John Wm. Pease to be the palace of the new bishopric of Newcastle-upon-Tyne, Nov. 1881.

BENZOLE, or BENZINE, a compound of hydrogen and carbon, discovered by Faraday in the oils of portable gas (1825), obtained by Mitscherlich from benzoic acid (1834) and by C. B. Mansfield in coal tar (1848), the latter of whom unfortunately died in consequence of being severely burnt while experimenting on it (26 Feb. 1855). Benzole has become useful in the arts. Chemical research has produced from it *aniline* (*which see*), the source of the celebrated modern dyes, mauve, magenta, and many others; see *Alizarine* and *Indigo*.

Aromatic essences and perfumes have been obtained from benzole by Perkin, Tiemann, Harrmann, and others. Febrifuge medicines, by O. Fischer, Dewar, McKendrick and others, in 1881; and saccharine, a principle 220 times sweeter than cane sugar, by Fahlberg and Remsen, patented in Britain in 1886; a convenient preparation in liquid form by Messrs. Allen and Hanbury, London, 1893.

BEOWULF, an ancient Anglo-Saxon epic poem, describing events which probably occurred in the middle of the 5th century, supposed to have been written subsequent to 597. An edition by Kemble was published in 1833. It has been translated by Kemble, Thorpe, and Wackerbarth. An excellent translation by Wm. Morris and A. J. Wyatt (1895).

BERBICE (S. America), settled by the Dutch, 1626, who surrendered it to the British, 23 April, 1796, and 22 Sept. 1803; and finally in 1814. It was united to Demerara and named British Guiana, 1831. Coolie riot, mob fired on, 6 killed, reported 8 May, 1903.

BERDITSCHEFF, Kiev, S. Russia. At the burning of a circus here about 300 persons perish, 13 Jan. 1883.

BERENGARIANS, followers of Berengarius, archdeacon of Angers, who, about 1049, opposed the Romish doctrine of transubstantiation, or the real presence in the Lord's supper. Several councils of the church condemned his doctrine, 1050-79. After much controversy he recanted about 1079, and died grieved and wearied in 6 Jan. 1088.

BERESINA, a river in Russia, crossed by the French main army after its defeat by the Russians, 25-29 Nov. 1812. The French lost upwards of 20,000 men, and their retreat was attended by great calamity and suffering.

BERG (W. Germany), on the extinction of its line of counts, in 1348, was incorporated with Juliers. Napoleon I. made Murat grand-duke in 1806. The principal part is now held by Prussia.

BERGAMO (N. Italy), a Lombard duchy, was annexed to Venice, 1428; which chiefly held it till it revolted, and was joined to the Cisalpine republic, 1797. It was awarded to Austria in 1814, and ceded to Sardinia, 1859.

BERGEN (Norway), founded 1070; was the royal residence during the 12th and 13th centuries. Population 1891, 53,686; 1900, 72,251.

BERGEN (in Germany), BATTLE OF, between the French and allies, the latter defeated, 13 April, 1752.—(In HOLLAND) 1. The allies under the duke of York were defeated by the French, under gen. Brune, with great loss, 19 Sept. 1799. 2. In another battle, fought 2 Oct. same year, the duke gained a victory over Brune; but on the 6th, the duke was defeated before Alkmaer, and on the 20th entered into a convention, by which his army was exchanged for 6000 French and Dutch prisoners in England.

BERGEN-OP-ZOOM, in Holland. This place, whose works were deemed impregnable, was taken by the French, 16 Sept. 1747, and again in 1795. An attempt, made by the British under general sir T. Graham (afterwards lord Lynedoch), to carry the fortress by storm, was defeated; after forcing an entrance, their retreat was cut off, and a dreadful slaughter ensued; nearly all were cut to pieces or made prisoners, 8 March, 1814.

BERGERAC, France. Here John of Gaunt, then earl of Derby, defeated the French, in 1344, and here a temporary treaty of peace between the Catholics and Protestants, establishing liberty of conscience, was signed 17 Sept. 1577.

BERKELEY CASTLE, Gloucestershire, was begun by Henry I. in 1108, and finished in the next reign. Here Edward II. was cruelly murdered by the contrivance of his queen Isabella (a princess of France), and her paramour, Mortimer, earl of March, 21 Sept. 1327. Mortimer was hanged at the Elms, near London, 29 Nov. 1330; and Edward III. confined his mother in her own house at Castle Rising, near Lynn, in Norfolk, till her death, 1357.

The *Berkeley peerage* suit in the court of Chancery, due to a disputed marriage, lasted from 1416 to 1609.

In another suit owing to a disputed marriage in 1811, Thomas Moreton Fitz Hardinge Berkeley became 6th earl. Earl Fitz Hardinge died unmarried in 1857. His next brother Maurice's claim for the barony of Berkeley was not granted, 23 July, 1858. The committee of privileges of the house of lords met to consider the claims of earl Fitzhardinge and Mr. Randal Mowbray Thomas Berkeley for the Berkeley Peerage, 23 April; committee decided in favour of Mr. R. M. T. Berkeley, 31 July, 1891, thus confirming lord Eldon's decision in 1811.

BERLIN (capital of Prussia, in the province of Brandenburg), and since 1871, of the German empire, alleged to have been founded by the margrave Albert the Bear, about 1163. Its five districts were united under one magistracy, in 1714; and it was subsequently made the capital of Prussia and greatly improved by the sovereigns. It was taken and held by the Russians and Austrians, 9-13 Oct. 1760. Establishment of the Academy of Sciences, 1702; of the university, 1810. On 27 Oct. 1806, after the battle of Jena (14 Oct.), the French entered Berlin; and from this place Napoleon issued the famous *Berlin decree*, an interdict against the commerce of England, 20 Nov. It declared the British islands to be in a state of blockade, and ordered all Englishmen found in countries occupied by French troops to be treated as prisoners of war. On 5 Nov. 1808, Napoleon entered into a convention with Prussia, by which he remitted to Prussia the sum due on the war-debt, and withdrew many of his troops to reinforce his armies in Spain. See *Prussia*, 1866, 1871. Population in 1901, 1,901,567.

The railway to Magdeburg opened . . 10 Sept. 1841
The first constituent assembly held here 21 June, 1842
An insurrection commenced here . . March, 1848
Berlin was declared in a state of siege . 12 Nov. ,,
The continuation of this state was declared to be illegal without its concurrence by the lower chamber . . . . . . 25 April, 1849
A treaty of peace between Prussia and Saxony was signed . . . . . . 21 Oct. 1866
The monument of Victory, in memory of the wars with Denmark (1864), Austria (1866), and France (1870-1), solemnly uncovered . . 2 Sept. 1873
Meeting of chancellors of Germany, Austria, and Russia, 11, 12 May; they agree to an urgent note to Turkey on the eastern policy; expressed in a note dated 13 May; accepted by Italy and France; received in London, 15 May; its acceptance by the earl of Derby declined, as her majesty's government had not been consulted, 19 May; this note not presented through the revolution in Turkey . . . . . . 30 May, 1876
The "Berlin note" printed in the *Times* . 4 July, ,,
International fish and fishing exhibition opened by the crown prince . . . . 20 April, 1880
International hygienic exhibition burnt; great loss 12 May, 1882; opened 12 May, closed 15 Oct. 1883
National theatre burnt . . . . . 4 April, ,,
Statues of Wilhelm and Alexander von Humboldt uncovered in presence of the emperor . 28 May, ,,
Foundation of New German parliament-house laid by the emperor . . . . . 9 June, 1884
International art exhibition opened by the emperor 22 May, 1886
Monument to Frederick William IV. unveiled by the emperor . . . . . . 10 June, ,,
Queen Victoria warmly received here 24 April; meets prince Bismarck 25 April; left. 26 April, 1888
New museum of natural history opened by the emperor . . . . . . 2 Dec. 1889
Visit of the prince of Wales and prince George 21–28 March, 1890
Address from 30,000 Berlin citizens presented to prince Bismarck . . . . 22 June, ,,
International arts exhibition opened by the empress Frederick . . . . . . 1 May, 1891
Britain, Italy, Spain, well represented; a few French works sent. British artists and others receive gold medals . . . . 20 July, ,,
Suspension of Messrs. Hirschfeld & Wolff, bankers; great losses, about 4 Nov., suspension of Friedlander, Felix, & Siegmund Sommerfeld (Felix commits suicide) . . . . . 7 Nov. ,,
Socialist riots of the unemployed suppressed by the armed police, 25–27 Feb.; rioters sentenced to various terms of imprisonment . 19 March, 1892
New Protestant cathedral foundation laid in presence of the emperor . . . . 17 June, 1894
New parliament-house opened by the emperor 5 Dec. ,,
Monument to Luther unveiled by prince Leopold, 11 June, 1895
Foundation of a national memorial to the emperor William I., laid by William II., 18 Aug.; (see *Germany*, 22 March, 1897); dedication of the Memorial church to the emperor Frederick; statue of the empress Augusta unveiled by the emperor . . . . . . 21 Oct. ,,
Industrial exhibition opened by the emperor, 1 May, 1896; closed 15 Oct. 1896
Bi-centenary of the foundation of the Royal Academy of Arts celebrated, speech by the emperor, 2 May, ,,
Li Hung Chang, Chinese statesman, receives the order of the Red Eagle . . . 15 June ,,
The emperor unveils 3 of the 32 historical groups of marble statues which he is erecting in the Sieges-Allee, 22 March, 1898; the last unveiled 18 Dec. 1901
The Virchow pathological museum, containing 20,000 specimens, opened by prof. Virchow 27 June, ,,
Monument to prince Bismarck unveiled by the emperor . . . . . . 17 June, ,,
The Pekin astronomical instruments placed in the Orangery, Sans Souci park . . 11 Sept. ,,
Industrial depression, over 35,000 unemployed, meetings held . . . . . . 18 Nov. ,,
Pergamon museum opened, speech by the emperor 18 Dec. ,,
Elevated and underground electric railway opened 16 Feb. 1902
The emperor unveils the new "Rolandbrunnen" 25 Aug. ,,
State entry of the king of Italy (he gives about 400*l*. to the poor). . . . . 28 Aug. ,,
Wagner festival . . . . . . Oct. 1903

BERLIN CONGRESS ON THE EASTERN QUESTION.

Representatives (with resident ambassadors): *Germany*, prince Bismarck, president; *Russia*, prince Gortschakoff; *Turkey*, Alexander Carathéodori; *Great Britain*, lord Beaconsfield and marquis of Salisbury (lord Odo Russell ambassador); *Austria*, count Andrassy; *France*, M. Waddington; *Italy*, count Corti.
First meeting, 13 June; 20th and last meeting; treaty signed . . . . . . 13 July, 1878
Articles 1—12. Bulgaria constituted an autonomous principality, tributary to the sultan; the Balkans southern limit; the prince, to be elected by the population, approved by the sultan and other powers; public laws, and other details.
,, 13—22. New province of Eastern Roumelia constituted; partially autonomous; boundaries defined: Christian governor-general to be appointed by the sultan; to be organised by an Austrian commission; a Russian army of occupation, to remain nine months.
,, 23. Bosnia and Herzegovina to be occupied and administered by Austria-Hungary.
,, 24—30. Montenegro to be independent; new frontiers; Antivari annexed.
,, 31—39. Servia to be independent, with new frontiers.
,, 40—49. Roumania to be independent, losing part of Bessarabia to Russia, with compensation.
,, 50—54. Regulation of navigation of the Danube, &c.
,, 55—57. Legal reforms in Crete, &c.
,, 58. The Porte cedes to Russia Ardahan, Kars, and Batoum, and settles boundaries.
,, 59. Batoum to be a free commercial port.
,, 60. Alasgird and Bayazid restored to Turkey.
,, 61—62. The Porte engages to realise legal reforms, and to grant religious liberty, &c.
,, 63. The treaty of Paris (30 March, 1856), and of London (13 March, 1871), maintained when not modified by this treaty.
,, 64. Treaty to be ratified in three weeks time. Ratified . . . . . . 3 Aug. 1878
Circular respecting delay in fulfilling the treaty from earl Granville, the British foreign secretary, to the foreign powers . . . . May, 1880

BERLIN CONFERENCE (16 June—1 July, 1880).

The ambassadors: for Great Britain, lord Odo Russell (after. lord Ampthill); France, comte de St. Vallier, etc. president, prince Hohenlohe, German foreign minister.

They agree to a collective note presented to the sultan of Turkey (urging the surrender of Dulcigno and cession of provinces to Greece), which is presented . . . . . . 15 July, 1880

BERLIN CONFERENCE respecting the condition of the working classes proposed by the German emperor, 4 Feb. The delegates (with the ambassadors and ministers) meet . . 15 March, 1890

[Delegates: Great Britain, sir John Gorst; France, M. Jules Simon; Italy, senator Boccardo, and others. The conference opened by baron von Berlepsch, Prussian minister of commerce, elected president, 15 March, closed 29 March, 1890. Subjects discussed: regulation of labour in mines, of Sunday labour, and of the labour of children and youths. Recommendations adopted referred to the respective legislatures.]

For other Berlin conferences, see *Samoan Isles*, 1889, *West African Settlements*, *Dulcigno*, *Turkey and Greece*, 1880–1.

BERLIN WORK, see *Embroidery*.

BERMUDAS or SUMMERS' ISLES, a group in the North Atlantic ocean, discovered by Juan Bermudas, a Spaniard, in 1522, but not inhabited until 1609, when sir George Summers was cast away upon them. They were settled by stat. 9 James I., 1612. Among the exiles from England during the civil war was Waller, the poët, who wrote, while resident here, a poetical description of the islands. There was an awful hurricane here, 31 Oct. 1780, and by another, a third of the houses was destroyed, and the shipping driven ashore, 20 July, 1813. A large iron dry dock here, which cost 250,000*l.*, was towed from the Medway to the Bermudas, in June and July, 1869. Governors, sir Fred. E. Chapman, 1867; gen. J. H. Lefroy, March, 1871; Sir Robert Michael Laffan, Feb. 1877; died 22 March, 1882; lieut.-gen. T. L. J. Gallwey, 1882; lieut.-gen. N. Newdigate, July, 1888; lieut.-gen. T. C. Lyons, June, 1892; gen. sir George D. Barker, April, 1896; sir Henry Le Zuay Geary, Jan. 1902. Visited by the princess Louise, Jan. 1883. Royal engineer office at Prospect burnt down, 14 Jan. 1897. Rear-adm. Sampson and 2 U.S. warships warmly received at Bermuda, 19—24 Feb. 1899. Destructive cyclone, 12 Sept. 1899. The great floating dock arrived, 8 Aug. 1902. Severe hurricane in the islands, much damage done to property, 28 Sept. 1903. Population, 1890, 15,013; 1901, *estimated* 17,535.

BERNAL COLLECTION of articles of taste and vertù, formed by Ralph Bernal, Esq., many years chairman of committees of ways and means in the house of commons. He died 26 Aug. 1854. The sale in March, 1856, lasted 31 days, and enormous prices were given. The total sum realised was 62,680*l.* 6*s.* 8*d.*

BERNARD, MOUNT ST., so called from a monastery founded on it by Bernardine Menthon in 962. Velan, its highest peak, is about 8000 feet high, covered with perpetual snow. Hannibal, it is said, conducted the Carthaginians by this pass into Italy (218 B.C.); and by the same route, in May, 1800, Bonaparte led his troops to Italy before the battle of Marengo, 14 June. On the summit of Great St. Bernard is the ancient monastery still held by monks, who entertain travellers.

BERNARDINES, or WHITE MONKS, a strict order of Cistercian monks, established by St. Bernard of Clairvaux, about 1115.

BERNE, the sovereign canton of Switzerland, joined the Swiss League, 1352; the town Berne was made a free city by the emperor Frederick, May, 1218; it successfully resisted Rudolph of Hapsburg, 1288. It surrendered to the French under general Brune, 12 April, 1798. The town has bears for its arms, and some of these animals are still maintained on funds specially provided for the purpose. It was made capital of Switzerland, 1848. Population, 1888: canton, 536,679; town, 46,009; 1901, canton, 587,983; town, 64,864.

The 700th anniversary of the foundation of Berne by duke Berchtold V. of Zähnugen, celebrated 14–17 Aug. 1891

Meeting of the International Geographical congress 10–14 Aug. ,,

Labour riots: 80 men arrested . about 21 June, 1893

International Copyright Conventions held here 1884, 1886, 1896, 1901; see *Copyright*.

BERNE COPYRIGHT CONVENTION, see under *Copyright*.

BERRIDGE BEQUEST of 152,000*l.* for philanthropic purposes. Different sums were given to the National Society for Promoting Education and similar societies, to the Sanitary Institute of Great Britain, to the Plumbers' company, to King's College and University College, London, and other bodies, reported, 7 Oct. 1892.

BERRY (the ancient *Biturigum regis*), centra, France, held by the Romans since the conquest by Cæsar (58-50 B.C.) till it was subdued by the Visigoths; from whom it was taken by Clovis in A.D. 507. Erected into a duchy by John II. in 1360, incorporated into the royal domains 1601. The duc de Berry, son of Charles, and father of comte de Chambord, was assassinated 13 Feb. 1820.

BERSAGLIERI, the sharpshooters of the Sardinian army, first employed about 1848.

BERWICK-ON-TWEED, a fortified town on the north-east extremity of England, the theatre of many bloody contests while England and Scotland were two kingdoms; it was claimed by the Scots because it stood on their side of the river. Here John Baliol did homage for Scotland, 30 Nov. 1292. It was annexed to England in 1333; and after having been taken and retaken many times, was finally ceded to England in 1482. In 1551 it was made independent of both kingdoms. The town surrendered to Cromwell in 1648, and to general Monk in 1659. Since the union of the crowns (James I. 1603), the strong fortifications have been neglected. The borough was absorbed into Northumberland in 1885 in respect to parliamentary elections. By an explosion in a room for manufacturing cartridges, Mr. A. M. Caverhill, the proprietor, and 2 others were killed, and much damage done in the neighbourhood; 22 Aug. 1896. Population 1881, 13,998; 1891, 13,378; 1901, 13,437.

BESSARABIA, a frontier province of European Russia, part of the ancient Dacia. After being possessed by the Goths, Huns, &c., it was conquered by the Turks, 1474, seized by the Russians, 1770, and ceded to them in 1812. The part annexed to Roumania in 1856, was restored to Russia at the close of the war in 1878, in exchange for the Dobrudscha, by the treaty of Berlin, 13 July, and given up, 21 Oct. 1878. Severe drought, crops destroyed, May, 1899; serious disturbances, troops called out, 20 peasants killed at Bolgrad, early Aug. 1899; famine reported, May, 1901. Massacre of Jews at Kishineff, 19, 20 April, 1903. Pop. 1886, 1,612,175; 1897, 1,933,436.

BESSEMER, see *Steel* and *Steam Navigation*.

BETHELL'S ACT, see *Fraudulent*.

BETHLEHEM now contains a large convent, enclosing, as is said, the very birthplace of Christ; a church erected by the empress Helena in the form of a cross, about 325; a chapel, called the Chapel of the Nativity, where the manger in which Christ was laid is said to be preserved; another, called the Chapel of Joseph; and a third, of the Holy Innocents. Bethlehem is much visited by pilgrims.—The Bethlehemite monks existed in England in 1257.

BETHLEHEM HOSPITAL (so called from having been originally the hospital of St. Mary of Bethlehem), a royal foundation for the reception of lunatics, incorporated by Henry VIII. in 1547. The old Bethlehem Hospital, Moorfields, erected in 1676, pulled down in 1814, was built in imitation of the Tuileries at Paris. The present hospital in St. George's-fields was begun April, 1812, and opened in 1815. In 1856 extensive improvements were completed under the direction of Mr. Sydney Smirke.

BETHNAL GREEN, E. London, a poor populous parish; said to have been the seat of Henry de Montfort, hero of the "Blind Beggar of Bethnal Green" (*Percy Ballads*). Many churches have been erected by the instrumentality of the bishops of London and others, and the district has been much favoured by the baroness Burdett-Coutts. The East London Museum here, a branch of that at South Kensington, was opened by the prince of Wales, 24 June, 1872. Sir Richard Wallace lent to it for a time a collection of fine pictures and valuable curiosities collected by the marquis of Hertford (died 25 Aug. 1870). Sir Richard Wallace died 20 July, 1890. See *Wallace Collection*. The gardens opened 19 May, 1875. See *Parks*. Returns two M.P.s by Act of 1885. Population 1881, 126,961; 1891, 120,134; 1901, 129,681.

Boundary-street estate, buildings erected by the London county council (cost over 600,000*l*.), for the housing of 5,380 of the working-classes, opened by the prince and princess of Wales, lord Welby and others present, 3 March, 1900.

BETHUNE, France, an independent lordship since the 11th century, was annexed to the monarchy by the treaty of Utrecht, 1713, after several changes.

BETTERMENT, is a term in American law, applied to the improvement of property in any locality, by the expenditure of public money or otherwise, and it is therefore held, that such property ought to be called upon to contribute more to taxation. The question much discussed in 1889-90 in relation to the Strand Improvement bill.

The principle introduced in the London Improvement Bill, 26 June, 1893; referred to a committee by the lords, May, 1894; report favourable with conditions, July, 1894.

Worsement, the opposite principle to betterment, was introduced in the Tower-bridge South Approaches Bill, 27 May, 1895.

Betterment of London assoc. founded, president W. B. Richmond, early 1902.

BETTING-HOUSES, affording much temptation to gaming and consequent dishonesty, in the lower classes, were suppressed by an act passed in 1853 (16 & 17 Vict. c. 119). A *Pari-mutuel*, or mutual betting machine, in Aug., and the "Knightsbridge Exchange," a betting company, 2 Nov. 1870, were declared illegal, see *Races*. New Betting Acts passed, 1874 and 1892.

In 1874 this Act was applied to betting stations at races; legal proceedings against Mr. H. Chaplin, as steward of the Jockey Club, were quashed by the magistrates at Newmarket.

Betting reported to have greatly increased, 1889, 1895.

Mr. justice Hawkins and 5 other judges in the cases of Hawke *v.* Dunn and M'Inaney *v.* Hildreth, decide that bookmaking and betting in Tattersall's ring and similar enclosed places are illegal in accordance with the Betting Act of 1853; 13 March, 1897.

Powell *v.* the Kempton park racecourse company, a similar case to Hawke *v.* Dunn; decision reversed by the court of appeal; the house of lords sustains their appeal, 14 March, 1899.

House of lords committee report increase of betting, but in smaller amounts; localisation and restrictions advised, 4 July, 1902.

Bill to amend the Betting Acts of 1853 and 1874 introduced in house of lords by lord Davey 28 Apr. 1903; rejected: contents 39, not contents 48.

BEVERLEY, E. Yorkshire, the Saxon Beverlac, or Beverlega. St. John of Beverley, archbishop of York, founded a stately monastery here, and died 721; and on his account the town received honours from Athelstane, William I., and other sovereigns. It was disfranchised for corruption in 1870, after a long investigation. Population 1881, 11,425; 1891, 12,539; 1901, 13,183.

BEYROUT (the ancient Berytus), a seaport of Syria, colonised from Sidon. It was destroyed by an earthquake, 566; was rebuilt, and was alternately possessed by the Christians and Saracens; and after many changes, fell into the power of Amurath IV. It was taken during the Egyptian revolt by Ibrahim Pacha, in 1832. The total defeat of the Egyptian army by the allied British, Turkish, and Austrian forces, and evacuation of Beyrout (the Egyptians losing 7000 in killed, wounded, and prisoners, and twenty pieces of cannon), took place 10 Oct. 1840. Sir C. Napier was the English admiral engaged. Beyrout suffered greatly in consequence of the massacres in Syria in May, 1860. In Nov. 1860 above 27,000 persons were said to be in danger of starving. Population in 1885, 85,000; 1901, *about* 118,811. See *Syria*.

BHOOTAN, a country north of Lower Bengal, with whom a treaty was made 25 April, 1774. After fruitless negotiations, Bhootan was invaded by the British in Dec. 1864, in consequence of injurious treatment of an envoy. See *India*, 1864-5.

By an insurrection the Deb Rajah was deposed, Aug. 1885.

BHOPAL, capital of a native state in Central India, founded in 1723 by Dost Mohammed Khan, and made dependent on the British government in 1818. The able female sovereign, the begum Shah Jahán, received the grand cross of the Star of India in 1872. Bhopal was visited by the viceroy of India, Nov. 1891; when the begum welcomed him with a very loyal address; she died much regretted, 16 June, 1901, succeeded by her son, Nawab Nasrulla Khan.

BHURTPORE (India), capital of Bhurtpore, was besieged by the British, 3 Jan. 1805, and attacked five times up to 21 March, without success. After a desperate engagement with Holkar, the Mahratta chief, 2 April, 1805, the fortress was surrendered to general Lake. By a treaty, the rajah of Bhurtpore agreed to pay twenty lacs of rupees, ceded territories that had been granted to him, and delivered his son as hostage, 17 April, 1805. On the rajah's death, during a revolt against his son, Bhurtpore was taken by storm, by lord Combermere, 18 Jan. 1826; see *India*. The maharajah set aside for incapacity; the British resident governs provisionally, reported 17 March, 1895.

BIANCHI (Whites), a political party at Florence, in 1300, in favour of the Ghibelines or imperial party, headed by Vieri de' Cerchi, opposed the Neri (or Blacks), headed by Corso de' Donati. The latter banished their opponents, among whom was the poet Dante, in 1302. "Bianchi" were also male and female penitents, clothed in white, who travelled through Italy in Aug. 1399; and were suppressed by pope Boniface IX., 1400.

BIARCHY. When Aristodemus, king of Sparta, died, he left two sons, twins, Eurysthenes and Procles; and the people, not knowing to whom precedence should be given, placed both upon the throne, and thus established the first biarchy, 1102 B.C. The descendants of each reigned for about 800 years. *Herodotus.*

BIARRITZ, a bathing-place near Bayonne. Here resided the comtesse de Montijo and her daughter Eugénie, empress of the French, till her marriage, 29 Jan. 1853. It was frequently visited by the emperor and empress.

Visited by Queen Victoria . . . 7 March–2 April, 1889.

BIBERACH (Würtemberg). Here Moreau twice defeated the Austrians,—under Latour, 2 Oct. 1796, and under Kray, 9 May, 1800.

BIBLE (from the Greek *biblos*, a book), the name especially given to the Holy Scriptures. The Old Testament is said to have been collected and arranged by Ezra between 458 and 450 B.C. The Apocrypha are considered as inspired writings by the Roman Catholics, but not by the Jews and Protestants;* see *Apocrypha.*

OLD TESTAMENT.†

Genesis contains the history of the world	from B.C.	4004—1635
Exodus		1635—1490
Leviticus		1490
Numbers		1490—1451
Deuteronomy‡		1451
Job	about B.C.	1520
Joshua	from	1451—1420
Judges		1425—1120
Ruth		1322—1312
1st and 2nd Samuel		1171—1017
1st and 2nd Kings		1015— 562
1st and 2nd Chronicles		1004— 536
Book of Psalms (principally by David)		1063—1015
Proverbs written	about	1000— 700
Song of Solomon	about	1014
Ecclesiastes	about	977
Jonah	about	862
Joel	about	800
Hosea	about	785— 725
Amos	about	787
Isaiah	about	760— 698
Micah	about	750— 710
Nahum	about	713
Zephaniah	about	630
Jeremiah	about	629— 588
Lamentations	about	588
Habakkuk	about	626
Daniel	from	607— 534
Ezekiel	from	595— 574
Obadiah	about	587
Ezra	about	536— 456
Esther	about	521— 495
Haggai	about	520
Zechariah	about	520— 518
Nehemiah	about	446— 434
Malachi	about	397

NEW TESTAMENT.

GOSPELS by Matthew, Mark, Luke, and John,	B.C. 5—A.D. 33
Acts of the Apostles	A.D. 33—65
EPISTLES—1st and 2nd of Paul to Thessalonians abt.	54
To Galatians	58
1st Corinthians	59
2nd Corinthians	60
Romans	60
Of James	60
1st of Peter	60
To Ephesians, Philippians, Colossians, Hebrews, Philemon	64
Titus, and 1st to Timothy	65
2nd to Timothy	66
2nd of Peter	66
Of Jude	66
1st, 2nd, and 3rd of John after	90
Revelation	96

[The date and authorship of the various books are much disputed by Biblical critics. Consult "New Dictionary of the Bible" (Hastings), and "Encyclopædia Biblica"; see *Higher Criticism*, under *Rationalism.*]

The most ancient copy of the *Hebrew* Scriptures existed at Toledo, called the Codex of Hillel; it was of very early date, probably of the 4th century after Christ; some say about 60 years before Christ. The copy of Ben Asher, of Jerusalem, was made about 1100.

The reputed oldest copy of the Old and New Testament in *Greek*, is that in the *Vatican*, which was written in the 4th or 5th century. Mai's edition appeared in 1857. The next in age is the *Alexandrian Codex* (referred to the 5th century) in the British Museum, presented by the Greek patriarch to Charles I. in 1628. It has been printed in England, edited by Woide and Baber, 1786—1821.—*Codex Ephraemi*, or Codex Regius, ascribed to the 5th century, in the Royal Library, Paris: published by Tischendorf in 1843.

The *Codex Sinaiticus*, probably written in the 4th century, was discovered by M. Constantine Tischendorf, at St. Katherine's monastery in 1844 and 1859, and presented to the czar of Russia, at whose cost a splendid edition was published in 1862.

The Hebrew Psalter was printed at Bologna in 1477. The complete Hebrew Bible was first printed by Soncino in Italy in 1488, and the Greek Testament (edited by Erasmus) at Rotterdam, in 1516. Aldus's edition was printed in 1518; Stephens' in 1546; and the *textus receptus* (or received text) by the Elzevirs in 1624.

The Codex Bezæ Cantabrigiensis (Cambridge university press) admirably photographed by M. Dujardin's new process, 1899.

TRANSLATIONS.

The Old Testament, in *Greek*, termed the Septuagint (*which see*), generally considered to have been made by order of Ptolemy Philadelphus, king of Egypt, about 286 or 285 B.C.; of this many fabulous accounts are given.

Origen, after spending twenty-eight years in collating MSS., commenced his *polyglot* Bible at Cæsarea in A.D. 231; it contained the Greek versions of Aquila, Symmachus, and Theodotion, all made in or about the 2nd century after Christ.

The following are ancient versions:—*Syriac*, 1st or 2nd century; the old *Latin* version, early in the 2nd century, revised by Jerome, in 384; who, however, completed a new version in 405, now called the VULGATE (*which see*); the first edition was printed (without date) about 1456; the first dated 1462;—*Coptic*, 2nd or 3rd century; *Ethiopic*; *Armenian*, 4th or 5th century; *Slavonic*, 9th century; and the *Mæso-Gothic*, by Ulfilas, the apostle of the Goths, about 360, a manuscript copy

* In April, 1865, was published a proposal for raising a fund for exploring Palestine in order to illustrate the Bible by antiquarian and scientific investigation; see *Palestine.*

† The division of the Bible into *chapters* has been ascribed to archbishop Lanfranc in the 11th, and to archbishop Langton in the 13th century; but T. Hartwell Horne considers the real author to have been cardinal Hugo de Sancto Caro, about the middle of the 13th century. The division into sections was commenced by Rabbi Nathan (author of a Concordance), about 1445, and completed by Athras, a Jew, in 1661. The present division into *verses* was introduced by the celebrated printer, Robert Stephens, in his Greek Testament (1551) and in his Latin Bible (1556-7).

‡ Fragments of portions of this book, on leather, asserted to have been written about the 8th century B.C., obtained from Arabs in Jerusalem by M. Shapira, were exhibited in the British Museum, Aug. 1883, and after a critical examination by Dr. Ginsburg and others, declared to be forged. M. Shapira, probably insane, committed suicide at Rotterdam, 9 March, 1884. Dr. Harkavy, of St. Petersburg, published a report, about Aug. 1884, describing some apparently ancient Hebrew MS. rolls of Lamentations and other books, said to have been found by Jews in Rhodes about 1850.

of which, called the Codex Argenteus, is at Upsal. The Psalms were translated into *Saxon* by bishop Aldhelm, about 706; Cædmon's metrical paraphrase of a portion of the Bible, about 680; and the Gospels by bishop Egbert, about 721; parts of the Bible by Bede, in the 8th century.

Bible Translation Society, founded by Baptists and others, 24 March, 1840.

ENGLISH VERSIONS AND EDITIONS.

MS. paraphrase of the whole Bible at the Bodleian Library, Oxford, dated by Usher . . . 1290

Versions (from the Vulgate) by Wickliffe and his followers (above 170 MS. copies extant) . . 1356-84

[Part published by Lewis, 1731; by Baber, 1810; the whole by Madden and Forshall, at Oxford 1850.]

William Tyndale's version of Matthew and Mark from the Greek printed, 1524; of the whole New Testament, 1525; 6 editions . . 1525-30

Miles Coverdale's version of the whole Bible; printing finished . . . 4 Oct. 1535

[Ordered by Henry VIII. to be laid in the choir of every church, "for every man that will to look and read therein."]

T. Matthews' (said to be fictitious name for John Rogers) version (partly by Tyndale* and Coverdale) 1537

Cranmer's Great Bible (Matthews' revised), the first printed by authority 1539

[Bible reading prohibited] 1502-57

Geneva version, "Breeches Bible," (the first with figured verses), 1540-1557; published . . 1560

Archbishop Parker's called "The Bishops' Bible" (eight of the fourteen persons employed being bishops) 1568

Roman Catholic authorised version: New Testament, at Rheims, 1582; Old Testament, at Douay, 1609-10

King James's Bible, the present authorised version —revision began 1604; published 1611

[Dr. Benjamin Blayney's revised edition, 1769.]

Authorised Jewish English version . . . 1851-61

The *revision* of the English version now in use was recommended by the bishops in convocation, 10 Feb. 1870. The committee, including eminent scholars of various denominations, appointed in May, held their first meeting at Westminster Abbey 22 June, 1870.

Revision of the New Testament completed (103 sessions, or 407 days), 11 Nov. 1880; various editions published 17 May, 1881. Revision of the Old Testament completed, July, 1884. Published 19 May, 1885. *Holy Bible, Two-version Edition*: prepared by A. F. Buxton, 1900.

Paragraph Bibles published in England by John Reeve, 1808; by the Tract Society, 1848; at Cambridge, Massachusetts, by Dr. Coit, 1834.

Smallest Bible known ($4\frac{1}{2} \times 2 \times \frac{1}{2}$ inches: weight under $3\frac{1}{4}$ oz.), issued from Oxford University press, Oct. 1875.

Polychrome Bible (James Clarke), 3 vols. (6s. each) out of 20, Judges, Psalms, Isaiah, published, March, 1898.

A MS. of Wycliffe's Bible (date about 1410) sold for 1,200*l.*, 16 May, 1901.

The Temple Bible (authorised version), a set of small vols., edited by profs. Sayce, Davidson, and others, published, 1902.

MODERN TRANSLATIONS.†

	N. TEST.	BIBLE.
Flemish		1477
Spanish (Valencian)		1478
German	1522	1530
English	1526	1535
French		1487
Swedish	1526	1541
Danish	1524	1550
Dutch		1475
Italian		1471
Spanish	1543	1569
Russian (parts)	1519	1822

* He was strangled at Antwerp, 6 Oct. 1536, at the instigation of Henry VIII. and his council. His last words were, "Lord, open the king of England's eyes!" 14 editions of his Testament had then been published. His statue on the Thames embankment was uncovered 7 May, 1884.

† "*The Bible of Every Land*," ed. 1860, published by Messrs. Bagsters, London, is full of information respecting ancient and modern versions of the Bible.

	N. TEST.	BIBLE.
Welsh	1567	1588
Hungarian	1574	1589
Bohemian		1488
Polish	1551	1561
Virginian Indians	1661	1663
Irish	1602	1686
Georgian		1743
Portuguese	1712	1748
Manks	1748	1767
Turkish	1666	1814
Sanscrit	1808	1822
Modern Greek	1638	1821
Chinese	1814	1823
Japanese		1888

The British and Foreign Bible Society continue to make and print translations of the Bible in all the dialects of the world; see *Polyglot*.

BIBLE CHRISTIANS, a branch of the Methodists began in 1815, formerly termed Bryanites after Wm. O'Bryan, their leader. In the United Kingdom they number about 40,000 joined members; they are numerous in N. Zealand and Australia.

BIBLE DICTIONARIES. The most remarkable are Calmet's "Dictionary of the Bible," 1722–8; Kitto's "Cyclopædia of Biblical Literature," 1843 and 1851; Smith's "Dictionary of the Bible," 1860–3; and "New Dictionary of the Bible," general editor, dr. J. Hastings, 1898–1902; "Encyclopædia Biblica," 1899–1903, edited by canon Cheyne and dr. J. S. Black. See *Concordances*.*

BIBLE SOCIETIES. Among the principal and oldest societies which have made the dissemination of the Scriptures a collateral or an exclusive object, are the following:—

Society for Promoting Christian Knowledge . . 1698

Society for Propagating the Gospel in Foreign Parts 1701

Society in Scotland, for Promoting Christian Knowledge 1709

Society for Promoting Religious Knowledge among the poor 1750

Naval and Military Bible Society 1780

Sunday School Society 1785

French Bible Society 1792

British and Foreign Bible Society,† begun 1803; organised 1804. Inaugural meeting of centenary of the society held at the Mansion house under presidency of the lord mayor. Speeches by right hon. A. J. Balfour, lord Northampton (president), and others, 6 Mar. 1903. Centenary fund of 250,000 guineas started, the king contributes 100 guineas.

* "An Index to the Persons, Places, and Subjects occurring in the Holy Scriptures," compiled by B. Vincent, late editor of the present work (died 3 May, 1899), was published anonymously by the queen's printers in 1848. It is still (1903) printed as an addendum to many editions of the Bible.

† This society had issued 24,247,667 copies of the Bible or parts of it up to Jan. 1851: in May, 1863, the number had risen to 43,044,334; in 1867 to 52,669,089; in 1875 to 76,432,723; in March, 1881, to 91,014,448; in 1884 to 100,035,933; in 1887 to 112,253,547; in 1890, to 123,929,046; in 1892, 135,894,552; 1897, 155,529,954; in 1901, 175,038,965. The income of the year 1876 was £206,978; in the year 1880-1, £209,519; in 1886-7, £116,761; in 1889-90, £212,077; 1894-95, £233,362; 1897, £229,749; 1901, £236,292. In 1857 the society published a catalogue of their library, which contains a large number of remarkable editions of the Bible. The foundation-stone of the Bible-house, Queen Victoria-street, London, was laid by the prince of Wales, 11 June, 1866; opened 3 May, 1869. The society had promoted translations of the Bible into 367 languages or dialects in 1903. The rev. Wm. Wright, D.D., since 1876 the superintendent of the translation department and author of the "Brontës in Ireland," &c., died 31 July, 1899.

Hibernian Bible Society 1806
City of London Auxiliary Bible Society . . 1812
American Bible Society 1816
A bull from the pope, Pius VII., against Bible Societies appeared in 1817

BIBLIA PAUPERUM (the Bible for the poor), consisting of engravings illustrating scripture history, with texts, carved in wood, a "block book," printed early in the 15th century, was compiled by Bonaventura, general of the Franciscans, about 1260. A fac-simile was published by J. R. Smith, in 1859.

BIBLICAL ARCHÆOLOGY, SOCIETY FOR, established by Dr. Samuel Birch, and others, 1871. Besides a journal, it has published, "Records of the Past," translations from the Assyrian, Egyptian, and other languages, 1873-89.

BIBLIOGRAPHY, the Science of Books.

Gesner's "Bibliotheca Universale" appeared . . 1545
De Bure's "Bibliographie Instructive" . . . 1763
Peignot, Manuel. 1823
Horne, Introduction to the Study of Bibliography . 1824
English, Watt's Bibliotheca Britannica . . . ,,
German, Hinrich's Verzeichniss
French, Querard
Lorenz 1828-64
English Catalogues, by Sampson Low . . 1840-1903
Scriptural, Orme, Bibliotheca Biblica, 1824; Darling, Bibliographica 1835-1903
Classical, Fabricius, Clarke, and Dibdin. . . 1854-8
Lowndes, Bibliographer's Manual, 1834; new ed. by Bohn 1857-62
Brunet's Manuel du Libraire, 1st edit. 1810; 5th ed., with supplements . . . 1860-8
Allibone's Dictionary of English Literature, 1859-71; supplement by John F. Kirk . . 1891
Sonnenschein's "The Best Books" . 1887, 2nd ed. ,,
Bibliographical Society, London, founded by Mr. W. A. Copinger . . . Oct. 1892
"Bibliographica," parts I.—VI. published . . 1894-5

BIBLIOMANIA (or book madness) prevailed in 1811, when Dr. Dibdin's work with this title was published; see *Boccaccio*, and *Printing*, 1450-5.

BICOCCA, N. Italy. Lautrec and the French were here defeated by Colonna and the Imperialists, 29 April, 1522.

BICYCLE, see *Velocipede*. The earliest bicycles with cranks and pedals fixed to the front wheel date from 1855. In 1869 Michaux invented the ordinary cycle with a large front wheel. Mr. Starley's safety bicycle produced 1885. In 1888 Mr. Dunlop, a surgeon of Belfast, introduced the pneumatic tyre. (The idea had already been patented by W. Thompson in 1846.) The Dunlop Co. founded in 1889, in 1894 had a capital of 5,000,000*l*. The "free-wheel," recently introduced, largely adopted 1903. Cycling has become universal throughout the world.

BIDASSOA. The allied army under lord Wellington, having driven the French from Spain, effected the passage of this river 8 Oct. 1813, and entered France.

BIDDENDEN MAIDS. A distribution of bread and cheese to the poor takes place at Biddenden, Kent, on Easter Mondays, the expense being defrayed from the rental of twenty acres of land, in 1875 yielding about 20*l*. a year, the reputed bequest of the Biddenden maids, two sisters named Chulkhurst, said to have been joined together like the Siamese twins, and to have died in the 12th century. In 1656, Wm. Horner, the rector, was non-suited in an attempt to add the "Bread and Cheese lands" to his glebe.

BIGAMY. The Romans branded the guilty party with an infamous mark; and in England the punishment, formerly, was death. An act respecting it was passed 5 Edw. I. 1276. *Viner's Statutes.* Declared to be felony, without benefit of clergy, 1 James I. 1603. Punishable, by imprisonment or transportation, 35 Geo. III. 1794; by imprisonment, 24 & 25 Vict. c. 100 (1861).

BILBAO (N.E. Spain), founded about 1300; was taken by the French and held a few days, July, 1795. It was delivered from the Carlists by Espartero, assisted by the British, 24 Dec. 1836. It was besieged by Carlists from Feb. to May, 1874, when the siege was raised by marshal Concha, who entered Bilbao 2 May. Population, 1887, 50,772; 1897, 74,093.

Strike of ironworkers, riotous proceedings, conflict with the police, state of siege, and military occupation . . . . . 14—16 May, 1890
Great fire in the dockyard, estimated damage, 2,500,000 pesetas . . . . . 1 May, 1891
Great strike of miners, middle Jan., disturbances; intervention of the military; state of siege, 27 Jan.; work resumed, 8 Feb.; quiet restored 16 Feb. 1892
Meeting of the Iron and Steel Institute 1 Sept. 1896
The king lays first stone of the new harbour, 7 Sept. 1902

BILL OF EXCEPTIONS. The right of tendering such a bill to a judge, either to his charge, to his definition of the law, or to other errors of the court, at a trial between parties, provided by the 2nd statute of Westminster, 13 Edw. I. 1284, was abolished by the Judicature Act, 1875.

BILL OF PAINS, &c.; see *Queen Caroline*.

BILL OF RIGHTS, &c.; see *Rights*.

BILLIARDS (Old French *billard*, "a stick with a curved end"). The French ascribe the invention to Henrique Devigne, an artist, about 1571; the game was mentioned by Spenser about 1591, and by Shakspeare, 1607. It was described by Cotton in his "Compleat Gamester," 1674. Slate billiard tables were introduced in England in 1827; other changes since. American tournament (14 competitors) at the Egyptian hall, London, Jan. 1899. The game is now popular; tournaments frequently held.

The Champion Cup has been won since 1870: by W. Cook, 11 Feb. 1870, 25 May, 1871, 21 Nov. 1871, 4 Mar. 1872, 4 Feb. 1874; by J. Roberts, junr., 14 April, 1870; 30 May, 1870, 30 Jan. 1871, 24 May, 1875, 20 Dec. 1875, 28 May, 1877, 30 Mar.–1 April, 1885, 1-3 June, 1885; by J. Bennett, 28 Nov. 1870, 8 Nov. 1880, 12–13 Jan. 1881. From 1885 to 1898 J. Roberts, junr., held undisputed claim to the title of champion, when in the last-named year he was challenged by C. Dawson, the match taking place under the new rules regulating the "spot stroke" and "push stroke," the width of the pockets, and the distance of the billiard spot from the top cushion. The new rules, framed by the Billiard Association, came into force 1 Oct. 1898. A match of 18,000 up was played Mar.—April, 1899, between Roberts and Dawson, the former winning by 1,814 points.

The Highest Spot-barred Breaks are: 1,467 by T. Taylor *v.* H. McNeil, Royal Aquarium, 24 April, 1891; 2,539 by F. C. Ives, Humphrey's hall, Knightsbridge, 1–2 June, 1893; 1,392 by J. Roberts, junr. *v.* Diggle, at Manchester, 3–4 May, 1894; 985 by E. Diggle *v.* J. Roberts, junr., Argyll hall, 4 Jan. 1895.

Highest Breaks in Exhibition Matches (ordinary tables): 3,304 (93, 3, 150, 123, 172, 400 spots) by W. J. Peall, at Westminster Aquarium, 4–6 Nov. 1896; 1,989 (649 spots) by W. J. Peall, at Cambridge, 19 May, 1884; 1,709 (18, 543 spots) by W. J. Peall, at Westminster Aquarium, 3, 4 Nov. 1885; 1,621 (536 spots) by W. Mitchell, at Westminster Aquarium, 3 Nov. 1885;

1,413 (334, 449, 3 spots) by W. J. Peall, at Westminster Aquarium, 4, 5 Nov. 1886; 189 successive cannons by H. W. Stevenson, at Waverley Market, Edinburgh, 30 Jan. 1895.

Highest Breaks on Standard Tables: 985 (spot-barred) by E. Diggle, at Argyll hall, 4 Jan. 1895; 772 (spot and push barred) by C. Dawson, at Argyll hall, 20, 21 Oct. 1899; 791 by E. Diggle, at Brighton, 24, 25 Feb. 1902.

BILLINGSGATE, the fish-market in London, is said to have derived its name from Belinus Magnus, a British prince, the father of king Lud, 400 B.C., but Stow thinks from a former owner. It was the old port of London, and the customs were paid here under Ethelred II., A.D. 979. *Stow*. Billingsgate was made a free market, 1699. *Chamberlain*. Fish by *land*-carriage, as well as sea-borne, now arrives daily here. In 1849, the market was extended and improved, and a new one was erected in 1852, Mr. Bunning, architect. Another new one, erected by Horace Jones, founded 27 Oct. 1874; completed Sept. 1876; lit by electric light, 25 Nov. 1878. Billingsgate market was declared to be insufficient for the fish supply of the metropolis in the report of the commission appointed by the city corporation, presented to the common council, 11 Aug. 1881.

BILLS OF EXCHANGE were invented by the Jews as a means of removing their property from nations where they were persecuted, 1160. *Anderson*. Bills are said to have been used in England, 1307. The only legal mode of sending money from England, 4 Richard II. 1381. Regulated, 1698; first stamped, 1782; duty advanced, 1797; again, June 1801; and since. It was made capital to counterfeit bills of exchange in 1734. In 1825, the year of disastrous speculations in bubbles, it was computed that there were 400 millions of pounds sterling represented by bills of exchange and promissory notes. The present amount is not supposed to exceed 50 millions. The many statutes regarding bills of exchange were consolidated by act 9 Geo. IV. 1828. An act regulating bills of exchange passed 3 Vict. July, 1839. Great alterations were made in the law on the subject by 17 & 18 Vict. c. 83 (1854), and 18 & 19 Vict. c. 67 (1855). Days of grace were abolished in the case of bills of exchange payable on sight in Aug. 1871. Forgery of bills to obtain discount was detected by the bank of England, 28 Feb., after 102,217*l*. had been paid. The culprits (Americans) were tried and condemned to penal servitude for life, 26 Aug. 1873. See *Trials*, Aug. 1873.

A Bills of Exchange Act, declaring the law relating to acceptance, passed 16 April, 1878; new Act passed 18 Aug. 1882.

BILLS OF MORTALITY FOR LONDON. These bills were first compiled by order of Cromwell, about 1538, 30 Hen. VIII., but in a more formal and recognised manner in 1603, after the great plague of that year. No complete series of them has been preserved. They have been superseded by the weekly returns of the registrar-general, since 1837. See *Public Health*. The following show the numbers for London at decennial periods:—

	Christenings.	*Burials.*		*Christenings.*	*Burials.*
1780	16,634	20,507	1830	27,028	23,524
1800	19,176	23,068	1840	30,387	26,774
1810	19,930	19,892	1850	39,973	36,947
1820	26,158	19,348			

IN ENGLAND AND WALES.

	Births.	*Deaths.*		*Births.*	*Deaths.*
1840	502,303	356,634	1860	684,048	422,721
1845	543,521	349,366	1861	696,406	436,114
1849	578,159	440,839	1862	712,684	436,573
1853	612,391	421,097	1863	727,417	473,837
1856	657,453	390,506	1864	740,275	495,531

	ENGLAND AND WALES.		SCOTLAND.		IRELAND.*	
	Births.	*Deaths.*	*Births.*	*Deaths.*	*Births.*	*Deaths.*
1865,	748,069	490,909	113,126	70,821	144,970	93,154
1866,	753,870	500,689	113,639	71,273	146,237	93,598
1867,	768,349	471,073	114,115	69,024	144,318	93,911
1868,	786,858	480,622	115,673	69,386	146,108	86,803
1869,	773,381	494,828	113,395	75,789	145,659	89,573
1870,	792,787	515,329	115,423	74,067	150,151	90,695
1871,	797,428	514,879	116,127	74,644	151,665	88,720
1872,	825,907	492,265	118,873	75,741	149,292	97,577
1873,	829,778	492,520	119,738	76,857	144,377	97,537
1874,	854,956	526,632	123,795	80,676	141,288	91,961
1875,	850,607	546,453	123,693	81,785	138,320	98,114
1876,	887,968	510,315	126,749	74,122	140,469	92,324
1877,	888,200	500,496	126,824	73,946	139,659	93,543
1878,	891,906	539,872	126,707	76,775	134,117	99,629
1879,	880,389	526,255	125,736	73,329	135,328	105,089
1880,	881,643	528,624	124,652	75,795	128,086	102,906
1881,	883,642	491,935	126,214	72,301	125,847	90,035
1882,	889,018	516,654	126,182	72.966	122,648	88,500
1883,	890,722	522,997	124,462	76,867	118,163	96,228
1884,	906,750	530,828	129,041	75,128	118,875	87,154
1885,	894,270	522,750	126,110	74,603	115,951	90,712
1886,	903,866	537,276	127,927	73,622	113,927	87,292
1887,	886,331	530,758	124,418	74,546	112,400	88,585
1888,	879,868	510,971	123,269	71,174	109,557	85,868
1889,	885,944	518,353	122,783	73,238	107,841	82,908
1890,	869,937	562,248	121,530	78,978	105,254	85,850
1891,	914,157	587,925	125,986	83,578	108,116	85,999
1892,	897,957	559,684	125,011	75,568	104,234	90,044
1893,	914,189	569,923	127,040	79,641	106,031	82,822
1894,	890,289	498,827	124,367	71,113	105,354	83,528
1895,	921,860	568,758	126,454	81,864	106,113	84,395
1896,	917,201	527,929	129,153	70,634	107,641	75,700
1897.	921,693	541,487	128,877	79,144	106,664	83,839
1899,	928,640	581,824	130,656	89,548	103,900	79,699
1900,	927,062	587,459	131,355	82,267	101,459	87,506
1901,	929,270	551,316	132,178	80,103	100,956	79,126

IN LONDON AND SUBURBS (52 OR 53 WEEKS).

		Births.		*Deaths.*
1854		84,684		73,697
1856		86,833		57,786
1858	(*Females*, 43,400)	88,620	(*Females*, 31,319)	63,882
1862		97,114		66,950
1864		102,187		77,723
1867	(*Females*, 54,862)	112,264		70,588
1868	(53 weeks)	115,744		74,908
1869		111,930		77,933
1870		113,449		77,278
1871		112,535		80,332
1872		117,200		70,893
1873	(53 weeks)	121,100		76,334
1874		121,394		76,606
1875		122,871		81,513
1876	(*Females*, 62,095)	127,015		77,411
1878		129,184		83,695
1879		134,096		85,540
1880	(*Females*, 64,659)	132,173	(*Females*, 39,426)	81,128
1885		132,952		80,946
1887		133,359		82,449
1888	(52 weeks)	131,080		78,848
1889		132,223		76,026
1890		128,161		87,689
1891		134,003		90,216
1892		131,535		87,749
1893		132,975		91,536
1894		130,553		77,039
1898		132,432		83,936
1900		130,868		84,103

BILLS OF SALE, an act to consolidate and amend the law for preventing frauds upon creditors by secret bills of sale of personal chattels (41 & 42 Vict. c. 31) passed 22 July, 1878, amended, 1882.

BI-METALLISM, the system of having two standard metallic currencies in a country, gold and silver, much advocated by MM. H. Cernuschi and E. Laveleye, and others since 1867. By 56 Geo. III. c. 68 (1816), it was enacted that "gold coins only should be legal tender in all payments of more than 40s." in this country; the tender of

* Approximative registration defective

silver being previously unlimited. A bi-metallic currency was established in France in 1803. It was recommended for Germany in 1879, and was discussed at the *Monetary Conference* at Paris, April, 1881. The unrestricted coinage of silver was suspended in the countries termed the Latin Union in 1873.

The Bimetallic League hold a conference at Manchester . . . . 4 April, 1888
The marquis of Salisbury and Mr. Goschen declare their neutrality to a deputation, 30 May, 1889; 11 May, 1892
Mr. Samuel Smith's resolution proposing an international conference on bi-metallism negatived by the commons, 183—87 . . . . . 18 April, 1890
The Bimetallic League declare that their chief object is to secure the opening of the mints of the leading nations, to the unrestricted coinage of silver and gold at a fixed ratio, Nov. 1890; annual meeting 2 March, 1892, and since. See *Monetary Conferences*.
The commons rejects bi-metallism . 28 Feb. 1893
Annual meeting of the Bi-metallic League at Manchester, 6 Feb. 1894; London . . 3 April, 1895
International bi-metallic conference at the Mansion-house, London . . . . 2 May, 1894
A bi-metallic league formed in Paris . 23 March, 1895
The principle accepted in Germany, April, May, 1895; United States, *which see* . . . May ,,
The Gold Standard Defence Association founded in the summer of 1895; the German bi-metallist league meets in Berlin, professes co-operation with England . . . . 7 Nov. ,,
International bi-metallic conference meets at Paris 10 Dec. ,,
A resolution, proposing a conference with foreign powers respecting the currency, adopted by the commons, 26 Feb. 1895; a similar resolution, adopted after powerful speeches in defence of the gold standard, by sir M. Hicks Beach and sir J. Lubbock . . . . . 17 March 1896
Statement of the Bi-metallic League (*Times*) 13 April international congress held at Brussels, 20 April; resolutions favouring bi-metallism adopted 24 April ,,
A gold standard adopted by Japan from Oct. 1897, announced . . . . 1 March 1897
Memorial of London bankers and merchants to the government against bi-metallism, 15 Oct.; an international conference at Washington declined by the British government, announced, 22 Oct.; the Bi-metallic League protests to the government against any modification of the gold standard . . . . 22 Oct. ,,
Major L. Darwin's "Bimetallism" was published in 1898.

BINARY ARITHMETIC, that which counts by twos, for expeditiously ascertaining the property of numbers, and constructing tables, was invented by Leibnitz of Leipsic, about 1703. For the *Binary theory* in chemistry, see *Compound Radical*.

BINOMIAL ROOT, in Algebra, composed of only two parts connected with the signs *plus* or *minus*; a term first used by Recorda, about 1550, when he published his Algebra. The celebrated *binomial theorem* of Newton is said to have been discovered in 1663.

BIOGRAPHY (from the Greek *bios*, life, and *graphō*, I write), defined as "history teaching by example." The book of *Genesis* contains the biography of the patriarchs; and the Gospels that of Christ. Plutarch wrote the Lives of Illustrious Men; Cornelius Nepos, Lives of Military Commanders; and Suetonius, Lives of the Twelve Cæsars (all three in the first century after Christ); Diogenes Laërtius, Lives of the Philosophers (about 205).—Boswell's Life of Johnson (published in 1790) is the most remarkable English biography. Mr. John Wilson Croker's edition appeared in 1831. A magnificent edition, edited by Rev. Alex. Napier, published by Messrs. Bell, Feb. 1884. An excellent edition by Dr. George Birkbeck Hill (Clarendon Press), published June, 1887.

Important Dictionaries.—Biographie Universelle, 85 vols., 1811-62; Nouvelle Biographie Générale, 46 vols., 1852-66; General Biographical Dictionary, by Alex. Chalmers, 32 vols., 1812-17; New General Biographical Dictionary, by H. J. Rose, 12 vols., 1848; Biographia Britannica, 7 vols., 1747; Dictionary of National Biography, edited by Leslie Stephen and afterwards by Sidney Lee, vol. i. published by Smith, Elder & Co., 1 Jan. 1885; vol. xliii. 1895; vol. lv, 1898; 2 supplementary vols. 1898; last vol., lxiii., 29 June, 1900; epitome and index, April, 1903.

BIOLOGY, the science of life and living things, expounded by Treviranus, of Bremen, in his "Biology, the philosophy of living nature," published 1802-5. Biology includes zoology, anthropology, botany, and ethnology (*which see*). Herbert Spencer's "Principles of Biology," published 1864-67; revised, 1898. Prof. T. H. Huxley, born 4 May, 1825, died 29 June, 1895, published "Practical instruction in Biology," 1875. In 1831 about 70,000 animals were known and described; in 1903, about 350,000.

A society for the Biological Investigation of the Coasts of the United Kingdom, established by the Royal Society and others 31 March, 1884; president, professor Huxley; incorporated as the Marine Biological Association; patron the prince of Wales; fine laboratory at Plymouth opened 30 June, 1888. See *Naples*, 1872. Annual reports issued. See *Cell Theory*.
Albert von Kölliker, eminent biologist, born at Zurich, 6 July, 1817.
G. J. Romanes died 1894, see *Species*.
Dr. St. George Mivart died, aged 72, 1 April, 1900.
Internat. conference for research, at Copenhagen, 22 July, 1902. Mr. F. J. Quick bequeaths over 50,000*l*. for research, Jan. 1903.

BIRCH TREE. The black (*Betula nigra*), brought from North America, 1736. The birch tree known as the *Betula pumila*, introduced into Kew gardens, England, by Mr. James Gordon, from North America, 1762. *Hardy's Annals*.

BIRDS were divided by Linnæus into six orders (1735); by Blumenbach into eight (1805); by Cuvier into six (1817); and by Huxley into three (1867). The most remarkable works are those published by John Gould, F.R.S.; they consist of 44 folio volumes of coloured plates, &c. They now include the birds of Europe, Asia, Australia, Great Britain, and New Guinea, besides monographs of the humming-birds, &c., 1889-92. John Gould died 3 Feb. 1881. "An Analytical Index" of his works by Dr. R. Bowdler Sharpe was published May, 1893. Dr. John Latham's "Synopsis of Birds," 1781-90. John James Audubon's "Birds of America," 1826-40. See *Wild Birds*.

"British Ornithologists' Union" founded 1858; published the "Ibis" 1859, *et seq.*
A morphological classification of birds (based on Huxley's), put forth by professors Parker and Newton; Encyclopædia Britannica, 9th ed. . 1875
International Congress of Ornithologists, at Vienna, April 7–11, 1884; at Budapest . . . May 17, 1891
A "Plumage League" formed by lady Mount-Temple, rev. F. O. Morris and others to check the destruction of wild birds, whose plumage is used for ornament . . . . . . Dec. 1885
Mr. W. Yarrell's "British Birds," 4th edition published in . . . . ,,
Twenty-ninth annual bird show at the Crystal palace, 27 Feb.—2 March, 1892; 30th, 11–15 Feb. 1893; a special show . . . . 4 Oct. 1898
The rev. F. O. Morris, author of "A History of British Birds," 3rd edition, 6 vols. 1891, died 10 Feb. 1893
Mr. Alfred Newton's and others "Dictionary of Birds," completed . . . . . April 1897

Agitation against the slaughter of birds, egrets, &c., for the sake of their feathers . . . Aug. *et seq.*, 1898
International agreement on the continent (Italy excepted) for the protection of birds useful to agriculture, signed, Paris . . . 19 March, 1902
Lieut. Boyd Alexander discovers 32 new species in Fernando Po . . . . Dec. ,,

See *Selborne Society*.

BIRKBECK LITERARY AND SCIENTIFIC INSTITUTION, Bream's buildings, W.C., the present name of the mechanics' institution founded by Dr. Birkbeck in 1823. Foundation stone of new building laid by the Duke of Albany, 23 April, 1883. New building opened with an address by Dr. Tyndall, 22 Oct. 1884; formally by Prince of Wales, 4 July, 1885. Additional rooms through the liberality of Mr. Ravenscroft, opened 1 Dec. 1900; he bequeathed 5,000*l.* to found a scholarship, June, 1902.

A run on the *Birkbeck bank* caused a temporary panic; well met by Mr. Ravenscroft, manager, supported by other banks . about 12–15 Sept. 1892
Mr. Francis Ravenscroft, the founder of the bank in 1851, died aged 73 . . . . . 15 June, 1902

BIRKENHEAD (Cheshire), a modern town on the Mersey, opposite to Liverpool. The great dock here was projected by Mr. John Laird, constructed by Mr. Rendell, and opened in Aug. 1847 by lord Morpeth. In 1861 Birkenhead was made a parliamentary borough, and Mr. Laird was elected first representative. He died 29 Oct. 1874. Birkenhead received a charter of incorporation in 1878. Population in 1831, 200; in 1861, 51,649; in 1871, 65,971; in 1881, 84,006; 1891, 99,184; 1901, 110,926. See *Wrecks*, 1852.

BIRMAN EMPIRE or **EMPIRE OF AVA**, see *Burmah* and *India*.

BIRMINGHAM (Warwickshire) existed in the reign of Alfred. There were "many smythes" here in the time of Henry VIII. (*Leland*), but its great importance commenced in the reign of William III. See *Population*.

Grammar school founded by Edward VI. 1552
Besieged and taken by prince Rupert 1643
Button manufactures established 1689
Soho works established by Matthew Boulton about 1764; and steam engine works about . . . 1774
Birmingham Canal originated 1767
Dr. Ash's hospital founded, 1766; first Birmingham musical festival for it 1768
Riots against Dr. Priestley and others commemorating the French Revolution, much property destroyed . . . . . 14 July, 1791
Theatre destroyed by fire . . . . 7 Aug. 1792
Theatre burnt . . . . . Jan. 1820
Political Union, formed by T. Attwood . Feb. 1831
Birmingham made a borough by Reform Act (2 members) 1832
Town-hall built 1833
Political Union dissolved itself . . 10 May, 1834
Birmingham and Liverpool railway opened as the Grand Junction . . . . 4 July, 1837
London and Birmingham railway opened its entire length . . . . . 17 Sept. 1838
Great Chartist riot; houses burnt . 15 July, 1839
Town incorporated, and Police Act passed . ,,
Meeting of British Association . . 29 Aug. ,,
Queen's College incorporated 1843
Corn Exchange opened . . . . 27 Oct. 1847
British Association (meet again) . . 12 Sept. 1849
Queen's College organised . . . . Jan. 1853
Birmingham and Midland Institute incorporated . 1854
Public park opened (ground virtually given by Mr. Adderley) . . . . . 3 Aug. 1856
New music-hall opened . . . . 3 Sept. ,,
Another park opened by the duke of Cambridge, 100,000 persons present (ground given by lord Calthorpe) . . . . . 1 June, 1857
Death of G. F. Muntz, M.P. . . . 30 July, ,,
John Bright elected M.P. 10 Aug. 1857, and April, 1859
The queen and prince consort visit Birmingham, Warwick &c., for the first time, and open Aston park . . . . . 14-16 June, 1858
The Free Library opened . . . . . 4 April, 1861
Factory explosion: 9 killed . . . . 23 June, 1862
People's park purchased by corporation . Sept. 1864
New Exchange opened . . . . . 2 Jan. 1865
The bank of Attwoods and Spooner stops payment and causes much distress . . . 10 March, ,,
Meeting of British Association (3rd) . . 6 Sept. ,,
Stoppage of the "Banking Company" . 13 July, 1866
First annual horse show . . . . . ,,
Great Reform meeting . . . . . ,,
Violent riots through the lectures of Murphy, an anti-popery orator, at a tabernacle 17, 18 June, 1867
An additional M.P. given to Birmingham by Reform Act . . . . . 15 Aug. ,,
Meeting of Nat. Social Science Association, 7 Oct. 1868
First club house here opened . . . 3 May, 1869
Erdington orphan houses, endowed by Josiah Mason, a manufacturer of steel-pens; begun 1858; finished . . . . . July, ,,
National Education League meet . . 12, 13 Oct. ,,
Explosion at Kynoch's cartridge-factory, Witton, many deaths and injuries . . . 17 Nov. 1870
Explosions at Messrs. Ludlow's cartridge-factory at Witton, 17 killed and 53 injured, several dying soon after: noon, 9 Dec.; 33 dead up to 13 Dec.; 51 up to 26 Dec. . . . . . ,,
Prince Arthur opens Royal Horticultural Exhibition . . . . . 25 June, 1872
Sir Josiah Mason (knighted 1872) endows a college for practical science 1873
Cannon-hill park (presented to the town by Miss Rylands) opened . . . . 1 Sept. ,,
Speech of Mr. Bright (after re-election on resuming office as chancellor of duchy of Lancaster) to about 16,000 persons in Bingley hall . 22 Oct. ,,
Statue of Priestley (in commemoration of his discovery of oxygen) unveiled by prof. Huxley 1 Aug. 1874
Visit of the prince and princess of Wales, 3 Nov. ,,
Foundation of sir Josiah Mason's college laid by himself and Mr. Bright . . . 23 Feb. 1875
Birmingham Philosophical Society founded 28 Feb. 1876
Wm. Dudley bequeaths 100,000*l.* for charitable purposes in Birmingham . . . . March, ,,
Annual meeting of the Royal Agricultural Society 17-24 July, ,,
Great Western arcade opened . . . 28 Sept. ,,
Mr. W. E. Gladstone addresses about 30,000 persons in Bingley hall . . . . 31 May, 1877
Birmingham liberal federation formed . May, June, ,,
Fire at Mr. Denison's, confectioner; Mrs. Denison and 3 others perish, 26 Aug.; verdict at inquest, arson, criminal unknown . . . 30 Sept. 1878
Central library, comprising the chief free reference library and the Shakspeare library, Cervantes collection, &c., with priceless treasures, destroyed by fire . . . . . 11 Jan. 1879
Death of sir Josiah Mason . . . 16 June, 1881
Discovery of nitro-glycerine manufacture carried on by Alfred Whitehead (arrested); box conveyed to London seized 4 April; a large quantity, made into dynamite, at great risk burnt in a field 8 April, 1883

[See *Dynamite* April, 1884.]

Festival in honour of John Bright, 25 years M.P. for Birmingham . . . . 11-15 June, ,,
Statue of the queen, by T. Woolner (to accompany that of the prince consort, by Foley), in the Free Library, uncovered . . . . 9 May, 1884
Great reform demonstration, Mr. Bright and Mr. Chamberlain present . . . . 4 Aug. ,,
Great Conservative demonstration at Aston (sir Stafford Northcote, lord Randolph Churchill, and others), prevented by brutal rioters; a free fight; many wounded and much damage of property . . . . . 13 Oct. ,,
Statue of sir Josiah Mason unveiled by sir John Lubbock . . . . . 1 Oct. 1885
The prince of Wales opens a suburban hospital and new art gallery . . . . 27-28 Nov. ,,
Meeting of the British Association here (4th) 1 Sept. ,,
Returns seven M.P.s by act passed . . 25 June, ,,
An industrial exhibition opened . . 26 Aug. 1886
The queen lays foundation stone of the "Victoria (Law) Courts"; about 500,000 persons out; no

disturbance or casualties, 23 March; Mr. T. Martineau, the mayor, knighted . 25 March, 1887
Miss Rylands presents 2,000*l.* to enlarge Victoria park . . . . . . Oct. ,,
Birmingham Liberal Unionist Association; Mr. Chamberlain elected president . . 28 May, 1888
Mr. Ph. Muntz, an eminent townsman, died 25 Dec. ,,
Birmingham created a city . . . . 14 Jan. 1889
Death of Miss Louisa Ann Rylands, great benefactress to the town, aged 75 . . . 28 Jan. ,,
Death of Mr. John Bright, M.P. . 27 March, ,,
His son, Mr. J. Albert Bright, elected his successor as M.P. . . . . 15 April, ,,
The Victoria law courts opened by the prince of Wales . . . . 21 July, 1891
Alderman Thomas Avery and his wife bequeathed 11,000*l.* to hospitals, &c.; reported . 23 Feb. 1894
The Birmingham canal burst its banks near Wolverhampton . . . . . . 10 July, ,,
Visit of the duke and duchess of York; foundation stone laid of a new general hospital . 8 Sept. ,,
Birmingham chamber of arbitration inaugurated 8 Nov. ,,
Death of the rev. Dr. R. W. Dale, aged 76, congregationalist minister, educationist 13 March, 1895
The title of lord conferred on the mayor . May 1896
The princess Christian opens the new building of the general hospital . . . . 7 July 1897
New meat market opened by sir James Smith, lord mayor . . . . . . 27 Oct. ,,
Mr. Chamberlain's speech, 13 May; censured in Europe, as to Gt. Britain's isolation, &c. May, 1898
Establishment of a Birmingham university with faculties in arts, science, medicine, and commerce, 95,244*l.* donations (50,000*l.* from Mr. Andrew Carnegie, May, 1899), total fund, 325,000*l.* Charter granted 1900 . . . . . July, ,,
Mr. Richard Cadbury, philanthropist, born about 1836, died . . . . . . 22 March, 1899
Mr. Richard Chamberlain (ex-mayor 1879) bequeaths over 50,000*l.* to charities; dies . . 2 April, ,,
Turner exhibition opened here, in the gallery, 22 July, ,,
Death of Mr. F. Schnadhorst, an eminent liberal organizer, aged 59 . . . . . . 2 Jan. 1900
Sir John Zaffray, public benefactor, dies, aged 81, 4 Jan. 1901
Scheme for a 2,000,000 shilling fund for Birmingham proposed at a meeting of clergy and laity, 8 Jan. ,,
Diamond jubilee statue of the queen presented by Mr. H. Barber, unveiled . . . 10 Jan. ,,
Serious damage by a canal burst . . 28 Sept. ,,
Mr. Chamberlain opens a new temperance hall, 14 Oct. ,,
Demonstration against Mr. Lloyd-George, M.P., in Victoria-square, some rioting, 1 death, 18 Dec. ,,
Mr. Chamberlain, chancellor of the university court; the lord mayor elected vice-chancellor, 31 May; prof. sir Oliver Lodge appointed principal, 23 June; 50,000*l.* from Sir James Chance (died about 7 Jan. 1902) and land valued at 20,0 0*l.* from lord Calthorpe and son, July; parliamentary grant 2,000*l.*; total fund 420,000*l.* in hand, Jan. 1902
The Lightwoods estate acquired as a public park, 28 Oct. ,,
Farewell banquet and torchlight procession in honour of Mr. Chamberlain on his departure to S. Africa . . . . 17 Nov. ,,
Important speech by Mr. Chamberlain at the town hall on the Colonies and preferential tariffs 15 May 1903
Lord Roberts receives the freedom of the city, 18 July, ,,
Birmingham musical festival, 13 Oct.; Dr. Elgar's new oratorio, *The Apostles*, produced . 14 Oct. ,,

BIRTHS. The births of children were taxed in England, viz.: birth of a duke, 30*l.*; of a common person, 2*s.*, 7 Will. III. 1695. Taxed again, 1783. The instances of four children at a birth are numerous; but it is recorded that a woman of Königsberg (3 Sept. 1784), and the wife of Nelson, a tailor, of Oxford-market, London (Oct. 1800), had five children at a birth. The queen usually presents a small sum of money to a poor woman giving birth to three or more living children at one time. See *Bills of Mortality* and *Registers*.

BISHOP (Greek *episcopos*, overseer), a name given by the Athenians to those who had the inspection of the city. The Jews and Romans had also like officers. St. Peter, styled the first bishop of Rome, was martyred 65. The presbyter was the same as a bishop. *Jerome*. The episcopate became an object of contention about 144. The title of pope was anciently assumed by all bishops, and was exclusively claimed by Gregory VII. (1073-85).

BISHOP OF LONDON'S FUND, see under *Church of England*, 1864, *et seq.*; amount received up to 31 Dec. 1878, 603,718*l.*

A special appeal was made by the bishop, 27 May, 1886; 23,074*l.* 19*s.* 4*d.* received in 1888; 277,85*l.* 10*s.* 1889; 17,000*l.* 1890; 1894, 24,541*l.*; 1895, 22,243*l.*; 1896, 23,558*l.*; 1897, 22,877*l.* (1,000*l.* from lord Iveagh, Feb. 1895); 1898, 20,793*l.* 3*s.* 2*d.*; (5,000*l.* from the duke of Westminster, Nov. 1899) 1899, 26,198*l.*; 1900, 26,744*l.*; 1901, 28,795*l.* 16*s.* 1*d.*; 1902, 27,800*l.*

BISHOPS IN ENGLAND* were coeval with the introduction of Christianity. The see of London is mythically said to have been founded by Lucius, king of Britain, 179. Restitutus, bishop of London, is said to have been present at the council of Arles, 314. The early dates given below are doubtful.

Bishops made barons 1072
Intervention of the pope in regard to bishops, 13th century
The *Congé d'Elire* of the king to choose a bishop originated in an arrangement by king John.
Bishops were elected by the king's *Congé d'Elire*, 25 Henry VIII. 1534
Bishops to rank as barons by stat. 31 Hen. VIII. . 1540
Seven were deprived for being married . . . 1554
Several suffered martyrdom under queen Mary, see *Protestants* 1555-6
Bishops excluded from voting in the house of peers on temporal concerns, 16 Charles I. . . . 1641
Several protest against the legality of acts of parliament passed while they are deprived of votes, 28 Dec.; committed to the tower . . 30 Dec. ,,
The order of archbishops and bishops abolished by the parliament . . . . . 9 Oct. 1646
Bishops regain their seats . . . . Nov. 1661
Seven bishops (Canterbury, Bath, Chichester, St. Asaph, Bristol, Ely, and Peterborough) sent to the tower for not reading the king's declaration for liberty of conscience (intended to bring the Roman Catholics into ecclesiastical and civil power), 8 June; tried and acquitted, 29-30 June, 1688
The archbishop of Canterbury (Dr. Sancroft) and five bishops (Bath and Wells, Ely, Gloucester, Norwich, and Peterborough) suspended for refusing to take the oaths to William and Mary, 1689; deprived 1690
Retirement of bishops: The bishops of London and Durham retired on annuities 1856
The bishop of Norwich resigned 1857
The Bishops' Resignation (for Infirmity) Act (authorising the appointment of bishop coadjutors) passed, 11 Aug. 1869; made perpetual by Act passed . . . . 14 June, 1875
Bishopric of St. Albans created, and dioceses of London, Winchester, and Rochester re-arranged, 38 & 39 Vict. c. 34; passed . . . . 29 June, ,,
Bishopric of Truro founded, 39 & 40 Vict. c. 54; passed . . . . 11 Aug. 1876
The Bishoprics Act, 41 & 42 Vict. c. 68, authorises the endowment of four new bishoprics, Liverpool, Newcastle, and Wakefield (York), and Southwell (Canterbury). The number of bishops in parliament is not to be increased . 16 Aug. 1878

* Bishops have the titles of *Lord* and *Right Rev. Father in God*. The archbishops of Canterbury and York have the title of *Grace*. The bishops of London, Durham, and Winchester have precedence of all bishops; the others rank according to seniority of consecration.

Confirmation of election of bishops, discussions in convocation . . . . . 26, 27 Jan. 1897

See *Canterbury, Archbishops*, 1896.

ENGLISH BISHOPRICS.

Sees.	*Founded.*	*Sees.*	*Founded.*
London (*abpc.*)	(?) 179	Cornwall and Devonshire (afterwards Exeter, 1050)	909
York (*abpc.*)	4th cent.	Wells	,,
Sodor and Man	4th cent.	Selsey about 681; removed to Chichester	about 1082
Llandaff	5th cent.	Bath	1088
St. David's	5th cent.	Ely	1108
Bangor*	about 516	Carlisle	1132
St. Asaph	about 560	Peterborough	1541
Canterbury (*abpc.*)	598	Gloucester †	,,
Rochester	604	Bristol † (re-constituted 1897)	1542
London (*see London*)	604	Chester	,,
East Anglia (afterwards Norwich, 1091)	630	Oxford	,,
Lindisfarne, or Holy Island (afterwards Durham, 995)	634	Ripon	1836
West Saxons, (afterwards Winchester, 705)	635	Manchester	1847
Mercia (afterwards Lichfield, 669)	656	St. Alban's	1876
Hereford	676	Truro	1877
Worcester	680	Liverpool	1880
Lindisse (afterwards Lincoln, 1067)	,,	Newcastle	1882
Sherborne (afterwards Salisbury, 1042)	705	Southwell	1884
		Wakefield	1888

BISHOPS IN IRELAND are said to have been consecrated in the 2nd century; see *Church of Ireland*.

Prelacies were constituted, and divisions of the bishoprics in Ireland made, by cardinal Paparo, legate from pope Eugene III. 1151

Several prelates deprived by queen Mary . . . 1554

Bp. Atherton suffered death ignominiously . . 1640

Two bishops deprived for not taking the oaths to William and Mary 1691

Church Temporalities Act, for reducing the number of bishops in Ireland, 3 & 4 Will. IV., c. 37, passed 14 Aug. 1833

[By this statute, of the four archbishoprics of Armagh, Dublin, Tuam, and Cashel, the last two were to be abolished on the decease of the then archprelates, which has since occurred; and it was enacted that eight of the then eighteen bishoprics should, as they became void, be henceforth united to other sees, which was accomplished in 1850; so that the Irish church at present consists of two archbishops and ten bishops.]

Ossory	founded 402	Ferns	about 598
Trim	432	Cloyne	before 604
Killala	about 434	Cork	about 606
Armagh, 445; *abpc.*	1152	Glendalough	before 612
Emly	about 448	Derry	before 618
Elphin	450	Kilmacduach	about 620
Ardagh	454	Lismore	about 631
Clogher	before 493	Leighlin	632
Down	about 499	Mayo	about 665
Ardfert and Aghadoe	before 500	Raphoe	before 885
Connor	about ,,	Cashel, before 901; *abpc.*	1152
Tuam, about 501; *abpc.*	1152	Killaloe, *abpc.*	1019
Dromore	about 510	Waterford	1096
Kildare	before 519	Limerick	before 1106
Meath	520	Kilmore	1136
Achonry	530	Dublin, *abpc.*	1152
Louth	534	Kilfenora	before 1254
Clonmacnois	548	(For the new combinations, see the separate articles.)	
Clonfert	558		
Ross	about 570		

* An order in council, Oct. 1838, directed the sees of Bangor and St. Asaph to be united on the next vacancy in either, and Manchester, a new see, to be created thereupon; this order, as regarded the union of the sees, was rescinded 1846.

† The sees of Bristol and Gloucester were united, 1836, separated, 1884. See *Bristol* 1884, *et seq.*

BISHOPS IN SCOTLAND were probably nominated in the fourth century.

The Reformers, styling themselves "the Congregation of the Lord," having taken up arms and defeated the queen-mother, Mary of Guise, called a parliament, which set up a new form of church polity on the Genevese model, in which bishops were replaced by "superintendents" . . . 1560

Episcopacy restored by the regent Morton (see *Tulchan Bishops*) 1572-3

Three prelates for Scottish sees consecrated at Lambeth (John Spottiswood, Gawin Hamilton, and Andrew Lamb) for Glasgow, Galloway, and Brechin . . . . . . 21 Oct. 1610

Episcopacy abolished, the bishops in a body deposed, and four excommunicated, by a parliament, elected by the people (covenanters), which met at Glasgow . . . . Dec. 1638

Episcopacy restored; an archbishop (James Sharp) and three bishops consecrated by Sheldon, bishop of London . . . . . . 15 Dec. 1661

The Scottish convention expelled the bishops; abolished episcopacy; declared the throne vacant; drew up a claim of right; and proclaimed William and Mary . . . . . . 11 April, 1689

Episcopacy formally abolished, and the bishops' revenues sequestrated . . . . . 19 Sept. ,,

The Episcopal church was thus reduced to the condition of a Nonconformist body, at first barely tolerated. It opened its first congress, 19 May, 1874

Bishop Rose connected the established episcopal church of Scotland with that form of it which is now merely tolerated, he having been bishop of Edinburgh from 1687 till 1720, when, on his death, Dr. Fullarton became the first post-revolution bishop of that see. Fife (now St. Andrews, so called in 1844) now unites the bishopric of Dunkeld (re-instituted in 1727) and that of Dunblane (re-instituted in 1731). Ross (of uncertain date) was united to Moray (re-instituted in 1727) in 1838. Argyll and the Isles never existed independently until 1847, having been conjoined to Moray and Ross, or to Ross alone, previously to that year. Galloway has been added to the see of Glasgow.

Orkney, founded.	Uncertain.	Edinburgh	1633
Isles	360	POST-REVOLUTION BISHOPS.	
Galloway	before 500	Edinburgh	1720
St. Andrews, 800; *abpc.*	1470	Aberdeen and the Isles	1721
Glasgow, about 560; *abpc.*	1488	Moray (and Ross)	1727
Caithness	about 1066	Brechin (*primus* 1886)	1731
Brechin	before 1155	Glasgow (and Galloway)	,,
Moray	1115	St. Andrews (Dunkeld, Dunblane, &c.)	1733
Ross	1124	Argyll and the Isles	1847
Aberdeen	1125		
Dunkeld	1130		
Dunblane	before 1153		
Argyll	1200		

Romanist Bishoprics revived by Pope Leo XIII. 4 March, 1878

Scotch Protestant bishops protest . . 13 April, ,,

BISHOPS, AMERICAN. The first was Samuel Seabury, consecrated bishop of Connecticut by four nonjuring prelates, at Aberdeen, in Scotland, 14 Nov. 1784. The bishops of New York and Pennsylvania were consecrated in London, by the archbishop of Canterbury, 4 Feb. 1787, and the bishop of Virginia in 1790. Several American bishops formed part of the Pan-Anglican synod, at Lambeth, 24-27 Sept. 1867. The first *R. C.* bishop of the United States was Dr. Carroll, of Maryland, in 1780.

BISHOPS, COLONIAL, &c.* By 15 & 16 Vict. c. 52 (1852), and 16 & 17 Vict. c. 49 (1853),

* Between 1847-59, Miss (now baroness) Burdett Coutts gave 60,000*l.* to endow colonial bishoprics. In 1866 she petitioned parliament, on account of some of the bishops professing independence of the church of England. Since then, colonial bishops have been appointed without intervention of the civil power. Much discussion

the colonial bishops may perform all episcopal functions in the United Kingdom, but have no jurisdiction. 90 colonial bishops in 1902.

Nova Scotia	1787
Quebec	1793
Calcutta	1813
Barbados	1824
Jamaica	1824
Madras	1835
Australia (see *Sydney*)	1836
Montreal	,,
Bombay	1837
Newfoundland	1839
Toronto	,,
Gibraltar	1841
New Zealand (see *Christchurch*)	,,
Antigua	1842
Guiana, S. America	,,
Huron, Canada	,,
Tasmania	,,
Colombo, Ceylon	1845
Fredericton, N. Bruns.	,,
Adelaide, S. Australia	1847
Cape Town	,,
Melbourne	,,
Newcastle, N. S. W.	,,
Sydney (*Metropolis of Australia*)	,,
Rupert's Land	1849
Victoria, Hong Kong	,,
Sierra Leone	1852
Graham's-town	1853
Natal, S. Africa	,,
Mauritius	1854
Labuan (joined with Singapore, and so-called)	1855
Christchurch, N. Z.	1856
Perth, W. Australia	,,
Wellington, N. Z.	1858
Nelson, N. Zealand	,,
Brisbane, Queensland	1859
British Columbia	,,
Goulbourn, N. S. W.	,,
St. Helena	,,
Waiapu, N. Z.	,,
Melanesia	1860
Ontario, Canada	1861
Nassau, Bahamas	,,
Grafton, Australia	1863
Dunedin, New Zealand	1866
Maritzburg, S. Africa	1869
Auckland, New Zeald.	,,
Bathurst	,,
Falkland Isles	1869
Huron	1871
Trinidad	1872
Ballarat	,,
Moosonee	,,
Algoma	1873
St. John's, Kaffraria	,,
Athabasca	,,
Saskatchewan	1874
Niagara	1875
Rangoon	1877
Transvaal	,,
Lahore	,,
Pretoria	,,
North Queensland	1878
Travancore and Cochin	1879
New Caledonia (B. C.)	,,
New Westminster	,,
Riverina	1883
Mackenzie River	1884
Qu'Appelle	,,
Mombasa	1889
Chota Nagpur	1890
Travancore and Cochin	,,
Bloemfontein	,,
Selkirk	1891
Zululand	,,
Lebombo	1892
Tinnevelly	1896
Osaka, *Japan*	,,
Uganda	1897
Keewatin	1900
Koolenay	,,
Carpentaria (Australia)	,,
Nagpur	1902
Calgary	,,

MISSIONARY BISHOPS.

Jerusalem	1841
Honolulu *	1861
Zanzibar	1863
Equatorial Africa and Niger Territory	1864
Madagascar	1870
North China	1872
Corea	1889
Mid-China	1892
W. Equatorial Africa	1893
Western China	1895
Likoma	,,

BISHOPS, SUFFRAGAN, to assist metropolitans, existed in the early church. Twenty-six, appointed by Henry VIII. 1534, were abolished by Mary, 1553, and restored by Elizabeth, 1558. The last appointed is said to have been Sterne, bishop of Colchester, 1606. The appointment of suffragan bishops was revived in 1869, and archdeacon Henry Mackenzie, suffragan bishop of Nottingham (diocese of Lincoln), was consecrated 2 Feb. 1870, and archdeacon Edward Parry, suffragan bishop of Dover (diocese of Canterbury), 23 March, 1870. Others have been appointed since; there were 9 in 1889; 16 in 1892; 24 suffragans in 1903. See *Suffragan*.

BISLEY COMMON, Surrey, see *Volunteers*, 1889.

BISMUTH was recognised as a distinct metal by Agricola, in 1529. It is very fusible and brittle, and of a yellowish white colour.

BISSEXTILE, see *Calendar* and *Leap Year*.

took place in 1867, through the deposition of Dr. Colenso, bishop of Natal, by his metropolitan, Dr. Gray, bishop of Capetown, and the attempts of the latter to consecrate a new bishop, in opposition to the law; see under *Africa*, and *Church of England*.

* Transferred to the American Church, Jan. 1902.

BITHYNIA, an ancient province in Asia Minor, is said to have been invaded by Thracian tribes, some named Bithyni, who gave it the name of Bithynia. It was subject successively to the Assyrians, Lydians, Persians, and Macedonians. Most of the cities were rebuilt by Grecian colonists.

Dydalsus revolted and reigned, about	B.C. 430-440
Botyras, his son, succeeds	378
Bas, or Bias, son of Botyras, 376; repulses the Greeks	
Zipætes, son of Bias, resists Lysimachus	328
He dies, leaving four sons, of whom the eldest, Nicomedes I., succeeds (he invites the Gauls into Asia)	326
He rebuilds Astacus, and names it Nicomedia	278
Zielas, son of Nicomedes, reigns . . . about	264
Intending to massacre the chiefs of the Gauls at a feast, Zielas is detected in his design, and is himself put to death, and his son Prusias I. made king, about	250
Prusias defeats the Gauls, and takes cities	228
Prusias allies with Philip of Macedon, and marries Apamea, his daughter	223
He receives and employs Hannibal, then a fugitive, 187; who poisons himself to escape betrayal to the Romans	208
Prusias II. succeeds	183
Nicomedes II. kills his father Prusias and reigns	180
Nicomedes III., surnamed Philopator	149
Deposed by Mithridates, king of Pontus	91
Restored by the Romans	88
Bequeaths his kingdom to the Romans	84
Pliny, the younger, pro-consul	74
The Oghusian Tartars settle in Bithynia . . . A.D.	103
The Othman Turks take Prusa, the capital (and make it the seat of their empire till they possess Constantinople)	1231
	1327

BITONTO (Naples). Here Montemar and the Spaniards defeated the Germans, 27 May, 1734, and thereby acquired the kingdom of the Two Sicilies for Don Carlos.

BLACK ACT, 9 Geo. I. c. 22 (1722), was passed to punish armed persons termed *blacks*, going about in disguise with their faces blacked, robbing warrens and fish-ponds, cutting down plantations, killing deer, &c. By this act, sending anonymous letters demanding money, &c., was made felony.

BLACK AND WHITE, a weekly illustrated paper, first published 6 Feb. 1901, price 6*d*.

BLACK ART, see *Alchemy*, *Witchcraft*.

BLACK ASSIZE, see under *Oxford*.

BLACK BOOK (*Liber Niger*), a book kept in the exchequer, which received the orders of that court. It was published by Hearne in 1728.

A book doubtfully said to have been kept in monasteries, wherein details of the enormities practised in religious houses were entered for the inspection of visitors, under Hen. VIII. 1535. The name was given to the list of pensioners, printed 1831; and to other books. See *Italy*, 1876. The title *Black Book* was given to a list of Habitual Criminals, 1869-76; published by lieut.-col. Du Cane of Brixton, March, 1877.

BLACKBURN, Lancashire, so called in Domesday-book. The manufacture of a cloth called Blackburn cheque, carried on in 1650, was superseded by Blackburn greys. In 1767, James Hargreaves, of this town, invented the spinning-jenny, for which he was eventually expelled from the county. About 1810 or 1812, the townspeople availed themselves of his discoveries, and engaged largely in the cotton manufacture, now their staple trade. Blackburn murder, see *Trials*, July, 1876. See *Riots*, 1878. Population, 1881, 104,014; 1891, 120,064; 1901, 127,527.

The prince of Wales laid the foundation of a technical school, 9 May, 1888.

Blackburn mission to China respecting trade, Messrs. Nevile and Bell and Mr. Bourne reached Shanghai, autumn of 1896, report published 1898.

BLACK CABINET, see under *Cabinet* (note).

BLACK DEATH, see *Plagues*, 1340, 1866, 1894, *et seq.*

BLACK FLAG, customary to hoist one after an execution: the one adopted by pirates, see *Buccaneers*, *Piracy*, and *Tonquin*, 1883.

BLACK FRIARS, see *Dominicans*.

BLACKFRIARS BRIDGE, London. The first stone of the late bridge was laid 31 Oct. 1760, and it was completed by Mylne, in 1770. It was frequently repaired, 1834-50, and began to sink. In 1864 it was pulled down, and a temporary bridge erected. The foundation of a new five-arched bridge, designed by Mr. Joseph Cubitt, was laid by lord mayor Hale, 20 July, 1865, and the bridge was opened by the queen 6 Nov. 1869. The first railway train (London, Chatham, and Dover) entered the city of London over the *new railway bridge*, Blackfriars, 6 Oct. 1864. Another railway bridge opened 7 Jan. 1884.

BLACK FRIDAY, 11 May, 1866, the height of the commercial panic in London, through the stoppage of Overend, Gurney, & Co. (limited), on 10 May. Messrs. John Henry and Edmund Gurney, and their partners, committed for trial for conspiracy to defraud, 21 Jan. 1869, were tried and acquitted, 13-23 Dec. 1869. On Friday, 21 Nov. 1890, a temporary panic was produced by the embarrassments of Messrs. Baring Brothers.

BLACK HAND, see *Spain*, 1883.

BLACKHEATH, Kent, near London. Here Wat Tyler and his followers assembled 12 June, 1381; and here also Jack Cade and his 20,000 Kentish men encamped, 1 June, 1450; see *Tyler* and *Cade*. Here the Cornish rebels were defeated and Flammock's insurrection quelled, 22 June, 1497. The ancient cavern, on the ascent to Blackheath, popularly termed "the retreat of Cade," and of banditti in the time of Cromwell, was re-discovered in 1780. Several daring highway robberies were committed near the heath, and the youthful culprits punished, in 1877. Murder of Mrs. Arabella C. Tyler at Kidbrook-park-road, 14 Aug. 1898. See *Trials*.

BLACK-HOLE, see *Calcutta*, 1756.

BLACK LEAD, see *Graphite*.

BLACKLEGS. A name commonly given to cheating gamblers, was unjustly given to non-unionist workmen by the unionists and others during the labour agitation in 1889 and 1890.

BLACK LETTER, employed in the first printed books in the middle of the 15th century. The first printing types were Gothic; but they were modified into the present Roman type about 1469: Pliny's Natural History was then printed in the new characters.

BLACK LIST, name given to printed lists of insolvents, bankrupts, and other matters affecting the credit of firms and individuals, published in London, weekly or bi-weekly, drawn from public registers. The legality of issuing information of this kind has been questioned, but, in the case of the *Scottish Mercantile Society's Record* in 1848, the house of lords found "such publication" was not slanderous. Private lists of a searching kind issued to subscribers were first started by Mr. Thos. Perry of Cornhill, Stubbs' being the best known of the kind. Similar systems widely used in America and elsewhere. *Chambers.*

Since the licensing act of 1902, confirmed drunkards who have been before the magistrates several times, are placed on the "*Black List*," and their names and photographs are sent round to publicans, who are forbidden to supply them with intoxicating liquors.

BLACK-MAIL, a compulsory payment for protection of cattle, &c., made in the border counties was prohibited by Elizabeth in 1601. It was exacted in Scotland from the lowlanders by the highlanders, till 1745. It checked agricultural improvement. The term *black-mail* has been applied to the payments of new commercial companies for notices respecting them in certain newspapers, 1889-90.

Five men convicted and sentenced for black-mailing (Andrew Grant and Herbert Coulton—penal servitude for life) . . . . . July 5, 1897
Richard, Edward, and Leonard Chrimes sentenced to several years penal servitude for blackmailing women . . . . 20 Dec. 1898
Oliver Fletcher sentenced to 7 years and John Cox to 9 months imprisonment . . . 15 April, 1899

BLACK MONDAY, Easter Monday, 14 April, 1360, "so full dark of mist and hail, and so bitter cold that many men died on their horsebacks with the cold." *Stow.* In Ireland, Black Monday was the day on which a number of the English were slaughtered at a village near Dublin, in 1209.

BLACK MONEY, base foreign coin so termed, 1335.

BLACK MOUNTAIN EXPEDITIONS, see *India*, 1888 and 1891.

BLACK MUSEUM, at Scotland Yard, is a collection of relics connected with crime, begun in 1874.

BLACKPOOL, Lancashire, a watering place. The foundation-stone of an Eiffel Tower was laid here 25 Sep. 1891. Population in 1851, 1664; 1881, 14,229; 1891, 23,846; 1901, 48,000.

BLACK PRINCE, EDWARD, eldest son of king Edward III., born 15 June, 1330; victor at Poitiers, 19 Sept. 1356; at Najara, 3 April, 1367; died 8 June, 1376.

BLACK REPUBLIC, see *Hayti*.

BLACK ROD has a gold lion at the top, and is carried by the usher of the order of the knights of the garter (instituted 1349), instead of the mace. He also keeps the door when a chapter of the order is sitting, and during the sessions of parliament attends the house of lords and acts as their messenger to the commons. Gen. sir M. Biddulph, G.C.B.

BLACK SEA, THE EUXINE (*Pontus Euxinus* of the ancients), a large internal sea between the S. W. provinces of Russia and Asia Minor, connected with the sea of Azoff by the straits of Yenikalé, and with the sea of Marmora by the channel of Constantinople.

This sea was much frequented by the Greeks and Italians, till closed to all nations by the Turks after the fall of Constantinople in 1453.
The Russians obtained admission by the treaty of Kainardji . . . . . 10 July, 1774
It was partially opened to British and other traders, (since which time the Russians gradually obtained the preponderance). 1779
Entered by the British and French fleets, at the requisition of the Porte, after the destruction of the Turkish fleet at Sinope by the Russians, 30 Nov. 1853 . . . . . . 3 Jan. 1854

A dreadful storm in this sea raged, and caused great loss of life and shipping, and valuable stores for the allied armies. See *Russo-Turkish War*. 13 to 16 Nov. 1854

The Black Sea was opened to the commerce of all nations by the treaty of 1856.

The article of the treaty of Paris, 30 March, 1856, by which the sea was opened to the commerce of all nations, and interdicted to any ships of war; and the erection of military maritime arsenals forbidden, was repudiated by a Russian circular, dated . . . . 31 (19) Oct. 1870

After some correspondence, the meeting of a conference on the subject, in London, was agreed to by all the powers concerned in the treaty . . ,,

The conference met in London 17 Jan. 1871, and a treaty was signed by which the neutralization of the sea was abrogated; but it was agreed by a special protocol, that no nation shall liberate itself from the obligations of a treaty without the consent of the others who signed it . . 13 March, 1871

Blockade of the Black Sea declared by Turkey during the war . . . . about 3 May, 1877

Revival of the Black Sea Fleet: *Tchesma*, ironclad launched by the Czar at Sebastopol (others to follow) . . . . 18 May, 1886

The Black Sea territory reorganized as a Russian province by decree; announced . . 4 Aug. 1896

BLACKS, or *Neri*; see *Bianchi*.

BLACKWALL (London), the site of fine commercial docks and warehouses. See *Docks*. The Blackwall railway was opened to the public, 4 July, 1840; the eastern terminus being at Blackwall wharf, and the western in Fenchurch street. See *Tunnels*, 1891, *et seq*. and *Navy*, June, 1898.

BLACK WATCH, armed companies of the loyal clans (Campbells, Monros, &c.) employed to watch the highlands from about 1725 to 1739, when they were formed into the celebrated 42nd regiment, enrolled as "The Royal Highland Black Watch." Their removal for foreign service probably facilitated the outbreak in 1745. They wore dark tartans, and hence were called *Black Watch*. They distinguished themselves in the Ashantee war, Jan. Feb. 1874, in Egypt, 1882-5, in S. Africa 1899-1902.

BLACKWATER, Battle of, in Ireland, 14 Aug. 1598, when the Irish chief O'Neil defeated the English under sir Henry Bagnall. Pope Clement VIII. sent O'Neil a consecrated plume, and granted to his followers the same indulgence as to crusaders.

BLACKWOOD'S Edinburgh Magazine established, 1817; "William Blackwood and Sons' Magazine," by Mrs. Oliphant, published 1897.

BLADENSBURG, see *Washington*, 1814.

BLANC, see *Mont Blanc*.

BLAND ACT, see *United States*, Feb. 1878.

BLANDFORD'S ACT, 19 & 20 Vict. c. 104, for augmentation of benefices, &c. passed, 1856.

BLANK VERSE, see *Verse*.

BLANKETEERS. A number of operatives who, on 10 March, 1817, met in St. Peter's field, near Manchester, many of them having blankets, rugs, or great coats rolled up and fastened to their backs. This was termed the Blanket meeting. They proceeded to march towards London, but were dispersed by the magistracy. It is stated that their object was to commence a general insurrection. See *Derby*. Eventually the ringleaders had an interview with the cabinet ministers, and a better understanding between the working classes and the government ensued.

BLANKET SCANDAL, see under *South African War*.

BLANKETS are said to have been first made at Bristol by Thos. Blanket, in the 14th century. This is doubtful.

BLASPHEMY was punished with death by the law of Moses (*Lev.* xxiv.) 1491 B.C.; and by the code of Justinian, A.D. 529. It is punishable by the civil and canon law of England, regulated by 60 Geo. III. c. 8 (1819). Daniel Isaac Eaton was tried and convicted in London of blasphemy, 6 March, 1812. Robert Taylor, a protestant clergyman, was tried twice for the same crime. He was sentenced to two years' imprisonment, and largely fined, July, 1831. In Dec. 1840, two publishers of blasphemous writings were convicted.

BLASTING GELATINE (a mixture of nitro-glycerine and gun-cotton), a violent explosive prepared by Alfred Nobel, and modified by professor Abel, 1879. See *Nobel Bequest*.

BLAZONRY. Bearing coats-of-arms was introduced and became hereditary in France and England about 1192, owing to the knights painting their banners with different figures, thereby to distinguish them in the crusades. *Dugdale*. See *Heraldry*.

BLEACHING was known in Egypt, Syria, India, and Gaul. *Pliny*. An improved chemical system was adopted by the Dutch, who introduced it into England and Scotland in 1768. There were large bleach-fields in Lancashire, Fife, Forfar, and Renfrew, and in the vale of the Leven, in Dumbarton. The application of the gas chlorine to bleaching is due to Berthollet's discovery, about 1785. Its combination with lime (as chloride of lime) was devised by Mr. Tennant, of Glasgow, who took out a patent for the process in 1798, and by his firm it is still extensively manufactured. In 1822 Dr. Ure published an elaborate series of experiments on this substance. A new and more rapid process invented by Mr. Jacob Baynes Thompson, tried at Bolton, and reported successful, April, 1884. Improvements made by Mr. William Mather, 1885. The manufacture of bleaching powder was cheapened by Mond's process, in which the wasted chlorine is utilized, by Messrs. Brunner, Mond & Co., reported, Oct. 1892. In 1860 bleaching and dyeing works were placed under the regulations of the Factories Act.

BLENHEIM (or Plintheim) a village in Bavaria on the left bank of the Danube, near the town of Hochstett, the site of a battle fought 2 Aug. (new style, 13), 1704, between the English and confederates, commanded by the duke of Marlborough, and the French and Bavarians, under marshal Tallard and the elector of Bavaria. The latter were defeated with the loss of about 12,000 killed, and 13,000 prisoners (including Tallard). Bavaria became the prize of the conquerors. The British parliament gave Marlborough the honour of Woodstock and hundred of Wotton, and erected for him the house of Blenheim.*

BLIND. The first public school for the blind was established by Valentine Haüy, at Paris in 1784. The first in England was at Liverpool, in 1791; in Scotland, at Edinburgh, in 1792; and the

* On 5 Feb. 1861, a fire broke out at this place, which destroyed the "Titian Gallery" and the pictures; the latter, a present from Victor Amadeus, king of Sardinia, to John, the great duke of Marlborough. Pictures, library, and other valuables sold 1885-6.

first in London in 1799. Printing in raised or embossed characters for the use of the blind was begun at Paris by Haüy in 1786. The whole Bible was printed at Glasgow in raised Roman characters about 1848. Louis Braille, born near Paris, Jan. 1809, died 1852, became blind from an accident at the age of three. He adapted from M. Barbier's system his own simple and beautiful one of dots, for reading and writing, now bearing his name, which he published in 1829 and fully developed in 1834. The Braille musical notation is also much used. A sixpenny magazine for the blind, edited by the late rev. W. Taylor, F.R.S., so eminent for his forty years' exertions on behalf of these sufferers, was published in 1855-6. He aided the establishment of a college for the blind of the upper classes at Worcester, in 1866. There is hardly any department of human knowledge in which blind persons have not obtained distinction.* Laura Bridgman, born in 1829, became dumb and blind two years after. She was so well taught by Dr. Howe, of Boston, U.S., as to become an able instructor of blind and dumb persons; she died 24 May, 1889. By the census of 1851, there were in Great Britain, 21,487 blind persons; 11,273 males, 10,214 females; about one in 975 blind. The number of the blind in Great Britain has proportionally decreased since 1851, according to the census, 22,800 in 1881. In 1881 about one in 1138 blind. Royal Normal College and Academy of Music for the Blind, established 1873, at Norwood, Surrey, mainly by the exertions of Mr. Francis Joseph Campbell, an American, himself blind, and an able teacher, aided by the marquis, aft. duke, of Westminster, purchased for 22.000*l*. by the London school board for the education of the blind, Jan. 1896. Mr. Campbell ascended Mont Blanc in 1880. There were 29 Societies for the blind in London in 1889.

Royal Commission on the condition of the blind; extended to the deaf and dumb, Jan. 1886.

According to the census of 1881, the number of blind in the United Kingdom was about 32,101, England and Wales 22,832, Scotland 3,158, Ireland 6,111, England and Wales, 1891, 23,467. The royal commission to enquire into their condition was appointed 28 July, 1885, and on the 20th Jan. 1886, additional members were appointed, and its inquiries were extended to the deaf, dumb, and imbecile in the United Kingdom, Paris, Germany, Switzerland, and Italy. The commission, after 116 sittings, and many visitations and examinations of witnesses, issued their first report July, 1889. The number of the deaf under instruction in the United Kingdom was in 1851 1,300, in 1888 3,138. The commission met with great uncertainty in regard to idiots and imbeciles.

The *Weekly Summary*, a newspaper for the blind, published in London on Wednesdays, started in June, 1892.

Elementary Education (Blind and Deaf Children) Act, passed in 1893.

Death of Dr. Wm. Moon, inventor of the largely adopted system of printing for the blind, 10 Oct. 1894.

International congress for improving the condition of the blind, opened at Brussels . . 6 Aug. 1902

M. Dussand's new writing system for the blind reported . . . . Aug. 1902

BLINDING by consuming the eyeballs with lime or scalding vinegar, was a punishment inflicted anciently on adulterers, perjurers, and thieves. In the middle ages the penalty was frequently changed from total blindness to a diminution of sight. A whole army of Bulgarians was deprived of sight by the emperor Basil, 104. Several of the eastern emperors had their eyes torn from their heads.

BLISTERS, used by Hippocrates (460-357 B.C.), made, it is said, of cantharides (*which see*).

BLIZZARD, an old term applied in the Midland counties to the snow-blast, also signifying anything blazing, blinding, or stifling. Of late years violent snow-storms have been termed blizzard in the United States of North America, as well as in Britain. See *Storms*, 11-13 Jan.; and 11-13 March, 1888, and since.

BLOCKADE is the closing an enemy's ports to all commerce; a practice introduced by the Dutch about 1584. The principle recognized by the European powers is that every blockade, in order to be binding, must be effective. Cadiz blockaded 1797-9; the Elbe was blockaded by Great Britain, 1803; the Baltic, by Denmark, 1848-49 and 1864; the gulf of Finland by the Allies, 1854; and the ports of the Southern States of North America by president Lincoln, April 19, 1861. See *Orders in Council*, and *Berlin*. Part of the east coast of Africa was blockaded by England and Germany on account of the slave trade, 2 Dec. 1888—1 Oct. 1889: see *Zanzibar*.

BLOCK BOOKS, see *Printing*.

BLOCKS employed in the rigging of ships were much improved in their construction by Walter Taylor, about 1781. In 1801, Mark I. Brunel invented a mode of making blocks by machinery, which was put into operation in 1808, and in 1815 was said to have saved the country 20,000*l*. a year.

BLOEMFONTEIN CONFERENCE, see *Orange Free State*, 1899.

BLOIS, France, the Roman Blesum. The count Guy II. sold it with his domains to Louis duke of Orleans in 1391, and eventually it accrued to the crown. The states-general were held here 1576 and 1588, on account of the religious wars; and here Henry duke of Guise was assassinated by order of the king, Henry III., 23 Dec. 1588. The empress Maria Louisa retired here in 1814.

BLOOD. The circulation of the blood through the lungs was known to Michael Servetus, a Spanish physician, in 1553. Cæsalpinus published an account of the general circulation, of which he had some confused ideas, improved afterwards by experiments, 1569. Paul of Venice, or Father Paolo (real name Peter Sarpi), discovered the valves which serve for the circulation; but the honour of the positive discovery of the circulation belongs to William Harvey, between 1619 and 1628. *Freind*. A memorial window in the church at Folkestone, his birthplace, was uncovered 9 April, 1874, and a statue at the same place, 6 Aug. 1881.

Eating Blood was prohibited to Noah, *Gen.* ix., to the Jews, *Lev.* xvii., &c., and to the Gentile converts by the apostles at an assembly at Jerusalem, A.D. 52, *Acts* xv.

Blood-Drinking was anciently tried to give vigour to the system. Louis XI. in his last illness, drank the warm blood of infants, in the vain hope of restoring his decayed strength, 1483. *Hénault*.

* James Holman, the "*blind traveller*" (born 1786, died 1857), visited almost every place of note in the world. His travels were published in 1825. In April, 1858, a blind clergyman, rev. J. Sparrow, was elected chaplain to the Mercers' Company, London, and read the service, &c., from embossed books.

Viscount Cranborne (blind) was the author of many interesting historical essays. He died in June, 1865. On 13 July, 1865, Henry Fawcett, the blind professor of political economy at Cambridge, was elected M.P. for Brighton; for *Hackney*, 1874 and 1880; and was appointed postmaster-general, April, 1880, died 6 Nov. 1884. Miss Alice King, blind at 7 years of age, learnt 7 languages by ear, novelist, beneficent to the poor, died aged 55, early May, 1894.

In the 15th century an opinion prevailed that the declining vigour of the aged might be repaired by TRANSFUSING into their veins the blood of young persons. It was countenanced in France by the physicians about 1668, and prevailed for many years, till the most fatal effects having ensued, it was suppressed by an edict. "An English physician (Louver, or Lower) practised in this way; he died in 1691." *Freind.* It was attempted again in France in 1797, and more recently there, in a few cases, with success; and in England (but the instances are rare) since 1823. Tried at Philadelphia, U.S., April, 1877; in London, unsuccessful, 10 May, 1877.

BLOOD'S CONSPIRACY. Blood, a discarded officer of Oliver Cromwell's household, with his confederates, seized the duke of Ormond in his coach, intending to hang him, and had got him to Tyburn, when he was rescued by his friends, 6 Dec. 1670. Blood afterwards, in the disguise of a clergyman, attempted to steal the regal crown from the Jewel-office in the Tower, 9 May, 1671; yet, notwithstanding these and other offences, he was not only pardoned, but had a pension of 500*l.* per annum settled on him by Charles II. 1671. He died 24 Aug. 1680.

"BLOODY ASSIZES," held by Jeffreys in the west of England, in Aug. 1685, after the defeat of the duke of Monmouth in the battle of Sedgmoor. Upwards of 300 persons were executed after short trials; very many were whipped, imprisoned, and fined; and nearly 1000 were sent as slaves to the American plantations.

BLOOMER COSTUME, see a *note* to article *Dress.*

BLOOMSBURY GANG, a cant term applied to an influential political party in the reign of George III., who met at Bloomsbury House, the residence of the duke of Bedford. The marquis of Stafford, the last survivor, died 26 Oct. 1803.

BLOREHEATH (Staffordshire), where, 23 Sept. 1459, the earl of Salisbury and the Yorkists defeated the Lancastrians, whose leader, lord Audley, was slain with many Cheshire gentlemen. A cross commemorates this conflict.

BLOWING-MACHINES, the large cylinders, used in blowing machines, were erected by Mr. Smeaton at the Carron iron works, 1760. One equal to the supply of air for forty forge fires was erected at the king's dockyard, Woolwich. The *hot-air blast*, a most important improvement, causing great economy of fuel, was invented by Mr. James B. Neilson, of Glasgow, and patented in 1828. He died 18 Jan. 1865.

BLOW-PIPE. An Egyptian using one is among the paintings on the tombs at Thebes. It was employed in mineralogy, by Antony Von Swab, a Swede, about 1733, and improved by Wollaston and others. In 1802, professor Robert Hare, of Philadelphia, increased the action of the blow-pipe by the application of oxygen and hydrogen. By the agency of Newman's improved blow-pipes, in 1816, Dr. E. D. Clarke fused the earths, alkalies, metals, &c. Works on the blow-pipe by Plattner and Muspratt, 1854; G. Plympton, 1874, and W. A. Ross, 1880–8.

BLUE was the favourite colour of the Scotch covenanters in the 17th century. Blue and orange or yellow, became the whig colours after the revolution in 1688; and were adopted on the cover of the whig periodical, the "Edinburgh Review," first published in 1802. The Prussian blue dye was discovered by Diesbach, at Berlin, in 1710. Fine blues are now obtained from coal-tar; see *Aniline*. BLUE-COAT SCHOOLS, so called in reference to the costume of the children. The *Blue-coat school*, formerly in Newgate-street, London, was instituted by Edward VI. in 1552; see *Christ's Hospital*. BLUE-STOCKING, a term applied to literary ladies, was originally conferred on a society comprising both sexes (1760, *et seq.*). Benjamin Stillingfleet, the naturalist, an active member, wore blue worsted stockings; hence the name. The beautiful Mrs. Jerningham is said to have worn blue stockings at the *conversaziones* of Mrs. Montague. *Blue Ribbon Army*, see *Temperance*, 1882.

BLUE-BOOKS, reports and other papers printed by order of parliament, are so named on account of their wrappers; 70 vols. were printed for the lords, and 76 vols. for the commons in 1871. The official colour of France is *yellow*, Spain *red*, Germany *white*, Italy *green*, Portugal *white*, United States, N.A., *green*, Austria, *red*.

BLUMENAU, Lower Austria; on 22 July, 1866, the Austrians in possession of this place were attacked by the Prussians on their march towards Vienna, a severe conflict was interrupted by the news of the armistice agreed to at Nikolsburg; and the same evening Austrians and Prussians bivouacked together.

BOARD OF ADMIRALTY, AGRICULTURE and FISHERIES CONTROL, GREEN-CLOTH, HEALTH, TRADE, EDUCATION, &c., see under *Admiralty*, &c.

BOATS. Flat-bottomed boats brought into use by Barker, a Dutchman, about 1690; see *Life-Boat*. A mode of building boats by the help of the steam-engine was invented by Mr. Nathan Thompson of New York in 1860, and premises were erected for its application at Bow, near London, in 1861. Charles Clifford's valuable Boat-lowering apparatus was invented 1856. See *Canal-Boats* and *Life-Boats*.

Boat Voyage. Alfred Johnson, a young man, started from America in the *Centennial*, a boat 20 feet long, on 15 June, and landed at Abercastle, Pembrokeshire . . . . . . 11 Aug. 1876

Two young sailors crossed the Atlantic in the *City of Bath*, a boat 14 feet long: arriving at Falmouth . . . . 24 Aug. 1882

Mr. Terry formed a boat on the framework of a tricycle, and on it went from London to Dover, crossed the Channel to Calais and proceeded to Paris . . . . July, 1883

Submarine boats, one is said to have been invented about 1578; and one tried in the Thames early in the seventeenth century, and one at Plymouth in 1774. Robert Fulton's experiments in this direction were not accepted (early nineteenth century). Unsuccessful attempts made by several European powers in 1851, and since. Nordenfelt's submarine boat first constructed at Stockholm in 1883, to be employed in naval warfare, exhibited at Landskrona in presence of officers sent by all the great powers 23 Sept. 1885; the boat, made of steel, 64 feet long; motive power, steam; crew of 3 or 4 men, breathe for six hours by means of sealed up compressed air; the boat may be raised or sunk at the will of the crews and by means of torpedoes may cause the destruction of any vessel. The boat was successfully tried in Southampton water, 19–20 Dec. 1887; the *Péral*, Spanish submarine torpedo boat, launched 8 Sept. 1888; *Gustave Zédé*, named after the constructor of the *Gymnote* (1886), successful trip between Toulon and Marseilles, mid Jan. 1899; submarine boats tried successfully at Cherbourg, 7 Jan. 1901; 1st British launched at Barrow, 63 ft. long, 11 ft. 9 in. wide, 2 Oct. 1901; the *Silure*, launched at Cherbourg, 29 Oct. 1901; 4th British launched at Barrow . . 23 May, 1902

Lieut. Isaac Peral's submarine boat, travelled for one hour under water near Cadiz 7 June; he was ennobled by the government . . 16 June, 1890
The *Sapolio*, a boat 15 feet long, with capt. William Andrews crossed the Atlantic from N. America in 68 days, arriving at Huelva . . 27 Sept. 1892
Lieut. H. R. Sayce, of Bristol, crossed the English Channel in his patent collapsible life-boat; weight under 35 lbs., length, 8½ ft. 17 June, 1893
Mr. J. M. Porter crossed from Folkestone to Boulogne in a canoe, 14 ft. 6 ins. long, in 10 hours 29 Aug. ,,
Mr. Sayce in a canvas boat, supported by air bags, designed by himself, crossed from Dover to Calais in 10½ hours . . . . 19 June, 1894
Mr. John Ruck, accompanied by Mr. R. E. Wicker, crossed from Dover to Calais in a tandem cycle boat in 7 hrs. 15 min. . . . 12 May, 1895
Harbro and Samuelson, Norwegians, cross the Atlantic from New York in a rowing boat 16 ft. long, in 55 days; arrive at Scilly . 1 Aug. 1896
Capt. Slocum alone in the *Spray*, 9 tons reg. net. 12·70 gross, sails round the world 1898
Capt. H. Blackburn crossed the Atlantic in a small boat, alone, in 38 days, reaching Lisbon, 21 July, 1901
Exhibition of boats and boating apparatus at Earl's court, opened . . . . . 1 March, 1902
Mr. and Mrs. Bradley crossed the Atlantic in a sailing boat, 16 ft. long, from Nova Scotia, arrived at Dover . . . . 21 July, ,,

BOAT-RACES; see *Doggett*, and *University*. First regatta on the Thames, 1775. Rowing clubs formed 1800–18. Leander in 1819. Oxford University boat club in 1839. Cambridge University boat club 1829. (First Oxford and Cambridge University boat-race, 10 June, 1829.) Henley regatta founded 1839. Royal Thames regatta started 1843. London rowing club formed 1856. The Amateur rowing association founded 1876. International race at Cork: English won, 23 July, 1902.

BOCCACCIO'S DECAMERONE, a collection of a hundred stories or novels (many very immoral), severely satirising the clergy, feigned to have been related in ten days, during the plague of Florence in 1348. Boccaccio lived 1313-75. A copy of the first edition (that of Valdarfer, in 1471) was knocked down at the duke of Roxburgh's sale, to the Duke of Marlborough, for 2260*l.*, 17 June, 1812. This copy was afterwards sold by public auction, for 875 guineas, 5 June, 1819.

BODLEIAN LIBRARY, Oxford, founded in 1598, and opened in 1602, by sir Thos. Bodley (died, 28 Jan. 1612). It is open to the public, and claims a copy of all works published in this country. In 1868, it contained about 250,000 volumes; in 1885, 432,417 volumes (MSS. 26,598.) For rare works and MSS. it is said to be second only to the Vatican. Mr Macray's "Annals of the Bodleian library," 1868. Tercentenary celebrated 8–9 Oct. 1902.

BŒOTIA, a division of Greece, north of Attica, known previously as Aonia, Messapia, Hyantis, Ogygia, and Cadmeis. Thebes, the capital, was celebrated for the exploits and misfortunes of its kings and heroes. The term Bœotian was used by the Athenians as a synonym for dulness; but unjustly,—since Pindar, Hesiod, Plutarch, Democritus, Epaminondas, and Corinna, were Bœotians. The early history and dates are mythical; see *Thebes*.

Arrival of Cadmus, founder of Cadmea (*Hales*, 1494; *Clinton*, 1313) . . . . B.C. 1493
Reign of Polydore 1459
Labdachus ascends the throne 1430
Amphion and Zethus besiege Thebes, and dethrone Laïus 1388
Myth of Œdipus; he kills in an affray his father Laïus; confirming the oracle foretelling his death by the hands of his son, 1276; resolves the Sphinx's enigmas 1266
War of the Seven Captains 1225
Thebes besieged and taken 1213
Thersander reigns 1198; slain 1193
The Thebans abolish royalty (ages of obscurity follow). . . . . about 1120
The Thebans fight with the Persians against the Greeks at Platæa 479
The Spartans aiding the Thebans defeat the Athenians near Tanagra. 457
Battle of Coronea, in which the Thebans defeat the Athenians 447
The Thebans, under Epaminondas and Pelopidas enrol their Sacred Band, and join Athens against Sparta 377
Epaminondas defeats the Lacedæmonians at Leuctra, and restores Thebes to independence . 371
Pelopidas killed at the battle of Cynoscephalæ . 364
Epaminondas gains the victory of Mantinea, but is slain 362
Philip, king of Macedon, defeats the Thebans and Athenians near Chæronea 338
Alexander destroys Thebes, but spares the house of Pindar 335
The Bœotian confederacy dissolved by the Romans 170
Bœotia henceforth partook of the fortunes of Greece: and was conquered by the Turks under A.D. Mahomet II. 1456

BOERS (peasants), a name given to the Dutch settlers, in South Africa, since the 16th century, who still retain their national character. Discontented with the British rule in the Cape since 1814, large bands of them in 1835-7 *trekked* or emigrated northwards, and founded the Orange Free State (1836), and the Transvaal Republic (1848), after much fighting with the natives. See *Transvaal* 1891.

BOG OF ALLEN, the name given to an extensive series of bogs in Ireland, on the E. side of the Shannon.

BOGOTÀ, SANTA FÉ DE, capital of New Grenada (*which see*), founded 1538.

BOGS, probably the remains of forests, covered with peat and loose soil. An act for the drainage of Irish bogs, passed March, 1830. The bog-land of Ireland has been estimated at 3,000,000 acres; that of Scotland at upwards of 2,000,000; and that of England at near 1,000,000 of acres. In Jan. 1849, Mr. Rees Reece took out a patent for certain valuable products from Irish peat. Candles and various other articles produced from peat have been since sold in London. Fuel for railway engines and other purposes was made from peat (April, 1873); and a peat, coal, and charcoal company established.

A considerable trade is carried on in Dublin in bog-oak jewelry and ornaments, originated on the occasion of the visit of Geo. IV. to Ireland, 1821.

Much destruction has been caused by the motion of bogs. Leland (about 1546) speaks of Chat Moss doing so.

Mischief was done at Enaghmore, Ireland, 3 Jan. 1853; and farm houses and fields near Dunmore were covered, Oct. 1873. Through heavy rains and the percolation of water, the Knocknageeha bog a mile long and a ¼ mile broad at Rathmore in E. Kerry gave way, and swept everything in its course for about 2 miles; the Donnelly family (8 persons) at Quarry-lodge, on lord Kenmare's estate, submerged; salmon fishery in the river Flesk, and small farmers ruined, 28, 29 Dec. 1896; bog slip near Liscannor, West Clare, much damage and live-stock lost, 11, 12 Nov. 1901.

BOGUE FORTS, see *China*, 1841.

BOHEMIA, formerly the Hercynian forest (Boiemum, *Tacitus*), derives its name from the Boii, a Celtic tribe. It was governed by dukes (Borzivoi the first, 891), till Ottocar assumed the title of king, 1198. The kings at first held their territory from the empire: and the crown was elective till it came to the house of Austria, in which it is now hereditary. Prague, the capital, is famous for sieges and battles. Population in 1857, 4,705,525; in 1870, 5,140,544; in 1890, 5,843,250; 1900, 6,318,280; see *Prague*. For Bohemians, see *Gypsies*.

The Czechs (Slavonians) conquer Bohemia about 5th century.
City of Prague founded 759
Introduction of Christianity 894
Bohemia conquered by the emperor Henry III. who spreads devastation through the country . . 1041
Ottocar (Premislas) I., first king of Bohemia . . 1198
Ottocar II. rules over Austria, and obtains Styria, &c., 1253; refuses the imperial crown . . . 1272
Ottocar vanquished by the emperor Rudolph and deprived of Austria, Styria and Carniola, 1277; killed at Marchfeld . . . . . 26 Aug. 1278
King John (*blind*), slain at the battle of Crecy . . 1346
John Huss and Jerome of Prague, two of the first reformers, burnt for heresy; which occasions an insurrection 1415, 1416
Ziska, leader of the Hussites, takes Prague, 1419; dies of the plague 1424
Albert, duke of Austria, marries the daughter of the late emperor and king, and receives the crowns of Bohemia and Hungary 1437
The succession infringed by Ladislas, son of the king of Poland, and George Podiebrad, a protestant chief 1440–1458
Ladislas, king of Poland, elected king of Bohemia, on the death of Podiebrad 1471
The emperor Ferdinand I. marries Anne, sister of Louis the late king, and obtains the crown . . 1527
The emperor Ferdinand II., oppressing the protestants, is deposed, and Frederic the elector-palatine, elected king . . . . 5 Sept. 1619
Frederic, totally defeated at Prague, flees to Holland . . . . . . 9 Nov. 1620
Bohemia secured to Austria by treaty 1648
Silesia and Glatz ceded to Prussia 1742
Prague taken by the Prussians 1744
Prussians defeat Austrians at Prague . . 6 May, 1757
Revolt of the peasantry 1775
Edict of Toleration promulgated 1781
The French occupy Prague 1806
Insurrection at Prague, 12 June; submission, state of siege raised . . . . 20 July, 1848
The Prussians enter Bohemia, which becomes the seat of war (see *Germany*, 1866) . 24 June, 1866
Agitation of the Czechs, who require the emperor to be crowned king of Bohemia with the crown of St. Wenceslas at Prague . . . autumn, 1867
Riots at Prague; habeas corpus act suspended, 10 Oct. 1868
Bohemian agitation for self-government; addresses to the emperor . . 14 Sept. and 5 Oct. 1870
Manifesto of the emperor . . . 14 Sept. 1871
Bohemian deputies absent from the reichsrath, Dec. ,,
The "Young Czech" party defeated in the elections July, 1874
Czech deputies enter reichsrath . . 8 Oct. 1879
The motion of the Young Czechs in the assembly for the coronation of the emperor as king of Bohemia negatived, after several days' warm debate . . . . . . 6 Nov. 1889
Peaceful settlement of the disputes between Czechs and Germans, in a conference, by the intervention of the emperor . . . . . 17—19 Jan. 1890
Peace confirmed at a meeting of the diet 19 May, ,,
Strike of about 6,000 miners at Nürschau; fight with military; five men killed . .19—29 May, ,,
The diet re-opened 14 Oct., the Young Czechs obstruct legislation . . . . Oct. ,,
Meeting of the diet; the Young Czech party obstructive; the reconciliation of Germans and Czechs delayed . . . . . Nov. ,,
The Brüx mine inundated through heavy rains, 87 colliers perish, announced . . 30 Nov. ,,
The emperor intervenes to promote the passing of the compromised bill by the diet; the Young Czechs require autonomy like Hungary middle Dec. ,,
Gradual dissolution of the Old Czech party (moderates) . . . . Dec. ,,
The Austrian government determine to make no more concessions to the Czechs; announced to the diet . . . . 5 Jan. 1891
Useful legislation in the diet obstructed by the Young Czechs, about . . . . 16 Jan. 1891
The Young Czechs victorious in the elections; Dr. Rieger, the venerable leader of the Old Czechs, and his party, totally defeated, 2—4 March; he retires from public life (died 3 March, 1903), March, ,,
The emperor visits Prague to promote peace between the Germans and Czechs, 26 Sept.—1 Oct. ,,
Explosion of a bridge at Rosenthal, over which the emperor was expected to pass . 30 Sept. ,,
The government compromise discussed in the diet and strongly opposed . . . 24 March, 1892
Fire in the great silver mine, Birkenberg, near Przibram, about 319 deaths . . 31 May ,,
Disagreements in the diet; ordered to be closed, 17 May, 1893
Disturbances of workmen at Prague and Brünn, suppressed . . . . . . 18 June ,,
Repression of the Young Czech agitation in Prague, about . . . . 12 Sept. ,,
Amnesty granted for political offences; announced (see *Prague*, Dec. 1897) . . . . 5 Nov. 1895
New language ordinance issued . . . Jan. 1898
Palacky (Czech historian) centenary of birth celebrated . . . . . . 19 June, ,,
Strike riots at Machod, 7 Jewish shops sacked and burnt, troops called out . . 5, 6 April, 1899
Card. count Schoenborn, abp. of Prague, died, aged 55, about . . . . . 25 June, ,,
Fatal riots at Graslitz, troops called in, 20 Aug. ,,
Language ordinances repealed, announced 17 Oct. ,,
The emperor warmly received at Prague, 12–18 June, 1901
Diet elections completed, Czech majority, 17 Oct. ,,
Budget and language question discussed in the diet . . . . 24 July, 1902

Bohemian language is the Czech, one of the most cultivated of the Slavonic dialects, it is also spoken in Moravia and N. Hungary; its literature divides itself into three periods. From the earliest time to the burning of Huss, 1415; from 1415 to Josef II.'s edict of toleration, 1781; and thence to the present time. The Bible translated during the 13th and 14th centuries. Thomas of Stitny, *theo.* and *rh.* 1373–1400; John Huss, *theo.* 1369–1415; A. J. Puchmajer, *p.* 1795–1814; Polak's poem, "Sublimity of Nature," 1819; Dr. Polacky's history completed in German, 1867; in Bohemian, 1876.

KINGS.

1198. Premislas Ottocar I.
1230. Wenceslas III.
1253. Premislas Ottocar II.
1278. Wenceslas IV., king of Poland.
1305. Wenceslas V.
1306. Rudolph of Austria.
1307. Henry of Carinthia.
1310. John of Luxemburg (killed at Crecy).
1346. Charles I., emperor (1347).
1378. Wenceslas VI., emperor.
1419. Sigismund I., emperor.
1438. Albert of Austria, emperor.
1440. Ladislas V.
1458. George von Podiebrad.
1471. Ladislas VI., king of Hungary (in 1490).
1516. Louis, king of Hungary (killed at Mohatz).
1526. Bohemia united to Austria under Ferdinand I. elected king. See *Germany*, emperors.

BOHEMIAN BRETHREN, a body of Christians in Bohemia, appear to have separated from the Calixtines (*which see*), a branch of the Hussites in 1467. Dupin says "They rejected the sacraments of the church, were governed by simple laics, and held the scriptures for their only rule of faith. They presented a confession of faith to king Ladislas in 1504 to justify themselves from errors laid to their charge." Luther, in 1533, testifies to their purity of doctrine, and Melanchthon commends their discipline. They were dispersed during the religious wars of Germany in the 17th century.

BOHN'S LIBRARIES. Mr. H. G. Bohn began the publication of his "Standard Library" in 1846. This was followed by the classical, antiquarian, scientific and illustrated libraries, above 600 volumes. These were bought by Messrs. Bell and Daldy in 1864, who have added many other volumes. Mr. Bohn died 22 Aug. 1884, aged 90. His pictures, china, and works of art by sale, realized 45,000*l.* in 1885.

BOII, a Celtic people of N. Italy, who emigrated into Italy, and were defeated at the Vadimonian lake, 283 B.C. They were finally subdued by Scipio Nasica, 191 B.C.

BOILERS, Steam. Many lives have been lost by their explosions. 23 persons were killed at Glasgow iron-works, 5 March, 1879; and 21 killed at the Birchill ironworks, near Walsall, 15 May, 1880. Boilers Explosion Act, passed 1882, amended in 1890. See also *Navy Boilers*.

By the explosion of a defective neglected boiler at Mr. Mattison's bedding manufactory, Rhodeswell Road, Stepney, 4 men were killed and 17 persons injured, 31 May, 1886.

The annual average of explosions in six years ending June, 1888, was 47; deaths 30.

1871–1890, 1,005 persons killed; June, 1892–93, 20 deaths; June, 1893–94, 24 deaths; June, 1894–95, 43 deaths; June, 1895–96, 25 deaths; June, 1896–97, 27 deaths; 1898–99, 36 deaths; 1900–01, 33 deaths; 1901–2, 30 deaths.

Committee of inquiry issue report favouring legal inspection, 20 July, 1900.

BOILING TO DEATH, made a capital punishment in England, by stat. 22 Hen. VIII., 1531 (repealed in 1547). This act was occasioned by seventeen persons having been poisoned by Richard Rosse, otherwise Coke, the bishop of Rochester's cook, two of whom died. Margaret Davy, a young woman, suffered in the same manner for a similar crime, 28 March, 1542. *Stow.*

BOIS-LE-DUC, Dutch Brabant, the site of a battle between the British and the French republican army, in which the British were defeated, and forced to abandon their position and retreat to Schyndel, 14 Sept. 1794. This place was captured by the French, 10 Oct. following; it surrendered to the Prussian army, under Bulow, in Jan. 1814.

BOKHARA, the ancient Sogdiana, after successively forming part of the empires of Persia, of Alexander, and Bactriana, was conquered by the Turks in the 6th century, by the Chinese in the 7th, and by the Arabs about 705. After various changes of masters it was subdued by the Uzbek Tartars, its present possessors, in 1505. The British envoys, colonel Stoddart and captain Conolly, were murdered at Bokhara, the capital, by the khan, about 17 June, 1842. Bokhara was visited by Dr. Joseph Wolff in 1844. In the war with Russia, begun in 1866, the emir's army was defeated several times in May, *et seq.* Peace was made 11 July, 1867. The Russians were again victors, 25 May, 1868, and occupied Samarcand the next day. Further conquests were made by the Russians, and Samarcand was secured by treaty, Nov. 1868. A new political and commercial treaty with Russia was published Dec. 1873. The right of the present khan, Saïd-Abdul-Ahad, since 1885, to the government being disputed, he appealed to Russia for protection Dec. 1890. Population 1891, estimated 1,250,000; 1894, 2,130,000. The emir visits Russia: at Moscow, 8 Jan., at St. Petersburg, 13 Jan.–9 Feb. 1893; again, May-June, 1898. See *Asia*.

BOLIVIA, a republic in South America, formerly part of Peru, population in 1875, about 2,000,000; in 1880, 2,325,000; 1890, 1,189,800; 1897 (estimated) 2,000,000.

The insurrection of the ill-used Indians, headed by Tupac Amaru Andres, took place here . . . 1780–2
The country declared its independence . . 6 Aug. 1824
Secured by the victory of Ayacucho . . 9 Dec. ,,
Took the name of Bolivia, in honour of general Bolivar . . . . 11 Aug. 1825
First congress met . . . . . . 25 May, 1826
General Sucre governed ably 1826-8
Slavery abolished 1836
Santa Cruz ruled 1828-39
Gen. Velasco, president. . . . . . 9 Feb. 1839
José Ballivian, president . . . . . . in 1841
Gen. Belzu . . . . until 1855
Free-trade proclaimed 1853
General Cordova, president 1855-7
Succeeded by José Maria Linares . . 31 March, 1859
George Cordova, constitutional president . . 1860
Succeeded by José M. de Acha . . . . May, 1861
General Melgarejo defeats the troops of president De Acha . . . . 28 Dec. 1864
Becomes dictator of the republic . . . Feb. 1865
Puts down an insurrection under Belzu, March, ,,
Totally defeats Arguedas at Viacha and publishes an amnesty . . . . 24 Jan. 1866
Suppresses a revolt . . . . . . 17 Oct. ,,
Proclaims an amnesty . . . . . 21 Dec. 1867
Civil war 1867–70
The president, A. Morales, 1871; said to have been murdered . . . . Jan. 1873
President, Dr. Tomas Frias . . . . 14 Feb. 1874
Corral's insurrection suppressed . . . . Sept. ,,
General Hilarion Daza, president . . . 4 May, 1876
Bolivia joins Peru in war against Chili (see *Chili*) April, 1879
Revolution; Daza deposed; flees; Campero president . . . . 1 June, 1880
Peace with Chili; conditions finally settled . Dec. 1883
Aniceto Arce (president 15 Aug.) suppresses a revolution . . . . Oct. 1888
Insurrection of gen. Camacho suppressed, sen. Don Mariano Baptista declared president . 8 Aug. 1892
Ultimatum addressed to Peru, demanding satisfaction, within 24 hours, for invasion of territory during the civil war, 10 July; Bolivian minister recalled; invasion of Peruvian troops, reported, 15 July; the dispute to be referred to arbitration . . . . 23 Aug. 1895
Sen. Matta, the Chilian minister, assassinated by José Cuellar, 15 Aug.; died . . 16 Aug. 1896
Severo Fernandez Alonso assumes the presidency; reported . . . . 20 Aug. ,,
Revolutionary outbreak; government forces defeated near La Paz . . . . 17 Jan. 1899
The Corocoro mining works attacked by the Indians, the manager kills his wife and colleague and himself to avoid surrender; reported . . 8 Feb. ,,
Revolutionists victorious; gen. Pando enters Oruro, pres. Alonso flies; reported . . 21 April, ,,
Frontier line of Cunha to Gomez adopted, Sep. ,,
Gen. Pando elected president . . . 24 Oct. ,,
Rupture with Brazil: Bolivians defeated by Brazilians in the Acre territory, state of siege declared . . . . 9 Nov. 1902
Arbitration treaty with Peru respecting boundaries signed . . . . 2 Jan. 1903
Modus vivendi re Acre disputes signed . March ,,

BOLLANDISTS, see *Acta Sanctorum*.

BOLOGNA (central Italy), the ancient Felsina, afterwards Bononia, a city distinguished for its architecture, made a Roman colony, 189 B.C. Population 1890, 143,607; 1901, 152,009.

A university said to have been founded by Theodosius, about 433; really in 1116
Bologna joins the Lombard League 1167
Pope Julius II. takes Bologna; enters in triumph 11 Nov. 1506
It becomes part of the states of the Church . . 1513
In the church of St. Petronius, remarkable for its pavement, Cassini drew his meridian line (over one drawn by Father Ignatius Dante in 1575) . 1653

Bologna was taken by the French, 1796; by the Austrians, 1799; again by the French, after the battle of Marengo, in 1800; and restored to the pope in 1815
A revolt suppressed by Austrian interference . . 1831
Rebellion, 1848; taken by Austrians . 16 May, 1849
The Austrians evacuate Bologna: and cardinal Ferretti departs: the citizens rise and form a provisional government . . . . . 12 June, 1859
Which decrees that all public acts shall be headed "Under the reign of king Victor Emmanuel," &c. 1 Oct. ,,
He enters Bologna as sovereign . . . 2 May, 1860
Exhibition opened by the king and queen . 6 May, 1888
The king unveils statue of Victor Emmanuel, 11 June; establishment of the University celebrated . . . . 11–16 June, ,,
Serious affray between the army and the populace through caricatures in a Bologna paper, 1, 2 Aug. 1891

BOLOMETER (Greek *bolos*, a throw or cast), an electrical instrument, invented by prof. S. P. Langley, of U.S., who also terms it an "actinic balance." It is much more sensitive to radiant heat than the thermopile (*Nature*, 3 Nov. 1881). By its means he made discoveries in the ultra red rays of the spectrum.

BOLTON, Lancashire, was stormed by prince Rupert, 1644. It was an early seat of the cotton manufacture. Cotton velvets were made here in 1756, and muslins in 1782. Temple Opera-house burned 16 April, 1882. Bayley's cotton works burned, several persons killed, and many injured; about 60,000*l*. worth damaged, 16 Aug. 1882. See *Strikes* 1887, 1890. Population 1881, 105,414; 1891, 115,002; 1901, 168,205.

Theatre Royal burnt, 4 Jan.; 100*l*. reward for discovery of suspected incendiary, about 5 Jan. 1888. Robert Preston sentenced to twelve years' penal servitude for arson, 7 Feb. 1888.
Great fire at the co-operative stores, estimated damage 50,000*l*., 1 June, 1902; part of messrs. Blair & Sumner's bleachworks gutted, estimated damage 40,000*l*. 30 Aug. 1902.

BOMARSUND, a strong fortress on one of the Aland isles in the Baltic sea, taken by sir Charles Napier, commander of the Baltic expedition, aided by the French military contingent under general Baraguay d'Hilliers, 15 Aug. 1854. The governor Bodisco, and the garrison, about 2000 men, became prisoners. The fortifications were destroyed.

BOMBAY, the most westerly and smallest of our Indian presidencies, was visited by the Portuguese in 1509, and acquired by them in 1530. It was given (with Tangier in Africa, and 300,000*l*. in money) to Charles II. as the marriage portion of the infanta Catherine of Portugal, 1662. In 1668, it was granted to the East India company, who had long desired it, "in free and common socage," as of the manor of East Greenwich, at an annual rent of 10*l*. Confirmed by William III. 1689. The two principal castes at Bombay are the Parsees (descendants of the ancient Persian fire-worshippers) and the Borahs (sprung from early converts to Islamism). They are both remarkable for commercial activity. Population: presidency, 1881, 16,469,199; 1891, 18,873,342; 1901, 25,500,000 (city and island, 776,006).

First British factory established at Ahmednuggur . 1612
Mr. Gyfford, deputy-governor, 100 soldiers, and other English, perish through the climate, Oct. 1675—Feb. 1676
Captain Keigwin usurps the government . . 1681-84
Bombay made chief over the company's settlements 1687
The whole island, except the fort, seized and held for a time by the mogul's admiral. 1690
Bombay becomes a distinct presidency . . 1708
Additions to the Bombay territory:—Bancot river, 1756; island of Salsette 1775
Bishopric established 1837
Lord Elphinstone governor 1853
The benevolent sir Jamsetjee Jejeebhoy, a Parsee (who erected several hospitals, &c.), dies 15 April, 1859
His son sir Cursetjee, visits England 1860
Sir G. R. Clerk, governor . . . . ,,
Rioting against the income-tax suppressed Nov. Dec. ,,
Sir Henry Bartle Frere, governor . . . March, 1862
Greatly increased prosperity through the cotton trade, leads to immense speculation . . Nov. 1864
Reported failure of Mr. Byramjee Cama, a Parsee, for 3,300,000*l*.; other failures, and great depression; the projected international exhibition in 1867 abandoned . . . . May, 1865
Recovering from commercial crisis . . . Aug. ,,
Mr. (after sir) W. R. Seymour Fitzgerald, appointed governor, Nov. 1866; arrived . . . 28 Feb. 1867
Held a durbar of native princes, at Poona . 6 Oct. 1868
Grand reception of the duke of Edinburgh, 11 March, 1870
Sir Philip Wodehouse, governor . . . April, 1872
Riots: Mahometans attack Parsees for publishing part of Washington Irving's "Life of Mahomet"; lives lost and property destroyed . 13-15 Feb. 1874
Culprits punished by the British . . . . . ,,
The prince of Wales warmly received, 8 Nov. 1875; sailed from here for home . . . 13 March, 1876
Meeting of loyal Mahometans to petition the queen in favour of the Sultan . . . . 24 Sept. ,,
Sir Richard Temple, governor . . . . early 1877
Dreadful famine, relieved by government and by British subscriptions . . . . ,,
Statue of the prince of Wales (given by sir Albert Sassoon), uncovered . . 26 or 27 June, 1879
Sir James Fergusson nominated governor . Feb. 1880
A patriotic fund to relieve sufferers by Afghan war, liberally subscribed to by natives and others, Aug. ,,
Lord Reay appointed governor . . . . Dec. 1884
Native troops sail for the Soudan . . 23 Feb. 1885
For the Crawford Case, see *India* 1889
George R. Canning, Lord Harris, appointed governor (Lord Reay having resigned), 18 Nov., 1889; arrives . . . . 11 April, 1890
An epidemic prevails resembling influenza, Feb.–March, ,,
The duke of Connaught commander-in-chief of Bombay, with the duchess, much esteemed, leaves for home . . . . 13 March, ,,
Prince Albert Victor of Wales lands at Bombay, 9 Nov. 1889, after a tour in India; departs for England . . . . 28 March, ,,
Lady Dufferin's hospital for women opened by the viceroy . . . . 24 Oct. ,,
The collapse of a large ill-built house in the city; about 30 persons killed . . . . . 17 Dec. ,,
Great fire at Poonah, over 200 houses destroyed 12 Jan. 1891
Destructive floods through heavy rains about 29 July, ,,
The viceroy opens the new Bombay waterworks, great undertaking, designed by major Tulloch 31 March, 1892
62 persons drowned in the great tank . 17 April, 1893
Banking difficulties . . . . March–May, ,,
Gen. sir John Hudson, commander of Bombay army, killed by a fall from his horse, 9 June; succeeded by major-gen. C. E. Nairne . Aug. ,,
Hindoo and Mahometan rioting quelled by troops end of June; renewed; about 60 persons killed; mosques and temples desecrated, 11, 13 Aug.; 1,500 arrests . . . . 15 Aug. ,,
(Riots attributed to the Cow Protection Society.)
Bombay and Madras Armies Act passed . 5 Dec. ,,
Lord Sandhurst appointed governor, Dec. 1894, arrived . . . . 18 Feb. 1895
Statue of Lord Reay unveiled by lord Sandhurst, 19 Dec. ,,
Lord Sandhurst cuts the first sod of the Ahmadabad-Prantij railway . . . . . . 14 Feb. 1896
Sir Albert Sassoon, an eminent benefactor of the city, born 1818, died at Brighton . 24 Oct. ,,
Epidemic of bubonic plague in Bombay city; remedial measures adopted; segregation of patients, &c., Oct.; panic and exodus, scarcity of food, rioting and bloodshed at Sholapur, 8 Nov. 1896; great mortality among cattle, no fodder Jan. 1897

Population returning, 30 April; mortality about normal . . . . 28 May, 1897
Many persons inoculated by Dr. Haffkine; a monthly salary granted him by government, May, ,,
Death of surgeon-major Robt. Manser, of the Jamsetjee hospital, active investigator of the plague 6 Jan. ,,
Lieut. C. E. Ayerst shot dead while driving, and Mr. W. C. Rand, Poona plague commissioner, mortally wounded near Poona . . 22 June, ,,
Seditious leaflets circulated in Poona and Bombay, June; incendiary articles in native journals against the government, &c., reported 24 June, ,,
Punitive police force occupies Poona 30 June, ,,
Meeting of citizens, firm speech of Mr. Lamb, magistrate . . . . 30 June, ,,
The brothers Natu (two Brahmins) imprisoned and deported for disloyalty to the British government under a lettre de cachet law of 1827; (released May, 1898;) other native editors arrested 28, 29 July, ,,
Large peaceful meeting of Mahomedans and Hindus at Poona . . . . 2 Aug. ,,
Plague increasing in Bombay and Poona, Aug.-Nov. ,,
Trial of Mr. Tilak for seditious writing begins, 8 Sept.; sentenced to 18 months' imprisonment, 14 Sept.; appeal rejected, 24 Sept.; others convicted . . . . Nov. ,,
Reconstruction of the city, sanitation, etc., supported by government . . . . . Oct. ,,
Serious riot in Gujarat, 5 sepoys killed; reported 13 Jan. 1898
Destructive riots against the plague measures at Sinnar, a hospital assistant killed; 150 arrests 29 Jan. ,,
Damodar Chapekar confesses to the murder of Mr. Rand and lieut. Ayerst (see above, 22 June), 4 Oct. 1897; tried, sentenced to death . . 3 Feb. ,,
Great increase of plague since Dec. 1897; exodus and stagnation of business; 71,000 deaths from Sept. 1896, to end of Feb. 1898; serious rioting with loss of life, troops called out; many arrests, 9–11 March; town quiet, 14 March; plague riot in Garshanker, a village, 9 rioters killed, 29 April, ,,
Dr. Haffkine reports 8,200 persons inoculated during the winter, 1897—8.
Plague commission (prof. T. R. Fraser, F.R.S.), president, arrives 26 Nov. 1898; see *India*, Nov. 1898 and Nov. 1901; exodus of natives continues, Feb. 1899; 3rd epidemic, average deaths daily 350 (lord Sandhurst actively superintends relief measures), 6 camps and 26 plague hospitals in Bombay, segregation successful, total deaths 94,000, up to . . . . 3 March, 1899
Two Brahmins named Dravid, witnesses against Chapekar, see above, assassinated at Poona, 8 Feb. ,,
Vasudev Chapekar and two others sentenced to death for the murder of Mr. Rand and lieut. Ayerst; Salhe, an accomplice, to 10 years imprisonment . . . . 5 March, ,,
Lieut.-gen. sir Chas. Nairne, late commander-in-chief, died, aged 62 . . . . . 19 Feb. ,,
Serious caste riots in the Tinnevelli and Madura districts, 150 villages attacked, houses burnt, 25 persons killed, 6–13 June; quiet restored, 22 June, ,,
Failure of the monsoon, famine relief started mid. Sept. ,,
See *India*, 1900, 1901, 1902.
Plague increasing; many deaths reported, 20 Dec. 1899; high mortality, 376 deaths on 12 Jan. 1900, 408 deaths on . . . . 6 Feb. 1900
Sir Stafford Northcote appointed governor, Oct. 1899; made a peer Jan. 1900; arrives . 16 Feb. ,,
Cholera mortality high, specially in famine-stricken districts, May, *et seq.*; 6,669 deaths in week ending . . . . 23 June, ,,
Plague reappears in Bombay; many deaths, 13 Feb.; 400 deaths . . . . . . 25, 26 Feb. 1901
Sir Dinshaw M. Petit, eminent Parsee millionaire and benefactor, died, aged 78 . . 5 May, ,,
Land revenue bill passed by the legislative council, 25 Aug. ,,
Good rainfall, rapid decrease of famine relief, reported . . . . 2 Sept. ,,
Lord Lamington appointed governor in succession to lord Northcote . . . . . . Aug. 1903
Departure of lord Northcote (see *Australia*) 5 Sept. ,,

BOMBS (iron shells filled with gunpowder), said to have been invented at Venlo, in 1495, and used by the Turks at the siege of Rhodes in 1522. They came into general use in 1634, having been previously used only by the Dutch and Spaniards. Bomb-vessels were invented in France in 1681. *Voltaire*. The *shrapnel* shell (invented by colonel Henry Shrapnel, who died in 1842) is a bomb filled with balls, and a lighted fuse to make it explode before it reaches the enemy.

BONA, Algeria; an early station of the French African company, till 1789. It was taken by the French from the Arabs, 6 May, 1832.

BONAPARTE, or **BUONAPARTE, FAMILY.** The name appears at Florence and Genoa in the 13th century; in the 15th a branch settled in Corsica. See Table in Vincent's "Dictionary of Biography."

CHARLES BONAPARTE, born 29 March, 1746, died 24 Feb., 1785. He married in 1767, Letitia Ramolina (born 24 Aug., 1750, died Feb. 1836); ISSUE,

1. JOSEPH, born 7 Jan. 1768, made king of Two Sicilies, 1805; of Naples alone, 1806; of Spain, 1808; resides in United States, 1815; comes to England, 1832; settles in Italy, 1841; dies at Florence, 28 July, 1844.
2. NAPOLEON I., emperor, born 15 Aug. 1769 (see *France*.)
3. LUCIEN, prince of Canino, born 1775; at first aided his brother Napoleon, but opposed his progress towards universal monarchy. He was taken by the English on his way to America, and resided in England till 1814. He died at Viterbo, 30 June, 1840. His son Charles (born 1803, died 1857) was an eminent naturalist. Charles Napoleon, prince of Canino, born 1839, died about 12 Feb. 1899. His granddaughter, Mme. Studolmine Bonaparte Wyse (Rattazzi), a brilliant woman and writer, died, aged about 71, 6 Feb. 1902. Louis Lucien, an eminent philologist, born in 1813; published his translations of parts of the Bible in several English dialects; received a pension of 250*l.* from the British government; died 3 Nov. 1891.
4. LOUIS, born 2 Sept. 1778; made king of Holland, 1806; died 15 July, 1846. By his marriage with Hortense Beauharnais (daughter of the empress Josephine), in 1802, he had three sons: 1. Napoleon Louis (born 1803, died 1807); 2. Louis Napoleon (born 1804, died 1831); and
   3. CHARLES-LOUIS-NAPOLEON, born 20 April, 1808; educated under the care of his mother at Aremberg, Switzerland, and at Thun, under general Dufour; took part in the Carbonari insurrection in the Papal States in March, 1831
   Attempted a revolt at Strasbourg, 30 Oct. 1836.
   Sent to America, 13 Nov. 1836.
   Repairs to London, 14 Oct. 1838.
   Lands at Boulogne with fifty followers, 6 Aug. 1840.
   Condemned to imprisonment for life, 6 Oct. 1840.
   Escapes from Ham, 25 May, 1846.
   Arrives at Boulogne, 2 March, 1848.
   Elected deputy, 8 June; and takes his seat, 27 Aug.
   see *France* 1848-71: died at Chislehurst, 9 Jan. 1873.
   Son: Napoleon Eugène Louis Jean Joseph; born 16 March, 1856; educated at military academy, Woolwich; killed in Zululand, June 1, 1879.
   Both buried at Chislehurst; removed to a mausoleum at Farnborough, 9 Jan. 1888.
5. JEROME, born 15 Nov. 1784; king of Westphalia, 1 Dec. 1807-1814; [married: I. Elizabeth Paterson, in America, 24 Dec. 1803; son Jerome, born at Camberwell, London, 7 July, 1805 (she died, aged 94, 4 April, 1879). II. Princess Catherine, of Würtemberg, 12 Aug. 1807.] Made governor of the Invalides, 1848; and marshal, 1850; died 24 June, 1860; his children—
   Mathilde, born 27 May, 1820; married to prince A. Demidoff in 1841.
   Napoleon, born 9 Sept. 1822; married princess Clotilde of Savoy, 30 Jan. 1859, died 17 March, 1891: issue, Victor, born 18 July, 1862; Louis, born 16 July, 1864; Marie, born 20 Dec. 1866; prince Victor separates from his father; accepted as chief by the Bonapartists; the father publishes painful correspondence, June, 1884. Expelled from France (see *France*) May–June, 1886; disinherited March, 1891; accepted as head of the family 31 March, 1891.

BOND, Dutch for league, a name adopted by the Dutch-speaking population of Southern Africa, see *Afrikander* and *Boers*. BONDS, see *Foreign*.

BONDAGE, see *Villanage*.

BONDED WAREHOUSES, see *Excise*.

BONES. The art of softening bones was discovered about 1688, and they were used in the cutlery manufacture, &c., immediately afterwards. The declared value of the bones of cattle and of other animals, and of fish (exclusive of whale-fins) imported into the United Kingdom from Russia, Prussia, Holland, Denmark, &c., amounted to 363,613*l.* in 1851, to 659,416*l.* in 1871, to 741,899*l.* in 1877, to 617,748*l.* in 1883, to 313,765*l.* in 1887, to 449,526*l.* in 1890. Bone-dust has been extensively employed in manure since the publication of Liebig's researches in 1840.

BONE-SETTING cannot be said to have been practised scientifically until 1620. *Bell.*

The ignorant "bone-setters" often did good and often harm; the principle upon which they acted is now adopted by surgeons: and is set forth in Dr. Wharton Hood's work on "The Setting and Treatment of Joints," 1871.

Mr. John Hutton, an eminent (unprofessional) "bone-setter," died July, 1887.

BON MARCHÉ (cheap). Name given by some shopkeepers in London to their mode of selling goods to the poor at very small profits; now applied to great establishments in London, Paris, and many large provincial towns. The system was originated at Paris by Mdme. Boucicault, originally a shop-girl; about 1842, she, with her husband, opened a shop in the time of deep distress for meeting the wants of the poorest people. In time her business greatly increased with enlarged premises, and she adopted the system of the division of profits with her employed. She realised a large fortune, and became a munificent benefactress of the city. She died in Dec. 1887, worth it is said four million pounds sterling. M. Crespin de Vidouville, a similar eccentric character, died at Paris 20 Feb. 1888.

BONN, a town on the Rhine (the Roman Bonna), was in the electorate of Cologne. It has been frequently besieged, and was assigned to Prussia in 1814. The academy founded by the elector in 1777, made a university 1784; abolished by Napoleon; re-established and enlarged, 1818. Here Albert, our late prince consort, was entered as a student, May, 1837. Population 1890, 39,801; 1900, 50,737.

BONNY RIVER, Guinea, West Africa; a seat of the palm oil trade; king George visited England in 1878. A sanguinary battle was fought between the king Oko Jumbo and the people of New Calabar, who were defeated, 9 April, 1882. Peace made by British intervention on Aug. 14, 1882.

King Oko Jumbo visited London, summer 1885; left 15 July, 1885; his death reported Aug. 1891.

Government offices, etc., destroyed by fire at Old Calabar, 24 Nov. 1895.

Death of king Duke, the last of the Old Calabar kings, at Duketown, early Nov. 1896.

See *Niger Coast Protectorate*.

BONS HOMMES, hermits of simple and gentle lives, appeared in France about 1257; in England about 1283. The prior of the order was called *le bon homme* by Louis VI.

BOOK (Anglo-Saxon, *boc*; German, *buch*). Books were originally made of boards, or the inner bark of trees: afterwards of skins and parchment. Papyrus, an indigenous plant, was adopted in Egypt. Books with leaves of vellum were invented by Attalus, king of Pergamus, about 198 B.C., at which time books were in volumes or rolls. The MSS. in Herculaneum consist of papyrus, rolled and charred and matted together by the fire, and are about nine inches long, and one, two, or three inches in diameter, each being a separate treatise. The first PRINTED BOOKS (see *Printing*) were printed on one side only, the leaves being pasted back to back. See *Libraries*.

Title-pages to printed books in England were not introduced till shortly before 1490, they were used by Wynkyn de Worde, but not by Caxton, in the 15th century. Mr. A. W. Pollard's "Last words on Title-pages," appeared in 1891. See *Printing*.

Books of astronomy and geometry were ordered to be destroyed in England as being infected with magic, 6 Edw. VI. (*Stow*) 1552

Anne's act, 1709, relating to the price of books, repealed 1739

2032 volumes of new works, and 773 of new editions, were published in London in 1839

3359 new works, and 1159 new editions, and 908 pamphlets, were published in 1852

3553 volumes were published in 1864

Published in Great Britain:—

	New Works.	New Editions.		New Works.	New Editions.
1870	4775		1887	4410	1276
1871	3547	1288	1888	4960	1631
1872	3419	1100	1889	4694	1373
1874	3351	961	1890	4414	1321
1875	3573	1331	1891	4429	1277
1876	2931	1957	1892	4915	1339
1877	3049	2046	1893	5129	1253
1878	3730	1584	1894	5300	1185
1879	4294	1540	1895	5581	935
1880	4293	1415	1896	5234	1339
1881	4110	1296	1897	6244	1682
1882	3978	1146	1898	6008	1508
1883	4732	1413	1899	5971	1596
1884	4832	1541	1900	5760	1389
1885	4307	1333	1901	6044	
1886	3984	1226	1902	7381	

The production of a Universal Catalogue of books printed in the United Kingdom, proposed by the Society of Arts, in the "Journal" . 11 April, 1879

See *Bibliography*.

PRICES OF BOOKS.—Jerome (who died 420) states that he had ruined himself by buying a copy of the works of Origen. A large estate was given by Alfred for a book on cosmography, about 872. The *Roman de la Rose* was sold for about 30*l.*; and a homily was exchanged for 200 sheep and five quarters of wheat. Books frequently fetched double or treble their weight in gold. They sold at prices varying from 10*l.* to 40*l.* each in 1400. A copy of *Macklin's Bible*, ornamented by Mr. Tomkins, was declared worth 500 guineas. *Butler.* A yet more superb copy was insured in a London office for 3000*l.* See *Boccaccio's Decamerone*.

Petrarca by Bernardino di Novara, 1488, at the Sunderland sale bought by B. Quaritch for 1950*l.*, 11 Nov. 1882; he gave for sir John Thorold's Mazarin bible, 3900*l.* 13 Dec.; and his "Psalmorum Codex," 4950*l.* . . . . 19 Dec. 1884

BOOK-BINDING.—The book of St. Cuthbert, a very early ornamental book, is supposed to have been bound about 650

A Latin Psalter was bound in oak boards, 9th, century.

A MS. copy of the four Evangelists, the book on which our kings from Henry I. to Edward VI. took their coronation oath, was bound in oaken boards, nearly an inch thick . . . . . .

Velvet was the covering in the 14th century; and silk soon after. Vellum was introduced early in the 15th century; it was stamped and ornamented about 1100

Leather came into use about the same time.

The rolling machine, invented by Mr. Wm. Burr, was substituted for the beating-hammer, and gas stoves began to take the place of the charcoal fires used to heat the gilder's finishing tools, about 1830
Cloth binding superseded the common boards generally about 1831
Caoutchouc or india-rubber backs to account-books and large volumes were introduced in . . . 1841
The use of thin metal plates instead of pasteboard introduced 1886
"Bookbindings" by Eyre and Spottiswoode 1895
"English book-bindings in the British museum," 1896, and "Foreign book-bindings," by W. Y. Fletcher 1897
Exhibition at the Society of Arts, opened 24 Jan. *et seq.* 1898

CHEAP BOOKS.—Mrs. (aft. lady) Brassey's "Voyage of the Sunbeam," Nov. 1881, published for sixpence (she died, 14 Sept. 1887); and Martin's "Life of the Prince Consort," for 2s. 6d. Autumn 1881

BOOK-HAWKING SOCIETIES (already in Scotland) begun in England in 1851 by archdeacon Wigram (afterwards bishop of Rochester). The hawkers vend moral and religious books in a similar manner to the French colporteurs.
"Books about Books," a series, 1893, *et seq.* Mr. W. J. Hardy's "Book Plates," 1893, *et seq.*
A Book Plate or Ex Libris society was formed in 1891; exhibitions held in London . . 1894–5
"The Book-hunter in London," by Mr. Wm. Roberts, is full of information . . Nov. 1895
H. B. Wheatley's "Prices of Books" published, Aug. 1898
"Book Prices Current. Prices at which Books have been sold at auction." Vol. 1, 1887; vol. 16, Oct. 1902

BOOK-KEEPING. The system by double-entry, called originally Italian book-keeping, was taken from the course of algebra published by Burgo, in the 15th century, at Venice. John Gowghe, a printer, published a treatise "on the kepyng of the famouse reconynge . . . Debitor and Creditor," London, 1543. This is our earliest work on book-keeping. James Peele published his *Book-keeping* in 1569. John Mellis published "A Briefe Instruction and Manner how to Keepe Bookes of Accompts," in 1588. Improved systems were published by Benjamin Booth in 1789 and by Edw. Thos. Jones in 1821 and 1831.

BOOK OF COMMON PRAYER, see *Common Prayer*. "*Book of the Dead*," see *Dead*. *Book of Sports*, see *Sports*. *Book Post*, see *Post*.

BOOK SOCIETY, 28, Paternoster-row, established for the gratuitous distribution of bibles and good books, 1750.

BOOKS, National, Coloured. See under *Blue-Books*.

BOOKSELLERS, at first migratory like hawkers, became known as *stationarii*, from their practice of having booths or stalls at the corners of streets and in markets. They were long subject to vexatious restrictions, from which they were freed in 1758.

The earliest bookseller's catalogue is said to be that published by Andrew Maunsell, of Lothbury, dedicated to queen Elizabeth, 1595.
"Booksellers' Provident Institution" founded 1837; "Retreat," Abbot's Langley, Herts, 1843.
The *Bookseller*, a monthly newspaper of British and foreign literature, published in 1858; with it was incorporated *Bent's Literary Advertiser*, established in 1802.

BOOKSELLERS' ASSOCIATION. For upwards of 100 years publishers associated to bring out works of reference and books of a popular character. This kind of partnership was usually agreed at a trade dinner of the associated booksellers. This custom developed into the trade dinners given annually by leading publishers, at which prices and issues of important works were settled. Messrs. Longman & Co.'s last dinner was in 1872, John Murray's in 1887, Messrs. Bentley & Son, 1897. On 29 Dec. 1828, the chief publishers in London formed themselves into an association and fixed the amount of discount to be allowed, and restricted the retail booksellers from selling copies of works under the full publishing price. A dispute arose which was referred to lord chief justice Campbell, at Stratheden house, 14 April. 1852. His lordship gave judgment against the association, which led to its dissolution, 19 May following. The London Booksellers' society was formed; the inaugural dinner took place 2 Oct. 1890. Association of booksellers of Great Britain, conferences held 1895.

BOOTHIA FELIX, a large peninsula, N.W. point of America, discovered by sir John Ross in 1830, and named after sir Felix Booth, who had presented him with 20,000*l.* to fit out his polar expedition. Sir Felix died at Brighton in Feb. 1850.

BOOTHISM, see *Salvation Army*.

BOOTS, said to have been the invention of the Carians, were mentioned by Homer, 907 B.C., and frequently by the Roman historians. A variety of forms may be seen in Fairholt's "Costume in England." An instrument of torture termed "*the boot*" was used in Scotland upon the covenanters about 1666.

A new system of boot-making introduced by Mr. M. L. Lion and Mr. F. Cutlan, reversing the ordinary method, July, 1887.
See *Strikes*, March, 1890, Aug. 1892, *et seq.* 6 March–19 April, 1895.
National conference of the boot and shoe trade at Leicester, Jan. 1894.
Leicester arbitration board dissolved, 28 Feb. 1895.
Boots and shoes of our ancestors, as exhibited by the Cordwainers' company, by W. H. Button, 1898.
Great competition in the trade due to large American and foreign imports in recent years still continues in 1903.

BORAX (Boron), known to the ancients, used in soldering, brazing, and casting gold and other metals, was called *chrysocolla*. Borax is produced naturally in the mountains of Thibet, and was brought to Europe from India about 1713. Homberg in 1702 discovered in borax *boracic acid*, which latter in 1808 was decomposed by Gay-Lussac, Thénard, and H. Davy, into oxygen and the previously unknown element, *boron*. Borax has lately been found in Saxony. It is now largely manufactured from the boracic acid found in certain lagoons in Tuscany. Very largely used as an antiseptic and in preservation of perishable foods, 1903.

BORDEAUX (W. France), the Roman Burdigalla, in Aquitania, was taken by the Goths, 412; by Clovis, 508. It was gained by Henry II. on his marriage with Eleanor of Aquitaine, 1151. Edward the Black Prince brought John, king of France, captive to this city after the battle of Poictiers, 19 Sept. 1356, and here held his court eleven years: his son, our Richard II., was born at Bordeaux, 1366. After several changes Bordeaux finally surrendered to Charles VII. of France, 14 Oct. 1453. The fine equestrian statue of Louis XV. was erected in 1743. Bordeaux was entered by the victorious British army after the battle of Orthez, fought 27 Feb. 1814.—13 vessels were burnt and others injured in the port through the ignition and explosion of petroleum spirit, 28 Sept. 1869. The French delegate government and the representatives of foreign powers removed here from Tours, 11 Dec. 1870. M. Gambetta remained for a time with the army of the Loire. By the "pacte de Bordeaux," between the different parties of the national assembly, M. Thiers became chief of the executive power, 17 Feb. 1871. The French Association for the Advancement of Science held its first meeting here, 5 Sept. 1872; M. Quatrefages, president. Great fire in the pine forests, 10 persons perish, about 28 Aug. 1891. The Bordeaux wines, Medoc, Claret, etc. largely exported; see *Vines*, 1881–91, and *Wine*. Population, 1891, 238,899; 1901, 257,471.

BORNEO, an island in the Indian Ocean, the largest in the world except Australia and New Guinea, was early known to the Chinese.

The Dutch trade here in 1604; establish factories, 1609; abandon them, 1623; re-establish them . 1776
Sarawak settled by sir James Brooke; appointed rajah 1841
The pirates of Borneo chastised by the British in 1813, and by captain Keppel in . . March, 1843
By a treaty with the sultan, through the instrumentality of sir J. Brooke, the island of Labooan, or Labuan (N. W. of Borneo), and its dependencies, incorporated with the British empire, and formally taken possession of in presence of the Bornean chiefs . . . . 2 Dec. 1846
James Brooke, rajah of *Sarawak* (1846), governor of Labuan and consul-general of Borneo, visits England and receives many honours . . Oct. 1847
He destroys many of the Bornean pirates . . . 1849
Labuan made a bishopric; the bishop (F. J. MacDougall) consecrated at Calcutta, the first English bishop consecrated out of England . 18 Oct. 1855
The Chinese in Sarawak rise in insurrection and massacre a number of Europeans; sir J. Brooke escapes by swimming across a creek; he speedily returns with a force of Malays, &c., and chastises the insurgents, of whom 2000 are killed, 17, 18 Feb. 1857
He comes to England to seek help from the government, without success 1858
His health being broken up, an appeal for a subscription for him made . . . . ,,
Deputation of merchants waits on the earl of Derby recommending the purchase of Sarawak, which is declined . . . . 30 Nov. ,,
Sir J. Brooke returns to Borneo . . . 20 Nov. 1860
Returned to England; died, succeeded by his nephew, sir Charles Johnson Brooke (born 3 June, 1829) . . . . 11 June, 1868
The rajah of Sarawak, with an expedition of Malays and Dyaks, defeats and punishes a marauding decapitating tribe of Dyaks . . . . June, 1870
British North Borneo company gazetted, 8 Nov.; threatened protest of Spanish government Nov. 1881
Meeting of committee in London . . . 3 Oct. 1882
Freedom of trade in the archipelago settled by Great Britain, Germany, and Spain, 1877; further with Spain 1884
Sultan Hasim Jalilal Alam succeeds . . . May, 1885
North Borneo reported prosperous . . . May, ,,
Rebels defeated . . . 10 Feb., war over April, 1889
Rajah Brooke, of Sarawak, annexes the Limbang region of Brunei on . . . . 17 March, 1890
He proclaims his son, Charles Vyner Brooke, aged 17, his heir, as Rajah Muda: announced 7 Aug. 1891
North Borneo, with Sarawak and Brunei, constituted a British protectorate, 1885; governor, Charles V. Creagh, 1892; Leicester Paul Beaufort 1895
Mat Salleh, native chief, and 60 rebels attack and burn Gaja, 50 mi. north of Labuan; the treasury looted; Mr. Neubronner and two others taken prisoners, 11 July, 1897: rescued; flight of rebels . . . . 16 July, 1897
Ambong attacked by Mat Salleh, residency burnt down, rebels retreat to the hills . 13 Nov. ,,
Expedition of about 50 police, under adjutant Jones, Mr. Hewitt, the resident, and two officers, attack the rebel fort; adj. Jones and 6 Sikhs killed . . . . 13 Dec. 1897
Fort Ranau taken, 105 rebels killed . . 9 Jan. 1898
Final submission of Mat Salleh . . 19, 22 April, ,,
Gov. Beaufort and Mr. Fraser well received by Mat Salleh . . . . 23 Jan. 1899
British N. Borneo company occupy the Tambunan country by native request . . . . . July, ,,
Native rising under Mat Salleh; capt. Harrington captures 2 forts and villages . . 8, 9 Jan. 1900
Mat Salleh's fort bombarded, 21 Jan. *et seq.*; he and many others killed, 31 Jan.; the fort and many prisoners taken . . . . . 1 Feb. ,,
Kudat raided, but recaptured. . . . 28 April, ,,
The rajah of Sarawak's Trusun expedition reported successful . . . . 31 May, ,,
Mr. Hugh Clifford, governor . Jan.—21 Sept. ,,
Mr. E. W. Birch, C.M.G., appointed governor . . 1901
Railway opened from Jesselton, W. Coast, to Beaufort (60 m.) . . . . . . end March, ,,
Telegraphic communication between Kudat and London completed; reported . . 14 May, 1902
Strong punitive expedition under the rajah Mudah, Mr. Vyner Brooke, against Bantin, a Dyak chief, attacked by cholera, over 1000 deaths, 9–19 June, ,,
Rajah of Sarawak subdues the Dyak tribes, 2 Apr. 1903

BORNOU, an extensive kingdom in central Africa, explored by Denham and Clapperton (sent out by the British government), in 1822. The population is estimated by Denham at 5,000,000, by Barth at 9,000,000. Rabah, an adventurer who had subdued the kingdom; defeated and killed by the French at Kusli, reported, 20 July, 1900. *See French W. Africa* and *Niger Coast*, 1901-2.

BORODINO, a Russian village on the river Moskwa, near which a sanguinary battle was fought, 7 Sept. 1812, between the French under Napoleon, and the Russians under Kutusoff; 240,000 men being engaged. Each party claimed the victory; but the Russians retreated, leaving Moscow, which the French entered, 14 Sept.; see *Moscow*.

BORON, see *Borax*.

BOROUGH or **BURGH**, anciently a fortified town (*burh*), now means an incorporated city or town. They are all (except city of London) governed under the Municipal Corporations Act, 1882. County boroughs were incorporated under the Local Government Act, 1888. Parliamentary boroughs are the electoral divisions which send members to parliament, since the election of burgesses in the reign of Henry III. (1265). They do not of necessity coincide with the Municipal boroughs which give them their name. Charters were granted to towns by Henry I. 1132; which were remodelled by Charles II. in 1682-4, but restored in 1688. 22 new English boroughs were created in 1553. Burgesses were first admitted into the Scottish parliament by Robert Bruce, 1326; and into the Irish, 1365; see *Constituency*.

BOROUGH-BRIDGE (W. R. of York). Here Edward II. defeated the earls of Hereford and Lancaster, 16 March, 1322. Lancaster was mounted on a lean horse, led to an eminence near Pontefract, and beheaded.

BOROUGH-ENGLISH, an ancient tenure by which the younger son inherits. It is mentioned as occurring 834, prevailing in some old boroughs in Middlesex, Kent, Surrey, Sussex and Somerset. Abolished in Scotland by Malcolm III. in 1062.

BOSCOBEL, near Donington, Shropshire. Charles II. (after his defeat at Worcester, 3 Sept. 1651), disguised in the clothes of the Pendrills, remained from 4 to 6 Sept. at White Ladies; on

7 and 8 Sept. he lay at Boscobel house, near which exists an oak, said to be the scion of the Royal Oak in which the king was part of the time hidden with col. Careless. *Sharpe*. The "Boscobel Tracts" were first published in 1660. In 1861 Mr. F. Manning published "Views," illustrating these tracts. W. H. Ainsworth's "Boscobel," a story with authentic details, published 1872.

BOSNIA, in European Turkey, formerly part of Pannonia, was governed by chiefs till a brother-in-law of Louis king of Hungary was made king, 1376. He was defeated by the Turks in 1389, and became their vassal. Bosnia was incorporated with Turkey in 1463. Many efforts have been made by the Bosnians to recover their independence. A rebellion, begun in 1849, was quelled by Omar Pasha in 1851. The Bosnians joined the insurgents in Herzegovina, Sept. 1875; revolt was subdued, Aug. 1877. See *Turkey*.

About 100,000 Bosnian fugitives said to be in Austrian territories . . . July, 1878
Proclamation of the emperor before his troops enter Bosnia (in conformity with the *treaty of Berlin*, 13 July) . . . . . . 27 July, „
Advance of the Austrians, 29 July, vigorously resisted by the Bosnian begs, aided by Turks 4-6 Aug. „
The Bosnians defeated between Zepce and Maglai, 7, 8 Aug. „
The Austrians occupy Travnik, the old capital, 11 Aug.; slightly repulsed . . . 16 Aug. „
Victories of Philippovich at Han Belalovich, 16 Aug.; of Tegethoff . . . . 18 Aug. „
Serajevo, the capital, bombarded and taken by storm 19 Aug.; other successes . . 30 Aug., 5 Sept. „
The fortress Trebinje voluntarily surrenders 7 Sept. „
Behacs firmly resists, 10 Sept.; taken 19 Sept. „
Senkovics, a strong fortress, with arms and ammunition, taken . . . . 21 Sept. „
Zwornik, a stronghold, surrenders about 25 Sept. „
Livno bombarded and taken . . . 28 Sept. „
Other places surrender . . . about 12 Oct. „
Resistance ended; general amnesty issued about 9 Nov. „
Austrian loss estimated 5000 killed, wounded, missing . . . . . . Nov. „
The country settled, gradual political reforms Jan. *et seq.* 1880
Population, 1,504,091; announced, Feb. 1889; steadily increasing, country progressing and good budget reported . . . . 20 May, 1902
Baron Burian appointed Imperial Minister of Finance and Administrator . reported 29 July, 1903

BOSPHORE EGYPTIEN, see *Egypt*, 1885.

BOSPHORUS, THRACIAN (now Channel of Constantinople). Darius Hystaspes threw a bridge of boats over this strait when about to invade Greece, 493 B.C. See *Constantinople*.

BOSPORUS (or also **BOSPHORUS**) **CIMMERIAN**. The name given by the ancients to the strait which leads from the Black Sea to the Sea of Azov. Called also the straits of Kertch or Yenikalé. The history of the kingdom is involved in obscurity. It was named Cimmerian, from the *Cimmeri*, who dwelt on its borders, about 750 B.C.

The Archænactidæ from Mitylene rule . . B.C. 502-480
They are dispossessed by Spartacus I. . . . 438
Seleucus, 431; Satyrus I. 407
Leucon, 393; Spartacus II., 353; Parysades . 348
Eumelus, aiming to dethrone his brother Satyrus II., is defeated; but Satyrus is killed . 310
Prytanis, his next brother, ascends the throne, but is murdered by Eumelus . . . 309
Eumelus puts to death all his relations, 309; and is killed 304
The Scythians conquer Bosporus . . . 285
Mithridates VI., of Pontus, conquers Bosporus . 80
He poisons himself; and the Romans make his son, Pharnaces, king 63
Battle of Zela, gained by Julius Cæsar over Pharnaces II. (Cæsar writes home, *Veni, vidi, vici*, "I came, I saw, I conquered") 47
Asander usurps the crown . . . . . „
Cæsar makes Mithridates of Pergamus king . . „
Polemon conquers Bosporus, and favoured by Agrippa, reigns 14
Polemon killed by barbarians of the Palus Mæotis A.D. 33
Polemon II. reigns . . . . . . „
Mithridates II. reigns 41
Mithridates conducted a prisoner to Rome, by order of Claudius; Cotys I. king . . . 49
A list of kings given by some writers ends with Sauromates VII. 344

BOSTON, Lincolnshire; a trading seaport, growing in importance since making of docks, &c., 1882-1900; made a staple for wool, 1357; St. Botolph's church with a lofty tower, was erected about 1309. Population 1881, 14,941; 1891, 14,953; 1901, 15,583.

BOSTON, Massachusetts, United States, built about 1627. Here originated that resistance to the British authorities which led to American independence. The act of parliament laying duties on tea, papers, colours, &c. (passed June, 1767) greatly excited the indignation of the citizens of Boston. Population 1890, 448,477; 1900, 560,892.

"Boston News Letter," first American newspaper, appeared . . . . . . 24 April, 1704
The duties on paper, &c., were suspended, that on tea, retained; the citizens of Boston seize the tea in three vessels in the harbour, and cast it into the sea . . . . . . 16 Dec. 1773
Boston seaport shut by the English parliament, until restitution should be made to the East India Company for the tea lost . . 25 March, 1774
Arrival of gen. Gage as commander-in-chief of the Colonies, with troops . . . . 13 May, „
The town besieged by the Americans, and 400 houses destroyed 1775
Battle of Bunker Hill, between the royalists and independent troops; the latter defeated, 17 June, „
The city evacuated by the king's troops . April, 1776
Industrial exhibition opened . . . . Oct. 1856
Great peace jubilee; concert of about 10,371 voices and 1094 instruments, with anvils, bells, &c., begun . . . . 15 June, 1869
International peace jubilee; chorus about 20,000; orchestra, 1000; with military bands and other performers of different nations, including the British grenadier guards' band; a day allotted to each nation . . . 17 June—4 July, 1872
Tremendous fire; great loss of life and property: about 80 acres of buildings burnt; 959 houses (125 dwellings); 35 persons killed. 9, 10, 11 Nov. „
Great fire; many buildings destroyed; estimated loss 5,000,000 dollars. Two firemen killed 28 Nov. 1889
Many buildings destroyed by fire; five deaths, estimated loss, 3,000,000 dollars . 10 March, 1893
Another fire, 500 families homeless, 15-16 May, and a great fire in warehouses, estimated loss, above 1,000,000 dollars . . . . . 17 May, 1894
Destructive blizzard, city blocked, 200 horses killed 31 Jan. 1898
Boston has the longest railway station in the United States, opened 1898. Street electric tramways (and subway), and an elevated line carry 50,000,000 people annually, completed . 1901

BOSWORTH FIELD, Leicestershire, the site of the thirteenth and last battle between the houses of York and Lancaster, 22 Aug. 1485, when Richard III. was defeated by the earl of Richmond, afterwards Henry VII., and slain, through the desertion of sir Wm. Stanley. It is said that Henry was crowned on the spot with the crown of Richard found in a hawthorn bush near the field.

BOTANY. Aristotle is considered the founder of the science (about 347 B.C.). *Historia Plantarum* of Theophrastus was written about 320 B.C. Authors on botany became numerous at the close of the 15th century. Fuchsius, Bock, Bauhin, Cæsalpinus, and others, wrote between 1535 and 1600. The system and arrangement of the great Linnæus (see *Linnæan system*) was made known about 1735; and Jussieu's system, founded on Tournetort's, and called "the natural system," in 1758. At Linnæus's death, 1778, the species of plants actually described amounted in number to 11,800. The number of species now recorded cannot fall short of 100,000. J. C. Loudon's "Encyclopædia of Plants," a most comprehensive work, first appeared in 1829. De Candolle's "Prodromus Systematis Naturalis Regni Vegetabilis" (of which Vol. I. appeared in 1818), was continued by his son Alphonse, who died aged 86, April, 1893. An International Botanical congress was opened in London, 23 May, 1866, professor A. De Candolle president; another at Amsterdam, 13 April, 1877. Robert Brown, who accompanied Flinders in his survey of New Holland in 1803, died 10 June, 1858, aged 85, was long acknowledged to be the chief of the botanists of his day.

Linnæan Society instituted 1788, incorporated 1802.
Royal botanic society's jubilee fête, 15 July, 1889.
International botanical congress at Genoa, 5 Sept. 1892; Paris, 1 Oct. 1900; at Geneva, 7 Aug. 1901.
Dr. Wm. Williamson, geol. botanist, d. 23 June, 1895.
Charles Naudin, French botanist, died 19 March, 1899; J. G. Agardh, Swedish, born 1813, died 17 Jan. 1901.
Nature study exhibition opened by the duke of Devonshire, 23 July, 1902; laboratory opened Jan. 1903.
New botanical and horticultural laboratory in connection with Botanical society school opened 1 April, 1903.

BOTANIC GARDENS.

	Established about		*Established about*
Padua	1545	Kew, 1760; greatly improved	1841-65
Montpellier	1558	Cambridge	1763
Leyden	1577	Coimbra	1773
Leipsic	1580	St. Petersburg	1785
Paris (Jardin des Plantes)	1624	Calcutta	1793
Jena	1629	Dublin	1800
Oxford	1632	Horticultural Society's, Chiswick	1821
Upsal	1657	Royal Botanic Society's, Regent's Park	1839
Chelsea	1673-86	Royal Horticultural Society's; see *Horticulture*	1860
Edinburgh	1680		
Vienna	1753		
Madrid	1755		

BOTANY BAY, Australia, discovered by captain Cook, 28 April, 1770, received its name from the great variety of plants growing on the shore. It was fixed on for a colony of convicts from Great Britain, which was however established at Sydney, near Port Jackson. The first governor, captain Arthur Phillip, who sailed from England in May, 1787, arrived at the settlement in Jan. 1788. The colony was eventually established at Port Jackson, about thirteen miles to the north of the bay; see *New South Wales*, and *Transportation*.

BOTHIE SYSTEM, a system which prevails in the eastern and north-eastern districts of Scotland of building the outhouses (barns, stables, byres, &c.) of a farmstead in the form of barracks, in which the unmarried male servants reside.

BOTHWELL BRIDGE, Lanarkshire. The Scotch covenanters, who took up arms against the intolerant government of Charles II., and defeated the celebrated Claverhouse at Drumclog, 1 June, 1679, were totally routed by the earl of Monmouth at Bothwell Bridge, 22 June, 1679, and many prisoners were tortured and executed.

BOTTLE-CONJURER. In accordance with a wager, a person having advertised that he would jump into a quart bottle at the Haymarket theatre, on 16 Jan. 1749, the house was densely crowded and besieged by thousands anxious to gain admittance. The pickpockets had a rich harvest, and the duped crowd nearly pulled down the edifice.

BOTTLES in ancient times were made of leather. The art of making glass bottles and drinking-glasses was known to the Romans at least before 79; for these articles and other vessels have been found in the ruins of Pompeii. Bottles were made in England about 1558. A bottle which contained two hogsheads was blown, we are told, at Leith, in Scotland, in Jan. 1747-8; see *Glass*.

Ashley's patent for making glass bottles by automatic machinery . . . . . 13 Nov. 1886
Bottles largely made of paper in Chicago . . . 1887
Screw-stoppered bottles in universal use for aërated waters 1903

BOUILLON, Belgium, formerly a duchy, was sold by Godfrey its ruler, to Albert, bishop of Liège, to obtain funds for the crusade, 1095. It was seized by the French in 1672, and held by them till 1815, when it was given to the king of the Netherlands, as duke of Luxemburg. It was awarded to Belgium after the Revolution of 1830.

BOULANGISTS, see *France*, 1886-91.

BOULEVARDS (Bulwarks), sites of old fortifications in Paris and other French towns, now planted with rows of trees. The practice has been adopted in London and its suburban roads, 1875, *et seq.* See *Playground*.

BOULOGNE, an important seaport in Picardy, N. France, added to Burgundy, 1435; to France, 1447. Here Henry VIII. and Francis I. concluded a treaty to oppose the Turks, 28 Oct. 1532. Boulogne was besieged by Henry VII. 2 Oct. 1492, for a few days; taken by Henry VIII. on 14 Sept. 1544, but restored for a sum of money, 1550. Its trade is growing; in 1902 the exports and imports amounted to over 19,000,000*l* The fishing fleet (many steamers) earn over 500,000*l*. annually. Population 1901, 49,083.

Lord Nelson attacked a flotilla here, disabling ten vessels and sinking five . . . . 3 Aug. 1801
In another attempt he was repulsed with great loss, captain Parker of the *Medusa* killed . 18 Aug. „
Bonaparte assembled 160,000 men and 10,000 horses, and a flotilla of 1300 vessels and 17,000 sailors to invade England in 1804; the coasts of Kent and Sussex were covered with martello towers and lines of defence; and nearly half the adult population of Britain was formed into volunteer corps; sir Sidney Smith unsuccessfully attempted to burn the flotilla with fire machines called catamarans . . . . . . 2 Oct. 1804
The army removed on the breaking out of war with Austria 1805
Congreve-rockets used in another attack, and set the town on fire . . . . . 8 Oct. 1806
Louis Napoleon (afterwards emperor) made a fruitless descent here with about 50 followers, 6 Aug. 1840
As emperor, he reviewed the French troops destined for the Baltic, 10 July, 1854; and entertained prince Albert and the king of the Belgians, 5 Sept. 1854
Statue of Edw. Jenner here inaugurated 11 Sept. 1865
Pilgrimages here to adore an image of the Virgin and Child, said to have been miraculously brought in a boat in 633 1857-75
Law authorising construction of a new deep-sea harbour, by M. Stoecklin (in 15 years), cost about 680,000*l*.; passed 19 June; first stone laid, by M. Freycinet . . . . . . 9 Sept. 1878
Great fire, shipping and timber destroyed, 29 Sept. 1895
British association entertained by the French association at the town hall, a monument of Dr. Duchesne, eminent scientist, and a plaque in memorial of the poet Campbell, unveiled, 21 Sept. 1899

Pres. Loubet lays first stone of the new dock 6 July, 1903

BOUNDARY ACTS. *Commissioners* were appointed by the Reform Bill, passed 15 Aug. 1867. Viscount Eversley, Russell Gurney, sir John T. B. Duckworth, sir Francis Crossley, and John Walter, first sat 16 Aug. England and Wales were divided into 18 districts, and other arrangements made. Another boundary act was passed 13 July, 1868.

Boundary commissioners appointed to carry out the redistribution of seats bill Nov. 1884. Work completed . . . . 10 Feb. 1885

[Sir John Lambert (chairman), hon. T. H. W. Pelham, sir F. R. Sandford, Mr. J. T. Henley, lieut.-col. R. O. Jones, and Major H. Tulloch.]

Boundaries commission appointed by the Local Government (Boundaries) Act passed 16 Sept. . 1887

[Earl Brownlow (chairman), Lord Edmond Fitzmaurice, Lord Basing, sir Henry Selwyn Ibbetson and Mr. Hibbert.]

BOUNTIES, premiums granted to the producer, exporter, or importer of certain articles; a principle introduced into commerce by the British parliament. The first granted on corn, in 1688, were repealed in 1815. They were first legally granted in England for raising naval stores in America, 1703, and have been granted to the herring fishery, on sail-cloth, linen, and other goods. See *Queen Anne's Bounty* and *Sugar*.

BOUNTY MUTINY, took place on board the *Bounty*, an armed ship which quitted Otaheite, with bread-fruit trees, 7 April, 1789. The mutineers put their captain, Bligh, and nineteen men into an open boat, with a small stock of provisions, near Annamooka, one of the Friendly isles, 28 April, 1789; these reached the island of Timor, south of the Moluccas, in June, after a voyage of nearly 4000 miles. Some of the mutineers were tried 15 Sept. 1792; six were condemned and three executed. For the fate of others, see *Pitcairn's Island*.

BOURBON, House of (from which came the royal houses of France, Spain, and Naples), derives its origin from the Archambauds, lords of Bourbon in Berry.

Robert, count of Clermont, son of Louis IX. of France, married the heiress Beatrice in 1272; died 1317; and their son Louis I. created duke of Bourbon and peer of France by Charles IV. . . 1327

The last of the descendants of their *elder* son Peter I., Susanna, married Charles, duke of Montpensier, constable of Bourbon, who, offended by his sovereign Francis I., entered into the service of the emperor Charles V., and was killed at the siege of Rome . . . . . . 6 May, 1527

From James, the *younger* son of Louis I., descended Antony, duke of Vendôme, who married (1548) Jeanne d'Albret, daughter of Henry, king of Navarre. Their son, Henry IV., born at Pau, 14 Dec. 1553, became king of France . 31 July, 1589

The crown of Spain was settled on a younger branch of this family, 1700, and guaranteed by the peace of Utrecht (*Rapin*). 1713

Bourbon Family Compact (a defensive alliance between France, Spain, and the Two Sicilies concluded by M. de Choiseul) . . 15 Aug. 1761

The Bourbons expelled France, 1791; restored 1814; again expelled on the return of Bonaparte from Elba, and again restored after the battle of Waterloo, 1815. The elder branch was expelled once more, in the person of Charles X. and his family, in 1830, in consequence of the revolution of the memorable days of July in that year.

Orleans branch ascended the throne in the person of the late Louis Philippe, as "king of the French," 9 Aug. 1830; deposed, 24 Feb. 1848; and his family also was expelled.

The Bourbon family fled from Naples (6 Sept. 1860), and Francis II. lost his kingdom: expelled from Spain, Sept. 1868; restored by Alfonso XII. 31 Dec. 1874; see *France*, *Spain*, *Naples*, *Orleans*, *Parma*, *Condé*, and *Legitimists*.

The fusion of the parties supporting the comte de Chambord with the Orleanists, said to be accomplished, 5 Aug. 1873. The comte de Chambord, last of the elder branch, died aged nearly 63, 24 Aug. 1883

See *France* and *Orleans*.

BOURBON, Isle of (in the Indian ocean), discovered by the Portuguese about 1542. The French are said to have first settled here in 1649. It surrendered to the British, under admiral Rowley, 8 July, 1810, and was restored to France in 1815. An awful hurricane in Feb. 1829, did much mischief. Bourbon was named "l'Ile de la Réunion" in 1848; population, 1892, 171,731.

BOURGOGNE, LA, see *Wrecks* footnote, 4 July, 1898.

BOURIGNONISTS, a sect founded by Antoinette Bourignon, who, in 1658, took the Augustine habit and travelled in France, Holland, England, and Scotland; in the last she made many converts about 1670. She maintained that Christianity does not consist in faith and practice, but in inward feeling and supernatural impulse. A disciple named Court left her a good estate. She died in 1680, and her works, 21 volumes 8vo, were published 1686.

BOURNOUS, the Arabic name of a hooded garment worn in Algeria, which has been introduced in a modified form into England and France since 1847.

BOUVINES (N. France), the site of a desperate battle, 27 July, 1214, in which Philip Augustus of France was victorious over the emperor Otho and his allies, consisting of more than 150,000 men. The counts of Flanders and Boulogne were taken prisoners, and the earl of Salisbury, brother of king John.

BOVILL'S ACT, 23 & 24 Vict. c. 34, 1860, relates to petitions of right.

BOVRIL, "Ox-strength." The name given to a preparation of lean beef from which the water, about 75 per cent., has been excluded; and the albumen and fibrine, the nutritive parts retained by processes gradually invented by Mr. J. Lawson Johnston, who began his experimental researches in Canada about 1872. Bovril is now largely manufactured by a company having its head quarters in London.

BOWLS or Bowling, an English game as early as the 13th century. Henry VIII., Charles I. played at it, and also Charles II. at Tunbridge. *Grammont*. Bowling clubs are general throughout England. Public bowling greens are provided in Finsbury-park, Clissold-park and other London recreation grounds, 1903.

BOW-STREET, see *Magistrates*.

Bow Street Runners, a name popularly given to the special officers attached to each police office of the metropolis, commonly called "Robin Redbreasts" from their red waistcoats. They were famous for the detection of hidden crimes, especially Townsend, who was a favourite of King George III. and his family, Limberham, Macmanus, Jealous, Forester and others. They were superseded by the new police established in 1829

BOWS and Arrows, see *Archery*.

BOXING, or Prize-Fighting, the *pugilatus* of the Romans, once a favourite sport with the British, who possess strong arms, giving them superiority in battles decided by the bayonet.

Broughton's amphitheatre, behind Oxford-road, built 1742

Schools opened in England to teach boxing . . 1790
Mendoza opened the Lyceum in the Strand in . 1791
Boxing was much patronised from about 1820 to 1830
Tom Winter (nicknamed Spring), beside other victories, beat Langan (for 1000*l.*) . . 8 June, 1824
John Gully, originally a butcher, afterwards a prize-fighter, acquired wealth, and became M.P. for Pontefract (1832–37) died . 9 March, 1863
Desperate conflict at Farnborough between Thomas Sayers, the Champion of England, a light Sussex man, about 5 feet 8 inches high, and John Heenan, the "Benicia Boy," a huge American, in height 6 feet 1 inch. Strength, however, was matched by skill; and eventually the fight was interrupted, 17 April Both men received a silver belt 31 May, 1860
Tom King beat Mace, and obtained the champion's belt, &c. 26 Nov. 1862
He beat Goss, 1 Sept., and Heenan (nearly to death) 10 Dec. 1863
A trial, in consequence of the last fight, ensued: the culprits were discharged, on promising not to offend again . . . . . 5 April, 1864
Wormald obtained the championship after a contest with Marsden . . . . . 4 Jan. 1865
Contest for championship between Mace and O'Baldwin, a giant; prevented by the arrest of Mace, 15 Oct. 1867
Railways prohibited carrying persons going to a prize-fight, 31 & 32 Vict. c. 119 . . . 1868
Prize-fight in St. Andrew's hall (formerly Tavistock chapel), London, W.C., stopped . 27 March, 1882
Attempted revival of pugilism in London, 1889—90; Queensberry rules drawn up by the marquis of Queensberry and generally adopted about . 1890
A fight between Slavin and M'Auliffe, pugilists from Australia, at the Ormonde club, Walworth, stopped, the gloves to be used being considered insufficient, 23 Sept.; fight took place 27 Sept.; the men committed for trial, 10 Oct.; the jury disagree . . . . . 17 Nov. „
Fitzsimmons, of Cornwall, beats Corbett, of Denver 1897
Walter Croot, after an encounter with James Barry at the Nat. Sporting club, from 10.15 p.m. 6 Dec. till 12.15 a.m. 7 Dec., died 9 a.m. . . Dec. 1897
Jeffreys, of Ohio, beat Fitzsimmons, 12,000*l.* divided between them 1899
Thos. Turner dies after a contest, 17 Nov. 1898; Michael Riley fatally injured at the Nat. Sporting club, 29 Jan. 1900; an American pugilist fatally injured there . . . . . 22 April, 1901
Sullivan, an eminent prize-fighter in 1903
Winners of the Amateur Boxing Association Championship 1902:—*Bantam weights* (8st. 4lb. and under), A. J. Milner; *Feather weights* (9st. and under), C. J. Clarke; *Light weights* (10st. and under), A. Warner; *Middle weights* (11st. 4lb. and under), E. Mann; *Heavy weights* (any weight), F. Parks.

BOXTEL (in Dutch Brabant), where the British and allied army, commanded by the duke of York, was defeated by the French republicans, who took 2000 prisoners and eight pieces of cannon, 17 Sept. 1794.

BOX-TREE, indigenous to this country, and exceedingly valuable to wood-engravers. In 1815 a large box-tree at Box-hill, Surrey, was cut down, and realised a large sum. Macculloch says, that "the trees were cut down in 1815, and produced upwards of 10,000*l.*" About 1820 the cutting of trees on the hill produced about 6000*l.*

BOY-BISHOP. During the middle ages a choir-boy was frequently elected on St. Nicholas' day, 6 Dec., and held office till the 28th. The custom was suppressed in England in July, 1542; but lingered for some time after.

BOYCOTTING, see *Ireland*, 1880, *et seq.* Condemned by the Pope, 20 April, 1888. A Boycott fund to assist capt. Boycott (died 21 June, 1897) in his trouble was subscribed 1880-1. Boycotting very prevalent in Tipperary, 1889-90.

BOYDELL'S LOTTERY for his Shakspeare gallery of paintings got up (1786), by alderman Boydell, lord mayor of London. Every ticket was sold at the time the alderman died, 12 Dec. 1804, before the decision of the wheel.

BOYLE LECTURES, instituted by his will (18 July, 1691), by Robert Boyle (son of the great earl of Cork), a philosopher, distinguished by his genius, virtues, and benevolence, who died 30 Dec. 1691. Eight lectures (in vindication of the Christian religion) are to be delivered. The office of lecturer is tenable for three years.

BOYNE, a river in Ireland, near which William III. defeated his father-in-law, James II., 1 July, 1690. The latter lost 1500 (out of 30,000) men; the Protestant army lost about a third of that number (out of 36,000). James fled to Dublin, thence to Waterford, and escaped to France. The duke of Schomberg was killed by mistake by his own soldiers as he was crossing the river, and here also was killed the rev. George Walker, who defended Londonderry, in 1689. Near Drogheda is a splendid obelisk, 150 feet in height, erected in 1736 by the Protestants of the empire in commemoration of this victory.

BOYNE, man-of-war of 98 guns, destroyed by fire at Portsmouth, 4 May, 1795, by the explosion of the magazine; numbers perished. Portions were recovered June, 1840.

BOYS' BRIGADE, inaugurated 1884, by Mr. W. A. Smith, with the object of promoting habits of obedience, self-control and Christian manliness among lads of 12 to 16 years of age. The companies of the brigade are formed in connection with the Sunday schools, churches and missions of religious bodies in all parts of the United Kingdom. The boys wear a simple uniform, and are exercised in military drill. The total number enrolled (1902) in the United Kingdom was 50,000, with 4000 officers The movement has extended to the United States and the colonies; the total strength throughout the world being 85,000. The Prince of Wales is the patron, and the Archbishop of Canterbury the vice-patron of the brigade.
Demonstration in the Albert hall under presidency of major-general Baden-Powell . . . May, 1903

BOYTON'S SWIMMING APPARATUS. See under *Life Boat*, &c.

BRABANT, part of Holland and Belgium, an ancient duchy, part of Charlemagne's empire, fell to his son Charles, 806. It became a separate duchy (called at first Lower Lorraine) in 959. It descended to Philip II. of Burgundy, 1429, and in regular succession to the emperor Charles V. In the 17th century it was held by Holland and Austria, as Dutch Brabant and the Walloon provinces, and underwent many changes through the wars of Europe. The Austrian division was taken by the French in 1746 and 1794. It was united to the Netherlands in 1814, but South Brabant was given to Belgium, 1830. The heir of the throne of Belgium is styled duke of Brabant; see *Belgium*.

BRACELETS are of great antiquity, and have been worn by almost every nation, savage or civilised. Bracelets were in use in Egypt at a very early period. Frequent mention is made in the Bible of this custom. Greek and Roman women wore this ornament, and a kind of bracelet (*armillæ*) was conferred on the Roman soldier as a reward for bravery. Bracelets constituted the chief ornament of the ancient German tribes, and are frequently found in ancient graves.

BRACHYGRAPHY, see *Stenography*.

BRADFIELD RESERVOIR, see *Sheffield*, 1864.

BRADFORD, West Riding of Yorkshire, an ancient seat of the woollen manufacture; made a parliamentary borough in 1832; has thriven since 1851. Bradford returns three M.P.'s by Act passed 25 June, 1885; made a city June, 1897. See *Poisoning*. Population, 1881, 194,495; 1891, 216,361; 1901, 279,767.

New town-hall was opened . . . . 9 Sept. 1873
British Association met here . . . . 17 Sept. „
Statue of Sir Titus Salt unveiled . . . 1 Aug. 1874
Statue of R. Cobden unveiled . . . 25 July, 1877
New technical school opened by the prince of Wales 23 June, 1882
Fall of chimney of New Lands mills; 54 killed, 250 injured . . . . . . 28 Dec. „
Statue of Mr. W. E. Forster, long M.P. for Bradford, unveiled by the marquis of Ripon . 17 May, 1890
Strike of about 15,000 operatives at the Manningham mills, Dec. 1890; ended . . . 27 April, 1891
Rioting suppressed by military . 13, 14 April, „
Fire at Messrs. Sutcliffe and Sons' cotton mills, etc., damage, about 20,000*l*. 27 Nov. 1893
Lord Masham offers 47,000*l*. to found an institute in Lister park as a memorial of Dr. Cartwright, May, 1898
Greenhill Mills burnt, damage 40,000*l*. . 11 March, 1903

BRADLAUGH CASE, see *Parliament*, 1880-5. Mr. Charles Bradlaugh, M.P. for Northampton, died 30 Jan. 1891, aged 57.

BRADSHAW'S RAILWAY GUIDE was first published by Mr. G. Bradshaw, assisted by Mr. W. J. Adams, in Dec. 1841. The *Continental Bradshaw* was established in 1848.

The beginning of railway guides is involved in obscurity. Mr. Bradshaw issued his first railway time tables in two forms, one for the Liverpool and Manchester district, and one for London and the Birmingham district, 19 and 25 Oct. 1839. His Railway Companion appeared in 1840; (F. Madan, *Athenæum*) . . . . . Dec. 24, 1887

BRAGANZA, a city in Portugal, gave title to Alfonso, natural son of John I. of Portugal (in 1422), founder of the house of Braganza. When the nation, in a bloodless revolution in 1640, threw off the Spanish yoke, John duke of Braganza, was called to the throne as John IV., and his descendants have since reigned over *Portugal*.

BRAHMINS, Hindoo priests, the highest of the four castes. Pythagoras is thought to have learned from them his doctrine of the *Metempsychosis*; and it is affirmed that some of the Greek philosophers went to India on purpose to converse with them. The Brahmins derive their name from Brahmah, one of the three beings whom God, according to their theology, created, and with whose assistance He formed the world. See *Vedas* and *Buddhism*.

BRAHMO SOMAJ, see *Deism*.

BRAIN, see under *Craniology* and *Nerves*.

BRAINTREE CASE (in Essex) decided in 1842 by Dr. Lushington, who determined that a minority in a parish vestry cannot levy a church rate.

BRAKES, see under *Railways*.

BRAMHAM (W. R. York): near here the earl of Northumberland and lord Bardolf were defeated and slain by sir Thomas Rokeby, the general of Henry IV., 19 Feb. 1408; and Fairfax was defeated by the royalists under the earl of Newcastle, 29 March, 1643.

BRANDENBURG, a city in Prussia, founded by the Slavonians, who gave it the name of *Banber*, which signified *Guard of the Forest*, according to some; others explain the name as Burg, or city, of the *Brenns*. Henry I., surnamed the Fowler, after defeating the Slavonians, fortified "Brannibor," 926, as a rampart against the Huns, and bestowed the government on Sigefroi, count of Ringelheim, with the title of margrave, or protector of the marches or frontiers. The emperor Sigismund gave perpetual investiture to Frederick IV. of Nuremburg, of the house of Hohenzollern, ancestor of the royal family of Prussia, made elector in 1417. For a list of the margraves since 1134, see *Prussia*. Population, 1890, 37,823; 1900, 49,263.

BRANDY (German *Branntwein*, burnt wine), the spirit distilled from wine. Alcohol appears to have been known to Raymond Lully in the 13th century, and to have been manufactured in France early in the 14th. It was at first used medicinally, and miraculous cures were ascribed to its influence. In 1852, 3,959,452; in 1866, 5,621,930; in 1870, 7,942,965; in 1874, 3,378,057; in 1876, 7,913,092; in 1877, 2,962,697; in 1879, 5,024,668; in 1883, 2,202,344; in 1888, 2,655,004; in 1889, 2,858,774; in 1890, 3,100,450; in 1893, 2,739,455; in 1896, 2,749,624; in 1900, 2,596,265; 1901, 2,434,970 gallons of foreign spirits were imported into the United Kingdom. In 1901, 55,306,438 gallons of spirits were manufactured in Britain. Manufacture of genuine French brandy has almost ceased.

BRANDYWINE, a river in N. America, near which a battle took place between the British, under Howe, and the Americans under Washington, in which the latter (after a day's fight) were defeated with great loss, 11 Sept. 1777. Philadelphia fell into the possession of the victors.

BRASS. That mentioned in the Bible was most probably bronze. When Lucius Mummius burnt Corinth to the ground, 146 B.C., he found immense riches, and during the conflagration, it is said, all the metals in the city melted, and running together, formed the valuable composition described as *Corinthian Brass*. This is well doubted, for the Corinthian artists had long before obtained great credit for their method of combining gold and silver with copper. *Du Fresnoy*. Some of the English sepulchral engraved *brasses* are said to be as old as 1277; a white brass produced by Mr. P. M. Parsons, about 1875.

BRAVO CASE. Mr. Charles Delauney Turner Bravo, barrister, died suddenly and mysteriously (at Balham, county of London), suicide suspected, 18 April, 1876; open verdict at inquest; new inquest ordered, 26 June, 1876; began 10 July. Verdict: "Wilful murder by administration of tartar emetic; but not sufficient evidence to fix the guilt upon any person," 11 Aug. 1876.

BRAY, Berks. Fuller says that its vicar, Symon Symonds, was twice a papist and twice a Protestant—in the reigns of Henry VIII., Edward VI., Mary, and Elizabeth (1533–1558). Upon being called a turn-coat, he said he kept to his principle, that of "living and dying the vicar of Bray." The story is doubted. The modern song refers to the political changes of the 17th and 18th centuries. BRAY, the "Irish Brighton," a beautiful seaside town 13 miles S.E. of Dublin, with esplanade a mile long. Pop. 6,888.

BRAY'S ASSOCIATES for founding clerical libraries and supporting negro schools. This society began in 1723, by Dr. Thomas Bray, rector of Sheldon, appointing trustees to expend 900*l.* bequeathed by Mr. D'Allone for the instruction of negroes. In 1733 these trustees received their present name, and their fund was increased by legacies in 1767 and 1768.

Dr. Bray, who was one of the founders of the Society for Propagating the Gospel, and who had acted energetically as commissary in Maryland for the bishop of London, about 1696, died 15 Feb. 1730, bequeathing part of his books to Sion College and part to found a parochial library, under certain conditions, complied with at Maidstone; and also money for other religious purposes. The associates assist schools and libraries in the colonies, and parochial libraries at home.

BRAZEN BULL, said to have been contrived by Perillus, at Athens, for Phalaris, tyrant of Agrigentum, 570 B.C. It had an opening in the side to admit the victims, and a fire was kindled underneath to roast them to death. Phalaris ordered the artist to make the first experiment. Pindar (522–422 B.C.) speaks of the cruelties of Phalaris, but later writers give him a different character.

BRAZIL, an empire in South America, was discovered by Vincent Pinzon, 26 Jan. 1500. Pedro Alvarez de Cabral, a Portuguese, driven upon its coasts by a tempest, April following, called it the land of the Holy Cross; but it was subsequently named Brazil, on account of its red wood. The French having seized on Portugal in 1807, the royal family and nobles embarked for Brazil, and landed 7 March, 1808. The dominant religion is Roman Catholic; but others are tolerated. Constitution of 25 March, 1824; modified 12 Aug. 1834 and 12 May, 1840. Population in 1888, 14,002,335, estimated; 1891, 17,000,000. See *Portugal*.

The emperor was deposed and a Federal republic, styled THE UNITED STATES OF BRAZIL, proclaimed 15, 16 Nov. 1889 (*see below*); a new constitution was promulgated, 22 June, 1890 and 24 Feb. 1891. It consists of a president, elected for 4 years, secretaries of state, a senate and a house of representatives.

Brazil explored by Amerigo Vespucci . . . about 1504
Divided into captaincies by the king of Portugal . 1530
Martin de Souza discovers Rio, and founds the first European colony at San Vincente 1531
Jews banished from Portugal to Brazil 1548
San Salvador (Bahia) founded by Thomé de Souza . 1549
French protestants occupy bay of Rio Janeiro . 1555–60
Sebastian founded 1567
Brazil, with Portugal, becomes subject to Spain . 1580
James Lancaster captures Pernambuco . . . 1593
The French establish a colony at Maranham . . 1594
Belem founded by Calderia 1615
The French expelled . . . . „
The Dutch seize the coast of Brazil, 1630; and hold Pernambuco 1630
Defeated at Guararapès, 1646; give up Brazil . . 1661
Gold mining commences 1693
Destruction of Palmares 1697
The French assault and capture Rio Janeiro . 1710–11
Diamond mines discovered in Sezzo Frio . . . 1729
Jesuits expelled 1758–60
Capital transferred from Bahia to Rio Janeiro . 1763
Royal family of Portugal arrive at Brazil, 7 March, 1808
First printing-press established . . . . „
Brazil becomes a kingdom 1815
King John VI. returns to Portugal, and dom Pedro becomes regent 1821
Brazil declares its independence . . . 7 Sept. 1822
Pedro I. crowned emperor . . . . 1 Dec. „
New constitution ratified . . . 25 March, 1824
Independence recognised by Portugal . 29 Aug. 1825
Revolution at Rio Janeiro; abdication of dom Pedro I. . . . . . . 7 April, 1831
Abolition of slave trade decreed (not effected till 1852) . . . . „
Reform of the constitution, 12 Aug. 1834 and 12 May, 1840
Pedro II. declared of age . . . . 23 July, „

Steam-ship line to Europe commenced . . . 1850
Suppression of the slave-trade; railways commenced 1852
Rio Janeiro lit with gas 1854
The British ship *Prince of Wales* wrecked at Albardas, on coast of Brazil, is plundered by some of the natives, and some of the crew killed, about 7 June, 1861
Reparation long refused; reprisals made; five Brazilian merchant ships being seized by the British . . . . 31 Dec. 1862
The Brazilian minister at London pays 3,200*l.* as an indemnity, under protest . . . 26 Feb. 1863
The Brazilian government request the British to express their regret for reprisals; declined; diplomatic intercourse suspended . . 5–28 May, „
Dispute between the governments respecting the arrest of some British officers at Rio Janeiro (17 June, 1862) referred to the arbitration of the king of the Belgians, who decides in favour of Brazil, 18 June, „
New ministry formed; F. J. Furtado, president—prospect of reconciliation with Gt. Britain, 30 Aug. 1864
U. S. war-steamer *Wachusett* seizes the confederate steamer *Florida* in the port of Bahia, while under protection of Brazil, 7 Oct.; after remonstrance, Mr. Seward, U.S. foreign minister, apologises. [The *Florida* (inadvertently) sunk?] 26 Dec. „
War with Uruguay—the Brazilians take Paysandú, and march upon Monte Video . . . 2 Feb. 1865
The comte d'Eu and princess Isabella (on marriage tour) land at Southampton . . . 7 Feb. „
Lopez, president of Paraguay, declares war against the Argentine Republic . . . . April, „
Treaty between Brazil, Uruguay, and the Argentine Republic against Paraguay, governed by Lopez, signed . . . . 1 May, „
Scientific expedition under Agassiz favoured by the emperor . . . . July, „
Amicable relations with England restored . Aug. „
The emperor joins the army against Lopez Aug. „
The allies under Flores defeat the Paraguayans at Santayuna on the Uruguay . . 18 Sept. „
Uruguayana surrenders to the allies . 18 Sept. „
Indecisive battle between the allies and the Paraguayans, at Paso de la Patria . about 25 Feb. 1866
Paraguayans defeated on the Parana 16, 17 April, „
Victory of the allies at Estero Velhaco, 2 May; indecisive battle there . . . . 24 May, „
Bombardment of the allied camp on the Parana 14 June, „
Two days' fight at Tuyuty; allies defeated, 16, 18 July, „
Fruitless meeting of president Lopez with the chiefs on proposals of peace . . . . 12 Sept. „
The allies attack the fortress of Curupaiti; defeated with severe loss . . . . 17–19, 22 Sept. „
The allies' camp bombarded, 18 Oct.; the Paraguayans repulsed at Tuyuty . . . 30 Oct. „
The Brazilians take Corumba . . . 13 June, 1867
The duke of Edinburgh visits Rio de Janeiro 15–22 July, „
The Paraguayans victors, 24 Sept.; severely defeated 3 and 21 Oct. „
Proposals for peace by Lopez declined . . Oct. „
Severe defeat of Paraguayans before Tuyuty 3 Nov. „
Freedom decreed to slaves belonging to the nation who shall become soldiers . . . 6 Nov. „
Three monitors pass Curupaiti, on the Paraguay, 17 Feb.; 6 ironclads force the passage of Humaitá; they find Asuncion abandoned . . 21 Feb. 1868
Fierce resistance of the Paraguayans; Lopez said to have armed 4000 women . . . . June, „
After several conflicts Lopez is totally defeated at Villeta, and flies . . . . . 11 Dec. „
The comte d'Eu appointed general of the allied army 24 March, 1869
The allies surprise and capture Rosario and garrison 8 May, „
Lopez defeated in severe conflicts, 12, 16, 18, 21 Aug. „
Lopez defeated and killed near the Aquidaban, 1 March, 1870
Treaty of peace with Paraguay, quite subdued 20 June, „
The count and countess d'Eu arrive in England, 13 Sept. „
New ministry under viscount St. Vincent, 29 Sept. „

The emperor and empress come to Europe, and visit public and scientific institutions, manufactories in Great Britain and other countries, June–Aug. 1871
Gradual slave emancipation bill passed by the senate; great rejoicings . . . 27, 28 Sept. ,,
The emperor and empress, after visiting the continent, return to Brazil . . . 31 March, 1872
Treaty with the Argentine republic . . . Jan. 1873
Prosecution of the archbishop of Pernambuco and other prelates, for infraction of the constitution Sept.–Dec. ,,
In a settlement of German emigrants at Porto Alegre, a number of fanatics, popularly termed *Mucker* (hypocrites), headed by Jacobina Maurer, a prophetess who claimed to be a female Christ, and her priest Hans Georg Maurer, attempt to convert their neighbours by force, and desolate the property of those who refuse. She and nearly all her band are killed after several conflicts with their neighbours, aided by the military 21–26 July, 1874
Great bank failures at Rio Janeiro . . May, 1875
Duke de Caixias president of ministry . 25 June, ,,
Emperor and empress at opening of Philadelphia Exhibition, 10 May, 1876; travelled in Europe, &c., returned to Rio Janeiro . . Sept. 1877
A ministerial crisis respecting emancipation of slaves (see under *Slavery*) . . . Sept. 1884
The emperor supports his minister Dantas; 1,200,000 slaves in Brazil . . . . . ,,
Resignation of Dantas, anti-slavery minister, on account of minority in the chamber . 5 May, 1885
The new minister Seraiva introduces a gradual emancipation bill . . . . 12 May, ,,
Ministry resigns, succeeded by Baron de Cotegipe, about 20 Aug. ,,
Bill for gradual abolition of slavery passed by senate and deputies . . . . Sept. ,,
New ministry under Sen. de Oliviera . March, 1888
Bill for total abolition of slavery passed by the chambers, 10–14 May; decree issued (about 700,000 persons freed) . . . . May, ,,
The emperor visits Europe; arrives at Paris, 20 July, 1887; returns to Rio Janeiro . 22 Aug. ,,
The emperor fired at by Adriano Valte, a Portuguese republican; not injured . . 15 July, 1889
Revolution at Rio de Janeiro, begun by the army; baron de Ladario, minister of marine, wounded; a republic proclaimed; marshal Deodoro da Fonseca, chief of a provisional government; people quiet; the emperor imprisoned, refuses to submit, 15, 16 Nov.; the emperor and family forcibly conveyed to the *Alagoas;* sail for Europe . 18 Nov. ,,
The emperor, at St. Vincent, refuses the offer of the provisional government to give him 500,000*l.* a year . . . . Nov. ,,
Official announcement that the republic will respect all state engagements . . . 18 Nov. ,,
All the provinces support the republic, separate governments organizing; suffrage conferred on all who can read and write; the republic blessed by the Abp. of Brazil, reported . . 23 Nov. ,,
The republic recognized informally by France; the United States of N.A. and Switzerland, about 29 Nov. ,,
The emperor and family arrive at Lisbon, received by the king . . . . . 7 Dec. ,,
Decree fixing the general elections for 15 Sept. and a meeting of the constituent assembly for 15 Nov. 1890 . . . . . . 20 Dec. ,,
Decree banishing the emperor and his family and viscount de Ouro Preto, the late premier, and recalling the grant to the emperor and suspending his annual allowance . . . . 20 Dec. ,,
Mutiny of two artillery regiments at Rio suppressed with much bloodshed; about 20 ringleaders shot; several citizens arrested . . 18–20 Dec. ,,
Sudden death of the empress at Oporto . 28 Dec. ,,
Decree for the separation of church and state, 7 Jan 1890
The emperor arrives at Cannes . . 16 Jan. ,,
The republic formally recognized by the United States N.A. . . . . 29 Jan. ,,
Issue Bank of the United States of Brazil, established . . . . . . 5 Feb. ,,
Serious disturbances in Rio Grande in opposition to government financial measures, 1 May, *et seq.;* rioting checked by the police; military government appointed . . . 13 May, *et seq.* ,,
New constitution promulgated . . 22 June 1890
The republic formally recognised by Great Britain, about 20 Oct. ,,
The first congress of the republic meets; the president transfers to it the powers of the provisional government . . . . . . 15 Nov. ,,
Decree rescinding the banishment of the late imperial ministers . . . . . 20 Nov. ,,
Secret decree to encourage immigration, 29 June, published in Warsaw, 26 Dec. 1890, about 25,000 Polish emigrants said to be received . Jan. 1891
The first republican ministry (sen. J. C. de Faria Alvim and others), resigns . . 20 Jan. ,,
New cabinet formed by sen. Uchoa . . 22 Jan. ,,
Reciprocal treaty of commerce with the United States N. A. . . . . . 5 Feb. ,,
A new constitution passed by the Constituent Assembly, 23 Feb.—promulgated . . 24 Feb. ,,
Marshal Deodoro da Fonseca elected president for four years, gen. Floriano Peixoto vice-president, 25 Feb., installed . . . . 26 Feb. ,,
The legislative session opens; cheerful speech of the president . . . . . 15 June, ,,
The British Foreign office warns emigrants against invitations to Brazil . . . . Aug. ,,
The congress, having passed a law opposing the veto of president Fonseca, is dissolved by him, and martial law proclaimed, 3 Nov.; he assumes the dictatorship . . . . 4 Nov. ,,
The provinces of Rio Grande do Sul and Grao Para declare their independence. . . 10 Nov. ,,
Insurrection in Rio Grande spreading; the governor, sen. J. Castilho, deposed, 13 Nov.; provisional government established under sen. Assis, about 15 Nov. The junta holds all the province, and prepares to resist the dictator Fonseca, reported 17 Nov., about 30,000 men in arms; Fonseca's proposals rejected by the junta, 19 Nov. ,,
Bresident Fonseca proclaims the election of a new congress for 29 Feb. to meet on 3 May, 1892, 21 Nov. ,,
Insurrection of the navy and others against president Fonseca; he resigns and is succeeded by gen. Floriano Peixoto; no bloodshed, 23 Nov.; he issues a manifesto declaring the re-establishment of legality . . . . . 25 Nov. ,,
Death of the ex-emperor Pedro II. at Paris 5 Dec. ,,
Gen. Rocha Osorio appointed governor of Rio Grande . . . . . . 6 Dec. ,,
Disturbances in Rio de Janeiro province suppressed with bloodshed . . . . 8 Dec. ,,
Revolution in São Paulo, begun 13 Dec., the governor resigns . . . . . 15 Dec. ,,
Meeting of congress; the president's message satisfactory . . . . . . 18 Dec. ,,
Revolution in Espiritu Santo; vice-governor deposed . . . . . . 19 Dec. ,,
Sen. Silveira Martinez appointed governor of Rio Grande . . . . about 26 Dec. ,,
Commercial treaty with Portugal signed . 15 Jan. 1892
Mutiny at the fortress of Santa Cruz; 2 forts captured by the rebels, who demand the restoration of Deodoro da Fonseca; the mutiny suppressed by government troops . . 19 Jan. *et seq.* ,,
The chambers prorogued till May . . Jan. ,,
Revolt of the province of Matto Grosso, 12 April; suppressed . . . . . June, ,,
The *Solimoes,* armour-clad war-vessel, founders off Cape Polonio, Uruguay, about 100 men drowned, 21 May, ,,
Death of gen. Deodoro da Fonseca . 23 Aug. ,,
Insurrection in Rio Grande do Sul, suppressed 4 Nov. ,,
Outrages on Italians in Rio Grande, Nov., Dec. 1892; reparation claimed . about 25 Jan. 1893
Disturbances in Rio Grande, conflict at Inhanduhy, reported . . . . . . 7 May, ,,
Revolution in Santa Catharina, indecisive fighting, 29–31 July; peace restored . . 3 Aug. ,,
Revolt of 3 cruisers under adm. Custodio de Mello against military government, bombardment of Rio de Janeiro stopped by the foreign admirals, 7 Sept. ,,
Bombardment of Rio, many killed 14–25 Sept. ,,
[The insurgents hold the arsenal at Nictheroy, adm. de Mello commands 6 warships and other vessels.]

Pres. Peixoto calls on the provinces for troops to defend Rio . . . . 17 Sept. 1893
The state of Santa Catharina, Itaqui in Rio Grande, and other frontier towns declare for the rebels . . . . 4 Oct. „
The commanders of foreign warships protest against the bombardment of Rio, 8 Oct.; continued firing on the forts . . 9 Oct. *et seq.* „
Government forces defeated in several parts of Rio Grande . . . . . . 12–21 Oct. „
Sen. Frederico Lorena appointed provisional president, by adm. de Mello, reported . 23 Oct. „
Daily bombardment of Nictheroy, &c. . 27 Oct. „
Collision between the *Republica* and *Rio de Janeiro* (transport), about 500 lives lost, reported 27 Oct. „
Explosion of a powder magazine at Rio, 3 British naval officers killed, others missing, reported, 6 Nov. „
Renewed bombardment of Nictheroy . 4–10 Nov. „
The insurgents hoist the imperial flag, and are joined by adm. Saldanha da Gama and other important persons . . . . . 7 Nov. „
The insurgent vessel *Javary* sunk by firing from fort Saõ João . . . . . . 22 Nov. „
Indecisive warfare . . . . . 3–15 Dec. „
Renewed bombardment of Rio . . . 28 Dec. „
Insurgent successes in Rio Grande . . Jan. 1894
Adm. de Mello organizes a government in the state of Parana . . . . Jan. „
The insurgents hold possession of the harbour of Rio; the foreign naval commanders telegraph to their governments for instructions . 25 Jan. „
Difficulties between the American fleet under adm. Benham and adm. da Gama's fleet, shots fired on both sides . . . . 29 Jan. „
Adm. Benham declaring that he acted only for the protection of American ships, his conduct approved by the U.S.A. government, and hostilities are suspended . . . . 30 Jan. „
The British government maintains neutrality, Feb. „
The blockade of Rio de Janeiro raised . 3 Feb. „
Indecisive engagements near Nictheroy, much bloodshed. . . . . . 9–12 Feb. „
Severe fighting in Parana . . . . . Feb. „
Explosion on the insurgent war vessel *Venus*, the commander and 32 men killed, reported 27 Feb. „
Insurgents defeated in Rio Grande, reported, 2 March, „
Dr. Prudente de Moraes elected president, 1 March, „
Terms of surrender proposed by adm. da Gama, rejected by marshal Peixoto; the firing of the government forts on the insurgent forts and ships not returned; ships deserted, and unconditional surrender of the insurgents . 13 March, „
Two Portuguese warships allowed to depart with adm. da Gama and 70 officers, 18 March; arrive at Buenos Ayres (to be conveyed to Portuguese territory) . . . . 26 March, „
The state of Parana in the hands of the insurgents under gen. Saraiva . . . . . . March, „
Adm. de Mello is proclaimed president at Desterro, reported . . . . 23 March, „
The insurgents defeated in Rio Grande with heavy loss, reported . . . . . . 10 April, „
Adm. de Mello and squadron surrender to the Argentine republic at Buenos Ayres, as political refugees; the *Republica* and other ships given up to the Brazilian minister . . . 16 April, „
Adm. da Gama and 220 insurgents escape from the Portuguese transport to Montevideo, and join the insurgents in the south, 26 April; others taken to Ascension island . . 27 April, „
The president's message to congress, declares the country settled, reported . . . 7 May, „
Diplomatic relations with Portugal broken off with respect to the escaped insurgents, reported, 14 May, „
Brazilian refugees, 148, arrive at Lisbon . 31 May, „
Gen. Saraiva defeated with great loss by the government forces under gen. Lima, near Passo Fundo, Rio Grande . . . . 27 June, „
Gen. Saraiva defeated and mortally wounded at Cavory . . . . 10 Aug. „
State of siege abolished by the president, reported, 1 Sept. „
Dr. Prudente Jose de Moraes assumes office as president; grants a political amnesty . 15 Nov. „

Amnesty to deserters during the revolt granted, 2 Jan. 1895
Explosion on board a pleasure steamer off the port of Nictheroy, 120 lives lost . . . 7 Jan. „
A new 5 per cent. internal currency loan announced (well taken up) . . . . . . 21 Feb. „
Renewal of the war in Rio Grande, gen. Sampaio defeated near the Uruguay frontier . 28 Feb. „
Rupture with Portugal settled, through British influence . . . . 14 March, „
Claims of Italy for compensation for Italian losses during the civil war . . . . 2 May, „
Congress re-opened by the president . 4 May, „
Defeat of the rebels at Cuareim; suicide of admiral da Gama, 26 June; armistice till 9 July, announced, 3 July; peace negotiations; treaty signed; reported, 23 Aug.; death of gen. Peixoto, late president . . . . . . 29 June, „
Amnesty bill to rebels in the late revolt in Rio Grande do Sul; signed by the president, 21 Oct. „
Congress opened by the president, large deficit; revision of the tariff, &c., proposed . 14 May, 1896
Disputes with Italy; Italians attacked by the mob at San Paulo, several persons killed, 24 Aug.; conflicts at Rio, 25 Aug.; order restored, 27 Aug. „
Italian squadron for S. American waters; appointed, 31 Aug.; Italian claims settled, 19 Nov. „
The president, through ill-health, transfers his duties temporarily, to the vice-president, Dr. Manuel V. Pereira, 10 Nov. 1896; resumes his functions . . . . 4 March, 1897
Monarchist newspaper offices destroyed by a mob at Rio de Janeiro, and the proprietor sen. Gentil Castro assassinated . . . . 8 March, „
Insurrection of the "Fanatics" under Antonio Conselheiro in Bahia; government forces defeated at Canudos; gen. Moreira Cesar, 32 officers, and 600 men, killed, and their arms captured, 3 March, „
8,000 Fanatics defeated by the troops at Canudos in Bahia, much slaughter; reported 7 June, „
Canudos, the stronghold of the Fanatics, after a long siege, captured by government troops; much slaughter, Antonio Conselheiro killed, 6 Oct. „
Attempt to assassinate president Moraes by Marcellino de Mello (who commits suicide, 24 Jan. 1898); general Bittencour, killed, 5 Nov. (attributed to newspaper attacks on the government); their offices destroyed by the mob . 7 Nov. „
Five conspirators sentenced to long imprisonment, 5 Nov. 1898; capt. Diocteano and 2 others sentenced to 30 years' imprisonment, reported, 5 July, 1899.
Jacobin attacks on an Italian colony Esperito Santo, 6 Italians killed; reported . 8 Nov. „
Suspected conspiracy, a state of siege proclaimed; convicts in revolt at Rio; reported, 10 Nov.; martial law enacted, till 23 Feb. 1898 12 Nov. „
Internal public loan at 6 per cent.; announced, 27 Nov. „
The Franco-Brazilian arbitration treaty passed by the senate; approved by the president 8 Dec. „
Congress closed . . . . . . 10 Dec. „
Police report incriminating 20 persons, including Dr. Manuel V. Pereira, vice-pres., in the attempt to assassinate the president (*see above*, 5 Nov.); published, 12 Jan. 1898; he protests his innocence and refuses to appear before the court, in an address issued . . . . . 28 Feb. 1898
Dr. Campos Salles elected president . 2 March, „
The 4 per cent. loan of 1890 converted into 5 per cent. currency bonds . . . . 1 July, „
British proposal to submit the Guiana boundary question to arbitration, accepted . March, 1899
Naval and military arsenals abolished, 3,970 soldiers disbanded, loans redeemed, expenditure reduced . . . . April, „
Congress opened by the president . . 3 May, „
Pres. Roca of Argentina visits Rio . 8, 18 Aug. „
Congress closed . . . . . . 22 Nov. „
Financial crisis: the Banco da Republica suspends payment on cheques, 12 Sept. 1900; the bank placed under government control by law passed 20 Sept. 1900; re-opened . . . . 5 Nov. 1900

Brazil and French Guiana frontier dispute (200 years) settled in favour of Brazil, by the Swiss Federal council, about 3,000 sq. miles allotted to France . . . . 1 Dec. 1900

Congress opened . . . . 3 May, 1901

The government's financial policy much praised 17 Sept. „

Rodriguez Alves installed president, reform scheme issued . . . . 15 Nov. 1902

Dr. Prudente de Moraes, ex-pres., died . 3 Dec. „

Agreement with Bolivia *re* Alve dispute, signed March, 1903

Congress opened . . . . 3 May „

EMPERORS OF BRAZIL.

1822. Dom Pedro (of Portugal); abdicated in favour of his infant son, 7 April, 1831; died 24 Sept. 1834.

1831. Dom Pedro II. (born 2 Dec. 1825); assumed the government, 23 July, 1840; crowned, 18 July. 1841; married, 4 Sept. 1843, princess Theresa of Naples (born 14 March, 1822; died 28 Dec. 1889). Pedro II. deposed 15 Nov. 1889; died at Paris 5 Dec., buried in the cathedral at St. Vincent, Lisbon, 12 Dec. 1891.

Heiress. Isabella, born 29 July, 1846; married (15 Oct. 1864) Louis comte d'Eu, son of the duc de Nemours (born 29 April, 1842).

Heir. Pedro, born 15 Oct. 1875.

BREACH OF PROMISE; see *Marriage*.

BREAD. Ching-Noung, the successor of Fohi, is reputed to have been the first who taught men (the Chinese) the art of husbandry, and the method of making bread from wheat, and wine from rice, 1998 B.C. *Univ. Hist.* Baking of bread was known in the patriarchal ages: see *Exodus* xii. 15. It became a profession at Rome, 170 B.C. After the conquest of Macedon, 148 B.C., numbers of Greek bakers came to Rome, obtained special privileges, and soon obtained a monopoly. During the siege of Paris by Henry IV., owing to famine, bread, which had been sold whilst any remained for a crown a pound, was at last made from the bones of the charnel-house of the Holy Innocents, A.D. 1594. *Hénault.* In the time of James I., barley bread was used by the poor; and now in Iceland, cod-fish, beaten to powder, is made into bread; potato-bread is used in Ireland. The London Bakers' Company was incorporated in 1307. Bread-street was once the London market for bread. Until 1302, the London bakers were not allowed to sell any in their own shops. *Stow.* Bread was made with yeast by the English bakers in 1634. In 1856 and 1857 Dr. Dauglish patented a mode of making "aërated bread," in which carbonic acid gas is combined with water and mixed with the flour, and which is said to possess the advantages of cleanliness, rapidity, and uniformity. In 1862 a company was formed to encourage Stevens' bread-making machinery. An act for regulating bakehouses was passed in July, 1863. A strike of the journeymen bakers of the metropolis, 23 Sept., was settled by concessions, 9 Oct. 1872. A *Bread Reform League* formed; meeting at the Mansion house, London, 17 Dec. 1880. The Bread Union, limited, established in London, Sept. 1889; failure, Oct. 1890. Delegated meeting of working bakers in London, demanding increased pay and shorter time of labour, 5 Sept.; strike averted by concessions, Nov. 1889.

National school for bakers and confectioners inaugurated at a meeting at the Agricultural Hall, 21 Sept. 1899

New bakery at the Borough Polytechnic opened, 9 Sept. 1902

Quartern Loaf (4lb. 5½oz.)

Year	Price
1735	5½d.
1745	4¾
1755	5
1765	7
1775	6½
1785	6¼
1795	12¼
1800	17½d.
1800	[For 4 weeks, 22½d.
1805	12½
1810	15½
1812 Aug.	21½
1814	12½
1820	11

Four-pound Loaf (best)

Year	June.	Dec.
1822	10d.	
1825	11	
1830	10½	
1835	7	
1840	9	
1845	7½d.	7½d.
1850	7	6½
1854	10	11
1855	11	10½
1856	11	10½
1857	9½	8½
1858	8	7
1859	8	7½
1860	8½	9
1861	9	9
1862	9	8
1863	8	7
1864	7	7
1865	7	8
1866	8½	9
1867	10	10½
1868	10	8½
1869	8	7½
1870	7½	8½
1871	9	9
1872	9½	10
1873	8	8
1874 (*medium*).	8	6½
1875	6	7
1876	6½	7
1877	7½	7
1878	7	6
1879	6	7
1880	7	7
1881	6	7
1882	6½	6½
1883		6½
1884	6½	6
1885	5½	5½
1886	6	6
1887	6	5½
1888	5½	6
1889	6	6
1890	6	6
1891	6½	6½
1892	6	5½
1893	5½	5½
1894	5	5
1895	5	5
1896	5	6
1897	—	6½
1898	—	7½
1899	4½	5
1900	5	—
1902	5	5½
		Oct.
1903	5½	5½

ASSIZE OF BREAD. The first statute for the regulation of the sale of bread was 3 John, 1203. The chief justiciary, and a baker commissioned by the king, had the inspection of the assize. *Matthew Paris.* The assize was further regulated by statute in 51 Hen. III. 1266, and 8 Anne, 1710. Bread Act, Ireland, placing its sale on the same footing as in England, 1 Vict. 1838. Bread was directed to be sold by weight in London in 1822; the statute "Assessa Panis" was repealed in 1824; and the sale of bread throughout the country was regulated in 1836.

In France the old laws were superseded, and a law enabling the municipalities to fix the price of bread (still unrepealed) was passed, July, 1791.

BREAD-FRUIT TREE, a native of the South Sea islands. A vessel under captain Bligh was fitted out to convey some of these trees to various British colonies in 1789 (see *Bounty*), and again in 1791. The number taken on board at Otaheite was 1151. Some were left at St. Helena, 352 at Jamaica, and five were reserved for Kew Gardens, 1793. The tree was successfully cultivated in French Guiana, 1802.

BREADSTUFFS. Confectioners and Bakers' International Exhibition (11th Annual), Agricultural Hall, 5–12 Sept. 1903. The figures following show the relative proportions of the supplies of breadstuffs, wheat and flour (*tons*), received from British possessions and foreign countries during the period 1895–1902:—

India: 1895, 440,000; 1896, 106,000; 1897, 29,000; 1898, 477,000; 1899, 410,000; 1900, *nil*; 1901, 167,000; 1902, 442,000.

Canada: 1895, 255,000; 1896, 315,000; 1897, 347,000; 1898, 387,000; 1899, 436,000; 1900, 400,000; 1901, 429,000; 1902, 611,000.

Australia: 1895, 179,000; 1896-7, *nil*; 1898, 11,000; 1899, 151,000; 1900, 146,000; 1901, 310,000; 1902, 211,000.

New Zealand: 1899, 35,000; 1900, 57,000; 1901, 69,000; 1902, 8,000.

Total British Possessions: 1895, 874,000; 1896, 421,000; 1897, 376,000; 1898, 875,000; 1899, 1,032,000; 1900, 603,000; 1901, 975,000; 1902, 1,272,000.

FOREIGN.

United States: 1895, 2,266,000; 1896, 2,639,000; 1897, 2,707,000; 1898, 3,104,000; 1899, 3,104,000; 1900, 2,871,000; 1901, 3,343,000; 1902, 3,248,000.
Argentina: 1895, 572,000; 1896, 250,000; 1897, 47,000; 1898, 201,000; 1899, 576,000; 1900, 938,000; 1901, 415,000; 1902, 227,000.
Russia: 1895, 1,153,000; 1896, 863,000; 1897, 756,000; 1898, 320,000; 1899, 126,000; 1900, 225,000; 1901, 129,000; 1902, 331,000.
Austria-Hungary: 1895, 91,000; 1896, 96,000; 1897, 79,000; 1898, 51,000; 1899, 72,000; 1900, 81,000; 1901, 56,000; 1902, 48,000.
Other Foreign Countries: 1895, 407,000; 1896, 713,000; 1897, 469,000; 1898, 170,000; 1899, 108,000; 1900, 212,000; 1901, 135,000; 1902, 270,000.
Total Foreign: 1895, 4,489,000; 1896, 4,561,000; 1897 4,058,000; 1898, 3,846,000; 1899, 3,893,000; 1900 4,327,000; 1901, 4,078,000; 1902, 4,124,000.

BREAKWATERS. The first stone of the Plymouth breakwater was lowered 12 August, 1812. It stretches 5280 feet across the sound, is 360 feet in breadth at the bottom and more than 30 at the top, and consumed 3,660,000 tons of granite blocks, from one to five tons each, up to April, 1841, and cost a million and a half sterling. The architects were Mr. John Rennie and his son sir John. The first stone of the lighthouse on its western extremity was laid 1 Feb. 1841. Breakwaters have been constructed at Holyhead, Portland, Dover, Middlesborough, &c. A great barrier, about two-thirds of a mile long, erected to defend the hæmatite iron mines near the Daddon estuary, was completed by Messrs. Lucas & Aird, sir John Coode being the engineer, Oct. 1890. A breakwater in connection with extension of Admiralty pier is in progress (1903), much damaged by gale of 10 Sept. 1903.

BREAST-PLATE. One was worn by the Jewish high priest, 1491 B.C. (*Exod.* xxxix.) Goliath "was armed with a coat of mail," 1063 B.C. (1 *Sam.* xvii.) Breast-plates dwindled to the diminutive gorgets. Ancient breast-plates are mentioned as made of gold and silver.

BRECHIN, Scotland; sustained a siege against the army of Edward III., 1333. The battle of Brechin or Huntly-hill was fought between the earls of Huntly and Crawford, the latter defeated, 18 May, 1452. The see of Brechin was founded by David I. in 1150. One of its bishops, Alexander Campbell, was made prelate when but a boy, 1556. The bishopric, discontinued soon after the revolution in 1688, was revived in 1731.

BREDA, Holland, was taken from the Spaniards by prince Maurice, of Nassau, in 1590; retaken by the Spaniards, under Spinola, June, 1625; and by the Dutch, Oct. 1637. The "*Compromise* of Breda" was a proposal to Philip II., deprecating his harsh measures in the Netherlands, presented and refused in 1566. Our Charles II. resided here at the time of the restoration, and here he issued his *declaration* of a free general pardon, and promised religious toleration, 14 April, 1660; see *Restoration*. Breda was taken by the French in 1793. The French garrison was expelled by the burgesses in 1813. Population, 1890, 22,536.

BREECHES. Among the Greeks, this garment indicated slavery. It was worn by the Dacians, Parthians, and other northern nations; and in Italy, it is said, was worn in the time of Augustus Cæsar. In the reign of Honorius, about 394, the *braccarii*, or breeches-makers, were expelled from Rome. The "Geneva Bible," termed the "Breeches Bible" (from the rendering in *Gen.* iii. 7), published 1560.

BREECH-LOADERS, see under *Cannon* and *Firearms*.

BREED'S HILL, see *Bunker's Hill*.

BREHON LAWS, the ancient jurisprudence of Ireland, said to have been administered by hereditary judges called *Brehons*. It was enacted by the statute of Kilkenny, that no English subject should submit to the Brehon laws, 40 Edw. III., 1366. These laws, however, were recognised by the native Irish till 1650. A translation of them was proposed in 1852, and a commission appointed. The publication of the "Ancient Laws of Ireland" by the government, began 1865; completed, by vol. vi., glossary, July, 1902.

BREITENFELD, see *Leipsic*.

BREMEN (N. Germany), said to have been founded in 788, and long an archbishopric, and one of the leading towns of the Hanseatic League, was allowed a seat and a vote in the college of imperial cities in 1640. In 1648 it was secularised and erected into a duchy and held by Sweden till 1712, when it was taken possession of by Denmark, by whom it was sold to Hanover in 1731. It was taken by the French in 1757, who were expelled by the Hanoverians in 1758. Bremen was annexed by Napoleon to the French empire in 1810; but its independence was restored in 1813, and all its old franchises in 1815. It became a member of the North German Confederation in 1866. International agricultural exhibition opened 13 June, 1874. Population of the province, 1871, 122,402; 1885, 165,628; 1890, 180,443: of the city, 125,684; 1900, 224,882; city, 163,297. See *Hanse Towns*. For the explosion at Bremerhaven (the port of Bremen), 11 Dec. 1875, see *Dynamite*. The statue of the emperor, William I. unveiled by William II. 18 Oct. 1893. Hermann H. Meier, founder of N. German Lloyd, died, aged 88, 18 Nov. 1898.

BRENNEVILLE, N.W. France. Here Henry I. of England defeated Louis VI. of France, who supported William Cliton, son of Robert, duke of Normandy, 20 Aug. 1119.

BRENTFORD, county town of Middlesex. Here Edmund Ironside defeated the Danes, May, 1016. It was taken by Charles I., after a sharp fight, 12 Nov. 1642. Cowper and others alluded to its "two kings on one throne." Falstaff ("Merry Wives of Windsor") disguises himself as a "fat woman of Brentford."—*Chambers*. New market opened 24 May, 1893. New workhouse cost 100,000*l*., opened 4 Nov. 1902. Population, 1881, 11,805; 1891, 13,736; 1901, 15,171.

BRESCIA, N. Italy (the ancient Brixia), became important under the Lombards, and suffered by the wars of the Italian Republics, being attached to Venice. It was taken by the French under Gaston de Foix, Feb. 1512, when it is said 40,000 of the inhabitants were massacred. It was retaken 26 May, 1516. It surrendered to the Austrian general Haynau, 30 March, 1849, on severe terms. It was annexed to Sardinia in 1859.

BRESLAU, in Silesia, was burnt by the Mongols in 1241, and conquered by Frederick II. of Prussia, Jan. 1741. A fierce battle took place here between the Austrians and Prussians, the latter under prince Bevern, who was defeated 22 Nov. 1757. Breslau was taken; but was regained 21 Dec. same year. It was besieged by the French, and surrendered to them, Jan. 1807, and again in 1813. Statue of the emperor William I. unveiled by

William II.; visit of the czar and czarina, review and banquet, 5 Sept. 1896. Population of the city, 1895, 378,250; 1900, 422,738.

BRESSA PRIZE. Dr. Cesare Antonio Bressa, by will of 4 Sept. 1835, bequeathed property to the Royal Academy of Sciences, Turin, to give a prize every two years for some important discovery or valuable work published relating to physics, natural history, geography, history, statistics, &c. The first prize (about 1200*l.*) was to be awarded in 1879 to a foreigner; the second to an Italian, and so on alternately. The prize awarded to the late M. Pasteur in 1888.

BREST, a seaport, N. W. France, possessed by the English A.D. 1378. Lord Berkeley and a British fleet and army were repulsed here with dreadful loss in 1694. The magazine burnt, to the value of some millions of pounds sterling, 1744. The marine hospitals, with fifty galley slaves, burnt, 1766. The magazine again destroyed by fire, 10 July, 1784. From this great depôt of the French navy, numerous squadrons were equipped against England, among them the fleet which lord Howe defeated on 1 June, 1794. England maintained a large blockading squadron off the harbour from 1793 to 1815; but with little injury to France. It is now a chief naval station, and is considered impregnable. Failure of sardine fishery, British subscriptions in aid of fishermen, Jan. 1902. Population in 1901, 81,948.

BRETAGNE, see *Brittany*.

BRETHREN, see *Bohemian* and *Plymouth Brethren*.

BRETIGNY, PEACE OF, concluded with France, 8 May, 1360, by which England retained Gascony and Guienne, and acquired other provinces; renounced her pretensions to Maine, Anjou, Touraine, and Normandy; was to receive 3,000,000 crowns, and to release king John, long a prisoner. The treaty not being carried out, the king remained and died in England.

BRETON, see *Cape Breton*, and *Brittany*.

BRETWALDA (wide-ruling chief), one of the kings of the Saxon heptarchy, chosen by the others as a leader in war against their common enemies. The title was bestowed upon Egbert, 828; see *Britain*. Palgrave, Kemble, and Freeman differ in regard to this title.

BREVIARY (so called as being an abridgment of the offices used in the Roman Catholic service), contains the seven canonical hours, viz., matins about midnight; lauds (when not joined to matins, about 3 a.m.), primes (about 6), tierce (about 9), sexts (about 12), nones (about 3 p.m.), vespers (4 or 6), complines (about 9). *Lord Bute* published a translation of the breviary, 1879. The breviary is ascribed to pope Gelasius I. about 492. It was first called the *custos*, and afterwards the breviary; came into use among the ecclesiastical orders about 1080; and was reformed by the councils of Trent and Cologne, and by Pius V., Urban VIII., and other popes. The quality of type in which the breviary was first printed is said to have given the name to the printing type called *brevier*.

The Sforza Horæ, "Book of Hours," a collection of illuminated MSS. of the 15th and 16th centuries, formerly the property of the emperor Charles V. and his successors, was eventually acquired by Mr. Malcolm, of Poltallock, who gave it in 1893 to the British Museum, which already possessed the breviaries of Isabella the Catholic, and her daughter Joan. Forty-six "Books of Hours" sold in the "Ashburnham" library, 7 Dec. 1897; an early 15th-century "Book of Hours" realised 640*l.*, 4 July, 1901.

BREWERS are traced to Egypt. Brewing was known to the Greeks, Romans, and to our Anglo-Saxon ancestors. *Tindal.* "One William Murle, a rich maltman or bruer, of Dunstable, had two horses all trapped with gold, 1414." *Stow.* In Oct. 1851, there were 2305 licensed brewers in England, 146 in Scotland, and 97 in Ireland; total, 2548: these are exclusive of retail and intermediate brewers. There were 40,418 licensed brewers in the United Kingdom in 1858; the revenue from whom to the state was in that year 81,030*l.* In 1858 in England there were 205 great brewers; see *Ale*, *Porter*, and *Vacuum*.

In 1880 the brewers' licence (for sale) was made 1*l.*, not for sale, 6*s.*; a duty was laid upon beer calculated upon the specific gravity of the wort (43 & 44 Vict. c. 20); now (1903) 7*s.* 9*d.* per barrel.

Annual Brewers' exhibition at the Agricultural Hall, London, began 1879.

BRIAR'S CREEK (N. America), near which the Americans, 2000 strong, under general Ashe, were totally defeated by the English under general Prevost, 3 March, 1779.

BRIBERY forbidden (*Deut.* xvi. 19). Samuel's sons were guilty of it, 1112 B.C. (1 *Sam.* viii. 3). Thos. de Weyland, a judge, was banished for bribery in 1288; he was chief justice of the common pleas. William de Thorpe, chief justice of the king's bench, was convicted of bribery in 1351. Another judge was fined 20,000*l.* for the like offence, 1616. Mr. Walpole, secretary-at-war, was sent to the Tower for bribery in 1712. Lord Strangford was suspended from voting in the Irish house of lords, for soliciting a bribe, Jan. 1784.

BRIBERY AT ELECTIONS. In 1854 an important act was passed consolidating and amending previous acts relating to this offence, from 7 Will. III. (1695) to 5 & 6 Vict. c. 184.

Messrs. Sykes and Rumbold fined and imprisoned for bribery . . . . 14 March, 1776
Messrs. Davidson, Parsons, and Hopping, imprisoned for bribery at Ilchester . . 28 April, 1804
Mr. Swan, M.P. for Penryn, fined and imprisoned, and sir Manasseh Lopez sentenced to a fine of 10,000*l.* and two years' imprisonment for bribery at Grampound . . . . Oct. 1819
The members for Liverpool and Dublin unseated . 1831
The friends of Mr. Knight, candidate for Cambridge, convicted of bribery . . . . . . 20 Feb. 1835
Elections for Ludlow and Cambridge made void . 1840
Sudbury disfranchised, 1848; St. Albans also . . 1852
Elections at Derby and other places declared void for bribery 1853
Corrupt Practices Act passed 1854
In Cooper *v.* Slade, it was ruled that the payment of travelling expenses was bribery . 17 April, 1858
Gross bribery practised at Gloucester, Wakefield, and Berwick 1859
Mr. Wm. H. Leatham convicted of bribery at Wakefield . . . . 19 July, 1860
Government commissions of inquiry respecting bribers, sat at Great Yarmouth, Totnes, Lancaster, and Reigate; and disgraceful disclosures were made . . . . Aug.–Nov. 1866
The boroughs were disfranchised by the Reform bill, passed . . . . 15 Aug. 1867
The Parliamentary Elections Act enacted that election petitions should be tried by a court appointed for the purpose, passed . 31 July, 1868
First trials under this act; Mr. Roger Eykyn (at Windsor) was declared duly elected, 15 Jan., and sir H. Stracey (at Norwich) was unseated, 18 Jan. 1869
Dr. Kinglake, Mr. Fenelly, and others, were sentenced to be fined for bribery in parliamentary elections . . . . 10 May, 1870

Beverley, Bridgewater, Sligo, and Cashel disfranchised for bribery and corruption . . . 1870
Much corruption during the elections of April; members for Oxford, Chester, Boston, and other places, unseated 1880
Stringent Act against it, brought in by sir H. James, attorney-general, was passed in . . . 1881
Public Bodies Corrupt Practices Act . . . 1889
See *Corrupt Practices.*

BRIC-À-BRACS (French), old curiosities, such as cabinets, pieces of ironwork, &c. The collecting began about the time of queen Anne, 1702–14. The publication of *Bric-à-Brac*, a monthly price-list, began in 1869. See *Strawberry Hill, Hamilton* and *Spitzer Fonthill.*

BRICKS were used in Babylon, Chaldæa, Egypt (cf. Ex. i. 12, 14), Greece, and Rome; in England by the Romans. The size was regulated by order of Charles I., 1625. Taxed, 1784. The number of bricks which paid duty in England in 1820 was 949,000,000; in 1830, above 1,100,000,000; in 1840, 1,400,000,000; and in 1850, 1,700,000,000. The duties and drawbacks of excise on bricks were repealed in 1850. In 1839 Messrs. Cooke and Cunningham brought out their machinery for brick-making. Clayton & Co., of London, 1861, Bradley & Craven, of Wakefield, and many others followed. Brick-making by steam is now almost universal. 18,000 bricks made in ten hours.

BRIDEWELL, once a palace of king John, near Fleet-ditch, London, 1210, was given to the city for a workhouse by Edward VI., 1553.* The New Bridewell prison, erected in 1829, was pulled down in 1864; that of Tothill-fields was rebuilt in 1831.

BRIDGE, a fashionable card game, which at the present time (1903) is played extensively. The excessive gambling associated with the game and the heavy losses incurred by players in "society" circles, especially among ladies, has given rise to considerable scandal.

BRIDGES were first of wood. There are ancient stone bridges in China. Abydos is famous for the bridge of boats which Xerxes built across the Hellespont, 480 B.C. Trajan's magnificent stone bridge over the Danube, 4770 feet in length, was built in A.D. 105. *Brotherhoods for building bridges* existed in S. France about 1180. The Devil's bridge in the Canton of Uri was built on two high rocks; and many stories have been invented to account for it. At Schaffhausen an extraordinary bridge was built over the Rhine, 400 feet wide: there was a pier in the middle of the river, but it is doubtful whether the bridge rested upon it; a man of the lightest weight felt the bridge totter under him, yet waggons heavily laden passed over without danger. The bridge was destroyed by the French in 1799. See *Hammersmith, London, Waterloo, Blackfriars, Southwark, Forth, Tay, Tower, Westminster*, and other bridges, in separate articles. The chief Thames bridges were freed from toll 24 May, 1879, and 26 June, 1880.

Triangular bridge at Croyland abbey referred to in a charter dated 943
London bridge: one existed about 978; one built of wood, 1014; one by Peter of Colechurch, 1176–1209; new bridge finished (widened 1901–3). . 1831

* Of the old buildings little remains: merely offices and a few cells for refractory City apprentices. By the Charity Commissioners' scheme (1860) the annual income (14,682*l.* in 1876) is devoted to the maintenance of two industrial schools: for boys, at Witley, Surrey; for girls, at St. George's fields.

A stone bridge erected at Bow, near Stratford, by queen Matilda . . . . about 1100–18
Bishop's bridge, Norwich 1295
The first large iron bridge erected over the Severn, Shropshire 1777
Sunderland bridge by Wilson, 100 feet high, an arch with a span of 236 feet . . 1796
The chain suspension bridge at Menai Strait . . 1825
Old Westminster, opened, 1750; old Blackfriars, 1769; Waterloo, 1817; Southwark, 1819; Hungerford, 1845; Chelsea, 1858; Vauxhall, 1816.
A railway bridge 2½ miles long projected over the Firth of Forth (not executed) . . Dec. 1864
The very wide Victoria bridge, over the Thames (by which the London, Chatham and Dover railway enters the Victoria station, Pimlico); founded by lord Harris . . 22 Feb. 1865
For details see separate articles, and also *Tubular bridge, Newcastle, Niagara, Victoria bridge, &c.*
New York and Brooklyn bridge, 5862 feet long; 1600 central span; 130 feet high; July, 1872, *et seq.*
Tay bridge (*which see*) 1871–7; Forth bridge (see under *Forth*) 1879–89
The great railway bridge over the Severn (about ¾ mile long), connecting the Forest of Dean with Sharpness Point, the port of Gloucester (cost 1,000,000*l.*), was formally opened . 17 Oct. 1879
Great railway bridge over the Volga, near Syzlan, Saratoy government, built . . . 1877-80
Suspension bridge from New York to Brooklyn (5989 feet long) opened . . . 24 May, 1883
The Gokteik viaduct, Shan hills, Burmah, the highest railway bridge in the world, completed, 13 Dec. 1900

BRIDGEWATER, seaport of Somersetshire, was incorporated by king John, in 1200. Coasting trade about 160,000 tons, 1902. In the civil war it was taken by the parliamentary forces, 23 July, 1645. Here stood an ancient castle in which the ill-advised duke of Monmouth lodged when proclaimed king in 1685. The town was disfranchised for bribery, 1870. Population, 1881, 12,007; 1891, 12,429; 1901, 15,209.

BRIDGEWATER CANAL, the first great work of the kind in England, was begun by the duke of Bridgewater, the father of canal navigation in this country, in 1759, and opened 17 July, 1761. James Brindley was the engineer. It commences at Worsley, seven miles from Manchester; and at Barton Bridge is an aqueduct which, for upwards of 200 yards, conveys the canal across the river Irwell. The length of the canal is about twenty-nine miles. The duke's canals connected the Thames, Humber, Severn and Mersey; and London, Hull, Bristol, and Liverpool.

BRIDGEWATER TREATISES. The rev. Francis, earl of Bridgewater, died in April, 1829, leaving by will 8,000*l.* to be given to the author or authors, appointed by the president of the Royal Society, who should write an essay "on the power, wisdom, and goodness of God, as manifested in the creation." The essays (by sir Charles Bell, Drs. T. Chalmers, John Kidd, William Buckland, William Prout, Peter M. Roget, and the revs. William Whewell and William Kirby) were published 1833–35.

BRIEFS are the letters of the pope despatched to princes and others on public affairs, and written short, without preface or preamble, and on paper; in which particulars they are distinguished from *bulls*. Briefs are sealed with red wax and the seal of the fisherman, or St. Peter in a boat, and always in the presence of the pope. Letters of the English sovereign, called "briefs," authorising collections in churches for charitable purposes, abolished in 1828. "Church Briefs," by Mr. W. A. Bewes, published Feb. 1897. A lawyer's brief is an abridgment of his client's case. It is endorsed with the title of the Court and the action, and with the names of the counsel and the solicitor, and marked with the proper fee.

BRIENNE (N. E. France). Here the allied armies of Russia and Prussia, under Blücher, were defeated by the French, 29 Jan. 1814.

BRIGANDAGE. See *Italy*, 1861 *et seq.*; *Greece*, 1870; *Spain*, 1870; and *Turkey*.

BRIGHT'S DISEASE, a degeneration of the tissues of the kidneys into fat, investigated about 1830 by Dr. Richard Bright.

BRIGHTON, formerly Brighthelmstone, a fishing town, Sussex, was made a place of fashionable resort by the prince of Wales, afterwards George IV. Brighton returns two M.P.'s by Act of 1885. Population, 153,691, 1901.

At Shoreham, near Brighton, Charles II. embarked for France after the battle of Worcester . . . 1651
Visit of the prince of Wales 1782
He founded the Pavilion 1784; it was greatly enlarged and made to resemble the Kremlin at Moscow, 1784–1823; sold to the town for 53,000*l.*, . 1849
The Block-house swept away . . . . 26 March, 1786
Part of the cliff fell; great damage . . 16 Nov. 1807
Chain-pier, 1134 feet long, 13 wide, completed . 1823
Brighton made a parliamentary borough . . 1832
The railway to London opened . . 21 Sept. 1841
Collision of trains in Clayton tunnel, 23 persons killed and many injured . . . 25 August, 1861
Volunteer reviews here on Easter Monday, 1862; and often since, see under *Volunteers*.
New "West" pier erected 1865–6
Great aquarium inaugurated by prince Arthur, 30 Mar.; and formally opened by the mayor, 10 Aug. 1872
British Association meet here . . 14 Aug. ,,
Free library, museum, and picture gallery, opened 12 Sept. 1873
Inauguration of statue of sir John Cordy Burrows, great benefactor to the town . . . 14 Feb. 1878
About 2000 French and Belgian singers and musicians meet . . . . 5 Sept. 1881
Grand concert room, &c., burned . . 8 Oct. 1882
New town hall, Hove, opened . . . 13 Dec. ,,
Electric railway tried . . . . . 4 April, 1884
Preston park (purchased for 60,000*l.* aided by legacy from W. E. Davis) opened by the mayor . 8 Nov. ,,
Railway to Devil's Dyke opened . . 1 Sept. 1887
International exhibition of arts and manufactures at Hove opened . . . . 21 Oct. 1889
New terraces, sheltered walk, halls, &c., opened by the mayor . . . . . . 25 May, 1890
Museum of British birds, bequeathed to the town by Mr. E. T. Booth, opened by the mayor, 3 Nov. ,,
Visit of the prince of Wales to lay the foundation stone (extension) of the Sussex county hospital 29 Feb. 1896
Visit of the duke and duchess of York; see *Teachers* 9 April ,,
New electric railway on the shore opened 28 Nov. ,,
Chain pier completely destroyed by a gale, and other damage . . . . . 4 Dec. ,,
Steep grade railway on the Devil's Dyke opened 24 July, 1897
Statue of the queen by prof. Nicoli, presented by mayor (sir John Blaker), unveiled . 8 Dec. ,,
New pier with marine palace, 1,700 feet long, opened 20 May, 1899
Bronze statue of queen Victoria, unveiled . 9 Feb. 1901
Public art galleries, museum, news-rooms and library, cost 40,000*l.*, opened . . . 5 Nov. 1902

BRILL OR BRIEL, Holland. A seaport, seized by the expelled Dutch confederates, became the seat of their independence, 1572. Briel, given up to the English in 1585 as security for advances made by queen Elizabeth to Holland, was restored in 1616.

BRISBANE, capital of Queensland, on the river Brisbane, Australia, was founded by Oxley, in 1823, settled as a penal station in 1825 by sir J. Brisbane, and made a bishopric in 1859, when the colony was constituted. Spacious dry dock opened at S. Brisbane in 1881. By the capsizing of the steamer *Pearl* about 40 persons were drowned on the Brisbane river, 13 Feb. 1896. Population in 1887 (with suburbs), 73,649; 1891, 93,657; 1901, 119,428. For the great floods, see *Queensland*, 1893.

BRISSOTINS, see *Girondists*.

BRISTOL (W. England) is mentioned in 430 as a fortified city. It was called Caer Oder, a city in the valley of Bath; and, sometimes Caer Brito, the British city, and by the Saxons Brightstowe, pleasant place. Gildas and Nennius speak of Bristol in the 5th and 7th centuries. From the 12th to the 18th century it was, next to London, the most flourishing port in England; it has since been surpassed by Liverpool. See under *Orphan-houses*. An industrial and fine art exhibition for Somerset and Gloucester opened 2 Sept. 1884. Population 1901, 329,990. Bristol returns four M.P.'s by Act of 1885.

Taken by the earl of Gloucester, in his defence of his sister Maud, the empress, against king Stephen 1138
Eleanor of Brittany (daughter of Geoffrey, son of Henry II.) dies in the castle after 39 years' imprisonment 1241
Church of St. Mary Redcliff built 1292, restored 1376; again 1470; spire completed . . 1872
Bristol made a distinct county by Edward III. . 1373
Bishopric founded by Henry VIII. . . . 1542
Taken by prince Rupert, 26 July, 1643; by Cromwell, 10 Sept. 1645
Edwd. Colston's hospital, a free school, and other charities established [his birthday, 13 Nov. kept annually] 1708
[Annual dinners: the Dolphin Society (conservative) since 1749; the Anchor Society (liberal) since 1768; Grateful Society (neutral) since 1757.]
New charter 1710
Act passed for new exchange, 1723; erected . . 1741
Bread riots 1753
Bridge built . . . . May, 1760
Attempt to set the shipping on fire . . 22 Jan. 1777
Riot on account of a toll; the troops fire on the populace, and many are wounded . 25 Oct. 1793
Docks built 1804–9
Riot on the entrance of sir Charles Wetherell, the recorder, into the city, he being opposed to the reform bill; the mansion house, the bishop's palace, several merchants' stores, some of the prisons (the inmates liberated), nearly 100 houses burned, and above 500 persons killed by the military or perished . . . . 29–31 Oct. 1831
Trial of rioters (four executed; 22 transported), 2 Jan.; suicide of col. Brereton, during trial by court-martial . . . . . . 9 Jan. 1832
Meeting of British Association . . . Aug. 1836
Railway to London completed . . 30 June, 1841
Clifton suspension-bridge opened . . 8 Dec. 1864
Industrial Exhibition opened . . . 19 Sept. 1865
British Association, 2nd meeting 1875
Proposed foundation of a college for science and literature here for the south and west of England; meeting, 13 June, 1874; medical school added; opened as University College . . . 10 Sept. 1876
Great fire; Clutterbuck's, drysalters, &c., loss between 80,000*l.* and 100,000*l.* . . . 24–25 May, ,,
Avonmouth dock opened . . . . 24 Feb. 1877
Merchant venturers' technical college, founded . 1885
Statue of Mr. Samuel Morley, long M.P. for Bristol, unveiled . . . . . 22 Oct. 1887
Explosion of 300 barrels of naphtha on board the Jersey ketch *The United*; 3 deaths . 21 Nov. 1888
Great flood; damage about 100,000*l.* . 8–9 March, 1889
Trade paralyzed by strikes; settled by compromise Oct.–Dec. ,,
About 10,000 of the boot trade locked out, 23 Dec., 1889; settled by compromise . about 20 Jan. 1890
Dock and other strikes; rioting checked by the police and military . . . . 23 Dec. 1892

Visit of the duke of Devonshire; speech against Irish home rule bill . . . . 6 April, 1893
Art and industrial exhibition opened by the mayor (Mr. Barker) . . . . 28 Aug. ,,
Statue of Edmund Burke presented by sir Wm. Wills, unveiled by the earl of Rosebery . 30 Oct. 1894
Wesleyan chapel, Redland-road, burnt down, 24 Oct. 1896
Visit of lord Dufferin; receives the freedom of the city and lays the foundation of the Cabot tower, 24 June, 1897; opened by him . . 6 Sept. 1898
Colston-hall and Messrs. Clarke's factory burnt down . . . . 1 Sept. ,,
British association, 3rd meeting . . 7 Sept. ,,
Mr. Vincent Stuckey Lean, dies 24 March; bequeaths 50,000*l.* for free libraries and 29,000*l.* to other charities . . . . . 29 March, 1899
The queen opens the Convalescent (Diamond Jubilee) Home (site presented by Mr. E. P. Wills, K.C.B., 1899); Mr. Herbert Ashman, knighted . . . . 15 Nov. ,,
Exhibition of Jamaican products and industries opened . . . . 11 April, 1901
The prince of Wales cuts the first sod of the Royal Edward dock at Avonmouth . . . 5 March, 1902
The dock entrances and clearances each amount to about 1,250,000 tons . . . . . . ,,
Mr. M. Whitwill, philanthropist, etc., died 6 Aug. 1903
Church congress held . . . . . 13–16 Oct. ,,

BRISTOL, SEE OF, one of the six bishoprics erected by Henry VIII. out of the spoils of the dissolved monasteries, 1542. The cathedral was the church of the abbey of St. Austin, founded here by Robert Fitz-Harding, son to a king of Denmark, and a citizen of Bristol, 1148. The see is valued in the king's books at 338*l.* 8*s.* 4*d.* Paul Bushe, provincial of the Bons-hommes, was the first bishop, in 1542—deprived for being married, 1554. The see of Bristol was united by an order in council with that of Gloucester, in 1836, but in 1884 an act was passed to provide for their again becoming separate bishoprics. Amendment, 1894, and 1896. Subscriptions received Aug. 1896; the bishopric reconstituted by an order in council, 7 July, 1897. The cathedral (under repair since 1844) was reopened in 1861; a new nave opened 23 Oct. 1877; restoration of the Lady Chapel, tower, etc., proceeding 1893, *et seq.*, the choir reopened, 5 May, 1895; a beautiful reredos unveiled, mid Oct. 1899.

BISHOPS OF BRISTOL.

1803. Hon. G. Pelham, translated to Exeter, 1807.
1807. John Luxmoore, translated to Hereford, 1808.
1808. Wm. Lort Mansell, died, 27 June, 1820.
1820. John Kaye, translated to Lincoln, 1827.
1827. Robert Gray, died 28 Sept. 1834.
1834. Joseph Allen, the last bishop, translated to Ely in June, 1836. (In October the diocese was united with Gloucester.)
1897 (Re-constituted). George Forrest Browne, D.D. (bp. suff. of Stepney), elected 16 Sept. 1897.

BRITAIN (called by the Romans Britannia,* from its Celtic name Prydain (*Camden*). The earliest records of the history of this island are the manuscripts and poetry of the Cambrians. The Celts, the ancestors of the Britons and modern Welsh, were the first inhabitants of Britain. It is referred to as the Cassiterides or tin-islands by Herodotus, 450 B.C.; as Albion and Ierne (England and Ireland) by Aristotle, 350 B.C., and Polybius, 260 B.C. Britain, including England, Scotland, and Wales, was anciently called Albion, the name of Britain being applied to all the islands collectively—Albion to only one. (*Pliny*). See *Albion, England, Scotland,* and *Wales.* Early history and dates doubtful.

* The Romans eventually divided Britain into *Britannia Prima* (country south of the Thames and Severn); *Britannia Secunda* (Wales); *Flavia Cæsariensis* (between the Thames, Severn, and Humber); *Maxima Cæsariensis* (between the Humber and Tyne); and *Valentia* (between the Tyne and Firth of Forth). The figure of Britannia on coins was first struck by the Romans. See *Copper,* 1665.

Divitiacus, king of the Suessones, in Gaul, said to have supremacy over part of Britain . . . B.C. 57
First invasion of Britain by the Romans, under Julius Cæsar . . . . . . 26 Aug. 55
Second invasion; he defeats Cassivelaunus, British general 54
Cymbeline (Cunobelin), king of Britain . . . 4
Aulus Plautius defeats the Britons . . . A.D. 43
He and Vespasian reduce S. Britain . . . 47
Caractacus defeated by Ostorius, 50; carried in chains to Rome 52
Romans defeated by Boadicea, queen of the Iceni; 70,000 slain, and London burnt: she is defeated by Suetonius: 80,000 slain, place uncertain . 61
Agricola, governor, conquers Anglesey, and overruns Britain in seven campaigns, and reforms the government 78–84
He defeats the Caledonians under Galgacus; surrenders the islands 84
The emperor Adrian visits Britain, 120; and builds a wall from the Tyne to the Solway . . 121
Lucius, king of the Britons, *said* to have sent an embassy on religious affairs to pope Eleutherius, about 181
The Britons (allies of Albinus) defeated at Lyons by Severus 197
Southern Britain subdued and divided by the Romans into two provinces 204
Severus keeps his court at York, then called Eboracum, 208; finishes his wall, and dies at York, 4 Feb. 211
Carausius usurps the throne of Britain . . . 286
He is killed by Allectus, another usurper . . 294
Constantius recovers Britain and kills Allectus . 296
St. Alban and 17,000 Christians martyred (*Bede*) . 304
Constantius, emperor of Rome, dies at York, 25 July, 306
British bishops at the council of Arles . . . 314
Scots and Picts invade Britain, 360; routed by Theodosius 368
Romans gradually withdraw from Britain . 402–436
Reign of Vortigern 425
The Saxons and Angles aid in expelling the Picts and Scots 429
The Romans quit Britain 436
The Anglo-Saxon invaders drive the Britons into Wales and Cornwall 449–455
Many Britons settle in Armorica (Brittany) . 388–457
The Saxon Heptarchy; Britain divided into seven or more kingdoms 457
Ella invades South Britain, 477; founds kingdom of Sussex 491
Supposed reigns of Vortimer, 464; Vortigern again, 471; Aurelius Ambrosius, 481; and Arthur Pendragon 500
Great Saxon invasion under Cerdic 495
The renowned king Arthur said to reign . . 500–532
Arrival of St. Augustin (or Austin), and re-establishment of Christianity 597
Cadwallader, last king of the Britons, reigns . . 678
Lindisfarne church destroyed by the Northmen . . 794
Egbert, king of Wessex, virtually KING OF ENGLAND 827

KINGS OF THE HEPTARCHY,* see *Bretwalda.*
KENT. [*The shire of Kent.*]

454. Hengist. [473, Saxon Chronicle.]
488. Æsc, Esca, or Escus, son of Hengist; in honour of whom the kings of Kent were for some time called Æscings.
512. Octa, son of Æsc.
542. Hermenric, or Ermenric, son of Octa.
560. St. Ethelbert; first Christian king (styled *Rex Anglorum*).
616. Eadbald, son of Ethelbert.
640. Ercenbert, or Ercombert, son of Eadbald.
664. Ecbert, or Egbert, son of Ercenbert.
673. Lothar, or Lothair, brother of Ecbert.
685. Edric; slain in 687. [The kingdom now subject to various leaders.]
694. Wihtred, or Wihgtred.

* The term "Octarchy" is sometimes used; Northumbria being divided into Bernicia and Deira, separate kingdoms.

725. Eadbert,
748. Ethelbert II., } sons of Wihtred, succeeding each other.
760. Alric,
794. Edbert, or Ethelbert Pryn; deposed.
796. Cuthred, or Guthred.
805. Baldred; who lost his life and kingdom to
823. EGBERT, king of Wessex.

SOUTH SAXONS. [*Sussex and Surrey.*]

491. Ella, a warlike prince, succeeded by
514. Cissa, his son, whose reign was long and peaceful, exceeding 70 years.
[The South Saxons then fell into an almost total dependence on the kingdom of Wessex.]
648. Edilwald, Edilwach, Adelwach, or Ethelwach.
686. Authun and Berthun, brothers, reigned jointly; vanquished by Ina, king of Wessex, 689; kingdom conquered in 725.

WEST SAXONS. [*Berks, Hampshire, Wilts, Somerset, Dorset, Devon, and part of Cornwall.*]

519. Cerdic.
534. Cynric, or Kenric, son of Cerdic.
560. Ceawlin, son of Cynric; banished; dies in 593.
591. Ceolric, nephew to Ceawlin.
597. Ceolwulf.
611. } Cynegils, and in
614. } Cwichelm, his son, reigned jointly.
643. Cenwal, Cenwalh, or Cenwald.
672. Sexburga, his queen, sister to Penda, king of Mercia; of great qualities; probably deposed.
674. Escwine, with Centwine; on his death,
676. Centwine rules alone.
685. Cædwallo: went to Rome, to expiate his deeds of blood, and died there.
688. Ina or Inas, a brave and wise ruler; journeyed to Rome; left an excellent code of laws.
728. Ethelheard, or Ethelard, related to Ina.
740. Cuthred, brother to Ethelheard.
754. Sigebright, or Sigebert, having murdered his friend Cumbran, governor of Hampshire, was slain by one of his victim's retainers.
755. Cynewulf, or Kenwulf, or Cenulpe, a noble youth of the line of Cerdic; murdered.
784. Bertric, or Beorhtric; poisoned by drinking of a cup his queen had prepared for another.
800. EGBERT, afterwards sole monarch of England, and Bretwalda.

EAST SAXONS. [*Essex, Middlesex, and part of Herts.*]

526, 527, or 530, Erchenwin, or Erchwine.
587. Sledda; his son.
597. St. Sebert, or Sabert; son, first Christian king.
614. Saxred or Sexted, or Serred, jointly with Sigebert and Seward; all slain.
623. Sigebert II. surnamed the little; son of Seward.
655. Sigebert III. surnamed the good; brother of Sebert: put to death.
661. Swithelm (or Suidhelm), son of Sexbald.
663. Sigher, or Sigeric, jointly with Sebbi, or Sebba, who became a monk.
693. Sigenard, or Sigehard, and Suenfrid.
700 Offa; became a monk at Rome.
709. Suebricht, or Selred.
738. Swithred, or Swithed; a long reign.
792. Sigeric; died in a pilgrimage to Rome.
799. Sigered.
823. Kingdom seized by EGBERT of Wessex.

NORTHUMBRIA. [*Lancaster, York, Cumberland, Westmoreland, Durham, and Northumberland.*]

*** Northumbria was at first divided into two governments, *Bernicia* and *Deira;* the former stretching from the Tweed to the Tyne, and the latter from the Tyne to the Humber.
547. Ida, a valiant Saxon.
560. Adda, his eldest son; king of Bernicia.
,, Ella, king of Deira; afterwards the sole king of Northumbria (to 587).
567. Glappa, Clappa, or Elapea; Bernicia.
572. Heodwulf; Bernicia.
573. Freodwulf; Bernicia.
580. Theodoric; Bernicia.
588. Ethelric; Bernicia.
593. Ethelfrith, surnamed the Fierce.
617. Edwin, son of Ella, king of Deira in 590; a great prince. Slain in battle with Penda, of Mercia.
634. Eanfrid rules in Bernicia, and Osric in Deira; both put to death.
635. Oswald slain in battle.
642. Osweo, or Oswy; a reign of great renown.
670. Ecfrid, or Egfrid, king of Northumbria.
685. Alcfrid, or Ealdferth.
705. Osred, or Ealdferth.
716. Cenric; sprung from Ida.
718. Osric, son of Alcfrid.
729. Ceolwulf; died a monk.
737. Eadbert, or Egbert; retired to a monastery.
757. Oswulf, or Osulf; slain in a sedition.
759. Edilwald, or Mollo; slain by Alred
765. Alred, Ailred, or Alured; deposed
774. Ethelred, son of Mollo; expelled.
778. Elwald, or Celwold; deposed and slain.
789. Osred, son of Alred; fled.
790. Ethelred restored; afterwards slain.
794. Erdulf, or Ardulf; deposed.
806. Alfwold.
808. Erdulf restored.
809. Eanred.
841. Kingdom annexed by EGBERT.

EAST ANGLES. [*Norfolk, Suffolk, Cambridge, Ely.*]

526. Uffa lands.
571 or 575. Uffa; a German, said to be first king.
578. Titilus, or Titulus; son of Uffa.
599. Redwald, son of Titilus; the greatest prince of East Angles.
624. Erpwald, Eorpwald, or Eordwald.
627. Richbert.
629. Sigebert, half-brother to Erpwald.
632. Egfrid, or Egric; cousin to Sigebert.
635. Anna, or Annas; a just ruler; killed.
654. Ethelric, or Ethelhere; slain in battle.
655. Ethelwald; his brother.
664. Aldulf, or Aldwulf.
713. Selred, or Ethelred.
746. Alphwuld.
749. Beorna and Ethelred, jointly.
758. Beorna alone.
761. Ethelred.
790. Ethelbert, or Ethelbryght; treacherously put to death in Mercia in 792, when Offa, king of Mercia, overran the country, which was finally subdued by EGBERT.
870. St. Edmund (vassal king) slain by the Danes.

MERCIA. [*Gloucester, Hereford, Chester, Stafford, Worcester, Oxford, Salop, Warwick, Derby, Leicester, Bucks, Northampton, Notts, Lincoln, Bedford, Rutland, Huntingdon, and part of Herts.*]

586. Crida, or Cridda, a noble chieftain.
593. [Interregnum—Ceolric.]
597. Wibba, a valiant prince, his son.
615. Ceorl, or Cheorl; nephew of Wibba.
626. Penda; fierce and cruel; killed in battle.
655. Peada, son of Penda; killed to make way for
656. Wulfhere (brother); slew his two sons.
675. Ethelred; became a monk.
704. Cenred, or Cendred; became a monk at Rome.
709. Ceolred, Celred, or Chelred; son of Ethelred.
716. Ethelbald; slain in a mutiny by his successor.
755. Beornred, or Bernred; himself slain.
,, Offa; formed the great dyke near Wales.
794. Egfrid, or Egferth, son of Offa; died suddenly.
,, Cenulph Cenwulf, or Kenulph; slain.
819. Kenelm, or Cenelm, a minor; reigned five months killed by his sister Quendreda.
,, Ceolwulf, uncle to Kenelm; expelled.
821. Beornwulf; killed by his own subjects.
823. Ludecan; a valiant ruler; slain.
825. Withlafe, or Wiglaf.
838. Berthulf, or Bertulf.
852. Burhred, or Burdred.
874. Ceolwulph; deposed by the Danes, 877.
[The kingdom merged into that of England.]

BRITANNIA, see *Britain.*

BRITANNIA TUBULAR BRIDGE, see *Tubular Bridge.*

BRITANNY, or BRETAGNE (N. W. France), the ancient Armorica (*which see*), formed part of the kingdom of the Franks. The Bretons still retain much of their ancient Celtic language and customs (1891). Sardine fishery fails 1902. See *Brest*.

Nomenoë revolts and becomes the first count . . 841
Britanny ravaged by Northmen, 907; ceded to them 921
Geoffroy I., the first duke 992
Alan V., 1008; Conan II. 1040
Hoel V., 1066; Alan VI. 1084
Conan III. 1112
Hoel VI. expelled; Geoffroy of Anjou duke . . 1155
Conan IV. duke, 1156; on the death of Geoffroy, cedes Britanny to Henry II. of England, and betroths his daughter, Constance, to Henry's son, Geoffroy (both infants) 1159
Geoffroy succeeds, 1171; killed at a tournament . 1186
His son, Arthur, dies mysteriously at Rouen, his uncle John suspected; his daughter, Eleanor, imprisoned at Bristol (for 39 years) . April, 1203
Alice, daughter of Constance by her second husband, Guy de Thours, proclaimed duchess, 1203; marries Peter of Dreux, made duke 1213
John I., duke, 1237; John II. 1286
John III., 1312; dies without issue 1341
The succession disputed between John of Montfort (John IV.) supported by Edward of England, and Charles of Blois, made duke by Philip VI. of France. John is made prisoner; his wife, Jane, besieged at Hennebonne, holds out, and is relieved by the English, 1343; John dies . . 1345
Charles of Blois defeated and slain at Auray, 29 Sept.; John V., son of Montfort, duke 1364
John VI., duke, 1399; Francis I. 1442
Peter II., 1450; Arthur III. 1457
Francis II., 1458; takes part with the Orleanists in France; defeated at St. Aubin, 28 July, 1488; dies 1488
Anne, his daughter and heiress, marries 1st, Charles VIII. of France, 1491; 2nd, Louis XII., 1499; her eldest daughter, Claude (born 1499), marries Francis, count of Angoulême, 1514; king of France . . . . 1 Jan. 1515
Britanny formally united to the monarchy . . . 1532
Britanny held by the Spaniards, 1591; recovered by Henry IV. 1594
The Bretons take part in the Vendean insurrection (see *La Vendée*) in 1791

BRITISH, see *Architects; Antiquaries; Banks, Joint Stock; Guiana, Honduras, National, Medical, Orphans, Societies*.

BRITISH ACADEMY, for the promotion of historical, philosophical and philological studies; first meeting held at the British museum, 17 Dec. 1901; petition to the king for incorporation, signed by 127 eminent men, issued *London Gazette*, 14 Jan. 1902; royal charter granted, list of 49 fellows; lord Rosebery, visc. Dillon, Mr. A. J. Balfour, Mr. John Morley, Mr. Lecky (d. 22 Oct. 1903), and others, lord Reay elected president 28 Nov. 1902.

BRITISH AMERICA (see *America*) comprises the Dominion of Canada, in which are included British Columbia, North-west Territories, the provinces of Manitoba, Ontario, Quebec, New Brunswick, Nova Scotia and Prince Edward Island, and that portion not in the Dominion, viz., Newfoundland and its dependency, Labrador.

Delegates from the first six provinces met at Quebec on 10 Oct., and agreed to the basis of a Federal union, with the queen as the executive (represented by the governor-general), a legislative council of 96 members for life, and a house of commons of 194 members, 20 Oct. 1864.
The secretary for the colonies, Mr. Cardwell, expressed his approval of the plan, 3 Dec. 1864.
The plan opposed by New Brunswick and Nova Scotia, 7 March, 1865.
Messrs. Cartier and Galt came to England to advocate it, April, 1865.
The British North America act: the Dominion of Canada to be divided into 4 provinces, viz.: Ontario, formerly Upper Canada; Quebec, formerly Lower Canada; Nova Scotia and New Brunswick, brought into parliament by the earl of Carnarvon, 19 Feb., passed 29 March, 1867.
(The British government guaranteed a subsidy of 3,000,000*l.* to complete the intercolonial railway.)
By the British North America act, the parliament of Canada may establish new provinces, 29 June, 1871.
BRITISH AMERICAN, see *George, St., Sons of.*

BRITISH AND FOREIGN—Bible Society, established 1804 (see under *Bible*);—School Society, 1808;—Sailors' Society, 1818.

BRITISH ASSOCIATION for the Advancement of Science, was established by sir David Brewster, sir R. I. Murchison, &c., in 1831. Professor John Phillips was secretary till 1863. It holds annual meetings; the first of which was held at York on 27 Sept. 1831. One of its main objects is "to promote the intercourse of those who cultivate science with each other." It appoints commissions and makes pecuniary grants for scientific research; and publishes annually a volume containing Reports of the proceedings; about 66 local societies are now in union (1895). Kew observatory presented to the association by the queen in 1842. Superintendents, Francis Ronalds, the first; John Walsh, 1852; Balfour Stewart, 1859. It was purchased for the Royal Society by Mr. J. P. Gassiot, in 1871. See *Women*, 1900.

1.	York Meeting	1831	40.	Liverpool (3rd)	1870
2.	Oxford	1832	41.	Edinburgh (3rd)	1871
3.	Cambridge	1833	42.	Brighton	1872
4.	Edinburgh	1834	43.	Bradford	1873
5.	Dublin	1835	44.	Belfast (2nd)	1874
6.	Bristol	1836	45.	Bristol (2nd)	1875
7.	Liverpool	1837	46.	Glasgow (3rd)	1876
8.	Newcastle	1838	47.	Plymouth (2nd)	1877
9.	Birmingham	1839	48.	Dublin (3rd)	1878
10.	Glasgow	1840	49.	Sheffield	1879
11.	Plymouth	1841	50.	Swansea (2nd)	1880
12.	Manchester	1842	51.	York (3rd) *Jubilee*	1881
13.	Cork	1843	52.	Southampton (2nd) 23 Aug.	1882
14.	York (2nd time)	1844	53.	Southport, 19 Sept.	1883
15.	Cambridge (2nd)	1845	54.	Montreal	1884
16.	Southampton	1846	55.	Aberdeen (2nd) 9 Sept.	1885
17.	Oxford (2nd)	1847	56.	Birmingham (4th)	1886
18.	Swansea	1848	57.	Manchester (3rd) (most successful)	1887
19.	Birmingham (2nd)	1849	58.	Bath (2nd), 5 Sept.	1888
20.	Edinburgh (2nd)	1850	59.	Newcastle (3rd)	1889
21.	Ipswich	1851	60.	Leeds (2nd), 2 Sept.	1890
22.	Belfast	1852	61.	Cardiff	1891
23.	Hull	1853	62.	Edinburgh (4th)	1892
24.	Liverpool (2nd)	1854	63.	Nottingham (2nd)	1893
25.	Glasgow (2nd)	1855	64.	Oxford (4th), 8 Aug.	1894
26.	Cheltenham	1856	65.	Ipswich, 11 Sept.	1895
27.	Dublin (2nd)	1857	66.	Liverpool (4th), 16 Sept.	1896
28.	Leeds	1858	67.	Toronto, 18 Aug.	1897
29.	Aberdeen	1859	68.	Bristol	1898
30.	Oxford (3rd)	1860	69.	Dover 13 Sept.	1899
31.	Manchester (2nd)	1861	70.	Bradford	1900
32.	Cambridge (3rd)	1862	71.	Glasgow 11 Sept.	1901
33.	Newcastle (2nd)	1863	72.	Belfast 10 Sept.	1902
34.	Bath	1864	73.	Southport 9 Sept.	1903
35.	Birmingham (3rd)	1865			
36.	Nottingham	1866			
37.	Dundee	1867			
38.	Norwich	1868			
39.	Exeter	1869			

PRESIDENTS.—1. Viscount Milton; 2. Dr. Buckland; 3. Prof. Sedgwick; 4. Sir Thos. Brisbane; 5. Provost Bartholomew Lloyd; 6. Marquis of Lansdowne; 7. Earl of Burlington; 8. Duke of Northumberland; 9. Rev. W. Vernon Harcourt; 10. Marquis of Breadalbane; 11. Professor Whewell; 12. Lord Francis Egerton; 13. Earl of Rosse; 14. Dean Peacock; 15. Sir J. F. W. Herschel; 16. Sir R. I. Murchison; 17. Sir R. H. Inglis; 18. Marquis of Northampton; 19. Rev. Dr. T. R. Robinson; 20. Sir D. Brewster; 21. Prof. G. B. Airy; 22. Col. E. Sabine; 23. Mr. W. Hopkins; 24. Earl of Harrowby; 25. Duke of Argyll; 26. Dr. C. G. B. Daubeny; 27. Rev. Dr. Humphry Lloyd; 28. Prof. R. Owen; 29. Prince Albert; 30. Lord Wrottesley; 31. Wm. Fairbairn; 32. Prof. R. Willis; 33. Sir Wm. Armstrong; 34. Sir Charles Lyell; 35. Prof. John Phillips; 36. W. R. Grove; 37.

Duke of Buccleuch; 38. Dr. J. D. Hooker; 39. Prof. G. G. Stokes; 40. Prof. T. H. Huxley; 41. Sir Wm. Thomson; 42. Dr. W. B. Carpenter; 43. Prof. A. W. Williamson; 44. Prof. J. Tyndall; 45. Sir John Hawkshaw; 46. Prof. Thos. Andrews; 47. Prof. Allen Thomson; 48. Dr. Wm. Spottiswoode; 49. Dr. G. Allman; 50. Prof. A. C. Ramsay; 51. Sir J. Lubbock; 52. Dr. C. Wm. Siemens; 53. A. Cayley; 54. Lord Rayleigh; 55. Sir Lyon Playfair; 56. Sir John William Dawson; 57. Sir Henry E. Roscoe, M.P.; 58. Sir Frederick Bramwell; 59. Professor W. H. Flower; 60. Sir F. A. Abel; 61. Dr. W. Huggins; 62. Sir A. Geikie; 63. Dr. B. Sanderson; 64. Marquis of Salisbury; 65. Sir Douglas Galton; 66. Sir Joseph Lister; 67. Sir John Evans; 68. Sir Wm. Crookes; 69. sir Michael Foster; 70. sir Wm. Turner; 71. prof. Arthur Rucker (knt. 1902); 72. prof. James Dewar; 73. sir Norman Lockyer.

BRITISH CHURCH, see *Church of England*.

BRITISH COLUMBIA (N. America). In June, 1858, news came to California that in April gold had been found in abundance on the mainland of North America, a little to the north and east of Vancouver's Island. A great influx of gold-diggers (in a few weeks above 50,000) from all parts was the consequence; and Mr. Douglas, governor of Vancouver's Island, evinced much ability in preserving order. The territory with adjacent islands was made a British colony with the above title, and placed under Mr. Douglas. The colony was nominated and the government settled by 21 & 22 Vict. c. 99 (Aug. 1858), and a bishop nominated in 1859. Visited by the marquis of Lorne and princess Louise, 20 Sept. 1882.—For a dispute in July, 1859, see *United States*. Vancouver's Island was incorporated with the colony in 1866, and Victoria was made the capital, 24 May, 1868. Recent lieut.-governors: Frederick Seymour, 1864; Anthony Musgrave, 1869; J. W. Trutch, 1871; C. F. Cornwall; Hugh Nelson, Feb. 1892; Hon. Edgar Dewdney, Oct. 1892. Hon. T. R. McInnes, 1897; sir Henri Joly de Lotibinière, 22 June, 1900. The colony was annexed to Canada, 1871. Population, 1891, 92,767; 1901, 190,000.

Disputes with Canada respecting the non-construction of railways, middle of 1876
Visit of lord Dufferin, gov.-gen. of Canada . Aug. ,,
Anti-Chinese legislation and oppression stopped by the Privy Council in England 1884–8
Visit of lord Stanley, gov.-gen. 26 Oct. 1889
Visit of the duke and duchess of Connaught, 21 May, 1890
Destructive floods with loss of life, caused by the overflow of the Frazer River, reported 30 May, 1894
New coal mines opened and towns built in the Kootenay district, during 1895, reported April, 1896; and rapid development of gold mining, reported Aug. *et seq.*; 336 companies, 345,000,000 dollars capitalization, in 1896–8
Snow slides on the Chilkoot and Dyea trails, over 100 deaths . . . . . . 3–10 April, 1898
Great fire at New Westminster, thousands homeless 10, 11 Sept. ,,
Bill prohibiting aliens from acquiring mining claims becomes law . . . . . 18 Jan. 1899
Anti-Japanese laws disallowed by an order in council. . . . . . . 5 June, ,,
The Semlin ministry dismissed by the lieut.-gov. 27 Feb. ,,
Legislative assembly prorogued. . . 1 March, 1900
Elections: the government defeated . 9 June, ,,
Mr. J. Dunsmuir forms a cabinet . 27 June, ,,
Legislature opened by the governor . 18 July, ,,
The church, mission buildings, schools, etc., at Metlakahtla burnt down . . . . 22 July, ,,
Mineral production greatly increased . during 1901

BRITISH EAST AFRICA, see under *Africa*. BRITISH SOUTH AFRICA COMPANY, see *Zambesi*.

BRITISH ECONOMIC ASSOCIATION, see *Economy*.

BRITISH EMPIRE, see *England*, etc. BRITISH EMPIRE LEAGUE, established to maintain the unity of the Empire, and to succeed the late Imperial Federation League, *which see*: the duke of Devonshire, pres.; Sir J. Lubbock (now lord Avebury), chairman, May, 1895; inaugural meeting at the Mansion house, London, 29 Jan. 1896. Annual meetings; banquet in honour of the colonial troops in S. Africa and of the Australian delegates, London, the prince of Wales, lord Salisbury, and others present, 30 April, 1900; annual meeting, 7 July, 1902, the duke of Devonshire presided, sir E. Barton and sir Gordon Sprigg, colonial premiers, present; annual meeting, 20 July, 1903, lord mayor presided, the duke of Devonshire spoke on Mr. Chamberlain's visit to S. Africa and promotion of trade within the empire.

BRITISH GUIANA AND HONDURAS, see *Guiana* and *Honduras*.

BRITISH INSTITUTE of Preventive Medicine, see *Preventive Medicine*.

BRITISH INSTITUTION (for the encouragement of British artists, Pall-mall, founded in 1805) opened 18 Jan. 1806, on a plan formed by sir Thomas Bernard. In the gallery (erected by alderman Boydell, to exhibit the paintings executed for his edition of Shakspeare), were from time to time exhibited pictures by the old masters, deceased British artists and others, till 1867, when the lease of the premises expired. The fund of 16,200*l.* in the hands of earl Powis and other trustees, to be devoted to the promotion of the fine arts, had accumulated to 24,610*l.* in 1884.

BRITISH LEGION, raised by lord John Hay, col. De Lacy Evans, and others to assist queen Isabella of Spain against the Carlists in 1835, defeated them at Hernani, 5 May, 1836, and at St. Sebastian's, 1 Oct.

BRITISH MEDICAL ASSOCIATION, see *Medical*.

BRITISH MUSEUM, originated with the grant by parliament (5 April, 1753) of 20,000*l.* to the daughters of sir Hans Sloane, in payment for his fine library, and vast collection of the productions of nature and art, which had cost him 50,000*l.* The library contained 50,000 volumes and valuable MSS., and 69,352 articles of virtù enumerated in the catalogue. Montagu-house was obtained by government as a place for their reception. The museum (including the Cottonian, Harleian, and other collections) was opened 15 Jan. 1759, and has since been enormously increased by gifts, bequests, and purchases.* The old royal library was given by George II., 1757. A list of the more important additions is given below. See *Mummies*, 1898.

* The total expenditure by the government on the British Museum for the year ending 31 March, 1860, was 78,445*l.*; 1867, 110,756*l.*; 1877, 108,947*l.*; 1884, 152,133*l.* The number of visitors to the general collection in 1851 (exhibition year), 2,524,754; in 1859, 517,895; in 1862 (exhibition year), 895,077; in 1863, 440,801; in 1866, 516,550; 1871, 418,094; 1875, 663,891; in 1878, 448,516; in 1879, 606,394; in 1880, 665,688; in 1882, 767,402; in 1883, 660,557; in 1896, 581,906; 1901, 718,674; 1902, 845,369. The number of visitors to the collection in the Natural History Museum in 1884, 375,231; at Bloomsbury in 1884, 468,873; in 1887, 501,256; in 1889, 504,537; in 1890, 463,833; 1893, 538,560; 1896, 453,956; 1901, 417,691; 1902, 433,619. Additions to library in 1880, 27,543 volumes and pamphlets (including books of music and volumes of newspapers); in 1894, 38,378 books only. Expenditure *on purchases*, 1753–1875, 1,070,934*l.* Readers in 1883, 152,983; 1893, 194,102; 1896, 191,363; 1901, 200,035; 1902, 211,244.

New buildings erected by sir R. Smirke . . 1823-47
Iron railing completed 1852
The great reading-room erected by Sydney Smirke, according to a plan by Mr. Antonio Panizzi, the librarian (cost about 150,000*l.*; height of dome, 106 feet; diameter, 140 feet; contains about 80,000 volumes, and accommodates 300 readers), opened to public . . . . . . 18 May, 1857
Incorporation of the four library catalogues into one alphabet begun; three copies made . . . 1861
The proposed separation of the antiquarian, literary, and scientific collections, was disapproved by a commission in 1860; and a bill to remove the natural history collections to South Kensington rejected by the commons . . . 19 May, 1862
Number of books (estimated) 1,600,000 . Jan. 1870
,, ,, ,, 1,350,000 (50,000 MSS.) 1884
6000*l.* voted for a Natural History Museum at South Kensington . . . . 2 Aug. 1870
Photographs of above 5000 objects of antiquity (supplying evidence of man's progress in civilisation), published for about 116*l.* . . . Aug. 1872
Castellani collection of gold ornaments, gems, bronzes, &c., purchased for 52,000*l* 1872-3
The museum partly opened daily after 11 Feb. 1879
Electric light adopted in the reading-room for evenings in the winter months . . 20 Oct. ,,
The White bequest (60,000*l.*) 1880
The new *British Museum for Natural History*, South Kensington; building completed, Nov. 1880; part of the collection opened 18 April 1881: *directors*, sir Richard Owen, 1856 (K.C.B. 1892), professor W. H. Flower, 1884 (K.C.B., 1892; resigned July, 1898; died, 1 July, 1899; succeeded by professor E. Ray Lankester, 1898); opened on Sundays, 17 May *et seq.*, 1896. Professor Owen died 18 Dec. 1892. At a meeting of the Royal Society, the prince of Wales in the chair, it was resolved to place a marble statue of the professor in the hall of the Natural History museum, of which he was the chief originator, 21 Jan. 1893; statue, by T. Brock, placed, March, 1897; collections enriched by explorers from all parts of the world. Statue of prof. Huxley (by Onslow Ford, R.A.) unveiled by the prince of Wales, 28 April, 1900
John Gould's humming-birds, &c., bought April, ,,
New buildings in Montague-street, founded (by means of Mr. Wm. White's legacy of 63,941*l.*) 23 Sept. 1882
New Assyrian room (including Mr. Rassam's collection) opened . . . . . . Jan. 1884
New catalogue printing, Dec. 1881, *et seq.*; new catalogues of the bible issued . . Dec. 1892
The Marquis of Tweeddale's ornithological library presented by capt. Wardlaw Ramsay . Oct. 1887
New galleries opened; glass and pottery, 1888; Greek sculpture, 1889; mummies, etc. . . 1898
Electric light set up in the public galleries, opened in the evenings, 8 to 10 . . . . 1 Feb. 1890
Gallery of Religions in the museum at Bloomsbury, opened . . . . . . 19 Feb. 1894
Mr. J. B. Martin and his wife, Mrs. Victoria Woodhull Martin *v.* the trustees of the British Museum and Mr. E. M. Thompson, librarian, for giving out books containing libels against Mrs. Martin, relating to the Beecher scandal (see *United States*, 1874–5), queen's bench division; verdict of the jury, the defendants acted with *bona fides* and not negligently, but did not (by their officers) discharge their duties with proper care, caution and judgment, damages, 20s. 23–27 Feb.; judgment given by baron Pollock for the defendants, with costs; appeal granted 3 March, dismissed . . . . . . 19 April, ,,
British Museum Purchase of Land (of the duke of Bedford) Act, passed . . . . . 17 Aug. ,,
George Bullen, C.B., library assistant, 1838; keeper of printed books, 1875–90; died . 10 Oct. ,,
Sir Charles Thos. Newton, keeper of antiquities, 1868–85, died . . . . . . 28 Nov. ,,
Mr. Reginald Stuart Poole, keeper of coins, 1870–93, died . . . . 8 Feb. 1895
The Malcolm collection of early drawings and engravings presented by Mr. Wm. Mitchell, July, ,,
Mr. H. Seebohm bequeaths his collection of bird skins and skeletons to the Nat. Hist. department, Kensington . . . . ,,
The museum opened from 2.30 to 7 p.m. on Sundays . . . . . . 17 May *et seq.* 1896
"Catalogue of birds in the museum," 27 vols., begun 1874, completed . . . March, 1899
Exhibition of Rembrandt's drawings and etchings March, ,,
Dr. Richard Garnett, keeper of printed books, 1851–99, retires . . . . . March, ,,
Mr. Vincent Stuckey Lean bequeaths 50,000*l.* for the library and reading-room, see *Bristol*, March, ,,
Dr. C. D. Fortnum, a trustee, dies 6 March, bequeaths a fund for the building of the "Fortnum galleries" for the Frank's collection, etc.; see *Ashmolean museum.*
Antiquities from Benin city and other parts of W. Africa presented by lord Salisbury . spring, ,,
300 notable books added to the library . 1890–99
"The Royal library of Assyria," about 23,000 tablets, from Nineveh, catalogued (5 quarto vols.) by Dr. Carl Bezold, see *Times* 14 April, 1900
The "General Catalogue of Printed Books" began 1881, completed . . . . . . early ,,
British museum act passed . . 20 June, 1902
Lord Cheylesmore's (died 10 July) bequest of 14,000 English mezzotint portraits to the nation placed here.

IMPORTANT ADDITIONS (*bought or given*). (*Edwards.*)
Those marked * were gifts or bequests.

*Solomon Da Costa, Hebrew Library . . . 1759
*G. Thomason, collection (political) from Geo. III. 1762
*Solander, fossils 1766
*Birch, library and MSS. . . . . . . ,,
Hamilton vases, &c. 1772
*Musgrave library 1790–95
*Cracherode library 1799
Hatchett minerals . . . . ,,
*Alexandrian collection (from Geo. III.) . . 1802
Lansdowne MSS. (catalogue published 1819) . . 1807
Townley marbles 1805–17
Greville minerals 1810
Roberts, English coins . . . . . . ,,
Hargrave library 1813
Phigaleian marbles 1815
Elgin marbles 1816
Burney library 1818
*Banks' archæological collections . . . ,,
*King George III.'s library, given by George IV. 1823–5
*Payne Knight's collections 1824
*Sir J. Banks' library and collections . . . 1827
*Egerton MSS. 1829
*Arundelian MSS. 1831
Mantell, fossils 1839
Syriac MSS. 1841–7
*Lycian marbles (by sir C. Fellows) . . . 1845
*Grenville library, collected by right hon. Thos. Grenville (20,240 vols.) 1847
Morrison's Chinese library . . . . . ,,
Assyrian collections (by A. Layard) . . . 1851–60
Halicarnassian and Cnidian marbles (by C. T. Newton) 1855–60
Carthaginian antiquities (by N. Davis) . . . 1859
Cyrene marbles (by Smith and Porcher) . . . 1860
Cureton, Oriental MSS. 1864
Duke of Blacas museum (bought for 48,000*l.*) . . 1866
*Abyssinian antiquities 1868
*Slade collection (glass, &c.) . . . . . ,,
*Mr. George Smith's (of *Daily Telegraph*) Assyrian collections 1873
*Elamite antiquities, by col. Ross . . . 1876
*Urns, implements, ornaments, &c., from 234 British barrows (see *Barrows*), by rev. canon Greenwell 1879
About 300 Babylonian tablets purchased . June 1882
*Osbert Salvin and F. du Cane Godman's collection of American birds, &c. 1885
*Indian birds and eggs from Mr. A. O. Hume . ,,
*The marquis of Tweeddale's collection of birds given by capt. Wardlaw Ramsay . . . Oct. 1887
*Mr. Octavius Morgan's collection of watches, clocks, keys, rings, &c., reported . . Oct. 1888
A great present of books and photographs from the Sultan of Turkey . . . . . May, 1894
The collection of sir Augustus Wollaston Franks, late keeper of antiquities, bequeathed . . . 1897

Baron Ferdinand de Rothschild's cinque-cents collection, value 300,000*l.*, "the Waddesdon bequest room," bequeathed . . . . Jan. 1899
Hardwicke papers and MSS. . . . 18 Feb. "

PRINCIPAL LIBRARIANS.

Dr. Gowin Knight 1753
Dr. Matthew Maty 1772
Dr. Charles Morton 1776
Joseph Planta 1799
Henry Ellis 1827
Antonio Panizzi 1856
J. Winter Jones 1866
Edward Augustus Bond, Aug. 1878; resigned June, 1888; K.C.B. 1 Jan. 1898; died . . 2 Jan. 1898
Sir Edward Maunde Thompson 1888

BRITISH NATIONALITY, see *Naturalization.*

BRITISH ORCHESTRAL SOCIETY, established 1872.

BRITISH PRODUCE Supply Association: directors, the earl of Winchilsea, lord Kesteven, and others; started early in 1896, for the purchase, sale, &c., of British agricultural produce. Local bodies forming, Aug.; central depôt, Long Acre, opened 21 Oct. 1896.

BRITONS, ANCIENT, Society of, established 1715, see *Wales;* 178th anniversary celebrated 1 March, 1893.

BRITTANY, see *Britanny.*

BRITTON, an ancient treatise on English law written in French by or in the name of king Edward I. about 1291. Coke attributed the work to John le Breton, bishop of Hereford, who died in 1275. An edition of "Britton," with a translation in English by Mr. F. Nicholls, was published in 1865.

BROAD ARROW. All attempts to ascertain the origin of this mark have been fruitless. It is stated that timber trees fit for shipping in the forest of Dean in 1639 were marked with the crown and broad arrow. It is said to have been the device of viscount Sydney, earl of Romney, master-general of the ordnance, 1693-1702. *Brewer.*

"BROAD BOTTOM" ADMINISTRATION. The Pelham administration (*which see*) was so called because formed by a coalition of parties, Nov. 1744.

BROAD CHURCH SCHOOL, in the Church of England, had its origin in a reaction from the Tractarian movement (see *Tractarianism* and *Puseyism*), influenced by German rationalism and the growth of the scientific and critical spirit. It became prominent in 1836 through the lectures of Dr. Hampden, and still more through the "Theological Essays" of the late F. C. Maurice in 1853, and found fuller expression in "Essays and Reviews," issued in 1860, written by Dr. Temple (late Archbishop of Canterbury), Dr. Rowland Williams, Professor Jowett, Baden Powell, Mark Pattison, H. B. Wilson, and C. H. Goodwin. These essays, with the exception of that on the "Education of the World" by Dr. Temple, were of a destructive critical nature, dealing with the subjects of the inspiration of the Scriptures, miracles, the Pentateuch, creeds and kindred subjects, and aroused a storm of hostile criticism from the bishops and "orthodox" members of the Church. The publication (1862 *et seq.*) of Dr. Colenso's work on the Pentateuch gave rise to still further controversy (see *Church of England*, May 20, 1863, *et seq.*). Although not numerically a strong party, the influence of broad-churchism has made itself felt among all sections of the Church, and includes among its past and present adherents such names as Dr. Arnold, dean Stanley, canon Kingsley, Aug. William and Julius C. Hare, Stopford Brooke, bishop Westcott, canon Driver, bishop Moorhouse, H. R. Haweis, canon Cheyne, dean Robinson, canon Henson, and other able and distinguished men. The attitude of the Broad Church school may be thus briefly stated. It pays little attention to either dogma or ceremony; it seeks to extend the liberty of belief within the Church to its greatest possible extent; it attaches great importance to the social Christian virtues and purity of life, adopting the precepts rather than the dogmas of religion. The "Churchmen's Union" (*which see*), an association of clergy holding "broad" views, but not necessarily members of the Broad Church school, was formed at the Bradford Church Congress, 1898.

BROCADE, a silken stuff, variegated with gold or silver, and enriched with flowers and figures, originally made by the Chinese; the manufacture was established at Lyons in 1757.

BROCCOLI, said to have been brought to England from Italy in the 16th century.

BROKERS, both of money and merchandise, were known early in England. See *Appraisers.* They are licensed, and their dealings regulated by law in 1695-6, 1816, and 1826. The dealings of *stockbrokers* were regulated in 1719, 1733, and 1736, and subsequently; see *Pawnbroker*, and *Barnard's Act.* Brokers in the city of London placed under the supervision of the lord mayor and aldermen, in 1707, were relieved from it by an act passed 9 Aug. 1870.

BROMINE (from the Greek *brōmos*, a stink), a poisonous volatile liquid element discovered in salt water by M Balard in 1826. It is found in combination with metals and mineral waters.

BRONTOMETER, thunderstorm measurer, an apparatus invented by M. M. Richard, of Paris, and commended by Mr. J. Symons, in *Nature*, July, 1890.

BRONZE was known to the ancients, some of whose bronze statues, vessels, &c., are in the British Museum. The bronze equestrian statue of Louis XIV., 1699, in the Place Vendôme at Paris (demolished 10 Aug. 1792), the most colossal ever made; it contained 60,000 lbs. Bronze is composed of copper and tin, with sometimes a little zinc and lead. The present *bronze coinage*, penny, half-penny, and farthing (composed of 95 parts of copper, 4 tin, 1 zinc), came into circulation Dec. 1860.

BROOKLYN, a city on Long Island, in the state of New York, first settled in 1636, organised by the Dutch governor of New Amsterdam, and named Breukelen, after a place in Holland. It contains many fine churches and public buildings, and a large naval yard. Incorporated in 1834. Population in 1810, 4402; in 1830, 15,396; in 1850, 96,838; in 1890, 806,343; see *New York*, 1900.

Brooklyn theatre burnt, about 300 perish . 5 Dec. 1876
The bridge from New York to Brooklyn (see *New York*), begun 3 Jan. 1870; opened . 24 May, 1883
St. James's cathedral destroyed by lightning 11 or 12 June, 1889
Brooklyn and other towns consolidated with New York, 27 Feb. 1894; act takes effect . 25 March, 1897
Strike of tram car men; rioting; military called out, 20 Jan.; further conflicts, with bloodshed, 21-25 Jan.; subsiding . . . . 26 Jan. 1895
City Hall much injured by fire . . . 26 Feb. "

BROOKS'S CLUB, first a gaming club in Pall Mall kept by Almack and afterwards by Brooks in 1764, gradually became the Whig club, and was removed to St. James's Street in 1778, now Liberal and social, 650 members.

BROTHERHOODS, see *Hermandad*, *Santa*, and *Lay Brotherhood*.

BROUGHAM, a popular vehicle said to have been invented in 1839, and so named in consequence of its adoption by lord Brougham. *Brougham's Act*, 13 & 14 Vict. c. 21; see *Acts*, and *Bankrupt*.

BROWN INSTITUTION, Battersea, with an hospital for quadrupeds and birds useful to man, established by means of a bequest of Thomas Brown of Dublin; opened 2 Dec. 1871. First professor, Dr. Burdon Sanderson (bart. June 1899); Dr. Greenfield, professor, Dec. 1878; Dr. C. S. Roy, professor, 1885; Professor Victor Horsley, 1889; C. S. Sherrington, M.D., was professor in 1895.

BROWN'S INSURRECTION, see *United States*, 1859.

BROWNIAN MOTION. So called from Robert Brown, the celebrated botanist, who in 1827, by the aid of the microscope, observed in drops of dew a motion of minute particles which at first was attributed to rudimentary life, but was afterwards decided to be due to currents occasioned by inequalities of temperature and evaporation.

BROWNING SOCIETY, for the study and discussion of the works of Robert Browning, inaugurated at University college, London, 28 Oct. 1881; dissolved, 1893. Mr. Browning died 12 Dec. 1889, aged 77. "The Browning Cyclopædia," by Edward Berdoe, published 19 Dec. 1891. "Browning Studies," edited by Dr. Berdoe, published 1895. Browning settlement founded in Walworth, 1895. See *Faraday*, 1901. Browning club and coffee tavern opened here, 14 June, 1901.

BROWNISTS or BARROWISTS, the first Independents (*which see*), named after Robert Brown, a schoolmaster in Southwark, about 1580. John Penry, Henry Barrow, and other Brownists were cruelly executed for alleged sedition, 29 May, 1593.

BRUCE'S TRAVELS. James Bruce, the "Abyssinian traveller," set out in June, 1768, to discover the source of the Nile. Proceeding first to Cairo, he navigated the Nile to Syene, thence crossed the desert to the Red Sea, and, arriving at Jedda, passed some months in Arabia Felix, and after various detentions reached Gondar, the capital of Abyssinia, in Feb. 1770. On 14 Nov. 1770, he obtained a sight of the sources of the Blue Nile. He returned to England in 1773, and died 27 April, 1794.

BRUGES, Belgium, in the 7th century was capital of Flanders, and in the 13th and 14th centuries almost the commercial metropolis of the world. It suffered much through an insurrection in 1488, and the consequent repression. It was subjected to France in 1794, to the Netherlands in 1814, and to Belgium in 1830. Population, 1890, 47,331; 1900, 52,867.

BRUMAIRE REVOLUTION, see *Directory*, 1799.

BRUNANBURG (supposed by some to be near Ford, Northumberland). Anlaf, with an army of Northmen from Ireland, and Constantine III. king of Scots, landed at the mouth of the Humber, and were defeated with very great slaughter at Brunanburg by Athelstan, 937.

BRUNDISIUM (now Brindisi), S. Italy, a Greek city, taken by the Romans, B.C. 267; and made a colony, 244. Here Virgil died 22 Sept. 19 B.C.

BRÜNN, capital of Moravia, since 1641; was entered by the French under Murat, 18 Nov. 1805, and by the Prussians, 13 July, 1866. Population, 1890, 95,342; 1900, 108,944.

BRUNSWICK CLUBS, established to maintain the house of Hanover and the Protestant ascendency in church and state, began in England at Maidstone, 18 Sept. 1828; in Ireland at the Rotunda in Dublin, 4 Nov. same year. Other cities formed similar clubs.

BRUNSWICK, HOUSE OF. The duchy of Brunswick, in Lower Saxony, was conquered by Charlemagne, and governed afterwards by counts and dukes. Albert-Azzo II. marquis of Italy and lord of Este, died in 1097, and left by his wife Cunegonde (the heiress of Guelph duke of Carinthia in Bavaria), a son, Guelph, who was invited into Germany by Imitza, his mother-in-law, and invested with all the possessions of his wife's step-father, Guelph of Bavaria; see *Bavaria*. His descendant, Henry the Lion, married Maud, daughter of Henry II. of England, and was the founder of the Brunswick family. His dominions were very extensive; but having refused to assist the emperor Frederick Barbarossa in a war against pope Alexander III., through the emperor's resentment he was proscribed at the diet at Wurtzburg, in 1180. The duchy of Bavaria was given to Otho of Wittelsbach, ancestor of the family of Bavaria; the duchy of Saxony to Bernard Ascanius, founder of the house of Anhalt; and his other territories to different persons. On this, he retired to England; but at the intercession of our Henry II. Brunswick and Luneburg were restored to him. The house of Brunswick in 1409 divided into several branches. Brunswick was included by Napoleon in the kingdom of Westphalia in 1806, but was restored to the duke in 1815.—Population of the duchy of Brunswick in 1871, 312,170; 1875, 327,493; 1880, 349,367; 1885, 372,452; 1890, 403,788; city, 101,047; 1900, 464,251; city, 128,231. Brunswick joined the North German Confederation, 18 Aug. 1866.

DUKES OF BRUNSWICK.

1136. Henry, duke of Bavaria.
1139. Henry the Lion (son).
1195. Henry the Long and William (sons).
1213. Otho I. (son of William).
1252. Albert I. (son of preceding).
1278. Albert II. (son).
1318. Otho, Magnus I., and Ernest (sons).
1368. Magnus II. (Torquatus) (son of Magnus I.)

DUKES OF BRUNSWICK-WOLFENBUTTEL.

First Branch.

1409. Henry I. (son of Magnus II.)
1416. William I. and Henry II. (sons).
1482. Frederic and William II. } sons of William I.
1495. Henry III. and Eric } sons of William I.
1514. Henry IV. (son of Henry II.)
1568. Julius (son of preceding).
1589. Henry Julius (son).
1613. Frederic-Ulric (son), died without issue.

Second Branch.

1634. Augustus (son of Henry of Luneburg).
1666. Rodolph-Augustus; who associated his next brother, Anthony-Ulric, in the government, from 1685; died, 1704.
1704. Anthony-Ulric now ruled alone; became a Roman Catholic in 1710; died in 1714.
1714. Augustus-William (son).
1731. Lewis-Rodolph (brother).
1735. Ferdinand-Albert, duke of Brunswick-Bevern, married Antoinette-Amelia, daughter of Lewis-Rodolph, and succeeded him.

1735. Charles (son).
1780. Charles-William-Ferdinand (son); a great general (served under his uncle Ferdinand in the Seven Years' War, 1756-1763); married princess Augusta of England; was mortally wounded at the battle of Auerstadt, 14 Oct., and died 10 Nov. 1806; succeeded by his fourth son (his elder sons being blind, abdicated).
1806. William-Frederick, whose reign may be dated from the battle of Leipsic in Oct. 1813; fell at Quatre-Bras, commanding the *avantgarde* under the duke of Wellington, 16 June, 1815; succeeded by his eldest son.
1815. Charles-Frederick-William, (very eccentric); assumed government 30 Oct. 1823. [Revolution at Brunswick; the duke (declared incapable of reigning by the German diet) retired to England, 7 Sept. 1830; died at Geneva, bequeathing his immense property to that city, 18 Aug. 1873.]
1830. William, brother; born 25 April, 1806; succeeded provisionally, 7 Sept. 1830; and, on the demand of the Germanic diet, definitively, 20 April, 1831; *unmarried;* died, deeply lamented, 18 Oct. 1884. (His magnificent palace was destroyed by fire, 24 Feb. 1865.) His jubilee celebrated 25 April, 1881. Succession claimed by the duke of Cumberland (set aside by the diet, 30 June, & 20 Oct. 1885); regency assumed, 18 Oct. 1884. Prince Albert of Prussia, born 8 May, 1837, nephew of the emperor of Germany, elected regent 21 Oct.; accepts about 24 Oct.; warmly received in Brunswick, 2 Nov. 1885.
See under *Cumberland*, 1892.

DUKES OF BRUNSWICK-LUNEBURG.

1409. Bernard (son of Magnus II., duke of Brunswick, *see above*).
1434. Otho and Frederic (his sons).
1478. Henry (son of Otho).
1532. Ernest I. (son of Otho). His sons were
1546. Henry (founder of *second branch* of Brunswick-Wolfenbuttel) and William, whose seven sons cast lots to determine who should marry. The lot fell on GEORGE, sixth son. Four of the brothers reigned, viz. :—
1592. Ernest II. }
1611. Christian. } no issue.
1633. Augustus. }
1636. Frederic II. }
1648. Christian-Lewis (son of the George *above-mentioned.*)
1665. George-William (brother of Christian-Lewis), dies in 1705; leaving as heiress SOPHIA-DOROTHEA, his daughter, who married in 1682 her cousin, prince GEORGE-LEWIS of Hanover, afterwards George I. of England (son of Ernest of Hanover, youngest son of the *above-mentioned* George).
(See *Hanover* and *England.*)

BRUNSWICK THEATRE, Well-street, East London, built to replace the Royalty (burnt down 11 April, 1826), was opened 25 Feb. 1828. On the 29th the building was destroyed by the falling in of the walls, too much weight being attached to the heavy iron roof. Fortunately the catastrophe happened in the day-time (during a rehearsal of "Guy Mannering"), and only twelve persons perished.

BRUSSELS, once capital of Austrian Brabant, now of Belgium (since 1831), was founded by St. Gery, of Cambray, in the 7th century. It is celebrated for its fine lace, carpets, and tapestry. The *Hôtel de Ville* was erected early in the 15th century; has a turret 364 feet in height; and on its top is a copper figure of St. Michael, 17 feet high, which turns with the wind; see *Belgium*. Population, 1890, 182,305; 1900, 570,844 (including suburbs).

Cathedral of St. Gudule (begun 1010?) completed . 1273
Made capital of the Low Countries 1507
Ruled tyrannically by Alva 1567
"Union of Brussels" to expel the Spaniards . 1577-78
Bombarded by marshal Villeroi; 14 churches and 10,000 houses destroyed . . . . Aug. 1695
Taken by the French, 1701; by Marlborough, 1706; by Saxe, 16 Feb. 1746, and by Dumouriez, Nov. 1792
The revolution commences . . . . 25 Aug. 1830
The costly furniture of 16 houses demolished in consequence of a display of attachment to the house of Orange . . . . 5 April, 1834
Maritime conference to obtain uniform meteorological observations held here 1853
International philanthropic congress . . . Sept. 1856
International association for social science meet 22-25 Sept. 1862
Brussels Conference. The Society for the Amelioration of the condition of prisoners of war sent circulars (dated 28 March) to the great powers. On 17 April Russia issued a programme for consideration at the conference, consisting of 71 articles, embracing all the "usages of war." Lord Derby (for Great Britain), in a despatch, declined the discussion of international law, 4 July. General sir Alfred Horsford was sent delegate for Great Britain without active powers: reserving liberty of action. The congress was opened 27 July; baron Jomini (from Russia) president. The United States not represented. The sittings were secret. The conference closed without important results, 28 Aug. 1874. British Report published in *London Gazette* . . . . 24 Oct. 1874
Belgian Industrial exhibition opened . . 5 Sept. „
International exhibition of objects relating to public health and safety, opened by the king, 26 June; a congress met . . . 27 Sept.—2 Oct. 1876
International congress of commerce and industry, 6—10 Sept. 1880
Commercial Museum opened . . about 17 Dec. 1882
The magnificent new Palace of Justice opened by the king . . . . 15 Oct. 1883
The parliament houses burnt; valuable library destroyed; loss about 480,000*l*. . . . 6 Dec. „
Industrial exhibition opened . . . . 29 Dec. „
International Exhibition opened 19 May, by the king, 7 June; closed . . . . . 11 Nov. „
Théâtre de la Bourse burnt . . . . 7 Jan. 1889
Anti-slavery conference meets . 18 Nov. *et seq.* „
Arrival of Mr. H. M. Stanley from Africa; entertainment by the king, &c. . . 19-25 April, 1890
Great fire at the palace of the Duc d'Arenberg, formerly the residence of the Egmont family, many of whose relics are destroyed . 24 Jan. 1892
The International Colonial Institute founded; lord Reay, M. Léon Say and others present . 8 Jan. 1894
A formidable explosion in a house in the Rue Royal; estimated loss, 500,000f. . . . 18 June, „
A large hall and buildings in the market burnt; attributed to explosives . . . . . 11 July, „
Decree signed changing the city's name to "Bruxelle port de mer" . . . . . 19 Oct. 1895
Opening of the international exhibition (British art well represented, a Congo village, 200 natives, etc.), deferred in consequence of the death of the duchesse d'Alençon, see *Paris*, 4 May; opened by the king, 10 May; visit of the lord mayor, sir G. Faudel-Phillips, 31 July; entertained by the king, 1 Aug.; closed . . . . 20 Oct. 1897
Monument to Charles Rogier, the Belgian patriot of 1830, unveiled . . . . . 25 July, „
Socialist demonstration by the labour party, 15 Aug. „
International colonial congress opened . 16 Aug. „
Death of Mdme. Auguste Couvreur, *Times* correspondent . . . . 23 Oct. „
The city boundaries extended for shipping warehouses, etc. 1900

BRUTTIUM (now Calabria Olta), S. Italy. The Bruttians and Lucanians defeated and slew Alexander of Epirus at Pandosia, 326 B.C. They were conquered by Rome, 277.

BUBBLE COMPANIES, see *Companies, Law's Bubble*, and *South-sea Bubble*.

BUCCANEERS, cruel piratical adventurers, French, English, and Dutch, who commenced their depredations on the Spaniards of America soon after the latter had taken possession of that continent and the West Indies. Their numbers were much increased by a twelve years' truce between the Spaniards and Dutch in 1609, when many of the discharged sailors joined the buccaneers. The first levy of ship-money in England in 1635 was to defray the expense of chastising these pirates. The principal commanders of the first buccaneers were Montbar, Lolonois, Basco, and Morgan. Van Horn, of Ostend, captured Vera Cruz, 1603; Morgan took Panama, 1670; Gramont seized Campeachy, 1685; and Pointis took Carthagena, 1697; all gained enormous booty. The buccaneer confederacy was broken up through the peace of Ryswick, 10 Sept. 1697.

BUCENTAUR, the vessel in which the doge of Venice used to proceed to wed the Adriatic, from the 12th to the 18th century.

BUCHANITES (in Scotland): followers of Mrs. Buchan, who about 1779 pretended to be the woman of *Rev.* xii., and promised to conduct them to the new Jerusalem, &c. She died in 1791, and her followers dispersed.

BUCHAREST (in Wallachia). Preliminaries of peace were ratified at this place between Russia and Turkey, it being stipulated that the Pruth should be the frontier of the two empires; signed 28 May, 1812. The subsequent war between these powers altered many of the provisions of this treaty. Bucharest was occupied by the Russians, Turks, and Austrians successively in the Crimean war. The last quitted it in 1856. It is now capital of the kingdom of Roumania, established 26 March, 1881. Population, 1885, 221,000; 1899, 282,071.

BUCKHURST PEERAGE, see *Trials*, 1876.

BUCKINGHAM PALACE, the London residence of the sovereign. Old Buckingham-house was built on the "Mulberry-gardens," by John Sheffield, duke of Buckingham, in 1703. In 1761 it was bought by George III., who in 1775 settled it on his queen, Charlotte. She made it her town residence; and here all her children, except the eldest, were born. Here were married the duke of York and princess Frederica of Prussia, in 1791; the duke of Gloucester and princess Mary, 1816; the prince of Hesse-Homburg and princess Elizabeth, 1818; and the duke of Cambridge and princess of Hesse the same year. The house was pulled down in 1825, and the present palace commenced on its site. After an expenditure of nearly a million sterling, it was completed, and occupied by queen Victoria, 13 July, 1837. Further improvements were made in 1853. The marble arch, taken down from the exterior of this palace, was re-erected at Cumberland-gate, Hyde-park, 29 March, 1851.

BUCKLES were worn instead of shoe-strings in the reign of Charles II., and soon became fashionable and expensive; about 1791 they fell out of use. Ornamental buckles became fashionable, 1873.

BUDA (or OFEN), the ancient Aquincum, on the W. bank of the Danube opposite Pesth, and with it (termed Buda-Pesth) the capital of Hungary. It was taken by Charlemagne in 799; and sacked by Solyman II. after the battle of Mohatz, when the Hungarian king, Louis, was killed, and 200,000 of his subjects carried away captives, 1526. Buda was sacked a second time, when the inhabitants were put to the sword, and Hungary was annexed to the Ottoman empire, 1541. Retaken by the Imperialists, under the duke of Lorraine, and the Mahometans delivered up to the fury of the soldiers, 1686. It suffered much in 1848; was entered without resistance by the Austrians, 5 Jan. 1849; stormed, 20 May; given up by Russians to Austrians, July, 1849. Here the emperor Francis Joseph was crowned king of Hungary, 8 June, 1867; see *Hungary*. Buda-Pesth constituted the capital of Hungary, Nov. 1873; equal to Vienna, June, 1892. Great loss of life (about 120) and property by a storm, 26 June, 1875; another storm, 11 July following. Population of Buda-Pesth, 1890, 506,384; 1900, 732,222.

The anniversary of the re-capture of the citadel of Buda from the Turks after ten weeks' siege on 2 Sept. 1686, was enthusiastically celebrated on 2 Sept. 1886.
Many drowned in the Danube, through the breaking of the ice, 4 Jan.; destructive inundations through rising of the Danube, 13 March *et seq.*, 1891.
Congress of nationalities of E. Europe, 10 Aug. 1895.
Millennial national exhibition opened, 2 May, 1896.
Riots of unemployed, 200 arrests, 21 Dec. 1901.
English art, etc., exhibition opened, 30 Sept. 1902.
Students' riots, 20 March, 1903.

BUDDHISM, the chief religion in Asia beyond the Ganges, and in China, Japan, and Ceylon, originated with Gautama Siddartha, the Sakya Muni, generally termed Buddha, or "the enlightened," a prince of Kapalivastu in Central India, said to have been born 623, and to have died 543 B.C.

In July, 594 B.C., disgusted with the behaviour of the Brahmins, he retired from the world for a time, and on coming forth, preached a new religion so successfully that it predominated in India till the 10th century, A.D.*
Buddhism inculcates strict morality; it forbids killing, stealing, adultery, lying, and drunkenness, and every shade of these vices, and declares charity or love to be the source of all virtues. Some writers assert that Buddhism includes belief in the transmigration of souls, and the absorption of good souls into God himself, from whom they have emanated; others reckon annihilation or eternal sleep (the Nirvâna) amongst Buddhist tenets.
A form of Buddhism, termed the religion of Fö, exists in China, besides the system of Confucius and Laot-se. It is said to have been introduced in the reign of Ming-ti, A.D. 68-81.
"Le Bouddha et ses Religions," by M. J. B. St. Hilaire, was published in 1860. Mr. T. Rhys Davids' "Buddhism," in 1878.
The Buddhists in the world are estimated at 455,000,000.
Buddhism in Japan reported to be declining, 3,737 temples in Kioto, the old capital, and 3,555 in 1889.
Mr. Brian Houghton Hodgson, eminent writer on Buddhism, etc., died, aged 94, 30 May, 1894.
The king of Siam subscribes to the publication of a translation of Buddhist sacred books, 1895.
The reputed birthplace of Buddha and other antiquities discovered, 1897-8; a well-preserved *stupa* containing the ashes and relics of Buddha, authenticated by a direct inscription, discovered at Piprâva, Nepal frontier, presented to the government by Mr. Wm. Peppé, who present it to the king of Siam, Jan. 1898.

BUDE LIGHT (so named from Bude in Cornwall, the residence of Mr. (aft. sir) Goldsworthy Gurney, its inventor), consisted of two or more concentric argand gas or oil burners, one rising above another, fed by oxygen gas in place of air; patents 1839 and 1841.

BUDGET (from the French *bougette*, Latin *bulga*, a small bag), a term applied to the English chancellor of the exchequer's annual statement of the finances of the country, from the documents having been formerly presented in a leather bag. The budgets of sir R. Peel in 1842 (including the income-tax) and 1846 (free trade), and of Mr. Gladstone in 1860 (in connection with the treaty with France), were very important. A surplus of about 6,000,000*l.* was announced by sir Stafford Northcote, 16 April, 1874. See *Revenue*. Mr. Childers in his budget proposed the reduction of consols from 3 to 2½ per cent. for capital raised to 108*l.*, and the coinage of 10*s.* pieces worth 9*s.* to meet the loss by wear of gold coinage. Coinage bill withdrawn 10 July, 1884.

* Mr. (aft. sir) Edwin Arnold's "Light of Asia," a poem, in 1879.

Budget of Mr. Childers, 30 April, 1885, to provide for estimated expenditure of 88,872,600*l.*, and a vote of credit for 11,000,000*l.* on account of war in the Soudan, and probable war with Russia.

Income tax raised to 8*d.* Increase of duty on beer and spirits, succession duties, duty on property of corporate bodies.

Bill rejected on second reading (264–252), 8–9 June; modified by Sir M. Hicks-Beach, new duties given up, and 4,000,000*l.* exchequer bills, 16 July, 1885.

Mr. Goschen's budget introduced 21 April, 1887, included abstraction of 2,000,000*l.* from the sinking fund, reduction of income tax from 8*d.* to 7*d.*, and of tobacco duty from 3*s.* 6*d.* to 3*s.* 2*d.*; a grant in aid of local rates, &c.

Mr. Goschen's budget introduced 26 March; aiming at a permanent equitable adjustment of imperial and local taxation; income tax reduced to 6*d.*; resolutions adopted 9 April; Mr. Gladstone's amendment on the succession duties rejected (310–217) 23 April; act passed 16 May, 1888.

Mr. Goschen's budget introduced 15 April, 1889, provided for the increased expenditure for the army and navy, by dealing with the consolidated fund and slightly increasing the succession and beer duties.

Mr. Goschen's budget, surplus, 3,549,000*l.*; house duty reduced to 2*d.*, 4*d.*, and 6*d.*, 540,000*l.*; additional duty on spirits, 6*d.* per gallon—resolutions carried 17–22 April, 1890.

Mr. Goschen's budget introduced 23 April, 1891: surplus, 1,756,000*l.*; proposed grant for free (or assisted) education from 1 Sept., about 2,000,000*l.* a year; resolutions agreed to, 27 April, 1891.

Mr. Goschen's budget introduced 11 April, 1892: surplus, 1,067,000*l.*; the duties on sparkling wines equalised to 2*s.* a gallon, 16 May, 1892.

Sir Wm. Harcourt's budget introduced, 24 April, 1893; deficit, 1,574,000*l.*, met by addition of 1*d.* to the income tax, making it 7*d.*; passed 12 May, 1893.

Sir Wm. Harcourt's budget introduced 16 April, 1894; deficit, 507,000*l.*, income tax, raised from 7*d.* to 8*d.*; appropriation of sinking fund, death or estate duties, additional duties on beer (6*d.* per barrel), spirits (6*d.* per gallon); Finance Act, passed 31 July, 1894.

Sir Wm. Harcourt's budget: receipts, 94,684,000*l.*, expenditure, 94,588,000*l.*, surplus, 766,000*l.*; the additional spirit duty dropped, 2 May, 1895; act passed 30 May, 1895.

Sir Michael Hicks-Beach's budget: receipts, 101,974,000*l.*; surplus 1895–6, 4,210,000*l.*; expenditure, 97,764,000*l.* 16 April, 1896; estimated expenditure, 1896–7, 100,047,000*l.*; relief from the death duties, relief of agriculture, reduction of the land-tax, etc.; Finance Act passed, 7 Aug. 1896.

Budget: receipts, 103,360,000*l.*; estimated expenditure, 101,791,000*l.*; estimated surplus, 1,569,000*l.*; disposal of surplus, 1897–8, navy, S. Africa garrison, post-office, etc., 29 April, Finance Act passed, 15 July, 1897.

Budget: receipts, 108,615,000*l.*; estimated expenditure, 106,829,000*l.*; estimated surplus, 1,786,000*l.*; reduction of income-tax, death duties, land tax, tobacco duty, 21 April; Finance Act passed, 1 July, 1898.

Budget, 1899-1900: receipts, 129,757,000*l.*; expenditure, 133,810,000*l.*; deficit, 13,882,000*l.* (reduction of the national debt by 2,000,000*l.*) and met by increase of stamp and wine duties; Finance Act passed, 20 June, 1899.

Budget, 1900-1901, introduced, 5 March: receipts, 130,385,000*l.*; expenditure, 183,592,000*l.* (army, 61,499,000*l.*); deficit, 53,207,580*l.*; provided for by treasury bills, 8,000,000*l.*, and war loan about 43,000,000*l.*, income tax raised from 8*d.* to 1*s.*; additional duties on beer, spirits, tea (raised to 6*d.*), tobacco, stamps, &c.; Finance Act, royal assent, 9 April, 1900.

Budget: receipts (estimated), 132,255,000*l.*; expenditure, 187,612,000*l.*; deficit, 55,357,000*l.*, to be met by 2*d.* on the income tax (14*d.*), a ½*d.* per lb. on sugar, and 1*s.* per ton on exported coal; war loan, 30,000,000*l.*; 60,000,000*l.* asked for in consols, 18 April; Finance Act, royal assent, 26 July, 1901.

Budget: receipts (estimated), 147,785,000*l.*; expenditure, 174,609,000*l.*; deficit about, 23,924,000*l.*, to be met by the consols loan, 29,920,000*l.*; and a 1*d.* on the income tax (15*d.*), 3*d.* and 5*d.* per cwt. on imported corn and flour; sinking fund, 4,640,000*l.*, restored; new loan, 32,000,000*l.*, and draft on exchequer balances about 3,500,000*l.*, 14 April; Finance Act passed, 4 July, 1902.

Budget: receipts (estimated), 144,270,000*l.*; expenditure, 143,954,000*l.*; estimated surplus, 316,000*l.*; reduction of income tax, 4*d.* (11*d.*); corn and flour duty, 3*d.* and 4*d.* per cwt., repealed from 1 July, 1903; Finance Act, royal assent, 30 June, 1903.

BUENOS AYRES, a province of S. America, now part of the Argentine republic. The country was explored by Sebastian Cabot in 1526, and the capital, Buenos Ayres, founded by don Pedro de Mendoza in 1535. In 1585 the city was rebuilt and recolonised; and made a bishopric, 1620; and a viceroyalty, 1775. La Plata, the new capital, founded by Dr. Rocha, the governor, 24 Nov. 1882; made seat of government April, 1884. Population in 1888: province, 3,793,800; city, 500,000; 1900, 821,291. See *Argentine Confederation.*

A British fleet and army, under sir Home Popham and gen. Beresford, take the city, 27 June; it is retaken by the Spaniards, 12 Aug.; by the British 29 Oct. 1806

Monte Video taken by storm by sir Samuel Auchmuty, 3 Feb.; evacuated . . . . . 7 July, 1807

General Whitelock and 8000 British enter Buenos Ayres; were repulsed with great slaughter 5 July; retired from the country on degrading terms, 6 July, „

[He was cashiered for inefficiency.]

Independence of the province declared 19 July, 1816

Recognised as forming part of the Argentine confederation . . . . . Feb. 1822

[A prey to civil war through the violent intrigues of Rosas, Oribe, Urquiza, and others, for many years.]

Urquiza overthrows Rosas, and is made provisional dictator 1851

Oribe defeated by general Urquiza, to whom Buenos Ayres capitulates . . . . 3 Feb. 1852

Rosas flees, arrives at Plymouth . . 25 April, „

Urquiza deposed, 10 Sept.; invests the city; after some successes he retires . . . Dec. „

Constitution voted . . . . . 23 May, 1853

Buenos Ayres secedes from the Argentine confederation, and is recognised as an independent state; the first governor, Dr. D. Pastor Obligado, elected 12 Oct. „

Dr. Valentin Alsina elected governor . . May, 1857

War breaks out; Urquiza, general of the forces of the Argentine confederation, has an indecisive conflict with the Buenos Ayres general Mitre 23 Oct. 1859

A treaty signed, by which Buenos Ayres is re-united with the Argentine confederation . 11 Nov. „

Fresh contests: Mitre defeats Urquiza in an almost bloodless contest at Pavon; Urquiza retires 17 Sept. 1861

National congress at Buenos Ayres . 25 May, 1862

Mitre installed president . . . 12 Oct. „

Jesuits' college and archbishop's palace burnt down, and several priests killed, by a great mob; martial law proclaimed . . . . 28 Feb. 1875

General amnesty bill passed . . . . Aug. 1883

International exhibition . . 6 May *et seq.* 1890

New docks opened by the president . . 24 June 1897

(See *Argentine Republic.*)

BUFFALO, a city in New York state, founded in 1801; incorporated 1832; burned by the British during the war, 1813. Population, 1832, 15,000; 1890, 255,664; 1900, 352,387. Pan-American Exhibition, opened 20 May, 1901; president McKinley shot at and wounded here by Leon Czolgosz, 5 Sept. 1901. See *Niagara*, 1896.

BUFFOONS were originally mountebanks in the Roman theatres. Their shows were discouraged by Domitian, and abolished by Trajan, 98; see *Jesters.*

BUFFS, this famous regiment took its name from the distinguishing colour of its uniform—coats faced with buff, and waistcoats, breeches and stockings of the same hue. The "Old Buffs" were raised in 1689 (it is stated by some that they were raised by Charles II., and were called the "Holland regiment"). At one period they were known as the "Buff Howards," from Howard, their colonel (1737-1749). The "Old Buffs" formed the 3rd regiment of foot. The "Young Buffs," the old 31st foot, were raised 1702, and are now known as the Kent (East) regiment. Their uniform is scarlet with buff facings. The "Rothshire Buffs," the old 78th regiment, form the 2nd battalion of the Seaforth Highlanders (the duke of Albany's). *Brewer*.

BUILDING. In early times men dwelt in caves; wood and clay were the first building materials. Building with stone was early among the Tyrians. In Ireland a castle was built of stone at Tuam by the king of Connaught, in 1161; and it was "so new and uncommon as to be called the *Wonderful Castle*." Building with brick was introduced by the Romans into their provinces. Alfred encouraged it in England in 886. It was adopted by the earl of Arundel, about 1598, London being then almost wholly built of wood; see *Architecture*.

Building acts were passed by Elizabeth in 1562, 1580, and 1592; and by Charles II. in 1667. Recent acts are very numerous. The Building Act for the Metropolis, 7 & 8 Vict. c. 84 (1844), was amended in 1855, 1860, 1869, 1871, 1878, and 1882.
Building societies, formed to enable a person to purchase a house by paying money periodically to a society for a certain number of years, instead of paying rent to a landlord, began about 1836, when an act was passed for their regulation. Their nature and objects having been considerably changed, a new act was passed 30 July, 1874, another, 1894. Building Societies in United Kingdom: 1877, 715; 1882, 1,606; 1887, 2,197; 1900, 2,239; 1891, England and Wales: 2,262; Scotland, 61; Ireland, 59; 1895, England and Wales: 2,181; Scotland, 136; Ireland, 56; 1898, England and Wales: 2,219; 1899, 2,124; 1900, 2,031; Scotland, 144; 1899, 136; 1900, 139; Ireland, 62; 1899, 65; 1900, 69.
Annual meetings of the Building Societies Association held 3 Feb. 1892; 19 Jan. 1893, *et seq.*
London and General Bank established in 1882 under the influence of Mr. Jabez Balfour, in connection with the Liberator Permanent Building and Investment Society, which was founded in 1868, and closely combined with the Land Allotment Company and several other companies, forming what is termed the "Balfour group." This body, professing to have a capital of 7,000,000*l.*, by means of prospectuses, false accounts and balance-sheets, attracted thousands of shareholders and depositors. Estates were purchased, speculations undertaken, dividends were paid out of fictitious profits, and large sums were absorbed by managing directors. The bank and companies failed Oct. 1892; official liquidators were appointed. An appeal was made for the poorer sufferers, and a committee was appointed Dec. 1892; 30,226*l.* received up to 18 Oct. 1893; much relief given to the sufferers, reported May, 1894; total, 114,360*l.*; about 92,000*l.* expended, reported . . . . 10 April, 1903
Mr. Jabez Spencer Balfour, M.P. for Burnley, accused of fraud connected with this society; absconds 14 Dec. 1892; at Buenos Ayres, April, 1893; is arrested near Buenos Ayres, Jan. 1894; negotiations for extradition; sails for England, 7 April, 1895; arrives . . . . . 6 May, 1895
Mr. S. Wheeler's (official receiver) scheme for liquidation, accepted . . . . . . 6 June, ,,
Total liabilities, 8,360,804*l.*; supposed assets, 3,033,154*l.*; 23,000 shareholders; 28,000 creditors, (Sir R. Webster's statement) . . . 25 Oct. ,,
The failure caused great national distress.
See *Trials*, March, 1893–1895; *Strikes*, 1899.

BULGARIA, the ancient Mœsia Inferior, a principality tributary to Turkey. The Bulgarians were a Slavonian tribe, who harassed the Eastern empire and Italy from 499 to 678, when they established a kingdom. They defeated Justinian II., 687; but were subdued, after several conflicts, by the emperor Basil, in 1018. After defeating them in 1014, and taking 15,000 Bulgarian prisoners, he caused their eyes to be put out, leaving one eye only to every hundredth man, to enable him to conduct his countrymen home. The kingdom was re-established in 1186; but after several changes was conquered by Bajazet and annexed to the Ottoman empire, 1396. Bulgaria was a chief site of the Russo-Turkish war (*which see*), 1877-8. Population of Bulgaria and Eastern Roumelia, 3,154,375 in 1888, 3,733,189 in 1900. Capital, Sofia (*which see*).

The Bulgarians said to support the revolt in Herzegovina (*which see*) 1875-6
Insurrection in Bulgaria, quickly suppressed with great cruelty ("*Bulgarian Horrors*," see *England*, 1876; *Daily News*); see *Turkey* . May–Sept. 1876
Zankoff and Balabanow, Bulgarian delegates, received in London . . . . . . 9 Oct. ,,
Bulgaria constituted an autonomous principality, tributary to the sultan, by the Berlin treaty (*which see*) . . . . 13 July, 1878
First parliament (or sobranje) opened at Tirnova by prince Dondoukoff Korsakoff; the new constitution brought forward . . . . . 22 Feb. 1879
Prince Alexander of Hesse elected prince as Alexander I. . . . . 29 April, ,,
Visits the European courts; received by queen Victoria . . . . 5 June, ,,
Takes the oaths to the constitution at Tirnova 9 July, ,,
Bulgaria said to be quitted by the Russians 17 July, ,,
Ministerial difficulties; parliament dissolved 18 Dec. ,,
The prince announces the summoning a national assembly, and threatens to resign . . 9 May, 1881
Zankoff and other liberal ministers arrested for insulting the prince in their election addresses (soon released) . . . . . . 21 June, ,,
Elections for national assembly; voters said to be coerced . . . . . . 27 June *et seq.* ,,
Meeting of the assembly; the prince's proposals unanimously accepted; he promises reforms and adherence to the constitution . . . 13 July, ,,
The late liberal ministers, Zankoff and Slaviekoff, temporarily arrested . . . about 23 July, ,,
Amnesty for political offences proclaimed 12 Sept. ,,
New council of state established . about 28 Sept. ,,
New ministry under gen. Skobeloff and M. Kypriak 15 March, 1883
The prince virtually dictator; opposes Russia, under whose influence a liberal reaction against the prince takes place, and a new constitution is proposed; the national assembly meets 16 Sept. ,,
Manifesto of the prince restoring the Tirnova constitution; Zankoff minister . . . . 20 Sept. ,,
Col. Redigher, war minister, and other Russian officers summarily dismissed by the prince, 26 Oct. ,,
Peaceful relations with Russia re-established about 15 Nov. ,,
Changes in the constitution proposed by government adopted . . . . . . 17 Dec. ,,
Disputes with Servia respecting refugees and boundaries . . . . . . May, June, 1884
M. Zankoff's ministry resigns; succeeded by Karaveloff . . . . July ,,
Raids of Servians repelled; the Bulgarian government protests . . . . . Sept. Oct. ,,
Disputes with Servia unsettled . . . . Dec. ,,
Re-union with Roumelia (termed South Bulgaria April, 1886) declared; about 18 Sept.; all Bulgaria arming; action suspended on advice of the powers of Europe . . . . about 15 Oct. 1885
Declaration of war by Servia 13 Nov.; circular to the powers alleging Bulgarian aggression; denied by prince Alexander, 14 Nov.; Bulgaria invaded at four points; skirmishes, several killed and wounded, and small places occupied by Servians; prince Alexander appeals to Turkey for help, 14 Nov. ,,
Desperate fighting: Servians take positions at Raptcha, Bulgarians retreat to Slivnitza; 400 Bulgarians captured; 50 Servians killed 15 Nov. ,,

Servian attack repulsed, 16 Nov.; renewed with artillery with success, many Bulgarian prisoners, 17 Nov. 1885

Bulgarians defeated between Kula (*Adlie*) and Widdin . . . . 17 Nov. ,,

The Bulgarians bravely defend the Dragoman pass, attacked by 40,000 Servians, but retire at night . . . . 15 Nov. ,,

Prince Alexander submits to the Porte and orders evacuation of Eastern Roumelia . . 19 Nov. ,,

Prince Alexander and the Bulgarians attack the Servians at Slivnitza; severe fighting; king Milan and the Servians retire, leaving 400 prisoners . . . . 17–19 Nov. ,,

Bulgarians totally defeat the Servians near the Dragoman pass 21–22 Nov. 1885; near Zaribrod, which is occupied by prince Alexander . 23 Nov. ,,

Estimated Servian loss 6,000 killed and wounded, 17–21 Nov. ,,

Servians retreat to Pirot, 24 Nov.; prince Alexander enters Servia, defeats Servians and occupies Pirot after severe conflict, 26–27 Nov.; siege of Widdin, Bulgarian sally repulsed . 27 Nov. ,,

Cessation of hostilities through Austrian intervention . . . . 28 Nov. ,,

Servian proposals rejected . . about 2 Dec. ,,

Sir W. M. White at Constantinople supports the Bulgarian union . . . . Nov.–Dec. ,,

Protocol signed by International Commission; Pirot in Servia and Widdin in Bulgaria to be evacuated; armistice to last till 1 March, 21 Dec. ,,

The powers in a collective note call upon the Balkan rulers to disarm; refused by Greece and Servia . . . . about 16 Jan. 1886

Virtual (not nominal) union of Eastern Roumelia with Bulgaria; prince Alexander representing the sultan, his suzerain, for five years; Jan.; Decree promulgated . . . . 2 Feb. ,,

Peace between Bulgaria and Servia signed at Bucharest 3 March; ratified 17 March; by the sultan . . . . 13 March, ,,

Prince Alexander demands governorship for life, about 15 March, 1886; not agreed to . March, ,,

The conference of powers at Constantinople; Turco-Bulgarian convention protocol nominating prince Alexander governor of Eastern Roumelia for five years signed 5 April; accepted with reservation by prince Alexander . 8 April, ,,

Bulgarian assembly opened; Eastern Roumelian deputies present . . . . . . 14 June, ,,

Conspiracy at Sofia, prince Alexander carried off a prisoner . . . . 21–23 Aug. ,,

Provisional government formed by M. Zankoff and others . . . . 21 Aug. ,,

Their proclamation disavowed by the army and people at Sofia, Philippopolis and other places . ,,

M. Stefan Stamboloff a lawyer, an ardent Bulgarian, elected deputy at Tirnova, 1879, president of the sobranje . . . . ,,

A loyalist provisional government formed at Tirnova by Stamboloff and others, which issues manifesto in the prince's name . . 23 Dec. ,,

The prince landed at Keni Russi in Russian Bessarabia . . . . ,,

Conflicts with M. Zankoff's supporters . . . ,,

The rebel government prisoners or fugitives, 25 Aug. ,,

Return of prince Alexander; triumphant reception at Rustchuk: he issues a proclamation, 29 Aug. 1886; arrives at Philippopolis, 1 Sept., at Sofia 3 Sept. M. Zankoff and others released; prince Alexander submits to Russia, announces his intention to abdicate, 4 Sept.; regency appointed Stamboloff, Mutkuroff, and Karaveloff . 6 Sept. ,,

Prince Alexander leaves Sofia with simple dignity, 8 Sept.; Sofia in a state of siege . . . . . ,,

The revolting soldiers degraded and officers arrested, about 8 Sept. ,,

Arrival of gen. Kaulbars as Russian agent, intimidating policy . . . . 25 Sept. ,,

M. Tisza, Hungarian Prime Minister, declares for maintenance of the treaty of Berlin and Bulgarian independence . . . . 30 Sept. ,,

M. Radoslavoff, premier, and ministry, firmly resist general Kaulbars, 4 Oct.; his mission in the provinces unsuccessful . . . . . . Oct. ,,

Elections for the sobranje (parliament); majority for the regency (about 400 to 20), 78 Zankoffists 10 Oct. ,,

Gadban Effendi, Turkish envoy, impugns the elections and requires delay of the meeting of the sobranje; resisted by the regency . 20 Oct. 1886

Russian war ships at Varna; state of siege renewed at Sofia. . . . . 28 Oct. ,,

The sobranje opened; the rebel officers released 1 Nov. ,,

Gen. Kaulbars threatens to retire if Russians are ill-treated; 100 Russian sailors land at Varna, 1, 2 Nov. ,,

Captain Nabokoff's attempt to create an insurrection in favour of the czar at Bourgas quickly suppressed . . . . 4 Nov. ,,

Prince Waldemar of Denmark elected prince by the sobranje 10 Nov. (declined 13 Nov.); resignation of the regent M. Karaveloff 10 Nov.; succeeded by M. Zivkoff . . . . 13 Nov. ,,

Important speeches of the marquis of Salisbury (9 Nov.) and of count Kalnoky against Russian aggression . . . . 13 Nov. ,,

Gen. Kaulbars' ultimatum unanswered; he and Russian consuls quit Bulgaria . 20 Nov. *et seq.* ,,

Prince Ferdinand of Saxe-Coburg invited for election as prince by Bulgarian delegates, 15 Dec.; prince Nicholas of Mingrelia recommended by Russia . . . . ,,

The delegates (MM. Stoiloff, Grekoff, and Caltcheff) visit various courts; not received at St. Petersburg; received unofficially at Vienna and Berlin Dec.; London (favorably) 29 Dec. 1886; Paris 9 Jan.; Rome 18 Jan.; Constantinople 29 Jan. 1887

Military revolt at Silistria, col. Kristeff shot; quickly suppressed . . . . 1, 2 March, ,,

Military insurrection at Rustchuk; fighting, many killed and wounded 3 March; suppressed by the militia and people 4 March; several ringleaders executed 6 March; many imprisoned 8–9 March, ,,

Sofia in a state of siege; MM. Karaveloff, Nikoforoff and 22 others arrested 4 March; released 6 April, ,,

Reported execution of 14 rebels at Rustchuk, 11 March, ,,

M. Mantoff, prefect of Rustchuk, shot at at Bucharest . . . . 31 March, ,,

Prince Alexander definitively declines re-election, about 12 June, ,,

Meeting of the sobranje at Tirnova 4 July; unanimous election of prince Ferdinand of Saxe-Coburg and Gotha as prince 7 July; he accepts conditionally 8 July; the ministers and regency resign, announced 9 July. M. Stoiloff forms a ministry 12 July; the regency on request withdraw resignation . . . . about 14 July, ,,

Prince Ferdinand arrives at Tirnova, and signs the constitution, &c., and issues a proclamation, 14 Aug.; the Russian government protests against this . . . . 15 Aug. ,,

The prince well received at Philippopolis 21 Aug.; and at Sofia . . . . 22 Aug. ,,

The sultan declares prince Ferdinand's position illegal . . . . 22 Aug. ,,

Stamboloff forms a strong ministry . . 1 Sept. ,,

Proposed mission of general Ernroth (Russian) opposed by the powers early . . . Sept. ,,

State of siege closed; the opposition to the government active . . . . Sept. ,,

The *Bulgaria* publishes a libellous statement respecting the German Consul, Herr Löper, Aug.; contradiction published by intervention of the Bulgarian government, and the paper suppressed Sept.; matter referred to the German government about 14 Sept.; pacific settlement announced . . . . 21 Sept. ,,

Elections for the sobranje; majority for the ministry (260—32); riots at Plevna, suppressed with bloodshed, 10 killed . . . . 9 Oct. ,,

Sobránje opened by the prince . . . 27 Oct. ,,

Insurrection at Eski-Zagra suppressed, 17 soldiers killed . . . . . . announced 16 Nov. ,,

Russian note to the sultan and the powers declaring the illegality of prince Ferdinand's position, Russia supported by France and Germany; Austria, England and Italy maintain reserve; middle Feb.–March 1888; the Porte telegraphs to M. Stamboloff that prince Ferdinand's position is illegal, 6 March; no answer returned . March, 1888

Temporary resignation of the ministry, 13–24 June, ,,

Prince Ferdinand's first anniversary . 14 Aug. ,,

M. Stamboloff reconstitutes his ministry, about 22 Dec. 1888

About 60 eminent men arrested by M. Stamboloff for petitioning the Exarch at Constantinople, as favouring M. Zankoff . 5–6 Feb. 1889
Death of Zacharia Stoianoff, president of the sobranje, eminent patriot, at Paris . 15 Sept. „
Prince Ferdinand visits Germany [M. Stamboloff appointed regent] . . . . . . 8 Oct. „
The Russian prince Dolgoroukoff visits Sofia, intrigues with the Zankoffists, and is expelled 8–12 Oct. „
Loan of 25,000,000 francs at 6 per cent. obtained on the railways announced . . . . 20 Oct. „
Prince Ferdinand, after a successful tour, during which he visited Paris, 16 Oct., Vienna, 27 Oct., returns to Sofia ; the parliament opened, 3 Nov. „
Russian circular note to the powers stating that the terms of the loan are contrary to the treaty of Berlin ; this is denied by the Bulgarian government ; the loan fully subscribed for five or six times at Vienna, Berlin, &c. . . . . Jan. 1890
Major Panitza, a high army official, and six others arrested on a charge of plotting against the prince and government (in 1887 *et seq.*) . . 1 Feb. „
More arrests ; M. Stamboloff acts as prefect of police . . . . 7 Feb. „
Trial of major Panitza and 14 others, charged with conspiring to overthrow the government and assassinate prince Ferdinand and his ministers : 9 officers, 4 civilians, and capt. Kalobkoff, a Russian, also arraigned. Court-martial opened 15 May ; sentences, major Panitza to be shot ; capt. Kalobkoff nine years' imprisonment ; lieut. Rifoff and M. Arnodoff six years, 4 officers three years, one man five months, the rest acquitted 30 May ; sentences confirmed on appeal, 19 June, „
Major Panitza* shot at Sofia . . . 28 June, „
The government sends a courteous but firm note to the Porte requesting the recognition of prince Ferdinand and religious autonomy to the Macedonian Bulgarians . . . . . 26 June, „
[Answer deferred, July, 1890.]
3 Bulgarian bishops in Macedonia appointed by the Porte about . . . . . . 31 July, „
Disapproved by the Greek patriarch, who resigns about . . . . 5 Aug. „
Kalobkoff, the Russian intriguer, released and expelled from Bulgaria about . . 25 Aug. „
Elections : great majority for the government, Sept. „
The prince opens the sobranje with a firm speech, 27 Oct. „

He is partially recognised by the Porte . 5 Feb. 1891
Detection of a plot by major Bendereff against the government, reported . . . . 17 March, „
M. Beltcheff, minister of finance, assassinated in the street in the presence of M. Stamboloff (for whom it was thought he was taken) about 8 P.M. 27 March ; many arrests . . . 28 March, „
Connection with major Bendereff's conspiracy suspected, 28 March ; above 150 arrests up to April, „
Archiepiscopal palace at Sofia searched by order of M. Stamboloff ; documents and letters carried off, 30 Aug. „
The sobranje votes by acclamation a pension of 50,000 francs to prince Alexander of Battenberg (count Hartenau), reported . . . 13 Dec. „
Rupture with France, on account of the expulsion of M. Chadourne, a journalist, accused of publishing injurious intelligence. . . 15 Dec. „
Rupture with France settled by explanation and apology, about . . . . . . 21 Jan. 1892
Dr. Vulkovitch, Bulgarian agent at Constantinople, stabbed 24 Feb. ; died . . . . 26 Feb. „
Government note to the Porte complaining of plots, &c., delivered . . . . . . 13 April, „
Plot at Rustchuk ; bombs discovered, 22 April ; many arrests . . . . April, May, „
The prince, during a tour, visits Britain, 30 May ; received by the queen at Balmoral, 6–8 June ; leaves . . . . 11 June, „
Trial of 18 persons connected with the conspiracy against prince Ferdinand and the assassination of M. Beltcheff (27 March, 1891), 30 June–18 July ; sentences, imprisonment : M. Petko Karaveloff, ex-premier and regent, 5 years ; Ghorghi Velikoff, 15 years ; three persons, 9 years ; one, 5 years ; one, 3 years : one, 16 months ; six acquitted ; Sweetoslaw Milaroff, Constantin Popoff, Toma Gheorghieff, and Alexander Karaguloff sentenced to death, 18 July ; executed . 27 July, 1892
M. Stamboloff, invited by the sultan, warmly received at Constantinople . . . 12–14 Aug. „
First Bulgarian exhibition opened at Philippopolis by prince Ferdinand, 27 Aug. ; closed . 13 Nov. „
Dispute with Greece respecting Greek schools and the new Bulgarian education law 21 Sept. *et seq.* ; the question referred to the powers, about 27 Sept. ; the schools re-opened . . . 1 Oct. „
The sobranje opened by the prince with a cheerful speech . . . . 27 Oct. „
Loan of 142,780,000 francs for railways authorised, about 22 Nov. „
Revision of the constitution ; Ferdinand and his heirs to remain R. C. ; bill introduced . 16 Dec. „
The bill passed permitting prince Ferdinand and his first successor to be Romanists, the next to belong to the Greek church . . . 19 Dec. „
M. Zankoff issues a fruitless manifesto against the prince and government . . about 24 Feb. 1893
The metropolitan Clement arrested for exciting the people against the government in a sermon at Tirnova . . . . 26 Feb. „
Russian circular to the powers against Bulgarian changes . . . . . . about 15 March, „
Ilia Gheorghieff convicted as an accomplice in the murder of M. Beltcheff . . . . 22 March, „
[Acquitted and discharged, 3 Nov.]
Marriage of prince Ferdinand to princess Marie Louise of Parma at Florence . . 20 April, „
Meeting of the grand sobranje, 15 May ; the new constitution passed 27 May ; proclaimed 29 May, „
Public entrance of the prince and princess into Sofia ; great festivities . . . 10, 11 June, „
The metropolitan, M. Clement, sentenced to banishment for his sermon (26 Feb.), 22 July ; commuted to 3 years' imprisonment . 10 Nov. „
Government majority in the elections . 30 July, „
The first Bulgarian steamship navigation company inaugurated at Varna . . . . 29 Aug. „
The sobranje opened by prince Ferdinand, 27 Oct. „
Discovery of a plot to assassinate prince Ferdinand ; arrest of lieut. Ivanoff and others, reported, 1 Dec. „

Bill restricting the press passed ; the sobranje adjourns . . . . 1 Jan. 1894
Trial of lieut. Luka Ivanoff and Stojan Ivanoff began 26 Jan. ; Luka sentenced to 15 years' and Stojan Ivanoff to 3 years' imprisonment, 30 Jan. „
Archbishop Clement's appeal dismissed, 21 Feb. ; pardoned by the prince . . . 15 March, „
Resignation of M. Stamboloff and ministry, 29 May, „
M. Stoiloff forms a new ministry . . 31 May, „
Rioting at Sofia, checked by the police . 1 June, „
Prince Ferdinand, in a warm complimentary rescript, expresses deep regret at the retirement of M. Stamboloff . . . . . 12 June, „
M. Stamboloff, for uttering remarks against prince Ferdinand, is prosecuted and bailed . 5 Sept. „
The sobranje opened by prince Ferdinand, 27 Oct. „
M. Stoiloff reconstitutes his ministry . 21 Dec. „
Amnesty for political offences granted, with some exceptions . . . . 30 Dec. „
The sobranje closed . . . . . . 1 Jan. 1895
M. Zankoff returns to Sofia ; warmly received by the people, 4 Jan. ; and the prince . 9 Jan. „
Elections ; government majority . . 4 Feb. „
Prosecution of M. Stamboloff ; in ill health ; his passport refused . . . . . May, „
Frontier conflicts and disputes with Turkey, Macedonian agitation reported . . . 19 June, „
Rupture with Turkey, M. Dimitroff (minister) recalled . . . . 23 June, „
Bulgarian note to the powers . . . 8 July, „
M. Stamboloff with his friend M. Petkoff attacked and dreadfully wounded in his carriage by three assassins, 15 July ; he dies 3 A.M., 18 July ; much sympathy expressed to Madame Stamboloff by queen Victoria and other foreign powers ; 19 July, „

* He was born at Tirnova, 1852 ; became an advocate ; he distinguished himself as leader of a volunteer band in the Servo-Bulgarian war ; was favoured by prince Alexander, and unwillingly submitted to prince Ferdinand.

public funeral: address by M. Petkoff, socialist rioting . . . . 20 July 1895

Bulgarian mission well received by the czar at St. Petersburg, 17 July; no reconciliation with prince Ferdinand; returns to Sofia . 4 Aug. „

The sobranje opened with a favourable speech by prince Ferdinand . . . . . . 31 Oct. „

Communication of reconciliation of the Russian government with prince Ferdinand, in consequence of his assent to the conversion of prince Boris to the Greek church . . . 8 Feb. 1896

M. Stoiloff honourably received by the sultan, who sends representatives to the prince's conversion, 9 Feb.; conversion of prince Boris from the Roman to the Greek church; solemn ceremony; the czar as sponsor represented by gen. Kutuzoff, 14 Feb.; the sobranje presents 500,000 francs to prince Boris, to remain in the bank till his majority . . . . 14 Feb. „

Prince Ferdinand recognized by all the powers; announced 19 Feb.; warmly received by the sultan at Constantinople, 26 March; receives Turkish honours, April; arrives in St. Petersburg, receives honours from the czar, 18, 21 April; at Paris, receives the cordon of the legion of honour, 25 April; arrives at Berlin, 30 April; receives honours, May; received at Belgrade by the king of Servia, 7 May; returns to Sofia . . . . 9 May „

Dissolution of the sobranje ordered, 22 Oct.; reopened with a speech from the prince . 13 Dec. „

Trial of persons implicated in the murder of M. Stamboloff, 21 Dec.; Mdme. Stamboloff summoned to the court, asserts the innocence of the prisoners, and that the real assassins are known to the court, 27 Dec.; 1 prisoner acquitted, and 2 others sentenced to 3 years' imprisonment, 30 Dec. „

The sultan grants three new bishoprics in Macedonia; announced . . . . . . 24 April 1897

Explosion at a cartridge factory near Rustchuk, about 81 deaths . . . . . . 6 Aug. „

The sobranje opened, 27 Oct.; closed . 27 Dec. „

Raids, murders, &c., by Arnauts, in various districts, reported . . . . . . 14 Dec. „

Three new bishoprics granted by the sultan, 4 Jan. 1898

Capt. Boitcheff and M. Novilitch, prefect of police, convicted of the murder of Anna Simon, and sentenced to death . . . . . . 25 Jan. „

Strong appeals to the sultan respecting torturing of prisoners, outrages, &c., at Kossova, and demanding the dismissal of Turkish officials, 31 Jan. and 3 Feb.; rejected by the Porte . 12 Feb. „

The public debt converted into a 3 per cent. loan of about 290,000,000f. . . . . . 20 Dec. „

The Macedonian committee memorialise the powers in favour of reforms, autonomy, &c. . . Jan. 1899

M. Stoiloff's ministry resigns, 28 Jan.; M. Grekoff forms a conciliation cabinet . . 31 Jan. „

Death of princess Marie Louise, much lamented, 31 Jan. „

Elections: government majority (104) . 7 May, „

Cabinet crisis: M. Grekoff, premier, resigns, early Oct.; new ministry, M. Ivantchoff premier and foreign minister . . . . . . 13 Oct. „

New railway, branch line to the Danube between Roman, Plevna, and Shumla, opened by the prince . . . . 20 Nov. „

Fatal rioting round Rustchuk quelled by the military, martial law proclaimed early May, 1900

Lawlessness and reign of terror against resident Roumanians in Sofia, many political murders; see *Roumania* . . . . . July, Aug. „

New railway from Rustchuk to Tirnova, opened by prince Ferdinand . . . . . 21 Oct. „

The sobranje opened by the prince, 28 Oct.; closed, 12 Dec. „

Frequent changes of ministry . . Oct. *et seq.* „

New French loan, 120,000,000f., reported 1 Jan. 1901

Elections (reported unsatisfactory), 10 Feb.; ministry resigns . . . . 26 Feb. „

Turkish troops ordered to the frontier owing to the Macedonian agitation . . . . . 26 Feb. „

M. Karaveloff forms a joint cabinet with the Zankoffists . . . . 4 March, „

Prince Ferdinand opens the sobranje, financial situation serious . . . . 7 March, „

The porte demands the dissolution of the Macedonian committee, March; the leaders are arrested in Sofia . . . . . 5 April, 1901

M. Stoiloff, ex-premier, born 1856, dies . 6 April, „

Impeachment of ex-ministers by the budget committee . . . . 24 May, „

Visit of the grand-duke Alexander and Russian fleet, at Varna . . . . . . 12 July, „

Sarafof, ex-president of the Macedonian committee, and 3 others charged with assassination (see *Roumania*), tried, and acquitted . . 12, 14 Aug. „

Prince Ferdinand opens the sobranje with a hopeful speech, 28 Oct.; resigns . . . 16 Dec. „

Contract for a loan of 125,000,000f. from a Paris bank, signed, 13 Dec.; withdrawn government resigns . . . . 16 Dec. „

M. Ivantcheff, ex-premier, and 3 colleagues impeached on charges of treason, &c., by the sobranje, 6 Sept., which closed . . 8 Sept. „

Financial and ministerial crisis; proposed French loan rejected, the sobranje suspended; the ministry resigns . . . . . . 24, 27 Dec. „

M. Daneff forms a cabinet, 3 Jan.; supplies rejected, the sobranje dissolved . . . . 5 Jan. 1902

Conflict with Turkish troops in Kossova, 10 Bulgarians killed . . . . . mid. Jan. „

M. Kantcheff, minister of public instruction, assassinated by a discharged schoolmaster, who afterwards committed suicide . . . 6 Feb. „

Elections: small government majority . 3 March, „

Cabinet (Zankoffists) reconstructed, M. Daneff premier and foreign minister . . 22 March, „

Bulgarian band destroyed by Turkish troops at Patili; reported . . . . . . 3 July, „

Budget passed, deficit over 6,000,000f. . 8 Aug. „

Split in the Macedonian congress at Sofia, col. Zoutcheff president . . . . . 10 Aug. „

Macedonian band captured near Sofia . mid. Aug. „

Cols. Zoutcheff and Nicoloff charged with aiding revolutionary bands, arrested 1, 2 Sept.; escaped, 23 Sept. „

Bulgarian raids into Macedonia (*which see* 1903), 9, 11 Oct. „

Anti-Greek riots at Varna . . . . 4 Nov. „

Visit of king of Roumania . . . . . 11 Nov. „

M. Daneff announces resignation of cabinet on account of internal differences . . . 14 Nov. „

Reconstructs cabinet. M. Daneff premier and foreign minister . . . . . . 17 Nov. „

Government grant of 50,000f. voted for Macedonian refugees; budget, 1903, estimated surplus 335,029f. . . . . 17 Dec. „

Count Lamsdorff, Russian foreign minister, negotiates on the Macedonian question . 26, 28 Dec. „

M. Karaveloff, thrice premier, died, aged 58, 6 Feb. 1903

Macedonian committees in Sofia suppressed, leaders arrested . . . . 14 Feb. „

Vote of confidence in the government carried after two days' debate . . . . . . 19 Feb. „

Fatal rioting near Sofia . . . . . . 11 Mar. „

Gen. Paprikoff (war) resigns, crisis, 7 March; the ministry resigns, 27 March, but returns, with col. Savoff war minister . . . 31 March, „

Gen. Paprikoff created inspector-gen. of the army, about 7 April, „

Sobranje prorogued after longest session in annals of the Principality . . . . . 13 April, „

Prince Ferdinand visits Mentone . . 16 April, „

Foundation-stone of a mausoleum for Russian officers killed at Plevna, 1877, laid . 25 April, „

Resignation of cabinet, a Stamboloffist cabinet, gen. Petroff premier . . . . . 15 May, „

Anti-Greek revolt suppressed with great severity, May-June, „

Bulgarian government addresses note to the great powers, protesting against the cruelties of the Porte in Macedonia, and threatening action unless the powers intervene, reported . 14 Sept. „

See *Macedonia* and *Addenda*.

PRINCE.

Alexander (Joseph) I. (son of prince Alexander, uncle of Louis IV., grandduke of Hesse), born 5 April, 1857; elected 29 April, 1879; deposed (*see above*) 4th Sept. 1886; declines re-election 12 June, 1887; dies . . . . . 17 Nov. 1893

Ferdinand, duke of Saxe-Coburg and Gotha, born 26 Feb. 1861; elected 7 July; married princess Marie Louise (daughter of Robert, duke of Parma,

b. 17 Jan. 1870; died 31 Jan. 1899), 20 April, 1893; *heir*, Boris (son), born, 18 Jan. 1894; Cyril, born 17 Nov. 1895; Clementina, born 30 Jan, 1899

BULL, or EDICT OF THE POPE. The bulla is properly the seal, either of gold, silver, lead, or wax. On one side are the heads of Peter and Paul; and on the other the name of the pope, and year of his pontificate. A bull against heresy was issued by Gregory IX. in 1231. Pius V. published a bull against Elizabeth, 25 April, 1570; in 1571 bulls were forbidden to be promulgated in England. The bull *Unigenitus* (beginning with this word) against the Jansenists was issued by Clement XI., 1713; confirmed by Benedict XIII., 1725. The Golden Bull of the emperor Charles IV., so-called from its golden seal, was made the fundamental law of the German empire, at the diet of Nuremburg, 1356; see *Brazen Bull*. Pius IX. published an encyclical letter censuring modern errors, 8 Dec. 1864; see under *Rome*; see *Stocks*.

BULL-BAITING or BULL-FIGHTING, was an amusement at Stamford in the reign of John, 1209; and at Tutbury, 1374. In the *Sports of England*, we read of the "Easter fierce hunts, when foaming boars fought for their heads, and lusty bulls and huge bears were baited with dogs"; and near the *Clink*, London, was the Paris, or Bear Garden, so celebrated in the time of Elizabeth for the exhibition of bear-baiting, then a fashionable amusement. A bill to abolish bull-baiting was thrown out in the commons, chiefly through the influence of Mr. William Windham, who made a speech in favour of the custom, 24 May, 1802. It was made illegal in 1835; see *Cruelty to Animals*. Bull-fights were introduced into Spain about 1260; abolished there, "except for *pious* and *patriotic* purposes," in 1784. Bull-fights are very common in Spain. A bull-fight at Lisbon, attended by 10,000 spectators, on Sunday, 14 June, 1840; one took place at Havre, 5 July, 1868. Somewhat theatrical fights with Spanish bulls, at the Agricultural Hall, London, were stopped 28 March, 1870, for cruelty. At a bull-fight at Marseilles about 17 persons were killed, and 230 injured, by the fall of wooden stands, Sunday, 14 Aug., 1881. A bull-fight at Nimes (since prohibited), 12 June, 1884.

A bull-fight at the Hippodrome, Paris, for sufferers by inundations in S. France, very successful, no casualties, Spanish ambassador present, 16 Jan. 1887
Bull-fights formed part of the entertainments at Paris during the universal exhibition in 1889; renewed with restrictions . . . May *et seq.* 1890
Prohibited in France . . . . . 25 Sept. 1894
Rioting at Marseilles through restrictions at a bull-fight . . . . 9 Aug. 1896
Several bull-fights at Boulogne, English visitors present . . . . . . Aug.-Sept. 1899
Collapse of a stand at a bull-fight at Pedreguer, Alicante, 12 deaths, 200 injured . 13 Nov. 1900

BULLETS of stone were in use 1514. Iron ones are mentioned in the *Fœdera*, 1550. Leaden bullets were made before the close of the 16th century. The conoidal cup rifle-ball was invented by capt. Minié, about 1833. Other and greatly improved bullets have been since devised for use with modern rifles, such as the Martini-Henry, the Enfield-Martini, the Mauser, the Mannlicher, and the Lee-Metford. The *dum-dum* bullet, so named from its having been invented and manufactured at the arsenal of that name near Calcutta, flattens out on striking an object. A bullet, a modification of the Lee-Metford bullet, having similar properties as the dum-dum, was issued to the army in 1899, but was not used, it being considered that it came, like the dum-dum, under the category of "explosive bullets," condemned by the Geneva Convention.

A *bullet-proof* coat or cuirass invented by Mr. Dowe at Vienna: successfully tested at Mannheim; reported efficient but heavy 13 March, 1894: tested at the Alhambra, London, in the presence of the duke of Cambridge, and other officers; report as to practical value indecisive, 23 May, 1894. The Prussian war office, after various trials, declare the cuirass to be worthless . 3 Sept. 1894
Mr. Maxim's bullet-proof cuirass; indecisive trials at Erith, 2 June, and at the Aquarium 9 June, 1895
Mr. Loris' bullet-proof and dagger-proof cuirasses exhibited at the Crystal palace . . 20 Aug. ,,
Capt. Boynton's bullet-proof shield tried at Sheffield, 15 Sept. ,,

BULLION, uncoined gold and silver. The "Bullion Report" of a parliamentary committee in 1810, principally guided by Mr. Horner and Mr. (afterwards Sir R.) Peel, established the conclusion that paper money is always liable to be over-issued, and consequently depreciated, unless it be at all times immediately convertible into gold. This principle has been adopted in British monetary arrangements; see *Bank of England*.

VALUE OF BULLION IMPORTED INTO GREAT BRITAIN.

	Gold.	Silver.
1858	£22,793,126	£6,700,064
1868	17,136,177	7,716,418
1870	18,806,728	10,648,940
1874	18,081,019	12,298,169
1876	23,475,975	13,578,269
1878	20,871,410	11,551,545
1879	13,368,675	10,786,863
1880	9,454,861	6,799,022
1881	9,963,006	6,901,402
1882	14,376,559	9,242,925
1883	7,755,800	9,468,002
1884	10,744,408	9,633,495
1886	13,392,256	7,471,639
1887	9,955,326	7,819,438
1888	15,787,588	6,213,940
1889	17,914,039	9,185,400
1890	23,568,049	10,385,659
1891	30,275,620	9,315,598
1892	21,583,232	10,746,382
1893	24,834,727	11,913,395
1894	27,572,347	11,005,417
1895	36,009,329	10,666,332
1896	24,468,580	14,329,116
1899	32,533,497	12,727,989
1900	26,190,873	13,322,300
1901	20,715,628	11,501,678
1902	21,629,049	9,764,296

BULL-RUN BATTLES, see *Manassas*.

BULWER-CLAYTON TREATY, concluded 19 April, ratified 4 July, 1850, by which sir Henry Lytton Bulwer for the British, and Mr. Clayton for the American government, declared that neither should obtain exclusive control over the proposed ship canal through Central America, or erect any fortification on any part of the country. Disputes afterwards arose with respect to this treaty, and the connection of Great Britain with the Mosquito territory (*which see*), which were settled in 1857.

Its abrogation was proposed by the Americans in 1880, on account of De Lesseps' plan for a canal in Central America. The treaty was finally superseded by the Hay-Pauncefote Isthmian canal treaty, signed by Mr. Hay and lord Pauncefote at Washington, 18 Nov.; ratified 16 Dec. 1901.

BUNDSCHUH, see *Jacquerie*.

BUNHILL-FIELDS (originally Bonhill-Field), a burial-ground near Finsbury-square, E. London, termed by Southey the "Campo Santo of the Dissenters;" first used in 1665. Here were interred Thomas Goodwin (1679), John Owen (1683), Isaac Watts (1748), John Bunyan (1688), George

Fox, the Quaker (1690), general Fleetwood, son-in-law of Cromwell (1692), and Daniel De Foe (1731). *Cunningham.* An act for the preservation of the ground as an open space was passed, 15 July, 1867, and it was re-opened by the lord mayor, 14 Oct., 1869; and a monument to De Foe, subscribed for by boys and girls, was inaugurated, 16 Sept. 1870.

BUNKER HILL, more properly Breed's hill (near Boston, U.S.). Here the British (nearly 3000), after severe loss, compelled the revolted Americans (about 5000) to retreat, after a desperate conflict, 17 June, 1775. Ralph Farnham, who was present at the battle, died on 28 Dec. 1860, aged 104½ years. He was introduced to the prince of Wales when in America. Centenary of the battle celebrated June, 1875.

BUONAPARTE, see *Bonaparte*.

BURFORD CLUB, the appellation given (according to Mr. Layer, the barrister, a conspirator, see *Layer*) by the Pretender and his agents to a pretended Jacobite club, of which lord Orrery was chairman, and lord Strafford, sir Henry Goring, earl Cowper, Mr. Hutcheson, the bishop of Rochester, sir Constantine Phipps, general Webb, lord Bingley, lord Craven, Mr. Dawkins, lord Scarsdale, lord Bathurst, Mr. Shippen, and lord Gower, were members. This story was set aside by the solemn declarations of lord Cowper and lord Strafford. The list of this club was published in the *Weekly Journal*, printed in Whitefriars; but when Read, the printer, was ordered to appear at the bar of the house, he absconded. March, 1722. *Salmon*.

BURGESSES, from the French *Bourgeois*, a distinction coeval in England with corporations. They were called to parliament in England, 1265; in Scotland in 1326; and in Ireland about 1365. Burgesses to be resident in the places they represented in parliament, 1 Hen. V. (1413); see *Borough*.

BURGH, see *Borough*. Burgh Convention, see under *Home Rule*.

BURGHERS AND ANTI-BURGHERS. In 1732 Ebenezer Erskine and others seceded from the church of Scotland. Differing in regard to the interpretation of the burgess oath, they divided into two sections with the foregoing names in 1747. In 1820 they were reunited as the United Associate Synod of the Secession church, which, on 13 May, 1847, joined the Relief church, together forming the United Presbyterian church.

BURGLARY was a capital offence till 1829. Formerly he who convicted a burglar was exempted from parish offices, 1699; Statute of Rewards, 5 Anne, 1706; and 6 Geo. I. 1720. Receivers of stolen plate and other goods to be transported, 10 Geo. III. 1770. Persons having upon them picklock-keys, &c., to be deemed rogues and vagabonds, 13 Geo. III. 1772-3. The laws with respect to burglary were amended by Mr. (afterwards sir Robert) Peel's acts between 1823 and 1829; by the criminal laws of 1861; and by Act passed, 14 Aug. 1896. Insurance policies against burglaries issued by many insurance companies, 1903.

Burglaries and housebreaking in England and Wales, 1885-6, 3,545; 1886-7, 3,852; 1888-9, 3,620; 1889-90, 3,401; 1890-1, 3,418; 1891-2, 3,986. Changes made in the return, 1893, 7,390; 1894, 6,740; 1895, 4,166; 1896, 5,922; 1897, 6,179; 1898, 6,703; 1899, 5,581; 1900, 6,289; 1901, 7,057.

Capture of a gang of burglars with a large amount of stolen property at the Queen's Head tavern, Wharf road, City road, London, 8 Nov. 1891. Frederick Clark and 7 others were convicted and sentenced to various terms of penal servitude, 18, 19 Jan. 1892. It was stated that they had been concerned in 86 burglaries.

Harry Jackson, 41, detected and convicted of burglary at Denmark-hill, by the identification of finger prints he had left on a window-sill, sentenced to 7 years penal servitude, 13 Sept. 1902.

BURGOS (Spain), the burial place of the Cid, 1099. Lord Wellington entered Burgos on 19 Sept. after the battle of Salamanca (fought 22 July, 1812). The castle was besieged by the British and allied army, but the siege was abandoned 21 Oct. same year. The fortifications were blown up by the French, 12 June, 1813. Population 1887, 31,301; 1897, 30,856.

BURGUNDY, a large province in France, derives its name from the Burgundians, a Gothic tribe who overran Gaul in 275, and were driven out by the emperor Probus: they returned in 287, and were defeated by Maximin. In 413 they established a KINGDOM, comprising the present Burgundy, large parts of Switzerland, with Alsace, Savoy, Provence, &c. Gondicar, their leader, the first king. It was conquered by the Franks, 534.—The *second* kingdom, consisting of a part of the first, began with Gontran, son of Clotaire I. of France, in 561. The kingdoms of Arles, Provence, and Transjurane Burgundy, were formed out of the old kingdom.—DUCHY. In 877 Charles the Bald made his brother-in-law Richard the first duke of Burgundy. In 938, Hugh the Great, count of Paris, founder of the house of Capet, obtained the duchy. His descendant, Henry, on becoming king of France, conferred it on his brother Robert, in whose family it remained till the death of Philippe de Rouvre, without issue, in 1361. In 1363, king John of France made his fourth son, Philip, duke; see *Austria* and *Germany*.

DUKES.

1363. Philip the Bold; marries Margaret, heiress of Flanders, 1369.

1404. John the Fearless (son); joined the English invaders of France; privy to the assassination of the duke of Orleans in 1407; see *Armagnac;* himself assassinated at Montereau, in presence of the dauphin, Sept. 1419.

1419. Philip the Good (son), the most powerful duke.

1467. Charles the Bold; married to Margaret of York, sister to Edward IV., 9 July, 1468; invaded France, 1472; Switzerland, 1476; killed in an engagement with the Swiss, before Nancy, 4 Jan. 1477.

1477. Mary (daughter); married, 19 Aug. 1477, to Maximilian of Austria; died, 27 March, 1482.

1479. Louis XI. annexed Burgundy to France. The other dominions fell to Austria.

BURIALS. Abraham buried Sarah at Machpelah, 1860 B.C., *Gen.* xxiii. Places of burial were consecrated under pope Calixtus I. in A.D. 210. *Eusebius.* The Greeks had their burial-places at a distance from their towns; the Romans near the highways; hence the necessity for inscriptions. The first Christian burial-place, it is said, was instituted in 596; burial in cities, 742; in consecrated places, 750; in churchyards, 758. Many of the early Christians are buried in the catacombs at Rome; see *Catacombs*, *Cemeteries*, and *Dissenters*.

Vaults erected in chancels first at Canterbury . . 1075

Woollen shrouds only permitted to be used in England 1666

Linen scarfs introduced at funerals in Ireland, 1729; and woollen shrouds used 1733

Burials taxed 1695

A tax enacted on burials in England—for the burial of a duke 50*l.*, and for that of a common person 4*s.*—under Will. III. 1695, and Geo. III. . . . 1783

Acts relating to metropolitan burials passed . 1850-6-

Parochial registers of burials, births, and marriages, instituted in England by Cromwell, lord Essex, about 1538. *Stow.*
"*Earth to earth*" system of burial advocated by Mr. Seymour Haden; wicker-coffins exhibited at Stafford-house . . . . 17 June, 1875
Consecrated burial grounds in England, 13,673; closed, 1411 1877
Burials Act (permitting any Christian service in a parish churchyard) passed . . . . 7 Sept. 1880
New bill read second time in the commons, 6 March, 1895
"The London Burial-grounds: Notes on their history from the earliest times to the present day," by Mrs. Basil Holmes, published . . 1896
New burial act (many reforms) passed . . . 1900

See *Dissenters.*

BURKING, a new species of murder, committed in Britain, thus named from Burke, the first known criminal by whom it was perpetrated. His victims were killed by pressure or other modes of suffocation, and the bodies, which exhibited no marks of violence, were sold to the surgeons for dissection. He was executed at Edinburgh, 28 Jan. 1829. A monster named Bishop was apprehended in Nov. 1831, and executed in London 5 Dec. with Williams, one of his accomplices, for the murder of a poor friendless Italian boy, named Carlo Ferrari. They confessed to this and other similar murders.

BURLINGHAME TREATY, promoted by Mr. Anson Burlinghame and a Chinese embassy, and signed at Washington 4 July, 1868. It authorised mutual immigration. California prospered through Chinese labour; but depression in 1879-80 led to a demand for its expulsion and abrogation of the treaty.

BURLINGTON ARCADE, Piccadilly, opened 20 March, 1819.

BURLINGTON FINE ARTS CLUB, for exhibiting works of art, and promoting intercourse between artists, amateurs, &c., founded 1866, 500 members.

BURLINGTON HEIGHTS. After a fierce contest here between the British and the United States American forces, 6 June, 1813, the British carried the heights.

BURLINGTON HOUSE, Piccadilly, London, was built by Denham for lord Burlington, about 1664; and rebuilt by lord Burlington, the architect, about 1731. It was bought for 140,000*l.* by the government, authorised by vote of the house of commons, on 27 July, 1854. It became the home of the Royal, Linnean, and Chemical societies in 1857 (who occupied new rooms in 1873), and of the Antiquaries, Geological, and Royal Astronomical societies in 1873. In 1866, sites for buildings for the University of London and the Royal Academy were granted in the grounds of Burlington House. The entrance, colonnade, &c., were removed in 1868, and the exhibition of the Royal Academy was first opened here 3 May, 1869. Burlington charity school near here, founded 1699.

BURMAH, or BURMESE EMPIRE, founded in the middle of the 18th century by Alompra, the first sovereign of the last dynasty. Our first dispute with this formidable power in 1795 was amicably adjusted by general Erskine. Hostilities were commenced by the British in 1824, and they took Rangoon on May 11. The fort and pagoda of Syriam were taken in 1825. After a short armistice, hostilities were renewed, 1 Dec. same year, and pursued until the successive victories of the British led to the cession of Aracan, and to the signature of peace, 24 Feb. 1826. For the events of this war, and of the war in 1851, see *India.* Pegu was annexed to our Indian empire, 20 Dec. 1852. The war ended 20 June, 1853. Population of Upper Burmah, reported in 1892, over 3,000,000; in 1901, 3,849,833; Lower Burmah, nearly 4,750,000 in 1892; 5,371,328 in 1901. Capitals of Burmah: lower, Rangoon; upper, Mandalay; northern, Bhamo.

Rebellion against the king (of Upper Burmah) suppressed by British aid . . about Sept. 1866
Treaties with Great Britain . . 1862 and 25 Oct. 1867
Burmese embassy in England, 6 June; introduced to the queen . . . . . . 21 June, 1872
The king Mindone suspected of inciting Chinese to attack British expedition to West China (see *India*) . . . . Feb. 1875
Sir Douglas Forsyth's mission to the king; arrives at Mandalay, 14 June; submission of the king announced about 18 June; he refuses permission for British troops to march as a convoy through his territories to China; sir D. Forsyth retires, June, ,,
Col. Duncan sent to Mandalay . . about Aug. ,,
The king eventually acceded to the British demands: announced . . . . . Oct. ,,
The king dies, about 5 Sept., announced 2 Oct. 1878
His successor, Thebau (Wongyee prince of Thebau) kills many of the royal family and their friends . . . . Feb. 1879
The British resident and others quit Mandalay, 8 Oct. ,,
The king, attacked by small-pox, commits fresh atrocities . . . . . . 12 April, 1880
Prince Nyoung's rebellion, May, June, suppressed; he enters British territory . . 27 June, ,,
Political massacres at Mandalay recommenced, announced . . . . . . 21 April, 1882
Destructive fire at Mandalay, announced 11 April, 1883
Another great fire . . . . . . 9 April, 1884
Misgovernment; massacres at Mandalay, 21 Sept.; prospect of British intervention . . Oct. ,,
Town of Bhamo violently captured by the Chinese, 8-10 Dec. ,,
Captain Terndrup of the steamer *Kahbyor* rescues missionaries and others . . 12-13 Dec. ,,
Treaty between France and Burmah signed at Paris 15 Jan. 1885
Bhamo recaptured by the Burmese about 16 March, ,,
French negotiations with the king . . Oct. ,,
Dispute between the half mad king and the Bombay and Burmah Trading Association; communication from British commissioner, dated 28 Aug., insolently rejected; envoy not received; the king refuses the arbitration of the viceroy of India; the commissioner of British Burmah asks for 8,000 men . . . . about 13 Oct. ,,
Ultimatum sent by lord Dufferin requiring equitable settlement of the dispute; reception of a British resident with a guard; protection of British subjects, &c.; rejection; proclamation of war about 8 Nov.; advance of the army under gen. Harry N. D. Prendergast . . 9 Nov. ,,
Burmese war steamer captured 16 Nov.; Minhla and Gurgyong forts taken, 3 hours attack, lieut. Robt. A. Dury killed and 8 others, 17 Nov. ,,
The army advances; Magwe captured, 20 Nov.; Pagan and Myingyan. . . . . 28 Nov. ,,
The king sends flag of truce; agrees to surrender himself, his army, and Mandalay; Ava forts occupied 27 Nov.; gen. Prendergast enters Madalay without resistence . . 28 Nov. ,,
Native rioting with bloodshed quelled . Dec. ,,
Sharp engagement at Nyadan, stockades taken, 2 Dec. ,,
Great quietness in Mandalay . . . 9 Dec. ,,
Dacoit pillaging outside Mandalay, Dec.; sharp conflicts with several bands, and some officers killed . . . . . Dec. 1885; Jan. 1886
Thebau and court sent to Madras, arrived 14 Dec. 1885
Reported massacre of three servants of the Bombay and Burmah Co. at Kendat on the Chindwin river . . . . Nov. ,,

Thebau's brother issues a proclamation against British rule; arrival of Mr. Bernard establishing provisional government . . 18 Dec. 1885
General Prendergast warmly received at Bhamo, 28 Dec. ,,
Rebels defeated at Moutshobo by major Williamson . . . . . . 29 Dec. ,,
Tynedah Mengyle, Thebau's minister, accused of murder, sent to Rangoon; two pretenders to the throne appear with the dacoits . . Jan. 1886
Surgeon Heath killed 9 Jan.; Alompra, a pretender, captured, Jan.; tried and shot . Feb. ,,
Burmese defeated at Kadol, 16 Jan; and at Kunnah; 36 rebels killed; the rebel princes flee, 19 Jan. ,,
Insurgents defeated by major Williamson on the Mas river . . . . . 27 Jan. ,,
Lord Dufferin, the viceroy, arrives at Mandalay 12 Feb.; well received 13 Feb.; leaves about 23 Feb. ,,
400 rebels surprised and defeated at Yindawango; 68 killed . . . . . 18 March, ,,
40 rebels killed near Zemethen . about 26 March, ,,
General Prendergast leaves Mandalay . 31 March, ,,
Rebels defeated 5 April; British repulsed 17 April, ,,
The Alhompra pretender Myinzaing prince attempts to burn Madalay; the palace greatly injured, 15 April, ,,
Successful expedition of col. Fitzgerald; insurgent chiefs surrender . . . . May, ,,
Defeat of insurgents at Ngape by Mr. Phayre 6–7 June; Mr. Phayre killed . . . . 8 June, ,,
Captain Dunsford killed in a conflict with 500 dacoits at Salen . . . . . 12 June, ,,
Major Hailes repulsed with loss by the Burmese, near Tummoo . . . . . . 19 June, ,,
BRITISH BURMAH, including Aracan, Pegu, and Tenasserim, constituted 1862. Sir Arthur Phayre, the able first commissioner, died 15 Dec. 1885. *Upper Burmah* annexed by proclamation of the viceroy, lord Dufferin, 1 Jan. 1886 (the Shan states partially independent). Upper and Lower Burmah united in one province under Mr. C. Bernard as chief commissioner, Feb. 1886; he issues a pacific proclamation, 6 March; he assumes office at Mandalay, 12 March; all Burmah included in British India by decree . 15 May, ,,
Increase of dacoity in Upper and Lower Burmah; two additional regiments and four commissioners ordered to be sent to Burmah . . July, ,,
The Myentzeen prince offers 200*l.* for Sir C. Bernard's head . . . . . . 13 July, ,,
Convention with China; many concessions; signed at Pekin . . . . 24 July, ,,
Lieut. Huggins defeats insurgents, who lose 150 killed and wounded . . . . 26 July, ,,
Several sharp engagements; major Aitkinson killed . . . . 1 Aug. ,,
Reinforcements ordered from India . . Aug. ,,
Sharp engagement at Lazay near Isagain . 9 Aug. ,,
Inundation of Mandalay by the Irrawaddy; great loss of life and property, 16 Aug. Subsiding, 25 Aug. ,,
Serious fighting . . . . . . 16 Sept. ,,
General Macpherson, commander-in-chief, arrives at Mandalay, 17 Sept.; dies of fever on the Irrawaddy near Prome, 20 Oct.; succeeded by general sir Frederick Roberts . . . . 21 Oct. ,,
Minhla burnt by the rebels . . . . 2 Nov. ,,
Several skirmishes; British successful with some loss of officers . . . . 9–14, 21 Nov. ,,
General sir Frederick Roberts arrives at Mandalay 18 Nov. ,,
Colonel Holt captures position at Puzan Myang; leader of the rebels, Thamban, and his son killed . . . . 23 Nov. ,,
Conflict near Pakoka; col. Gatacre and Bombay lancers disperse the rebels . . . 12 Dec. ,,
Expeditions against Boshway and Hla-Oo, dacoit chiefs; their strongholds captured and bands dispersed by gen. Low and major Symonds, Nov.–Dec. ,,
Dacoits defeated in skirmishes . . 10–12 Dec. ,,
In a proclamation the Bhuddist archbishop recommends submission to Great Britain, about 31 Dec. ,,
Attack on Boshway's camp; he escapes, announced 24 Jan. 1887
General Roberts after great success leaves Burmah, succeeded by general Arbuthnot . . Feb. 1887
Band of dacoits repulsed by Hyderabad cavalry after hard fighting, announced . 8 Feb. ,,
The queen's jubilee celebrated at Mandalay, 15–16 Feb. ,,
Woontho Tsawbwa, an important chief, submits, about 5 March, ,,
Death of Hla-Oo, reported . . . . April, ,,
Numerous petty fights; dacoits defeated, March, ,,
Boshway's party defeated, he escapes . 9 March, ,,
Col. Dance defeats dacoits . . . 22 March, ,,
Successful skirmishes with the dacoits . April, ,,
Octama defeated with loss of 23 men . 20 April, ,,
Dacoits defeated by Madras lancers in Toundwingee district . . . . 23 April, ,,
Skirmishes at Sidotia; captain A. W. Rendle killed, 30 April; renewed skirmishes . 2–4 May, ,,
The Limbin prince, the last legitimate Alaungpaa prince, surrenders . . . . . 23 May, ,,
Desultory war with dacoits . . . . June, ,,
New roads and a railway constructing . Sept. ,,
Camp near Chindwin captured; major Kennedy and captain Beville killed, and about 50 dacoits, 16 Oct. ,,
Discontent in Mandalay through taxation, &c., Nov. 1887; quietness restored . . Jan. 1888
About 20,000 effective military police established in Burmah; renewed fighting . . Jan. ,,
Mr. Chan-Toon, a Burmese, as a law student in the Middle Temple gains all the principal prizes, June, ,,
Boh Sway and many followers killed, announced 27 July, ,,
Dacoits defeated and two of their chiefs killed 25 Oct. ,,
Victorious conflicts of gen. Collett with native chiefs; many of the enemy killed . 1 Jan. 1889
The dacoits defeated in several conflicts . Jan. ,,
Sawlon captured by gen. Collett . . 9 Jan. ,,
Rebel position near Popa stormed by the Rifle Brigade under major Francis Howard 9 Feb. ,,
Railway to Rangoon formally opened at Mandalay 27 Feb. ,,
Khama, the capital of the Lepu Kachyens, and 17 villages destroyed by the British troops, announced . . . . 9 March, ,,
Gen. Wolseley's expedition against the Phunkan Tsawbwa starts 13 April; he captures a village, 18 April; returns to Bhamo, May; dacoits very active, successful in some severe conflicts April–May, ,,
A great fire at Mandalay, 450 houses burnt 11 May ,,
Mr. Dyson, assistant commissioner, and others, killed in an unsuccessful attack upon the dacoits, reported . . . . 2 June ,,
Savage tribes beyond the frontier of Burmah Proper; incited by rebel Burmese chiefs; reduced to submission by the police and military Jan.–June, ,,
Frequent engagements with bands of dacoits June–July, ,,
Rebel chief Boh Kyee Tha defeated and killed and arms captured by Rifle Brigade Mounted Infantry under lieuts. K. J. Mackenzie and H. G. Majendie 23 July, ,,
Mr. C. A. MacDonnell appointed chief commissioner in the absence of sir C. Crosthwaite, announced . . . . 3 Aug. ,,
Gen. Gordon at Mandalay organizing an expedition against the Chins and other border tribes about 22 Sept. ,,
Improved condition of the country under sir C. Crosthwaite's administration reported . Sept. ,,
Successful attacks on the Chins by capt. Gookhas 16, 17, 19 Oct. ,,
The Mingoon prince on the frontiers . . 3 Nov. ,,
Interned by the French at Saigon . . Nov. ,,
Prince Albert Victor of Wales at Rangoon, 20 Dec.; at Mandalay . . . . . 24 Dec. ,,
Three Chin villages destroyed by British . Dec. ,,
Mr. MacDonnell retires after successful government Dec. ,,
Repulse of the attack of the Chins on the British advanced camp, a stockade captured and destroyed, reported . . . . . . 30 Dec. ,,
Lowsaing captured . . . . . . 15 Jan. 1890
Dacoits very troublesome; destructive attack of rebels on Sandoway, Aracan coast, repulsed by police, reported . . . . . . 22 Feb. ,,

The dacoits burn Kangyi, chastised by police, reported . . . . 2 March, 1890
Conspiracy to burn Mandalay and set Moungba, an Alhompra pretender, on the throne, discovered and arrests made . . . . . . 9 March, ,,
Major Blundell's expedition from Bhamo, to punish Kan Hlaing, chief of the Swesaing Tonhon Kachyens, for raids on British territories, and for harbouring the Alhompra pretender Sawyauni. Starts 15 Dec., severe fighting 23 Dec., after further successes the expedition returned to Bhamo . . . . April, ,,
Gen. Gordon (successful) relinquishes his command; succeeded by brigadier Wolseley . . June, ,,
Many dacoit gangs surrender, two eminent chiefs captured, reported . . . . 21 June, ,,
Boh Yanyun, a dacoit leader, surrenders to Mr. M'Donald, his life being assured . July, ,,
Many intercessions for him, 9 Aug.; transported for life about . . . . . . 23 Aug. ,,
Great floods, Mandalay in danger, about . 9 Aug. ,,
Gen. Wolseley concludes peace with the Sinyin Chins; tribute paid, and prisoners exchanged, reported . . . . 2 Sept. ,,
Mr. (aft. sir) Alex. Mackenzie appointed to succeed sir C. Crosthwaite as chief commissioner, reported 31 Oct.; arrives at Rangoon . . 3 Dec. ,,
In Upper Burmah Kanlaing, a rebel chief with a large following, appears at Manwaing about 3 Dec. ,,
Mr. Wetherell, political officer, killed by the Chins in an ambush, at Yokwa . . . 21 Dec. ,,
Dacoit raids and murders reported about 24 Dec. ,,
A strong punitive force sent against the Chins and others, reaches Thetta; after a repulsed attack, Thetta surrenders; lieut. James and two men killed about . . . . 2 Jan. 1891
Expedition against the Shan state, Momeik, to punish outrages, about 17 Jan. fighting; a village burnt, many natives killed and wounded about 28 Jan. ,,
Major Nixon, lieut. Jameson, adjutant and two Sepoys killed by a mad Pathan at Fort Stedman in the Shan states . . . . 11 Feb. ,,
The Kanhow chiefs chastised for raids; submit; restore captives and pay fines to capt. Rundall; five villages attacked and destroyed, reported 15 Feb. ,,
Insurrection in Wuntho, a frontier state; pretended objections to the railway; capt. Smith present with 400 Europeans; reinforcements ordered; arrive . . . . 19 Feb. ,,
Proclamation issued, deposing the Tsawbwa of Wuntho for his attacks, and annexing his territory 22 Feb. ,,
Gen. Wolseley takes the command in Wuntho, 26 Feb.; the rebels at Okpho attacked, above 50 killed, arms and ammunition captured . . ,,
British force at Kawlin, 600 men (200 Europeans); capt. Hastings punishes the Panchaung Chins for their raids, destroying villages, &c., reported 23 Feb. ,,
The Kanhow Chins subdued by capt. Rundall, surrender captives and pay fines . . 24 Feb.
Wuntho occupied by Major Smyth, without opposition, 25 Feb.; the villagers lay down their arms; the Tsawbwa flies; his palace burnt; capt. Alex. Hutchinson defeats rebels near Okhau, after five hours' fighting [he died of his wounds]; Kanhoco chiefs, raiders, submit about . . 25 Feb. ,,
The Tsawbwa solicits pardon, which is promised on speedy surrender, but not re-instatement, about 27 Feb. ,,
More villages surrender about . . . . . ,,
Gen. Stedman leaves for England; in four years he created an effective army of military police (about 20,500) . . . . 28 Feb. ,,
Gen. Wolseley holds a durbar at Wuntho, well attended, British flag hoisted . . 3 March, ,,
Advance of gen. Wolseley and col. Macgregor into the Wuntho territory; the two Tsawbwas retreat, reported . . . . 11 March, ,,
Several fights with the Chins, with casualties reported . . . . 6 April, ,,
Disturbances on the trade route between Bhamo, reported . . . . 9 April, ,,
Gen. Wolseley returns to Mandalay, the campaign ended . . . . 4 May, ,,
Alarming deficiency of rain in Upper Burmah, Aug.; fall of rain in some places, Sept.; investigation by sir A. Mackenzie; his minute published 15 Sept.; relief works begun, early Sept.; prospects improved . . . . Oct. 1891
Gen. Wolseley transferred to Belgaum . . Nov. ,,
Boh Le, a dacoit leader, killed, and his band captured or dispersed by lieut. Magrath, assistant-commandant at Katha, reported . . 31 Dec. ,,
Major Yule captures Sadon after two days' fighting 6 Jan. 1892
Successful operations of lieut. Macnabb in the Chin country . . . . Jan. ,,
Severe fighting in Upper Burmah; the Kachins repulsed in their attack on Sadon by lieut. Harrison; successful advance of major Yule 19 Feb. *et seq.* ,,

[Sadon re-named Fort Harrison.]

Joined by capt. Davies at Sadon, about 25 Feb. ,,
Continued fighting at Sadon . . 28 Feb. *et seq.* ,,

[Kachins, a warlike but not intractable tribe, inhabiting the hilly tracts east of head waters of the Irrawaddy in Upper Burmah, adjoining Chinese provinces.]

Boh Minlaung, famous Aracan dacoit, captured at Kudoung about 26 Feb.; sentenced to death with others about . . . . . . 14 March, ,,
Mr. Chan Toon, a Burmese barrister, made a judge about . . . . 28 Feb. ,,
Falam, headquarters of the Tashons, occupied by the British about . . . . . 17 March, ,,
Great fire at Mandalay, destroying the telegraph office and a large part of the city; estimated loss 1,000,000*l*. . . . . . . 30–31 March, ,,
Sentence of death upon the Minlaung prince and others confirmed . . . . . 30 March, ,,
Sir A. Mackenzie ill, leaves for England; Mr. F. W. Fryer appointed deputy . . about May, ,,
Famine greatly relieved . . . . . May, ,,
Amnesty to the Tswabwa of Wuntho and his followers; he enters China about . . 15 May, ,,
Lieut. Nightingale repulses an attack on Lwekaw, in the S. Shan states . . . 25 June, ,,
Rising of the Chins; 7 sepoys killed in a conflict near Fort White. The Chins retire on the arrival of lieut. Henegan with 50 sepoys. Fort White reinforced by lieut. Wardell . . 14 Oct. ,,
Chin rising checked; several villages burnt Nov.–Dec. ,,
Exploring expedition to the Chinese frontier, &c.; conflicts with the Kachins, a warlike tribe, Dec. ,,
Capt. Morton killed during a conflict . 6 Jan. 1893
Chins punished for raids . . . . . Jan. ,,
The Kachins repulsed in their attacks on Sima (re-named Fort Morton), by capt. Atkinson, 17–30 Jan.; they are defeated at Meungyn 4 Feb. *et seq.*; lieut. Williams killed at North Theinni, reported 12 Feb.; major Hammans reduces the Siyin and Nwengal Chins to submission in North Theinni and round Sima, 20–24 Feb.; disarmament of the Chins, reported 13 March; an old dacoit gang, led by Tanka, captured, reported 21 July, ,,
The viceroy warmly received at Rangoon, 18 Nov., Mandalay, &c.; leaves Rangoon . . 11 Dec. ,,
Frontier convention with China signed . March, 1894
Punitive expedition under Mr. W. N. Porter against the Kaswa Chins for their murderous raid on Naingtaung (Feb.) . . . . . 24 March, ,,
Total submission of the Siyin Chins . May, ,,
The Chins completely disarmed and the country quieted . . . . June, ,,
Thetta occupied without resistance . 3 Jan. 1895
Thonze, ruler of the Shan state, removed; Sawke, son of Thebaw Tswabwa, appointed . . Jan. ,,
Expedition against the Sana Kachins, no opposition; reported . . . . . . 5 Jan. 1896
Major G. D. Atkinson died of fever . . 17 Feb. ,,
Sir Fred. Wm. R. Fryer, chief commissioner, holds a durbar at Mandalay, and bestows honours on the northern Shan chiefs; reported . 19 Jan. ,,
Capt. Eliott successful in some sharp skirmishes with the tribes in the Wa country . 22 March ,,
Punitive expedition against the Yindu Chins for raids, 19 March; very successful, captives released, &c., announced . . . . 11 Jan. 1897

Failure of crops, relief works started, Oct.-Nov. 1896; famine in Upper Burmah; 30,000 on relief works Dec., 17,000 reported 25 April, 1897; end of famine announced . . . . Dec. 1897

Burmah placed under a lieut.-governor (Sir F. W. Fryer) with a local legislative council, from 1 May, 1897; first meeting . . . 4 Nov. „

Exploring party (Upper Irawaddy) under lieut. Eldred Pottinger attacked, 2 killed . 22 May „

New Anglo-Chinese frontier agreement modifying the trade convention of 1894, and ceding to Great Britain the Shan state of Kokang, &c., signed at Peking . . . . . . 5 June „

Mr. Scott, superintendent of the Shan states, falls into an ambuscade in the Wa country, the Was driven back with heavy loss, 6 British killed, reported . . . . 4 July „

Attack of 25 Burmans on Mandalay fort repulsed, 4 killed, 14 captured . . . . 11 Oct. „

Delimitation of the Burmo-Chinese frontier begins at the Taping river, 8 Dec. 1897; completed by Mr. Scott in Yun-nan, reported . . 5 July, 1899

Sir Fred. Fryer holds a durbar at Rangoon, peace and prosperity reported . . . . 25 July, 1898

Lord Elgin well received at Rangoon and other places . . . . . . 16 Nov.–10 Dec. „

Capt. Wingate reaches Rangoon by a new overland route from Shanghai . . . . 27 April, 1899

Sir F. Fryer holds a durbah at Rangoon, several Burmese decorated; suppression of dacoitism; record rice crop, reported . . . 16 Jan. 1900

Burmo-Chinese boundary commission attacked at Monghem, on the Galween, major Kiddle and Mr. A. Sutherland killed by the Was at Meng-tun 8 Feb. „

British exploring party under Mr. Hertz and capt. Taylor attacked by Chinese at Hapang; 71 Chinese killed, stockades, &c., captured; British loss slight . . . . 13 Feb. „

Further fighting; 60 Was killed, reported 2 March „

Sir Fred. Fryer opens the Gokteik viaduct and railway to Thibaw . . . . . 1 June, 1901

The viceroy tours through Upper Burmah, at Kindat, 23 Nov.; holds a large durbar at Mandalay, and notes the increasing revenue, peaceful progress and development of the country; 28 Nov.; welcomed at Rangoon, receives deputations . . . . 9, 10 Dec. „

Sir Hugh S. Barnes, new governor, arrives at Rangoon . . . . 4 April, 1903

BURNETT PRIZES, to be awarded every 40 years to the authors of the two best essays on "The evidence that there is a Being all powerful, wise, and good, by whom everything exists, &c.," were founded by Mr. Burnett, a Scottish gentleman, who died 1784, bequeathing moneys for the purpose. Various amounts have been paid to Dr. W. L. Brown, to rev. J. B. Sumner, afterwards archbishop of Canterbury, 1815; to rev. R. A. Thompson, and to Dr. J. Tulloch, 1855; Prof. G. G. Stokes, 1885. The establishment of a Burnett lectureship in Aberdeen by the trustees (the lecturer to be chosen in 1883) was sanctioned Aug. 1880. Prof. W. Robertson Smith's lectures on the "Religion of the Semites," were published in 1889.

BURNHAM BEECHES, Bucks, the picturesque remains of an ancient forest, were purchased for public use by the corporation of London in 1879. Dedicated 3 Oct. 1883.

BURNING ALIVE was inflicted among the Romans, Jews, and other nations, and was countenanced by bulls of the pope; see *Witches*. Many persons have been burned alive as heretics. Sir William Sawtre, priest of St. Osyth, London, suffered 12 Feb. 1401. In the reign of Mary numbers were burned; see *Protestants*. Elizabeth Gaunt, an Anabaptist, was burnt at Tyburn for treason (concealing rebels under Monmouth), 23 Oct. 1685.

BURNING THE DEAD was practised among the Greeks and Romans, and Homer gives descriptions. It was very general about 1225 B.C., and was revived by Sylla about 78 B.C. It is still practised in parts of the East Indies, and has been advocated in this country by the eminent surgeon sir Henry Thompson, and others, 1873; see *Suttees*, *Barrows*.

Professor L. Brunetti exhibited his plan and results at the Vienna exhibition 1873

Cremation societies founded in London, Vienna, and Berlin, &c. . . . . 13 Jan. 1874

Lady Dilke cremated at Dresden . . . 10 Oct. „

A crematorium erected at Milan, Jan. 1883; in Paris 1884

Cremation increasing at Rome . . . . . „

Mr. Justice Stephen decides that it is legal, March, „

The erection of a crematorium at Woking stopped by authorities, summer 1879; afterwards permitted and first used, 26 March, 1885; again 21 Oct. 1885; and 25 Jan. 1886; and others occasionally.

Dr. Cameron's bill for the regulation of cremation rejected by the commons (149–79), 30 April, 1884.

The Cremation society of England in Feb. 1892, reported that at Woking there had been 3 cremations in 1885; 10 in 1886; 13 in 1887; 28 in 1888; 46 in 1889; 54 in 1890; in 1891, 99; 1892, 104; 1898, 240; 1900, 301; 1901, 273; 1902, 275. Among these were that of the marquis of Ely, 13 April, 1889; sir Tindal Robertson, M.P., 10 Oct. 1889; baron Huddleston, 11 Dec. 1890; Mr. A. W. Kinglake, 8 Jan. 1891; the duke of Bedford, 16 Jan. 1891; lord Bramwell, 13 May, 1892; sir Samuel W. Baker, 4 Jan. 1894; sir A. H. Layard, 9 July, 1894; Sergius Stepniak, 28 Dec. 1895; Mr. George Du Maurier, 10 Oct. 1896; Dr. George Harley, 30 Oct. 1896; sir B. Ward Richardson, 27 Nov. 1896; Miss Matilde Blind, 1 Dec. 1896; sir Isaac Pitman, 28 Jan. 1897; sir Spencer Wells, 8 Feb. 1897; Elizabeth, dowager-duchess of Bedford, 26 April, 1897; Frances Anna Maria, dowager Countess Russell, 20 Jan., 1898; lord Sackville Cecil, 2 Feb. 1898; sir Edward Burne-Jones, 20 June, 1898; sir Wm. Flower, 5 July, 1899; lord Farrer, 14 Oct. 1899; Mr. Grant Allen, 27 Oct. 1899; Mr. Jacob Bright, 10 Nov. 1899; the duke of Westminster, 24 Dec. 1899; Mr. Sims Reeves, 31 Oct. 1900; the rev. H. R. Haweis, 4 Feb. 1901; Miss Kate Greenaway, 12 Nov. 1901; William E. Henley, 14 July, 1903; major-gen. D. Strong, 15 July, 1903; lt.-gen. the hon. C. W. Thesiger, 1 Aug. 1903; countess of Galloway, 21 Aug. 1903. Golders Green:—Quintin Hogg, founder of Polytechnic Instn., 21 Jan. 1903; rev. Norman Macleod Ferrers, D.D. Camb., 5 Feb. 1903; lord Edward W. Manners, 4 March, 1903; lady Richardson, 19 May, 1903; Mrs. Forrest Browne, wife of ld. bishop of Bristol, 25 June, 1903; sir Vincent H. Kennett Barrington, 17 July, 1903; sir P. H. Edlin, K.C., D.L., retd. chairman London qr. sessions, 22 July, 1903; Benjamin L. Farjeon, author, 25 July, 1903; sir Henry Rae Reid, bart., 8 Sept. 1903; rt. hon. W. E. H. Lecky, 26 Oct. 1903. Cremations carried out from 1 Jan.—7 Sept. 1903: Golders green, 103; Woking, 105; total, 208.

Cremation greatly increasing in France and Italy, 1890.

International Cremation Conference at Berlin, 4 Aug. 1890. Similar societies formed in Great Britain.

Dr. W. Price cremated in a field adjoining his house at Llantrissant, 31 Jan. 1893: Miss Emily Faithfull near Manchester, 4 June. 1895.

Cremations near New York in 9 years (to 1894), 1,262; in United States during 1901, 3,613.

Crematorium opened at Liverpool, 11 Sept. 1890; at Hendon, 22 Nov. 1902. Cremation acts passed, 6 Aug. 1900, and 24 Feb. 1902. Came into force 1 April, 1903.

First *municipal* crematorium opened by the mayor in Hull, 2 Jan. 1901. Foundation stone laid of City of London crematorium at Ilford cemetery, 14 Oct. 1903.

BURNING-GLASS AND CONCAVE MIRRORS. Their power was known to Archimedes, and it is mythically stated that by their aid he burnt a fleet in the harbour of Syracuse, 214 B.C. Their powers were increased by Settalla; Tschirnhausen,

1680; Buffon, 1747; and Parker and others more recently. The following experiments were made about 1800, with Mr. Parker's lens or burning mirror, which cost 700*l.*, and is said to have been the largest ever made. It was sold to capt. Mackenzie, who took it to China, and left it at Pekin.

Substances fused.	*Weight.*	*Time.*
Pure gold	20 grains	4 seconds.
Silver	20 ,,	3 ,,
Copper	33 ,,	20 ,,
Platina	10 ,,	3 ,,
Cast iron (a cube)	10 ,,	3 ,,
Steel	10 ,,	12 ,,
A topaz	3 ,,	45 ,,
An emerald	2 ,,	25 ,,
A crystal pebble	7 ,,	6 ,,
Flint	10 ,,	30 ,,
Cornelian	10 ,,	75 ,,
Pumice stone	10 ,,	24 ,,

Green wood takes fire instantaneously; water boils immediately; bones are calcined; and things not capable of melting at once become red-hot, like iron.

BURSE, see *Exchange*.

BURTON CRESCENT, London. Here Mrs. Rachael Samuel, a widow living alone, was murdered in the night 11 Dec. 1878. No robbery. Mary Donovan, a charwoman, was arrested and discharged, 10 Jan. 1879. In a house here also, Mary Ann Yates was found murdered, 9 March, 1884.

BURWELL FIRE. A number of persons assembled to see a puppet-show in a barn at Burwell, near Newmarket, 8 Sept. 1727 A candle having set fire to a heap of straw, seventy-six individuals perished, and others died of their wounds.

BURY ST. EDMUND'S, Suffolk, named from St. Edmund, king of East Anglia, who was murdered by the Danes on 20 Nov. 870, and buried here, and to whose memory its magnificent abbey was founded. Magna Charta was prepared here by the barons on 20 Nov 1214. Henry VI. summoned a parliament in Feb. 1447, when Humphry, duke of Gloucester, was imprisoned, and died here, it is supposed by poison. It was almost consumed by fire in 1608, and was desolated by plague in 1636. Population 1881, 16,111; 1891, 16,630; 1901, 16,255.

BURYING ALIVE. In Bœotia, Creon ordered Antigone, the sister of Polynices, to be buried alive, 1225 B.C. The Roman vestals were subjected to it for any levity that excited suspicion of their chastity. The vestals buried alive on a charge of incontinence, were Minutia, 337 B C.; Sextilla, 274 B.C.; Cornelia, A.D. 92. Lord Bacon gives instances of the resurrection of persons who had been buried alive; Duns Scotus being of the number. The two assassins of Capo d'Istria, president of Greece, were sentenced to be immured in brick walls built around them up to their chins, and to be supplied with food in this species of torture until they died, Oct. 1831.

BUSACO, or **BUZACO** (Portugal). Here the British, under lord Wellington, repulsed the French under Massena, 27 Sept. 1810. The latter lost one general and 1000 men killed, two generals and about 3000 men wounded, and several hundred prisoners; the loss of the allies did not exceed 1300; the British retreated to the lines of Torres Vedras, too strong for Massena to force, and the armies remained in sight of each other to the end of the year.

BUSHEL. This measure was ordered to contain eight gallons of wheat, 12 Henry VIII., 1520; the legal Winchester bushel was regulated 9 Will. III. 1697; the imperial corn bushel of 2218·192 cubic inches is to the Winchester of 2150·42 as 32 to 31. Regulated by act 5 Geo. IV., June, 1824, which act came into operation 1 Jan. 1826.

BUSHIRE (on the Persian Gulf), attacked by sea by sir H. Leeke, and by land by general Stalker, was taken 10 Dec. 1856. The place proved stronger than was expected, and was bravely defended. Brigadier Stopford and col. Malet were killed in a previous attack on the fort at Reshire, 9 Dec. The loss of the British was four officers killed, and one wounded; five men killed, and thirty-five wounded.

BUSHRANGERS, Australian highwaymen, formerly escaped convicts. Morgan, a desperate robber and murderer, was surrounded and shot April, 1865. The "Kelly gang" seized and pillaged the town of Jerilderie, New South Wales, 8-10 Feb. 1879. Ned Kelly and some of his gang were captured and taken to Melbourne, 27, 28 June, 1880.

BUSSORAH, see *Bassorah*.

BUSTS. Lysistratus, the statuary, was the inventor of moulds, from which he cast wax figures, about 328 B.C. *Pliny*. Busts from the face in plaster of paris, were first taken by Andrea Verrochi, about A.D. 1466. Smaller busts and statuettes are now accurately produced from larger ones by machinery.

BUTCHERS. Among the Romans there were three classes: the *Suarii* provided hogs, the *Boarii* or *Pecuarii* oxen and sheep, which the *Lanii* or *Carnifices* killed. The butchers' company in London is ancient, though not incorporated till 1606. See *Provisions*.

BUTE ADMINISTRATION. John earl of Bute,* tutor of prince George (afterwards George III.), formed an administration in May, 1762, which, after various changes, resigned 8 April, 1763. It was severely attacked by Junius and John Wilkes.

John earl of Bute, *first lord of the treasury.*
Sir Francis Dashwood, *chancellor of the exchequer.*
Earl Grenville, *president of the council.*
Duke of Bedford, *privy seal.*
Earl of Halifax, *admiralty.*
Earl of Egremont and George Granville, *secretaries of state.*
Lord Ligonier, *ordnance.*
Henry Fox, afterwards lord Holland, *paymaster of the forces.*
Viscount Barrington, *treasurer of the navy.*
Lord Sandys, *first lord of trade.*
Duke of Marlborough, earl Talbot, lord Huntingdon, lord Anson, lord North, &c.

BUTTER is said to have been used by the Arabs in early times, but not by the Greeks and Romans, who had excellent oil. It is not mentioned as food by Galen A.D. 130-200. It has long been used by northern nations. Various statutes have passed respecting its package, weight, and sale; the principal of which are the 36th & 38th Geo. III. and 10 Geo. IV. 1829. In Africa, vegetable butter is made from the fruit of the shea tree, and is of richer taste, at Kebba, than any butter made from cow's milk. *Mungo Park.* The import duties of 5*s.* per cwt. on foreign butter (producing in 1859, 104,587*l.* on 421,354 cwts.) were repealed in 1860. Butter imported, 1846, 257,385 cwt.; 1856, 513,329 cwt.; 1866, 1,165,081 cwt.; 1870, 1,159,210 cwt.;

* John Stuart, earl of Bute, born 1713; secretary of state, March, 1761; prime minister, May, 1762; died 10 March, 1792.

1874, 1,619,808 cwt.; 1876, 1,659,492 cwt.; 1877, 1,637,403 cwt.; 1885, 2,401,373 cwt.; 1889, (butter), 1,927,842 cwt.; (margarine) 1,241,690 cwt.; 1890 (butter), 2,027,717 cwt.; (margarine) 1,079,856 cwt.; 1893 (butter) 2,327,474 cwt.; (margarine) 1,299,970 cwt.; 1896, 3,037,718 cwt.; (margarine) 925,934 cwt.; 1898, 3,209,153 cwt.; (margarine) 900,615 cwt.; 1899, 3,389,851 cwt.; (margarine) 953,175 cwt.; 1900, 3,378,516 cwt.; (margarine) 920,412 cwt.; 1901, 3,702,890 cwt.; (margarine) 962,127 cwt.; 1902, 3,974,933 cwt.; (margarine) 966,170 cwt.

Butterine, a composition of fats as a substitute for butter, sold in London 1885, and declared to be wholesome by eminent chemists. Bills to change the name to oleomargarine, and check its sale, brought in and withdrawn 1885-6. The Butterine Defence Association formed 1886.

By the Margarine Act, 1887, butterine and other substances like butter must be termed *margarine* on and after 1 Jan. 1888. The term "*butter*" is restricted to the product of milk or cream or both by this act.

Butter manufactured from cocoa-nuts in Mannheim, &c., coming into use, 1888; much imported into India, from whence the nuts are largely brought, 1889 *et seq.*

BUTTONS, an early manufacture in England; those covered with cloth were prohibited, to encourage the manufacture of metal buttons, 8 Geo. I. 1721. Buttons largely employed to ornament ladies' dresses, 1873 *et seq.* Birmingham is the chief centre of the button trade in England. The manufacture of buttons is carried on extensively in France, but in recent years Germany has become a formidable competitor, especially with the cheaper kinds. New York and Philadelphia are the seats of button-making in the United States. Large quantities of buttons are manufactured from the corozo nut (vegetable ivory), mother-of-pearl, glass, various kinds of wood, metal, bone, and horn. Machinery is now much used in making buttons.

BUXAR, a town in Bengal, near which, on 23 Oct. 1764, major, afterwards sir Hector Monro (with 857 Europeans and 6215 sepoys) gained a great victory over the troops of the nabob of Oude, &c., 50,000 in number; 6000 of these were killed, and 130 pieces of cannon were taken. The loss of the English was trifling.

BY-LAWS, or **BYE-LAWS**, private ordinances, made by subordinate communities, such as corporations. These laws must not militate against the law of the land. By 5 & 6 Will. IV. 1834, those made by corporate bodies become valid, if not disallowed by the king's council within forty days after their enactment.

BYE PLOT (also termed Surprise or Surprising Plot), planned by George Brooke, brother of lord Cobham, sir Griffin Markham, lord Grey of Wilton and two Romanist priests, to seize James I. to compel him to change his ministers and to grant toleration of their religion, &c. The conspirators were apprehended July, 1603. This plot was connected with the "Main plot," *which see.*

BYNG, HON. ADMIRAL JOHN, was charged with neglect of duty in an engagement with the enemy off Minorca, 20 May, 1756, condemned for an error of judgment, and shot on board the *Monarch* at Spithead, 14 March, 1757.

BYRON'S VOYAGE. Commodore Byron left England on his voyage round the globe, 21 June, 1764, and returned 9 May, 1766. He discovered the populous island in the Pacific Ocean which bears his name, 16 Aug. 1765. Though brave and intrepid, such was his general ill-fortune at sea, that he was called by the sailors of the fleet "Foulweather Jack."

BYRON NATIONAL MEMORIAL. Its erection determined on, at a meeting in London, 16 July, 1875; Mr. Disraeli in the chair. About 3000*l.* were subscribed. The statue by Richard Claude Belt, placed on a pedestal near Hamilton-place, Hyde-park, was uncovered privately by lord Houghton, 24 May, 1880. "The works of lord Byron," an enlarged edition revised and illustrated, by Ernest Hartley Coleridge, Letters and Journals 6 vols.; Poetry, 6 vols.; 1898-1903.

BYTOWN, Canada, was named after col. By, the British surveyor, 1823-6. In 1854 its name was changed to Ottawa, after the river on which it is situated, and in 1858 it was made the capital of the Dominion. See *Ottawa.*

BYZANTIUM, now *Constantinople*, and *Stamboul*, in the ancient Thrace, founded by a colony of Megarians, under Byzas, 667 B.C.; but various dates and persons are given. It was taken successively by the Medes, Athenians, and Spartans. In 340 B.C., in alliance with the Athenians, the Byzantines defeated the fleet of Philip of Macedon. During the wars with Macedon, Syria, &c., it became an ally of the Romans, by whom it was taken, A.D. 73. Rebelling, it was taken after two years' siege, and laid in ruins by Severus in 196. It was refounded by Constantine in 324, and dedicated on 22 May, 330, all the heathen temples being destroyed; and from him it received its name; see *Constantinople.* BYZANTINE ART flourished from the time of Constantine to about 1204. The BYZANTINE or Eastern empire really commenced in 395, when Theodosius divided the Roman empire; see *East.* The "Byzantine Historians," from 325 to 1453, were published at Paris, 1645-1711; and at Venice, 1722-33.

C.

CAABA, the shrine of the sacred black stone, kept in a temple at Mecca, and venerated by the Arabs, long before the Christian era. Its guardians, the tribe of Koreish, were defeated by Mahomet, by whose followers it is still venerated.

CABAL. In English history the term has been applied to the cabinet of Charles II. 1667-73; the word Cabal being formed from the initials of their names: sir Thomas, afterwards lord Clifford (C); the lord Ashley (A), (afterwards earl of Shaftesbury); George Villiers, duke of Buckingham (B); Henry, lord Arlington (A); and John, duke of Lauderdale (L). The term had been previously applied to a secret faction or cabinet.

CABBAGES. Some new kinds were brought to England from Holland about 1510, it is said by sir Arthur Ashley of Dorset, and introduced into Scotland by Cromwell's soldiers.

CABBALA, a Jewish system of philosophy or theosophy, deriving its name from a Hebrew word, signifying reception or tradition, said to have been given by God to Adam, and transmitted from father to son by his descendants. It is said to have been lost at the Babylonian captivity (587 B.C.), but to have been revealed again to Ezra. Its supporters assert that the cabbalistic book "Sohar," or "Splendour," a mystic commentary on the Pentateuch, was first committed to writing by Simon Ben Jochai, A.D. 72-110. The true date of the books containing the cabbala is now considered to range from 9th to the 14th centuries, and their origin to be the mingling of talmudism with the Greek philosophy termed Neo-Platonism. Some of their dogmas are akin to Christian tenets, such as the trinity, the incarnation, &c. The cabbala exercised much influence upon the mental development of the Jews, and even captivated the greatest thinkers of the 16th and 17th centuries.

CABEIRA (Asia Minor). Here Mithridates, king of Pontus, was defeated by Lucullus, 71 B.C.

CABINET COUNCIL. There were councils in England as early as the reign of Ina, king of the West Saxons, 690; Offa, king of the Mercians, 758; and in other reigns of the Heptarchy. State councils are referred to Alfred the Great. *Spelman;* see *Administrations*.*

CABLES. A machine was invented in 1792 for making them, by which human labour was reduced nine-tenths. Chain cables were introduced into the British navy about 1812; directions for testing them enacted, 1864 and 1874. "*Cable Farm*," see *Agriculture*, 1894.

CABOCHIENS, an armed Burgundian faction, including 500 butchers, named from their leader Simonet Caboche, a skinner, 1412. They ruled Paris with violence, and constrained the doctors of the Sorbonne to become their allies and the dauphin to recognise them as the "White Hoods," and reformers. They were exterminated by the citizens, in 1418.

* Cabinet Noir, or "Dark Closet," the chamber in which letters entrusted to the French post were opened for state purposes. The system, which began with Louis XI., was organised under Louis XV.; and is said to have been discontinued in 1868. The Spanish government have a similar system—"Gabinete negro.

CABRIOLETS (*vulgo* Cabs), one-horsed vehicles, were introduced into the streets of London in 1823, when the number plying was twelve. In 1831 they had increased to 165, and then the licences were thrown open. The number in 1862 running in the metropolis exceeded 6000 (of which about 1800 only plied on Sunday). Previous to throwing open the trade, the number of hackney carriages was limited to 1200, when there were few omnibuses. Number in 1871 was 7818; in 1881, 9652; 1893, 7,193 hansoms; 3,613 clarences: 1896, 7,585 hansoms, 3,449 clarences: 1901, 7,454 hansoms; 3,719 clarences. See *Hackney Coaches*.

Mr. Joseph Aloysius Hansom, architect, invented his patent safety cab about 1833. He died 29 June, 1882.

Cab Strike.—On 28 June, 1853, an act (called Mr. FitzRoy's act) was passed for "the better regulation of metropolitan stage and hackney carriages, and for prohibiting the use of advertising vehicles," by which the cab fares were reduced to 6*d.* a mile. It came into operation 11 July, and on the 27th a general strike of the London cabmen took place. Much inconvenience was felt, and every kind of vehicle was employed to supply the deficiency. Some alterations having been made in the act, the cabs re-appeared on the stands on the 30th.

Cabmen's clubs began at Paddington in . . Feb. 1859

A London General Cab Company published its prospectus, professing a reformed system, July, 1862

Cabs running in London: in 1855, 3296; in 1867, 6149; in 1874, 7864; in 1877, about 8000.

Cab Tragedy.—S. H. Hunt, a servant of Butler and McCulloch's, seedsmen, Covent-garden, London, poisoned his wife and children in a cab, on 7 Nov. 1863; and himself on 9 Nov. at his own house, just before his apprehension.

The cabmen in Paris strike against a company; above 3000 vehicles stopped, 16 June; fierce attack on men who give in; strike subsides 23 June, 1865

Second Cab Strike.—Metropolitan Streets Act, 30 & 31 Vict. c. 17 (passed 20 Aug.) required hackney carriages to carry lamps; and changed lowest fare from 6*d.* to 1*s.* The cab-proprietors and drivers struck at 4 p.m., 3 Dec.; but by the intervention of lord Elcho, an arrangement was made with Mr. Gathorne Hardy, the home secretary, and the strike ceased . . . . 4 Dec. 1867

Third Cab Strike to compel railway companies to discontinue privileged cabs; unsuccessful, 5-9 Sept. 1868

Licences on cabs reduced from 19*l.* and 17*l.* to 42*s.* by act of 1869 . . . . 1 Jan. 1870

Cab-drivers' Benevolent Association founded . . "

First *Cabmen's Shelter* opened by hon. A. Kinnaird at St. John's-wood, 6 Feb. 1875; others soon after. *Cabmen's Mission Hall*, King's-cross, London, N., opened 12 Nov. 1875. Thirty-nine *Shelters* in 1888

Disputes about wages; lock-out of 100 drivers (hansom), 27 June, 1882, closed; proposed establishment of Cab-drivers' Co-operative Cab company, about 29 July, 1882.

Strike of the Shrewsbury-Talbot Cab company's men . . . . April, 1891

Strike of about 300 other cabmen 14 April; demonstration in Hyde-park 19 April; strike gradually subsided . . . . "

The cab distance-recorder and fare-indicator of Messrs. W. C. Owen and W. Grimes described, *Times* . . . . 29 Sept. "

The newly-formed London Cab-drivers' union orders a strike against the proprietors, which begins 16 May, 1894; little public inconvenience; about 7000 men on strike; mediation of Mr. Asquith; meetings at the house of commons,

5 June *et seq.*; terms to last till 1 April, 1895; accepted . . . . 11 June, 1894
London Cab Act passed . . . . . 7 Aug. 1896
Strike of about 1,300 London cab-drivers against the privilege system at railway stations, 22 Sept.; gradual failure of the strike, Nov.; practically over . . . . . 25 Dec. ,,
Mass meeting of cab-drivers in Trafalgar-square to protest against the privilege system at railway termini . . . . 16 Jan. 1897
Electric cabs. See *Carriages*, 1897.
Crawlers forbidden in Bond street, Strand, and other great thoroughfares, 1 Feb. 1899; 23 new stands, and 17 abolished . . . 14 Feb. 1899
Taxameter (fare-meter) cabs parade along the Embankment, etc., 18 April; another fare-meter devised . . . . May, ,,
Fifty motor hansom cabs of the London Express Motor Service, Ltd., for London traffic, announced . . . . Sept. 1903

CABUL, or **Cabool**, on the river Cabul, about 1774, by Timsur Shah, was made capital of Afghanistan. A British mission received at Cabul, 1893; see ***Afghanistan***; great fire at the bazaar, 150 shops burnt, 4 deaths, 6, 7 Sept. 1897.

CACHET, see *Lettres de Cachet*.

CADDEE, or **League of God's House**, the league of independence in Switzerland, formed by the Grisons to resist domestic tyranny, 1396 to 1419. A second league of the Grisons was called the Grise or Gray League, 1424. A third league, the League of Ten Jurisdictions, was formed in 1436; see *Grisons*. They united in 1471.

CADE'S INSURRECTION. In May, 1450, Jack Cade, an Irishman, who assumed the name of Mortimer, laid before the royal council the complaint of the commons of Kent. He headed about 20,000 Kentish men, who armed "to punish evil ministers, and procure a redress of grievances." He defeated and slew sir Humphry Stafford, at Sevenoaks, 27 June, entered London in triumph, and beheaded the lord treasurer, lord Saye, and several other persons of consequence, 3 July. When the insurgents lost ground, a general pardon was proclaimed, and Cade, deserted by his followers, fled. A reward having been offered for his apprehension, he was discovered, and refusing to surrender, was slain by Alexander Iden, sheriff of Kent, 11 July.

CADET'S COLLEGE, see *Sandhurst*.

CADIZ (W. Spain), anciently Gadiz, the Roman Gades; said to have been built by the Phœnicians, about 1100 B.C. Population in 1887, 62,531; 1897, 70,177.

One hundred vessels of the Spanish armada destroyed in the port by sir Francis Drake . 1587
Cadiz was taken by the English under the earl of Essex, and plundered . . . . 15 Sept. 1596
Vainly attacked by sir George Rooke . . . 1702
Bombarded by the British . . . . July, 1797
Blockaded by lord St. Vincent for two years . 1797-9
Again bombarded by the British . . . Oct. 1800
A French squadron of five ships of the line and a frigate surrender to the Spanish and British, 14 June, 1808
Besieged by the French, but the siege was raised after the battle of Salamanca . . . July, 1812
Insurrection, 1819; massacre of many inhabitants by the soldiery . . . . . 9, 10 March, 1820
Taken by the French in Oct. 1823, and held till . 1828
Declared a free port 1829
Insurrection against the queen began with the fleet here (see *Spain*) . . . . . 17 Sept. 1868
Republican insurrection suppressed with bloodshed, 5-13 Dec. ,,
Naval exhibition opened . . . . 15 Aug. 1887
Strike riots, shops pillaged, people injured, 11 Dec. 1901

CADMIUM, a metal, discovered by Stromeyer and Hermann in 1818.

CADOUDAL, see *Georges*.

CÆCILIAN SOCIETY, instituted in London, in 1785, for the performance of sacred music, especially Handel's. At first it met at private houses, afterwards at various city company halls, and finally at Albion hall, Moorfields, till its dissolution in 1861. Mr. Z. W. Vincent, the first conductor, held the office for upwards of thirty years. Out of this society, which was the predecessor of the Sacred Harmonic Society, came many eminent professional musicians.

CAEN (N. France), a place of importance before 912, when it became the capital of the possessions of the Normans, under whom it flourished. It was taken by the English in 1346 and 1417; but was finally recovered by the French 1 July, 1450. Here were buried William the conqueror (1087), and his queen (1083).

CAERLEON, Monmouthshire, a Roman station, and made the seat of an archbishopric by Dubritius. His disciple and successor, St. David (522), is said to have removed it to Menevia, now St. David's, 577.

CAERNARVON (N. Wales). In the castle (founded in 1282) Edward II. was born, 25 April, 1284; and the town was then chartered by Edward I. The town suffered by the civil war of Charles, but was finally retained for the parliament. The North Wales Training College destroyed by fire, 20 Dec. 1891. Population, 1881, 10,258; 1891, 9,804; 1901, 9,760.

CÆSAREA, the Roman capital of Judea, built by Herod the Great, 10 B.C. Eusebius the historian was bishop about 315.

CÆSARS, see *Rome; Emperors*. The Era of the Cæsars or Spanish Era, is reckoned from 1 Jan. 38 B.C., being the year following the conquest of Spain by Augustus. It was much used in Africa, Spain, and the south of France; but by a synod held in 1180 its use was abolished in all the churches dependent on Barcelona. Pedro IV. of Arragon abolished the use of it in his dominions in 1350. John of Castile did the same in 1383. It was used in Portugal till 1415, if not till 1422. The months and days of this era are identical with the Julian calendar; and to turn the time into that of our era, subtract thirty-eight from the year; but if before the Christian era, subtract thirty-nine.

CÆSIUM (Latin, bluish), a rare alkaline metal, found in some mineral waters by Bunsen in 1861, by means of the "Spectrum analysis," *which see*.

CAFEINE (English Caffeine), an alkaline body, discovered in coffee by Runge in 1820, and in tea (and named théine) by Oudry in 1827. The identity of the two was proved by Jobst and Mulder in 1828.

CAFFRARIA, and Caffre War, see ***Kaffraria***.

CAGLIARI, see *Naples*, note.

CAGOTS, an outcast race in the Pyrenees, supposed to be descendants of the ancient Goths. They have been subjected to superstitious persecution so lately as 1755.

CAI-FONG, the old capital of China, was besieged by 100,000 rebels, in 1642. The commander of the relieving forces, in order to drown the enemy, broke down its embankments. All the besiegers and 300,000 of the citizens perished.

ÇA IRA! the burden of a popular song, during the French revolution, first heard at Paris, 5 Oct. 1789:

"Ah! ça ira, ça ira, ça ira! Malgré les mutins, tout réussira." An after addition was "Les aristocrates à la lanterne!"
("It will proceed! &c. In spite of mutineers, all will succeed." "Hang the aristocrats!")

CAIRO, or **GRAND CAIRO**, the modern capital of Egypt, remarkable for its mosques, and the sepulchres of its Fatimite caliphs; see *Egypt, Cholera.*

Partially built by the Saracens . . . 969
Taken by the Turks from the Egyptian sultans . . 1517
Ruined by an earthquake and a great fire, when 40,000 persons perished . . . . . June, 1754
Taken by the French under Napoleon Bonaparte; they enter the city . . . 23 July, 1798
Taken by the British and Turks, when 6000 French capitulated . . . . 27 June, 1801
Massacre of the Mamelukes . . . . 1 March, 1811
Visit of the prince of Wales . . . March, 1862
Riots against Nubar Pasha and the British ministers 18 Feb. 1879
After their victory at Tel-el-Kebir, 13 Sept. 1882, the British entered Cairo the next day.
Electric tramway opened, 1 Aug. 1898.
Population 31 Dec. 1878, 327,462; 1897, 576,400. See *Cholera*, 1883.
Visit of the duke and duchess of Connaught, 9 Feb. 1899
First stone of the Nat. bank laid by the Khedive 4 March, ,,
Museum of Egyptian antiquities opened 15 Nov. 1902
Powder magazine explosion, 18 deaths . 18 Nov. ,,

CALABAR, OLD and NEW, rivers in West Africa, see *Bonny*.

CALABRIA (the ancient Messapia of S. E. Italy), was conquered by the Romans, 266 B.C. It formed part of the kingdom of the Ostrogoths under Theodoric, A.D. 493; was re-conquered (for the Eastern empire) by Belisarius, 536; subdued by the Lombards and joined to the duchy of Benevento, 572. After various changes, it was conquered by Robert Guiscard, the Norman, 1058, who obtained the title of duke of Calabria, and eventually that of king of Naples. Population, 1890, 1,309,554; see *Naples*.

CALAIS (N. W. France), fortified by Baldwin IV., count of Flanders, 997; taken by Edward III. after a year's siege, 4 Aug. 1347. It was retaken by the duke of Guise, in the reign of Mary, 7 Jan. 1558, and its loss so deeply touched the queen's heart, as to cause some to say it occasioned her death, which occurred soon afterwards, 17 Nov. same year. "When I am dead," said the queen, "Calais will be found written on my heart." It was taken by the Spaniards, April, 1596, restored, 1598. About 12 persons drowned in a house by bursting of a reservoir, 30 Jan. 1882. The new harbour and docks were opened by president Carnot, 3 June, 1889; see *Tunnels*.

Great strike of lace-workers, Sept. 1890; ended by concession of the masters . . . 30 Oct. 1890
Hogarth's picture of the "Gate of Calais" given to the National Gallery by the duke of Westminster . . . . Dec. 1895

CALATRAVA, see *Knighthood*.

CALCIUM, the metallic base of lime, was discovered at the Royal Institution, London, by Humphry Davy in 1808.

CALCULATING MACHINES. To avoid errors in computing and printing logarithms and tables of figures, machines to calculate and print have been devised. Pascal, when nineteen years of age, invented one about 1650. The construction of Mr. C. Babbage's differential machine was commenced at the expense of government in 1823, and continued till 1833, when the work was suspended after an expenditure of 17,000*l*. The portion completed was placed in the library of King's College, London; it is now at South Kensington. Professor Clifford, in his lecture at the Royal Institution, 24 May, 1872, stated that Babbage expended 20,000*l*. upon his machines, and that the analytical machine was nearly finished, and would eventually be much used. "Babbage's Calculating Engines: a Collection of Papers relating to them," was published by his son, Gen. Babbage, in 1889. C. Babbage died 1871, aged 78. In 1857, Messrs. E. and G. Scheutz, two Swedish engineers, published in London specimen tables, calculated and printed by machinery constructed between 1837 and 1843, after a study of the account of Mr. Babbage's machine. Messrs. Scheutz brought their machine to England in 1854. It was bought for 1000*l*. by Mr. J. F. Rathbone, an American merchant, to be presented to Dudley observatory in his own town, Albany. In 1857, Messrs. Scheutz were engaged to make one for the British government, which was completed. Mr. Wiberg's machine, exhibited at Paris, Feb. 1863, was much commended. Tables constructed by means of Scheutz's machine, and edited by Dr. W. Farr, were published by the government in 1864. The arithmometer, patented by M. Thomas (de Colmar) in 1822 (?), exhibited at the International exhibitions, 1851 and 1862, is said to be in use in assurance offices. Geo. B. Grant described a simpler machine in the "American Journal of Science," Oct. 1874. Other machines have been constructed since.

The "calculating boy," George P. Bidder, born 14 June, 1806; noted in 1815 *et seq.*; president of the institution of civil engineers, 1860–61; died . . . . 20 Sept. 1878
An "arithmometer," for adding up figures and printing, was invented by Mr. Burroughs in the United States, and introduced into this country by Mr. H. E. Winter in 1893
M. Jacques Inaudi, a young Italian, eminent in mental arithmetic, visited Paris and London in the spring of . . . . ,,

CALCUTTA, capital of Bengal and British India; the first settlement of the English here was made in 1689. Population, 1881, 766,298; 1891, 840,130; 1901 (including suburbs), 1,026,987.

Purchased as a zemindary, and Fort William built 1698
Made the head of a separate presidency . . . 1707
The fort attacked and taken by an army of 70,000 horse and foot, and 400 elephants (147 of the British crammed into the "Black-hole prison," a dungeon, 18 feet square, from whence 23 only came forth the next morning alive) (monument unveiled by the Viceroy, 19 Dec. 1902), 20 June, 1756
Calcutta retaken by Clive . . . 2 Jan. 1757
Supreme court of judicature established . . . 1773
Asiatic society founded 1784
College founded 1801
Bishopric of Calcutta instituted by act, July, 1813; first bishop, Thomas F. Middleton 1814
Bishop's college founded 1820
Cathedral founded 1840
An industrial exhibition opened . . . . 25 Jan. 1855
Great cyclone, followed by a "bore" or spring tide in the Hooghly; water rises 30 feet high; immense damage done to shipping and houses; about 60,000 persons said to have perished . 5 Oct. 1864
Another cyclone; about 30,000 small houses unroofed, much small shipping injured; and the crops in Lower Bengal destroyed (about 90,000 persons drowned; 75,000 die of cholera), 1 Nov. 1867
Visited by the king of Siam . . . . Jan. 1872
Visited by the prince of Wales, 25 Dec. 1875—3 Jan. 1876
Statue of lord Mayo unveiled by him . . 1 Jan. ,,

Statue of the queen given by the maharajah of Burdwan, unveiled . . . . 1 Jan. 1878
International exhibition opened by the viceroy, the marquis of Ripon, the duke and duchess of Connaught present, 4 Dec. 1883; closed 10 March, 1884
Destructive cyclone; the *Sir John Lawrence* and the tug *Retriever* lost, about 700 lives lost, 23 May *et seq.* 1887
About sixty persons killed by the collision of a ferry steamer with a tug-boat near Calcutta 6 Nov. 1888
Visit of prince Albert Victor of Wales, great festivities . . . . . . 3–13 Jan. 1890
Fatal religious riot, May, 1891; trial of rioters, 5 Aug. 1891
Statue of the marquis of Dufferin unveiled, 8 Dec. ,,
Cyclone; 64 men drowned while unloading the *Germania*, reported . . . 29 May, 1893
Destructive earthquake, the cathedral, churches, and other buildings damaged; 8 natives killed in a panic, 5 p.m. . . . . . 12 June, 1897
Serious Mahometan riots at Chitpur; troops called out, 11 rioters killed; quelled by the police, 29, 30 June, and 1 July; compromise effected . . . . . . 2 July, ,,
Statue of lord Roberts unveiled . . 2 March, 1898
Rev. J. E. C. Welldon, bishop . . Aug. 1898–1902
Statue of queen Victoria unveiled . 19 March, ,,
Coronation festivities; 60,000 poor feasted, 27 Jan. 1903
Imperial Library opened by Lord Curzon 30 Jan. ,,
See *Bengal* and *India*.

CALEDONIA, the Roman name for part of Scotland, north of the wall of Antoninus, so termed by Tacitus, who died 99. Venerable Bede says that it retained this name until 258, when it was invaded by a tribe from Ireland, and called *Scotia*. The ancient inhabitants appear to have been the Caledonians and Picts, tribes of the Celts, who passed over from the opposite coast of Gaul. About the beginning of the 4th century of the Christian era they were invaded (as stated by some authorities) by the Scuyths or Scythins (since called Scots), who, having driven the Picts into the north, settled in the Lowlands, and gave their name to the whole country; see *Scotland*.

Caledonian monarchy, mythically said to have been founded by Fergus I. . . . . about B.C. 330
The Picts from England settle in the south . . 140
Agricola, the Roman, invades Caledonia . A.D. 79
He defeats Galgacus, and builds a wall between the Forth and Clyde 84
Wall of Antoninus built 140
Ulpius Marcellus repels their incursions . . 184
Christianity introduced in the reign of Donald I. . 201
The Caledonians invade South Britain, 207; repelled by the emperor Severus, who advances to the Moray Frith 209
Caledonia invaded by the Scuths, or Scotti, from Ireland, about 306
Caledonian monarchy revived by Fergus II. . . 404
Kenneth II., king of the Scotti, subdues the Caledonians and Picts, and founds one monarchy, named *Scotland* . . . . . . 838 to 843

CALEDONIAN ASYLUM, Royal, for children of indigent respectable Scotch parents, established in 1815, at Caledonian road, London. Some 200 children are maintained and educated. Princess Henry of Battenberg laid the first stone of the new building at Bushey, 10 May, 1902, to which the asylum was removed 26 May, 1903. The Caledonian Society of London holds annual festivals, 25 Jan., Burns's birthday.

CALEDONIAN CANAL, from the North Sea to the Atlantic Ocean. The act for its construction received the royal assent 27 July, 1803; and the works were commenced same year. The nautical intercourse between the western ports of Great Britain and those also of Ireland to the North Sea and Baltic, is shortened in some instances 800, and in others 1,000 miles. A sum exceeding a million sterling was granted by parliament from time to time; and safe navigation for ships was opened 1 Nov. 1822. It has not been successful commercially Annual income from tonnage, 1 May, 1859, 5,080*l.*; expenditure, 6,951*l.*; annual income, April, 1866–7, 6,541*l.*; expenditure, 6,698*l.*; receipts, April, 1890–91, 7,530*l.*; expenditure, 10,001*l.*

CALENDAR, see *Jewish Era* and *Calendar*. The Roman calendar was introduced by Romulus, who divided the year into ten months, comprising 304 days, 738 B.C. This year was of fifty days' less duration than the lunar year, and of sixty-one less than the solar year, and its commencement did not correspond with any fixed season. Numa Pompilius, 713 B.C., added two months; and Julius Cæsar, 46 B.C., to make it more correct, fixed the solar year at 365 days 6 hours, every fourth year being bissextile or leap-year; see *Leap-year*. This calendar was defective, as the solar year consists of 365 days, 5 hours, 49 minutes, and not of 365 days 6 hours. The pontiffs erroneously inserted on intercalary day each *third* instead of each *fourth* year, so that they had inserted 12 instead of nine 29 Febs, up to B.C. 8; Augustus Cæsar ordained that there should be no leap-year for 12 years, until this was rectified. The difference in the 16th century amounted to 10 entire days, the vernal equinox falling on 11th instead of 21st March. To obviate this error, pope Gregory XIII. ordained, in 1582, that *that* year should consist of 355 days only (5 Oct. became 15 Oct.); and to prevent further irregularity, it was determined that a year ending a century should not be bissextile, with the exception of that ending each fourth century; thus 1700, 1800 and 1900 have not been bissextile, but the year 2000 will be a leap-year. In this manner three days are retrenched in 400 years, because the lapse of eleven minutes makes three days in about that period. The year of the calendar is thus made as nearly as possible to correspond with the true solar year, and future errors of chronology are avoided. See *New Style* and *French Revolutionary Calendar*. The Greek and Russian calendars retain the old style, 1895.

CORRESPONDENCE OF CALENDARS WITH A.D. 1903.

Julian period 6616
Year of the world (Jewish year) 2 Oct. 1902 5663–64
Hegira 1320
Foundation of Rome (Varro) 2652
United States Independence 127–128
Year of king Edward VII. 2–3
Comte, in his "Systeme de Politique Positive" (instituting the "Religion of Humanity"), published a calendar of 13 months, dedicated successively to Moses, Homer, Aristotle, Archimedes, Cæsar, Paul, Charlemagne, Dante, Guttenberg, Shakespeare, Descartes, Frederic, and Bichat; an eminent person was commemorated every day.

CALENDER, a machine used in glazing various kinds of cloth was introduced into England by the Huguenots, who were driven by persecution from France, Holland, and the Netherlands to these countries, about 1685. *Anderson.*

CALENDS were the first days of the Roman months. The *Nones* of March, May, July, and Oct., fell on the 7th; and their *Ides* on the 15th. The other months had the *Nones* on the 5th and the *Ides* on the 13th. As the Greeks had no *Calends*, "on the Greek Calends," *ad Græcas Calendas*, meant *never*.

CALICO, cotton cloth, named from Calicut, a city of India, visited by the Portuguese in 1498. Calico was first brought to England by the East India Company in 1631. Calico-printing and the Dutch loom engine were first used in 1676, when a

Frenchman established a factory at Richmond, near London. *Anderson.* Calicoes were prohibited to be printed or worn in 1700; and again in 1721 a penalty of 5*l.* was laid on the wearer, and 20*l.* on the seller of calico. In 1831, by the exertions of Mr. Charles Poulett Thompson, afterwards lord Sydenham, and others, the consolidated duty of 3½*d.* on the square yard of printed calico was taken off. Since 1834, the manufacture has been greatly increased by the applications of science. Printing cylinders are made by electric deposition, dyes are artificially made from coal tar products, by the discoveries of Liebig, Hofmann, Perkin, and others; see *Cotton* and *Dyeing*.

John Mercer, a great improver of calico-printing, died 30 Nov. 1866.

CALICUT (now Kolikod), S.W. India, the first Indian port visited by Vasco da Gama, 20 May, 1498. It was seized by Hyder Ali, 1766; taken by the English, 1782; destroyed by Tippoo Saib, 1789; ceded to the English, 1792.

CALIFORNIA (from the Spanish, *Caliente Fornalla*, hot furnace, in allusion to the climate), was discovered by Cortez in 1537; others say by Cabrillo in 1542; and visited by sir Francis Drake, who named it New Albion, in 1579. California was admitted into the United States in 1850. The population in 1856 was 506,067; in 1880, 864,694; in 1890, 1,208,130; 1900, 1,485,053. State capital, Sacramento. San Francisco is the largest city.

The Spanish establish missionary and military stations 1698
California becomes subject to Mexico . . 1823
After a bloodless revolution, it becomes virtually independent 1836
Occupied by the army of the United States . . 1846
Gold discovered in great abundance by capt. Sutter and Mr. Marshall . . . . . Sept. 1847
Ceded to the United States 1848
Made a sovereign state 1850
Numerous murders in San Francisco—Lynch law prevailing 1853-60
Adhered to the union during the war . . . 1861-4
Suffered much damage by an earthquake, 21 Sept. 1868
Bank of California, long very prosperous, stops through unsuccessful speculations, suspected suicide of "the prince," Wm. C. Ralston, manager . . . . about 25 Aug. 1875
Great opposition to increasing Chinese immigration, March, 1876
Political agitation caused by Dennis Kearney against cash payments . . . . Aug. 1878
New constitution (excluding Chinese from citizenship; altering taxation to favour the working-classes; restricting companies, &c.) promoted by Dennis Kearney, the agitator; passed 8 May, 1879
Political disorders; Mr. de Young, an editor, dangerously wounds rev. Mr. Kallock, the elected mayor . . . . Aug. ,,
Violent reaction against Kearney, who flees for his life . . . . July, 1880
Anti-Chinese bill passed; resident Chinese may remain, immigrants prohibited . 13 March, 1891
Towns and villages in the Sacramento valley suffer by an earthquake . . . . 19 April, 1892
California international exhibition (midwinter fair) at San Francisco, opened by gov.-gen. Markham, 27 Jan. 1894
Sacramento occupied by Federal troops in consequence of the *Pullman* railway strike, 11 July; mail train wrecked on a bridge by strikers, several deaths, 11 July; martial law, bloodshed, 13 July, ,,
Suicide of a Chinese murderer at Oakland by blowing up the magazine of the California fuse works; 6 deputy sheriffs and several women also killed . . . . 18 July, 1898
Successful biological survey of mount Shasta (14,450 feet), under Dr. Merriam, new peaks named, 5 new species of plants and 8 of mammals discovered in 1898-99
A large reflector set up at S. Pasadena, concentrates the solar rays, by which steam is produced in a boiler, and a motor driven that pumps water from a well for irrigation, reported successful, April, 1901
Los Alamos suffers by an earthquake . 31 July, 1902

CALIPER COMPASS, whereby the bore of cannon, small arms, &c., is measured, is said to have been invented by an artificer of Nuremberg in 1540.

CALIPH (Arabic), Vicar, or Lieutenant, the title assumed by the sophi of Persia, as successor of Ali, and, since 1517, by the sultan of Turkey, as successor of Mahomet, and sovereign of Mecca and Medina. The caliphat began with Abubeker, the father of the prophet's second wife. Sir Wm. Muir's "Caliphate" published 1891.

CALIPHS OF ARABIA.

632. Abubeker.
634. Omar I.
644. Othman.
655. Ali.
661. Hassan.
The OMMIADES ruled 661-750.
The ABBASIDES ruled 750-1258.
In 775 they were styled caliphs of Bagdad.
Haroun-al Raschid ruled 786-809.

See *Ommiades* and *Abbasides*.

CALIPPIC PERIOD, invented by Calippus, about 330 B.C., to correct the Metonic cycle, consists of four cycles, or of seventy-six years, at the expiration of which he incorrectly imagined the new and full moons return to the same day of the solar year. This period began about the end of June, third year of 112th Olympiad, year of Rome 424, and 330 B.C.

CALIXTINS, 1. A sect derived from the Hussites, about 1420 demanded the cup (Greek, *Kalix*) in the Lord's supper. They were also called Utraquists as partaking of both elements. They were reconciled to the Roman church at the council of Basle, 1433. 2. The followers of George Calixtus, a Lutheran, who died in 1656. He wrote against the celibacy of the priesthood, and proposed a re-union of Catholics and Protestants based on the Apostles' creed.

CALI YUGA, the Hindoo era of the Deluge, dates from 3101 B.C. (according to some, 3102), and begins with the entrance of the sun into the Hindoo sign Aswin, now on 11 April, N.S. In 1600 the year began on 7 April, N.S., from which it has now advanced four days, and from the precession of the equinoxes, is still advancing at the rate of a day in sixty years. The number produced by subtracting 3102 from any given year of the Cali Yuga era will be the Christian year in which the given year begins.

CALLAO (Peru). After an earthquake, the sea retired from the shore, and returned in mountainous waves, which destroyed the city in 1687, and on 28 Oct. 1746. The attempt of the Spanish admiral Nuñez to bombard Callao, 2 May, 1866, was defeated by the Peruvians; blockaded by Chilians, April 1880, see *Chili*. Population, 1876, 33,502.

CALLIGRAPHY (beautiful writing). Callicrates is said to have written an elegant distich on a sesamum seed, 472 B.C. In the 16th century Peter Bales wrote the Lord's Prayer, Creed, and Decalogue, two short Latin prayers, his own name, motto, day of the month, year of our Lord, and of the reign of queen Elizabeth (to whom he presented them at Hampton Court), all within the circle of a silver penny, enchased in a ring and border of gold, and covered with crystal, so accurately done, as to be plainly legible. *Holinshed.*

CALMAR, UNION OF. The treaty whereby Denmark, Sweden, and Norway were united under one sovereign, Margaret, queen of Sweden and Norway, "the Semiramis of the north;" June, 1397, see *Sweden*. The union was dissolved by Gustavus Vasa in 1523.

CALMUCKS, see *Tartary*.

CALOMEL ("beautiful black"), a compound of mercury, sulphuric acid, and chloride of sodium, first mentioned by Crollius early in the 17th century. The first directions given for its preparation were by Beguin in 1608.

CALORESCENCE. In Jan. 1865 Professor Tyndall rendered the ultra-red rays of the spectrum of the electric light visible by causing a focus of them to impinge on a plate of platinum, which they raised to a white heat. He termed the phenomenon Calorescence; see *Fluorescence*.

CALORIC, see *Heat*.

CALOTYPE PROCESS (from the Greek *kalos*, beautiful), by which negative photographs are produced on paper, is the invention of Mr. Henry Fox Talbot about 1840. Also called TALBOTYPE. See *Photography*.

CALOYERS (meaning *good old men*). The monks of the Greek church, of the order of St. Basil. Their most celebrated monastery in Asia is at Mount Sinai, endowed by Justinian (died 565); the European one is at Mount Athos.

CALPEE, India. Sir Hugh Rose defeated the mutineers here, and took the town, 22, 23 May, 1858.

CALVARY, MOUNT, the place where the Re- destination, particular redemption, total depravity, irresistible grace, and the certain perseverance of the saints.

CAMALDULES or **CAMALDOLITES,** a religious order founded at Camaldoli near Florence, by Romuald about 1022.

CAMBAY, see *India*, 1890.

CAMBERWELL, south London. The grammar school was established (Mr. W. Minet) by the rev. E. Wilson, 29 Sept. 1715. The ancient church was burnt 7 Feb. 1841. Camberwell returns 3 members to parliament by the acts of 1884-85. The public library presented by Mr. George Livesey, opened by sir E. Clarke, 18 Oct. 1890. Fine art gallery, library and lecture-hall, gift of Mr. Passmore Edwards; central free public library opened by the prince of Wales and the duke and duchess of York, 9 Oct. 1893. New mission hall opened by princess Christian, 18 Oct. 1902. Houses wrecked by a cyclone, 29 Oct. 1898. Population, 1891, 235,312; 1901, 259,258.

CAMBIUM REGIS; see *Royal Exchange*.

CAMBODIA, or Camboja, an ancient state in central Asia, formerly subject to Annam and later to Siam. The country was called Khmer, and the remains of early sculptures, temples, &c., exhibit evidences of a high civilization. The people are of Hindu origin and akin to the Siamese, the religion being Buddhism. Population, estimated, 1901, 1,500,000. Capital, Pnompenh since 1866; population, 1894, 50,000.

The kingdom visited by the Portuguese, Spaniards and Dutch, 16th century; dismembered 17th century. Disastrous voyage and death of M.

CAMBRIC first made at Cambray; worn in England, and accounted a great luxury, 1580. *Stow.* Its importation restricted in 1745; prohibited in 1758; re-admitted, 1786; prohibited 1795.

CAMBRIDGE, supposed to be the Roman *Camboricum* and the Saxon *Granta bricsir*, frequently mentioned by the earliest British historians, was burnt by the Danes in 870 and 1010. See table in *Population*, *Rede Lecture* and *Torres*.

Fortified by William I. 1070
Plundered by the barons 1088
In Wat Tyler's and Jack Straw's rebellion, the rebels enter the town, seize the university records and burn them in the market-place 1381
Garrisoned by Cromwell 1642
Cambridge Philosophical Society established in 1819, and chartered 1832
Railway to London opened . . . . June, 1845
Fitzwilliam museum, endowed 1816; founded 1837; completed 1847
British association met here . . . 1833, 1845, 1862
Visit of prince and princess of Wales . 2–4 June, 1864
Royal Agricultural society show . 25 June *et seq.* 1894
Training college for women teachers, costing over 10,000*l.*, opened by the marquis of Ripon, 19 Oct. 1895
Houses wrecked by cyclone . . . . 29 Oct. 1898
Small pox epidemic, 146 cases, 15 deaths . . 1903

CAMBRIDGE UNIVERSITY.

The early history is traditional till the 12th century. Sigebert, king of the East Angles, is mythically said to have set up a school about 630. Scholars are said to have collected here and to have been favoured by Henry I., 1110. Henry III. granted the first charter in 1231, about which time the students began to live together in hostels which afterwards became colleges named after saints. It is said that there were 27 hostels in 1280. The university was incorporated in 1571, and sent two members to parliament in 1603. University tests act passed, 16 June, 1870. University commission respecting property was appointed 6 Jan. 1872. Universities act, making many changes was passed . . . . . . 10 Aug. 1877
St. Paul's Hostelry for Indian students, chartered 18 July, 1883
New Museum of Classical Art and Archæology opened . . . . 6 May, 1884
Henry Fawcett, M.P., postmaster-general, buried at Trumpington . . . . 10 Nov. ,,
Miss A. F. Ramsay, of Girton, senior and alone in the first division of the classical tripos; Miss B. M. Hervey, of Newnham, alone in the first division of the mediæval and modern languages tripos, 18 June, 1887
Prof. G. G. Stokes, Bart., elected M.P. for the university, 17 Nov. 1887; his jubilee as Lucasian professor celebrated (died 1 Feb., 1903) 1, 2 June, 1899
Miss G. P. Fawcett, Newnham (daughter of the late professor), above the senior wrangler in mathematics . . . . 7 June, 1890
The senate supports the compulsory study of Greek (525–185) . . . . 29 Oct. 1891
Establishment of an engineering school, proposed Dec. ,,
New science buildings, for engineering, &c., opened by lord Kelvin . . 28 Oct. 1893; 15 May, 1894
"Companions of St. John," an eccentric secret society, founded by the rev. E. J. Heriz-Smith, about 1892; much criticised . . . early in 1896
Depressed financial condition, reported by the duke of Devonshire, chancellor . *Times*, 23 April, 1897
Controversy respecting granting degrees for women; see *Women*, 1896-7 . March *et seq.* ,,
Cambridge university association formed, meeting at Devonshire house, 31 Jan. 1899; new endowment fund, total 67,000*l.* (10,000*l.* from Mr. W. Astor) . . . . Oct. 1900
The "John Hopkinson" wing of the engineering laboratory at the university erected by his family (see *Switzerland*), Aug. 1898; opened . 2 Feb. ,,
Lord Acton's Library (about 65,000 vols.) presented to the university by Mr. John Morley 20 Oct. 1902
"The Cambridge Modern History," vol. 1 pub. Jan. 1903
Mr. F. J. Quick bequeathed over 50,000*l.* for biological research, reported . . . . 14 Jan. ,,

COLLEGES.

Peterhouse College, founded by Hugo de Balsham, bishop of Ely 1257
Pembroke College, founded by the countess of Pembroke 1347
Gonville and Caius, by Edmund Gonville . . . 1348
Enlarged by Dr. John Caius 1558
Corpus Christi, or Benet 1352
King's College, by Henry VI. 1441
Queens' College, by Margaret of Anjou, 1448; and Elizabeth Woodville 1449
Jesus College, by John Alcock, bishop of Ely . . 1496
Christ's College, founded 1442; endowed by Margaret, countess of Richmond, mother of Henry VII. 1505
St. John's College, endowed by Margaret, countess of Richmond 1511
Magdalene College, by Thomas, baron Audley . . 1519
Trinity College, by Henry VIII. 1546
Emmanuel College, by sir Walter Mildmay . . 1584
Sidney-Sussex College, founded by Frances Sidney, countess of Sussex 1598
Downing College, by sir George Downing, by will, in 1717; its charter 1800
Ridley Hall (theological), foundation-stone laid, 17 Oct. 1879
Selwyn College, founded . . . . . 1 June, 1881

THREE HALLS.

Clare Hall, or College, first founded by Dr. Richard Baden in 1326; destroyed by fire and re-established by Elizabeth de Bourg, sister to Gilbert, earl of Clare . . . . . . about 1342
Trinity Hall, by Wm. Bateman, bishop of Norwich, 1350
St. Catharine's College or Hall, founded . . . 1473
[*Cambridge University Calendar.*]

CHANCELLORS.

Charles, duke of Somerset, elected 1688
Thomas, duke of Newcastle 1748
Augustus Henry, duke of Grafton 1768
H.R.H. William Frederick, duke of Gloucester . 1811
John, marquis Camden 1834
Hugh, duke of Northumberland 1840
The Prince Consort [died Dec. 14, 1861] 28 Feb. 1847
William, duke of Devonshire [died 21 Dec. 1891] 31 Dec. 1861
Spencer C., duke of Devonshire . . . 4 Jan. 1892

PRINCIPAL PROFESSORSHIPS. FOUNDED

Divinity (Lady Margaret, mother of Henry VIII.) 1502; Regius 1540
Laws, Hebrew, Greek and Physic . . . . ,,
Arabic 1632
Mathematics (Lucasian) 1663
Music 1684
Chemistry 1702
Astronomy 1704, 1749
Anatomy 1707
Modern History, Botany 1724
Natural and Experimental Philosophy . . . 1783
Mineralogy 1808
Political Economy 1863
Slade (fine art) 1869
Agriculture 1899

CAMBRIDGE UNION SOCIETY begun as a debating club at the "Red Lion" in 1811; settled in its new building in 1886. Dr. Whewell was president in 1817. Lord Houghton, sir Alex. Cockburn, lords Macaulay and Lytton were early members.

DUKES OF CAMBRIDGE.

George Augustus, electoral prince of Hanover, created duke 9 Nov. 1706; king as George II., 11 June, 1727, see *England*.
Adolphus Frederick, fifth son of George III., born 24 Feb. 1774, created duke 27 Nov. 1801; viceroy of Hanover, 1816–37; died 8 July, 1850.
George William Frederick Charles, son, born 26 March, 1819; duke, 8 July, 1850; colonel, 3 Nov. 1837; commanded the first division in the Crimean war; general commanding in chief, 5 July, 1856; commander-in-chief by patent, 1887; resigned from Nov. 1895; a marble bust of the duke was unveiled in his presence in the Guildhall, London, and an address of thanks, in a gold casket, presented to him in recognition of his public services, 19 Oct. 1896.

See *England* (royal family) end.

CAMBRIDGE, a city in Massachusetts; first settled in 1630. The "Bay Psalm book," said to be the first book printed in British America, was published here in 1640. See *Harvard College*. Population in 1870, 39,364; 1890, 70,028; 1900, 91,886.

CAMBUSKENNETH, near Stirling (Central Scotland). Here Wallace defeated the English under Warrenne and Cressingham, 10 Sept. 1297.

The abbey, one of the richest in Scotland, was founded by king David I. in 1147, was spoiled and the fabric nearly destroyed by the reformers in 1559.

CAMDEN (S. Carolina). Here 16 Aug. 1780, lord Cornwallis defeated the revolted Americans under Gates. At a second battle (also called Hobkirk's hill), between general Greene and lord Rawdon, the Americans were again defeated, 25 April, 1781. Camden was evacuated and burnt by the British, 13 May, 1781.

CAMDEN SOCIETY, established 1838, in honour of the distinguished historian and antiquary (1551-1623), publishes British historical documents. 1517 volumes have been issued, 1895.

CAMDEN TOWN, N.W. London, begun by land let for building 1400 houses by earl Camden in 1791; received his name a few years after.

CAMEL, DAY OF THE, 4 Nov. 656 (according to some 658 or 659) when Talha and Zobeir, rebel Arab chiefs were defeated and slain by the caliph Ali. Ayesha, Mahomet's widow, friend of the chiefs, was present in a litter, on a camel, hence the name.

A *camel corps* was raised during the Soudan campaigns of 1884-5. It consisted of about 1,000 camels, controlled by British cavalry and marines.

CAMERA LUCIDA, invented by Dr. Hooke about 1674; another by Dr. Wollaston in 1807. CAMERA OBSCURA, or dark chamber, constructed, it is said, by Roger Bacon in 1297; improved by Baptista Porta, about 1500; and remodelled by sir Isaac Newton; see *Photography*. *The Camera Club* (photographers), founded 1885, holds annual meetings.

CAMERON'S ACT, DR., see *Debt*, 1880.

CAMERONIANS, a name frequently given to the Reformed Presbyterian church of Scotland, the descendants of the covenanters of the 17th century, the established church, 1638-50.* Charles II. signed the League and Covenant in 1650, in hopes of recovering his kingdoms, but renounced it in 1661, and revived episcopacy. A revolt ensued in 1666, when many covenanters were slain in battle (in the Pentland hills, &c.), and many refusing to take the oaths required, and declining to accept the king's *indulgence*, died on the scaffold, after undergoing cruel tortures. The name *Cameronian* is derived from Richard Cameron, one of their ministers, who was killed in a skirmish, in 1680. On 22 June in that year he and others issued at Sanquhar a declaration for religious liberty. The bi-centenary was kept in 1880. In 1689 they raised a body of soldiers to support William III., who enrolled them under the command of lord Angus, as the 26th regiment, since so famous, now designated the Cameronians (the Scottish Rifles). In 1712 they renewed their public covenants, and are described in one of their tracts as "the suffering anti-popish, and anti-prelatical, anti-erastian, true presbyterian church of Scotland." They have now between thirty and forty congregations in Scotland.—The *Cameron Highlanders* ("the Queen's Own") formerly the 79th foot, raised in 1793 by Allan Cameron, were not connected with the Cameronian movement.

* They were frequently called *hill-men* or *mountain men*, and *society people* (from the places and modes of worship to which they were frequently reduced), and McMillanites, from John McMillan, their first minister, after their secession from the church of Scotland on account of its subserviency to the English government, and its declining from its original rigid principles. They assumed the name of the "Reformed Presbyterian Church," on May 5, 1876, and soon after united with the Free Church of Scotland.

CAMEROONS. Mountains and river, S. W. Africa. Dr. Nachtigall founded a German colony here, Aug., which was recognised Oct. 1884. He died 24 April, 1885. To it was annexed the British colony Victoria, 28 March, 1887.

A German expedition in 1889 left the Cameroons under the command of lieut. Morgan with 250 men, to investigate the inland district of the Niger tributaries; after suffering many privations and troubles with the men, and losing over 100 men, lieut. Morgan and his party were brought from the Benue river to Akassa by an agent of the royal Niger company, reported 20 March, 1891

Occasional fighting with the natives, capt. von Gravenreuth killed, reported . . . Nov. ,,

Mutiny of 60 Dahomey soldiers, assisted by 40 women; the women flogged by order of Herr Leist, 15 Dec.; the rising suppressed by the crew of the *Hyæna* and others, 21 Dec. 1893; Herr Leist is recalled to Berlin, April; tried, censured, but acquitted, 16 Oct. 1894; a higher court sentence him to expulsion from the public service, &c. . . . . April, 1895

Major Leutwein appointed chief commander in S. W. Africa; major von François commander of the troops, reported . . . . 20 March, 1894

Hendrik Witbooi's stronghold stormed, 27 Aug.; he surrenders unconditionally; reported 14 Sept. ,,

Buea captured by the Germans after slaughter of the natives, reported . . . . . 17 Feb. 1895

Bakoko tribes defeated: Jaunde occupied without resistance, reported . . . . . 7 June, ,,

Native outbreak suppressed . . . . Jan. 1896

Two engagements near Gobabis, natives repulsed, with loss, by capt. Estorff . . . . 5 April, ,,

Capt. Estorff defeats the Hottentots and Hereros, near Gobabis . . . . . 18, 19 April, ,,

The insurrection of Hottentots suppressed by major Leutwein; reported . . . 19 June, ,,

A large tract of land acquired by the Germans, June, ,,

Rebellion in the south, repressed . . May, 1898

Capt. Kamptz captures the native usurper in the Tibati country . . . . . 25 Aug. 1899

Rebel raids into Kribi, Batanga, repulsed after some days' fighting, 21-26 Sept.; English and other factories looted by the Bulis, native rising, reported, 14 Nov.; 2 Germans murdered, reported, 14 Jan.; punitive expedition sent, officers wounded, reported . . . . 23 March, 1900

Military operations in Adamawa, chiefs submit, reported . . . . 9 July, 1902

CAMISARDS (from *chemise*, Latin *camisa*, a shirt, which they frequently wore over their dress in night attacks), a name given to the French Protestants in the neighbourhood of the Cevennes (mountain chains in S. France), who after enduring much severe persecution in consequence of the revocation of the edict of Nantes, 22 Oct. 1685, took up arms in July, 1702, to rescue some imprisoned brethren. They revenged the cruelties of their enemies, and maintained an obstinate resistance against the royalist armies commanded by marshal Montrevel, and other distinguished generals, till 1705, when the insurrection was suppressed by marshal Villars. After futile conciliatory efforts, several of the heroic leaders suffered death rather than surrender. Cavalier, an able general, unable to carry out a treaty made with Villars, seceded in 1704, entered the British service, and died governor of Jersey, 1740.

CAMLET, formerly made of silk and camel's hair, but now of wool, hair, and silk. Oriental camlet first came here from Portuguese India, in 1660. *Anderson.*

CAMORRA, a secret society of plunderers and ratteners, exacting money from shopkeepers and traders, in Naples (said to have originated from the extreme destitution of the lower classes); tolerated under the Bourbons; checked by the king of Italy; about 80 Camorristi seized and transported, Sept.-Oct. 1874. Many Camorristi seized in the markets at Naples, 30 Aug. and 1 Sept. *et seq.*, 1877. 179 of these tried at Bari, mid-April, May, 1891. The Camorristi are said to be the highest grade of the society named "Mala Vita."

159 members of the Mala Vita society arrested at Taranto . . . . March, 1892

CAMP (Lat. *castra*, English camp is derived from Lat. *campus*, a plain), the name given to the place and the aggregate body of tents or huts in the field. Encampments are mentioned about 1490 B.C. (Numbers ii.). The Lacedæmonians among the Greeks were the first who cultivated the art of forming military camps, the form of which was circular. The Romans, whose camps were square and entrenched, attained to a high degree of skill in this science. Polybius, who accompanied Scipio the younger in many campaigns, gives a very full description of the Roman camp. As described by this historian the camp of a consular army accommodated 16,800 foot and 1,800 horse soldiers, and was elaborately constructed. Vestiges of Roman camps exist at the present day in various parts of England and Scotland. The introduction of gunpowder greatly modified the construction and area of camps. Artillery of the most improved type, and strong detached forts, constitute the chief defensive feature of entrenched camps. The vast size of European armies of the present day necessitate the accommodation of troops in cantonments or bivouacs, but in expeditions in hot climates, with flying columns, tents are used. If occupied for one or two nights only camps are called "flying camps," if for a longer period "standing camps." Camps of exercise of large extent are established at Aldershot (*q.v.*), Colchester, Shorncliffe, the Curragh, Kildare (*q.v.*). A camp was formed in Hyde-park in 1745 and 1814, and at the Alexandra Palace and Hampton Court for the Indian and Colonial troops, 1901-1902 (see *Coronation*).

CAMPAGNA, near Rome. Its drainage and planting were authorised by the Italian senate, 31 May, 1878; works completed, July, 1895.

CAMPANIA (S. Italy), was occupied by Hannibal and various cities declared in his favour 216 B.C.; conquered by the Romans, 213. Its capital was Capua (*which see*).

CAMPBELL'S ACTS, introduced by John Campbell, lord chancellor. 1. Against libels and slanders, 6 & 7 Vict. c. 96 (1843), and 8 & 9 Vict. c. 75 (1845). 2. To compel railway companies to make compensation for injuries by culpable accidents, 9 & 10 Vict. c. 93 (1846). 3. Against obscene publications, prints, &c., 20 & 21 Vict. c. 83 (1857). In accordance with the second act, the family of a gentleman killed through the breaking of a rail, obtained a verdict for 13,000*l.* from the Great Northern railway company. On appeal the sum was reduced.

CAMPBELLITES, or Rowites, a name given to the followers of the rev. John McLeod Campbell, minister of Row, Dumbartonshire, who, on 24 May, 1831, was deposed by the general assembly of the church of Scotland for teaching the universality of the atonement, and other doctrines contrary to the church's standard. Dr. Campbell established a congregation in Glasgow in 1833. The "Disciples of Christ," *which see*, are also sometimes termed Campbellites.

CAMPEACHY-BAY (Yucatan, Central America), discovered about 1517, and settled by Spaniards in 1540; taken by the English in 1659; by the buccaneers in 1678; and by the freebooters of St. Domingo in 1685. These last burnt the town and blew up the citadel. The English logwood-cutters made their settlement here about 1662.

CAMPERDOWN: south of the Texel, Holland, near which admiral Duncan defeated the Dutch fleet, commanded by admiral De Winter; the latter losing fifteen ships, either taken or destroyed, 11 Oct. 1797. The British admiral was made lord Duncan of Camperdown. He died suddenly on his way to Edinburgh, 4 Aug. 1804.

CAMPO FORMIO (N. Italy). Here a treaty was concluded between France and Austria; the latter yielding the Low Countries and the Ionian Islands to France, and Milan, Mantua, and Modena to the Cisalpine republic, 17 Oct. 1797. By a secret article the emperor gained the Venetian dominions.

CAMPO SANTO (Holy Field), a burial-place. That at Pisa, surrounded by an arcade erected by archbishop Ubaldo, about 1300, is celebrated for the frescoes painted on the walls by Giotto, Memmi, and others.

CAMPUS RAUDIUS, near Verona, N. Italy. Here the Cimbri were defeated with great slaughter by Marius and Catulus, 101 B.C.

CANAAN (Palestine), is considered to have been settled by the Canaanites, 1965 B.C. (*Clinton*, 2088). Abram, by divine command, went into the land of Canaan, B.C. 1921, Gen. xii. The land was divided among the Israelites by Joshua, 1445 (*Hales*, 1602).

CANADA (N. America), was discovered by John and Sebastian Cabot, 24 June, 1497. In 1524, a French expedition under Verazani formed a settlement named New France, and in 1535 Jacques Cartier (a Breton mariner), ascended the St. Lawrence as far as the site of Montreal; see *Montreal* and *Quebec*. Canada has been termed "the Dominion," since its incorporation with the other North American colonies, 1 July, 1867. Mr. Castell Hopkin's "Encyclopædia of Canada," an elaborate work, with articles by the chief literary men of the country, vol. 2 pub. March, 1899.

Besides the governor-general there are the lieut.-governors of Ontario, Quebec, Nova Scotia, Cape Breton Island, New Brunswick, Manitoba, Prince Edward Island, British Columbia, and Western Territories, 1892; N.W. territories, 1897.

Population: 1857, Lower Canada, 1,220,514; Upper Canada, 1,350,923; of the Dominion, 1871, 3,788,614; 1881, 4,359,933; 1891, nearly 5,000,000; 1901, 5,369,666.

1886-7, revenue, 7,364,916*l.*; expenditure, 7,326,920*l.*; 1890, revenue, 39,879,925 dollars; expenditure, 35,994,031 dollars; 1893, revenue, 38,168,609 dollars; expenditure, 36,814,053 dollars; 1894-95, revenue, 36,374,693 dollars; expenditure, 37,585,025 dollars; 1896-7, revenue, 37,829,778 dollars; expenditure, 38,349,759 dollars; 1900, surplus, 8,054,715 dollars; 1901, 5,648,333 dollars.

1886-7, imports, 23,197,035*l.*; exports, 18,393,660*l.*; 1890, imports, 121,858,241 dollars; exports, 96,749,149 dollars; 1893, imports, 129,094,268 dollars; exports, 118,564,352 dollars; 1897, imports, 111,294,021 dollars; exports, 123,959,835 dollars; 1901-02, imports, 202,791,595 dollars; exports, 211,725,563 dollars.

First permanent settlement: Quebec founded . . 1608
Canada taken by the English, 1629; restored . . 1632
War begins in 1756; Canada conquered by the English, 1759 (see *Quebec*), confirmed to them by the treaty of Paris, signed . . . 10 Feb. 1763
Legislative council established; the French laws confirmed, and religious liberty given to Roman Catholics . . . 1774
The Americans under Montgomery invade Canada, and surprise Montreal, Nov. 1775; expelled by Carleton . . . March, 1776
Canada divided into Upper and Lower . . . 1791
The "clergy reserves" established by parliament—one-seventh of the waste lands of the colony appropriated for the maintenance of the Protestant clergy (during the debates on this bill the quarrel between Mr. Burke and Mr. Fox arose) . . . „
Canada made a bishopric . . . 1793
United States army, under general Hull, invades Canada, 12 July, 1812, crossing at Detroit, repulsed at River Canard, about 3 miles from Amherstburgh, retreated across to Detroit and surrendered to gen. Brock . . 16 Aug. 1812
Americans take York, 27 April; Fort George, 27 May, 1813; defeated at Lundy's Lane, 25 July, 1814; peace signed at Ghent . . 24 Dec. 1814
Opposition to Canada clergy reserves . . 1817 *et seq.*
Treaty with United States respecting fisheries . 1818
First railway in Canada opened . . July, 1836
The Papineau rebellion commences at Montreal by a body called *Fils de la Liberté* . . . 1837
The rebels routed and dispersed at Toronto, 7 Dec. „
Earl of Durham appointed gov.-gen. . 16 Jan. 1838
Lount and Mathews (rebels) hanged . 12 April, „
Lord Durham's ordinance prohibiting the return of banished rebels to Canada under pain of death, 28 June; censured by the home government; he annuls the ordinance by proclamation, 9 Oct.; justifies his conduct, resigns, and returns to England (where he died in 1840) . Oct. „
Rebellion appears in Beauharnais, 3 Nov.; the insurgents at Napierville, under Nelson, routed, 6 Nov.; rebellion suppressed . . 17 Nov. „
Sir John Colborne, governor . . Dec. „
Acts relating to government of Lower Canada, passed in Feb. 1838, and . . . Aug. 1839
Chas. Poulett Thompson (afterwards lord Sydenham), governor . . . Sept. „
Upper and Lower Canada re-united . 10 Feb. 1840
Sir Chas. Bagot, governor . . . Oct. 1841
Sir Chas. T. (aft. lord) *Metcalfe*, governor Feb. 1843
Earl Cathcart, governor . . . March, 1846
Earl of Elgin, gov.-general . . . Oct. „
Riots in Montreal; parliament house burnt 26 April, 1850
Canada clergy reserves abolished by the British parliament . . . 9 May, 1853
Concluded a reciprocity treaty with United States, 7 June, 1854
The Grand Trunk railroad of Canada (850 miles), from Quebec to Toronto, opened 12 Nov. 1856
On reference made to the queen, Ottawa, formerly Bytown, appointed the capital; this decision unpopular . . . Aug. 1858
Canada raises a regiment of soldiers (made one of the line, and called the 100th) . . . „
The prince of Wales presents the colours at Shorncliffe . . . 10 Jan. 1859
The prince of Wales, the duke of Newcastle, &c., arrived at St. John's, Newfoundland, 24 July; visit Halifax, 30 July; Quebec, 18 Aug.; Montreal, and opens the Victoria railway bridge, 25 Aug.; Ottawa, 1 Sept.; leave Canada, 20 Sept.; after visiting the United States embark at Portland, 20 Oct.; and arrive at Plymouth . 15 Nov. 1860
Lord Monck assumes office as gov.-gen. . 28 Nov. 1861
In consequence of the *Trent* affair (see *United States*, 1861), 3000 British troops sent to Canada; warlike preparations made . . . Dec. 1861
British N. American association founded in London Jan. 1862
Cartier's ministry defeated on Militia bill; Mr. J. Sandfield Macdonald, premier . . 20-23 May, „
The assembly vote only 5000 militia and 5000 reserve towards the defence of the country; this causes discontent in England . . . July, „
Mr. J. Macdonald again premier . . . 20 May, 1863
New Militia bill passed . . . . Sept. „
Military measures in progress . . . Sept. 1864
Meeting of about 20,000 volunteers; delegates from N. American colonies at Quebec, to deliberate on the formation of a confederation, 10 Oct.; agree on the bases . . . 20 Oct. „
Between 20 and 30 armed confederates quit Canada and enter the little town of St. Alban's, Vermont; rob the banks, steal horses and stores, fire, and kill one man and wound others, and return to Canada, 19 Oct.; 13 are arrested, 21 Oct.; but are discharged, on account of some legal difficulty, by Judge Coursol . . . 14 Dec. „
Great excitement in United States, general Dix proclaims reprisals; volunteers called out in Canada to defend the frontiers; president Lincoln rescinds Dix's proclamation . . Dec. „
The confederation scheme rejected by New Brunswick . . . . . 7 March, 1865
The British parliament grant 50,000*l.* for defence of Canada . . . . 23 March, „
The St. Alban's raiders discharged, 30 March; Mr. Seward gives up claim for their extradition. April, „
Messrs. Galt and Cartier visit England to advocate confederation . . . . April, „
The threatened invasion of the Fenians, 9 March; 10,000 volunteers called out . . 15 March, 1866
The renewal of reciprocity treaty declined by United States . . . . 17 March, „
The Canadian parliament opened, for the first time, at Ottawa; the Habeas Corpus act suspended; many Fenians flee; 35,000 men under arms (see *Fenians*) . . . . 8 June, „
Discovery of gold in Hastings county, Canada west, Nov. „
Act for the union of Canada, Nova Scotia, and New Brunswick under the name of the Dominion of Canada, with parliament, to consist of the Queen, a senate of 72 members, and a house of commons of 181 members, passed . . 29 March, 1867
Canada railway loan act passed . 12 April, „
Lord Monck sworn in as viceroy of Canada, by virtue of the act for the union of the British provinces in North America . . 2 July, „
New parliament meets at Ottawa (John Alex. Macdonald premier) . . . 6 Nov. „
Reported agitation against the new confederation in Nova Scotia . . . . Jan. 1868
Murder of Mr. D'Arcy McGee . . . 7 April, „
A Fenian raid into Canada vigorously repelled by the militia . . . about 24 May, „
Visit of prince Alfred . . . Sept. *et seq.* „
Sir John Young (aft. *lord Lisgar*) appointed governor-general in room of lord Monck (resigned), arrives . . . . 27 Nov. „
Hudson's Bay territories purchased, subject to conditions, for 300,000*l.* (see *Hudson's Bay*) Nov. 1869
In consequence of the resistance of some of the settlers (see *Rupert's Land*), an expedition, under colonel Wolseley, arrived at Fort Garry, and a conciliatory proclamation was issued 23 July, 1870
Rupert's Land formed into a province, named Manitoba; Mr. Adams G. A. Archibald named the first governor . . . . . Aug. „
Canada defences loan act passed . . 9 Aug. „
Disputes with United States respecting fishing, Nov. „
Opposition to the fishery clauses in the treaty of Washington . . . . June, 1871
By the British North America act, the parliament of Canada may establish new provinces, 29 June, „
British Columbia united to the "Dominion" . . „
Departure of last battalion of royal troops . Nov. „
A liberal ministry constituted under Mr. Edward Blake . . . . 23 Dec. „
Lord (aft. *earl of*) *Dufferin* appointed governor-general; inaugurated . . . 25 June 1872

Sir George Cartier, statesman, died . . . 20 May, 1873

Mr. Arch, on behalf of British labourers, visits Canada . . . . . . autumn ,,

The ministry of sir John Alexander Macdonald charged with corruption connected with the Pacific railway; the parliament suddenly prorogued by lord Dufferin . . . . 13 Aug. ,,

Commission of inquiry . . . . Sept. ,,

Parliament meets, 23 Oct.; the ministry resigns, 5 Nov.; Mr. Alex. Mackenzie forms a ministry, 7 Nov. ,,

New reciprocity treaty rejected by the U.S. senate, 4 Feb. 1875

The Canadian and United States fishery commission (sir Alexander Galt for Canada, Mr. E. T. Kellogg for United States, and M. Delfoss, Belgian U.S. minister) meet at Halifax, 15 June; award 5,500,000 dollars to Canada, Mr. Kellogg dissenting . . . . . . 23, 24 Nov. 1877

American fishermen in Fortune Bay attacked for breaking laws respecting fishing . . 6 Jan. 1878

Elections: great majority against the government, about . . . . 19 Sept. ,,

The *marquis of Lorne* appointed governor-general, 14 Oct. ,,

Resignation of ministry; sir John Macdonald forms a new one about . . . . . . 19 Oct. ,,

Halifax award paid . . . . 21 Nov. ,,

The marquis of Lorne and princess Louise land at Halifax . . . . 25 Nov. ,,

The Queen's telegram, "Delighted at reception, say so" . . . . 1 Dec. ,,

A protectionist budget passed . . . 15 Mar. 1879

Dominion industrial exhibition at Ottawa opened by the marquis of Lorne. . . . . 24 Sept. ,,

Fortune Bay affair (Jan. 1878), compensation refused by the earl of Salisbury, granted by lord Granville, but rules affirmed . . . . 26 Oct. 1880

Return of Canadian prosperity affirmed by the marquis of Lorne . . . . . . 9 Dec. ,,

Contract for new Pacific railway ratified by the assembly 1 Feb.; work commenced . . May, 1881

Victoria steamer sunk on the Thames, great loss of life (see *Wrecks*) . . . . . 24 May, ,,

Fortune Bay affair; 15,000*l*. awarded . 28 May, ,,

Successful progress of the governor-general through the dominion . . . . . July—Oct. ,,

The marquis of Lorne arrives at Birkenhead 14 Nov. 1881; returns to Canada . . 21 Jan. 1882

Pacific railway bill passed. . . . 20 April, ,,

Society for the Advancement of Literature and Science founded in Ottawa by the marquis of Lorne . . . . 25 May, ,,

Elections: a protectionist majority . . June, ,,

Western territory beyond Manitoba divided into four new districts: Assiniboia, Saskatchewan, Alberta, and Athabasca: by order in council July, ,,

Marquis of Lorne returns to Ottawa from a visit to British Columbia, Washington, &c. . 31 Jan. 1883

New parliament meets . . . . . 8 Feb. ,,

The *marquis of Lansdowne* arrives at Quebec as governor-general . . . . . . 22 Oct. 1884

Canada offers military assistance in the Soudan Feb. 1885

Insurrection in N. W. Territories (see *Manitoba*), March, ,,

Insurrection in N.W. territories, headed by Louis Riel, of Batoche (see *Hudson's Bay*, 1870), supported by French half-breeds and Indians, claiming political and social rights alleged to have been promised in 1870; government stores seized, &c., about 24 March. Capt. Crozier attacks and kills many rebels, but retreats. Col. Irvine evacuates and burns Fort Carleton . . 25–27 March, ,,

Troops despatched from various parts of the dominion . . . . . . March, April, ,,

Battleford besieged by Indians . . . 1 April, ,,

Col. Irvine at Prince Albert waiting help 1 April, ,,

Col. Otter occupies Battleford without opposition 24 April, ,,

Gen. Middleton defeats rebels at Fish Creek after severe conflict, and suffering much by an ambush of sharpshooters . . . . 24 April, ,,

Skirmishing at Cut Knife Creek . . . 1 May, ,,

Gen. Middleton attacks Batoche on the Saskatchewan river, well defended by Riel, with rifle-pits, &c. British success greatly due to the skill and courage of capt. Howard, U.S., in using the Gatling gun, which mowed down the enemy (Batoche captured) . . . . . . 9 May, 1885

The Indian chief Poundmaker captures a supply train, 31 waggons; defeated in an engagement but supplies not recovered . . . 14 May, ,,

Riel surrenders to gen. Middleton's scouts; many of his followers surrender . . . 15 May, ,,

1500 Indians under Big-Bear and Poundmaker hold out, reported . . . . . . 15 May, ,,

Surrender of the Indian chiefs; Poundmaker surrenders . . . . 26 May, ,,

General Strange attacks Big-Bear's entrenched camp, about 20 miles from Fort Pitt, but retreats in good order . . . . . . 28, 29 May, ,,

Big-Bear's army divided, pursued by generals Middleton and Strange; his escape reported 7 June, ,,

captured 3 July; sentenced with others to imprisonment . . . . 27 Sept ,,

Canadian Pacific Railway completed about 2900 miles; first through train from Montreal to Vancouver . . . . 8 Nov. ,,

[First public daily train 28 June, 1886.]

Message of congratulation from the Queen to the people of Canada . . . . . . 6 Nov.

Trial of Louis Riel at Regina 20 July; convicted 1 Aug.; 28 prisoners plead guilty to treason felony 5 Aug.; appeal for Riel on ground of insanity disallowed 10 Sept.; appeal dismissed by privy council, London, 22 Oct.; Riel executed near Regina . . . . 16 Nov. ,,

French demonstrations against the government at Montreal and Quebec without rioting 17 Nov. ,,

Eight Indian murderers hanged at Battleford 27 Nov. ,,

Seizure of American vessel for illegal fishing in the Bay of Fundy announced about 24 April; released about 27 April, ,,

David J. Adams, U.S. fishing vessel, seized at Digby, Nova Scotia, for alleged illegal practices, announced 8 May (captain fined 19 July); the Americans seize the *Sisters*, a Canadian smack, in retaliation (released 30 May); Mr. Bayard, U.S. minister, appeals to the British government for release of *David J. Adams;* Canadian armed fleet sent out; new legislation at Ottawa May, 1886 ,,

Seizure and counter-seizure of 35 vessels . . 1886–7

General amnesty to all persons implicated in the rebellion, except murderers . . . 9 July, 1886

Dissolution of Parliament . . . . 17 Jan. 1887

Sir Alexander Campbell appointed high commissioner for Canada in London in succession to sir Charles Tupper . . . . Feb. ,,

Elections, majority for government 49, 23 Feb.; House opened . . . . . . 13 April, ,,

Fisheries Retaliation Bill passed by the United States congress . . . . . 3 March, ,,

Mr. Wm. O'Brien, editor of *United Ireland*, arrives at Montreal on a mission 11 May; visits Ottawa, Toronto, &c.; generally unsuccessful, and frequently stoned; left . . . . . 28 May, ,,

Joint commission on fisheries dispute (3 British, including Mr. J. Chamberlain, and 3 United States) appointed . . . . about 30 Aug. ,,

British vessels seized by United States authorities in N. Pacific waters . . . 2, 9, 12, 17 Aug. ,,

Great railway bridge over the St. Lawrence at Lachine completed . . . . . . 30 July, ,,

Arrangements made for a fortnightly mail service, &c., from London to the East by the Pacific Railway by government subsidies . . Sept. ,,

Treaty respecting fisheries signed at Washington, U.S. (see *Fisheries*) . . . . 15 Feb. 1888

The senate refuses to ratify . . . 21 Aug. ,,

The *David J. Adams* and *Ella Doughty*, the American fishing vessels, released . . . 28 Feb. ,,

The bill for trade reciprocity with United States negatived after 15 days' debate . . 7 April, ,,

The marquis of Lansdowne leaves Canada 23 May; succeeded by *Lord Stanley of Preston* (see *Salisbury Admin.*); who took the oath . . . 11 June, ,,

Commissioners report the capability of the great Mackenzie basin, &c. (about 1,260,000 square miles) for colonization; announced . . Sept. ,,

Proposed extension by Manitoba of the Red River railway across the Pacific railway; opposed by the Canadian Pacific Company as interfering with their monopoly, and disallowed by the Dominion parliament; a compromise agreed to;

the Manitoba government determine to proceed; the Canadian company resists, Oct.; conflict between the men, the company successful, 26 Oct.; decision of the supreme court in favour of Manitoba announced 23 Dec.; leave given to cross the line . . . . 28 Jan. 1889

Proposal of a petition to the Queen to give the governor-general independent action in foreign affairs negatived by parliament (94–66) . 18 Feb. ,,

Jesuits' estate act, restoring property to them, much opposed by Protestants in Quebec; their petition against the act disallowed by government . . . . Aug. ,,

Destructive storm from Ontario to Quebec, 14 Jan. 1890

Parliament opened, general prosperity announced 16 Jan. ,,

The commons of the dominion unanimously vote a resolution of adhesion to the mother country; a copy to be sent to the queen . . 29 Jan. ,,

The Manitoba railway named the Great Northern railway of Canada . . . . . . Jan. ,,

Crowfoot, the lawyer chief of the Blackfeet Indians dies, sending a message of thanks for kindness received from the government . . 26 April ,,

Resignation of gen. Middleton, commander of militia (under censure) . . about 24 June, ,,

David Crockett, U.S. schooner, seized for illegal fishing, near Prince Edward Island, released on bond, reported . . . . 28 Sept. ,,

John Reginald Birchall, an educated Englishman, tried at Woodstock, Ontario, for the murder in Niagara swamp, of Mr. F. J. Benwell (whom he had decoyed from England into a farming partnership), 17 Feb. Birchall wrote a forged letter to Col. Benwell, requesting him to send 500*l.* to his son: evidence circumstantial; eight days' trial; Birchall convicted 11.45 p.m., 29 Sept.; executed . . . . 14 Nov. ,,

The Indians of Ontario and Quebec, at a meeting on 21 Nov., agree to petition the government to release them from the political franchise, and to permit them to elect their own chiefs as formerly, still remaining subject to the queen; petition presented, and reserved for consideration, Dec. 1890; parliament dissolved . . . . 4 Feb. 1891

Sir John Macdonald, the premier, and the conservatives, propose reciprocity with the United States, restricted to natural products; Mr. Laurier and the liberals propose unrestricted reciprocity . . . . ,,

Elections; estimated result, for the government, 124; for the opposition, 91 . . . 5 March, ,,

The Canadian Pacific railway completed by giving an entrance to New York over the New York central lines, by agreement between the companies . . . . 28 March, ,,

The new parliament opened by lord Stanley, 30 April, ,,

Death of sir John Macdonald, aged 76, greatly lamented, 6 June; public funeral at Kingston, 10, 11 June, ,,

The hon. John Joseph C. Abbott becomes premier, 14 June, ,,

[K.C.M.G. 24 May.]

Motion in favour of unrestricted reciprocity with the United States, after 15 days' debate, rejected in the commons, by a government majority of 26, 29 July, ,,

Great strike in the lumber mills at Ottawa begins 14 Sept. ,,

Sir Hector Louis Langevin, minister of public works, and his friend, the hon. Thomas McGreevy, an active ministerialist M.P., and other officials, charged by Mr. Tarte, M.P., a journalist, with corruption in relation to contracts for government works in 1890; the matter referred to the standing committee on privileges and elections, which met 21 July; sir H. Langevin makes his defence, 11 Aug.; his resignation as minister accepted, 7 Sept.; Mr. T. McGreevy makes damaging admissions, and retires to the United States; the committee in their report exonerate sir H. Langevin from all charges, except that of negligence; they censure Mr. T. McGreevy, and certain officials, 14 Sept. ,,

Report adopted by the house . . . 25 Sept. ,,

The St. Clair tunnel connecting the Canadian and the United States railways running to Chicago opened by sir Henry Tyler, chairman of the Grand Trunk railway . . . . . 19 Sept. 1891

Lady Macdonald created a peeress as baroness Macdonald of Earnscliffe . . . . Oct. ,,

Very large crop of wheat in the N.W. territories, end of Nov. ,,

In consequence of the restriction of Newfoundland in its supply of herring bait to Canadian fishermen, the Dominion government imposes a duty on imported Newfoundland fish . . 8 Dec. ,,

Mr. Nicholas Conolly and Mr. Thomas McGreevy committed for trial . . . . . 24 Dec. ,,

Lachute, on the Canadian Pacific line, burnt, 7 Jan. 1892

Meeting at Washington of the representatives of Canada and the United States to consider reciprocity, no result . . . . . 10–15 Feb. ,,

Negotiations broken off . . . . . 20 June, ,,

The dominion parliament opened by lord Stanley of Preston . . . . 24 Feb. ,,

Difficulty with Newfoundland ended; return to the *status* of 1889 . . . . . . 21 May, ,,

Mr. Thomas McGreevy sentenced to 12 months' imprisonment . . . . April, ,,

The hon. Alexander Mackenzie, originally a Scotch mason, came to Canada and gradually rose till he became liberal premier, 1873–8; he passed several important acts and promoted great public works; visited Great Britain and was received at Windsor, 1875; died aged 70 . . . . . 17 April, ,,

Motion for a new reciprocity tariff with Great Britain, adopted by the commons at Ottawa (98—64) . . . . 25 April, ,,

Death of sir William Ritchie, chief justice and statesman . . . . about 25 Sept. ,,

Resignation of sir John Abbott, premier, 25 Nov.; succeeded by sir John S. D. Thompson Nov. ,,

Department of trade and commerce to be created Dec. ,,

The sentence of Mr. Thomas McGreevy reduced from 12 to 9 months' imprisonment . 17 Dec. ,,

Parliament opened; prosperity reported, 26 Jan.; closed . . . . 2 April, 1893

Treaty for reciprocal trade between France and Canada signed at Paris . . . . 9 Feb. ,,

Lord Stanley of Preston becomes earl of Derby 21 April, ,,

The *earl of Aberdeen* appointed governor-general, May; arrives at Ottawa . . . 25 Sept. ,,

Meetings of the liberal convention at Ottawa for promoting tariff reform, reciprocity, and an elective senate, &c. . . . . . mid June, ,,

Sir Alexander Galt, statesman, aged 76, died, 19 Sept.; Sir John Abbott, aged 72, died . 30 Oct. ,,

Mr. Thomas McGreevy and Mr. N. K. Conolly sentenced at Ottawa to 1 year's imprisonment for conspiracy to defraud the government, 22 Nov. 1893; released . . . . Feb. 1894

New tariff bill, favouring trade with Great Britain, introduced . . . . . . 27 March, ,,

Annual meeting of the Canadian Imperial Federation League held at Ottawa . . . 29 May, ,,

Intercolonial conference opened at Ottawa (see *Colonies*) . . . . . 28 June–9 July, ,,

The earl and countess of Aberdeen close an extensive tour in W. Canada . . . . 23 Nov. ,,

Death of sir John Thompson (born 10 Nov., 1844), of heart disease, at Windsor Castle, after being sworn in as privy councillor, 12 Dec.; state funeral at Halifax, St. Mary's Cathedral, R.C., the earl and countess of Aberdeen, and other eminent persons present, 3 Jan. 1895.

New ministry formed by Mr. Mackenzie Bowell 14 Dec. ,,

See *Behring Straits* and *Manitoba* . . . March, 1895

Opening of parliament, federation with Newfoundland (*which see*), proposed . . . 19 April, ,,

Report of royal commission on the liquor traffic, with recommendations; prohibition disapproved of; issued . . . . 25 April, ,,

Budget announced, 1895–6; probable deficit, 4,500,000 dollars, to be met by increased taxation . . . . 3 May, ,,

Tottenham partially destroyed by fire, estimated damage, 150,000 dollars . . . . 18 June, ,,

First exhibition at Regina, N.W. Canada, opened by the gov.-general . . . . . 30 July,

Franco-Canadian commercial treaty ratified 7 Oct. 1895
The imperial government agrees to grant 75,000*l.* per annum to support a fast mail service and Pacific cable between Gt. Britain and Canada; announced . . . . 19 Nov. ,,
Thanksgiving day for a bountiful harvest 21 Nov. ,,
A draft bill amending the Copyright Act of 1889 (a compromise) brought forward . . . 25 Nov. ,,
"Bell river," the name given to a large river discovered by sir Robert Bell, near the upper Ottawa, reported . . . . . . Nov. ,,
The earl and countess of Aberdeen return to Ottawa after a long visit to the Far West, 7 Dec. ,,
Discontent with the premier, sir Mackenzie Bowell; 7 ministers resign . . . . . . 5 Jan. 1896
Ministry reconstituted . . . . . 15 Jan. ,,
Sir Charles Tupper, jun., secretary of state 16 Jan. ,,
Total force of all ranks, 28,962, reported by the militia department . . . . . 30 Jan. ,,
"British empire league" meeting held at Ottawa . . . . 4 March, ,,
The Catholic Schools remedial (Manitoba) bill read second time, 112—94, 39 hours sitting, 20 March; debate on the third reading, religious and political differences, after 129 hours continuous sitting the house adjourned, 6–11 April; after 59 more hours the debate suspended, 16 April; parliament prorogued . . . . . 23 April, ,,
Sir Mackenzie Bowell resigns, 27 April; new ministry formed by sir Charles Tupper . 1 May, ,,
Royal society of Canada (unification of time, etc., considered) met at Ottawa . . . 19 May, ,,
Elections: victory of Mr. Wilfrid Laurier (French origin) and the liberals . . . 23 June, ,,
Resignation of sir Charles Tupper . 8 July, ,,
Mr. Laurier made president of the privy council 11 July; premier . . . . 13 July, ,,
New parliament opened at Ottawa by the earl of Aberdeen, 20 Aug.; liberal majority in first conflict (34) . . . . . . 22 Sept. ,,
Lord Russell of Killowen arrives at Montreal, 27 Aug; at Ottawa . . . . . 2 Sept. ,,
The dispute with Manitoba to be settled by arrangement; reported . . . . . 6 Sept. ,,
Strike on the Canadian Pacific railway, 28 Sept.; ended by compromise . . . . 7 Oct. ,,
Parliament prorogued . . . . . 5 Oct. ,,
About 21,341 immigrants arrive during the year; reported . . . . 17 Dec. ,,
The "United empire association" started at Ottawa; announced . . . . . 3 Jan. 1897
War eagle mine in British Columbia purchased, by a Toronto syndicate for 850,000 dollars . Jan. ,,
Parliament opened by lord Aberdeen 25 March, ,,
Budget: new tariff, favouring and strengthening the union with Gt. Britain and colonies; opposing the United States; increase on spirits and tobacco, reduction on iron, steel and taxation, proposed; 22 April; passed, at Ottawa 18 June, ,,
Sir Donald Smith, high commissioner, made a peer (lord Strathcona) . . . . . 21 June, ,,
Mr. Laurier, sir Richard Cartwright, and sir Oliver Mowat made, G.C.M.G. . . . . 21 June, ,,
Parliament prorogued . . . . . 29 June, ,,
The alien labour laws in the United States enforced against Canadians, causes much indignation; reported; 7 July; retaliation enforced; announced . . . . . . 14 July, ,,
Gold discovered in the N.W., in the Yukon districtand (on the Klondyke by Geo. McCormack, 17 Aug. 1896), about 250,000 square miles rapid development; new government mining regulations, July; great rush to the Klondyke goldfields; much suffering at Dawson city, site belonging to Joseph Ladue, provisions scarce, miners leaving, Aug.; starvation averted (major Walsh appointed governor, early 1898) . Dec. ,,
Steamer from Klondyke, with 35 miners and 200,000 dollars of gold, arrives at Victoria, B.C., 20 Aug.; [nearly 1,000,000 dollars in value arrived there, 15 July, 1898] . . . . ,,
Sir Wilfrid Laurier warmly welcomed on his return from England . . . . . 30 Aug. ,,
Bush fires (300 squ. mi.); 3 villages destroyed, 20 mi. S. of Ottawa; 5 deaths; reported 6 Oct. ,,
Discovery of a rich vein of gold, near Wawa lake; reported . . . . . . Oct. ,,

New government mining regulations in the Yukon district; issued . . . . . 17 Jan. 1898
Gold discovered in the Hay, Buffalo, and other rivers that run into the Great Slave lake . Jan. ,,
Parliament opened, with a cheerful speech, 3 Feb. ,,
Resignation of the earl of Aberdeen (to leave in Oct.) announced . . . . . 13 May, ,,
Parliament prorogued . . . . . 13 June, ,,
Lord Herschell, sir Wilfrid Laurier, sir R. Cartwright, and sir L. H. Davies (Canada) appointed British high commissioners for the international commission between United States and Canada, 29 June. Mr. Chas. Fairbanks and four others appointed U.S. commissioners, 16 July; meet at Quebec . . . . . . 23 Aug. *et seq.* ,,
The earl of Minto appointed to succeed the earl of Aberdeen as governor-gen. . . . July, ,,
A pier of the Ottawa and New York railway bridge fell, 14 deaths . . . . . . 6 Sept. ,,
A statue of Samuel Champlain, founder of Quebec in 1608, unveiled there by lord Aberdeen, 21 Sept. ,,
Farewell banquet to lord and lady Aberdeen, 1 Nov.; they leave Quebec on the arrival of lord and lady Minto . . . . . 12 Nov. ,,
Serious fires at Dawson city, 14 Oct. (again, 25 April and 3 July, 1899) . . . . . ,,
Postage rate reduced from 3 to 2 cents to U.S.N.A. and all parts of Canada . . . . Dec. ,,
Father Chiniquy, born 30 July, 1809, a great temperance leader, seceded from Romanism 1858, dies . . . . 16 Jan. 1899
Archibald Lampman, poet, born 17 Nov. 1861, dies 11 Feb. ,,
Internat. commission (U.S. and Canada) adjourns; disputed questions, Alaskan boundary, &c., remitted to the two governments, 20 Feb.; lord Herschell, the president, dies suddenly, 1 March, ,,
Parliament opened by the governor . 16 March, ,,
Sir Charles Tupper's motion for a judicial inquiry into the administration of the Yukon, defeated, majority of 50 . . . . . . 30 June, ,,
Dominion day (32nd) kept from the Atlantic to the Pacific . . . . 1 July, ,,
The hon. Wm. Eli Sanford, "wool king," born 1838, drowned in the Muskoka lakes, Ontario 10 July, ,,
Serious riots due to a tram strike in London, Ontario, troops called out . . 8, 9 July, ,,
Government redistribution bill rejected by the senate, 36—14 . . . . . 20 July, ,,
Canada's contribution to the Pacific cable to Australia and New Zealand (cost 1,700,000*l.*) sanctioned . . . . 25 July, ,,
Sir Wilfrid Laurier's resolution of sympathy with the imperial government's S. African policy adopted unanimously in both houses, 31 July, 1 Aug. ,,
Sir James D. Edgar, speaker of the commons, author of "This Canada of ours," and other poems, born 1841, died . . . . 31 July, ,,
The Soulanges canal (1,435 miles 14 ft. navigation), from Quebec to lake Superior, opened 9 Oct. ,,
Ministry reconstituted; the hon. G. W. Ross, premier . . . . 21 Oct. ,,
Provisional boundary between Canada and Alaska, proposed by U.S.N.A., accepted by Great Britain, 20 Oct. ,,
The hon. Peter Mitchell, one of the "Fathers" of Canadian federation, born 1818, died 25 Oct. ,,
Departure of troops for S. Africa from Quebec, 30 Oct. ,,
Sir Wm. Dawson, born 1820, eminent naturalist and writer, principal and prof. nat. phil. of McGill university, Montreal, in 1855, dies 19 Nov. ,,
Lord Strathcona's offer to raise and maintain 400 men for service in S. Africa accepted . 12 Jan. 1900
Great fire in Dawson city, Klondike, estimated damage 400,000 dols. . . . . . 10 Jan. ,,
Lord Minto reviews the 2nd battalion of Canadian M.R. for S. Africa at Ottawa . . . 19 Jan. ,,
Parliament opened by lord Minto, 1 Feb.; address passed, 6 Feb.; great speech by sir Wilfrid Laurier on Canada and Great Britain . 7 Feb. ,,
Loyal mass meeting at Toronto . . . 20 Feb. ,,
Sir Wilfrid Laurier speaks warmly in favour of the S. African war; vote of confidence, 119–10, 13 March ,,

Mr. Fielding introduces the budget with an eloquent speech, reports great prosperity in 1899, the first year in which the preferential tariff, 25 per cent. reduction in favour of the United Kingdom, was in full force . . . 23 March, 1900

Attempt to blow up a lock on the Welland canal, between lakes Erie and Ontario, 21 April: 3 men convicted and sentenced to life imprisonment . . . 24 May, „

HULL, a suburb of Ottawa, nearly destroyed by fire, and part of Ottawa also burnt; 8 deaths, 18,000 homeless, 5,000 unemployed; estimated damage 3,000,000*l.*, 26, 27 April; queen's message of sympathy, 27 April; see *Mansion House*; relief fund at Ottawa, 952,182 dols. (8 Jan. 1901) 27 April „

Forest fires in N. Ontario, many settlers ruined May, „

Copyright bill passed both houses of parliament, announced . . . . 10 July „

Parliament prorogued; many laws passed during session . . . 18 July „

Great fire at Paris (Ontario); 40 houses burnt; estimated damage over 300,000 dol. . . 12 Sept. „

Dissolution of parliament . . . 9 Oct. „

Lord and lady Minto's successful tour through Western Canada to the Pacific (over 10,000 miles) completed . . . . . . 16 Oct. „

Demonstrations in honour of lord Strathcona at Montreal . . . . . . 19 Oct. „

Elections: large government majority . 7 Nov. „

Canadian troops under col. Otter warmly thanked by the queen at Windsor for their services in S. Africa . . . . 30 Nov. „

Universal mourning on the death of the queen 22 Jan. 1901

Lord Strathcona's Regiment of Horse presented with colours and medals by the king in London 15 Feb. „

Dr. Geo. Mercer Dawson, eminent geologist, born 1849, died . . . . . . 2 March, „

Sir Wilfrid Laurier upholds British policy in S. Africa, an adverse motion rejected, 144—3 12 March, „

Budget: large surplus, 8,054,715 dol. for 1900, 14 March, „

May 24 made a Bank holiday and called *Victoria Day* by bill passed . . . . . . 9 May, „

Parliament prorogued . . . . 23 May, „

Sir Thomas Galt, late chief justice in Ontario, dies, aged 86 . . . end June „

ROYAL TOUR: the duke and duchess of Cornwall warmly received at Quebec, the duke made LL.D. of the Laval university, 16 Sept.; review of troops, 17 Sept.; a loyal welcome at *Montreal*, 5 Iroquois chiefs with their squaws presented; the medical hall at McGill university opened, degrees conferred, 18, 19 Sept.; received at Ottawa by lord Minto, presented with an address at the parliament house, 20 Sept.; the duke unveils a statue of queen Victoria and presents war medals, etc., to the troops, 21 Sept.; celebrations and festivities at Winnipeg, 26 Sept.; at Regina, N.W. Territory, 27 Sept.; at Calgary war medals presented and an Indian encampment visited, 28 Sept.; warmly welcomed at Vancouver, 30 Sept., and Victoria, 1 Oct.; at Toronto 11,000 troops reviewed, lieut. Cockburn receives the V.C., 11 Oct.; London and Niagara visited, 12 Oct.; Hamilton, Kingston, and other cities visited, 14–16 Oct.; St. John, New Brunswick, 17 Oct.; "unrivalled among the naval ports of the world" were the duke's words on arriving at Halifax, Nova Scotia, 19 Oct.; see *Newfoundland*, 21 Oct. „

Canadian manufacturers' assoc. meets at Montreal, lord Strathcona, sir W. Laurier, and others present; resolutions adopted . . 6 Nov. „

Parliament opened by the governor . 13 Feb. 1902

Royal commission recommends prohibition of further immigration of Chinese labourers . Feb. „

Mr. Fielding's budget: estimated surplus (1902) 5,800,000 dol. . . . . 17 March, „

Meeting of 60 chambers of commerce on imperial trade at Toronto . . . . 4 June, „

Great sympathy with the king's illness 24 June, „

Lord Dundonald, new commander of militia, enthusiastically received . . . 25 July, „

Canadian coronation arch in Whitehall, London, erected by the government, June; finely illuminated . . . . . . 9–12 Aug. 1902

Sir Wilfrid Laurier visits England and France during summer „

Lord Minto reviews the Nat. Guards (New York State) . . . . . . 1 Sept. „

Visit of sir E. Barton, sir J. Forrest, and other Australians . . . . early Sept. „

Russian immigrants of the Dukhobor sect leaving their settlements in East Assiniboia migrate into Manitoba: they are compelled by the government to return . . . . . Oct. „

Pacific cable completed . . . . . Nov. „

American syndicate purchased 2,000,000 acres in the North-West to settle 12,500 citizens, reported 14 Nov. „

Railway collision in Ontario, 28 lives lost . 26 Dec. „

Alaska boundary treaty signed . . 24 Jan. 1903

Report of Canadian department of Indian affairs 1901–02, showing distinct progress . issued Feb. „

Paardeberg day celebrated in all the principal cities by gathering of S. African veterans . 27 Feb. „

New Brunswick general election, government secures 38 out of 46 seats . . . 28 Feb. „

Resolution advocating home rule for Ireland carried in the Dominion parliament by 102 votes to 41. Decennial redistribution bill introduced

Great floods around Montreal, much damage done. Toronto opera house destroyed by fire, 150,000 dols. loss . . . . . . 25 March „

Official return of Ontario *plébiscite*, taken 4 Dec. recording 199,692 in favour of the Liquor Act, 103,482 against, requisite majority required to bring the Act in force not obtained, published Feb. „

Sir W. Laurier introduced bill for the readjustment of the constituencies, based on census of 1901 1 April „

New provisions of Canadian customs tariff relating to German goods came into force . 16 April „

Budget estimated surplus, 1903, 13,350,000 dols. 16 April „

Sir Oliver Mowat, statesman, dies, aged 82; see *Ontario* . . . . . . 19 April „

Volcanic explosion in Rocky Mountains coal-mining region, 75 lives lost . . . 29 April „

Dock strike at Montreal, causing much inconvenience to shipping . . . 7–10 May „

Great fire at Ottawa, 1,200 people homeless, 10 May, and at St. Hyacinthe, 1,000,000 dols. damage, many shops and 250 houses burnt . 20 May „

Extension of the earl of Minto's governorship for another year from October, 1903, announced end May „

Ministry of Brit. Columbia dismissed by lt.-governor. Mr. R. McBride, leader of the opposition, forms new government, himself as premier and chief commissioner . . early June „

Great forest fires reported from Manitoba and in Eastern Canada . . . . early June „

Drought of 66 days in Montreal section broken 12 June „

House of commons rejected by 102 to 50 votes motion declaring for a fiscal policy adequately and firmly protective of national and Canadian interests . . . . . . late June „

Resignation of Mr. Blair, minister of railways and canals . . . . . . mid-July „

Great victory of conservatives in Manitoba elections . . . . 20 July „

Federal government, in view of future development of the North-West, adopts scheme of new railway from Moncton, New Brunswick, *viâ* Quebec, to Winnipeg, 2,000 miles, at cost of 12,000,000*l.*, to be constructed under specially appointed commissioners, line to be leased for 50 years to Grand Trunk Pacific co. early July, agreement between government and company signed . 27 July „

Bill for construction of the new transcontinental railway introduced in the house of assembly by sir W. Laurier . . . . . 30 July „

Fifth congress of chambers of commerce of the empire under presidency of lord Brassey, opened at Montreal . . . . . 17 Aug. „

Canadian government steamer *Neptune* sails for Hudson Bay and Arctic regions on a botanical, geological and natural history expedition, 22 Aug. „

Government's transcontinental railway proposals passed by the Dominion house of commons by 117 votes to 71 . . . . end Aug. 1903
Lord Lyveden and members of the British parliamentary party, on tour of investigation in Canada and the United States, arrive at Quebec, end Aug. Entertained by mayor of Montreal 1 Sept. „
36 hours' sitting of house of commons in consequence of opposition declining to pass clause 2 of the Grand Trunk Pacific agreement until government furnishes fuller information, 3-4 Sept. „
Ontario conservative convention re-affirms its vote for preferential trade within the empire, mid Sept. „
Reports of serious reduction of yield of crops by storms officially contradicted, and stating that 90 to 95 per cent. of estimated crop for 1903 (57,000,000 bush.) will be marketed . 18 Sept. „
Alaska award signed at London . . 20 Oct. „

CANAL BOATS, used as dwellings; an act passed for their registration and regulation, 14 Aug. 1877 (40 & 41 Vict. c. 60); amended, 1884. M. Rigoni's application of mechanical traction to canal boats by means of an endless cable of Bessemer steel, set in motion by fixed engines; tried between Antwerp and Liège, Sept. 1882.

CANALS (artificial watercourses). The imperial canal in China, commenced in the 13th century, is said to pass over 2000 miles, and to 41 cities; see *Ganges, Suez, Panamá, Punjaub*, and *Germany*, 1899.

The canal of Languedoc (Canal du Midi) which joins the Mediterranean with the Atlantic Ocean, was completed 1681
Orleans from the Loire to the Seine commenced . 1675
Burgundy canal 1775
That between the Baltic and the North Sea, at Kiel, opened 1785
That of Bourbon, between the Seine and Oise, commenced 1790
Seine and Loire, opened 1791
That from the Cattegat to the Baltic . 1794–1800
The great American Erie canal, 363 miles in length, was commenced 1817
That of Amsterdam to the sea 1819–25
Ganges canal completed 1854
Canal between Amsterdam and the North Sea opened . . . . . . 1 Nov. 1876
Grand canal connecting the Atlantic and Mediterranean (between Bordeaux and Narbonne) proposed . . . . . May, 1884
Baltic and North Sea canal (61 miles long) proposed Jan. 1884; completed, see *Baltic* and *Kiel*, 1895.
Inland navigation congress at Brussels opened 25 May, 1885
Manchester ship canal (see *Manchester*) . „
Railway and Canal Traffic Act passed . 10 Aug. 1888
Fourth international congress on inland navigation, Manchester, 28–31 July, 1890; fifth, Paris, 21 July, 1892
Joint parliamentary committee sitting . June, 1893
Canals protection (London) act, passed . 25 July, 1898
Canal embankment in the Stour valley gave way, near Dudley port; market flooded; much damage 9 Sept. 1899
The Michigan-Mississippi (cost over 30,000,000 dol.) opened . . . . . . 1 Jan. 1900
Palontnotchnie canal, from the mouth of the Danube through Russian territory, opened 5 Oct. „

BRITISH CANALS.

The first was by Henry I., when the Trent was joined to the Witham, 1134.
Francis Mathew in 1656, and Andrew Yarranton in 1677, in vain strongly urged improvement in internal navigation.
In England there are said to be 2800 miles of canals, and 2500 miles of rivers, taking the length of those only that are navigable—total, 5300 miles. (Mr. Porter, in 1851, says 4000 miles.)
In Ireland there are 300 miles of canals; 150 of navigable rivers; and 60 miles of the Shannon, navigable below Limerick; in all, 510 miles. *Williams.*
The prosperity of canals, for a time largely checked by the formation of railways, is now greatly revived; and railways are connected with them (1878-1889).

INLAND NAVIGATION.

New river commenced 1609
Brought to London 1613
Thames made navigable to Oxford 1624
Kennet navigable to Reading 1715
Caermarthenshire canal 1756
Droitwich to the Severn . . . . . . „
Duke of Bridgewater's navigation (first great canal) commenced (see *Bridgewater*) 1759
Northampton navigation 1761
Dublin to the Shannon (the Grand) . . 1765–1788
Stafford and Worcester, commenced . . . „
Grand Trunk (Trent and Mersey) commenced by Brindley 1766
Forth to Clyde, commenced 1768
Birmingham to Bilston . . . . . . „
Oxford to Coventry, commenced 1769
Lea made navigable from Hertford to Ware, 1739; to London 1770
Leeds to Liverpool . . . . „
Monkland (Scotland), commenced . . . . „
Ellesmere and Chester 1772
Basingstoke canal begun . . . . . . „
Liverpool to Wigan 1774
Stroud to the Severn 1775
Staffordshire canal, begun 1776
Stourbridge canal, completed . . . . „
Runcorn to Manchester . . . . . . „
Mersey, opened 1777
Chesterfield to the Trent . . . . . „
Belfast to Lough Neagh 1783
Severn to the Thames, completed 1789
Forth and Clyde, completed 1790
Bradford, completed . . . . . . „
Grand Junction, begun . . . . . . „
Birmingham and Coventry . . . . . „
Monasterevan to Athy 1791
Worcester and Birmingham . . . . . „
Manchester, Bolton, and Bury . . . . „
Warwick and Birmingham 1793
Crinan, Argyllshire, cut 1793–1801
Barnsley, cut 1794
Rochdale, act passed . . . . . . „
Huddersfield, act passed . . . . . . „
Derby, completed . . . . „
Hereford and Gloucester 1796
Paddington Canal begun 1798
Kennet and Avon, opened 1799
Peak-forest canal, completed 1800
Thames to Fenny Stratford . . . . . „
Buckingham canal 1801
Grand Surrey, act passed . . . . . „
Brecknock canal 1802
Caledonian canal begun 1803
Ellesmere aqueduct 1805
Ashby-de-la-Zouch, opened . . . . . „
Royal Military canal, Hythe to Rye . . . 1807
Aberdeen, completed . . . . . . „
Glasgow and Ardrossan, opened 1811
Leeds and Liverpool, opened 1816
Wye and Avon . . . . „
Edinburgh and Glasgow Union 1818
Sheffield, completed 1819
Regent's canal, opened 1820
Caledonian canal, completed . . 30 Oct. 1822
Birmingham and Liverpool, begun 1826
Gloucester and Berkeley, ship-canal, completed . 1827
Norwich and Lowestoft navigation opened . . . 1831
Manchester ship canal opened 1894
Medway and Thames canal projected 1902

CANARY ISLANDS (N. W. Africa), known to the ancients as the *Fortunate Isles*. They were re-discovered by a Norman named Bethencourt, about 1400; his descendants sold them to the Spaniards, who became masters, 1483. The *canary-bird*, a native of these isles, brought to England about 1500. Teneriffe is the largest island. *Ferro*, the most south-western, was appointed the French meridian by Louis XIII. in 1632. Destructive floods in N. Canary, estimated damage, 70,000*l.*, reported 22 Feb. 1896.

CANCER HOSPITAL (Free), Brompton, S.W. London, was founded in 1851 by the late Dr. William Marsden (born Aug. 1796), who actively superintended it till his death, 16 Jan. 1867. The foundation-stone of the building was laid by Miss (afterwards Baroness) Burdett Coutts, an early liberal benefactor, 30 May, 1859. See *Free Hospital*, founded by Dr. Marsden in 1828, and *Middlesex Hospital*, 1900; Dr. John Gilman, in Chicago, reports treatment of the disease with Röntgen rays, Nov. 1901–1903.

CANCER RESEARCH FUND, had its origin in 1901 for the investigation of the cause, nature, and treatment of cancer. 100,000*l.* stated to be necessary as capital. 5,000*l.* contributed by Goldsmiths' company, and 25,000*l.* from other sources, appeal in *Times*, 18 April, 1902. Scheme adopted by Roy. Colleges of Physicians and Surgeons, 4 July. First meeting of executive committee held, London, 30 July (*Times*, 31 July). Dr. E. T. Bashford appointed superintendent of cancer research, and visited Germany to inquire into position of investigation in that country. First annual meeting, 30 July, 1903. Address by Mr. A. J. Balfour. Beneficial effects of Röntgen rays on superficial cancer reported, no progress made in treatment of malignant growths. About 74,000*l.* received to Sept. 1903, including 20,000*l.* contributed by Mr. W. Waldorf Astor. President, the prince of Wales. Offices, Examination hall, Victoria embankment.

CANDAHAR, a province of Afghanistan held by Duranis and Ghilzais. Candahar, the capital, is said to have been founded by Alexander the Great (334–323 B.C.) After being subject to successive rulers of India, it was made capital of Afghanistan by Ahmed Shah, 1747, but the seat of government was transferred to Cabul in 1774.

Taken and held by the British 7 Aug. 1839 to 22 May, 1842
Gen. Nott (with major Rawlinson and major Lane) defeated the Afghans near here . Jan. and June, „
The government of Candahar conferred on Shere Ali (a cousin of the late ameer Shere Ali), with the title of *Wali*, by the viceroy of India . April, 1880
Shere Ali resigned, and went to Calcutta in Dec. „
After the disaster of Maiwand, 27 July, 1880, Candahar was held by British during the winter 1880-1
In the house of lords on the earl of Lytton's motion to retain Candahar, 165 voted for its retention, 76 against . . . . . 5 March, 1881
The house of commons, on Mr. Stanhope's motion for retention, 336 voted against it; 216 for it, 24–26 March, „
Candahar evacuated by the British, 16–21 April, „
Sirdar Kashim Khan (on behalf of Abdur-rahman, ameer of Cabul) enters Candahar . 16 April, „
Invasion of Ayoob Khan; he defeats the ameer's army at Karez-i-Atta, 26 July; enters Candahar 30 July, „
After a severe conflict, 22 Sept., the ameer enters Candahar . . . . . 30 Sept. „

See *Afghanistan*.

CANDIA, the mediæval name (now disused) of Crete, of which Candia is the capital, an island in the Mediterranean Sea, mythically celebrated for its 100 cities, its centre Mount Ida, the laws of its king Minos, and its labyrinth to secure the Minotaur. It was conquered by the Romans 68 B.C. Population estimated 1889, 210,000; 1897, 250,000; 1900, 301,577 (including 33,422 Mahometans).

Seized by the Saracens . . . . . A.D. 823
Re-taken by the Greeks 961
Sold to the Venetians . . . . Aug. 1204
Rebelled; reduced 1364
Gained by the Turks, after a twenty-four years' siege, during which about 30,000 men perished . 1669
Ceded to the Egyptian pacha 1830
Restored to Turkey 1840
Insurrections suppressed, 1841; by conciliation . 1858
Persecution of the Christians . . 31 July, 1859
The Christians demand redress of grievances, June, 1866
They establish a "sacred battalion" . 12 Aug. „
Publish an address to the powers protecting Greece, 21 Aug. 1866
The Cretan general assembly proclaim the abolition of the Turkish authority in Candia, and union with Greece . . . . . 2 Sept.
Commencement of hostilities: the Turkish army commanded by Mustapha Pacha . . 11 Sept. „
Greeks victorious in several conflicts, Sept. and Oct. „
The Greek steamer *Panhellenion* begins to convey volunteers, &c., to Candia . . . . Oct. „
Monastery of Arkadi besieged; blown up by the defenders; great loss on both sides . 26 Nov. „
Proposition of Austria, Prussia, Italy, and Switzerland to the sultan to give up Candia, 28 March; declined . . . . . 31 March, 1867
Many defenceless villages said to be burnt June, „
Collective note from Russia and other powers urging the Porte to suspend hostilities . 15 June, „
Indecisive conflicts . . . . . July, „
The *Arkadi* Greek steamer, after running the blockade 22 times, landing Greek volunteers, and bringing away women and children, destroyed by the Turkish vessel *Izeddin* . . . 10 Aug. „
Assembly of delegates meet the vizier . 22 Sept. „
Insurrection subsides; the grand vizier arrives, 28 Sept.; proclaims an amnesty, and promises reforms . . . . . 5 Nov.
Successful blockade running by the Greeks; Omar Pasha, the Turkish general, resigns his command in the island . . . . . Nov. „
The delegates' demands granted . . . 11 Dec. „
The war renewed (indecisive) . . . . Feb. 1868
The *Petropaulakes* landed about 2500 men on opposite sides of the isle, 10 Dec., but failed in their attempt to unite; after several skirmishes, in which they lost about 650 men, all surrendered, (and were sent to Greece) . . . 26 Dec. „
The provisional government surrendered 30 Dec. „
The new Turkish governor, Omer Fenizi, arrived, and the blockade ended . . . 8 March, 1869
The "Organic statute," a scheme of reform, compiled . . . . . about 1871
Insurrection announced, with provisional government . . . . . about 20 Dec. 1877
Union with Greece proclaimed, 31 Jan.; decreed by a general assembly . . . 11 Feb. 1878
Insurrection unsubdued; anarchy; Berlin treaty declares for enforcing legal and political reforms, 13 July, „
Pacification by Mukhtar Pasha through concession of self-government, &c. . . . . Oct. „
The Pact of Halepa drawn up under British influence, sanctioned by the porte . . . Nov. „
Insurrection on account of religious difficulties 8 Feb. 1884
The christian notables appeal to the sultan for a christian governor, and to Greece and other powers for mediation . . about 1 March, „
Photiades, reappointed governor for five years announced . . . . . 6 March, „
Temporary disturbances, order restored 1–6 May, 1887
Anarchy through party strife of Christians and Mahometans, May–June; Turkish troops sent to Crete, 13 June; provisional government formed to restore order . . . . . 13 June, 1889
Mahmoud Djellalledin pasha, Turkish commissioner, well received; agitation calmed by his inquiries, June 14 *et seq.* An insurgent assembly demands a constituent assembly, judicial reforms, and dismissal of the governor, the people neutral about 1 July; the sultan sends 20,000*l.* T., 6 July; Mahmoud Djellalledin pasha informs a deputation that their demands must be referred to the sultan, 8 July; he is suddenly recalled, 8 July, „
Asserted influence of Greek agitators, 22 July; insurrection increasing; call for annexation to Greece, or British protection, about 25 July; Djavad pasha arrives to take command of the troops . . . . . 1 Aug. „
Riza pasha appointed temporary governor, with extra powers for repressing disorder . 4 Aug. „
Fighting going on, villages burnt, reported 5 Aug. „
Note from the Greek government to the powers, urging intervention in Crete, 6 Aug.; they decline, leaving the settlement to the Sultan, 9–12 Aug.; about 17,000 Turkish troops in Crete, reported . . . . . 7 Aug. „

Riza Pasha, the governor, recalled; replaced by Shakir pasha, who arrives with plenary powers, 23 Aug.; proclaims martial law . . 14 Aug. 1889

Partial submission of the insurgents; amnesty promised . . . . . . 17 Aug. ,,

Tranquillity gradually restored by Turkish moderate firmness . . . . . . Sept. ,,

The Notables address the sultan, thanking him for his good government . . . 28 Jan. 1890

Turkish circular to the great powers, reporting the pacification of Crete, 6 March; amnesty, except to 18 persons convicted of crimes, announced . . . . 11 March, ,,

Great return of refugees from Greece about 10 May, ,,

Djevad pasha appointed governor about 7 July, in room of Shakir pasha . . . . . ,,

Mahmoud Djellalledin pasha appointed governor (Djevad pasha having been made grand vizier) about . . . . . . 8 Sept. 1891

Disturbances; several conflicts with the Turkish troops . . . . . . Oct. *et seq.* 1892

Turkhan pasha appointed governor; discontent among the people, reported . 13 Aug. 1894

Alexander Karatheodory pasha (a Christian) appointed governor . . . . March, 1895

Reforms demanded by the assembly; refusal of the Porte; reported . . . . 12 Nov. ,,

Sanguinary conflict between Turkish troops and Cretans at Kampos . . . 20 Nov. ,,

Turkish troops defeated with heavy loss at Vryses, in Apokorona . . . . 10 Dec. ,,

Reinforcements sent; prisoners released by request of the Greek consul; reported . . 26 Dec. ,,

Renewed conflicts and murders between Turks and Christians, intervention of the Greek government; reported . . . . . 23 Feb. 1896

Karatheodory, gov.-general, resigns, 27 Feb.; succeeded by Turkhan pasha . . . 6 March, ,,

General amnesty proclaimed . . . 18 March, ,,

Serious conflicts between Turks and Christians, many killed; reported . . . 23 April, ,,

Krape, in the mountains of Sphakia, held by the Cretan reform committee; negotiations between the Greek government and the porte; reported 7 May, ,,

Turkish garrison besieged at Vamos, 17 May; continued hostilities; siege raised by Abdullah pasha, the new governor . . . 30 May, ,,

Turkhan pasha recalled . . . . 21 May, ,,

Massacre of Christians in Canea without provocation by the Turkish soldiery . . . 24 May, ,,

H.M.S. *Hood* and other foreign warships arrive 26 May, *et seq.* ,,

Turkish troops burn and sack Tsivara and other villages; reported . . . . . 1 June ,,

Anarchy and destruction over the western portion of the island; increased excesses by the Turks; state of siege proclaimed; reported . . 4 June, ,,

Turkish troops defeated at Aghia . . . 11 June, ,,

Galata and other villages looted and burnt by the Turks, 6–10 June; subscriptions at Alexandria for relief of the sufferers . . . . June, ,,

Protest of the foreign consuls submitted to the governor-gen. . . . . . 12 June, ,,

The Cretan relief committee at Athens appeal to the world for assistance . . . 15 June, ,,

The Turkish proclamation promising reforms, etc., discredited; the Cretans demand securities 19 June, ,,

Frequent encounters and massacres by Turkish troops, reported . . . . 19-21 June, ,,

Georgi Pasha Berovitch, prince of Samos, appointed governor-general of Crete, reported . 28 June, ,,

The Cretan committee issue a circular calling for a provisional government and union with Greece 29 June, ,,

The powers recommend that the porte should grant a Christian governor-general, the revival of the Halepa constitution, the immediate convocation of the assembly, and a general amnesty; all granted . . . . 3 July, ,,

The Christian deputies arrive at Canea 11-12 July, ,,

The assembly opened by the governor . 13 July ,,

Desultory fighting near Candia, Retimo, and other places . . . . July, ,,

Villages destroyed, 3 Aug.; anarchy and rioting at Heraklion, 4 Aug.; 30,000 Mahometans enter the town, flight of Christians . . 5-9 Aug. ,,

Reform committee dissolved; new revolutionary assembly formed at Canea; they profess submission to the premier and deputies, and await the action of the powers, reported . . 9 Aug 1896

The monastery of St. John at Anopolis attacked and burnt, 32 men, women, and children and 3 monks killed, churches and other villages burnt . . . . 8 Aug. ,,

Zihni pasha, special commissioner, and Ibrahim pasha, military commander, arrive in Canea 13 Aug. ,,

Four Christian villages and two monasteries sacked 11 Aug. ,,

Greek officers and volunteers land on the W. and E. coasts . . . . . 16 Aug. *et seq.* ,,

Fighting at Tenedos in Candia, reported . 16 Aug. ,,

Turkish troops besieged by Christians at Kasteli, reported . . . . 24 Aug. ,,

The ambassador's scheme of reforms; political independence of the island, etc.; Christian governor for 5 years to be appointed; accepted by the porte, 25, 29 Aug.; by the Cretan deputies, 1 Sept. and by the insurgents . . . 6 Sept. ,,

Devastation and massacre at Platania, near Canea, reported . . . . 29 Aug. ,,

New "organic statute" comprising the scheme of reforms, promulgated . . . . 2 Sept. ,,

Georgi Pasha Berovitch re-appointed as the first Christian governor-gen., reported 11 Sept. ,,

Three villages looted and burnt in Monofatsi by armed Mahometans from Candia, reported 27 Sept. ,,

Saadeddin pasha, the sultan's envoy, recalled, through the remonstrances of the ambassadors, announced . . . . 15 Dec. ,,

Organisation of temporary gendarmerie proceeding . . . . 13 Jan. 1897

Anarchy and murders at Heraklion, Retimo, Galata, and Canea, villages burnt . 14 Jan.–5 Feb. ,,

Exodus of 5,000 refugees in foreign war vessels to the Piræus and Greek islands . . 6-7 Feb. ,,

Canea desolate; 2 entire streets, the bishop's house and schools destroyed, 20 lives lost; fires suppressed by bluejackets from the British fleet ,,

Major Bor appointed commandant of the gendarmerie; arrives and takes active measures; chief offices guarded by marines . . 7 Feb. ,,

Mahometans capture rifles from the arsenal at Heraklion; panic among the Christians 7 Feb. ,,

Desperate fight at Kisamo Kasteli; women and children killed; 22 Mahometans killed . 7 Feb. ,,

H.M.S. *Revenge*, flagship of rear-admiral Harris, arrives at Retimo and H.M.S *Trafalgar* at Heraklion; conflicts at Sitia, villages burnt and eastern districts blockaded by Christians, reported . . . . 9-10 Feb. ,,

Mahometans plunder Heraklion . . 11 Feb. ,,

Desultory fighting; flotilla of torpedo boats, under prince George of Greece, arrives at Canea 12 Feb. ,,

Halepa declared neutral territory by the Cretan insurgents and the foreign consuls, announced 12 Feb. ,,

Georgi Pasha Berovitch, governor-gen., resigns to Mushavir Ismail Bey, and takes refuge on the Russian flagship off Halepa, 13 Feb.; Ibrahim pasha, military gov. also resigns . . 14 Feb. ,,

The Greek consuls leave Canea and other places; Canea bombarded by the Christians, frequent conflicts, with much bloodshed . . . 14 Feb. ,,

Naval occupation of Canea, Heraklion, and Retimo by the allied powers; the Greek commodore called on to withdraw . . . . 15 Feb. ,,

Greek forces, under col. Vassos, land at Columbari; fighting reported near Heraklion . 15 Feb. ,,

Col. Vassos issues a proclamation in the name of king George; the fort of Aghia attacked and captured, 400 Mahometans taken prisoners, two Greek officers killed . . . . . 16 Feb. ,,

The porte appeals to the powers to intervene 16 Feb. ,,

The Italian admiral, on behalf of the powers, warns the Greek commodore that any attack on the seaports will be repelled by force; the Greek government concurs and the Greek consulate is reopened; the Greek army remains in the interior 17 Feb. ,,

Massacre of prisoners at Sitia by Christians, 18 Feb. ,,

Photiades Karatheodery pasha made governor, and Saadeddin pasha military commander; Turkey preparing for war . . . . . 18 Feb. 1897
Massacre of 104 Mahometans at Sarakina in Selino, including 23 women and 61 children, reported 18 Feb. ,,
The Greek army attacks the Turkish outposts at Platania; the tower of Bukolies captured by the Greeks, 7 Greeks killed, reported . . 19 Feb. ,,
The foreign consuls reject the proclamation of col. Vassos concerning the annexation of Crete by Greece . . . . . 18 Feb. ,,
Circular note from lord Salisbury to the powers recommending autonomy for Crete, announced 18 Feb. ,,
Col. Vassos proclaims the occupation of Crete by Greece at Retimo and Candia . . 20 Feb. ,,
Insurgents take possession of the heights above Halepa, and are fired on from the Turkish outposts and bombarded by the foreign squadron, 21 Feb., 3 men killed (Turks afterwards declared to be the aggressors); constant firing kept up by the Turks on the insurgents and on the Greek outposts at Platania but not returned 22, 23 Feb. ,,
Turks and Mahometans (2,000) besieged at Candano . . . . Feb. ,,
Seven days' armistice agreed to in Selino 22 Feb. ,,
The zone of protection under the powers extended 25 Feb. ,,
The Christians blockaded at Hierapetra, liberated by the Italian warship *Etna*; announced 25 Feb. ,,
Sharp fight at Malaxa and near Retimo with bloodshed . . . . . . 27, 28 Feb. ,,
Union with Greece demanded by the insurgents, Tewfik pasha, new military governor, arrives 28 Feb. ,,
Fort Stavros captured by the Cretans, 3,000 Turks prisoners; reported . . . . 1 March, ,,
Mutiny of the Turkish gendarmerie at Canea suppressed, Suleiman Bey (col.) and 2 others killed 2 March, ,,
Collective and identical note from the powers informing the Greek government of their decision to give autonomy to Crete under Turkish suzerainty, and withdrawal of the Greek forces within 6 days demanded . . . . . 2 March, ,,
The Greek government declines to accede to the request of the powers . . . 8 March, ,,
Death of Mgr. Timotheos, archbishop of Candia on landing at the Piræus, 2 March; state funeral, 3 March, ,,
Declaration of neutrality and unanimity by the foreign admirals . . . . 4 March, ,,
Turkish outrages continue . . . . 8 March, ,,
Col. Vassos ordered by his government to avoid conflicts, desultory fighting at Akrotiri, on the east coast; Greeks ordered to quit Canea 8 March ,,
Sir A. Biliotti, British consul, with a mixed foreign force under capt. Rainier, of H.M.S. *Rodney*, rescues the besieged Mahometans (about 2,000) in Candano . . . . . . 9 March, ,,
Greek volunteers (500) landed . . . 11 March, ,,
The fortress of Spinalonga bombarded by insurgents and Greeks . . . . . 12 March, ,,
The interior of Crete held by Greeks and insurgents; Mahometans rescued by detachments from the warships from Kisamo Kasteli 14 March, ,,
International gendarmerie disbanded, col. Bor leaves Canea . . . . . 15 March, ,,
The Greek fleet leaves Cretan waters . 16 March, ,,
Autonomy proclaimed in Crete . . . 17 March, ,,
Col. Chermside appointed British military commissioner in Crete . . . . . 17 March, ,,
Blockade of the island by the six powers, begun 21 March; the Greek government protests 26 March, ,,
Conflicts near Candia, Malaxa, and Retimo 16–23 March, ,,
British and foreign troops landed 23–24 March, ,,
Desperate fighting between Turks and insurgents at Malaxa; Malaxa bombarded by the foreign fleet . . . . 25 March, ,,
Turkish troops fire on a body of insurgents with a flag of truce . . . . . 28 March, ,,
Fort Butsunaria occupied by a foreign contingent 29 March, ,,
Desultory fighting near Retimo and Canea; insurgents driven back, 2 killed, by the foreign bombardment; Fort Izedin occupied by a foreign contingent; villages burnt by Turkish troops 30, 31 March, 1897
Mahometans attack the insurgents near Canea, and are afterwards disarmed by European troops 3–4 April, ,,
Turks repulsed near Retimo . . . 5 April, ,,
Fruitless negotiations . . . . . 8–18 April, ,,
Insurgents bombarded by the warships at Kisamo-Kasteli; refugees taken away by foreign ships 9 April, ,,
Insurgents bombarded by the Turkish warships, Kalyves destroyed . . . . . 15 April, ,,
Bashi-bozouks disarmed at Canea . . 15 April, ,,
Relaxation of the blockade; 65,000 persons in receipt of relief . . . . 24–28 April, ,,
Greek army recalled; leaves . . . 9–26 May, ,,
Insurgents retire after a severe conflict with Bashi-bozouks at Elia; major Mustapha bey killed 9–26 May, ,,
Insurgents gradually disarming . . . May, ,,
Mahomedan raid from Candia, Christian village burnt, 14 persons killed. . . . 29 May, ,,
The insurgents institute a provisional government; reported . . . . . . 2 June, ,,
Mahomedan outrages on Christians near Candia, Kani-Kasteli and other places burnt, many killed, 22–25 June; another raid . . . . 7 July, ,,
The Christian delegates style their body at Armeni the "General insurrectionary assembly of Cretans," Dr. Sphakianaki president, and present a document to the foreign admirals announcing their constitution . . . . . . 14 July, ,,
Conflicts between Bashi-bozouks and Christians; reported . . . . 13 July, ,,
Mahometan outrages, murders, &c. 15, 16 July, ,,
Mahometans prohibited from carrying arms, 16 July; 20 arrested and taken on board five European ships . . . . . 18 July, ,,
Djevad pasha arrives as military commander at Canea . . . . 24 July, ,,
An assembly of deputies proclaim their acceptance of autonomy 1 Aug.; notified to the admirals Nov. ,,
An international commission appointed as a court of summary jurisdiction for the island, reported 15 Aug.; M. Vandenbrook (France) president 21 Aug. ,,
The porte protests to the powers against the commission; announced . . . . 21 Sept. ,,
Suda placed under the jurisdiction of capt. Amoretti; reported . . . . . 26 Sept. ,,
Col. Schäffer chosen by the powers as gov.-general of Crete; reported 22 Oct.; opposed by the porte, 27 Oct.; and dropped . . 29 Nov. ,,
International court holds its first sitting at Canea 3 Nov. ,,
Appeal from the Cretan assembly to the powers for relief from tribute to the sultan through poverty; reported 6 Dec.; again . . . . . 27 Dec. ,,
Perivolaki besieged by insurgents to avenge a murder: reported. . . . . 8 Dec. ,,
Great excitement in Canea through the murder of a Christian merchant, 13 Dec.; public funeral 15 Dec. ,,
International committee of consuls agree to Bozo Petrovitch (Montenegrin), proposed as governor, about 19 Dec. 1897; rejected; prince George of Greece proposed by Russia, Great Britain and France, 29 Dec.; opposed by the sultan, Germany, and Austria, Jan. 1898 (deferred).
Distress in the island increasing . . . Dec. ,,
Fifteen Christians killed by an ambuscade of Bashi-bozouks; announced . . . . . 28 Dec. ,,
The Cretan assembly address a memorial to the powers against the ambassadors' proposals for the government of the island . . . Jan. 1898
Candia pillaged by Bashi-bozouks; reported 20 Jan.; 20 of them taken prisoners and embarked on H.M.S. *Hood*; Edhem pasha appointed governor of Candia in consequence of the protests of the admirals . . . . 23 Jan. ,,
Memorial from the Cretan assembly respecting the raids, &c., to the admirals . . . 24 Jan. ,,
Mahomedan raids at Retimo, and great distress; reported . . . . 31 Jan. ,,
Refugees (506) starving near Candia, relief afforded by officers and men of H.M.S. *Anson* . Feb. ,,

German and Austrian troops withdrawn from Canea . . . 16 March and 12 April, 1898
Turkish cordon removed from Canea; outposts taken by international troops, 2 April; peaceable meetings of Christians and Mahometans at markets instituted by Sir A. Biliotti, near Candia, under British protection . . . 6 April *et seq.* ,,
The admirals decide that the island shall be divided into 4 provinces under the 4 powers, 10 April; military tribunals instituted . . . . May, ,,
Modus vivendi committee of the national assembly, under supervision of the admirals, carries on the government, June; the porte protests against the provisional *régime* arranged by the 4 powers (the Cretan assembly to govern the interior and the admirals the coast towns), 8 July, ,,
British troops attacked in Candia by Mahometans and Turkish troops dissatisfied with the measures taken by the admirals, 4 hours fighting, lieut. Robt. Haldane and 12 British soldiers and marines killed, 42 (6 mortally) wounded, about 500 Christians massacred, 29 Bashi-Bozouks and 4 Turkish soldiers killed; Mr. L. A. Calocherino, British vice-consul, and his servants, massacred, the town looted and set fire to by Bashi-Bozouks, 6 Sept.; foreign consulates looted and burnt, 7 Sept.; Edhem pasha, the governor, held responsible for the massacre by his inaction (succeeded by col. Chevki, 29 Sept.); foreign reinforcements landed, martial law proclaimed, 9 Sept. ,,
Two British soldiers murdered by Bashi-Bozouks 10 Sept. ,,
Adm. Noel (K.C.M.G., Nov.) in H.M.S. *Revenge*, arrives, 12 Sept.; British ultimatum: surrender of ringleaders, Turkish disarmament, &c., 13 Sept.; demands acceded to, reinforcements arrive, 14 Sept.; prisoners transferred to British warships, 16 Sept.; a stringent ultimatum despatched to the sultan by the four powers 5 Oct.; accepted, 16, 20 Oct.; 17 murderers hanged at Candia by British authority, 19, 29 Oct., 7 Nov.; 2 shot, 22 Nov.; others sentenced to life imprisonment . . . . 30 Nov. ,,
Turkish troops evacuate the island . 19 Oct.–Nov. ,,
Exodus of Mahometans . . . . 7 Nov. ,,
Ismail Bey, ex-civil gov.-gen. of Crete, leaves, 11 Nov. ,,
General peace and order; British administration in Candia and 6 provinces very successful, 21 Nov. ,,
Internat. court-martial opened at Candia, 3 Turks sentenced to death . . . . 21 Nov. ,,
Prince George of Greece appointed by the 4 powers high commissioner of Crete for 3 years under the sultan's suzerainty, 26 Nov.; agreed to by the porte . . . . 7 Dec. ,,
Sir A. Biliotti returns to Candia from a tour of the 6 provinces under British governors, 1 Dec. ,,
Mahometan petition to the queen, begging for British protection, and that sir H. Chermside may remain . . . . . . 6 Dec. ,,
Blockade of Crete abolished . . . 5 Dec. ,,
The executive committee resign, their demands being granted . . . . . . 7 Dec. ,,
Prince George well received at Canea; the Christians express gratitude to England and the queen . . . . . . 21 Dec. ,,
Prince George visits the mosque, 22 Dec.; lays the foundation-stone of new Christian schools (given by the czar) at Canea . . . . 26 Dec. ,,
Adm. sir Gerard Noel presented with an address of gratitude; leaves . . . . . 27 Dec. ,,
Commission appointed to draw up a constitution, inaugural meeting, prince George presides, 12 Jan. 1899
Sir Edward Law (financier) received by the prince at Canea . . . . . . 9 Jan. ,,
Prince George warmly received at Retimo, *fêtes*, &c.; visits the monastery of Arcadi; opens 2 new schools . . . . 21, 22, 23 Jan. ,,
Prince George opens the assembly; new constitution voted; M. Sphakianaki elected president, 20, 21 Feb. ,,
Great decrease in crime and contraband trade March, ,,
Amnesty granted to political offenders (between 16 Sept. 1896 and 9 Dec. 1898), with some exceptions . . . . April, ,,
M. de Bloney, a Swiss, financial adviser to prince George, arrives . . . . . 8 April, 1899
Loan of 9,000,000 drachma, 3 per cent., voted by the assembly, reported . . . . 27 April, ,,
The princess of Wales visits Crete . 27-30 April, ,,
The first administrative (autonomous) council (4 Christians and 1 Mahometan) formed . 30 April, ,,
Prince George visits Candia; festivities, &c., 12-14 May; he returns to Halepa after a successful tour in the Retimo district . . . 21 May, ,,
Mahometan emigration continues . . . May, ,,
Cretan exploration fund formed; prince George patron; excavations under the direction of Messrs. Evans and Hogarth (British school at Athens); the palace of Minos at Knossos and the "Labyrinth" (about 2,000 B.C.) discovered, &c. . . . . . . May, *et seq.* ,,
The British resign, 21 July; Cretan government begins at Candia, 24 July; the Russians evacuate Retimo . . . . 27 July, ,,
Queen of Greece welcomed at Canea, 19 Sept.-5 Oct. ,,
Anniversary of prince George's arrival in Crete, celebrated . . . . . . 21 Dec. ,,
Prince George visits Europe to negotiate for union with Greece, Oct. 1900; returns . 15 Dec. 1900
Union with Greece rejected by the powers, 22 Feb. 1901
M. Venezelo, councillor, suggests a temporary principality in Crete; is dismissed from office, April, ,,
Prince George opens the assembly; resolution appealing for union with Greece passed by the chamber, 31 May; again refused by the powers, the *status quo* to be maintained . 18 June, ,,
Further excavations: the palace of Phæstos in the south revealed 1900–1901
Prince George re-appointed high commissioner for 3 years . . . . 15 Dec. ,,
Three years' excavations at Knossos completed; another Mycenæan palace discovered near Phæstos . . . . 24 May 1902
Four Mussulman boatmen murdered at Sphakia, reported . . . . 9 June, ,,
Elections give the government a majority, early Apr. 1903
Further discoveries at Knossos reported . 11 Apr. ,,

CANDLEMAS DAY, 2 Feb. is kept in the church in memory of the purification of the Virgin, who presented the infant Jesus in the Temple. From the number of candles lit (it is said in memory of Simeon's song, *Luke* ii. 32, "a Light to lighten the Gentiles," &c.), this festival was called Candlemas, as well as the Purification. Its origin is ascribed by Bede to pope Gelasius in the 5th century, by others to the Roman emperor Justinian, 541. Some antiquarians trace a connection between the Christian festival with the great feast of expiation and purification called *Februa*, held 15 Feb. in ancient Rome. The practice of lighting the churches was forbidden by order of council, 2 Edw. VI. 1548; but is still continued in the church of Rome. Candlemas is a Scotch quarter-day.

CANDLES. The Roman candles were composed of string surrounded by wax, or dipped in pitch. Splinters of wood fatted were used for light among the lower classes in England, about 1300. Wax candles were little used, and dipped candles were usually burnt. The Wax Chandlers' company was incorporated 1483. Mould candles are said to be the invention of the sieur Le Brez, of Paris. Spermaceti candles are of modern manufacture. The Chinese make candles from wax obtained from the candleberry-tree (*myrica cerifera*). The duty upon candles made in England, imposed in 1709, amounted to about 500,000*l.* annually when it was repealed in 1831. Improvements in the manufacture of stearine candles, due to the researches on oils and fats by Chevreul, 1811-23. He died 9 April, 1889, aged 102. The plaited wick introduced by Cambacères 1825, improved by Wilson 1844, did away with snuffing. At Price's manufactory at Lambeth, the principles involved in many patents are carried into execution; including those of Gwynne (1840), Jones and Price (1842), and Wilson in 1844, for candles which require no snuffing. When tallow was high in price palm and cocoa-nut oils were for a time extensively used. The discovery of paraffin by Dr. James Young, 1847-50, introduced a material which has practically superseded all others. Price's patent candle company, established 1847, incorporated by act of parliament 1848 and 1857, have the largest candle-making works in the world. In 1870 the manufacture of candles from a mineral substance named *ozokerit* began. *Cricklite* in vogue, 1903.

CANDLESTICKS (or *lamp-stands*) with seven branches were regarded as emblematical of the priest's office, and were engraven on their seals, cups, and tombs. Bezaleel made "a candlestick of pure gold" for the tabernacle, B.C. 1491 (*Exod.* xxxvii. 17). Candlesticks were used in Britain in the days of king Edgar, 959 ("silver candelabra and gilt candelabra well and honourably made").

CANDY or **KANDY** (Ceylon), was taken by a British detachment, 20 Feb. 1803, who capitulated 23 June following, on account of its unhealthiness, and many were treacherously massacred at Colombo, 26 June. The war was renewed in Oct. 1814; the king was made prisoner by general Brownrigg, 19 Feb. 1815; and the sovereignty was vested in Great Britain, 2 March, 1815. Candy has many objects of interest; among these are the governor's house, one of the finest structures in Ceylon, and the Buddhist temple, "the palace of the tooth," containing, it is said, a tooth of Gautauma the Buddha, the most sacred spot in the Buddhist world.

CANICULAR PERIOD, see *Dog-star*.

CANNÆ (Apulia). Here, on 2 Aug. 216 B.C., Hannibal with 50,000 Africans, Gauls, and Spaniards, defeated Æmilius Paulus and Terentius Varro, with 88,000 Romans, and their allies. This great army was nearly annihilated, the far greater part being slain on the field, including the consul Æmilius Paulus, his chief officers, above 80 senators, with many other persons of high rank. Hannibal is said to have lost about 6,000 men. The other consul, Varro, who had escaped with some cavalry, conducted himself with so much discretion and firmness after the battle, that the senate, instead of blaming him for the defeat, thanked him for not despairing of the Roman Commonwealth.

CANNES, a fashionable watering place and seaport of France, in the department of Alpes-Maritimes, situated on a bay of the Mediterranean (22 miles N.W. of Nice). Founded by the Romans between *Via Aurelia* and the sea. Held as a fief by the convent of the Lérins during the middle ages. In 1580 it was devastated by the great plague, and during the religious wars it was sacked by the duke of Savoy. Napoleon landed at Cannes on his return from Elba, 1815. Its rise as a watering place is due to lord Brougham, who in 1834 selected Cannes as a health resort. The duke of Albany died at the Villa Nevada, 28 March, 1884, and the late queen Victoria visited Cannes in 1887 to inspect the Albert Memorial church of St. George of England, built in memory of the prince. During the winter it is frequented by visitors of all nationalities. Population, 19,385.

CANNIBAL, an Indian term, thought to be a form of Carribal; as Columbus, in 1493, found the Caribs of the West Indies gross cannibals. *Anthropophagi* (man-eaters) are mentioned by Homer and Herodotus; and the practice still exists in some of the South Sea Islands and other savage countries. For *Mignonette* case, see *Wrecks*, 1884. Superstitious cannibalism practised in Hayti, 1884.

A number of Melanesian labourers said to have killed and eaten the entire crew of a ship conveying them to Apia, Navigators Island . . Dec. 1886

Lieut. de Magnée and party reported to have been killed and eaten by cannibals at Port Boni, 14 June 1902

CANNING ADMINISTRATION.* The illness of lord Liverpool, Feb., led to the formation of this administration, 24-30 April, 1827. Mr. Canning died 8 Aug. following: see *Goderich*.

George Canning, *first lord of the treasury and chancellor of the exchequer.*
Earl of Harrowby, *president of the council.*
Duke of Portland, *lord privy seal.*
Viscount Dudley, viscount Goderich, and Mr. Sturges Bourne, *foreign, colonial, and home secretaries.*
W. W. Wynn, *president of the India board.*
Wm. Huskisson, *board of trade.*
Lord Palmerston, *secretary at war.*
Lord Bexley, *chancellor of the duchy of Lancaster.*
Duke of Clarence, *lord high admiral.*
Lord Lyndhurst, *lord chancellor, &c.*
Marquis of Lansdowne, *without office; afterwards home secretary.*
Earl of Carlisle, *woods and forests.*

CANNON. Gibbon describes a cannon employed by Mahomet II. at the siege of Adrianople, 1453; see *Artillery*.

The first cannon cast in England was by Hugget, at Uckfield, Sussex, 1543.

Mons Meg, a large cannon (above 13 ft. long, 20 inches calibre) in Edinburgh castle, said to have been cast at Mons in Hainault, in 1486, but more probably forged at Castle Douglas, Galloway, by three brothers named M'Kim, and presented by them to James II. at the siege of Thrieve castle, 1455. It was removed to London, 1754; but, at the request of sir Walter Scott, restored to Edinburgh, 1829.

A cannon of Mahomet II., dated 1464, presented to the British government by the sultan of Turkey, and placed in the Artillery Museum, Woolwich, 1868.

Moolk-e-Maedan, an Indian bronze gun of Beejapoor, calibre 23 inches; 17th century.

At Ehrenbreitstein castle, opposite Coblentz on the Rhine, is a cannon, eighteen feet and a half long, a foot and a half in diameter in the bore, and three feet four inches in the breech; the ball for it weighs 180lb., and its charge of powder 94lb. It was made by one Simon 1529

In Dover castle is a brass gun (called queen Elizabeth's pocket pistol), 24 feet long, a present from Charles V. to Henry VIII.

Fine specimens in the Tower of London.

A leathern cannon fired three times in the King's park, Edinburgh. *Phillips* . . . 23 Oct. 1788

The Turkish piece, now in St. James's park, was taken by the French at Alexandria; but was retaken, and placed in the park . . March, 1803

Messrs. Horsfall's monster wrought-iron gun was completed in May, 1856, at Liverpool. Its length is 15 feet 10 inches, and its weight 21 tons 17 cwt. 1 qr. 14lb. Its cost was 3500*l*. With a charge of 25lb. it struck a target 2000 yards' distance. It has been since presented to government.

Rifled ordnance committee appointed . 20 Aug. 1858

Great improvements made in the construction of cannon, by Messrs. Whitworth, Mallet, Armstrong, and others. Mr. Wm. G. Armstrong knighted . . . . 18 Feb. 1859

* George Canning was born 11 April, 1770; became foreign secretary in the Portland administration, 1807; fought a duel with ld. Castlereagh and resigned, 1809; president of the India board in 1820; disapproved of the queen's trial and resigned in 1821; appointed governor-general of India in 1822, soon after foreign secretary till 1827, when he became premier. He died 8 Aug. same year.

He had been working for four years on gun-making, and had succeeded in producing "a *breech-loading* rifled wrought-iron gun of great durability and of extreme lightness, combining a great extent of range and extraordinary accuracy." The range of a 32-lb. gun, charged with 5lb. of powder, was a little more than 5 miles. The accuracy of the Armstrong gun is said at equal distances to be fifty-seven times more than that of our common artillery, which it greatly exceeded also in destructive effects. The government engaged the services of sir W. Armstrong for ten years (commencing with 1855) for 20,000*l.*, as consulting engineer of rifled ordnance . . . 22 Feb. 1859

A parliamentary committee on ordnance was appointed 20 Feb., and reported . . 23 July, 1860

His gun said to be very effective in the attack on the Chinese forts at Taku . . 21 Aug. ,,

Mr. Whitworth's guns and rifles greatly commended 1860-70

An *American* cannon, weighing 35 tons, stated to be the largest in the world, cast 1860

Great endeavours made to improve the construction of cannon, to counterbalance the strength given to ships of war by iron plates. Trials at Shoeburyness, Essex 1862

Targets of the thickness of the iron sides of the *Warrior*, three 5-inch plates of wrought iron bolted together, pierced three times by 156lb. shot from an Armstrong gun smooth bore, 300lb., muzzle-loaded with charges of 40lb. of powder, twice, and once of 50lb. . . 8 April, ,,

The Horsfall gun, mentioned above, with a charge of 75lb. of powder and a shot of 270lb., smashed a Warrior target . . . . . 16 Sept. ,,

Mr. Whitworth's shells sent through 5½-inch iron plates and wood-work behind . . 12 Nov. ,,

Sir W. Armstrong resigned his appointment 5 Feb. 1863

Clark's target destroyed . . . 7 July, ,,

Armstrong's gun "Big Will" tried and pronounced to be perfect; weight, 22 tons; length, 15 feet; range with shot weighing 510lb., 748 to 4187 yards 19 Nov. ,,

Reed's target tried successfully . . 8 Dec. ,,

The competitive trial between the Armstrong and Whitworth guns began . . 1 April, 1864

Iron-plate commission experiments close 4 Aug. ,,

Capt. Palliser, afterwards sir W., by experiment, has shown that iron shot cast in cold iron moulds instead of hot sand, is much harder, and equals steel; he also suggested the lining cast-iron guns with wrought-iron exits, which is stated to be successful . . . . . . ,,

He received 24,000*l.* from the government, besides other remuneration . . . . ,,

The competitive trials of Armstrong's and Whitworth's cannon upon the *Alfred* target-ship at Portsmouth closed . . . 15 Nov. ,,

"Hercules target," 4 ft. 2 in. thick, 11½ inches of iron, resists 300 pounders . . . June, 1865

National Artillery Association (see *Artillery*) . . ,,

Duel between the *Bellerophon*, with a 12½-ton 9-inch rifled naval service gun with steel bolts (250 lb.), and powder charge of 48lb., and the single gun turret of the *Royal Sovereign* by capt. Cowper Coles: the equilibrium of the turret base undisturbed by any amount of pounding . 15 June, 1866

At Shoeburyness Palliser's chilled metal shot (250lb.) by 43lb. of powder in a 9-inch muzzle-loading wrought-iron Woolwich rifle gun, is sent through a target of 8 inches rolled iron, 18 inches teak, and ⅝ inch iron, and about 20 feet beyond, 13 Sept. ,,

[His patent is dated 27 May, 1863. Mr. James Nasmyth had previously suggested the use of chilled iron.]

Many experiments made with cannon and targets at Shoeburyness 1867

The American 15-inch naval gun, with a cast-iron spherical shot 453lb., greatly damages an 8-inch target; other experiments at Shoeburyness, 23 July, ,,

Continued experiments at Shoeburyness; Plymouth model fort, with 15-inch solid shield-plates, tried with 23-ton gun of 12-inch bore, bearing 600lb. Palliser shot; exterior of fort destroyed; interior intact;—the 10-inch English gun shown to be superior to American and Prussian great guns . . . 16-24 June, 1868

Capt. Moncrieff's protected barbette gun-carriage (in which the recoil is utilized for reloading), tried at Shoeburyness and proved successful . 2 Oct. ,,

Contest at Shoeburyness: the iron targets of Brown of Sheffield resist the Whitworth guns, 2 March, 1870

Palliser shot said to have failed in the *Hercules*. 20 Jan. ,,

"Woolwich Infant," 35 tons; largest gun then ever made; length 16 feet 3 inches; formed of a steel tube with coiled breech piece; designed to fire a 700lb. projectile, with 120lb. charge; made at Woolwich in 1870; when tried in Dec. 1871, the inner tube cracked; others made . . . 1872

Duel between the *Hotspur* (with 25-ton 12-inch rifle gun, heaviest afloat, with Palliser's 600lb. shot, and 85lb. of powder), and the *Glatton* iron-clad, whose turret plates successfully resisted the attack (animals in the turret uninjured), 5 July, ,,

Col. Moncrieff's hydro-pneumatic carriage for artillery invented about April; the principle claimed by sir Wm. Armstrong for hydraulic machine 11 Nov. ,,

Woolwich Infant.—Experimental gun constructing at Woolwich; 80 tons; 27 feet long; for 1650 lb. shot; 300 lb. of powder . . . May, 1874

81-ton gun tried at Woolwich; shot 1250 lb.; 190 lb. of powder; 12 men rammed in the charge; shot penetrated 50 feet of sand; tried successfully 18 Sept. 1875, 24-26 July, with 370 lb. of powder 4 Aug. 1876

Gen. von Uchatius's steel bronze cannon making at Vienna, . Sept. 1875; reported successful, Sept. ,,

Sir Wm. Armstrong's 100-ton gun for Italy tried successfully at Spezzia, 2000 lb. shot and 330 lb. powder . . . . . . 21 Oct. ,,

81-ton (or 80-ton) gun tried at Shoeburyness for sea-range, with 1760 lb. Palliser shell 27 Sept. *et seq.* 1876, and 1 Feb. 1877

Four 100-ton guns by Armstrong ordered by government . . . . . . March, 1878

A 100-ton gun tried at Woolwich, 13 June; finally proved . . . . . 16 July, 1879

Great guns by Krupp successfully tried at Meppen, Hanover . . . . . . 5-8 Aug. ,,

[He has supplied thousands of cannon to different governments; he died, aged 77, 14 July, 1887.]

Breech-loading cannon ordered to be made Dec. ,,

Experiments with the 38-ton *Thunderer* gun (see *Navy*, 1879), 9 Dec. 1879; exploded when double-charged . . . . 3 Feb. 1880

One of Armstrong's 100-ton guns in the *Duilio* near Naples exploded . . . . 6 March, ,,

A Krupp gun, of 130 tons, cast for Italy . Oct. 1884

Mr. Hiram Stevens Maxim's machine-gun, in which the recoil is utilised for reloading and refiring until the store of ammunition is exhausted (described in "Nature," 5 March, 1885) ,,

Sir Wm. Armstrong's 111-ton gun tried at Woolwich, length 43 ft. 8 in., charge 960 lbs. of gunpowder, weight of projectile 1800 lbs., range of about 8 miles . . . . June, 1887

Manufacture of guns largely removed from Woolwich; about 56 per cent. transferred to private firms announced . . . . . . Nov. 1888

Zalinski gun for the projection of dynamite adopted by the United States for coast defence, Feb. 1889; by the British Government . . . Feb. 1890

The Graydon torpedo projector announced March, 1889

Messrs. Krupp, of Essen, make a gun weighing 270,000 lbs., for Cronstadt; reported 10 March, 1890

Lieut. James W. Graydon, late of U. S. Navy, invents the Graydon dynamite gun, in which dynamite shells are discharged by means of condensed air, the force of the dynamite being moderated by means of non-conductors of heat; one of these guns manufactured by Messrs. Taunton & Co., of Birmingham . . . Jan. 1891

The Maxim-Nordenfelt Gun Company *v.* Mr. Thorsten Nordenfelt, on appeal; he is prohibited carrying on business . . . . 18 Dec. 1892

The Giffard gun, in which the propelling agent is liquefied carbonic acid gas, the invention of M. Paul Giffard, a French engineer; the gas is said to be cheaply manufactured, liquefied, and stored; many experiments on the continent reported

successful, 1889-90; M. Giffard exhibited and discharged rifles, illustrating his inventions in London before a number of distinguished persons 18 July; tried at Nottingham . 3 May, 1893
The Hotchkiss Ordnance Company, registered 1887; their weapons were used with effect in suppressing the Indian revolt in the United States, Dec. 1890; one of their improved guns successfully tried at Exeter . . 12 April, 1897
Messrs. Vickers, Sons, and Maxim (Limited), new quick-firing gun tried successfully at Eynsford, lord Roberts and others present . 6 June, 1898
The Colt machine quick-firing gun tried at Runnymede, duke of Cambridge present . 20 July, 1899
Death of lord Armstrong, aged 90 . 27 Dec. 1900
See *Artillery*, 1903.

CANOE. In the "Rob Roy" a very lightly constructed canoe, "giving the pleasure of a yacht without the expense," Mr. J. Macgregor, in 1865, travelled about a thousand miles on the rivers and lakes of Europe. His second cruise was on the Baltic. He explored the Suez canal, Nov., and the rivers of Syria, Dec. 1868, and the canals and lakes of Holland in the summer of 1871. The "Octoroon" (16 feet long, 23 inches broad) crossed the Channel from Boulogne to Dover, in 11 hours, 19 Aug. 1867. The Royal canoe club founded, 1866. The prince of Wales president, 1876.

Mr. Fowler crossed from Boulogne to Sandgate standing in an india-rubber twin canoe (the *Podoscaphe*), in 12 hours . . . . . 19 Aug. 1878
M. Felix Cauchois crossed from Dover to Calais in a canoe 14 ft. long and 2 ft. wide . 9, 10 Sept. 1900
An ancient Irish canoe, 52 ft. long, found in a bog near Tuam . . . . end Dec. 1901

CANON, a piece of music in two or more parts, imitating each other. "Non nobis, Domine," by Birde (died 1523) is an early specimen.

CANON OF SCRIPTURE, see *Bible*.

CANONBURY TOWER, Islington, N. London, relic of ancient priory, built by Prior Bolton, of the order of St. John of Jerusalem, said to have been visited by queen Elizabeth.

CANONICAL HOURS, see *Breviary*.

CANONISATION of pious men and martyrs as saints, was instituted by pope Leo III., 800. *Tallent*. Every day in the calendar is now a saint's day. The first canonisation by papal authority was of St. Udalricus, Ulric, in 993. Previously canonisation was the act of the bishops and people. *Hénault*. On 8 June, 1862, the pope canonised 27 Japanese, who had been put to death on 5 Feb. 1597, near Nagasaki, and 25 others, on 29 June, 1867. Among persons canonised by pope Pius IX. in Oct. 1872, was the late queen of Naples. Sir Thomas More, Bishop John Fisher, and others were canonised, Jan. 1887. See *Popes*, 1881. Francis Xavier Binachi of the Order of the Barnabites canonised, 22 Jan. 1893. Anthony Zaccaria, born 1502, died 1539, founder of the Barnabites, and Peter Fourier, born 1565, died 1640, canonised at St. Peter's, Rome, 27 May, 1897.

CANONS, APOSTOLICAL, ascribed to the Apostles by Bellarmin and Baronius, by others to St. Clement, are certainly of much later date (since 325). The Greek church allows 85, the Latin 50 of them. The first Ecclesiastical Canon was promulgated 380. *Usher*. *Canon law* of the church. Gratian compiled a text-book of the canon law as it existed in his time, about 1130-50; it was introduced into England about 1154; see *Decretals*. The present *Canons and Constitutions of the Church of England*, collected from former ordinances, were established in 1603 by the clergy in convocation, and ratified by king James I., 1604. A new body of canons formed by the convocation in 1640, were declared unlawful by the commons, 16 Dec. 1641.—An intermediate class of religious, between priests and monks, in the 8th century, were termed *canons*, as living by a rule. *Canons* in some of our cathedrals and collegiate churches resemble the prebendaries in others. The endowment of canonries was facilitated by the Cathedrals Act, 1873.

CANOPUS, see *Alexandria*.

CANOSSA, a castle in Modena. Here h emperor Henry IV. of Germany, submitted to penance imposed by his enemy, pope Gregory VII. (Hildebrand), then living at the castle, the residence of the great countess Matilda. Henry was exposed for several days to the inclemency of winter, Jan. 1077, till the pope admitted him, and granted absolution. Matilda greatly increased the temporal power of the papacy by bequeathing to it her large estates, to the injury of her second husband, Guelph, duke of Bavaria. A Canossa monument, near Harzburg, against the papacy, was inaugurated 26 Aug. 1877.

CANTERBURY (Kent), the *Durovernum* of the Romans, and capital of Ethelbert, king of Kent, who reigned 560-616. He was converted to Christianity by Augustin, 596, upon whom he bestowed many favours, giving him land for an abbey and cathedral, dedicated to Christ, 602. St. Martin's church is said to be the oldest Saxon church in Britain. The riot at Boughton, near Canterbury, produced by a fanatic called Tom or Thom, who assumed the name of sir William Courtenay, occurred 28-31 May, 1838; see *Thomites*. The railway to London was completed in 1846.—The ARCHBISHOP is primate and metropolitan of all England, and the first peer in the realm, having precedency of all officers of state, and of all dukes not of the blood royal. Canterbury had formerly jurisdiction over Ireland, and the archbishop was styled a patriarch. This see has yielded to the Church of Rome 18 saints and 9 cardinals; and to the civil state of England, 12 lord chancellors and 4 lord treasurers. This see was made superior to York, 1073; see *York*. The revenue is valued in the king's books at 2816*l*. 7*s*. 9*d*. *Beatson*. Present income, 15,000*l*. The *Cathedral* was sacked by the Danes, 1011, and burnt down 1067; rebuilt by Lanfranc and Anselm, and the choir, completed by the prior Conrad in 1130, and in which Becket was murdered, 1170, was burnt 1174. It was rebuilt by William of Sens (1174-78), and by "English William," 1178-84. A new nave was built and other parts, 1378-1410. The great central tower was erected by prior Goldstone about 1495. The gorgeous shrine of Becket was stripped at the reformation, and his bones burnt. Here were interred Edward the Black Prince, Henry IV., cardinal Pole, and other distinguished persons. Part of the roof was destroyed by an accidental fire, and the edifice narrowly escaped, 3 Sept. 1872. The clock-tower was nearly on fire, 2 June, 1876. Restoration of the cathedral and cloisters. Chapter-house re-opened by the prince of Wales and others, 29 May, 1897. See *Huguenots*. Dr. Beaney, of Melbourne, bequeaths 10,000*l*. to the city, announced July, 1891. Population, 1881, 21,848; 1891, 23,026; 1901, 24,868. Great fire at the barracks; estimated damage about 13,000*l*., 16 Nov. 1891.

By the *Archbishop's court* which existed before the Reformation, Thos. Watson, bishop of St. David's, was deprived for simony, 3 Aug. 1699. Dr. E. King, bishop of Lincoln, was cited before this court by

Read and others, and appeared before the archbishop and the bishops of London, Winchester, Rochester, Oxford, and Salisbury (he was prosecuted for ritualistic practices connected with the holy communion 4 Dec. 1887 *et seq.*) 12 Feb. He protested against the jurisdiction of the court, and the case was adjourned 13 Feb.; court adjourns 27 March; met and decided to uphold its jurisdiction, 13 May, 1889.

The trial of the bishop of Lincoln before the archbishop and other bishops at Lambeth began (sir Horace Davey and others for the promoters of the suit, Dr. Phillimore and others for the bishop) 4-7, 20-25 Feb. 1890

All the charges against the bishop were dismissed except two; his practices of breaking the bread and taking the cup "not before the people," and making the sign of the cross while pronouncing absolution and benediction, were declared to be unjustifiable additions to the ceremonies of the church, and were ordered to be discontinued (no costs allowed on either side) . . 21 Nov. ,,

An appeal to the judicial committee of the Privy Council, July, 1891; was dismissed . 2 Aug. 1892

Mr. H. B. Wilson's saw-mills destroyed by fire, loss about 2,000*l*. . . . . 27 Aug. 1896

Lord George Hamilton unveils a memorial to 41 Kentish martyrs burnt in the reign of queen Mary . . . . 10 June, 1899

Royal museum, institute and library (built by aid of Dr. Beaney's bequest of 10,000*l*., 1897) opened by the mayor . . . . 11 Sept. ,,

Visit of members of the French and British associations (see *Dover* and *Boulogne*) . 20 Sept. ,,

Princess Louise and the duke of Argyle unveil a memorial to officers and men who fell in India, 1895–98 . . . . 12 June, 1900

Lord Roberts and general sir John French receive the freedom . . . . 26 Aug. 1902

Death of dean Farrar, aged 71 . . . 22 Mar. 1903

Dr. Wace, dean . . . . ,,

Archbishops of Canterbury.

602-605. St. Augustine, or Austin, died 26 May.
605-619. St. Lawrence
619-624. St. Mellitus.
624-630. Justus.
631-653. St. Honorius.
655-664. Deusdedit (Adeodatus).
668-690. Theodore of Tarsus.
693-731. Berhtuald.
731-734. Taetwine.
735-741. Nothelm.
741-758. Cuthbert.
759-762. Breogwine.
763-790. Jaenbehrt, or Lambert.
790-803. Æthelheard.
803-829. Wulfred.
829. Fleogild.
830-870. Ceolnoth.
870-889. Æthelred.
891-923. Plegemund.
923 (?) Æthelm.
928-941. Wulfelm.
941-958. Odo.
959-988. St. Dunstan, d. 19 May.
988-989. Æthelgar.
990-995. Sigeric.
995-1006. Ælfric.
1006-1011. St. Ælphage, murdered by the Danes, 19 April.
1013-1020. Lyfing, or Ælfstun.
1020-1038. Æthelnoth.
1038-1050. St. Eadsige.
1050-1052. Robert of Jumiéges.
1052-1070. Stigand: deprived.
1070-1089. St. Lanfranc, d. 24 May.
1093-1109. Anselm.
[See vacant 5 years.]
1114-1122. Radulphus de Turbine.
1123-1136. William de Curbellio.
1139-1161. Theobald.
1162-1170. Thomas à Becket: murdered 29 Dec.
[See vacant.]
1174-1184. Richard.
1184-1190. Baldwin.
1191. Reginald Fitz-Joceline, died 26 Dec.
[See vacant.]
1193-1205. Hubert Walter. [Reginald the sub-prior, and John Grey, bishop of Norwich, were uccessively chosen, but set aside.]
1206-1228. Stephen Langton, died 6 July.
1229-1231. Richard Weathershed.
1233-1240. Edmund de Abingdon.
1240-1270. Boniface of Savoy.
1272-1278. Robert Kilwarby (resigned).
1279-1292. John Peckham.
1293-1313. Robert Winchelsey.
1313-1327. Walter Reynolds.
1327-1333. Simon de Mepham.
1333-1348. John Stratford.
1348-1349. John de Ufford.
1349. Thomas Bradwardin.
1349-1366. Simon Islip.
1366-1368. Simon Langham (resigned).
1368-1374. Wm. Whittelsey.
1375-1381. Simon Sudbury, beheaded by the rebels, 14 June.
1381-1396. William Courtenay.
1397-1398. Thos. Fitzalan or Arundel (attainted).
1398. Roger Walden (expelled).
1399-1414. Tho. Arundel (restored).
1414-1443. Henry Chicheley.
1443-1452. John Stafford.
1452-1454. John Kemp.
1454-1486. Thomas Bouchier.
1486-1500. John Morton.
1501-1503. Henry Deane or Denny.
1503-1532. Wm. Warham.
1533-1556. Thos. Cranmer (burnt 21 March).
1556-1558. Reginald Pole, d. 17 Nov.
1559-1575. Matt. Parker, d. 17 May (see *Nag's Head*).
1576-1583. Edm. Grindal, d. 6 July.
1583-1604. John Whitgift, d. 29 Feb.
1604-1610. Rd. Bancroft, d. 2 Nov.
1611-1633. Geo. Abbot, d. 4 Aug.
1633-1645. Wm. Laud (beheaded, 10 Jan.).
[See vacant 16 years.]
1660-1663. Wm. Juxon, d. 4 June.
1663-1677. Gilb. Sheldon, d. 9 Nov.
1678-1691. Wm. Sancroft (deprived 1 Feb.), d. 24 Nov. 1693.
1691-1694. John Tillotson, d. 22 Nov.
1695-1715. Thos. Tenison, d. 14 Dec.
1715-1737. Wm. Wake, d. 24 Jan.
1737-1747. John Potter, d. 10 Oct.
1747-1757. Thos. Herring, d. 13 Mar.
1757-1758. Matt. Hutton, d. 19 Mar.
1758-1768. Thos. Secker, d. 3 Aug.
1768-1783. Fred. Cornwallis, d. 19 Mar.
1783-1805. John Moore, d. 18 Jan.
1805-1828. Chas. Manners Sutton, d. 21 July.
1828-1848. Wm. Howley, d. 11 Feb.
1848-1862 John Bird Sumner, d. 6 Sept.
1862-1868. Chas. Thos. Longley, d. 27 Oct.
1868-1882. Archibald Campbell Tait, d. 3 Dec. 1882.
1882-1896. Edward White Benson (trans. from Truro), d. suddenly 11 Oct.; state funeral in the cathedral, 16 Oct. 1896; memorial unveiled by the duchess of Albany, 8 July, 1899.
1896-1902. Frederick Temple (trans. from London, Oct.), elected 25 Nov.; confirmed 22 Dec. 1896; d. 23 Dec. 1902.
1903. Randall Thomas Davidson (trans. from Winchester), enthroned 12 Feb. 1903.

CANTERBURY (New Zealand), a Church of England settlement founded in 1850. Population in 1854, 6000, in 1868, 54,000; 1901, 143,041. Large quantities of mutton are annually exported to Great Britain. Canterbury mutton is of a fine quality and commands a large sale.

CANTERBURY TALES, by Geoffrey Chaucer, were written about 1364; and first printed about 1475 or 1476 (by Caxton). A copy dated 1478 sold for 1020*l*., 26 Feb. 1896. Chaucer Society established 1867.

CANTHARIDES, venomous green beetles (called Spanish flies), employed to raise blisters. This use is ascribed to Aretæus of Cappadocia, about 50 B.C.

CANTICLES, these are the Benedictus, Magnificat, Nunc dimittis, &c., in the Book of Common Prayer, and especially the "Song of Solomon."

CANTILEVER, a large bracket used in architecture and bridge building, primitively in Japan, India, and China. It is defined as "a structure overhung from a fixed base." The principle was adopted in the Forth bridge and the Mississippi bridge (*which see*).

CANTON, founded about 200 B.C., the only city in China with which Europeans were allowed to trade, till the treaty of 29 Aug. 1842. Merchants arrived here in 1517. English factory established, 1680. A fire destroying 15,000 houses, 1822. An inundation swept away 10,000 houses and 1000 persons, Oct. 1833. Canton was taken by the British in 1857; restored, 1861. See *China* 1835, 1839, 1856, 1861. The "flower-boats" burnt, about 100 persons missing, 31 Aug. 1894. Population estimated at 1,600,000 in 1890.

CANTOR LECTURES, scientific courses given annually at the rooms of the Society of Arts. The expenses are defrayed by a legacy from Dr. Theodore Edward Cantor, of the Indian civil service; who died about 1859. The lectures began 7 Dec. 1863.

CANULEIAN LAW, permitting the patricians and plebeians to intermarry, was passed at Rome 445 B.C.

CAOUTCHOUC or INDIA RUBBER, an elastic resinous substance that exudes by incisions from several trees that grow in South America, Mexico, Africa, and Asia, especially *Castilloa Hevea* or *Siphonia elastica*, and *Ficus elastica*.

Observed at Hayti by Columbus (*Herrera*) . . . 1493
Described by Torquemada 1615
Discovered by La Condamine in Quito (termed by natives *cahout-chou*); brought to Europe about 1735
Dr. Priestley said that he had seen "a substance excellently adapted to the purpose of wiping from paper the marks of a black lead pencil." It was sold at the rate of 3s. the cubic half-inch . . 1770
India-rubber cloth was made by Samuel Peal and patented 1791
Caoutchouc discovered in the Malay Archipelago, 1798; in Assam 1810
Vulcanised rubber formed by combining India rubber with sulphur, which process removes the susceptibility of the rubber to change under atmospheric temperatures, was patented in America, by Mr. C. Goodyear 1839
Invented also by Mr. T. Hancock (of the firm of Macintosh & Co.), and patented 1843
Mr. Goodyear invented the hard rubber (termed Ebonite) as a substitute for horn and tortoise-shell 1849
A mode of retaining India rubber in its natural fluid state (by applying to it liquid ammonia) patented in England for the inventor, Mr. Henry Lee Norris, of New York 1853
See under *Printing*.
African caoutchouc imported into England . . 1856
Caoutchouc imported in 1850, 7617 cwts.; in 1856, 28,765 cwts.; in 1864, 71,027 cwts.; in 1866, 72,176 cwts.; in 1870, 152,118 cwts.; in 1874, 129,163 cwts.; in 1876, 158,692 cwts.; in 1879, 150,601 cwts.; in 1883, 229,101 cwts.; in 1887, 237,511 cwts.; in 1888, 220,350 cwts.; in 1889, 236,310 cwts.; in 1890, 264,008 cwts.; 1893, 293,373 cwts.; 1899, 449,651 cwts.; 1900, 513,286 cwts.; 1901, 466,474 cwts.

CAPE BRETON, a large island, E. coast of N. America, said to have been discovered by Cabot, 1497; by the English in 1584; taken by the French in 1632, but was afterwards restored; and again taken in 1745, and re-taken in 1748. The fortress, Louisburg, was captured by the English 26 July, 1758, when the garrison were made prisoners, and eleven French ships were captured or destroyed. The island was ceded to England, 10 Feb. 1763; incorporated with Nova Scotia 1819. Population in 1881, 84,262; 1891, 86,914. Lieut.-governor, hon. M. B. Daly (1891). Chief town, Sidney. Population, 1901, nearly 18,000.

CAPE-COAST CASTLE, in Upper Guinea, S. W. Africa. Settled by the Portuguese in 1610; taken by the Dutch 1643; demolished by admiral Holmes in 1661. All the British factories and shipping along the coast were destroyed by the Dutch admiral, De Ruyter, in 1665. It was confirmed to the English by the treaty of Breda, in 1667. See *Ashantees* and *Gold Coast*.

CAPE FINISTERRE (N. W. Spain). Off this cape admirals lord Anson and Warren defeated and captured a French fleet under De la Jonquière, 3 May, 1747.

CAPE HORN, or HOORN, on the last island of the Fuegian archipelago, the southernmost point of America, was discovered and named by Schouten, 1616, after his birth-place in the Netherlands.

CAPE LA HOGUE, see *La Hogue* (correctly, Hague).

CAPEL COURT, see under *Stocks*.

CAPE OF GOOD HOPE, a promontory on the S. W. point of Africa, called "Cabo Tormentoso" (the stormy cape), the "Lion of the Sea," and the "Head of Africa," discovered by Bartholomew de Diaz in 1487. Its present name was given by John II. of Portugal, who augured favourably of future discoveries from Diaz having reached the extremity of Africa. Population of "Cape Colony" in 1856, 267,096; in 1881, 720,984; in 1891, 1,527,224; Dec. 1901, estimated 2,433,000. Cape Town and suburbs, population, 1888, 60,000; 1902, 167,200. For governors, see *below*.

The cape was doubled, and the passage to India discovered by Vasco da Gama . . 19 Nov. 1497
CAPE TOWN, the capital, founded by the Dutch . 1650
Colony taken by the English under admiral Elphinstone and general Clarke . . . 16 Sept. 1795
Restored at the peace of Amiens . . 25 March, 1802
Taken by sir D. Baird and sir H. Popham 9 Jan. 1806
Finally ceded to England . . . . 13 Aug. 1814
British emigrants arrive . . . . . March, 1820
The Kaffirs make irruptions on the British settlements, and ravage Grahamstown; see *Kaffraria*, Oct. 1834
Bishopric of Cape Town founded; Dr. Robert Gray, first bishop 1847
The inhabitants successfully resist the attempt to make the cape a penal colony . . 19 May, 1849
Territories north of Great Orange river placed under British authority, 3 Feb. 1848; annexed as the Orange river territory . . . . March, 1851
The constitution granted to the colony promulgated and joyfully received . . . . 1 July, 1853
General Prætorius, chief of the Transvaal republic, died . . . . Aug. ,,
The British jurisdiction over the Orange river territory abandoned, 30 Jan.; a free state was formed; see *Orange river* . . . March, 1854
The first parliament meets at Cape Town 1 July, ,,
The Kaffirs much excited by a prophet named Umhla-kaza; by the exertions of sir George Grey, the governor, tranquillity maintained . Aug. 1856
The cape visited by prince Alfred in . July, 1860
The first railway from Cape Town, about 58 miles long, opened . . . . . . about Dec. ,,
Governor, sir Philip E. Wodehouse 1861
Disputes between bishops of Cape Town and Natal; see *Church of England* 1863-5
Cape Town visited by the duke of Edinburgh, 17 Aug. 1867
Discovery of diamonds; leads to disputes between the free states and the tribes; see *Diamonds* 1867-70

Large tracts of territory devastated by fire Feb. 1869
Death of Moshesh, an eminent chief of the Basutos, friendly to the British . . . . 11 March, 1870
New harbour, breakwater, and docks at Cape Town inaugurated by the duke of Edinburgh, 12 July, „
Sir Henry Barkly appointed governor . Aug. „
Energy of sir Henry Barkly, in repressing aggressions of the president of the Orange river territory . . . . March, 1871
Colony of Griqualand constituted . . 27 Oct. „
The British flag erected amidst the diamond fields with great acclamation . . . . . 17 Nov. „
Great success in the diamond fields; robbery of diamonds valued between 35,000*l.* and 40,000*l.*; oppression of the natives stopped by sir H. Barkly, Aug. 1872
Death of bishop Gray, deeply lamented . 1 Sept. „
Macomo, an eminent Kaffir chief, died . 11 Sept. 1873
Insurrection of Langalibalele, a chief, suppressed (See *Natal*) . . . . Nov. Dec. „
South African Confederation (*which see*), proposed by earl of Carnarvon; opposed by Mr. Molteno and his cabinet, May; long debate commenced on it in the Cape parliament . . . . 11 Nov. 1875
Earl of Carnarvon, in a despatch, proposes that the conference on the confederation shall be transferred to England, 22 Oct.; much resented Nov. „
Earl of Carnarvon's despatch expressing earnest desire for the confederation, and proposing a meeting of delegates in London, their decision not to be conclusive, 15 Nov.; parliament prorogued . . . . 26 Nov. „
Conference of delegates in London began; earl of Carnarvon, not Mr. Molteno, present . 5 Aug. 1876
Sir H. Bartle E. Frere appointed governor and lord high commissioner for South Africa . . Nov. „
He opens a successful exhibition at Cape town 5 April, 1877
Transvaal republic (*which see*) annexed 12 April, „
Troublesome disputes between tribes (Fingoes and Galekas); lead to war (see *Kaffraria*) . Sept. „
The minister Molteno opposes employing imperial troops in the Kaffir war . Jan., Feb. 1878
Mr. Molteno's ministry dismissed; one formed by Mr. J. Gordon Sprigg, about 12 Feb.; reported successful . . . . April, „
Kaffir war ended; amnesty to surrendering rebels announced . . . . 2 July, „
Thanksgiving day for restoration of peace 1 Aug. „
Zulu war begins (see *Zululand*) . . 12 Jan. 1879
Insurrection in the Transvaal (*which see*) Dec. „
Telegraphic communication with Great Britain completed; telegram from the queen to sir Bartle Frere and others . . . . . 25 Dec. „
Government proposition for conference of delegates to promote federation, rejected by the assembly about 24 June, 1880
War with Basutos . . . . . . June, „
Recall of sir Bartle Frere, 1 Aug.; announced in parliament . . . . 2 Aug. „
Opinions [as to his policy and that of the home government greatly differed.]
Sir Hercules G. R. Robinson appointed governor and Lord High Commissioner for South Africa 21 Aug. „
Resignation of Mr. Sprigg's ministry, through narrow escape of vote of censure; succeeded by Mr. Scanlen and Mr. Molteno . 6, 7 May, 1881
Settled difficulty with Transvaal (*which see*) . 1883-4
Ministry defeated, resigns; Mr. Upington, new minister . . . . 7 May, 1884
They agree to support the imperial government in repressing the Boer filibusters . . . Oct. „
Railway to Kimberley opened by sir H. Robinson 28 Nov. 1885
The houses of parliament opened . . . „
The Pondos invade Xesibeland 20 Oct.; peace announced . . . . 9 Dec. 1886
New ministry; sir J. Gordon Sprigg prime minister about 25 Nov. „
New registration act disfranchising many natives passed; much opposed Aug.–Sept.; supported by the home government . . . . . . Oct. 1887
The South African Jubilee Exhibition opened at Grahamstown by sir Hercules Robinson, 15 Dec. „
Conference of delegates from Cape Colony, Natal, and the Orange Free State held at Cape Town; a customs union and railway extension proposed; a movement towards S. African federation; conference closed . . . . 18 Feb. 1888
Sir H. Brougham Loch appointed governor and high commissioner for South Africa about 22 June, 1889; arrives 13 Dec. He unveils a statue of the queen in front of the houses of parliament, Cape Town . . . . 21 Jan. 1890
Defeat of the ministry on the great railway schemes about 5 July; resignation of sir J. Gordon Sprigg, under whom the colony prospered 10 July, „
New ministry formed by Mr. Cecil John Rhodes, the "diamond king," founder of the British South Africa company . . . . . . 17 July, „
Failure of the Cape of Good Hope bank after long run on it; much alarm throughout the colony, 24 Sept.; reported deficiency, 464,000*l.*, 16 Oct. „
South African Language Association, 1st Congress opened at Cape Town . . . . . 31 Oct. „
Sir Henry Loch and Mr. Rhodes visit London to discuss South African affairs with the government, 2–27 Feb. Satisfactory results reported 6 March, 1891
Great fire at Cape Town; the exhibition buildings and other places destroyed . . . 21 Feb. 1892
Sir H. B. Loch opens the junction railway between Cape Colony and the Free State . 10 March, „
A new franchise act opposed by the coloured population (1892), not vetoed by the queen, Feb. 1893
Mr. Cecil Rhodes returns from a visit to England, 8 March; he resigns; reconstructs his ministry, including sir J. Gordon Sprigg . . . 4 May, „
Vote disapproving Mr. Cecil Rhodes' continuance as premier and a director of the S. Africa company, rejected (57–2) . . . . . . 22 June, „
Mr. Cecil Rhodes arrives at Cape Town after his tour through Mashonaland and Matabeleland, reports the conquest of Matabeleland . 3 Jan. 1894
Sir Henry B. Loch arrives in England, 21 April; returned to Cape Town . . . . . 7 Nov. „
Budget: surplus, 334,161*l.* . . . . . 14 June, „
Mr. Cecil Rhodes made privy councillor . 2 Feb. 1895
Sir Hercules Robinson appointed to succeed sir Henry Loch, Feb.: warmly received at Cape Town . . . . 30 May, „
Sir Charles Mills, agent-general for the colony, 1882, *et seq.*, a brave soldier and able financier, born in 1825, died . . . . . 31 March, „
Wm. Lippert, formerly manager of the Union bank of Cape Town, sentenced to 7 years' penal servitude for forgeries on the bank amounting to 200,000*l.* . . . . 25 April, „
British Bechuanaland annexed by the assembly, 11 June and 1 Aug. „
Mr. Cecil Rhodes accused of complicity with Dr. Jameson's action: see *Transvaal*, Jan. 1896; resigns; 6 Jan.; succeeded by sir John Gordon Sprigg . . . . 6 Jan. 1896
Sir H. Robinson returns from his successful visit to the Transvaal (*which see*) . . . 16 Jan. „
Mr. Cecil Rhodes arrives in London, 4 Feb; interview with Mr. Chamberlain, 6 Feb.; leaves for Rhodesia . . . . 10 Feb. „
Loyal colonial league, formed to maintain the British supremacy in some of the frontier towns; reported . . . . 28 April, „
Parliament opened . . . . . . 1 May, „
Sir H. Robinson leaves for England; 20 May; created Baron Rosmead, July (1896); returns to Cape Town . . . . 31 Aug. „
Petition for the reinstatement of Mr. Cecil Rhodes, 13,000 signatures, transmitted to Mr. Chamberlain . . . . 22 Sept. „
Mr. Cecil Rhodes warmly received at Cape Town; 30 Dec.; sails for England . . . . 6 Jan. 1897
Lord Rosmead resigns, succeeded by sir Alfred Milner; announced . . . . . . 15 Feb. „
Great meeting in favour of Mr. Cecil Rhodes, and against the evidence of Mr. Schreiner at the S. Africa committee, London . . . 29 March, „
Explosion of two cases of blasting gelatine, at a mine; 30 deaths . . . . . . 14 April, „
Mr. Rhodes arrives at Cape Town; well received, 20 April, „
Lord Rosmead leaves for England . 21 April, „

Sir J. Gordon Sprigg's budget; estimated surplus, 227,000*l*. . . . . . . 29 April, 1897
Vote of censure on the ministry, defeated by the speaker's casting vote . . . 30 April, „
Sir Alfred Milner arrives at Cape Town; cordially received . . . . . . 5 May, „
Solemn fast (13 June), owing to the spread of rinderpest, proclaimed . . . . 28 May, „
Suicide of Mr. B. I. Barnato, by leaping overboard from the *Scot* (insane); a highly successful speculator in gold and diamonds, and very influential in Africa and London . . . 14 June, „
Diamond jubilee celebration throughout S. Africa; rejoicings at Cape Town . . 20 June *et seq.* „
Sir J. Gordon Sprigg (in London) authorized by the Cape parliament, offers Mr. Goschen, first lord of the admiralty, to present the cost of a 1st class battleship, as a contribution from Cape Colony, 10 July; proposed to take the form of the payment of the yearly interest (abt. 25,000*l*.); announced . . . . 16 Dec. „
Colonial tour of sir Alfred Milner; 30 Aug.–26 Sept. „
Sigcau, the Pondo chief, claims 1,500*l*. from the government as damages for false imprisonment; announced . . . . 30 Dec. „
Legislative council dissolved . . . . Jan. 1898
Galishwe, rebel chief, captured by capt. Denison; 30 Aug. 1897; sentenced to 10 years' imprisonment . . . . 11 Feb. „
The Graaf Reinet-Middelburg railway, opened by sir A. Milner . . . . . 3 March, „
The Customs union conference opened at Cape Town . . . . 12 April, „
Telegraphic communication established between Cape Town and Blantyre . . . 20 April, „
Parliament opened 20 May; Mr. Schreiner's motion of want of confidence voted, 22–23 June; parliament prorogued, 28 June; opened by sir A. Milner, 10 Oct.; Mr. Schreiner's vote of want of confidence carried, 39–37, 11 Oct.; (ministry resigns) new one under Mr. Schreiner, 14 Oct. „
Death of general sir W. Goodenough, commander-in-chief, 24 Oct.; succeeded by general Butler, who arrives at Cape Town . . . 30 Nov. „
Redistribution act, 16 new seats; total, 95 members, passed . . . . . . 7 Dec. „
Imperial navy contribution bill (30,000*l*. annually) passed without debate . . . . 9 Dec. „
Customs union convention comes into operation, 3 Jan. 1899
Parliament prorogued . . . 11 April, 14 July, „
The Swellendam railway opened by sir A. Milner, 12 April; he leaves Cape Town for Natal (*which see*), 29 May; returns, his Transvaal policy, "equality all round," warmly supported . . . June, „
Van Riebeck's statue, presented by Mr. Rhodes, unveiled at Cape Town . . . . 18 May, „
Parliament opened, with queen's speech, 14 July, „
Demonstration to Mr. Rhodes on his return to Cape Town . . . . . . 18 July, „
General sir F. Forestier-Walker arrives to take command of troops . . . . 6 Sept. „
General sir Redvers Buller received with great rejoicing at Cape Town (see *South African War*), 31 Oct. „
Loyal meeting of Mahomedans at Cape Town, 30 Oct. „
Sir A. Milner's proclamation of equality to British and Dutch alike, issued . . . 23 Nov. „
Field-marshal lord Roberts and lord Kitchener arrive at Cape Town . . . . 10 Jan. 1900
Disaffection among the Dutch in Cape Colony, increasing . . . . Jan. „
Dr. W. Hiddingh bequeaths 30,000*l*. to the Cape university, with a site for new buildings, and 10,000*l*. to the South Africa college, reported mid. Jan. „
The City of London imperial volunteers reviewed by lord Roberts, 31 Jan.; 2nd detachment arrives . . . . 3 Feb. „
Rapid rally of volunteers, Brabant's Horse and others, in a few weeks . . . Jan.-Feb. „
Great rejoicings at the relief of Kimberley (see *South African War*), 15 Feb.; the surrender of general Cronje, 27 Feb., and the relief of Ladysmith . . . . 28 Feb. „
Public meeting of Irishmen, loyal message to the queen . . . . 16 March, „
Great fire in Grave-street, Cape Town, building gutted . . . . 25 March, 1900
Sir George White (the defender of Ladysmith) warmly received at Cape Town . 27 March, „
Loyal mass meetings in Cape Town and elsewhere, March–April, „
Many Cape rebels sentenced to various terms of imprisonment . . . . . . 23 April, „
Mr. David Gill, astronomer-royal at the Cape, made K.C.B. . . . . . . 24 May, „
Annexation of the Orange Free State proclaimed at Cape Town . . . . . . 28 May, „
Ministerial crisis, disruption of the Bond party, Mr. Schreiner, premier, upholds the policy of sir A. Milner and home government, 11, 12 June; he resigns, 13 June; sir J. Gordon Sprigg forms a (progressive) cabinet, Mr. Rose-Innes, att.-gen.; Mr. Graham, col. sec. . . . 18 June, „
Parliament opened by sir A. Milner . 19 July, „
Sir J. Gordon Sprigg's budget statement, deficit 69,000*l*.; estimated revenue for 1900, 7,252,000*l*.; expenditure, 7,225,026*l*. . . . . 21 Aug. „
Royal hospitals commission arrives, first meeting held at Cape Town . . . . . 21 Aug. „
Letters found at Pretoria and Bloemfonteim, written by leading South Africans in Cape Colony and English M.P.'s to Boer officials, published as a parliamentary paper . . . . 23 Aug. „
The annexation of the Transvaal announced in the house of assembly . . . . . 3 Sept. „
General Baden-Powell, hero of Mafeking, received with great enthusiasm at Cape Town, 7–12 Sept. „
Treason bill read third time in the house of assembly, 46—37, 21 Sept., and the legislative council, 12—8 . . . . . . 28 Sept. „
Transvaal concessions commission began work in South Africa, end of Aug.; meets at Cape Town (see *Transvaal*, Oct., June, and Nov. 1901), 2 Oct. „
South African league congress opened with a cheerful speech by Mr. Rhodes, he is re-elected president . . . . 10, 13 Oct. „
Parliament prorogued . . . . . 13 Oct. „
General Buller warmly received at Cape Town, 23, 24 Oct. „
Afrikander congress at Worcester; resolutions against the war and demanding the independence of the Boer republics carried, 6 Dec.; presented to sir A. Milner . . . . . . 12 Dec. „
Lord Roberts presented with a sword of honour and addresses at Cape Town . . 8–11 Dec. „
Boer raids, see *South African War*, Dec. 1900 *et seq.*
Proclamation calling for volunteers (loyal response), issued . . . . . . 1 Jan. 1901
Serious plague epidemic, many deaths, Feb.–May, „
Sir Walter F. Hely-Hutchinson appointed governor, Jan.; arrives . . . . . 6 March, „
Martial law proclaimed in the Paarl district, April, „
Mr. Malan, editor of *Ons Land*, and two others sentenced to 6 months, and Mr. Cartwright, editor of the *South African News*, to a year's imprisonment for seditious libel . 19, 22 April, „
Sir A. Milner leaves for Pretoria, 28 Feb.; returns to Cape Town, presented with an address of confidence (over 10,000 signatures), leaves for England, 4–8 May; made a peer (lord Milner of St. James' and Cape Town) . . . 24 May, „
Parliament prorogued . . . . . 7 June, „
Sir W. Hely-Hutchinson well received on tour by the Dutch in the west, returns to Cape Town, 8 June, „
South African constabulary formed, reported successful . . . . 4 July „
Duke and duchess of Cornwall welcomed at Cape Town, receive 95 addresses and many gifts, 19 Aug.; Khama, Lethorodi, and over 100 chiefs presented, 20 Aug.; the duke installed chancellor of the university, children's fête, &c., 21 Aug.; foundation-stones laid for the new cathedral and a nurses' home, 22 Aug.; the Boer prisoners present several serviette rings and a brooch made from Kruger coins to the duke and duchess, who left . . . . 23 Aug. „
Lord Milner returns to Cape Town . 27 Aug. „
Martial law extended through the colony, 9 Oct. „
Life assurance offices in Cape Town burnt, estimated damage 200,000*l*. . . . 11 Oct. „

Mr. Marais charged with violating certain regulations in the Paarl district under martial law, and imprisoned, Aug.; his claim to be tried by a civil tribunal rejected by the supreme court, and again by the judicial committee of the privy council, London . . . . 18 Dec. 1901

The governor's eastern tour (1,200 miles) very successful, reported . . . . 6 Feb. 1902

Mass meeting at Cape Town, the mayor, chairman, to protest against Continental and pro-Boer slanders on British troops in South Africa, 8 Feb.; another by Germans. . . . 10 Feb. „

Mr. Cecil Rhodes, statesman, philanthropist, and millionnaire, "a great empire builder," born 5 July, 1853; died, greatly mourned, 26 March, 1902; laid in state, impressive funeral ceremonies at Cape Town (see *Rhodesia*) . 3 April, „

Princess Radziwill convicted of forging promissory notes; sentenced to 2 years' detention in a house of correction . . . . . . 30 April, „

Mr. Seddon, the New Zealand premier, visits Cape Town . . . . 26 May, „

Peace rejoicings . . . . 12 June, „

Sir J. Gordon Sprigg (G.C.M.G. 26 June, 1902) opposes the suspension of the constitution, 2 June, „

Thanksgivings for the conclusion of peace and public holiday . . . . . 8, 9 June, „

Cold and storm general, cattle and sheep perish, June, „

Proclamation calling on rebels to surrender before 10 July, issued . . . . 11 June, „

Meetings in favour of the suspension of the constitution . . . . 6, 21, 23 June and 4, 5 July, „

Lord Kitchener (visct., 26 June) enthusiastically received, presented with an address, leaves for England . . . . 23 June, „

Great fire in Cape Town, 5 buildings gutted, 27, 28 June, „

Cape Town illuminated at news of the king's progress towards recovery . . . . . 3 July, „

Petition for the temporary suspension of the Cape constitution, signed by 42 members of the Cape parliament and over 34,000 others, negatived by Mr Chamberlain, but the speedy summoning of the legislature agreed to, in order to pass the necessary legislation . . . . . 5 July, „

Peace thanksgivings in Dutch churches, 13 July, „

Ex-pres. and Mrs. Steyn leave for England; Mrs. Steyn receives a purse of 1,000*l.* from the ladies of Cape Town, about . . . . . 16 July, „

Cape Town cathedral memorial fund meeting held (see *England*) . . . . 17 July, „

Generals Louis Botha, Delarey, and De Wet well received, 23–29 July; sail for Europe . 30 July, „

Sir J. Gordon Sprigg returns from England, 29 July, „

Cape Town sword of honour presented to lord Kitchener by the lord mayor, in London, 31 July, „

Sir W. Hely-Hutchinson opens the new railway at Caledon . . . . 1 Aug. „

The first *train de luxe* from Bulawayo reaches Cape Town in 74 hours . . . . 13 Aug. „

Parliament opened by the governor . 20 Aug. „

Split in the progressives; Dr. Smartt elected leader . . . . 20 Aug. „

Dr. Jameson denounces the proposed colonial commission of inquiry into martial law . 28 Aug. „

Smallpox reported in Cape Town . . 29 Aug. „

Violent gale at Algoa Bay and Port Elizabeth, great loss of life and shipping . . . 1 Sept. „

Conference of Dutch loyalists at Paarl, Aug.; petition of grievances presented . . . 2 Sept. „

Breach between sir Gordon Sprigg and the progressives . . . . Aug.–Sept. „

Budget: estimated surplus (1902–3), 286,227*l.*; navy grant increased to 50,000*l.* per ann., 9 Sept. „

Budget, 1901–2, deficit, 2,291,942*l.*; estimated revenue, 1902–3, 10,350,000*l.* . . . 10 Sept. „

Indemnity bills passed . . . . . 11 Sept. „

Royal commission (lord Alverstone, Mr. Justice Bigham, and others) reviews martial law sentences at Cape Town, 26 Aug. *et seq.*; leaves for the north . . . . 12 Sept. „

Martial law repealed; peace preservation Act proclaimed . . . . 17 Sept. „

African Gold Farms Company (ltd.) holding 2,000,000 acres, 600,000*l.* capital, 100,000*l.* reserve, floated by Messrs. Barnato bros. at Johannes- . . . . 2 Jan. 1903

Cape Town branch of progressive association formed. Enthusiastic welcome to Dr. Jameson, who stated that he hoped the S. African league and progressive association would work side by side to carry out progressive cause, and suggested amalgamation with the league. Mr. Rudyard Kipling heartily received . . . . 26 Jan. 1903

Carl van der Merwe, former Boer landrost, committed for trial on charges of flogging the Kaffir Esau . . . . end Jan. „

Mr. Chamberlain at Cape Town, enthusiastic reception, 10 Feb.; receives deputations from S. African league, the progressive parliamentary committee, and other bodies; entertained at lunch by government at Groot Constantia, 20 Feb.; Rondebosch, 21 Feb.; addresses great gathering of children under auspices of the league of children of the empire; important interview with leading members of S. African party, a new association which has taken the place of the Bond; receives deputation of loyal Dutchmen of Cape Colony, headed by sir Henry Juta; farewell banquet at Cape Town, 23 Feb., urges the importance of amity and co-operation for the interests of the empire, concluding with the remark, "All the divergent races which went to make up the British empire had as their motto, 'One life, one flag, one fleet, one empire.'" Leaves Cape Town for England . . . 24 Feb. „

Bond congress opened at Somerset East . 30 April „

Passes resolution urging a colonial commission of inquiry into the administration of martial law. Revision of the constitution of the Bond agreed to. Mr. Theron elected president . . 1 May „

Bill authorising expenditure of over 2,000,000*l.* on new railways introduced in Cape assembly, late June „

Appointment of members of legislative council of the Transvaal and Orange River Colonies announced . . . . late June „

Customs convention accepted by house of assembly . . . . 29 June „

Attorney-general announced refusal of government to appoint a commission to inquire into martial law . . . . 29 June „

Optimistic budget speech by sir J. Gordon Spriggs dwelling upon enormous growth of imports and exports. Expenditure to June, 1903, 10,738,484*l.* leaving surplus of 1,028,682*l.* Estimated revenue for 1903–04, 11,725,000*l.*, expenditure, 11,585,232*l.* 13 July „

Revenue, 3,160,658*l.*, expenditure, 3,332,907*l.*, 1886–7; imports, 5,036,135*l.*, exports, 7,719,385*l.*, 1887; 1889–90, actual revenue, 4,430,050*l.*; expenditure, vote, 3,878,925; 1892–93, revenue, 6,416,149*l.*, expenditure, 5,734,503*l.*, imports, excluding specie, 11,364,836*l.*, exports, ditto, 12,956,554*l.*; 1900, imports, 19,678,336*l.*; exports, 8,147,670*l.*; Dec. 1901, imports, 23,990,543*l.*; exports, 10,873,273*l.* 1902, imports, 34,190,500*l.*: exports, 17,436,131*l.* Revenue, 1899–1900, 6,565,752*l.*; expenditure, vote, 6,667,651*l.* Revenue, 1901, 7,957,499*l.*

For recent wars, see *Basutoland*, *Zululand*, and *Transvaal*.

CAPE ST. VINCENT (S.W. Portugal). Sir George Rooke, with twenty-three ships of war, and the Turkish fleet, was attacked by Tourville, with 160 ships, off Cape St. Vincent, when twelve English and Dutch men-of-war, and eighty merchantmen, were captured or destroyed by the French, 16 June, 1693.—Sir John Jervis, with the Mediterranean fleet of fifteen sail, defeated the Spanish fleet of twenty-seven ships of the line off this cape, taking four ships and sinking others, 14 Feb. 1797. For this victory sir John was raised to the peerage as earl St. Vincent. Nelson was engaged in this battle. Near this cape the fleet of dom Pedro, under admiral Charles Napier, captured dom Miguel's fleet, 5 July, 1833.

CAPETIANS, the third race of the kings of France, named from Hugo Capet, count of Paris and Orleans, who seized the throne on the death of

Louis V., called the Indolent, 987. *Hénault.* The first line of the house of Capet ended with Charles IV., in 1328, when Philip VI. of Valois ascended the throne; see *France.*

CAPE VERD ISLANDS (N. Atlantic Ocean), belonging to Portugal, were known to the ancients as Gorgades, but not to the moderns till discovered by Antonio de Noli, a Genoese navigator in the service of Portugal, 1446, 1450, or 1460. Population, 1885, 110,926; 1900, 147,424.

CAPILLARITY (the rising of liquids in small tubes, and the ascent of the sap in plants) is said to have been first observed by Niccolo Aggiunti of Pisa, 1600-35. The theory has been examined by Newton, La Place, and others. Dr. T. Young's theory was put forth in 1805, and Mr. Wertheim's researches in 1857.

CAPITAL PUNISHMENT, see *Death* and *Crime.*

CAPITATION TAX, see *Poll-tax.*

CAPITOL, said to have been so called from a human head (*caput*) found when digging the foundations of the fortress of Rome, on Mons Tarpeius. Here a temple was built to Jupiter Capitolinus. The foundation was laid by Tarquinius Priscus, 616 B.C.; the building was continued by Servius Tullius; completed by Tarquinius Superbus, but not dedicated till 507 B.C. by the consul Horatius. It was destroyed by lightning 6 July, 183; burnt during the civil wars, 83; rebuilt by Sylla, and dedicated again by Lutatius Catulus, 69; again burnt A.D. 69, 80; rebuilt 70, 82; sacked by Genseric, June, 455. The Roman consuls made large donations to this temple, and the emperor Augustus bestowed on it 2000 pounds weight of gold, of which metal the roof was composed: its thresholds were of brass, and its interior was decorated with shields of solid silver. The *Capitoline games*, instituted 387 B.C. to commemorate the deliverance from the Gauls, were revived by Domitian, A.D. 86. The Campidoglio contains palaces of the senators, erected on the site of the Capitol by Michael Angelo soon after 1546. The corner-stone of the *capitol* at Washington, U.S.A., was laid 18 Sept. 1793.

CAPITULARIES, laws of the Frankish kings, commencing with Charlemagne (801). Collections have been published by Baluze (1677) and others.

CAPITULATIONS: a name given to the judicial rights granted by treaties to foreign consuls in Turkey, beginning with Genoa in 1453. The English capitulations, 1675, contain most favoured nation clauses, and were maintained till April, 1870, when Nubar Pasha, Egyptian minister of foreign affairs, persuaded the great powers to substitute mixed international courts and a uniform code. The capitulations were finally abolished July, 1872.

CAPPADOCIA, Asia Minor. Its early history is involved in obscurity.

Pharnaces said to have founded the kingdom	B.C. 744
Cappadocia conquered by Perdiccas, regent of Macedon; the king, Ariarathes I., aged 82, crucified	322
Recovers its independence	315
Conquered by Mithridates of Pontus	291
Held by Seleucus, 288; independent	288
Ariarathes V., Philopator, reigns, 162; dethroned by Holophernes, 158, but restored soon after by the Romans; killed with Crassus in the war against Aristonicus	130
His queen, Laodice, poisons five of her sons; the sixth (Ariarathes VI.) is saved; she is put to death	,,
Ariarathes VI. murdered by Mithridates Eupator; who sets up various pretenders; the Roman senate declares the country free, and appoints Ariobarzanes I. king	B.C. 93
He is several times expelled by Mithridates, &c., but restored by the Romans; dies	64
Ariobarzanes II. supports Pompey, and is slain by Crassus	42
Ariarathes VII. deposed by Antony	36
Archelaus is favoured by Augustus, 20 B.C.; but accused by Tiberius, he comes to Rome and dies there oppressed with age	A.D. 15
Cappadocia becomes a Roman province	17
Invaded by the Huns	515
And by the Saracens	717
Recovered by the emperor Basil I.	876
Conquered by Soliman and the Turks	1074
Annexed to Turkish Empire	1360

CAPPEL (Switzerland). Here the reformer Ulric Zwinglius was slain in a conflict between the catholics and the men of Zurich, 11 Oct. 1531.

CAPRI (Capreæ), an island near Naples, the sumptuous residence of Augustus, and particularly of Tiberius, memorable for the debaucheries he committed during his last years, 27-37. Remains of his famous triremes which lie at the bottom of lake Nemi, discovered, in 1897. Capri was taken by sir Sydney Smith, 12 May, 1806.

CAPS, see *Hats.*

CAPS AND HATS. About 1738, Sweden was much distracted by two factions thus named, the former in the interest of the Russians, and the latter in that of the French. They were broken up and the names prohibited by Gustavus III. in 1771, who desired to exclude foreign influence. His assassination by Ankarström, 16 March, 1792, set aside all his plans for the improvement of Sweden.

CAPSTAN, used to work ships' anchors, is said to have been invented, but more probably was only improved, by sir Samuel Morland, who died 30 Dec. 1695.

CAPTAIN, H.M.'s iron-clad turret ship, capsized during a squall, 12.15 A.M., 7 Sept., 1870. Capt. Hugh Burgoyne, capt. Cowper Coles, who designed the vessel, and 481 persons perished. See under *Navy of England.* Subscriptions for relief of the widows and orphans of the lost up to 17 Nov., 34,894*l.*; 3 Dec., 38,004*l.*; 31 Dec., about 46,000*l.*; May, 1871, about 55,000*l.*; 25 June, 1871, about 55,700*l.* Total, 57,824*l.* The fund was transferred to the Royal Commission of the Patriotic Fund.

CAPUA, capital of Campania, took the part of Hannibal when his army wintered here after the battle of Cannæ, 216 B.C., and it is said became enervated. In 211, when the Romans retook the city, they scourged and beheaded all the surviving senators; the others had poisoned themselves after a banquet previous to the surrender of the city. Only two persons escaped; one woman who had prayed for the success of the Romans, and another who succoured some prisoners. During the middle ages Capua was successively subjugated by the Greeks, Saracens, Normans, and Germans. It was restored to Naples in 1424, and captured by Cæsar Borgia, 24 July, 1501; was taken by Garibaldi 2 Nov. 1860.

CAPUCHIN FRIARS, Franciscans, so named from wearing a *Capuchon*, or cowl hanging down upon their backs. The order was founded by Matthew Baschi, about 1525; and established by the pope Clement VII. 1529. The capuchin confessors of the queen Henrietta introduced here 1630, were imprisoned by the parliament, 1642.

CAR. The invention is mythically ascribed to Erichthonius of Athens. Covered cars (*currus arcuati*) were used by the Romans. The *lectica* (a soft cushioned car), next invented, gave place to the *carpentum*, a two-wheeled car, with an arched covering, hung with costly cloth. Still later were the *carrucæ*, in which the officers of state rode. Triumphal cars, introduced by Tarquin the Elder, were formed like a throne. See *Carriages* and *Motor Car*.

CARACAS (S. America), part of Venezuela, discovered by Columbus 1498. It was reduced by arms, and assigned as property to the Welsers, German merchants, by Charles V.; but for their tyranny, they were dispossessed in 1550, and a crown governor appointed. The province declared its independence, 9 May, 1810. In the city Leon de Caracas, on 26 March, 1812, nearly 12,000 persons perished by an earthquake. Population, 1889, 72,429. See *Venezuela*.

CARAITES, see *Karaites*.

CARASMIA, see *Khiva*.

CARBERRY HILL (S. Scotland). Here lord Hume and the confederate barons dispersed the royal army under Bothwell, and took Mary queen of Scots prisoner, 15 June, 1567. Bothwell fled.

CARBO-DYNAMITE, a powerful explosive of the nitro-glycerine class, invented by Messrs. Reid and Borland, was tried in 1888, and in July, 1889 was said to be practically perfect.

CARBOLIC ACID (or phenic acid), obtained by the distillation of pit-coal, by Laurent, 1846-7, is a powerful antiseptic. It is largely manufactured for surgical purposes, and has been advantageously used at Carlisle and Exeter in the deodorisation of sewage (1860-1); and as a disinfectant during the prevalence of cholera in London in 1866. It was successfully used for embalming by professor Seely in 1868. Professor F. Crace Calvert, a great manufacturer of this acid, died 1873.

CARBON was shown to be a distinct element by Lavoisier in 1788. He proved the diamond to be its purest form, and converted it into carbonic acid gas by combustion.

CARBONARI (charcoal-burners), a powerful secret society in Italy, which derived its origin, according to some, from the Waldenses, and which became prominent early in the present century. It aimed at the expulsion of foreigners from Italy, and the establishment of civil and religious liberty. In March, 1820, it is said that 650,000 joined the society, and an insurrection soon after broke out in Naples, general Pépé taking the command. The king Ferdinand made political concessions, but the influence of the allied sovereigns at Laybach led Ferdinand to annul them and suppress the liberal party, Jan. 1821, when the Carbonari were denounced as traitors.

CARBONIC ACID GAS, a gaseous compound of carbon and oxygen, found in the air, and a product of combustion, respiration, and fermentation. The Grotto del Cane yields 200,000 lbs. per annum. No animal can breathe this gas. The briskness of champagne, beer, &c., is due to its presence. It was liquefied by atmospheric pressure by Faraday in 1823. On exposing the liquid to the air it becomes solid, resembling snow, through vaporisation. See under *Cannon*, 1889-90.

CARCHEMISH, see *Hittites*.

CARDIFF, S. Wales, here was an ancient Welsh and Norman castle founded in 1080, where Robert, duke of Normandy, eldest son of William I., is said to have been imprisoned from 1106 till his death 10 Feb. 1135. The prosperity of the town has been greatly increased by the construction of a canal (1794) and railroad, and by docks, &c., promoted by the Marquis of Bute. Population, 1881, 82,761; 1891, 128,849; 1901, 164,420. Cardiff University College, established, 1883.

Stoppage of a savings bank (established in 1819) through the embezzlements of the actuary, the late Mr. R. E. Williams, effected through the neglect of the trustees; defalcations about 37,000*l.* April 1886. Report of the hon. E. Lyulph Stanley issued, *Times*, 22 Dec. 1887.
Mr. Peter Davies, a trustee, was declared to be liable for a part of the bank losses . 27 March, 1890
Church Congress met here . . . . 1 Oct. 1889
Seamen's Congress . . . . . . 8 Oct. ,,
Cardiff building society, established 1865, defalcation of 37,000*l.*, partly through the long-continued embezzlement of the funds by Arthur J. Robbins, a clerk, the loss re-imbursed partly by the defaulter and his family, the remainder by the secretary and directors—reported January. Robbins sentenced to five years' penal servitude. 25 March, 1890
Strike of railway servants, see *Strikes* . 8 Aug. ,,
New bridge over the Taff opened by the Duke of Clarence . . . . . 17 Sept. ,,
See *Shipping*, Feb. 1891; and *Strikes* . . ,,
Meeting of British Association . . 19 Aug. ,,
Strike of about 4,000 men of the building trades 30 April—3 June, 1892
The Merchants' Exchange at the Pier-head, and 30 offices destroyed by fire; great loss . 19 Nov. ,,
Remains of a Roman villa, etc., discovered by Mr. John Storrie, reported . . . 26 Sept. 1894
Industrial and fine arts exhibition opened by lord Windsor, 2 May; visit of prince and princess of Wales . . . . . . 27 June, 1896
Anti-ritualist demonstration . . . . 26 July, 1899
Grain warehouses burnt, over 40,000*l.* damage, 21 Feb. 1903

CARDIGAN BAY, see *Fishguard*.

CARDINALS, princes in the church of Rome, the council of the pope, and the conclave or "sacred college," at first were the principal priests or incumbents of the parishes in Rome, and said to have been called *cardinales* in 853. They began to assume the exclusive power of electing the popes about 1179. They first wore the red hat to remind them that they ought to shed their blood for religion, if required, and were declared princes of the church by Innocent IV., 1243 or 1245. Paul II. gave the scarlet habit, 1464; and Urban VIII. the title of Eminence in 1623 or 1630. In 1586 Sixtus V. fixed their number at 70; but there are generally vacancies. In 1860 there were 69 cardinals. In 1873, 5 of the order of bishops; 34 priests; 6 deacons; 45 in all. Nine cardinals (one a Bonaparte) were made, 13 March, 1868.* Eleven new cardinals appointed, 12 March, 1877. In 1885, 6 cardinal bishops, 35 priests, 11 deacons; in all 52. In Jan. 1894, there were 72 cardinals, 9 bishops, 52 priests and 14 deacons; 9 cardinals created, 29 Nov. 1895; 4 created, 23 June, 2 on 30 Nov. 1896; 4 on 19 April; 3 French, 20 May, 1897; 10 Italian, 2 foreign, created, 15 April, 1901; 3 created, 9 June, 1902; 58 cardinals in March, 1903.

* *British Cardinals:* Henry Stuart, created 1747; Charles Erskine, 1801; Thomas Weld, 1830; Charles Acton, 1839; Nicholas Wiseman, 30 Sept. 1850—65; Henry Edward Manning, 1875—14 Jan. 1892; Edward H. Howard, 12 March, 1877, died 16 Sept. 1892; John Henry Newman, 12 May, 1879—11 Aug. 1890; Ewd. McCabe, 27 March, 1882 (d. 11 Feb. 1885); Herbert Vaughan (d. 19 June, 1903) and Michael Logue, 16 Jan. 1893.

CARDROSS CASE, see *Trials*, 1861.

CARDS, PLAYING. The origin of the game is uncertain. It is said to have been brought to Viterbo in 1379. Cards were illuminated for Charles VI. of France, 1392, then depressed in mind. W. A. Chatto's work on the "History of Playing Cards," published, 1848. Piquet and all the early names are French.—Cards first taxed in England 1710. 428,000 packs were stamped in 1775, and 986,000 in 1800. In 1825, the duty being then *2s. 6d.* per pack, less than 150,000 packs were stamped; but in 1827 the stamp duty was reduced to *1s.*, and 310,854 packs paid duty in 1830. Duty was paid on 239,200 packs in the year ending 5 Jan. 1840; and on near 300,000, year ending 5 Jan. 1850. By an act passed in 1862 the duty on cards was reduced to *3d.* per pack. and the sellers were required to take out a licence, *1l.*; duty paid 1901-2, 23,323*l*. See also *Christmas*.

CARIA (Asia Minor), was conquered by Cyrus, 546 B.C.; by Dercyllidas, a Lacedæmonian, 397; his successor Hecatomnus became king, 385 B.C.; for his son Mausolus the *Mausoleum* was erected (*which see*). Caria was annexed by the Romans, 129 B.C. It is now part of the Turkish empire.

CARIBBEE ISLANDS, see *West Indies*.

CARICATURES were drawn by the ancient Egyptians, Greeks, and Romans. Bufalmaco, an Italian painter, about 1330, drew caricatures and put labels to the mouths of his figures with sentences. Modern caricature began with Hogarth (1697-1764). The caricatures of Gillray, Rowlandson, Cruikshank, H. B. (John Doyle $\frac{ID}{ID}$ = HB), Richard Doyle, John Leech, John Tenniel, Du Maurier, Pellegrini, "F.C.G." are justly celebrated. "Punch" was first published in 1841. See *Charivari* and *Punch*. Mr. T. Wright published a "History of Caricature," 1865; and "the Life and Works of James Gillray," 1873. Mr. J. Grego published T. Rowlandson's Works and Life, 1880. Mr. Alfred Bryan, a clever caricaturist in black-and-white, died, aged 47, 17 May, 1899. Phil May died, aged 39, 5 Aug. 1903.

CARIGNAN, a small town about twelve miles from Sedan, department of Ardennes, N.E. France. At the plain of Douzy near this place and the encampment of Vaux, a part of MacMahon's army, retreating before the Germans, turned round and made a stand, 31 Aug. 1870. After a long, severe engagement, in which the same positions were taken and retaken several times, the Germans turned the flank of their enemies, who were compelled to fall back upon Sedan, where they were finally overcome, 1 Sept.

CARILLONS, see *Bells*.

CARINTHIA, a Bavarian duchy, annexed to the territories of the duke of Austria, 1336. Population, 1890, 361,008; 1900, 367,344.

CARISBROOKE CASTLE (Isle of Wight), said to have been a British and Roman fortress. Its Norman character has been ascribed to William Fitz-Osborne, earl of Hereford in William I.'s time. Here Charles I. was imprisoned Nov. 1647 to Nov. 1648; and here his daughter Elizabeth, aged fifteen, died, 8 Sept. 1650; museum opened, 11 Aug. 1898; visited by the king, 2 April, 1902.

CARIZMIANS (fierce shepherds living near the Caspian), having been expelled by the Tartars, invaded Syria in 1243. The union of the sultans of Aleppo, Hems, and Damascus was insufficient to stem the torrent, and the Christian military orders were nearly exterminated in a single battle in 1244. In Oct. they took Jerusalem. They were totally defeated in two battles in 1247.

CARLAVEROCK CASTLE (S. Scotland), taken by Edward I., July, 1300, the subject of a contemporary poem published, with illustrations, by sir Harris Nicolas in 1828.

CARLISLE (Cumberland), a frontier town of England, wherein for many ages a strong garrison was kept. Just below this town the famous Picts' wall began, which crossed the whole island to Newcastle-upon-Tyne, and here also ended the great Roman highway. Of the great church, called St. Mary's, a large part was built by David, king of Scotland, who held Cumberland, Westmoreland, and Northumberland, from the crown of England. The castle, destroyed by the Danes, 875, restored in 1092 by William II., was the prison of Mary queen of Scots in 1568.—Taken by the parliamentary forces in 1645, and by the young Pretender, 15 Nov. 1745; retaken by the duke of Cumberland, 30 Dec. same year; partly destroyed by fire, 18 Jan. 1890.—The *see* was erected by Henry I. in 1132, and made suffragan to York. The cathedral had been founded a short time previously, by Walter, deputy for William Rufus. It was almost ruined by Cromwell, 1648, and partially repaired after the Restoration. It was reopened in 1856 after renovation, costing 15,000*l*. The see has been held by one lord chancellor and two lord treasurers; it is valued in the king's books at 530*l*. 4*s*. 11*d*. per annum. Present income 4500*l*. "Home for Art and Science," with a library at Tullie House established by the corporation, cost about 20,000*l*., opened by the mayor, 8 Nov. 1893. Prince Christian receives the freedom, and unveils a statue of queen Victoria, 7 July, 1902. Population of the city 1881, 36,585; 1891, 39,176; 1901, 46,000.

BISHOPS OF CARLISLE.

1791. Edward Venables Vernon, trans. to York, 1807.
1808. Samuel Goodenough, died 12 Aug. 1827.
1827. Hugh Percy, died Feb. 1856.
1856. Hon. H. Montagu Villiers, trans. to Durham, May, 1860.
1860. Hon. Samuel Waldegrave, died 1 Oct. 1869.
1869. Harvey Goodwin; consecrated Jan. 1870, died 25 Nov. 1891.
1891. John W. Bardsley, translated from Sodor and Man, Dec.

CARLISLE ADMINISTRATION, see *Halifax*.

CARLISTS, see *Spain*, 1830-40, 1872-6, and 1898. The legitimists of Europe subscribed to their cause 1873-6. A committee in London supplied arms and money.

CARLOVINGIANS, OR CAROLINGIANS, the second dynasty of the French kings, 752-987. Charles Martel (715-741) and Pepin his son (741-752) were mayors of the palace. The latter became king 752; see *France*.

CARLOW (S. E. Ireland). The castle, erected by John, 1180, surrendered after a desperate siege to Rory Oge O'Moore, in 1577; again to the parliamentary forces, in 1650. Here the royal troops routed the insurgents 24 May, 1798.

CARLOWITZ, Austria. Here was concluded a treaty of peace between Turkey and the allies, Germany, Russia, Poland, and Venice, 26 Jan. 1699, in consequence of the great defeat of the Turks by prince Eugene at Zenta, 11 Sept. 1697, by which Hungary was finally secured to Austria.

CARLSBAD (or Charles's Bath), in Bohemia, the celebrated springs, said to have been discovered by the emperor Charles IV. in 1370.—On 1 Aug. 1819, a congress was held here, when the great powers decreed measures to repress the liberal press, &c. Destructive gale and inundations, estimated damage, 2,500,000 florins, 23–25 Nov. 1890.

CARLSRUHE, capital of Baden, built by margrave Charles William, 1715. A revolution here was suppressed by Prussian aid, June, 1849, and the grand-duke returned 18 Aug. Population, 1890, 73,496; 1900, 97,164.

CARLTON CLUB, Pall Mall (Conservative), established by the duke of Wellington and others, 1831-2; present house opened 1855.

CARLYLE CLUB. Formed in 1881 for the purpose of affording to disciples and students of Thomas Carlyle a means of meeting together and of discussing the religious, political, and social problems treated of in his writings. His statue on the Thames-embankment, Chelsea, was unveiled by Prof. Tyndall 26 Oct. 1882. Centenary of Carlyle's birth, exhibition of a loan collection of portraits, &c., at his house, Chelsea (purchased by a trust fund); celebrated, 4 Dec. 1895.

CARLYLE SOCIETY, founded in 1879, consists of students and admirers of Carlyle's works, desirous of extending his influence; they meet monthly to read papers, &c. They have a branch at Montreal.

CARMAGNOLE, a Piedmontese song and dance, written about Aug. 1792; popular in France during the reign of terror, 1793-4. The chorus was "Dansons la Carmagnole: vive le son du canon!"

CARMATHIANS, a Mahometan sect. Carmath, a Shiite, about 890, assumed the title of "the guide, the director," &c., including that of the representative of Mahomet, St. John the Baptist, and the angel Gabriel. His followers subdued Bahrein in 900, and devastated the east. Dissensions arose amongst themselves, and their power soon passed away.

CARMAUX STRIKE, see *France*, Aug. 1892.

CARMELITES, or **WHITE FRIARS,** of Mount Carmel, one of the four orders of mendicants with austere rules, founded by Berthold about 1156, and settled in France in 1252. *Hénault*. Their rules were modified about 1540. They claimed succession from Elijah. They had numerous monasteries in England, and a precinct in London without the Temple, west of Blackfriars, is called Whitefriars to this day, after a community of their order, founded there in 1245. A Carmelite church at Kensington was founded by archbishop Manning, July, 1865. The Carmelites, as well as other orders, were expelled from their houses in France in Oct. 1880.

CARNARVON, see *Caernarvon*.

CARNATIC, a district of Southern Hindostan, extending along the whole coast of Coromandel. Hyder Ali entered the Carnatic with 80,000 troops, in 1780, and was defeated by the British under sir Eyre Coote, 1 July and 27 Aug. 1781; and decisively overthrown 2 June, 1782. The Carnatic was overrun by Tippoo in 1790. The British acquired entire authority over the Carnatic by treaty, 31 July, 1801; see *India*.

CARNATION, so called from the original species being of a flesh colour (*carnis*, of flesh). Several varieties were first planted in England by the Flemings, about 1567. *Stow*.

CARNEIAN GAMES, observed in many Grecian cities, particularly at Sparta (said to have been instituted in the 5th century B.C. in honour of Apollo, surnamed Carneus), lasted nine days.

CARNIVAL (*Carni vale*, Italian, *i.e. Flesh farewell!*), a festival time in Italy and other catholic countries before beginning Lent. The "Battle of Flowers," a sport, probably of heathen origin, is played at this time, in S. France and Italy.

CAROLINAS (N. America). Said to have been discovered by Sebastian Cabot in 1498, or by De Leon in 1512. Raleigh formed a settlement at Roanoke in June, 1585, which was broken up in 1586. About 850 English settled here about 1660; and Carolina was granted to lord Clarendon and others in 1663. The cultivation of rice was introduced by governor Smith in 1695, and subsequently cotton. A constitution drawn up by John Locke was abandoned. The province was divided into North and South in 1729; see *America*. The Carolinas being slave states, great excitement prevailed in them in Nov. 1860, on account of Abraham Lincoln's election to the presidency of the United States, he being strongly opposed to slavery. South Carolina began the secession from the United States, 20 Dec. 1860: North Carolina followed, 21 May, 1861; see *United States*, 1861-5. Both re-admitted to the Union 25 June, 1868. Embezzlements of South Carolina "official ring" (state government) disclosed; prosecutions, Sept., Oct. 1877. Increasing disaffection between the whites and negroes, riots and fighting at Charlotte, N. Carolina, 15 April, 1891. Population 1880, N. Carolina, 1,399,750; S. Carolina 995,577; 1890, N. Carolina, 1,617,947; 1900, 1,893,810; S. Carolina, 1,151,149; 1900, 1,340,316. Capitals, North, Raleigh; South, Columbia; chief city, Charleston, founded 1680.

Severe conflict at Bakersville, N. Carolina, after the lynching of a prisoner; the officers and many of the mob killed . . . . 3 Jan. 1893
Destructive cyclone (over 1000 deaths reported) S. Carolina . . . . . . 28 Aug. ,,
Riots at Darlington, S. Carolina, against a law restricting the sale of alcoholic liquors except by state official dispensaries; 5 men killed; martial law, 30 March, 1894; the law declared unconstitutional by the Supreme Court, 5 April; end of martial law . . . . . . 6 April, 1894
Convention against the negro race: disfranchisement, &c., adopted . . . Sept.—Nov. 1895
Mr. Gonzales, editor of the *State* newspaper, mortally wounded by Mr. Tillman, lieut.-gov. of S. Carolina . . . . 15 Jan. 1903

CAROLINE ISLANDS (S. Pacific), said to have been discovered by the Portuguese, 1525; also by the Spaniard, Lopez de Villalobos, 1545, and named after Charles II. of Spain, 1686. The Jesuits laboured in them in vain, 1710-33. The claims of Spain, uncontested till the protest of England in 1875, were virtually given up by Spain in 1876. The Germans occupied some of the islands, against which Spain protested in Aug. 1885. Spanish vessel arrived at the island of Yap, 21 Aug.; the Germans land and set up their flag without resistance, 24 Aug. See *Spain*. The dispute referred to the pope; the sovereignty awarded to Spain, with commercial concessions to Germany and Great Britain; agreement signed, 25 Nov.; confirmed at

Rome, 17 Dec. 1885. Anglo-Spanish protocol signed, 8 Jan. 1886. Missionaries imprisoned; natives kill the governor, announced 28 Sept. 1887. See *Spain*, 1899.

Massacre of 28 Spanish soldiers at Yap, and defeat of others sent to punish . . . 10 Aug. 1890
The natives were punished by a Spanish expedition; 150 were killed, and a village burnt. The Spanish lost 7 men killed; reported . . 13 Oct. „
Dissensions between the Spaniards, the natives, and the American missionaries, reported Dec. 1890; about 300 persons killed during the war up to . . . . Jan. 1891
After several reverses, 500 Spaniards subdue the natives, reported . . . . . Feb. „
The islands explored by Mr. Fred. W. Christian, his report published 1898
Spanish garrison at Ponape massacred by native forces and Henry Nanopi chosen ruler, reported, 30 Dec. „
The islands ceded to Germany (see *Spain*), June, 1899; the Spanish garrison leaves early Dec. „

CARP, a fresh-water or pond fish, was, it is said, first brought to these countries about 1525. *Walton*. It is mentioned by lady Juliana Berners in her book printed 1496.

CARPENTARIA, gulf of N. Australia, discovered about 1627, and said to have been named in honour of Pieter Carpentier, a retired governor of the Dutch Indies.

CARPETS are of ancient use in the East. The manufacture of woollen carpets was introduced into France from Persia, in the reign of Henry IV., between 1589 and 1610. Some artisans who had quitted France in disgust established the English carpet manufacture, about 1750. A cork-carpet company was formed in 1862.

CARPET-BAGGERS, a name given to adventurers in the southern states of North America, who, after the conclusion of the war, in 1865, endeavoured, from interested motives, to promote the political predominance of the negroes. Their influence counteracted by the conciliatory measures of president Hayes, 1877-8.

CARPI (N. Italy). Here prince Eugène and the Imperialists defeated the French 9 July, 1701.

CARPOCRATIANS, followers of Carpocrates, a Gnostic, in the 2nd century.

CARRACK or **KARRACK** (Italian, *Caracca*), a large ship in the middle ages. The Santa Anna, the property of the knights of St. John, of about 1700 tons, sheathed with lead, was built at Nice about 1530. It was literally a floating fortress, and aided Charles V. in taking Tunis in 1535. It contained a crew of 300 men and 50 pieces of artillery.

CARRAGEEN, a seaweed, *Chrondus crispus*, with flat fronds of a deep purple-brown colour, found with some other allied species on rocks and stones on the shores of Britain and northern Europe. After being gathered it is washed in fresh water and dried and bleached in the open air, when it becomes whitish and transparent. It is used for making soups, jellies, size, &c., and is regarded as a beneficial article of diet for invalids. It takes its name from Carragheen, near Waterford, in Ireland, and is also known as *Irish Moss*.

CARRARA, a town in N. Italy, province Massa-Carrara, near which are the celebrated marble quarries (now about 400), which have been worked about 2,000 years. Population in 1881, 11,869; of which the greater part are marble workers. Disturbances attributed to anarchists, checked by the military with loss of life, and a state of siege proclaimed, 16 Jan. *et seq.* 1894. Many arrested and imprisoned, 5 Feb. 1894; Carlo Gattini sentenced to 25 years, and Pietro Gattini to 12 years' solitary confinement, and 5 others to varying terms of imprisonment, 17 Feb. 1894; state of siege raised, 3 June, 1894.

CARRIAGES, see *Chariots*. Rude carriages were known in France in the reign of Henry II., A.D. 1547; in England in 1555. Henry IV. of France had one without straps or springs. They were made in England in the reign of Elizabeth, and then called whirlicotes. The duke of Buckingham, in 1619, drove six horses; and the earl of Northumberland, in rivalry, drove eight. Carriages were let for hire in Paris, in 1650, at the Hôtel Fiacre: hence the name, *fiacre; see Car, Cabriolets, Coaches* and *Licence duty*.—Annual licence duty for carriages: 4 wheels, *2l. 2s.*; under 4 cwt. or less than 4 wheels, 15*s*. Carlo Bianconi successfully introduced *cars* into Ireland about 1815: he died, nearly 90, 16 Sept. 1875. G. A. Thrupp's "History of Coaches" published, 1877. The duties on carriages altered by Customs Act, 1888.

The motor-car club formed to promote the horse less carriage industry, exhibited specimens of such carriages at the Imperial institute; locomotion obtained by compressed air, gas, oil combustion, steam, &c., or electricity, 15 Feb. 1896
International exhibition of carriages (horseless, &c.) opened at the Crystal palace by lord mayor Wilkin. . . . . 2 May „
Light locomotives on highways, act passed 14 Aug. „
Motor-cars licensed to run in Paris, Aug. 1896; public service of cars, opened . . 3 June, 1898
Regulations respecting motor-cars issued by the local government board come into force 14 Nov. „
Great meet of motor-cars near Whitehall-place, lord Winchilsea, Mr. Harry Lawson and others present, movements impeded by crowds and vehicles; 24 cars start, 10.30 a.m., 13 of the club's cars arrive at Brighton between 12.30 and 6 p.m.; 20 cars from Brixton arrived during the evening, 14 Nov. 1896; another meet 8 June, „
A van started by Messrs. Thornycroft at Chiswick, 30 Dec. 1896, arrived at Cardiff . 2 Jan. 1897
An electrical omnibus, Radcliffe-Ward system, successful trial trip in London . 9 Jan. „
A motor-car race from Paris to Trouville, about 108 miles, won by M. Gille's car in 4 hours 20 minutes . . . . 15 Aug. „
Electric cabs started in London, 19 Aug.; reported successful . . . . . . Sept. „
Mr. F. Lanchester's improved motor-car goes from Birmingham to London in 6½ hours . March, 1899
Motor-car display at the Crystal Palace, races, &c., 6 May, „
Automobile club show at Richmond opened by prince Edward of Saxe-Weimer, 17 June; exhibition at the Agricultural hall opened . 3 July, „
65 automobile vehicles leave London for a 1,000-mile trial, 23 April; 46 return, 12 May, 1900; gold medal awarded to the 12-h.p. Panhard (Hon. C. S. Rolls) . . . . . . early July, 1900
Motor-car race, left Paris about 3.30 a.m., 27 June; won by M. Fournier, at Berlin, 11.46 a.m., 29 June, 1901
Motor-cars to carry passengers at omnibus fares from Piccadilly-circus to Putney, started, 18 Sept. „
International automobile exhibition opened at Paris, M. Loubet present . . . 10 Dec. „
Motor war-car invented by Mr. F. R. Simms, exhibited at the Crystal palace . 4 April, 1902
Motor-car exhibition at the Agricultural hall, Islington . . . . 19 April, „
International motor race, Paris-Vienna, emperor's prize won by M. Renault . . . 1 July, „
Mr. S. F. Edge wins the Paris to Innsbruck motor race, announced . . . . 5 July, „

Motor-car expedition round the world left London end April, Berlin 31 Aug., arrived in St. Petersburg . . . . . 26 Sept. 1902
Stanley Automobile exhibition, Earl's Court, 16–27 Jan. Motor-car show, Crystal palace . 30 Jan. 1903
Paris to Madrid race began on Sunday, May 23; 3 persons on the road killed and 4 automobilists. The Spanish government prohibited the cars from crossing the frontier, Sunday . May 23 „
Gordon-Bennett Internat. race in Ireland authorised by act of parliament; 5 cars completed the course of 370¾ miles; Jenatzy (Germany) winner, 6h. 39m. . . . . . 2 July, „
Motor-car bill introduced in the house of lords, 6 July; royal assent . . . 14 Aug. „
Act to be in force from Jan. 1, 1904, to Dec. 31, 1906.
See *Motor Cars*.

CARRICKFERGUS (Antrim, Ireland). Its castle is supposed to have been built by Hugh de Lacy in 1178. The town surrendered to the duke of Schomberg 28 Aug. 1689. The castle surrendered to the French admiral Thurot, Feb. 1760; see *Thurot*.

CARRIERS ACT, 11 Geo. IV. & 1 Will. IV. c. 68, 1830.

CARROCIUM, a vehicle containing a crucifix and a banner, usually accompanied Italian armies in the middle ages. The Milanese lost theirs at Cortenuova, 27 Nov. 1237.

CARRON IRONWORKS, on the banks of the Carron, in Stirlingshire, established in 1760, are still (1903) the most extensive in the kingdom. The pieces of ordnance called *Carronades* or *smashers*, invented by gen. Melville, were first made at these works in 1779, but are now superseded.

CARROTS and other edible roots were imported from Holland and Flanders, about 1510.

CARS, see *Carriages*.

CARSE, a Scottish name for low alluvial lands, usually clayey and fertile, adjoining rivers.

CARTEL (challenge), a name given to the powerful coalition of the conservatives and national liberals, which for five years formed the government majority, 23, in the German Imperial parliament. The majority was lost by the elections, Feb., March, 1890.

CARTES DE VISITE. The small photographic portraits thus termed are said to have been first taken at Nice, by M. Ferrier, in 1857. The duke of Parma had his portrait placed upon his visiting cards, and his example was soon followed in Paris and London.

CARTESIAN DOCTRINES, promulgated by René Descartes, the French philosopher, in 1637. His metaphysical principle is, "I think, therefore I am;" his physical principle, "Nothing exists but substance." He accounts for all physical phenomena on his theory of vortices, motions excited by God, the source of all motion. He was born 1596, and died at Stockholm, the guest of queen Christina, in 1650.

CARTHAGE (N. coast of Africa near Tunis), founded by Dido or Elissa, according to the legend adopted by Virgil in the Æneid, some time in the 9th century B.C.; 878, 853, 826 are mentioned. She fled from her brother Pygmalion, king of Tyre, who had killed her husband, and took refuge in Africa. Towns subject to Carthage were gradually founded along the coast, and colonies in Spain and Sicily. Carthage disputed the empire of the world with Rome, which occasioned the Punic wars. The Carthaginians bore the character of a faithless people, hence the term *Punic faith*. Cato the censor ended his speeches in the senate with *Delenda est Carthago!* "Carthage must be destroyed!" Many councils were held here, A.D. 200-535.

First alliance of Carthaginians and Romans . B.C. 509
The Carthaginians in Sicily defeated at Himera by Gelon; the elder Hamilcar perishes . . . 480
They send 300,000 men into Sicily 407
Take Agrigentum 406
Defeated at the siege of Syracuse, see *Sicily* . . 396
The Carthaginians land in Italy 379
The *first* Punic war begins (lasts 23 years) . . 264
The Carthaginians defeated by the Roman consul Duilius in a naval engagement near Mylæ . . 260
War in Sicily; Roman victories . . 264 *et seq.*
Regulus with an army crosses to Africa, and defeats the Carthaginians; his hard terms of peace rejected 256
Xanthippus defeats Regulus 255
Hasdrubal defeated by Metellus at Panormus . 250
Regulus, prisoner, accompanies an embassy to Rome to propose peace, which he opposes; he returns to Carthage, and dies there . . . „
Long siege of Lilybæum . . . . 250 *et seq.*
Hamilcar Barca, successful commander in Sicily 247 *et seq.*
The great Hannibal born 247
Roman naval victory near the Ægates; treaty of peace; Sicily lost by Carthage . . . 241
Hasdrubal founds New Carthage (Carthagena) . 242
War between the Carthaginians and African mercenaries 241
Hamilcar Barca sent into Spain: takes his son, Hannibal, at the age of nine years, having first made him swear an eternal enmity to the Romans 238
Hamilcar killed 229
Hasdrubal assassinated 221
Hannibal conquers Spain, as far as the Iberus . 219
The *second* Punic war begins (lasts 17 years) . 218
Hannibal crosses the Alps, and enters Italy . „
He defeats the Roman consuls at the Ticinus and Trebia, 218; at the lake Trasimenus, 217; and at Cannæ (*which see*) . . . 2 Aug. 216
The two Scipios in Spain, at first successful, defeated and slain by the young Hasdrubal, Hannibal's brother 212
The Romans take Syracuse, 212; and expel the Carthaginians from Sicily 210
Hannibal unable to relieve Capua, closely besieged, marches to Rome, but does not attack it; Capua surrenders, and is severely punished . . 211
Philip, king of Macedon, prevented from joining Hannibal . . . . . about „
Publius Scipio carries war into Spain and takes New Carthage 210
Hasdrubal arrives with an army; defeated and slain at the Metaurus 207
Carthaginians expelled from Spain by Scipio . . 206
Scipio arrives in Africa, and gains victories . . 204
Hannibal recalled to Carthage 203
Totally defeated at Zama (*which see*) . . . 202
End of the second Punic war 201
Hannibal reforms the state, and prepares for a fresh contest with Rome, but is exiled, and takes refuge with Antiochus III., king of Syria, whom he incites against Rome, after whose defeat, 190, he resided at the court of Prusias, king of Bithynia, till he took poison, when about to be surrendered to the Romans . . . . about 183
The *third* Punic war: Scipio invades Africa . 149
Carthage taken and burned, by order of the Senate July, 146
Colony settled at Carthage by C. Gracchus about 116
Its rebuilding planned by Julius Cæsar . . 46
And executed by his successors . . 19 *et seq.*
The new city becomes a Christian bishopric A.D. 200
Cyprian holds a council here 252
Taken by Genseric the Vandal . . 9 Oct. 439
Retaken by Belisarius 533
Ravaged by the Arabs 647
Taken and destroyed by Hassan, the Saracenic governor of Egypt 698
Carthaginian antiquities (excavated by Mr. Nathan Davis) brought to the British museum . . 1861
His excavations about to be renewed . Aug. 1876
Mr. Bosworth Smith's "Carthage," published . 1878

CARTHAGENA, or **New Carthage** (S.E. Spain), built by Hasdrubal, the Carthaginian general, 242 B.C.; taken by surprise by Publius Scipio Africanus, 210 or 209. The modern Carthagena was taken by a British force under sir John Leake, June, 1706; retaken by the duke of Berwick, Nov. It was the last place held by the Intransigentes and Internationalists of Spain; was besieged by general Martin Campos, about 22 Aug. 1873. Bombardment begun 26 Nov., taken by general Lopez Dominguez, 12 Jan. 1874. See *Spain*.—Carthagena, in Columbia, South America, was taken by sir Francis Drake in 1585; pillaged by the French buccaneers in 1697; bombarded by admiral Vernon in March, 1741; and unsuccessfully besieged, April, 1741. Population, 1884, 75,980; 1897, 86,245.

CARTHUSIANS, a religious order (springing from the Benedictines) founded by Bruno of Cologne, who retired with six companions about 1084, to Chartreuse (*which see*), in the mountains of Dauphiné. Their austere rules were formed by Basil VII., their general. In France in 1880 the majority of the order refused to "seek authorisation" to remain in their monasteries, were expelled, and sought refuge in England and other countries. They appeared in England about 1180, and a monastery was founded by sir William Manny, 1371, on the site of the present Charter-house, London; see *Charter-house*. The Carthusian powder of father Simon, at Chartreuse, was first compounded about 1715.

CARTOONS, large chalk drawings preparatory to oil painting. Those of Raphael (twenty-five in number) were designed (for tapestries) in the chambers of the Vatican under Julius II. and Leo X. about 1510 to 1516. The seven preserved were purchased in Flanders by Rubens for Charles I. of England, for Hampton-court palace in 1629. They were removed to South Kensington 28 April, 1865.—The tapestries executed at Arras from these designs are at Rome. They were twice carried away by invaders, in 1526 and 1798, and were restored in 1815.—The Cartoons for the British houses of parliament were exhibited in July, 1843.

RAPHAEL'S CARTOONS.

1. The Miraculous Draught of Fishes.
2. The Charge to Peter.
3. Peter and John Healing the Lame at the Gate of the Temple.
4. The Death of Ananias.
5. Elymas the Sorcerer Struck with Blindness.
6. The Sacrifice to Paul and Barnabas, at Lystra.
7. Paul Preaching at Athens.

CASAMICCIOLA, Ischia. See *Earthquakes*, 4 March, 1881, and 28 July, 1883.

CASHEL (Tipperary, Ireland). Cormack Cuillinan, king and bishop of Cashel, was the reputed founder or restorer of the cathedral, 901. In 1152 bishop Donat O'Danergan was invested with the pall; see *Pallium*. Cashel was valued in the king's books, 29 Henry VIII. at 66*l*. 13*s*. 4*d*. Irish money. By the Church Temporalities Act, 1833, it ceased to be archiepiscopal, and was joined to Waterford and Lismore.

CASHMERE, also *Kashmir*, in the valley of the Himalayas: was subdued by the Mahometans under Akbar, in 1586; by the Afghans in 1752; by the Sikhs, 1819; and by the treaty of Lahore, 9 March, 1846, ceded to the British, who gave it to the Maharajah Gholab Singh, as tributary sovereign. The true Cashmere shawls, first brought to England in 1666, are well imitated at Bradford and Huddersfield. Shawls of Thibetan wool, for the omrahs, cost 150 rupees each, about 1650. Population, 1881, 1,534,972; 1891, 2,543,000; 1901, 2,906,000.

Gholab dies, succeeded by his son Runbeer, a favourer of education, 1857; who assists in suppressing the Indian mutiny and receives further guarantees . . . . March, 1860
The prince of Wales warmly received by the maharajah at Jummoo . . . . . . 20 Jan. 1876
Dreadful famine (partly due to continued destructive snowstorms, Oct. 1877—May, 1878) summer, 1879
The maharajah dies 12 Sept. 1885; succeeded by his son Pertab Singh; the power of the British resident greatly increased; the country virtually subject to the viceroy of India, through incompetence and folly of the maharajah . . 1888–9
The viceroy of India informs the maharajah that if he reform he may be restored to power . Aug. 1889
Increased prosperity of the country reported Nov. 1890
Visit of the viceroy of India; honourably received at Srinagar, the capital . . . . 23 Oct. 1891
Increased powers given to the maharajah . Oct. ,,
See *India*, Dec. 1891.
See *Earthquakes*, 1885.
Destructive floods, with loss of life; part of Srinagar swept away, reported, 30 July, 1893; destructive fire there . . . . . . 29 Oct. 1898

CASPIAN SEA, between Europe and Asia. The Trans-Caspian Railway (Russian) from the sea to Samarcand, opened May, 1889, was reported successful in Nov. 1892.

CASS'S CHARITY. Sir John Cass, a citizen of London, in 1709 bequeathed property to found a Church of England school in the parish of St. Botolph, Aldgate, which has existed from 1710 to the present time, with some alterations. The value of the property having enormously increased, the charity commissioners proposed a scheme involving important changes, Feb. 1893, opposed by the parishioners, 15 May, 1893.

CASSANO (N. Italy). Site of an indecisive conflict between prince Eugène of Savoy and the French, 16 Aug. 1705.

CASSATION, Court of, the highest court of appeal in France, was established 10 Nov. 1790, by the national assembly.

CASSEL, formerly the capital of Hesse-Cassel, Central Germany, acquired importance through becoming the refuge of French protestants after the revocation of the edict of Nantes, 1685. It was the capital of Jerome Bonaparte, king of Westphalia, 1807-13, and Wilhelmshöhe, a neighbouring castle, became the residence of Napoleon III. after his surrender to the king of Prussia, 2 Sept. 1870, arriving at 9.35 P.M. 5 Sept. He went to England in 1871. Population, 1890, 72,461; 1900, 106,001.

CASSITERIDES, see *Scilly Isles*.

CASTALIA, see under *Steam*.

CASTEL-FIDARDO, near Ancona, Central Italy. Near here general Lamoricière and the papal army of 11,000 men were totally defeated by the Sardinian general, Cialdini, 18 Sept. 1860. Lamoricière with a few horsemen fled to Ancona, then besieged. On 29 Sept. he and the garrison surrendered, but were shortly after set at liberty.

CASTES, distinct sections of society in India. In the laws of Menu (see *Menu*), the Hindus are divided into the Brahmans, or sacerdotal class; the Kshatrya or Chuttree, military class; the Vaisya, or commercial class; and the Sudras, or sooders, servile class. "Hindu Castes and Sects," by J. N. Bhattacharya, published 1896.

CASTIGLIONE (N. Italy). Here the French under Augereau defeated the Austrians, commanded by Wurmser, with great loss, 5 Aug. 1796.

CASTILE (Central Spain). A Gothic government was established here about 800.—Roderick, count of Castile, 860; Ferdinand, a count, became king, 1035. Ferdinand, king of Arragon, married Isabella, queen of Castile, in 1474, and formed one monarchy, 1479; see p. viii., and *Spain*.

CASTILLEJOS (N. Africa). Here on 1 Jan. 1860, was fought the first decisive action in the war between Spain and Morocco. General Prim, after a vigorous resistance, repulsed the Moors under Muley Abbas, and advanced towards Tetuan.

CASTILLON, Guienne (S. France). Here the army of Henry VI. of England was defeated by that of Charles VII. of France, and an end put to the English dominion in France, Calais alone remaining, 17 or 23 July, 1453. Talbot, earl of Shrewsbury, was killed.

CASTLEBAR (Ireland). About 1100 French troops, under Humbert, landed at Killala, and assisted by Irish insurgents here, compelled the king's troops under Lake to retreat, 27 Aug. 1798; but were compelled to surrender at Ballinamuck, 8 Sept.

CASTLEPOLLARD (Ireland). At an affray at a fair here between some peasantry and a body of police, thirteen persons lost their lives, and many were wounded, 23 May, 1831.

CASTLES. The castle of the Anglo-Saxon was a tower keep, either round or square, and ascended by a flight of steps in front. William I. erected 48 strong castles. Several hundreds, built by permission of Stephen, between 1135 and 1154, were demolished by Henry II., 1154. Many were dismantled in the civil wars. Richborough, Studfall, and Burgh are existing specimens of Roman castles.

CASUAL POOR ACT, 45 & 46 Vict. c. 36, passed 18 Aug. 1882; another bill withdrawn 23 June, 1892.

CAT. The generally received opinion that our domestic cat is derived from the European wild cat is doubted by Mr. T. Bell (1827). Rüppell (died 1794) found a wild cat in Nubia, whose conformation agreed with that of the Egyptian cat mummies. See *Mummies*. Cats fetched high prices in the middle ages, and were protected by law in Wales, about 948. Great cat shows are annually held at the Crystal palace; the 35th, 1903. A cat interrupted the debates in the commons, 9 July, 1874. A cat asylum formed at Battersea, Dec. 1882; and at Hampstead, Jan. 1896; removed to Camden town, 1900; 49,373 lost cats received up to Jan. 1902.

A discussion respecting the use of the "cat of nine tails" took place in the commons, and navy *cats* and others were inspected (see *Flogging*), 5 July, 1879

First annual international show at St. Stephen's hall, Westminster . . . . 19 Jan. 1899

CATACLYSMISTS, see *Continuity*.

CATACOMBS. The early depositories of the dead. The first Christians at Rome met for worship in the catacombs; and here are said to have been the tombs of the apostles Peter and Paul. Belzoni in 1815-18 explored many Egyptian catacombs, built 3000 years ago. He brought to England the sarcophagus of Psammetichus, formed of oriental alabaster, exquisitely sculptured. In the Parisian catacombs (formerly stone quarries), human remains from the cemetery of the Innocents were deposited in 1785; and many of the victims of the revolution in 1792-4, are interred in them.—On 31 May, 1578, some labourers digging on the Via Salaria, two miles from Rome, discovered the celebrated catacombs, of which an account with engravings was published by Antonio Bosio, in his "Roma Sotteranea" (1632), and by Aringhi (1659), and others. John Evelyn saw them in 1645. Elaborate accounts have been published recently by De Rossi; an abstract of whose researches will be found in the "Roma Sotteranea" of the Rev. J. S. Northcote and W. R. Brownlow, 1869 and 1879.

CATALOGUES, see *Libraries, Books, Scientific Papers*.

CATALONIA (N.E. Spain), was settled by the Goths and Alani, about 409; conquered by the Saracens, 712; recovered by Pepin, and by Charlemagne (788). It formed part of the Spanish marches and the territory of the count of Barcelona (*which see*). The natives were able seamen: being frequently unruly, their peculiar privileges were abolished in 1714. See *Barcelona*.

CATALYTIC FORCE. The discovery in 1819 by Theuard of the decomposition of peroxide of hydrogen by platinum, and by Döbereiner in 1823 of its property to ignite a mixture of hydrogen and oxygen, formed the groundwork of the doctrine of catalytic force, also termed "action of contact or presence," put forth by Berzelius and Mitscherlich. Their view has not been adopted by Liebig and other chemists.

CATAMARANS (or carcases), fire-machines for destroying ships; tried in vain by sir Sydney Smith, 2 Oct. 1804, on the Boulogne flotilla destined by Bonaparte to invade England.

CATANIA (the ancient Catana), a town near Etna, Sicily, was founded by a colony from Chalcis, about 730 B.C. Ceres had a temple here, open to none but women. Catania was almost totally overthrown by an eruption of Etna in 1669, and in 1693 was nearly swallowed up by an earthquake: in a moment more than 18,000 of its inhabitants were buried in the ruins. An earthquake did great damage, 22 Feb. 1817. In Aug. 1862, the town was held by Garibaldi and his volunteers, in opposition to the Italian government. He was captured on 29 Aug. Population in 1890, 109,687; 1901, 149,694.

CATAPHRYGIANS, heretics in the second century who followed the errors of Montanus. They are said to have baptized their dead, forbidden marriage, and mingled the bread and wine in the Lord's supper with the blood of young children.

CATAPULTÆ, military engines of the crossbow kind, for throwing huge stones as well as darts and arrows; said to have been invented by Dionysius, the tyrant of Syracuse, 399 B.C.

CATCH CLUB, NOBLEMEN AND GENTLEMEN'S, formed in 1761, included eminent musicians of the time. Prizes were given occasionally; sometimes, since 1821, for a composition, a gold or silver cup.

CATEAU CAMBRESIS (N. France), where, on 2, 3 April, 1559, peace was concluded between Henry II. of France, Philip II. of Spain, and Elizabeth of England. France ceded Savoy, Corsica, and nearly 200 forts in Italy and the Low Countries to Philip.

CATECHISMS are said to have been compiled in the 8th or 9th century. Luther's were published 1520 and 1529. The catechism of the church of England in the first book of Edward VI., 7 March, 1549, contained merely the baptismal vow, the creed, the ten commandments, and the Lord's prayer, with explanations; but James I. ordered the bishops to add an explication of the sacraments, 1612. The catechism of the council of Trent was published in 1566; those of the Assembly of Divines at Westminster (one termed the *shorter catechism*), 1647 and 1648; Evangelical Free Church catechism, published, 5 Jan. 1899.

CATHARI (from the Greek *katharos*, pure), a name given to the Novatians (about 251), Montanists, and other early Christian sects. See *Puritans*.

CATHAY, an old name for China.

CATHEDRAL, the chief church of a diocese, as containing the *cathedra*, or seat of the bishop, obtained the name in the 10th century.

A conference of the higher clergy to consider cathedral institutions held at Lambeth, 1 March, 1872
The act 3 & 4 Vict. c. 113, for the regulation of cathedrals passed in 1840, amended and the endowment of canonries facilitated in . . . 1873
A royal commission to inquire respecting cathedral churches appointed (abp. of Canterbury, lord Cranbrook, Mr. Beresford Hope, and others), July; met in . . . . . . Aug. 1879
Report issued recommending more flexibility in services, with use of nave, &c. . . . Feb. 1882
Final report issued . . . . . . April, 1885

CATHERINE. The order of knights of St. Catherine was instituted in Palestine, 1063. An order of ladies of the highest rank in Russia was founded by Peter the Great, 1714, in honour of the bravery of his empress Catherine. They were to be distinguished, as the name implied (from *katharos*, pure), for purity of life and manners; see *Docks* and *Katharine*.

CATHOLIC ASSOCIATION, see under *Roman Catholics*.

CATHOLIC LEAGUE formed by English churchmen more Romanistic than the English Church Union, June, 1882.

CATHOLIC MAJESTY. This title was given by pope Gregory III. to Alphonso I. of Spain, 739, and to Ferdinand V. and his queen in 1474 by Innocent VIII. on account of their zeal for religion, and their establishment of the Inquisition.

CATHOLICS, see *Roman Catholics*.

CATHOLIC UNION, and **CATHOLIC TRUTH** Society, see *Roman Catholics*. 1868.

CATILINE'S CONSPIRACY. Lucius Sergius Catiline, a dissolute Roman noble, having been refused the consulship (65 B.C.), conspired to kill the senate, plunder the treasury, and set Rome on fire. This conspiracy was timely discovered and frustrated. A second plot (in 63), was detected by the consul Cicero, whom he had resolved to murder. Catiline's daring appearance in the senate-house, after his guilt was known, drew forth Cicero's celebrated invective, "Quousque tandem, Catilina!" on 8 Nov. On seeing five of his accomplices arrested, Catiline fled to Gaul, where his partisans were assembling an army. Cicero punished the conspirators at home, and Petreius routed their forces; Catiline being killed in the engagement, Jan. 62 B.C.

CAT ISLE, see *Salvador*.

CATO, SUICIDE OF. Considering freedom as that which alone "sustains the dignity of man," and unable to survive the independence of his country, Cato stabbed himself at Utica, 46 B.C.

CATO-STREET CONSPIRACY: a gang of desperate men, headed by Arthur Thistlewood, assembled in Cato-street, Edgware-road, and proposed the assassination of the ministers of the crown, at a cabinet dinner. They were betrayed and arrested, 23 Feb. 1820, and Thistlewood, Brunt, Davidson, Ings, and Tidd, were executed as traitors, on 1 May.

CATTI, a German tribe, attacked but not subdued by the Romans A.D. 15, and 84; absorbed by the Franks, 3rd century.

CATTLE. The importation of horned cattle from Ireland and Scotland into England was prohibited by a law, 1663; but the export of cattle from Ireland became very extensive. In 1842 the importation of cattle into England from foreign countries was subjected to a moderate duty, and in 1846 they were made duty free; and since then the numbers imported have enormously increased.* Horned cattle imported into the United Kingdom 1849, 53,480; 1853, 125,523; 1855 (war), 97,527; 1860, 104,569; 1865, 283,271; 1866, 237,739; 1867, 177,948; 1868, 136,688; 1869, 220,190; 1870, 202,172; 1874, 193,862; 1876, 271,576; 1877, 201,193; 1879, 247,768; 1881, 319,374; 1883, 474,750; 1887, 295,961; 1888, 377,088; 1889, 555,222; 1890, 642,596; 1892, 502,237; 1896, 562,553; 1900, 495,645; 1902, 419,488. See under *Sheep*, *Smithfield*, *Foreign Cattle-market*.

A cattle plague began in Hungary; extended over Western Europe, destroying 1½ million cattle 1711-14
A severe cattle plague raged in England and west Europe (about 3 million cattle perish) . . 1745-56
The privy council ordered diseased beasts to be shot, and their skins destroyed; granting moderate compensation . . . . 12 March, 1746
Great disease among foreign cattle; excluded from this country by prohibitions . . . April, 1857
The cattle plague appears at Laycock's dairy, Barnsbury, London, N.; rapidly spreads, about 24 June, 1865
27,432 beasts had been attacked; 12,680 died; 8,998 slaughtered, up to . . . . . 21 Oct. ,,
A royal commission to inquire into the causes of cattle plague and suggest remedies met first, 10 Oct.; report of majority considered the disease to have been imported, and recommend slaughter of animals, and stringent prohibition of passage of cattle across public roads, &c., 31 Oct. 1865; second report, 6 Feb.; 3rd report . 1 May, 1866
Orders in council for regulating the cattle plague (in conformity with the act of 1850), 23 Nov. and 16 Dec. 1865; and . . . . . . 20 Jan. ,,
Disease raging; official report; cattle attacked, 120,740; killed, 16,742; died, 73,750; recovered, 14,162; unaccounted for, 16,086 . . 1 Feb. ,,
Cattle Disease Acts passed 20 Feb. and 10 Aug. ,,
Orders in council making uniform repressive measures throughout the country . . 27 March, ,,
The disease materially abates . . . . April, ,,
Privy council return: cattle attacked, 248,965; killed, 80,597; died, 124,187; recovered, 32,989; unaccounted for, 11,192 . . . . . 22 June, ,,
The disease nearly "stamped out" . . 27 Oct. ,,
Order in council directing that foreign cattle be landed only at certain ports (after 13 Nov.), there to be subjected to quarantine . . . . 10 Nov. ,,
Cattle plague re-appears in Cheshire and Lancashire and Yorkshire . . . . . . Dec. ,,
Re-appears at Barnsbury (see 24 June, 1865), 46 animals slaughtered . . . . . 2 Feb. 1867
Re-appearance in various places . . June, July, ,,

* Sale of 30 of duke of Devonshire's shorthorn bulls for 19,923*l.*, about Sept. 1878.

Contagious Diseases (Animals) Act renewed 1867; amended 1869
Order of council permitting cattle to be removed from the metropolis . . . . 25 July, 1868
New general orders issued . . . . . Aug. 1869
Prevalence of "foot-and-mouth disease" in England . Aug. 1869—Dec. 1870; June, July, 1871
Disease appears at Kaiserslautern, rear of the German army; cautionary regulations promulgated by the privy council . . . . . 9 Sept. 1870
New foreign cattle market determined on, Nov. 1870; opened Dec. 1871; suffers by great fire, about 10,000*l.* lost . . . 18 Sept. 1883
Foot-and-mouth disease in England . July, Aug. 1872
Appearance of the plague in German cattle; further importation suspended . . . about 3 Aug. ,,
Cattle-plague appears at Pocklington, Yorkshire; vigorously treated, 3 Sept.; stringent order from the privy council . . . . . . 7 Sept. ,,
Live cattle imported to Glasgow from America by Mr. Bell . . . . July, 1873
Foot-and-mouth disease in some English counties, Aug.—Sept. 1875
Re-appearance of cattle-plague in England; restrictions in London and other places; much cattle killed . . . . Jan.—May, 1877
Cattle-plague commission enlarged, 3 May; plague said to be stamped out; restrictions removed, 26 June; fresh cases in London; restrictions resumed 13 July; removed . . . 31 July, ,,
New Cattle Contagious Diseases Act passed 16 Aug. 1878
Order in council prohibiting importation of living cattle from eastern half of Europe after 1 Jan. 1879; imports permitted from some countries, cattle to be slaughtered; (no restriction respecting some countries) . . . . . 6 Dec. ,,
Foot-and-mouth disease in E. Lancashire, Aug. 1881; in Staffordshire, Aug. 1882; Norfolk Oct. 1882
International cattle show at Hamburg . July, 1883
Foot-and-mouth disease prevailing in English midland counties, July; in Kent . July, *et seq.* ,,
Severe at Odessa . . . . Oct. 1883—May, 1884
Abating in England through suspension of fairs, &c., announced . . . . . . April, ,,
Cattle-men of United States; above 12,000 delegates hold a convention at St. Louis, organize a national live stock association, and recommend the formation of a national trail ten miles wide for the passage of cattle from the Red River to the Northern boundary of the States 18-22 Nov. ,,
Contagious Diseases Act (amended) 1884, 1886, 1890, 1892, and 1893
Foot-and-mouth disease stamped out, *Earl Spencer*, 28 May; favourable reports . . . Dec. 1886
Cattle disease in Leicestershire . . . . June 1889
Foot-and-mouth disease in Germany; importation into England checked. . . . . Oct. ,,
Pleuro-pneumonia and anthrax in the United Kingdom . . . . . . reported 6 Feb. 1890
Foot-and-mouth disease at the Metropolitan cattle market detected in some Danish cattle; all slaughtered, 4-6 Feb. The sale of live cattle temporarily suspended, 8 Feb. The disease soon after appeared in Kent, Surrey, W. R. Yorkshire, Chester, Westmoreland, Edinburgh, Glasgow, Paisley, and was vigorously stamped out by the action of the board of agriculture . Feb.-July, 1892
Pleuro-pneumonia in Dundee and other places, Oct. ,,
Importation of live Canadian cattle prohibited Oct. ,,
Foot-and-mouth disease in N. London; movement of cattle prohibited, 2 Jan.; the disease disappears 7 Jan.; order rescinded, 16 Jan. 1893, reappears in Essex, Cambridgeshire and Kent Nov. 1894
Consolidation Act passed in . . . . . . ,,
Great spread of rinderpest in S. Africa, April *et seq.* ,,
Diseases of Animals Act, ordering immediate slaughter of diseased foreign cattle when landed, passed . . . . 20 July ,,
In 1894 three-fourths of the live cattle and nearly six-sevenths of the fresh beef imported into the United Kingdom came from the United States; still increasing . . . . ,,
Dr. Koch in Cape Town renders cattle immune by means of a mixture of serum and rinderpest blood; announced, 12 Feb. *et seq.* 1897; Dr. Kolle's and Dr. George Turner's treatment by injection very successful, reported (Roy. Soc.), 30 Nov. 1898
Boycotting practised by certain butchers and salesmen against farmers and others in Scotland, respecting the sale of cattle, checked by an agreement, the result of conferences between the board of agriculture, the Scottish chamber of agriculture, and some of the leading salesmen *Times*, 28 and 29 Nov. ,,
Outbreak of foot-and-mouth disease in Norfolk and Suffolk . . . . Jan., Feb. 1900
Rinderpest in S. Africa successfully checked by inoculation . . . . Sept. 1901
Dr. Remo Guzzi's cure for foot-and-mouth disease by injections of a solution of corrosive sublimate successful in Italy, reported. . . 12 Nov. ,,
Board of Agriculture issues order revoking the Foreign Animals Amendment Order of 1900, which prohibited the landing in the United Kingdom of animals from the Argentine republic and from Uruguay . . . . . 3 Feb. 1903

CATTLE AND SHEEP IN THE UNITED KINGDOM AND ISLANDS.

	Cattle.	*Sheep.*		*Cattle.*	*Sheep.*
1866	8.570,000	26,380,000	1881	9,905,013	27,896,273
1868	9,083.416	35,607,812	1882	9,832,417	27,448,220
1869	9,078,282	34,250,272	1883	10,097,943	28,347,560
1870	9,235,052	32,786,783	1884	10,422,762	29,376,787
1871	9,346,216	31,403,500	1885	10,868,760	30,086,200
1872	9,718,505	32,246,642	1886	10,872,811	28,955,240
1873	10,153,670	33,982,404	1887	10,639,960	29,401,750
1874	10,281,036	34,837,597	1888	10,268,600	28,938,716
1875	10.162,787	33,491,948	1890	10,789,858	31,667,195
1876	9,997,189	32,252,579	1894	10,780,796	30,037,818
1877	9,731,537	32,220.067	1896	10,942,423	30,853,809
1878	9,761,288	32,571,018	1901	11 437,217	30,755,950
1879	9,961,536	32,237,958	1902	11,338,180	29,981,446

CATTLE SHOW, see *Smithfield.*

CAUBUL, see *Cabul.*

CAUCASUS, a lofty mountain, a continuation of the ridge of Mount Taurus, between the Euxine and Caspian seas. The passes near the mountain were called *Caucasiæ Portæ*, and it is supposed that through them the Sarmatians or Huns invaded the provinces of Rome, A.D. 447. Population of the province, 1885, 7,824,567; 9 Feb. 1897, 9,723,553: see *Circassia.*

Two explorers, Mr. W. F. Donkin and Mr. H. Fox, and their guides lost . . . . about 1 Sept. 1888
Alpine club search party find only some of their property . . . . 29 July, 1889
Agricultural exhibition opened at Tiflis 27 Sept. ,,
Violent rioting against the cattle sanitary laws suppressed by the military in Borgustan, reported . . . . 22 Aug. 1894
Brigandage and murder in Batum and Elizabetpol, reported . . . . 7 Nov. 1896
Prince Galitzin, gov.-gen. 1896, issues reports, see *Times* . . . . 5 April, 1899
Glacier disaster in the Ghenal Don valley, 32 lives lost . . . . mid July, 1902
Brigandage and lawlessness . . . . . Jan. 1903

CAUCUS. An American term applied to a private meeting of the leading politicians of a party to agree upon the plans to be pursued during an election or session of congress. This institution is now a very powerful antagonist to public opinion. The word is said to be derived from "ship"-caulkers' meetings. A "caucus club" is mentioned by John Adams, in 1763. *Bartlett.* Similar meetings are occasionally held in London by conservatives and liberals; one was held by Mr. Gladstone respecting the ballot bill, 6 July, 1871. Jealousy respecting the system was aroused in 1878.

The Birmingham Liberal association began in 1868 a powerful caucus, systematized by Mr. Schnadhorst, very efficient 1873 *et seq.*; a similar conservative association since formed; a network of similar societies exist throughout the kingdom Autumn 1885

The London Liberal and Radical council, actually a caucus, active in . . . November, 1885
10,500*l*. presented to Mr. Schnadhorst by the Liberals, 9 March, 1887; he retired from politics, Nov. 1894, died . . . . . 2 Jan. 1900

CAUDINE FORKS, according to Livy, the *Furculæ Caudinæ* (in Samnium, S. Italy), were two narrow defiles or gorges, united by a range of mountains on each side. The Romans went through the first pass, but found the second blocked up; on returning they found the first similarly obstructed. Being thus hemmed in by the Samnites, under the command of C. Pontius, they surrendered at discretion, 321 B.C. (after a fruitless contest, according to Cicero). The Roman senate broke the favourable treaty. C. Pontius, taken prisoner in the third Samnite war, was executed at Rome, 290.

CAULIFLOWER, said to have been brought from Cyprus to England about 1603.

CAUSTIC, in Painting, a method of burning colours into wood or ivory, invented by Gausias of Sicyon. He painted his mistress Glycerē sitting on the ground making garlands with flowers; the picture was hence named *Stephanoplocon*. It was bought by Lucullus for two talents, 335 B.C. *Pliny*.

CAUTIONARY TOWNS (Holland), (the Briel, Flushing, Rammekins, and Walcheren), were given to queen Elizabeth in 1585 as security for their repaying her for assistance in their struggle with Spain. They were restored to the Dutch republic by James I. in 1616.

CAVALIER. The appellation given to the supporters of the king during the civil war, from a number of gentlemen forming themselves into a body-guard for the king in 1641. They were opposed to the Roundheads, or parliamentarians.

CAVALRY. Used by the Canaanites in war, 1450 B.C. (*Josh.* xi. 4). Attached to each Roman legion was a body of 300 horse, in ten turmæ; the commander always a veteran.—The Persians had 10,000 horse at Marathon, 490 B.C.; and 10,000 Persian horse were slain at the battle of Issus, 333 B.C. *Plutarch*. In the wars with Napoleon I. the British cavalry reached to 31,000 men. Our cavalry force, in 1840, was 10,733. In 1867, cavalry of the line, 10,023; in depôts, 838; in India, 5421; total, 17,599; in 1880, total 17,245; 1903-4, 554 officers, 1337 non-commissioned, 14,271 rank and file; in India, total 5,635; voted household cavalry 60,900*l*., line 419,000*l*. *Cavalry Manœuvres* on the Berkshire Downs, eight regiments, director, sir Evelyn Wood; general in command, sir Baker Russell, Sept. 1890. The manœuvres are now annually repeated near Aldershot, Aug.-Sept. see *Horse Guards, &c.* "Achievements of Cavalry," by gen. sir Evelyn Wood, published 1897.

CAVENDISH COLLEGE, Cambridge (founded in 1871 to give cheap university education to youths younger than those admitted at other colleges, and leaving earlier for business), was inaugurated by the duke of Devonshire, 26 Oct. 1876. New buildings opened by the marquis of Hartington, 16 Nov. 1889; closed since 1891.

CAVENDISH EXPERIMENT. In 1798 the hon. Henry Cavendish described his experiment for determining the mean density of the earth, by comparing the force of terrestrial attraction with that of the attraction of leaden spheres of known magnitude and density, by means of the torsion balance. *Brande*. The Cavendish Society, for the publication of chemical works, which ceased with Gmelin's Chemistry (1848-72), was established 1846.

CAVES are frequently mentioned in the Bible as dwellings, refuges, and burying-places. Mr. W. B. Dawkins' "Cave-hunting; Researches on the Evidence of Caves respecting the Early Inhabitants of Europe," was published 1874. Oreston cave, Devon, discovered 1816; Kirkdale, Yorkshire, 1821; Kent's Hole, Torquay, *which see*, 1825; Brixham cave, 1858; Wookey Hole, Somerset, 1859; and many others, have been well explored, including the caves in the valley of the Lesse in Belgium, of the Pyrenees and Perigord in France, and the Kesserloch, Thaingen, Switzerland. The remains of extinct mammalia found in these caves furnish proof of the antiquity of man.

CAWNPORE, a town in India, on the Doab, a peninsula between the Ganges and Jumna. During the mutiny in June, 1857, it was garrisoned by native troops under sir Hugh Wheeler. These broke out into revolt. An adopted son of the old Peishwa Bajee Rao, Nana Sahib, who had long lived on friendly terms with the British, came apparently to their assistance, but joined the rebels. He took the place after three weeks' siege, 26 June; and in spite of a treaty massacred great numbers of the British, without respect to age or sex, in the most cruel manner. General Havelock defeated Nana Sahib, 16 July, at Futtehpore, and retook Cawnpore, 17 July. Sir Colin Campbell defeated the rebels here on 6 Dec. following. A column was erected here, in memory of the sufferers, by their relatives of the 32nd regiment. In Dec. 1860, Nana was said to be living at Thibet; and in Dec. 1861 was incorrectly said to have been captured at Kurrachee; see *India*, 1857. Population, 1901, 197,170.

CAXTON SOCIETY, established for the publication of chronicles and literature of the Middle Ages, published sixteen volumes, 1844-54. *Caxton Celebration*, see under *Printing*, 1877.

CAYENNE, French Guiana (S. America), settled by the French, 1604-35. It afterwards came successively into the hands of the English (1654), French, and Dutch. The last were expelled by the French in 1677. Cayenne was taken by the British, 12 Jan. 1809, but was restored to the French in 1814. Here is produced the *Capsicum baccatum*, or cayenne pepper. Many French political prisoners were sent here in 1848.

CECILIAN SOCIETY, see *Cæcilian*.

CEDAR CREEK and MOUNTAIN, Virginia, U.S. On 19 Oct. 1864, gen. Sheridan converted the defeat of the Federals by the Confederates under Longstreet into a complete victory. At Cedar Mountain gen. Stonewall Jackson defeated Banks, 9 Aug. 1862.

CEDAR TREE. The red cedar (*Juniperus virginiana*) came from North America before 1664; the Bermudas cedar from Bermudas before 1683; the Cedar of Lebanon (*Pinus Cedrus*) from the Levant before 1683. In 1850 a grove of venerable cedars, about 40 feet high, remained on Lebanon. The cedar of Goa (*Cupressus lusitanica*) was brought to Europe by the Portuguese about 1683; see *Cypress*.

CELERY is said to have been introduced into England by the French marshal, Tallard, during his captivity in England, after his defeat at Blenheim by Marlborough, 2 Aug. 1704.

CELESTIAL GLOBE, see *Globes*.

CELIBACY (from *cœlebs*, unmarried) was preached by St. Anthony in Egypt about 305. His early converts lived in caves, &c., till monasteries were founded. The doctrine was rejected in the council of Nice, 325. Celibacy was enjoined on bishops only in 692. The decree was opposed in England, 958-978. The Romish clergy generally were enjoined a vow of celibacy by pope Gregory VII. in 1073-85, and its observance was established by the council of Placentia, held in 1095. Marriage was restored to the English clergy in 1547. The marriage of the clergy was proposed, but negatived at the council of Trent (1563); also at a conference of the old catholics at Bonn, June, 1876. Sir Bartle Frere termed the Zulu army "a *celibate* man-slaying machine," 1878.

CELL THEORY (propounded by Schwann in 1839) supposes that the ultimate particles of all animal and vegetable tissues are small cells. Some of the lowest forms of animal and vegetable life are composed of merely a single cell, as the great majority of the Protozoa and Protophyta. Prof. Virchow proved in his Croonian lecture in London that all new cells proceed from old ones, 16 March, 1893, see *Protoplasm*.

CELLULOID, see *Ivory*.

CELTIBERI, see *Numantine War*.

CELTS, or KELTS, a group of the Aryan family; see *Gauls*. Chiefly by the exertions of Prof. John S. Blackie a Celtic professorship at the university of Edinburgh was founded 1876; 11,937*l*. subscribed April, 1879. One was established at Oxford in 1876; see *Gaelic*.

CEMETERIES. The burying-places of the Jews, Greeks, Romans, were outside their towns (*Matt*. xxvii. 60). Many public cemeteries resembling "Père La Chaise" * at Paris, have been opened in all parts of the kingdom since 1856; see *Catacombs*, *Bunhill-fields*.

PRINCIPAL METROPOLITAN CEMETERIES.

Kensal-green cemetery, 53 acres; consecrated, 2 Nov.	1832
South Metropolitan and Norwood cemetery, 40 acres; consecrated . . . . . 6 Dec.	1837
Highgate and Kentish-town cemetery, 22 acres; opened and consecrated . . . . 20 May,	1839
Abney Park cemetery, Stoke Newington, 30 acres; opened by the lord mayor . . . . 20 May,	1840
Westminster, or West London cemetery, Kensington-road; consecrated . . . . 15 June,	,,
Nunhead cemetery, about 50 acres; consecrated 29 July,	,,
City of London and Tower Hamlets cemetery, 30 acres; consecrated	1841
London Necropolis and National Mausoleum, at Woking, Surrey, 2000 acres; the company incorporated in July, 1852; opened . . . Jan.	1855
City of London cemetery, Ilford; opened, 24 June, and many others since.	1856
Acts respecting burials passed	1850-57

CENIS, MOUNT, see under *Alps*.

CENSORS, Roman magistrates, to survey and rate the property, and correct the manners of the people. The two first censors were appointed, 443 B.C. Plebeian censors were first appointed, 131 B.C. Cato, the censor, elected 184 B.C., strenuously endeavoured to restrain the luxury and vice of the patricians. The office, abolished by the emperors, was revived by Decius, A.D. 251; see *Press*.

* Père La Chaise was the favourite and confessor of Louis XIV., who made him superior of a great establishment of the Jesuits on this spot, then named Mont Louis. The house and grounds were bought for a national cemetery, which was laid out by M. Brongniart, and first used on 21 May, 1804.

CENSUS. The Israelites were numbered by Moses, 1490 B.C.; and by David, 1017 B.C.; Demetrius Phalereus is said to have taken a census of Attica, 317 B.C. Servius Tullius is traditionally said to have enacted that a general estimate of every Roman's estate and personal effects should be delivered to the government upon oath every five years, 566 B.C. A census of the people is stated to have been taken at Florence in 1527; at Venice, 1584; in France, 1700; in Sweden, 1749; and in the United States, N.A., 1790. In England the proposal for a census in 1753 was opposed as profane and subversive of liberty. In the United Kingdom the census is now taken at decennial periods since 1801; 1811, 1821, 1831, 1841, 1851, 1861 (7 April), 1871 (3 April), 1881 (3 April), 1891 (5 April), 1901 (31 March). See *Population*. For the latest census of other countries, see TABLE at the beginning of this work.

CENTAL, a new name given to the 100-lbs. weight, *London Gazette*, 7 Feb. 1879.

CENTENARIANS, see *Longevity*.

CENTRAL AFRICA, see under *Africa*.

CENTRAL AMERICA, see *America, Central*. A large American steamer of this name was wrecked during a gale in the gulf of Mexico, 12 Sept. 1857. Of about 550 persons only 152 were saved; several of these after drifting on rafts above 600 miles. The loss of about 2½ million dollars in specie aggravated the commercial panic in New York shortly after. The captain and crew behaved heroically.

CENTRAL ASIA. See under *Asia*.

CENTRAL CRIMINAL COURT, established in 1834. Commissions are issued to the fifteen judges of England (of whom three attend in rotation at the Old Bailey) for the periodical delivery of the gaol of Newgate, and the trial of offences of greater degree, committed in Middlesex and parts of Essex, Kent, and Surrey; the new district is considered as one county.

CENTRAL PROVINCES OF INDIA, constituted out of territories from the North-West provinces and Madras in 1861 and placed under a chief commissioner. Population in 1881, 9,838,791; 1891, 10,761,630; 1901, 9,845,318. Capital, Nagpur, population, 1891, 117,910. Chief commissioners, Alex. Mackenzie (1887); A. Patrick MacDonnell (1891); J. Woodburn (1895); C. J. Lyall (1895); A. H. L. Fraser (1901).

CENTURION, the captain, head, or commander of a subdivision of a Roman legion, which consisted of 100 men, and was called a *centuria*. By the Roman census each hundred of the people was called a centuria, 556 B.C.

CENTURY. The Greeks computed time by the Olympiads, beginning 776 B.C., and the Roman church by Indictions, the first of which began 24 Sept., A.D. 312. The method of computing time by centuries commenced from the incarnation of Christ, and was adopted in chronological history first in France. *Dupin*. See *Dictionaries*, 1889.

CEPHALONIA, the ancient Cephallenia, one of the Ionian islands, was taken from the Ætolians by the Romans, 189 B.C., and given to the Athenians by Hadrian, A.D. 135; see *Ionian Isles*.

It was held successively by the eastern emperors, by the Franks in the 12th century, by the princes of Achaia, 1224; by the Turks, 1479; by the Venetians 1500–1797
Mr. P. A. Vagliano, of Bayswater (died 25 Jan. 1902), bequeathed 500,000*l.* for charities in the island.

CEPHISUS, a river in Attica, near which Walter de Brienne, duke of Athens, was defeated and slain by the Catalans, 1311.

CERBÈRE, a French gun-brig, with a crew of 87 men, and seven guns, in the harbour of L'Orient, within pistol-shot of three batteries, was captured in a most daring manner by lieut. Jeremiah Coghlan, in a cutter with 19 companions aided by two boats, one of which was commanded by midshipman Paddon. The prize was towed out under a heavy but ineffectual fire from the batteries, 26 July, 1800. *Nicolas.*

CEREMONIES, MASTER OF THE, an office instituted for the more honourable reception of ambassadors and persons of quality at court, 1 James I. 1603. The order maintained by the master of the ceremonies at Bath, "Beau Nash," the "King of Bath," led to the adoption of the office in ordinary assemblies; he died in his 88th year, 1761. *Ashe.*

CERES, a planet, 160 miles in diameter, was discovered by M. Piazzi, at Palermo, 1 Jan. 1801; he named it after the goddess highly esteemed by the ancient Sicilians.

CERESUOLA (N. Italy). Here Francis de Bourbon, count d'Enghien, defeated the imperialists under the marquis de Guasto, 14 April, 1544.

CERIGNOLA (S. Italy). Here the great captain Gonsalvo de Cordova and the Spaniards defeated the duc de Nemours and the French, 28 April, 1503.

CERINTHIANS, followers of Cerinthus, a Jew, who lived about A.D. 80, are said to have combined Judaism with pagan philosophy.

CERIUM, a very rare metal, discovered by Klaproth and others in 1803.

CEUTA (the ancient Septa), a town on N. coast of Africa, stands on the site of the ancient Abyla, the southern pillar of Hercules. It was taken from the Vandals by Belisarius for Justinian, 534; by the Goths, 618; by the Moors about 709, from whom it was taken by the Portuguese, 1415. With Portugal, it was annexed in 1580 to Spain, which power still retains it. See *Morocco*, 1893.

CEYLON (the ancient Taprobane), an island in the Indian Ocean, called by the natives the seat of paradise. It became a seat of Buddhism, 307 B.C., and was known to the Romans about 41 A.D. Population 1873, 2,323,760; 1881, 2,758,165; 1891, 3,008,239; 1901, 3,576,990. Imports, 72,340,662 Rs.; exports, 74,195,367 Rs., in 1893; imports, 122,339,758; exports, 94,962,277, in 1900.

The Mahavansa, a metrical chronicle in Pali, gives the history of Ceylon from 543 B.C. down to 432 A.D., which has been continued to 1756. Buddhism was established as the national religion B.C. 307
The usurpation of the Malabars 237
Wyjayo Bahu re-establishes a native dynasty A.D. 1071
Prakrama Bahu, a great prince, reigns . 1153 *et seq.*
Wars with the Malabars, 12th and 13th centuries.
Invaded by the Portuguese Almeyda . . . 1505
The Dutch landed in Ceylon, 1602; and captured the capital, Colombo 1603
Frequent conflicts; peaceful commercial relations established (the Portuguese having been expelled) 1664
Intercourse with the British begun 1713
A large portion of the country taken by them in 1782; was restored 1783
The Dutch settlements seized by the British: Trincomalee, 26 Aug.; Jaffnapatam . . Sept. 1795
Ceylon was ceded to Great Britain by the peace of Amiens 1802
British troops treacherously massacred or imprisoned by the Adigar of Candy, at Colombo: see *Candy* . . . . 26 June, 1803
Complete sovereignty of the island assumed by England 1815
Bishopric of Colombo founded 1845
The governor, lord Torrington, absolved from a charge of undue severity in suppressing a rebellion . . . . . . May, 1851
Prosperity of Ceylon greatly increased under the administration of sir H. Ward . . . 1855-60
Sir J. E. Tennent's work, "Ceylon," appeared . 1859
Sir Hercules G. Robinson appointed governor, 7 March, 1865
The duke of Edinburgh visited Ceylon . April, 1870
Wm. H. Gregory, M.P., appointed governor, 9 Jan. 1872
Visit of the prince of Wales . . . . 1 Dec. 1875
Sir J. R. Longden appointed governor . Nov. 1876
Sir Arthur Hamilton Gordon . . . . Feb. 1883
Sir Arthur E. Havelock . . . . 12 March, 1890
Sir Joseph West Ridgeway . . . . Sept. 1895
Death of Mr. Henry Trimen, F.R.S., eminent botanist . . . . . . 16 Oct. 1896
Increased revenue and diminished debt, public works and railways much promoted, announced 6 Nov. 1897
First sod of the Colombo graving dock cut by the governor . . . . . . 1 March, 1899
Sir J. Ridgeway returns; Colombo decorated, addresses presented . . . 25 Nov. ,,
Cambridge expedition, under Mr. S. Gardiner, to the Maldives and Laccadives to investigate the coral reefs, &c.; 300 islands visited . 1899–1900
Boer prisoners (5,127) deported from S. Africa located here 1900–1
The duke and duchess of Cornwall warmly received, 12-16 April, 1901
Queen's statue unveiled at Colombo . 25 June, 1902
Rev. E. A. Copeland consecrated bishop of Colombo 30 Aug. 1903

CHÆRONEA (Bœotia). Here Greece was ruined by Philip; 32,000 Macedonians defeating 30,000 Thebans, Athenians, &c., 6 or 7 Aug. 338 B.C. Here Archelaus, lieutenant of Mithridates, was defeated by Sylla, and 110,000 Cappadocians were slain, 86 B.C.; see *Coronea.*

CHAIN BRIDGES, see *Suspension Bridges.*

CHAIN-CABLES, PUMPS, AND SHOT. Iron chain-cables were in use by the Veneti, a people intimately connected with the Belgæ of Britain in the time of Cæsar, 57 B.C. These cables came into use, generally in the navy of England, in 1812. Acts for the proving and sale of chain-cables and anchors were passed in 1864, 1871, and 1874.—CHAIN SHOT, to destroy the rigging of an enemy's ship, were invented by the Dutch admiral, De Witt, in 1666.—CHAIN-PUMPS were first used on board the *Flora*, British frigate, in 1787.

CHALCEDON, Asia Minor, opposite Byzantium, colonised by Megarians, about 684 B.C. It was taken by Darius, 505 B.C.; by the Romans, 74 B.C.; plundered by the Goths, A.D. 259; taken by Chosroes, the Persian, 609; by Orchan, the Turk, 1338. Here was held the "Synod of the Oak," 403; and the fourth general council, which annulled the act of the "Robber Synod," 8 Oct. 451.

CHALCIS, see *Eubœa.*

CHALDÆA, the ancient name of Babylonia, but afterwards restricted to the S. W. portion. The Chaldæans were devoted to astronomy and astrology; see *Dan.* ii. &c.—The CHALDÆAN REGISTERS of celestial observations, said to have commenced

2234 B.C., were brought down to the taking of Babylon by Alexander, 331 B.C. (1903 years).

CHALGROVE (Oxfordshire). At a skirmish here with prince Rupert, 18 June, 1643, John Hampden, of the parliament party, was wounded, and died 24 June. A column was erected to his memory, 18 June, 1843.

CHALLENGER, see *Deep Sea Soundings*.

CHALONS-SUR-MARNE (N.E. France). Here the emperor Aurelian defeated Tetricus, the last of the pretenders to the throne, termed the Thirty Tyrants, 274; and here in 451 Aëtius defeated Attila the Hun, compelling him to retire into Pannonia.

CHAM, see *Charivari*.

CHAMBERLAIN, early a high court officer in France, Germany, and England. The office of chamberlain of the exchequer ceased in 1834.

JOINT-HEREDITARY LORD GREAT CHAMBERLAINS OF ENGLAND.—The sixth great officer of state, whose duties, among others, relate to coronations and public solemnities. The office was long held by the De Veres, earls of Oxford, granted by Henry I. in 1101. On the death of John De Vere, the sixteenth earl, Mary, his sole daughter, marrying lord Willoughby De Eresby, the right was established in that nobleman's family by a judgment of the house of peers, 2 Charles I. 1625. On the death of his descendant, unmarried, in July, 1779, the house of lords and twelve judges concurred that the office devolved to lady Willoughby De Eresby, and her sister the lady Georgina Charlotta Bertie, as heirs to their brother Robert, duke of Ancaster, deceased; and that they had powers to appoint a deputy to act for them, not under the degree of a knight, who, if his majesty approved of him, might officiate accordingly. *Beatson*. This dignity was for some time held jointly by the lord Willoughby De Eresby and the marquis of Cholmondeley, descendants of John de Vere, earl of Oxford. Lord Willoughby De Eresby died without issue 27 Aug. 1870, and lord Aveland, his sister's son, was appointed to act. The marquis of Cholmondeley died 16 Dec. 1884, and was succeeded by his grandson, George H. H., the present marquis, 1884; re-appointed, 2 Sept. 1901; again by the king, 21 June, 1902. Lady Willoughby De Eresby died 26 July, 1879, was succeeded by her sons, the earl of Ancaster and lord Carrington (earl, 1895).

LORD CHAMBERLAIN OF THE HOUSEHOLD.—An ancient office. The title is from the French *Chambellan*, in Latin *Camerarius*. Sir William Stanley, knt., afterwards beheaded, was lord chamberlain, 1 Henry VII. 1485. A vice-chamberlain acts in the absence of the chief; the offices are co-existent. *Beatson*. The earl of Lathom, 1885; lord Carrington, 1892; earl of Lathom, 1895 (died aged 61, 19 Nov. 1898); the earl of Hopetoun, Dec. 1898; the earl of Clarendon, Sept. 1900.

The Chamberlain of London is an ancient office.

CHAMBERLAIN'S, MR., TOUR IN SOUTH AFRICA, see under *Cape Colony*, *Natal*, *Transvaal*.

CHAMBERS, see *Commerce*, *Agriculture*, *Shipping*.

CHAMBERS' JOURNAL was first published at Edinburgh in Feb. 1832. Jubilee kept 4 Feb. 1882. Robt. Chambers died 17 Mar. 1871. William died 20 May, 1883. Chambers' Encyclopædia, see under "*Encyclopædia*."

CHAMBRE ARDENTE (fiery chamber), an extraordinary French tribunal so named from the punishment frequently awarded by it. Francis I. in 1535, and Henry II. in 1549, employed it for the extirpation of heresy, which led to the civil war with the Huguenots in 1560; and in 1679 Louis XIV. appointed one to investigate the poisoning cases which arose after the execution of the marchioness Brinvilliers.

CHAMBRE INTROUVABLE, a name given to the chamber of deputies, elected in France in 1815, on account of its ignorance, incapacity, and bigoted reactionary spirit.

CHAMPAGNE, an ancient province, N. E. France, once part of the kingdom of Burgundy, was governed by counts from the 10th century till it was united to Navarre, count Thibaut becoming king, in 1234. The countess Joanna married Philip IV. of France, in 1284; and in 1361 Champagne was annexed by their descendant king John. The effervescing wine termed *Champagne* became popular in the latter part of the 18th century.

CHAMP DE MARS, an open square in front of the Military school at Paris, with artificial embankments on each side, extending nearly to the river Seine. The ancient assemblies of the Frankish people, the germ of parliaments, held annually in March, received this name. In 747, Pepin changed the month to May. Here was held, 14 July, 1790 (the anniversary of the capture of the Bastile), the "federation," or solemnity of swearing fidelity to the "patriot king" and new constitution: great rejoicings followed. On 14 July, 1791, a second great meeting was held here, directed by the Jacobin clubs, to sign petitions on the "altar of the country," praying for the abdication of Louis XVI. A commemoration meeting took place, 14 July, 1792. Another constitution was sworn to here, under the eye of Napoleon I., 1 May, 1815, at a ceremony called the *Champ de Mai*. The prince-president (afterwards Napoleon III.) had a grand review in the Champ de Mars, and distributed eagles to the army, 10 May, 1852. Here also was held the international exhibitions opened 1 April, 1867, and 1 May, 1878, see *Paris*.

CHAMPERTY, see *Barratry*.

CHAMPIONS OF CHRISTENDOM, see *Seven Champions of Christendom*.

CHAMPION OF THE KING OF ENGLAND (most honourable), an ancient office, since 1377 has been attached to the manor of Scrivelsby, held by the Marmion family. Their descendant, sir Henry Dymoke, the seventeenth of his family who held the office, died 28 April, 1865; succeeded by his brother John; he died, and his son Henry Lionel succeeded, who died Dec. 1875; succeeded by Francis Seaman Dymoke, who died 2 June, 1893; succeeded by his son, Mr. Francis Seaman Dymoke. An account of the champions, and the Marmion and Dymoke families, is given by the rev. Samuel Lodge, in his "Scrivelsby," 1893. At the coronation of the English kings, the champion used to challenge any one that should deny their title. The Dymoke suit of armour presented to the king, 13 June, 1901.

CHAMPLAIN, see *Lake Champlain*.

CHANCELLOR OF ENGLAND, LORD HIGH, the first lay subject after the princes of the blood royal. Anciently the office was conferred upon some dignified ecclesiastic termed *Cancellarius*, or doorkeeper, who admitted suitors to the sovereign's presence. Arfastus or Herefast, chaplain to the king (William the Conqueror) and bishop of Elmham, was lord chancellor in 1067. *Hardy*. Thomas à Becket was made chancellor in 1154. The first person qualified by education, to decide causes upon his own judgment, was sir Thomas More, appointed in 1529, before which time the officer was rather a state functionary than a judge. Sir Christopher Hatton, appointed lord chancellor in 1587, was very ignorant, on which account the first reference was made to a master in 1588. The great seal has been frequently put in commission; the lord chancellor's powers enlarged over legal officials by act passed in 1881; in 1813 the office of *Vice-Chancellor* was established; see *Keeper*, and *Vice-Chancellor*.—Salary, 6000*l.*; as speaker of house of lords, 4000*l.*

LORD HIGH CHANCELLORS.

1487. John Moreton, archbishop of Canterbury.
1504. William Warham, aft. archbishop of Canterbury.
1515. Thomas Wolsey, cardinal and abp. of York.
1529. Sir Thomas More.
1532. Sir Thomas Audley, keeper.
1533. Sir Thomas Audley, chancellor, aft. lord Audley.
1544. Thomas, lord Wriothesley.
1547. William, lord St. John, keeper.
,, Richard, lord Rich, lord chancellor.
1551. Thomas Goodrich, bishop of Ely, keeper.
1552. The same; now lord chancellor.
1553. Stephen Gardiner, bishop of Winchester.
1556. Nicholas Heath, archbishop of York.
1558. Sir Nicholas Bacon, keeper.
1579. Sir Thomas Bromley, lord chancellor.
1587. Sir Christopher Hatton.
1591. The great seal in commission.
1592. Sir John Puckering, lord keeper.
1596. Sir Thomas Egerton, lord keeper.
1603. Sir T. Egerton, lord Ellesmere, chancellor.
1617. Sir Francis Bacon, lord keeper.
1618. Sir Francis Bacon, cr. ld. Verulam, ld. chancellor.
1621. The great seal in commission.
1625. John, bishop of Lincoln, lord keeper.
,, Sir Thomas Coventry, afterwards lord Coventry, lord keeper.
1640. Sir John Finch, afterwards lord Finch.
1641. Sir Edward Lyttelton, afterwards lord Lyttelton, lord keeper.
1643. The great seal in the hands of commissioners.
1645. Sir Richard Lane, royal keeper.
1646. In the hands of commissioners.
1649. In commission for the commonwealth.
1653. Sir Edward Herbert, king's lord keeper.
1654. In commission during the commonwealth.
1660. Sir Edward Hyde, lord chancellor, afterwards created lord Hyde, and earl of Clarendon.
1667. Sir Orlando Bridgman, lord keeper.
1672. Anthony Ashley, earl of Shaftesbury, lord chancellor.
1673. Sir Heneage Finch, lord keeper.
1675. Heneage, now lord Finch, lord chancellor, afterwards earl of Nottingham.
1682. Sir Francis North, cr. lord Guilford, lord keeper.
1685. Francis, lord Guilford,; succeeded by
,, George, lord Jeffreys, lord chancellor.
1689. In commission.
1690. Sir John Trevor, knt., sir William Rawlinson, knt., and sir George Hutchins, knt., commissioners or keepers.
1693. Sir John Somers, lord keeper.
1697. Sir John Somers, cr. lord Somers, chancellor.
1700. Lord chief justice Holt, sir George Treby, chief justice, C. P., and chief baron, sir Edward Ward, lord keepers.
,, Sir Nathan Wright, lord keeper.
1705. Right hon. William Cowper, lord keeper, afterwards lord Cowper.
1707. William, lord Cowper, lord chancellor.
1710. In commission.
,, Sir Simon Harcourt, cr. lord Harcourt, keeper.
1713. Simon, lord Harcourt, lord chancellor.
1714. William, lord Cowper, lord chancellor.
1718. In commission.
,, Thomas, lord Parker, lord chancellor; afterwards earl of Macclesfield.
1725. In commission.
1725. Sir Peter King, cr. lord King, chancellor.
1733. Charles Talbot, cr. lord Talbot, chancellor.
1737. Philip Yorke, lord Hardwicke, lord chancellor.
1756. In commission.
1757. Sir Robert Henley, afterwards lord Henley, *last lord keeper*.
1761. Lord Henley, lord chancellor, afterwards earl of Northington.
1766. Charles, lord Camden, lord chancellor.
1770. Hon. Charles Yorke, lord chancellor.
[Created lord Morden; died by suicide within three days, and before the seals were put to his patent of peerage.]
1770. In commission.
1771. Henry Bathurst, lord Apsley; succeeded as earl Bathurst.
1778. Edward Thurlow, created lord Thurlow.
1783. Alexander, lord Loughborough, and others, commissioners.
,, Edward, lord Thurlow, again.
1792. In commission.
1793. Alexander Wedderburne, lord Loughborough, lord chancellor.
1801. John Scott, lord Eldon.
1806. Hon. Thomas Erskine, created lord Erskine.
1807. John, lord Eldon, again.
1827. John Singleton Copley, created lord Lyndhurst.
1830. Henry Brougham, created lord Brougham.
1834. Lord Lyndhurst, again.
1835. Sir Charles Christopher Pepys, master of the rolls, vice-chancellor Shadwell, and Mr. justice Bosanquet, C. P., commissioners.
1836. Sir Charles Christopher Pepys, created lord Cottenham, lord chancellor. 16 Jan.
1841. Lord Lyndhurst, a third time. 3 Sept.
1846. Lord Cottenham, again lord chancellor, 6 July.
1850. Lord Langdale, master of the rolls, sir Launcelot Shadwell, vice-chancellor of England, and sir Robert Monsey Rolfe, B.E., commissioners of the great seal. 19 June.
,, Sir Thomas Wilde, lord Truro. 15 July.
1852. Sir Edward Sugden, lord St. Leonards. 27 Feb.
Robt. Monsey Rolfe, lord Cranworth. 28 Dec.
1858. Sir Frederic Thesiger, lord Chelmsford. 26 Feb.
1859. John, lord Campbell, 18 June; died 23 June, 1861.
1861. Richard Bethell, lord Westbury. 26 June. Resigned 4 July, 1865.
1865. Robert Monsey Rolfe, lord Cranworth, again, 6 July. Resigned June, 1866.
1866. F. Thesiger, lord Chelmsford, again. 6 July. Resigned Feb. 1868.
1868. Hugh Cairns, lord Cairns. 29 Feb.
,, William Page Wood, lord Hatherley; died 10 July, 1881.
1872. Roundell Palmer, lord Selborne. 15 Oct.
1874. Hugh Cairns, lord Cairns. 21 Feb.; died 2 April, 1885.
1880. Roundell Palmer, lord (aft. earl) Selborne. 28 April.
1885. Sir Hardinge Giffard (lord Halsbury). 24 June.
1886. Sir Farrer Herschell (lord Herschell). 6 Feb.
,, Hardinge Giffard, lord Halsbury. 26 July.
1892. Lord Herschell, 18 Aug.
1895. Lord Halsbury, 25 June (visc. Tiverton, earl of Halsbury, Jan. 1898).

CHANCELLOR OF IRELAND, LORD HIGH. The earliest nomination was by Richard I., 1189, when Stephen Ridel was elevated to this rank. The office of vice-chancellor was known in Ireland in 1232, Geoffrey Turvillo, archdeacon of Dublin, being so named. The Chancery and Common Law Offices (Ireland) act was passed 20 Aug. 1867.

LORD HIGH CHANCELLORS OF IRELAND.

Patent.
1690. Sir Charles Porter. 29 Dec.
1697. Sir John Jeffreyson, Thomas Coote, and Nehemiah Donellan, lords keepers. 12 Jan.
,, J. Methuen. 11 March.
,, Edward, earl of Meath, Francis, earl of Longford, and Murrough, viscount Blessington, lords keepers. 21 Dec.
1702. Lord Methuen, lord chancellor. 26 Aug.
1705. Sir Richard Cox, bart., 6 Aug.; resigned in 1707.
1707. Richard Freeman. June.
1710. Robert, earl of Kildare, archbishop (Hoadley) of Dublin, and Thomas Keightley, commissioners. 28 Nov.
1711. Sir Constantine Phipps. 22 Jan. Resigned Sept. 1714.
1714. Alan Brodrick, afterwards viscount Middleton. 11 Oct. Resigned May, 1725.
1725. Richard West. June.
1726. Thomas Wyndham, afterwards lord Wyndham of Finglas. 21 Dec.

1739. Robert Jocelyn, afterwards lord Newport and visct. Jocelyn. 7 Sept.; died 25 Oct. 1756.
1757. John Bowes, afterwards lord Bowes of Clonlyon. 22 March; died 1767.
1768. James Hewitt, afterwards viscount Lifford. 9 Jan. died 28 April, 1789.
1789. John, baron Fitzgibbon, afterwards earl of Clare. 20 June; died 28 Jan. 1802.
1802. John, baron Redesdale. 15 March. Resigned Feb. 1806.
1806. George Ponsonby. 25 March; resigned April, 1807.
1807. Thomas Manners Sutton, lord Manners, previously an English baron of the exchequer. May. Resigned Nov. 1827.
1827. Sir Anthony Hart, previously vice-chancellor of England. 5 Nov. Resigned Nov. 1830.
1830. William, baron Plunket. 23 Dec. Resigned Nov. 1834.
1835. Sir Edward Burtenshaw Sugden. 13 Jan. Resigned April, 1835.
,, William, baron Plunket, a second time. 30 April. Resigned June, 1841.
1841. John Campbell. June. Resigned Sept. 1841.
,, Sir Edward Sugden, afterwards lord St. Leonards, a second time. Oct. Resigned July, 1846.
1846. Maziere Brady. 16 July. Resigned Feb. 1852.
1852. Francis Blackburne. March. Resigned Dec.
1853. Maziere Brady, again. Jan.
1858. Joseph Napier. Feb.
1859. Maziere Brady, again. June.
1866. Francis Blackburne. July. Resigned March, 1867.
1867. Abraham Brewster. 24 March.
1868. Thomas, lord O'Hagan. Resigned, Feb. 1874.
1875. John T. Ball. 1 Jan.
1880. Thomas, lord O'Hagan. April. Resigned 9 Nov. 1881.
1881. Hugh Law, died 10 Sept., 1883.
1883. (in commission) 22 Sept., sir Edwd. Sullivan. 5 Dec., 1883; died 13 April, 1885.
1885. John Naish, about 25 April.
,, Edward Gibson, lord Ashbourne. 24 June.
1886. John Naish, about 2 Feb.
,, Edward Gibson, lord Ashbourne, 26 July.
1892. Samuel Walker, Aug.
1895. Lord Ashbourne. 25 June.

CHANCELLOR OF THE EXCHEQUER, see *Exchequer*.

CHANCELLOR OF SCOTLAND, LORD, The laws of Malcolm II. (1004) say:—"The chancellar sall at al tymes assist the king in giving him counsall mair secretly nor the rest of the nobility. . . The chancellar sall be ludgit neir unto the kingis grace, for keiping of his bodie, and the seill, and that he may be readie, baith day and nicht, at the kingis command." *Sir James Balfour.* Evan was lord chancellor to Malcolm III., Canmore, 1057; and James, earl of Seafield, afterwards Findlater, was the last lord chancellor of Scotland, the office having been abolished in 1708; see *Keeper*.

CHANCELLOR'S AUGMENTATION ACT, passed 1863, enabled the lord chancellor to sell the advowson of certain livings in his gift for augmenting poor benefices.

CHANCELLORSVILLE, Virginia, U.S., a large brick hotel, once kept by a Mr. Chancellor, was the site of severe sanguinary conflicts between the American federal army of the Potomac under general Hooker, and the confederates under general Lee. On 28 April, 1863, the federal army crossed the Rappahannock; on 2 May, general "Stonewall" Jackson furiously attacked and routed the right wing, but was mortally wounded by his own party firing on him by mistake. Gen. Stuart took his command, and after a severe conflict on 3 and 4 May, with great loss to both parties, the federals were compelled to recross the Rappahannock. The struggle was compared to that at Hougomont during the battle of Waterloo. Jackson died 10 May.

CHANCERY, COURT OF, is mythically said to have originated with Alfred (871-901) or William I. (1066-1087). Its power was probably derived from the council of state, under which it acted, and of which it became gradually independent. Its acts were frequently complained of by the commons in the 14th and 15th centuries. Its professed object was to render justice complete, and to moderate the rigour of other courts that are bound to the strict letter of the law. It gives relief to or against infants, notwithstanding their minority; and to or against married women, notwithstanding their coverture; and all frauds, deceits, breaches of trust and confidence, for which there is no redress at common law, are relievable here. *Blackstone*; see *Chancellors of England*. The delays in chancery proceedings having long given dissatisfaction, the subject was brought before parliament in 1825, and frequently since; which led to the passing of important acts in 1852, 1853, 1855, 1858, and 1867, to amend the practice in the court of chancery. See *Accountant*, *County Courts*, and *Supreme Court*, *Berkeley*.

The *Chancery division* of the high court of justice now consists of the lord chancellor and six judges, an additional judge, sir G. Farwell, having been appointed, Oct. 1899. The chancery taxing office, the bankruptcy and other taxing departments, amalgamated with the central office, 11 Jan. 1902.

Chancery forgery case, see under *Trials*, 4 Feb. 1888.

CHANDOS CLAUSE, see *Counties*.

CHANNEL ISLANDS, a group about 80 miles south of England, see *Jersey, &c.*

CHANNEL STEAMERS, see under *Steam*.

CHANNEL TUNNEL COMPANY, registered 15 Jan. 1872; see *Tunnels*.

The construction of a channel bridge from Dover to Calais was proposed in Paris, 1889, by MM. Schneider and Hersent, and sir John Fowler and Mr. (afterwards sir Benjamin) Baker, and discussed in 1890.

M. Bunau Varilla, of Paris, engineer, publishes his plans for a mode of communication between Dover and Calais, consisting of a pier or viaduct half a mile long, on each side connected by a tunnel, and estimated cost 10,000,000*l*. . May, 1890

Sir E. J. Reed proposed the construction of a tubular railway, above the bed of the sea . 1890-1

In relation to a proposed Channel bridge, a new survey of the Straits of Dover was undertaken; a report on the scheme was published 26 Dec. 1890

Meeting held; no further development announced, 2 Dec. 1902

CHANTING is attributed to Ambrose, about 386. About 602, Gregory the Great added tones to the Ambrosian chant, and established singing schools. M. Gevaet, of Brussels, in Oct. 1889, asserted that this statement is legendary and that it was Gregory III. (731-741) who made the change. Chanting was adopted by some dissenters about 1859.

John Marbeck's "Book of Common Praier noted" (1559) is the first adaptation of the ancient Latin music to the Reformed Church; Clifford's "Common Tunes" for chanting, 1664.

The Plainsong and Mediæval Music Society was founded in 1888.

"The Sarum Gradual and the Gregorian Antiphonale Missarum," edited by W. H. Frere, 1896.

CHANTREY LEGACY, see *Royal Academy*.

CHANTRY, a chapel endowed with revenue for priests to sing mass for the souls of the donors;

see *Chanting*. Chantries were abolished in England in 1545.

CHAPEL. There are free chapels, chapels of ease, the chapel royal, &c. *Cowell.* The gentlemen pensioners (formerly poor knights of Windsor, who were instituted by the direction of Henry VIII. in his testament, 1546-7) were called knights of the chapel; see *Poor Knights of Windsor*.—The Private Chapels Act passed 14 Aug. 1871. The place of conference among printers, and the conference itself, are by them called a *chapel*, it is said, because the first work printed in England by Caxton was executed in a ruined chapel in Westminster-abbey.

CHAPLAIN, a clergyman who performs divine service in a chapel, for a prince or nobleman. About seventy chaplains are attached to the chapel royal. The chief personages invested with the privilege of retaining chaplains are the following, with the number that was originally allotted to each rank, by 21 Hen. VIII. c. 13 (1529):—

Archbishop	8	Knight of the Garter	3
Duke	6	Duchess	2
Bishop	6	Marchioness	2
Marquis	5	Countess	2
Earl	5	Baroness	2
Viscount	4	Master of the Rolls	2
Baron	3	Royal Almoner	2
Chancellor	3	Chief Justice	1

CHAPLETS, the string of beads used by the Roman Catholics in reciting the Lord's prayer, Ave Maria, &c.; see *Beads*.

CHAPTER. Anciently the bishop and clergy lived in the cathedral, the latter to assist the former in performing holy offices and governing the church, until the reign of Henry VIII. The chapter is now an assembly of the clergy of a collegiate church or cathedral. *Cowell.* The *chapter-house* of Westminster-abbey was built in 1250. By consent of the abbot, the commoners of England held their parliaments there from 1377 until 1547, when Edward VI. granted them the chapel of St. Stephen.

CHAR-ASIAB, the heights before Cabul; held by Afghan mutineers, were gallantly carried by general Baker, with the 72nd Highlanders and 5th Ghoorkas, 6 Oct. 1879. The enemy was totally defeated with severe loss. Capt. Young, Dr. Duncan, and lieut. Fergusson were killed, and about 70 of the British force killed and wounded. The British were falsely accused of cruelty after the victory.

CHARCOAL AIR-FILTERS were devised by Dr. John Stenhouse, F.R.S., in 1853. About the end of the last century Löwitz, a German chemist, discovered that charcoal (carbon) possessed the property of deodorising putrid substances, by absorbing and decomposing offensive gases. Air-filters, based on this property, have been successfully applied to public buildings, sewers, &c. Dr. Stenhouse also invented charcoal respirators. See *Fireman's Respirators*.

CHARING CROSS. At the village of Charing stood the last of the memorial crosses erected in memory of Eleanor, queen of Edward I., in conformity with her will. She died, 28 Nov. 1290. The cross remained till 1647, when it was destroyed as a monument of popish superstition. The present cross was erected for the South Eastern railway company in 1865 by Mr. E. M. Barry. The houses at Charing-cross were built about 1678; alterations began in 1829. The first stone of Charing-cross hospital was laid by the duke of Sussex, 15 Sept. 1831. Hungerford-bridge (or Charing-cross bridge) was opened 1 May, 1845; taken down July, 1862, and the materials employed in erecting Clifton suspension bridge, beginning March, 1863; see *Clifton*.—CHARING-CROSS RAILWAY. The first train passed over it, 2 Dec. 1863, and it was opened to the public on 11 Jan. 1864. The new railway bridge, built of iron with brick piers, was constructed by Mr. (aft. sir John) Hawkshaw. The foot-bridge was opened toll free 5 Oct. 1878. Pleistocene fossils found in excavations for Drummond's banking house: cave lion, mammoth, Irish deer, rhinoceros, &c. Autumn, 1882.

Charing-cross-road, from Tottenham-court-road to Charing-cross, was opened by the duke of Cambridge, 26 Feb. 1887.

CHARIOTS are frequently mentioned in the Bible, those of Joseph are mentioned *Gen.* l. 9, B.C. 1689. Chariot-racing was a Greek exercise. War-chariots were effectively used by the Gauls in Italy. Cæsar relates that Cassivelaunus, after dismissing his other forces, retained no fewer than 4000 war-chariots about his person; see *Carriages*, &c.

CHARITABLE BEQUESTS, &c. Boards for their recovery were constituted in 1764 and 1800, and a board for Ireland (chiefly prelates of the established church), in 1825. The Roman Catholic Charitable Bequests Act passed in 1844, and an act for the better administration of Charitable Trusts in 1853, when commissioners were appointed, who have from time to time published voluminous reports. Amendment acts were passed 1855 and 1871. 1,200,000*l.* bequeathed 1892; 1,390,136*l.*, 1899; 2,016,600*l.*, 1900; 1,926,850*l.*, 1901; 4,443,200*l.*, 1902.

CHARITABLE BRETHREN, an order founded by St. John of God, and approved by pope Pius V. 1572; introduced into France 1601; settled at Paris, 1602. *Hénault.*

CHARITABLE FUNDS INVESTMENT ACT passed, 1 Aug. 1870.

CHARITABLE LOANS (Ireland) act passed, 30 July, 1900.

CHARITABLE RELIEF, society for organizing, established about 1867. There are 40 offices, where applications are received and inquiries made (1889). Reported successful, 1881, in which year about 14,000 persons were assisted. Annual meetings held; 23,603 new cases dealt with; 1,089 persons in receipt of pensions in 1895; 14,555 applications; about 50,000*l.* expended in relief 1902. A conference of representatives of this and similar societies was held at Oxford on 1, 2 Oct. 1890. See *Mendicity*, *Charity Organisation Society*.

CHARITABLE TRUSTEES' INCORPORATION ACT passed, 27 June, 1872.

CHARITABLE TRUSTS ACTS, 1853-69, amended in 1887 and 1894.

CHARITABLE USES, statute of, 43 Eliz. c. 4 (1601), passed "to redresse the misemployment of landes, goodes, and stockes of money, heretofore given to charitable uses." The law respecting the conveyance of land for charitable uses was amended in 1861.

CHARITIES AND CHARITY SCHOOLS, see *Education*. The Charity Commission reported to parliament that the endowed charities alone of Great Britain amounted to 1,500,000*l.* annually in 1840. Charity schools were instituted in London to prevent the seduction of the infant poor into Roman Catholic seminaries, 3 James II., 1687-8. Mr. Low's "Charities of London" was published 1862, and frequently since (1903). Mr. W. F. Howe's "Classified Directory to the Metropolitan Charities," published annually, 1875 *et seq.* The house of lords, on appeal in a special case (the Moravian Brethren), decide that religious and charitable societies are exempt from income tax, 20 July, 1891.

First charity commission originated by Mr. (afterwards lord) Brougham in 1816, appointed in 1818; issued reports in 38 vols. (income of charities, 1,209,395*l.*) 1819-40
New commissioners appointed 1853; office, Gwydyr house, Whitehall; powers increased . . 1860
A meeting was held at the Mansion house, London, to consider objections to charity electioneering, without immediate result . . . . 30 Oct. 1873
Additional commissioners appointed through abolition of the Endowed Schools commission . . 1874
The Charity Voting association held its first annual meeting . . . . . . 18 Feb. 1875
The Metropolitan charities received about 3,195,181*l.* in 1874; 4,114,489*l.* in 1875; 4,447,436*l.* in 1884; 4,918,652*l.* in 1889-90; 5,638,270*l.* in 1896-7; 6,431,062*l.* in 1900-01.
The Charity Commissioners' scheme for the Campden estates, Kensington; much opposed; confirmed by Chancery . . . . . 27 May, 1881
The earl of Shaftesbury, who died 1 Oct. 1885, and lord Kinnaird, who died 26 April, 1887, were eminent supporters of philanthropic institutions.
The City of London Parochial Charities Act, passed 20 Aug. 1883, places the parochial charities at the disposal of the Charity Commissioners; they recommended the application of the funds of the City Parochial Charities (about 50,000*l.* a year) to the general benefit of the poor of London . . Sept. 1887
Their scheme issued Sept., which was opposed by the London County Council. . . . . Dec. 1889
Mr. Henry Quinn bequeaths 50,000*l.* to London charities 1888
Gross income of parochial charities in 1879-80, London, 116,960*l.*; Westminster, 33,173*l.*
Resolution in the commons passed, recommending parliamentary control over the Charity commission, 30 March, 1894; a select committee of the Commons on the working of the Charity commission sat May, 1894; another resolution stopped, 23 April, 1895; the annual report shows that they held in trust 18¾ millions sterling, end of 1897—total: 21,616,912*l.* . . . . 31 Dec. 1901
Mr. Alfred Marriott, died 28 July, bequeaths 250,000*l.* to charities, 1896; Mr. Edw. Mackeson bequeaths about 100,000*l.*, 12 March, 1898; Mrs. Marian Leigh, of Halifax, bequeaths over 29,000*l.* to various institutions, announced . 26 April, 1900
Sir H. Barron bequeaths 27,000*l.* to benefiting institutions in London and Ireland . Dec. "
Mr. S. Lewis bequeaths about 1,000,000*l.* to hospitals and charities . . . . . mid Jan. 1901
Mr. F. T. Freeman bequeaths 120,000*l.* (estimated) 3 Feb. 1902
Mr. C. Gassiot bequeaths about 421,000*l.* to hospitals and charities . . . . . 16 May, "
Mr. R. Stokes bequeaths in all about 60,000*l.* to King's College hospital, announced . 29 Jan. 1903
See also *Cancer Research* and *Hospitals.*

CHARITY CHILDREN of London; meetings began at St. Andrew's, Holborn, 1704; held at other churches in 1801 and since at St. Paul's, with intermissions; no meeting in 1878 and since, the erections interfering with the ordinary services.

CHARITY ORGANISATION SOCIETY, see under *Poor.*

CHARIVARI (French for "clattering of pots and pans," &c., noise made to annoy obnoxious persons), the name assumed by the French illustrated satirical journal, first published 1 Dec. 1832, edited by Louis Desnoyers, Altaroche, and Albert Clerc. Among the artists were "Cham," a name taken by the comte de Noë, who contributed from 1842 till his death, 6 Sept. 1879. See *Punch,* "the London Charivari."

CHARLEROI, in Belgium; fortified and named by the Spanish governor Rodrigo, 1666. Several great battles have been fought near this town, especially in 1690 and 1794; see *Fleurus.* Charleroi was besieged by the prince of Orange, 1672 and 1677; but he was soon obliged to retire. Near here, at Ligny, Napoleon attacked the Prussian line, making it fall back upon Wavres, 16 June, 1815.

CHARLES-ET-GEORGES, a French vessel, professedly conveying free African emigrants (but really slaves), seized by the Portuguese, in Conducia bay, 29 Nov. 1857, sent to Lisbon, and condemned as a slaver. The French government sent two ships of war to the Tagus, and the vessel was surrendered under protest; but the emperor of France gave up the free emigration scheme.

CHARLESTON (South Carolina), founded by people from old Charlestown, 1680. The English fleet here was repulsed with great loss, 28 June, 1776. It was besieged by the British troops at the latter end of March, 1780, and surrendered 13 May following with 6000 prisoners; it was evacuated, 14 Dec. 1782. Great commotion arose here in Nov. 1860, through the election of Mr. Lincoln for the presidency, he being opposed to slavery. On 12, 13 April, 1861, the war began by the confederates bombarding Fort Sumter; see *United States.* In Dec. 1861, the federals sank a number of vessels laden with stone in order to choke up the entrance to Charleston harbour. Unsuccessful attacks were made on Charleston by the federals between April, 1863, and 17 Feb. 1865, when the confederates were compelled to retire; and the federals replaced their standard on fort Sumter, 14 April, the day on which president Lincoln was assassinated.

About three-fourths of the city destroyed by an earthquake, 10 p.m. 31 Aug. 1886; 96 persons killed.
Population, 1890, 54,955; 1900, 55,807.

CHARLESTOWN (Massachusetts) was burnt by the British forces under general Gage, 17 June, 1775. Charlestown taken by the British, 7 May, 1779.

"CHARTE CONSTITUTIONNELLE," the French political constitution acknowledged by Louis XVIII., 4-10 June, 1814. The infraction of this constitution led to the revolution of 1830. The amended "Charte" was promulgated by Louis Philippe, 14 Aug. 1830; and set aside by the revolution of 1848.

CHARTER-HOUSE (a corruption of Chartreuse, *which see*), London, formerly a Carthusian monastery, founded in 1371 by sir Walter de Manny, one of the knights of Edward III., now an extensive charitable establishment. The last prior, John Houghton, was executed as a traitor, for denying the king's supremacy, in May, 1535. After the dissolution of monasteries in 1539, the charter-house passed through various hands till 1 Nov. 1611, when it was sold by the earl of Suffolk to Thomas Sutton for 13,000*l.*, who obtained letters patent directing that it should be called "the hospital of king James, founded in the Charter-house," and that "there should be for ever 16 governors," &c. On the foundation are 80 poor brothers and 44 poor scholars. Sutton died, 12 Dec. 1611. The expenditure for 1853-4 was 22,396*l.*; the receipts, 28,908*l.*; receipts in 1885, 30,364*l.* This school was affected by the Public Schools Act, 1868. In Sept. 1872, the school was opened in new buildings, at Godalming, Surrey. The old buildings, adapted for the Merchant Taylors' (day) school, were opened by the prince of Wales, 6 April, 1875. The buildings for the poor "brethren" were also modified, and in Nov. entirely new arrangements for them were proposed. Bill proposing removal of the "brethren" (55), who are to become annuitants with additions; and erection of buildings on the site of the old buildings and land (four acres), a total reversal of Sutton's will, introduced; opposed; withdrawn 7 May, 1886. The "Charter-house past and present," by Dr. Wm. Haig Brown, head master, published 1879.

CHARTER-PARTY, a covenant between merchants and masters of ships relating to the ship and cargo, said to have been first used in England about 1243.

CHARTERS, granted to corporate towns to protect their manufactures by Henry I. in 1132; modified by Charles II. in 1683; the ancient charters restored in 1698. Alterations were made by the Municipal Reform Act in 1835. See *Magna Charta* and *Boroughs*. Ancient Anglo-Saxon charters are printed in Kemble's "Codex Diplomaticus," 1829.

CHARTISTS, the name assumed by large bodies of the lower classes, shortly after the passing of the Reform Bill in 1832, from their demanding the people's *Charter*,* the six points of which were *Universal Suffrage, Vote by Ballot, Annual Parliaments, Payment of the Members, the abolition of the Property Qualification* (which was enacted, June, 1858), and *Equal Electoral Districts*. In 1838 the chartists assembled in various parts of the country, armed with guns, pikes, and other weapons, and carrying torches and flags. A proclamation was issued against them, 12 Dec. Their petition (agreed to at Birmingham, 6 Aug. 1838) was presented to parliament by Mr. T. Attwood, 14 June, 1839. They committed great outrages at Birmingham, 15 July, 1839, and at Newport (*which see*), 4 Nov. 1839. They held for some time a sort of parliament called the "National Convention," the leading men being Feargus O'Connor, Henry Vincent, Mr. Stephens, &c. On 10 April, 1848, they proposed to hold a meeting of 200,000 men on Kennington-common, London, to march thence in procession to Westminster, and present a petition to parliament; but only about 20,000 came. The bank and other establishments were fortified by military, preventive measures adopted, and not less than 150,000 persons of all ranks (including Louis Napoleon, afterwards emperor) were voluntarily sworn to act as special constables. The chartists dispersed after slight encounters with the police, and the monster petition, in detached rolls, was sent in cabs to the house of commons. From this time the proceedings of the chartists became insignificant.

CHARTREUSE, LA GRANDE, chief of the monasteries of the Carthusian order, situated among the rugged mountains near Grenoble, in France, was founded by Bruno of Cologne, about 1084. At the revolution in 1792, the monks were expelled and their valuable library destroyed. They returned to the monastery after the restoration of 1815. In Nov. 1880 they declined to accept indulgence from the decrees for expelling the religious orders from France. The monks of the Grande Chartreuse locked themselves in their fortress and awaited expulsion by force. This took place on the 29th April, 1903.

* Wm. Lovett, its alleged author, died Aug. 1877.

CHARTS AND MAPS. Anaximander of Miletus is said to have been the inventor of geographical and celestial charts, about 570 B.C. Modern sea-charts were brought to England by Bartholomew Columbus to illustrate his brother's theory respecting a western continent, 1489. The first tolerably accurate map of England was drawn by George Lilly, who died in 1559. Gerard Mercator published an atlas of maps in 1595; see *Mercator*. The daily papers published in their columns maps illustrating the wars of 1870-1, 1876-7, &c.

Atlases. Ab. Ortelius, Epitome Theatri Præcipuarum Orbis Regionum Delineationes, &c., 1595. J. Speed, "Prospect, &c., of the world and of Great Britain's Empire," 1646. J. B. D'Anville, Atlas, 1761–1807. W. Faeden, "General Atlas," 1790. A. Arrowsmith, "Comparative Atlas," 1828. Maps of the Society for the Diffusion of Useful Knowledge, 1844–56. A. K. Johnston, "Physical Atlas," 1849; "Royal Atlas," 1861 and 1878. Stanford's "London Atlas of Geography," 1887; "The *Times* Atlas," 1896, and many others. Rand, M'Nally & Co.'s "Indexed Atlas of the World," Chicago and New York, autumn 1892. Scheme for a map of the world, on a uniform scale of 1—1,000,000, proposed by prof. A. Penck, of Vienna, 1891; maps on this scale since published by the Royal Geographical Society of parts of Africa, Asia, etc. The Howard Vincent map of the British Empire, reduced edition for use in barrack rooms and lower decks of H.M. ships, club rooms, &c., pub. by W. & A. K. Johnston, 1903.

CHASSEPOT RIFLE, a modified needle-gun, and a breech-loader (named after its inventor, Alphonse Chassepot), adopted by the French government in 1866. In April, 1867, 10,000 had been issued to the troops. In his report on the battle of Mentana (*which see*), 3 Nov. 1867, gen. De Failly said, "The chassepot has done wonders." It was generally considered successful in the war, 1870-1. "The range of the chassepot being 1800 paces, and that of the needle-gun only between 600 and 700, the Germans in all their charges had to traverse 1200 paces before their arms could be used to purpose." Many Germans were armed with the chassepot after the surrender of the French army at Sedan, 2 Sept. 1870.

CHÂTEAUDUN, an old city, N. C. France, the residence of the heroic Dunois, who died 1468. Here were massacred, 20 July, 1183, about 7000 Brabançons, fanatic mercenaries who had been hired to exterminate the Albigenses by the cardinal Henry, abbot of Clairvaux, in 1181. They had become the scourge of the country, and the "Capuchons" were organised for their destruction. Châteaudun was captured by the Germans after a severe conflict of about nine hours, 18 Oct. 1870. Barricades had been erected in the town, and the Garde Mobile fought bravely. The town was re-occupied by the French, 6 Nov.

CHATHAM (Kent), a principal station of the royal navy; the dockyard, commenced by queen Elizabeth, has been greatly extended. The Chatham *Chest*, for the relief of the wounded and decayed seamen, originally established here by the queen and admirals Drake and Hawkins, in 1588, was removed to Greenwich in 1803. On 10 June, 1667, the Dutch fleet, under admiral De Ruyter, sailed up to this town, and burnt several men-of-war; but the entrance into the Medway is now defended by Sheerness and other forts, and additional fortifications were made at Chatham. On 8-11 Feb. 1861, a violent outbreak of the convicts was suppressed by the military, and many rioters flogged. About 1000*l.* worth of property was destroyed, and many persons were seriously hurt.

New docks and a basin, said to be the largest and finest in the world, opened by Mr. Goschen, 21 June, 1871. Additional docks completed, 1883. New municipal buildings opened by lord Rosebery, 23 Jan. 1900. Theatre Royal, opened July, 1897, burnt down, estimated damage 30,000*l.*, 16 May, 1900. Naval barracks, erected at cost of 500,000*l.*, completed, 30 April, 1903; see *Navy*, for launch of battleships. Pop. in 1891, 31,711; 1901, 35,659.

CHATHAM ADMINISTRATION,* succeeded the first Rockingham administration in Aug. 1766: after several changes it terminated Dec. 1767. See *Grafton*.

Earl of Chatham, *first minister and lord privy seal.*
Duke of Grafton, *first lord of the treasury.*
Lord Camden, *lord chancellor.*
Charles Townshend, *chancellor of the exchequer.*
Earl of Northington, *lord president.*
Earl of Shelburne and general Conway, *secretaries of state.*
Sir Charles Saunders (succeeded by Sir Edward Hawke), *admiralty.*
Marquis of Granby, *ordnance.*
Lord Hillsborough, *first lord of trade.*
Viscount Barrington, *secretary at war.*
Lord North and sir George Cooke, *joint paymasters.*
Viscount Howe, *treasurer of the navy.*
Duke of Ancaster, lord le Despencer, &c.

CHATILLON (on the Seine, France). Here a congress was held by the four great powers allied against France, at which Caulaincourt attended for Napoleon, 4 Feb. 1814: the negotiations for peace were broken off on 19 March following.

CHAT MOSS (Lancashire), a peat bog, twelve miles square, in most places so soft as to be incapable of supporting a man or horse, over which George Stephenson, the railway engineer, carried the Liverpool and Manchester railway, after overcoming difficulties considered invincible. The road (literally a floating one) was completed by 1 Jan. 1830, when the first experimental train, drawn by the Rocket locomotive, passed over it. See *Bogs*.

CHATTANOOGA (Tennessee). Near here the federal generals, Sherman and Thomas, defeated the confederate general Bragg, after storming the entrenchments, 24-25 Nov. 1863. Bragg retreated into Georgia, and Longstreet into Virginia.

CHAUMONT (on the Marne, France), TREATY OF, entered into between Great Britain, Austria, Russia, and Prussia, 1 March, 1814. This treaty was succeeded by that of Paris, 11 April, by which Napoleon renounced his sovereignty; see *Paris*.

CHAUVINISM, a term said to be derived from Chauvin, the principal character in Scribe's "Soldat Labourour," a veteran soldier of the first empire, filled with intense admiration for Napoleon and for all that belonged to him. Scribe was born 24 Dec. 1794, died 20 Feb. 1861.

CHEAP TRAINS ACT, 7 & 8 Vict. c. 85, 1844. Another act passed, Aug. 1883; still (1903) the governing statute. See *Railways*.

CHEATS were punishable by pillory, imprisonment, and fine, and a rigorous statute was enacted against them in 1542. Persons cheating at play, or winning at any time more than 10*l.* or any valuable thing, were deemed infamous, and were to suffer punishment as in cases of perjury, 9 Anne, 1711. *Blackstone.*

CHEE-FOO CONVENTION, see *China*, 1876.

CHEESE is mentioned by Aristotle, about 350 B.C. It is supposed by Camden and others that the English learned cheese-making from the Romans. Wilts, Gloucester, and Cheshire make vast quantities. In 1140 we imported from abroad about 10,000 tons; in 1855, 384,192 cwt.; 1866, 872,342 cwt.; 1870, 1,041,281 cwt.; 1876, 1,531,204 cwt; 1881, 1,840,090 cwt.; 1887, 1,836,789 cwt.; 1890, 2,244,974 cwt.; 1893, 2,077,462 cwt.; 1896, 2,244,525 cwt.; 1899, 2,384,069 cwt.; 1900, 2,705,878 cwt; 1901, 2,586,837 cwt.; 1902, 2,546,384 cwt. Exported: 1876, 17,411 cwt.; 1880, 11,903 cwt.; 1885, 12,708 cwt.; 1890, 12,211 cwt.; 1893, 10,917 cwt.; 1896, 10,333 cwt.; 1902, 51,863 cwt. The duty on foreign cheese, producing annually about 50,000*l.*, was taken off in 1860.

The Cheddar system of cheese-making, named after a village in Somersetshire, has been largely adopted in the British colonies and the United States during the present century.

CHELSEA (Middlesex). A council held here 27 July, 816. *Nicolas.* A theological college here, founded by James I. in 1609, was converted by Charles II. in 1682 to an asylum for wounded and superannuated soldiers. The erection was carried on by James II., and completed by William III. in 1690. The projector was sir Stephen Fox, grandfather of the orator C. J. Fox; the architect was sir Christopher Wren; and the cost 150,000*l.* In 1850 there were 70,000 *out-* and 539 *in-pensioners.*—The physic garden of sir Hans Sloane, at Chelsea, was given to the Apothecaries' company, 1721.—The Chelsea waterworks were incorporated, 1722.—The first stone of the Military Asylum, Chelsea, was laid by Frederick duke of York, 19 June, 1801.—The bridge, constructed by Mr. T. Page to connect Chelsea with Battersea-park, was opened March, 1858. The Chelsea embankment was opened by the duke and duchess of Edinburgh, 9 May, 1874. See *Trials*, July, 1870 and 1872. Cremorne public gardens closed, 1877. The Albert-bridge was opened 31 Dec. 1872; both freed from toll, 24 May, 1879. The parliamentary borough of Chelsea, created by the Reform act, 15 Aug. 1867, consisted of Chelsea, Kensington, Fulham, and Hammersmith. By the act of 1855, Chelsea alone returns 1 member. The Chelsea Savings Bank suspended payment; liabilities to be sustained by trustees, 18 Jan. 1890. Free library opened by earl Cadogan, 21 Jan. 1891. Thos. Carlyle's house, Cheyne-row, opened as a museum, with personal relics, 26 July, 1895. New drill-hall opened by the prince of Wales, 16 May, 1902; Chelsea physic garden opened by lord Cadogan, 25 July, 1902. Population, 1881, 88,128; 1891, 96,272; 1901, 73,856.

CHELTENHAM (Gloucestershire). Its celebrated mineral spring was discovered in 1718. The king's well was sunk in 1778; and other wells by Mr. P. Thompson in 1806. Magnesian salt was first found in the waters in 1811. The theatre was erected in 1804 Grammar school and almshouses, endowed by Richard Pates, 1574. Cheltenham was incorporated, 1876. Population, 1881, 43,972; 1891, 42,914; 1901, 49,439.

CHELTENHAM COLLEGE was founded in 1841, mainly by Mr. George Simon Harcourt and capt. James Shrubb Tredell for a classical, mathematical, and general

* William Pitt, earl of Chatham (the "*great commoner*"), born 15 Nov. 1708, entered parliament in 1735; became secretary of state (virtually the premier) in the Devonshire administration, Nov. 1756, secretary in the Newcastle administration, Jan. 1757. In 1766 he became premier, lord privy seal, and afterwards earl of Chatham, which lord Chesterfield called *a fall upstairs*. He opposed the taxation of the American colonies, but protested against the recognition of their independence, 7 April, 1778, and died 11 May following.

education in strict conformity with the principles of the church of England; among the pupils have been Lord Plunket, archbishop of Dublin, sir Henry James, aft. lord James of Hereford, prince Alamayn, son of Theodore negus of Abyssinia, prince Louis Napoleon, and prince Francis of Teck. The college was visited, and the prizes distributed, by the duke of Cambridge; 29 June, 1883; and by the duchess of Teck, 28 June, 1886; incorporated 1894

Art gallery, the gift of the baron de Ferrieres, with his fine collection of Dutch and Belgian pictures, opened . . . 26 Oct. 1899

Princess Henry of Battenberg unveils a bust of queen Victoria by the countess Feodora Gleichen at the Ladies' college . . . . 16 Nov. „

CHEMICAL SOCIETIES. One formed in London in 1780 did not long continue. The present Chemical society of London was established in 1841 (jubilee celebrated at Burlington house, 24 Feb. 1891) [Mr. J. J. Tustin gave 1,000 guineas to the society's Research fund, Jan. 1897], banquet to past presidents, prof. Dewar in the chair, 11 Nov. 1898; that of Paris in 1857; that of Germany at Berlin, 1867; that of America, 1876. The *Institute of Chemistry of Great Britain* formed, professor Edward Frankland first president, 1877 (died 9 Aug. 1899); first meeting, 1 Feb. 1878; chartered, Oct. 1885. *Chemical Industry Society* founded 4 April, 1881.

CHEMICAL RESEARCH LABORATORIES founded by Mr. Henry S. Wellcome, in King-street, Snow-hill, for investigations in pure and applied chemistry; opened, 18 June, 1900.

CHEMICAL UNION of manufacturers of bleaching powders, alkalies, &c., was projected July, 1890. The union, named the united alkali company, advertised shares for sale to the amount of 1,250,000*l.*, Feb. 1891.

CHEMICAL WORKS. Royal commission appointed to inquire into the management of chemical works, to ascertain the effect of gases and vapours given off, and the means of prevention: the commissioners were lord Aberdare, earl Percy: professors Abel, A. Williamson, Roscoe, and others, 18 July, 1876. In their report, issued Aug. 1878, they recommended increased inspection and more stringent regulations. See *Alkalies*.

CHEMISTRY was introduced into Spain by the Moors, about 1150. The Egyptians and Chinese claim an early acquaintance with chemistry. The first chemists were the Alchemists (see *Alchemy*); but chemistry was not a science till the 17th century; during which its study was promoted by Bacon, Hooke, Mayow, and Boyle. In the early part of the 18th century, Dr. Stephen Hales laid the foundation of *Pneumatic Chemistry*, and his contemporary Boerhaave combined the study of chemistry with medicine. These were succeeded by Bergman, Stahl, Black, &c. In 1772, Priestley published his researches on air, having discovered the gases oxygen, ammonia, &c.; and thus commenced a new chemical era. He was ably seconded by Cavendish, Scheele, Lavoisier, Chaptal, and others. The 19th century opened with the brilliant discoveries of Davy, continued by Dalton, Faraday, Thomson, &c. *Organic Chemistry* has been very greatly advanced by Berzelius, Liebig, Dumas, Laurent, Hofmann, Cahours, Frankland, Williamson,* and others, since 1830; see *Pharmacy*, *Electricity*, *Galvanism*. For the analytical processes termed "*Spectrum analysis*," invented by Kirchhoff and Bunsen (1861), and "*Dialysis*" (1861), and "*Atmolysis*" (1863), invented by Mr. T. Graham, see those articles.—The *Royal College of Chemistry*, Oxford-street, London, was established in 1845 (now at South Kensington)—Henry Watts' great "Dictionary of Chemistry," begun 1863, has supplements; new edition, 1890-94; he died 30 June, 1884. M. Ad. Wurtz's equally great "Dictionnaire de Chimie," 1868-85. Prof. T. E. Thorpe's Dictionary of Applied Chemistry, 1890-93. Von Meyer, "A History of Chemistry," 1892. Eighth internat. congress of applied chemistry at Berlin, 4 June, 1903.

CHEQUE BANK, opened in Pall Mall East, 23 July, 1873. It issued cheques for sums from 1*l.* upwards to suit persons not having a banker. The plan was due to Mr. James Hertz. He died 23 Feb. 1880. The bank is now (1903) in liquidation, owing to extensive forgeries of its cheques.

CHEQUES, see *Drafts*.

CHERBOURG, the great naval fortress and arsenal of France on the coast of Brittany, about 60 or 70 miles equi-distant from Portsmouth and Plymouth. It was captured by our Henry V. in 1418, and lost in 1450. Under the direction of Louis XIV., some works were erected here by the great Vauban, which with some shipping, &c., were destroyed by the British, 6, 7 Aug. 1758. The works, resumed by Louis XVI., were interrupted by the revolution. The breakwater, commenced in 1783, resumed by Napoleon I. about 1803, and completed in 1813, forms a secure harbour, affording anchorage for nearly the whole navy of France, and protected by strong fortifications. On 4, 5 Aug. 1858, the railway and the Grand Napoleon docks were opened, the latter in the presence of the queen of England and court. The British fleet visited Cherbourg, 15-17 Aug. 1865, receiving much hospitality. Presidents Grévy, Léon Say, and Gambetta visit Cherbourg; launch of a man-of-war, &c., 8-11 Aug. 1880; visit of president Loubet, 18 July, 1900.

CHERITON DOWN (Hants). Here sir Wm. Waller defeated the royalists under lord Hopton, 29 March, 1644.

CHERRY, the *Prunus cerasus* (from Cerasus, a city of Pontus, whence the tree was brought by Lucullus to Rome, about 70 B.C.), first planted in Britain, it is said, about 100. Fine kinds were brought from Flanders, in 1540, and planted in Kent.

CHERSON, see *Kherson*.

CHERSONESUS, see *Crimea*.

CHESAPEAKE. At the mouth of this river a contest took place between the British admiral Graves and the French admiral De Grasse aiding the revolted states of America; the former was obliged to retire, 5 Sept. 1781. The Chesapeake and Delaware were blockaded by the British fleet in the American war of 1812, and the bay was, at that period, the scene of great hostilities of various results.

CHESAPEAKE, an American frigate, in Boston bay, commanded by capt. Lawrence (50 guns, 376 men), struck to the *Shannon*, British frigate (38 guns, 330 men) commanded by capt. Philip Vere Broke, after a severe

* In 1828 Wöhler produced artificially *urea*, a body hitherto known only as a product of the animal organism. Since then, acetic acid, alcohol, grape sugar, various essential oils, similar to those of the pine-apple, pear, garlic, &c., have been formed by combinations of the gases, oxygen, hydrogen, and carbonic acid. The barrier formed by chemists between organic and inorganic bodies is thus broken down. Indigo artificially formed by Bäyer, 1878.

action of eleven minutes, 1 June, 1813. Eleven minutes elapsed between the firing of the first gun and the boarding, and in four minutes more the *Chesapeake* was the *Shannon's* prize. Capt. Lawrence died of his wounds. Adm. sir Provo W. P. Wallis, who succeeded in the command of the *Shannon*, when capt. Broke was disabled, born 1791, died 13 Feb. 1892.

CHESHUNT COLLEGE, Herts, founded by Selina, countess of Huntingdon, for the education of ministers of her "connexion," Calvinistic methodists. The college was first opened at Trevecca-house, Talgarth, near Brecon, by the countess and George Whitefield, 1768. It was removed to Cheshunt in 1792. She died 17 June, 1791. Trevecca college is still used by the Calvinistic methodists, 1890.

CHESS. An ancient game of eastern origin, probably brought into Europe by the Arabs; the invention is doubtfully ascribed to India, China, Persia and Egypt.

Caxton printed "the Game and Playe of the Chesse" 1474
A chess-club formed at Slaughter's coffee-house, St. Martin's-lane 1747
The automaton chess-player of Maelzel, worked by a hidden person, was exhibited in . . . 1769
M. F. A. Danican, known as Philidor, played three matches blindfolded at the Salopian; he died . 1795
The London Chess-club founded in 1807, and St. George's 1833
Herr Paulsen played ten games at once, of which he won five, and lost one; three were drawn, and one not played out . . . . . . Dec. 1861
International chess congresses: 1, 2, London (*winner*, M. Anderssen, of Breslau), 1851, 1862; 3, Paris, (M. Kolisch), 1867; 4, Paris (M. Anderssen), 1870; 5, Vienna (M. Steinitz), Aug. 1873.
Automaton chess-player at the Crystal-palace (a youth concealed in box perforated with holes) exhibited 1873
Howard Staunton, a great player, died . . June, 1874
J. J. Löwenthal, eminent Hungarian player, died 20 July, 1876
J. H. Zukertort of Riga, gains first prize at the International Chess Congress, Paris, June, July, 1878
"Mephisto," a mechanical chess-player, exhibited at the Westminster Aquarium . . 2 Oct. ,,
Chess Congress at New York . . . Jan. 1880
Chess tournament at Wiesbaden, 9 July, 1880; at Berlin, 30 Aug. 1881 (1st prize, Mr. Blackburne); at Vienna, first prize, M. Steinitz . 24 June, 1882
In London (M. Zukertort, 1st prize), 26 April—23 June 1883
M. J. H. Zukertort died aged 46 . . 20 June, 1888
International chess tournament, New York, closed; equal prizes awarded to Herr Weiss (Vienna) and M. Tschigorin (Russia) . . . 27 May, 1889
One at Amsterdam, 28 Aug. 1889; at Manchester, (1st prize, Dr. Tarrasch, of Nuremberg), 25 Aug.–8 Sept. 1890; at Dresden, Dr. Tarrasch, 18–29 July, 1892; Leipsic, Sept. 1894; Hastings, Aug. 1895; St. Petersburg, Jan.; Nuremburg, Aug.; Budapest, Sept. 1896. Match between 10 English and 10 U.S.N.A. players by cable, London, won by English, 5½ to 4½ games, 12, 13 Feb. 1897; another won by the British (5½ to 4½), 18, 19 March, 1898. England and American match by cable, Newnes trophy won by the Americans, 11 March, 1899; again won by the Americans, 24 March, 1900; another ends in a draw, 20 April, 1901; Americans win, 15 March, 1902.
Games, in which the pieces were replaced by living men, were played at St. Leonards, Sussex, 14 Jan. 1891
"The Hastings Chess Tournament, 1895," edited by Horace F. Cheshire, published . . . 1896
Death of Wilhelm Steinitz, a noted player, aged 64, 12 Aug. 1900
Americans win an inter-university match (by cable), 4½ to 1½ . . . 26 April, 1902
Games played by wireless telegraphy between steamers to and from United States . . . 1903
Third and last vol. of Mr. M. Morgan's "Chess Digest," a complete survey of the whole field of chess, and giving the openings of 15,000 games, published Feb. ,,
Monte Carlo tournament: Dr. Tarrasch, winner 20 games; Maroczy, 19; Pillsbury, 18½; Teichmann, 16½; 14 players . . . . Mar. 1903
Seventh American Chess Congress to be held at the World's Fair, Louisiana, U.S., 1904. Open to all the world, announced . . . . Oct. ,,

CHESTER (England, N. W.), the British Caerleon and the Roman Deva, the station of the twentieth legion, *Valeria Victrix*, quitted by them about 406. The city wall was first built by Edelfleda, about 908; and Hugh d'Abrinces, called Lupus, the earl, nephew of William I., rebuilt the Saxon castle in 1084, and the abbey of St. Werburgh. Chester was incorporated by Henry III. and made a distinct county. The palatine jurisdiction was abolished by parliament, 23 July, 1830. The SEE, anciently part of Lichfield, one of whose bishops, Peter, removing the seat hither in 1075, occasioned his successors to be styled bishops of Chester; but it was not made a distinct bishopric until Henry VIII. in 1541 raised it to this dignity, and allotted the church of the abbey of St. Werburgh for the cathedral. After extensive repairs, the cathedral was re-opened, 25 Jan. 1872. This see is valued in the king's books at 420*l*. 1*s*. 8*d*. per annum. Present income 4500*l*. Population, 1881, 36,794; 1891, 37,105; 1901, 41,603.

Taken, after three months' siege, for the parliament 1645
Fatal gunpowder explosion 1772
Royal Agricultural Society's show . . July, 1858
Exchange and town hall burnt . . 30 Dec. 1862
A projected attack of Fenians on Chester castle was defeated by the vigilance of the authorities and the arrival of the military . . 11, 12 Feb. 1867
New town hall opened by the prince of Wales 15 Oct. 1869
Cathedral re-opened after restoration by sir Gilbert G. Scott . . . . . . 7 Aug. 1876
Ancient tower of St. John's Church fell 15 April, 1881
Foundation stone of Grosvenor Museum and School of Art laid by the duke of Westminster 3 Feb. 1885 . . . . . opened 6 Aug. 1886
Royal Agricultural Society's show . 19 June, 1893
Town-hall council chamber burnt . 27 March, 1897
Remains of a Roman basilica, date about 300 A.D., discovered . . . . July, ,,

RECENT BISHOPS OF CHESTER.

1800. Henry Wm. Majendie, trans. to Bangor, 1809.
1810. Bowyer Edward Sparke, trans. to Ely, 1812.
1812. George Henry Law, trans. to Bath, 1824.
1824. Chas. J. Blomfield, trans. to London, Aug. 1828.
1828. John Bird Sumner, trans. to Canterbury, 1848.
1848. John Graham, died 15 June, 1865.
1865. William Jacobson. Resigned Jan.; died 13 July, 1884.
1884. Wm. Stubbs, Feb.; translated to Oxford, July, 1888.
1888. Francis John Jayne, elected 26 Jan.

CHESTER LE STREET. It is stated that a bishopric founded in Holy Island was removed to this place in 875, and to Durham, 995; see *Durham*.

CHEVY CHASE, see *Otterburne*.

CHICAGO, 912 m. from New York, Illinois, United States, a flourishing city settled in 1831; incorporated 1837; population, 1867, above 200,000; in 1880, 503,185; 1890, 1,099,859; 1901, 1,750,000.

Chicago was nearly destroyed by fire, occasioned by the upsetting of a paraffin lamp . . 7–11 Oct. 1871
About 250 persons perished, and 98,500 were rendered destitute. The loss was reckoned at 290,000,000 dollars. Large sums were collected for relief of the sufferers in London (10,000*l*. in a few hours) and other British cities, as well as in North America. The area of the fire was computed at from three to five square miles, and about 25,000 buildings were destroyed. The heart of the city was composed of old wooden buildings. The city was rebuilt most energetically 1872

Another great fire; many homeless . 14 July, 1874
A convention of Irish National Delegates met 19–22 Aug. 1886
Socialist riots with bloodshed on 4 May, 1886. See *United States*. 11 Nov. 1887
The World's Columbian Exposition, 1893; Chicago chosen as the site (7 m. from the city, 586 acres, with many lagoons) . . . . 25 Feb. 1890
Mr. Thomas W. Palmer, of Michigan, chosen as the president of the fair . . . . . 27 June „
Mr. George R. Davis elected director-general, 19 Sept. „
President Harrison announces the day of opening to be 1 May, to close 31 Oct. 1893.
Congress votes 2,500,000 dollars for expenses 5 Aug. 1892
Solemn dedication of all the buildings (400), "White City" (central dome, 275 ft. high), with prayers by John Ireland, archbishop of St. Paul, and Charles H. Fowler, bishop of California; a dedicatory ode by Miss Harriet F. Monroe, several addresses, an oration by Mr. Chauncey Depew, and much music, in the presence of the hon. L. P. Morton, vice-president of the United States, the members of the government, and other officials, foreign representatives, many eminent persons, and about 100,000 spectators, in the manufactures and liberal arts building, 21 Oct. 1892 (the fourth centenary of the landing of Columbus). See *America*, 1492.
[President Harrison was absent through the illness of his wife, who died 25 Oct.]
The exhibition opened by president Cleveland in the presence of a distinguished company, including the duke of Veragua and family, a lineal descendant of Columbus, with great rejoicings; by pressing a button the president started a vast amount of machinery; Handel's "Hallelujah Chorus" was sung, and followed by other demonstrations (about 300,000 persons present), noon . . . . 1 May, 1893
The British exhibition in Victoria house included work sent by the queen and princess Beatrice, and specimens of works of art and manufactures from all parts of the world; literary, scientific, and other congresses, and also a "world's parliament of religions," were held; catalogues were published . . . . . July *et seq*. „
Hotels and other buildings destroyed by a great wave at Chicago . . . . 7 April, „
Great fire at a warehouse in the grounds, 17 deaths, 10 July; Senate hotel burnt, 8 deaths, 14 Aug. „
"British day" at the fair; processions, &c. 19 Aug. „
Great fire in S. Chicago, 5,000 homeless . 24 Aug. „
"Chicago day" at the fair; 713,646 paying visitors (6 killed by the crush) . . . 9 Oct. „
The fair closed without festivities owing to the murder of the mayor, Mr. Carter H. Harrison (28 Oct.), 30 Oct.; Prendergast, the murderer, executed, 13 July, 1894.
Total number of visitors, 23,529,400; estimated surplus for stockholders, 1,000,000 dollars 31 Oct. „
Medals awarded to artists: United States N.A., 90; British, 72; Germany, 81; Austria, 26; Italy, 15; Spain, 29; Sweden, 16; Denmark, 12; Holland, 27; Japan, 38; France did not compete.
Sculptors: United States, 14; British, 6; Germany, 19; Italy, 12; Austria, 5; Spain, 6; Sweden, 3; Denmark, 3, and Japan, 7.
Financial success reported, surplus, 1,404,841 dollars, 26 Nov.
About 40,000 men out of work; much distress, reported . . . . . . 11 Dec.
A destructive fire in the buildings of the fair 8 Jan. 1894
A number of the exhibition buildings, covering 80 acres, burnt by incendiaries; several deaths, 5 July; conflicts between the troops and rioters, chiefly foreigners; several deaths and much destruction of property . . 6–8, 11 July,
President Cleveland proclaims martial law; gen. Miles at the head of Federal troops, 8 July; improved traffic under military protection, 9 July, „
Mr. Eugene Debs and other officers of the American Railway Union indicted for obstructing the mails and other offences; bailed for large sums . . . . . . 10, 11 July, „
Strike declared over, 13 July; 17 lives lost, and 4,000,000 dollars property (railway) destroyed, reported . . . . 14 July, „
Mr. Debs and other leaders of the railway strike sentenced to terms of imprisonment, Dec.; released on bail . . . . . . Jan. 1895
Irish national convention, see *United States* Sept.–Oct. „
Mr. George M. Pullman, millionaire, inventor of the Pullman car system, 1863 (see *Railways*, 1874), died, aged 66 . . . . 19 Oct. 1897
The coliseum, a large building, burnt down: 9 deaths; estimated loss, 700,000 dollars 25 Dec. „
Peace jubilee, pres. McKinley present . 16-20 Oct. 1898
Collapse of the new Colliseum in course of erection, over 12 deaths . . . . . 28 Aug. 1899
Corner-stone of new Federal building laid by pres. McKinley, naval and military review . 9 Oct. „
Great sanitary works, canal (29 mi. long), 7 yrs. in construction, cost about 6,000,000*l*., from lake Michigan, by way of the Illinois and Mississippi, to the Gulf of Mexico, completed . early Jan. 1900
Anarchist meeting stopped by the police, some rioting . . . . . . 5 Aug. „
Mr. J. D. Rockfeller gives 1,250,000 dol. to the university, reported . . . . 17 April, 1902
St. Luke's sanatorium burnt, over 8 deaths, 9 June, „
Lincoln hotel burnt, 14 deaths . . . 4 Dec. „

CHICAMAUGA ("the stream of death"), near Chattanooga, Tennessee, North America. Near here the confederates under general Bragg, aided by Longstreet, totally defeated the federals under Rosencrans, 19, 20 Sept. 1863. The loss was severe on both sides. The credit of the victory was attributed to Longstreet; its fruitlessness to Bragg.

CHICHESTER (Sussex), built by Cissa, about 540. The cathedral was completed about 1108, burnt with the city in 1114, and rebuilt by bishop Seffrid about 1187. The present cathedral was erected during the 13th century. The spire fell 20 Feb. 1861; the foundation of a new one was laid 2 May, 1865, completed June, 1866. The cathedral re-opened after repairs, 14 Nov. 1867. The bishopric originated thus: Wilfrid, archbishop of York, compelled to flee by Egfrid, king of Northumberland, preached the gospel in this country, and built a church in the Isle of Selsey, about 673. In 681 Selsey became a bishopric, and so continued until it was removed to Chichester, then called Cissan-Caester, from its builder, Cissa, by Stigand, about 1082. This see has yielded to the church two saints, and to the nation three lord chancellors. It is valued in the king's books at 677*l*. 1*s*. 3*d*. per annum. Present income, 4500*l*. The borough was absorbed into Sussex, 1885. Population, 1881, 8,114; 1891, 7,842; 1901, 12,241.

RECENT BISHOPS OF CHICHESTER.

1798. John Buckner, died 2 May, 1824.
1824. Robert J. Carr, trans. to Worcester, Sept. 1831.
1831. Edward Maltby, translated to Durham, 1836.
1836. Charles Otter, died 20 Aug. 1840.
1840. Philip Nicholas Shuttleworth, died 7 Jan. 1842.
1842. Ashurst Turner Gilbert, died 21 Feb. 1870.
1870. Richard Durnford, died, aged 92, 14 Oct. 1895.
1895. Ernest Roland Wilberforce, trans. from Newcastle, Nov. 1895.

"CHICHESTER" training-ship for homeless London boys, established chiefly by the earl of Shaftesbury and Mr. Williams, in connection with the refuges for destitute children, Great Queen-street. 50 boys placed in it, 18 Dec. 1866; reported highly successful. The baroness Burdett-Coutts gave 5000*l*. in 1874. H.M.S. *Arethusa* was devoted to a similar object, through the instrumentality of the same persons, 3 Aug. 1874. The *Goliath* training ship was burnt, 22 Dec. 1875; several lives were lost. See *Wrecks*, 1875.

CHICKAHOMINY BATTLES, see *Fair-oaks*, and *United States*, June, 1862.

CHICORY, the wild endive, or *Cichorium Intybus* of Linnæus, grows wild in calcareous soils. It was for many years so largely mixed with coffee in England that it became a matter of serious complaint, the loss of revenue being estimated at 100,000*l*. a year. An excise order was issued, interdicting the mixture of chicory with coffee, 3 Aug. 1852. The admixture, however, has since been permitted, provided the word "chicory" be plainly *printed* on each parcel sold. In 1860 a duty of 3*s*. per cwt. was put upon English-grown chicory until April, 1861; it is now 13*s*. 3*d*. per cwt. (1903).

CHIGNON, French for the "back-hair" of ladies. In directions for full dress in 1783, it is said: "The hair large and the chignon low behind." *Lady's Magazine*. Large chignons began to be worn in England in 1866; discontinued 1875.

CHILDERMAS DAY, 28 Dec., of ancient observance by the Roman Church, in memory of the slaughter of the Holy Innocents. (*Matt*. ii.)

CHILDREN. Many ancient nations exposed their infants,—the Egyptians on the banks of rivers, and the Greeks on highways,—when they could not support or educate them; in such cases, they were protected by the state. The old custom of English parents selling their children to the Irish for slaves, was prohibited by Canute, about 1017. See *Emigration, Foundling, Factory Acts, and Infanticide*.

Children's Dangerous Performances Act (earl de la Warr's act) passed: much needed . 24 July, 1879
By the new factory act the age of child-labour was raised from 10 to 11 . . . . . 5 Aug. 1891
National Society for the Prevention of Cruelty to Children, founded 8 July, 1884, to protect them from neglect, ill-usage, and immorality. (A similar society established in Liverpool, 19 April, 1883, was very efficient.) See *Trials* . 19 Oct. 1893
Frequent prosecutions by the society, 1894–1903; Mr. W. Astor gives 10,000*l*. to the society, end Sept. 1901.
Prevention of cruelty to, and protection of children act passed, 26 Aug. 1889; acts consolidated . 1894
State Children's Aid Association, visc. Peel chairman, supported by abp. of Canterbury and others, started Dec. 1896. Annual meetings.
New poor law board in relation to diseased children; 55 members, to be elected by the guardians of the unions; subject to the local government board; proposed, Jan.; adopted . . 1 Feb. 1897
Childhood Society, for the scientific study of the mental and physical conditions of children. Report based on the observation of 100,000 school children examined individually, 1888–94, issued 1896. Appeal for funds by sir Douglas Galton, *Times* . . . . 1 March, ,,
Internat. congress for the protection of children, presidents earl Beauchamp and sir Jas Crichton-Browne, opened by the lord mayor at the Guildhall . . . . 15 July, 1902
Nat. Society's new central offices in Leicester-square opened by Lord Alverstone . . 4 Feb. 1903
Employment of Children Act . . . . Aug. ,,

CHILI, or CHILE, a republic of S. America, discovered by Magellan, who landed at Chiloé, 1520. It was explored by Diego de Almagro, one of the conquerors of Peru, 1536. Capital, Santiago, founded 1541. Chili was subdued, but not wholly, in 1546. Population in 1865, 1,068,447; 1885, 2,527,320; 1896, 3,300,000; 1900, about 3,110,000; and about 50,000 Indians.

Chili declares its independence of Spain, 18 Sept. 1810
War with varying success: decisive victory gained by San Martin over the royal forces at Chacabuce, 12 Feb. 1817; the province declared independent, 12 Feb. 1818
Peace with Spain 1826
Present constitution established . . . 22 May, 1833
Manuel Montt elected president . . . 18 Oct. 1851
Insurrection headed by Pedro Gallo, Dec. 1858, suppressed . . . . April, 1859
José J. Perez, president . . . 18 Sept. 1861
Conflagration of the Jesuits' church at Santiago (see *Santiago*), more than 2,000 persons perished 8 Dec. 1863
Rupture between Chili and Bolivia respecting the "Guano" isles . . . . 1 March, 1864
Disputes with Spain respecting Peru settled by the Spanish minister, 20 May, disavowed by his government . . . . . . 25 July, ,,
Religious toleration enacted. . . . . July, 1865
J. J. Perez again proclaimed president; vigorous prosecution of the war . . . . Oct. ,,
The Spanish admiral Pareja appears before Valparaiso claiming satisfaction for Chilian intervention in the war with Peru, 17 Sept.; refused, 21 Sept.; he declares a blockade, 24 Sept.; Chili declares war against Spain, 29 Sept.; joins Peru, 5 Dec. ,,
The Spaniards bombard Valparaiso . 31 March, 1866
End of the blockade . . . . . 14 April, ,,
J. J. Perez re-elected president . . 18 Sept. ,,
F. Errazuriz elected president . . 18 Sept. 1871
Gold mines discovered near Iquique . . Oct. ,,
The *Tacna* (capt. Hyde), overloaded, left Valparaiso, 7 March; soon after sank; 19 (some children) drowned; captain and officers saved; he was reprimanded at Valparaiso, and set free; afterwards seized by orders of the Chilian government at Lota; eventually released and *compensated* 1874
International exhibition provisionally opened at Santiago, 26 Sept.; to the public . 31 Oct. 1875
Anibal Pinto, president (till 1881) . 18 Sept. 1876
Bolivian forts seized by the Chilians . Dec. 1878
Chili refuses to recognise a treaty between Peru and Bolivia (6 Feb. 1873) respecting boundaries; they declare war against Chili . . . . April, 1879
The Chilian wooden vessels *Esmeralda* and *Covadonga* blockade Iquique; the Peruvian ironclad turret ships (with rams) *Huascar* and *Independencia* attempt relief; *Esmeralda* sunk by *Huascar* (about 110 perish); *Independencia* runs ashore while chasing *Covadonga*; capt. Pratt and 6 men climb up *Huascar* and are killed fighting on the deck . . . . 21, 23 May, ,,
Huascar enters port of Iquique, and captures 2 vessels . . . . 29 July, ,,
Blockade of Iquique raised; announced 4 Aug. ,,
Huascar captured by Chilian fleet off Mejillones, after 6 hours' gallant fight; the admiral and many officers killed . . . . . 8 Oct. ,,
Pisagua bombarded and captured by Chilians, 2 Nov. ,,
Combined Peruvian and Bolivian army defeated near Iquique (which surrenders), Nov.; again near Tarapaca, which is taken . about 27 Nov. ,,
Naval engagement; dashing conduct of Peruvian vessels . . . . 27 Feb. 1880
Callao blockaded by Chilians; alarm at Lima, about 18 April, ,,
Battle of Tacna; it is captured by Chilians, 26 May, ,,
Arica taken by the Chilians . . . 8 June, ,,
Pierola dictator of Peru; declares for perseverance in the war; excitement at Lima; levy *en masse*. 28 June, ,,
Chilian transport *Loa* sunk by torpedo, by a Peruvian launch apparently laden with fruit; Callao greatly shaken . . . . . . 3 July, ,,
Chilian vessel *Covadonga* bombarding town, sunk by Peruvian torpedoes off Chancay; about 115 perish (severe reprisals) . . . . 14 Sept. ,,
Chilians storm Lurin, 4 Jan.; defeat the Peruvians at Chorillos, 13 Jan.; at Miraflores, 15 Jan.; occupy Lima without resistance, Pierola flees, about 17 Jan.; Callao taken soon after . Jan. 1881
Conditions of peace reported; cession of territory; 750 million dollars indemnity; occupation of Callao; working of mines till indemnity paid; announced . . . . 30 Jan. ,,
England and France requested to mediate by Peru Feb. ,,

Treaty of peace between Spain confirmed . Sept. 1881
Calderon elected president, announced . 1 Sept. ,,
President; Domingo Santa-Maria . . . 18 Sept. ,,
Treaty of peace with Bolivia . . . 25 Jan. 1882
Peace protocol between Chili and Peru, agreed to March, ,,
War resumed; skirmishes; Chilians generally successful . . . July, ,,
Peruvians defeated by Chilians in several engagements, 13, 15, and 16 July, also 8 Aug. . . . ,,
Concepcion burned, announced . . . 19 July, ,,
Reported peace; cession of Tarapaca and Tacna 28 Sept. ,,
Negotiations fail, announced . . . 8 Oct. ,,
Peace said to be signed; Peru cedes Tacna and Arica to Chili for 10 years, reported 25 May, 1883
Severe battle, Peruvians defeated with great loss at Huamachuca . . . 10 July, ,,
Peruvian leaders defeated at Huanchuco by col. Grostiago . . . 19 July, ,,
Peace with Peru signed at Ancon . . . 20 Oct. ,,
Lima evacuated . . . 23 Oct. ,,
Señor Don José Manuel Balmaceda, president 18 Sept. 1886
After much agitation, great electoral reforms carried Oct. 1890
The congress issues a declaration deposing the president for treason against the constitution, tyranny, and misuse of the public money, and designates sen. Jorge Montt as its assistant in restoring the due observance of the constitution. 1 Jan. 1891
The navy (under capt. J. Montt) revolts against the president; the army remains faithful to him about 7 Jan. ,,
Valparaiso, held for the president, blockaded by the navy; frequent skirmishes; contradictory reports . . . 16 Jan. ,,
Small British squadron sent to Chilian waters about 17 Jan. ,,
The navy blockades the coast . . . 20 Jan. ,,
Coronel bombarded by the navy, reported 25 Jan. ,,
The congressists take Pisagua . . . 26 Jan. ,,
A French squadron ordered to the Chilian coast about 28 Jan. ,,
The government troops re-take Pisagua; the congressists occupy Talta . . . about 1 Feb. ,,
Fighting at Castro; congressists defeated; 130 killed . . . reported 4 Feb. ,,
Insurrection confined to the chief harbours 5 Feb. ,,
Pisagua and Iquique burned by bombardment, reported . . . 13 Feb. ,,
The president's troops defeated at Dolores, 15 Feb., and Iquique . . . 19 Feb. ,,
The congressists defeated at Pisagua . 22 Feb. ,,
Iquique bombarded by the congressists; the British admiral Hotham intervenes to save women and children; capt. Lambton, of the *Warspite*, passes through a heavy fire to obtain an armistice; the town and troops surrender to the congressists 20 Feb. ,,
Tarapaca taken by the congressists reported 27 Feb. ,,
Conflicting news . . . Jan., Feb., March, ,,
The troops at Pisagua declare for the congressists, reported . . . 3 March, ,,
The president's troops defeated at Pozo Almonte, 4 March; the province of Tarapaca held by the congress party . . . about 8 March, ,,
Part of the army joins the congress party, which holds all southern Chili, reported . 12 March, ,,
Col. Robles, with the president's troops, totally defeated; he is killed after the engagement at Pozo Almonte, 4 March. The province of Tarapaca held by the congress party . . . 8 March, ,,
The port of Antofagasta taken by the congressist fleet . . . 18–23 March, ,,
Tacna and Arica occupied by the congressists without resistance . . . 7 April, ,,
A provisional government or junta established by the congress party, at Iquique . . 10 April, ,,
Part of the regular army (2,450) crosses the Argentine territory to reach Santiago, reported 14 April, ,,
Newly-elected congress (his nominees) opened by the president; his conduct reported very tyrannical . . . 21 April, ,,
The congressist ironclad *Blanco Encalada*, in Caldera Bay, Atacama, sunk by Balmaceda's torpedo boats early . . . 23 April, 1891
Revolt of troops at Coquimbo, to the congressists. 25 April, ,,
The congressist cruiser *Magellanes*, in Valparaiso harbour, beats off a fierce attack of three government torpedo boats . . . 28 April, ,,
Capiapo, the capital of Atacama, occupied by the congressists, reported . . . 29 April, ,,
President Balmaceda invites foreign mediation, reported . . . 6 May, ,,
Negotiations between the government and the congressists fail . . . about 8 May, ,,
The *Itata*, and *Robert* and *Minnie*, private transports, supply the congress party with contraband articles from New York, 15 April *et seq.*; they are chased by the U.S. cruiser *Charleston*, early May,
Amicable arrangement between the congressists and the United States respecting the *Itata*, reported . . . 20 May, ,,
Balmaceda's ships, *Condell* and *Imperial*, bombard Iquique . . . 22 May, ,,
The officers and crew of Balmaceda's torpedo launch *Giralda*, shot for suspected desertion 30 May, ,,
The statements respecting the various conflicts and movements of the two parties very uncertain and frequently contradictory . May, June, ,,
The congressional provisional junta at Iquique issues decrees respecting the state finances 22 May, ,,
The *Itata* surrenders to the American cruisers at Iquique . . . 4 June, ,,
The provisional junta at Iquique issues a circular note to the powers denouncing president Balmaceda as a dictator, and asking to be recognised as a belligerent, 7 May, published . 11 June, ,,
Balmaceda's squadron bombards Pisagua, 8 June; Iquique . . . 9 June, ,,
Reported reign of terror in Santiago through the tyranny of president Balmaceda . . 25 June, ,,
The congressists occupy Huasco . . 2 July, ,,
Sen. Pedro Montt and sen. Varas, on behalf of the congressists, declare that the financial dealings of president Balmaceda will not be recognised by them . . . 10 July, ,,
The ten conspirators who attempted to blow up Balmaceda's ships at Valparaiso shot . 14 July, ,,
The judges and legal officers of the republic discharged by Balmaceda and replaced by his ignorant partisans; no security for foreigners, reported . . . 21 July, ,,
The congress party occupy the Atacama province 25 July, ,,
The congressist army, about 10,000, with batteries, &c., commanded by col. Canto, land at Quinteros Bay, 20 Aug., and after a night's march, they completely defeat Balmaceda's army at Colmo; the congressists have about 300 killed; Balmaceda has about 1,000 killed, 21 Aug.; they advance and take Salto, 24 Aug.; and Quilpue, 25 Aug.; march toward Valparaiso, receiving large numbers of deserters from the enemy, and encamp in a farm-house . . . 27 Aug. ,,
Battle of Placilla: Balmaceda's army totally defeated; about 1,000 killed and 3,000 prisoners; congressists, 400 killed; the battle lasted from 7.30 to 10.30, and the congressists took possession of Valparaiso at 1 P.M. . . 28 Aug. ,,
Santiago occupied by the congressists, who restore constitutional government . . 30 Aug. ,,
Temporal resistance at Coquimbo; several of Balmaceda's officers shot . . reported 1 Sept. ,,
The great powers recognise the congressist provisional government . . about 16 Sept. ,,
National holiday with great rejoicings, 16–20 Sept. ,,
Balmaceda's funds being exhausted he issues state notes to the amount of 12,000,000 pesos, he also seizes bars of silver valued at 4,500,000 pesos, the metallic reserve of the paper currency and illegally offers it for sale, without effect Feb. *et seq.*; he then forms a new congress to support him, April; and negotiates for the purchase of a steamer at Montevideo without effect; Mr.

Kennedy, British minister at Santiago, places at Balmaceda's disposal H.M.S. *Espiegle* to convey the silver bars to Montevideo, June *et seq.*; 338 silver bars transferred to H.M.S. *Moselle*, which conveys them to Southampton . 16 Sept. 1891
Litigation ensued between the republic of Chili and the London and River Plate Bank, who had advanced money on the bars of silver to Balmaceda. Finally the court of appeal in London awarded the silver to the company . . . . 7 Aug. 1894
Balmaceda concealed at the Argentine Legation in Santiago; commits suicide, leaving a justificatory letter, and is secretly buried . . 19 Sept. 1891
Two ironclad cruisers, the *Presidente Pinto* and *Presidente Errazuriz*, constructed for Balmaceda at Bordeaux; col. Villagran with 114 soldiers claims them for him, 6 April; an embargo on these vessels raised by order of a French law court, 8 July; the vessels leave Bordeaux, and after endeavouring to enlist men at several ports in Europe, July, Aug., are given up at the end of the war to the new provisional government, Sept. *et seq.* ,,
Election of senate and deputies . about 21 Oct. ,,
Mr. Patrick Egan, the U.S. minister, charged with breach of neutrality by favouring Balmaceda's party during the war . . . . . . Oct. ,,
At Valparaiso some of the populace assault the boats' crews of the U.S. ship *Baltimore*; 2 of the crew killed, 16 Oct.; the U.S. government demands reparation; the Chilian government promises investigation . . . . . 29 Oct. ,,
The case against the *Itata* dismissed by the U.S. court . . . . 3 Nov. ,,
Señor Jorge Montt elected president . . 4 Nov. ,,
Amnesty granted to the followers of Balmaceda, 24 Dec. ,,
A liberal-conservative ministry constituted; sen. Barros Luco premier . . . . . 31 Dec. ,,
The Chilian rioters sentenced (some to imprisonment and some to penal servitude), for assaulting the sailors of the *Baltimore*, 3 Jan.; the president apologises to the U.S.A. government for the incident . . . . Jan. 1892
After further correspondence the Chilian government accepts the stringent U.S.A. ultimatum, 25-30 Jan. ,,
The first congress closes after progress . 30 Jan. ,,
A new ministry constituted under sen. Edouardo Matte . . . . . . about 13 March, ,,
New ministry formed by sen. Barros Luco, 11 June, ,,
Mr. P. Egan concludes a convention between Chili and the United States . . . . . . Aug. ,,
Resignation of the cabinet . . . about 8 Nov. ,,
Balmacedist plots in the army suppressed, Nov. Dec. ,,
Amnesty granted to Balmaceda's partisans, with some exceptions . . . . reported 8 Feb. 1893
Mr. Patrick Egan replaced by Mr. James D. Porter as minister for U.S.A. . . . . 30 March, ,,
Disturbances; martial law proclaimed in Santiago, Valparaiso and Aconcagua . reported 10 April, ,,
New ministry; sen. Pedro Montt premier 26 April, ,,
Arbitration commission on the claims of the United States against Chili, at Washington; award to the States, 240,564 dollars; other claims not accepted, 24 April; paid 9 Oct.; finance of president Montt reported successful . . . Aug. 1894
Resignation of sen. MacIver's ministry, 5 Nov.; succeeded by sen. Ramon B. Luco . . 7 Dec. ,,
The congress house at Santiago burnt . 18 May, 1895
Congress opened; revived prosperity . 2 June, ,,
Resignation of the ministry, 6 July; new ministry formed by sen. Recabarren . . . 29 July, ,,
National guard established; announced 14 April, 1896
Gen. Federico Errazuriz elected president, 25 July, ,,
The ministry resigns, 8 Nov.; new liberal cabinet 17 Nov. ,,
Elections: government majority . . 13 March, 1897
Frequent changes of ministry . . June–Dec. ,,
Boundary disputes with Argentina referred to the arbitration of queen Victoria, early July, 1897 (settled Oct. 1898).
Financial panic; banks closed, 7 July; a moratorium, 30 days, ordered, 10 July; paper money authorised . . . . . 20 July, ,,
Convention with Peru relating to the retrocession of Tacna and Arica, adopted . . . 26 Sept. 1898
See *Peru*, April, 1898.
Frauds discovered at the arsenal; suicide of señ. Navarro, chief accountant . . . . 13 Oct. ,,
Puña de Atacama award settled by compromise, 24 March, 1899
Frequent changes of ministry . . Dec.–Sept. ,,
Naval arsenal at Talcahuano burnt; estimated loss 50,000 dol. . . . . 30 June, ,,
Severe storms and tidal wave at Valparaiso; railway wrecked; great damage; at Santiago villages destroyed . . . . 8–15 Aug. ,,
Congress opened by the president, with a cheerful speech . . . . 1 June, 1900
Compulsory military service, with some exceptions, decreed . . . . . . 5 Sept. ,,
Coalition cabinet formed, señ. Fontecilla premier, 4 Nov. ,,
Boundary protocol signed by Chili and Argentina, 27 Dec. ,,
Pres. Errazuriz resigned from illness, 1 May; he died . . . . 12 July, 1901
Señ. Arias Sanchez, Ecuador consul, assassinated in Valparaiso . . . . 17 July, ,,
Señ. German Riesco proclaimed president 25 July, ,,
New ministry, señ. Barros Luco, premier 11 Sept. ,,
Frontier dispute with Argentina, Dec.; question to be submitted to British arbitration . 26 Dec. ,,
British commission, sir Thos. Holdich and others, to delimit the Argentine-Chilian frontier, arrive 1 March, 1902
Naval arsenal at Valparaiso burnt down, 15 March, ,,
Treaties with Argentina for arbitration under king Edward, limitation of naval armaments, boundaries, &c., signed at Santiago, 28 May; approved by the chamber of deputies . 12 Aug. ,,
Congress opened . . . . . . 1 June, ,,
Bursting of a reservoir at Las Palmas (35 deaths, and many houses destroyed) . . . 11 July, ,,
Battleships.—*Constitucion*, launched at Newcastle-on-Tyne; *Libertad*, at Barrow . 14, 15 Jan. 1903
Crisis, 6 Apr.; Señ. Ramon Barros Luco forms a coalition cabinet . . . . . . 8 Apr. ,,
Pisaqua, a nitrate port, nearly destroyed by fire, mid-Apr. ,,
Labour troubles at Valparaiso, resulting in strikes and arson; conflict between troops and strikers ,,

CHILLED SHOT, see *Cannon*, 1864-6.

CHILLIANWALLAH, BATTLE OF, India, between the Sikh forces in considerable strength, and the British commanded by lord (afterwards viscount) Gough, fought 13 Jan. 1849. The Sikhs were completely routed, but the loss of the British was very severe: 26 officers were killed and 66 wounded, and 731 rank and file killed, and 1446 wounded. The Sikh loss was 3000 killed and 4000 wounded.* On 21 Feb. lord Gough attacked the Sikh army, under Shere Singh, in its position at Goojerat, with complete success; and the whole of the enemy's camp fell into the hands of the British.

CHILTERN HUNDREDS (viz. Burnham, Desborough, near Stoke), an estate of the crown on the chain of chalk hills that pass from east to west through the middle of Buckinghamshire. The stewardship is a nominal office, with a salary of 25*s.*, conferred on members of parliament when they wish to vacate their seats. The strict legality of the practice is questioned. The practice began in 1750. "The Chiltern Hundreds," by A. J. Foster, published 1897.

CHIMBORAZO, highest point in the Andes, South America (altitude 21,068 feet); was as-

* The duke of Wellington (commander-in-chief) did not think the victory complete. Gough was superseded, and sir Charles Napier sent out (March, 1849), who did not arrive in India till Gough had redeemed his reputation.

cended by Humboldt, 23 June, 1802, by Boussingault and Hall, 16 Dec. 1831; by Edward Whymper, 3 July, 1880. See *Andes*.

CHIMNEY-TAX, see *Hearth*.

CHIMNEYS. Chafing-dishes were in use previous to the invention of chimneys, which were first introduced into Britain about 1200. Chimneys were general in domestic architecture in the 14th century. At the chemical works, Glasgow, is a chimney (there termed a *stalk*) 420 feet in height; the height of the monument in London being 202 feet; of St. Paul's, 404 feet.

Act to regulate *chimney-sweeping*, 28 Geo. III. . . 1789
The *chimney-sweeping machine* was invented by Smart 1805
A statute regulating the trade, the apprenticeship of children, the construction of flues, preventing calling "sweep" in the streets, &c., passed . . 1834
By 3 & 4 Vict. c. 85 (1840), it is not lawful for master sweeps to take apprentices under sixteen years of age; and no individual under twenty-one to ascend a chimney after . . . . 1 July, 1842
Enforcement of this law made more stringent . . 1864
Joseph Glass, inventor of the sweeping machine now in general use, *not patented*, died 29 Jan. 1868
New chimney-sweepers' acts passed . 1875 and 1894
By the fall of a chimney at Marsh Mills, Cleckheaton, Yorkshire, 15 persons were killed, 24 Feb. 1892

CHINA (TSING), the "Celestial Empire," in Eastern Asia, for which the Chinese annals claim an antiquity of from 80,000 to 100,000 years B.C. The three religions are Confucianism, Taoism, and Buddhism, which see. Mr. B. C. Boulger's "History of China," 3 vols., 1881-84. Professor Legge has published "Chinese Classics" and a translation of the Chinese "sacred books." Population (as stated at Pekin) in 1888, 303,241,969; 1890, 360,250,000; 1897, 303,241,969; 1903, 426,447,000.

The early condition of China was tribal, which gradually merged into a vast feudal system, nominally ruled by many contemporaneous dynasties, dated from 2205 B.C. The king of Ts'in put down all other rulers and assumed the title of *Hwang Ti*, or emperor, declaring that "as there is but one sun in the sky, there should be but one ruler in the nation" 221
Principal dynasties: Han, 206 B.C.–220 A.D.; T'ang, 618–906; Sung, 960–1279; Yüan, the Mongol, 1280–1367; the Ming, 1368–1643; the Ch'ing, or Ts'ing, Manchû Tartar, 1643 to the present date. *Legge*.

Supposed age of Confucius (Kungfutze), the philosopher . . . . B.C. 551–479
Stupendous wall of China completed 211
Literature and the art of printing encouraged . B.C. 202
Battle between Phraates and the Scythians; the Chinese aided the latter, and ravaged the coasts of the Caspian: their first appearance in history (*Lenglet*) 129
The religion of Laot-se begun 15
A form of Buddhism, or the religion of Fŏ, introduced . . . . . . about A.D. 68–81
Nankin becomes the capital 420
The atheistical philosopher, San-Shin, flourishes . 449
The Nestorian Christians permitted to preach . 635
They are proscribed and extirpated 845
China ravaged by Tartars, 9th to 11th centuries.
Seat of government transferred to Pekin . . . 1260
Marco Polo introduces missionaries . . . 1275
Kublai Khan establishes the Yuen or Mongol dynasty . . . . about ,,
Ming dynasty 1368
Canal, called the Yu Ho, completed . . about 1400
Europeans first arrive at Canton 1517
Macao is granted to the Portuguese . . . 1536
Jesuit missionaries are sent from Rome . . . 1575
The country is conquered by the eastern or Manchu Tartars, who establish the present reigning Tsing dynasty 1616–43
Tea brought to England 1660
An earthquake throughout China, buries 300,000 persons at Pekin alone 1662
Galdan, a prince of Jangaria, conquers Kashgaria and becomes supreme in Central Asia, 1678; checked by Kang-hi, 1689; totally defeated . 1695
Commerce with East India Company begins . . 1680
Jesuit missionaries preach 1692
Commercial relations with Russia 1719-27
The Jesuits expelled 1724-32
Another general earthquake destroys 100,000 persons at Pekin, and 80,000 in a suburb . . . 1731
Successful war in Central Asia; Davatsi and his opponent Amursana, subdued by Keen-lung, 1755 *et seq.*; Kashgar, Khokand, the Khirgez, &c. annexed 1760
In a salute by one of our ships in China, a gun was inadvertently fired, which killed a native; the government demanded the gunner; he was soon strangled 1785
Earl Macartney's embassy arrives at Pekin; his reception by the emperor . . . . 14 Sept. 1793
[This embassy threw light on the empire; it appeared to be divided into 15 provinces, containing 4402 walled cities; the population of the whole was given at 333,000,000: its annual revenues at 66,000,000*l.*; and the army, including the Tartars, 1,000,000 of infantry and 800,000 cavalry; the religion Pagan, and the government absolute. Learning, and the arts and sciences, were encouraged, and ethics studied.]
He is ordered to depart . . . . . . 7 Oct. ,,
And arrives in England . . . . . . 6 Sept. 1794
The affair of the Company's ship *Neptune*, when a Chinaman was killed 1807
Edict against Christianity 1812
Chinese rule in Central Asia weakened . . . ,,
Lord Amherst's embassy; he leaves England 8 Feb. 1816
[His lordship failed in the objects of his mission, having refused to make the prostration of the *kotou*, lest he should thereby compromise the majesty of England.]
Temporary insurrections in Kashgar . 1826, *et seq.*
Exclusive rights of the E. I. Co. cease . 22 April, 1834
Free-trade ships sail for England . 25 April, ,,
Lord Napier arrives at Macao to superintend British commerce . . . . . 15 July, ,,
Affair between the natives and two British ships of war; several Chinese killed . . 5 Sept. ,,
Lord Napier dies, and is succeeded by Mr. (afterwards sir John) Davis . . . . . 11 Oct.
Opium dispute begins; the trade prohibited by the emperor . . . . Nov. ,,
Chinese seize the *Argyle* and crew . . . 31 Jan. 1835
Opium burnt at Canton by Chinese . . 23 Feb. ,,
Captain Elliot, chief British commissioner, 14 Dec. 1836
A British commissioner settled at Canton, March, 1837
Admiral Maitland arrives at Macao . . 12 July, 1838
Commissioner Lin orders seizure of opium, 18 March; British and other residents forbidden to leave Canton, 19 March: the factories surrounded and outrages committed . . 24 March, 1839
Captain Elliot requires British subjects to surrender to him all opium, promising them full value of it, 27 March; half of it is given up as contraband to the Chinese, 20 April; the remainder (20,283 chests) surrendered, 21 May; captain Elliot and the British merchants leave Canton, 24 May; the opium destroyed by the Chinese . 3 June, ,,
Affair between the British and American seamen and the Chinese; a native killed . . . 7 July ,,
Hong-Kong taken . . . . 23 Aug. ,,
The British boat *Black Joke* attacked, and the crew murdered, 24 Aug.; the British merchants retire from Macao . . . . . . 26 Aug. ,,
Affair at Kow-lung between British boats and Chinese junks . . . . . . 4 Sept. ,,
Attack by 28 armed junks on the British frigates *Volage* and *Hyacinth*: several junks blown up 3 Nov. ,,
The British trade with China ceases, by an edict of the emperor, and the last servant of the company leaves this day . . . . . . 6 Dec. ,,
Edict of the emperor interdicting all trade and intercourse with England for ever . 5 Jan. 1840
The *Hellas* ship attacked by armed junks, 22 May, blockade of Canton by a British fleet, by orders from sir Gordon Bremer, 28 June; the *Blonde* with a flag of truce fired on at Amoy, 2 July;

Ting-hai, in Chusan, surrenders, 5 July; blockade established along the Chinese coast, 10 July; Mr. Staunton carried off to Canton . . 6 Aug. 1840
Captain Elliot, on board a British steam-ship, enters the Peiho river, near Pekin . 11 Aug. ,,
The ship *Kite* lost on a sand-bank, and the captain's wife and a part of the crew are captured by the natives, and confined in cages . . 15 Sept. ,,
Lin finally degraded; Keshin appointed imperial commissioner, 16 Sept.; capt. Elliot's truce with him . . . . 6 Nov. ,,
British plenipotentiaries off Macao . . 20 Nov. ,,
Admiral Elliot's resignation announced . 29 Nov. ,,
Mr. Staunton released . . . . . 12 Dec. ,,
Negotiations cease, owing to breach of faith on the part of the Chinese emperor . . 6 Jan. 1841
Chuen-pe and Tae-coc-tow, and 173 guns (some sent to England) captured . . . . 7 Jan. ,,
Hong-Kong ceded by Keshin to Great Britain, and 6,000,000 dollars agreed to be paid within ten days to the British authorities . . 20 Jan. ,,
Hong-Kong taken possession of . . . 26 Jan. ,,
The emperor rejects Keshin's treaty, 11 Feb; hostilities resumed, 23 Feb.; Chusan evacuated, 24 Feb.; rewards proclaimed at Canton for the bodies of Englishmen, dead or alive: 50,000 dollars to be given for chiefs . . 25 Feb. ,,
Bogue forts taken by sir G. Bremer; admiral Kwan killed; 459 guns captured . . . 26 Feb. ,,
The British squadron proceeds to Canton, 1 March; sir H. Gough takes command of the army, 2 March; hostilities again suspended, 3 March; and again resumed, 6 March; Keshin degraded by the emperor . . . . . 12 March ,,
Flotilla of boats destroyed, Canton threatened, the foreign factories seized, and 461 guns taken by the British forces . . . . 18 March, ,,
New commissioners from Pekin arrived at Canton, 14 April, ,,
Hong Kong Gazette first published . . 1 May, ,,
Capt. Elliot prepares to attack Canton . 17 May, ,,
Heights behind Canton taken . . 25 May, ,,
The city ransomed for 6,000,000 dollars; 5,000,000 paid down; hostilities cease . . 31 May, ,,
British forces withdrawn, 1 June; and British trade re-opened . . . . . 16 July, ,,
Arrival at Macao of sir Henry Pottinger, who, as plenipotentiary, proclaims the objects of his mission; capt. Elliot superseded . 10 Aug. ,,
Amoy taken, and 296 guns destroyed . 27 Aug. ,,
The Bogue forts destroyed . . . 14 Sept. ,,
Ting-hae taken, 136 guns captured, and Chusan re-occupied by the British, 1 Oct.; they take Chin-hae, 10 Oct.; Ning-po, 13 Oct.; Yu-yaou, Tsze-kee, and Foong-hua . . . 28 Dec. ,,
Chinese attack Ning-po and Chin-hae, and are repulsed with great loss, 10 March; 8000 Chinese are routed near Tze-kee . . 15 March, 1842
Cha-pou attacked; defences destroyed 18 May, ,,
The British squadron enters the river Kiang 13 June; capture of Woosung and of 230 guns and stores 16 June; Shang-hae taken, 19 June, ,,
The British armament anchors near the "Golden Isle," 20 July; Chin-Keang taken; the Tartar general and many of the garrison commit suicide, 21 July; the advanced ships reach Nankin, 4 Aug.; the whole fleet arrives, and the disembarkation commences, 9 Aug.; Keying arrives at Nankin, with full powers to treat for peace, 12 Aug. ,,
Treaty of peace signed before Nankin, on board the *Cornwallis* by sir Henry Pottinger for England, and Keying Elepoo* and Neu-Kien on the part of the Chinese emperor—[Conditions: lasting peace and friendship between the two empires; China to pay 21,000,000 of dollars; Canton, Amoy, Foochoofoo, Ningpo, and Shang-hai to be thrown open to the British, and consuls to reside at these cities; Hong-Kong to be ceded in perpetuity to England, &c.; Chusan and Ku-lang-su to be held by the British until the provisions are fulfilled †] 29 Aug. ,,

* He took part (it was said without authority) in arranging the treaty of Tien-tsin in June, 1858. He was in consequence condemned to death—by suicide.

† The non-fulfilment of this treaty led gradually to the war of 1856-57.

The ratification signed by queen Victoria and the emperor formally exchanged . . . 22 July, 1843
Canton opened to the British . . . 27 July, ,,
Appointment of Mr. Davis in the room of sir Henry Pottinger . . . . 16 Feb. 1844
Bogue forts captured by the British . 5 April, 1847
Hong-Kong and the neighbourhood visited by a violent typhoon; immense damage done to the shipping; upwards of 1000 boat-dwellers on the Canton river drowned . . . . . Oct 1848
H.M. steam-ship *Medea* destroys 13 pirate junks in the Chinese seas. . . . . 4 March, 1850
Rebellion breaks out in Quang-si . . . Aug. ,,
Appearance of the pretender, Tien-teh* March, 1851
Defeat of Leu, the imperial commissioner, and destruction of half the army . . . 19 June, 1852
Successful progress of the rebels; the emperor applies to the Europeans for help, without success, March and April, 1853
The rebels take Nankin, 19, 20 March; Amoy, 19 May; Shang-hae . . . . 7 Sept. ,,
And besiege Canton without success Aug.-Nov. 1854
The scanty accounts are unfavourable to the rebels, the imperialists having retaken Shang-hae, Amoy, and many important places 1855
Outrage on the British lorcha *Arrow*, in Canton river † . . . . 8 Oct. 1856
After vain negotiations with commissioner Yeh, Canton forts attacked and taken . 23 Oct. ,,
A Chinese fleet destroyed and Canton bombarded, by sir M. Seymour . . . 3, 4 Nov. ,,
Imperialists defeated, quit Shang-hae . . 6 Nov. ,,
The Americans revenge an attack by capturing three forts . . . . . . 21-23 Nov. ,,
Rebels take Kuriking . . . . 25 Nov. ,,
Other forts taken by the British . . . Dec. ,,
The Chinese burn European factories . . 14 Dec. ,,
And murder the crew of the *Thistle* . 30 Dec. ,,
The Mahometans of Panthay, in Yunan, become independent during Tae-ping rebellion . . ,,
A-lum, a Chinese baker, acquitted of charge of poisoning the bread . . . . 2 Feb. 1857
Troops arrive from Madras and England; and lord Elgin appointed envoy . . . . March, ,,
No change on either side: Yeh said to be straitened for money; the imperialists seem to be gaining ground upon the rebels . . . . May, ,,

* The emperor Taou-Kwang, who died 25 Feb., 1850, during the latter part of his reign, became liberal in his views, and favoured the introduction of European arts; but his son, the late emperor, a rash and narrow-minded prince, quickly departed from his father's wise policy, and adopted reactionary measures, particularly against English influence. An insurrection broke out in consequence, Aug. 1850, and quickly became of alarming importance. The insurgents at first proposed only to expel the Tartars; but in March, 1851, a pretender was announced among them, first by the name of Tien-teh (Celestial Virtue), but afterwards assuming other names. He is stated to have been a native of Quang-si, of obscure origin, but to have obtained some literary knowledge at Canton about 1835, and to have become acquainted at that time with the principles of Christianity from a Chinese Christian, named Leang-afa, and also from the missionary Roberts in 1844. He announced himself as the restorer of the worship of the true God, Shang-ti, and derived many of his dogmas from the Bible. He declared himself to be the monarch of all beneath the sky, the true lord of China (and thus of all the world), the brother of Jesus, and the second son of God, and demanded universal submission. He made overtures for alliance to lord Elgin in Nov. 1860. His followers were termed *Taepings*, "princes of peace," a title utterly belied by their atrocious deeds. The rebellion was virtually terminated, 18 July, 1864, by the capture of Nankin, the suicide of the Tien-Wang, and the execution of the military leaders.

† It was boarded by the Chinese officers, 12 men out of the crew of 14 being carried off and the national ensign taken down. Sir J. Bowring, governor of Hong-Kong, being compelled to resort to hostilities, applied to India and Ceylon for troops. On 3 March, 1857, the house of commons, by a majority of 19, censured sir John for the "violent measures" he had pursued. The ministry (who took his part) dissolved the parliament; but obtained a large majority in the new one.

Total destruction of the Chinese fleet by commodore Elliot, 25, 27 May; and sir M. Seymour and commodore Keppel . . . . 1 June, 1857
Blockade of Canton . . . . . Aug. ,,
Stagnation in the war—lord Elgin departs to Calcutta, with assistance to the English against the Sepoys, 16 July; returns to Hong-Kong 25 Sept. ,,
Gen. Ashburnham departs for India, and gen. Straubenzee assumes the command . . . 19 Oct. ,,
Canton bombarded and taken by English and French, 28, 29 Dec. 1857; who enter it . 5 Jan. 1858
Yeh* sent a prisoner to Calcutta . . . . Jan. ,,
The allies proceed towards Pekin, and take the Pei-ho forts . . . . 20 May, ,,
The expedition arrives at Tien-tsin . 20 May, ,,
Negotiations commence, 5 June; treaty of peace signed at *Tien-tsin* by lord Elgin, baron Gros, and Keying (who signed the treaty of 1842)—[Ambassadors to be at both courts; freedom of trade; toleration of Christianity; expenses of war to be paid by China; a revised tariff; term *I* (*barbarian*) to be no longer applied to Europeans] 26, 28, 29 June, ,,
Lord Elgin visits Japan, and concludes an important treaty with the emperor . . 28 Aug. ,,
The British destroy about 130 piratical junks in the Chinese seas . . . . Aug. and Sept. ,,
Lord Elgin proceeds up the Yang-tse-Kiang to Nankin, Jan.; returns to England . May, 1859
Mr. Bruce, the British envoy, on his way to Pekin, is stopped in the river Pei-ho (or Tien-tsin); admiral Hope attempting to force a passage, is repulsed with the loss of 81 killed, and about 390 wounded . . . . . . 25 June, ,,
The American envoy Ward arrives at Pekin, and refusing to submit to degrading ceremonies, does not see the emperor . . . . 29 July, ,,
Commercial treaty with America . . 24 Nov. ,,
The English and French prepare an expedition against China . . . . . . Oct. ,,
Lord Elgin and baron Gros sail for China, April 26; wrecked near Point de Galle, Ceylon, 23 May; arrive at Shang-hae . . . . 29 June, 1860
The war begins: the British commanded by sir Hope Grant, the French by general Montauban. The Chinese defeated in a skirmish near the Pei-ho 12 Aug. ,,
The allies repulse the Taeping rebels attacking Shang-hae, 18-20 Aug.; and take the Taku forts, losing 500 killed and wounded; the Tartar general San-ko-lin-sin retreats . . . . . 21 Aug. ,,
After vain negotiations, the allies advance towards Pekin; they defeat the Chinese at Chang-kia-wan and Pa-li-chiau . . . . . 18 & 21 Sept. ,,
Consul Parkes, captains Anderson and Brabazon, Mr. de Norman, Mr. Bowlby (the *Times'* correspondent), and 14 others (Europeans and Sikhs), advance to Tung-chow, to arrange conditions for a meeting of the ministers, and are captured by San-ko-lin-sin; capt. Brabazon and abbé de Luc beheaded, and said to be thrown into he canal; others carried into Pekin 21 Sept. ,,
The allies march towards Pekin; the French ravage the emperor's summer palace, 6 Oct.; Mr. Parkes, Mr. Loch, and others, restored alive, 8 Oct.; capt. Anderson, Mr. De Norman, and others die of ill-usage . . . . 8-11 Oct. ,,
Pekin invested; surrenders, 12 Oct.; severe proclamation of sir Hope Grant . . . 15 Oct. ,,
The bodies of Mr. De Norman and Mr. Bowlby solemnly buried in the Russian cemetery, Pekin, 17 Oct.; the summer palace (Yuen-ming-yuen) burnt by the British, in memory of the outraged prisoners . . . . 18 Oct. ,,
Convention signed in Pekin by lord Elgin and the prince Kung, by which the treaty of Tien-tsin is ratified; apology made for the attack at Pei-ho (25 June, 1859); a large indemnity to be paid immediately, and compensation in money given to the families of the murdered prisoners, &c.; Kowloon ceded in exchange for Chusan, and the treaty and convention to be proclaimed throughout the empire . . . . 24 Oct. 1860
Allies quit Pekin . . . . . . 5 Nov. ,,
Treaty between Russia and China—the former obtaining free trade, territories, &c. . 14 Nov. ,,
First instalment of indemnity paid . . 30 Nov. ,,
Part of the allied troops settled at Tien-tsin; consulate established . . . . 5 Jan. 1861
Adm. Hope examines Yang-tse-Kiang, &c. . Feb. ,,
English and French embassies established at Pekin, March, ,,
The emperor Heinfung dies . . . 21 Aug. ,,
Canton restored to the Chinese . . 21 Oct. ,,
Ministerial crisis; several ministers put to death, Nov.; Kung appointed regent . . 13 Dec. ,,
Advance of the rebels; they seize and desolate Ning-po and Hang-chow . . . . . Dec. ,,
They advance on Shang-hae, which is placed under protection of the English and French, and fortified . . . . Jan. 1862
Rebels defeated in two engagements . April, ,,
English and French assist the government against the rebels—Ning-po retaken . . 10 May, ,,
French admiral Protet killed in an attack on rebels, 17 May, ,,
Captain Sherard Osborne permitted by the British government to organise a small fleet of gunboats to aid the imperialists to establish order July, ,,
Imperialists gain ground, take Kah-sing, &c. Oct. ,,
Tungani (Mahometan) revolt in Central Asia; massacre of Buddhists . . . . . . ,,
Commercial treaty with Prussia ratified 14 Jan. 1863
The Imperialists under col. Charles Gordon defeat the Taepings under Burgevine, &c. . Oct. ,,
Gordon captures Sowchow (after a severe attack, 27, 28, Nov.); the rebel chiefs treacherously butchered by the Chinese . . . 4, 5 Dec. ,,
Capt. Osborne came to China; but retired in consequence of the Chinese government departing from its engagements . . . . . 31 Dec. ,,
Gordon's successes continue . Jan. to April, 1864
Repulsed; he takes Chang-chow-foo 23 March, ,,
He takes Nankin (a heap of ruins); Hun-seu-tseun, the Tien-wang, the rebel emperor, commits suicide by eating gold leaf, 30 June; Chang-wang and Kan-wang, the rebel generals, are "cut into a thousand pieces" . . . . . 18 July, ,,
Great mortality among British troops at Kowloon, Jan. 1865
The Taepings hold Ming-chow; the Mahometan rebellion (Douganese) progressing in Honan, Jan.–March, ,,
Taepings evacuate Ming-chow . . . 23 May, ,,
Rebellion in the north advancing . . . June, ,,
A rebellion of the Nien-fei in the north; Pekin in danger . . . . July, ,,
The Chinese general San-ko-lin-sin defeated and slain; his son more successful . . July, ,,
Prince Kung chief of the regency again . 7 Nov. ,,
Sir Rutherford Alcock, ambassador at Pekin, 26 Nov. ,,
Chinese newspaper "Messenger of the Flying Dragon," appears in London . . 14 Jan. 1866
Great victory over the Nien-fei announced at Canton 13 March, ,,
Chinese commissioners visit London . June, ,,
Rivalry of two great political chiefs in China, Li-Hung Chang and Tsen-kwo-fan . . July, ,,
Reported victory over the Nien-fei over the imperialists . . . . Dec. 1867
Mahomed Yakoob Beg defeats the Tungani, becomes supreme in Kashgar, 1866; is recognised by Europe . . . . ,,
The rebels seize Ningpo . . . . . Oct. 1868
The people at Yang-chow, incited by the "literati" (learned classes) destroy the Protestant mission-houses, 22 Aug.; redress not obtained; a British squadron proceeds to Nankin, 8 Nov.; the viceroy Li-Hung-Chang is superseded, and the British demands acceded to . . . 14 Nov. ,,
Chinese embassy (Mr. Anson Burlinghame, Chin Kang, and Sun Chia Su) received by president Johnson at Washington, 5 June; they sign a treaty (see *Burlinghame*); 4 July; arrive in London, Sept.; received by the queen . 20 Nov. ,,
Chinese embassy received by the emperor at Paris 24 Jan. 1869

* He died peacefully at Calcutta, 9 April, 1859. He is said to have ordered the beheading of about 100,000 rebels.

Pekin visited by the duke of Edinburgh, incognito, Oct. 1869
Supplementary convention to the treaty of Tien-tsin (June, 1858) for additional commercial freedom, signed . . . . 24 Oct. „
Burlinghame dies at St. Petersburg . 22 Feb. 1870
Successful rebellion of Mahometans in north-west provinces reported . . . . . . May, „
Cruel massacre of the French consul at Tien-tsin, Roman catholic priests, sisters of Mercy (22 persons), besides many native converts, and above 30 children in the orphanage, by a mob, with, it is said, the complicity of the authorities: the missionaries were accused of kidnapping children, 21 June, „
Increased hatred of the people to foreigners at Tien-tsin; lukewarm proceedings of the government against the murderers . . . . July, „
Ma, a viceroy of Nankin, favourable to Europeans, assassinated . . . . about 22 Aug. „
Chapels destroyed at Fatshan . . 21 Sept. „
The French ultimatum refused; the murderers of the nuns unpunished; Chinese warlike preparations reported . . . . 26 Sept. „
Judicious mandate from the mandarin Tseng-kwo-fan, exculpating the missionaries, and condemning their massacre . . . . . . Oct. „
16 coolies beheaded, 15 Sept., and 23 exiled; indemnity to the sufferers by the outrage ordered; reported . . . . . . 26 Oct. „
End of the difficulty announced . . . 3 Nov. „
Chung-how, an envoy, arrives in London . Aug. 1871
Memorial addressed to the Chinese government by Mr. Hart, inspector of customs, recommending changes in civil and military administration, autumn,
The young emperor married . . . . 16 Oct. „
Received at Paris; apologizes for Tien-tsin massacres, and reports redress . . . . 23 Nov. „
Russia annexes Kuldja . . . . . „
Wm. Armstrong Russell consecrated Anglican bishop of North China . . . . . Dec. „
The emperor's majority; he assumes the government . . . . 23 Feb. 1873
Talifoo, capital of the insurgent Panthay Mahometans, captured; thousands massacred . Feb. „
Foreign ministers for the first time received by the emperor . . . . 29 June, „
Dispute with Japan, see *Formosa*, July–Aug.; settled by treaty . . . . . . 31 Oct. 1874
The *Spark* sails from Canton to Macao; capt. Brady and Mr. Mundy, and a foreign crew and passengers; pirates, who came on board secretly, kill captain and others, and carry off booty, while on voyage; the wounded crew manage to reach Macao . . . . 22 Aug. „
Death of the emperor . . . . . . 12 Jan. 1875
Proclamation of his successor, Tsai-tien, son of Chun, 7th son of Taou-Twang (nephew of Kung), 4 Feb. „
Exploring expedition under col. Horace Browne to open a passage from Burmah into S. W. China, Dec. 1874; Mr. Margary and 5 Chinese going before, killed at Manwyne, 21 Feb.; col. Browne and his troops repulse an attack by Chinese, but retreat to Rangoon, 22 Feb.; some of the party missing . . . . 12 March, „
Through negotiations of Mr. Wade, the Chinese government promise due reparation; announced Sept. „
Edict permitting intercourse between chiefs of departments and foreign ministers, about 4 Oct.; enjoining proper treatment of foreigners, 11 Oct. „
Telegram from Mr. Wade; he has obtained necessary guarantees, satisfaction for the murder of Mr. Margary, and concessions for foreign trade 18 Oct. „
Gen. Lee-see-ta-hee ordered for trial, 11 Feb.; Margary's murderers said to be executed, 5 May, 1876
First railway in China, from Shang-hae to Oussoon (Woosung), (11 miles); trial trip, 16 March (at first opposed); publicly opened . 30 June, „
Mr. Grosvenor and others, sent to inquire respecting the murder of Mr. Margary, arrive at the place and report the proposed punishment of the murderers . . . . June, „
Chee-foo convention between sir Thos. Wade and Li-Hung-Chang; difficulties in the negotiations removed (the government agree to compensation to Mr. Margary's family; removal of commercial grievances; opening of four ports; proper official intercourse); said to be signed, 13 Sept.; ratified . . . . 17 Sept. 1876
War against the Tungani; Manas captured; great massacre of rebels . . . . . 6 Nov. „
Accredited Chinese envoy (Quo-ta-Zhan) lands at Southampton . . . . . . 21 Jan. 1877
Decree of equal rights to Chinese Christians, 1 Feb. „
Dreadful famine in northern provinces . . . „
Four more Chinese ports opened . . . 1 April, „
Opium smoking interdicted after 3 years; announced . . . . Aug. „
The railway from Shang-hae bought to be stopped, 31 Oct.; resumed . . . . . . Dec. „
Quo-ta-Zhan (or Kuo-ta-Jên) first accredited minister at London; Liu-ta-Jên at Berlin about Nov. „
Yakoob Beg of Kashgaria totally defeated by the Chinese general, Tso-tsung-tang; is assassinated, May; Kashgar and other towns captured; end of war . . . . Dec. „
The Chinese minister's first grand evening reception 19 June, 1878
Destruction of mission property at Wu-shih-shan by a fanatical mob, unrestrained by the mandarins 30 Aug. „
Famine abating; 48,303*l.* for relief collected in England . . . . Sept. „
The Shang-hae railway plant removed to Formosa . . . . „
Chinese immigrants virtually excluded from Australia by a poll-tax . . . . . . „
Rebellion in Kwang-si, announced . . . Oct. „
Chung-How, ambassador at St. Petersburg, demands the surrender of Kuli Beg, a fugitive from Kashgar, and restitution of the territory . . Dec. „
Rebellion in Hainan, in Canton province; Li-Yang-tsai, who invades Annam, claims the throne by descent; reported . . . . Jan. 1879
Marquis Tsêng, the new Chinese ambassador, arrives in London, 28 Feb.; presents his credentials to the queen . . . . 20 March, „
Treaty with Russia, who agrees to evacuate the Kuldja territory, China to pay an indemnity about June, „
Li-Yang-tsai, rebel chief, captured; announced 2 Dec. „
Chung-How, the late Chinese ambassador at St. Petersburg, imprisoned and the treaty disavowed spring, 1880
Chinese from Kashgar said to invade Russian territory . . . . May, „
Prospect of war; col. Gordon goes to China from Bombay . . . . June, „
Li-Hung-Chang, governor of metropolitan provinces, fortifies approaches to the capital, June; visited by col. Gordon . . . . . July, „
Chung-How released; proposed war with Russia given up; announced . . . . 15 July, „
Thomas duke of Genoa sails up the Yang-tse-Kiang in an Italian vessel . . . . . April, „
Peace with Russia, who makes concessions negotiated by marquis Tsêng; treaty signed 19 Aug. 1881
Complication with France respecting Tonquin (see *Tonquin*) . . . . Sept. 1883
Mr. Logan sentenced to seven years' penal servitude for killing a coolie at Canton . . Sept. „
Canton greatly excited against foreigners . Oct. „
Correspondence of France and China respecting Tonquin published in the *Times*, both firm 29 Oct. „
Warm reception of sir Henry Parkes as British ambassador . . . . Sept. „
China issues a circular claiming Annam as a dependency . . . . Nov. „
Coup d'état at Pekin effected by prince Chun, father of the reigning emperor, who becomes dictator; prince Kung, and the viceroy Li-Hung-Chang, deposed . . . . 11 April, *et seq.* 1884
The marquis Tsêng recalled from Paris, announced 2 May, „
Replaced by Li-Fong-Pao . . . about 8 May, „
Treaty with France, signed by capt. Fournier and Li-Hung-Chang, at Tientsin; French protectorate of Annam and Tonquin recognized; three southern provinces opened to commerce . . . 11 May, „
The Chinese break the treaty by attacking the French marching to occupy Langson (see *Tonquin*) „

The French demand evacuation of the Tonquin frontier forts, and 10,000,000*l.* indemnity . July, 1884

The war party at Pekin oppose the empress and Li-Hung-Chang the viceroy . . . July, ,,

The frontier towns to be surrendered, the indemnity refused, announced . . . . 30 July, ,,

China offers reduced indemnity . . . Aug. ,,

Kelung in Formosa bombarded and forts destroyed by alleged treachery by adm. Lespès 5, 6 Aug. ,,

Adm. Courbet at Foochow . . . . 10 Aug. ,,

Negotiations at Shanghai . . . . Aug. ,,

France declines mediation of the powers; France issues a circular to the powers 17 Aug. ,,

Indemnity claimed by France, reduced to 3,200,000*l.* 19 Aug.; refused by China . . . . ,,

The French ambassador, Semallé, leaves Pekin; war ensues . . . . . 21 Aug. ,,

Adm. Courbet with his fleet sails up the Min river unattacked; destroys the Chinese fleet with much slaughter, 23 Aug.; bombards the arsenal at Foochow, and dismantles the forts; destroys the forts and batteries, &c., at Mingan and Kinpai; French killed, about 7; Chinese said to be about 1000 . . . . . . 26-28 Aug. ,,

Li-Hung-Chang deprived of his highest offices about 28 Aug. ,,

Chinese declaration of war, in a manifesto to the people, announced . . . . 6 Sept. ,,

H.M. gun-boat *Zephyr* fired on by mistake, 6 Sept.; Chinese apologise . . . 18 Sept. ,,

Chinese said to be defeated at Kinpai Pass, about 16 Sept. ,,

Europeans, at Shanghai and other places, protest against the war . . . . . Sept. ,,

Li-Hung-Chang reappointed viceroy about 24 Sept. ,,

Adm. Courbet captures Kelung 1 Oct.; adm. Lespès bombards Tamsui, 2 *et seq.* Oct.; lands; retires 8 Oct. ,,

N. and W. Formosa blockaded . . . 23 Oct. ,,

Kelung occupied by French; little resistance 8 Oct. ,,

1000 Chinese defeated near Tamsui, 2 Nov.; repulsed in attack on Kelung, announced 12 Nov. ,,

Fruitless mediation of earl Granville with marquis Tsêng, announced . . . . 10 Dec. ,,

Reported Chinese defeat near Kelung . . 13 Dec. ,,

The native press, originally official (*Pekin Gazette*, ancient), becomes political and popular . ,,

Foreign Enlistment Act proclaimed at Hong Kong 23 Jan. 1885

French attack near Kelung, Chinese works carried 25 Jan. ,,

Chinese defeated with much loss . 31 Jan. ,,

Two Chinese junks sunk by French torpedoes, 15 Feb. ,,

Bombardment of Chin-hae, at the mouth of the Yung-Kiang river . . . . 2 March, ,,

Siege of Tuyen Quan, much slaughter 2-3 March, ,,

Several forts at Kelung captured, Sanguinary conflicts . . . . 4-12 March, ,,

Sir Harry Parkes, ambassador, dies . 22 March, ,,

Pescadores Islands captured . . 30-31 March, ,,

Preliminaries of peace, through intervention of sir Robt. Hart, signed at Pekin about 6 April; treaty signed 9 June; ratified . . . . 28 Nov. ,,

Sir Robert Hart, British ambassador, 23 June; resigns about . . . . . . 31 Aug. ,,

Formosa evacuated about . . . 23 June, ,,

Introduction of railways authorized—new policy about Aug. ,,

Disputes with Japan settled; reported . Aug. ,,

The emperor agrees to receive a papal agent to protect R. C. missionaries . . . July, ,,

Death of Tso Tsung-Tang, a great statesman and guardian of the king . . . 4 Sept. ,,

Sir John Walsham British minister . 7 April, 1886

Liu-shin-fun, ambassador for Great Britain, arrives 28 April, ,,

M. Agliardi appointed Internuncio . 14 July, ,,

The scheme suspended by the Pope through French opposition . . . . . about 15 Sept. ,,

Convention with many concessions by the British government respecting the Burmese frontiers and trade signed at Pekin . . . 24 July, ,,

The French consent to the transfer of the Pehtang Cathedral from its contiguity with the palace Nov. ,,

The Chinese annul the French protectorate over all christians . . . . . . Nov. ,,

Decanville railway successfully opened 21 Nov. 1886

General proclamations for protection of christian missionaries and converts, excluding foreign protection . . . . Jan. 1887

Remarkable presents from the emperor to sir Halliday Macartney, secretary of the British and other legations (for good services to China) received in London . . . . Feb. ,,

The emperor, aged 16, assumes the government 7 Feb. ,,

Convention between Great Britain and China, respecting Burmah and Thibet, signed 24 July, and ratified . . . . . . 25 Aug. ,,

Chinese fleet of five ironclads (three constructed in Britain) at Spithead; sail for China under admiral Lang with others lent by the Admiralty Sept. ,,

Commercial treaty with France, 1886; signed and ratified . . . . Aug. ,,

Reported convention of Li-Hung-Chang, the viceroy, with count Mitkiewicz and an American syndicate for introduction of railways, telegraphs, telephones, &c., and a loan, Aug.; repudiated by the Chinese government . . . . Oct. ,,

Overflow of the Hoang Ho, or Yellow River, causing immense destruction; about 1,500 populous villages destroyed, and the important city Chuhsien Chen narrowly escaped with loss of suburbs; millions of persons said to have perished; famine imminent; the government active in providing relief . . . . . Sept.–Oct. ,,

Treaty with United States to allow Chinese immigration for 20 years with some exceptions (lawful marriage and children, property worth 1,000 dollars, &c.) signed 14 March, 1888; China refuses the ratification . . . . Sept. 1888

The empress-mother announces her resignation of the administration of government, which is to be assumed by the emperor . . 27 July, ,,

The Chinese Exclusion Act vigorously carried out at San Francisco, and at other places middle Oct. ,,

Railway from Tientsin to Taku opened . Nov. ,,

Conventions with Italy and Germany for them to protect their missionaries . . announced Dec. ,,

New R. C. cathedral at Pekin consecrated 8 Dec. ,,

Great famine in consequence of inundations of the Yangtsze and Yellow River valleys announced Jan. 1889; relief money sent from London, above 30,000*l.* (gratefully acknowledged) (see *Mansion House Fund*) 1889

Riots at Chin-Kiang, the British consulate and foreigners' houses burnt . . . . 4, 5 Feb. ,,

Marriage of the Emperor . . . . 25 Feb. ,,

Hsieh Ta Jên appointed minister for London, Paris, Brussels, and Rome, announced . 4 June, ,,

Luchow, in the province of Szechuen, destroyed by fire, about 1,200 persons perish . 27 June, ,,

The Yellow River bursts its banks at Shantung, and inundates the country, and countless lives are lost, reported . . . . . 26 July, ,,

Great inundations in North China through typhoons; about 5,000 persons perish, reported 30 Aug. ,,

The Yellow River again burst its banks, causing much destruction about . . . 22 July, ,,

Insurrection in the province of Fuhkien; suppressed; 100 insurgents killed; announced 9 Sept. ,,

The construction of a trunk railway from Pekin to Hankow, 700 miles, proposed . . . Aug. ,,

The project postponed through opposition Dec. ,,

Insurrection in the Amour district of Manchuria; reported success of the rebels; they seize the town Lan-pei-tuan; imperialists defeated in battles; announced . . . . . Dec. ,,

Collapse of a temple theatre at Hangting, near Shantung; about 250 persons killed 13 Oct. ,,

Imperial decree for reforms in the army and civil services; promoted by the emperor . Jan.–Feb. 1890

Convention for the opening of the Chung-King to commerce signed at Pekin . . 31 March, ,,

Death of the marquis Tsêng, eminent statesman 12 April, ,,

The duke and duchess of Connaught honourably received in Canton and Shanghai . . May, ,,

Great floods at Pekin, Tungchow and Tientsin; business stopped, 3 Aug.; renewal of the Yellow River inundations early Sept.; also in the provinces Shantung and Chihli; great loss of life and prospect of famine reported . . 16 Oct. 1890

Explosion of the government powder magazine at Canton, killing many persons and destroying 200 houses, 15 Aug.; a similar explosion at Taiping-Fu, 300 persons killed, reported . 7 Nov. ,,

Massacre of many native Christians at Jongtuytsin and other places by a fanatical society reported . . . . Dec. ,,

An imperial decree, granting audience of the emperor to representatives of foreign powers issued . . . . 12 Dec. ,,

The first audience . . . . . 5 March, 1891

Death of prince Chung, father of the emperor, reported . . . . 2 Jan. ,,

Disastrous floods in Shue-Shang, Wen-Chuan, and other districts, about 1,000 lives lost, early Feb. ,,

Anti-European riots at Wuhu; much destruction; British consulate wrecked; the consul and his wife escape; quiet restored by force, 12, 13 May, ,,

Increased popular anti-foreign agitation throughout China, June; the diplomatic body appeal to the government; the emperor issues a decree for the protection of foreigners and punishment of aggressors about . . . . . . 15 June, ,,

French church and orphanage at Woosieh destroyed by fire . . . . 9 June, ,,

Loss of life and much destruction by the rising of the Yang-tse-Kiang about . . . . 21 July, ,,

Continued persecution of foreigners; the imperial decree ineffectual; the diplomatic body press the government about . . . . . . 18 Aug. ,,

The Kolao Hui, a secret society, strongly opposed to foreigners and Christianity, active, summer, ,,

The American mission at Ishang destroyed, 11 Sept. ,,

The outrages against foreigners increase; the diplomatic body report to their respective governments about . . . . 15 Sept. ,,

Great Britain, France, Germany and the United States, N.A., unite for the common support of their people against Chinese violence, reported 21 Sept. ,,

Compensation paid to the sufferers in Wuhu by the viceroy about . . . . 23 Oct. ,,

British squadron and other vessels at Nagasaki and other ports about . . . . . 23 Oct. ,,

A *modus vivendi* with the Chinese authorities arranged by the European ministers, reported 11 Nov. ,,

Insurrection in Mongolia and N. China against foreigners and native Christians; reported massacres, Nov.; suppressed by government troops after battles, with much slaughter 28, 29 Nov. ,,

Agreement of the Hunan societies against Europeans, &c., published at Shanghai about 7 Dec. ,,

Memorials of the viceroys of Nanking and Hukuang (attributing the anti-foreign outrages to baseless rumours circulated by conspirators) issued Dec. ,,

The government pays indemnities amounting to 100,000*l.* to Christian missions and others, and punishes Chinese officials and offenders . Dec. ,,

Mr. Christopher Gardner, British consul, and Dr. Griffith John, missionary, assert that the anti-foreign outbreaks originated with the local mandarins, aided by Chanhan (or Chou Han), an eminent Hunan scholar and writer of offensive placards, &c., reported . . . . . Dec ,,

The rebels in the north, headed by Li Hung, defeated by Yulu, reported . . . . 3 Jan. 1892

Mr. Nicholas R. O'Conor appointed British minister at Pekin about . . . . . . 4 March, ,,

Chanhan, the agitator, ordered to be arrested, 25 March; not arrested; the right of audience by the emperor requested by the foreign ministers, rejected, early . . . . April, ,,

Bill for the stringent exclusion of Chinese immigrants from the United States, N. A., passed by congress . . . . early May, ,,

Renewed outrages on European missionaries 27 April, reported . . . . . 14 June, ,,

Great fire at Tchang; about 50 junks destroyed and 200 lives lost . . . . 4 Sept. ,,

Great inundation by the Yellow River; 12 towns said to be destroyed; reported . . 23 Sept. ,,

Mr. O'Conor, British minister, warmly received informally by the emperor . . . 13 Dec. ,,

The ancestors of sir Halliday Macartney raised to mandarins, reported . . . . . Dec. ,,

Famine in N. Shen-si reported . . 8 March, 1893

The Chinese exclusion (immigration) act in the United States comes into effect; (107,475 in the States) . . . . 5 May, ,,

Kung Chao-quan appointed minister at St. James's, reported . . . . 29 June, ,,

Chinese exclusion amended bill passed by the U.S. senate . . . . 2 Nov. ,,

Insurrection in Manchuria reported . 31 May, 1894

Gen. Ting sent to suppress the rising, and to redress grievances, reported 4 June; rebellion subsides . . . . 14 June, ,,

War with Japan, see *Corea* . . . . . July, ,,

Murderous outrages on missionaries; murder of the rev. James Wylie, presbyterian, by soldiers at Liao-Yang; the murderers beheaded and officers degraded, reported . . . . 15 Sept. ,,

Treaty between China and United States ratified Aug. ,,

Great fire in Chung King; many deaths 25 Aug. ,,

Disorganization of the government and its resources reported . . . . Aug. ,,

Prince Kung returns to power, announced Oct. ,,

Imperial edict for the protection of foreigners and missionaries . . . . 15 Oct. ,,

Li Hung Chang (minister) superseded by prince Kung with enlarged powers . . . 4 Nov. ,,

Rebellion at Wu-hu; admiral Fremantle proceeds there, reported . . . . 10 Dec. ,,

Prince Kung appointed president of the grand council, virtually dictator; Li Hung Chang returns to power . . . . 13 Dec. ,,

Risings in S.W. Kwang-tung, government troops repulsed, reported . . . . . 22 March, 1895

Treaty of peace with Japan, concluded; see *Corea*, 17 April; ratifications exchanged . 8 May, ,,

Foreign mission houses at Chengtu and Szechuan destroyed by rioters; missionaries safe 29, 31 May, ,,

Loan of 16,000,000*l.* sterling from France and Russia, reported . . . . June, ,,

Treaty with France respecting boundaries, commerce, etc., signed at Pekin . . . 25 June, ,,

Loan of 400,000,000*f.* 4 per cent. guaranteed by Russia, signed at Pekin, 4 July, at St. Petersburg, 6 July, ,,

Massacre of British missionaries (the rev. R. W. Stewart, 8 ladies and 2 children) at Whasang, near Ku-cheng by a fanatical sect called Vegetarians . . . . 1 Aug. ,,

British and American missions attacked, hospitals destroyed at Fatshan . . . . . 7 Aug. ,,

The British government demands immediate redress 17 Aug. ,,

Japan demands an indemnity for giving up the Liao-tong peninsula; evacuations to begin on first payment, Aug.; supplementary treaty signed . . . . 8 Nov. ,,

The Chinese government acting with the foreign consuls; arrests and punishes criminals; reported . . . . Aug. ,,

Additional outrages reported in Aug.; 10 members of the Vegetarian society and others convicted about 28 Aug.; 7 criminals executed at Kucheng . . . . 17 Sept. ,,

Insurrection of the Dungans, Chinese troops defeated near Su-chau, gen. Soui beheaded; reported . . . . 22 Sept. ,,

British ultimatum demanding the degradation of the viceroy of Szu-chuan and others, 28 Sept.; accepted by China . . . . . . 30 Sept. ,,

China agrees to pay compensation to Germany for the plundering of a mission station at Swatau; an agreement concluded at Shanghai for a crown concession to Germany at Han-kau, 6 Oct.; and at Tien-tsin; reported, 30 Oct. . . . . . ,,

The viceroy of Fo-kien agrees to the trial and punishment of those convicted in the Ku-cheng massacres, owing to the arrival of the British admiral; reported . . . . . . 15 Oct. ,,

An explosion on the transport *Kung Pai*, near Kinchau, 500 soldiers killed . . . 14 Oct. ,,

Lan-chau-fu, capital of Kansu, captured by Mahomedans; reported . . . . . . 31 Oct. ,,

Li-Hung-Chang charged with orders to suppress the insurrection; mutiny of troops at Kiu-kiang Khiang . . . . Nov. ,,

Sir C. M. Macdonald appointed British envoy and minister at Pekin, Jan.; arrives . 22 April, 1896

Anglo-German loan for 16,000,000*l.* at 5 per cent. signed at Pekin . . . . . 24 March 1896
Sir Robert Hart appointed superintendent of posts and telegraphs; reported . . . 30 March „
China enters the postal union . . . . 2 April „
M. Gérard, French mini ter, recalled . 2 April „
Mahomedan rebellion: a town in Kansu captured by the Dungans; reported . . . 25 May „
Li-Hung-Chang, grand secretary, received by the Czar at St. Petersburg, 4 May; travels in Germany—Berlin (honoured), Essen, etc., visits prince Bismarck, 25 June; at the Hague, 4 July; Brussels, 8 July; Paris, 13 July; London and other cities, 1–21 Aug; received by the marquis of Salisbury, 4 Aug.; received and decorated by the queen at Osborne, 5 Aug.; arrives at New York, 28 Aug., received by pres. Cleveland, 29 Aug.; Canada: Toronto, 7 Sept.; leaves Victoria, full of gratitude, 16 Sept.; Yokohama, 27 Sept.; Pekin 20 Oct.; appointed minister for foreign affairs . . . . 26 Oct. „
Second payment of war indemnity to Japan at the bank of England (4,400,506*l.*) . . . . 8 May „
Tidal wave at Hai-chau, 4,000 lives lost 26 July, „
Reparation granted for the injuries done to French missionaries, at Kwei-chau, since 1886 Sept. „
Sun Wen or Sun Yat Sen, medical student, detained at the Chinese legation, London, on suspicion of being a conspirator, 11 Oct.; released by the intervention of lord Salisbury . . . 23 Oct. „
Ministers appointed in London, Washington, Berlin, and St. Petersburg; announced . . 24 Nov. „
Chinese Eastern, or Russian Manchurian railway; see *Russia*; Dec. 1896.
Baron von Wahlborn appointed first Austro-Hungarian minister at Pekin; announced; 10 Jan. 1897
Sheng Ta-jên, director of railways; contract for the construction of the Han-Kau railway signed with a Belgian syndicate . . . 30 May, „
Chang Yin-huan, special envoy, arrives in England, 26 May, „
Prince Oukhtomsky's mission to Pekin; well received . . . . May, „
New Russian bank opened at Pekin . 27 May, „
The West river opened to foreign trade . 4 June, „
Reparation demanded by Germany for the recent murder of 2 German missionaries; troops landed at Kiao-chau bay: the Chinese retired, 14 Nov.; indemnity, 200,000 taels (about 35,000*l.*), etc., refused; 29 Nov.: [Kiao-chau, ceded to Germany, with adjacent territory, 99 yrs. lease; 5 Jan.: ratified; 24 Jan. 1898.]
Russian fleet, arrives at Kinchau, near Port Arthur, with China's approval . . . . . 18 Dec. „
Li Hung Chang recalled to power . 3 Jan. 1898
Negotiations with Gt. Britain and Russia, respecting loans, fail . . . . Jan., Feb. „
Trains blown up with dynamite, by the insurgents, near Nuevitas; 3 deaths; reported . 25 Jan. „
Japan claims payment of the indemnity, 9 Feb. (11,008,857*l.* paid by the bank of England on behalf of China, 7 May).
Inland waters to be opened to British and other steamers, with regulations, in June . 20 Feb. „
Père Favier (30 years resident) consecrated as bishop at Pekin . . . . . 20 Feb. „
Chinese loan of 16,000,000*l.* at 4½ per cent., between Hong-kong and other banks; ratified . 3 March, „
German-Chinese agreement relating to privileges in Shan-tung, signed . . . . . 6 March, „
Four ports opened to trade, April; see *Russia*, *England*, and *France*, 1898.
The Yangtsze trade regulations, drawn up by sir Robert Hart, agreed to . . . . 13 May, „
Death of prince Kung, aged 68 . . 29 May, „
Wei-hai-wei, occupied by the British, 30 May; convention signed . . . . . 1 July „
Successful steam navigation of the Yangtsze rapids (750 miles) by Mr. Little. . . May, „
Prince Henry and the German squadron visits Kiao-chau, 5 May; received by the emperor and empress at Pekin . . . . 15–18 May, „
Serious riots at Sha-shi, Japanese consulate and other offices, &c., destroyed, 9 May; indemnity, &c., paid . . . . . . 12 July, „
Indemnity and concessions granted to France for the murder of père Berthollet . . 7 June, „
Convention signed at Pekin leasing extension of boundaries to Hong-kong . . . . 9 June, 1898
Rebellion in Kwang-tung; a magistrate and his wife killed; reported . . . 10 June, „
Concession for Grand-central railway from Hankau to Pekin secured by Franco-Belgian syndicate; reported . . . . 15 June, „
Contract signed at Pekin, authorizing the Anglo-Italian syndicate to work coal and iron mines in Honan, &c., for 60 years . . 21 June, „
Typhoon at Port Arthur, 130 Chinese sailors drowned; reported . . . . 23 June, „
Riots in Shanghai concerning the sale by the French local authorities of the Ning-po guild cemetery, French marines and police fire on the mob, 14 natives killed, 16 July; provisional agreement, quiet restored, . . . 18 July, „
Contract for Russian loan for the Pekin Hankau railway ratified . . . . 12 Aug. „
Black Flag rising in Kwang-si; British consul at Wu-chau telegraphs for gunboats, 28 June; a magistrate and many officials killed; nine towns captured, and troops defeated near Wu-chau, reported 12 July; further conflicts reported, 19 Aug. „
Li Hung Chang dismissed from the Tsung-li-Yamên by decree . . . . 7 Sept. „
Reforms progressing; reported . . . Sept. „
American and French missions attacked at Ho-chau, 50 miles from Chung-king; reported, Sept. 1898 [indemnity paid to the United States, Jan. 1899].
Coup d'état, regency of the empress restored, reactionary policy, flight of Kang-Yu-Wei, reformer (saved by British consuls, and conveyed to Hong-kong) . . . . 22 Sept. „
The marquis Ito visits Pekin, received by the emperor . . . . 20 Sept. „
Six members of the reform party executed 28 Sept. „
Great fire at Han-kau, 1000 deaths reported, 1 Oct. „
Violent insults to Europeans, 1 Oct.; foreign escorts arrive at Pekin . . . . 7 Oct. „
Reformers in office dismissed . . . 10 Oct. „
Lord Charles Beresford, on a commercial mission, arrives at Pekin, 16 Oct.; well received at Chinese ports; returns to Hong-kong, advocates the "open door" (*which see*), 3 Jan. 1899.
French missionary and converts massacred at Pak-lung; indemnity demanded by France . 20 Oct. „
Military outrages on Englishmen near Pekin, railway work stopped, 23, 24 Oct.; Chinese troops removed . . . . . . 15–27 Nov. „
Yellow river floods in Shan-tung, villages destroyed, early Nov.; Li Hung Chang sent to concert preventive measures, 30 Nov. [his report issued, end of March, 1899].
Chinese force (1000) enrolled under British officers at Wei-hai-wei . . . . . mid-Nov. „
M. de Giers, new Russian minister, arrives, 24 Nov.
Mr. W. S. Fleming, British missionary, murdered at Pang-hai, 4 Nov. (2 murderers executed and 3 officials degraded, Jan. 1899; further reparation demanded, June, July).
Anti-Christian riot in Hu-pei, French priest killed Dec. „
Great distress reported . . . . . Dec. „
Rebels defeated at Sah-chiao-tsang . . 27 Dec. „
Edict initiating administrative reforms issued 30 Dec. „
Tseng-ho, governor of Hu-pei, in favour of reforms, degraded . . . . Jan. 1899
Insurrection in An-hui. . . . . . Jan. „
Hu Yu Fen, director of northern railways, dismissed, Jan.; sir Claude Macdonald insists on an investigation, 31 Jan.; Hu Yu Fen is acquitted, 7 Mar. „
Russian troops (1300) at Port Arthur and neighbourhood, Feb.; fight between Russians and Chinese at Ta-lien-wan, many Chinese killed, reported . . . . 19 Feb. „
2800 miles of railway granted to British investors Feb. „
Sig. Martino, Italian minister, demands a naval station at Sammun bay, &c., 28 Feb.; refused, 3 March; ultimatum presented to China,

rejected, 11, 12 March; sig. Martino recalled, and his action disavowed by his government, 14 Mar. 1899

Yu Hsien, founder of the anti-foreign and anti-Christian sect, the "Boxers," made governor of Shantung . . . . Mar. ,,

Boundary of territory leased by Russia near Port Arthur settled, mid. March; anti-foreign dis-disturbances by the Boxers' (Red Fist) and the Big Knife societies, in Shantung, March; German punitive expedition, villages burnt, Yi-chau occupied . . . . April, ,,

Anglo-Russian agreement with regard to railway extension in Manchuria and the Yang-tsze-kiang, &c., signed at St. Petersburg . . 28 April, ,,

Extension of the cosmopolitan settlement at Shanghai, agreed to, 20 June (ratified Dec.)

Anglo-German Tien-tsin–Chin-kiang railway loan, 7,400,000*l.* (5 per cent.), ratified at Pekin, 18 May, ,,

French consulate and other houses at Mong-tsze destroyed in a riot . . . . . . 22 June ,,

Marqu. Salvago-Raggi, new Italian minister, arrives 24 June ,,

German railway works raided (18 June) near Kiao-chau, troops sent, 17 Chinese killed. 23–26 June ,,

Two Russian engineers and 10 Cossacks killed by brigands in Niu-chwang . . . . June ,,

Burmo-Chinese boundary completed . . July, ,,

Imperial edict against the malpractices of revenue officials issued . . . . . . 12 July, ,,

Ta-lien-wan declared a free port . . 13 Aug. ,,

Fight between Chinese troops and brigands at Cokton on the West River, many killed mid-Aug. ,,

Russian province of Kwang-tung placed under a gov.-gen. . . . . early Sept. ,,

Yano Fumio, Japanese minister at Pekin, recalled mid-Oct. ,,

Two French naval officers massacred near Mon-tao; villages seized by adm. Courregolles; the Chinese repulsed with loss . . 15–18 Nov. ,,

Indemnity demanded by M. Pichon, Nov. [paid 16 Jan. 1900.]

Li Hung Chang appointed minister of commerce, Nov., and viceroy of Canton . . . Dec. ,,

Rev. Mr. Brooks massacred by rioters in Shan-tung, officials degraded and 2 of the murderers beheaded, by edict issued 5 Jan. 1900; another edict evasive as to the suppression of the "Boxers" and other anti-Christian societies, issued . . . . 11 Jan. 1900

Coup d'état by the empress-dowager, edict issued, naming Po Ching (14), son of prince Tuan, the heir-designate. . . . . 24 Jan. ,,

Foreign ministers demand the suppression of the Boxers and other hostile secret societies 27 Jan. ,,

Negotiations, edicts issued without effect Feb.–Mar. ,,

Boundary convention of Kwang-chau-wan, 99 years' lease to France, ratified, reported . . 4 Mar. ,,

Extension of the French settlement in Shanghai mid-March ,,

The "open door" in China for the world's commerce successfully promoted by Mr. Hay, U.S.A. sec. of state . . . . March, ,,

Treacherous attacks on the Wei-hai-wei boundary commission repulsed by Chinese under col. Bower and capt. Watson . . . . . . 5, 6 May ,,

Massacre of native Christians by Boxers between Pao-ting-fu and Pekin . . . . mid-May ,,

Troops sent to the disturbed areas; 6 leaders arrested in Pekin . . . . . 21 May, ,,

Insurrection spreads; railway property, &c., destroyed; Chinese employés killed . 27 May, ,,

Feng-tai railway station burnt by the Boxers; refugees arrive at Pekin . . . . 28 May ,,

Evasive edict, practically encouraging the Boxers, issued . . . . 29 May ,,

Emphatic protests *re* the Boxer movement from the legations to the Yamên . . 20–30 May, ,,

Foreign marine guards (340; 75 British), arrive at the Pekin legation . . . . 31 May, ,,

Pao-ting-fu refugees attacked by Boxers, 4 killed and many missing . . . . . 31 May, ,,

Mr. Norman and Mr. Robinson, missionaries, and 5 converts murdered at Yung-ching . 2 June, ,,

Huang-tsun station burnt, employés killed by the Boxers . . . . 4 June, ,,

German and Austrian guards arrive in Pekin, 3–5 June, 1900

Foreign reinforcements land at Tien-tsin, 5 June, ,,

Railway communication stopped at Pekin, anti-foreign movement still spreading, another evasive edict issued . . . . 6 June, ,,

Massacres and destruction of railway and mission stations spreading from Pekin district to other provinces . . . . 7, 8 June, ,,

Imperial edict decreeing a massacre of foreigners, issued 9 June (changed into a protective edict by 3 members of the Tsung-li-Yamên, who were afterwards cruelly executed, 14 Aug.).

The Tsung-li-Yamên reorganised under prince Tuan and 3 Manchus . . . . . . 10 June, ,,

Adm. sir Edw. Seymour's force defeats the Boxers at Lang-fang . . . . . . 11 June, ,,

M. Sugiyama, Japanese chancellor, murdered by Chinese troops in Pekin . . . . 11 June, ,,

Massacre of native converts and foreign employés in Pekin, buildings burnt . . 13, 14 June, ,,

Disbandment of troops in the Taku forts demanded by allies, 16 June; the forts open fire on allied fleets, but are captured . . . . 17 June, ,,

Tien-tsin foreign settlement fiercely attacked, 17 June, ,,

Stern message from France to the viceroy of Yun-nan, respecting the safety of the missions there, 18 June, ,,

Adm. Seymour repels the enemy at Lang-fang, 14, 18 June, ,,

Mr. James Watts (C.M.G., May, 1901) carries despatches from Tien-tsin to Ta-ku . 19 June, ,,

Foreign legations ordered to quit Pekin 19 June, ,,

Baron von Ketteler murdered by Chinese troops in Pekin, the legations besieged (*see* below) 20 June, ,,

The dowager-empress and prince Tuan issue anti-foreign decrees . . . . 22 or 23 June, ,,

Seymour captures arsenal near Tien-tsin, 22 June; Chinese driven back, capt. Beyts killed, 23 June, ,,

Tien-tsin foreign garrison hard pressed, 21 June; relieved by allies after hard fighting, 23 June, ,,

Seymour, returns to Tien-tsin . . . 26 June, ,,

Edict issued at Pekin virtually declares war on all foreigners, and their expulsion ordered, 26 June, ,,

Arsenal N.E. of Tien-tsin captured by the allies, 27 June, ,,

Insurrection spreads to Manchuria in the north and Shantung in the south, slaughter of Chinese near Tien-tsin, reported . . . . 29 June ,,

Imperial edict disclaims responsibility for the fighting and throws all blame on the Europeans, 29 June, ,,

Adm. Seymour's advance to Pekin checked, retires to Tien-tsin. . . . . 29 June, ,,

Joint proclamation by the Nankin and Wu-chang viceroys, generally satisfactory, issued 3 July, ,,

Chinese attack on foreign settlements of Tien-tsin repulsed . . . . 3, 4 July, ,,

Anarchy in Manchuria, missions destroyed, bishop Guillon, R.C., and others, burned alive in the cathedral of Mukden . . . . . . July ,,

Edict from Pekin ordering the extermination of foreigners, issued . . . . . . July, ,,

British government announces that it will hold the authorities in Pekin responsible for injuries to foreigners . . . . 5 July, ,,

Li Hung Chang maintains order in Canton, frequent executions of robbers and pirates, reported, 6 July, ,,

Co-operation of the powers, Japan allowed a free hand, about . . . . . . 6 July, ,,

British government assures the viceroy of Nankin of support in quelling disorder in the Yang-tsze region . . . . 8 July, ,,

Massacre of about 54 missionaries, men, women, and children, at Tai-ynen-fu in Shan-si, by Yu-Hsien, the governor's, orders, 28 June and 9 July, ,,

Li Hung Chang made viceroy of Chi-li . 9 July, ,,

Fierce fighting at Tien-tsin, 6 July; the allies seize an arsenal, about 386 Chinese killed, 9 July; Chinese attack on the railway station repelled with heavy loss . . . . . . 11 July, ,,

TIEN-TSIN, native city and forts, captured, a fort and 48 guns seized by the Japanese, 13, 14 July. [Allies casualties about 800; 26 British of the naval contingent alone killed and 149 wounded during the 4 weeks' fighting].

Fighting on the Russian frontier of the Amur, Blagovestchensk bombarded . . 16 July, 1900

Li Hung Chang confers with the governor in Hong-kong . . . . 18 July, ,,

Russians rout the Chinese on the Amur, 18, 19 July, ,,

Capt. Watts-Jones and 10 or 12 Europeans murdered at Kwei-hua-cheng by the governor's order, about . . . . . 20 July, ,,

Li Hung Chang arrives at Shanghai . 21 July, ,,

The emperor appeals in vain for mediation to France, Germany, America, and Japan, 19, 21 July, ,,

Further massacres of missionaries and others in Shan-si at Pao-ting-fu, Chu-Chau, and other places in the north . . . . . 21 July, ,,

Severe fighting at Niu-Chwang . 19-26 July, ,,

British successes near Wei-hai-wei, reported 23 July, ,,

Gen. Zakharoff captures San-sung in Manchuria, 28 July, ,,

Two progressive Yamên ministers beheaded in Pekin by the empress's order, and the exiled Chang-Yin-Huan, G.C.M.G., executed in Kash-garia . . . . . . 29, 31 July, ,,

The Russians seize Hailar, Harbin relieved, Chinese defeated at Blagovestchensk, Sakhalin, and Niu-chwang captured . . . . . 3, 4 Aug. ,,

Allies advance to Pekin, Japanese victory, Chinese driven out of Pei-tsang, many killed, 4, 5 Aug.; Yang-tsun captured . . . . . 6 Aug. ,,

British troops land at Shanghai . . 9 Aug. ,,

Frequent executions of pirates in Canton . Aug. ,,

Bengal lancers charge Tartar cavalry at Ho-si-pou with success . . . . . . 9 Aug. ,,

Allies occupy Tung-chau, enemy fled . 12 Aug. ,,

Emperor, empress, and court fly from Pekin after ordering the execution of 5 pro-foreign members of the Yamên . . . . . . 14 Aug. ,,

Russians seize both banks of the Amur, massacre of about 4,800 Chinese by Gribsky and his Cossacks at Blagovestschensk . . 14 Aug. ,,

[SIEGE OF THE PEKIN LEGATIONS begins; total guards: 18 officers, 389 men; the British legation filled with refugees; outposts fiercely attacked; prof. J. Huberty and others killed, 20 June; sir Claude Macdonald takes command at the British legation, the Hanlin academy burnt by Chinese, 22 June; the Japanese repulse a fierce attack, many Chinese killed, 24 June; combined attack of Boxers and troops repulsed with severe loss, 27 June; brilliant sortie, many Chinese killed, 3 July; captain Strouts killed, 16 July; armistice concluded, but siege continued, 17 July; the allies relieve the legations after a rapid march and much fighting, general Gaselee and his Sikhs arrive first, followed by the Americans, amid the wildest joy, 3 p.m., 14 Aug. (total casualties during the siege, about 67 killed, 120 wounded, and 5 other deaths); the queen sent a message of thankfulness and sympathy, 20 Aug.]

PEI-TANG R. C. bishopric, in Pekin, nobly defended by mgr. Favier, 133 priests, and 42 French and Italian marines, with about 3,000 refugees, 20 June, till relieved by the Japanese and allies, 17 Aug. [Total deaths during the siege, 400.]

Imperial city entered, palace gates held by allies, 17 Aug. ,,

Forbidden city closely guarded by allies, 17 Aug. ,,

Boxers defeated near Tien-tsin, 300 killed, 64 captured . . . . 19 Aug. ,,

British force defeats Chinese and Boxers in the park, Pekin . . . . . 20 Aug. ,,

Sir Robert Hart resumes his office in Pekin, 21 Aug. ,,

Li Hung Chang's peace overtures rejected by the powers . . . . . . 22 Aug. ,,

The allies forbid looting, and call on the Chinese to return, 22 Aug.; they march through the Forbidden city and occupy the imperial palace, 28 Aug. ,,

Continued Russian successes in Manchuria, 24-29 Aug. ,,

Wholesale massacres of missionaries and native converts at Fu-chau-fu, 15 Aug., and many other places . . . . . . July-Aug. ,,

Four Boxer leaders executed at Tien-tsin, 30 Aug. ,,

Boxers routed round Pekin . . early Sept. 1900

British troops occupy Feng-tai, near Pekin, early Sept. ,,

Liang-hsiang, S.W. of Pekin, stormed by German marines and Bengal lancers, 500 Boxers killed, 11 Sept. ,,

20 Germans killed in an encounter with Boxers near Pekin . . . . . . 13 Sept. ,,

Boxers routed, and over 200 killed by Americans and Bengal lancers, at Mo-tao . . mid-Sept. ,,

Total allies in Pekin, 62,000 (22,000 Russians, 19,000 Japanese, and 5,000 British) . 14 Sept. ,,

Accident to British party while destroying gunpowder at Tung-chau, 16 deaths and 22 wounded, 14 Sept. ,,

Boxers defeated at Pa-ta-chu . . . 17 Sept. ,,

Ti-lin occupied by the allies and afterwards burnt, mid-Sept. ,,

Russians occupy the Manchurian frontier and 6 towns, columns penetrating the interior, much slaughter, reported . . . . . 18 Sept. ,,

Punitive expeditions of the allies against the Boxers, reported effective . . . 21 Sept. ,,

Pei-tang and Lutai captured with heavy losses by the allies . . . . . . 20, 21 Sept. ,,

Anti-Christian riots in the south, converts slaughtered, reported . . . . 21 Sept. ,,

Boxers routed by the British, 15 m. S. of Pekin, 25 Sept. ,,

Kirin, a rich town in Manchuria, occupied by the Russians, 24 Sept.; An-shan-jan captured, 26 Sept. ,,

Degradation and punishment of prince Tuan and 4 others, ordered by imperial edict (reported a forgery, 15 Oct.) . . . . . 25 Sept. ,,

Count von Waldersee appointed commander-in-chief of the allies, Aug.; arrives at Tien-tsin, 27 Sept. ,,

Shan-hai-kwan forts surrender to the British 29 Sept. ,,

Russian garrison in Pekin reduced . . 29 Sept. ,,

The German emperor, in reply to the emperor Kwang-su's message, states that he cannot regard the murder of baron von. Ketteler as expiated by *certain ceremonies*, refers to the massacres of missionaries, and insists on full reparation for the crimes committed and punishment of the guilty officials . . . . . . 1 Oct. ,,

Mukden taken by the Russians . . . 1 Oct. ,,

Summer palace looted by the Russians, Sept.; occupied by the British and Italians . . 3 Oct. ,,

French note, demanding punishment of the chief culprits, prohibition of the import of arms, indemnities for states, societies, or persons, establishment of permanent legation guards at Pekin, dismantlement of the Taku forts, and military occupation of certain points between Tien-tsin and Taku (accepted as the basis of negotiations), issued . . . . . . 4 Oct. ,,

Pekin–Tien-tsin railway held by the British; Russian claim to left bank of river at Tien-tsin disputed . . . . 8 Oct. ,,

The Czar announces that no part of China shall be annexed by Russia . . . . . 8 Oct. ,,

Conference of ministers in Pekin: Chinese proposals pronounced inadequate, 8 Oct.; punishment of guilty officials, payment of an indemnity, dismantling of Taku and other forts, abolition of the Tsung-li-Yamên and appointment of one minister for foreign affairs, provision for rational intercourse with the emperor, &c., agreed to as a basis of negotiations . . . . . 10 Oct. ,,

Prince Ching, Li Hung Chang, Liu Kun-yi, and Chang Chih-tung appointed peace negotiators, by edict . . . . 13 Oct. ,,

Chinese camp, 3 officers and 200 men, captured in Manchuria . . . . . . 14 Oct. ,,

Imperial court reported at Si-ngan-fu . . 15 Oct. ,,

Anti-dynastic rebellion in S. China, reported mid Oct. ,,

Reactionary Manchus appointed to high posts in Yang-tsze districts . . . . . Oct. ,,

Anglo-German agreement—chief points: the "open door" and the integrity of China to be maintained . . . . 16 Oct. ,,

Allies (4000, under gens. Campbell and Bailloud) enter Pao-ting-fu . . . . 15-21 Oct ,,

Sir Claude Macdonald, by his own wish, translated to Tokio, Japan; sir E. Satow arrives at Pekin 20 Oct. 1900

Death of Kang Yi, instigator of the Boxer movement and chief secretary of state, confirmed 24 Oct. ,,

Rebels victorious in Kwai-sin, much slaughter, reported . . . . 25 Oct. ,,

Sir C. Macdonald leaves Pekin amid regret 25 Oct. ,,

Punitive expeditions by the allies, villages destroyed . . . . Oct. ,,

242 missionaries (mainly British), with their wives and children, murdered during the Boxer rising in 1900.

The governor and 13 headmen beheaded at Pao-ting-fu for the murder of missionaries and others; city bastions and temple destroyed . 27 Oct. ,,

Boxers defeated near Shun-i-hsien . 31 Oct. ,,

Fatal explosion at Nankin, the Yamên destroyed, reported . . . . 2 Nov. ,,

Kunan-sien captured by an Italo-German column, 2, 3 Nov. ,,

Explosion at Tiu-lin, 5 soldiers and many Chinese killed . . . . 6 Nov. ,,

Russian excesses, indiscriminate slaughter, 5000 Chinese thrown into the Amur . Oct.–Nov. ,,

Illusory punishments on guilty princes and officials decreed . . . . 13 Nov. ,,

China resumes the civil government of Manchuria under Russian protection . . . . Nov. ,,

The emperor writes to the German emperor owning that punishment of the guilty officials would be just . . . . 14 Nov. ,,

Count Yorck's column occupies Kalgan, Chinese fly, 18 Nov. [he died 25 Nov.] 1900.

Yu-chang, governor of Hu-pei (Oct.), dismissed through sir E. Satow, and one friendly to foreigners appointed . . . . mid-Nov. ,,

Anti-Christian riots in Kwang-si, reported 19 Nov. ,,

Boxers defeated in several small actions, and the Ming tombs occupied, reported . 19 Nov. ,,

Che-kiang, governor, to whom was due the Chu-chau massacre of 20 missionaries (9 British) and others, dismissed . . . . . . 28 Nov. ,,

The astronomical instruments, erected over 2 centuries ago by the Jesuits, seized by the Germans 29 Nov. ,,

Russians exterminate brigands and Chinese troops in Manchuria . . . . . Nov.–Dec. ,,

Districts round Pekin placed under the allies 19 Dec. ,,

Yu-Hsien, ex-governor of Shan-si, executed 19 Dec. ,,

Gen. Bailloud defeats Boxers and Chinese, many killed, near Pei-chau, town burnt . 22 Dec. ,,

Joint note, after long negotiations, demanding China's compliance to "12 irrevocable conditions," preliminary to the withdrawal of the allies from Pekin and provinces, signed by the ministers in Pekin, 20 Dec.; presented, 22 Dec.; accepted by the emperor in his decree . 27 Dec. ,,

German operations in Chi-li, indiscriminate punishment, 5–15 Dec.; much criticised . 28 Dec. ,,

En-hai, the murderer of baron von Ketteler, executed in Pekin . . . . 31 Dec. ,,

Russian *de facto* protectorate over Feng-tien and Mukden; Manchuria-Russo-Chinese agreement signed, about . . . . . . 31 Dec. ,,

Germans defeat the Boxers in Chi-li, about 200 killed . . . . 3–5 Jan. 1901

Col. Tulloch's punitive expedition to Kao-li-ying successful, returns to Pekin . . . 6 Jan. ,,

Peace protocol signed at Pekin, 14 Jan.; ratified by the emperor . . . . . 17 Jan. ,,

New judicial system, under Chinese, instituted by the allies in Pekin . . . . . . Jan. ,,

The Russians hand over the Shan-hai-kwan–Pekin railway to the Germans . . . . Jan. ,,

Kwei-chau rebels defeated by Chinese, reported 24 Jan. ,,

Russian operations against the Hungus in Manchuria . . . . Jan. ,,

Imperial government reform decree, issued, 30 Jan. ,,

Explosion at Shan-hai-kwan, 40 Japanese killed, reported . . . . . . 30 Jan. ,,

Edict suppressing anti-foreign societies, under penalty of death . . . . . . 1 Feb. ,,

8 Boxer leaders executed at Han-kau, reported, 16 Feb. 1901

The court, after much evasion and delay, and threatened by a foreign military expedition, accepts the demands of the powers, punishment of guilty officials conceded . . 20 Feb. ,,

Prince Tuan sentenced to life-imprisonment, Duke Lan and gen. Tung-fuh-siang banished, prince Chuang and 2 others ordered to commit suicide, and 2 others to be executed, by edicts, 13, 21 Feb. ,,

Germans rout the Chinese W. of Pao-ting-fu, 21 Feb. ,,

Chi-hsiu and Hsu-Cheng-yu executed in Pekin, 26 Feb. ,,

N. China railway restored to the British, 21–28 Feb. ,,

Anglo-Russian dispute over a railway siding at Tien-tsin, 15 March; British reinforcements arrive, matter referred to arbitration, 22, 23 March, ,,

Rev. J. Stonehouse murdered by Chinese near Lo-fa, on the Tien-tsin line, about . 23 March, ,,

Manchurian convention, opposed by the powers and rejected by the emperor, end of March; withdrawn by Russia . . . . . 5 April, ,,

The Winter palace nearly destroyed by fire, gen. von Schwarzhoff killed . . . 17 April, ,,

The privy council replaced by a "general board of state affairs," by edict . . 23 April, ,,

Sharp fighting near Ching-wang-tao, maj. Browning and a sepoy killed; enemy defeated by the allies near Shan-hai-kwan . about 23 April, ,,

Chinese routed by Germans at the Great Wall, 23, 24 April, ,,

British capture 16 Krupp guns, &c., reported, 26 April, ,,

New Chinese board appointed to consider reforms, April *et seq.* ,,

Famine in Shan-si spreading, great mortality, April, ,,

German raids on the borders of Shan-si . April, ,,

The viceroy of Canton abolishes the privileges of the Manchus . . . . . . 1 May, ,,

Fresh fighting in Manchuria, reported . 1 May, ,,

M. Beau succeeds M. Pichon as French minister, 19 May, ,,

Six out of the 11 chief criminals reported to have met their death; punishments demanded by all the powers, Russia excepted, in 107 cases, 21 May, ,,

Trade prosperous in Canton . . mid-May, ,,

Boxers dispersed, 110 killed near Pao-ting-fu, reported . . . . 22 May, ,,

Departure of foreign troops . . . May *et seq.*, ,,

Edict favouring reform in official business and increasing taxation, reported . . 30 May, ,,

Count von Waldersee leaves Pekin for Germany, 3 June, ,,

Great fire in the Forbidden city at Pekin, 4 June, ,,

"Allied villagers" new anti-foreign movement spreading, reported . . . . . 24 June, ,,

Russian civil administrator installed at Niu-chwang . . . . June, ,,

Chinese government partially resumed in the British section of Pekin . . . 1 July, ,,

New Russian concession at Tien-tsin opened, 13 July, ,,

General Gaselee leaves Pekin . . 14 July, ,,

Destructive floods in the Yang-tsze districts, 1 June; many deaths (over 10,000,000 homeless), 15–24 July, ,,

Sixtieth ministerial meeting in Pekin; Chinese indemnity of 450,000,000 taels at 4 per cent. finally agreed upon, 26 July; notified to Chinese envoys . . . . 28 July, ,,

Edict forbidding examinations in all cities where foreigners were massacred or cruelly treated, 19 Aug. ,,

British famine relief mission leaves Pekin for Shan-si . . . . mid-Aug. ,,

Sir E. Satow demands the punishment of the authors of the Chu-chau massacre, when Mr. and Mrs. Thompson, their children, Miss Desmond, and 5 other English missionaries, Wu, a Chinese magistrate, and 31 others, were barbarously killed, about 21 July, 1900 [4 high officials banished, 15 others executed, 9 banished and 7 imprisoned, reported, 13 Sept.].

Prince Chun's mission received at Potsdam (see *Germany*), 4 Sept. 1901; Chinese envoy sent to Japan, *which see* . . . . . . Sept. 1901

Peace protocol with China signed by the 11 foreign ministers), 15 Aug.; by prince Ching and envoys (see *Times*, 10 Oct. 1901) . . . 7 Sept. ,,

The Summer palace occupied by the British and Italians, 12 Oct. 1900; transferred to the Chinese, 14 Sept. ,,

The Japanese and Americans hand over the Forbidden city to the Chinese; the evacuation of Pekin completed . . . . 17 Sept. ,,

Total German losses during the expedition to China, 676, including deaths from disease, reported, 23 Sept.; French casualties, 433, 61 killed . . . . Oct. ,,

Many reform edicts issued . . . . Oct. ,,

The Basel mission at Piang-tong, N.E. Kwang-tung, burnt by Triad rebels, end Sept.; rebels routed near Swatau with great slaughter by gen. Wu, 1 Oct.; another station destroyed in the Hsing-ning district, reported . . 5 Oct. ,,

The court leaves Si-ngan-fu for Pekin . 6 Oct. ,,

The Chinese maintain peace and order in Pekin, N. China, and railways, mines, &c., active, Oct. ,,

Welsh barracks burnt at Tien-tsin, 2 deaths, 1 Nov. ,,

Yang-tsze valley reported peaceful and prosperous, 5 Nov. ,,

Death of Li Hung Chang, diplomatist, friend of Russia, aged about 78, 7 Nov.; succeeded by Yuan Shih-kai, an able man, as governor of Chi-li . . . . 8 Nov. ,,

Missionary work and reform encouraged by the viceroys of Shan-si, Shan-tung, and Yang-tsze, reported . . . . 7 Sept. ,,

Imperial edicts favouring reorganisation and reforms issued; Pu Chun, heir-apparent, disinherited, but styled *duke* . . . 30 Nov. ,,

Sir Robert Hart appointed one of the guardians of the heir-apparent . . . mid. Dec. ,,

Rising in N. Chi-li suppressed, daily executions of rebels in Pekin . . . . . mid. Dec. ,,

Impressive funeral to the Christians massacred in 1900, and public atonement made by the officials of Tung-chau and 50 villages . . 20 Dec. ,,

Two missionaries and 3 converts murdered in Kan-su, Dec.; officials degraded by edict issued 31 Dec.; Tung-fuh-siang ordered to be beheaded, Jan. 1902

THE IMPERIAL COURT returns to Pekin; the dowager-empress again supreme . . 7 Jan. ,,

Edicts protecting missionaries and native Christians, and ordering punishment of officials complicated in the Boxer movement, issued, 14 Jan. ,,

A French priest and 2 converts murdered in Kwang-tung . . . . . . 16 Jan. ,,

Foreign ministers received at court, 22 Jan.; the ladies received by the dowager-empress, who expressed regrets for late events, and desire for progress . . . . 1 Feb. ,,

Marriage between Chinese and Manchus legalised; the custom of foot-binding deprecated by edicts, 1 Feb. ,,

United States of America note protesting against Russian encroachments in Manchuria . 1 Feb. ,,

Yung-lu appointed first grand secretary by edict, 2 Feb. ,,

European professors dismissed from the Imperial university . . . . 8 Feb. ,,

Conflicts in Manchuria between Russians and Tunguses . . . . . . Jan.–Feb. ,,

German mission in Kwang-tung destroyed by Chinese, reported . . . . . 10 Feb. ,,

Anglo-Japanese agreement, maintaining the *status quo*, the "open door" policy, independence and territorial integrity of China and Corea, signed in London, 30 Jan., issued . . . 11 Feb. ,,

Sir Robt. Hart and mgr. Favier received in court, 24 Feb. ,,

Marshal Su defeats the rebels at Lang-chau, Kwang-si; 2 French officers murdered on the frontier, reported . . . . . . 12, 13 March, ,,

Franco-Russian joint declaration, the integrity of China to be maintained . . . 19 March, ,,

Edict issued degrading 2 magistrates in consequence of a rebellion and murder of 14 converts in S. Honan . . . . . . 25 March, ,,

Chinese attack on a Russian post in Kwan-tung, Manchuria, defeated . . . . 26 March, 1902

Riots at Ta-ming-fu in Chi-li, many killed, reported . . . . . . 29 March, ,,

Manchurian convention revised, the *status quo* to be maintained, Russia to withdraw gradually in 18 months, signed and ratified . . 8, 9 April, ,,

Kwang-si rebels severely defeated . early April, ,,

Russian force inflicts terrible loss on a robber band on the Mukden frontier, reported, 12 April, ,,

N. China railway restored to China, agreement signed by sir E. Satow, Yuan Shih-kai, and Hu Yu-fen . . . . . . 29 April, ,,

The emperor and empress-dowager return to Pekin from a pilgrimage (cost over a million taels) to the Eastern Tombs . . . . 29 April, ,,

Imperial postal service gradually supersedes private agencies, reported . . . 30 April, ,,

Anti-indemnity riots at Ching-ting-fu, French missionary murdered, reported . . . 2 May, ,,

Rebels totally defeated by the troops at Nan-ning, 5 May, ,,

Export duty on tea reduced, to about ½*d.* per lb. (5 per cent.), reported . . . . 12 May, ,,

Chou-fu, treasurer of Chi-li appointed governor of Shan-tung . . . . . about 30 May, ,,

Grand duke Cyril (Russian) received with highest honours at Pekin . . . . 6 June, ,,

Sir Ernest Satow agrees to a *pro rata* reduction of the final indemnity claims to about 2 per cent., reported . . . . 12 June, ,,

Anglo-French syndicate secures a mining concession (60 years) in Yun-nan . . . 15 June, ,,

Russia withdraws from the Tien-tsin foreign government, announced . . . 20 June, ,,

Kai Chi, Chinese cruiser, blown up by an explosion in the powder-magazine near Nankin, 150 lives lost . . . . 22 June, ,,

Boxer movement in Sze-chuan, Methodist chapel destroyed, 10 converts killed; English and American missions at Tien-ku-chao destroyed, and a missionary killed, reported, 23, 27 June, ,,

Yuan Shih-kai's plan for the reorganisation of Manchuria, published . . . . 30 June, ,,

Chinese accept the conditions for the restoration of Tien-tsin . . . . . 19 July, ,,

Native steamer capsized on the West river, 200 deaths, reported . . . . . 23 July, ,,

Chang Chih-tung, viceroy of Wun-chang, appointed imperial commissioner of trade, about 29 July, ,

Tariff revision completed by China, Great Britain, and 8 powers . . . . . 29 July, ,,

Order restored in Sze-chuan, over 300 rioters killed; rebel leader in S. Chi-li captured and executed . . . . end July, ,,

The viceroy of Sze-chuan deposed . early Aug. ,,

Great mortality from cholera in Manchuria, July–Aug. ,,

Floods in Shan-tung, great distress . . Aug. ,,

Rebels defeated with great slaughter in Sze-chuan, 12 Aug. ,,

Tien-tsin transferred to the Chinese . 15 Aug. ,,

Protocol tariff signed by the British and 6 other powers . . . . 16 Aug. ,,

Rev. H. R. Lowis and rev. J. R. Bruce murdered by rioters at Cheu-chau, in Hu-nan (Lin-Hann-Yu, a mandarin, executed 17 Nov.) 15 Aug. ,,

Sir James Mackay's (G.C.M.G. 9 Nov.) British treaty, abolishing *likin* dues on all goods, native or foreign, and substituting other import and export duties, &c., signed after long negotiations . . . . 5 Sept. ,,

Evacuation of Shanghai completed by departure of last detachment of German troops . 3 Jan. 1903

Shanghai Taotai makes half-year's indemnity payments on a silver basis. Foreign ministers, except U.S. representative, sign joint note that protocol adopted by the bankers' commission provides for payment of the indemnity in gold: failure to fulfil obligation must entail grave consequences . . . . 7 Jan. ,,

Telegraphic returns from treaty ports show customs revenue for 1902 over 30,000,000 taels, as compared with 25,500,000 taels in 1901. Total of Shanghai 10,000,000 taels . . . early Jan. ,,

Agreement for construction of a railway from Shanghai to Nankin, in substitution for the preliminary contract of May 1898, concluded with

government by British and Chinese corporation, early Jan. 1903
Memorial arch erected at Pekin by Chinese government as atonement for murder of baron von Ketteler in 1900, formally dedicated by prince Chun in presence of baron Goltz and large number of foreigners and natives . . 18 Jan. „
Russia presents 7 demands as conditions for carrying out the Manchurian convention, and the evacuation of Niu-chwang and the two southern provinces of Manchuria. Chief provisions: No new treaty ports to be opened in Manchuria, and no new foreign consuls permitted; all customs revenues to be paid into Russo-Chinese bank; no portion of Manchuria to be alienated to any other power; none but Russians to be employed in any administrative capacity, civil or military, in Manchuria; reported . . . . 23 April, „
Demand rejected by China . . . 29 April, „
Imperial decree sanctioning construction of the Shanghai-Nankin railway; to be completed in 5 years from date of signing final contract, 11 June, „
Pekin and North Chi-li suffering from severest drought known for many years; reported 11 June, „
Settlement of a Chinese customs at Dalny, on the Russian frontier of leased territory . 12 June, „
Negotiations with Japan for revision of commercial treaty, in consequence of the insistence of Japan on clause in treaty opening Mukden, Taku-shen, and other Manchurian centres to foreign trade, announced . . 12 June, „
Report of U.S. consul at Niu-chwang on trade of Manchuria in 1902. Increase of foreign imports for last 10 years from 100 to 500 per cent., reached highest point in 1902; total import and export trade about 8,000,000*l*. . mid-June, „
Secret agreement between China and Russia regarding Manchuria, reported . . 22 June, „
Ratification of Mackay treaty announced on way to Pekin . . . . . . 28 June, „
Wang Chi-chung, the notorious governor of Kwangsi, marshal Su, and other high officials of that province, removed by imperial decree, mid-July, „
Negotiations for opening the ports desired by Japan and U.S. reported to be successful, end July, „
Ratifications of Anglo-Chinese commercial treaty exchanged . . . . . . 28 July, „
Chinese journalist and reformer, Shen Chien, beaten to death by order of government, 31 July, „
Protest of British government . . . 7 Aug. „
See also *Addenda*.

CHINESE EMPERORS.

1627. Chwang-lei.
1643. Shun-che (first of the Tsing dynasty).
1662. Kang-hi, an able sovereign; consolidated the empire, compiled a great Chinese dictionary.
1723. Yung-ching.
1736. Keen-lung, warlike; fond of art; greatly embellished Pekin.
1795. Kea-king.
1820. Taou-Kwang.
1850. Hieng-fung, 25 Feb.
1861. Ki-tsiang (altered to Toung-chi) 21 Aug.; born 27 April, 1856; married 16 Oct. 1872; died 12 Jan. 1875.
1875. Tsai T'ien (altered to Kwang Su), aged 4, 12 Jan.; married, 21 Feb. 1889.

[China was ruled by two empresses (Tsze An and Tsze Chi), 1861–1881; and by one (Tsze Chi, born 1834), a powerful woman, 1881 *et seq.*
1887. The emperor nominally assumed the government, 7 Feb.

CHINA GRASS, or RHEA; a prize of 5000*l*. was offered by the Indian government for machinery to prepare and cleanse the fibre, 11 Jan. 1870. Mr. John Greig's machine was exhibited in Edinburgh, Dec. 1871. Various unsuccessful machines and processes were tried; eventually Mr. Gomess invented processes by which a variety of fabrics can be manufactured, and a Rhea Fibre Treatment company was formed in London, with associations in India, Europe, and America, reported Aug. 1896.

CHINA PORCELAIN, introduced into England about 1531; see *Pottery*.

CHINA ROSE, &c. The *Rosa indica* was brought from China, and successfully planted in England, 1786; the Chinese apple-tree, or *Pyrus spectabilis*, about 1780.

CHINCHA ISLES, see *Peru*, 1864–5.

CHINCHONA, see *Jesuits*.

CHINESE WALL, said to have been completed about 211 B.C. Reported in 1879 to be 1728 miles long, 18 feet wide, 15 feet thick at the top.

CHINS and Lushais, savage tribes living in the mountainous region between Lower Bengal and Upper Burmah, of very primitive habits.

For their raids and chastisements, see *Burmah*, 1889–95, and *India*, 1890–2.
A conference of the authorities concerned at Calcutta, to consider the best means of keeping in order the Chins near Upper Burmah and the Lushais near Assam and Bengal; the transference of the southern Lushais from Bengal to Assam, recommended Jan. 1892; this is effected, 1 April, 1893

CHIOS (now SCIO), an isle in the Greek Archipelago, revolted against Athens, 412 and 357 B.C. It partook of the fortunes of Greece, being conquered by the Venetians, A.D. 1124; by the crusaders, 1204; by the Greek emperor, 1329, by the Genoese, 1346; and finally by the Turks in 1594. A dreadful massacre of about 40,000 inhabitants by the Turks took place 11 April, 1822, during the Greek insurrection.

About 4000 perished by an earthquake; the town Chio and many villages were destroyed, 3 April; many shocks since up to . . 12 April, 1881

CHIPPAWA (Upper Canada). Here the British under Riall were defeated by the Americans under Brown, 5 July, 1814. The Americans were defeated by the British under Drummond and Riall at Lundy's Lane, 3 miles from Chippawa, 25 July, following; Riall was wounded and taken prisoner.

CHIROMANCY, see *Palmistry*.

CHITRAL, a small frontier state in Kafiristan, N. India, subject to the maharajah of Cashmere, and under British influence.

Murder of the mehtar reported . . 30 Aug. 1892
His younger son, Afzul-ul-Mulk, seizes the government, reported . . . . . . 17 Oct. „
He is murdered by his uncle, Sher Afzul Khan, who usurps the government, reported . 25 Nov. „
Sher Afzul defeated by Nizam-ul-Mulk; flees to Afghanistan, about . . . . 12 Dec. „
Nizam-ul-Mulk recognized by the British . Jan. 1893
Dr. Robertson, British Agent, with a mission arrives at Chitral; well received, 28 Jan. leaves June „
Civil war reported . . . . . . 1 June, 1894
Nizam-ul-Mulk, able and educated, murdered by his brother, Amir-ul-Mulk, who seizes the government, reported . . . . . 10 Jan. 1895
Invasion of Umra Khan of Jandol . . Jan. „
Dr. Robertson arrives at Chitral, and temporarily recognises Amir-ul-Mulk as mehtar . 31 Jan. „
Umra Khan retreats to Drosh fort . 22 Feb. „
Shuja-ul-Mulk made temporary mehtar by Mr. Robertson: Amir-ul-Mulk under surveillance, 2 March, „
Sher Afzul escapes from Cabul and joins Umra Khan, reported, 8 March; British proclamation against Umra Khan issued . 19 March, „
A detachment of 60 men marching to relieve lieutenants Fowler and Edwards at Reshun is attacked in a defile at Karagh by a large body of tribesmen, 8 March; they retreat, fighting desperately; capt. Claye Ross, aged 33, and 40 Sikhs killed, 10 March; lieut. Jones and 14 men fell back on Boni and thence to Mastuj . . March, „

Malakand pass held by tribesmen; stormed by the relief force under major-gen. sir Robt. Low; enemy's loss heavy, British slight . 3 April, 1895
Successful advance of the British; the enemy again repulsed with loss . . . . 4 April, ,,
Lieuts. Fowler and Edwards with a small party, after seven days' vigorous defence, are captured by treachery, and held prisoners by Umra Khan at Barwa, reported . . . . . 6 April, ,,
The British cross the Swat river; enemy driven back with loss . . . . . . 7 April, ,,
Loyal offers of support to the British from native chiefs . . . . 9 April, ,,
Col. Kelly's force crosses the Shandur Pass (12,000 ft. high) and reaches Laspur, 7 April; enemy defeated near Gasht; lieut. Jones relieved at Mastuj . . . . 9 April, ,,
The Panjkora river crossed . . 9 April, *et seq.* ,,
Lieut.-col. F. D. Battye, of the Guides, and three Sepoys, killed in a skirmish while reconnoitring at Sado on the Panjkora; enemy lost heavily, 13 April, ,,
Capt. A. L. Peebles, aged 27, fatally wounded at Panjkora . . . . 14 April, ,,
Lieut. Edwards released; arrives in camp 14 April; lieut. Fowler and other prisoners arrive, 16 April, ,,
Col. Kelly defeats the tribesmen at Sanoghar, 12 April, ,,
About 3,000 of the enemy repulsed near Miankalai, and Munda fort occupied; flight of Umra Khan, 17, 18 April, ,,
Umra Khan surrenders to Gholam Hyder, Afghan commander, near Asmar . . . 24 April, ,,
Siege of Chitral fort by combined forces of Umra Khan and Sher Afzul; bravely defended by the British, Sikhs, etc.; 463 combatants, under capts. Campbell (wounded), C. V. Townshend, lieuts. Gurdon and Harley, 3 March, *et seq.*; capt. John Macdonald Baird, mortally wounded, 3 March; successful sally by lieut. Harley, etc., 8 killed; enemy's loss, about 60, 17 April; flight of the enemy, the siege raised (British loss during the siege, 40), 18 April. (Six months' additional pay presented to the garrison, May.) Arrival of col. Kelly's force after a brilliant march from Gilgit, 20 April, ,,
Order restored in Chitral, reported . 29 April, ,,
Sher Afzul surrenders to the Khan of Dir, who brings him with followers into camp at Dir, 27 April, ,,
Umra Khan and Mahomed Shah Khan sent to Cabul, 4 May; imprisoned by the Ameer . June, ,,
Native night attacks on the British camp at Munda, sentry James Green killed; 7 coolies killed at Kambat . . . . 14 May, ,,
Arrival of sir R. Low at Chitral; Shuja-ul-Mulk, mehtar, present . . . . . . 17 May, ,,
Honours and promotions of officers, etc. gazetted, 16 July, ,,
Dr. Robertson made K.C. of the star of India.
Jandol to be given up to native government; Chitral to be retained by the British, announced 10 Aug. ,,
"The Relief of Chitral," by capts. G. J. and F. E. Younghusband, published . . . . autumn, ,,
With reference to the maintenance of the military road to Chitral, see *Times*, 11 Dec. 1897.

CHIVALRY arose out of the feudal system in the latter part of the 8th century (*chevalier*, or knight, being derived from the *caballarius*, the equipped feudal tenant on horseback). From the 12th to the 15th century it tended to refine manners. The knight swore to accomplish the duties of his profession, as the champion of God and the ladies, to speak the truth, to maintain the right, to protect the distressed, to practise courtesy, to fulfil obligations, and to vindicate in every perilous adventure his honour and character. Chivalry expired with the feudal system. See *Knighthood* and *Tournaments*. By letters patent of James I. the earl-marshal of England had "the like jurisdiction in the *courts of chivalry*, when the office of lord high constable was vacant, as this latter and the marshal did jointly exercise," 1623.

CHLORAL HYDRATE, a crystalline compound of the marsh gas series, discovered by Liebig in 1831, which, when taken dissolved in water, produces deep sleep, but not insensibility to pain. This property was discovered by Oscar Liebreich, and reported to the French Academy of Sciences, 16 Aug. 1869. Its use requires great caution, particularly if weakness of the heart is suspected. The lamented death of prof. John Tyndall was caused by an overdose of chloral given by mistake for sulphate of magnesia, 4 Dec. 1893.

CHLORALUM, or chloride of alumina, a compound of chlorine and alumina, an antiseptic disinfectant, invented by Dr. Gamgee about 1870. It is safe and efficacious, and useful in medicine for gargles, washing wounds, &c.

CHLORINE (Greek *chloros*, pale green), a gas first obtained by Scheele in 1774, by treating manganese with muriatic (hydrochloric) acid. Sir H. Davy, in 1810, stated this gas to be an element, and named it chlorine. Combined with sodium it forms common salt (chloride of sodium), and combined with lime it forms the bleaching powder and disinfectant, chloride of lime; see *Bleaching*. In 1823 Faraday condensed chlorine into a liquid.

The supposed dissociation of oxygen from chlorine by heat by V. and H. Meyer of Zurich, was announced Aug. 1879. Afterwards chlorine was proved to exist in two similar states at high temperatures.

CHLOROFORM (the ter-chloride of the hypothetical radical formyl) is a compound of carbon, hydrogen, and chlorine, and was made from alcohol, water, and bleaching powder. It was discovered by Soubeiran in 1831, and independently by Liebig in 1832; and its composition was determined by Dumas in 1834. Chloroform was first applied as an anæsthetic experimentally by Mr. Jacob Bell in London, in Feb., and dr. Simpson of Edinburgh in Nov. 1847: its jubilee was celebrated by the society of Anæsthetists, 18 Nov. 1897; and was administered in England on 14 Dec. 1848, by Mr. James Robinson, surgeon-dentist. A committee of the Royal Medical and Chirurgical Society in July, 1864, after examining statistics, reported that the use of anæsthetics had in no degree increased the rate of mortality.

By the invitation of the Nizam through the *Lancet*, Dr. Lauder Brunton arrived at Hyderabad, 21 Oct., 1889; and there with other medical men investigated experimentally on the peculiar action of chloroform. They came to the conclusion that the danger of its use was not specially due to its effect upon the heart, but upon respiration, which could be easily obviated by proper caution. The Nizam remitted 1,000*l.* for the expenses of the commission. *Lancet* Jan. March, 1890
Full report issued (estimated cost 10,000*l.*), Dec. 1891; book published . . . . Aug. 1896

CHOBHAM COMMON, in Surrey. A military camp was formed here on 14 June, 1853, by a force between 8000 and 10,000 strong.

CHOCOLATE, made of the cocoa berry, introduced into Europe (from Mexico and the Brazils) about 1520, was sold in the London coffee-houses soon after their establishment, 1650.

CHOCZIM, Bessarabia, S. Russia. Here the Turks were totally defeated by John Sobieski, king of Poland, 11 Nov. 1673; and by the Russians, 30 April and 13 July, 1769.

CHOIR. This was separated from the nave of the church in the time of Constantine. The choral service was first used in England at Canterbury, 677; see *Chanting*.

CHOLERA MORBUS (Asiatic cholera) was described by Garcia del Huerto, a physician of Goa, about 1560. It appeared in India in 1774, and at other times, and became endemic in Lower Bengal in 1817, whence it gradually spread, till it reached Russia in 1830, and Germany in 1831, carrying off more than 900,000 persons in 1829-30. In England and Wales in 1848-9, 53,293 persons died of cholera, and in 1854, 20,097; see *Germ Theory of Disease*.*

Cholera appears at Sunderland . . . 26 Oct. 1831
And at Edinburgh . . . . . . 6 Feb. 1832
First observed at Rotherhithe and Limehouse, London, 13 Feb.; and in Dublin . 3 March, „
Deaths reported in England in 1831-2, 52,547.
Mortality very great, but more so on the Continent; 18,000 deaths at Paris, between March and Aug. „
Cholera rages in Rome, the Two Sicilies, Genoa, Berlin, &c., in . . . . July and Aug. 1837
24,014 deaths in Palermo in 17 weeks . . . „
Another visitation of cholera in England: the number of deaths in London, for the week ending 15 Sept. 1849, was 3,183; the ordinary average, 1,008; and the number of deaths by cholera from 17 June to 2 Oct. in London alone, 13,161. The mortality lessened and the distemper disappeared about 13 Oct. 1849
Newcastle-upon-Tyne, Hexham, Tynemouth, and other northern towns, suffer much from cholera, Sept. 1853
It rages in Italy and Sicily; above 10,000 are said to have died at Naples; it was also very fatal to the allied troops at Varna . . autumn, 1854
Cholera very severe for a short time in the southern parts of London, and in Soho and St. James's, Westminster . . . . . Aug. and Sept. „
Raging in Alexandria, June; abated . July, 1865
Prevailing in Ancona (843 deaths) Aug., subsiding, Sept. „
Very severe in Constantinople, nearly 50,000 deaths, Aug.; subsides after the great fire . 6 Sept. „
Cases at Marseilles, Toulon, and Southampton, end of Sept. „
Cholera prevalent at Marseilles, Paris, Madrid, and Naples . . . . . . July-Oct. „
An international meeting at Constantinople, to consider preventive measures, proposed, Oct. 1865, met 18 Feb. 1866. At the last sitting the conclusions adopted were that cholera may be propagated, and from great distances; and a number of preventive measures were recommended, 26 Sept. 1866
Cholera appears at Bristol, 24 April; at Liverpool, 13 May; at Southampton . . . July, „
Cholera severe in east of London: 346 deaths in week ending . . . . 21 July, „
House to house visitation; Metropolitan Relief Association formed; large subscriptions received (Queen's 500l.) . . . . . July and Aug. „
Cholera subsides . . . . . . Sept. „
Very severe at Naples . . . . Sept. „
Cholera Relief Committee closes . . 31 Oct. „
Cholera declared to be extinct in London 1 Dec. „
Cholera in Rome, Naples, and Sicily, Aug.-Sept.; in Switzerland . . . . . Oct. 1867
Alarm of approaching cholera, July; said to be severe in Königsberg in Prussia . . Aug. 1871
Cholera severe in Vienna, Aug.; Paris . . Sept. 1873
Egypt, at Damietta, June; at Cairo about 16 July; Alexandria about 1 Aug.; the disease abating, Aug.; deaths up to 31 Aug.—27,318, including 140 among British troops; cholera lingering at Alexandria, Sept. *et seq.*; no cases . 31 Dec. 1883
France, June; registered deaths: Toulon, 880, 18 June—26 Oct.; Marseilles, 1700, 27 June—26 Oct.; estimated total deaths in Paris, nearly 900, Sept.—Nov.; the disease appeared at Arles, Nantes, Yport, and other places; total deaths in France estimated 5000 up to . . 15 Sept. 1884
Italy. Cholera severe at Turin, 7 Aug.; spreading 19 Aug., increasing at Spezzia, &c., 23, 24 Aug., and at Naples and Turin 2 Sept.; very many deaths at Genoa 24 Sept.—8 Oct.; very severe at Naples (visited by the king) 2 Sept.—2 Nov. 1884
Spain, 1884. Cholera appears in Alicante 1 Sept. *et seq.*; much panic: at Toledo, Madrid, and other places Sept., Oct. . . . . . . „
Spain (Grenada, Malaga, Valencia, Murcia, &c.), 91,000 deaths (998 in Madrid) . May to 11 Sept. 1885
Official returns for all Spain, 12,337 deaths, March to 7 July . . . . „
Total since outbreak 61,521 . . . . 22 Aug. „
Gibraltar, 191 deaths in . . . . Sept. „
Palermo, Sicily, 2,540 deaths . 7 Sept. to 31 Oct. „
Marseilles, 1,250 deaths, 1 Aug. to 1 Sept.; gradually diminished up to . . . . 16 Sept. „
Toulon, slight outbreak, 6 deaths 20 Aug.; 32, 26 Aug.; gradually diminished till . . 18 Sept. „
Italy, 1886, Brindisi province, 4—31 July: *Venice*, a few deaths, May-Aug.; *Ravenna*, about 178 deaths, Aug., *Fiume*, about 55 deaths, July; *Bologna*, about 95 deaths, Aug.; *Barletta*, total about 611 deaths . . . . . . Aug. 1886
Japan. 37,000 deaths . . . . Jan.-Sept. „
Hungary, principally Pesth and Szegedin. 966 cases; 409 deaths . . . . Oct.-Dec. „
Trieste. 882 cases, 544 deaths . . 7 June-Oct. „
Istria. 671 cases, 374 deaths . . 13 July-Oct. „
Naples, Brindisi, &c. Temporary outbreak . Sept. „
Great epidemic of cholera in India 1887; N.W. Provinces, 30,780 deaths in . . . . Aug. 1887
Sicily, provinces, July-Oct. 1887; deaths daily varied from 1 to 27.
Messina. Deaths daily rose from 1 to 63; Sept.—Oct. „
Palermo, Sept. Deaths daily varied from 2 to 11; Sept. . . . . „
Malta. Deaths daily varied from 4 to 10, Aug.-Sept. „
Cholera in Mesopotamia, 5,983 cases in autumn, 1889; 3,000 fatal cases in Bussorah, reported 21 Jan.; it passed off in the spring, but returned in July-Aug. 1890
Cholera severe at Mecca, &c. (about 30,000 deaths), Arabia, July-Aug.; at Jeddah and in Syria, Aug. „
Cholera appears at Riebla de Rugal, a village in Valentia, Spain, 13 May; continues in the province and neighbourhood; 2,840 deaths reported up to . . . . March, „
Cholera severe at Guatemala, S.A., 1,200 deaths in seven weeks . . . reported 14 Dec. „
The progress of cholera greatly checked by the exertions of the International Quarantine board at Tor in Egypt . . . . . autumn, 1891
France. On the coast, 217 deaths . 1 Jan.-19 April 1892
Cholera severe at Damascus, Aleppo, &c., in Syria; at Mecca (about 11,000 deaths), Oct. *et seq.*, 1891; at Benares, 130 deaths up to . . 23 April, „
The disease appeared in India in March; about 6,000 deaths in Cabul and 2,000 deaths in Herat were reported; and about 3,000 deaths in Cashmere up to . . . . . . 3 June, „
Nantes. About 17 deaths, reported . 29 Aug. „
Roumania. 594 deaths . . . 21 July-4 Sept. „
Hungary, Budapest, 153 deaths . Aug.-11 Sept. „
Rotterdam. About 30 deaths . . 11 Aug.-Oct. „
Galicia. 400 deaths . . . . Aug.-19 Sept. „
Brest, etc. 259 deaths . . . 1 Sept.-Oct. „
Palermo. 81 deaths . . . . 30 Sept.-8 Oct. „
Persia. Total deaths reported, 60,000, May-Oct. (deaths in Teheran rose from 20 to 800 daily, 7-21 Aug. and gradually decreased). „
Russia. The disease appeared in the south and thence traversed the empire, June. It was severe in Baku and neighbouring districts; St. Petersburg, total deaths up to 23 Oct. 1,150. All Russia, since outbreak, 260,000 deaths, 13 Dec.
France. Total deaths, 3,184 . . April-16 Oct. „
Hamburg State. Total deaths, 7,611 20 Aug.-27 Nov. „
Belgium. Total deaths, 564 . . 25 July-13 Oct. „
Great Britain. A few isolated cases, chiefly foreigners, some fatal . . . . . Aug.-Sept. „
England. Several deaths from choleraic disease at Grimsby, Hull, etc.; 11 deaths in Greenwich workhouse (Government report published April, 1895) . . . . Aug.-Oct. „
Spain, Bilbao, 99 deaths . . . 28 Sept.-19 Oct. „

* Dr. Ferran inoculates by microbes many persons; reported successful; stopped June; permitted 23 June; a commission reports it unsatisfactory, Oct. 1885. Many persons inoculated in India by Dr. W. M. Haffkine, June, 1893-4; successful reports, Jan. 1896, *et seq.*

Budapest. Total deaths, 395 . . 13 Nov. 1892
Mecca. 6,721 deaths . . . June–July 1893
Jeddah. 1,586 deaths . . . 29 June–7 July ,,
Smyrna. 42 deaths . . . Aug.–Sept. ,,
Teheran. About 700 deaths since 21 Sept.; extinct 31 Oct. ,,
Russia. 369 deaths in 14 provinces 1 Jan.–7 Feb. many deaths, June, July; total in all Russia, 1,209, 24–31 Aug. Moscow, 67 deaths, 8–12 Aug. St. Petersburg, 47 deaths, 6–9 Oct.; about 30 deaths daily, reported . . . 16 Dec. ,,
Germany, Nietleben, near Halle, 46 deaths Jan–6 Feb. ,,
Hamburg. 46 deaths . . 16 Sept.–2 Oct. ,,
Stettin. 41 deaths . . . 23 Sept.–Oct. ,,
Russia. Severe throughout the provinces and Polish frontier during the summer. Average deaths weekly, 2,500, reported . . 6 Sept. 1894
St. Petersburg. 1,014 deaths, 8 July–7 Sept.; decreasing . . . . . . Oct.–Dec. ,,
Galicia and *Bukovina.* Total deaths, 2,400, July–Aug., reported, 5 Sept.; decreasing; ceased Oct. ,,
Germany. 490 deaths reported . . May–Dec. ,,
Japan. 16,000 deaths up to . . . 22 Aug. 1895
Russia. Volkynia, 3,085 deaths, Aug.–14 Sept; Podolia, 64 deaths, 21 Aug.–14 Sept.; decreasing, Oct.; St. Petersburg, 31 deaths; reported 18 Nov. ,,
India. Inoculation for cholera successfully practised by dr. Haffkine in the north (42,445 cases); reported . . . . . . Sept. ,,
Egypt, Lower (English supervision). 14,498 deaths, 11 Oct. 1895–14 Aug. 1896; decreasing, Sept.; extinct . . . . 25 Oct. 1896
Nubia, P. & O. steamer, from Calcutta, outbreak due to fruit, &c., taken on board at Port Said, arrived at Plymouth Sound: 4 deaths . 2–9 Jan. 1897
N. W. India. Outbreak at relief works in native state of Rewa; 160 deaths in two days; reported 23 Feb. ,,
India. Karachi, native district, 1,099 deaths, May, 1899; severe in Bombay and the famine districts, May, *et seq.*; 6,669 deaths week ending 23 June; decreasing . . . . Aug. 1900
Afghanistan. Severe in Kabul and Djebal Abad, great mortality; total deaths in Kabul, 4,500, June–Aug. ,,
Mecca. 523 deaths, 10–24 March, 1,120 deaths since outbreak; 928 deaths and 61 at Jeddah week ending 31 March; 1,127 deaths in the Hedjaz week ending . . . . 31 March, 1902
Tokio . . . . 28 June, ,,
Manchuria. Severe at Harbin, over 100 deaths daily reported . . . . 2 Aug. ,,
Corea. Spreading in the South . . . Aug. ,,
Philippines. 3,091 deaths . . . 29 Sept, ,,
Egypt. Total deaths 31,540, reported . 3 Oct. ,,
Palestine. Severe in Jerusalem, Jaffa and Gaza Nov.-Dec. ,,

CHORAL HARMONISTS' SOCIETY, London, existed 1833-51.

CHORUS, a band of singers which formed an important part of the Greek dramas, beginning in the 6th century B.C., and has been continued in modern oratorios and operas.

CHOUANS, a name given to the Bretons during the war of La Vendée in 1792, from their chief Jean Cottereau, using the cry of the *Chat-huant*, or screech-owl, as a signal. He was killed in 1794. Georges Cadoudal, their last chief, was said to be connected with Pichegru in a conspiracy against Napoleon when first consul, and was executed in 1804.

CHRISM, consecrated oil, was used early in the ceremonies of the Greek and Roman churches, Musk, saffron, cinnamon, roses, and frankincense, are mentioned as used with the oil, in 1541. It was ordained that chrism should consist of oil and balsam only; the one representing the human nature of Christ, and the other his divine nature, 1596.

CHRIST, see *Jesus Christ*.

CHRIST CHURCH, see *Lincoln Tower* and *New Zealand*.

CHRIST'S HOSPITAL (the *Blue-Coat* school) was established in conformity with a grant made by Henry VIII. in 1547, by Edward VI. 1553, on the site of the Grey Friars' monastery. A mathematical ward was founded by Charles II. 1672. The *Times* ward was founded in 1841. Large portions of the edifice having fallen into decay, it was rebuilt: in 1822 a new infirmary was completed, and in 1825 (25 April) the duke of York laid the first stone of the magnificent new hall. On 24 Sept. 1854, the master, Dr. Jacob, in a sermon in the church of the hospital, censured the system of education and the general administration of the establishment, and many improvements have since been made. Rev. G. C. Bell, successor of Dr. Jacob, 12 Aug. 1868-1876. The subordinate school at Hertford, for 416 younger boys and 80 girls, was founded in 1683.—The annual income varies. The removal of the school to the country negatived by the governors, 26 April, 1870. The proposal that the buildings and ground should be purchased by the Mid-London Railway Company for 600,000*l*. was not carried out. The Charity Commissioners' scheme for the reformed administration of the hospital published in the *Times*, 9 March, 1885.

The appeal of the governors against the charity commissioners' scheme was submitted to the judicial committee of the privy council 18 June; the appeal was disallowed . . . 14 Dec. 1889
Royal assent to the new scheme given 15 Aug. 1890
The new governing body, the duke of Cambridge president, first met, 1 Jan., 1891, when the scheme came into operation; by it 700 boys, 150 junior boys, and 350 girls are provided for.
Site for the new buildings at Horsham, Sussex, purchased . . . . . . Nov. 1892
The long controversy between the governors and the charity commissioners settled by compromise: important changes to be made . June, 1896
Foundation stone of the new schools laid by the prince of Wales at West Horsham, 23 Oct., 1897; occupied by the boys . . . . 29 May, 1902
Old buildings demolished 1903

CHRISTIAN BROTHERS, an organised secret society which existed in London, 1525, for the distribution of English New Testaments and tracts. It mainly consisted of the middle and lower classes, and produced martyrs.

CHRISTIAN COMMUNITY, founded about 1685 by Huguenot refugees, re-organised by John Wesley and others in 1772, for visiting and preaching the gospel in workhouses, asylums, rooms, &c., and in the open air; and for distribution of tracts.

CHRISTIAN ENDEAVOUR, see *Young People's Society of Christian Endeavour*.

CHRISTIAN ERA, see *Anno Domini*. MOST CHRISTIAN KING; *Christianissimus Rex*, a title conferred by pope Paul II. in 1469 on the crafty Louis XI. of France.

CHRISTIAN EVIDENCE SOCIETY established by earl Russell, the bishop of London, and others to counteract "the current forms of unbelief among the educated classes," 1870. Lectures for this purpose were given in St. George's Hall in 1871, beginning with the archbishop of York, 25 April. Volumes of lectures and tracts for circulation are published. Annual meetings are held; income 1901-02, 1,166*l*.

CHRISTIAN KNOWLEDGE, SOCIETY FOR PROMOTING, founded 1698, to promote charity schools, and to disperse Bibles and religious tracts. 1877: income, for charitable purposes (including legacies of 16,000*l*.), 52,581*l*.; 1892: 41,000*l*.; income 33,887*l*., expenditure 54,256*l*., reported Dec. 1896; 10,000 members, income 39,000*l*., 1900. Bibles, &c., given away; churches and schools helped; bishoprics maintained, &c.

Offices removed from Lincoln's Inn-Fields to Northumberland avenue, opened 3 Nov., 1879.
Bi-centenary celebrated, meeting at the Guildhall, 8 March, 1898.

CHRISTIAN SCIENTISTS, a sect founded in the United States by Mrs. M. B. G. Eddy. In 1867 she taught that the Spirit of God being Love and Good, moral and physical evil are contrary to that Spirit, and that a true knowledge of God and Christ can therefore cure all disease mental and physical; in 1876 her adherents formed the Christian Scientists Association; in 1903 they are numerous in the United States, see *Mind-cure*.

CHRISTIAN SOCIALISM, had its origin in 1848, under the leadership of Frederick D. Maurice, Charles Kingsley, Tom Hughes, Vansittart Neale, J. M. Ludlow, and others, in the practical interest in social reform evoked by the evils of the factory system, the efforts for reform by the working classes, and the political ideals of the Chartists. It is represented at the present time by the Guild of St. Matthew, and the *Christian Social Union*, which has a large and increasing membership, and seeks by raising its ideal of Christian duty to increase the quantity and improve the quality of Christian influences on social legislation and administration.

CHRISTIAN SOCIAL UNION, see *Christian Socialism*.

CHRISTIAN UNITY, ASSOCIATION FOR THE PROMOTION OF, on the basis of the three creeds, formed by thirty members of the Greek, Roman, and English Churches, 8 Sept. 1857; 20th anniversary kept in London, 8 Sept. 1877. A meeting to promote the reunion of Christendom was held in London, 19 July, 1878, the bishop of Fredericton in the chair.

CHRISTIANIA, the capital of Norway, built in 1624, by Christian IV. of Denmark, to replace Opslo (the ancient capital founded by Harold Haardrade, 1058), which had been destroyed by fire. On 13 April, 1858, Christiania suffered by fire, the loss being about 250,000*l*. The university was established in 1811. New Storthing (parliament house) built 1861–2. Statue of Charles John XIV. unveiled, 7 Sept. 1875. Population, 1891, 150,444; 1900, 227,606.

Visit of the German emperor . . 1 July *et seq.* 1890
Destructive fire, 9 deaths . . . . 6 Aug. 1896
Dr. Henrik Ibsen's 70th birthday celebrated with great festivities . . . 21 March, 1898
National theatre opened by the king . 1 Sept. 1899

CHRISTIANITY. The name Christian was first given to the disciples of Christ at Antioch, in Syria, 43 (*Acts* xi. 26; 1 *Peter* iv. 6). The first Christians were divided into *episcopoi* (bishops or overseers) or *presbyteroi* (elders), *diaconoi* (ministers or deacons), and *pistoi* (believers); afterwards were added *catechumens*, or learners, and *energumens*, who were to be exorcised; see *Persecutions*.

Christianity preached in Jerusalem, A.D. 33; Samaria, 34; Damascus, 35; Asia Minor, 41; Cyprus, 45; Macedonia, 53; Athens, Corinth, &c., 54; Ephesus, 56; Troas, &c., 60; Rome . . . 63
Christianity said to be taught in Britain, about 64; and propagated with some success (*Bede*) . . 156
Christianity said to be introduced into Scotland in the reign of Donald I. about 212
Constantine the Great professes the Christian religion 312
Frumentius preaches in Abyssinia . . about 340
Introduced among the Goths by Ulfilas . . . 376
Into Ireland in the second century, but with more success after the arrival of St. Patrick . . 432
Christianity established in France by Clovis . . 496
Conversion of the Saxons by Augustin . . . 597
Introduced into Helvetia, by Irish missionaries . 643
Into Flanders in the 7th century.
Into Saxony, by Charlemagne 785
Into Denmark, under Harold 827
Into Bohemia, under Borsivoi 894
Into Russia, by Swiatoslaf . . . . about 940
Into Poland, under Meicislaüs I. 992
Into Hungary, under Geisa 994
Into Norway and Iceland, under Olaf I. . . . 998
Into Sweden, between 10th and 11th centuries.
Into Prussia, by the Teutonic knights, when they were returning from the holy wars . . . 1227
Into Lithuania; paganism was abolished about . . 1386
Into Guinea, Angola, and Congo, in the 15th century
Into China where it made some progress (but was afterwards extirpated, and thousands of Chinese Christians were put to death) 1575
Into India and America, in the 16th century.
Into Japan, by Xavier and the Jesuits, 1549; but the Christians were exterminated 1638
Christianity re-established in Greece 1628

CHRISTINOS, supporters of the queen-regent Christina against the Carlists in Spain during the war, 1833-40.

CHRISTMAS, a festival in commemoration of the nativity of Christ, the exact time of which is quite unknown. Its observation appears to have begun in the second century in different months, January, April or May; for two or three centuries the Eastern church kept the feast Jan. 6 (see *Epiphany*), whilst the Latin church observed it 25 Dec. The Armenians celebrate both feasts on 18 Jan. The holly and mistletoe used at Christmas are said to be the remains of the religious observances of the Druids; see *Anno Domini*.

Christmas Cards.—About 1862 pictures of robins, holly, &c., on cards, designed by Mr. John Leighton, were issued by Messrs. Goodall of London, playing-card makers. Artistic designs were introduced in 1865. Great improvements were made in Germany, France, and in London by Messrs. de la Rue, Marcus Ward, and others, 1879-1903.

CHRISTMAS ISLAND, in the Pacific Ocean, so named by captain Cook, who landed here on Christmas-day, 1777. He had passed Christmas-day at Christmas-sound, 1774. On the shore of Christmas Harbour, visited by him in 1776, a man found a piece of parchment inscribed: "*Ludovico XV. Galliarum rege, et d. Boynes regi a secretis ad res maritimas, annis 1772 et 1773.*" On the other side captain Cook wrote: "*Naves Resolution et Discovery de rege Magnæ Britanniæ, Dec. 1777,*" and placed it in a bottle.

Annexed to the Straits Settlements . . Jan. 1880

CHRISTMAS ISLAND (Indian Ocean), an ancient coral atoll, visited by H.M.S. *Egeria*, 1887; annexed by Great Britain, 1888; leased to sir John Murray and Mr. G. Clunies Ross, 1891; transferred to a company, 1897; scientifically explored by Mr. C. W. Andrews, a "Monograph" by him published, 1900. Sir John Murray's expedition to the island reported successful, March, 1901.

CHRISTOPHER'S, ST. (or St. Kitt's), a West India Island, discovered in 1493, by Columbus, who gave it his own name. Settled by the English and French, 1623 or 1626. Ceded to England by the peace of Utrecht, 1713. Taken by the French in 1782, but restored the next year. The town of Basseterre suffered from fires, 3 Sept. 1776; also 3 and 4 July, 1867, when the cathedral and nearly all the town were destroyed. About 200 lives lost by inundations, 11, 12 Jan. 1880. Population in 1891, 47,662; 1901, 46,446.

CHROMIUM (Greek, *chroma*, colour), a rare metal, discovered by Vauquelin in 1797. It is found combined with iron and lead, and forms the colouring matter of the emerald. Chromium is now (1903) prepared in large quantities in the electric furnace by a process discovered by Moissan in 1895.

CHROMO-LITHOGRAPHY, see *Printing in Colours*.

CHRONICLES. The earliest are those of the Jews, Chinese, and Hindoos. In Scripture there are two "Books of Chronicles"; see *Bible*. Collections of the British chronicles have been published by Camden, Gale, &c., since 1602; in the present century by the English Historical Society, &c. In 1858, the publication of "Chronicles and Memorials of Great Britain and Ireland during the Middle Ages," commenced under the direction of the Master of the Rolls (still going on, 1903). In 1845 Macray's "Manual of British Historians" was published. Some of the monkish chronicles are now discredited. "The Chronicle of Froissart," translated by lord Berners, vol. i., Jan. 1901.

CHRONOGRAM, an inscription on tombs, buildings, medals, &c. in which a date or epoch is expressed by letters (the Roman numerals) added together as they occur in the sentence. A large collection of "Chronograms," with translations and explanations, was published by Mr. James Hilton in 1882, 1885, and 1896.

CHRONOLOGY, the science of time; see *Eras and Epochs*. Valuable works on the subject are *l'Art de Vérifier les Dates*, compiled by the Benedictines (1783-1820). Playfair's Chronology, 1784; Blair's Chronology, 1753 (new editions by sir H. Ellis in 1844, and by Mr. Rosse, in 1856). The Oxford Chronological Tables, 1838. Sir Harris Nicolas' Chronology of History, 1833; new edition, 1852. Hales' Chronology, 2nd edition, 1830; Woodward and Cates' Encyclopædia of Chronology, 1872; Mr. H. Fynes-Clinton's Fasti Hellenici and Fasti Romani (1824-50).

CHRONOMETER, see *Clocks*, and *Harrison*.

CHRONOSCOPE, an apparatus invented by professor Wheatstone in 1840, to measure small intervals of time. It has been applied to the velocity of projectiles and of the electric current. A chronoscope was invented by Pouillet, in 1844, and by others since. Capt. Andrew Noble (engaged by sir William Armstrong) invented an apparatus for determining the velocity of a projectile in a gun; a second of time is divided into millionths, and the electric spark is employed in recording the rate of the passage. The apparatus was exhibited at Newcastle-on-Tyne in Aug. 1869, and in London in April, 1870.

CHRYSANTHEMUMS were introduced into England from China, about 1790; and many varieties since. Centenary celebrated in London, 11 Nov. 1890.

CHRYSOPOLIS, or SCUTARI (*which see*).

CHUNAR, or CHUNARGHUR, N.W. India, taken by the British, 1763, and ceded to them, 1768. Here was concluded a treaty between the nabob of Oude and governor Hastings, by which the nabob was relieved of his debts to the East India Company, on condition of his seizing the property of the begums, his mother and grandmother, and delivering it up to the English, 19 Sept. 1781. This treaty enabled the nabob to take the lands of Fyzoola Khan, a Rohilla chief, who had settled at Rampoor, under guarantee of the English. The nabob presented to Mr. Hastings 100,000*l.*; see *Hastings*.

CHURCH (probably derived from the Greek *kyriakos*, pertaining to the Lord, *Kyrios*), signifies both a collected body of Christians, and the place where they meet. In the New Testament, it signifies "congregation," in the original *ekklesia*. Christian architecture commenced with Constantine, who erected at Rome churches called basilicas (from the Greek *basileus*, a king); St. Peter's about 330. His successors erected others, and adopted the heathen temples as places of worship. Several very ancient churches exist in Britain and Ireland. See *Architecture; Choir* and *Chanting; Rome, Modern; Popes*.

CHURCH AND STAGE GUILD, was formed in 1880 to promote morality and temperance by the agency of theatrical performances.

CHURCH ARMY, constituted in 1882 under episcopal control. Founder, Rev. W. Carlile. It is a working-man's mission to working-men, and includes evangelists' and nurses' training homes, and labour homes for tramps and inebriates; one opened by the marquis of Lorne in Whitechapel, 25 April, 1896. Annual services and meetings are held. Income, 1902, 147,000*l.* The work of the Church Army is divided into Evangelistic and social departments. 66 colportage and mission vans carry on the work in the country, and the pioneer and tent mission hold missions in London and the provinces. Labour yards and relief depôts gave assistance to 68,000 cases in 1902. Head-quarters, 130, Edgware-road, London, W.

CHURCH ASSOCIATION, founded to maintain Reformation principles, 1865. Annual meetings are held in London and the provinces.

The prosecutions under the Public Worship Regulation Act, *which see*, have been supported by the Association.

CHURCH BUILDING. The society for promoting the enlargement, building, and repairing of churches and chapels, was established 1818, and incorporated 1828. A commission for building churches in populous places, appointed in 1820, was incorporated with the ecclesiastical commission about 1856.

CHURCH CONGRESSES, meet annually since 1861. See under *Church of England*.

CHURCH DEFENCE INSTITUTION; founded in 1859—the archbishop of Canterbury president. It does not meddle with doctrines.

The Oxford Laymen's League for defence of the national church founded Aug. 1886. Lord Selborne's "Defence of the Church of England against Disestablishment" published . 1 Dec. 1886
Great church defence meeting, Queen's Hall, London, the two abps., chairmen . 1 March, 1895
An appeal to raise 20,000*l.*, published, *Times*, 6 April, 1895
Annual meetings are now held.

CHURCH DISCIPLINE ACT (3 & 4 Vict. c. 86), passed 7 Aug. 1840, enables bishops to issue commissions of inquiry, and on conviction to inhibit clergymen from performing service, &c.

A new bill brought in by the archbishop of Canterbury, read second time, 15 March, 1888; another rejected (2nd reading) 310–156, 10 May, 1899

Two bills were brought forward in 1903, No. 1 "the Liverpool bill," by Mr. Austin Taylor, M.P. for the East Toxteth division of Liverpool, to compel obedience of the clergy to the vestries, and to abolish the episcopal veto, passed second reading 190 to 139 . . . 13 March, 1903
No. 2, introduced by Mr. C. A. Cripps, M.P. for the Stretford division, Lancs., gave the bishops increased power to enforce discipline, read the second time: for 80, against 56 . 13 May, ,,

CHURCH OF ENGLAND.* The earliest history is legendary. See *Bishops*. The following are leading facts in her history: for details, refer to separate articles; see *Clergy* and *Free Church*. In Sept. 1880, the archbishop of Canterbury said that he was *in communion with* 162 *bishops*. 288 bishops in the Anglican communion, announced, 1897.

Christianity probably introduced into Britain by Gaulish missionaries, and bishoprics founded in the 3rd and 4th centuries.
Restitutus, bishop of London, and Adelfius of Caerleon, said to have been present at the council of Arles 314
Rise and spread of the Pelagian heresy, 400 *et seq.*
The persecutions of the Saxon invaders, drive the Christian into Wales and Cornwall, 5th and 6th centuries.
The Saxons converted by Augustin and his companions, 597 *et seq.* He landed at Ebbs Fleet.
Dunstan establishes the supremacy of the monastic orders, about 960
The aggrandising policy of the Church, fostered by Edward the Confessor, checked by William I. and his successors . . . . . 1066 *et seq.*
Contest between Henry II. and Becket respecting "Constitutions of Clarendon" . . 1164-1170
Contest between national or English party and Roman party (chiefly Norman) 11th and 12th centuries
John surrenders his crown to the papal legate . 1213
Rise of the Lollards—Wickliffe publishes tracts against the errors of the church of Rome, 1356; and a version of the Bible, about . . 1383
The clergy regulated by parliament, 1529; they lose the first fruits 1534
The royal supremacy imposed on the clergy by Henry VIII., 1531; many suffer death for refusing to acknowledge it 1535
Coverdale's translation of the Bible commanded to be read in churches . . . . . ,,
"Six Articles of Religion" promulgated . . . 1539
First Book of Common Prayer issued . . . 1549
The clergy permitted to marry . . . . ,,
"Forty-two Articles of Religion" issued . . 1552
Restoration of the Roman forms, and fierce persecution of the Protestants by Mary . . 1553-8
The Protestant forms restored by Elizabeth; the Puritan dissensions begin . . . 1558-1603
Matthew Parker, consecrated abp. of Canterbury at Lambeth, by bps. Barlow, Hodgkins, and two others (see *Nag's Head*) . . 17 Dec. 1559
"Thirty-nine" Articles published 1563
Hampton Court conference with the Puritans . . 1604
New translation of the Bible published . . 1611
Book of Common Prayer suppressed and Directory established by parliament 1644
Presbyterians established by the Commonwealth . 1649
Act of Uniformity (14 Chas. II. c. 4) passed—2000 nonconforming ministers resign their livings . 1662

Attempts of James II. to revive Romanism; "Declaration of Indulgence" published . . . 1687
Acquittal of the seven bishops on a charge of "seditious libel" . . . . . . ,,
Comprehension bill for dissenters introduced . . 1688
The Non-juring bishops and others deprived; (they formed a separate communion) . . 1 Feb. 1691
"Queen Anne's Bounty," for the augmentation of poor livings 1704
Act for building 50 new churches passed . . 1710
Fierce disputes between the low church and the high church; trial of Henry Sacheverell, for seditious sermons; riots . . . . ,,
The Bangorian controversy begins 1717
John Wesley and George Whitefield commence preaching 1738
Rise of the Evangelical party in the church, under Newton, Romaine, and others, latter part of 18th century
Church of England united with that of Ireland at the Union 1800
Clergy Incapacitation Act passed 1801
Incorporated Church Building Society established, 6 Feb. 1818
Church Inquiry Commission, appointed 23 June, 1832
Ecclesiastical Commissioners incorporated by act, 13 Aug. 1836
Acts for building and enlarging churches, 1828, 1838
200 new churches erected in the diocese of London under bishop C. J. Blomfield . . . 1828-56
"Tracts for the Times" (No. 1-90) published (much controversy ensued) 1833-41
Church Pastoral Aid Society, founded . . . 1836
Additional Curates' Society, founded . . . 1837
New Church Discipline Act (3 & 4 Vict. c. 86) . 1840
For the Gorham and Denison cases, see *Trials*, 1849, 1856
Anglo-Continental Society (*which see*), founded . 1853
English Church Union, established . . . 1860
"Essays and Reviews" published, 1860; numerous Replies issued (see *Essays and Reviews*) . 1861-2
[The Church of England is now said to be divided into High, Moderate, Low (or Evangelical), and Broad Church: the last including persons who hold the opinions of the late Dr. Arnold, the Rev. F. D. Maurice, dean Stanley, canon Kingsley, and others.]
Church Congresses began at Cambridge, 1861; and at Oxford . . . . . . July, 1862
Dr. Colenso, bishop of Natal, publishes his work on "The Pentateuch," about Oct. 1862; the bishops, in convocation, declare that it contains "errors of the gravest and most dangerous character" . . . . . . 20 May, 1863
A Church Congress at Manchester 13, 14, 15 Oct. ,,
Bishop Colenso deposed by his metropolitan, Dr. Gray, bishop of Capetown. . . 16 April, 1864
"Oxford Declaration" (authorship ascribed to archdeacon Denison and Dr. Pusey), respecting belief in eternal punishment, drawn up and signed on 25 Feb., and sent by post to the clergy at large for signature: about 3000 are said to have signed; it was presented to the archbishop of Canterbury 12 May, ,,
Bishop of London's Fund, for remedying spiritual destitution in London, established 1863; the queen engages to give (in three years) 3000*l.*, and prince of Wales 1000*l.* . . . . . 7 March, ,,
100,456*l.* received; 72,003*l.* promised . 31 Dec. ,,
The queen engages to give 15,000*l.* in 10 years, April, 1865
Church Congress at Bristol . . . . Oct. 1864
Church of England Education Society, founded . ,,
Church Association (against popery and ritualism) established. 1865
District Churches Tithes act passed (rectories constituted) . . . . ,,
Bishop Colenso's appeal came before the privy council, which declared bishop Gray's proceedings null and void (since a colonial bishop can have no authority except what is granted by parliament or by the colonial legislature), 21 March, ,,
London Free and open Church Association, founded ,,
New form of clerical subscription proposed by a commission in 1864; adopted by parliament, July, ,,
Church Congress at Norwich . . . 3-7 Oct. ,,
Meeting in London of three English bishops, Dr. Pusey, and nearly 80 of the clergy and laity, with counts Orloff and Tolstse, and the Russian chap-

* The church consists of three *orders of clergy*—bishops, priests and deacons; 1903; two archbishops, 33 bishops, with 22 suffragans, 8 assistant bishops, about 100 colonial and missionary bishops, and about 23,000 clergy. The other dignitaries are chancellors, deans (of cathedrals and collegiate churches), archdeacons, prebendaries, canons, minor canons, and priest-vicars. In 1903, the number of ecclesiastical parishes or districts with churches or chapels was about 1400. Total revenue of the church, ancient endowments, 5,469,171*l.*; through private bounty (since 1703), 284,386*l.* Estimated total revenue of the church, 7,250,000*l.*, 1891. Benefices about 14,250*l.*, reported 1891. Voluntary offerings to the church for year ending Easter, 1901, 7,778,134*l.* 17*s.* 4*d.*; 1902, 8,217,316*l.* 5*s.* 5*d.*

lain, to consider on the practicability of uniting the English and Russian churches . 15 Nov. 1865
Bishop Colenso publicly excommunicated at Maritzburg cathedral, by bishop Gray . . 5 Jan. 1866
Bishop Gray declares himself independent, establishes synods, and calls his see "The Church of South Africa" . . . . . . early in „
The Church Missionary Society refuses to support colonial bishops, unless they keep within the formularies of the Church of England . early in „
Church Congress at York . . . . . 6 Oct. „
Much excitement caused by the progress of *ritualism (which see)* . . . Sept.-Nov. „
Bishop Colenso *v.* Gladstone and others (trustees of the Colonial Bishopric Fund) for withholding his salary. Verdict of master of the rolls, for plaintiff, with costs . . . . . . 6 Nov. „
Unqualified condemnation of ritualism by the bishops in convocation, 13 Feb.; the lower house concurred . . . . . . 15 Feb. 1867
The bishop of Salisbury (Dr. Hamilton) in a church asserts the doctrine of the supernatural gifts of priests, the Divine presence in the sacrament; public protest against it . . . 16 May, „
Trial in Court of Arches, Martin *v.* Mackonochie, respecting extreme ritualistic practices at St. Alban's, Holborn; case deferred . . 21 May, „
Royal Ritualistic Commission appointed to inquire respecting rubrics in the Prayer-Book, table of lessons, &c., 3 June; first report, censuring innovation, signed . . . . . . 19 Aug. „
Pan-Anglican Synod (*which see*) meets at Lambeth, 24-27 Sept. „
Church Congress at Wolverhampton . . 1 Oct. „
Meeting of ritualists in St. James's Hall, claiming liberty . . . . 19 Nov. „
Case of Martin *v.* Mackonochie, begun 4 Dec., lasted 14 days; resumed . . . 16-18 Jan. 1868
Proposal of bishop Gray of Capetown to consecrate Mr. Macrorie bishop of Natal in opposition to bishop Colenso, disapproved of by the English and Scotch bishops . . . . . . Jan. „
Bishop of London's Fund, received, 312,309*l.* 31 Jan. „
Martin *v.* Mackonochie decided; verdict for plaintiff; use of incense, mixing water with the wine, and elevation of the elements, in the sacrament, forbidden . . . . . . 28 March, „
Great meeting at St. James's hall, in defence of the Irish Church establishment; 23 bishops present, 6 May, „
District Churches Act, constituting vicarages (Bishop of Oxford's Act), passed . . . . „
Church Congress at Dublin . . . . 29 Sept. „
Sharp party contests at a special meeting of the Christian Knowledge Society . . . 8 Dec. „
Martin *v.* Mackonochie: appeal case; verdict for plaintiff, declaring certain ritualistic practices illegal . . . . 23 Dec. „
Warm meeting of ritualists at St. James's hall, 12 Jan. 1869
First meeting of a Church Reform Society (since named "Liturgical Revision Society"): Lord Ebury, chairman . . . . . 13 May, „
Church conference at Sheffield . . . 24 May, „
Church Congress at Liverpool . . . 5 Oct. „
Martin *v.* Mackonochie: defendant censured by privy council for evading sentence . . 4 Dec. „
Bishop of London's Fund: — 411,839*l.* received, July, 1870
"Clerical Disabilities Act" passed . . . Aug. „
Church Congress at Southampton . . . 11 Oct. „
Christian Knowledge Society votes 10,000*l.* to support Church schools . . . . 20 Oct. „
Rev. Mr. Mackonochie suspended from duty for three months by decree of privy council for evading former sentence . . . . 25 Nov. „
Rev. C. Voysey sentenced to be deprived for heresy; appeal to judicial committee of privy council disallowed (see *Voysey*) . . . . 10 Feb. 1871
Hebbert *v.* Purchas, of Brighton; verdict against defendant for offences against ecclesiastical law; considered a great defeat of the ritualists, and caused much excitement . . . . 23 Feb. „
Mr. Miall's resolution for disestablishing the church of England defeated in the commons—374-89, 9 May, „
Incumbents' Resignation Act passed . 13 July, „
Agitation for revival of diocesan synods, Sept.-Oct. „
Church Congress at Nottingham; closed 10 Oct. 1871
Sheppard *v.* Bennett (for teaching the divine presence in the sacrament); appeal to privy council, 28 Nov.; judgment adjourned . . . 2 Dec. „
Bishop of London's Fund—received 441,199*l.* 31 Dec. „
The convocation authorised to consider alterations in the Prayer Book . . . . . . Feb. 1872
Church reform meeting at St. James's hall; parochial councils recommended . . . 15 Feb. „
Rev. John Purchas, of Brighton, to be suspended from duties for one year, from . . 18 Feb. „
[He died 18 Oct.]
Conference of bishops, deans, and canons at Lambeth, to consider cathedral reform . 1 March, „
Sheppard *v.* Bennett; judgment for defendant, who is censured . . . . 8 June, „
Mr. Miall's motion for royal commission to inquire into the property of the church lost (295-94) 2 July, „
Church Congress at Leeds . . . . 8-11 Oct. „
Memorial (signed by 60,200 persons) against Romanist teaching, &c. in the church, presented at Lambeth to the archbishop by the church association . . . . 5 May, 1873
The archbishops in reply admit the danger, and recognize their duty, as well as the difficulties of action, saying, "We live in an age when all opinions and beliefs are keenly criticised, and when there is less inclination than ever was before to respect authority in matters of opinion. In every state, in every religious community, almost in every family, the effect of this unsettled condition may be traced." . . . . 1 June, „
Mr. Miall's motion for disestablishing the church, lost (356-61) . . . . 16 May, „
483 clergymen petition convocation for the licensing of duly qualified sacramental confessors, May, „
Church Congress, at Bath . . . . . 9 Oct. „
Archdeacon Denison, Dr. Pusey, canons Liddon and Liddell, and others, publish a declaration in favour of confession and absolution in *Times*, 6 Dec. „
Archdeacon Denison attacks the bishops in a Latin pamphlet, "Episcopatus Bilinguis" . . Dec. „
Public Worship Regulation Act (*which see*) brought in by the archbishops, 20 April; royal assent, 7 Aug. 1874
Meeting of lay and clerical delegates at Lambeth palace on church affairs . . . . 10 June, „
Addresses to the archbishops largely signed for and against the sanction of a distinctive dress for the minister during the celebration of the holy communion . . . . Sept. „
Church Congress at Brighton met . . 6 Oct. „
New society formed by bishops of Manchester, Carlisle, and Edinburgh, and others, to promote union with orthodox dissenters . . . . . . Oct. „
Bishop of London's Fund:—500,187*l.* received or promised . . . . Nov. „
Martin *v.* Mackonochie: new suit in court of arches (see 1870), 26 Nov.; Mackonochie to be suspended for 6 weeks and pay costs . . . 7 Dec. „
Pastoral of the archbishops and bishops (bishops of Salisbury and Durham excepted) to the clergy and laity (counselling moderation and forbearance,) dated 1 March, 1875
Mackonochie declines to appeal; excitement at his church; rev. A. Stanton and congregation celebrate holy communion at St. Vedast's, Foster-lane . . . . 27 June, *et seq.*
Church Congress at Stoke-upon-Trent . 5-9 Oct. „
Several clergymen secede to Rome . . . Oct. „
Public Worship Regulation Act: new court, under lord Penzance, meet at Lambeth-palace; first case the Parish of Folkestone *v.* rev. Charles Joseph Ridsdale, 4 Jan.; verdict for plaintiffs . 3 Feb. 1876
Reported negotiation of ritualistic ministers with Rome disclaimed by Mr. Mackonochie and about 100 others in *Times* . . . . . . 4 Feb. „
Church of England Working Men's Society established at St. Alban's, Holborn . . . 5 Aug. „
Church Congress at Plymouth . . . 3-9 Oct. „
"English Church Union" deny the authority of any secular court in matters spiritual, at a meeting, 16 Jan. 1877
Address to the archbishops and bishops (signed by Dr. Church, dean of St. Paul's, and other deans and canons) against the Public Worship Regula-

tion act, &c., requiring legislation respecting ecclesiastical affairs to be made by church synods and adopted by parliament . . 3 April, 1877
Both archbishops vote for permitting dissenters' funeral service in churchyards. . 17 May, ,,
Bishop of London's Fund received 571,597*l*. . June, ,,
Declaration of above 41,000 (clergy and laity) and proposed petition to the queen against judgment in the Ridsdale case . . . . July, ,,
96 peers (Duke of Westminster and others) address the archbishop of Canterbury against auricular confession, "Priest in Absolution," &c., about 9 Aug. ,,
17th *Church Congress* at Croydon, the archbishop of Canterbury president; very successful, 9-12 Oct. ,,
Pan-Anglican Congress (*which see*) meet at Lambeth, &c., . . . 2-27 July, 1878
Bishoprics Act authorising establishment of four new sees, passed . . . 16 Aug. ,,
18th *Church Congress*, at Sheffield, archbishop of York president . . . 1-4 Oct. ,,
New rubrics in Prayer-book agreed to by the convocation, 4 July; act for them passed by convocation . . . . . . Aug. 1879
19th *Church Congress* at Swansea . . 7 Oct. ,,
Dr. Julius v. the bishop of Oxford (for not prosecuting rev. Mr. Carter, of Clewer), queen's bench; verdict against the bishop in 1879; reversed on appeal by house of lords; (the bishop may but is not compelled to prosecute) . 22 March, 1880
20th *Church Congress*, at Leicester; friendly address from nonconformists . 28 Sept.—1 Oct. ,,
Rev. John Baghot de la Bere, jun., vicar of Prestbury, Gloucestershire, deprived for disobedience respecting ritualism, &c., by court of arches 21 Dec. 1880, and 8 Jan. 1881
Memorial to the archbishop of Canterbury, from five deans (Dr. Church, dean of St. Paul's, and other clergymen) in favour of toleration of divergence in ritualistic practice . . 10 Jan. ,,
Counter memorial from bishops Parry and Ryan, dean Close, and other deans and clergymen, opposing toleration of unscriptural practices 31 Jan ,,
Mr. Mackonochie's appeal to the house of lords dismissed; sentence of 3 years' suspension affirmed . . . . . 7 April, ,,
21st *Church Congress* at Newcastle-on-Tyne 4-10 Oct. ,,
Catholic league formed . . . . June, 1882
Death of Dr. E. B. Pusey . . . 16 Sept. ,,
22nd *Church Congress* at Derby . . 3-6 Oct. ,,
Rev. A. Mackonochie resigns living at St. Alban's, Holborn, at the request of abp. of Canterbury, 1 Dec. ,,
23rd *Church Congress* at Reading . . 2 Oct. 1883
"Official Year-book of the Church of England" first published . . . . . . ,,
Church School Company formed, 1883; first annual meeting . . . . . 21 Feb. 1884
24th *Church Congress* at Carlisle . . 30 Sept. ,,
Church of England Purity Society, see *White Cross Army* . . . . . . ,,
25th *Church Congress* at Portsmouth . 6 Oct. 1885
Agitation for disestablishment and disendowment preparatory to elections . . . . ,,
Address to the archbishops and bishops from important members of the university of Cambridge advocating church reform . . 30 Nov. ,,
See *Laymen, House of*, which first met . 16 Feb. 1886
Proposed disestablishment of the Church in Wales negatived in the Commons (241-229) . 9 March, ,,
26th *Church Congress* at Wakefield (Church reform discussed) . . . . 5 Oct. ,,
Proposed erection of a Church House for general business, meetings, &c.; committee appointed at Lambeth Palace . . . 18 Oct. ,,
Church Patronage Bill introduced; see *Patronage*, 13 May, ,,
27th *Church Congress* at Wolverhampton began 3 Oct. ,,
Church House Corporation, first annual meeting 21 July, 1888
28th *Church Congress* at Manchester; disputed questions boldly discussed . . 1 Oct. ,,
Declaration and remonstrance of clergy and laity adopted at a large meeting . . 13 Nov. ,,
Bishop of London's fund received 15,500*l*. in 1887; 23,000*l*. in 1888
29th *Church Congress* at Cardiff; position of Welsh church discussed . . . 1 Oct. 1889
"*Churchmen in council*," initiated in Zion College, May, 1889. Large meeting in Westminster town-hall to promote the relief of the church by obtaining for it, from the state, the power of settling its differences in doctrine and ritual in a liberal spirit, by the agency of convocation . 6 Feb. ,,
"*Protestant churchmen's alliance*," lord Grimthorpe president; object to promote the substitution of deprivation for imprisonment; support of the bishops reported; first general meeting 25 Feb. 1890
30th *Church Congress* at Hull . 30 Sept.-3 Oct. ,,
31st *Church Congress* at Rhyl; the bishop of St. Asaph president; the abps. of Canterbury and York present . . . . . 6 Oct. 1891
A declaration of faith in the divine inspiration and truth of the Holy Scriptures, on the testimony of the universal church, independently of human criticism, signed by dean E. M. Goulburn and 37 other eminent clergymen . *Times*, 18 Dec. ,,
32nd *Church Congress* at Folkestone; the abp. of Canterbury president . . . 4-7 Oct. 1892
Secession of a small body of clergy in consequence of the Lincoln judgment; see *Canterbury*, they propose to form a new evangelical sect . Aug. ,,
Meeting at the Mansion-house, London, convened by the bishops of London, Rochester, and St. Albans, to consider the spiritual needs of the metropolis . . . . . 17 Feb. 1893
Protest against the Lincoln judgment signed by 50 selected clergymen . . . 27 Feb. ,,
Great meeting of the bishops, clergy, laymen and churchwardens, in London to consider the (Welsh) Suspensory bill (*which see*), and defence of the National Church (convoked by the archbishop of Canterbury), 13 March; at the Albert hall, after a service in St. Paul's . 16 May, ,,
Many meetings throughout the country opposing the Welsh Suspensory bill . March, April, ,,
33rd *Church Congress* at Birmingham; the bp. of Worcester president, 3 Oct., 1893; (discussions on the proposed bishopric of Birmingham; parish councils bill; church disestablishment; cremation).
Declaration of the archbishops and bishops against the Welsh disestablishment bill . 17 May, 1894
34th *Church Congress* at Exeter, opened, the bishop of Exeter president; discussions on religious instruction, Church reform, &c. . 9-12 Oct. ,,
Letter from Cardinal Vaughan denying the validity of Anglican orders (5 Oct.), much controversy ensues; *Times*, 5 Oct. *et seq.*
The 250th anniversary of the execution of abp. Laud, celebrated at the church of All Hallows, Barking, London, E.C.; an exhibition of relics; addresses by the bp. of Peterborough and others 10 Jan. 1895
35th *Church Congress* at Norwich; the bishop of Norwich president . . . 8-11 Oct. ,,
Since the passing of the education act of 1870, the church has raised for her voluntary schools 13,144,775*l*., reported . . . . April, ,,
Inauguration of the "Church Reform league" at the Church House, Westminster . 27 Nov. ,,
Voluntary contributions in 1894 to support the church, 5,851,986*l*.. reported . . 20 Feb. 1896
Anglican church conference held at Vienna, 3 June, ,,
Anglican orders, see *Pope*, 1896-8.
Mr. Alfred Marriott, of Hopton, Dewsbury, bequeaths 400,000*l*. to the church and its societies; announced . . . . . . 3 Oct. ,,
36th *Church Congress* at Shrewsbury, the bishop of Lichfield president; discussions on church reform, clerical poverty, &c. (see *Clergy*) 6-9 Oct. ,,
37th *Church Congress* at Nottingham, the bishop of Southwell president . . 28 Sept.-1 Oct. 1897
R.C. celebration of the 13th centenary of the landing of St. Augustine at Ebbs Fleet, Ramsgate 12-17 Sept. ,,
"The Conversion of England" in relation to the landing of St. Augustine, a spectacular historical play by the rev. Henry Creswell, resembling the mystery plays (see *Drama*), said to have been first performed at St. Peter's, Vauxhall, in 1885; revived at Canterbury, anonymous actors, including clergy and laity, 17 Nov. 1897, and at the Church House, Westminster . 15 Jan. *et seq.* 1898

Agitation against ritualism, the so-called "Church crisis," the abp. of Canterbury and bps. and convocation censure changes in the worship contary to the Book of Common Prayer, 11 May; letter from the bp. of London to his clergy to the same effect . . . . *Times*, 27 June, 1898
38th *Church Congress* at Bradford; bp. of Ripon president; Churchmen's union founded, 27-30 Sept. ,,
Demonstrations by Mr. Kensit and others against ritualistic practices, in various churches, autumn, ,,
Anti-ritualistic meeting, lord Midleton in the chair, Church-house, Westminster . . . 11 Jan. 1899
See *Ecclesiastical courts*, 1899, and *Manchester*.
Anti-ritualistic meeting (chiefly nonconformists), lord Kinnaird in the chair, at the Albert hall, 31 Jan. ,,
National Protestant Church union present a memorial to the queen against ritualistic practices, 9 Feb. ,,
The use of the revised version of the Bible in church services, authorized . . . 10 Feb. ,,
Anti-ritualistic demonstrations at Liverpool, 31 March, ,,
Centenary of the Church Missionary society at Exeter-hall . . . . . . 10-15 April, ,,
See *English Church Union*, 1899.
Deputation representing over 10,000 laymen, expressing confidence and sympathy in the archbishops and bishops in their efforts to secure due observance of the rules prescribed by the Book of Common Prayer, received at Lambeth palace, 1 May, ,,
The abps. decide, *re* the appeal of the rev. H. Westall, of St. Cuthbert's, London, and the rev. E. Ram, of St. John's, Norwich, that incense and processional lights are prohibited by the ornaments rubric of the Church of England, 31 July, ,,
Lady Wimborne's ladies' anti-ritualistic league founded . . . . July, ,,
39th *Church Congress* at London, the bp. of London president; received at the Guildhall; congress held at the Albert hall, after services at St. Paul's, the Abbey, &c. . . . . . . 10-14 Oct. ,,
Protest signed by 13,794 lay members presented to the abp. of Canterbury by the duke of Newcastle, lord E. Churchill, and Mr. R. W. Burnie, against opinion of the 2 abps. regarding incense and processional lights; the abp. affirmed that he based his action entirely on the Book of Common Prayer, 19 Jan. 1900; reservation of the Sacrament pronounced unlawful by both abps. . 1 May, 1900
Davey *v.* Hinde: in the consistory court at Lewes, Dr. Tristram, chancellor, granted the petitioner an order for the removal of certain ornaments from the church of the Annunciation at Brighton, within 3 months . . . . 21 Aug. ,,
40th *Church Congress* at Newcastle-on-Tyne; very successful; the bp. of Newcastle, president; progress of the church, its policy in elementary education, and its autonomy, &c., discussed 25-28 Sept. ,,
Fulham round-table conference on "The doctrine of the Holy Communion, and its expression in ritual," 11-13 Oct.; see *Times* . . 27 Nov. ,,
The abps. and bps. appeal to the clergy for loyalty and obedience, *Times* . . . . . 21 Jan. 1901
41st *Church Congress* at Brighton . . 1-4 Oct. ,,
A "Petition of Right," against the appointment of canon Gore as bp. of Worcester, by the Church assoc. and the Nat. Protestant league . 28 Nov. ,,
King *v.* the abp. of Canterbury and the vicar-gen.: the lord chief justice and justices Wright and Ridley held that under act 25 Henry VIII. c. 20, the abp. or vicar-gen. could not question the fitness of a person nominated to a bishopric by the *crown;* the rules for a *mandamus* to the abp. of Canterbury and the vicar-gen. directing them to hear objections to the confirmation of canon Gore as bp. of Worcester were accordingly discharged . . . . 10 Feb. 1902
Death of rev. Wm. ("Father") Dolling, devoted high churchman . . . . . 15 May, ,,
Education bill (see under *Education*) excites much controversy; vigorous opposition to it by nonconformists; introduced . . . 24 May, ,,
42nd *Church Congress* held at Northampton, 7-11 Oct. ,,
Education bill received royal assent . . . 8 Dec. ,,
Death of Dr. Temple, abp. of Canterbury, aged 81, 22 Dec. 1902
Omission of "damnatory clauses" by dean and chapter of Westminster in cathedral services excites much discussion (see *Times*, 28 Jan.), Jan. 1903
Bp. of Stepney (Dr. Lang) delivers an address at Sion college on "The dangers of clericalism," 27 Jan. ,,
Official statement of the bp. of London regarding "reservation" published in *London Diocesan Magazine* . . . . 1 Feb. ,,
The rev. H. Myddleton Evans, vicar of St. Michael's, Shoreditch, against whom the bp. of London had decided to proceed under the Church Discipline act, 1840, resigns his benefice, 1 Feb. ,,
Dr. Randall Davidson, late bp. of Winchester, enthroned abp. at Canterbury . . 12 Feb. ,,
Death of Dr. Lyttleton, bp. suffr. of Southampton, 19 Feb. ,,
Deputation of unionist M.P.s to abps. at Lambeth, to call attention to lack of discipline and novel practices in church services; important speech by abp. of Canterbury . . . . 11 March, ,,
Death of Dr. Bradley, ex-dean of Westminster (dean 21 years) . . . . 13 March, ,,
Church Discipline bill No. 1, "the Liverpool bill," to compel observance of rubrics and abolish bishops' veto, passed second reading (house of commons), 190 to 139 . . . . 13 March, ,,
Death of Dr. Farrar, dean of Canterbury, aged 71, 22 March, ,,
Announcement made of proposed celebration of the Holy Communion on 6 May at St. Paul's cathedral in commemoration of those members of the guilds of the Holy Standard and St. Helena who died in the S. African war, 9 April, ,,
Death of prebendary Kitto, prominent evangelical, 13 April, ,,
Letter from lady Wimborne, president of the Ladies' Anti-Ritualistic league, to *Times*, protesting that the proposed service is a revival of the Roman use of prayers for the dead, and that prayers for the souls of the departed have been discontinued in the English church for 350 years, 17 April, ,,
Bp. Taylor Smith, chaplain-gen. to the forces, withdraws his membership of the guild as a protest against the proposed service, which is subsequently abandoned . . . . . April, ,,
Convocation of Canterbury opened. Upper house passes resolutions on church reform; lower house agrees to appoint a committee on the relation of the Church of England with other churches. House of laymen approved Church Discipline bill No. 2 . . . . 12 May, ,,
Convocation of York opened. House of laymen adopted resolution deploring the lack of discipline in the church, and urging that further powers be given to the bishops . . 13 May, ,,
Declaration drawn up by committee of high church clergy (Rev. Russell Wakefield, chairman), embodying statements of belief in regard to the obligations imposed on the clergy under the 36th canon; the authority of the ceremonial system provided by the first prayer-book of Edward VI., and the desirability of a complete restoration of the synodical action of the church, pending that, of obedience to the bishops, May, ,,
Remarriage of a divorced person at St. Mark's, North Audley-street, the subject of controversy between the bp. of London, the vicar of St. Mark's, and Dr. Tristram, chancellor of the diocese. Opinion of Mr. Dibden, new dean of Arches, in response to request of archbp. of Canterbury, published, *Times*. . . . 30 May, ,,
Convocations of Canterbury and York hold joint meetings and pass resolutions on the formation of a National Church council, and on the qualifications of electors for lay representatives, 10 July ,,
Abps. receive deputation representing the signatories to the clerical declaration on ritual: speech by the archbp. of Canterbury on the ornaments rubric, the authority of the privy council, and synodical action . . . . 11 July, ,,
Dr. Moorhouse, bp. of Manchester, intimates the resignation of his see at the end of October, late July, ,,
Death of Dr. Webber, bp. of Brisbane . 3 Aug. ,,

Death of canon Overton, eminent ecclesiastical historian . . . . . . Sept. 1903
43rd *Church Congress* held at Bristol . 13–16 Oct. ,,

See *Canterbury; Public Worship Regulation Act; Trials.*

CHURCH OF FRANCE. St. Pothinus is said to have preached Christianity to the Gauls about 160; became bishop of Lyons, and suffered martyrdom with others, 177. For the reformed church see *Huguenots* and *Protestants.*

A mission of seven bishops arrived in 245; followed by severe persecution 286-288
Christianity tolerated by Constantius Chlorus . 292
Council of Arles convoked by Constantine, about 600 bishops present; the Donatists condemned . 314
Christianity established by Clovis 496
Pragmatic sanction of St. Louis restraining the impositions of the pope; and restoring the right of electing bishops, &c. 1269
Pragmatic sanction of Bourges, declaring a general council superior to the pope, and prohibiting appeals to him 1438
Concordat of Leo X. and Francis I. annulling the pragmatic sanction . . . . . 18 Aug. 1516
Disputes between the Jesuits and Jansenists . 1640
Declaration of the clergy (drawn up by Bossuet) in accordance with the pragmatic sanctions, confirmed by the king . . . . . 23 March, 1682
The Jansenists excommunicated by the Bull Unigenitus 1713
Concordat with Pius VII. and Napoleon 1801 and 1813
The principles of the concordat of Leo X. restored by Pius VII. and Louis XVIII. 1827
The archbishop of Paris and other prelates resist dogma of papal infallibility at the council at Rome 1870
The clergy at first supported Napoleon III.; but opposed his Italian policy, 1852-70; energetically support MacMahon's ministry, in elections, Sept., Oct. 1877
18 archbishops, 77 bishops . . . . . . ,,
The abbé Bougaud asserts that there are 2658 parishes without priests, and 3000 parishes without churches 1878
Jesuits and other orders in France dissolved by decree . . . . 29 March, 1880
Many members af the Carthusian order, refusing to seek authorisation to remain in their monasteries, are expelled during 1880
Association law against unauthorised religious communities and tutelage promulgated, 1 July, 1901
Abrogation of the Falloix law, guaranteeing liberty of instruction, voted . . . 14 Feb. 1902
Action of government in closing schools for infringement of the association law approved by large majority of the chamber . . . 4 July, ,,
Protest of bishops and clergy against closing conventual schools; much excitement and hostile demonstrations . . . . end July, ,,
Bishops ordered by minister of interior and public worship to renounce the employment of Marists and Lazarists . . . . 3 Oct. ,,
Resolution carried supporting the government in closing conventual schools . . . . 17 Oct. ,,
Committee appointed by chamber to consider the question of the separation of church and state, 20 Oct. ,,
Seventy-four bishops petition government in favour of the religious orders; declared illegal, 28 Nov. ,,
Act of government in respect to their treatment of religious orders supported by large majority, 15 Jan. 1903
Dispute with Pope concerning appointment to vacant bishoprics . . . . Feb. ,,
Motion for suppression of budget of public worship rejected . . . . 21 March, ,,
Several bishops and various religious associations resist the measures of the government; the stipends of some of the clergy suspended; expulsion of orders . . . . 29 April, ,,
Anti-clerical demonstrations . . . . 17 May, ,,
Motion for the separation of church and state rejected by 278 to 247; policy of the government in their action toward the clergy approved, 313 to 237 . . . . 20 May, ,,

CHURCH OF ENGLAND TEMPERANCE SOCIETY. See *Temperance Societies.*

CHURCH OF IRELAND, founded by St. Patrick in the 5th century; accepted the Reformation about 1550; united with that of England as the United Church of England and Ireland in 1800; see *Bishops Ireland,* 1868, and *Armagh.*

"An act to put an end to the establishment of the church of Ireland," introduced into the house of commons by Mr. Gladstone, 1 Mar.; vote for second reading, 368; against 250; 2 A.M., 24 March; for third reading, 361; against, 247; 31 May, 1869
Introduced into the house of lords by earl Granville, 1 June; read third time, 12 July; some amendments by the lords accepted, others rejected; received royal assent [*to come into effect,* 1 Jan. 1871] . . . . 26 July, ,,
Address of bishops to the clergy and laity dated, 18 Aug. ,,
Meeting of the general synod of the Irish church in St. Patrick's cathedral, Dublin, for re-organization of the general council . . 14 Sept. ,,
Conference of the laity; duke of Abercorn chairman . . . . 13 Oct. ,,
Church of Ireland disestablished . . . 1 Jan. 1871
A *sustentation fund* established (well supported) ,,
First elected bishop (Dr. Maurice Day, bishop of Cashel) consecrated at St. Patrick's, Dublin, 14 April, 1872
The new ecclesiastical court meets; tries a case of ritual practices . . . . . . 26 June ,,
The Irish Church Act amended . . . June, ,,
Received for the sustentation fund, 33,573*l.* up to 31 Dec. ,,
The first bishop elected by clergy and laity of Kilmore, &c., archdeacon Darley (12 candidates), 23 Sept. 1874
Alleged migration of clergy to England . Autumn ,,
Warm discussion upon the revision of the liturgy, May, 1875

CHURCH OF NORTH AMERICA was established in Nov. 1784, when bishop Seabury, chosen by the churches in Connecticut, was consecrated in Scotland. The first convention was held at Philadelphia in 1785. On 4 Feb. 1787, bishops Provost and White were consecrated at Lambeth. The centenary was celebrated at Lambeth, 4 Feb. 1887. Two American bishops, Lyman and Potter, were present. In 1851 there were 37 bishops; in 1903 there were, in the United States, 58 dioceses, 82 bishops, 27 missionary bishops, and 4,776 priests and deacons, see *Pan-Anglican Synod.*

After much discussion, for several years, the church convention passed a stringent canon against ritualism, 27 Oct. 1847.

CHURCH OF SCOTLAND, see *Bishops in Scotland.* On the abolition of Episcopacy, in 1638, Presbyterianism became the established religion. Its formulary of faith, said to have been compiled by John Knox, in 1560, was approved by the parliament and ratified in 1567, finally settled by an act of the Scottish senate in 1696, and secured by the treaty of union with England in 1707; see *Discipline, Patronage,* and *Bishops.* The church is regulated by four courts—the general assembly, the synod, the presbytery, and kirk sessions; see *Presbyterians.* For important secessions, see *Burghers* (1732), and *Free Church* (1843).

The first general assembly of the church was held 20 Dec. 1560.

The general assembly constitutes the highest ecclesiastical court in the kingdom; it meets annually in Edinburgh in May, and sits about ten days. It consists of a grand commissioner, appointed by the sovereign, and delegates from presbyteries, royal boroughs, and universities, some being laymen. To this court all appeals from the inferior ecclesiastical courts lie, and its decision is final.

Patronage was abolished after 1 Jan. 1875, by act passed 7 Aug. 1874.

Prosecution of Rev. Wm. L. M'Farlan of Lenzie for heresy in "Scotch Sermons" (published 1880) by the Presbytery of Glasgow, Oct. 1880. Mr. Hastie, principal of the Church (Calcutta) Institution, 1878; dismissed for bad temper, &c., Nov. 1883; his appeal to the General Assembly, dismissed (193–90), 29 May, 1884.

Mr. Finlay's Bill for Promoting re-union of Presbyterian churches negatived by the Commons (202–177) 17 March, 1866.

Dr. Cameron's resolution for disestablishment negatived in the Commons, 30 March, 1886; (260–208) 22 June, 1888; (256–218) 2 May, 1890; (265–209) 24 May, 1892; his bill read, 1st time, 1893, 1895.

"Basis of Union" between the Church, the United Presbyterians, the Free Church, and some others, reported . . . . June, 1898

The Free and United Presbyterian churches of Scotland united as one under the title of the United Free Church of Scotland, by act adopted in Edinburgh (see *Glasgow*, Jan. 1903) . 31 Oct. 1900

Lord Mount-Stephens gives 40,000*l.* to increase the incomes of over 20 ministers in Aberdeenshire and Banffshire, July, 1901; Mrs. Elizabeth Carnegie bequeathed 38,000*l.* to various church schemes . . . . 8 July, 1902

CHURCH HOUSE. A corporation was established to commemorate the queen's jubilee of 1887, by the erection of a building in London for the general use of the clergy of England. The two houses of convocation meet in the Church House.

Charter obtained 23 Feb. 1888; on 7 July, 1888, 65,853*l.* had been subscribed, by means of which a site, with useful buildings, in Dean's Yard, Westminster, was purchased. A meeting was held on 21 July, 1888; the 1st general meeting of the corporation on their own premises was held on 26 June, 1890, the archbishop of Canterbury being in the chair. At a meeting at Norwich, 1 Feb. 1890, it was reported that 70,000*l.* had been subscribed.

The foundation stone of the great hall laid by the duke of Connaught, 24 June, 1891 (architect, sir Arthur Blomfield); opened by the duke of York, in the presence of the two archbishops and others . . . . 11 Feb. 1896

Henry Hoare Memorial hall (house of laymen) open; other buildings progressing 1903

CHURCH LADS' BRIGADE, a movement to influence the elder boys of a parish by combining systematic religious teaching with physical exercise based on military drill. Founded 1891. Income, 1902, 906*l.*, for general support of the work.

CHURCHMEN'S UNION, a broad church movement originated at the Bradford Church congress 1898. It has for its objects the restatement of belief in the light of scientific and biblical criticism, the spirit of tolerance in non-essentials, the rights of the laity, and the promotion of friendly relations with other Christian communities.

CHURCH MISSIONARY SOCIETY, founded 1799. Income, 1876, 195,116*l.*; 1887, 237,639*l.*; 1890, 260,282*l.*; 1902, 342,619*l.* Annual meetings are held. Mr. Eugene Stock's "History," 3 vols., pub. 1899; "Centenary vol.," pub. 1902.

CHURCH PASTORAL AID SOCIETY (Evangelical), instituted in 1836 to maintain curates and lay-agents in densely populated districts. Annual meetings are held. Income utilized 1902, 118,766*l* amongst 1006 workers.

CHURCH PATRONAGE, see *Patronage*.

CHURCH-RATES. The maintaining the church in repair belongs to the parishioners, who have the sole power of taxing themselves for the expense when assembled in vestry. The enforcement of payment, which is continually disputed by dissenters and others, belonged to the ecclesiastical courts. Many attempts were made to abolish church-rates before Mr. Gladstone's "Compulsory Church-rate Abolition" Bill, passed 31 July, 1868.

Church Rate Abolition for Scotland repealed in the Commons (204–143) . . . . . 11 July, 1877

CHURCH REFORM LEAGUE, for separation of Church and State, began at St. Alban's schools, Holborn, London, Rev. A. H. Mackonochie, president; 1876-7. Meeting at the Church House, Westminster, over 1,000 clergymen and about 1,000 laymen present, 18 Jan. 1899; another, 27 Feb. 1903.

CHURCH SERVICES were ordered by pope Vitelianus to be read in Latin, 663; by queen Elizabeth in 1558 to be read in English.

CHURCH-WARDENS, officers of the church, appointed by the first canon of the synod of London, in 1127. Overseers in every parish were also appointed by the same body, and they continue now nearly as then constituted. *Johnson's Canons.* Church-wardens, by the canon of 1603, are to be chosen annually, and are elected at the Easter vestry.

CHURCHING OF WOMEN is the act of returning thanks in the church by women after child-birth. It began about 214. *Wheatley;* see *Purification.*

CHURCHYARDS, are by common law the freehold of the rector of the parish, who has power to prohibit the erection of monuments, &c. See *Consecration* and *Burials.*

CHUSAN, a Chinese isle; see *China*, 1840-1, 1860.

CIBORIUM, in early Christian times, was a protection to the altar-table, first a tabernacle, and afterwards a baldachin over the altar, and also a canopy used at solemn processions. Ciborium also means the vessel in which the eucharist is received.

CIDER (*Zider*, German), when first made in England, was called wine, about 1284. The earl of Manchester, when ambassador in France, is said to have passed off cider for wine. It was subjected to the excise in 1763, *et seq.* The duty was taken off in 1830. Many orchards were planted in Herefordshire by lord Scudamore, ambassador from Charles I. to France. John Philips published his poem "Cider" in 1706. The National association of Cidermakers founded, in London, Oct. 1894. "Cider," a monthly periodical, appeared in 1895. Great increase of manufacture of cider in France, through failures of the grape crops; reported 1896.

CIGAR SHIP, see under *Steam*, 1866.

CIGARS, see *Tobacco.*

CILICIA, in Asia Minor, partook of the fortunes of that country. It became a Roman province about 64 B.C., and was conquered by the Turks, A.D. 1387.

CIMBRI, a Teutonic race from Jutland, invaded the Roman empire about 120 B.C. They defeated the Romans under Cneius Papirius Carbo, 113 B.C.; the consul Junius Silanus, 109; the consul Cassius Longinus (who was killed) near the lake of Geneva, 107; and the united armies of the consul Cn. Mallius and the proconsul Servilius Caepio near the Rhone, 105. Their allies, the Teutones, were defeated by Marius in two battles at Aquæ Sextiæ (Aix) in Gaul; 200,000 were killed, and 70,000 made prisoners, 102 B.C. The Cimbri were defeated by Marius and Catulus, at Campus Raudius, when about to enter Italy; 120,000 were killed, and 60,000 taken prisoners,

101 B.C. They were afterwards absorbed into the Teutones or Saxons.

CIMENTO (Italian, *experiment*). The "Accademia del Cimento," at Florence, held its first meeting for making scientific experiments, 18 June, 1657. It was patronised by Ferdinand, grand duke of Tuscany. The Royal Society of London was founded in 1660, and the Academy of Sciences at Paris in 1666. The *Nuovo Cimento*, a scientific periodical, published at Pisa, began in 1855.

CINCHONA, or CHINCHONA, see *Jesuits' Bark*.

CINCINNATI. A society established by officers of the American army soon after the peace of 1783, "to perpetuate friendship, and to raise a fund for relieving the widows and orphans of those who had fallen during the war." On the badge was a figure of Cincinnatus as symbolising Washington and other patriots who had left their rural affairs to fight for their country. The people dreaded military influence, and the society dissolved itself.

CINCINNATI, the chief city of the state of Ohio, North America, founded 1789. This flourishing city desolated by an inundation caused by the rising of the river Ohio, 13 Feb. 1883. Several lives were lost, and about 50,000 rendered homeless. Ample relief afforded. About 50 persons killed and 150 wounded in an attack on the gaol to execute murderers (especially Wm. Berner); new court-house burnt, 28-30 March, 1884; one regiment refused to march. Ten persons killed by a tramway accident, 15 Oct. 1889. Population in 1880, 255,139; in 1890, 296,908; 1900, 405,000.

CINEMATOGRAPH, see *Kinematograph* and *Kinetoscope*, March, 1896, and *Vivograph Pictures*.

CINNAMON, a species of laurel, is mentioned among the perfumes of the sanctuary (*Exodus* xxx. 23) 1491 B.C. It was found in the American forests by don Ulloa, 1736, was cultivated in Jamaica and Dominica 1788, and is now grown in Ceylon.

CINQUE-CENTO (five hundred); *ter cento*, &c.; see note to article *Italy*.

CINQUE PORTS, on the south coast of England, were originally *five* (hence the name)—Dover, Hastings, Hythe, Romney, and Sandwich; Winchelsea and Rye were afterwards added. *Jeake*. Their jurisdiction was vested in barons, called wardens. These ports, instituted by Saxon monarchs, were constituted by William I. and succeeding kings, who required them to supply ships to defend the coast. Nearly all the harbours, except Dover, have been destroyed by the action of the sea. The latest lord-wardens: the duke of Wellington, 1828-52; the marquis of Dalhousie, 1852-60; lord Palmerston, 1861-65; earl Granville, appointed Dec. 1865, died 31 March, 1891; W. H. Smith, May, died 6 Oct.; the marquis of Dufferin and Ava, about 4 Nov. 1891; resigned; the marquis of Salisbury, Oct. 1895; died 22 Aug. 1903. Their peculiar jurisdiction was abolished in 1855.

CINTRA (Portugal). Here was signed an agreement on 22 Aug. 1808, between the French and English the day after the battle of Vimeira. As it contained the basis of the convention signed on 30 Aug. following, it has been termed the convention of Cintra. By it Junot and his army were permitted to evacuate Portugal free, in British ships. The convention was publicly condemned, and a court of inquiry was held at Chelsea, which exonerated the British commanders. Both Wellington and Napoleon justified sir Hew Dalrymple.

CIPHER, a secret manner of writing. Julius Cæsar and Augustus when writing secret despatches are said to have employed the second or third letter instead of the first, and the same sequence with regard to the others. This cipher was in use till the reign of Sixtus IV. (1471-84), when the secret was divulged by Leon Battista Alberti, and a new sort of cipher sprang up. The father of Venetian cipher was Zuan Soro, who flourished about 1516. *Rawdon Brown*. Cipher telegrams, see *Transvaal*, 29 April, 1896.—See *Cryptograph*.

CIRCASSIA (Asia, on N. side of the Caucasus). The Circassians, said to be descended from the Albanians, were unsubdued, even by Timour. In the 16th century they acknowledged the authority of the czar Ivan II. of Russia, and about 1745, the princes of Kabarda took oaths of fealty. Many Circassians became Mahometans in the 18th century.

Circassia surrendered to Russia by Turkey by the treaty of Adrianople (but the Circassians, under Schamyl, long resist) . . . 14 Sept. 1829
Victories of Orbelliani over them, June, Nov., Dec. 1857
He subdues much country, and expels the inhabitants . . . . . . April, 1858
Schamyl, the great Circassian leader, captured, and treated with much respect . . . 7 Sept. 1859
About 20,000 Circassians emigrate to Constantinople, suffer much distress, and are relieved, 28 April, 1860
Vaidar, the last of the Circassian strongholds, captured, and the grand duke Michael declares the war at an end . . . . 8 June, 1864
Many thousand Circassians emigrate into Turkey; partially relieved by the sultan's government, June, *et seq.* „
Schamyl and his son at the marriage of the czarowitch, 9 Nov. 1866; he dies . . . March, 1871
Revolt against Russia; suppressed. Many Circassians flee to Turkey and join the army, July, Aug. 1877

CIRCENSIAN GAMES were combats in the Roman circus (at first in honour of Consus, the god of councils, but afterwards of Jupiter, Neptune, Juno, and Minerva), said to have been instituted by Evander, and established at Rome, 732 B.C. by Romulus. Tarquin named them Circensian; their celebration continued from 4 to 12 Sept.

CIRCLE. The quadrature, or ratio of the diameter of the circle to its circumference, has exercised the ingenuity of mathematicians of all ages. Archimedes, about 221 B.C., gave it as 7 to 22; Abraham Sharp (1717) as 1 to 3 and 72 decimals; and Lagny (1719) as 1 to 3 and 122 decimals.

CIRCLES OF GERMANY (formed by Maximilian I. about 1500, to distinguish the members of the diet of the empire) were, in 1512, Franconia, Bavaria, Upper Rhine, Suabia, Westphalia, and Lower Saxony; in 1512, Austria, Burgundy, Lower Rhine, the Palatinate, Upper Saxony and Brandenburg were added. In 1804 these divisions were annulled by the establishment of the Confederation of the Rhine, in 1806 (*which see*).

CIRCUITS IN ENGLAND were divided into three, and three justices were appointed to each, 1176. They were afterwards divided into four, with five justices to each division, 1180. *Rapin*. They have been frequently altered. England and Wales were formerly divided into eight—each travelled in spring and summer for the trial of civil and criminal cases, the larger towns are visited in winter for trials of criminals only; this is called "going the circuit." The circuits were settled by order in council, 5 Feb. 1876. There are monthly sessions for the city of London and county of Middlesex.

The circuit system was much modified by the council of judges, with the object of retaining more judges in London, and economising their labour, 10 June, 1884.

The system was again changed, three circuits being adopted in place of four with a few exceptions; (civil and criminal Feb., July; criminal Oct.) Dec. 1887.

CIRCULAR IRONCLADS. The design is attributed to the Russian admiral Popoff; died March, 1898; one of these, named after himself, was launched at the port of Nicolaieff, 7 Oct. 1875. The admiral stated that he derived the idea from the works and views of Mr. E. J. Reed, late constructor of the British navy, who has expressed his approbation of the admiral's works.

CIRCULATING LIBRARY. Stationers lent books on hire in the middle ages. The public circulating library in England, opened by Samuel Fancourt, a dissenting minister of Salisbury, about 1740, failed; but similar institutions at Bath and in London succeeded, and others were established throughout the kingdom. There was a circulating library at Crane-court, London, in 1748, of which a catalogue in two vols. was published.—No books can be taken from the British Museum except for judicial purposes, but the libraries of the Royal Society and the principal scientific societies, except that of the Royal Institution, London, are circulating.—The London Library (circulating) which was founded 24 June, 1840, is of great value to literary men.—Of the subscription libraries that founded by Chas. E. Mudie, in New Oxford-street, is remarkable for the large quantity and good quality of the books: several hundreds, sometimes thousands, of copies of a new work being in circulation. It began in 1842, and grew into celebrity in Dec. 1848, when the first two volumes of Macaulay's History of England were published, for which there was an unprecedented demand, supplied by this library. The hall was opened in Dec. 1860. Mr. C. E. Mudie died 28 Oct. 1890, aged 72. Other libraries are:—The Grosvenor Gallery Library; W. H. Smith (exchanges made at railway stations); Mitchell's Royal Library; Law Lending Library; Day's Library, and Cawthorn and Hutt's Library. The "Tabard," with numerous exchange depôts, 1903.

CIRCULATION OF THE BLOOD, see *Blood*.

CIRCUMCISION (instituted 1897 B.C.) was the seal of the covenant made by God with Abraham. It was practised by the ancient Egyptians, and is still by the Copts and some oriental nations. The Festival of the Circumcision (of Christ), originally the octave of Christmas, is mentioned about 487. It was introduced from the Roman missal into the first English prayer-book in 1549.

CIRCUMNAVIGATORS. Among the most daring human enterprises at the period when it was first attempted, was the circumnavigation of the earth in 1519-22.

Magellan or Magalhaens, a native of Portugal, in the service of Spain, sailed from San Lucar, 20 Sept. 1519; with three ships passed the Straits named after him, 28 Nov. 1520; he was killed in a conflict on the Philippine Isles, 17 April, 1521: Juan Sebastian del Cano in the *Vittoria*, the only remaining ship of five, reached San Lucar 6 Sept. 1522
Grijalva, Spaniard 1537
Alvaradi, Spaniard . . . . ,,
Mendana, Spaniard 1567
Sir Francis Drake, first English 1577-80
Cavendish, first voyage 1586-88
Le Maire, Dutch 1615-17
Cuiros, Spaniard 1625
Tasman, Dutch 1642
Cowley, British 1683
Dampier, English 1689
Cooke, English 1708
Clipperton, British 1719
Roggewein, Dutch 1721-23
Anson (*afterwards* lord) 1740-44
Byron, English 1764-66
Wallis, British 1766-68
Carteret, English 1766-69
Bougainville, French 1766-9
James Cook 1768-71
On his death the voyage was continued by King . 1779
Portlocke, British 1788
King and Fitzroy, British 1826-36
Belcher, British 1836-42
Wilkes, American 1838-42
The steamer *Ionic* sailed from New Zealand to Plymouth and back in 86 days. . . 24 Aug. 1883
Arawa sailed from Plymouth to New Zealand and back in 73 days, 5h. 4m. . 28 March-12 July, 1885
Lady Brassey published "Voyage in the *Sunbeam*" (yacht) in 1876, 1878; she died at sea . Sept. 1887
The *Sunbeam*, after voyage of 36,000 miles, arrived at Portsmouth . . . . . . 14 Dec. ,,

See *North East and West Passage* and *Deep Sea Soundings*.

CIRCUS (Greek, Hippodrome). There were eight (some say ten) buildings of this kind at Rome; the largest the *Circus Maximus*, was built by the elder Tarquin, 605 B.C. It was an oval figure: length three stadia and a half, or more than three English furlongs; breadth 960 Roman feet. It was enlarged by Julius Cæsar so as to seat 150,000 persons, and was rebuilt by Augustus. Julius Cæsar introduced into it large canals of water, which could be quickly covered with vessels, and represent a sea fight. *Pliny*; see *Amphitheatres*, *Factions* and *Hippodrome*.

CIRRHA, a town of Phocis (N. Greece), for sacrilege, razed to the ground in the Sacred War, 586 B.C.

CISALPINE REPUBLIC, including the territories of Milan, Mantua, Modena, Bergamo, Ferrara, Bologna, Ravenna, &c. (N. Italy), formed by the French in May, 1797, from the *Cispadane* and *Transpadane* republics, acknowledged by the emperor of Germany by the treaty of Campo Formio (*which see*), 17 Oct. following. It received a new constitution in Sept. 1798; was remodelled, and named the Italian republic, with Napoleon Bonaparte president, 1802; and merged into the kingdom of Italy in March, 1805; see *Italy*.

CISPADANE REPUBLIC, with the Transpadane republic, merged into the Cisalpine republic, Oct. 1797.

CISTERCIANS (the order of Citeaux), a powerful order of monks founded about 1098 by Robert, a Benedictine, abbot of Molesme, named from Citeaux, in France, the site of the first convent, near the end of the 11th century. The monks observed silence, abstained from flesh, lay on straw, and wore neither shoes nor shirts. They were reformed by St. Bernard; see *Bernardines*. The Feuillants, and the nuns of Port Royal, the Recollets (reformed Cistercians), and the monks of La Trappe, emanated from this order. Their earliest establishment in England (1128) was Waverley Abbey, Farnham.

CITATE. The Russian general Gortschakoff, intending to storm Kalafat, threw up redoubts at Citate, close to the Danube, which were stormed by the Turks under Omer Pacha, 6 Jan. 1854. The fighting continued on the 7th, 8th and 9th, when the Russians were compelled to retire to their former position at Krajowa, having lost 1500 killed and 2000 wounded. The loss of the Turks was estimated at 338 killed and 700 wounded.

CITIZEN. It was not lawful to scourge a citizen of Rome. *Livy.* In England a citizen is a person who is free of a city, or who doth carry on a trade therein. *Camden.* Various privileges have been conferred on citizens as freemen in several reigns.—The wives of citizens of London (not being aldermen's wives, nor gentlewomen by descent) were obliged to wear minever caps, being white woollen knit three-cornered, with the peaks projecting three or four inches beyond their foreheads; aldermen's wives made them of velvet, 1 Eliz. 1558. *Stow.*—On 10 Oct. 1792, the convention decreed that "citoyen" and "citoyenne" should be the only titles in France.

CITY. (Latin *civitas*, French *cité*, Italian *città*.) Originally signified a state. Cities were incorporated in Spain, France, and England in the 11th and 12th centuries. A city has been usually, but not always, the seat of a bishop. Truro and St. Albans were made cities in 1877, Newcastle in 1882, and Liverpool in 1883, having become bishoprics. Birmingham was made a city, Jan. 1889.

CITY AND GUILDS OF LONDON INSTITUTE (see *Education*, 1878-81). Foundation stone of Central Institution, South Kensington, laid by the prince of Wales, the president, 18 July, 1881.

CITY'S CASH. The City have published a tabulated statement of the receipts and payments of that portion of their property known as "the City's Cash" during the years 1893–1902. The receipts in that time amounted to 7,621,890*l.*—viz., in 1893, 711,428*l.*; in 1894, 718,722*l.*; 1895, 509,545*l.*; 1896, 733,123*l.*; 1897, 1,010,835*l.*; 1898, 1,508,614*l.*; 1899, 436,408*l.*; 1900, 464,396*l.*; 1901, 611,636*l.*; and 1902, 917,478*l.* The principal totals in the decade were the following:—rents, 1,838,470*l.*; interest, 50,893*l.*; markets, 1,859,645*l.*; corn and fruit dues, 6,197*l.*; mayor's court fees, 66,719*l.*; betting penalties, 1,807*l.*; justiciary fees, 23,467*l.*; and loans raised for markets, &c., 3,563,954*l.* The payments in the same period were as follows:—1894, 717,629*l.*; 1895, 729,355*l.*; 1896, 499,753*l.*; 1897, 740,539*l.*; 1898, 1,004,048*l.*; 1899, 422,677*l.*; 1900, 489,859*l.*; 1901, 625,006*l.*, and 1902, 955,938*l.*, making a total for the ten years of 7,716,510*l.* Among the chief items of expenditure were:—income-tax, 118,050*l.*; charges on markets, 1,532,016*l.*; expenses of the magistracy, 111,436*l.*; City police, 356,781*l.*; administration of justice, 82,072*l.*; allowances to ten lord mayors, 101,000*l.*; expenses of the Mansion-house, 74,941*l.*; salaries to officers, 327,267*l.*; charitable donations and pensions, 197,185*l.*; donations for public and other purposes, 43,000*l.*; technical education, 3,900*l.*; receptions of royal and illustrious guests, &c., 21,000*l.*; celebration of coronation, 27,680*l.*; celebration of Queen Victoria's diamond jubilee, 9,786*l.*

CITY CHURCH PROTECTION SOCIETY, founded to preserve old churches, 1879.

CITY GUILDS REFORM ASSOCIATION held fifth annual meeting, 2 Sept. 1880. It had recommended the appointment of the royal commission of inquiry of 1880.

CITY LIBRARY AND MUSEUM, see *Guildhall.*

CITY OF GLASGOW BANK, see under *Banks.*

CITY OF LONDON COLLEGE (for young men) established 1861; began in 1848 as Metropolitan Evening Classes.

CITY OF LONDON COURT, the name given to the Sheriffs' Court (established 1517) by the County Courts act of Aug. 1867.

CITY OF LONDON SCHOOL, established by parliament in 1834 (based on an endowment by John Carpenter in 1442) was opened first in Honey-lane. The foundation of the new buildings on the Victoria Embankment laid 14 Oct. 1880; opened, 1883.

CITY OF PARIS, Atlantic steamer, see *Wrecks*, March, 1890.

CITY OF REFUGE, the name given to each of the six cities of Canaan set apart by the Mosaic law as places of refuge to which the person who had committed unintentional homicide might flee (see Num. xxxv., Deut. xix., Josh. xx.). If the elders of the city recognised the manslayers' claim for asylum, he was secure from the avenger, until his right to protection was judicially decided. The cities of refuge on the west side of Jordan were Hebron, Shechem, and Kedesh; on the east Golan, Ramoth-Gilead, and Bezer.

CITY ROAD, from London to Islington, was projected by Mr. Dingler, and cut out about 1760.

CIUDAD RODRIGO, a strong fortified town in Spain invested by the French, 11 June, 1810, and surrendered to them 10 July. It remained in their possession until it was stormed by the British, under Wellington, 19 Jan. 1812.

CIVIL CLUB (at the New Corn Exchange Tavern, Mark-lane), was established 19 Nov. 1669, for the purpose of promoting fellowship, mutual assistance, and the revival of trade after the interruption to business in consequence of the fire, Sept. 1666.

Only one person of the same trade or profession can be a member of this club, and the members pledge themselves to give "preference to each other in their respective callings." The club meets monthly, and the members dine together four times a year. Its officials are a treasurer, stewards, auditors, a secretary (all merchants of London), and a chaplain.

CIVIL ENGINEERS, see *Engineers.*

CIVIL LAW. See *Codes.* Civil law was restored in Italy, Germany, &c., 1127. *Blair.* It was introduced into England by Theobald, a Norman abbot, afterwards archbishop of Canterbury, in 1138. It is now used in the spiritual courts only, and in maritime affairs; see *Doctors' Commons*, and *Laws.*

CIVIL LIST. This now comprehends the revenue awarded to the kings of England in lieu of their ancient hereditary income. The entire revenue of Elizabeth was not more than 600,000*l.*, and that of Charles I. was about 800,000*l.* After the revolution a civil list revenue was settled on the new king and queen of 700,000*l.* (in 1660), the parliament taking into its own hands the support of the forces both maritime and military. The civil list of George II. was increased to 800,000*l.*; and that of George III., in the 55th year of his reign, was 1,030,000*l.*

In 1831, the civil list of the sovereign was fixed at 510,000*l.*, and in December, 1837, the civil list of the queen was fixed at 385,000*l.*

Prince Albert obtained an exclusive sum from parliament of 30,000*l. per ann.* . . . 7 Feb. 1840
Sir H. Parnell's motion for inquiry into the civil list led to the resignation of the Wellington administration . . . . . 15 Nov. 1830
A select committee was appointed by the house of commons for the purpose . . . . 2 Feb. 1860
See *Crown Lands.*
A select committee appointed to consider the provision to be made for the king and the royal family, 11 March, 1901; the civil list of the king fixed at 470,000*l.*; total, with annuities and pensions for members of the royal family, 543,000*l.* 9 May; act passed . . . . . 25 June, 1901

CIVIL PROCEDURE ACTS, 42 & 43 Vict. c. 59, passed 15 Aug. 1879 (it abolishes outlawry in civil proceedings); and 44 & 45 Vict. c. 59, passed 27 Aug. 1881.

CIVIL SERVICE. Nearly 17,000 persons were employed in this service under the direction of the treasury, and the home, foreign, colonial, post, and revenue offices, &c. In 1855, a commission reported most unfavourably on the existing system of appointments, and on 21 May commissioners were appointed to examine into the qualifications of the candidates, who report annually. By an order of council, 4 June, 1870, the system of competitive examination was made general after 1 Oct. 1870. The civil service superannuation act passed in April, 1859. Civil service for the year (ending 31 March)—

Year.	*Cost.*	*Year.*	*Cost.*
1855	£7,735,515	1891–2	£17,060,875
1865	10,205,413	1892–3 (estimate)	17,310,920
1867	10,523,019	1893–4	18,129,929
1871	13,176,659	1894–5	20,021,785
1877 (estimate)	15,779,779	1895–6	19,297,744
1880	15,155,522	1896–7	19,795,040
1881	15,432,442	1897–8	20,167,968
1883–4	17,253,004	1898–9	21,792,646
1884–5	17,243,254	1899–1900	22,179,665
1885–6	17,678,149	1900–1	22,846,308
1886–7	18,008,691	1901–2 (net)	23,637,620
1888–9	18,037,730	1902–3	26,443,145
1889–90	15,739,092	1903–4	20,205,000
1890–1	15,660,959		

A select committee to inquire into this expenditure issued its report, June, 1874. Important changes made, by order in council, 12 Feb. 1875. See *Public Departments Commission.* Further changes in the lower, now named *second* division; salaries limited, to be from 70*l.* to 250*l.* a year, 4 Feb. 1890. The fourth and last report of the Royal Commission on Civil Establishments, dated 30 July, issued 28 Aug. 1890. Parliamentary return, issued Jan. 1903, shows that the total number of persons employed in the civil service on 31 March, 1902, was 107,782, including 77,035 employed in the postal service, and 8,869 in the Admiralty.

CIVIL WARS, see *England, France, United States, Chili,* &c.

CIVILISATION. The opinion that the civilisation of mankind was gradually developed from a low savage state is advocated by sir John Lubbock in his "Origin of Civilisation," 1870, and by Mr. Edward B. Tylor in his "Primitive Culture," 1871.

CLAIM OF RIGHT. A document agreed to by the Scottish Convention parliament at Edinburgh asserting the constitutional liberties of the kingdom, accepted by King William III. and Queen Mary II. at Whitehall, 11 May, 1689.

CLAIMANT, The. See *Trials,* 1871-4; see *France,* 1874.

CLAIRVOYANCE, see *Hypnotism* and *Mesmerism.*

CLAMEURS, see *Haro.*

CLANS are said to have arisen in Scotland, in the reign of king Malcolm II., about 1008. The legal power of the chiefs and other remains of heritable jurisdiction were abolished in Scotland, and liberty was granted to clansmen in 1747, in consequence of the rebellion of 1745. The following is a list of all the known clans of Scotland, with the badge of distinction anciently worn by each. The chief of each clan wears two eagle's feathers in his bonnet, in addition to the badge. *Chambers.* A history of the clans by Wm. Buchanan was published in 1775.

Name.	*Badge.*	*Name.*	*Badge.*
Buchanan	Birch.	M'Kenzie	Deer-grass.
Cameron	Oak.	M'Kinnon	St. John's wort.
Campbell	Myrtle.	M'Lachlan	Mountain-ash.
Chisholm	Alder.	M'Lean	Blackberry heath.
Colquhoun	Hazel.	M'Leod	Red whortleberries.
Cumming	Common sallow.	M'Nab	Rose blackberries.
Drummond	Holly.	M'Neil	Sea-ware.
Farquharson	Purple foxglove.	M'Pherson	Variegated box-wood.
Ferguson	Poplar.	M'Quarrie	Blackthorn.
Forbes	Broom.	M'Rae	Fir-club moss.
Frazer	Yew.	Menzies	Ash.
Gordon	Ivy.	Munro	Eagle's feathers.
Graham	Laurel.	Murray	Juniper.
Grant	Cranberry heath.	Ogilvie	Hawthorn.
Gun	Rosewort.	Oliphant	Great maple.
Lamont	Crab-apple tree.	Robertson	Fern, or brechans.
M'Alister	Five-leaved heath.	Rose	Briar-rose.
M'Donald	Bell-heath.	Ross	Bear-berries.
M'Donnell	Mountain-heath.	Sinclair	Clover.
M'Dougall	Cypress.	Stewart	Thistle.
M'Farlane	Cloud-berry bush.	Sutherland	Cat's-tail grass.
M'Gregor	Pine.		
M'Intosh	Box-wood.		
M'Kay	Bull-rush.		

CLAN-NA-GAEL (brotherhood of Gaels), an Irish secret oath-bound society, originating out of the Fenian brotherhood in 1870, it became the heart of the Irish National League in the United States, of which it was the extreme violent part. Its action much restrained by the influence of Messrs. Parnell, Sexton, and other members of the Irish Parliamentary party who originated a "new departure." It obtained the support of the Irish peasantry by promising to obtain them their farms without rent. The ultimate object of the Clan-na-Gael is said to be the establishment of Ireland as a perfectly independent state; it is termed a dynamite party ("Parnellism and Crime," series III., June, 1887).

For murder of Dr. Cronin, &c., see *United States,* 1889.
The Clan-na-Gael at Chicago declare against any form of violence . . . . reported Feb. 1890

CLAPHAM SECT, a name given to the evangelical party in the Church of England, first by the rev. Sydney Smith, in the latter part of the 18th century. The rev. Henry Venn was vicar of Clapham, and several of its eminent members lived there. The sect included Wm. Wilberforce, Zachary Macaulay (father of the historian), and the Rev. W. Romaine.

Memoirs of some appear in sir James Stephen's "Ecclesiastical Biography," 1849.

CLARE AND CLARENCE (Suffolk). Richard de Clare, earl of Gloucester, is said to have seated here a monastery of the order of Friars Eremites, the first of this kind of mendicants who came to

England, 1248. *Tanner*. Lionel, third son of Edward III., becoming possessed of the honour of Clare, by marriage, was created duke of *Clarence*. The title has ever since belonged to a branch of the royal family.

DUKES OF CLARENCE.

1362. Lionel, born 1338, died, 1369; see *York*.
1411. Thomas (second son of Henry IV.), born 1389: killed at Baugé, 1421.
1461. George (brother of Edward IV.), murdered, 1478.
1789. William (third son of George III.), afterwards king William IV.
1890. Albert Victor Christian Edward, eldest son of the prince of Wales, *see under Wales*, created duke of Clarence and Avondale and earl of Athlone, about 23 May; died 14 Jan., 1892. See *England*, 1892.

CLARE was the first place in Ireland since 1689 that elected a Roman Catholic M.P.; see *Roman Catholics*. At the election, held at Ennis, the county town, Mr. Daniel O'Connell was returned, 5 July, 1828. He did not sit till after the passing of the Catholic Emancipation Act, in 1829, being re-elected 30 July, 1829.

CLARE, NUNS OF ST., a sisterhood, called Minoresses, founded in Italy by St. Clare and St. Francis d'Assisi, about 1212. They were also called Urbanists; their rule having been modified by pope Urban IV., who died 1264. This order settled in France about 1260, and in England, in the Minories without Aldgate, London, about 1293, by Blanche, queen of Navarre, wife of Edmund, earl of Lancaster, brother of Edward I. At the suppression, the site was granted to the bishopric of Bath and Wells, 1539. *Tanner*.

CLAREMONT (Surrey), the residence of the princess Charlotte (daughter of the prince-regent, afterwards George IV., married to prince Leopold of Saxe-Coburg, 2 May, 1816): here she died in childbirth, 6 Nov. 1817. The house was built by sir John Vanbrugh, and was the seat successively of the earl of Clare, of lord Clive, lord Galloway, and the earl of Tyrconnel. It was purchased of Mr. Ellis by government for 65,000*l*. for the prince and princess of Saxe-Coburg; and the former, the late king of Belgium, assigned it to prince Albert in 1840. The exiled royal family of France resided at Claremont, 4 March, 1848; and the king, Louis Philippe, died there, 29 Aug. 1850. Bought by Queen Victoria, March, 1882. The duchess of Albany lived here for a time, returned 27 April, 1903.

CLARENCIEUX, the second king-at-arms, said to have been nominated by Thomas, son of Henry IV., created duke of Clarence, 1411. His duty was to arrange the funerals of baronets, knights, esquires, and gentlemen, on the south side of the Trent, from whence he is also called sur-roy or south-roy.

CLARENDON, CONSTITUTIONS OF, were enacted at a council held 25 Jan. 1164, at Clarendon, in Wiltshire, to retrench the power of the clergy. They led to Becket's quarrel with Henry II., were annulled by the pope, and abandoned by the king, April, 1174. The following is approximative:

I. All suits concerning advowsons to be determined in civil courts.
II. The clergy accused of any crime to be tried by civil judges.
III. No person of any rank whatever to be permitted to leave the realm without the royal licence.
IV. Laics not to be accused in spiritual courts, except by legal and reputable promoters and witnesses.
V. No chief tenant of the crown to be excommunicated, nor his lands put under interdict.
VI. Revenues of vacant sees to belong to the king.
VII. Goods forfeited to the crown not to be protected in churches.
VIII. Sons of villeins not to be ordained clerks without the consent of their lord.
IX. Bishops to be regarded as barons, and be subjected to the burthens belonging to that rank.
X. Churches belonging to the king's see not to be granted in perpetuity against his will.
XI. Excommunicated persons not to be bound to give security for continuing in their abode.
XII. No inhabitant in demesne to be excommunicated for non-appearance in a spiritual court.
XIII. If any tenant *in capite* should refuse submission to spiritual courts, the case to be referred to the king.
XIV. The clergy no longer to pretend to the right of enforcing debts contracted by oath or promise.
XV. Causes between laymen and ecclesiastics to be determined by a jury.
XVI. Appeals to be ultimately carried to the king, and no further without his consent.

CLARENDON PRESS, OXFORD. The building was erected by sir John Vanbrugh, in 1711-13, the expense being defrayed out of the profits of lord Clarendon's History of the Rebellion, the copyright of which was given to the university by his son. The original building was converted into a museum, lecture-rooms, &c., and a new printing-office erected by Blore and Robertson, 1825-30.

CLARIONET, or **CLARINET**, a wind instrument of the reed kind, said to have been invented by Johann Christopher Denner, in Nuremberg, about 1690. Mr. James Clinton's "combination" clarinet was exhibited at the Royal College of Music, 7 July, 1896. A tenor clarinet, called the *basset-horn*, is used in orchestral music.

CLASSIS. The name was first used by Tullius Servius (the sixth king of ancient Rome), in making divisions of the Roman people, 573 B.C. The first of the six classes were called *classici*, by way of eminence, and hence authors of the first rank (especially Greek and Latin) came to be called *classics*.

CLAVECIN, French for *harpsichord*. See *Pianoforte*.

CLAVICHORD, a keyed-stringed musical instrument of various forms in use in France, Spain, and Germany, in the 16th and 17th centuries. See *Virginals*, *Spinet*, *Harp* and *Piano*.

CLAVICYTHERIUM, an upright musical instrument, probably resembling the harpsichord, used in the 16th century.

CLAVIER, German for *pianoforte* (*which see*).

CLAY'S ACT, SIR WILLIAM, 14 & 15 Vict. c. 14 (1851), relates to the compound householders.

CLAYTON-BULWER TREATY, see *Bulwer*.

CLEARING-HOUSE. In 1775, a building in Lombard-street was set apart for the use of bankers, in which they might exchange drafts, bills, and securities, and thereby save labour and curtail the amount of floating cash requisite to meet the settlement of the different houses, if effected singly. By means of transfer tickets, transactions to the amount of millions daily are settled without the intervention of a bank note. In 1861, the clearing-house was used by 117 companies, and in May, 1864, it was joined by the Bank of England. In the year ending 30 April, 1868, 3,257,411,000*l*. passed through the clearing-house; 30 April, 1873, 6,003,335,000*l*.; 1877-8, 3,066,533,000*l*.; 1880-1, 5,909,989,000*l*.; 31 Dec. 1887, 6,077,097,000*l*.;

1890, 7,801,000,000*l.*; 1892, 6,482,000,000*l.*; 1893, 6,478,000,000*l.*; 1896, 7,575,000,000*l.*; 1899, 9,150,000,000*l.*; 1900, 8,960,000,000*l.*; 1901, 9,561,169,000*l.*; 1902, 10,028,742,000*l.* The *Railway clearing-house* in Seymour-street, near Euston-square, established 2 Jan. 1842, is regulated by an act passed in 1850. The jubilee was celebrated Jan. 1892. *Clearing House Act* (Ireland) 1860, and the *Cotton Brokers Bank*, at Liverpool. New York clearing-house, the first started in America, 1853; Vienna, 1864; Paris, 1872; Berlin, 1883. A clearing-house for the systematic relief of the *unemployed* in London was constituted at the Polytechnic Institution, Regent Street, in 1892.

CLEMENTINES, apocryphal pieces, attributed to Clemens Romanus, a contemporary of St. Paul, and said to have succeeded St. Peter as bishop of Rome. He died 102. *Niceron*. Also the decretals of pope Clement V. who died 1314, published by his successor. *Bowyer*. Also Augustine monks, each of whom having been a superior nine years, then merged into a common monk.—CLEMENTINES were the adherents of Robert, son of the count of Geneva, who took the title of Clement VII. on the death of Gregory XI., 1378, and URBANISTS, those of pope Urban VI. Christendom was divided by their claims: France, Castile, Scotland, &c., adhering to Clement; Rome, Italy, and England, to Urban. The schism ended in 1409, when Alexander V. was elected pope, and his rivals resigned; see *Anti-Popes*.

CLEOPATRA'S NEEDLE, see *Obelisks*.

CLEPSYDRA, a water-clock; see *Clocks*.

CLERGY (from the Greek *kleros*, a lot or inheritance) in the first century were termed presbyters, elders, or bishops, and deacons. The bishops (*episcopoi* or *overseers*), elected from the presbyters, in the second century assumed higher functions (about 330), and, under Constantine, obtained the recognition and protection of the secular power. Under the Lombard and Norman-French kings in the 7th and 8th centuries, the clergy began to possess temporal power, as owners of lands; and after the establishment of monachism, a distinction was made between the regular clergy, who lived apart from the world, in accordance with a *regula* or rule, and the *secular* (worldly) or beneficed clergy. The English clergy write *clerk* after their names in legal documents. See *Church of England* (note) and *Bishops*.

The clergy were first styled clerks, owing to the judges being chosen after the Norman custom from the sacred order, and the officers being clergy: this gave them that denomination, which they keep to this day. *Blackstone*.

As the Druids kept the keys of their religion and of letters, so did the priests keep both these to themselves; they alone make profession of letters, and a man of letters was called a clerk, and hence learning went by the name of clerkship. *Pasquier*.

BENEFIT OF CLERGY, *Privilegium Clericale*, arose in the regard paid by Christian princes to the church, and consisted of: 1st, an exemption of places consecrated to religious duties from criminal arrests, which was the foundation of sanctuaries; 2nd, exemption of the persons of clergymen from criminal process before the secular judge, in particular cases, which was the original meaning of the *privilegium clericale*. The *benefit of clergy* was afterwards extended to everyone who could read; and it was enacted, that there should be a prerogative allowed to the clergy, that if any man who could read were to be condemned to death, the bishop of the diocese might, if he would, claim him as a clerk, and dispose of him in some places of the clergy as he might deem meet. The ordinary gave the prisoner at the bar a Latin book, in a black Gothic character, from which to read a verse or two; and if the ordinary said, "*Legit ut Clericus*" ("He reads like a clerk"), the offender was only burnt in the hand; otherwise, he suffered death, 3 Edw. I. (1274).

The privilege was restricted by Henry VII. in 1489, and abolished, with respect to murderers and other great criminals, by Henry VIII., 1512. *Stow*.

The reading was discontinued by 5 Anne, c. 6 (1706).

Benefit of Clergy was wholly repealed by 7 & 8 Geo. IV. c. 25 (1827).

CLERGY CHARITIES.

William Assheton, an eminent theological writer, was the first proposer of a plan to provide for the families of deceased clergy. He died Sept. 1711. *Watts's Life of Assheton*.

Festival of the "*Sons of the Clergy*," held annually at St. Paul's cathedral, instituted about 1655; from it sprang the charity called the "Sons of the Clergy" (clergy orphan and widow corporation), incorporated, 1 July, 1678.

Clergy Orphan corporation, 1749.

Friend of the Clergy corporation, 1849.

St. John's foundation school for sons of poor clergy, 1852.

Poor Clergy Relief corporation, established 1856; incorporated 1867.

There are several other charities for relatives of the clergy. See *Bromley College*.

The clergy prevented from being members of parliament by 41 Geo. III. c. 63, 1801.

A bill to repeal this act was lost in the commons (110 to 101), 11 May, 1881.

Clergy discipline (immorality) bill introduced by the archbishop of Canterbury, 23 Feb.; passed 27 June, 1892

Poverty of the Clergy in 1895, 400 benefices under 50*l.* a year, 3,500 less than 100*l.* a year . . Oct. 1896

1,400, at 65*l.* a year, reported . . . 4 July, 1898

Queen Victoria Clergy fund. The queen sends 1,000*l.*, Xmas, 1897; meeting of the council, lord Ashcombe in the chair, at the Church house; total fund, 63,137*l.*, 25,000*l.* to be voted to affiliated dioceses, 25 Feb. (total 145,000*l.*) . . 1898

See *Church and Clerical Aid Society*.

CLERICAL DISABILITIES, an act passed 9 Aug. 1870, relieves persons who have been admitted priests or deacons of certain clerical disabilities upon their resigning their ecclesiastical offices and preferments, and declares them incapable of officiating henceforward.

CLERICAL SUBSCRIPTION ACT, 28 & 29 Vict. c. 122, passed 5 July, 1865, simplified and modified the oaths to be taken by the clergy when ordained.

CLERK OF ARRAIGNS, see *Arraignment*.

CLERKENWELL, a parish, N. E. London, so called from a well (*fons clericorum*) in Ray-street, where the parish clerks occasionally acted mystery-plays: once before Richard II. in 1390. Hunt's political meetings in 1817 were held in Spa-fields in this parish. In St. John's parish are the remains of the priory of the knights of St. John of Jerusalem. Clerkenwell prison was built in 1615, in lieu of the noted prison called the Cage, which was taken down in 1614; the then Bridewell having been found insufficient. The prison called the House of Detention, erected in 1775, was rebuilt in 1818; again 1844. For the explosion here, see *Fenians*, Dec. 1867. At Clerkenwell-close formerly stood the house of Oliver Cromwell, where some suppose the death-warrant of Charles I. was signed, Jan. 1649.

Free library in Skinner street (site given by Skinners' company) opened by the lord mayor . 10 Oct. 1890

Rosebery avenue opened by the earl of Rosebery 21 July, ,,

Hugh Myddelton School on site of "House of Detention," opened by the prince of Wales 13 Dec. 1893

New town-hall opened by the earl of Rosebery 14 June, 1895

Visit of the prince of Wales (see *John, St.*, knights of) . . . . 11 June, 1902

CLERMONT (France). Here was held the council under pope Urban II. in 1095, in which the first crusade against the infidels was determined upon, and Godfrey of Bouillon appointed to command it. In this council the name of pope is said to have been first given to the head of the Roman Catholic church, exclusively of the bishops who used previously to assume the title. Philip I. of France was (a second time) excommunicated by this assembly. *Hénault.*

CLEVEDON COURT, Somersetshire, the mediæval seat of sir Arthur Hallam Elton; destroyed by fire 27 Nov. 1882—damage about 20,000*l.*

CLEVELAND, see *Steel*, a town in Ohio, U.S.; the Euclid Avenue opera house burnt down, 29 Oct, 1892; population in 1880, 160,146; 1890, 261,353; 1900, 381,768.

CLEVELAND IRON DISTRICT, see *Middlesbrough.*

CLEVES (N. E. Germany). Rutger, count of Cleves, lived at the beginning of the 11th century. Adolphus, count of Mark, was made duke of Cleves by the emperor Sigismund, 1417. John William, duke of Cleves, Berg, Juliers, &c., died without issue, 25 March, 1609, which led to a war of succession. Eventually Cleves was assigned to the elector of Brandenburg in 1666; seized by the French in 1757; restored at the peace in 1763, and now forms part of the Prussian dominions.

CLIFTON SUSPENSION-BRIDGE, over the Avon, connecting Gloucestershire and Somersetshire, constructed of the removed Hungerford-bridge, was completed in Oct. and opened 8 Dec. 1864. It is said to have the largest span (702 feet) of any chain bridge in the world. In 1753 Alderman Vick, of Bristol, bequeathed 1000*l.* to accumulate for the erection of a bridge over the Avon. In 1831 Brunel began one, which was abandoned after the expenditure of 45,000*l.*

CLIMACTERIC, the term applied to certain periods of time in a man's life (multiples of 7 or 9), in which it was affirmed notable alterations in the health and constitution of a person happen. The *grand climacteric* is 63.

CLIMATE. The condition of a place in regard to natural phenomena of the atmosphere as temperature, moisture, &c., see *Meteorology.*

International Congresses on Climatology met at Paris Oct. 1889, and Rome in 1892; at Liège, 25 Sept. 1898.
Dr. Lombard's Traité de Climatologie published 1877–80; he died at Geneva, aged nearly 92, 22 Jan. 1895.
Pan-Russian congress on climate in reference to health, opened by the grand duke Paul . Jan. 1899
Internat. Congress; Grenoble . . . . 29 Sept. 1902

CLINICAL SOCIETY OF LONDON, for the cultivation of practical medicine and surgery, established in Dec. 1867; first president, sir Thomas Watson. See *Lectures* (clinical).

CLIO. The initials C. L. I. O., forming the name of the muse of history, were rendered famous from the most admired papers of Addison, in the *Spectator*, having been marked by one or other of them, signed consecutively, in 1713. *Cibber.*

CLISSOLD PARK, Stoke Newington, London, N., purchased by the Charity Commissioners and the Metropolitan Board of Works, &c., for public use, 1887. See *Parks.*

CLITHEROE CASE, see *Wives*, 1891.

CLOACA MAXIMA, the chief of the celebrated sewers at Rome, the construction of which is attributed to king Tarquinius Priscus (600 B.C.) and his successors.

CLOCK. The clepsydra, or water-clock, was introduced at Rome from the east about 158 B.C. by Scipio Nasica. Toothed wheels were applied to them by Ctesibius, about 140 B.C. Clocks said to have been found by Cæsar on invading Britain, 55 B.C. The only clock supposed to be then in the world was sent by pope Paul I. to Pepin, king of France, A.D. 760. Pacificus, archdeacon of Genoa, invented one in the 9th century. Originally the wheels were three feet in diameter. The earliest complete clock of which there is any certain record was made by a Saracen mechanic in the 13th century. Alfred is said to have measured time by wax tapers, and to have used lanterns to defend them from the wind, about 887.

The scapement ascribed to Gerbert 1000
A great clock put up at Canterbury cathedral cost 30*l.* 1292
A clock constructed by Richard, abbot of St. Alban's . . . . about 1326
John Visconti sets up a clock at Genoa . . . 1353
A striking clock in Westminster 1368
A perfect one made at Paris, by Vick 1370
The first portable one made 1530
In England no clock went accurately before that set up at Hampton-court (maker's initials N. O.) 1540

. . . . "Like a German clock,
Still a-repairing; ever out of frame;
And never going aright."
Shakspeare, "Love's Labour's Lost," 1598

The *pendulum* is said to have been applied to clocks by the younger Galileo, 1639; and by Richard Harris (who erected a clock at St. Paul's, Covent-garden) 1641
Christian Huyghens said he made his pendulum clock previously to 1658
Fromantil, a Dutchman, improved the pendulum about 1659
Repeating clocks and watches invented by Barlow, about 1676
Spiral pendulum spring invented by Robert Hooke, about 1658; cylinder and escapement, by Thos. Tompion 1695
The dead beat, and horizontal escapements, by Graham, about 1700; compensating pendulum . 1715
The spiral balance spring suggested, and the duplex scapement, invented by Dr. Hooke; pivot holes jewelled by Facio; the detached-scapement, invented by Mudge, and improved by Berthould, Arnold, Earnshaw, and others in the 18th century.
Harrison's time-piece (*which see*) constructed . 1735
Clocks and watches taxed, 1797; tax repealed . 1798
Church clocks illuminated: the first, St. Bride's, London . . . . 2 Dec. 1826
The Horological Institute established . . . 1858
The great Westminster clock set up . . 30 May, 1859
See Paul's, St.
266,750 clocks and 8,621 watches imported into the United Kingdom in 1857; 258,628 clocks, 372,420 watches in 1870; 687,271 clocks in 1877; 839,934 in 1886
The duty came off 1861
Messrs. Barraud and Lund's electric system of synchronising clocks: city of London circuit of 108 clocks in action . . . . . Nov. 1878
Victor Popp of Vienna applies compressed air as a motive power to clocks; announced . March, 1881
See *Electric Clock*, under *Electricity.*

CLOGHER (Ireland). St. Macartin, a disciple of St. Patrick, fixed a bishopric at Clogher, where he also built an abbey "in the street before the royal seat of the kings of Ergal." He died in 506. Clogher takes its name from a golden stone, from which, in times of paganism, the devil used to pronounce juggling answers, like the oracles of *Apollo Pythius. Sir James Ware.* In 1041 the cathedral was built anew, and dedicated to its founder. Clogher merged, on the death of its last prelate (Dr. Tottenham), into the archiepiscopal see of Armagh, by the act of 1833.

CLONFERT (Ireland). St. Brendan founded an abbey at Clonfert in 558: his life is extant in jingling monkish metre in the Cottonian library at Westminster. In his time the cathedral, famous in ancient days for its seven altars, was erected; and Colgan makes St. Brendan its founder and the first bishop; but it is said, in the Ulster Annals, under the year 571, "*Mæna*, bishop of Clonfert-Brenain, went to rest." Clonfert, in Irish, signifies a wonderful den or retirement. In 1839 the see merged into that of Killaloe; see *Bishops*.

CLONTARF (near Dublin), the site of a battle fought on Good Friday, 23 April, 1014, between the Irish and Danes, the former headed by Bryan Boroimhe, monarch of Ireland, who defeated the invaders, after a long and bloody engagement, was wounded, and soon afterwards died. His son Murchard also fell with many of the nobility; 13,000 Danes are said to have perished in the battle.

CLOSTERSEVEN (Hanover) **CONVENTION OF**, was entered into 8 Sept. 1757, between the duke of Cumberland, third son of George II., hardly pressed, and the duke of Richelieu, commander of the French. By it 38,000 Hanoverians laid down their arms, and were dispersed. The treaty was disavowed by the king, and soon broken; the duke resigned all his commands.

CLOSURE, see *Clôture*.

CLOTH, see *Woollen Cloth* and *Calico*.

CLÔTURE, the power of closing a debate in the French chamber of deputies, exercised by the president. A similar power, termed *Closure*, was given to the speaker of the House of Commons, 11 Nov. 1882; first enforced 24 Feb. 1885; the closure made part of a standing order, 18, 19 March, 1887. By a new rule the power of closure was given to a house of 100, 28 Feb. 1888; and was frequently exercised in 1888, and since. See *Parliament*, 1887 and 1893.

CLOUD, ST., a palace near Paris, named from prince Clodoald or Cloud, who became a monk there in 533, after the murder of his brothers, and died in 560. The palace was built in the 16th century, and in it Henry III. was stabbed by Clement, 1 Aug. (died 2 Aug.) 1589. This palace, long the property of the dukes of Orleans, was bought by Marie Antoinette in 1785. It was a favourite residence of the empress Josephine, of Charles X. and his family, and of the emperor Napoleon III. It was burnt during the siege of Paris, having been fired upon by the French themselves, 13 Oct. 1870. The ruins were cleared away, and the site sold, July, 1892.

CLOUDS consist of minute particles of water, often in a frozen state, floating in the air. In 1803 Mr. Luke Howard published his classification of clouds, now generally adopted, consisting of three primary forms—cirrus, cumulus, and stratus; three compounds of these forms; and the nimbus or black rain clouds (cumulo cirro-stratus.) A new edition of Howard's Essay on the Clouds appeared in 1865. Important international cloud work by prof. F. H. Bigelow; 10 standard types of clouds defined by the international cloud committee, taken during 1896; published by the U.S. Weather Bureau, 1900.

CLOVESHOO (now Cliff), Kent. Here was held an important council of nobility and clergy concerning the government and discipline of the church, Sept. 747; and others were held here, 800, 803, 822, 824.

CLOYNE (S. Ireland), a bishopric, founded in the 6th century by St. Coleman, was in 1431 united to that of Cork, and so continued for 200 years. It was united with that of Cork and Ross, 1834; see *Bishops*.

CLUBMEN, associations founded in the southern and western counties of England, to restrain the excesses of the armies during the civil wars, 1642–9. They professed neutrality, but inclined towards the king, and were considered enemies by his opponents.

CLUBS, originally consisted of a small number of persons of kindred tastes and pursuits, who met together at stated times for social intercourse. The club at the Mermaid tavern, established about the end of the 16th century, consisted of Raleigh, Shakspeare, and others. Ben Jonson set up a club at the Devil tavern. Addison, Steele, and others, frequently met at Button's coffee-house, as described in the *Spectator*. Some odd clubs are described in No. 9 of that journal, 10 March, 1710–11. The present London clubs, some comprising 500, others about 6000 members, possess handsome, luxuriously furnished edifices in or near Pall Mall. The members obtain choice viands and wines at moderate charges, and many clubs possess excellent libraries, particularly the Athenæum (*which see*). The annual payment varies from 3*l*. 3*s*. to 11*l*. 11*s*.; the entrance fee from 5*l*. 5*s*. to 42*l*. A bill for the registration of clubs was read a second time in the commons, 22 March, 1893. The following are the *principal clubs*; several are described in separate articles:—

Rota (*political*)	1659
Civil Club (*professional and commercial*) 19 Nov.	1669
White's (*Tory*), at White's Coffee-house, 1698; revived	1888
Kit-Cat (*literary*)	1700
Dilettanti (*fine arts*)	1734
Beef Steak	1735
Royal Society (*scientific*) before	1743
Cocoa Tree	1746
Boodle's	1762
Literary Club (*which see*), termed also "The Club," and Johnson's Club	1764
Brooks's, originally Almack's (*Whig*)	,,
Royal Naval	1705
Arthur's	,,
Alfred (*literary*)	1808–51
Roxburghe, London	1812
Guards	1813
United Service	1815
Travellers'	1819
Union	1821
United University	1822
Bannatyne, *Edinburgh*	1823
Athenæum (*which see*)	1824
Oriental	,,
United Service (Junior)	1827
Wyndham	1828
Maitland, *Glasgow*	,,
Oxford and Cambridge	1829
Carlton (*Conservative*), founded by the duke of Wellington and others	1831
Garrick	,,
City of London Club	1832
Abbotsford, *Edinburgh*	1835
Reform (*Liberal*)	1836
Parthenon	,,
Army and Navy	1837
Etching, *London*	1838
Spalding, *Aberdeen*	1839
Conservative	1840
Gresham	1843

National	1845
Whittington (founded by Douglas Jerrold and others)	1846
East India United Service	1847
Savage	1857
St. James's	,,
Naval and Military	1862
Grafton	1863
Arts	,,
Junior Carlton	1864
Thatched House	1865
Cobden Club	1866
Savile	1868
City Carlton	,,
Marlborough	1869
Lyric	1870
St. Stephen's	,,
Universities	1871
Scientific	1874
Wanderers	,,
Devonshire (*Liberal*)	,,
City Liberal Club	,,
Verulam (*Literary and Scientific*)	,,
Byron	1875
Hanover Square	1876
New Athenæum Club	1878
Eighty Club	1880
National Liberal Club	1882
Constitutional	1883
Grosvenor, Bond Street	,,
Imperial and American	1885
Camera	,,
National Conservative	1886
National Union	1887
Arts and Letters	1889
Thirteen Club	,,
Amphitryon, Albemarle Street, W.	1890
Cavalry	,,
Golfers	1893
Automobile	1897
Colonial	1899
Oxford and Cambridge Musical	,,
Boz (*literary*), Dickensonian	1900
O.P. club (playgoers and others connected with the drama)	,,
Imperial Service	1901
Auxiliary Forces	1902

See *Working Men's Clubs*; *Ladies' Clubs*, in London 1898, *et seq.*: University, New Somerville, Alexandra, Pioneer, Writers' and others.

CLUBS, FRENCH. The first arose about 1782. They were essentially political, and greatly concerned in the revolution. The *Club Breton* became the celebrated *Club des Jacobins*, and the *Club des Cordeliers* comprised among its members Danton and Camille Desmoulins. From these two came the *Mountain* party which overthrew the Girondists in 1793, and fell in its turn in 1794. The clubs disappeared with the Directory in 1799. They were revived in 1848, but did not attain to their former eminence, and were suppressed by decrees, 22 June, 1849, and 6 June, 1850. *Bouillet.*

CLUB-FOOT, a deformity due to the shortening of one or more of the muscles, although attempted to be relieved by Lorenz in 1784, by cutting the tendo Achillis, was not effectually cured till 1831, when Stromeyer of Erlangen cured Dr. Little by dividing the tendons of the contracted muscles with a very thin knife.

CLUGNY or **CLUNY, ABBEY OF,** in France, formerly most magnificent, founded by Benedictines, under the abbot Bern, about 910, and sustained afterwards by William, duke of Berry and Aquitaine. English foundations for Cluniac monks were instituted soon after.

CLYDE AND FORTH WALL was built by Agricola, 84. The Forth and Clyde CANAL was commenced by Mr. Smeaton, 10 July, 1768, and was opened 28 July, 1790. It forms a communication between the seas on the eastern and western coasts of Scotland.

CNIDUS, in Caria, Asia Minor: near here Conon the Athenian defeated the Lacedæmonian fleet, under Peisander, 394 B.C.

COACH (from *coche*, Spanish). Beckmann states that Charles of Anjou's queen entered Naples in a *caretta* (about 1282). Under Francis I. there were but two in Paris, one belonging to the queen, the other to Diana, the natural daughter of Henry II. There were but three in Paris in 1550; and Henry IV. had one without straps or springs. John de Laval de Bois-Dauphin set up a coach on account of his enormous bulk. The first coach seen in England was about 1553. Coaches were introduced by Fitz-Alan, earl of Arundel, in 1580. *Stow.* A bill was brought into parliament to prevent the effeminacy of men riding in coaches, 43 Eliz. 1601. *Carte.* Repealed 1625. The coach of the duke of Buckingham had six horses, that of the earl of Northumberland eight, 1619. The coach-tax commenced in 1747. Horace Walpole says that the present royal state coach (first used 16 Nov. 1762) cost 7,528*l.* The lord mayor's old state coach was not used 9 Nov. 1867; see *Car*, *Carriages*, *Chariots*, *Hackney Coaches*, *Mail Coaches*, &c. G. Thrupp's "History of Coaches" published 1877.

A coachmakers' exhibition, London, opened 2 June, 1879.

A private university teacher is termed a "*Coach.*" Dr. Edward John Routh, of Cambridge, out of 631 pupils produced 27 senior wranglers, 1858–88. On his retirement his old pupils presented his portrait to his wife, 3 Nov. 1888. Mr. Walter Wren, eminent *coach*, died Aug. 1898.

COAL.* It is contended, with much seeming truth, that coal, although not mentioned by the Romans in their notices of Britain, was yet in use by the ancient Britons. *Brandt.* Henry III. is said to have granted a licence to dig coals near Newcastle-upon-Tyne in 1234; some say earlier, and others in 1239. Sea-coal was prohibited from being used in and near London, as being "prejudicial to human health;" and even smiths were obliged to burn wood, 1273. *Stow.* In 1306 the gentry petitioned against its use. Coal was first made an article of trade from Newcastle to London, 4 Rich II. 1381. *Rymer's Fœdera.* Notwithstanding the many previous complaints against coal as a public nuisance, it was at length generally burned in London in 1400; but it was not in common use in England until the reign of Charles I. 1625. Coal was brought from Dublin to Newry in 1742. Coal declared a contraband of war by Great Britain, April, 1898.

1700 consumed in London	317,000	chald.
1750	510,000	,,
1800	814,000	,,
1810	980,372	,,
1820	1,171,178	,,
1830	1,588,360	,,
1835	2,299,816	tons.
1840	2,638,256	,,
1850	3,638,883	,,

Coal and fuel exported: value: 1856, 2,826,582*l.*; 1869, 5,165,668*l.*; 1873, 13,188,511*l.*; 1878, 7,330,474*l.*; 1883, 10,645,919*l.*; 1887, 10,169,991*l.*; 1888, 11 345,299*l.*; 1889, 14,781,990*l.*; 1890, 19,020,269*l.*; 1893, 14,375,476*l.*; 1900, 38,619,856*l.*; 1901, 30,434,744*l.*

The coal-fields of Great Britain are estimated at 5400 square miles; of Durham and Northumberland,

* There are five kinds of fossil fuel: anthracite, coal, lignite, bituminous shale, and bitumen. No satisfactory definition of coal has yet been given. The composition of *wood* is 49·1 carbon, 6·3 hydrogen, 44·6 oxygen; of *coal* 82·6 carbon, 5·6 hydrogen, 11·8 oxygen.

723 square miles. *Bakewell.* In 1857 about 65¼ millions of tons were extracted (value about 16,348,676*l.*) from 2095 collieries; about 25 millions are consumed annually in Great Britain. 1882, collieries, 3,759.

Coal obtained in Great Britain and Ireland :—

Year	Tons	Year	Tons
1854.	64,661,401 tons.	1865.	98,150,587 tons.
1861.	83,635,214 ,,	1866.	101,630,544 ,,
1862.	81,638,338 ,,	1867.	104,500,480 ,,
1863.	86,292,215 ,,	1868.	103,141,157 ,,
1864.	92,787,873 ,,	1869.	107,427,557 ,,

Year	Tons		Value
1870.	110,431,192	tons. ...... value.	27,607,798*l.*
1871.	117,352,028	,, ... ,,	35,205,608*l.*
1872.	123,497,316	,, ... ,,	46,311,143*l.*
1873.	127,016,747	,, ... ,,	47,631,280*l.*
1874.	125,067,016	,, ... ,,	45,849,194*l.*
1875.	131,867,105	,, ... ,,	46,163,486*l.*
1876.	133,344,826	,, ... ,,	46,670,668*l.*
1877.	134,610,763	,, ... ,,	47,113,767*l.*
1878.	132,654,887	,, ... ,,	46,429,210*l.*
1879.	134,008,228	,, ... ,,	46,902,879*l.*
1880.	146,818,622	,, ... ,,	62,395,414*l.*
1881.	154,184,300	,, ... ,,	65,528,327*l.*
1882.*	156,499,977	,, ... ,,	44,118,409*l.*
1883.	163,737,327	,, ... ,,	46,054,143*l.*
1884.	160,757,779	,, ... ,,	43,446,183*l.*
1885.	159,351,418	,, ... ,,	41,139,408*l.*
1886.	157,518,482	,, ... ,,	38,145,930*l.*
1887.	162,119,812	,, ... ,,	39,092,830*l.*
1888.	169,935,219	,, ... ,,	42,971,276*l.*
1889.	176,916,724	,, ... ,,	56,175,426*l.*
1890.	181,614,288	,, ... ,,	74,953,997*l.*
1891.	185,479,126	,, ... ,,	74,099,816*l.*
1892.	181,786,871	,, ... ,,	66,050,451*l.*
1893.	164,325,795	,, ... ,,	55,809,808*l.*
1894.	188,277,525	,, ... ,,	62,730,179*l.*
1895.	189,661,362	,, ... ,,	57,231,213*l.*
1896.	195,361,260	,, ... ,,	57,190,147*l.*
1898.	202,042,303	,, ... ,,	64,169,382*l.*
1899.	220,094,781	,, ... ,,	83,481,137*l.*
1900.	225,181,300	,, ... ,,	121,652,596*l.*
1901.	219,046,945	,, ... ,,	102,846,552*l.*

United States, 41,752,609 tons, obtained in 1872

Mr. Sopwith, in 1855, computed the annual product of the coal-mines of Durham and Northumberland at 14 million tons :—6 millions for London, 2½ millions exported, 2½ millions for coke, 1 million for colliery engines, &c., and two millions for local consumption.

By a stipulation in the commercial treaty of 1860, in consequence of the French government greatly reducing the duty on imported coal, the British government (it is thought by many imprudently) engaged to lay no duty on exported coal for ten years. In 1859 about 7,000,000 tons of British coals were exported, of which 1,391,009 tons went to France; over 8,000,000 tons sent in 1900.

A commission (consisting of the duke of Argyll, sir R. I. Murchison, Dr. John Percy, professor Ramsay, and others) appointed to investigate into the probable quantity of coal in the coal-fields of the United Kingdom, &c. 28 June, 1866, reported 27 July, 1871 :—

	TONS
Attainable quantity of coal known .	90,207,000,000
Probable available coal in other places	56,273,000,000
	146,480,000,000

Total coal production in 1901, 789,000,000 tons.

Another commission appointed . . . . Dec. 1901

44½ million tons exported to the colonies and foreign countries; reported . . . . . . Dec. 1897

Sale of Coal Regulation Act 1831

The duties on the exportation of British coal, which had existed since the 16th century, were practically repealed 1834

Sir R. Peel imposed a duty of 4*s.* a ton in 1842; caused much dissatisfaction; repealed . . . 1845

Women were prohibited from working in English collieries in 1842

* The plan adopted for obtaining the value of the coal produced was changed in 1882.

The consumption of coal in France in 1780, only 400,000 tons, rises to 6,000,000 tons in . . . 1845

The United States produced between 8 and 9 millions of tons: Belgium, 5,000,000; and France, 4,500,000, 1855

An Act for the regulation and inspection of mines passed 1860

Duplicate shafts act passed 1862

Coal-pitmen's strikes frequently occur; a long and severe one arose in Staffordshire in 1864; near St. Helen's, March, 1868; in S. Wales . Jan.-March, 1873

Coal-mines regulation act, tending to check the supply, passed 10 Aug. 1872; act amended . . . 1886

By another act preceding acts were consolidated, the employment of women and boys under 12 underground was prohibited, the qualifications of managers is to be tested by examiners, and other regulations made . . . . 6 Sept. 1887

A coal-cutting machine at work, producing about 70 tons in 8 hours (work of 40 men); requires attendance of 3 or 4 men . . *Times*, 6 Feb. 1873

reported successful in Northumberland . Nov. ,,

Great dearth of coal in London (see *Strikes*), best coal 52*s.* a ton . . . . . 15 Feb. ,,

Duty on Coal brought to London, 9*d.* a ton, and 4*d.* a ton for London improvements; produced 381,249*l.* . . . . ,,

Parliamentary committee respecting coal first met 24 March, ,,

Exhibition of coal-raising machinery at Salford, Manchester, opened . . . . . 30 Jan. 1874

Royal Commission on spontaneous combustion of coal (Mr. H. C. Childers, professor Abel, &c.) met 11 Nov. 1875; report issued; alludes to danger of absorption of oxygen, need of ventilation, &c. Aug. 1876

A commission to inquire into the causes and remedies for explosions was appointed (including Messrs. Warington W. Smyth, Tyndall, F. A. Abel, and others) . . . . . Feb. 1879

[Preliminary report issued Nov. 1881; final report 15 March, 1886.]

A great reduction of accidents through improved management announced . . . . . Nov. 1881

A new method of blasting by quick-lime-cartridges invented by Smith and Moor much recommended 1882

Increase of wages obtained in consequence of the miners conference at Manchester . Jan.-Feb. 1883

Yorkshire Miners' Association (Benjamin Pickard and others) demand diminution of time of labour, and decrease of output in order to raise the price of coal . . . . Feb. ,,

Government circular issued, recommending the use of Fleus's apparatus for rendering foul air respirable after explosions (see *Diving*) March, ,,

Important meeting of delegates from about 17,000 miners requiring 15 per cent. increase of wages at Ardwick . . . . 6 Nov. ,,

Pit-brow women employed outside of coal mines in Lancashire and South Wales; an attempt to prohibit this negatived by the commons 23 June, 1887

Messrs. Ashworth and Kneen patent a furnace which saves about 35 per cent. of coal and consumes smoke, autumn 1887.

Proposed formation of "The Coal Owners and Consumers Co-operative Association" March, 1889

Coal-field discovered near Dover . . . 15 Feb. 1890

Federation of colliery owners proposed (except S. Wales, Northumberland, and Durham) in opposition to strikes, &c. . . 31 Jan., 11 Feb. ,,

The colliers' demand for advance of 10 per cent. pay, resisted . . . . 11 Feb. ,,

The miners' delegates (40) at Westminster (representing 350,000) threaten a general strike if the advance of 10 per cent. is not conceded before 15 March . . . . 15 Feb. ,,

The strike begins . . . . 15 March ,,

Meeting of delegates from both parties; and immediate advance of 5 per cent. on Aug. 1 agreed to; strike closes . . . . 20 March, ,,

Royal commission appointed to inquire into the effect of *coal dust* in relation to explosions in mines (Mr. J. Chamberlain, lord Rayleigh, prof. Dixon, and others); first meeting . 6 March, 1891

The Northumberland coal-miners agree to a reduction of 5 per cent. on their wages . . 2 Jan. 1892

The new "sliding scale" agreed to, 1 Jan., adopted at Cardiff and Aberdare . . . . 4 Jan. ,,

The representatives of the National Miners' Federation at Manchester, recommend a temporary suspension of work (12–26 March), to raise the prices and maintain the rate of pay to miners; generally accepted, except in South Wales, Northumberland, Durham, Worcestershire, Staffordshire, and Scotland . . . . . . Feb. 1892

Prices raised in London, &c., temporary panic . 29 Feb. *et seq.* ,,

Strike of the Durham coal-miners against the proposed 10 per cent. reduction of wages, 11 March; 92,588 said to be out, 16 March; the men agree to accept 7½ or 10 per cent. reduction; the coal-owners require 13½ per cent.; compromise effected by the intervention of bishop Westcott at a meeting at Auckland Castle, 10 per cent. accepted by both parties, 1 June; manufactures on the Tyne and Wear much suspended March—June, ,,

The reduction of 5 per cent. on wages accepted by the Northumbrian miners, 3 Nov. 1892, *et seq.*; by the Durham miners . 13 March, 1893

Strike of about 3,000 colliers at the Forest of Dean against reduced wages, 8 July; return to work 18 Sept. ,,

The midland coal-owners propose a reduction of 25 per cent. on the excess wages paid in 1888 *et seq.* Meetings of coal-owners and miners held in London; the miners reject the reduction and arbitration, 21 July. Strike of about 200,000 miners begins against reduction, 24 July *et seq.*; strike extends to N. Wales, Yorkshire, and N.W. Scotland, 9 Aug.; about 35,000 men out, mid. Aug. Strike collapsing in Wales; rioting checked by the military in Derbyshire, S. Yorkshire Notts. . . . . Aug.—Sept. ,,

Resumption of work at old wages in some parts Oct.; joint conference at Westminster, 4–6 Nov; no result; by advice of Mr. Gladstone, a joint conference meets at the foreign office, the earl of Rosebery chairman: result, a board of conciliation of 14 delegates from each side and a chairman, with a casting vote, to be appointed for a year; work to be resumed at once at the old rate of wages till 1 Feb. 1894 (the strike lasted 16 weeks) . . . . 17 Nov. ,,

Destruction of the works at lord Masham's colliery, Featherstone, near Pontefract, by rioters; intervention of the military; James Gibbs and James Duggan killed, and many wounded 7 Sept. ,,

Royal commission of inquiry (lord Bowen and others), 19–25 Oct.; report issued justifying the conduct of the magistrates and military . 8 Dec. ,,

200*l.* awarded to the relatives of the men killed, reported . . . . March, 1894

The strike occasions much stoppage of work in the country, and great distress through the rise of the price of coal . . . . . Sept.—Nov. 1893

Strike of miners in the Pas de Calais and Belgium, &c. (see *France*) . . . . Sept.—Oct. ,,

Strike of Scotch coal-miners for an advance of 1*s.* per day, 22 Nov.; about 100,000 men out of work, 4 Dec.; end of strike by compromise . 11 Dec. ,,

The formation of a coal-trust for the United Kingdom, proposed by sir George Elliot and others, by the co-operation of coal-owners, bankers, &c. as a company—*Times*, 20 Sept.; scheme favourably received at a conference in Newcastle-on-Tyne, Nov.; sir George Elliot, originally a pit-lad, gradually rose through his great abilities to be a wealthy proprietor; died, aged 78, 23 Dec. ,,

Joint conference of masters and men at Westminster to consider the formation of a board of conciliation; the selection of a chairman referred to the speaker of the house of commons 13 Dec. ,,

The increase of 5 per cent. recently granted to Northumberland miners raised to 7½ per cent. 13 Jan. 1894

Miners' conciliation board: 2nd meeting in London, 15 Jan.; lord Shand nominated chairman by the speaker, reported 26 Jan.; accepted at a meeting 14 Feb.; 4th meeting; lord Shand present; rules adopted . . . . 3 April, ,,

Wages to be reduced 10 per cent. from 1 Aug. 1894 to 1 Jan. 1896; settled at a meeting of the conciliation board . . . . 19 July, ,,

Strike of about 5,000 in the Wigan district 1 Aug. ,,

Great strike of Scotch miners (about 65,000) began 26 June; negotiations fail; contributions for their support from the British miners' federation received; work gradually resumed: end of the strike . . . . . . 22 Oct. 1894

. Wales coal trade sliding-scale, arrangement settled for 18 months . . . 28 March, 1895

Coal Mines Regulation Act of 1887 amended 1894; and 1896.

Coal strikes: see *United States*, April—June, 1894.

Earl of Durham sells his collieries, shipping, &c., co. Durham, to Messrs. Joicey and Co.; reported, 20 May, 1896

London Coal combination: 8 firms form a company, headed by Wm. Cory and Son . Sept. ,,

Death of Mr. Wm. Armstrong, aged, 84; mining engineer, "Father of the coal trade" 3 Nov. ,,

"Our Coal resources," by Edw. Hull; published 1897

Discussion respecting the output of coal . Dec. ,,

The use of dangerous explosives in coal mines prohibited; order issued . . . . 20 Dec. ,,

United States, 198,250,000 tons output in 1897, April, 1898; 267,542,444 in 1900. See *Strikes* April, 1898

Lord James of Hereford chairman of conciliation board, 16 Dec.; wages to be increased 5 per cent., April, 1899, and 2½ per cent. from Oct.; decided, 10 Feb. 1899, further advance; wages now 46¼ per cent. above those of 1879 . . . May, 1900

"Annals of Coal Mining and the Coal Trade," by R. L. Galloway . . . . . . Feb. 1899

Coal struck at Barham, Kent, 24 March; and at Ropersole, near Dover . . . early April, ,,

The world—723,239,000 tons output in 1899.

Sir Wm. Thos. Lewis, founder of the sliding scale system, resigns his over 50 years' leadership of the S. Wales coal-owners' association . July ,,

Sir M. Hicks Beach imposed 1*s.* per ton duty on exported coal . . . . . . 18 March, 1901

Demonstrations against the proposed coal tax, April, ,,

Royal commission appointed, Mr. W. L. Jackson (made a peer, lord Allerton, June, 1902), chairman, to inquire into the coal supplies of the United Kingdom . . . . . . end Dec. ,,

Strike of winding enginemen in W. Monmouthshire, 14,000 colliers affected . . . 31 Dec. ,,

Lord James of Hereford awards a 10 per cent. reduction in wages from July . . . 16 June, 1902

Decrease of wages (mines and quarries), 1,075,000*l.* in 1901, reported . . . . 27 Aug. ,,

Welsh miners' demonstration at Mountain Top, Cefn Glass, in favour of a conciliation board, 13 Sept. ,,

Crisis in South Wales, 31 Dec.; settlement effected 24 Jan. 1903

ACCIDENTS.—About 1000 lives are lost annually by explosion and accidents in mines. (1856-76). 1877, 1208 lost: 1878, 1413; 1879, 973 lost; 1880, 1318 lost; 1881, 954 lost; 1882, 1126 lost; 1883, 1054 lost; 1884, 942 lost; 1885, 1150 lost; 1886, 953; 1887, 995; 1888, 888; 1889, 1,110; 1890, 1,206; 1891, 1,030; 1896, 1,025; 1897, 930; 1898, 908; 1899, 916; 1900, 1,012; 1901, 1,131; 1902, 1,018.

More men employed than formerly, consequently more deaths at explosions (1886). Pits deeper than formerly. Dust as well as after-damp causes explosions.

In 1858, by explosions in coal-mines, 52 persons perished at Bardsley; 20 at Duffryn, near Newport; 52 at Tyldesley, near Leeds; and about 36 in different parts of the country.

1859—5 April, 26 lives were lost at the chain colliery, near Neath, through the irruption of water.

1860—76 lives were lost on 2 March, at Burradon, near Killingworth; 145 at the Risca mine, near Newport, Mon., 1 Dec.; and 22 at the Hetton mine, Northumberland, 20 Dec.

1861—11 June, 21 lives were lost through an inundation in the Claycross mines, Derbyshire.

85 lives were lost at Lalle coal-mine, in France, in Oct. 1861.

1862—47 lives were lost at Gethin mine, Merthyr Tydvil, S. Wales, 19 Feb.; at Walker, near Newcastle-on-Tyne, 15 lives lost, 22 Nov.; Edmund's Main, near Barnsley, 60 lives lost, 8 Dec.

1863—13 lives lost at Coxbridge, near Newcastle, 6 March; 39 lives lost at Margam, S. Wales, 17 Oct.; 14 lives lost at Maesteg, S. Wales, 26 Dec.

1865—6 lives lost at Claycross, 3 May; 24 at New Bedwellty pit, near Tredegar, 16 June; explosion at Gethin mine, Merthyr Tydvil, 30 lives lost, 20 Dec.

1866—Explosion at Highbrook colliery, near Wigan, Lancashire, about 30 lives lost, 23 Jan.; at Dukinfield near Ashton, 37 lives lost, 14 June; at Pelton Fell colliery, near Durham, about 24 lives lost, 31 Oct.; at Oaks colliery, Hoyle-mill, near Barnsley, about 360 persons killed, 12 Dec.; 28 searchers killed (including Mr. Parkin Jeffcock, mining engineer) by fresh explosion, 13 Dec.; at Talke-of-the-hill, Staffordshire, about 80 persons perish, 13 Dec.

1867—Explosion at Garswood colliery, near St. Helen's, 14 lives lost, 29 Aug.; Shankhouse colliery, Cramlington, Northumberland, flooded, 1 man drowned, 1 Nov.; explosion at Ferndale colliery, Rhondda valley, Glamorganshire, about 178 lives lost: attributed to naked lights, 8 Nov.

(For still more fatal accidents, see *Lundhill* and *Hartley*.)

47 lives lost in a mine near Jemmapes, Belgium, 6 Aug. 1868.

1868. Explosions: at Green pit, near Ruabon, 11 persons killed, 30 Sept.; at Arley mine, Hindley-green, near Wigan, 62 killed, 26 Nov.; at Norley mine, near Wigan, about 7 killed, 21 Dec.; at Haydock collieries, near St. Helen's, 26 deaths, 30 Dec.

1869. Brierly pit, near Stourbridge, inundated 17 March, many lost;—some rescued, 20, 21 March. Explosions at Highbrook colliery, near Wigan, about 33 persons perished, 1 April: at Ferndale colliery, Glamorganshire, about 60 lost, 10 June; Haydock pit, St. Helen's, about 58 lost, 21 July; Moss Coal Company's pit, near Hindley, about 30 lost, 22 Nov.

1870. Explosions—at Silverdale colliery, Staffordshire, 19 killed, 7 July; Llansamlet, near Swansea, 19 killed, 23 July; Brynn-hall, near Wigan, about 19 killed, 16 Aug.

1871. Explosions, Renishaw park colliery, Eckington, near Sheffield, 27 killed, 10 Jan.; Pentre colliery, Rhondda valley, 38 killed, 24 Feb.; Victoria, near Ebbw Vale, Monmouthshire, about 19 killed, 2 March; Moss Pits, near Wigan, 70 killed, 6 Sept.; Grisons, Belgium, 30 killed, 27 Sept.; Gelly pit, Aberdare, 4 killed, 4 Oct.; Seaham, 30 killed, 25 Oct.

1872. Explosions—Llynvi valley near Bridgend, 11 killed, 11 Jan.; Black lake colliery, S. Staffordshire, 8 killed, (through carelessness), 25 Jan.; Morley main, near Dewsbury and Leeds, 7 Oct. about 34 deaths: great carelessness and bad discipline; Rains mine, Pendlebury, 6 killed, 6 Nov.; Monceaux, department of Saône et Loire, about 38 killed, 8 Nov.; Pelsall-hall, Walsall, about 22 drowned by influx of water from an old working, 14 Nov.

1873. Explosion at Talke colliery, N. Staffordshire Coal and Iron Company's works, about 20 killed, 18 Feb.; Drummond colliery, Nova Scotia, explosion and fire, about 75 perished, 13 May; Shamokin, Pennsylvania, U.S., 15 killed, 18 June; Meshes colliery, near Wigan, 6 killed, 21 Nov.

1874. Explosions—Astley pit, Dukinfield, near Manchester, 54 killed, (attributed to gross ignorance or culpable carelessness), 14 April; Saw-mills pit, near Wigan, 15 killed, 18 July; Rawmarsh colliery near Rotherham, explosion through naked lights, about 23 killed, 20 Nov.; Bignall hall colliery, near Dudley, Staffordshire, 17 killed, 24 Dec.

1875. Explosions—Aldwarke Main, near Rotherham, 7 killed, 5 Jan.; Ruffery colliery, Dudley, 4 killed, 6 Jan.; Bunker's Hill, North Staffordshire, (through a gunpowder fuze), 43 deaths, 30 April; Donnington Wood, Shropshire, 11 killed, 11 Sept.; Ashton Vale, near Bedminster, 4 killed, 7 Oct.; Haigh, near Wigan, Alexandra pit (accident with descending cages), 7 killed, 3 Dec.; Powell Duffryn, New Tredegar, 22 killed, 4 Dec.; Llancolly, Pentyrch, (naked light), 12 killed, 5 Dec.; Swaithe main, near Barnsley, about 140 killed, 6 Dec.; Methley junction, near Leeds, 6 killed, 9 Dec. Explosion at a colliery near Mons, Belgium, about 110 killed, 14 Dec.

1876. Explosions—Talke, North Staffordshire, 5 killed, 5 Jan.; St. Etienne, France, about 30 killed, 4 Feb. Birley, near Sheffield, 6 killed, 26 June; Abertillery, Monmouthshire, 17 killed, 18 Dec.

1877. Explosions, &c.—Stonehill, near Bolton, about 18 killed, 23 Jan.; Darcy Lever, near Bolton, about 10 killed, 7 Feb.; Tyldesley, near Bolton, 7 killed, 6 March; New Worcester pit, Swansea, 18 or 19 killed, 8 March. *Inundation*—Tynewydd mine, near Pontypridd, S. Wales, several drowned, 11 April, several rescued by excavation after ten days' imprisonment; great heroism shown, see *Albert Medals*, 20 April; Mr. Thomas, manager, accused of culpable negligence, after inquest on 5 deaths, 17 May.—King Pit, Pemberton, near Wigan, about 33 perished (including Mr. Walker, the manager, and two overlookers attempting rescue) 11 Oct.; High Blantyre, near Glasgow, Messrs. Dixon's pits, above 200 perished, 22 Oct.; South Kirby, near Barnsley, rope broke, 4 killed, 29 Oct.

1878. Explosions, &c.—High Blantyre, 6 perished, 9 March; Kilsyth, Stirlingshire, Barnard Pit, 16 immured. March; Kearsley, near Bolton, about 43 perished, 12 March; Apedale, near Chesterton, N. Staffordshire, about 30 perished, 27 March; Wood Pits, Florida mine, Haydock, near Wigan, about 189 perished, 7 June; Ebbw Vale colliery, Abercarne, 12 miles from Newport, Monmouthshire, about 268 out of 387 perished, 11 Sept.

1879. Explosions, &c.—Dinas pit, Rhondda valley, Glamorganshire, about 63 perish, 13 Jan.; "Deep Drop" pit, near Wakefield, 19 perish, 4 March; Victoria colliery, Snydale, near Wakefield; rope of descending cage broke, 8 killed, 7 March; Cwmavon, Glamorganshire; chain broke, 6 killed, 24 June; High Blantyre collieries, Dixon & Co., 28 killed, 2 July; Lady pit, Silverdale, N. Staffordshire, 8 deaths, 12 Sept.; Wann Llwyd, Ebbw Vale, Monmouth, 3 killed, 22 Sept. Shortheath, near Wolverhampton, 6 killed, 12 Nov.; Scowcrofts, Kearsley, near Bolton, 7 deaths, 25 Dec.

1880. Explosions, &c.—Leycett, near Newcastle-under-Lyme, about 73 deaths, 21 Jan.; *Anderlaüs* (France), about 20 deaths, 1 April; Risca, 6 miles from Newport, Mon., about 120 deaths 15 July; Seaham, near Sunderland, Durham, 164 deaths, 8 Sept.; Pen-y-graig, S. Wales, 101 perished, 10 Dec.

1881. Explosions.—Whitfield colliery, Chell, N. Stafford, 20 killed, 7 Feb.; Hanley, Staffordshire, about 5 killed, 21 Nov.; Cockerill colliery, Belgium, 66 perished, about 9 Dec.; Abram colliery, near Wigan, about 48 perished, 19 Dec. (13 explosions, with loss of 99 lives).

1882. Explosions—Coedlae, Glamorganshire, 6 lives, 11 Feb.; Trimdon Grange colliery, 74 perished, 16 Feb.; Blaina, Monmouthshire, 5 deaths, 27 Feb.; Lumley, near Fencehouses, Durham, fall of shaft, about 100 imprisoned, 14 March; Tudhoe colliery, Weardale, Durham, 37 lives lost, 18 April; West Stanley, Durham, 13 lives lost, 19 April; lord Lonsdale's colliery, near Whitehaven, 4 killed, 25 April; Baxterley mine, near Atherstone, Warwickshire, about 32 lives lost, 2 May; Victoria colliery, Brantcliff, Morley, near Leeds, 7 killed, 1 May; Claycross, above 45 deaths, 7 Nov.

1883. Explosions.—Wharncliffe colliery, near Barnsley, 17 deaths, 19 Oct.; Fair Lady pit, near Leycett, Newcastle-under-Lyme, 22 Oct.; Moor-fields colliery, near Accrington, Lancashire, about 68 deaths, 7 Nov.

1884. Explosions, &c.—Gamant, Cwmamman, South Wales; rope broke; cage fell; 11 killed, 16 Jan.; Rhondda valley, Glamorganshire, explosion, about 11 perished, Jan.; Pochin colliery, near Tredegar, 14 deaths, 8 Nov.

1885. Explosions, &c.—Usworth, near Newcastle-on-Tyne; about 42 deaths, 2 March; Camphausen, near Saarbrück, about 140 perish, 17 March; Dombrau, Ostrau, Moravia, about 41 deaths, 27 March; Fenton colliery, near Stoke-on-Trent, 8 deaths, 7 April; Houghton-le Spring, about 12 perish, 3 June; Clifton Hall, near Pendlebury, Lancashire, about 177 perish, 9.30 A.M. 18 June; Burley, Apedale, N. Stafford, 9 killed, 20 June; Mardy colliery, Pontypridd, S. Wales, 200 entombed, 81 deaths, 23 Dec. (Explosions in Britain 16, deaths 322.)

1886. Explosions, &c.—Easton colliery, Bristol, 4 killed, 19 Feb.; Werfa old pit, Abernant, near Aberdare, 3 killed, 27 March; Woodend or Bedford colliery, near West Leigh, S.W. Lancashire, explosion, 38 deaths, 13 Aug.; Bedminster colliery, near Bristol, 10 killed, 10 Sept.; Braysdown colliery, near Radstock, 3 killed, 14 Sept.; Schalke, in Westphalia, 45 perish, 24 Sept.; Pope and Pearson's colliery, Altofts, near Wakefield, 22 deaths, 2 Oct.; Taunton colliery near Ashby-de-la-Zouch, Mr. Lakin, the owner, and three others killed by choke-damp, 6 Oct.; Albion colliery, near Pontypridd, four killed, Nov.; Elemore colliery, Durham 28 deaths, 2 Dec.; Houghton Main colliery, near Barnsley, 10 men killed by fall of a cage, 30 Dec.

1887. Explosions, &c.—Ynyshir colliery, Rhondda valley, Wales, about 39 lives lost, 18 Feb.; Mons colliery, Belgium, about 87 perish, 5 March; Bulli (Sydney), 85 perish, 23 March; Victoria colliery, Nanaimo, Vancouver Island, over 170 perish, 4 May; Udston colliery, near Glasgow, 73 perish, 28 May;

Gelsenkirchener, Prussia, above 60 perish, 8 June; Walker, near Newcastle, 8 killed, 24 Oct.

1888. St. Helen's colliery, Workington, about 30 lives lost, 19 April; Aber colliery, Glamorgan, 5 lives lost, 20 May; Aveyron, France, 40 lives lost, 3 Nov.; Dour, Belgium, 21 lives lost, 13 Nov.

1889. Hyde colliery, Cheshire, 23 lives lost, 18 Jan.; Brynnally colliery, near Wrexham, 20 lives lost, 13 March. Explosion of fire-damp in Verpilleux mine, near St. Etienne, about 184 deaths, 3 July; Shell colliery, N. Staffordshire, explosion, 3 deaths, 17 Aug.; Penicuik colliery (Mauricewood pit), Midlothian, fire discovered, 2 men escaped, 63 reported to have perished, 5 Sept.; Mossfield colliery, Adderley Green, Longton, N. Staffordshire, 59 deaths, 16 Oct.; Hebburn colliery, near Newcastle-on-Tyne, 6 deaths, 4 Nov.

1890. Explosions, &c.—Glynn Pit, near Pontypool, 5 deaths, 23 Jan.; Llanerch colliery, near Abersychan, Monmouthshire, 176 deaths (relief subscribed nearly 26,000*l.*), 30 April; colliery near Decize, Nièvre, France, about 44 deaths, 18 Feb.; Morfa colliery, Tarbach, Glamorganshire, 87 deaths, 10 March; Hill Farm mine, Pennsylvania, 34 perish, 16 June; Pelissier mine, St. Etienne, S. France, about 100 lives lost, 29 July; Mayback pit, near Wendel, 24 deaths, 15 Sept.

1891. Explosions, &c.—Sladderhill pits, Apedale, near Newcastle-under-Lyme, about 10 lives lost, 2 April; Malago Vale, Bedminster, 10 deaths, 31 Aug.; Abergwynfi, Avon Valley, S. Wales, 7 men killed by accident to machinery, 30 Sept.; St. Etienne, France, explosion through fire-damp, about 73 deaths, 6 Dec.

1892. Explosions, &c.—Anderlues colliery, Mons, Belgium, about 153 killed, 11 March; Ravenswharf, near Dewsbury, 6 men drowned by flooding of a pit, 4 Aug.; Ynisceiyn colliery in Ystradgynlais, Brecon, derangement of machinery, 7 deaths, 24 Aug.; Park Slip colliery, Tondu, Aberkenfig-cefn, near Bridgend, S. Wales, out of 151 persons there were 116 deaths, 26 Aug.; Mr. Asquith, the home secretary, visited the place 28 Aug.; Agrappe colliery, Frameries, Belgium, 25 deaths, 1 Sept.; Bamfurlong, near Wigan, fire, 16 deaths, 14 Dec.

1893. Explosions, &c.—Kings, near Como, Colorado, 27 deaths, 10 Jan.; Pontypridd, Wales, accident, 7 men killed, 23 Jan.; Fortschritt mine, Dux, Bohemia, about 17 deaths, 24 Jan.; near Recklingshausen, 18 deaths, 1 Feb.; fire at the Great Western colliery, Pontypridd, Rhondda valley, 61 deaths, 11 April; Combs colliery, Thornhill, near Dewsbury, 139 deaths, 4 July; Dortmund, Germany, firedamp, 50 deaths, reported 20 Aug.

1894. Explosions, &c.—Disastrous explosions in Silesia (*which see*), 14 June, 1894, and 1895; explosion at the Albion colliery, 3 miles from Pontypridd, S. Wales, about 286 deaths, 23 June.

1895. Explosions, &c.—Colliery flooded at Audley, N. Staffordshire, 77 lives lost, 14 Jan.; explosion (firedamp) at Monteeau-les-Mines, 33 lives lost, 4 Feb.; Radstock, Somerset, 7 deaths, 6 Feb.; Denny, near Stirling, 13 deaths, 26 April; near Bochum, Germany, 33 deaths, 25 July; Tyldesley, near Manchester, Mr. Kay, manager, and 4 others killed, 1 Oct.; Blackwell, Derbyshire, 7 deaths, 11 Nov.

1896. Explosions, &c., at Tylors Town colliery, S. Wales, 57 deaths, 27 Jan.; Brancepeth pit, co. Durham, 20 deaths, 13 April; Micklefield colliery, near Leeds, 66 deaths, 30 April; relief fund, 50*l.* from the Queen, total over 20,000*l.* reported 6 Oct.; at Rochebelle, near Alais, France, 25 deaths, 2 June; Neath colliery, Glamorgan, 6 deaths, 4 Aug.; gen. Blumenthal colliery, Westphalia, about 25 deaths, 19 Nov.; colliery flooded at Abernant, S. Wales, 6 men drowned, 9 Dec.; Reschitza colliery, Hungary, about 36 killed, reported, 20 Dec.

1897. Explosion, &c.. at Broadoak, near Loughor, S. Wales, 5 deaths, 5 Jan.; 10 men killed by the fall of a cage at Garth colliery, Glamorganshire, 11 June.

1898. Whitwick, Leicestershire, a "gob" fire, 35 deaths, 19 April; explosion, firedamp, near Mons., 13 deaths, 25 May; Drumley pit, Ayr, 6 deaths, 9 Sept.

1899. Explosions, &c., at St. Helens, fall of roof, 3 deaths, 20 Feb.; Caledonia mine, Cape Breton, 11 deaths, 16 June; Brandon colliery, Durham, 5 deaths, 15 Aug.; Llest coalpit at Pontyrhyl, near Cardiff, 19 deaths, 18 Aug. (due to naked lights); Couchard mine, near St. Etienne, chain broke, 16 deaths, 28 Aug.

1900. Explosions, &c.—Haydock colliery, 8 deaths, 29 June; No. 5 pit, near Kilmarnock, 6 deaths, 17 Aug.; Glenavon colliery, Glamorgan, flooded, 5 deaths, 24 Oct.; Preston colliery. N. Shields, 3 deaths, 16 Nov.; Fénelon pit, Aniche, Dep. du Nord, 16 deaths, 28 Nov.

1901. Explosions, &c.—Beath colliery, Dunfermline, 7 deaths from "white damp," 15 Feb.; Orrell, near Wigan, 4 deaths, 10 April; Croft pit, Whitehaven colliery, 4 deaths, 17 April; at Wasmes, near Mons, 19 deaths, 26 April; Universal colliery, near Caerphilly, 81 deaths, 24 May; Talk-o'-th'-hill colliery, Staffordshire, 4 deaths, 27 May; Dayton, Ohio, about 30 deaths, 27 May; Donibristle, Fifeshire, 14 entombed, 8 deaths, 26 Aug. [Mr. Andrew Carnegie gave 4 of the rescuers 100*l.* apiece, 2 Sept.]; at Llanbradach colliery, S. Wales, 8 deaths, 10 Sept.

1902. Explosions, &c.—Milfraen colliery, S. Wales, 5 men killed by a cage tilting, 4 March; Edge-green shaft, near Wigan, 9 killed, 6 April; Fraterville colliery, Tennessee, estimated deaths over 200, 19 May; Crow's Nest Pass, Ferme, British Columbia, about 150 deaths, 23 May; Dowlais, S. Wales, 8 deaths, 3 June; Rolling Mill mine, Pennsylvania, 105 deaths, 10 July; Mt. Kembla, New S. Wales, over 85 deaths, 31 July; Abertysswg, S. Wales, 16 deaths, 3 Sept.; Coleford, Forest of Dean, 4 deaths, 4 Sept. 3 saved, 9 Sept.; Tirpentwys, Pontypool, winding accident, 8 deaths, 1 Oct.; Fauldhouse, Linlithgow, fire, 4 deaths, 21 Oct.; Donisthorpe cage accident, 2 deaths, 25 Oct.; cage accident, Treharris, S. Wales, 5 deaths, 11 Nov.; Uspensk, Russia, fire, 58 deaths, about 27 Dec.

1903. Explosion and fire, Hanna, Wyoming, 175 deaths, 30 June.

See also *Wyoming*, 1895, and *Utah*, 1900.

See *Mansion-house Funds*.

COAL-EXCHANGE, London, established by 47 Geo. III. c. 68 (1807). The present building (a most interesting structure) was erected by Mr. J. B. Bunning, and opened by prince Albert 30 Oct. 1849

COAL-WHIPPERS' BOARD, to protect the men employed in unloading coal-vessels from publicans, formed by an act of parliament in 1843, lasted till 1856, when the coal-owners themselves established a whipping office. The use of steam machinery in discharging cargoes has diminished the employment of coal-whippers.

COAL DUES, on coal entering the port of London for metage are mentioned in 1444. The right of the Corporation to 4*d.* per chaldron was established in 1591. The amount of the tax and the term of levying it have been frequently changed since 1694. In 1831, the tax was directed to be levied on all coals entering London by water or railways, to be regulated by weight and not by measure. The tax of 13*d.* per ton by the act of 1868 extended to 5 July, 1889. The receipts in 1885 amounted to 449,343*l.* Latterly the money was expended on extensive City improvements. Much discussion on the subject, 1887-9.

An act for the abolition of these dues received the royal assent 9 July, 1889. Provision was made for the continuance of these dues another year to enable the corporation to pay debts due for the Holborn Viaduct and various city improvements. They ceased 5 July, 1890. Tax of 1*s.* per ton on exported coal, 18 March, see *Budget*, 26 July, 1901.

COALING STATIONS, for supplying ships of the navy and the mercantile marine, are established by the British government at important parts of the empire. Many of these stations are fortified, and in the event of war would be of the first importance to the navy as points of refuge, defence, and repair, as Aden, Hong Kong, Singapore, St. Helena, Simon's Town, and other stations.

COAL TAR, see *Tar* and *Benzole*.

COALITIONS AGAINST FRANCE generally arose through England subsidising the great powers of the continent. See *Treaties*.

Austria, Prussia and Great Britain 1793

Great Britain, Germany, Russia, Naples, Portugal, and Turkey, signed . . . . . 22 June, 1799

Great Britain, Russia, Austria, and Naples, 5 Aug. 1805
Great Britain, Russia, Prussia, and Saxony, 6 Oct. 1806
England and Austria . . . . 6 April, 1809
Russia and Prussia; the treaty ratified at Kalisch 17 March, 1813

COALITION MINISTRIES, see *Aberdeen*, *Grenville II.*, *Pelham*, *Portland*, and *Salisbury, III.*

COAST GUARD. In 1856, the raising and governing this body was transferred to the admiralty. A coast brigade of artillery was established in Nov. 1859.—COAST VOLUNTEERS, see under *Navy of England.* The importance of electric coast communication in time of storms, &c., was much discussed in 1892. A royal commission on the subject met 18 June, 1892, see *Lighthouses.* Good results from electric communications, reported Oct. 1892, see *Hydrophone.*

COASTING TRADE of Great Britain thrown open to all nations by 17 Vict. c. 5, 1854.

COBALT, a rare mineral found among the veins of ores, or in the fissures of stone, at an early date, in the mines of Cornwall, where the workmen call it mundic. *Hill.* It was distinguished as a metal by Brandt, in 1733.

COBDEN CLUB, instituted to spread and develop Cobden's principles; held first dinner, W. E. Gladstone in the chair, 21 July, 1866. The statue of Richard Cobden, at Camden Town, was inaugurated, 27 June, 1868. 12 out of 14 cabinet ministers were members July, 1880.

At a meeting of the club, 12 May, 1890, earl Granville in the chair, an address was presented to Mr. T. B. Potter, founder and hon. secretary for 30 years (dies 6 Nov. 1898); and Mr. W. E. Gladstone gave a discourse on free trade.

Increased activity of the club consequent on Mr. Chamberlain's fiscal proposals and campaign. Meetings organised under the auspices of the club, and literature disseminated in support of free trade June *et seq.* 1903

COBURG, see *Saxe-Coburg.*

COCA, a powerful narcotic existing in the *Erythroxylon Coca*, a South American plant known in 1580; men taking a little of this are enabled to endure hard labour without any food for six or seven days and nights. Dr. Mantegazza's prize essay in German was published at Vienna in 1849. Cocaine, an anæsthetic obtained from this plant, is used in operations of the eye and mucous membranes. The habitual use of cocaine produces *cocaism*, which induces deterioration of the moral sense and various nervous conditions.

COCCEIANS, a small sect founded by John Cocceius, of Bremen, in the seventeenth century. He held, amongst other opinions, that of a visible reign of Christ in this world, after a general conversion of the Jews and all other people to the Christian faith. He died in 1665.

COCHEREL (near Evreux, N. W. France). Here Bertrand du Guesclin defeated the king of Navarre, and took prisoner the captal de Buch, 16 May, 1364.

COCHIN (India), held by the Portuguese, 1503; by the Dutch, 1663; by Hyder Ali, 1776; taken by the British, 1796; ceded to them, 1814.

COCHIN CHINA, previously province of Annam, was acquired by the French in 1861–62, and their sovereignty recognized by treaty, 25 Aug. 1884; by China, 9 June, 1885. Population, 1885, 1,792,933. Capital, Saigon; population, 1895, 17,235. Lieut.-gov. M. Ducos (1895); M. Picanon, 1900. See *Indo-China.*

COCHINEAL INSECT (*Coccus cacti*), deriving its colour from feeding on the *cactus*, became known to the Spaniards soon after their conquest of Mexico in 1518. Cochineal was brought to Europe about 1523, but was not known in Italy in 1548, although the art of dyeing then flourished there. In 1858 it was cultivated successfully in Teneriffe, the vines having failed through disease. 260,000 lbs. of cochineal were imported into England in 1830; 1,081,776 lbs. in 1845; 2,360,000 lbs. in 1850; 3,034,976 lbs. in 1859; 47,790 cwt. in 1870; and 32,094 cwt. in 1877; 30,017 cwt. in 1881; 21,440 cwt. in 1883; 10,089 cwt. in 1887; 7,808 cwt. in 1890; 4,471 cwt. in 1893; 5,697 cwt. in 1896; 3,823 cwt. in 1899. The use of cochineal has been much replaced by the coal tar colours. Duty repealed 1845.

COCKER'S ARITHMETIC. Edward Cocker, an eminent penman, born 1631, died 1675, compiled a book which first appeared in 1677, edited by John Hawkins.

COCKERTON CASE, see under *Education*, 20 Dec., 1900.

COCK-FIGHTING, practised by the Greeks, was brought by the Romans into England. William Fitz-Stephen, in the reign of Henry II., describes cock-fighting as the sport of school-boys on Shrove-Tuesday. It was prohibited by Edward III. 1365; by Henry VIII.; and by Cromwell, 1653, and latterly in 1849. Part of the site of Drury-lane theatre was a cock-pit in the reign of James I.; and the Cock-pit at Whitehall was erected by Charles II. Formerly there was a *Cock-pit-Royal* in St. James's Park; but the governors of Christ's Hospital would not renew the lease for the building. Cock-fighting is now forbidden by law. On 22 April, 1865, 34 persons were fined at Marlborough-street police-office, for being present at a cock-fight. It was popular in New York, 1873.

COCK-LANE GHOST, an imposition practised by William Parsons, his wife, and daughter, by means of a female ventriloquist, during 1760 and 1761, at No. 33, Cock-lane, London, was at length detected, and the parents were condemned to the pillory and imprisonment, 10 July, 1762.

COCOA or CACAO, the kernel or seed of *Theobroma cacao* (Linn.), was introduced into this country shortly after the discovery of Mexico, where it is an article of diet. From cocoa is produced chocolate. The cocoa imported into the United Kingdom, chiefly from the British West Indies and Guiana, was in 1849, 1,989,477 lbs.; in 1855, 7,343,458 lbs.; in 1861, 9,080,288 lbs.; in 1866, 10,308,298 lbs.; in 1870, 14,793,950 lbs.; in 1876, 20,443,591 lbs.; in 1879, 26,155,788 lbs.; in 1887, 27,352,568 lbs.; in 1890, 28,112,210 lbs; in 1893, 32,982,005 lbs.; in 1896, 38,281,803 lbs.; in 1898, 42,833,993 lbs.; in 1899, 43,473,241 lbs.; in 1900, 52,647,318 lbs.; 1901, 51,798,802 lbs.

COCOA-NUT TREE (*Cocos nucifera*, Linn.), supplies the Indians with almost all they need, as bread, water, wine, vinegar, brandy, milk, oil, honey, sugar, needles, clothes, thread, cups, spoons, basins, baskets, paper, masts for ships, sails, cordage, nails, covering for their houses, &c. *Ray.* In Sept. 1829, Mr. Soames patented his mode of procuring stearine and elaine from cocoa-nut oil. It is said that 32 tons of candles have been made in a month from these materials at the Belmont works, Lambeth.

CODES, see *Laws.* Alfrenus Varus, the civilian, first collected the Roman laws about 66 B.C.; and

Servius Sulpicius, the civilian, embodied them about 53 B.C. The Gregorian and Hermoginian codes were published A.D. 290; the Theodosian code commenced by order of Theodosius II. in 429; and published for the eastern empire in 438. In 447 he transmitted to Valentinian his new constitution spromulgated as the law of the west in 448. The celebrated code of the emperor Justinian in 529—a digest from this last made in 533; see *Basilica*. Alfred's code, a selection from existing laws, is the foundation of the common law of England, 887.—The CODE NAPOLEON, the civil code of France, was promulgated from 1803 to 1810. The emperor considered it his most enduring monument. It was prepared under his supervision by the most eminent jurists, from the 400 systems previously existing, and has been adopted by other countries. For Code telegrams, see *Telegraphs*.

A conference of jurists and publicists to consider an international code held at Brussels, July, Aug. 1874
The new German civil code, after much preparation, was passed by the parliament . . . 1 July, 1896

CODEX, see under *Bible, Alexandrian*, &c.

CODFISH, see *Holland*, 1347.

COD-LIVER OIL was recommended as a remedy for chronic rheumatism by Dr. Percival in 1782, for diseases of the lungs about 1833, and by professor Hughes Bennett in 1841. De Jongh's treatise on cod-liver oil was published in Latin, 1844; in English, 1849.

COERCION BILLS, see *Ireland*, 1881 and 1887.

CŒUR DE LION or **THE LION-HEARTED**, a surname given to Richard I. of England, on account of his courage, about 1192; and also to Louis VIII. of France, who signalised himself in the crusades, and in his wars against England, about 1223.

COFFEE. The tree was conveyed from Mocha in Arabia to Holland about 1616; and carried to the West Indies in 1726. First cultivated at Surinam by the Dutch, 1718. The culture was encouraged in the plantations about 1732, and the British and French colonies now grow coffee abundantly. Its use as a *beverage* is traced to the Persians. It came into great repute in Arabia Felix, about 1454; and passed thence into Egypt and Syria, and thence (in 1511) to Constantinople, where a coffee-house was opened in 1551. M. Thevenot, the traveller, first brought it to France, 1662. *Chambers*. See *Cafeine*.

Coffee brought into England by Mr. Nathaniel Canopus, a Cretan, who made it his common beverage at Balliol college, Oxford. *Anderson* . 1641
The first coffee-house in England was kept by a Jew, named Jacobs, in Oxford 1650
Mr. Edwards, an English Turkey merchant, brought home with him Pasqua Rosee, a Greek servant, who opened the first coffee-house in London, in George-yard, Lombard-street . . . 1652
Pasquet afterwards went to Holland, and opened the first house in that country. *Anderson*.
Rainbow coffee-house, Temple-bar, represented as a nuisance 1657
Coffee-houses suppressed by proclamation, 1675; the order revoked on petition of the traders . 1676
Licences to sell coffee abolished . . . 1869
Duty on coffee reduced to 1½*d*. the pound from 2 May, 1872
The quantity of coffee imported into these realms in 1852, 54,935,510 lbs.; in 1860, 82,767,746 lbs.; in 1866, 127,044,816 lbs.; in 1873, 183,397,576 lbs.; in 1876, 1,361,642 cwts.; in 1879, 1,600,386 cwts.; in 1883, 1,407,134 cwts.; in 1887, 1,045,698 cwts.; in 1890, 864,454 cwts.; in 1896, 713,468 cwts.; in 1898, 922,252 cwts.; in 1899, 974,991 cwts.; in 1900, 759,656 cwts.; 1901, 958,464 cwts.

Coffee Palaces, founded by Dr. Barnardo to replace public-houses for working-men. The "Edinburgh Castle," Limehouse, the first opened, 1873; the "Dublin Castle," Mile End 1876
Coffee Taverns, many opened in London . 1877–1889
Coffee Public-house National Society, formed April, 1879; opened a house at Shadwell . 28 June, 1879
Coffee disease prevalent in Ceylon, &c. autumn, 1882
M. Raoul reports the destructive, nearly universal ravages of *Hemilia Vastatrix* . . June, 1888

COFFERER OF THE HOUSEHOLD, formerly an officer of state, and a member of the privy council, who had special charge of the other officers of the household. Sir Henry Cocks was cofferer to queen Elizabeth. In 1782 the office was suppressed.

COFFINS. Athenian heroes were buried in coffins of cedar; owing to its aromatic and incorruptible qualities. *Thucydides*. Coffins of marble and stone were used by the Romans. Alexander is said to have been buried in one of gold; and glass coffins have been found in England. *Gough*. Patent coffins were invented in 1796; air-tight metallic coffins advertised at Birmingham in 1861.

COIF. The serjeant's coif was introduced before 1259, to hide the tonsure of such clergymen as chose to remain advocates in the secular courts, notwithstanding their prohibition by canon. *Blackstone*. The coif was at first a thin linen cover gathered together in the form of a skull or helmet, the material being afterwards changed into white silk, and the form eventually into the black patch at the top of the forensic wig, which is now the distinguishing mark of the degree of serjeant-at-law. *Foss's Lives of the Judges*.

COIMBRA was made the capital of Portugal by Alfonso, the first king, 1139, and remained so for about 250 years; many of the early kings of Portugal are interred here. The only Portuguese university was transferred from Lisbon, where it was originally established 1288, to Coimbra in 1308; finally settled in 1527. In a convent here, Alfonso IV. caused Iñez de Castro, at first mistress and afterwards wife of his son Pedro, to be cruelly murdered in 1355. Fatal riots against the rates mid-March, 1903. Population, 13,369.

COIN. Homer speaks of brass money, 1184 B.C. The invention of coin is ascribed to the Lydians, whose money was of gold and silver. Both were coined by Pheidon, tyrant of Argos, about 862 B.C. Money was coined at Rome under Servius Tullius, about 573 B.C. The most ancient known coins are Macedonian of the 5th century B.C. Brass money only was in use at Rome previously to 269 B.C. (when Fabius Pictor coined silver). Gold was coined 206 B.C. Iron money was used in Sparta, and iron and tin in Britain. *Dufresnoy*. In the earlier days of Rome the heads were those of deities, or of those who had received divine honours. Julius Cæsar first obtained permission of the senate to place his portrait on the coins, and the example was soon followed. The Britons and Saxons coined silver.—Rev. Roger Ruding's "Annals of the Coinage of Great Britain," published 1817-40.—The gold and silver coinage in the world is about 250,000,000*l*. silver, and 150,000,000*l*. gold. *Times*, 25 June, 1852. See *Gold, Silver, Copper* and *Guineas*, and other coins under names. An international conference relative to a universal system of coinage met at Paris in 1867; and a royal commission was appointed in London, Feb. 1868. £ for *libræ*, Roman pound of 12 ounces; *s*. for *solidi* (Anglo-Saxon *scill* or *scilling*); *d*. for *denarii*, the Roman penny.

The first coinage was at Camalodunum, or Colchester.

Coin was made sterling in 1216, before which time rents were mostly paid in kind, and money was found only in the coffers of the barons. *Stow.*

Coinage reformed by Edward VI. 1547-53

Queen Elizabeth caused the *base coin* to be recalled and genuine issued 1560

During the reigns of the Stuarts the coinage was greatly debased by clipping, &c. A commission (Charles Montague, aft. earl of Halifax, lord Somers, sir Isaac Newton, and John Locke) was appointed by William III. to reform the coinage; an act was passed, withdrawing the debased coin from circulation, and 1,200,000*l.* was raised by window-tax duty to defray the expense . 1695-96

Broad-pieces called in, and re-coined into guineas . 1732

The gold-coin brought into the Mint by proclamation, amounted to about 15,563,593*l.*; the expense of collecting, melting, and recoining it, was 754,019*l.* 1773-6

Act for weighing gold coin passed . . 13 June, 1774

The coin of the realm valued at about 12,000,000*l.* in 1711. *Davenant.* At 16,000,000*l.* in 1762. *Anderson.* It was 20,000,000*l.* in 1786. *Chalmers.* 37,000,000*l.* in 1800. *Phillips.*

New silver coinage 1816

English and Irish money assimilated . . 1 Jan. 1826

The gold is 28,000,000*l.*, and the rest of the metallic currency is 13,000,000*l.* *Duke of Wellington* . 1830

Metallic currency calculated to reach 45,000,000*l.* . 1840

Estimated as approaching, in gold and silver, 60,000,000*l.* 1853

Silver coined in London, value 11,108,265*l.* 15*s.* 1816-40

Ditto. value 2,440,614*l.* 1837-47

Light gold called in 1842

Napier's coin-weighing machine at the bank of England constructed 1844

The law respecting coinage offences consolidated . 1861

The first gold coins on certain record, struck 42 Hen. III. 1257

Gold florin first struck, Edw. III. (*Camden*) . . 1337

He introduced gold 6*s.* pieces, and nobles of 6*s.* 8*d.* (hence the lawyer's fee), afterwards half and quarter nobles 1344

Edw. IV. coined angels with a figure of Michael and the dragon, the original of George and the dragon 1465

Sovereigns first minted 1489

Shillings first coined (*Dr. Kelly*) . . . 1503 or 1504

Crowns and half-crowns coined 1553

Irish shillings struck 1560

Milled shilling of Elizabeth 1562

First large copper coinage, putting an end to the circulation of private leaden pieces, &c. . . 1620

Modern milling introduced 1631

Halfpence and farthings 1665

Copper coined by government 1672

Guineas (value 20*s.*), 2-guinea and 5-guinea pieces, 1663-64

Quarter-guinea coined, 3 Geo. I. 1716

Two-penny copper pieces 1797

Gold 7*s.*-pieces authorised . . . 29 Nov. „

Sovereigns, new coinage, St. George and dragon, designed by Pistrucci 1817

Four-penny pieces (see *Groat*) coined . . . 1836-56

Three-penny pieces: 3,299,208 coined . . . 1861

Half-farthings coined 1843

Silver florin (2*s.*) 1849

No crowns (1848-78) or half-crowns coined . . 1848-73

Bronze coinage issued, 1 Dec., 1860; a new penny issued in 1895

Coinage act passed, 4 April, 1870; amended 5 Aug. 1891

St. George and dragon sovereigns re-issued 14 Jan. 1871

Half-crowns again coined; recommended by bankers 1874

New die for gold coin finished . . . March, 1882

The bankers complain of great loss, by receiving light gold coins 1882-3

See *Budget*, 1884.

Sale of Mr. Whittall's great collection of Greek and other coins, 1,668 lots realized 3,951*l.* . July, 1884

Proclamation against importation of foreign bronze coins [to be received with slight reduction at post offices up to May 31] . . . 25 March, 1887

Proclamation respecting changes in coinage, viz., in pieces value of 5*l.*, 2*l.*, 1*l.*, 10*s.*, 5*s.*, 2*s.* 6*d.*, 2*s.*, 1*s.*, and 6*d.*; also Maundy monies value of 4*d.*, 3*d.*, 2*d.*, & 1*d.* New coin ordered, double florin 4*s.*; new effigy and designs 13 May; new coinage issued 20 June, 1887

The importation of imitation coins was prohibited by act passed . . . . . 26 Aug. 1889

Mr. Goschen introduces a bill for the withdrawal of light gold coin issued before June, 1837, and the substitution of coin of full weight provisionally, at the expense of the mint, July; passed 30 Aug. „

[The offer expired 13 Jan., extended to 31 March, 1890.]

The coinage committee (sir John Lubbock, sir Frederick Leighton, the deputy-master of the mint, and others) recommends that new designs by various artists be adopted for the sovereign and other coins, gold and silver; report presented, March, 1892

Permission to Victoria, Australia, to coin silver, granted with conditions . . . . Sept. „

Proclamation for the issue of the new coinage, 30 Jan. *London Gazette* . . . . 14 Feb. 1893

[Designs: *obverse* of all coins, the queen's head as modelled by Mr. Brock; *reverse* of 5*l.*, 2*l.*, 1*l.*, 10*s.*, 5*s.*, St. George and the dragon, by Pistrucci; 2*s.* 6*d.* by Mr. Brock; 2*s.* and 1*s.* by Mr. Poynter, 6*d.* and 3*d.* as at present.]

New Coinage Act passed . . . . 28 March, „

Proclamation for the issue of the new silver coinage, 14 Jan., *London Gazette*, 1902.

AMOUNT OF MONEY COINED.

Elizabeth		£5,832,000
James I.		2,500,000
Charles I.		10,500,000
Cromwell		1,000,000
Charles II.		7,524,100
James II.		3,740,000
William III.		10,511,900
Anne		2,691,626
George I.		8,725,920
George II.		11,966,576
George III.	gold	74,501,586
George IV.		41,782,815
William IV.		10,827,603

[The quantity of gold that passed through the Mint, since the accession of queen Elizabeth in 1558, to the beginning of 1840, is 3,353,561 pounds weight, troy. Of this, nearly one-half was coined in the reign of George III., namely, 1,593,078 pounds weight, troy.]

Victoria, from 1837 to 1848, gold, 29,886,457*l.*; weight, 746,452 lbs.; silver, 2,440,614*l.*; copper, 43,743*l.* 1848-1852, gold, silver, and copper, 19,838,377*l.*

Gold coined in 1853 (when Australian gold came in), 12,664,125*l.*; in 1854, 4,354,201*l.*; in 1855, 9,245,264*l.*; Australian colonies authorized to coin gold, 1855; in 1856, 6,476,060*l.*

Coined in 1859, 1,547,603 sovereigns; 2,203,813 half-sov.

Coined from 1 July, 1854, to 31 Dec. 1860: gold, 27,632,039*l.*; silver, 2,432,116*l.*

Coined in 1861: gold, 8,190,170*l.*; silver, 209,484*l.*; copper (bronze), 273,578*l.* 13*s.* 4*d.*

Coined in 1862: gold, 7,836,413*l.*; silver, 148,518*l.*; copper, 352,800*l.*

Coined in 1866: gold, 5,076,676*l.*; silver, 493,416*l.*; copper, 50,624*l.*

Coined in 1869: gold, 7,372,204*l.*; silver, 76,428*l.*; copper, 20,832*l.*

Coined in 1873 (less than 1872): gold, sovereigns, 2,382,835; half-sovereigns, 1,001,733*l.*; silver, (*number of pieces*) florins, 5,965,740; 1*s.*, 6,486,480; 6*d.*, 4,395,600; 4*d.*, 4158; 3*d.*, 4,059,528; 1*d.*, 7920. Copper: 1*d.*, 8,494,080; ½*d.*, 3,584,000; ¼*d.*, 3,215,600.

Coined in 1876 (work stopped five months through breakdown of machinery), gold, sovereigns, 3,318,705*l.*; half-sovereigns, 1,401,943*l.* 10*s.*; silver, half-crowns, 79,200*l.*; florins, 60,786*l.*

In 1877, 30,131,130 pieces; value 1,567,936*l.* 15*s.* 6½*d.*

Value of coinage in ten years (1867-76). Gold, 46,802,517*l.*; silver, 5,642,406*l.*; bronze, 401,309*l.*

1879: *Gold*, sovereigns, 17,525; half-sovereigns 35,050; total value, 35,050*l.* 3*s.* 0*d.* *Silver*, half-crowns, 901,296; florins, 1,354,320; shillings, 3,611,520; sixpences, 3,326,400; fourpences, 4,158; threepences, 2,966,568; twopences, 4,752; pence, 7,920; total value, 549,054*l.* *Bronze*: Pence, 7,848,964; halfpence, 3,584,000; farthings, 4,300,800; total value, 44,650*l.* 13*s.* 4*d.*

Net loss to the Mint in 1878, 51,543*l.*; in 1879, 27,955*l.*

1880: *Gold*, 4,150,052*l.* *Silver*, 761,508*l.* *Copper*, 19,264*l.*; total, 4,930,824*l.*

1883: *Gold*, 1,403,713*l.* *Silver*, 1,274,328*l.* *Copper*, 33,450*l.*; total, 2,711,491*l.*

		l.		*l.*		*l.*
1887 :	*Gold,*	1,908,686	*Silver,*	861,498	*Copper,*	45,173
1889 :	*Gold,*	7,500,700	*Silver,*	2,178,888	*Bronze,*	66,950
1890 :	*Gold,*	7,680,156	*Silver,*	1,694,688	*Bronze,*	90,285
1891 :	*Gold,*	6,723,648	*Silver,*	1,000,548	*Bronze,*	89,535
1892 :	*Gold,*	13,907,840	*Silver,*	849,932	*Bronze,*	58,556
1893 :	*Gold,*	9,266,251	*Silver,*	1,008,971	*Bronze,*	46,664
1894 :	*Gold,*	5,678,100	*Silver,*	942,856	*Bronze,*	33,485
1895 :	*Gold,*	3,810,636	*Silver,*	1,196,168	*Bronze,*	40,995
1896 :	*Gold,*	4,984,800	*Silver,*	1,235'161	*Bronze,*	122,860
1897 :	*Gold.*	1,820,497	*Silver,*	982,001	*Bronze,*	107,230
1898 :	*Gold,*	5,780,446	*Silver,*	1,312,306	*Bronze,*	84,555
1899 :	*Gold,*	9,011,011	*Silver,*	1,616,246	*Bronze,*	139,065
1900 :	*Gold,*	13,103,793	*Silver,*	2,013,381	*Bronze,*	168,295
1991 :	*Gold,*	2,599,000	*Silver,*	914,201	*Bronze,*	120,280
1002 :	*Gold,*	6,908,000	*Silver,*	937,202	*Bronze,*	148,399

COINAGE. Originally the metal was placed between two steel dies, and struck by a hammer. In 1553, a mill, invented by Antoine Brucher, introduced into England, 1562. An engine invented by Balancier, 1617. Great improvements effected by Boulton and Watt, at Soho, 1788. The erection of the Mint machinery, London, began 1811. The machinery was re-organised in 1869.

COLCHESTER (Essex), *Camulodunum*, a Roman station, obtained its first charter from Richard I., 1189. Its sixteen churches and all its buildings sustained great damage at the ten weeks' siege, June-Aug. 1648. Two of its defenders, sir George Lisle and sir Charles Lucas, were tried and shot after surrendering. The baize manufacture was established here, 1660. *Anderson.* The railway to London was opened in 1843. A great fire; several business establishments destroyed, about 25,000*l.* damage, 18 Aug. 1882. Foundation stone of a new town hall laid by the duke of Cambridge, 31 Oct., 1898; opened by lord Rosebery, who was presented with the freedom of the city, 15 May, 1902. Treasure trove of 10.000 silver groats discovered, early July, 1902. Population in 1881, 28,374; 1891, 34,559; 1901, 38,323. See *Earthquakes*, 22 April, 1884.

COLCHIS, N.W. Asia, now Mingrelia. See *Argonautic Expedition.*

COLD. On 3 Jan. 1854, the thermometer in London marked 8° below zero, Fahrenheit; on 25 Dec. 1860, it fell (on the grass) at Nottingham, to 13·8° Fahr. *Mr. Lowe.* From 23 to 30 Dec. the cold was excessive. On 4 Jan. 1867, the thermometer stood at 3° below zero at Hammersmith and Hornsey, near London; on 7 Jan., at 55° above.

Very cold Nov. 1878—May 1879, and Nov. 1879—Feb. 1880.

The December of 1879 said to be the coldest since 1796.

Temperature said to have been on 19 Jan. 13° Fahr. at Stepney, London, 1881; Cambridge, 4° Fahr.; Oxford, 9° Fahr.; London, 16° Fahr. 21 Dec. 1890.

The summer of 1888 exceptionally cold in Europe; London, 11 July, temperature from 42·8° to 55·7° (Jan. 1, 1877, from 49·3° to 54·0° Fahr.)—*G. J. Symons.*

Very cold throughout the continent; the Danube, Elbe, Rhine, Seine and other rivers frozen; heavy falls of snow, Jan. 1891.

Temperature in London, night, 17–18 Feb. 1892, 17·5° Fahr.; 16° Fahr. 26 Dec. 1892; 15·8° 14 Feb., 1902.

Whilst liquefying gases, at the Royal Institution, professor Dewar obtained the temperature of —213° Cent., June, 1884. The liquefaction of carbonic acid was obtained at —180° Cent.; oxygen —184° Cent.; air —192° Cent.; nitrogen —198° Cent. He stated the zero of absolute temperature to be about —273° Cent. June, 1885. He liquefied hydrogen at 240° Cent. 10 May, 1898, and solidified it at 16° Cent. absolute scale, reported Jan. 1900.

See *Air, Frosts, Ice, Congelation, Regelation* and *Provisions.*

COLDINGHAM, near Berwick, is celebrated for the heroism of its nuns, who, on the attack of the Danes, to disfigure themselves, cut off their noses and lips. The Danes burnt them all, with the abbess Ebba, in their monastery, 870.

COLDSTREAM GUARDS. General Monk, before marching from Scotland into England to restore Charles II., raised this regiment at Coldstream, at the confluence of the Leet and Tweed, 1660. For its services in suppressing Venner's insurrection in 1661, it was not disbanded, but constituted the 2nd regiment of foot guards. Col. Ross-of-Bladensburg's "History of the Coldstream Guards, published Dec. 1896.

COLENSO CONTROVERSY, see *Church of England*, 1862-8.

COLEY'S FLUID, a fluid obtained by the culture of the bacilli of erysipelas, streptococci, and staphylococci, used in the treatment of cancer.

COLIN, see *Kolin.*

COLISEUM or COLOSSEUM, at Rome, an elliptical amphitheatre, of which the external diameter is 1641 Italian feet, supposed to have been able to contain 80,000 spectators of the fights with wild beasts, and other sports in the arena. It was erected between 75 (some say 77) and 80, by the emperors Vespasian and Titus, at an expense sufficient to have built a metropolis. Its remains are very imposing. Excavations have been made since 1874.

COLLAR, a very ancient ornament. The Roman hero Titus Manlius slew a gigantic Gaul in single combat, and put his *torques* (twisted chain or collar) on his own neck, and was hence surnamed Torquatus, 361 B.C. A collar is part of the ensigns of the order of knighthood. That of the order of the garter is described, and its wearing enjoined, in the statutes of Henry VIII., 24 April, 1522; but a collar had been previously worn. *Ashmole.* The collar of SS. was adopted by Henry IV., and became a Lancastrian badge; some consider the letters stand for "souveraigne," in reference to his claim to the crown. Some writers consider SS. to be in honour of St. Simplicius, a martyr. The order of the Collar or Necklace (or Annonciada) was instituted by Amadeus VI. of Savoy, about 1360.

COLLECTIVISTS, a name adopted by some socialists, who opened their fourth congress at Calais, 13 Oct., 1890. Collectivism is a name given to a scheme for reconstituting society, by union of individuals together for mutual benefit, in 1894.

COLLECTS, short prayers, very ancient, introduced into the Roman service by pope Gelasius, about 493, and into the English liturgy in 1548. The king of England coming into Normandy, appointed a collect for the relief of the Holy Land, 1166. *Rapin.*

COLLEGES, from the Latin *collegium*, assemblages of persons for sacred, civil, literary or scientific purposes. University education preceded the erection of colleges, which were foundations to relieve the students from the expense of living at lodging-houses and at inns. Collegiate or academic degrees are said to have been first conferred at the university of Paris, 1140; but some authorities say not before 1215. In England, it is contended that the date is much higher, and some hold that Bede obtained a degree formally at Cambridge, and John de Beverley at Oxford, and that they were the first doctors of these universities; see *Cambridge, Oxford, Aberdeen, Queen's Colleges, Heralds, Working Men's Colleges, Preceptors*, &c. Some grammar-schools are termed colleges.

	FOUNDED A.D.
Birmingham, Queen's College	1853
Cheshunt College	1792
City of London	1861
Doctors' Commons, civil law	1670
Dulwich College	1619
Eton College	1441
Firth College, Sheffield	1879
Glasgow College, now University	1451
Gresham College	1581
Haileybury, or East India College . 1806; closed	1858
Highbury College	1826
Highgate	1564
King's College, London	1829
Maynooth College	1705
Military College, Sandhurst	1799
Music, Royal College of; see *Music*	1883
Naval College, Osborne	1903
Naval College, Portsmouth	1722
New College, St. John's Wood	1850
Owens College, Manchester	1870
Physicians, London	1518
Physicians, Dublin	1667
Physicians, Edinburgh	1681
St. Andrews, Scotland	1410
Sion College, incorporated	1630
Stonyhurst, Lancashire (Jesuit)	1794
Surgeons, London	1745
Surgeons, re-incorporated	1800
Surgeons, Dublin	1786
Surgeons, Edinburgh (new)	1803
Trinity College, Dublin	1591
University College, London	1826
University, Sheffield	1903
Winchester College	1387

College de France, the name given about 1793 to the College Royal, which in the 16th century was formed by the incorporation of the "king's readers" or professors, and settled at Paris, independently of the universities. The college was much favoured by the Directory and Napoleon I. It is supported by the state, and the lectures, by eminent men, are free.

COLLIERY ACCIDENTS, see under *Coal*.

COLLISIONS, see *Seas*, and *Railways*.

COLLODION, a film obtained from the solution of gun-cotton in ether. The *iodised* collodion extensively employed in photography, was invented by Mr. F. Scott Archer, and announced in the "Chemist," in March, 1851. On the premature death of himself and wife, a pension of 50*l.* per annum was granted by government to his three orphan children.

COLLYRIDIANS, Arab heretics who offered *collyrides*, little cakes, to the Virgin Mary as a goddess in the 4th century.

COLMAR, W. Germany; an imperial city 13th century; taken by the Swedes, 1632; by Louis XIV. of France, who destroyed the fortifications, 1673; ceded to France, 1697; with Alsace, restored to Germany, 1871.

COLNEY HATCH, Middlesex. County lunatic asylum here erected, 1851, see *Fires*, 27 Jan. 1903.

COLOGNE (*Colonia Agrippina*), on the Rhine, the site of a colony founded by the empress Agrippina, about 50; an imperial town, 957; a member of the Hanseatic league, 1260. Many ecclesiastical councils held here, 782-1536. The Jews were expelled from it in 1485, and the Protestants in 1618, and it then fell into decay. Cologne was taken by the French under Jourdan, Oct. 1794. The archbishopric secularised, 1801; assigned to Prussia, 1814. Population in 1885, 161,401; in 1895, 321,564; 1900, 372,229.

The cathedral, termed *dom* (containing many supposed relics, such as the heads of the magi or three kings, bones of the 11,000 virgins, &c.) founded by abp. Conrad von Hochstade or Hochstettin; architect Gerhard von Riehl or Rile . 15 Aug. 1248
Building intermittent; suspended . 1509
Great collections made for resuming it by Prussia 1814 *et seq.*
Repairs completed; new buildings founded 4 Sept. 1842
The body of the cathedral opened in the presence of the king, 600th anniversary of the foundation 15 Aug. 1848
International industrial exhibition opened by the crown prince . 2 June, 1865
Dispute between the king and the chapter respecting the electing an archbishop, settled; the pope appoints Melchers . Jan 1866
Congress of Old Catholics meet (*which see*) 20, 22 Sept. 1872
Archbishop Melchers arrested . 30 March, 1874
A colossal statue of Frederick-William III., 22 feet high, with pedestrian figures at the base (Blucher, Humboldt, and others), the work of Blaser and Calendrelli, subscribed for by Rhinelanders; unveiled by the emperor William I. 26 Sept. 1878
The cathedral solemnly opened by the emperor and other German sovereigns, 15 Oct. 1880. For the new bell see *Bells*, 1887.
A statue of the emperor William I. unveiled by the emperor William II. . 18 June, 1897
Destructive tornado . 7 Aug. 1898

COLOMBIA, a republic of S. America, formed of states which declared their independence of Spain, 5 July, 1811. A long war ensued. Estimated population of the present state, in 1888, 4,000,000; 1895, abt. 5,000,000. Capital, Bogota.

Union of New Grenada and Venezuela . 17 Dec. 1819
The royalists defeated at Carabobo . 24 June, 1821
Bolivar named dictator . 10 Feb. 1824
Alliance between Colombia and Mexico 30 June ,,
Independence of Colombia recognised . 1825
Alliance with Guatemala . March, ,,
Congress at Lima names Bolivar president, Aug.; dictator . 23 Nov. 1826
Padilla's insurrection . 9 April, 1828
Conspiracy of Santander against Bolivar 25 Sept. ,,
Venezuela separates from Grenada . Nov. 1829
Bolivar resigns, 4 April; dies . 17 Dec. 1830
Santander dies . 26 May, 1840
The republic now named Colombia instead of New Grenada; president, general E. Salgar . 1871
Manuel Murillo Toro, president . 1 April, 1872
Santiago Perez, president . 1 April, 1874
Aquileo Parra, president . 1 April, 1876
General Trujillo, president, proclaimed, 1 April, 1878
General R. Nuñez, president, proclaimed, 1 April, 1880
President Zyaldua died . Dec. 1882
T. E. Otálora, president . 1 April, 1883
Rafael Nuñez elected president Sept. 1883; again 7 Aug. 1886
Insurrection; government troops defeated at Tunja announced 9 Jan. 1885; peace restored 10 Jan. 1885
Fresh insurrection; government troops defeated at Barranquilla, announced 2 March; rebels defeated about 13 July; rebellion over, reported 31 July, ,,
Death of president Nuñez, 18 Sept.; Miguel a Caro became president . Oct. 1894
Insurrection at Bogota, 31 Jan.; rebels defeated at Corozal; gen. Salmiento surrenders, reported 9 Feb.; amnesty granted . 16 Feb. 1895
Government forces defeated at Cucuta with great loss; the city captured . reported 4 March, ,,
Rebels defeated at Ensiso . 15 March, ,,
Government forces defeated . 24 June, ,,
Quinto Calveron, president . Oct. 1896
An Italian squadron under admiral Candiani anchors off Cartagena to enforce payment of an award given by president Cleveland to signor Cerruti for robbery and imprisonment (March, 1897) mid July, 1898; controversy settled, reported. 16 July, 1899
Insurrection suppressed, rebels defeated, Oct.–25 Nov. ,,
Death of señ. Sanclemente, president, 1898; *et seq.*, reported . 8 Jan. 1900
J. M. Marroquin, vice-president. . Jan. ,,

Rebels defeated before Cartagena, and dispersed 13, 16 May, 1900
Cucuta held by the rebels and Venezuelan invaders, taken by gen. Gonzales Valencia, reported, 25 July „
Rebels routed after 2 days' fighting at Girardo Point, reported . . . . . 19 Dec. „
Rebels defeated outside Panama . . 12 Jan. 1901
Insurrection, severe fighting near Colon, 28, 29 July, „
Relations strained with Venezuela, *which see*; American mediation accepted, but refused by gen. Castro . . . . . . early Sept. „
Colombia invaded by Venezuelans, who are totally routed near La Hacha . . . . 14 Sept. „
Insurgents defeated near Ambaleg, much slaughter, 5 Oct. „
Insurrection, the Liberals attack and capture Colon, 19 Nov.; fierce fighting near Colon, the insurgents defeated, 24 Nov.; they surrender at Colon 29 Nov.; Honda attacked, fierce fighting, insurgents defeated with loss . . . 9 Dec. „
Naval fight at Panama, Dr. Alban, the governor of Panama, killed . . . . . 20 Jan. 1902
Insurgents repulsed with great loss 20 miles from Bogota, reported . . . . . 26 Jan. „
Aguadulce attacked by gen. Herrera, great slaughter; gen. Castro abandons the town and breaks through the Liberal lines . . 23–27 Feb. „
Peace treaties signed, general amnesty for political offences, reported . . . . 25 June „
Fresh outbreak, terrible fighting at Aguadulce, 29–31 July; 2,000 men surrender there; desperate fighting elsewhere, and great slaughter, 5–8 Sept. „
Civil war ends, peace signed . . about 22 Nov. „
(See *New Grenada*, *Venezuela*, and *United States* 22 Jan., 1903.

COLOMBO (Ceylon), fortified in 1638 by the Portuguese, who were expelled by the Dutch in 1666; the latter surrendered it to the British, 15 Feb. 1796; see *Ceylon*, 1803, 1845.

COLON (:). The colon and period were adopted by Thrasymachus about 373 B.C. (*Suidas*), and known to Aristotle. The colon and semicolon (;) first used in British literature in the 16th century. For Colon, a S. American seaport, see *Panama*.

COLONEL (from Italian *colonna*, a column), the highest regimental military officer. The term had become common in England in the 16th century.

COLONIAL, see under *Colonies*.

COLONIAL COLLEGE, THE, was founded 1887 to train youths for colonial life. The course of instruction is scientific and practical, and includes veterinary science, hygiene, surveying, farming, fruit culture, dairy keeping, and other branches of agricultural knowledge. The college is at Hollesley Bay, Suffolk, with an estate of 2000 acres. Since its opening some 600 students have received instruction at the college.

COLONIES. The Phœnician and Greek colonies, frequently founded by political exiles, soon became independent of the mother country. The Roman colonies, on the contrary, continued in close connection with Rome itself; being governed almost entirely by military law.—The COLONIES OF GREAT BRITAIN partake of both these characters. The N. American colonies revolted in consequence of the attempt at taxation without their consent in 1764. The loyal condition of the present colonies now is due to the gradual relaxation of the pressure of the home government. The population of the British colonies in all parts of the world was estimated, in 1861, at 142,952,243; in 1888, 275,520,216; in 1902 400,000,000. The revenue of the colonies was estimated in 1865 to be 51,492,000*l.*, the expenditure, 59,353,000*l.*; in 1902, 144,000,000*l.* The act for the abolition of slavery in the British colonies, and for compensation to the owners of slaves (20,000,000*l.* sterling), was passed in 1833. All the slaves throughout the British colonies were emancipated on 1 Aug. 1834. Germany and other powers showed great desire for colonization in 1884-5 *et seq.* See *Holland* and *Germany*.

Resolution of House of Commons recognises the claims of colonies to protection from consequences of imperial policy, but "is of opinion that colonies exercising rights of self-government ought to undertake the main responsibility of providing for their own internal order and security, and ought to assist in their own external defence" 1862

Chief Colony, or Possession.		*Date of Settlement, &c.*
Aden		1838
African Forts		about 1618
Anguilla	Settlement	about 1666
Antigua	Settlement	1632
Ascension	Occupied	1815
Australia, South	Settlement	1834
Australia, W. (Swan river)	Settlement	1829
Bahama Island	Settlement 1629, *et seq.*	
Barbadoes	Settlement	1605
Basutoland		1871
Bechuanaland		1885
Bengal	Settlement	about 1652
Berbera		1884
Berbice	Capitulation,	Sept. 1803
Bermudas	Settlements 1609, *et seq.*	
Bombay	See *India*	1662
British Burmah (Upper Burmah, 1885)	See *Pegu*	1862
British Columbia	Settlement	1858
Brunei		1888
Canada	Capitulation,	Sept. 1759-60
Cape Breton	Ceded	1763
Cape Coast Castle	By cession	1667
Cape of Good Hope	Capitulation	Jan. 1806
Ceylon	All acquired	1815
Cyprus	Ceded (under conditions)	1878
Demerara and Essequibo	Capitulation	Sept. 1803
Dominica	Ceded by France	1763
Elmina and Dutch Guinea	By cession	Feb. 1872
Falkland Islands	See *Falkland Islands*	1833
Fiji	Ceded	1874
Gambia	Settlement	1631
Gibraltar	Capitulation	Aug. 1704
Gold Coast	Settlement	about 1618
Gozo	Capitulation,	Sept. 1800
Grenada	Ceded by France	1763
Griqualand, S. Africa	Settlement	27 Oct. 1871
Guiana, British	Capitulation	1803
Heligoland	Capitulation	1807
Honduras	By treaty	1670
Hong-Kong (Victoria)	Ceded	1841
Jamaica	Capitulation	1655
Keeling Islands		1857
Kermadec Islands		1886
Labuan	See *Borneo*	1846
Lagos	Ceded	1861
Leeward Isles		1626–1763
Madras	See *India*	1639
Malacca (under *Bengal*)		
Malta	Capitulation	Sept. 1800
Mashonaland		1890
Matabeleland		1890
Mauritius	Capitulation	Dec. 1810
Montserrat	Settlement	1632
Natal	Settlement	1823
Nevis	Settlement	1628
New Brunswick	Settlement	1622-1713
Newfoundland	Settlement	about 1500
New Guinea		1884
New South Wales	Settlement	1787
New Zealand	Settlement	1840
Niger districts		1885
Norfolk Islands		1787
North Borneo		1840
Nova Scotia	Settlement	1622
Orange Free State (Orange River Colony)	Conquered	1901
Pegu	Conquered	1852
Port Phillip	See *Victoria*.	
Prince Edward Island	Capitulated	1745
Prince of Wales Island (Penang)	Settlement	1786

Queensland, N. S. Wales	Settlement	1860
Sarawak		1888
Sierra Leone	Settlement	1787
[United with other settlements as West Africa, Feb. 1866.]		
Singapore	Purchased	1819
Socotra		1886
St. Christopher's	Settlement	1623
St. Helena	Capitulated	1600
St. Lucia	Capitulation June,	1803
St. Vincent	Ceded by France	1763
Swan River	See *West Australia.*	
Tasmania	See *Van Diemen's Land.*	
Tobago	Ceded by France	1763
Tortola	Settlement	1666
Transvaal	Annexed, 1877; conquered	1901
Trinidad	Capitulation Feb.	1797
Van Diemen's Land	Settlement	1803
Vancouver Island	Settlement	1781
Victoria (Port Phillip)	Settlement	1850
Victoria	See *Hong-Kong.*	
Virgin Isles	Settlement	1666
Windward Isles		1605–1803
Zululand		1886

Colonial bishoprics fund, established . . . 1841

Colonial Branch Army Act passed . . . 1866

Colonial Clergy Act, 37 & 38 Vict. c. 77, passed 7 Aug. 1874, removes certain disabilities of persons not ordained by bishops of the united church of England and Ireland.

Colonial and Continental Church Society (formerly "Colonial Church Society"), took its name 1 May, 1861. It deals with colonial dioceses and British residents on the continent.

Colonial Defences Commission (including the earl of Carnarvon, Mr. Childers, and others), appointed about . . . 12 Sept. 1879

Works recommended by government; expenditure imperial and local . . . 1884

Colonial Naval Defence Act, to enable the Colonies to take effectual measures for their defence against attacks by sea, was passed in . . . 1865

Colonial Society, established to promote the interests of the colonies, lord Bury, president, held its first meeting 26 June, 1868, and first annual meeting 28 June, 1869, when it assumed the title "Royal." On 7 March, 1870, it became "*The Royal Colonial Institute;*" incorporated 1882. The "Proceedings" are published. 4208 fellows, income 7142*l.* in 1901. A colonial congress met at Amsterdam 19 Sept. 1883.

The formation of a *National and Colonial League* was resolved on at a meeting in London 5 Jan. 1870

Colonial Exhibition. An Exhibition of the products, manufactures, and arts of India and the colonies in London in 1886; Royal Commission 8 Nov. 1884; great exertion of the prince of Wales and sir P. C. Owen; opened with great splendour by the Queen; ode by lord Tennyson, set to music by sir A. Sullivan, sung 4 May, 1886; visited by 5,550,745 persons; closed 10 Nov. A surplus of 35,235*l.*, of which 5964*l.* supplied the deficit on the Inventions exhibition, and 25,000*l.* supplied to the funds of the Imperial Institute, leaving a reserve of 4279*l.*; meeting of commission, 30 April 1887. Testimonial for his exertions was presented to sir Philip Cunliffe Owen, 18 Dec. . . . 1886

Mr. E. Stanhope, colonial secretary, proposes a conference of agents-general on colonial defence and communication with Great Britain . Dec. „

Colonial conference; first meeting of representatives of all the colonies; president, sir H. T. Holland, colonial secretary, the marquis of Salisbury and other ministers present; questions discussed, defence of colonies, coaling stations, &c., cable communication, new harbours, employment of Imperial naval and military officers, relations with foreign powers, postal regulations, legal affairs, census returns, &c., 4 April, 1887. Results of the conference successful; closed 9 May. The delegates received by the Queen at Windsor, 4 May, 1887

Lord George Hamilton's plan for colonial defence accepted by Australia, &c. . about 22 April, „

Naval Defence Act passed at Melbourne with royal assent, 24, 25 Nov.; accepted by Tasmania, New South Wales, South Australia, and New Zealand 1 Dec.; deferred by Queensland . Dec. 1887

Canadian co-operative colonization company founded . . . 1889

The committee of the commons on colonization appointed in 1889; sir James Fergusson, chairman, issued a report, with sensible recommendations, about . . . 18 March, 1891

Burke's "Colonial Gentry," vol. i. published Sept. „

The title of "honourable" assumed by certain colonial officials approved by the queen . June, 1893

Imperial and inter-colonial conference opened at Ottawa; the earl of Aberdeen present; delegates from Australia, Canada, Cape Colony, and other colonies, the earl of Jersey for the home government, 28 June; Mr. Mackenzie Bowell elected president; imperial unity strongly advocated, 29 June; closing sitting, 9 July; lord Jersey's report published . . . Dec. 1894

Colonial boundaries act passed . . . 6 July, 1895

Despatch of Mr. Chamberlain to colonial governors on the great importance of the development of commerce . . . 28 Nov. „

Large sums voted by the colonies in reference to the queen's diamond jubilee (20 June), 1897; celebrations and rejoicings throughout all the colonies and British possessions, 20 June *et seq.* 1897

Mr. Laurier, from Canada, and 10 other colonial premiers, received by the duke of Devonshire at Liverpool, 12 June; visit Edinburgh, 14 June; Glasgow, 15 June; Birmingham, 21 June; Paris, 19 July, „

Banquet to the premiers, the prince of Wales present, at the Imperial institute, London, 18 June, „

The eleven premiers made privy councillors; 21 June; entertained by the lord mayor at the Mansion house; lord Salisbury, and a distinguished company, present, 1 July; received by the queen at Windsor . . . 7 July, „

Colonial and Indian troops entertained and reviewed by the queen at Windsor, 2 July; by the prince and princess of Wales, at Buckingham palace . . . 3 July „

Colonial loans act passed . . . 9 Aug. 1899

Troops sent from each colony to S. African war, Oct. *et seq.* „

Colonial marriages (deceased wife's sister) act passed . . . 6 Aug. 1900

Colonial stock act, royal assent . . . 8 Aug. „

Death of the queen, universal mourning, . 22 Jan. 1901

The king sends his thanks for sympathy, declaring that *with God's blessing he would solemnly work for the welfare of the great empire over which he had been called to reign;* . . . 4 Feb. „

International colonial institute at the Hague opened . . . 28 May, „

Colonial acts confirmation bill passed . 16 Aug. „

Government's policy in S. Africa approved; admiration for Mr. Chamberlain and British troops throughout the colonies . . . Feb. 1902

Peace thanksgivings . . . 8 June, „

Colonial premiers received by the prince and princess of Wales at St. James's palace 10 July; by the king, 12 Aug.; entertained throughout the country . . . June–Sept. „

Colonial conferences with Mr. Chamberlain, London, 30 June, *et seq.*; resolutions passed regarding preferential tariffs and subsidies to steamship lines, military defence and political relations of the empire; contracts for army and navy supplies; reduction of postal rates; united contribution to the queen Victoria memorial; 10th and final meeting resolutions were adopted on commercial relations of the empire and in favour of the metric system of weights and measures, 11 Aug. „

Colonial and Indian troops in London, see *Alexandra Park*, June; visit the fleet at Spithead, 30 June; special service at the Abbey, 17 Aug.; leave end . . . Aug. „

Total troops sent to S. Africa, 1899–31 May, 1902, 30,238; total returned to colonies after the war, 12,294, reported . . . 4 Sept. „

Sir H. Norman unveils a memorial tablet to 16 fellows of the Royal Colonial Institute who fell in the S. African war . . . 17 Feb. 1903

Mr. Chamberlain's tour to colonies in S. Africa: he leaves England 25 Nov. 1902, and arrives home 14 March, 1903
The inter-imperial tariff scheme advocated by Mr. Chamberlain, and his subsequent resignation, arouses much interest in the colonies, and meets with general approval . . . 15 May *et seq.* „
See *Bishops (Colonial), Imperial Defence, Imperial Institute, Secretaries, Nurses,* and separate articles.

COLORADO (so called from its coloured ranges), a territory of the United States of North America, was organised 2 March, 1861; proclaimed a state, Aug. 1876; capital, Denver City. Population in 1880, 194,327; 1890, 412,198; 1900, 539,700.

Gold found here, 1858, and much copper and lead. La Sal Mining Co. shipped 3500 tons higher grade silver and copper ores, 1902.
Women enfranchised, Nov. 1893.
Strike of miners at Cripple Creek, with cruel outrages; 11 deaths, 26 May; troops called out, 27 May; the country controlled by a rebel encampment on Bull Hill, 1 June; skirmish with the troops, 7 June; the strikers yield, 9 June, 1894.
3 Italians shot by a mob in connection with the murder of a deputy-sheriff (Mr. Lixon) at Walsenburg; order restored, 10–14 March, 1895.
Mining strike, rioting with bloodshed; militia called out, 21 Sept. 1896.
Collision on the Rio Grande railway, near Newcastle, 25 deaths, 10 Sept. 1897.
Irrigation act passed by congress, March 1, 1902.
Tenth Nat. Irrigation congress, Colorado springs (value of irrigated land, 40·77 dol. per acre), Oct. 6, 1902.
New mint, May 1, 1902.

COLORADO BEETLE, so called from its striped colouring, was first found in Wisconsin, was described by Thomas Say, and named *Doryphora decemlineata,* in 1824, when he found it near the Upper Missouri. It soon took to feeding on potatoes, as they were planted, and gradually proceeded eastward through Nebraska, Iowa, Illinois, Ohio, &c., to the New England states, destroying the crops, 1859 *et seq.* In 1873 it reached New York, and the Atlantic seaboard in 1874, swarming there in 1876, and attacking Canada. The fear of its invading Britain led to an order in council respecting its destruction, &c., 14 Aug. 1877. Very few specimens arrived. Discovered among potatoes at Tilbury dock, crops, and grass promptly destroyed in the infected area, reported, 3 Sept. 1901; again there May, 1902.

COLOSSEUM, see *Coliseum.* The building in Regent's Park, London, was planned by Mr. Hornor, a land surveyor, and commenced in 1824, by Peto and Grissell, from designs by Decimus Burton. The chief portion was a polygon of 16 faces, 126 feet in diameter externally: the walls were three feet thick at the ground: the height to the glazed dome 112 feet. On the canvas walls of the dome was painted the panoramic view of London, completed in 1829 from sketches by Mr. Hornor taken from the summit of St. Paul's cathedral in 1821-2. The picture covered above 46,000 square feet, more than an acre of canvas. The different parts were combined by Mr. E. T. Parris, who in 1845 repainted the whole. In 1848 a panorama of Paris was exhibited; succeeded, in 1850, by the lake of Thun in Switzerland; in 1851 the panorama of London was reproduced. In 1848 the theatre, with the panorama of Lisbon, was added. In 1831, when Mr. Hornor failed, the establishment was sold for 40,000*l.* to Messrs. Braham and Yates. In 1843 it was bought by Mr. D. Montague for 23,000 guineas. *Timbs.* After having been long closed, the building was opened to the public at Christmas, 1856, at one shilling. Under the charge of Dr. Bachhoffner, it continued open till the spring of 1864, when it was again closed. The sale of the site was announced 1870. It was announced in Dec. 1871, that a company was about to transform the building and grounds into club-chambers, baths, a winter garden, &c. In 1874, it was sold; large mansions have been erected on the site.

COLOSSUS OF RHODES, a brass statue of Apollo, seventy cubits high, esteemed one of the wonders of the world, was erected at the port of Rhodes in honour of the sun, by Chares of Lindus, disciple of Lysippus, 290 or 288 B.C. It was thrown down by an earthquake about 224 B.C. The figure is said mythically to have stood upon two moles, a leg being extended on each side of the harbour, so that a vessel in full sail could enter between. The statue was in ruins for nearly nine centuries, and had never been repaired; when the Saracens, taking Rhodes, pulled it to pieces, and sold the metal, weighing 720,900 lbs., to a Jew, who is said to have loaded 900 camels in transporting it to Alexandria about 653. *Dufresnoy.*

COLOUR is to light what pitch is to sound, according to the undulatory theory of Huyghens (about 1678), established by Dr. T. Young, and others. The shade varies according to the number of vibrations. 458 millions of millions of vibrations in a second attributed to the red end of the spectrum: to the violet, 727; see *Spectrum.** See *Blue-Books* for National official colours. *Photography.*

COLSTON DAY, Nov. 13, see *Bristol.*

COLUMBIA, a federal district round the city of Washington in Maryland; established 1800. Slavery was abolished in 1862. Population in 1880, 177,624; 1890, 230,392; 1900, 278,718; see *British Columbia.*

COLUMBIA MARKET, Bethnal Green, E. London; erected by Mr. Darbishire, architect, in the pointed Gothic style, and inaugurated by Miss (now lady) Burdett-Coutts, the proprietor, 28 April, 1869. It cost her 200,000*l.* It was opened as a wholesale fish-market, 21 Feb. 1870, but was not successful. On 3 Nov. 1871, lady Burdett-Coutts presented the market to the corporation of London, and on 18 July, 1872, she received publicly the freedom of that city.

The market did not succeed, and the buildings were restored to the donor . . . . . 4 Dec. 1874
Again opened on liberal terms under superintendence of Great Eastern, Great Northern, and Midland railway companies . . . . 15 Dec. 1875
Reported failure; proposed use as a co-operative store . . . . April, 1878
Re-opened as a fish-market . . . . 17 July, 1883
Market a failure, the building subsequently converted into industrial dwellings.

COLUMBIUM, a metal discovered by C. Hatchett, in a mineral named columbite, in 1801. It is identical with niobium, and not with tantalum, as supposed by some chemists. *Watts.*

COLUMBUS, capital of Ohio, U.S.A., founded in 1812, is the seat of important manufactures. Population, 1870, 31,274; 1890, 88,150; 1900, 125,560. *Columbus celebrations,* see *Spain, United States, Genoa, Chicago, &c.,* 1892.

* Some persons (about 65 out of 1154) cannot distinguish between colours, and are termed *Colour blind.* The defect said to have been first described by Priestley, *Phil. Trans.* 1777. In 1859, professor J. Clerk Maxwell invented spectacles to remedy this defect, which is also called "Daltonism," after John Dalton, the chemist, to whom scarlet appeared drab-colour. Dr. George Wilson, "Researches on Colour-Blindness," 1847; Dr. Joy Jeffries, "Colour Blindness," 1879. The Royal Society commission appointed in March to consider colour blindness, reported in May, 1892; Holmgren's method of testing by the use of skeins of coloured wool was recommended.

COMBAT, SINGLE. Trial by this commenced by the Lombards, 659. *Baronius.* It was introduced into England for accusations of treason, if neither the accuser nor the accused could produce good evidence; see *Appeal of Battle.*

A battle by single combat was fought before the king, William II., and the peers, between Geoffrey Baynard and William, earl of Eu, who was accused by Baynard of high treason; and Baynard having conquered, Eu was deemed convicted, and blinded and mutilated, 1096.

A combat proposed between Henry of Bolingbroke, duke of Hereford (afterwards Henry IV.), and Thomas, duke of Norfolk, was forbidden by Richard II. Sept. 1398.

A trial was appointed between the prior of Kilmainham and the earl of Ormond, the former having impeached the latter of high treason, quarrel taken up by the king, decided without fighting, 1446.

A combat was proposed between lord Reay and Mr. David Ramsey, in 1631, but the king prevented it.

In a combat in Dublin castle, before the lords justices and council, between Connor MacCormack O'Connor and Teig Mac-Gilpatrick O'Connor, the former had his head cut off, and presented to the lords, 1553.

COMBINATION. Laws were enacted from the time of Edward I. downwards, regulating the price of labour and the relations between masters and workmen, and prohibiting the latter from *combining* for their own protection. The combination laws consolidated in 1799 and 1800 were repealed in 1825, due protection being given to both parties. The act was amended in 1859 by 22 Vict. c. 34, when the subject was much discussed, in consequence of the strike in the building trades, see *Trades Unions* and *Strikes.*

COMBS, found in Pompeii; Combmakers' company incorporated, 1636 or 1650.

COMBUSTION, see *Spontaneous.*

COMÉDIE FRANÇAISE, Paris, established 1680.

At the death of Molière in 1673, his company of actors, at the Palais Royal, separated into two bodies. The fusion of these formed the French National Theatre, founded by Louis XIV. by a decree 18 Aug., first performance 25 Aug. 1680; the actors, 15 men, and 12 women, being the best of the time. The theatre was much depressed in the king's last years; revived under Louis XV.; ceased in 1799; restored in 1803; and established in the Théâtre Français, Paris.

The company visited London in 1879; first appearance at the Gaiety, 2 June, 1879; eminent actors, Madame Sarah Bernhardt, MM. Got (died 21 March, 1901), Delaunay, and Coquelin, and Mlles. Brohan and Favart.

The 200th anniversary of the establishment celebrated 21 Oct., *et seq.* 1880.

The Théâtre Français burnt down, Mlle. Henriot, a young actress, killed, 8 March, 1900. New theatre opened, state performance, 29 Dec. 1900.

COMEDY. Thalia is the muse of comedy and lyric poetry. Susarion and Dolon, the reputed inventors of theatrical exhibitions, 578 B.C., performed the first comedy at Athens, on a waggon or movable stage, on four wheels, for which they were rewarded with a basket of figs and a cask of wine; see *Arundelian Marbles,* and *Drama.*

Comedy, for libel, prohibited at Athens, 440 B.C.

Aristophanes called the prince of ancient comedy, 434 B.C., and Menander that of the new, 320 B.C.

Of Plautus, 20 comedies are extant; he flourished 220 B.C.

Statius Cæcilius wrote upwards of 30 comedies; flourished at Rome 180 B.C.

Comedies of Lælius and Terence first acted 154 B.C.

First regular comedy performed in England about A.D. 1551.

It was said of Sheridan that he wrote the best comedy (the *School for Scandal*), the best opera (the *Duenna*), and the best afterpiece (the *Critic*), in the English language (1775-1779).

COMETS (Greek *come,* a hair). See *Astron. Soc.* Mr. Hind, in his little work on comets, gave a chronological list (1852). The identity and periodicity of comets are considered in Mr. G. F. Chambers' Handbook of Astronomy, 1889-90, and in Mr. W. T. Lynn's "Remarkable Comets," 10th edition, 1902. Amédée Guillemin's "World of Comets," by J. Glaisher, published 1877. The spectrum analysis of Donati (1864), Dr. Wm. Huggins, and Dr. William Allen Miller in 1866, *et seq.,* and others, indicate in comets the presence of gaseous matter in a state of incandescence. There are 20 *known* periodical comets, 1889.

The Chinese annalists give early accounts of comets.

Aristotle describes one which appeared, B.C. 371.

At the birth of the great Mithridates two [probably only one] large comets appeared, which were seen for seventy-two days together, whose splendour eclipsed that of the mid-day sun, and occupied the fourth part of the heavens, about 134 B.C. *Justin.*

A grand comet seen, 1264. It is considered to have reappeared in 1556, with diminished splendour; and was expected to appear again about Aug. 1858 or Aug. 1860. *Hind.*

A remarkable one seen in England, June, 1337. *Stow.*

Tycho Brahé demonstrated that comets are extraneous to our atmosphere, about 1577.

A comet observed by Tycho Brahé and others in 1596.

A comet which terrified the people from its near approach to the earth was visible from 3 Nov. 1679 to 9 March, 1680. It enabled Newton to demonstrate that comets, as well as planets, are subject to the law of gravitation, and most probably move in elliptic orbits, 1704.

A comet first seen by Klinkenberg at Haarlem, 9 Dec. 1743.

HALLEY'S COMET, 1682. Named after one of the greatest astronomers of England. He first proved that many of the appearances of comets were but the periodical returns of the same bodies, and he demonstrated that the comet of 1682 was the same with the comet of 1456, 1531, and 1607, deducing this fact from a minute observation of the first-mentioned comet, and being struck by its wonderful resemblance to the comets described as having appeared in those years: Halley, therefore, first fixed the identity of comets, and predicted their periodical returns. *Vince's Astronomy.* The revolution of Halley's comet is performed in about 75 years; it appeared (as he had predicted) in 1758, and came to its perihelion on March 13; its last appearance was 1835; its next will be 1910.

A most brilliant comet appeared in 1769, which passed within two millions of miles of the earth, first seen by Messier 8 Aug. This beautiful comet, moving with immense swiftness, was seen in London; its tail stretched across the heavens like a prodigious luminous arch, 36,000,000 miles in length.

The computed length of that which appeared in 1811, and which was so remarkably conspicuous, was, on 15 Oct. according to the late Dr. Herschel, upwards of 100,000,000 miles, and its apparent greatest breadth, at the same time, 15,000,000 miles. It was visible all the autumn to the naked eye. *Philos. Trans. Royal Soc.* for 1812. Another comet, Dec. 1823.

ENCKE'S COMET was observed by Méchain in 1786, Miss Caroline Herschel in 1795, and Thulis in 1805; rediscovered by Pons, 26 Nov. 1818, but justly named by astronomers after professor Encke, for his success in detecting its orbit, motions, and perturbations; it is, like the preceding one of the three comets which have appeared according to prediction, and its revolutions are made in 3 years and 15 weeks. Thirteenth return observed at Copenhagen by M. d'Arrest, 20 July, 1863; observed in England, 14 Oct. 1871; seen 13 April, 1875; in New South Wales, 3 Aug. 1878; visible at Washington, &c., 18–21 Sept. 1881; imperfectly seen in Italy by Cerulli and others, 1 Nov. 1894; seen at Cambridge, Mass., 6 Aug.; and at Heidelberg, 9, 10 Aug. 1901.

BIELA'S COMET has been an object of fear to many on account of the nearness with which it has approached, not the earth, but a point of the earth's path; it was first discovered by M. Biela, an Austrian officer, 27 Feb. 1826. It is one of the three comets whose re-appearance was predicted, its revolution being performed in

6 years and 38 weeks. Its second appearance was in 1832, when the time of its perihelion passage was 27 Nov.; its third was in 1839; its fourth in 1845; and its fifth in 1852; it has since vanished.

Comet discovered by M. Faye at Paris, Nov. 1843; reappears every 7 years. Brorsen's comet discovered by him in 1846.

DONATI'S COMET, so called from its having been first observed by Dr. Donati, of Florence, 2 June, 1858, being then calculated to be 228,000,000 miles from our earth. It was very brilliant in England in the end of September and October following, when the tail was said to be 40,000,000 miles long. On the 10th of October it was nearest to the earth; on the 18th it was near coming into collision with Venus. Opinions varied as to this comet's brilliancy compared with that of 1811.

THE GREAT COMET of 1861 was first seen by Mr. Tebbutt at Sydney, in Australia, 13 May; by M. Goldschmidt and others in France and England on 29, 30 June. The nucleus was about 400 miles in diameter, with a long bush-like tail, travelling at the rate of 10,000,000 miles in 24 hours. On 30 June, it was suggested that we were in the tail—there being "a phosphorescent auroral glare."

A tailless comet was discovered in the constellation Cassiopœia, by M. Seeling, at Athens, on 2 July, and by M. Tempel, at Marseilles, 2 and 3 July, 1867.

A comet detected at Marathon, N.Y., by Mr. Swift, 15 July, and by Rosa, at Rome, on 25 July, 1862. It was visible by the naked eye in August and September.

Six telescopic comets were observed in 1863, and several in 1864.

A fine comet appeared in the southern hemisphere, and was visible in South America and Australia, in Jan.-Feb. 1865.

M. Babinet considered that comets had so little density that the earth might pass through the tail of one without our being aware of it, 4 May, 1857.

Schiaparelli, of Milan, discovered that the August meteors move round the sun in an orbit almost identical with the third comet of 1862.

One discovered at Bonn by Dr. Winnecke, 13 June, 1858.

Several small comets discovered by various astronomers, 1873-81.

COGGIA'S COMET, discovered by him at Marseilles, 18 April, became visible (near Polar star) in London about 4 July; gradually increased in brightness, and passed out of sight in a few weeks, in Europe; and appeared brilliant at Melbourne, 1 Aug. 1874.

A bright comet appeared in the southern hemisphere, large nucleus, fan-shaped tail; visible in the southern hemisphere, May; in London, 22 June *et seq.* 1881.

DENNING'S comet appears 4 Oct. 1881.

Another at Madeira, at Ealing, near London, &c. (probably that of 1843 and 1880) 17 Sept. 1882; at Paris, 27 Sept.; seen at Vienna, 29 Sept. 1882.

New comet discovered by prof. Barnard at Lick, 16 July, 1884.

New comet discovered at Heidelberg by Dr. Max Wolf, 17 Sept. 1884.

Another discovered by M. Fabry of Paris 3 Dec. 1885; by Mr. Brooks of New York Jan. 1886.

Three comets visible, Brooks', Fabry's, and Barnard's, Jan.; increasing in brightness, May, 1886.

New comet discovered by Mr. Finlay of the Cape observatory 26 Sept. 1886.

One discovered by Mr. Brooks at Geneva, New York, 6 July, 1889.

A comet observed by Mr. Brooks at New York, 19 March; one by prof. Denning at Bristol, 23 July; one by prof. Zona at Palermo, 15 Nov. 1890.

Tempel Swift's comet (1869 and 1880) seen by Mr. Denning, 30 Sept., 1 Oct. 1891.

A comet observed by prof. Lewis Swift, 7 March; one by Mr. W. F. Denning near Bristol, 18 March, 1892.

Winnecke's comet observed by Dr. Spitaler, 18 March, 1892; one discovered by Mr. Edwin Holmes at Islington, London, 6 Nov. 1892.

A comet *a* discovered by Mr. Denning at Bristol, 26 March, 1894.

A comet *b* discovered by Mr. Gale, of Sydney, 3 April, 1894.

Numerous telescopic comets observed at different places in 1892–4.

Temple's comet (discovered by him at Milan, 3 July, 1873) seen again by Mr. Finlay at the Cape, 8 May, 1894; one discovered by Mr. E. Swift in California, 21 Nov. 1894.

One discovered by prof. L. Swift, California, 20 Sept. 1895; one discovered by Mr. Perrine at the Lick observatory, U.S.A., 16–17 Nov. 1895; one by prof. Brooks at Geneva, New York, 21 Nov. 1895.

One by Mr. Perrine at Lick, 14 Feb. 1896; one *b* discovered by prof. Swift at S. Carolina, 13 April, 1896; one by Mr. W. Sperra, Ohio, 31 Aug. 1896; one by M. Giacobini, 4 Sept. 1896; two near the sun by prof. L. Swift at Lick, 20 Sept. 1896 one *f* discovered by Mr. Perrini at Lick, California, 2 Nov. 1896; one *g* discovered by him at Lick, 9 Dec. 1896.

One *a* discovered by Mr. Perrine at Lick, 16 Oct. 1897; one *b* discovered by him there, 8 Dec., and another 20 March, 1898; one by M. Giacobini, Nice, 18 June, 1898.

One *a* discovered by prof. L. Swift, California, 3 March, 1899; Tuttle's periodical comet *b* (first discovered by Méchain in 1790) detected by Dr. Wolf, 5 March; one *e* discovered by M. Giacobini, 30 Sept. 1899.

One *a* discovered by him, 31 Jan. 1900; one *b* by M. Borelly at Marseilles, and Mr. Brooks at Geneva, N.Y. 23 July, 1900; one *c* by M. Giacobini at Nice, 20 Dec. 1900.

One *a* by Mr. A. Hill at Queenstown, S. Africa, and by Mr. Tattersall at Cape Leeuwin, Australia, 24 April, 1901.

One *a* by Mr. Brooks at Geneva, 15 April, 1902; *b* by Mr. Perrine at Lick, 1 Sept, 1902; *c* by Mr. Grigg at Mames, N.Z., 22 July, 1902; *d* by M. Giacobini, Nice, 2 Dec. 1902; and *a* by him, Nice, 15 Jan. 1903.

COMMANDER-IN-CHIEF, an office in the British army occasionally vacant. When the duke of Wellington resigned the office, on becoming prime minister, in 1828, his successor, lord Hill, became commander of the forces, or general commanding-in-chief.

By Order in Council the duties of the Commander-in-Chief were defined and published . 2 Feb. 1888

CAPTAINS-GENERAL.

Duke of Albemarle	1660
Duke of Monmouth	1678
Duke of Marlborough	1690
Schomberg, duke of Leinster	1691
Duke of Ormond	1711
Duke of Marlborough, again	1714
Duke of Cumberland	1744
Duke of York	1799

COMMANDERS-IN-CHIEF.

Duke of Monmouth	1674
Duke of Marlborough	1690
Duke of Schomberg	691
Duke of Ormond	1711
Earl of Stair	1744
Field-Marshal Wade	1745
Lord Ligonier	1757
Marquis of Granby	1766
Lord Amherst, general on the staff	1778
Gen. Seymour Conway	1782
Lord Amherst, again	1793
Frederick, duke of York	11 Feb. 1795
Sir David Dundas	25 March, 1809
Frederick, duke of York, again	29 May, 1811
Duke of Wellington 22 Jan.—5 May;	27 Aug. 1827
Lord Hill, general commanding-in-chief	25 Feb. 1828
Duke of Wellington, again	15 Aug. 1842
Viscount Hardinge (died 24 Sept. 1856), general commanding-in-chief	28 Sept. 1852
Duke of Cambridge, ditto 15 July, 1856; appointed commander-in-chief by patent, 1887; resigned from	1 Nov. 1895
Lord Wolseley (for five years)	Nov. 1895
Lord Roberts (earl, Jan. 1901) assumed command	Jan. 1901

COMMEMORATION, see *Encænia*, *Jubilee*, 1887 and 1897.

COMMENDAM, "a benefice or church living, which being void, is commended to the charge of some sufficient clerk, to be supplied until it may be conveniently supplied with a pastor." *Blount*. By 6 & 7 Will. IV. c. 77 (1836), future bishops were prohibited from holding *in commendam* the livings they held when consecrated.

COMMERCE early flourished in Arabia, Egypt, and among the Phœnicians, see the description of Tyre, 588 B.C., *Ezek.* xxvii. In later times it was spread over Europe by a confederacy of maritime cities, 1241 (see *Hanse Towns*); by the discoveries of Columbus; and by the enterprises of the Dutch and Portuguese; see *Exports, Imports, and articles connected with this subject.*

The first *treaty of commerce* made by England with any foreign nation was entered into with the Flemings, 1 Edw. I. 1272. The second was with Portugal and Spain, 2 Edw. II. 1308. *Anderson;* see *Treaties.* Hertslet's Collection, in 16 vols. 8vo, published 1828-85, has a copious index.

An important commercial treaty was concluded with France (see *French Treaty*) 1860

Chambers of Commerce originated at Marseilles in the 14th century, and similar chambers were instituted in all the chief cities in France, about 1700

These chambers suppressed in 1791; restored by decrees . . . . 3 Sept. 1851

A chamber of commerce was started by John Weskett, merchant, he receiving payment, about 1782

The chamber of commerce at Glasgow was established 1783; at Edinburgh, 1785; Manchester, 1820; Hull, 1837; at Liverpool (mainly through the exertions of Professor Leone Levi) . . 1849

Associated (twenty-seven) chambers of commerce (not including Liverpool, Manchester, and Glasgow) met at Westminster for interchange of opinions on various questions, 21 Feb. 1865; annual and other meetings held since: Hull, 19 Sept. 1889; London, 25 March, 1890; 3 March, 1891; 8 March, 1892; 12 March 1895; 24 March, 1896; 9-11 March, 1897; 15 March, 1898; 14 March, 1899; 13 March, 1900 (special meeting in Paris, opened 5 Sept. 1900); London, 12 March, 1901; 4 March, 1902; 3 March, 1903.

Congress of chambers of the empire, 1886; 28 June, 1892; 9 June, 1896.

COMMERCIAL EDUCATION: conference at the Mansion House to promote the scheme put forth by the London chamber of commerce, 5 Feb. 1890; another at the Guildhall, 9 July, 1898; reported successful Nov. 1899; 6th international congress at Venice, 4 May, 1899.

The London chamber of commerce constituted, Sept. issued prospectus, about 10 Oct. 1881; 600 members first general meeting . . . 25 Jan. 1882

First annual meeting, 24 Jan. 1883 (publishes its report of its special commission on secret commissions prevalent in all trades and said to be increasing . . . . March, 1899

International Congress of Commerce at Brussels, 6-10 Sept. 1883; one at Philadelphia, mid. Oct.–Nov. 1899; one at Ostend . . 26 Aug. 1902

The International Congress of Commercial Law met at Antwerp, 1885; Brussels . . 30 Sept. 1888

Australasian chamber of commerce founded in London . . . . 4 July, 1901

Commercial Travellers' schools, Pinner, founded 1845;—Benevolent Institution, Finsbury . . 1849

Commercial Travellers' Association founded in Manchester, 1883, has many branches in the country. See *London Chamber of Arbitration.*

Commercial Court. The judges of the Queen's Bench resolved, May, 1894, "That a Commercial Court should be constituted from amongst themselves; in 1895 they laid down rules for procedure. It is not authorised by act of parliament, as a matter of convenience it is much resorted to 1903

COMMERCIAL INTELLIGENCE OFFICE, a branch of the board of trade, instituted Oct. 1899, "to provide the public with accurate information on all tariff and trade matters." Statistics of wages, the conditions and hours of labour, state of the labour market and the social condition of the working classes are collected, with statistics relating to strikes and industrial questions. The *Labour Gazette* containing such information is published monthly.

COMMISSION, see *High Commission, Court of.*

COMMISSIONNAIRES, street messengers in Paris. Those in London were originally pensioned soldiers wounded either in the Crimea or India, first employed in the west-end. They were appointed by a society, founded 13 Feb. 1859 by capt. Edward Walter, which is now under the patronage of the king and the commander-in-chief. The charges are regulated by a tariff. In Jan. 1861 the society commenced the gratuitous issue of a Monthly Advertising Circular. In March, 1864, there were 250 commissionnaires in London; in Nov. 1866, about 340; in Oct. 1872, 500; in Feb. 1887, 1,650; 1 Jan. 1895, 2,151; 2,450 in June, 1898; 1 Jan. 1902, 2,709. On 17 June, 1865, capt. Edward Walter resigned, and a permanent system of administration was formed. In 1865 commissionnaires were first engaged as private night-watchmen. A testimonial (piece of plate) from the officers of the army and navy was presented to captain Walter, 14 June, 1884; knighted, 1887. The corps was inspected by lord Roberts at Chelsea, 18 June, 1893. Annual inspection, 1894, *et seq.* Commissionnaires have been introduced in the colonies, beginning at Sydney, Feb. 1888.

COMMITTEES, Standing and Grand, were directed to be appointed by the new rules for procedure passed by the House of Commons in 1882, for facilitating the progress of legislation. The first grand committee (on trade, shipping, &c.) met 9 April, 1883; another (on law, &c.) soon after.

These Committees were re-appointed by the new rule (13). March 1888, *and since.* See *Scotland,* April 1894, May 1895.

COMMON COUNCIL OF LONDON. The city parliament, consists of 206 members elected annually on St. Thomas' day, 21 Dec. by the freemen householders of the 26 wards and their aldermen. This court, which appears to have been gradually organized in the 12th century, is mentioned in a charter granted by John, 1214. See *Plough Monday.* A *Common Hall* is held occasionally. The common council supported the prince of Orange in 1688, and queen Caroline in 1820. It vigorously opposed the scheme for amalgamation with the London County Council, 1893.

COMMON LAW OF ENGLAND, an ancient collection of unwritten maxims and customs (*leges non scriptæ*), of British, Saxon, and Danish origin, which has subsisted immemorially in this kingdom; and although somewhat impaired by the rude shock of the Norman conquest, has weathered the violence of the times. At the parliament of Merton, 1236, "all the earls and barons," says the parliament roll, "with one voice answered, that they would not change the laws of England, which have hitherto been used and approved;" eminently the law of the land; which has been supported by the reports of the decisions of the courts of law and the statutes passed by parliament; see *Bastard.* The process, practice, and mode of pleading in the superior *courts of common law,* were amended in 1852 and 1854.

COMMON PLEAS, COURT OF, IN ENGLAND, in ancient times followed the king's person, and is distinct from that of the King's Bench; but on the grant of *Magna Charta* by king John, in 1215, it was fixed at Westminster. In 1833 the mode of procedure in all the superior courts was made uniform. In England, no barrister under the degree of serjeant could plead in the court of common pleas; but in 1846 the privilege was extended to barristers practising in the superior courts at Westminster. Sat last, July, 1875. By an order in council, 16 Dec. 1880, the courts of exchequer and common pleas were abolished and were consolidated into one called the "Queen's bench division," under the lord chief justice of England. By the Act 44 and 45 Vict., sec. 68, passed 27 Aug. 1881; the lord chief justice was endowed with the powers of the chief justice of common pleas and the chief baron of the exchequer.

CHIEF JUSTICES. (*England.*)

1558. Sir Anthony Browne.
1559. Sir James Dyer.
1582. Sir Edmund Anderson.
1605. Sir Francis Gawdy.
1606. Sir Edward Coke.
1613. Sir Henry Hobart.
1626. Sir Thomas Richardson.
1631. Sir Robert Heath.
1634. Sir John Finch.
1639. Sir Edward Lyttleton.
1640. Sir John Bankes.
1648. Oliver St. John.
1660. Sir Orlando Bridgman, afterwards lord keeper.
1668. Sir John Vaughan.
1675. Sir Francis North, afterwards lord keeper Guildford.
1683. Sir Francis Pemberton.
,, Sir Thomas Jones.
1686. Sir Henry Bedingfield.
1687. Sir Robert Wright.
,, Sir Edward Herbert.
1689. Sir Henry Pollexfen.
1692. Sir George Treby.
1701. Sir Thomas Trevor, afterwards lord Trevor.
1714. Sir Peter King, afterwards lord chancellor King.
1725. Sir Robert Eyre.
1736. Sir Thomas Reeve.
1737. Sir John Willes.
1761. Sir Charles Pratt, afterwds. lord chancellor Camden.
1766. Sir John Eardley Wilmot.
1771. Sir William de Grey, afterwards lord Walsingham.
1780. Alexander Wedderburne, aft. ld. ch. Loughborough.
1793. Sir James Eyre.
1799. Sir John Scott, afterwards lord chancellor Eldon.
1801. Sir Richard Pepper Arden (lord Alvanley) 22 May.
1804. Sir James Mansfield, 21 April.
1814. Sir Vicary Gibbs, 24 Feb.
1818. Sir Robert Dallas, 5 Nov.
1824. Sir Robert Gifford, 9 Jan.; (lord Gifford); afterwards master of the rolls.
,, Sir William Draper Best, afterwards lord Wynford, 15 April.
1829. Sir Nicolas C. Tindal, 9 June; died July, 1846.
1846. Sir Thomas Wilde, 11 July; afterwards lord chancellor Truro.
1850. Sir John Jervis, 16 July; died 1 Nov. 1856.
1856. Sir Alex. Cockburn, Nov.; ch. j. Q. B. June, 1859.
1859. Sir William Erle, June; retired Nov. 1866.
1866. Sir William Bovill, 29 Nov.; died 1 Nov. 1873.
1873. John Duke Coleridge, Lord Coleridge, Nov.; removed to queen's bench, Nov. 1880.

The last chief justice of the common pleas (see *Supreme Court of Judicature Act*, 1881).

CHIEF JUSTICES. (*Ireland.*)

1691. Richard Pyne, 5 Jan.
1695. Sir John Hely, 10 May.
1701. Sir Richard Cox, 4 May.
1703. Robert Doyne, 27 Dec.
1714. John Forster, 30 Sept.
1720. Sir Richard Levinge, 13 Oct.
1724. Thomas Wyndham, 27 Oct.
1726. William Whitshed, 23 Jan.
1727. James Reynolds, 8 Nov.
1740. Henry Singleton, 11 May.
1754. Sir William Yorke, 4 Sept.
1761. William Aston, 5 May.
1765. Richard Clayton, 21 Feb.
1770. Marcus Patterson, 18 June
1787. Hugh Carleton, afterwards viscount Carleton, 30 April.
1800. John Toler, afterwards lord Norbury, 22 Oct.
1827. Lord Plunket, 18 June.
1830. John Doherty, 23 Dec.
1850. James Henry Monahan, 23 Sept.; died 8 Dec. 1878.
1876. Sir Michael Morris (Lord Morris and Killanin), Jan.; died, 8 Sept. 1901. *The last of the chief justices.*

COMMON PRAYER, BOOK OF, was ordered by parliament to be printed in the English language on 1 April, 1548. It was voted out of doors by parliament, and the Directory (*which see*) set up in its room in 1644, and a proclamation was issued against it in 1647. With a few changes the English Common Prayer-book is used by the episcopal churches in Scotland, Ireland, and North America.

The King's Primer published 1545
First book of Edward VI. printed . . 7 March, 1549
Second book of Edward VI. 1552
First book of Elizabeth (*revised*) 1559
King James's book . *ditto* 1604
Scotch book of Charles I. 1637
Charles II.'s book (*Savoy Conference*) now in use . 1662

[The original MS. of this book, signed by convocation in 1661, and annexed to the act of uniformity in 1662, was in time detached and lost, and not found till 1867; photographs were published by the queen's printers and the universities early in 1891; reproduced in type, 1893.]

The *State services* (which had never formed part of the Prayer-book, but were annexed to it at the beginning of every reign) for 5 November (Gunpowder treason), 30 Jan. (Charles I.'s execution), and 29 May (Charles II.'s restoration), were ordered to be discontinued; 17 Jan. 1859.

Changes in the Lectionary or calendar of lessons were recommended in the third report of the Ritual Commission, 12 Jan. 1870. A bill for sanctioning these changes passed the house of lords, but was dropped in the house of commons through want of time, Aug.; passed . 13 July, 1871
[The old tables might be used till 1 Jan. 1879.]

The fourth report of the Ritual Commission disclosed great difference of opinion amongst the commissioners . . . . Aug. 1870
Shortened services and other changes were authorized by the New Uniformity Act, passed 18 July, 1872
Public Worship Regulation Act (to check ritualism) passed . . . . . . Aug. 1874
The Wesleyan Methodists who had used the Prayer-book appoint a committee to revise it . Aug. ,,
The Prayer Book revision society petition the abp. of Canterbury for changes . . Jan.-Feb. 1883
The name of St. Patrick to be inserted in the calendar, resolved on . . . . 25 April, 1900
Coronation Prayer Book issued . mid-June, 1902
Slight alterations adopted. See *Times* . 11 Mar. 1903

COMMONS, HOUSE OF, originated with Simon de Montfort, earl of Leicester, who by the Provisions of Oxford ordered returns to be made of two knights from every shire, and deputies from certain boroughs, to meet such of the barons and clergy as were his friends, with a view thereby to strengthen his own power in opposition to that of his sovereign Henry III., 1258. *Stow*; see *Parliament*. In 1859 Mr. Newmarch estimated the constituency of England and Wales at 934,000. It was largely increased by the reform act of 1867:—Registered parliamentary electors, 1872: England and Wales, boroughs, 1,250,019; counties, 801,109. Scotland, burghs, 49,025; counties, 79,919. Ireland, boroughs, 171,912; counties, 175,439. Total, 2,526,423. By the Franchise Act of 1884, the electors of the United Kingdom were increased to about 5,000,000, and many changes were made by the Redistribution Act of 1885 (disqualified persons about 7,000,000), 1,911,955 voters in boroughs in England and Wales; and 2,579,403 in counties in 1888. The present house of Commons (counties, boroughs, and universities): England, 465; Wales, 30; Scotland, 72; Ireland, 103 members (1903). See under *Reform*.

Parliamentary electors: England and Wales: 1875, 2,301,266; 1878, 2,416,222; 1883, 2,632,223. Scotland, 1875, 289,789; 1883, 226,511. Ireland, 1875, 230,436; 1883, 322,967; total, 1878, 2,952,005. Electorate, 1889:

England and Wales, 4,501,851; Scotland, 571,911; Ireland, 763,145; total, 5,836,907; United Kingdom, total, 6,528,629, in 1898; total, 6,891,093 in 1903.

By the reform act of 1884, the county franchise was made uniform with that of the boroughs, and about 2,000,000 voters were added.

By the acts of 1884–5, 670 members: elections, July, 1892, reported: Liberals, 270; Parnellites, 9; anti-Parnellites, 72; Labour members, 4; Conservatives, 268; Liberal-Unionists, 47. 12 Aug. 1895: Conservatives, 340; Liberal-Unionists, 71—411; Liberals and Radicals, 177; anti-Parnellites, 70; Parnellites, 12—259. Unionist majority, 152; (137, 7 Feb. 1899); total 670.

Elections, 27 Sept. *et seq.* 1900: Conservatives, 334 Liberal-Unionists, 68; Liberals and Labour members, 186; Irish Nationalists, 82. Unionist majority, 134; total 670; 3 Dec. 1900.

	Old House.	Members.		*By the Reform Act of 1832.**	Members.		*By the Acts of 1867 and 1868.*	Members.
	ENGLAND.			ENGLAND.			ENGLAND.	
202	Cities or boroughs	403	187	Cities or boroughs	323	186	Cities or boroughs †	286
40	Counties	82	40	Counties	144	40	Counties	171
2	Universities	4	1	Isle of Wight	1	1	Isle of Wight	1
			2	Universities	4	3	Universities	5
244		489	230		472	230		463
	WALES.			WALES.			WALES.	
12	Cities or boroughs	12	14	Cities or boroughs	14	14	Cities or boroughs	15
12	Counties	12	12	Counties	14	12	Counties	15
24		24	26		28	26		30
	SCOTLAND.			SCOTLAND.	Members.		SCOTLAND.	Members.
15	Cities or burghs	15	21	Cities or burghs	23	22	Cities or burghs	26
33	Counties	30	33	Counties	30	33	Counties	32
						4	Universities	2
48		45	54		53	59		60
	IRELAND.			IRELAND.			IRELAND.	
33	Cities or boroughs	35	33	Cities or boroughs	39	33	Cities or boroughs †	39
32	Counties	64	32	Counties	64	32	Counties	64
1	University	1	1	University	2	1	University	2
66		100	66		105	66		105
382	Total	658	376	Total	658	381	Total	658

COMMONS. In 1685, of the 37,000,000 acres of land in England, about 18,000,000 were moorland, forest, and fen. In 1727, about 3,000,000 acres more had been brought into cultivation; and from that time to 1844, by means of 4000 private acts of parliament, about 7,000,000 acres more were enclosed. Since the inclosure act of 1845, which established commissioners, another 1,000,000 acres have been enclosed.

Act for improvement, protection, and management of commons near the metropolis, passed . Aug. 1866

The Commons Preservation Society established 1865 elected Wm. Cowper, president . . . Feb. 1867

Metropolitan commons act, to prevent inclosure in the neighbourhood of London, passed, 1866 and 1869

It is stated that there are 900,000 acres of common land capable of cultivation in England and Wales, Aug. 1874

Act for the regulation of commons, passed 11 Aug. 1876

Mr. de Morgan, active opponent of enclosures, imprisoned for contempt of court (The Rolls) . Jan. 1878

Metropolitan Board of Works authorised to secure commons, &c. by act passed . . 16 Aug. ,,

About 14,000 acres of land near London preserved by the agency of the Commons Preservation Society reported at the annual meeting on 10 Dec. 1886

Law of commons amendment act requires consent of the board of agriculture before inclosure . 1893

By the ranges act, passed in 1891, power was given to any lord of the manor to acquire possession of any part of any common over which his rights extend, in order that the secretary of state for war may establish ranges for rifle practice, &c., with regulations.

New commons act (to preserve open spaces for the public) passed, 1899.

COMMONWEALTH OF ENGLAND, the term applied to the interregnum between the death of Charles I. and the restoration of Charles II. A republic was established at the execution of Charles I., 30 Jan. 1649,—a new oath called the "Engagement" was framed, which all officials were obliged to take.* *Salmon.* Oliver Cromwell was made protector, 16 Dec. 1653 (see *Naseby*); succeeded by his son Richard, 3 Sept. 1658. Monarchy was restored 8 May, and Charles II. entered London, 29 May, 1660. COMMONWEALTH of AUSTRALIA constitution act, royal assent, 9 July, 1900, see *Australasia*.

COMMUNALISTS, or COMMUNISTS, propose to divide France into about a thousand small thoroughly independent states, with councils elected by all the population, Paris to be the ruling head. They declare that capital and its holders must be adapted to nobler uses, or cease to exist. Their creed is stated to be atheism and materialism. They are intimately connected with the Interna-

* In 1844 Sudbury, and in 1852 St. Alban's, were disfranchised for bribery and corruption; each having previously returned two members; the aggregate number of the house then became 654. In 1861, the forfeited seats were thus distributed by act of parliament—two additional to the west riding of York, one additional to South Lancashire, and one to a newly-created borough, Birkenhead.

† Disfranchised and replaced, 1867: Lancaster, Yarmouth, Totnes, and Reigate. —Disfranchised, 1870: Beverley and Bridgwater, each two members; Cashel and Sligo, each one member: 652 members, 1878; 12 members short, through void elections, Aug. 1880.

* By this oath they swore to be true and faithful to the Commonwealth, without king or house of lords. The statues of Charles were next day demolished, particularly that at the Royal Exchange, and one at the west end of St. Paul's; and in their room the following inscription was conspicuously set up: —"*Exit Tyrannus Regum ultimus, Anno Libertatis Angliæ Restitutæ Primo, Anno Dom.*, 1648, Jan. 30."

tional Society of workmen (see *Workmen*), and with the communists or socialists (1871-3).*

COMMUNES, in France, are territorial divisions under a mayor. In the 11th century the name was given to combinations of citizens, favoured by the crown, against the exactions of the nobles. In 1356 Stephen Marcel, during the English invasion, vainly endeavoured to establish a confederation of sovereign cities, having Paris as the governing head; and for six months it was really governed by a commune in 1588. After the insurrection of July, 1789, the revolutionary committee which replaced the city council took the name of "commune of Paris," Péthion being mayor. It met at the Hôtel de Ville, and was definitively constituted, 21 May, 1791. It had great power under Robespierre, and fell with him 17 July, 1794; being replaced by twelve municipalities. The commune of Paris was proclaimed 28 March, 1871, during the insurrection, which began 18 March, and ended with the capture of the city by the government troops, 28 May following. 2245 communists were pardoned by decree issued 17 Jan. 1879; and many others afterwards. A number re-entered Paris, 4 September following. For the events of the communal rule in Paris, see *France*, 1871. See *Socialism*.

COMMUNION, a name given to the ordinance of the Lord's Supper, 1 *Cor.* x. 16. Communicating under the form of bread alone is said to have had its rise in the west, under pope Urban II., 1096. The cup was first denied to the laity by the council of Constance, 1414-18. The fourth Lateran council, 1215, decreed that every believer should receive the communion at least at Easter. The communion service of the church of England was set forth in 1549.

COMMUTATION, see *Tithes*.

COMORN, see *Komorn*.

COMORO ISLANDS, see *Madagascar*, 1891.

COMPANIES.† The London trade companies were gradually formed out of the trade or craft guilds, mainly by the exertions of Walter Harvey, mayor, in 1272, who is said to have been very active in enlarging and maintaining the liberties and privileges of the city. The original religious element in the companies gradually disappeared. Among the earliest commercial companies in England may be named the Steelyard society, established 1232. The second company was the merchants of St. Thomas à Becket, in 1248. *Stow*. The Merchant Adventurers, incorporated by Elizabeth, 1564. Mr. Edward Arnold's *Early Chartered Companies*, published July, 1896. The following are the city companies of London; the first twelve are the chief, and are styled "the honourable." Many companies are extinct, and many dates are doubtful. An inquiry into their affairs was partially resisted by them in 1835. In 1869 the gross income of the endowed charities of the city companies was stated to be above 99,000*l*. A motion in the commons for inquiry into the revenues and other affairs of 89 companies, by Mr. W. H. James, withdrawn, 23 May, 1876. A commission of inquiry was appointed (the earl of Derby, duke of Bedford, lords Coleridge and Sherbrooke, sir R. A. Cross, &c.), 14 July, 1880. Five reports issued with recommendations for reform, 1884-5.

In 1884, 7319 liverymen and about 10,000 freemen, estimated annual income about 750,000*l*., expended in maintenance, education, and charities; about 75,000*l*. spent in entertainments.

Grants from the companies to the City Guilds of London Institute (Goldsmiths 46,000*l*., Drapers 43,000*l*., Clothworkers 37,000*l*., Fishmongers 34,000*l*., Mercers 22,000*l*., Grocers 10,000*l*.); for technical education, &c. (Drapers 60,000*l*., Goldsmiths 85,000*l*., Mercers 60,000*l*.) and others promised 1878-88.

1. Mercers . . 1393
2. Grocers . . . 1345
3. Drapers . . 1438
4. Fishmongers (salt, 1433; stock, 1509); united . . . 1537
5. Goldsmiths . . 1327
6. Skinners . . . ,,
7. Merchant Taylors. 1326
8. Haberdashers . 1448
9. Salters . . . 1558
10. Ironmongers . 1464
11. Vintners . . . 1363
12. Cloth-workers . 1480

———

13. Dyers . . . 1471
14. Brewers . . 1438
15. Leather-sellers . 1444
16. Pewterers . . 1473
17. Barber-Surgeons . 1462
18. Cutlers . . . 1415
19. Bakers . . . 1509
20. Wax-chandlers . 1483
21. Tallow-chandlers . 1462
22. Armourers and Braziers . . 1453
23. Girdlers . . 1448
24. Butchers . . . 1606
25. Saddlers . . 1272
26. Carpenters . . 1477
27. Cordwainers . 1438
28. Painter-stainers . 1581
29. Curriers . . 1606
30. Masons . . . 1677
31. Plumbers . . 1611
32. Inn-holders . . 1515
33. Founders . 1614
34. Poulterers . . 1504
35. Cooks . . . 1482
36. Coopers . . . 1501
37. Tilers and bricklayers . . 1568
38. Bowyers . . . 1621
39. Fletchers . . 1536
40. Blacksmiths . . 1571
41. Joiners . . . 1571
42. Weavers . . . 1184
43. Woolmen . . 1484
44. Scriveners . . 1617
45. Fruiterers . . 1606
46. Plasterers . . 1501
47. Stationers . . 1556
48. Broderers . . 1561
49. Upholders . . 1626
50. Musicians . . 1604
51. Turners . . ,,
52. Basket-makers . 1569
53. Glaziers . . 1631
54. Horners . . . 1638
55. Farriers . . 1684
56. Paviors . . . 1479
57. Loriners . . 1712
58. Apothecaries . . 1617
59. Shipwrights . 1605
60. Spectacle-makers. 1629
61. Clock-makers . 1631
62. Glovers . . . 1639
63. Comb-makers . 1635
64. Felt-makers . . 1604
65. Framework knitters . . . 1663
66. Silk-throwsters . 1629
67. Silk-men . . 1608
68. Pin-makers . . 1636
69. Needle-makers . 1656
70. Gardeners . . 1605
71. Soap-makers . 1638
72. Tinplate-workers. 1671
73. Wheelwrights . 1670
74. Distillers . . . 1638
75. Hatband-makers . 1664
76. Patten-makers . 1671
77. Glass-sellers . . 1664
78. Tobacco-pipe makers . . 1619
79. Coach and Harness makers . 1677
80. Gunmakers . . 1637
81. Gold and Silver wire-drawers . 1693
82. Bowstring-makers 1440
83. Card-makers . 1628
84. Fan-makers . . 1709
85. Wood-mongers . 1605
86. Starch-makers . 1632
87. Fishermen . . 1687
88. Parish clerks . 1223
89. Carmen . . . 1606
90. Porters . . 1154
91. Watermen . . 1556

COMPANIES ACTS: one passed 1862, was amended and continued, 20 Aug. 1867; both amended by acts, 2 July, 1877, 15 Aug. 1879, and Aug. 1898. The important companies winding-up act was passed 18 Aug. 1890; amended 1893.

By the last act, unlimited banking companies were regulated in regard to their issue of notes, audit of accounts, &c. The acts of 1862, 1867, 1877, and 1879 were amended by 43 Vict. c. 19 (1880), in 1883 and 1886. Committee appointed by the board of trade to inquire

---

* M. Dufaure, in opposing the amnesty, 17 May, 1876, asserted that the outbreak was organised by about 7000 communists and 1500 foreigners; 40,000 persons were inculpated; 10,000 tried; 25,000 dismissed. See *France*.

† Bubble companies have been formed, commonly by designing persons. Law's bubble, in 1720-1, was perhaps the most extraordinary of its kind, and the *South Sea Bubble*, in the same year, was scarcely less memorable for its ruin of thousands of families. Many companies were established in these countries in 1824 and 1825, and turned out to be *bubbles*. Immense losses were incurred by individuals, and the families of thousands of speculators were totally ruined. Many railway enterprises (1844-5) were termed *bubbles*. Lord chief justice Russell stated that from 1891-7, over 28 millions sterling had been lost to the community in connection with dishonest company promotions, 9 Nov. 1898. See *Law's Bubble; South Sea; Railways; Joint-Stock Companies*.

into the working of companies acts: lord Davey, Mr. justice Chitty, and others, Nov. 1894; the report recommends important changes, Aug. 1895.

Legality of a "one man company" affirmed on appeal, by the house of lords, in the case of Salomon (pauper) *v.* Aron Salomon, 16 Nov.; *Times*, 17, 18 Nov. 1896.

Companies act (for the regulation of limited companies, limited liability, and the discovery of fraud), passed, 8 Aug. 1900.

Companies registered in the United Kingdom 1862–1902, 83,915; nominal capital 6,305,578,902*l*. Of these 3033, with nominal capital 156,714,468*l*., were registered in 1902. By the official return of the Registrar, 33,259 joint-stock companies were believed to be carrying on business, April 1902; paid-up capital, including vendors' shares, 1,805,141,161*l*.

COMPASS, MARINER'S, said to have been early known to the Chinese, 1115 B.C., and brought to Europe by Marco Polo, a Venetian, 1260, A.D. Flavio Gioja, of Amalfi, a navigator, of Naples,* is said to have introduced the suspension of the needle, 1302. The compass is also said to have been known to the Swedes in the time of king Jarl Birger, 1250. Its variation was discovered first by Columbus, 1492; afterwards by Sebastian Cabot, 1540. The compass box and hanging compass used by navigators were invented by William Barlowe, an English divine and natural philosopher, in 1608; see *Magnetism*. The *measuring* compass was invented by Jost Bing, of Hesse, in 1602. The compass of sir William Thomson (lord Kelvin), patented in 1876, is considered the best. The Evoy compass, constructed so as to be unaffected by the magnetism inseparable from an iron ship, reported successful, Feb. 1900.

COMPETITIVE EXAMINATIONS, see *Civil Service*.

COMPIEGNE, a French city north of Paris, the residence of the Carlovingian kings. During the siege, Joan of Arc was captured by the Burgundians, 25 May, 1430, and given up to the English for money. The emperor Napoleon III. and the king of Prussia met here on 6 Oct. 1861.

COMPLUTENSIAN BIBLE, see *Polyglot*.

COMPOSING-MACHINES, see *Printing* and *Times*.

COMPOSITE ORDER, a mixture of the Corinthian and Ionic, and also called the Roman order, is of uncertain date.

Composite Portraits. By means of photography in 1877-8, Mr. Francis Galton combined from 2 to 9 separate portraits; the result was generally an improvement on the features of the components.

COMPOUND HOUSEHOLDERS (in regard to the payment of rates) were constituted by the Small Tenements act of 1851. Their position, with regard to the suffrage, caused much discussion during the passing of the Reform act in 1867; and their claims were rejected.

COMPOUND RADICAL, in organic chemistry, is a substance which, although containing two or more elements, in ordinary circumstances performs the part of an element. The Radical or Binary theory was propounded by Berzelius, 1833, and by Liebig, 1838; and modified in the nucleus theory of Aug. Laurent, 1836. The first compound radical isolated was cyanogen (*which see*), by Gay-Lussac, in 1815; see *Amyl*, *Ethyl*, and *Methyl*.

* The statement that the *fleur-de-lis* was made the ornament of the northern point of the compass in compliment to Charles, the king of Naples at the time of the discovery, has been contradicted.

COMPREHENSION BILL. Passed by the house of lords in 1689, it proposed changes likely to induce nonconformists to join the church of England — it was dropped in the commons, being unsatisfactory to all parties.

COMPROMISE, see *Breda*.

COMTE PHILOSOPHY, see *Positive Philosophy*.

CONCEPTION, IMMACULATE. A festival (on 8 Dec.) appointed in 1389, observed in the Roman Catholic Church in honour of the Virgin Mary's having been conceived and born immaculate, or without original sin. Opposition to this doctrine was forbidden by decree of pope Paul V. in 1617, confirmed by Gregory XV. and Alexander VII. *Hénault*. On 8 Dec. 1854, pope Pius IX. promulgated a bull, declaring this dogma to be an article of faith, and charging with heresy those who should doubt it or speak against it.—The CONCEPTIONISTS were an order of nuns in Italy, established in 1488; see *Santiago*.

CONCERT OF EUROPE, termed by lord Salisbury, "inchoate federation," 9 Nov. 1897; gradually formed by the ambassadors at Constantinople, with regard to the troubles in Turkey, Candia, and Greece, 1896–7.

CONCERTINA, a musical instrument invented by prof. afterwards sir Charles Wheatstone, about 1825, and improved by Mr. G. Case. The sounds are produced by free vibrating metal springs.

CONCERTS. The Filarmonia gave concerts at Vicenza in the 16th century. The first public subscription concert was performed at Oxford in 1665; the first in London is said to have been in 1672, by John Banister, afterwards by Thomas Britton till his death, 1714. The Academy of Ancient Music, which introduced concerts in London, began in 1710; the Concerts of Ancient Music in 1776; and the present Philharmonic Society in 1813; see others, under *Music; Crystal Palace;* and *Handel*. Colossal peace concerts were held at Boston, U.S., 15 June, &c. 1869; 17 June to 4 July, 1872; see *Boston*.

Concerts Spirituels at Paris, organized by Anne Dannican Philidor, began in Passion week, 18 March, 1725: closed in 1791; re-established, 1805; replaced by the Concerts du Conservatoire, begun 9 March, 1828.

Jullien's Popular Concerts, with monster quadrilles, began at Drury Lane Theatre 8 June, 1840; a farewell series, 1859. He greatly promoted the taste for classical music.

Promenade Concerts revived at Covent Garden Theatre, autumn, 1880 *et seq.*; Queen's Hall, 1895, *et seq.*

CONCHOLOGY, the science of shells, is mentioned by Aristotle and Pliny. It was first reduced to a system by John Daniel Major, of Kiel, who published his classification of the *Testacea* in 1675. Lister's system was published in 1685; and that of Largius in 1722. Johnson's Introduction (1850) and Sowerby's Manual of Conchology (1842) are useful. Forbes and Hanley's "British Mollusca and their Shells" (1848-53) is a magnificent work. "British Conchology," by J. G. Jeffreys, published in 1862-9.

CONCILIATION COUNCILS, see *Councils*. Conciliation (trade disputes) act passed, 7 Aug. 1896.

CONCLAVE (L. *con* together, *clavis* a key). A meeting of persons shut up to consult in privacy. The term is now specially used to signify the assembly of cardinals locked up in apartments of the Vatican till they have elected a pope. The practice is said to have been instituted by Alexander III. in 1179. Clement IV. having died at Viterbo in 1268, the cardinals were unable to agree in the choice of a successor. In 1271 they were on the point of breaking up, when the magistrates, by the advice of St. Bonaventura, shut the gates of their city, and locked up the cardinals, upon which Gregory X. was elected. This pope in 1274, with aid from a council, formulated rules for the seclusion of cardinals during a papal election, which, with slight alterations, are still adhered to. Small cells are erected in a hall of the Vatican, with access to the Sistine chapel, in which the votes (by ballot) are cast. All doors but one are built up, every possible outlet being strictly guarded. The day after the death of a pope the cardinals are locked up in these apartments and do not come out until from amongst their number a pope has been chosen. The latest conclave was on July 31, 1903, when the Sacred college to the number of 62 cardinals entered the conclave; on Aug. 4 Cardinal Sarto (who has taken the name of Pius X.) was elected pope in succession to Leo XIII.

CONCORD (Massachusetts, N. America). Near here was fought the battle of Lexington (*which see*), 19 April, 1775.

CONCORDANCE. An index or alphabetical catalogue of all the words and also a chronological account of all the transactions in the Bible. The first concordance was made under the direction of Hugo de St. Caro, who employed as many as 500 monks upon it, 1247. *Abbé Lenglet.* It was based on one compiled by Anthony of Padua. Thomas Gibson's "Concordance of the New Testament" published, 1535. John Marbeck's "Concordance" (for the whole Bible), 1550. Two Concordances (with royal privileges), by Rob. F. Herrey, appeared in 1578. Cruden's Concordance was published in London in 1737. Dr. Robert Young's valuable "Analytical Concordance to the Bible," 1879-80. The Index to the Bible, published by the King's printers and others, prepared by B. Vincent, 1848, still in use 1903.

Verbal indexes accompany good editions of the ancient classics. An index to *Shakspeare*, by Ayscough, appeared in 1790; another by Twiss in 1805; and Mrs. Cowden Clarke's (late Mary Novello) concordance to *Shakspeare's* Plays (on which she spent 16 years' labour) in 1847. *Shakspeare*-Lexicon by Dr. A. Schmidt, 2 vols. 1874-5. Mrs. Horace Furness's concordance to *Shakspeare's* Poems, 1874. Todd's verbal index to *Milton*, 1809. Cleveland's concordance to *Milton*, 1867. Other concordances are—to *Burns*, by Reid, 1889; to *Cowper*, by Neve, 1887; to *Dante's Divina Commedia*, by Fay, 1888; to *Homer*, by Dunbar, 1880; to *Pope*, by Abbott, 1875; to *Shelley*, by Ellis, 1892.

CONCORDAT. An instrument of agreement between a prince and the pope, usually concerning benefices. The concordat between the emperor Henry V. of Germany and pope Calixtus II., in 1122, has been regarded as the fundamental law of the church in Germany. The concordat between Napoleon Bonaparte and Pius VII., signed at Paris, 15 July, 1801, re-established the Catholic church and the papal authority in France. Napoleon was made in effect the head of the Gallican church, as bishops were to have their appointments from him, and their investiture from the pope. Another concordat between the same persons was signed at Fontainebleau, 25 Jan. 1813. These were almost nullified by another, 22 Nov. 1817. A concordat, signed 18 Aug. 1855, between Austria and Rome, by which a great deal of the liberty of the Austrian church was given up to the papacy, caused much dissatisfaction. In 1868 it was virtually abolished by the legislatures of Hungary and Austria.

CONDÉ, Louis I. de Bourbon, prince of, brother of Antony of Bourbon, king of Navarre, was born 7 May, 1530; representative of an ancient race, taking their name from the town of Condé, distinguished in the wars of the time, a leader of the Huguenots, taken prisoner at the battle of Jarnac, and killed by the baron de Montesquieu (1569). Louis II. de Bourbon, "the Great Condé," born, 8 Sept. 1621, commander of the French forces in the Thirty Years war, defeated the Spaniards at Rocroi, a brilliant victory (1643), and others, 1644-8. Retired finally to Chantilly, about 1675, and died, 11 Dec. 1686. "Histoire des princes de Condé," by the duc d'Aumale, published 9 vols., 1865-96.

CONDENSATION, see *Gas, Beer, Milk.*

CONDOTTIERI, *conductors* or leaders of mercenaries, termed free companies or lances, which became so troublesome in Italy, that the cities formed a league to suppress them in 1342. Many ravaged France after the peace of Bretigny, in 1360.

CONDUITS. Two remarkable conduits, among a number of others in London, existed early in Cheapside. The "great conduit" was the first cistern of lead erected in the city, and was built in 1825. At the procession of Anna Boleyn, on the occasion of her marriage, it ran with white and claret wine all the afternoon, 1 June, 1533. *Stow.*

CONFEDERATE STATES OF NORTH AMERICA. The efforts of the Southern States for the extension of slavery, and the zeal of the Northern States for its abolition, with the consequent political dissensions, led to the great secession of 1860-1. On 4 Nov. 1860, Abraham Lincoln, the Republican or Abolitionist candidate, was elected president of the United States. Hitherto, a president in the interest of the South had been elected. On 20 Dec., South Carolina seceded from the Union; and soon after Alabama, Florida, Mississippi, Georgia, Louisiana, Texas, Virginia (except West Virginia), Arkansas, Tennessee, and North Carolina also. Jefferson Davis was inaugurated president of the Southern Confederacy at Montgomery in Alabama, 18 Feb. 1861. For the events of the war which ensued, and the restoration of the Southern States to the Union, see *United States*, 1861-5. Jefferson Davis's "Rise and Fall of the Confederate Government," 2 vols., published June, 1881; he died, aged 81, 6 Dec. 1889.

CONFEDERATION AT PARIS, 14 July, 1790; see *Champ de Mars* and *Bastille.*

CONFEDERATION OF THE RHINE, the League of the Germanic States, formed by Napoleon Bonaparte, 12 July, 1806, when he abolished the Holy Roman Empire, and the emperor of Germany became emperor of Austria. In Dec. it consisted of France, Bavaria, Wurtemberg, Saxony, and Westphalia; seven grand duchies; six duchies; and twenty principalities. The princes collectively engaged to raise 258,000 troops to serve in case of war, and established a diet at Frankfort. This league terminated with the career of Bonaparte in 1814; and in 1815 it was replaced by the *Germanic Confederation* (*which see*, and *Germany*).

CONFERENCES, ECCLESIASTICAL. One was held at Hampton Court palace, between the prelates of the church of England and the puritan ministers, in order to effect a general union, at the instance of the king, James I., 14, 16, 18 Jan. 1604. It led to the new translation of the Bible, now in general use in England; executed in 1607-11. Some alterations in the church liturgy were agreed upon: but these not satisfying the dissenters, nothing more was done.—Another conference of the bishops and presbyterian ministers, with the same view, was held in the *Savoy*, 15 April to 25 July, 1661. The dissenters' objections were generally disallowed, but some alterations were recommended in the Prayer-book. See *Wesleyans* and *Congresses*.

CONFESSIONAL, see *Auricular Confession*.

CONFESSIONS OF FAITH, or **CREEDS**; see *Apostles'*, *Nicene* (325), and *Athanasian* (about 434) *Creeds*. J. R. Lumby's "History of the Creeds," published 1874.

The confession of faith of the Greek church was presented to Mahommed II. in 1453. This gave way in 1643 to one composed by Mogila, metropolitan of Kiev, which is the present standard of the Russo-Greek church.
The creed of Pius IV., composed of the Nicene creed, with additional articles which embody all the peculiar dogmas of the Roman Catholic church, published by the council of Trent . . . 1564
The church of England retains the Apostles', Nicene, and Athanasian creeds, with articles:—42 in 1552; reduced to 39 1563
The confession of Augsburg (that of the Lutherans) was drawn up principally by Melancthon, in 1530, and has since undergone modifications, the last of which is called the "Form of Concord" . 1579
The Westminster confession was agreed to in 1643; and adopted by the presbyterian church of Scotland; see *Westminster* . . . 1647
The congregational dissenters published a declaration of faith 1833

CONFIRMATION, or "laying on hands," was practised by the Apostles in 34 and 56 (*Acts* viii. 17; xix. 6), and was general, according to some church authorities, in 190. In the church of England it is the public profession, with laying on of hands by a bishop, of the Christian religion by an adult person, who has been baptized in infancy. It is made a sacrament by the church of Rome.

CONFLANS (near Paris), **TREATY OF**, between Louis XI. of France and the dukes of Bourbon, Brittany, and Burgundy, 5 Oct. 1465. By its provisions Normandy was ceded to the duke of Berry, and an end was put to the "War of the Public Good." It was confirmed by the Treaty of Peronne, 1468.

CONFUCIANISM, the doctrines or system of morality taught by Confucius K'ung Fû-tze, or "the Master K'ung" (B.C. 551-479), which has been long adopted in China as the basis of jurisprudence and education. It inculcates no worship of a god, and doubts a future state.

CONGE D'ÉLIRE (permission to elect), the licence given by the sovereign as head of the church, to chapters and other bodies, to elect dignitaries, particularly bishops; the right asserted by Henry VIII., 1535. After the interdict of the pope upon England had been removed in 1214, king John made an arrangement with the clergy for the election of bishops.

CONGELATION, the act of freezing. Dr. Cullen produced ice by rapid evaporation of water by an air pump. Ice was produced in summer by means of chemical mixtures, by Mr. Walker, in 1783. In 1810 Leslie used an air-pump in combination with a vessel of sulphuric acid. Numerous freezing mixtures have been discovered since. Intense cold is produced by the aërification of liquefied carbonic acid gas. Ice-making machines invented by Jacob Perkins 1834, John Gorrice 1848, and others. In 1857 Jas. Harrison patented a machine for manufacturing ice for commercial purposes, by means of ether and salt water, and made large blocks. In 1860, M. Carré devised a method of freezing to 60° below zero by making water in a close vessel absorb and give off the gas ammonia. Siebe's ice-making machine, an improvement on Harrison's, exhibited in use 1861-30. R. Reece liquefied ammonia by compression and vaporised it in a closed vessel surrounded with the liquid to be cooled, 1868. Prof. Linde of Munich followed up this principle and produced an ammonia compression machine, 1873. Compression machines, ammonia or carbonic, are now 1903 in general use.

CONGESTED DISTRICTS BOARD (Ireland), constituted by the purchase of land act, 5 Aug. 1891, amended 1893, 1894. Land purchased, works undertaken, &c.; reported Nov. 1895. Reports issued, 1896, 1897, 1898. Another act (Ireland) passed, 1 Aug. 1899. Congested districts act (Scotland) passed, 1897.

CONGO RIVER, S.W. Africa. The mouths of the Congo were discovered by the Portuguese in 1484, and they have ever since claimed territories on its banks, having founded settlements, and sent missionaries, with temporary success. Dr. Livingstone explored the Congo, 1867-71. The natives on its bank and on the creeks having rifled the *Geraldine*, and committed other acts of piracy, were chastised by an expedition under commodore sir Wm. Hewett, 3-11 Sept. 1875. Several villages and chiefs' houses were destroyed.

For Mr. H. M. Stanley's expeditions in connection with the Belgian government, and his settlements, see *Africa*, 1876, *et seq.*
M. de Brazza's expedition; his treaty with the king of Congo ratified by the French government . . . . . 21 Nov. 1882
Colonies formed; national jealousies excited; regret of the disinterested king of the Belgians; the British government partly recognize the rights of the Portuguese, Jan., with certain modifications (afterwards set aside) . . . . . March, 1883
Sir F. Goldsmid, chief of an expedition connected with the International African Association favoured by Belgium, starts summer . . . ,,
The French seize fresh territories, 28 March, 1883; burn a village, March, *et seq.*
Mr. Stanley had peaceably founded 12 stations and opened up 4500 miles of rivers to trade and civilization, reported 12 July; he advocates a British protectorate, Sept.; M. de Brazza's settlements reported unsuccessful . . . . Sept. ,,
Circular from the Portuguese government asserting rights over the mouth of the Congo, published in *Times* . . . . . 5 Nov. ,,
Sir F. Goldsmid ill; returns to England; reports; Gen. (Chinese) Gordon appointed by the king of Belgium to act on behalf of the International African Association on the Congo for the suppression of slavery, and support of commerce, Jan.; but is sent by the British government to the Soudan . . . . . 18 Jan. 1882
Mr. Stanley returns to Stanley Pool . 21 Jan. ,,
British agreement with Congo, announced 5 Feb. ,,
British interest secured by treaty with Portugal; signed . . . . Feb. ,,
The International African Association (captain Strauch, president), aiming at the suppression of slavery, has 30 stations, announced 9 April; its flag recognized by United States, 22 April; it formulates itself as a federal state, and is said to enter into engagements with France, regarded as presumptuous, but justified by the Association, May–June, ,,
Recognized by Great Britain, Italy, and other powers, Dec. 1884, *et seq.*
Colonel sir Francis de Winton appointed administrator-general of the Congo territories June, ,,

Free trade in the Congo valley declared by the West African conference (*which see*) . Dec. 1884

The Mouth of the Congo occupied by the Portuguese 15 Jan. 1885

Treaty between the Association and France respecting the delimitation of territory, signed 5 Feb. ,,

King Leopold II. takes the title of Independent Sovereign of the State about . . 30 April ,,

Mr. H. M. Stanley's book "Congo, and the Founding of its Free State" published . . May ,,

Conference at Berlin (which met 1884–5) ratifying the recognition of the Congo State by the Powers 19 April, 1886

Stanley Falls Station evacuated . . . Dec. ,,

Leopoldville, at Stanley Pool, founded by Mr. H. M. Stanley in 1881 reported prosperous . . 1887

Stanley Falls Station re-occupied . . 4 June, 1888

The state appeals to Belgium for an annual subsidy of 1,500,000 francs for ten years about 12 Aug. 1889

Prosperity of the country reported (Mr. Janssen governor-general) . . . . . Sept. ,,

Supreme council of the Congo State, king Leopold president, held its first sitting at Brussels, 18 Dec. ,,

The Belgian government agree to lend to the Congo State 5,000,000 francs at once, and 2,000,000 francs annually for the next 10 years without interest, July; the bill passed by the chamber, 11 July, by the senate . . . . . . 30 July, 1890

The budget shows a deficit of 7,000,000 francs 17 April, 1892

The killing of M. de Poumayrac in debatable land causes a territory dispute between France and Belgium; the Congo state declines responsibility; arbitration proposed and deferred, July, Aug.; the French demand indemnity and evacuation of the land, 7 Aug.; the death of M. Poumayrac and some of his party, attributed to indiscreet dealings with the natives . Sept. ,,

Rising of the Arabs in the Upper Congo, and massacre of Europeans, anti-slavery agents, &c., including M. Hodister, an able officer of the Katanga company about 15 May. (See *Katanga*.) ,,

Major de Wahis appointed governor about 26 Aug. ,,

Exploring expedition of M. Van den Kerckhoven, a Belgian, with above 1,000 men, which started in 1891, reported arrival at Wadelai . about 25 Aug. ,,

Lieut. Dhanis severely defeats the slave traders under Sefu, son of Tippoo Tib, and takes many prisoners . . . . 22 Nov. ,,

Expedition under lieut. Dhanis against the Arabs of Munie Moharra . . . . . Jan. 1893

Dynamite explosion on a railway between Emposi and Matadi, about 50 persons killed, reported, 16 Jan. ,,

Expedition for the relief of capt. Jacques [reported safe, 25 Oct. 1892], engaged in the suppression of the slave trade, organized in Brussels . Feb. ,,

The Arabs defeated by lieut. Chaltin; 80 slaves released, reported . . . . . 26 Feb. ,,

Successful expedition of M. Delcommune up the Lukuga to the Congo; important discoveries, about 29 Sept. 1892, *et seq.*, reported . March, ,,

Capt. Bia, who started on an expedition 19 Dec. 1891, from Lupongo in the Lomami valley after exploring lakes Mweru and Bangeweolo, died, 30 Aug. 1892; reported . . . . . March, ,,

Nyangwe taken by capt., aft. baron, Dhanis 4 March, ,,

Gradual suppression of the Arab slave-traders, and subjection of the country to the Congo Free State . . . . . . March, April, ,,

The Ponthier expedition leaves Antwerp, 6 March; reached Boma . . . . . . 30 March, ,,

M. van den Kerckhoven killed, reported 5 May, succeeded by capt. Delanghe, reported July ,,

Defeat of Rumaliza at Kassango by baron Dhanis with heavy loss, 20 Oct.; capt. Ponthier dies of his wounds . . . . 25 Oct. ,,

Said ben Abadi, the murderer of Emin Pasha, taken and shot, reported . . . 16 Nov. ,,

Sefu killed in battle . . . . 17 Nov. ,,

A new district constructed on the Upper Congo, the capital to be Nyangwe, reported . 28 Nov. ,,

First section of the Congo railway (24 m.) opened 4 Dec. ,,

Gov.-gen. in Boma, M. Wahis . . . . Dec. ,,

Friendly relations with natives, reported 12 Jan. 1894

Rumaliza defeated by baron Dhanis and lieut. Lothaire, 14 Jan., reported . . . March, 1894

An attack of the Mahdists on Mundu, Upper Nile, repulsed by capt. Delanghe; capt. Bonvalet and M. Devos killed . . . . 18 March, ,,

Anglo-Belgian treaty settling the boundaries of the Congo State and the British possessions, signed at Brussels . . . . 12 May, ,,

French claims set forth, *Times* . . . 19 June, ,,

A dispute with Germany settled by compromise 22 June, ,,

Capt. Jacques, leader of the Anti-slavery committee, warmly welcomed in Brussels . 23 June, ,,

Agreement with France signed . . . 14 Aug. ,,

Baron Dhanis, commander of the expedition to Katanga, warmly received at Antwerp . 11 Oct. ,,

Annexation of the Congo State to Belgium proposed by the government at Brussels . . 4 Jan. 1895

Settlement between Belgium and France as to the right of pre-emption with regard to the Congo State . . . . 5 Feb. ,,

The debt of the State adopted by Belgium 27 June, ,,

Excitement respecting capt. Lothaire's execution of Mr. Stokes, ivory dealer, after a court martial (1 Jan.), charged with selling arms, &c. . Aug. ,,

Capt. Lothaire summoned to give explanations to Col. Wahis, governor-gen. of the Congo . Sept. ,,

150,000 francs paid as indemnity to the British government for Mr. Stokes' family; 100,000 francs to the German government; announced, 14 Nov. ,,

Complete defeat of the rebels at Luluaburg by maj. Lothaire . . . . 18 Oct. ,,

Zemio, on the Mbomu river, occupied by the French; reported . . . . . 2 Dec. ,,

Skirmish at Congo-ute, lieut. Liebrecht and M. de Valdere killed; reported . . . . 5 Jan. 1896

Arrival of maj. Lothaire at Boma, 27 March; his trial begun, 25 April; acquitted, on the ground that Stokes was inciting to civil war by allying himself with Kibonge, a native chief, and placing himself at the head of an armed troop, 27 April; Mr. Arthur, British consul at Boma, appeals against the finding of the court . . 15 May, ,,

Maj. Lothaire arrives at Brussels, 5 June; second trial there, 3 Aug.; acquitted, 6 Aug. (resigns, announced 6 Aug. 1897).

Royal warrant withdrawing the proposal of annexation of the State read in the chamber, Brussels 10 June, ,,

The German government claims indemnity for robbery of traders; reported . . 21 June, ,,

First half of the Congo railway inaugurated 22 July, ,,

Revolt of natives quelled at Trebu; about 27 July, ,,

Successful expedition of baron Dhanis in the Upper Nile; Lado occupied, and an alliance concluded with the natives; reported . . 2 Sept. ,,

Baron Dhanis appointed governor-gen. . 4 Sept. ,,

A European committee for protection of natives appointed by the Belgian government, with regulations; reported . . . . . 20 Sept. ,,

White population, 1,325 (899 Belgian), 1 Jan. 1896; ,,

A native educational military colony established and declared successful; pacification of the river tribes and others; reported . . . 21 May, ,,

Mutinous native troops defeated at Kohoa, in Munsa, by capt. Michaux . . . 11 Nov. ,,

Capt. Chaltin totally defeats the Mahdists and occupies Rejaf; lieut. Bardlea killed . 17 Feb. 1897

Mutiny of native troops at Ndirfa, commander Leroi and other officers killed; reported, 4 March, ,,

Baron Dhanis' Batetela soldiers mutiny on their way to put down the rebellion; lieut. Julien and two officers killed; mutiny suppressed and the country subjugated, reported . . . Sept. ,,

Col. Wahis, governor-gen., arrives in Brussels, 27 May; justificatory letter in *Times* . 31 May, ,,

Frequent raids; British fort on Salt lake destroyed 17 June, ,,

Lado captured by capt. Chaltin; reported . July, ,,

Lieut. Henry totally defeats the Batetela rebels near Lake Albert Nyanza . . . 15 July, ,,

Rebels totally defeated by lieut. Dorme 23 March, 1898

Prosperity reported, May; a loan to meet expenses for public works concluded by the king, at Brussels . . . . June, ,,

Lieut. Chargois' column attacked by mutineers on Lake Tanganyika, and compelled to retreat, the enemy finally routed and 25 killed, end of April, ,,

Lieut. Dubois' expedition of 100 men to occupy Lake Rivu, surprised by rebels and 31 killed, he himself deserted afterwards by his men and killed; reported . . . . . . 7 July, 1898
Dervish attack on Rejaf repulsed, MM. Desnenx and Bartholi killed . . . 3, 4 June, „
Lieut. Glorie defeats the Batatelas at Givesé, 17 June, „
The Batatelas defeat the Belgians, 3 officers and 200 men killed at Sungula, 4 Nov.; Kabambaré captured, 5 whites killed, 14 Nov.; Kabambaré re-occupied by the troops after severe fighting, 31 Dec.: rebels defeated by baron Dhanis, Feb. 1899
The Budjas defeated by maj. Lothaire, reported, Feb. „
Capt. Maurice Bell, in an expedition against the Aruwimis, killed by cannibals, Jan.; 100 natives killed by a punitive expedition and many made prisoners . . . . May, „
Baron Dhanis defeats the rebels near Sungula, much bloodshed, 20 July; rebels again defeated, 8–12 Oct. „
Alleged atrocities by the Zappo Zaps, villages burnt and natives massacred, reported early, 1900
Lieut. Weylants and M. Rabe massacred by the Budjas near Zambeta . . . . 4 March, „
Explorations in Katanga, down the Kasai to lake Dilolo under lieut. Lemaire, reported - 4 April, „
Provisional agreement between Germany and the Congo state regarding territory near lake Kivu, signed at Brussels . . . . . 10 April, „
Revolt at Chinkakassa, fort seized by mutineers, 17 April; but recaptured by the Boma troops, rebels fled . . . . 19 April, „
Batatela mutiny ended, mutineers surrender, Oct. „
Much slaughter of natives, villages burnt, for refusing to work rubber . . . . . Nov. „
Colonel Bartels appointed governor-general, reported . . . . 21 Dec. „
Lacroix and Mathys sentenced to 15 and 12 years' imprisonment for murdering natives in Katanga, Nov.; confirmed . . . . Feb. 1901
Rebellion in Kassai, Jan., suppressed . mid-Feb. „
Native rising in the Welle district, April; revolt quelled . . . . mid-July, „
Batatelas severely defeated, 35 Congo troops killed, Nov. „
Concession reported to be obtained for a railway between the northern borders of Rhodesia across the Congo territory to lake Kasali,—*Times* . 22, 25 April 1902
Taxes on religious, charitable, and scientific institutions lowered, by decree . . . . 1 July, „
Debate in the house of commons on the administration of the Congo territory, and ill-treatment of the natives, 20 May; correspondence of British government with Belgium respecting the question; blue book published 1903

CONGREGATION OF THE LORD, a name taken by the Scotch reformers, headed by John Knox, about 1546. Their leaders (the earls of Glencairn, Argyle, Morton, and others) called "lords of the congregation," signed the first bond or covenant which united the protestants under one association, 3 Dec. 1557. *Tytler*.

CONGREGATIONALISTS, see *Independents*.

CONGRESS. An assembly of princes or ministers for the settlement of the affairs of nations or of a people. The following are the most remarkable congresses of Europe:—

Münster	1643-8
Nimeguen	1676-8
Ryswick	1697
Utrecht	1713
Soissons	1728
Antwerp	8 April, 1793
Rastadt	9 Dec. 1797-9
Chatillon	5 Feb. 1814
Vienna	3 Nov. „
Aix-la-Chapelle	9 Oct. 1818
Carlsbad	1 Aug. 1819
Troppau	20 Oct. 1820
Laybach	6 May, 1821
Verona	25 Aug. 1822
Paris	16 Jan.—22 April, 1856
Frankfort (see *Germany*)	16-31 Aug. 1863
Constantinople	23 Dec. 1876—20 Jan. 1878
Berlin	13 June—13 July, „

See *Alliances, Church, Conventions, Peace, &c.*

The first general CONGRESS of the UNITED STATES of AMERICA, preparatory to their declaration of independence, when strong resolutions were passed, also a petition to the king, and an address to the people of England, was held, 5 Sept. 1774. The second was held, 10 May, 1775; the third, when the independence was declared . 4 July, 1776
The first federal American congress, under the constitution, was held at New York; George Washington, president . . . . . . March, 1789
The first congress of the seceding southern states was held at Montgomery, Alabama, 4 Feb.; it elected Jefferson Davis president of the confederate states on 9 Feb. For political reasons it adjourned on 24 May, to meet at Richmond, in Virginia, on . . . . . . 20 July, 1861
In 1863, the emperor Napoleon invited the sovereigns of Europe to a congress; which was declined by England 25 Nov., and only conditionally acceded to by other powers. He proposed a congress on the affairs of Italy and Rome in Nov. 1867, without effect.

CONGREVE ROCKETS, see *Rockets*.

CONIC SECTIONS. Their properties were probably known to the Greeks, four or five centuries before the Christian era, and their study was cultivated in the time of Plato, 390 B.C. The earliest treatise on them was written by Aristæus, about 330 B.C. Apollonius's eight books were written about 240 B.C. The parabola was applied to projectiles by Galileo, the ellipse to the orbit of planets by Kepler, and to comets by Newton.

CONJURATION, see *Witchcraft*.

CONJURERS, see under *Wizard*.

CONNAISSANCE DES TEMPS, the French nautical almanack, continuing Hecker's Ephemerides, was first published by Picard, 1679.

CONNAUGHT, W. Ireland; long a nominal kingdom, divided into counties, 1590. Prince Arthur, third son of queen Victoria, born 1 May, 1850, was created duke of Connaught, 23 May, 1874; being the first royal prince whose leading title was Irish.

The Duke of Connaught's Establishment Act, passed 8 Aug., 1878, made the same provision for the duke, as for his brother Alfred; see *Edinburgh*. The duke was married to the princess Louise Margaret of Prussia, 13 March, 1879. See *England* (Royal Family).
The condition of the peasantry was greatly benefited by the construction of light railways, introduced by Mr. A. J. Balfour, the Irish chief secretary . . . . 1890 *et seq.*

CONNECTICUT, a New England state of N. America. The settlements of 1635 and 1638 were united by charter in 1665. Capital Hartford. Population 1880, 622,700; 1890, 746,258; 1900, 908,424.

Trestle bridge accident, car overturned, 35 deaths, reported . . . . 7 Aug. 1899
Great fire at Waterbury, buildings destroyed, over 3,000,000 dols. damage . . . . . 2 Feb. 1902

CONNOR, Ireland. The bishopric was united to that of Down, 1442. The first prelate, Ængus Macnisius, died 507. The united sees were added to Dromore on the death of its last bishop, 1842, in accordance with the Irish church temporalities act, 1833.

CONQUEST, the era in British history, when William duke of Normandy overcame Harold II. at the battle of Hastings, 14 Oct. 1066, and obtained the crown which he asserted had been bequeathed to him by Edward the Confessor (Edgar being the rightful heir). William has been erroneously styled the *Conqueror*, for he succeeded to the crown of England by *compact*. He defeated Harold, who was himself a usurper, but a large portion of the kingdom afterwards held out against him; and he, unlike a conqueror, took an oath to observe the laws and customs of the realm, in order to induce the submission of the people. Formerly our judges were accustomed to reprehend any gentleman at the bar who said casually William the Conqueror, instead of William I. *Selden*. Maclise exhibited forty-two drawings on the events of the Norman conquest, in May, 1857. E. A. Freeman's "History of the Norman Conquest," 6 vols, 1870-9, is valued. He died, aged 69, 16 March, 1892.

CONSCIENCE CLAUSE, see *Education*, 1863, 1902-3.

CONSCIENCE, COURTS OF, or OF REQUESTS for recovery of small debts, constituted by a stat. of Hen. VII. 1493, and re-organised by stat. 9 Hen. VIII. 1517. These courts were improved and amended by various acts; their jurisdiction in London reached to 5*l.* and (until superseded by county-courts) to 40*s.* in other towns. The practice was by summons, and if the party did not appear, the commissioners had power to apprehend and commit; see *County Courts*.

CONSCIENCE, LIBERTY OF, a principle of genuine Christianity (1 *Cor.* x. 29); repudiated by Romanism, proclaimed by James II. for political purposes, 1687.

CONSCRIPT FATHERS (*patres conscripti*), the designation given to the Roman senators, because their names were written in the registers of the senate.

CONSCRIPTION, a mode (derived from the Romans) adopted for recruiting armies on the continent. On 5 Sept. 1798, a military conscription was ordained in France, comprehending all the young men from 20 to 25 years of age: from whom selections were made. A conscription for 350,000 men took place in Jan. 1813, after the disastrous Russian campaign, and in Dec. same year, another for 300,000 after the battle of Leipsic. Estimated conscription, 1793-1813, 4,103,000. The law of 1818 (modified in 1824, 1832, and 1868) required a certain annual contingent for each department. The conscription was enlarged and modified by the army bill which was enacted in Feb. 1868. The reorganisation of the army began in 1871, after the fatal war with Germany. Substitutes were allowed under certain conditions. Conscription for Great Britain was advocated and strongly opposed in 1875.

CONSECRATION. Aaron and his sons were consecrated priests, 1490 B.C. (*Lev.* viii.) The Jewish tabernacle was dedicated, 1490 B.C., and Solomon's temple, 1004 B.C. (1 *Kings* viii.) The consecration of churches began in the 2nd century. Anciently the consecration of popes was deferred until the emperor had given his assent to their election. Gregory IV. desired to have his election confirmed by the emperor Louis, in 828. *Hénault*. The consecration of churches, places of burial, &c., is admitted in the reformed religion. An act relating to the consecration of churchyards, passed 20 Aug. 1867, was amended in 1868. A form of consecration was adopted by convocation, but not sanctioned by the crown, April, 1712. It is generally used but is not compulsory.—*Burn*. The form of consecrating bishops in the church of England is set forth in the prayer-book of 1549.—*Stow*.

CONSERVATION OF FORCE. The doctrine that no physical force can be created or destroyed, but may be transferred, maintained by Faraday, Grove, Helmholtz, Tyndall, and other scientists; see *Correlation*.

CONSERVATIVES, a name said to have been invented by John Wilson Croker,* an earnest Tory, in 1830, assumed by a party, whose leading principle is the preservation of our national institutions. It was termed a new cant word by T. B. Macaulay in *Edinburgh Review*, July, 1832. Sir Robert Peel acknowledged himself a conservative when reproached by the Irish party in parliament with being an Orangeman; but the party that afterwards separated from him called their principles conservative in contradistinction to his,—his policy and measures being changed.—The *Conservative Club* was founded in 1840; see *Protectionists* and *Clubs*. The party in the north of the United States which supported the president in his conciliatory efforts to re-establish the Union, Jan. 1866, were termed "Conservatives." A great meeting of the National Union of Conservative Associations was held at the Crystal Palace, 24 June, 1872. The party in the minority at the elections in 1868 obtained a majority at those in Feb. 1874, and came into office. They were again in a minority at the general election, and resigned 22 April, 1880. The marquis of Salisbury was elected leader of the party, 9 May, 1881, succeeding the earl of Beaconsfield, who died 19 April previous. Constitutional club (central) formed in London, President, the late marquis of Salisbury. House opened 8 Aug. 1883. *National Conservative Clubs*, established in 1866. See *Derby* and *Disraeli*, *Fourth Party*, *Liberals* (1886), *National Union*. *Salisbury administrations*, 1885, 1886, 1895, 1900-02. *Balfour administration*, 1902.

- The national union of conservative associations met at Salisbury, 25 July, 1889; Liverpool, 1890; Birmingham, 24 Nov. 1891; Sheffield, 13 Dec. 1892; Cardiff, 28 Nov. 1893; Newcastle-on-Tyne, 13 Nov. 1894; Brighton, 18 Nov. 1895; Rochdale, 17 Nov. 1896; London, 16 Nov. 1897; London, 18 Dec 1900; Wolverhampton, 26 Nov. 1901; Manchester, 14 Oct. 1902; Sheffield . 1 Oct. 1903
- The marquis of Salisbury addresses 10,000 conservatives at Exeter . . . . 2 Feb. 1892
- Testimonial of 10,000*l.* presented by lord Salisbury from the conservative party to capt. Middleton, the chief conservative agent, at a meeting 19 March, 1896
- Great meeting at the Albert hall; speech by lord Salisbury . . . . 16 Nov. 1897
- The national union of conservative associations for Scotland, annual meetings; Glasgow . 2 Dec. ,,
- Associated clubs, 936; 375,000 members . May, 1901
- Mr. Balfour opens a new club at Fulham 19 July, 1902
- Mr. Balfour expounds the fiscal policy of the government at great meeting of the National union at Sheffield, and pays a high tribute to Mr. Chamberlain . . . . 1 Oct. 1903
- Sir John Dorrington's resolution in support of Mr. Balfour's policy unanimously carried at conference . . . . 2 Oct. ,,

CONSERVATOIRES, a name given to establishments for the cultivation of music and the arts on the continent. One was established at Naples in 1537. The singing school at Paris, founded in 1784, and closed in 1789, was re-opened in 1793 as the "Institut National de Musique," and after being reorganised, was re-named "Conservatoire de Musique" in 1795, and flourished under Cherubini (1822-42). "The Conservatoire des Arts et Métiers" was established in 1784. It includes a museum and library, and lectures are given to workmen there.

* Quarterly Review, vol. xlii. p. 276, Jan. 1830.

CONSERVATORS OF THE PUBLIC LIBERTIES. Officers chosen in England to inspect the treasury and correct abuses in administration, 28 Hen. III. 1244.—*Rapin*. Conservators were appointed to see the king's peace kept.—*Pardon*. Conservators were formerly appointed in every seaport to take cognisance of all offences committed against the peace upon the main sea out of the liberty of the Cinque Ports.—*Bailey*.

CONSISTORIES for regulating ecclesiastical discipline and divine worship in the Lutheran church in Germany, were established at the reformation—the first at Wittenberg in 1542; other consistories were established after the peace of Augsburg in 1555.

CONSISTORY COURT, anciently joined with the hundred court; and its original, as divided therefrom, is found in a law of William I., 1079, quoted by lord justice Coke. The chief and most ancient consistory court of the kingdom belongs to the see of Canterbury, and is called the Court of Arches (*which see*).

CONSOLIDATED FUND was formed by combining the "aggregate," "general," and "South Sea funds," 1786. On 5 Jan. 1816, the exchequers of Great Britain and Ireland, previously separate, were amalgamated, forming "the consolidated fund of the United Kingdom." Acts are passed annually for the appropriation of the fund.

CONSOLS, see *Stocks*.

CONSORZIO NAZIONALE, see *Italy*, 1866.

CONSPICUOUS SERVICE CROSS; naval decoration, instituted, 28 June, 1901.

CONSPIRACIES. Among the recorded conspiracies, real or supposed, the following are the most remarkable: see *Rebellions*.

Of the duke of Gloucester against Richard II. . . 1397
Of the earl of Cambridge and others against Henry V. 1415
Of Anthony Babington and others against Elizabeth. (See *Babington*) 1586
Of Lopez, a Jew, and others 1594
Of Patrick York, an Irish fencing-master hired by the Spaniards to kill the queen . . . . . "
Of Walpole, a Jesuit, and Edward Squyer to poison the queen 1598
Tyrone's insurrection in Ireland 1599
The Gunpowder plot (*which see*) 1605
Tyrone's conspiracy to surprise the castle of Dublin, 1607
Of Penruddock (1655) and of Syndercombe and others to assassinate Oliver Cromwell . Jan. 1657
Insurrection of the Fifth-monarchy men against Charles II. 1661
Of Blood, who seized the duke of Ormond, wounded him, and would have hanged him, Dec. 1670; and who afterwards attempted to steal the regalia. 9 May, 1671
The pretended conspiracy of the French, Spanish, and English Jesuits to assassinate Charles II., revealed by the infamous Titus Oates, Dr. Tongue, and others . . . . . . Aug. 1678
The Meal-tub plot (*which see*) 1679
The Rye-house plot to assassinate the king on his way to Newmarket. (See *Rye-house Plot*). . . 1683
Of lord Preston, the bishop of Ely, and others to restore James II. . . . . . Jan. 1691
Of Granville, a French chevalier, to murder king William in Flanders 1692
The Assassination plot (*which see*) frustrated . . 1696
Of Simon Fraser, lord Lovat, against queen Anne. (See *Rebellions*) 1703
Of the marquis Guiscard . . . . . March, 1711
Of James Sheppard, an enthusiast, to assassinate George I. 1718
Of counsellor Layer and others, to bring in the Pretender 1722
Of the Corresponding Society, &c. (*which see*) . 1706-8
Of colonel Despard 1802
Of Robert Emmett, in Dublin, when lord Kilwarden was killed . . . . . 23 July, 1803
Of Thistlewood and others, to assassinate the king's ministers. (See *Cato-street*) 1820
Of the Sepoys in India. (See *India*) . 10 May, 1857
Of the Fenians 1858-68
Major Panitza against prince Ferdinand, see *Bulgaria* . . . . . . Feb. *et seq.* 1890
Of Servian revolutionists against king Alexander of Servia and queen Draga (see *Servia*) . 9 June, 1903

See *Rebellions, Chartists, &c.*

CONSPIRACY AND PROTECTION TO PROPERTY ACT, passed 13 Aug. 1875; relates to trade disputes, breaches of contract, &c.

CONSTABLE OF ENGLAND, LORD HIGH. The seventh great officer of the crown, and, with the earl marshal, formerly a judge of the court of chivalry, called, in the time of Henry IV., *curia militaris*, and subsequently the court of honour. The power of this officer was so great, that in 1389 a statute was passed for abridging it, and also the power of the earl marshal (*which see*). The office existed before the conquest, after which it went by inheritance to the earls of Hereford and Essex, and next in the line of Stafford. In 1521 it was forfeited by Edward Stafford, duke of Buckingham, attainted for high treason, and has never since been granted to any person, otherwise than *pro hâc vice* (for this occasion), to attend at a coronation or trial by combat. The only instance of a trial by combat being *ordered* since this office fell into the hands of the crown, was that commanded between lord Reay and Mr. David Ramsey, in Nov. 1631; but the king prevented it.

LORD HIGH CONSTABLES AT CORONATIONS.

Queen Anne, Wriothesly, duke of Bedford . . . 1702
George I., John, Duke of Montague 1714
George II., Charles, duke of Richmond 1727
George III., John, duke of Bedford 1761
George IV. } Arthur, duke of Wellington . . 1821
William IV. } Arthur, duke of Wellington . . 1831
Victoria } Arthur, duke of Wellington . . 1838
Edward VII., Alexander, duke of Fife . . . 1902

CONSTABLE OF SCOTLAND, LORD HIGH. The office was instituted by David I. about 1147. The holder had the keeping of the king's sword, which the king, at his promotion, delivered to him naked (and hence the badge of the lord high constable is a naked sword); and the absolute command of the king's armies while in the field, in the absence of the king. The office was conferred heritably in 1314 on sir Gilbert Hay by Robert Bruce. One of Hay's descendants was made Earl of Erroll, and with his family the office still remains, being expressly reserved by the treaty of union in 1707. The present earl of Erroll is the twenty-third lord high constable (1892).

CONSTABLES of Hundreds and Franchises, instituted in the reign of Edward I., 1285, are now called high constables. There are three kinds of constables, *high, petty, and special;* the high constable's jurisdiction extends to the whole hundred; the petty constable's to the parish or liberty for which he is chosen; and the special constable is appointed for particular emergencies (as in April, 1848, on account of the Chartists). The general appointment of parish constables was made unnecessary by an act passed Aug. 1872. See *Special Constables* and *Tower*.

CONSTABULARY FORCE. For that of London, see *Police*. The constabulary of Ireland act passed in 1823, when this species of force was embodied throughout the country. Several subsequent acts were consolidated in 1836.

CONSTANCE, a city in Baden (S. Germany). Here was held the seventeenth general council, 1414-18, which condemned John Huss; and here he was burnt, 6 July, 1415; see *Hussites*.

CONSTANTINA, the ancient capital of Numidia, was taken by the French, 13 Oct. 1837. During the assault on 12 Oct. the French general Damremont was killed. Achmet Bey retired with 12,000 men, as the victors entered Constantina.

CONSTANTINOPLE (formerly Byzantium) (*which see*), now *Stamboul*, derives its name from Constantine the Great, who removed the seat of the Eastern Empire here, dedicating it 11 May, 330. See *Eastern Empire*. Population, 1897, abt. 1,136,000.

General ecclesiastical councils against heresy were held here in 381, 553, 680, and 869.
Seized by Procopius 365
The city suffered much from religious dissensions, and was burnt during the "Nika" conflicts . . 532
Rebuilt by Justinian with great splendour . . . ,,
St. Sophia dedicated 537
Resisted the Saracens successfully . . 675, 718
And the Russians 865, 904, 941, 1043
Taken by the Latins 1203, 1204
Recovered by the Greeks 1261
Vainly besieged by Amurath the Ottoman, June—Aug. 1422
Taken by Mahomet II. after 53 days' siege, 29 May, 1453
CONFERENCE on Turkish Affairs; representatives: *Great Britain*, marquis of Salisbury; *Russia*, general Ignatieff; *France*, Chaudordy; *Austria*, Zichy; *Germany*, Von Werther; *Italy*, Corti; ordinary meetings began . . . . 23 Dec. 1876
Turkey rejected the propositions and the conference closed . . . . 20 Jan. 1877
Treaty of peace with Russia: 12 articles: Turkey accepted modifications of treaty of San Stefano (*which see*); an indemnity of about 802,500,000 francs to be paid by Turkey (settlement deferred); Russian troops to quit within 40 days, &c.; signed 8 Feb. 1879
By the falling down of a barracks at Beykoi about 200 soldiers said to be killed, about 9 Feb. 1880
Conference of European powers respecting Egypt constituted (see *Egypt*) . . . . 23 June, 1882
Great fire, thousands homeless . . . . 5 Oct. 1883
Great fire, about 900 houses destroyed 12 July, 1890
Grand opening of the new station of the Orient (European Turkish) railway . . . 4 Nov. ,,
Great fire at Cadikeui, about 3,000 persons homeless . . . . 22 Feb. 1893
Collision of a palace steamer with an Admiralty steamer at Seraglio Point; 54 persons drowned 2 April, ,,
Representation of the city at *Olympia*, London, opened, 26 Dec. 1893, *which see*.
Destructive earthquakes in the city and neighbourhood, about 200 lives lost, 10, 15, 19 July; public subscriptions opened by the Sultan 16 July, 1894
The German emperor's fountain (designed by him) unveiled by baron von Bieberstein . 27 Jan. 1901
See *Turkey*, *Germany*, Oct. 1898.

ERA OF CONSTANTINOPLE has the creation placed 5508 years B.C. It was used by the Russians until the time of Peter the Great, and is still used in the Greek church. The civil year begins 1 Sept., and the ecclesiastical year in March; the day is not exactly determined. To reduce it to our era, subtract 5508 years from January to August, and 5509 from Sept. to the end. *Nicolas.*

CONSTELLATIONS. *Arcturus*, *Orion*, the *Pleiades*, and *Mazzaroth*, are mentioned in *Job* ix. 9, and xxxviii. 31, about 1520 B.C. Homer and Hesiod notice constellations; but our first direct knowledge was derived from Claudius Ptolemæus, about A.D. 140. Hipparchus (about 147 B.C.) made a catalogue of forty-eight constellations, and others were added by Tycho Brahe, Hevelius, Halley, and others. The number at present acknowledged is 29 northern, 45 southern, and 12 zodiacal.

CONSTITUENCIES, see *Commons, House of*.

CONSTITUENT, see *National Assembly*.

CONSTITUTION OF ENGLAND. It comprehends the whole body of laws by which the British people are governed, and to which it is presumptively held that every individual has assented. *Lord Somers*. This assemblage of laws is distinguished from the term government in this respect—that the constitution is the rule by which the sovereign ought to govern at all times; and government is that by which he does govern at any particular time. *Lord Bolingbroke*. The king of England is not seated on a solitary eminence of power: on the contrary, he sees his *equals* in the co-existing branches of the legislature, and he recognises his superior in the law. *Sheridan*. Hallam's "Constitutional History of England" was first published in 1827; May's in 1861-3; Stubbs' in 1875; Sir William R. Anson's "Law and Custom of the Constitution," published 1886–92.

CONSTITUTIONALIST PARTY, a name assumed by a combination of Conservatives and seceded Whigs, Aug. 1867, and used during the severely contested elections, Nov. 1868. The *Constitutional Union* held its first anniversary 20 June, 1881. Dinner, 14 June, 1890.

Constitutional Press Corporation.—An active conservative body, autumn, 1881.
Constitutional Club established 1883.

CONSTITUTIONS OF FRANCE, enacted 1789-91, 1795, 1799, (charter) 1814, 1848, 1852, 1875.

CONSUBSTANTIATION, see *Transubstantiation*.

CONSULS (meaning colleagues), ROMAN: at the expulsion of the Tarquins, a republic was established, to be ruled by two prætors or consuls elected annually: the first being Lucius Junius Brutus and Lucius Tarquinius Collatinus, husband of the injured Lucretia, 509 B.C. The consular power was in emergencies superseded by dictators and tribunes.

Government of the Decemviri . . B.C. 451—449
Three Military Tribunes with consular power . . 444
A Plebeian elected consul 366
[In the reign of Tiberius the consuls were nominated by the senate, and the appointment became henceforth honorary.]
The French consulate established when the directory was abolished: Bonaparte, Siéyès, and Roger Ducos made provisional consular commissioners, 10 Nov.; Bonaparte, Cambacérès, and Lebrun made consuls . . . . . . 13 Dec. 1799
Bonaparte was made first consul for 10 years, 6 May, and for life, 2 Aug. 1802; emperor . 18 May, 1804
Commercial agents were first distinguished by the name of *consuls* in Italy. Lorenzo Strozzi was appointed by Richard III. 1485
A British consul first appointed in Portugal . . 1633
The Associations of Foreign Consuls in London held a banquet at the Hôtel Métropole, 22 Feb. 1890, and others since. Mr. Alfred C. de Rothschild elected president . . . . . July, 1894

CONSUMPTION, see *Tuberculosis*.

CONTAGIOUS DISEASES ACT for naval and military stations first passed in 1864; followed by others in 1866, 1868, and 1869. They gave rise to great opposition and much agitation in the country. Their operation was suspended in consequence of a resolution of the house of commons, 20 April, 1883, and they were repealed, 16 April, 1886; see *India*, 22 July, 1897. For contagious diseases of animals, see *Cattle*.

CONTEMPORARY REVIEW, first appeared Jan. 1866; editor Dean Alford.

CONTINENTAL SYSTEM, the name given to Napoleon's plan to exclude the British merchandise from the entire continent. It began publicly with his *Berlin decree*, 20 Nov. 1806, confirmed by the *Milan decree*, 17 Dec. 1807. This led to the *Orders in Council* (*which see*).

CONTINUITY. Mr. (after sir) W. R. Grove, in his address as president of the British Association, on 22 Aug. 1866, at Nottingham, expounded the opinion held by many philosophers, that all the past changes in the world have been produced by the continuous action of the causes now in operation—that "continuity is a law of nature, the true expression of the action of Almighty Power."

Those who hold this opinion are termed Uniformitarians; their opponents are termed Cataclysmists, who attribute the changes to the violent action of fire and water.

CONTRABAND OF WAR, a term said to have been first employed in the treaty of Southampton between England and Spain in 1625. During the struggle between Spain and Holland, both powers acted with much rigour towards ships of neutrals conveying goods to the belligerents. This provoked the resistance of England. A milder policy was adopted by the treaty of Pyrenees, 1650; and by the declaration of Paris, 26 April, 1856. The subject was much discussed during the North American conflict, 1861-4, and in April, 1898.

CONTRACTING OUT, see *Employer's Liability*.

CONTRACTORS with Government, disqualified from sitting in parliament, 1782.

CONTRE-DANSE (English, *country-dance*), a dance, so called from the dancers being opposite each other, was introduced into France (probably from England) about 1715, *et seq*.

CONTRIBUTIONS, VOLUNTARY, to a vast amount have been several times made by the British people in aid of the government.. One, in 1798, to support the war against France, amounted to two millions and a half sterling. Several men of wealth, among others sir Robert Peel, of Bury, Lancashire, subscribed each 10,000*l.*: and 200,000*l.* were transmitted from India in 1799; see *Patriotic Fund*. For *India, &c.*, see *Mansion House*.

CONTROL, BOARD OF. Mr. Pitt's bill, establishing this board for the purpose of aiding and controlling the executive government of India, and of superintending the territorial concerns of the company, was passed 18 May, 1784. Act amended and the board remodelled, 1793. The president of the board was a chief minister of the crown, and necessarily one of the members of the cabinet. This board was abolished in 1858, when the government of India was transferred from the company to the crown; see *India Bills* and *India*.

CONTROL DEPARTMENT, in the British army, was divided into the commissariat and transport department, and the ordnance store department; the old title was abolished; order issued 11 Dec. 1875.

CONVALESCENT INSTITUTION (Metropolitan), at Walton-on-Thames, with children's branches at Hendon and Mitcham, was established in 1840; a branch at Bexhill, Sussex, was founded in 1880. A convalescent hospital for the east of London was founded at Snaresbrook in 1866, greatly due to Mr. and Mrs. Charlesworth and Mrs. Gladstone. Homes at Ramsgate, 1866; Waltham, 1867; Margate, 1875, &c. See *Bartholomew, St.*, 1881. There were 42 such institutions in 1888. 100,000*l.* for the establishment of a general hospital convalescent home offered by a secret benefactor (Peter Reid), himself, sir W. S. Savary, and W. H. Cross to be joint trustees, 30 Dec. 1889; 50,000*l.* more presented, announced 18 March, 1890. The Police Seaside Home, W. Brighton, patroness the countess of Chichester, established 1890. The Surrey Convalescent Home, erected through an anonymous gift of 25,000*l.*, opened by the duke of Cambridge, 27 July, 1891. Mr. Henry Harben gives 20,000*l.* to erect a home for working men at Littlehampton, April, 1895. Others established throughout the country.

CONVENTICLES, private assemblies for religious worship, held by dissenters from the established church; but first applied to the schools of Wickliffe. 35 Elizabeth, c. 1 (1593) passed "to prevent and suppress seditious conventicles," was re-enacted by 16 Charles II. c. 4 (1664) and by 22 Charles II. c. 1 (1670). Persons attending them were liable to severe punishment. The statutes were repealed by the toleration act, 24 May, 1689.

CONVENTION PARLIAMENTS, assembled without the king's writ upon extraordinary occasions. One on 25 April, 1660, voted the restoration of Charles II. A second met 22 Jan. 1689; offered the crown to William and Mary 13 Feb.; and dissolved in Feb. 1690; see *National Convention*.

CONVENTIONS, see *Treaties*.

CONVENTS were first founded, according to some authorities, 270. The first in England was erected at Folkestone, by Eadbald, in 630. *Camden*. The first in Scotland was at Coldingham, where Ethelreda took the veil in 670. They were founded earlier in Ireland. They were suppressed in England in various reigns, particularly in that of Henry VIII. A very great number have been suppressed in Europe in the present century. The king of Prussia secularised all the convents in the duchy of Posen. Dom Pedro put down 300 convents in Portugal in 1834; and Spain abolished 1,800 convents. Many were abolished in Italy and Sicily in 1860, 1861, and 1866, and many in Russia 31 July, 1832, and Nov. 1864.

In 1597 lady Mary Percy founded a convent at Brussels, which flourished there till 1794, when the nuns were compelled to remove to England. They were received by bishop Milner, and placed at Winchester, at which place they remained till their removal to East Bergholt, in Suffolk, June, 1857. This was the first English conventual establishment founded on the continent after the Reformation.

By the Emancipation act of 1829, 10 Geo. IV., the establishment of convents and other religious communities in the United Kingdom was prohibited, but this enactment has been a dead letter . . 1829

There were in 1832, 16 convents in England; in 1870, 233; and 70 monasteries in Great Britain.

A select committee to investigate into the revenues of British convents appointed by the commons, 10 May, 1870; reappointed . . . . Feb. 1871

The committee reported the evidence heard . June, ,,

Mr. Newdegate's motion for an inquiry respecting these institutions was negatived . . 12 June, 1874

Large convent at Bournemouth, in connection with Church of England, opened . . 3 Oct. 1875

A Carmelite convent, specially patronised by the duke of Norfolk and family, at St. Charles's Square, Notting Hill, London, W., opened by Cardinal Manning . . . . 29 Sept. 1878

Many convents in France abolished, by decree 29 March, 1880

CONVERSION, see *National debt*, 1888.

CONVEYANCING ACT (Scotland) passed 7 Aug. 1874. The conveyancing and law of property act (England), 44 & 45 Vict. c. 41, passed 22 Aug. 1881.

CONVICTS, see *Transportation*.

CONVOCATION, the ancient general assembly of the clergy of the nation, convened by the sovereign's writ, to consult on the affairs of the church; the writ is directed to the archbishop of each province requiring him to summon all the bishops, archdeacons, &c. The convocation is divided into two houses, the upper, consisting of bishops; and lower, of deans, prebendaries, archdeacons, and members (termed proctors) elected from the inferior clergy. The clergy were summoned to meet the king by writ, 23 Edw. I. 1294. The power of the convocation was limited by a statute of Henry VIII., in whose reign the convocation was reorganised. The two houses of convocation were deprived of various privileges in 1718, and ceased to meet. The annual meetings of the clergy held during the sitting of parliament were revived in the province of Canterbury 1852, and York 1861, and fruitless attempts have been made to obtain the power of dealing summarily with ecclesiastical affairs; but in Feb. 1872, convocation was authorised to deliberate respecting alterations in the Liturgy; upon which it acted, 5 March; again in 1879. Petition to the queen for reform of convocation, Nov. 1882.

Convocation relieved from the jurisdiction of the secular courts by Richard III., 1484. The Archbishop of York's claim for this in regard to elections (in the case of Canon Tristram) confirmed by the Queen's Bench Division, Nov. 1887. See *Laymen, House of*, which first met 16 Feb. 1886.

CONVOLVULUS. The Canary Convolvulus (*Convolvulus canariensis*) came to England from the Canary Isles, 1690. The Many-flowered, 1779.

COOKERY, an art connected with civilised life. Animals granted as food to Noah, 2348 B.C., the eating of blood expressly forbidden (*Gen.* ix. 3, 4). In 1898 B.C. a calf was cooked by Abraham to entertain his guests (*Gen.* xviii. 7, 8). "The Forme of Cury" (*i.e.* cookery) is dated 1390. An English cookery-book was printed 1498. "The art of cookery made plain and easy," by a lady (Hannah Glasse), 1st edition, 1747; see *Cottager's Stove*, Encyclopædia of Practical Cookery, edited by T. F. Garrett, 1898. "Mrs. Beeton's Book of Household Management," new edit. 1903.

The Cooks' Company, London, chartered 1482, celebrated the anniversary Aug. 1882. Since 1887 the company have given instruction to girls, and prizes for proficiency.

Military Cookery.—Capt. Grant devised a system of cooking for the camp at Aldershot, which has continued in successful operation for the service of between 12,000 and 14,000 men. From April to August, in 1857, the plan was subjected to the severe test of cooking for 92,000 men, who marched in and out of the encampment during that period. The consumption of fuel requisite for this system of cooking was one half-pound of coal per man per day, and the official report states the cost to be one halfpenny per man per week for the three daily meals.

Self-supporting *Cooking Dépôts* for the working classes were set up at Glasgow (by Mr. Thomas Corbett), 21 Sept. 1860; and proved successful in Manchester, London, and other places soon after.

Three medals were awarded to the Norwegian self-acting cooking apparatus (Sorenson's patent) at the Paris Exhibition, 1867. Cooking is effected by boiling water, the heat of which is maintained by enclosing it in a non-conducting substance.

A *School of Cookery* was opened at the international exhibition, South Kensington, 14 April, 1873.

A *National Training School for Cookery*, proposed 17 July, 1873, was established in 1874.

COOK'S EXCURSIONS. Mr. Thomas Cook in 1841 began his tourist system by arranging with the Midland railway company for the conveyance of a party of 570 from Leicester to Loughborough and back at 1s. a-head.

He gradually extended his scheme through the United Kingdom, and thence to the continent. In 1856 he conducted his first touring party from Harwich to the Rhine, returning home *viâ* Paris. Mr. Cook died 18 July, 1892, aged 83.

Mr. J. M. Cook appointed government agent for passenger traffic on the Nile, 1870; his firm transported the British army to the second cataract during the campaign, 1884-5; entrusted with the arrangements for the German emperor's visit to Palestine, 1898. His system, applied to America, India, Egypt, and the Holy Land, has largely developed, and branch offices are now established in all parts of the world. A banking business, with numerous English and foreign branches, is in active operation, and special facilities are afforded for the conveyance of the luggage and goods of travellers. An extensive fleet of steamers is maintained on the Nile, together with a large engineering staff at Boulac. Mr. J. M. Cook died, aged 65, 4 March, 1899.

COOK ISLANDS, a group of seven islands in the S. Pacific, subject to New Zealand since 1888; formally annexed by lord Ranfurly, governor of New Zealand, 8 Oct. 1900. Population, about 7,300.

COOK'S VOYAGES. James Cook, accompanied by Mr. (afterwards sir) Joseph Banks, sailed from England in the *Endeavour* on his first voyage, 30 July, 1768; and returned home after having circumnavigated the globe, arriving at Deal 12 June, 1771. The chief object of the expedition, at the request of the Royal Society, was the observation of the transit of Venus over the sun's disk, which was effected, 3 June, 1769. Captain Cook sailed to explore the southern hemisphere, 13 July, 1772, and returned 30 July, 1775. In his last expedition (begun 12 July, 1776) he was killed by the savages of Owhyhee, 14 Feb. 1779. His ships, the *Resolution* and *Discovery*, arrived at Sheerness, 4 Oct. 1780. A literal transcription of capt. Cook's journal of his first voyage in the *Endeavour*, edited by capt. W. J. L. Wharton, published by Elliot Stock in 1893.

COOLIES, the hill tribes of India, have been recently much employed as labourers in Australia and California, especially since 1861; and about 30,000 of them were conveyed by M. Kootmanschap, to assist in making the great Pacific railway. His proposal in 1869 to replace the negroes in the Southern States of North America for the cultivation of cotton, was not accepted. "The Coolie, his Rights and Wrongs," by E. Jenkins, was published 1871. Coolie emigration has been the subject of negotiation between the British and Chinese governments since 1855.

COOMASSIE, see *Ashantee*.

COOPERAGE, an ancient art, probably suggested for preserving wine. The coopers of London were incorporated in 1501.

CO-OPERATIVE SOCIETIES are composed of working men, having for their object the sale of articles of daily consumption to the members at low prices. The Rochdale Equitable Pioneers Society began in 1844, with a capital of 28*l.* In 1860, the business done amounted to 152,063*l.*, the profits being 15,906*l.* These societies (332 in 1862) are registered pursuant to 13 & 14 Vict. c. 115 (1849). On 31 Dec. 1866, 749 industrial, provident, and co-operative societies were registered; 1,273, 1885; 1,683, 1892; 1,845, 1897; 1,843, 1899; in United Kingdom. By an act passed in 1867 they are bound to make a return. The fourth congress of delegates from the Co-operative Societies of

Great Britain and Ireland met at Bolton, April 1, 1872; fifth at Newcastle, 12 April, 1873; sixth at Halifax, 6 April, 1874; seventh in London, 29 March, 1875; eighth at Glasgow, 17 April, 1876; ninth at Leicester, 2 April, 1877; twelfth, Newcastle, 17 May, 1880; thirteenth, at Leeds, 6 June, 1881; fourteenth, Oxford, 29 May, 1882; fifteenth, Edinburgh, 14 May, 1883; sixteenth, Derby (co-operation in production proposed), 2 June, 1884; seventeenth at Oldham, May, 1885; eighteenth at Plymouth, 14 June, 1886; at Carlisle, 28 May, 1887; at Dewsbury, 21 May, 1888; at Ipswich, 10 June, 1889; at Glasgow, 26 May, 1890; at Lincoln, 18 May, 1891; 24th at Rochdale, 4 June, 1892; at Bristol, 20 May, 1893; at Sunderland, 12 May, 1894; at Huddersfield, 1 June, 1895; Woolwich, exhibition of manufactures produced by co-operation, 23 May, 1896; Perth, 5 June, 1897; Peterborough, 30 May, 1898; Liverpool, 22 May, 1899; Cardiff, 4 June, 1900; Middlesbrough, 27 May, 1901; Exeter, 19 May, 1902. A national trade society in opposition to co-operation was formed in 1872.

Co-operative *production*. The co-operative productive federation; annual meeting at the Crystal palace, 20 Aug. 1897; 16 Aug. 1898; 14 Aug. 1900; 16 Aug. 1901.

CO-OPERATIVE COTTON-MILLS in south Lancashire were reported successful in 1875.

OUSEBURN CO-OPERATIVE ENGINEERING WORKS, established 1871, failed through want of capital: wound up 1875.

Much discontent among London tradesmen on account of the numerous co-operative stores, 1878—80.

Co-operative farming begun in Northamptonshire, 1886.

Establishment of a Co-operative Dwellings Association in London, proposed, 1887.

The Tenant Co-operators (Limited) started Jan. 1888.

The International Co-operative Congress opened at Bologna, 1 Oct. 1888; London, 19 Aug. 1895; and Paris, Oct. 1896; Delft, 1897; Paris, 1900; Manchester, 21 July, 1902.

The Co-operative Union included 1,500 societies with a share capital of 11,000,000*l*. . Nov. 1890

National Co-operative Festival at the Crystal Palace, 15 Aug. 1891; 17 Aug. 1894; 18 Aug. 1896; 17 Aug. 1897; 14 Aug. 1899 . 25 Aug, 1902

COORG, a province, S. India. War broke out between the rajah and the East India Company 1832, which ended by col. Lindsay defeating and deposing the rajah, 10 April, 1834, and his territories were soon after annexed by the British. In 1853 the rajah brought his daughter to be educated in England, where she was baptized. She married a col. Campbell, and died a few years after. Chief commissioner, Col. P. D. Henderson, 1892.

COPENHAGEN (Denmark), built by Waldemar I., 1157, made the capital, 1443; the university founded 1479. In 1728, more than seventy of its streets and 3,785 houses were burnt. Its palace, valued at four millions sterling, was wholly burnt, Feb. 1794, when 100 persons lost their lives. In a fire which lasted forty-eight hours, the arsenal, admiralty, and fifty streets were destroyed, June, 1795. A new national theatre was founded by the king, 18 Oct. 1872.—Copenhagen was bombarded by the English under lord Nelson and admiral Parker; and in their engagement with the Danish fleet of twenty-three ships of the line, eighteen were taken or destroyed by the British, 2 April, 1801. Again, after a bombardment of three days, the city and Danish fleet surrendered to admiral Gambier and lord Cathcart, 7 Sept. 1807. The capture consisted of eighteen sail of the line, fifteen frigates, six brigs, and twenty-five gun-boats, and immense naval stores. Population, with suburbs, 1880, 273,727; 1890, 375,251; 1901, 378,235. See *Denmark*.

The czar and the kings of Denmark and Greece, and other royal persons, breakfast with Mr. Gladstone, Mr. Tennyson, and others on board the *Pembroke Castle*, 18 Sept. 1883.

The royal castle of Christiansborg, burnt; Thorwaldsen's works saved, 3, 4 Oct. 1884.

International Exhibition opened by the king, 18 May 1888.

The "Marble Church," founded as a tercentenary memorial of the Danish-Norwegian dynasty, 30 Oct. 1749; half finished till 1874; completed by M. C. F. Tietgen; consecrated by the primate of the Danish church in the presence of the king and the royal family, 19 Aug. 1894.

New free port opened, 9 Nov. 1894.

An international monument to Dr. Hans Meyer unveiled by sir Felix Semon, 25 Oct. 1898.

M. Carl Jacobsen presents his art collection to the city, Jan. 1899.

Explosion at the military laboratory at Refshalet, 8 deaths, 23 May, 1899.

National monument unveiled in commemoration of the Danish-German war, 1848-50; the king, king of Greece, the czar and czarina, the empress Alexander, the princess of Wales, present, 12 Sept. 1899.

The 700th anniversary of bishop Absalon's death (founder of the city) celebrated, 21 March, 1901.

Serum institute for study of bacteriology opened 9 Sept. 1902.

COPENHAGEN FIELDS (N. London). Here the Corresponding Society met on 26 Oct. 1796; and the Trades' Union, 21 April, 1834. The fields are now chiefly occupied by the Metropolitan Cattle-market, opened 13 June, 1855.

COPERNICAN SYSTEM, so called from its author Nicolas Copernicus, born at Thorn, 19 Feb. 1473, died 24 May, 1543. A few days before his death the printing of his book on the "Revolution of the Celestial Bodies" was completed. The system, which resembles that attributed to Pythagoras, was condemned by a decree of pope Paul V. in 1616; not revoked till 1818 by Pius VII.

COPLEY MEDAL, see *Royal Society*.

COPOPHONE, a musical instrument, consisting of a series of glass tumblers, connected with a sounding board. The sounds are produced by moving wet fingers along the edge of the glasses. It was played on at parties in London in June, 1875, by Chevalier Furtado Coelho, the inventor.

COPPER. One of the six primitive metals, said to have been first discovered in Cyprus. *Pliny*. We read in the Scriptures of two vessels of fine copper (or brass), "precious as gold," 457 B.C. (*Ezra* viii. 27). The mines of Fahlun, in Sweden, are most surprising excavations. In England, copper-mines were discovered in 1561, and there are upwards of fifty mines in Cornwall, where mining has been increasing since the reign of William III. In 1857, 75,832 tons of copper ore were imported, and 25,241 tons extracted. In 1865, 198,298 tons of copper ore were extracted from British mines, and 11,888 tons smelted: 82,562 tons were imported. In 1856, 24,257 tons of pure copper (worth 2,983,611*l*.); in 1869, 8291 tons (worth 644,065*l*.); in 1875, 4593 tons (worth 413,284*l*.); in 1876, 4694 tons (worth 391,130*l*.); in 1879, 3462 tons (worth 222,507*l*.); 1883, 2,620 tons (worth 181,067*l*.); 1887, 889 tons (worth 42,850*l*.); 1888, 1,456; 1889, 905; 1890, 936; 1893, 425 (20,522*l*. value); 1896, 556 tons (28,180*l*. value); 1898, 640 (35,523*l*. value); 1900, 765 (59,995*l*. value); 1901 (37,661*l*. value), were produced in the United Kingdom. The Burra-Burra copper-mines, in S. Australia, discovered 1842, brought great prosperity.

COPPER MONEY. The Romans, prior to the reign of Servius Tullius, used rude pieces of copper for money; see *Coin*.

In England copper money was made at the instance of sir Robert Cotton, in 1609; but was first really coined (when Miss Stewart sat for the figure of Britannia) 1665
Its regular coinage began in 1672, and it was largely issued in 1689
In Ireland, copper was coined as early as 1339; in Scotland in 1406; in France in 1580
Wood's coinage (*which see*) in Ireland commenced in 1723
The copper coinage was largely manufactured at Birmingham, by Boulton and Watt, in . . . 1792
Penny and two-penny pieces were extensively issued 1797
The half-farthing was coined, but disused (see *Farthing*) 1843
10,000*l.* voted towards replacing the copper coinage, July, 1855
Bronze coinage (*which see*) issued . . . Dec. 1860
A French Syndicate formed to raise the price of copper by a monopoly. Price of copper recently very low . . Feb. 1888; continued March 1889
Collapse and financial panic (see *France*) March ,,
COPPER-PLATE PRINTING was first invented in Germany, about 1450; and rolling-presses for working the plates, about 1545
Messrs. Perkins, of Philadelphia, invented a mode of engraving on soft steel, which, when hardened, will multiply copper-plates and fine impressions indefinitely (see *Engraving*) 1819
COPPER SHEATHING first applied to the bottom of H.M.S. *Alarm*, at Woolwich, 1761; all the navy copper-bottomed by 1780
Electrotyping with copper printing types and casts from woodcuts, began . . . . about 1850
COPPER-ZINC COUPLE, a Voltaic arrangement made by Dr. J. H. Gladstone and Mr. A. Tribe in 1872, in which a mixture of the two metals is finely subdivided, with the points of junction exposed, so as to promote the decomposition of any binary liquid into which small pieces are immersed; the resistance of the liquid being greatly reduced. The couple is formed by immersing zinc foil in a solution of sulphate of copper; the copper being deposited on the zinc in minute particles. By this couple impurities in water are readily detected, many peculiar analyses have been made, and new organic bodies formed.

COPPERAS, a mineral composed of copper or iron combined with sulphuric acid (vitriol), found in copper-mines, commonly of a green or blue colour; said to have been first produced in England by Cornelius de Vos, a merchant, in 1587.

COPPERHEADS, a name given about 1863 to such members of the Democrat party in the United States as were in favour of peace with the South on any terms.—Copperhead is a poisonous serpent, also named dumb-rattle snake, red viper, &c.

COPTIC CALENDAR, see *Diocletian*.

COPTIC PSALTER, see *Psalms of David*.

COPTS, in Egypt, the supposed descendants of the ancient Egyptians, mingled with Greeks and Persians. The Catholic branch of the Copts number about 600,000, and belong chiefly to the Jacobite or monophysite sect. "The Ancient Coptic Churches of Egypt," by Alfred J. Butler, published 1884. The Catholic patriarchate of Alexandria for the Copts re-established by the pope, after about 7 centuries' interruption; bp. Kyrillos Macarius appointed vicar Apostolic, Dec. 1895; enthroned as Cyril the second, 21 July, 1899. Two Coptic bishops for Upper and Lower Egypt consecrated at Cairo, 29 March, 1896.

COPYHOLDERS, who hold an estate by a copy of the rolls of a manor made by a steward of the lord's court. They were enfranchised by 5 Vict. c. 35, 1841. By the Reform act in 1832, copyholders to the amount of 10*l.* became entitled to a vote for the county. The copyhold acts were amended by 21 & 22 Vict. c. 94 (1858) and 1887, consolidated, 1894.

COPYING-MACHINES (for letters, &c.) were invented by James Watt in 1778; patented in May, 1780; and 150 machines were sold before the end of the year. Wedgwood's "manifold writer" was patented in 1806; and in 1855 Terry patented a copying machine to be combined with the cover of a book. Other inventions patented since.

COPYRIGHT. Decree of the Star-chamber regarding it, 1556. Every book and publication ordered to be licensed, 1585.

Ordinance forbidding the printing of any work without the consent of the owner 1649
The first *copyright act* (for 14 years, and for the author's life if then living), 8 Anne 1709
This act confirmed by a decision of the house of lords, and the claim of perpetual copyright overruled . . . . 22 Feb. 1774
Later acts extended the author's right to 28 years, and if living at the end of that time, then to the remainder of his life.
Protection of copyright in prints and engravings, 17 Geo. III. 1777
Copyright protection act (for 28 years, and the remainder of the author's life if then living), 54 Geo. III. 1814
Dramatic authors' protection act, 3 Will. IV. c. 15 . 1833
Act for preventing the publication of lectures without consent, 6 Will. IV. c. 65 1835
International copyright bill, 1 Vict. c. 59 . . . 1838
5 & 6 Vict. c. 45 (Talfourd's or lord Mahon's act), to amend the copyright act passed 1842
(By this act, the right is to endure for the life of the author, and for seven years after his death; but if that time expire earlier than 42 years, the right is still to endure for 42 years, for which term also any work published after the author's death is to continue the property of the owners of the manuscript.)
The colonies' copyright act, 10 & 11 Vict. c. 95, 1847
Canada copyright act, passed . . . . 2 Aug. 1875
Royal commission on copyright nominated: earl Stanhope, chairman, 22 Sept., 1875; report (signed 24 May) issued . . . . . autumn, 1878
Warne & Co. *v.* Seebohm; verdict for the plaintiffs prohibiting printing and the representation of a dramatised form of "Little Lord Fauntleroy," a story by Mrs. F. Hodgson Burnett, . 10 May 1888
Copyright (Musical Compositions) act . . 5 July ,,
Copyright for articles in newspapers affirmed, see *Trials*, 2 June, 1892, and Aug., Nov. 1899. Copyright (literary) bill (amended) text issued, *Times*, 10 Aug. 1899
Musical copyright (summary proceedings) act came into operation . . . . 1 Oct. 1902
Springfield *v. Evening Standard* for alleged infringement of copyright in a paragraph contributed by plaintiff to the *Daily Mail*; nonsuited 27 July, 1903

COPYRIGHT FOR DESIGNS, ETC.

Protection granting security for two months to new designs applied by printing to linens, calicoes, and muslins, 1787; extended to three months . 1794
A copyright of 14 years conferred on sculpture, 1798 and 1814
The designs act of Geo. III. made to embrace printed designs on wool, silk, and hair; and 12 months' copyright granted to designs applied to all tissues except lace and those already provided for; for the modelling, embossing, and engraving of any manufacture not being a tissue; and for the shape or configuration of any article 1839
By 5 & 6 Vict. c. 100, all existing designs acts repealed (except that for sculpture), and provision made for including all ornamental designs under 13 classes, and conferring upon them terms of protection, varying from nine months to three years 1842
[Fees on registration vary from 1*s.* to 1*l.*]
The "non-ornamental designs act," securing the configuration of articles of utility (fee 10*l.*), passed in 1843
By the "designs act," the Board of Trade is empowered to extend the copyright for an additional term of three years 1850

Copyright of photographs secured by the act protecting works of art, passed in . . July, 1862
Another copyright of designs act passed 13 Aug. 1875
Registration of designs and trade marks, amalgamated with the patent office . . Sept. ,,
S. Franklin ordered to pay 23*l.* in fines and costs for selling unauthorised reproductions of paintings by well-known artists . . . 14 July, 1899
Copyright (artistic) act passed . . 6 Aug. 1900

INTERNATIONAL COPYRIGHT.

Acts passed to secure to authors, in certain cases, the benefits of international copyright (1 & 2 Vict. c. 59, and 15 Vict. c. 12), and conventions have, in consequence, been entered into with France, Prussia, &c. . . . . 1838 and 1852
The question of a foreigner possessing a copyright in this country was finally decided in the negative by the house of lords, who reversed the decision of the court of exchequer, on an appeal by the defendant in the case of Boosey *v.* Jeffrey. (In 1831, Mr. Boosey purchased the copyright of Bellini's opera, *La Sonnambula*, from which Mr. Jeffrey published a cavatina. Six of the judges were for protecting foreign copyrights, and seven of a contrary opinion.) . . . . Aug. 1854
International copyright bill introduced into American house of representatives . . 21 Feb. 1868
In the case of Routledge *v.* Low, the house of lords on appeal decided in favour of the copyright of a foreign author . . . . . . 29 May, ,,
Copyright association of England, founded by eminent London booksellers . . 19 March, 1872
The subject discussed at the literary congress, Paris, opened . . . . . . 18 June, 1878
International copyright congress at Berne opened, 8 Sept. 1884
Another (artistic) Brussels, 29 Sept. 1884; again at Berne. 1886
International copyright act passed, 1886; modified at Paris, 4 May, 1896; ratified . . 9 Sept. 1897
International copyright convention signed at Berne 9 Sept., 1886; ratified at Berne 5 Sept., 1887; by Great Britain, Germany, France, Italy, Spain, Belgium and Switzerland (not Austria), Holland, United States, by Denmark, 12 Dec. 1902.
International copyright bill passed by the United States: by the house, 3 Dec. 1890; by the senate, 18 Feb.; by the president . 4 March, 1891
For books (which must be set up and printed in the United States), works of art, such as pictures, engravings, photographs, etchings, lithographs, &c., musical compositions, statuary, models, or designs: the act came into effect . . 1 July, ,,
Convention with Great Britain adopted by the Austrian diet . . . . . . 9 Dec. 1893
The house of lords on appeal decides that the sketches in the *Daily Graphic*, of living pictures, produced at the Empire theatre, were not an infringement of copyright . . . 17 Dec. 1894
An act passed in Canada injurious to English copyright; protest of the incorporated society of authors; Mr. Hall Caine visits Canada and proposes a *modus operandi* by licences, 25 Oct. 1895; he reports the prospect of a compromise, London 27 Jan. 1896
International congress on copyright met at Berne, 22 Aug. ,,
A service of plate, &c., presented by sir John Lubbock, on behalf of the copyright association, to Mr. Daldy, in recognition of his services to the cause of copyright . . . . . 9 Dec. 1897
Anglo-German and Anglo-Prussian agreements declared null and void by the withdrawal of Germany 16 Dec. ,,
International literary and artistic copyright congress at Berne . . . . . . 8 Aug. 1901

CORBIESDALE, Caithness (N. Scotland). Here, on 27 April, 1650, the gallant marquis of Montrose was defeated by the covenanters. He was taken soon after, treated with great contumely, and hanged at Edinburgh, on 21 May.

CORCYRA (now *Corfu*, chief of the Ionian Isles), a colony founded by the Corinthians about 734 B.C. It had frequent wars with the mother country; one about the possession of Epidamnus (431 B.C.) led to the Peloponnesian war. It was subdued by the Romans, 230. At the decline of the eastern empire it fell into the hands of the Venetians about A.D. 1386. The Turks attacked Corfu in 1716, but were gallantly repulsed, and retired, 18 Aug. 1717. It was taken from the French by the allied Russian and Turkish fleets 3 March, 1799, and formed (with the other isles) into the Ionian republic; see *Ionian Isles*.

CORDELIERS, friars of the order of St. Francis d'Assisi (the Minorites), instituted about 1223. They are clothed in coarse grey cloth, having a girdle of cord, hence the name, first given to them by St. Louis of France, about 1227. Several members of the French revolutionary party, termed "Cordeliers," established at Paris Dec. 1790 (Hebert, Cloots, &c.), were executed 24 March, 1794.

CORDITE, so named from its resemblance to cords; a smokeless explosive, invented 1889, by sir F. A. Abel (died 6 Sept. 1902) and prof. James Dewar, patented and assigned by them to the secretary of war, 1890. Several inventions were submitted to the explosives committee. Cordite was chosen and reported successful in 1892. Sir F. Abel and Prof. Dewar exonerated from charges brought forward in the commons, 11 Sept. 1893.

An action was brought by the Nobel's explosives company against the government (represented by Dr. Wm. Anderson, head of the works at Woolwich Arsenal) for infraction of Mr. Nobel's patent relating to ballistite (1888). The trial in the Chancery division before Mr. Justice Romer began 30 Jan., verdict for the defendant, 14 Feb. 1894. Appeal to the lords dismissed . . 28 Feb. 1895
Maxim-Nordenfelt guns and ammunition company and Hiram Stevens Maxim *v.* sir Wm. Anderson (died 11 Dec. 1898), for an alleged infringement of a smokeless powder patent (1889) in making cordite; long trial; judgment virtually for the defendant, 5 March, 1897; and again . 9 July, 1897
See Gunpowder.

CORDOVA, the Roman Corduba (S. Spain), founded about 152 B.C., taken by the Goths A.D. 572, and made the capital of an Arab kingdom by Abderahman in 756, who founded the great mosque (now the cathedral) 786. It was the birthplace of Seneca and Lucan, and of the Arabian physician Averrhoës. It was rescued from the Arabs by Ferdinand III. of Castile in 1236, was taken by the French under Dupont and disgracefully ravaged 7-9 June, 1808; surrendered to Joseph Bonaparte Jan. 1810; abandoned by the French in 1813; plundered by the Carlists, Oct. 1836. Population, 1887, 55,614; 1897, 57,313. Explosion in a mine at Belmez, 75 deaths, 18 March, 1898.

COREA, or **KOREA**, a peninsula, E. Asia, tributary to China, and from which foreigners were rigidly excluded till June, 1882, when four ports were opened to commerce by the agency of the United States of America and China by treaty. For the dispute with Americans see *United States*, June, 1871. King, Yi Huing, Jan. 1864; proclaimed emperor, 3 Oct. 1897. Capital, Seöul. Population, 10,528,937 (last government census).

Anti-foreign insurrection; outrages, 11 of the Japanese legation killed, 23 July; Japanese preparations for war with Corea on account of injuries, announced . . . . . Aug. 1882
War averted by compensations, reparation, and peace . . . . Sept. ,,
Treaty with Great Britain signed . 26 Nov. 1883
Another insurrection; the king attacked in his palace, and his ministers massacred by Coreans and Chinese, 4-6 Dec.; peace restored by intervention of Japanese . . . about 13 Dec. 1884

Difficulty between Japan and China settled by European mediation, Jan.; Japan predominant Feb.; treaty . . . . . . 18 April, 1885
British flag set up at Port Hamilton, as a station, announced 13 May 1885; decided to be kept, Nov. 1886
Port Hamilton restored to Corea, subject to China Jan. 1887
China reasserts by proclamation her suzerainty over Corea . . . . Dec. ,,
Corea endeavours to enter into independent diplomatic relations with United States and European Powers . . . . May, 1888
Treaty with Russia . . . . . . 8 Aug. ,,
The Rev. Charles James Corfe consecrated bishop of Corea . . . . 1 Nov. 1889
Rebellion, reported . . . . . 5 June, 1894
Suppressed by foreign assistance . . 14 June, ,,
Invasion of Japanese troops, Seöul occupied, 25 June, ,,
China remonstrates . . . . . . 27 June, ,,
The king renounces all subjection to China, and calls on the Japanese for help . . 30 June,
Foreign intervention to stop the war unsuccessful, June, ,,
Japan demands extensive reforms, and claims observance of treaty of 1885; opposed by China, July, ,,
Hostilities begin between China and Japan; the *Kowshing*, a British despatch boat (capt. Galsworthy) conveying Chinese troops, attacked by Japanese warships and sunk off Asan, capt. Galsworthy escaped to the Japanese: many killed, 25 July, ,,
Japanese victories at Chan-hon and at Asan under gen. Oshima . . . . 29 July, ,,
Much conflicting intelligence . . . . Aug. ,,
Chinese declaration of war . . . . . 4 Aug. ,,
Japanese army increased, they hold Seöul and some provinces, guerilla warfare; treaty of alliance between Japan and Corea signed at Seöul, 26 Aug. ,,
Asan recaptured . . . . 30 Aug. ,,
The emperor of China transmits a justificatory circular to the great powers, 23 Aug.; reported, 10 Sept. ,,
The Chinese surrounded and defeated with great loss at Ping-Yang, on the Tatong river; gen. Tso (Chinese) killed . . . . . 15, 16 Sept. ,,
Great naval battle at the mouth of the Yalu river; much slaughter, 8 Chinese vessels destroyed, 17 Sept. ,,
Disorganization of Chinese commissariat, &c., reported . . . . 1 Oct. ,,
Japanese occupy Wi-ju, without resistance, reported . . . . 9 Oct. ,,
The British proposals for mediation, considered premature by the great powers, reported, 14 Oct. ,,
Indecisive battle near Wi-ju, great slaughter, 22 Oct. ,,
The Japanese cross the Yalu and enter Manchuria; Chinese fort taken after sharp fighting . 25 Oct. ,,
Kiu-lien-tcheng taken by marshal Yamagata, 26 Oct. ,,
Gens. Yeh and Wei (Chinese) tried at Shanghai for cowardice, &c., at Ping-Yang, 15 Sept., and degraded . . . . 30 Oct. ,,
Tung-huan-tcheng surrenders . . . . 31 Oct. ,,
Kinchou and Talienwan captured . . . 6, 7 Nov. ,,
Prince Kung acknowledges the defeat of China, and requests foreign intervention . . 3 Nov. ,,
Chinese routed at the Namquan Pass . . 9 Nov. ,,
Port Arthur, a strong naval arsenal, taken by the Japanese under marshal Oyama by storm, 20, 21 Nov. ,,

[Great massacre of Chinese after the battle, owing to their having killed some captive Japanese, 21–26 Nov.]

Vigorous attack of Chinese on marshal Yamagata's army at the Fen-Shiu pass repulsed . 25 Nov. ,,
Corean insurgents severely defeated . 28 Nov. ,,
Kinchou re-occupied by marshal Oyama . 3 Dec. ,,
Fuchou taken without resistance . . 5 Dec. ,,
Chinese defeated at Kinkuahu and Yih-man-shan, 10, 14 Dec. ,,
Hai-tcheng taken by gen. Katsura . . 13 Dec. ,,
Chinese defeated under gen. Sung by gen. Katsura, near Hai-tcheng . . . . 19 Dec. ,,
Rebellion of the Tonghaks: 3 towns burnt, rebels defeated, 23 Dec.; again defeated . 8 Jan. 1895
Japan refuses an armistice . . . . . 5 Jan. ,,
The independence of Corea proclaimed by the king at Seöul . . . . 7 Jan. ,,
Desolation in Manchuria; Chinese routed at Kai-phing . . . . 10 Jan. ,,
Tung-chou bombarded and taken . . 18, 19 Jan. ,,
Yung-tcheng and Ning-hai occupied . 20, 24 Jan. ,,
Bombardment of Wei-hai-wei and the island fortress Leu-kung-tau by adm. Ito and marshal Oyama, began, 30 Jan.; fierce fighting; adm. Ting, gen. Chang, capt. Liu surrender ships and forts under honours of war, and commit suicide from grief and shame (great respect shown to their memory) . . . . 12 Feb. ,,
Adm. McClure accepts the Japanese conditions, 13 Feb. ,,
Japanese successful advances . . . . Feb. ,,
Niu-chuang and port of Ying-kow taken after fierce fighting by gen. Nodzu . . . 4, 6 March, ,,
Denshodai burnt by the Japanese; much slaughter, 9 March, ,,
Li Hung Chang, Chinese minister plenipotentiary, with Mr. Foster, American adviser, sent to treat for peace; received by visc. Mutsu, Japanese minister, at Shimonoseki in Manchuria 19 March, ,,
Li Hung Chang fired at in the face by Koyama, a young Japanese, a lunatic . . . . 24 March, ,,
Haichow, on the Kiangsu coast taken . 24 March, ,,
The Pescadores Islands taken . . 26–31 March, ,,
Armistice (21 days) proclaimed at Tokio 29 March, ,,
See *Formosa*, 31 March, 1895.
Peace signed; conditions: the independence of Corea; Japan retains conquered places, the Pescadores and part of the Liao-tung peninsula, Liao, and Formosa: an indemnity of 200,000,000 taels; 4 new ports opened to commerce. Li Hung Chang departs . . . . . 17 April, ,,
The ministers of Russia, Germany, and France protest against the annexation of Chinese continental territory to the Japanese empire by the treaty . . . . 23 April, ,,
Japan abandons the claim to the Liao-tung peninsula, 6 May: ratifications of the treaty exchanged, 8 May, ,,
Armistice prolonged for 5 days; negotiations proceeding . . . . May, ,,
Li Yo Shun, Corean minister, sentenced to penal servitude for life, and 5 officials to death, for murder and treason . . . . . 13 May, ,,
Government unsettled . . . . . . 21 May, ,,
Count Inouye employed by Japan to promote reforms . . . . May *et seq.* ,,
Mutiny of Corean soldiers; the palace invaded by an anti-reform mob; the queen and 2 ladies murdered, reported 8 Oct.; H.M.S. *Edgar* ordered to Chemulpho, 13 Oct.; visct. Miura and other Japanese ministers and soldiers recalled from Seöul, reported . . . . 18 Oct. ,,
Evacuation of the Liao-tong peninsula by the Japanese . . . . 30 Nov. ,,
Withdrawal of Japanese troops completed; reported . . . . 7 Jan. 1896
Insurrection at Seöul, the king and his son take refuge in the Russian legation; Russian marines landed at Chemulpho, march to Seöul, 10, 11 Feb. ,,
Two Corean ministers executed for treason; anti-Japanese cabinet formed; Russian influence predominant . . . . 14 Feb. ,,
Fighting between the Japanese and rebels near Fusan; reported . . . . . . 23 March, ,,
Concession to work for gold granted to a Russian company; reported . . . . . . 17 May, ,,
Russian slow policy reported successful . 7 Nov. ,,
The king leaves the Russian legation for the new palace . . . . 20 Feb. 1897
Treaty between Russia and Japan providing for the maintenance of the independence of Corea under their military protection; text published, 24 Feb. ,,
Financial improvement under Mr. M'Leavy Brown, chief commissioner (in unison with M. Alexieff, Russian); more ports open to foreign trade; reorganization of the army by the Russians, &c.; reported . . . . 8 Oct. ,,
Solemn burial of the queen (*see above*, Oct. 1895), the emperor and others present . . 22 Nov. ,,

Six British warships arrive at Chemulpho to support Mr. M'Leavy Brown . . 31 Dec. 1897
"Korea and her Neighbours," by Mrs. Bishop (Isabella L. Bird), published 1898
M. Alexieff and Russian drill instructors recalled, with 3,300*l.* compensation . . 25 March, ,,
Convention signed between Russia and Japan respecting Corea . . . . April, ,,
Plot against the government discovered at Seöul, officials arrested, reported . . 11 July, ,,
Attempt to poison the emperor and crown prince frustrated, reported, 16 Sept. 1898; Tim Khunyuk, interpreter at the Russian legation, executed on a false charge, his wife and others tortured, 10, 12 Oct.; the minister of justice dismissed, 13 Oct. ,,
Political riot at Seöul, 23 deaths, reported, 23 Nov. ,,
Seöul and Chemulpho railway taken over by Japan, Jan. 1899 (opened 5 July, 1900).
Cabinet dismissed and 2 ministers banished on account of changes in provincial offices, March, 1899
Ports (3) on the E. coast leased to Russia for 12 years . . . . May, ,,
Japanese influence again paramount in Seöul, Aug. ,,
Russia obtains an exclusive settlement at Masampho harbour, agreements signed . . 30 March, 1900
Two Corean officials, under Japanese protection, suspected of complicity in the murder of the queen (1895), tortured and put to death . May, ,,
Judicial officials punished to appease Japan, mid-June, ,,
Disturbances in the north, reported . mid-Aug. ,,
Railway loan with France concluded . 16 April, 1901
Land at Masampho leased to Japan by government . . . . May, ,,
Two missionaries and 6 converts murdered at Quelpart, reported . . . . 2 June, ,,
[Three ringleaders sentenced to death, others imprisoned, reported, 4 Dec.]
Japanese expansion and trade progressing, reported July, ,,
Anglo-Japanese agreement, the *status quo* and independence of Corea to be maintained; see *China* . . . . . . signed, 30 Jan. 1902
Corea gives its adhesion to the Geneva convention, 8 Jan. 1903
Russian demand for concession to Russo-Chinese bank of the Seöul-Wi-ju railway rejected, 25 Feb. ,,
Dispute with Japan (see *Japan* and *Russia*), June, *et seq.* ,,

CORFU, see *Corcyra*.

CORINTH (Greece), a city said to have been built 1520 B.C. and named Ephyra. It was defended by an elevated fortress called Acrocorinth, surrounded with strong walls, and Cicero named it the *Eye of Greece*.—For *Corinth*, in North America, see *United States*, 1862, 1863.

The Isthmian games, traditionally said to have been instituted by Sisyphus, who founded a kingdom . . . . . . B.C. 1326
Return of the Heraclidæ, or Dorians 1107
Their dynasty established by Aletes . . . 1074
The Corinthians invent ships called *triremes* (with three benches of oars) . . . 786 or 758
Reign of Bacchis, 925; oligarchy of Bacchidæ 747-657
Thelestes deposed; the government of Prytanes instituted; Automenes, the first, about 745
The Corinthian colonies of Syracuse and Corcyra founded . . . . . about 734
Revolt of the Corcyreans: they defeat the Corinthians at sea 664
Cypselus, a despot, sets aside the Prytanes . . 655
His son Periander rules, and favours learning . 627-585
Psammetichus deposed, and a republic formed . 580
The Corinthians engaged in the Persian war . 480
Defeated in war with the Corcyreans . . 435
The Corinthian war (*which see*) . . . 395
Timoleon kills his usurping brother Timophanes . 344
Acrocorinth (citadel) taken by Aratus, and annexed to the Achæan League 243
The Roman ambassadors first appear at Corinth 228
Greeks defeated at Cynoscephalæ . . . 197
Corinth sacked by Lucius Mummius, who sends to Italy the first fine paintings there seen (*Livy*) B.C. 146
Rebuilt by Julius Cæsar 46
Visited by St. Paul (*Acts* xviii.) . . . A.D. 54
His two *Epistles to the Corinthians* . . about 59, 60
Ravaged by Alaric 396
Plundered by Normans from Sicily 1146
Taken by Turks, 1446; by Venetians, 1687; by Turks, June, 1714; from whom it was finally taken by the Greeks in 1823
Nearly destroyed by an earthquake . . 21 Feb. 1858
A concession granted for 99 years to a French company to cut the isthmus for a canal; to be completed in six years, by MM. E. G. Piat and Chollet, April, 1870; concession transferred to baron de Lesseps and gen. Turr . . . . 28 May, 1881
Cutting begun in presence of the king and queen 5 May, 1882
Work actively proceeding; stopped through claims of a Paris company . . . . 1 April, 1889
The company at Paris dissolved, 12 Feb., 1890; the scheme transferred to a Greek company, capital of 200,000*l.*; agreement signed by M. Tricoupis, about 18 March; the work resumed, 22 June, 1890; the canal opened in the presence of the king and royal family, 6 Aug. 1893. The canal blocked through a landslip, 27 Nov. 1894; navigation restored . . . . . . 17 Dec. 1894

CORINTHIAN ORDER, the richest of the orders of ancient architecture, called by Scamozzi the virginal order, is attributed to Callimachus, 540 B.C.; see *Abacus*.

CORINTHIAN WAR, began 395 B.C.; received this name because mostly in the neighbourhood of Corinth; waged by a confederacy of the Athenians, Thebans, Corinthians, and Argives, against the Lacedæmonians. It was closed by the peace of Antalcidas, 387 B.C. The most famous battles were at Coronea and Leuctra (*which see*).

CORIOLI, a Latin city, capital of the Volscians, taken by the Romans, 493 B.C. The exploits of Caius Marcius or Coriolanus against it are deemed mythical.

CORK (S. Ireland), built in the 6th century. The principality of the M'Cartys was converted into a shire by king John, as lord of Ireland. The foundation of the SEE is ascribed to St. Barr, or Finbarr, early in the 7th century. About 1431, this see and Cloyne were united; but in 1678 they were separated, Ross having been added to Cork 1582. Cork and Cloyne were reunited (by the act of 1833) 1835. Population of the city, 1881, 80,124; 1891, 75,070; 1901, 75,978.

Garrisoned by Henry II. 1172
First charter, from Henry II. 1185
Supported Perkin Warbeck, who landed here . . 1492
A large part of the town burnt 1621
Taken by Cromwell 1649
Marlborough besieged and took Cork from king James, when the duke of Grafton, a son of Charles II., was slain 1690
The cathedral was rebuilt by the produce of a coal duty, between the years . . . 1725 & 1735
Explosion of gunpowder here . . . 10 Nov. 1810
One of the three colleges, endowed by government pursuant to act 8 & 9 Vict. c. 66, passed 31 July, 1845, was inaugurated in this city (see *Queen's Colleges*) . . . . . . 7 Nov. 1849
Railway to Dublin finished 1850
Cork industrial exhibition opened, 10 June, and closed . . . . . . 11 Sept. 1852
For a seditious speech in favour of the Fenians (*which see*), on 27 April, 1869, the mayor was compelled to resign (an act for his disability having been introduced into parliament) . 11 May, 1870
Riots, partially connected with a strike, suppressed 26, 28 June, ,,
New protestant cathedral consecrated . 30 Nov.
Industrial exhibition opened, 3 July; closed 13 Oct. 188

Cork Defence Union, against National League formed . . . . Oct. 1885

Strike of the employed, of the City of Cork Steam Packet Co. (14 weeks), ends with submission 27 Jan. 1891

Mr. Matthew Honan bequeaths 158,000*l.* to found a hospital in Cork for aged men, etc. . April, 1894

Destructive floods, with loss of life . 24–27 Dec. 1895

Visit of the lord-lieut. the earl of Cadogan . Sept. 1896

Strike on the Cork, Bandon, and S. Coast railway Jan., Feb. 1898

The title of *lord* bestowed on the mayor . April, 1900

International exhibition (cost 30,000*l.*) opened by lord Bandon, street pageant, &c., the lord mayors and mayors of Ireland present . . . 1 May, 1902

The duke of Connaught opens a new bridge over the St. Hern branch of the Lee, 7 May; the duke and prince Henry of Prussia visit the exhibition, 8 May; state visit of the lord-lieutenant and countess Cadogan, 29 May; international boatrace, Anglo-German, English won lord O'Brien's cup, 23 July, ,,

International exhibition opened by lord Dudley, 28 May, 1903

Visit of king and queen . . . . . . 1 Aug. ,,

Exhibition, total visitors, 1,400,000, closed 1 Nov. ,,

CORK-TREE, *Quercus suber*, a species of the oak; part of its bark used for stopping bottles. The Egyptians made coffins of cork. The tree grows in great abundance on the Pyrenean mountains, and in other parts of Spain, in France, and in the north of New England. It was brought to England about 1690. A cork carpet company was formed in 1862.

Life-preserving clothes made of cloth into which cork is interwoven, invented by Wm. Jackson, tried successfully on the Thames . . 3 Sept. 1886

CORN. The origin of its cultivation is attributed to Ceres, who, having taught the art to the Egyptians, was deified by them, 2409 B.C. *Arundelian Marbles.* The art of husbandry, and the method of making bread from wheat, and wine from rice, is attributed by the Chinese to Ching Noung, the successor of Fohi, and second monarch of China, 1998 B.C. *Univ. Hist.* Corn provided a common article of food from the earliest ages of the world, and baking bread was known in the patriarchal ages; see *Exodus* xii. 15. The first importation of corn, of which we have a note, was in 1347. A law restricting it was made in 1361, and similar legislation followed. Bounties were granted on its importation into England in 1689. See *Wheat.*

CORN LAWS.

The restrictions on the importation of corn felt, in consequence of the increase of manufactures, about 1770; relaxed 1773

Mr. Robinson's act passed, permitting importation when wheat is 80*s.* a quarter 1815

During the discussions on this bill, mobs assembled in London, and many of the houses of its supporters were damaged, 28 Jan.; and a riot in Westminster continued . . . . 6-9 March, ,,

A corn bill, after passing in the commons, defeated in the lords, by a clause proposed by the duke of Wellington, carried by a majority of 4 . 1 June, 1827

The act (called the *sliding* scale) whereby wheat was allowed to be imported on payment of a duty of 1*l.* 5*s.* 8*d.* per quarter, whenever the average price of all England was under 62*s.*; from 62*s.* to 63*s.*, 1*l.* 4*s.* 8*d.*; and so gradually reduced to 1*s.*, when the average price was 73*s.* and upwards, passed 15 July, 1828

The act 5 Vict. c. 14, the second "sliding scale act," regulating the duty on wheat as follows, with sliding duties, also, on other articles of corn, passed . . . . 29 April, 1842

Average per quarter. Shillings.	Shillings.	Duty: £	s.	d.
———	under 51	1	0	0
51 and	under 52	0	19	0
52 and	under 55	0	18	0
55 and	under 56	0	17	0
56 and	under 57	0	16	0
57 and	under 58	0	15	0
58 and	under 59	0	14	0
59 and	under 60	0	13	0
60 and	under 61	0	12	0
61 and	under 62	0	11	0
62 and	under 63	0	10	0
63 and	under 64	0	9	0
64 and	under 65	0	8	0
65 and	under 66	0	7	0
66 and	under 69	0	6	0
69 and	under 70	0	5	0
70 and	under 71	0	4	0
71 and	under 72	0	3	0
72 and	under 73	0	2	0
73 and	upwards	0	1	0

See *Anti-Corn Law League.*

The CORN IMPORTATION Bill (introduced by sir Robert Peel), 9 & 10 Vict. c. 22 (by which the duty on wheat was reduced to 4*s.* when imported at or above 53*s.*, until 1st Feb. 1849; after which day the duty became 1*s.* per quarter only, on all kinds of grain imported into the United kingdom, at any prices), received the royal assent . 26 June, 1846
[Jubilee address to right hon. C. P. Villiers, an early earnest advocate for the repeal, 27 June, 1896.]

The 1*s.* duty repealed by act passed . 24 June, 1869

Duty on imported corn, 3*d.* per cwt., and flour, 5*d.* per cwt., passed; see *Budget* . . . 4 July, 1902

Duty remitted; see *Budget* . . . . 22 June, 1903

CORN EXCHANGE, Mark-lane, London, erected at an expense of 90,000*l.* (replacing one established in 1747), was opened . . . . . 24 June, 1828

Corn Exchange Benevolent Society, founded . . 1864

The Society of Arts gave a prize to Mr. W. A. Gibbs for his essay on harvesting corn in wet weather 23 Nov. 1868

CORNELL UNIVERSITY, Ithaca, New York: for the study of the applied sciences, agriculture, engineering, &c.; partially on a self-supporting system; founded by Ezra Cornell in 1868, that "any person may find instruction in any study." He had risen from poverty to wealth by patenting his inventions. The university is well-appointed, includes Sage college for women, and has a staff of 150 professors and tutors and about 1700 students.

CORNER, a term applied in America to the paralysis of trade and manufactures, produced by speculators purchasing in anticipation grain, petroleum, cotton, &c. (termed *futures*). The *cotton corner* at Liverpool in Sept. 1881 led to the stopping of looms in Lancashire, &c., by way of counteraction. The corner ended 30 Sept. 1881. Mr. Morris Ranger, a great cotton speculator, failed 31 Oct. 1883, causing much disaster.

Another "cotton corner" proposed in June 1887 was resisted by the joint action of the manufacturers and operatives. A "cotton corner" in Liverpool was resisted and closed, 30 Sept. 1889. See *Trusts.* A "wheat corner" in Chicago since 1895, collapsed, June, 1898. "Cotton corner," New York, 1903.

CORNWALL, S. W. extremity of England. On the retreat of the ancient Britons after the Saxon conquest, Cornwall is said to have been formed into a kingdom, and to have existed many years under different princes, among whom were Ambrosius Aurelius, and the celebrated Arthur. Cornwall is said to have been made an earldom by Alfred. The eldest son of the British sovereign is born duke of Cornwall. See *Stannary Courts.* Before the reform of 1832, Cornwall sent 44 members to parliament, in 1886 it sent 7.

Bishopric of Cornwall, founded, 909; united to Devonshire, 1040; removed to Exeter . . . 1046
Cornwall given by the conqueror to Robert de Mortein, his half-brother, 1068; killed . . . 1087
William, his son, dispossessed by Henry I. . . 1104
Reginald de Dunstanville, natural son of Henry I., earl 1140
John Plantagenet, son of Henry II., earl, about 1189
Richard Fitz-Count, son of Reginald, earl, 1215; resigned 1220
Richard, son of king John, 1225; elected king of the Romans, 1256; died . . . 2 April, 1272
Edmund, son, earl, 1272; died without issue . . 1300
Piers de Gaveston, earl, 1308; beheaded, 19 June, 1312
John, son of Edward II., earl, 1330; died with issue 1336
Cornwall made a *duchy*, by Edward III., for Edward his eldest son, afterwards created prince of Wales 17 March, 1337
Insurrection of Cornishmen under lord Audley, Thomas Flammock, and others, against taxes; they march to London; defeated at Blackheath 22 June, 1497
Insurrection in Devon and Cornwall against the Protestant liturgy, defeated by lord Russell, Aug. 1549
Dolly Pentreath, said to have been the last person who spoke Cornish, died aged 102 [contradicted] 1778
Rev. R. Polwhele's "History of Cornwall" published 1803-8
Prince and princess of Wales visit Cornwall, July, 1865
Stoppage of the Cornish Bank (Tweedy & Co.) established 1771 . . . . . 4 Jan. 1879
Duchy of Cornwall Act passed 1893, amended . 1893
A neolithic cemetery discovered during excavations at Harlyn bay; see *Athenæum* . 22 Sept. 1900
Receipts from the duchy, 1866, 77,755*l.*; 1877, 87,895*l.*; 1887, 99315*l.*—paid to the prince of Wales, 1866, 53,403*l.*; 1877, 69,339*l.*; 1887, 60,290*l.* Receipts from the duchy in 1888, 107,572*l.*; 104,188*l.* for 1889; 100,680*l.* for 1891; 131,081*l.* for 1901; 130,206*l.* for 1902.

CORONATION. Leo I., emperor of the East, was crowned by Anatolius, patriarch of Constantinople, being the first instance of a Christian sovereign receiving his crown from the hands of a priest, 457. Majorian, emperor of the West, is said to have been crowned in the same year in a similar manner.

Charlemagne crowned emperor of the west by the pope Leo III. (using the words "*coronato a Deo,*" "crowned by God") . . . . . 25 Dec. 800
Edward I., son of Alfred, crowned . 16 May, 902
William I. crowned at Westminster . . 25 Dec. 1066
Anointing at coronations introduced into England 872, and Scotland 1097
Coronation of Henry III., in the first instance without a crown, at Gloucester. A plain circle was used on this occasion in lieu of the crown, which had been lost with the other jewels and baggage of king John, in passing the marshes of Lynn, or the Wash, near Wisbeach 28 Oct. 1216
Henry VII., 30 Oct. 1485; Henry VIII., 24 June 1509; Edward VI. received as king, 28 Jan. 1547; Mary, 1 Oct. 1553; Elizabeth, 13 Jan. 1559; James I., 25 July, 1603; Charles I., 2 Feb. 1626; Charles II., 23 April, 1661; James II., 23 April 1685
William and Mary crowned by Compton, bishop of London, as Sancroft, archbishop of Canterbury, would not take the oaths, 11 April, 1689; Anne, 23 April, 1702; George I., 20 Oct. 1714; George II., 11 Oct. 1727; George III., 22 Sept. 1761; George IV., 19 July, 1821; William IV., 8 Sept. 1831; Victoria, 28 June, 1838; Edward VII., 9 Aug. 1902

CORONATION CHAIR. In the cathedral of Cashel, formerly the metropolis of the kings of Munster, was deposited the *Lia Fail*, or Fatal Stone, on which they were crowned. Tradition says, that in 513 Fergus, a prince of the royal line, having obtained the Scottish throne, procured the use of this stone for his coronation at Dunstaffnage, where it continued until the time of Kenneth II., who removed it to Scone; and in 1296 it was removed by Edward I. from Scone to Westminster; the present chair being made to receive it.

A CORONATION OATH was administered by Dunstan, archbishop of Canterbury, to Ethelred II., in 978. An oath, nearly corresponding with that now in use, was administered in 1377. The oath prescribed by 1 Will. & Mary, c. 6 (1689) was modified in 1706, and again in 1821 on account of the union of the Churches of England and Ireland. See *Accession*.

CORONEA, BATTLES OF. I. (or Chæronea). The Athenians were defeated and their general Tolmides slain in a battle with the Bœotians at Coronea near Chæronea, 447 B.C. II. The Athenians, Thebans, Argives, and Corinthians having entered into a league, offensive and defensive, against Sparta, Agesilaus, after diffusing the terror of his arms, from his many victories, even unto Upper Asia, engaged the allies at Coronea, a town of Bœotia, and achieved a great victory over them, 394 B.C.

CORONERS, officers of the realm, mentioned in a charter, 925. Coroners for every county in England were first appointed by statute of Westminster, 3 Edw. I. 1275. *Stow.* They are chosen for life by the freeholders, and their duty is to inquire into the cause of unnatural death, upon view of the body. By an act passed in 1843, coroners are enabled to appoint deputies to act for them in case of illness. The act amended 1887. Laws respecting coroners amended 1860 and 1892—20,315 coroners' inquests were held in England and Wales in 1859:—

1860 . .	21,178	1879 . .	27,039	1890 . .	32,027
1861 . .	21,038	(18,233 males.)		(20,997 males.)	
1862 . .	20,591	1880 . .	26,569	1891 . .	32,816
1863 . .	22,757	(18,131 males.)		(21,459 males.)	
1864 . .	24,787	1881 . .	27,451	1892 . .	32,254
1865 . .	25,011	(18,548 males.)		(20,975 males.)	
1866 . .	24,926	1882 . .	27,502	1893 . .	33,227
1867 . .	24,648	(18,673 males.)		(21,575 males.)	
1868 . .	24,774	1883 . .	28,725	1894 . .	32,059
1869 . .	24,709	1884 . .	28,603	(21,029 males.)	
(17,191 males.)		(19,280 males.)		1895 . .	34,688
1870 . .	25,376	1885 . .	28,181	(22,139 males.)	
1871 . .	25,898	(18,863 males.)		1897 . .	33,289
1872 . .	25,705	1886 . .	28,940	(21,476 males.	
1873 . .	26,427	(19,329 males.)		1898 . .	34,541
1874 . .	27,184	1887 . .	30,030	(22,256 males.)	
(18,875 males.)		(19,814 males.)		1899 . .	37,026
1875 . .	28,587	1888 . .	29,057	(24,036 males.)	
1876 . .	26,845	(19,120 males.)		1900 . .	37,076
1877 . .	26,287	1889 . .	29,675	(24,089 males.)	
1878 . .	27,628	(19,700 males.)			

CORONETS, caps or inferior crowns of the nobility. The coronets for earls were first allowed by Henry III.; for viscounts by Henry VIII.; and for barons by Charles II. *Baker.* But authorities conflict. Sir Robert Cecil, earl of Salisbury, was the first of the degree of earl who wore a coronet, 1604. It is uncertain when the coronets of dukes and marquises were settled. *Beatson.*

CORPORATE REUNION. See *Order*.

CORPORATIONS. Numa, in order to break the force of the two rival factions of Sabines and Romans, is said to have instituted separate societies of manual trades. *Plutarch.*—MUNICIPAL CORPORATIONS IN ENGLAND. Bodies politic, authorised by the king's charter to have a common seal, one head officer, or more, and members, who are able, by their common consent, to grant or receive in law any matter within the compass of their charter. *Cowell.* Charters of rights were granted by the kings of England to various towns; by Edward the Confessor, Henry I., and succeeding monarchs, subject to tests, oaths, and conditions. *Blackstone.* The Corporation and Test act, passed in 1661, was repealed in May, 1828. The Corporation Reform act, for the regulation of municipal corporations (London not included) in England and Wales, 5 & 6 Will. IV. c. 76 (1835), was amended in 1869. The Irish Municipal Corporation act, 4 Vict. c. 108, passed in 1840, was amended in 1861. The Corrupt Practices (Municipal Elections) act, was passed 6 Aug. 1872. The law relating to municipal elections amended by act passed 19 July, 1875. Municipal Elections, Corrupt and Illegal Practices act passed 14 Aug. 1884. Royal commission on 110 unreformed municipal corporations appointed in 1876; report issued 17 Feb. 1880. Bill for their reform introduced by sir Charles Dilke, 21 Feb. 1883. A consolidation act passed 1882; amended 1893. Property qualification bill rejected in commons (173—167), 2 April, 1879. The London Government act, 1899, constituted 28 London boroughs; first elections of councillors to these held 1 Nov. 1900; second elect ons, 2 Nov. 1903.

Jubilee of the passing of the Act of 1835 celebrated 9 Oct. 1885

The association of municipal corporations met, 5 Dec. 1884; it met at the Guildhall, London; 219 towns represented, 12 March, 1890; again, 13 March, 1891; 10 March, 1892; 23 Feb. 1893; 10 March, 1894; 21 March, 1895; 13 March, 1896; 27 Feb. 1897; 26 March, 1898; 25 March, 1899; 31 March, 1900; 22 March, 1901; 21 March, 1903.

The municipal electrical association, first meeting at Whitehall . . . . 10 June, 1896

CORPULENCE, Remarkable Instances of.

Mr. Edward Bright, a tallow-chandler and grocer, of Maldon, in Essex, who died in his 29th year, is said to have weighed 616 pounds. Seven persons of the common size were with ease enclosed in his waistcoat; buried at All Saints, Maldon 12 Nov. 1750

Daniel Lambert, supposed to have been the heaviest man that ever lived, died in his 40th year, at Stamford, in Lincolnshire, weighing 52 stone 11 pounds; (10 stone 4 pounds more than Mr. Bright) . . . . 21 June, 1809

James Mansfield, died at Debden, aged 82, weighing 34 stone . . . . 9 Nov. 1856

Mr. Wm. Banting published a letter on corpulence, recommending, from his own experience, as a remedy, great moderation in the use of sugar and starch in diet. 50,000 copies of this letter were speedily sold or given away 1863

CORPUS CHRISTI (*Fête Dieu* in France), a festival in the Roman church, in honour of the Lord's supper, kept on the Thursday after Trinity Sunday (*which see*). It was instituted by pope Urban IV. between 1262 and 1264, and confirmed by the council of Vienne in 1311.

CORPUS JURIS CIVILIS, see *Justinian Code.*

"CORRELATION of the PHYSICAL FORCES," a book by Mr. (afterwards sir) W. R. Grove, F.R.S., who in 1842 enunciated the theory of the correlation or mutual dependence and convertibility into each other of all the forces of nature (viz., heat, light, electricity, magnetism, chemical affinity, and motion). This theory has been fully established by experimental researches, see *Heat*, *Electricity*, &c. Sir W. R. Grove was present at the Faraday Centenary, *which see*, 17 June, 1891.

CORRESPONDING SOCIETY of LONDON, was formed about 1791, to spread liberal opinions and check the severity of the British government, then much alarmed by the French revolution. Horne Tooke and other members were tried for treason and acquitted, Oct. 1794; see *Trials*, 1794. The meetings of the society at Copenhagen-fields and elsewhere, in 1795 and 1796, were termed treasonable.—On 21 April, 1798, Messrs. O'Connor, O'Coigley, and others, were tried for corresponding with the French directory; and James O'Coigley was executed as a traitor (protesting his innocence) on 7 June.

CORROSIVE SUBLIMATE, see *Mercury.*

CORRUPT PRACTICES ACTS, respecting elections for members of parliament, were passed in 1854, and continued in following years. An act relating to Scotland was passed in 1890. See *Bribery at Elections and Corporations.*

By an act passed in 1881 elections at Boston, Canterbury, Chester, Gloucester, Macclesfield, and Oxford, were temporarily suspended; and Messrs. May and Main (Macclesfield), Mr. Edwards (Deal), Mr. Olds (Sandwich), and others were sentenced to imprisonment varying from 2 to 9 months . . . . 29 Nov. 1881

Petition for their release signed (in vain) by 43,841 persons . . . . . about 23 Dec. „

The act 46 & 47 Vict. c. 51, passed 25 Aug. 1883, strictly prohibits hiring carriages and illegal payments; amended 6 July, 1895. In 1880 the election by about 3,000,000 electors cost about 3,000,000*l*. In 1885 the election by 5,670,000 electors cost 780,000*l*.

CORSICA, an island in the Mediterranean Sea (called by the Greeks *Cyrnos*), held by the French. The ancient inhabitants had the character of robbers, liars, and atheists, according to Seneca. Corsica was colonised by Phocæans 564 B.C., and afterwards held by the Carthaginians, from whom it was taken by the Romans, 238 B.C. It has been held by Vandals, A.D. 456; by Saracens 852; by Pisans, 1077. It was dependent upon Genoa from 1559 till 1768, when it was ceded to France.

During a revolt erected into a kingdom under Theodore Neuhoff, its first and only king 1736

He came to England, was imprisoned in the King's Bench prison for debt, and long subsisted on private friends, but released; he gave in his schedule the kingdom of Corsica to his creditors, and died in Soho 1756

The earl of Orford wrote the following epitaph, for a tablet near his grave in St. Anne's church, Dean-street:—

> "The grave, great teacher! to a level brings
> Heroes and beggars, galley-slaves and kings.
> But Theodore this moral learn'd ere dead;
> Fate pour'd its lesson on his living head,
> Bestow'd a kingdom and denied him bread."

Pascal Paoli chosen for their general by the Corsicans 1753

Defeated by the count de Vaux, he fled to England 1769

Napoleon Bonaparte born at Ajaccio (5 Feb. 1768, baptismal register; doubtful) . . 15 Aug. „

The people acknowledge George III. of England for king . . . . 17 June, 1794

Sir Gilbert Eliott made viceroy, and opened a parliament 1795

A revolt suppressed, June; the island relinquished by the British, 22 Oct.; the people declare for the French 1796

A statue to Napoleon I. inaugurated by prince Napoleon Jerome . . . . . . 15 May, 1865

Visit by the empress and imperial prince 4 Sept. 1869

Gen. Paoli's remains buried at Old St. Pancras cemetery, London, exhumed and transferred and re-interred in Corsica . . . 31 Aug. *et seq.* 1889

Corsica visited by president Carnot 21-23 April, 1890

Election riots at Linguizzota, several deaths, 20 Oct. 1901

CORTE NUOVA, near Milan, N. Italy. Here the emperor Frederic II. defeated the Milanese after a severe conflict, 27 Nov. 1237.

CORTES, the Spanish parliament, originating in the old Gothic councils. The cortes were assembled after a long interval of years, 24 Sept. 1810; and settled the new constitution, 16 March, 1812, which was set aside by Ferdinand VII., who banished many members of the assembly in May, 1814. The cortes were reopened by him March, 1820, dissolved Oct. 1823; again assembled April, 1834, and have since been regularly convened. The cortes of Portugal assembled by virtue of Dom Pedro's charter, 30 Oct. 1826; they were suppressed by Dom Miguel in 1828, and restored in 1833.

CORUNNA (N. W. Spain). The British army, about 15,000 men, under the command of sir John Moore, had just accomplished their retreat when they were attacked by the French, whose force exceeded 20,000: the enemy were completely repulsed. British loss estimated 800, French, 3,000, 16 Jan. 1809. Sir John was struck by a cannon-ball, which carried away his left shoulder and part of the collar-bone, and he died universally lamented. The remains of the army embarked at Corunna, under sir David Baird, 17 Jan.

CORUS (Corupedion, or Cyropedium), a plain in Phrygia, Asia Minor, where the aged Lysimachus was defeated by Seleucus, and slain, 281 B.C. These two were the only survivors of Alexander the Great's generals.

CORVÉE, forced labour and service under the feudal system in France, was partially reduced by Louis XVI., at the instigation of Turgot, 27 June, 1787; by the constituent assembly, 18 March, 1790, and totally abolished by the convention, 17 July, 1792. Forced labour of the peasantry (fellaheen) abolished in Egypt 17 Dec. 1889.

CORYPHÆUS, the principal person of the chorus in ancient tragedy. The name is said to have been given to Tysias, or Stesichorus, who first instructed the chorus to dance to the lyre, 556 B.C.

COSMOGRAPHY, see *Astronomy* and *Geography*.

COSMOPOLIS, an international review containing articles in English, French, and German by eminent writers. No. I., Jan. 1896, includes articles by R. L. Stevenson, Andrew Lang, Henry James, Edmund Gosse; MM. Paul Bourget, Jules Lemaitre; prof. Mommsen, F. Spielhagen, and others.

COSPATRICK, emigrant vessel, burnt, see *Wrecks*, 1874.

COSSACKS, warlike people inhabiting the confines of Poland, Russia, Tartary, and Turkey. They at first lived by plundering the Turkish galleys and the people of Anatolia; but were formed into a regular army by Stephen Bathori, about 1576, to defend the frontiers of Russia from the Tartars. They joined the Russians in 1654, and in the great war against France (1813-15) formed a valuable portion of the Russian army; and also in the Russo-Turkish wars of 1853-56; 1877-79.

COSSOVA, a plain in Servia. Here Amurath I. totally defeated the Christian army (Servians, Hungarians, &c.), 15 June, 1389; but was himself killed by an expiring soldier. Here John Huniades was defeated by a Turkish army four times larger than his own, 17 Oct. 1448.

COSTA RICA, a republic in Central America, part of Guatemala, declared independent 15 Sept. 1821. With the other republics of Central America formed a single state 1 July, 1823; compact dissolved 1840; constitution of 22 Dec. 1871 adopted 26 April, 1882. It has been much disturbed by the American filibusters, see *Nicaragua* and *America, Central*. Population, 1892, 243,205. Capital, San José; population, 1892, 19,326. Constitution, 27 Dec. 1859. On 14 Aug. 1859, the president Juan Mora was suddenly deposed, and Dr. José Montealegre made president; Dr. J. Ximenes president 3 April, 1863, was succeeded by Dr. Joseph Castro, 8 May, 1866, deposed; J. Jimenez, governor, Nov. 1868; Vicente Quadra proclaimed president 12 March, 1871; J. M. Guardia, 1871 for 1872-6; Aniceto Esquivel, 8 May, 1876; Vicente Herrera, 31 July, 1876, resigned: succeeded by Thomas Guardia, Oct. 1877; died July, 1882, succeeded by Prospero Fernandez; died March, 1885, succeeded by Bernardo Soto 12 March, 1885; by J. J. Rodriguez, 8 May, 1890. Population, 1885, estimated, 213,785; 1892, 243,205; 1901, 313,000.

President Rodriguez declares himself dictator and arrests opponents . . . . . 13 Sept. 1892

Sen. Rafael Iglesias, elected president, 3 April, 1894; attempted assassination of pres. Iglesias by Arava, an anarchist, who was arrested with 24 accomplices, reported . . . . . 28 Sept. 1894

Sen. Iglesias re-elected president . . 8 May, 1902

COSTERMONGERS, itinerant dealers in fruit, vegetables, fish, &c., deriving their name, it is said, from *costard*, a favourite apple. The London costermongers are useful in relieving the markets when glutted; and it was said in 1860, that 3,000,000*l*. passed through their hands annually. Previous to fasting and thanksgiving days, they sell the appointed forms of prayers in great numbers. On 22 Nov. 1860, they held a meeting in order to represent to the city authorities the hardships they felt by the police restricting their means of livelihood; and the Metropolitan Streets Act was modified, 7 Dec. 1867.

Their moral and physical condition has been much improved of late years, greatly through the instrumentality of the earl of Shaftesbury, who constituted himself a costermonger, and owned a barrow in 1874.

Much agitation among the costermongers of south London by the prohibition against their trading in the London-road, Southwark . . June, 1903.

COSTUME, see *Dress*.

COTOPAXI, see *Andes*.

COTTAGE. The term was originally applied to a small house without land, 4 Edw. I. 1275. "No man may build a cottage, except in towns, unless he lay four acres of land thereto," &c., 31 Eliz. 1589. This statute was repealed, 15 Geo. III. 1775. By returns to the tax office, in 1786, the number of cottages was 284,459. The number in 1800 was 428,214; the number in 1840 was about 770,000. In 1860 the public attention was much drawn to the deplorable state of cottages in many parts of the country, and the law of settlement was altered in 1865. Mr. Disraeli (afterwards lord Beaconsfield) said that "every cottage should have a tank, an oven, and a porch."

Cottage Improvement Society, founded 12 April, 1861, 7, Adam-street, Strand. Some of the society's models appeared in the International Exhibitions —in London, 1862; in Paris 1867
See *Shaftesbury Park*.

The *Cottager's Stove*, designed by captain John Grant, registered and presented by him to the metropolitan association for improving the dwellings of the industrious classes . . . . . . Dec. 1849

A Cottage Garden Society established about 1846 still exists 1886

COTTAGE HOSPITALS: much advocated by Dr. Horace Swete in 1870. Many since then have been established: including one by the baroness Burdett-Coutts, 1878; one at Wood Green, erected by Mr. J. Passmore Edwards, opened 15 June, 1895; one at Caterham, Queen Victoria memorial, 2 June, 1903.

COTTON, a vegetable wool, the produce of the *Gossypium*, a shrub indigenous to the tropical regions of India and America. Indian cotton cloth is mentioned by Herodotus, was known in Arabia in the time of Mahomet, 627, and was brought into Europe by his followers. It does not appear to have been in use among the Chinese till the 13th century; to them we are indebted for the cotton fabric termed nankeen. Cotton was the material of the principal articles of clothing among the Americans when visited by Columbus. It was grown and manufactured in Spain in the 10th century; and in the 14th century was introduced into Italy. Indian muslins, chintzes, and cottons were so largely imported into England in the 17th century, that in 1700 an act of parliament was passed, prohibiting their introduction. Cotton became the staple commodity of England in the present century. About 1841 the "cotton" or "Manchester" interest began to obtain political influence, which led to the repeal of the corn laws in 1846. Failure of Mr. Morris Ranger, a great cotton speculator, and others at Liverpool announced 31 Oct. 1883. Cotton manufacture introduced into Bombay about 1868 gradually becomes very successful, reported Dec. 1889. See *Calico*, *Muslin*, *Corner*, *Strikes*.

Act for collection of cotton statistics passed 25 June, 1868

John Rylands, the head of the company of Rylands & Sons which employs 12,000 hands died aged 87 11 Dec. 1888

n Lancashire and Cheshire the mills put on half time, to limit the production and check speculations to raise the price of cotton, &c. about 15 July, 1889

Cotton mills fully engaged . . . . 5 Nov. "

Strike and lock-out of cotton-spinners throughout Lancashire (not Manchester), 16 April *et seq.*; dispute settled by compromise . . 6 May, 1892

Depression in the cotton industry caused by the American cotton "corner" 1903

Fustian and *Velveteen* made of cotton, about 1641.

Calico sheeting, &c. The fly-shuttle was invented by John Kay, of Bury, 1738; the drop-box by Robert Kay, 1760; spinning by rollers (also attributed to John Wyatt) patented by Louis Paul, 1738; the spinning-jenny, by Hargreaves, 1767; the water-frame, by Arkwright, 1769; the power-loom, by Rev. Dr. Edmund Cartwright, 1785; the dressing machine, by Johnson and Radcliffe, 1802-4; another power-loom, by Horrocks, 1803-13. A combing machine was patented by Joshua Heilmann, in 1845.

British muslin (totally superseding that of India) is due mainly to the invention of the MULE (*which see*) by Samuel Crompton, 1774-9; and to the self-acting mule of Mr. Roberts, 1825.

Calico Printing commenced 1764.

The *Steam-Engine* first applied to the cotton manufacture (by Boulton and Watt), 1785.

Bleaching by means of chloride of lime introduced by Mr. Tennant, of Glasgow, 1798.

Stockings. The stocking-frame was invented by William Lee, in 1589. *Cotton stockings* were first made by hand about 1730; Jedediah Strutt obtained a patent for Derby ribbed stockings in 1758; and Horton patented his knotter frame in 1776; Crompton's mule was employed in making thread for the stocking manufacture about 1770.

Cotton-Lace—Bobbin-net. The stocking-frame of Lee was applied to lace-making by Hammond, about 1768; the process perfected by John Heathcoat, 1809.

See *Factory system*.

COTTON FIBRE IMPORTED INTO THE UNITED KINGDOM.

	lb.		*lb.*
1697	1,976,359	1868	1,328,761,616
1710	715,008	1870	1,339,367,120
1730	1,545,472	1872	1,408,837,472
1765	3,870,392	1874	1,566,864,432
1782	11,828,039	1875	1,492,351,168
1790	31,500,000	1876	1,487,858,848
1800	56,000,000	1877	1,355,281,200
1810	132,500,000	1879	1,469,358,464
1820	151,500,000	1881	1,679.068,384
1830	264,000,000	1883	1,734,333,552
1840	592,500,000	1885	1,425,816,336
1860	1,390,938,752	1887	1,791,437,312
1861	1,256,984,736	1889	1,937,462,240
1862	523,973,296	1890	1,793,495,200
1863	670,084,128	1893	1,416,780,064
1864	894,102,384	1900	1,760,206,672
1865	978,502,000	1901	1,829,710,064
1866	1,377,514,096		

American Cotton. Previous to 1795, our cotton fibre came from the East and West Indies, the Levant, and a little from the United States. About 1786, the growth of cotton began in Georgia. In 1793, Eli Whitney, an American, invented the *saw-gin*, a machine by which cotton wool is separated from the pod and cleaned with great ease and expedition.* This led to such increased cultivation that the United States soon exported 1,500,000 lb. of cotton:—

From the United States, N.A.

1795	5,250,000 lb.	1875	841,333,472 lb.
1820	89,999,174	1876	932,800,176
1830	210,885,358	1877	912,244,592
1840	487,856,504	1879	1,082,462,080
1847	364,599,291	1881	1,210,980,288
1859	961,707.264	1883	1,239,410,592
1860	1,115,890,608	1885	1,050,546,000
1861	819,500,528	1887	1,256,894,464
1866	520,057,440	1889	1,423,811,872
1870	716,248,848	1890	1,316,756.896
1871	1,038,677,920	1892	1,405,528,208
1872	625,600,080	1893	1,055,855,360
1873	832,573,616	1900	1,365,298,928
1874	874,926,864	1901	1,480,785,936

Cotton imported from India: 1856, 463,000 bales; official value, 3,572,329*l.*; in 1865, 1,266,520 bales; value, 25,025,856*l.*; in 1866, 1,847,770 bales; value, 25,270,547*l.*; in 1874, 412,025,040 lb.; in 1876, 275,856,336 lb.; in 1877, 193,856,320 lb.; in 1879, 181,347,601 lb.; 1881, 198,577,680 lb.; 1883, 260,698,480 lb.; 1885, 145,130,048 lb.; 1887, 276,506,720 lb.; 1888, 170,238,768 lb.; 1889, 273,810,880 lb.; 1890, 238,746,704 lb.; 1892, 68,877,984 lb.; 1900, 36,832,320 lb.; 1901, 37,740,976 lb.

Australian Cotton said by Manchester manufacturers to be superior to the best American cotton, Jan. 1861.

A company formed at Manchester to obtain cotton from India, Africa, and other places (arose out of the *Cotton Supply Association*, formed in 1857), Sept. 1860.

Since 1861, the cultivation of cotton in India, Egypt, Italy, &c. has greatly increased.

Cotton imported from Egypt in 1856, 34,399,008 lb.; in 1870, 143,710,448 lb.; in 1876, 199,245,312 lb.; in 1877, 176,558,256 lb.; in 1879, 158,232,032 lb.; 1881, 175,317,072 lb.; 1883, 170,685,200 lb.; 1885, 177,515,520 lb.; 1887, 176,608,096 lb.; 1889, 191,750,720 lb.; 1890, 181,266,176 lb.; 1892, 261,492,784 lb.; 1900, 312,448,864 lb.; 1901, 282,132,368 lb.

Exhibition of cotton states, opened at Atlanta; reported Sept. 1895.

EXPORTS OF COTTON GOODS, YARN, &C., FROM UNITED KINGDOM.

	Official Value.		*Official Value.*
1697	£5,915	1862	£36,750,971
1701	23,253	1864	54,882,329
1751	45,986	1866	74,565,426
1780	355,000	1870	71,416,345
1790	1,662,369	1874	73,247,625
1800	5,406,501	1876	67,641,286
1820	20,509,926	1879	63,974,053
1847	23,333,225	1881	72,744,531
1860	52,012,430	1883	76,445,757
1861	46,872,489	1885	66,976,887

* A trial of various kinds of cotton gins, under the direction of Dr. Forbes Watson, took place at Manchester, 28 Nov.-23 Dec. 1871.

	Official Value.		Official Value.
1887 . .	£70,959,766	1890 . . .	£52,089,442
(including mixtures of cotton and wool.)		1891	60,230,256
		1893 . . .	54,699,367
1888(cotton only)	60,329,051	1900	62,009,150
1889 . . .	58,793,448	1901 . . .	65,708,582

COTTON FAMINE.

The supply of cotton from North America nearly ceased, in consequence of the secession of the southern states from the union in 1860-61. In 1852, Mr. T. Bazley warned the country on the danger of trusting to this source. In May, 1862, he stated that through its failure the loss of the labouring classes was 12,000,000*l.* sterling a year, and estimated the loss, including the employing classes, at nearly 40,000,000*l.* a year.

At a meeting of noblemen and gentlemen, connected with the cotton manufacturing districts, at Bridgewater-house, St. James's, on 19 July, 1862, the earl of Derby in the chair, 10,000*l.* were subscribed to the *Cotton District Relief Fund.* The viceroy of Egypt, in London at the time, gave 1000*l.*, and the queen gave 2000*l.* on 24 July. Liberal subscriptions flowed in from all parts. On 28 Aug.. the lord mayor had received 41,902*l.*

In the Lancashire district (population about 4,000,000) there were receiving parish relief, Sept. 1861, 43,500 persons; in Sept. 1862, 163,498. *Earl of Derby*, 2 Dec. 1862.

In July, 1863, about the value of 700,000*l.* remained of the donations which had been received in money and goods, amounting to about 1,900,000*l*

On 9 Feb., 1863, the "George Griswold" arrived, containing contributions of provisions, &c., from North America, for the relief of the sufferers in Lancashire.

The Union Relief Act (passed Aug. 1862, and continued in 1863) gave much relief by enabling overseers to borrow money to be expended in public works to be executed by the unemployed workmen.

In Oct. 1864, much distress still existed, and fears were entertained for the approaching winter—90,000 more paupers than ordinary in cotton districts. *Times*, 18 Jan. 1865.

In June, 1865, Mr. Farnall, the special commissioner, (appointed in May, 1862) was recalled by the poor-law board and the famine was declared to be ended. 1,000,000*l.* had been expended in two years. The executive of the Central Relief Fund held their last meeting, 4 Dec. 1865.

"The Coal Question," by Wm. Stanley Jevons, published 1865.

The account of the fund was made up in 1873. The balance, above 130,000*l.*, was proposed to be appropriated to the foundation of a convalescent hospital for Lancashire.

A memorial window (the gift of the cotton operatives of Lancashire, who subscribed to commemorate the munificence of the metropolis to them during the cotton famine, 1861-4) unveiled in Guildhall, 15 July, 1868.

COTTON FACTORIES regulated by acts of parliament passed in 1825, 1831, 1833, 1844, and 1889. The hours of labour were limited, and the employment of children under nine years of age prohibited. In 1846, 1724 cotton mills employed 197,500 persons. In 1862, the persons employed were stated to be 451,000; 315,000 in Lancashire. Excitement through 5 per cent. reduction of wages in Lancashire, &c., Sept. 1883; strike; dispute settled, 27 Sept. 1883. Great strike of about 4,400 cotton spinners in Lancashire against 5 per cent. reduction of pay, 7 Nov. 1892; settlement; reduction of wages 7*d.* in the pound; arrangement to avoid strikes and lock-outs, 24 March, 1893.

Great meeting in Manchester against the re-imposition of the Indian cotton duties, 8 Jan. 1895; 5 per cent. duties on Lancashire goods imported into India, 8 Jan. 1895; another in London, 14 Feb. 1895. Lancashire's case against the Indian import duties by Mr. Holt S. Hallett, published Feb. 1895.

The masters' demand for a 5 per cent. reduction in wages referred to arbitration, 11 Nov. 1897; arbitration refused by the men in Bolton district at meetings, 23, 29 Nov.; reduction of wages resisted by the men, 6 Dec.; abandoned by the masters, 7 Dec. 1897.

Conference of cotton trade employers at Manchester, 8 March, 1898; 2 meetings at Manchester, advance of 7*d.* in the pound agreed to, 18 Feb. 1899.

New system of quotation adopted at Liverpool, prices quoted in decimals without discount, 1 Oct. 1902.

See *India*, 1894.

COTTON OIL, largely manufactured from the seeds in the south of the United States. Imported to the United Kingdom 1900, 13,262 tons, value 290,197*l.*; 1902, 12,360 tons, value 310,069*l.*

COTTONIAN LIBRARY, formed by sir Robert Bruce Cotton, 1600, *et seq.* He died 6 May, 1631. It was rescued from the republicans during the protectorate, 1649-60, and was secured to the public by a statute in 1700. It was removed to Essex-house in 1712; in 1730 to Dean's-yard, Westminster (where on 23 Oct. 1731, a part of the books sustained damage by fire); to the British Museum in 1757.

COTTON-WOOL, see *Respiration.* Dr. Percy, in 1874, applied cotton-wool to filter the air for ventilating the houses of parliament.

COULMIERS, a village ten miles west of Orleans, central France. Here the Bavarians, under general Von der Tann, were defeated by the French army of the Loire, under general d'Aurelle de Paladines, who took about 2000 prisoners, 9 Nov. 1870, and regained Orleans.

COUNANI, a territory between Brazil and French Guiana. The ridiculous attempt to found an independent Republic failed here (M. Jules Gros, president), Aug.-Sept. 1887. An arrangement respecting this territory was made between France and Brazil in 1862, for police purposes.

COUNCIL OF JUDGES. See *Judges.*

COUNCIL OF OFFICERS, of the army, constituted by Cromwell and termed "New Model" 1642, abolished by Charles II. 1660.

COUNCILS. King Alfred, in about 886, is said to have so arranged the business of the nation, that all resolutions passed through three councils. The first was a select council which considered all affairs to be laid before the second council, bishops and nobles appointed by the king, like the present privy council. The third was a general assembly of the nation, called, in Saxon, Wittenagemót, in which quality and offices gave a right to sit. In these three councils we behold the origin of the cabinet, privy councils, and parliaments; see *Cabinet, Common* and *Privy Councils*, &c.

COUNCILS, FRENCH. The Council of ANCIENTS, consisting of 250 members, together with the council of FIVE HUNDRED, instituted at Paris, 1 Nov. 1795: the executive was a Directory of FIVE. Bonaparte dispersed the council of Five hundred at St. Cloud, 9 Nov. 1799, declaring himself, Roger Ducos, and Siéyès, consuls *provisoires*; see *France.*

COUNCILS OF THE CHURCH. The following are among the most memorable. Those numbered are the *Œcumenical* or *General* Councils. *Sir Harris Nicolas* in his "Chronology of History," enumerates 1604 councils, and gives an alphabetical list.

Of the church at Jerusalem (*Acts* xv.) 50
Of the western bishops at Arles, in France, to suppress the Donatists; three fathers of the English church attended . . . 314
I. First Œcumenical or General, at Nice (Constantine the Great presided), decreed the consubstantiality of the Son of God, condemned Arianism, and composed the Nicene creed 325
At Tyre, against Athanasius 335

The first at Constantinople, when the Arian heresy gained ground 337
At Rome, in favour of Athanasius 342
At Sardis: 370 bishops attended; Arians condemned 347
At Rimini: 400 bishops attended; Constantine obliged them to sign a new confession 359
II. Constantinople: oriental council; 150 orthodox bishops present when it met; presided over 1st by Meletius, 2nd by Gregory Nazianzen, 3rd by Nectarius; added to the Nicene creed; declared the bishop of Constantinople next in rank to Rome; Constantinople being New Rome . . 381
III. Ephesus: Cyril of Alexandria presided; anathematised and deposed Nestorius; protested against any addition to the original Nicene creed 431
IV. Chalcedon: 520 bishops present; declared the two natures of Christ, Divine and Human, as defined by Leo of Rome; accepted and decreed the Constantinopolitan addition to the Nicene creed 451
V. Constantinople: Eutyches, patriarch of Constantinople, presided; condemned the three chapters (written by Theodore of Mopsuestia, Theodoret, and others); Vigilius, bishop of Rome, protested, but afterwards assented . . . 553
VI. Constantinople: pope Agatho presided; against Monothelites . . 7 Nov. 680, to 16 Sept. 681
Authority of the six general councils re-established by Theodosius 715
VII. Second Nicene: 350 bishops attended; against Iconoclasts . . . 24 Sept. to 23 Oct. 787
VIII. Constantinople: the emperor Basil attended; against Iconoclasts and heresies 5 Oct. 869, to 28 Feb. 870
At Clermont, convened by Urban II. to authorise the crusades: 310 bishops attended . . 1095
IX. First Lateran: right of investiture settled by treaty between pope Calixtus II. and the emperor Henry V. . . . . 18 March to 5 April, 1123
X. Second Lateran: Innocent II. presided; preservation of temporalities of ecclesiastics, the principal subject; 1000 fathers of the church attended . . . . 20 April, 1139
XI. Third Lateran, against schismatics 5 to 19 March, 1179
XII. Fourth Lateran: 400 bishops and 1000 abbots attended; Innocent III. presided; against Albigenses, &c. . . . . . . 11 to 30 Nov. 1215
XIII. Lyons; under pope Innocent IV.: emperor Frederick II. deposed . 28 June to 17 July, 1245
XIV. Lyons; under Gregory X.: temporary union of Greek and Latin churches 7 May to 17 June, 1274
XV. Vienne in Dauphiné: Clement V. presided, and the kings of France and Aragon attended; order of Knights Templars suppressed 16 Oct. 1311; 3 April and 6 May, 1312
XVI. Pisa: Gregory XII. and Benedict XIII. deposed; Alexander elected 5 March to 7 Aug. 1409
XVII. Constance: Martin V. elected pope; and John Huss and Jerome of Prague condemned to be burnt 1414-1418
XVIII. Basel 1431-1443
XIX. Fifth Lateran: begun by Julius II. . . 1512
Continued under Leo X. for the suppression of the pragmatic sanction of France, against the council of Pisa, &c., till 1517
XX. Trent: held to condemn the doctrines of the reformers, Luther, Zuinglius, and Calvin. (See *Trent*.) . . . . . 13 Dec. 1545, to 3 Dec. 1563
XXI. Rome: summoned by an encyclical letter, 8 Sept. 1868; met . . . . . . 8 Dec. 1869
Present: 6 archbishop-princes, 49 cardinals, 11 patriarchs, 680 archbishops and bishops, 28 abbots, 29 generals of orders—803 in all . . ,,
There were held four public sessions, and between 90 and 100 congregations. New canons were issued 24 April, 1870, and after much discussion and opposition, the infallibility of the pope as head of the Church was affirmed by 547 placets against 2 non-placets, and promulgated, 18 July, 1870
Many bishops withdrew from the discussion. The council then adjourned to 11 Nov. (see *Rome*.)
See under *Church of England*, 1903.

COUNCILS OF CONCILIATION, to adjust differences between masters and workmen, established by licence of the secretary of state, by virtue of an act passed 15 Aug. 1867; and by the Arbitration (Masters and Workmen) act passed 1872. Both these acts were repealed by the "Conciliation act" passed 7 Aug. 1896; in pursuance of which conciliation and arbitration boards may be constituted and registered as such, by intervention of the board of trade.

The labour conciliation board of the London chamber of commerce, constituted to promote amicable methods of settling labour disputes, &c. 6 Feb. 1890
London conciliation board with separate committees of delegates . . about 6 March ,,
Meeting of delegates of labour organisations at the offices of the chamber of commerce . 29 Oct. ,,
Successful conciliation conferences in Yorkshire mining districts . . . . Oct. ,,
First meeting of the London board . 12 Dec. ,,
Active in 1891. First annual report issued 16 Jan. 1892
Annual meetings; from . . . . 15 April, 1896
See *Coal*, 1893-94 and *Strikes*.

COUNSEL are supposed to be coëval with the *curia regis*. Advocates are referred to the time of Edward I., but are mentioned earlier. Counsel who were guilty of deceit or collusion were punishable by the statute of Westminster, 13 Edw. I. 1285. Counsel were allowed to persons charged with treason by act 8 Will. III. 1696. An act to enable persons indicted for felony to make their defence by counsel, passed Aug. 1836; see *Barristers* and *King's Counsel*.

COUNTERPOINT (in music), the art of combining melodies in harmony. The earliest known specimen of contrapuntal writing is by Adam de la Halle in the 12th century.

COUNTESS OF HUNTINGDON'S CONNEXION; see *Whitefieldites*.

COUNTIES or SHIRES. The division of this kingdom into counties began, it is said, with king Alfred; but some counties bore their present names above a century before. The division of Ireland into counties took place in 1562. Lord-lieutenants were appointed in 1549 in England, and in 1831 in Ireland. Counties first sent members to parliament, before which period knights met in their own counties, 1285. CHANDOS CLAUSE, Sect. 20 of the Reform act, 2 Will. IV. c. 45 (1832), inserted by the motion of the marquis of Chandos. By it occupiers as tenants of land not situate in a borough, paying an annual rent of 50*l*., became entitled to a vote for the knight of the shire. It increased the number of tory voters, and in consequence several attempts were made to repeal it. It was superseded by the Reform act of 15 Aug. 1867.

By the Winter Assizes Act, 1876, certain counties were united (by order in council, first time, 23 Oct. 1876) to facilitate more speedy trials of prisoners.
"The Victoria History of the Counties of England," began 1900

COUNTRY DANCE, see *Contre-Danse*.

COUNTRY PARTY, see *Court Party*.

COUNTY CONVENTIONS, see *Ireland* 1885.

COUNTY COUNCILS, see *Local Government Act*. At the first elections in Jan. 1889, a large number of the nobility, gentry, and justices, were elected.

The Councils assume their powers 1 April 1889; see *London County Councils*. The time of election was changed from Jan. to March, by act passed 5 Aug. 1891.
County Council Magazine started . . . . Feb. 1889

County Councils Association held their first meeting at Westminster . . . . 23 May, 1890
Others since.

COUNTY-COURTS or schyremotes, in the time of the Saxons, were important tribunals. Alfred is said to have divided England into counties, and counties into hundreds; but county-courts seem to have existed much earlier.

County-Courts, for the recovery of debts under 20*l.*, superseding courts of requests, instituted by 9 & 10 Vict. c. 95 . . . . 26 Aug. 1846
The counties of England and Wales are divided into sixty districts, each district having a county-court, with a barrister as judge, and juries when necessary. Their jurisdiction extended by 13 & 14 Vict. c. 61, to sums not exceeding 50*l.* . . . 1850
Their proceedings facilitated in 1852 and 1854; 60 county-courts in England and Wales . . 1868-72
In 1850 plaints entered at the courts of the sixty circuits were 306,793, for 1,265,115*l.*; in 1857, 744,652 plaints for 1,937,745*l.*; of the 217,173 causes tried, 4297 were for sums between 20*l.* and 50*l.*
From 1847 to 1858 judgment was obtained in these courts for 8,309,236*l.*
Equity powers, like those of the court of chancery, in cases relating to sums under 500*l.*, conferred on these courts, to begin . . . . . 1 Oct. 1865
Their jurisdiction still further enlarged . 20 Aug. 1867
Admiralty jurisdiction conferred on them by act passed July, 1868, amended . . . Aug. 1869
County Court Acts amended by acts passed 2 Aug. 1875 and 1887
A County Boards Bill, withdrawn . . . July, 1879
New regulations, respecting procedure, &c., came into operation . . . . . . 28 April, 1886
Amendment Act passed . . . . . 13 Aug. 1888
Mr. Francis Bayley, judge at Westminster, 1849-93, died, aged 90 . . . . 4 May, 1893
Mr. Commissioner R. M. Kerr, judge of the City of London court, died, aged 83 . . . 21 Nov. 1902

COUNTY FRANCHISE, a bill for giving votes to labourers and others, annually brought in by Mr. (afterwards sir) G. O. Trevelyan. The object was effected by the reform acts of 1884-5. See *Household Suffrage*.

COUNTY OFFICERS AND COURTS, Ireland: an act to amend the law respecting them passed 14 Aug. 1877.

COUP D'ÉTAT, in France (see *France*, 2 Dec. 1851); *Pronunciamiento* in Spain; changes in the government effected by force, either by the ruler, the army, or the populace. The Speaker's *Coup d'état*, see *Parliament*, 2 Feb., 1881. See *Brazil*, Nov. 1889; *Servia*, April, 1893; and 10 June, 1903.

COURIERS. Xenophon attributes the first to Cyrus; and Herodotus says that they were common among the Persians; see *Esther* iii. 15, about 510 B.C. The Greeks and Romans had no regular couriers till the time of Augustus, when they travelled in cars, about 24 B.C. Couriers or posts are said to have been instituted in France by Charlemagne about A.D. 800. Couriers for letters were employed by Louis XI. of France, 1463. *Henault*. See *Post-office*.

COURLAND, a duchy of Livonia, conquered by Danes, 1218; by Teutonic knights, 1239; subjected to Poland in 1561, conquered by Charles XII. of Sweden in 1701; Ernest Biren, duke, 1737; his son, Peter, 1769; annexed to Russia, March, 1795. Population, 1886, 682,792. Libau, on the Baltic, was constituted a military and commercial port; the first stone was laid by the czar, 24 Aug. 1893.

COURSING, see *Dogs*.

COURT BARON, an ancient court which every lord of a manor may hold by prescription. In it duties, heriots, and customs are received, and estates and surrenders are passed. Its jurisdiction was restricted in 1747 and 1833. By the Small Debts Act, 1856, lords of the manor may give up holding these courts.

COURT CIRCULAR, conservative weekly paper; established 26 April, 1856.

COURT DRESS, see *Dress*.

COURT JOURNAL, fashionable journal, established 1829.

COURT LEET, an ancient court of record, belonging to a hundred, instituted for punishing encroachments, nuisances, fraudulent weights and measures, &c. The steward is judge, and all residing within the hundred (peers, clergymen, &c., excepted) are obliged to do suit within this court.

COURT OF HONOUR. In England the court of chivalry, of which the lord high constable was a judge, was called *Curia Militaris*, in the time of Henry IV., and subsequently the Court of Honour. In Bavaria, to prevent duelling, a court of honour was instituted in April, 1819. Mr. Joseph Hamilton for many years ardently laboured to establish a similar institution in Britain.

COURT OF JUSTICIARY, HIGH, in Scotland, constituted by a commission under the great seal, 1671, ratified 1672. The procedure in this court was amended by an act passed in 1868. See *Court of Session*.

COURT OF REQUESTS, see *Conscience*.

COURT OF REVIEW, see *Bankruptcy*.

COURT OF SESSION, the highest civil tribunal in Scotland, was instituted by James V. by statute, 17 May, 1532, its origin being ascribed to the regent, duke of Albany. It consisted of 14 judges and a president, and replaced a committee of parliament. In 1830 the number of judges was reduced; and the court now consists of the lord president (termed lord justice general), the lord justice-clerk, and 11 ordinary judges. In 1867 the necessity of renovating this court was asserted by high legal authority; and an act to amend its procedure was passed 31 July, 1868. The lord president, the right hon. John Inglis, appointed, Feb. 1867; died 20 Aug., succeeded by James P. B. Robertson, Sept. 1891; and subsequently by John Blair Balfour.

COURT PARTY—COUNTRY PARTY, politicians in the parliaments of England, beginning about 1620. At the end of the 17th century the latter embodied toryism and high church principles, maintained the rights of "the land," as opposed to whiggism and the trading interests. Its most distinguished statesman was sir Thomas Hanmer (the *Montalto* of Pope's Satires), who died in 1746. *Ashe*.

COURTRAI (Belgium). Here Robert, count of Artois, who had defeated the Flemings in 1297, was defeated and slain by them, 11 July, 1302. The conflict was named the "Battle of Spurs," from the number of gilt spurs collected.

COURT THEATRE, Sloane-square, Chelsea, opened 25 Jan. 1871; Miss Litton first manager.

COURTS MARTIAL are regulated by the Mutiny act, first passed in 1690. The powers of these courts were much discussed in 1867, in consequence of the measures used to suppress the negro insurrection in Jamaica, Oct. 1866. See *Army*, 1 Jan. 1887, 1893.

COURTS OF JUSTICE were instituted at Athens, 1507 B.C. (see *Areiopagus*); by Moses, 1491 B.C. (*Exod.* xviii. 25), and in Rome. For these realms, see *Chancery*, *Common Pleas*, *Exchequer*, *King's Bench*, &c. The citizens of London were privileged to plead their own cause in the courts of judicature, without employing lawyers, except in pleas of the crown, 41 Hen. III. 1257. *Stow*. The rights of the Irish courts were established by the British parliament in April, 1783. See *Supreme Court*.

COURTS OF LAW FEES ACT, passed 20 Aug. 1867, directs the application of surplus fees towards providing new courts of justice. Acts for building these courts were passed in 1865 and 1866. See *Law Courts*.

COURTS OF SURVEY, consisting of a judge and two assistants, for appeals respecting unseaworthy ships, were directed to be appointed in certain ports and districts by the Merchant Shipping Act, 39 & 40 Vict. c. 80 (15 Aug. 1876). They sat in 1877.

COUTRAS (S. W. France). Here Henry of Navarre totally defeated the duc de Joyeuse and the royalists, 20 Oct. 1587.

COVENANTERS, those persons who in the reign of Charles I. having signed the solemn league and *covenant*, engaged to stand by each other in opposition to the projects of the king in 1638. The COVENANT or league between England and Scotland (the preceding one modified), solemnly adopted by the parliament, 25 Sept. 1643; was accepted by Charles II. 16 Aug. 1650, but repudiated by him on his restoration in 1661, when it was declared to be illegal by parliament, and copies of it ordered to be burnt. See *Cameronians* and *Bothwell Bridge*.

The covenant consisted of six articles:

1. The preservation of the reformed church in Scotland and the reformation of religion in England and Ireland.
2. The extirpation of popery, prelacy, schism, &c.
3. The preservation of the liberties of parliament and the king's person and authority.
4. The discovery and punishment of all malignants, &c.
5. The preservation of "a blessed peace between these kingdoms:"
6. The assisting all who enter into the covenant:

"*This will we do as in the sight of God.*"

COVENT GARDEN (London), corrupted from "Convent Garden," having been the garden of St. Peter's convent. The square was built about 1633, and the piazza on the north side and the church were designed by Inigo Jones. The fruit and vegetable markets were rebuilt in 1829-30, from designs by Mr. Fowler (the ground belonging to the duke of Bedford). In the 17th century, Covent Garden was a very fashionable quarter of London. Frequent allusions are made at it by the playwriters of the time of Charles II.; and Dryden lays a scene of one of his plays here. It is depicted also by Hogarth.

COVENT GARDEN THEATRE sprang out of one in Lincoln's-inn-fields, through a patent granted 14 Chas. II. 1662, to sir William Davenant, whose company was denominated the "duke's servants," as a compliment to the duke of York, afterwards James II.; see under *Theatres*.—The theatre was burnt down 5 March, 1856, during a *bal masqué* held by Mr. Anderson, the wizard of the north. The present theatre by E. Barry was opened 15 May, 1858. The *Floral Hall* adjoining it was opened 7 March, 1860, with the volunteers' ball.

COVENTRY ACT passed, to prevent malicious maiming and wounding, 6 March, 1671, in consequence of sir John Coventry, K.B., M.P., being maimed in the streets of London, by sir Thomas Sandys and others, adherents of the duke of Monmouth, 21 Dec. 1670. Repealed 1828.

COVENTRY (Warwickshire). Leofric, earl of Mercia, lord of Coventry, is said to have relieved it from heavy taxes, at the intercession of his wife Godiva, on condition of her riding naked through the streets, about 1057. Processions in her memory took place in 1851; 23 June, 1862; 4 June, 1866; 20 June, 1870; 4 June, 1877; 6 Aug. 1883; and 2 Aug. 1892. The legend is probably fabulous. A parliament was held here in the reign of Henry IV. called *parliamentum indoctum*, or the unlearned parliament, because lawyers were excluded, 1404; and in the reign of Henry VI. another met, called *parliamentum diabolicum*, from the acts of attainder passed against the duke of York and others, 20 Nov. 1459. The town was surrounded with strong walls, three miles in circumference, and twenty-six towers, which were demolished by order of Charles II. in 1662. The ribbon-makers here suffered much from want of work in the winter of 1809-10. Its chief manufactures are ribbons, watches and bicycles, of which industry it is now the chief centre; cotton, worsted, and woollen goods, silk dyeing and art metalwork. The BISHOPRIC was founded by Oswy, king of Mercia, 656, and had the double name of Coventry and Lichfield, which was reversed by later bishops. It was so wealthy, that king Offa, by the favour of pope Adrian, made it archiepiscopal; but this title was laid aside on the death of that king. In 1075 the see was removed to Chester; in 1102 to Coventry; and afterwards to its original foundation, Lichfield, but with great opposition from the monks of Coventry. Coventry merged into the bishopric of Lichfield (*which see*). In 1888, under the Local Government act, Coventry was reconstituted a county, a privilege it possessed from 1451 to 1842. Population, 1881, 44,831; 1891, 52,720; 1901, 69,877.

Rioting on the levying of the "vicar's rate" . . . 11 Sept. 1882
New park, gift of Mr. D. Spencer, opened . . . 11 Oct. 1883
Messrs. Humber's cycle manufactory burnt and adjoining houses damaged; estimated loss, 100,000*l*. . . . 17 July, 1896
Premises of Mr. Hills, builder, and Messrs. Phillips and Marriott, brewers, burnt, estimated damage, 40,000*l*. . . . 15 Dec. 1899

COW-POCK INOCULATION; see *Small Pox* and *Vaccination*.

CRABS. The size at which they are to be sold is determined by the Fisheries Act, 1877.

CRACOW, a city in Austrian Poland. The Poles elected Cracus for their duke, who built Cracow with the spoils taken from the Franks about 700. It was their capital, 1320-1609. Cracow was taken by Charles XII. in 1702, and taken and retaken several times by the Russians and other confederates. The sovereign was crowned at Cracow until 1764. The Russians, who had taken it 1768, were expelled by Kosciusko, 24 March, 1794; but it surrendered to the Prussians, 15 June same year, and in 1795 was awarded to Austria. Cracow was formed into a republic, June, 1815. Occupied by 10,000 Russians, who followed here the defeated Poles, Sept. 1831. Its independence was extinguished: and it was seized by the emperor of Austria, and incorporated with his empire, 16 Nov. 1846, which was protested against by England, France, Sweden, and Turkey; see *Poland*. A dreadful fire laid the greater part of the city in ashes, 18 July, 1850. The discovery on 22 July, 1869, of Barbare Abryk, a nun, secluded for 21 years in a convent cell, led to violent rioting. Population, 1890, 76,025; 1900, 73,168.

New university (includes the Polish academy, founded 1872), a fine gothic building . . 1881-7
The Catholic Bishop raised to the rank of prince of the Empire, and primate of Poland . . Jan. 1889
The body of Adam Mickiewicz, the Polish poet, brought from France, re-interred here . 4 July, 1890
Polish congress of natural science and medicine . about 10 July, 1891

CRANES are of very early date, for the engines of Archimedes may be so called. In 1857 a crane had been erected at Glasgow capable of lifting 50 tons. One in Woolwich arsenal in 1881 lifted 400 tons. See *Derricks.*

CRANIOLOGY (or PHRENOLOGY), the study of the external form of the human skull, as indicative of mental powers and moral qualities. Dr. Gall, the propounder, was a German physician, born March, 1758, and his first observations were among his schoolfellows. Afterwards he studied the heads of criminals and others, and eventually reduced his ideas to a system, marking out the skull like a map. His first lecture was given at Vienna in 1796; but in 1802 the Austrian government prohibited his teaching. In 1800 he was joined by Dr. Spurzheim; who divided "the mental and moral faculties" of Gall into two orders, "feelings and intellect," and in 1810-12 they published at Paris their work on the "Anatomy and Physiology of the Nervous System, and of the Brain in particular." Gall died in 1828. The researches of Gall and Spurzheim led to increased study of the brain. Combe's "Phrenology" was first published in 1819. Phrenological societies were formed early in London and Edinburgh; and in 1832, there were in existence some 30 phrenological societies, and several journals devoted to the subject. Various modifications in the localisation of the faculties were made by pupils of Gall, among them the American phrenologists, the Fowlers, and S. R. Wells.

Phrenology was refuted by Lord Jeffrey in the *Edinburgh Review*, in 1826, and more recently by Dr. W. B. Carpenter. Professor David Ferrier reported the results of researches tending to prove localisation of certain faculties in the brain to the British Association, Sept. 1873. He published his work "The Functions of the Brain," 1876; 2nd edition 1887.
"Brain," a quarterly journal, began in 1878.

CRANMER, LATIMER, AND RIDLEY, martyrdom of, see *Protestants*, note.

CRANNOGES, see *Lake-dwellings.*

CRANNON or CRANON, Thessaly, N. Greece. Near here the Macedonians under Antipater and Craterus defeated the confederated Greeks, twice by sea, and once by land, 322 B.C. The Athenians demanded peace, and Antipater put their orators to death, among whom was Hyperides, who, that he might not betray the secrets of his country when under torture, cut out his tongue, and Demosthenes is said to have taken poison shortly after.

CRANWORTH'S ACT, LORD, to simplify the practice of conveyancers, 23 & 24 Vict. c. 145 (1860).

CRAONNE (N. France). Here Victor and Ney defeated the Prussians under Blücher after a severe contest, 7 March, 1814.

CRAPE. It is said some crape was made by Ste. Badour, when queen of France, about 680. It is said to have been first made at Bologna.

CRAVANT, see *Crevant.*

CRAYFORD (Kent). Hengist the Saxon is said to have defeated the Britons here, 457.

CRAYONS, coloured substances made into paste, and dried into pencils, were known in France about 1422; and improved by L'Oriot, 1748.

CREASOTE, or KREASOTE (discovered by Reichenbach about 1833), a powerful antiseptic and coagulator of albuminous tissue, is obtained by the destructive distillation of wood and other organic matters. It has been used for the preservation of meat, timber, &c.

CREATINE (from the Greek *kreas*, flesh), the chemical principle of flesh, was discovered in 1835 by E. Chevreul, and has been investigated by Liebig, Gregory, and others.

CREATION OF THE WORLD. The date given by the English bible, and by Usher, Blair, and some others, is 4004 B.C. There are about 140 different dates assigned to the Creation, varying from 3616 to 6984 B.C. Dr. Hales gives 5411; see *Eras.*

Haydn's *Creation* (oratorio), composed 1796—8; first performed (in London, at Covent Garden Theatre), 28 March, 1800; in Paris, 24 Dec. same year.

CRÈCHES, establishments for temporarily receiving the young children of working mothers begun at Paris, about 1844; in London (in Rathbone-place, &c.) about 1863; others since.

CRECY, or CRESSY (N. France), where Edward III. and his son, Edward the Black Prince, and an army of about 36,800, obtained a great victory over Philip, king of France, with about 130,000, 26 Aug. 1346. John, king of Bohemia (nearly blind); James, king of Majorca; Ralph, duke of Lorraine (sovereign princes); and a number of French nobles, together with 30,000 private men, were slain, while the loss of the English was very small. The crest of the king of Bohemia (three ostrich feathers, with the motto *Ich dien*—in English, "I serve") has since been adopted by princes of Wales.

CRÉDIT FONCIER, &c. A plan of providing loans to landowners was introduced by Frederick the Great of Prussia, in 1763, in some of the Prussian provinces, as the best method of alleviating the distresses of the landed interest caused by his wars. The system consists of lending money to landowners on the security of their estates, and providing the loan capital by the issue of debentures charged upon the aggregate mortgaged estates. There are two modes of carrying out this scheme: (1) by means of an association of landowners; (2) by means of a proprietary public company. The former obtains in Eastern Prussia, but the latter is exclusively found in Western Europe.

Crédit Foncier companies have been founded in Hamburg (1782), Western Prussia (1787), Belgium (1841), France (1852), England (1863). Similar companies were formed in all the states of Europe, in India, and in our colonies and dependencies. *A. G. Henriques.* See *France*, May, 1890.

CRÉDIT MOBILIER: a joint-stock company with this name was established at Paris by Isaac and Emile Péreire, and others, 18 Nov. 1852.

It took up or originated trading enterprises of all kinds, applying to them the principle of *commandite*, or limited liabilities; and was authorised to supersede or buy in any other companies (replacing their shares or bonds with its own scrip), and also to carry on the ordinary business of banking. The funds were to be obtained by a paid-up capital of 2⅜ millions sterling, the issue of obligations at not less than 45 days' date or sight, and the receipt of money on deposit or current account. The society apparently prospered; but was

considered by experienced persons a near approach to Law's bank of 1716.
Several of the directors failed, Sept. 1857, no dividend paid . . . . May, 1858
Many companies based on its principles established in London 1863
Emile and Isaac Péreire withdrew from the management; the company failed, and the capital was said to have disappeared . . . . . Oct. 1867
The high court of appeal decided that MM. Péreire and other directors were responsible for their acts, and that damages should be given to the shareholders . . . . 1 Aug. 1868
Emile Péreire died 6 Jan., 1875; Isaac died 12 July, 1880

CREEDS, see *Confessions of Faith*. J. R. Lumby's *History of the Creeds* appeared 1874.

CREMATION, see *Burning the Dead*. Crematoria, or buildings for reducing the dead human body to ashes are now (1903) established at Woking, Golder's Green, Hendon, Hull, Manchester, Liverpool, Glasgow, and other places. On the continent there are crematoria at Rome, Milan, Cremona, Padua, and other cities.

CREMERA, BATTLE OF, see *Fabii*.

CREMONA (N. Italy), a city founded by the Romans, 221 B.C. It became an independent republic in 1107, but was frequently subjugated by its neighbours, Milan and Venice, and partook of their fortunes. In Nov. 1859 it became part of the kingdom of Italy. Cremona was eminent for violin makers from about 1550 to 1750.

CREOSOTE, see *Creasote*.

CRESCENT, a symbol of sovereignty among the Greeks and Romans, and the device of Byzantium, now Constantinople, whence the Turks adopted it. The Crescent has given name to three orders of knighthood; founded by Charles I. of Naples, 1268; by René of Anjou, in 1448; by the sultan Selim, in 1801.

CRESPY (N. France). Here was signed a treaty between Charles V. of Germany and Francis I. of France, 18 Sept. 1544. The former renounced Burgundy, and the latter Italy.

CRESTS are ascribed to the Carians. Richard I. (1189) had a crest on the helmet resembling a plume of feathers. The English kings had generally crowns above their helmets: that of Richard II. 1377, was surmounted by a lion on a cap of dignity; see *Crecy*. Alexander III. of Scotland, 1249, had a plume of feathers; and the helmet of Robert I. was surmounted by a crown, 1306; and that of James I. by a lion. 1424. In the 15th and 16th centuries, the crest was described to be a figure placed upon a wreath, coronet, or cap of maintenance. *Gwillim*. Fairbairn's "Book of Crests," edited by A. C. Fox-Davies, published Nov. 1892. The badge of the Red Dragon added to the prince of Wales's crest, Dec. 1901.

CRETAN DISTRESS FUND, founded in London by the duke of Westminster and others, *Times*, 8 Feb. 1897.

CRETE, see *Candia*.

CREVANT-SUR-YONNE (N. France), was besieged by John Stuart, earl of Buchan, with a French army, July, 1423, and relieved by the earl of Salisbury with an army of English and Burgundians. After a severe contest, the French were totally defeated.

CREVELDT, near Cleves (W. Prussia). Here on 23 June, 1758, prince Ferdinand of Brunswick defeated the French under the count of Clermont.

CREWE, Cheshire, the site of a great junction and works of the London and North-Western railway since 1840. The company presented a beautiful park to the town in 1887-88. Crewe was incorporated in 1877. Great fire at the railway works; estimated damage under 3,000*l*., 28 March, 1892. Population, 1881, 24,385; 1891, 28,761; 1901, 42,074.

CRICKET, an ancient English game, said to be identical with the "club ball" of the 14th century; mentioned in 1598. Rules were laid down in 1774 by a committee of noblemen and gentlemen, including the duke of Dorset and sir Horace Mann. In 1861 the All England Eleven gained and lost games in Australia; in Sept. 1868, they beat the New York Twenty-two. In 1873-4 they were beaten at Melbourne.

Eleven Australians visited England, and after gaining ten games and losing five, gained one against "Players of All England," . . . . 3 Sept. 1878
Thirteen Australians visited England in May 1880; they won 21 out of 37 matches, and lost 4; the others were drawn or indecisive; they were victors in a match with the "Players of England" at the Crystal Palace . . . 27, 28, 29 Sept. 1880
The Australians, previously victorious, were defeated at Manchester by N. England team 16 Sept. 1882
England beats Australia . . . . 23 July, 1884
Australia wins 12 out of 20 matches in . . . . ,,
North of England beat Australians . . 3 Sept. ,,
English cricketers in Australia victorious . Jan. 1885
Frequent contests with the Australians with varied success . . . . 1885—8
Lord Sheffield and his English eleven at Adelaide, in 26 matches, win 13, lose 2, 11 drawn . March, 1892
Suicide of Mr. Scotton, eminent cricketer, 9 July, 1893
A good cricket year through the long drought; eighth visit of Australians, 36 matches, 18 won, 10 lost, and 8 drawn . . . . April—Sept. ,,
Victory of the English eleven over "All Australia" at Melbourne . . . . 6 March, 1895
Dr. W. G. Grace, aged 46, completed his hundredth "hundred" score at Bristol, in a match between Gloucester and Somerset, mid-May, 1895; national testimonial subscribed for . . June *et seq.* ,,
3rd and last test match (England and Australia) at Kennington Oval, won by the English by 66 runs 12 Aug. 1896
Australians generally victors in the counties ,,
Prince Ranjitsinhji, an eminent player, publishes "The Jubilee book on Cricket" . . Aug. 1897
First test match between England and Australia won by the English, at Sydney, 17 Dec. 1897; 2nd by the Australians, 5 Jan. 1898; 3rd by them, 19 Jan.; 4th by them, 2 Feb.; 5th by them, 2 March; other matches played . . 1898
George Giffen's "With Bat and Ball" published ,,
George Ulyett, famous player, born 1851, died 18 June; J. D. Walker, famous Harrow player, died 6 July . . . . ,,
Strong team of Australians visit England; 5 test matches: *one* won by the Australians at Lords by 10 wickets, 17 May; the rest drawn, May-Sept. 1899
Richard Daft, the famous Notts cricketer, died, aged 64 . . . . 18 July, 1900
Mr. Wm. Yardley, fine batsman, and writer of burlesques, died . . . . . 29 Oct. ,,
George Lohmann, famous player, died, aged 36, 1 Dec. 1901
Australians win 3 out of 4 test matches against Mr. MacLaren's English eleven in Australia, Feb. 1902; the English won the return match at Adelaide . . . . 18 March, 1902
First test match, at Birmingham, ends in a draw, 31 May; 2nd won by Australia, 10 June; 3rd and 4th by them, Manchester, 5, 26 July; 5th by England at the Oval . . . . . 13 Aug. ,,
Meeting of M.C.C., proposal to widen the wicket carried, but not by the requisite two-thirds majority . . . . 6 April, 1903
Result of season's county matches, 1903, Middlesex champion county.

CRIME. About 1856 it was computed that a fifteenth part of the population of the United Kingdom lived by crime. The increase in education and manufactures is gradually reducing this proportion. From 1848 to 1865 there had been no commitment for political offences, such as treason or sedition. The returns of thirty-two years showed that crime absolutely and relatively diminished (Sept. 1866). "Judicial Statistics" for England and Wales, with abundant details, published by the government annually, began with the year 1856; the new series (in two parts, civil and criminal, published separately) began in 1893; comparative tables, 1857-96. See *Murder*, *Executions*, *Trials*, *Poisoning*, *Prevention of Crime*, *Anthropology*, &c.

CONVICTIONS (BY TRIAL) IN ENGLAND AND WALES.

	Persons.	Cap. Off.		Persons.	Cap. Off.
1847	21,542	—	1875	10,954	33
1849	21,001	66	1876	12,195	32
1850	20,537	49	1877	11,942	34
1851	21,579	70	1878	12,473	20
1852	21,304	61	1879	12,525	34
1853	20,756	55	1880	11,214	28
1854	23,047	49	1881	11,353	23
1855	19,971	50	1882	11,699	22
1856	14,734	69	1883	11,347	23
1857	15,307	54	1884	11,134	38
1858	13,246	53	1885	10,500	25
1859	12,470	52	1886	10,686	35
1860	12,068	48	1887	10,338	35
1861	13,879	50	1888	10,561	36
1862	15,312	29	1889	9,348	20
1863	15,799	29	1890	9,242	24
1864	14,726	32	1891	9,055	19
1865	14,740	20	1892	9,607	22
1866	14,254	26	1893	9,694	28
1867	14,207	27	1894	9,518	29
1868	15,033	21	1895	3,010	19
1869	14,340	18	1896	3,972	19
1870	12,953	15	1898	9,133	27
1871	11,946	13	1899	8,608	29
1872	10,862	30	1900	7,975	20
1873	11,089	18	1901	8,631	28
1874	11,509	26			

See *Executions*.

Act for improving the administration of criminal justice passed 7 Aug. 1851.

The Criminal Justice Act authorises justices, with the consent of prisoners, to pass sentence for short periods, instead of committing them to trial, 1855.

Cost of criminal prosecutions in England and Wales: 1856, 194,912*l.*; 1878, 148,103*l.*; 1883, 144,026*l.*; 1886, 141,329*l.*; year ending 31 March, 1890, 131,202*l.* *Ticket-of-leave* system instituted by 16 & 17 Vict. c. 99, passed in 1853; see *Transportation*. 2666 persons were liberated on *tickets-of-leave* in 1856.

On 17 Feb. 1857, of 126 persons thus liberated, 58 were believed to be living honestly.

In 1861, 1862, and 1863, the system was considered to have failed through the numerous crimes committed by *ticket-of-leavers*; it was modified by the Penal Servitude act, in 1864.

Sentences to penal servitude, 1869, 2006; in 1870, 1788; 1886, 910; 1887, 948; 1890, 729; 1891, 751; 1892, 894; 1893, 960; 1896, 255; 1898, 473; 1899, 736; 1900, 728.

Criminal classes at large in England and Wales: estimated number, 1869-70, 45,800; 1878-9, 35,469; 1886-7, 28,729; 1887-8, 28,103; 1888-9, 27,136; 1889-90, 26,406; 1890-1, 25,627; 1891-2, 25,220; 1899 (habitual criminals), 5,749; 1900, 5,256.

"Statistical Criminal Act" passed . . . 11 Aug. 1869

Prevention of crimes act passed (see *Evidence*) Aug. 1871 and 1898.

Great decrease in crimes in relation to the increase of population 1861-1897

Confirmed by lord Coleridge for 1874-84 . 19 Jan. 1885

The number of female convicts fallen in ten years from 1477 to 706, announced . . . 4 Nov. 1887

CRIME—International Congress for the prevention and repression of crime met in the Middle Temple, London . . . . 3 July, 1872

Third international congress opened . . 25 Aug. 1891

Convict Supervision Office, good results reported by Mr. J. Monro 1886

A committee on the identification of criminals advocate the adoption of M. Bertillon's anthropometrical system and Mr. Francis Galton's method of classifying finger-prints, March; adoption ordered . . . . Sept. 1894

Internat. congress St. Petersburg, 17 Sept.; Moscow, 23 Sept. 1902

Summary convictions in 1893 in England and Wales, 649,371; in 1900, 760,704. Pardons granted, 439 in 1893; 35,144 in 1900.

CRIMES ACTS, see *Prevention*.

CRIMEA, or CRIM TARTARY, a peninsula in the Euxine or Black Sea, the ancient *Taurica Chersonesus*, colonised by the Greeks about 550 B.C. The Milesians founded the kingdom of Bosporus, now Kertch, which about 108 B.C. formed part of the dominion of Mithridates, king of Pontus, whose descendants continued to rule the country under Roman protection till the irruption of the Goths, Huns, &c. about A.D. 258. About 1237 it fell into the hands of the Mongols under Genghis Khan; soon after the Venetians established commercial stations, with a lucrative trade, but were supplanted by the Genoese, who were permitted to rebuild and fortify Kaffa, about 1261. In 1475 Mahomet II. expelled the Genoese, and subjected the peninsula to the Ottoman yoke; permitting the government to remain in the hands of the native khans, but closing the Black Sea to Western Europe. In 1774, by the intervention of the empress Catherine II., the Crimea recovered its independence: but on the abdication of the khan in 1783, the Russians took possession of the country, after a war with Turkey, and retained it by the treaty of Jassy, 9 Jan. 1792. The Crimea (now Taurida), was divided into eight governments in 1802. War having been declared against Russia by England and France, 28 March, 1854, large masses of troops were sent to the East, which, after remaining some time at Gallipoli, and other places, sailed for Varna, where they disembarked 29 May. An expedition against the Crimea having been determined on, the allied British, French, and Turkish forces, amounting to 58,000 men (25,000 British), commanded by lord Raglan and marshal St. Arnaud, sailed from Varna, 3 Sept. and landed on the 14th, 15th, and 16th, without opposition, at Old Fort, near Eupatoria, about 30 miles from Sebastopol. On the 20th they attacked the Russians, between 40,000 and 50,000 strong (under prince Menschikoff), entrenched on the heights of Alma, supposed to be unassailable. After a sharp contest the Russians were totally routed. See *Alma* and *Russo-Turkish War*. Peace was proclaimed in April, 1856, and the allies quitted the Crimea 12 July following.

CRIMINAL LAW PROCEDURE (IRELAND) ACT, (see *Ireland*) 50 & 51 Vict. c. 20, passed 19 July, 1887, provides for summary jurisdiction by magistrates, special juries, change of place of trial, proclamation of districts, prohibition of dangerous associations, and continuance of 44 & 45 Vict. c. 5, and 49 & 50 Vict. c. 24.

Mr. Dillon's motion for 2nd reading of repeal bill rejected, 220-141, 19 April, 1899.

Act for Scotland passed 16 Sept. 1887 to simplify and amend the Criminal Law of Scotland.

CRIMINAL LAWS OF ENGLAND. Their great severity, pointed out by sir Samuel Romilly, sir James Mackintosh, and others, about 1818, was considerably mitigated by sir R. Peel's acts, passed 1826-8. The criminal law acts were consolidated by 24 and 25 Vict. cc. 94-100, 1861. Some defects were amended by an act passed in 1867. The punishment of death is now virtually restricted to treason and wilful murder. See *Evidence*.

Sir J. F. Stephen's "Digest of the Criminal Laws" published, 1877; and "History of the Criminal Law of England," published 1883
Bill for amending law relating to indictable offences (resembling a digest and code) brought in by sir John Holker, attorney-general . 14 May, 1878
Referred to royal commission (justices Blackburn and Lush and sir James F. Stephen . 8 July, „
The bill brought in and withdrawn 1879
Criminal Law Amendment Act (relating to women) passed . . . . 14 Aug. 1885

CRIMINOLOGY, as a branch of anthropology which treats of crime and criminals, is based on the researches of Dr. Lambroso, of Turin, the author of "L'Uomo Delinquente," published 1875 (several editions). In this work he expounds his theory of criminology, and indicates the physical and mental defects by which the habitual criminal is characterised. The treatment of criminals at Elmira, with the view to their reclamation, is based upon criminal anthropology.

CRIMISUS, a river in Sicily, near which Timoleon defeated the Carthaginians, 339 B.C.

CRIMPING-HOUSES were used to entrap persons into the army; hence the name of "crimp sergeant." Some of them in London were destroyed by the populace, in consequence of a young man who had been enticed into one being killed in endeavouring to escape, 16 Sept. 1794.

CRINAN CANAL, Argyleshire, cut through Kintyre peninsula, 1793-1801: 15 locks; saves about 115 miles.

CRINOLINE (a French word, meaning stuff made of *crin*, hair) is the modern name of the "fardingale" of the time of queen Elizabeth, hoop-like petticoats made of whalebone, &c., revived in France and England since 1855. They have frequently occasioned loss of life, by coming in contact with fire and machinery. In No. 116 of the *Tatler*, published 5 Jan. 1710, is an amusing trial of the hoop-petticoat then in fashion.

A "No Crinoline League" was originated by "John Strange Winter" (Henrietta E. V. Stannard), a popular writer, in the view of a revival of crinolines, and was well supported . . . Jan. 1893

CRIPPLEGATE (London), was so-called from the lame beggars who sat there, so early as the year 1010. The gate was new built by the brewers of London in 1244; and was pulled down and sold for 91*l*. in July, 1760. The poet Milton was buried in the church near it, 12 Nov. 1674. Cripplegate institute (founded by the duke of York, July, 1894) opened by the lord mayor, 4 Nov. 1896. See *London* and *Fires*, Nov. 1897.

CRIPPLES' HOME, Marylebone-road, established 1851, for crippled girls to be taught suitable trades. The Cripples' Nursery, Old Quebec-street and Margate, was established 1862.

CRISPIN AND CRISPIANUS are said to have been two saints, born at Rome, from whence they travelled to Soissons, in France, to propagate the Christian religion. They worked as shoemakers; but the governor of the town discovering them to be Christians, ordered them to be beheaded, about 288. Their day is 25 Oct.

CRITERION THEATRE, Regent's Circus, Piccadilly, opened by Spiers and Pond, 21 March, 1874.

CRITH (from the Greek *krithē*, a barleycorn or small weight), a term suggested by Dr. A. W. Hofmann (about 1864) to express the volume-weight of gases; a cube containing 1 litre of hydrogen (0·0896 gramme) to be the unit. Hydrogen being 1 crith, oxygen will be 16, nitrogen 14 criths.

CRITICS. The first society of them was formed 276 B.C. *Blair*. Varro, Cicero, Apollonius, and Aristarchus were ancient critics. In modern times the *Journal des Sçavans* was the earliest periodical critical work. It was originated by Denis de Sallo, ecclesiastical councillor in the parliament of France, and was first published at Paris, 30 May, 1655, and is still continued. Jean Le Clerc's "Ars Critica," published 1696, is said to be the earliest systematic treatise. The first work of this kind in England was the *Review* of Daniel Defoe (the term being invented by himself), published in Feb. 1703. The *Works of the Learned* began 1710, and the *Waies of Literature* in 1714; discontinued in 1722. See *Reviews*.

The legality of fair criticism was established in the English courts, in Feb. 1794, when an action that excited great attention, brought by an author against a reviewer for a severe critique upon his work, was determined in favour of the defendant on the principle that criticism is allowable, however sharp, if just, and not malicious. See *Trials*, 1875.

CROATIA, conquered by Coloman, king of Hungary, in 1102, was with that country united to Austria in 1526.

The Croatian diet abolished . . . . Nov. 1861
The Croats protest against incorporation with Hungary . . . . 25 May, 1867
Their diet (including Croatia and Sclavonia), at Agram dissolved . . . . . 27 May, „
The union of Croatia with Hungary recognised by a Croatian deputation . . . . . 27 May, 1868
Croatian delegates enter the Hungarian diet 24 Nov. „
The emperor and empress visit Agram 9-10 March, 1865
Riots in Agram and other places against the Jews, complicated with Sclavonic jealousy of Hungary, and desire for autonomy, Aug.; the ban superseded by gen. Ramberg, special commissioner about 6 Sept. 1883
Conflicts with the military, 8-10 Sept.; ten rioters killed . . . . 20 Sept. „
Agitation increasing; demand for separation from Hungary . . . . . . about 22 Sept. „
38 rioters sentenced to imprisonment, &c. 30 Sept. „
Count Khün-Hedervary, appointed ban 4 Dec. „
The diet opened at Agram—important meeting 17 Dec. „
Continued political disagreements 1884
Diet dissolved . . . . 22 Jan. „
Again dissolved . . . . 27 Aug. „
The separatist movement said to be totally quelled by the ban after much resistance . . Nov. 1887
Visit of the emperor to Agram; warmly received mid-Oct. 1895
Disturbances, agitation against the Magyars; 3 officials murdered by peasants in Lasinia, martial law, reported . . . . 29 Sept. 1897
Ferry-boat wrecked on the Kulpa river, 23 deaths; reported . . . . 16 Sept. 1901
Riots in Agram, houses and shops wrecked, troops called out, over 100 persons injured, 31 Aug., 1 Sept.; capt. Wittas beaten by the mob, martial law proclaimed . . . . 3 Sept. 1902
Further rioting . 27-30 Mar. and later in July 1903

CROCKERY-WARE see *Pottery*.

CROFTERS and Cottars, the holders of small portions of land, and the labourers in the highlands and islands of Scotland.

A royal commission appointed 22 March, 1883 (Francis baron Napier and others), to inquire into their condition, issue their report and describe their state as not being worse than formerly, but acknowledge the existence of many startling grievances relating to the tenure of land, high rents, the deficiency of education, of postal communication, of roads, &c. They recommend, among other remedies, the revival of the ancient highland townships with common

privileges, limiting the power of the superior lords, &c. . . . . 28 April, 1884
Highland Land Law Reform Association began to work . . . . March, 1883
Agitation begun at Dingwall by the Highland Land Law Reform Association . . . . . Sept. 1884
Seditious circulars threatening violence; troops conveyed to Skye; tranquillity restored by free church ministers . . . . . . 15 Nov. „
Meeting at Inverness of chief landlords; conciliatory favourable changes proposed . . 14 Jan. 1885
Act giving crofters fixity of tenure, enlargement of holdings, and state-aid to fisheries 25 June 1886; amended 1888
Riotous resistance to ejectments at Greenhill Farm, &c., Isle of Tiree, Hebrides; 50 police repulsed by 300 men; marines sent to the Isle 25 July; order restored; six crofters apprehended up to 8 Aug. sentenced to three months' imprisonment, 14 Dec. 1886
Raid of 2,000 cottars on Park and Aline deer forests in the Island of Lewis, 22 Nov.; stopped 23 Nov. 1887
Riots at Stornoway, Lewis; the fences of the sheep farm of Mr. Samuel Newall destroyed and the sheep dispersed; severe conflict between the crofters and the police and military; many wounded; the rioters dispersed with difficulty 9 Jan. 1888, many arrested; 16 sentenced to imprisonment . . . . 3 Feb. 1888
Lewis reported quiet . . . . . . 28 Jan. „
Crofters colonization commission appointed by Imperial and Canada governments . . 28 Dec. „
The Canadian settlements reported prosperous, March 1891; moderate report . . . Oct. 1896
Royal commission to consider the means of enlarging the crofters holdings appointed about 25 Nov. 1892; report issued . . . . . . May, „
New crofters holding bill read 2nd time (commons) 11 June, 1895

CROIX, ST., a W. India Island, purchased from the French by Christian VI. king of Denmark, in 1733; taken by sir Alexander Cochrane, 22 Dec. 1807; restored in 1814.

CROMLECHS, ancient monuments, formerly considered to be Druidical altars, but now believed to be connected with burials. One still exists in Anglesey: similar structures have been found in Ireland, India, Arabia, and other countries.

CRONIN CASE. See *United States*, 1889.

CRONSTADT, Russia, founded by Peter the Great, 1710, and received its name (Crown-town) in 1721. It was not attacked by the fleets in the war with Russia, 1854-5. Connected with St. Petersburg since 1884 by the Cronstadt ship canal. Murder of the governor, rear-admiral Ragvozoff, and suicide of Peninsky, the murderer, a discharged official, 17 Aug. 1894.

CROOK, a bishop's pastoral staff or crook, distinct from the crosier. Many pastoral staffs have been presented to English bishops from 1872-1903.

CROPREDY BRIDGE, near Banbury, Oxfordshire. Here the royalists defeated sir William Waller and the army of the parliament, 29 June, 1644.

CROQUET. This game, which became common in Britain about 1850, is said to be a revival of the old *Pall Mall* (*which see*). It was practically superseded by Lawn Tennis, 1877-97, but since the latter date has been much played. The hoops used in the game as at present (1903) are much narrower than those formerly in use, and the game generally has been made more scientific.

CROSIER, a staff surmounted by a cross, borne before an archbishop, was in use in the 4th century. The bearing a crosier before ecclesiastics is mentioned in the life of St. Cæsareus of Arles about 500. The term "crozier" is sometimes erroneously applied to the pastoral staff of a bishop, which terminates in an ornamental curve or crook.

CROSS. That on which the Redeemer suffered on Mount Calvary, was said to have been found at Jerusalem, with two others, deep in the ground, by the empress Helena, mother of Constantine I., 3 May, 326 (termed the *Invention of the Cross*); commemorated annually on that day. It was carried away by Chosroes, king of Persia, on the plundering of Jerusalem; but was recovered by the emperor Heraclius (who defeated him in battle), 14 Sept. 615, and that day has since been commemorated as "the festival of the Exaltation of the Cross," established in 642.

It is asserted by church writers that a great shining cross was seen in the heavens by Constantine, and that it led him to adopt it on his standard, with the inscription *"In hoc signo vinces,"* "Under this sign thou shalt conquer." With this (Labarum) he advanced to Rome, where he vanquished Maxentius, 27 Oct. 312. *Lenglet.*
Signing with the Cross was first practised by Christians to distinguish themselves from the Pagans, about 110
In the time of Tertullian, it was deemed efficacious against poison, witchcraft, &c. 260
Crosses in churches and chambers were introduced about 431; and set up on steeples about . . 568
12 crosses in honour of queen Eleanor were set up in the places where her hearse rested, between 1290 (when she died) and 1307; repaired crosses remain at Teddington, Waltham, and Northampton . 1892
Crosses and idolatrous pictures were removed from churches, and crosses in the streets demolished by order of parliament 1641
Maids of the Cross were a community of young women who made vows of poverty, chastity, and obedience, instituted in 1625
The order of *Ladies of the Star of the Cross* was instituted by the empress Eleonora di Gonzaga, wife of Leopold I., in 1668

CROSSED CHEQUES, see *Drafts*.

CROTONA (S. Italy), a city founded by the Achæan Greeks about 710 B.C. Here Pythagoras taught about 520. The Crotons destroyed Sybaris, 510.

CROWN. An Amalekite brought Saul's crown to David, 1056 B.C. (2 *Sam.* i.) The first Roman who wore a crown was Tarquin the Elder, 616 B.C. The crown was first a fillet tied round the head; afterwards it was formed of leaves and flowers, and also of stuffs adorned with jewels. See *Tiara*.

The crown of Alfred had two little bells attached (872); it is said to have been long preserved at Westminster, and may have been that described in the parliamentary inventory taken in 1649.
Athelstan's crown resembled an earl's coronet, 929.
William I. wore his crown on a cap, adorned with points, 1066.
Richard III. introduced the crosses, 1483.
Henry VII. introduced the arches, 1485.
The crown and regalia of England were pledged to the city of London by Richard II. for 2000*l*. in 1386: see the king's receipt on redeeming them. *Rymer.*
The crown of Charles II., made in 1660, is the oldest existing in England; see *Blood's Conspiracy*.
The *Imperial State Crown of England* was made by Rundell and Bridges, in 1838, principally with jewels taken from old crowns. It contains one large ruby, 1 large sapphire, 16 sapphires, 11 emeralds, 4 rubies, 1363 brilliants, 1273 rose diamonds, 147 table diamonds, 4 drop-shaped pearls, and 273 pearls. *Professor Tennant.*
Mr. Cyril Davenport's "The English Regalia in the Tower of London" published July, 1897, with photographs, &c.
Queen Alexandra's coronation crown of diamonds (3,688), 22 oz. 15 dwt. in weight, designed and executed by Messrs. Carrington, 1902.

CROWN OF INDIA, Imperial Order of, instituted by Queen Victoria (to commemorate the assumption of the title of empress, 1 Jan. 1877), for princesses of the royal family, distinguished Indian and British ladies, and wives of viceroys and governors and secretaries of state for India; 31 Dec. 1877. Twelve ladies (the late marchioness of Salisbury and others) invested, 29 April, 1878.

CROWN LANDS. The revenue arising from those in England is now nearly all subject to parliament, which annually provides for the support of the sovereign and government about 375,000*l.* The revenue of the duchy of Cornwall belongs to the prince of Wales even during his minority. Henry VII. (1485) resumed those lands which had been given to their followers by the sovereigns of the house of York. The hereditary estates of the crown were largely bestowed on their courtiers by the sovereigns — especially by the Stuarts. The income of the crown, formerly derived from lands, royalties, &c., now belongs to the state exchequer, see *Civil List*. The crown lands act passed, 1894. In the year ending 31 March, 1891, the receipts were 515,737*l.* 3*s.* 10*d.*, the expenditure 87,121*l.* 19*s.* 6*d.*; 1899, 430,000*l.*; 1900, 450,000*l.*; 1901, 500,000*l.*; 1902, 455,000*l.*; 1903, 435,000*l.*

CROWNS in gold were coined by Henry VIII., 1522. Crowns and half-crowns of silver were coined in England by Edward VI. in 1553. None were coined in 1861, and they were gradually withdrawn from circulation. The coinage of half-crowns was resumed in 1874, after an inquiry as to their utility. The coinage of silver crowns recommenced in 1887.

CROWS. An act passed for their destruction in England, 24 Hen. VIII. 1532. Crows were anciently employed as letter-bearers, as carrier-pigeons are now.

CROYDON, Surrey, granted to Lanfranc, archbishop of Canterbury, about 1070. Archbishop Whitgift's hospital was founded in 1596. The fine old parish church was burnt, 5, 6 Jan. 1867. Croydon incorporated by charter, 15 Feb. 1883. Polytechnic institution opened by the archbishop of Canterbury, 22 Dec. 1891. New Grand theatre opened by Mr. Beerbohm Tree and company, 6 April, 1896. Visit of the prince and princess of Wales; town hall, courts of justice, and free library opened, 19 May, 1896. Electric tramway opened, 26 Sept. 1901. Population, 1881, 78,811; 1891, 102,697; 1901, 133,885.

CROYLAND or CROWLAND, Lincolnshire. The foundation of an abbey here was ascribed to king Ethelbald, 716. Its history, by Ingulph, printed by Peter of Blois, 1684, of which a translation by H. T. Riley was published by Mr. Bohn, 1854, is generally considered fabulous.

CROZIER, see *Crosier*.

CRUCIFIX, the cross with the figure of Christ attached to it, first known in the fourth, came into general use in the eighth century.

CRUCIFIXION. A mode of execution common among the Assyrians, Egyptians, Persians, Carthaginians, Greeks, and Romans. Ariarathes, of Cappadocia, aged 80, vanquished by Perdiccas, and discovered among the prisoners, was flayed alive, and nailed to a cross, with his principal officers, 322 B.C. Jesus Christ was crucified 3 April, A.D. 33. *Usher*. (15 April, A.D. 29, *Clinton*; 28 March, A.D. 31, *Hales*; *probably* 7 April, A.D. 30, *Lynn*). Crucifixion was ordered to be discontinued by Constantine, 330. *Lenglet*.

CRUELTY TO ANIMALS, see *Animals*, *Children*, and *Vivisection*.

CRUSADES (French *Croisades*), wars undertaken to drive the infidels from Jerusalem and the "Holy Land." Peter Gautier, the Hermit, an officer of Amiens, on his return from pilgrimage incited pope Urban II. to expel infidels from the city where Christ had taught. Urban convened a council of 310 bishops at Clermont in France, at which the ambassadors of the chief Christian potentates assisted, and gave Peter the commission to summon Europe to a general war, 1094. The first crusade was published; an army of 300,000 men was raised, of which Peter had the direction, and Godfrey de Bouillon the command, 1095. The warriors wore a red cross upon the right shoulder: and their motto was *Volonté de Dieu*, "God's will."
—The French government have published some of the Historians of the Crusades (1844-86).

I. Crusade (1095) ended by Jerusalem being taken by assault, 15 July, 1099, and Godfrey de Bouillon made king.
II. Preached by St. Bernard in 1146, headed by emperor Conrad II., and Louis VII. of France. Crusaders defeated; Jerusalem lost in 1187.
III. Emperor Frederick Barbarossa, &c., in 1188, joined by Philip II. of France and Richard I. of England, in 1190. Glorious, but fruitless.
IV. 1195, by emperor Henry VI.; successful till his death in 1197.
V. Proclaimed by Innocent III., 1198. Baldwin, count of Flanders, attacked the Greeks, and took Constantinople in 1203. His companions returned.
VI. In 1216. In 1229, emperor Frederick II. obtained possession of Jerusalem on a truce for ten years. In 1240, Richard, earl of Cornwall, arrived at Palestine, but soon departed.
VII. By Louis IX. (St. Louis), 1248, who was defeated and taken prisoner at Mansourah, 5 April, 1250; released by ransom; truce of ten years.
VIII. and last, in 1270, by the same prince, who died of a contagious disease, at Carthage, in Africa, 2 Aug. Prince Edward, afterwards Edward I. of England, was at Acre, 1271. In 1291, the soldan took Acre, and the Christians were driven out of Syria.

CRUTCHED FRIARS, who bore the figure of the cross on their back and breast; from which circumstance they derived their name, a corruption of *croisiers*, "cross bearers," an order founded at Bologna about 1169. They are also called Trinitarians. They had a monastery in London in a district still called Crutched Friars.

CRUZ, see *Santa Cruz*.

CRYOLITE, a Greenland mineral, a fluoride of aluminium and sodium, employed in procuring metallic aluminium in 1855.

CRYOPHORUS, an instrument (invented by Dr. Wollaston about 1812) to demonstrate the relation between evaporation at low temperatures and the production of cold.

CRYPTOGRAPH, an apparatus for writing in cipher, invented by sir Charles Wheatstone, and made known in 1868, in which different key-words may be employed, and it is said, absolute secrecy ensured. A cryptographic machine was patented, 1860. See *Cipher*.

A system of secret writing described in "Archiv der Mathematik" 1795
Professor J. F. Lorenz published a system at Magdeburg 1806
Joseph Ludwig Kluber published "Kryptographik" 1809
Messrs. Thos. De la Rue published Mr. Wm. Henry Rochfort's system of secret writing termed "Arcanography," resembling Lorenz's . 1836

Mr. A. L. Flamm patented an improvement upon this system . . . . . about Oct. 1875
Mr. Weir's cryptograph, in which type-writing is employed, exhibited London . . . 19 Oct. 1889

CRYPTON, a new gas discovered by prof. Ramsay by means of the spectroscope, reported, 6 June, 1898.

CRYSTALLOGRAPHY is the science relating to the symmetrical forms assumed by substances passing from the liquid to the solid state. Romé de Lisle published his "Essai de Cristallographie," in 1772; but René-Just Haüy is regarded as the founder of the modern school of crystallography (1801). *Whewell.* Dana, Dufresnoy, and Miller, are eminent modern writers on this subject.

CRYSTAL PALACE, Hyde Park, London; see *Exhibition of* 1851.

CRYSTAL PALACE, Sydenham. The Exhibition building of 1851 having been surrendered to Messrs. Fox and Henderson on 1 Dec. 1851, the materials were sold for 70,000*l.* to a company, who soon after commenced re-erecting the Crystal Palace on its present site, near Sydenham in Kent, under the direction of sir Joseph Paxton, Owen Jones, Digby Wyatt, and others. The proposed capital of 500,000*l.* (in 100,000 shares of 5*l.* each) was increased in Jan. 1853 to a million pounds. In Feb. 1887, it was stated that the total expenditure had been 3,004,737*l.*; receipts, 4,409,969*l.*; paid for debentures, &c., 1,405,232*l.*; number of visitors above 50,000,000. Bill for new financial arrangements passed.

First column raised by S. Laing, M.P. . 5 Aug. 1852
During the progress of the works as many as 6400 men were engaged at one time. By the fall of scaffolding, 12 men were killed . . 15 Aug. 1853
Dinner given to professor Owen and others in the interior of the model of the iguanodon, constructed by Mr. Waterhouse Hawkins 31 Dec. ,,
The palace opened by the queen . 10 June, 1854
Grand musical *fête* on behalf of the Patriotic Fund, 28 Oct. ,,
The palace visited by the emperor and empress of the French, &c. . . . . 20 April, 1855
First grand display of the great fountains, before the queen and 20,000 spectators . 18 June, 1856
The receipts were 115,627*l.*; the expenditure, 87,872*l.*, not including payments for preference shares, &c., in year ending . . 30 April, 1857
The preliminary Handel festivals (see *Handel*), 15, 17, 19 June, 1857; and . . . . 2 July, 1858
On the Fast day (for the Indian mutiny) rev. C. Spurgeon preached here to 23,000 persons; 476*l.* were collected, to which the C.P. company added 200*l.* . . . . 7 Oct. 1857
Centenary of the birth of Robert Burns celebrated: the directors awarded 50*l.* to a prize poem on the subject, which was obtained by Miss Isa Craig, 25 Jan. 1859
The Handel festival . . . . 20, 22, 24 June, ,,
Festival kept in honour of Schiller, 10 Nov. 1859; of Mendelssohn . . . . . . 4 May, 1860
London charity children sing here . 6 June, ,,
3000 Orpheonistes (French musical amateurs) perform choral music, 25 June; the Imperial band of Guides perform, 26 June; both dine in the palace, 30 June, ,,
115 brass bands perform . . . . 10 July, ,,
Annual rose show began . . . . ,,
North wing injured by a gale of wind, 20, 21 Feb. 1861
Haydn's "Creation" performed (Costa, conductor) 1 May, ,,
Blondin's performances on an elevated rope begin here (he plays on violin, cooks, simulates falling, &c.) . . . . 1 June, ,,
Successful Handel festival: a new arched roof constructed for the orchestra: about 4000 vocal and instrumental performers . 23, 25, 27 June, 1862
Successful Handel festival . . 26, 28, 30 June, 1865
North wing, containing tropical department, the Alhambra, and other courts, destroyed by fire (about 150,000*l.* damage) . . 30 Dec. 1866
Prince of Wales present at a grand concert to raise funds to restore the palace . . . 26 June, 1867
Visit of the viceroy of Egypt (gives 500*l.*), July; of the sultan (gives 1000*l.*) . . . . 16 July, ,,
Conservative working men's demonstration 11 Nov. ,,
Meeting of shareholders decide by ballot that free tickets shall not be issued to admit non-shareholders on Sundays . . . . . 31 Dec. ,,
North wing restored and re-opened . . 15 Feb. 1868
An Aeronautical Exhibition opened . 25 June, ,,
Protestant meeting to defend the Irish Church, 17 Aug. ,,
Reception of the vicomte de Lesseps . . July, 1870
Death of Mr. Robert K. Bowley, fourteen years manager of the company . . . 25 Aug. ,,
Successful Handel festival . . 19, 21, 23 June, 1871
The grand duke Wladimir of Russia entertained here by the prince of Wales . . 26 June, ,,
Cat show, native and foreign . . 13 July, 2 Dec. ,,
Dividend on stock, 1½ per cent. . . . . Dec. ,,
Inauguration of the great aquarium by professor Owen . . . . Jan. 1872
Lecture by professor Flower . . . . 12 Jan. ,,
Bird show opens . . . . 10 Feb. ,,
Thanksgiving festival for the recovery of the prince of Wales . . . . 1 May, ,,
Dog show opens . . . . 4 June, ,,
Meeting of National Union of Conservative and Constitutional Associations . . . . 24 June, ,,
National music meetings; competition and concerts, 27 June—6 July, ,,
Scottish southern gathering, sports . 25 July, ,,
National cat show . . . . . 26—29 Oct. ,,
Bird show . . . . 22 Feb. 1873
Grand commemoration of the opening of the palace; the Paxton memorial unveiled . . 10 June, ,,
Visits of the shah of Persia . 30 June, 3 July, ,,
National music meetings . 3, 5, 8, 10, 12 July, ,,
Resignation of Mr. (aft. sir) George Grove, many years secretary, announced Sept., succeeded by capt. (aft. major) Flood Page . . . . Dec. ,,
Visit of the czar . . . . . . 16 May, 1874
Handel festival; successful . . 22, 24, 26 June, ,,
Visit of the sultan of Zanzibar . . . 19 June, 1875
National music meeting . . . . 1-10 July, ,,
Visit of the king and queen of Greece and prince and princess of Wales . . . . . 19 July, 1876
Great clock completed . . . . . . Nov. ,,
Handel festival, 25, 27, 29 June, 1877; 21, 23, 25 June, 1880
Great damage done by bursting of a water tank, no lives lost . . . . 30 Sept. ,,
International Woollen exhibition, opened by the duke of Connaught . . . . . 2 June, 1881
Handel festivals, 15, 18, 20, 22 June, 1883; 19, 22, 24, 26 June, 1885; 22, 25, 27, 29 June, 1888; 19, 22, 24, 26 June, 1891; June, 1894; 1897; 1900.
London International Universal Exhibition opened by the lord mayor . . . . 23 April 1884
Insolvency of the Company; the chairman appointed receiver . . . . . . Feb. 1887
Jubilee fêtes . . . . . . 22 June *et seq.* ,,
Visit of the Shah of Persia . . . . . 6 July, 1889
Grand fête of the unionists of the metropolis; Mr. Goschen, Mr. A. J. Balfour present 28 June, 1890
International exhibition of mining and metallurgy 28 July–11 Oct. ,,
Visit of the German emperor and empress; review of the fire-brigade (see *Germany*) . 11 July, 1891
Tonic Sol-fa jubilee largely attended . 18 July ,,
Electrical exhibition opened . . . 9 Jan. 1892
African exhibition opened . . 18 May *et seq.* 1895
Visit of Li-Hung-Chang . . . . 10 Aug. 1896
The Victorian exhibition opened by the princess Christian . . . . 6 May 1897
National temperance fête and choral festival, about 40,000 present . . . . 6 July, 1898
Crystal Palace Act passed . . . . 25 July ,,
English and foreign paintings, new collection, opened . . . . 11 May, 1899
First pony show in England held here, 10-12 July, ,,
Historical loan exhibition of musical instruments, &c., opened . . . . . . 7 July, 1900

Commemoration concert of Sir Arthur Sullivan's works (see *Music*, 1900), conducted by Mr. Manns, 8 Dec. 1900
Bird show (42nd; about 3,000 birds), opened, 8 Feb. 1901
Lord Roberts opens a naval and military exhibition, 23 May, ,,
National cat show, 1200 entries . . 29 Oct. ,,
Motor-car exhibition opened . . . . 14 Feb. 1902
American exhibition opened . . . 31 May, ,,
Coronation gift (in aid of hospitals) ball, 2 July, ,,
Peace festival: "British and American concert," 5 July, ,,
Labour association co-operative exhibition, 20 Aug. ,,
Visit of the shah of Persia . . . . 23 Aug. ,,
Brass band contest, 1,000 *g.* cup awarded to Black Dyke from W. Yorkshire . . . . 27 Sept. ,,
Automobile show opened . . . . 30 Jan. 1903
Report of directors for 1902; gross receipts, 126,795*l.*; expenditure, 106,578*l.*; total admissions, 2,963,613, largest record since palace opened 1854 Mar. ,,
First meeting of the Aero club . . . 25 April ,,
Handel festival . . . 20, 22, 25, 27 June ,,
Centenary celebration of Sunday School union 8 July ,,

See *Handel Festivals* and *Fireworks*.

CTESIPHON (afterwards Al Madayn), on the Tigris, the splendid capital of Parthia, was taken by Trajan in 116; and by Septimius Severus (who made 100,000 captives), 198. Its defences deterred Julian from the siege, 363. It was taken by Omar and the Saracens, 637, and utterly destroyed, and Cufa near it built with the remains.

CUBA (its original name), an island (W. Indies) discovered by Columbus on his first voyage, 28 Oct. 1492, settled by Velasquez, 1511-12. Havana, the capital, settled 1519. Population, 1880, 1,521,684; 1899, 1,572,000.

The buccaneer Morgan took the Havannah; see *Buccaneers* 1669
A British expedition lands and remains, 20 July—20 Nov. 1741
The Havana taken by admiral Pococke and lord Albemarle, 1762; restored at the peace of Paris, 10 Feb. 1763
Cuba opened to the trade of the world . . . 1818
"Lone Star" society (*which see*), for the acquisition of Cuba, &c. formed 1848
The president of the United States (Taylor) published a strong proclamation, denouncing the object of the invaders . . . 11 Aug. 1849
Expedition of general Lopez and a large body of Americans, with the view of wresting this island from the dominion of Spain, landed at Cuba, (defeated) . . . . 17 May, 1850
Cuba again invaded by Lopez and others 13 Aug. 1851
They are defeated and taken; 50 shot, and Lopez garotted at Havannah . . . . . 1 Sept. ,,
The president of the United States again issued a proclamation against an intended expedition against Cuba . . . . . . 31 May, 1854
Messrs. Buchanan, Mason, and Soulé, United States envoys, met at Ostend and Aix-la-Chapelle, and reported, recommending the purchase of Cuba, Oct. ,,
The Spanish minister in cortes declared that the sale of Cuba would be "the sale of Spanish honour itself" . . . . 19 Dec. ,,
Insurrection of Creoles, headed by Carlos Manuel de Cespedes, for expulsion of Spaniards after the revolution in Spain—Volunteer force raised to aid Lersundi, the governor. . . . Sept.—Nov. 1868
A filibusters' attack on Cuba repelled . 17 May, 1869
The United States decide not to recognise the insurgents as belligerents . . . . . June, 1870
About 2,000 lives lost by a hurricane, about 14 Oct. ,,
The captain-general De Rodas resigned, and left Cuba . . . . 15 Dec. ,,
Insurrection subdued, but enduring; the volunteers very insubordinate; military despotism; occasional reign of terror; massacres . Jan.—Nov. 1871
Don Gonzalo Castañon murdered by Cubans; his tomb desecrated by medical students, 25 Nov.; eight tried and shot at Havana . . 27 Nov.
Mr. F. Delano sent by the United States government to report on the state of Cuba . . . 9 Dec. 1871
The merciless war still continues; no quarter given, Dec. ,,
Suspended hostilities through the establishment of the Spanish republic . . . . . Feb. 1873
Much fighting reported . . . . . . June, ,,
The *Virginius*, American schooner, while conveying men and arms from New York to the insurgents in Cuba, is captured by the Spanish gun-boat *Tornado*, 31 Oct.; conveyed to Cuba; above 90 insurgents and sailors (some British and Americans) tried; many insurgents, and about 6 British and 30 Americans shot . . . . 4–7 Nov. ,,
After much correspondence the *Virginius* was surrendered to the Americans, 19 Dec.; she foundered on her way to New York . about 26 Dec. ,,
Bascones defeats the marquis Santa Lucia and 5000 insurgents at Naranjo . . . . . Feb. 1874
Gen. Martinez Campos appointed governor, with plenary powers . . . . Oct. 1876
The struggle going on, but more subdued, summer 1877
A "Cuban league" in the United States, said to be formed to obtain recognition of the insurgents as belligerents, &c. . . . . . . Sept. ,,
Estrada, the Cuban president, said to be captured, Oct. ,,
Reported surrender of many insurgents 23, 24 Dec. ,,
Surrender of the insurgent government; end of the insurrection announced . . . 21 Feb. 1878
Amnesty declared, with freedom to slaves presenting themselves before 31 March (slavery to be abolished gradually) . . . . . March, ,,
Campos and Jovellar enter Havana triumphantly 14 June, ,,
Insurrection, state of siege; amnesty promised, 19 Sept. 1879
Insurgents totally defeated at Placeta; announced 3 Dec. ,,
Bill for gradual emancipation of the slaves passed by the Spanish Senate, 21 Dec., 1879; by chambers of Deputies (230—10, 21 Jan.); promulgated 18 Feb. 1880
Cuba reported tranquil . . . . . Sept. ,,
Surrender of gen. Maceo and other insurgents to the Spaniards at Gibraltar (see *Spain*), Aug. and Dec. 1882, and March, 1883
Aguerro calls on Cubans to revolt about 26 Sept. ,,
Unsuccessful American filibustering expeditions Spring, 1884
Gen. Aguerro at the head of forces in Cienfuegos April, ,,
Some insurgents defeated . . about 23 April, ,,
Last vestige of slavery abolished by the queen's decree . . . . 6 Oct. 1886
Destructive cyclone, with great loss of life by inundations, &c.; about 1,000 lives lost . 4 Sept. 1888
The governor-general Salamanca dies, succeeded by Gen. Rodriguez Arias . . . . . Feb. 1890
Cuba suffers much by the M'Kinley tariff bill, and appeals to the queen-regent for help . 7 Jan. 1891
Temporary insurrection near Holgium . May, 1893
Gov.-gen. Calleja in 1894
Insurrection in Santiago, reported Feb.; frequent conflicts . . . . March, 1895
Vinales captured by the rebels, reported 9 March, ,,
The rebels defeated with great loss . 16 March, ,,
Gen. Calleja resigns, reported . . 28 March, ,,
Government troops defeated in Santa Clara, 26, 28 March, ,,
Rebels twice defeated; Varona, a leader, killed, April, ,,
Arrival of marshal Campos . . . 16 April, ,,
Insurgents defeated near Palmarito with heavy loss, 12 April, ,,
Gen. Salcedo defeats the insurgents under gen. Maceo in Parra Hueco . . . . . 28 April, ,,
Spanish troops severely defeated . . 19 April, ,,
Guerilla warfare; Spanish army inefficient; conflicting reports . . . . May, ,,
The insurgents defeated near Guantanamo after a desperate fight; the Spanish commander, lieut.-col. Bosch, killed . . . . . 13 May, ,,
The insurgents capture Cristo . . . 16 May, ,,
Gen. Salcedo defeats the insurgents in Puerto Principe; their leader, Jose Marti, killed, 21 May, ,,

Extension of the insurrection, aided secretly by S. Americans and others . . . . June, 1895
Frequent indecisive conflicts . . June, July, ,,
Yellow fever epidemic, great mortality . July, ,,
Gen. Martinez Campos attacked by insurgents near Bayamo, gen. Santo Cildes, and other officers and men killed . . . . 12 July, ,,
Cuba demands autonomy under Spain . July, ,,
Guerrilla warfare and much disease . Aug. ,,
Gen. Salcedo resigns; leaves for Spain, 9 Aug.; several towns taken by insurgents; few authentic details received, Aug.; the insurgent delegates proclaim a federal republic, and the Autonomista party petition the Spanish government for a constitution resembling the Dominion of Canada . . . . . . Aug. ,,
Continued fighting: government reinforcements arrive, 16 Sept.; the insurgent leader Cantero killed in a skirmish, reported 17 Sept.; defeat of the insurgents, Mejon, their leader, killed at Limpias; reported . . . . 1 Oct. ,,
Antonio Maceo defeated at Holguin, 30 Sept.; violent storms and floods, with loss of life and property . . . . . 6 Oct. ,,
Insurgents defeated; 15, 20 Oct.; 25, 29 Nov. 11 Dec. ,,
Capt. Borrega's party (72) surprised by 800 insurgents near Puerto Principe, lieut. Ardieta and 29 Spaniards killed; capt. Borrega and 4 men escaped, the rest taken prisoners . Dec. ,,
Insurgents under Gomez, severely defeated by gen. Campos at Coliseo; 24 Dec.; repulsed with heavy loss in several encounters; reported . 31 Dec. ,,
Spaniards defeated near Colon; Havana nearly surrounded by the insurgents, Fort Victoria surrenders . . . . 4 Jan. 1896
Gen. Campos defeats the insurgents near Havana, 6 Jan.; guerilla warfare: with varying results 14 Jan. ,,
Gen. Martinez Campos recalled (leaves Havana, 21 Jan.); succeeded by gen. Weyler . 19 Jan. ,,
The *Hawkins* U.S. filibustering steamer from Philadelphia wrecked, 75 miles off Long island, 10 deaths; reported; 28 Jan.; see United States, 29 Jan. ,,
Main body of Gomez's army defeated with heavy loss, at St. Lucia . . . . . 29 Jan. ,,
Fierce fight on the borders of Havana, the Spanish column, under gen. Canella saved by aid, many killed . . . . 1 Feb. ,,
Gen. Canella defeats the united bands of Maceo and others (6,000), near Candelaria; reported, 8 Feb. . . . . ,,
Two Spanish forces mistake each other for insurgents, many killed . . . . 24 March, ,,
The Spaniards entrapped and defeated by Maceo, near Lechuzo; reported . . . . 4 April, ,,
U. S. filibustering schooner *Competitor* captured, 5 men sentenced to death; 8 May; intervention of the U. S. government . . . . 10 May, ,,
Guerilla warfare: general ruin, trade and manufactures stopped; reported . . . 15 May, ,,
Insurgents defeated by gen. Valdes near Consolacion; 26 May; again by gen. Castellano, near Puerto Principe; 14 June; desultory fighting; Juan Zayas, insurgent leader, killed July, Aug. ,,
Reinforcements, 14,000, arrive . . . 12 Sept. ,,
Business paralysed; forced paper currency; notes refused . . . . 19 Sept. ,,
Indecisive engagements . . . . . 2–7 Oct. ,,
Fighting, with loss on both sides, at Soroa, Pinar del Rio, near Guanajay; Reyes, the rebel leader, and other officers killed; reported . 27 Oct. ,,
Guaimaro, in Puerto Principe, surrendered to the insurgents, under Calixto Garcia . . 7 Nov. ,,
Insurgents defeated by gen. Castellano, at San Miguel and other places; early Nov.; again defeated, and their leader, Francisco Abad, killed; the town of Pagsanjuan captured by the Spaniards; reported . . . . 24 Nov. ,,
Col. Aldea defeats insurgents (300 killed) in Matanzas; reported . . . . . . 5 Dec. ,,
Antonio Maceo, insurgent leader, killed in a hot fight, and suicide of Francisco Gomez at San Pedro, in Havana . . . . . 7 Dec. ,,
Convoy captured by insurgents under Calixto Garcia, 6 Spanish officers and 158 men killed, near Manzanillo; reported . . . 27 Dec. ,,
Filibustering expedition of the *Three Friends* failed, 2 boats wrecked and 51 deaths; reported, 1 Jan. 1897
Bainoa completely destroyed by the insurgents 4 Jan. ,,
Bands of insurgents dispersed with heavy loss in Havana and Santa Clara; Col. Luque defeats Maximo Gomez at Arroyo Blanco, 106 killed and 205 submit . . . . 5 Jan. ,,
Reform scheme drawn up by sen. Canovas, signed by the queen-regent at Madrid, 4 Feb. 1897 (refused by the Cubans, who demand independence).
Spaniards surprised by insurgents, 40 killed; reported . . . . 22 Feb. ,,
Insurgents' camps, &c. destroyed in Pinar del Rio, many killed; reported . . . . 7 March, ,,
Lenient policy entered on, American prisoners released; reported . . . . . 12 March, ,,
Gen. Rius Rivera, insurgent leader in the Ten years' war, wounded at Cabezadas and taken prisoner, with col. Bacallao; reported . . 29 March, ,,
Filibustering expedition under capt. Roloff landed by the *Laurada* at Banes . . . . March, ,,
Gen. Weyler's campaign destructive and indecisive, situation little changed since April, 1896; pacification of the west of the island . 29 April, ,,
Application of reforms by royal decree, published at Havana . . . . 6 June, ,,
Train blown up with dynamite by insurgents, about 100 killed, near Havana; reported . 10 June, ,,
Gen. Weyler proclaims an amnesty to all who surrender . . . . 6 July, ,,
Frequent conflicts, 225 rebels and 21 of the troops killed . . . . 1–10 July, ,,
Desultory fighting, 202 insurgents killed, 700 surrender; 20 Spanish killed; reported . 16 Aug. ,,
Victoria de las Lunas besieged by the insurgents under Garcia, 14 Aug.; captured . . 28 Aug. ,,
Señ. Domingo Mendez Capote elected president of the Cuban Insurgent Republic at Havana; announced . . . . 12 Sept. ,,
Gen. Weyler recalled, and succeeded by marshal Blanco . . . . 7 Oct. ,,
Gen. Weyler signs a general amnesty; reported 11 Oct. ,,
The *Triton*, an overloaded steamer, wrecked off Pinar del Rio; 181 deaths . . . 16 Oct. ,,
Frequent encounters, 101 insurgents killed; 224 submit to the authorities; reported 26 Oct. ,,
Decrees granting constitutional rights to Cubans, etc., approved by council; 6 Nov.; published; 27 Nov.; at Havana . . . . . 17 Dec. ,,
Guisa, in Santiago, captured by the insurgents (mostly escaped convicts), under Calixto Garcia; great excesses committed; Spanish loss heavy; announced . . . . 2 Dec. ,,
Insurgents defeated near Manzanillo; Maximo Gomez defeated in Santa Clara; reported, 8 Dec. ,,
33 out of 60 filibustering expeditions frustrated by the United States during the rebellion; reported, 9 Dec. ,,
Fort Guamo besieged by insurgents, under Rabi, 11 days; siege raised on the arrival of Spanish column; loss on both sides; reported, 11 Dec. ,,
Several engagements: 303 insurgents killed, 400 captured, and 69 surrendered; 3 Spanish officers and 23 soldiers killed (during 10 days) Dec. ,,
Col. Ruiz sent to Aranguren, rebel chief, to induce him to surrender and accept autonomy; is executed by his orders; reported . . 19 Dec. ,,
Gen. Gonzalez Munoz appointed capt.-gen. of Puertorico . . . . 23 Dec. ,,
First cabinet under the autonomy scheme: señ. Jose M. Galvez, president; established, 1 Jan. 1898
Lieut.-col. Soto, major Nuñez, and other insurgent leaders, with their men, submit, declaring themselves satisfied with the new autonomous *régime*; reported . . . . 9 Jan. ,,
The insurgent gen. P. Delgado killed by his own followers, and several leaders surrender Jan. ,,
Gen. Masso, insurgent, with 11 officers and 100 men surrenders to gen. Aguirre in Santa Clara; 115 rebels killed, and 379 surrendered, 34 prisoners; 12 Spanish killed (in 2 weeks); reported, 21 Jan. ,,
Maximo Gomez's 2nd squadron surrenders; reported . . . . 23 Jan. ,,
Marshal Blanco publishes manifesto of the new autonomous government . . . 24 Jan. ,,
Aranguren, insurgent chief, and 4 men surprised and killed near Tapaste; reported . 27 Jan. ,,

Real power still in the hands of the gov.-gen.; eastern provinces still dominated by the insurgents, Jan.; they demand absolute independence of the island . . . . . . March, 1898
Train blown up by dynamite by insurgents in Santiago de Cuba, 5 deaths; reported . 7 Feb. ,,
Desperate fighting at Najasa, Cartagena and Camagnez, Calixto Garcia defeated by gen. Luque, March; Garcia dies in Washington, 11 Dec. ,,
An armistice granted; see *United States* and *Spain* April, ,,
Gen. Lee, U. S. embassador, leaves Havana 10 April, ,,
Blockade of Cuba by the U.S. fleet; ordered 22 April, ,,
The first Cuban autonomous congress opened by gen. Blanco . . . . 4 May, ,,
Starvation round Havana, many deaths, Gen. Fernandez appointed acting governor . 13 May, ,,
Gen. Blanco issued a proclamation to loyal Cubans to hold out to the end . . . 7 July, ,,
Gen. Blanco holds a meeting in Havana of generals and officers on the question of peace negotiations or extension of the war . . . . . 12 July, ,,
He issues a proclamation maintaining the Spanish army to be intact . . . . 22 July, ,,
Havana occupied by U. S. troops . . . 7 Oct. ,,
Mutiny of Spanish troops at Havanah, order restored . . . . 14 Nov. ,,
Gen. Blanco leaves, succeeded by gen. Castellanos, 30 Nov. ,,
The remains of Columbus exhumed and taken to Spain, see *Havana* . . . 26 Sept.–Dec. ,,
Gen. Brooke arrives in Havana (Cuba to be divided into 7 military departments), 27 Dec.; American flag hoisted . . . . 1 Jan. 1899
New tariff, 6 per cent. average reduction, 1 Jan. ,,
Gen. Gomez, insurgent leader, accepts the U. S. terms; 3,000,000 dol. to be distributed to the soldiers . . . . Feb. ,,
The Cuban assembly votes disbandment of the army and its own dissolution (21–1), reported, 1 April, ,,
President McKinley issues a proclamation regarding a system of Cuban self-government, a census to be taken, &c. . . . . . . 17 Aug. ,,
Cuban constitutional convention opened, reported 5 Nov.; American terms accepted . . June, 1901
Seńs. Estrada Palma and Estevez chosen president and vice-president of the Cuban republic, about 23 Feb. 1902
Seń. Palma's ministry formed, announced, 17 May, ,,
Transfer of Cuba to the new republican government under American suzerainty; gen. Wood, retiring U. S. governor, and troops leave Havana, 20 May, ,,
Bill passed for loan of 4,000,000 dol. at 5 per cent., high duties on wine, coal, &c. . . . 6 Aug. ,,
Commercial treaty with U.S.A. signed . 12 Dec. ,,
Internat. chamber of commerce established Feb. 1903
Treaty with U.S. ratified by Cuban senate, 28 Mar. ,,
Permanent treaty between Cuba and U.S. signed; secures the right of U.S. to intervene for the preservation of the independence of the republic, end of May ,,
Treaty providing for perpetual naval bases for U.S. and placing Isle of Pines under Cuban sovereignty signed . . . . . reported mid-July ,,

See also *United States*; *Spanish-American War*.

CUBIT, a measure by which the ark of Noah was measured (2448 B.C.). It was the distance from a man's elbow to the extremity of the middle finger. According to Arbuthnot, the Hebrew cubit was a little under 22 inches, the Roman cubit 17½ inches, and the English cubit 18 inches.

CUCKING-STOOL (or DUCKING-STOOL), for shrews: one at Kingston-on-Thames was used in April, 1745; and another at Cambridge in 1780. *Chambers.*

CUCUMBERS, noticed by Virgil and other ancient poets, were brought to England from the Netherlands about 1538.

CUDDALORE (India), on the coast of the Carnatic, was acquired by the English in 1681. It was reduced by the French in 1758, but recaptured in 1760 by sir Eyre Coote. Again lost in 1781, it underwent a destructive siege by the British under general Stuart, in 1783, which was continued until peace was signed, when it reverted to them, 1784.

CUENCA, New Castile, Spain, 80 miles from Madrid, attacked by the Carlists 13 July, and captured 14 July, 1874. The garrison and the inhabitants were barbarously used. General Lopez Pinto rescued the prisoners, 19 July.

CUIRASS, a part of Greek and Roman armour. The skins of beasts, and afterwards tanned leather, formed the cuirass of the Britons until the Anglo-Saxon era. It was afterwards made of iron and brass. The cuirass was worn by cavalry in the reign of Henry III. 1216 *et seq*. Napoleon had several regiments of cavalry wearing cuirasses; and most European armies have picked corps of such. For bullet-proof cuirasses, see *Bullets*, 1894.

CULDEES, said to derive their name from *cultores Dei*, worshippers of God, monks in Scotland and Ireland, who had their principal seat at St. Andrews. It is said that in 1185 at Tipperary there was a Culdean abbey whose monks were "attached to simple truth and pure Christian worship, and had not yet conformed to the reigning superstition." They were eventually subjected to the papal yoke.

CULLEN'S-WOOD (Ireland). An English colony from Bristol inhabiting Dublin, went to divert themselves at Cullen's-wood, when the O'Byrnes and O'Tooles fell upon them, and destroyed 500 men, besides women and children, 30 March, 1209 (on Easter, afterwards called *Black* Monday).

CULLODEN, near Inverness, where the English, under William, duke of Cumberland, defeated the Scottish headed by Charles Edward Stuart, the young Pretender, 16 April, 1746. The Scots lost 2500 men killed upon the field, or in the slaughter which occurred in the cruel pursuit, while the loss of the English did not far exceed 200. Prince Charles, who wandered among the wilds of Scotland for six months, while 30,000*l*. were offered for taking him, at length escaped from Uist to Morlaix, and died at Rome, 3 March, 1788.

CULTURE, according to Mr. Matthew Arnold ("The Apostle of Culture, 'sweetness and light,' and the opponent of Philistinism"); is the knowledge of "the best that has been thought and said in the world" (1880). The writings of John Ruskin and Matthew Arnold are said to have greatly promoted culture, and refinement in literature and art among all classes in Great Britain.

CULTUR-KAMPF, see *Kultur-Kampf*.

CULVERIN, cannon so called from the French *couleuvrine*, said to have been introduced into England from a French model in 1534. It was originally five inches and a quarter diameter in the bore, and carried a ball of eighteen pounds. *Bailey.*

CUMÆ (S. Italy), a Greek colony, said to have been founded 1050 B.C., probably too early, and to have been the residence of the ancient Sibyl. It was taken by the Samnites 420 B.C., and was annexed by the Romans 338 B.C.

CUMBERLAND, a N.W. county of England, was granted to Malcolm I. of Scotland in 945, by king Edmund, "on condition that he should be his fellow-worker." It was seized by William I., but restored to Malcolm III., "who became his man," 1072. William the Lion, after his defeat at Alnwick, resigned Cumberland to Henry II., and it was finally annexed to England in 1237. Brandelhow park, Keswick, opened 16 Oct. 1902.

DUKES.

1726. William Augustus, second son of George II., died 13 Oct. 1765.
1766. Henry Frederic, son of Frederic, prince of Wales, died 18 Sept. 1790.
1799. Ernest Augustus, fifth son of George III.; became king of Hanover, 20 June, 1837; died 18 Nov. 1851.
1851. George V., the ex-king of Hanover; died 12 June, 1878.
1878. Ernest Augustus, son; born 21 Sept. 1845, married princess Thyra of Denmark, 21 Dec., 1878. Issue, George William, born 28 Oct. 1880, and five other children. Prince Christian, born 4 July, 1885, died 3 Sept. 1901.

A rescript from the emperor William II. was issued 12 March, 1892, restoring the Guelph fund (the accumulated property of king George V.), which had been sequestrated in 2 March, 1868, to his son, the duke of Cumberland, on certain conditions, the duke having stated in a letter to the emperor, dated 10 March, "that he had no intention of engaging in any undertaking which would threaten the peace of the German Empire.' The Guelph Fund bill for making the necessary arrangements, was passed by the Prussian diet, 31 March–6 April, 1892.

The affair settled; the duke retains the Guelph museum, library, and gardens for the benefit of the public, March, 1893. See *Brunswick*.

CUMBERLAND, The, see *Naval Battles*, 1811.

CUMULATIVE VOTE, in parliamentary elections, proposed by Mr. Robert Lowe,* 4 July, during the debates on the reform bill; and rejected, 5 July, 1867, by 314 to 173. By the act passed 15 Aug. 1867 (30 & 31 Vict. c. 102), it was enacted that at a contested election for any county or borough represented by three members, no person shall vote for more than two candidates. The cumulative vote was used in the election of the London school board, 29 Nov. 1870.

CUNAXA, in Mesopotamia, near the Euphrates, where Cyrus the younger was defeated and slain by his brother Artaxerxes II., against whom he had conspired (401 B.C.), narrated in Xenophon's Anabasis. His Greek auxiliaries were successful; see *Retreat of the Greeks*.

CUNEIFORM INSCRIPTIONS (from *cuneus*, Latin for a wedge), in characters resembling arrow-heads, inscribed on bricks or clay-tablets, found at Babylon, Behistun, &c., have lately been deciphered by English and foreign scholars, who date some of them as far back as 2000 B.C. See *Assyria, Babylon, Behistun*.

CUNNERSDORF (in Prussia). On 12 Aug. 1759, Frederick II. king of Prussia, with 50,000 men, attacked the Austrian and Russian army of 90,000 in their camp near this place, and at first gained considerable advantages; but pursuing them too far, the Austrians and Russians rallied, and gained a complete victory. The Prussians lost 200 pieces of cannon and 30,000 men in killed and wounded.

CUPOLA SHIPS, see *Navy of England*, 1861.

CUPPING, a mode of blood-letting. The skin is scarified by lancets, and a glass cup in which the air has been rarified by heat, is immediately applied to it, when the blood usually flows into the cup. This operation was well known to the ancients, and is described by Hippocrates (413 B.C.) and Celsus (20 B.C.). It was common in England about 1820.

* "At any contested election for a county or borough represented by more than two members, and having more than one seat vacant, every voter shall be entitled to a number of votes equal to the number of vacant seats, and may give all such votes to one candidate, or may distribute them among the candidates as he thinks fit.'

CURAÇOA (correctly, Curaçao), an island in the Caribbean sea, settled by the Spaniards about 1527, was seized by the Dutch in 1634. In 1800 the French, settled on part of this island, quarrelled with the Dutch, who surrendered it to a British frigate. It was restored to the Dutch in 1802; taken from them by the British in 1807, and again restored in 1814. The name of a well-known and esteemed liqueur manufactured chiefly in Holland from the dried peel of the curaçoa orange, by a process of maceration and distillation with spirit and water. A cheap imitation is made from whisky and the peel of bitter oranges.

CURATES were of early appointment as coadjutors in the Romish church, and are mentioned in England in the 7th century. Among the acts passed for the relief of this laborious class of the clergy are the 12th Anne, 1713, and 36th, 53d, and 58th Geo. III., and especially the beneficent act, 2 Will. IV. Oct. 1831. It appeared by parliamentary reports on ecclesiastical revenues, that there were in 1831, 5230 curates in England and Wales, whose stipends amounted to 424,695*l*. The greatest number of curates in one diocese was Lincoln, 629; and the smallest that of St. Asaph, 43. The Pastoral Aid Society was established in 1836; the Society for promoting the Employment of Additional Curates, in 1837; the Curates' Augmentation Fund, 1866. The Curates' Alliance, a reforming body, issued its first annual report, Dec. 1882.

CURFEW BELL (from the French *couvre feu*), was revived or introduced in England by Will. I. 1068. On the ringing of the curfew at eight o'clock in the evening all fires and candles were to be extinguished under a severe penalty. *Rapin*. The curfew was modified 1 Hen. I. 1100. The practice has been continued to the present time at Sandwich in Kent, and some other places (1891).

CURIATII, see *Rome*, 669 B.C.

CURLING, a Scotch national game with stones on the ice, said to have been introduced from the Low Countries in the 16th century. The Duddingstone curling club was instituted 1795. The royal Caledonian curling club, founded in 1838, owns a large artificial pond at Strathallan, Perthshire. A party of Scottish curlers visited Nova Scotia, New Brunswick, and Canada, and played a number of matches with colonial teams, Dec. 1902–Feb. 1903.

CURRAGH, see *Kildare*.

CURRANTS, from *Corinth*, whence, probably, the tree was first brought to us about 1533. The name is also given to a small kind of dried grape, brought from the Levant and Zante. The duty on these currants (44*s*. 4*d*. per cwt. in 1834) has been reduced to 7*s*.; reduced to 2*s*. 17 April, 1890. The hawthorn currant (*Ribes Oxyacanthoides*) came from Canada in 1705, see *Greece* 1903.

CURRENCY ACTS. See under *Bank of England*, 1797-1823, and *Gold*, 1816. Those of sir Robert Peel were passed in 1819 and in 1844.

Royal commission appointed to inquire into the depreciation of silver, relative values of the precious metals, &c., Messrs. A. J. Balfour (chairman), (succeeded by lord Herschell), J. Chamberlain, L. Courtney, L. Cohen, W. H. Houldsworth, Sir John Lubbock, D. M. Barbour, J. W. Birch (Bank of England), Sir T. Farrer, C. W. Fremantle (deputy master of the mint) and J. R. Bullen Smith, about 7 Sept. 1886.

In their final report, issued 6 Nov. 1888, the commissioners were found to be greatly divided in opinion respecting bi-metallism, a paper currency, etc.

Mr. H. Chaplin advocates his "thirty shilling" theory Jan. 1889.

Mr. W. A. Shaw publishes his "History of Currency (1252–1894)," Feb. 1895.

CURSITOR BARON. This office, formerly attached to the court of exchequer, was abolished in 1856, on the death of the right hon. George Bankes.

CURTATONE, near Mantua, N. Italy. Here the Austrians, under Radetzky, crossed the Mincio, and defeated the Italians after a severe conflict, 29 May, 1848.

CUSHEE PIECES, invented by Richard Leake, the master-gunner of the *Royal Prince* man-of-war, renowned for bravery shown in the engagement with the Dutch admiral Van Tromp, in 1673.

CUSTOM is a law not written (*lex non scripta*), established by long usage and consent, and is distinguished from *lex scripta*, or the written law. It is the rule of law when it is derived from 1189 downwards. Sixty years' custom is binding in the civil law, and forty years' in ecclesiastical cases.

CUSTOMS were collected upon merchandise in England, under Ethelred II. in 979. The king's claim to them by grant of parliament was established 3 Edw. I. 1274. The customs were farmed to sir Thomas Smith for annual sums varying from 14,000*l.* to 50,000*l.* in the reign of Elizabeth. *Stow.* They were farmed by Charles II. for 390,000*l.* in 1666. *Davenant.* In 1671 commissioners were appointed. The customs were consolidated by Mr. Pitt in 1787. Between 1820 and 1830 so many reductions and consolidations were made in the customs department, that above a quarter of a million was saved in salaries, though the work had enormously increased.—Acts consolidating the customs duties were passed in 1853, 1854, and 1860, whereby the number of articles in the tariff and the amount of the customs were greatly reduced. Many changes have been made since; by the Customs Act of 1890, the laws were amended and the duties modified; see *Revenue*. The disqualification of custom-house officers and officers of excise from voting for the election of members of parliament in 1782, was removed in 1867–8.

The laws respecting the customs were amended by an act passed 21 Aug. 1871, and consolidated by acts passed, 24 July, 1876; amended, 1887 and 1898

Customs in		Customs in year ending 31 March.	
1580	£14,000	1877	£19,896,386
1592	50,000	1878	20,043,180
1614	148,000	1879	20,348,064
1622	168,000	1880	19,169,605
1642	500,000	1881	19,210,466
1684	530,000	1882	19,275,668
1720	1,555,600	1883	19,682,671
1748	2,000,000	1884	19,653,352
1808	9,973,240	1885	20,557,819
1823	11,498,762	1886	19,722,302
1830	17,540,323	1887	20,135,855
1835	18,612,906	1888	19,579,476
1840	19,915,296	1889	20,067,000
1845	20,196,856	1890	20,424,000
1850	20,442,170	1891	19,480,000
1855	21,630,081	1892	19,736,000
1860	24,391,084	1893	19,885,339
1864	23,234,356	1894	19,698,698
1867	22,299,306	1895	20,115,000
1869	22,434,737	1896	20,756,000
1870	21,449,843	1897	21,254,000
1871	20,238,880	1898	21,798,000
1872	20,225,892	1899	20 850,000
1873	20,976,236	1900	23,800,000
1874	20,323,325	1901	26,270,959
1875	19,349,280	1902	31,046,869
1876	20,196,691	1903	34,433,000

The customs in Ireland, a sack of wool, 3*d.*; a last of hides, 6*d.*; a barrel of wine, 2*d.* 1224

The Customs business of Ireland was transferred to the London board . . . . . 6 Jan. 1830

Custom-house. A custom-house was erected in London on a large scale, 1304; and a yet larger in 1559; burnt down in 1666; a new one, built by Charles II., burnt down in 1718, again rebuilt; and once more burnt down, and immense property and valuable records destroyed . . 12 Feb. 1814

The present edifice opened . . . 12 May, 1817

Dublin Custom-house commenced in 1781; opened in 1791. The eastern wing of its warehouse was destroyed by fire, with property to the amount of 400,000*l.* . . . . . 9 Aug. 1833

International conference on customs tariffs at Brussels . . . . . 1–5 July, 1890

Changes in the duties made in 1894

The customs duties are described in the Finance Act, passed annually.

CUSTOMS PARLIAMENT, see *Zollverein*.

CUSTOS ROTULORUM, keeper of the rolls or records of the sessions of the peace, previously nominated by the lord chancellor, was in 1545 directed to be appointed by a bill signed by the king. The act was confirmed in 1689.

CUSTOZZA, near Verona, N. Italy. Here the Italians were defeated by marshal Radetzky, 23 July, 1848; and here they were again defeated, 24 June, 1866, after a series of desperate attacks on the Austrian army. The Italians were commanded by their king, Victor Emmanuel, and the Austrians by the archduke Albrecht. The Italian loss was computed to be 720 killed, 3112 wounded, and 4315 missing; the Austrian loss, 960 killed, 3690 wounded, and nearly a thousand prisoners. The Italians soon recrossed the Mincio.

CUTCH (Kachh), W. India, a principality under the government of Bombay. In consequence of the depredations of the natives, the East India government resorted to hostile measures, which resulted in a stringent treaty with the rao in Jan. 1816. In 1819 he was deposed for misgovernment, and replaced by his infant son, supported by a British contingent. The traffic in children, detected in Dec. 1835, was suppressed by the British. Many persons perished by an earthquake in July, 1819. *Thornton.*

CUTLERY, see *Steel*. *Cutlers' Feast*, see *Sheffield*, 1889.

CUTTACK (Katak), E. India, a British province ceded to the E. I. company in 1803. Cuttack, the capital, was taken by col. Harcourt, 14 Oct. same year. The Mahrattas conquered it in 1750. *Thornton.*

CUTTING-OUT MACHINES. Wearing apparel was first cut out by machinery in England by Messrs. Hyams in 1853. The machine, invented by Mr. Frederick Osbourn, consists of a reciprocating vertical knife working through a slot in the table that supports the pile of cloth to be cut. The cloth being pressed up to the edge of the knife by the attendant, the knife will sever it in the direction of the lines marked on the upper layer.

CUZCO, capital of Peru, was entered by Pizarro in Nov. 1533, and taken by him in Aug. 1536, after five months' siege.

CYANOGEN, a colourless gas (composed of nitrogen and carbon), irritating to the nose and eyes, derived from Prussian blue, was first obtained in the free state by Gay Lussac in 1815, being the first instance of the isolation of a compound radical.

CYCLE of the sun, a period of twenty-eight years, which having elapsed, the dominical or

Sunday letters return to their former place, and proceed in the former order according to the Julian Calendar; that of the moon is nineteen lunar years and seven intercalary months, or nineteen solar years. The cycle of Jupiter is sixty years. The Paschal cycle, or the time of keeping Easter, was first calculated for the period of 532 years by Victorius, 463. *Blair*. See *Metonic Cycle, Calippic Period.*

CYCLE AND CYCLING, see *Velocipede*.

CYCLONE PULVERIZER, an apparatus invented by Messrs. Raymond, Bros., of America, in imitation of the violent action of air in cyclones, for pulverizing various substances. It is said to have been successfully applied in crushing gold quartz. Exhibited in London in May 1888.

CYCLONES, circular whirlwinds, or hurricanes, common in the East and West Indian and Chinese seas, varying from 200 to 500 miles in diameter. Many details respecting them will be found in Reid's "Law of Storms," published 1838.

Great cyclone in India; see *Calcutta* . 5 Oct. 1864
Captain Watson, of the *Clarence*, observing the barometer falling, and foretelling the approach of the cyclone, saved his ship by steering out of its range . . . . ,,
Great cyclone in the Bahamas, at Nassau, New Providence, above 600 houses and many churches and other buildings thrown down; between 60 and 70 persons killed, and a great many ships dismantled . . . . 1, 2 Oct. 1866
A cyclone desolated Antigua, St. Kitts, and other isles; religious and manufacturing buildings destroyed, and thousands made homeless, 21 Aug. 1871
Destructive cyclone near Madras; ships lost, 1 May, 1872
Destructive cyclone, S. E. Bengal; Calcutta barely escaped; about 215,000 persons perished, 31 Oct. 1876
Destructive cyclone near Aden, about 50,000*l.* damages reported; ships sunk, &c., . 3 June, 1885
Destructive cyclone at Calcutta 23 May *et seq.* 1887
Destructive cyclone in W. Indies, 100 deaths at Montserrat, 1500 injured, total deaths 2000, 7–12 Aug. 1899
Cyclone in Huelva, Spain, much damage done, 29 April 1900
Destructive cyclone at Mafeking . . 29 Aug. ,,
Destructive cyclone at Columbia, Tennessee 20 Nov. ,,
Destructive cyclone over south and west of United States, many deaths . . . . . 10 Mar. 1901
Cyclone at Leruka, Fiji Is. . . . . 13 Mar. ,,
Cyclone in Majorca . . . . . 27 Aug. 1902
Destructive cyclone at Yokohama, 200 deaths, 29 Sept. ,,
Cyclone in Jamaica, much damage, 50,000*l.* granted by government for relief of planters . 10 Aug. 1903
See *Virgin Isles, Storms, which see, Bengal, Madrid*, 1886 *et seq.*

CYCLOPÆDIA, see *Encyclopædia*.

CYCLOPEAN MASONRY, a term given to very ancient buildings in Greece, Italy, and Asia Minor, probably the work of the Pelasgi, more than 1000 B.C.

CYDER, see *Cider*.

CYMBAL, the oldest known musical instrument, made of brass. Cymbals were used by the ancient Egyptians, Assyrians, Hebrews and other nations, 2 Sam. vi. 5, B.C. 1047.

CYMMRODORION SOCIETY was established in Sept., 1751, to instruct the ignorant and relieve distressed Welsh. It was suspended in 1781, and revived 24 June, 1820, for literary purposes. The society was re-established in 1877 for promotion of literature and the arts in Wales.

CYMRI or **KYMRI** (hence Cambria), the great Celtic family to which the Britons belonged, and which came from Asia and occupied a large part of Europe about 1500 B.C. About A.D. 640 Dyvnwal Moelmud reigned "*King of the Cymry;*" see *Wales*.

CYNICS, a sect of philosophers founded by Antisthenes (about 396 B.C., *Diog. Laert., Clinton*), who professed to contemn all worldly things, even sciences, except morality; and lived in public with little shame. Diogenes, the eminent cynic, died 323 B.C.

CYNOSCEPHALÆ (*dogs' heads*, so named from the shape of the heights), in Thessaly, where Pelopidas and the Thebans defeated Alexander tyrant of Pheræ and the Thessalians, 364 B.C. Pelopidas was slain. Here also the consul Flaminius totally defeated Philip V. of Macedon, 197 B.C., and ended the war.

CYPRESS, *Cupressus sempervirens*, a tree found in the isle of Cyprus. The Athenians buried heroes in coffins made of this wood, of which Egyptian mummy-chests were also fabricated. The ancients planted it in cemeteries. The cypress was brought to England about 1441. The deciduous cypress, *C. disticha*, came from North America before 1640.

CYPRUS, a large island in the Mediterranean, near the coasts of Asia Minor and Syria; present capital, Levkosia or Nikosia; sea-ports, Larnaka and Famagosta. Here the ancients found copper (*æs Cyprium*), silver, and precious stones. The country was fertile, and abounded with trees in ancient times; and under Venice its commerce was important. Population in 1881, 186,173; 1891, 209,291; 1901, 237,022.

The Phœnician colonists introduced the worship of Ashtaroth (the Greek Astarte or Aphrodite, the Roman Venus)
Conquered by Amasis, king of Egypt; revolted at the invasion of Cambyses, and submitted to Persia . . . . B.C. 525
Revolted, and subjected 500-499
Partly independent under Evagoras and Nicocles, kings of Salamis . . . . . . 387 *et seq.*
Supported Alexander the Great . 333
Taken from Demetrius by Ptolemy of Egypt . . 295
Became a Roman province 58
Visited by Paul and Barnabas (*Acts* xiii.) . A.D. 45
Great revolt of the Jews . 117
Seized by the Arabs, 646; recovered by Greeks 648
Isaac Comnenus, king . 1184
Seized by Richard I. of England, 1191; given by him to Guy de Lusignan, as king . . 1192
"Order of the Sword" established (ceased with 8th king) 1195
Guy's descendant, Catherine de Cornaro, sold it to Venice 1487
Cyprus conquered by the Turks with great barbarity 1570-1
Insurrections suppressed, 1764; with massacre . 1823
General di Cesnola, a Genoese, the American consul, by excavations, discovers many Babylonian, Egyptian, Phœnician, and Greek gold and silver ornaments, and other relics (sold to the New York museum) . . . . . 1866 *et seq.*
His work, "Cyprus: its Ancient Cities, Tombs, and Temples," published in London . Dec. 1877
The island given up to Great Britain for administration by the Anglo-Turkish convention 4 June, 1878
Possession taken by admiral lord John Hay, 12 July; by sir Garnet J. Wolseley, as lord high commissioner . . . . . . 22 July, ,,
Much sickness, with deaths, reported Aug.—Sept. ,,
Orders for the government by a lord high commissioner, given at court . . . 14 Sept. ,,
Sir G. J. Wolseley's decree for compulsory labour on public works, dated . . . . 16 Dec. ,,
He is sent to S. Africa; succeeded by sir Robert Biddulph . . . . June, 1879
The British buy the Government lands, except the Sultan's estates, early in . . . . . ,,
Increased general prosperity reported (in Blue Book) . . . . . . Aug. 1880

Sir R. Biddulph reports that the British government is popular, but the finances depressed, Aug.; 78,000*l.* voted for Cyprus . . 28 Aug. 1881
New pier at Limasol opened by Sir R. Biddulph 6 Oct. ,,
New constitution announced . . 24 March, 1882
Elective legislative council opened by sir R. Biddulph . . . . July, 1883
Long continued destructive ravages of locusts, greatly checked by the skill and energy of Mr. S. Brown, reported . . . . . Sept. 1884
Sir R. Biddulph reports great prosperity and increased revenue (194,051*l.*, expenditure 111,685*l.*). General health good . . . . 31 March, ,,
Sir H. E. Bulwer nominated as high commissioner, Aug. 1885; arrived . . . . . 9 March, 1886
Cyprus Society, London, formed for the establishment of a hospital at Kyrenia and other objects, June, 1888
Archæological excavations; discoveries on the site of the temple of Aphrodite, inscriptions, &c.; reported . . . . Sept. ,,
Long drought in 1887–8; bad harvest, great distress, relieved by government . . July, 1889
An excellent harvest, prosperity increasing, and reduced taxation, reported by sir R. Biddulph . 18 Dec. ,,
Sir Walter J. Sendall appointed high commissioner Feb. 1892
Locust campaigns of 1891, 1892, reported successful, March, 1893–5; 4,802*l.* expended in 1894.
Dr. Max Ohnefalsch-Richter reports the miscellaneous results of excavations in various places since 1885 undertaken by direction of the German emperor (to be published in 1895) for the Berlin museum . . . . Nov. ,,
Disastrous floods (22 deaths) at Limasol, 12 Nov.; estimated loss, 50,000*l.*, reported . 29 Nov. ,,
Excavations at Amathus supported by the British museum . . . . 1893 *et seq.*
Mass meetings demanding union with Greece and abolition of Turkish tribute . . . 5 May, 1895
Locust campaign 7,639*l.* expended; reported, Oct. 1896
Sir Wm. Haynes Smith appointed high commissioner, Nov. 1897; arrives . . . 4 June, 1898
Increase of revenue and prosperity . . Aug. 1900
British annual grant of 30,000*l.* voted . 26 May, 1902
Long drought . . . . May 1903

CYR, ST., near Versailles. Here a college for ladies was founded by madame De Maintenon in 1686, and here she died, 15 April, 1719. It was made a military college in 1803; suppressed in 1886.

CYRENAIC SECT, founded by Aristippus the Elder, 365 B.C. They taught that the supreme good of man is pleasure, particularly that of the senses; and that even virtue ought to be commended only because it gave pleasure.

CYRENE (N. W. Africa), a Greek colony, founded by Battus about 630 B.C. Aristæus, who was chief of the colonists here, gave the city his mother's name. It was also called Pentapolis, on account of its five towns; namely, Cyrene, Ptolemais, Berenice, Apollonia, and Arsinoë. It was conquered by Ptolemy Soter I., who placed many Jews here (286 B.C.). Cyrene was left by Ptolemy Apion to the Romans, 96 B.C. It is now a desert. Some Cyrenaic sculptures were placed in the British Museum in July, 1861.

CYROPEDIUM, see *Corus*.

CYZICUS (Asia Minor). In the Peloponnesian war, the Lacedæmonian fleet under the command of Mindarus, assisted by Pharnabazus, the Persian, was encountered by the Athenians under Alcibiades, and defeated with great slaughter, near Cyzicus; Mindarus being slain: 410 B.C. *Plutarch.*

CZAR, more properly *tsar* or *tzar*, the title of the emperor of Russia, probably derived from Cæsar, a title said to have been assumed by Ivan Basilowitz after defeating the Tartars, about 1482. The empress is termed czarina or tsarina, and the eldest son cesarevitch or tsarevitch; the spelling still varies.

CZECHS, the most westerly branch of the Slavic family of nations, which about 480 migrated to Bohemia and Moravia (*which see*). The antagonism between the Germans and Czechs is milder in Moravia than in Bohemia. Their representatives entered the reichsrath at Vienna, 8 Oct., 1879, see *Hungary* 1903.

D.

DACCA, N. E. India, a province acquired by the East India Company in 1765, and ruled under them by a Nawab till its annexation in 1845. *Thornton.*

DACIA, a Roman province (included Temeswar and parts of Hungary, Transylvania, Wallachia, Moldavia, and Galicia), after many contests, was subdued by Trajan, 106, when Decebalus, the Dacian leader, was killed. Dacia was abandoned to the Goths by Aurelian, in 270; subdued by the Huns, 376: by Scythians, 566; by Charlemagne, and by the Magyars, in the 9th century.

DACOITS, hereditary robbers of North India, formerly employed in war by native sovereigns.

It is stated that between 1818 and 1834, one tribe alone, in 118 "dacoitees," or expeditions, killed 172 persons, and obtained plunder valued at 115,000*l.* In 1838 lord Auckland did much to suppress the dacoits, and many settlements were broken up, but they are not quite extinct in Bengal and Burmah. Several dacoitees were suppressed in 1879. See *Burmah.*

DAFOUR, see *Soudan*, 1884.

DAGHESTAN (a mountain country S. W. Asia), was conquered by the czar Peter, 1723; restored to Persia, 1735; re-annexed to Russia by Alexander I., 1813.

DAGUERREOTYPE PROCESS, invented by Daguerre, and published 1838; see *Photography.*

DAHLIA, a flower discovered in Mexico by Vincent Cervantes in 1784, and brought to Europe about 1787, and cultivated by the Swedish botanist, Dahl. About 1814 it was introduced into France and England; André Thouine suggested improvements in its culture, and it soon became a favourite. Georgi introduced it at St. Petersburg; hence it is known in Germany as the *Georgina.* The National Dahlia Society, annual exhibition at the Crystal palace, 1 Sept. 1893.

DAHOMEY, a negro kingdom, West Africa, became known to Europeans early in the last century, when Trudo Andati or Guadjor Trudo, a man of energy and talent, was king. He died in 1732, and was succeeded by a series of cruel tyrants, a large part of whose revenue was derived from the slave-trade. *Abbeokuta*, a robbers' haunt in 1825, has, since 1829, become a strong-walled town, inhabited by free blacks; and was consequently opposed by the king of Dahomey. His army has been severely defeated in its attacks on this place, and in one on 16 March, 1864, a great number of his Amazons (female celibates) were slain. Dahomey has been visited by captain Burton and other travellers, who have described the royal sanguinary customs. Capital of Dahomey, Abomey.

Trade opened with Dahomey and settlements made by M. Régis, of Marseilles 1840–50
The king ordered to pay a fine (for an outrage on Mr. Turnbull at Whydah, 23 Jan.) . . March, 1876
He refuses in insulting terms, April; the coast about to be blockaded . . . . July, ,,
The king threatens massacre of Europeans if attacked . . . . Aug. ,,
He makes concessions; blockade removed 12 May, 1877
Renewed massacres of natives ("customs") and outrages on foreigners at Whydah; reported 26 Sept. 1878
The king attacks Lagos, kills many and takes about 1000 prisoners . . . . . . 10 May, 1885
Dahomey placed under the protectorate of Portugal at the request of the king . . . 7 Oct. ,,
The Dahomey troops repulsed in an attack upon the French settlements at Zebo, on Lake Denham, by commandant Ferrillon, 100 killed . . reported 24 Feb. 1890
The king after losing about 1,000, retires with his army . . . . . reported 12 March ,,
Porto Novo and Kotonou well held by the French 5 April ,,
The Dahomey coast blockaded by the French from 4 April ,,
The French repulsed in a conflict with the king reported 22 April ,,
The king's army near Porto Novo; French reinforcements from Senegal landed, April; his troops retreat after an engagement with severe loss 23 April ,,
The king in a letter to president Carnot justifies his retention of French merchants at Whydah for meddling with politics . received about 28 April ,,
Whydah bombarded by the French vessel *Kerguelin* 29, 30 April; Commander Fournier demands the surrender of 13 Frenchmen, in prison since Feb., 3 May; they are surrendered, and Dahomeyan prisoners released . . . . . . 5 May ,,
The new king Behanzin installed; he writes to president Carnot desiring a just peace . 12 May ,,
Peace with France concluded . . reported 6 Oct. ,,
The king's continued aggressions and threats lead to war, April; the French chamber votes 3,000,000 francs for an expedition to protect Porto Novo and Kotonou, and avenge injuries . . 11 April, 1892
French reinforcements from Senegal arrive at Kotonou . . . . 20 April, ,,
Porto Novo and Kotonou besieged, reported 23 May, ,,
Col. Dodds (aft. Gen.) commander of the French expedition, arrives at Kotonou, 28 May; Whydah occupied by 4,000 French troops, 11 June; the coast blockaded, 16 June; several villages bombarded, about 5 July; the coast bombarded, 9 Aug. *et seq.*; Taku captured, 20 Aug.; Katagu taken, 24 Aug.; reinforcements from France arrive, 24 Aug.; about 4,000 Dahomeyans defeated with heavy loss in an attack on gen. Dodds' column at Dogba; French loss slight; commandant Faurax killed, 17 or 19 Sept.; Dahomeyans again defeated . . 4, 19 Oct. ,,
An attack of 4,000 Dahomeyans defeated with severe loss, by gen. Dodds, reported . 30 Sept. ,,
The Dahomeyans, commanded by king Behanzin, routed near Poguessa; capt. Falamine, lieut. Amelot, and 7 French killed . . 4 Oct. (?) ,,
Sabovi occupied by the French without resistance, 10 Oct.; successful advance of gen. Dodds, with loss on both sides . . . . . . 13–15 Oct. ,,
The Dahomeyans defeated with great loss, 20, 21, 26 Oct. ,,
The fortress of Muates taken, 2 Nov.; the Dahomeyan army disperse after 4 hours' fighting, 3 Nov.; Cana and Dioxoue taken . . 4 Nov. ,,
French loss during the campaign, 215 men, reported . . . . 7 Nov. ,,
King Behanzin proposes inadmissible terms of peace, about 15 Nov.: he burns palaces, &c., and retires . . . . 16 Nov. ,,
Gen. Dodds occupies Abomey, 17 Nov., and proclaims the deposition of Behanzin; the chiefs and people submit . . . . . 18 Nov. ,,
Gen. Dodds at Porto Novo . . . . . 27 Nov. ,,
Whydah and other towns occupied . 3–6 Dec. ,,

Blockade of the coast raised . . . . 19 Dec. 1892
Behanzin on the Mahi with 2,000 men about 9 Jan. 1893
King Behanzin issues to all nations a justificatory manifesto, 2 March; proffers submission to France under conditions . reported 2 May, „
Gen. Dodds arrives at Marseilles . . 11 May, „
Message from king Behanzin to president Carnot charging the French with treachery . . June, „
Gen. Dodds and 400 officers at Kotonou . 31 Aug. „
Advance successfully into the interior 27 Oct. *et seq.* „
Flight of Behanzin and submission of the chiefs; gen. Dodds arrives at Youneton . 12 Nov. „
Behanzin's envoys at Paris not received by pres. Carnot . . . . 12 Nov. „
The Dahomeyans defeated at Badagha . 4 Dec. „
Gouthili chosen as king of Allada, and recognised by gen. Dodds and the chiefs at Goho . 15 Jan. 1894
Behanzin surrenders unconditionally, 25 Jan.; sent to Martinique, Feb.; arrives . . 30 March, „
M. Ballot appointed civil governor . . 22 Feb. „
Gen. Dodds returns to France; col. Dumas assumes command . . . . . 24 April, „
M. Ballot well received on his tour through the country; nominates a new station, Carnotville, reported . . . . 2 Oct. „
The Kotonou canal, between Porto Novo and Godomey, constructed by native labour, opened 8 Jan. 1895
Successful explorations by lieut. Baud, treaties signed with chiefs, reported . . . 8 Aug. „
Convention for the delimitation of the French and German possessions in the *Hinterland*, signed at Paris . . . . 23 July, 1897
The Franco-German boundary commission opposed, natives defeated with heavy loss near Lama, reported . . . . 21 Sept. 1899
Behanzin's brother made king of Abomey, afterwards deposed and imprisoned at Porto Novo, reported . . . . 5 June, 1900

DAHRA (Algeria). On 18 June, 1845, above 500 Kabyles at war with the French were suffocated in a cave, a fire having been kindled by order of general Pelissier, afterwards duke of Malakoff. They had fired on a messenger bearing an offer of a truce. The massacre was condemned by marshal Soult, but justified by marshal Bugeaud.

DAILY CHRONICLE. Built up by Edward Lloyd on the *Clerkenwell News* (founded 1855), which he purchased in 1877. It is an active progressive liberal paper. In 1891 a "literary page" was added. Since 1901 it has adopted a liberal imperialistic policy.

DAILY EXPRESS. Independent morning paper, price ½*d*. Founded 1900.

DAILY GRAPHIC. Illustrated morning paper, price 1*d*. Founded 1 Jan. 1890.

DAILY MAIL. The first halfpenny morning paper. It gives the latest news of the world in a condensed form. It claims a daily circulation of 1,000,000. Founded 4 May, 1896.

DAILY MIRROR, a new morning paper intended as a journal for women, but not for women exclusively. Up-to-date telegrams, and bright paragraphs of news of interest to women are among its special features. Founded 2 Nov. 1903.

DAILY NEWS, liberal commercial newspaper, established 21 Jan. 1846. Price reduced to 1*d*. 1868. During the Franco-Prussian war 1870 *et seq.*, the circulation rose to 150,000 weekly. In 1870 it absorbed the *Morning Star* (founded 1856). Charles Dickens was the first editor. From 1868 the paper was under the management of Mr. (afterwards sir) John R. Robinson. He retired in 1901 on the re-organisation of the newspaper under a new proprietorship.

DAILY TELEGRAPH, established 29 June, 1855, as a 2*d*. paper, by colonel Sleigh. In Sept. it was bought by Mr. J. M. Levy, who on 17 Sept. reduced the price to 1*d*. Under the management of Mr. (bart. 1892, ld. Burnham, 1903) Edw. Lawson, it has become one of the most influential of the London papers. Liberal till 1878, from 1886 it has been unionist. The *Daily Telegraph* in times of need raises large funds, which are distributed free of cost. Its "Shilling" fund for our soldiers' widows and orphans, 236,000*l*. collected up to 31 Dec. 1900; over 7 million donors; see *Mansion House War Fund.*

DAIRY FARMERS' ASSOCIATION, British, established 24 Oct. 1876. No. 1 of a journal published Sept. 1877. *Dairy Shows,* exhibitions at Agricultural Hall, 1877 *et seq.*

Establishment of *dairy schools* in Great Britain . 1888

DAKOTA (North America), organised as a territory of the United States, 2 March, 1861. Capital Yankton. North and South Dakota were made States in 1889.

About 100,000 persons destitute in North Dakota through failure of the crops . . . 30 Oct. 1889
The Sioux reserves in S. Dakota, about 9,000,000 acres, opened to settlers by proclamation; immediately occupied . . . . . Feb. 1890
For the rising of the Sioux, see *Indians*, 1890–91.
President Harrison proclaims the opening of 1,600,000 acres in the Fort Berthold Indian Reservation, North Dakota . . . 21 May, 1891
Great fire at Fargo, N. Dakota, many deaths, about 2,000 homeless . . . . . 7–8 June, 1893
Mr. Taylor, state treasurer of S. Dakota, bankrupt, absconds; the National bank stops payment, reported . . . . 10 Jan. 1895
Population, 1890: N. Dakota, 182,719; S. Dakota, 328,808; 1900: N. Dakota, 319,146; S. Dakota, 401,570.

DALECARLIANS (Sweden), revolted against Christian of Denmark, 1521, and placed Gustavus Vasa on the throne of Sweden.

DALMATIA, an Austrian province, N. E. of the Adriatic Sea, conquered and made a province by the Romans, 34 B.C. The emperor Diocletian erected his palace at Spalato (erroneously written Spalatro), and retired there, A.D. 305. Dalmatia was held in turns by the Goths, Hungarians, and Turks, till its cession to Venice in 1699. By the treaty of Campo Formio in 1797 it was given to Austria, but in 1805 it was incorporated with Italy, and gave the title of duke to marshal Soult. In 1814 it reverted to Austria. An insurrection opposed to the new military law broke out at Bocche di Cattaro, and a conflict with the troops at Dragali took place, 10 Oct. 1869. Several regiments were sent there, but the insurgents obtained several successes during the month. A deputation offered submission, 2 Nov., and the operations against them were suspended about the end of the month. Population, 1890, 527,426; 1900, 591,597.

DAMARALAND (S.W. Africa), a territory rich in minerals and pasture, occupied by German settlers and missionaries since 1840. The native population is estimated at 80,000.

During a German expedition Mr. Luderitz acquired lands at Angra Pequeña from the chiefs; Dr. Gœring, who also had obtained land, transferred his rights to Mr. Robert Lewis, a British subject, long known in the country, whose claims were set aside by the German colonial company of S.W. Africa, and he and his party were expelled. His claims set forth at Berlin by the British government in 1885, were disallowed, and the question was still under discussion . . autumn, 1892

South-West Africa company formed in London to develop Damaraland . . . . . Sept. 1892
Agreement made between the German and English companies . . . . . about 15 Nov. „
Capt. François, with a German force of 200, storms Witbooi's stronghold, with much slaughter, including women and children . . . 12 April, 1893
Continual fighting with the natives, much bloodshed, reported . . . . . Feb. 1894
Natives subdued by lieut. Leutwein and a murderer shot, reported . . . . . 9 April, „
Hottentot rising: Germans repulsed, and 2 killed, near Coyamus, 5 July, 1897; rebels defeated, with great loss, lieut. Herzog and 2 others killed; reported . . . . . 10 Aug. 1897
Revolt of several tribes, owing to the enforced stamping of guns, 11 Germans killed, reported 1 Oct. 1898

DAMASCUS (Syria), a city in the time of Abraham; 1913 B.C. (*Gen.* xiv.), now the capital of a Turkish pachalic. Population, 1885, 150,000; 1901, *about* 140,487.

Taken by David (1040 B.C.), but retaken shortly after; made the capital of Syria under Benhadad and his successors . . . . . B.C. 930
Recovered by Jeroboam II. . . . . about 822
Taken by Tiglath-Pileser, king of Assyria . . 740
From the Assyrians it passed to the Persians, and from them to the Greeks, under Alexander . 333
To the Romans . . . . . about 64
Paul, converted, preaches here (*Acts* ix.) . A.D. 35
Taken by the Saracens, 633; by the Turks in 1075; destroyed by Tamerlane . . . Jan. 1401
Taken by Ibrahim Pacha 1832
The disappearance of a Greek priest, named father Tommaso, from here, 1 Feb. 1840, led to the torture of a number of Jews, suspected of his murder, and to a cruel persecution of that people, which caused remonstrances from many states of Europe 1840
Damascus restored to Turkey 1841
In consequence of a dispute between the Druses and Maronites, the Mahometans massacred above 3000 Christians and destroyed the houses, rendering vast numbers of persons homeless and destitute; a large number were rescued by Abd-el-Kader, who held the citadel 9, 10, 11 July, 1860
Justice executed for these crimes by Fuad Pacha: 160 persons executed, including the Turkish governor; and 11,000 persons made soldiers, Aug.-Sept. „
The great Omeyyad mosque destroyed by fire, 14 Oct. 1893. See *Syria*, 1895–6.
Damascus-Hauran Railway opened, July, 1894; the Beirut-Damascus line opened, Aug. 1895; financial failure, reported 1899
Visit of the German emperor and empress, warm reception . . . . . . 7 Nov. 1898

DAMASK LINENS and SILKS, first manufactured at Damascus, have been beautifully imitated by the Dutch and Flemish. The manufacture was brought to England by artisans who fled from the persecutions of Alva, 1571-3. The DAMASK ROSE was brought here from the south of Europe by Dr. Linacre, physician to Henry VIII., about 1540

DAMIENS' ATTEMPT. Louis XV. of France was stabbed with a knife in the right side by Damiens, a native of Arras, 5 Jan. 1757. The culprit endured the most excruciating tortures, and was then broken on the wheel, 28 March.

DAMIETTA (Lower Egypt) was taken by the crusaders, 5 Nov. 1219; lost 1221; retaken by Louis IX., 5 June, 1249; surrendered as his ransom when a prisoner, 6 May, 1250. The present town was built soon after. See *Egypt*, Sept. 1882. Population, 1888, 34,044.

DAMON AND PYTHIAS (or Phintias), Pythagorean philosophers. Damon was condemned to death by the tyrant Dionysius of Syracuse, about 387 B.C. He obtained leave to go and settle some domestic affairs, promising to return at the appointed time of execution, and Pythias became his surety. When Damon did not appear, Pythias surrendered, and was led to execution; but at this critical moment Damon returned. Dionysius remitted the sentence, and desired to share their friendship.

DANAI: an ancient name of the Greeks derived from Danaus, king of Argos, 1474 B.C.

DANCE OF DEATH. The triumph of death over all ranks of men was a favourite subject with the artists of the middle ages, and appears in rude carvings and pictures in various countries.

The *Chorea Machabæorum* or *Danse Macabre*, the first printed representation, published by Guyot Marchand, a bookseller of Paris . . . 1485
Holbein's *Dance of Death* (concerning the authorship of which there has been much controversy), printed at Lyons in 1538, and at Basil . . . 1594
Many editions have since appeared; one with an introduction and notes published by Mr. Russell Smith 1849
The term *Dance of Death* was also applied to the frenzied movements of the Flagellants, who had sometimes skeletons depicted on their clothing, about the end of the 14th century.
Dancing mania, accompanied by aberration of mind and distortions of the body, was very prevalent in Germany in 1374, and in the 16th century in Italy, where it was termed Tarantism, and erroneously supposed to be caused by the bite of the Tarantula spider. The music and songs employed for its cure are still preserved.

DANCING was practised by the Curetes, 1534 B.C. *Eusebius.* The Greeks combined the dance with their dramas, and pantomimic dances were introduced on the Roman stage, 22 B.C. *Usher.* Dancing by cinque paces was introduced into England from Italy, A.D. 1541. In modern times the French introduced *ballets analogues* in their musical dramas. The country dance (*contre-danse*) is of French origin, but its date is not precisely known. *Spelman.* See *Morice Dance*, *Quadrille*, and *Waltz*.

Establishment of a national training school for dancing, by Mr. Mapleson; second annual distribution of prizes, &c. . . . . 21 Sept. 1878

DANE-GELD, or DANEGELT, a tribute paid to the Danes to stop their ravages in England; first raised by Ethelred II. in 991, and again in 1003; and levied after the expulsion of the Danes to pay fleets for clearing the seas of them. The tax was suppressed by Edward the Confessor in 1051; revived by William I. 1068; and formed part of the revenue of the crown, until abolished by Stephen, 1136. Every hide of land, *i.e.* as much as one plough could plough, or as *Bede* says, as much as could maintain a family, was taxed at first 1*s.*, afterwards as much as 7*s.* Camden says that once 24,360*l.* was raised.

DANES, or NORTHMEN; see *Denmark*. During their attacks upon Britain and Ireland they made a descent on France, where, in 895, under Rollo, they received presents under the walls of Paris. They returned and ravaged the French territories as far as Ostend in 896. They attacked Italy in 903. Neustria was granted by the king of France to Rollo and his Normans (North-men), hence Normandy, in 911. The invasions of England and Ireland were as follows:—

First hostile appearance of the Danes 783
They land near Purbeck, Dorset 787
Descend in Northumberland: destroy the church at Lindisfarne; are repelled, and perish by shipwreck . . . . . . 8 Jan. 794
They invade Scotland and Ireland . . . 795, 796

They enter Dublin with a fleet of 60 sail, and possess themselves of Dublin, Fingal, &c. . . . 798
They take the Isle of Sheppey . . . 832
Defeated at Hengeston, in Cornwall, by Egbert . 835
They land in Kent from 350 vessels, and take Canterbury and London 851
They descend on the north, and take York . . 867
They defeat the Saxons at Merton 871
They take Wareham and Exeter 876
They take Chippenham: but 120 of their ships are wrecked 877
Defeated: Guthrum, their leader, becomes Christian, and many settle in England . . . 878
Alfred enters into a treaty with them . . . 882
Their fleet destroyed by Alfred at Appledore . 894
Defeated near Isle of Wight 897
They invade and waste Wales 900
Defeated by Edward the Elder 922
They defeat the people of Leinster . . . 956
Ravage Cornwall, Devon, and Dorset . . . 859
And ravage Essex and Suffolk 990
Said to assume the title *lord dane* about . . 991
Their fleet defeated after a breach of treaty, purchased by money 992
Anlaf and Sweyn ravage Kent and the south (erroneously said to have been paid 16,000*l.* for peace) 994
A general massacre of the Danes, by order of Ethelred II. . . . . 13 Nov. 1002
Sweyn revenges it, and receives 36,000*l.* (as an annual tribute) to depart 1003
Their fleet anchors at Isle of Wight 1006
They make fresh inroads, and defeat the Saxons in Suffolk, 1010; sack Canterbury, and kill the inhabitants, 1011; receive 48,000*l.* as tribute, and murder Alphege, archbishop 1012
Vanquished at Clontarf, Ireland (see *Clontarf*) . 1014
Conquest of England completed; Canute king . . 1017
They settle in Scotland 1020
They land again at Sandwich, carrying off much plunder to Flanders 1047
Defeated by Harold II. at Stamford-bridge, 25 Sept. 1066
They burn York, and kill 3000 Normans . . . 1069
Once more invade England to aid a conspiracy; but compelled to depart 1074

DANGEROUS ASSOCIATIONS (IRELAND) BILL; see *Roman Catholic Association*.

DANGEROUS GOODS: act regulating their deposit and carriage passed 6 Aug. 1866.

DANGEROUS PERFORMANCES, see *Children*.

DANNEWERKE, or **DANNAWIRKE**, a series of earthworks, considered almost impregnable, stretching across the long narrow peninsula of Schleswig, Holstein, and Jutland—said to have been constructed during the "stone age," long before the art of metal-working. It was rebuilt in 937 by Thyra, queen of Gormo the Old, for which she was named "Dannabod," the pride of the Danes. It was repaired by Olaf Tryggveson between 995 and 1000. Near here the Prussians, helping the duchies, defeated the Danes, 23 April, 1848. The retreat of the Danes from it, 5 Feb. 1864, occasioned much dissatisfaction at Copenhagen.

DANTE'S DIVINA COMMEDIA was first printed in 1472. He was born 14 May, 1265, died at Ravenna, 14 Sept. 1321. A festival in his honour, at Florence, was opened by the king, 14 May, 1865, when a large statue of Dante by Pazzi of Ravenna was uncovered. An exhibition of objects relating to Dante and his works collected by Mr. P. H. Wicksteed in Dr. Williams' library, Gordon-square, London, April, 1893. Dante's complete works, published at Oxford, edited by Dr. E. Moore, 1894. Dante society founded, annual meetings, sir Theodore Martin, pres., 1899.

MM. Sardou and Morreau's *Dante* produced at Drury-lane theatre . . . . . 30 April 1903

DANTZIC (N. Germany), a commercial city in 997; according to some authorities, built by Waldemar I. in 1165. Poland obtained the sovereignty of it in 1454. It was seized by the king of Prussia, and annexed in 1793. It surrendered to the French, May, 1807; and by the treaty of Tilsit was restored to independence, under the protection of Prussia and Saxony, July, 1807. Dantzic was besieged by the allies in 1812; and surrendered 1 Jan. 1814. By the treaty of Paris it reverted to the king of Prussia. By the Vistula breaking through its dykes, 10,000 head of cattle and 4000 houses were destroyed, and many lives lost, 9 April, 1829. Population, 1895, 125,605; 1900, 140,539.

DANUBE (German, Donau; anciently Ister and Danuvius), the largest river in Europe, except the Volga, rises in the Black Forest and falls into the Black Sea. Trajan's bridge at Gladova was destroyed by Adrian, to prevent the barbarians entering Dacia. Steam navigation was projected on this river by count Szechenyi, in 1830, and in that year the first steam-boat was launched at Vienna, and the Austrian company was formed shortly after. The Bavarian company was formed 1836. A canal between the Danube and the Maine was completed by Louis I. of Bavaria. Charlemagne, in the 8th century, contemplated uniting the Danube and Rhine by a canal. At the peace of 30 March, 1856, the free navigation of the Danube was secured, and an independent European commission appointed to make it navigable from Isaktchi to the sea, which has worked with good effect. The British government, in 1868, lent 135,000*l.* to complete the works. The treaty respecting the navigation of the Danube renewed for twelve years, 13 March, 1871. The river suddenly took possession of a new bed near Vienna, 17 April, which was formally opened 30 May, 1875.

In the Russo-Turkish war the Russians crossed the Danube and entered Bulgaria. (See *Russo-Turkish War, II.*) . . . . June, 1877
The navigation of the Danube was regulated by Articles 50—54 of Berlin treaty . . 13 July, 1878
A conference of the powers respecting the Danube held in London, 8 Feb. *et seq.*; treaty signed restoring rights to Russia, 10 March: ratified 15 Aug. 1883
Huge rocks in that portion of the Lower Danube called the "Iron Gates" blown up; M. Baross, the Hungarian minister of communications, set fire to the first mine, 5 Sept., 1889; the explosion of the rocks recommenced . . 15 Sept. 1890
New canal being cut . . . . June, 1893 *et seq.*
Foundation of a great bridge at Tchernavoda; laid by Charles, king of Roumania, 21 Oct. 1890; work going on 1892
Inauguration of the great bridge at Tchernavoda, in presence of the king of Roumania, royal family and dignitaries . . . . . 26 Sept. 1895
The Iron Gates Canal opened by the emperor, in presence of the kings of Roumania and Servia, at Orsova, 27 Sept. 1896; opened for navigation, 1 Oct. 1898

DANUBIAN PRINCIPALITIES; WALLACHIA and MOLDAVIA (capitals, Bucharest and Jassy) were united and named ROUMANIA, 1859. Population of the two, 1860, 3,864,848; 1866, 4,424,961; 1887, 5,500,000; 1899, 5,912,520. These provinces formed part of the ancient Dacia (*which see*).

Part of Moldavia ceded to Russia 1812
The provinces having participated in the Greek insurrection in 1821, were severely treated by the Turks; but by the treaty of Adrianople were placed under the protection of Russia . . . 1829
The Porte appointed as hospodars prince Stirbey for Wallachia, and prince Ghika for Moldavia, June, 1849

They retire from their governments when the Russians enter Moldavia. See *Russo-Turkish War*. 2 July, 1853

The Russians quit the provinces and the Austrians enter, Sept. 1854; retire . . . . March, 1857

The government of the principalities finally settled at the Paris conference: (there were to be two hospodars, elected by elective assemblages, and the suzerainty of Turkey was to be preserved), 19 Aug. 1858

Alexander Couza elected hospodar of Moldavia, 17 Jan.; of Wallachia . . . . . 5 Feb. 1859

The election acknowledged by the allies 6 Sept. „

The definitive union of the provinces (under the name of Roumania) proclaimed and acknowledged by the Porte . . . . . . Dec. 1861

[For continuation, see *Roumania*.]

DARDANELLES, the classic *Hellespont*, derives its name from Dardanus, an ancient city in the Troad, and called after the ancient Dardani. Two castles (Sestos, in Roumania, and Abydos, in Anatolia), built by the sultan Mahomet IV. in 1659, command the entrance of the strait of Gallipoli, and recall the story of Hero and Leander (see *Hellespont*).—The passage of the strait was achieved by the British squadron under sir John Duckworth, 19 Feb. 1807; but he repassed them with great loss, 3 March, the castles of Sestos and Abydos hurling down stone-shot upon the British ships. The allied English and French fleets passed the Dardanelles at the sultan's request, Oct. 1853; see *Hellespont* and *Xerxes*.

DARIC, a Persian gold coin, issued by Darius, hence its name, about 538 B.C. About 556 cents. *Knowles*. It weighed two grains more than the English guinea. *Dr. Bernard*.

DARIEN, ISTHMUS OF, central America, discovered by Columbus, 1494. In 1694, William Paterson, founder of the Bank of England, published his plan for colonising Darien. A company was formed in 1695, and in 1698-9, three expeditions sailed thither from Scotland, where 400,000*l*. had been raised. The first consisted of 1200 young men of all classes, besides women and children. The enterprise not having been recognised by the English government, the settlements were threatened by the Spaniards, to whom they were finally surrendered, 30 March, 1700. Paterson and a few survivors from famine and disease, had set off shortly before the arrival of the second expedition. Several years after, 398,085*l*. were voted by parliament to the survivors as "Equivalent money." 18,000*l*. were also voted to Paterson; but the bill was rejected in the house of Lords. See *Panamá*. The *average breadth*, 40 miles; least breadth, 30 miles

DARJEELING, a British district in the Himalayas, ceded about 1824. The capital Darjeeling, is used as a sanitarium. The cultivation of tea is flourishing, and the population rapidly increasing (1889.)

See *Landslips*, 1899.

DARK AGES, a term applied to the *Middle Ages*; according to Hallam, comprising about 1000 years—from the invasion of France by Clovis, 486, to that of Naples by Charles VIII., 1495. During this time learning was at a low ebb. Hallam's "View of the State of Europe during the Middle Ages," published 1818. Supplemental Notes, 1848.

DARLINGTON. An ancient town S. Durham, chartered and made a parliamentary borough 1867. The opening of the Stockton and Darlington railway 27 Sept. 1825, the first railway to convey passengers, gave the impulse to the prosperity of the borough. The handsome collegiate church of St. Cuthbert, founded 1160 by bishop Pudsey, and restored in 1869 by sir Gilbert Scott, is a fine specimen of Early English architecture. To the free library, opened 1885, Mr. Edward Pease gave 10,000*l*. The Royal Agricultural Society show was opened here, 22 June, 1895. Population 1871, 21,730; 1881, 35,102; 1891, 38,060; 1901, 45,000. See under *Railways*, 1825 and 1875.

DARMSTADT, capital of Hesse-Darmstadt, made a city 1330, became the residence of the landgraves, 1567. The ducal palace built 1568 *et seq.* Memorial to the grand duchess Alice, unveiled 12 Sept. 1902. Population, 1890, 56,503; 1900, 72,381; see *Hesse*, 1894.

DARTFORD (Kent). Here commenced the insurrection of Wat Tyler, 1381. A convent of nuns, of the order of St. Augustin, endowed here by Edward III. 1355, was converted by Henry VIII. into a royal palace. The first paper-mill in England was erected at Dartford by sir John Spielman, a German, in 1590 (*Stow*), and about the same period was erected here the first mill for splitting iron bars. The powder-mills here were blown up four times between 1730 and 1738. Various explosions have since occurred, in some cases with loss of life to many persons: 12 Oct. 1790; 1 Jan. 1795; and others recently. Population, 1881, 10,163; 1891, 11,962; 1901, 18,643.

DARTMOOR, South Devon, a tract of land, 20 miles long, 9 to 12 miles broad, subject to the duchy of Cornwall. The Dartmoor Preservation Association hold their annual meeting at Plymouth, 26 Oct. 1885. *Dartmoor Prison*, founded Mar. 1806. Seven prisoners of war were shot 6 April, 1815, after an insurrection. The autumn military manœuvres at Dartmoor, Aug. 1873, were unsuccessful.

A mutiny here was checked with loss of life of one prisoner . . . . 12 Nov. 1880

Wm. Carter, convict, shot dead while attempting to escape . . . . 24 Dec. 1896

DARTMOUTH (Devon). Burnt by the French in the reigns of Richard I. and Henry IV. In a third attempt (1404), the invaders were defeated by the inhabitants, assisted by the valour of the women. The French commander, Du Chastel, three lords, and thirty-two knights, were made prisoners. In the war of the parliament, Dartmouth was taken after a siege of four weeks, by prince Maurice, who garrisoned the place for the king (1643); but it was retaken by general Fairfax in 1646. The duke and duchess of York visited the *Britannia* training ship (where the duke was a a naval cadet), 6 July, 1899. The king, accompanied by the queen and princess Victoria, laid the stone for the new Britannia naval college, 7 March, 1902. Population, 1881, 5,725; 1891, 6,038; 1901, 6,037.

DARWINISM, see *Development* and *Species*.

DATES were affixed to grants and assignments 18 Edw. I. 1290. Before this time it was usual at least to pass lands without dating the deed of conveyance. *Lewis*. Numerous instruments of assignment enrolled among our early records establish this fact. The date is determined by the names of the parties, particularly that of the grantor: the possession of land was proof of the title to it. *Hardie*. A useful glossary of the dates given in old charters and chronicles will be found in Nicolas's "Chronology of History." J. J. Bond's "Handy-Book for Verifying Dates," published 1866.

DAUPHINÉ,* S.E. France, successively held by the Allobroges, Burgundians, and Lombards; was, about 732-4, delivered from the invading Saracens by Charles Martel. After forming part of the kingdom of Arles, it was much subdivided among counts. One of these, Humbert II., ceded Dauphiné and the Viennois to Philip VI., in 1343, for his eldest son, on the condition that the prince should be styled *dauphin*, which took effect in 1349, when Humbert became a monk. Louis Antoine, duke of Angoulême, son of Charles X., the last dauphin who assumed the title at his father's accession, 16 Sept. 1824, died 3 June, 1844.

DAVENTRY, Northamptonshire, an old municipal borough, situated at the sources of the Avon and Nene. Charles I. spent a few days at Daventry just before the battle of Naseby (14 June, 1645). Near here Lambert, having escaped from the Tower, was defeated and retaken, in his attempt to enkindle the war, by Monk, 21 April, 1660. Danes or Borough hill, near the town, is one of the largest Roman camps in England. The dissenting academy removed here from Northampton in 1752, was transferred to Wymondley in 1789, thence to London as Coward College, and finally united with Homerton and Highbury Colleges as New College, in 1850.

DAVENPORT, see *Plymouth*.

DAVID, the capital of Chiriqui in Panama, on the Rio David, a centre of stockraising and tobacco industries. Population 1901, 10,000 (about).

DAVID'S, ST. (S. W. Wales), the ancient Menapia, now a poor decayed place, but once the metropolitan see of Wales, and archiepiscopal. When Christianity was planted in Britain, three archbishops' seats were appointed, viz. London, York, and Caerleon upon Usk, in Monmouthshire. That at Caerleon being too near the dominions of the Saxons, was removed to Mynyw, and called St. David's, in honour of the archbishop who removed it, 522. St. Sampson was the last archbishop of the Welsh; for he, withdrawing himself on account of a pestilence to Dôle, in Brittany, carried the pall with him. In the reign of Henry I. the archbishops submitted to the see of Canterbury. *Beatson*. Present income 4500*l*.

BISHOPS.

1800. Lord George Murray, died 3 June, 1803.
1803. Thomas Burgess, trans. to Salisbury, June, 1825.
1825. John Banks Jenkinson, died 7 July, 1840.
1840. Connop Thirlwa; resigned June, 1874; died 27 July, 1875.
1874. Wm. Basil Jones, consecrated 24 Aug.; died, 14 Jan. 1897.
1897. John Owen, Feb.; consecrated 1 May.

DAVID'S DAY, ST., 1 March, is annually commemorated by the Welsh, in honour of St. David. Tradition states that on St. David's birthday, 540, a great victory was obtained by the Welsh over their Saxon invaders; and that the Welsh soldiers were distinguished, by order of St. David, by a leek in their caps.

DAVIS'S STRAIT (N. America), discovered by John Davis, 11 Aug. 1585, on his voyage to find a N. W. passage, 1585-87. He made two more voyages for the same purpose, and five voyages to the East Indies. In the last he was killed by Japanese pirates, on the coast of Malacca, 27 or 29 Dec. 1605.

DAVY JONES, a familiar name by which seamen designate an evil spirit. *Davy Jones's locker* is an equivalent phrase for the ocean. The name has been derived from Jonah the prophet, and from *duffy*, a W. Indian negro spirit.

DAVY LAMP, &c., see *Safety Lamp*.

DAVY MEDAL. Funds were furnished by the sale of sir Humphry Davy's plate. It was first awarded by the Royal Society to Professors Bunsen and Kirchhoff in 1877 for their discovery of *spectrum analysis* (*which see*). Davy-Faraday Research Laboratory, see *Royal Institution*.

DAVYUM. It is a metal of the platinum group, discovered by Sergius Kern, 28 June, 1877, in the residuum of platinum ore; hard, infusible, and rather ductile.

DAY. Day began at sunrise among most of the northern nations, at sunset among the Athenians and Jews; and among the Romans at midnight as with us. The Italians in some places, reckon the day from sunset to sunset, making their clocks strike twenty-four hours round. The Chinese divide the day into twelve parts of two hours each. The *astronomical day* begins at noon, is divided into twenty-four hours (instead of two parts of twelve hours). Thus the astronomical day 8 Dec. begins at noon of 8 Dec. and ends at noon 9 Dec. At Greenwich, from 1 Jan. 1885, the day of 24 hours began at midnight; the reckoning was recommended for railways, &c. A system of universal time for all countries was put forth by Mr. Sandford Fleming, of Canada. The Washington Prime Meridian Conference adopted a resolution declaring the universal day to be the mean solar day, beginning, for all the world, at the moment of mean midnight of the initial meridian, coinciding with the beginning of the civil day, and that meridian to be counted from zero up to 24 hours, 21 Oct. 1884. The scheme for universal time was advocated by Mr. W. H. M. Christie, the Astronomer Royal, at the Royal Institution, 19 March, 1886. A *lawful day* is a day on which a writ may be executed; Sundays, Christmas Day, and Good Friday are excepted.

DEACONS (literally *servants*), an order of Christian ministers, began with the Apostles, about 53. (*Acts* vi.) Their qualifications are given by St. Paul (65), 1st *Timothy* iii. 8—14. Mr. John Andrews, master of Shrewsbury High School, was ordained at Lichfield Cathedral a *permanent* deacon in conformity with a resolution passed in the Upper House of Convocation, Feb. 1884; his duties being to assist the priest in the communion service, &c., 18 Dec. 1887.

DEACONESSES, or ministering widows, have their qualifications given in 1 *Tim.* v. 9, 10 (65). Their duties were to visit the poor and sick, assist at the agapæ or love feasts, admonish the young women, &c. The office was discontinued in the Western church after the 6th century, and in the Greek church about the 12th. In 1836 a deaconesses' house was founded by pastor Fliedner at Kaiserswerth, near Düsseldorf; many since on the continent. The appointment of deaconesses, subject to the parochial clergy, was advocated by the bishop of Ely about 1853, and some were appointed. The Diocesan Deaconess Institution, London, was established in 1861. The office adopted by the church of Scotland, 1887.

* One of the counts of Vienne placed a dolphin (dauphin) in his coat-of-arms, and assumed the title of dauphin.

DEAD. Prayers for their benefit were probably offered up in the 2nd century, being referred to by Tertullian, who died 220. The practice was protested against by Aerius, and defended by Epiphanius, who died 403. It is generally objected to by the church of England, but is not expressly forbidden; so decided by sir Herbert Jenner in the Court of Arches (*Phillimore, Eccl. Law*, 1873-6).

Book of the Dead, a collection of prayers and exorcisms written in Egyptian hieroglyphic or hieratic characters, composed for the benefit of the pilgrim soul in his journey through Amenti (the Egyptian Hades). Portions of these papyri were placed with the mummy in his tomb. They are said to form fully one half of the thousands which are extant. The "Book of the Dead" is dated from the 4th dynasty 3733–3566 B.C. After much toil a pure text with illustrations was published by M. Edouard Naville, 1886. Translations in several European languages have appeared. A facsimile of the Papyrus of Ani in the British Museum was printed in 1890. Mr. E. A. Wallis Budge's editions, with translations, 1895, 1897, 1899, and 1901.

DEAD WEIGHT LOAN acquired its name from its locking up the capital of the Bank of England, which in 1823 advanced 11,000,000*l.* to the government (to construct new ordnance, &c.). The latter engaged to give an annuity of 585,740*l.* for 44 years, which ceased in June, 1867.

DEAF AND DUMB. The first systematic attempt to instruct the deaf and dumb was made by Pedro de Ponce, a Benedictine monk of Spain, on Jerome Cardan's system, about 1570. See *Blind*.

Bonet, a monk, published a system at Madrid . . . 1620
Dr. Wallis published a work in England on the subject . . . 1650
The first regular academy for the deaf and dumb in Britain opened in Edinburgh . . . 1773
In modern times the abbé de l'Epée (1712-89), and his friend and pupil the abbé Sicard of Paris (1742—1822); the rev. Mr. Townsend and Mr. Baker, of London; Mr. Thos. Braidwood of Edinburgh; and surgeon Orpen of Dublin, have laboured with much success in promoting the instruction of the deaf and dumb.
The asylum for deaf and dumb children, opened in London through the exertions of Mr. Townsend in 1792; one in Edinburgh by Mr. T. Braidwood, in 1810; and Birmingham by Mr. T. Braidwood . 1815
The asylum at Claremont, Dublin, opened . . . 1816
A college for the deaf and dumb established at Washington, U.S., under the presidency of Dr. E. M. Gallaudet, and empowered by government to grant degrees . . . 1864
A deaf and dumb debating club (Wallis club) closed its third session . . . April, 1869
The foundation stone of St. Saviour's church, near Oxford street, London, for the deaf and dumb, laid by the prince of Wales . . . 5 July, 1870
In 1851, there were in Great Britain, 12,553 deaf and dumb out of a population of 20,959,477.
Oral Teaching.—Mr. Wm. Van Praagh introduced the so-called German system into this country in July, 1867; published his "Plan for the Establishment of Day Schools [in preference to boarding-houses] for the Deaf and Dumb" (in which they are to be taught by speech and lip teaching only; the finger alphabet and artificial signs being rigidly excluded), in 1871. By the help of the baroness Meyer de Rothschild and others, the "Association for the Oral Instruction of the Deaf and Dumb" was founded in 1871, and a day-school opened at 12, Fitzroy-square . 16 July, 1872
Training college and school founded at Ealing . 1877
The Royal Association for the Deaf and Dumb, London, founded in 1840, and re-organised 1854. It provides instruction and entertainment under clerical direction.
Washington Deaf and Dumb college confer degree of LL.D. on prof. A. Graham Bell, the inventor of the telephone and influential advocate of the oral system . . . 1880
International congress at Milan; great majority in favour of oral teaching of deaf-mutes . Sept. 1880
International congress at Brussels. 13 Sept. *et seq.* 1883
Teachers' college founded . . . 1885
The rev. R. A. Pearce, a mute, was a clergyman at Winchester . . . 1893
Report of the royal commission on the education of the deaf and dumb issued . . . 1899
15,246 deaf and dumb in England and Wales, census . . . 1901

DEAL, a cinque port with Sandwich, 1229; a fishing village in the reign of Henry VIII.; its strong castle built 1539 by Henry VIII. Deal was incorporated and made independent of Sandwich, 1699. Iron promenade pier erected 1864. Victoria Hospital, new wing opened by lady George Hamilton, 28 July, 1899. Population, 1901, 10,427.

DEAN, FOREST OF, Gloucestershire, anciently wooded quite through, and in the last century, though much curtailed, was twenty miles in length and ten in breadth. It was famous for its oaks, the material of our ships of war. Riots in this district, when more than 3000 persons assembled in the forest, and demolished upwards of fifty miles of wall and fence, throwing open 10,000 acres of plantation, took place on 8 June, 1831. The Dean forest (mines) act passed 16 Aug. 1871.

DEAN (decanus), a name commonly given to the arch-presbyter, or eldest presbyter, in the 12th century; originally a military title, an officer over ten soldiers. In the church of England the dean and chapter of a cathedral nominally elect the bishop and form his council. By 13 & 14 Car. II. (1662), a dean must be in priest's orders; previously the office had occasionally been held by a layman, with special dispensation. The ancient office of "rural dean" has been much revived since 1850. The Deans' and Canons' resignation act passed 13 May, 1872. The Five Deans' memorial, and counter memorial, see *Church of England*, 1881. See *Arches*.

DEATH, ordained as the punishment for murder, 2348 B.C. (*Gen.* ix. 6.)

The Jews generally stoned their criminals (*Lev.* xx. 2) . . . B.C. 1490
Draco's code punished every offence with death . 621
It was limited to murder by Solon . . . 594
Mithridates, a Persian soldier, who boasted that he had killed Cyrus the Younger, at the battle of Cunaxa, was by order of Artaxerxes exposed to the sun for eighteen days
Maurice, the son of a nobleman, was hanged, drawn, and quartered for piracy, the first execution in that manner in England, 25 Hen. III. . A.D. 1241
The punishment of death was abolished in a great number of cases by sir Robert Peel's acts, 4 to 10 Geo. IV . . . 1824-9
By the criminal law consolidation acts, death was confined to treason and wilful murder . . 1861
The commission on capital punishment (appointed 1864) issued their report (recommending that penal servitude be substituted for death in some cases where murder was unpremeditated, and that executions should not be public) . Dec. 1865
Capital punishment restricted in Italy . April, „
Proposed abolition in Belgium negatived, 18 Jan. 1867
"Capital Punishment within Prisons Bill" passed May, 1868. First case, 13 Aug. 1868: see *Executions*
Abolition of the punishment of death in Great Britain proposed by Mr. Gilpin in the commons; negatived (127 to 23), 21 April, 1868; negatived (118 to 58), 29 July, 1869; negatived (167-54), 24 July, 1872; (155-50), 12 June, 1877; (263-64), 13 March, 1878; proposed by Mr. (aft. sir J.) Pease, negatived (175-79), 22 June, 1881; again 10 May, 1882; again (117-62) . . . 11 May, 1886
Capital punishment abolished in Russia by Catherine II., except for treason . . . 1767

Capital punishment abolished in Tuscany, 1859, Roumania, 1864; Portugal, 1867; Saxony, 1 April, 1868; Holland, 1870. In 17 out of 21 cantons of Switzerland, 1874; Italy, 1888; New York . . 1890
Practically ceased in Belgium, Prussia, Bavaria, Denmark, and Sweden, though not abolished.
In France 126 convictions for murder—4 executed, in one year; similar proportion in Italy.
Abolished in some of United States. Maine, 1876; Rhode Island, Michigan, and Wisconsin, since; in others, virtually ceased.
Capital punishment by electricity (electrocution) ordered to be adopted by the State of New York from . . . . 1 Jan. 1889
The execution of William Kemmler by electricity was ordered, but deferred, on appeal . 11 Oct. „
Execution by electricity declared constitutional by the court of appeals . . . . 22 March, 1890
Execution stopped by *habeas corpus* . 29 April „
Effected with some difficulty . . . 6 Aug. „
Four men executed by electricity at Sing-Sing, N.Y. (others since) . . . . . . 7 July, 1891
Three men electrocuted at Clinton prison, Dannemora, N.Y. . . . . 1 Oct. 1903

Modes of execution (1903):—Austria, gallows, public; Bavaria, guillotine, private; Belgium, guillotine, public; Brunswick, axe, private; China, sword or cord, public; Denmark, guillotine, public; Ecuador, musket, public; France, guillotine, public; Great Britain, gallows, private; Hanover, guillotine, private; Italy, capital punishment abolished; Netherlands, gallows, public; Oldenburg, musket, public; Portugal, gallows, public; Prussia, sword, private; Russia, musket, gallows, or sword, public; Saxony, guillotine, private; Spain, garotte, public, till Dec. 1894; Switzerland, fifteen cantons, sword, public; two cantons, guillotine, public; two cantons, guillotine, private; United States (other than New York), gallows, mostly private.
See *Beheading, Ravaillac, Damiens, Boiling, Burning, Hanging, Forgery, and Campbell's Acts.*
Medical certificates of death; select committee of the commons, first meeting 14 April; report issued, proving great laxity . . . . 1 Sept. 1893
Death penalty abolished for 55 out of 60 crimes in the Federal code . . . . . . 5 Jan. 1897

DEATH DUTIES, a name given to the estate duties (*which see*).

DEATHS, Registers of, see *Bills of Mortality, Public Health,* and *Registers.*

DEBATES IN PARLIAMENT. See *Reporting.*

DEBATING SOCIETIES; several formed in the last century. The celebrated Oxford Union Society was founded in 1823, and many orators have been trained by it.

DEBT, NATIONAL. See *National Debt.*

DEBTORS have been subjected to imprisonment in almost all countries and times. In the eighteen months subsequent to the panic of Dec. 1825, as many as 101,000 writs for debt were issued in England. In the year ending 5 Jan. 1830, there were 7114 persons sent to the several prisons of London; and on that day, 1547 of the number were yet confined. On the 1st of Jan. 1840, the number of prisoners for debt in England and Wales was 1732; in Ireland the number was under 1000; and in Scotland under 100. The operation of statutes of relief, and other causes, considerably reduced the number of imprisoned debtors. When the new Bankruptcy act (abolishing imprisonment for debt except when fraudulently contracted) came into operation in Nov. 1861, a number of debtors who had been confined were released. Arrest of Absconding Debtors bill, 14 & 15 Vict. c. 52, 1852. In 1863 nearly 18,000 persons were imprisoned by order of the county courts for contempt: average time, 15 days, amount of debt, 3*l.* 10*s.* Agitation against this imprisonment, Dec. 1892; select committee of lords on the subject met May, 1893. By an act passed 9 Aug. 1869, the imprisonment of fraudulent debtors was abolished, with certain exceptions, and nearly a hundred debtors were released by a judge's order in Jan. 1870. An act to facilitate the arrest of absconding debtors, passed 9 Aug. 1870. Imprisonment for debt in Ireland was abolished by an act passed 6 Aug. 1872, and in Scotland (after 31 Dec.) by Dr. Cameron's Act, passed 7 Sept. 1880. See *Arrest, King's Bench, Bankrupts, Insolvents, Fleet,* and *National Debt.*

7978 persons were committed to gaol by the county courts in 1871; 4438 in 1874. Imprisonment for debt was virtually abolished by the Bankruptcy Act of 1883, which relieved small debtors; 7,808 imprisoned in 1898; 8,494 in 1902.

DEBUSSCOPE, an instrument of French origin, somewhat similar to the kaleidoscope, said to be useful for devising patterns for calico-printers, &c., made its appearance in 1860.

DECAMERONE (10 *days*), see *Boccaccio.*

DECAPITATION, see *Beheading.*

DECALOGUE (Greek *deka* ten, and *logos* a word), the ten commandments (Ex. xx., Deut. v.), called by the Jews the "ten words" (Ex. xxxiv. 28). The division of the decalogue varies among the Jews and the Christian churches.

DECCAN (Dekhan or Dakhan), S. India, was invaded by the Mahometans in 1294. The first independent sultan was Alaudin. The natives revolted, and the dynasty of Bahmani was founded by Hasan Ganga in 1347. About 1686-90, Aurungzebe I. recovered the Deccan, but soon lost great part of it to the Mahrattas. The Nizam al Mulk, his viceroy, became independent in 1717. A large part of the Deccan was ceded to the English in 1818.

DECEMBER (from *decem*, ten), the tenth month of the year of Romulus, commencing in March. In 713 B.C. Numa introduced January and February before March, and thenceforward December became the twelfth of the year. In the reign of Commodus, A.D. 181—192, December was called, by way of flattery, Amazonius, in honour of a courtesan whom that prince had loved, and had had painted like an Amazon. The English commenced their year on the 25th December, until the reign of William I.; see *Year.* For 2 Dec. revolution see *France,* 1851.

DECEMVIRI, or Ten Men, appointed to draw up a code of laws, to whom for a year the whole government of Rome was committed, 451 B.C. The laws they drew up were approved by the senate and general assembly of the people, written on ten metallic tables, and set up in the place where the people met (*comitium*). Two more tables were added by a second decemvirate, 450 B.C. The tyrannical conduct of Appius Claudius, one of the Decemviri, towards Virginia, who was stabbed by her father Virginius to save her from slavery, led to a revolution, and the re-establishment of the consular government, 449 B.C.

DECENNALIA, festivals instituted by Augustus, 17 B.C., celebrated by the Roman emperors every tenth year of their reign, with sacrifices, games, and largesses. *Livy.* Celebrated by Antoninus Pius, A.D. 148.

DECIMAL SYSTEM of Coinage, Weights, &c., see *Metric System.*

DECIPIUM, a metal found by M. Delafontaine in the same earth with Philippium (*which see*); announced Nov. 1878.

DECLARATION, see *Independence*, *Rights*, and *Accession*.

DECORATED STYLE, see *Gothic*.

DECORATIVE ART. Its principles, enunciated by A. W. Pugin, in his "Designs," in 1835, have been advanced by Owen Jones, Redgrave, and others. Owen Jones's elaborate "Grammar of Ornament" was published in 1856. A Decorative Art society, founded in 1844, existed for a short time only.

DE COURCY'S PRIVILEGE, that of standing covered before the king, granted by king John to John de Courcy, baron of Kingsale, and his successors, in 1203. He was the first Irish nobleman created by an English sovereign, 27 Hen. II. 1181, and was entrusted with the government of Ireland, 1185. The privilege was allowed to the baron of Kingsale by Will. III., Geo. III., and by Geo. IV. at his court held in Dublin, in Aug. 1821. The present baron, Michael Constantine De Courcy, premier baron of Ireland, b. 1855, succeeded 1895, is the 33rd in succession.

DECRETALS. They formed the second part of the canon law, or collection of the pope's edicts and decrees and the decrees of councils. The first acknowledged to be genuine is a letter of Siricius to Himerus, a bishop of Spain, written in the first year of his pontificate, 385. *Howel.* Certain false decretals were used by Gregory IV. in 837. The decretals of Gratian, a Benedictine (a collection of canons), were compiled in 1150. *Hénault.* Five books were collected by Gregory IX. 1227; a sixth by Boniface VIII. 1297; the Clementines by Clement V. in 1313; employed by John XXII. in 1317; the Extravagantes range from 1422 to 1483.

DEDICATION of the Jewish tabernacle took place 1490 B.C.; of the temple, 1004 B.C.; of the second temple, 515 B.C. The Christians under Constantine built new churches and dedicated them with great solemnity, in A.D. 331, *et seq.* The dedication of BOOKS (by authors to solicit patronage or testify respect) existed in the time of Mæcenas, 17 B.C., the friend and counsellor of Augustus, and a patron of Horace (*Ode* I. 1).

DEED, a written contract or agreement. The formula, "I deliver this as my act and deed," occurs in a charter of 933. *Fosbrooke.* Deeds in England were formerly written in Latin or French; the earliest known instance in English is the indenture between the abbot of Whitby and Robert Bustard, dated at York in 1343; see *English Language.*

DEEMSTER, the name given to the two judges who, in the Isle of Man, act as chief justices of the island. One presides over the northern and the other over the southern division. Mr. Hall Caine's novel *The Deemster* gives much interesting information about this office. In Scotland, the deemster, dempster, or doomster, was the title of an official attached to the High Court of Justiciary, whose office it was to pronounce the sentence of death on condemned persons. The office was united to that of executioner.

DEEP-SEA SOUNDINGS. Much new and interesting information respecting the animal life and temperature of the deep sea was acquired by the dredgings on the coast of Norway by M. Sars, and by those of Dr. W. B. Carpenter and prof. (aft. sir) Wyville Thomson on our own coasts, near the Faroe isles, in 1868 and 1869, and in the Mediterranean by Dr. Carpenter in 1870. Living animals have been found at a depth of three miles. On 21 Dec. 1872, Dr. Wyville Thomson and a party of scientific men sailed in H.M.S. *Challenger* (Capt. G. S. Nares), to examine into the physical chemical, geological, and biological condition of the great ocean basins and the direction of their currents. Deepest sounding then known was taken in the Atlantic, north of St. Thomas's, 3875 fathoms (4 miles, 710 yards), 24 March, 1873. On 10 Dec. 1874, capt. Thompson succeeded capt. Nares, who took the command of the new Arctic expedition. The *Challenger* returned, with valuable collections, 25 May, 1876, after a voyage of above 80,000 miles. The "Voyage" was published by sir C. Wyville Thomson in Dec. 1877; and fifty volumes of reports, with many illustrations, had been published, in 1895. The *Challenger* expedition was warmly promoted by Mr. Robert Lowe (afterwards lord Sherbrooke), chancellor of the exchequer, 1868-73. A Norwegian expedition explored the northern seas 16 July—18 Aug. 1877; an Italian expedition in the Mediterranean started 2 Aug. 1881.

Explorations carried on in the eastern Mediterranean for the academy of Vienna; the greatest depth, 2¼ miles, is between Molla and Cerigo . March, 1891
The greatest known ocean depth was said to be 4,475 fathoms south of the Ladrone Islands.
Adm. W. J. Wharton stated that the soundings taken by H.M.S. *Penguin* in the S. Pacific, Feb. 1896, exceeded 5,000 fathoms; *Times* 29 Feb. 1896
Exploration by the Danish cruiser *Ingolf* round Iceland, 2 years . . . . . . 20 Aug. ,,
Expedition under Mr. G. Murray in the *Oceana* to determine the vertical distribution of oceanic life off W. coast of Ireland . . 5 Nov.-2 Dec. 1898
German government deep sea expedition in the *Valdivia* to the Canaries, Cape of Good Hope, and Antarctic, leaves Aug. 1898, returns . 30 April, ,,
Sir John Murray states greatest depth to be 5,155 fathoms, E. of Friendly isles, S. Pacific, 14 Sept. 1899
Internat. conferences on sea exploration, at Stockholm, 15-23 June, 1899; at Christiania, May, 1901
The *Albatross*, prof. Agassiz's, explorations in the Pacific, deepest sounding 4,813 fathoms, lat. 16° 38' N. . . . . . . Aug. *et seq.* 1899
The *Siboga*, Dutch expedition under Herr Max Weber, in the Indian archipelago, 3,560 fathoms taken . . . . 7 March, 1899-27 Feb. 1900
The *Nero*, U.S. ship, in the N. Pacific, between Midway island and Gaam, made 2 soundings, 5,160 and 5,269 fathoms, in . . . . . ,,
Annual deep sea explorations by the prince of Monaco. 4th cruise in the *Princess Alice*, W. Mediterranean and Atlantic . 18 July-Sept. 1902
See also *N.E. and N.W. Passages*, Jan. 1903.

DEER are mentioned in a will of one Athelstan, dated 1045. Professor Owen thinks that fallow deer are not native, but were introduced here at an early period. There are now in England 334 deer parks, the oldest being probably lord Abergavenny's at Eridge, Sussex. See Evelyn Shirley's "Account of Deer Parks," July, 1867. Large numbers of deer are kept at the royal parks of Windsor and Hampton court.

DEERHOUND, an English yacht, while conveying arms to the Carlists, seized by the Spanish government vessel *Buenaventura*, off Biarritz, and captain and crew imprisoned, 13 Aug.; released about 18 Sept. 1873.

DEFAMATION is punishable by fine and imprisonment by statute of 1843. The jurisdiction of the ecclesiastical courts on this subject was abolished by 18 & 19 Vict. c. 41 (1855). See *Libel*.

DEFENCE, see *Church Defence*, *National Defence*, and *Naval and Military adm.* 1895.

DEFENCE ACT, a complete conscription act, authorising a levy *en masse*, 1803, was unsuccessful; new measures were taken in 1807-8. The *Defence of the Realm Act* passed 28 Aug. 1860, in consequence of the unsettled state of Europe, and the doubtful policy of the emperor Napoleon; see *Fortification*, *Colonies*, and *Imperial defence*. Other defence acts passed 1865 and 1873; see also *Naval Defence Acts*.

"DEFENCE GOVERNMENT" in France, formed on 4 Sept. 1870, when the emperor was deposed and a republic proclaimed, gen. Trochu president; it included Gambetta, Simon, &c. It resigned, after Paris had capitulated, 5, 6 Feb. 1871. See *France*.

DEFENDER OF THE FAITH (*Fidei Defensor*), a title of the British sovereign, conferred by Leo. X. on Henry VIII. of England, 11 Oct. 1521, for the tract against Luther on behalf of the Church of Rome (then accounted *Domicilium fidei Catholicæ*).

DEFENDERS, a faction in Ireland, which arose out of a quarrel between two residents of Market-hill, 4 July, 1784. Each was soon aided by a large body of friends, and many battles ensued. On Whit-Monday, 1785, an armed assemblage of one of the parties (700 men), called the *Nappagh Fleet*, prepared to encounter the *Bawn Fleet*, but the engagement was prevented. They subsequently became religious parties, Catholic and Presbyterian, distinguished as *Defenders* and *Peep-o'-day-boys*: the latter were so named because they usually visited the dwellings of the Defenders at daybreak in search of arms; see *Diamond*.

DEGREES. Eratosthenes attempted to determine the length of a geographical degree about 250 B.C. See *Geodesy*, *Latitude*, and *Longitude*. *Collegiate degrees* are coeval with universities. Masters and doctors existed, 826. See *Lambeth Degrees*. Those in law are traced up to 1149; in medicine, to 1384; in music, to 1463. Middle class examinations for degrees were instituted at Oxford, 18 June, 1857; at Cambridge, 24 Nov. 1857; girls were allowed to compete for degrees, Oct. 1863; other universities since. See *Women*, 1896–7 *et seq.*

DEI GRATIA, see *Grace of God*.

DEIRA, a part of the Anglo-Saxon kingdom of Northumbria; see under *Britain*.

DEISM, THEISM, or MONOTHEISM (Latin, *deus*; Greek, *theos*, God), the belief in one God, in opposition to polytheism and to the doctrine of the Trinity. About the middle of the 16th century some gentlemen of France and Italy termed themselves *deists*, to disguise their opposition to Christianity by a more honourable appellation than that of Atheism (*which see*). The most distinguished deists were Herbert, baron of Cherbury, in 1624; Hobbes, Tindal, Morgan, lord Bolingbroke, Gibbon, Hume, Holcroft, Paine, and Godwin.

A high-caste Brahmin, Rammohun Roy, founded a Brahmin monotheistic church in 1830, termed the Brahmo Somaj. He died at Bristol 27 Nov. 1833. His reforming work was revived in 1842 by Debendra Nath Tangore. In 1858 Bal oo Keshub Chunder Sen joined the society, and became a most energetic propagandist, advocating also social reform; being much opposed, he formed the new Brahmo Somaj of India in 1866
Keshub Chunder Sen was received at a public meeting in London as a reformer, 12 April, and subsequently preached in a Unitarian chapel, Finsbury, London 1870
Schism in his church; new church formed (Society of God) 1880
He died at Calcutta . . . . . 8 Jan. 1884
Protap Chunder Mozoomdar, a leader of the Brahmo Somaj, visited Chicago, where he attended the world's parliament of religions, in . 1893

See *Unitarians* and *Voysey*.

DEITIES, see *Mythology*.

DELAGOA BAY, S. E. Africa, claimed by Great Britain and Portugal. Having been referred to arbitration, the southern portion was awarded to Portugal by marshal MacMahon, Aug. 1875.

The importance of the port was greatly increased by the discovery of gold in the Transvaal districts. The South African Republic promoted a railway to be constructed by German and Dutch capitalists. The acquisition of the bay by Great Britain strongly advocated . . . Dec. 1887
The Portuguese government on 14 Dec. 1883, granted a concession to a Portuguese company for the construction of a railway from the bay to the Transvaal territory. The prospectus of the East African railway company (capital 500,000*l.*) was issued 7 March, 1887. As the railway was not completed in the specified time, the works were confiscated by the Portuguese government, 25 June, *et seq.*, who cancelled the concession (see *Portugal*) . . . . . . 26 June, 1889
The British and United States governments remonstrate with Portugal. . . . April, 1890
The completed railway inaugurated . 28 April „
The Portuguese government accepts the principle of arbitration; the governments request the Swiss government to appoint three jurists to form a court of arbitration . . reported 2 May „
The Portuguese government pays 28,000*l.* to the British government for the railway company provisionally . . . . . . reported July „
The court of arbitration meets at Berne . 8 Aug. „
A notice of the facts sent to Berne, 12 Nov. 1892; meetings in Feb. 1896; report issued . April, 1898
Portuguese routed in the Bileni district; reported 30 July, 1897
Plague epidemic, 49 deaths at Magude, reported, 14 Sept. 1899
The Delagoa railway award delivered at Berne: Portugal to pay Great Britain and United States governments 612,560*l.* at 5 per cent. simple interest per ann. from 25 June, 1899, to the date of payment, total amounting to about 950,000*l.*; costs of arbitration to be paid by the 3 governments . . . . . . 29 March, 1900

See *Lourenco Marques*, 1894.

Natural resources of Delagoa bay and harbour to be developed by Portuguese authorities, announced, Jan. 1903

DELAWARE, one of the United States of North America, named after lord de la Warre, governor of Virginia, who entered the bay 1610. It was settled by Swedes, sent there by Gustavus in 1627; acquired by the Dutch, 1655; ceded to the English, 1664. Capital, Dover. Population, 1880, 146,608; 1890, 168,493; 1900, 184,735.

By an explosion at Messrs. Dupont's powder mills near Wilmington 13 persons were killed, 7 Oct. 1890; explosion in a pulp mill at Wilmington, 13 deaths, 6 missing, reported . . 21 Aug. 1902

DELEGATES, COURT OF. Appeals to the pope in ecclesiastical causes having been forbidden (see *Appeals*), such causes were for the future to be heard in this court, established by Henry VIII. 1533. *Stow.* This court was abolished in 1832, and appeals now lie to the Judicial Committee of the Privy Council, according to 3 & 4 Will. IV. c. 41 (1833); and 6 & 7 Vict. c. 38 (1843). See *Arches*.

DELEGATIONS, in the Austro-Hungarian Monarchy, established in 1867, composed of 60 Austrian and 60 Hungarian members.

DELFT (S. Holland), a town founded by Godfrey le Bossu, about 1074; famous for "Delft earthenware;" first manufactured here about 1310. The sale of delft greatly declined after the introduction of potteries into Germany and England. Grotius, jurist, was born here, 10 April, 1583; tercentenary celebrated 10 April, 1883. His statue erected, 17 Sept. 1886. And here William, the great prince of Orange, was assassinated by Gerard, 10 July, 1584; tercentenary celebrated 10 July, 1884. Population, 1890, 29,022; 1900, 31,878.

DELHI, the once great capital of the Mogul empire, and chief seat of the Mahometan power in India; it was taken by Timour in 1398. It is now in decay, but contained a million of inhabitants in 1700. In 1739, when Nadir Shah invaded Hindostan, he entered Delhi; 100,000 of the inhabitants perished by the sword, and plunder to the amount of 62,000,000*l*. sterling is said to have been collected. Similar calamities were endured in 1761, on the invasion of Abdalla, king of Candahar. In 1803, the Mahrattas, aided by the French, took Delhi; but were defeated by general Lake, 11 Sept., and the aged Shah Aulum, emperor of Hindostan, was restored to his throne with a pension; see *India*, 1803. On 10 May, 1857, a mutiny arose in the sepoy regiments at Meerut. It was soon checked; but the fugitives fled to Delhi on 11 May, and, combined with other troops here, seized the city; proclaimed a descendant of the Mogul king, and committed frightful atrocities. The rebels were anxious to possess the chief magazine, but after a gallant defence it was exploded by order of lieut. Willoughby, who died of his wounds shortly after. The other heroes of this exploit were lieutenants Forrest and Rayner, and the gunners Buckley and Scully. Delhi was shortly after besieged by the British, but was not taken till 20 Sept. following. The final struggle began on the 14th; brigadier (aft. sir) Archdale Wilson, the commander, much aided by col. R. Baird Smith. Much heroism was shown; the gallant death of Salkeld at the explosion of the Cashmere gate created much enthusiasm. The old king and his sons were captured soon after: the latter were shot, and the former after a trial was sent for life to Rangoon, where he died 11 Nov. 1862. See *India*, 1857. A camp formed at Delhi by the earl of Mayo, the viceroy, Dec. 1871, was visited by the king of Siam, Jan. 1872. The prince of Wales visited Delhi, 11 Jan. 1876. Queen Victoria was proclaimed empress of India here with much magnificence, many Indian princes being present, 1 Jan. 1877. Great fire, 2000 houses burnt, 19 April, 1883. Pop. 1901, 208,575.

Foundation-stone of Dufferin Hospital laid by lord Dufferin . . . . 2 Nov. 1885
Riots by collisions at Hindoo and Mahommedan festivals quelled by the military 5 Oct. *et seq.* 1886
Great fire, 300 houses destroyed . 11–12 May, 1889
Fanatical riots quelled . . about 8 April, 1892
Railway collision, 50 persons killed or injured; reported . . . . . . 27 July, 1896
Statue of queen Victoria unveiled . . 26 Dec. 1902
Proclamation of Edward VII. king and emperor, see *India*, Jan. 1903.

"DELICATE INVESTIGATION" into the conduct of the princess of Wales (afterwards queen of England, as consort of George IV.), was commenced by a committee of the privy council, under a warrant of inquiry, dated 29 May, 1806. The members were lord Grenville, lord Erskine, earl Spencer, and lord Ellenborough. The inquiry, of which the countess of Jersey, sir J. and lady Douglas, and other persons of rank, were the prompters, led to the publication called "The Book"; afterwards suppressed. The charges against the princess were disproved in 1807 and in 1813; but not being permitted to appear at court, she went on the continent in 1814; see *Queen Caroline*.

DELIUM, Bœotia, N. Greece, the site of a celebrated temple of Apollo. Here, in a conflict between the Athenians and the Bœotians, in which the former were defeated, Socrates the philosopher is said to have saved the life of his pupil Xenophon, 424 B.C.

DELLA CRUSCA ACADEMY of Florence merged into the Florentine in 1582.—The DELLA CRUSCA SCHOOL, a term applied to some English residents at Florence, who printed inferior sentimental poetry and prose in 1785. They came to England, where their works, popular for a short time, were severely satirised by Gifford in his "Baviad" and "Mæviad" (1792-5).

DELOS, a Greek isle in the Ægean sea. Here the Greeks, during the Persian war, 477 B.C., established their common treasury, which was removed to Athens, 461. Excavations, resulting in interesting discoveries, were made in the island by the French in 1883.

DELPHI (N. Greece), celebrated for its enigmatical oracles delivered by the Pythia or priestess in the temple of Apollo, which was built, some say, by the council of the Amphictyons, 1263 B.C. The Pythian games were first celebrated here 586 B.C. The temple was burnt by the Pisistratidæ, 548 B.C. A new temple was raised by the Alcmæonidæ. The Persians (480 B.C.) and the Gauls (279 B.C.) were deterred from plundering the temple by awful portents. It was, however, robbed and seized by the Phocians 357 B.C., which led to the sacred war, and Nero carried from it 300 costly statues, A.D. 67. The oracle was consulted by Julian, but silenced by Theodosius.

An ancient hymn to Apollo, the words and musical notation, inscribed on two tablets, recently discovered, sung in the presence of the king and queen, &c., at Athens . . . . 29 March, 1894
Excavations by the French school of archæology; discoveries of the remains of the temple of Apollo, April, 1894; a great statue of Apollo and altar (date about 480 B.C.) . . May, ,,

DELPHIN CLASSICS, a collection of thirty-nine Latin authors in sixty volumes, made for the use of the dauphin (*in usum Delphini*), son of Louis XIV., and published in 1674-91. Ausonius was added in 1730. The duc de Montausier, the young prince's governor, proposed the plan to Huet, bishop of Avranches, the daupbin's preceptor; and he, with other learned persons, including Madame Dacier,* edited all the Latin classics except Lucan. Each author is illustrated by notes and an index of words. An edition of the Delphin classics, with additional notes, &c., was published by Mr. Valpy of London, 1818, *et seq.*

DELTA, the island formed by the alluvial deposits between the mouths of the Nile, so named by the Greeks from its resemblance to their letter Δ (our D).

DELTA METAL, a modern bronze resembling gold, containing a small proportion of iron, invented by Mr. A. Dick: watch cases were made of it at Geneva in 1885.

DELUGE, THE, which was predicted by Noah, is described in *Genesis* vi. vii. viii.; dated by Usher and the English Bible 2348 B.C. The

* This beautiful and gifted woman translated *Callimachus* at the age of 23; and also *Anacreon, Sappho, Plautus, Terence,* and *Homer*. She died in 1720.

following are the epochs of the deluge, according to Dr. Hales:—

Septuagint	B.C. 3246	Clinton	B.C. 2482
Jackson	3170	Playfair	2352
Hales	3155	Marsham	2344
Josephus	3146	Petavius	2329
Persian	3103	Strauchius	2293
Hindoo	3102	Hebrew	2288
Samaritan	2998	Vulgar Jewish	2104
Howard	2698		

Traditional deluges described in the classics: in Bœotia and Attica in the reign of Ogyges, 18th century B.C.; in Thessaly in the reign of Deucalion, 1503 B.C.; the dates are conjectural.

DEMERARA, ESSEQUIBO, AND BERBICE, colonies in British Guiana, South America, founded by the Dutch, 1580, were taken by the British, under major-general Whyte, 22 April, 1796, but were restored at the peace of Amiens, March, 1802. They again surrendered to the British under general Grinfield and commodore Hood, Sept. 1803, and became English colonies in 1814. See *Guiana, British.*

Riot of coolies, conflict with police, 6 killed, 7 wounded . . . . 6 May, 1903

DEMISE OF THE CROWN ACT, royal assent, 2 July, 1901, making fresh appointments to offices held under the crown unnecessary after the death of the sovereign.

DEMOCRATIC FEDERALS, a political party, proposed by Mr. Joseph Cowen, M.P. for Newcastle, opposed to the policy of the government of Mr. Gladstone, 5 April, 1881.

DEMOCRATS, advocates for government by the people themselves (*demos*, people, and *kratein*, to govern), a term adopted by the French republicans in 1790 (who termed their opponents *aristocrats*, from *aristos*, bravest or best). The name *Democrats* was adopted by the pro-slavery party in N. America (the southern states), and the abolitionists were called *Republicans*. Into these two great parties a number of smaller ones were absorbed at the presidential election in 1856. In 1860, the Republicans formed "Wide-awake" clubs for electioneering purposes, and succeeded in getting their candidate, Abraham Lincoln, elected president, 4 Nov., which led to civil war; see *United States*, 1860.

In the autumn of 1874, the democrats, free-traders, and opponents of negro-rule, once more obtained the majority in the elections for the next congress; a reaction in their favour against the republicans, protectionists, then powerful; see *United States*, 1875-7. Governor Grover Cleveland, democrat, elected president, 4 Nov. 1884; not re-elected, being replaced by general Benjamin Harrison, republican . . . . 5 Nov. 1888

Mr. Cleveland was re-elected president, 8 Nov. 1892, the democrats having obtained a majority in the new congress and the senate, the first time since 1860. The democrat party was much disorganized by the election of Mr. M'Kinley, republican; see *United States*, Nov. 1896 *et seq.*

DEMOGRAPHY. A modern term, signifying "the natural history of society." *Quetelet.* See *Hygiene.*

DEMONOLOGY, see *Devil Worship.*

DENAIN (N. France). Here marshal Villars defeated the Imperialists, 24 July, 1712.

DENARIUS, the chief silver coin among the Romans, weighing the seventh part of a Roman ounce, and value 7¾*d.* sterling, first coined about 269 B.C., when it exchanged for ten ases (see *As*). In 216 B.C. it exchanged for sixteen ases. A pound weight of silver was coined into 100 denarii. *Digby.* A pound weight of gold was coined into twenty denarii aurei in 206 B.C.; and in Nero's time into forty-five denarii aurei. *Lempriere.*

DENHAM MURDERS, see *Trials*, 1870.

DENIS, ST., an ancient town of France, near Paris, famous for its abbey and church; the former abolished at the revolution, the latter the place of sepulture of the French kings, from its foundation by Dagobert, about 630; the remains of the saint Denis were placed there in 636. On 6, 7, 8 Aug. 1793, the republicans demolished most of the royal tombs, and in Oct. following, the bodies were taken from coffins and cast into a pit; the lead was melted, and the gold and jewels taken to Paris. By a decree of Bonaparte, dated 20 Feb. 1806, the church (which had been turned into a cattle-market) was ordered to be cleansed out and redecorated as "the future burial-place of the emperors of France." On the return of the Bourbons, more restorations were effected, and the duc de Berri and Louis XVIII. were buried here. The damage sustained in the war of 1870-1 has been well repaired. Near St. Denis the Catholics defeated the Huguenots, but lost their leader, the constable Montmorency, 10 Nov. 1567.

DENISON'S ACT (18 & 19 Vict. c. 34), provided "for the education of the children of persons in receipt of out-door relief:" passed 26 June, 1855.

DENMAN'S ACT, LORD, 6 & 7 Vict. c. 85 (1843), related to juries and witnesses, permitting them to affirm instead of taking an oath. It is superseded by the oaths act 1888.

DENMARK (N. Europe). The most ancient inhabitants were Cimbri and Teutones, who were driven out by the Jutes or Goths. The Teutones settled in Germany and Gaul; the Cimbrians invaded Italy, where they were defeated by Marius. The peninsula of Jutland obtained its name from the Jutes; and the name of Denmark is supposed to be derived from *Dan*, the founder of the Danish monarchy, and *mark*, a German word signifying country. For their numerous invasions of Britain, &c., see *Danes*. Population of the kingdom of Denmark in 1860, 1,600,551; of the duchies of Schleswig, Holstein, and Lauenburg, 1,004,473; of the colonies, 120,283. By the treaty of peace, signed 30 Oct. 1864, the duchies were taken from Denmark; Schleswig and Holstein were to be made independent, and Lauenburg was to be incorporated, by its desire, with Prussia. For the result, see *Gastein* and *Prussia*, 1866. Population of the monarchy, 1870, 1,784,741; 1880, 1,969,039; of the colonies, 1880, 127,200; 1900 (including Faröe Isles), 2,185,335. Revenue, 1889-90, 3,192,009*l.*; 1893-94, 3,088,089*l.*; 1896-7, 3,624,185*l*; 1901-2, 5,379,528*l.* Imports, 1890, 17,057,000*l.*; 1892, 18,029,845; 1901, 22,101,766*l.*; exports, 1890, 12,990,000*l.*; 1892, 14,017,696*l.*; 1896, 15,771,053*l.*; 1901, 16,222,333*l.*

[The early dates are doubtful.]

Reign of Skiold, alleged first king . . . B.C. 60
The Danish chronicles mention 18 kings to the time of Ragnar Lodbrog, killed in an attempt to invade England . . . . A.D. 794
Canute the Great conquers Norway . . . 1016-28
By the union of Calmar, Denmark, Norway, and Sweden made one kingdom under Margaret, 12 July, 1397
Copenhagen made the capital 1440
Accession of Christian I. (of *Oldenburg*), from whom the late royal family sprang 1448
Christian II. deposed; independence of Sweden under Gustavus Vasa acknowledged . . . 1523
Lutheranism introduced in 1527; established by Christian III. 1536

Danish East India Company established 1612
Christian IV. chosen head of the Protestant league against the emperor 1629
Charles Gustavus of Sweden invades Denmark, besieges Copenhagen, and makes conquests . . 1658
The crown made hereditary and absolute . . 1665
Frederick IV. takes Holstein, Schleswig, Tonningen, and Stralsund; reduces Weismar, and drives the Swedes from Norway . . . . . 1716 *et seq.*
Copenhagen nearly destroyed by fire . . . 1728
The peaceful reign of Christian VI. . . . 1730-46
Plot of the queen dowager against the ministers and Matilda (sister of our George III. and queen of Christian VII., a weak monarch). Matilda, entrapped into a confession of criminality to save the life of her supposed lover, Struenzee, condemned to imprisonment for life in the castle of Zell. 18 Jan. 1772
Count Struenzee and Brandt beheaded 28 April, ,,
Queen Matilda dies, aged 24 1775
Christian VII. becomes deranged, and prince Frederick is appointed regent 1784
One-fourth of Copenhagen burnt . . . 9 June, 1795
Admirals Nelson and Parker bombard Copenhagen (*which see*). (Confederacy of the North, see *Armed Neutrality*, dissolved.) 2 April, 1801
Admiral Gambier and lord Cathcart bombard Copenhagen; the Danish fleet surrenders . 7 Sept. 1807
Peace of Kiel: Pomerania and Rügen annexed to Denmark for Norway . . . 14 Jan. 1814
Pomerania and Rügen ceded to Prussia for Lauenburg 1815
Commercial treaty with England 1824
Frederick VI. grants a new constitution . . . 1831
Christian VIII. declares the right of the crown to Schleswig, Holstein, &c. . . . 11 July, 1846
Accession of Frederick VII. 20 Jan.; he proclaims a new constitution, uniting the duchies more closely with Denmark . . . . . 28 Jan. 1848
Insurrection in the duchies: a provisional government founded . . . . . 23 March, ,,
The rebels seize fortress of Rendsburg 24 March, ,,
They are defeated near Flensburg 9 April, ,,
The Danes defeated by the Prussians (helping the duchies) near Dannawerke, Schleswig . 23 April, ,,
The North sea blockaded by Denmark . 1 Aug. ,,
Hostilities suspended: the European powers recommend peace . . . . . . 26 Aug. ,,
Hostilities recommence . . . . 25 March, 1849
Victory of the Danes over the Holsteiners and Germans . . . . 10 April, ,,
Several conflicts with varying success . June, ,,
The king sanctions a new liberal constitution, 5 June, ,,
Armistice renewed at Malmo . . . 10 July, ,,
Separate peace with Prussia . . . . 2 July, 1850
Integrity of Denmark guaranteed by England, France, Prussia, and Sweden . . . . 4 July, ,,
Battle of Idstedt, and defeat of the Schleswig-Holsteiners by the Danes . . . . 25 July, ,,
Protocol signed in London by the ministers of all the great powers . . . . 23 Aug. ,,
Bombardment of Friedrichstadt by the Holsteiners, and the town almost destroyed, but not taken, 29 Sept. to 6 Oct. ,,
Proclamation of the stadtholders of Schleswig-Holstein, placing the rights of the country under the protection of the Germanic confederation 10 Jan. 1851
The integrity of the Danish monarchy and the independence of Schleswig and its old union with Holstein guaranteed by treaty . . . 18 Feb. 1852
Austrians evacuate Holstein, &c. . . 2 March, ,,
Treaty of European powers. [The succession in the line of Sonderburg-Glücksburg settled, and the integrity of the Danish kingdom guaranteed. Christian, duke of Augustenburg-Holstein, renounced his rights for a compensation in money.] 8 May, ,,
The king promulgates a new constitution, 29 July, 1854; adopted . . . . . 1 Oct. 1855
The sound dues abolished for a compensation (see *Sound*) . . . . . . 14 March, 1857
Dissension between the government and the duchies, Oct. 1857-62
Fortification of Copenhagen decreed 27 March, 1858
New ministry appointed 3 Dec. 1859; resigns 9 Feb.; bishop Monrad forms a ministry . . 24 Feb. 1860
The assembly of Schleswig complain that the promise of equality of national rights in 1852 has not been kept, 11 Feb.; protest against the annexation to Denmark . . . . . 1 March, 1860
The Prussian chamber of deputies receive a petition from Schleswig, and declare that they will aid the duchies, 4 May; at which the Danish government protests . . . . . . 16 May, ,,
Correspondence ensues between the Prussian, Danish, and British governments; the Danish government declare for war, if German forces enter the duchies . . . . . . Jan. 1861
Warlike preparations in Denmark . . . Feb. ,,
Decimal coinage adopted . . . . June, ,,
Agitation in favour of union of Denmark with Sweden, June; the king of Sweden visits Denmark, and is warmly received . . 17 July, 1862
Earl Russell recommends the government to give to Holstein and Lauenburg all that the Germanic confederation desire for them, and to give self-government to Schleswig . . . 24 Sept. ,,
M. Hall, the Danish minister, declines to accede; stating that to do so would imperil the existence of the monarchy itself . . . . 20 Nov. ,,
Princess Alexandra of Denmark married to the Prince of Wales at Windsor . . 10 March, 1863
The king grants, by patent, independent rights to Holstein, but annexes Schleswig . 30 March, ,,
Austria and Prussia protest against it . 17 April, ,,
Further diplomatic correspondence . . . May, ,,
The king accepts the crown of Greece for his relative, prince William-George, and gives him sound political advice . . . . . . 6 June, ,,
Death of the crown prince Frederick-Ferdinand, the king's uncle . . . . . 29 June, ,,
The German diet demands annulment of the patent of 30 March; (Holstein and Schleswig to be united with the same right;) and threatens an army of occupation . . . . 9 July, ,,
The king replies that he will consider occupation to be an act of war . . . . . 27 Aug. ,,
Vain efforts for alliance with Sweden . Aug. ,,
Extra levy for the army decreed . . 1 Aug. ,,
New constitution (uniting Schleswig with Denmark) proposed in the rigsraad . . . . 29 Sept. ,,
Death of Frederick VII. and accession of Christian IX. . . . . 15 Nov. ,,
Prince Frederick of Augustenburg claims the duchies of Schleswig and Holstein . . 16 Nov. ,,
Great excitement in Holstein; many officials refuse to take oath to Christian . 21 Nov. *et seq.* ,,
Saxony, Bavaria, Hesse, and other German powers resolve to support the prince of Augustenburg, 26 Nov. *et seq.* ,,
New constitution affirmed by the rigsraad, 13 Nov.; signed by king, 18 Nov.; published, . 1, 2 Dec. ,,
The Austrian and Prussian ministers say that they will quit Copenhagen if the constitution of 18 Nov. is not annulled . . . . . Dec. ,,
Great excitement in Norway: proposals to support Denmark . . . . Dec. ,,
Prince Frederick's letter to the emperor Napoleon, 2 Dec.; an ambiguous reply . . . 10 Dec. ,,
Denmark protests against federal occupation 19 Dec. ,,
900 representatives of different German states meet at Frankfort, and resolve to support prince Frederick as duke of Schleswig and Holstein, and the inseparable union of those duchies . . 21 Dec. ,,
The federal execution takes place; a Saxon regiment enters Altona, 24 Dec.; and the federal commissioners assume administrative powers . 25 Dec. ,,
The Danes retire from Holstein, to avoid collision with federal troops . . 24 Dec. *et seq.* ,,
Prince Frederick enters Kiel, as duke of Schleswig and Holstein . . . . . . 30 Dec. ,,
The Danes evacuate Rendsburg . . 31 Dec. ,,
Ministerial crisis: Hall retires, and bishop Monrad forms a cabinet . . . . . 31 Dec. ,,
Dissension among Germans: the Austro-Prussian proposition rejected by the diet . . 14 Jan. 1864
Austria and Prussia demand abrogation of the constitution (of 18 Nov.) in two days, 16 Jan.; the Danes require six weeks' time . . 18 Jan. ,,
The German troops under marshal Wrangel enter Holstein . . . . 21 Jan. ,,
The Prussians enter Schleswig, and take Eckenforde, 1 Feb. ,,

They bombard Missunde, 2 Feb.; which is burnt, 3 Feb. 1864

The Danes abandon the Dannewerke to save their army, 5 Feb.; great discontent in Copenhagen, 6 Feb. ,,

The Danes defeated by Wrangel at Oever-see; Schleswig taken; pr. Frederick proclaimed, 6 Feb. ,,

The allies occupy Flensburg, 7 Feb.; commence their attack on Düppel . . . 13 Feb. ,,

The federal commissioners protest against the Prussian occupation of Altona . . . 13 Feb. ,,

The Prussians enter Jutland; take Kolding, 18 Feb.; Danes fortify Alsen . . . 18 Feb. *et seq.* ,,

A conference on Danish affairs proposed by England; agreed to by allies . . . 23 Feb. ,,

A subscription for the wounded Danes begun in London . . . 24 Feb. ,,

De Gertach, general of the Danes . . 1 Mar. ,,

Defeated at Sonderbygaard and Veil . 8 Mar. ,,

The rigsraad vote a firm address to the king, 26 Feb.; adjourned . . . 22 Mar. ,,

The Prussians bombard and take the village of Düppel, or Dybböl, 16, 17 March, and bombard Fredericia, 20 March; repulsed in an attack on the fortress . . . 28 Mar. ,,

The opening of the conference adjourned from 12 to 20 April, ,,

The Prussians take the fortress of Düppel, by assault, with much slaughter . . . 18 April, ,,

Meetings of the conference of London: result unfavourable to Denmark . . 25 April, *et seq.* ,,

The Danes retreat to Alsen; evacuate Fredericia and fortresses of Jutland . . . 29 April, ,,

Agreement for an armistice for one month from 12 May . . . 9 May, ,,

Jutland subjected to pillage for not paying a war contribution to Prussians . . 6 May, *et seq.* ,,

The Danes defeat the allies in a naval battle off Heligoland . . . 9 May, ,,

The armistice prolonged a fortnight . 9 June, ,,

The conference ends . . . 22 June

Hostilities resumed, 26 June; the Prussians bombard Alsen; take the batteries and 2400 prisoners, 29 June, ,,

The Monrad ministry resigns; count Möltke charged to form an administration . 8-10 July, ,,

Alsen taken;—Jutland placed under Prussian administration;—Prince John of Denmark sent to negotiate at Berlin . . . 9 July, ,,

Formation of the Bluhme ministry . . 11 July, ,,

Armistice agreed to . . 18 July, ,,

Conference for peace at Vienna . . 26 July, ,,

Treaty of peace signed at Vienna;—the king of Denmark resigns the duchies to the disposal of the allies, and agrees to a rectification of his frontier, and to pay a large sum of money to defray the expenses of the war . . 30 Oct. ,,

Proclamation of the king to the inhabitants of the duchies, releasing them from their allegiance, 16 Nov. ,,

Project of a new constitution presented to the chambers, 21 Dec.; rejected . . 25 Feb. 1865

New ministry formed under count Frijsenborg, 6 Nov.; a new constitution proposed, 7 Nov. 1865; approved by the two chambers, 19 and 27 July; sanctioned by the king . . 28 July, 1866

Princess Dagmar married to prince Alexander of Russia . . . 9 Nov. ,,

New rigsraad opened . . 12 Nov. ,,

The king visited England . . March, 1867

The Danish West Indies, St. Thomas and St. John, proposed to be sold to the United States for 1,500,000*l.* — proclamation in the islands dated 25 Oct. ,,

Proposed sale of St. Thomas's to the United States approved by the assembly (not carried out), 30 Jan. 1868

Marriage of the crown prince Frederic to the princess Louisa of Sweden . 28 July, 1869

New ministry formed by M. Holsteinborg, 20 May, 1870

Denmark remains neutral in the Franco-Prussian war; fruitless visit of the duc de Cadore to Copenhagen . . 4-11 Aug ,,

Birth of a son to the crown prince . . 27 Sept. ,,

Destructive hurricane over the kingdom; loss of life and property . . . 12, 13 Nov. ,,

Parliament opened . . . 1 Oct. 1871

War budget reduced . . . 18 Dec. ,,

Meeting of the "International" (see *Working Men*) at Copenhagen forbidden; chiefs arrested 5 May, 1872

Industrial exhibition opened . . 13 June, ,,

Statue of Frederick VII., at Copenhagen, solemnly inaugurated . . 6 Oct. 1873

A communistic party in the assembly (folkething) defeat the ministry, 4 Dec.; the king refuses to dismiss it . . 6 Dec. ,,

New ministry under Fonnesbeck . 14 July, 1874

The king visits Iceland (*which see*), July-Aug.; Edinburgh . . 16 Aug. ,,

Several ministerial changes . . 1875

J. B. S. Estrup, president of the ministry, 11 June, ,,

The folkething, defeating the government on the question of fortifications, is dissolved 29 March, ,,

New assembly meets, 15 May; votes no confidence in the ministry, 12 June; is adjourned, 24 June, 1876

Continued contest between the king and senate and the lower house . . Oct. ,,

Crisis respecting the supplies . Dec. ,,

The session closed without settling the budget, 4 April, 1877

Provision made by the king for it in accordance with the constitution . 12 April, ,,

Political crisis; an armistice agreed to . 8 Nov. ,,

Marriage of princess Thyra with the duke of Cumberland . . 21 Dec. 1878

The lower house dismissed by the king as incapable and idle . . about 10 May, 1883

Anna Kristiane Ludvigsen, author of patriotic songs, dies, aged 90 . . 27 July, 1884

Opposition of the lower house continues; legislation greatly stopped . . 1881-4

Elections: lower house, 82 liberals (opposition); 20 conservatives . . June, 1884

The king recommends unity in providing national defence . . about 30 Oct. ,,

The king refuses to dismiss his ministry, 21 March; closes parliament; decrees financial arrangement, 1 April, 1885

Importation and possession of arms and drill prohibited . . 5 May, ,,

M. Estrup fired at by Julius Rasmussen 21 Oct. ,,

The parliament condemns the restrictive press laws by great majority . . 21 Dec. ,,

M. Berg, president of the assembly, sentenced to six months' imprisonment for obstructing the police at a meeting . . Jan. 1886

Discord in parliament, which is closed . 8 Feb. ,,

Fusion of two parties forming the left of the Diet . . about 26 Oct. ,,

The folkething dissolved . 8 Jan. 1887

Amnesty granted to political prisoners on the king's 70th birthday . . 8 April, 1888

25th anniversary of the king's accession celebrated 15th Nov. ,,

The Budget rejected 16 Oct. 1885; 26 Jan. 1886; 1 April, 1887; 1 April, 1888; 1 April, 1889; 31 March, 1890; 1 April, 1891—the revenue collected by royal decree . . 1886-91

Elections for the folkething; the moderates successful . . 20 April, 1892

National celebration of the king's golden wedding, 26 May, ,,

New military bill introduced . about 27 Oct. ,,

Death of Christian Richardt, national poet, aged 61 Dec. ,,

The king decrees a provisional budget for 1892-3, 1 April, 1892; 1893-94 . . 1 April, 1893

The king and queen visit England, June; present at the marriage of the duke and duchess of York, 6 July; visit the queen at Windsor, 12 July; leave England . . 27 July, ,,

Anarchist club discovered in Copenhagen; some arrests . . 23 Feb. 1894

The ministerial budget accepted by the parliament; surplus, 2,830,000 kronen . 30 March, ,,

Messrs. Hunter & Erichsen, of Newcastle, *v.* M. Tietgen, in Copenhagen (15 years' suit); 13,000*l.* claimed for supplies for harbour works at Esbjerg from 1868-71; verdict for the plaintiffs reversed by the supreme court . . 1 June, ,,

The crown prince visits England . . June, ,,

Resignation of M. Estrup, 19 years autocratic premier; cabinet re-constructed, baron de Reedtz-Thott, premier . . 7 Aug. ,,

Death of M. Carl Plong, "Paul Rytter," poet and politician . . . . . . 27 Oct. 1894
Loan of 25,000,000 kroner, at 3 per cent., authorised 4 Dec. ,,
Electoral district (reform) bill passed . 20 Dec. ,,
The budget passed, with a surplus . 16 March, 1895
Parliamentary election; small radical majority 9 April, ,,
Parliament opened . . . . 7 Oct. ,,
Budget, with a surplus, passed . 31 March, 1896
Prince Charles, son of the crown prince, married to princess Maud of Wales at Buckingham palace 22 July, ,,
Count Frijs-Frijsenborg (premier 1865-70) died, aged 79 . . . . 12 Oct. ,,
Budget, with compromise; reported . 23 April, 1897
Cabinet crisis; premier, M. de Reedtz-Thott, resigns . . . . 11 May, ,,
New ministry; M. Hörring, premier . 23 May, ,,
Collision between a fast train and a standing excursion train at Gjentofte, near Copenhagen, 32 deaths, 99 injured; M. Holst and many members of associations killed . . . . 11 July, ,,
Debt conversion bill passed, authorizing a 3 per cent. state loan of 72,000,000 kroner . 26 Nov. ,,
Elections (lower house) radical victory . 5 April, 1898
Mr. E. Fane appointed British Minister (knt., 1899; died, 20 March, 1900) . . . . June ,,
The queen dies, much lamented, 29 Sept.; funeral at Copenhagen . . . . 15 Oct. ,,
See *Prussia*, Oct. 1898.
M. Bille, statesman and journalist, dies, aged 70, 11 Nov. ,,
Cabinet reconstructed, M. Bramsen (interior), col. von Schnack (war) . . . . . 28 Aug. 1899
General lock-out (40,000) in the building and engineering trades, 31 May, 1899; extended to other trades, Aug.; closed in favour of the employers, 5 Sept. ,,
Budget for 1900: revenue, 72,900,000 kroner; expenditure, 72,000,000 kroner, introduced, 3 Oct. ,,
Resignation of the Hörring cabinet . 22 March, 1900
The prince and princess of Wales arrive . 5 April, ,,
M. Schested (conservative) forms a cabinet, 27 April, ,,
Committee elected to examine the taxation laws, government majority of 1 . . . . 5 Dec. ,,
Sophus Schandorph, poet and novelist, born, 8 May, 1837, died . . . . . 1 Jan. 1901
General election: utter defeat of the conservatives and the ministry, reported . . . 4 April ,,
Ministerial crisis, early May; M. Schested remains in office . . . . 22 May, ,,
Constitutional day; anti-ministerial demonstrations . . . . 5 June, ,,
Cabinet resigns, 17 July; prof. Deuntzer forms a radical ministry . . . . . . 23 July, ,,
Radical deputation from all districts received by the king . . . . 1 Sept. ,,
Royal gathering at Fredensborg, Aug.; joined by the czar and czarina, 2-10 Sept.; king Edward arrives, 7 Sept.; he receives a deputation and an address in Copenhagen; he and the queen visit prof. Finsen's Light institute (see *Tuberculosis*, 1901), 13 Sept.; they leave . . . 23 Sept. ,,
Great fire at Kallundborg, 30 houses burnt; estimated damage, 2,000,000 kroner . 23, 24 Sept. ,,
Parliament opened by the king . . . 5 Oct. ,,
Bill authorising a new state loan passed . 12 Oct. ,,
Death of Mr. C. F. Tietgen, the great merchant, "the king of the Baltic," aged 72 . 19 Oct. ,,
Tercentenary of Tycho Brahe's death celebrated at Copenhagen, Prague, and Lund, in Sweden, 24 Oct. ,,
Death of M. Sophus Hogsbro, aged 79 . 15 Jan. 1902
Treaty for the sale of the Danish West Indies to the United States signed at Washington, 24 Jan.; rejected by the Landsthing . . . 16 May, ,,
President Loubet visits the king . . 25 May, ,,
Danish West Indian company formed, prince Waldemar president . . . . . 25 Oct. ,,
Government bill, repealing existing land taxes, providing a *pro ratâ* property tax, an income tax, a tax on capital, and the reform of commercial assessments adopted by large majority by the folkething . . . . May 1903

A.D.

SOVEREIGNS.

794. Sigurd Snogoje.
803. Hardicanute.
850. Eric I.
854. Eric II.
883. Gormo, the Old; reigned 53 years.
941. Harold, surnamed Blue Tooth.
991. Suenon, or Sweyn, the Forked-beard.
1014. Canute II. the Great, king of *Denmark and England*.
1035. Canute III., son (Hardicanute of England).
1042. Magnus, surnamed the Good, of Norway.
1047. Suenon, or Sweyn II. (Denmark only).
1073. [Interregnum.]
1076. Harold, called the Simple.
1080. Canute IV.
1086. Olaus IV. the Hungry.
1095. Eric I., styled the Good.
1103. [Interregnum.]
1105. Nicholas I. killed at Sleswick.
1135. Eric II., surnamed Harefoot.
1137. Eric III. the Lamb.
1147. { Suenon, or Sweyn III.: beheaded. Canute V. until 1157 (civil war).
1157. Waldemar, styled the Great.
1182. Canute VI., surnamed the Pious.
1202. Waldemar II. the Victorious.
1241. Eric IV.
1250. Abel: assassinated his elder brother Eric; killed in an expedition against the Frisons.
1252. Christopher I.: poisoned.
1259. Eric V.
1286. Eric VI.
1320. Christopher II.
1334. [Interregnum of seven years.]
1340. Waldemar III.
1375. [Interregnum.]
1376. Olaus V.
1387. Margaret, styled the "Semiramis of the North," queen of *Sweden, Norway, and Denmark*.
1397. Margaret and Eric VII. (Eric XIII. of Sweden.)
1412. Eric VII. reigns alone; obliged to resign both crowns.
1438. [Interregnum.]
1440. Christopher III. king of *Sweden*.
1448. Christian I. count of *Oldenburg;* elected king of *Denmark*, 1448; of *Sweden*, 1457; succeeded by his son.
1481. John; succeeded by his son,
1513. Christian II., called the Cruel, and the "Nero of the North;" he caused all the Swedish nobility to be massacred: dethroned for his tyranny in 1523; died in a dungeon in 1559.
[Sweden separated from Denmark.]

DENMARK AND NORWAY.

1523. Frederick I. duke of Holstein, son of Christian I.; a liberal ruler.
1533. Christian III. son of Frederick; established the Lutheran religion; esteemed the "Father of his People."
1559. Frederick II. son of Christian III.
1588. Christian IV. son.
1648. Frederick III.; changed the constitution from an elective to an HEREDITARY MONARCHY, vested in his own family, 1665.
1670. Christian V., son of Frederick III.; succeeded by his son.
1699. Frederick IV.; leagued with the czar Peter and the king of Poland against Charles XII. of Sweden.
1730. Christian VI. his son.
1746. Frederick V. his son: married the princess Louisa of England, daughter of George II.
1766. Christian VII. his son.
1784. Prince Frederick declared regent, in consequence of the mental derangement of his father.
1808. Frederick VI. previously regent, now king.
1814. Norway annexed to Sweden, 14 Jan.

DENMARK.

1839. Christian VIII. (son of Frederick, brother of Christian VII.)
1848. Frederick VII. son of Christian VIII.; 20 Jan.; born 6 Oct. 1808; *separated* from his first wife Sept. 1837; from his second wife, Sept. 1846; married *morganatically* Louisa, countess of Danner, 7 Aug. 1850; died 15 Nov. 1863.

63. Christian IX. son of William, duke of Schleswig-Holstein-Sonderburg-Glücksburg; 15 Nov. succeeded by virtue of the protocol of London, 8 May, 1852, and of the law of the Danish succession, 31 July, 1853. He was born 8 April, 1818: married princess Louisa of Hesse-Cassel, 26 May, 1842 (born 7 Sept. 1817; died 29 Sept. 1898). [He is descended from Christian III. and she from Frederick V.; both from George II. of England.]

Heir: Frederick (his son), born 3 June, 1843; married princess Louisa of Sweden, 28 July, 1869. Sons: Christian, born 26 Sept., 1870; Charles, born 3 Aug. 1872, married princess Maud of Wales, 1896.

DENNEWITZ (Prussia), here a victory was obtained by marshal Bernadotte (afterwards Charles XIV., king of Sweden), over marshal Ney, 6 Sept. 1813. The loss of the French exceeded 13,000 men, several eagles, and cannon; of the allies, 6,000. The defeat of Napoleon at Leipsic, on the 18th of October following, closed this disastrous campaign.

DENOMINATIONS, The Three (presbyterians, congregationalists or independents, and baptists), were organised in 1727 as an association, with the privilege of direct appeal to the reigning sovereign of Great Britain.

DENTISTS, an act for regulating their education and registration, passed, 22 July, 1878. By this act "no one except qualified medical practitioners and those *bonâ fide* engaged in the practice of dentistry at the time of the act's passing can take or use the title 'dentist' or any title signifying that he is registered, under a penalty of 20*l*., and in future any person desiring to become a dentist must undergo a course of study, and have taken a degree or licence."

The Odontological Society (of Dentists), established 1856.
The Dental Hospital of London, Leicester-square, was established 1858, rebuilt and opened 1902. See *Odontology*.
Sir John Tomes, F.R.S., reformer of dental surgery, born 1815, died 29 July, 1895.

DEODAND (Latin, "*to be given to God*"): formerly anything which had caused the death of a human being became forfeit to the sovereign or lord of the manor, and was to be sold for the benefit of the poor. The forfeiture was abolished by 9 & 10 Vict. c. 62 (1846).

D'EON, Chevalier, who had acted in a diplomatic capacity in several countries, and been minister plenipotentiary from France in London, was affirmed to be a *female*, at a trial at the King's Bench in 1771, in an action to recover wagers as to his sex. He subsequently wore female attire; but at his death he was proved to be a male. His "True story," published by Ernest Vizetelly, 1896.

DEONTOLOGY, the knowledge of what is right, or the science of duty (from the Greek *to deon*, that which is proper), an element of the Utilitarian philosophy propounded by Jeremy Bentham in his "Deontology," published by Dr. Bowring in 1834.

DEPARTMENTS, see *France*.

DEPRESSION of Trade, see *Trade*, 1885.

DEPTFORD (near London). The hospital here was incorporated by Henry VIII. about 1512, and called the Trinity-house of Deptford Strond; the brethren of Trinity-house hold their corporate rights by this hospital. The dockyard, founded about 1513, was closed 31 March, 1869, having been purchased by Mr. T. P. Austin for 70,000*l*. He sold part of it to the corporation of London for 94,640*l*., for a market for foreign cattle, which was opened for use, 28 Dec. 1871. On 4 April, 1581, Queen Elizabeth dined at Deptford on board the *Golden Hind*, the ship in which Drake had made his voyage round the globe. The Deptford victualling-office was burnt 16 Jan. 1748-9; the store-house, 2 Sept. 1758; the red-house, 26 Feb. 1761; and the king's-mill, 1 Dec. 1755. Peter the Great of Russia lived at Evelyn's house, Say's-court, while learning ship-building, &c., in 1698. By the acts, 1884-5, Deptford returns one member to parliament, John Evelyn the first. Deptford park purchased from Mr. W. J. Evelyn for 36,031*l*. by the London county council; opened 7 June, 1897. Baths and washhouses opened by lord mayor, 20 April, 1898. Constituted a borough under the London Government act 1899.

DEPUTIES, Chamber of, the title borne by the French legislative assembly, from the restoration of the Bourbons in 1814 till Jan. 1852, when it was named "*Corps Législatif*."

DERBY was made a royal burgh by Egbert (about 828). Alfred expelled the Danes from it and planted a colony in 880. His heroic daughter, Ethelfleda, again expelled the Danes in 918. William I. gave Derby to his illegitimate son William Peveril. Lombe's silk-throwing machine was set up in 1718; and in 1756, Jedediah Strutt invented the Derby ribbed stocking-frame. The young Pretender reached Derby, 3 Dec. 1745, and retreated thence soon after. The new town-hall was opened 29 May, 1866. The midland counties fine art exhibition was held here, and was opened by the duke of Devonshire, 5 May, 1870. Mr. M. T. Bass gives 25,000*l*. for a museum and library, and an endowment of 3000*l*. for an art gallery announced, Jan. 1882. Art gallery, the gift of Mr. M. Bass and others, opened 4 Nov. 1882. Queen Victoria laid the foundation-stone of the Derbyshire Royal Infirmary, 21 May, 1891. Population, 1881, 81,168; 1891, 94,146; 1901, 105,785.

Derby Trials. Brandreth, Turner, Ludlam senior, Ludlam junior, Weightman, and others, Luddites, convicted at a commission of high treason, 15 Oct. 1817; and Brandreth, Turner, and the elder Ludlam executed, 7 Nov. following. 23 others were tried.
21 prisoners indicted at Derby for the murder of several miners in the Red-soil mine; acquitted on the ground that the mischief was not wilful, 23 March, 1834.
The new Grand Theatre burnt; 3 deaths . 6 May, 1886.
Mr. Ernest T. Hooley, sets aside 15,000*l*. per ann. for the poor of his district, to be distributed annually by local committees, in commemoration of the 60th year of the queen's reign . . Jan. 1897
New county court buildings opened by lord chancellor Halsbury . . . . . . 9 April, „
Municipal technical college opened by the duke of Devonshire . . . . 19 Jan. 1899
Miss Eliz. Turner bequeaths bulk of her estate to establish almshouses and for other charitable objects of the city . . . . . . Jan. 1903

DERBY ADMINISTRATIONS: the first formed after the resignation of lord John Russell, 21 Feb. 1852 (facetiously termed the "*who who administration*," from the duke of Wellington's inquiry).

FIRST ADMINISTRATION, 27 Feb. 1852.

First lord of the treasury, Edward, earl of Derby.*
Lord chancellor, lord St. Leonards (previously sir Edward Sugden).
President of the council, earl of Lonsdale.

* Born 1799; M.P. for Stockbridge (as hon. E. G. S. Stanley) in 1820; chief secretary for Ireland, 1830-33; secretary for the colonies, 1833-4, and 1841-5; termed the "Rupert of debate" by lord Lytton in "the New Timon," 1845; succeeded his father as earl of Derby, 30 June, 1851; resigned 25 Feb. 1868; died 23 Oct. 1869.

Lord privy seal, marquis of Salisbury.
Home, foreign, and colonial secretaries, Spencer Horatio Walpole, earl of Malmesbury, and sir John Pakington.
Chancellor of the exchequer, Benjamin Disraeli.
Board of control, John Charles Herries.
Board of trade, Joseph Warner Henley.
Postmaster-general, earl of Hardwicke.
Secretary-at-war, William Beresford.
First commissioner of works and public buildings, lord John Manners.
Robert Adam Christopher, lord Colchester, &c.
[Defeated on the budget, 16 Dec.; resigned 17 Dec. 1852; succeeded by the Aberdeen administration.]

SECOND ADMINISTRATION, 25 Feb. 1858.

First lord of the treasury, earl of Derby.
Lord chancellor, lord Chelmsford (previously sir F. Thesiger).
Chancellor of the exchequer, Benjamin Disraeli.
Secretaries—foreign, earl of Malmesbury; *home*, Spencer H. Walpole (resigned March, 1859), T. Sotheron Estcourt; *colonies*, lord Stanley; in June, 1858, sir E. Bulwer Lytton; *war*. col. Jonathan Peel.
Presidents—of the council, marquis of Salisbury; *of board of control (India)*, 1, earl of Ellenborough (who resigned in May, 1858; he had sent a letter, on his own authority, censuring the proclamation of lord Canning to the Oude insurgents; the government hardly escaped a vote of censure); 2, in June, 1858, lord Stanley;—*board of trade*, Mr. Joseph W. Henley (resigned in March, 1859): earl of Donoughmore;—*board of works*, lord John Manners.
Lord privy seal, earl of Hardwicke.
First lord of the admiralty, sir John S. Pakington.
Postmaster, lord Colchester.
Chancellor of the duchy of Lancaster, duke of Montrose.
[This ministry resigned in consequence of a vote of want of confidence, 11 June, 1859; it was succeeded by the Palmerston-Russell cabinet (*which see*).]

THIRD ADMINISTRATION, CONSTITUTED 6 July. 1866.

First lord of the treasury, Edward, earl of Derby.
Lord chancellor, Frederick, lord Chelmsford.
President of council, Richard, duke of Buckingham; succeeded by John, duke of Marlborough, 8 March, 1867.
Lord privy seal, James, earl of Malmesbury.
Secretaries—home, Spencer Horatio Walpole, resigned; Gathorne Hardy, 17 May, 1867;—*foreign*, Edward, lord Stanley;—*colonies*, Henry, earl of Carnarvon, resigned; Richard, duke of Buckingham and Chandos, 8 March, 1867;—*war*, lieut.-gen. sir Jonathan Peel, resigned; sir John Somerset Pakington, 8 March, 1867;—*India*, Robert, lord Cranborne, resigned; sir Stafford Henry Northcote, 8 March, 1867.
Chancellor of the exchequer, Benjamin Disraeli.
First lord of admiralty, sir John S. Pakington; succeeded by Henry Thomas Corry, 8 March, 1867.
Chief commissioner of works, &c., lord John Manners.
President of board of trade, sir Stafford Northcote; succeeded by Charles Henry, duke of Richmond, March, 1867.
Chief secretary for Ireland, Richard, lord Naas (afterwards earl of Mayo)
President of poor-law board, Gathorne Hardy; succeeded by Wm. Reginald, earl of Devon (*not in cabinet*), 17 May, 1867.
Horatio Spencer Walpole, *without office*, died 1898.
The above formed the cabinet, Feb. 1868.
Postmaster-general, James, duke of Montrose.
Lord chamberlain, Orlando, earl of Bradford.
Chancellor of the duchy of Lancaster, William, earl of Devon; succeeded by colonel John Wilson Patten, June, 1867.
Lord-lieutenant of Ireland, James, earl (afterwards marquis) of Abercorn.
The earl of Derby resigned through ill-health, 25 Feb. 1868; and Mr. Disraeli reconstituted the ministry, see *Disraeli*.]

DERBY DAY (see *Races*), generally (not always) the Wednesday in the week preceding Whitsunday, the second day of the grand spring meeting at Epsom. The Derby was won by prince Regent in 1816, and by the Duke of York in 1822. Mr. Henry Hall, who painted 43 consecutive winners of the Derby, died 22 April, 1882.

RECENT WINNERS OF "THE DERBY" AT EPSOM.

1846. Pyrrhus.
1847. Cossack.
1848. Surplice.
1849. Flying Dutchman.
1850. Voltigeur.
1851. Teddington.
1852. Daniel O'Rourke.
1853. West Australian.
1854. Andover.
1855. Wild Dayrell.
1856. Ellington.
1857. Blink Bonny.
1858. Beadsman.
1859. Musjid.
1860. Thormanby.
1861. Kettledrum.
1862. Caractacus.
1863. Macaroni.
1864. Blair Athol.
1865. Gladiateur, 31 May (a horse reared in France, the property of the comte de la Grange. He also won the St. Leger at Doncaster, 13 Sept.).
1866. Lord Lyon (16 May).
1867. Hermit (22 May).
1868. Blue Gown (27 May).
1869. Pretender (26 May).
1870. Kingcraft (1 June).
1871. Favonius (24 May).
1872. Cremorne (29 May).
1873. Doncaster (28 May).
1874. George Frederick (3 June).
1875. Galopin (26 May).
1876. Kisber, or Mineral Colt (Hungarian, owner, Alex. Baltazzi), 31 May.
1877. Silvio (30 May).
1878. Sefton (5 June).
1879. Sir Bevys (baron Rothschild's), 28 May.
1880. Bend Or (duke of Westminster's) May 26.
1881. Iroquois (Mr. Lorillard's, an American), 1 June.
1882. Shotover (duke of Westminster's), 24 May.
1883. St. Blaise (sir Fredk. Johnstone's), 23 May.
1884. St. Gatien (J. Hammond's), and Harvester (sir J. Willoughby's), 28 May.
1885. Melton (ld. Hastings) 3 June.
1886. Ormonde (duke of Westminster), 26 May.
1887. Merry Hampton (Mr. Abington), 25 May.
1888. Ayrshire (duke of Portland), 30 May.
1889. Donovan (duke of Portland), 5 June.
1890. Sanfoin (sir James Miller), 4 June.
1891. Common (sir F. Johnstone), 27 May.
1892. Sir Hugo (lord Bradford), 1 June.
1893. Isinglass (Mr. H. M'Calmont), 31 May.
1894. Ladas (lord Rosebery), 6 June.
1895. Sir Visto (lord Rosebery), 29 May.
1896. Persimmon (prince of Wales, present at the race), 3 June.
1897. Galtee More (Mr. J. Gubbins), 2 June.
1898. Jeddah (Mr. J. W. Larnach), 25 May.
1899. Flying Fox (duke of Westminster).
1900. Diamond Jubilee (prince of Wales, present at the race), 30 May.
1901. Volodyovski (Mr. W. C. Whitney, an American), 5 June.
1902. Ard Patrick (Mr. J. Gubbins), 4 June.
1903. Rock Sand (sir Jas. Miller), 27 May.

DERELICT LAND TRUST, formed by subscription to promote the cultivation of farms in Ireland from which the tenants have been evicted for non-payment of rent. "Plantations" in county Wexford were formed in 1889.

A report of a committee respecting derelict vessels in the Atlantic recommend no definite action, except prompt reporting of such when discovered . . . . 30 Nov. 1894

DERMATOLOGY, the science of the skin and its diseases.

The International dermatological congress met at Paris in 1889; at Vienna, 5 Sept. 1892; in London, Aug. 1896.

DERRICKS are lofty, portable crane-like structures, used on land and water for lifting enormous loads, and in some cases depositing them at an elevation. They are extensively used in the United States, and were introduced into England as floating derricks for raising sunken vessels, by their inventor, A. D. Bishop, in 1857.

DERRY (N. Ireland), a bishopric first at Ardfrath; thence translated to Maghera; and in 1158 to Derry. The cathedral, built in 1164, becoming ruinous, was rebuilt by Londoners, who settled here in the reign of James I. The see is valued in the king's books at 250*l.* sterling; but it has been one of the richest sees in Ireland. *Beatson.* The see was united to Derry, 1834; see *Bishops; Londonderry*.

DERVISH. (Persian, signifying "poor.") The dervishes of the present time, fanatical enthusiasts, unrecognized by orthodoxy, originated in Persia, whence they spread over the Mahommedan world. The khalifa Abdulla killed at Om Debrikat 24 Nov. 1899. Dervish trophies and relics exhibited at Whitehall, 22 Nov. *et seq.* 1898. See *Soudan.*

DESCENT OF MAN, see *Development.*

"DESERTED VILLAGE," a poem, by Dr. Oliver Goldsmith, first published, May, 1770.

DESICCATING APPARATUS, see under *Hay.*

DESIGN, SCHOOLS OF, established by government, began at Somerset-house, London, 1 Jan. 1837. In 1852 the head school was removed to Marlborough-house, and became eventually "the department of science and art," transferred to South Kensington in 1857. It is under the direction of the committee of council on education and arts. See *Copyright,* Sept. 1896.

DESPARD'S CONSPIRACY. Colonel Edward Marcus Despard, a native of Ireland, Broughton, Francis, Graham, Macnamara, Wood, and Wratten conspired to kill the king, and establish a republic, on the day of opening parliament, 16 Nov. 1802. Above 30 persons including soldiers were taken in custody; of those tried, 20 Jan. 1803, Despard and six others were executed, 21 Feb. He had been a distinguished officer under Nelson.

DESTITUTE CHILDREN'S DINNER SOCIETY, established in 1867, to give weekly meat dinners. 16,822 dinners given in 1869; 147,858 dinners in 58 dining rooms in 1870; 114,000 dinners in 42 dining rooms, year 1876-7; 170,000 dinners in 49 rooms, 1878-9; now about 283,000 annually. In 1890, the co-operation of several societies was effected.

DESTRUCTIVE INSECTS (to crops), an act passed to prevent their introduction and spreading in Great Britain, 14 Aug. 1877. See *Colorado.*

DETECTIVE POLICE, see *Police,* and *Trials.*

DETROIT, Michigan, U.S.A., the oldest city in the west, was built by the French about 1610. It is eminent for large metal works. Population in 1880, 116,340; 1890, 205,876; 1900, 285,704.

DETTINGEN (Bavaria), **BATTLE OF,** 16 (or 27 O. S.) June, 1743, between the British, Hanoverian, and Hessian army (52,000), commanded by king George II. of England and the earl of Stair, and the French army (60,000), under marshal Noailles and the duc de Grammont. The French passed a defile, which they should have merely guarded. The duc de Grammont with his cavalry charged the British foot with great fury, but was so received that he was obliged to give way, and to repass the Maine, losing 3000 men. Handel's "Dettingen Te Deum," first performed, 27 Nov 1743.

DEUTERONOMY. See *Bible,* note.

DEVELOPMENT (or Evolution). Wolff put forth a theory of epigenesis in 1759; Lamarck, the naturalist, in 1809, propounded a theory that all animals had been developed from "monads," living minute particles; see *Species* and *Vestiges.* Buffon held a similar doctrine. In 1827 Ernst von Baer of Königsberg demonstrated that all mammals are developed from a minute egg not a hundredth of an inch in diameter. Mr. C. Darwin's views are given in his "Origin of Species," 1859; and "Descent of Man," 1871. He supposes that man was gradually evolved from the lowest created form of animal life. Hæckel, his most advanced follower, published in German a "History of Creation," 1873; a translation in English, 1875. Mr. Alfred Wallace published his work on Natural Selection in 1870. See *Evolution.*

The theory of the development of living beings out of the substance of the earth was put forth by Lucretius in his "De Rerum Naturæ," about 57 B.C.

"We cannot teach, we cannot pronounce it to be a conquest of science, that man descends from the ape or from any other animal. We can only indicate it as a hypothesis."—*Professor Virchow,* 1877.

"The primitive monads were born by spontaneous generation in the sea."—*Professor Hæckel,* 1878.

The Royal Society's Darwin medal was first awarded to Mr. Alfred Russel Wallace in 1890.

DEVIL WORSHIP. Devil, Greek, *diabolos,* false accuser; Hebrew, *satan,* an adversary; *abaddon,* destroyer, &c. The worship of devils is frequently mentioned in the Bible (*Lev.* xvii. 7; 2 *Chron.* xi. 15; 1 *Cor.* x. 20; *Rev.* ix. 20, &c.) Mr. Layard describes the Yezidees as recognising one supreme being, yet reverencing the devil as a king or mighty angel, to be conciliated (1841).

Mr. Moncure Conway's "Demonology and Devil-Lore," first published Dec. 1878.

DEVIZES, a borough, Wiltshire; the castle here was founded by bp. Roger, about 1107; and was for some time royal property until Cromwell besieged and ruined it. The remains were sold by the executors of the last holder, Mr. R. V. Leach, for 8,000*l.* in August, 1888. At Roundway Down, near here, sir William Waller and the parliamentarians were defeated, 13 July, 1643. Population of the town 1901, 6,532; of the borough, 13,070.

Visit of the prince of Wales; centenary of the royal Wiltshire yeomanry . . . 24 May, 1893

DEVOLUTION, a term applied in 1886-8 to the transfer of business of minor importance in the parliament to grand or other committees (see *Committees*).

DEVONPORT, see *Dockyards* and *Plymouth.*

DEVONSHIRE, the country of the Damnonii or Dumnonii. Odun, earl of Devon, in 878, defeated the Danes, slew Ubbo or Hubba their chief, and captured his magic standard. A bishopric of Devonshire was founded in 909; see *Exeter.*

Richard de Redvers, first earl of *Devon,* son of Baldwin, sheriff of Devonshire, died 1137.

William Courtenay, the present earl, is descended from Robert de Courtenay and Mary de Redvers, daughter of William de Redvers, earl of Devon in 1184.

William Cavendish, created first *earl of Devonshire,* 1618.

William Cavendish (his great grandson), created first *duke of Devonshire,* 1694.

His descendant, William Cavendish, born 27 April, 1808; became earl of Burlington, 1834; and 7th duke of Devonshire, 1858; chancellor of the university of London, 1836; of the university of Cambridge, 1861. See *Barrow-in-Furness, Eastbourne,* and *Owens College.* The duke died 21 Dec., 1891. Spencer C. Cavendish, the 8th duke, was born 23rd July, 1833. See *Gladstone. Administrations* 1st and 2nd; elected chancellor of the University of Cambridge, 4 Jan., 1892, see also *Salisbury* and *Balfour.*

DEVONSHIRE AND PITT ADMINISTRATION, formed 16 Nov. 1756; dismissed 5 April, 1757.

First lord of the treasury, William, duke of Devonshire.
Chancellor of the exchequer, hon. Henry Bilson Legge.
Lord president, earl Granville (lord Carteret).
Privy seal, earl Gower.
Secretaries of state, earl of Holdernesse and Wm. PITT (afterwards earl of Chatham, the virtual *premier*).

George Grenville, earl of Halifax, dukes of Rutland and Grafton, earl of Rochfort, viscount Barrington, &c. The great seal in commission.

"DEVOUT LIFE." "Introduction à la Vie dévote," written by St. François de Sales, and published 1608. He was born 21 Aug. 1567; bishop of Geneva, 1602; died, 28 Dec. 1622.

DEW, the modern theory respecting it was put forth by Dr. Wells in his book, 1814.

DEWANGIRI, see *India*, 1865.

DIADEM, the band or fillet worn by the ancients instead of the crown, and consecrated to the gods. At first it was made of silk or wool, set with precious stones, and was tied round the temples and forehead, the two ends being knotted behind, and let fall on the neck. Aurelian was the first Roman emperor who wore a diadem, 272. *Tillemont*.

DIALECTICAL SOCIETY, LONDON, for the philosophical consideration of all subjects, with a view to the discovery and elucidation of truth, was established in 1866. The members at one time included profs. Huxley and W. K. Clifford, sir Andrew Clark, visct. Amberley, Mr. George Henry Lewes, W. A. Hunter, Sir John Lubbock, Miss Frances Power Cobbe, and Dr. Alice Vickery. The report of their committee on spiritualism was published in Nov. 1871. The Society ended 29 Sept. 1894. See *Wales*, 1890.

DIALECTS, see *English Language* and *Wales*, 1890.

DIALS. "The sun-dial of Ahaz," 713 B.C. (*Isa.* xxxviii. 8). A dial invented by Anaximander, 550 B.C. *Pliny*. The first dial of the sun seen at Rome was placed on the temple of Quirinus by L. Papirius Cursor, when time was divided into hours, 293 B.C. *Blair*. Dials set up in churches about A.D. 613. *Lenglet*. Mrs. Alfred Gatty's "Book of Sun Dials" was published in 1872.

DIALYSIS, an important method of chemical analysis, depending on the different degrees of diffusibility of substances in liquids, was made known in 1861, by its discoverer, professor Thomas Graham, then master of the mint.

DIA-MAGNETISM, the property possessed by nearly all bodies of behaving differently to iron, when placed between two magnets. The phenomena, previously little known, were reduced to a law by Faraday in 1845, and confirmed by Tyndall and others.

DIAMOND, a hamlet, Armagh, N. Ireland, where was fought the "battle of the Diamond," 21 Sept. 1795, between the "Peep-o'-day-boys" and the "Defenders," and many of the latter were killed. To commemorate this conflict the first Orange Lodge was formed immediately after. See *Defenders*.

DIAMOND JUBILEE, see *Jubilee*, 1897.

DIAMONDS were first brought to Europe from the East, where the mine of Sumbulpoor was the first known. Golconda, in India, now in ruins, was a celebrated diamond mart. The mines of Brazil were discovered in 1728. From these last a diamond, weighing 1680 carats, or fourteen ounces, was sent to the court of Portugal, and was valued by Mr. Romeo de l'Isle at 224 millions; by others at 56 millions, and at 3½ millions; its true value (not being brilliant) was 400,000*l*.

The great RUSSIAN diamond weighs 193 carats, or 1 oz. 12 dwts. 4 gr. troy. The empress Catherine II. offered for it 104,166*l*. 13*s*. 4*d*., besides an annuity for life to the owner of 104*l*. 13*s*. 4*d*., which was refused; but it was afterwards sold to Catherine's favourite, count Orloff, for the first-mentioned sum, without the annuity, and was by him presented to the empress on her birthday, 1772; it is now in the sceptre of Russia.

The PITT (or Regent) diamond weighed 136 carats, and after cutting, 106 carats: it was sold to the king of France for 125,000*l*. in 1720.

The PIGOTT diamond (bought by Mr. Pitt, grandfather of Wm. Pitt) was sold for 9500 guineas, 10 May, 1802.

The diamond called the KOHINOOR, KOH-I-NUR, or MOUNTAIN OF LIGHT, has a legendary history, and is said to have belonged in turn to Shah Jehan, Aurungzebe, Nadir Shah, the Afghan rulers, and afterwards to the Sikh chief Runjeet Singh. Upon the abdication of Dhuleep Singh, the last ruler of the Punjab, and the annexation of his dominions to the British empire, in 1849, the Kohinoor was surrendered to the queen. It was accordingly brought over and presented to her, 3 July, 1850. It was shown in the Great Exhibition, 1851. Its original weight was nearly 800 carats, but it was reduced by the unskilfulness of the artist, Hortensio Borghese, a Venetian, to 279 carats. Its shape and size resembled the pointed half (rose cut) of a small hen's egg. The value is scarcely computable, though two millions sterling have been mentioned as a justifiable price, if calculated by the scale employed in the trade. This diamond was re-cut in 1852, and now weighs 102¼ carats.

The SANCI diamond, which belonged to Charles the Bold, duke of Burgundy, was bought by sir C. Jejeebhoy from the Demidoff family for 20,000*l*. in Feb. 1865.

Mr. Porter Rhodes's great diamond (weighing 150 carats; alleged value 60,000*l*.) found at Kimberley 12 Feb. 1880, exhibited by Mr. Streeter, Bond-street, London, Nov. 1881.

Ancient diamond said to have belonged to the Mogul emperors of India, date of engraved characters possibly 1200, shown by Mr. Bryce Wright, Jan. 1882.

A diamond, termed the STAR OF THE SOUTH, was brought from Brazil in 1855, weighing 254½ carats, half of which was lost by cutting.

Diamonds were discovered in Cape Colony, S. Africa, in March, 1867. A fine one, termed the "Star of South Africa," brought to England in 1869, was purchased by Messrs. Hunt and Roskell. After cutting, it weighed 46½ carats, and was valued at 25,000*l*., in June, 1870.

Rich diamond fields discovered near the Vaal and Orange rivers, Sept. 1870.

Great influx of diggers, and many fine diamonds found, Nov. Value of 141 diamonds found in 1869, 7405*l*.; of 5661 found in 1870, 124,910*l*.; about 2,000,000*l*. said to be exported in 1877. See *Griqua-land, West*.

The largest African diamond found, weighing 302 carats, at Kimberley, named "*Victoria*," 27 March, 1884.

Several magnificent South African diamonds have since been discovered—one said to weigh 400 carats, reduced by cutting to 180. 1884–8.

Estimated value of South African diamonds up to 1886, 40,000,000*l*.

By a fire and panic in De Beer's mine, Kimberley, about 220 perish, 11 July, 1888.

Diamonds discovered in British Guiana by Mr. Kaufmann, spring, 1891.

A diamond weighing 655 carats found in the Jagersfontein mine in the Orange Free State, 26 Nov. 1895.

Application of the mechanical or saving process to rough diamonds, by which parts from the rough stone can be cut to any size desired and converted into small brilliants, effects great change in diamond-workers' trade. See *Annual report of Amsterdam Chamber of Commerce*, issued Jan. 1903.

DIAMOND NECKLACE AFFAIR.—In 1785, Bœhmer, the court jeweller of France, offered the queen Marie Antoinette, a diamond necklace, for 56,000*l*. The queen desired the necklace, but feared the expense. The countess de la Motte (of the ancient house of Valois) forged the queen's signature, and by pretending that the queen had an attachment for him, persuaded the cardinal de Rohan, the queen's almoner, to conclude a bargain with the jeweller for the necklace for 56,000*l*. De la Motte thus obtained the necklace and made away with it. For this she was tried in 1786, and sentenced to be branded on the shoulders and imprisoned for life.

She accused in vain the celebrated Italian adventurer, Cagliostro, of complicity in the affair, he being then intimate with the cardinal. She made her escape and came to London, where she was killed by falling from a window-sill, in attempting to escape an arrest for debt.—De Rohan was tried and acquitted, 14 April, 1786. The public in France at that time suspected the queen of being a party to the fraud. Talleyrand wrote at the time, that he should not be surprised if this miserable affair overturned the throne.

Diamond Robbery. See *Trials*, 1871; *Jewels*.

Diamonds valued at 50,000*l*. stolen from the post-office at Capetown about 20 March, 1880.

Artificial Diamonds: those prepared by Mr. MacTear of Glasgow, examined by Mr. Story Maskelyne, and declared not to be diamonds, 30 Dec. 1879; acknowledged by Mr. MacTear, Jan. 1880.

Diamonds said to have been made by J. Ballantine Hannay at Glasgow, announced in *Times*, 20 Feb. 1880.

Diamonds said to have been made at Paris, 1880.

For the "imperial diamond" case, see *Trials*, Dec. 1891.

Sir Wm. Crookes, who visited the Kimberley and other mines in 1896, in a lecture on "Diamonds" at the Royal institution, 11 June, 1897, explained M. Moissan's method of manufacturing artificial diamonds from molten iron in a carbon crucible, and exhibited specimens on the screen of others made by prof. Roberts-Austen and himself. See *Royal Institution Proceedings*, 1897.

Mr. Justice Byrne stops the sale of the 44½ carat Tavernier blue or Hope diamond, May; his decision affirmed on appeal, 15 July, 1899.

INFLAMMABILITY OF DIAMONDS.

Boetius de Boot conjectured that the diamond was inflammable, 1609. When exposed to a high temperature it gave an acrid vapour, in which a part of it was dissipated, 1673. *Boyle.*

Sir Isaac Newton concluded from its great refracting power, that it must be combustible, 1675.

Averani demonstrated, by concentrating the rays of the sun upon it, that the diamond was exhaled in vapour, and entirely disappeared, while other precious stones merely grow softer, 1695.

It has been ascertained by Guyton, Davy, and others, that diamonds contain nothing but pure charcoal, or carbon. Diamonds were charred by the intense heat of the voltaic battery—by M. Dumas, in Paris, and by professor Faraday, in London, in 1848.

DIANA, TEMPLE OF (at Ephesus), accounted one of the seven wonders of the world, was built at the common charge of all the Asiatic states, 552 B.C.; the chief architect being Ctesiphon. Pliny says that 220 years were employed in completing it. It was 425 feet long, 225 broad, and was supported by 127 columns (60 feet high, each weighing 150 tons of Parian marble), furnished by so many kings. It was set on fire, on the night of the birth of Alexander the Great, by Herostratus or Eratostratus, who confessed that his sole motive was the desire of transmitting his name to future ages, 356 B.C. The temple was rebuilt, but again burnt by the Goths, in their naval invasion, A.D. 256 or 262. In April, 1869, Mr. J. T. Wood discovered the site of the second temple; and since then sculptured marble columns have been removed to the British Museum. Diana was the Roman name of the Greek *Artemis*.

DICE. The invention of dice is mythically ascribed to Palamedes, of Greece, about 1244 B.C. The game of tali and tessera among the Romans was played with dice. Stow mentions two entertainments given by the city of London, at which dice were played. Act to regulate the licences of makers, and the sale of dice, 9 Geo. IV. 1828.

DICHROOSCOPE, an optical apparatus, described by the inventor, professor Dove of Berlin, in 1860, who intended it to represent interferences, spectra in coloured lights, polarisation of light, &c.

DICTATORS were supreme and absolute magistrates of Rome, appointed to act in critical times. Titus Lartius, the first dictator, was appointed, 501 B.C. Caius Marcius Rutilus was the first plebeian dictator, 356 B.C. This office became odious by the usurpations of Sylla and Julius Cæsar; and after the death of the latter, the Roman senate, on the motion of the consul Antony, passed a law forbidding a dictator to exist in Rome, 44 B.C. The dictator was also called master of the people, and had under him a master of the horse.

DICTIONARY. A standard dictionary of the Chinese language, containing about 40,000 characters, most of them hieroglyphic, or rude representations, somewhat like our signs of the zodiac, was perfected by Pa-out-she, who lived about 1100 B.C. *Morrison;* see *Encyclopædias, Music*, &c.

A Latin one was compiled by Varro, born . . B.C. 116

Varro's work "de Linguâ Latinâ"; he died . . 28

The "Onomasticon," a collection of vocabularies in Greek, by Julius Pollux, was published about A.D. 177

The "Catholicon," an attempt at a Latin Lexicon, by Friar Johannes Balbus Januensis, printed at Mentz 1460

The first noted polyglot dictionary, perhaps the first, is by Ambrose Calepini, a Venetian friar, in Latin; he wrote one in eight languages. *Niceron.* about 1500

John E. Avenar's *Dictionarium Hebraicum* was published at Wittenberg in 1589. Buxtorf's great work, *Lexicon Hebraicum*, &c., appeared . . 1621

The *Lexicon Heptaglotton* was published by Edmund Castell, in 1669

The great English dictionary by Samuel Johnson appeared in 1755

Francis Grose's Dictionary of the Vulgar Tongue (or Slang) was compiled in 1768

"Slang Dictionary," by Albert Barrère and Charles G. Leland, 2 vols., 1889–90; new edition (reduced) published 1897

The following academies have published large dictionaries of their respective languages: the French academy, (the first, edited by Vaugelas,) 1694; new editions, 1718, 1740, 1762, 1835, and 1878; the Spanish, 1726; the Italian academy (della Crusca) 1729; and the Russian . . . 1789-94

Schwan's great German-French dictionary appeared 1782

Richardson's English dictionary appeared . . 1836

Lemprière's Classical Dictionary, which first appeared in 1788, is now superseded by Dr. W. Smith's classical series 1842-93

The Philological Society of London issued proposals for a "New English dictionary," on the historical method, 1859; after some delay the work was vigorously revived; editor, Dr. J. H. Murray 1879

[About 5000 authors, dating from 1150 to 1883, have been read by about 13,000 persons (British and American), who made about 3,000,000 extracts. Part I., entitled "The Oxford English Dictionary," published Feb. 1884, was considered highly successful, and a specimen of the grandest lexicographical work ever produced. Vol. V. to K completed 1901. Instalments of Vols. VI., VII., and VIII., R—Reactive, July, 1903.]

The great German dictionary, by Jacob and Wilhelm Grimm . . . . 1854 *et seq.*

Mr. Hensleigh Wedgwood's Dictionary of English Etymology 1859-67

Smith's Dictionary of the Bible was published . 1860-3

The earliest known English-Latin dictionary is the *Promptorium Parvulorum*, compiled by Galfridus Grammaticus, a preaching friar of Norfolk, in 1440; and printed by Pynson, as *Promptorius Puerorum*, in 1499. A new edition, carefully edited by Mr. Albert Way, from MSS., was published by the Camden Society . . . 1843-65

Liddell and Scott Greek lexicon, founded on Passow, 1843; 7th edition 1883

The great French dictionary, by E. Littré, 1863-72; supplement 1877

The "Bonâ Fide French and English Dictionary" (4½ inches by 2⅜, weight 4 oz.), printed by Bellows, 1873 *et seq.*

The Imperial Dictionary of the English language, by John Ogilvie. New edition by Charles Annandale, 4 vols. published 1882; new edition . 1895
Rev. W. W. Skeat's "Etymological Dictionary of the English language" published 1882-4
"The Century Dictionary:" an encyclopedic lexicon of the English language, edited by Prof. W. D. Whitney, 6 vols. 1889-91
The "Stanford Dictionary of Anglicised words and phrases," edited by C. A. M. Fennell . . . 1893
A "Standard Dictionary of the English language." 200 specialist authors; chief editor, Dr. Isaac K. Funk; 2 vols. New York 1894-95
The "Dictionary of National Biography" (see *Biography*) 1885-1900
Chambers' "Twentieth Century Dictionary of the English language," edited by the rev. Thomas Davidson, published . . . . Nov. 1901
"Dictionary of Philosophy and Psychology," edited by Jas. M. Baldwin, vol. I. . . early 1902
The "English Dialect Dictionary," edited by Dr. Wright, Part XVIII. published . . early 1903

DIDYMIUM, a rare metal, discovered by Mosander in 1841. It is found associated with lanthanum and cerium. Declared to be a compound by Mr. (aft. sir) W. Crookes in 1888.

DIEPPE (N. France). This town was bombarded by an English fleet, under admiral Russell, and laid in ashes, July, 1694. It was again bombarded in 1794; and again, together with the town of Granville, by the British, 14 Sept. 1803.

"DIES IRÆ" ("Day of Wrath"), a Latin mediæval hymn on the day of judgment, is ascribed to various authors, amongst others to pope Gregory the Great (died about 604); St. Bernard (died 1153); but is generally considered to have been composed by Thomas of Celano (died 1255), and to have been used in the Roman service of the mass before 1385.

DIET OF THE GERMAN EMPIRE (in which the supreme court of authority of the empire may be said to have existed) was composed of three colleges: one of electors, one of princes, and one of imperial towns, and commenced with the edict of Charles IV. 1356; see *Golden Bull; Würzburg* (1180); *Nuremberg* (1467); *Worms* (1521); *Spires* (1529); *Augsburg* (1530); *Ratisbon* (1541); *Frankfort* (1806, *et seq.*); and *Germany*.

DIETHEROSCOPE, an apparatus for geodesy and teaching optics, constructed by G. Luvini, of Tunis, and announced, April, 1876.

"DIEU-DONNÉ," the name given in his infancy to *Louis le Grand*, king of France, the queen, his mother, having been barren for 23 years previously, 1638. Also to the comte de Chambord, son of the duchess of Berri, born 29 Sept. 1820, died 24 Aug. 1883. His father was assassinated, 14 Feb. 1820. One of the popes (672) was named *Adeodatus* or God's gift.

DIEU ET MON DROIT ("God and my right"), the royal motto of England, was the parole of the day, given by Richard I. of England to his army at the battle of Gisors, in France, 20 Sept. 1198, when the French army was signally defeated. "*Dieu et mon droit*" appears to have been first assumed as a motto by Henry VI. (1422-1461); see *Semper Eadem*.

DIFFERENTIAL ENGINE, see *Calculating Machine*.

DIFFUSION OF GASES. In 1825, Döbereiner observed the transmission of hydrogen gas through a crack in a glass vessel, and professor Thomas Graham discovered the passage of gases through porous porcelain, graphite, and other substances, and established laws in 1832, and to him we are indebted for the discovery of *Atmolysis* and *Dialysis*. He died 16 Sept. 1869.

DIFFUSION OF USEFUL KNOWLEDGE SOCIETY, which published a number of books relating to history, science, and literature, and an atlas, in a cheap form, ridiculed as the "Sixpenny Sciences," was established by Lord Brougham, Mr. William Tooke, Mr. Charles Knight, and others. It published its "Library" 1827-48, and patronised the publication of the Penny Magazine and the Penny Cyclopædia. Its proceedings were suspended in 1846. The Royal Institution of Great Britain was established in 1799, for "the Promotion, Diffusion, and Extension of Science and Useful Knowledge."

DIGEST. The first collection of Roman laws under this title was prepared by Alfrenus Varus, the civilian, of Cremona, 66 B.C. *Quintil.* The "Digest," so called by way of eminence, was the collection made by order of the emperor Justinian, 529: it made the first part of the Roman law and the first volume of the civil law. Quotations from it are marked with a ff. *Pardon.* The "Digest of Law" commissioners signed their first report 13 May, 1867, recommending the immediate preparation of a digest of the English common law, statute law, and judicial decisions.

DIGITS (*digitus*, finger), any whole number under 10: 1, 2, &c., are the nine digits; see *Arithmetic*. In astronomy, the digit is a measure used in the calculation of eclipses, and is the twelfth part of the luminary eclipsed.

DIJON, E. France, the ancient capital of Burgundy, is said to have been founded by Julius Cæsar, fortified by the emperor Marcus Aurelius, and named *Divio*, about 274. It has been several times captured in war; and a castle was erected here by Louis XI. Dijon became the capital of the dukes of Burgundy about 1180. It was attacked by the Germans, under general Beyer, 30 Oct. 1870. The heights, &c. were taken by prince William of Baden, and the town surrendered on 31 Oct. Memorial to pres. Carnot unveiled by pres. Loubet, 21 May, 1899. Population in 1901, 70,428.

DILAPIDATIONS, see *Ecclesiastical*.

DILETTANTI, SOCIETY OF, established in 1734 by the viscount Harcourt, lord Middlesex, duke of Dorset, and others who had travelled and who were desirous of encouraging a taste for the fine arts in Great Britain. The society published, or aided in publishing, Stuart's Athens (1762-1816), Chandler's Travels (1775-6), and several other finely illustrated works. The members dine together from time to time at the Thatched-house tavern, St. James's. Mr. R. P. Pullan, on behalf of this society, excavated the temple of Bacchus at Teos, of Apollo Smintheus in the Troad, and of Minerva Polias at Priene, between 1861-70. Published "Antiquities of Ionia," 4 parts, 1769-1881. "History of the Society of Dilettanti," by Lionel Cust, published May, 1898.

DINAS, see *Accidents* under *Coal*, and *Mansion House*.

DINNERS, see *Destitute* and *Jubilees*.

DIOCESE. The first division of the Roman empire into dioceses, at that period civil governments, is ascribed to Constantine, 323; but Strabo remarks that the Romans had the departments called dioceses long before. In England the principal dioceses are coeval with the establishment of

Christianity; of 28 dioceses, 20 are suffragan to the diocese of Canterbury, and six to that of York; see *Bishops*, and the sees severally. Diocesan conferences of the clergy and laity now frequent.

DIOCLES' CODE, drawn up by him for Syracuse, where he was a popular leader, 412 B.C. It was highly approved, and copied by other nations, and remained in force till superseded by the Roman laws, after the conquest, 212 B.C.

DIOCLETIAN ERA (called also the era of Martyrs, on account of the persecution in his reign) was used by Christian writers until the introduction of the Christian era in the 6th century, and is still employed by the Abyssinians and Copts. It dates from the day on which Diocletian was proclaimed emperor at Chalcedon, 29 Aug. 284.

DIONYSUS, the Greek god of wine, poetry, and music, called Bacchus after the 5th century B.C. His worship was introduced from Greece into Rome, and his festivals, termed Dionysia and Bacchanalia, were finally suppressed by the senate on account of their dissolute character. The Greek drama is said to have arisen out of the Bacchic festivals, 168 B.C.

DIOPTRIC SYSTEM (from the Greek, *dia*, through, and *optomai*, I see), an arrangement of lenses for refracting light in lighthouses, devised by Fresnel, about 1819, based on the discoveries of Buffon, Condorcet, Brewster, and others; see *Lighthouses*.

DIORAMA. This admired exhibition was first opened by MM. Bouton and Daguerre in Paris, 11 July, 1822; in London, 29 Sept. 1823. It was not successful commercially here, and was sold in 1848. The building in Regent's-park was purchased by sir S. M. Peto, and opened on May 2, 1855, as a Baptist chapel.

DIPHTHERIA (from the Greek *diphthera*, leather), a disease resembling croup which has the essential character of developing a false membrane on the mucous membrane connected with the throat. It was named *diphtheritis* by Brétonneau of Tours in 1820. From its prevalence in Boulogne, it has been termed the Boulogne sore-throat; many persons were affected with it in England at the beginning of 1858. The princess Alice, grand-duchess of Hesse-Darmstadt, died of this disease, 14 Dec. 1878, after nursing her husband and children.

Often epidemic in London, &c., 1891–1901; origin and propagation uncertain.

Dr. Roux of Paris successfully applied the anti-toxin treatment of disease to diphtheria in 1894 by injecting into the patient's blood the serum of the blood of a horse previously rendered *immune* by a course of injections of the weak virus of diphtheria.

The treatment has been gradually developed from the discoveries of Löffler, Behring, Koch, and others in Germany. The Goldsmiths' company grant 1000*l.* for the prosecution of researches on the subject . . . . Nov. 1894

Anti-toxin successfully used . . . . 1895 *et seq.*

Dr. Roux awarded the Prix Osiris of 100,000*f.* by Institute of France in recognition of his scientific labours in bacteriology . . . . April, 1903

DIPLOMACY, the art of managing the relations of foreign states by means of ambassadors, envoys, consuls, chargés d'affaires, &c.; see *Ambassadors* and *Consuls*. New regulations for the British diplomatic service were issued 5 Sept. 1862.

DIPLOMAS. The wholesale fraudulent sale of diplomas of M.D., &c., for 10*l.*, by a Dr. Buchanan, dean of the American University of Philadelphia, and others, was detected in 1880. He attempted escape by a sham suicide, but was captured, prosecuted, and imprisoned.

DIPLOMATICS, the foreign term for the science of palæography or ancient writings. Valuable works on this subject have been compiled by Mabillon (1681), De Vaines (1774), Astle (1781), De Wailly (1838), and other antiquaries.

DIPTYCH, a two-leaved tablet of metal, ivory, or other material, used by the Greeks and Romans. In the Christian church in its early days it was customary to inscribe the names of deceased bishops on diptychs. This practice was extended to include other distinguished persons who had deserved well of the church, and from it arose the calendars and martyrologies of a later period. The earliest dyptichs in existence belong to the 5th century.

"DIRECTORY FOR THE PUBLIC WORSHIP OF GOD" was drawn up at the instance of the parliament by an assembly of divines at Westminster in 1644, after the suppression of the Book of Common Prayer. The general hints given were to be managed with discretion; for the Directory prescribed no form of prayer or manner of external worship, and enjoined the people to make no responses except *Amen*. It was adopted by the parliament of Scotland in 1645, and many of its regulations are still observed by presbyterians.

DIRECTORY, THE FRENCH, established by the constitution of the 5th of Fructidor, an III. (22 Aug. 1795), and nominated 1 Nov., was composed of five members (MM. Lépeaux, Letourneur, Rewbel, Barras, and Carnot). On 18 Fructidor, 4 Sep. 1797, two directors (Carnot and Barthélemy) were deposed, and afterwards, with other officials, transported to Cayenne for favouring royalty. The directory ruled in conjunction with two chambers, the Council of Ancients and Council of Five Hundred (*which see*), till the revolution of the 18th of Brumaire (9, 10 Nov. 1799). It was deposed by Bonaparte, who, with Cambacérès and Lebrun, assumed the government as three consuls, himself the first, 13 Dec. 1799; see *Consuls*.

DIRECTORY, the first LONDON, is said to have been printed in 1677. The "Post-office Directory" first appeared in 1800.

Directories of most of the English counties and of Scotland now published at short intervals.

Thom's Official Directory, Ireland, 60th year, 1903.

Messrs. Kelly's "Directory of the Merchants, Manufacturers, and Shippers of the United Kingdom," was first published in 1877; at first triennially, now annually.

DIRECTORS' LIABILITY ACT, relating to prospectuses, &c., of public companies, passed 18 Aug. 1890.

"DISCIPLES OF CHRIST" (also called CAMPBELLITES) profess adherence to pure Scriptural doctrine and practice, reject human creeds and formularies, and admit to their communion all who recognise Christ's obedience and death, as "the only meritorious cause of the sinner's acceptance with God;" and are baptized (by immersion) in his name.

The term Campbellite originated through their first church at Brush Run, in America, having been set up by a Scotch presbyterian preacher from Ireland, named Thomas Campbell, and his son Alexander. In 1812 they renounced infant baptism, and were rebaptized by immersion. Their number in America is said to be about 600,000; and in the United Kingdom, where the movement began independently and simultaneously, about 5000. They have also churches in the British colonies.

DISCIPLINE, ecclesiastical, originally conducted spiritually according to the divine commands in *Matt.* xviii. 15, 1 *Cor.* v., 2 *Thess.* iii. 6, and other texts, was gradually changed to a temporal character, as it now appears in the Roman, Greek, and other churches. The "First Book of Discipline" of the presbyterian church of Scotland was drawn up by John Knox and four ministers in Jan. 1560-1. The more important "Second Book" was prepared with great care in 1578 by Andrew Melville and a committee of the leading members of the general assembly. It lays down a thoroughly presbyterian form of government, defines the position of the ecclesiastical and civil powers, &c.

DISCOUNT, see under *Bank of England.*

DISEASE, see *Pathology* and *Cattle*, and articles on several diseases.

DISEASES OF ANIMALS IN GREAT BRITAIN. The following returns under the Diseases of Animals acts show the number of animals suffering from anthrax, glanders and rabies in Great Britain in the years respectively. *Anthrax:* outbreaks, 1894, 494; 1898, 556; 1902, 687; animals affected 1894, 1,000; 1898, 845; 1902, 1,042. *Glanders:* outbreaks, 1894, 965; 1898, 748; 1902, 1,162; animals affected, 1894, 1,437; 1898, 1,385; 1902, 2,073. *Rabies in dogs*, cases reported, 1893, 93; 1898, 17; 1902, 13. *Swine fever:* outbreaks, 1894, 5,682; 1898, 2,514; 1902, 1,688; swine slaughtered, 1894, 56,296; 1898, 43,756; 1902, 8,263. The board of agriculture announced Jan. 1903, that no case of foot and mouth disease had been confirmed in the United Kingdom or Channel Islands since May, 1902, and that there was reason to believe that the disease had been stamped out.

DISESTABLISHMENT. See *Church of Ireland.*

DISPENSARIES, to supply the poor with medical advice and medicines, began in London. The Royal General Dispensary, London, was established in St. Bartholomew's Close, in 1770. The Western Dispensary was founded 1789. There are now (1903) over 100 dispensaries in London, many of these are provident institutions. Garth's satiric poem, "The Dispensary," published 1699.

DISPENSATIONS, ecclesiastical, were first granted by pope Innocent III. in 1200. These exemptions from the discipline of the church, with indulgences, absolutions, &c., led eventually to the Reformation in Germany in 1517.

DISPENSING POWER OF THE CROWN (for setting aside laws or their power) asserted by some of our sovereigns, especially by Charles II. (in 1672 for the relief of nonconformists) and by James II. principally to enable Roman Catholics to hold civil and military offices, in 1686-8, was abolished by the bill of rights, 1689. It has been on certain occasions exercised, as in the case of embargoes upon ships, the Bank Charter act, &c.; see *Indemnity.*

DISRAELI ADMINISTRATIONS.* On the resignation of the earl of Derby through ill-health, 25 Feb., 1868, Mr. Disraeli reconstituted the ministry, 29 Feb. (see *Derby Administrations*, III.). As the elections gave a large majority to the liberal party, Mr. Disraeli's ministry resigned 2 Dec. He declined to take office with the then house of commons when Mr. Gladstone resigned, 12 March, 1873, and the latter resumed office.

FIRST ADMINISTRATION, 29 Feb. 1868.

First lord of treasury, Benjamin Disraeli.
Lord chancellor, Hugh MacCalmont, lord Cairns.
Lord president of the council, John, duke of Marlborough.
Lord privy seal, James, earl of Malmesbury.
Secretaries—home, Gathorne Hardy;—*foreign*, Edward, lord Stanley;—*colonies*, Richard, duke of Buckingham and Chandos;—*war*, sir John S. Pakington;—*India*, sir Stafford Henry Northcote.
Chancellor of exchequer, George Ward Hunt.
First lord of admiralty, Henry Thomas L. Corry.
Chief commissioner of works, lord John Manners.
President of board of trade, Charles Henry, duke of Richmond.
Chief secretary for Ireland, Richard, earl of Mayo; made viceroy of India, Oct.; succeeded by col. J. Wilson Patten, 7 Nov. 1868.
President of poor-law board, Wm. Reginald, earl of Devon.
The above formed the Cabinet.
Postmaster-general, James, duke of Montrose.
Lord great chamberlain, Orlando, earl of Bradford.
Chancellor of duchy of Lancaster, col. John Wilson Patten; succeeded by col. Thos. E. Taylor, 7 Nov. 1868.
Lord lieutenant of Ireland, James, earl (afterwards marquis) of Abercorn.

MR. DISRAELI'S LETTER of 30 Oct. 1873, to lord Grey de Wilton, severely censuring the Gladstone ministry as having "harassed every trade, worried every profession, and assailed or menaced every class, institution, and species of property in the country;" and also stating that the country has "made up its mind to close this career of plundering and blundering;" was published 7 Oct. 1873. (See *Gladstone Administration.*)

SECOND ADMINISTRATION, received seals, 21 Feb. 1874.

First lord of the treasury, Benjamin Disraeli (earl of Beaconsfield, 16 Aug. 1876),—and *lord privy seal*, Aug., 1876 to Jan. 1878).
Lord chancellor, Hugh MacCalmont, lord Cairns.
Lord president of the council, Charles Henry, duke of Richmond.
Lord privy seal, James, earl of Malmesbury; resigned, 12 Aug. 1876; earl of Beaconsfield, Aug. 1876; Algernon, duke of Northumberland, 4 Feb. 1878.
Secretary of state for foreign affairs, Edward, earl of Derby; resigned;—Robert, marquis of Salisbury, 28 March, 1878.
Secretary of state for India, Robert, marquis of Salisbury;—Gathorne Hardy, created viscount Cranbrook, 2 April, 1878.
Secretary of state for the colonies, Henry, earl of Carnarvon; resigned, 24 Jan. 1878; sir Michael Hicks-Beach, 4 Feb. 1878.
Secretary of state for war, Gathorne Hardy; col. Fred. Arthur Stanley, 2 April, 1878.
Secretary of state for home department, Richard Assheton Cross.
First lord of the admiralty, George Ward Hunt, died 29 July, 1877; Wm. Henry Smith, 7 Aug. 1877.
President of board of trade, sir Charles Adderley, resigned, created baron Norton, April, 1878;—Dudley Ryder, viscount Sandon.
Chancellor of the exchequer, Sir Stafford Northcote.
Postmaster-general, lord John Manners.
(The above formed the Cabinet.)

* Benjamin Disraeli (son of Isaac Disraeli, author of the "Curiosities of Literature," &c.), born 21 Dec. 1805 published "Vivian Grey," 1825; M.P. for Maidstone, 1837-41; Shrewsbury, 1841-7; Bucks, 1847-76. Chancellor of Exchequer (see *Derby administrations*). Feb. 1852; Feb. 1858; July, 1866; installed lord rector of Glasgow university, 19 Nov. 1873; created earl of Beaconsfield, Aug. 1876; plenipotentiary at the Berlin Congress, 13 June—13 July, 1878; K.G. invested by the queen, 22 July, 1878; received freedom of London, 3 Aug. 1878; ("at the pinnacle of ministerial renown; the favourite of his sovereign, and the idol of society,"—*Times*, 8 Aug. 1878); see *People's Tribute;* resigned (through liberal majority in elections), 22 April, 1880; published "Endymion," Dec., 1880; died 19 April, 1881, buried at Hughenden; prince of Wales and many present, 26 April; monument in Westminster abbey voted, 9 May, 1881. Mrs. Disraeli created viscountess Beaconsfield, 28 Nov. 1868; died 15 Dec. 1872.

Lord lieutenant of Ireland, James, duke of Abercorn. resigned Dec. 1876; John, duke of Marlborough, Dec. 1876.
Chief secretary for Ireland, sir Michael Edward Hicks-Beach (entered the cabinet, Nov. 1876): succeeded by James Lowther, Feb. 1878.
Vice-president of council (education), Dudley, viscount Sandon; lord George Hamilton, April, 1878.
Chancellor of duchy of Lancaster, col. Thos. E. Taylor.
Commissioner of woods and forests, lord Henry Lennox, resigned July, 1876; Gerard James Noel, 14 Aug. 1876.

DISSECTION, see *Anatomy*.

DISSENTERS. (For dates of foundation of various dissenting churches, see *Nonconformists*.) An association of baptist, independent, and presbyterian ministers styled "The general body of Protestant dissenting ministers resident in and about London and Westminster" was organised July 1727. This body has direct access to the throne, with kissing of hands. The secretary, 1903, is the rev. W. H. King. "Dissenting deputies," laymen, founded Nov. 1732. Chairman, 1903, W. S. Caine, M.P. The great act (9 Geo. IV. c. 17) for the relief of dissenters from civil and religious disabilities was passed 9 May, 1828. By this act, called the Corporation and Test Repeal act, so much of the several acts of preceding reigns as imposed the necessity of receiving the sacrament of the Lord's Supper as a qualification for certain offices, &c., was repealed. By 6 & 7 Will. IV. c. 85 (1836), dissenters acquired the right of solemnising marriages at their own chapels, or at a registry office. Another act passed in 1898, by which, under certain regulations, marriages may be solemnized in nonconformist places of worship if duly registered for that purpose, without the presence of a registrar. The act does not apply to Scotland or Ireland, nor to marriages of the Society of Friends, or of Jews. See *Worship in England* and *Independents*.

A Burials bill to permit the ministers of dissenters to officiate at funerals in churchyards several times rejected; in the commons 248 to 234, 21 April, 1875; 279 to 248, 3 March, 1876; earl Granville's resolution in the lords rejected 148 to 92, 15 May, 1876.
Lord Harrowby's additional clause to the government burials bill (permitting dissenters to have religious services in churchyards), was supported by the archbishops, and carried against government, (127-111,) 18 June; the bill withdrawn, 25 June, 1877.
Mr. Osborne Morgan's resolution for reforming burial laws (*i.e.* permitting other services), rejected (242-227), 15 Feb. 1878.
Act to amend the burial laws, permitting dissenters to have their own service or no service in churchyards; passed commons (258-79), 13 Aug., royal assent, 7 Sept. 1880.
The Rev. W. H. Fremantle having proposed to preach at Dr. Parker's city temple, and the bishop of London having disapproved, the opinion of two counsel (Messrs. Fitzjames Stephen and Benjamin Shaw) was taken. They declared it to be illegal for the clergy of the English church to take part in worship of dissenters, June, 1875.
Several episcopal clergymen take part in the dedication services of Christ church (formerly Surrey chapel), Blackfriars, middle of July, 1876.
Great dissatisfaction expressed by nonconformists, and strenuous opposition to the Education bills of 1902 and 1903 (see *Education*). Their cause championed by Dr. Clifford and others, March 1902, *et seq.*
Many nonconformists refuse to pay the Education rate, their goods distrained upon. Passive resistance movement (*which see*) started, March 1903.

DISSOLVING VIEWS. Henry Langdon Childe, the alleged inventor, died 15 Oct. 1874, aged 92.

DISTAFF (or Rock), the staff to which flax or any substance to be spun is fastened. The art of spinning with it at the small wheel, first taught to English women by Anthony Bonavisa, an Italian. *Stow.* St. Distaff's or Rock day was formerly the first free day after the Epiphany (6th Jan.), because the Christmas holidays were over and women's work was resumed.

DISTILLATION, and the various processes dependent on it, are believed to have been introduced into Europe by the Moors about 1150; see *Alcohol, Brandy*. The distillation of spirituous liquors was in practice in Great Britain in the 16th century. *Burns*. The processes were improved by Adam of Montpellier in 1801. M. Payen's work (1861) contains recent improvements. An act to prevent the use of stills by unlicensed persons was passed in 1846. 118 licences to distillers were granted in the year ending 31 March, 1858, for the United Kingdom.

M. Raoul Pictet announces a method of distillation by use of ice made by the air-pump, April, 1881.
System introduced in Russia rendering distillation a government monopoly, reported, April, 1901.

DISTINGUISHED SERVICE ORDER, for army and navy officers established 9 Nov.; first investiture, 17 Dec. 1886.

DISTRICT AUDITORS ACT, 42 Vict. c. 6 (28 March, 1879), regulated their appointment, duties, and payment.

DISTRICT CHURCHES ACTS. By the one passed in 1865 certain new churches were constituted rectories, and by another act, passed in 1868 (the Bishop of Oxford's act) the new parishes not rectories were ordered to be styled vicarages. See under *Parishes*.

DITCH, see *Expedition*.

"DIVERSIONS OF PURLEY" ("*Epea Pteroenta*," flying words) a collection of grammatical treatises by John Horne Tooke, published in 1786, named from the residence at Purley, near Wandsworth, Surrey.

DIVIDENDS OF PUBLIC STOCKS. By an act passed 11 Aug. 1869, these may be paid by post if the recipients desire it, as railway dividends are.

DIVINATION was forbidden to the Jews, B.C. 1451. (*Deut.* xviii. 9.) It was common among their neighbours: and is described by *Ezekiel* (xxi. 21) 493 B.C.

DIVINE RIGHT OF KINGS, the absolute and unqualified claim of hereditary sovereigns to the obedience of their subjects, a doctrine which is generally considered to be foreign to the genius of the English constitution, was defended by many persons of otherwise opposite opinions, *e.g.*, by James I., by Hobbes the free-thinker (1642), by Salmasius (1640), by sir Robert Filmer (about 1653), in his *Patriarcha*, published in 1680, and by the High Church party generally about 1714; but opposed by Milton (1651), Algernon Sydney, and others. The comte de Chambord, the last of the elder branch of the Bourbons, and the last consistent holder of the divine right of kings, died 24 Aug. 1883. See *France*, 1872, *et seq.*

DIVING-BELL (first mentioned, though obscurely, by Aristotle, about 325 B.C.) was used in Europe about A.D. 1509. It is said to have been used on the coast of Mull, in searching for the wreck of part of the Spanish Armada, before 1662. Halley (about 1716) greatly improved this machine, and was, it is said, the first who, by means of a diving-bell, set his foot on the ground at the bottom of the sea. Smeaton made use of the diving-bell in improving Ramsgate harbour, 1779-88. Mr. Spalding and his assistants going down in a diving-bell in Ireland were drowned, 1 June, 1783. The *Royal George* man-of-war, which was sunk off Portsmouth in 1782, was first surveyed by means of a diving-bell in May, 1817. Latterly it has been employed in submarine surveys and harbour works. The "*talpa marina*," or sea-mole, a diving machine for laying down torpedoes, &c., being a cylinder provided with compressed air sufficient for two persons for 50 hours, was invented by Toselli, a Venetian, and was successfully tried in the bay of Naples, 26 Aug. 1871. *Diving Dress*, a close dress made by Mr. Siebe 1839. M. Cabirol, maker of one, died Dec. 1874.

Mr. Fleuss invented a helmet with a mouthpiece into which he introduced enough oxygen to last five hours, and thus was enabled to remain under water several hours. He exhibited his method at the Polytechnic Institution, London, Nov. 1879, and at the Society of Arts, 6 May, 1880.

DIVINING ROD (*virgula divina, baculatorius*), formed of wood or metal, was formerly believed, even by educated persons, to have the property of indicating the position of minerals and springs of water. Instances were alleged in 1851 by Dr. H. Mayo, in his work on "Popular Superstitions"; and upheld by Mr. B. Tompkins, in his "Theory of Water Finding by the Divining rod," published, 1899.

DIVINITY, see *Theology* and *Mythology*.

DIVORCE was permitted by the law of Moses (*Deut.* xxiv. 1), 1451 B.C., but forbidden by Christ except for unchastity (*Matt.* v. 31, 32). It was put in practice by Spurius Carvilius Ruga at Rome, 234 B.C. At this time morals were so debased that 3000 prosecutions for adultery were enrolled. Divorces are of two kinds; one, *à vinculo matrimonii* (total divorce); the other *à mensâ et thoro* (from board and bed). Divorces were attempted to be made of more easy obtainment in England in 1539. The Judicature act, 1873, constituted the probate, divorce, and admiralty division of the High Court of Justice, with two judges. See *Supreme Court* and *Probate*.

Bill to prevent women marrying their seducers brought into parliament 1801

The commissioners on the law of divorce issued their first report . . . . . . April, 1857

In 1857 there had been in England, since the Reformation, 317 divorces by act of parliament; in Scotland, by the law, 174 divorces since 1846.

From the establishment of the divorce court, to March, 1859, 37 divorces had been granted out of 288 petitions; from Nov. 1860 to July, 1861, 164.

By 20 & 21 Vict. c. 85, the jurisdiction of the ecclesiastical courts respecting divorce, &c., was abolished, and the Divorce and Matrimonial Causes court instituted, to consist of three judges, the judge of the Probate court to be one (if possible) . . . . "

A full court sat—lord Campbell, chief baron Pollock, sir Cresswell Cresswell (judge of the Probate court) when five marriages were dissolved . 10 May, 1858

The act, amended by acts passed in consequence of the increase of the business of the court . 1858-6

An act respecting divorces in Scotland passed . . 1861

Sir C. Cresswell died in July; sir James P. Wilde (afterwards lord *Penzance*) successor . Sept. 1863

Lord Penzance retired, Oct.; succeeded by sir James Hannen, Nov. 1872; sir Francis H. Jeune, 30 May, 1892

See *Appeal*, *Probate* and *Supreme Court*.

The *Divorce Amendment act* passed 21 July, 1868.

Between 1856 and 1867 1279 dissolutions of marriage and 213 judicial separations were decreed.

Divorces 1858-87, 7321. In 1858, 200; 1868, 200; 1878, 403; 1887, 450; 1888-93 (inclusive), 2,094; 188 judicial separations; 1898, 5,949.

On appeal, the House of Lords decide that proceedings may be taken for divorce from a wife insane (see Mordaunt case, *Trials*, 1870) . 22 June, 1874

Sebright case, 1886, see *Trials*.

Divorce legalised by the French Republic; about 7000 divorces in Paris alone 1793-4; prohibited by the civil code, yet Napoleon I. divorced Josephine 16 Dec. 1809; again prohibited 1816; again legalised (with conditions) by M. Naquet's bill, passed July; many suits instituted, Aug. 1884; 7,051 divorces in 1896; 9,053 in 1899; 2,254 judicial separations 1899

Total up to end of 1889, 15,521.

In the United States of N.A. in twenty years (1867-86), there were 328,716 divorces. To check divorce by reforming the law, the National Divorce League addressed congress . . . 1889

Bills greatly facilitating divorce passed by the parliaments of New South Wales and Victoria, vetoed by the colonial office 1888-9

A divorce bill for Victoria, having received the assent of the home government, the bishops of Victoria forbid their clergy marrying divorced persons . . . . . . May, 1890

See *Church of England*, 1903.

DIZIER, St. (N.E. France). Here a siege was sustained for six weeks against the army of the emperor Charles V., 1544. The allies here defeated Napoleon, 27 Jan. and 26 March, 1814.

DOBRUDSCHA, the N.E. corner of Bulgaria; in 1854, the scene of the earlier incidents of the Russo-Turkish war (*which see*). At the close of the war of 1877-8 it was given to Roumania in exchange for the part of Bessarabia restored to Russia, and occupied 26 Dec. 1878.

DOCETÆ, a sect of the 1st century, said to have held that Jesus Christ was God, but that his body was an appearance, not a reality.

DOCKS OF ENGLAND. The following are the principal commercial docks:—

Commercial Docks, Rotherhithe, originated about 1660. West India Docks commenced 3 Feb. 1800; opened 27 Aug. 1802, when the "Henry Addington" West Indiaman, first entered them, decorated with the colours of the different nations of Europe.

London Docks were commenced 26 June, 1802, and opened 20 Jan. 1805.

East India Docks commenced 1803; opened 4 Aug. 1806.

St. Katharine's Docks began 3 May, 1827; and 2500 men were daily employed on them until they were opened, 25 Oct. 1828.

Royal Victoria Docks (in Plaistow marshes) completed and opened Nov. 1855; great enlargement proposed, July, 1876; completed and named Royal Albert Docks by the duke and duchess of Connaught, 24 June, 1880.

Magnificent docks at Liverpool and Birkenhead erected 1810-57.

Millwall Docks, near London, opened, 14 March, 1868.

A great floating iron dry dock, which cost 250,000*l.*, was launched at North Woolwich, 3 Sept. 1868; and towed from the Medway by two ships of war, 23 June, and arrived at the Bermudas (in thirty-six days), 30 July, 1869; another sent arrived 8 Aug. 1903.

The construction for floating docks for repairing ships advocated by lord Brassey, Jan. 1887.

Erection of docks at Tilbury determined on 30 Sept. 1881; begun 8 July, 1882; opened 17 April, 1886.

New Barry docks, 7 miles west of Cardiff, Bristol channel (cost 850,000*l.*), opened 18 July, 1889.

For dock labourers' strike, see *Strikes*, Aug.-Sept. 1889.

The wharfingers and other employers of labour resolve to form a union, 4 Feb. 1890.

The Port of London Docks, &c., Association, &c., resolve to employ any men they please, 12 Feb. 1890.

The dock companies employ free and union labour, without much resistance, 3 Nov. *et seq.* 1890.

A co-operative system working well, Nov., Dec., 1890.

Renewal of strikes; the unionists opposing the engagement of federation men, see under *Shipping*, Feb. 1891

The fourth annual dockers congress held at Bristol; Mr. Tom Mann president, 11–16 Sept. 1893; fifth congress at Grimsby, 24 May, 1894.
Floating dock for Durban, launched, Wallsend-on-Tyne, 8 Aug. 1903.

ROYAL DOCK-YARDS.

Woolwich, an extensive one in 1509; closed 1 Oct. 1869.
Deptford dock-yard founded about 1513, closed 31 March, 1869.
Chatham dock-yard was founded by queen Elizabeth. Three grand docks constructed at a cost of about 2,000,000*l.* independent of cost of convict labour, 1866-83.
Portsmouth dock-yard established by Henry VIII.
Plymouth dock, now Devonport, about 1689. Great fire here, by which the *Talavera*, of 74 guns, the *Imogene* frigate, of 28 guns, and immense stores, were destroyed; the relics and figure-heads of the favourite ships of Boscawen, Rodney, Duncan, and other naval heroes, which were preserved in a naval museum, were also burnt: the loss was estimated at 200,000*l.*, 27 Sept. 1840. Great fire, damage 20,000*l.* 8 Feb. 1882.
Sheerness dock-yard was built by Charles II. after the insult of the Dutch, who burnt our men-of-war at Chatham in 1667. A fire occurred at Sheerness dock-yard, on board the *Camperdown*, 9 Oct. 1840.
Milford-Haven dock-yard, 1790; removed to Pembroke in 1814.—See *Hull*.
Southampton large graving dock, length 750 ft., width, quay level, 112 ft. 6 in., depth 35 ft.; opened by the prince of Wales, 3 Aug. 1895.
See also *St. Margaret's Hope*.

DOCTOR. Doctor of the Church was a title given to Athanasius, Basil, Gregory Nazianzen, and Chrysostom in the Greek church; and to Jerome, Augustin, Ambrose, and Gregory the Great in the Latin church; see *Fathers*. Afterwards the title of doctor only was conferred on certain persons with distinguishing epithets, viz.: Thomas Aquinas (Angelicus), Bonaventura (Seraphicus), Alexander de Hales (Irrefragabilis), Duns Scotus (Subtilis), Roger Bacon (Mirabilis), William Occam (Singularis), Joseph Gerson (Christianissimus), Thomas Bradwardine (Profundus), and so on. *Doctor of the Law*, was a title of honour among the Jews. The degree of doctor was conferred in England, 8 John, 1207. *Spelman*. Some give it an earlier date, referring it to the time of the Venerable Bede and John de Beverley, the former of whom, it is said, was the first that obtained the degree at Cambridge in the 8th century.

DOCTORS' COMMONS, the college for the professors of civil and canon law in the 8th century. In February, 1568, Dr. Henry Hervie, dean of the arches and master of Trinity-hall (a seminary founded at Cambridge chiefly for the study of the civil and canon laws), procured from the dean and chapter of the diocese of London a lease of Montjoy-house and buildings in the parish of St. Benet, Paul's wharf, for the accommodation of the society. Other courts being held here, the whole place received the appellation of "DOCTORS' COMMONS." The original college was destroyed in the great fire of 1666; in 1672 it was rebuilt on the old site. After the great fire, until 1672, the society held its courts at Exeter-house in the Strand. It was incorporated by charter in June, 1768. *Coote*. The buildings of the College of Advocates, which included all the courts of Doctors' Commons, (arches, admiralty, consistory, &c.) were purchased by the Metropolitan Board of Works, and were pulled down in April, 1867, for the new Queen Victoria Street; some new buildings were erected. Till 1857 the causes taken cognizance of here were blasphemy, divorces, bastardy, adultery, penance, tithes, mortuaries, probate of wills, &c.; see *Ecclesiastical Courts, Civil Law*, &c.

The wills were removed to Somerset-house, where the office was opened 24 Oct. 1874.

DOCTRINAIRES, a name given since 1814 to a class of politicians in France (Guizot, Molé, the duc de Broglie and others), who upheld constitutional principles, in opposition to arbitrary monarchical power. The party came into office in 1830 under Louis-Philippe, and fell with him in 1848. The term has been applied in this country to the writers in the "Westminster Review" (1824, *et seq.*), Bentham, Molesworth, and others.

DODONA, Epirus. The temple of Jupiter here, renowned for its ancient oracle, delivered by the sound of wind in a grove of trees, was destroyed by the Ætolians, 219 B.C. The foundations of the temple, with other relics, were discovered in 1883, by the excavations of M. Carapanos.

DODSON'S ACT (brought forward by Mr. John G. Dodson, and passed 1 Aug. 1861) provides that votes for electing members of parliament for the universities may be recorded by means of polling papers. The act was amended in 1868.

DOG, the, was worshipped by the Egyptians and hated by the Hebrews. The greyhound and mastiff are represented in the Assyrian sculptures in the British Museum. V. Shaw's "Book of the Dog" (new edition), 1881; J. H. Walsh's "Dogs of the British Islands," (new edition), 1878.

Statute against dog stealing, 10 Geo. III. . . 1770
Dog-tax imposed, 1796; and again in 1808; 12*s.* a year realised 219,313*l.*, in 1866
Assessed taxes on dogs repealed, 29 Mar. 1867; an annual excise duty of 5*s.* imposed on all dogs more than six months old, to begin on 5 April, 1867; increased to 7*s.* 6*d.* . . . . 1 June, 1878
Employment of dogs in drawing carts, &c., abolished in London, 1839; in the United Kingdom . 1854
Several clubs have been formed to improve the breeds.
Dog shows held in London in 1861; since 1862 at the Agricultural Hall, the Crystal Palace, Royal Aquarium, Westminster, and other places. Great show at Earl's Court, 15 Dec. 1897; another under Kennel Club rules, Agricultural Hall, 11 Feb. 1903.
"Dogs' temporary home" opened, Hollingsworth-street, London, N., 1861; removed to Battersea in 1871; about 2200 animals have been sheltered in a year; adapted for cats, 1882. 22,000 dogs received in 1894; 28,937 in 1897; 21,391 in 1901; a home at Hackbridge, Surrey, opened by the duke of Portland, 29 Oct. 1808.
Lethal chamber, invented by sir B. Ward Richardson, used when death is required.
As a nuisance, dogs at large unmuzzled in the metropolis were ordered to be seized by the police . . . . . . July to 27 Nov. 1868
A new act, more stringent, passed . . 24 July, 1871
Coursing is the term applied to racing between hounds. Master McGrath, an excessively fleet hound, the property of Lord Lurgan, thrice won the Waterloo cup; was sent for the queen to see, 1 Mar., and died . . . . 24 Dec. "
"Help," the railway dog (a colley), by mute appeals, collected above 200*l.* for the railway men's orphan fund . . . . Jan.—Sept. 1884
The muzzling of dogs in the metropolis ordered by the police ceased, 31 Dec. 1886; a similar order made in 1889; ceased, 31 Dec. 1890, rabies having greatly diminished. Increase of rabies reported in 1895-6. Muzzling ordered for 17 Feb. *et seq.* 1896; ceased 2 Feb. 1897; new order, with special muzzle, 6 April, 1897; ceased 27 Oct. 1899. Report of committee of 30 April, 1896, presented Feb. 1897.
"Miss Scottie, an intelligent collie, exhibited at the Westminster aquarium . . . 23 July, 1894
National canine defence league; Mr. B. Bryan hon. sec. in 1897
Dog regulation bill introduced . . . . March, 1898
Dog licences (7*s.* 6*d.* each) issued in financial year 1871-2, produced 279,425*l.*; in 1875-6, 343,257*l.*; in 1876-7, 349,613*l.*; in 1877-8, 372,699*l.*; in 1881-2,

342,836*l.*; 1887–8, 354,278*l.*; 1893-4, 466,081*l.*; 1894–5, 446,469*l.*; 1901-2, 571,802*l.*

Number of dogs licensed in United Kingdom: in 1866, 445,656; in 1876, 1,362,176; 1900 (Gt. Britain), 1,777,543.

Rabies reported extinct in England and Scotland in 1900

New order regarding the muzzling and importation of dogs, issued . . . . . 14 Dec. 1901

"Tim," the Paddington railway dog, collected over 796*l.* 7*s.* 2*d.* since 1892 for railway servants' widows' and orphans' fund; died of old age, 8 Sept. 1902

Waterloo cup, won by Messrs. Fawcett's "Father Flint" . . . . 20 Feb. 1903

DOG-DAYS. The canicular or dog-days now commence on 3 July and end 11 Aug; other dates were formerly given. The rising and setting of Sirius or the dog-star with the sun has been erroneously regarded as the cause of excessive heat and of consequent calamities.

DOGE or **DUKE**: Venice was first governed by a doge named Anafesto Paululio, or Paoluccio, 697; see *Venice*. The Genoese chose their first doge, Simone Boccanegra, in 1339. *Muratori.*

DOGGER-BANK (German Ocean). Here a gallant but indecisive battle was fought between the British, under admiral sir Hyde Parker, and the Dutch, 5 Aug. 1781.

DOGGETT'S COAT AND BADGE. Thomas Doggett, an eminent actor of Drury-lane, at the first anniversary of the accession to the throne of George I., 1 Aug. 1715, gave a waterman's coat and silver badge to be rowed for by six young watermen in honour of the day, and bequeathed at his death, in 1722, a sum of money to continue the custom. Rowed for 1 Aug. every year.

DOIT. The ancient silver Scottish penny, of which twelve were equal to a penny sterling. The circulation of "doydekyns" (small Dutch coins) was prohibited by statute in 1415.

DOLLAR, the German *thaler*. Stamped Spanish dollars (value 4*s.* 9*d.*) were issued from the Mint in March, 1797, but called in Oct. following. The dollar is the principal silver coin in the United States of North America, value about 4*s.* British money.

DOLLY'S BRAE, see *Riots*, 1849.

DOM and **DUOMO**, see *Cologne* and *Milan*.

DOM-BOC or **DOOM-BOOK** (*Liber Judicialis*), the code of law compiled by king Alfred from the West-Saxon collection of Ina and other sources. Alfred reigned from 871 to 901.

DOMES'-DAY BOOK or **DOOM'S-DAY** [*Domus Dei* book, *Stow*] (*Liber Censualis Angliæ*), a book of the general survey of England, commenced in the reign of William I., 1080 (some say 1085), and completed in 1086. It was intended to be a register to determine the right in the tenure of estates*; and from it the question whether lands be ancient demesne or not, is sometimes still decided. The book, formerly kept in the Chapter-house of Westminster, is now in the Public Record Office. It consists of two volumes, a greater and less, wherein all the counties of England, except Northumberland, Durham, Westmoreland, and Cumberland, are surveyed. "This Dome's-day book was the tax-book of kinge William." *Camden.* The taxes were levied according to this survey till 13 Hen. VIII., 1522, when a more accurate survey was taken, called by the people the New Doom's-Day-Book. Domes'-day Book was printed in 2 vols., folio, and issued in 1783; 2 supplemental vols., including an introduction by sir Henry Ellis, were issued in 1816. Photo-zinco-graphic copies of various counties have been published since 1861. The eighth centenary of the completion of the original Doomsday Book, celebrated in London, 25-29 Oct. 1886. In Sept. 1872, government ordered a return of all the owners of land in England and Wales—in fact, a new Domes'-Day-Book; the work to be done by the Local Government Board.

The return for Scotland 1872-3, was published by government, April, 1874; for England and Wales (exclusive of the metropolis) in 1875; for Ireland, 1876.

"Domesday Book," &c., by prof. F. W. Maitland, published Feb. 1897.

* Sir Martin Wright says, "to discover the quantity of every man's fee, and to fix his homage," *i.e.*, the question of military aid he was bound to furnish.

DOMESTIC ECONOMY, or the study of food and clothing, was introduced into the government educational department in 1874; the congresses begun at Birmingham, 16 July, 1877; and others since.

DOMINGO, ST., see *Hayti* and *Dominican Republic*.

DOMINICA (W. Indies), discovered by Columbus in his second voyage, on Sunday, 3 Nov. 1493. It was taken by the British in 1761, and confirmed to them by the peace of Paris, Feb. 1763. The French took Dominica in 1778, but restored it at the subsequent peace in 1783. Their admiral Villeneuve ineffectually attacked it in 1805. It suffered great damage by a hurricane in 1806, and also 4-5 Sept. 1883. Failing prosperity; changes in the administration to be made, reported 5 Oct. 1894; imperial assistance accepted, July, 1898. Population, 1881, 28,211; 1891, 26,841; 1901, about 29,000. See *Leeward Isles*.

DOMINICAL LETTER, noting the Lord's day, or Sunday. The seven days of the week, reckoned as beginning on the 1 Jan., are designated by the first seven letters of the alphabet, A (1 Jan.), B, C, D, E, F, G; and the one of these which denotes Sunday is the Dominical letter. If the year begin on Sunday, A is the Dominical letter; if on Monday, G; on Tuesday, F; and so on. Generally to find the Dominical letter call New Year's day A, the next B, and go on thus until you come to the first Sunday, and the letter that answers to it is the Dominical letter; in leap years count two letters. The letters for 1893, A; 1894, G; 1895, F; 1896, E D; 1897, C; 1898, B; 1899, A; 1900, G; 1901, F; 1902, E; 1903, D; 1904, C B; 1905, A. The letter or its number (figure of 1 for A, &c.) used in ancient charters.

DOMINICALS. See *Exeter*.

DOMINICAN REPUBLIC or San Domingo, formerly the Spanish part of the island of Hayti, the oldest European settlement, founded in 1494, by Bartolomeo Columbus. The capital, San Domingo, contains the cathedral and Columbus's residence. See *Hayti*, 1844, *et seq.* Population, 1887, 504,000; 1902 (estimated), 500,000. President, Ulises Heureaux, 20 July, 1886-99; assassinated at Moca, 26 July, 1899; succeeded by señ. Juan Jimenez, Nov. 1899; short revolution, the president resigned; succeeded by señ. Vasquez, 2 May, 1902.

DOMINICANS, formerly a powerful religious order (called in France, Jacobins, and in England, *Black friars*), founded to put down the Albigenses and other heretics by St. Dominic, approved by

Innocent III. in 1215, and confirmed by Honorius III. in 1216, under St. Augustin's rules and the founder's particular constitution. In 1276 the corporation of London gave the Dominicans two streets near the Thames, where they erected a large convent, whence that part is still called Blackfriars. A Dominican establishment at Haverstock hill, near London, was consecrated 10 Oct. 1867.

DOMINION OF CANADA, see *Canada*.

DOMINOES, "a sport imported from France a few years back." *Strutt's Sports*, 1801. Now very popular, much played in restaurants, clubs, &c.

DONATISTS, an ancient strict sect, formed about 313-318, by an African bishop, Donatus, who was jealous of Cæcilian, bishop of Carthage: it became extinct in the 7th century. The Donatists held that the Father was above the Son, and the Son above the Holy Ghost. Their discipline was severe, and those who joined them were re-baptized.

DONAUWERTH (Bavaria). Here the French and Bavarians were defeated by the duke of Marlborough, after a severe conflict, 2 July, 1704.

DONCASTER (Yorkshire), the Roman *Danum*, the Saxon *Donne ceastre*. The races here (held annually in September) began about 1703; see *Races*. Royal Agricultural Society met here 22-26 June, 1891. Population, 1881, 21,139; 1891, 25,936; 1901, 28,928.

DONGOLA, a town on the Nile, 750 miles S. of Cairo, subject to Egypt. See *Soudan*, 1883, 1885, 1896. The town and province re-conquered for Egypt by sir H. H. Kitchener in the campaign of 1896. New Dongola rapidly built and fortified, reported 19 Nov. 1896; reported prosperous by sir H. H. Kitchener, 17 Jan. 1897. Government organized. Population, about 60,000.

DONKEY SHOW. An exhibition of donkeys and mules belonging to the upper and lower classes took place at the Agricultural Hall, Islington, 9 Aug. 1864; and since.

DON QUIXOTE, by Saavedra Miguel de Cervantes (born 1547; died 1616). The first part of this work appeared in 1605, and the second part in 1608. It is said that upwards of 12,000 copies of the first part were circulated before the second was printed. *Watts*. First English translation, by Thos. Shelton, was published in 1612.

DOOM'S-DAY BOOK, see *Dome's-day Book*

DORADO, see *El Dorado*.

DORCHESTER (Oxfordshire) was once a bishopric, founded about 636. The first bishop Birinus, the apostle of the West Saxons (*which see*), was succeeded in 650 by Agilbert. In 659 the see was divided by the king. Dorchester remained with Agilbert, and Wina, established at Winchester, in 660 obtained the whole. The see of Dorchester was revived about 764. In 1072 the bishop Remigius de Feschamp removed the see to Lincoln.

DORCHESTER (Dorsetshire), the Roman *Durnovaria*, the Saxon *Dorneeaster*. Here are found remains of a Roman theatre and of a British camp. Splendid specimen of villa pavement discovered, Aug. 1899. Here Jefferies held his "bloody assize" (after Monmouth's rebellion), 3 Sept. 1685. Much excitement was caused by six labourers of Dorchester being sentenced to transportation 17 March, 1834, for administering illegal oaths. Population, 1881, 7,567; 1891, 7,946; 1901, 10,000.

DORIANS, Greeks, who claimed descent from Dorus, son of Helien; see *Greece*. The return of the Dorians, named Heraclidæ, to the Peloponnesus is dated 1104 B.C. They sent out many colonies. To them we owe the Doric architecture, the second of the five orders.

DORKING, Surrey, an ancient town; the manor having been given by the Conqueror to earl Fitzwarren. An imaginary battle of Dorking in which the German invaders totally defeat the British army is the subject of a clever article, attributed to gen. sir George Chesney, in Blackwood's Magazine for May, 1871. It provoked much controversy, and caused the publication of several pamphlets. Population, 1881, 6,328; 1891, 7,132; 1901, 7,670.

DORMANS (N. E. France). The Huguenots and their allies, under Montmorency, were here defeated by the duke of Guise, 10 Oct. 1575.

DORT, or **DORDRECHT**, an ancient town in Holland. Here happened an inundation of the Meuse in 1421, through the breaking down of the dykes. In the territory of Dordrecht 10,000 persons perished; and more than 100,000 round Dollart, in Friesland, and in Zealand. The independence of the thirteen provinces was declared here in 1572, when William Prince of Orange was made stadtholder. A Protestant synod sat at Dort 13 Nov. 1618, to 25 May 1619; to which deputies were sent from England, and from the reformed churches in Europe, to settle the difference between the doctrines of Luther, Calvin, and Arminius, principally upon points of justification and grace. This synod condemned the tenets of Arminius. Population, 1900, 38,884.

DORYLÆUM (Phrygia). Soliman, the Turkish sultan of Iconium, having retired from the defence of Nicæa his capital, was here defeated with great loss by the crusaders 1 July, 1097. *Michaud.*

DOTEREL, H.M.S., destroyed by explosion, 26 April, 1881. See under *Navy*.

DOUAY (N. France), the Roman Duacum, was taken from the Flemings by Philip the Fair in 1297; restored by Charles V. in 1368. It reverted to Spain, from which it was taken by Louis XIV. in 1667. It was captured by the duke of Marlborough in June, 1710; and retaken by the French 8 Sept. 1712. This town gives its name to the Roman Catholic English version of the Bible authorised by the pope, the text being explained by notes of Roman divines. The Old Testament was published by the English college at Douay in 1609; the New had been published at Rheims in 1582. The English college for Roman Catholics was founded in 1568 by William Allen, afterwards cardinal. *Dodd.* For 335 years most English and Irish priests were trained here. The Benedictine monks, professors and students, were expelled from France 18 July, 1903; the college transferred to St. Mary's Roman Catholic college at Wolverhampton.

DOURO, a river (separating Spain and Portugal), which, after a desperate struggle between Wellington's advanced guard under Hill, and the French under Soult, was successfully crossed by the former on 12 May, 1809. So sudden was the movement, that Wellington at 4 o'clock sat down to the dinner prepared for the French general. *Alison.*

DOVER (Kent), the Roman Dubris. Near here Julius Cæsar is said to have first landed in

England, 26 Aug., 55 B. C., and its original castle to have been built by him soon after; but this is disputed. The works were strengthened by Alfred and succeeding kings, and rebuilt by Henry II. The earliest named constable is Leopoldus de Bertie, in the reign of Ethelred II., followed by earl Godwin, Odo the brother of William I., &c. In modern times, this office, and that of warden of the Cinque Ports, have been frequently conferred on the prime minister for the time being,—*e.g.*, lord North, Mr. Pitt, lord Liverpool, and the duke of Wellington. The earl of Dalhousie, late governor-general for India, appointed in Jan. 1853, died 19 Dec. 1860. Lord Palmerston, appointed constable March, 1861, died 18 Oct. 1865. Earl Granville appointed Dec. 1865, died 31 March, 1891. W. H. Smith, appointed May, died 6 Oct. 1891. The marquis of Dufferin and Ava, about 4 Nov. 1891 (died 12 Feb. 1902). Marquis of Salisbury appointed 1895, died 22 Aug. 1903. See *Tunnels*. Population, 1901, 41,782.

The priory was commenced by archbishop Corboyl, or Corbois, about 1130
At Dover, king John resigned his kingdom to Pandolf, the pope's legate . . . . 13 May, 1213
The pier projected by Henry VIII. 1533
Charles II. landed here from his exile 26 May, 1660
Iniquitous secret treaty with France signed here May, 1670
The foot barracks burnt by accident . 30 July, 1800
Admiralty pier commenced 1844
Railway to London opened . . . . 7 Feb. „
A submarine telegraph laid down between Dover and Calais by Brett . . . . . 28 Aug. 1850
A telegraph between Dover and Calais opened, 13 Nov. 1851
Part of the cliff fell, 27 Nov. 1810; and 13 Jan. 1853
Easter volunteer review here . . . 22 April, 1867
Suffragan bishop, Edward Parry, D.D. 1870
Dover College inaugurated by earl Granville 4 Oct. 1871
Dover and Deal railway begun by earl Granville, 29 June, 1878; opened . . . . . June, 1881
New municipal buildings and park opened 14 July, 1883
Coal-field discovered under the cliffs, 15 Feb. 1890; the colliery flooded, 8 deaths . . . 6 March, 1897
Construction of a new harbour proposed by the admiralty, Oct. 1890; first stone of new works laid by the prince of Wales . . . 20 July, 1893
Discovery of closed-up caves and passages, under the east cliff; closed up again . . early March, 1891
Mr. W. F. Smith presents to the nation the valuable relics of William Pitt, the duke of Wellington, and other lord wardens, which had become the property of his late father, Mr. W. H. Smith, and which were preserved in Walmer Castle . April, 1892
New pier opened . . . . . . 22 May, 1893
Discovery of great water springs . . 11 Sept. 1896
Parts of Shakespeare's cliff fell, 5, 6 Feb. 1897; coast-guard station removed, 8 Feb.; more fell 9 March, 1897
Fire at the castle, one wing gutted . . 14 Dec. „
Foundation stone of soldiers' Victoria hall and institute laid by lord Roberts, 8 Dec. 1898; opened by Mr. G. Wyndham . . . 15 Sept. 1899
British association meets here, 13–20 Sept.; 300 members of the French association and others from Boulogne, received by sir Michael Foster, 16 Sept. „
Dover harbour works, first block laid by Messrs. Pearson . . . . 15 Dec.
The shah of Persia arrives . . . 17 Aug. 1902
German officers of the *Stein* training ship entertained by the mayor at a banquet . . . 21 Aug. „
Lord Roberts presented with the freedom, 28 Aug. „
Prince of Wales's pier, costing 600,000*l.*, opened to public . . . . 1 Jan. 1903
Inauguration of Dover as port of call for Hamburg-American liners; congratulatory telegram by Emperor of Germany . . . . . 27 July „

DOWER, the gifts of a husband to a wife before marriage (*Genesis* xxxiv. 12). The portion of a man's lands or tenements which his wife enjoys for life after her husband's death. By the law of king Edmund, a widow was entitled to a moiety of her husband's lands or tenements for her life, 941. The widows of traitors, but not those of felons, are debarred their dower by statute 5 Edw. VI. 1551. By the Dower act passed in 1833, the power of the wife over her dower was much diminished.

DOWN (N. E. Ireland). An ancient see, first bishop St. Cailan, in 499. At the instance of John de Courcy, the conqueror of Ulster, the cathedral, consecrated to the Trinity, was re-dedicated to St. Patrick about 1183. The sepulchre of St. Patrick (buried here in 493, in the abbey of Saul, founded by himself) brought this place into great repute. The see was united with that of Connor in 1441 (see *Connor*); and the see of Dromore was united to both by the Irish Church Temporalities act, 3 & 4 Will. IV. c. 37, Aug. 14, 1833. The cathedral of Downpatrick was destroyed by lord Grey, lord deputy of Ireland; for this and other crimes he was impeached and beheaded in 1541. *Beatson.*

DOWNS, see *Naval Battles*, 1652-3.

DRACO'S LAWS (enacted by him when archon of Athens, 621 B. C.), on account of their severity, were said to be written in blood. Idleness was punished as severely as murder. This code was set aside by Solon's, 594 B. C.

DRAFTS (or cheques). In 1856, drafts crossed with a banker's name were made payable only to or through the same banker. This act was passed in consequence of a decision to the contrary in the case of Carlon *v.* Ireland, 12 Dec., 1855. In 1858 the crossing was made a material part of a cheque, but bankers are not held responsible when the crossing does not plainly appear, and a penny stamp was ordered to be affixed to drafts on bankers, commencing 25 May. In the case of Simmonds *v.* Taylor, May, 1858, it had been decided that the crossing formed no part of the draft. The crossing had been erased, and the money paid to the holder of the draft, who had stolen it.

The "*Cheque-bank*," established for issuing drafts for limited amounts, opened 23 July, 1873; after many years' successful working it failed owing to extensive forgeries; still in liquidation, 1903.
The payment of a stolen draft crossed on one banker and presented by another banker declared legal; Smith *v.* Union Bank of London: verdict for defendants, 29 Nov. 1875.
Crossed Cheques act passed, Aug. 15, 1876.

DRAGONNADES. The fierce persecution of the Protestants in the reign of Louis XIV. by dragoons, by the minister Louvois, 1684, was consummated by the revocation of Henry IV.'s edict of Nantes, 22 Oct. 1685, which drove 50,000 families from France. *Duruy.*

DRAGOON. A cavalry soldier with infantry arms; the name is of doubtful origin, the Roman *Draconarii* were horse soldiers, who bore dragons for ensigns. Charles de Cossé, Marshal of Brisac, instituted French dragoons about 1600. The oldest British regiment, the Scots Greys, was enrolled in 1683.

DRAINAGE OF LAND, in England, is of early date—remains of British works being still extant in the Fens district. Cornelius Vermuyden, the Dutch engineer, was invited to England in 1621, and amidst much opposition, he and his successors drained the districts termed the Great Levels; see *Levels*. In the present century great progress has been made in drainage. In 1861 was passed "an act to amend the laws relative to the drainage of land for agricultural purposes;" see *Sewers*.

DRAKE'S CIRCUMNAVIGATION. Sir Francis Drake sailed from Falmouth 13 Dec. 1577, circumnavigated the globe, and returned to England after many perils, 3 Nov. 1580. He was vice-admiral under lord Howard, high admiral of England, in the conflict with the Spanish Armada, 19 July, 1588. He died at Panamà, 28 Jan. 1596, during an expedition against the Spaniards.

DRAMA, both tragedy and comedy, originated with the Greeks, rudimentary forms being gradually combined with the periodical choral performances in honour of the gods, the stories being derived from sacred legends. The early dates given below are doubtful. See *Theatre*.

The first comedy performed at *Athens*, by Susarion and Dolon, on a movable scaffold about B.C. 580 or 562
The chorus introduced 556
Tragedy first represented at Athens by Thespis, on a waggon (*Arundelian Marbles*) 535
Thespis of Icaria performed at Athens "Alcestis," and was rewarded with a goat (*tragos*). *Pliny* . ,,
GREEK DRAMA.—*Tragedy:* Æschylus, introduced trilogies (sets of 3 plays), with unity of time and place, several actors, scenery aud other improvements; wrote 70 tragedies, 7 extant: *Persæ, Agamemnon, Prometheus*, &c. B.C. 525–456
Sophocles, highly moral, wrote 113 tragedies; about 81 represented, 7 extant: *Antigone, Œdipus Tyrannus*, &c. . . . . B.C. 495–406
Euripides, lower moral tone and other changes; wrote 75 or 92 plays; 18 extant: *Alcestis, Medea, Hecuba, Iphigenia, Orestes*, &c. . . B.C. 480–400
Comedy: Aristophanes, a strong conservative, exhibited the common life and politics of Athens, and satirized the sophists; wrote 54 plays, 11 extant: *the Knights, Clouds, Wasps, Birds, Frogs*, &c. B.C. about 444–380
Cratinus: 21 comedies, only fragments extant B.C. 519–422
Menander, Epicurean moralist; above 100 comedies, only fragments extant . . B.C. 342–291
Anaxandrides, wrote many comedies approved by Aristotle; died . . . . . . B.C. 340
[Acted in Greek at Cambridge; "Agamemnon" of Æschylus and "Ajax" of Sophocles, Nov. 1882; "Birds" of Aristophanes, 28 Nov. 1883. The "Eumenides" of Æschylus 1 Dec. 1885; "Œdipus Tyrannus" of Sophocles, 22 Nov. 1887; "Ion" of Euripides, 25 Nov. 1890; "The Frogs" of Aristophanes at Oxford, about 24 Feb. 1892; "The Knights," 24 Feb. 1897; "Iphigenia in Tauris" of Euripides, at Cambridge, 30 Nov.–5 Dec. 1894; "The Wasps" of Aristophanes, 19 Nov. 1897; Mr. Todhunter's "Helena in Troas," written in English, and successfully performed in the Greek style at Hengler's circus near Oxford Street, W., 17 May, 1886.]
LATIN DRAMA, derived from the Greek.
Livius Andronicus, a freed Greek slave of Tarentum, wrote Latin dramas; of 14 the titles and fragments have been preserved; his first play acted at Rome about . . . . . B.C. 240
T. Maccius Plautus wrote about 130 plays; 20 extant: *Miles, Trinummus*, &c.; very national and popular, about . . . . . . B.C. 254–184
P. Terentius or Terence, a freed slave, educated by his master, translated 108 of Menander's comedies, and imitated them; 6 of his own comedies extant: *Andria, Hecyra, Heauton-timoroumenos*, (the self-tormentor) *Eunuchus, Phormio, Adelphi* B.C. 195–159
L. Annæus Seneca, the philosopher, wrote 10 tragedies: *Hippolytus, Oedipus, Medea, Agamemnon*, &c.; killed by Nero . . . A.D. 65
The high-class drama declined under the emperors till its extinction, when it had degenerated into gross buffoonery
A latin play of Plautus or Terence is annually performed at Westminster school in conformity with the statute of queen Elizabeth.
The MODERN DRAMA, ENGLISH, was gradually developed from the services of the church in the 12th and 13th centuries, and appeared in the form of a miracle or mystery plays, based upon the bible history and legends of the saints. They were originally performed in churches, and afterwards in market-places and open fields. The Coventry, Chester and other mysteries, published by the Shakspeare Society, in 1843–7. See *Church of England*, 1897. John Skelton and others wrote Moralities about 1500; Nicholas Udall, 1540; The tragedy of Gorboduc or Ferrex & Porrex by Thos. Sackville and Thos. Norton, interludes by John Heywood . . . . . . 16th century
The drama patronized by queen Elizabeth and the Stuarts . . . . 1558 *et seq.*
See article *Shakspeare's Plays*.
Dramatists: Robert Greene, 1560(?)–92; Christopher Marlowe, 1564–93; Wm. Shakspeare, 1564–1616; Ben Jonson, 1574–1637; Francis Beaumont, 1586–1616; John Fletcher, 1576–1625; Philip Massinger, 1584–1640; John Ford, 1586–1639; sir Wm. Davenant, 1603–68; John Milton, 1608–74.
The Puritans condemned the stage; Wm. Prynne published his "Histrio-Mastix," the "Player's Scourge," 1633. The theatres closed during the commonwealth 1649–60
Dramatists: John Dryden, 1631–1701; sir G. Etherege, 1636–1689; Thos. Shadwell, 1640–92; W. Wycherley, 1640 (?)–1715; Thos. Otway, 1651–85; Nat. Lee, 1655–92; Thos. Southerne, 1659–1746; Mrs. Susannah Centlivre, 1667–1723; sir Wm. Congreve, 1670–1729; Colley Cibber, 1671–1757; sir John Vanbrugh, 1672 (?)–1726; Geo. Farquhar, 1678–1707; Nicholas Rowe, 1687–1715.
Bp. Jeremy Collier published his "Short view of the Immorality and Profaneness of the English Stage" 1697
Dramatists: Henry Fielding, 1707–54; David Garrick, 1716–79; S. Foote, 1720(?)–77; O. Goldsmith, 1728–74; Richard Cumberland, 1732–1811; R. B. Sheridan, 1751–1816; Joanna Baillie, 1762–1851; J. Sheridan Knowles, 1784–1862; Lord Byron, 1788–1824; Edward Bulwer, lord Lytton, 1806–73; Alfred, lord Tennyson, 1809–92; Francis Talfourd, 1827 (?)–62; T. W. Robertson, 1829–71; Oscar Wilde, 1856–1900; A. W. Pinero, *b.* 1855; Henry A. Jones, *b.* 1851; Stephen Phillips, *b.* 1866; James M. Barrie, *b.* 1860; Sydney Grundy, *b.* 1848.
Act for the revision of plays, and for licensing them previous to performance 1737
Authors' Dramatic Copyright Protection act, 3 Wil. IV. c. 15 to June, 1833; extended to operas, 1 July 1842
School of dramatic art, Argyll-street, London, W., opened . . . . 4 Oct. 1882
See *Theatres*, &c.
FRENCH DRAMA.—Adam de la Halle is said to have originated the comic opera in "Robin et Marion," and the modern comedy in "Adam" or "Jus de la Feuillie," . . . . . . 13th century
Chronical plays and Moralities or Allegorical plays 14th and 15th centuries
At the Renaissance French tragedy copied Seneca rather than the Greek poets and was much influenced by the Italian and Spanish dramatists.
Stephen Jodelle, 1532–73; Paul Scarron, 1610(?)–60; J. B. Poquelin, aft. Molière, 1662–73; P. J. de Crebillon, 1674–1762; Peter Corneille, 1606–84; Jean Racine, 1639–99; F. M. Arouet de Voltaire, 1694–1778; Alfred de Musset, 1810–57; A. E. Scribe, 1791–1861; Alexandre Dumas, 1802–70; Victor Hugo, 1802–85; Alexandre Dumas (fils), 1824–95; Edouard Pailleron, 1834–99; Edmond Rostand, *b.* 1868; Jules Barbier; Victorien Sardou, *b.* 1831 1825–1903
Great influence of Romanticism . . . 1830, *et seq.*
Opera bouffe . . . . 1852, *et seq.*
ITALIAN DRAMA, began with the Renaissance.
J. G. Trissino (imitated Seneca), 1478–1550; Nich. Machiavelli, 1469–1527; L. Ariosto, 1474–1533
Rise of the Opera; P. Metastasio, 1698–1782; C. Goldoni, 1707–93; V. Alfieri, 1749–1803; C. Gozzi, 1772–1806; A. Manzoni . . 1784–1873
SPANISH DRAMA.—National not classical. Popular Don Juan stories.
Dramatists.—Lope de Vega, 1568–1635; Pedro Calderon, 1601–87; much copied in England and France.

The "Passion-play" is still performed.

GERMAN DRAMA.—Sacred dramas and the passion play performed before 1300

The "Passion of Christ," a *miracle-play*, still frequently performed at Ober-Ammergau in Bavaria, is said to have had its origin after a pestilence in 1633

This play was witnessed by the prince of Wales and other distinguished persons in the summer and autumn, 1871.

Performances, 17-26 May, 25 Sept. 1880; and frequently since, 28 Sept. *et seq.* 1890; 20 May, 1900.

Its proposed performance at the Westminster Aquarium, 4 Nov., was stopped by the disapprobation of many . . . . . . Oct. 1878

Dramatists: Gotthold E. Lessing, 1729–81; J. C. F. von Schiller, 1759–1805; A. F. F. von Kotzebue, 1761–1819; J. W. von Goethe, 1749–1832; A. W. Iffland 1759–1814

Translation of Shakespeare by Ch. M. Wieland, published 1762–66, and by August W. von Schlegel and J. W. Tieck . . . 1797–1810

SCANDINAVIAN DRAMA. — *Dramatists*, Holberg, Heiberg, Ochlenschläger, Ibsen, Björnson.

DRAMATIC COLLEGE, for the benefit of distressed actors and their children, was proposed 21 July, 1858, at the Princess's theatre, by Messrs. C. Dickens, Thackeray, C. Kean, B. Webster, and others. Mr. Henry Dodd's offer of land and money, with certain stipulations, was declined Jan. 1859. The first stone of the buildings at Maybury, near Woking, was laid by the prince consort, 1 June, 1860; and on 29 Sept. 1862, seven annuitants were installed. The central hall was opened by the prince of Wales, 5 June, 1865. The queen was the patron. The viceroy of Egypt was present at the annual fête at the Crystal Palace, July 1867, and gave 500*l.* to the college. The scheme was unsuccessful. On 12 Nov. 1877, it was determined to close the college, and provide for the inmates. The buildings were sold by private contract about 23 July, 1880.

DRAMATIC REFORM ASSOCIATION, started at Manchester, Jan. 1878.

DRAPIER'S LETTERS, by dean Swift, published in 1723–4 against *Wood's Halfpence* (*which see*).

DRAUGHTS, a game resembling chess, played upon a checkered board divided in 64 black and white squares. Its origin is unknown. Strutt, in *Sports and Pastimes*, calls it a modern game. but it was played in Europe in the 16th century. Paul de Mallet wrote a treatise on draughts, which was published in Paris 1668. A game resembling draughts is depicted on the Egyptian monuments, and the Greeks and Romans played a similar game. *Checkers* is the common name for draughts in America, and in France it is called *jeu des dames*.

DRAWING SOCIETY (made Royal, 1892) of Great Britain, formed in July, 1888, to promote the teaching of drawing in schools. There are annual exhibitions.

DREADNOUGHT. In this ship, which was engaged in the battle of Trafalgar, 21 Oct. 1805, was established a hospital for the seamen of all nations (whose sovereigns are subscribers), by the Seamen's Hospital Society established 1821. The old vessel was replaced by others. The removal of the men to Greenwich hospital was proposed in 1867; effected, April, 1870.

DREAMS are mentioned in Scripture, *e. g.*, Joseph's and Pharaoh's, 1715 B. C. (*Gen.* xxxvii. and xli.), and Nebuchadnezzar's, 603 and 570 B. C. (*Daniel* ii. and iv.), and were regarded as direct messages from the spiritual world. The first attempt to interpret dreams and omens is ascribed to Amphictyon of Athens, 1497 B.C.

DRED SCOTT CASE; see *United States*, 1857.

DREDGING; see *Deep Sea*.

DREPANUM (Sicily). Near this place the Carthaginian admiral Adherbal totally defeated the Roman fleet under Publius Claudius, 249 B. C.

DRESDEN, termed the German Florence, became the capital of Saxony in 1548.* Population in 1885, 246,086; 1895, 336,440; 1900, 397,300.

Alliance of Dresden between Saxony and Denmark and Russia . . . . . . 28 June, 1709

Peace of Dresden between Hungary, Prussia, and Saxony . . . . . . 25 Dec. 1745

Taken by Frederick of Prussia in 1756; by the Austrians 1759

Bombarded in vain by Frederick . . July, 1760

Held by Austrians . . . . June–July, 1809

Severe contests between the allied army under the prince of Schwarzenberg, and the French commanded by Napoleon . . . 26, 27 Aug. 1813

The allies, 200,000 strong, attacked Napoleon in his position at Dresden, and the event had nearly proved fatal to them, but for an error in the conduct of general Vandamme. They were defeated with dreadful loss, and were obliged to retreat into Bohemia; but Vandamme pursuing them too far, his division was cut to pieces, and himself and all his staff made prisoners. In this battle, general Moreau received his mortal wound, while in conversation with the emperor of Russia 27 Aug. "

Marshal St. Cyr, and 25,000 French troops, surrendered Dresden to the allies . . 11 Nov. "

During a political commotion the king abdicated, and prince Frederick, his nephew, was declared regent . . . . . . 9 Sept. *et seq.* 1830

An insurrection 3 May; suppressed . . 6 May, 1849

DRESS. The attire of the Hebrew women is censured in *Isaiah* iii., about 760 B.C. Excess in dress among the early Romans was restrained by sumptuary laws: and also in England by numerous statutes, in 1363, 1465, 1570, &c. (see *Cap*). *Stow.* F. W. Fairholt's "Costume in England" (1846) contains a history of dress with numerous illustrations derived from MSS., the works of Strutt, &c. J. R. Planché's elaborate "Cyclopædia of Costume" first appeared in 1876. A "dress-making company" was established in London, 6 Feb. 1865, with the view of improving the condition of the workwomen.

Sir Walter Raleigh wore a white satin-pinked vest, close-sleeved to the wrist, and over the body a doublet finely flowered, and embroidered with pearls, and in the feather of his hat a large ruby and pearl drop at the bottom of the sprig in place of a button. His breeches, with his stockings and ribbon garters, fringed at the end, all white; and buff shoes, which, on great court days, were so gorgeously covered with precious stones as to have exceeded the value of 6600*l.*; and he had a suit of armour of solid silver, with sword and belt blazing with diamonds, rubies, and pearls.

King James's favourite, the duke of Buckingham, had his diamonds tacked so loosely on, that when he chose to shake a few off on the ground, he obtained all the fame he desired from the pickers-up, who were generally *les Dames de la Cour*.

The *court dress* of civilians, previously that of the time of the Georges, was modified by the lord chamberlain, lord Sydney, in 1869.

The BLOOMER COSTUME, introduced into America in 1849, by Mrs. Amelia Jenks Bloomer, and worn there by many of the women. It resembled male attire, being an

* *Dresden china* was invented by John Frederick Böttger (or Böttcher), an apothecary's boy, about 1709. He died 13 March, 1719. A costly service, each piece exquisitely painted, with battles, &c., was presented to the duke of Wellington by the king of Prussia, in 1816.

open-fronted jacket and loose trowsers, the latter wide like those of the Turk, but gathered in at the ankles. The Bloomer dress was adopted by a few females in the west of London, in August, 1851; but though recommended by some American ladies in popular lectures, it was soon totally discontinued. Mrs. Bloomer warmly advocated the enfranchisement of women and other important reforms. She was born at Homer, New York, in 1818, and died at Council Bluffs, Iowa, 30 Dec. 1894.

A dress exhibition opened in Piccadilly, London, 19 May, 1883.

Rational Dress Association active, May, 1883, *et seq.*

Mr. Charles Worth, dressmaker, born at Bourne, Lincolnshire, in 1825; at the age of 20 went to Paris, and there, by great energy and skill, established a business, employing latterly 1,200 hands; greatly influencing fashion; he is said to have been very charitable; he died 10 March, 1895.

DREUX (N. W. France). Here the Huguenots were defeated, and their general Condé taken prisoner; and the catholic leader Montmorenci was captured by the protestants; the slaughter was great on both sides, 19 Dec. 1562. Here is the burying-place of the Orleans family since 1816. The duke of Guise, aged 18, the last surviving child of the duc d'Aumale, was buried here 27 July, 1872. The bodies of king Louis Philippe and others of his family were brought here from England and buried, 9 June, 1876.

DREYFUS CASE: see *France*, 1894 *et seq.* Capt. Alfred Dreyfus was arrested 15 Oct., tried by court-martial *in camera*, convicted from the *bordereau* (secret documents from the war office) of high treason, and sentenced to life-imprisonment, 23 Dec. 1894; publicly degraded, protesting his innocence, 5 Jan. 1895; sent first to the Ile de Ré, mid Jan., and to the Ile du Diable, Feb. 1895.

Col. Picquart, urging an inquiry into the case, Sept., is dismissed from the war office and replaced by col. Henry . . . . 16 Nov. 1896

M. Scheurer-Kestner (died 19 Sept. 1899), vice-pres. of the senate, intercedes for Dreyfus . Sept. 1897

Maj. Esterhazy, charged with having written the *bordereau*, demands an inquiry . . 19 Nov. ,,

M. Méline, premier, declares in the senate, "*Il n'y a pas d'affaire Dreyfus*" . . . 7 Dec. ,,

Maj. Esterhazy is acquitted by court-martial, 11 Jan. 1898

Col. Picquart (brought from Tunis to answer Esterhazy's charges, Nov. 1899) is rearrested and sent to Mont Valérien . . . 13 Jan. ,,

M. Zola's letter, *J'accuse* (defending Dreyfus and demanding a new trial), appears in the *Aurore*, 13 Jan. ,,

Col. Picquart secretly examin d at Mont Valérien, 1 Feb.; and retired from the army . 25 Feb. ,,

Col. Henry confesses to forgery against Dreyfus, is arrested, and commits suicide in prison, 31 Aug. ,,

Esterhazy flies from France . . . . 9 Sept. ,,

Col. du Paty de Clam placed on the retired list, 13 Sept. ,,

Col. Picquart liberated by the civil court, 21 Sept.; is rearrested by gen. Zurlinden's orders, 22 Sept. ,,

The Dreyfus case submitted for revision to the court of cassation . . . 26 Sept. *et seq.* ,,

The secret *dossier* communicated to the court, 27 Dec. ,,

M. Quesnay de Beaurepaire, president, resigns, 8 Jan. 1899

Vote of confidence in the chamber for the ministry and the court of cassation . . . 12 Jan. ,,

Esterhazy, under a safe-conduct, gives evidence, 24 Jan.; leaves Paris before concluding . 1 Feb. ,,

Revision (adjunction) bill passed by the senate, 158–131 . . . . 28 Feb. ,,

Esterhazy confesses that he wrote the *bordereau* under col. Sandherr's instructions . 2 June, ,,

The court orders a fresh trial . . 3 June, ,,

Col. Picquart is released, charges dismissed, 9, 13 June, ,,

Dreyfus brought back and taken to Rennes, 1 July, ,,

Esterhazy states that gens. Gonse, de Boisdeffre, and Billot knew the *bordereau* that condemned Dreyfus to be a forgery . . . . 13 July, 1899

Court-martial at Rennes opens, 7 Aug.; M. Labori, Dreyfus's counsel, shot at and wounded on his way to the court . . . . . 14 Aug. ,,

Major Hartmann's technical criticism of the *bordereau* and its ante-dating (the change in the date shown by M. Lamothe), conclusive in favour of prisoner's innocence . . . . . 2 Sept. ,,

M. Labori's request for the evidence of military attachés refused . . . . . 6 Sept. ,,

The declarations of prince Münster (Dec. 1894 and Jan. 1895), and count von Bülow (24 Jan. 1898), that neither the German embassy in France nor any German agent had ever had relations of any kind with Dreyfus, published officially in the *Imperial Gazette*, Berlin . . . . 8 Sept. ,,

M. Demange maintains Dreyfus's innocence and Esterhazy's guilt in an eloquent speech, but *the judges, after an hour and a-half's absence, by a majority of 5–2, pronounce him* guilty, *with extenuating circumstances*, and sentence him to 10 years' imprisonment . . . . 8, 9 Sept. ,,

Great indignation at the sentence and sympathy with the prisoner; meetings held in his favour in all parts of the world; see *Times*, 9 Sept. *et seq.* ,,

M. Zola's letter, "The Fifth Act," appears in the *Aurore* . . . . . . 12 Sept. ,,

Capt. Dreyfus is *pardoned* by pres. Loubet, after a cabinet council, and released . 19, 20 Sept. ,,

[Many books were written on the case. "Five Years of my Life," by Alfred Dreyfus, translated by James Mortimer, was published, April, 1901.]

M. Jaurès unsuccessfully urges in the chamber of deputies the re-opening of the Dreyfus case, 6–7 April, 1903

DRILL REVIEW of children; see *Education*, 1870.

DRILLING-MACHINES, in agriculture. One was invented by Jethro Tull, early in the last century.

DRINK, see *Drunkards*.

DRINKING-FOUNTAINS. Several were erected in Liverpool in 1857. The Metropolitan Drinking Fountain Association was formed in London in April, 1859, by lord John Russell, the earl of Carlisle, Mr. S. Gurney, and others. The first of the numerous fountains since erected is that near St. Sepulchre's church, Skinner-street, 21 April, 1859. The magnificent fountain in Victoria-park, London, was inaugurated by the donor, Miss (afterwards baroness) Burdett-Coutts, 28 June, 1862. A remarkable drinking-fountain (the gift of the maharajah of Vizianagram) was inaugurated in Hyde-park, 29 Feb. 1868; another in Regent's-park, the gift of a Parsee, Aug. 1869.—324 in the metropolis, June, 1877; 437 fountains, 438 troughs, July, 1880; 672 drinking fountains, 726 troughs, July, 1890; 725 fountains, 729 troughs, June, 1903; 609 fountains, 924 troughs.

The fountain at the Royal Exchange, with the statue of Charity (cost, by subscription, 150*ol.*), finished Oct. 1879; many fountains erected since.

DROGHEDA (Ireland, E.), formerly Tredagh, a place of great importance, having the privilege of coining money. Here was passed Poynings' law (*which see*) in 1494. In the reign of Edward VI. an act was passed for the foundation of a university here. The town was besieged several times in the contests between 1641 and 1691, and Cromwell took it by storm, and put the governor, sir A. Aston, and the whole of the garrison, to the sword, 12 Sept. 1649. More than 3000 men, most of them English, perished. It surrendered to William III. in 1690. Population, 1901, 12,765.

DROMORE, Bishopric of (N. E. Ireland), founded by St. Coleman, first bishop, about 556. By an extent returned 15 James I., this see was valued in the king's books at 50*l.* Jeremy Taylor was bishop of Down and Connor in 1660, and of this see in 1661. In 1842 Dromore was united to Down by the Irish Church Temporalities act of 1833.

DRONTHEIM, capital of Norway, founded by Olaf I. about 998.

DROUGHT. The great suffering occasioned by drought, frequent in the eastern countries, is exemplified by Jeremiah, chap. xiv., about 601 B.C. Absolute droughts are rare in this country. According to Mr. G. J. Symons, there was partial drought in London, 16 April–30 May and 9 Aug.–5 Sept. 1880. "Of these long partial droughts I can trace only eight in the 93 years, viz.:—1800, June 6 to Aug. 19; 1817, March 8 to May 13; 1835, June 27 to Sept. 2; 1840, Feb. 5 to May 7; 1844, March 11 to June 23; 1852, Feb. 1 to April 28; 1854, Feb. 5 to April 26; 1893, Feb. 28 to May 16."—*Times*, 11 May, 1893. Almost absolute drought in S.E. England, 1 March–18 June, 1893; storms and rain in various places, 19 June; very little rain July–Sept.; great scarcity of fodder, and failure of root crops. Drought in *S. Italy*, *France* and *Spain*, 1893. Very little rain from mid April–July, 1895. Great drought in Gt. Britain and the continent to mid Oct. 1898. Drought in England, common fires frequent, June–28 Aug. 1899. See *Madras*, *Heat*, *United States*.

DROWNING, an ancient punishment. The ancient Britons are said to have inflicted death by drowning in a quagmire. *Stow*. It is said to have been inflicted on eighty intractable bishops near Nicomedia, A.D. 370; and to have been adopted as a punishment in France by Louis XI. The wholesale drownings of the royalists in the Loire at Nantes, by command of the brutal Carrier, Nov. 1793, were termed *Noyades*. 94 priests were drowned at one time. He was condemned to death in Dec. 1794. Societies for the *recovery of drowning persons* were first instituted in Holland, in 1767. The second society is said to have been formed at Milan, in 1768; the third in Hamburg, in 1771; the fourth at Paris, in 1772; and the fifth in London, in 1774. The motto of the Royal Humane Society in England is: *Lateat scintillula forsan*—"A small spark may perhaps lie hid." François Texier, of Dunkerque, after saving 50 lives at different times, was drowned in a storm, Oct. 1871.

Drowned in inland waters in England and Wales, 1877, 2662; found drowned in 1893, 1,114; in 1894, 1,149; in 1895 1,178. In United Kingdom in 1880, 4044.

DRUGS, sales regulated by Sale of Food and Drugs Act, passed 11 Aug. 1875. See *Pharmacy*.

DRUIDS. Priests, among the ancient Germans, Gauls, and Britons, so named from their veneration for the oak (Brit. *derw*). They administered sacred things, were the interpreters of the gods, and supreme judges. They headed the Britons who opposed Cæsar's first landing, 55 B.C., and were exterminated by the Roman governor, Suetonius Paulinus, A.D. 61.

DRUM. It was used by the Egyptians and other ancient nations; and brought by the Moors into Spain. The drum, or drum capstan, for weighing anchors, was invented by sir S. Morland, in 1685. *Anderson*.

DRUMCLOG (W. Scotland). Here the covenanters defeated Graham of Claverhouse, on 1 June, 1679. An account of the conflict is given by Walter Scott, in "Old Mortality."

DRUMCONDRA, see *Roman Catholic*.

DRUMMOND CASTLE, Castle Line steamer, Donald Currie co., from the Cape and Natal, struck on the *Pierres Vertes*, Molène island, off Ushant, abt. midnight, 16 June, 1896, Captain W. Pierce, 103 of the crew, and 147 passengers drowned. Perfect order and much heroism was displayed during this great calamity. Mr. Marquardt, passenger, and 2 sailors were saved by 3 Breton fishermen. Much humanity was shown by the natives of Ushant, Molène and neighbourhood in regard to the burials and the relatives of the sufferers; above 9,387*l.* received for the relatives, 22 June; total, 25,409*l.*, 3 May, 1897. Board of trade inquiry, calamity attributed to neglect of precautions, 27 July. Waterworks to be built in Molène, and a church clock and steeple at Ushant, with 1,600*l.* subscribed in England to commemorate French sympathy; reported 24 Jan. 1897. Silver medals distributed by sir Edmund Monson and Mr. Gosselin to 247 persons at Brest, with a message from the queen, 27, 29 April; others awarded by her June, 1897. 5,000 francs subscribed by the English for a harbour at Port Sall, Finistère: announced 13 March, 1898.

DRUMMOND LIGHT; see *Lime-light*.

DRUNKARDS were to be excommunicated in the early church, 59 (1 *Cor.* v. 11). In England, a canon law forbade drunkenness in the clergy, 747. Constantine, king of Scots, punished it with death, 870. By 21 James I., c. 7, 1623, a drunkard was liable to a penalty of five shillings, or six hours in the stocks. See *Temperance* and *Tee-totaler*.

A commission to inquire into the prevalence of intemperance granted by the lords on the motion of the archbishop of Canterbury, 30 June, 1876; report neutral respecting alcohol, recommends trial of modified Gothenburg system (*which see*), issued . . . . 18 March, 1879

A society for promoting legislation for the control and cure of habitual drunkards formed . 22 Sept. 1876

The establishment of an industrial home for intemperate females proposed at the Mansion house, London . . . . 29 Oct. 1877

Habitual Drunkards (inebriates) bill, passed 30 July, 1879; amended 1888; Habitual Inebriates Act, passed (reported successful, Oct. 1901) 12 Aug. 1898

Society for the study and cure of Inebriates, established . . . . 25 April, 1884

Drink Bill, Mr. Wm. Hoyle computes that the nation in 1860 spent in intoxicating liquors, 85,276,870*l.*; in 1876, 147,288,760*l.*; in 1879, 128,143,863*l.* In 1880, for beer, 67,881,673*l.*; British spirits, 28,457,486*l.*; foreign spirits, 10,173,014*l.*; wine, 14,287,102*l.*; British wines, &c., estimated 1,500,000*l.*; total, 122,299,275*l.*

Total drink bill 1881, 127,074,460*l.*; 1884, 126,349,256*l.*; 1885, 123,268,906*l.*; Dr. Dawson Burns computes in 1886, 122,389,045*l.*; 1887, 124,347,369*l.*; 1888, 124,603,939*l.*; 1889, about 132,103,000*l.*; 1890, 139,495,470*l.*; 1891, 141,220,675*l.*; 1892, 140,886,262*l.*; 1893, 138,854,829*l.*; 1894, 138,737,828*l.*; 1895, 142,414,812*l.*; 1896, 148,972,230*l.*; 1897, 152,281,723*l.*; 1898, 176,967,349*l.*; 1899, 185,927,227*l.*; 1900, 184,881,196*l.*; 1901, 181,738,245*l.*, expenditure per head 4*l.* 7*s.* 8½*d.*; 1902, 179,499,817*l.*, expenditure per head 4*l.* 5*s.* 6¾*d.*

A departmental committee, respecting habitual drunkards, which sat in 1892, presented its report, with recommendations, to the commons, 8 May, 1893

Royal Victoria Home for inebriate women, at Horfield, founded in 1895; Brentry reformatory and many others since; reports on retreats and reformatories issued by Home office for 1899 (22 institutions end of 1900) . . . Jan. 1901

Farnfield reformatory for female drunkards opened, end of Aug. 1900; hopeful report issued . Aug. 1901
152,200 prosecutions for drunkenness in England and Wales . . . . ,,
France, a temperate nation, yet from statistics, stands as the greatest consumer of alcohol among European nations, *Times*, 19 Feb. 1902, also Dr. Hyslop, British Medical association . Aug. 1903
Licensing act, 1902, came into force . 1 Jan. ,,
See *Black List*.

DRURY-LANE THEATRE derives its origin from a cock-pit, which was converted into a theatre in the reign of James I. It was rebuilt and called the Phœnix; and Charles II. granted an exclusive patent to Thomas Killigrew, 25 April, 1662. The actors were called "the king's servants," and ten of them, called gentlemen of the great chamber, had an annual allowance of ten yards of scarlet cloth, with lace; see under *Theatres*. *Drury-lane Theatrical Fund*, established, 1766.

DRUSES, a warlike people dwelling among the mountains of Lebanon, derive their origin from a fanatical Mahometan sect which arose in Egypt about 996, and fled to Palestine to avoid persecution. They now retain hardly any of the religion of their ancestors: they eat pork and drink wine, and do not practise circumcision, pray, or fast. In the middle of 1860, in consequence of disputes (in which doubtless both parties were to blame), the Druses attacked their neighbours the Maronites (*which see*), whom they massacred, it was said, without regard to age or sex. Peace was made in July; but in the meantime a religious fury seized the Mahometan population of the neighbouring cities, and a general massacre of Christians ensued. Fuad Pacha with Turkish troops, and general Hautpoul with French auxiliaries, invaded Lebanon in Aug. and Sept. The Druses surrendered, giving up their chiefs, Jan. 1861. See *Damascus* and *Syria*.

DRYING MACHINES, see under *Hay*.

DUALIN, an explosive substance (said to be from four to ten times more powerful than gunpowder), composed of varying proportions of cellulose (woody fibre), nitro-starch, nitro-mannite, and nitro-cellulose; invented by Carl Ditmar, a Prussian, and made known in 1870. This name is also given to another explosive compound, invented by Mr. Nobel, composed of ammonia and sawdust, acted on by nitro-sulphuric acid.

DUALISM, a term applied to the equally-matched conflicting powers of good and evil in the Persian mythology, the Hormuzd and Ahriman of Zoroaster: is also applied to the principles of the advocates for a separate government of Hungary under the emperor of Austria; effected in 1867.

DUBLIN, capital of Ireland, anciently called Ashcled, said to have been built 140. Auliana, daughter of Alpinus, a lord or chief among the Irish, having been drowned at the ford where now Whitworth-bridge is built, he changed the name to Auliana, by Ptolemy called Eblana (afterwards corrupted into Dublana). Alpinus is said to have brought "the then rude hill into the form of a town," about 155; see *Ireland* and *Trinity Colleges*. Dublin returns 4 M.P.'s by Act passed 25 June, 1885. Population in 1881, 249,602; in 1891, 254,709; 1901, 289,108.

Christianity introduced by St. Patrick . . . 448
Dublin environed with walls by the Danes . . 798
Named by king Edgar in the preface to his charter "*Nobilissima Civitas*" 964
Battle of Clontarf (*which see*) . . . 23 April, 1014
Dublin taken by Ramond le Gros, 1170, for Henry II. who soon after arrives 1171
Charter granted by this king 1173
Christ church built by the Danes, 1038; rebuilt about . . . . 1180—1225
Slaughter of 500 British by the Irish citizens near Dublin (see *Cullens Wood*) 1209
Assemblage of Irish princes, who swear allegiance to king John 1210
Foundation of Dublin castle laid by Henry de Loundres, 1205; finished 1213
John de Decer first provost; Richard de St. Olave and John Stakebold first bailiffs (see *Mayor*) . . 1308
Thomas Cusack, first mayor 1409
Besieged by the son of the earl of Kildare, lord deputy 1500
Christ church made a deanery and chapter by Henry VIII. (see *Christ Church*) 1541
Bailiff changed to sheriffs; John Ryan and Thomas Comyn, first 1548
Trinity college founded 1591–2
Charter granted by James I. 1609
Convocation which established the Thirty-nine articles of religion 1614
Besieged by the marquis of Ormond, defeated at battle of Rathmines (*which see*) . 2 Aug. 1649
Cromwell arrives in Dublin with 9000 foot and 400 horse . . . . Aug. ,,
Chief magistrate styled lord mayor 1665
Blue coat hospital incorporated 1676
Essex bridge built by sir H. Jervis 1670
Royal hospital, Kilmainham, founded . . . 1683
James II. arrives in Dublin, 24 March; proclaimed 4 May, 1689
Great gunpowder explosion 1693
Lamps first erected in the city 1698
Infirmary, Jervis-street, founded 1728
Parliament-house begun 1729
Foundling hospital incorporated 1739
St. Patrick's spire erected (see *St. Patrick*) . . 1749
Royal Dublin Society originated, 1731; incorpd. . . ,,
Hibernian society . . . . ,,
Marine society 1765
Queen's bridge first erected, 1684; destroyed by a flood, 1763; rebuilt 1756
Act for a general pavement of the city . . . 1768
Royal exchange begun, 1769; opened . . . 1773
Order of St. Patrick instituted 1779
Bank of Ireland instituted (see *Bank*) . . . 1783
Police established by statute . . . . . ,,
Royal academy incorporated 1786
Custom house begun, 1781; opened . . . ,,
Dublin library instituted 1791
Fire at the parliament house . . . . . ,,
Carlisle bridge erected 1792
City armed association 1794
New Four law courts opened 1796
The rebellion; arrest of lord Edward Fitzgerald, in Thomas-street . . . . ,,
Union with England (see *Union*) . . 19 May, 1798
Emmett's insurrection . . . . 1 Jan. 1801
Hibernian Bible society . . . . 23 July, 1803
Bank transferred to College-green 1806
Dublin institution founded 1808
Riot at the theatre 1811
Visit of George IV. . . . . . 16 Dec. 1814
Theatre Royal opened . . . . . 12 Aug. 1821
The "Bottle riot" . . . . ,,
Hibernian academy . . . . . 14 Dec. 1822
Dublin lighted with gas . . . . 16 Aug. 1823
Great custom-house fire . . . . . 5 Oct. 1825
Railroad to Kingstown . . . . . 9 Aug. 1833
British Association meet here 1834
Dublin new police act . . . . . 6 Aug. 1835
Cemetery, Mount Jerome, consecrated . 4 July, 1836
Royal arcade burnt . . . . . 19 Sept. ,,
Poor-law bill passed . . . . . 25 April, 1837
Awful storm raged . . . . . 31 July, 1838
O'Connell's arrest (see *Trials*) . . . 6 Jan. 1839
He is found guilty, 12 Feb.; liberated in Sept. 14 Oct. 1843
His death at Genoa 1844
Arrest of Mitchell, of the "United Irishman" newspaper . . . . . . 15 May, 1847
State trial of Wm. Smith O'Brien and Meagher in Dublin . . . . 13 May, 1848
[These persons were afterwards tried at Clonmel, and found *guilty*.] . . . . 15 May, ,,
Trial of Mitchell; *guilty* . . . . . 26 May, ,,

"Irish Felon" newspaper first published, 1 July, 1848
"Nation" and "Irish Felon" suppressed, 29 July, ,,
Conviction of O'Doherty . . . . . 1 Nov. ,,
The queen visits Dublin . . . 6 Aug. 1849
Royal exchange opened as a city hall . 30 Sept. 1852
Dublin industrial exhibition, which owed its existence to Mr Dargan who advanced 80,000*l.* for the purpose, was erected by Mr. (afterwards sir) John Benson, in the Dublin society's grounds, near Merrion-square. It consisted of one large and two smaller halls, lighted from above. It was opened by earl St. Germains, the lord-lieutenant . . . . 12 May, 1853
Visited by the queen and prince Albert, 30 Aug.; and closed on . . . . 1 Nov. ,,
Acts passed to establish a national gallery, museum, &c. . 10 Aug. 1854; and 2 July, 1855
British Association meet here (2nd time) . 26 Aug. 1857
Arrival of lord Eglinton—disgraceful contest between the Trinity college students and the police; the latter severely blamed . . 12 March, 1858
Fine art exhibition proposed, 20 July, 1860; opened by the lord-lieutenant, the earl of Carlisle, 24 May, 1861; visited by the prince of Wales, 1 July; and by the queen and prince consort . 22 Aug. 1861
National association for social science met, 14-22 Aug. ,,
Demonstration at the funeral of the rebel M'Manus, 10-12 Nov. ,,
Lord Rosse installed as chancellor of the university, 17 Feb. 1863
Statue of Oliver Goldsmith inaugurated by the lord-lieutenant, 5 Jan.; who opens the national gallery of Ireland . . . . . 30 Jan. 1864
New Richmond hospital, to be called the "Carmichael School of Medicine," founded by lord Carlisle (Mr. Carmichael, the surgeon, bequeathed 10,000*l.* to it) . . . . . 29 March, ,,
Industrial exhibition opened by the lord chancellor, 25 May, ,,
The O'Connell monument founded . . 8 Aug. ,,
St. Patrick's cathedral restored by Mr. Benjamin L. Guinness; re-opened . . . 24 Feb. 1865
The international exhibition opened by the prince of Wales . . . . . . 9 May, ,,
The newspaper "The Irish People" seized, and several Fenians taken in custody. (See *Fenians*, and *Ireland*.) . . . . . 15 Sept. ,,
International exhibition closed . . . 9 Nov. ,,
Great fire: Mrs. Delany and five others burnt; fire-brigade blamed . . . . . 7 June, 1866
Great banquet to John Bright . . . 30 Oct. ,,
Meeting of Royal Agricultural Society of Ireland, 27 Aug. 1867
Two policemen shot (probably by Fenians), 31 Oct. ,,
Funeral demonstration for Allen, Gould, and Larkin, the Fenians . . . . . . 8 Dec. ,,
Visit of prince of Wales (see *Ireland*) . 15 April, 1868
Sir Benjamin L. Guinness, benefactor, died 19 May, ,,
Church congress held . . 29 Sept.—2 Oct. ,,
Public entry of earl Spencer as lord-lieut. . 16 Jan. 1869
Smith O'Brien's statue unveiled . . 26 Dec. 1870
State funeral of lord mayor Bulfin (died in office), 16 June, 1871
Fine art and industrial exhibition opened by the duke of Edinburgh . . . . 5 June, 1872
Closed by the lord-lieutenant, earl Spencer, 30 Nov. ,,
Spencer dock inaugurated by the lord-lieutenant, 15 April, 1873
Great fire; rioting suppressed by the military, 7 June, ,,
Conference on "Home Rule" in the Rotondo, 18-21 Nov. ,,
International Rifle Match Irish and Americans; Americans won . . . . . 29 June, 1875
Statue of Henry Grattan unveiled . . 6 Jan. 1876
Entry of the duke of Marlborough, new lord lieutenant . . . . . . 10 Jan. 1877
Freedom of city given to Mr. W. E. Gladstone, 7 Nov. ,,
Christ church cathedral thoroughly restored by Mr. G. E. Street, at the expense of Mr. Henry Roe (above 250,000*l.*), re-opened . . . 1 May, 1878
British Association meets here (3rd time) . 14 Aug. ,,
Death of cardinal Paul Cullen, r.c. abp. of Dublin (since 1851), 24 Oct.; successor, monsignor McCabe, elected . . . . . . 28 Nov. ,,
Centenary of birth of Thomas Moore celebrated, 28 May, 1879

Theatre Royal burnt down, Mr. Egerton, the manager, and 5 others, perish . . . . 9 Feb. 1880
Great convention of the land league; Mr. Parnell declares for abolition of landlordism . 15 Sept. 1881
Phœnix park murders (see *Ireland*) . . 6 May, 1882
Statue of D. O'Connell unveiled, and the Exhibition of Irish Arts and Manufactures (not patronised by the queen and loyalists) opened by the lord mayor Dawson, 15 Aug. 1882, closed 6 Jan. 1883.
Discovery of the assassination plot (see *Ireland*) Feb. 1883
A futile attempt to blow up Ship-street barracks 25 April, 1884
Visit of the duke of Edinburgh with the Channel fleet warmly received end of Aug. . . . . ,,
Grand review of the troops in the Phœnix park by the duke of Cambridge . . . . 30 Sept. ,,
Death of cardinal M'Cabe . . . . 11 Feb. 1885
The prince and princess of Wales enthusiastically received, 8 April; he lays foundation of Museum of Science and Art, &c. . . . 10 April, ,,
Dr. Wm. J. Walsh appointed R.C. archbishop by the pope . . . . June, ,,
Entry of the marquis of Londonderry, lord-lieut., 18 Sept. 1886
Princes Albert Victor and George of Wales arrive at Dublin 27 June; review in Phœnix Park 28 June; received deputations, jubilee cathedral service and State banquet, &c., 29 June; left 30 June, 1887
The lord mayor, T.D. Sullivan, appears in full state at the police court to answer charge of offence against the Crimes Act by publication in his paper, the "Nation"; discharged through insufficient evidence 6 Oct.; on appeal the objection set aside by the Exchequer Division 10 Nov.; sentenced to two months' imprisonment as first-class misdemeanant . . . . . . 2 Dec. ,,
Great Unionist meeting in Leinster Hall to receive lord Hartington and Mr. Goschen . 29 Nov. ,,
Mr. T. Sexton, M.P., lord mayor . . 2 Jan. 1888
Great meeting of Irish Nationalists to receive the marquis of Ripon and Mr. John Morley, M.P., amid great enthusiasm . . . . 2 Feb. ,,
Dublin barracks built about 1708; enteric fever long prevalent, greatly increased in 1888; government inspection, special inquiry by Mr. Rogers Field, aided by Drs. Dupré and Klein, ordered Nov.; interim report with recommendations dated 25 Feb.; issued . . . . . April, 1889
The earl of Zetland sworn in lord lieut. . 5 Oct. ,,
Mr. E. Kennedy, lord mayor . . . 1 Jan. 1890
Strike of servants of Great S. and W. railway company at Dublin, 25 April; closed by the efforts of Abp. Walsh and others . . . . 3 May, ,,
The earl of Zetland opens the new museum of Science and Art and the National Library . . 29 Aug. ,,
Mr. Joseph Meade, lord mayor . . . 1 Jan. 1891
Mr. C. S. Parnell dies at Brighton, 6 Oct., buried in Glasnevin cemetery; solemn funeral 11 Oct. ,,
Explosion at Dublin castle attributed to nitro-glycerine; much destruction but no one injured 31 Dec. ,,
Mr. James Shanks, lord mayor . . . 1 Jan. 1892
Telephonic communication with Belfast opened 5 April, ,,
Great Unionist meeting . . . . . 23 June, ,,
Tercentenary of the foundation of Trinity college celebrated . . . . 5–9 July, ,,
New city market, shops, &c. destroyed by fire, very great loss, 27 Aug.; public meeting to raise a fund for restoration . . . . 29 Aug. ,,
Mr. Shanks, lord mayor . . . . . Dec. ,,
Explosion outside the detective office, Dublin castle; Patrick Synnott, a detective, killed, and others injured, 11 P.M. . . . . . . 24 Dec. ,,
The lord mayor of London, Stuart Knill, R. C., visits Dublin, 31 Dec., and receives the freedom of the city, 2 Jan.; leaves . . . . 3 Jan. 1893
See *Ireland* . . . . 15 March, and 8 April, ,,
Explosion of a bomb near the Four Courts; windows broken . . . . 6 May, ,,
Mr. V. B. Dillon, lord mayor . . 1 Jan. 1894, 1895
Annual military tournament at Ballsbridge, 8–15 June, ,,
Entrance of earl Cadogan, lord lieut. . 22 Aug. ,,
Mr. M'Coy elected lord mayor . . . . 2 Dec. 1896
Mr. W. E. H. Lecky elected M.P. for Dublin university . . . . 6 Dec. ,,

Great part of the college of St. Columba, Rathfarnham, destroyed by fire (re-opened 17 May, 1898) 7 Dec. 1896
State banquet at the castle inaugurating the queen's diamond jubilee . . . 13 March, 1897
Revival of the ancient musical festival held at Tara in the 12th century . . . . . . May, „
Rioting of Parnellites on jubilee day, 22, 23 June, „
Army manœuvres: great review by lord Roberts in the Phœnix park . . . . . 17 Aug. „
Arrival of the duke and duchess of York, warm reception, 18 Aug.; opened the Irish Textile exhibition, 19 Aug.; received various honours, 20 Aug.; at the Dublin horse show, 25 Aug.; left Dublin, 28 Aug.; see *Ireland*, 1897.
Mr. Tallon elected lord mayor . . . . . Dec. „
The Burlington hotel, St. Andrew-street, burnt, one death . . . . 1 Feb. 1898
Sir John Arnott bequeaths 40,000*l*. to charities in Cork and Dublin . . . . . April, „
Sir Robert Sexton (Unionist) nominated lord mayor 4 July, „
Messrs. Sealy & Co., government printers, burnt, state documents destroyed . . . 12 Oct. „
Lord Iveagh gives 250,000*l* for the Bull-alley area (poor neighbourhood), his scheme embodied in a bill, *Times* . . . . 23 Dec. „
Dublin county council (see *Ireland*) 1899
Alderman Tallon re-elected lord mayor . 23 Jan. „
Duke and duchess of York visit the lord-lieut., 10–24 April; well received at the Punchestown races . . . . 11 April, „
Dr. Wm. Frazer, eminent physician and antiquarian, born 1824, died 17 April, and Dr. Thomas Nedley, a great humourist, died, aged 80, 25 April, „
Third musical Feis Ceoil, concerts, exhibitions, &c., 15–20 May, „
High death-rate, city area, 42·4 per 1,000, week ending . . . . 9 Sept. „
First stone of the Parnell monument laid, 8 Oct. „
Commission appointed to inquire into the public health of Dublin, death-rate (47·9), &c., 6 Jan., 1890; meets . . . . 13 Feb. 1900
The queen visits Dublin (see *Ireland*) 14–26 April, „
Councillor Pile nominated lord mayor, 4 Sept. 1899; made a baronet . . . . . April, „
Death of prof. G. Fitzgerald, aged 50, eminent scientist . . . . 21 Feb. 1901
Mr. T. C. Harrington, M.P., installed as lord mayor; some hostility shown at Trinity college, 18 March, „
Messrs. Todd, Burns' drapers' premises in Mary-street burnt . . . . . . 1 Jan. 1902
Mr. Timothy Harrington, M.P., re-elected lord mayor . . . . 23 Jan. „
Messrs. J. Redmond, M.P., and P. A. M'Hugh, M.P. (see *Ireland*, 22 April, 1901), presented with the freedom . . . . . 3 April „
Prince Henry of Prussia, with naval squadron, visits Dublin . . . . . . 17 May „
Lord Cadogan opens the Roberts-house for lions in the Zoological gardens . . . . 20 May, „
Trinity college graduates' memorial (cost 25,000*l*.) opened by lord Cadogan . . . . 30 May, „
New organ given by lord Iveagh dedicated in St. Patrick's cathedral . . . . . 18 June, „
Mr. Edw. Martyn gives 10,000*l*. to the choir at the pro-cathedral, Marlborough-street . 30 July, „
Lord and lady Cadogan leave amid great demonstrations of goodwill . . . . 12 Aug. „
Lord Dudley installed lord-lieut. . . 16 Aug. „
Horse show at Ballsbridge opened; visited by Mr. Wyndham, chief sec., the duke and duchess of Connaught, Mr. Seddon and sir A. Hime, colonial premiers . . . . 26, 27, Aug. „
Crimes act extended to Dublin . . . 31 Aug. „
Mr. T. Harrington, M.P., 3rd time lord mayor, 23 Jan. 1903
Destructive gale, 1 death, many injured . 26 Feb. „
Mr. Campbell elected M.P. for the university, 5 March „
The king and queen visit Dublin . . 21 July, „

DUBLIN, Archbishopric of. It is supposed that the bishopric of Dublin was founded by St. Patrick, in 448. Gregory, bishop in 1121, became *archbishop* in 1152. It was united to Glandalagh in 1214. George Browne, an Augustine friar of London (deprived by queen Mary in 1554), was the first Protestant archbishop. Dublin has two cathedrals, St. Patrick's, said to have been founded 1190, restored 1865; Christ Church, built about 1038, made a cathedral in 1541. The revenue was valued, in the king's books, 30 Henry VIII., at 534*l*. 15*s*. 2*d*. Irish. Kildare, on its last avoidance, was annexed to Dublin, 1846; recent protestant archbishops: Richard Whately, 1831, dies 8 Oct. 1863; Richard Chenevix Trench, Nov. 1863, resigns 28 Nov. 1884 (dies 28 March, 1886); Wm. Conyngham, lord Plunket, 18 Dec. 1884, dies 1 April, 1897; succeeded by Dr. J. F. Peacocke, 17 June, 1897. See *Bishops*. For R.C. abps. see *Dublin*.

DUBLIN UNIVERSITY, see *Trinity College, Dublin*.

DUCAT, a coin so called because struck by dukes. *Johnson*. First coined by Longinus, governor of Italy. *Procopius*. First struck in the duchy of Apulia, 1140. *Du Cange*. Coined by Robert, king of Sicily, in 1240.

DUCKING-STOOL; see *Cucking-stool*.

DUDLEY GALLERY. The exhibition held since 1865 in the Egyptian Hall was removed to a new building in Piccadilly, under the direction of the Dudley Gallery Art Society, established in 1883.

DUELLING took its rise from the judicial combats of the Celtic nations. The first formal duel in England, between William count of Eu and Godfrey Baynard, took place 1096. Duelling in civil matters was forbidden in France, 1305. Francis I. challenged the emperor Charles V. 1528 without effect. The fight with small swords was introduced into England, 1587. Proclamation that no person should be pardoned who killed another in a duel, 1679.* Duelling was checked in the army, 1792; and has been abolished in England, by the influence of public opinion, aided by the prince consort. A society "for the discouraging of duelling" was established in 1845. "The British Code of Duel," published in 1824, was approved by the duke of Wellington and others. See *Battle, Wager of, Combat,* and *Jarnac*.

MEMORABLE DUELS.

Between beau Fielding and sir Henry Dutton Colt, 14 Feb. 1695-96. The baronet was wounded, but disarmed his antagonist. Sir H. D. Colt was adjutant to prince Rupert, and M.P. for Westminster. Bridgewater house stands on the site of the duel.
Between the duke of Hamilton and lord Mohun, fought . . . . 15 Nov. 1712
[This duel was fought with small swords, in Hyde-park. Lord Mohun was killed upon the spot, and the duke expired of his wounds as he was being carried to his coach.]
Capt. Peppard and Mr. Hayes; latter killed . 1728
Messrs. Hamilton and Morgan; former killed . 1748
S. Martin wounded Mr. Wilkes, M.P. . 16 Nov. 1763
Lord Byron killed Mr. Chaworth . . 26 Jan. 1765
Lord Townsend wounded lord Bellamont, 1 Feb. 1773
Comte d'Artois wounded by duc de Bourbon, at Paris . . . . 21 March, 1778
Mr. Donovan and capt. Hanson; the latter killed, 13 Nov. 1779
Charles James Fox wounded by Mr. Adam, 30 Nov. „

* "As many as 227 official and memorable duels were fought during my grand climacteric."—*Sir J. Barrington*. A single writer enumerates 172 duels, in which 63 individuals were killed and 96 wounded; in three of these cases both the combatants were killed, and 18 of the survivors suffered the sentence of the law. *Hamilton*.

Col. Fullerton wounded lord Shelburne, 22 March, 1780
Rev. Mr. Allen killed Lloyd Dulany . . 18 June, 1782
Col. Thomas killed by col. Gordon . 4 Sept. 1783
Lord Macartney wounded by major-general Stuart, 8 June, 1786
Mr. M'Keon killed George N. Reynolds, 1787; executed . . . . . . 16 Feb. 1788
Mr. Purefoy killed col. Roper . . . . . Dec. ,,
Duke of York and col. Lennox, aft. duke of Richmond (for an insignificant cause) 26 May, 1789
Sir George Ramsay and captain Macrea: sir George killed 1790
Mr. Curran and major Hobart . . 1 April, ,,
Mr. Macduff and Mr. Prince; latter killed 4 June, ,,
Mr. Harvey Aston and lieut. Fitzgerald; the former severely wounded . . . 25 June, ,,
Mr. Anderson killed Mr. Stevens . . 20 Sept. ,,
Mr. Julius killed Mr. Graham . . 19 July, 1791
Mr. John Kemble and Mr. Aiken; no fatality, 1 March, 1792
Earl of Lonsdale and captain Cuthbert; no fatality 9 June, ,,
M. de Chauvigny wounded Mr. Lameth . 8 Nov. ,,
Wm. Pitt and Geo. Tierney . . . 27 May, 1796
Lord Valentia wounded by Mr. Gawler . 28 June, ,,
Mr. Carpenter killed by Mr. Pride . 20 Aug. ,,
Henry Grattan wounded Isaac Corry . 15 Jan. 1800
Lieut. Willis killed major Impey . . 26 Aug. 1801
George Ogle and Bernard Coyle; no fatality . . 1802
Sir Richard Musgrave and Mr. Todd Jones; sir Richard wounded . . . 8 June, ,,
Capt. Mac Namara killed col. Montgomery, 6 April, 1803
Gen. Hamilton and col. Aaron Burr (in America); the general killed 1804
Capt. Best killed lord Camelford 6 (died 10) March, ,,
Surgeon Fisher killed lieut. Torrens . 22 March, 1806
Baron Hompesch wounded Mr. Richardson, 21 Sept. ,,
Sir Francis Burdett and Mr. Paull; both wounded 5 May, 1807
Mr. Alcock killed Mr. Colclough; and lost his reason 8 June, ,,
M. de Granpré and M. Le Pique, in balloons, near Paris, and the latter killed . . 3 May, 1808
Major Campbell and captain Boyd; latter killed (former hanged, 2 Oct. 1808) 23 June, ,,
Lord Paget and captain Cadogan; neither wounded 30 May, 1809
Lord Castlereagh wounded Geo. Canning 21 Sept. ,,
Mr. Clarke killed George Payne . . 6 Sept. 1810
Ensign de Balton killed capt. Boardman, 4 March, 1811
Lieut. Stewart killed lieut. Bagnal . 7 Oct. 1812
Mr. Edward Maguire killed lieut. Blundell, 9 July, 1813
Captain Stackpole (of "Statira" frigate) and lieut. Cecil; the captain killed (arose on account of words spoken four years previously) . April, 1814
Mr. D. O'Connell killed Mr. D'Esterre . 31 Jan. 1815
Colonel Quentin and colonel Palmer . 7 Feb. ,,
Mr. O'Connell and Mr. Peel; an affair, no meeting 31 Aug. ,,
Major Greene and Mr. Price, in America; the latter killed, greatly lamented 1816
Lieut. Conroy killed lieut. Hindes . 8 March, 1817
Major Lockyer killed Mr. John Sutton . 10 Dec. ,,
Mr. O'Callaghan killed lieut. Bayley . 12 Jan. 1818
Mr. Grattan and the earl of Clare . 7 June, 1820
Mr. Henshaw and Mr. Hartinger; both desperately wounded . . . . . 18 Sept. ,,
Mr. Christie killed Mr. Scott . . . 16 Feb. 1821
M. Manuel and Mr. Beaumont . 9 April, ,,
Mr. James Stuart killed sir Alexander Boswell, 26 March, 1822
The duke of Buckingham and the duke of Bedford; no fatality . . . . . . 2 May, ,,
Gen. Pepe wounded gen. Carascosa . 28 Feb. 1823
Mr. Westall killed capt. Gourlay . . . 1824
Mr. Beaumont and Mr. Lambton: no result 1 July, 1826
Mr. Hayes killed Mr. Bric . . 26 Dec. ,,
Rev. Mr. Hodson wounded Mr. Grady . Aug. 1827
Duke of Wellington and the earl of Winchelsea; no injury . . . . . 21 March, 1829
Capt. Helsham killed lieut. Crowther . 1 April, ,,
Mr. W. Lambrecht killed Mr. O. Clayton . 8 Jan. 1830
Capt. Smith killed Mr. O'Grady . . 18 March, ,,
Mr. Storey wounded Mr. Matthias 22 Jan. 1833
Sir John W. Jeffcott and Dr. Hennis; the latter wounded, and died on the 18th 10 May, ,,
Lord Alvanley and Mr. Morgan O'Connell 2 shots each . . . . 4 May, 1835
Sir Colquhoun Grant and lord Seymour; no fatality 29 May, 1835
Mr. Roebuck, M.P., and Mr. Black, editor of the "Morning Chronicle;" 2 shots each . 19 Nov. ,,
Capt. Dickson wounded gen. Evans . . 8 April, 1836
Mr. Ruthven and Mr. Scott; and Mr. Ruthven and Mr. Close (Mr. Scott's second); the latter wounded 23 May, ,,
Emile de Girardin killed Armand Carrel (both journalists) . . . . . . 24 July, ,,
The earl of Cardigan and captain Tuckett; 2 shots each; the latter wounded; (the earl was tried in the house of lords and acquitted, 16 Feb. 1841) 12 Sept. 1840
Captain Boldero and hon. Craven Berkeley; no fatality . . . . . . 15 July, 1842
Lieut. Munroe killed col. Fawcett 1 (died 3) July, 1843
Lieut. Hawkey killed lieut. Seton 20 May, 1845
Duc de Grammont Caderousse kills Mr. Dillon at Paris, for a newspaper attack . . . Oct. 1862
Paul de Cassagnac and M. Lissagaray, journalists; (latter run through) . . . . 4 Sept. 1868
Don Enrique de Bourbon killed by the duc de Montpeusier, near Madrid, much provocation, 12 Mar. 1870
Paul de Cassagnac (wounded) and M. Ranc, Paris, 7 July, 1873
Prince Soutza kills N. Ghika at Fontainebleau, 27 Nov. ,,
MM. Gambetta and De Fortou; neither hit 21 Nov. 1878
Duels (often nominal) still frequent in France 1875-84
Capt. Fournier and H. Rochefort, for attack in *Intransigeant;* both slightly wounded 10 Oct. 1884
M. Habert killed M. Felix Dupuis (artist), who resented satirical verses, Paris . 29 April, 1888
Gen. Boulanger, seriously, and M. Floquet slightly wounded (see *France*) . . . 13 July, ,,
Capt. Mayer killed by marq. de Mores, Paris, 23 June, 1892
M. Hippolyte Percher (*Harry Alis*) killed by M. le Chatelier, near Paris: see *Egypt* . 1 March, 1895
Agitation against duelling, see *Germany* April, *et seq.* 1896
Sig. F. Cavalotti killed by sig. F. Macola, 6 March, 1898
M. Marlier, a municipal councillor, killed by M. Ferrette, a deputy, Paris . . 4 Oct. 1900
M. Max Régis slightly wounded by M. Laberdesque, 8 June, 1901
Duels still occur in Germany, lieut. Blaskowitz killed by lieut. Hildebrand . . 4 Nov. ,,
An influential appeal against duelling, 300 signatures, published in Vienna . . 7 Dec. ,,
Herr Falkenhagen mortally wounds Landrath von Bennigsen, 16 Jan., and is sentenced to 6 years' imprisonment . . . . . . 17 Feb. 1902

DUFFERIN FUND, LADY, see *India*, 1887.

DUKE, from Latin *dux*, a leader. In England, during Saxon times, the commanders of armies were called dukes, *duces*. *Camden*. In *Genesis* xxxvi. some of Esau's descendants are termed *dukes*. *Duke-duke* was a title given to the house of Sylvia, in Spain, on account of its possessing many duchies.

Edward the Black Prince made *duke of Cornwall* 17 March, 1337
Robert de Vere was created marquis of Dublin and *duke of Ireland*, 9 Rich. II. 1385
Robert III. created David, prince of Scotland, duke of Rothsay, a title which afterwards belonged to the king's eldest son, 1398, and is now borne by the prince of Wales.
Cosmo de' Medici created *grand-duke* of Tuscany, the first of the rank, by pope Pius V. . . 1569
The dukes of Buccleuch, Grafton, Richmond, and St. Albans are descendants of Charles II.

DUKHOBORTSY, see *Spiritual Combatants*.

DULCIGNO, a port in Albania on the Adriatic.

Taken by Turks 1571
In the 17th century a den of pirates, and the residence of Sabbatai Zewi, a Smyrnese Jew, who declared himself to be the Messiah, became Mahometan; and died 1676
Taken by Venetians; and held for a short time 1722

The Montenegrins take it by storm; but give it up 1878
Assigned to them by the Berlin conference June, July; seized by 8000 Albanians, who expelled the Turks Sept.; the Sultan signed the decree for its cession to Montenegro, 12 Oct.; after a slight conflict with Albanians, 22 Nov., occupied by Dervish Pasha, 24 Nov., and surrendered to the Montenegrins . 26, 27 Nov. 1880

DULWICH COLLEGE (Surrey) called God's-gift college, founded by Edward Alleyn, an eminent comedian, was completed and solemnly opened 13 Sept. 1619. Alleyn was its first master, and died in 1626. In 1686 Wm. Cartwright, an actor, gave a library and some portraits, and on 20 Dec. 1810 sir Francis Bourgeois bequeathed his collection of pictures, the gallery for which was erected by sir John Soane, and opened in 1812. Sir Francis died 8 Jan. 1811. In 1857, an act was passed by which the college was reconstituted. Two schools were established; and the number of the almspeople increased. The annual income, about 20,000*l*., is derived from Dulwich manor. The new school buildings, founded 26 June, 1866, were opened by the prince of Wales, 21 June, 1870. The Endowed Schools Commissioners put forth a draft scheme for remodelling the charity about Oct. 1872; and another scheme was approved 18 Aug. 1882. Four parishes are benefited by the charity, St. Luke's, Middlesex; St. Botolph's, Bishopsgate; St. Saviour's, Southwark; and St. Giles's, Camberwell. Dulwich Park, 72 acres, presented to the public by the governors of the college, opened by the earl of Rosebery, 26 June, 1890. Mr. Wm. Young, governor and benefactor; his history of the college, including many documents, 2 vols. 4to, was published in 1890. Mr. Young, born 1815, died in New York, 10 May, 1896.

DUM-DUM BULLETS, see *Bullets*.

DUMB, see *Deaf and Dumb*.

DUMBLANE or DUNBLANE (Perth), an ancient city, near which took place a conflict called the battle of Sheriffmuir, between the royalist army under the duke of Argyll, and the Scots rebels under the earl of Mar, 13 Nov. 1715. Both claimed the victory.

DUNBAR (Haddington). Here the Scottish army and king John Baliol were defeated by Warrenne, earl of Surrey, 27 April, 1296, and Scotland was subdued. Near here also Cromwell obtained a signal victory over the Scots, in arms for Charles II. 3 Sept. 1650. Population, 1901, 3.581.

DUNCIAD, the celebrated satirical poem by Alexander Pope, was published in 1728.

DUNCOMBE PARK, N. R. Yorkshire, the magnificent mansion of the earl of Feversham, with valuable treasures (really a museum open to the public), was destroyed by fire, 11 Jan. 1879.

DUNDALK (Louth, Ireland). On 5 Oct. 1318, at Foughard near this place, was defeated and slain Edward Bruce, who had invaded Ireland in 1315. The walls and fortifications of Dundalk were destroyed in 1641. It was taken by Cromwell in 1649. The first cambric manufacture in Ireland was established in this town by artisans from France in 1727. Population, 1901, 14,308.

DUNDEE (E. Scotland), on the Tay. The site was given by William the Lion (reigned 1165—1214) to his brother David, earl of Huntingdon, who built or strengthened the castle, and erected a large church, the tower of which, 156 feet high, still remains. Charter granted by Robert I. 1327. The town was taken by the English in 1385; pillaged by Montrose, 1645; stormed by Monk in 1651; and visited by queen Victoria in 1844. It has thriven since 1815, through its extensive linen manufactories; at one of these (Edwards's) a steam explosion took place on 15 April, 1859, when twenty persons were killed. Claverhouse, viscount Dundee (killed 1689), had a house here. See *Population*.

The Baxter park, the gift of sir David Baxter, opened by earl Russell . . . . 9 Sept. 1863
The British association met here . . 4 Sept. 1867
While preparing for building the great Tay bridge of the N. British railway six men were killed, 27 Aug. 1873
The Albert Institution opened by the earl of Dalhousie . . . . 1 Nov. ,,
The Queen-street calendering works burnt, loss between 15,000*l*. and 20,000*l*. . . 20 Dec. ,,
New wet dock (Victoria) opened by lord Strathmore . . . . 16 Aug. 1875
The Tay bridge (*which see*) completed Aug. 1877; opened, 31 May, 1878; destroyed by a gale; between 80 and 90 lives lost, 7.15 p.m. 28 Dec. 1879
Statue of Burns unveiled . . . 16 Oct. 1880
Armistead's flax warehouse burnt, loss about 10,000*l*. . . . . . . 16 Jan. 1883
Great demonstration in favour of the government and franchise bill . . . 20 Sept. 1884
Mr. T. H. Cox gives 12,000*l*. for the establishment of a medical school in connection with the college . . . . . . 13 Dec. 1885
Mr. J. M. Keiller gives 10,500*l*. for the free library, museum and picture gallery as a jubilee offering 24 Dec. ,,
The old theatre, newly renovated, burnt . 6 Oct. 1888
Rt. Hon. C. T. Ritchie, a native, president of the Local Government Board, made a burgess 13 Oct. ,,
Dundee created a city . . . . . Dec. ,,
The Victoria art galleries, opened by the marquis of Lorne . . . . . 26 Oct. 1889
The freedom of the city given to Mr. H. M. Stanley 14 June, 1890
Rt. hon. E. Baxter, statesman and benefactor, dies aged 65 . . . . . 10 Aug. ,,
The freedom of the city given to Mr. Gladstone 29 Oct. ,,
The provost ordered to be styled "lord provost" 11 Feb. 1892
Historical exhibition opened by the earl of Strathmore . . . . . . 23 Dec. ,,
Strike of jute workpeople against reduction of wages; 24,000 idle, 1 May, *et seq.*; strike ended by a compromise . . . . 5 May, 1893
Ernest Hassberger, merchant, charged with forgery to the amount of 112,821*l*. 12*s*. 6*d*., 17 Aug.; pleaded guilty, 24 Aug.; sentenced to 8 years' penal servitude . . . 28 Aug. 1894
University college founded by sir D. Baxter; professor appointed Nov. 1882. Munificent additions made to the funds by Miss Mary Ann Baxter, sister of sir David, 1882 [she died 19 Dec. 1884]; college opened by earl of Dalhousie 5 Oct. 1883. Mrs. Margaret Harris bequeaths 35,000*l*., reported . . . . . . Oct. ,,
Strike of jute-workers, early Aug.; about 30,000 out, 23 Aug.; end of the general strike 2 Sept. 1895
Address to the czar on his way to Balmoral, 22 Sept. 1896
The university college united with the university of St. Andrew's; announced . . . Jan. 1897
Proposed erection of hospitals to commemorate the queen's reign; 13,000*l*. received . 8 Feb. ,,
Death of Mr. Alex. Crawford Lamb, author of "Dundee and its Antiquities" . . 29 April, ,,
Mr. John M. Keiller, benefactor, died, aged 48, 2 Jan. 1899
Duke of Connaught inaugurates the Victoria hospital for incurables, and a statue of the queen in Albert-square . . . . 26 Aug. ,,
Strike and lock-out in the jute trade . 8–23 Sept. ,,
Mr. Balfour presented with the freedom 28 Sept. ,,
Memorial to J. B. Lindsay, the pioneer in wireless telegraphy, unveiled by sir W. Preece . 14 Sept. 1901
Mr. Andrew Carnegie gives 11,000*l*. for a central library, and 25,000*l*. to branch libraries 23 Oct. ,,

Dundee sanatorium for consumptives (site presented by the late lord Airlie) opened . 26 Sept. 1902

DUN ECHT, Aberdeenshire, seat of the earl of Crawford, who erected an observatory here. In the autumn, 1888, he presented to the nation his valuable instruments, set up at the new Royal Observatory in Edinburgh, 1896. The earl issued the 179th, and last, "Dun Echt Circular," Feb. 1890.

On 3 Dec. 1881, it was discovered that the body of the late earl had been stolen from the mausoleum in the grounds; it was found near the spot, 18 July, 1882, through information given by Chas. Soutar, who was convicted of stealing it, 24 Oct. 1882

DUNES, see *Dunkirk*.

DUNGAN-HILL (Ireland). Here the English army, commanded by colonel Jones, signally defeated the Irish, of whom 6000 are said to have been slain, while the loss on the side of the English was inconsiderable, 8 Aug. 1647.

DUNKELD (Perthshire) was made a bishopric by David I. in 1127; the ancient Culdee church, founded by king Constantine III., becoming the cathedral. The beautiful bridge over the Tay, erected by Thomas Telford, was opened in 1809.

DUNKIRK (N. France), founded in the 7th century, was taken by the Spaniards, Sept. 1652, and retaken from them by the English and French after Turenne's victory over them under Condé on the *dunes* (or sands), 14 June, 1658, and put into the hands of the English, 25 June following. It was sold by Charles II. for 500,000*l*. to Louis XIV., 17 Oct.; restored 1662, and was one of the best fortified ports in the kingdom; but the works were demolished in conformity with the treaty of Utrecht in 1713. The works were ordered to be demolished at the peace of 1763; but in 1783 they were again resumed. The English besieged Dunkirk; the duke of York, defeated by Hoche, retired with loss, 7 Sept. 1793. It was made a free port in 1816. Large dock works constructed in 7 years, inaugurated; 13 Sept. 1896. Pres. Loubet opens a new town-hall, 17 Sept. 1901; receives the czar and czarina, 18 Sept. 1901. Dockers' and miners' strike, rioting 22, 23 Oct., 1902.

DUNMOW (Essex), famous for the tenure of the manor (made by Robert Fitz-Walter, 1244), "that whatever married couple will go to the priory and kneeling on two sharp-pointed stones, will swear that they have not quarrelled nor repented of their marriage within a year and a day after its celebration, shall receive a flitch of bacon."

The earliest recorded claim for the bacon was in 1445, since when to 1855 it is said to have been demanded only five times.

The last claimants previous to 1855 were John Shakeshanks and his wife, 20 June, 1751; they made a large sum by selling slices of the flitch to witnesses of the ceremony (5000 persons).

Flitches were awarded to Mr. and Mrs. Barlow, of Chipping-Ongar, and the Chevalier Chatelaine and his lady, 19 July, 1855.

The lord of the manor opposed the revival, but Mr. W. Harrison Ainsworth, the novelist, and some friends, defrayed the expense, and superintended the ceremonials.

A flitch was awarded in 1860 and 9 July, 1873; on 17 July, 1876, to James Henry and Mary Boosey; to others 23 July, 1877; to 3 couples, 3 Aug. 1896; to 2 couples, 2 Aug. 1897; to 2 couples, 3 Aug. 1903.

DUNSE (S. Scotland). Here on 18 June, 1639, by treaty between the Scots commission and Charles I., their demands were acceded to, and they agreed to disband their army. Disputes arose, and the treaty was not carried into effect.

DUNSINANE (Perthshire). On the hill was fought the battle between king Macbeth formerly the thane of Glammis, and Siward, earl of Northumberland, 27 July, 1054. Edward the Confessor had sent Siward on behalf of Malcolm III., whose father Duncan, the usurper had murdered. Macbeth was defeated, and it was said was pursued to Lumphanan, in Aberdeenshire, and there slain, 1056 or 1057.

DUOMO, see *Milan*, *Florence*.

DUPES (day of), 11 Nov. 1630, when Richelieu energetically and adroitly frustrated the plan for his ruin, formed by the queen Marie de Medicis and Gaston, duke of Orleans, and others, during the king's illness.

DUPLEX TELEGRAPHY. See *Electric Telegraph* under *Electricity*.

DÜPPEL or **DYBÖL**. See under *Denmark*, 1864.

DUPPLIN (Perthshire). Here Edward Balliol and his English allies totally defeated the Scots under the earl of Mar, 11 Aug. 1332, and obtained the crown for three months.

DURBAN, the seaport of the colony of Natal, and during the S. African war of 1899-1902 the port of entry for British troops and supplies. It was originally laid out by the Dutch, and since 1842, when the British took possession of the colony, has been greatly improved. The government railway runs to Pietermaritzburg, and an extension to Johannesburg and the Transvaal was completed in 1895. The inner harbour of 4,700 acres has been made accessible to vessels of deep draught, by extensive works carried out 1883-95. The bar which formerly prevented large vessels from entering the harbour is now (1903) in process of being removed. The principal residential part of Durban is the hilly district near the town called the Berea, with which it is connected by a series of tramways. Durban has numerous public buildings, including a town hall, museum, library, and theatre, and there are also public parks, and botanical and town gardens. New floating dock 1903. Population 1900, 48,410.

DURBAR, an East Indian term for an audience-chamber or court. On 18 Oct. 1864, a durbar was held at Lahore by the viceroy of India, sir John Lawrence, at which 604 of the most illustrious princes and chieftains of the north-west province were present, magnificently clothed. Similar ones were held in 1866, 1867, 27 March, 1869, Umballah. Imperial coronation durbar at Delhi, see *India*, Jan., 1903.

Sir Seymour Fitzgerald, governor of Bombay, held a great durbar of the princes of Western India at Poona . . . . 6 Oct. 1868

The earl of Mayo, the viceroy, held a solemn durbar at Ajmere in Rajpootana . . . . 22 Oct. 1870

The marquis of Ripon's grand durbar (as viceroy) at Lahore (after Afghan war) . . . . 15 Nov. 1880

The earl of Dufferin, viceroy, held a grand durbar at Rawul Pindi, at which the Ameer of Afghanistan and the Duke of Connaught were present, 8 April, 1885

Sir Auckland Colvin, lieut.-governor of the N.W. Provinces, held a grand durbar at Meerut 10 March, 1888

A durbar at Quetta by the viceroy, the marquis of Lansdowne, 19 Nov. 1889; at Agra . 24 Nov. 1890

At Lahore, by the viceroy, the earl of Elgin, 30 Nov. 1894

DURHAM, an ancient city, the *Dunholme* of the Saxons, and *Durême* of the Normans. The BISHOPRIC was removed to Durham from Chester-le-street in 995; whither it had been transferred from Lindisfarne, or Holy Island, on the coast of Northumberland, in 875, in consequence of the invasion of the Danes. The bones of St. Cuthbert, the sixth bishop, were brought from Lindisfarne, and enshrined in a church erected by bp. Aldune in 995, on the site of which the present cathedral was begun by bp. Wm. Abbot of St. Carilef, about 1093, and the work was continued by his successors till 1500. This see, deemed the richest in England, was valued in the king's books at 2821*l.* Present income 8000*l.* Population, 1881, 14,932; 1891, 14,863; 1901, 14,659.

College founded (abolished at the Reformation) . 1290
Near Durham was fought the decisive battle of *Neville's cross* (see *Strikes*) . . . . 17 Oct. 1346
Durham ravaged by Malcolm of Scotland, 1070; occupied by the Northern rebels 1569
By the Scots 1640
Cromwell quartered his Scotch prisoners in the cathedral 1650
Cromwell established a college, 1657; which was suppressed at the Restoration 1660
The palatine privileges, granted to the bishop by the Danish Northumbrian prince Guthrum, taken by the crown . . . . . June, 1836
The *University*, located in the ancient castle, established in 1813, opened Oct. 1833; chartered June, 1837
Certain new ordinances, recommended by a commission, 1862, set aside 1863
Cathedral renovated; re-opened . . 18 Oct. 1876
See *Coal* (strike, 1892).
During some excavations superintended by canon Greenwell interesting remains of the ancient cathedral were discovered in 1894–5
Philosophical society founded about the end of . 1896
Visit of the prince of Wales . . . 26 Nov. 1897

RECENT BISHOPS.

1791. Hon. Shute Barrington, died in 1826.
1826. Wm. Van Mildert (the last prince bishop), died 21 Feb. 1836.
1836. Edward Maltby, resigned in 1856; died 3 July, 1859, aged 90.
1856. Charles Thomas Longley; became archb. of York, May, 1860.
1860. Hon. H. Montagu Villiers (translated from Carlisle); died 10 Aug. 1861.
1861 Charles Baring, resigned 3 Feb., 1879; died 14 Sept. 1879.
1879. Joseph Barber Lightfoot, died 21 Dec. 1889.
1890. Brooke Foss Westcott, D.D., March, consecrated 1 May; died 27 July, 1901.
1901. C. Glyn Moule, elected 21 Sept.

DURHAM LETTER, see *Papal Aggression*.

DUST. A controversy respecting the connection between dust and disease originated with a lecture on the subject by professor Tyndall at the Royal Institution, 21 Jan. 1870, when he demonstrated the presence of organic matters in the dust of the atmosphere in conformity with the experiments of Pasteur and other eminent philosophers. See *Germ Theory* and *Vivisection*. The agency of dust in promoting fires and explosions was asserted by Faraday in relation to coal mines in 1845, and by Rankine and Macadam in relation to flour mills in 1872. Professor F. A. Abel's discourse on Some of the Dangerous Properties of Dusts, 28 April, 1882. Mr. Aitken's dust-counting apparatus was set up on Ben Nevis, Feb. 1890.

DUTCH CHURCH, see *Augustin or Austin Friars*.

DUTCH PLAYS, "Annie Mie," by Rosier Faassen, and others, were performed at the Imperial Theatre, Westminster, 7 June *et seq.*, 1880. Madame Catherine Beersman's acting was much approved.

DUTCH REPUBLIC, see *Holland*.

DUTIES, see *Customs, Excise, &c.*

DUTY, see *Whole* and *Deontology*.

DUUMVIRI, two Roman patricians appointed by Tarquin the Proud 520 B.C. to take care of the books of the Sibyls, which were supposed to contain the fate of the Roman empire. The books were placed in the Capitol, and secured in a chest under the ground. The number of keepers was increased to ten (the Decemviri) 365 B.C., afterwards to fifteen, the added five called *quinque viri*.

DWARFS, OR PIGMIES, are described by several ancient classical writers. Herodotus gives an account of a race of pigmies living in Libya and the Syrtes, to which Aristotle and Pliny also refer. Mr. H. M. Stanley, in his journey across Africa in 1888, came upon a dwarfish race, which he thought might be descended from that mentioned by Herodotus. Mr. Arthur B. Lloyd crosses the great pigmy forest and descends the Aruwimi to the Congo, Sept.–Nov. 1898. "The Land of the Pigmies," by capt. Guy Burrows, published Jan. 1899. Philetas of Cos, distinguished about 330 B.C., as a poet and grammarian, was jocularly said to have carried weights to prevent his being blown away. He was preceptor to Ptolemy Philadelphus. *Ælian.* Julia, niece of Augustus, had a dwarf named Coropas, two feet and a hand's-breadth high; and Andromeda, a freed-maid of Julia's, was of the same height. *Pliny.*

MODERN DWARFS.—John d'Estrix, of Mechlin, was brought to the duke of Parma, in 1592, when he was 35 years of age, having a long beard. He was skilled in languages, and not more than three feet high.

Geoffrey Hudson, an English dwarf, when a youth of 18 inches high, was served up to table in a cold pie, before the king and queen, by the duchess of Buckingham, in 1626. He challenged Mr. Crofts to fight a duel, but the latter came armed with a squirt. At another meeting the dwarf shot his antagonist dead, 1653.

Count Borowlaski, a Polish gentleman, of great accomplishments and elegant manners, well known in England, where he resided for many years, was born in Nov. 1739. His growth was at one year of age, 14 inches; at six, 17 inches; at twenty, 33 inches; and at thirty, 39. He had a sister, named Anastasia, seven years younger than himself, and so much shorter that she could stand under his arm. He visited many of the courts of Europe, and died in England in 1837.

Charles Heywood Stratton (termed general Tom Thumb), an American, was exhibited in England, by Mr. P. T. Barnum, 1846. In Feb. 1863, in New York, when 25 years old and 31 inches high, he married Lavinia Warren, aged 21, 32 inches high. He, his wife and child, and commodore Nutt, another dwarf, came to England in Dec. 1864, and remained here some time. Died 15 July, 1883.

Mr. Collard, aged 22, smaller than Stratton, sang at concerts in London, and was termed the "Pocket Sims Reeves," May, June, 1873.

Several dwarfs (said to be smaller than the preceding) exhibited at the Westminster Aquarium, July, 1878.

Che-mah, a Chinese, 42 years old, 25 inches high, exhibited at the Westminster Aquarium, 11 June, 1880.

Lucia Zarate, born 2 Jan. 1863, in Mexico, weight 4¾ lbs., and general Mite, Francis Joseph Flynn, born 2 Oct. 1864, in New York State, height 21 inches, weight 9 lbs., were both exhibited in Piccadilly. 22 Nov. 1880, *et seq.* Milly Edwards exhibited in London, July, 1882, 15 years of age, weighing 7 lbs.; Miss Edwards and "general Mite" were married at Manchester, 28 May, 1884.

"Princess Topaze," of French parentage, born at Buenos Ayres, stated to be 16 years old, to weigh 15 lbs., height 20 inches, with symmetrical proportions, exhibited at the Westminster aquarium, 30 Jan. *et seq.* 1893.

E. J. Wood's "Giants and Dwarfs," 1868.

DYEING is attributed to the Tyrians, about 1500 B.C. The English are said to have sent fine goods to be dyed in Holland, till the art was brought to them probably in 1608. "Two dyers of Exeter were flogged for teaching their art *in the north*" (of

England), 1628. A statute against abuses in dyeing passed in 1783. The art has been greatly improved by chemical research. A discovery of Dr. Stenhouse in 1848 led to M. Marnas procuring *mauve* from lichens; and Dr. Hofmann's production of aniline from coal-tar, has led to the invention of a number of beautiful dyes (mauve, magenta, red, green, black, &c.); see *Aniline*.

DYNAMICS is the science which treats of matter and motion recently substituted for "*mechanics*," *which see*. Professor W. K. Clifford's "Elements of Dynamics," 2 vols., 1878-87.

DYNAMITE, a new explosive compound, consisting of 25 parts of silicious earth saturated with 75 parts of nitro-glycerine (*which see*). It is suitable for mining purposes, and was tried and approved at Merstham 14 July, 1868. It was invented by Alfred Nobel to obviate danger. Its manufacture is very dangerous. Mr. Nobel died, 10 Dec. 1896; and bequeathed a fund of about 434,093*l*. to promote science. A preparation called "Safety" Dynamite, invented by Herr von Dahmen, who by the addition of a simple substance renders dynamite uncongealable, thus avoiding the danger of thawing in cold weather, 1889. Dynamite which cannot be frozen, invented by Herr Edward Liebert, of Berlin (very important, many deaths having been caused by thawing frozen dynamite); reported Aug. 1890. See *New York*, 28 Dec. 1892; *Cannon*, 1891; and *Nobel Bequest*.

Snyder dynamite projectile; experiments at Aberdare, S. Wales; British and foreign officers present; reported fairly successful 5 Oct. 1891.

Thirteen men killed by explosion of dynamite in a railway tunnel at Cymmer, S. Wales, 21 April. 1876.

A man named Thomson, Thomassin, or Thomas, consigned a cask of dynamite to Bremerhafen, to be conveyed by the North German Lloyd steamer *Mosel*. With it he sent a clock-work machine, which would in eight days give the cask a blow powerful enough to explode the dynamite and destroy the ship. From some cause the machine went off and exploded in the dock, killing above 80 and wounding about 200 persons, chiefly emigrants and their friends, 11 Dec. 1875. Thomson committed suicide, dying 16 Dec. 1875, after confessing his crime, his object being to obtain the paltry sum for which he had insured his goods. It appears that similar machines were known in 1873.

Use of dynamite for killing oxen tried and advocated, summer, 1877.

Its use in fisheries prohibited by parliament, 14 Aug. 1877.

A parcel containing 27 cartridges of dynamite placed on the London and N. W. Railway, between Bushey and Watford (perpetrators not discovered), night 12-13 Sept. 1880.

Failure of attempt at explosion at the *Times* office, 15 Mar. 1883.

Thomas Callan, *alias* Scott, of Lowell, Massachusetts, and Michael Harkins, of Philadelphia, both residing in Islington, charged with conspiring together to cause a dynamite explosion, a large quantity of dynamite having been found in their dwellings in Islington 21 Nov.; committed 19 Dec. (Cohen, a co-conspirator died 19 Oct.) 1887; as secondaries sentenced to fifteen years' penal servitude 1-3 Feb. 1888; Thomas Callan released, 20 Jan. 1893.

Zalinski gun for the projection of dynamite adopted by the United States for coast defence Feb. 1889.

Lieut. Graydon's safe dynamite for use in shells, &c., announced April, 1889.

See *Explosions* and *Glasgow*, 1883.

The violent Irish party in America termed *Dynamitards*, April, 1883. Many said to be settled in Paris. Report refers to two associations—one under O'Donovan Rossa (failing), another named Clan-na-gael—2 men said to have been killed; 25 convicted and imprisoned; issued 1886.

O'Donovan Rossa said to have been succeeded by Dr. Hamilton Williams at New York (see *Fenians*) 14 Dec. 1887.

Portmanteaus, containing dynamite, with clock-work of American make, which had failed, found at Charing-cross and Paddington stations, 28 Feb., and at Ludgate-hill station, 1 March, 1884.

FitzGerald arrested in London, 10 April, 1884.

Dennan, or Daley, with three infernal machines, arrested at Birkenhead.

James Francis Egan and Patrick Hogan arrested at Birmingham, 11 April, 1884.

[Treasonable papers about Irish republic, &c., discovered in Egan's garden.]

Wm. M'Donnell arrested at Wednesbury, 1 May, 1884.

Daly sentenced to penal servitude for life; released, 20 Aug. 1896; Egan to 20 years, for treason-felony; M'Donnell discharged on recognizances, 1 Aug. 1884.

[James F. Egan discharged, 21 Jan. 1893.]

Explosion at Nobel's dynamite factory near Stevenston, Ayr; ten lives lost, 8 May, 1884; again, 6 men killed, 24 Feb. 1897.

Explosion of a bomb at the house of the hon. Reginald Brett, M.P., 2, Tilney-street, Mayfair; the door and windows shattered, 4 Nov. 1894.

Explosion of a large cargo of dynamite on board the *Elizabeth* (capt. Reymers) at Salmorth, on the Rhine, near Düsseldorf; 13 lives lost; the *Hoop* burnt and other boats sunk; houses and property destroyed, 19 March, 1895.

Dynamo-machines, see *Electricity*, 1866.

Release of dynamitards (see *Trials*, 11, 14 June, 1883), Aug. 1896, and 1898.

Dynamite plot organized in the United States, by Fenians and others, against the queen and the czar in Gt. Britain. A bomb factory discovered at Antwerp. P. J. Tynan, "No. I.," arrested at Boulogne, 13 Sept. 1896; his extradition demanded by the British government on the charge of the murder of Mr. Burke (6 May, 1882), 24 Sept.; extradition refused by the French government, 14 Oct.; Tynan is released, 15 Oct.; returns to New York, 27 Oct. Kearney, *alias* Wallace, and Haines, arrested at Rotterdam, 12, 13 Sept.; shipped to New York; 5 Oct. Edward Bell, *alias* Ivory, arrested in Glasgow, 12 Sept.; at Bow-st., 17 Sept.; committed, 20 Nov. 1896; acquitted, 20 Jan. 1897.

Rolla Richards, sentenced to 7 years' imprisonment for having caused a bomb explosion at a New-cross post-office (Aug, 1894), 9 April, 1897.

Explosion in a train at Aldersgate-station; empty compartment wrecked, 1 death, 26 April, 1897

Dynamite explosion in the Eiger tunnel (Jungfrau railway), 6 deaths, 26 Feb. 1899.

Dynamite explosions at the Avigliana factory near Turin, 10 deaths, 30 injured, 16 Jan. 1900.

Explosion at Nobel's dynamite works, Perranporth, Cornwall, 3 deaths, others injured, 16 Jan. 1902.

See *Macedonia*, 1903.

DZOUNGARIA, a region of Central Asia, N. of China, with about 2,000,000 inhabitants, fierce, warlike Mahometans. After being long tributary to China, they rebelled in 1864, massacred the Chinese residents, and set up their countryman Abel Oghlan as sultan. As he was unable to restrain predatory attacks upon the Russians, the czar declared war in April, 1871. After a brief campaign in May and June, and several conflicts in which the Russians were victors, the sultan surrendered to general Kolpakoviski, 4 July, and the country was annexed to the Russian empire.

E.

EAGLE, an ancient coin of Ireland, made of a base metal, and current in the first years of Edward I. about 1272, was so named from the figure impressed upon it. The *American* gold coinage of eagles, half eagles, and quarter eagles, began 6 Dec. 1792; an eagle is of the value of 10 dollars, or about *2l. 1s.*—The *standard of the eagle* was borne by the Persians, at Cunaxa, 401 B.C. The Romans carried gold and silver eagles as ensigns, and sometimes represented them with a thunderbolt in their talons, on the point of a spear, 102 B.C. Charlemagne added the second head to the eagle for his arms, to denote that the empires of Rome and Germany were united in him, A.D. 802. The eagle was the standard of Napoleon I. and Napoleon III.; as well as of Austria, Russia, and Prussia; see *Knighthood.*

EARL (Latin, *comes*), introduced at the conquest, superseded the Saxon ealdorman, and continued the highest rank in England, until Edward III. created dukes in 1337 and 1351, and Richard II. created marquises (1385), both above earls. Alfred used the title of earl as a substitute for king. William Fitz-Osborn was made earl of Hereford by William the Conqueror, 1066. Gilchrist was created earl of Angus, in Scotland, by king Malcolm III. in 1037, and sir John de Courcy created baron of Kingsale and earl of Ulster in Ireland, by Henry II. 1181.

Earl Marshal of England, the eighth great officer of state. This office, until it was made hereditary, always passed by grant from the king. Gilbert de Clare was created lord marshal by king Stephen, 1135. The last *lord* marshal was John Fitz-Alan, lord Maltravers. *Camden.* Richard II. in 1397 granted letters patent to the earl of Nottingham by the style of *earl* marshal. In 1672, Charles II. granted to Henry lord Howard the dignity of hereditary earl marshal. The earl marshal's court was abolished in 1641. (See *Howard.*)

Earl Marischal of Scotland was an officer who commanded the cavalry, whereas the constable commanded the whole army; but they seem to have had a joint command, as all orders were addressed to "our constable and marischal." The office was never out of the Keith family. It was reserved at the Union, and when the heritable jurisdictions were bought, it reverted to the crown, being forfeited by the rebellion of George Keith, earl marischal, in 1715.

EARL DE LA WARR'S ACT, see *Children.*

EARLY CLOSING ASSOCIATION established 1842, to abridge the hours of labour, and to abolish Sunday trading.

Frequent meetings. Congress Feb. 1888.
Sir John Lubbock's Early Closing Bill for shops (8 p.m. and 10 p.m on Saturdays) rejected by the commons (278–95), 2 May, 1888.

EARLY ENGLISH TEXT SOCIETY began to publish in 1864.

EARRINGS were worn by Jacob's family, 1732 B.C. (*Gen.* xxxv. 4).

EARTH, see *Globe.* "Earth to Earth" discussion in 1875; advocacy of cremation, see *Burials.*

EARTHENWARE, see *Pottery.*

EARTHQUAKES. Kircher, Des Cartes, and others supposed that there were many vast cavities under ground which have a communication with each other, some of which abound with water, others with exhalations, arising from inflammable substances, as nitre, bitumen, sulphur, &c. Dr. Stukeley and Dr. Priestley attributed earthquakes to electricity. They are probably due to steam generated by subterraneous heat. An elaborate Catalogue of earthquakes (from B.C. 1606 to A.D. 1842), with commentaries on the phenomena, by R. and J. W. Mallet, was published by the British Association in 1858. In 1860 the velocity of their propagation was estimated by Mr. J. Brown at between 470 and 530 feet per second.* Prof. John Milne, at the Royal Institution, London, 12 Feb. 1897, described his important researches in seismology, with special reference to Japan; his "Seismology" published Nov. 1898. See *Seismometer.*

One which made Eubœa an island . . . . B.C. 425
Helice and Bura in Peloponnesus swallowed up 373
Duras, in Greece, buried with all its inhabitants; and 12 cities in Campania also buried . . . 345
Lysimachia and its inhabitants buried about . . 283
Ephesus and other cities overturned . . . A.D. 17
One accompanied the eruption of Vesuvius when Pompeii and Herculaneum were buried . . 79
Four cities in Asia, two in Greece, and two in Galatia overturned . . . . . . 105 or 106
Antioch destroyed 115
Nicomedia, Cæsarea, and Nicea overturned . . 126
In Asia, Pontus, and Macedonia, 150 cities and towns damaged 157
Nicomedia again demolished, and its inhabitants buried in its ruins 358
One felt by nearly the whole world 543
At Constantinople; its edifices destroyed, and thousands perished 557
In Africa; many cities overturned 560
Awful one in Syria, Palestine, and Asia; more than 500 towns were destroyed, and the loss of life surpassed all calculation 742
In France, Germany, and Italy 801
Constantinople overturned; all Greece shaken . . 936
One felt throughout England 1089
One at Antioch; many towns destroyed . . . 1114
Catania, in Sicily, overturned, and 15,000 persons buried in the ruins 1137
One severely felt at Lincoln 1142
In Syria, &c., 20,000 perished 1158
At Calabria; one of its cities and all its inhabitants overwhelmed in the Adriatic sea . . Sept. 1186
In Cilicia, 60,000 perished 1268
One again felt throughout England; Glastonbury destroyed 1274
In England; the greatest known there . 14 Nov. 1318
At Naples; 40,000 persons perished . . 5 Dec. 1456
Constantinople; thousands perished . . 14 Sept. 1509
At Lisbon; 1500 houses and 30,000 persons buried in the ruins; several neighbouring towns engulfed, 26 Feb. 1531
One felt in London; part of St. Paul's and the Temple churches fell . . . . 6 April, 1580
In Japan; several cities made ruins, and thousands perish . . . . 2 July, 1596
In Naples; 30 towns or villages ruined; 70,000 lives lost . . . . . . 30 July, 1626
Awful one at Calabria . . . . 27 March, 1638
Ragusa ruined; 5000 perished . . . 6 April, 1667
At Schamaki, lasted 3 months; 80,000 perished . „

* Mrs. Somerville states that about 255 earthquakes have occurred in the British Isles; all slight. To avoid the effects of a shock predicted by a madman, for the 8th of April, 1750, thousands of persons, particularly those of rank and fortune, passed the night on the 7th in their carriages and in tents in Hyde-park.

At Rimini; above 1500 perished . . . 14 April, 1672

One severely felt at Dublin, &c. . . . 17 Oct. 1690

One at Jamaica, which totally destroyed Port Royal, whose houses were engulfed 40 fathoms deep, and 3000 perished . . . 7 June, 1692

One in Sicily, which overturned 54 cities and towns, and 300 villages; of Catania and its 18,000 inhabitants, not a trace remained; more than 100,000 lives were lost . . . . Sept. 1693

Aquila, in Italy, ruined; 5000 perished 2 Feb. 1703

Jeddo, Japan, ruined; 200,000 perished . . . ,,

In the Abruzzi; 15,000 perished . . 3 Nov. 1706

At Algiers; 20,000 perished May and June, 1716

Palermo nearly destroyed; nearly 6000 lives lost 1 Sept. 1726

Again in China; and 100,000 people swallowed up at Pekin . . . . 30 Nov. 1731

In Naples, &c.; 1940 perished . . . 29 Nov. 1732

Lima and Callao demolished; 18,000 persons buried in the ruins . . . . . . 28 Oct. 1746

In London, &c., a slight shock . . 19 Feb. 1750

Port-au-Prince, St. Domingo, ruined . 21 Nov. 1751

Adrianople nearly overwhelmed . . 29 July, 1752

At Grand Cairo; half of the houses and 40,000 persons swallowed up . . . . Sept. 1754

Quito destroyed . . . . . . April, 1755

Kaschan, N. Persia, destroyed; 40,000 perished, 7 June, ,,

Great earthquake at LISBON. In about eight minutes most of the houses and upwards of 50,000 inhabitants were swallowed up, and whole streets buried. The cities of Coimbra, Oporto, and Braga, suffered dreadfully, and St. Ubes was wholly overturned. In Spain, a large part of Malaga became ruins. One half of Fez, in Morocco, was destroyed, and more than 12,000 Arabs perished there. The island of Madeira was affected; and 2000 houses in the island of Mitylene, in the Archipelago, were overthrown. This awful earthquake extended 5000 miles; even to Scotland . . . . 1 Nov. ,,

In Syria, extended over 10,000 square miles; Baalbec destroyed; here 20,000 perished . 30 Oct. 1759

Comorn, Pesth, &c., much damaged . 28 June, 1763

At Martinico; 1600 persons perished . Aug. 1767

At Guatemala; Santiago, with its inhabitants, swallowed up . . . . . . 7 June, 1773

A destructive one at Smyrna . . 3 July, 1778

At Tauris; 15,000 houses thrown down, and multitudes buried 1780

Messina and other towns in Italy and Sicily overthrown: thousands perished . . . 5 Feb. 1783

Ezinghian, near Erzeroum, destroyed, and 5000 persons buried in its ruins . . 23 July, 1784

St. Lucia, W. Indies; 900 perished . 12 Oct. 1788

At Borgo di San Sepolcro; many houses and 1000 persons swallowed up . . . 30 Sept. 1789

In Naples; Vesuvius overwhelmed the city of Torre del Greco . . . . . . June, 1794

The whole country between Santa Fé and Panamà destroyed, including Cuzco and Quito; 40,000 people buried in one second . . . 4 Feb. 1797

Cumana, S. America, ruined . . 14 Dec. ,,

At Constantinople, which destroyed the royal palace, and many buildings . . . . 26 Sept. 1800

From Cronstadt to Constantinople . 26 Oct. 1802

A violent one felt in Holland . end of Jan. 1804

At Frosolone, Naples; 6000 lives lost . 26 July, 1805

At the Azores; a village of St. Michael's sunk, and a lake of boiling water appeared in its place, 11 Aug. 1810

Awful one at Caracas (*which see*) . 26 March, 1812

Several throughout India; district of Kutch sunk; 2000 persons buried . . . . 16 June, 1819

Genoa, Palermo, Rome, and many other towns greatly damaged; thousands perish . . ,,

Aleppo destroyed; above 20,000 perish; shocks on 10 and 13 Aug., and 5 Sept. 1822

Coast of Chili permanently raised . 19 Nov. ,,

Very violent at Palermo and other parts of Sicily 5 March, 1823

Violent shocks at Granada, in Spain; buildings destroyed . . . . 15-17 May, 1826

Island of Ischia; 28 men killed in Casamicciola; many buildings destroyed 2 Feb. 1828

In Spain; Murcia and numerous villages devastated; 6000 persons perish . . . . 21 March, 1829

Canton and neighbourhood; above 6000 perished, 26, 27 May, 1830

In the duchy of Parma; 40 shocks at Borgotaro; and at Pontremoli many houses thrown down 14 Feb. 1834

Concepcion, &c., in Chili, destroyed . 20 Feb. 1835

In Calabria, Cosenza and villages destroyed; 1000 persons buried . . . . . . 29 April, ,,

In Calabria; 100 perish at Castiglione . 12 Oct. ,,

At Martinique; nearly half of Port Royal destroyed; nearly 700 persons killed, and the whole island damaged . . . . 11 Jan. 1839

At Ternate; the island made a waste, and thousands of lives lost . . . . . . 14 Feb. 1840

Awful and destructive earthquake at mount Ararat, in one of the districts of Armenia; 3137 houses were overthrown, and several hundred persons perished . . . . 27 July, ,,

Great earthquake at Zante, where many persons perished . . . . 30 Oct. ,,

At Cape Haytien, St. Domingo, which destroyed nearly two-thirds of the town; between 4000 and 5000 lives were lost . . . . 7 May, 1842

At Point à Pitre, Guadaloupe, which was entirely destroyed . . . . 8 Feb. 1843

At Rhodes and Macri, when a mountain fell in at the latter place, crushing a village, and destroying 600 persons . . . . . 28 Feb.—7 March, 1851

At Valparaiso, where more than 400 houses were destroyed . . . . 2 April, ,,

In South Italy; Melfi almost laid in ruins; 14,000 lives lost . . . . 14 Aug. ,,

Philippine isles; Manilla much injured 16-30 Sept. 1852

In N.W. of England, slight . . . 9 Nov. ,,

Thebes, in Greece, nearly destroyed . . 18 Aug. 1853

St. Salvador, S. America, destroyed . 16 April, 1854

Anasaca, in Japan, and Simoda, in Niphon, destroyed; Jeddo much injured . . . 23 Dec. ,,

Broussa, in Turkey, nearly destroyed . 28 Feb. 1855

Several villages in Central Europe destroyed, 25, 26 July, ,,

Jeddo, Japan, nearly destroyed . . 11 Nov. ,,

At the island of Great Sanger, one of the Moluccas, volcanic eruption and earthquake; nearly 3000 lives lost . . . . 2 March, 1856

In the Mediterranean: at Candia, 500 lives lost; Rhodes, 100; and other islands, 150 . 12 Oct. ,,

In Calabria,* Montemurro and other towns destroyed, and about 10,000 lives lost . 16 Dec. ,,

Corinth nearly destroyed . . . . 21 Feb. 1858

At Quito; about 5000 persons killed, and an immense amount of property destroyed, 22 March, 1859

Erzeroum, Asia Minor; thousands perished, 2 June—17 July, ,,

At San Salvador; many buildings destroyed, no lives lost . . . . 8 Dec. ,,

In Cornwall, slight . . 21 Oct. 1859; 13 Jan. 1860

At Mendoza, South America; about two-thirds of the city and 7000 lives lost . . 20 March, ,,

In Perugia, Italy; several lives lost . 8 May, 1861

In Greece; N. Morea, Corinth, and other places injured . . . . 26 Dec. ,,

Guatemala; 150 buildings and 14 churches destroyed . . . . 19 Dec. 1862

Rhodes; 13 villages destroyed, about 300 persons perished, and much cattle and property lost, 22 April, 1863

Manilla, Philippine isles; immense destruction of property; about 1000 persons perish 2, 3 July, ,,

Central, west, and north-west of England, at 3 *h.* 22 *m.* A.M. 6 Oct. ,,

At Macchia, Bendinella, &c., Sicily; 200 houses destroyed, 64 persons killed . . 18 July, 1865

Slight earthquake near Tours and Blois, in France. 14 Sept. 1866

Argostoli, Cephalonia; above 50 perished 4 Feb. 1867

At Mitylene; about 1000 killed . 8, 9 March, ,,

Djocja, Java above 400 perished; town destroyed, 10 June, ,,

The cities of Arequipa, Iquique, Tacna, and Chencha, and many small towns in Peru and Ecuador destroyed; about 25,000 lives lost, and 30,000

* In the course of 75 years, from 1783 to 1857, the kingdom of Naples lost, at least, 111,000 inhabitants by the effects of earthquakes, or more than 1500 per year, out of an average population of 6,000,000 !—*Lacaita.*

rendered homeless; loss of property estimated at 60,000,000*l*. . . . . . 13–15 Aug. 1868
[About 11,000*l*. collected in London to relieve the sufferers.]
Slight earthquake in W. England and S. Wales; felt at Bath, Swansea, &c. . . . 30 Oct ,,
In Santa Maura, an Ionian isle, the town Santa Maura destroyed; about 17 persons perished, 28 Dec. 1869
At Quebec, not much damage . . . . 20 Oct. 1870
In Calabria; several villages destroyed, early in Oct. ,,
N. W. England; houses shaken, crockery broken, evening, 17 March; slight in Yorkshire, 22 March, 1871
California; several small towns destroyed; about 30 killed . . . . . . 26, 27 March, 1872
Lehree, Eastern Catchi, Sind frontier, India, destroyed; about 500 killed . . 14, 15 Dec. ,,
San Salvador nearly destroyed; about 50 killed; the rest escaped through timely warning 19 March, 1873
North of Italy: at Feletto, near Conegliano, Venetia, church destroyed; about 50 killed; lives lost at Belluno, &c.; shock felt at Venice, Verona, &c. . . . . 29 June, ,,
Azagra, Spain: 200 killed by a landslip 22 July, 1874
Antigua and other places in Guatemala destroyed; great loss of life . . . . . . 3 Sept. ,,
Kara Hissar and other places in Asia Minor; great destruction of life . . . . . 3–5 May, 1875
Smyrna, and neighbourhood; many perish, 12 May, ,,
San José de Cucuta and other towns near Santander on the boundary of Colombia, destroyed: about 14,000 lives said to be lost . 16–18 May ,,
Lahore and vicinity, India; several killed 12 Dec. ,,
At Scheibs on the Danube, felt throughout Austrian empire . . . . 17 July, 1876
Earthquake and great tidal wave near Callao; went southward; much shipping and several towns destroyed; not much mortality . . 9, 10 May, 1877
Cua, Venezuela, nearly destroyed, about 300 killed, loss about 30,000*l*. . . . . . 14 April, 1878
Shocks felt at Cologne and other parts of Germany; and Holland; houses much shaken; bells rung, &c. 9–11 A.M. . . . . 26 Aug. ,,
Aci Reale, Catania, Sicily, 5 villages destroyed, 10 persons killed . . . . . . 17 June, 1879
Severe shock at Brieg in Switzerland, felt at Berne, Zurich, Geneva, &c., several killed . 4 July, 1880
Manilla, &c., Philippines, cathedral destroyed, several killed, many hurt . . . 18–24 July, ,,
Smyrna and neighbourhood, many houses destroyed, 2 persons killed . . . . . 29, 30, July, ,,
Valparaiso; at Illapel, Chili, about 200 perish, 13 Sept. ,,
South Austria, much damage with loss of life, at Agram, &c. . . . . 10-16 Nov.—8 Dec. ,,
Slight shocks at Inverary and other places W. Scotland . . . . 28 Nov. ,,
Berne, and other places, Switzerland, houses split up, &c. . . . . . . 27 Jan. and 3 March, 1881
Severe shocks in South Italy, much destruction and loss of life at Casamicciola, a town in the Isle of Ischia, 289 houses destroyed, 114 lives lost, about 36,000*l*. loss, 4 March; more destruction by another shock . . . . 15 March, ,,
Scio—the town and several villages destroyed, about 4000 perish, much destitution ensues, successive shocks, beginning 1.30 P.M. . . . 3 April, ,,
Panamá; railway partially destroyed 7, 9, 10 Sept. 1882
A slight shock in Cornwall and Devon . 25 June, 1883
Casamicciola, and several villages in the island of Ischia, almost entirely destroyed, 1990 lives lost, 28 July; slight shocks since; one severe 3 Aug. ,,
[Great exertions of the military; many remarkable preservations.]
Anatolia, coast of Asia Minor; Ischesne and about 30 small towns and villages destroyed, about 100 lives lost and 30,000 destitute; Smyrna much shaken . . . . . . about 16 Oct. ,,
Shocks felt at Gibraltar . . 20 Oct. *et seq.* ,,
Severe shocks in eastern counties of England, proceeding from N.E. to S.W., centre Colchester, where the congregational church steeple fell, as well as many chimneys; damages estimated at 10,000*l*.; much destruction in neighbouring villages; many inhabitants rendered homeless; Langenhoe church wrecked; much damage at Abberton; a child killed at Rowhedge; an invalid died; the shock felt more or less distinctly at Coggeshall, Sudbury, Ipswich, Cambridge, Bishop's Stortford, Northampton, Leicester, Woolwich, Sheerness, different parts of London, Hampstead, &c. . . . . 22 April, 1884
[See *Mansion House Funds.*]
Severe shocks for several days on Asiatic shore of sea of Marmora; about 20 deaths reported 19 May, ,,
A violent shock on the Island of Kishm, near the mouth of the Persian Gulf; 12 villages destroyed; about 200 people killed . . . 19–20 May, ,,
Slight shocks in the Alban hills, near Rome 7 Aug. ,,
Slight shocks throughout United States, from Washington to New York . . . 10, 11 Aug. ,,
At Genoa, 27 Nov.; at Marseilles, Lyons, &c. 29 Nov. ,,
Severe shocks in Andalusia, Malaga; many houses destroyed, about 266 persons killed; felt at Madrid 25 Dec. ,,
Several towns destroyed: Alhama, Granada, many killed; Periana, about 900 killed . 26, 27 Dec. ,,
Shocks, intermitting . . . . . 26-31 Dec. ,,
Slight shocks in Carinthia and Styria . 28 Dec. *et seq.* ,,
Shocks, 1-27 Jan., much camping out . . 1885
Slight shocks in Styria . . . . 27, 28 Jan. ,,
Slight shocks at Alhama . . . . 12 Feb. ,,
Alarming shocks at Malaga and other towns, 27 Feb. ,,
Stated number of victims in province of Granada, 690 (see *Spain*, 1884–5) . . . . 28 Feb. ,,
Slight shocks at Rome 9 April; in Granada 11 April, ,,
Severe shock at Srinagur, Cashmere; 87 killed 30-31 May; successive shocks, 3.081 deaths, 70,000 dwellings destroyed, reported up to 20 June; slight shocks up to . . . . 8 July, ,,
Sikuch, in the Caucasus, destroyed about 12 June, ,,
Shocks in Yorkshire . . . . . 18 June, ,,
Three shocks in Bengal; a village near Nattore sunk; announced . . . . . . 25 July, ,,
Shocks in Central Asia, Vernoe, Tashkend, &c., above 54 killed . . . . about 2 Aug. ,,
Shocks in Algeria, about 30 killed at Msila 3–5 Dec. ,,
Shocks at Amatitlan, Guatemala . . 18 Dec. ,,
Severe shock at Granada, &c. . . 14 March, 1886
Severe shocks in the Morea, Ionian Islands, Malta, and neighbourhood; Filiatra, Gargaliano, and Pyrgos on the mainland destroyed; 300 lives lost 27 Aug. ,,
Shocks throughout United States, chiefly in South Carolina, Georgia, and Alabama; three-fourths of Charleston destroyed, 96 persons perish; Savannah, Washington; 17 shocks at Charleston 31 Aug.; other shocks on Atlantic coast 2, 3 Sept.: slight shocks occasionally 3–14 Sept. and 22 Oct. ,,
Severe shocks from Corsica to Lyons and Geneva, and from Milan to beyond Marseilles; centre point Nice and neighbourhood; buildings thrown down and much damage, 5.37 to 9 A.M.; about 12 deaths in French territory and 2,000 in Italy 23 Feb.; San Remo district 300 killed; slight shocks . . . . 24 Feb. 1887
Slight shocks near Mentone . . . 11 March, ,,
Violent shocks at Montezuma, &c., San Francisco, about 170 perish; announced . . 8 May, ,,
Violent long-continued earthquake at Tokio, Japan 15 Jan. ,,
Earthquake at Vernoe and Almatensky, Turkestan; about 140 perish; announced . . 13 June, ,,
Earthquake shocks in Hawaii (*Owhyhee*); 167 persons perish . . . . . 5 May *et seq.* ,,
Violent earthquake shocks at Athens and neighbourhood . . . . 4 Oct. ,,
Destruction of Bisignano, Cosenza, Calabria, by earthquake, about 25 lives lost, about 4,000 homeless . . . . 4 Dec. ,,
Slight shock all over Scotland . . . 2 Feb. 1888
Earthquake at Yunnan, China, 4,000 persons killed March, ,,
Slight shocks in Annandale, Scotland . 19 July, ,,
Several severe shocks in New Zealand, without loss of life . . . . 1 Sept. ,,
Shocks at Vostitza, Greece, damage estimated at 2,000,000 drachmas . . . . . 10 Sept. ,,
Destructive shocks at Costa Rica, with loss of life, cathedral and palace destroyed 29, 30 Dec. ,,

Slight earthquake at Edinburgh, little damage, 18 Jan. 1889
Earthquake in Asia Minor . . . 17 Jan. ,,
Slight shock in East Lancashire . . 10 Feb. ,,
Shock at Djarkend, government of Semiretchinsk; half the town destroyed . reported 12 July, ,,
Earthquakes in Japan, *which see* . 28 July, ,,
Shocks at Inverness and Forres, buildings damaged 15 Nov. ,,
The town of Joana, in Java, greatly injured, 12 lives lost . . . . 12 Dec. 1890
Algeria—Gouraya and Villebourg villages nearly destroyed, about 40 natives perish . 15 Jan. 1891
Adil-Djevas in Van, Armenia; 146 houses destroyed 3 April, ,,
Violent shocks in Italy, especially in the province of Verona, where there is much damage and some loss of life, 7 June, *et seq.*; continued slighter shocks . . . . . . 11–14 June, ,,
San Salvador, *which see*, Central America, great destruction of life and property . . 9 Sept. ,,
Very destructive earthquake in Japan, *which see* 28 Oct. ,,
Shocks of earthquake in New South Wales, Victoria, and Tasmania . . . . about 27 Jan. 1892
San Cristobal, Mexico, every building destroyed, thousands homeless . . . . 30 July, ,,
Shocks in W. and S. W. England, from Swansea to Cornwall and Ireland; little damage; boats injured by tidal wave . . . 17, 18 Aug. ,,
Many shocks in Eastern Europe; slight damage; 14 Oct., near Naples . . . 16 Nov. ,,
Violent shocks at Zante. See *Ionian Islands*, 31 Jan. *et seq.* 1893
Destructive earthquake in Samothrace; reported 14 Feb. ,,
Shocks at New York, *which see* . . . 7 March, ,,
Severe shocks at the foot of Mount Etna 1 April, ,,
Destructive shocks in Servia, Bulgaria, and Hungary; several villages destroyed . 8–10 April, ,,
Severe shocks at Thebes, *which see* end of May, ,,
Destructive shocks with loss of life at Mattinata, Italy, and in Stromboli, with a volcanic eruption, 12 Aug. ,,
Slight shocks in S. Wales and N. Cornwall, and E. coast of Ireland . . . . . 2 Nov. ,,
Destructive shocks in Kuchan (Persia); 12,000 deaths reported, 17 Nov.; and at Samarcand, 19 Nov. ,,
Severe shock at Montreal, *which see* . . 27 Nov. ,,
Shocks in New York and Vermont . 27 Nov. ,,
Shock at Larissa; considerable damage 19 March, 1894
Severe shocks throughout Greece; *which see* 20 April—7 May, ,,
Shocks at Pontypridd, Cardiff, and other places, S. Wales . . . . . . 2 May, ,,
Shocks at Wellington, &c., New Zealand 21 May, ,,
Violent shocks at Constantinople, *which see* 10–16 July, ,,
Shocks in Macedonia, Old Servia, E. Bulgaria, with loss of life; reported . . 27 July, ,,
Severe shocks in Sicily; 6 persons killed at Zafarana; 4 at Aci San Antonio . . . 8 Aug. ,,
Slight shock at Athens and other places, 26 Aug.; and at Bucharest, &c., reported . . 2 Sept. ,,
Severe shocks in Japan, *which see* . 22 Oct. ,,
Shocks in Argentina, *which see* . . 27 Oct. ,,
Destructive shocks in S. Italy and Sicily, *which see*, 16 Nov., 1894; again, with loss of life, 23 March, 1895
Shocks in Austria-Hungary and Italy; over 300 miles' extent; 2 deaths; see *Trieste* and *Laybach* 14, 17 April, ,,
Shocks in Florence, Bologna, Parma, Pisa, Siena, Placentia, and many villages, with loss of life, 18 May; other shocks . . . . . 6 June, ,,
Paramythia in Epirus, destroyed; great loss of life; reported . . . . . 24 May, ,,
Earthquake at Brüx, Bohemia, no deaths, 2,462 persons homeless . . . . . 19 July, ,,
Severe shock at Laibach . . . . 19 Sept. ,,
Shocks at and near Rome . . . 1 Nov. ,,
Destructive shocks in Persia, *which see*, 2–5 Jan. 1896
Destructive shocks (seismic waves) in Japan, *which see* . . . . . 15–17 June, ,,
Severe shocks in Iceland, *which see*, 26, 27 Aug., and 5, 6 Sept. ,,

Shocks in many parts of England and Wales, felt in London, 5 A.M. . . . . 17 Dec. 1896
Severe shock in Kishim, Persian gulf, *which see*, 10, 11 Jan. 1897
Severe shocks, with loss of life, in Guadeloupe, &c., W. Indies . . . . 29 April, ,,
Shocks in Calcutta, Assam, India, *which see*, Hughli, Dacca, and many other places, 5 P.M. 12 June, ,,
See *Philippines* . . . . . . 1 July, ,,
Slight shocks in Italy, and other places . Sept. ,,
Shocks near Smyrna, with loss of life, 22 Dec. ,,
Destructive shocks at Balikesri, in Asia Minor, with loss of life . . . . 29 Jan. 1898
Severe shocks in Antigua, St. Kitts, Guadeloupe, and Montserrat . . . . . 4 March, ,,
Shocks at Parma, and elsewhere, 4 March; along the Antrodoco valley, in Italy, with loss of life 27 June, ,,
Shocks in the Peloponnesus, much damage, 21 Jan. 1899
Again, 5 villages destroyed in Kyparinia . 24 Jan. ,,
Shocks at Mexico, many injured, serious damage, 24 Jan. ,,
At Yokohama, with loss of life . . . 7 Mar. ,,
45 shocks in 5 hours at Montserrat, great damage, 17 May, ,,
Shocks in S.E. Austria and W. Hungary, 11 June; and in Kohat, Allahabad, with some loss of life, 12 June, ,,
Shocks in Westphalia, with damage . . 14 July, ,,
Rome, Frascati, Marino, and other towns on the Alban hills, buildings damaged, 19 July; Lisbon, 8.55 P.M. . . . . . . 13 Aug. ,,
Severe shocks at Aidin, 2 villages destroyed, Asia Minor, over 1600 deaths, many injured . 20 Sept. ,,
Frequent shocks at Yakutat in Alaska, 3–17 Sept. ,,
See *Landslips*, 24 Sept. 1899.
Violent shocks in Ceram, Dutch E. Indies, many killed, reported . . . . 12 Oct. ,,
Six villages destroyed and 7 others damaged in the province of Tiflis, Russia, about 1,000 deaths, 31 Dec. ,,
Sharp shock at Safed, in Syria . . . 5, 6 Jan. 1900
Slight shock in Venetia . . . 4 Mar. ,,
Severe shock at Caracas, Guaronas destroyed, 25 deaths . . . . . . 30 Oct. ,,
Further shocks and 3 villages destroyed 31 Oct. ,,
Shocks in S. Russia and Turkey, lighthouse destroyed at Cape Kaliakra, in the Black Sea 31 Mar. 1901
Shocks in Scotland N. of the Forth, severe near the Grampians . . . . 18 Sept. ,,
Severe shocks at Kishnieff, in Bessarabia, 24 Sept. ,,
Shocks at Gallarate and elsewhere in Italy, 1 death, 30 Oct. ,,
Shocks in Utah, U.S. . . . 13, 14 Nov. ,,
Severe shocks (50) in Erzerum, Armenia, buildings destroyed, 22 deaths . . . . 8–12 Nov. ,,
Severe shocks in the Cheviot district, New Zealand, township destroyed, 1 death . 16–18 Nov. ,,
Severe shocks at Chilpancingo and Chilapa, Mexico, buildings wrecked, 17 deaths, many injured, 16, 17 Jan. 1902
Schemacha and district in Transcaucasia, 2,000 killed and injured, large numbers homeless (czar gave 150,000 roubles for relief) . 13–18 Feb. ,,
Kiangri, in Asia Minor, destroyed, 4 killed, 100 injured . . . . 12 Mar. ,,
Shocks in Greece, reported . . . 31 May, ,,
Shocks at Irkutsk and round lake Baikal, 12 April, ,,
Fearful shocks in Guatemala, Quezaltenango, and 8 towns destroyed, and many other places ruined, about 900 deaths, 8.25 P.M. . . . 18 April, ,,
Severe shock at Shemakha . . . . 3 May, ,,
St. Pierre, in Martinique, suddenly destroyed, with 30,000 inhabitants, by fearful eruption of the volcano Mont Pelée . . . 8 May ,,
The Souffrière volcano, in St. Vincent, about the same time became active, 2,000 perished.
Slight shock near Camborne, Cornwall . 4 June, ,,
Shocks in Syracuse and province, 14 June; in Calabria, Italy . . . . . 22 June, ,,
Shocks in Salonika and Adrianople . . 5 July, ,,
Mont Pelée again in violent eruption, earthquake shocks . . . . . 8–11 July ,,
Severe shocks in St. Vincent, W. Indies, 10, 17, 22 July, ,,

Destructive shocks at Bandar Abbas, India 9, 10, 25 July, 1902
Shocks in Nebraska, Iowa, S. Dakota . 28 July, ,,
Severe shocks at Los Alamos, California, 28, 31 July and 1 Aug. ,,
Shocks at Leiria in Portugal, 3, 4 Aug.; and at Carrara, Italy . . . . 4 Aug. ,,
Severe shock at Skagway, New York . 10 Aug. ,,
Shocks in Kashgar, July, 667 deaths, 1,000 injured 22–23 Aug. ,,
Shocks in Mindanao, Philippines . about 26 Aug. ,,
Shock at Carupano, Venezuela . . 30 Aug. ,,
Shock at Pau, Pyrenees . . . . 8 Sept. ,,
Shocks at Oran, Algeria, and at Oned Marsa 17 Nov. ,,
Severe shocks at Andijan, in Ferghana, Turkestan, 10,000 deaths, 15,000 houses destroyed . 16 Dec. ,,
Shock in Syracuse . . . . . 28 Dec. ,,
Shock in West Jamaica . . . . . 5 Feb. 1903
Shocks in Saxony and Bohemia . . 5, 6 March ,,
Severe shocks in Dominica . . . 7 March ,,
Shocks in the Austrian Alps . .19, 20 March ,,
And from Landau to Wörth . . . 23 March ,,
Shocks in Derbyshire, Staffordshire, Notts and E. Lancs., buildings, &c. damaged mid-day 24 March ,,
Shock in Jerusalem; slight damage . 30 March ,,
Shocks in Catania . . . . . . 3 April ,,
Shocks in Van, Armenia; Melazgvird, and other villages destroyed, 785 deaths, many cattle and sheep killed . . . . . . 29 April ,,
Shocks in Derbyshire villages . . . 3 May ,,
Shocks at Carnarvon, Bangor and district 19 June ,,
Violent shocks at Erlau, Hungary, much damage 26 June ,,

EAST AFRICA PROTECTORATE, ETC., see under *Africa* (*British E.*), *Slave Trade*, and *Zanzibar*.

EAST ANGLES, the sixth kingdom of the Heptarchy, commenced by Uffa, 526; ended with Ethelbert in 792; see *Britain*. The bishop's see founded by St. Felix, who converted the East Angles in 630, was eventually settled at Norwich (*which see*) about 1094.

EASTBOURNE, a town on the coast of Sussex. Roman remains found here. Incorporated July, 1883. Many buildings have been erected by the duke of Devonshire, who died 21 Dec. 1891. Town hall opened 9 Oct. 1884. Population 1881, 22,014; 1891, 34,977; 1901, 44,000.

The Sunday processions of the salvation army, forbidden by a clause in the Eastbourne Improvement act of 1885, were continued 1890–1. Elkanah Clarkson and 8 others convicted of holding an unlawful assembly, 3 Dec. 1891. The judgment set aside, 23 Jan. 1892. An act to repeal the clause, passed June, 1892.
The prince of Wales opens the Sussex agricultural show, 17 July, 1899.
Russian exhibition, held by the Russian reformation society, opened, 1 Sept. 1899.
Lord Rosebery opens the Hampden park and king's drive, 12 Aug. 1902.
First stone of technical institute laid, 25 April, 1903.
Visit of the king, 11–13 July, 1903.

EAST END JUVENILE MISSION established 1866, to reclaim destitute children, see *Barnardo's Homes*.

EAST-END MURDERS, see *Whitechapel*.

EASTER, instituted about 68, the festival observed by the church in commemoration of Our Saviour's resurrection, so called in England from the Saxon goddess *Eostre*, whose festival was in April. After much contention between the eastern and western churches, it was ordained by the council of Nice, 325, to be observed on the same day throughout the whole Christian world. But the eastern and western churches generally differ; they coincided in 1882. "Easter-day is the Sunday following that fourteenth day of the calendar moon which happens upon or next after the 21st March: so that, if the said fourteenth day be a Sunday, Easter-day is not that Sunday but the next." Easter-day may be any day of the five weeks which commence with March 22 and end with April 25. The dispute between the old British church and the new Anglo-Saxon church respecting Easter was settled about 664.—Easter Sunday, 1893, 2 April; 1894, 25 Mar.; 1895, 14 April; 1896, 5 April; 1897, 18 April; 1898, 10 April; 1899, 2 April; 1900, 15 April; 1901. 7 April; 1902, 30 March; 1903, 12 April; 1904, 3 April; 1905, 23 April.

EASTER ISLAND, in the Pacific Ocean, was discovered by Davis in 1686; it was visited by Roggewein, April 1722, and from him obtained the name it now bears; it was visited by captain Cook, March 1774. At the south-east extremity is the crater of an extinguished volcano, about two miles in circuit and 800 feet deep.

Prehistoric remains; about 555 stone images were examined by Mr. paymaster Thomson, of the U.S. navy, who gave a report to the national museum at Washington, Sept. 1892. The decaying population was then about 155.

EASTERN (or GREEK) CHURCH, see *Greek Church*.

EASTERN EMPIRE. After the death of the emperor Jovian, in Feb. 364, the generals at Nice elected Valentinian as his successor, who, in June, made his brother Valens emperor of the west; the final division was in 395, between the sons of Theodosius. The eastern empire ended with the capture of Constantinople, and death of Constantine XIII., 29 May, 1453; see *Turkey*.

Nestorius, the bishop, nominated the first patriarch of Constantinople . . . . . 9 July, 381
Theodosius the Great succours Valentinian II., the western emperor, and defeats the tyrant Maximus, at Aquileia 388
Valentinian II. slain by Arbogastes the Frank, who makes Eugenius emperor 392
Eugenius defeated and slain by Theodosius, who re-unites the two empires . . . . 6 Sept. 394
Death of Theodosius; the empire *finally divided* between his sons—Arcadius receives the east, Honorius the west . . . . . . 17 Jan. 395
Constantinople walled by Theodosius II. . 413
Alaric the Goth begins to ravage the empire ,,
Violent religious dissensions; Theodosius II. establishes schools, and revives learning . . 425
The Theodosian code promulgated . . 438
The councils of Ephesus, 431, 449; of Chalcedon . 451
Frequent sanguinary conflicts between the Blues and Greens, circus factions at Constantinople, 498-520
The Justinian code published 529
War with Persia; beginning of the victorious career of Belisarius, the imperial general . . 529-531
He suppresses the "Nika" ("conquer") insurrection of the circus factions; 30,000 Greeks slain, and Constantinople burnt 532
Dedication of St. Sophia 537
Victories of Belisarius in Africa, Italy, and the East 533-541
Recalled through Justinian's jealousy, 542; again, 548; again, 549; disgraced 562
Beginning of the Turkish power in Asia . . . 545
The Slavonians ravage Illyria 551
Narses defeats Totila and the Goths near Rome . 552
Disaffection of Narses 561
Death of Belisarius, aged 84; of Justinian (83) . 565
Victories of Maurice and Narses in the East, 579 *et seq.*
Severe contests with the Avars 594-620
Narses burnt at Constantinople 606
The flight (Hejira) of Mahomet from Mecca to Medina, where he establishes himself as a prophet and prince . . . . 16 July, 622
Victorious career of Heraclius II. . . . 622 *et seq.*
He recovers his lost territories 627
The Saracens invade the empire, 632; defeat Heraclius at Aiznadin, 633; at Yermuk, 636; take Alexandria, 640; and the Greek provinces in Africa 648

Constans purchases peace with them 660
They besiege Constantinople seven times . . . 672-677
The Bulgarians establish a kingdom in Mœsia (now Bulgaria), 678; they ravage the country up to Constantinople 711
The Saracens vainly invest Constantinople, 716, 718; defeated 720
Leo III. the Isaurian, forbids the worship of images: (this leads to the Iconoclast controversy, and eventually to the separation of the eastern and western churches) 726
A great invading Arab force (90,000) defeated by Acronius 739
The monasteries dissolved 770
Destruction of images throughout the empire decreed, 754; image-worship restored by the empress Irene (for which she was canonized) . . . 787
The empire loses the exarchate of Italy, 752; Dalmatia, 825; Sicily and Crete 827
Image-worship persecuted, 830; restored, 842; forbidden at Constantinople by one council, 869; restored by another 879
South Italy annexed to the empire 890
Five emperors reigning at one time 928
Naples added to the empire 928
Basil subdues the Bulgarians 987, 1014
Bulgaria annexed to the empire 1018
The Turks invade Asia Minor 1068
The Normans conquer South Italy 1080
The first crusade; Alexis I. recovers Asia . . . 1097
The Venetians victorious over the Greeks . . . 1125
The Hungarians repelled, 1152; peace made with the Normans in Sicily 1156
Wars with the Turks and the Venetians . . . 1172
Cyprus lost to the empire 1190
The fourth crusade begins 1202
Revolt of Alexis against his brother Isaac; the crusaders take Constantinople, and restore Isaac and his son Alexis IV. . . . 19 July, 1203
Alexis Ducas murders Alexis IV. and usurps the throne; the crusaders take Constantinople, kill Alexis, and establish the Latin empire, under Baldwin, count of Flanders . . . . 9 May, 1204
Empire of Nice founded by Theodore Lascaris . . ,,
Kingdom of Epirus and Ætolia established . . 1208
Constantinople recovered, and the empire re-established by Michael Palæologus . . 25 July, 1261
Establishment of the Turkish empire in Asia, under Othman I. 1299
The Genoese trade in the Black sea 1303
The Turks ravage Mysia, &c., 1340 and 1345; and settle in the coast of Thrace 1353
The sultan Amurath takes Adrianople, and makes it his capital, 1362; and, by treaty, greatly reduces the emperor's territories 1373
All the Greek possessions in Asia lost . . . 1390
Sultan Bajazet defeats the Christians under Sigismund of Hungary, at Nicopolis. . 28 Sept. 1396
The emperor Manuel vainly solicits help from the western sovereigns 1400
A Turkish pacha established at Athens . . . 1401
The Greek empire made tributary to Timour, 1402; who subjugates the Turkish sultan, and dismembers his empire, 1403; death of Timour, on his way to China 1405
Dissension amongst the Turks defers the fall of Constantinople, 1403-12; Mahomet I. aided by the emperor Manuel, becomes sultan . . . 1413
Amurath II. in vain besieges Constantinople, 1422; peace made 1425
John Palæologus visits Rome and other places, soliciting help in vain 1437-40
Accession of Constantine XIII., last emperor . . 1448
Accession of Mahomet II. 1451; begins the siege of Constantinople, 6 April; takes it . 29 May, 1453
(He granted the Christians personal security and free exercise of their religion.) See *Turkey*.

EMPERORS OF THE EASTERN EMPIRE.

364. Valens.
379. Theodosius I. the Great.
395. Arcadius, the son of Theodosius.
408. Theodosius II. succeeded his father.
450. Marcian, a Thracian of obscure family.
457. Leo I. the Thracian.
474. Leo II. the Younger, died the same year.
,, Zeno, called the *Isaurian*.
491. Anastasius I. an Illyrian, of mean birth.
518. Justin I. originally a private soldier.
527. Justinian I. founder of the Digest.
565. Justin II. nephew of Justinian.
578. Tiberius II. renowned for his virtues.
582. Maurice, the Cappadocian: murdered with all his children, by his successor,
602. Phocas, the Usurper, a centurion, whose crimes and cruelties led to his own assassination in 610.
610. Heraclius, by whom Phocas was dethroned.
641. (Heracleonas) Constantine III. reigned a few months; poisoned by his step-mother Martina.
,, Constans II.: assassinated in a bath.
668. Constantine III. (or IV.) Pogonatus.
685. Justinian II. son of the preceding; abhorred for his exactions, debaucheries, and cruelties: dethroned and mutilated by his successor,
695 Leontius: dethroned and mutilated by Tiberius Aspimar.
698. Tiberius III. Aspimar.
705. Justinian II. restored. Leontius and Tiberius degraded in the Hippodrome, and put to death. Justinian slain in 711.
711. Philippicus-Bardanes: assassinated.
713. Anastasius II.: fled on the election of Theodosius in 716; afterwards delivered up to Leo III. and put to death.
716. Theodosius III.
718. Leo III. the Isaurian.
[In this reign (726) commences the great Iconoclastic controversy; the alternate prohibition and restoration of images involves the peace of several reigns.]
741. Constantine IV. (or V.) Copronymus, son of the preceding; succeeded by his son.
775. Leo IV.
780. Constantine V. (or VI.) and his mother Irene.
790. Constantine, alone, by the desire of the people, Irene having become unpopular.
792. Irene again, jointly with her son, and afterwards alone, 797; deposed for her cruelties and murders, and exiled.
802. Nicephorus I. Logothetes: slain.
811. Stauracius: reigns a few days only.
,, Michael I.: defeated in battle, abdicates the throne, and retires to a monastery.
813. Leo V. the Armenian: killed in the temple at Constantinople on Christmas-day, 820, by conspirators in the interest of his successor.
820. Michael II. the Stammerer.
,, Theophilus, son of Michael.
842. Michael III. Porphyrogenitus, and the Sot, son of the preceding; murdered by his successor,
867. Basil I. the Macedonian.
886. Leo VI. the Philosopher.
911. Alexander and Constantine VI. (or VII.) Porphyrogenitus, brother and son of Leo, the latter only six years of age; the former dying in 912, Zoë, mother of Constantine, assumes the regency.
919. Romanus Lecapenus, usurper, associates with him his sons:
920. Christopher, and
928. Stephen and Constantine VII. (or VIII.)
[Five emperors now reign: Christopher dies, 931; Romanus exiled by his sons Constantine and Stephen, who are themselves banished the next year.]
945. Constantine VII. (or VIII.) reigns alone: poisoned by his daughter-in-law, Theophania, 959.
959. Romanus II. son of preceding: contrived his father's death; banished his mother, Helena.
963. Nicephorus II. Phocas: married Theophania, is predecessor's consort, who has him assassinated.
969. John I. Zimisces, celebrated general: takes Basil II. and Constantine VIII. (or IX.), sons of Romanus II., as colleagues; John dies, supposed by poison, and
976. Basil II. and Constantine VIII. reign: the former dies in 1025; the latter in 1028.
1028. Romanus III. Argyropulus: poisoned by his profligate consort Zoë, who raises
1034. Michael IV. the Paphlagonian, to the throne: on his death Zoë places
1041. Michael V. Calaphates, as his successor: Zoë dethrones him, has his eyes put out, and marries

1042. Constantine IX. (or X.) Monomachus and Zoë reign jointly: Zoë dies, 1050.
1054. Theodora, widow of Constantine.
1056. Michael VI. Stratiotes, or Strato: deposed.
1057. Isaac I. Comnenus: abdicates.
1059. Constantine X. (or XI.) Ducas.
1067. Eudocia, consort of the preceding, and Romanus IV. Diogenes, whom she marries, reign to the prejudice of Michael, Constantine's son.
1071. Michael VII. Parapinaces, recovers his throne, and reigns jointly with Constantine XI. (or XII.)
1078. Nicephorus III.; dethroned by
1081. Alexis or Alexius I. Comnenus, succeeded by
1118. John Comnenus (Kalos), his son, died of a wound from a poisoned arrow.
1143. Manuel I. Comnenus, son of John.
1180. Alexis II. Comnenus, son of the preceding, under the regency of the empress Maria, his mother.
1183. Andronicus I. Comnenus, causes Alexis to be strangled, and seizes the throne; put to death by
1185. Isaac II. Angelus-Comnenus, who is deposed, imprisoned, and deprived of his eyes by his brother,
1195. Alexis III. Angelus, the Tyrant: deposed, and his eyes put out; died in a monastery.
1203. Isaac II. again, with his son, Alexis IV.; deposed.
1204. Alexis V. Ducas, murders Alexis IV.; is killed by the crusaders.

LATIN EMPERORS.

1204. Baldwin I. earl of Flanders, on the capture of Constantinople by the Latins, elected emperor; made a prisoner by the king of Bulgaria and never heard of afterwards.
1206. Henry I. his brother: dies in 1217.
1216. Peter de Courtenay, his brother-in-law.
1221. Robert de Courtenay, his son.
1228. Baldwin II. his brother, a minor, and John de Brienne, of Jerusalem, regent and associate emperor.
1261. [Constantinople recovered, and the empire of the Franks or Latins terminates.]

GREEK EMPERORS AT NICE.

1204. Theodore Lascaris I.
1222. John Ducas Vataces.
1255. Theodore Lascaris II., his son.
1259. John Lascaris, and (1260) Michael VIII. Palæologus.

GREEK EMPERORS AT CONSTANTINOPLE.

1261. Michael VIII. now at Constantinople: puts out the eyes of John, and reigns alone.
1282. Andronicus II. Palæologus the Elder, son of preceding: deposed by
1328. Andronicus III. the Younger, his grandson.
1341. John Palæologus I. under the guardianship of John Cantacuzenus: the latter proclaimed emperor at Adrianople.
1347. John Cantacuzenus abdicates.
1355. John Palæologus I. restored.
1391. Manuel II. Palæologus, his son: succeeded by his son and colleague.
1425. John Palæologus II. The throne claimed by his three brothers.
1448. Constantine Palæologus XII. (XIII. or XIV. some of the other emperors being called *Constantine* by some writers) killed, when Constantinople was taken, 29 May, 1453.

EASTERN QUESTION. In the 19th century related especially to the affairs of the Turkish empire and its connection with its neighbours; see *Turkey* and *Russo-Turkish wars*. An Eastern Question association was formed in London, Dec. 1876, the duke of Westminster president. The eastern question became again prominent through the troubles in the Balkan, see *Bulgaria* and *Servia*, 1889-92. *Armenia* and *Turkey*, 1893 *et seq*. *Crete*, 1896-97. *Macedonia*, 1903.

EASTERN ROUMELIA, see *Roumelia*.

EAST INDIA ASSOCIATION, for the advocacy of the interests of all the inhabitants of India, founded 7 Nov. 1866. A journal is published and meetings held. The maharaja of Gwalior gives 1,000*l*. to the association, Aug. 1902.

EAST INDIA STOCK DIVIDEND REDEMPTION ACT passed 15 May, 1873. It finally abolished the company on 1 June, 1874, and made needful arrangements.

EAST INDIES, see *India*.

EAST LONDON MUSEUM, see *Bethnal Green*.

EAST SAXONS, see under *Britain*.

EBELIANS, a German revivalist sect, which began at Königsberg in Prussia, about 1836, its leaders being archdeacon Ebel and Dr. Diestel, who were tried and condemned for unsound doctrine and impure lives in 1839. The sentence was annulled in 1842, it is said by royal influence. The sect is popularly termed "Mucker," German for hypocrites. Their theory and practice of spiritual marriage is described by Mr. Hepworth Dixon in his "Spiritual Wives," 1868.

EBIONITES, heretics, in the 1st century, a branch of the Nazarenes, were of two kinds: one believed that Our Saviour was born of a virgin, observed all the precepts of the Christian religion, but added the ceremonies of the Jews; the other believed that Christ was born after the manner of all mankind, and denied his divinity. Photinus revived the sect in 342.

EBONITE (vulcanised india-rubber), see *Caoutchouc*.

EBRO, a river in Spain—the scene of a signal defeat of the Spaniards by the French, under Lannes, near Tudela, 23 Nov. 1808; and also of several important movements of the allied British and Spanish armies during the Peninsular war (1809—1813).

ECBATANA, capital of Media; the date of foundation is unknown; Herodotus ascribes it to Deioces about 700 B.C.; it was taken by Cyrus 549, and became the summer residence of himself and his successors.

"ECCE HOMO," "Behold the man" (John xix. 5). A study of the human character of Jesus Christ (the supernatural element being excluded), a work of much spiritual reverence and literary excellence. It was published anonymously in 1865, and caused great excitement; the authorship was attributed to many eminent persons, but eventually assigned to prof. John Robert Seeley, without his contradiction. He was made Regius professor of modern history at Cambridge in 1869, and K.C.M.G. in 1894. He published "Natural Religion" in 1882, and the "Expansion of England" in 1883. He was born in 1834, and died 13 Jan. 1895.

ECCLESIASTICAL ASSESSMENTS (Scotland) act passed, 1900.

ECCLESIASTICAL COMMISSIONS: appointed by queen Elizabeth, 1559; by James I. in Scotland, 1617; by the English parliament in 1641; and by James II. to coerce the universities in 1687. A Church Inquiry Commission, appointed 23 June, 1832, reported June, 1835. The present Ecclesiastical Commissioners (bishops, deans, and laymen) for the management of church property, were appointed in Feb. 1835; incorporated in 1836; and their proceedings regulated in 1840 and 1841. The law relating to them was amended in 1868;

annual reports issued. Since 1840 (when the common fund was first created) the commissioners have augmented and endowed over 5,900 benefices by annual grants, capital sums, lands, &c., equivalent to a capital sum of about 32,188,000*l.* for year ended 31 Oct. 1902.

ECCLESIASTICAL COURTS. There existed no distinction between lay and ecclesiastical courts in England until 1085, after the Norman conquest; see *Arches* and *Consistory Courts.* Till the establishment of the Divorce and Probate courts (*which see*) in 1857, the following were the causes cognisable in ecclesiastical courts: blasphemy, apostasy from Christianity, heresy, schism, ordinations, institutions to benefices, matrimony, divorces, bastardy, tithes, incest, fornication, adultery, probate of wills, administrations, &c.

A royal commission of inquiry respecting these courts agreed to, house of lords; 7 March, 1881, appointed. Report issued, Aug. 1883.

ECCLESIASTICAL DILAPIDATIONS, law respecting, amended by acts passed in 1871 and 1872.

ECCLESIASTICAL GAZETTE, Church of England semi-official journal; sent gratuitously to all dignitaries and incumbents; established 10 July, 1838.

ECCLESIASTICAL STATE, or STATES OF THE CHURCH, see *Rome, Modern.*

ECCLESIASTICAL TITLES ACT, 14 & 15 Vict. c. 60 (1851), repealed 24 July, 1871; see *Papal Aggression.*

ECCLESIOLOGICAL SOCIETY, formed in 1839, was originally the Cambridge Campden Society, mainly established by the 2nd earl of Gainsborough (Charles George Noel) for the proper restoration of ancient churches.

ECHO. The time which elapses between the utterance of a sound and its return must be more than one-twelfth of a second, to form an echo. The whispering gallery of St. Paul's is a well-known example. The *Echo*, independent evening paper, price ½*d.*, established Dec. 1868.

ECKMUHL (Bavaria), the site of a battle between the main armies of France (75,000) and Austria (40,000); Napoleon and marshal Davoust (hence prince d'Eckmühl) defeated the archduke Charles, 22 April, 1809.

ECLECTICS (from Greek, *eklego*, I choose), ancient philosophers (called *Analogetici*, and also *Philalethes*, the lovers of truth), who, without attaching themselves to any sect, chose what they judged good from each: of them was Potamon of Alexandria, about A.D. 1. Also a Christian sect, who considered the doctrine of Plato conformable to the spirit of Christianity.

ECLIPSE (the race-horse), see *Races.*

ECLIPSES. Their revolution was calculated by Calippus, the Athenian, 336 B.C. The Egyptians said they had accurately observed 373 eclipses of the sun, and 832 of the moon, in the period from Vulcan to Alexander, who died 323 B.C. The theory of eclipses is said to have been known to the Chinese before 120 B.C.; they record an eclipse 776 B.C. The first eclipse recorded in history happened 19 March, 721 B.C., at 8*h.* 40*m.* P.M., according to Ptolemy; it was lunar, and was observed with accuracy at Babylon. See *Sun.*

A list of eclipses to the year 2000 is given in "*L'Art de Vérifier les Dates.*"

The Royal Astronomical Society published a volume of "Observations made during total solar eclipses," 1880.

"Recent and Coming Eclipses," by sir Norman Lockyer, published Oct. 1897.

"Remarkable Eclipses," by W. T. Lynn, 6th edition, published Nov. 1902.

ECLIPSES OF THE SUN.

Eclipse recorded in the Assyrian tablets B.C. . . 661

The Nineveh eclipse (recorded, according to sir Henry Rawlinson, on a Nineveh tablet in the British Museum) . . . 15 June, B.C. 763

That predicted by Thales; see *Halys* (*Pliny*, lib. ii. 9), believed to have occurred . . 28 May, 585

[Sir G. B. Airy thinks the date should be 610: others say 603 or 584 B.C. It is the one recorded by Herodotus as interrupting a battle between the Medes and Lydians.]

The alleged eclipse at the time of Xerxes' expedition against Greece, 480 B.C., is much disputed, and the darkness was probably meteorological.

One at Athens (*Thucydides*, lib. iv.) . . B.C. 424

Eclipse of Agathocles (*Airy*) . . . . 15 Aug. 310

Total one: three days' supplication decreed at Rome (*Livy*) 188

One observed at Constantinople . . . . A.D. 968

At the battle of Sticklestadt . . . 29 July, 1030

Mythical reports: in France, when it was dark at noon-day (*Du Fresnoy*), 29 June, 1033; in England a total darkness (*W. Malmsb.*), 20 Mar. 1140; again, the stars visible at ten in the morning (*Camden*) . . . . . . 23 June, 1191

Total eclipse, visible in England; the darkness so great that the stars shone, and the birds went to roost at noon . . . . 3 May, 1715

Last total eclipse observed in England; seen near Salisbury . . . . 22 May, 1724

Remarkable one, central and annular in the interior of Europe . . . . . . 7 Sept. 1802

Total eclipses—17 July, 1833; 8 July, 1842; 28 July, 1851.

An annular eclipse; it was seen and photographed at Oundle; but not seen well at other places 15 March, 1858

Total eclipse of the sun; well seen by sir G. B. Airy, astronomer royal, and others in Spain; Mr. Warren de la Rue took photographs, 18 July, 1860

Total eclipse of the sun of the longest possible duration; (the Royal Society provided means for its observation in India, by col. Walker, Mr. Herschel, and others) . . . . . 18 Aug. 1868

During the solar eclipse, 18 Aug. 1868, as observed in India, M. Janssen invented a method of studying the phenomena of the sun at any time, by employing several spectroscopes, whereby the spectrum is lengthened and the dazzling brilliancy diminished. Mr. Joseph Norman Lockyer had suggested a similar method of observation in 1866, but did not use it till 20 Oct. 1868, being then not aware of M. Janssen's discovery.

The solar eclipse well observed in North America, 7 Aug. 1869

Two expeditions to observe the solar eclipse of 22 Dec. 1870, sent out by the British government, were not successful . . . . 22 Dec. 1870

The solar eclipse well observed at Ceylon and in southern India, 12 Dec. 1871; and in North America, 29, 30 July, 1878; and in Egypt 17 May, 1882

[The same eclipses (about 70) recur in a period of 18 years 10⅓ days.]

Except the total eclipse, 12 Aug. 1999, there can be no total eclipse of the sun visible in England for 250 years: *July*, 1871. *Hind.*

Grand eclipse, well seen by astronomers at Caroline island, &c., Pacific . . . . 6 May, 1883

Eclipse of the sun well seen in North America, &c., 16 March; seen in New Zealand . . 8 Sept. 1885

Solar eclipse 29 August, 1886; British expedition to island of Grenada (West Indies) authorized by Government April; eclipse well observed and photographed at Grenada 1886

Eclipse of 19 Aug. not well observed through unfavourable weather, except at Moscow and other places in Russia and Germany . . . 1887

Solar eclipse observed in California . . 1 Jan. 1889

Eclipse Dec. 22 observed, Salut isle, near Demerara, by Father Stephen J. Perry, who died at sea . . . . . . 27 Dec. 1889
Partial eclipse visible in N. America . 20 Oct. 1892
Total eclipse, 15, 16 April, 1893, well observed; British, prof. Thorpe at Fundium on the Salum River, W. Africa; Mr. Albert Taylor and Mr. Wm. Shackleton at Para Cura, Brazil; American, prof. Pickering at Minas Aris, Brazil; prof. Schaeberle at Valparaiso; French, M. Bigourdan at Joal in Senegal; M. Deslandres and M. Colulesco, Senegal.
Total eclipse; visible in the Indian Ocean and E. Africa . . . . . . 29 Sept. 1894
Total eclipse, 9 Aug. 1896; British expedition at Vadsö, Norway; Dr. A. Common, sir Robert Ball, professor J. N. Lockyer, and others; unfavourable weather, scientific results meagre.
A party conveyed in sir George Baden-Powell's (he died 20 Nov. 1898) yacht *Otaria*, Dr. Stone (Radcliff observer), Mr. Shackleton, lieut. Vernon Webb, and others, arrived at Karmakul, Novaya Zemlya, 72° 23' N. lat. 3 Aug.; successful observations, many photographs taken 9 Aug. 1896
Baron Kaulbars obtains excellent results at Tornea, N. Finland; successful observations also in Siberia. *Nature*, 13, 27 Aug. . . . 3 Sept. ,,
Expeditions to Yezo in Japan, unsuccessful . ,,
Total eclipse about 7 A.M., 22 Jan. 1898; well observed at six stations in India, at Viziadrug, by sir Norman Lockyer and others, totality lasted 1 min. 30 secs., magnificent results, published; at Buxar, near Benares, the rev. J. M. Bacon, with apparatus supplied by Mr. Nevil Maskelyne, obtained what was said to be the first "animated photograph" of any celestial phenomenon; at Sahdol the astronomer royal, prof. Turner, and others; 103 secs. of totality; programme successfully carried out . 22 Jan. 1898
Mr. Christie gave an illustrated discourse on the "Eclipse" at the Royal institution . 22 April, ,,
Total eclipse over the S.E. of the United States, Portugal, and Spain to Algiers . . 28 May, 1900
Valuable results obtained by Mr. Christie and others at Ovar, Portugal; sir Norman Lockyer and party near Alicante; prof. Turner, Messrs. Maunder, Wesley, and others at Algiers; and prof. Todd at Tripoli; and other parties in America; 106 secs. of totality at Cape Henry, Virginia; longest near the middle of the Atlantic.
Total eclipse seen by Mr. Dyson in Sumatra, and by Mr. Maunder in Mauritius . . 18 May, 1901
An annular solar eclipse well observed at Cairo, 11 Nov. ,,
Total eclipse over the region of the south pole, 21 Sept. 1903

OF THE MOON.

The first, observed by the Chaldeans at Babylon (*Ptolemy* iv.) . . . . . . B.C. 721
A total one observed at Sardis (*Thucydides* vii.) . 413
Again, in Asia Minor (*Polybius*) . . . 219
One at Rome, predicted by Q. Sulpitius Gallus (*Livy* xliv.) 168
One terrified the Roman troops and quelled their revolt (*Tacitus*) . . . . . A.D. 14
Total eclipse, well observed at Greenwich, &c. 11 March, 1895
Total eclipse, well observed in Dublin . 28 Dec. 1898
One well seen near London . . . 16 Dec. 1899
Total eclipse at Cape Town and Berlin, partial in England . . . . . . 22 April, 1902

ECNOMUS, see *Himera*.

ECOLE POLYTECHNIQUE, a military academy at Paris, established in 1794, and reorganised and given its present name on 1 Sept. 1795. The "Journal" (which began in 1795) contains profound mathematical papers. The school was reorganised 4 Sept. 1816. The pupils helped to defend Paris in 1814 and 1830. Centenary festival, 17, 18, 19 May, 1894.

ECONOMIC MUSEUM (or Museum of Domestic and Sanitary Economy), at Twickenham, open free, was established chiefly by the agency of Mr. Thos. Twining, in 1860. It originated from the Paris exhibition of 1855. *Economic Review*, No. 1, published Jan. 1891.

ECONOMIST, London weekly journal, devoted to financial matters, first appeared 2 Sept. 1843.

ECONOMISTES, a philosophical sect, founded by François Quesnay (1694—1774), who exalted agriculture above all other arts; he asserted that it gave two things, the support of the labourer and an excess of value which belonged to the proprietor of the land ("product net"), and which alone should be taxed. He also favoured great freedom for industry and trade. His "Physiocratie" (1768) and other works were at the time very popular, even at court, and are said to have influenced Adam Smith, author of "The Wealth of Nations."

ECONOMY, see *Political Economy* and *Societies*, 1902.

The British Association for the Advancement of Economic Knowledge was founded 20 Nov. Mr. (aft. visct.) G. J. Goschen elected first president, 23 Nov. 1890. A quarterly journal was founded 1893

ECORCHEURS (Flayers), bands of armed adventurers who desolated France and Belgium during the 15th century, beginning about 1435. Amongst their leaders were Chabannes, comte de Dammartin, the bastard of Armagnac, and Villandras; and they at one time numbered 100,000. They are said to have stripped their victims to their shirts, and flayed the cattle. They were favoured by the English invasion and the civil wars.

ECRASITE, an explosive invented by Siersch and Kubin, Austrian engineers, impervious to damp, shock, or fire, Oct. 1889.

ECUADOR, see *Equator*.

EDDAS (thought formerly to mean *Oldemoder*, or "mother of mothers," by others, "art"), two books of songs and sagas (prose and verse) containing the Scandinavian mythology (or history of Odin, Thor, Frea, &c.), written by skalds or bards about the 10th, 11th or 12th centuries. Translations have been made into French, English, &c. "The Prose, or Younger Edda," by George Dasent, was published in 1842. MSS. of the Eddas exist at Copenhagen and Upsal. The "Saga Library," published by Mr. B. Quaritch, includes texts, with translations by Wm. Morris, Eiriker Magnússon, and Snorri Sturluson, 1891 *et seq.*

EDDYSTONE (or EDYSTONE) **LIGHTHOUSE**, off the port of Plymouth, erected by the Trinity-house to enable ships to avoid the Eddystone rock. The first lighthouse was commenced under Mr. Winstanley, in 1696; finished in 1699; and destroyed in the dreadful tempest of 27 Nov. 1703, when Mr. Winstanley and others perished. A wooden one, by Rudyerd, was built by order of parliament, and all ships were ordered to pay one penny per ton inwards and outwards towards supporting it, 1708. This lighthouse was burnt 4 Dec. 1755; and one on a better plan, erected by Mr. Smeaton, finished 9 Oct. 1759. The woodwork of this, burnt in 1770, was replaced by stone.

The foundation having given way, a new one was designed by Mr. (aft. sir) James N. Douglass, engineer of the Trinity House. The foundation-stone was laid by the duke of Edinburgh in the presence of the prince of Wales, 19 Aug. 1879. The corner-stone was placed by the duke on 1 June, 1881. Successfully lit, 3 Feb. 1882; opened by the duke, 18 May, 1882.

Smeaton's lighthouse memorial tower erected at Plymouth; founded by duke of Edinburgh, 20 Oct. 1882; inaugurated, 24 Sept. 1884.

EDEN, ship burnt; see *Wrecks*, 1873.

EDESSA (now Orfah), a town in Mesopotamia, said by some to have been built by Nimrod; by Appian, to have been built by Seleucus. It became famous for its schools of theology in the 5th century. It was made a principality by the crusaders, and was taken by the Saracens, 1145; by Nur-ed-deen, in 1144; and the Turks in 1184. Its ancient kings or rulers were named Abgarus and Mannus.

EDGECOTE, see *Banbury*.

EDGEHILL FIGHT (23 Oct. 1642), Warwickshire, between the royalists under prince Rupert and the parliament army under the earl of Essex, was the first important engagement in the civil war. Charles I. was present, and the earl of Lindsay, who headed the royal foot, was mortally wounded. The king lost 5,000 dead. The action was indecisive, though the parliament claimed the victory.

EDICT OF NANTES, by which Henry IV., of France granted toleration to his protestant subjects 13 April, 1598, was confirmed by Louis XIII. in 1610, and by Louis XIV. in 1652. It was revoked by Louis XIV. 22 Oct. 1685. This act cost France 50,000 Protestant families, and gave to England and Germany thousands of industrious artisans. It also caused a fierce insurrection in Languedoc. See *Camisards*. Some of the refugees settled in Spitalfields, where their descendants yet remain; others settled in Soho and St. Giles's, and pursued the art of making crystal glasses, and carried on the silk manufacture and jewellery, then little understood in England.

EDICTS, public ordinances and decrees, usually set forth by sovereigns; originated with the Romans. The PERPETUAL EDICT: Salvius Julianus, of Milan, a civilian at Rome (author of several treatises on public right), was employed by the emperor Adrian to draw up this body of laws for the prætors, promulgated 132.

EDINBURGH, the metropolis of Scotland, derives its name—in ancient records *Edinbure* and *Dun Edin*, "the hill of Edin"—from its castle, founded or rebuilt by Edwin, king of Northumbria, who, having greatly extended his dominions, erected it for the protection of his newly acquired territories from the incursions of the Scots and Picts, 626. But it is said the castle was first built by Camelon, king of the Picts, 330 B.C. It makes a conspicuous appearance, standing on a rock 300 feet high at the west end of the old town, and, before the use of great guns, was a fortification of considerable strength. Edinburgh returns 4 M.P.'s by act passed 25 June, 1885. "Municipal Edinburgh" (historical and official), published June, 1895. See *Population*.

Christianity introduced (reign of Donald I.) . . . 201
City fortified, and castle rebuilt by Malcolm Canmore . . . 1074
St. Giles's church founded (845?) . . . 1120
Improved by David I. . . . 1124 to 1153
Holyrood abbey founded by David I. . . . 1128
Edinburgh constituted a burgh . . . about ,,
Castle held by England . . . 1174-86
A parliament held here under Alexander II. . . . 1215
City taken by the English . . . 1296
Grant of the town of Leith to Edinburgh . . . 1329
Surrenders to Edward III. . . . 1355
St. Giles's church destroyed . . . 1385
Rebuilt . . . 1387
City burnt by Richard II., 1385; and by Henry IV. 1401
The parliament hall, Edinburgh castle, built by James I. . . . about 1434
James II. first king crowned here . . . 1437
Execution af the earl of Athol . . . ,,
Annual fair granted by James II. . . . 1447
City strengthened by a wall . . . 1450
Charter of James III. . . . 1477
Edinburgh made the metropolis by James III. . 1482
Royal College of Surgeons incorporated . . . 1505
Received charter from James IV. . . . 1508
[The palace of Holyrood was built in the reign of James IV.]
High school founded . . . about 1518
A British force, landing from a fleet of 200 ships, burns both Edinburgh and Leith . . . May, 1544
Leith is again burnt, but Edinburgh is spared . 1547
Tolbooth built . . . 1561
Marriage of queen Mary and lord Darnley . . . 1565
David Rizzio murdered . . . 1566
Lord Darnley blown up in a private house by gunpowder . . . 10 Feb. 1567
Mary marries James, earl of Bothwell . 15 May, ,,
Mary's forced resignation; civil war . . . 1570
Death of John Knox . . . 1572
University chartered; see *Ed. University* 14 April, 1582
Bothwell's attempt on Holyrood-house . 27 Dec. 1591
Riot in the city; the mob attacks the king . 1596
James VI. leaves Edinburgh as king of England, 5 April, 1603; he revisits it . . . 16 May, 1617
George Heriot's hospital founded by his will . 1624
Charles I. crowned at Edinburgh . . . June, 1633
Edinburgh made a bishopric . . . ,,
Riots in Greyfriars church at the reading of the English Liturgy . . . 23 July, 1637
Parliament house finished . . . 1640
Charles again visits the city . . . 1641
The castle is surrendered to Cromwell . . . Dec. 1650
"*Mercurius Caledonius*," first Edinburgh newspaper, appeared 1661
Coffee-houses first opened . . . 1677
Merchants' company incorporated . . . 1681
College of Physicians incorporated . . . 1681
Earl of Argyll beheaded . . . 30 June, 1685
African and East India company incorporated . 1695
Bank of Scotland founded . . . ,,
Union of the kingdoms . . . 1707
Royal bank founded . . . 1727
Board of trustees of trade and manufactures appointed . . . ,,
Royal Infirmary incorporated . . . 1736
Affair of Captain Porteous (see *Porteous*) 7 Sept. ,,
Medical Society instituted . . . 1737
The young Pretender occupies Holyrood 17 Sept. 1745
Battle of Preston Pans . . . 21 Sept. ,,
Modern improvements, "New town," commenced . 1753
Magistrates assigned gold chains . . . 1754
Royal Exchange completed . . . 1761
Foundation of the North Bridge, 21 Oct. 1763; completed . . . 1772
Theatre Royal erected . . . 1769
Great fire in the Lawn-market . . . 1771
Register-office, Princes-street, commenced . . 1774
Calton-hill observatory founded . . 25 July. 1776
Great commotion against popery . . 2 Feb, 1779
Society of Antiquaries . . . 1780
Royal Society of Edinburgh incorporated . . 1783
South Bridge commenced . . . 1 Aug. 1785
Royal College of Surgeons incorporated . . 1786
First stone of present university laid 16 Nov. 1788
Robertson, the historian, dies here 11 June, 1793
Bridewell, Calton-hill, erected . . . 1799
Holyrood, an asylum to Louis XVIII. and his brother, afterwards Charles X. . . 1795 to ,,
New Bank of Scotland commenced . 3 June, 1801
"*Edinburgh Review*" first published . 10 Oct. 1802
New system of police established . . . 1805
Alarming riots here . . . 31 Dec. 1811
Nelson's monument completed . . . 1815
Gas company incorporated . . . 1818
Water company incorporated . . . 1819
Professor Playfair dies . . . 20 July, ,,
Society of Arts instituted . . . 1821
Union Canal completed . . . 1822
George IV.'s visit; foundation of the national monument . . . 15-27 Aug. ,,
Royal Institution erected . . . 1823
Destructive fires . . . June and Nov. 1824

Scottish Academy founded 1826
Lord Melville's monument erected 1828
Edinburgh and Dalkeith railway opened . July, 1831
Statue of George IV. erected 1832
Death of sir Walter Scott . . . 21 Sept. ,,
Chambers's Edinburgh Journal published . . . ,,
Association of the Fine Arts 1833
The British Association meets here . . 8 Sept. 1834
Edinburgh and Granton railway begun . . . 1836
Art-union of Scotland 1837
Monument to sir Walter Scott commenced . . . 1840
Society of Arts, founded 1821; incorporated . . 1842
Edinburgh and Glasgow railway opened . Feb. ,,
Queen Victoria visits Edinburgh, &c., 31 Aug.–15 Sept. ,,
Secession, and formation of the Free Church, 18 May, 1843
New College instituted . . . . ,,
North British railway commenced 1844
The monument to the political martyrs of 1793-4 laid by Mr. Hume . . . . . . 21 Aug. ,,
Granton pier, &c., constructed by the duke of Buccleuch 1835-44
Sir Walter Scott's monument completed . . . 1845
Edinburgh Philosophical Association (established 1832) re-organised as the Edinburgh Philosophical Society 1846
N. British railway opened . . . . 18 June, ,,
British Association (2nd time) meets . 31 July, 1850
The queen again visits Edinburgh . 29 Aug. ,,
Prince Albert lays the foundation-stone of the Scotch national gallery . . . . 30 Aug. ,,
Meeting to vindicate Scottish rights . 2 Nov. 1853
Old buildings near Lawn-market burnt . 5 Aug. 1857
Act passed for building new Post-office . . July, 1858
National gallery opened . . . 21 March, 1859
Agitation against Ministers' annuity tax . Sept. ,,
Lord Brougham elected chancellor of the university, Edinburgh . . . . 1 Nov. ,,
Ministers' tax abolished, and other arrangements made which did not give satisfaction: riots ensued . . . . Nov. ,,
20,000 volunteers reviewed by the queen in Queen's Park . . . . 7 Aug. 1860
Industrial museum act passed . . . 28 Aug. ,,
Edinburgh visited by empress Eugénie, 20 Nov. ,,
The prince consort lays foundation of new Post-office and industrial museum . . . 23 Oct. 1861
Fall of a house in High-street, 35 persons killed, 24 Nov. ,,
Accident on Edinburgh and Glasgow railway—17 killed; above 100 wounded . . . 13 Oct. 1862
Lord Palmerston's visit . 31 March—4 April, 1864
Theatre royal burnt: George Lorimer, dean of guild, and seven persons, killed by fall of wall, while endeavouring to extricate others, 13 Jan. 1865
Statues of Allan Ramsay and John Wilson inaugurated . . . . 25 March, ,,
New Post-office opened . . . . . 7 May, 1866
National museum of science and art opened by prince Alfred (who is created duke of Edinburgh, &c., the first royal prince whose leading title was Scotch, 24 May) . . . . . . 19 May, ,,
Great reform demonstration . . . . 17 Nov. ,,
Explosion in the Canongate, at Hammond's, a firework-maker's: 5 killed, many injured . 9 Oct. 1867
Visit of Mr. Disraeli, chancellor of the exchequer, conservative demonstration . . . 29, 30 Oct. ,,
Meeting to propose restoration of St. Giles's cathedral . . . . 1 Nov. ,,
Visit of John Bright, made freeman . 3 Nov. 1868
The annuity tax abolition act passed . 9 Aug. 1870
The prince of Wales installed as patron of the Freemasons of Scotland, 12 Oct.; laid the foundation of the new royal infirmary . . 13 Oct. ,,
Meeting of British Association (3rd) . . 2 Aug. 1871
Scott centenary celebrated . . (9 for 15) Aug. ,,
Restoration of St. Giles's cathedral begun, 17 June, 1872
Lady Burdett-Coutts made a burgess . 15 Jan. 1873
The earl of Derby elected lord rector of the university . . . . 14 Nov. 1874
Theatre Royal destroyed by fire . . . 6 Feb. 1875
Advocates' library injured by fire . . 3 March ,,
Southminster theatre burnt . . . . 14 March ,,
Freedom of city given to rt. hon. W. E. Forster, 5 Nov. ,,
Earl of Derby's address as lord rector, . 17 Dec. ,,
Statue of Dr. Livingstone unveiled . . 15 Aug. 1876
Albert Memorial inaugurated by the queen, 17 Aug. ,,
Fire at Leith Walk, 7 killed through fall of a house, 20 Dec. 1877
Messrs. Nelson's printing-office burnt; great loss, 10 April, 1878
Statue of Dr. Chalmers, by Steell, unveiled 27 July ,,
Marquis of Hartington installed lord rector, 31 Jan. 1879
New waterworks (Portmore reservoir at the Moorfoot Hills) opened by the lord provost 13 June, ,,
St. Mary's cathedral (episcopal) founded by the duke of Buccleuch, 1874; consecrated 30 Oct. ,,
New dock at Leith opened by the duke of Edinburgh 26 July, 1881
About 40,000 Scottish volunteers reviewed in the queen's park by the queen . . . . 25 Aug. ,,
Fishery exhibition opened . . . . 11 April, 1882
Academy of Music for Scotland (at Edinburgh) founded . . . . Sept. ,,
Freedom of the city given to the marquis of Salisbury . . . . 27 Nov. ,,
A severe snowstorm; locomotion stopped; frost 9–18 Dec. ,,
Death of William Chambers, bookseller, restorer of St. Giles's [which is reopened 23 May] 20 May, 1883
Sir Stafford Northcote lord rector of the university 3 Nov. ,,
Theatre Royal again destroyed by fire . 30 June, 1884
Mass meeting to support the government and the franchise bill . . . . 12 July, ,,
Visit of the prince and princess and family 22 Aug. ,,
Demonstration in favour of the government; speeches of Mr. Gladstone . . 30 Aug. and 1, 2 Sept. ,,
The ancient cross restored by Mr. W. E. Gladstone, Nov. 1885
International Industrial exhibition opened by prince Albert Victor, 6 May; visited by the queen, grand civic demonstration 18 Aug. 1886; 2,740,000 visitors; closed . . . . 31 Oct. 1886
Jubilee gifts of Dr. R. H. Gunning for prizes, &c. to Royal Society of Edinburgh, Society of Antiquaries of Scotland, University of Edinburgh, Royal Colleges of Physicians and Surgeons, Edinburgh, Ben Nevis observatory, &c. announced July, 1887
The Heriot-Watt College inaugurated; address by Sir F. Bramwell . . . . . . 10 Jan. 1889
Slight earthquake. . . . . 18 Jan. ,,
Naval and Military exhibition opened 18 June, ,,
Freedom of the city presented to Mr. C. S. Parnell (18,000 municipal electors protest against it) 20 July, ,,
[His name erased from the roll, 1891.]
National Association for the advancement of Art congress meets . . . . 28 Oct.—2 Nov. ,,
International Industrial exhibition, buildings erected at Merchiston and S.W. suburb; nearly 90 acres occupied; the exhibition opened by the duke and duchess of Edinburgh, the duke of Buccleuch, lord Kingsburgh, the provosts of Glasgow, Leith, Perth, Aberdeen, Dundee, and Manchester, and other eminent persons were present, 1 May; visited by the lord mayor of London in state, 20 June; closed 31 Oct. . . . 1890
The exhibition was not successful financially 13 Nov. ,,
The free public library (for which Mr. Andrew Carnegie gave 50,000*l.*) opened by the earl of Rosebery . . . . 9 June, ,,
Mr. H. M. Stanley, the African explorer, receives the freedom of the city . . . . . 11 June, ,,
The parliament Hall restored; see *Parliament of Scotland* . . . . Feb. 1891
Statue of Wm. Chambers (subscribed for) in Chambers-street: unveiled . . . . 5 March ,,
Dr. James A. Russell elected lord provost 6 Nov. ,,
Banquet to Mr. G. J. Goschen . . . 20 Nov. ,,
Fire at the house of Prof. Copeland, astronomer royal for Scotland, valuable instruments and books much damaged . . . . 8 March, 1892
Meeting of British Association (4th) . 3 Aug. ,,
Mass meeting opposing the Irish home rule bill, 17 March, 1893
Alexander Howland Smith sentenced to 12 months' imprisonment for forging literary documents of Burns and others . . . . . . 27 June, ,,
Wedding of the duke and duchess of York; festive demonstrations . . . . . . 6 July, ,,
Congress of the British Institute of Public Health; the lord provost and the lord mayors of London and Dublin present . . . . . 27 July, ,,

Visit of the duke and duchess of York, 2 Oct; he receives the freedom of the city and wedding gifts . . . . 3 Oct. 1893
Great speech of the earl of Rosebery, the premier, 17 March, 1894
Death of John Stuart Blackie, prof. of Greek at the university; aged 86, 2 Mar.; public funeral 6 March, 1895
New royal observatory on Blackpool hill, with collection of instruments from the earl of Crawford's Dun Echt observatory, opened by lord Balfour of Burleigh, the earl of Crawford, sir Robert Ball, and others present . . . . 7 April, 1896
Address to the czar on his way to Balmoral 22 Sept. ,,
Speech of lord Rosebery on the eastern question, and his resignation of leadership of the Liberals 9 Oct. ,,
Lord Rosebery opens the first of four public halls and free libraries, erected by a bequest of Mr. Thomas Nelson, publisher . . . . 10 May 1897
The new North-bridge (steel) opened by the lord provost, sir A. M'Donald . . . . 15 Sept. ,,
The M'Ewan hall presented to the university of Edinburgh by Mr. W. M'Ewan, M.P.; opened by Mr. A. J. Balfour . . . . . . 3 Dec. ,,
Lords Wolseley and Lister presented with the freedom of the city . . . . . 15 June, 1898
Mr. John Findlay, philanthropist, dies . 16 Oct. ,,
Lords Dufferin and Kitchener presented with the freedom of the city . . . . . 29 Nov. ,,
The prince of Wales, the president, visits the Highland and agricultural society's show, and receives the freedom of the city . . . . 5, 6 July, 1899
Lord Dufferin elected lord rector of the university 4 Nov. ,,
Mr. T. Aitken gives 40,000*l.* to the royal infirmary Jan. 1900
Death of sir Thomas Grainger-Stewart, eminent physician, aged 63 . . . . . . 3 Feb. ,,
Princess Henry of Battenberg opens the new pavilion of the royal infirmary . . . 26 Oct. ,,
Prof. Peter G. Tait, an eminent scientist, dies, aged 70 . . . . 4 July, 1901
Physiological laboratory, in memory of prof. Hughes Bennett, at the university, opened, 20 July ,,
Lord Rosebery opens a horticultural show, 11 Sept. ,,
Mr. Chamberlain in a speech upheld the conduct of the war in S. Africa, and protested against foreign slanders of the army . . . . 25 Oct. ,,
Mr. David McCosh bequeathed 50,000*l.* to the royal infirmary, and the rest of his estate to other charities; Mr. J. Murdoch nearly 70,000*l.* to indigent bachelors and widowers . . Dec. ,,
Mr. J. A. Molleson, bequeaths 17,500*l.* to charities, and the residue of his estate, valued 130,463*l.*, after certain legacies, to the Edinburgh infirmary, reported . . . . 7 March, 1902
Prof. Ivison Macadam and Mr. Jas. Forbes, student, shot by Daniel McClinton in the royal college of surgeons, 24 June; McClinton found guilty of culpable homicide and sentenced to life imprisonment . . . . 18 Sept. ,,
Colonial premiers presented with the freedom of the city, &c. . . . . . . 26 July ,,
Indian troops entertained by the city, 30 July—1 Aug. ,,
Messrs. Dobson, Molle & Co., stationers and printers, premises burnt, a fireman killed, estimated damage 30,000*l* . . . . 20 Aug. ,,
The king and queen visit the city 11 May; hold a court at Holyrood, 12 May; open the Colinton hospital . . . . 13 May, 1903

EDINBURGH, Bishopric of, was created by Charles I. when in Scotland in 1633; and William Forbes, minister of Edinburgh, first bishop. The king allotted the parishes of the shires of Edinburgh, Linlithgow, Haddington, and a part of Berwick and of Stirlingshire, to compose the see. The sixth and last prelate was Alexander Ross, who was ejected on the abolition of episcopacy, at the period of the revolution, in 1689. Edinburgh became a post-revolution bishopric in 1720; see *Bishops*.

EDINBURGH, Duke of, Alfred Ernest, second son of late queen Victoria, born 6 Aug. 1844, created duke of Edinburgh and earl of Kent 24 May, 1866, with an annuity of 15,000*l.*; this annuity he resigned on becoming grand duke of Saxe-Coburg-Gotha, announced Dec. 1893.

The duke was married to Marie Alexandrovna, the grand duchess of Russia, 23 Jan. 1874. [The queen was empowered by parliament, 5 Aug. 1873, to grant an additional annuity of 10,000*l.* to the duke on his marriage, and an annuity of 6,000*l.* to the grand duchess if she should survive the duke.] For biography and issue, see *England*, Royal Family; and Saxe-Coburg-Gotha, 1893. He died 6 Feb. 1899.

EDINBURGH REVIEW (by Francis Jeffrey, rev. Sydney Smith, Henry Brougham, and other whigs) published first on 10 Oct. 1802; editors: Sydney Smith (first three numbers); Jeffrey, 1803; Macvey Napier, 1829; Wm. Empson, 1847; sir George Cornewall Lewis, 1852; Henry Reeve, 1855; died, aged 82, 21 Oct. 1895; his "Life and Correspondence" published, Sept. 1898.

EDINBURGH UNIVERSITY. A college was commenced by the town council of Edinburgh, in 1581, for which queen Mary had given the site of ancient religious houses, and Robert Reid, bishop of Orkney, the funds in 1558. The university was chartered 14 April, 1582. On 24 Oct. 1582 the university was chartered by James VI., afterwards James I. of England. The first principal was appointed in 1585. The foundation-stone of the new buildings was laid by Francis, lord Napier, grandmaster of the masons of Scotland, 16 Nov. 1789. The constitution of the university was modified by act of parliament in 1858. In 1845, the library contained upwards of 80,000 volumes, besides numerous curious and rare MSS. and documents. Dr. Lyon Playfair elected the first M.P. for Edinburgh and St. Andrew's universities in conformity with the act of 1868, 4 Dec. 1868. Great movement to extend the university; meeting in London: large subscriptions, 7 Dec. 1874. The tercentenary of the university was celebrated by a distinguished assembly, 16–18 April, 1884. Students' union formed to promote recreation, discussion, comfort, &c. Fancy fair opened for its support by the marquis of Lorne, 30 Nov. 1886. Miss Jane Jeffrey, of Portobello, bequeaths 5,000*l.* for scholarships, announced Nov. 1887. University gathering to promote the University extension scheme, 24 Sept. *et seq.* 1889. Mr. A. J. Balfour, M.P., elected chancellor of the university, 30 Oct. 1891. Mr. G. J. Goschen's address (on Imagination) as lord rector, 19 Nov. 1891; lord Balfour of Burleigh elected lord rector; 7 Nov. 1896; sir Robert Finlay, att.-gen., elected lord rector 1 Nov. 1902.

Sir Wm. Fraser bequeaths 25,000*l.* to found a chair of Ancient History and Palæography, and about 38,000*l.* for other purposes; he died, 13 March, 1898.

EDLINGHAM BURGLARY, see *Trials*, Nov. 1888.

EDMUNDS' CASE, see under *Patents*.

EDOM, see *Idumæa*.

EDUCATION, the art of developing the physical, intellectual, and moral faculties of man, has occupied the greatest minds in all ages: Socrates, Plato, Aristotle, Cicero, Quintilian, Bacon, Milton, Locke, Rousseau, &c. In England the earliest schools for the lower classes were those attached to the monasteries; for the higher classes halls and colleges were gradually founded; see *Arts*, *Colleges*,

Schools, Oxford, Cambridge, Endowed Schools, Ascham Society, Technical and Physical Education, &c.

William of Wykeham planted the school at Winchester, whence arose his colleges at that place and Oxford 1373
Eton college founded by Henry VI. 1443
After the reformation, education was greatly promoted, and many grammar schools were erected and endowed by Edward VI. and Elizabeth . 1535-65
Christ's hospital, the bluecoat school, established 1553
Westminster school founded by Elizabeth . . 1560
Foundation of Rugby school by Lawrence Sheriff, 1567; of Harrow school by John Lyon . . 1571
The Charterhouse founded by Thomas Sutton . 1611
Many charity schools founded in opposition to Romish ones . . . . about 1687
Parish schools appointed by the parliament of Scotland 1697
Queen Anne, a zealous friend of education, founded the Greycoat school, Westminster, and cordially supported parochial charity schools (one established at St. Margaret's, Westminster, 1688) . 1698
Nearly 2,000 of these schools established in Great Britain and Ireland, principally by the instrumentality of the Society for the Promotion of Christian Knowledge 1698-1741
Robert Raikes set up *Sunday schools* . . about 1781
In 1833 there were 16,828 of these schools, with 1,548,890 scholars.
Joseph Lancaster, a young Quaker, began to instruct the children of the poor 1796
He had 90 pupils before he was 18 years old, and 1000 pupils in 1798
National education greatly promoted in the French empire by Napoleon, ably assisted by M. Cuvier, the eminent naturalist . . . . . 1802 *et seq.*
Sunday School Union formed 1802
To provide teachers, Lancaster invented the monitorial system. In consequence of his exertions the present British and Foreign School Society was founded with the name of the "Royal Lancasterian Institution," &c. 1805
This, being unexclusive, was followed by the institution of the Church of England "National Society for Educating the Poor," on Dr. Bell's system 1811
Infant schools began . . . . . . about 1815
The Charity commission, appointed at the instance of Mr. (afterwards lord) Brougham, published their reports on education, in 37 volumes folio, 1819-40
Irish national school system (to accommodate both Roman Catholics and Protestants) organised mainly by archbishop Whately and the Roman Catholic archbishop Murray 1831
City of London School, Honey-lane, opened . . 1834
The Home and Colonial School Society was instituted 1836
In 1834, the government began ANNUAL GRANTS (the first 20,000*l.*), which continued till the committee of the Privy Council on education was constituted for the distribution of the money . 1839
The Voluntary School Society and the Congregational Board of Education formed . . about 1843
Ragged School Union established 1844
Educational Times, monthly, established . Oct. 1847
Out of a population of 17,927,609, there were 2,466,481 day scholars 1851
A great educational conference took place at Willis's rooms, the prince consort in the chair, 22-24 June, 1857
The Industrial Schools act passed in . . . ,,
Middle class examinations from the university of Oxford began, June, 1858. The examiners granted the degree of A.A. to many persons at Liverpool, Leeds, &c.; similar examinations from Cambridge took place in the autumn, and are to be continued 1858
Four establishments for international education in England, France, Germany, and Italy proposed; the idea is attributed to Mr. Cobden and M. Michel Chevalier 1862
Report of commissioners on popular education (appointed 1858), published 18 March, 1861, led to the minute of the committee of the Privy Council on education, establishing a revised code of regulations; Mr. Lowe's, adopted 21 July, 1861, to come into operation, after 31 March, 1862. It decreed regular examinations of the pupils, payment by results, evening schools for adults, and other changes, which raised a storm of opposition from the clergy and school masters. The subject was much discussed in parliament (25, 28 March, 1862); but eventually a compromise was effected, 5 May, 1862
Official instructions for the administration of the revised code issued . . . . . . Sept. ,,
"*Conscience clause*," founded on the Endowed Schools act, March, 1860, introduced by the committee of Council on education for parishes where only one school is required. It provided for the admission of children of dissenters, and exempted them from religious teaching, and attendance at public worship . . . . Nov. 1863
(Report, 10 June, 1865.)
It has been much opposed by the clergy ever since, and created much controversy in . . . 1866-7
College and Public School Commission report, signed . . . . 16 Feb. 1864
Royal Commission appointed, to inquire into the state of education in Scotland. First meeting at Edinburgh . . . . 14 Nov. ,,
Miss (aft. baroness) Burdett-Coutts proposes the establishment of small village-schools, to be taught by "ambulatory" teachers . . Jan. 1865
Parliamentary committee appointed to inquire into the best mode of benefiting schools unassisted by the state . . . . 28 Feb. ,,
Training ship established for homeless boys of London; 50 boys placed there by Boys' Refuge committee. See *Chichester* . . . 18 Dec. 1866
Foundation of the London College of the International Education Society laid by the prince of Wales . . . . 10 July, 1867
Committee appointed at a meeting for establishment of higher *schools for middle classes* in London, by means of funds of lapsed charities, &c., 7 Nov.; nearly 28,000*l.* subscribed by end of Dec. 1865; 51,349*l.* received . . . . Oct. 1866
The subscribers incorporated by charter; their first school opened by lord mayor and others in Bath-street, St. Luke's, 1866; great prosperity reported at the annual meeting . . . . 18 March, 1867
Resolutions moved in the lords by earl Russell (asserting that every child has a right to education, and recommending appointment of a cabinet minister of education), withdrawn . . 2 Dec. ,,
Important report of schools inquiry commissioners signed . . . . 2 Dec. ,,
Conference at Manchester recommend compulsory education, to be paid for by rates . 15 Jan. 1868
Public Schools bill brought into the commons 7 Feb. ,,
Public Elementary Education bill brought into the lords by duke of Marlborough, 24 March; withdrawn . . . . 18 May, ,,
Mr. (aft. sir Joseph) Whitworth's offer to found 30 scholarships of annual value of 100*l.* each, for instruction of young men in mechanics, &c., 18 March, accepted by the lords of the council 27 Mar. ,,
Foundation of the first new building for a middle class school in London laid by the lord mayor, Lawrence (*very successful*, 1873) . . . 15 Dec. ,,
Public Schools act (modifying the government of Eton, Winchester, Westminster, Charterhouse, Harrow, Rugby, and Shrewsbury schools) passed 31 July, 1868; amendment acts . 9 Aug. 1869-70-73
New statutes for them issued . . Oct.—Nov. 1869
National Education League (advocating compulsory secular education by the state), first met at Birmingham (*see below*, 1877) . . . 12, 13 Oct. ,,
National Education Union for supplementing the present denominational system, first met at Manchester . . . . 3 Nov. ,,
Conference at the Society of Arts to reconcile the League and the Union . . . . . 7 Feb. 1870
Scientific instruction and advancement commission appointed . . . . 19 May, ,,
First "drill-review" of London charity schools, and others, at the Crystal Palace . . . 21 June, ,,
Elementary Education bill introduced by Mr. W. E. Forster, 17 Feb.; after much discussion, and opposition from secularists and some dissenters, it passed, and received the royal assent . 9 Aug. ,,
[Religious instruction with the parents' consent: reading in the Bible, without catechisms, or sectarian formularies, 1870.]

[By the compromise of 8 March, 1871, the reading of the Bible, with instruction in the principles of religion and morality suitable to children, was permitted.]

[The act was amended in 1872, 1873, and 1876.]

[Mr. Forster died, aged 67, 5 April, 1886; his statue on the Victoria embankment unveiled 1 Aug. 1890.]

10,000*l.* voted by the Christian Knowledge Society in aid of Church of England schools . 20 Oct. 1870

First election of Metropolitan school-board (*which see*) (lord Lawrence, chairman) . . 29 Nov. ,,

Regulations for school-boards issued . 21 Dec. ,,

New revised code discussed . . . March, 1871

London school-board education scheme proposed, 23 June, ,,

At the London school-board, after sharp discussion, the religious difficulty respecting payment for poor children at denominational schools settled for a year . . . . 2 Nov. ,,

Arrangements for erecting or adapting buildings for new schools made by London school-board, Dec. ,,

Conference of masters of grammar schools at Highgate . . . . 28 Dec. ,,

Mr. Dixon's and the nonconformists' censure on the Elementary Education act; negatived in the commons, 355-94 . . . . . 5 March, 1872

Scientific instruction: royal commission appointed, May, 1870; reported . . April, 1871, April, ,,

Education (Scotland) act passed . . 10 Aug. ,,

The London school-board determine to open separate schools for dirty unruly children . . 20 Nov. ,,

"Society for Organization of Academical Study," proposed by sir B. C. Brodie, Dr. Carpenter, Prof. Rolleston, and others at a meeting, 16 Nov. ,,

Irish University bill introduced by Mr. Gladstone, 13 Feb. 1873

First London board-school (at Whitechapel) opened, 12 July, ,,

College for northern counties at Knutsford; foundation laid . . . . 24 Sept. ,,

College for higher education of women, opened at Girton, *which see* . . . . . . Oct. ,,

Great meeting for religious denominational education at St. James's hall . . . . 6 Nov. ,,

Second Metropolitan school-board elected; religious party the strongest (Mr. (after. sir) Charles Reed, M.P. chairman) . . . . 27 Nov. ,,

The universities nominate a board for the examination of pupils from public schools . Dec. ,,

Mr. Dixon's compulsory attendance bill rejected (320-156) . . . . . . 1 July, 1874

Result of first university examination of 221 schools: Winchester, 34 certificates; Manchester, 27; Marlborough, 15; Eton, 13; Sherborne, 11; Wellington college, 10; Rugby, 6, &c.; Christ's Hospital and others, 1; published . . . Sept. ,,

London school-board occupy their new building on Victoria Embankment . . . . 30 Sept. ,,

Classes for cookery, laundry-work, and housewifery introduced, into board schools . . . 1875

New code of raised standards for schools issued, March, ,,

Newnham college at Cambridge for women opened, 18 Oct. ,,

First annual conference of teachers . . 14 Jan. 1876

Mr. Dixon's bill for universal school-boards and compulsory education rejected by the commons (281-260) . . . . April, ,,

Another Elementary Education act introduced by lord Sandon, 18 May; a clause permitting unnecessary school-boards to be suppressed, introduced by Mr. Pell, carried, 24 July; 3rd reading (119-46), 5 Aug. (considered reactionary); royal assent . . . . 15 Aug. ,,

International congress on education at Philadelphia, July, ,,

Third Metropolitan school board elected; majority against denominational school systems (sir Charles Reed, chairman) . . . . . 30 Nov. ,,

National Education League dissolved . 28 March, 1877

Election of school attendance committees under the new act . . . . . . April, ,,

Intermediate Education act for Ireland passed 16 Aug. 1878

Education act (Scotland) amended . 16 Aug. ,,

Revised code, 7 Feb. 1877; 2 April, 1878; April, 1879

161st metropolitan board school opened by sir Charles Reed, at Portland-town . 23 June, 1879

The Queen *v.* sir Charles Reed; the Queen's bench decide that the school board has power to borrow money . . . . 27 June, ,,

Fourth Metropolitan school board elected (sir Charles Reed, chairman) . . 27 Nov. ,,

Ascham Society (*which see*) formed 1880

Important decision respecting *school fees* and attendance, see *Trials* . . . . 27 June, 1881

Death of sir Charles Reed, 25 March; succeeded by Mr. Edward North Buxton . . . . ,,

Changes in the code; circular issued . . Aug. 1882

Education Society, formed in July, 1875, for examining and propounding the principles upon which the practice of education should be founded, by professor Alexander Bain, Dr. J. H. Gladstone, and others. Branches have been formed in Dublin, and other places.

Lord Aberdare Mr. W. E. Forster sir John Lubbock, and others form a committee to instruct electors of school board . . . 23 Oct. ,,

Fifth Metropolitan school board elected (old policy affirmed; E. N. Buxton, chairman) . 24 Nov. ,,

The Boys' Public Day school company founded, 5 Dec. 1882; first school opened . 12 Sept. 1883

Art for schools, proposed societies formed in London and the provinces . . . . . ,,

International Educational Conference at South Kensington opened . . . . . 4 Aug. 1884

New education code (much attacked) comes into operation, 3 April, 1884; revised instructions issued . . . . June, 1885

Dr. (after sir) Crichton Browne's report on over-pressure in primary and secondary schools, with Mr. Fitch's memorandum against it published Sept. 1884; denied after investigation report 16 July, ,,

H. T. Holland (after lord Knutsford) appointed vice-president of council . . about 25 Aug. ,,

Sixth Metropolitan school board elected, 2 Nov. (new economical policy), rev. J. R. Diggle elected chairman . . . . . . 3 Dec. ,,

New scheme for enforcing payment of fees stated to be inquisitorial and partially ineffectual Oct. 1886

About 30,000 elementary scholars entertained in Hyde Park, see *Jubilee* . . . . 22 June, 1887

Royal commission on elementary education in England and Wales, sir R. A. Cross (chairman), earl of Harrowby, Dr. Temple (bishop of London), cardinal Manning, Mr. A. J. Mundella, sir John Lubbock, sir F. Sandford, and others. First report issued 4 Sept. 1886. Final report Aug. 1888

Majority report for aiding voluntary schools from the rates and development of moral and religious education, June; opposite opinions reported by the minority . . . . July, ,,

The government declines to interfere with the settlement of 1870 . . . . . . Nov. ,,

School accommodation in the eleven divisions reported sufficient . . . . . . Oct. ,,

Seventh Metropolitan school board elected, 26 Nov.; rev. J. R. Diggle elected chairman . . 4 Dec. ,,

New code introducing many changes brought forward . . . . 19 March 1889

Committee on relieving children coming to school unfed, 2 Nov.: London Schools Dinner association formed, by combination of several societies, Dec. ,,

Bill for enforcing new education code, withdrawn, 22 July, 1889; new code with important changes brought forward by sir William Hart-Dyke, March; bill passed . . . . . 25 July, 1890

Number of voluntary schools largely increased since 1870 . . . . . reported April, 1891

Grant for free, or assisted education, 2,000,000*l.* annually, proposed by Mr. Göschen 23 April, ,,

A new Elementary Education act (reducing or abolishing school fees) passed 5 Aug., comes into operation . . . . 1 Sept. ,,

Eighth Metropolitan school board elected—moderates, 34; progressives, 193 . 26 Nov. ,,

Mr. Joseph R. Diggle re-elected chairman 3 Dec. ,,

Irish free education act passed . . 27 June, 1892

The City of London school for girls, founded by Mr. Wm. Ward's bequest of 20,000*l.*, in 1881;

buildings erected on the Victoria embankment; first stone laid . . . . . . 30 Nov. 1892
Departmental committee on secondary education appointed; Mr. A. H. Dyke Acland, chairman, Jan. 1893
Important circular respecting the school buildings regulating their area, ventilation, &c., issued 21 Jan. ,,
New education code issued . . 27 March, ,,
First meeting in the new board-room, Victoria embankment . . . . . . 28 Sept. ,,
[Protest against government interference.]
Important conference at Oxford to promote secondary education . . . . . 10–11 Oct. ,,
A majority of the committee recommends the adherence to biblical teaching; "Christian religion and morality" . . . . Dec. ,,
Royal commission on secondary education appointed; Mr. J. Bryce, M.P., chairman, sir J. T. Hibbert, M.P., prof. Jebb, M.P., lady Frederick Cavendish, E. C. Maclure, dean of Manchester, sir Henry Roscoe, M.P., Mrs. Henry Sidgwick and others . . . . about 1 March, 1894
Association of school boards of England and Wales; first annual meeting held in London; the rev. E. C. Maclure, dean of Manchester, president . . . . 3 April, ,,
School boards: England, 2,079; Wales, 313; April, ,,
In consequence of charges against some teachers, a circular from the school board to teachers, respecting instruction in the *Christian* religion, with suggestions for maintaining the provisions of the education act of 1870, and the *compromise* of 1871, with indulgence to non-assenting teachers, was issued, 13 April; much controversy followed . . . . . April, *et seq.* ,,
Ninth Metropolitan school board elected: moderates (Mr. Diggle's party), 29; progressives (various opinions), 26 . . . 22 Nov. ,,
Annual report; metropolitan school board; 31 March; 430 schools; 488,039 scholars; 1,220 head teachers, and 6,974 assistants; total expenditure, 2,033,565*l.*; reported . . . Nov. ,,
Lord George Hamilton elected chairman by the moderates, 6 Dec.; resigned, 3 Oct. 1895 (succeeded by the marquis of Londonderry, 31 Oct. 1895).
Death of Miss Frances Mary Buss, aged 67; promoter of female education . . . . 24 Dec. ,,
A committee to consider the condition of the voluntary schools appointed by the archbishops of Canterbury and York; viscount Cross, chairman, bishop of London, dean Gregory, and others, Nov., 1893; report issued; complaint of pressure by the education department and the great need of money support . . . Jan. 1895
(A similar appeal set forth by the R. C. clergy, Jan. ,,
Death of Mr. Thos. Twining of Twickenham, eminent supporter of education, aged 88 16 Feb. ,,
New revised code for schools, presented to parliament . . . . 27 Feb. ,,
Disputes respecting religious teaching in the London school board . . . . Oct. ,,
Report of the commission on secondary education, with recommendations issued . . 31 Oct. ,,
Sir John Gorst's education (England and Wales) bill read first time, 31 March, 1896 (decentralizing) nonconformist manifesto against the bill, issued, 18 April; 1,238 amendments having been proposed, the bill was withdrawn . 22 June 1896
School boards in England and Wales, 2,487, 1 April ,,
Estimated sum required for 1896–7, 1,800,926; rate, 12·31*d.* . . . . . . 25 June, ,,
Annual report: metropolitan school board (the number of committees and their members reduced) 448 schools; 511,566 scholars; 10,703 teachers; total expenditure, 2,337,156*l.*—reported, *Times* . . . . . . 2 Oct. ,,
Voluntary schools (aid grant) bill (much opposed in the commons), royal assent . 8 April 1897
The Act of 1870 amended by act passed; 3 June, ,,
Vote of 7,306,910*l.* for public education (England and Wales), an increase of 339,000*l.* on 1896, passed . . . . 17 June, ,,
Imperial education congress at the exhibition, Earl's Court, lord Loch, chairman 12–15 July 1897
Report of Messrs. Sadler and J. W. Edwards on elementary education (progress and results) since 1833, issued, ... Aug. ,,
Voluntary schools associations formed . Aug. ,,
Annual report: metropolitan school board, 459 schools; 512,025 scholars; 11,004 teachers; grant 423,657*l.*—*Times* . . . . 1 Sept. ,,
Elementary education act, amendment of section 97, passed . . . . 3 June ,,
"Studies in board schools" by Chas. Morley, published, autumn . . . . . . ,,
Tenth Metropolitan school board elected: 29 progressives, 21 moderates, Mr. J. R. Diggle, *not elected* . . . . 25 Nov. ,,
Lord Reay and Mr. Lyulph Stanley elected chairman and vice-chairman . . . . 2 Dec. ,,
Revised education code, issued . . March, 1898
School boards: England, 2,165; Wales, 337, April, ,,
Vote of 8,520,175*l.* for public education (England and Wales) passed . . . . . 17 June, ,,
London county council to be responsible for science and art in co. of London, announced 17 Feb. 1899
Invalid and crippled children's schools started, one in Tavistock place, London, opened Feb. ,,
New code of regulations issued . . . March ,,
Education of children (half-timers) act passed 13 July ,,
Board of education act passed . . . 9 Aug. ,
Elementary education (defective and epileptic children) act passed . . . . . Aug. ,,
Committee of council on education (England and Wales) issue their report for 1898–99: see *Times*, 31 Oct. ,,
The proposal to provide meals for underfed children at the charge of the ratepayers rejected, 35–14, 30 Nov. ,,
English education exhibition at the imperial institute opened by the prince of Wales, the duke of Devonshire presiding . . . . 5 Jan. 1900
Report of the sub-committee (L.S.B.) on underfed children, their recommendations adopted 1 March ,,
New board of education, under the act of 1899, the duke of Devonshire appointed president, sir George Kekewich, secretary . . 30 March ,,
New education code issued . . . . May ,,
London school board: receipts for 1899–1900, 2,795,000*l.*; expenditure, 2,965,000*l.*; estimated receipts for 1900–1901, 2,933,000*l.*; expenditure, 2,938,000*l.* . . . . 5 July ,,
Education act and an elementary education act passed . . . . 8 Aug. ,,
Education rate London 14*d.* in the pound, increased expenditure . . . . . Oct. ,,
Eleventh Metropolitan school board elected (28 progressives, 25 moderates, and 2 Roman catholics) 29 Nov. ,,
Lord Reay and Mr. L. Stanley re-elected chairman and vice-chairman . . . . 6 Dec. ,,
"Regina *v.* Cockerton," Messrs. justices Wills and Kennedy declare it illegal for school boards to provide at the ratepayers' expense science and art classes, and the education of adults in evening continuation schools [appeal dismissed with costs, 1 April, 1901] . . . . . 20 Dec. ,,
Reports issued by the board of education on continental systems of technical and commercial education, 1899, see *Times* . . . 25 Dec. ,,
School boards: England and Wales, in 1900, 5691.
Revised education code, dealing with higher elementary schools, issued . . . . April, 1901
Vote of 9,747,716*l.* for England and Wales passed 30 July ,,
Education bill (No. 2) passed . . . 9 Aug. ,,
London evening continuation schools, 395 schools opened; 146,971 pupils, 19th session, 1900–1901.
Sir John Gorst made president of the British association's new section of educational science, early Sept. ,,
Annual report, London school board (902,528 scholars; 3,122,762*l.*) 1901–2, issued 16 Dec.

Education bill, powers and duties of school boards and control of all secular instruction transferred to local authorities; religious training to be according to a parent's faith; read 2nd time, commons (402–165), 8 May; and 7th clause *re* managers, &c., passed, after long debates (220–98), 7 Aug. 1902

Vote of 9,921,852*l.* passed.

London school board: expenditure, 3,122,762, 1900–1; 887,301 children; estimated expenditure, 3,250,000*l.*, 1902–03; reported . 12 June ,,

Miss Rosamund Davenport-Hill, 18 years on the London school board, died, aged 77 . 5 Aug. ,,

Vacation school at the Passmore Edwards settlement, London, very successful . . . Aug. ,,

London School board expenditure, 1901–2, 3,118,500*l.* . . . . 30 Oct. ,,

Education bill passed commons, 152 majority, 3 Dec.; royal assent . . . . . 18 Dec. ,,

Agitation by nonconformists against payment of education rates; plan of "passive resistance" started, 1903. See *Passive Resistance*.

Meeting of English Church union to discuss the Education act . . . . . . 20 Jan. 1903

Carnegie trustees issue regulations for the endowment of post-graduate study and research by means of scholarships, fellowships, and grants, mid Feb. ,,

Circular issued by Board of Education to local authorities to the effect that wherever possible April 1 be appointed as the day on which the new Education act comes into operation, early March, ,,

Report of the Royal Commission on University Education in Ireland issued . . 11 March, ,,

London Education bill, first reading (commons), 7 April, ,,

Great demonstration in Hyde park against London Education bill . . . . . 23 May, ,,

Another in St. James's hall, speech by sir H. Campbell-Bannerman; letter from Mrs. Humphry Ward read, protesting against the bill . 11 June, ,,

Conference on matters of special interest to universities throughout the empire held in London, 10 July, ,,

Great Free Church meeting at the Royal Albert hall to protest against the bill . . . 11 July, ,,

Regulations for the instruction and training of pupil-teachers and students in training colleges; practically a new scheme for training pupil-teachers, issued by Board of Education, mid-July, ,,

Death of sir Joshua Fitch, eminent educationalist, 31 years H.M. inspector of schools, aged 79, 14 July, ,,

London Education bill read the third time, 228—118, 22 July; royal assent . . . . . 14 Aug. ,,

London School board, expenditure 1902–3, 3,250,486*l.*

The grant for Public Education in Great Britain, in 1851, was 150,000*l.*; 1856, 451,213*l.*; 1860, 798,167*l.*; 1861, 803,794*l.*; 1864, 705,404*l.*; 1867, 705,865*l.* England, 1872, 1,554,560*l.*; 1877, 1,910,000*l.*; 1882, 2,749,863*l.*: 1884, 3,016,167*l.* For Ireland, 1860, 270,722*l.*; 1861, 285,377*l.*; 1863, 316,770*l.* From 1839 to 1860, 3,655,067*l.* were granted for education. The grant for education, science, and art, in 1861, was 1,358,996*l.*; for 1867-8, 1,487,554*l.*; 1874-5, 2,228,470*l.*, (in addition, 3,060,566*l.*, were locally raised); 1876-7, England, 707,055*l.*; Scotland, 438,227*l.*; Ireland, 649,949*l.*; for year 1876-7 (United Kingdom), 3,349,397*l.*; 1879-80 (Great Britain), 2,854,938*l.*; United Kingdom, 1880-1, 3,730,329*l.*; 1882-3, 3,955,737*l.*; 1884-5, 4,410,195*l.*; 1886-7, 4,780,945*l.*; 1888-9, 5,042,614*l.*; 1889-90, 5,098,304*l.*; 1890-1, 5,244,447*l.*; 1891-2, 6,216,956*l.*; 1892-3, 7,051,884*l.*; 1893-4, 8,409,972*l.*; 1896–7, 9,538,029*l.*; 1898, 8,567,746*l.*; 1899, 8,753,986*l.*; 1900, 9,747,716*l.*

Primary schools in Great Britain: in 1854, 3825; in 1860, 7272; in 1870, 10,949; in 1877, 18,118; in 1879, 20,169; in 1880, 20,670; in 1881, 21,136; in 1882, 21,362; in 1883, 21,630; 1884, 21,892; 1885, 21,976; 1886, 22,114; 1887, 22,265; 1888, 22,326; 1889, 22,426; 1890, 22,495; 1893, 22,581; 1896, 22,931; 1900, 23,204; 1901, 23,257.

Annual grant for primary schools in Great Britain: in 1861, 813,442*l.*; in 1865, 636,806*l.*; in 1870, 840,336*l.*; in 1878, 2,463,283*l.*; in 1879, 2,732,067*l.*; in 1880, 2,854,067*l.*; 1881, 2,978,224*l.*; 1882, 3,101,028*l.*; 1883, 3,247,725*l.*; 1884, 3,403,415*l.*; 1885, 3,664,174*l.*; 1886, 3,802,009*l.*; 1887, 3,945,038*l.*; 1888, 4,011,464*l.*; 1889, 4,167,884*l.*; 1890, 4,259,080*l.*; 1891, 4,392,126*l.*; 1894, 7,368,056*l.*; 1896–7, 8,406,997*l.*; 1900, 10,049,398*l.*; 1901, 10,241,532*l.*; 1902, 10,550,591*l.*

Metropolitan school board children on the rolls: 1871, 1,117; 1873, 50,606; 1876, 146,031; 1878 (Christmas), 207,289; 1883, 293,811; 1888, 420,914; 1890, 443,143; 1893, 477,689; 1894, 488,038; 1895, 832,966; 1896, 839,737; 1897, 609,026; 1899, 888,466; 1902, 887,301.

ÉGALITÉ (*Equality*), see *Orleans*.

EGGS. The duty on imported eggs was repealed in 1860, whereby the revenue lost about 20,000*l.* a year. Number imported into Great Britain. *Thousands*, 1879, 766,433; 1887, 1,090,088; 1890, 1,233,730; 1893, 1,322,102; 1898, 1,730,952; 1900, 2,025,849; 1901, 2,048,612; 1902, 18,966,795. Great quantities are now brought from Italy by the St. Gothard railway.

EGLINTOUN TOURNAMENT, see *Tournament*.

EGYPT,* N.E. Africa, the earliest known seat of civilization, the hieroglyphic and Coptic Kemi, Hebrew Mazor (Lower Egypt), Mizraim (Upper and Lower Egypt), Greek name Egypt, Arabic for all Egypt Misr or Masr. Population, 1882, about 6,806,381; 1897, about 9,700,000.

For our present knowledge of the early history of Egypt we are almost wholly indebted to discoveries in the nineteenth century, and to the interpretation of monumental inscriptions, and the papyri found in the tombs. The most recent investigators are Brugsch, Maspero, Lepsius, De Rougé, Mariette, Chabas, Lieblein, Birch, Naville, Le Page, Renouf, and Petrie, with some others; A. Erman's "Egyptian Grammar," English translation, by J. H. Breasted, published about July, 1894; "History of Egypt," by W. M. Flinders Petrie, vol. I. 1894; E. A. Wallis Budge's "First steps in Egyptian for beginners," 1896; "History of Egypt under Roman rule," by J. G. Milne, edited by prof. Flinders Petrie, vol. 5 pub. 1899; vol. 7, "Under the Ptolomies," by Dr. Mahaffy, pub. 1899; see *Egypt exploration Fund and Rosetta stone, &c.*

Manetho a high-priest of On or Heliopolis in the second century B.C., at the request of king Ptolemy Philadelphus, wrote a history of Egypt, divided into 30 dynasties from Menes to the Persian conquests; of his work lists only have been preserved, by Julius Africanus, a writer who lived about 300 A.D. Eusebius died about 340, Georgius Syncellus, 800.

The fabulous god kings, including the sun god, Osiris god of Hades, and Isis his wife, Typhon, Horus the last, were said to have reigned 13,900 years, the demi-gods and manes 4,000 years. See *Pharaoh*.

The following table of Dynasties, including the more important kings, is derived from various sources. the names and dates vary. B. stands for Brugsch, and M. for Mariette.

I. Thinite (from This, near Abydus) M. 5004; B. 4400 B.C.

Mena or Menes; first known king and law-giver, founder of Memphis. M. 5004; B. 4455. His tomb and remains, etc., discovered at N'gada by M. de Morgan in the spring of 1897, and placed in the museum at Gizeh. Tola or Athothis—Ouenephes I., conjectured to have built the Steppe pyramid of Sakkarah.

II. Memphite. M. 4751; B. 4133.

* Three magnificent works on Egypt have been published: in France (commenced by Napoleon, and the savans who accompanied him to Egypt), *Description de l'Egypte*, 1809-22; in Italy, Rosellini's *Monumenti dell' Egitto*, 1832-44; and in Prussia, K. R. Lepsius' *Denkmäler aus Ægypten*, 1848-56. All these are in the Library of the Royal Institution of Great Britain, London.

Kakaoo or Kaiechos. The worship of Apis the bull established at Memphis. B. 4100.
III. Memphite (monumental history properly begins). M. 4449; B. 3966.
Seneferoo—soldier, architect and patron of literature and art.
IV. Memphite. M. 4235; B. 3733.
Shoofoo or Khufa, the Cheops of Herodotus, built the great pyramid of Geezeh. M. 4235; B. 3733. The great limestone rock at the foot of the Libyan mountains was converted into a man-headed lion, termed by the Greeks Sphinx. Khafra built the second Gizeh pyramid. B. 3666. Menkaura (Mycerinus III.). B. 3633. High state of civilization and art, and the vast cemetery of Memphis erected. The book or ritual of the dead (papyri) found in tombs.
V. Memphite. M. 3951; B. 3566.
Raencoser. B. 3433. Katkara. B. 3366. Unas truncated pyramid near Sakkárah built. B. 3333.
VI. Memphite (history nearly a blank to the 11th dynasty). M. 3703; B. 3300.
Pepi I.—powerful—long reign. B. 3233. Romantic story of queen Nitocris in Herodotus.
VII. Memphite. B. 3100.
Petty kings.
VIII. Memphite.
IX. Heracleopolite. M. 3358.
X. Heracleopolite. M. 3249.
XI. Theban. M. 3064.
Sankhkara, expedition to Ophir and Punt (S. Arabia?). B. 2500.
XII. Theban (Egypt very prosperous). B. 2466.
Amenemhat I. M. 3064; B. 2466.
Osirtasen I. (obelisk of On or Heliopolis erected).
Osirtasen II. (memorial temple discovered in 1889).
Osirtasen III., important national works, excavated the lake Moeris and made the labyrinth and the Nilometer. B. 2300.
XIII. Theban. M. 2851; B. 2233.
Sebekhotep, name of several kings.
XIV. Xoite. M. 2398.
XV. Hyksos or Shepherd kings. M. 2214.
Invaders from Asia take Memphis and settle in Lower Egypt.
XVI. Hyksos or Shepherd kings.
XVII. Hyksos or Shepherd kings.
Nub—arrival of Joseph. B. 1750.
Dynasties XIII.—XVII. history very obscure; probably Theban kings reigned in southern, while the Hyksos reigned in Lower Egypt.
XVIII. Theban. M. 1703; B. 1700.
Achmes I. conquers the Hyksos. M. 1703; B. 1700 Amenhotep I. B. 1666. Thothmes I. B. 1633. Thothmes II. and Hatasoo, sister. B. 1600. Thothmes III., great king, victor in western Asia, &c., his exploits recorded in his temple at Karnak. B. 1600. Amenhotep II. B. 1566. Thothmes IV. B. 1533. Amenhotep III. victorious in Ethiopia; the Colossi or vocal Memnon bear his name. B. 1500. Amenhotep IV. introduced Semetic worship. Two or three heretical successors. Haremhebi or Horus restores the old worship. See *Thebes*, 1898.
XIX. Theban. M. 1462; B. 1400.
Rameses I. M. 1462; B. 1400. Seti or Sethos (Menetah I.) victorious in Asia; made first canal from the Red sea to the Nile; many monuments of him at Karnak, &c. B. 1333. Rameses II. son, the legendary Sesostris, took Salem, conquered Ethiopia, and set up a fleet, his epoch about 1322. Maneptah son, probably the Pharoah of the Exodus, 1300; Seli II. and two or three unimportant kings.
XX. Theban. M. 1288; B. 1200.
Rameses III. (Rhampsinitus of Herodotus) victorious, cultivated navigation and commerce. M. 1288; B. 1200. Inglorious line of kings named Rameses.
XXI. Tanite. M. 1110; B. 1100.
History obscure—Hirhor, high priest of Amen, probably first of priest kings—Assyrian governors.
XXII. Bubasite. M. 980; B. 966. Shashank or Sheshonk I., Shishak, 1 *Kings* XIV., 25–28.
XXIII. Tanite, probably only three petty kings. M. 810; B. 766.
XXIV. Saite. M. 721; B. 733.
Bocchoris (Bokenranef), taken prisoner by Sabaco, king of Ethiopia, and burnt alive. During the last three dynasties, the Ethiopians appear to have ruled in the south.
XXV. Karnak. Ethiopian. M. 715; B. 700.
Shabat or Sabaco. M. 715; B. 700. Takaraka or Tirhakah (2 *Kings* XIX. 9). B. 693. Egypt frequently invaded by the Assyrians; subdued and divided into 12 governments.
XXVI. Saite. M. 665; B. 666.
Psammetichus I. (Greek), one of the governors under the Assyrians, restored the monarchy and revived art. M. 665; B. 666. Necho II. son, attempted the construction of a canal across the Isthmus of Suez, defeated Josiah king of Judah at Megiddo (II. *Kings* xxiii. 29); defeated by Nebuchadnezzar at Carchemish, 612. Psammetichus II.; inglorious. B. 596. Uahbra or Hophra (*Jer.* xliv. 30) son; went to help Zedekiah, but deserted him. B. 591. Apries loses the conquests and is strangled by Amasis, who has a long prosperous reign and increased intercourse with the Greeks. B. 572. Psammetichus III. son (defeated by Cambyses, son of Cyrus, king of Persia). B. 528.
XXVII. Persian. M. 527; B. 527.
Cambyses, conquers Egypt; his army perished in an expedition against Ethiopia. M. 527; B. 527. Darius I. Hystaspes, greatly favoured Egypt, 521. Xerxes I. severe (Egyptian revolt subdued), 486. Artaxerxes I. Longimanus (another revolt), 465. Darius II. Nothus, 424. Egypt regained its independence by Armyrtæus, 424.
XXVIII. Saite. M. 406.
Armyrtæus, 406.
XXIX. Mendesian. M. 399; B. 399.
Nepherches and Achoris maintain Greek alliance.
XXX. Sebennyte. M. 378; B. 378.
Nectanebes I. Nectanebes II. conquered by Artaxerxes Ochus, king of Persia.
XXXI. Persia 340.
Darius III. Codomanus—defeated by Alexander the Great and killed.

Alexander conquered Egypt and founded Alexandria, 332
The empire divided, 323. One of Alexander's generals, Ptolemy I. (the son of Lagus) Soter became king of Egypt, 323.
Ptolemy II. Philadelphus (with his father) 285; alone [the museum of Alexandria founded; the Septuagint version of the Hebrew Scriptures made; the Pharos completed] 283–247
Ambassadors first sent to Rome 269
Ptolemy III. Euergetes, 247; overruns Syria, and returns laden with spoils 246
Ptolemy IV. Philopator . . . . . Nov. 222
Battle of Raphia; Ptolemy defeats Antiochus, king of Syria 217
Ptolemy V. Epiphanes . . . . . Nov. 205
Embassy to Rome 200
Ptolemy VI. Philometor . . . . . Oct. 181
At the death of Philometor, his brother Physcon (Ptolemy VII. Euergetes) marries his queen, and on the day of his nuptials murders the infant son of Philometor in its mother's arms . Nov. 146
His subjects, wearied by his cruelties and crimes, compel him to flee 130
He defeats the Egyptians and recovers his throne, 128; dies 117
Ptolemy VIII. Soter II. and Cleopatra his mother, ,,
Alexander I. and Cleopatra 107
Ptolemy VIII. restored 89
Revolt in Upper Egypt; Thebes destroyed after a siege of three years (*Diod. Siculus*) 82
Alexander II. and Cleopatra I. 81
Ptolemy IX. Auletes 80
Berenice and Tryphæna 58
Auletes restored, 55: leaves his kingdom to Ptolemy and Cleopatra 51
During a civil war between Ptolemy and Cleopatra II., Alexandria is besieged by Cæsar, and the library nearly destroyed by fire (*Blair*) . . . 47
Cæsar defeats the king, who, in crossing the Nile, is drowned; and the younger Ptolemy and Cleopatra reign 46
Cleopatra poisons her brother, and reigns alone . 43
She appears before Marc Antony, to answer for this crime; fascinated by her beauty, he follows her into Egypt 41
Cleopatra in Syria 36
Antony defeated by Octavius Cæsar at the battle of Actium (*Blair*) . . . . . . 2 Sept. 31
Octavius enters Egypt; Antony and Cleopatra kill themselves; and the kingdom becomes a Roman province . . . . Sept. 30

Egypt visited by Adrian, 122; by Severus . A.D. 200
Monachism begun in Egypt by Antony 305
Destruction of the temple and worship of Serapis, 389
Egypt conquered by Chosroes II. of Persia . . . 616
Invasion of the Saracens under Amrou . June, 638
Conquest of Alexandria . . . . 22 Dec. 640
Cairo founded by the Saracens 969
Conquest by the Turks 1163-91
Government of the Mamelukes established . . 1250
Selim I., emperor of the Turks, conquers Egypt . 1567
It is governed by beys till a great part of the country is conquered by the French, under Bonaparte (see *Alexandria*) 1798-99
The invaders dispossessed by the British, and the Turkish government restored 1801
Mehemet Ali massacres the Mamelukes, and obtains the supreme power . . . . 1 March, 1811
Arrival of Belzoni, 1815; he removes statue of Memnon, 1816; explores temples, &c. . . . 1817
Formation of the Mahmoud canal, connecting Alexandria with the Nile 1820
Mehemet Pasha revolts and invades Syria . . . 1831
His son Ibrahim takes Acre, 27 May; overruns Syria; defeats the Turks at Konieh . 21 Dec. 1832
He advances on Constantinople, which is entered by Russian auxiliaries, 3 April; war ends with convention of Kutayah . . . . 4 May, 1833
Mehemet again revolts, claiming hereditary power; Ibrahim defeats the Turks at Nezib 24 June, 1839
England, Austria, Russia, and Prussia undertake to expel Ibrahim from Syria; Napier bombards Beyrout, 10 Oct.; Acre taken by the British and Austrian fleets, under sir R. Stopford, 3 Nov.; the Egyptians quit Syria . 21 Nov., *et seq.* 1840
Peace restored by treaty; Mehemet made hereditary viceroy of Egypt, but deprived of Syria 15 July, 1841
Ibrahim Pacha dies (see *Suez*) . . . 10 Nov. 1848
The Suez canal begun 1858
Commercial treaty with Great Britain signed 19 April, 1861
Hereditary succession and right of coining money granted; but tribute raised from 400,000*l.* to 750,000*l.* . . . . 27 May, ,,
Malta and Alexandria telegraph opened . 1 Nov. ,,
The viceroy Saïd visits Italy, France, and England, May to Sept.; returns to Alexandria . 1 Oct. 1862
Sultan of Turkey visits Egypt . . . 7 April, 1863
Increased cultivation of cotton in Egypt . 1863-67
At the demand of the sultan, the viceroy sends troops to repress the insurgents in Arabia, May, 1864
Opening of part of the Suez canal (*which see*), 15 Aug. 1865
Direct succession to the viceroyalty granted by the Porte . . . . 21 May, 1866
Egyptian legislative chamber opened with a speech from the viceroy . . . . . 27 Nov. ,,
Viceroy invested with Order of the Bath (as G.C.B.) by lord Clarence Paget . . . . 30 Jan. 1867
Designated "sovereign" by the sultan . 9 June, ,,
The viceroy visits Paris . . . 16 June-5 July, ,,
He arrives in London 6 July; received by the queen at Windsor, 8; by lord Derby, 10; by the lord mayor, 11; departs . . . . 18 July, ,,
The viceroy (now termed the Khedive) visited England . . . . 22 June, 1869
Present at the inauguration of the Suez canal, 17 Nov. ,,
The differences between the sultan and himself respecting prerogatives arranged, the viceroy giving up the power of imposing taxes and of contracting loans . . . . . . Dec. ,,
Sir Samuel Baker appointed sole commander of a military expedition to suppress the slave-trade up the Nile, with absolute authority over the country south of Gondokoro (for four years from 1 April, 1869) . . . . . . 10 May, ,,
Departure from Khartoum . . . 8 Feb. 1870
Many delays and impediments; proceeds to explore White Nile . . . . 11 Aug. ,,
Arrives at Gondokoro, 15 April; names it Ismailia, and officially annexes it to Egypt . 26 May, 1871
War with the warlike and treacherous Baris of Belinian; beats them in several engagements, July-Sept. ,,
Supported by his model corps, "the forty thieves," he quells disaffection and mutiny in his troops, Oct. ,,
Sends vessels with women, children, and sick, to Khartoum . . . . 3 Nov. 1871
Makes peace with the Baris, and returns to Gondokoro . . . . 19 Nov. ,,
Advances south; suffers much by negro treachery, and inefficiency of his Egyptian troops: heroism of lady Baker . . . . . Jan.-Feb. 1872
Arrives at the African Paradise, Faliko: meets there his enemy, Abou Saoud, the slave-dealer, 6 March; at Masindi, in Unyoro . 25 April, ,,
Received by Kabba Rega, the young king, who attempts to poison Baker's party, and attacks them in the night; he is defeated, and Masindi burnt . . . . 8 June, ,,
The khedive's son, prince Hassan, made D.C.L. at Oxford . . . . 13 June, ,,
The khedive visits the sultan: Constantinople rejoices . . . . 25 June, ,,
Baker marches to Foweera; received by Raongi, enemy of Kabba Rega, 18 July; returns to Faliko, and suppresses an insurrection of slave-dealers, probably incited by Abou Saoud . . 2 Aug. ,,
Slave-trade apparently subdued; "peace and prospect of prosperity" . . . . 31 Dec. ,,
The sultan, by a firman, renders the khedive practically independent; (he must not coin money, make treaties, or build ironclads) . 8 June, 1873
First Egyptian budget produced; asserted revenue, 10,166,000*l.*; expenditure, 9,040,000*l.* . Oct. ,,
Baker returns to Gondokoro, 1 April; receives honours from the khedive at Cairo, 25 Aug.; arrives in London . . . . . . 9 Oct. ,,
Col. Gordon appointed his successor; Abou Saoud his subordinate . . . . ,,
Baker's work, "Ismailia," published . . Nov. 1874
The first stone of the new port laid by the khedive, 15 May, 1871
Mr. Acton and Mr. Pennell employed to arrange finances of Egypt . . . . spring of 1875
International court of justice opened by the khedive, 28 June ,,
The khedive's shares of Suez canal (*which see*) purchased by the British government; announced, Nov. ,,
Egyptian expedition into Abyssinia surprised and defeated with much slaughter . . . 16 Oct. ,,
Rt. hon. Stephen Cave sent on special mission to Egypt . . . . Dec. ,,
War with Abyssinia (*which see*) 1875-7
New (Gregorian) style adopted; mixed courts opened . . . . 1 Jan. 1876
Resignation of Nubar Pasha, able minister of commerce, announced . . . . . 4 Jan. ,,
Mr. Cave's report—(refers to waste and extravagance; great works undertaken with insufficient means; loss by adventurers; military expenditure; and necessity for intervention of superior power to restore credit and restrain expenditure); sent 13 March; published in *Times* . . 4 April, ,,
The khedive decrees consolidation of his debt, 91,000,000*l.*, at 7 per cent., and a sinking fund, 7 May; decrees signed . . 14 and 25 May ,,
His son Hassan received by the queen . 27 June, ,,
Decisions of the international law court not accepted by the government; the court closed by M. Haakman; he is superseded . . . July, ,,
Mr. Goschen with M. Joubert (on behalf of the khedive's creditors), arrive at Cairo, 14 Oct.; their scheme accepted (debt of about 91,000,000*l.* to be reduced to about 59,000,000*l.*, interest of 7 per cent. to be reduced to about 6 per cent.); agreement signed about 10 Nov. announced (termed since, "Goschen decree") . . . . 18 Nov. ,,
Ismail Sadyk, autocratic finance minister, suspected of conspiracy; resigns insolently; seized and banished . . . . Nov. ,,
Mr. Goschen's report approved by a meeting in London . . . . 28 Nov. ,,
Col. Gordon, after successful administration, returns to England . . . . . . Feb. 1877
Peace with Abyssinia negotiating by col. Gordon, June; terms said to be accepted . . . Oct. ,,
Bad report respecting Egyptian finances, Feb.; commission appointed . . . . . March, 1878
Egypt at peace; all soldiers at home . 20 April, ,,

Confidence restored by decree for payment of official salaries . . . . . 12 May, 1878

Nubar Pasha again minister . . . . 15 Aug. ,,

The khedive accepts the terms of the commission; he and his family give up landed property to the state . . . . Aug. ,,

Mr. Rivers Wilson appointed finance minister; and M. de Blignières, minister of works, soon after, Sept. ,,

Attacks on them and Nubar Pasha by discontented officers at Cairo dispersed . . . 18 Feb. 1879

Nubar Pasha resigns . . . . . 19 Feb. ,,

Definitive peace between the khedive and Abyssinia, announced . . . . . Feb. ,,

Prince Tewfik, president of the council, and Nubar Pasha, foreign minister, about . . 5 March, ,,

Mr. Rivers Wilson and M. de Blignières remonstrate with the khedive . . . . . 6 April, ,,

He puts forth a new financial scheme; Tewfik Pasha, Mr. Rivers Wilson, and M. de Blignières, dismissed: new ministry under Cherif Pasha formed about . . . . 7 April, ,,

Col. Gordon's lieutenant, Gessi (Nov. 1878), completely defeats the rebel slave-dealers in the Soudan, Central Africa . . . . 5 May, ,,

England and France in a note require the appointment of European ministers, about . 5 May, ,,

England, France, Germany, Austria, and Italy, recommend the khedive to abdicate, about 20 June, ,,

He refers to the sultan, who declines to interfere, the khedive offers to pay his debts in full 22 June ,,

The khedive deposed by the sultan, prince Tewfik, his son, proclaimed his successor . 26 June, ,,

The khedive leaves for Naples . . . 30 June, ,,

Tewfik succeeds as khedive . . . . 8 Aug. ,,

Mr. Baring and M. de Blignières appointed comptrollers-general . . . . 4 Sept. ,,

New ministry, Riaz Pasha, &c., announced 9 Sept. ,,

Col. Gordon negotiating with Abyssinia to prevent war, reported successful . . . Oct. ,,

He resigns governorship of the Soudan, Oct., 1879; accepted . . . . Jan. 1880

Peace with Abyssinia announced . end of June, ,,

Public festivities at Cairo on anniversary of the khedive's accession . . . about 26 June, ,,

International committee on the debt appointed, 4 April; issue a report, on which is based a law of liquidation in 99 articles, approved by the khedive . . . . 17 July, ,,

New ministry appointed, the khedive president, 18 Aug. ,,

General prosperity reported . . . . . Oct. ,,

Military revolt (for pay) at Cairo vigorously checked by Mr. E. Malet (British minister 1879) and baron de Ring . . . . 1-11 Feb. 1881

Decree for abolition of slavery . . end of July, ,,

Insurrection in the Soudan (*which see*) . . July, ,,

British pacific interference . . about 11 Aug. ,,

Ministerial crisis; the khedive calls for Riaz Pasha Aug. ,,

Ahmed Arabi Bey and about 4,000 soldiers surround the khedive's palace, demanding increased pay—agreed to; Cherif Pasha made minister 9 Sept. ,,

Negotiations of Cherif and the consuls with the troops succeed; tranquillity restored 11-13 Sept. ,,

Envoys from the sultan received by the khedive 7 Oct. ,,

Jealousy of England and France, the envoys leave Cairo . . . . 18 Oct. ,,

Important letter from earl Granville to s Edwd. Malet . . . . 4 Nov. ,,

The khedive opens the chamber of delegates with excellent speech . . . . . 26 Dec. ,,

Arabi Bey appointed under-secretary of war Jan. 1882

English and French note in support of the khedive about 7 Jan. ,,

Deputies demand entire control of the ministry, about 19 Jan.; dead lock . . . . 27 Jan. ,,

Resignation of Cherif Pasha, 2 Feb.; new ministry under Mahmoud Pasha . . . 3 Feb. *et seq.* ,,

M. Blignières resigns . . . . . March ,,

Alleged conspiracy of Circassian officers to assassinate Arabi Pasha . . . about 10 April, ,,

43 persons convicted of conspiracy to kill Arabi Pasha, and dethrone the khedive; exiled 28 April; sentence confirmed by khedive . . 9 May ,,

Political crisis continues, 9-13 May; the khedive firm; ministry submits, about 16 May; English and French squadron arrive at Alexandria, 20 May; Arabi Pasha refuses to resign, 23 May; ultimatum of English and French consuls; Arabi Pasha to retire; khedive's authority to be restored, &c. 25 May, 1882

Ministry resigns; Cherif Pasha appointed, May the officers resist; Arabi Pasha reinstated, 27-28 May; anarchy; Europeans quitting the country, 29 May; 6,000 Egyptian soldiers said to be massacred . . . . . . June, ,,

Dervish Pasha and others sent to Cairo by the sultan, 4 June; well received at Cairo 8 June ,,

Commencement of a rebellion; riots at Alexandria; Arabs attack Europeans; quelled by Egyptian troops, with great loss of life (about 60 Europeans killed), town ravaged, and deserted 11 June, ,,

Panic at Cairo and Alexandria; many arrests 15, 16 June, ,,

About 37,000 Europeans in Egypt . . . . ,,

Ragheb Pasha forms a ministry; about 20,000 Europeans said to be leaving Egypt. . June, ,,

The powers agree to a conference at Constantinople; Turkey objects . . . . . . 19 June, ,,

Conference opened . . . . . 24 June, ,,

Great emigration from Alexandria to Malta June, ,,

Dervish Pasha's favourable report . . 27 June, ,,

30,000 Arabs said to be starving at Alexandria 29 June, ,,

Arabi Pasha decorated by the sultan . . about 28 June, ,,

The English and French admirals protest against the fortifying of Alexandria . about 4 July, ,,

British subjects warned to quit Egypt . about 6 July, ,,

Bombardment of forts of Alexandria threatened by adm. sir Beauchamp Seymour, if works threatening the British fleet are not stopped . 9 July, ,,

Ships entering Suez canal cautioned by adm. Seymour . . . . 10 July, ,,

Bombardment begun by the *Alexandra*, 7.5 A.M.; vessels engaged: *Monarch*, *Invincible*, *Penelope*, *Téméraire*, and *Inflexible*; gunboats, *Condor*, *Cygnet*, *Bittern*, *Decoy*, &c., very effective; forts Mexs, Marabout, &c., silenced; 10 sailors from *Invincible* land and spike guns of fort Mexs; object of bombardment fully obtained; the bombardment ceases 5.30 P.M. Egyptians fought well; heavy loss in forts and part of the town, British loss, 6 killed, including lieut. Jackson of the *Inflexible*, and 28 wounded . . 11 July, ,,

Defiant letter of Arabi Pasha to Mr. Gladstone, 2 July, received . . . about 12 July, ,,

The sultan protests against the bombardment; Austria, Germany, and Russia said to approve about 12 July, ,,

1,000 marines sent from Malta to Alexandria about 12 July, ,,

Gaining time by a flag of truce, Arabi Pasha and part of his army abandon Alexandria and retreat into the interior; he releases convicts, who with the Arab mob plunder and set fire to the city, and massacre, it is said, *many christians*, 12 July, ,,

Conflagration increasing (about a mile long); about 800 marines land to maintain order as police 13 July, ,,

European portion entirely destroyed . 13 July, ,,

The khedive escapes assassination, and gains over part of Arabi Pasha's army; views the city 12, 13 July, ,,

English marines active . . . . . 14 July, ,,

Fire dying out; order restored; shops re-opened; foreign marines enter city . . . 15 July, ,,

The khedive at his palace Ras-el-Tin guarded by British marines; degrades Arabi Pasha from his offices; sends for Cherif Pasha, Riaz Pasha, and others . . . . . . about 16 July, ,,

About 5,000 soldiers land at Alexandria . 17 July, ,,

Identical note from the six powers inviting the Porte to intervene to support the khedive and restore order . . . . 18 July, ,,

Arabi Pasha with his army said to be intrenched at Kafr-Douar . . . . . . 18 July, ,,

Arabi Pasha attempts to cut off water supply; denounces the khedive, and calls on the people about 20–21 July, 1882
Proclamation of the khedive declaring Arabi a rebel, &c.; reported anarchy at Cairo . about 23 July, ,,
Skirmish with the Arabs by sir A. Alison; he takes about 60 prisoners, and holds Ramleh 24 July, ,,
Arabi proclaims a Jihad or holy war, said to have 30,000 men . . . . . . about 24 July, ,,
British troops landed at Alexandria . 24 July, ,,
Troops sent to Egypt from England and India about 25 July, ,,
Withdrawal of French fleet ordered . 31 July, ,,
The duke of Connaught sails in the *Orient* for Egypt . . . . 31 July, ,,
Indecisive skirmish of outposts . . . . 2 Aug. ,,
Sir Evelyn Wood sails for Egypt . . . 3 Aug. ,,
Town of Suez occupied by British marines 3 Aug. ,,
Reconnaissance; sharp skirmish near Mahmoudieh canal; Gen. Sir A. Alison commanding; British success; lieut. Howard Vyse and 3 others killed; about 30 wounded; Egyptian loss about 300 5 Aug. ,,
Prof. Palmer, capt. Gill, and lieut. Charrington start from Suez to buy camels of the Bedouins, &c. . . . . 7 Aug. ,,
Arrival of duke of Connaught and officers at Alexandria . . . . 10 Aug. ,,
The conference agrees to the international protection of the Suez canal, and adjourns *sine die*, 14 Aug. ,,
Sir Garnet Wolseley lands at Alexandria and assumes the command; the khedive gives up power to the British commanders to establish order . ,,
Troops, &c., under gen. Willis embark as if for Aboukir, but proceed eastward, and occupy Port Said, Ismailia, and Kantara; thus command the canal, 19-20 Aug.; skirmishes near Mahmoudieh canal, sir Evelyn Wood successful; the enemy shelled out of Nefiche . . . . . 20 Aug. ,,
Total British force in Egypt, 31,468 men of all ranks . . . . 20 Aug. ,,
Chaloux-el-Terraba captured by sailors, &c., great Egyptian loss . . . . . . 20 Aug. ,,
Twenty-six ironclads at Alexandria . 20 Aug. ,,
Successful skirmishes; gen. Hamley, &c., from Ramleh; capt. Hastings and maj. Kelsey repel Egyptians, who suffer heavy loss, 20 Aug.; sir G. Wolseley's proclamation to the Arabs 21 Aug. ,,
Arrival of gen. Macpherson with the Indian troops at Suez . . . . 21 Aug. ,,
Advance from Ismailia of two squadrons of household cavalry, with two guns, and detachment of 19th hussars, mounted infantry, &c., on Nefiche met by above 10,000 Egyptians with much artillery . . . . 24 Aug. ,,
Cavalry and artillery engagement; enemy routed; capture of 5 Krupp guns, and train of ammunition and provisions, Egyptian camps at Tel-el-Mahuta and Mahsameh occupied; British loss, 6 killed, 30 wounded . . . . 25 Aug. ,,
Suez canal held by the British . . . 26 Aug. ,,
Kassassin occupied by Gen. Graham with above 2,000 infantry . . . . . . 26 Aug. ,,
Mustapha Fehmy, Arabi Pasha's second in command, captured while reconnoitring (sent to the khedive) . . . . 27 Aug. ,,
Gen. Graham at Kassassin vigorously attacked by 13,000 Egyptians; signals for assistance, rendered by Gen. Drury Lowe with household cavalry; brilliant charge and capture of 11 guns (afterwards lost), rout of the enemy; disorderly flight; British loss, 7 killed, 70 wounded . 28 Aug. ,,
Military convention with Turkey about to be signed . . . . 29 Aug. ,,
Arabi Pasha strengthening his intrenchments near Tel-el-Kebir (said to have about 28,000 men) about 31 Aug. ,,
Artillery duel at Ramleh, little result . 4 Sept. ,,
Arabi Pasha's estimated forces: infantry, 44,600; cavalry, 1802; guns, 143; Bedouins 30,500 . ,,
Vigorous attack on the British camp at Kassassin repelled with severe loss, 4 guns taken, 6 British killed . . . . 9 Sept. ,,
Siege train sent in the *Copia* . . . . 9 Sept. 1882
Capture of Tel-el-Kebir, *which see*; total defeat of the Egyptians; flight of Arabi Pasha; surrender of Zagazig with railway trains, &c. 13 Sept. ,,
The British enter Cairo; Arabi Pasha and his officers surrender unconditionally; about 10,000 Egyptian soldiers lay down their arms 14 Sept. ,,
Sir Garnet Wolseley and British troops enter Cairo; warmly received . . . . . . 15 Sept. ,,
Surrender of Kafr Douar; about 500 Egyptians march to Damietta . . . . 16, 17 Sept. ,,
The khedive dissolves the Egyptian army 17 Sept. ,,
Surrender of Aboukir, 17 Sept.; re-establishment of the khedive's authority . . . 19 Sept. ,,
Abd-el-Al holding Damietta with about 7,000 men, 21 Sept.; British expedition sent against him, 22 Sept.; he surrenders to sir Evelyn Wood 23 Sept. ,,
Triumphal entry of the khedive into Cairo, 25 Sept. ,,
Valentine Baker Pasha nominated commander of a new Egyptian army (10,900) . end of Sept. ,,
Cairo railway station partly burned by explosion of shells, large amount of stores and ammunition destroyed; 4 persons killed, about 15 wounded 28 Sept. ,,
18,000 British troops "march past" the khedive at the Abdin palace . . . . . 30 Sept. ,,
12,000 British to remain in Egypt, sir A. Alison commander . . . . 30 Sept. ,,
Return of the troops; warmly received in London 21 Oct. *et seq.* ,,
The prophet said to hold all the country south of Khartoum . . . . 25 Oct. ,,
Murder of prof. Palmer, capt. Gill and lieut Charrington . about 10 Aug. announced 26 Oct. ,,
Thanks of Parliament voted to army and navy:—Admiral sir Beauchamp Seymour (created lord Alcester); Admiral John Miller Adye; vice-admiral William Montagu Dowell; lieutenant-generals George Harry Smith Willis, sir Edward Bruce Hamley; major-general sir Archibald Alison; rear-admirals sir William Nathan Wrighte Hewett, sir Francis William Sullivan, Anthony Hiley Hoskins; major-generals his royal highness Arthur duke of Connaught, William Earle, sir Henry Evelyn Wood, Gerald Graham, George Byng Harman, Drury Curzon Drury-Lowe, sir Herbert Taylor Macpherson . . . 26 Oct. ,,
An amnesty of officers signed by the khedive 24 Oct. ,,
Lord Dufferin arrives at Cairo . . . 7 Nov. ,,
Anglo-French control abolished . . . 9 Nov. ,,
British troops from Egypt with Indian contingent reviewed by the queen at St. James's Park 18 Nov. ,,
Queen's thanks published 21 Nov.; distributes medals, &c., at Windsor . . . 21 Nov. ,,
Trial of Arabi Pasha; secret examination of witnesses (his defence supported by Mr. Wilfrid Blunt) . . . . Nov. ,,
Pleads guilty of rebellion; sentence of death commuted to banishment for life . . . 3 Dec. ,,
General amnesty and release of political prisoners about 1 Dec. ,,
Letter from Arabi Pasha to Mr. Wilfrid Blunt, expressing gratitude to, and confidence in, England 4 Dec.; *Times*, 5 Dec. ,,
Mahoud and other rebel leaders sentenced to banishment . . . . 7 Dec. ,,
Riaz Pasha resigns; succeeded by Nubar Pasha 7, 8 Dec. ,,
Arabi Pasha and others to be sent to Ceylon 9 Dec. ,,
Sir Evelyn Wood, appointed commander of the new Egyptian army, arrives at Cairo . 22 Dec. ,,
Nine of the murderers of professor Palmer and others captured . . . . about 30 Dec. ,,
Arabi and others sailed for Ceylon, 27 Dec.; arrived 10 Jan. 1883
End of the dual control . . . . . 11 Jan. ,,
British circular to the powers laid before the Porte, &c. (the Suez Canal to be free, with restrictions in time of war; formation of Egyptian army, &c.) . . . . 11 Jan. *et seq.* ,,
All the powers accept proposals except France and Turkey . . . . . about 27 Jan. ,,
Sir Auckland Colvin appointed financial adviser 24 Jan. ,,

Trial of professor Palmer's murderers; several confess; 5 executed . . . . 28 Feb. 1883
Lord Dufferin's report on reorganization of Egypt published . . . . 20 March, ,,
Constitution signed by the khedive, 30 April; promulgated . . . . . . 1 May, ,,
Lieut.-gen. Alison replaced by gen. F. C. Stephenson May, ,,
Major Evelyn Baring nominated resident . May, ,,
Suleiman Sami convicted of the firing, massacre, and plundering at Alexandria (11 June, 1882), hanged . . . . 9 June, ,,
Greatly improved condition of the country. June, ,,
The ex-khedive Ismail in London . . 28 June, ,,
Parliamentary grants to lord Alcester (Seymour), 25,000*l.*, lord Wolseley, 30,000*l.* . . 29 June, ,,
Eruption of cholera (see *Cholera*) . . . . ,,
British force reduced to 6,763 . . . Aug. ,,
Council of state nominated . . . . 24 Sept. ,,
The khedive grants a general amnesty, about 10 Oct. ,,
New council of state opened by Cherif Pasha, 30 Oct. ,,
Departure of part of the British troops countermanded on account of the destruction of gen. Hicks' army (see *Soudan*) . . . . . Nov. ,,
The khedive proposes reduction of his court expenses . . . . 1 Jan. 1884
The British government require a limitation of the line of defence in regard to the Soudan 6 Jan. ,,
Cherif Pasha and his ministry resign; Nubar Pasha (an Armenian christian) becomes minister, about 7 Jan. ,,
Loan of 950,000*l.* to the khedive by Messrs. Rothschild . . . . . . about 30 Jan. ,,
Disorder in the government and finances reported, 20 March, ,,
British army: total killed, 255; July 1882 to March, ,,
Resignation of Nubar Pasha in opposition to Mr. Clifford Lloyd, 6 April; both remain in office, 11 April, ,,
Chaos at Cairo; sir Evelyn Baring comes to London ,,
Conference of the powers, respecting Egyptian finance proposed by England accepted by Germany, Austria, Russia, Italy, France, and Turkey, May, ,,
Need of loan of 8,000,000*l.* to meet several years' deficits, indemnification for damages at Alexandria (3,950,000*l.*), civil and Soudan war expenses, &c. . . . . May, ,,
Proposed relaxation of the international law of liquidation . . . . May, ,,
Mr. Clifford Lloyd leaves . . . May and June, ,,
Select committee by examination discovers serious defects in the commissariat and transport systems during the war of 1882, announced . . June, ,,
Conference of six great powers on Egyptian affairs meets (see *London Conferences*) . . 28 June, ,,
Conference adjourns, without result, *sine die*, 2 Aug. ,,
Credit for 300,000*l.* voted to assist gen. Gordon, 5 Aug. ,,
Lord Northbrook, as high commissioner, and lord Wolseley as commander-in-chief, sail 31 Aug. arrive at Cairo . . . . 9 Sept. ,,
Suspension of the international law of liquidation in regard to the sinking fund, from 18 Sept. to 25 Oct. decreed, with consent of lord Northbrook 20 Sept. ,,
France, Germany, Austria, Russia, and Italy protest, 25 Sept. *et seq.* but tacitly acquiesce Oct. ,,
Lord John Hay and the fleet arrive at Alexandria, 24 Sept. ,,
Egyptian army reduced to 4000 men, announced, 24 Oct. ,,
Lord Northbrook leaves Egypt . . . 28 Oct. ,,
Arrives in London . . . . 3 Nov. ,,
British force in Egypt and Soudan, about 16,000 men, Nov. ,,
Action of the *caisse* (commission) of the public debt against the Egyptian government for suspension of the sinking fund; the court condemns it to refund, 9 Dec.; the khedive appeals Dec. ,,
Great improvements in irrigation, conducted by col. Scott Moncrieff 1884-5
Reply of France and other powers to the British proposals respecting the financial condition of Egypt, 17 Jan.; English reply . . 24 Jan. 1885
Prince Hassan, brother of the khedive, appointed high commissioner in the Soudan about 15 Feb. ,,
Egyptian financial scheme; convention agreed to by the Powers signed, 18 March [reduction of interest on debt, loan of 9,000,000*l.* on international guarantee, &c.]; adopted by the Commons on Mr. Gladstone's resolution (294-246), 27-28 March, 1885
Gen. Grenfell succeeds sir E. Wood as commander-in-chief . . . about 1 April, ,,
Bosphore Egyptien, a Cairo newspaper, suppressed by decree, 29 Feb. 1884; carried into effect, for publication of a proclamation of the Madhi, on 9 April, 1885; the French government much offended by the manner of suppression; the dispute settled by British intervention, announced, 28 April, 1885; paper reappears, 20 May, 1885; stopped . . . . 5 Sept. ,,
Sir F. Stephenson, commander-in-chief of British army . . . . 6 July, ,,
Lord Wolseley arrives in London . . 13 July, ,,
Payment of indemnity begins . . . 16 Aug. ,,
Telegraph system freed from Eastern company, through Mr. Floyer . . . about 12 Sept. ,,
Turkish convention with sir H. D. Wolff on Egyptian affairs; departure of the British deferred till their work be accomplished, signed 24 Oct. ,,
Sir H. D. Wolff arrives at Cairo on commission 29 Oct. ,,
High commissioners, Ghazi-Mukhtar Pasha and sir H. D. Wolff, ... Nov. ,,
British forces in Egypt, exclusive of Indians and Egyptians, 14,000 . . . . . . 1 Dec. ,,
Mukhtar arrives at Cairo . . . . . 27 Dec. ,,
Immense increase in postal communications . . 1880-6
Ancient necropolis discovered at Assouan by general Grenfell . . . . . . Feb. 1886
Discovery of petroleum at Jebel Zeit on the Red Sea, March; probable success reported about 24 April, ,,
Ismail Pasha claims 5,000,000*l.* arrears of annual payments for surrendered estates . . June ,,
The khedive's two sons presented to the queen at Windsor . . . . 6 July, ,,
Reduction of the British army begins . Jan. 1887
Improvement in the state of the country reported Feb. ,,
Neutralisation of Egypt and defence of the Suez canal proposed to the sultan by sir H. Drummond Wolff . . . . . . (?) 9 Feb. ,,
Anglo-Turkish convention respecting Egypt signed at Constantinople; (British troops to leave in three years; Turkish troops to intervene or British to return; Suez canal to be neutral, etc.,) 28 May; ratified by queen Victoria, June; not ratified by the Sultan; sir H. D. Wolff leaves Constantinople . . . . 15 July, ,,
Sudden death of general Valentine Baker Pasha, aged 62 . . . . 17 Nov. ,,
Major Dormer appointed commander of the British army . . . . Dec. ,,
Ismail Pasha permitted to reside at Constantinople Dec. ,,
General prosperity of the country; surplus in the budget . . . . Jan. 1888
The exorbitant claims of the ex-khedive on the Egyptian government reduced and liberally settled by the influence of sir Edgar Vincent and Mr. Marriott, Q.C., the judge advocate general; he receives 100,000*l.* with much land Jan. ,,
Death of prince Hassan . . . . . 22 March ,,
Mr. Limperopoulos's claim for 2,910*l* (Egyptian) on Gordon bonds said to have been issued at Khartoum, disallowed . . . . . May, ,,
Nubar Pasha dismissed; Riaz Pasha succeeds (see *Soudan*) . . . . 8 June ,,
The Caisse de la Dette (general reserve fund) established . . . . 13 June, ,,
Sir Edgar Vincent's proposal to convert the Egyptian preference debt of 22,000,000*l.* at 5 per cent. to a loan at 4 per cent. not accepted by the French government, unless a time be fixed for the evacuation of Egypt by the British 27 June, *et seq.* 1889
Sir Edgar Vincent resigns the office of financial adviser to the khedive, 21 Aug.; succeeded by Mr. Elwin Palmer, director-general of accounts . Sept. ,,

The prince of Wales and prince George received by the khedive at Cairo, 1 Nov.; review of the British and Egyptian armies; the prince suddenly takes the command of the British; during the march past he salutes the Khedive, 2 Nov.; leaves Egypt . . . . 5 Nov. 1889
Mr. Palmer's budget, surplus 150,000*l.* after reduced taxation, announced, . . . 18 Nov. ,,
The Equatorial province lost by the retirement of Emin Pasha, through the mutiny of his officers 1888–89
Abolition of forced labour (*corvée*) of the peasantry (fellaheen), a tax proposed to the general assembly, 15 Dec., bill passed . . . . . . 17 Dec. 1889
Negotiations with France respecting the conversion scheme (see June, 1889), again fails Jan. 1890
New commercial treaty with Great Britain (signed 29 Oct. 1889) from . . . . . 1 Jan. ,,
National accounts for 1889, declared surplus 196,000*l.* . . . . 28 Jan. ,,
Prince Albert Victor of Wales visits the Khedive at Cairo, reviews the army, &c. 7–15 April ,,
The French government assents to the conversion of the preference debt, under conditions which are accepted by the Egyptians reported 7 May ,,
The first settlement was effected at Paris by Tigrane pasha, Mr. Elwin Palmer, and M. Ribot, 21 May; the assent of the other great powers reported 2 June, the khedive's decree authorizing the conversion issued . . . . . 7 June ,,
Mr. Justice Scott's plan for the decentralization of justice and creation of local courts, adopted by decree . . . . reported 3 July ,,
Annual meeting of the society (formed in 1888) for the preservation of the monuments of ancient Egypt; London . . . . 9 July ,,
Death of Hussein Bey, son of Ismail Pasha, aged 50 27 July ,,
The corvée tax for 1890 not to be collected . . reported 17 Aug. ,,
Highly favourable report of the results of British occupation since 1882 . . . . . Aug. ,,
Much needed judicial reforms recommended by Mr. Justice Scott, of Bombay, Jan., opposed by a commission . . . . 2 Feb. 1891
Return of the khedive from a successful five weeks' tour (during which he visited Wady-Halfa); Cairo illuminated . . . . 8 Feb. ,,
Discovery of the vast tomb of a high priest of Ammon, W. of Thebes, see under *Mummies* . announced Feb. ,,
Sir Evelyn Baring recommends to the khedive the nomination of Mr. Justice Scott as judicial adviser and president of a judicial committee of three (one Italian and one Egyptian) for the supervision of the local tribunals, about 11 Feb. ,,
The khedive assents; officially announced 16 Feb. ,,
Revenue returns for 1890, about 10,250,000*l.*, said to be the largest ever received . . . 18 Feb. ,,
The judicial changes disapproved by France, about 20 Feb. ,,
Count d'Aubigny, the French minister, recalled, and disgraced, leaves . . . . 1 March, ,,
Resignation of Riaz Pasha, the premier, for ill-health 12 May ,,
New ministry under Mustapha Fehmy Pasha (influence of the khedive increased) . . 13 May ,,
Sir Colin Moncrieff reports the beneficial results of the great improvements in irrigation, 5 March; published . . . . June, ,,
The khedive's palace, the Abdin, greatly injured by fire, 22–23 July; the British troops thanked for their help . . . . 24 July, ,,
Great increase in the crops of cotton and cereals, and in railway receipts; large surplus revenue; proposed reduction of taxation . end of Nov. ,,
Sudden death of the khedive Tewfik; much lamented . . . . 7 Jan. 1892
His eldest son, Abbas, recognised by the Porte, 8 Jan.; state reception at Cairo . . 16 Jan. ,,
Reduction of the salt tax, 40 per cent., ordered about 28 Jan. ,,
The khedive opened the general assembly with a cheerful speech . . . . . . 30 Jan. ,,
Arrival of Ahmed Eyoub Pasha at Cairo with the sultan's firman for the investiture of the khedive 4 April; the reading delayed through proposed changes relating to Mount Sinai, which are settled satisfactorily through British influence; the firman read in public . . . . . 14 April, 1892
New railway bridge over the Nile, opened by the khedive . . . . 5 May ,,
Justice Scott's judicial reforms, reported very successful . . . . 22 May ,,
Sir Evelyn Baring created a peer (baron Cromer) . ,,
Budget for 1893, estimated revenue, 10,267,000*l.*; surplus, 472,000*l.* . . . . . 22 Nov. ,,
The Khedive suddenly dismisses the premier, Mustapha Pasha Fehmy and his colleagues, supporters of the English reforms, and nominates Fakhri Pasha and others, anti-reformers, 15 Jan.; Lord Cromer, for the British government protests, 17 Jan.; the Khedive expresses regret, and proposes the appointment of Riaz Pasha and others, which is accepted by lord Cromer, 18 Jan. 1893
Popular agitation, 22 Jan.; the British army of occupation (about 3,000 under major-gen. Walker) increased; end of the crisis . . . 27 Jan. ,,
The khedive opens the railway extension to Girgeh, 5 Feb. ,,
Budget: surplus, 788,000*l.*; taxation greatly reduced under British management, about 13 Feb. ,,
A French squadron arrives at Alexandria; the admiral received by the khedive . 15 April, ,,
The khedive visits the sultan at Constantinople; receives honours . . . . . 10–27 July, ,,
Budget surplus, 740,000*l.*, further reduction of taxation . . . . Dec. ,,
The khedive opens the steam tramway connecting Ismailia and Port Said (50 miles) . 2 Dec. ,,
The khedive reviews the troops at Wady Halfa, &c., 19 Jan. 1894
He retracts his censures on the troops under British officers, declares his high approval, and dismisses Maher Pasha, war minister 26 Jan. ,,
Gen. Kitchener and Mr. John (justice) Scott made K.C.M.G. . . . . Feb. ,,
Resignation of Riaz Pasha; new ministry formed by Nubar Pasha . . . . . 14–16 April, ,,
The first national exhibition of art and industry, at Alexandria, opened by the khedive 22 April, ,,
A strike of coal porters at Port Said, 21 May, closed . . . . 26 May, ,,
The construction of a Nile reservoir at Assuan, ordered by the khedive and his council, 3 June; sir Benjamin Baker appointed technical adviser, 10 Dec. ,,
Tour of the khedive; Nubar Pasha appointed regent . . . . 21 June, ,,
The khedive arrives at Constantinople, 25 June; honoured by the sultan, July; visits Italy and Switzerland, July; at the Hague . 8 Aug. ,,
Death of prof. Heinrich Karl Brugsch Pasha, Egyptologist; born 1827; died . . 9 Sept. ,,
Important reforms in the civil administration introduced by lord Cromer; Mr. J. L. Gorst, influential adviser . . . . . 28 Oct. ,,
Gen. sir H. H. Kitchener starts for Wady Halfa on a tour of inspection; reported . . . . 1 Feb. 1895
Government accounts for 1894: revenue, 10,562,000*l.*; expenditure, 9,756,000*l.*; announced . 10 Feb. ,,
Intrigues against the Nubar Pasha ministry; serious disorders at Alexandria, *which see* Feb. ,,
Contract of marriage with Ikbal Hanem signed by the khedive . . . . . . 19 Feb. ,,
A decree creating a special tribunal to deal with offences against the British issued . 22 Feb. ,,
Fall of 25 per cent. in the value of the cotton crop, &c. . . . . 24 Feb. ,,
Agreement with the khedive and lord Cromer 25 Feb. ,,
The khedive reviews the army of occupation at Cairo . . . . 27 Feb. ,,
M. Hippolyte Percher, *alias* Harry Alis, French journalist in Egypt and France; a sharp opponent of lord Cromer and the British occupation; killed in a duel near Paris by M. le Chatelier, whom he had attacked in the *Debats* 1 March, ,,
Death of Ismail Pasha, ex-khedive at Constantinople, 2 March; state funeral at Cairo 12 March, ,,
Slatin Bey, an Austrian, 12 years prisoner of the Mahdi, escapes; warmly received at Cairo; made pasha . . . . 19–21 March ,,

Visit of the Mediterranean squadron, under sir Michael Culme-Seymour to Alexandria, warmly received, 26 May; inspected by the khedive, 27 May; banquet given by the khedive 28 May, 1895
An Egyptian committee held at Paris, to effect the British evacuation and obtain equal rights for all nations; president, M. Deluns-Montaud; M. Deloncle an active member . . . 18 June ,,
Resignation of Nubar Pasha, premier and great reformer; Mustapha Fehmy Pasha, friend to the British, appointed president of the council and minister of the interior . . . . 11 Nov. ,,
A new Anglo-Egyptian anti-slavery convention sanctioned by the khedive . . . 21 Nov. ,,
See *Cholera*, 1895 *et seq.*
General improvement and tranquillity in the provinces reported by sir Elwin Palmer (K.C.B. Jan. 1897) . . . . . . 9 Feb. 1896
The assembly opened by the khedive . 10 Feb. ,,
Government accounts for 1895: revenue, 10,568,000*l.*; expenditure, 9,480,000*l.* . 13 March, ,,
Advance of 9,000 troops under sir H. H. Kitchener up the Nile to Dongola, to check the dervishes and relieve Kassala (see *Soudan*), 19 March, *et seq.* ,,
Mr. John Morley's vote of censure on the government in the commons negatived, 288–145 20 March, ,,
The cost of the Nile expedition (500,000*l.*) to be borne by the Caisse de la Dette (Egyptian reserve fund); opposed by France and Russia, 26 March; money paid . . . . . . 1 April, ,,
The mixed tribunal (founded by Nubar pasha) gives judgment against the Egyptian government, 8 June; the government appeals against the decision to the court of Alexandria, 8 foreign judges, 17 Nov.; the money ordered to be refunded to the Caisse de la Dette, with interest, 6 Dec. 1896 [the money voted by British parliament, 5 Feb. 1897].
Concession for light railways (70 yrs.) granted to an English company . . . . . 26 March, ,,
The Beit-el-mal (native court) abolished, and other reforms made; reported . . . . 15 May, ,,
Tour of the khedive in Switzerland, &c.; Mustapha Fehmy pasha appointed regent . . 9 Aug. ,,
Return of lord Cromer and sir E. Palmer to Cairo 23 Sept. ,,
Important legal reforms passed by the council 22 Nov. ,,
Surplus revenue for 1896, 1,345,000*l.* reported 8 Feb. 1897
Decrease of crime in 1896, reported . . 28 Feb. ,,
Foundation stone of the new museum at Cairo laid by the khedive . . . 5 April ,,
Medals presented at Cairo to British officers and men of the Dongola expedition . . 3 May, ,,
Sir Francis Grenfell takes command of the army of occupation, Cairo . . . . 7 Oct. ,,
Reform of the native penal code . . Dec. ,,
Horticultural and agricultural exhibition opened by the khedive at Cairo . . 14 Jan. 1898
The Egyptian government sells to the firm of Allen, Alderson & co. 11 steamers, floating dock, &c., at Alexandria and Suez, for 150,000*l.* . 30 Jan. ,,
Contract (5 years) concluded with Messrs. John Aird & co. for the construction of dams across the Nile at Assuan and Assuit, about 20 Feb. ,,
Grants to the government from the general reserve fund of 922,000*l.* for public works . 1 March ,,
Receipts, 11,092,564*l.*; expenditure, 10,559,257*l.*, for year ending, 31 Dec. 1897; . 6 March ,,
Foundation stone of the native palace of justice at Cairo laid . . . . . 17 March ,,
Sir J. Scott, judicial adviser 1890–8, decorated by the khedive, on his retirement 17 April, ,,
Internat. comm. to discuss modifications in the code of the mixed tribunals meets at Cairo 5 Dec. ,,
Prince Ahmed Safeddin sentenced to 7 years' imprisonment for attempting to murder prince Fuad, 29 June; reduced to 5 years . 14 Dec. ,,
Sir Edwin Palmer appointed governor of the national bank of Egypt (capital to be 1,000,000*l.*), 11 July, ,,
An English board of education formed at Cairo, reported . . . . . . 1 Dec. ,,
Major-gen. the hon. R. A. J. Talbot commander of the British troops; col. sir Francis Wingate, chief of the Egyptian army, appointed . Dec. ,,
Nubar Pasha, ex-premier, able reformer, see *Capitulations*, an Armenian Christian, born 1825, died in Paris, ... 14 Jan.
Soudan convention signed at Cairo . 19 Jan. ,,
The duke of Connaught lays the foundation stone of the Nile reservoir dam at Assuan, 12 Feb.; gives 25*l.* and lays first stone of the English church of St. Mark . . . . 27 Feb. ,,
Decree signed reforming the court of appeal, May, ,,
Reform of the Grand Cadi's court; Mahomet Abdul, progressive and capable, appointed grand mufti . . . . 3 June, ,,
Sir W. E. Garstin's report suggesting improvement of the Nile channel, irrigation, and the management of forests on the Blue Nile and in the Bahr-el-Ghazal, issued . 23 June, ,,
International commission of judicial reform, 1898, see *Times* . . . . . . 17 July, ,,
Sir J. G. Rogers, head of the sanitary department, successful in suppressing the plague in Egypt, resigns, and is succeeded by Pinching Bey, end Oct. ,,
The khedive unveils statue of Ferdinand de Lesseps at Port Said (see *Suez Canal*) . 17 Nov. ,,
Mixed tribunals prolonged 5 years; decree signed, 30 Jan. 1900
Mutiny in Turah prison near Cairo repressed, 4 March, ,,
The khedive visits England (*which see*), 27 June–4 July, ,,
Revenue for 1900: surplus, 1,552,000*l.*; reported, 27 Feb. 1901
The duke and duchess of Cornwall visit Port Said, 30, 31 March, ,,
Arabi Pasha released (exiled 1882), May; returns a staunch friend to Britain, reported . 30 Sept. ,,
The khedive's tour (see *Soudan*, Dec. 1901); views the great Nile dam at Assuan, sir Benjamin Baker and sir John Aird present . 9 Dec. ,,
Surplus revenue for 1901, 700,000*l.* . 12 April, 1902
Saadeddin Pasha, governor of Gharbieh, charged with torturing natives, accused of stealing, dismissed from service, 13, 14 April; other officials punished . . . . . . 24 April, ,,
Great fire at Mit Gamr, 1,000 houses, 200 shops destroyed, 50 deaths. . . . . 1 May, ,,
Mr. Chamberlain received by the khedive 8 Dec ,,
Nile dam at Assuan opened, see *Nile* . 10 Dec. ,,
First Egyptian medical congress held . 19-24 Dec. ,,
Zifteh barrage between Cairo and the sea opened 7 March, 1903
Surplus for 1902, 716,000*l.* over expenditure, real surplus over 2,000,000*l.* reported . 13 April, ,,
The khedive visits London . 24 June—3 July, ,,

KHEDIVES OR HEREDITARY VICEROYS (nearly independent).

1806. Mehemet Ali Pasha; abdicated Sept. 1848; dies 2 Aug. 1849.
1848. Ibrahim (adopted son), Sept.; dies 9 or 10 Nov. 1848.
,, Abbas (his son), 10 Nov.; dies 14 July, 1854.
1854. Saïd (brother), 14 July; dies 18 Jan. 1863.
1863. Ismail (nephew), 18 Jan. (born 31 Dec. 1830); deposed by the sultan at the request of England, France and other powers, 26 June, 1879; died 2 March, 1895.
1879. Mechmet Tewfik, born Nov., 1852, invested with the star of India by the prince of Wales, 25 Oct. 1875; proclaimed 26 June, invested 14 Aug.; died 7 Jan. 1892.
1892. Abbas Hilmi, born 14 July, 1874; heir, Abdul Mouneim Bey, born 20 Feb. 1899.

EGYPT EXPLORATION FUND, originated by Miss Amelia B. Edwards, and promoted by sir Erasmus Wilson, first president (died 8 Aug. 1884), and Mr. R. S. Poole, secretary, 1881; hon. secretary, 1892; died 8 Feb., 1895. Its object is to promote excavations in order to elucidate the history and arts of ancient Egypt and biblical history. Miss Edwards, a learned Egyptologist, hon. secretary, died 15 April, 1892. She bequeathed property to endow a professorship of Egyptology in University College, London. Annual meetings.

Mr. W. M. Flinders Petrie was the first Edwards professor; first lecture given, 14 Jan. 1893.

M. Edouard Naville's explorations began 19 Jan. 1883. The excavations conducted by M. Naville, 1883-4, led to many important discoveries, including the site of Goshen. Mr. W. M. F. Petrie examined more than twenty sites in 1884-5, and made remarkable discoveries. Some of the results were given to British and foreign museums. Makes discoveries, including Naucratis, which was a flourishing Greek commercial and manufacturing city, on the Canopic arm of the Nile, about 550 B.C., and declined after the Persian invasion and the founding of Alexandria 332 B.C. Explorations carried on by Mr. F. Llewellyn Griffith at Tanis, 1886; Mr. Petrie, in the mounds of Tel-Defenneh, discovered the remains of "Pharaoh's house in Tahpanhes" (588 B.C.; *Jeremiah* xliii., 8-11), May, 1886.

Mr. Ernest A. Gardner reported the results of his excavations in the spring at Naucratis, and exhibited relics with statuettes, pottery, &c., obtained from the sites of temples, cemeteries, &c., 6 July, 1886. M. Naville's explorations at the city of Onia and the "Mound of the Jews," continued spring 1887. He discovers the great temple of Bubastis (about B.C. 1300), granite monolithic columns, sculpture, &c., April–June 1887; resumes his excavations March, 1888.

Exhibition of Egyptian antiquities at the Egyptian Hall, Piccadilly; by Mr. Flinders Petrie, of his excavations at Fayûm, July, 1888.

Mr. Petrie forces an entrance into the sepulchral chamber of the pyramid of Anenemhat III. at Hawara, Jan.; exhibits the results of his explorations, at the Oxford Mansions, London, mummies, ornaments, implements, &c., Sept. 1889 *et seq.*

The archæological survey of Egypt approved by the government; began in 1890

A monograph on the results of M. Naville's excavations at Bubastis in 1887-9, was published in the "Memoirs" . . . . . Feb. 1891

Mr. Petrie discovers fragments of a lost play of Euripides, of the Phædo of Plato and other writers, which have been published by Professor Mahaffy after study by himself and Professor Sayce, reported July, 1891. Mr. Petrie's "Ten Years' Digging in Egypt, 1881 to 1891," published . May 1892

Mr. F. Petrie exhibits in London results of his latest researches . . . . 17 Sept.–Oct. ,,

Important discoveries by M. de Morgan in the brick pyramid of Dahsur; reported . March, 1894

"Atlas of Ancient Egypt," published . . June, ,,

M. Naville reports the result of his recent labours at Tmei-el-Amdid, &c., near the site of Mendes, including Greek and Roman remains, 14 Dec.; again . . . . . . 8 July, 1895

Results of Professor Flinders Petrie's explorations (11 weeks in 1894), exhibited in University College, Gower St., July, 1894. At the royal society in Edinburgh he described the discovery (30 miles N. of Thebes, by excavations), of an entirely distinct race of men, which probably existed about 3000 B.C.; possibly Amorites or Libyans, not negroes; human remains found in the cemeteries; no mummies, writings, or hieroglyphs; the relics included good pottery, flint and metal implements, &c., 17 April, 1895; fresh discoveries reported, April, 1896; exhibition at the British museum, July, 1896; another of the joint work of Mr. Flinders Petrie and Mr. J. E. Quibell; the "Logia" of our Lord, and the oldest MS. of Thucydides, discovered by Messrs. Grenfell and Hunt at Oxyrhynchus (Behnesa), 12 Jan., 18, 10 March, 1897; antiquities and papyri from the Fayûm and Oxyrhynchus (Dec. 1898), and others from Naucratis, found by Mr. Hogarth, exhibited at Burlington house (fresh papyri at Oxyrhynchus, 1903) . 5-12 July, 1899

"The Temple of Mut in Asher," by the Misses Benson and Gourlay; an account of its excavation, &c., 1894-97, published . . . . . ,,

Many discoveries, excavations carried on by six different institutions, 1899-1900; first dynasty (Merneit), &c., royal tombs discovered by prof. Flinders Petrie at Abydos and others there of the 12th, 18th, and 3rd dynasties by Mr. Garstang (see *Times*, 24 April, 1900); important Ptolemaic papyri found by Messrs. Grenfell and Hunt at Umm-el-Baragât (Tebtunis), south of the Fayûm, (part 1 pub. Jan. 1903) . . 3 Dec. 1899–Jan. 1900

Mr. Garstang discovers the royal tomb of Neter-Kha in Upper Egypt, reported . . Feb. 1901

Professor Flinders Petrie states the recent discoveries at Abydos to have settled the continuous order of 17 kings and the very foundations of Egyptian history, 7 Nov. 1902; exhibitions in Gower Street . July, 1901; July, 1902; July, 1903

Professor Flinders Petrie's lecture on "The beginnings of the Egyptian Kingdom" at the British Association . . . . . 10 Sept. ,,

EGYPTIAN ERA, &c. The old Egyptian year was identical with the era of Nabonassar, beginning 26 Feb. 747 B.C., and consisted of 365 days only. It was reformed 30 B.C., at which period the commencement of the year had arrived, by continually receding to the 29th Aug., which was determined to be in future the first day of the year. To reduce to the Christian era, subtract 746 years 125 days. The canicular or heliacal period of the Egyptians and Ethiopians (1460 years) began when Sirius or the dog star emerged from the rays of the sun, on 20 July, 2785 B.C., and extended to 1325 B.C. This year comprised 12 months of 30 days, with 5 supplementary days.

EGYPTIAN HALL, Piccadilly, erected in 1812 by G. F. Robinson for Bullock's natural history collections, which were sold in 1819; since used for exhibitions, concerts, &c. See *Dudley Gallery*.

EHRENBREITSTEIN (Honour's broad-stone), a strong Prussian fortress on the Rhine, formerly belonged to the electors of Treves. It was often besieged. It surrendered to the French general Jourdain, 24 Jan. 1799. The fortifications were destroyed on its evacuation, 9 Feb. 1801, at the peace of Luneville. The works have been restored since 1814.

EIDER, a river separating Schleswig from Holstein, was passed by the Austrians and Prussians, 4 Feb. 1864. *Eider*, German steamer, see *Wrecks*, 1892.

EIDOGRAPH, see *Pantograph*.

EIDOPHONE, see ADDENDA.

EIFFEL TOWER, see *Paris*, 1889. Re-opened 30 March, 1890.

EIGHT HOURS. In 1889-95 there was much agitation among the working classes in Britain and on the Continent, in favour of limiting the working day to eight hours. This was one of the objects of the demonstrations in May, 1890-92, see *Working Men*.

The factories and shops act (an 8 hrs. working day for women), passed at Melbourne . . . 1890

The limitation adopted by some trades in England; by the bookbinders of London . . Nov. 1891

Great meeting in Hyde park to support the movement . . . . . . 1 May, 1892

The marquis of Salisbury and Mr. A. J. Balfour receive a deputation of workmen; they deprecate legislation as premature . . . 11 May, ,,

The eight hours' system opposed by the Durham miners (nearly 41,000), reported 26 Oct. 1892; but approved by the annual conference at Birmingham . . . . Jan. 1893

The mines (eight hours) bill rejected by the commons (272-160), 23 March, 1892; 2nd reading, 3 May, ,,

Mr. W. Mather, M.P., of the Salford ironworks, gave a favourable report of the results of a year's trial of the 48 hours' week . . 28 March, 1894

The adoption of the eight hours' system in some of the government works; reported . . March, ,,

A resolution for an eight hours' working day passed by the international miners' congress at Berlin, 17 May, 1894; again at Aix-la-Chapelle 25 May 1896

Miner's eight hours bill, 25 April, withdrawn Aug. 1896; rejected . . . . 5 May, 1897
Eight hours' day demanded by engineers; see *Strikes* . . . . . . 3 July, *et seq.* ,,
Resolution in favour of legislative limitation of labour hours to 8 per day, and making this a test question at all elections passed at Trades Union congress . . . . 10 Sept. 1903

EIGHTY CLUB. Established in 1879 and 1880, to promote political education and to stimulate liberal organisation by Mr. Albert Grey, Sir Henry James, and lord Richard Grosvenor. Mr. Gladstone, president, 1887. The club adopted Home Rule, and 80 Liberal Unionists seceded, 18 May, 1887.

EIKŌN BASILIKĒ ("the Portraiture of His Sacred Majesty in his Solitudes and Sufferings"), a book of devotion formerly attributed to king Charles I., but now generally believed to have been written partially, if not wholly, by bishop Gauden, and possibly approved by the king: it was published in 1648–9, and 44 English editions and 10 in foreign languages, printed in 1649; 68 in all up to the present time. By direction of the parliament, Milton published a reply entitled "Iconoclastes," or Image-breaker.

EIRENICON. Peace manifesto, see *Russia*, Aug. 1898; and *Peace*, 1898 *et seq.*

EISENACH DECLARATION, see *Germany*, 1859.

EISTEDDFOD, at Llanelly Aug. 4-8, 1903, see *Bards*.

ELAM, see *Persia*.

EL ARISCH, Egypt, captured by the French under Reynier, 18 Feb. 1799. A convention was signed here between the grand vizier and Kleber for the evacuation of Egypt by the French, 28 Jan. 1800. He beat the Turks at Heliopolis on 20 March; and was assassinated on 14 June following.

ELBA, Isle of (on the coast of Tuscany), taken by admiral Nelson in 1796; but abandoned 1797. Elba was conferred upon Napoleon (with the title of emperor) on his relinquishing the throne of France, 5 April, 1814. He secretly embarked hence with about 1200 men in hired feluccas, on the night of 25 Feb. 1815, landed in Provence, 1 March, and soon after recovered the crown; see *France*, 1815. Elba was resumed by the grand duke of Tuscany, July, 1815; was annexed to Sardinia, 1860, and included in the kingdom of Italy in 1870; population in 1893 about 24,000.

ELBE, North German Lloyd Steamer, see *Wrecks*, 30 January, 1895, and 21 July, 1902.

ELCHINGEN, Bavaria. Here Ney beat the Austrians, 14 Oct. 1805, and was made duke of Elchingen.

ELCHO SHIELD, see under *Volunteers*.

ELDERS (in Greek, *presbuteroi*), in the early church equivalent with *episcopoi*, or bishops (see 1 *Tim.* iii. and *Titus* i.), who afterwards became a distinct and superior order. Elders in the presbyterian churches are laymen.

Elders' Widows Fund, established by the East India Company, in 1820, to provide for widows and orphans of some of its servants, was closed in 1860. In 1878 an act was passed to transfer the surplus money to the provident fund, &c.

ELDON'S ACT, see *Bankrupts*.

EL DORADO (the "Gilded Man"). When the Spaniards had conquered Mexico and Peru, they began to look for new sources of wealth, and having heard of a golden city ruled by a king or priest, smeared in oil and rolled in gold dust (which report was founded on a merely annual custom of the Indians), they organised various expeditions into the interior of South America, which were accompanied with disasters and crimes, about 1560. Raleigh's expeditions in search of gold in 1596 and 1617 led to his fall.

ELEASA, Palestine. Here Judas Maccabæus was defeated and slain by Bacchides and Alcimus, and the Syrians, about 161 B.C. (1 *Macc.* ix.)

ELEATIC SECT, founded at Elea in Sicily, by Xenophanes, of Colophon, about 535 B.C., whither he had been banished on account of his wild theory of God and nature. He supposed that the stars were extinguished every morning and rekindled at night; that eclipses were occasioned by a partial extinction of the sun; that there were several suns and moons for the convenience of the different climates of the earth, &c. *Strabo.* Zeno (about 364) was an Eleatic.

ELECTIONS PETITIONS. The laws respecting them were consolidated in 1828, 1839, and 1844. An act passed in 1848 was amended in 1865. By the act of 1868, 3 new judges were appointed, and three to be selected from all the judges to try election cases; justices Willes and Blackburn, and baron Martin were first appointed, Nov. 1868.

ELECTOR PALATINE, see *Palatinate*.

ELECTORS for members of parliament for counties were obliged to have forty shillings a-year in land, 8 Hen. VI. 1429. Among the acts relating to electors are the following: Election Act for the City of London passed 1724; Act depriving excise and custom-house officers and contractors with government of their votes, 1782; see *Customs*. Act to regulate polling, 1828. Great changes were made by the *Reform Acts* of 1832, 1867, 1868, and 1885. County elections act, 1836; see *Bribery*. The forty-shilling freeholders in Ireland lost their privilege in 1829. By Dodson's act, passed in 1861, university electors are permitted to vote by sending balloting papers. Hours of polling in metropolitan boroughs extended (from 8 A.M. to 8 P.M.) by act passed 25 Feb. 1878.

Mr. Shaw Lefevre's Plural Voting (Abolition) bill, based on the principle, "one man, one vote," rejected by the commons (243–196) . . 18 May, 1892
Mr. Stansfeld's Electors' Qualification and Registration bill (removing certain vexatious clauses), read a 2nd time . . . . . . 25 May ,,

ELECTORS of Germany. In the reign of Conrad I. king of Germany (912-918), the dukes and counts, from being merely officers, became gradually independent of the sovereign, and subsequently elected him. In 919 they confirmed the nomination of Henry I. duke of Saxony by Conrad as his successor. In the 13th century seven princes (the archbishops of Mentz, Treves, and Cologne, the king of Bohemia, the electors of Brandenburg and Saxony, and the elector Palatine), assumed the exclusive privilege of nominating the emperor. *Robertson.* An eighth elector (Bavaria) was made in 1648; and a ninth (Hanover) in 1692. The number was reduced to eight in 1777 (by the elector palatine acquiring Bavaria) and increased to ten at the peace of Luneville, in 1801. On the dissolution of the German empire, the crown of Austria was made hereditary, 1804-1806; see *Germany*.

ELECTRIC CLOCK; see *Electricity*, 1889.

ELECTRICAL ENGINEERS, see under *Telegraphs*.

ELECTRICITY, from the Greek *ēlektros*, electrum, amber. The electrical properties of rubbed amber are said to have been known to Thales, 600 B.C.; and Pliny, 70 A.D.; see *Magnetism*, *Electrical transmission of force*, p. 328, and *Niagara*.

The *Electrician* first published, 1861.

"The Intellectual Rise in Electricity: a History," by Dr. Park Benjamin, published, 1895. "Electric Movement in Air and Water," by lord Armstrong, published, June, 1897.

Electrical measurements: the following terms (after great electricians, suggested by sir Chas. Bright), were adopted by the electrical congress at Paris, 22 Sept. 1881: ohm, volt, ampère, coulomb, and farad. Important resolutions were passed by the international conference on electrical units at Paris (the "congress ohm" agreed to), April-May, 1884

Capital punishment by electricity adopted by the state of New York . . . . from 1 Jan. 1889

An electrical standard committee (consisting of lord Raleigh, sir Wm. Thomson and others) appointed, Dec. 1890; it was recommended that new denominations of standards be made, and determined with reference to the centimetre, gramme, and second, of the Board of Trade; the ohm to be the standard of resistance; the ampère, the standard of electrical current; the volt, the standard of electrical pressure; all being scientifically defined . . . 20 Feb. 1891

The committee's report printed Aug., 1891, supplementary report . . . . . . 29 Nov. 1892

Joint parliamentary committee on "Electrical Disturbances," viscount Cross, chairman June, 1893

FRICTIONAL OR STATIC ELECTRICITY

Gilbert records that other bodies besides amber generate electricity when rubbed, and that all substances may be attracted 1600

Otto von Guericke constructed the first electric machine (a globe of sulphur), about . . . 1647

Boyle published his electrical experiments . . 1676

Stephen Gray, aided by Wheeler, discovered that the human body conducts electricity, that electricity acts at a distance (motion in light bodies being produced by frictional electricity at a distance of 666 feet), the fact of electric induction, and other phenomena 1720-36

Dufay originated his dual theory of two electric fluids: one *vitreous*, from rubbed glass, &c., the other *resinous*, from rubbed amber, resin, &c.; and showed that two bodies similarly electrified repel each other, and attract bodies oppositely electrified, about 1733

Desaguliers classified bodies as electrics and non-electrics 1742

The Leyden jar (vial or bottle) discovered by Kleist, 1745, and by Cunæus and Muschenbroek, of Leyden: Winckler constructed the Leyden battery . 1746

Important researches of Watson, Canton, Beccaria and Nollet 1740-7

Franklin announced his theory of a single fluid, terming the vitreous electricity *positive*, and the resinous *negative*, 1747; and demonstrated the identity of the electric spark and lightning, drawing down electricity from a cloud by means of a kite . . . . . . June, 1752

At a pic-nic, he "killed a turkey by the electric spark, and roasted it by an electric jack before a fire kindled by the electric bottle" . . . 1748

Professor Richman killed at St. Petersburg, while repeating Franklin's experiments Aug. 1753

Beccaria published his researches on atmospheric electricity, 1758; and Æpinus his mathematical theory 1759

Electricity developed by fishes investigated by Ingenhousz, Cavendish, and others, about . . 1773

Lichtenberg produced his electrical figures . . 1777

Electro-Statics: Coulomb applied the torsion balance to the measurement of electric force . . 1785

Electro-Chemistry— water decomposed by Cavendish, Fourcroy, and others 1787-90

Discoveries of Galvani and Volta (see *Voltaic Electricity*, below) 1791-3

Œrsted, of Copenhagen, discovered electro-magnetic action (see *Electro-Magnetism*, next page) . 1819

Thermo-Electricity (currents produced by heat), discovered by Seebeck: it was produced by heating pieces of copper and bismuth soldered together, 1821; the Thermo-electrometer invented by sir Wm. Snow Harris, 1827; the Thermo-multiplier constructed by Melloni and Nobili, 1831. [Marcus constructed a powerful thermo-electric battery in 1865.]

Mr. C. V. Boys exhibits his very sensitive quartz-fibre thermopile at the Royal Institution, see *Moon* . . . . 14 June, 1889

Dr. Giraud's thermo-electric stove reported successful in London and Paris . . . May, 1893

Faraday produced a spark by the sudden separation of a coiled keeper from a permanent magnet (see *Magneto-Electricity*, next page) . . 1831

Wheatstone calculated the velocity of electricity, on the double fluid theory, to be 288,000 miles a second; on the single fluid theory, 576,000 miles a second 1834

Mr. W. G. Armstrong (aft. lord, died 27 Dec. 1900), discovered, and Faraday explained, the electricity of high pressure steam, which produces the hydro-electric machine 1840

ELECTRIC MACHINES. Otto von Guericke obtained sparks by rubbing a globe of sulphur, about 1647; Newton, Boyle, and others used glass, about 1675; Hawksbee improved the machine, about 1709; Bose introduced a metallic conductor, 1733; Winckler contrived the cushion for the rubber, 1741; Gordon employed a glass cylinder, 1742; for which a plate was substituted about 1770; Canton introduced amalgam for the rubber, 1751; Van Marum constructed an electric machine at Haarlem, said to have been the most powerful ever made, 1785; the Rev. A. Bennet invented the "doubler of electricity," 1786; Carvallo discovers that metals when insulated, acquire slight charges of electricity, 1787; Nicholson constructs an influence machine, 1788; modified by Ronalds, 1823; Dr. H. M. Noad set up at the Panopticon, Leicester-square, London, a very powerful electric machine and Leyden battery [in possession of Mr. Edwin Clark, 1862] . . . 1855

The *Hydro-Electric* machine, by Armstrong, was constructed 1840

Holtz's induction machine 1865

The ELECTROPHORUS, a useful apparatus for obtaining frictional electricity, was invented by Volta in 1775, and improved by him in . . 1827

C. F. Varley's "reciprocal electrophorus" invented

Sir William Thomson's "electric replenisher" described . . . . Jan. 1862

The Carré machine invented 1868

Mr. Apps's great inductorium, or induction coil, giving the largest sparks ever seen, exhibited at the Royal Polytechnic Institution . 29 March, 1869

The Voss machine introduced 1880

Mr. James Wimshurst invents a "continuous electrophorus" (very successful), and an "influence machine" 1882

ELECTROSCOPE and ELECTROMETER, as the terms signify, are apparatus for ascertaining the presence and quantity of electrical excitation. Pith-balls were employed in various ways as electroscopes by Gilbert, Canton, and others. Dr. Milner invented an electrometer similar to Peltier's, 1783. The gold leaf electrometer was invented by rev. A. Bennet, 1789, and improved by Singer, about 1810; Lane's discharging electrometer is dated 1767; Henley's, 1772; Bohnenberger's electroscope, 1820; Peltier's induction electrometer, about 1848; sir Wm. Thomson's quadrant electrometer, ... about, 1857

GALVANISM, OR VOLTAIC-ELECTRICITY, ELECTROLYSIS, AND ELECTRO-MAGNETISM.

(See *Electro-Physiology*.)

Sulzer noticed a peculiar sensation in the tongue when silver and lead were brought into contact with it and each other 1762

Madame Galvani observed the convulsion in the muscles of frogs when brought into contact with two metals, in 1789; and M. Galvani, after studying the phenomena, laid the foundation of the galvanic battery 1791

Volta announced his discovery of the "Voltaic pile," composed of discs of zinc and silver, and moistened card 1800

Mr. W. Cruikshank's experiments . . . . . ,,

By the voltaic pile, Nicholson and Carlisle decomposed water, and Dr. Henry decomposed nitric acid, ammonia, &c. . . . . . . ,,

Transfer of acids and alkalies by Hisinger and Berzelius 1803

Behrens formed a dry pile of 80 pairs of zinc, copper, and gilt paper 1805

By means of a large voltaic battery in the Royal Institution, London, Davy decomposed the alkali potash, and evolved the metal potassium, (soda and other substances soon after) . 6 Oct. 1807

Zamboni constructed a dry pile of paper discs, coated with tin on one side and peroxide of manganese on the other 1809

Children's battery fused platinum, &c. . . ,,

J. W. Ritter constructed his "secondary pile" about 1812

Davy exhibited the voltaic arc 1813

Wollaston's thimble battery ignited platinum wire. 1815

Multipliers or rheometers, popularly termed "galvanometers," invented by Ampère and by Schweigger, 1820; by Cumming, 1821; De la Rive, 1824; Ritchie (torsion), 1830; Joule (magnetic), 1843. Sir William Thomson has made many improvements since 1856; he described his reflecting galvanometer, and similar apparatus in the report of the British Association in 1867. Very large galvanometer made by prof. Wm. A. Cornell, of New York . . . . . Aug. 1885

Faraday described his discovery of electro-magnetic rotation . . . . Jan. 1822

Georg Simon Ohm enunciated his formulæ relating to the galvanic current, 1827; proposed erection of a statue of Ohm, at Munich, on the centenary of his birth, 16 March, 1789 . . . Feb. 1889

Improvement in constructing the *Voltaic battery* made by Wollaston, 1815; Becquerel, 1829; Sturgeon, 1830; J. F. Daniell, 1836; Grove (nitric acid, &c.), 1839; Jacobi, 1840; Smee, 1840; Bunsen (carbon, &c.), 1842; Grove (gas battery), 1842.

Faraday read the first series of his "Experimental Researches on Electricity" at the Royal Society, 21 Nov. 1831

Faraday demonstrated the nature of electro-chemical decomposition, and the principle that the quantity and intensity of electric action of a galvanic battery depend on the size and number of plates employed 1834

Wheatstone invented his electro-magnetic chronoscope 1840

Copper-Zinc Couple (*which see*) constructed by Dr. J. H. Gladstone and Mr. A. Tribe . . . 1872

Batteries; Bichromate of potash battery; a modification of Dr. Leeson's; very powerful; now much used. (Gaston Planté's lead battery, powerful, 1860.) Chloride of silver battery (14,400 cells)—results of its discharge published by Drs. Warren de la Rue and Hugo Müller. Powerful results exhibited at Royal Institution, London, 21 Jan., 1881

Dr. Byrne's pneumatic battery (air blown in), very effective, announced 1878
See under *Electric Lighting*.

Mr. Coad's primary battery, put forth in 1884, greatly improved, exhibited in Soho square, London, W., Jan.; Major Renard's primary battery exhibited in London, Jan.; Mr. Weymersch's primary battery exhibited . . . . Feb. 1890

Continuous to alternating current transformer, invented by sir David Salomons and Mr. L. Pyke; exhibited . . . . . . 1 Dec. 1892

Electric Accumulator, or secondary battery, a modification by M. Faure, of Gaston Planté's powerful lead battery of 1860, was exhibited at Paris, May, 1881. In June a box, one cubic foot in size, containing four cells, inclosing thin sheets of lead surrounded with felt saturated with dilute acid, &c., was conveyed from Paris to London. Sir Wm. Thomson found it to possess the electric energy of one million foot-pounds; and said, in a letter to *The Times* of 9 June, 1881: "This solves the problem of storing electricity in a manner and in a state useful for many important applications" . . 6 June, 1881

Electro-Magnetism began with Œrsted's discovery of the action of the electric current on the magnetic needle, 1819; proved by Ampère, who exhibited the action of the voltaic pile upon the magnetic needle, and of terrestrial magnetism upon the voltaic current; he also arranged the conducting wire in the form of a helix or spiral, invented a galvanometer, and imitated the magnet by a spiral galvanic wire 1820

Arago magnetised a needle by the electric current, and attracted iron filings by the connecting wire of a galvanic battery . . . . . . ,,

The first electro-magnet 1825

Induction of electric currents discovered by Faraday and announced 1831. (sir W. H. Preece made experiments, showing how induced currents (from wire to wire) might be utilized in electric telegraphy, Nov., 1892).

Becquerel invented an electro-magnetic balance . 1831

Faraday discovered the electro-magnetic rotative force developed in a magnet by voltaic electricity, 1831; experiments on the induction of a voltaic current, &c. 1834–5

Sturgeon made a bar of soft iron magnetic by surrounding it with coils of wire, and sending an electric current through the wire 1837

Induction coil made by Professor G. C. Page of Salem, Mass. . . . . ,,

Joseph Henry announced his discovery of secondary currents . . . . . . 2 Nov. 1838

Breguet used electro-magnetic force to manufacture mathematical instruments, about 1854

Magneto-Electricity (the converse of Œrsted's discovery of electro-magnetism), discovered by Faraday, who produced an electric spark by suddenly separating a coiled keeper from a permanent magnet; and found that an electric current existed in a copper disc rotated between the poles of a magnet (paper read to the Royal Society, 24 Nov.) 1831

The *Magneto-Electric* machine arose out of Faraday's discovery, and was first made at Paris by Pixii, 1832; and in London by Saxton . . . 1833

Magneto-electricity applied to electro-plating by Woolwich 1842

Ruhmkorff's magneto-electric induction coil constructed, about 1850

Siemens' armature produced 1854

Principle of accumulation by successive action discovered by Wilde; 1865, by mutual action (by which permanent steel magnets are dispensed with), independently by Wheatstone and Siemens, 1866

Dr. H. Wilde's description of his machine (a powerful generator of dynamic electricity, by means of permanent magnets) and the magneto-electric machine (constructed in 1865) sent to the Royal Society by professor Faraday and reported, 26 April, ,,

The light (resembling bright moon-light) exhibited on the top of Burlington house . 2 March, 1867

Dynamo-magneto-electric machines, by Wheatstone and Siemens, described at the Royal Society, 14 Feb.; by Ladd . . . . 14 March, ,,

"*Faraday as a Discoverer*," by Professor Tyndall, published . . . . . . March, 1868

Trial of Siemens' dynamo-magneto *electric light* in the torpedo service at Sheerness reported successful . . . . 18 Dec. 1871

Gramme's magneto-electric machine described . 1875

Two of Siemens' machines ordered for the Lizards, announced 1878

Mr. W. Groves' electro-induction balance . . 1879

International Electrical Congress at Paris with exhibition . . . . . 15 Aug.–15 Nov. 1881
[Medals and other honours awarded to England.]

Mr. E. J. Atkins' method of separating metals from their alloys by electrolysis, announced . Nov. 1883

Decomposition of common salt by electrolysis and the production thereby of alkali and bleaching powder very successful, discovered by H. Y. Castner (died Oct. 1899).

APPLICATIONS—ELECTRIC TELEGRAPH.* See *Telegraph*.

The transmission of electricity by an insulated wire was shown by Watson and others 1747

Telegraphic arrangements were devised by Lesarge, 1744; Betancourt, 1787; Cavallo, 1795; Salva, 1796; Sœmmering, exhibited 29 Aug. 1809; Ronalds 1816

Ampère invents his telegraphic arrangement, employing the magnetic needle and coil, and the galvanic battery 1820

F. (aft. sir Francis) Ronalds publishes an account of his electric telegraph (died, aged 85, 8 Aug. 1873) 1823

Professor Wheatstone constructs an electro-magnetic apparatus, by which 30 signals are conveyed through nearly four miles of wire . June, 1836

Telegraphs invented by Schilling, Gauss, and Weber (magneto-electric), 1833; by Steinheil and by Masson, 1837; by Morse (died 1872). . . . 1837

The magnetic needle telegraph patented by (aft. sir) Wm. F. Cooke and (aft. sir) Charles Wheatstone. (The Society of Arts Albert gold medal was awarded to them in June, 1867) . 12 June, ,,

Mr. Robert Stirling Newall, of Gateshead, patented his wire rope used for submarine telegraphs . . 1840

Mr. Cooke set up the telegraph line on the Great Western Railway, from Paddington to West Drayton, 1838-9; on the Blackwall line, 1840; and in Glasgow 1841

Wheatstone's alphabetical printing telegraph patented . . . . ,,

The first telegraph line in America set up from Washington to Baltimore 1844

The murderer Tawell apprehended by means of the telegraph 1845

The electric telegraph company established (having purchased Cooke and Wheatstone's telegraphic inventions) 1846

Gutta-percha suggested as an insulator by Faraday 1847

Professor Charles Wheatstone drew plans of a projected *submarine telegraph* between Dover and Calais 1840

Mr. John Watkins Brett (on behalf of his brother, Jacob Brett, the inventor and patentee), submitted a similar plan to Louis Philippe without success 1847

He obtained permission from Louis Napoleon to make a trial, 1847; took place . . 28 Aug. 1850

The connecting wires (27 miles long) were placed on the government pier in Dover harbour, and in the *Goliath* steamer were coiled about 30 miles in length of telegraphic wire, enclosed in a covering of gutta-percha, half an inch in diameter. The *Goliath* started from Dover, unrolling the telegraphic wire as it proceeded, and allowing it to drop to the bed of the sea. In the evening the steamer arrived on the French coast, and the wire was run up the cliff at cape Grisnez to its terminal station, and messages were sent to and fro between England and the French coast. But the wire, in settling into the sea-bottom, crossed a rocky ridge, and snapped in two, and thus the enterprise for that time failed.

New arrangements were soon made, and on a scale of greater magnitude; and the telegraph was opened; the opening and closing prices of the funds in Paris were known on the London stock exchange within business hours, and guns were fired at Dover by communication from Calais; this cable was laid by the late T. R. Crampton, 13 Nov. 1851

Duplex Telegraphy—two messages transmitted along a single wire at the same time in opposite directions first accomplished by Dr. Gintl, Austrian, 1853; by Messrs. Siemens, 1857; in the same direction, by Stark, of Vienna, 1855; apparatus perfected by Stearns, an American, and also by Muirhead and Taylor for long cables; applied to British telegraphs 1873

Quadruplex Telegraphy—four messages along one wire; successful experiments between London and Liverpool . . . . 25 Sept. 1877

Mr. T. A. Edison's quadruplex instrument, by which four messages, two from each end, may be transmitted upon one wire simultaneously, and professor Delaney's synchronous multiplex instrument by which six messages may be so transmitted on one wire, were exhibited at the Post Office Jubilee Fête . . . . . 2 July, 1890

Professor Elisha Gray's teleautograph exhibited at the Royal society . . . . 13 June, 1894

Prof. Hughes in 1879-80 and in 1888 telephoned messages across space. Capt. Jackson succeeding in getting Morse signals across the Air, Dec. 1895

Wireless Telegraphy—Sir W. H. Preece, C.B., F.R.S., at the Royal Institution, 4 June, 1897, after some remarks on the propagation of waves in the ether; described and illustrated his own method of "Signalling through Space without Wires," by means of electro-magnetic waves of low frequency and two parallel circuits, established on each bank of a river. This system was successfully used in 1895, to telegraph across the Sound of Mull, when the submarine cable had broken down. Sir Wm. Preece next exhibited and explained the apparatus by which Hertzian waves of high frequency are utilized in the new system invented by Mr. Marconi, a young Italian, who brought it to England, in July, 1896, and who assisted at the lecture.—*Times*, 7 June, 1897. By Marconi's system, signals had been transmitted across the Bristol Channel, between Penarth and Brian Down, about 9 miles. Sir Wm. Preece considered the invention valuable for shipping and lighthouse purposes. Further experiments by the Post Office authorities between Dover and Fort Burgoyne, 17 Sept., *et seq.* 1897; 2nd by Prof. Slaby with balloons (13½ mi.) March, 1898. Very successful experiments between the S. Foreland lighthouse and the E. Goodwin lightship (12 mi.). Current not affected by stormy weather, mid Jan. 1899; again 30 Jan.; the first Press message, by Marconi's system, from Wimreux, near Boulogne, to S. Foreland; messages sent across the Channel in all weathers, 28-31 March. Lord Rayleigh and members of trinity house inspect Sig. Marconi's system at S. Foreland, messages worked well, 6 April; Mr. Ritchie (pres. Board of Trade) witnessed similar demonstrations, 15 April; experiments in the presence of a French commission between a moving ship and the land, messages sent between the French gunboat *Isis*, the S. Foreland, the E. Goodwin lightship and Boulogne. It was clearly shown by a new device discovered by Sig. Marconi that not only can moving ships communicate with each other at sea, but that the messages can be concentrated on the point intended to be reached, 24 April; similar experiments carried on before the Chinese minister and others, 25 April; the E. Goodwin lightship being run into and damaged by *F. F. Matthews*, steamer, a wireless message from the lightship to the S. Foreland procured assistance, 28 April; again of practical use in an accident to a seaman, 18 May; experiments by Prof. Tuma between 2 balloons at Vienna, fairly successful, 14 July; messages sent from Dover town-hall to S. Foreland and E. Goodwin lightship, 16 Aug.; experiments with the Popoff system arranged under conditions of warfare, successfully carried on between the Black Sea fleet and the Crimean shore, reported, 25 Sept.; rapid development, successful long-distance transmissions from the Poldhu station at the Lizard, Cornwall, to St. Catherine's, Isle of Wight, 22 Jan. 1901; across the Atlantic to St. John's, Newfoundland, 13, 14 Dec.; and at night 2000 mi. to and from the ship *Philadelphia*, 25 Feb. 1902. Correspondence as to whether Prof. Oliver Lodge (in 1894) or Sig. Marconi (about June, 1902) was the first inventor, *Times*, 5 and 15 July, 1902. Messages sent from the Lizard received by the *Carlo Alberto*, Italian cruiser, at Kronstadt, 1,600 mi., 14 July, 1902; and from there to the Mediterranean, Aug.-Sept. Various patents taken out by sir O. Lodge,

* Sir W. H. Preece, F.R.S., president of the Institution of Electrical Engineers, at a meeting on 26 Jan. 1893, described the amazing progress of the applications of electricity since 1850, in telegraphy, railway signaling, telephony, lighting, chemistry, transmission of power, and traction. In relation to our press, Sir Wm. Preece stated that in 1871, 21,701,968 words were transmitted by telegraph, and in 1891, 600,409,000.

M. Righi Branley, Popoff, Slaby, Arco, Braun, Solari, Guarini Cervera, Ducretet, Castelli, Rutherford, Jackson, and Willoughby Smith . 1902
Messages (sent from Cape Breton to Poldhu, Cornwall) exchanged between the king and lord Minto, gov.-gen. of Canada, and the king of Italy; also by the Canadian government to the *Times*, congratulating the British people on the accomplishment by Signor Marconi, of the *greatest feat which modern science has as yet achieved*, 21 Dec. 1902; used successfully between Aldershot and the Channel squadron off Portsmouth . 12 Jan. 1903
President Roosevelt sends a greeting to king Edward . . . . 19 Jan. „
Two telegrams from the United States received by "Marconigraph," Poldhu . 28, 29 March, „
25 stations now erected, 8 in England . April, „
Messrs. Taft and Williams's method of finding ore by electricity tried successfully at Prestatyn, N. Wales. . . . . . . 26 March, „
The Orling-Armstrong system shown at the Alexandra palace . . . . 2 April „
Application of X rays and Finsen or ultra-violet rays, reported beneficial in lupus, cancer, etc., *Times* . . . . 19 May, „
Italian legation begin installation of Marconi system at Pekin to communicate direct with ships in the gulf of Pe-chi-li, reported. . . . 11 June, „
International conference on wireless telegraphy opened in Berlin . . . . 4 Aug. „
"History of Wireless Telegraphy," by J. J. Fahie, pub. 1899.

Communications complete between Dover and Ostend and between Portpatrick and Donaghadee, (laid by sir Chas. Bright), May, 1853. "The late sir Charles Bright was the first to lay a cable in deep water," lord Kelvin, ... 30 Oct., 1896
Holyhead and Howth . . . . . June, 1854
Paris and Bastia . . . . . . Nov. „
London and Constantinople . . . . May, 1858
Cromer and Emden . . . . „
Aden and Suez . . . . May, 1859
Malta and Alexandria . . . . 28 Sept. 1861
England and Bombay, opened . . 1 March, 1865
Marsala, Sicily, and La Calle, Algeria. . 21 June, „

Over-house electric telegraphs (first erected at Paris) set up between their premises in the City and West-end by Messrs. Waterlow, in 1857, extended throughout London 1859-73
House's printing telegraph, 1846; Bain's electro-chemical telegraph, 1846; Hughes's system, 1855; the American combination system (of the preceding), which can convey 2000 words an hour, adopted by the American telegraph company, Jan. 1859
Wheatstone's automatic printing telegraph patented 1860
It was stated that there were in work 15,000 miles of electric telegraph wire in Great Britain; 80,000 on the continent of Europe; and 48,000 in America; and altogether about 150,000 miles laid down in the world . . . . July, 1862
Bonelli's typo-electric telegraph, made known and company established, 1860; and tried between Liverpool and Manchester, 1863; promised revival, June, 1864
An "electric telegraph" conference, at which 16 states (not Great Britain) were represented, met at Paris, see *Telegraph* . . . . March, 1865
The Telegraph Act (see *Telegraph*) passed 31 July, 1868
It enabled H.M.'s postmaster-general to acquire, work, and maintain electric telegraphs; postal telegraphy began . . . . . 5 Feb. 1872
Result of the "Derby" race sent to Calcutta in five minutes . . . . 24 May, 1871
Society of Telegraph Engineers established, 28 Feb. 1872
Statue of Morse at New York uncovered 10 June, „
Messages rise from 6,000,000 to 20,000,000 a year . 1875
The "shilling telegraph" said not to pay . July, „
A new international telegraphic convention came into operation . . . . . . 1 Jan. 1876
Direct line between New Zealand and London, completed 18 Feb.; communication between lord mayor and mayors of Wellington and Dunedin, 23 Feb. „

ATLANTIC TELEGRAPH. A plan to unite Europe and America by telegraph was entered at the government registration office in June, 1845, by Mr. J. Watkins Brett and Mr. Jacob Brett, who made proposals to the government, which were not accepted. This scheme was carried out by a company in 1858, with the concurrence of the British and American governments.
2500 miles of wire were manufactured, and tested in March, 1857
The laying it down commenced at Valentia, in Ireland on . . . . 5 Aug. „
The vessels employed were the *Niagara* and *Susquehanna* (American vessels), and the *Leopard* and *Agamemnon* (British vessels). After sailing a few miles the cable snapped. This was soon repaired; but on 11 Aug. after 300 miles of wire had been *paid out*, it snapped again (and the vessels returned to Plymouth) . . . . 11 Aug. „
A second attempt to lay the cable failed through a violent storm, ... 20–21 June, 1858
The third voyage was successful. The junction between the two continents was completed by the laying down of 2050 miles of wire from Valentia, in Ireland, to Newfoundland; the engineer, sir Chas. Bright was knighted, aged 26. The first two messages, on 5 Aug., were from the queen of England to the president of the United States and his reply . . . . . . 5 Aug. „
This event caused great rejoicing in both countries; but, unfortunately, the insulation of the wire gradually became more faulty, and after 271 messages had been sent and received the power of transmitting intelligence utterly ceased owing to the employment of too high battery power, 4 Sept. „
A new company was formed 1860
First cable to India laid by sir Chas. Bright for the government in 1864
The *Great Eastern* steamer, engaged to lay down 2300 miles of wire, with 25,000 tons burden, sailed for Valentia, Ireland, from the Thames, sir Samuel Canning, engineer in charge for contractors, sir C. Bright and Mr. Latimer Clark, consulting engineers to the company, accompanied by professor Wm. Thomson and Mr. Cromwell F. Varley, as electricians, 15 July, 1865
After connecting the wire with the land, the *Great Eastern* sailed from Valentia . . 23 July, „
Telegraphic communication with the vessel (interrupted by two faults, due to defective insulation, caused by pieces of metal pressed into the gutta-percha coating, which were immediately repaired) finally ceased on 2 Aug. The apparatus for raising the wire proving insufficient, the vessel returned, and arrived at the Medway 19 Aug. „
Atlantic telegraph company reconstituted as the Anglo-American telegraph company limited, March, 1866
The *Great Eastern*, with a new cable, sailed from the Medway, 30 June; the shore-end at Valentia was spliced with the main cable, and the *Great Eastern* sailed, 13 July; 1200 miles of cable had been laid, 22 July; the cable was completely laid at Heart's Content, Newfoundland, and a message sent to lord Stanley, 27 July; message from the queen to president of the United States sent, 28 July, "From the queen, Osborne, to the president of the United States, Washington. The queen congratulates the president on the successful completion of an undertaking which she hopes may serve as an additional bond of union between the United States and England." To which he replied . . . . 30 July, „
The lost cable of 1865 recovered, 2 Sept.; and its laying completed at Newfoundland . 3 Sept. „
The *Great Eastern* arrived at Liverpool 19 Sept. „
Baronetcies conferred on Messrs. Curtis Lampson, John Pender, Daniel Gooch, R. R. Glass, Samuel Canning: prof. Wm. Thomson and capt. James Anderson, chief promoters of the company, were knighted . . . . . . Oct. „
[It was stated (in Sept. 1866) that the engineer of the cable passed signals through 3700 miles of wire by means of a battery formed in a lady's thimble.]

The U. S. congress voted a gold medal to Cyrus Field, for his exertions connected with Atlantic telegraphs . . . . 7 March, 1867
At a dinner given to Cyrus Field at Willis's Rooms, London, telegraphic messages were exchanged between the company and lord Monck, viceroy of Canada and president Johnson . 1 July, 1868
French Atlantic Telegraph company formed; French government grant concession for 20 years, from 1 Sept. 1869, to baron (1871) Julius de Reuter and baron Emile d'Erlanger, see *Reuter* . 8 July, ,,
Anglo-Danish telegraph (Newbiggin to Copenhagen) completed . . . . . . 31 Aug. ,,
European end of the French Atlantic cable laid at Brest, 17 June; the American end at Duxbury, Massachusetts . . . . . . 23 July, 1869
Reported union between the Anglo-American and French Atlantic telegraph companies . Jan. 1870
Telegraph between Bombay and Suez completed ,,
Telegraph between Adelaide and Port Darwin, Australia, completed . . . 22 Aug. 1872
Message from the mayor of Adelaide received by the lord mayor of London, and replied to, 21 Oct. ,,
The *fourth* Atlantic telegraph cable laid by the *Great Eastern*, from Valentia, Ireland, to Heart's Content, Newfoundland 8 June–3 July, 1873
The Brazil telegraph cable completely laid, 22 Sept. ,,
"*Faraday*," a great electric cable ship, built for Siemens Brothers, launched at Newcastle (see *Steam*), 17 Feb.; sails to lay the "Direct United States Company's" cable, 16 May; laid shore-end in Nova Scotia, 31 May; in New Hampshire, 8 June; connected with Newfoundland, July . 1874
The *sixth* Anglo-American telegraph laid by the *Great Eastern* . . . . . Aug.–Sept. ,,
E. A. Cowper's Writing telegraph: quick plain writing (36 miles), exhibited at Royal Institution, &c. [an improved one by J. Hart Robertson exhibited in London, 1887] . . . . . May, 1879
South African line laid between Mozambique and Natal, 23 Aug.; connected with Capetown; telegrams sent by the queen to sir Bartle Frere and others, 25 Dec.; opened to the public 29 Dec. ,,
The new French Transatlantic Cable to be laid from Brest to St. Pierre by the *Faraday*, sailed June; connected with Halifax, Oct. 1879; line from Paris to New York opened . 1 June, 1880
International Congress of Electricians opened at Paris, 15 Sept.; exhibition . 11 Aug.-20 Nov. 1881
New Atlantic Cable laid by the *Faraday* 22 Aug. *et seq.* ,,
Telegraph from England to Panama completed Sept. 1882
Many submarine cables laid down . . *et seq.* ,,
International Sub-marine Conference, Paris, 16 Oct. ,,
Cromwell Fleetwood Varley, electrical engineer, who patented many inventions, died . 2 Sept. 1883
International Conference for protection of submarine cables, Paris, closed; convention agreed to, 26 Oct. 1883: signed at London, 14 March; signed for 26 states at London, at Paris 26 March, 1884; another conference . . . . 1 Dec. 1886
The *Volta*, an electric launch (37 feet long, 7 feet beam) built of steel, constructed by Messrs. Stephens, Smith & Co. of Millwall, designed by Mr. A. Reckenzaun, crossed from Dover to Calais and back by means of one charge of the accumulators; about 4 hours crossing . . 13 Sept. ,,
Electric boat for communicating light to powder houses, &c.; invented by Thomas Webb; launched at Waltham Abbey . . . Aug. ,,
Arrangements invented for transmitting telegraphic messages from railway trains in motion without contact with the ordinary wires 1887
A central laboratory of electricity inaugurated at Grenelle, Paris, by the International society of electricians 1888
Sir Charles Bright, an eminent engineer, who laid many telegraph cables, died, . . 3 May, ,,
Electric omnibus invented by Mr. Radcliffe Ward, running in London . . . . Feb. 1889
Messrs. Moore & Wright announce their *column printing telegraph* in which messages are produced resembling type writing . . . April ,,
The Metropolitan electric supply company propose six central stations, W. & W.C. . April ,,
International Electro-Technical congress at Frankfort-on-Maine, opened . . . . 8 Sept. 1891
Electrical exhibition at the Crystal Palace, near London, opened . . . . . 9 Jan. 1892
Electrical Exhibition at St. Petersburg, opened 23 Jan. ,,
Great progress made, messages and returns sent all round the world in a few minutes from New York, during an electrical exposition . June, 1895
Sir John Pender, an energetic promoter of submarine telegraphy, born 1815, died . 7 July, ,,
Meetings of sir J. Wolfe Barry, sir Robert Herbert, and Mr. Chas. Bright, committee of the Sub-marine Telegraph Memorial, to establish a memorial to sir John Pender and to promote an international memorial recording the jubilee of submarine-telegraphy in 1901; subscriptions invited . . . . 30 Oct., 10, 27 Nov. ,,
Submarine telegraph cable between Emden and Vigo, opened, reported . . . 24 Dec. ,,
All British Pacific Cable scheme reported to the Colonial Office by Mr. Chas. Bright . May, 1897
"Sub-marine Telegraphs," by Mr. Chas. Bright, published . . . . . . Nov. 1898
New cable laid between Brest and England, reported . . . . . . 3 Aug. 1899
Successful experiments in rapid telegraphing in Buda Pesth and Berlin, 220 words sent in 10 secs. Sept. ,,
German-American Cable, between Emden and New York, opened . . . . 1 Sept. 1900
Sub-marine cable between Cornwall and St. Vincent, Cape de Verd Islands, opened . 30 Jan. 1901
Cable from S. Africa to W. Australia, opened, Oct. ,,
Committee to consider the cable communications of the empire, presided over by lord Balfour, evidence given by sir E. A. Sassoon, sir J. D. Pender, sir Sandford Fleming, Mr. Chas. Bright, and others 1901–2
Pacific Cable bill passed, 16 Aug. 1901; amendment bill passed . . . . . 7 Aug. 1902
All British Pacific Cable from Vancouver to Queensland, connecting New Zealand, Norfolk Island, and Australia, first section completed at Doubtless Bay, 25 March, 1902; the king receives a message from Fiji, 10 April; last link completed at Suva, Fiji, 31 Oct.; a telegraphic girdle round the world, touching foreign soil only at Madeira and St. Vincent; a message travels the whole circuit in 30 minutes, *Times* . 1 Nov. ,,
ELECTRIC CLOCK, &c. Professor Wheatstone invented an electro-magnetic telegraph clock in 1840. Clocks worked by electricity, invented by Mr. Alexander Bain, Mr. Shepherd, and others, appeared in the exhibition of 1851. An electric clock, with four dials, illuminated at night, was set up for some time in front of the office of the electric telegraph company, in the Strand, London, July, 1852. A time-ball was set up by Mr. French, in Cornhill, in 1856. In 1860, Mr. C. V. Walker so connected the clock of the Greenwich observatory with that of the South-eastern station, London, that they could be controlled by electricity.
Lowne's electric clock reported successful mid-May, 1903

ELECTRIC LIGHT.

Humphry Davy produced electric light with carbon points 1800
Apparatus for regulating the electric light were devised in 1846, and shown by W. Staite's patents, 1846, 1849; Staite (at Sunderland, 25 Oct. 1847), and Petrie in 1848; by Foucault soon after.
Jules Duboscq's *Electric Lamp* (the most perfect of the kind) appeared at the Paris exhibition in 1855; and was first employed by professor Tyndall, at the Royal Institution, London, for illustrating lectures on light and colours . . . 1856
The works of new Westminster bridge were illuminated by Watson's electric light 1858
The *Magneto-Electric* light (the most brilliant artificial light yet produced), devised by Prof. Holmes, successfully tried at the South Foreland lighthouse, Dover . . . . . 1858 and 1859
The French government ordered eight lighthouses to be illuminated by electric light . . April, 1861
M. Serrin, of Paris, exhibited his improved electric lamp 1862

Electric Candle, invented by Paul Jablochkoff (an electric current passed through two carbons side by side with a slip of kaolin between them, produces a steady, soft, noiseless light; the carbons burn like wax); reported to the Academy of Sciences, Paris, by M. Dénayrouze . . . Oct. 1876
The electric light successfully employed for photography by Mr. H. Van der Weyde . . . . ,,
Head, Wrightson, & Co., of Stockton-on-Tees, use Siemens' electric light for bridge building . . ,,
At the Magasin du Louvre, 8 electric lights replaced 100 Carcel gas-burners; as manageable as coal gas supply; tried at West India docks 15 June, 1877
Tyndall's experiments at S. Foreland, demonstrate superiority of Siemens' dynamo-electric machine, Aug. 1876–July, ,,
Gramme's machine (light equal to 758 candles) . ,,
Serrin's and Jablochkoff's lights improved by Rapieff, a Russian; taken up by Mr. E. J. Reed, M.P.; a small magneto-electric machine, worked by steam; conducting wires replace the gasworks and pipes . . . . . . July, 1878
Mr. Stayton reports, that the light is much dearer than gas, and not suitable for street lighting in London . . . . Sept. ,,
Electric light tried at Westminster palace, 28 March, ,,
Two of Siemens' dynamo-magneto-electric machines ordered for the Lizards lighthouses . . . ,,
The Gaiety theatre lit by light from Lontin's machine and modification of Jablochkoff's Aug. ,,
Hippolyte Fontaine's treatise on Electric Lighting, 1877; translated by Paget Higgs, published . ,,
Mr. T. A. Edison announces at New York his discovery of a method of producing a great number of lights and much mechanical power from a Ritchie inductive coil, a dynamo-electric machine, which he terms "telemachon," which may be worked by water-power or steam; this causes a panic among gas companies in London, and depression in value of shares . . Sept., Oct. ,,
Edison's plans of subdividing lights filed at patent office . . . . 23 Oct. ,,
National Electric Light company forming Nov. ,,
Richard Werdermann's electric light subdivided; a number of jets lit simultaneously; shown by British telegraph company . . . . 2 Nov. ,,
Electric light used for large workshops at Woolwich, &c., throughout the country . . . Nov. ,,
Times machine-room lit by six lights from one current; Rapieff system . . . . Oct.–Nov. ,,
Three systems trying at New York by Edison, Sawyer, and Brush . . . . . . Nov. ,,
Wallace lamp (American), introduced by Mr. Ladd, autumn, ,,
Jablochkoff candle tried at Westgate-on-Sea, by Mr. E. F. Davis, 2–26 Dec.; light successful; difficulty in practice; given up . . . Dec. ,,
Formation of nitric acid in the air by electric light; announced by Mr. T. Wills, 13 Dec. 1878; of hydro-cyanic or prussic acid by prof. J. Dewar, autumn, 1879
Machines of Farmer & Wallace, Lontin, De Meritens, Browning, Carré, and others in use in London . . . . ,,
Light given up at Billingsgate market, about 30 Jan. ,,
Siemens' light successful at the Albert Hall, 13 Feb. ,,
Edison obtains beautiful light from platinum which fuses; used 600-horse power to obtain 20,000 lights at one station; failure announced, March; his patent registered . . . . 23 April, ,,
Exhibition of lights at Royal Albert Hall opened by the prince of Wales . . . . . 7 May, ,,
M. Jamin's electric candle exhibited at Academy of Sciences, Paris . . . about 17 March, ,,
A continuous current dynamo-magneto-electric machine patented by lord Elphinstone and C. W. Vincent (since improved)
A committee of the House of Commons appointed "to consider whether it is desirable to authorize municipal corporations or other local authorities to adopt any schemes for lighting by electricity" (Dr. Lyon Playfair, chairman), reports: "The energy of one-horse power may be converted into gaslight, and yields a luminosity equal to 12-candle power. But the same amount of energy transformed into electric light produces 1,600-candle power. . . . Scientific witnesses considered that in the future the electric current might be extensively used to transmit power as well as light to considerable distances, so that the power applied to mechanical purposes during the day might be made available for light during the night. . . . There seems to be no reason to doubt that the electric light has established itself for lighthouse illumination, and is fitted to illumine large symmetrical places, such as squares, public halls, railway stations, and workshops. . . . Compared with gas, the economy for equal illumination does not yet appear to be conclusively established. . . . Gas companies, in the opinion of your committee, have no special claims to be considered as the future distributors of electric light . . . Your committee, however, do not consider that the time has yet arrived to give general powers to private electric companies to break up the streets, unless by consent of the local authorities."—*Times*. . . . . 19 June, 1880
Electric light placed on Thames Embankment, in British Museum, at Victoria Station, &c. Dec. ,,
System of C. F. Brush (American), exhibited in London, said to be simple and trustworthy 23 Dec. ,,
Dr. C. William Siemens reports to Royal Society, that electric light acts like solar light on vegetation . . . . . . 2 March, ,,
Electric lights set up for trial on Thames Embankment, north side (Jablochkoff system), 13 Dec. 1878; Waterloo Bridge, 10 Oct. 1879; continued, April, ,,
Mr. J. W. Swan exhibits his system of dividing light, &c., at Newcastle-on-Tyne (aft. in London) 20 Oct. ,,
Trial of three systems in London: Lontin's, Southwark bridge, &c.; Brush, Blackfriars' bridge, &c.; Siemens', Guildhall, &c. . . . 31 March, 1881
Swan's incandescent lamp set up in Earnock colliery, Hamilton, Lanarkshire, 9 Aug.; also in the Savoy Theatre, London, successfully, opened 10 Oct.
Junior Carlton Club first lit by the electric accumulator . . . . 16 Sept. ,,
Godalming lit by electric light produced by water wheels driven by the Wey, Sept.; reported successful . . . . 15 Dec. ,,
New lamp (the sun) by Louis Clerc, a combination of the arc and incandescent systems . June, 1882
The electric "sun" lamp and power company was formed . . . . July, ,,
Electric lighting act passed . . . . 18 Aug. ,,
The Ferranti system of electric lighting (invented by Sir William Thomson, Mr. S. Ziani de Ferranti, and Mr. Alfred Thomson) successfully tried, Dec. ,,
International electrical and gaslight exhibition at the Crystal Palace opened . . . . 13 Dec. ,,
Electric light applied by Bell Brothers, Newcastle, to their mines . . . . . . Dec. ,,
Elphinstone and Vincent machine advertised for sale . . . . ,,
Mr. J. E. H. Gordon's great dynamo machine exhibited at Woolwich . . . . 25 Oct. ,,
Messrs. G. C. V. Holmes, F. E. Burke, and F. Cheesewright's invention for the use of the electric light in railways tried on Great Northern line, reported successful . . . . 25 Oct. ,,
St. Matthew's Church, Brixton, lit by electricity 28 Oct. ,,
Gaulard-Gibbs' system of secondary generators announced April; inaugurated on the Metropolitan railway . . . . . . Nov. ,,
H. T. Barnett's secondary battery tried at the Great Western station . . . Oct. *et seq.* ,,
Mr. O. C. D. Ross's improved galvanic battery for light and motion 1883–4
Domestic electric lighting by the Beeman, Taylor and King system tried at Colchester 11 June, 1884
Electric light employed in Liverpool and Manchester trains . . . . . . Aug. ,,
Electric lighting successful at the Fisheries, 1883, and Health exhibitions . . . . . ,,
Brighton successfully lit by the Hammond-Wright system; described . . . . . Nov. ,,
Upward's primary battery (an advance); use of acid dispensed with . . . . July, 1886
The Edison & Swan united electric light company *v.* Woodhouse & Rawson for infringement of patent for carbon filaments; verdict for plaintiffs 20 May, ,,

Affirmed on appeal, judge Cotton dissentient 31 Jan. 1887

Kensington & Knightsbridge electric lighting company's first station opened . . Jan. ,,

Mr. Edison's "Pyro-Magnetic" dynamo, in which heat is directly transformed into electricity without the intervention of steam-engine or other machinery, announced to the American association . . . . Sept ,,

Duc de Feltre's suggestion for the employment of windmills to produce electric light by working dynamo machines; experiments made at Cap de la Hève . . . . Sept. ,,

Mr. Urquhart's new portable electric lamp, weighing 4 lb. 2 oz., adapted for coal mines, &c.; exhibited in London . . . . Dec. ,,

Schanschieff's primary battery; applicable to lighting, miners' lamps &c. . . . autumn ,,

Proposal to light part of the city by the Anglo-American Brush system submitted to the commissioners of sewers, deferred . . 21 Feb. 1888

Electric light only in theatres in Spain, ordered by royal decree . . . . . . 31 March, ,,

Erection by the London electric supply corporation of works at Deptford to supply the metropolis with electric light, ... ,,

The Edison & Swan united electric light company *v.* Holland and others; 21 days' trial; divided verdict, Edison's patent of 1879 declared invalid. Cheeseborough patent of 1878 maintained 16 July, 1888. Edison's patent declared valid on appeal, 18 Feb. 1889

The house-to-house electric supply company founded 1888; the first station at West Brompton opened 24 Jan., about nine stations established and others in preparation . . . . . Feb. ,,

The city of London from Fleet street to Aldgate about to be electrically lighted . . Feb. ,,

The electric light had been adopted at Milan, Rome, Paris, Tours, Marseilles, New York and other great cities up to . . . . . . June, 1890

Fourteen companies have been established to supply electricity in the Metropolis alone up to Feb. 1891

The first permanent electric lights in the city of London set up in Queen Victoria street from the Mansion-house to Blackfriars . . summer, ,,

Electric light extension acts brought in, . . 1892

Several explosions in St. Pancras and other places in the electrical supply street boxes, attributed to the presence of sodium and escaped coal-gas; remedies suggested by the Board of Trade Feb. 1895

Revised regulations respecting electric lighting issued by the Board of Trade, about, 5, Feb. 1896

J. A. Berly's "Universal Electrical Directory," nearly 1,000 pages, price 6*s.*, for . . . . ,,

Prof. Nernst's new electric lamp described by Mr. Jas. Swinburne at the Society of Arts 8 Feb. 1899

Mr. Thos. Edison's machine for generating electricity direct from coal without dynamos or engines, reported . . . . . . 1 Sept. 1900

ELECTRIC LOOM. M. Bonelli, of Turin, in 1854, devised a plan of employing magnets and electro-magnets in weaving, thereby superseding the tedious and costly Jacquard system of cards. His loom was set up in London in 1859, and lectured upon at the Royal Institution by professor Faraday . . . . 8 June, 1860

Electric Pen (for copying, &c.), invented by Mr. T. A. Edison; an electric writing company was established; active in 1877-8

Lamp-lighting by Electricity.—Mr. St. George Lane Fox's invention tried at Fulham, and reported successful, autumn 1877; doubtful . . . 1879

ELECTROPHONE, invented by Dr. Strethill Wright, for producing sound by electric currents of high tension: one laid before the Royal Scottish Society of Arts. See *Telephone* . 25 April, 1864

ELECTRO-TINT. Mr. Palmer, of Newgate-street, London, patented inventions by which engravings may be copied from engraved plates, and the engraving itself actually produced, by electrical agency, and one process he termed glyphography 1841

ELECTRO-TYPE OR DEPOSIT. Mr. W. Cruikshank's experiments, 1800; Mr. Spencer. in England, and professor Jacobi, in Russia, made the first successful experiments in this art in 1837 and 1838. Since then, Mr. A. Smee and others have perfected the processes. In 1840, Mr. Rob. Murray applied black-lead to non-metallic bodies as a conducting surface. In 1840, Mr. Ruolz and Mr. Elkington applied it to gilding and silver plating. Since 1850, printing types and wood-cuts, and casts from them, have been electrotyped with copper, and the process is now largely adopted in the arts.

Messrs. C. Wheatstone and F. A. Abel experiment on the application of electricity to *military purposes.* 1861

An *Electric safety lamp* made by MM. Dumas and Benoit; exhibited at Paris . . . 8 Sept. 1862

The Electro-block company established, 1860; by their processes the enlargement and reduction of engravings, obtained by india-rubber, can be immediately transferred to a lithographic stone, and multiplied. Leech's engravings, so enlarged, were coloured by himself, and exhibited in . ,,

OZONE, generated by a current produced by Wild's magneto-electric machine, employed to bleach sugar, at Whitechapel (Edward Beane's patent) . . . . Aug. 1868

Electric furnace, formed in the electric arc, by C. Wm. Siemens, fuses platinum, iridium, etc., shown at Royal Institution . . . 12 March, 1880

Electric light applied by him to grow vegetables and fruit in greenhouses . . . . . ,,

The electric welding syndicate exhibit at Hoxton, Professor Elihu Thomson's process of welding metals by electricity (discovered in 1887, and shown in New York) . . . . . Jan. 1890

Machines at work at Crewe . . . . April, ,,

ELECTRIC RAILWAY by Werner Siemens and Halske, opened near Berlin . . . 12 May, 1881

Siemens' *motive machines* 6 inches square, 2 inches deep; Tissandier's *electrically propelled balloon;* Menier's *ploughing machine*, 11 Aug.; *electric tramway* set up in Paris . . . . Aug. ,,

Siemens' new electric railway tried at Berlin about 7 Nov. ,,

International electrical exhibition, Crystal Palace, completed, inaugurated by the duke of Edinburgh, 25 Feb.; closed . . . . . 3 June, 1882

First electric tramway cars run at Leytonstone, Essex . . . . 4 March, ,,

New electric railway opened at Berlin . . 1 May, ,,

Electric congress at Paris opened . . 11 Oct. ,,

A boat ("*Electricity*") with screw-propeller moved by power, provided by electric accumulators (built by the Electrical Storage Company), sails from Millwall to London Bridge . . 28 Sept. ,,

Siemens' electrical tramway between Portrush and Giant's Causeway completed, Dec. 1882; opened by earl Spencer . . . . . . 28 Sept. 1883

Electric tramcars first run from Kew to Hammersmith . . . . 10 Mar. ,,

Electrical exhibition at Westminster Aquarium opened . . . . 14 Mar. ,,

International electric exhibition at Vienna 16 Aug.–3 Nov. ,,

Electric exhibition at Philadelphia opened, 8 Sept. 1884

Electrical transmission of force; M. Marcel Deprez experiments at Creil (1876–86), supported by M. Rothschild, reported successful:—mechanical power transmitted 35 miles for industrial purposes . . . . 23 July, 1886

Elieson company's electric engines reported successful at Stratford; tramcars driven five miles Oct. *et seq.* ,,

Electrical traction on tramways at Northfleet; successful demonstration . . . . 14 March, ,,

Successful trial of an electric tramcar on a new principle, at Birmingham . . . . 23 Oct. 1889

Mr. M. Immisch's electric motors employed successfully in pumping and hauling at St. John's colliery, Normanton and other places . Nov. ,,

The City & South London electric railway opened by the prince of Wales 4 Nov., *to the public,* 18 Dec. 1890

Mr. Nikola Tesla, at the Royal Institution, exhibited his alternate-current electric motor, by which currents are transformed by rapidly changing their direction to and fro into mechanical power. It was stated that, with the increase of physical power, the effect upon the human frame is diminished . . . . 3, 4 Feb. 1892

[By means of Mr. Tesla's apparatus, the force of about 77·7 horse power was transmitted from the rapids of the Neckar to Frankfort-on-Maine, 110 miles, Sept. 1891.] See *Niagara*.

See *Liverpool*, 1893.

M. Heilmann's electric motor traction-engine on the Western railway in France, attained the speed of 65 miles an hour . . . . 9 May, 1894

Trial trip from Paris to Mantes of an electric locomotive devised by M. Heilmann . 12 Nov. 1897

Central London electric railway (Bank to Shepherd's Bush) opened by the prince of Wales . 27 June, 1900

Electrification of Mersey railway completed 1 May, 1903

South London electric tramways system opened by prince of Wales . . . . 15 May, ,,

ELECTRO-PHYSIOLOGY. Aristotle and Pliny refer to the powers of the torpedo; Walsh and Ingenhouss, the discoveries of Galvani in 1790, and the researches of Matteucci about 1830, have greatly advanced the science.

Fowler experimented on animals with galvanism, 1793; and Aldini, 1796, who produced muscular contractions in a criminal recently executed, 1803: Ure did the same. 1818

Du Bois Reymond lectured on animal electricity at the Royal Institution, and showed the existence of an electric current, developed by action of the human muscles, in . . . . May, 1855

Dr. Burdon Sanderson (bart. 1899) announced his discovery of electricity in plants to the British Association at Bradford . . . . Sept. 1873

Executions by electricity, see under *Death*.

ELECTRIC LIGHTING ACT, 45 & 46 Vict. c. 56, passed 18 Aug. 1882. Amendment act passed 1888 (extending the monopoly of electric light companies from 21 to 42 years). Regulations of the Board of Trade published 18 May, 1889. Professor Fleming reported in 1894, that London was supplied by 13 companies, and about 700,000 incandescent electric lamps were in use, and about 425,000 lamps in the provinces. Electric lighting is now generally adopted throughout the civilised world, 1903.

ELECTRO-CHEMICAL SOCIETY, ounded in America, at Philadelphia, pres., prof. J. W. Richards, 3–5 April, 1902. Another in London. The "Faraday," Mr. Swan, pres., 1903.

ELECTROCUTION, a method of execution by means of electricity. See under *Death*.

ELECTROLYSIS, see *Electricity*, 1883.

ELEGY. Elegiac verse (consisting of a hexameter and pentameter alternately) was the first variation from the hexameter or epic measure, used by Tyrtæus and other early poets. The elegies of Ovid and Catullus are celebrated. Gray's "Elegy, written in a country churchyard," was published in 1749.

ELEMENTARY EDUCATION ACT, 33 & 34 Vict. c. 75, passed 9 Aug. 1870; amended in 1872. Clause 25, which authorizes payments to support denominational schools, much objected to by dissenters; bill to repeal it rejected by the commons (373–128), 10 June, 1874. Another act (for agricultural districts, &c.,) brought in by lord Sandon, 18 May, 1876; royal assent, 15 Aug. 1876. Another combining act passed 5 Aug. 1891. Other acts passed, 8 Aug. 1900. See *Education*.

ELEMENTS were formerly reckoned as four: earth, air, fire and water. Lavoisier enunciated the principle that all bodies which cannot be proved to be compounded are elements, and to be treated as such. Mr. W. Crookes, (knt. 1897), F.R.S., in a lecture at the Royal Institution, London, by delicate experiments demonstrated that yttrium is a compound body, and expounded a theory that all the elements have been evolved from what he termed *Protyle*, 18 Feb. 1887. Above twelve new elements said to have been discovered in rare earths by MM. Krüss and Nilson by the spectroscope in 1887. Mr. Crookes declared Didymium to be a compound body. See *Table*, and separate articles. The chemical elements were stated to be about 54 in 1834, about 77 in 1881, about 80, 1903.*

LIST OF 63 ELEMENTS, 1872 (*Odling*).

Date	Element	Discoverer
—	Gold	☉
—	Silver	☽
—	Mercury	☿
—	Copper	♀
—	Iron	♂
—	Tin	♃
—	Lead	♄
1490.	Antimony	B. Valentine.
1530.	Bismuth	Agricola ?
1541.	Zinc	Paracelsus.
—	Carbon	
—	Sulphur	
1669.	Phosphorus	Brandt.
1702.	Borax, boron	Homberg.
1733.	Arsenic }	G. Brandt.
,,	Cobalt }	
1741.	Platinum	Woods.
1751.	Nickel	Cronstedt.
1736 to 1758	Soda -ium	Duhamel.
	Potash	
	Lime	Marggraf.
	Silex	
	Alumina	Bergmann, and
	Magnesia	Scheele.
1766.	Hydrogen	Cavendish.
1771.	Fluor -ine	Scheele.
1772.	Nitrogen	Rutherford.
1774.	Chlorine { (doubtful, see *Chlorine*) }	Scheele.
,,	Oxygen	Priestley.
,,	Manganese	Gahn.
,,	Baryta -ium	
1778.	Molybdenum	Scheele.
1781.	Tungsten	Delhuart
1782.	Tellurium	Müller.
1789.	Uranium	Klaproth.
,,	Zirconia -ium	
1791.	Titanium	Gregor.
1793.	Strontia -ium	Hope.
1794.	Yttria -ium	Gadolin.
1797.	Chromium	Vauquelin.
1798.	Glucina -um	
1802.	Tantalum	Hatchett.
1803.	Cerium	Klaproth.
,,	Palladium	Wollaston.
,,	Rhodium	
,,	Iridium	Descotils & Smithson Tennant.
,,	Osmium	
1811.	Iodine	Courtois.
1817.	Lithium	Arfwedson.
,,	Selenium	Berzelius.
1818.	Cadmium	Stromeyer.
1826.	Bromine	Balard
1828.	Thorinum	Berzelius.
1830.	Vanadium	Sefstrom.

* Mr. Joseph Norman Lockyer, in a paper read at the Royal Society, 12 Dec. 1878, expressed doubts of the elementary character of some of the following substances based on his spectroscopic experiments. His views were not supported by the researches of professors Dewar and Liveing, 1880–81. See *Chlorine*. Professor Mendeléef classified the elements into 7 groups or families; each having special properties. His "Principles of Chemistry (in English), published 1898.

1839.	Lanthanum	Mosander.
1841.	Didymium	
1843.	Erbium	
1844.	Ruthenium	Claus.
1846.	Niobium	H. Rose.
1859.	Cæsium	Bunsen.
,,	Rubidium	
1861.	Thallium	Crookes.
1863.	Indium	Reich and Richter.
1875.	Gallium	Lecoq de Boisbaudran.
1877.	Davyum (?)	Kern.
,,	Neptunium	Hermann.
,,	Ilmenium (?)	
1878.	Philippium	Delafontaine.
1879.	Norwegium	Tellef Dahll.
,,	Mosandrum (?)	Lawrence Smith
,,	Decipium (?)	Delafontaine.
,,	Scandium (?)	
,,	Ytterbium (?)	Marignac.
,,	Holmium	Soret.
,,	Thulium	
,,	Uralium	A. Guyard.
,,	Vesbium	Scacchi.
1886.	Germanium	

Helium discovered, 1895; Neon, Krypton, and Xenon in 1898. Radium (*which see*), 1903.

See *Argon* and *Air*.

ELEPHANT, in the earliest times trained to war. The history of the Maccabees informs us, that "to every elephant they appointed 1000 men armed with coats of mail, and 500 horse: and upon the elephants were strong towers of wood, &c." The elephants in the army of Antiochus were provoked to fight by showing them the "blood of grapes and mulberries." The first elephant said to have been seen in England was one of enormous size, presented by the king of France to our Henry III. in 1238. *Baker's Chron.* Polyænus states that Cæsar brought one to Britain 54 B.C., which terrified the inhabitants greatly. See *Knighthood.* 13 elephants in lord mayor's procession, 9 Nov. 1876.

Chunee, an elephant 13 feet high, in Cross's menagerie, Exeter Change, London, becoming dangerous, was shot, receiving 180 musket balls before he fell, 1 March, 1826.

A young elephant brought into Court of Exchequer to show his peaceful character, in a suit for damages for frightening a pony at the Alexandra Palace, 18 July, 1879.

Barnum, the American showman, bought, for 2,000*l.*, the large male African elephant Jumbo, 6 tons weight, of the Zoological Society, Regent's Park, London. Jumbo refused to go 18 Feb. After much trouble he was removed in the night, 22–23 March, and placed in the *Assyrian Monarch*, 24 March; arrived at New York, 9 April, 1882; killed on the railway, 15 Sept. 1885.

A so-called white elephant (little differing from others), "Toung Taloung," bought from the king of Siam, shown at the Zoological gardens, London, 17 Jan. to 12 March, 1884; burnt with Alice, "Jumbo's wife," and others at the destruction of Mr. Barnum's show and menagerie at Bridgeport, U.S., by fire, 20 Nov. 1887.

"Jung Pasha" given to the "Zoo" by the Prince of Wales in 1876; died 8 March, 1896.

"Jingo," the tallest elephant in England, sold by the Zoological Soc. to Mr. Bostock, of U.S.A.; pined away and died at sea, 12 Mar. 1903.

"Lita," a pet elephant in the Dublin Zoological gardens, killed his keeper, and was shot, 11 June, 1903.

ELEUSINIAN MYSTERIES. The institution of these annual secret religious ceremonies in honour of Demeter (Ceres) at Athens, is traditionally attributed to Cadmus, 1550; to Erechtheus, 1399; or to Eumolpus, 1356 B.C. If any one revealed them, he was to be put to death. They were introduced from Eleusis into Rome, lasted about 1800 years, and were abolished by Theodosius A.D. 389. The laws were—1. To honour parents; 2. To honour the gods with the fruits of the earth; 3. Not to treat brutes with cruelty. Cicero makes the civilisation of mankind one of the beneficial effects of the Eleusinian mysteries. During the excavations carried on by the Greek archæological society on the site of Eleusis in 1895, interesting ancient relics were discovered.

ELGIN MARBLES, derived chiefly from the Parthenon, a temple of Minerva, on the Acropolis at Athens, of which they formed part of the frieze and pediment, the work of Phidias, under the government of Pericles, about 440 B.C. Thomas earl of Elgin began the collection of these marbles during his mission to the Ottoman Porte, in 1802; and from him they were purchased by the British government for 35,000*l.* and placed in the British Museum, in 1816. The ship conveying them was wrecked near Cerigo, and Mr. W. R. Hamilton, who was on board, remained several months at Cerigo, and recovered them from the sea.

ELGUETA, N. Spain; near here the Carlists defeated the republicans under gen. Sorna, and took 600 prisoners, 5-6 Aug. 1873.

ELINGA, W. Spain. Here P. Scipio Africanus totally defeated the Carthagenians under Hasdrubal Gisco, which led to their expulsion from the country, 206 B.C.

ELIS, a Greek state termed the "Holy Land," in the Peloponnesus, founded by the Heraclidæ, 1103 B.C. Here Iphitus revived the Olympic games, 884, which were regularly celebrated after Corœbus gained the prize in 776. Elis surrendered many towns to the Spartans in war, 400. After various changes, Elis joined the Achæan league, 274; and with the rest of Greece was subjugated by the Romans in 146.

ELIZABETHAN SOCIETY. Lecture by the president, Mr. Sidney Lee, on "Thomas Nash," 5 Dec. 1894.

Elizabethan Stage Society, founded in 1895 to promote the performance of Shakespeare's plays in a manner resembling that of his time; "Twelfth Night" was so performed, under the direction of Mr. Wm. Poel, at Burlington Hall, London, 21 June; "Comedy of Errors," at Gray's Inn, 6 Dec., 1895; Marlowe's "Faustus," July, 1896. Other plays since, "Tempest," at the Mansion House, 2 Nov. 1897; Ben Jonson's "Alchemist," 24 Feb.; Mr. Algernon Swinburne's "Locrine," 20 March; Edw. Fitzgerald's adaptation of Calderon's "La Vida es Sueño," 15 May, 1899; "Everyman," a fine 15th-century morality play (copied from the original MS. in the library of Lincoln cathedral), revived first in the Charterhouse, London, 13, 20, 27 July, 1901, performed afterwards with great effect at Oxford, Brighton, Cheltenham, St. George's hall, and the Imperial theatre, closed, 9 July, 1902, and at the Coronet theatre, 5 Ap. 1903; a reprint issued with notes by Mr. Bullen, 1902. Marlowe's "Edw. II." performed at Oxford, 10 Aug. 1903.

ELL (so named from *ulna*, the arm) was fixed at 45 inches, by king Henry I. in 1101. The old French ell, or *aune*, was 46·790 inches.

ELLISON GALLERY. In April, 1860, Mrs. Elizabeth Ellison (in conformity with the wish of her deceased husband, Richard), presented to the South Kensington Museum a series of 50 original water-colour drawings, by the first masters.

ELLORA or **ELORA**, Central India; remarkable for its very ancient rock-cut temple; excavated according to Hindoo legends nearly 7000 years ago; but more probably about 800 A.D. The town was ceded to the British by Holkar in 1818, and transferred by them to the Nizam of the Deccan in 1822.

ELMINA (originally named La Mina, from the gold found here), and Dutch Guinea, W. Africa, were ceded by the Dutch government by treaty, signed Feb. 1872, and consolidated with the West African settlements; first governor, Mr., after Sir John, Pope Hennessy, April, 1872. See *Ashantees*.

EL-OBEID, Battle of, 3-5 Nov. 1884. See *Soudan*.

ELOPEMENT. A wife who departs from her husband, loses her dower by the statute of Westm. 1285—unless her husband, without coercion of the church, be reconciled to her. Earlier laws punished elopement with death when adultery followed.

ELPHIN (Ireland). St. Patrick founded a cathedral near Elphin, in the 5th century, and placed over it St. Asicus, whom he created bishop, and who soon after filled it with monks. After many centuries, Roscommon, Ardcarn, Drumclive, and others of less note, were also annexed to Elphin, which became one of the richest sees in Ireland. It is valued in the king's books, by an extent returned 28 Eliz., at 103*l.* 18*s.* sterling. The see was united to Kilmore in 1841, under the provisions of the Church Temporalities act, passed Aug. 1833.

ELSINORE, Zealand, Denmark, formerly the station for receiving the Sound dues (*which see*). Population, 1890, 11,082.

ELSWICK, a township of Newcastle-on-Tyne. the site of the great works of lord Armstrong & Co. The engineering department began about 1847, the ordnance works in 1857, see *Cannon*. Since then the naval construction has been largely carried on. About 14,000 workmen employed in 1888 and about 19,000 in 1896. The works were visited by the Chinese grand secretary, Li Hung Chang, who specially examined the *Esmeralda*, 1st class cruiser, completed for the Chilian Republic, 20 Aug. 1896. Great fire at the works, estimated damage, 150,000*l.*, 10 June, 1899.

EL-TEB, Battle of, 29 Feb. 1884. See *Soudan*.

ELY, an island in Cambridgeshire, on which a church was built about 673, by Etheldreda, queen of Egfrid, king of Northumberland; she also founded a religious house, filled it with virgins, and became herself first abbess. The 1200th anniversary was celebrated 17-21 Oct. 1873; about 60,000*l.* had then been spent on the restoration of the cathedral. The Danes ruined the convent about 870; but a monastery was built in 879, on which king Edgar and succeeding monarchs bestowed great privileges and grants of land; whereby it became the richest in England. Richard, the eleventh abbot, wishing to free himself from the bishop of Lincoln, made great interest with Henry I. to get Ely erected into a bishopric, 1108, and his successor Hervæus was the first prelate, 1109. It is valued in the king's books at 2134*l.* 18*s.* 5*d.*; present stated income, 5500*l.* Population in 1881, 8,171; 1891, 8,017; 1901, 64,435.

RECENT BISHOPS.

1781. James York, died 26 Aug. 1808.
1808. Thomas Dampier, died 13 May, 1812.
1812. Bowyer Edward Sparke, died 4 April, 1836.
1836. Joseph Allen, died 20 March, 1845.
1845. Thomas Turton, died 7 Jan. 1864.
1864. Edward Harold Browne, translated to Winchester, Aug. 1873.
1873. James Russell Woodford, Aug.; died 24 Oct. 1885.
1885. Lord Alwyne Compton.

ELY CHAPEL, Holborn, London, erected in the 14th century, sold for 5250*l.*, 29 Jan. 1874; acquired by the R. C. fathers of the order of Charity, 1874; and finely restored at the expense of the duke of Norfolk and others, opened as St. Etheldreda's chapel, 23 June, 1876.

ELZEVIR, or **ELSEVIER**, a family of printers, in Holland, whose reputation is based on fine pocket editions of the classics.

Louis, the founder, was born in 1540; began business at Leyden in 1580; he printed about 150 works, and died 4 Feb. 1617. His sons (especially Bonaventure) and grandsons, were celebrated for their work.

EMANCIPATION, see *Roman Catholics* and *Slavery*. The Emancipation Society for slaves lasted 1862-5.

EMANUEL HOSPITAL, Westminster, founded in 1594 by lady Anne Dacre for aged people and children. Its original annual income had increased from 360*l.* to about 4000*l.* in 1870, when changes in the disposition of the funds were proposed by the Charity Commissioners, and some effected. Through reduction of income to about 800*l.* the buildings decay, and the number of inmates decrease, reported Jan. 1890. The proposed change of site much opposed, 1892.

EMBALMING. The ancient Egyptians believing that their souls, after many thousand years, would reinhabit their bodies, if preserved entire, embalmed the dead. Some of the bodies, called *mummies*, buried 3000 years ago, are still perfect. "The physicians embalmed Israel," 1689 B.C. *Gen.* l. 2; see *Mummies*. Carbolic acid was successfully employed by professor Seely in America, in 1868.

The most perfect specimens of *modern embalming* are preserved in the museum of the royal college of surgeons. one being the body of the wife of Van Butchell, preserved by John Hunter by injecting camphorated spirits of wine, &c., into the arteries and veins; and the other the body of a young woman, who died about 1780 of consumption, in the Lock hospital. The method of embalming royal personages in modern times is fully described in Hunter's "Posthumous Works." He died in 1793.—During the American War (1861-5), many soldiers' bodies were embalmed and sent home.

Improvements in embalming made by Prof. Laskowski of Geneva, 1885.

EMBANKMENTS of earth were erected by the ancients for preservation from their enemies and the inundations of the tide. Those of the Egyptians and Babylonians are described by Herodotus and Strabo. To the Romans are attributed the first dykes of Holland, and the embankments of Romney Marsh, considered to be the oldest in Britain. In 1250 Henry III. issued a writ enforcing the support of these works; and his successors followed his example. James I. greatly encouraged the embankment of the Thames. Sir W. Dugdale's "History of Embanking" first appeared in 1662; see *Drainage*, *Levels*, and *Thames*. Since 1830, millions of pounds have been expended in embankments for railways.

EMBARGO, from the Spanish *embargar*, to detain, applied to the restraining ships from sailing. This power is vested in the crown, but is rarely exercised except in extreme cases, and sometimes as a prelude to war. The most memorable instances of embargo were those for the prevention of corn going out of the kingdom in 1766; and for the detention of all Russian, Danish, and Swedish ships in the several ports of the kingdom, owing to the armed neutrality, 14 Jan. 1801; see *Armed Neutrality*.

EMBER WEEKS, instituted, it is said, by pope Callixtus I. (219-223), to implore the blessing of God on the produce of the earth by prayer and fasting, in which penitents used to sprinkle the ashes (embers) of humiliation on their heads. In the English church the *Ember days* are the Wednesday, Friday, and Saturday, after the following days—the first Sunday in Lent, Whit-sunday, 14 Sept. (Holy Cross), and 13 Dec. (St. Lucia).

EMBROIDERY is usually ascribed to the Phrygians; but the Sidonians excelled in it, and it is mentioned in 1491 B.C. *Exodus* xxxv. 35 and xxxviii. 23. See *Bayeux Tapestry*. Embroidery is now done by machinery. The first embroidery machine is said to have been invented by John Duncan of Glasgow in 1804. Heilman's embroidery machine was patented by Köchlin. *Berlin Wool-work* has been much improved of late years by the production of more elegant patterns, first published by Mr. Wittich in Berlin, about 1810.

EMERALD, a precious stone, of a green colour, found in the East and in Peru. It has been erroneously alleged that there were no true emeralds in Europe before the conquest of Peru; but there is one in the Paris Museum, taken from the mitre of pope Julius II. who died in 1513, and Peru was not conquered till 1545. It is stated that there were mines at Gebel Zabâra worked by Egyptians, 1800 B.C.

EMERGENCY MEN, a name given to the more energetic members of the Irish Defence Association; and especially to the men engaged in carrying out evictions in Ireland. See *Mansion House Funds*, 1881.

EMESA, now Hems, Syria, renowned for a temple of the sun, the priest of which, Bassianus, was proclaimed emperor with the name Heliogabalus or Elagabalus, 218. His atrocities led to his assassination, 11 March, 222.

EMIGRANTS. The French aristocracy and clergy (*émigrés*) began to leave their country in July, 1789, at the breaking out of the revolution: their estates were confiscated in Dec. A large number returned in 1802, by an amnesty granted after the peace of Amiens. Many were indemnified after the restoration in 1815.

EMIGRATION. Phœnician and Greek emigrants colonised the coasts of the Mediterranean and the Black Sea; see *Magna Græcia*, *Marseilles*, &c. The discovery of America opened a vast field for emigration, which was restrained by Charles I. in 1637. It has been greatly encouraged since 1819. Regulations for emigration were made in 1831, and in Jan. 1840, the Colonial Land and Emigration Board was established. Emigration much promoted through want of employment in London, 1869-70; from Ireland, by act passed, 1883. Much emigration from Great Britain and Germany to America, 1881-5. Fare of steerage passengers from Britain to America by steamers reduced to about 4*l.* Jan. 1883.

The "Order of the Sons of St. George," at Philadelphia, which was established to succour emigrants, still exists. (See under *George, St.*) It published a letter dissuading unsuitable emigration . . . . 31 July, 1874

Meetings at the Mansion House to promote State-directed emigration of the unemployed 5 April, 1882

A tax of 2s. per head levied in United States on immigrants; act passed by congress in opposition to the government and steam ship companies Aug. „

Association formed to promote State-directed emigration and colonization . . . . 10 Aug. 1883

About 2,000 deserted children domesticated in Liverpool, and sent to Canada by the agency of Mr. Samuel Smith and Mrs. Birt, reported Dec. 1886

Emigrants' Information Office, London, opened 7 Oct. 1886; reported to be highly successful May, 1888

The Self-Help Emigration Society, supported by the earls of Aberdeen and Roden, lords Monkswell and Dorchester and other gentlemen, established in 1884. Up to 1898, about 6,000 emigrants had been assisted by the society; received the grant of 11,500 acres in Ontario and a section near Winnipeg, announced . . . . 13 Jan. 1898

Decrease of emigration, lowest in 1894 (35,959), since 1851

Emigration from the United Kingdom, in 1815, 2081; in 1820, 25,729; in 1830, 56,907; in 1840, 90,743; in 1850, 280,843; in 1860, 128,469; in 1866, 204,882; in 1870, 256,940; in 1871, 252,435; 1872, 295,213; 1873, 310,612; 1874, 241,014; 1875, 173,809. Of British origin only, 1876, 109,469; 1877, 95,195; 1878, 112,902; 1879, 164,274; 1880, 227,542; 1881, 243,002; 1882, 279,366; 1883, 320,118; 1884, 242,179; 1885, 207,644; 1886, 232,900; 1887, 281,487; 1888, 279,928; 1889, 253,795; 1890, 218,116; 1891, 218,507; 1892, 210,042; 1893, 208,814; 1894, 156,030; 1895, 185,181; 1896, 161,925; 1897, 146,460; 1898, 140,644; 1899, 146,362; 1900, 168,825; 1901, 171,715; 1902, 205,910. See *Immigration*.

	1846.	1851.
From England	86,611	254,970
„ Scotland	3,427	18,646
„ Ireland	38,813	62,350
	128,851	335,066

Emigration from the United Kingdom from 1815 to 1897: to the United States, 9,892,597; to British N. America, 2,236,392; to Australasia, 1,777,876; to the Cape of Good Hope and Natal, 339,687; to all other places, 468,450.

Emigration to North American colonies, West Indies, Cape of Good Hope, New South Wales, Swan River, Van Diomen's Land, &c., in 1820-30, 154,291; in 1830-40, 277,695.

To the Cape and Natal in 1897, 28,801; 1898, 19,756; 1899, 14,432; 1900, 20,857; 1901, 23,254; 1902, 43,224.

To North American Colonies, in 1842, 54,123; in 1847, 109,680; in 1856, 16,378; in 1861, 12,707; in 1863, 18,083; in 1864, 12,721; in 1866, 13,255; in 1867, 15,503; in 1868, 21,062; in 1869, 33,891; in 1870, 35,295; 1871, 32,671; 1872, 32,205; 1873, 37,208; 1874, 25,450. Of British origin, 1876, 9335; 1877, 7720; 1878, 10,652; 1879, 17,952; 1880, 20,902; 1881, 23,912; 1882, 40,441; 1883, 44,185; 1884, 31,134; 1885, 19,838; 1886, 24,745; 1887, 32,025; 1888, 34,853; 1889, 28,269; 1890, 22,520; 1892, 23,254; 1893, 24,732; 1897, 22,669; 1898, 17,640; 1899, 16,410; 1900, 18,818; 1901, 15,868; 1902, 26,407.

To United States, in 1842, 63,852; in 1847, 142,154; in 1857, 126,905; in 1861, 49,764; in 1863, 146,813; in 1864, 147,042; in 1866, 161,000; in 1867, 159,275; in 1868, 155,532; in 1869, 203,001; in 1870, 196,075; 1871, 198,843; 1872, 233,747; 1873, 233,073; 1874, 148,161. Of British origin, 1876, 54,554; 1877, 45,481; 1878, 54,694; 1879, 91,806; 1880, 1[illegible]6,570; 1881, 176,104; 1882, 181,903; 1883, 191,573; 1884, 155,280; 1885, 137,687; 1886, 152,710; 1887, 201,526; 1888, 195,986; 1889, 168,771; 1890, 152,413; 1891, 156,395; 1892, 150,039; 1893, 148,949; 1897, 132,048; 1898, 80,494; 1899, 92,482; 1900, 102,955; 1901, 104,257; 1902, 108,501.

To Australia and New Zealand, in 1842, 8534; in 1845, 830; in 1850, 16,037; in 1852 (*gold discovery*), 87,881; in 1853, 61,401; in 1854, 83,237; in 1855, 52,309; in 1856, 44,584; in 1857, 61,248; in 1861, 23,738; in 1863, 53,054; in 1864, 40,942; in 1866, 24,097; in 1867, 14,466; in 1868, 12,809; in 1869, 14,901; in 1870, 17,065; in 1871, 12,227; 1872, 15,876; 1873, 26,428; 1874, 53,958. Of British origin, 1876, 32,196; 1877, 30,138; 1878, 36,479; 1879, 40,959; 1880, 24,184; 1881, 22,682; 1882, 37,289; 1883, 71,264; 1884, 44,255; 1885, 39,395; 1886, 43,076; 1887, 34,183; 1888, 31,127; 1889, 28,294; 1890, 21,179; 1892, 15,950; 1893, 11,203; 1897, 12,396; 1898, 10,693; 1899, 11,467; 1900, 16,001; 1901, 15,376; 1902, 14,408.

To other places, in 1854, 3366; in 1859, 12,427; in 1868, 6922; in 1870, 8505; 1871, 8694; 1872, 13,385; 1873

13,903; 1874, 13,445; 1875, 173,809. Of British origin, 1876, 13,384; 1877, 11,856; 1878, 11,077; 1879, 13,557; 1880, 15,886; 1881, 20,304; 1882, 19,733; 1883, 13,096; 1884, 11,510; 1885, 10,724; 1886, 12,369; 1887, 13,753; 1888, 17,962; 1889, 28,461; 1890, 22,004; 1891, 20,987; 1892, 20,799; 1893, 23,930; 1897, 17,366; 1898, 12,061; 1899, 11,571; 1900, 11,848; 1901, 13,385; 1902, 13,370.

EMILY ST. PIERRE, see *United States*, 1862.

EMINENCE, a title conferred upon cardinals by pope Urban VIII. Jan. 10, 1631, as more honourable than "Excellency." Previously cardinals had the title of *Illustrissimi*. *Ashe*. The grand-master of Malta also obtained this title. *Pardon*.

EMIN PASHA RELIEF. The committee for the purpose appointed, 1887.

Sir William Mackinnon, chairman, lord Kinnaird, Mr. W. Burdett-Coutts and others. See *Soudan* 1886–7, and *Africa* (*German East*).

The German committee at Berlin, dissolved itself Dec. 1890

Emin Pasha murdered Oct. 1892, reported, May—Sept. 1893

"His Life and Work," by George Schweitzer, published . . . . Sept. 1898

EMIR, a title of the caliphs among the Turks and Persians, first awarded to the descendants of Mahomet's daughter Fatima, about 650. To such only was originally given the privilege of wearing the green turban.

EMISSION THEORY of Light (advocated by Newton, about 1672), supposes that individual particles pass from the luminous body to the eye, and that each ray of light passes from the sun to the earth. It is opposed to the *Undulatory Theory* (*which see*), now generally received.

EMLY, an Irish see, said to have been founded by St. Patrick. Emly was called Imelaca-Ibair: St. Ailbe was the first bishop in 448. In 1568, the see was united to Cashel (*which see*). It is now an inconsiderable village.

EMPALEMENT. This mode of executing criminals, mentioned by Juvenal, and often inflicted in Rome, is still used in Turkey and Arabia. In England the dead bodies of murderers were sometimes staked in this manner, previously to being buried; abolished, 1823. See *Suicide*.

EMPEROR, from *Imperator* (ruler), a title conferred on victorious Roman generals.

Augustus Cæsar the first Roman emperor . B.C. 27

Valentinian I. first emperor of the west, and Valens, first emperor of the east . . . . A.D. 364

Charlemagne first emperor of Germany, crowned by Leo. III. 800

Othman I. founder of the Turkish empire, the first emperor of Turkey 1299

The Czar the first emperor of Russia 22 Oct. 1721

Napoleon Bonaparte first emperor of the French 1804

Napoleon III., his nephew, founded the second French empire, Dec. 1852, deposed . 4 Sept. 1870

Iturbide, emperor of Mexico, Feb. 1822; shot 19 July, 1824

Dom Pedro IV. of Portugal the first emperor of Brazil 1825

Faustin I. the first emperor of Hayti, in 1849: deposed 1859

Maximilian I. emperor of Mexico, 10 April, 1864; shot . . . . 19 June, 1867

EMPEROR'S HYMN (of Austria), words by L. L. Hauschka, music by Joseph Haydn, first sung, 12 Feb. 1797.

EMPIRE. *Empire City*, a name given to New York. *Empire Club*, Constitutional, established 10 Oct. 1881, founded 1883; closed 1886. *Empire Route* to the east, by the Canadian Pacific Railway; term applied 1887.

EMPIRICS, a sect of physicians, formed in the 3rd century before Christ, who contended that all reasoning respecting the animal economy was useless, and that experience and observation were the only foundations of medicine. The sect adopted the principles of Acron of Agrigentum, who flourished about 430 B.C. *Empiricism*, the name applied to a school in philosophy, which admits of nothing as true but what is the result of experience.

EMPLOYERS OF LABOUR, National Federation of Associated, formed in London about 10 Dec. 1873. The founders were said to employ about 2,000,000, principally in N.W. and N. England. Their object was to counteract the influence of trade unions. The first annual meeting held 24 Feb. 1875.

Iron trades employers' association issued a circular proposing increase in hours of labour, Dec. 1878. See *Coal Strikes*, 1890.

EMPLOYERS' LIABILITY ACT (to make compensation for personal injuries suffered by workmen not by their own fault), passed for 7 years, 7 Sept. 1880; effects neutral (1884). New act passed 24 Dec. 1888. The stringent application of the spirit of these laws by the decision of the house of lords in the case of Smith *v.* Charles Baker & Sons on appeal was strongly enforced 21 July, 1891.

New bill introduced, 20 Feb. 1893; re-introduced 8 Nov.; the commons reject a clause for enabling workmen to contract out of the act by arrangement with employers, 10 Nov.; the clause maintained by the lords, 29 Jan.; the bill withdrawn 20 Feb. 1894

Workmen's Compensation Act passed, after much discussion . . . . 6 Aug. 1897

EMPLOYERS AND WORKMEN ACT, passed 13 Aug. 1875, relates to legal settlement of disputes, &c.

EMPLOYMENTS of the people as shown in the census of 1891; blue book, published Nov. 1895.

EMPRESS of India (Imperatrix Indiæ), addition to the royal titles of the late Queen Victoria, proclaimed in London, 1 May, 1876.

ENAMELLING was practised by the Egyptians, Chinese, and other nations, and was known in England in the time of the Saxons. At Oxford is an enamelled jewel, which belonged to Alfred, and which, as appears by the inscription, was made by his order, in his reign, about 887. Limoges enamelled ware was popular in the 16th century. Magnificent specimens by Lepec, Elkington, Emanuel, and others, appeared at the exhibition at Paris, 1867. See *Mosaic*. On 19 June, 1862, madame Rachel (Levison or Leverson) sued captain Carnegie for 928*l*. for *enamelling his wife's face*, and was nonsuited; see *Trials*, 1868. She was convicted of fraud in 1878; and died in prison 12 Oct. 1880. See *Trials*.

ENCÆNIA, Greek festivals kept on days on which cities were built and temples consecrated; and in later times, as at Oxford, at the celebration or commemoration of founders and benefactors. *Oldisworth*. The public commemoration at Oxford suspended in 1875; restored, 21 June, 1876. They were the origin of church-wakes in England, about 600. They were also feasts celebrated by the Jews on the 25th of the ninth month, in commemoration of the Maccabees cleansing the temple, which had been polluted by Antiochus Epiphanes, 131 B.C.

ENCAUSTIC PAINTING, enamelling by fire. Painting with burnt wax is said to have been known to Praxiteles about 360 B.C. This art was revived by M. Bachelier, 1749, by count Caylus, 1765, and by Miss Greenland, 1785 and 1792.

ENCLOSURE, see *Inclosure*.

ENCRATITES, followers of Tatian, about 170, denounced marriage, and abstained from flesh, and from wine even at the Lord's supper.

ENCUMBERED ESTATES ACT, passed July 1849, to enable owners of land or leases in Ireland, subject to encumbrance, to apply to commissioners appointed under it to direct a sale of such property. These commissioners held their first court in Dublin, 24 Oct. 1849, and their last 28 July, 1858, a new court being established under the Landed Estates act. The number of estates sold, up to 1858, was 2380, producing twenty-two millions of pounds. In 1854 a similar act was passed for the West Indies.

ENCYCLICAL LETTER, see *Rome*, 1864 *et seq.*

ENCYCLOPÆDIA or **CYCLOPÆDIA**, a general dictionary of art, science, and literature. This name has been given to a work by Abulpharagius in the 13th century.

"De Proprietatibus Rerum," an encyclopædic work in Latin, attributed to Bartholomeus Anglicus, a Franciscan (proved to be incorrectly named *Glanville*), was written about 1248 and 1267, and translated into several languages. The first English version, by John of Trevisa, a Wycliffite, in 1397, was printed between 1495–1582, and was doubtless the source from which Shakspeare, Spenser, and other writers derived much of their knowledge of natural history, &c., "Mediæval lore: being classified Gleanings," from this work, edited by Robert Steele, published, 1893.

Chinese cyclopædia, 6109 vols. (all the valuable books then existing), printed by order of the emperor between 1661-1721
A copy bought for British Museum 1877
Alsted's Encyclopædia 1620
Louis Moreri's Dictionnaire Historique 1673
Hofmann's Lexicon Universale 1677
Corneille's Dictionnaire des Arts 1694
Bayle's Dictionnaire 1696
Lexicon Technicum of John Harris (earliest English encyclopædia) 1704; supplements 1710, 1741
Ephraim Chambers' Cyclopædia 1728
Zedler's Universal Lexicon 1732-50
Encyclopédie (by Didérot and D'Alembert) 1751-80
[The contributors were termed ENCYCLOPEDISTES, and their daring writings are believed to have hastened the French revolution in 1789.]
Encyclopædia Britannica (1st edition by William Smellie) 1771
[The 8th completed 1861 (sale 5,000); 9th (sale 50,000) 1875-89, reprint issued 1898; *The Times* supplement to the 9th edition, edited by sir Donald Mackenzie Wallace, pres. Hadley, Yale university, Mr. Hugh Chisholm, and others, 35th vol. index vol. published April 1903
Encyclopædia Biblica, edited by the rev. T. K. Cheyne and J. Sutherland Black 1899-1903
The Jewish Encyclopædia (edited by Dr. Isidore Singer, over 400 writers engaged), vol. i. published, Aug. 1901; vol. vii . . . . . Sept. ,,
Encyclopédie Méthodique (by Pancoucke) 1782-1832
Chambers' Cyclopædia (edited by Rees) 1785
Rees' Cyclopædia 1802-19
Brockhaus's Conversations Lexicon, 1st edition 1818
[New editions frequent.] 13th, 1883 *et seq.*
Encyclopædia Metropolitana 1817-45
Cabinet Cyclopædia (a collection of treatises) 1829-46
Penny Cyclopædia 1833-46
Knight's English Cyclopædia (4 divisions) 1853-61-70
Chambers' Encyclopædia, 1859-68; 1874-5; 1888-93; 1901
Ersch and Gruber's Allgemeine Encyclopädie, began 1818, 164 vols. published 1889
American cyclopædia, by Geo. Ripley and Charles A. Dana, 17 vols. 1873-8, continued as "The Annual Cyclopædia" to last vol. 1903
Globe encyclopædia, completed 1879
Encyclopædic Dictionary completed 1889
Meyer's Konversations Lexicon, 1840 (latest edition) 1903
The "Grande Encyclopédie" begun 1885, 31 vols. 200,000 articles, 12 illustrations, 150 maps, completed . . . . . June, 1903

ENDERBY LAND, see *Southern Continent*.

ENDOSMOSIS. M. Dutrochet, about 1826, found that if two fluids, gases or vapours, of unequal density, are separated by an animal or vegetable membrane, the denser will attract the less dense through the medium. This property he called *endosmose*, when the attraction is from the outside to the inside, and *exosmose* when it operates from the inside to the outside. Many natural phenomena are thus more clearly understood. *Brande.*

ENDOWED SCHOOL COMMISSION (consisting of lord Lyttelton, canon Robinson, and others), was appointed under the act 32-33 Vict. c. 50 (2 Aug. 1869). It threw open many endowments to the nation, and carried out reforms, being frequently much opposed. By an act passed 7 Aug. 1874, its duties were transferred to the charity commissioners, two new commissioners (Mr. Longley, lord Clinton), and canon Robinson being appointed. The commissioners had dealt with 74 schools; prepared schemes for 66; leaving about 660 to be dealt with; Aug. 1874.

ENDOWED SCHOOLS ACT, containing the "Conscience Clause," passed 1860; another similar act passed 2 Aug. 1869. A committee reported on the working of the act, June, 1887.

ENERGY. In an address to the British Association at York, 1 Sept. 1881, sir William Thomson described the sources of all the energy in nature available to man for the production of mechanical effect, as tides, food, fuel, wind and rain, all except the tides derived from the sun.

ENFIDA CASE, see *Tunis*.

ENFIELD, N. Middlesex; a manor belonging to the duchy of Lancaster, is mentioned in Domesday, and was given to De Mandeville by William I. after 1066. After various changes it became the property of the crown by the marriage of Mary, heiress of the Bohuns, to Henry duke of Lancaster, afterwards king Henry IV. 1399. Edward VI. gave it to his sister Elizabeth, who resided here in 1552, in a palace, part of which still remains. The grammar school was founded about 1586. The ancient chase was dischased and enclosed, after 1 Jan. 1779. Population, 1881, 18,944; 1891, 31,532; 1901, 42,738.

Sir Redvers Buller presented with an address and a silver inkstand by the Enfield ladies . 23 Sept. 1901

ENFIELD MUSKET, see *Fire-arms*.

ENGEN, Baden. Here Moreau defeated the Austrians, 3 May, 1800.

ENGHIEN or **STEENKIRK** (S. W. Belgium). Here the British under William III. were defeated by the French under marshal Luxemburg, 24 July, 1692.—The duc d'Enghien, a descendant of the great Conde, was seized in Baden by order of Bonaparte, conveyed to Vincennes, and, after a hasty trial, shot by torch-light, immediately after condemnation, 21 March, 1804. The body was exhumed, 20 March, 1816.

ENGINEERS, Military, formerly called Trench-masters. Sir William Pelham officiated as trench-master in 1622; the chief engineer was called camp-master-general in 1634. Capt. Thomas Rudd had the rank of chief engineer to the king about 1650. The corps of engineers was formerly a civil corps, but was made a military force, and directed to rank with the artillery, 25 April, 1787. It has a colonel-in-chief, 16 colonels-commandant, and 16 colonels. *Civil Engineering* became important in the middle of the last century, when Smeaton began the Eddystone lighthouse, and Brindley the Bridgewater canal. Since then the Rennies, Telford, the Stephensons and Brunels, Locke, and others have constructed breakwaters, docks, bridges, railways, tunnels, &c., which are the marvel of our age.

"*Engineering* is the art of directing the great sources of power in nature for the use and convenience of man." (*Thos. Tredgold*, died 1829.)

The first society of Civil Engineers formed by Smeaton and others, afterwards termed the *Smeatonian Society* of Civil Engineers 1793

Institution of Civil Engineers established 2 Jan. 1818; obtained a charter, 3 June, 1828; 5728 members . . . . April, 1889

Institution of Mechanical Engineers, which had its head-quarters in Birmingham, moved to London, 1877; annual meetings are held; established . 1847

The Society of Engineers, established for the advance of the science and practice of engineering, May 1854; John Corry Fell, president, 1899. Annual meetings held.

Civil and Mechanical Engineers' Society founded . 1859

Isambard Kingdom Brunel, projector of the *Great Eastern*, aged 53, died 15 Sept.; Robert Stephenson, railway engineer, aged 59, died 12 Oct. ,,

Engineers' Amalgamated Society, in 1867, consisted of above 30,000 members; annual income, 86,000*l.*; disbursed to disabled workmen, &c., about 50,000*l.*, amassed capital, about 125,000*l.*

Engineer, weekly journal, established . 4 Jan. 1856

Engineering, weekly journal, established . Jan. 1866

Newcastle strike (see *Newcastle*) . May—Oct. 1871

Strike of engineers in London (18 firms) 7 Feb.—4 Oct. 1879

College of Practical Engineers, Muswell hill, near London, opened by sir Henry Bessemer, sir Joseph Whitworth, Dr. C. Wm. Siemens, and others . . . . Sept. 1881

Engineering exhibition, Agricultural Hall, London 5–21 July, 1883

Sir Charles Bright, the pioneer of Atlantic cable-laying, born 1832, died 1888
See *Electricity*.

Mr. T. A. Walker, contractor for the Manchester ship canal and other great works, dies . 25 Nov. 1889

Sir John Hawkshaw, engineer of the Severn tunnel, dies aged 80. . . . . . . 2 June, 1891

Sir John Coode, eminent for breakwaters and other works born 1816, died . . . . 2 March, 1892

Mr. Thomas Hawksley, F.R.S., eminent throughout the world for waterworks, gasworks, sanitation, &c., died, aged 86 . . . . 23 Sept. 1893

Death of Mr. Edwin Clark, inventor of the railway block signalling system, hydraulic graving dock, &c., aged about 80 . . . . . . 22 Oct. 1894

Death of Mr. James Henry Greathead, inventor of the Greathead shield, constructor of tunnels, &c. . . . . 21 Oct. 1896

Continued disputes between the Employers' national federation and the Amalgamated society of engineers, respecting hours of labour, &c. Feb. 1897

Circular issued by 7 societies demanding an 8 hours' day without reduction of pay . . . April, ,,

See *Strikes* . . . . July, ,,

Sir John Fowler, eminent railway engineer (born 1817) died . . . . 20 Nov. 1898

Sir Douglas Galton, eminent engineer (born 1822) and Mr. Jeremiah Head, mechanical and consulting engineer (born 1835) died 10 March . . . 1899

Sir James Wright, late engineer-in-chief of the navy (under his régime great changes in the naval steam machinery, etc., took place), died, aged 75, 17 April, ,,

Mr. John Nixon, mining and civil engineer, successful in many enterprises in S. Wales, invented many machines, *Billy Fairplay*, etc.; one of the founders of the sliding scale system, born 1815, died . . . . 3 June ,,

Mr. Edw. Case, whose system of groyning for sea walls has been successful round the U.K. and at Ostend, died . . . . 23 Sept. ,,

Internat. engineering congress meets in Glasgow, 3 Sept. 1901

Mr. Barlow, F.R.S., see *Tay bridge*, died 12 Nov. 1902

ENGLAND (from *Angles* and *lond*, land), so named, it is said, by Egbert, first king of the English, in a general council held at Winchester, 829; or by Athelstan, 925. See *Anglo-Saxons*. England was united to Wales, 1283; to Scotland in 1603; they have had the same legislature since 1707, when the three were styled Great Britain. James I. first adopted the title of king of England, Scotland, afterwards Great Britain, France, and Ireland. After the treaty of Amiens, signed 27 March, 1802, France was omitted from the royal style. Ireland was incorporated with them, by the act of legislative union, 1 Jan. 1801, as the United Kingdom of Great Britain, France, and Ireland. The British empire is computed to contain about 11,500,000 square miles of territory, with 407,000,000 inhabitants in 1899. Statistical details are given under the respective headings, *Army*, *Navy*, *Revenue*, *Population*, &c. Population of England and Wales, 1891, 29,001,018. For previous history, see *Britain*, *Histories of England*, by Rapin (in English), 1725-31; Thomas Carte, 1747-55; David Hume, 1755-62; Tobias Smollett, 1757-65; John Lingard, 1819-30; Charles Knight, 1856-62; J. R. Green, 1874-80. Parts by T. B. Macaulay, Earl Stanhope, J. A. Froude, Miss H. Martineau, and others. "The Victoria History of the Counties of England," a national survey of England at the commencement of the 20th century, Mr. H. Arthur Doubleday and Mr. Laurence Gomme, joint editors, supported by a committee, the marqu. of Lorne and many others, first series, illustrated, with maps, etc., issued March, 1899. See *Chronicles*, *Imperialism*, and *Style*.

Egbert, "king of the English," 828; defeats the Welsh, Danes, &c., at Hengestdown . . . 835

Alfred, king, 871; after many vicissitudes, vanquishes the Danes 871-896

He frames a code of laws, 890; forms a militia and navy, surveys and subdivides the country, and promotes education (many statements mythical). 896

Athelstan's great victory over the Danes, Scots, &c. at Brunanburg 937

Predominance of Dunstan; he promotes monachism and the celibacy of the clergy, about . . . 952

Ethelred compounds with the Danes for peace . 991

Causes their massacre . . . . . . 13 Nov. 1002

Avenged by Sweyn, king of Denmark: Ethelred flees to Normandy 1003

Sweyn dies, and Ethelred returns, 1014; dies . . 1016

Canute the Dane sole monarch 1017

Edward the Confessor king; Saxon dynasty restored 1042

Harold II. crowned, 6 Jan.; defeats the Norwegians, 25 Sept.; defeated and slain at Hastings by William of Normandy . . . . . . 14 Oct. 1066

William I. crowned . . . . . . 25 Dec. 1066

The northern counties rebel; ravaged from the Humber to the Tyne 1069-70

Introduction of the feudal system, about . . . 1070
Justices of peace appointed . . . 1076
Domesday book compiled 1085-6
WILLIAM II. crowned . . . . 26 Sept. 1087
The crusades begin 1096
HENRY I. crowned, restores Saxon laws, &c 5 Aug. 1100
Defeats his brother Robert, and gains Normandy . 1106
Prince William and nobles drowned . 25 Nov. 1120
STEPHEN crowned . . . . 26 Dec. 1135
Civil war between the empress Maud, Henry's daughter, and Stephen; her friends the Scots defeated at the battle of the Standard 22 Aug. 1138
She lands in England, and is successful . . 1139
Crowned at Winchester . . . 3 March, 1141
Defeated; retires to France 1147
Concludes a peace with Stephen 1153
HENRY II. crowned . . . . 19 Dec. 1154
Constitutions of Clarendon enacted . . Jan. 1164
Arrogance of Becket; murdered . . 29 Dec. 1170
Conquest of Ireland 1171, 1172
England divided into six circuits for the administration of justice 1176
English laws digested by Glanville, about . . 1181
RICHARD I. crowned . . . 3 Sept. 1189
He joins the crusades 1191
Defeats Saladin 1192
Made prisoner by duke of Austria, and sold to Henry VI. of Germany . . . Dec. ,,
Ransomed for about 300,000*l.* 1194
JOHN crowned . . . . . May, 1199
Normandy lost to England 1204
England put under an interdict 1208
Magna Charta granted . . . 15 June, 1215
HENRY III. crowned . . . 28 Oct. 1216
The Barons' war (*which see*) 1262-8
Simon de Montfort, earl of Leicester, summoned two parliaments; one including knights of the shire, 1264 (the other first including burgesses); the first regular parliament met . . Jan. 1265
EDWARD I. crowned . . . . 20 Nov. 1272
Wales subdued, united to England . . . 1283
Death of Roger Bacon 1292
Scotland subdued, 1296; revolts 1297
EDWARD II. crowned . . . . 8 July, 1307
Defeated by Bruce at Bannockburn 24 June, 1314
Insurrection of the barons against his favourites 1308, 1315, 1325
EDWARD III. crowned . . . 25 Jan. 1327
Defeat of the Scots at Hallidown-hill . . . 1333
Invades France; victorious at Crecy 26 Aug. 1346
Takes Calais 1347
Order of the Garter instituted 1349
Victory at Poictiers . . . 19 Sept. 1356
Peace of Bretigny . . . . 8 May, 1360
Law pleadings in English 1362
RICHARD II. crowned . . . 22 June, 1377
Insurrection of Wat Tyler suppressed . 15 June, 1381
Death of Wickliffe 1385
HENRY IV. crowned . . . 30 Sept. 1399
Order of the Bath instituted by Henry IV. . . ,,
Insurrection of the Percies and the Welsh . . 1402-5
HENRY V. crowned . . . 21 March, 1413
France invaded by Henry V. who gains the battle of Agincourt . . . . . 25 Oct. 1415
Treaty of Troyes; the French crown gained . 1420
HENRY VI. crowned at Paris . . . Dec. 1430
Appearance of the maid of Orleans; the conquests in France lost, except Calais 1429-31
Cade's insurrection . . . . June, 1450
War of the Roses (see *Roses* and *Battles*) . 1455-71
EDWARD IV. deposes Henry VI. 4 March, 1461
Printing introduced by Caxton 1471
EDWARD V. accession . . . 9 April, 1483
Murdered in the Tower (soon after) . . . ,,
RICHARD III. deposes Edward V. 25 June, 1483
Valuable statutes enacted 1484
HENRY VII. accession; Richard defeated and slain at Bosworth Field . . 22 Aug. 1485
Yeomen of the guard, the first appearance of a standing army in England instituted . . ,,
Henry marries Elizabeth, daughter of Edward IV. . 1486
Insurrection of Lambert Simnel quelled . . 1486-7
Court of Star-Chamber instituted . . . 1487
Insurrection of Perkin Warbeck quelled . . 1492-8
Gardening introduced into England, principally from the Netherlands, about 1502
Death of prince Arthur . . . . . 2 April, 1502
HENRY VIII. accession . . . 22 April, 1509
Rise of Wolsey 1514
Henry VIII.'s interview with Francis I. at Ardres (see "*Field of the Cloth of Gold*") . 4-25 June, 1520
First map of England drawn by G. Lilly, about . ,,
Henry VIII. becomes "Defender of the Faith" . . 1521
Fall of Wolsey; he dies . . . 29 Nov. 1530
Henry VIII. marries Anne Boleyn privately, 14 Nov. 1532 or January 1533; divorced from Catherine, 23 May, 1533
Henry VIII. styled "Head of the Church" . . 1534
The pope's authority in England is abolished . ,,
Sir Thomas More beheaded . . . 6 July, 1535
Queen Anne Boleyn beheaded . . 19 May, 1536
Queen Jane Seymour dies . . . 24 Oct. 1537
Monasteries suppressed 1538
Statute of Six Articles passed 1539
Abbots of Glastonbury, Reading, &c. executed . ,,
The first authorised edition of the Bible (Cranmer's) printed . . . . ,,
Cromwell, lord Essex, beheaded 1540
Anne of Cleves divorced . . . 9 July, ,,
Queen Catherine Howard beheaded . . . 1542
The title of "king of Ireland" confirmed to the English sovereigns 1543
Henry marries Catherine Parr . . 12 July, ,,
EDWARD VI. accession, 28 Jan.; promotes the Reformation (Somerset, protector) . . . 1547
Book of Common Prayer authorised . . . 1548
Somerset deprived of power, 1549; beheaded . . 1552
MARY, accession, 6 July; restores popery . . 1553
Execution of lady Jane Grey and her friends . 1554
Mary marries Philip of Spain; persecutes the Protestants . . . . ,,
Ridley, Latimer, and Cranmer burnt . 1555 and 1556
Calais re-taken by the French . . 7 Jan. 1558
ELIZABETH, accession; the church of England re-established . . . . . 17 Nov. ,,
Mary, queen of Scots, lands in England, 1568; executed . . . . . . 8 Feb. 1587
The Spanish armada repulsed . . . . July, 1588
Devereux, earl of Essex, beheaded . 25 Feb. 1601
JAMES I. accession; union of the two crowns 24 March, 1603
Styled "king of Great Britain" . . 24 Oct. 1604
The Gunpowder Plot . . . . . Nov. 1605
The present translation of the Bible completed . 1611
Baronets first created . . . . May, ,,
The Overbury murder . . . 15 Sept. 1613
Shakespeare dies . . . . 23 April, 1616
Raleigh beheaded . . . . 29 Oct. 1618
Book of Sports published . . . 24 May, ,,
CHARLES I. accession . . . 27 March, 1625
Death of lord Bacon . . . . 9 April, 1626
Duke of Buckingham assassinated . 23 Aug. 1628
Hampden's trial respecting "ship money" . . 1637
Contest between the king and parliament; impeachment and execution of lord Strafford . . . 1641
Attempted "arrest of the five members" (John Hampden, John Pym, Sir Arthur Hasilrigge, Denzil Holles, and Wm. Strode) . . 4 Jan. 1642
Civil war begins; see *Battles* . . 23 Oct. ,,
Archbishop Laud beheaded . . . 10 Jan. 1645
Charles defeated at Naseby . . 14 June, ,,
He flees to the Scotch, 5 May; is given up, 21 Sept. 1646
Execution of Charles I. . . . . 30 Jan. 1649
Cromwell's victory at Worcester . . 3 Sept. 1651
OLIVER CROMWELL protector of the Commonwealth . . . . . . 16 Dec. 1653
Naval victories of Blake 1652-7
RICHARD CROMWELL, protector . . 3 Sept. 1658
Richard resigns . . . . . 25 May, 1659
CHARLES II.: monarchy re-established principally by gen. Monk . . . 29 May, 1660
Act of uniformity passed; church of England restored 1662
The great plague 1665
The great fire of London . . . 2, 3 Sept. 1666
Disgrace of lord Clarendon . . . . Nov. 1667
Secret treaty with France signed at Dover May, 1670
Death of John Milton . . . . 8 Nov. 1674
Oates's "popish plot" creates a panic . 13 Aug. 1678
Sir Edmundbury Godfrey found murdered, 17 Oct. ,,
Many Roman Catholics executed 1678-9
The Habeas Corpus act, for protecting English

subjects against false arrest and imprisonment, passed . 27 May, 1679

Violent reaction, many protestants executed; London humbled . 1681

"Rye-house plot;" William, lord Russell (executed 21 July), and Algernon Sydney executed . 1683

JAMES II. accession . 6 Feb. 1685

Duke of Monmouth's rebellion defeated at Sedgemoor, 6 July; he is beheaded . 15 July, ,,

Acquittal of the seven bishops . 30 June, 1688

Abdication of James II. . 11 Dec. ,,

WILLIAM III. and MARY proclaimed by the convention parliament . 13 Feb. 1689

National debt begins . 1693

Bank of England incorporated . 27 July, 1694

Death of the queen regnant, Mary . 28 Dec. ,,

Peace of Ryswick . 1697

Death of James II. in exile . 6 (16) Sept. 1701

ANNE, accession . 8 March, 1702

Victory of Marlborough at Blenheim . 2 Aug. 1704

Union of the two kingdoms . 1 May, 1707

Sacheverell riots . 1710

Treaty of Utrecht, advantageous to Great Britain 11 April, 1713

GEORGE I. of Hanover, accession . 1 Aug. 1714

The Scots' rebellion quelled . 1715

South-sea bubble . 1720

Death of the duke of Marlborough . 16 June, 1722

Order of the Bath revived (*which see*) . 1725

GEORGE II. accession . 11 June, 1727

Death of Newton . 20 March, ,,

George II. at the victory of Dettingen . 16 June, 1743

Second Scots' rebellion: prince Charles-Edward gains Edinburgh, 17 Sept.; victor at Prestonpans, 21 Sept. 1745

Victory at Falkirk, 18 Jan.; defeated totally at Culloden . 16 April, 1746

Death of prince Frederick Louis, son of George II. and father of George III. . 20 March, 1751

New style introduced into England, 3 Sept. (made 14) 1752

Seven years' war begins . May, 1756

Conquest of India begins, under colonel (afterwards lord) Clive (see *India*) . 1757

Victory and death of general Wolfe (see *Quebec*) . 1759

GEORGE III. accession . 25 Oct. 1760

His marriage with Charlotte Sophia, of Mecklenburg Strelitz, 8 Sept.; crowned . 22 Sept. 1761

Peace of Paris; Canada gained . 10 Feb. 1763

Isle of Man annexed to Great Britain . 1765

Death of the Old Pretender, the "chevalier de St. George" . 30 Dec. ,,

Royal marriage act passed . 1772

American war begins (see *United States*) . 1775

Death of earl of Chatham . 11 May, 1778

"No Popery" riots . 2-7 June, 1780

Separation of America from England . 30 Nov. 1782

Margaret Nicholson's attempt on the life of George III. . 2 Aug. 1786

Trial of Warren Hastings begins . 13 Feb. 1788

Death of the Young Pretender, at Rome, 3 March, ,,

The king's illness made known . 12 Oct. ,,

He recovers, and goes to St. Paul's to make thanksgiving . 23 April, 1789

First coalition against France . 26 June, 1792

Habeas Corpus act suspended . 23 May, 1794

Howe's victory . 1 June, ,,

Marriage of the prince of Wales with the princess Caroline of Brunswick . 8 April, 1795

Warren Hastings acquitted . 23 April, ,,

Princess Charlotte of Wales born . 7 Jan. 1796

Cash payments suspended . 25 Feb. 1797

Death of Edmund Burke . 9 July, ,,

Irish rebellion . May, 1798

Habeas Corpus act again suspended. ,,

Battle of the Nile; Nelson victor . 1 Aug. 1798

Hatfield's attempt on the king's life . 15 May, 1800

Union of Great Britain with Ireland . 1 Jan. 1801

Nelson's victory at Copenhagen . 2 April, ,,

Habeas Corpus act again suspended . 19 April, ,,

Peace of Amiens concluded . 1 Oct. ,,

War against France under Bonaparte . 18 May, 1803

Nelson's victory and death at Trafalgar . 21 Oct. 1805

Death of Mr. Pitt . 23 Jan 1806

"Delicate investigation" (*which see*) . May, ,,

Lord Melville impeached, 29 April; acquitted 12 June, ,,

Death of Charles James Fox . 13 Sept. ,,

Orders in council against Berlin decree . 7 Jan. 1807

Abolition of the slave trade by parliament, 25 Mar. ,,

Victory and death of sir J. Moore. (See *Corunna*) 16 Jan. 1809

Duke of York impeached by col. Wardle . Jan. ,,

Jubilee celebrating king's accession . 25 Oct. ,,

Unfortunate Walcheren expedition . Aug.–Nov. ,,

Disappearance of Mr. Benjamin Bathurst, diplomatist at Perleberg, N. Germany; suspected assassination by French . 25 Nov. ,,

Sir Francis Burdett's arrest, and riots . 6 April, 1810

Death of princess Amelia; king's malady returns, 2 Nov. ,,

Great commercial embarrassment . Dec. ,,

REGENT—The prince of Wales . 5 Feb. 1811

Luddite riots . Nov. ,,

Assassination of Mr. Perceval, premier . 11 May, 1812

Earl of Liverpool premier . 9 June, ,,

War with America commenced . 18 June, ,,

Peace with France, &c. . 14 April, 1814

Visit of the emperor of Russia and king of Prussia to England . 7 June, ,,

Centenary of the house of Hanover . 1 Aug. ,,

Peace with America (treaty of Ghent) . 24 Dec. ,,

Battle of Waterloo (close of French war), 18 June, 1815

Princess Charlotte marries prince Leopold, of Saxe-Coburg . 2 May, 1816

Death of R. B. Sheridan . 9 July, ,,

Spa-fields meeting (*which see*) . 2 Dec. ,,

Green-bag inquiry (*which see*) . 2 Feb. 1817

Habeas Corpus act suspended . 24 Feb. ,,

Cash payments resumed . 22 Sept. ,,

Princess Charlotte dies in childbirth . 6 Nov. ,,

Queen Charlotte dies at Kew . 17 Nov. 1818

Queen Victoria born . 24 May, 1819

Manchester reform meeting (Peterloo) . 16 Aug. ,,

Duke of Kent dies . 23 Jan. 1820

GEORGE IV. accession . 29 Jan. ,,

Cato-street conspirators arrested, 23 Feb. executed, 1 May, ,,

Trial of queen Caroline . 19 Aug. to 10 Nov. ,,

Coronation of George IV. . 19 July, 1821

Queen Caroline dies at Hammersmith . 7 Aug. ,,

Lord Byron dies . 19 April, 1824

Commercial panic . 1825-6

Duke of York dies . 5 Jan. 1827

Mr. Canning, premier, 30 April; dies . 8 Aug. ,,

Battle of Navarino . 20 Oct. ,,

Roman Catholic Relief bill passed . 13 April, 1829

Political panic in London;—riots . Nov. ,,

WILLIAM IV. accession . 26 June, 1830

Mr. Huskisson killed at the opening of the Liverpool and Manchester railway . 15 Sept. ,,

Grey administration formed . Nov. ,,

King opens new London bridge . Aug. 1831

The cholera morbus in England . 26 Oct. ,,

Reform bill rejected by the lords, 7 Oct.; fatal Bristol riots . 29 Oct. ,,

English Reform act passed . 7 June, 1832

Assault on William IV. by a discharged pensioner at Ascot . 19 June, ,,

Sir Walter Scott dies . 21 Sept. ,,

S. T. Coleridge dies . 25 July, 1834

Slavery ceases in the colonies . 1 Aug. ,,

Corporation reform act passed . 9 Sept. 1835

VICTORIA, accession; Hanover separated from Great Britain . 20 June, 1837

Coronation of queen Victoria . 28 June, 1838

Beginning of war with China . March, 1839

Penny postage begins . 10 Jan. 1840

Marriage of the queen with prince Albert of Saxe-Coburg . 10 Feb. ,,

Oxford's assault on the queen . 10 June, ,,

Prince of Wales born . 9 Nov. 1841

King of Prussia visits England . 24 Jan. 1842

John Francis fires at the queen . 30 May, ,,

Bean presents a pistol at her . 3 July, ,,

Income tax act passed . Aug. ,,

Queen embarks for Scotland (1st visit) . 29 Aug. ,,

Peace of Nankin (with China) . Dec. ,,

Death of duke of Sussex . 21 April, 1843

Queen's visit to the Orleans family at Château d'Eu, 2 Sept. ,,

Emperor of Russia visits England . 1 June, 1844

King Louis Philippe's visit (see *France*) . 6 Oct. ,,

Tractarian or Puseyite controversy . 1844-5

Anti-corn-law agitation . 1845

Queen's visit to Germany . . . . 9 Aug. 1845
Peel's new tariff, 1845; railway mania . . Nov. ,,
Commercial panic . . . . March, 1846
Corn laws repealed . . . . 26 June, ,,
Chartist demonstration in London . . 10 April, 1848
Cholera re-appears in England in . . 1848 and 1849
Queen embarks on her visit to Ireland . 1 Aug. ,,
Adelaide, queen dowager, dies . . . 2 Dec. ,,
"Exhibition of 1851" announced . . 3 Jan. 1850
Death of Wordsworth (aged 80) . . 23 April, ,,
Pate's assault on the queen . . 27 June, ,,
Death of Sir Robert Peel (aged 62) . . 2 July, ,,
Duke of Cambridge dies . . . 8 July, ,,
Queen's visit to Belgium . . . 21 Aug. ,,
Great excitement occasioned by the pope's establishment of a Roman Catholic hierarchy in England, Nov. ,,
Sixth census of United Kingdom (see *Population*) (27,637,761) . . . . 30 March, 1851
The first "Great Exhibition" opened . 1 May, ,,
Australian gold arrives . . . Dec. ,,
Death of the poet Thomas Moore . . 26 Feb. 1852
John Camden Neild, an eccentric miser, bequeathed about 250,000*l.* to the queen; he died 30 Aug. ,,
Slight earthquake at Liverpool, &c. . 9 Nov. ,,
Death of Wellington (aged 83), Sept. 14; public funeral . . . . 18 Nov. ,,
Camp at Chobham . . . 14 June-19 Aug. 1853
Death of sir Charles Napier, conqueror of Scinde, 29 Aug. ,,
English and French fleets enter Bosphorus, 22 Oct. ,,
Protocol signed between England, France, Austria, and Prussia, for re-establishment of peace between Russia and Turkey . . . 5 Dec. ,,
Many meetings on eastern question, favourable to Turkey . . . . Sept. to Dec. ,,
Great strike at Preston; 14,972 hands unemployed at one time . . 15 Oct. 1853, to 1 May, 1854
Queen reviews Baltic fleet . . . 11 March, ,,
Treaty of alliance between England, France, and Turkey signed . . . 12 March, ,,
War declared against Russia (see *Russo-Turkish War*) 28 March, ,,
Fast day on account of the war . . 26 April, ,,
Marquis of Anglesey dies . . . 28 May, ,,
King of Portugal visits England . . June, ,,
Crystal Palace opened by the queen . 10 June, ,,
Cholera prevails in the south and west of London, Aug. and Sept. ,,
Thanksgiving for abundant harvest . . 1 Oct. ,,
Great explosion and fire at Gateshead and Newcastle, 6 Oct. ,,
Meeting of Parliament . . . . 12 Dec. ,,
Resignation of Aberdeen ministry . . 29 Jan. 1855
Formation of Palmerston ministry . . Feb. ,,
Death of Joseph Hume (aged 78) . . 20 Feb. ,,
Sebastopol inquiry committee named . 23 Feb. ,,
Visit of emperor and empress of French, 16 to 21 April, ,,
Loan of 16 millions agreed to . . . April, ,,
Distribution of Crimean medals . . 18 May, ,,
Metropolitan cattle market opened . 13 June, ,,
Agitation and rioting concerning Sunday trading bill, which is withdrawn . . 2 July, ,,
The queen and prince visit Paris . . 18 Aug. ,,
Peace with Russia proclaimed, 19 April; thanksgiving day, 4 May; illuminations, &c. 29 May, 1856
War with China (*which see*) . . . Oct. ,,
War with Persia (*which see*) . . . Nov. ,,
Mutiny of Indian army begins (see *India*) . March, 1857
Dissolution of parliament, 21 March; new parliament meets . . . . 30 April, ,,
Death of duchess of Gloucester (aged 81), the last of George III.'s children . . 30 April, ,,
Opening of the Fine Arts exhibition at Manchester, 5 May, ,,
Educational conference in London, prince Albert in the chair . . . . 22 June, ,,
Victoria crosses (*which see*) distributed by the queen in Hyde-park . . . 26 June, ,,
Meetings for relief of sufferers by the mutiny in India [by 15 Nov. 260,000*l.* raised] 25 Aug. ,,
Great commercial panic; relieved by suspension of Bank Charter Act of 1844 . 12 Nov. ,,
Parliament meets . . . . 3 Dec. ,,
Marriage of princess royal to prince Frederick-William of Prussia . . . . 25 Jan. 1858
Excitement respecting attempted assassination of Louis Napoleon, 14 Jan.; indiscreet addresses of French colonels, published . . 27 Jan. 1858
"Conspiracy to Murder" bill (introduced by lord Palmerston, 8 Feb.) rejected, 19 Feb.; Palmerston ministry resigns . . . . 22 Feb. ,,
Derby-Disraeli administration formed . 26 Feb. ,,
Dr. Simon Bernard acquitted of conspiracy against the life of Louis Napoleon . . 17 April, ,,
The Jewish Disabilities bill passed . . 23 July, ,,
The India bill passed . . . . 2 Aug. ,,
The queen visits Birmingham, 15 June; Cherbourg, 4, 5 Aug.; the princess royal (at Potsdam), 12 Aug. &c.; and Leeds . . . Sept. ,,
Excitement about the confessional; public meetings held against it . . 12 July and 18 Sept. ,,
The Association for the Promotion of Social Science meet at Liverpool . . . 12 Oct. ,,
Excitement respecting the Italian war; proclamation for manning the navy . . 30 April, 1859
Thanksgiving for suppression of Indian mutiny, 1 May, ,,
Declaration of neutrality of England . . 12 May, ,,
Proclamation for the organisation of volunteer rifle corps; many formed . . . May-Oct. ,,
The Derby ministry defeated on the Reform bill; dissolve parliament, 23 April; again defeated, they resign 11 June; the Palmerston-Russell administration formed . . . 18 June, ,,
The Handel commemoration . . 20, 22, 24 June, ,,
The income-tax increased to provide for the defences of the country . . . . July, ,,
Lord Macaulay dies (aged 59) . . . 28 Dec. ,,
Commercial treaty with France, signed 23 Jan.; approved by parliament . . . March, 1860
Sir Charles Barry dies (aged 65) . . 12 May, ,,
The queen reviews 18,000 volunteers in Hyde-park, 23 June, ,,
National rifle shooting match at Wimbledon (see *Volunteers*) . . . . . 2-7 July, ,,
The earl of Derby reviews about 11,000 Lancashire volunteers at Knowsley . . . 1 Sept. ,,
The queen and prince visit their daughter in Prussia Sept. ,,
Peace with China signed . . . . 24 Oct. ,,
Thos. Cochrane, earl of Dundonald, dies (aged 82) 31 Oct. ,,
Prince of Wales visits Canada and United States, 24 July-20 Oct.; returns . . . 15 Nov. ,,
Severe cold (see *Cold*) . . Dec. 1860, and Jan. 1861
Charter granted for Exhibition of 1862 . 14 Feb. ,,
Death of duchess of Kent (aged 75) . 16 March, ,,
Excitement about "Essays and Reviews" . . . ,,
Seventh census taken (29,192,419) . . 8 April, ,,
King of Sweden and his son visit London . Aug. ,,
Great excitement through capt. Wilkes (of U.S. navy) forcibly taking Messrs. Slidell and Mason from the Royal British Mail steamer *Trent* (see *United States*) . . . . 8 Nov. ,,
Death of the prince consort of "typhoid fever, duration 21 days," 14 Dec.; buried (see *Albert Memorial*) . . . . . 23 Dec. ,,
The United States' government release Messrs. Slidell and Mason . . . . 28 Dec. ,,
Second great International Exhibition opened by the duke of Cambridge . . . . 1 May. 1862
Inundations in Norfolk (see *Levels*) . . . May, ,,
Marriage of princess Alice to Louis of Hesse, 1 July, ,,
Prince Alfred declared king of Greece at Athens (throne declined) . . . . 23 Oct. ,,
Final closing of international exhibition . 15 Nov. ,,
Remains of the prince consort transferred to the mausoleum at Frogmore . . . 18 Dec. ,,
Great distress in the cotton manufacturing districts begins, April: contributions received, central relief fund, 407,830*l.*; Mansion-house fund, 236,926*l.* 20 Dec. 1862
Rupture with Brazil . . . . . Jan. 1863
Prince Alfred elected king of Greece . . 3 Feb. ,,
Princess Alexandra of Denmark enters London, 7 March; married to the prince of Wales, 10 March, ,,
The British, French, and Austrian governments remonstrate with Russia on cruelties in Poland, 7 April, ,,
Inauguration of the Great Exhibition memorial to the prince consort in the Horticultural gardens, London . . . . 11 June.

Arrival of captains Grant and Speke from exploring the source of the Nile . . . June, 1863

Great decrease of distress in cotton districts Oct. „

Earthquake in central and N.W. England . 6 Oct. „

The government declines the French emperor's proposal for a congress of sovereigns . . . Nov. „

Death of William Thackeray (aged 52) . . 24 Dec. „

Birth of prince Albert-Victor of Wales . 8 Jan. 1864

Final judgment of the judicial committee of the privy council that the government had no authority to seize the *Alexandra* (Confederate) steamer 8 Feb. „

Garibaldi's visit to England . . . 3-27 April, „

The Ionian isles made over to Greece . 1 June, „

European conference at London on the Schleswig-Holstein question; no result, 24 April—25 June, „

Great excitement through the murder of Mr. Briggs in a first-class carriage on the North-London railway . . . . 9 July, „

Great explosion of gunpowder at the Belvedere magazine, near Woolwich . . . . 1 Oct. „

Death of John Leech (aged 47). . 29 Oct. „

Death of Richard Cobden (aged 61) . . 2 April, 1865

Prince George of Wales born . . . 3 June, „

Resignation of lord-chancellor Westbury . 4 July, „

General election; majority for Palmerston administration . . . . 10 July, &c. „

Visit of Abd-el-Kader; departs . . 6 Aug. „

Prevalence of a cattle plague, June-Oct.; royal commission appointed; met . . 10 Oct. „

English fleet visits Cherbourg, 15 Aug.; French fleet visits Portsmouth . . . 29, 30 Aug. „

Fine art and industrial exhibitions opened in London and the provinces . . July-Sept. „

Death of lord Palmerston, 18 Oct.; public funeral 27 Oct. „

Earl Russell premier . . . . 3 Nov. „

Important commercial treaty with Austria signed 16 Dec. „

New parliament opened by the queen . . 6 Feb. 1866

New reform bill introduced by Mr. Gladstone, 12 Mar. „

Commercial panic in London . . 11 May *et seq.* „

International botanical congress opened . 22 May, „

Defeat of the government on the reform bill, 18 June; resignation of ministers . 26 June, „

Marriage of princess Helena to prince Christian of Schleswig-Holstein . . . . . 5 July, „

The third Derby cabinet formed . . 6 July, „

The Atlantic telegraph completely laid, and messages sent to lord Stanley . . 27 July, „

The cable of 1865 recovered, and communication established with Valentia, 2 Sept.; and with Newfoundland . . . . . . 8 Sept. „

Projected attack of Fenians on Chester prevented by the authorities . . . 11, 12 Feb. 1867

The queen laid foundation of the Albert hall of arts at S. Kensington . . . . 20 May, „

Visit of the viceroy of Egypt . . . 6-18 July, „

Visit of the Belgian volunteers (see *Belgium*), 10-22 July, „

Visit of the Sultan (see *Turkey*) . . 12-23 July, „

"Early Years of the Prince Consort," published end of . . . . July, „

New Reform act passed (see *Reform*) . . 15 Aug. „

Michael Faraday, natural philosopher (nearly 76), died . . . . 25 Aug. „

Preparations for the expedition to Abyssinia (see *Abyssinia*) . . . . . . Aug. „

Fenian outrages; rescue of prisoners at Manchester (see *Fenians*) . . . . 18 Sep., „

Synod of bishops at Lambeth (see *Pan-Anglican*) 24-27 Sept. „

Meeting of parliament respecting Abyssinian war, 19 Nov. „

Fenian explosion at Clerkenwell prison, London, 13 Dec. „

Special constables called for; 113,674 (in the U.K.) sworn in by . . . . . 28 Jan. 1868

"Leaves from our Journal in Scotland," &c., by the queen, published . . . . Jan. „

Resignation of earl of Derby, 25 Feb.; the Disraeli ministry formed . . . 29 Feb. „

The queen holds a drawing-room again 12 March, „

Mr. Gladstone's resolution for disestablishing the Irish church; adopted by the commons, 30 April, „

Death of lord Brougham, aged 89 . . 7 May, „

Arrival of the duke of Edinburgh from Australia 26 June, 1868

Irish and Scotch reform acts passed . 13 July, „

Nearly 21,000 extra deaths attributed to the hot summer (23 July said to be the hottest) 1 July—30 Sept. „

Parliament dissolved 11 Nov., new parliament meets 10 Dec. „

Resignation of Disraeli ministry, 2 Dec.; Gladstone ministry take office . . . 9 Dec. „

Convention with the United States respecting the Alabama claim signed (afterwards rejected by the States) . . . . . . 14 Jan. 1869

New parliament meets for business . . 16 Feb. „

Irish Church bill introduced into the commons, 1 March; royal assent . . . 26 July, „

The earl of Derby dies (aged 70) . . . 23 Oct. „

Parliament meets . . . . . . 8 Feb. 1870

Charles Dickens dies (aged 58) . . . 9 June, „

Earl of Clarendon dies (aged 70) . . 27 June, „

Irish land bill brought in, 15 Feb., received royal assent . . . . 8 July, „

Neutrality in Franco-Prussian war (*which see*) proclaimed . . . . 19 July, „

2,000,000*l.* voted to increase the army by 20,000 men 1 Aug. „

Foreign enlistment act passed, 1 Aug.; stringent proclamation of neutrality issued . . 9 Aug. „

Parliament prorogued . . . . 10 Aug. „

Treaty with Prussia and France for neutrality of Belgium signed . . . . . 9, 11 Aug. „

Long drought: bad hay harvest: good wheat harvest . . . . Mar.–Aug. „

Earl Granville repels the charge of violating neutralities made by the Prussian government, 1-15 Sept. „

The queen's consent to the marriage of the princess Louise to the marquis of Lorne announced 24 Oct. „

Foot and mouth disease prevalent among cattle Aug.–Nov. „

Election of elementary school-boards . . Nov. „

Excitement through the Russian note respecting the Black sea (see *Russia*) . . . Nov. „

Foundation of new Post-office laid . 16 Dec. „

Resignation of Mr. Bright announced . 20 Dec. „

Parliament meets . . . . . 9 Feb. 1871

Marriage of the princess Louise and the marquis of Lorne . . . . . . 21 March, „

Royal Albert Hall, Kensington, opened by the queen 29 March, „

Eighth census taken (31,817,108) . . 3 April, „

Death of sir John F. Herschel, astronomer and philosopher (aged 79) . . . 11 May, „

Death of George Grote, historian of Greece (aged 77) 18 June, „

First annual International Exhibition at South Kensington, opened 1 May, closed . . 30 Sept. „

Black Sea conference met 17 Jan., closed (neutralisation of Black Sea abrogated, &c.) . 13 March, „

Disestablishment of the Church of England bill rejected in the commons (374—89), 1 May; parliament prorogued . . . . . 21 Aug. „

Illness of the queen at Balmoral, 4 Sept.; recovery 13 Sept. „

Serious illness of the prince of Wales from typhoid fever, Dec.; began to recover . . 14 Dec. „

Letter from the queen and princess to the people, thanking them for sympathy . . 26 Dec. „

Thanksgivings for recovery of prince of Wales 21 Jan. 1872

Excitement respecting the American claims under the treaty of Washington . . . . Feb. „

Meeting of parliament . . . . . 6 Feb. „

The queen, prince and princess of Wales, and court and parliament go in state to St. Paul's; national thanksgiving for recovery of the prince of Wales; London decorated; illuminations, &c.; a successful day . . . . 27 Feb. „

The queen in a public letter, gazetted 1 March, says, "Words are too weak for the queen to say how very deeply touched and gratified she has been by the immense enthusiasm and affection exhibited towards her dear son and herself," dated 29 Feb. „

The queen, while entering Buckingham Palace, threatened by Arthur O'Connor, aged about 18,

who presents an unloaded pistol, with a paper to be signed; immediately apprehended . 29 Feb. 1872
The queen sailed for Germany, and stayed several weeks . . . . 23 March–7 April, ,,
Strikes among agricultural labourers in Warwickshire and other counties; union formed, 29 March, ,,
Arthur O'Connor pleads guilty (sentenced to imprisonment and flogging) . . 9 April, ,,
Correspondence between the British and American governments respecting the claims for indirect losses, which the former rejects . 3 Feb.–May, ,,
Supplemental treaty proposed; accepted by U.S. senate, 25 May; further discussion in parliament; unsatisfactory correspondence; the U.S. congress adjourns . . . . 10 June, ,,
Strikes among builders and other trades . June, ,,
Final meeting of arbitrators; damages awarded; see *Alabama* . . . . 14 Sept. ,,
New commercial treaty with France signed at London . . . . 5 Nov. ,,
Continued rain; floods in Midland counties . Dec. ,,
Death of Edward Bulwer Lord Lytton, orator, poet, and novelist, aged 66 . . . 18 Jan. 1873
Strikes among colliers, Jan.; great dearth of coal; the best, 52*s.* a ton in London . . 15 Feb. ,,
Resignation of Mr. Gladstone on account of a defeat in the Commons on the Dublin university bill (287—284), 13 March; resumes office, 17 March, ,,
Visit of the shah of Persia . 18 June–5 July, ,,
Proposed marriage of duke of Edinburgh to grand-duchess Marie of Russia announced by the queen, 17 July; Annuity bill for the duke passed, 5 Aug. ,,
Judicature Act passed . . . . 5 Aug. ,,
Severely contested elections: conservative reaction, Sept.–Oct. ,,
Marriage of duke and duchess of Edinburgh, 23 Jan. 1874
Parliament dissolved . . . . 26 Jan. ,,
General election; conservative majority about 50, Feb.; Gladstone ministry resigns, 17 Feb.; Disraeli ministry formed . . . 21 Feb. ,,
Close of the Tichborne trial (see *Trials*) . 28 Feb. ,,
Meeting of parliament . . . 5 March, ,,
The duke and duchess of Edinburgh enter London, 12 March, ,,
Sir Garnet Wolseley returns from his successful expedition against the Ashantees . 21 March, ,,
Visit of the czar of Russia . . 13-21 May, ,,
Public worship regulation act passed . 7 Aug. ,,
Fruitful season; excellent corn crop . Aug.–Sept. ,,
The queen receives a testimonial of gratitude from the French nation for British assistance during the war (see *France*) . . . . 3 Dec. ,,
Meeting of parliament . . . . 5 Feb. 1875
Moody and Sankey, American revivalists, arrive in London, 9 March; sail from Liverpool (see *Revivals*) . . . . 4 Aug. ,,
Parliament prorogued . . . . 13 Aug. ,,
Railway jubilee at Darlington . . 27 Sept. ,,
Departure of the prince of Wales for India, 11 Oct. ,,
The khedive's shares in the Suez canal bought by the British government (see *Suez*) 1 Nov., announced . . . . 25 Nov. ,,
Parliament opened by the queen in person, 8 Feb. 1876
The queen sails for Germany (all her sons abroad), 28 March; returns . . . 22 April, ,,
Royal titles bill received royal assent . 27 April, ,,
The queen proclaimed "empress of India," 1 May, ,,
Arrival of prince of Wales at Portsmouth, 11 May, ,,
Parliament prorogued . . . . 15 Aug. ,,
Great heat; failure in fruit crops; harvest beneath average. . . . . middle Aug. ,,
Great excitement and many public meetings respecting the Turkish atrocities in Bulgaria, Aug.–Oct. ,,
Mr. Gladstone's "Horrors in Bulgaria" published, 6 Sept. ,,
National conference against war to defend Turkey, St. James's hall . . . . 8 Dec. ,,
Parliament opened by the queen . . 8 Feb. 1877
Proclamation of neutrality in Russo-Turkish war, 30 April, ,,
Debate on Mr. Gladstone's resolutions:—1st. That this house found much cause for dissatisfaction and complaint in the conduct of the Ottoman Porte, with regard to the despatch written by the earl of Derby, 21 Sept. 1876, and relating to the massacres in Bulgaria, (for the resolution, 225; against, 354) . . . . 7-14 May, ,,
Fleet sent to Besika bay . . . . 3 July, 1877
Statue of king Alfred by count Gleichen, at Wantage, unveiled by the prince of Wales, his descendant . . . . . 14 July, ,,
Early meeting of parliament on account of Russo-Turkish war . . . . 17 Jan. 1878
Vote of 6,000,000*l.* asked for before entering into conference respecting eastern affairs, 24 Jan.; debate . . . . 31 Jan. ,,
Liberal amendment withdrawn on report of Russian advance on Constantinople, 7 Feb.; vote passed (204-124) . . . . 8 Feb. ,,
Warlike policy of the ministry; resignation of lord Carnarvon, 24 Jan.; and earl of Derby (see *Disraeli Administration*) . . . 28 March, ,,
Message of the queen, respecting calling out the reserves, &c., 2 April; adopted by parliament, April, ,,
Earl of Salisbury's circular, indicting the Treaty of San Stefano, 2 April; moderate reply of Gortschakoff, printed . . . 10 April, ,,
Indian troops ordered to Malta, about . 17 April, ,,
Censured by the opposition; debate in commons; for government, 347; against, 226 . 20-23 May, ,,
Earl Russell died, aged 85 . . . 28 May ,,
The ministry announce the meeting of a European congress on the eastern question to meet on 13 June; the earl of Beaconsfield and the marquis of Salisbury to attend for England. (See *Berlin*), 3 June, ,,
Anglo-Turkish convention (see *Turkey*) signed, 4 June, ,,
The conference meets at Berlin (*which see*) 13 June; treaty signed . . . . 13 July, ,,
10,000*l.* a year voted for the duke of Connaught for his proposed marriage with princess Louise Margaret of Prussia . . . . 25 July, ,,
Debate on the Berlin treaty, in the commons; great speech of Mr. Gladstone, 30 July; majority for government (338—195) . 29 July–3 Aug. ,,
Parliament prorogued . . . . 16 Aug. ,,
Meeting of parliament on account of Afghan war, 5 Dec. ,,
Majority for ministers on vote of censure, lords (201-65), 10 Dec.; commons (328-227) . 13-14 Dec. ,,
Death of princess Alice by diphtheria at Darmstadt, after attendance on her husband, the grand-duke, and children, 7.30 A.M. . . . 14 Dec. ,,
Severe winter, many persons unemployed . Dec. ,,
Parliament adjourned (to 13 Feb.) . . 17 Dec. ,,
The Queen in a letter thanks her subjects for their sympathy with her loss of a dear child, who was "a bright example of loving tenderness, courageous devotion, and self-sacrifice to duty," dated 26 Dec. ,,
Edward Byrne Madden (? lunatic) arrested for threatening to attack the Queen in letters to the Home Office, 12 Dec. 1878; judged insane, 13 Jan. 1879
1,500,000*l.* voted for Zulu war . . . 27 Feb. ,,
Expedition sent (between 8,000 and 9,000 men, 1,800 horses, &c.), ... Feb.–March, ,,
Marriage of duke and duchess of Connaught at Windsor . . . . . 13 March, ,,
The Queen at Paris, 26 March, arrives at Baveno, on Lago Maggiore . . . 28 March, ,,
Proposed censure of government respecting Zulu war, &c., negatived, lords (156-61), 25 March; commons (306-246) . . 31 March–1 April, ,,
Great depression of trade (attributed to bad harvest, famine, pestilence, war, and over-trading) 1878-9
Commons debate on the budget, for government, 303; against, 230 . . . 28-29 April, ,,
Cold and very wet summer, little sunshine, failure of corn and fruit crops . . . autumn, 1879
Severe weather, Nov. very cold, 1-12 Dec. and Jan., much fog 1880
Parliament opened by the Queen, 5 Feb., dissolved 23 Feb. ,,
General election, great liberal majority, 30 March–16 April; resignation of ministry . 22 April, ,,
Gladstone ministry formed . . . 29 April, ,,
New parliament meets 29th April, Bradlaugh difficulty (see *Parliaments*) . . 3 May *et seq.* ,,
Fine autumn, good average harvest, improved trade, Oct. ,,
Early meeting of parliament on account of Ireland, 6 Jan. 1881

Successful review of about 52,000 volunteers by the queen at Windsor . . . . . 9 July, 1881
Parliament prorogued . . . . 27 Aug. ,,
Wet autumn; deficient harvest; much depression Sept. ,,
Court and general mourning for death of gen. Garfield, president of United States 21-27 Sept ,,
Gradual revival of trade . . 1 July-30 Oct. ,,
Great hurricane throughout England, causing destruction of life, property, and shipping, 13-15 Oct. ,,
Very mild winter . . . . . Nov.-Feb. 1882
Meeting of parliament . . . . 7 Feb. ,,
The queen shot at, at Great Western railway station, Windsor, by Roderick Maclean, aged 27; 2nd March; he is committed for trial for high treason 10 March, ,,
The queen's letter of thanks for general sympathy dated . . . . . . 12 March, ,,
She sails for Mentone, 14 March; arrives, 16 March; leaves it, 12 April; at Windsor, 14 April, ,,
The queen dedicates Epping Forest to the use of the people for all time . . . . . 6 May, ,,
Parliament adjourned, and meets on 24 Oct.; prorogued . . . . 2 Dec. ,,
New law courts, London, opened by the queen 4 Dec. ,,
Great excitement through attempted explosion of Local Government office . . 15 March, 1883
Detection of secret manufacture of explosives at Birmingham, 4 April; arrest of Alfred Whitehead, Thos. Gallagher, physician, Wm. Norman, H. H. Wilson, H. D. E. and Henry Dalton, otherwise John O'Connor . . . . 5-6 April, ,,
Other arrests in Liverpool, Glasgow, and London about 6-7 April, ,,
Parliament prorogued . . . . . 25 Aug. ,,
The queen publishes "More Leaves from my Journal in the Highlands" . . . 11 Feb. 1884
Egypt and the Soudan: censure of the government for its "vacillating and inconsistent policy," voted by the lords (181-81) 12 Feb.; rejected by the commons (311-262) . . . 12-20 Feb. ,,
Prince Leopold, duke of Albany, dies, aged nearly 31, 28 March; buried at Windsor . . 5 April, ,,
The queen starts for Darmstadt . . . 16 April, ,,
The queen in a letter expresses her deep sense of the loving sympathy of her subjects in all parts of her empire and also of foreign countries with herself and the duchess of Albany . 14 April, ,,
The queen present at the marriage of her granddaughter princess Victoria of Hesse to prince Louis of Battenburg at Darmstadt, 30 April; returned to Windsor . . . . . . 7 May, ,,
Vote of censure of the government for not supporting Gordon negatived in the commons (303-275) 12-14 May, ,,
Parliament prorogued . . . . . 14 Aug. ,,
Good harvest, continued fine weather . July, Aug. ,,
Parliament meets . . . . 23 Oct.-6 Dec. ,,
Franchise bill passed, see under *Reform* . 6 Dec. ,,
Prince Albert Victor Edward of Wales comes of age . . . . 8 Jan. 1885
Parliament meets . . . . . . 19 Feb. ,,
Ordered that the militia be embodied and soldiers stopped from entering the reserve . 18 Feb. ,,
Vote of censure on the government respecting Egypt, passed by the lords (189-58); negatived by the commons (302-288) . . . . 27, 28 Feb. ,,
Day of mourning for general Gordon and the killed in the Soudan . . . . . . 13 March, ,,
Reserves to be called out in prospect of war with Russia . . . . 27 March, ,,
The queen visits Aix-les-Bains, &c. 1 April-2 May, ,,
(See *Ireland, Parliament, and Revenue.*)
Redistribution of Seats Act (see under *Reform*) passed . . . . 25 June, ,,
Vigorous preparations for war: vote of credit for 11,000,000*l.* passed by the commons (see *Russia*) 27 April, ,,
Resignation of the Gladstone ministry on account of minority on the Budget bill (264-252) 8-9 June, ,,
Ministry of the marquis of Salisbury formed 24 June, ,,
Parliament prorogued . . . . . 14 Aug. ,,
Very dry summer, average harvest . . ,,
The earl of Shaftesbury, a great philanthropist, dies, aged 84 . . . . 1 Oct. ,,
Agitation for the disestablishment of the Church, &c. autumn, 1885
Dissolution of parliament . . . . 18 Nov. ,,
Elections: about 333 Liberals, 251 Conservatives, 86 Parnellites . . . . 23 Nov.-18 Dec. ,,
The new parliament meets 12 Jan.; opened by the queen . . . . 21 Jan. 1886
Resignation of the Salisbury administration (*which see*) . . . . 27 Jan. ,,
Gladstone's third administration formed 2-6 Feb. ,,
Long winter; severe cold, Feb.; heavy snowstorms in N.E. counties; railway trains snowed up several days . . . . . 1, 2, 3 March, ,,
Mr. Gladstone introduces his bill to "make better provision for the future government of Ireland" 8 April, ,,
Colonial and Indian Exhibition (the first great national exhibition) opened at South Kensington by the queen . . . . 4 May, ,,
International exhibition of navigation, commerce, &c., at Liverpool opened by the queen 11 May, ,,
Queen Victoria's jubilee year begins . 20 June, ,,
Excessively cold spring and summer . . . ,,
Very hot part of June and July . . . ,,
Parliamentary election on Mr. Gladstone's Irish policy (reported, 316 conservatives, 191 Gladstonians, 78 unionists, 85 Parnellites) . July, ,,
The Gladstone administration resigns . 20 July, ,,
The second Salisbury administration (*which see*) formed 26 July; the marquis of Hartington and friends decline to form a coalition ministry 31 Dec. ,,
Revival of trade and commerce, last half of ,,
Meeting of parliament . . . . . 28 Jan. 1887
The queen starts for the Riviera 29 March; visits Cannes, Aix-les-Bains, &c. 1 April *et seq.*; returns to England . . . . . 29 April, ,,
The queen attends the jubilee service at Westminster Abbey (see *Jubilee*) 21 June; she issues a letter to the nation expressing her profound gratitude for the very kind reception by the vast multitude during her progress to, and return from the Abbey, and her high admiration for the excellent order preserved . . . . 24 June, ,,
Severe drought; 35 rainless days in some parts (11 weeks) . . . . June-mid. Aug. ,,
Very early harvest . . . . . summer, ,,
Parliament prorogued . . . . 16 Sept. ,,
Amicable conventions respecting Suez canal and New Hebrides, signed at Paris . . 24 Oct. ,,
Meeting of parliament . . . . . 9 Feb. 1888
The queen starts for Florence 21 March; at Florence 24 March; at Innsbrück 23 April; at Berlin 24 April; in London . . . 27 April, ,,
Local Government Act (*which see*) passed 13 Aug. ,,
Parliament adjourns till 6 Nov. . . . 13 Aug. ,,
The queen's visit to Glasgow . . 18, 19 Aug. ,,
Cold wet summer, very fine autumn 1888; very mild weather, London much warmer than at Constantinople, Paris, &c. . . . . 4 Dec. ,,
Parliament meets 6 Nov.; adjourns . . 24 Dec. ,,
Epidemic of measles throughout the country, winter, 1888-9
Parliament meets . . . . . . 21 Feb. 1889
The queen started for Biarritz 5 March: meets the queen-regent of Spain at San Sebastian 27 March; returns . . . . 3 April, ,,
Death of Mr. John Bright, M.P. (aged 78), orator, "tribune of the people," free-trader (see *Anti-Corn Law League*), fearless, honest, independent 27 March; "one of the noblest figures that we have ever known in Parliament"—*Lord Hartington* . . . . 29 March, ,,
Great improvement in trade and revenue Jan.-April ,,
Warren de la Rue, D.C.L., F.R.S., astronomer, chemist, and physicist, aged 74, died . 19 April, ,,
The queen visits the prince of Wales at Sandringham . . . . . . 23-27 April *et seq.* ,,
Parliament prorogued . . . . . 30 Aug. ,,
The emperor William II. visits the queen, see *Germany* . . . . 1-8 Aug. ,,
The queen visits Wales (*which see*) . 23 Aug. ,,
Fine summer and autumn; excellent hay and moderate corn harvests and good wool season . ,,
Envoys from the sultan of Zanzibar, received by the queen at Balmoral . . . . . 20 Oct. ,,

Many strikes, and much agitation respecting labour and wages in London and throughout the country Aug.–Dec. 1889
Great revival in trade . . . June–Dec. ,,
Epidemic of influenza (*which see*) . . . Jan. 1890
Parliament meets . . . . . 11 Feb. ,,
The queen visits Aix-les-Bains 26 March–22 April; at Darmstadt receives the empress Frederick, the emperor William II. and others of her family 23–29 April, ,,
At Windsor . . . . . . 30 April, ,,
The queen visits Aylesbury and baron Ferdinand de Rothschild at Waddesdon Manor . 14 May, ,,
The ex-queen Isabella of Spain visits the queen at Windsor, and attends the state Ball, Buckingham Palace, 20 May; leaves England . . 29 May, ,,
Anglo-German Agreement (*which see*) respecting East Africa, signed at Berlin . . 1 July ,,
Return of Mr. H. M. Stanley (see *Soudan*) . . 26 April, 1887–90
The queen inaugurates the Empress dock at Southampton . . . . . . 26 July, 1890
The emperor William II. visits the queen at Osborne, inspects the fleet, &c. . 4–8 Aug. ,,
Anglo-French Agreement (*which see*) respecting Africa, signed . . . . . 5 Aug. ,,
Parliament prorogued . . . . . 18 Aug. ,,
Anglo-Portuguese Agreement settled 20 Aug.; not ratified (see *Portugal*) . . . . Nov. ,,
Meeting of parliament . . . . . 25 Nov. ,,
Parliament meets after the recess . . 22 Jan. 1891
The queen present at the launch of the *Royal Sovereign*, great battleship, and of the *Royal Arthur*, first class cruiser; Portsmouth 26 Feb. ,,
The queen visits Grasse, a French town near Cannes, in the Alpes-Maritimes . 25 March–28 April, ,,
Destructive snow-storm in the S. and S.W. counties (see *Storms*) 9, 10 March; close of nearly six months' winter (see *Frosts*) 25 March . . ,,
Death of earl Granville, eminent statesman, aged 75 31 March, ,,
The empress Frederick visits England 27 Feb.–8 April. ,,
Visit of the German emperor and empress very successful (see *Germany*) . 4–13 July, ,,
Visit of the prince of Naples (see *Italy*) 22 July–Aug. ,,
The queen receives Veldtman, a Fingoe chief, and his presents . . . . . . 7 Aug. ,,
Visit of the French fleet to Portsmouth (see *France*) 19 Aug. ,,
Prince George of Wales attacked by typhoid fever, 10 Nov., recovery . . . . . 23 Dec. ,,
The duke of Clarence and Avondale attacked with influenza and pneumonia, 10 Jan., died at Sandringham, 14 Jan. Universally lamented; military funeral at Windsor . . . . 20 Jan. 1892
Letter from the queen, to the empire (*London Gazette*, 2 Feb.)

"OSBORNE, *January* 26, 1892.

"I must once again give expression to my deep sense of the loyalty and affectionate sympathy evinced by my subjects in every part of my empire on an occasion more sad and tragical than any but one which has befallen me and mine, as well as the nation. The overwhelming misfortune of my dearly loved grandson having been thus suddenly cut off in the flower of his age, full of promise for the future, amiable and gentle, and endearing himself to all, renders it hard for his sorely stricken parents, his dear young bride, and his fond grandmother to bow in submission to the inscrutable decrees of providence.

"The sympathy of millions, which has been so touchingly and visibly expressed, is deeply gratifying at such a time, and I wish, both in my own name and that of my children, to express from my heart, my warm gratitude to *all*.

"These testimonies of sympathy with us, and appreciation of my dear grandson, whom I loved as a son, and whose devotion to me was as great as that of a son, will be a help and consolation to me and mine in our affliction.

"My bereavements during the last thirty years of my reign have indeed been heavy. Though the labours, anxieties, and responsibilities inseparable from my position have been great, yet it is my earnest prayer that God may continue to give me health and strength to work for the good and happiness of my dear Country and Empire while life lasts. "VICTORIA, R.I."

The seventh session of the queen's twelfth parliament opened . . . . . 9 Feb. 1892
The queen visits Costebelle, a suburb of Hyères, an ancient town in Provence 13 miles from Toulon, 21 March–25 April; at Darmstadt, 26 April–2 May, ,,
Dissolution of parliament, 28 June; general election: conservatives, 268; liberal unionists, 47 (315); liberals (Gladstonians), 270; Parnellites, 9; anti-Parnellites, 72; labour members, 4 (355); total 670 . . . . . . 23 July, ,,
See *Commons*.
Death of Robert Lowe, viscount Sherbrooke, statesman, aged 80 . . . . . 27 July, ,,
Visit of the German emperor . . 1–8 Aug. ,,
Meeting of parliament, 4 Aug.; want of confidence in the Salisbury ministry voted (350—310), 11 Aug.; the ministry resigns . . 13 Aug. ,,
Mr. Gladstone's ministry constituted . 18 Aug. *et seq.*
Parliament prorogued . . . . . ,, ,,
See *Gladstone*.
Death of Alfred, lord Tennyson, poet laureate, aged 83, 6 Oct.; buried in Westminster Abbey, 12 Oct. ,,
Agricultural depression through bad harvest and low prices of corn and cattle . . Oct. ,,
Sir Richard Owen, naturalist, &c., aged 88; died, 18 Dec. ,,
Opening of parliament; the queen's speech; announces the Irish home rule bill, 31 Jan.; introduced . . . 13 Feb. (see *Ireland*) 1893
Meetings with eminent speakers against the home rule bill, throughout the country; petitions and subscriptions . . . . March, April, ,,
Visit of the empress Frederick . 1 Feb.–4 April, ,,
Death of Edward Henry, earl of Derby, statesman, aged 66 . . . . . . 21 April, ,,
Great unionist meeting at the Albert-hall; see *Ireland* . . . . 22 April, ,,
The queen visits Florence . 23 March–26 April, ,,
The Imperial institute, *which see*, inaugurated by the queen . . . . . . 10 May, ,,
Very dry season, see *Rainfall* . March–June, ,,
M. Albert Decrais appointed French ambassador end of . . . . June, ,,
The queen unveils the statue of herself (as in 1837), by the princess Louise, in Kensington gardens, 28 June, ,,
Marriage of the duke of York and the princess Victoria Maud (May) of Teck, at St. James's palace, in the presence of the queen and royal family, the king and queen of Denmark, the cesarevitch, other royal persons, 4 Indian princes, and a ranee, ambassadors, foreign representatives, eminent official persons; the duke and duchess of York drove through London from Buckingham palace to Liverpool St. station, and arrived at Sandringham in the evening . . . . . 6 July, ,,
[Ode on the marriage by Lewis Morris] National fête . . . . 6–8 July, ,,
Message of thanks from the queen to the nation, for hearty sympathy in relation to her grandson's wedding, Windsor castle . . . . 10 July, ,,
Very early harvest in Mid., S. and E. counties, about 15 July, ,,
Heat wave, especially in the south, see *Heat*, mid. August: open weather, moderate rains, favourable to grass and roots . . . . autumn, ,,
Parliament adjourns, 22 Sept.; meets again 2 Nov. ,,
Death of professor John Tyndall, aged 73 . 4 Dec. ,,
See *Royal Institution*.
Manchester ship canal, public opening . 1 Jan. 1894
Visit of the empress Frederick to Osborne, 2 Feb.–19 March, ,,
Resignation of Mr. Gladstone as premier, succeeded by the earl of Rosebery . . . 3 March, ,,
Parliament prorogued, 5 March; re-opened 12 March, ,,
The queen visits Florence . 16 March–16 April, ,,
Death of eminent judges: lord Hannen, 29 March; lord Bowen . . . . . 10 April, ,,
The queen at Coburg, 17 April; at Windsor 29 April, ,,
The queen inaugurates the Manchester ship canal, 21 May, ,,
Birth of prince Edward Albert Christian, &c. of York . . . . 23 June, ,,
Parliament prorogued . . . . . 25 Aug. ,,
Fairly good hay and corn harvest reported 11 Sept. ,,
Henry, earl Grey, able statesman, born 28 Dec. 1802, died . . . . 9 Oct. ,,

James Anthony Froude, historian, born 23 April, 1818, died . . 20 Oct. 1894
Death of lord Randolph Churchill; (born 13 Feb. 1849) . . . . . . 24 Jan. 1895
See *Salisbury adm.*, 1885–6.
Meeting of parliament . . . . . . 5 Feb. ,,
Intense cold, see *Frost* . . . . Jan.–Feb. ,,
The queen at Nice, 15 March–23 April; Darmstadt, 23 April; at Sheerness . . . 30 April, ,,
The empress Frederick visits England, 7 Feb.–23 March, ,,
Gross revenue for 1894–5: 94,683,762*l.*; (expenditure 16 March) 94,181,000*l.*, reported . 1 April, ,,
"Apostolic letter of pope Leo XIII. to the English people;" see *Pope* . . . . 14 April, ,,
Visit of prince Nasrullah Khan; see *Afghanistan*, 24 May ,,
Resignation of the Rosebery ministry . 22 June, ,,
New cabinet formed by the marquis of Salisbury, 4th administration . . . 25 June *et seq.* ,,
Parliament dissolved, 8 July; meets (see *Commons*) 12 Aug.–5 Sept. . . . . ,,
Visit of the German emperor to the queen, the fleet at Cowes . . . . . . 5 Aug. ,,
Reassuring speech of the marquis of Salisbury at the lord mayor's banquet in reference to Turkey, &c., unity of the great powers, the sultan warned . . . . 9 Nov. ,,
Death of gen. the rt. hon. sir Henry Ponsonby, private secretary to the queen since 1870, 21 Nov. ,,
Visit of the king of the Belgians and princess Clementine to the queen . . . 3–9 Dec. ,,
For dispute with the United States, see *Venezuela*, 1895. Falls on the Stock Exchange, London, 17, 18 Dec. ,,
Revival of trade and increased revenue . Jan. 1896
General displeasure at the German emperor's message to pres. Kruger respecting the defeat of Dr. Jameson, see *Transvaal* . . . 4 Jan. ,,
Naval force ordered to Delagoa bay . . 7 Jan. ,,
The Australian and Tasmanian governments send a telegram to lord Salisbury approving the action of his government and promising cordial support, 12 Jan.; for which lord Salisbury returns his hearty thanks . . . . . 14 Jan.
The prince of Wales visits the colonial office and declares his support of Mr. Chamberlain, 11 Jan. ,,
Sir Frederick, lord Leighton, painter, sculptor and scholar, born, 3 Dec., 1830; died, 25 Jan., 1896; public funeral at St. Paul's . . . 3 Feb. ,,
Death of prince Henry of Battenberg, 20 Jan., buried at Whippingham, see *Ashantees* 5 Feb. ,,
Letter from the queen thanking the nation for its sympathy . . . . . . 14 Feb. ,,
Dr. Jameson and his troopers (350 officers and men) arrive at Plymouth, 23 Feb.; at London, 25 Feb.; for trial, see *Transvaal*, 1896, *footnote*.
The queen's visit to Nice, 11 March; she receives the emperor and empress of Austria, 13 March; leaves . . . . 29 April, ,,
Budget: revenue, 101,974,000*l.*; expenditure, 97,764,000*l.* . . . . . 16 April, ,,
Sir Hercules Robinson arrives in London, 7 June, ,,
Marriage of princess Maud of Wales and prince Charles of Denmark, at Buckingham palace, 22 July, ,,
Visit of Li Hung Chang, see *China* 1 Aug. *et seq.* ,,
Lord Rosebery proposes non-party public meetings respecting the Armenian massacres, *Times*, 14 Sept. ,,
He resigns the leadership of the Liberal party through differences with Mr. Gladstone and others on the Eastern question . . 6 Oct. ,,
Meetings held at London, Liverpool, Birmingham, and Manchester, urging the Government to take stronger measures . . 15 Sept. *et seq.* ,,
Congratulations received by the queen from London and other places on having reigned longer than any British sovereign . . 23 Sept. 1896
Visit of the empress Frederick 31 Jan.–15 March, 1897
Lady Wallace bequeaths her husband's collection of pictures, &c., to the nation, conditionally, see *Bethnal Green* and *Wallace Collection*, announced . . . . 25 Feb. ,,
The queen leaves Windsor for Nice, 10 March; interview with pres. Faure at Noisy-le-Sec, 11 Mar.; arrives at Nice, 12 March; returns to Windsor, 30 April ,,
Col. Hay, U.S. ambassador, and Mrs. Hay received by the queen . . . . . . 3 May 1897
Completion of the 60th year of the queen's reign, see *Jubilees (Diamond)* . . 20 June, *et seq.* ,,
Grand naval review at Spithead, see *Navy*, 26 June ,,
The queen returns her sincere thanks for all congratulations, 28 June and again . 15 July ,,
Death of princess Mary of Cambridge, duchess of Teck, active philanthropist, 27 Oct.; funeral at Windsor . . . . 3 Nov. ,,
Close of the 7 months' engineering dispute, 28 Jan. 1898
See *Strikes.*
Count de Rascon, Spanish ambassador, received by the queen . . . . . . 19 Feb. ,,
The queen arrives at Nice, 10 March; at Windsor, 1 May, ,,
A lease of Wei-hai-wei granted by China to Great Britain . . . . 2 April, ,,
Death of Mr. Gladstone, see *Gladstone adm.* 19 May, ,,
Baron Francesco de Renzis appointed Italian ambassador, Sept. 1898; dies . . . 28 Oct. 1900
M. Paul Cambon, French ambassador, received by the queen . . . . . . 9 Dec. 1898
Split in the liberal party, *which see* . . Dec. ,,
Mr. Joseph Choate appointed U.S. ambassador, 11 Jan. 1899
Visit of the empress Frederick, Dec. 1898–14 Jan. ,,
The queen leaves Windsor for Cimiez, 11 March; returns 5 May; see *Kensington Palace* and *S. Kensington*; her 80th birthday celebrated throughout the empire and all parts of the world, 24 May; her thanks for congratulations, &c. . . . . 25 May, ,,
Tercentenary of the birth of Oliver Cromwell celebrated, see *Naseby* . . . . 25 April, ,,
The queen's message to Parliament; vote of 30,000*l.* to lord Kitchener for services in the *Soudan*, carried, with vote of thanks to the officers and men, 5–8 June, ,,
Transvaal crisis: parliament affirms the duty of the imperial power to protect the Uitlanders against oppression, and demands the *minimum* of reforms laid down by sir A. Milner, 28 July; parliament prorogued, 9 Aug.; mobilisation of troops, reserves called out, well responded to, 7 Oct. *et seq.*; steady growth of national prosperity during 1898 99; meetings throughout the country and empire supporting the government's policy in S. Africa, 13 Oct.; gen. sir Redvers Buller leaves to take command in S. Africa, 14 Oct.; parliament summoned, 17 Oct.; great speech of Mr. Chamberlain, 19 Oct.; firm speech by lord Salisbury at the Guildhall, "his faith in the British soldier unbounded' . . . 9 Nov. ,,
Tercentenary of Cromwell's birth, his statue in front of Westminster-hall unveiled; large meeting in Queen's-hall, addresses by lord Rosebery and others . . . . 14 Nov. ,,
German emperor and empress and two sons visit the queen at Windsor . . . 20–25 Nov. ,,
The government's call for volunteers and yeomanry for S. Africa eagerly responded to, 17 Dec. *et seq.* ,,
Duke of Westminster dies, aged 74—a "many-sided" man and a good landlord . . . 22 Dec, ,,
Lord Roberts leaves to take command in S. Africa, 23 Dec. ,,
Country prosperous and trade flourishing year ended . . . . 31 Dec. ,,
Death of the duke of Teck, aged 62 . . 21 Jan. 1900
Fine speech of Mr. Chamberlain in the Commons, 5 Feb. ,,
Budget, *which see*, 1900–1901, deficit 53,207,000*l.*, passed . . . . 9 April, ,,
Centenary of the death of the poet Cowper, celebrated at Olney, Bucks . . . 25 April, ,,
The queen visits London "to see her people," 7–10 March; leaves Windsor for Dublin, see *Ireland*, 2 April; returns to Windsor . 27 April, ,,
Attempt on the life of the prince of Wales at Brussels, see *Wales*, 4 April; his letter of thanks for world-wide sympathy, *Times* . . 28 April, ,,
Unbounded rejoicings on the relief of Mafeking (17 May) . . . . . . 18–21 May, ,,
Visit of the khedive, 21 June; received by the duke of York in London, June 27; by the queen at

Windsor, 28, 29 June; entertained at the Guildhall, the prince of Wales and lord Salisbury present, 3 July; leaves . . . 4 July, 1900

Prince Alfred (Duke of Edinburgh), duke of Saxe-Coburg and Gotha, dies, near Coburg, aged 55 (see *Admirals*) . . . . . 30 July, ,,

Death of lord Russell of Killowen, lord chief justice, aged 68 . . . . . . 13 Aug., ,,

Letters from Mr. Labouchere, Mr. Ellis, Dr. Clark, and others to Boer officials found in S. Africa, published as a parliamentary paper, and greatly discussed . . . 23 Aug. *et seq.* ,,

Gen. sir John Adye, who in 64 years had served in the Crimea, India, and Egypt, died, aged 81, 26 Aug. ,,

Parliament prorogued, 8 Aug.; dissolved, 25 Sept.; 4th Salisbury administration, cabinet reconstructed . . . . 12 Nov. ,,

Sir Arthur Sullivan, popular composer (see *Savoy* and *Opera*) dies, aged 58 . . . . 22 Nov. ,,

New parliament meets (see *Commons*) . 3 Dec. ,,

The queen's message of gratitude to her soldiers in S. Africa, see *Times*, 19 Dec. 1900; lord Roberts received by the queen at Osborne, and created an earl and K.G., 2 Jan.; by the prince and princess of Wales and others at Paddington, and escorted to Buckingham palace . . 3 Jan. 1901

Death of the Queen at Osborne after a few days' illness, the German emperor, her children and grandchildren being with her 6.30 p.m., 22 Jan. ,,

[Universal sorrow and mourning throughout the world and empire.]

King Edward VII. accession. The king holds a council at St. James's palace, and declares "that it will be his constant endeavour to walk in his mother's footsteps," . . . . . 23 Jan. ,,

Parliament meets; many touching tributes to the late queen's memory by lord Salisbury, Mr. Balfour, and others . . . . 25 Jan. ,,

Funeral of Queen Victoria: the remains conveyed on board the royal yacht *Alberta* from Cowes to Portsmouth, through a long line of British and foreign warships, on a calm sea and in a glorious sunset, 1 Feb.; borne in stately procession, with an escort of kings and princes, through the west of London to Paddington, thence to Windsor, and after a service in St. George's Chapel, placed in the Albert Memorial Chapel, 2 Feb.; removed with solemn ceremonial to the Royal Mausoleum at Frogmore . 4 Feb. ,,

Memorial services held throughout the world, 3 Feb. ,,

The king's messages: "To my people," "To my people beyond the seas," and "To the people and princes of India," thanking them for their loyalty and affection, which *inspired him with courage and hope solemnly to work for the promotion and security of the great empire over which he had been called to reign*, issued . . 4 Feb. ,,

The German emperor (made a field-marshal in the army and the crown prince a K.G.) warmly greeted in London, leaves . . . 5 Feb. ,,

The king and queen open parliament in state, 14 Feb. ,,

The king visits the empress Frederick in Germany, 27 Feb.–3 March. ,,

Meeting at the Guildhall in aid of the "Queen Victoria Memorial," the mayors and provosts of the U.K. invited to join (see *Mansion-house*), 7 March, ,,

Sig. Albert Pansa appointed Italian ambassador, March, ,,

The duke and duchess of Cornwall start on their colonial tour in the *ss. Ophir* . 16 March, ,,

Budget: revenue, 132,255,000*l.*; expenditure, 187,612,000*l.* . . . . 18 April, ,,

Sir Alfred Milner, high commissioner of S. Africa, met by lord Salisbury and others at Waterloo, great demonstrations; received by the king and made a peer . . . . . 24 May, ,,

Lord Wantage, V.C., a great supporter of the volunteers and administrator of war relief funds, etc., dies, aged 69 . . . . 10 June, ,,

The king presents S. African war medals to lords Roberts and Milner and some 3,200 officers and men, London . . . . . 12 June, ,,

Pro-Boer meeting in the Queen's hall, London (Mr. Labouchere, M.P., chairman), addressed by the Afrikander Bond delegates and others; some disturbance in and outside . . 19 June, 1901

Mr. Asquith, in a firm speech to a liberal meeting in London, repudiates the resolutions and opinions of the Pro-Boers . . . 20 June, ,,

Blue-book issued on S. African war, see *Times*, 9 July, and *London* . . . . 10 July, ,,

Mass meeting at the Guildhall in favour of the government's S. African policy (similar meetings held throughout the country) . . 10 July, ,,

Budget, which *see*: deficit about 55,347,000*l.*, passed . . . . . . 25 July, ,,

Vote of 100,000*l.* to lord Roberts for his eminent services in S. Africa, passed . . 31 July, ,,

Great unionist demonstration at Blenheim palace, speakers Mr. Chamberlain, Mr. Balfour and others . . . . 10 Aug. ,,

Parliament prorogued . . . . . 18 Aug. ,,

King Alfred millenary, celebration (see *Winchester*), 18 Sept. ,,

The duke and duchess of Cornwall warmly welcomed after their successful tour (40,000 mi.), at Portsmouth and London . . . 1, 2 Nov. ,,

Count Hatzfeldt, 16 years German ambassador, resigns, 30 Oct.; died, aged 70, 22 Nov.; succeeded by count Wolff-Metternich . Nov. ,,

Lord Rosebery at Chesterfield urges the liberals to throw off their own *Toryism*, and offers his services; appealing solely to the tribunal of *public opinion* . . . . . . 16 Dec. ,,

The marquis Ito, eminent Japanese statesman, arrives, 24 Dec.; received by the king . 27 Dec. ,,

Mr. Chamberlain's frank, manly speech at Birmingham a check to Anglophobia (see *Germany*), 20 Jan. 1902; highly approved . . 11 Jan. 1902

Dutch government's proposals for negotiations with the Boers in S. Africa presented, 25 Jan.; firmly declined by the British Government 29 Jan.; correspondence issued . 4 Feb. ,,

Lord Salisbury unveils a statue of queen Victoria at the Jun. Constitutional club, and speaks nobly and forcibly as to the end of the war, 5 Feb. ,,

Lord Dufferin, an eminent diplomatist and administrator (see *Canada* 1872 and *India* 1884), died, aged 75 . . . . . 12 Feb. ,,

Mr. Chamberlain presented with an address, see *London* . . . . . . 13 Feb. ,,

Death of lord Kimberley, K.G. 1885, liberal statesman, 50 years in office, aged 76 . . 8 April, ,,

Budget (*which see*): receipts, 147,785,000*l.*; expenditure, 174,609,000*l.* . . . . 14 April, ,,

New loan on consols, 320,000,000*l.*, see *Stocks*, over subscribed . . . . . 16–18 April, ,,

Lord Pauncefote, great diplomatist (see *United States* 1889 *et seq.*, and *Peace*), dies, aged 74, 24 May, ,,

Peace signed at Pretoria, 31 May; universal rejoicings . . . . . . 1, 2 June, ,,

Thanksgivings for the conclusion of peace, 8 June; Jewish services . . . . 11 June, ,,

Mr. Samuel Butler, author of "Erewhon," died, aged 66 . . . . . . 18 June, ,,

Lord Acton, prof. of modern history, Cambridge, eminent scholar, died, aged 68 . . 19 June, ,,

The king and queen warmly welcomed in London, 23 June, ,,

Grave illness of the king from *perityphlitis*; "Will my people ever forgive me?" were his first words on recovering consciousness after a critical operation; universal anxiety, sorrow and sympathy; coronation ceremonies (26 June) and most other festivities postponed . . . . 24 June, ,,

Bank holidays; festivities of a modified kind held by the king's desire (chiefly in the provinces) 26, 27 June, ,,

The king made an admiral of the German navy, 26 June, ,,

Intercessory services at St. Paul's and elsewhere, 26–29, June, ,,

Coronation bonfires throughout the country, 30 June, ,,

Grand colonial and Indian reviews (the duke of Connaught in command) held by the prince of Wales, the queen, and many foreign princes and distinguished guests present, London, 1, 2 July, ,,

The king sends a kind message to his soldiers and people, "having heard the cheering with gratification in his sick-room" . . . 3 July, 1902
Royal and other eminent foreign guests arrived in London, 23 June; many left 28 June—3 July, „
The king pronounced *out of danger*; his dinner to the poor of London, *which see*. . . 5 July, „
Colonial reception held by the prince and princess of Wales at St. James's Palace . . 10 July, „
Lord Kitchener welcomed from S. Africa (see *London* and *Southampton*) . . . . 12 July, „
Lord Salisbury (see *Salisbury administration*), over 13½ years prime minister and lord privy seal, 4 times foreign secretary, resigns . 11 July, „
Mr. Arthur J. Balfour (leader of the commons and first lord of the treasury) made prime minister and lord privy seal . 12–14 July, „
The king taken in his yacht to Cowes . 15 July, „
Meeting at the Church-house, Westminster, in aid of the Cape Town Cathedral memorial fund (over 16,000*l*. received), princess Christian present, lord Roberts presided . . . 17 July, „
Debate in the commons on the case of sir Redvers Buller, his message to sir George White at Ladysmith, Spion Kop, &c. . . . 17 July, „
Mr. Balfour's speech at Fulham, warm tributes to lord Salisbury and Mr. Chamberlain . 19 July, „
The king and queen heartily welcomed in London, 6 Aug. „

Letter from the king to his people :—

"On the eve of my coronation, an event which I look upon as one of the most solemn and important in my life, I am anxious to express to my people at home, and in the colonies, and in India my heartfelt appreciation of the deep sympathy which they have manifested towards me during the time that my life was in such imminent danger.

"The postponement of the ceremony owing to my illness caused, I fear, much inconvenience and trouble to all those who intended to celebrate it; but their disappointment was borne by them with admirable patience and temper.

"The prayers of my people for my recovery were heard; and I now offer up my deepest gratitude to Divine Providence for having preserved my life and given me strength to fulfil the important duties which devolve upon me as the sovereign of this great empire.

"Signed, EDWARD R. & I.,
"Buckingham Palace, 8th August, 1902."

Ministerial changes: see *Balfour administration*, 8 Aug. 1902
Parliament adjourns . . . . . 8 Aug. „
Coronation of king Edward VII. and queen Alexander at the abbey; many colonial statesmen and Indian princes present; great rejoicings and celebrations throughout the empire and world, 9 Aug. „
The king presents Osborne house, *which see*, to the nation . . . . . . 9 Aug. „
Thanksgiving services held for the king's recovery, 10 Aug. „
The lord mayor, visc. Duncannon, and sir Savile Crossley present to the king a coronation gift (115,000*l*.) from some of his subjects; see *Hospitals*, 11 Aug. „
The queen presents S. African war medals to many (male and female) of the Imp. Yeo. Hospital staffs, at Devonshire house . . 11 Aug. „
The king receives the Indian princes and colonial premiers, 12 Aug., and holds investiture parades of the colonial and Indian troops, London, 12, 13 Aug. „
The Indian princes, in a letter to the lord mayor, express warm gratitude for the kindness received, and their loyalty and affection for the British nation, *Times* . . . . . . 15 Aug. „
Coronation naval review; over 100 vessels at Spithead . . . . 16 Aug. „
The Boer generals Botha, De Wet, and Delarey, received by lords Kitchener and Roberts and Mr. Chamberlain at Southampton, and by *enthusiastic* crowds in London, 16 Aug.; by the king and queen at Cowes, 17 Aug.; they leave for the continent . . . . 18 Aug. „
Visit of the shah of Persia . . . 17–25 Aug. „
The king inspects the fleet . . . . 18 Aug. „
Cruise of the king and queen; Weymouth, Pembroke, Isle of Man, Arran, Hebrides, Dunrobin, &c. . . . . 21 Aug.–8 Sept. 1902
Maj.-gen. sir J. M. Heriot-Maitland, who served in China, Egypt, Soudan, and India, died, aged 65, 27 Aug. „
Sir Frederick Abel, eminent chemist, died, aged 75, and Philip J. Bailey, the author in 1839 of "Festus," died, aged 86 . . . 6 Sept. „
Mr. Brodrick (war secretary), lord Roberts, gens. Kelly-Kenny and Ian Hamilton, visit Germany, *which see* . . . . 5 Sept. „
Baron de Staal, Russian ambassador, retires, Sept. „
Nonconformist agitation against the Education bill . . . . Aug.–Oct. „
Conference between Mr. Chamberlain and the Boer generals; the Vereeniging terms signed (31 May) unaltered, 5 Sept.; parliamentary paper issued, 10 Sept. „
Royal commission of inquiry into the conduct of the S. African war, *which see* . . . Oct. „
Parliament meets . . . . . 16 Oct. „
Royal progress through London, thanksgiving service at St. Paul's, and review of the Guards from S. Africa . . . . . . 25, 26, 27 Oct. „
Liberal demonstration at the Alexandra palace, sir H. Campbell-Bannerman and Mr Asquith chief speakers, resolution passed against the Education bill . . . . . . 1 Nov. „
Grant of 8,000,000*l*. voted for the Transvaal and Orange River Colony . . . . 5 Nov. „
Visit of the emperor of Germany . . 8–20 Nov. „
Death of prince Edward of Saxe-Weimar, G.C.B., aged 79; served in the Crimea, 1854-55; a general, 1879; commander of forces in Ireland, 1885-90; field-marshal, 1897 . . . . . 16 Nov. „
Death of Mr. G. A. Henty, journalist and writer of boys' books, aged 69 . . . . . 16 Nov. „
Count Benckendorff appointed Russian ambassador, 18 Nov. „
Mr. Chamberlain accompanied by Mrs. Chamberlain, leaves on his mission to S. Africa, 25 Nov. „
Visit of the king of Portugal . 17 Nov. to 8 Dec. „
Great poverty and distress in London and other cities; thousands unemployed; funds started; reported . . . . 13 Dec. „
Death of Dr. Temple, archbishop of Canterbury, aged 81 . . . . 23 Dec. „
Queen's dinner, 629 widows and 836 children of soldiers who fell in S. African war . 27 Dec. „
Dr. Davidson, abp. of Canterbury . 12 Feb. 1903
The king opens parliament, address agreed to (lords) . . . . 17 Feb. „
Death of lt.-col. F. R. Henderson, author of "Stonewall Jackson," &c. aged 49 . 5 Mar. „
Inaug. meeting of the centenary of the British and Foreign Bible society held at mansion house, the lord mayor presiding; speeches by Mr. Balfour, lord Northampton, and others . 6 March, „
Mr. and Mrs. Chamberlain welcomed home, 14 Mar. „
Naval estimates, "statement of First Lord of the Admiralty," 1903-04, 34,457,000*l*., those of 1903 being 31,255,000*l*., also "statement of work, 1902-03" with appendix, issued . . 9 March, „
Army estimates for 1903-04, including special expenditure for S. Africa, China and Somaliland, 34,500,000*l*. . . . . . . 9 March, „
The queen presents sprays of shamrock to the Irish guards at the tower, St. Patrick's day, 17 March, „
Dr. Farrar, dean of Canterbury, died, aged 71, 22 March, „
Maj.-gen. sir Hector Macdonald, "Fighting Mac," after brilliant services in Afghanistan, Egypt, the Soudan, and S. Africa, found dead in Paris, 25 March, „
M. Curie's (and Mdme. Curie's) discovery of the remarkable properties of radium (see *Radium*), announced . . . . March, „
Mr. Chas. Booth's "Life and Labour of the People in London," third series, "Religious Influences," published mid April „
London Education bill first reading (house of commons) . . . . 7 April, „
Royal commission of inquiry *re* food imports, &c. during war; lord Balfour of Burleigh, chairman, the prince of Wales, and others, appointed, April, „

Budget statement, 1903-4, final surplus 316,000*l.*, 23 April, 1903
Mr. Robert W. Hanbury, M.P., president of the board of agriculture, died . . . 28 April, ,,
MM. Sardou and Morreau's new play *Dante* produced at Drury lane theatre . . . 30 April, ,,
Stockbrokers' walk to Brighton; 87 competitors, won by E. F. Broad; time 9 hrs. 30 min. 1 sec., 1 May, ,,
Sale of the Gambart collection of pictures, realized 31,014*l.* . . . . . 2-4 May, ,,
King's tour to Lisbon, 7 Apr.; Gibraltar, 8-13 Apr.; Malta, 16-21 Apr.; Sicily, 21-22 Apr.; Naples, 23 Apr.; Rome, 27 Apr.; visits the pope at the Vatican, 29 Apr.; Paris, 1-4 May; leaves Cherbourg and arrives in London . . 5 May, ,,
Transvaal loan, 35,000,000*l.*, 3 per cent., issued; well taken up . . . . . 7 May, ,,
King and queen visit Scotland . . 11-15 May, ,,
Mr. Chamberlain's speech on preferential tariffs, at Birmingham . . . . . 15 May, ,,
Earl of Onslow appointed president of the board of agriculture . . . . . about 19 May, ,,
Mr. Chamberlain's inter-imperial tariff scheme much discussed in England and on the continent; generally approved in the colonies (see under *Preferential Tariffs*) . . May-June, *et seq.* ,,
Fatal fire at Eton college, 2 scholars burnt to death; message of condolence from the king and queen . . . . . . 1 June, ,,
Death of sir Edmund Du Cane, K.C.B., long director of prisons and chairman of prison commissioners, aged 73 . . . . . 7 June ,,
Lord Rosebery speaks at Liberal league dinner against the tariff scheme . . . 12 June, ,,
The king receives Mr. Austen Chamberlain, M.P., and nearly 300 members of the international telegraph convention, at Windsor . . . 15 June, ,,
Cardinal Vaughan, archbishop of Westminster, dies, aged 71 . . . . 19 June, ,,
Khedive visits England, arrives . . . 24 June, ,,
British academy holds its first annual meeting at Burlington house . . . . . 28 June, ,,
Death of viscount Colville of Culross, lord chamberlain to the queen, aged 84 . . . 1 July ,,
Centenary of the Sunday School union, great international bazaar, Portman rooms, opened by lady Aberdeen, 2 July; speech by Mr. Choate, U.S. ambassador, at public meeting, 6 July; festival at the Crystal palace . . . 8 July ,,
M. Loubet, president of the French republic, visits the king; arrives at Dover 6 July; reception and luncheon at the guildhall, presented with an address of welcome; king and prince of Wales dine with the president at the French embassy; state performance at royal opera, 7 July; present at review by the king of the first army corps, Aldershot, state ball at Buckingham palace, July; returns . . . . . . 9 July, ,,
Death of Mr. Whistler, distinguished artist, 17 July, ,,
Visit of United States squadron to Portsmouth; entertainments to adm. and officers 6-17 July, ,,
Tariff Reform league inaugurated. . . 21 July, ,,
Irish Land bill passed the third reading by 317 votes to 20 (see *Addenda*) . . . . 21 July, ,,
Visit of the king and queen to Ireland 20-25 July, ,,
The duke of Marlborough appointed under-secretary for the colonies . . . . about 23 July, ,,
Royal naval college at Osborne, I. of W., opened by the king . . . . 4 Aug. ,,
Death of Mr. Phil May, clever caricaturist . 5 Aug. ,,
Lond. Education bill (see *Addenda*) royal assent 14 Aug.
Death of Lord Salisbury, aged 73 (see *Salisbury Administration*) . . . . . . 22 Aug. ,,
Royal Commission on S. Afric. war, report 25 Aug. ,,
Mr. Balfour's pamphlet, "Economic Notes on Insular Free Trade," published 15 Sept. ,,
Resignation of Mr. Chamberlain, Mr. Ritchie, and lord Geo. Hamilton, announced . . 18 Sept. ,,
Death of the duke of Richmond and Gordon, aged 85 . . . . 27 Sept. ,,
Lord Milner arrives in England . . 28 Sept. 1903
Death of sir Michael Herbert, British ambassador to the United States . . . . 30 Sept. ,,
Letters of resignation of Mr. Ritchie and lord Geo. Hamilton published . . . . . 1 Oct. ,,
Meeting of the National Conservative association at Sheffield, great speech at public meeting by Mr. Balfour, who declares his policy on the fiscal question . . . . . . 1 Oct. ,,
Duke of Devonshire's resignation, and new cabinet appointments announced (for names see under *Balfour Administration* in *Addenda*) 6 Oct. ,,
Mr. Chamberlain opens his "fiscal campaign" by a great speech on "Colonial Preference" at St. Andrew's hall, Glasgow, enthusiastic reception (60,000 applications made for tickets of admission), 6 Oct. ,,
Mr. Chamberlain speaks at Greenock on "Retaliation" in British trade (see *Preferential Tariffs*), 7 Oct. ,,
Dr. Knox, bishop suffragan of Coventry, appointed to see of Manchester, vacant Nov. 1 . 7 Oct. ,,
Mr. John Morley's biography of Mr. Gladstone published . . . . 8 Oct. ,,
Death of Mr. J. C. Horsley, R.A . . 18 Oct.
Death of Lord Rowton . . . . 9 Nov. ,,

[For other events see *Addenda*.]

KINGS AND QUEENS OF ENGLAND.

BEFORE THE CONQUEST.

827. Egbert, styled "king of England" in 828.
837. Ethelwolf; his son.
857. Ethelbald; his son.
860. Ethelbert; brother.
866. Ethelred; brother.
871. Alfred the Great; brother; born 849; died 25 or 26 Oct. 900 or 901; some say 899.
901. Edward the Elder; son; died 925.
925. Athelstan; eldest son; died 17 Oct. 940.
940. Edmund I., fifth son of Edward the Elder; died from a wound received in an affray, 26 May, 946.
946. Edred; brother; died 955.
955. Edwy, eldest son of Edmund; died of grief in 958.
957. Edgar the Peaceable; brother; died 1 July, 975.
975. Edward the Martyr, his son, stabbed at Corfe Castle, at the instance of his step-mother Elfrida, 18 March, 979.
979. Ethelred II.; half-brother; retired.
1013. Sweyn, proclaimed king; died 3 Feb. 1014.
1014. Canute the Great; his son.
1014. Ethelred restored in Canute's absence; died 24 April, 1016.
1016. Edmund Ironside, his son, divided the kingdom with Canute; murdered at Oxford, 30 Nov. 1016; reigned seven months.
1017. Canute sole king; married Emma, widow of Ethelred; died 12 Nov. 1035.
1035. Harold I.; son; died 17 Mar. 1040.
1039. Hardicanute, son of Canute and Emma; died of repletion at a marriage feast, 8 June, 1042.
1042. Edward the Confessor, son of Ethelred and Emma; died 5 Jan. 1066.
1066. Harold II., son of earl Godwin; reigned nine months; killed near Hastings, 14 Oct. 1066.

THE NORMANS.*

1066. William the Conqueror; crowned 25 Dec.: died at Rouen, 9 Sept. 1087.

---

* The REGNAL DATES are those given by sir H. Nicolas. The early Norman and Plantagenet kings reckoned their reigns from the day of their coronation; the later Plantagenets from the day after the death of their predecessor. With Edward VI. began the present custom of beginning the reign on the day of the death of the preceding sovereign.

ROYAL ARMS OF ENGLAND.

William I., William II., and Henry I.—two lions or leopards passant.
Stephen—sagittarius, the archer, one of the signs of the zodiac (*traditional*).
Henry II. to Edward II. Three lions passant.
Edward III. and his successors quartered the preceding with fleurs de lys, the arms of France.

Queen, Matilda, daughter of Baldwin, earl of Flanders; married in 1054; died in 1083.

1087. William II. Rufus; reign began 26 Sept.; killed by an arrow, 2 Aug. 1100.

1100. Henry I. Beauclerc, his brother; reign began 5 Aug.; died of a surfeit, 1 Dec. 1135.

Queens, Matilda, daughter of Malcolm III. king of Scotland; married 11 Nov. 1100; died 1 May, 1119. 2. Adelais, daughter of Godfrey, earl of Louvaine; married 29 Jan. 1129; died 1151.

1135. Stephen, earl of Blois, nephew of Henry; reign began 26 Dec.; died 25 Oct. 1154.

Queen, Matilda, daughter of Eustace, count of Boulogne; married in 1128; died 3 May, 1151.

[Maud, daughter of Henry I. and rightful heir to the throne; born 1101; betrothed, in 1109, at eight years of age, to Henry V. emperor of Germany, who died 1125. She married, secondly, Geoffrey Plantagenet, earl of Anjou, 1130. Was set aside from the English succession by Stephen, 1135; landed in England and claimed the crown, 1139. Crowned, but soon after defeated at Winchester, 1141; concluded a peace with Stephen, which secured the succession to her son Henry, 1153; died 1165.]

THE PLANTAGENETS.

1154. Henry II. *Plantagenet*, grandson of Henry I. and son of Maud; reign began 19 Dec.; died 6 July, 1189.

Queen, Eleanor, the repudiated queen of Louis VII. king of France, and heiress of Guienne and Poitou; married to Henry, 1151; died 26 June, 1202; see *Rosamond*.

1189. Richard I. *Cœur de Lion*, his son; reign began 3 Sept.; died of a wound, 6 April, 1199.

Queen, Berengaria, daughter of the king of Navarre; married 12 May, 1191; survived the king.

1199. John, the brother of Richard; reign began 27 May; died 19 Oct. 1216.

Queens, Avisa, daughter of the earl of Gloucester; married in 1189; divorced. 2. Isabella, daughter of the count of Angoulême: she was the young and virgin wife of the count de la Marche: married to John in 1200. Survived the king, on whose death she was re-married to the count de la Marche.

1216. Henry III. son of John; reign began 28 Oct.; died 16 Nov. 1272.

Queen, Eleanor, daughter of the count de Provence; married 14 Jan. 1236; survived the king; and died in 1291, in a monastery.

1272. Edward I. son of Henry, surnamed *Longshanks;* reign began 20 Nov.; died 7 July, 1307.

Queens, Eleanor of Castile; married in 1253; died of a fever, on her journey to Scotland, at Grantham, in Lincolnshire, 1290. 2. Margaret, sister of the king of France; married 12 Sept. 1299, survived the king, dying in 1317.

1307. Edward II. son of Edward I.; reign began 8 July; dethroned 20 Jan. 1327; *murdered* at Berkeley castle, 21 Sept. following.

[An inscription in the castle of Melazzo, Piedmont, states that he escaped from Berkeley castle, was sheltered by Pope John XXII. at Avignon. After long wandering, resided secretly in this castle 1330-33. *Reported* by count Negra, Oct., 1890.]

Queen, Isabella, daughter of the king of France; married in 1308. On the death, by the gibbet, of her favourite Mortimer, she was confined for the rest of her life in her own house at Risings, near Lynn, and died in 1357.

1327. Edward III. his son; reign began 25 Jan.; died 21 June, 1377.

Queen, Philippa, daughter of the count of Hainault; married in 1326; died 15 Aug. 1369.

1377. Richard II. son of Edward the Black Prince, and grandson of Edward III.; reign began 22 June; dethroned 29 Sept. 1399; said to have been *murdered* at Pomfret castle, 10 Feb. 1400.

Queens, Anne of Bohemia, sister of the emperor Wenceslaus of Germany; married in Jan. 1382; died 7 June, 1394. 2. Isabella, daughter of Charles VI. of France; married when only seven years old, 1 Nov. 1396. On the deposition of her husband she returned to France; married the duke of Orleans and died 13 Sept. 1409.

HOUSE OF LANCASTER.

1399. Henry IV. cousin of Richard II.; reign began 30 Sept.; died 20 March, 1413.

Queens, Mary, daughter of the earl of Hereford; she died before Henry obtained the crown, in 1394. 2. Joan of Navarre, widow of the duke of Bretagne; married 1403; survived the king; died 1437.

1413. Henry V. his son; reign began 21 March; died 31 Aug. 1422.

Queen, Catherine, daughter of the king of France; married 30 May, 1420. She outlived Henry, and was married to Owen Tudor, grandfather of Henry VII., in 1423; died 1437.

1422. Henry VI. his son; reign began 1 Sept.; deposed 4 March, 1461; said to have been *murdered* by Richard, duke of Gloucester, in the Tower, 20 June, 1471.

Queen, Margaret, daughter of the duke of Anjou; married 22 April, 1445; survived the king; died 25 Aug. 1481.

HOUSE OF YORK.

1461. Edward IV.; died 9 April, 1483.

Queen, Elizabeth, daughter of sir Richard Woodville, and widow of sir John Grey, of Groby; married 1463 or 1464. Suspected of favouring the insurrection of Lambert Simnel; and closed her life in confinement, 8 June, 1492.

1483. Edward V. his son; deposed 25 June, 1483, and said to have been *murdered* in the Tower; reigned two months and thirteen days.

" Richard III. brother of Edward IV.; began to reign, 26 June; *slain* at Bosworth, 22 Aug. 1485.

Queen, Anne, daughter of the earl of Warwick, and widow of Edward, prince of Wales, murdered 1471. She is said to have been poisoned by Richard (having died suddenly, 16 March, 1485), to make way for his intended marriage with princess Elizabeth of York.

HOUSE OF TUDOR.

1485. Henry VII. (son of Edmund Tudor, earl of Richmond, and Margaret, daughter of John Beaufort, duke of Somerset, legitimated descendant of John of Gaunt, duke of Lancaster); began to reign 22 Aug.; died 21 April, 1509.

Queen, Elizabeth of York, princess of England, daughter of Edward IV.; married 18 Jan. 1486; died 11 Feb. 1503.

1509. Henry VIII. his son; began to reign, 22 April; died 28 Jan. 1547.

Queens, Catherine of Aragon, widow of Henry's elder brother, Arthur, prince of Wales; married 11 June, 1509; mother of queen Mary; repudiated, and afterwards formally divorced, 23 May, 1533; died 7 Jan. 1536.

2. Anne Boleyn, daughter of sir Thomas Boleyn, and maid of honour to Catherine; privately married, before Catherine was divorced, 14 Nov. 1532, or Jan. 1533; mother of queen Elizabeth; beheaded at the Tower, 19 May, 1536.

3. Jane Seymour, daughter of sir John Seymour, and maid of honour to Anne Boleyn; married 20 May, 1536, the day after Anne's execution; mother of Edward VI. of whom she died in childbirth, 24 Oct. 1537.

4. Anne of Cleves, sister of William, duke of Cleves; married 6 Jan. 1540; divorced 10 July, 1540; died 1557.

Henry V. used only 3 fleurs de lys.

Mary I. quartered the preceding with the arms of her husband Philip II. of Spain.

UNITED KINGDOM.

James I. and his successors combined the arms of England and France (1st and 4th quarter); 2nd, the lion rampant of Scotland; 3rd, the harp of Ireland. He introduced the unicorn as a supporter of the arms.

George I., George II. and George III. introduced the arms of Brunswick.

In 1801 the arms of France were omitted. In 1816 the arms were modified through Hanover being made a kingdom.

VICTORIA. In 1837 the arms of Hanover were omitted. The arms are now: 1st and 4th quarters, 3 lions passant for England; 2nd, lion rampant for Scotland; 3rd, harp for Ireland. Also EDWARD VII., 1901.

5. Catherine Howard, niece of the duke of Norfolk; married 28 July, 1540; beheaded, 12 Feb. 1542.

6. Catherine Par or Parr, daughter of sir Thomas Parr, and widow of Nevill, lord Latimer; married 12 July, 1543; survived the king, after whose death she married sir Thomas Seymour, created lord Sudley; died 5 Sept. 1548.

1547. Edward VI. son of Henry VIII. (by Jane Seymour), died 6 July, 1553.

1553. Jane, daughter of the duke of Suffolk, and wife of lord Guildford Dudley; proclaimed queen on the death of Edward; ten days afterwards returned to private life; was tried 13 Nov. 1553; beheaded 12 Feb. 1554, when but 17 years of age.

1553. Mary, daughter of Henry (by Catherine of Aragon), married Philip of Spain, 25 July, 1554; died 17 Nov. 1558.

1558. Elizabeth, daughter of Henry (by Anne Boleyn), died 24 March, 1603.

HOUSE OF STUART.

1603. James I. of England and VI. of Scotland, son of Mary, queen of Scots; died 27 March. 1625.

Queen, Anne, princess of Denmark, daughter of Frederick II.; married 20 Aug. 1590; died March, 1619.

1625. Charles I. his son; *beheaded* at Whitehall, 30 Jan. 1649.

Queen, Henrietta-Maria, daughter of Henry IV. king of France; married 13 June, 1625; survived the king; died in France 10 Aug. 1669.

1649. COMMONWEALTH. Oliver Cromwell made protector, 16 Dec. 1653; died 3 Sept. 1658; grant for the erection of his statue at Westminster voted by the commons, 14 June; vote withdrawn, 17 June, 1895. See *Naseby*.

1658. Richard Cromwell, his son, made protector, 4 Sept.; resigned 22 April, 1659.

1660. Charles II. son of Charles I.; died 6 Feb. 1685.

Queen, Catherine of Braganza, infanta of Portugal, daughter of John IV. and sister of Alfonso VI.; married 21 May, 1662; survived the king; returned to Portugal; died 21 Dec. 1705.

1685. James II. his brother; *abdicated* by flight, 11 Dec. 1688; died in exile, 6 (16) Sept. 1701.

[*1st Wife*, Ann Hyde, daughter of Edward Hyde, earl of Clarendon; married Sept. 1660; died 1671; mother of queens Mary II. and Anne.]

Queen, Mary Beatrice, princess of Modena, daughter of Alphonso d'Este, duke; married 21 Nov. 1673; in 1688 retired with James to France; died at St. Germains, 1718.

1689. William III. prince of Orange, *king*, and Mary, *queen*, daughter of James II.; married 4 Nov. 1677; began their reign, 13 Feb. 1689; Mary died 28 Dec. 1694.

1694. William III.; died of a fall from his horse, 8 March, 1702.

1702. Anne, daughter of James II.; married George, prince of Denmark, 28 July, 1683; succeeded to the throne, 8 March, 1702; had seventeen children, all of whom died young (William, duke of Gloucester, born 24 July, 1689, died 30 July, 1700); lost her husband, 28 Oct. 1708; died 1 Aug. 1714.

HOUSE OF HANOVER. (See *Brunswick* and *Este*.)

1714. George I. elector of Hanover and duke of Brunswick-Luneburg; son of Sophia, who was daughter of Elizabeth, the daughter of James I.; died 11 June, 1727.

Queen, Sophia-Dorothea, daughter of the duke of Zell; died in prison, 2 Nov. 1726.

1727. George II. his son; died 25 Oct. 1760.

Queen, Wilhelmina Carolina Dorothea, of Brandenburg Anspach; married 1705; died 20 Nov. 1737.

1760. George III. grandson of George II.; died 29 Jan. 1820.

Queen, Charlotte Sophia, daughter of the duke of Mecklenburg-Strelitz; married 8 Sept. 1761; died 17 Nov. 1818.

1820. George IV. his son; died 26 June, 1830.

Queen, Caroline Amelia Augusta, daughter of the duke of Brunswick; married 8 April, 1795; died 7 Aug. 1821 (see article *Queen Caroline*)

1830. William IV. brother of George IV.; died 20 June, 1837.

Queen, Adelaide Amelia Louisa Theresa Caroline, sister of the duke of Saxe-Meiningen; married 11 July, 1818; died 2 Dec. 1849.

1837. *Alexandrina VICTORIA, only daughter of Edward duke of Kent (fourth son of king George III.),† *born* 24 May, 1819; *succeeded* to the throne on the decease of her uncle, William IV. 20 June, 1837; *crowned* at Westminster, 28 June, 1838; *married* (10 Feb., 1840) to her cousin,

Francis-ALBERT-Augustus-Charles-Emmanuel, duke of Saxony, prince of Saxe-Coburg and Gotha; *born* 26 Aug. 1819, naturalized, 24 Jan. 1840; (ordered to be styled *Prince Consort* 25 June, 1857;) elected chancellor of the university of Cambridge, 28 Feb. 1847; *died* 14 Dec. 1861.

ISSUE.

1. VICTORIA-Adelaide-Mary-Louisa, princess royal, *born* 21 Nov. 1840 (she died 5 Aug. 1901); *married* to prince Frederick-William, of Prussia, 25 Jan. 1858 (dowry 40,000*l*. and annuity of 8000*l*.) (he died 15 June, 1888). *Issue:* William, *born* 27 Jan. 1859; and 5 other children living.

2. ALBERT-EDWARD (now Edward VII.), prince of Wales, duke of Saxony, duke of Cornwall and Rothsay, earl of Chester, Carrick, and Dublin, baron of Renfrew, and lord of the Isles, *born* 9 Nov. 1841; *married* princess Alexandra of Denmark (*born* 1 Dec. 1844) 10 March, 1863. *Issue:* Albert Victor, *born* 8 Jan. 1864; *died* 14 Jan. 1892; George, *born* 3 June, 1865 (*married* princess Victoria Mary (*May*) of Teck, 6 July, 1893; see *Wales*. Louise, *born* 20 Feb. 1867; Victoria, *born* 6 July, 1868; Maud, 26 Nov. 1869; Alexander John, *born* 6 April, *died* 7 April, 1871. (See *Wales*.)

3. ALICE-Maud-Mary, *born* 25 April, 1843; *married* prince Louis (since grand duke) of Hesse-Darmstadt (*which see*), 1 July, 1862 (dowry 30,000*l*., annuity 6000*l*.); *d*. of diphtheria, 14 Dec. 1878. *Issue:* Victoria, 5 April, 1863; and 6 other children.

4. ALFRED-Ernest, *born* 6 Aug. 1844; entered the *Euryalus* as midshipman, 31 Aug. 1858; created duke of Edinburgh, &c. 24 May, 1866; visited Cape of Good Hope, Aug.; Australia, Nov. 1867; escaped assassination by a Fenian at Port Jackson, 12 March, 1868; visited Japan, China, and India, 1869; *married* archduchess Marie of Russia (*born* 17 Oct. 1853), 23 Jan. 1874; commander of the Channel fleet, Nov. 1883; of the Mediterranean fleet, Feb. 1886; at Davenport, Aug. 1890; he became duke of Saxe Coburg Gotha (*which see*) 22 Aug. 1893; *died* suddenly near Coburg, 30 July, 1900. *Issue:* Alfred, *born* 15 Oct. 1874; *died*, 6 Feb. 1899; Mary, 29 Oct. 1875; *married* to prince Ferdinand of Roumania (*which see*) 10 Jan. 1893; Victoria, 25 Nov. 1876; *married* to Ernest Louis, grand-duke of Hesse (*which see*) 19 April, 1894; Alexandrina, 1 Sept. 1878; *married* to the prince of Hohenlohe-Langenburg, 20 April, 1896; Beatrice, 20 April, 1884.

5. HELENA-Augusta-Victoria, *born* 25 May, 1846; *married* to prince Christian of Schleswig-Holstein, 5 July, 1866. *Issue:* Christian Victor, *born* 14 April, 1867; *died* at Pretoria, 29 Oct. 1900; and 4 other children.

6. LOUISE-Carolina-Alberta, *born* 18 March, 1848; *married* to John, marquis of Lorne (*born* 6 Aug. 1845), 21 March, 1871.

* On 1 Nov. 1858, the queen was proclaimed throughout India as "Victoria, by the grace of God, of the united kingdom of Great Britain and Ireland and of the colonies and dependencies thereof, in Europe, Asia, Africa, America, and Australasia, QUEEN, defender oft he faith," &c. "Empress of India" added to the royal style by proclamation, 28 April, 1876 (see *Style, Royal*). The colonial conference in May, 1887, recommended that the title of her majesty should, in recognition of the unity of the empire, be "Queen of the United Kingdom of Great Britain and Ireland, and of the Colonies and Dependencies thereof." She died 22 Jan. 1901. "The queen Victoria Memorial (8) volumes," compiled from the current records of the newspaper press, both illustrated and non-illustrated, preface by sir George Birdwood, issued Jan. 1902. A biography by Sidney Lee, Dec. 1902.

† He was born 2 Nov. 1767; and died 23 Jan. 1820; he married Victoria-Maria-Louisa (widow of the prince of Leiningen, sister of Leopold, king of the Belgians, and aunt to the prince consort), 29 May, 1818. She was born 17 Aug. 1786; and died 16 March 1861.

7. ARTHUR-William-Patrick-Albert, *born* 1 May, 1850; created duke of Connaught, earl of Sussex and Strathearn, 23 May, 1874; *married* 13 March, 1879, princess Louise Margaret of Prussia (*born* 25 July, 1860). *Issue*: Margaret, *born*, 15 Jan. 1882; Arthur Frederick, *born* 13 Jan.. 1883; Victoria Patritia, 17 March, 1886. Commander-in-chief at Bombay, 1886 *et seq.*; commander of the S. Military District, Aug. 1890.

8. LEOPOLD-George-Duncan-Albert, *born* 7 April, 1853: voted 15,000*l.* a year by parliament, 23 July, 1874; created baron Arklow, earl of Clarence, and duke of Albany, 24 May, 1881; *married* princess Helene, 4th daughter of the prince of Waldeck-Pyrmont, 27 April, 1882. 10,000*l.* additional income granted, 21 April, 1882; *died* at Cannes, 28 March, 1884. *Issue*: Alice Mary, born 25 Feb., 1883; Leopold Charles, *born* 19 July, 1884.

9. BEATRICE-Mary-Victoria-Feodore, *born* 14 April, 1857; *married* prince Henry Maurice of Battenberg (*born* 5 Oct. 1858) 23, July, 1885; he *died*, see *Ashantees*, 20 Jan. 1896. *Issue*: Alexander Albert, *born* 23 Nov. 1886; Victoria Eugénie, 1887; Leopold, 1889; and Maurice, 1891.

First greatgrandchild; Feodore, *born* 12 May, 1879; daughter of Charlotte, daughter of princess royal Victoria, and prince Bernard of Saxe-Meiningen. See *Germany*, children of William II.

THE QUEEN'S AUNT and COUSINS, Augusta, duchess widow 8 July 1850, of duke) of Cambridge, *born* 25 July, 1797; *married* 1 June, 1818; *died* 6 April, 1889.
Her son, George, duke of Cambridge, commander-in-chief 1887–1895, *born* 26 March, 1819 [*wife* Mrs. Fitz-George, *died*, aged 74, 12 Jan. 1890].
Her daughters, Augusta, grand duchess of Mecklenburg-Strelitz, *born* 19 July, 1822; *married* 28 June, 1843; and the princess Mary of Cambridge, *born* 27 Nov. 1833; *married* to the prince Francis, now duke, of Teck, 12 June, 1866; *died*, 27 Oct. 1897 (he died 21 Jan. 1900). *Issue*: Adolphus, Francis and Alexander George; her daughter, Victoria Mary (*May*), *married* to the duke of York, see *England*, 6 July, 1893.

1901. Edward VII., the reigning king, WHOM GOD PRESERVE.

THE PRESENT ROYAL FAMILY OF GREAT BRITAIN.

The KING ALBERT EDWARD, eldest son of queen Victoria, *born* 9 Nov. 1841; *married* princess Alexandra of Denmark (*born* 1 Dec. 1844), 10 March, 1863; *succeeded* to the throne on the death of his mother, queen Victoria, 22 Jan. 1901.

ISSUE.

1. ALBERT-VICTOR, *born* 8 Jan. 1864; went to sea with his brother, prince George, in *H.M.S. Bacchante*, visited West Indies, &c., 1879–82; their diaries published, 1885; he receives the freedom of London, 29 June, 1885; opens the new Alexandra docks at Belfast, 20 May, 1889; successful tour in India (*which see*) 9 Nov. 1889—28 March, 1890; visits Egypt, 7–12 April; in London, 2 May; created duke of Clarence and Avondale, &c., 23 May, 1890; engaged to princess Victoria Mary (May) of Teck, announced, 5 Dec. 1891; died at Sandringham, 14 Jan. 1892; military funeral at Windsor, 20 Jan.; his parents in a telegram express their deep gratitude for the universal sympathy throughout the empire, 20 Jan. 1892. "Memoir" of the duke, by James Edmund Vincent, published by authority, 5 Dec. 1893. See *England*, 26 Jan. 1892.

2. GEORGE Frederick, *born* 3 June, 1865, created duke of York, earl of Inverness and baron Killarney, 24 May, 1892; *married* princess Victoria Mary (May) of Teck, 6 July, 1893; takes the title of duke of Cornwall, Jan. 1901; made prince of Wales and earl of Chester, 9 Nov. 1901. *Issue*: Edward Albert Christian, *born* 23 June, 1894; Albert Frederick, *born* 14 Dec. 1895; Victoria Alexandra, *born* 25 April, 1897; Henry William, *born* 31 March, 1900; George, *born* 20 Dec. 1902. See *Wales*.

3. LOUISE, princess royal, *born* 20 Feb. 1867; *married* Alexander William George, duke of Fife, 27 July, 1889. *Issue*: Alexandra, *born* 17 May, 1891; Maud, *born* 3 April, 1893.

4. VICTORIA, *born* 6 July, 1868.

5. MAUD, *born* 26 Nov. 1869; *married* her cousin, prince Charles, *second* son of the crown prince of Denmark, 22 July, 1896; Alexander Edward, *born* 2 July, 1903.

6. ALEXANDER JOHN, *born* 6 April; *died* 7 April, 1871.

ENGLISH CHURCH UNION, established 1860, when it consisted of 210 members; there were 22,100 in 1888. Its object is to defend the Church of England and its ancient constitution, doctrine and liturgy, and her right to regulate her own affairs; and has supported clergymen who have suffered for so doing. Annual meetings are held. The union earnestly protested against the Welsh disestablishment bill, May, 1894.

ENGLISH LANGUAGE is traced from the Frisian variety of the Teutonic or Germanic branch of the great Indo-European family. "The English tongue possesses a veritable power of expression, such as, perhaps, never stood at the command of any other language of man." *Grimm.*

Celtic prevailed in England . . . . A.D. 1
Latin introduced . . . . . . about . 1
Saxon prevails (Beowulf; Cædinon; Alfred) 450-1066
Latin re-introduced by missionaries . . . 596
Norman-French combining with English . 1066-1250
William I. and his successors used English in their laws, &c.; it was superseded by Latin in the reign of Henry II. Norman-French was not used in law-deeds till the reign of Henry III.
Early English 1250-1500
The present English settled in the 16th century.
Law pleadings were made in English by order of Edward III. instead of in French 1362
The English tongue and English apparel were ordered to be used in Ireland, 28 Hen. VIII. . . 1536
The English language was ordered to be used in all law-suits, and the Latin disused . . May, 1731
Percentage of ANGLO-SAXON words in the English bible, 97; Swift, 89; Shakspeare and Thomson, 85; Addison, 83; Spenser and Milton, 81; Locke, 80; Young, 79; Pope, 76; Johnson, 75; Robertson, 68; Hume, 65; Gibbon, 58. *Marsh.*
Of 100,000 English words, 60,000 are of Teutonic origin; 30,000 Greek and Latin; and 10,000 from other sources.
Early English Text Society began publishing . . 1864
English Dialect Society, established to print old glossaries, May, 1873; many publications, 1893: 77 vols. up to 1896. The society much aided by the late prince Louis Lucien Bonaparte, see *Bonaparte*.
English greatly used in the East, Japan, China, &c.
Dr. S. A. Allibone's great "Critical Dictionary of English Literature," published in 1859 and 1871; he died 12 Sept., 1889, supplement by John F. Kirk 1891
The "English Dialect Dictionary," edited by Dr. Joseph Wright, aided by a government grant of 600*l.* Part I. published July 1896; vol. I. published . . . . June, 1898
"The Works of Geoffrey Chaucer," edited by Alfred Pollard, Frank Heath, Mark Liddell, and W. S. Cormick, published 1899

PRINCIPAL BRITISH AND AMERICAN AUTHORS.

d. dramatist; *e.* essayist; *h.* historian; *hum.* humorist; *m.* miscellaneous; *n.* novelist; *nat.* naturalist; *p.* poet; *t.* theologian; *tr.* traveller; *pol.* political; *ph.* philosopher.

	Born.	*Died.*
John Wickliffe, *t.*	1324	1384
Geoffrey Chaucer, *p.*	1328 or 1340	1400
John Gower, *p.*	about 1320	1402
Paston Letters, 1460-1482		
Wm. Caxton	1421	1491
Sir Thomas More, *h. p.*	1482	1535
Sir Philip Sidney, *n. p.*	1554	1586
Holinshed's Chronicles, 1586.		
John Fox, *t. h.*	1517	1587
Edmund Spenser, *p.*	about 1553	1598
Richard Hooker, *t.*	1553	1600
Wm. Shakspeare, *d.*	1564	1616
Walter Raleigh, *h. p.*	1552	1618
Francis Bacon, *ph.*	1561	1626
George Herbert, *p.*	1593	1633

	Born.	Died.
Ben Jonson, *d.*	1574	1637
Philip Massinger, *d.*	1584	1640
Edmund Waller, *p.*	1605	1687
Jeremy Taylor, *t.*	1613	1667
Abraham Cowley, *p.*	1618	1667
John Milton, *p.*	1608	1674
Isaac Barrow, *t.*	1630	1677
Thomas Hobbes, *phil.*	1588	1679
Samuel Butler, *p.*	1612	1680
John Bunyan, *t.*	1628	1688
John Dryden, *p.*	1631	1700
John Locke, *ph.*	1632	1704
Joseph Addison, *e.*	1672	1719
Matthew Prior, *p.*	1664	1721
Richard Steele, *e.*	1671	1729
Daniel De Foe, *n. pol.*	1663	1731
John Gay, *p.*	1688	1732
Alexander Pope, *p.*	1688	1744
Jonathan Swift, *n. p.*	1667	1745
James Thomson, *p.*	1700	1748
Henry Fielding, *n. d.*	1707	1754
Sam. Richardson, *n.*	1689	1761
Edward Young, *p.*	1681	1765
Laurence Sterne, *n.*	1713	1768
Mark Akenside, *p.*	1721	1770
Thomas Gray, *p.*	1716	1771
Tobias Smollett, *n.*	1720	1771
Oliver Goldsmith, *n. p.*	1728	1774
David Hume, *h. ph.*	1711	1776
Samuel Johnson, *e. n. p.*	1709	1784
Benjamin Franklin, *ph. pol.*	1706	1790
William Robertson, *h.*	1721	1793
Edward Gibbon, *h.*	1737	1794
Robert Burns, *p.*	1759	1796
Edmund Burke, *pol.*	1729	1797
William Cowper, *p.*	1731	1800
John Keats *p.*	1795	1821
Percy B. Shelley, *p.*	1792	1822
George lord Byron, *p.*	1788	1824
George Crabbe, *p.*	1754	1832
Walter Scott, *n. p.*	1771	1832
Samuel T. Coleridge, *p. ph.*	1772	1834
Charles Lamb, *e.*	1775	1834
William Cobbett, *pol. e.*	1762	1835
Robert Southey, *p. h.*	1774	1842
Thomas Arnold, *h.*	1795	1843
Thomas Campbell, *p.*	1777	1844
Sidney Smith, *e. pol.*	1771	1845
Thomas Hood, *hum.*	1799	1845
Fred. (capt.) Marryat	1792	1848
Edgar Allan Poe, *p.*	1809	1849
Maria Edgeworth, *n.*	1769	1849
Wm. Wordsworth, *p.*	1770	1850
J. Fenimore Cooper, *n*	1798	1851
Joanna Baillie, *p.*	1763	1851
Thomas Moore, *p. m.*	1780	1852
John Wilson, *p. e.*	1785	1854
Samuel Rogers, *p.*	1763	1855
Charlotte Brontë, *n.*	1816	1855
E. T. Channing, *m.*	1790	1856
Henry Hallam, *h.*	1778	1859
Thomas de Quincey, *e.*	1786	1859
Leigh Hunt, *e.*	1784	1859
William Prescott, *h.*	1796	1859
Washington Irving, *n. h.*	1783	1859
T. B. Macaulay, *h. p.*	1800	1859
Eliz. (Barrett) Browning	1809	1861
Sir Francis Palgrave, *h.*	1788	1861
Abp. Richd. Whately, *ph.*	1787	1863
Wm. M. Thackeray, *n.*	1811	1863
W. S. Landor, *m.*	1775	1864
Nathl. Hawthorne, *n.*	1804	1864
W. Whewell, *m.*	1794	1866
Chas. F. Browne ("Artemus Ward")	1833	1867
Henry lord Brougham, *pol. h.*	1778	1868
Charles Dickens, *n.*	1812	1870
Sir J. Herschel, *ph.*	1792	1871
George Ticknor, *h.*	1791	1871
G. Grote, *h.*	1794	1871
Edwd. Bulwer-Lytton, lord Lytton, *p. n.*	1805	1873
John Stuart Mill, *ph.*	1806	1873
Bryan W. Procter ("Barry Cornwall"), *p.*	1790	1874
Arthur Helps, *e.*	1813	1875
Charles Kingsley, *m.*	1819	1875
Harriet Martineau, *m.*	1802	1876
Marian Evans ("George Eliot") *n. p.*	1820	1880
Benjamin Disraeli, lord Beaconsfield, *n.*	1805	1881

	Born.	Died.
Thomas Carlyle, *h. e.*	1795	1881
H. W. Longfellow, *p.*	1807	1882
Dante Gabriel Rossetti, *p.*	1828	1882
Charles Darwin, *nat.*	1809	1882
Anthony Trollope, *n.*	1815	1882
R. W. Emerson, *e. p.*	1803	1882
Sir Henry Taylor, *p.d.*	1800	1886
Matthew Arnold, *p. m.*	1822	1888
W. G. Palgrave, *tr.*	1826	1888
George Bancroft, *h.*	1800	1891
W. E. Gladstone, *m.*	1809	1898
O. W. Holmes, *e. p. n.*	1809	1894
Alfred Tennyson (lord, 1883), *p*	1809	1892
Thomas A. Trollope, *n.*	1810	1892
Robert Browning, *p.*	1812	1889
Sir Theodore Martin, *h. p. m.*	1816	
Mrs. M. Oliphant, *n.*	1828	1897
James Anthony Froude, *h. m.*	1818	1894
J. R. Lowell, *hum. p. pol.*	1819	1891
John Ruskin, *art critic*	1819	1900
Herbert Spencer, *ph.*	1820	
John Tyndall, *m.*	1820	1893
E. A. Freeman, *h.*	1823	1892
Francis Turner Palgrave, *p.*	1824	
T. H. Huxley, *m.*	1825	1895
Lord Lytton, *p. m.*	1831	1891
Edwin Arnold (aft. sir), *p.*	1832	
Wm. Morris *p.*	1834	1896
A. C. Swinburne *p.*	1837	
Robert Buchanan, *p.*	1841	1901
R. L. Stevenson, *n.*	1850	1894
Wm. Wilkie Collins, *n.*	1824	1889
A. W. Kinglake, *h.*	1812	1891
Walter Whitman, *Am. p.*	1819	1892
John Greenleaf Whittier, *Am. p.*	1807	1892
John A. Symonds, *h.*	1840	1893
Augusta Webster, *p.*	1840	1894
Baroness Tautphœus (*b* Montgomery), *n.*		1893
Francis Parkman, *Am. h.*	1823	1893
Charles Merivale, *h.*	1808	1893
Henry Morley, prof.	1822	1894
George Meredith, *p. n.*	1828	
Edmund Yates, *n.*	1831	1894
Augusta de Grasse Stevens, *Am. n.* about	1865	1894
Christina Georgina Rossetti, *p.*	1830	1894
Sir John Robert Seeley, *h. ph.*	1834	1895
Joseph Henry Shorthouse, *n. e.*, author of "John Inglesant"	1834	1903
Sir Walter Besant, *n.*	1836	1901
Sir Lewis Morris, *p.*	1832	
Mrs. Mary Anne Everett-Green (Wood), *h.*	1818	1895
Alfred Austin, *p.*	1835	
Harriet Beecher Stowe, *n.*	1812	1896
Coventry Patmore, *p.*	1823	1896
Jean Ingelow, *p.* and *n.*	1820	1897
Sir John Skelton (Shirley), *h. e.*	1831	1897
Francis Wm. Newman, *e.*	1805	1897
James Payn, *n. e.*	1830	1898
William Black, *n.*	1841	1898
Grant Allen, *n. e.*	1848	1899
R. D. Blackmore, *n.*	1825	1900
Sir William Hunter, *h.*	1840	1900
H. D. Traill, *e.*	1842	1900
Charlotte M. Yonge, *n.*	1823	1901
William Stubbs, *h.*	1825	1901
Aubrey de Vere, *p.*	1814	1902
S. R. Gardiner, *h.*	1829	1902
Stephen Phillips, *p.*	1866	
Arthur Conan Doyle, *n.* (knt. June, 1902)	1859	
Leslie Stephen, *e.* (K.C.B. June, 1902)	1832	
Sir Gilbert Parker, *p.* (Canadian)	1862	
Marie Corelli, *n.*	1864	
Rudyard Kipling, *m.*	1865	
H. Rider Haggard, *m.*	1856	
Mrs. Humphry Ward (Mary A. Arnold), *m.*	1851	
Thomas Hardy, *n. p.*	1840	
George Gissing, *n.*	1857	
H. G. Wells, *n. e.*	1866	
Robt. S. Hichens, *e. n.*	1864	
Edward F. Benson, *n.*	1867	
Henry W. Lucy ("Toby, M.P."), *hum.*	1845	
Andrew Lang, *e.*	1844	
Stanley J. Weyman, *n.*	1855	
Israel Zangwill, *m.*	1864	
Sabine Baring-Gould, *n.*	1834	
James Matthew Barrie, *n. d.*	1860	
Chas. Dudley Warner, *hum. & p.*	1829	1900

	Born.	Died.
Bret-Harte, *hum.* and *n.*	1839	1902
John Fiske, *phil.* and *hist.*	1842	1901
Justin MacCarthy, *h. n. pol.*	1830	
Samuel Clemens ("Mark Twain")	1835	
Wm. D. Howells, *n.*	1837	
Henry James, *n.*	1843	
F. Marion Crawford, *n.*	1845	
Anthony Hope Hawkins (Ant. Hope)	1863	

"ENGLISHMAN," a newspaper edited by Dr. Kenealy, published in April, 1874, soon after the conviction of the claimant of the Tichborne estates (see *Trials*, 1873-4). For its libellous character, the editor was disbenched by the society of Gray's Inn, 1 Aug. 1874; ordered to give up his chambers by vice-chancellor, 29 June, 1876. He died 16 April, 1880.

ENGRAVING on signets is mentioned *Exod.* xxviii. 11 (B.C. 1491). Engraving on plates and wood began about the middle of the 15th century. Engraving on glass was perfected by Bourdier, of Paris, 1799. The copyright to engravings has been protected by several statutes; among the principal are the acts 16 & 18 Geo. III. 1775 and 1777; and the acts 7 & 8 Vict. 6 Aug. 1844, and 15 Vict. 28 May, 1852. A process of enlarging and reducing engravings by means of sheets of vulcanised india-rubber, was shown by the electro-printing block company in 1860; see *Lithography* and *Photo-Galvanography* In "Lyra Germanica," published in 1861, are illustrations engraved upon blocks photographed from negatives taken by John Leighton, F.S.A.

ENGRAVING ON COPPER. Prints from engraved copper-plates made their appearance about 1450, and were first produced in Germany. Masso, surnamed Finiguerra, is considered to have been the first Italian engraver, about 1440. (See *Niello.*)

The earliest date known of a copper-plate engraving is 1461.

Rolling-presses for working the plates invented in 1545.

Of the art of *etching* on copper by means of *aqua-fortis*, Francis Mazzuoli, or Parmegiano, is the reputed inventor, about 1532. *De Piles.*

Etching was practised by Albert Dürer, and most especially by Rembrandt. Its revival began about 1860. Eminent modern etchers:—Messrs Lalanne, P. G. Hamerton, F. Seymour Haden, Bracquemond, Jacquemart, Martial, and others. The Etching Club was established in 1838.

Mr. Lumb Stocks, R.A., line engraver, born 1812, died April, 1892.

Royal Society of Painter-etchers formed; opened an exhibition, April, 1881; annual exhibitions, 27 Feb. 1893, *et seq.*

ENGRAVING ON WOOD, long known in China, began in Europe with the *brief-mahlers* or manufacturers of playing-cards, about 1400 (see *Printing*). The art is referred by some to a Florentine, and by others to Reuss, a German; it was greatly improved by Dürer (1471-1528) and Lucas van Leyden (1497). It was much improved in England by Bewick and his brother, and pupils, Nesbitt, Anderson, &c. 1789 *et seq.* The earliest wood engraving which has reached our times is one representing St. Christopher carrying the infant Jesus over the sea: it bears date 1423.

Mr. W. J. Linton's "Masters of Wood Engraving," with 250 fine examples, published July, 1890.

International society of wood engravers; 2nd annual dinner, 27 April, 1894. Mr. George Dalziel, eminent wood engraver, died, aged 86, 4 Aug. 1902.

ENGRAVING ON SOFT STEEL, to be hardened afterwards, was introduced into England by Messrs. Perkins and Heath, of Philadelphia, 1819.

ohn Pye, "father of English landscape engraving," born 1782; died 6 Feb. 1874.

MEZZOTINTO is said to have been discovered by col. von Siegen, who engraved a portrait of princess Amelia of Hesse in mezzotinto in 1643: it was improved by prince Rupert in 1648; and by sir Christopher Wren, about 1662. See *British Museum*, 1902.

Aquatinta, by which a soft and beautiful effect is produced, was invented by the celebrated French artist St. Non, about 1662; he communicated his invention, to Le Prince. Barabbe of Paris was distinguished for his improvements in this kind of engraving, 1763. *Chiar'-oscuro* engraving originated with the Germans, and was first practised by Mair, one of whose prints bears date 1491 (see *Zinc.* &c.).

ENLISTMENT. No persons enlisting as soldiers or sailors are to be sworn in before a magistrate in less than twenty-four hours after, and they are then at liberty to withdraw upon their returning the enlistment or bounty money, and 21*s.* costs. Enlistment is now entirely voluntary. In 1847 the term of enlistment was limited to ten years for the infantry, and twelve years for the cavalry, artillery, and royal marines; and in 1867, to twelve years; see *Army*, 1867 and 1879, and *Foreign Enlistment*.

ENNISKILLEN (N. W. Ireland). This town made an obstinate defence against the army of Elizabeth, 1595, and resisted James II., 1689. 1500 Enniskilleners met his general M'Carthy at Newton Butler with 6000 men (of whom 3000 were slain, and nearly all the rest made prisoners), they losing but twenty men, 30 July, 1689. The dragoon regiment, the "Inniskillingers," was originally recruited here.

ENOCH, BOOK OF, an apocryphal work, quoted by the fathers, disappeared about the 8th century. A MS. Ethiopic version was found in Abyssinia by Bruce, and brought to England in 1773. Of this, archbishop Laurence published an English translation in 1821, and the Ethiopic text in 1838. Mr. R. H. Charles published in 1893 an emended English translation from prof. Dillmann's Ethiopic text, with introduction, notes, &c.

ENSILAGE (from *silo*, a pit), a system of preserving corn and green fodder for cattle in pits made air and water tight, practised by French and other agriculturists; described by M. Goffart and by professor Thorold Rogers, M.P., in his "Ensilage," published 1883. Ensilage reported successful at Peckforton, Cheshire, 27 Nov. 1883; commended by the prince of Wales and others at a meeting of the Institute of Agriculture, 17 March, 1884; ensilage has been found successful in India, 1884. Favourable reports of a private practical and scientific commission issued, 5 Aug. 1885; and 14 May, 1886; opinions differ as to economy. Ensilage with building silos practised in 1887.

ENSISHEIM (E. France). Here Turenne defeated the Imperial army, and expelled it from Alsace, 4 Oct. 1674.

ENTAIL of estates began with the statute of Westminster, 1285. Subsequent legislation broke the entail in cases of treason (1534), when the estate is to revert to the crown, and of bankruptcy (1833 and 1849), when it is to be sold. The law of entail in Scotland was amended in 1875.

ENTERTAINMENT OF THE PEOPLE SOCIETY, for the very poor, held first concert at the board school room, Saffron-hill, London, Saturday, 12 April, 1879.

ENTOMOLOGY, the science of insects, now mainly based upon the arrangement of Linnæus, 1739. Ray's "Methodus Insectorum," 1705; "Insectorum Historia," 1710. The Entomological Society of London was instituted 3 May, 1833; was made Royal, Aug. 1885. Prof. John O. Westwood, one of the founders, died, aged 87, 2 Jan. 1893. A National Entomological Exhibition at the Westminster Aquarium was opened 9 March, 1878. Miss Ormerod, honorary consulting entomologist to the Royal Agricultural Society, 1882–1892; her 24th last annual report respecting insects issued March, 1901 (she died 19 July, 1901, aged 73). Prof. Charles Valentine Riley, eminent agricultural entomologist of the United States, born 1843, killed by an accident, 14 Sept. 1895.

ENVELOPES for letters are mentioned by Swift, 1726. Stamped adhesive envelopes came into general use shortly after the establishment of the penny postal system, 10 Jan. 1840. Machinery for their manufacture was patented by Mr. George Wilson in 1844; and by Messrs. E. Hill and Warren de la Rue, 17 March, 1845.

ENVOYS AT COURTS, in dignity below ambassadors, enjoy the protection, but not the ceremonies of ambassadors. Envoys extraordinary are of modern date. *Wicquefort.*

EOZOÖN CANADENSE, asserted to be the earliest known form of life, and a species of foraminifera, found by professor J. W. Dawson, of Montreal, in Laurentian limestone in 1858, see *Geology.*

EPACT (Greek, *added*) is the excess of the solar month above the lunar synodical month, 1 day, 11 hours, 15 minutes, 57 seconds, the lunar month being only 29 days, 12 hours, 44 minutes, 3 seconds; and the excess of the solar year above the lunar synodical year (nearly 11 days), the lunar year being 354 days. The epact of any year indicates the moon's age on the 1st Jan. in that year. The number of the Gregorian epact for 1893, 12; 1894, 23; 1895, 4; 1896, 15; 1897, 26; 1898, 7; 1899, 18; 1900, 0; 1901, 10; 1902, 21; 1903, 2; 1904, 13; 1905, 24.

EPERNAY (N.E. France), seat of the trade in champagne, was taken from the League by Henry IV., 26 July, 1592, when marshal Armand Biron was killed.

EPHESUS (in Asia Minor), a city said to have been founded by the Carians and Leleges, burnt by the Amazons, rebuilt by the Ionians about 1043 B.C. It was subdued by Cyrus in 544 B.C.; revolted from the Persians, 501 B.C. and was destroyed by an earthquake in A.D. 17. See *Diana, Temple of*, and *Seven Churches.* Paul preached here A.D. 55, 56 (*Acts* xviii. xix.) His epistle to the Ephesians is dated A.D. 64. The third general council was held here in 431. After investigation, begun in 1863, Mr. J. T. Wood discovered the site of the temple of Diana in April, 1870; and about 60 tons of marble were shipped at Smyrna for the British Museum, Jan. 1872, part of which arrived in the summer. Mr. Wood published an illustrated account of his discoveries in 1876. The site of the temple was purchased for the British Museum. Mr. J. T. Wood resumed his excavations, summer, 1883.

EPHORI, powerful magistrates of Sparta, five in number, said to have been first created by Theopompus to control the royal power, about 757 B.C.

EPIC POEMS (from Greek *epos*, a song), narratives in verse. Eminent examples:—

Homer's "Iliad" and "Odyssey" (*Greek*), between 8th and 10th century B.C. (see *Homer*).
Mâhâ-bârhata, Sanscrit, very ancient; by several authors; the longest epic known (220,000 lines).
Virgil's "Æneid" (*Latin*) about . . . B.C. 19
Ovid's "Metamorphoses" (*Latin*), about . A.D. 1
Lucan's "Pharsalia" (*Latin*), before . . . 65
Dante (died 1321), "Divina Commedia" (*Italian*) published 1472
Ariosto, "Orlando Furioso" (*Italian*) . . . 1516
Camoens' "Lusiad" (*Portuguese*) . . . 1569
Tasso, "Jerusalem Delivered" (*Italian*) . . . 1581
Spenser's "Faery Queen" 1590–6
Milton's "Paradise Lost" 1667
Voltaire, "Henriade" (*French*) 1728
Walter Scott, "Lay of the Last Minstrel," 1805; "Marmion," 1808; "Lady of the Lake" . . 1810
Byron, "Childe Harold," 1812; "Don Juan" . 1818–23
R. Browning, "Ring and the Book" . . . 1868–9
A. Tennyson, "Idylls of the King" . . . 1859–85

EPICUREAN PHILOSOPHY. Epicurus of Gargettus, near Athens, about 306 B.C., taught that the greatest good consists in peace of mind springing from virtue, as tending to prevent disquiet: but the name epicurean is frequently given to those who derive happiness from sensual pleasure. (See *Atoms.*)

EPIDAURUS (Greece), celebrated for the temple of Asclepius, or Æsculapius, god of medicine, and enriched by gifts from persons healed. The Romans sent an embassy to seek the help of the god during a pestilence, and his worship was introduced at Rome, 293 B.C. The temple was visited by Æmilius Paulus, after his conquest of Macedonia, 167 B.C.

EPIDEMIC PREVENTION ACT, 46 & 47 Vict. c. 59, passed 25 Aug. 1883.

EPIDEMIOLOGICAL SOCIETY OF LONDON, established in 1850; has done valuable work. Dr. Charles Creighton's "History of Epidemics in Britain," 3 vols. 1895.

EPIGENESIS, see *Spontaneous Generation.*

EPIGRAMS. Marcus Valerius Martialis, the Latin epigrammatist, who flourished about A.D. 83, is allowed to have excelled all others, ancient or modern. The following epigram on Christ's turning water into wine (*John* iii.) is an example:—"Vidit et erubuit lympha pudica Deum." "The modest water saw its God, and blushed." *Crashaw* (died 1650).

"The Epigrammatists," a collection by rev. H. P. Dodd, published 1870 and 1875.

EPIPHANY (appearance), a feast (Jan. 6), termed Twelfth Day, celebrates the manifestation of the Saviour, by the appearance of the star which conducted the Magi to the place where he was to be found; early observed, but became a separate feast, 813. *Whately.*

EPIRUS (Northern Greece). Its early history is very obscure.

The first Pyrrhus (Neoptolemus) settled in Epirus, after the Trojan war, 1170 B.C., and was killed in the temple of Delphi . . . about B.C. 1165
Alexander the first king invades Italy to assist the Tarentines against the Lucanians, &c., is defeated and slain at Pandosia . . . B.C. 326
Pyrrhus the Great reigns, 295; he takes Macedon from Demetrius; is compelled to yield to Lysimachus 287
Invited by the Tarentines, invades Italy, see *Rome*, 281–275
Temporary success in Sicily . . . . 279 *et seq.*
He takes Macedon from Antigonus . . . 273
He unsuccessfully invades Sparta; enters Argos, and is killed by a tile, thrown by a woman . . 272
Philip unites Epirus to Macedon . . . 220
Its conquest by the Romans 167

* * * * * * *

Epirus annexed to the Ottoman empire . A.D. 1466
An insurrection against the Turks put down . 1854

EPISCOPACY, see *Bishops.*

EPISTEMOLOGY. A science of the sciences. See "*Groundwork of Science*," by Dr. St. George Mivart, published 1899; he died, 1 April, 1900.

EPISTLES or **Letters.** An Egyptian letter about 1300 B.C. is translated in "Records of the Past," vol. 6. A letter was sent to Joab by David by the hands of Uriah, about 1035 B.C. (2 *Sam.* xi. 14); see under article *Bible*. Horace Walpole, renowned for his letters, was born 5 Oct. 1717; died 2 March, 1797. The collection entitled "Elegant Epistles," commencing with Cicero, was published in 1790. It ends with an essay on letter writing by Dr. Johnson. Prof. Walter Raleigh in his lectures on "English Letter-Writers," at the Royal Institution, March, 1898, referred to the Paston letters, lady Mary Wortley Montagu, lord Chesterfield, Pope, Swift, Cowper, Byron and Keats.

EPITAPHS were inscribed on tombs by the Egyptians, Jews, Greeks, and Romans. Mr. T. J. Pettigrew published a collection entitled "Chronicles of the Tombs," in 1857.

EPITHALAMIUM, a nuptial song at marriage. Tisias, the lyric poet, is said to have been the first writer of one. He received the name of Stesichorus, from the alterations made by him in music and dancing, about 536 B.C. *Bossuet.*

EPOCHS, points of time made remarkable by some event, from which subsequent years are reckoned by historians and chronologers; see *Eras*.

See *Anno Domini, Hegira,* &c.

EPPING FOREST, see *Forests*, note.

EPSOM (Surrey). The mineral springs were discovered in 1618. The races began about 1711, and have been held annually since 1730. See *Derby Day*. Population, 1881, 6,916; 1891, 8,417; 1901, 10,915.

EQUALISATION of rates (London) act passed, 25 Aug. 1894.

EQUATION of **Time.** See *Geodesy*.

EQUATOR or **Ecuador,** a South American republic, formerly Quito and other provinces, part of Columbia, 1821; independent in 1831, when the Columbian republic was divided into three; the other two being Venezuela and New Granada. The population of Equator in 1885, 1,004,651; 1897, about 1,270,000.

Presidents: general Franco, 21 Aug. 1859; defeated in battle by general Flores, Aug. 1860; G. G. Moreno, Jan. 1861; Geronimo Carrion, 4 Aug. 1865; disputes with the chambers; resigns Dec. 1867
Dr. Xavier Espinosa was elected president, 13 Sept. ,,
Dr. Gabriel Garcia Moreno, president, . end of 1872
President Moreno assassinated, 6 Aug.; state of siege proclaimed, Sept. 1875; Veintimille, president . . . . Sept. 1876
Revolt; constitutional army under Aparicio defeated at Galte . . . . 14 Dec. ,,
Eruption of Cotopaxi . . . . . 25 June, 1877
Alfaro dictator . . . . Jan. 1883
Jose Maria Placido Caamano, president 12 Feb. 1884
Revolution at Esmeraldas under Eloy Alfaro 4 Nov. 1886
Señor Antonio Flores, president, 30 June, 1888; Sen. Luis Cordero . . . . . . 30 June, 1892
The *Sucre* gunboat blown up at Guayaquil; the commander and 14 men killed . . 31 May, 1895
Insurrection under gen. Vernaza, reported 16 Aug. ,,
Quito taken by gen. Eloy Alfaro, made dictator, rep. 28 Aug. 1895; elected president, reported, 15 Jan. 1897
Rebels routed at San Aneaja . . 24 Jan. 1899
Gen. Plaza succeeds gen. Alfaro as president, 31 Aug. 1901

See *Earthquakes*, 1868.

EQUATORIAL AFRICA. See *Soudan*, 1886.

EQUESTRIAN ORDER in Rome was established with Romulus, about 750 B.C.; see *Knighthood*.

EQUINOX. When the sun in his progress passes through the equator in one of the equinoctial points, the day and night are equal all over the globe. This occurs twice in the year: about 21 March, the *vernal* equinox, and 22 Sept., the *autumnal* equinox. The equinoctial points move backwards about 50 seconds yearly, requiring 25,000 years to accomplish a complete revolution. This is called the *precession* of the equinoxes, which is said to have been observed by the ancient astronomers.

EQUITY, Courts of, are those of the lord chancellor, the vice-chancellors, and the master of the rolls, their office being to correct the operations of the literal text of the law, and supply its defects by reasonable construction not admissible in a court of law. The supreme court of session in Scotland combines the functions of law and equity. In 1865 equity powers were conferred on the county courts for cases respecting sums under 500*l*. See *Supreme Court*, in which law and equity are combined.

ERAS. The principal are more fully noticed in their alphabetical order.

Common Era (English Bible, *Usher*, &c.) . B.C. 4004
Era of the Jews 3761
Era of *Constantinople*, 1 Sept. 5508; of *Antioch*, 1 Sept. 5492
Alexandrian or *Mundane* era . . 29 Aug. 5502
Julian era . . . . 1 Jan. 4713
Era of *Abraham* . . . . . . 1 Oct. 2015
Era of *Nabonassar*, after which the astronomical observations made at Babylon were reckoned, began 26 Feb. 747
Era of the *Seleucidæ* (used by the Maccabees), commenced 312
The *Olympiads* belong to the Grecians, and date from 1 July, 776 B.C.
The Romans reckoned from the founding of their city, A.U.C. (*anno urbis conditæ*) 753
Era of *Tyre* . . . . 19 Oct. 125
Cæsarean era of Antioch . . . 1 Sept. 48
Spanish Era (of the conquest of Spain), the 16th year of the emperor Augustus (see *Cæsars*), long used by the Spaniards . . . . . A.D. 1 Jan. 38
Actian era . . . . B.C. 1 Jan. 30
Pontifical or *Ecclesiastical* Indiction, 25 Dec. or 1 Jan. 6
Vulgar Christian era . . . . . A.D. 1 Jan. 1
Era of *Diocletian* or Martyrs, began . . 29 Aug. 284
The Mahometans began their era from the *Hegira*, or flight of their prophet from Mecca 16 July, 622
Armenian era . . . . . . A.D. 7 July, 552
Era of *Yezdegird III*. or *Persian* era A.D. 16 June, 632
Era of *Vicramaditya*, used in India, began B.C. . 57

See *Creation, Cali Yuga, Anno Domini, Calendar*.

ERASTIANISM, the opinions of Thomas Lieber (latinised *Erastus*), a German physician (1524-83), who taught that the church had no right to exclude any person from church ordinances, to inflict excommunication, &c. Persons who acknowledge the jurisdiction of the civil power in spiritual matters and the law of patronage are now termed Erastians.

ERASURES. By order of sir John Romilly, master of the rolls, in 1855, no document corrected by erasure with the knife was to be henceforth received in his court. The errors must be corrected with the pen. It is so in the army courts.

ERDINGTON ORPHANAGE, &c.; see *Orphans'-houses*.

ERFURT (Central Germany), was founded in 476; and its university established about 1390.

Erfurt was ceded to Prussia in 1802. It capitulated to Murat, when 14,000 Prussian troops surrendered, 16 Oct. 1806. In this city Napoleon and Alexander met, and offered peace to England, 27 Sept. 1808. The French retreated to Erfurt from Leipsic, 18 Oct. 1813. A German parliament met here in March and April, 1850. Population, 1890, 72,371; 1900, 85,190.

ERICSSON'S CALORIC ENGINE, see *Heat*, note.

ERIVAN (Armenia), in the 16th century the residence of the shahs of Persia, was taken by the Turks in 1553 and 1582; but recovered by Abbas the Great, 1604. After being several times captured, it was ceded to Persia, 1769. It was taken by Paskiewitch in 1827, and annexed to Russia by treaty in Feb. 1828.

ERYTHREA, a new Italian colony on the Red Sea, established by royal decree, 2 Jan. 1890. Military occupation to be restricted to Massowah, announced, May, 1897; Sig. F. Martini appointed governor, 21 Nov. 1897. See *Massowah* and *Italy*, 1898, and 26 Nov. 1901.

ERZEROUM (Asiatic Turkey), a city built by Theodosius II., 415; taken by the Seljuk Turks in the 13th century, and by the Ottoman Turks in 1517. It was captured by the Russian general Paskiewitch, June, 1829, but restored in 1830. It was almost totally destroyed by earthquakes, 2 June to 17 July, 1859. Population in 1885, 60,000.

ESCHEAT, the reverting of any land or tenements to the lord of the fee, or to the state, through failure of heirs; formerly also through attainder of the tenant, which last was abolished by the Felony Act, 1870.

ESCOMBRERA BAY, BATTLE OF; see *Spain*, 11 Oct. 1873.

ESCURIAL, properly **ESCORIAL** (25 miles N.W. of Madrid), the magnificent palace of the sovereigns of Spain, termed the eighth wonder of the world, was commenced by Philip II. in 1563, and completed in 1586, at a cost of about 10,000,000*l.* It is built in the form of a gridiron in honour of St. Lawrence, on whose day (10 Aug. 1557) the Spaniards gained the victory of St. Quentin. According to Francisco de los Santos the total length of all its rooms and apartments is above 120 English miles. The Escurial comprises a church, mausoleum, monastery, palace, library, and museum. It was struck by lightning and caught fire 11.30 p.m. 1 Oct. 1872, and was much damaged; but the grand library and other treasures were preserved.

ESPARTO, from the Latin *spartum*, *stipa tenacissima* of Linnæus, a Spanish grass used by Romans for whip-thongs, and now largely employed in paper-making. In 1856 about 50 tons, in 1870 above 100,000 tons, and in 1902, 198,292 tons, were imported into Britain. The price has risen considerably in recent years. Living plants were received at Newcastle, July, 1867.

ESPIERRES (Belgium). At Pont-à-Chin, near this village, the French, under Pichegru, attacked the allied English and Austrian army (100,000 men), commanded by the duke of York, and were repulsed after a long and desperate engagement, losing the advantages gained by the victory at Turcoing, 22 May, 1794.

ESPRIT, SAINT (or Holy Ghost), the title of an order of knighthood, founded by Henry III. of France in 1578, and abolished in 1791.

ESQUIRES, among the Greeks and Romans, were armour-bearers to, or attendants on a knight. *Blount.* In England the king created esquires by putting about their necks the collars of SS, and bestowing upon them a pair of silver spurs. John de Kingston was created a squire by patent, 13 Richard II., 1389-90. There are now legally esquires by birth, by creation, and by holding some office, but the title is very loosely given by courtesy.

"ESSAYS AND REVIEWS," by six clergymen and one layman of the church of England (the Rev. Drs. Fred. Temple and Rowland Williams, professor Baden Powell, H. B. Wilson, Mark Pattison, and professor B. Jowett, and Mr. C. W. Goodwin) were published in an 8vo vol. in March, 1860. The book did not excite much attention at first, but having been severely censured for heterodox views by nearly all the bishops and many of the clergy, it created much excitement in 1861, and was condemned by convocation 24 June, 1864. The ecclesiastical courts sentenced the revs. R. Williams and H. B. Wilson to suspension for one year, and costs, 15 Dec. 1862; but on appeal the sentence was reversed by the judicial committee of the privy council, 8 Feb. 1864. The most remarkable amongst the works put forth in opposition (in 1862) are the "Aids to Faith," edited by the bishop of Gloucester (W. Thomson, aft. abp. of York), and "Replies to Essays and Reviews," edited by the bishop of Oxford (S. Wilberforce). The election of Dr. Temple to the see of Exeter was much opposed on account of his essay in this collection; see *Church of England*, 1869 and *Broad Church*.

ESSENES, an ascetic Jewish sect at the time of Christ.

ESSEN, a town in Rhenish Prussia, which began with the Benedictine nunnery, about 873. Among the iron and steel manufactories, the chief are those of Krupp, established 1810, in which were employed 74 men in 1848, and 46,000 in 1902, when the works contained 1,600 furnaces, 600 steam-hammers, 497 steam-engines, and other great apparatus. A Christian miners' congress held, 424 delegates present; opposed to the social democrats, 26 Aug. 1894. See *Cannon*. Population, 1890, 78,723; 1900, 118,863. See *Westphalia*, 1889.

ESSEX, KINGDOM OF; see under *Britain*.

EARLS OF ESSEX (from *Nicolas*).

Geoffrey de Mandeville, created earl of Essex by Matilda, was slain . . . . . 14 Sept. 1144
Humphrey de Bohun, succeeded by right of his mother, Mary, sister of William, who died without heir 1182
Humphrey de Bohun, died without heir . . 1376
Thomas of Woodstock, son of Edward III. 1372; murdered 1397
Henry Bourchier (grandson) 1461
Henry Bourchier, grandson; died without heir (earldom extinct) 1532
Thomas Cromwell, 1539; beheaded 1540
William Parr, 1543; attainted 1543
Walter Devereux, 1572; died 1576
Robert Devereux, lord lieut. of Ireland, 1599; censured for misgovernment; conspired against the government; beheaded, 25 Feb. 1601
Robert, son; died without heir 1646
Arthur Capel, ancestor of the present earl . . 1661
An industrial colony for loafers and tramps at Hadleigh (abt. 3,000 acres) founded by gen. Booth in 1890, reported very successful, *Times*, 22 Aug. 1899

See *Storms*, June, 1897; *Trials* 1903.

ESSLING, BATTLE OF, see *Asperne*.

ESTATE DUTY, replacing the legacy, probate and succession duty, was, by the finance act (*which see*), passed 31 July, 1894, 1895 and 1896.

Rates on 100*l.*–500*l.*, 1 per cent.; 500*l.*–1,000*l.*, 2 per cent.; 1,000*l.*–10,000*l.*, 3 per cent; 10,000*l.*–25,000*l.*, 4 per cent.; 25,000*l.*–50,000*l.*, 4½ per cent.; 50,000*l.*–75,000*l.*, 5 per cent., &c.; 1,000,000*l.*, 8 per cent.

Estate duty, net receipts, year ending 31 March, 1896, 11,600,000*l.*; 1897, 10,830,000*l.*; 1898, 11,100,000*l.*; 1899, 11,400,000*l.*; 1900, 14,020,000*l.*; 1901, 12,980,000*l.*; 1902, 14,200,000*l.*; 1903, 13,850,000*l.*

ESTE, House of. Boniface, count of Lucca and duke of Tuscany, about 811, is said to have descended from Odoacer, king of Italy. From Boniface sprang Albert Azzo II. marquis of Italy and lord of Este, born about 996, who married—first, Cunegonda of the house of Guelf, by whom he had Guelf, duke of Bavaria, the ancestor of the house of Brunswick (see *Bavaria* and *Brunswick*); and secondly, Gersonda, by whom he had Fulk, the ancestor of the Estes, dukes of Ferrara and Modena.

ESTELLA, N. Spain. In a conflict at Peña Mura, near this place, 25-28 June, 1874, the republicans were repulsed, and their general, Manuel de Concha (aged 66), killed, by the Carlists, 27 June.

ESTHONIA or **Revel**, a Russian province, said to have been conquered by the Teutonic knights in the 12th century; after various changes it was ceded to Sweden by the treaty of Oliva, 3 May, 1660, and finally to Russia by the peace of Nystadt, 30 Aug. 1721, having been conquered by Peter in 1710. Population, 1886, 395,979; 1897, 413,724.

ÉTATS, see *States*.

ETCHING, see *Engraving*.

ETHER was known to the earliest chemists. Nitric ether was first discovered by Kunkel, in 1681; and muriatic ether, from the chloride of tin, by Courtanvaux, in 1759. Acetic ether was discovered by count Lauraguais, same year; and hydriotic ether was first prepared by Gay-Lussac. The phosphoric ether was obtained by M. Boullay. The discovery that by *inhaling ether* the patient is rendered unconscious of pain, is due to Dr. C. T. Jackson, of Boston, U. S. Mr. Thomas Morton, of the same place, first introduced it into surgical practice, under Dr. Jackson's directions (1846); see *Chloroform*, and *Amylene*. The drinking of ether as an intoxicant greatly increased in the north of Ireland, was checked by the enforcement of the Poisons Act of 1870, in regard to its sale, Oct. 1891. The term "ether" was applied to the transparent celestial space by the German astronomer Encke, about 1829, when studying the elements of Pons' comet, discovered in 1818. Ether is now believed by scientists to be the medium by which heat, light, electricity, etc., are transmitted through space. See *Wireless Telegraphy* under *Electricity*, 1897 *et seq.*

ETHICS (Greek term for *Morals*). The works of Plato, Aristotle, and Confucius, contain heathen systems; the New Testament is that of Christianity. Paley's Moral Philosophy appeared in 1785, and Whewell's Elements of Morality in 1845. An Ethical Society existed in London, 1890. Mr. Herbert Spencer's "Principles of Ethics," 2 vols., published in sections, 1879–93. Moral instruction league formed in London, 7 Dec. 1897. The late Prof. Wallace's lectures and essays on Natural Theology and Ethics, published April, 1899 (edited by Master of Balliol).

ETHIOPIA. The name was applied anciently rather vaguely to countries the inhabitants of which had *sun-burnt* complexions, in Asia and Africa; but is now considered to apply properly to the modern Nubia, Sennaar, and Northern Abyssinia. Many pyramids exist at Napata, the capital of Meroë, the civilised part of ancient Ethiopia.

The Ethiopians settle near Egypt . . . B.C. 1615
Zerah, the Ethiopian, defeated by Asa . . . 941
A dynasty of Ethiopian kings reigned over Egypt 765 to 715
Tirhakah, king of Ethiopia, marches against Sennacherib 710
Unsuccessful invasion of Cambyses . . . 525-522
Ptolemy III. Euergetes extended his conquests in Ethiopia 225
Candace, queen of Meroë, advancing against the Roman settlement at Elephantine, defeated and subdued by Petronius . . . A.D. 22-23

ETHIOPIAN EQUATORIAL PROVINCES, M. Leontieff appointed gov.-gen. by the emperor Menelik, rep. Aug. 1897.

ETHNIKE HETAIRIA, an enthusiastic Greek national society, founded Nov. 1894; a revolutionary movement made by them in Macedonia summer, 1896; their forces were reported to have begun the war with Turkey. See *Greece*, 10 April, 1897, *et seq.*; denied by them, Dec. 1897.

ETHNOLOGY, a branch of Anthropology, is defined as the science "which determines the distinctive characters of the persistent modifications of mankind, their distribution, and the causes of the modifications and distribution." The study of the relations of the different divisions of mankind to each other is of recent origin. Balbi's Ethnographic Atlas was published in 1826, and Dr. Prichard's great work, *Researches on the Physical History of Mankind*, 1841-7. The Ethnological Society, established in 1843, published transactions. On 17 Jan. 1871, it was amalgamated with the Anthropological Society, (*which see*) and named the Anthropological Institute. Dr. R. G. Latham's works, on the Ethnology of the British Empire, appeared in 1851-2. Professor T. H. Huxley gave lectures on Ethnology at the Royal Institution, London, in 1866-7. Annual reports of the Bureau of Ethnology, Washington, U.S., began to be published, 1879. The International Congress of the Ethnographic Sciences met at Paris Sept. 30, 1889.

ETHYL, a compound radicle, a colourless gas, with a slightly ethereal odour, a compound of carbon and hydrogen, first obtained in the free state by professor (aft. sir; died 9 Aug. 1899) Edw. Frankland in 1849. Several of its compounds with metals take fire in the air.

ETNA, Mount (Sicily). Here were the fabled forges of the Cyclops: and it is called by Pindar the pillar of heaven. Eruptions are mentioned by Diodorus Siculus as happening 1693 B.C., and Thucydides speaks of three eruptions as occurring 734, 477, and 425 B.C. There were eruptions, 125, 121, and 43 B.C. *Livy.*

Eruptions, A. D. 40, 254, and 420. *Carrera.*
One in 1012. *Geoffrey de Viterbo.*
One overwhelmed Catania, when 15,000 inhabitants perished in the burning ruins . . . 1169
Eruptions, 1329, 1408, 1445, 1536, 1537, 1564, *et seq.*
In 1669, when tens of thousands of persons perished in the streams of lava which rolled over the whole country for forty days.
Eruptions in 1766, 1787, 1809, 1811, and in May, 1830, when several villages were destroyed, and showers of lava reached near to Rome.
The town of Bronte was destroyed . 18 Nov. 1832
Violent eruption occurred in . . Aug. and Sept. 1852
An eruption began on 1 Feb., and ceased in July 1865
Violent eruptions began 28 Nov. 1868, and 29 Aug. 1874
Violent eruption . . 26 May—7 June, 1879

Eruption . . . . . . 22 March—4 April, 1883
A violent eruption, with earthquakes; much damage . . . . 18 May—4 June, 1886
Destructive eruptions, with earthquake shocks, 9 July–2 Sept. (variations) 1892
Railway round Etna opened (about 62 m. long.) 29 Sept. 1895
Eruptions, the observatory damaged by falling débris . . . . . . 19, 25 July, 1899

ETON COLLEGE (Buckinghamshire), founded by Henry VI. in 1440, and designed as a nursery to King's College, Cambridge. John Stanbery, confessor to Henry VI. (bishop of Bangor, in 1448), was nominated the first provost. One of the provosts, William Waynflete, (bishop of Winchester, 1447) greatly promoted the erection of the buildings. Besides about three hundred noblemen's and gentlemen's sons, there were seventy king's scholars on the foundation, who, when properly qualified, were formerly elected, on the first Tuesday in August, to King's College, Cambridge, and removed there when there were vacancies, according to seniority. The establishment of the *Montem* is nearly coeval with the college. It consisted in the procession of the scholars, arrayed in fancy dresses, to Salt-hill once in three years; the donations collected on the road (sometimes as much as 800*l.*) were given to the senior or best scholar, their captain, for his support while studying at Cambridge. The montem was discontinued in 1847. The college system was modified by the Public Schools act, 1868. In 1873 election Saturday ceased, the scholars to be students at Cambridge being chosen there. In 1880 there were 853 students; in 1891, 1,007.

The birthday of George III. is annually celebrated 4 June, 1738
The Queen laid the corner stone of the new school buildings . . . . . . 18 May, 1889
Ninth jubilee of the foundation of the college celebrated . . . . . . 24 June, 1891
The statue of bishop Waynflete, first head master, unveiled by Dr. R. D. Durnford, bishop of Chichester . . . . . . 6 June, 1893
Fatal fire resulting in the death of two scholars, the iron-barred windows of their bedroom preventing their escape. The king and the queen sent messages of sympathy and condolence, 1 June, 1903
Population of Eton in 1891, 2,409; 1901, 3,301.

ETRURIA (or TUSCIA, hence the modern name Tuscany), a province of Italy, whence the Romans, in a great measure, derived their laws, customs, and superstitions. Herodotus asserts that the country was conquered by a colony of Lydians. The subjugation of this country forms an important part of early Roman history. It was most powerful under Porsena of Clusium, who attempted to reinstate the Tarquins, 506 B.C. Veii was taken by Camillus, 396 B.C. A truce between the Romans and Etrurians for forty years was concluded, 351 B.C. The latter and their allies were defeated at the Vadimonian lake, 310, with the Boii their allies, 283 B.C., and totally lost their independence about 265 B.C. The vases and other works of the Etruscans still remaining show the degree of their civilisation. Napoleon I. established a kingdom of Etruria, 1801, and suppressed it 1807, see *Tuscany*.—"The Cities and Cemeteries of Etruria," by George Dennis, published 1848 and 1878 (died, aged 83, 18 Nov. 1898). *Etruria*, Staffordshire, the site of Josiah Wedgwood's porcelain works, &c., was founded in 1771.

EUBŒA, the largest island in the Ægean sea. Two of its cities, Chalcis and Eretria, were very important, till the former was subdued by Athens, 506 B.C. and the latter by the Persians, 490. After the Persian war, Eubœa became wholly subject to Athens, and was its most valuable possession. It revolted in 445, but was soon subdued by Pericles. After the battle of Chæronea, 338, it became subject to Macedon. It was made independent by the Romans in 194; but was afterwards incorporated in the province of Achaia. It now forms part of the kingdom of Greece.

EUCALYPTUS GLOBULUS, or Blue Gum Tree, a very fast growing Tasmanian evergreen, of the order *Myrtaceæ*. From the extraordinary power of its roots of absorbing moisture, and the salutary aromatic odour of its leaves, it has been found highly beneficial in counteracting the malaria of marshy districts of hot climates, and hence has been named the fever-destroying tree. M. Ramel first sent seeds from Melbourne to Paris in 1854, and subsequently seeds were distributed over the south of Europe, the north and south of Africa, and elsewhere. He died in 1881.

So rapid is the growth of this tree, that a forest may be formed in twenty years. It sometimes reaches the height of 350 feet, with a circumference of 100 feet, rivalling *Wellingtonia gigantea*, which see.
The timber, bark, and oils of the Eucalyptus are highly valuable, and professor Bentley says that the genus is one of the most important to man in the vegetable kingdom. In 1874 its medicinal value was said to have been exaggerated.

EUCHARIST, thanksgiving, an early name for the Lord's Supper; see *Sacrament*.

EUCLID'S ELEMENTS. Euclid, a native of Alexandria, flourished about 323-283 B.C. The *Elements* are not wholly his; for many of the demonstrations were derived from Thales, Pythagoras, Eudoxus, and others; Euclid reduced them to order, and probably inserted many theorems of his own. The *Elements* were first printed at Basil by Simon Grynæus, in 1533. Euclid is said to have told king Ptolemy that there was no royal road to geometry.

EUDIOMETER, an apparatus to ascertain the purity of atmospheric air, or the quantity of oxygen gas or vital air contained in it; one was invented by Marsilio Landriani, and described by him in his "Ricerche," 1775; Dr. Priestley is said to have first used Fontana's eudiometer in 1770. *Gmelin*.

EUGENICS, see *Heredity*.

EUGUBINE TABLES, seven tablets of brass, probable date about 400 B.C., (with inscriptions relating to sacrifices, &c., four in Umbrian, two Latin, and one partly in both dialects), were discovered in 1444 at Gubbio, the ancient Eugubium or Iguvium. The inscriptions are accurately given by Lepsius, in his "Inscriptiones Umbricæ et Oscæ," 1841.

EUNUCHS, first mentioned among the Egyptians and Assyrians, and said to have been first employed by Semiramis, queen of Assyria, about 2007 B.C. Eunuchs frequently attained to political power in the later Eastern empire.

EUPATORIA (KOSLEFF), a sea-port on the west coast of the Crimea. After the allied French, English, and Turkish armies landed in the Crimea, 14 Sept. 1854, a detachment under captain Brock occupied this place, which was afterwards reinforced by the Turks. It was attacked 17 Feb. 1855, by 40,000 Russians under Liprandi. The latter were repulsed with the loss of 500 men by the Turks, whose loss was only 50, among which, however, was Selim Pasha, the commander of the Egyptian contingent.

EUPHRATES, the largest river in Western Asia. It rises in Armenia, and has two branches.

On its banks are the remains of numerous ancient cities, such as Babylon and Birs Nimrûd. The Euphrates Valley Railway, as a speedy means of reaching India, has been much advocated, especially by the late general Chesney, who published his survey of the Euphrates and Tigris in 1850. A parliamentary commission reported on it, Aug. 1872, when it was also considered at the meeting of the British association at Brighton. The construction would cost from five to ten millions sterling, and its advantages are considered rather hypothetical by the best judges.

EUPHUISM, an affected style of language, prevalent in the time of Elizabeth, arose from "Euphues; the Anatomy of Wit," by John Lyly, published in 1581.

EURASIAN PLAIN, the great central plain of Europe and Asia, so named by ethnologists (1865). The offspring of a European father and an Asiatic mother is termed Eurasian. The degraded condition of the Eurasians, which has caused much anxiety, especially at Calcutta, was discussed early in 1891. The Marchioness of Dufferin was deeply interested in the matter about 1884.

EUROPE, the smallest of the three divisions of the old continent, really an appendage of Asia; area, nearly 3,800,000 square miles; population, 301,700,000 (1872); 310,675,966 (1877); 330,321,680 (1884) 333,054,908 (1888); 357,379,000 (1891); nearly 370,000,000 (1898). For the history, see *Greece*, *Rome*, and the modern kingdoms.

EUROPEAN ASSURANCE COMPANY, see *Insurance*.

EURYDICE, H.M.S. frigate, foundered in a squall off Dunnose, near Ventnor, Isle of Wight, 24 March, 1878; see *Navy* and *Wrecks*, 1878.

EURYMEDON, a river in Pamphylia, near which Cimon, son of Miltiades, destroyed the fleet of the Persians at Cyprus, and defeated their land forces, 469 B.C.

EUSTACE, ST. (Lower Canada). The rebels were defeated here, 14 Dec. 1837, and compelled to surrender their arms. Their chiefs fled.

EUSTATIUS, ST., a West India island, settled by the Dutch, 1632; taken by the French in 1689; by the British in 1690; again by the British forces under Rodney and Vaughan, 3 Feb. 1781. It was recovered by the French under the marquis de Bouillé, 26 Nov. same year; captured by the British, 1801, 1810; restored to the Dutch, 1814.

EUSTON SQUARE MYSTERY, see *Trials*, July, 1879. Euston hall, Suffolk (seat of the earl of Grafton), almost entirely destroyed by fire, 5 April, 1902.

EUTAW SPRINGS (S. Carolina). Here the Americans were defeated by the British under Arnold, 8 Sept. 1781.

EUTYCHIANS, so called from Eutyches, an abbot of Constantinople, who asserted in 446 that there was but one nature in Christ, the human having been absorbed in the divine. This doctrine was condemned by councils—at Constantinople in 448, and at Chalcedon in 451. It has been also called *Monophysite* (of one nature), and *Jacobite*, from Jacobus Baradæus, its zealous defender in the 6th century. It is the form of Christianity now existing among the Copts and Armenians.

EUXINE, see *Black Sea*.

EVACUATION TREATY see *France*, Sept. 1871.

EVANGELICAL, a term applied to a portion of the clergy of the church of England (also called the low church), who profess to preach the gospel more purely than their brethren termed the high church party; see *Church of England* and *Free Church*.

The Evangelical Alliance was founded by sir Culling Eardley Smith and others at Liverpool in 1845, with the view of promoting unity among all denominations of Protestant Christians against Romanism and infidelity.

At a general meeting held in London 19 Aug. 1846, 921 members were present from all parts of the world.

Since 1845, annual meetings have been held in various towns in the United Kingdom.

General international conferences have been held: London, 1851; Paris, 1855; Berlin (received by the king), Sept., 1857; Geneva, 1861; Amsterdam, 1867; New York, Oct., 1873; Basle, 1879; Copenhagen, 1885; Florence, 4 April, 1891; Exeter-hall, London, 29 June, 1896.

A conference in connection with the Evangelical Alliance met at Washington, U.S. 9 Dec. 1887.

The "Evangelical Church" in Germany began with a fusion of the Lutherans and Calvinists in Nassau in 1817: followed by similar movements in different parts of Germany, 1818-22.

A conference termed *Reunion* was held at Grindelwald, Switzerland, to promote a protestant union, July; it closed 15 Sept. 1892; at Lucerne, Sept. 1893; when annual conferences were decided upon.

EVANGELISTS, preachers of the "gospel," or good news; see *Gospels*.

EVELINA HOSPITAL, Southwark, established in 1869 by baron Ferdinand de Rothschild, in memory of his wife. Renovated and enlarged 1903.

EVENING SCHOOLS for adults of the lower classes were strongly recommended by bishop Hinds in 1839, and by the committee of the Privy Council on Education in 1861. One was set up at Bala in Wales by the rev. T. Charles in 1811. See under *Recreation*.

EVESHAM (Worcestershire), where prince Edward, afterwards Edward I., defeated the barons headed by Simon de Montfort, earl of Leicester, 4 Aug. 1265, when the earl, his son Henry, and most of his adherents were slain. Henry III. at one period of the battle was on the point of being cut down by a soldier who did not know him, but was saved by exclaiming, "Do not kill me, soldier; I am Henry of Winchester, thy king!" This victory broke up the combination of the barons.

EVICTIONS (in Ireland), 482,000 persons evicted from 1849-82, 119,000 reinstated as caretakers, see *Ireland*, 1886 *et seq*. Many evicted tenants made terms with their landlords, and returned to their farms, 1891-2.

Eviction commission appointed, see *Ireland*, 14 Oct. 1892
Report recommending reinstatement, &c., presented to the commons . . . . 9 March, 1893
24,000 evictions in Ireland from 1 Oct. 1881, to 30 Sept. 1887; 8,975 from 1 Oct. 1887, to 30 June, 1894; about 4,000 . . . . . . Aug. 1894
Bill for the compulsory reinstatement of evicted tenants in Ireland; passed by the commons, 7 Aug.; rejected by the lords (249—30), 14 Aug., 1894; by the commons, 26 Feb. 1896; again rejected by the commons . . . . 12 April, 1899

EVIDENCE, LAW OF, regulated by 14 & 15 Vict., c. 99 (1851), 16 & 17 Vict., c. 83 (1853), 32 & 33 Vict., c. 68 (1869).

Mr. Labouchere's application for a mandamus of the Court of Queen's Bench to compel sir Robert Carden to hear irrelevant evidence, refused 20 Nov. 1879
Documentary Evidence Acts, passed . May 14 1895

Prisoners in certain criminal cases were permitted for the first time in England to give evidence on their own behalf in 1872, and the practice has been legalised with good effect by 26 acts up to 1897.

The Evidence in Criminal Cases Act which makes this practice uniform in all cases, was passed 12 Aug. 1898

EVIL MAY-DAY (1 May, 1517), thus called on account of the violence of the apprentices and populace, directed against foreigners, particularly the French. The rioters were headed by one Lincoln, who, with 15 others, was hanged; and 400 more in their shirts, and bound with ropes, and halters about their necks, were carried to Westminster; but they crying "Mercy, mercy!" were all pardoned by the king, Henry VIII.

EVOLUTION THEORY includes the nebular theory and Mr. Darwin's doctrine of natural selection; see *Development*, and *Progressionists*.

In 1877 three forms of evolution were discussed:—1. That of all animals gradually from the lowest form, the amœba, up to man, in opposition to the Biblical account of the creation; 2. that of every animal from protoplasm in a cell, or egg; 3. that of all the parts of an animal from its blood. "Organic Evolution cross-examined, or some suggestions on the great secret of Biology," by the duke of Argyll, published April, 1890.

Mr. Alfred Wallace's work on "Natural Selection," published 1870; he was awarded the first Darwin medal by the Royal society, 1890.

EXALTATION, see *Cross*.

EXAMINATIONS of candidates for employment in the civil service has been enforced since 1855. Mr. Gladstone in 1862 said that the present might be termed the "age of examinations;" see *Civil Service*.

A strong protest against the system, fully signed, *Nineteenth Century*, Nov. 1888.

EXAMINER, liberal weekly journal, established Jan. 1808; last number, 26 Feb. 1881.

EXAMINER OF STAGE PLAYS, an office under the lord chamberlain, held by Mr. E. F. S. Pigott, appointed 25 Aug. 1874; died 23 Feb.; succeeded by Mr. G. A. Redford, March, 1895. His more recent predecessors were, George Colman, Chas. Kemble, John Mitchell Kemble, and Mr. Wm. Bodham Donne (1857-74).

EXARCHS, appointed by the Byzantine emperors of the East, to govern central Italy after its conquest by Belisarius and Narses, 548-553. They rule Ravenna from 568 to 752, when Eutychus, the last, was overcome by Astolphus the Lombard. The Exarch in the church was next in dignity to the patriarch.

EXCHANGE, formerly *Bourse*, the Royal Exchange being "Britain's Burse;" that at Paris is still named "*La Bourse*," from *bursa*, a purse. One called *Collegium Mercatorum* existed at Rome, 493 B.C. The Exchange at Amsterdam was reckoned the finest structure of the kind in the world. See *Royal Exchange*, and *Bills of Exchange*. The new building of the Baltic Mercantile and Shipping Exchange, on the site of Jeffrey's square, St. Mary Axe, covering 27,500 sq. ft., opened by the lord mayor 21 April, 1903.

EXCHEQUER, an ancient institution, consisting of officers with financial and judicial functions: the chancellor of the exchequer, the financial officer, formerly sat in the court of exchequer above the barons. The first chancellor was Eustace de Fauconbridge, bishop of London, in the reign of Henry III. about 1221. Sir Robert Walpole was the last chancellor of the exchequer who acted judicially (in 1735). The legal function of the chancellor was abolished by the Judicature act, Aug. 1873. Charles II. seized on the Goldsmiths' funds in the exchequer to prepare for war, 2 Jan. 1672. The English and Irish exchequers were consolidated by parliament in 1817; see *Chancellors of the Exchequers*, and *Tally Office*.

EXCHEQUER BILLS. The government securities, so called, said to have been invented by Montague, afterwards earl of Halifax, were first issued in 1697, and first circulated by the bank in 1796. These bills, of which more than twenty millions sterling are often in circulation, are in effect accommodation notes of government, that are issued in anticipation of taxes, at daily interest; and being received for taxes, and paid by the bank in lieu of taxes, in its dealings with the exchequer, they usually bear a premium. Amount in circulation, 56,974,780*l*. in 1817; in 1854, 16,008,700*l*.

Robert Aslett, a cashier of the bank of England, tried for embezzling exchequer bills, and found *not guilty*, on account of the invalidity of the bills, though the actual loss to the bank amounted to 342,697*l*., 18 July, 1803.

Mr Beaumont Smith tried for forging exchequer bills to the amount of 350,000*l*.; pleaded guilty; sentenced to transportation, 4 Dec. 1841.

EXCHEQUER BONDS, a species of public securities, introduced by Mr. W. E. Gladstone, in 1853, have not been well received.

TELLERS OF THE EXCHEQUER. Besides chamberlains of the exchequer, clerks of the pells, and auditor of the exchequer (offices which have all been discontinued since their last avoidance in Oct. 1826, or by surrender or abolition, in Oct. 1834), there were the four lucrative offices of *tellers* of the exchequer, also abolished, 10 Oct. 1834.

John Jeffreys Pratt, earl, afterwards marquis Camden, was appointed a teller of the exchequer, in 1780, and held the appointment until his death, in 1840. During nearly half of this long term he relinquished the income (amounting in the whole to upwards of a quarter of a million sterling) and placed it at the service of the state, as it annually accrued.

COMPTROLLER-GENERAL OF THE EXCHEQUER. This office was created on the abolition of the offices of the auditor and the four tellers of the exchequer, and the clerk of the pells, mentioned in the preceding paragraph. The first comptroller-general was sir John Newport, appointed 11 Oct. 1834.—34,438*l*. *per annum* have been saved to the state by the retrenchments in this department of the government.

COURT OF EXCHEQUER CHAMBER. Erected by Edward III. in 1357. It was remodelled by Elizabeth, in 1584, and then made to comprise the judges of all the courts. This court is for error from the judgments of the courts of queen's bench, common pleas, and exchequer of king's pleas in actions commenced therein. Re-modelled by act 2 Geo. IV. & 1 Will. IV. c. 70 (23 July, 1830).

The Exchequer office, Westminster, was instituted by Henry IV. in 1399.

"The Red Book of the Exchequer," an ancient record of feodaries, edited by Hubert Hall, 3 vols., published Oct. 1897.

CHANCELLORS OF THE EXCHEQUER.

Henry Addington (aft. lord Sidmouth)	21 March,	1801
Wm. Pitt (*premier*)	16 May,	1804
Lord Henry Petty (afterwards marquis of Lansdowne)	10 Feb.	1806
Spencer Perceval	31 March,	1807
And *premier* 6 Dec. 1809 (assassinated 11 May, 1812)		
Nicholas Vansittart (aft. lord Bexley) .	9 June,	1812
Fred. J. Robinson (afterwards lord Goderich and earl of Ripon)	31 Jan.	1823
George Canning (*premier*)	April,	1827
John C. Herries	17 Aug.	,,
Henry Goulburn	26 Jan.	1828
Viscount Althorp (aft. earl Spencer) .	22 Nov.	1830
Sir Robert Peel (*premier*)	10 Dec.	1834
Thos. Spring Rice (aft. lord Monteagle)	18 April,	1835
Francis T. Baring (afterwards baronet) .	26 Aug.	1839
Henry Goulburn	3 Sept.	1841

Charles Wood (afterwards baronet, lord Halifax, 1866) . . . . . . 6 July, 1846
Benjamin Disraeli . . . . . . 21 Feb. 1852
William Ewart Gladstone . . . . 28 Dec. ,,
Sir George Cornewall Lewis . . . . 5 March, 1855
Benjamin Disraeli, again . . . . 27 Feb. 1858
William Ewart Gladstone, again . . . June, 1859
Benjamin Disraeli, again . . . . 6 July, 1866
George Ward Hunt . . . . . 29 Feb. 1868
Robert Lowe . . . . . . 9 Dec. ,,
William Ewart Gladstone (and *premier*) . Aug. 1873
Sir Stafford Northcote . . . . 21 Feb. 1874
William Ewart Gladstone (and *premier*) 28 April, 1880
Hugh Culling Eardley Childers . . . Dec. 1882
Sir Michael Hicks-Beach . . . 24 June, 1885
Sir William V. Harcourt . . . about 6 Feb. 1886
Lord Randolph Henry Churchill (resigned) 26 July, ,,
George Joachim Goschen . . . . 3 Jan. 1887
Sir William V. Harcourt . . . . 18 Aug. 1892
Sir Michael Hicks-Beach (resigned 1902) . July, 1895
Chas. T. Ritchie, resigned 18 Sept. 1903 . 8 Aug. 1902
J. Austen Chamberlain . . . . 9 Oct. 1903

EXCHEQUER, COURT OF (*Curia Regis*), instituted by William I. on the model of the Transmarine Exchequer of Normandy, in 1079; according to some authorities, by Henry I. It included the common pleas until they were separated, 16 John, 1215. *Coke's Reports.* The exchequer is so named from a chequered cloth which anciently covered the table where the judges and chief officers sat.* Here are tried all causes relating to the king's revenue; such as are concerning accounts, disbursements, customs, and fines imposed, as well as all matters at common law between subject and subject. The judges are styled barons, first appointed 1234. There were a chief and four puisne barons: the fifth judge having been added 23 July, 1830. The office of Cursitor Baron was abolished in 1856. For changes, see *Supreme Court*. The ancient court sat for last time, 10 July, 1875. The Exchequer division was abolished in 1881; in Ireland in 1887. See *Supreme Court Judicature Act*, passed 27 Aug. 1881.

CHIEF BARONS.

1689. Sir Robert Atkins. 10 April.
1695. Sir Edward Ward. 10 June.
1714. Sir Samuel Dodd. 22 Nov.
1716. Sir Thomas Bury. 11 June.
1722. Sir James Montagu. 9 May.
1723. Sir Robert Eyre. 5 Dec.
1725. Sir Geoffrey Gilbert. 1 June.
1726. Sir Thomas Pengelly. 29 Oct.
1730. Sir James Reynolds. 30 April.
1738. Sir John Comyn. 7 July.
1740. Sir Edmund Probyn. 24 Nov.
1742. Sir Thomas Parker. 29 Nov.
1772. Sir Sidney Stafford Smythe. 29 Oct.
1777. Sir John Skynner. 17 Dec.
1787. Sir James Eyre. 26 Jan.
1793. Sir Archibald Macdonald 12 Feb.
1813. Sir Vicary Gibbs. 8 Nov.
1814. Sir Alexander Thomson. 24 Feb.
1817. Sir Richard Richards. 22 April.
1824. Sir William Alexander. 9 Jan.
1831. John, lord Lyndhurst. 18 Jan. Previously lord chancellor; again lord chancellor, 1834.
1834. Sir James Scarlett, 24 Dec. Lord Abinger, Jan. 1835.
1844. Sir (Jonathan) Frederick Pollock. 15 April.
1866. Sir FitzRoy Kelly. 16 July, [died 17 Sept. 1880.]
The last of the chief barons.

Sir Charles Edward Pollock, last of the barons, queen's remembrancer, born 1823, son of the chief baron, sir J. Frederick Pollock, died 21 Nov. 1897. Master George Pollock, senior master and king's remembrancer retires, succeeded by lord Dunboyne, Dec. 1901.

* In process of time the court of exchequer became gradually enlarged in its jurisdiction, until at length it was not merely a revenue court and one at common law between subject and subject, but one in which suits in equity were also instituted. In fact, until the act 5 Vict. c. 5 (1841), the court of exchequer possessed a triple jurisdiction; but by this statute its equity business was transferred to the court of chancery.

CHIEF BARONS OF EXCHEQUER IN IRELAND.

1690. John Hely. 5 Dec.
1695. Robert Doyne. 10 May.
1703. Nehemiah Donnellan. 27 Dec.
1706. Richard Freeman. 25 June.
1707. Robert Rochfort. 12 June.
1714. Joseph Deane. 14 Oct.
1715. Jeffrey Gilbert. 16 June.
1722. Bernard Hale. 9 June.
1725. Thomas Dalton. 2 Sept.
1730. Thomas Marlay. 29 Sept.
1741. John Bowes. 21 Dec.
1757. Edward Willis. 11 March.
1766. Anthony Foster. 5 Sept.
1777. James Dennis (aftds. baron Tracton). 3 July.
1782. Walter Hussey Burgh. 2 July.
1783. Barry Yelverton (afterwards viscount Avonmore). 29 Nov.
1805. Standish O'Grady (aft. viscount Guillamore) 5 Oct
1831. Henry Joy. 6 Jan.
1838. Stephen Woulfe. 20 July.
1840. Maziere Brady. 11 Feb.
1846. David Richard Pigott; 1 Sept., died 22 Dec. 1873.
1874. Christopher Palles. Jan.
The last of the chief barons.

EXCISE. The system was established in England by the Long Parliament in 1643, duties being levied on wines, beer, &c., and tobacco, to support the army against Charles I. It was continued under Charles II. Sir Robert Walpole's plan for extending the excise and introducing the bonding system was withdrawn through vehement opposition in 1733. Farming the excise duties led to many evils, see *Smugglers*. *Bonded warehouses* for the temporary storage of exciseable goods, authorised in 1802, were begun in 1823. The system was modified in 1882. Bonds for the payment of the duties are entered into by the importers. The old excise office was built on the site of Gresham college in 1774; the present is at Somerset-house. The officers of excise and customs were deprived of their votes for returning members to parliament in 1782; but received them again in 1868. In 1849 the boards of excise, stamps and taxes, were united, as "*the board of commissioners of inland revenue.*" Notwithstanding the abolition of the excise duty upon numerous articles, and the reduction of duty upon various others, of late years, the total excise revenue, so far from having decreased, has progressively advanced (1847 and 1861 excepted) in its aggregate annual amount. Additional excise duties were charged by 17 & 18 Vict. c. 27, July 3, 1854. The excise duties were further modified in 1860–94; see *Revenue*.

REVENUE FROM EXCISE.

Great Britain.

Year	Amount	Year	Amount
1744 . .	£3,754,072	1877 to Mar. 31.	£27,681,523
1786 . . .	5,540,114	1878 ,, ,,	27,710,514
1808. . .	19,867,914	1879 ,, ,,	27,186,021
1820 . . .	26,364,702	1880 ,, ,,	25,218,303
1827 (*United*		1881 ,, ,,	25,372,183
Kingdom) .	20,995,324	1882 ,, ,,	27,170,798
1830. . .	18,644,385	1883 ,, ,,	26,982,916
1834 . . .	16,877,292	1884 ,, ,,	27,048,051
1837 . .	14,518,142	1885 ,, ,,	26,501,612
1840 . . .	12,607,766	1886 ,, ,,	25,441,922
1845. . .	13,585,583	1887 ,, ,,	25,212,883
1847 . . .	12,883,678	1888 ,, ,,	25,625,520
1848. . .	13,919,652	1890 ,, ,,	24,160,000
1850 . . .	15,278,208	1891 ,, ,,	24,788,000
1858 to Mar. 31.	17,901,545	1892 ,, ,,	25,717,425
1860 ,, ,,	20,240,467	1893 ,, ,,	25,283,134
1865 ,, ,,	19,428,324	1894 ,, ,,	25,246,861
1868 ,, ,,	20,190,338	1895 ,, ,,	26,050,000
1869 ,, ,,	20,475,740	1896 ,, ,,	26,800,000
1870 ,, ,,	21,879,238	1897 ,, ,,	27,460,000
1871 ,, ,,	22,833,907	1898 ,, ,,	28,300,000
1872 ,, ,,	23,386,064	1899 ,, ,,	29,200,000
1873 ,, ,,	25,904,450	1900 ,, ,,	32,100,000
1874 ,, ,,	27,115,969	1901 ,, ,,	33,100,000
1875 ,, ,,	27,254,132	1902 ,, ,,	31,600,000
1876 ,, ,,	27,569,323	1903 ,, ,,	32,100,000

EXCLUSION BILL (to exclude the duke of York, afterwards James II., from the throne), was passed by the commons, but rejected by the lords in 1680. The revival of the question led to the dissolution of parliament in 1681.

EXCOMMUNICATION, or separation from Christian communion (*Matt.* xviii. 17; 1 *Cor.* v., &c.), was instituted to preserve the purity of the church. The Roman church excommunicated by *Bell, Book, and Candle* (*which see*). See *Interdict*.

Gregory VII. excommunicated the emperor Henry IV., and absolved his subjects from their allegiance 1077

Innocent III. excommunicated John of England, placing the country under an interdict . 1208-14

Gregory IX. excommunicated the emperor Frederick II. four times between . . . 1228-45

Louis XII. of France was excommunicated by Julius II. 1510; Luther by Leo X. 1521; Henry VIII. of England by Paul III. in 1535; and Elizabeth by Pius V. . 25 April, 1570

The emperor of France, the king of Sardinia, and others, were virtually excommunicated (but not by name) on account of the annexation of the Romagna by Sardinia . . . . 29 March 1860

EXECUTIONS, see *Crime*. In the reign of Henry VIII. (38 years) it is said that no less a number than 72,000 criminals were executed. *Stow*. In the ten years between 1820 and 1830, there were executed in England alone 797 criminals; but as our laws became less severe, the number of executions decreased. In the three years ending 1820, the executions in England and Wales amounted to 312; in the three years ending 1830, they were 178; in the three years ending 1840, they were 62. The place of execution in London (formerly generally at Tyburn) was in front of Newgate from 1783 to 1868, when an act was passed directing executions to take place within the walls of prisons. The dissection of the bodies of executed persons was abolished in 1832, see *Death*, 1868.

John Calcraft, born 1800, executioner for London, 1828-1871, died 13 Dec. 1879; his successor, Wm. Marwood, died 4 Sept. 1883; he was succeeded by Berry; said to have resigned March, 1892; Jas. Billington, in 1894; died 15 Dec. 1901; succeeded by his son.

EXECUTIONS IN LONDON.

1820, 43;—1825, 17;—1830, 6;—1835, 0;—1836, 0;—1837, 2;—1838, 0;—1839, 2;—1840, 1;—1842, 2;—1843, 0;—1844, 1;—1845, 3;—1846, 2.

IN ENGLAND.

	England.	London.		England.	London.
1847	8	1	1874	22	5
1848	12	2	1875	18	1
1849	15	0	1876	22	6
1850	6	0	1877	23	4
1851	10	0	1878	15	1
1852	9	1	1879	17	3
1853	8	1	1880	13	4
1854	5	0	1881	11	0
1855	7	2	1882	11	0
1856	15	2	1883	14	1
1857	13	1	1884	16	2
1858	11	1	1885	12	3
1859	9	1	1886	19	0
1860	12	1	1887	21	3
1861	15	1	1888	16	1
1862	16	2	1889	14	0
1863	22	1	1890	16	3
1864	19	8	1891	11	2
1865	8	2	1892	17	5
1866	12	1	1893	16	1
1867	10	2	1894	18	1
1868	12	2	1895	10	1
1869	10	3	1896	19	6
1870	6	2	1898	11	0
1871	3	0	1899	15	6
1872	15	1	1900	13	6
1873	10	0	1901	15	0

EXECUTIONS OF REMARKABLE CRIMINALS.*

Gunpowder plot conspirators, Digby, R. Winter, Grant, and Bates, 30 Jan.; T. Winter, Rookwood, Keys, and Fawkes, 31 Jan.; Henry Garnett, jesuit; at London . . . . . . 3 May, 1606

John Felton, murder of duke of Buckingham; Tyburn . . . . . . 28 Nov. 1628

James, duke of Monmouth, treason; Tower-hill, 15 July, 1685

Charnock, King, and Keys, 18 March; sir John Friend, and sir Wm. Perkins ("assassination plot") . . . . 3 April, 1696

Capt. Wm. Kidd and three others, piracy 23 May, 1701

James, earl of Derwentwater, and William, earl of Kenmure, rebellion; Tower-hill . . 24 Feb. 1716

John Price, the hangman; murder, Bunhill-row, 21 May, 1718

Jack Sheppard, thief; Tyburn . . 16 Nov. 1724

Richard Turpin, highwayman; York 7 or 10 April, 1739

Lord Balmerino and others, rebellion; Tower-hill, 18 Aug. 1746

Lord Lovat, rebellion; Tower-hill . 9 April, 1747

Richard Wm. Vaughan, first forger of Bank of England notes . . . . . . 11 May, 1758

Eugene Aram, murder; York . . . 6 Aug. 1759

Earl Ferrers, murder of his steward; Tyburn, 5 May, 1760

Theodore Gardelle, murder; Haymarket 4 April, 1761

John Perrott, fraudulent bankrupt; Smithfield, 11 Nov. ,,

John M'Naughten, esq., murder of Miss Knox; Strabane . . . . 13 Dec. ,,

Elizabeth Brownrigg, murder of her apprentice; Tyburn . . . . 14 Sept. 1767

Daniel and Robert Perreau, wine merchants, forgery; Tyburn . . . . 17 Jan. 1776

Rev. Dr. Dodd, found guilty of forging a bond, in the name of lord Chesterfield for 4200*l.*; the highest influence was exerted to save him, but when the case came before the council, the minister of the day said to George III., "If your majesty pardon Dr. Dodd, you will have murdered the Perreaus;" Tyburn 27 June, 1777

Rev. Henry Hackman, murder of Miss Reay, mistress of earl of Sandwich; Tyburn . 19 April, 1779

Capt. John Donellan, murder of sir Theodosius Boughton; Warwick . . . 2 April, 1781

Christian Murphy (or Bowman), a woman; strangled and burnt for coining . . . 18 March, 1789

Richard Parker and others, mutiny at the Nore, 30 June, 1797

Mrs. Phepoe, celebrated murderess; Old Bailey, 11 Dec. ,,

Sir Edward Crosbie, high treason; Ireland, 4 June, 1798

Messrs. Sheares, high treason; Dublin 12 July, 1799

Galloping Dick, highwayman; Aylesbury, 4 April, 1800

Governor Joseph Wall, murder of serjeant Armstrong; Old Bailey . . . . . 28 Jan. 1802

Mr. Crawley, murder of two females; Dublin, 10 March, ,,

George Foster, murder of wife and child; Old Bailey, 18 Jan. 1803

Colonel Despard and others, high treason; Horse-monger-lane . . . . . . 21 Feb. ,,

John Hatfield (a rank impostor, who married, by means of the most odious deceit, the celebrated "Beauty of Buttermere"), forgery; Carlisle, 3 Sept. ,,

Robert Emmett, high treason; Dublin 20 Sept.

Richard Patch, murder of Mr. Bligh; Horsemonger-lane . . . . 8 April, 180

John Holloway, Owen Haggerty, murder of Mr. Steele; Old Bailey (28 of the spectators of this execution were trodden to death, and numbers were pressed, maimed and wounded), 23 Feb. 1807

T. Simmons, the man of blood, murder; Hertford, 7 March, 1808

Major Campbell, murder of capt. Boyd in a duel; Armagh . . . . 2 Oct. ,,

Capt. Sutherland, murder; Execution dock, 29 June, 1809

Richard Armitage, forgery; Old Bailey 24 June, 1811

John Bellingham, murder of Mr. Perceval; Old Bailey . . . . 18 May, 1812

* For some other executions, see *England*, 1535-6, 1618-41-45-83; and *Oates's Plot*.

Philip Nicholson, murder of Mr. and Mrs. Bonar; Pennenden-heath . . . . . 23 Aug. 1813
Francis Tuite, murder of Mr. Goulding; Dublin, 9 Oct. ,,
Charles Callaghan, murder of Mr. Merry; Horsemonger-lane . . . . . . 2 April, 1814
William Sawyer, murder of Jack Hacket; Old Bailey, 15 May, ,,
Eliza Fenning, administering poison; Old Bailey, 26 July, 1815
[Universally believed to be innocent; she denied her guilt on the scaffold; and thousands accompanied her funeral. In the "Annual Register" for 1857, p. 143, it is stated on the authority of Mr. Gurney, that she confessed the crime to Mr. James Upton, a baptist minister, shortly before her execution.]
John Cashman, Spa-fields riots; Skinner-street, 12 March, 1817
Murderers of the Lynch family. Wild-goose Lodge affair; Ireland . . . . . . 19 July, ,,
The three Ashcrofts, father and sons, murder; Lancaster . . . . 8 Sept. ,,
Brandreth and others, high treason; Derby, 7 Nov. ,,
Charles Hussey, murder of Mr. Bird and his housekeeper; Pennenden-heath . . . . 3 Aug. 1818
John Scanlan, esq., murder of Ellen Hanley; Limerick . . . . 16 March, 1820
Arthur Thistlewood, John Brunt, James Ings, John Davidson, Richard Tidd (see *Cato-street*); Old Bailey . . . . 1 May, ,,
John Chennell, Thomas Calcraft, murder of Mr. Chennell, senr.; Godalming . . . 17 Aug. ,,
Josiah Cadman, forgery; Old Bailey . 21 Nov. 1821
Samuel Greenwood, highway robbery; Old Bailey, 27 Dec. 1822
John Thurtell, murder of Mr. Weare; Hertford, 9 Jan. 1824
John Wayte, forgery; Old Bailey . . 24 Feb. ,,
Henry Fauntleroy, banker, forgery; Old Bailey, 30 Nov. ,,
Wm. Probert (an accomplice of Thurtell's in the murder of Mr. Weare; he became approver), horse-stealing; Old Bailey . . 20 June, 1825
Spitalfields' gang, highway robbery; Old Bailey, 29 Nov. 1826
Chas. Thos. White, arson; Old Bailey . 2 Jan. 1827
Edward Lowe, coining (the last coiner drawn on a sledge to the scaffold); Old Bailey 22 Nov. ,,
Catherine Walsh, murder of her child; Old Bailey, 14 April, 1828
William Rea, highway robbery; Old Bailey, 4 July, ,,
Captain Charles Montgomery was ordered for execution this day for forgery; but he took a dose (an ounce and a half) of prussic acid, to save himself from the ignominy of the gallows, and was found dead in his cell . . . . . . 4 July, ,,
William Corder, murder of Maria Marten; Bury St. Edmunds . . . . 11 Aug. ,,
Joseph Hunton, quaker, forgery; Old Bailey, 8 Dec. ,,
Wm. Burke, murderer (see *Burking*); Edinburgh, 28 Jan. 1829
Anne Chapman, murder of her child; Old Bailey, 30 June, ,,
Stewart and wife, murder; Glasgow . 24 July, ,,
Thomas Maynard, the last executed for forgery; Old Bailey . . . . 31 Dec. ,,
Mr. Comyn, arson; Ennis . . . 18 March, 1830
John Any Bird Bell, a boy of 14 years of age, for the murder of Richard Taylor, aged 13, Maidstone 1 Aug. 1831
John Bishop, Thomas Williams, murder of a poor Italian boy (see *Burking*); Old Bailey, 5 Dec. ,,
John Smith, James Pratt, unnatural crime; Old Bailey . . . . 8 April, 1835
Maryanne Burdock, remarkable case of poisoning; Bristol . . . . 15 April, ,,
John Pegsworth, murder; Old Bailey 7 March, 1837
James Greenacre, murder of Hannah Brown; Old Bailey . . . . 2 May, ,,
William Lees, murder of his wife; Old Bailey, 16 Dec. 1839
François Benj. Courvoisier, murder of lord W. Russell; Old Bailey . . . . . 6 July, 1840
Josiah Misters, wounding Mr. Mackreth; Shrewsbury . . . . 3 April, 1841
Robert Blakesley, murder of Mr. Burdon; Old Bailey . . . . 15 Nov. ,,
John Delahunt, murder of Thomas Maguire; Dublin, 5 Feb. 1842
Daniel Good, murder of Jane Jones; Old Bailey, 23 May, ,,
John Hulme, Samuel Bonsall, William Bland, murder of Miss Goddard; Derby . 4 April, 1843
William Crouch, murder of his wife; Old Bailey, 27 May, 1844
James Tapping, murder of Emma Whiter; Old Bailey . . . . 24 March, 1845
John Tawell, murder of Sarah Hart; Aylesbury, 28 March, ,,
Thomas Henry Hocker, murder of Mr. Delarue; Old Bailey . . . . 28 April, ,,
Joseph Connor, murder of Mary Brothers; Old Bailey . . . . 2 June, ,,
John Platts, murder of Collis; Derby . 1 April, 1847
Catherine Foster, murder of her husband; Bury St. Edmunds . . . . . . 17 April, ,,
James Bloomfield Rush, murder of Messrs. Jermy, sen. and jun.; Norwich . . . 21 April, 1849
Fred. George Manning, and his wife, Maria Manning, murder of O'Connor; Horsemonger-lane, 13 Nov. ,,
James Barbour, murder; York . . . 15 Jan. 1853
Hy. Horler, murder of wife; Old Bailey . 15 Jan. ,,
Grant, Quin, and Coomey, murder of Thomas Bateson; Monaghan . . . . . 9 April, 1854
Emanuel Barthelemy, murder of Mr. Moore and C. Collard; Old Bailey . . . . 22 Jan. 1855
William Bousfield, murder of his wife and three children; Old Bailey . . . . 31 March, 1856
William Palmer (of Rugeley), murder of J. P. Cook by poison; Stafford . . . . 14 June, ,,
William Dove, murder of his wife by poison; York 9 Aug. ,,
Joseph Jenkins, *alias* Robert Marley, murder of Cope, a shopman, in Westminster; Old Bailey, 15 Dec. ,,
William Jackson, murder of two children; Chester, 20 Dec. ,,
Lagava, Bartelano, and Pettrick, murder of two officers and piracy; Winchester . . 23 Dec. ,,
Dedea Redaines, murder of two girls at Dover; Maidstone . . . . 1 Jan. 1857
Thomas Mansell (after seven months' respite), murder of a soldier; Maidstone . 6 July, ,,
Capt. H. Rogers, murder of A. Rose, a black, with great cruelty; Liverpool . . 11 Sept. ,,
Thomas Davis, murder of wife; Old Bailey, 16 Nov. ,,
John William Beale, murder of Charlotte Pugsley, his sweetheart; Taunton . . . 12 Jan. 1858
John Thomson, *alias* Peter Walker, murder of Agnes Montgomery by poison—discovered by a child; Paisley . . . . 14 Jan. ,,
Christian Sattler, a German, murder of inspector Thain; Old Bailey . . . . 8 Feb. ,,
Giovanni Lani, murder of Héloïse Thaubin; Old Bailey . . . . 26 April, ,,
John B. Bucknall, murder of his grandfather and grandmother; Taunton . . . 24 Aug. ,,
Wm. Burgess, murder of his daughter; Taunton, 4 Jan. 1859
Joseph Castle, murder of his wife; Bedford, 31 March, 1860
William Youngman, murder of sweetheart, Mary Streeter, and mother and two brothers, on Aug. 16; Horsemonger-lane . . . . 4 Sept. ,,
James Mullins, murder of Mrs. Emsley, at Stepney; Old Bailey . . . . . . 19 Nov. ,,
James Johnson, murder of two non-commissioned officers; Winchester . . . . . . 1 Jan. 1861
Matthew and Charles Wedmore, murder of their aunt; Taunton . . . . . 5 April, ,,
Martin Doyle, barbarous attempted murder (*last execution for this crime*); Chester 27 Aug. ,,
Wm. Cogan, murder of wife; Old Bailey, 14 Oct. ,,
Thomas Jackson, a soldier, murder of sergeant John Dickson; Winchester . . 27 Dec. ,,
Wm. Charlton, engine-driver, murdered Jane Emmerson, to obtain the money she had saved for her funeral; Carlisle . . . 15 March, 1862
G. J. Gilbert, brutal murder of Miss M. S. Hall, on her way to church; Winchester . . 4 Aug. ,,
William Taylor, murder of Mr. Meller from revenge; he previously killed his own children; Kirkdale, 13 Sept. ,,

Catherine Wilson, murder of Mrs. Soames by poison [and of several other persons]; Old Bailey, 20 Oct. 1862

William Ockold (aged 70), murder of his wife, after 50 years' marriage; Worcester . . 2 Jan. 1863

Noah Austen, murder of Mr. Allen; Oxford, 24 March, „

Robert A. Burton, murder of a boy; Maidstone, 11 April, „

Edward Cooper, murder of his deformed son; Shrewsbury 11 April, „

Dennis Delane, hired Beckham and Walsh to murder his landlord, F. Fitzgerald . . 13 April, „

John Ducker, murder of Tye, a policeman; Ipswich, 14 April, „

Wm. Hope, violation and murder of Mary Corbett; Hereford 15 April, „

D. MacPhail and G. Woods, murder of Mrs. Walne; Kirkdale . . . . 25 April, „

Joseph Brooks, murder of Davy, a policeman; Old Bailey . . . . 27 April, „

Joseph Kelly, murder of Fitzhenry, a schoolmaster; Wexford . . . . 11 Aug. „

Thomas, Alvarez, Hughes, and O'Brien, ferocious murderers; Liverpool . . . 11 Sept. „

Alice Holt, murder of her mother; Chester, 28 Dec. „

Samuel Wright, murder of his paramour, 12 Jan. 1864

John Lyons and four others (foreigners); murder and piracy; Old Bailey 22 Feb. „

Charles Bricknell, murder of his sweetheart, 1 Aug. „

Franz Müller, murder of Mr. Briggs in a railway carriage (see *Trials*); Old Bailey 14 Nov. „

Ferdinand Kohl, murder of M. Fuhrkop; Chelmsford . . . . 26 Jan. 1865

Edw. William Pritchard, M.D., murder of wife and her mother; Glasgow . . . 28 July, „

John Currie, murder of major De Vere; Maidstone, 12 Oct. „

Stephen Forward, *alias* Ernest Southey, murder of wife and four children; Maidstone 11 Jan. 1866

Mary Ashford, murder of husband; Exeter, 28 March, „

John Wm. Leigh, murder of wife's sister; Brighton, 10 April, „

Robert Coe, murder of a young man for his wages, 30*s.*; Swansea . . . 12 April, „

John Grant, a soldier, murder of a boy; Exeter, 15 Aug. „

J. R. Jeffreys murder of his son (aged 7); Old Bailey, 9 Oct. „

Jas. Langhurst, brutal murder of Harriet Sax (6 years old) 16 April, 1867

Hubbard Lingley, murder of his uncle, Benj. Black; Norwich . . . . 26 Aug. „

George Britten, murder of his wife; Taunton, 29 Aug. „

John Wiggins, murder of his concubine, Agnes Oakes; Old Bailey . . . 15 Oct. „

Louis Bordier, murder of his concubine, Mary Ann Snow; Horsemonger-lane 15 Oct. „

Wm. O'Meara Allen, Wm. Gould (or O'Brien), and Michael Larkin, Fenians, for murder of Brett, a policeman; Salford 23 Nov. „

Frederick Baker, murder of a little girl, whom he afterwards cut up; Winchester . 24 Dec. „

Wm. Worsley, murder of Wm. Bradbury; Bedford, 31 March, 1868

Frances Kidder, murder of her husband's child; Maidstone 2 April, „

Timothy Faherty, for murder of his sweetheart, Mary Hanmer (for rejecting him), and

Miles Weatherill, murder of Rev. Mr. Plow, of Todmorden, and his maid (for revenge); Manchester; 4 April, „

Frederick Parker, murder of Daniel Driscoll; York, 4 April, „

John Mapp, murder of little girl; Shrewsbury, 9 April, „

O'Farrell, for attempting to assassinate the duke of Edinburgh; Sydney, N.S. Wales 21 April, „

Richard Bishop; murder of Alfred Cartwright; Maidstone . . . . 30 April, „

Michael Barrett, Fenian; for Clerkenwell explosion; THE LAST PUBLIC EXECUTION IN ENGLAND; Old Bailey . . . . . . 26 May, „

Thomas Wells, murder of Mr. Walsh, stationmaster at Dover; (*the first private execution*), 13 Aug. 1868

William Sherward, for murder of his wife, Norwich (see *Norwich*) . . . 20 April, 1869

Josiah Detheridge, murder of warder in Portland prison; Dorchester . 12 Aug. „

Wm. Taylor, soldier; murder of his corporal; Exeter, 11 Oct. „

Frederick Hinson, murder of his concubine, Maria Death, and of Wm. Douglas Boyd, her paramour, at Wood Green, Middlesex; Old Bailey, 13 Dec. „

Wm. Mobbs, purposeless murder of a child; Aylesbury . . . . . 28 March, 1870

Walter Millar, murder of Rev. Elias Huelin and Ann Boss (at Chelsea); Old Bailey . 1 Aug. „

John Owen or Jones, for murder of a family (7 persons) at Denham; Aylesbury . 8 Aug. „

Thomas Ratcliffe; murder of a warder in Portland prison; Dorchester . . . 15 Aug. „

Margaret Waters; murder of infants; baby-farming case; Horsemonger-lane 11 Oct. „

Patrick Durr; murder of his wife; Manchester, 26 Dec. „

Wm. Bull; brutal murder of an old woman; Bedford . . . . . 3 April, 1871

Michael Campbell; murder of Mr. Galloway at Stratford; Springfield gaol, Essex . 24 April, „

Richard Addington; murder of wife; Northampton, 31 July, „

Frederic Jones; murder of Emily Gardner, through jealousy; Gloucester . . 8 Jan. 1872

Edward Roberts; murder of Ann Merrick, who refused to marry him; Oxford 18 March, „

Wm. Fred. Horry; murder of wife; Lincoln, 1 April, „

Charles Holmes; murder of wife; Worcester, 12 Aug. „

Thomas Moore, murder of wife; James Tooth, soldier, murder of drummer; Francis Bradford, soldier, murder of comrade; Maidstone, 13 Aug. „

Christopher Edwards; murder of wife; Stafford, 13 Aug. „

Wm. Lace; murder of wife; Taunton 26 Aug. „

Augustus Elliott; murder of paramour; Old Bailey, 9 Dec. „

Mich. Kennedy; murder of wife; Manchester, 30 Dec. „

Edwd. Handcock; murder of wife; Warwick, 7 Jan. 1873

Richard Spencer; murder of paramour; Liverpool, 8 Jan. „

Hugh Slane and John Hayes; murder of Joseph Waine; Durham . . . . . 13 Jan. „

Mary Ann Cotton; murder of child (see *Poisoning*); Durham 24 March, „

Henry Evans, at Aylesbury; and Benjamin Hudson, at Derby, for murder of their wives 4 Aug. „

Thos. Hartley Montgomery, murder of Mr. Glasse, Omagh 26 Aug. „

James Connor; murder of James Gaffney; Liverpool 8 Sept. „

Charles Dawson, William Thompson, and Edward Gough; murders; Durham; Thos. Corrigan; m. of mother; Liverpool 5 Jan 1874

Edward C. Butt; murder of Miss Phipp, through jealousy; Edwin Bailey and Ann Barry; murder of child; Gloucester 12 Jan. „

Thos. Chamberlain; murder; Northampton 30 March, „

James Godwin; murder of wife; Newgate, 25 May, „

Frances Stewart; murder of grandchild; Newgate, 29 June, „

Thos. Macdonald; murder of paramour; Exeter, 10 Aug. „

Wm. Jackson; murder of sister; York . 18 Aug. „

James H. Gibbs; murder of wife; Usk . 24 Aug. „

Henry Flanigan; murder of aunt; Mary Williams; murder of Nicholas Manning; Liverpool, 31 Aug. „

John W. Coppen; murder of wife; Horsemonger-lane . . . . 13 Oct. „

Private Thos. Smith, 20th Hussars; murder of Capt. Bird, in revenge for slight punishment; Winchester 16 Nov. „

Robert Taylor; m. of Mrs. Kidd; Stafford 29 Dec. „

James Cranwell; murder of Emma Bellamy; Newgate. Michael Mullen, John McCrave, and Wm. Worthington; Liverpool . . . 4 Jan. 1875

Richard Coates; murder of girl, 10 years old; Chelmsford . . . . . 29 March, „

John Morgan; murder of comrade; Maidstone; John Stanton; m. of uncle; Stafford 30 March, 1875

Alfred T. Heap, quack; murder of Margaret McKivett; Liverpool . . . . . 19 April, ,,

Wm. Hole; murder of wife; Bristol . 26 April, ,,

Jeremiah Corkery; murder of policeman; Warwick, 27 July, ,,

McHugh, Gilligan, and Pearson (woman); murders; Durham . . . . 2 Aug. ,,

Peter Blanchard; murder of Louisa Hodgson; Lincolnshire . . . . . . 9 Aug. ,,

Philip Lebrun; murder of sister; Jersey, 12 Aug. ,,

Wm. McCullogh; murder of Wm. Watson; and Mark Fiddler; murder of wife; Lancaster, 16 Aug. ,,

Wm. Baker and Edward Cooper; murders; Liverpool . . . . 6 Sept. ,,

Henry Wainwright; murder of Harriet Lane, his mistress (see *Whitechapel*); Newgate, 21 Dec. ,,

Wm. Smedley; murder of Elizabeth Firth, his mistress; Armley, near Leeds . . 21 Dec. ,,

John William Anderson; murder of wife; Newcastle-on-Tyne . . . . 22 Dec. ,,

Richard Charlton; m. of wife; Morpeth 23 Dec. ,,

George Hunter; murder of fellow-workman; Morpeth . . . . . . 28 March, 1876

Thos. Fordred; murder of Ann Bridger; Maidstone . . . . . . 4 April, ,,

George Hill; murder of his illegitimate child, and nearly of its mother; Hertford . 10 April, ,,

Edward Deacon; murder of wife; Bristol, 24 April, ,,

John Webber; murder; Cardiff . 26 April, ,,

Henry Webster; murder of wife; Norwich, 1 May, ,,

"Lennie" mutineers and murderers: Matteo Cargalis, Pascalis Caludis, George Kaida, and Giovanni Carcaris; Newgate . . 23 May, ,,

John Williams; shot his brother-in-law; Durham, 26 July, ,,

James Parris; murder of a child; Maidstone 1 Aug. ,,

Wm. Fish; murder of a child (see *Trials*); Richard Thompson, murder of J. H. Blundell: Liverpool; 14 Aug. ,,

C. E. Baumbos (see *Mutinies*); and Crowe (see *Ireland*): Cork . . . . 25 Aug. ,,

John Ebelthrift; murder of wife; Newgate 26 Aug. ,,

Charles O'Donnell; murder of wife; Newgate 11 Dec. ,,

Robert Browning; murder of Emma Rolfe, aged 16; Cambridge . . . . . . 14 Dec. ,,

Silas Barlow; murder of Ellen Sloper, paramour; Horsemonger-lane; James Dalgleish; murder of Sarah Wright; Carlisle . . 19 Dec. ,,

John Thomas Green; murder of wife; Leicester, 20 Dec. ,,

Wm. Flanagan; murder of paramour; Manchester 21 Dec. ,,

Isaac Marks, Jew; murder of Fredk. Barnard, for revenge; (Newington murder); Horsemonger-lane 2 Jan. 1877

Henry & Francis George Tidbury; murder of two policemen; Reading . . . 12 March, ,,

Wm. Clark (or Slenderman); murder of Henry Walker, gamekeeper; Lincoln 26 March, ,,

John McKenna; murder of wife; Manchester 27 March, ,,

James Bannister; murder of wife; Chester 2 April, ,,

John Henry Johnson; murder of Amos White; through jealousy; . . . . 3 April, ,,

Frederick Baker; murder of Mary Saunders; jealousy; Warwick . . . 17 April, ,,

John Henry Starkey; murder of wife; Leicester; Henry Rogers; murder of wife; Stafford 31 July, ,,

Henry Leigh; murder of child; Chester 13 Aug. ,,

Caleb Smith; murder of nominal wife (Eliza Osborne); Horsemonger-lane . . 14 Aug. ,,

John Goulding and Patrick McGovern; murders; Liverpool . . . . . 21 Aug. ,,

John Lynch; murder of wife; Newgate . 15 Oct. ,,

Thos. Pratt; murder of paramour; Newgate 12 Nov. ,,

Wm. Hussell; murder of wife; Exeter . 19 Nov. ,,

Henry March; murder of employer and fellow-workman; Norwich . . . . 20 Nov. ,,

Thos. Gray; murder of Ann Mellors, who refused him; Nottingham . . . 21 Nov. ,,

Cadwallader Jones; murder of paramour; Dolgelly, 23 Nov. ,,

James Sachwell, John Upton, and John Wm. Swift; brutal murder of an old man; Leicester 27 Nov. ,,

Geo. Pigott; murder of Florence Galloway; Manchester . . . . . . 4 Feb. 1878

James Caffyn; murder of Maria Barber; Winchester . . . . 11 Feb. 1878

James Trickett; murder of wife; Liverpool 12 Feb. ,,

John Brooks; murder of Caroline Woodhead; Nottingham . . . . 13 Feb. ,,

Harry Rowles; murder of sweetheart; Oxford 1 April, ,,

Vincent Knowles Walker; murder of woman; York, 15 April, ,,

Charles J. Revell; murder of wife; Chelmsford, 29 July, ,,

Robert Vest; ship steward; murder of Wm. Wallace, a pilot; Durham . . . 30 July, ,,

Thos. Cholerton; murder of paramour; Nottingham . . . . 12 Aug. ,,

Selina Wadge; murder of illegitimate child; Bodmin . . . . 15 Aug. ,,

Thomas Smithers, murder of woman, Wandsworth, 8 Oct. ,,

Patrick John Byrne; murder of two brother sergeants; Northampton . . . 12 Nov. ,,

Joseph Garcia, Spanish sailor, murder of William Watkins and his wife and three children, Usk, 18 Nov. ,,

James McGowan; murder of wife; Manchester; 19 Nov. ,,

Henry Gilbert; murder of illegitimate child; Huntingdon . . . . . . 25 Nov. ,,

Stephen Gambrill; murder of Arthur Gillow while defending his machinery (Wednesborough) Maidstone . . . . 4 Feb. 1879

Enoch Whiston; murder of Alfred Meredith; Worcester . . . . . . 10 Feb. ,,

Wm. McGuiness; murder of wife; Lancaster 11 Feb. ,,

Charles Peace; murder of A. Dyson Leeds; (see *Trials*, 1878-9) . . . . . . 25 Feb. ,,

James Simms; American seaman; murder of woman; Newgate . . . 24 March ,,

Edwd. Smart; murder of woman; Gloucester, 12 May ,,

Wm. Cooper; murder of Ellen Mather; Manchester, 20 May, ,,

Catherine Churchill; murder of husband; Taunton, 26 May, ,,

John Darcy; murder of Wm. Mitechalle; York; 27 May, ,,

Thomas Johnson; murder of Eliza Patten; Liverpool . . . . . . 28 May, ,,

Catherine Webster; murder of Mrs. Julia Martha Thomas; Wandsworth; (see *Richmond*), 29 July, ,,

Annie Took; murder of nurse-child; Exeter, 11 Aug. ,,

James Dilley; murder of illegitimate child; Newgate . . . . . . 25 Aug. ,,

John Ralph; murder of Sarah Vernon; Birmingham . . . . . . 26 Aug. ,,

Henry Bedingfield; murder of Eliza Rudd; Ipswich, 3 Dec. ,,

Charles Shurety; murder of child; Newgate, 5 Jan. 1880

Wm. Cassidy; murder of wife; Manchester, 17 Feb. ,,

Hugh Burns and Patrick Kearns; murder of Patrick Tracey at Widnes; Liverpool 2 March, ,,

John Wingfield; murder of his wife; Newgate, 22 March, ,,

Wm. Dumbleton; murder of John Edmunds; Aylesbury . . . . . . 10 May, ,,

John Henry Wood; murder of John Coe; York; 11 May, ,,

John Wakefield; murder of a child; Derby 16 Aug. ,,

Wm. Brownless; murder of sweetheart; Durham; 16 Nov. ,,

Wm. J. Distin; murder of paramour; Bristol; 22 Nov. ,,

Thos Wheeler; murder of Edward Anstee, near St. Albans . . . . . . 29 Nov. ,,

George Pavey; murder of Ada Shepherd, aged 11; and Wm. Herbert, murder of Jane Messenger, sister-in-law; Newgate . . . 13 Dec. ,,

Wm. Stanway; murder of Ann Mellor; Chester; 21 Feb. 1881

James Williams; murder of Eliz. Bagnall; Stafford; 22 Feb. ,,

Albert Robinson; murder of wife; Derby 28 Feb. ,,

Albert Moore; murder of old woman; Maidstone; 17 May, ,,

James Hall; murder of wife; Leeds . 23 May, ,,

Joseph P. McEntee; murder of wife; Liverpool; 31 May, ,,

Thos. Brown; murder of Eliza Caldwell; Nottingham . . . . 15 Aug. ,,

George Durling; murder of Fanny Musson, Maidstone . . . . 23 Aug. 1881
John Aspinal Simpson; murder of girl; Manchester . . . . 28 Nov. ,,
Percy Lefroy Mapleton; murder of F. T. Gold in a Brighton railway carriage; Lewes . 29 Nov. ,,
Alfred Gough; murder of a little girl; Derby ,,
Robert Templeton; murder of landlady; Manchester . . . . 13 Feb. 1882
Dr. G. H. Lamson; murder of Percy M. John (*see* Wimbledon); Wandsworth . . 28 April, ,,
Thos. Fury; murder of Maria Fitzsimons in 1869; Sunderland . . . . . . 16 May, ,,
Wm. Geo. Abigale; murder of girl; Norwich, 22 May, ,,
Osmond Otto Brand; murder of apprentice at sea; Leeds . . . . . . 23 May, ,,
Charles Gerrish; murder of fellow pauper; Wilts ,,
Wm. Turner; murder of wife; Liverpool, 21 Aug. ,,
Wm. Meager Bartlett; murder of infant; Bodmin, 13 Nov. ,,
Edward Wheatfill; cruel murder of Peter Hughes, aged 16; York . . . . 27 Nov. ,,
Bernard Mullarkey; murder of Thomas Cruise; Liverpool . . . . 4 Dec. ,,
Charles Taylor; murder of wife; Wandsworth, 12 Dec. ,,
Louisa Jane Taylor; murder of Mrs. Tregillis; Wandsworth . . . . . . 2 Jan. 1883
Abraham Thomas, a butler; murder of Mrs. C. Leigh; Manchester . . . . 12 Feb. ,,
James Anderson; murder of wife; Lincoln, 19 Feb. ,,
Thomas Garry; murder of John Newton; Lincoln 7 May ,,
Patrick Carey, or John White; murder of Thomas Eastam and Mary Moran; Chester . 8 May ,,
George White; murder of wife; and Joseph Wedlake, murder of Mark Cox; Taunton . 21 May, ,,
James Burton; murder of Elizabeth Sharpe; Durham . . . . 6 Aug. ,,
Henry Powell; murder of master's son, J. H. D. Bruton; Wandsworth . . . . 6 Nov. ,,
Thomas Lyons; murder of his child . 13 Nov. ,,
Peter Bray; murder of Thomas Pyle; Durham, 19 Nov. ,,
Thomas Riley; murder of Elizabeth Alston; Manchester . . . . 26 Nov. ,,
Henry Dutton; murder of Hannah Henshaw; Liverpool . . . . 3 Dec. ,,
Patrick O'Donnell; murder of James Carey, the informer; Newgate . . . . 17 Dec. ,,
Charles Kite; murder of Albert Miles; Taunton, 25 Feb. 1884
Michael Maclean; murder of Spanish sailor; Liverpool . . . . 10 March ,,
Mary Leffley; murder of husband; Lincoln, 26 May, ,,
Joseph Lawson; murder of sergeant Smith; Durham 27 May, ,,
Peter Cassidy; murder of wife; Liverpool, 19 Aug. ,,
Joseph Laycock; murder of wife and 4 children; Leeds . . . . 26 Aug. ,,
Thos. Henry Orrock; murder of policeman Cole; Newgate . . . . 6 Oct. ,,
Thomas Harris; murder of wife; Newgate 6 Oct. ,,
Kay Howarth and Henry Hammond; Swindell's murder; Manchester . . . . 24 Nov. ,,
Ernest Ewerstadt and Arthur Shaw; murder of women . . . . 8 Dec.
Horace Robert Jay; murder of a girl; Wandsworth 13 Jan. 1885
Henry Kimberley; murder of Mrs. Palmer; Birmingham . . . . 17 March, ,,
John Lee, murder of police-inspector Simmons Chelmsford . . . . . . 18 May, ,,
Moses Shrimpton, murder of policeman; Worcester, 25 May, ,,
Henry Alt, murder of C. Howard; Newgate, 13 July, ,,
Joseph Tucker, murder of Elizabeth Williamson; Nottingham . . . . . . 3 Aug. ,,
Thomas Boulton, murder of niece; Stafford, 17 Aug. ,,
Henry Norman, murder of wife; Newgate 5 Oct. ,,
John Hill and John Williams, murder of Ann Dickson; Hereford . . . . 23 Nov. ,,
Robert Goodale, murder of wife; *head severed through long drop*; Norwich . . . 30 Nov. ,,
Daniel Minahan, murder of wife; Newgate 7 Dec. ,,
George Thomas, murder of woman; Liverpool 8 Dec. ,,

John Horton, murder of his father; Devizes 1 Feb. 1886
Anthony Benjamin Rudge, John Martin, and James Baker, murder (see *Trials*); Carlisle 8 Feb. ,,
Joseph Baines, murder of wife; Lancaster 9 Feb. ,,
John Thurston, murder of H. Springall; Norwich 10 Feb. ,,
George Saunders, murder of wife; Ipswich 16 Feb. ,,
Owen M'Gill, murder of wife; Cheshire 22 Feb. ,,
Thomas Nash, murder of child; Swansea March, ,,
David Roberts, murder of David Thomas; Cardiff 2 March, ,,
Albert Edward Brown, and James Whelan, for murders; Winchester . . . . 31 May, ,,
Edward Hewitt, murder of wife; Gloucester 15 June, ,,
William Samuel, murder of Wm. Mabbott; Shrewsbury . . . . . . 26 July, ,,
Mary Ann Britland, murder of Mrs. Dixon; Manchester . . . . 9 Aug. ,,
Patrick Judge, murder of wife; Newcastle 16 Nov. ,,
James Murphy, poacher, murder; York 29 Nov. ,,
James Banton, murder of police constable; Leicester . . . . 30 Nov. ,,
George Harmer, murder of an old man; Norwich 13 Dec. ,,
Thomas Leatherbarrow, murder of woman; Manchester. . . . . 15 Feb. 1887
Thomas Bloxham, murder of wife; Leicester 14 Feb. ,,
Edward Pritchard, murder of Allen; Gloucester 17 Feb. ,,
Richard Insole, murder of wife; Lincoln 21 Feb. ,,
Benjamin Terry, murder of wife; Nottingham 22 Feb. ,,
Elizabeth Berry, murder of daughter; Liverpool 14 March, ,,
Joseph King, murder of woman and child; Newgate 21 March, ,,
Thomas William Carroll, murder of Lydia Green (see *Trials*); Newgate . . . 18 April, ,,
Charles Smith, murder of wife; Cowley near Oxford . . . . 9 May, ,,
Henry William Young, murder of child; Dorchester . . . . 16 May, ,,
Walter Wood, murder of wife; Manchester 31 May, ,,
Alfred Sowery, murder of sweetheart; Lancaster 1 Aug. ,,
Israel Lipski, murder of woman; Newgate 22 Aug. ,,
Henry Hobson, murder of Ada Stodhart; Leeds 22 Aug. ,,
Thomas H. Bevan, murder of woman; Chester 17 Aug. ,,
William Wilton, murder of wife; Lewes 29 Aug. ,,
William Hunter, murder of a child; Carlisle 14 Nov. ,,
Joseph Walker, murder of wife; Oxford 15 Nov. ,,
Joseph Morley, murder of woman; Chelmsford 21 Nov. ,,
Enoch Wadley, murder of woman; Gloucester 28 Nov. ,,
Thomas Payne, murder of his sister-in-law; Warwick . . . . 6 Dec. ,,
David Rees, murder of Thomas Davies; Carmarthen 13 March, 1888
Alfred Scandrett and James Jones, murder of Philip Ballard; Hereford . . 20 March, ,,
George Clarke, murder of stepdaughter; Winchester 27 March, ,,
William Arrowsmith, murder of his uncle; Shrewsbury . . . . . . 28 March, ,,
John Alfred Gell, murder of Mrs. Mary Miller; Manchester . . . . . . 15 May, ,,
James William Richardson, murder of Wm. Berridge; Leeds. . . . 22 May, ,,
Robert Upton, murder of wife; Oxford 17 July, ,,
Thomas Wyre, murder of son; Worcester 18 July, ,,
John Jackson, murder of warder Webb; Manchester, 7 Aug. ,,
Arthur T. Delaney, murder of wife; Derby 10 Aug. ,,
George Sargeant, murder of wife; Chelmsford 15 Aug. ,,
George N. Daniels and Harry B. Jones, murders; Birmingham . . . . . . 28 Aug. ,,
Levi Richard Bartlett, murder of wife; Newgate 13 Nov. ,,
Samuel Crowther, murder of John Willis; Worcester 11 Dec. ,,
William Waddell, murder of woman; Durham 18 Dec. ,,
Charles Bulmer, murder of wife; Leeds . 1 Jan 188

Thomas Clews, murder of woman; Stafford 1 Jan. 1889
George Nicholson, murder of wife; Warwick 8 Jan. ,,
William Gower, aged 18, and Charles Joseph Dobell, aged 19, confessed to murder of Bensley C. Lawrence, timekeeper at saw-mills at Tunbridge Wells; Maidstone . . . . 2 Jan. ,,
Ebenezer Samuel Jenkins, murder of his sweetheart; Wandsworth . . . . . 6 March, ,,
Samuel Rylands, murder of little girl; Shepton Mallet gaol . . . . . . 13 March, ,,
Thomas Allen, a Zulu; murder of F. G. Kent; Swansea . . . . 10 April, ,,
John Witney, murder of wife; Bristol 11 April, ,,
George Horton, murder of little daughter; Derby, 21 Aug. ,,
Benjamin Purnell, murder of wife; Devizes, 9 Dec. ,,
William Dukes, murder of Mr. Gordon; Bury, 24 Dec. ,,
Robert West and Frederick Brett, wife murder; Leeds . . . . 31 Dec. ,,
William Thomas Hook, wife murder; Maidstone, 31 Dec. ,,
Charles Lister Higginbotham, murder of landlady, 7 Jan. 1890
Joseph Boswell and Samuel Boswell, for murder of Frank Stephens, gamekeeper; Worcester, 11 March, ,,
William Row, for the murder of Lily McClarence; Newcastle-on-Tyne . . . . 12 March, ,,
Thomas Neal, murder of wife; Newgate, 26 March, ,,
Richard Davies, murder of father (see *Trials*), Knutsford, Cheshire . . . 8 April, ,,
William Chadwick, murder of Walter Davies; Liverpool . . . . 15 April, ,,
Daniel Stewart Gorrie, murder of fellow-workman; Wandsworth . . . . 10 June, ,,
George Bowling, murder of Eliza Nightingale, with whom he lived, Wandsworth 29 July, ,,
Felix Spicer, murder of two children; Knutsford, 22 Aug. ,,
James Harrison, murder of wife; Leeds 26 Aug. ,,
Frederick Davis, murder of wife; Birmingham, 26 Aug. ,,
François Manteau, murder of François De Grave; Newgate . . . . 27 Aug. ,,
Mary Eleanor Wheeler, otherwise Pearcey, for murder of Mrs. Hogg (see *Trials*); Newgate, 23 Dec. ,,
Thomas Macdonald, murder of Miss Alice Holt, schoolmistress, near Bolton; Liverpool; Robert Kitching, murder of policeman Weedy; York, 30 Dec. ,,
Alfred Turner, murder of sweetheart, Mary Moran; Manchester . . . . . . 19 May, 1891
Franz Joseph Münch, murder of James Hickey; Wandsworth . . . . 21 July, ,,
Arthur Spencer, murder of Mary Ann Garner; Lincoln . . . . 28 July, ,,
Walter Lewis Turner, murder of Barbara Waterhouse, 5 years old; Leeds . . 18 Aug. ,,
Thomas Sadler, murder of Wm. Wass; Chelmsford . . . . 18 Aug. ,,
Robert Bradshaw, murder of wife; Wandsworth, 19 Aug. ,,
John Conway, murder of Nicholas Martin, a youth; Liverpool . . . . . . 20 Aug. ,,
Edward H. F. Watts, murder of wife; Winchester, 26 Aug. ,,
Harry Dainton, murder of wife at Bath; Shepton Mallett . . . . 15 Dec. ,,
John William Johnson, murder of Margaret Addison; Durham . . . . . . 22 Dec. ,,
Charles Saunders, murder of child; Hereford, 23 Dec. ,,
James Stockwell, murder of Catherine Dennis; Armley, Yorkshire . . . . 5 Jan. 1892
James Muir, murder of Abigail Sullivan; Newgate, 1 March, ,,
Frederick Eggleton and Charles Rayner, poachers, murder of two gamekeepers, Joseph Crawley and William Puddlephat; Oxford . 17 March, ,,
Joseph Wilson, murder of Marion Greaves Crossman; Carlisle . . . . . 22 March, ,,
John Noble, murder of woman; London, 29 March, ,,
George H. Wood, murder of Edith Jeal; Lewes, 26 April, ,,
Harry Pickering, murder of wife; Leeds 14 June, ,,
John Gurd, *alias* Louis Hamilton, murder of Henry Richards; Devizes . . 26 July, 1892
John G. Wenzel, murder of Joseph Joyce, a police officer; and James Taylor, murder of wife; Newgate . . . . 16 Aug. ,,
Patrick Gibbons, murder of mother; Liverpool 17 Aug. ,,
Moses Culworth, murder of wife; Leeds 18 Aug. ,,
John J. Banbury, murder of Emma Oakley; Wandsworth . . . . . . 11 Oct. ,,
Thomas Neill, otherwise Cream (see *Trials*); Newgate . . . . 15 Nov. ,,
Joseph Mellor, murder of wife; Manchester 20 Dec. ,,
Thomas Edwards, murder of Mary Conolly; Usk 22 Dec. ,,
Cross Duckworth, murder of Alice Barnes, a child; Walton . . . . 3 Jan. 1893
Andrew G. M'Rae, murder of Annie Pritchard at Althorp; Northampton . . 10 Jan. ,,
Albert Manning, murder of Jane E. Flew; Gloucester . . . . . . 16 March, ,,
Edward Hemmings, murder of wife; Leeds 4 April, ,,
Richard Sabey, murder of Louisa Johnson; Northampton . . . . 18 July, ,,
Aimé Meunier, (extradited) murder of an old woman; Worcester . . . . 19 July, ,,
George S. Cooke, police-constable, murder of Maud Merton; Newgate . . . . . 25 July, ,,
Charles Squires, murder of child; Shepton Mallet, 10 Aug. ,,
John T. Hewitt, murder of Wm. Masfen; Stafford 15 Aug. ,,
John Davis, murder of police-sergt. Eves; Chelmsford . . . . 16 Aug. ,,
Emanuel Hamar, murder of an old woman, Catherine Tyrer; Manchester . . 28 Nov. ,,
John Carter, murder of wife; Reading . 5 Dec. ,,
George Mason, murder of sergt. James Robinson; Winchester . . . . 6 Dec. ,,
Henry Rumbold, murder of a woman named Rushby, at Lincoln . . . . 19 Dec. ,,
James Wyndham, murder of his father; Gloucester 21 Dec. ,,
William Harris, *alias* Haynes, murder of Florence Clifford; Warwick . . . . . 1 Jan. 1894
George Thomas, murder of Mary Jane Jones; Carmarthen . . . . . . 13 Feb. ,,
Walter Smith, murder of Catherine Cross, hospital nurse; Nottingham . . . . 27 March, ,,
Margaret Walber, murder of her husband, Liverpool . . . . 2 April, ,,
Philip Garner, murder of wife; Leeds 3 April, ,,
Frederick W. Fenton, murder of Florence Elborough; Birmingham . . . 4 April, ,,
John Langford, murder of Elizabeth Steven; Liverpool . . . . 22 May, ,,
Samuel Elkins; Winchester . . . . 18 July, ,,
William Crossley, murder of Mary Ann Allen; Manchester . . . . . . 31 July, ,,
Paul Koczula (24), murder of Mrs. Rasch in Shaftesbury avenue; Newgate . . 14 Aug. ,,
Alfred Dews, murder of infant son: Leeds 21 Aug. ,,
James Wilshaw Whitehead, murder of wife, Manchester . . . . 27 Nov. ,,
Thomas Richards (sailor), murder of Mary Davies, at Borth, 21 Sept.; Carmarthen . 29 Nov. ,,
James Canham Read, murder of Florence Dennis at Southend, June; Chelmsford . . 4 Dec. ,,
John Wm. Newell, murder of wife in Aug.; Leicester 9 Dec. ,,
Samuel George Emery (20), soldier, murder of Mary Ann Marshall; Newcastle-on-Tyne . 11 Dec. ,,
Cyrus Knight (45), murder of wife, and Wm. Rogers, murder of a woman; Winchester . 12 Dec. ,,
Edmund Kesteven, murder of Sarah Ann Oldham; Nottingham . . . . . . 26 March, 1895
Wm. Miller, murder of Edw. Moyse; Liverpool 4 June, ,,
Joseph Canning (32), murder of Jane Youell; Wandsworth . . . . 18 June, ,,
Henry Tickner (42), soldier, murder of wife, Wandsworth . . . . 2 July ,,
Robert Hudson, murder of wife and child, York, 13 Aug. ,,
Thomas Bond, murder of Fredk. Bakewell and George Hackett, Stafford . . . 20 Aug. ,,

Richard Wingrove, murder of Jane Eagle; Newgate, 19 Nov. 1895

Arthur Covington (27), murder of Effie Burgin (20), Bedford 3 Dec. ,,

Elijah Winstanley, murder of detective Kidd (Wigan), Liverpool 17 Dec. ,,

Henry Wright (35), murder of Mary E. Reynolds, her 2 sons and grandson, Nottingham 24 Dec. ,,

Patrick Morley (38), murder of wife, Leeds 31 Dec. ,,

Wm. James Morgan, murder of wife; Wandsworth, 4 Feb. 1896

Alfred Chipperfield (26), murder of wife; Newgate, 25 Feb. ,,

Wm. Seaman, Albert Millsom and Henry Fowler, Newgate, 9 June; see *Trials*, April, May, 1896.

Amelia E. Dyer, Newgate, 10 June; see *Infanticide*, May, 1896.

Charles T. Woodridge, murder of wife; Reading, 7 July, ,,

Samuel E. Smith, murder of corporal Robert Payne; Winchester 21 July, ,,

Philip Matthews, murder of his child; Winchester, 21 July, ,,

Frederick Burden, murder of Angelina Faithful; Winchester 21 July, ,,

Joseph Hirst, murder of child; Manchester, 4 Aug. ,,

Wm. Pugh (21), murder of Elizabeth Boot (19); Derby 5 Aug. ,,

Samuel Wilkinson, murder of an old woman, named Kaye; John Rose, murder of wife; Nottingham, 11 Aug. ,,

Joseph Robt. Ellis (22), murder of wife; Leeds, 25 Aug. ,,

James Jones, murder of Edw. White; Newgate, 6 Oct. ,,

Carlsen, Swedish sailor, murder of Julia Wood; York 22 Dec. ,,

Joseph Allcock (26), murder of wife; Nottingham, 23 Dec. ,,

Henry Brown, murder of wife; Wandsworth, 5 Jan. 1897

Robt. Hayman, murder of Esther Allchin; Maidstone 9 Feb. ,,

George Paterson, murder of a woman; Glasgow, 7 June, ,,

Joseph Bowser, murder of wife; Lincoln 27 July, ,,

Joseph Robinson (33), murder of wife; and Walter Robinson, murder of his cousin, Sarah Pickles; Leeds 17 Aug. ,,

Thomas Lloyd, murder of wife; Liverpool, 18 Aug. ,,

William Betts (47), murder of father; Maidstone, 16 Dec. ,,

George W. Howe (33), murder of Joseph K. Pickup; Manchester 22 Feb. 1898

John Herdman, murder of Jane Calder or Souter; Edinburgh 14 March, ,,

Charles Smith (33), murder of wife; Durham, 22 March, ,,

Private Kenny (Wilfrid Kreutze), (27), a Prussian, murder of private Goodwin; Clonmel gaol, 5 April, ,,

Walter Horsford (26), murder of Mrs. Annie Holmes, widow, Cambridge. See *Poisons* 28 June, ,,

James Watt, murder of wife; Norwich 12 July, ,,

William Wilkes, murder of wife; Chelmsford, 18 July, ,,

Thomas Jones, murder of Mary Bruton; Carnarvon 3 Aug. ,,

Joseph Lewis, murder of Robert Scott; Swansea, 30 Aug. ,,

John Ryan, murder of police-constable James Baldwin; Newgate 15 Nov. ,,

Thomas Daley, murder of a woman named Penfold; Maidstone 13 Dec. ,,

John Cotton, murder of wife; Derby 21 Dec. ,,

Johann Schneider, *alias* Mandelkow, murder of Conrad Berndt; Newgate 3 Jan. 1899

Patrick Holmes, murder of Ellen Lawlor (70); Kilkenny 7 Jan. ,,

Thomas Kelly (24), murder of his father; Armagh 10 Jan. ,,

Philip King, murder of wife and mother-in-law; Armagh 13 Jan. ,,

George Robertson, murder of Mary Kenealey (4): Newgate 28 Mar. ,,

Frederick Andrews, murder of Frances Short; Wandsworth 3 May, ,,

Josiah Cornelius Parker, murder of Mary Elizabeth Meadows; Northampton 11 July, 1899

Charles Maidment (22), murder of Dorcas Houghton (18); Winchester 18 July, ,,

Mary Ann Ansell (21), murder of sister, by sending her poisoned cake; St. Albans 19 July, ,,

Edward Bell, murder of wife by strychnine; Lincoln 25 July, ,,

Elias Torr, murder of daughter (26); Nottingham, 9 Aug. ,,

Frederick Preston (22), murder of Emily Mears, 3 Oct. ,,

Robert Ward (27), murder of 2 daughters, 4 Oct. ,,

George Nunn (18), murder of Eliza Dixon; Ipswich, 21 Nov. ,,

Charles Scott (28), murder of Eliza O'Shea; Reading 28 Nov. ,,

Samuel Crozier (55), murder of wife; Chelmsford, 5 Dec. ,,

Michael Dowdle, murder of wife; Manchester, 6 Dec. ,,

Louise Masset, murder of son ($3\frac{1}{2}$); Newgate. See *Trials*, Dec. 198 9 Jan. 1900

Ada Chard Williams (24), murder of a child; Newgate 6 March, ,,

Henry Grove (26), murder of Henry Smith (84); Newgate 22 May, ,,

Alfred Highfield (22), murder of Edith Poole, 17 July, ,,

Wm. James Irwin (61), murder of wife; Newgate, 14 Aug. ,,

Mellor, murder of his 2 children, and Chas. Blackhouse (23), murder of a policeman; Leeds, 16 Aug. ,,

William Lacey, a negro, murder of wife; Cardiff, 21 Aug. ,,

Charles Blewitt, murder of wife; Leeds, 28 Aug. ,,

John Parr (19), murder of Sarah Willett; Newgate, 2 Oct. ,,

Wm. Burrett, murder of wife; Chelmsford, 3 Oct. ,,

Joseph Holden (57), murder of grandson; Manchester 4 Dec. ,,

John Bowes (50), murder of wife; Durham, 12 Dec. ,,

James Bergin (28), murder of sweetheart, Margaret Morrison; Liverpool 27 Dec. ,,

Sampson S. Salmon (32), murder of cousin, Lucy Smith; Newgate 19 Feb. 1901

John Toole, murder of Lizzie Brennan; Dublin, 7 March, ,,

George Henry Parker (23), murder of Mr. W. Pearson. See *Railways*, 17 Jan. 1901. 19 March, ,,

Herbert John Bennett, murder of wife; Norwich, 21 March, ,,

Joseph A. Shufflebotham, a miner, murder of wife; Stafford 2 April, ,,

Valeri Giovanni, seaman, murder of Victor Baileff on the high seas; Bodmin 9 July, ,,

Chas. T. R. Watkins, a pilot, murder of Fred. Hamerton; Maidstone 30 July, ,,

Ernest Wickham (30), clerk, murder of Amy Russell in the street at Brixton; Wandsworth, 13 Aug. ,,

John Joyce, murder of an old man, John Nugent; Birmingham 20 Aug. ,,

Martial Faugeron (23), murder of Herman Jung; Newgate 19 Nov. ,,

Patrick M'Kenna, murder of wife; Manchester, 3 Dec. ,,

John and Robert Miller, uncle and nephew, murder of Joseph Ferguson; Newcastle 7 Dec. ,,

John G. Thompson, murder of Maggie Lieutand; Durham 10 Dec. ,,

Alick Claydon, murder of wife; Northampton, 13 Dec. ,,

John Harrison (31), murder of a woman, Wright; Liverpool 24 Dec. ,,

Harold Apted (20), murder of Frances Eliza O'Rourke ($7\frac{1}{2}$); Maidstone; and Richard Wigley (54), murder of Mary E. Bowen; Shrewsbury, 18 March, 1902

Arthur Richardson (26), murder of his aunt; Hull, 25 March, ,,

Chas. Robert Earl (55), murder of Margaret Pamphilon; Wandsworth 29 April, ,,

George Woolfe (21), murder of Charlotte Cheeseman; Newgate . . . . . 6 May, 1902
Thomas Marsland (21), murder of wife; Liverpool, 20 May, „
Samuel Middleton, murder of wife; Worcester, 15 July, „
Wm. Churcher, murder of Sophia Hepworth; Winchester . . . . 22 July, „
John Bedford, murder of Nancy Price; Derby, 30 July, „
Wm. Lane, murder of a woman, Dyson; Stafford, 12 Aug. „
George Hibbs, murder of a woman, Tye; Wandsworth . . . . 13 Aug. „
John McDonald (23), a hawker, murder of Henry Groves; Pentonville . . . . . 30 Sept. „
Henry Williams, murder of his child, Margaret Andrews; Pentonville . . . . . 11 Nov. „
Patrick Leggett, murder of his wife; Glasgow, 12 Nov. „
Henry Mack, 29, murder of Esther Elizabeth Bedford; Manchester . . . . 2 Dec. „
William Chambers, 47, murder of his wife and mother-in-law; Bedford . . . . 4 Dec. „
Thomas F. Barrow, 49, murder of Emily Coates his stepdaughter; Pentonville . . 9 Dec. „
Jeremiah Callaghan, 42, murder of a woman; Usk, Monmouthshire . . . . . 12 Dec. „
William Brown, 42, murder of his wife; Wandsworth: Samuel Walton, 31, murder of his wife, mother-in-law, and infant daughter: Thomas Nicholson, 24, murder of a little girl; Durham, 16 Dec. „
Wm. J. Bolton, 44, murder of Jane Allen; Hull, 23 Dec. „
George Place, miner, murder of Elizabeth Chetwynd, her mother, and infant child; Warwick: James Doherty, farmer, murder of his son; Sligo, 30 Dec. „
Joseph Taylor, murder of John Daly; Kilkenny: Mary Daly, his accomplice; Tullamore, 7, 9 Jan. 1903
Annie Walters, 54, and Amelia Sach, 29, for baby-farming murders . . . . . 3 Feb. „
William Hughes, reservist, murder of his wife; Ruthin, N. Wales . . . . . . 17 Feb. „
Edgar Edwards, murder of the Darby family; Wandsworth . . . . . . 3 March, „
Samuel H. Smith, murder of Lucy M. Lingard; Lincoln . . . . 10 March, „
Severino Klosowski, *alias* Chapman, murder of Maud Marsh by antimonial poisoning; Wandsworth . . . . 7 April, „
William G. Hudson, 26, soldier, murder of Harry Shoot, his comrade; Manchester . 12 May, „
Gustav Rau and William Smith, *alias* Dirk Herlaar, Germans, murder of the captain and 6 of the crew of the *Veronica*; Liverpool . 2 June, „
Samuel H. Dougal, ex-soldier, murder of Camille Cecile Holland (Moat farm, Clavering, Essex); Chelmsford . . . . 14 July, „
Wm. Joseph Tuffen, 23, murder of his wife Caroline; Wandsworth . . . . . 11 Aug. „

See *Addenda*.

EXETER (Devonshire), said to have been named *Augusta* from having been occupied by the second Augustan legion commanded by Vespasian: its present name is derived from *Excestre*. It was for a considerable time the capital of the West Saxon kingdom. The BISHOPRIC anciently comprised two sees: Devonshire (founded about 909) and Cornwall. The church of the former was at Crediton, of the latter at Bodmin, and afterwards at St. German's. About 1040 the sees were united. St. Petroc was the first bishop of Cornwall, before 900; Eadulphus, the first bishop of Devonshire, 905; and Leofric, the first bishop of Exeter, in 1049. The cathedral originally belonged to a monastery founded by Athelstan: Edward the Confessor removed the monks to his new abbey of Westminster, and gave their church for a cathedral to the united see, 1049; the see was valued in the king's books at 500*l*. *per annum*. Present stated income, 4200*l*. Population, 1881, 37,665; 1891, 37,580; 1901, 46,940.

Alfred invested the city, held by the Danes, and compelled them to capitulate . . . . 877 & 894
Exeter sacked by Sweyn 1003
Besieged by William the Conqueror 1067
The castle surrendered to king Stephen . . . 1136
The city first governed by a mayor 1200
The celebrated nunnery founded 1236
The ancient bridge built 1250
Edward I. holds a parliament here 1286
The Black Prince visits Exeter 1371
The duchess of Clarence takes refuge in the city . 1469
Besieged by sir William Courtenay . . . . „
City assaulted by Perkin Warbeck 1497
Exeter constituted a county of itself 1536
Welsh, the vicar of St. Thomas's, hanged on the tower of his church, as a Cornish rebel . 2 July, 1549
Annual festival established . . . . . 6 Aug. „
The guildhall built 1593
Prince Maurice takes Exeter for king Charles I. Sept. 1643
It surrenders to the parliamentarians . April, 1646
The canal to Topsham cut 1675
A mint established by James II. 1688
Water-works erected 1694
The sessions-house built 1773
The new bridge built 1778
The theatre erected 1783
Lunatic asylum founded 1795
County gaol built 1796
Devon and Exeter institution for the promotion of science established 1803
Subscription library founded 1807
New city prison built 1818
The last of the ancient gates removed . . . „
The subscription rooms opened 1820
The public baths erected 1821
Mechanics' institution opened 1825
New cemetery commenced 1837
Railway to Bristol opened . . . . 1 May, 1844
Great fire, 20 houses burnt . . . . 2 Aug. „
Another great fire . . . . . . 26 April, 1847
Inauguration of a statue of John Dinham, who died June, 1864, bequeathing 24,000*l*. to charities, 26 March, 1866
Bread and meat riots; suppressed . 4-5 Nov. 1867
Albert Memorial Museum given up to the town council . . . . 21 April, 1870
A new reredos, by sir Gilbert Scott (see *Reredos*), set up in the cathedral (1873): ordered to be removed by decision of the bishop and justice Keating, 15 April; this decision reversed by the court of arches (sir R. Phillimore), 6 Aug. 1874; the privy council decided that the reredos should remain . . . . . . 24 Feb. 1875
The church-tax "dominicals," or "sacrament-money," said to be of the nature of tithes; distraints for payment; much excitement . Oct. „
Destructive fire on the quay, of warehouses, &c. 22 Dec. 1882
Theatre Royal burnt during first performance of *Romany Rye*; panic and loss of about 127 lives; gallery exit insufficient 5 Sept.; (Percy S. M. Gosset, M.A., assistant master of Bradford college, Berks, and Robert M. Tamplin, B.A., victims) the coroner's jury censure the licensing magistrates and Mr. Phipps the architect 21 Sept. 1887
Captain Shaw agrees, and points out twelve serious defects in the construction, *Times* . 16 Nov. „
A new theatre opened . . . . . 7 Oct. 1889
Visit of the marquis of Salisbury; he addresses about 10,000 persons in a temporary building, 2 Feb. 1892
Church congress meets here . . . . 9 Oct. 1894
The duke and duchess of York open a new wing of the Albert memorial museum and visit the cathedral and hospital . . . . . 4 July, 1899
Sir Redvers Buller receives the freedom . 22 Nov. 1900
The lord mayor of London opens a manual school; is entertained by the citizens at a banquet, 12 Sept. 1902

RECENT BISHOPS.

1803. John Fisher, translated to Salisbury in 1807.
1807. Hon. George Pelham, trans. to Lincoln, Sept. 1820.
1820. William Carey, translated to St. Asaph, March, 1830.
1830. Christopher Bethell, translated to Bangor, 1830.
1830. Henry Philpotts, died 18 Sept. 1869.
1869. Frederick Temple, elected 11 Nov., and enthroned (after much opposition from some of the clergy) 29 Dec. 1869; translated to London, Jan. 1885.
1885. E. H. Bickersteth, resigned Nov. 1900.
1900. Herbert E. Ryle, 3 Dec. 1900, trans. to Winchester Feb. 1903.
1903. Archibald Robertson, Feb. 1903.

EXETER CHANGE (London), was built about 1680, on part of the site of Exeter house, the palace of Walter Stapleton, bishop of Exeter and lord treasurer in 1319, beheaded by order of the queen-regent, Isabella, in 1326. It was entirely demolished at the period of the Strand improvements, in 1829. The new Exeter Change, built by the marquis of Exeter near its site, opened in 1845, was pulled down in 1862, for the Strand Music-hall, now Gaiety theatre.

EXETER COLLEGE (Oxford) was founded by Walter Stapleton, bishop of Exeter in 1314. The college buildings mainly consist of a quadrangle in the later Gothic style.

EXETER HALL (Strand, London), erected in 1830-1 for the meetings of religious and philanthropic institutions, concerts, oratorios, and musical societies, a large and magnificent apartment with a splendid orchestra and organ, and having rooms attached for committees, &c., opened 29 March, 1831. See under *Music*. Religious services were held here in 1856 by the Rev. C. Spurgeon, and in 1857 by ministers of the church of England, on Sundays.

The Sacred Harmonic Society met here 1831-80; last concert, "Israel in Egypt," 30 April, 1880.

The hall was purchased for the Young Men's Christian Association for 25,000*l.* July 1880; re-opened (jubilee), 29 March, 1881.

EXHIBITION OF 1851 (THE GREAT EXHIBITION). The original idea of a *National* Exhibition* is attributed to Mr. F. Whishaw, secretary of the Society of Arts in 1844. It was not taken up till 1849, when prince Albert, president of the society, said, "Now is the time to prepare for a Great Exhibition, an exhibition worthy of the greatness of this country; not merely national in its scope and benefits, but comprehensive of the whole world; and I offer myself to the public as their leader, if they are willing to assist in the undertaking."

Royal commission appointed . . . . 3 Jan. 1850
A subscription list opened, headed by the queen for 1000*l.*
Civic banquets in support of the plan, at London, 21-22 March; and at York . . . . 25 Oct. ,,
The building † commenced . . . . 26 Sept. ,,
Many persons admitted into it in Jan.; it is virtually transferred to the royal commissioners by the contractors, Messrs. Fox and Henderson, Feb. 1851
Reception of goods began 12 Feb., and the sale of season tickets . . . . . . 25 Feb. ,,
The Exhibition opened by her majesty . 1 May, ,,
The number of exhibitors exceeded 17,000, of whom 2918 received prize medals and 170 council medals. The articles exhibited in arts, manufactures, and the various produce of countries, defied calculation.
The palace continued open above 23 weeks, altogether 144 days (1 May to 15 Oct.) within which time it was visited by 6,170,000 persons, averaging 43,536 a day, whose admission at the respective prices of one pound, half-a-crown, and one shilling, amounted to 505,107*l.* including season tickets, leaving a surplus, after payment of expenses, of about 150,000*l.** . . . . . ,,
The greatest number of visitors in one day was 109,760 (8 Oct.); and at one time (2 o'clock, 7 Oct.) there were 93,000; these persons were assembled at one time, not in an open area, like a Roman amphitheatre, but within a windowed and floored and roofed building. There is no like vast assemblage recorded in either ancient or modern annals, as having been gathered together, it may be said, in *one room.*
The Exhibition was closed to the public . 11 Oct. ,,
A memorial statue of the prince consort by Joseph Durham, placed in the gardens of the Royal Horticultural Society, uncovered in the presence of the prince and princess of Wales . 10 June, 1863
Prince of Wales elected president of the Royal Commission of 1851, in room of the king, who had held that office since 1870 . . 10 Feb. 1903

See *Crystal Palace.*

EXHIBITION OF 1862 (INTERNATIONAL). A proposal in 1858 for another great exhibition, to be held in 1861, was withdrawn in consequence of the war in Italy in 1859, &c. The scheme was revived in April 1860, when the prince consort engaged to guarantee 10,000*l.* if 240,000*l.* should be subscribed for by other persons.

A charter granted to the following commissioners: earl Granville, the marquis of Chandos, C. W. Dilke, jun., and Thomas Fairbairn . 22 Feb. 1861
The guarantee fund amounted to 349,000*l.* in Nov. 1860, and to 452,300*l.* . . . . 22 Aug. 1862
The building,† erected at South Kensington, by Messrs. Kelk and Lucas, according to a design by capt. Fowke, made over to the commissioners, 12 Feb. 1862

---

* Industrial exhibitions began with the French; *Expositions* having been organised and opened at Paris in 1798, 1801, 1802, 1806, 1819, 1823, 1827, 1834, 1839, 1844, and 1849, the last, being the eleventh, exceeding all the preceding in extent and brilliancy. The first exhibition of the kind in this country was the National Repository, opened under royal patronage in 1828, near Charing-cross. It was not successful. Other exhibitions were opened at Manchester in 1837, at Leeds in 1839, and at Birmingham in 1849. Exhibitions have since been held at Cork, Dublin, Manchester, New York, Paris, Montreal, Florence, Constantinople, Bayonne, Melbourne, Vienna, Philadelphia, and many other places (*which see*).

† The palace, with the exception of the flooring and joists, was entirely of glass and iron. It was designed by Mr. (aft. sir Joseph) Paxton (who died 8 June, 1865), and the contractors were Messrs. Fox and Henderson, to whom it was agreed to pay 79,800*l.*, or 150,000*l.* if the building were permanently retained. It cost 176,030*l.* 13*s.* 8*d.* Its length was 1851 feet, corresponding with the year; the width 408 feet, with an additional projection on the north side, 936 feet long, by 48 wide. The central portion was 120 feet wide and 64 feet high, and the great avenues ran east and west through the building; the transept near the centre was 72 feet wide and 108 feet high. The entire area was 772,784 square feet, or about 19 acres. Four galleries ran lengthways, and others round the transept. The ground-floor and galleries contained 1,000,000 square feet of flooring. There were altogether 4000 tons of iron in the structure, and 17 acres of glass in the roof, besides about 1500 vertical glazed sashes.

* This was placed in the hands of commissioners, who have promoted the South Kensington museum, and in 1876 proposed the establishment of a science library.

† The main building occupied about 16 acres of ground, and the annexes 7 acres. The south front was 1150 feet long and 55 feet high, and over the east and west fronts rose the two domes 260 feet high. The interior was decorated by Mr. John G. Crace. The building was given up to Messrs. Kelk and Lucas on 31 Dec. 1862, the house of commons having refused to purchase it for 80,000*l.* 2 July, 1863; and the pulling down commenced on 6 July. The domes and other parts of the structure were purchased or erection in Alexandra-park Muswell-hill near London (north).

The Exhibition opened by the duke of Cambridge and royal commissioners . . . . 1 May, 1862
The fine arts department included a noble collection of paintings and sculptures.
The jurors' award of medals was announced in the building . . . . . 11 July, ,,
The Exhibition was closed 1 Nov., when the total number of visitors (exclusive of attendants) had been 6,117,450.
The Exhibition reopened on 3 Nov. for the sale of goods exhibited; was finally closed 15 Nov. ,,
The success of the Exhibition was much impaired by the *decease of the prince consort*, 14 Dec. 1861, and the breaking out of the civil war in the United States of America. The foreign exhibitors in 1851 were 6566; in 1862, 16,456.
Exhibitors at London, in 1851, 14,000; at Paris, in 1855, 24,000; at London, in 1862, 29,000; at Paris, in 1867, 50,000. See also *Paris*, 1839 and 1900.

EXHIBITIONS, INTERNATIONAL. A meeting was held 4 April, 1870, the prince of Wales in the chair, to promote annual international exhibitions at South Kensington, to commence 1 May, 1871.

I. 1871. Fine arts, pottery, manufactures, &c.; opened by the prince of Wales, 1 May; closed 30 Oct. [34 countries contributed; total number of visitors, 1,142,154.]
II. 1872. Fine arts, machinery; and raw materials; opened by the duke of Edinburgh, 1 May; closed 19 Oct.
III. 1873. Fine arts; manufactures (silk, steel, surgical instruments, &c.; carriages for rails or tramways; food); scientific inventions and new discoveries; opened 14 April; closed 31 Oct.
IV. Fine arts; manufactures and raw materials, engineering, and recent scientific inventions; opened, 6 April; closed, 31 Oct. 1874.
[The annual exhibitions having proved unsuccessful, the building was appropriated by the East India Museum].
Exhibition of 1884, held at the Crystal Palace, opened on 23 April.
See *Fisheries, Forests, Sanitation*, and *Great Britain*.
INTERNATIONAL HEALTH EXHIBITION, 8 May–30 Oct. 1884
EXHIBITION of the products, manufactures and arts of India and the colonies at South Kensington (See under *Colonies*) . . . . 4 May–10 Nov. 1886

EXODUS (Greek, *way out*), a term applied to the departure of the Israelites from Egypt, 1491 B.C.; and described in the book of *Exodus*. Chronologers vary in the date of this event: the LXX. give 1614; Hales, 1648; Wilkinson, 1495; Bunsen, 1320 or 1314.

EX OFFICIO INFORMATIONS are those filed by the attorney-general, *by virtue of his office*, without applying to the court where they are filed for leave, or giving the defendant an opportunity of showing cause why they should not be filed. *Cabinet Lawyer*. They were used by the Liverpool administration about 1817-19. William Hone was tried on criminal information, 18-20 Dec., 1817, and acquitted. The British bank directors were thus tried, 1857.

EXPEDITIONS. Many are described under their respective heads.

Expedition of "the Nations" or "the Ditch"; the third expedition of the Koreish (*which see*) against Mahomet, named from the nations who marched under their leader Abu Sophian, and from the ditch which was drawn before the city. They were principally vanquished by the fury of the elements. *Gibbon*. 625.

BRITISH EXPEDITIONS.

France, near Port l'Orient . . . . 1 Oct. 1746
Cherbourg . . . . 7 Aug. 1758
St. Malo; 4000 men lost . . . . Sept. ,,
Quiberon Bay (*French emigrants*) . . . 1796
Ostend (*all made prisoners*) . . . May, 1798
Helder Point and Zuyder Zee . . . . Sept. 1799
Ferrol, in Spain . . . . . . Aug. 1800
Egypt (*Abercrombie*) . . . . . . March, 1801
Copenhagen . . . . Sept. 1807
Walcheren (*unfortunate*) . . . . . July, 1809
Bergen-op-Zoom . . . . . . 8 March, 1814
Crimea . . . . Sept. 1854
Abyssinia . . . . . Oct. 1867-April, 1868
Against the Ashantees (*which see*) . . 12 Sept. 1873
See *Egypt, India, Soudan, Niger, Somaliland*, &c.

EXPENDITURE, see under *Revenue*.

EXPLOSIONS, see *Boilers, Coal*, and *Gas*.

Criminal Explosions, close to the local government office, Charles Street, Westminster; great damage, no loss of life; 9 p.m.; 15 March, 1883.
Explosions (by nitro-glycerine?) 30 Oct. 1883, on Metropolitan District railway, between Charing Cross and Westminster stations; some damage; no persons injured. Metropolitan railway, near Praed Street Station; two third class carriages shattered; above 62 persons injured, 8.13 p.m. Capt. Majendie and prof. Abel consider it to have been caused by dynamite thrown from a railway carriage.
Victoria Station, Pimlico, building much injured, property destroyed, and two men hurt by an explosion in the cloak-room, 1.3 a.m., 27 Feb. 1884.
9.20, 30 May, 1884. Detective department, Scotland Yard, Whitehall; wall blown down, windows broken; public house wrecked, many persons injured, two seriously. 9.20 p.m. Junior Carlton club house and Sir W. W. Wynn's, St. James's Square, much damage, some persons injured.
Sixteen cakes of dynamite and fuse found at foot of Nelson's monument, Trafalgar Square, 30 May, 1884.
Explosion at Genoa, 10 June; at Madrid, 18 June, 1884.
Failure of attempt to explode S.W. end of London Bridge, about 6 p.m., 13 Dec., 1884.
Explosion in Metropolitan railway near Gower Street, (by a bomb shell), about 9 p.m., 2 Jan. 1885.
Three explosions, *see Parliament, Westminster Hall*, and *Tower*, 24 July 1885.
Mr. Richards, at Broadstairs, killed by explosives sent by parcels post, 22, 23 July, 1893.
Kurtz's chemical works, St. Helens, Lancashire, destroyed by explosion of potassium chlorate; 5 deaths, 20 injured; estimated damage, 100,000*l*., 12 May, 1899.
Explosion at a hat factory, Denton, near Manchester, 14 deaths, 14 Jan. 1901.
Explosion at Chilworth gunpowder works, near Guildford, 6 deaths, 12 Feb. 1901.

EXPLOSIVES: see *Gunpowder, Gun Cotton, Nitro-Glycerine, Dynamite, Dualine, Lithofracteur, Glyoxiline, Blasting, Gelatine, Bellite, Roburite, Helloffite, Melenite, Silotvor, Cordite, Ballistite, &c.* A committee to examine into the nature and properties of various explosives suitable for artillery was appointed by government in 1871-88. Col. Vivian D. Majendie, chief inspector of explosives to the Home Office, 1871, died, 24 April, 1898; succeeded by Capt. M. B. Lloyd. Explosives have been much studied by sir F. A. Abel of Woolwich since 1881 (died 6 Sept. 1902).

Professor Osborne Reynolds produced a new explosive, 75 parts chlorate of potash, 25 sulphuria, a product of coal gas; the ingredients kept apart till required; announced 1878.
The manufacture and use of explosives greatly increased 1885–6.
Carbo-dynamite, a new explosive, invented by Mr. W. F. Reid and Mr. W. D. Borland; announced April, 1888.
Schnebelite, a smokeless explosive (chlorate of potash, &c.), invented by the Abbé Schnebele, tried at Nunhead, Surrey, 21 Sept., 1893; at Argenteuil, 24 Jan., 1894; 29 smokeless powders known in 1895.
Tonite, or cotton powder; by its misuse in blasting a wreck in the Solent, 7 men were killed, 19 July, 1894.

EXPLOSIVES ACT, passed 14 June, 1875, amends the law with respect to the manufacturing, keeping, selling, carrying, and importing gunpowder, nitro-glycerine, and other explosive substances. Amendment act passed 1882.

A committee appointed in 1875; 20th annual report issued, 1895.

In consequence of the attempt at explosion in London in March, a new act to watch over the manufacture of explosives and punish possessors for felonious purposes, &c., passed by both houses, 9 April; royal assent, 10 April, 1883. The authors of attempted explosions are punishable with penal servitude for life.

EXPORTS. Edward III. by his encouragement of trade turned the scale so much in favour of English merchandise, that, by a balance taken in his time, the exported commodities amounted to 294,000*l.* and the imported to only 38,000*l.*; see *Revenue.* The declared value is of much less amount than the official.

OFFICIAL VALUE OF EXPORTS FROM GREAT BRITAIN TO ALL PARTS OF THE WORLD, VIZ.:—

Year	Value	Year	Value
1700	£6,097,120	1830	£66,735,445
1750	10,130,991	1835	78,376,732
1775	16,326,363	1840	97,402,726
1800	38,120,120	1845	131,564,503
1810	45,869,839	1850	175,126,706
1820	51,733,113	1851	190,397,810

DECLARED VALUE OF BRITISH AND IRISH PRODUCE EXPORTED.

Year	Value	Year	Value
1851	£74,448,722	1879	£191,531,758
1853	98,933,781	1880	223,060,449
1855	95,688,085	1881	234,022,678
1856	115,826,948	1882	241,467,162
1857	122,155,237	1883	239,799,473
1859	130,440,237	1884	233,025,242
1860	135,891,227	1885	213,115,114
1861	125,102,814	1886	212,725,200
1862	123,992,264	1887	221,913,910
1863	146,602,342	1888	234,534,912
1865	165,835,725	1889	248,935,195
1866	188,917,536	1890	263,530,585
1867	180,961,923	1891	247,235,150
1868	179,677,812	1892	227,077,053
1869	189,953,957	1893	218,094,865
1870	199,586,822	1894	216,005,639
1875	223,465,963	1895	226,128,240
1876	200,639,204	1896	240,145,551
1877	198,893,065	1901	280,022,376
1878	192,848,914	1902	283,540,000

Exports of all kinds to foreign countries, in 1875, 152,373,800*l.*; in 1876, 135,779,980*l.*; n 1877, 128,969,715*l.*; 1878, 126,611,428*l.*; 1879, 130,529,647*l.*; 1880, 147,806,267*l.*; 1881, 154,658,083*l.*; 1882, 156,640,727*l.*; 1883, 156,321,921*l.*; 1884, 152,149,296*l.*; 1885, 135,120,194*l.*; 1886, 137,053,799*l.*; 1887, 146,543,654*l.*; to British possessions in 1875, 71,092,163*l.*; in 1876, 64,859,224*l.*; in 1877, 69,923,350*l.*; 1878, 66,237,486*l.*; 1879, 61,002,111*l.*; 1880, 75,254,179*l.*; 1881, 79,364,595*l.*; 1882, 84,826,435*l.*; 1883, 83,477,552*l.*; 1884, 80,875,946*l.*; 1885, 77,929,626*l.*; 1886, 75,506,637*l.*; 1887, 75,135,849*l.*; 1888, 150,293,399*l.*; 1890, 176,160,202*l.*; 1891, 161,279,062*l.*; 1892, 152,446,884*l.*; 1893, 146,079,764*l.*; 1898, 90,110,736*l.*; 1899, 94,249,596*l.*; 1900, 102,024,054*l.*; 1901, 113,118,364*l.*; 1902, 283,423,966*l.*

EXTENSION, see *University.*

EXTINCTEUR, see *Fire-Annihilator.*

EXTRACT OF MEAT, obtained by Liebig in 1847; a company was formed to manufacture it in South America in 1866.

EXTRADITION TREATIES. The extradition of criminals formed part of the Ashburton treaty (*which see*), 9 Aug. 1842. Between Great Britain and France, 1843. In Dec. 1865, the French government gave notice of withdrawing from it in six months. It was renewed, with modifications, for six months, 21 May, 1866. A new act was passed, 9 Aug. 1870; amended in 1873. New act passed, 6 July, 1895. The treaty of Aug. 1876, amended 13 Feb. 1896. Similar treaties have been concluded with other powers; with Austria, 3 Dec. 1873 (amended 1901); Switzerland, 4 April, 1874; Holland, Aug. 1874; with Spain, 1878. Applications for extradition: 35 to England in 1896; 74 to, 8 by England, 1898; 51 to, 7 by England, 1899; 53 to, 20 by England, 1900; 63 to, 20 by England, 1901.

In 1866, M. Lamirand, charged with forgery and fraud against the Bank of France, fled to America. He was pursued, and was arrested at Montreal, on 1 Aug., under the governor-general's warrant. On 15 Aug., while his examination was still pending, he petitioned the governor-general not to warrant his surrender before he could apply for a writ of *habeas corpus*, and was assured on 17 Aug. that ample time should be allowed for this purpose. On 22 Aug. he was finally committed; and on 24 Aug. his petition for a writ of *habeas corpus* was presented to judge Drummond, twenty-four hours' notice having been given to the representatives of the crown and the Bank of France. After arguments had been heard and the case adjourned until the following day, he was surreptitiously carried off the same night by train to Quebec, and hurried on board a steamer bound for Europe, by virtue of an extradition warrant, purporting to be signed by the governor-general at Ottawa, on 23 Aug. He was conveyed to France, and on 5 Dec. was tried, found guilty, and condemned to ten years' imprisonment. These circumstances led to much discussion, and the Canadian authorities were censured for irregularity and want of discretion. The discussion ended by Lamirand declining British intervention.

Dispute with United States respecting the surrender of Ezra D. Winslow, a forger, by Great Britain, which is refused unless it is agreed that the prisoner shall only be tried for the offence for which he has been committed (according to the treaty) April, 1876

Mr. Hamilton Fish, the American foreign secretary, stands on Ashburton treaty of 1842, wherein no stipulation is mentioned; although it is found in other treaties with other governments.

Winslow was discharged, 15 June; and Brent, another fugitive, a few days after . . . . . ,,

The British Government yield, 27 Oct.; Brent recaptured, Dec. 1876. Winslow, claimed by Swiss government, escapes through flaw in the treaty; decision of queen's bench . . . 2 Nov. 1877

Stringent treaty, for anarchists and political offenders, between Russia and Prussia 13 Jan. 1885

Similar treaty between Germany and Russia proposed 12 Feb. 1885; accepted . . April, ,,

Enlarged treaty between United States and Great Britain proposed 1886; deferred till Dec. 1888; rejected by the senate (38–15) . . . 1 Feb. 1889

New treaty ratified by the senate, 18 Feb. 1890; it is an enlargement of the Ashburton treaty of 1842, proclaimed at Washington and gazetted in London . . . . 25 March, 1890

Extradition treaty between England and Russia April, 1887; with Portugal, 17 Oct. 1892; Roumania, 21 March, 1893; Argentine Republic, 7 Dec. 1893

Extradition treaty between France and Holland ratified . . . . 26 Dec. 1895

New treaty between United Kingdom and the Netherlands . . . . 26 Sept. 1898

Extradition treaty between Spain and the U.S.N.A., Aug. 1900; between Italy and Argentina ratified, 11 Oct. 1900

Extradition treaty between Great Britain and Servia . . . . 5 Feb. 1901

EXTRAVAGANTES, see *Decretals.*

EXTREME UNCTION, see *Anointing.*

EYLAU (Prussia), where, on 7-8 Feb. 1807, was fought between the French and Russians one of the most bloody contests of the war. Napoleon commanded in person. Both armies by this and other battles were so much reduced, that the French retired to the Vistula, and the Russians on the Pregel.

EYRE (old French for *ire*, to go on), the itinerant court of justices, the justices in eyre, was instituted by Henry II. 1176; and when the forest laws were in force, its chief-justice had great dignity. These justices were to go their circuit every third year, and punish all abuses committed in the king's forests. The last instance of a court being held in any of the forests is said to have been in 1671. *Beatson.*

F.

F's, Three (that is, "fixity of tenure, fair rents, and free sale"), term much used respecting Irish land question in 1880-1. Sir Stafford Northcote termed them "fraud, force, and folly," and they were much opposed by lord Dufferin and others.

FABII. A noble family at Rome, said to have derived their name from *faba*, a bean, because some of their ancestors cultivated this pulse; or to have descended from Fabius, a son of Hercules. According to the legend, the whole family, on behalf of the state carried on the war against the Veientes. During a march to Rome, they were surprised, and all the grown up males (306) were slain 477 B.C. From a boy detained at Rome, arose the noble Fabii of the following ages. Fabius *Cunctator* (the delayer) kept Hannibal in check for some time without coming to an engagement, 217-216 B.C.

FABLES. "Jotham's fable of the trees (*Judges* ix., about 1209 B.C.) is the oldest extant, and as beautiful as any made since." *Addison.* Nathan's fable of the poor man (2 *Sam.* xii., about 1034 B.C.) is next in antiquity. The earliest collection of fables extant is of eastern origin, and preserved in the Sanscrit. The fables of Vishnu Sarma, or Pilpay, are the most beautiful, if not the most ancient in the world. *Sir William Jones.* Professor Max Müller traced La Fontaine's fable of the Milkmaid to a very early Sanscrit collection. Æsop's fables (*which see*) supposed to have been written about 565 or 620 B.C., were versified by Babrius, a Greek poet, about 130 B.C. (*Coray*), and turned into prose by Maximus Planudes, a Greek monk, about 1320, who added other fables and appended a worthless life of Æsop. The fables of Phædrus in elegant Latin-iambics (about A.D. 8), of La Fontaine (1700) and of Gay (1727) are justly celebrated.

FACIAL ANGLE (that contained by one line drawn horizontally from the middle of the ear to the edge of the nostrils, and another from the latter point to the ridge of the frontal bone) was invented by Peter Camper to measure the elevation of the forehead. In negroes this angle is about 70°; in Europeans varies from 75° to 85°. Camper died 7 April, 1789. His book on "Characteristic Marks of Countenance" was published in 1791.

FACTIONS of the Circus among the Romans, were parties that fought on chariots in the circus, and who were distinguished by colours, as green, blue, red, and white; Domitian added gold and scarlet, about A.D. 90.

Nika sedition.—In Jan. 532, a conflict took place at Constantinople, lasting five days, when about 30,000 lives were lost, and Justinian was mainly indebted for his life and throne to the heroism of his empress Theodora. The blues and greens united for a day or two against the emperor, taking *Nika!* (overcome) for a watchword. The blues soon turned, and massacred nearly all the greens. The conflict was suppressed by Belisarius with difficulty, and the games were abolished for a time.

FACTORY SYSTEM was gradually developed by Arkwright and others, 1774, *et seq.*, to carry on the cotton manufacture, which has been greatly increased by the invention of machinery. The work had been previously executed by working men in cottages by the hand or stock cards, loom, and spinning wheel. Factories have immensely increased in this country since 1815. The Factory act, regulating the hours of labour, &c., was passed in 1833 and amended 1834 and 1844. Similar acts have been passed since; and an act for the extension of the principles of the Factory acts was passed in 1867 in relation to women and children employed in manual labour; short time on Saturdays was enacted. Other acts were passed in 1870-1878.

The Act of 1878 (like that of 14 July, 1874) relates to sanitary provisions, safety from machinery, hours of employment, meal hours, women and children, holidays, education of children, accidents, &c., passed 27 May, 1878. Consolidating act passed in 1883.

The earl of Shaftesbury, the energetic promoter of this legislation, died 1 Oct. 1885, aged 84.

New Factories and Workshops Act passed 5 Aug. 1891; amendment act passed, 6 July, 1895.

Mr. Alexander Redgrave, chief inspector of factories in 1851, retired, and was succeeded by Mr. F. H. Whymper, Sept. 1891.

Factory and Workshop act (laundry clause omitted), royal assent, 17 Aug. 1901; amended by act passed 20 March, 1902.

FACULTIES, COURT OF, giving powers to the archbishops of Canterbury and York, 25 Hen. VIII. cap. 21, 1534. Master lord Penzance, 1876.

FAENZA, central Italy, the ancient Faventia, submitted to the emperor Frederick I., 1162; was taken by Frederick II., 12 April, 1241; held by the pope, 1275; by the Bolognese, 1282; by Cæsar Borgia, 1501; by Venice, 1504; by the papacy, 1509; by the French, 1512. After various changes early in the 16th century it was acquired by the papacy and retained till the annexation by Sardinia, 1859. Faience pottery owes its name to this place, where it was invented.

"FAERIE QUEEN," by Edmund Spenser; a part was published in 1590; the whole, 1611.

FAHRENHEIT, see *Thermometer*.

FAINÉANTS, see *Mayors of the Palace*.

FAIRLOP OAK, with a trunk 48 feet in circumference, the growth of five centuries, in Hainault forest, Essex, was blown down in Feb. 1820. Beneath its branches an annual fair was long held on the first Friday in July, which originated with the eccentric Mr. Day, a pump and block maker of Wapping, who, having a small estate in the vicinity, annually repaired here with a party of friends, to dine on beans and bacon.

FAIROAKS, near the Chickahominy, Virginia, the site of two sanguinary indecisive battles between the Confederates, under general Joseph Johnson, and the Federal army of the Potomac, under general M'Clellan, 31 May and 1 June, 1862.

FAIR TRADE LEAGUE, NATIONAL, founded by lord Dunraven, Mr. Sampson Lloyd, Mr. David Maclver, and others, agriculturists and merchants, who issued a circular in Aug. 1881. It is opposed to what it considers unfair free trade.

They advocate recurrence to duties on foreign corn and manufactures, but not on raw materials.

Unsuccessful in the parliamentary election of 1885.
Meeting of the league 28 April and 2 Nov. 1887.
The National Association for the Preservation of Agriculture and other industries held a meeting in London 8 Dec. 1887.

FAIRS AND WAKES, of Saxon origin, were instituted in Italy, about 500; in England by Alfred, 886. *Spelman*. Wakes were established by order of Gregory VII. in 1078, and termed *Feriæ*, at which the monks celebrated the festival of their patron saint: the vast resort of people occasioned a great demand for goods, wares, &c. Fairs were established in France about 800 by Charlemagne, and encouraged in England about 1071 by William the Conqueror. Many statutes were made for the regulation of fairs (1328—1868). The "Fairs Act," passed 25 May, 1871, provides for the abolition of fairs; in 1872, Charlton and Blackheath fairs, and in 1873 Clapham fair, were abolished as nuisances. See *Frosts*.

An "old English fair" was opened at the Royal Albert Hall by princess Christian, to aid the Chelsea Hospital for Women, 9 June, 1881. See *Markets*.

FAITH, see *Defender*. "Faith-healing," see *Peculiar People*.

FALCK LAWS, see *Prussia*, 1873.

FALCONRY OR HAWKING in England cannot be traced with certainty before the reign of king Ethelbert, the Saxon monarch, 858. *Pennant*. The grand seignior at one time kept six thousand falconers in his service. Juliana Berners' book on "Hawkynge and Huntynge" was printed in 1496; see *Angling*. Recent attempts have been made to revive falconry. Hawking was practised in Thrace. *Aristotle*.

FALCZI, on the Pruth, Turkey. Here was concluded a *Peace* between Russia and Turkey, 21 July, 1711, the Russians giving up Azof, and all the possessions on the Black Sea to the Turks. The Russians were saved from imminent destruction by the address of Catherine the empress. In 1712 the war was renewed, and terminated by the peace of Constantinople, 16 April, 1712.

FALERII, a city of the Falisci, an Etruscan people who joined the Veientes against Rome, and were beaten by Cornelius Cossus, 437 B.C. It is recorded that when the city was besieged by Camillus in 394, a schoolmaster offered to betray to him the children of the principal citizens. On his refusal, the citizens from gratitude surrendered. They opposed Rome during the first Punic war; and in 241 the city was taken and destroyed.

FALERNIAN WINE, celebrated by Virgil and Horace, was the produce of Falernus, or, as called by Martial, Mons Massicus, in Campania. Horace in his *Odes* boasts of having drunk Falernian wine that had been, as it were, born with him, or which reckoned its age from the same consuls, 14 B.C.

FALKIRK (Stirlingshire, Scotland), the site of a victory by the English under Edward I. over the Scots, commanded by Wallace, part of whose forces deserted him. It is said from 20,000 to 40,000 Scots were slain, 22 July, 1298. A battle was fought at Falkirk Muir between the royal forces under Hawley, and prince Charles Edward Stuart, in which the former were defeated, 17 Jan. 1746.

FALKLAND ISLANDS, a group in the South Atlantic, belonging to Great Britain, seen by Americus Vespucius, 1502, and visited by Davis, 1592; explored by Hawkins, 1594; taken possession of by France, 1764. The French were expelled by the Spaniards; and in 1771, Spain resigned them to England. Not having been colonised by us, the republic of Buenos Ayres assumed a right to these islands, and a colony from that country settled at Port Louis; but owing to a dispute with America, the settlement was destroyed by the latter in 1831. In 1833 the British flag was hoisted at Port Louis, and a British officer has since resided there. Population in 1888, 1,890. Governors, Wm. C. F. Robinson, 1866; col. George A. K. D'Arcy, 1870; Thos. F. Callaghan, 1876; Thos. Kerr, 1880; Sir Roger T. Goldsworthy, Feb. 1891; Mr. W. Grey-Wilson, March, 1897. Falkland Islands created a crown colony, March, 1892. Population 1892, 1,789; 1901, 2,043.

FALLING STARS, see *Meteors*.

FAMILISTÈRE, see *Fourierism*.

FAMILY COMPACT, see *Bourbon*.

FAMILY OF LOVE, a society, called also Philadelphians, from the love they professed to bear to all men, assembled at Brew-house yard, Nottingham. Their founder, David George, an Anabaptist of Holland, propagated his doctrines in Switzerland, where he died in 1556. The tenets of the society were declared impious, and George's body and books ordered to be burned by the hangman. In England a sect with a similar title was repressed by Elizabeth, 1580; but existed in the following century. See *Agapemone*.

FAMINES. The famine of the seven years in Egypt began 1708 B.C. *Usher; Blair*.

Famine at Rome, when thousands of people threw themselves into the Tiber . . . . . B.C.	436
Awful famine in Egypt . . . . . A.D.	42
At Rome, attended by plague	262
In Britain; people ate the bark of trees	272
In Scotland; thousands died	306
In England; 40,000 perished	310
Awful one in Phrygia	370
In Italy, when parents ate their children (*Dufresnoy*)	450
In England, Wales, and Scotland	739
Again, when thousands starve	823
Again, which lasts four years	954
Awful one throughout Europe	1016
In England, 21 William I.	1087
In England and France: this famine leads to a pestilential fever, which lasts from . . . 1193 to	1195
Another famine in England	1251
Again, so dreadful that the people devoured the flesh of horses, dogs, cats, and vermin	1315
One occasioned by long rains	1335
One in England and France (*Rapin*) . . .	1353
Again, one so great, that bread was made from fern-roots (*Stow*)	1438
One throughout these islands	1565
Awful one in France (*Voltaire*)	1693
One general in these realms	1748
One which devastates Bengal	1770–1
At Cape de Verde; 16,000 persons perish . . .	1775
One grievously felt in France	1789
One severely felt in England	1795
Again, throughout the kingdom	1801
At Drontheim, owing to Sweden intercepting the supplies	1813
Scarcity of food severely felt by the Irish poor, 1814, 1816, 1822, 1831, 1846, in consequence of the failure of the potato crop. Grants by parliament, to relieve the suffering of the people, were made in the session of 1847, the whole amounting to ten millions sterling.	
In N.W. India; above 800,000 perish . . .	1837-8
In N.W. India; thousands perish . . .	1860-1
In Bengal and Orissa; about 1,000,000 perish .	1865-6
In Rajpootana, &c.; about 1,500,000 perish .	1868-9
In Persia very severe	1871-2
In Bengal, through drought. (See *India*) .	1874
In Asia Minor	1874-5
In Bombay, Madras, Mysore, &c.; about 5,000,000 perish (see *India* and *Mansion-house*) . .	1877

In N. China; very severe; 9,500,000 said to have perished (45,503l. collected in England for relief) 1877-8
In Cashmere (*which see*) 1879
Very severe in Tauris, &c., Asia Minor . July, 1880
Asia Minor 1887
China (*which see*), 1887-9; since in Kwang-si . . 1903
In Madras 1889-92
Montenegro . . . . ,,
Japan 1890
Very severe throughout Russia 1891-2
In Russia (*which see*) 1899, 1901-2
India (*which see*), Bombay, Rajputana, 1892; again (very severe), 1896-8; again . Sept. 1899—Jan. 1901

FAN. Used by the ancients; *Cape hoc flabellum, et ventulum huic sic facito,* "Take this fan, and give her thus a little air." *Terence's Eunuchus*, 166 B.C.—Fans, together with muffs, masks, and false hair, were first devised by the harlots in Italy, and were brought to England from France. *Stow.* In the British Museum are Egyptian fan-handles.

Great competitive exhibition of fans at Drapers' hall, London, opened . . . . 2 July, 1878
"English Fans and Fan Leaves, collected and described," by lady Charlotte Schreiber; a magnificent work was published by Mr. John Murray. It includes historical, allegorical and satirical pictures, Jan. 1889; her work on foreign fans was published April, 1891. Lady Schreiber was granted the freedom of the Fanmakers' Company, London 17 Dec. 1891
Exhibition of fans at Drapers' hall, London, opened 8 May, 1889. Similar exhibitions . . 1890 *et seq.*

FARADAY MEMORIALS, &c. Professor Michael Faraday, natural philosopher and chemist (see *Electricity*), died 25 Aug. 1867. A public meeting was held at the Royal Institution, 21 June, 1869, the prince of Wales in the chair, to take measures to provide a public monument to him. A sufficient sum having been subscribed, the production of a statue was entrusted to Mr. Foley. The statue was placed at the Royal Institution, London, in 1876. From the same fund a marble bust was provided and placed in the National Portrait Gallery, 1886. The "*Faraday Medal,*" to be given to distinguished foreign philosophers by the Chemical society, was awarded to M. Dumas, June, 1869; to professor Cannizzaro, May, 1872; to Dr. A. W. Hofmann, March, 1875; to professor A. Wurtz, and given to him after his lecture, 12 Nov. 1878; to professor H. Helmholtz, April, 1881; professor Demetri Mendeleef, June, 1889; lord Rayleigh, March, 1895, see *Argon*. For "*Faraday,*" steamship, see *Steam*. The centenary of the birth of Michael Faraday (22 Sept. 1791) was celebrated at the Royal Institution on 17 June, 1891; the prince of Wales, vice-patron R. I., in the chair; discourse by professor lord Rayleigh; on 26 June the duke of Northumberland, president, in the chair; discourse by professor James Dewar.

The "Michael Faraday" Board school, in Faraday-st., Walworth, opened by the marquis of Londonderry, 13 May, 1897; the marble bust of Faraday in the boys' hall of the school is a copy of one by Matthew Noble. It was presented by the managers of the Royal Institution of Gt. Britain, and was unveiled by their treasurer, sir James Crichton-Browne, M.D., F.R.S., at a public meeting, 15 Nov. 1897, Gen. F. J. Moberly, vice-chairman of the London school board in the chair; died, 26 Jan. 1898. The "Michael Faraday" home of rest for the poor at East Dulwich (the house given by Miss Isabel Faraday), opened . 25 Oct. 1901

FARADISATION, the medical application of the magneto-electric currents which Faraday discovered in 1837. Apparatus for this purpose was first made by M. Pixii, and employed by Dr. Neef of Frankfort. "*Farad,*" name taken for a unit of electric capacity, 1875.

FARCE, a short comic drama, usually of one or two acts. One by Otway is dated 1677. The best English farces (by Foote, Garrick, Bickerstaff, &c.) appeared from about 1740 to 1780. This species of dramatic entertainment originated in the droll shows which were exhibited by charlatans and their buffoons in the open streets; see *Drama*.

FARMERS' ALLIANCE, an organization of agricultural reformers; held a provisional meeting 27 May, and a conference 2 July, 1879. It was active during the elections of April, 1880. A Farmers' Alliance for Scotland was founded at Aberdeen, 1 Dec. 1881. The Farmers' Alliance in the United States, N.A., begun about 1873, became influential and elected about 23 representatives for Congress, Nov. 1890, see *United States, N.A.*

The Farmers' Club was established in 1843 for discussions on agricultural subjects.
"A Farmer's Year, 1898," by H. Rider Haggard, published 1899.

FARMERS-GENERAL, see *Fermiers*.

FARMERS' UNION, National, established at Leamington, by lord Walsingham and others, to oppose the Agricultural Labourers' Union, June, 1874.

FARNESE FAMILY became important through the elevation of Alexander Farnese to the papacy as Paul III. He gave his natural son Peter the duchy of Parma, and his descendants ruled till the death of Antony without issue in 1731. Alexander prince of Parma was governor of the Netherlands in 1579.

FARRIERS, see under *Horse, Horseshoeing*.

FARRINGDON-MARKET, erected by the corporation of London, near the abolished Fleet-market, was opened 20 Nov. 1829. After several changes it was re-opened as a Fish Market in 1882. The scheme was altogether unsuccessful, occasioning great loss to the corporation; abandoned, 1892.

FARTHING, an early English coin. Farthings in silver were coined by king John, in copper by James I. and Charles I.; the Irish farthing of John's reign (1210) is rare. Farthings were coined in England in silver by Henry VIII. First coined in copper by Charles II. 1665; and again in 1672, when there was a large coinage of copper money. Half-farthings were first coined in 1843; see *Queen Anne's Farthings*. A single copy of the "Penny-a-week Country Daily Newspaper" (conservative), No. 1, sold for ¼d., 25 June, 1873. The *Farthings Act*, 21, 22 Vict. c. 75, 1858, relates to the payment for portions of a mile travelled by third class railway trains.

FARTHINGALE, see *Crinoline*.

FASHODA, on the White Nile (Upper Nile valley), occupied by capt. (aft. major) Marchand, with 8 officers and 120 Sengalese (who had crossed from the French Congo, overcoming great obstacles), 10 July, 1898; see *Africa*; Dervish attack repulsed, 25 Aug.; see *Soudan*, 19 Sept., 1898. Diplomatic correspondence, blue book published, 9 Oct.; the Marchand mission recalled by the French government, 4 Nov.; they leave Fashoda, 11 Dec. 1898. Lieut.-col. Jackson appointed governor, 21 Jan. 1899.

FASTI CAPITOLINI, marble tablets dug up in the forum at Rome, 1547, contain a list of the consuls and other officers from the year of Rome 250 to 765. Other fragments were found in 1817 and 1818. The "Fasti Consulares," from 509 B.C. to

A.D. 235, are given at the end of Smith's "Dictionary of Greek and Roman Antiquities."

FASTS, observed by most nations from the remotest antiquity; by the Jews (2 *Chron.* xx. 3); by the Ninevites (*Jonah* iii.); see *Isai.* lviii. A fast was observed by the Jews on the great day of atonement. *Lev.* xxiii. 1490 B.C. Moses fasted 40 days and nights on Sinai, *Exod.* xxiv. 1491 B.C. The first Christian ministers were ordained with fasting (A.D. 45) *Acts* xiii. 2. Annual fasts, as that of Lent, and at other stated times, and on particular occasions to appease the anger of God, began in the Christian church, in the second century, 138. The Mahometan fast is termed *Ramadan* (*which see*). Fast days are appointed by the Reformed churches in times of war and pestilence (as 21 March, 1855, for the Russian war, and 7 Oct. 1857, for the Indian mutiny). The Jeynes, *which see*, have religious fasts of 30 to 40 days' duration. See *Abstinence*.

FATHERS OF THE CHURCH. The following are the principal:—

FIRST CENTURY. *Greek.*
Apostolical.

Hermas . .
Barnabas . .
Clemens Romanus, *d.* 100
Ignatius . . . *d.* 115
Polycarp . *d.* abt. 169

SECOND CENTURY. *Greek.*

Justin Martyr, *d.* abt. 166
Irenæus . *d.* abt. 200
Athenagoras.

THIRD CENTURY. *Greek.*

Clemens Alexandrinus . *d.* abt. 217
Hippolytus . . *d.* 230
Origen . . *d.* abt. 253

Latin.

Tertullian . *d.* abt. 220
Minutius Felix, *fl.* abt. 230
Cyprian . . *d.* abt. 258

FOURTH AND FIFTH CENTURIES. *Greek.*

Eusebius . *d.* abt. 340
Athanasius . *d.* 373
Ephrem Syrus, *d.* abt. 378
Basil . . . *d.* 379
Cyril of Jerusalem *d.* 386
Gregory Nazianzen . *d.* 389
Macarius . *d.* abt. 391
Gregory Nyssen *d.* abt. 394
Epiphanius . *d.* 403
John Chrysostom . *d.* 407
Cyril of Alexandria *d.* 444
Theodoret . . *d.* 457

Latin.

Arnobius . . . *fl.* 303
Lactantius . *d.* abt. 330
Ambrose . . . *d.* 397
Jerome . . . *d.* 420
Augustine . . . *d.* 430

FATIMITES, see *Ali* and *Mahometanism*.

FATS are oils solid at ordinary temperatures. The researches of Chevreul since 1811 on their chemical nature are very important; see *Candles*.

FAUGHARD, see *Foughard*.

FAUSTUS, a professor of magic, renowned in chap books, flourished about the end of the 15th century. Christopher Marlowe's powerful tragedy "Dr. Faustus," was published in 1616. Goethe's dramatic poem, "Faust," appeared in 1790.

FEASTS AND FESTIVALS. The "Feasts of the Lord," viz., those of the Passover, Pentecost, Trumpets, and Tabernacles, were instituted 1490 B.C. (*Leviticus* xxiii.)

Feast of Tabernacles, celebrated upon the dedication of the Temple of Solomon, 1004 B.C.
Hezekiah (726 B.C.) and Josiah (623) kept the feast of Passover in a most solemn manner.
In the Christian Church the feasts of Christmas, Easter, Ascension, and the Pentecost or Whitsuntide (*which see*), are *said* to have been ordered to be observed by all Christians in the 1st century.
Rogation days appointed 469.
Jubilees in the Romish Church were instituted by Boniface VIII. in 1300; see *Jubilees*.
For fixed festivals observed in the Church of England, as settled at the Reformation, *et seq.*, see Book of Common Prayer.
Feasts of Charity; see *Agapæ*.

FEBRUARY (from *Februus*, an Italian divinity), the second month of the year, in which were celebrated Februa, feasts on behalf of the manes of deceased persons. This month, with January, was added to the year by Numa, about 713 B.C. The February of 1886, said to be the coldest for 27 years—continued frost. *February* 24, 25 *Constitution*, see *France*, 1875.

FECIALES or **FETIALES**, twenty in number, heralds of Rome, to denounce war or proclaim peace, appointed by Numa, about 712 B.C.

FEDERAL STATES are those united by treaty as one state, without giving up self-government—as in Switzerland. The people of the Northern United States of America during the great conflict in 1861-5 were styled *Federals*; their opponents *Confederates*. See *Imperial Federation*.

Federal council of Australasia Act introduced by the earl of Derby 23 April, passed 14 Aug. 1885.
See *Australia*, 1885 *et seq.*, *Argentine*, *Brazil*, &c.

FEEJEE, see *Fiji*.

FÉLIBRIGE. A literary septennial festival held in Provence by *félibres*, writers in prose and verse in the langue d'oc, founded in 1854, in honour of seven eminent troubadours.

FELO DE SE, see *Suicide*.

FELONY, in English law (says Blackstone, in 1765), comprises every species of crime which occasions the forfeiture of land and goods. An act to abolish forfeitures for treason and felony, and to otherwise amend the law relating thereto, passed 4 July, 1870.

FEMALE MEDICAL SCHOOL, London, held its first session in 1865, when courses of lectures were given. Dr. Mary Walker attended Middlesex hospital in 1866. She gave an autobiographical lecture at St. James's Hall, 20 Nov. 1866. In 1869 the decision that "ladies should be admitted to study medicine in the university of Edinburgh," led to disturbances. Schools of medicine for women have been since established in London, Edinburgh, Glasgow, Dundee, Dublin, Belfast and Cork. Many women now (1903) registered as practitioners; many in India and other countries; see *Physic*, 1865, *et seq.*

Female Orphan Asylum, Beddington, Surrey, established 1758
Female Orphans' Home, Hampton, Middlesex . . 1855
Female Servants' Home Society 1836
Female Aid Society 1836

FEMALE SUFFRAGE, &c., see *Women*.

FENCIBLE LIGHT DRAGOONS, a body of cavalry raised voluntarily in various counties of England and Scotland in 1794, to serve during the war in any part of Great Britain. This force (between 14,000 and 15,000), which did its duty with much judgment during a period of intense popular excitement, was disbanded in 1800.

FENCING was introduced into England from France. Fencing-schools having led to duelling in England, were prohibited in London by statute 13 Edw. I. 1285. In 1859 there were eight teachers of fencing in London; in 1872, ten.

FENIANS (the name of ancient Irish national heroes, *Fionna*), a "brotherhood" in the United States and Ireland united to liberate Ireland and establish a republic.* The agitation was begun, it is said, by Stephens in March, 1858, and in 1864 enlistments and secret drillings took place. A convention was formed in 1863 in America. The movement is opposed by the Roman Catholic clergy. See *Ireland*.

* *Fenian oath.* "I promise by the divine law of God to do all in my power to obey the laws of the society F. B., and to free and regenerate Ireland from the yoke of England. So help me God."

Riot between the Fenians and their opponents at the Rotondo, Dublin . . . . . 22 Feb. 1864
25 persons arrested in Dublin, and the newspaper the *Irish People* (established Sept. 1863) seized, 15 Sept.; others arrested at Cork, &c. 16-30 Sept. 1865
The Fenians in America publish an address, stating that officers were going to Ireland to organise an army of 200,000 men . . . . . Sept. ,,
Fenians arrested at Manchester . . . 21 Sept. ,,
A ship with gunpowder seized at Liverpool Sept. ,,
Allocution of the pope, condemning secret societies 30 Sept. ,,
Evidence that 5000*l.* and 2000 pike-heads had been received from America in . . . Sept. ,,
O'Donovan and 5 others committed for high treason 2 Oct. ,,
33 Fenians committed for trial up to . 14 Oct. ,,
A Fenian provisional government at New York, and a congress of 600 members held at Philadelphia Oct. ,,
Fenians in United States said to have raised 200,000*l.* Oct. ,,
Capture of James Stephens, Irish head-centre, 11 Nov.; he escapes from gaol . . . 24 Nov. ,,
Fierce disputes between the senate and O'Mahony, the head-centre, who is charged with corruption and deposed; Mr. Roberts appointed his successor Dec. ,,
380,000 Fenians reported in the United States Jan. 1866
Habeas Corpus act suspended in Ireland; about 250 suspected persons arrested immediately 17 Feb. ,,
Great mass meeting at New York, threatening to invade Canada . . . . . 4 March, ,,
Fenian schooner *Friend* captures British schooner *Wentworth*, and scuttles her near Eastport, N. A. 1 May, ,,
James Stephens arrives at New York . 10 May, ,,
Col. O'Niel and Fenians cross the Niagara and enter Canada, 31 May; a conflict ensued with the volunteers, with bloodshed . . . . 2 June, ,,
The American generals Grant and Meade capture many retreating Fenians . . 2 June *et seq.*
Sweeny and others arrested . . 6, 7 June, ,,
President Johnson's proclamation against the Fenians . . . . . . 7 June, ,,
Spear and others cross the boundary near Vermont, 7 June; the corps demoralised; many return 9 June, ,,
Much dissension among the Fenians, July, *et seq.* ,,
They exercise much influence in the elections in America in . . . . . Oct. ,,
TRIALS IN CANADA.—Col. Lynch and Rev. John MacMahon (sentenced to be hanged on 13 Dec.) reprieved . . . . . 24-26 Oct. ,,
James Stephens, "central organiser of the Irish republic," said to sail from America . 24 Nov. ,,
The British government offer 2000*l.* for his apprehension . . . . . Nov. ,,
Meaney, a delegate, arrested in London . 1 Dec. ,,
Arms and ammunition seized in Dublin, Cork, and Limerick; many arrests . . . Dec. ,,
Gen. Millen, head of the Fenian military department, denounces Stephens "as a cheat and a rascal," and declares the cause for the present hopeless, but exhorts to watchfulness for an opportunity 3 Dec. ,,
Sweeny (released) rejoins the U.S. army . . Jan. 1867
22 convictions at Toronto . . . . Jan. ,,
67 Fenians from Liverpool arrested in Dublin 12 Feb. ,,
Irruption of Fenians into Chester; compelled to retire . . . . . . 11, 12 Feb. ,,
Outbreak in Kerry; Killarney threatened; capt. Moriarty and others captured . . . 12 Feb. ,,
Attack on coastguard station, Cahirciveen, 12 Feb.; movement collapsed . . . . 16 Feb. ,,
Kilmallock police barrack defended for three hours by 14 constables, who drove off 200 armed Fenians, with loss, by a sally . . . . 5 March, ,,
General Massey captured . . . 4 or 6 March, ,,
Rising at Midleton in Cork; Daly, a leader, killed; rails of South and Midland railway taken up 6 March, ,,
Proclamation of the Irish republic sent to the *Times* and other papers . . . . 6 March, ,,
Fenian rising near Dublin; telegraph destroyed; attack on the police station at Tallaght repelled; several shot, 208 prisoners taken into Dublin, 7 March, 1867
1000 Fenians hold market-place at Drogheda, but retreat at the approach of police . 7 March, ,,
Capt. Maclure captured . . . . 31 March, ,,
Special commission to try 230 Fenians; Whiteside, ch.-just.; Deasy and Fitzgerald, begin (Massey, Keogh, Corydon, and McGough, approvers) 9 April, *et seq.* ,,
Burke and Doran sentenced to death, 1 May; reprieved . . . . . . 26 May, ,,
Many convictions of treason (M'Afferty, M'Clure, and others) and treason-felony, and many discharged . . . . May, ,,
Trials at Limerick begin . . . . 11 June, ,,
President Roberts retires; the party in the United States said to be demoralised . . . July, ,,
Many Fenians tried and convicted July and Aug. ,,
Several imprisoned Fenians released and sent to America . . . . Aug. and Sept. ,,
Fenian congress at Cleveland, Ohio . . Sept. ,,
Kelly and Deasy, two Fenians, remanded for further examination, rescued from the prisoners' van, near Manchester; and Brett, a policeman, shot for refusing to give up his keys . 18 Sept. ,,
Many persons taken up; 23 committed on charge of murder—tried, 5 condemned to death (2 reprieved); 7 sentenced to 7 years' imprisonment 29 Oct.-12 Nov. ,,
Allen, Gould, and Larkin executed at Salford, 23 Nov. ,,
Funeral demonstration in London . . 24 Nov. ,,
Trials of Halpin and others at Dublin, Oct.-Nov. ,,
Funeral demonstrations for Allen, &c., at Cork, 1 Dec.; Dublin and Limerick . . 8 Dec. ,,
Address of the president and senate of the Fenian brotherhood of America to the "liberty-loving people of England," dated New York, 12 Dec. ,,
Reunion of the Roberts and Stephens parties under a new president . . . about 20 Dec. ,,
Premeditated explosion of Clerkenwell house of detention, London, to release Burke and Casey, leading Fenians, at 3.45. (A cask of gunpowder was fired close to the prison wall; Timothy Desmond, Jeremiah Allen, and Ann Justice captured on suspicion) . . . . . . 13 Dec. ,,
[*Consequences of the explosion.*—"Six persons were killed 'outright,' six more died from its effects, according to the coroner's inquests; five, in addition, owed their deaths indirectly to this means; one young woman is in a madhouse, 40 mothers were prematurely confined, and 20 of their babes died from the effects of the explosion on the women; others of the children are dwarfed and unhealthy. One mother is now a raving maniac; 120 persons were wounded; 50 went into St. Bartholomew's, Gray's Inn-lane, and King's College Hospitals; 15 are permanently injured, with loss of eyes, legs, arms, &c.; besides 20,000*l.* worth of damage to person and property." —*Times*, 29 April, 1868.]
Capt. Mackay and others rifle a Martello tower, 27 Dec. ,,
Audacious seizure of arms and ammunition in a gunsmith's shop in Cork . . . . 30 Dec. ,,
12 suspected Fenians captured at Merthyr Tydvil, 31 Dec. ,,
Mullany, a prisoner, turns queen's evidence, and accuses Barrett or Jackson (captured at Glasgow, 14 Jan.) of firing the barrel at Clerkenwell, 28 Jan. 1868
Attack on Martello tower near Waterford 28 Jan. ,,
Capt. Mackay arrested at Cork, 7 Feb.; much rioting there . . . . . 11, 12 Feb. ,,
Conviction of Patrick Lennon, a leader, 12 Feb. ,,
Habeas corpus act susp. till 1 March, 1869 Feb. ,,
Mullany and Thompson convicted as accessories in murder of Brett . . . . 18 March, ,,
Capt. Mackay convicted; sentenced to 12 years' imprisonment . . . . 20 March, ,,
O'Farrell, a Fenian, wounds the duke of Edinburgh at Port Jackson, 12 March; sentenced to death, 31 March, ,,
Mr. Darcy M'Gee, M.P., shot dead by a Fenian at Ottawa . . . . 7 April, ,,

Trial of Wm. and Timothy Desmond, Nicholas English, John O'Keefe, Michael Barrett, and Ann Justice, for murder (Clerkenwell outrage) begun 20; acquittal of Justice, 23; of O'Keefe, 24; and of the two Desmonds and English, 27. Conviction of Barrett . . . . . . 27 April, 1868
Richard Burke, a leader, convicted of treason-felony, 30 April, „
Michael Barrett (for causing the Clerkenwell explosion) executed . . . . . 26 May, „
O'Donovan Rossa and others released, behave violently . . . . March, 1869
The government declines to release others, 18 Oct. „
Manifesto from John Savage, executive officer, Dec. „
Fenian raid into Canada vigorously repelled by the militia, and their general, O'Neill, captured by the U. S. marshal . . . . . 26 May, 1870
Formation of the Clan-na-Gael (*which see*) . . „
Michael Davitt and John Wilson convicted of treason-felony for endeavouring to transmit arms secretly to Ireland (detected March) . 18 July, „
Captured Fenian generals (Thompson and Starr) in United States, sentenced to imprisonment for breach of neutrality laws . . . . July, „
President Grant's proclamation against Fenian raids into Canada . . . . 13 Oct. „
Letter from Mr. Gladstone announcing early release of Fenian convicts . . . . . 15 Dec. „
The convicts released . . . . Jan. 1871
The released convicts welcomed in the United States . . . . Jan. „
The Fenians favour the French in the war, Aug. 1870-Feb. „
Fenian raid into Manitoba suppressed by United States troops, and general Neill arrested; see *Ireland* . . . . . . about 12 Oct. „
Gen. Cluseret (a short time in the service of the Fenians) publishes an account of them in *Fraser's Magazine*: he says, "Their insurrection was foolishly planned and still more foolishly executed," and strongly advises reconciliation with England . . . . July, 1872
Great demonstration near Drogheda . 20 Sept. 1874
Escape of Fenian prisoners from West Australia in the *Catalpa*, American ship, 17 April; arrived at New York . . . . . 19 Aug. 1876
O'Mahony, head-centre, dies at New York; grand funeral service . . . . . 6 Feb. 1877
Davitt and other Fenian convicts released Jan. to Sept. 1878
Davitt prominent during the land league agitation, 1880-81
Arrested and committed to prison . 3, 4 Feb. 1881
Elected M.P. for co. Meath, 22 Feb., election annulled . . . . . . 28 Feb. 1882
Seizure of arms and ammunition, St. John Street Road, Clerkenwell; Thomas Walsh arrested 17 June „
Committed for trial, 17 July; sentenced to 7 years' penal servitude . . . . . 9 Aug. „
Detection of a murderous Fenian plot in Dublin, carried out by a band termed the "Irish Invincibles," said to be connected with the Land League 19 Jan.—17 Feb. 1883
Plot to explode public buildings in England concocted in New York, by O'Donovan Rossa, a chief of the Fenian Brotherhood, Wm. J. Lynch (Norman) sent to England; conveys explosives from Birmingham to London (see *Birmingham*), gives evidence at Bow-street . . . 19 April, „
Great convention at Philadelphia opened, 25 April; denounced by O'Donovan Rossa, who revives the Irish Revolutionary Brotherhood . 6 May, „
See *Dynamite* and *Explosions*.
Centre of Fenian organisation discovered at Paris; Frederick Allen apprehended . . . . Oct. „
Capt. Thos. Phelan stabbed (not killed) as a suspected traitor by Richard Short—in Rossa's house, in New York, 9 Jan.; O'Donovan Rossa shot in the street by Lucilla Yseult Dudley, an English widow, 2 Feb.; Phelan and he recover, in the same hospital, Feb.; Short acquitted, 6 May; Mrs. Dudley declared insane . 30 June, 1885
Threatening Fenian manifesto sent to Mr. Gladstone and others from Paris . about 19 Feb. „
Great Fenian congress held in Paris . . 23 Feb. „
James Stephens expelled from France . March, „
Fenianism becomes prominent in Ireland autumn 1887
The brotherhood expels O'Donovan Rossa about 8 Dec. 1886; said to be succeeded by Dr. Hamilton Williams at New York, having 200,000*l.* to be employed in war against England by means of dynamite explosions, &c.; statement in *Times* 14 Dec.; stated to be absurd . . 14 Dec. 1887
Meeting of the old Fenian Brotherhood at New York; they decide to discard Mr. Parnell and all leaders, and to maintain only military organisation 14 July, 1891
Michael Davitt elected M.P. for N. Meath, July; unseated, see *Ireland*, 23 Dec. 1892; elected for N.E. Cork, 8 Feb. 1893; retires . . 26 Oct. 1899
See *Dynamite*, Sept. 1896.
"Recollections of Fenians and Fenianism," by John O'Leary, published 1897
James Stephens, founder of the conspiracy of the 'Sixties, born 1824, died, near Dublin, 29 March, 1901
James Cahill, one of the Fenian gang of 1867, died in Massachusetts . . . . . 25 Aug. 1902

FERE-CHAMPENOISE (France). Here the French army under Marmont, Mortier, and Arrighi, were surprised and defeated by the allies under the prince of Schwarzenberg, 25 March, 1814, after a heroic resistance. Paris surrendered six days after.

FERGHANA, see *Khokand*.

FERIÆ LATINÆ, solemn Roman festivals, said to have been instituted by Tarquin the Proud, about 534 B.C. The principal magistrates of forty-seven towns of Latium assembled on a mount near Rome, and with the Roman authorities offered a bull to Jupiter Latialis.

FERKEH, in the Soudan. Here the army of the dervishes was skilfully surprised and totally defeated by gen. sir H. H. Kitchener, 7 June, 1896, when on his march toward Dongola. The battle lasted from 5 to 7 a.m. The enemy's loss was about 1,000, including Hammuda, the commander, many emirs, and about 500 prisoners. Egyptian loss, 20 killed. The enemy fought with desperate valour. Early in the action about 300 dervishes were surrounded, and refusing to surrender were nearly all killed.

FERMENTATION, termed by Gay-Lussac one of the most mysterious processes in nature: he showed that in the process, 45 lbs. of sugar are resolved into 23 of alcohol and 22 of carbonic acid. His memoir appeared in 1810. In 1861 Pasteur brought forward evidence to show that fermentation depends on the presence of minute organisms in the fermenting fluid, and that the source of all such organisms is the atmosphere. For his researches he was awarded an annual pension of 120,000 francs in 1874.

FERMIERS GÉNÉRAUX, officers who farmed the French revenues previous to 1789, frequently with much oppression. Lavoisier and 27 of these were executed 8 May, 1794.

FERNDALE COLLIERY EXPLOSION; 8 Nov. 1867; about 178 lives lost. See under *Coal*.

FERNS (Ireland), an ancient bishopric, once archiepiscopal. St. Edæn was seated here in 598. Leighlin and Ferns were united in 1600; and by the Church Temporalities Act, passed Aug. 1833, both were united to the bishopric of Ossory. See *Ossory*.—FERNS, an order of cryptogamous plants, much cultivated in Wardian cases; *which see*, and also *Nature-Printing*.

FEROZESHAH (India). The British, commanded by sir Hugh Gough, attacked the entrenchments of the Sikhs, and carried their first line of works, 21 Dec. 1845; but night coming on, the operations were suspended till daybreak, wher their second line was stormed by general Gilbert, and 74 guns captured. The Sikhs advanced to retake their guns, but were repulsed with great loss, and retreated towards the Sutlej, 22 Dec.; and recrossed that river unmolested, 27 Dec. The British loss was reckoned at 2415.

FERRARA, formerly part of the exarchate of Ravenna, under the emperors of the East. It was subdued by the Lombards in the 8th century, and taken from them about 752 by Pepin, who gave it to pope Stephen II. About 1208 it fell into the hands of the house of Este (*which see*), and became the principal seat of the literature and fine arts in Italy. Pope Clement VIII. obtained the sovereignty in 1598, on the death of the duke Alphonso II., the last legitimate male of the Este family. His illegitimate nephew, Cæsar, became duke of Modena. The French under Massena took Ferrara in 1796; but it was restored to the pope in 1814. An Austrian garrison held it from 1849; it retired in June, 1859, and the people rose and declared for annexation to Sardinia, which was accomplished in March, 1860. The centenary of the university, founded in 1392, celebrated 18 April, 1892.

FERRARS' ARREST. In March, 1542, Mr. George Ferrars, a member of parliament, while in attendance on the house was taken in execution by a sheriff's officer for debt, and committed to the Compter prison. The house despatched their serjeant to require his release, which was resisted, and an affray taking place, his mace was broken. The house in a body repaired to the lords to complain, when the contempt was adjudged to be very great, and the punishment of the offenders was referred to the lower house. On another messenger being sent to the sheriffs by the commons, they delivered up the senator, and the civil magistrates and the creditor were committed to the Tower, the inferior officers to Newgate, and an act was passed releasing Mr. Ferrars from liability for the debt. The king, Henry VIII., highly approved of all these proceedings, and the transaction became the basis of that rule of parliament which exempts members from arrest. *Holinshed.*

FERRO, see *Canary Isles.*

FERROL (N.W. Spain). Upwards of 10,000 British landed near Ferrol under the command of sir James Pulteney, in Aug. 1800. They gained possession of the heights; but, despairing of success, on account of the strength of the works, sir James re-embarked his troops. His conduct was much condemned. Soult captured Ferrol, 27 Jan. 1809. An insurrection of about 1500 men in the arsenal here broke out, headed by brigadier Pozas and capt. Montojo, who raised the red flag, 11 Oct.; they dispersed or surrendered when about to be attacked, 17 Oct. 1872.

FESCENNINE VERSES were rude extemporary dialogues, frequently licentious, in favour among the ancient Etruscans at weddings, and still popular in Italy.

FESTIVALS, see under *Feasts, Clergy, Music.*

FÊTE DE DIEU, a feast of the Roman church in honour of the real presence in the Lord's Supper, kept on the Thursday after Trinity Sunday. See *Corpus Christi.* Berengarius, archbishop of Angers, opposed the doctrine of transubstantiation, and to atone for his crime a yearly procession was made at Angers, called *la fête de Dieu*, 1019.

FÊTE DE VERTU, an annual assemblage, chiefly of young persons, to whom were adjudged rewards for industry and virtue. These fêtes, held at Nuneham, in Oxfordshire, begun by lady Harcourt in 1789, were continued till her death.

FEUDAL LAWS. The tenure of land by suit and service to lord or owner, partly in use in England by the Saxons, was mainly established by William I. in 1066. The kingdom was divided into baronies, which were given on condition of the holders furnishing the king with men and money. The vassalage, limited by Henry VII., 1495, was abolished by statute, 1660. The feudal system was introduced into Scotland by Malcolm II. in 1008, and the hereditary jurisdictions were finally abolished in that kingdom, 1746-7. The feudal laws, established in France by Clovis I. about 486, were discountenanced by Louis XI. in 1470. "Feudal Aids, 1284-1431," vol. i., County returns, published by the Public Record Office. May, 1899.

FEUILLANTS, a religious order founded by Jean de la Barrière in 1577 at the abbey of Feuillant, near Toulouse, and settled in Paris in 1587. The *Feuillant club*, formed in Paris by La Fayette and others in 1789, to counteract the intrigues of the Jacobins, was so named from the convent where they met. A body of Jacobins burst into their hall and obliged them to separate, 25 Dec. 1791; and the club was broken up in 1792.

FEVER, see *Scarlet Fever*; 11 fever hospitals in London and neighbourhood; the Southern (for convalescents), at Carshalton, in course of construction, 1903.

FEZ (in the ancient *Mauritania*, Africa), founded by Edris, a descendant of Mahomet, about 787, was long capital of the kingdom of Fez. After long-continued struggles, it was annexed to Morocco about 1550. Leo Africanus describes it as containing more than 700 temples, mosques, and other public edifices, in the 12th century. Jewish quarter burnt, many deaths, Sept. 1896. Prison reforms well carried out, many prisoners freed, &c., Nov. 1901—Sept. 1902. See *Morocco.*

FICTIONS, see *Romances.*—FICTIONS IN LAW were invented by the lawyers in the reign of Edward I. as a means of carrying cases from one court to another, whereby the courts became checks to each other. *Hume.* Lord Mansfield, in the court of King's Bench, emphatically declared that "no fiction of law shall ever so far prevail against the real truth, as to prevent the execution of justice:" 31 May, 1784. They have been mostly abolished in the present century.

"FIDELIO," Beethoven's single opera; composed in 1804, produced at Vienna, 20 Nov. 1805.

FIDENÆ, a Sabine city, frequently at war with Rome. It was finally captured and the inhabitants enslaved, 426 B.C., by the Romans, whose ambassadors they had slain.

FIEF, see *Feudal Laws.*

FIELD. The country gentleman's weekly paper, devoted to natural history, sports, &c., first appeared 1 Jan. 1853.

FIELD OF MARCH AND MAY, see *Champ.*—FIELD OF THE CLOTH OF GOLD, a plain near Ardres, near Calais, in France, on which Henry VIII. met Francis I. of France, 7-25 June, 1520. The nobility of both kingdoms displayed their magnificence, and many involved themselves in debt. Paintings of the embarcation and interview are at Windsor castle.

FIELD-MARSHAL, see *Marshal*.

FIERY-CHAMBER, see *Chambre Ardente*.

FIESCHI'S ATTEMPT ON LOUIS-PHILIPPE, see *France*, 1835.

FIFE. A maritime county E. Scotland, containing St. Andrews, Dunfermline, and other towns with ruined abbeys. Alexander William George Duff, born 10 Nov. 1849, created duke of Fife, 1889, married princess Louise Victoria of Wales (*which see*), 27 July, 1889. His house, Mar Lodge, built about 1825, was destroyed by fire 14 June, 1895.

FIFTH-MONARCHY MEN, about 1645, supposed the period of the Millennium to be just at hand, when Jesus Christ should descend from heaven, and erect the fifth universal monarchy. They proceeded so far as to elect him king at London. Cromwell dispersed them, 1653. *Kearsley*. Another rising with loss of life was suppressed, 6 Jan. 1661. Thos. Venner, a cooper, their leader, and 16 others, were executed soon after.

FIFTH PARTY, a term applied to the advocates of temperance in the House of Commons (about 60), Feb. 1884.

FIG-TREE (*Ficus carica*) brought from the south of Europe, before 1548. The Botany-Bay fig, *Ficus australis*, brought from N. S. Wales in 1789.

FIGURES, see *Arithmetic*.

FIJI or VITI ISLES, in the Pacific Ocean, about 1500 miles from Sydney. Discovered by Tasman, Dutch navigator, in 1643. There are above 200 isles; 80 inhabited; the largest about 360 miles in circumference. Capital Suva.

Population in 1887, 124,658; including 2,105 Europeans; 1893, 122,712; 1901, 117,870. 1890, revenue, 66,817*l.*; expenditure, 60,826*l.*; imports, 206,757*l.*; exports, 364 531*l.*; 1893, revenue, 76,774*l.*; expenditure, 85,982*l.*; imports, 276,398*l.*; exports, 355,631*l.*; 1,424*l.* surplus March, 1898; revenue, 111,569*l.*; expenditure, 100,022*l.*, 1900.

The islands offered by the king, Thakombau, and chiefs to the British government, but not accepted July, 1859

The house of commons granted 1680*l.* for expenditure in them; and European settlements made . 1860

Annexation to Great Britain proposed in parliament; declined 25 June, 1872; but unconditional cession to the British government accepted by sir Hercules Robinson, July: and announced by him . . . . 25 Oct. 1874

His club sent as a present to the queen by the king Thakombau . . . . ,,

Sir Arthur Hamilton Gordon, first governor . . 1875

About 50,000 deaths by epidemic measles early in ,,

Outbreak of cannibal devil-worshippers suppressed by the military; about 20 ringleaders executed about June, 1876

Sir George Wm. Des Vœux, governor . . Oct. 1880

King Thakombau died . . . Feb. 1883

Sir Charles Bullen Hugh Mitchell, governor Sept. 1886

Sir John Bates Thurston, high commissioner of the Western Pacific, Dec., 1887, *et seq.*; died about 8 Feb. 1897

Rising of some of the tribes suppressed, reported 9 July, 1894

Shipping and buildings destroyed by a hurricane; many lives lost . . . . . . 6 Jan. 1895

Sir G. T. M. O'Brien appointed governor, March, 1897; Sir H. M. Jackson . . . April, 1902

FILES are mentioned (1 *Sam.* xiii. 21) 1093 B.C. The manufacture of them has attained to great perfection, by means of file-cutting machinery. That set up by Mr. T. Greenwood of Leeds, in 1859, was invented by M. Bernot of Paris. It is said that the price of files made by it is reduced from 32*d.* to 4*d.* per dozen.

FILIBUSTERS (properly *Flibustiers*), a name given to the freebooters who plundered the coasts of America in the 16th and 17th centuries; see *Buccaneers* and *Nicaragua*, *Cuba*, 1896-7.

FILIOQUE, ("and from the Son"), inserted in the Nicene creed, in respect to the procession of the Holy Ghost from the Father and the Son, by the second council at Constantinople, 381; was rejected, by the Greek church, 431; accepted by the Spanish, 447, and by the Roman 883. The omission of the phrase was considered at the Old Catholic Conference at Bonn, Aug. 1875. See *Athanasian Creed* and *Nice*.

FILTERERS. A plan for purifying corrupted water was patented by Wm. Woolcott in 1675. Other modes followed. James Peacock's method of filtration was patented in 1791; and many others since: Ransome's, 1856.

Apparatus for freshening salt water, brought forward by Grant, 1849; by Macbride, 1849; Gravely, 1858. Dr. Normandy's greatly improved apparatus, 1859, much used in the royal navy.

FINANCE ACTS passed 31 July, 1894; 30 May, 1895; 7 Aug. 1896; 15 July, 1897; 1 July, 1898; 20 June, 1899; 9 April, 1900. See *Budget*, *Estate Duty*, *Customs*, *Excise*, *Income Tax*.

FINANCES of Great Britain, &c., see *Revenue* and other articles.

A select committee of the commons, consisting of Mr. Goschen, chancellor of the exchequer, Mr. J. Morley, Mr. A. J. Balfour, Mr. Childers, lord R. Churchill and others, was appointed to consider the present Financial Relations between England, Scotland, and Ireland, 13 Aug. 1890. Returns presented for the years ending 31 March, 1890, 1891, 1892, 1893, *et seq.*

FINANCE ACT, the title given in 1894 to the act, granting certain duties of customs and inland revenue, &c.; passed annually.

The "Statistical Abstract," published annually by the government, contains much financial information.

Royal commission to inquire into the financial relations of Gt. Britain and Ireland appointed 26 May, 1894; report, with recommendations signed, 24 June, 1896. Final, report, 5 Sept., 1896. See *Ireland*, Dec. 1896, and July, 1898.

FINE ARTS, see *Arts*, *Paintings*, *Sculpture*, *Engraving*, &c.

FINES AND RECOVERIES, conferring the power of breaking ancient entails and alienating estates, began in the reign of Edward IV., but was not, properly speaking, law, till Henry VII., by correcting some abuses that attended the practice, gave indirectly a sanction to it, 1487. Fines and recoveries were abolished in 1833.

FINISTERRE, see *Cape Finisterre*.

FINLAND, a Russian grand duchy, in the middle of the 12th century was conquered by Eric IX. of Sweden, who introduced Christianity. It was several times taken by the Russians (1714, 1742, and 1808), and restored (1721 and 1743); but in 1809 they retained it by treaty; see *Abo*. Its political constitution was confirmed by the Czar in 1800, 1825, and 1855. It was made nearly autonomous in 1883. Population in 1862, 1,746,229; in 1867, 1,830,853; 1875, 1,912,647; 1889, 2,388,404; 1897, about 2,572,801; 1902, abt. 2,700,000. During a dreadful famine, whole villages were starved. Elias Lönnrot, editor of the ancient national epic, "Kalevala" (1834-49), died 1884. Triennial Diet opened with constitutional speech sent by the Czar,

19 Jan. 1885. The Czar warmly received at Helsingfors, Aug. 1885.

Discontent of the chambers and people at expected changes by the Russian government . . Jan. 1891
Rescript of the czar to the governor-general, assuring the people of the maintenance of their ancient rights and privileges . . about 18 March, „
The czar visits Finland, coolly received . July, „
A new stringent press law enforced . 1 Oct. „
Famine in N.W. Finland; much suffering . Dec. „
Statue of the czar Alexander II. unveiled at Helsingfors by count Heyden, gov.-gen., 30 April, 1894
Count Heyden resigns, reported . 13 Jan. 1897
Triennial diet opened at Helsingfors, financial measures adopted, imperial speech read by gov.-gen. Gontscharoff . . . . . . 25 Jan. „
Zacharias Topelius, author and poet, born 14 Jan. 1818; died . . . . . . 12 March 1898
Agitation against changes in the constitution, Oct. „
Gen. Bobrikoff, gov.-gen, arrives . 12 Oct. „
Diet opened with a speech from the throne, 24 Jan. 1899
Russification of Finland, revision of laws, discussion in parliament restricted by imperial rescript, issued . . . . 3 Feb. „
Political crisis continues . . . . . March, „
Deputation of over 500 Finlanders petitioning for their constitutional rights, not received by the czar at St. Petersburg . . 16–18 March, „
Army reform to be introduced during 10 years, reported . . . . May, „
Diet closed by imperial edict . . . 1 June, „
Failure of crops and floods reported . June, „
An international deputation petitioning the czar to spare the liberties of Finland (800 eminent signatories) not received, 1 July; warmly welcomed at Helsingfors . . . . . . 2 July, „
An imperial (autocratic) rescript issued . 2 July, „
M. von Plehwe, a Russian, appointed secretary of state . . . . . . early Sept. „
Mr. Eugene Wolff, 13 yrs. British vice consul at Viborg, resigns, owing to complaints from the Russian govmt. regarding his part in the political agitation, early Sept. (banished, April, 1903); similar resignations in other parts; officials from St. Petersburg appointed, Oct.; press restrictions . . May, 1899—Jan. *et seq.* 1900
Triennial diet opened at Helsingfors . 27 Jan. „
Imperial rescript, to enforce the measures taken to solidify the empire and Finland, issued . 14 Feb. „
Protest against the new military law, 1899, and infringement of constitutional rights, published in England . . . . April, „
The *Nya Pressen*, newspaper, suppressed 29 June, „
Russian ordered to be the official language 26 June, „
Petition of the diet regarding the present administration in Finland, 27 Aug.; rejected by the czar . . . . early Sept. 1901
Monster petition, 471,131 signatures, against the new army law of 12 July, and other edicts, issued . . . . 30 Sept. „
Disturbance during a levy of recruits at Helsingfors; repressed by Cossacks . . 18 April, 1902
Emigration largely increasing . . . April, „
The senate placed under control of the gov.-gen., and other restrictive laws published . end Sept. „
Statue of Elias Lönnrot, patriot, unveiled at Helsingfors . . . . 28 Oct. „
Several judges and governors dismissed . Feb. 1903
Famine, great distress, reported . 18 March, „
Gen. Bobrikoff's power absolute. New rules signed by the czar . . . . . . 2 April, „
Count Mamerheim, baron Born and others banished . . . . 27 April, „

FINNIAN, see *Fenians*.

FINSBURY PARK, London, N. In 1866, land was purchased, and preparations for the park began; and it was opened 7 Aug. 1869.

FIRE. Heracleitus about 596 B.C. maintained that the world was evolved from fire, which he deemed to be a god omnipotent. Fire was worshipped by the Persians and other ancient nations, see *Guebres* and *Parsees*.

FIRE-ANNIHILATOR, an apparatus invented by Mr. T. Phillips, and made known by him in 1849. When put in action, steam and carbonic acid are formed, which extinguish flame. It was not successful commercially. *L'Extincteur* was invented by Dr. F. Carlier, and patented by A. Vignon in July, 1862. It is an iron cylinder filled with water and carbonic acid gas, generated by bicarbonate of soda and tartaric acid. The apparatus was developed and improved by Mr. W. B. Dick, in his Manual and Chemical Fire-Engines, which give a continuous flow of water and gas, patented April, 1869.

The "Mata Fuego," or "Fire-killer," of M. Banolas of Paris, was successfully exhibited at the Alexandra Palace, 16 Oct., 1880. Great bodies of flame were almost instantaneously extinguished.
The Harden Grenade Fire Extinguisher tried successfully near Farringdon-road, London, 24 July, 1884.
The Draper-Hetherington sprinkler reported successful, Nov. 1888.
Col. Imchessetsky's "Uralite" successfully tested, London, 15 Aug. 1902.
See *Antipyrogene* and *Asbestos*.

FIRE-ARMS, see *Artillery*, *Cannon*, *Needle-gun*, *Chassepot*, and *Pistols*. The first small fire-arms were a species of cannon, borne by two men.

Fire-arms made at Perugia, in Italy . . . 1364
Employed by the Burgundians at Arras . . . 1414
Edward IV., when he landed at Ravenspur, is said to have been accompanied by 300 Flemings, armed with hand-guns 1471
At Morat, the Swiss are said to have had 10,000 arquebusiers (men armed with fire-arms) . . 1476
Fire-arms said to have been used at the siege of Berwick 1521
The petronel (from *poitrine*, the chest) or arquebus came into use, 1480; and the musket employed in the armies of the emperor Charles V. about . „
All these were of very rude construction, being first discharged by a lighted match, afterwards, about 1517, by a wheel-lock, then by the flint.
The match-lock and wheel-lock superseded by the flint-lock, about 1692
The rev. Mr. Forsythe patented the percussion principle of igniting gunpowder in muskets, by means of detonating powder . . April, 1807
Percussion caps came into use between . 1820 & 1830
Percussion musket; pattern 1842
Artillery carbine; pattern . . . . . „
Regulation rifle musket; pattern . . . 1851
Application of machinery in small arms factory established at Enfield (the old musket *Brown Bess* superseded) . . . . . . Jan. 1857
Mr. Jacob Snider's system of breech-loading invented in 1859; presented to the British government; finally adopted, 1866. He received 1000*l.* for expenses in June; died 25 Oct. . . . 1866
100,000 breech-loaders said to have been ordered by the British government . . . . July, „
New government advertises for propositions for conversion of Enfield rifles into breech-loaders, Aug. „
"Chassepot" guns in use in France . 1 Oct. „
War-office advertises for proposals for breech-loading rifles, to replace those in use 22 Oct. „
Nine systems selected for further trial; 1000*l.* to be awarded to the best . . . . June, 1867
Snider's rifle reported very successful at Wimbledon, July, „
61,682 new arms had been made at Enfield; 175,550 converted to Sniders, up to . . . Dec. „
The "Money-Walker" rifle (patented by Mr. Mowbray-Money and lieut.-col. Walker), tried and approved . . . . . 18 June, 1868
A report in favour of the Martini-Henry rifle issued [adopted] . . . . . March, 1869
An act to grant a duty of excise on licences to use guns, passed . . . . . . 9 Aug. 1870
Complaints respecting the Martini-Henry rifle (for weight and recoil) . . . . . Aug. 1874
Magazine rifles came into use in Germany 1870–1; the Mauser rifles used there in 1887, which

contain enough ammunition for five or more almost simultaneous discharges, were coming into general adoption in Europe in 1887
An improved form (firing from 6 to 9 shots successively) determined upon by the small arms committee, Dec. 1887; ordered to be made for general use, announced (name, Lee-Metford) . Nov. 1888
This magazine rifle censured in the *Times*, defended by Mr. Stanhope and the War office . *Times*, 15 Nov. 1890
The merits of the Lee-Speed magazine rifle discussed, Feb.; and also the French Berthier magazine rifle . . . . . . Nov. 1891
Herr von Mannlicher (Austrian) produces a new repeating rifle, said to be light and effective, Aug. 1892
Wm. Ellis Metford, who developed the rifle to its present perfection by his discovery of the principle of shallow grooves, died . . 14 Oct. 1899
The "Hylard" rifle, invented by Mr. Hylard, tried successfully at Runnymede . . 11 Nov. 1901

See *Mitrailleuse*, *Gatling* and *Hyposcope*.

FIRE-BRIGADE. The "London Fire-engine Establishment," an amalgamation of the engines of the different companies, was established in London in 1832 by Mr. Charles Bell Ford, director of the Sun Fire-office. It then had 80 men and 19 stations. In May, 1862, a commission recommended the establishment of a fire-brigade, which was effected by the Metropolitan Fire-brigade Act, in 1865. The establishment then gave up its plant to the Metropolitan Board of Works, and was afterwards taken over by the London County Council under the Local Government Act of 1888. The fire-brigade is supported by a rate, and by contributions from government and from the insurance offices. In 1889, 591 me nand 55 land fire-engine stations; 1902, 985 officers and men and 78 (land) stations. Captain Eyre M. Shaw recommended a large increase of the establishment, April, 1889; which was carried into effect in 1890. Annual reviews.

Capt. Eyre M. Shaw, C.B., appointed chief officer of metropolitan fire brigade in succession to Mr. James Braidwood (see *Fires*, 1861) 1861
Great fire-brigade exhibition at Oxford, with men and appliances representing the united kingdom 31 May, 1887
The success of a similar exhibition with the presentation of medals by the prince and princess of Wales at the Horse Guards Parade, Westminster, was greatly marred by insufficient arrangements for the preservation of order . . . 27 May, 1889
The London County Council orders the appointment of 138 additional firemen and 4 new stations with the usual appliances. . . . early Aug. ,,
Review of the brigade at Crystal Palace by the German Emperor . . . . . . 11 July, 1891
Capt. Shaw announces his intention to resign 26 June; (made K.C.B.), 31 Oct.; succeeded by capt. James S. Simonds (previously second in command), 22 Dec. 1891; requested to resign, 16 June, 1896; succeeded by commander L. de L. Wells . . . . 3 Nov. 1896
French fire-brigades congress at Havre, about 160 of the English fire-brigade present mid-Aug. 1892
International fire tournament and exhibition in London, 12 June 1893
Roll of honour of men killed while on duty (James Braidwood and others), unveiled 23 Oct. ,,
The national fire-brigade union holds annual meetings; 400 brigades and 30,000 men . 4 March, 1895
International congress at Amsterdam . 24–28 Sept. ,,
Tournament and exhibition, &c., at the Agricultural hall . . . . 19 June, 1896
Fire-brigades of the United Kingdom reviewed by the queen at Windsor . . . . . 25 June, 1897
The London fire brigade to be recruited from any source, not only from sailors . 18 July, 1889 *et seq.*
Internat. congress opened in Berlin . . 6 June, 1901
Internat. fire exhibition opened, Earl's Court, 6 May, 1903
Capt. J. de Courcy Hamilton appointed chief officer on resignation of commander Wells . 28 July, ,,

FIRE-DAMP INDICATOR, a small apparatus, about the size of a chronometer, invented by Mr. G. F. Ansell, and patented by him in 1865, by which the presence of very small quantities of fire-damp or light carburetted hydrogen gas may be detected in mines. It is an application of the law of the diffusion of gases.

FIRE-DETECTOR and **ALARUM,** a mechanical and chemical apparatus invented by prof. Grechi, which causes a bell to be rung and exhibits coloured light, when the temperature of a room is greatly increased. It was tried at the International exhibition, London, 4 June, 1873.

Pearson's automatic fire-indicator, practically a Sixe's thermometer, reported successful, *Times*, 7 Dec. 1897

FIRE-ENGINES are said to have been invented by Ctesibius, 250 B.C. They are mentioned by Pliny, A.D. 70. A "water-bow" was patented by Thos. Grent in 1632, one was constructed by John Van der Heyden, about 1663. Bramah's engine was patented in 1793. Mr. John Braithwaite constructed a steam fire-engine in 1830. A trial of steam fire-engines took place at the Crystal Palace, Sydenham, on 1, 2, 3 July, 1863, when prizes were awarded to a large one by Merryweather and a small one by Shand and Mason.

W. Dennis's portable self-acting pneumatic fire-engine was tried successfully at gas-works near the Thames . . . . . . 30 Nov. 1876

FIRE-ESCAPES were patented by David Marie (1766), and Joachim Smith (1773). The Royal Society for the Protection of Life from Fire was first established in 1836; its object was not fully attained till 1843, when it was re-organised, beginning with six escape stations in London; in 1859 it possessed 67; in 1866, 85; in 1902, 192; 56 horsed escapes; 37 fire escape stations. In Aug. 1867, the plant of the society was virtually presented to the Board of Works, in consequence of the passing of the Metropolitan Fire Brigade Act, 1865, and subsequently passed to the London County Council (see *Fire Brigade*). The fatal fire in Queen Victoria-street, 9 June, 1902, occasioned an inquiry respecting the adequacy of the fire escapes in use. Versmann's composition for rendering washing dresses *fire-proof* was published about 1860. The British Fire Prevention Committee reported an incorporated scientific society, under the Board of Trade, March, 1899.

FIRE INSURANCE, see *Insurance*.

FIREMAN'S RESPIRATOR, the invention of Dr. Tyndall (1870-71), is a combination of his respirator of cotton-wool moistened with glycerine, and Dr. Stenhouse's charcoal respirator. Armed with this apparatus a man may remain a long time in the densest smoke.

The Loeb respirator was tried in smoke and poisonous vapour, and was reported efficacious at Westminster . . . . . . July, 1888

FIRE, ROYAL SOCIETY FOR PROTECTION FROM. See *Fire-Escapes*.

FIRE-SALVAGE CORPS formed, in 1865, by the London Fire Insurance Offices.

FIRE-SHIPS. Among the most formidable contrivances of this kind ever used, was an explosion vessel to destroy a bridge of boats at the siege of Antwerp, in 1585. The first use of them in the British navy was by Charles lord Howard of Effingham, in the engagement with the Spanish Armada, July, 1588. *Rapin.*

FIRE-WATCH or **Fire-Guard**, of London, was instituted Nov. 1791.

FIRE-WORKS are said to have been made by the Chinese in remote ages. They were invented in Europe at Florence about 1360; and were exhibited as a spectacle in 1588.

Macaulay states that the fire-works let off in England at the peace of Ryswick, in 1697, cost 12,000*l.*

Very grand fire-works were let off from a magnificent building erected in the Green-park, London, at the peace of Aix-la-Chapelle, Nov. 1748.

Exhibition of fire-works in Paris, 31 May, 1770, in honour of the marriage of the dauphin, afterwards Louis XVI.; nearly 1000 persons perished by pressure and drowning, through a panic.

The display of fire-works, under sir Wm. Congreve, at the general peace, and the centenary of the accession of the Brunswick family to the throne, 1 Aug. 1814

Another at the coronation of William IV., 8 Sept. 1831.

A grand display of this kind (at a cost of 10,000*l.*) to celebrate the peace with Russia, 29 May, 1856.

In consequence of explosions frequently occurring at fire-work makers (particularly one on 12 July, 1858, at Mr. Bennett's in the Westminster-road, Lambeth, when five lives were lost, and about 300 persons seriously injured, and much property destroyed), it was determined to enforce 9 & 10 Will. III. c. 7 (1697), an act to prevent the throwing and forming of squibs, serpents, and other fire-works. An act regulating the making of fire-works was passed in 1860.

Ralph Fenwick, a maker, his wife, and six others, Broad-street, Lambeth, killed by explosion 4 Nov. 1873.

Mr. C. T. Brock, the greatest pyrotechnist of the time, has a manufactory at Nunhead; exhibits at the Crystal Palace, &c., and abroad, 1871, *et seq.*

FIRES in London. The conflagration of a city, with all its tumult of concomitant distress, is one of the most dreadful spectacles which this world can offer to human eyes. *Dr. Johnson.* Fires (false alarms) act passed, 6 July, 1895.

A great part of the city destroyed, including St. Paul's cathedral . . . . . . 962 & 1087

One at London-bridge, began on the Southwark side, and was communicated to the other side, and hemmed in a numerous crowd; about 3000 were drowned, and a great part of the city, north and south, burned 1212

The Great Fire, whose ruins covered 396 acres, extended from the Tower to the Temple-church, and from the north-east gate to Holborn-bridge. It began in a baker's house in Pudding-lane, behind Monument-yard, and destroyed, in the space of four days, 88 churches (including St. Paul's), the city gates, the Royal Exchange, the Custom-house, Guildhall, Sion college, and many other public buildings, besides 13,200 houses, laying waste 400 streets. About 200,000 persons encamped in Islington and Highgate fields; only 8 deaths reported. (See *Monument.*) . . 2-6 Sept. 1666

In Southwark, 60 houses burnt 1676

In Wapping, 150 houses burnt, 50 lives lost . . 1715

Custom-house burnt 1718

At Shadwell, 50 houses burnt . . . 10 Sept. 1736

In Cornhill ward, 200 houses burnt; this fire began in Change-alley, and was the most terrible since the great fire of 1666 . . . 25 March, 1748

At Covent Garden, 50 houses burnt 1759

In Smithfield, 28 houses burnt 1761

At Shadwell, 30 houses burnt . . . . ,,

In Throgmorton-street, 20 houses . . . 1774

At Wapping, 20 houses 1775

At Hermitage-stairs, 31 houses 1779

At Horselydown, 30 houses, besides many warehouses and ships . . . 30 April, 1780

Newgate, &c., by the Gordon mob . . June, ,,

In the Strand, 40 houses burnt 1781

In Aldersgate-street, 40 houses; the loss exceeding 100,000*l.* . . . . . . 5 Nov. 1783

The Opera-house . . . . 17 June, 1789

At Rotherhithe, 20 houses . . . 12 Oct. 1790

Again, when many ships and 60 houses were consumed . . . . . . 14 Sept. 1791

Pantheon, Oxford-street . . . 14 June, 1792

At Wapping, 630 houses, and an East India warehouse, in which 35,000 bags of saltpetre were stored: the loss 1,000,000*l.* (tents for the sufferers were lent by the government) . 21 July, 1794

Astley's amphitheatre . . . . 17 Sept. ,,

St. Paul's church, Covent-garden . . 11 Sept. 1795

At Shadwell, 20 houses burnt . . . 1 Nov. 1796

In the Minories, 30 houses . . . 23 March, 1797

In the King's Bench, 50 residences . 14 July, 1799

Near the Customs, three West India warehouses; loss 300,000*l.* . . . . . 11 Feb. 1800

At Wapping, 30 houses . . . . 6 Oct. ,,

In Store-street, Tottenham-court-road, immense property destroyed . . . . 27 Sept. 1802

The great tower over the choir of Westminster abbey burnt . . . . . . 9 July, 1803

Astley's again, and 40 houses . . . 1 Sept. ,,

Frith-street, Soho, lasted several days, many houses destroyed . . . . 2 Dec. ,,

Surrey Theatre . . . . . . 12 Aug. 1805

Covent-garden Theatre . . . . . 20 Sept. 1808

Drury-lane Theatre . . . . . 24 Feb. 1809

In Conduit-street; Mr. Windham, in aiding to save Mr. North's library, received an injury which caused his death . . . . . 9 July, ,,

Bury-street, St. Mary-axe, great fire . 12 June, 1811

Custom-house: warehouses, and public records destroyed . . . . 12 Feb. 1814

At Rotherhithe, 60 houses and several ships destroyed; loss 80,000*l.* . . . . 16 March, 1820

At Mile-end; loss 200,000*l.* . . . 22 Jan. 1821

In Smithfield; loss 100,000*l.* . . . 14 Aug. 1822

Royalty Theatre, Wellclose-sq., destroyed 11 April, 1826

In Red Lion-street, 15 houses . . . 6 June, 1828

Argyle rooms destroyed . . . . 5 Feb. 1830

English opera-house, &c., burnt . . . 16 Feb. ,,

Houses of parliament consumed . . . 16 Oct. 1834

Fenning's-wharf, London-bridge, &c.; loss 250,000*l.* 30 Aug. 1836

The Royal Exchange destroyed . . . 10 Jan. 1838

At Wapping, 12 houses . . . . 16 June, 1840

Camberwell church . . . . . 7 Feb. 1841

Astley's theatre again . . . . . 8 June, ,,

At the Tower; the armoury and 280,000 stand of arms, &c., destroyed . . . . 30 Oct. ,,

Raggett's hotel, Dover-street, Piccadilly; several eminent persons perished . . . 27 May, 1845

Several houses in New-square, Lincoln's inn, 14 Jan. 1849

Olympic Theatre . . . . . . 29 March, ,,

One in St. Martin's-lane (at a publican's named Ben Caunt), three lives lost . . . 15 Jan. 1851

Fire at Duke-street, London-bridge; property lost estimated at 60,000*l.* . . . . 19 Feb. ,,

At the Rose and Crown, Love-lane, City, four lives lost . . . . 18 May, ,,

Foot of London-bridge, four large hop warehouses burnt; loss 150,000*l.* . . . . 23 June, ,,

Collard and Co., pianoforte makers, Camden-town; loss 60,000*l.* . . . . . . 19 Dec. ,,

The warehouses of Messrs. Pawson, St. Paul's churchyard, burnt . . . . . 24 Feb. 1853

Works of Gutta Percha Company, near City-road; loss 100,000*l.* . . . . . 5 June, ,,

Kirkman's pianoforte manufactory . . 10 Aug. ,,

Messrs. Scott Russell and Co.'s works, Millwall; loss 100,000*l.* . . . . . 10 Sept. ,,

Premises of Messrs. Savill and Edwards, printers, Chandos-street, destroyed . . . 30 Sept. ,,

Premises of Townend and Co., Bread-street, destroyed; loss about 100,000*l.* . . 31 Dec. ,,

Messrs. Cubitt's premises, Pimlico . . 17 Aug. 1854

Whittington club-house . . . . 3 Dec. ,,

Premises of Messrs. Routledge, Messrs. Rennie, &c., Blackfriars-road; loss, one life and 150,000*l.*, 16 Feb. 1855

Of Etna steam battery at Messrs. Scott Russell's works; loss about 120,000*l.* . . . . 3 May, ,,

Pavilion Theatre . . . . . . 13 Feb. 1856

Covent-garden Theatre . . . . . 5 March, ,,

Messrs. Scott Russell's (third fire), much valuable machinery destroyed . . . . 12 March, ,,

Messrs. Dobbs' premises, Fleet-street . 1 April, ,,

Shad Thames flour-mill; loss about 100,000*l.*, 17 July, ,,

Messrs. Broadwood's, pianoforte makers, Westminster . . . . 12 Aug. ,,

Premises of Messrs. Almond, army accoutrement makers, and others, in St. Martin's-lane; estimated loss 20,000*l.* . . . . . . 9 Nov. 1856
Messrs. Pickford's premises, at Chalk Farm station, 9 June, 1857
Gilbert-street, Bloomsbury; 15 lives lost, 28 March, 1858
Fresh-wharf; 25,000*l.* of silk . . 21 June, ,,
London docks; great explosion; man killed by fright; loss about 150,000*l.* . 29 June, ,,
Limehouse; Messrs. Forest, Dixon's, &c., premises destroyed, and Blackwall railway arches; insured, 19-20 July, ,,
Gt. James-st., Marylebone; six lives lost, 26 Feb. 1859
Messrs. Hubbuck and Co., Lime-street; one life and a large amount of property . . 20 May, ,,
West Kent wharf and New Hibernia wharf; destroyed property valued at 200,000*l.*; fire lasted nearly a month; commenced . . 17 Aug. 1860
St. Martin's-hall, built for Mr. Hullah, and other premises, destroyed . . . . . 26 Aug. ,,
Thames iron-works, Blackwall . . 31 Aug. ,,
Kilburn church, Maida-hill, destroyed 29 Nov. ,,
Surrey music-hall destroyed . . 11 June, 1861
Cotton's wharf and depôt and other wharves near Tooley-street, containing oil and other combustible substances, took fire about half-past 4 P.M., 22 June, and continued burning for a month. (Several persons were killed, including James Braidwood, the able superintendent of the London fire-brigade; the loss of property was estimated at 2,000,000*l.*) . . . . ,,
Davis's wharf, Horselydown, burnt; loss about 15,000*l.* . . . . . . 1 Aug. ,,
Near Paternoster-row; Messrs. Longman's, booksellers, Messrs. Knight's, tallow-melters, and others; loss above 50,000*l.* . . 4 Sept. ,,
Mr. Price's, Fountain-court, Strand, three lives lost, 3 Jan. 1862
At Campden-house, Kensington, pictures and other valuable property of Mr. Woolley destroyed (see *Trials*, 1863) . . . 23 March, ,,
Mr. Dean's, Berkeley-street, Clerkenwell, three lives lost . . . . . . 5 May, ,,
Mr. Joel's, Fore-street, City, four lives lost, 21 May, ,,
Mr. Boor's, druggist, Bishopsgate-street; explosion; two lives lost . . . 7 June, ,,
Great Cumberland-street, Hyde-park; Mr. S. Barrett and two daughters burnt . 15 Aug. ,,
Messrs. Price's oil-mills, Blackfriars bridge, burnt; great loss of property . . . 20 Nov. ,,
Ancient Austin-friars church, City, partially destroyed . . . . . . 22 Nov. ,,
Mr. Chard's, Portland-street, Soho; six lives lost, 26 Dec. ,,
Messrs. Capel's, Seething-lane, City; great destruction of property . . . 18 April, 1863
Warehouses of Messrs. Grant and others, between Wood-street and Milk-street; property worth about 100,000*l.* destroyed . . . 19 Dec. ,,
Meriton's wharf, Dockhead; immense loss of property . . . . . . 7 June, 1864
Royal Savoy chapel, Strand, destroyed 7 July, ,,
Haberdashers'-hall and Messrs. Tapling and others' warehouses . . . . . 19 Sept. ,,
Messrs. Barry, Sufferance wharves, Dockhead; great loss . . . . . 25, 26 Nov. ,,
Surrey Theatre destroyed . . . 30, 31 Jan. 1865
Saville-house (where George III. was born), Leicester-square . . . . . 28 Feb. ,,
Poulterers' arms, Leadenhall market; two lives lost . . . . 13 June, ,,
Messrs. Meeking and Co., Holborn; damage 30,000*l.* 24 June, ,,
Messrs. Sotheby and Co., auctioneers; valuable library destroyed . . . . 29 June, ,,
Great fire at Beale's wharf; about 18,000*l.* damage, 30 Oct. ,,
Immense fire at St. Katharine's-docks . 1 Jan. 1866
Holland and Hennen's premises, Duke-street, Bloomsbury, destroyed . . . 26 Aug. ,,
Great fire in Haydon-square, Minories; depôt of N. W. Railway company, and other warehouses; great loss . . . . . . 11 Sept. ,,
Standard Theatre, Shoreditch, burnt down, 21 Oct. ,,
In Hampstead-road, thirteen lives lost . 5 Nov. ,,
North wing of the Crystal palace destroyed, 30 Dec. ,,
Quebec-street, Oxford-street; six lives lost, 11 March, 1867
Rotherhithe, 16 or 17 houses burnt; about 100 persons destitute . . . . 12 Sept. 1867
Her Majesty's theatre, Royal opera-house, destroyed: see *Opera* . . . 6 Dec. ,,
Oxford music-hall, Oxford-street, partially destroyed . . . . . . 11 Feb. 1868
Above 20 shops burnt in Portman-market, Marylebone . . . . 23 Feb. ,,
Hubbard and Stutters' hop-warehouses; and many small houses destroyed . . . 10 Aug. ,,
Northumberland house, Strand; valuable pictures, &c., injured . . . . . 19 Aug. ,,
Adelaide rooms, Strand, destroyed . 14 March, 1869
All Saints church, Walworth, destroyed 27 April, ,,
Mrs. Jago's, Pentonville-hill; 3 perish 5 June, ,,
Moscow-road, Bayswater; through explosion of fireworks; 7 persons perish . . 1 Oct. ,,
Mr. McMicken's, Newington-butts; 4 lost 10 Oct. ,,
Old Star and Garter hotel, Richmond; Wm. Lever, the manager, killed . . . 12 Jan. 1870
Mr. Hill's, upholsterer's, Waterloo-road; 6 children suffocated . . . . . 23 July, ,,
Church-street, Rotherhithe; 3 lives lost 23 Aug. ,,
Cecil-house, Cecil-street, Strand; Mr. Forbes burnt; architectural books, &c., of Mr. G. G. Scott destroyed . . . . . . 4 Sept ,,
Mr. Bush's, manufacturing chemist, Liverpool-street, Bishopsgate; 4 lives lost . 27 Sept. ,,
Chapel-street, Edgware-road, 4 lives lost; Crouch-end, Hornsey, 3 lives lost . . 5 March, 1871
Pavilion-road, Chelsea; 5 deaths . 26 March, ,,
Gray's-inn-road; James Ford, a fireman, lost his life after saving 6 . . . . 7 Oct. ,,
Thames-street; Nicholson's and other warehouses destroyed; great loss . . . 24 Oct. ,,
Oxford music-hall; quite destroyed . 1 Nov. 1872
City flour-mills, Upper Thames-street; 1 fireman killed . . . . 10, 11, 12 Nov. ,,
Grosvenor-mews, Bond-street, 6 killed . 27 May, 1873
Alexandra-palace, Muswell-hill, destroyed, 1 life lost . . . . 9 June, ,,
Silver-street, Stepney; 2 killed . 10 Sept. ,,
Lloyd's newspaper printing-office, Whitefriars, destroyed . . . . 4 p.m. 29 Dec. ,,
Pantechnicon (*which see*), Knightsbridge; much valuable property destroyed . . 13, 14 Feb. 1874
Carnaby-street, W.; 2 lives lost . . 15 Feb. ,,
Latta's great hop warehouse, Bermondsey, destroyed . . . . 28 Dec. ,,
Rimmel's perfumery manufactory, Beaufort-house, Strand, destroyed . . . 19 March, 1875
W. Walker's cabinet manufactory, Bunhill-row, E.C., destroyed; estimated loss 30,000*l.* 14 Sept. ,,
Mr. H. A. Hankey's new mansion, near St. Anne's gate, St. James's park, destroyed; about 60,000*l.* damage . . . . 7, 8 Oct. ,,
East London Rice and Flour Mills, Devonshire-street; and 18 other buildings . 3 Jan. 1876
Chick's Great Western Pantechnicon . 2 June, ,,
Messrs. Warner's and other premises, Brook's-wharf, Upper Thames-street . 15-18 June, ,,
Little Windmill-street, Haymarket; about 80,000*l.* damage; many poor sufferers . 15 July, ,,
Bridgman's saw-mills, St. Luke's, destroyed 24-25 July, ,,
Grant & Co.'s printing-office, &c., Turnmill-street, Clerkenwell; about 100,000*l.* loss 10, 11 Aug. ,,
Mill-street, Hanover-square, W., three lives lost 18 Sept. ,,
New wharf flour-mills, &c., Rotherhithe, destroyed; above 80,000*l.* loss . 8 Oct. ,,
Near Old Kent-road, two lives lost; suspected arson . . . . 2 Nov. ,,
House of Correction, Clerkenwell, mill-house, &c.; no prisoners injured or escaped 24 March, 1877
Charing-cross restaurant, one life lost 21 May, ,,
Little Britain, E.C., a paraffin lamp upset; four lives lost . . . . . . 9 July, ,,
250, Mile End-road, two lives lost . . 23 Oct. ,,
Scottish Corporation hall, Crane-court, Fleet-street (built by Wren), burnt many valuable portraits, &c. . . . . 14 Nov. ,,
Watson's wharf, Wapping, loss abt. 30,000*l.* 31 Dec. ,,
Manchester warehouses, Watling-street; Crocker & Co.; and others; about 200,000*l.* loss 12 Jan. 1878
Elephant and Castle theatre destroyed 26 March, ,,
Price and Co., oil-merchants, &c. . . 3 Sept. ,,

Messrs. Tylor's, brass-founders, &c., Newgate-street, great loss . . . . 2-3 Jan. 1879

New East London Theatre, Whitechapel-road, several houses injured . . . . . 16 March, ,,

Wesley's chapel, City-road, nearly destroyed, caused by heating apparatus . . . . . 7 Dec. ,,

Holborn, Roworth's printing office . . 19 April, 1880

Messrs. Hodgkinson's, chemists, and others, four perish . . . . 30 April, ,,

The Duke's Theatre, Holborn, burnt. . 4 July, ,,

Whitechapel church, recently rebuilt, destroyed, 26 Aug. ,,

Trinity-lane, Thames-street, large block of buildings, and much property destroyed . . 3 Feb. 1881

Cöoperative stores, Haymarket, destroyed; loss about 20,000*l*. . . . . . . 23 April, ,,

Mr. Allen's, stationer, 96, Walworth-road, 4 deaths, 26 April, ,,

422, Portobello-road, Notting-hill, 6 deaths, 16 May; (Wm. Nash, shopkeeper, charged with arson and murder; convicted, but reprieved) . 30 May, ,,

Messrs. T. Foster and Co.'s warehouses, Cheapside; much property destroyed: checked by firemen and good building . . . . . 1 Sept. ,,

Dowgate dock warehouse; ald. Breffit's 3 Sept. ,,

Park theatre, Camden Town, destroyed 10 Sept ,,

Morson and Son, chemical works, explosion; 2 killed 17 Jan. 1882

Philharmonic Theatre, Islington, interior destroyed 6 Sept. ,,

Whiteley's great stores, Westbourne Grove, W., about 100,000*l*. damage . . . . 17 Nov. ,,

The Royal Alhambra Theatre destroyed; 3 men killed . . . . 7 Dec. ,,

Wood-street, &c., premises of Foster, Porter, and Co., Rylands, Silber, and Fleming, and others. A large block of buildings destroyed, estimated loss nearly 2,000,000*l*.: 1 death . 8-10 Dec. ,,

St. Ann's restaurant and warehouses in Cheapside destroyed . . . . 15 Dec. ,,

St. John's Presbyterian church, Forest-hill, destroyed . . . . 17 Dec. ,,

Another fire at Whiteley's . . . . 26 Dec. ,,

Windsor-street, E.C., 5 deaths . . 16 Jan. 1883

Newnham-street, Edgeware-road, 5 deaths 14 April, ,,

Messrs. Kegan, Paul, and Co.'s premises, and other buildings (16 firms), Paternoster-square 17 April, ,,

Freemason's-hall much injured . . . 3 May, ,,

Lunatic asylum, Southall-park, W., Dr. Boyd and 5 others perish . . . . . . 14 Aug. ,,

Hay warehouses at Foreign-cattle-market, Deptford; damage, about 18,000*l*. . . 18 Sept. ,,

Great fire at Haggerston, beginning at Messrs. Lines, timber merchants, saw mills and eleven small houses destroyed; 40 families homeless 5-9 Nov. ,,

Messrs. Silver and Co., premises near Cornhill 17 Jan. 1884

Premises of Messrs. Pardon, printers, &c., Messrs. Williams, Faudel, and Phillips, Smith Brothers, and others, Lovell's-court, Paternoster-row, destroyed, 7.30 P.M.; by great exertions fire quelled, 11 P.M. . . . . 2 April, ,,

Bell hotel, Old Bailey; three young women lamentably perish, about 2.30 A.M. . . 23 April, ,,

Another fire at Whiteley's stores, loss about 150,000*l*. 26 April, ,,

East End Aquarium, menagerie, and waxwork, &c., Bishopsgate, destroyed; lioness, bear, monkeys, and other animals perish, 8.30 A.M. 4 June, ,,

Wapping, Messrs. E. H. Cousens and Co., warehouses and others; damage about 100,000*l*. 19-20 July, ,,

Mr. Abrahams, hatter, 33, Wilton-road, Pimlico, 7.45 A.M., 4 deaths . . . . . 12 Aug. ,,

Messrs. Hodgson's envelope manufactory, Little Trinity-lane, destroyed, about 10,000*l*. loss, 9.45 A.M. . . . . 15 Aug. ,,

Jones's wharf; great destruction of timber 17 Dec. ,,

Holles-street, Clare-market, 4 deaths . 31 Dec. ,,

Mr. H. Chandler's, 194, Union-st., Borough; 5 lives lost, including Alice Ayres, who courageously saved 3 children, ... 23-24 April, 1885

Japanese village burnt; 1 life lost . . 2 May, ,,

Jackson and Graham's upholstery workshops, near Oxford-st . . . . . . 6 May, ,,

Messrs. Groom's wood-yard at Camberwell destroyed . . . . 9 May, 1885

India Museum, South Kensington, much injured 12 June, ,,

Mr. W. Whiteley's establishment at Westbourne-grove, over 100,000*l*. damage, (? incendiary) 17 June. ,,

St. John's-road, Hoxton; 3 lives lost . 26 Aug. ,,

Charterhouse buildings, &c., Clerkenwell; 14 houses destroyed; loss 20,000*l*. . . 8 Oct. ,,

Anton, Brenda & Co., Japanese merchants, Houndsditch; damage 25,000*l*. . . . 15 Feb. 1886

"Three Compasses," Beak-street, W.; 3 lives lost; 2.20 a.m. . . . . 28 April, ,,

"Jacob's Well," Shoreditch; 3 lives lost 12 May, ,,

Grandison-road, Battersea; 2 lives lost 30 Nov. ,,

Knightrider-street, city; several houses and St. Mary Magdalene church destroyed . 2 Dec. ,,

24, Grafton-street, W., and adjoining buildings 18-19 Dec. ,,

103, 104, Wood-street, city . . . . 1 Jan 1887

22, Newman-street, Oxford-street; 4 lives lost 26 June, ,,

Mr. W. Whiteley's establishment and neighbouring houses destroyed by fire; estimated damage 500,000*l*.; 3 lives lost; 3,000*l*. reward for discovery of incendiary . . . . . 6-9 Aug. ,,

Messrs. Kindon & Powell's oil-cloth manufactory burnt, loss about 50,000*l*. . . . 6 Dec. ,,

Grand Theatre, Islington, totally destroyed in an hour, 12.55 a.m. . . . . . 29 Dec. ,,

No. 274, Strand; 2 boys perish; Sunday, 18 Sept.; Leon Serné, the father, and John Henry Goldfinch tried for murder, 13 Dec.; acquitted 15 Dec. 1887. Leon Serné sentenced to twenty years' penal servitude; Goldfinch acquitted 21 Jan. 1888

Houndsditch, 4 persons (foreigners) perish, 20 Jan. ,,

Bay-tree tavern, No. 5, St. Swithin's-lane 12 May, ,,

Messrs. Garrould's, drapers, &c., Edgware-road, 6 women perish; 6 a.m. 30 May; jury censures the kitchen-maid for carelessness with a lucifer-match, and two fire-brigade men for neglect of duty . . . . 11 June, ,,

Messrs. Doulton's potteries, Lambeth; great part of the works destroyed, damage 15,000*l*. 11 Dec. ,,

Farringdon meat market, thirty shops destroyed 6 Jan. 1889

Ward's Wharf, Commercial-rd., Lambeth; damage about 20,000*l*. . . . . . . 7-8 Feb. ,,

Messrs. W. & D. Gibb's great soap-works, Milton-street and surrounding premises destroyed, estimated damage 250,000*l*. . . . 6 May, ,,

Messrs. W. H. & F. Croker, builders, and Messrs. Bonsey, corn merchants, extensive buildings near Great Dover-street, Borough . . 7 July, ,,

Messrs. Burroughs and Wellcome, manufacturing chemists, Bell-lane, Wandsworth, fireman Jacobs suffocated; (long inquest) . . . . 11 Oct. ,,

The Salvation army offices, Queen Victoria-street, upper floors destroyed . . . . . 3 Dec. ,,

Block of buildings in Charterhouse-square, W. Smithfield (Mr. Burgess, printer, Messrs. Ruddiman, Johnston & Co., publishers, & Mr. Ferranti, electrical engineers); great destruction . 25 Dec. ,,

Forest-gate District Industrial school, London, E., partly destroyed; 26 boys, aged between 7 and 12 years, suffocated; many escaped through the energy of Mr. Charles Duncan, the superintendant, and other officials, early 1 Jan.; inquest, verdict, accidental death with strong recommendations . . . . 20 Jan. 1890

Premises of Messrs. James & Pike, mantle manufacturers, back of the General Post-office, partly destroyed, estimated loss 40,000*l*. . . 3 Feb. ,,

Premises of Messrs. Gay, Armstrong & Co., skin merchants, Westminster-bridge-road, 2 lives lost 18 Feb. ,,

Sir W. A. Rose & Co.'s great oil mills, Bankside, Southwark, destroyed; London illuminated by the blazing oil; no loss of life, two firemen injured, horses rescued . . . . 24 April, ,,

Old Sun, coal wharf, Messrs. Ray, destroyed 29 Aug. ,,

Messrs. Rowley & Brock, hat-makers, premises in Cloth-fair destroyed, by the combustion of naphtha; 8 deaths, 3 men and 5 women, about 1 P.M. . . . . 13 Oct. ,,

Messrs. Vogan & Co.'s granaries, &c., Mill-street, Dockhead, destroyed; great fire . . 9 Nov. 1900
Wellington barracks, Westminster, much injured; six persons hurt; no deaths through the gallant and orderly conduct of the soldiers [two children died afterwards] . . . . . 12 Nov. ,,
Messrs. Lever, Wright & Co., furriers, Bunhill-row; great loss . . . . . 28 Nov. ,,
Herbert-passage, Strand; four lives lost 21 Dec. ,,
Messrs. Davidson, paper manufacturers, Upper Thames-street, Queen Victoria-street, &c., Messrs. Frankau, fancy goods importers, Revillon Frères, furriers, and other firms in Upper Thames street, and Queen Victoria street; a large block of buildings wholly or partially destroyed, tenanted by Messrs. C. Davidson, paper-makers, Messrs. Revillon, furriers, and 16 other firms; St. Benet's church, damaged; estimated loss 500,000*l.* midday, 30 Dec. ,,
Hope's chemical works, Hackney-wick, destroyed . 30 Dec. ,,
Messrs. Morgan & Company, carriage builders, Long-acre, and others; loss about 50,000*l.* 13 Feb. 1891
Messrs. J. Tylors, engineers, Newgate-street, and other premises, workshops destroyed; serious loss to workmen . . . . . . 21 March, ,,
Messrs. Payton & Co., tea dealers, Tower-hill, and other premises, greatly damaged 11 April, ,,
M. C. Duffy & Son, saw-mills, Stork's-road, Bermondsey, destroyed and about 24 private houses damaged; inhabitants compelled to leave their homes hastily; much suffering; 5 A.M.—6 P.M. 29 April, *et seq.* ,,
House of John, Lord Romilly, 38, Egerton-gardens, Brompton, W., through the upsetting of a large spirit-lamp; his lordship and two servants suffocated and others injured . . . . 23 May ,,
Mr. Louis Tussaud's waxwork exhibition, Regent-street, destroyed by fire . . . 20 June, ,,
25, Duncan-square, Hackney; 3 lives lost, 20 Aug. ,,
Tooley-street; wharves, occupied by Messrs. Leach and others, and several warehouses destroyed, 4-5 Oct., enormous loss; fire still burning, 24 Oct. ,,
401, West Ferry-road, Millwall; 5 deaths 16 Oct. ,,
Satchwell-rents, Bethnal-green-road; Mr. J. D. Rawlins' timber yard and other premises destroyed . . . . 12 Nov. ,,
Premises of Messrs. Everleigh and others in Fore-street, E.C. . . . . . . 9, 10 Dec. ,,
Messrs. Rothschild and others, 11, Silk-street, Cripplegate, City, E.C. . . . . 14 Dec. ,,
3, Cheyne-row, Chelsea, 2 lives lost . 15 Dec. ,,
Mr. Minnis and others, Lavender-hill, Battersea; 2 lives lost . . . . . . 19 Dec. ,,
Messrs. Shoolbred's workshops and other premises, Mitford-place, Tottenham-court-road . 22 Dec. ,,
Premises of Bottle Seal company, Eagle-wharf-road, N. . . . . . . 23 Dec. ,,
Premises of A. Wicklow and others, Bermondsey-street, S.E. . . . . . . 24 Dec. ,,
Mumford's flour mills, Albert Embankment, near Vauxhall-bridge; nearly destroyed . 27 Jan. 1892
Premises of Messrs. Grindley & Co. and others, Upper North-street, Poplar . . 27–29 Jan. ,,
J. Latham, timber-merchant, premises in Curtain-road, E.C., many houses destroyed or injured, causing much distress . . . 8–11 March, ,,
House of Mr. Weston, butcher, 10, Lillie-road, Fulham; his wife, 2 children and Miss Glover burnt to death. 18 March, ,,
Mr. G. Odone's restaurant, 152, Victoria-street, Westminster, 3 lives lost 29 March, ,,
Messrs. Eyre & Spottiswoode, the queen's printers, premises at Little New-street-hill, Fetter-lane, much injured and property destroyed (about 15,000*l.*) . . . . 4 April, ,,
Premises of Page & Pratt and other firms, Great Saffron-hill, E.C., destroyed or much injured 10 April, ,,
Scott's supper-rooms, Coventry-street, Haymarket, 4 youths perish . . . . 9 May, ,,
Union-street, W.C., Mary Ann Flood perishes in vainly endeavouring to save a child . 7 May, ,,
Mr. S. Burrows' dancing academy, Hargrave-park-road, Upper Holloway; Wm. Smart and Wm. Abernethy, firemen, killed . 10 June, ,,
Jewin-street and crescent, Aldersgate-street, premises belonging to the Goldsmiths' company, tenanted by the London Printing and Publishing Alliance, and others . . . 29 Aug. 1892
Destruction of Messrs. Sheppard & Co.'s large warehouses on the New Sun wharf, and other premises, Narrow-street, Ratcliff-highway 24, 25 Oct. ,,
Great fire in the London and India docks, Wapping; large warehouses destroyed . 25–28 Nov. ,,
23, Tower-street, Westminster-bridge-road; 4 deaths 26 Jan. 1893
Messrs. Darell, timber merchants, Globe wharf, Mile-end-road; saw-mills, much timber, &c., destroyed . . . . . 2–4 March, ,,
Premises of Messrs. Judd & Co., printers, and many others, St. Andrew's-hill, E.C., and Carter-lane; much destruction . . . . 31 March, ,,
Messrs. Wm. Cubbitt's works, Gray's-inn-road; estimated loss, nearly 100,000*l.* . 17 June, ,,
W. Brown & Co., wholesale stationers, and others, 38–40, St. Mary-axe, E.C., and other places 18 July, ,,
129, Whitechapel High-street, premises of Messrs. Brooke, Bond & Co., tea blenders, and others, 18 July, ,,
Messrs. Beauchamp Bros.' general stores, Brompton-road, S.W. . . . . 18 July, ,,
62, Fulham Palace-road; Mr. Wale (oilman) and 4 children burnt . . . . . 4 Sept. ,,
High-street, Whitechapel; Mr. Hermann (pastry cook) and 4 women burnt . . 19 Sept. ,,
Messrs. Thomson & Co., perfume manufacturers, &c., Old Bailey and adjoining buildings, Fleet-lane, &c.; 1 fireman killed . . 15–16 Nov. ,,
British Xylonite company's premises, High-street, Homerton; 1 death . . . . 29 Dec. ,,
Stacey-street, W.C.; 2 women burnt . 30 Dec. ,,
11, Northampton-street, Clerkenwell, by the upsetting of a paraffin lamp; 5 deaths 24 March, 1894
Great fire at the London docks . . 3–5 April, ,,
Tabernacle-street, Nos. 62–78; Messrs. Lebus, Harris & Co., cabinet-makers and others; over 30 buildings destroyed or seriously damaged, 21–22 June, ,,
Minories; premises of the Terrabona (tea) company, and Messrs. Martin, Pulvermann & Co. and others; also at Messrs. T. J. Brodie, printers, Clerkenwell-road . . . . . 10 Nov. ,,
At 8, Clegg-street, Wapping; 3 deaths 24 Nov. ,,
Premises of Messrs. Harper, upholsterers, and others, Cygnet-street, E. . . . 3, 4 Dec. ,,
French laundry, Nos. 412, 414, Edgware-road; totally destroyed; Mdm. Martin, the proprietor, and 7 others perished; 1–2 A.M. . . 2 Jan. 1895
Fire at the S. W. India docks; block of buildings destroyed . . . . . . 8–10 Feb. ,,
Destructive fires in Wood-street and Jewry-street 9 March, ,,
In Hermit-road, Canning-town, through bursting of a lamp; 5 children suffocated . . 5 April, ,,
Messrs. Goode, printers, Clerkenwell-green, 30 Aug. ,,
Mr. A. Houston's house, 65, Queen's-cresc., N.W.; 3 deaths . . . . 12 Jan 1896
The Cambridge music-hall burnt down 28 Jan. ,,
7, Church-street, Soho (lodging-house), 3 A.M.; 9 lives lost . . . . . . 16 Feb. ,,
Messrs. Ashby & Horner, builders, Love-lane, Shadwell . . . . . . 24 Feb. ,,
Messrs. Clozenberg, cabinet-makers, Charlotte-street; warehouses in Pavey-st., E.C. 10–12 June, ,,
Messrs. Davies & Evans, oil and colourmen, Mare-street, Hackney; 4 deaths . . 17 June, ,,
Premises of Gt. Western R. Co., Paddington, 22 June, ,,
Rudyard-place, Bermondsey; 4 deaths . 10 July, ,,
Messrs. Street's cabinet factory, New-inn-yard, Shoreditch. . . . . 10–11 Sept. ,,
Portman chapel, Baker-street, much injured by fire . . . . 25 Oct. ,,
8, Clarence-street, Bethnal-green, Eliza Hollington, burnt to death . . . . . 2 Nov. ,,
274, Caledonian-road, Islington, Mr. and Mrs. Jones, and 3 others, burnt . . . 3 Nov. ,,
Messrs. Shand, Mason & Co., engineering works, Blackfriars, burnt, ... 7–9 Nov. ,,
The belfry tower of St. George's church, Hanover-square, burnt, through fusion of electric wires, 18 Nov.

Lodging-house, 18, Dorset-street, W.; 4 deaths, 23 Nov. 1896

28, Aintree-street, Fulham; 3 deaths . 30 Nov. ,,

Messrs. Moss & Co., timber merchants, Hoxton-street, Hoxton . . . . . . 4 Jan. 1897

60, Grosvenor-street, W., the house of the dowager countess De La Warr, who narrowly escaped, burnt down; 1 death . . . . 26 Jan. ,,

Messrs. Walker & Hall, silversmiths, &c., Shoe-lane, warehouse gutted . . . . 1 Feb. ,,

Messrs. Maple & Co., Little Camden-street, Camden Town, warehouse (block E), destroyed, 6, 7 Feb. ,,

Explosion of gas and fire at a hop warehouse, &c., Chapel-street, Borough; 2 deaths . 15 Feb. ,,

Wareham-street, Hoxton, caused by a lamp at a bedside; 3 deaths . . . . 6 March, ,,

Messrs. Gleaney & Ray's printing premises, Gate-street, Lincoln's-inn-fields, burnt 26, 27 April, ,,

At a coffee-house, Caledonian-road, Islington; 2 deaths . . . . . . 26 April, ,,

Destructive fire: Messrs. King, publishers; Messrs. Plimpton, cabinet-makers; and other warehouses burnt; Curtain-road, Shoreditch . . 13 June, ,,

196, Regent's-park-road, Hannah Bush, burnt to death . . . . 7 July, ,,

113, Drury-lane, 2 persons burnt, and 1 killed by a fall . . . . 4 Aug. ,,

Fire in a stable, King Edward-street, Whitechapel; 4 horses burnt . . . . . 7 Aug. ,,

Messrs. Carter, Paterson & Co., carriers, Goswell-road, buildings, &c., destroyed. . 31 Oct. ,,

CITY FIRE: over 4 acres, 2½ acres burnt out, 17 streets affected: began at Messrs. Waller & Brown, Well-street, Cripplegate, at 12.50 P.M., 19, 20 Nov.; no lives lost; estimated loss, about 2,000,000*l.* (insurance loss, 1,000,000*l.*); over 100 warehouses destroyed; 4,000 persons thrown out of work; relief fund opened, 22 Nov. (795*l.* surplus given to the fire brigade, 15 March, 1898); inquest at the Guildhall, began 6 Dec.; verdict: the fire attributed to the wilful ignition of goods by person or persons unknown, 12 Jan. 1898

Dixie-street, Bethnal-green, the Jarvis family (mother and 9 children), burnt . . 26 Dec. ,,

Morning-lane, 188, Hackney; 2 deaths 25 Jan. ,,

Destructive fire (druggists), High Holborn, 10 Feb. ,,

Sir Henry Irving's theatrical stores, Bear-lane, Southwark, burnt . . . . . 18 Feb. ,,

London Gen. Omnibus Co.'s stores, stables, &c., burnt, Bell-lane, Spitalfields . . 2 March, ,,

The Tabernacle (Spurgeon's), Newington Butts, burnt . . . . 20 April, ,,

Messrs. McDougall's premises, flour merchants, Milwall Docks, burnt . . . . 19–21 Sept. ,,

Messrs. Hudden, iron and tin workers, warehouse, 72, Clerkenwell-road, burnt; 1 death 14 Dec. ,,

Bedfordbury, Covent Garden; 2 deaths 5 Feb. 1899

Cork warehouse, 73, 74, 75 Minories; much damage, 9 Feb. ,,

Messrs. Tucker, Johnson & Co., printers, premises burnt, Southwark . . . . . 19 Feb. ,,

L. Schwabacher's premises, Bread-street, Cheapside . . . . 20 Feb. ,,

Messrs. Keiller's jam factory, Silvertown, 3, 4 April, ,,

Destructive fire, glass warehouse, &c., Farringdon-road . . . . 13 April, ,,

Hyde Park-court, Albert-gate, residential flats, 17 April, ,,

Millwall docks, large stores burnt . . 24 April, ,,

Donald Currie & Co.'s offices, &c., Orchard-place, Blackwall, E.; much damage . 12, 13 May, ,,

16 fires in London . . . . . . 13 May, ,,

Messrs. Spottiswoode & Co., printers, 54, Gracechurch-street; much damage . . 1 June, ,,

Victoria docks, iron warehouse burnt down, *Banffshire* s.s. and barges, &c.; much damage; 1 death . . . . 1, 2 June, ,,

Messrs. Young Bros., forage merchants, Crinan-street, King's-cross; 25 horses burnt . 17 June, ,,

Western Electrical Co.'s premises, N. Woolwich; buildings destroyed . . . . . 21 July, ,,

W. Keen's chair factory, and 2 rows of cottages, High Wycombe; great loss . . . 21 July, ,,

Bull-stairs wharf, Messrs. Sadler & Co., Blackfriars, 22 July, ,,

209, Long-lane, Bermondsey, Messrs. W. Clarke & Co.; much loss . . . . . . 23 July, ,,

Messrs. A. McKenzie, coach builders, Walnut-tree-walk, Lambeth; buildings destroyed . 4 Oct. 1899

Houndsditch, engineering workshop; 1 death, 7 Oct. ,,

West Ham technical institute, Stratford, burnt; estimated damage, 80,000*l.* . . . 23 Oct. ,,

Willow-tree inn, Ball's-pond-road, Islington; 5 little children burnt . . . . . 13 Nov. ,,

Watson-street, Plaistow; 4 young children killed, 20 Nov. ,,

11 deaths . . . . 11–24 Nov. ,,

Messrs. E. Carr & Sons, sack manufacturers, 14 to 20, The Grange, Bermondsey . . 22 Nov. ,,

Messrs. Isbister & Co. and Ballantyne & Co., printers, and other premises, Tavistock-street, Strand . . . . 8, 9 Dec. ,,

Great fire, Messrs. Haggis, timber yards, and Messrs. Mowlem, contractors, and dwelling-houses, Caledonian-road . . . . 9 Dec. ,,

Messrs. Weber, Wolf, boot factories; Messrs. Lifttree, Emil & Co.; great damage; Banner-street, St. Luke's . . . . . 10 Dec. ,,

147, St. George-street, E., oilshop; 5 children burnt to death . . . . 11 Dec. ,,

St. Paul's-road, Camden Town; 2 ladies named Poole burnt . . . . . . 22 Dec. ,,

Business premises (Messrs. Lloyd and others), Featherstone-street, Old-street, City, destroyed, 13 Jan. 1900

Grand Theatre, Islington, much damaged by fire, 26 Feb. ,,

Large timber yards and buildings, Millwall, burnt, 26 March, ,,

Warehouses, Hay's wharf, Tooley-street, 22, 23 April, ,,

St. Luke's mission church, the Board school, and Messrs. Kellett's premises, Willesden, burnt; estimated damage, 30,000*l.* . . . 26 April, ,,

Blyth's wharf, Limehouse, Mr. Richardson's premises, iron merchant (uninsured), destroyed, 9, 10 June, ,,

Victoria docks, south jetty . . . 9, 10 Oct. ,,

6, Sturge-street, Southwark; Mr. Poulton and 2 sons killed . . . . . . 15 Oct. ,,

Model dwellings, Spitalfields; 7 persons injured, 6 Nov. ,,

Printer's premises, Colley's Patents (limited), and Cooke & Co., 147–150 Gt. Saffron-hill, burnt, 24 Nov. ,,

Day's drug stores, Borough-road, Southwark, 4 Dec. ,,

Chemical works at Blackwall, destroyed. 10 Feb. 1901

Fatal fire, 8 deaths . . . . 14–17 Feb. ,,

A. C. Horsley's premises, Melior-street, Bermondsey, and other buildings, burnt, 9, 10 March, ,,

11, Barnsbury-street; Mr. Kelly, aged 80, burnt, 23 March, ,,

Wandsworth and Putney gasworks, Wandsworth; 1 death . . . . 1 April, ,,

363, Brixton-road, S.W.; Fred. G. Baldock, a fireman, aged 29, suffocated . . 15 April, ,,

8, Upper Bedford-place, Russell-square; 1 death; and 69, St. John-street-road; 2 deaths . 2 May, ,,

Naphtha fire in White-post-lane, Hackney-wick; 3 deaths; many injured . . . 27 July, ,,

London docks fire . . . . . . 1, 2 Aug. ,,

Warehouse, 48, Fore-street, E.C. . . 13 Aug. ,,

Warehouse, Tower-hill, E.C. . . . 17 Aug. ,,

Marmion Works, Lavender-hill, S.W., destroyed; other houses damaged . . . . 23 Aug. ,,

Warehouses, Nos. 6 and 8, Royal Albert docks, gutted . . . . 29 Aug. ,,

Messrs. Lascelles' factory, and other premises, Bunhill-row, City, burnt . . . 8 Sept. ,,

Messrs. White, Tomkins & Courage's premises destroyed, Rotherhithe-street, Bermondsey; estimated damage, 70,000*l.* . . . 15 Sept. ,,

Globe Express Co., Errol-street, E.C.; 4 horses burnt . . . . 1 Oct. ,,

Messrs. E. Carr's factory, Bermondsey; Messrs. Emery's (draper's) premises, Bow-road, E., burnt down; 2 deaths . . . . . 14 Oct. ,,

Oilshop gutted, Judd-street, King's-cross; 3 deaths . . . . 6 Nov. ,,

Blouse factory, 14, London-wall, gutted, 7, 8 Nov. ,,

GREAT FIRE in Gresham-street, City, the warehouses of 53 firms affected; over 50,000*l.* loss; 11.22 p.m., 25 Nov.—5 p.m. . . . 26 Nov. 1901

LEATHER MARKET, Bermondsey, Messrs. Margetson's factory, &c., 24 Nov.; Messrs. Strong & Rawle, fellmongers, 25 Nov.; and Messrs. Tebbitt's premises destroyed; Messrs. Christy's much damaged . . . Nov. 30 ,,

Messrs. J. Barringer's oil factory, Hackney-wick, destroyed . . . . . . 30 Dec. ,,

Fatal fire, 24, Church-street, Plaistow; 3 deaths, 17 Jan. 1902

Fatal fires in private houses; 5 deaths . 1 Feb. ,,

Messrs. Valentine & Norrish's premises, Wandsworth-road, S.E., burnt; 3 deaths . 4 March, ,,

Messrs. Rogers, 423, Hackney-road, E.; 7 deaths, 19 April, ,,

BARBICAN: about 40 buildings damaged, some totally destroyed; estimated insurance loss, 250,000*l.* . . . . . . 21, 22 April, ,,

Lever-street, St. Luke's; 2 deaths, 2 injured, 30 April ,,

Henshaw-street, Walworth; 3 deaths . 10 May, ,,

Welsbach Incandescent Light Co., Palmer-street, Westminster, great fire . . . . 20 May, ,,

Messrs. N. Levy & Co.'s boot factory, burnt, High-street, Shoreditch . . . . 8 June, ,,

Electric Lighting Co., Queen Victoria-street, City; 9 girls and a boy killed (C. J. Jayne's heroic efforts to save life fruitless); some injured, 9 June, ,,

Messrs. Olney, Amsden & Sons, haberdashery warehouse, Falcon-street, burnt out . 13 Aug. ,,

Messrs. Roperstone & Lehap's cabinet works, Vallance-road, Whitechapel, gutted . 30 Aug. ,,

Bermondsey, 78, Jamaica-road; 1 death . 9 Sept. ,,

Messrs. Dixon & Hayne's furniture depository, Harrow-road, Paddington, gutted; great loss, over 170,000*l.*, tapestries, &c. (uninsured), 11 Sept. ,,

Gatesborough-street, Shoreditch, cabinet factory, 14 Sept. ,,

Victoria dock, wharf, acme wood flooring premises, burnt out; estimated damage, 30,000*l.* 18 Sept. ,,

Messrs. T. Smith & Co.'s warehouse, Finsbury-square, gutted . . . . . . 18 Sept. ,,

Messrs. Piggott & Co., Booth-street, Spitalfields, gutted . . . . 3 Oct. ,,

Messrs. Redmayne & Co., silk mercers, 19, 20 New Bond-street; estimated damage, 34,000*l.*, 26, 27 Oct. ,,

Royal Mint-street, Minories, 3 deaths . 22 Nov. ,,

Tarpaulin factory destroyed, 57 Glengal-road, S.E. 24 Nov. ,,

[19 deaths from fires in London, in 7 days, Nov. 7–24]

Ben Jonson-road, Stepney, draper's shop, Mrs. Schlesinger and 5 of her children burned to death . . . . 29 Dec. ,,

Messrs. McMurray's paper mills, S. Wandsworth, burned . . . . 17–18 Jan. 1903

COLNEY HATCH ASYLUM, wooden annexe destroyed in about an hour, 51 women killed, the rest saved with great difficulty . . . . 27 Jan. ,,

Destitute poor asylum, Banner-street, St. Luke's, 1 death . . . . 28 Feb. ,,

Civil Service stores, Haymarket . 13–14 March, ,,

9 Sumner-street, Clerkenwell, 2 deaths . 9 April, ,,

Baltic-place, Golden-lane, 1 death . . 17 April, ,,

Battersea-rise, S.W. 1 death . . . 19 May, ,,

ETON COLLEGE, at boarding-house of Mr. R. S. Kindersley, 2 scholars burned to death, iron-barred windows preventing their egress. Messages of condolence from the king and queen, 1 June, ,,

Destructive fire at goods warehouse of Midland railway co. in St. Pancras-road, Somers-town, 28 June, ,,

Panton-street, Haymarket, at foreign produce importers . . . . 18 Aug. ,,

Corrugated iron buildings in Limehouse basin of the W. India docks . . . . . 1 Sept. ,,

Charing Cross-road, builders' merchant, much damage to adjoining property . . 10 Sept. ,,

Furrier's warehouse, Queen-street, Cheapside, 10 Sept. ,,

Confectionery factory at Camberwell, and adjoining premises of the London Essence co. 26 Sept. ,,

There were 953 fires in 1854; 1113 in 1857; 1114 in 1858 (38 lives lost); 1183 in 1861. 1303 fires in 1862; 1404 in 1863; and 1715 in 1864. In 1866, 1338 fires (326 serious); in 1867, 1397 fires (245 serious); in 1868, 1668 fires (235 serious); in 1869, 1572 fires (199 serious); in 1870, 1946 fires (276 serious); in 1871, 1842 (207 serious); in 1872, 1494 (120 serious); in 1873, 1548 (166 serious: 35 lives lost); in 1874, 1573 (154 serious: 23 lives lost); in 1875, 1529 (163 serious: 29 lives lost); in 1876, 1632 (166 serious: 35 lives lost); in 1877, 1533 (159 serious: 29 lives lost); in 1878, 1659 (170 serious); in 1879, 1718; 1880, 1871 (162 serious; 33 lives lost); in 1881, 1991 (167 serious: 40 lives lost); 1882, 1926 (164 serious: 36 lives lost); 1883, 2144 (184 serious: 39 lives lost); 1884, 2,289 (194 serious: 42 lives lost); 1885, 2,270 (160 serious; 47 lives lost); 1886, 2,149 (151 serious; 49 lives lost); 1887, 2,363 (175 serious; 55 lives lost); 1888, 1,884 (121 serious; 48 lives lost). In but few cases were the premises totally destroyed. 1889, 2,338 (153 serious, 44 lives lost); 1890, 2,555 (153 serious, 61 lives lost); 1891, 2,892 (193 serious, 47 lives lost); 1892, 3,146 (177 serious, 64 lives lost); 1893, 3,410 (180 serious, 82 lives lost); 1894, 3,061 (151 serious, 82 lives lost); 1895, 3,633 (142 serious, 91 lives lost); 1896, 3,616 (122 serious, 106 lives lost); 1897, 3,500 (168 serious, 87 lives lost); 1899, 3,846; 1900, 3,385 (115 serious, 74 lives lost); 1901, 3,684 (99 serious, 97 lives lost); 1902, 3,574 (76 serious, 116 lives lost).

FIRST-FRUITS were offerings which made a large part of the revenues of the Hebrew priesthood. First-fruits (called ANNATES, from *annus*, a year), in the Roman church, originally the profits of one year of every vacant bishopric, afterwards of every benefice, were first claimed by pope Clement V. in 1306, and were collected in England in 1316; but chronologers differ on this point. In the 26th of Henry VIII. 1534, the first-fruits were assigned, by parliament, to the king and his successors. Mary gave the Annates to the popes (1555); but Elizabeth resumed them (1559). They were granted, together with the tenths, to the poor clergy, by queen Anne, in 1703. The offices of First-fruits, Tenths, and Queen Anne's Bounty were consolidated by 1 Vict. c. 20, 1838; see *Augmentation of Poor Livings*. Annates were long resisted in France, but not totally suppressed till 1789.

FIRST OFFENDERS' PROBATION ACT, permits the conditional release of First Offenders in certain cases, passed 8 Aug. 1887.

FIRTH COLLEGE: see *Sheffield*, 1879.

FISH, FISHERIES, &c. Laws for the protection of fisheries were enacted by Edward I. in 1284, and by his successors. The rights of the English and French fishermen were defined by treaty in 1839; see *Ichthyology, Herring, Whale, Newfoundland Fisheries, Oysters, Trawling*. The known species of fish are about 8525. *Günther*, 1880.

Fishmongers' company of London (salt) 1433; (stock) 1509; united 1536

Fishing towns regulated by an act passed in . . 1542

Fishing on our coast forbidden to strangers . . 1609

The Dutch paid 30,000*l.* for permission to fish on the coasts of Britain 1636

Corporation of Free British fisheries instituted . 1750

Fish-machines, for conveying fish by land to London, set up in 1761; and supported by parliament 1764

The British Society of Fisheries established in London in 1786

The Irish Fishery Company formed in . Dec. 1818

In 1849, two peasants, Remy and Gehin, obtained medals for their exertions in cultivating fish in France, and the government set up an establishment for this purpose at Huningue, under M. Coumes.

In 1860 great progress had been made by M. Coste and others.

Commission to examine into British fisheries was appointed in 1860, and acts to amend the law relating to fisheries in Great Britain and Ireland were passed 1861-2-3-8-9

In April, Mr. Ponders placed in the Thames 76,000 young fish (salmon, trout, char, and grayling); and on 17 April, Mr. Frank Buckland demonstrated the importance of fish culture before the members of the Royal Institution, London . . 1863

In 1853 Mr. Buist began the culture of fish at Stormontfield, Perthshire: reported highly successful, Sept. 1866

Act for the protection of freshwater fish passed, 8 Aug. 1878

International fish and fishing exhibition at Berlin, opened by the Crown Prince . . . 20 April, 1880

National fisheries exhibition at Norwich, opened by the prince of Wales . . . 18—30 April, 1881

International exhibition at Edinburgh opened 11 April, 1882

National Fish Culture Association established . 1883

London Central Fish Market, Smithfield, opened 10 May, „

International fisheries exhibition, South Kensington, London, opened and closed by prince of Wales, 14 May—31 Oct. 1883. 335 gold medals (160 to Great Britain) awarded, and other testimonials. Receipts, 140,346*l.* 13*s.*; surplus, 15,243*l.* 2,703,051 persons admitted.

Sea Fisheries Act, 46 & 47 Vict. c. 22, relates to international convention concerning fisheries in North Sea. Sea Fisheries (Ireland) Act also passed . . . . 2 Aug. „

International fisheries, Vienna, opened 29 Sept. 1884

Aquaculture.—Mr. W. Oldham Chambers (in *Times*, 10 Nov.) advocated the formation of ponds in waste lands for the cultivation of carp and other fish. Sir Lyon Playfair recommends the scheme to be taken up by government *Times*, 11 Nov. „

A convention with France respecting sea fisheries, signed at Paris, 11 Nov. 1867; ratified by the "Sea Fisheries Act," passed, 13 July, 1868; amended 1884; convention signed . 14 Nov. 1885

Introduction of American salmon-trout tried at Burghley park in . . . . „

Board of trade inquiry ordered concerning the injuries done to British drift-net fishing by foreign trawlers in the north seas (see *Trawling*) Nov. 1886

First stone of a new fish market laid, Farringdon-street, London . . . . . . 13 Dec. „

Conference at Fishmongers' hall respecting railway charges, &c. . . . . . . 2 Feb. 1887

Fishing school established at Baltimore (which see) Ireland . . . . 17 Aug. „

Many attacks on British fishermen by foreigners, Aug.; one by Belgians near Southwold 8 Sept. „

Intervention of the king of the Belgians . Sept. „

Conference on sea fisheries at Fishmongers' hall opened . . . . . . 20, 23 March, 1888

New central fish market, Farringdon-street, opened 7 Nov. „

Mr Francis Day, the author of important works on British and foreign fishes, died . 10 July, 1889

The Sea Fisheries of the United Kingdom, produce fish 12,678,000 cwt., value 5,608,000*l.* „

The Royal Provident Fund for Sea Fishermen, founded 1884, incorporated 1891

International declaration respecting the North Sea fisheries, ratified by act passed . . 21 July, „

Piscatorial exhibition at the Royal Aquarium, Westminster, middle Feb. *et seq.* (annual exhibitions) 1892

Conference on sea-fishing industry at Fishmongers' hall . . . . 22–24 March, 1893

A select committee of the commons on sea fisheries, Mr. Marjoribanks chairman; first meeting, 2 May; report issued . . . . . 17 Aug. „

North Sea Fisheries Act passed . . . . „

The Sea Fisheries regulation (Scotland) bill passed by the commons, amendments by the lords, 16 Feb.; the bill dropped, 19 Feb. 1894; act passed 6 July, 1895

International conference called by the National Sea Fisheries Protection Association opened at Fishmongers' hall, London, 1 July, 1890; annual meetings . . . . . 21 March, 1894 *et seq.*

Fishery board for Scotland established 1882; its powers were extended by an act passed 3 July, 1894

Riotous opposition to Sunday fishing of the east coast boats; boats boarded by the Newlyn fishermen and their cargoes thrown into the sea, Mounts Bay, Cornwall; troops sent by the admiralty and war office, 19 May; at a mass meeting of W. Cornwall fishermen the matter referred to government . . . . 21 May, 1896

The successful Howietoun hatchery, Stirlingshire, was founded by sir James Gibson Maitland, about 1873; he died, aged 49 . . 19 Nov. 1897

Fisheries disaster, see *Mansion house* . April, 1899

International fisheries conference meets at Stockholm, 15–23 June, 1899; Christiania, 6–11 May, 1901; Copenhagen . . . . 22 July, 1902

Internat. fishery exhibition, Vienna . . 6 Sept. „

Sea fisheries, United Kingdom, produce 17,902,000 cwt. fish, value 9,296,000*l.* . . . . . . „

FISHERIES DISPUTES, &c. The fisheries on the North American coast were settled by treaty, between Great Britain and the United States in 1818, the privileges of the latter extended to 1866 by treaty in 1854, and renewed for ten years, 1871, and again to 1885. On the failure of negociations, the restrictions of 1818 were revived March, 1886. A *joint commission* was appointed, Rt. hon. J. Chamberlain (chief), hon. sir Lionel S. West afterwards lord Sackville, British minister, and sir Charles Tupper, Aug. 1887, received at Washington 19 Nov., met 22 Nov. *et seq.* 1887

Treaty (with a *modus vivendi* till ratified) was signed at Washington, 15 Feb. 1888; passed by Canadian parliament, 2 May; royal assent, 16 May; United States senate refuse to ratify 21 Aug. 1888

FISHGUARD (Pembroke). On 22 Feb. 1797, 1400 Frenchmen landed in Cardigan Bay. On the 24 Feb. they surrendered to lord Cawdor with the Castlemartin yeomanry, and some countrymen, armed with scythes and pitchforks, near Fishguard.

FITZWILLIAM MUSEUM (Cambridge), founded by Richard viscount Fitzwilliam, who died in 1816, and bequeathed his collection of books, pictures, &c., to the university, with 100,000*l.* to erect a building to contain them. The building was begun by G. Basevi in 1837, and finished by Cockerell some years after.

FIUME (meaning river), the port of the kingdom of Hungary, on the Adriatic; a very ancient town, built on the supposed site of Tersatica, destroyed by Charlemagne about 799, and afterwards known as Vitopolis, Cività Sancti Viti ad Flumen, and finally Fiume. After being successively subjected to the Greeks, Romans, the eastern emperors, and the pope, it was transferred to the house of Austria. It was captured by the French early in the century, from whom it was taken by the English in 1813, and given to Austria in 1814. It was transferred to Hungary in 1822; to the Croats in 1848; restored to Hungary in 1868. A new port and railways have been recently constructed (1877). Visit of the emperor of Austria, entertained by admiral Hoskins and the British fleet, 23 June *et seq.* 1891.

Great fire at the railway station; heavy loss; 13, 14 Aug. 1894.

Disastrous floods, 1 death, 20 Oct. 1898.

FIVE FORKS, near Richmond, Virginia. Here general Sheridan turned the front of the Confederates, and defeated them after a fierce struggle, 1 April, 1865.

FIVE HUNDRED, Council of, established by the new French constitution, 22 Aug. 1795, was unceremoniously dissolved by Napoleon Bonaparte, 10 Nov. 1799.

FIVE MEMBERS, see under *England*, 4 Jan. 1642.

FIVE MILE ACT, 17 Chas. II. c. 2 (Oct. 1665), forbade Nonconformist teachers who refused to take the non-resistance oath, to come within five miles of any corporation where they had preached since the act of oblivion (unless they were travelling), under the penalty of 40*l.* They were relieved by Will. III. in 1689.

FLADENHEIM, or **Flatcheim,** Saxony. Here Rodolph of Swabia defeated the emperor Henry IV., 27 Jan. 1080.

FLAG. The flag acquired its present form in the 6th century, in Spain; it was previously small and square. *Ashe.* It is said to have been introduced there by the Saracens, before whose time the ensigns of war were extended on cross pieces of wood; see *Carrocium.* The *honour-of-the-flag salute* at sea was exacted by England from very early times; but it was formally yielded by the Dutch in 1673, at which period they had been defeated in many actions. Louis XIV. obliged the Spaniards to lower their flag to the French, 1680. *Hénault.* After an engagement of three hours between Tourville and the Spanish admiral Papachin, the latter yielded by firing a salute of nine guns to the French flag, 2 June, 1688. *Idem;* see *Salute at Sea*, and *Union Jack.*

The comte de Chambord definitively declined to give up the white flag for the tricolor (see *France*), 5 July, 1871 and 27 Oct. 1873.

FLAGELLANTS, at Perouse, about 1268, during a plague, they maintained there was no remission of sins without flagellation, and publicly lashed themselves. Clement VI. declared them heretics in 1349: and 90 of them and their leader, Conrad Schmidt, were burnt, 1414. In 1574, Henry III. of France became a flagellant for a short time.

FLAGEOLET, a musical instrument said to have been invented by Juvigny, about 1581; double flageolet patented by Wm. Bainbridge, 1803; improved 1809 and 1819.

FLAMBEAUX, Feast of, see *Argos.*

FLAMINIAN WAY, the great road from Rome to Ariminum in Umbria, made under the direction of C. Flaminius, when censor in 221 B.C., when he also constructed the Flaminium circus. In 217 he was defeated and killed at the battle of the Trasimene lake, when resisting the march of Hannibal.

FLAMMOCK'S REBELLION, see *Rebellions*, 1497.

FLANDERS, the principal part of ancient Belgium, which was conquered by Julius Cæsar, 51 B.C. It became part of the kingdom of France, A.D. 843, and was governed by counts subject to the king, from 862 till 1369, the first being Baldwin, *Bras de Fer*, who is said to have introduced the cloth manufacture. In 1204, Baldwin IX. became emperor at Constantinople. In 1369, Philip duke of Burgundy married Margaret, the heiress of count Louis II. After this, Flanders was subjected successively to Burgundy (1384), Austria (1477), and Spain (1555). In 1580 it declared its independence, but afterwards returned to its allegiance to the house of Austria. In 1713 it was included in the empire of Germany. France obtained a part of Flanders by treaty in 1659 and 1679. See *Burgundy* and *Belgium.*

FLANNEL, see *Woollen.*

FLASHING SIGNALS, see under *Fog.*

FLATBUSH, Battle of, see *Long Island.*

FLATTERY, CAPE (W. coast of North America), so named by captain Cook, because at a distance it had the deceptive appearance of a harbour, 1778.

FLAVIAN CÆSARS, the Roman emperors Vespasian, Titus, and Domitian, 66-96.

FLAX. The manufacture in Egypt in very early times was carried thence to Tyre about 588 B.C., and to Gaul about 1 B.C.; and thus reached Britain. It was ordered to be grown in England, by statute, 24 Hen. VIII. 1533. For many ages the core was separated from the flax, the bark of the plant, by the hand. A mallet was next used; but the old methods of breaking and scutching the flax yielded to a water-mill which was invented in Scotland about 1750; see *Hemp.* The duty imposed on imported flax, 1842, was repealed 1845. In 1851 chevalier Claussen patented a method of "cottoning" flax.

FLAYERS, see *Ecorcheurs.*

FLEECE, see *Golden Fleece.*

FLEET, see *Navy of England.*

FLEET PRISON, MARKET, &c. (London), were built over the small river Fleta, now used as a common sewer. In the reign of Henry VII. this river is said to have been navigable to Holborn-bridge.

Fleet Prison was founded in the first year of Richard I., and was allotted for debtors, 1640; and persons were committed here who had incurred the displeasure of the Star-Chamber, and for contempt of the court of Chancery. It was burnt during the Gordon riots, 7 June, 1780, and rebuilt 1781-2. It was pulled down in 1845 (and the debtors removed to the Queen's Bench prison). The site was sold to the London, Dover, and Chatham railway company for 60,000*l* on 2 June, 1864. Last vestige removed . . . . . Feb. 1868

Fleet-market, originally formed in 1737, was removed, and the site named Farringdon-street in 1829. A new (Farringdon) market was opened 20 Nov. 1829. The granite obelisk in Fleet-street, to the memory of alderman Waithman was erected 25 June, 1833

Fleet Marriages. Between the 19th of October, 1704, and 12 Feb. 1705, there were celebrated 295 marriages in the Fleet without licence or certificate of banns. 20 or 30 couples were sometimes joined in one day, and their names concealed by private marks, if they chose to pay an extra fee. Pennant says that in his youth he was often accosted with, "Sir, will you please to walk in and be married?" Painted signs, of male and female hands conjoined, with the inscription, "Marriages performed within," were common along the building.

This abuse abolished by the Marriage Act . . 1753

FLEETS: Effective Fighting Strength, 1902.—Great Britain, total 225 (57 *battleships*, 134 *cruisers*); France, 98 (35 *b.*, 42 *c.*); Russia, 49 (23 *b.*, 17 *c.*); Italy, 47 (10 *b.*, 20 *c.*); Germany, 51 (24 *b.*, 23 *c.*); United States, 35 (16 *b.*, 19 *c.*); Japan, 29 (8 *b.*, 20 *c.*).—"The Naval Annual," T. A. Brassey, April, 1902.

35 ships completed and passed into the British navy since April, 1901; 75 ships under construction (including 24 armoured cruisers and 14 battleships) during 1902; announced, 29 May, 1902.

FLEETWOOD, see *Hythe*.

FLENSBORG, N. Germany. Here the Danes defeated the Slesingers and Germans, 9 April, 1848. It was entered by the Germans, 7 Feb. 1864.

FLETA, an ancient English law treatise, an abridgment of Bracton, dated about 1290, said to have been composed *in Fletâ*, in the Fleet prison, by some lawyer.

FLEUR-DE-LIS, the emblem of France, said to have been brought from heaven by an angel to Clovis, he having made a vow that if he proved victorious in a pending battle with the Alemanni near Cologne, he would embrace Christianity, 496. It was the national emblem till the revolution in 1789, when the tricolor (white, red, and blue) was adopted. The comte de Chambord declared his adherence to the old national flag, 5 July, 1871 and 27 Oct. 1873.

FLEURUS (Belgium), the site of several battles.

Between the Catholic league under Gonzales de Cordova, and the Protestant union (indecisive) 30 Aug. 1622
The prince of Waldeck defeated by marshal Luxemburg . . . . 1 July, 1690
The allies under the prince of Coburg, defeated by the French revolutionary army commanded by Jourdan, who was enabled to form a junction with the armies of the Moselle, the Ardennes, and the north. (The French used a balloon to reconnoitre the enemy's army, which, it is said, contributed to their success) . . . . 26 June, 1794
Here Napoleon defeated Blucher at the battle of Ligny (*which see*) . . . . . . 16 June, 1815

FLIES. An extraordinary fall of these insects in London covered the clothes of passengers, 1707. *Chamberlain.* In the United States of America the *Hessian fly*, so called from the notion of its having been brought there by the Hessian troops in the service of England in the War of Independence, ravaged the wheat in 1777. Before and during the severe attack of cholera at Newcastle in Sept. 1853, the air was infested with small flies.

FLINTS, see *Man*.

FLOATING BATTERIES, see *Batteries*, and *Gibraltar*, 1781.

FLOATING DOCKS, see *Docks*.

FLODDEN FIELD (Northumberland). The site of a battle on 9 Sept. 1513, between the English and Scots; in consequence of James IV. of Scotland having taken part with Louis XII. of France against Henry VIII. of England. James, many of his nobles, and upwards of 10,000 of his army, were slain; while the English, who were commanded by the earl of Surrey, lost only persons of small note.

FLOGGING by the Jewish law was limited to forty stripes, "lest thy brother should seem vile unto thee," 1451 B.C. (*Deut.* xxv. 3). Wm. Cobbett in 1810, and John Drakard in 1811, were punished for publishing severe censures on flogging in the army. Flogging was made a punishment for attempts at garrotting in 1863; and for juvenile criminals, 1847 and 1850; for burglars carrying revolvers proposed; the bill enacting it was withdrawn 2 Aug. 1889.

Flogging in the army much diminished by orders 9 Nov. 1859
First-class seamen not to be flogged, except after a trial, Dec. 1859; more diminished . March, 1867
By an amendment on the clause in the mutiny bill, flogging abolished in the army in time of peace April, 1868
New regulations for the navy issued . 18 Dec. 1871
Proposed total abolition negatived in commons (120-60), 20 June, 1876; (164-122), 10 April, 1877; (239-56) . . . . . . 20 May, 1879
By the Army Discipline Act (42 & 43 Vict. c. 33), flogging reduced, and may be commuted by imprisonment . . . . ,,
Total abolition of flogging by Army Discipline Act April, 1881
Substitutes for flogging (handcuffing, &c.) announced . . . . . . Oct. ,,

21 soldiers flogged	1869	41 soldiers flogged	1878
61 sailors ,,	,,	8 sailors ,,	,,

Flogging inflicted for cases of robbery with violence, 65 cases in 1894; 75 in 1895.

FLOODS, see *Inundations*.

FLORAL HALL, adjoining Covent-garden theatre, is a large conservatory, 220 feet long, 75 feet wide, and 55 feet high, designed by Mr. E. M. Barry, and was opened with the volunteers' ball, 7 March, 1860. It was used as a flower-market, 22 May–Aug. 1861. Here was held the West London industrial exhibition, 1 May to 2 Aug. 1865.

FLORALIA, annual games at Rome in honour of Flora, early instituted but not celebrated with regularity till about 174 B.C.

FLORENCE (*Florentia*), capital of Tuscany (*which see*), and from 1864 to 1871, of Italy, is said to have been founded by the soldiers of Sylla (80 B.C.), and enlarged by the Roman triumviri. In its palaces, universities, academies, churches, and libraries, are to be found the rarest works of sculpture and painting in the world. The Florentine academy and *Academia della Crusca* (established 1582) were instituted to enrich literature and improve the language of Tuscany; the latter was so named, because it rejects like *bran* all words not purely Tuscan: both are now united under the former name. Population, 1890, 191,453; 1900, 204,950.

Destroyed by Totila . . . . . . about 541
Rebuilt by Charlemagne . . . . . about 800
Becomes an independent republic . . about 1198
Wars of the Guelphs and Ghibellines . 1215 *et seq.*
Dante born here . . . . . . 14 May, 1265
Arti or guilds established 1266
Factions of the Bianchi and Neri 1300
Great plague, the Black Death 1348
The influence of the Medici begins with Cosmo de' Medici, "the father of his country" . about 1420
Death of Lorenzo de' Medici . . . 8 April, 1492
Republic proclaimed, 1493; Niccolo Machiavelli, chief secretary, 1498 till the fall . . . 1512
Savonarola strangled and burnt . . . 23 May, 1498
Appointment of Alexander de' Medici as perpetual governor 1530
Cosmo de' Medici created grand-duke of Tuscany; makes Florence his capital: see *Tuscany* . . 1569
Revolution at Florence . . . . 27 April, 1859
Annexation to Sardinia voted by people, 11, 12 March; the king enters Florence . 7 April, 1860
The king opens the exhibition of the industrial products of Italy . . . . . 15 Sept. 1861
Florence decreed the capital of Italy till the acquisition of Rome . . . . . 11 Dec. 1864
The king and court remove there . . 13 May, 1865
The Dante festival (the 600th anniversary of his birth) opened by the king . . 14 May, ,,
Inauguration of a national rifle-meeting; the king fires the first shot . . . . 18 June, ,,
First assembly of Italian parliament here 18 Nov. ,,
The government removes to Rome as capital of Italy July, 1871
Fourth centenary of Michel Angelo Buonarroti kept . . . . 12 Sept. 1875

Torchlight procession; shell thrown among crowd; 5 killed . . . . . 18 Nov. 1878

The brick duomo, begun by Arnulfo, 1294; dedicated by pope Eugenius IV., 1436; was completed by Brunelleschi, 1447; the façade was cased with marble by the Italian government and uncovered in presence of the king . . . 12 May, 1887

Other renovations of public buildings carried on 1883–6

Visit of Queen Victoria . . 24 March–22 April, 1888

Equestrian statue of king Victor Emmanuel unveiled . . . . . . 20 Sept. 1890

Visit of queen Victoria, 23 March—26 April, 1893: 16 March—16 April, 1894; visit of the king and queen of Italy . . . . . 10 April, 1894

The national museum and other buildings greatly damaged by an earthquake . . . 18 May, 1895

Fine arts exhibition opened by the king and queen 10 Dec. 1896

Fifth centenary of Amerigo Vespucci and Paolo Toscanelli, who visited America in 1498, celebrated, 17 April, *et seq.* 1898

FLORES, or Isle of Flowers (one of the Azores, *which see*), discovered by Vanderberg in 1439; and settled by the Portuguese in 1448.

FLORIDA, a peninsula, one of the southern states of North America, first discovered by Sebastian Cabot in 1497. It was visited by Juan Ponce de Leon, the Spanish navigator, April 4, 1512, in a voyage he had undertaken to discover a fountain whose waters had the property of restoring youth to the aged who tasted them! Florida was conquered by the Spaniards under Ferdinand de Soto in 1539; but the settlement was not fully established until 1565. It was plundered by sir Francis Drake in 1585; and by Davis, a buccaneer, in 1665. It was invaded by the British in 1702; and again by gen. Oglethorpe in 1740; ceded to the British crown in 1763; taken by the Spaniards in 1781; and guaranteed to them in 1783. Capital, Tallahassee. Population in 1880, 269,493; 1890, 391,422; 1900, 528,542.

The Americans purchase Louisiana from the French and claim West Florida 1801

The Spaniards compelled to cede all Florida to the United States . . . . . 24 Oct. 1820

Florida admitted as a state 1845

Seceded from the Union, Dec. 1860; readmitted (see *United States*) 1865

A ship canal proposed; company organised May 1883

After long neglect, this beautiful and fertile wilderness warmly taken up by British and American capitalists 1883-4

Yellow fever prevailed here, autumn of . . . 1888

Remains of pre-historic villages, pottery, &c., discovered on the east coast; reported by Dr. De Witt Webb . . . . . May, 1894

Destructive cyclone, many deaths . . 3–5 Aug. 1899

Great fire in Jacksonville, 148 blocks burnt, several deaths . . . . . 3 May, 1901

FLORIN, a coin first made by the Florentines. A *florin* was issued by Edward III. which was current in England at the value of 6*s*. in 1337. *Camden.* This English coin was called floren after the Florentine coin, because the latter was of the best gold. *Ashe.* The florin of Germany is in value 2*s*. 4*d*.; that of Spain, 4*s*. 4½*d*.; that of Palermo and Sicily, 2*s*. 6*d*.; that of Holland, 2*s*. *Ayliffe.* Silver florins (value 2*s*.) were issued in England in 1849.

FLOUR, COLONIAL AND FOREIGN, see *Food-stuffs*.

FLOWERS. Many of our present common flowers were introduced into England from the reign of Henry VII. to that of Elizabeth (1485-1603). The art of preserving flowers in sand was discovered in 1633. A mode of preserving them from the effects of frost in winter, and hastening their vegetation in summer, was invented in America, by Geo. Morris, in 1792. A very great number have been introduced from America, Australia, the Cape, &c., during the present century. Many of the dates in the following list, given in botanical works, are doubtful.

"Battle of Flowers," see *Carnival.*

London Flower-girl Brigade formed by baroness Burdett-Coutts and others . . . autumn 1880

Acacia, N. America, before 1640
Allspice shrub, Carolina 1726
Aniseed tree, Florida, about 1766
Arbor Vitæ, Canada, before 1596
Arctopus, Cape of Good Hope 1774
Auricula, Switzerland 1567
Azarole, S. Europe, before 1640
Bay, Royal, Madeira 1665
Bay, sweet, Italy, before 1548
Camellia, China 1811
Canary bell-flower, Canaries 1696
Canary Convolvulus, Canaries 1690
Carnation, Flanders 1567
Ceanothus, blue, New Spain 1818
Chaste tree, Sicily, before 1570
Christ's thorn, Africa, before 1596
Chrysanthemums, China . . . . 1763 or 1790
Convolvulus, many flowered 1779
Coral tree, Cape 1816
Coral tree, bell-flowered, Cape 1791
Coral tree, tremulous, Cape 1789
Creeper, Virginian, N. America 1629
Dahlia, China 1803
Dryandria, New Holland . . . . ,,
Evergreen Thorn, Italy 1629
Everlasting, giant-flowered, Cape 1781
Everlasting, giant, Cape 1793
Fernbush, sweet, N. America 1714
Fox-glove, Canaries 1698
Fuchsia fulgens, Mexico, about 1835
Geranium, Flanders 1534
Gillyflower, Flanders 1567
Gold-plant, Japan 1783
Golden-bell-flower, Madeira 1777
Hawthorn, American, before 1683
Heaths, Cape 1774-1803
Honeyflower, great, Cape 1688
Honeysuckle, Chinese, China 1806
Honeysuckle, fly, Cape 1752
Honeysuckle, trumpet, N. America 1656
Hyssop, S. Europe, before 1548
Jasmine, Circassia, before 1548
Jasmine, Catalonia, East Indies 1629
Judas tree, S. Europe, before 1596
Laburnum, Hungary 1576
Laurel, Alexandrian, Portugal, before 1713
Laurustine, S. Europe, before 1596
Lavender, S. Europe, before 1568
Lily, Italy, before 1460
Lily, gigantic, N. South Wales 1800
Lily, red coloured, S. America 1623
Loblolly bay, N. America, before 1739
Lupine tree, Cape, about 1793
Magnolia (see *Magnolia*), N. America 1688
Magnolia, dwarf, China 1786
Magnolia, laurel-leaved, N. America 1734
Maiden-hair, Japan 1714
Mignonette, Italy 1528
Milk-wort, giant-flowered, Cape 1713
Milk-wort, showy, Cape 1814
Mock orange, S. Europe, before 1596
Mountain tea, N. America, before 1758
Myrtle, candleberry, N. America 1699
Myrtle, woolly-leaved, China 1776
Nettle tree, S. Europe, before 1596
Oleander, red, S. Europe . . . . ,,
Olive, Cape, Cape 1730
Olive, sweet-scented, China 1771
Paraguay tea, Carolina, before 1724
Passion-flower, Brazil 1692
Passion-flower, orange, Carolin 1792
Petunia, S. America 1823
Pigeon-berry, N. America 1736
Pink, from Italy 1567
Ranunculus, Alps 1528
Roses, Netherlands 1522
Rose, China, China 1789
Rose, damask, S. Europe, about 1543
Rose, the Japan, China 1793

Rose, the moss, before 1724
Rose, the musk, Italy 1522
Rose, the Provence, Flanders 1567
Rose, sweet-scented guelder, from China 1821
Rose, tube, from Java and Ceylon 1629
Rose without thorns, N. America, before 1726
Rosemary, S. Europe 1548
Sage, African, Cape 1731
Sage, Mexican, Mexico 1724
St. Peter's wort, N. America 1730
Sassafras, N. America, before 1663
Savin, S. Europe, before 1584
Snowdrop, Carolina 1756
Sorrel-tree, N. America, before 1752
Sweet-bay, S. of Europe, before 1548
Tamarisk plant, Germany 1560
Tea tree, China, about 1768
Tooth-ache tree, from Carolina, before 1739
Trumpet-flower, N. America 1640
Trumpet-flower, Cape 1823
Tulip, Vienna 1578
Verbena, S. America 1827
Victoria Regia, Guiana 1838
Virginian creeper, N. America 1629
Virgin's bower, Japan 1776
Wax-tree, China 1794
Weeping willow, Levant, before 1692
Winter-berry, Virginia 1736
Youlan, China 1789

FLUORESCENCE. When the invisible chemical rays of the blue end of the solar spectrum are sent through uranium glass or solutions of quinine, horse-chestnut bark, or stramonium datura, they become luminous. This phenomenon was termed "fluorescence" by its discoverer, professor Stokes, in 1852. By means of fluorescence Drs. Bence Jones and Dupré detected the presence of quinoidine in animal tissues; see *Calorescence*.

FLUORINE, a gaseous element, obtained from fluor spar; first collected over mercury by Priestley. Its property of corroding all vessels is so great that it is separated with great difficulty. It was named by Ampère in 1810. Its chemical history was further elucidated by Davy (1809), Berzelius (1824), and succeeding chemists. The corroding property of fluoric acid was employed in the arts in 1760, by Schwankhard of Nuremberg. *Gmelin*.

Fluorine liquefied by M. Moissan and prof. Dewar at about 210c, May *et seq.*, 1897; paper read at Paris, 21 Oct. 1897; solidified by them . early 1903

FLUSHING, a seaport of the Netherlands, on the isle of Walcheren. For the siege, see *Walcheren Expedition*. It was fortified by Napoleon I., but the works were finally dismantled in 1867. The port improved, and new dock opened by the king of Holland, 8 Sept. 1873.

FLUTE. The transverse flute, incorrectly termed the "German" instead of the Swiss flute, was known to the ancients. It was described by Michael Pretorius, of Wolfenbuttel, in 1620, and by Mersenne of Paris, in 1636. It was much improved by the French in the 17th century, by Quantz, Tacet, Florio, Potter, Miller, Nicholson, and others in the 18th. In the present century also the Nicholsons, Boehm of Munich, Godfrey of Paris, Carter, Rockstro, and Rudall and Rose of London, have greatly contributed to the perfection of this instrument. See *Flageolet*.

Mr. Benjamin Wells, a great player, died, aged 73, 6 Sept. 1899

FLUXIONS, a branch of the higher mathematics, invented by Newton, 1665, similar to the differential calculus described by Leibnitz, 1684. A fierce controversy ensued as to the priority of the discovery. The finest applications of the calculus are by Newton, Euler, La Grange, and La Place. The first elementary work on fluxions in England is a tract of twenty-two pages in *A New Short Treatise of Algebra, together with a Specimen of the Nature and Algorithm of Fluxions*, by John Harris, M.A. London, 1702.

FLYING, ARTIFICIAL. In Greek mythology, Dædalus is said to have attached wings of wax to the body of his son Icarus, who, neglecting the advice of his father, flew so high that the sun melted his wings, and he fell into the Icarian sea. Archytas is said to have made a flying dove, about 400 B.C. Friar Bacon maintained the possibility of the art of flying, and predicted it would be a general practice, 1273. Bishop Wilkins says (1651), it will yet be as usual to hear a man call for his *wings* when he is going on a journey, as it is now to hear him call for his boots! Borelli (about 1670) showed the futility of these speculations. About 1800 sir George Cayley experimented on the subject, and in 1843 Mr. Henson invented a flying machine; but nothing has been devised capable of serving a practical purpose. The motion of birds in relation to aëronautics was much discussed by scientific men in 1867-8. At a meeting of the Aëronautical society, 26 March, 1868, it was stated that a member had actually, by his muscular force, aided by apparatus, risen from the ground and flown horizontally. Dr. James Pettigrew published his elaborate researches on flying, 1867-71. M. Von Groof, a Belgian, "the flying-man," descended from a balloon by means of a parachute resembling wings, in 1874: but was killed by falling through failure of his apparatus at Chelsea, 9 July.

Mr. Simmonds' flying-machine (combining an umbrella and kite), at Chatham, carried sand bags about 100 feet high and fell, 15 Dec. 1875.
Mr. H. C. Linfield tried his steam flying machine on the railway near West Drayton, 29 Aug. 1883.
Mr. Horatio Phillips' aerial machine, weighing 330 lbs., to be sustained in its course by induced currents, tried at Harrow, May, 1893.
A flying machine constructed by Mr. Maxim, tried at Bexley, Kent. It is reported to have conveyed himself and two men with water and fuel a distance of about 500 ft., 31 July, 1894; another trial, 5 July, 1895.
Mr. Maxim, at the society of arts, described his experiments, 28 Nov. 1894.
Herr Otto Lilienthal's experiments with his machine, fairly successful, are described in "Nature," 30 Jan. 1896; he was killed by a fall while experimenting at Rhinow . . 9 Aug. 1896
Experiments by prof. Langley and others, reported "Æronautical Annual, 1896."
Flying machines, etc., exhibited at the meeting of the Æronautical Society . . . . 16 Dec. 1897
Mr. Percy Pilcher, inventor of a machine, after 4 previous ascents, killed by a fall while experimenting at Stamford hall, Market Harbro', 30 Sept. 1899
Prof. Langley's aerostat tested at Widewater, Virginia, U.S., after ascent of 60 ft. sank into the Potomac and was totally wrecked . 8 Oct. 1903

FLY SHEETS, see under *Wesleyans*.

FÔ, RELIGION OF, the form of Buddhism (*which see*) existing in China.

FOG. In 1862 much attention was paid to the subject of fog signals by the Royal commission on Lighthouses, &c. The use of bells, steam-trumpets, a battery of whistles blown by steam, the transmission of sound through water, the siren, &c., were considered. A fog horn blown by steam is in use at Dungeness lighthouse (1869). For Dr. Tyndall's experiments, see *Acoustics*.

Continued fogginess in London, Nov. 1879, to Feb. 1880, caused much mortality; very bad on 25 Dec. 1879
Fatal fogs, Dec. 1881, Jan. 1882; Jan. 1888, general over the British Isles and N. W. Europe.
Mr. De Cordova's fog signals announced . March, 1883

Prof. Holmes' siren fog horn tried in the Zuyder Zee, reported successful . . . Sept. 1883
Capt. Barker's marine safety signal code for merchant vessels; he indicates directions for sailing by combinations of short and long blasts of a fog horn . . . . 1879—1884
Improved fog signalling by sound set up at Ailsa Craig, mouth of the Clyde . . . 17 July, 1886
Adm. Colomb's systems of signalling by flashing lights at night, or by spurts of sound in fogs, invented 1858 *et seq.*, adopted 1868; these are considered highly valuable for manœuvring squadrons of ships, and also for the army 1890
Lord Middleton's application in the house of lords for the appointment of a royal commission respecting London fogs negatived . . . 12 Feb. 1892
Little fog in London, winter, 1891–2, except at Christmas; very bad then throughout England. ,,
General fog in the United Kingdom . 10–12 Nov. ,,
Remarkable absence of fog in London . winter, 1893–4
Mr. F. H. Berry's automatic marine fog signal tried on the *Dunera* in the docks, 15 July, 1895; an improved form exhibited . . . . 5 Dec. 1897
Dense fog, London, S. England, and Channel 18 Dec. ,,
Dense fog, London and elsewhere, several fatalities, 4–6 Nov.; in the Channel . . . 4–8 Nov. 1901

FOIX (S. France), a county established 1050, and united with Bearn, 1290. About 1494 Catherine de Foix, the heiress, married Jean d'Albret, whose descendant, Henry IV., as king of France, united Foix to the monarchy, 1589.

FOLK LORE, a general name given by Mr. W. J. Thoms, in 1846, to popular legends, fairy tales, local traditions, old outdying customs, superstitions, and similar matters. The formation of the Folk-lore society was advocated by Mr. W. J. Thoms in "*Notes and Queries*," 1 Dec. 1877; established in 1878. National congresses are held. See *Music*, 1899.

FOLKMOTE, or Folkmoot, Anglo-Saxon, a general assembly of the people to deliberate on general matters relating to the commonwealth, resembling the public meetings of later times. From these meetings, parliaments and other elective assemblies were gradually developed. The name was also given to local courts.

FONTS. Fonts are said to have been set up in churches in the sixth century.

FONTAINEBLEAU, near the Seine, France. The royal palace, founded by Robert le Pieux about 999, enlarged and adorned by successive kings, was completed by Louis Philippe, 1837-40. Fontainebleau was entered by the Austrians, 17 Feb. 1814. Here Napoleon resigned his dignity, 4 April, and bade farewell to his army, 20 April, 1814.

Peace between France, Denmark, &c. . 2 Sept. 1679
Treaty between Germany and Holland . 8 Nov. 1785
Treaty between Napoleon and Spain . 27 Oct. 1807
The decree of Fontainebleau for the destruction of British merchandise issued . . 19 Oct. 1810
Concordat between Napoleon and pope Pius VII. 25 Jan. 1813
80 acres of pines destroyed by fire . 28 Sept. 1895

FONTENAILLE, or Fontenay (*Fontanetum*), a village in Burgundy. Near here Charles the Bald and Louis the German totally defeated their brother the emperor Lothaire I. 25 June, 841. This victory, termed "the judgment of God," conduced to the formation of the French monarchy.

FONTENOY, near Tournay, in Belgium, the site of an obstinate sanguinary battle on 30 April (11 May, N.S.), 1745, between the French, commanded by marshal Saxe, and the English, Hanoverians, Dutch, and Austrians, commanded by the duke of Cumberland. The king Louis XV. and the dauphin were present. The success of the British at the commencement is still quoted as an illustration of the extraordinary power of a column; and the advance of the Austrians during several hours at Marengo (14 June, 1800) was compared to it by Bonaparte. The allies lost 12,000 men, and the French nearly an equal number; but the allies were compelled to retire. Marshal Saxe (ill of the disorder of which he afterwards died) was carried about to all the posts in a litter, assuring his troops that the day would be their own.

FONTHILL ABBEY, Wiltshire, founded in 1796, the mansion of William Beckford, author of "Vathek," and son of Alderman Beckford. He died 2 May, 1844. Within this edifice (which alone cost 273,000*l.*) were collected costly articles of virtu and art, and the rarest works of the old masters. The sale of the abbey and its contents to Mr. Farquhar took place in 1822; 7,200 catalogues at a guinea each were sold in a few days. On 21 Dec. 1825, the lofty tower fell, and in consequence the remaining buildings were sold.

FOOD, see *Provisions*. A Food Journal published 1870; continued several years. Sale of Food and Drugs act passed 11 Aug. 1875; another passed 9 Aug. 1899. Dr. Arthur Hill Hassall's "Food and its Adulterations" published 1854, and since. International food exhibition at Agricultural Hall, 13-20 Oct. 1880. National food reform society advocates abstinence from animal food, 1883. "Foods: Composition and Analysis," by A. W. Blyth, published 1882. Food and Temperance Drink exhibition, Westminster, opened 3 Dec. 1898. Food exhibition, Albert-hall, opened 21 April, 1903.

FOOD SUPPLY IN TIME OF WAR. The war in S. Africa and the important question of the security of the food supply of the United Kingdom in the event of hostilities with any one or more of the great powers directed public attention specially to this question. The subject was also brought forward in parliament and pressure was brought upon the government to institute an inquiry by a parliamentary committee or royal commission. In furtherance of this object an influential meeting was held at Stafford-house, 4 Feb. 1903, under the presidency of the duke of Sutherland, when *The Association to Promote an Official Inquiry into the Security of our Food Supply in Time of War* was formed. President, the duke of Sutherland; vice-president, lord Strathcona. Offices, 35, Parliament-street, Westminster.

Royal Commission appointed, prince of Wales president, lord Balfour of Burleigh chairman, April, 1903.

FOOLS, FESTIVALS OF, were held at Paris on the 1st of January, when, we are told, all sorts of absurdities were committed, from 1198 to 1438. Fools or licensed jesters were kept at court in England up to the time of Charles I. 1625.

FOOT AND MOUTH DISEASE, see *Cattle*.

FOOTBALL, an old English game (is said to have originated with the Britons), popular in the middle ages, censured and opposed by Edward II., 1314, and Edward III., 1349. Its suppression was attempted by Henry IV., 1401, Henry VIII., and Elizabeth, but the playing of the game continued till about 1650. It was revived in various forms during the last century by public schools and clubs, such as Sheffield and Hallam, 1857, Blackheath and Richmond, 1858.

The Football association was formed by the "dribbling clubs" in 1858, followed by the Rugby Football union in 1871. The game is now played in our colonies and the United States; annual matches. The League championship (association rules) 1903, won by Sheffield Wednesday; Southampton winning the Southern league competition, 1903.

FOOTPATH (National) *Preservation* society, founded under the patronage of the duke of Westminster and others, 1884. Annual meeting Jan. 1890.

FORBES MACKENZIE'S ACT, see *Scotland*, 1853.

FORCE, see *Conservation* and *Correlation*.

FOREIGN BOND-HOLDERS were incorporated by licence of the Board of Trade as an association 1 Aug. 1873. A fund was created for the protection of the investing public. Reports issued 1895-96. *Foreign consuls*, see *Consul*, 1896.

FOREIGN CATTLE MARKET. The city of London having been required to provide this market before 1 Jan. 1872, by the Contagious Diseases act (for Animals), 1869, the common council, 7 Nov. 1870, agreed to the expenditure of 160,000*l.* for the purpose. The site chosen, Deptford dockyard, was much opposed. The requisite alterations were made by Mr. Horace Jones, and the market was formally opened by the lord mayor, 28 Dec. 1871; for use on 1 Jan. 1872.

FOREIGN ENLISTMENT ACT, 59 Geo. III. c. 69 (1819), forbids British subjects to enter the service of a foreign state, without licence from the king or privy council, and prohibits the fitting out or equipping ships for any foreign power to be employed against any power with which our government is at peace; see *Trials*, 1862, 1863. In 1606, Englishmen were forbidden to enter foreign service, without taking an oath not to be reconciled to the pope. The act was suspended in 1835 on behalf of the *British Legion* (*which see*). The act passed 9 Aug. 1870 relates to illegal enlisting, shipbuilding, and expeditions.

FOREIGNERS, see *Alien* and *Law*. Foreigners in the United Kingdom: 1871, 113,779; in 1881, 135,640; the Germans being about one-third. Foreign prison-made goods act passed (prohibitory), 1897.

FOREIGN JURISDICTION ACTS, passed in 1843, 1865, and 1866, were extended and amended by 41 & 42 Vict. c. 67, passed 16 Aug. 1878; these acts were consolidated in 1890.

FOREIGN LEGION. Foreigners have frequently been employed as auxiliaries in the pay of the British government; see *Hessians*. An act (18 & 19 Vict. c. 2) for the formation of a foreign legion as a contingent in the Russian war (1855), was passed 23 Dec. 1854.* The queen and prince Albert reviewed 3500 soldiers, principally Swiss and Germans, at Shorncliffe, 9 Aug. 1855. On the peace in 1856, many were sent to the Cape of Good Hope; but not prospering, returned.

FOREIGN LOANS, see *Loans*.

FOREIGN MISSIONS, see *Missions*.

* The endeavour to enlist for this legion, in 1854, in the United States, gave great offence to the American government. Mr. Crampton, our envoy, was dismissed, 28 May, 1856, in spite of all the judicious pacific efforts of lord Clarendon. Lord Napier was sent out as our representative in 1857.

FOREIGN OFFICE was established at the re-arrangement of the duties of secretaries of state in 1782. It has the exclusive charge of British interests and subjects in foreign countries. The secretary for foreign affairs negotiates treaties, selects ambassadors, consuls, &c., for foreign countries, and grants passports. The new foreign office building in the Italian style (designed by Sir Gilbert Scott) was begun in 1864. A portion of it was inaugurated by Mr. Disraeli's reception, 25 March, and it was occupied by lord Stanley, 24 June, 1868. See *Administrations* under separate heads, and *Secretaries*.

Foreign Office Circular warning travellers and others that they will incur capture at their own risk Aug. 1881
Important changes in the departments Feb. 1883;
Sir Martin Gosseling made additional under secretary . . . . July, 1898

FOREIGN ORDERS. No British subject is permitted to accept a foreign order from the sovereign of any foreign country, or wear the insignia thereof, without his majesty's consent, by orders issued in 1812 and 1834;—regulations published in London Gazette, 10 May, 1855.

FORESTALLING was forbidden by statutes (in 1350, 1552, &c.), all repealed in 1844.

FORESTS. There were in England, even in the last century, as many as 68 forests, 18 chases, and upwards of 780 parks. See *New Forest*.*

International Forestry exhibition at Edinburgh, recommended by government, Nov. 1883; opened on 1 July; closed . . . . . 11 Oct. 1884
"The Forester," by J. Brown; new edition . . 1882
Parliamentary committee on forestry appointed, May, 1885 Planting of trees increased . 1888 *et seq.*
Committee on British forestry. Report . Jan. 1903
See *Gardening*, 1893.

FORESTS, CHARTER OF THE. *Charta de Foresta*, granted by Henry III. in 1217, was founded on *Magna Charta*, granted by king John, 15 June 1215. It was confirmed in 1225 and 1297. See *Woods*.

FORESTERS, Ancient Order of, a species of benefit society, founded on the principle that many can help one; all religious and political discussions are strictly avoided. The 54th High Court at Reading; number of members reported 690,000, 6 Aug. 1888. At Bournemouth, 5 Aug. 1889. At Hull, 4 Aug. 1890. At London, 1 Aug. 1891. Number of members reported Dec. 1891, 830,720; Dec. 1897,

* The commissioners appointed to enquire into the state of the woods and forests, between 1787 and 1793, reported the following as belonging to the crown, viz.:— In Berkshire, Windsor Forest and Windsor Great and Little Park. In Dorset, Cranburn Chase. In Essex, Waltham or Epping and Hainault Forest. In Gloucestershire, Dean Forest. In Hampshire, the New Forest, Alice Holt, Woolmer Forest, and Bere Forest. In Kent, Greenwich Park. In Middlesex, St. James's, Hyde, Bushey, and Hampton-court Parks. In Northamptonshire, the forests of Whittlebury, Salcey, and Rockingham. In Nottingham, Sherwood Forest. In Oxford, Whichwood Forest. In Surrey, Richmond Park. Several of these have been disforested since 1851, viz. Hainault, Whichwood, and Whittlebury. A committee of the house of commons respecting forests sat in 1863. Motion in parliament to preserve *Epping Forest* adopted 14 Feb. 1870; and the decision of the Master of the Rolls, 10 Nov. 1874, stopped the enclosures by the lords of manors. The lord mayor Stone visited the forest in state 14 Oct. 1875. The commissioners' new scheme was published July, 1876. *Memorial trees* were planted by the duke and duchess of Connaught, 16 Oct. 1880. The forest was dedicated to the use of the people by queen Victoria, 6 May, 1882. 28 acres of land at Yardley-hill, given by Mr. E. N. Buxton to the forest, opened by the duke of Connaught, 1 June, 1899.

895,769; Dec. 1901, 928,035; Dec. 1902, 932,827. Reported capital, 3,670,114*l.* 31 Dec. 1887; Dec. 1897, 6,117,072*l.*; Dec. 1901, 7,172,833*l.*; Dec. 1902, 7,437,444*l.*

FOREST GATE, Essex, see *Fires*, 1 Jan. 1890.

FORFARSHIRE STEAMER, on its passage from Hull to Dundee, on 6 Sept. 1838, was wrecked in a violent gale, and thirty-eight persons out of fifty-three perished. The Outer-Fern Lighthouse keeper, James Darling, and his heroic daughter Grace, ventured out in a tremendous sea in a coble, and rescued several of the passengers.

The "journal of William Darling" from 1795 to 1860, published in 1887, states that forty-three persons out of sixty-one perished.

FORGERY of deeds, or giving forged deeds in evidence, was made punishable by fine, by standing in the pillory, having both ears cut off, the nostrils slit up and seared, the forfeiture of land, and perpetual imprisonment, 5 Eliz. 1562. Since the establishment of paper credit many statutes have been enacted; the latest Forgery act passed 9 Aug. 1870. The Forged Transfer acts were passed to preserve purchasers of stock from losses by forged transfers, 1891 and 1892. Convictions for forgery and offences against the currency, 1887-8, 652; 1893, 440; 1894, 355; 1895, 341; 1896, 327; 1898, 351; 1899, 311; 1900, 255; 1901, 282.

Forgery first made punishable by death . . 1634
Forging letters of attorney made capital . . 1722
Mr. Ward, M.P., a man of wealth, expelled the house of commons for forgery, 16 May, 1726; and consigned to the pillory . . . 17 March, 1727
The first forger on the bank of England was Richard William Vaughan, once a linen-draper of Stafford. He employed a number of artists on different parts of the notes fabricated. He filled up twenty of the notes and deposited them in the hands of a young lady whom he was on the point of marrying, as a proof of his being a man of substance; no suspicion was entertained. One of the artists informed, and Vaughan was executed at Tyburn . . . . 1 May, 1758
Value of forged notes presented to the bank 1801-10 nominally 101,661*l.*
The bank prosecuted 142 persons for forgery or the uttering of forged notes 1817
Thos. Maynard, the *last person executed for forgery*, 31 Dec. 1829
Statutes reducing into one act all such forgeries as shall henceforth be punished with death . . 1830
The punishment of forgery with death ceases, except in cases of forging or altering wills or powers of attorney to transfer stock 1832
These cases also reduced to transportable offences 1837
A barrister, Jem Saward, and others, tried for forging numerous drafts on bankers 5 March, 1857
The law respecting forgery amended in . 1861 and 1870
For W. Roupell's case, see *Trials* Aug.–Sept. 1862
An elaborate system of bill forgery in London, discovered by the Bank of England 1 March, 1873
Ralph Cooper, "king of the forgers," sentenced to fifteen years for forging a cheque of 3,670*l.* on the London & Westminster bank . . 24 March, 1888
Major W. E. Heath's forgery detector, "The Planet," described in the *Times* . 1 Dec. 1896
Devonport, Freeman, and Gibbons pleaded guilty to having in their possession 200 forged 5*l.* Bank of England notes, and to conspiring to forge and utter 213 such notes; sentenced each to 14 yrs., Brown to 8 yrs., two others to 3 yrs., and one to 18 months' imprisonment, 16 May; see *Trials*, Dec. 1902

[See *Executions* (for forgery), 1776, 1777, *et seq.*]

Literary forgeries, see *Formosa; Ireland's Forgeries; Edinburgh*, 1893. Shipway pedigree case, see *Trials*, Nov. 1898; and *Germany*, Jan. 1899.

FORKS were in use on the Continent in the 13th and 14th centuries. *Voltaire*. This is reasonably disputed. In Fynes Moryson's *Itinerary*, reign of Elizabeth, he says, "At Venice each person was served (besides his knife and spoon) with a fork to hold the meat while he cuts it, for there they deem it ill manners that one should touch it with his hand." Thomas Coryate describes, with much solemnity, the manner of using forks in Italy, and adds, "I myself have thought it good to imitate the Italian fashion since I came home to England," 1608. Two-pronged forks were made at Sheffield soon after. Three-pronged forks are more recent. Silver forks, previously only used by the highest classes, came into more general use in England about 1814.

Mr. G. Smith found a bronze fork with two prongs at Kouyunjik, Assyria, 1873.
A "flesh-hook of three teeth" mentioned 1 Sam. ii. 13, about 1165 B.C.

FORMA PAUPERIS. A person having a just cause of suit, certified as such, yet so poor that he cannot meet the cost of maintaining it, has an attorney and counsel assigned him on his swearing that he is not worth 5*l.*, by stat. 11 Hen. VII. 1495.—This act has been remodelled, and now any person may plead *in formâ pauperis* in the courts of law.

FORMIC ACID, the acid of ants (*formicæ*). Its artificial production by Pelouze in 1831 was considered an event in the progress of organic chemistry.

FORMIGNI (N.W. France). Here the constable de Richemont defeated the English, 15 April, 1450.

FORMOSA, an island in the Pacific, 90 miles from the Chinese coast. The early Spanish and Dutch settlers were expelled by Chinese colonists about 1661. Amoy is the chief port. Savages hold the mountains. Mixed population, above 1,500,000. In May, 1874, the Japanese, with the consent of a Chinese mandarin, chastised the savage tribes here for massacring Japanese sailors on their proposed settlement on the isle. The Chinese threatened war if they did not quit within 90 days, 18 Aug. 1874. By British interposition the Japanese withdrew, an indemnity having been agreed on; treaty between Japan and China signed 31 Oct. 1874. Formosa flourished under the rule of Ting; removed in 1878. The plant of the Woosung railway brought here in 1878. George Psalmanazar published his fabricated description of Formosa in 1704. See *China*, 1884-5.

Severe fighting between the Chinese and the natives . . . . . . Dec. 1889; Feb. 1890
Nearly 200 Chinese soldiers massacred by an ambush, reported . . . . . 13 March, „
General rebellion . . . . May, „
Black flag outrages, British reinforcements sent; 18 Feb. 1895
Tai-wan-Foo, the capital, bombarded by the Japanese . . . . 30 March, „
Formosa ceded to Japan by the treaty of Shimonoseki . . . . 17 April, „
Sanguinary disturbances . . . 22 April *et seq.*
Adm. visc. Kabayama appointed governor by the Japanese . . . . 10 May, „
A Chinese independent republic proclaimed; gen. Tang as president; reported 25 May; collapsed; gen. Tang escaped, early June; Japanese land 31 May, *et seq.*; the port of Kelung captured 3 June, „
100 Chinese killed by explosion of a powder mill, reported 6 June, „
Japanese authority established at Taipehfu 7 June, „
British marines landed at Anping, under capts. Shubrick and Brabazon . . . . 19 June „

British marines withdrawn, 1 July; flight of foreigners; Chinese attack on Japanese garrison defeated with great loss, reported 11 July; Japanese attacked by the black flags about 16 July 1895
The island gradually subdued by the Japanese, reported . . . . Oct. „
Rising north-east of Tamsui, Tai-pei attacked by rebels . . . . . 28 Dec.—1 Jan. *et seq.* 1896
Japanese atrocities in South Formosa . 18 July, „
Rebels defeated and peace restored . . 11 Aug. „
Bubonic plague, reported . . . . 1 Oct. 1897
Government offices attacked and burnt by rebels, their villages afterwards burnt and great loss inflicted by the troops, reported . . 29 Sept. 1898
Rebellion suppressed, many killed . April–May, 1902
Insurgents' stronghold near Tai-nan captured, reported . . . . 29 Aug. „
Further conflicts . . . . . 4 Oct.- 2 Dec. „

FORNOVO (Parma, Italy). Near here Charles VIII. of France defeated the Italians, 6 July, 1495.

FORSTER'S ACT, see *Education*, 1870.

FORT DU QUESNE, N. America. Near here general Braddock was surprised by a party of French and Indians, his troops routed and himself killed, 9 July, 1755. The fort was named *Fort Pitt* after its capture by Forbes, 24 Nov. 1758. It is now *Pittsburg*.

FORT ERIE (Upper Canada). This fortress was taken by the American general Browne, 3 June, 1814. After several conflicts it was evacuated by the Americans, 5 Nov. 1814.

FORT GEORGE, Inverness, N.W. Scotland, was erected in 1747, to restrain the Highlanders.—FORT WILLIAM, besieged by them in vain in 1746, is now in ruins.

FORTH, a great river of Scotland, rising in Ben Lomond, and entering the North Sea as an estuary, termed the Firth of Forth. The FORTH AND CLYDE CANAL was commenced 10 July, 1768, under the direction of Mr. Smeaton, and opened 28 July, 1790. A communication was thus formed between the eastern and western seas on the coast of Scotland.

The FORTH RAILWAY-BRIDGE projected, and a raft launched in June, 1866.
Mr. (afterwards sir T.) Bouch, of Edinburgh, was engaged to prepare plans for a suspension-bridge, 1878.
The Forth bridge company accepted tenders from Wm. Arrol & Co. (1,250,000*l.*) for constructing bridge and railway, Oct. 1879; through Tay-bridge disaster, &c., the scheme was suspended and eventually abandoned by the company, 13 Jan. 1881.
The construction of the present FORTH BRIDGE was undertaken by the company supported by the North British, North Eastern, Great Northern, and Midland railway companies; the act was passed, June, 1882; engineers, Mr. John Fowler and Mr. Benjamin Baker, whose plans were based on the cantilever or bracket principle; Messrs. Wm. Arrol & Co. were the contractors. The rocky islet of Inchgarvie was of great importance in the construction of the bridge; the works began by building the foundations, Jan. 1883.
The last bolt was driven, 6 Nov. 1889; the strength of the bridge was tested by the passage of nearly 2,000 tons, steamed half way across, 21 Jan.; and officially tested for the board of trade, 20 Feb. 1890.
The first train which crossed the entire bridge was driven by the marchioness of Tweeddale, carrying a distinguished company, in five minutes, 24 Jan. 1890.
The prince of Wales after driving in the last rivet, in the presence of the duke of Edinburgh, the duke of Fife, prince George of Wales, the marquis of Tweeddale, the earl of Rosebery, and other distinguished visitors, including M. Eiffel, and other eminent engineers, said, "Ladies and gentlemen, I now declare the Forth bridge open," 1.30 P.M. 4 March, 1890.
The ceremony was followed by a banquet in a hall adjoining the works.
The length of the bridge (from North to South Queensferry), with the approaching viaducts, is one mile 1,005 yards; the highest part of the bridge is 361 feet; the clear headway under the centre of the bridge is 152 feet above high water. The greatest number of men employed at one time was 5,000. 56 lives were lost during the construction, in spite of great precautions.
Estimated cost 1,600,000*l.*, actual cost about 2,500,000*l.*
Mr. Matthew William Thompson, chairman of the Forth bridge and Midland railway companies, and Mr. John Fowler (died 20 Nov. 1898), were created baronets, Mr. Benjamin Baker, was made K.C.M.G., and Mr. William Arrol was knighted, 1890.
The bridge was opened for the ordinary railway trains, 2 June. 1890.
The bridge slowly crossed by the queen coming south, 19 June, 1891.
By the fall of scaffolding through high wind, 3 painters killed, 29 Sept. 1891.
The bridge firmly withstood a violent gale, 29 Jan. 1892.

FORTIFICATION. The Phœnicians were the first people to fortify cities. Apollodorus says that Perseus fortified Mycenæ, where statues were afterwards erected to him. The modern system was introduced about 1500. Albert Dürer wrote on fortification in 1527; and great improvements were made by Vauban, who fortified many places in France; he died 1707. The new fortifications of Paris were completed in 1846; see *Paris*. In Aug. 1860, the British parliament passed an act for the expenditure of 2,000,000*l.* in one year upon the fortifications of Portsmouth, Plymouth, Pembroke, and Portland, the Thames, Medway, and Sheerness, Chatham, Dover, and Cork, and on the purchase of a central arsenal establishment; the estimated expense being 9,500,000*l.* A committee to investigate our fortifications was appointed, 16 April, 1868.

FORTIS, a powerful explosive invented in Belgium about 1887, said to be well adapted for mining purposes. In May, 1890, it was manufactured by the Fortis Powder and Explosives company. Successful experiments at Liége, 8 Sept. 1891.

FORTNIGHTLY REVIEW, first published in 1865, edited by G. H. Lewes, succeeded by John Morley in 1867, and others. It was afterwards published monthly.

FORTUNATE ISLES, see *Canaries*.

FORTUNE BAY AFFAIR, see *Canada*, 1878, 1880-1, and *Newfoundland*.

FORTUNE-TELLING is traced to the early astrologers, by whom the planets Jupiter and Venus were supposed to betoken happiness. The Sibyllæ were women said to be inspired by Heaven; see *Sibyls* and *Gipsies*. In England the laws against fortune-telling were at one time very severe. A declaration was published in France, 11 Jan. 1680, of exceeding severity against fortune-tellers and poisoners, under which several persons suffered death. *Hénault*. Fortune-tellers, although liable by the acts of 1743 and 1824 to be imprisoned as rogues and vagabonds, still exist in England. See *Palmistry*.

FORTY-SHILLING FREEHOLDERS, see *Freeholders*.

FORTY-SHILLINGS' DAY, the name of a quaint custom annually kept up since 1718 on the feast of the Purification (2 Feb.), at Walton, in Surrey. William Glanville left 2*l.* each for 5 boys who should, placing their fingers upon his tomb in the churchyard, repeat the Creed, the Lord's Prayer, the Ten Commandments, and afterwards read 1 Cor. xv. and write out two verses of the chapter. The number of recipients has since been increased.

FORUM, at Rome, originally a market-place, became about 472 B.C. the place of assembly of the people in their tribes (the Comitia), and was gradually adorned with temples and public buildings.—Near FORUM TREBRONII, in Mœsia, the Romans were defeated by the Goths, Nov. 251. After a struggle in the morass, the emperor Decius and his son were slain and their bodies not recovered. See *Rome*, 1885, 1899–1902.

FOSSALTA, near Bologna, central Italy. Here Enzo or Enrico, titular king of Sardinia, natural son of the emperor Frederick II., was defeated and made prisoner, 26 May, 1249, and retained. He was kept in honourable captivity till his death, 14 March, 1272.

FOTHERINGHAY CASTLE (Northamptonshire), built about 1400. Here Richard III. of England was born in 1450; and here Mary queen of Scots was tried, 11-14 Oct. 1586, and beheaded, 8 Feb. 1587. It was demolished by her son, James I. of England, in 1604.

FOUDROYANT, Nelson's flagship 1798; purchased by Mr. J. R. Cobb, F.S.A., of Brecon, from a German firm, and brought to the Thames, 28 Nov. 1892; proposal to make her a Nelson museum unsuccessful, October, 1893. A company having failed, Mr. J. R. Cobb restored the vessel, 1895–96; it was moored off Woolwich, and open to visitors, 19 June, 1896; wrecked in a gale at Blackpool, crew saved, 16 June, 1897; destroyed in a gale, 28 Nov. 1897; Mr. Cobb died, 6 Dec. 1897.

FOUGHARD, near Dundalk, N. Ireland. Here Edward, brother of Robert Bruce, after invading Ireland in 1315, was defeated by sir John Bermingham, 5 Oct. 1318. Bruce was killed by Roger de Maupis, a burgess of Dundalk.

FOUNDLING HOSPITALS are ancient. A species of foundling hospital was set up at Milan in 787, and in the middle ages most of the principal cities of the continent possessed one. The French government in 1790 declared foundlings to be the "children of the state."

No foundling hospital in England when Addison wrote in 1713

London foundling hospital, projected by Thomas Coram, a sea-captain, incorporated, Oct. 1739; opened . . . . 2 June, 1756

Handel gave an organ; opened it . . 1 May, 1750

It succours about 500 infant children; Coram's statue was put up in 1856

Foundling hospital in Dublin instituted in 1704. Owing to great mortality, and from moral considerations, the internal department was closed by order of government . . 31 March, 1835

Foundling hospital at Moscow, founded by Catherine II. in 1772; about 12,000 children are received annually.

FOUNTAINE COLLECTION of Renaissance works, Faience, Limoges, Raffaelle, and Palissy enamelled ware, &c. (unequalled); and also a fine collection of coins, medals, carved ivory work, &c., formed by sir Andrew Fountaine, in the reigns of Anne and George I.; placed in Narford Hall, Norfolk, about 1730; sold by Christie and Manson for 91,112*l.*, 16-19 June, 1884; by the sale of ancient drawings, on 11 July, the sum was raised to 96,278*l.* Sir Andrew Fountaine died in 1873.

FOUNTAINS. The fountain of Hero of Alexandria was invented about 150 B.C. Among the remarkable fountains at Rome are the Fontana di Trevi, constructed for pope Clement XII. in 1735; the Fontana Paolina, erected for pope Paul V. in 1612; and Fontana dell' Acqua Felice, called also the Fountain of Moses. The fountains in the palace gardens at Versailles, made for Louis XIV., and the Grand Jet d'Eau, at St. Cloud, are exceedingly beautiful. There are above 100 public fountains in Paris, the most striking being the Château d'Eau on the Boulevard St. Martin (by Girard, 1811) and that at the Palais Royal. London is not remarkable for fountains; the largest are in Trafalgar-square, constructed in 1845, after designs by sir Charles Barry. There are beautiful fountains at Chatsworth, in Derbyshire, the seat of the duke of Devonshire. The magnificent fountains at the Crystal Palace, Sydenham, were first publicly exhibited on 18 June, 1856, in the presence of the queen and 20,000 spectators.

The fountain at Park-lane, London, W., the gift of Mrs. Brown, was inaugurated and uncovered, 9 July, 1875. It has statues of Chaucer, Shakspeare, and Milton, the work of Mr. Thomas Croft, and cost 5000*l.*

FOURIERISM, a social system devised by M. Charles Fourier (who died in 1837). The Phalanstery (from *phalanx*), an association of 400 families living in one edifice, was to be so arranged as to give the highest amount of happiness at the lowest cost. The system failed; caused, it is said, by the smallness of the scale on which it was tried.

The *Familistère*, a somewhat similar system, established by M. Godin, a manufacturer of stoves, &c., at Guise, N. France, was reported successful in Jan. 1886.

"FOUR MASTERS," a name given to Michael, Conary, and Cucogry O'Clery, and Ferfeasa O'Mulconry, who compiled from original documents the annals of Ireland from 2242 B.C. to A.D. 1616. An edition of these "Annals," printed from autograph MSS., with a translation edited by Dr. John O'Donovan, was published at Dublin in 1851. The "Four Masters" lived in the first half of the 17th century.

FOURTH ESTATE. Thomas Carlyle states that this term was applied to the newspaper press by Edmund Burke when speaking in the House of Commons. Burke died 9 July, 1797.

FOURTH PARTY, a name facetiously given to lord Randolph Churchill, sir Henry Drummond Wolff, Mr. (aft. sir) John Gorst, and a few other conservative members, active opponents of the government, also termed "free lances." The other parties were liberals, conservatives, and home-rulers (1880-5).

Lord Randolph Churchill and some of his friends desire to imitate radical organization (popular, responsible, and representative), advocating "tory democracy" . . . . . May, 1884

He and some others took office under the *Salisbury administration* . . . June, 1885

FOX, see *Reynard*.

FOX AND GRENVILLE ADMINISTRATION, see *Grenville Administration*.

FOX-GLOVE (folks' or fairies' glove), a handsome indigenous flower. The canary fox-glove (*Digitalis canariensis*) came from the Canary islands, 1698. The Madeira fox-glove came here in 1777. The fox-grape shrub (*vitus vulpina*), from Virginia, before 1656.

FOYERS, FALLS OF, WORKS, see *Aluminium*.

FRAGA, N.E. Spain. Near here the Christians, under Alfonso I. of Aragon, were defeated by the Moors, 17 July, 1134.

FRANC, the current silver French coin (value 10*d*.), superseded the *livre tournois* 1795.

FRANCE, the Roman *Gaul* (*which see*). In the 5th century it was conquered by the Franks, a people of Germany, then inhabiting Franconia, where they became known about 240. The country was gradually named *Franken-ric*, Franks' kingdom. For the dynastic changes, see list of sovereigns, *infra*. Previous to the revolution, France was divided into 40 governments. In 1790 it was divided into 83 departments, and subsequently into 130, including Corsica, Geneva, Savoy, and other places, chiefly conquests. In 1815 the departments were reduced to 86; in 1860 they were raised to 89 by the acquisition of Savoy and Nice,* reduced to 86 by the loss of Alsace and Lorraine. The political constitution has been frequently changed since 1789. For details of more important events, see separate articles. The title of king of France, adopted by the English sovereigns from Edwd. 3rd, 1340, was given up by Geo. 3 in 1802. Colonies.

The Franks settle in that part of Gaul, till late called Flanders . . . . . . about 418

Clovis, 481; defeats Syagrius and the Gauls at Soissons, 486; and the Alemanni at Tolbiac, near Cologne; and embraces Christianity . . . 496

He kills Alaric the Goth at the battle of Vouglé, near Poictiers, unites his conquests from the Loire to the Pyrenees, and makes Paris his capital 507

He proclaims the Salique law; and dies, leaving four sons 511

Frequent invasions of the Avars and Lombards 562-584

The mayors of the palace now assume almost sovereign authority 584

Charles Martel becomes mayor of the palace, and rules with despotic sway 714

Invasion of the Saracens, 720; defeated by Charles Martel, near Tours . . . . . 10 Oct. 732

Reign of Pepin the Short 752

Charlemagne, king, 768; conquers Saxony and Lombardy, 773-4 crowned emperor of the West. 25 Dec. 800

The Normans invade Neustria, 876; part of which is granted Rollo, as Normandy, by Charles the Simple 911

Reign of Hugh Capet 987

Paris made capital of all France 996

Letters of franchise granted to cities and towns by Louis VI. 1135

Louis VII. joins in the Crusades 1146

Philip Augustus defeats the Germans at Bouvines . 1214

Louis VIII., *Cœur de Lion*, frees his serfs . . . 1224

Louis IX. conducts an army into Palestine; takes Damietta, 1249; see *Crusades*; dies before Tunis, 25 Aug. 1270

Charles of Anjou conquers Naples and Sicily . 1266

His tyranny leads to the massacre called the Sicilian Vespers (*which see*) 1282

Philip the Fair's quarrels with the Pope . . 1301-2

Knights Templars suppressed 1307-8

Union of France and Navarre 1314

English invasion—Philip VI. defeated at Cressy, 26 Aug. 1346

Calais taken by Edward III. . . . . 3 Aug. 1347

Dauphiny annexed to France 1349

Battle of Poictiers (*which see*); king John taken (brought prisoner to England) . . 19 Sept. 1356

France laid under an interdict by the pope . . 1407

Battle of Agincourt (*which see*) . . . 25 Oct. 1415

Massacre of the Armagnacs by the Burgundians, June, 1418

Henry V. of England acknowledged heir to the throne 1420

Henry VI. crowned at Paris; duke of Bedford regent 1422

Siege of Orleans raised, by *Joan of Arc*, 8 May; battle of Patay; the English defeated 18 June, 1429

Joan of Arc burnt at Rouen . . . . 30 May, 1431

England lost all her possessions (but Calais) in France, between . . . . 1434 and 1450

"League of the public good" against Louis XI. by the nobles . . . . Dec. 1464–Oct. 1465

Edward IV. of England invades France . . . 1475

Charles VIII. conquers Naples, 1494; loses it . . 1496

League of Cambray against Venice 1508

Pope Julius II. forms the Holy League against France 1511

English invasion—battle of Spur . . 16 Aug. 1513

Interview on the *Field of the Cloth of Gold* between Francis I. and Henry VIII. of England . . . 1520

Francis I. defeated and taken at Pavia . 24 Feb. 1525

Peace of Cambray . . . . . . 5 Aug. 1529

Persecution of protestants begins 1530

Royal printing press established, 1531; Robert Stephens prints his Latin Bible 1532

Brittany annexed to France . . . . . ,,

League of England with the emperor Charles V.; Henry VIII. invades France 1544

Peace with England . . . . . 7 June, 1546

Successful defence of Metz by the duke of Guise . 1552

He takes Calais (*which see*) 1558

Religious wars; massacre of protestants at Vassy, 1 March, 1562

Guise defeats the Huguenots at Dreux 19 Dec. ,,

Guise killed at siege of Orleans, 18 Feb.; temporary peace of Amboise . . . . . 19 March, 1563

Huguenots defeated at St. Denis . . . 10 Nov. 1567

At Jarnac 13 March; at Moncontour . . 3 Oct. 1569

Massacre of St. Bartholomew . . . 24 Aug. 1572

"Holy Catholic League" established 1576

Duke of Guise assassinated by king's order, 23 Dec.; and his brother, the cardinal 24 Dec. 1588

Henry III. stabbed by Jacques Clement, a friar, 1 Aug.; died . . . . 2 Aug. 1589

Henry IV. defeats the league at Ivry 14 March, 1590

* *Population of France* in 1700, 19,669,320; in 1762, 21,769,163; in 1801, 27,349,003; in 1820, 30,451,187; in 1836, 33,540,910; in 1846, 35,401,761; in 1856, 36,039,364; in 1861, including the new departments, 37,382,225; in 1872 (after the war), 36,102,921. Population 31 Dec. 1876, 36,905,788; 18 Dec. 1881, 37,672,048; 1891, 38,343,192; 1901, 38,961,945. Population of the colonies (1876) (in *Asia*, Pondicherry, &c.; *Africa*, Algeria, Madagascar, &c.; *America*, Martinique, Guadaloupe, &c.; *Oceania*, the Marquesas, &c.), in 1858, 3,641,226; in 1872, about 5,621,000; in 1877, about 6,440,660; in 1901, about 44,260,000. [Alsace and Lorraine lost with population of 1,597,219 in 1871.] In May, 1862, the *Moniteur* asserted the effective army to be 447,000, with a reserve of 170,000: virtually raised to 1,200,000 in 1868; disposable force in 1869, about 1,350,000; in 1875, 1,750,000; in 1880, 2,423,164 men; effective army 1903, 1,000,000. Revenue, 1809-1, 126,611,900*l*.; 1891–2, 130,074,474*l*.; 1902–3, 142,995,072*l*.; expenditure, 1890–1, 126,595,261*l*.; 1891–2, 130,060,963*l*.; 1902–3, 142,535,957*l*.; 1890, imports, 218,080,000*l*.; 1893, 157,468,800*l*.; 1896, 151,944,000*l*.; 1900, 176,341,200*l*.; 1901, 174,600,000*l*.; exports, 1890, 193,600,000*l*.; 1893, 128,384,760*l*.; 1896, 136,036,000*l*.; 1900, 163,121,280*l*.; 1901, 160,520,000*l*.

Henry IV. becomes a Roman Catholic . 25 July, 1593

The league leaders submit to him . . Jan. 1596

He promulgates the edict of Nantes . 13 April, 1598

Silk and other manufactures introduced by him and Sully 1606-1610

Quebec in North America settled . . . 1608

Murder of Henry IV. by Ravaillac . . 14 May, 1610

Regency of Mary de Medici 1610-14

The states-general meet and complain of the management of the finances . . . 27 Oct. 1614

Rise of the Concinis, 1610; their fall and death . 1617

Navarre annexed to France 1620

Vigorous and successful administration of Richelieu, begins with finance 1624

Rochelle taken after a long siege 1628

"Day of Dupes;" Richelieu's energy defeats the machinations of his enemies . 11 Nov. 1630

Richelieu organises the *Académie de France* . 1634-5

His death (aged 58) . . . 4 Dec. 1642

Accession of Louis XIV., aged four years (Anne of Austria, regent) . . . . . 14 May, 1643

Administration of Mazarin; victories of Turenne, 1643-6

Civil wars of the Fronde . . . . 1648, &c.

Death of Mazarin, 9 March; Colbert financial minister 1661

War with Holland, &c 1672

Canal of Languedoc constructed . . . 1664-81

Peace of Nimeguen . . . . . 10 Aug. 1678

Edict of Nantes revoked . . . . 22 Oct. 1685

Louis marries Madame de Maintenon . . . ,,

War with William III. of England . . . 1689, &c.

Peace of Ryswick . . . . . 20 Sept. 1697

War of the Spanish succession . . Sept. 1701

French defeated at Blenheim . . 2 Aug. 1704

At Ramillies . . . . . 23 May, 1706

Peace of Utrecht (*which see*) . . 11 April, 1713

Dissensions of Jesuits and Jansenists; the bull *Unigenitus* . . . . . Sept. ,,

Accession of Louis XV.; stormy regency of the duke of Orleans . . . . . 1 Sept. 1715, &c.

Law's bubble in France (see *Law*) . . . 1716

French defeated at Dettingen . . 16 June, 1743

Successful campaign of marshal Saxe . . . 1746

Peace of Aix-la-Chapelle . . . . 18 Oct. 1748

Seven years' war begun . . . May, 1756

Damiens' attempt on life of Louis XV. . 5 Jan. 1757

Canada lost—battle of Quebec . . 13 Sept. 1759

The Jesuits banished from France, and their effects confiscated 1762

Peace of Paris: Canada ceded to England, 10 Feb. 1763

Louis XV. enslaved by madame du Barry . . 1769

Death of Louis XV. . . . . . 10 May, 1774

Famine riots at Versailles . . . May, 1775

The minister Turgot dismissed . . May, 1776

Ministry of Necker . . . . . Nov. ,,

Louis XVI. assists America to throw off its dependence on England, at first secretly 1778

Torture abolished in French judicature . . . 1780

Peace of Versailles with England . . 3 Sept. 1783

The diamond-necklace affair (*which see*) . . 1785

Meeting of the assembly of notables, 22 Feb. 1787; again . . . . . . 6 Nov. 1788

Opening of states-general (308 ecclesiastics, 285 nobles; 621 deputies, tiers état) . 5 May, 1789

The tiers état constitute themselves the National Assembly . . . . . 17 June, ,,

The French revolution commences with the destruction of the Bastille (*which see*) . 14 July, ,,

The National Assembly decrees that the title of the "king of France" shall be changed to that of the "king of the French" . . . 16 Oct. ,,

The property of the clergy confiscated . 2 Nov. ,,

Emigration of nobles . . . Oct.-Dec. ,,

Confederation of the *Champ de Mars*; France declared a limited monarchy; Louis XVI. swears to maintain the constitution . . 14 July, 1790

The silver plate used in the churches transferred to the mint and coined . . . 3 March, 1791

Death of Mirabeau . . . . 2 April, ,,

The king, queen, and royal family arrested at Varennes, in their flight . . . . 21 June, 1791

Louis (a prisoner) sanctions the National Constitution . . . . 15 Sept. ,,

War declared against the emperor . 20 April, 1792

The Jacobin club declare their sittings permanent, 18 June, ,,

The multitude, bearing the red bonnet of liberty, march to the Tuileries to make demands on the king . . . . . . 20 June, ,,

First coalition against France; commencement of the great French war . . . . June, ,,

[See *Battles*, 1792 to 1815.]

The royal Swiss guards cut to pieces; massacre of 5000 persons . . . . . 10 Aug. ,,

Revolutionary tribunal set up . . . 19 Aug. ,,

Decree of the National Assembly against the priests; 40,000 exiled . . . . . 26 Aug. ,,

Massacre in Paris; the prisons broken open, and 1200 persons (100 priests) slain . 2-5 Sept. ,,

Murder of the princess de Lamballe . 3 Sept. ,,

The National Convention opened . 17 Sept. ,,

Convention establishes a republic, 20 Sept.; proclaimed . . . . . . 22 Sept. ,,

Duke of Brunswick defeated at Valmy 20 Sept. ,,

The French people declare their fraternity with all nations who desire to be free, and offer help, 19 Nov. ,,

Flanders conquered . . . . . Dec. ,,

Decree for the perpetual banishment of the Bourbon family, those confined in the Temple excepted, 20 Dec. ,,

Louis imprisoned in the Temple distinct from the queen, and brought to trial, 19 Jan.; condemned to death, 20 Jan. Beheaded in the *Place de Louis Quinze* . . . . . . 21 Jan. 1793

Committee of public safety established 21 Jan. ,,

War with England and Holland declared 1 Feb. ,,

War in La Vendée . . . . . March, ,,

Reign of terror—proscription of Girondists, 31 May; establishment of convention 23 June, ,,

Marat stabbed by Charlotte Corday . 13 July, ,,

The queen beheaded . . . . 16 Oct. ,,

Execution of the Girondists . . . 31 Oct. ,,

Philip Egalité, duke of Orleans, who had voted for the king's death, guillotined at Paris (see *Orleans*), 6 Nov.; and madame Roland . 8 Nov. ,,

Worship of goddess of reason . 10 Nov. ,,

Adoption of new republican calendar 24 Nov. ,,

Execution of Danton and others, 5 April; of madame Elizabeth . . . . . . 12 May, 1794

Robespierre president, 4 June; he and 71 others guillotined . . . . . 28 July, ,,

Abolition of the Revolutionary Tribunal 15 Dec. ,,

Peace with Prussia . . . . . 5 April, 1795

Insurrection of the Faubourgs . . 20, 21 May, ,,

Louis XVII. dies in prison . . . 8 June, ,,

French directory chosen . . . . 1 Nov. ,,

Bonaparte's successful campaigns in Italy, 1796, &c.

Babeuf's conspiracy suppressed . . 12 May, ,,

Pichegru's conspiracy fails . . . May, 1797

Expedition to Syria and Egypt (*which see*) July, 1798

European coalition against France . . April, 1799

Council of Five Hundred deposed by Bonaparte, who is declared First Consul . . 10 Nov. ,,

He defeats the Austrians at Marengo . 14 June, 1800

His life attempted by the infernal machine, 24 Dec. ,,

The bank of France founded by Napoleon, aided by count Mollien . . . . . . ,,

Peace of Amiens (with England, Spain, and Holland) signed . . . . 25-27 March, 1802

Amnesty to the emigrants . . . . April, ,,

Legion of Honour instituted . . . 19 May, ,,

Bonaparte made consul for life . . 2 Aug. ,,

The bank of France established . . 14 April, 1803

Declaration of war against England 22 May, ,,

Conspiracy of Moreau and Pichegru against Bonaparte, 15 Feb.; Pichegru found strangled in prison (see *Georges*) . . . . . 6 April, 1804

Duc d'Enghien executed . . . 21 March, ,,

France made an empire; Napoleon proclaimed emperor, 18 May; crowned by the pope 2 Dec. ,,

He is crowned king of Italy . . . 26 May, 1805

Another coalition against France . . Aug. ,,

Napoleon defeats the allies at Austerlitz 2 Dec. ,,

And the Prussians at Jena . . . 14 Oct. 1806

And the Russians at Eylau . . . 8 Feb. 1807

His interview with the czar at Tilsit, 26 June; peace signed . . . . . . 7 July, 1807
His Milan decree against British commerce, 17 Dec. „
New nobility of France created . . 1 March, 1808
Abdication of Charles IV. of Spain and his son, in favour of Napoleon, 5 May; insurrection in Spain, 27 May, „
Commencement of the Peninsular war (see *Spain*), July, „
Alliance of England and Austria against France, April, 1809
Victories in Austria; Napoleon enters Vienna, May, „
Peace of Vienna . . . . . . 14 Oct. „
Divorce of the emperor and empress Josephine decreed by the senate . . . 16 Dec. „
Marriage of Napoleon to Maria Louisa of Austria, 1 April, 1810
Holland united to France . . . . 9 July, „
Birth of the king of Rome (since styled Napoleon II.), 20 March, 1811
War with Russia declared . . . . 22 June, 1812
Victory at Borodino . . . . . . 7 Sept. „
Disastrous retreat; French army nearly destroyed, Oct. „
Alliance of Austria, Russia, and Prussia against France . . . . March, 1813
The British enter France . . . . 7 Oct. „
Surrender of Paris to the allies . . 31 March, 1814
Abdication of Napoleon negotiated . . 5 April, „
Bourbon dynasty restored, and Louis XVIII. arrives in Paris . . . . 3 May, „
Napoleon arrives at Elba . . . . 4 May, „
The Constitutional Charter decreed . 4-10 June, „
Quits Elba, and lands at Cannes . 1 March, 1815
Arrives at Fontainebleau (*the 100 days*) 20 March, „
Joined by all the army . . . 22 March, „
The allies sign a treaty against him . March, „
He abolishes the slave trade . . 29 March, „
Leaves Paris for the army . . . . 12 June, „
Defeated at Waterloo . . . . 18 June, „
Returns to Paris, 20 June; abdicates in favour of his infant son . . . . 22 June, „
Intending to embark for America, he arrives at Rochefort . . . . . . 3 July, „
Louis XVIII. enters Paris . . . . 3 July, „
Napoleon surrenders to capt. Maitland, of the *Bellerophon*, at Rochefort . . . 15 July, „
Transferred at Torbay to the *Northumberland*, and with admiral sir George Cockburn sails for St. Helena . . . . 8 Aug. „
Arrives at St. Helena to remain for life 15 Oct. „
Execution of marshal Ney . . . 7 Dec. „
The family of Bonaparte excluded *for ever* from France by the law of amnesty . . 12 Jan. 1816
Duke of Berry murdered . . . . 13 Feb. 1820
Death of Napoleon I. (see *Wills*) . 5 May, 1821
Louis XVIII. dies; Charles X. king . 16 Sept. 1824
National Guard disbanded . . . 30 April, 1827
War with Algiers; dey's fleet defeated . 4 Nov. „
Seventy-six new peers created . . 5 Nov. „
Election riots at Paris; barricades: several persons killed . . . . . . 19, 20 Nov. „
The Villèle ministry replaced by the Martignac, 4 Jan. 1828
Béranger imprisoned for political songs . 10 Dec. „
Polignac administration formed . . 8 Aug. 1829
Chamber of deputies dissolved . . 16 May, 1830
Algiers taken . . . . . . 5 July, „
The obnoxious ordinances regarding the press, and reconstruction of the chamber of deputies, 26 July, „
Revolution commences with barricades 27 July, „
Conflicts in Paris between the populace (ultimately aided by the national guard) and the army, 28-30 July, „
Charles X. retires to Rambouillet; flight of his ministry, 31 July; he abdicates . . 2 Aug. „
The duke of Orleans accepts the crown as Louis-Philippe I. . . . . 7 Aug. „
The constitutional charter of July published, 14 Aug. „
Charles X. retires to England . . 17 Aug. „
Polignac and other ministers tried and sentenced to perpetual imprisonment . . . 21 Dec. „
The abolition of the hereditary peerage decreed by both chambers; the peers (36 new peers being created) concurring by a majority of 103 to 70, 27 Dec. 1831
The A B C (*abaissés*) insurrection in Paris suppressed . . . . 5, 6 June, 1832
Charles X. leaves Holyrood-house for the continent . . . . 18 Sept. „
Ministry of Soult, duke of Dalmatia . . 11 Oct. „
Bergeron and Benoit tried for an attempt on the life of Louis-Philippe; acquitted . 18 March, 1833
The duchess of Berry, who has been delivered of a female child, and asserts her secret marriage with an Italian nobleman, sent to Palermo, 9 June, „
Death of La Fayette . . . . . 20 May, 1834
Marshal Gerard takes office . . . . 15 July, „
M. Dupuytren dies . . . . . . 8 Feb. 1835
Duc de Broglie, minister . . . . Feb. „
Fieschi attempts the king's life . . 28 July, „
[He fired an infernal machine as the king and his sons rode along the lines of the national guard, on the boulevard du Temple. The machine consisted of twenty-five barrels, charged with various missiles, and lighted simultaneously by a train of gunpowder. The king and his sons escaped; but marshal Mortier, duke of Treviso, was shot dead, many officers dangerously wounded, and upwards of forty persons killed or injured.]
Fieschi executed . . . . . . 19 Feb. 1836
Louis Alibaud fires at the king on his way from the Tuileries, 25 June; guillotined . . 11 July, „
Ministry of count Molé, *vice* M. Thiers . 6 Sept. „
Death of Charles X. . . . . . 6 Nov. „
Attempted insurrection at Strasburg by Louis Napoleon (afterwards emperor), planned, it is said, by Filain de Persigny, 29-30 Oct.; he is sent to America . . . . 13 Nov. „
Prince Polignac and others set at liberty from Ham, and sent out of France . . . . 23 Nov. „
Meunier fires at the king on his way to open the French chambers . . . . 27 Dec. „
Amnesty for political offences . . . . 8 May 1837
"Idées Napoléoniennes," by prince Louis Napoleon, published 1838
Talleyrand dies . . . . 20 May, „
Marshal Soult at the coronation of the queen of England . . . . . . 28 June, „
Birth of the count of Paris . . . 24 Aug. „
Death of the duchess of Wurtemberg (daughter of Louis Philippe), a good sculptor . . 2 Jan. 1839
Insurrection of Barbès and Blanqui at Paris, 12 May, „
M. Thiers, minister of foreign affairs . 1 March, 1840
The chambers decree the removal of Napoleon's remains from St. Helena to France . . 12 May, „
[By the permission of the British government these were taken from the tomb at St. Helena (15 Oct. 1840), and embarked on the next day on board the *Belle Poule* French frigate, under the command of the prince de Joinville; the vessel reached Cherbourg on 30 November; and on 15 December the body was deposited in the Hôtel des Invalides. The ceremony was witnessed by 1,000,000 of persons; 150,000 soldiers assisted in the obsequies: and the royal family and all the high personages of the realm were present; all the relatives of the emperor were absent, being proscribed, and in exile or in prison. The body was finally placed in its crypt on 31 March, 1861.]
Descent of prince Louis Napoleon, general Montholon, and 50 followers, at Vimereux, near Boulogne, 6 Aug.; the prince sentenced to imprisonment for life . . . . . . 6 Oct. „
Darmès fires at the king . . . . 15 Oct. „
M. Guizot, minister of foreign affairs . 29 Oct. „
Project of law for an extraordinary credit of 140,000,000 of francs, for erecting the fortifications of Paris, 15 Dec. „
The duration of copyright to 30 years after the author's death, fixed . . . . 30 March, 1841
Bronze statue of Napoleon placed on the column of the grande armée, Boulogne . . 15 Aug. „
Attempt to assassinate the duke of Aumale (king's son) on return from Africa . . . 13 Sept. „
The duke of Orleans, heir to the throne, killed by a fall from his carriage . . . 13 July, 1842
The queen of England visits the royal family at Château d'Eu . . . . . . 2-7 Sept. 1843
An extradition treaty with England signed . . „

War with Morocco, May; peace . . 10 Sept. 1844
The king visits England; received by the queen 6 Oct.; installed K.G. 9 Oct.; departs . 13 Oct ,,
Attempt of Lecompte to assassinate the king at Fontainebleau . . . . . 16 April, 1846
Louis Napoleon escapes from Ham . 25 May, ,,
The seventh attempt on the life of the king: by Joseph Henri . . . . . . 29 July, ,,
Spanish marriages: marriage of the queen of Spain with her cousin, and of the duc de Montpensier with the infanta of Spain . . 10 Oct. ,,
Disastrous inundations in the south . . 18 Oct. ,,
The Praslin murder (see *Praslin*) 18 Aug. 1847
Death of marshal Oudinot (duke of Reggio) at Paris, in his 91st year, 13 Sept.; Soult made general of France, in his room . . . 26 Sept. ,,
Jerome Bonaparte returns to France after an exile of 32 years . . . . . 10 Oct. ,,
Surrender of Abd-el-Kader . . . 23 Dec. ,,
Death of the ex-empress, Maria Louisa, 18 Dec.; and of madame Adelaide . . 30 Dec. ,,
The grand reform banquet at Paris prohibited, 21 Feb. 1848
Revolutionary tumult in consequence; impeachment and resignation of Guizot, 22 Feb.; barricades thrown up, the Tuileries ransacked, the prisons opened, and frightful disorders committed, 23, 24 Feb. ,,
Louis Philippe abdicates in favour of his infant grandson, the comte de Paris, who is not accepted; the royal family and ministers escape, 24 Feb. ,,
A republic proclaimed from the steps of the Hôtel de Ville . . . 26 Feb. ,,
The ex-king and queen arrive at Newhaven in England . . . . . 3 March, ,,
Grand funeral procession in honour of the victims of the revolution . . . 4 March, ,,
The provisional government resigns to an executive commission, elected by the national assembly of the French Republic . . . 7 May, ,,
[The members of this new government were: MM. Dupont de l'Eure, Arago, Garnier-Pagès, Marie, Lamartine, Ledru-Rollin, and Crémieux. The secretaries: Louis Blanc, Albert, Flocon, and Marrast.]
The people's attack on the assembly suppressed, 15 May, ,,
Perpetual banishment of Louis Philippe and his family decreed . . . 26 May, ,,
Election of Louis Napoleon (to the national assembly) for the department of the Seine and three other departments . . . 13 June, ,,
Rise of the red republicans: war against the troops and national guard; more than 300 barricades thrown up, and firing continues in all parts of Paris during the night . . 23 June, ,,
The troops under Cavaignac and Lamoricière, with immense loss, drive the insurgents from the left bank of the Seine . . . . 24 June, ,,
Paris declared in a state of siege . . 25 June, ,,
The faubourg du Temple carried with cannon, and the insurgents surrender . . 26 June, ,,
[The national losses caused by this outbreak estimated at 30,000,000 francs; 16,000 persons killed and wounded, and 8000 prisoners were taken. The archbishop of Paris was killed while tending the dying, 26 June.]
Cavaignac, president of the council . . 28 June, ,,
Louis Napoleon takes his seat in the National Assembly . . . . . . 26 Sept. ,,
Paris relieved from a state of siege, which had continued four months . . . 20 Oct. ,,
Solemn promulgation of the constitution of 4 Nov., in front of the Tuileries . . 12 Nov. ,,
Louis Napoleon elected president of the French republic, 11 Dec.; proclaimed . . 20 Dec. ,,
[He had 5,587,759 votes; Cavaignac, 1,474,687; Ledru-Rollin, 381,026; Raspail, 37,121; Lamartine, 21,032; and Changarnier, 4,975.]
Military demonstration to stifle an anticipated insurrection of the reds . . . 29 Jan. 1849
Death of king Louis Philippe, at Claremont, in England . . . . . . 26 Aug. 1850
Liberty of the press restricted . . 26 Sept. ,,
Gen. Changarnier deprived of the command of the national guard . . . . . 10 Jan. 1851
Death of the duchess of Angoulême, daughter of Louis XVI., at Frohsdorf . . . 19 Oct. 1851
Death of marshal Soult . . . . . 26 Oct. ,,
Electric telegraph between England and France opened . . . . . . 13 Nov. ,,
Factious oppositions in the chamber; alleged plots Nov. ,,
Coup d'état planned by the prince-president, Persigny, and De Morny; carried out by C. de Maupas, minister of police, St. Arnaud, and others; legislative assembly dissolved; universal suffrage established, and Paris declared in a state of siege; the election of a president for ten years proposed, and a second chamber or senate, 2 Dec. ,,
MM. Thiers, Changarnier, Cavaignac, Bedeau, Lamoricière, and Charres arrested, and sent to the castle of Vincennes . . . . . 2 Dec. ,,
About 180 members of the assembly, with M. Berryer at their head, attempting to meet, are arrested, and Paris is occupied by troops. 2 Dec. ,,
M. Charles Baudin, a deputy, shot dead while protesting against the violation of the law 2 Dec. ,,
Sanguinary conflicts in Paris; the troops victorious, 3, 4 Dec. ,,
Consultative commission founded . . 12 Dec. ,,
Voting throughout France for the election of a president of the republic for ten years; affirmative votes 7,473,431, negative votes 641,351. 21, 22 Dec. ,,
Installation of the prince-president in the cathedral of Notre Dame; the day observed as a national holiday at Paris, and Louis Napoleon takes up his residence at the Tuileries, 1 Jan. 1852
Generals Changarnier, Lamoricière, and others, conducted to the Belgian frontier . . 9 Jan. ,,
83 members of the legislative assembly banished; 575 persons arrested for resistance to the *coup d'état* of 2 Dec., and conveyed to Havre for transportation to Cayenne . . . . 10 Jan. ,,
[The inscription "*Liberty, Fraternity, Equality,*" ordered to be forthwith erased throughout France, and the old names of streets, public buildings, and places of resort to be restored. The trees of liberty are everywhere hewn down and burnt.]
The national guard disbanded, reorganised anew, and placed under the control of the executive; the president appointing the officers . 10 Jan. ,,
A new constitution published . . 14 Jan. ,,
Decree obliging the Orleans family to sell all their real and personal property in France within a year . . . . 22 Jan. ,,
Second decree, annulling the settlement made by Louis Philippe upon his family previous to his accession in 1830, and annexing the property to the domain of the state . . . . 22 Jan. ,,
The birthday of Napoleon I. (15 Aug.) decreed to be the only national holiday . . . 17 Feb. ,,
The departments of France released from a state of siege . . . . . . 27 March, ,,
Legislative chambers installed . . 29 March, ,,
A crystal palace authorised to be erected in the Champs Elysées at Paris . . . 30 March, ,,
Plot to assassinate the prince-president discovered at Paris . . . . 1 July, ,,
President's visit to Strasburg . . . 19 July, ,,
M. Thiers and others permitted to return to France, 8 Aug. ,,
The French senate prays "the re-establishment of the hereditary sovereign power in the Bonaparte family" . . . . 13 Sept. ,,
Enthusiastic reception of the prince-president at Lyons . . . . 19 Sept. ,,
Infernal machine, to destroy the prince-president, seized at Marseilles . . . . 23 Sept. ,,
Prince-president visits Toulon, 27 Sept.; and Bordeaux, where he says "the empire is peace" (*l'empire c'est la paix*) . . . . 7 Oct. ,,
He releases Abd-el-Kader (see *Algiers*) . 16 Oct. ,,
He convokes the senate for November to deliberate on a change of government, when a *senatus consultum* will be proposed for the ratification of the French people . . . . . . 19 Oct. ,,
Protest of comte de Chambord . . . 25 Oct ,,

In his message to the senate, the prince-president announces the contemplated restoration of the empire, and orders the people to be consulted upon this change . . . . 4 Nov. 1852

Votes for the empire, 7,824,189; noes, 253,145; null, 63,326 . . . . . . 21 Nov. ,,

The prince-president declared emperor; assumes the title of Napoleon III. . . . 2 Dec. ,,

His marriage with Eugénie de Montijo, countess of Téba, at Notre-Dame . . . . 29 Jan. 1853

4312 political offenders pardoned . . . . 2 Feb. ,,

Bread riots . . . . Sept. ,,

Military camp at Satory, near Paris . . . Sept. ,,

Emperor and empress visit the provinces (many political prisoners discharged) . . . Oct. ,,

Francis Arago, astronomer, &c., died . . 2 Oct. ,,

Attempted assassination of the emperor—ten persons transported for life . . . . Nov. ,,

Reconciliation of the two branches of the Bourbons at Frohsdorf . . . . . . 20 Nov. ,,

Marshal Ney's statue inaugurated exactly 38 years after his death on the spot where it occurred, 7 Dec. ,,

War declared against Russia (see *Russo-Turkish War*) 27 March, 1854

Visit of prince Albert at Boulogne . . 5 Sept. ,,

Death of marshal St. Arnaud . . . 29 Sept. ,,

Emperor and empress visit London . 16-21 April, 1855

Industrial exhibition at Paris opened . 15 May, ,,

Queen Victoria and prince Albert visit France, 18-27 Aug. ,,

Attempted assassination of the emperor by Pianort, 28 April; by Bellemarre . . . . . 8 Sept. ,,

Death of count Molé . . . . . 24 Nov. ,,

Birth of the imperial prince; amnesty granted to 1000 political prisoners . . . 16 March, 1856

Peace with Russia signed . . . 30 March, ,,

Awful inundation in the south . . . June, ,,

[Subscriptions in London to relieve the sufferers amounted to 43,000*l.* Sir Jamsetjee Jejeebhoy, of Bombay, gave 500*l.* for the same purpose.]

Distress in money market . . . . 6 Oct. ,,

Sibour, archbishop of Paris, assassinated by Verger, a priest . . . . . . 3 Jan. 1857

Elections (3,000,000 voters to elect 257 deputies): gen. Cavaignac elected deputy, but declines to take the oath . . . . . 21, 22 June, ,,

Conspiracy to assassinate the emperor in Paris detected . . . . . . 11 July, ,,

Death of Béranger, popular poet . . 16 July, ,,

Longwood, the residence of Napoleon I. at St. Helena, bought for 180,000 francs . . . ,,

The conspirators Grilli, Bartolotti, and Tibaldi, tried, convicted, and sentenced to transportation, &c. . . . . . . 6, 7 Aug. ,,

Emperor and empress visit England . 6-10 Aug. ,,

The emperor meets the emperor of Russia at Stuttgart . . . . . . 25 Sept. ,,

Death of Eugène Cavaignac (aged 55) . 28 Oct. ,,

Death of Mdlle. Rachel (aged 38) . . 4 Jan. 1858

Attempted assassination of the emperor by Orsini, Pieri, Rudio, Gomez, &c., by the explosion of three shells (two persons killed, many wounded) 14 Jan. ,,

[Felix Orsini, a man of talent and energy, earnest to obtain Italian independence, was born Dec. 1819; studied at Bologna in 1837; joined a secret society in 1843; was arrested and condemned to the galleys for life in 1844; was released in 1846; took part in the Roman revolution in 1848, when he was elected a member of the assembly; and on the fall of the republic, fled to Genoa in 1849, and came to England in 1853. Entering into fresh conspiracies, he was arrested in Hungary, Jan. 1855, and sent to Mantua; he escaped thence and came to England in 1856, where he associated with Kossuth, Mazzini, &c.; delivered lectures, and where he devised the plot for which he suffered. In his will he acknowledged the justice of his sentence.]

Public safety bill passed—bold protest against it by Ollivier . . . . 18 Feb. ,,

France divided into five military departments; general Espinasse becomes minister of the interior, Feb. ,,

"*Napoleon III. et l'Angleterre*" published 11 Mar. ,,

Intemperate speeches in France against England—misconceptions between the two countries partially removed in . . . . . March, 1858

Republican outbreak at Chalons suppressed 9 March, ,,

Orsini and Pieri executed . . . 13 March, ,,

Simon Bernard, tried in London as their accomplice, acquitted . . . . . 12-17 April, ,,

Marshal Pelissier, ambassador to London, 15 April, ,,

Espinasse retires from ministry of the interior [he was killed at the battle of Magenta, 4 June, 1859] June, ,,

Queen of England meets the emperor; visits Cherbourg . . . . . . 4, 5 Aug. ,,

Conference at Paris respecting the Danubian principalities closes . . . . 19 Aug. ,,

Dispute with Portugal respecting the *Charles et Georges* (*which see*) settled . . . 23 Oct. ,,

Trial of comte de Montalembert . . . 25 Nov. ,,

[In Oct. 1858, the comte published a pamphlet entitled "*Un Débat sur l'Inde,*" eulogising English institutions and depreciating those of France. He was sentenced to six months' imprisonment and a fine of 3000 francs, but was pardoned by the emperor, 2 Dec. The comte appealed against the sentence of the court, and was again condemned; but acquitted of a part of the charge. The sentence was once more remitted by the emperor (21 Dec.). In Oct. 1859, the comte published a pamphlet entitled "*Pie IX. et la France en 1849 et 1859,*" in which England is severely censured for opposition to popery.]

Emperor's address to the Austrian ambassador (see *Austria*) . . . . . . 1 Jan. 1859

Marriage of prince Napoleon to princess Clotilde of Savoy . . . . . . 30 Jan. ,,

Publication of "*Napoleon III. et l'Italie*" . Feb. ,,

On the Austrians invading Sardinian territories, France declares war, and the French enter; the empress appointed regent; the emperor arrives at Genoa . . . . 12 May, ,,

Loan of 20,000,000 francs raised . . 21 May, ,,

Victories of the allies (French and Sardinians) at Montebello, 20 May; Palestro, 30, 31 May; Magenta, 4 June; Melegnano (Marignano), 8 June; Napoleon enters Milan, 8 June; victory of allies at Solferino . . . . . . 24 June, ,,

Armistice agreed on . . . . . 6 July, ,,

Meeting of emperors of France and Austria at Villa Franca . . . . 11 July, ,,

Peace agreed on . . . . . 12 July, ,,

Louis Napoleon returns to Paris . . 17 July, ,,

The emperor addresses the senate, 19 July; and the diplomatic body . . . . . 21 July, ,,

Reduction of the army and navy ordered . Aug. ,,

Conference of Austrian and French envoys at Zurich (see *Zurich*) . . . . . 8 Aug.-Nov. ,,

Amnesty to political offenders . . 17, 18 Aug. ,,

Violent attacks of the French press on England repressed . . . . Nov. ,,

"*Le Pape et le Congrès*" published; 50,000 sold in a few days . . . . Dec. ,,

Count Walewski, the foreign minister, resigns; M. Thouvenel succeeds him . . . Jan. 1860

The emperor announces a free trade policy; Mr. Cobden at Paris . . . . . 5 Jan. ,,

Commercial treaty with England signed . 23 Jan. ,,

L'Univers suppressed for publishing the pope's letter to the emperor. . . . . . 29 Jan. ,,

Treaty for the annexation of Savoy and Nice signed 24 March, ,,

The press censured for attacking England, 7 April, ,,

The emperor meets the German sovereigns at Baden 15-17 June, ,,

Jerome Bonaparte, the emperor's uncle, dies (aged 76) . . . . 24 June, ,,

The emperor, in a letter to count Persigny, disclaims hostility to England . . . 25 July, ,,

The emperor and empress visit Savoy, Corsica, and Algiers . . . . 1-17 Sept. ,,

New tariff comes into operation . . . 1 Oct. ,,

Public levying of Peter's pence forbidden, and free issue of pastoral letters checked . . . Nov. ,,

The empress visits London, Edinburgh, Glasgow, &c., privately . . . . . . Nov.-Dec. ,,

Important ministerial changes; greater liberty of speech granted to the chambers; two sets of ministers appointed—speakers and administrators; Pelissier made governor of Algeria; Persigny, minister of the interior; Flahault, English ambassador . . . . . Nov. & Dec. 1860
Passports for Englishmen to cease after 1 Jan. 1861 16 Dec. „
Six bishoprics vacant . . . . . Dec. „
Persigny relaxes the bondage of the press, Dec. 11; [but for a short time] . . . . 20 Dec. „
The emperor advises the pope to surrender his revolted provinces . . . . . 31 Dec. „
"*Rome et les Evêques*" published . . . 6 Jan. 1861
Jerome (son of Jerome Bonaparte and Elizabeth Paterson, an American lady) claims his legitimate rights; non-suited after a trial 25 Jan.–15 Feb. „
[The marriage took place in America, on 24 Dec. 1803; but was annulled, and Jerome married the princess Catherine of Würtemberg, 12 Aug. 1807; their children are the prince Napoleon and the princess Mathilde (see *Bonaparte*).]
Purchase of the principality of Monaco for 4,000,000 francs, Feb. 2; announced . . . 5 Feb. „
Meeting of French chambers, 4 Feb.; stormy debates in the chambers . . Feb. & March, „
"*La France, Rome, et l'Italie*" published 15 Feb. „
Angry reply to it by the bishop of Poitiers, who compares the emperor to Pilate . . 27 Feb. „
Failure of Mirès, a railway banker and loan contractor, &c.; he is arrested . . 17 Feb. „
Many influential persons suspected of participating in his frauds; the government promise strict justice . . . . . Feb. & March, „
Eugène Scribe, dramatist, dies (aged 80) 20 Feb. „
Speech of prince Napoleon in favour of Italian unity, the English alliance, and against the pope's temporal government . . . 1 March, „
Strong advocacy of the temporal government of the pope in the chambers; the French army stated to consist of 637,000 men . . . March, „
Circular forbidding the priests to meddle with politics 11 April, „
Liberal commercial treaty with Belgium . 1 May, „
Publication in Paris of the duc d'Aumale's severe letter to prince Napoleon, 13 April. Printer and publisher fined and imprisoned . . May, „
Declaration of neutrality in the American conflict 11 June, „
Official recognition of kingdom of Italy . 24 June, „
Visit of king of Sweden . . . . 6 Aug. „
Conflict between French and Swiss soldiers at Ville-la-Grande . . . . . 18 Aug. „
Mirès, the speculator, sentenced to five years' imprisonment . . . . . 29 Aug. „
Commercial treaty between France, Great Britain, and Belgium comes into operation . 1 Oct. „
Meeting of emperor and king of Prussia at Compiègne, 6 Oct.; and king of Holland . 12 Oct. „
French troops enter the valley of Dappes (Switzerland) to prevent an arrest . . 27 Oct. „
Convention between France, Great Britain, and Spain, respecting intervention in Mexico, signed (see *Mexico*) . . . . . 31 Oct. „
Embarrassment in the government finances; Achille Fould becomes finance minister, 14 Nov.; with enlarged powers . . . . . 12 Dec. „
The emperor reminds the clergy of their duty "towards Cæsar" . . . . . 1 Jan. 1862
French army lands at Vera Cruz . . . 7 Jan. „
The French masters of the province of Bienhoa, in Annam . . . . . 20 Jan. „
Fruitless meeting of French and Swiss commissioners respecting the Ville-la-Grande conflict 3 Feb. „
Fould announces his finance scheme (reduction of 4½ per cent. stock to 3 per cent., and additional taxes and stamp duties) . . . 24 Feb. „
Fierce debate in the legislative chamber, in which prince Napoleon takes part . . 27 Feb. „
French victories in Cochin-China (6 provinces ceded to France) . . . . . 28 March, „
The Spanish and British plenipotentiaries decide to quit Mexico: the French declare war against the Mexican government (for the events see *Mexico*) 16 April, „
Sentence against Mirès examined and reversed at Douai; he is released . . 21 April, 1862
Treaty of peace between France and Annam signed 3 June, „
Duke Pasquier dies (aged 96) . . . 5 July, „
New commercial treaty with Prussia . 2 Aug. „
Newspaper *La France*, opposed to Italian unity, set up by Lagueronnière . . . . . Aug. „
Ship *Prince Jerome*, with reinforcements for Mexico, burnt near Gibraltar; crew saved . . Aug. „
Camp at Chalons formed on account of Garibaldi's movements in Sicily; broken, when he is taken prisoner . . . . . 29 Aug. „
Great sympathy for him in France . . Sept. „
Treaty of commerce with Madagascar . 12 Sept. „
Drouyn de Lhuys made foreign minister in room of Thouvenel . . . . . 15 Oct. „
Baron Gros, ambassador at London in room of comte de Flahault, resigned . . 18 Nov. „
Serjeant Glover brings an action in the court of queen's bench against the comte de Persigny and M. Billault, claiming 14,000*l*. for subsidising the *Morning Chronicle* and other newspapers, 22 Nov. „
The emperor inaugurates "Boulevard Prince Eugène," Paris . . . . . 7 Dec. „
Great distress in the manufacturing districts through the cotton famine and the civil war in America Dec. „
Treaty of commerce with Italy signed . 17 Jan. 1863
Revolt in Annam suppressed . . . 26 Feb. „
Convention regulating the French and Spanish frontiers concluded . . . . 27 Feb. „
Resignation of Magne, the "speaking minister" in the assembly . . . . . 1 April, „
Dissolution of the chambers . . . 8 May, „
Persigny issues arbitrary injunctions to electors May, „
Thiers, Ollivier, Favre, and other opposition candidates elected in Paris . . 31 May–15 June, „
Changes in the ministry—resignation of Persigny, Walewski, and Rouland . . . 23 June, „
The empress visits queen of Spain at Madrid Oct. „
Baron Gros resigns, prince Tour d'Auvergne becomes ambassador at London . . . 14 Oct. „
Death of Billault (born 1805) "speaking minister" in legislative assembly, 13 Oct.; succeeded by Rouher, as "minister of state" . . 18 Oct. „
The emperor proposes the convocation of a European congress, and invites the sovereigns or their deputies by letter . . . . . 4 Nov. „
Thiers and his friends form a new opposition 9 Nov. „
The invitation to the congress declined by England 25 Nov. „
Thiers speaks in the chamber . . . 24 Dec. „
Arrest of Grego and other conspirators against the emperor's life, 3 Jan.; tried and sentenced to transportation and imprisonment . . 27 Feb. 1864
Convention between France, Brazil, Italy, Portugal, and Hayti, for establishing a telegraphic line between Europe and America . . 16 May, „
Death of marshal Pelissier, duke of Malakoff, governor of Algeria (born 1794) . . 22 May, „
Convention between France and Japan signed by Japanese ambassadors at Paris . . 20 June, „
Convention of commerce, &c., between France and Switzerland, signed . . . . 30 June, „
Prince Napoleon Victor, son of prince Napoleon Jerome and princess Clotilde, born . 16 July, „
Convention between France and Italy respecting evacuation of Rome, &c. . . . 15 Sept. „
Garnier-Pagès and 12 others who had met at his house for election purposes convicted as members of a society "of more than 20 members" 7 Dec. „
Death of the emperor's private secretary and old friend, Mocquard . . . . 9 Dec. „
Death of Proudhon (born 1809), who said "la propriété c'est le vol" . . . . 19 Jan. 1865
The clergy prohibited from reading the pope's encyclical letter of 8 Dec. in churches; much excitement; the archbishop of Besançon and other prelates disobey . . . . 5 Jan. „
The prince Napoleon Jerome appointed vice-president of the privy council . . . Jan. „
Decree for an international exhibition of the products of agriculture and industry and of the fine arts, at Paris, on 1 May, 1867 . . . . 1 Feb. „

Treaty with Sweden signed . . . . 14 Feb. 1865

The minister Duruy's plan of compulsory education rejected by the assembly . . . 8 March, ,,

Death of the duc de Morny, said to be half-brother of the emperor . . . . . 10 March, ,,

"Loi des suspects" (or of public safety) suffered to expire . . . . 31 March, ,,

Attempted assassination of a secretary at the Russian embassy . . . . . 24 April, ,,

The emperor visits Algeria . . . . 3-27 May, ,,

Inauguration of the statue of Napoleon I. at Ajaccio, with an imprudent speech by prince Napoleon Jerome, 15 May; censured by the emperor, 23 May; the prince resigns his offices 9 June, ,,

The English fleet entertained at Cherbourg and Brest, 15 Aug. *et seq.*; review of the fleets 15 & 21 Aug. ,,

The French fleet entertained at Portsmouth, 29 Aug.–1 Sept. ,,

Protest of the United States against French intervention in Mexico—prolonged correspondence (see *Mexico*) . . . . . Aug. 1865–Feb. 1866.

Count Walewski nominated president of the *corps législatif* . . . . 2 Sept. ,,

Death of general Lamoricière . . . . 11 Sept. ,,

The queen of Spain visits the emperor at Biarritz 11 Sept. ,,

Notice given of the abrogation of the extradition treaty in six months . . . . . 4 Dec. ,,

Riots of republican students at Paris (several expelled from the Academy of Medicine) . 18 Dec. ,,

Emperor opens chambers with a pacific speech 22 Jan. 1866

At Auxerre, Napoleon expresses his detestation of the treaties of 1815 . . . . 6 May, ,,

In a letter says that in regard to the German war, "France will observe an attentive neutrality" 11 June, ,,

The emperor of Austria cedes Venetia to France, and invites the emperor's intervention with Prussia 4 July, ,,

Empress of Mexico arrives at Paris . . 8 Aug. ,,

Note to the Prussian government desiring rectification of the French frontier to what it was in 1814; declared by Prussia to be inadmissible Aug. ,,

Resignation of M. Drouyn de Lhuys, foreign minister (succeeded by the marquis de Moustier) 2 Sept. ,,

Inundations in the south; railways destroyed, Sept. ,,

Pacific circular of the emperor sent to foreign courts . . . . 16 Sept. ,,

Death of M. Thouvenel, formerly foreign minister, 18 Oct. ,,

Commission appointed to inquire into the advisability of modifying the organisation of the army; the emperor president; report . . . 30 Oct. ,,

The French troops quit Rome . . . 3-11 Dec. ,,

Publication of letter from the comte de Chambord to his adherents in favour of the pope's temporal power, dated . . . . 9 Dec. ,,

Commercial treaty with Austria signed . 11 Dec. ,,

General opposition to the army organisation plan published . . . . 12 Dec. ,,

Richelieu's head, after many removals, deposited in the Sorbonne . . . . . . 17 Dec. ,,

Imperial decree announcing political reforms; interpellation in the chambers; relaxation of the restriction on the press . . . . 19 Jan. 1867

Ministerial changes; Rouher becomes minister of finance; Niel, of war, &c. . . . Jan. ,,

The chambers opened by the emperor . 14 Feb. ,,

Emile Girardin fined for libel in *La Liberté*, 7 March, ,,

Severe speech of Thiers on foreign policy, 18 March, ,,

International exhibition opened (see *Paris*), 1 April, ,,

Resignation of Walewski, president of the chamber, 29 Mar.; succeeded by M. Schneider 11 April, ,,

Scheme for organising the army rejected by committee . . . . May, ,,

Paris visited by the czar, 1-12 June; and the king of Prussia . . . . . . 5-14 June, ,,

Three provinces in Annam annexed to the French empire . . . . 25 June, ,,

International conference at Paris respecting monetary currency . . . . 17 June–9 July, 1867

The emperor distributes the prizes of the international exhibition . . . . . 1 July, ,,

Protectorate of France over Cambodia assured by treaty . . . . 15 July ,,

Law abolishing imprisonment for debt adopted by the senate . . . . . . 18 July, ,,

Meeting of the emperors of France and Austria at Salzburg . . . . . . 18–21 Aug. ,,

The emperor's letter recommending money to be expended in improving intercommunication by means of railways, canals, and roads, 15 Aug. ,,

Emperor of Austria visits Paris . 23 Oct.–2 Nov. ,,

French troops enter Rome (see *Rome*) . . 30 Oct. ,,

Garibaldians defeated at Mentana . . 3 Nov. ,,

Lord Lyons received as British ambassador 9 Nov. ,,

Pacific and liberal speech of the emperor on opening the chambers . . . . . 18 Nov. ,,

"*Napoleon III. et l'Europe en 1867,*" published, Nov. ,,

During a debate in the legislative assembly, Rouher, the minister, says, "We declare that Italy shall never seize upon Rome" (the government supported by 238 votes to 17) . . . . 5 Dec. ,,

12 persons convicted for belonging to a secret seditious society . . . . about 24 Dec. ,,

Friendly reception of foreign ministers . 1 Jan. 1868

New army bill (allowing 100,000 men to be added to the army annually; establishing a new national guard, &c.; giving the empire virtually an army of 1,200,000 men), passed in the *Corps législatif* (206 to 60) . . . . 1 Jan. ,,

Ten journals fined for printing comments on legislative debates . . . . . . end of Jan. ,,

M. Magne announces a deficiency in the budget; and a loan for 17,600,000*l*. . . . 29 Jan. ,,

The army bill passes the senate—125 to 1 (Michel Chevalier, who spoke warmly against it), 30 Jan.; becomes law . . . . 4 Feb. ,,

The "Arcadians" (new ultra-conservative party) oppose the new press law; fierce debates on it, Feb. ,,

New press law passed in legislative chamber, 240 to 1 (M. Berryer) . . . . . . March, ,,

"*Les Titres de la Dynastie impériale*" appeared, about 20 March, ,,

Riotous opposition to enlistments for "garde mobile" (new national guard) at Bordeaux, Toulon, and other towns . . 20 March *et seq.* ,,

Defeat of an attack on free trade in the chamber, May, ,,

New press law put in force; increasing facility for publishing new journals . . . . June, ,,

The assembly closes . . . . . 30 July, ,,

Rochefort's weekly satirical pamphlet *La Lanterne*, suppressed; he and his printer condemned to fine and imprisonment, escapes to Belgium, Aug. ,,

M. Berryer, the advocate (born 1790) died, 29 Nov. ,,

Ministerial changes; marquis de la Valette, foreign minister, in room of De Moustier; Forcade de la Roquette minister of the interior . . . Dec. ,,

The *Moniteur* replaced by the *Journal officiel*, 1 Jan. 1869

Meeting of the assembly . . . . . 18 Jan. ,,

De Moustier dies . . . . 5 Feb. ,,

Death of Lamartine (born Oct. 1792), 28 Feb.; of Troplong, president of the senate . 1 March, ,,

Dissolution of the legislative assembly of 1863, 26 April, ,,

Difference with Belgium respecting the Luxembourg railway settled . . . . 27 April, ,,

Fierce election riots at Paris, 9 June; the emperor and empress ride boldly through the boulevards, 11 June, ,,

The new legislative chamber meets; the opposition to the government more than trebled, 26 June, ,,

Message from the emperor announcing important political changes; introducing ministerial responsibility, &c., read 12 July; resignation of ministers, 13 July, ,,

New ministry: Forcade de la Roquette (interior); La Tour d'Auvergne (foreign); Chasseloup-Laubat, president, &c. . . . . 17 July, ,,

M. Rouher made president of the senate 20 July, ,,

French Atlantic telegraph completely laid 23 July. ,,

Marquis de la Valette appointed ambassador in London . . . . . July, 1869
The political changes announced to the senate, 5 Aug. ,,
Marshal Niel, war minister, aged 66 dies, 13 Aug. ,,
Centenary of the birth of Napoleon I.; amnesty granted to political offenders; increased pensions to survivors of the grand army; troops reviewed by the imperial prince (the emperor ill), 15 Aug. ,,
Ultra-liberal speech of prince Napoleon Jerome in the senate . . . . . 1 Sept. ,,
New constitution promulgated . . . 10 Sept. ,,
Père Hyacinthe (name Loyson), popular Carmelite preacher at Paris, protests against papal infallibility and encroachments, and resigns by letter, 20 Sept. ,,
Great excitement at Paris through discovery of Tropmann's murder of the Kinck family at Pantin, about 19 Sept. ,,
Proposed meeting of republicans at Paris (did not take place) . . . . . 26 Oct. ,,
Agitation against free trade . Oct., Nov., Dec. ,,
Journey of the empress to the East; arrival at Constantinople, 13 Oct.; at Alexandria, 13 Nov. ,,
Firm and temperate manifesto of the left (ultra republican opposition) issued . about 16 Nov. ,,
Henri Rochefort (of *La Lanterne*) elected a deputy for Paris . . . . . 22 Nov. ,,
The chambers opened by the emperor with a liberal speech . . . . . 29 Nov. ,,
Resignation of ministers announced . 27 Dec. ,,
New liberal ministry formed by Emile Ollivier (justice); Daru (foreign); Le Bœuf (war) . 3 Jan. 1870
Resignation of M. Haussmann—rebuilder of Paris—prefect of the Seine, . . about 6 Jan. ,,
Victor Noir, a journalist, killed by Pierre Bonaparte during an interview at Auteuil respecting a challenge sent to M. Rochefort . 10 Jan. ,,
Tropmann, the murderer, executed . 19 Jan. ,,
Great excitement amongst lower orders; prosecution of Rochefort for libel in his paper, the *Marseillaise;* he is sentenced to fine and imprisonment . . . . . 22 Jan. ,,
Barricades erected in Paris, and riots after the apprehension of Rochefort, 7 Feb.; soon quelled, 8, 9 Feb. ,,
Jules Favre's attack on the ministry in the chamber defeated (236 to 18) . 22 Feb.
Charles, comte de Montalembert, eminent author, dies (*see* 1858) . . . . . 13 March, ,,
Trial of Pierre Bonaparte at Tours; acquitted (but ordered to pay 1000*l.* to Noir's family); 21–27 March, ,,
Emperor's letter to Ollivier, agreeing to modification of the constitution of the senate 22 March, ,,
Senatus consultum communicated to the senate, 28 March; adopted . . . 20 April, ,,
Ministerial crisis: resignation of Daru and other ministers opposing the proposed *plébiscite,* 10 April, ,,
Proclamation of the emperor respecting changes in the constitution . . . . 24 April, ,,
Conspiracy against the emperor's life detected; Baurie (aged 22) and others arrested, about 30 April, ,,
Plébiscite to ascertain whether the people approve of above changes,—*yes,* 7,527,379; *no,* 1,530,909, 8 May, ,,
Ollivier ministry reconstructed, 13 April; duc de Grammont foreign minister . about 15 May, ,,
Rioting and barricades in Paris, 9, 10 May; about 100 arrested, many sentenced to imprisonment, 14 May, ,,
Speech by the emperor on receiving result of the *plébiscite* . . . . . 23 May, ,,
The Orleans princes address the legislative assembly, demanding their return to France, 19 June; opposed by 173 to 31 . . . 2 July, ,,
Discovery of a plot against the emperor's life, 5 July, ,,
Great excitement through the nomination of prince Leopold of Hohenzollern Sigmaringen for the Spanish throne; warlike speeches of the ministers, 5, 6, 7 July, ,,
The prince Leopold withdraws from candidature guarantees required by France from Prussia refused; France decides to declare war against Prussia, 15 July; declaration signed 17 July, 1870
[For events of the war, see *Franco-Prussian War.*]
The empress appointed regent . . . 23 July, ,,
The emperor joins the army . . . 28 July, ,,
Publication of the *Marseillaise* of Rochefort ceases, end of July, ,,
The government declare that they are only "at war with the policy of Bismarck" . . 2 Aug. ,,
Great excitement in Paris through the false announcement of a great victory . . 6 Aug. ,,
State of siege proclaimed in Paris after the great defeat of MacMahon at Wœrth . . 7 Aug. ,,
Decrees for the enlargement of the national guard, appealing to patriotism and deprecating discord, 7, 8 Aug. ,,
At Blois, the conspirators against the emperor's life sentenced to long imprisonments . 8 Aug. ,,
Energetic measures taken for the defence of Paris; Changarnier offers his services to the emperor; well received . . . . . . 8 Aug. ,,
The government appeals to France and Europe against Prussia . . . . 8 Aug. ,,
Stormy debate in the *corps législatif;* (M. de Kératry called on the emperor to abdicate; M. Guyot Montpeyroux said that the army were "lions led by asses"); resignation of Ollivier and his ministry . . . . . 9 Aug ,,
New ministry formed: General Cousin-Montauban comte de Palikao (distinguished in the war with China), minister of war, chief: M. Chevreau, minister of the interior; M. Magne, minister of finance; M. Clément Duvernois, minister of commerce and agriculture; admiral Rigault de Genouilly, minister of marine: baron Jerome David, minister of public works; prince de la Tour d'Auvergne, minister of foreign affairs; and others . . . . . . 10 Aug. ,,
Decree for the great augmentation of the army during the war, and appointing a "defence committee" for Paris . . . . 10 Aug. ,,
The Orleans princes (the duc d'Aumale, prince de Joinville, and duc de Chartres) proffer their services in the army; declined . . Aug. ,,
Extraordinary sitting of the *corps législatif* respecting the new levies . . Sunday, 14 Aug. ,,
Great disturbances at La Villette, a suburb of Paris: about 200 armed men attack the police, crying "Vive la république!" soon suppressed, and many arrested . . . . . 14 Aug. ,,
The government declare against any negotiations for peace . . . . . 14 Aug. ,,
Atrocious murder of M. Allain de Moneys, suspected of republicanism and Germanism; he was half killed by blows and then burnt to death by infuriated peasants at Hautefaye, Dordogne, not far from Bordeaux . . . . 16 Aug. ,,
General Trochu (Orleanist), energetic and able author of "l'Armée française en 1867," appointed governor of Paris, 17 Aug.: issues a stirring proclamation . . . . . . 18 Aug. ,,
A loan of 750 million francs announced, 21 Aug. ,,
Frequent diplomatic conferences at the British embassy respecting mediation . about 22 Aug. ,,
Confident statement of the national position by the ministry . . . . . 23 Aug. ,,
M. Thiers placed on the defence committee, about 26 Aug. ,,
Decree of gen. Trochu for the expulsion from Paris of all foreigners not naturalized . 28 Aug. ,,
Death of count Flahault de la Billarderie, chancellor of the legion of honour, aged 85 (served under Napoleon I., Louis Philippe, and Napoleon III.), 31 Aug. ,,
Deputation from 10,000 persons call on Trochu to assume the government: he declines, 8 p.m., 3 Sept. ,,
The news of the final defeat of MacMahon near Sedan, and the surrender of the emperor and the remainder of MacMahon's army (90,000) to the king of Prussia announced by comte de Palikao to the legislative assembly! Jules Favre declares for defending France to the last gasp, attacks the imperial dynasty, and proposes concentration of all power in the hands of general Trochu, amid profound silence . . . 3.35 a.m., 4 Sept. ,,
The ruin of MacMahon's army announced in the *Journal officiel* . . . . . . 4 Sept. ,,

On the proposition of Thiers the chamber appoints a commission of government and national defence, and orders the convocation of a constituent assembly, and adjourns . . 3.10 p.m., 4 Sept. 1870

At the resumption of the sitting of the assembly it is invaded by the crowd, demanding a republic; most of the deputies retire. Gambetta and other liberal members of the "left" proclaim the deposition of the imperial dynasty and the establishment of a republic . . . 4.15 p.m., 4 Sept. „

Last meeting of the senate; it declares adhesion to the emperor . . . . . 4 Sept. „

Proclamation of a "government of defence," general Trochu, president; MM. Léon Gambetta (interior), Jules Simon (public instruction), Jules Favre (foreign), Crémieux (justice), Jules Picard (finance), general Le Flo (war), Fourichon (marine), Magnin (agriculture), Dorian (public works), Etienne Arago (mayor of Paris), Kératry (police). 4 Sept. „

An informal meeting of the legislative assembly held, M. Thiers, president. M. Jules Favre reports to it the formation of the provisional government; some protest; Thiers recommends moderation, and the meeting retires, evening 4 Sept. „

The empress, the comte de Palikao, and other ministers secretly leave Paris and enter Belgium, evening, 4 Sept. „

Legislative chamber dissolved; senate abolished; regular troops and national guard fraternise; "perfect order reigns" . . . . 5 Sept. „

M. Favre calls on the United States of America for moral support . . . . . 5 Sept. „

The emperor Napoleon arrives at Wilhelmshöhe, near Cassel . . . 9.35 p.m., 5 Sept. „

The republican deputies in the Spanish cortes greet the republic . . . . . 5 Sept. „

Henri Rochefort added to the government 5 Sept. „

The red republican flag raised at Lyons 5 Sept. „

Victor Hugo and Louis Blanc arrive in Paris, 6 Sept. „

Jules Favre, in a circular to French diplomatic representatives, while professing desire for peace, says, "We will not cede either an inch of our territories or a stone of our fortresses" 6 Sept. „

Proclamation of general Trochu, saying that the defence of the capital is assured . . 6 Sept. „

The police replaced by national guards . 6 Sept. „

Proffered services of the Orleans princes again declined . . . . . . 6 Sept. „

The imperial correspondence seized, about 7 Sept. „

The government proclaim that to-day, as in 1792, the republic signifies the hearty union of the army and people for the defence of the country 7 Sept. „

The republic recognised by the United States, 8 Sept. „

The defence committee summon the king of Prussia to quit French territory without loss of time 8 Sept. „

Reappearance of the *Marseillaise*: Rochefort resigns editorship, and disclaims connection on account of a violent article; the paper ceases to appear soon after . . . . . . 8 Sept. „

Decree convoking the constituent assembly, to be composed of 750 members (to be elected on 16 Oct.) . . . . 8 Sept. „

The imperial prince at Hastings, 7 Sept., joined by the empress . . . . . . 8 Sept. „

Victor Hugo publishes an address to the Germans, appealing to their fraternal sentiments 9 Sept. „

Cattle plague began in Alsace and Lorraine Sept. „

The republic recognised by Spain, 8 Sept.; by Switzerland . . . . . . 9 Sept. „

M. Thiers arrives in London on a mission from the government . . . . . 13 Sept. „

Lyons said to be ruled by a "committee of safety;" red flag raised; reign of terror . . 13 Sept. „

Letter from M. Pietri, private secretary to the emperor, stating that "his master has not a centime in foreign funds" . . . 15 Sept. „

Elections for constituent assembly ordered to take place on 2 Oct. . . . . . 16 Sept. „

The academies of the institute protest against the bombardment of the monuments, museums, &c., in Paris . . . . . . 16 Sept. „

Diplomatic circular from M. Jules Favre: he admits he has no claim on Prussia for disinterestedness; urges that statesmen should hesitate to continue a war in which more than 200,000 men have already fallen; announces that a freely elected assembly is summoned, and that the government will abide by its judgment, and that France, left to her free action, immediately asks the cessation of the war, but prefers its disasters a thousand times to dishonour. He admits that France has been wrong, and acknowledges its obligation to repair by a measure of justice the ill it has done 17 Sept. 1870

A government delegation at Tours under M. Crémieux, the minister of justice; the foreign ambassadors proceed there . . . 18 Sept. „

Manifesto of the red republicans signed by general Cluseret, placarded in Paris . . about 18 Sept. „

Bronze statues of Napoleon ordered to be made into cannon . . . . . about 19 Sept. „

Stern proclamation of Trochu respecting the cowardice of the Zouaves on 19 Sept. . 20 Sept. „

M. Duruof in a post-balloon quits Paris with mail-bags, arrives at Evreux, and reaches Tours 23 Sept. „

The *Journal officiel* replaced by the *Moniteur universel* as the organ of the government, about 23 Sept. „

Esquiros struggles to maintain order at Marseilles 24 Sept. „

Failure of the negotiations for peace between count Bismarck and Jules Favre; manifesto of the government at Tours, calling on the people to rise and either disavow the ministry or "fight to the bitter end;" the elections for the assembly suspended . . . . Sept. 24 „

All Frenchmen between 20 and 25 years of age prohibited leaving France . . . about 26 Sept. „

Great enthusiasm in the provinces on the failure of the negotiations; "war to the knife" and *levée en masse* proclaimed by the prefects; efforts made to excite warlike ardour in Brittany by M. Cathelineau . . . . 26, 27 Sept. „

The duc d'Aumale consents to become a candidate for the representative assembly, and promises submission to the *de facto* government for defence about 27 Sept. „

Attempted insurrection of the red republicans at Lyons; order restored by national guards; general Cluseret disappears . . . . . 28 Sept. „

Great order in Paris maintained by the national guard; report from surgeon-major Wyatt, 28 Sept. „

All between 21 and 40 to be organised as a national garde mobile; all men in arms placed at the disposal of the minister of war . . . 30 Sept. „

The empress and her son residing at Camden-house, Chislehurst, Kent . . . . . Sept. „

The elections for the constituent assembly (753 members) ordered by the delegates at Tours to take place on 16 Oct. . . . 29 Sept.—1 Oct. „

Proclamations of general Trochu for maintaining order in Paris . . . . . about 1 Oct. „

Marseilles said to be unsettled: many arrested, 1 Oct. „

The elections deferred till they can be carried out throughout the whole extent of the republic, by order of the government at Paris . . 1 Oct. „

M. Crémieux becomes delegate minister of war at Tours in room of admiral Fourichon, still minister of marine . . . . 3 Oct. „

Gustave Flourens, heading five battalions of national guards, marches to the Hôtel de Ville and demands chassepots (not to be had) . 5 Oct. „

Suppression of the schools of the "brethren of the Christian doctrine" by the republicans: much dissatisfaction . . . . . . 8 Oct. „

All Frenchmen under 60 years of age forbidden to quit France . . . . . . 8 Oct. „

M. Gambetta escapes from Paris in a balloon, 7 Oct.; arrives at Rouen and declares for "a pact with victory or death," 8 Oct.; arrives at Tours and becomes minister of war as well as of the interior 9 Oct. „

Address from the comte de Chambord, saying that his whole ambition is to found with the people a really national government . . . 9 Oct. „

Battalions of amazons said to be forming in Paris 12 Oct. „

Blanqui, Gustave Flourens, Ledru-Rollin, Félix Pyat, and other red republicans defeated in their

attempts to establish the commune at Paris to supersede the government, 10, 11 Oct.: reconciliation effected by Rochefort . about 14 Oct. 1870
Riots at Honfleur; the people oppose the embarkation of cattle to England, 12 Oct.; similar riots at St. Malo . . . . . 15 Oct. ,,
M. Edmond Adam, prefect of police; replacing M. de Kératry, sent on a foreign mission, about 16 Oct. ,,
M. de Kératry quits Paris in a balloon, 12 Oct.; at Madrid fails in obtaining assistance from Prim 19, 20 Oct. ,,
Marseilles disturbed by red republicans; Esquiros still in office . . . . . 19 Oct. ,,
Publication of the imperial correspondence seized in the Tuileries . . . . . Oct. ,,
Decree for a loan of 10,000,000*l.* issued on behalf of the French government . . . 25 Oct. ,,
The imperial guard suppressed . . . 26 Oct. ,,
Circular of Gambetta stigmatising the surrender of Metz (on 27 Oct.) as a crime . . . 28 Oct. ,,
Death of M. Baroche in Jersey . . . 30 Oct. ,,
M. Thiers arrives in Paris with news of the surrender of Metz and the proposals for an armistice, 30 Oct. ,,
Riots in Paris: general Trochu threatened; the principal members of the defence government imprisoned in the Hôtel de Ville; Ledru-Rollin, Victor Hugo, and Gustave Flourens, and others, established as a committee of public safety and of the commune of Paris, under the direction of M. Picard; the national guard releases the government, and order is restored . 31 Oct. ,,
General Boyer, replying to Gambetta, says, "We capitulated with hunger" . . . 31 Oct. ,,
The empress arrives at Wilhelmshöhe; interview of Bazaine with the emperor . . . 31 Oct. ,,
Etienne Arago and other mayors of Paris resign, 1 Nov.; M. Jules Ferry, a member of the defence government, becomes mayor of Paris . Nov. ,,
Marshals Canrobert and Le Bœuf and many generals at Wilhelmshöhe . . . . 1 Nov. ,,
Proclamation of Gambetta calling on the army to avenge the dishonour at Metz . . 1 Nov. ,,
The government proclaim a *plébiscite* in Paris on 3 Nov. to ascertain whether the people maintain the power of the government of national defence 1 Nov. ,,
M. Rochefort, member of the defence government, resigns . . . . . 2 Nov. ,,
Result of the *plébiscite*:—for the defence government, 557,976; against, 62,638 . 3 Nov. ,,
Resignation of M. Esquiros at Marseilles, succeeded by M. Alphonse Gent . . . 3 Nov. ,,
The ex-empress returned to Chiselhurst . 3 Nov. ,,
Mobilisation of all able-bodied men between 20 and 40, ordered . . . . 4 Nov. ,,
Failure of the negotiations for an armistice 6 Nov. ,,
Félix Pyat and others arrested for the affair of 31 Oct. . . . . . 6 Nov. ,,
"France can do nothing now but carry on with such courage and strength as remain to her a war *à outrance.*"—*Guizot.* . . . 8 Nov. ,,
Decree for melting some of the church-bells to make cannon . . . . . 10 Nov. ,,
Alexander Dumas, novelist and dramatist, dies 10 Dec. ,,
The delegate government removed from Tours to Bordeaux . . . . . 11 Dec. ,,
Murder of lieut. Arnaud at Lyons by the people for resisting them . . . . 20 Dec. ,,
Trial of 21 peasants for murder of M. Moneys (see 16 Aug.): 4 condemned to death; others to imprisonment . . . about 23 Dec. ,,
Firm proclamation of Trochu at Paris . 30 Dec. ,,
Gambetta at Bordeaux declares that the government only holds office for defence of the country; demonstration in honour of the republic 1 Jan. 1871
Foreigners not permitted to leave Paris by the Germans . . . . . 19 Jan. ,,
Fierce speech of Gambetta at Lille, demanding continuance of the war . . . 22 Jan. ,,
Disturbances at Paris suppressed by the army, 23 Jan. ,,
Resignation of Trochu; Vinoy made governor of Paris . . . . . 24 Jan. ,,
Capitulation of Paris; armistice signed by Favre and Bismarck . . . . 28 Jan. ,,
Disavowed by Gambetta at Bordeaux . 31 Jan. ,,

Manifesto of the duc d'Aumale in favour of a constitutional monarchy . . . . . 1 Feb. 1871
Arrival of food from London to relieve Paris (see *Mansion-house*) . . . . . 3 Feb. ,,
The defence government publish their reasons for capitulation (2,000,000 people in Paris with only ten days' provisions), 4 Feb.; and annul Gambetta's decree, 4 Feb.; he and his ministry resign, 5, 6 Feb. ,,
Railway accident between Bandoz and St. Nizaire; explosion of casks of gunpowder; 60 killed; about 100 wounded . . . . 5 Feb. ,,
Four murderers of M. Moneys (16 Aug. 1870) executed . . . . . 8 Feb. ,,
Proclamation of Napoleon III. "Betrayed by fortune," he condemns the government of 4 Sept.; states that his government was four times confirmed in 20 years; submits to the judgment of time; saying "that a nation cannot long obey those who have no right to command" 8 Feb. ,,
General election of a national assembly . 8 Feb. ,,
M. F. P. J. Grévy elected president . . Feb. ,,
First meeting of the new national assembly, 12 Feb. ,,
Supplementary armistice signed . . 15 Feb. ,,
Garibaldi resigns his election, 13 Feb.; Grévy elected president by 519 out of 538 . 16 Feb. ,,
Termination of the war; the Belfort garrison (12,000) marches out with military honours, 16 Feb. ,,
"*Pact of Bordeaux:*" M. Thiers made chief of the executive power, by agreement of the different parties in the assembly, 17 Feb.; voted 18 Feb. ,,
Thiers ministry: Dufaure (justice); Jules Favre (foreign), Picard (interior), Jules Simon (public instruction), Lambrecht (commerce), gen. Leflo (war), admiral Pothuan (marine), De Larcy (public works) . . . . . 17 Feb. ,,
The French government recognised by the great powers of Europe . . . . 18 Feb. ,,
The duc de Broglie appointed French minister at London . . . . . 21 Feb. ,,
Negotiations for peace between Thiers and Bismarck . . . . . 22, 23, 24 Feb. ,,
Preliminaries of a treaty of peace accepted by MM. Thiers and Favre, and 15 delegates of the national assembly at Versailles (cession of parts of Alsace and Lorraine, including Strasbourg and Metz, and payment of five milliards of francs—200,000,000*l.*), 25 Feb.; signed . . 26 Feb. ,,
Intense excitement in Paris . . . 27 Feb. ,,
Preliminaries of the treaty accepted by the assembly (546 to 107); the fall of the empire unanimously confirmed; and the emperor stigmatised 1 Mar. ,,
A strong party of the national guard seize some cannons and transport them to Montmartre and Belleville, to defend themselves against the Germans entering Paris . . 1 March, ,,
The emperor of Germany reviews about 100,000 of his troops at Longchamps near Paris, 1 March, ,,
About 30,000 Germans enter Paris, 1 March; remain 48 hours; depart . . . 3 March, ,,
Impeachment of the defence government demanded by the party of the left (Victor Hugo, Louis Blanc, Quinet, and others) . 6 March, ,,
The ex-emperor protests against his deposition, 6 March, ,,
The army of the north and other special army corps dissolved . . . . 7-10 March, ,,
Meeting of national guard in Paris quelled, 10 March, ,,
The national assembly vote for removal to Versailles (461-104) . . . 10 March, ,,
Le Vengeur and four other violent journals suppressed in Paris by Vinoy . . 11 March, ,,
Blanqui, Flourens, and others condemned for insurrection of 31 Oct. 1870 . 12 March, ,,
Central committee of republican confederation of national guards (termed "the government of the Buttes") meet; depose Vinoy and appoint Garibaldi general-in-chief . . . 15 March, ,,
Insurrection at Paris: the regular troops take possession of the Buttes Montmartre and Belleville, for the assembly; the national guard attempt to recover them; after a brief conflict the troops fraternise with the insurgents, who capture and shoot generals Lecomte and Clément Thomas, and take possession of the Hôtel de Ville; barricades erected in Belleville and

other places; general Vinoy with the gendarmerie retire across the Seine . . . 18 March, 1871
The insurgents nominate a central committee of the national guard, headed by Assy, a workman, which takes possession of public offices; Thiers issues a circular, enjoining obedience to the assembly . . . . . . 19 March, ,,
The central committee order communal election in Paris, 19 March: and liberate about 11,000 political prisoners in Paris . . . 20 March, ,,
The national assembly meet at Versailles; propose conciliatory measures; and appoint a committee to support the government . . 20 March, ,,
Napoleon III. arrives at Dover . 20 March, ,,
The *Journal des Débats* and other papers renounce the central committee . . . . 20 March, ,,
The bank of France saved by the courage of the governor, marquis de Plœuc, and by the forbearance of citizen Beslay . . . . 20 March, ,,
The assembly appeal to the nation and the army, 21 March, ,,
Requisitions levied on the Paris shop-keepers, 21 March, ,,
Unarmed demonstration of the Friends of Order; they are fired on by the insurgents; 10 killed, 20 wounded . . . . . . 22 March, ,,
Lullier arrested by the central committee, 22 March, ,,
Admiral Saisset appointed commander of the national guard for the assembly . . 23 March, ,,
The 69th regiment of the line retire to Versailles, 23 March, ,,
The central committee appoint some of their delegates generals . . . . . 24 March, ,,
The insurgents hold central Paris; Saisset returns to Versailles . . . . . . 25 March, ,,
Municipal elections at Paris; 200,000 out of 500,000 vote; majority of two-thirds in favour of the insurgents . . . . . . 26 March, ,,
The government of the commune proclaimed at the Hôtel de Ville . . . . . 28 March, ,,
Meeting of the conference for the peace at Brussels, 28 March, ,,
Gustave Flourens, Blanqui, and Félix Pyat now at the head of the movement: they propose revival of the system of the Italian republics of the middle ages . . . . . . 29 March, ,,
The remission of part of the rents due by tenants ordered; the standing army to be named the national guard . . . . . 29 March, ,,
Reign of terror: "Paris has no longer liberty of the press, of public meeting, of conscience, or of person."—*Le Soir* . . . . . 1 April, ,,
Military operations commence 9 a.m.; action at Courbevoie; Flourens marches his troops to Versailles, *viâ* Rueil . . . . . 2 April, ,,
The corps d'armée of general Bergeret at the Rond Point, near Neuilly, stopped by the artillery of Mont Valérien; exchange of shot between Fort Issy and Fort Vanves, occupied by the insurgents, and Meudon . . . . . 3 April, ,,
General Duval made prisoner in the engagement at Châtillon and shot; death of Flourens at Chatou; Delescluze, Cournet, and Vermorel succeed Bergeret, Eudes, and Duval on the executive commission; Cluseret, delegate of war, and Bergeret, commandant of Paris forces . . 4 April, ,,
Communist insurrection at Marseilles suppressed, 4 April, ,,
General Cluseret commences active operations; military service compulsory for all citizens under 40; the archbishop of Paris arrested . 5 April, ,,
Extension of action to Neuilly and Courbevoie; severe decree concerning complicity with Versailles, and arrest of hostages; Dombrowski succeeds Bergeret as commandant of Paris; the guillotine burnt on the Place Voltaire . . . . . 6 April, ,,
Federals abandon Neuilly; commission of barricades created and presided over by Gaillard Senior; military occupation of the railway termini by the insurgents . . . . 8 April, ,,
Insurgents repulsed in an attempt to take Châtillon; forts Vanves and Montrouge disabled; Mont Valérien shells the Avenue des Ternes; Bergeret arrested by order of the commune, 9 April, ,,
Marshal MacMahon, commander-in-chief for the assembly, distributes his forces, and commences the investment of Fort Issy . . 11 April, ,,
Versailles batteries established on Châtillon; the Orleans railway and telegraph cut; communications of the insurgents with the south intercepted; decree ordering the fall of the column Vendôme . . . . 12 April, 1871
Publication of the reports of the sittings of the commune . . . . . . 13 April, ,,
The redoubt of Gennevilliers taken; the troops of Versailles advance to the Château de Bécon, a post of importance; Assy at the bar of the commune . . . . . . 14 April, ,,
The national assembly pass the new municipal bill (419-18) . . . . 14 April, ,,
Complementary elections; organisation of a court-martial under the presidence of Rossel, chief officer of the staff . . . . . 16 April, ,,
Capture and fortification of the Château de Bécon by the Versailles troops . . . 17 April, ,,
Station and houses at Asnières taken by the army of Versailles . . . . . 18 April, ,,
The communists appeal to the nation 19 April, ,,
Bagneux occupied by the Versaillais; reorganisation of commissions; Eudes appointed inspector-general of the southern forts; transfers his quarters from Montrouge to the palace of the Legion of Honour . . . . . . 20 April, ,,
The Versailles batteries at Breteuil, Brimborion, Meudon, and Moulin de Pierre trouble the federal fort Issy, and battery between Bagneux and Châtillon shells fort Vanves; truce at Neuilly from 9 a.m. to 5 p.m.; the inhabitants of Neuilly enter Paris by the Porte des Ternes, 25 April, ,,
Capture of Les Moulineaux, outpost of the insurgents, by the troops, who strongly fortify themselves on the 27th and 28th . . 26 April, ,,
Cemetery and park of Issy taken by the Versaillais in the night; freemasons make a new attempt at reconciliation; the commune levies a sum of two millions of francs from the railway companies, 29 April, ,,
A flag of truce sent to fort Issy by the Versaillais, calling upon the federals to surrender; general Eudes puts fresh troops in the fort, and takes the command; Cluseret imprisoned at Mazas by order of the commune; Rossel appointed provisional delegate of war . . . . 30 April, ,,
The Versaillais take the station of Clamart and the Château of Issy; creation of the committee of public safety; members: Antoine Arnauld, Léo Meillet, Ranvier, Félix Pyat, Charles Gérardin; alleged massacre of communist prisoners, 1 May, ,,
Lacretelle carries the redoubt of Moulin Saquet, 3 May, ,,
Colonel Rossel appointed to the direction of military affairs, defines the military quarters of Dombrowski, La Cécilia, Wroblewski, Bergeret, and Eudes . . . . . . 5 May, ,,
Central committee of the national guard charged with administration of war; the Chapelle expiatoire condemned to destruction—the materials to be sold by auction . . . . 5 May, ,,
Concert at the Tuileries in aid of the ambulances. Suppression of newspapers . . . 6 May, ,,
Battery of Montretout (70 marine guns) opens fire; Thiers exhorts the Parisians to rise against the commune . . . . . . 8 May, ,,
Morning; insurgents evacuate the fort Issy; the committee of public safety renewed; members: Ranvier, Antoine Arnauld, Gambon, Eudes, Delescluze; Rossel resigns . . . 8 May, ,,
Treaty of peace with Germany signed at Frankfort, 10 May, ,,
Cannon from the fort Issy taken to Versailles; decree for the demolition of M. Thiers' house; Delescluze appointed delegate of war 10 May, ,,
Thiers opposed; offers to resign; the assembly vote confidence in him (495-10) . . . 11 May, ,,
Troops take possession of the Couvent des Oiseaux at Issy, and the Lyceum at Vanves; Auber, the composer, dies, aged 89 . . . . 12 May, ,,
Triumphal entry of the troops into Versailles with flags and cannon taken from the convent; evacuation of the village of Issy completed; fort Vanves taken by the troops . . . . . 13 May, ,,
Vigorous cannonade from the batteries of Courbevoie, Bécon, Asnières, on Levallois and Clichy,

both villages evacuated; commencement of the demolition of house of M. Thiers . . 14 May, 1871
Report of the re-armament of Montmartre 15 May, ,,
The column Vendôme overthrown . . 16 May, ,,
Secession from the communist government; a central club formed; a battalion of women formed, 17 May, ,,
Stringent conscription in Paris . about 17 May, ,,
Silver ornaments in churches seized; explosion of a cartridge factory near the Champ de Mars; above 100 killed . . . . . 17 May, ,,
The assembly adopt the treaty of peace 18 May, ,,
Rochefort brought a prisoner to Versailles; last sitting of the commune . . . 21 May, ,,
Noon, explosion of the powder magazine of the Manége d'Etat-Major (staff riding-school); the hostages transferred from Mazas to La Roquette; Assy arrested in Paris by the Versaillais; the assembly votes the re-erection of the column Vendôme; M. Ducatel, at the risk of his life, having signalled that the way was clear, the Versailles troops enter Paris by the gates of St. Cloud and Montrouge, 2 p.m., 21 May; take possession of the south and west, and about 10,000 prisoners, after some conflicts . 22 May, ,,
Montmartre taken by Douai and Ladmirault: death of Dombrowski. Morning: Assy arrives at Versailles; execution of gendarmes and Gustave Chaudey at the prison of Sainte-Pélagie. Night: the Tuileries set on fire; Delescluze and the committee of public safety hold permanent sittings at the Hôtel de Ville . . 23 May, ,,
Morning: Palais Royal, Ministry of Finance, Hôtel de Ville, &c., set on fire. 1 p.m.. the powder magazine at the Palais du Luxembourg blown up; the committee of public safety organise detachments of fusee-bearers; petroleum pumped into burning buildings; Raoul Rigault shot in the afternoon by the soldiers. Evening: execution in the prison of La Roquette of the archbishop, abbé Deguerry, president Bonjean, and 64 others, hostages . . . 24 May, ,,
The forts Montrouge, Hautes-Bruyères, Bicêtre evacuated by the insurgents; the death of Delescluze reported; executions in the Avenue d'Italie of the Pères Dominicans of Arcueil, 25 May, ,,
26 priests and 38 gendarmes shot at Belleville by the insurgents; many women fighting, and casting petroleum into fires, shot . . 26, 27 May, ,,
The Buttes Chaumont, the heights of Belleville, and the cemetery of Père Lachaise carried by the troops; taking of the prison of La Roquette by the marines; deliverance of 169 hostages; the investment of Belleville complete; last position captured by MacMahon; fighting ends, 5 p.m., 28 May, ,,
Federal garrison of Vincennes surrendered at discretion . . . . 29 May, ,,
Reported results of seven days' fighting in Paris: *regular troops*, 877 killed, 645 wounded, 183 missing; *insurgents*, about 50,000 dead, 25,000 prisoners; nearly all the leaders killed or prisoners; about a fourth part of Paris destroyed 22-27 May, ,,
Estimated loss of property through the insurrection, 32,000,000*l*. . . . . . April, May, ,,
Thiers' decree for disarming Paris and abolishing the National Guard of the Seine . . 29 May, ,,
Victor Hugo expelled from Belgium . 30 May, ,,
Reported wholesale execution of prisoners by the marquis de Gallifet; Paris put under martial law; about 50,000 insurgents still at large . 30 May, ,,
Severe letter from prince Napoleon Jerome to Jules Favre, dated . . . . . . 31 May, ,,
Changes in the ministry; resignation (and reappointment of some) of those who had been members of the government of defence . 6 June, ,,
Solemn funeral of Darboy, archbp. of Paris 7 June, ,,
Abrogation of the laws of proscription by the assembly (484—103); elections of the duc d'Aumale and the prince de Joinville declared valid 8 June, ,,
Important speech of Thiers for maintaining the republic at present . . . . . 8 June ,,
Imposition of new taxes (463,000,000 francs) and a loan proposed by M. Pouyer Quertier . 12 June ,,
Gen. Trochu's powerful speech defending the "government of national defence" . 13, 14 June, ,,

Army of reserve ordered to be dissolved 14 June, 1871
Financial measures of M. Pouyer-Quertier opposed by Dufaure and the free-traders about 14 June, ,,
Theatres and public places reopened in Paris about 20 June, ,,
Letter from M. Guizot to M. Grévy recommending political moderation to all parties, and maintenance of the present government, published 22 June, ,,
The loan of 2 milliards francs (80,000,000*l*.) decreed 26 June; subscription opened, 27 June; about 4 milliards subscribed for in France alone 28 June ,,
132 members elected for the assembly; includes Gambetta, and a few legitimists and Bonapartists; the rest support the government . 2 July, ,,
Letter from the comte de Chambord at Chambord, professing devotion to France, and adhesion to modern policy and liberality; but declining to give up the white flag of Henry IV.; he retires to Germany to avoid all pretext for agitation, dated 5 July, ,,
The government said to have 500 votes in the assembly; bill for new taxes passed (483 to 5) 8 July, ,,
20,000,000*l*. part of the indemnity, paid to the Germans . . . . . . about 14 July, ,,
Prince Napoleon Jerome expelled from France (at Havre) . . . . 15 July, ,,
M. Devienne, president of the court of cassation, acquitted of blame for settling disputes relative to an imperial scandal (in Nov. 1860) . 21 July, ,,
Jules Favre, foreign minister, resigns about 23 July; succeeded by Charles de Remusat about 3 Aug. ,,
Full compensation for losses claimed by the invaded provinces refused by Thiers, who acknowledges no debt, but proposes to act generously . Aug. ,,
Trial of communist prisoners at Paris, begun about 8 Aug. ,,
Great dissensions in the assembly between the monarchists and republican parties; resignation of Thiers not accepted, 24 Aug.; prolongation of his power and the sovereign and constituent authority of the assembly voted (443 to 227) about 25 Aug. ,,
Thiers' powers prolonged, and nominated president of the French republic by the assembly; to continue till the assembly shall terminate its labours; (the Rivet-Vitet proposition), 491-93 31 Aug. ,,
French postage increased . . . . . Sept. ,,
Société de Prévoyance established to counteract the *Internationale*; becomes permanent . Sept. ,,
Ferré and Lullier sentenced to death, others to transportation or imprisonment, 2 Sept.; 3 women (pétroleuses) sentenced to death for throwing petroleum on fires . . . . . . 5 Sept. ,,
Bill for making the whole nation bear the losses of the invaded provinces adopted by the assembly 6 Sept. ,,
Rossel, communist general, sentenced to death 8 Sept. ,,
Message from Thiers to the assembly; consideration of the budget adjourned 12 Sept.; read 13 Sept. ,,
Disarmament of the national guard begun at Lyons, &c. . . . . 14 Sept. ,,
Bill introduced concerning treaty with Germany relating to tariff on goods from Alsace and Lorraine, and the reducing German troops in France to 50,000 men, 14 Sept.; adopted by the assembly (533-33); the session declared closed, 2 a.m. 17 Sept. ,,
Courts-martial on communists go on . . Sept. ,,
"Permanent Committee" of 25 of different parties appointed by the assembly to watch over the course of the government during the recess (17 Sept.-4 Dec.) . . . . 15 Sept. ,,
25,000 communists yet to be tried; about half to be set free . . . . 15 Sept. ,,
Evacuation of Paris forts by the Germans begun about 20 Sept. ,,
Rochefort (of "*La Lanterne*" and "*Le Mot d'Ordre*") sentenced to life-imprisonment . . 21 Sept. ,,
Difficulty in settling the Alsace and Lorraine treaty 21 Sept. ,,
M. Pouyer-Quertier, the French finance minister, arrives at Berlin . . . . . . 8 Oct. ,,
M. Lambrecht, minister of the interior, dies suddenly, 8 Oct.; succeeded by M. Casimir Perier 10 Oct. ,,

Tranquil election of above 2000 general councillors Oct. 1871

Convention for evacuation of 6 departments, and finance convention of Alsace and Lorraine signed, 12 and 13 Oct.; exchanged . . . 21 Oct. „

Count Benedetti publishes an apology, attacking the Prussian government; count Bismarck replies (in "Official Journal") disproving his assertions 22 Oct. „

Dispute with Tunis settled . . about 25 Oct. „

Prince Napoleon resigns his seat in the council-general of Corsica; and denounces intimidation 28 Oct. „

nsurrection in Algeria ended . . . Nov. „

Eight of the murderers of generals Lecomte and Thomas condemned . . . . 18 Nov. „

Rossel, Ferré, and Bourgeois, communist leaders, shot at Satory in presence of 3000 soldiers 28 Nov. „

Gaston Crémieux executed at Marseilles . 30 Nov. „

Territory held by Germans put into state of siege 4 Dec. „

Meeting of the national assembly . . 4 Dec. „

Sixteen political parties said to exist . . Dec. „

Thiers reads his message to the assembly; deprecates free trade, but proposes moderate protection of French manufactures . . 7 Dec. „

Sharp despatch from count Bismarck in reference to the acquittal of murderers of Germans at Melun and Paris . . . 7 Dec. „

After some discussion with M. Thiers, the duc d'Aumale and prince de Joinville take their seats in the assembly . . . 19 Dec. „

A committee of the assembly decide against the assembly removing to Paris . . 22 Dec. „

Joseph Lemettre condemned to death for 27 crimes (chiefly atrocious murders). . . 23 Dec. „

Income-tax proposed and negatived . . 28 Dec. „

Vautram, a government candidate, elected deputy for Paris, and not Victor Hugo . . 7 Jan. 1872

The duc de Persigny dies . . . 12 Jan. „

Long debate in the assembly; opposition to the proposed taxes on raw materials; government defeated (377-307) . . . . 19 Jan. „

Resignation of Thiers and the ministry opposed by the assembly; M'Mahon writes that the army will respect the orders of a majority of the assembly, but not obey dictatorship; Thiers resumes office 20 Jan. „

Death of Arlès Dufour, of Lyons, St. Simonian and free-trader . . . about 22 Jan. „

The government taxes voted . . . 22 Jan. „

Conviction of the assassins of archbishop Darboy and others (on 24 May, 1871), 1 to death 23 Jan. „

Manifesto of the comte de Chambord; his mind unchanged; he will not become a legitimate king by revolution . . . . . 29 Jan. „

Abrogation of the commercial treaties with Great Britain and Belgium determined on . Feb. „

Sardou's play, "Rabagas," satirising the radicals; causes much excitement . . . 1 Feb. „

Proposed return of the assembly to Paris negatived (377-318); resignation of Casimir Périer, minister of the interior . . . . 2 Feb. „

League for commercial liberty formed . . Feb. „

Five communists sentenced to death for murder of the Dominicans on 25 May . . 17 Feb. „

Blanqui condemned to transportation to a fortified prison . . . . about 17 Feb. „

M. Rouher elected a member of the assembly about 15 Feb. „

Universal subscription to pay the indemnity to the Germans begins . . . . Feb. „

Manifesto in favour of a constitutional monarchy signed by about 280 of the "Right," about 21 Feb. „

Assassins of generals Lecomte and Clément Thomas executed . . . . . 22 Feb. „

Janvier de la Motte, a prefect, prosecuted for forgery, &c., by government, acquitted; M. Pouyer-Quertier, who gives evidence in his favour, resigns, about 5 March, „

Joseph Lemettre executed . . 5 March, „

The treaty of commerce with Great Britain (1860), denounced (to cease in 12 months) 15 March, „

War budget of 27,000,000*l.* (formerly 10,000,000*l.*) proposed . . . . March, „

Publishers of "*Figaro*" convicted of libel against general Trochu; moderate punishment 2 April, „

Abolition of passports for British subjects announced . . . . . 10 April, 1872

Law against the International Society placarded 22 April, „

In a letter, the ex-emperor takes upon himself the whole responsibility of the surrender at Sedan 12 May, „

Rouher in the assembly repels the duc d'Audiffret Pasquier's severe attack on the empire 21 May, „

Three more condemned communists shot 25 May, „

The duc d'Aumale speaks in the chamber in favour of the army organisation bill . . . 28 May, „

Marshal Vaillant dies . . . . 4 June, „

Thiers threatens to resign at opposition in the chamber . . . . about 9 June, „

Interview of delegates of the majority (the right) in the assembly with Thiers (respecting his policy); much censured . . . . . 20 June, „

Budget for 1873; deficiency, 4,800,000*l.*; 8,000,000*l.* to be raised; Thiers advocates duty on raw materials, and opposes income-tax 26 June, *et seq.* „

The majority in the assembly propose MacMahon as president in room of Thiers . . . July, „

New convention between Germany and France respecting speedy payment of the indemnity and evacuation of territory, signed . . 29 June, „

Anniversary of the destruction of the Bastille celebrated by public dinners; important moderate speech by Gambetta at Ferté-sous-Jouarre, 14 July, „

Announcement of a public loan of 120,000,000*l.* at $6\frac{1}{4}$ per cent. . . . . . 26 July, „

Three communists (murderers of hostages) executed at Satory . . . . . 25 July, „

The loan subscribed for, nearly 12 times the amount, chiefly in France . . . . July, „

Thiers' financial measures carried (taxes on raw materials, &c.); the session of the assembly closed 3 Aug. „

Meeting of Guizot and Thiers at Val Richer 11 Sept. „

Three more communist murderers shot at Satory 15 Sept. „

Arrest of Edmond About at Saverne, by the Germans, on account of a newspaper article (written Oct. 1871), 14 Sept.; released . . 21 Sept. „

Attempted celebration of the anniversary of the establishment of the first French republic; banquet at Chambery stopped . . . 22 Sept. „

M. Thiers and the ministry in Paris . . Sept. „

Progress of Gambetta in the south; violent speech at Grenoble against Thiers . . . 27 Sept. „

Pilgrimage of about 20,000 persons to the grotto of the Virgin Mary at Lourdes, on account of alleged miracles (the Virgin was said to have appeared to two girls, 14 Feb. 1858) . . . 6 Oct. „

Report that the Russian minister remonstrated on Gambetta's speech at Grenoble . . . Oct. „

The supreme council of war constituted; includes MacMahon, Canrobert, duc d'Aumale, and other eminent generals; first meeting, Thiers present 9 Oct. „

Prince Napoleon and princess Clothilde come to Paris; expelled by order of the government (he protests) . . . . . . 12 Oct. „

Letter from the comte de Chambord to M. de la Rochette, protesting against a republic, and asserting that France can be saved by a monarchy alone; that she is catholic and monarchical, and cannot, therefore, perish; dated . 15 Oct. „

Elections for vacancies in the assembly; radical republicans mostly elected . . . 20 Oct. „

The Germans evacuate Haute Marne and other departments . . . . Oct., Nov. „

Banquet of monarchical party at Bordeaux 31 Oct. „

New commercial treaty with Great Britain signed at London . . . . . . 5 Nov. „

Re-assembling of the national assembly, 11 Nov.; Thiers in his message declares that the republic is the legal government; and that to exist it must be conservative; and proposes changes 12 Nov. „

Service of prayer on behalf of the assembly 17 Nov. „

Fruitless attack of general Changarnier on Thiers' policy and Gambetta's speech at Grenoble; motion to pass to order of the day; majority for government, 150; (300 did not vote) . 18 Nov. „

The result becomes the law of . . 19 Nov. „

M. Kerdrel proposes a commission to consider Thiers' proposals for changes; adopted 19 Nov.

Thiers threatens to resign; crisis . 19, 20 Nov. 1872
Report of the commission read by M. Batbie, claiming the right of the assembly to frame a constitution with a responsible ministry; the president not to speak in the assembly, &c.; he advocated "gouvernement de combat" . 26 Nov. ,,
Amendment proposed by Dufaure, minister of justice, accepting ministerial responsibility, rejected by the committee . . . . 28 Nov. ,,
M. Thiers addresses the assembly; declares he prefers the English to the American system; but that a monarchy in France is at present impossible; that he is faithful to the republic; and that he wishes to render it conservative; and that he has for two years served his country with boundless devotion; Dufaure's amendment carried by 370-334 (union of royalists with Bonapartists against the radicals) . . . . 29 Nov. ,,
Vote of censure on the home minister (Lanfranc) carried; 305-299; he resigns . . 30 Nov. ,,
Agitation respecting the appointment of the commission of 30, proposed by Dufaure; it consists of 19 for the right, 11 for the government, 6 Dec.; changes in the ministry announced . 8 Dec. ,,
Manifesto of the left, proposing a dissolution of the assembly by legal means . . . 10 Dec. ,,
Negatived by the assembly (490-201) . 14 Dec. ,,
Powerful speech of Thiers to the commission of 30 16 Dec. ,,
Execution of Poitevin, a traitor . . 23 Dec. ,,
Debt (before the war, about 460,500,000*l.*)—748,700,000*l.* . . . . Dec. ,,
Illness of the ex-emperor . . . . 4 Jan. 1873
Meeting of the national assembly . . 6 Jan. ,,
Death of Napoleon III. at Chislehurst . 9 Jan. ,,
Bonapartist manifesto; "the emperor is dead, but the empire is living and indestructible" 15 Jan. ,,
The "30 committee" considering Tallon's project for a constitution . . . . . . Jan. ,,
Three communist murderers shot at Satory 22 Jan. ,,
Reported recognition of the comte de Chambord as king by the Orleans princes . . . 26 Jan. ,,
Powerful speech of Thiers before the commission of 30 against their proposed changes . 2 Feb. ,,
The commission of 30 close their meetings 8 Feb. ,,
Letter of the comte de Chambord published; destroys all hopes of the fusion of the Bourbons . Feb. ,,
Debate begins on the report of the commission, which reserves the legislative rights of the present assembly, and the adherence to the provisional state in accordance with the "pacte de Bordeaux," 27 Feb.; powerful speech of Thiers in favour of this "truce of parties," adopted (475-199) . . . . 4 March, ,,
Convention for the total evacuation of the departments in Sept. on payment of indemnity, signed at Berlin . . . . . . 15 March, ,,
Declaration in the assembly "that M. Thiers has deserved well of his country" . . . 17 March, ,,
M. Grévy resigns the presidency on account of the conduct of the party of the right, 2 April; M. Buffet, a liberal Bonapartist, elected in opposition to Martel, the government candidate, 4 April, ,,
M. Barodet, radical, ex-mayor of Lyons, elected member of the assembly for Paris by a large majority over the minister de Remusat . 27 April, ,,
Changes in the ministry:—Casimir Périer, interior; W. H. Waddington, of Cambridge, public instruction (in room of De Goulard and Jules Simon) . . . . 18 May, ,,
Meeting of the national assembly, 19 May; the government introduce their constitutional bills, 21 May; the duc de Broglie leads an attack on the government, 23 May; speech of Thiers; the government defeated (362-348) at a sitting, 2 p.m., 24 May, ,,
Resignation of Thiers and his ministry accepted (368-339), 24 May; marshal McMahon, duc de Magenta (born 1808) elected president of the republic by 390 votes (the left did not vote); he accepts the office, declaring his independence of party, 24 May; in his message to the assembly he says, "The post in which you have placed me is that of a sentinel, who has to watch over the integrity of your sovereign power." . 26 May, ,,
The duc de Broglie chief of the new ministry 26 May, ,,

General Ladmirault succeeds MacMahon in the command of the army of Versailles . 3 June, 1873
Private circular of the minister to prefects requesting them to sound newspapers of his department; censured in the assembly . 11 June, ,,
The assembly (by a large majority) order the prosecution of Ranc, formerly a communist, now deputy for Lyons . . . . . 19 June, ,,
Visit of the Shah . . . . . . 5 July, ,,
Grand review of the renovated army at Paris, and assembly prorogued . . . . 10 July, ,,
Renewal of the Anglo-French treaty of 23 Jan. 1860 (till 30 June, 1877); signed 24 July; ratified 29 July, ,,
Evacuation of all the French territories by the Germans, except Verdun, by . . . 2 Aug. ,,
Fusion of the Legitimists and Orleanists; after an interview of the comte de Paris with the comte de Chambord; the latter recognised as chief 5 Aug. ,,
Odilon-Barrot died . . . . . . 6 Aug. ,,
The imperial prince Napoleon declares the policy of his family to be "Everything by the people for the people" . . . . . 15 Aug. ,,
Last instalment of 10,000,000*l.* of the indemnity of 200,000,000*l.* paid . . . . 5 Sept. ,,
About 2,700 communists yet to be disposed of Sept. ,,
Verdun quitted by the Germans . . 13 Sept. ,,
The last quitted the French territory . 16 Sept. ,,
Duc Decazes ambassador for London . . Oct. ,,
Letter from comte de Chambord to the vicomte de Rodez-Benavent; not explicit; shows tendency to concession; says, "I want the co-operation of all, and all have need of me" dated 19 Sept. ,,
Prince Napoleon Jerome joins the republican party, 26 Sept. ,,
Letter from Thiers to mayor of Nancy, censuring the fusionists, who "without the consent of France pretend to decide upon her destinies" 29 Sept. ,,
France divided into 18 new military regions; 18 generals appointed . . . . 30 Sept. ,,
Trial of marshal Bazaine, late commander of the army of the Rhine in 1870, for alleged treachery and misconduct at Metz; duc d'Aumale president of the court; begins . . . . . 6 Oct. ,,
Changes in the ministry; duc Decazes foreign and Changarnier war minister . . . 6 Oct. ,,
Rouher's letter to the Bonapartists against the monarchists . . . . 9 Oct. ,,
M. Remusat and 3 other republicans elected deputies . . . . 12 Oct. ,,
Ranc condemned to death *in contumaciam* 13 Oct. ,,
M. Lemoinne (in the *Journal des Débats*) says "The partisans of an absolute monarchy make a *tabula rasa* of history; for them nothing has occurred. If that be so, nothing will return" . 15 Oct. ,,
Manifesto of the monarchists proposing restoration of the monarchy, guaranteeing all necessary liberties, &c. . . . . . . 18 Oct. ,,
M. Léon Say and the left centre decline negotiation with the monarchists; who threaten abstention in the next elections, if successfully opposed 23 Oct. ,,
Letter from the comte de Chambord to M. Chesnelong; he says, "I retract nothing, and curtail nothing of my previous declarations. I do not wish to begin a reign of reparation by an act of weakness; if enfeebled to-day, I should be powerless to-morrow; I am a necessary pilot; the only one capable of guiding the ship to port, because I have for it a mission of authority." dated . . . . 27 Oct. ,,
M. Léon Say and the left centre say the moment has arrived for the organisation of a conservative republic . . . . 30 Oct. ,,
Meeting of national assembly; message from marshal MacMahon, requesting increased and prolonged power (ten years); this referred to a committee of 15; voted urgent (by 360 to 350) 5 Nov. ,,
M. Buffet re-elected president . . 6 Nov. ,,
Conspiracy at Autun to seize marchioness MacMahon; offenders convicted . . 7 Nov. ,,
Eight of the committee vote for prolongation of MacMahon's presidency for five years after date of meeting of the next legislature, under existing

conditions till the passing of constitutional laws; the others vote for ten years' prolongation without conditions . . . . 13 Nov. 1873
M. Laboulaye's report of the committee laid before the assembly; MacMahon's message suggesting 7 years' prolongation of his powers . 17 Nov. ,,
Warm debate in the assembly; majority of 68 for ministers, 18 Nov.; 7 years' power voted to marshal MacMahon (383-317), 19 Nov.; decree 20 Nov. ,,
Incognito visit of the comte de Chambord to Paris about 20 Nov. ,,
Ministry resigns, 20 Nov.; re-constituted; duc de Broglie, minister of interior; duc Decazes, foreign minister; announced . . 26 Nov. ,,
Committee of 30 for constitutional changes, completed . . . . 4 Dec. ,,
Holds its first meeting, Batbie, president 5 Dec.
Embassy to London declined by Guizot; accepted by the duc de la Rochefoucauld-Bisaccia Dec. ,,
Bazaine's trial ends; he is found guilty of capitulating with his army (of 170,000 men) in the open field; of negotiating dishonourably with the enemy, and surrendering a fortified place; sentence, death and degradation, 10 Dec.; commuted to 20 years' imprisonment . 12 Dec.
Peaceful republican demonstration in Paris at the funeral of Victor Hugo's second son, François, 28 Dec. ,,
Meeting of the assembly; majority against the nomination of mayors bill, through the legitimists (268-226), 8 Jan.; the ministry resign, 9 Jan.; vote of confidence in the ministry (379 to 329), 12 Jan.; the ministers resume office 13 Jan. 1874
Vote for ministers on the nomination of mayors bill (341-336) . . . . 17 Jan. ,,
The Ultramontane newspaper, *L'Univers* (edited by M. L. Veuillot), suspended for 2 months for attacks on Italy and Germany, about 19 Jan. ,,
Nomination of mayors bill passed, 21 Jan.; many mayors replaced . . . . . . Feb. ,,
A person calls himself comte Albert de Bourbon, and claims to be son of Louis XVII.; his claim rejected . . . . 27 Feb. ,,
Ledru-Rollin and Lepetit elected members of the national assembly . . . . 1 March, ,,
New electoral law presented by the committee; about 3 millions disfranchised . 11 March, ,,
Demonstration at Chiselhurst on prince Louis Napoleon's coming of age (at 18); 6000 Frenchmen present; he says that he waits the result of the 8th plébiscite . . . . 16 March, ,,
Gabriel Hugelmann, political spy and swindler, convicted and sentenced to 5 years' imprisonment . . . . 25 March, ,,
Ferrand, contractor (made about 80,000*l.* during war), fined and imprisoned, about . 25 March, ,,
Proposal of Dahirel, legitimist, of a law enacting that on 1 June the assembly should vote for either a monarchy or republic, negatived (330-256) . . . . 27 March, ,,
Assembly adjourns to 12 May . . 28 March, ,,
Two republican deputies elected 29 March, ,,
Reported escape of Rochefort, the communist, from New Caledonia . . announced 30 March, ,,
Death of Beulé, ex-minister . . . . 4 April, ,,
Newspapers warned not to attack the septennate 12 April, ,,
Clément Duvernois, ex-imperial minister, arrested for suspected fraud . . . . . 14 April, ,,
The assembly meets, 12 May; the ministry defeated on electoral law (381-317), resigns 16 May, ,,
M. Goulard failing to form a ministry, the president re-appoints the former without Broglie; nominal head, gen. De Cissey . . 22 May, ,,
Prince Hohenlohe, the new German ambassador, received by the president; mutual professions of peace . . . . 23 May, ,,
Rochefort and other communists arrive at San Francisco . . . . announced 21 May, ,,
Bourgoing, a Bonapartist, elected for Nièvre (asserted that he was devoted to the marshal) 24 May, ,,
Thiers addresses some Gironde friends; refers to the failure of his opponents; and recommends dissolution of the assembly . . 24 May, ,,
Electoral bill; assembly pass to second reading (393-318) . . . . 1 June, ,,
Ledru-Rollin's speech a failure . . 3 June, 1874
Hot disputes between republicans and Bonapartists; left centre demand the establishment of the republic, or dissolution of the assembly 8, 9 June, ,,
Bonnard, communist, condemned for murder, 25 Feb., shot . . . . 6 June, ,,
Electoral bill; age of electors fixed at 21, not 25 (defeat of ministry) . . . . 10 June, ,,
Gambetta having called the Bonapartists "*misérables*," is struck at a railway station by comte de Sainte Croix, 11 June, who is condemned to fine and imprisonment . . . . 13 June, ,,
Casimir Périer (leader of left centre) moves for recognition of the republic; MacMahon president till 20 Nov. 1880, and revision of the constitution; voted "urgent" (345-341) . 14, 15 June, ,,
Duc de Rochefoucauld-Bisaccia's motion for restoration of the legitimate monarchy negatived; he resigns British embassy . . . 15 June, ,,
Rochefort in London . . . . . 19 June, ,,
The "fusion" between legitimists and Orleanists ended; conflict now between republicans and Bonapartists . . . . June, ,,
Grand review of 60,000 men at Longchamps, near Paris . . . . 28 June, ,,
In his order of the day, marshal MacMahon declares that with the army he will maintain the authority of the land for the seven years 29 June, ,,
Casimir Périer's motion negatived by commission of thirty . . . . 29 June, ,,
Manifesto from comte de Chambord, saying, "France has need of monarchy. My birth has made me your king. . . The Christian and French monarchy is in its very essence limited (*tempérée*). It admits of the existence of two chambers: one nominated by the sovereign, the other by the nation. . . I do not wish for those barren parliamentary struggles, whence the sovereign too frequently issues powerless and enfeebled. . . I reject the formula of foreign importation, which all our national traditions repudiate, with its king who reigns and does not govern."—Signed, Henri V. . 2 July, ,,
"*L'Union*," legitimist paper, suspended for publishing the above . . . . . 4 July, ,,
M. Goulard, ex-minister, dies 4 July, ,,
Debate on the manifesto; legitimists defeated; ministers defeated on a motion in favour of the septennate, resign (368-331); their resignation not accepted by the marshal 8 July, ,,
He states, in a message to the assembly, his determination to maintain the law of 20 Nov., and exhorts them to pass the constitutional laws 9 July, ,,
"*Figaro*" suspended for 15 days for attacking the assembly . . . . 11 July, ,,
Reports of committee, by Ventavon (the bill proposes maintenance of the authority of the president of the republic; ministerial responsibility; two legislative assemblies; dissolution of the chamber of deputies by the president; &c.), suspended . . . . 16 July, ,,
Casimir Périer's motion for a republic rejected (375-333) . . . . . . 23 July, ,,
Malleville's motion for dissolution of the assembly rejected (374-332) . . . . ,,
The assembly adjourns (to 30 Nov.) . . 5 Aug. ,,
Marshal Bazaine escapes from the isle of Ste. Marguerite (see Dec. 1873) 10 p.m. [His wife asserted that he descended by an old gutter by means of a knotted rope; was received into a boat by her and her nephew, Alvarez de Rul, and conveyed to the steamer *Baron Ricasola*, which landed him at Genoa] . . . 9 Aug. ,,
Forcade de Roquette, a minister under the empire, dies, aged 53 . . . . . 16 Aug. ,,
MacMahon's progress in the N.W. provinces; well received . . . . . . 17 Aug. ,,
Vendôme column restored . . . 31 Aug. ,,
Comte de Jarnac, minister at London, arrives there 4 Sept. ,,
Death of M. Guizo . . . . . 12 Sept. ,,
Bazaine's defence sent by him to the *New York Herald*, dated 6 Sept., published in London 14 Sept. ,,

Trials for complicity in Bazaine's escape; col. Villette and others sentenced to imprisonment 17 Sept. 1874

Thiers, at Vizille near Grenoble, in reply to an address, says, "Since you cannot establish the monarchy, establish the republic, and do it frankly and sincerely" . . . 27 Sept. ,,

Poirier executed at Chartres for 5 murders 29 Sept. ,,

Severe note from Spanish government complaining of French neglect in regard to the Carlists on the Spanish frontier . . . . early Oct. ,,

Clément Duvernois, ex-imperial minister, convicted of fraud; 2 years' imprisonment 25 Nov. ,,

Political parties: Extreme right. Legitimists: adherents of Henry V. Moderate right: monarchists. Right centre: septennates, Imperialists or Bonapartists. Left centre: moderate republicans (chief, Thiers). Left: more pronounced. Extreme left: radicals (chief, Gambetta) . . . . Nov. ,,

St. Genest's pamphlet, "*L'Assemblée et la France,*" inciting to a *coup d'état* . . . end of Nov. ,,

Comte de Chambord requests his friends not to vote so as to prevent or delay the restoration of the monarchy . . . . . . Nov. ,,

Four ornamented volumes of addresses from towns, &c., in France, conveying thanks for relief during the war 1870-1 (inscribed on the outside, "*Britanniæ grata Gallia,*") with about 12,000,000 signatures, presented to the queen by M. D'Agiout and the comte de Serrurier [placed in the British Museum for inspection] . . . . . 3 Dec. ,,

The assembly meets; firm moderate message from MacMahon . . . . . . 3 Dec. ,,

Sudden death of M. Ledru-Rollin . . 31 Dec. ,,

President in his message having recommended the passing a bill for constituting a senate, motion against it passed (420 to 250), 6 Jan.; ministers' resignation not accepted . . . . . 7 Jan. 1875

Cost of the war (395,400,000*l.*) announced Jan. ,,

Emile Péreire, financier . . . died 6 Jan. ,,

A Bonapartist elected deputy for Hautes-Pyrénées 17 Jan. ,,

Nine days' debate on the new army bill . Jan. ,,

Stormy debate on Ventavon's bill for organising MacMahon's powers, 1st reading passed (557 to 146). . . . . 22 Jan. ,,

Laboulaye's amendment rejected (359-335) 29 Jan. ,,

Wallon's amendment (the president of the republic to be elected by absolute majority of the two chambers for 7 years, and to be eligible for re-election; the republic virtually established); passed 1 a.m. 31 Jan. ,,

Great satisfaction throughout the country Feb. ,,

Duprat's amendment carried (senate to be chosen by universal suffrage), 11 Feb.; third reading of the constitutional bill rejected (357-345); proposed dissolution of the assembly negatived (407-266), 12 Feb.; message from the marshal disapproving of last votes . . . 13 Feb. ,,

Senate bill (senate to consist of 300; 225 to be elected by the departments, 75 by national assembly) . . . . . . 22 Feb. ,,

Laws passed constituting French republic by union of moderate monarchists and republicans; legitimists and Bonapartists defeated; senate bill passed (448-244), 24 Feb.; final vote for republic, constitutional laws passed (436-262) 5 p.m. 25 Feb., published 1 March, ,,

New ministry under Buffet constituted; Buffet, interior; Dufaure, justice; Léon Say, finance; Wallon, instruction; De Meaux, agriculture and commerce; Cissey war; Decazes, foreign; Montaignac, marine; Caillaux, public works 10 March, ,,

Duc d'Audiffret Pasquier elected president of the assembly almost unanimously . . 15 March, ,,

Death of M. Jarnac-Chabot, ambassador at London 22 March, ,,

Assembly adjourns to 11 May . . 20 March, ,,

Edgar Quinet, author of "Les Jésuites," a staunch republican, died . . . . 27 March, ,,

Powerful speech of Gambetta at Belleville, defending the new constitution . . 23 April, ,,

Meeting of the assembly, 11 May; the ministry propose to refer a bill to the committee of 30; defeated; part of the committee resign, 18 May; new committee elected (republican majority) 26 May, 1875

Louis Blanc's speech against the conservative republic, 21 June; self-denying resolution of the left party (to avoid delaying the dissolution by speaking, &c.) . . . . . . June, ,,

Destructive inundations at Toulouse; about 1000 lives lost, with much property . 23 June, ,,

Election of baron de Bourgoing, a Bonapartist, annulled by the assembly, 13 July; warm defence of his party by Rouher (on the charge of there being a central committee of Bonapartists in Paris with branches in the provinces, actively endeavouring to overthrow the republic in 1874) 14 July, ,,

Fierce debate in assembly; Buffet defends the imperialistic prefects, and gains vote of confidence; the left not voting . . 15 July, ,,

H. Rochefort, after challenging Paul de Cassagnac, declines accepting the conditions of the combat at Geneva . . . . Aug. ,,

The assembly adjourns . . . . . 4 Aug. ,,

Naquet, an "irreconcilable" republican, attacks Gambetta for his moderation . end of Aug. ,,

Plon having lost by publishing "Julius Cæsar," by Napoleon III., sues the emperor's executors; fails; and is adjudged to pay costs . . Aug. ,,

L'Echo de Blois fined for libel on the duc d'Aumale 28 Aug. ,,

"*Les Responsabilités,*" pamphlet recommending the comte de Chambord to resign his rights to the crown . . . . Aug. ,,

Belgian and German pilgrimage to Lourdes (see 1872) . . . . Sept. ,,

Admiral De la Roncière Noury superseded for writing a letter animadverting on the republic (2 Sept.) . . . . 8 Sept. ,,

Alleged adhesion of the Orleanist party to the republic . . . . . about 10 Sept. ,,

Important speeches; M. Thiers at Arcachon defending his policy; advocating a conservative republic, and censuring delay; M. Rouher at Ajaccio, advocating imperialism and universal suffrage, and asserting that the nation will not accept the republic as a definite government 17 Oct. ,,

Important letter of Gambetta to his friends at Lyons (in favour of the conservative republic), said to be "too advanced for the moderate, and too moderate for the advanced." . . 25 Oct. ,,

Meeting of the assembly: duc d'Audiffret re-elected president . . . . . 4 Nov. ,,

The assembly virtually votes its dissolution before 31 March, 1876; 6 months' residence in a commune to give right to vote, 9 Nov., majority for ministers; the *scrutin d'arrondissement* adopted instead of *scrutin de liste* (357-326); able speech of Gambetta for the latter . . . 11 Nov. ,,

New Catholic University opened . . 17 Nov. ,,

Beginning of ballot for senators for life; duc d'Audiffret Pasquier elected; the result discloses a breach between the legitimists and Orleanists; government defeated . . 9 Dec. ,,

Committees on the bills relating to the press and the state of siege protest against them strongly about 13 Dec. ,,

Seventy-five senators for life (52 republicans) elected by the assembly . . . 9—21 Dec. ,,

Powerful speech of Buffet in favour of rigid press law and state of siege, 23 Dec.; much censured, but approved in a letter by MacMahon 24 Dec. ,,

Majority for ministers (376-303) . . 24 Dec. ,,

Solemn funerals of generals Clément Thomas and Lecomte, killed by the communists (18 March, 1871); violent recrimination in the assembly 27 Dec. ,,

Re-election to the assembly declined by the duc d'Aumale, 27 Dec.; by the prince de Joinville, 29 Dec. ,,

New press law (abolishing interdiction) passed; state of siege raised except in Paris, Versailles, Lyons, and Marseilles; proposal to raise it at Paris negatived (369-279) . . . 29 Dec. ,,

The assembly prorogued till 8 March, 1876 31 Dec. ,,

Powerful letter from Gambetta . . 31 Dec. ,,

Communist trials report: 9,596 convicted; 110 sentenced to death . . . . . . Dec. ,,

Ministerial crisis: difference between Buffet and Say respecting an electoral list; resignation of Say; withdrawn at MacMahon's request, 10 Jan. *et seq.;* the marshal issues a proclamation, countersigned by Buffet; he says, "I think that the constitution ought not to be revised before having been loyally worked. I shall fulfil to the end the mission entrusted to me." . . . 13 Jan. 1876

New Catholic university inaugurated at Paris by the archbishop . . . . . 10 Jan. ,,

Commencement of election of senators in departments . . . . 17 Jan. ,,

General prosperity; revenue for 1875 estimated 100,000,000*l*., said to be the highest ever received by any government . . . . Jan. ,,

Election of senators; mostly moderate republicans; Thiers for Belfort nearly unanimous; Buffet and Louis Blanc rejected; Victor Hugo elected 30 Jan. ,,

Resignation of Léon Renault, prefect of police, opposed to Buffet . . . . . 9 Feb. ,,

Election of deputies; great majority of republicans, 20 Feb.—5 March; resignation of Buffet, about 22 Feb.; Dufaure chief minister, with a modified cabinet . . . . . 24 Feb. ,,

Estimated result of elections: moderate republicans, 270; radicals, 60; Bonapartists, 92; Orleanists, 58; legitimists, 36 . . 7 March, ,,

Dufaure's ministry complete (including Decazes, Say, Waddington, de Cissey, &c.) about 9 March, ,,

Senate and assembly meet, 8 March; duc d'Audiffret Pasquier elected president of senate; M. F. P. Jules Grévy, president of assembly 13 March, ,,

Amnesty bill for communists introduced in the senate by Victor Hugo; in the assembly by Raspail . . . . . . 21 March, ,,

Proposed international exhibition, Paris, for 1 May, 1878 . . . . 5 April, ,,

Archbishop Guibert, of Paris, declines to give evidence concerning the election of comte de Mun as deputy . . . . . April, ,,

Gambetta president of budget committee for 1877 about 19 April, ,,

Queen Victoria in Paris; received by the president, 21 April, ,,

Death of Ricard, popular liberal minister of the interior, aged 48, 12 May; succeeded by M. De Mercère, under-secretary . . about 15 May, ,,

Debate on the amnesty to communists, 14 May; rejected (394-52), 17 May; Victor Hugo's speech in favour of amnesty; proposal rejected almost unanimously . . . . . 22 May, ,,

Funeral procession of Michelet at Paris 18 May, ,,

M. Buffet, ex-minister, elected life-senator 16 June, ,,

87 communists pardoned . . . . 28 June, ,,

Casimir Périer dies . . . . . 6 July, ,,

Nearly 2,000,000*l*. voted for public instruction 31 July, ,,

Chambers prorogued . . . . . 12 Aug. ,,

68 communists pardoned . . . . 17 Aug. ,,

Observatory at Puy de Dôme near Clermont inaugurated . . . . . . 22 Aug. ,,

New fortifications round Paris nearly completed, Sept. ,,

The assembly reopened, 30 Oct.; the duc Decazes' firm pacific speech . . . . . 3 Nov. ,,

Prince Napoleon Jerome becomes prominent in the assembly . . . . Nov. ,,

Resignation of Dufaure's ministry through defeats in the senate, &c. . . . . . 2 Dec. ,,

Pardons and commutations granted to many communist convicts . . . . . 2 Dec. ,,

New ministry: Jules Simon, president of the council and minister of interior; Martel, justice; others remain . . . . 12, 13 Dec. ,,

Estimated revenue 109,000,000*l*. . . . Dec. ,,

Chambers opened . . . . . . 9 Jan. 1877

Gambetta president of the budget . . 26 Jan. ,,

Above fifty prefects, hostile to the republic, removed . . . . Jan. ,,

Gen. Changarnier died, aged 83 . . 14 Feb. ,,

Paul de Cassagnac fined and imprisoned for libel against chamber of deputies in the "Pays," 5 April, ,,

Rochefort's "Lanterne" re-published . April, ,,

M. Jules Simon compelled to yield to Gambetta in the chamber . . . . . . 4 May, ,,

Peremptory letter of censure from marshal MacMahon to Jules Simon causes him and his ministry to resign . . . . . 16 May, 1877

The duc de Broglie forms a ministry (royalist and imperial), De Fourtou, interior; Cailloux, finance; Paris, public works; De Meaux, agriculture; Brunet, public instruction; (Decazes, foreign, and Berthaut, war, remain) . . 17 May, ,,

Gambetta's resolution in chamber in favour of parliamentary government carried, (355 - 154) 17 May; protest of 363 liberal deputies signed . 18 May, ,,

The marshal prorogues the chambers for a month; a firm manifesto issued by the left . 18 May, ,,

Many changes made in the prefects . 20 May, ,,

Thiers accepted as leader by the republicans; Broglie's circular for repressing the press issued about 29 May, ,,

Bonnet Duverdier, chief of municipality of Paris; arrested for speaking against the marshal, 1 June; sentenced to fine and imprisonment . 8 June, ,,

Meeting of chambers; stormy debate in second chamber, 16 June; vote against government carried (363-158) . . . . . 19 June, ,,

The deputies vote the necessary supplies, but not direct taxes . . . . . . 21 June, ,,

The senate votes dissolution of the chambers (150-130) 22 June; decreed . . . 25 June, ,,

The marshal, in an order of the day, after a review at Longchamps, says: "I appeal to the army to defend the dearest interests of the country," 2 July, ,,

Quarrels among Bonapartists (Rouher against Cassagnac) . . . . . July, Aug. ,,

Repressive measures towards the press, &c. July, Aug. ,,

Prosecution of Gambetta (and Murat, editor of the "République Française," in which it appeared) for a speech at Lille (29 July) in which he said the marshal must, if the elections be against him, "submit or resign" ("se soumettre ou se démettre") . . . . about 25 Aug. ,,

Thiers dies, aged 80; 3 Sept. public funeral; no disorder . . . . . . 8 Sept. ,,

Gambetta and Murat convicted; sentence 3 months imprisonment and fine of 80*l*. 11 Sept.; on appeal sentence affirmed . . . . . 22 Sept. ,,

The marshal's excursions to various places; reception differs . . . . . Aug. Sept. ,,

In his manifesto respecting the elections, he refers to his successful government, and says: "I cannot obey the injunctions of the demagogy; I can neither become the instrument of radicalism nor abandon the post in which the constitution has placed me" . . . . 19 Sept. ,,

Thiers' manifesto to electors (an historical defence of the republic and late chamber) published 24 Sept. ,,

The clergy energetically support the government Sept. Oct. ,,

Temperate manifesto of the left, 4 Oct.; of Grévy and Gambetta . . . . . . 7 Oct. ,,

Justificatory manifesto of the marshal, appealing to voters . . . . 11 Oct. ,,

Gambetta convicted for placarding his address; fine 150*l*. and 3 months' imprisonment 12 Oct. ,,

M. de Fourtou interferes very energetically in elections; foreign papers stopped, &c. . Oct. ,,

General election; quiet and dignified; results: defeat of Bonapartist and clerical parties; (of 506 official candidates about 199 elected; republicans, 320) . . . . . . 14 Oct. ,,

Final result: 325 republicans; 112 Bonapartists; 96 monarchists . . . . . 28 Oct. ,,

Ministry hold office till successors appointed; M. Pouyer-Quertier fails to form a ministry . Nov. ,,

Election of departmental councils who elect senators; majority for republicans . . 4 Nov. ,,

Meeting of chambers . . . . . 7 Nov. ,,

Census for 1876 announced: 36,905,788 (increase of 802,867 over 1872) . . . . 8 Nov. ,,

The marshal determines not to resign; his ministry agree to remain temporarily; announced 8 Nov. ,,

F. P. Jules Grévy re-elected president of the chamber of deputies now constituted . 10 Nov. ,,

Albert Grévy's resolution for the appointment of a commission of 33 to inquire into the conduct of the government respecting elections, 13 Nov.; carried after a warm debate (312-205) . 15 Nov. ,,

Debate in senate on M. Kerdrel's motion respecting

ministers; vote in their favour indirectly reflecting on Grévy's resolution, &c. (151-129) 19 Nov. 1877

Resignation of ministers announced . 20 Nov. ,,

New ministry formed under gen. Rochebouet, president; no member of it in the senate or assembly; termed "ministry of affairs" 23 Nov. ,,

No confidence in the new ministry voted in the second chamber (323-208) . . . 24 Nov. ,,

Important meeting of commercial men at Paris; petition to the marshal agreed on . 2 Dec. ,,

The chamber refuses to discuss the budget 4 Dec. ,,

The ministry resign; negotiations with Dufaure to form a parliamentary ministry fail; Batbie (see 26 Nov. 1872) also fails . . . 7-13 Dec. ,,

The marshal submits unconditionally 13 Dec. A thorough republican ministry formed under M. Dufaure, president of the council and minister of justice; De Marcère, interior; Waddington (protestant), foreign affairs; Bardoux, public instruction; general Borel, war; vice-admiral Pothuau, marine; Léon Say, finance; Teisserenc de Bort, commerce; De Freycinet, public works: announced; the marshal in his message accepts the will of the country . . . 14 Dec. ,,

Restrictions of the press removed; many prefects resign and others are removed 15 Dec. *et seq.* ,,

Death of gen. Aurelle de Paladines . 17 Dec. ,,

Budget voted; chambers adjourn . . 18 Dec. ,,

Limoges affair; gen. Rochebouet said to have issued orders to gen. de Bressoles for a military movement which he issued 12 Dec.; major Labordère denounces the orders as illegal, 13 Dec.; the orders nullified by the change of ministry, 14 Dec.; De Bressoles suspended for alleged mistake; Labordère cashiered; much excitement in Paris on account of suspected preparations for a *coup d'état* . . . . . . Jan. 1878

Legislative assembly meets . . 8 Jan. ,,

Gen. Ducrot dismissed from command for suspected connection with projected *coup d'état* 10, 11 Jan. ,,

Committee of 18 liberal deputies (formed in May) virtually dissolve . . . . 13 Jan. ,,

Break up of combined reactionary parties; the ministry generally successful . . March, ,,

International exhibition at Paris opened by the marshal president (see *Paris*) . . 1 May, ,,

Joan of Arc and Voltaire centenaries celebrated, 30 May, ,,

M. Waddington, foreign minister, a plenipotentiary at the Berlin Conference . 13 June—13 July ,,

Temporary strikes of workmen . . July, Aug. ,,

Republican success in electing departmental councils . . . . Aug. ,,

Solemn commemoration of death of Thiers at Nôtre Dame, &c. . . . . . . 3 Sept. ,,

Execution of Barré, stockbroker, and Lebiez, medical student, for murder of a milkwoman for her funded property . . . . 7 Sept. ,,

Review of 55,000 soldiers at Vincennes . 15 Sept. ,,

Powerful speech of Gambetta at Romans (department Drôme), proposing abolition of the exemption of theological students from military service, 18 Sept., and at Grenoble . . . 10 Oct. ,,

Dupanloup, bishop of Orleans, dies suddenly, 11 Oct. ,,

The assembly meets . . . . . 28 Oct. ,,

12,000 national lottery tickets of 1 franc sold (see *Lotteries*) . . . . . . up to Nov. ,,

Energetic manifesto of united Legitimists, Orleanists, and Bonapartists against republicans respecting election of senators . . 13 Nov. ,,

Elections of Paul de Cassagnac (7 Nov.) and M. Fortou invalidated by the Chamber, 18 Nov.; of Decazes . . . . 7 Dec. ,,

Letter from comte de Chambord to M. de Mun maintaining his rights; published . 25 Nov. ,,

All foreign commercial treaties *denounced* in view of a new tariff . . . . . 31 Dec. ,,

Elections for Senate; 64 republican, 16 opposition, 5 Jan. 1879

Compulsory resignation of gen. Borel, war minister, 13 Jan.; succeeded by gen. Gresley . 13 Jan. ,,

Meeting of chambers; M. Martel elected president of the senate . . . . . 15 Jan. ,,

Confidence in the ministry voted in chamber of deputies (223-121) . . . . 20 Jan. ,,

2,245 communists pardoned by decree, issued 17 Jan. ,,

Ministerial programme: pardons to communists; check of clerical influence upon education; dismissal of officials opposed to the republic, &c. 16 Jan. 1879

Drawing of the national lottery begun . 26 Jan. ,,

Budget: revenue, about 110,242,812*l.*; expenditure, 110,177,304*l.* . . . . Jan. ,,

Marshal MacMahon refuses to supersede military officers, 28 Jan. resigns; F. P. Jules Grévy elected president by the senate, and deputies united as "The National Assembly" (536 for Grévy; 99 for gen. Chanzy) . . . . . 30 Jan. ,,

Gambetta elected president of the chamber, 31 Jan. ,,

Resignation of Dufaure; 1 Feb. new ministry formed by M. Waddington; changes (see Nov. 1877); M. le Royer (keeper of seals and justice), Jules Ferry (public instruction), M. Lepère (agriculture), adm. Jauréguiberry (marine) . . . . 4 Feb. ,,

Communist amnesty bill passed by chamber of deputies . . . . 21 Feb. ,,

Resignation of M. de Marcère, minister of the interior (police scandals), 3 March; succeeded by M. Lepère . . . . . . 4 March, ,,

Admiral Pothuau, ambassador to England, March, ,,

Impeachment of De Broglie and Rochebouet (late ministers) recommended by a commission, 8 March, ,,

Impeachment negatived by the chamber (317-159); vote of censure passed (240-154) . 13 March, ,,

Proposed return of the assemblies to Paris; congress to be appointed (315-128) . . . 22 March, ,,

M. Ferry's education bills to check clerical influences, abolishing Jesuit colleges, &c. March, ,,

Pardon of 252 communists signed . 8 April, ,,

Blanqui (a convict) elected for Bordeaux 20 April, ,,

Pardon of 400 communists signed . 24 May, ,,

Prince Louis Napoleon killed while reconnoitering in Zululand . . . . . . 1 June, ,,

Blanqui's election annulled by the chamber (372-33), 4 June; pardoned and released . 11 June, ,,

Pardon of 288 more communists signed . 5 June, ,,

Violent opposition of Paul de Cassagnac; he is expelled the house for 3 days for abusing government . . . . 16 June, ,,

Congress of senate and deputies vote for their return to Paris (526-249) . . . 20 June, ,,

M. Ferry's law of superior public instruction passed by the deputies . . . . . 9 July, ,,

President Grévy's first grand military review at Longchamps . . . . 13 July, ,,

Fête of the republic . . . . . 14 July, ,,

Prince Napoleon Jerome coldly accepted as chief of the Bonapartists . . . . . 20 July, ,,

Comte de Chambord's letter: "With the co-operation of all honest men, and with the grace of God, I may save France, and will" . . 26 July, ,,

Chambers prorogued . . . . . 2 Aug. ,,

Treaties of commerce with England prolonged; signed . . . . 10 Oct. ,,

Humbert, an amnestied communist, elected to the municipal council, Paris, 11 Oct.; imprisoned for seditious speeches, &c., 22 Oct.; election annulled . . . . 4 Nov. ,,

About 60 mayors in La Vendée dismissed for celebrating comte de Chambord's birthday . Nov. ,,

The senate and assembly meet again at Paris, 27 Nov. ,,

Michel Chevalier, political economist, dies, 28 Nov. ,,

M. Waddington demands a vote of confidence, 2 Dec. ,,

[Republican sections: left centre, pure left, advanced left, extreme left.]

Ministerial majority (221-97); many abstainers, 4 Dec. ,,

Resignation of Lepère and Le Royer, ministers, 11, 12 Dec. ,,

Resignation of the Waddington ministry . 21 Dec. ,,

New ministry (more republican left) formed by M. de Freycinet; includes Jules Ferry (public instruction) and Lepère (interior); not Waddington or Léon Say . . . 28, 29 Dec. ,,

Gen. Farre, new war minister, dismisses heads of departments in War office . . . . Jan. 1880

Meeting of the Chambers . . . . 13 Jan. ,,

M. de Freycinet's moderate programme 16 Jan. ,,

Death (ex-foreign ministers): duc de Gramont, 16 Jan.; Jules Favre . . . . . 20 Jan. ,,

Budget for 1881 announced: estimated revenue, 110,935,000*l.*; 960,000*l.* more than for 1880; surplus, 1,300,000*l.* . . . . . . Feb. ,,

Death of M. Crémieux . . . . . 10 Feb. ,,

Plenary amnesty for communists rejected by the Chambers . . . . 12 Feb. 1880

Debate in senate: 7th clause of Ferry's education bill (abolishing Jesuit schools, &c.); Jules Simon speaks against it; rejected (148-129) 9 March, ,,

Decree dissolving order of Jesuits and other orders in France . . . . 29 March, ,,

Letter from prince Napoleon Jerome in favour of the decree; offends Bonapartists, about 5 April, ,,

Many bishops and others protest against the decree . . . . April, ,,

Pacific circular of M. de Freycinet respecting international relations . . . . . . 16 April, ,,

Ministerial defeat on public meetings bill; M. Lepère resigns, 15 May; M. Constans succeeds, 18 May, ,,

General Martel, president of senate, resigns; succeeded by M. Léon Say . . . 20 May, ,,

Amnesty bill for political offences, 19 June; presented by M. de Freycinet, 19 June; passed by the chambers (333-140) . . . . 21 June, ,,

Otaheite formally annexed to France . 29 June, ,,

Expulsion of religious orders (much officially opposed) carried into effect with Jesuits 30 June, ,,

Amnesty bill passed for all, except incendiaries and assassins, by senate (143-138) . . . 3 July, ,,

The president, Grévy, grants a general amnesty, 10 July; Rochefort warmly received in Paris, 12 July, ,,

First grand republican national fête . 14 July, ,,

Chambers prorogued . . . . . . 15 July, ,,

Elections of councils-general; great majority for republicans (anti-clerical and anti-Bonapartist), 1 Aug. ,,

MM. Grévy, Gambetta, and Léon Say, witness the launch of a man-of-war at Cherbourg, 8—11 Aug. ,,

M. de Freycinet, in a speech at Montauban, expresses disagreement with his colleagues respecting decree against religious orders; resigns, 19 Sept. ,,

New ministry: Jules Ferry (premier and public instruction), adm. Clouet (marine), Sadi-Carnot (public works), Barthélemy St. Hilaire (foreign); other offices unchanged . . . . 20 Sept. ,,

Two important letters from Guibert, abp. of Paris, to the president, recommending suspension of execution of the decree of 29 March against religious orders, delivered . . . 6, 15 Sept. ,,

Félix Pyat, editor of the *Commune*, sentenced to imprisonment and fine for justifying regicide, 19 Oct. ,,

Carmelites and other religious orders expelled, 16 Oct.—Nov. ,,

Meeting of the assembly: majority against the ministry (who resign) (200-166) . . . 9 Nov. ,,

The ministry withdraw their resignation on vote of confidence (240-149) . . . . 12 Nov. ,,

M. Baudry d'Asson, deputy, excluded 9 Nov.; refuses to retire from the chamber; forcibly expelled . . . . 11 Nov. ,,

Violent attacks of Rochefort (in *l'Intransigeant*) on Gambetta; crushing replies . . . Dec. ,,

Municipal council elections strongly in favour of the government . . . . . . 9 Jan. 1881

Meeting of the chambers . . . . . 20 Jan. ,,

Bill greatly freeing the press brought in 26 Jan. ,,

Projected loan of 40,000,000*l.* (public debt, about 1,200,000*l.*) immediately taken up for 30 times the amount . . . . March, ,,

Discussion respecting the *scrutin de liste* (*which see*), advocated by Gambetta; opposed by president Grévy, who yields . . 21, 22 March, ,,

Expedition to N. Africa to chastise the Kroumirs; invasion of Tunis . . . . March, April, ,,

Treaty with the bey signed (see *Tunis*) 12 May, ,,

Excitement at Marseilles and in Italy (*which see*), 13 May, *et seq.* ,,

M. Bardoux's bill for the *scrutin de liste* adopted by the chamber of deputies (243-235) . 18 May, ,,

The Tunis treaty ratified by the chamber (453-1), 23 May, ,,

Warm reception of Gambetta at Cahors and other places . . . . 25 May, ,,

Proposed revision of the constitution negatived in the chambers . . . . 31 May, ,,

The *scrutin de liste* rejected by the senate (148-114), 9 June, ,,

Adjournment of the chambers . . . . July, ,,

Election addresses. M. Rouher retires from political life (virtual end of Bonapartism), about 31 July; prince Napoleon Jerome advocates progress—"everything for and by the people"—about 31 July; speeches of M. Gambetta at Tours, Belleville, 12 Aug., advocating revision of the constitution, Aug.; M. Jules Ferry at Nancy deprecates division . about 11 Aug. 1881

Negotiations for treaty of commerce broken off; announced . . . . 16 Aug. ,,

Elections; triumph of Gambetta and moderate republicans; gain of about 44 members; hopeless minority of extremists of both kinds . 21 Aug. ,,

French treaty. French government propose meeting of the commissioners at Paris on 22 Aug.; England requests 3 months' extension of existing treaty; France declines; negotiations stopped; announced . . . . 18 Aug. ,,

Complications respecting Tripoli cleared up about 18 Aug. ,,

General elections; great republican majority; number of extremists on both sides much reduced 21 Aug. *et seq.* ,,

Negotiations respecting the commercial treaty resumed (France agrees to 3 months' extension of the treaty from 8 Nov.) . . . . 19 Sept. ,,

Capuchins and other orders relieved from their monastic vows by the pope . . . . Oct. ,,

Meeting of new chamber of deputies . 28 Oct. ,,

M. Brisson elected president . . . . 3 Nov. ,,

Treaty with the bey of Tunis confirmed by the chamber. Vote of censure on the Ferry ministry respecting Tunis war negatived by a great majority, 9 Nov.; the ministry resign . 10 Nov. ,,

New ministry gazetted; M. Gambetta (minister of foreign affairs and premier), M. Cazot (justice), M. Waldeck-Rousseau (interior), M. Allain-Targé (finance), general Campenon (war), M. Gougeard (marine), M. Paul Bert (education and worship), M. Raynal (public works), M. Rouvier (commerce and colonies), M. Cochery (posts and telegraphs), M. Devès (agriculture), and M. Proust (Arts) . . . . 12 Nov. ,,

Moderate declaration of Gambetta to the chambers (everything to be for France) . . . . 15 Nov. ,,

M. H. Rochefort acquitted of bitter libel against M. Roustan in *l'Intransigeant*; a virtual censure of the Tunis affair . . . . . 15 Dec. ,,

Anglo-French treaty negotiations stop; French concessions insufficient . . . . 30 Dec. ,,

Elections for senators; republicans gain 27; now 207—93; opposition announced . . 9 Jan. 1882

Much speculation; panic on the bourse, 19 Jan.; checked by resolution . . . . ,,

The *League of Patriots* established to support the army by encouraging military spirit, and support M. Gambetta . . . . ,,

Defeat of the government; rejection of the *scrutin de liste* (305—119); resignation of M. Gambetta, 26 Jan. ,,

New ministry: M. de Freycinet (president of the council and minister for foreign affairs), M. Léon Say (finance), M. Jules Ferry (public instruction), M. Goblet (interior and public worship), M. Humbert (justice), general Billot (war), admiral Jauréguiberry (marine), M. Varroy (public works), M. Tirard (commerce), M. Mahy (agriculture), M. Cochery (posts and telegraphs) 30, 31 Jan. ,,

Failure of the Union Générale company; continuance of panic . . . . 30 Jan. ,,

Arrest of Bontoux, president, and Feder, manager 2 Feb. ,,

Proposed revision of constitution negatived, 287—66 6 Feb. ,,

Anglo-French treaty renewed till 1 March, 6 Feb.; till 15 May . . . . 27 Feb. ,,

M. Tissot ambassador at London . . . March, ,,

New education bill passed; much government interference . . . . . . about 31 March, ,,

Commercial convention with Great Britain for ten years proposed . . . . April, ,,

Vote of confidence in the government (298—70) 1 June, ,,

Crisis: confidence in the ministry respecting Egypt voted (286—105) . . . . . . 20 July, ,,

Vote of credit for protection of Suez canal negatived on motion of M. Clémenceau (416—75); resignation of ministry . . . . . . 29 July ,,

The New French ministry, composed as follows: M. Duclerc (president of the council and minister for foreign affairs), M. Tirard (finance), M. Devès (justice), M. Fallières (interior), M. Pierre Legrand (commerce, and *ad interim* public works), general Billot (war), admiral Jauréguiberry (the navy), M. Cochery (post office and telegraphs), M. de Mahy (agriculture), M. Duvaux (public instruction) . . . . . . 1 Aug. 1882
Gambetta advocates activity in foreign affairs, and abstention in domestic; Clémenceau the reverse, July—Aug.; chambers prorogued . 9 Aug. ,,
Disturbance amongst the miners of the Saône and Loire . . . . . . about 17 Aug. ,,
The Bonapartists select prince Victor as their chief about 31 Aug. ,,
The compulsory education act comes into operation 2 Oct. ,,
Discovery of an organisation of anarchists (alleged origin at Geneva, and prince Krapotkine, member); tracts distributed by groups of young men throughout the country; attempted insurrection at Montceau-les-Mines suppressed . Aug. ,,
Many arrested [9 convicted, 22 Dec.] 21 Oct. ,,
Place of trial changed; dynamite explosions threatened . . . . . . about 26 Oct. ,,
Disturbances at Lyons; anarchy and panic; business and amusements suspended; the town said to be held by the mob . . . . 27 Oct. ,,
Government official note promising public security 27 Oct. ,,
Arrest connected with an explosion at a café (one man killed) on 23 Oct.; railway station held by troops . . . . 28 Oct. ,,
Much dynamite seized . . . . . . 29 Oct. ,,
Great distress in Lyons . . . . . . Oct. ,,
Panic subsiding in Paris, &c. . . 8 Nov. ,,
Opening of the chambers . . . . 9 Nov. ,,
Crown jewels (value about 100,000*l.*) stolen from the cathedral of St. Denis . . . 23 Nov. ,,
Treaty with the king of Congo negotiated by M. Brazza ratified . . . . . . 21 Nov. ,,
Death of Louis Blanc . . . . . . 6 Dec. ,,
MM. Bontoux & Feder, directors of the "Union Générale" (a financial company established in 1878, and patronised by the legitimists, clergy, and the middle classes), sentenced to imprisonment and fines for gross frauds, which caused very great universal distress (it stopped 28 Jan.) 20 Dec. ,,
Prince Krapotkine, anarchist, arrested about 21 Dec. ,,
Death of M. Gambetta, aged 44, after several weeks illness through an accidental wound, midnight, 31 Dec. ,,
His grand state funeral at Paris . . 6 Jan. 1883
Death of gen. Chanzy, aged about 60 . 5 Jan. ,,
Death of gen. Vinoy . . . . . . Jan. ,,
Trial of Krapotkine and about 50 anarchists begun at Lyons . . . . 8 Jan. ,,
He sentenced to 5 years' imprisonment and fine, others to imprisonment . . . 19 Jan. ,,
Gambetta's remains removed and re-buried at Nice 13 Jan. ,,
Prince Napoleon publishes a manifesto against the government; arrested . . . 16 Jan. ,,
M. Floquet's bill for expulsion of Bourbons and Bonapartes . . . . . . 16 Jan. ,,
Government bill of M. de Fallières for power to expel the same . . . . . 20 Jan. ,,
Ministerial crisis . . . . . 23 Jan. ,,
Expulsion bill adopted by committee . 25 Jan. ,,
M. Duclerc's ministry resigned . . 28 Jan. ,,
Ministry re-constituted under M. Fallières 29 Jan. ,,
M. Fabre's bill permitting princes to remain with deprival of civil rights, discussed, 29 Jan.; passed by the chamber (343–163) . . 1 Feb. ,,
Prince Napoleon's indictment quashed; released, 9 Feb. ,,
Expulsion bill rejected by the senate; amendment of MM. Say and Waddington adopted (165–127); princes to be expelled only after trial . 12 Feb. ,,
Resignation of M. Fallières and ministry 13 Feb. ,,
M. Barbey's bill empowering the president to expel princes when dangerous, adopted by the deputies, 15 Feb.; rejected by the senate . 17 Feb. ,,
M. Jules Ferry (opportunist) forms a ministry (Gambettist); M. Jules Ferry (premier and minister of public instruction), M. Challemel-Lacour (foreign affairs), M. Waldeck-Rousseau (interior), M. Martin Feuillé (justice), General Thibaudin (war), M. Charles Brun (marine), M. Tirard (finance), M. Raynal (public works), M. Meline (agriculture), M. Cochery (posts and telegraphs), M. Hérisson (commerce) . 21 Feb. 1883
Decree for retirement of the Orleanist princes from the army in virtue of the law of 1834 (the duc d'Aumale, the duc de Chartres, and the duc d'Alençon), approved by the deputies (295–103), 24 Feb. ,,
M. Clémenceau's motion for revision of the Constitution rejected by the deputies . 6 March, ,,
Open-air meeting of artisans out of work at Paris excited to violence by Louise Michel the anarchist and others; bakers' shops rifled; checked by police, 9 March; many arrested . 10 March, ,,
Louise Michel arrested . . . . 30 March, ,,
Trial of madame Monasterio and others for putting her daughter Fidelia in a mad-house, and ill-usage; case referred back to public prosecutor, March, ,,
Death of Louis Veuillot, ultramontane, editor of *l'Univers* . . . . . . 8 April, ,,
Marshal Bazaine publishes his defence at Madrid. ,,
Conversion of *Rentes* bill (5 to 4½) passed 27 April, ,,
Museum of revolution established at Versailles, 20 June, ,,
Louise Michel sentenced to 6 years' imprisonment, and others to different terms . 23 June, ,,
National fête; colossal statue of the Republic uncovered . . . . 14 July, ,,
M. Waddington, ambassador in London, appointed about 16 July, arrives . . . 23 July, ,,
The chambers close . . . . . . 2 Aug. ,,
The inauguration of the monument (by M. Barrias) erected at Courbevoie to commemorate the defence of Paris in 1870–1 . . . . 12 Aug. ,,
Death of the comte de Chambord, aged nearly 63 24 Aug. ,,
Statue of Lafayette unveiled at Lepuy . 6 Sept. ,,
Great royalist meeting at Paris; little excitement, 20 Sept. ,,
The king of Spain received by president Grévy at Paris; hooted by the mob . . 29 Sept. ,,
Gen. Thibaudin, minister of war, resigns, 5 Oct.; succeeded by gen. Campenon . . 9 Oct. ,,
M. Jules Ferry declares for a Republic of "common sense," and opposition to the extreme left at Rouen, 13 Oct.; and at Havre . 14 Oct. ,,
The government awards 1,000*l.* to Mr. Shaw (see *Madagascar*, 1883) . . . about 15 Oct. ,,
The chambers meet . . . . . 23 Oct. ,,
Correspondence between France and China respecting Tonquin published in *Times;* China firm in resisting French encroachments. . 29 Oct. ,,
Debate on Tonquin; votes of confidence in ministry (339–160) . . . 29–31 Oct.; 10, 18 Dec. ,,
M. Ferry becomes foreign minister on the retirement of M. Challemel-Lacour; other changes in the ministry . . . about 17–20 Nov. ,,
Government defeated on Algerian colonisation (249–211) . . . . 28 Dec. ,,
Death of M. Rouher, prime minister of Napoleon III. . . . . 3 Feb. 1884
Industrial crisis in Paris; defeat of the government; a committee of investigation into the condition of the working classes appointed (254–249) 4 Feb. ,,
Proposals for loan of 14,000,000*l.* issued 12 Feb. ,,
Government defeated on its seditious meetings bill, 16 Feb. ,,
Death of François Mignet, French historian, aged about 87 . . . . . . 24 March, ,,
Statue of Gambetta (by Falquières) at Cahors, unveiled by M. Jules Ferry . . . 14 April, ,,
Municipal elections: radicals rather more than opportunists; few of other parties . May, ,,
Bill for revision of the Constitution (abolition of life senators, &c.) brought in by M. Jules Ferry, 24 May, ,,
Prince Victor acknowledged chief of the Bonapartists; his father publishes painful correspondence . . . . June, ,,
Cholera prevalent in the south, &c. (see *Cholera*) June, *et seq.* ,,
Colossal statue of Liberty by Bartholdé given to the United States of America unveiled by M. Jules Ferry at Paris . . . . . 4 July,

Revision bill, modified by the senate, accepted by the deputies . . . . . . 31 July, 1884
Congress of senate and deputies meet at Versailles, M. Le Royer, president . . . 4 Aug. ,,
The revision of the Constitution accepted by the congress, 509–172 . . . 13 Aug. ,,
Excitement about the price of bread at Paris and other places . . . . . Oct., Dec. ,,
Wife of M. Clovis Hugues, a deputy, shoots Morin, a slanderous libeller, in the Palace of Justice; he dies; [she acquitted! 8 Jan. 1885] . 27 Nov. ,,
Credit for Tonquin war adopted by the deputies, 282–187, 28 Nov.; by the senate . 11 Dec. ,,
Trade Unions legalized . . . . ,,
Resignation of gen. Campenon, war minister, 3 Jan. succeeded by gen. Lewal . . . 5 Jan. 1885
Senatorial elections (67 republicans and 20 conservatives returned) . . . . 25–26 Jan. ,,
The Chamber votes for engagement of unemployed workmen on public works . . . 5 Feb. ,,
The Ferry ministry resign in consequence of defeat in the chamber . . . . . 30 March, ,,
New ministry formed by M. Brisson . 6 April, ,,
Peace with China, announced . . . 7 April, ,,
Duty on foreign corn voted by the senate 27 March, ,,
M. Ferry's ministry defeated on vote of credit for Chinese war (308–161); resigns . . 30 March, ,,
Vote of credit for 2,000,000*l.*, 31 March; for 6,000,000*l.* . . . . . . 7 April, ,,
New ministry; H. Brisson (president and justice), D. E. Freycinet (foreign), Allain Targé (interior), Goblet (public instruction and worship), gen. Campenon (war), adm. Galiber (marine), Clamageran, afterwards Sadi-Carnot (finance), and others 6 April, ,,
Bosphore Egyptien Affair. See *Egypt* . May, ,,
Anarchist demonstration at Père la Chaise; many wounded by the police . . 24 May, ,,
Death of Victor Hugo, poet, dramatist and novelist, aged 83, 22 May; buried in the Panthéon; procession 3 miles long, all Paris spectators 1 June, ,,
Scrutin de liste bill passed with the senate's amendments . . . . . . 8 June ,,
Death of admiral Courbet . . . . 11 June, ,,
Great excitement in Paris about Olivier Pain (see *Soudan*) . . . . Aug. ,,
Chambers prorogued 6 Aug.; parliamentary elections, 200 conservatives, 230 moderates or opportunists, 150 radicals . . . . 4 Oct. ,,
The ministers not re-elected resign . 6 Oct. ,,
M. de Freycinet shot at in the Place de la Concorde 29 Oct. ,,
New chamber meets . . . . . 10 Nov. ,,
Republican party disorganised . . . 10 Nov. ,,
The ministry propose retrenchment in colonial war expenditure, and consideration of church disestablishment . . . . . 16 Nov. ,,
Report of committee on Tonquin recommends vote of 19,000,000 francs instead of 75,000,000 proposed by government . . . . 16 Dec. ,,
Great commercial depression, attributed to government prodigality, &c. . . . . . . Dec ,,
Vote for government (274–270) . . 21–23 Dec. ,,
F. P. Jules Grévy elected president for seven years (457 for Grévy, 68 for M. Brisson) . 28 Dec. ,,
M. Brisson's ministry resigns . . . 29 Dec. ,,
New ministry; M. de Freycinet (president and foreign affairs), M. Demôle (justice), M. Sarrien (interior), M. Goblet (education), M. Sadi-Carnot (finance), general Boulanger (war), admiral Aube (marine and colonies), M. Baïhaut (public works), M. Develle (agriculture), M. Lockroy (commerce), M. Granet (posts and telegraphs) . . 7 Jan. 1886
Amnesty for political offenders granted . 14 Jan. ,,
The prefect of Eure (M. Barrème) assassinated in a railway carriage . . . . . 13 Jan. ,,
Riotous strike of 3,000 miners at Decazeville, in Aveyron, murder of M. Watrin, manager, end of Jan. ,,
New elections increase the Republican members to 400, the Right 184 . . . about 16 Feb. ,,
M. Sadi-Carnot's budget; proposed new loan of about 58,500,000*l.* (70,000,000*l.* really wanted) 17 March; the modified loan immediately subscribed for, 20,000,000*l.* passed by the deputies 21 April, ,,
Abp. Guibert of Paris, in a letter to president Grévy, protests against prohibiting monks and nuns to teach in schools . . about 1 April, ,,

M. Barthélemy's book, "Avant la Bataille," advocating the re-conquest of Alsace and Lorraine, published . . . . about 6 April, 1886
Grand reception of the comte de Paris on account of the marriage of his daughter with the duke of Braganza 15 May; causes republican jealousy May, ,,
Bills for giving discretionary power to expel the Orleans princes and prince Napoleon and son from France and confiscating their property, introduced in the chambers (M. Freycinet influenced by M. Clémenceau) 27 May; reported disagreement in the cabinet on the subject 2, 3 June; bill for immediate expulsion of heads of families and heirs of dynasties who have reigned in France passed by the chamber 11 June; and by the senate (137–122) 22 June; promulgated; the Bonapartes quit France 23 June; the comte de Paris and family leave; at Dover he issues a protest declaring monarchy to be the most suitable government for France, and places himself as head of the royalists . . . . 24 June, ,,
Death of Guibert, abp. of Paris . . . . 8 July, ,,
The duc d'Aumale remonstrates against the deprivation of his rank in the army; his expulsion from France voted 13 July; rev. W. J. Drought, English chaplain at Chantilly, expelled from France for delivering an address of sympathy to the duke . . . . Aug. ,,
Session closed . . . . 15 July, ,,
Celebration of the 100th birthday of M. Chevreul, chemist and physicist . . . . 31 Aug. ,,
Education bill permitting lay teachers only passed by the chamber . . . . . 28 Oct. ,,
Ministry defeated in the chamber (by 13 majority), resigns . . . . 3 Dec. ,,
New ministry: M. Goblet (president and interior), M. Flourens (foreign), M. Dauphin (finance), M. Berthelot (public instruction), M. Sarrien (justice), gen. Boulanger (war), adm. Aube (marine), M. Granet (posts and telegraphs), M. Lockroy (commerce), M. Millaud (public works), M. Develle (agriculture) . . . . Dec ,,
Continued deficit; budget rejected; amended one accepted by government . . . 22 Jan. 1887
Panic on the bourse through war rumours 1 Feb. ,,
Bill for increasing duty on foreign corn adopted by the chamber (318–248) 14 March; by the senate 25 March; duty on foreign cattle and meat raised March ,,
M. Schnaebell, commissary of police, arrested near Pagny-sur-Moselle, territory doubtful, and sent to Metz 20 April; charged with treason 22 April; statements contradictory; released by order of the emperor William . . . . 29 April, ,,
Sale of the crown jewels for 274,560*l.*, diamonds 289,000*l.*; the diamonds distributed between the Louvre and other museums . . 12–23 May, ,,
The Goblet ministry defeated on the budget bill (275–257); resigns . . . . . 17 May, ,,
MM. Freycinet, Floquet, Devès and Duclerc fail May, ,,
M. Rouvier forms a moderate ministry, consisting of M. Rouvier (finances, posts and telegraphs), M. Flourens (foreign affairs), M. Mazeau (justice), M. Fallières (interior), M. Spuller (public instruction and worship), M. Barbey (marine and colonies), gen. Ferron (war), M. Dautresme (commerce and public works), M. Barbe (agriculture) 30 May, ,,
Gen. Boulanger, the late war minister, issues a monitory order to the army . . . 30 May, ,,
Exemption of ecclesiastical students (seminarists) abolished in new army bill . . 25 June, ,,
Gen. Boulanger warmly received in his progress to Clermont Ferrand . . . . 9 July, ,,
Radical attack on the ministry defeated (382–120) 11 July, ,,
Pranzini, a sordid profligate, convicted of the murder of Marie Regnault and two other women 13 July; executed . . . . . 31 Aug. ,,
Session closed . . . . . . 22 July, ,,
Gen. Boulanger challenges M. Ferry for remarks in a speech about 29 July; seconds differ; no result. Aug. ,,
Mobilisation of 17th army corps, near Toulouse 31 Aug. ,,

Manifesto of the comte de Paris calling for the re-establishment of a constitutional monarchy by universal suffrage as specially needful for France 14 Sept. 1887

M. Brignon killed, and M. Wangen de Girolseck (French sportsmen) wounded by Kaufmann, a German soldier and gamekeeper, near the boundary in the Vosges 24 Sept.; German redress given, 2,500*l.* presented to Mad. Brignon announced 7 Oct.

Military scandal; gen. Caffarel of the war office convicted by a military tribunal of dishonourable conduct in trafficking with decorations 13 Oct. ,,

Gen. Boulanger under arrest for thirty days for remarks respecting the scandal . . . 14 Oct. ,,

Amicable conventions respecting Suez Canal and New Hebrides signed at Paris . . . 24 Oct. ,,

Prince Victor Napoleon issues a Bonapartist manifesto . . . . 25 Oct. ,,

The chambers meet . . . . 27 Oct. ,,

Lord Lyons, British ambassador, retires (appointed in 1867); [died 5 Dec.;] succeeded by the earl of Lytton . . . . Oct. ,,

Trial of gen. Caffarel and others; discharged 7 Nov. ,,

Gen. count D'Andlau and Madame Rattazzi sentenced to imprisonment and fines for trafficking in decorations . . . . . . 14 Nov. ,,

M. Wilson, son-in-law of the president, implicated; also charged with tampering with documents Nov. ,,

The old four-and-a-half per cent. rentes converted to three per cents. accepted . . . Nov. ,,

M. Rouvier defeated in the chamber on a motion of M. Clémenceau (317–227); the ministry resigns; M. Grévy refuses to resign 19 Nov.; but is compelled by the combination of opposite parties; the Rouvier ministry retains office; on their announcing that M. Grévy defers his resignation the chamber immediately adjourns (531–3) 1 Dec.; receives M. Grévy's resignation . . 2 Dec. ,,

National assembly at Versailles; congress of senators and deputies (833); M. Sadi-Carnot ("moderate independent") elected president (616); general Saussier, an unwilling candidate (148); (MM. Ferry and de Freycinet withdrawn) 3 Dec. ,,

M. Goblet fails to form a ministry 9 Dec.; M. Fallières fails . . . . . . 10 Dec. ,,

Attempted assassination of M. Ferry by Aubertin, a lunatic, in the lobby of the chamber of deputies, a narrow escape . . . . . 10 Dec. ,,

The tribunals find no case against M. Wilson 13 Dec. ,,

New ministry: M. Tirard (finance and premier), M. Flourens (foreign affairs), M. Fallières (justice), M. Sarrien (interior), M. Faye (education and worship), M. de Mahy, afterwards adm. Krantz, Jan. 1888 (marine and colonies); M. Loubet (public works), M. Dautresme (commerce), M. Viette (agriculture), gen. Logerot (war) 13 Dec. ,,

The session of the chambers closed . . 18 Dec. ,,

Mr. Archibald M'Neill, journalist, wounded and drowned (suspected murder) at Boulogne 20 Dec. 1887; Vermersch arrested . . . . Jan. 1888

Gen. Boulanger deprived of his command for insubordination in visiting Paris against orders; announced . . . . . 15 March, ,,

Death of M. L. H. Carnot, father of the president, aged 86 . . . . . . 16 March, ,,

Trial of M. Wilson for traffic in decorations; sentenced to two years' imprisonment, loss of civil rights for five years, and fine of 3,000 francs, 1 March; sentence quashed by court of appeal 26 March, ,,

Gen. Boulanger tried by court of five generals; sentenced to retirement 26 March; confirmed 27 March, ,,

M. Tirard's ministry defeated when opposing urgency for revision of constitution (268–234), resigns . . . . 30 March, ,,

M. Floquet forms a ministry: M. Charles Floquet president of the council and minister of the interior), M. de Freycinet (war), M. Goblet foreign affairs), admiral Krantz (marine and the colonies), M. Peytral (finance, posts, and telegraphs), M. Edouard Lockroy (public instruction, fine arts, and worship), M. Deluns Montaud (public works), M. Ferrouillat (justice), M. Pierre Legrand (commerce and industry), M. Viette (agriculture) . . . . . . 3 April, 1888

Gen. Boulanger begins to form a party; elected deputy for the Dordogne (59,500–35,750) 8 April; for the Nord (172,528–75,901) . . 15 April, ,,

Rise of an anti-parliamentary party, a mixture of conservatives, radicals, &c. . . . . April, ,,

After vote of confidence in the ministry (379–177), it is defeated on the revision question (340–215) 19 April, ,,

A committee advises postponement of revision; riots between students and Boulangists 20 April, ,,

Great circulation of gen. Boulanger's (alleged) "German Invasion, no. 1" 8 May; soon fell off 18 May, ,,

Royalist banquet at the château de Mons, near St. Étienne; powerful speech of general de Charette 27 May, ,,

Gen. Boulanger's motion in the chamber for urgency in the revision of the constitution rejected (377–186) . . . . 4 June, ,,

The manifesto of the comte de Paris to the mayors of communes against the republic signed 6 July, ,,

Gen. Boulanger in the chamber demands dissolution, firmly resisted by M. Floquet; the general accuses M. Floquet of falsehood, resigns his seat, and leaves the House in great excitement, 12 July; duel, gen. Boulanger seriously, and M. Floquet slightly wounded, 13 July; gen. Boulanger reported convalescent . . . 20 July, ,,

Unveiling of the Gambetta monument at Paris by president Carnot . . . . . 13 July, ,,

National fête passes quietly . . . 14 July, ,,

67,000,000 francs voted for the defence of Brest, Toulon and Cherbourg . . . . 17 July, ,,

Session of chambers closed . . . . 18 July, ,,

Gen. Boulanger defeated in elections for Ardèche &c. July, ,,

Funeral of Eudes the communist; rioting suppressed; no deaths . . . . . 8 Aug. ,,

Diplomatic dispute with Italy respecting Massowah (MM. Goblet and Crispi). . . . Aug. ,,

Gen. Boulanger elected for the Nord, Somme, and Charente . . . . . . 19 Aug. ,,

Death of marshal Bazaine, aged 77 . . 23 Sept. ,,

Decree of president Carnot and M. Floquet respecting resident foreigners and immigrants 2 Oct.; registration causes much annoyance; time prolonged to 1 Jan. 1889 . . . . 28 Oct. ,,

The *League of the Rose* formed to promote the re-establishment of the monarchy . . autumn, ,,

The chambers re-open; M. Floquet introduces a bill for the revision of the constitution, which is declared urgent 15 Oct.; much dissatisfaction 16 Oct. *et seq.* ,,

Graduated tax on incomes above 2,000 francs proposed by M. Peytral . . . . 22 Oct. ,,

Increase of Boulangist demonstrations . Oct. ,,

Prado, *alias* count Linska de Castillon, and other names, a daring unprincipled adventurer, the husband and associate of many women, whom he had robbed of jewelry, &c., and some of whom he was strongly suspected to have murdered, is convicted of the murder and robbery of diamonds of Marie Aguétant, an unfortunate in Paris (14 Jan. 1886) . . . . . . 14 Nov. ,,

M. Numa Gilly tried for defamation against the budget committee; acquitted for want of evidence 17 Nov. ,,

Festival of the *League of Patriots* (Boulangists) 25 Nov. ,,

Demonstration at Paris in honour of M. Baudin, a deputy killed on the barricades 2 Dec. 1851, 2 Dec. ,,

Powerful speech of M. Challemel-Lacour on the demoralization of parliament by reckless faction 19 Dec. ,,

Prado executed (see 14 Nov.) . . . . 28 Dec. ,,

Windfall of 1,218,000 francs to the government (see *Tontine*) . . . . Dec. ,,

Gen. Boulanger elected for the department of the Seine (244,000); M. Jacques, advanced republican, (162,000) . . . . . . 27 Jan. 1889

M. Floquet has majority of 62 in the chamber 31 Jan. ,,

Bill for replacing the *scrutin de liste* by the *scrutin d'arrondissement* carried in the chamber (268–222) 11 Feb.; in the senate (228–54) . . 13 Feb. ,,

The ministerial scheme for the revision of the constitution rejected (307–218); they resign 14 Feb. 1889

Dissension between the opportunists and the radicals . . . . Feb. ,,

M. Meline fails to form an opportunist ministry 18 Feb. ,,

M. Tirard forms a mixed ministry, including several ex-premiers: M. Tirard (premier and minister of commerce), M. Constans (interior), M. Spüller (foreign), M. de Freycinet (war), M. Rouvier (finance), M. Thévenet (justice), adm. Jaurès (died 13 March; succeeded by admiral Krantz) (marine), M. Fallières (education), M. Yves Guyot (public works), M. Faye (agriculture) 21, 22 Feb. ,,

The *League of Patriots*, established in 1882, becoming seditious and connected with Boulangism, suppressed by the government 28 Feb.; alleged number 240,000; protest about 2 March; MM. Déroulède, Laguerre, and others, committee of the League, prosecuted; trial 2 April; each fined 100 fr. . . . . 6 April, ,,

Fall in the shares of the Comptoir d'Escompte de Paris through speculations in copper (*which see*), Feb.; suicide of M. Denfert-Rochereau, the manager, 5 March; panic; checked by the intervention of government and bank of France, 9 March; supported by Messrs. Rothschild and other bankers, March; reconstituted successfully March-May, ,,

Decree of expulsion of the duc d'Aumale revoked 7 March; the duc received by M. Carnot, 12 March, ,,

Manifesto of gen. Boulanger to the Nord against the government . . . . . 18 March, ,,

He escapes to Brussels 1, 2 April; his trial for conspiracy by the senate proposed; issues manifesto 5 April; expects expulsion; arrives in London 24 April, ,,

The senate meets as a high court for his trial 12 April, ,,

M. Chevreul, chemist, dies aged 102 . 9 April, ,,

M. Carnot, the president, opens the "Revolution Exhibition" of relics, at Paris . 18 April, ,,

Great Royalist banquet at Paris . . . 1 May, ,,

Centenary celebration of the meeting of the States General (afterwards the Constituent Assembly) 5 May, 1789—president Carnot in the presence of a grand assembly in the "Hall of Mirrors," Versailles, delivers a eulogium on the revolution 5 May, ,,

[On his way to Versailles, the president's carriage was fired at by a semi-lunatic named Perrin—sentenced to four months' imprisonment 28 May] ,,

The Universal Exhibition opened by the president (see *Paris*) . . . . . . 6 May, ,,

New army bill reducing the term of service from five years with exemptions to three years, nominally without exemptions, passed by the chamber July 9, ,,

M. Quesnay de Beaurepaire hands in the indictment against gen. Boulanger . . . . . 7 July, ,,

Sale (at Paris) of the pictures, tapestries, china, &c., of M. Secrétan (ruined by speculations in copper); enormous prices realised, 1–4 July; 17 of M. Secrétan's pictures were sold by Messrs. Christie in London for 27,824*l.* 10*s.* . 13 July, ,,

Anniversary of the fall of the Bastille celebrated in France, the United States, &c. . . 14 July, ,,

Bill prohibiting a man to be candidate for more than one place in the chamber passed by the senate . . . . 15 July, ,,

Cantonal elections: republicans, 752; conservatives, 497; gen. Boulanger, 12 . . 28 July, ,,

The chamber votes 2,400,000*l.* for the increase of the navy (3 ironclads, &c.); the session closed 15 July, ,,

Indictment against gen. Boulanger, charging him when director of infantry in 1882, with courting popularity by corruption, &c., and when minister of war in 1886 with malversation of public money, and plotting against the state, with count Dillon, H. Rochefort and other confederates; they are cited to appear before the High Court of Justice on 6 Aug.; non-appearance to be followed by loss of civil rights and sequestration of property 17, 28 July, ,,

Gen. Boulanger appeals to the people in reply to the indictment . . . . 6 Aug. ,,

The trial of gen. Boulanger, count Dillon, and H. Rochefort begins . . . . . 8 Aug. 1889

Sentenced to deportation to a fortress, and payment of costs of the trial . . . . . 14 Aug. ,,

The comte de Paris, prince Gerome Napoleon, his son Victor, and gen. Boulanger set forth their claims for political power . . . Aug. ,,

Elections of the chamber of Deputies; decisive victory of the government 22 Sept. and 6 Oct. ,,

[112 Monarchists, 62 Bonapartists, 325 Republicans, 41 Boulangists, 32 uncertain Liberals. Gen. Boulanger's election was annulled.]

The universal exhibition closed . . . . 6 Nov. ,,

The new chamber opened, 12 Nov.; M. Floquet elected president . . . . . 18 Nov. ,,

Moderate statement by M. Tirard . . 19 Nov. ,,

The Boulangist demonstration easily quelled 12 Nov. ,,

Supreme naval council created by decree . 6 Dec. ,,

Gen. Boulanger's election, and that of several Boulangists, for Montmartre, annulled by the chamber (370—123) . . . . . 9 Dec. ,,

Three Boulangist deputies expelled from the chamber for disorderly conduct . . 20 Jan. 1890

The duke of Orleans (aged 21) comes to Paris, and offers to enter the army; arrested, 7 Feb.; sentenced to two years' imprisonment for breaking the exile law of 1886, 12 Feb.; taken to Clairvaux 25 Feb. ,,

Miners' strike at St. Etienne, 2,700 out . 20 Feb. ,,

Resignation of M. Constans, minister of the Interior, succeeded by M. Léon Bourgeois 1 March, ,,

M. Tirard and his cabinet defeated in the senate, resign . . . . 14 March, ,,

New ministry, M. de Freycinet (premier and war minister), M. Rouvier (finance), M. Constans (interior), M. Bourgeois (public instruction), M. Ribot (foreign), M. Fallières (justice and public worship), M. Jules Roche (commerce), M. Deville (agriculture), M. Barbey (marine), M. Guyot (public works) . . . . . . March, ,,

M. Carnot's tour in S. France, Corsica, &c. 16—27 April ,,

The Boulangists totally defeated in the Paris municipal elections . . . . . . 27 April, ,,

Suspected anarchist plot: the marquis de Mores, Louise Michel, and about 300 others arrested, 28 April—2 May; the marquis and others liberated 3 May, *et seq.* ,,

The labour day of the working classes passes off tranquilly at Paris, &c. . . . . 1 May, ,,

Strike of thousands of workmen at Croix, Roubaix and Tourcoing, in the Nord; serious rioting suppressed by the military, 1, 2 May; strikes subsiding . . . . 8 May, ,,

War with Dahomey, *which see* . . Feb., May, ,,

Trial of M. Secrétan and other directors of the Comptoir d'Escompte for fraud, &c., *see above* Feb. 1889—5 May, ,,

M. Secrétan sentenced to 6 months' imprisonment and fine of 10,000 francs; the others received less sentences . . . . 28 May, ,,

Gen. Boulanger submits to the government; the Boulangist committee dissolves . . 21 May ,,

17 Russian Anarchists or Nihilists, engaged in the manufacture of explosives at Raincy, arrested 29 May, *et seq.* ,,

All discharged except 8 . . . . 25 June, ,,

The duke of Orleans pardoned and expelled from France . . . . 3 June, ,,

Revelations respecting the affairs of the Crédit Foncier; investigation ordered by government, 9 May, ,,

Explanations given by M. Christophle, May; the inspectors' report stated that the establishment had departed from its original object and gone into banking, &c., without proper precautions, but that it is stable . . . . 21 June, ,,

Trial of 8 Russian Nihilists, 4 July; 6 men convicted sentenced to 3 years' imprisonment; Landesen the instigator (absent) to 5 years' imprisonment, two women acquitted . 5 July, ,,

Close of the session . . . . . 6 Aug. ,,

Anglo-French agreement (*which see*) signed in London . . . . 5 Aug. ,,

Violent cyclone in the department of the Aude; great destruction of vines, 15 Aug. also at Dreux . . . . 18 Aug. ,,

"Les Coulisses du Boulangisme," by M. Mermeix, published by him in the *Figaro*, describing an alleged conspiracy of Royalists, early Sept.; causes much excitement and involves the author in several duels, in one of which he is wounded 15 Sept. 1890
Destructive storms and floods in the departments of Gard, Ardèche and Herault, with loss of life 21—24 Sept. ,,
Meeting of chamber of deputies . . . 20 Oct. ,,
The Union for the promotion of Free Trade in Raw Materials, &c., formed in Paris . . . Oct. ,,
Assassination of gen. Michael Seliverskoff, aged 69, wealthy retired Russian general and formerly a minister of secret police, at the Hôtel de Bade, Paris, 18 Nov.; died . . . 19 Nov. ,,
Mme. Duc Quercy, MM. Labruyère and Grégoire sentenced to imprisonment for aiding the escape of Padlewski, the suspected murderer of gen. Seliverskoff (19 Nov.) . . . 23 Dec. ,,
The French Africa Committee formed; expeditions proposed . . . . . . Nov. ,,
The government defeated in the chambers on a financial question (303—248) . . 28 Nov. ,,
Cardinal Lavigerie and other prelates declare their adhesion to the republic, with the approval of the pope . . . . Dec. ,,
Parliamentary session opened . . . 13 Jan. 1891
Vote of censure on the ministry relative to the loan of gold by the Bank of France to the Bank of England, during the Baring crisis (see *London*, 15 Nov. 1890), negatived (419—29) 17 Jan. ,,
Communication between Paris and London by telephone (*which see*) . . . . 18 March, ,,
The performance of Sardou's new play *Thermidor* (*which see*), stopped by order of the ministry 27 Jan. ,,
Michel Eyraud sentenced to death, and Gabrielle Bompard sentenced to 20 years' penal servitude, for murder of Toussaint Gouffé, a process-server, whom they had inveigled to their rooms, about 25 July, 1889. His decomposed body was found at Millery (Rhone), 13 Aug., to which place it had been carried in a trunk. Gabrielle confessed to the police, Jan. 1890. Eventually, Eyraud was brought from the Havanah, Cuba, to Paris (five days' trial at Paris), 20 Dec. 1890; executed 3 Feb. ,,
Royalist demonstration in Paris in honour of the duke of Orleans . . . . . . 7 Feb. ,,
The empress Frederick visits Paris, chiefly on behalf of the Berlin International Exhibition of Fine Arts; many French works promised, afterwards withdrawn, through popular opposition, chiefly of the Boulangists and others 18—27 Feb. ,,
Financial panic in Paris, through embarrassment of the Société des Dépôts et Comptes Courants, relieved by the Bank of France and others 12 March, ,,
Death of prince Napoleon, son of Jerome (see *Bonaparte*) . . . . 17 March, ,,
Annual banquet of the Republican Association at the Elysée . . . . . . 21 March, ,,
Census of the population taken . . . 12 April, ,,
"Labour day" generally quiet; some excitement at Paris—dynamite explosion, little damage; fighting at Lyons, Marseilles and other places 1 May, ,,
Riots at Fourmies (Nord) suppressed by the military; 14 persons killed and about 40 wounded 1 May, ,,
Many strikes in the department of the Nord, about 6 May, ,,
National fête celebrated . . . . . 14 July, ,,
A protectionist customs tariff adopted by the chamber (385—111) . . . . 18 July, ,,
A French naval squadron under admiral Gervais warmly received at Cronstadt . . . 23 July, ,,
Visited by the Czar, 25 July. The French officers received at St. Petersburg, 28 July. The fleet leaves Cronstadt, 4 Aug. The fleet (*Marengo* flagship, with Admiral Gervais), 6 other vessels, and 2 torpedo boats arrive in Osborne Bay, near Portsmouth, 5.30 P.M., 19 Aug. Admiral Gervais and officers presented to the queen at Osborne, and dined with her, 20 Aug The fleet inspected by the queen; admiral Gervais and officers dine with admiral the earl of Clanwilliam and officers at Portsmouth . . . . . . 21 Aug. 1891
Dinner with the duke of Connaught, 24 Aug.; departure of the fleet . . . . 26 Aug. ,,
Death of ex-president M. Jules Grévy, aged about 84 9 Sept. ,,
Suicide of gen. Boulanger in a cemetery near Brussels* . . . . . . 30 Sept. ,,
M. de Giers, the Russian foreign minister, visits M. Carnot, M. de Freycinet, and M. Ribot . 20, 21 Nov. ,,
Death of Robert, earl of Lytton, British ambassador, much regretted, at Paris . 24 Nov. ,,
Xavier Gouthe Soulard, archbishop of Aix, sentenced to a fine of 3,000 francs, for writing an insulting protest against a circular of M. Fallières the minister of public worship, respecting pilgrimages . . . . 24 Nov. ,,
New customs bill issued; it authorised the government to prolong or modify the treaties expiring 15 Feb. 1892 . . . . 3 Dec. ,,
M. de Freycinet takes his seat as a member of the French Academy . . . . . 10 Dec. ,,
Stormy debate in the chamber on church and state; the government support the concordat (*which see*); majority for government (243—223). 11–13 Dec. ,,
The marquis of Dufferin and Ava appointed British ambassador at Paris, announced . 12 Dec. ,,
Death of Mons. Freppel, bishop of Angers, powerful champion of the French church . 22 Dec. ,,
Walter Bedwell and John S. Cooper convicted of acting as British spies in relation to the arsenal at St. Etienne; sentenced to fine and imprisonment . . . . 26 Dec. ,,
The new tariff bill passed by the senate . 26 Dec. ,,
Best vintage since 1884; reported . . . Jan. 1892
M. Constans, a minister, having been attacked by M. Laur, a Boulangist deputy, strikes him as he leaves the tribune; his apology accepted by the chamber . . . . 19 Jan. ,,
The new "minimum" tariff comes into operation with Great Britain and some other powers, 1 Feb.; the "maximum" tariff to be enforced in Spain, Portugal, Italy, Roumania, and the United States Feb. ,,
The De Freycinet cabinet defeated in a debate on the Associations bill (relating to church and state), resign . . . . 18 Feb. ,,
Encyclical of the pope to the French bishops enjoining submission to the government of the republic . . . . 16 Feb. ,,
76 French bishops accept the declaration of cardinal Lavigerie and four other cardinals, Dec. 1890, recognizing the republic 26 Jan—19 Feb. ,,
MM. Rouvier and Bourgeois successively fail to form a ministry . . . . . 23–26 Feb. ,,
New ministry; M. Loubet (premier and minister of interior), M. de Freycinet (war), M. Ribot (foreign affairs), M. Rouvier (finance), M. Bourgeois (public instruction), M. Ricard (justice and public worship), M. Cavaignac (marine), M. Develle (agriculture), M. Jules Roche (commerce), M. Viette (public works) . . . 28 Feb. ,,
The ministerial declaration accepted by the chamber (341 to 91) . . . . . . 3 March, ,,
Death of Etienne Arago, statesman and dramatist (brother of the astronomer), aged 90 . 7 March, ,,
Dynamite explosions in the Boulevard St. Germain, in Paris, attributed to the anarchists 11 March *et seq.* ,,
Explosion at the Lobau barracks, buildings injured, 15 March, ,,
Bill introduced to punish the authors of explosions with death, 15 March; several arrests 17 March, ,,
The marquis of Dufferin received as ambassador by president Carnot . . . . . 21 March, ,,
A bomb factory in Paris discovered, 23 March; other explosions at the houses of legal officials in Rue de Clichy, 6 injured . . 27 March, ,,
Ravachol, otherwise Léon Léger (real name said to be Francis Königstein), a notorious anarchist,

* Georges Ernest J. M. Boulanger, born at Rennes, 29 April, 1837; entered the army 1856; served with distinction in Algeria, Italy, Cochin China, and at Paris, 1870–1; brigader-general, 1880; sent on a mission to America, 1881; general of division at Tunis, 1884; minister of war, 7 Jan. 1886 (*see above*), 1887–1891.

arrested in the Café Véry in the Boulevard Magenta, through the agency of Lhérot, a waiter, and M. Véry . . . . . . 30 March, 1892
The anti-dynamite bill passed by the senate, 31 March, ,,
Louis Anastey, who murdered his benefactress, Madame Dellard, mother of baron Dellard, at Paris, 4 Dec. 1891, executed . . 9 April, ,,
The chamber votes 300,000,000 francs for an expedition against Dahomey . . . . 11 April, ,,
Order for the prosecution of the archbishop of Avignon and the bishops of Nîmes, Montpellier, Valence, and Viviers, for their concerted addresses to the Catholic electors in opposition to the state, about 22 April, ,,
Many anarchists arrested at Paris, Lyons, and other places, 51 in Paris, reported . . 22 April, ,,
The restaurant of M. Véry wrecked by explosion: he and 4 others seriously wounded (MM. Véry and Hamonod died, May) . . 25 April, ,,
Trial of anarchists; Ravachol and Simon sentenced to penal servitude for life, 3 others acquitted, 26, 27 April, ,,
"Labour day" at Paris, &c., very orderly through precautions . . . . . . 1 May, ,,
The stipends of several bishops stopped on account of their pastorals, &c. . . . . May, ,,
Many suspected anarchists released 7 May, *et seq.* ,,
Public funeral of M. Véry; the premier, M. Loubet, present . . . . . . 13 May, ,,
The proceedings of the government approved by the chamber . . . . . . 21 May, ,,
Tour of president Carnot; present at the Nancy fêtes . . . . 5, 6 June, ,,
The duc de la Rochefoucauld's declaration of submission to the pope in matters of the faith, but not in state affairs, signed by 40 of the 70 royalist deputies . . . . 9 June, ,,
Ravachol, on his confession of robbing and murdering Jean Rivollier, an aged hermit at Varizelle, sentenced to death at Montbrison, 23 June; executed . . . . 11 July, ,,
M. Godefroy Cavaignac, minister of marine, resigns (censured in relation to Dahomey); succeeded by M. Burdeau . . . . . . 11 July, ,,
M. Ressmann, new Italian ambassador, received by the president . . . . . 11 July, ,,
Government protest against the presence of Protestant missionaries in Algeria, about . 5 July, ,,
Decree signed for the Universal exhibition, 5 May –31 Oct. 1900 . . . . . . 13 July, ,,
Naval manœuvres near Brest, &c. 24 July, *et seq.* ,,
Faugoux and three other anarchists, sentenced to penal servitude (for 20, 10, 6, 5 years) for stealing dynamite . . . . 28 July, ,,
Disputes between the coal mining company at Carmaux, in the department of Tarn, and their workmen respecting the dismissal of M. Calvignac, a socialist workman and secretary of the miners' union, who had been elected mayor, and consequently neglected his work; a general strike with much rioting ensues, Aug.–Sept.; great meeting at Paris to support the strike 7 Sept.; strikers supported by deputies of the chamber, Sept.; government intervention ineffectual . . . . 11, 12 Oct. ,,
Resignation of the marquis de Solages, manager of the Carmaux mines, reported . . 14 Oct. ,,
Attack on the government, respecting Carmaux, in the chamber, defeated, 18 Oct.; arbitration accepted, 21 Oct.; M. Loubet, the premier, the arbitrator, decides that M. Calvignac should be reinstated as a workman with leave of absence while mayor; that all the strikers, except those in prison for violence, should be taken back, and that the manager, M. Humblot, should be reinstated, 26 Oct.; this award rejected by the miners, 26–27 Oct.; work resumed by advice 3 Nov. ,,
Centenary of the proclamation of the first republic celebrated by the people at Paris, Lyons, and other cities . . . . . . 22 Sept. ,,
Death of Ernest Renan, scholar and philosopher, aged 69, 2 Oct.; state funeral . . 7 Oct. ,,
Bill regulating the labour of women and children in factories (first introduced in 1879, and much discussed), passed . . . . . 29 Oct. ,,
A metal boiler containing dynamite found near the door of the offices of the Carmaux mining company, in the Avenue de l'Opéra, Paris: when conveyed by the police to an adjoining station, explodes, killing 6 persons, 8 Nov.; M. Loubet, the premier, speaks at their funeral . 11 Nov. 1892
Abolition of duty on wine, beer, cider, and other "hygienic" drinks, and an increase of the spirit duties adopted by the chamber [bill passed, 21 Dec. 1892; by the senate, 26 June, 1893] . 15 Nov. ,,
Death of gen. de Failly, aged 81, about . 15 Nov. ,,
Jean Pierre François, anarchist (a companion of Ravachol), in London, extradited to Paris 16 Nov. ,,
Press bill to check anarchical publications: confidence in the ministry voted (329–228), 18 Nov.; the bill much softened, passed . . 19 Nov. ,,
Prosecution of the directors of the Panama canal company, *which see* . . . 25 Nov. *et seq.* ,,
Death of cardinal Lavigerie, aged 67, near Algiers, 26 Nov. ,,
The Loubet ministry, opposing the exhumation of Baron Jacques Reinach, late director of the Panama company, defeated in the chamber (293–195), resigns . . . . . . 28 Nov. ,,
The ministry reconstituted by M. Ribot, 5 Dec.; declaration and vote of confidence (307–104), 8 Dec. ,,
The Panama committee invested with judicial powers . . . . 9 Dec. ,,
The body of baron Jacques Reinach exhumed for autopsy at Nivillers, 11 Dec.; natural death reported . . . . 28 Dec. ,,
M. John Lemoinne, journalist, long connected with the *Journal des Débats*, aged 77, dies 15 Dec. ,,
Duel between M. Déroulède and M. Clémenceau, no injury . . . . 22 Dec. ,,
Tariff war with Switzerland, *which see*, 1 Jan. *et seq.* 1893
Reconstruction of the ministry by M. Ribot (M. de Freycinet not included) . . . 11 Jan. ,,
The Socialist union, *which see*, started at Paris 14 Jan. ,,
The new president, M. Casimir-Perier, opens the chamber . . . . 12 Jan. ,,
Foreign journalists ordered to be expelled for writing against the Russian ambassador, &c. mid-Jan. ,,
Centenary of the execution of Louis XVI. celebrated by Royalists and Jacobins . . . 21 Jan. ,,
Bill to protect savings banks against political alarms, passed . . . . . 3 Feb. ,,
M. Cavaignac's motion for sustaining prosecution of official corruption, adopted by the chamber (446 (?)–3) . . . . 8 Feb. ,,
Treaty for reciprocal trade with Canada, signed at Paris . . . . 9 Feb. ,,
Attack on the ministry; confidence voted (315–186) 16 Feb. ,,
A Panama procession at the carnival at Basle, 14 Feb.; gives offence in France, 21 Feb.; apology made about . . . . 22 Feb. ,,
M. Jules Ferry elected president of the senate 24 Feb.; died, aged nearly 61, 17 March; state funeral . . . . 22 March, ,,
Death of H. A. Taine, philosopher and historian, aged 64 . . . . 5 March, ,,
Great public excitement at the disclosures 10, 11 March; the ministry supported by the chamber and senate (see under *Panama*) . 13, 14 March, ,,
Farewell dinner to M. Waddington at the Mansion house, London, 4 March; his wife receives a memorial gold pendant with gems, 17 March; they leave England . . . . . 8 May, ,,
M. Challemel-Lacour elected president of the senate, 27 March, ,,
Manifesto of the comte de Paris attacking the Republic in relation to the Panama affairs, 23 March, ,,
Herr Otto Brandes, a German journalist, expelled for libelling Ernest Carnot; his family insulted by a mob (for which the government apologised), 28 March, ,,
Resignation of the Ribot ministry through amendments of the budget . . . . 30 March, ,,
M. Méline fails to form a cabinet . . 1, 2 April ,,
New ministry; premier and minister of interior, M. Dupuy; foreign affairs, M. Develle; finance, M. Peytral; commerce, M. Terrier; education, M. Poincaré; justice, M. Guérin; agriculture, M. Viger; public works, M. Viette; war, gen. Loizillon; marine, adm. Rieunier; colonies, M. Delcassé . . . . 3 April ,,

M. Meissonier presents many of his paintings by his will to the state, reported . . April 1893
Arton, an anarchist, is sentenced to 20 years' hard labour and 400,000 francs fine, for complicity in frauds and dynamite explosions . 23 May, ,,
Unveiling of the statue of Théophraste Renaudot, the first French journalist, editor of the *Gazette de France*, 30 May, 1631 (still publishing), at Paris . . . . 4 June, ,,
Statue of D. F. Arago, philosopher, at Paris, unveiled . . . . 11 June, ,,
Severe drought, the crops suffer . . June, ,,
M. Millevoye, a Boulangist, accuses M. Clémenceau and others of complicity in the publication in the *Cocarde* of forged documents alleged to have been stolen from the British embassy; after a stormy debate, the chamber passes to the order of the day (389–4), 22 June; Norton, for forgery, sentenced to 3 years' imprisonment; Ducret to 1 year . . . . 5, 6, Aug. ,,
M. Albert Decrais appointed ambassador at St. James's . . . . . end of June, ,,
Death of Duc d'Uzés, chief of an expedition in Portuguese Congo, reported . . 2 July, ,,
M. Henri Guy de Maupassant, eminent novelist, dies . . . . 6 July, ,,
Dispute with Siam (*which see*) . . June, July, ,,
The national fête passes quietly . . 13 July, ,,
Letter from the pope to the catholics, severely censuring malcontents, 3 Aug.; published, 11 Aug. ,,
Much suffering through wave of intense heat, mid-Aug. ,,
Conflicts between French and Italian salt-workers at Aigues-Mortes; see *Italy*, 16 Aug. *et seq.*
Four French warships launched, at St. Nazaire, Nantes, Brest, Cherbourg . . end of Aug. ,,
Destructive forest fires in the country round Mont de Marsan (Landes) . . . . 23–28 Aug. ,,
General election; for government, 292; socialists, 187; "Rallied" (to republicanism), 35; monarchists, 58; M. Clémenceau and M. Floquet rejected; many socialists, M. Réné Goblet, leader, elected for Paris . . . . . 20 Aug.–3 Sept. ,,
The coal-miners in the Pas de Calais, &c., demand increase of wages; leads to a strike of about 42,000 men . . . . 18 Sept. ,,
Strike ends by submission . . . . 4 Nov. ,,
Visit of the Russian fleet to Toulon, &c.; see *Russia* . . . . . . 13–29 Oct. ,,
Death of marshal MacMahon, aged 85 (honourable and brave), 17 Oct.; state funeral at the Invalides; large attendance of government officials, foreign ministers and troops . Sunday, 22 Oct. ,,
The *Jauréguiberry*, battle-ship, launched at Toulon, 27 Oct. ,,
Death of M. Gounod, musical composer, 18 Oct.; state funeral . . . . . . 27 Oct. ,,
Death of M. Tirard, ex-premier, aged about 66, 4 Nov. ,,
The new chamber opens . . . . 14 Nov. ,,
Difference between M. Carnot and the ministry; M. Dupuy resigns, after a crisis . 26 Nov. ,,
New ministry:—(premier and foreign office) M. Casimir-Perier, (finance) M. Burdeau, (interior) M. Raynal, (education and public worship) M. Spuller, (justice) M. Antonin Dubost, (war) gen. Mercier, (marine) vice-adm. Lefevre, (public works) M. Jonnart, (commerce) M. Marty, (agriculture) M. Viger . . . . 3 Dec. ,,
M. Dupuy elected president of the chamber, 5 Dec. ,,
A bomb thrown at the president in the French chamber during the debate, by Auguste Vaillant, an anarchist, who was apprehended and confessed; many injured, order maintained, 9 Dec. ,,
A restrictive press law in relation to anarchists passed by the chamber (413–63) . . 11 Dec. ,,
Sympathetic messages from the British and other governments received by M. Dupuy 12 Dec. *et seq.* ,,
The "Rallied" agree to call themselves "Independent republicans" . . about 13 Dec. ,,
Nearly 2,000 domiciliary visits on anarchists in Paris and provinces; many arrests and seizure of explosives . . . . . . 1 Jan. *et seq.* 1894
Vaillant, when sentenced to death, cried out, "Vive l'Anarchie," 10 Jan.: executed 4 Feb. ,,

Death of M. Wm. Henry Waddington, aged 67, 13 Jan. 1894
Bill for the conversion of the $4\frac{1}{2}$ per cent. rentes to $3\frac{1}{2}$ per cent. passed by the senate . . 17 Jan. ,,
M. Maurice Charnay sentenced to 6 years' imprisonment for publishing "Le catéchisme du soldat," inciting to mutiny . . . 27 Jan. ,,
Chanzy, armoured cruiser, launched at Bordeaux 24 Jan. ,,
Revue de Paris first publication; editors, MM. Ganderax Long and Darmesteter . . 2 Feb. ,,
Emile Henry, an anarchist, aged 20, throws a bomb into the café of the Terminus hotel; many injured, 2 deaths . . . . . . 12 Feb. ,,
Another bomb explosion in a private house; several injured, and a woman killed . 19 Feb. ,,
Increased pursuit and arrests of anarchists Feb., March, ,,
M. Jean Grave sentenced to 2 years' imprisonment and a fine, for writing "La société mourante" and "l'Anarchie" . . . . . 24 Feb. ,,
Duty on corn, 7 f. per quintal, passed by the senate . . . . 27 Feb. ,,
Joseph Pauwels killed by his own bomb at the Madeleine . . . . . . 15 March, ,,
The establishment of a colonial ministry passed by the senate (225–32) . . . . 19 March, ,,
M. Boulanger created colonial minister, 21 March, ,,
An explosion of a bomb at the café Foyot in Paris; several persons injured . . . . 4 April, ,,
Budget introduced; deficit, 139,000,000f., met by conversion of the debt, increased taxation, &c. 16 April, ,,
Emile Henry, anarchist (*see above*, 12 *Feb.*) convicted, 28 April; executed . . . 21 May, ,,
Navy estimates, 277,000,000 (issued), increase, 10,000,000 . . . . . . 30 April, ,,
Fêtes in honour of Joan of Arc at Orleans, Marseilles, &c. . . . . . . 6–8 May, ,,
Defeat of the ministry in the chamber by the radicals in relation to the restraining of workmen on state railways from attending a congress (251—217); resigned . . . . 23 May, ,,
New ministry: premier, interior, and public worship, M. Dupuy; justice, M. Guérin; finance, M. Poincaré; education, M. J. Leygues; war, gen. Mercier; marine, M. Felix Faure; colonies, M. Delcassé; public works, M. Barthou; commerce, M. Lourties; agriculture, M. Viger; foreign, M. Hanotaux . . . . 29 May, ,,
The ministry declare a moderate policy - 31 May ,,
M. Casimir-Perier elected president of the chamber 2 June ,,
Discussion in the chamber on the Anglo-Belgian treaty . . . . 7 June ,,
1,900,000f. voted by the senate for African reinforcements . . . . 12 June, ,,
President Carnot warmly received at Lyons; stabbed in his carriage on his way to the theatre by Caserio Santo Hieronymo, 9.30 p.m., 24 June; dies at 12.45 a.m. . . . . . . 25 June, ,,
Profound emotion in the senate and the chamber at the announcement . . . . 26 June, ,,
Deep expressions of sympathy with the French government and nation from queen Victoria, the prince of Wales, and the parliament; from the president of the United States, and the European powers, transmitted . . . 25 June *et seq.* ,,
M. Casimir-Perier, president of the chamber, elected president of the republic by the senate and chamber . . . . 27 June, ,,
National state funeral of M. Carnot at the Panthéon after service at Notre Dame. Present: president Casimir-Perier, the ministry, diplomatic body, the legislature, &c.; memorial services held in the European capitals . . . . 1 July, ,,
Requiem and mass at the French chapel, Leicester-square; the prince of Wales, the Dukes of York, Saxe-Coburg, and Cambridge, the ministry and the diplomatic body, cardinal Vaughan and others, present . . . . . . 2 July, ,,
M. Dupuy and his cabinet agree to remain in office 1 July; gazetted . . . . . 2 July, ,,
M. Burdeau elected president of the chamber 5 July, ,,
374 pardons granted by president Casimir-Perier July, ,,

New anti-anarchist bill passed by the chamber, 26 July; by the senate . . . 27 July, 1894
Carnot ironclad launched at Toulon . 12 July, ,,
Joseph Constant Meunier arrested in London; extradited to Paris, 11 May; sentenced to 20 years penal servitude for complicity in blowing up the Véry restaurant, 25 April, 1892, &c. 27 July, ,,
Chamber prorogued . . . . . 28 July, ,,
Socialist-Radical manifesto . . 30 July, ,,
Caserio condemned, 3 Aug.; executed at Lyons 16 Aug. ,,
Three anarchists sentenced to imprisonment; 22 acquitted . . . . . 11 Aug. ,,
Execution of the abbé Bruneau at Laval for the murder of the abbé Fricot . . . 30 Aug. ,,
Death of the comte de Paris at Stowe, Bucks 8 Sept. ,,
Fire in the suburbs and adjoining forest near Cannes . . . . . . 10–12 Sept. ,,
Baron de Courcel succeeds M. Decrais as ambassador in London . . . 30 Sept. ,,
65,000,000f. voted, &c., for the Madagascar expedition (26 Nov.). by the senate . 6 Dec. ,,
Ferdinand de Lesseps, born 19 Nov., 1805; died 7 Dec. ,,
Death of M. Auguste Burdeau; aged 42; president of the chamber of deputies, of lowly origin, self-educated, an eminent professor, able statesman and a lover of England, 12 Dec.; state funeral at Paris . . . . 16 Dec. ,,
M. Brisson elected president of the chamber 18 Dec. ,,
Dreyfus Case (*which see*), 1894–1899. Capt. Alfred Dreyfus arrested 14 Oct (trial within closed doors), convicted of delivering to a foreign power in 1894 documents connected with the defence of France; sentenced to perpetual imprisonment in a fortress . . . 23 Dec. ,,
Resignation of M. Dupuy's ministry through an adverse vote in the chamber . . 14 Jan. 1895
Resignation of president Casimir-Perier . 15 Jan. ,,
In his letter to the senate and deputies he complains of the opposition to law and order, and "campaign of slander and insult."
His resignation generally censured . 16 Jan. ,,
M. Felix Faure, minister of marine in the Dupuy cabinet, long deputy for Havre, a firm moderate; elected president of the republic by 430 votes in the convention, against 361 for M. Brisson 17 Jan. ,,
M. Bourgeois fails to form a "concentration" cabinet . . . . . . 24 Jan. ,,
A ministry formed by M. Ribot (finance); (interior) M. Leygues; (justice) M. Trarieux; (foreign affairs) M. Hanotaux; (war) gen. Zurlinden; (marine) M. Combes; (public instruction) M. Poincaré; (public works) M. Dupuy-Dutemps; (commerce) M. André Lebon; (agriculture) M. Gadaud; (colonies) M. Chautemps . 26 Jan. ,,
The amnesty bill passed by the chamber . 28 Jan. ,,
Death of marshal Canrobert, aged 86; much respected in England; originally a private; of great courage; served in Algeria, Italy, Crimea, and the Franco-Prussian war, 28 Jan.; buried in the Invalides . . . . . 3 Feb. ,,
Return of Henri Rochefort; six years an exile 3 Feb. ,,
Count Tornielli, Italian ambassador, well received at Paris . . . . . . 18 Feb. ,,
M. Hippolyte Percher, "Harry Alis," killed in a duel near Paris by M. le Chatelier, see *Egypt* 1 March, ,,
The army estimates voted . . . 9 March, ,,
M. Hanotaux's moderate speech in the senate respecting English influence in Africa . 5 April, ,,
Budget amended by the senate passed 13 April, ,,
Tour of president Faure; warmly received on board H.M.S. *Australia*, 19 April; friendly demonstrations at Havre . . . 19, 20 April, ,,
Bursting of a dam on the Eastern canal at Bousey in the Vosges; two villages, and bridges swept away, 110 deaths; estimated damage above 50,000,000f. . . . . . 27 April, ,,
Exhibition of memorials and relics of the revolution and empire opened at Paris. . 30 April, ,,
The abbé Paul de Broglie, a benevolent priest, brother of the duc de Broglie, murdered in Paris by Maxence Amelot, a lunatic . . 11 May, ,,

Public expenditure reduced by 12,000,000f., 31 May, 1895
Pres. Faure decorated with the order of St. Andrew by order of the czar . . . . 17 June, ,,
An Egyptian committee formed, see *Egypt*, 18 June, ,,
Naval manœuvres at Toulon . . 1 July *et seq.* ,,
Duties on hygienic drinks dropped, on alcohol increased . . . . 6 July, ,,
Masséna, first-class ironclad, launched at St. Nazaire . . . . 24 July, ,,
Meetings of the clergy against the monastic tax, declared illegal . . . . . . July ,,
Explosive letter sent to baron Alphonse de Rothschild; opened by his confidential clerk, M. Jodkowitz, at the bank in Paris, who was much injured, 24 Aug.; fruitless arrests . 26 Aug. ,,
Strike in the works of the Carmaux company's glassworks, July; lock-out, 6 Aug.; works reopened to free hands, 26 Aug.; arbitration refused by M. Rességuier, director of the firm, 4 Nov.; end of strike by surrender . 22 Nov. ,,
A bomb, which did not explode, thrown at the Rothschild bank at Paris by Léon Bouteilhe, an anarchist, 5 Sept.; he is sentenced to 3 years' imprisonment . . . . . . 26 Sept. ,,
Visit of the lord mayor to Paris, 6 Sept.; received by president Faure . . . 7–16 Sept. ,,
M. Louis Pasteur, chemist, physicist, and biologist, born 27 Dec. 1822; died 28 Sept.; state funeral . . . . 5 Oct. ,,
Charlemagne, battleship, launched at Brest, 12 Oct. ,,
Treaty of peace with the Hovas, see *Madagascar* 1 Oct. ,,
M. Edmond Magnier, senator of the Var department, sentenced to one year's imprisonment for corrupt official practices . . . 19 Oct. ,,
Centenary of the establishment of the Institute of France; meeting of the 5 academies at the Sorbonne; foreign savants present . 24 Oct. ,,
Debate on the Carmaux strike in the chamber; government majority . . . 24–26 Oct. ,,
Resignation of the Ribot ministry through a vote of censure relating to a railway scandal (311–210) 28 Oct. ,,
The marquis de Nayve tried for the murder of his wife's illegitimate son, Hyppolyte Menaldo, aged 14 (in 1885), 28 Oct.; acquitted . . 4 Nov. ,,
Huahine and Bolabola, two islands in the S. Pacific, annexed by France . . . . . Oct. ,,
New cabinet (radical but pacific): premier and minister of interior, M. Bourgeois; finance, M. Doumer; justice, M. Ricard; war, M. Cavaignac; marine, M. Lockroy; public instruction, M. Combes; public works, M. Guyot-Dessaigne; commerce, M. Mesureur; colonies, M. Paul Guieysse; foreign affairs, M. Berthelot; agriculture, M. Vigo . . . . . . 31 Oct. ,,
A panic on the Bourse in Paris, due to speculation, averted by M. M. Rothschild and others, 9 Nov. ,,
Emile Arton, *alias* Baron, sentenced (in absence) to 20 years' penal servitude in connection with the Panama scandals, &c.; arrested in London, 16 Nov.; extradition ordered, 6 Dec.; sentenced to six years' imprisonment and fine, 10 July, 1896; sentence quashed on technical grounds on appeal, 6 Aug.; sentenced to 8 years' imprisonment, 6 Nov. 1896.
M. Barthélemy Saint-Hilaire, statesman, philosopher and savant, born 19 Aug. 1805; died, 24 Nov. ,,
M. Alexandre Dumas (fils), dramatist and novelist, born 29 July, 1824; died . . . 27 Nov. ,,
A moderate budget finally passed . . 28 Dec. ,,
Publication of No. 1 of the "Nineteen Hundred," a monthly journal in English promoting the coming exhibition of 1900 . . . . 1 Jan. 1896
Meeting of the senate and chamber . 14 Jan. ,,
M. Loubet elected president of the senate 16 Jan. ,,
M. Floquet born 1828; died . . . 18 Jan. ,,
The cabinet censured by a vote of the senate for an illegality of M. Ricard, 11 Feb.; compromise by the chamber . . . . . 13 Feb. ,,
M. Ambroise Thomas, musical composer, born 5 Aug. 1811; died 12 Feb. 1896. See *Opera*.
Debate in the chamber, M. Bourgeois supports M. Ricard; confidence in the ministry (309—185) voted . . . . 20 Feb. ,,
The senate, by a firm declaration, maintains its rights and withdraws from the conflict 21 Feb. ,,

The government income-tax replacing the house-tax passed by the chamber (5 days debate) (286—270) . . . . . . 26 March, 1896
Resignation of M. Berthelot; duties assumed by M. Bourgeois, 29 March; M. Sarrien, minister of interior, 30 March; confidence in the foreign policy voted in the chamber . . . 2 April, ,,
The senate votes no confidence in the ministry (who determine to retain office), 3 April; and refuses the vote on the Madagascar credits to the present ministry (171—90) . . . 21 April, ,,
M. Jean Baptiste Léon Say, eminent political economist, born 1826; died 22 April; public funeral . . . . 23 April, ,,
M. Bourgeois and his ministry resign with a protest, 23 April; the senate adopts the Madagascar credits . . . . . . 24 April, ,,
New cabinet (moderate): premier and minister of agriculture, M. Méline; justice, M. Darlan; foreign affairs, M. Hanotaux; interior, M. Barthou; finance, M. Georges Cochery; war, gen. Billot; marine, adm. Besnard; public instruction, M. A. Rambaud (resigned), M. Darlan, Sept.; commerce, M. Henri Boucher; colonies, M. André Lebon; public works, M. Turrel 29 April, ,,
Proposed revision of the constitution rejected by the chamber and senate . . . . 30 April, ,,
Differences between the duke of Orleans and the royalist committee, which disapproves of his proposed candidature for a seat in the chamber; his letter, *Times* . . . . . 19 May, ,,
Public demonstrations in honour of the czar's coronation . . . . 26, 27 May, ,,
Bill for the annexation of Madagascar and its dependent islands proposed by M. Hanotaux 30 May, ,,
Lord Dufferin's brilliant fête to the government, 3 June; leaves France . . . 29 June, ,,
Death of M. Jules Simon, philosopher and philanthropist, aged 82, 8 June; state funeral 13 June, ,,
The chamber prorogued . . . . . 11 July, ,,
National fête; the president fired at by a lunatic 14 July, ,,
Monument to pres. Carnot at Châlons-sur-Marne unveiled . . . . 16 Aug. ,,
Sir Edmund Monson appointed British minister; about 18 August; received . . . 8 Dec. ,,
The *Ernest Bazin* new roller ship (see *Steam*), launched at St. Denis . . . . 19 Aug. ,,
The *St. Louis* battleship, launched at Lorient, 8 Sept. ,,
Gaulois battleship, launched at Brest . Oct. ,,
Great vintage, reported . . . . . Sept. ,,
State visit of the czar and czarina; he gives 100,000f. to charities; 402 criminals released; see *Russia* . . . . . . 5–9 Oct. ,,
Death of gen. Trochu, see above, 1870–1 7 Oct. ,,
The king of Greece received by M. Faure 13 Oct. ,,
Death of M. Challemel-Lacour, statesman and scholar, aged 69 . . . . . . 26 Oct. ,,
The chamber and senate meet . . . . 27 Oct. ,,
Mdme. Furtado Heine, eminent philanthropist, born 1821, died . . . . . . 10 Dec. ,,
M. Loubet opens the senate, with an address, 15 Jan. 1897
M. Brisson opens the chamber of deputies 16 Jan. ,,
Vote of confidence passed in the chamber; reinforcements sent to Crete . . . 15 March, ,,
An MS. of Louis Philippe showing his great aversion to capital punishment (consequently seldom carried out), read to the French Academy by his son, the Duc d'Aumale, 18 March; died, [and bequeathed (dated 1889) to the Institut de France, in trust for the French nation, the château Chantilly, 24 mi. N. of Paris, with its large estate, Condé museum, and valuable art collections]; see *Orleans* . . . . . 6 May, ,,
Calamitous fire: see *Paris* . . . . 4 May, ,,
M. Gerault Richard, socialist, expelled from the chamber for disorderly conduct . . 5 June, ,,
Pres. Faure invited by the czar to Russia, 27 June, ,,
M. Henri Meilhac, popular dramatist, died, aged 67 . . . . 6 July, ,,
Duel between prince Henry of Orleans and the count of Turin; see *Italy* . . . 15 Aug. ,,
Pres. Faure received by the czar at Cronstadt, arrives at Peterhof, 23 Aug.; leaves, 26 Aug.; returns to Paris . . . . . . 31 Aug. 1897
Franco-Russian alliance confirmed . . Aug. ,,
The sovereigns of Belgium, Servia, Bulgaria, and Siam, at Paris . . . . . 8 Oct. ,,
The chambers reassemble . . . . 19 Oct. ,,
Excitement about the case of capt. Dreyfus (see *above*, Dec. 1894)
Government inquiry instituted . . . 16 Nov. ,,
M. Darlan, minister of justice, resigns, in consequence of a qualified vote of censure, 1 Dec.; succeeded by M. Millard . . . 2 Dec. ,,
Duties on wine, beer, and cider reduced 3 Dec. ,,
Debates in the chamber on the Dreyfus affair, 4, 7 Dec. ,,
Baron Mohrenheim, Russian ambassador, resigns, succeeded by prince Urussoff . . . Dec. ,,
Criminal investigations bill, an important reform (passed by the senate, Nov.), becomes law 10 Dec. ,,
M. Alphonse Daudet, novelist, died, aged 57, 16 Dec. ,,
Collision between two express trains, near Péage-de-Roussillon (Paris and Marseilles line), capt. Lota, professor at St. Cyr, M. Athelin and capt. Blouet killed; 15 injured . . . 24 Dec. ,,
Count Esterhazy tried by court martial for treason, 10 Jan., and acquitted . . . 11 Jan. 1898
Letter *J'accuse* to the president from M. Zola in the *Aurore*, denouncing the conviction of capt. Dreyfus on the strength of a single document which was kept secret, as illegal; and bringing charges against gens. Mercier, Billot (minister of war), and others; and asserting the Esterhazy court-martial to have knowingly acquitted a guilty man . . . . . . 13 Jan. ,,
Violent scene in the chamber on the discussion of the Dreyfus case, sitting closed . 22 Jan. ,,
Declarations of the government against further discussion in the chamber, adopted, 376–133, 24 Jan. ,,
Herr von Bulow, foreign secretary, asserts in the reichstag at Berlin, that there never had been any relations between ex-capt. Dreyfus and any German representative, 24 Jan.; Italy declares the same . . . . . . 31 Jan. ,,
Dr. Pean, eminent surgeon, founder of the International hospital, born, 1830, died . 29 Jan. ,,
M. Zola and M. Perreux (publisher of the *Aurore*), 15 days' trial, for defamation, with reference to the Esterhazy court-martial (see *above*, 13 Jan.); sentence, *maximum*: M. Zola, 1 year, and M. Perreux, 4 months' imprisonment, and 3,000f. fine each (*Times*, 24 Feb. 1898) . . 7–23 Feb. ,,
Interpellation in the chamber, government largely supported; "Disciplinary measures" introduced by M. Méline 24 Feb.; Col. Picquart and others punished for intervention . . . 25 Feb. ,,
Flachat, French liner, lost 16 Feb.; see *Wrecks* footnote; *La Bourgogne*, French liner, lost, 4 July, ,,
Prince Urussoff, Russian ambassador, received by the president . . . . . . 18 Feb. ,,
Lease of a bay S.E. coast, &c., granted by China 5 April; Kwang-chan-wan occupied . 22 April, ,,
M. Jules Marco, eminent geologist and explorer, died, aged 74 . . . . . . 18 April, ,,
General elections; government *net* majority (4), 8 May; the chamber meets 1 June; M. Méline resigns 15 June; M. Brisson forms a cabinet 28 June; the chambers meet . . 30 June, ,,
Anglo-French agreement (*which see*) . 14 June, ,,
Legal proceedings respecting M. Zola, 2 April; he escapes to England . . . . 18 July, ,,
Resignation of M. Méline's ministry, 15 June; several failures to form a cabinet; new ministry: premier and minister of the interior, M. Brisson; foreign affairs, M. Delcassé; finance, M. Peytral; justice, M. Sarrien; education, M. Léon Bourgeois; war, M. Cavaignac; marine, M. Lockroy; colonies, M. Trouillot; commerce, M. Maruéjouls; agriculture, M. Viger; public works, M. Tillaye . . . . 28 June, ,,
Col. Picquart arrested for disclosing state papers, 13 July; his trial postponed . . 21 Sept. ,,
"A History of the Dreyfus Case," by capt. Paul Marin, issued . . . . . . July, ,,
Abyssinian envoys, with a letter and presents to pres. Faure, received by him at Paris . 8 July, ,,
Railway accident near Lisieux, Normandy, 10 deaths . . . . 14 Aug. ,,

Lieut.-col. Henry, chief of the *Espionnage* department, after confessing to forgery of documents against Dreyfus, is arrested and commits suicide in prison . . . . 31 Aug. 1898
Proposed revision of the Dreyfus case agreed to; M. Cavaignac, minister of war, resigns, 3 Sept.; succeeded by gen. Zurlinden, 5 Sept.; he and M. Tillaye, both against revision of the Dreyfus case, resign, succeeded by gen. Chanoine (war) and M. Godin (public works), 17 Sept.; revision commission meets, 21 Sept. *et seq.*; divided in opinion; the Dreyfus case referred to the Cour de Cassation . . . . . . 27 Sept. ,,
Military manœuvres, grand review at Moulins pres. Faure and the duke of Connaught present, 16 Sept. ,,
The ministry, defeated by the anti-revisionists, resigns, 25 Oct.; new *conciliation* ministry: premier and minister of interior, M. Dupuy; foreign, M. Delcassé; finance, M. Peytral; war, M. de Freycinet; marine, M. Lockroy 31 Oct. ,,
For *Fashoda* and *Dreyfus Case*, see separate articles.
New commercial treaty with Italy, signed, 21 Nov. ,,
Bill allowing aid of counsel to accused in courts-martials passed the senate, 1 Dec. (by the chamber, 8 June, 1899); one abolishing public executions, adopted by the senate . 5 Dec. ,,
Demonstration in Paris against col. Picquart and in honour of the army, a stormy scene in the chamber, 12 Dec.; chambers closed . 24 Dec. ,,
"League de la Patrie Française" (anti-revision of the Dreyfus case) founded; manifesto issued, 1 Jan.; *L'Union Nationale*, opposition league, started . . . . Jan. 1899
M. Edouard Hervé, journalist, founder of the *Soleil* 1873, died, aged 64 . . . 4 Jan. ,,
The chambers opened, M. Deschanel elected president of the deputies; M. Loubet re-elected president in the senate . . . 10, 12 Jan. ,,
M. Adolphe Philippe Dennery, dramatist, born 17 June, 1811; bequeaths his Paris house and collections to the nation . . . . Jan. ,,
French maritime league founded . . . Jan. ,,
Comte de Chambrun, benefactor, founder of the "Musée Social," 1894, dies, aged 78 . 7 Feb. ,,
Anarchist disorder in Paris suppressed . 10 Feb. ,,
Criminal procedure bill passed by the chamber, 332–216 . . . . 10 Feb. ,,
Sudden death of pres. Faure, 16 Feb; public funeral, oration by M. Dupuy at Père Lachaise; MM. Déroulède (deputy) and Marcel-Habert arrested for inciting gen. Roget to a *coup d'état* (18 Feb.), 23 Feb. (acquitted, 31 May); M. Emile Loubet elected president of the republic at Versailles by 483 votes against 279 for M. Méline, 18 Feb. ,,
M. Méline elected president of the chamber, 25 Feb. ,,
M. Fallières of the senate . . . . 3 March, ,,
Domiciliary visits to royalist houses, &c., 25–28 Feb.; treasonable leagues dissolved and prosecuted . . . . . . March–April, ,,
Army estimates and budget passed by the chamber, 13 March, ,,
Comte de Chaudordy, diplomatist, born 1826, dies, 26 March, ,,
M. Pailleron, eminent dramatist (*Le Monde où l'on s'ennuie*, 1881), &c., born, 17 Sept. 1834; died about . . . . 20 April, ,,
Anglo-French convention (*which see*) signed in London, 21 March (1899), ratified . 30 May, ,,
M. de Freycinet (minister of war), after a stormy debate in the chamber, resigns, 5 May; succeeded by M. Krantz; M. Monestier taking office of public works . . . . . . 6 May, ,,
M. Francisque Sarcey, eminent dramatic critic, &c., born 1828, died 16 May; M. Henri Becque, dramatist and journalist (*Les Corbeaux*, *La Parisienne*, *L'Enfant Prodigue*, &c.), born, 9 April, 1837; died . . . . . . May, ,,
Major Marchand and force from Fashoda (*which see*) warmly received at Toulon; Marseilles, 30, 31 May; and Paris . . . . . . 1 June, ,,
Anti-Dreyfus demonstration at the Auteuil races; pres. Loubet assaulted, ringleaders arrested, 4 June, ,,
Stormy debate in the chamber; M. Largentaye, a royalist, suspended; ministerial declarations carried, 513–32 . . . . . . 5 June, 1899
Supplementary credit of 61,600,000f. for coast defences, France and colonies, voted . 9 June, ,,
Pres. Loubet well received at Longchamp races, 11 June, ,,
Difference in the chamber respecting the conduct of the police at Longchamp, 11 June; the ministry resigns . . . . . . 12 June, ,,
Baron F. de Christiani sentenced to 4 years' imprisonment for assaulting pres. Loubet at Auteuil, 7 others to fines and short imprisonment . . . . 13, 16 June, ,,
Adm. de Cuverville superseded for criticising defects in the defences; gen. de la Rocque removed from active service . 19, 22 June, ,,
New (concentration) cabinet: premier and minister of interior, M. Waldeck-Rousseau; war, gen. de Galliffet; marine, M. de Lanessan; justice, M. Monis; foreign affairs, M. Delcassé; commerce, M. Millerand; finance, M. Caillaux; education, M. Georges Leygues; public works, M. Pierre Baudin; colonies, M. Decrais; agriculture, M. Jean Dupuy . . . . 22 June, ,,
Ministerial declaration approved in the chamber, 263–237, and senate, 157–25 . . 26 June, ,,
Gen. Gilletta di San Giuseppe (Italian) charged with *espionage*, sentenced to 5 years' imprisonment and a fine of 5,000f., at Nice, 26 June; pardoned by pres. Loubet, 9 July; placed on half-pay . . . . 16 July, ,,
Stormy debate in the chamber; M. Déroulède's proposal for the revision of the constitution refused urgency, 379–70, 27 June; chamber prorogued . . . . 4 July, ,,
Victor Cherbuliez, novelist and critic, "Comte Kostia," born at Geneva, 1829; died . 1 July, ,,
Gen. Zurlinden, military governor of Paris, superseded by gen. Brugère . . . . 7 July, ,,
Suffren, 1st-class battleship, launched at Brest, displacement, 12,728 tons . . . 25 July, ,,
Gen. de Pellieux removed from the command of Paris (dies, aged 58, 15 July, 1900); gen. de Négrier dismissed from the supreme council of war for inciting to insubordination in the army, 26 July; succeeded by gen. Pierron . Aug. ,,
Pisson, tried *in camera* and condemned to 3 years' imprisonment and 500f. fine, for attempting to sell to foreigners documents relating to national defences . . . . 12 Aug. ,,
M. Paul Déroulède and others arrested on a charge of plotting against the republic, 12 Aug.; M. Jules Guérin, founder of the "Anti-Semitic league," resists arrest, and stands siege in the Rue de Chabrol, thoroughfare closed by police, 13 Aug. ,,
Anarchist demonstration in Paris, rioting, 380 persons injured, 2 churches pillaged, many arrests, 20 Aug. ,,
M. Jules Guérin surrenders in the Rue de Chabrol . . . . 20 Sept. ,,
Adm. Sallandrouze de Lamornaix, born, 1840, died suddenly on board the *Formidable* . 20 Sept. ,,
Strike at the Creuzot ironworks (20 days) ends with concessions to the men, by the arbitration of M. Waldeck-Rousseau (premier) . 7 Oct. ,,
Suppression of the embassy to the Vatican voted by the budget committee . . . 30 Oct. ,,
Gen. de Galliffet's army *reforms* sanctioned by the cabinet and president, see *Times* . 31 Oct. ,,
Major Esterhazy (see *Dreyfus Case*) tried for embezzlement (sends written defence); fine 500f. and sentenced to 3 years' imprisonment, 6 Nov. ,,
The chamber opens; interpellations against the government and the minister of war, 14 Nov.; vote of confidence, ministerial "acts of republican defence" approved, 320–215 . 16 Nov. ,,
Chambers opened, M. Deschanel re-elected president of the chamber, 308–221 . . 9 Jan. 1900
The *Aurora* petition, demanding "justice for Dreyfus," 44,760 signatures, sent to the president . . . . 17 Jan. ,,
The superior and 11 monks of the Assumptionist fathers charged with belonging to an illegal association and with issuing propaganda against the government, 22 Jan.; the community dissolved;

the superior and father Bailly, director of *La Croix* newspaper, and 10 others, fined, 24 Jan. [sentence confirmed by the court of appeal, 6 March].
The stipends of several bishops suspended by government . . . . . Jan. 1900
Senatorial elections, republican victory (99 seats, 92 gained by the government); nationalists: gen. Mercier and 2 others . . . . . 28 Jan. „
Senate meets, 1 Feb.; M. Fallières re-elected president . . . . . 5 Feb. „
MM. Buffet and Déroulède charged with conspiracy against the state, 9 Nov.; sentenced to 10 years' banishment; M. Jules Guérin to 10 years' detention in a fortress, 4 Jan.; M. Marcel Habert, banished for 5 years, 23 Feb. „
Death of count Benedetti, diplomatist (ambassador in Berlin, 1864–70), aged 83 . 28 March, „
Budget (good surplus) passed, 457–32; chambers adjourn . . . . . 12 April, „
Paris (international) exhibition opened by pres. Loubet . . . . . 14 April, „
Chamber meets, vote of confidence in the ministry carried, 286–237; amendment opposing a revival of the Dreyfus case carried, 457–78, 22 May; noisy scene in the chamber, government majority 47, 28 May; gen. de Galliffet (able war minister) in ill-health resigns, succeeded by gen. André, 29 May; amnesty bill (stopping further prosecutions connected with the Dreyfus case) passed by the senate . . . . . 2 June, „
Navy bill agreed to by the chamber . 30 June, „
M. Berthelot's vote of censure regarding military operations in S. Algeria rejected by the chamber, 458–60 . . . . . 2 July, „
Gen. André's firmness in maintaining discipline among the officers, supported by the chambers; gen. Delanne, chief of the staff, and gen. Jamont, generalissimo, resign; succeeded *at once* by gen. Pendezec and gen. Brugère . . 4 July, „
Chambers prorogued . . . . . 10 July, „
Abyssinian envoys received by pres. Loubet, 16 July, „
Grand naval review at Cherbourg, M. Loubet present . . . . . 19 July, „
The shah of Persia visits Paris, 28 July–11 Aug. [fired at by Salsou, an anarchist, 2 Aug.; Salsou sentenced to life-imprisonment, 10 Nov.; dies, Sept. 1901] . . . . . „
The *Framée*, torpedo-boat destroyer, sunk in collision with the *Brennus* war-ship off Trafalgar, 42 deaths, including all the officers . 11 Aug. „
Many strikes throughout France . . Aug. „
M. de Witte, Russian finance minister, arrives in Paris; pres. Loubet invested with the Russian Order of St. Andrew . . . . . 3 Sept. „
Army manœuvres closed by a review before pres. Loubet at Chartres . . . . . 20 Sept. „
Banquet to 22,000 mayors (23,000 guests) in the Tuileries gardens, fine speech by pres. Loubet, 22 Sept. „
The chambers meet: M. Waldeck-Rousseau (in the deputies) announces the religious associations bill and other important measures; vote of confidence passed, 316–237 . . . 6, 8 Nov. „
International exhibition in Paris (*which see*) closed, 12 Nov. „
Popular ovations to Mr. Kruger, ex-president of the Transvaal, at Marseilles, 22 Nov.; and Paris; received by pres. Loubet . . . 24 Nov. „
Prince Münster, German ambassador, resigns, Nov. „
Resolutions of sympathy to Mr. Kruger passed by the chamber and senate . . . 29, 30 Nov. „
The chamber adopts a resolution, counting on the government to repress slavery and cruelty in the colonies (government majority, 77) . 7 Dec. „
M. Zola's letter to pres. Loubet in the *Aurore* protests against the amnesty bill as a denial of justice . . . . . 22 Dec. „
Amnesty amendment bill, against a revival of the Dreyfus agitation and stopping prosecutions pending against M. Zola, col. Picquart and others, passed by the chamber, 155–2, after much debate, 19 Dec.; by the senate . 24 Dec. „
Death of the prince de Joinville, son of Louis Philippe, aged 82 . . . . . Dec. „
Paris municipality votes 100,000f. for the poor in celebration of the 20th century . 1 Jan. 1901
Chambers meet; MM. Deschanel and Fallières re-elected presidents . . . . . 8, 9 Jan. 1901
M. Waldeck-Rousseau's declaration that the pope has no power to intervene in state affairs, carried by a large majority . . . . . 14 Jan. „
M. Arthur Desjardins, eminent jurist and international lawyer, dies, aged 65 . . 15 Jan. „
Death of the duc de Broglie, historian, and statesman, aged 80 . . . . . 19 Jan. „
Army reorganisation, M. de Montebello's plan adopted by army committee . . early Feb. „
Prince Radolin, German minister, arrives in Paris, 20 Feb. „
Budget passed . . . . . 25 Feb. „
M. de Rodays, editor of the *Figaro*, wounded in a duel with count Boni de Castellane, near Paris, 16 March, „
M. Edmond Got, eminent actor, dies, aged 79, 21 March, „
The associations (21 clauses) bill (against unauthorized religious tutelage and communities) introduced 15 Jan., passed by the chamber after long debates, 303–224 . . . 29 March, „
Budget for 1902, deficit 8,000,000f. . 29 March, „
Prof. François Raoult, eminent chemist, born 10 May, 1830, dies . . . . . 1 April, „
Pres. Loubet visits Nice, and entertains the Italian fleet at Toulon . . . . . 8–10 April, „
Ex-queen Ranavolo, of Madagascar, visits Paris, 30 May, „
Eugène Manuel, inspector-gen. of education and popular poet, dies, aged 78 . . . 2 June, „
Scene in the chamber on Algerian affairs, M. Drumont, an anti-Semite, expelled . . 14 June, „
Moorish mission arrives in Paris . . mid June, „
Count de Lur-Saluces sentenced to 5 years' banishment for treason (with extenuating circumstances) . . . . . 6 June, „
Associations (religious) bill (amended by the senate) passed by the chamber, 313–149, 28 June; promulgated . . . . . 1 July, „
Prince Henry of Orleans, eminent explorer, dies at Saigon, aged 34 . . . . . 9 Aug. „
M. Edmond Audran, popular composer (*La Mascotte*, etc.), died, aged 59 . . . . 18 Aug. „
Sugar bounties reduced by 55 per cent. to cover 14,000,000f. deficit . . . . 25 Aug. „
Diplomatic rupture with Turkey, *which see*, Aug.–3 Sept. „
Pres. Loubet receives gen. Sakharoff and 6 Russian generals . . . . . 12 Sept. „
Meets the czar and czarina off Dunkirk; naval review held . . . . . 18 Sept. „
The czar and czarina arrive at Compiègne; view the manœuvres at Rheims; visit the cathedral and the Hôtel de Ville, 18, 19 Sept.; grand review (150,000 men) at Bethény; they leave 21 Sept. „
8,800 R.C. religious establishments out of a total of 16,468 apply for authorisation under the new associations law; the Jesuits, Passionists, Assumptionists, Benedictines and others leave France, many for England . . . July—3 Oct. „
MM. Tailhade & Grandidier sentenced to 12 and 6 months' imprisonment respectively for inciting to murder by an anarchist propaganda in the journal *Libertaire* . . . . . 10 Oct. „
Chambers opened; M. Basly's proposal for a *minimum* wage and an 8 hours' day for miners rejected, 290–245; and a motion to repeal the law against anarchists defeated, 402–132 . . 22 Oct. „
Debate on Franco-Turkish affairs, see *Turkey*, Aug.—Nov.; vote of confidence in the ministry, 305–77 . . . . . 4 Nov. „
M. de Lanessan (marine minister) abolishes compulsory attendance at mass, and prohibits the substitution of the religious service flag for the tricolour in the navy . . . . . Nov. „
Diplomatic relations with Turkey resumed 11 Nov. „
Railway bill (10 hours' day) passed by the chamber, 338–87 . . . . . 14 Nov. „
Jubilee of M. Berthelot, scientist, celebrated in the Sorbonne . . . . . 24 Nov. „
M. Hervé, professor in the Sens university, dismissed for anti-military newspaper articles; debate in the chamber, M. Leygues' speech defending the action of the authorities ordered to

be placarded, 13 Dec.; M. Roger-Ballu, fine art professor, also dismissed for insulting the government . . . . 19 Dec. 1901
Budget (amended), surplus 146,000f. reported mid Dec. ,,
The 3 per cent. loan of 265,000,000f. in connection with the Chinese indemnity passed by the chamber, 335–213, 28 Nov.; by the senate, 224–43, 6 Dec.; issued and subscribed about 25 times over . . . . 21, 22 Dec. ,,
M. Fouquier, brilliant journalist, died, aged 63, end Dec. ,,
M. Paul Deschanel again re-elected president of the chamber . . . . . . 14 Jan. 1902
Miners (eight hours) bill passed by the chamber, 5 Feb. ,,
Death of Mme. Clémence Royer, eminent *savant* and essayist, aged 72 . . . . . 6 Feb. ,,
Abrogation of the Falloux law, guaranteeing liberty of instruction, voted in the chamber, 289–239, 14 Feb. ,,
Centenary of Victor Hugo's birth celebrated in Paris, Brussels, and London . . . 26 Feb. ,,
Future chambers to last 6 instead of 4 years, voted by the chamber, 298–237 . . . 18 March, ,,
The chamber votes an amnesty for strikers, but rejects that for anarchists. . . . 21 March, ,,
Budget passed . . . . 29 March, ,,
Death of prof. Alfred Cornu, eminent scientist, aged 61 . . . . 14 April, ,,
Humbert-Crawford case, extensive frauds carried on for 20 years; sham litigation; proceedings finally instituted; M. and Mdme. Humbert escaped . . . . 8 May, ,,
Elections (ministerial majority, 88), 27 April–11 May, ,,
Destruction of St. Pierre, 8 May; see *Martinique*; 3 days' public mourning, general sympathy; relief fund started. . . . . . . 11 May, ,,
Death of M. Benjamin Constant, eminent painter, aged 55 . . . . 26 May, ,,
Death of Mme. Durand, "Henry Greville," novelist, aged about 60 . . . . . . 26 May, ,,
Pres. Loubet warmly received in Russia and Copenhagen, 20–25 May; holds a naval review at Dunkirk, 27 May; 220 convicts pardoned, or their sentences reduced . . . . 30 May, ,,
M. Waldeck-Rousseau, premier (in need of rest) and his ministry resign . . . . . 3 June ,,
M. Léon Bourgeois elected president of the chamber . . . . 6 June, ,,
New ministry: premier and minister of interior and public worship, M. Combes; justice, M. Vallé; foreign, M. Delcassé; war, gen. André; public works, M. Maruéjouls; agriculture, M. Mougeot; finance, M. Rouvier; marine, M. Pelletan; education, M. Chaumié; commerce, M. Trouillot; colonies, M. Doumergue; posts and telegraphs, M. Bérard . . . . . 7 June, ,,
M. Bourgeois opens the chamber of deputies, 10 June, ,,
Government policy, unsectarianism, fiscal reforms, &c.; vote of confidence passed . . . 12 June, ,,
Mme. Henry, widow of col. Henry (see *Dreyfus*) *v.* M. Reinach and the manager of the *Siècle*, for libel, damages for plaintiff 500f. . . 12 June, ,,
Cabinet council decides that no official is to be appointed until questioned as to politics, 20 June, ,,
The Humbert collection of pictures, Paris, realised 1,187,000f. . . . . . . 20, 21 June, ,,
Budget—estimated deficit 180,000,000f.; supplementary credits voted . . . 26, 27 June, ,,
Debate in the Chamber on the Humbert-Crawford frauds; vote of confidence in the government carried, 403–74, 27 June; discussed in the senate, 10 July, ,,
Debate in the chamber on the closing of R.C. schools for infringing the associations law; vote of confidence in the government carried, 333–206, 4 July, ,,
Conversion of the three-and-a-half per cent. rentes into three per cents. bill passed by the senate and made law, 9, 10 July; the closing of 2,500 catholic schools denounced in the chamber, wild uproar . . . . 11 July, ,,
Prince Komatsu, Japan, the crown prince of Siam, and Ras Makonnen, Abyssinian envoy, visit France . . . . July ,,
National fête, Paris illuminated . . . 14 July, 1902
Naval manœuvres in the Mediterranean, July—8 Aug. ,,
Protests of the episcopate against the closing of conventual schools, July; M. Combes' defence issued, 21 July; hostile demonstrations in Paris and elsewhere; M. Coppée, Lerolle, and Conti arrested . . . . . . 22, 23, 26 July, ,,
Col. Picquart is awarded 20,000f. damages for the libel in the *Echo de Paris* . . . 31 July, ,,
Revenue 64,000,000f. below the estimate, end July, ,,
Sir Wilfrid Laurier, Canadian premier, received by pres. Loubet, 26 Aug.; entertained at a banquet (leaves 2 Oct.) . . . . . . 1 Sept. ,,
Visit of the shah of Persia, 25 Aug.; and the Khedive . . . . 2 Sept. ,,
République battleship launched at Brest. 4 Sept. ,,
Lieut.-col. de Saint Remy arrested, 9 Aug., for refusing to assist at the closing of a conventual school as against his religious convictions, sentenced by court-martial to a day's imprisonment, 5 Sept.; placed on the retired list, 9 Sept.; maj. Le Roy Ladurie also dismissed . 26 Sept. ,,
Army manœuvres, the prince of the Asturias present, at Toulouse . . . . . 3–10 Sept. ,,
M. Émile Zola, eminent writer and novelist (see *Dreyfus case*), found suffocated in his bedroom, from a foul chimney (Mme. Zola was also unconscious, but recovered), 29 Sept.; imposing public funeral, Paris, ex-capt. Dreyfus present, 5 Oct. ,,
M. Rouvier's budget approved by the cabinet, 30 Sept. ,,
Coal strike in the north . . . . . 2 Oct. ,,
M. Combes calls on 22 bishops to renounce the employment of Lazarists and Marists . 3 Oct. ,,
Franco-Siamese treaty, ratification of frontier, signed . . . . 7 Oct. ,,
General coal strike declared (about 100,000 out), 8, 9 Oct.; riot at St. Etienne, 2 miners killed, 11 Oct.; Boer generals visit Paris, Oct. 13–15; chambers meet, budget estimates, large deficits for 1902; debate on the closing of conventual schools, 14, 16 Oct.; resolution supporting the government passed, 329–233 . . . 17 Oct. ,,
Committee appointed by the chamber to consider the question of separation of church and state, 20 Oct. ,,
M. Clémenceau upholds the government and criticises the concordat; resolution for the ministry carried, 163–90 . . . . 30 Oct. ,,
Vidal, the "woman-killer," sentenced to death, 5 Nov. ,,
Navy estimates, 306,000,000f., issued . 10 Nov. ,,
Strike ends in the north, reported . . 14 Nov. ,,
Change in parliamentary procedure voted by the chamber, 361–179 . . . . . . 17 Nov. ,,
Col. Picquart (charged with treason by the *Jour*) awarded 10,000f. . . . . . . 20 Nov. ,,
Petition of 74 bishops in favour of the religious orders declared illegal, reported . . 28 Nov. ,,
Two years' military service bill to come into operation 1904 . . . . 29 Nov. ,,
Brussels sugar convention ratified . . . 5 Dec. ,,
Colliers' strike over, award accepted, about 4 Dec. ,,
Violent scenes in the chamber, on an interpellation *re* the escape of the Humberts (swindlers); vote of confidence carried, 338–133 . . . 6 Dec. ,,
Visit of the king of Portugal, 18 Oct.–16 Nov.; again . . . . 8–10 Dec. ,,
Strike riots at Marseilles . . . . 11 Dec. ,,
The Humbert family arrested in Madrid. . 20 Dec. ,,
And brought to Paris . . . . . . 29 Dec. ,,
Report of new Panama canal company to sell concessions and property to the United States for 40,000,000 dols. and to verification of company's title adopted (Paris) . . . . . . 30 Dec. ,,
Senatorial elections; government gain 13 . 4 Jan. 1903
Chamber meets, M. Bourgeois re-elected president, and M. Jaurès, socialist leader, vice-president, 13 Jan. ,,
Interpellation *re* religious orders, government acts approved, 313–211 . . . . . . 15 Jan. ,,
Eight hours' day extended to naval establishments, 18 Jan. ,,
Death of M. de Blowitz, 30 years Paris correspondent of *The Times*, aged 78 . . . . 18 Jan. ,,
Brussels sugar convention ratified . . . 24 Jan. ,,

The czar gives 1,000*l.* to the Breton fishermen, 24 Jan. 1903

Dispute with the vatican concerning vacant bishopric nominations . . . . Feb. ,,

Scene in the chamber regarding the Humbert swindle, interpellation postponed . 13 Feb. ,,

Death of M. Gaston, Paris, eminent scholar and writer . . . . 6 March ,,

Debates on the religious orders, 54 refused authorization, ministerial vote carried . 12–18 March, ,,

Death of M. Ernest Legouvé, dramatist, aged 96, 14 March, ,,

Motion for the suppression of the budget of public worship rejected, M. Combes' declaration *re* church and state, approved . . 21 March, ,,

Budget passed with amendments . . 31 March, ,,

M. Jaurès in the chamber urges the re-opening of the Dreyfus case in a long speech . 6–7 April, ,,

Socialist congress at Bordeaux, M. Millerand, *opportunist*, remains a member by majority of 20, 14 April, ,,

President Loubet visits Algiers, confers honours on adm. Curzon-Howe, and other officers of the British squadron . . . . . . 15 April, ,,

At Tunis, 27 April; returns to Paris . 30 April, ,,

Government measures resisted by several bishops, and various religious associations; expulsions of religious orders continue . . . 29 April, ,,

King Edward warmly welcomed, Paris *en fête*; review of troops at Vincennes; races held at Longchamps; state banquet, &c. 1–2 May; the king confers honours on MM. Combes, Delcassé, Cambon, sir E. Monson, and others, 3 May; leaves. . . . . 4 May, ,,

Anti-clerical demonstrations held in various places 17 May, ,,

Debate in the chamber on the action of the government with regard to the religious bodies; motion for the separation of church and state rejected, 278–247; order of the day the government's policy, and counting on its firmness to repress the encroachments of the clergy, and the maintenance of religious liberty, adopted, 20 May, ,,

International exhibition, Limoges, May-Sept. opened . . . . May ,,

"Max O'Rell," Paul Blouët, author, and Paris correspondent of the *New York Journal*, died, aged 55 . . . . . . 24 May, ,,

Yellow book on relation between France and the Vatican, May, 1899–July, 1902, issued 22 June, ,,

Violent scene in the chamber during a debate on the religious question: expenditure of 256,000,000f. on the improvement of French ports and canals approved by the senate . . . . 23 June, ,,

President Loubet, on his return, sends a message to king Edward VII. expressing his warm gratitude for his reception in England: the king in reply expressed his ardent desire that the *rapprochement* between the two countries should be lasting . . . . 9 July, ,,

French senators and deputies received by the lord mayor and lady mayoress at the mansion house, 23 July; visit Windsor castle . . 24 July, ,,

Trial of the Humbert family for fraud begins at Paris . . . . 8 Aug. ,,

Terrible fire and explosion on the Underground railway in Paris caused by the fusion of the electric light wires, 84 lives lost . 10 Aug. ,,

Customs' official statement shows imports for 1902, 4,594,109,000f.; exports, 4,252,181,000f. mid Aug. ,,

M. and Mme. Humbert found guilty of forgery and swindling, and the Daurignacs for complicity in swindling; the Humberts sentenced to 5 years' solitary confinement, Romain Daurignac to 3 years', and Emile Daurignac to 2 years' inprisonment . . . . 22 Aug. ,,

Territory on the right bank of the Lower Senegal added to French colonial possessions, announced late Aug. ,,

Statue of Ernest Renan unveiled by M. Combes at Tréguier, Brittany . . . . . 13 Sept. ,,

Outbreak of bubonic plague at Marseilles, mid Sept. ,,

International Peace congress opened at Rouen, 22 Sept. ,,

[For other events see ADDENDA.]

SOVEREIGNS OF FRANCE.

MEROVINGIAN RACE.

Pharamond (his existence doubtful).

428. Clodion the Hairy; his supposed son; king of the Salic Franks.
447. Merovæus, or Mérovée; son-in-law of Clodion.
458. Childeric; son of Mérovée.
481. Clovis the Great, his son, real founder of the monarchy. His four sons divided the empire:
511. Childebert; Paris.
,, Clodomir; Orleans.
,, Thierry; Metz; and
,, Clotaire; Soissons.
534. Theodebert; Metz.
548. Theodebald; succeeded in Metz.
558. Clotaire I.; sole ruler. Upon his death the kingdom divided between four sons: viz.,
561. Charibert, ruled at Paris.
,, Gontram, in Orleans and Burgundy.
,, Sigebert, at Metz, and } Both assassinated by
,, Chilperic, at Soissons. } Fredegond.
575. Childebert II.
584. Clotaire II.; Soissons.
596. Thierry II., son of Childebert; in Orleans.
,, Theodebert II.; Metz.
613. Clotaire II.; became sole king.
628. Dagobert I. the Great, son of Clotaire II.; divided the kingdom between his two sons:
638. Clovis II., Burgundy and Neustria.
,, Sigebert II., Austrasia.
656. Clotaire III., son of Clovis II.
670. Childeric II.; sole king; assassinated, with his queen and his son Dagobert, in the forest of Livri.
,, Thierry III.; Burgundy and Neustria.
674. Dagobert II., son of Sigebert, in Austrasia; assassinated 679.
691. Clovis III. (Pepin, mayor of the palace, rules in his name; succeeded by his brother).
695. Childebert III., the Just; Pepin supreme.
711. Dagobert III., son of Childebert.
715. Chilperic II., deposed by Charles Martel, mayor of the palace.
717. Clotaire IV., of obscure origin, raised by Charles Martel to the throne; dies soon after; Chilperic is recalled from Aquitaine.
720. Chilperic II. restored; shortly afterwards dies at Noyon; succeeded by
,, Thierry IV., son of Dagobert III., surnamed *de Chelles*; died in 737. Charles Martel now reigns under the new title of "duke of the French." *Hénault.*
737. Interregnum, till the death of Charles Martel, in 741.
742. Childeric III., son of Chilperic II., surnamed the Stupid. Carloman and Pepin, the sons of Charles Martel, share the government.

THE CARLOVINGIANS.

752. Pepin the Short, son of Charles Martel; he is succeeded by his two sons,
768. Charles the Great (Charlemagne) and Carloman; Charles crowned EMPEROR OF THE WEST, by Leo III., 800. Carloman reigned but three years.
814. Louis I. *le Débonnaire*, EMPEROR; dethroned, but restored to his dominions.
840. Charles, surnamed the Bald, KING; EMPEROR in 875; poisoned by Zedechias, a Jewish physician.
877. Louis II., the Stammerer, son of Charles the Bald, KING.
879. Louis III. and Carloman II.; the former died in 882, and Carloman reigned alone.
884. Charles III. *le Gros*; a usurper, in prejudice to Charles the Simple.
887. Eudes, or Hugh, count of Paris.
898. Charles III. (or IV.), the Simple; deposed, and died in prison in 929; he married Edgiva, daughter of Edward the Elder, of England, by whom he had a son, King Louis IV.
922. Robert, brother of Eudes; crowned at Rheims; Charles killed him in battle. *Hénault.*
923. Rudolf or Raoul, duke of Burgundy; elected king, but never acknowledged by the southern provinces. *Hénault.*
936. Louis IV. *d'Outremer*, or Transmarine (from having been conveyed by his mother into England), son of Charles III. (or IV.); died by a fall from his horse.
954. Lothaire, his son; reigned jointly with his father from 952, and succeeds him at 15 years of age, under the protection of Hugh the Great; poisoned.

986. Louis V., the Indolent, son of Lothaire; also poisoned, it is supposed by his queen, Blanche; last of the race of Charlemagne.

THE CAPETS.

987. Hugh Capet, the Great, count of Paris, &c., eldest son of Hugh the Abbot, 3 July; he seizes the crown, in prejudice to Charles of Lorraine, uncle of Louis Transmarine. From him this race of kings is called Capevingians and Capetians. He died 24 Oct.
996. Robert II., surnamed the Sage; son; died lamented, 20 July.
1031. Henry I., son; died 29 Aug.
1060. Philip I. the Fair, *l'Amoureux;* son; succeeded at 8 years of age; ruled at 14; died 3 Aug.
1108. Louis VI., surnamed the Lusty, or *le Gros;* son; died 1 Aug.
1137. Louis VII.; son; surnamed the Young, to distinguish him from his father, with whom he reigned for some years; died 18 Sept.
1180. Philip II. (Augustus); son; succeeds at 15; crowned at Rheims in his father's lifetime; died 14 July.
1223. Louis VIII., *Cœur de Lion;* son; died 8 Nov.
1226. Louis IX.; son; called St. Louis; ascended the throne at 15, under the guardianship of his mother, who was also regent; died in his camp before Tunis, 25 Aug.
1270. Philip III., the Hardy; son; died at Perpignan, 6 Oct.
1285. Philip IV., the Fair; son; king in his 17th year; died 29 Nov.
1314. Louis X.; son; surnamed *Hutin*, an old word for headstrong, or mutinous; died 5 June.
1316. John I., posthumous son of Louis X.; born 15 Nov.; died 19 Nov.
,, Philip V. the Long (on account of his stature); brother of Louis; died 3 Jan.
1322. Charles IV., the Handsome; brother; died 31 Jan. 1328.

HOUSE OF VALOIS.

1328. Philip VI., de Valois, the Fortunate; grandson of Philip III.; died 23 Aug.
1350. John II. the Good; son; died suddenly in the Savoy in London, 8 April.
1364. Charles V., the Wise; son; died 16 Sept.
1380. Charles VI. the Beloved; son; died 21 Oct.
1422. Charles VII., the Victorious; son; died 22 July.
1461. Louis XI.; son; able but cruel; died 30 Aug.
1483. Charles VIII., the Affable; son; died 7 April.
1498. Louis XII., *Duke of Orleans;* the Father of his People; great-grandson of Charles V.; died 1 Jan.
1515. Francis I. *of Angoulême;* called the Father of Letters; great-great-grandson of Charles V.: died 31 March.
1547. Henry II.; son; received a wound at a tournament at the nuptials (by proxy) of his daughter Isabella with King Philip II. of Spain, accidentally inflicted by Montgomery, a Scotch nobleman in his service, 29 June; died 10 July, 1559.
1559. Francis II.; son; married Mary Stuart, queen of Scots; died 5 Dec.
1560. Charles IX.; brother; Catherine de Medicis, his mother, regent; died 30 May.
1574. Henry III.; brother; elected king of Poland; last of the house of Valois; stabbed by Jacques Clement, a Dominican friar, 1 Aug.; died 2 Aug. 1589.

HOUSE OF BOURBON.

1589. Henry IV., the Great, of Bourbon, king of Navarre; son-in-law of Henry II.; murdered by Francis Ravaillac, 14 May.
1610. Louis XIII., the Just; son; died 14 May.
1643. Louis XIV., the Great, *Dieudonné;* son; died 1 Sept.
1715. Louis XV., the Well-beloved; great-grandson; died 20 May,
1774. Louis XVI., his grandson; ascended the throne in his 20th year; married the archduchess Marie Antoinette, of Austria, May, 1770; dethroned, 14 July, 1789; guillotined, 21 Jan. 1793, and his queen, 16 Oct. following.

[Louis was executed Monday, 21 January, 1793, at eight o'clock A.M. On the scaffold he said, "Frenchmen, I die innocent of the offences imputed to me. I pardon all my enemies, and I implore of Heaven that my beloved France——" At this instant Santerre ordered the drums to beat, and the executioners to perform their office. When the guillotine descended, the priest exclaimed: "Son of St. Louis! ascend to heaven." The bleeding head was then held up, and a few of the populace shouted, "*Vive la République!*" The body was interred in a grave that was immediately afterwards filled up with quick lime, and a strong guard was placed around until it should be consumed.]

1793. Louis XVII., son of Louis XVI. He never reigned; and died in prison, supposed by poison, 8 June, 1795, aged 10 years 2 months. It is believed by some that he escaped to England, and lived there some time as Augustus Meves.* In 1874 a person calling himself Auguste de Bourbon claimed to be his son. In France also Albert de Bourbon, son of one Naundorff, claimed to be son of Louis XVII. At a trial in Paris, when Jules Favre was his counsel, the verdict was strongly against his claim, 27 Feb. 1874.

THE FIRST REPUBLIC.

1792. The NATIONAL CONVENTION (750 members), first sitting, 21 Sept.
1795. The DIRECTORY (Lareveillère Lépaux, Letourneur, Rewbell, Barras, and Carnot) nominated 1 Nov.; abolished, and Bonaparte, Ducos, and Siéyès appointed an executive commission, Nov. 1799.
1799. The CONSULATE. Napoleon Bonaparte, Cambacérès, and Lebrun appointed consuls, 24 Dec. Napoleon appointed consul for 10 years, 6 May, 1802; for life, 2 Aug. 1802.

FIRST EMPIRE. (See article *Bonaparte Family.*)
[Established by the senate 18 May, 1804.]

1804. Napoleon (Bonaparte) I.; born 15 Aug. 1769. He married,
1st, Josephine, widow of Alexis, vicomte de Beauharnais, 8 March, 1796 (who was divorced 16 Dec., 1809, and died 29 May, 1814);
2nd, Maria-Louisa of Austria, 2 April, 1810 (she died 17 Dec. 1847). Son, Napoleon Joseph, duke of Reichstadt, born 20 March, 1811; died, 22 July, 1832.
He renounced the thrones of France and Italy, and accepted the isle of Elba for his retreat, 5 April, 1814.
Again appeared in France, 1 March, 1815.
Was defeated at Waterloo, 18 June, 1815.
Abdicated in favour of his infant son, 22 June, 1815.
Banished to St. Helena, where he dies, 5 May, 1821. (See *France*, 1840.)

BOURBONS RESTORED.

1814. Louis XVIII. (*comte de Provence*), brother of Louis XVI.; born 17 Nov. 1755; married Marie-Josephine-Louise of Savoy; entered Paris, and took possession of the throne, 3 May, 1814; obliged to flee, 20 March, 1815; returned 8 July, same year; died without issue, 16 Sept. 1824.
1824. Charles X. (*comte d'Artois*), his brother; born 9 Oct. 1757; married Marie-Thérèse of Savoy; deposed 30 July, 1830. He resided in Britain till 1832, and died at Gratz, in Hungary, 6 Nov. 1836.
[His grandson, Henry, duc de Bordeaux, called comte de Chambord, son of the duc de Berry; born 29 Sept. 1820; married princess Theresa of Modena, Nov. 1846; no issue; styled himself Henri V. See *France*, 1870, *et seq.*]

HOUSE OF ORLEANS. (See *Orleans.*)

1830. Louis-Philippe, son of Louis-Philippe, duke of Orleans, called *Egalité*, descended from Philippe, duke of Orleans, son of Louis XIII.; born 6 Oct. 1773; married 25 Nov. 1809, Maria-Amelia, daughter of Ferdinand I. (IV.) king of the Two Sicilies; (she died 24 March, 1866). Raised to the throne as king of the French, 9 Aug. 1830; abdicated 24 Feb. 1848. Died in exile, in England, 26 Aug. 1850.
[*Heir:* Louis-Philippe, count of Paris; born 24 Aug. 1838.]

SECOND REPUBLIC, 1848.

The revolution commenced in a popular insurrection at Paris, 22 Feb. 1848. The royal family escaped by flight to England, a provisional government was established, monarchy abolished, and France declared a republic.

* He died insane, Jan. 1880.

Charles-Louis-Napoleon Bonaparte, declared by the National Assembly (19 Dec.) PRESIDENT of the republic of France; and proclaimed next day, 20 Dec.; elected for ten years, 22 Dec. 1851.

FRENCH EMPIRE REVIVED. (See *Bonaparte.*)

[1821. Napoleon II. (decreed to be so termed by Napoleon III. on his accession). Napoleon, Joseph, son of Napoleon I. and Maria-Louisa, archduchess of Austria; born 20 March, 1811: created king of Rome. On the abdication of his father he was made duke of Reichstadt, in Austria; and died at the palace of Schoenbrunn, 22 July, 1832, aged 21.]

1852. Napoleon III. formerly president of the French republic, elected emperor, 21, 22 Nov. 1852; proclaimed, 2 Dec. 1852; surrendered himself a prisoner to the king of Prussia at Sedan, 2 Sept. 1870; deposed at Paris, 4 Sept.; arrives at Wilhelmshöhe, near Cassel, 5 Sept.; deposition confirmed by the national assembly, 1 March; he protested against it, 6 March, 1871; died at Chislehurst, England, 9 Jan. 1873; buried there 15 Jan.

Empress: Eugénie-Marie (a Spaniard, countess of Téba), born 5 May, 1826; married 29 Jan. 1853.

Heir: Napoleon-Eugène-Louis-Jean-Joseph, son; styled Napoleon IV., born 16 March, 1856; killed in Zululand, 1 June, 1879; buried beside his father at Chislehurst (the prince of Wales and other princes present), 12 July, 1879 [both removed to mausoleum, Farnborough, 9 Jan. 1888]. See *Wills.*

At the celebration of the fête Napoleon, 15 Aug., 1873, the prince declared the policy of his family to be "Everything by the people, for the people."

[On 18 Dec. 1852, the succession, in default of issue from the emperor, was determined in favour of prince Jerome-Napoleon and his heirs male.]

THIRD REPUBLIC.

I. Louis Adolphe Thiers (born 16 April, 1797) appointed chief of the executive power, 17 Feb., and president of the French republic, by the national assembly, 31 Aug. 1871; resigned, 24 May, 1873; died, 3 Sept. 1877.

II. Marshal M. E. Patrice Maurice MacMahon, duc de Magenta, elected president, 24 May; nominated for seven years, 20 Nov. 1873, died 17th October, 1893.

III. François Paul Jules Grévy (born 15 Aug. 1813); elected 30 Jan. 1879; re-elected 28 Dec. 1885; resigned 2 Dec. 1887.

IV. Marie-François Sadi-Carnot (born 11 Aug. 1837); elected 3 Dec. 1887; assassinated 24—25 June, 1894.

V. Jean Pierre Paul Casimir-Perier, elected 27 June, 1894; resigned 15 Jan. 1895.

VI. François Felix Faure (born 20 Jan. 1841); elected 17 Jan. 1895; died, 16 Feb 1899.

VII. Emile Loubet (born 31 Dec. 1838); elected 18 Feb. 1899.

FRANCE, ISLE OF, see *Mauritius.*

FRANCHE COMTE, in upper Burgundy, E. France, was conquered by Julius Cæsar, about 45 B.C.; by the Burgundians, early in the fifth century, A.D.; and by the Franks about 534. It was made a county for Hugh the Black in 915, and received its name from having been taken from Renaud III. (1127-48), and restored to him. By marriage with the count's daughter, Beatrice, the emperor Frederick I. acquired the county, 1156. Their descendant, Mary of Burgundy, by marriage with the archduke Maximilian, conveyed it to the house of Austria, 1477. It was conquered by the French, 1668; restored by the treaty of Aix la Chapelle, 2 May, 1668; again conquered; and finally annexed to France by treaty, 1678.

FRANCHISE. A privilege or exemption from ordinary jurisdiction, and anciently an asylum or sanctuary where the person was secure. In Spain, churches and monasteries were, until lately, franchises for criminals, as formerly in England; see *Sanctuaries.* In 1429, the ELECTIVE FRANCHISE for counties was restricted to persons having at least 40*s.* a year in land, and resident; for recent changes, see *Reform.*

FRANCIS' ASSAULT ON THE QUEEN. John Francis, a youth, fired a pistol at queen Victoria as she was riding down Constitution-hill, in an open barouche, accompanied by prince Albert, 30 May, 1842. The queen was uninjured. Previous intimation having reached the palace of the intention of the criminal, her majesty had commanded that none of the ladies of her court should attend her. Francis was condemned to death, 17 June following, but was transported for life. He was liberated on ticket-of-leave in 1867.

FRANCISCANS. Grey or Minor Friars, an order founded by St. Francis d'Assisi, about 1209. Their rules were chastity, poverty, obedience, and very austere regimen. About 1220 they appeared in England, where, at the time of the dissolution of monasteries by Henry VIII., they had fifty-five abbeys or other houses, 1536-38.

FRANCISCO, SAN, the largest city in California, *which see.* The centenary of the foundation of the city by Franciscan monks, 8 Oct. 1776, was celebrated in 1876. The city suffered by earthquakes in 1868 and 1872. Mr. William Coleman, an eminent maintainer of public order, died, aged about 69, Dec. 1893. Mrs. Jane L. Stanford's deed of gift, &c., equal to 25,000,000 dol., to the Leland Stanford Jun. University, signed, 9 Dec. 1901. Population, 1880, 233,959; 1890, 298,997; 1900, 360,000.

FRANCONIA, or **FRANKENLAND** (on the Maine), formerly a circle of the German empire, part of Thuringia, was conquered by Thierry, king of the Franks, 530, and colonized. Its count or duke, Conrad, was elected king of Germany, 8 Nov. 911; and his descendant was the emperor Conrad III., elected 1138, and another duke. Franconia was made a distinct circle from Thuringia in 1512. At its subdivision in 1806 various German princes obtained a part; but in 1814 the largest share was awarded to Bavaria.

FRANCO-PRUSSIAN WAR originated in the emperor of the French's jealousy of the greatly increased power of Prussia, through the successful issue of the war with Denmark in 1864, and with Austria in 1866. The German Confederation was thereby annulled, and the North German Confederation established under the supremacy of the king of Prussia, to whose territories were further annexed Hanover, Hesse-Cassel, Nassau, Frankfort, and other provinces. This great augmentation of the power of Prussia was mainly due to the energetic policy of count Bismarck-Schönhausen, prime minister since Sept. 1862.

In a draft treaty, secretly proposed to the Prussian government by the French emperor in 1866: "1. The emperor recognises the acquisitions which Prussia has made in the last war; 2. The king of Prussia promises to facilitate the acquisition of Luxemburg by France; 3. The emperor will not oppose a federal union of the northern and southern states of Germany, excluding Austria; 4. The king of Prussia, in case the emperor should enter or conquer Belgium, will support him in arms against any opposing power; 5. They enter into an alliance offensive and defensive."

[This draft treaty was published in the *Times*, 25 July, 1870. After some discussion, its authenticity was admitted; count Bismarck asserting that it emanated entirely from the French emperor, and that the scheme had never been seriously entertained by himself.]

In March, 1867, a dispute arose through the French emperor's proposal for purchasing Luxemburg from the king of Holland, which was strongly opposed by Prussia, as that province had formed part of the dissolved Germanic Confederation; and the affair was only settled by a conference of the representatives of the great powers in London, at which the perfect neutrality of Luxemburg was determined, together with the withdrawal of the Prussian garrison and the destruction of the fortifications . . . . 7-11 May, 1867

Prince Leopold of Hohenzollern-Sigmaringen (connected with the Prussian dynasty, and brother of Charles, prince of Roumania), consented to become a candidate for the throne of Spain, 4 July, 1870

This was denounced by the French government. Threatening speeches were made in the French chamber by the duc de Grammont, the foreign minister, and eventually, after some negotiation and the intervention of Great Britain, prince Leopold, with the consent of his sovereign, declined the proffered crown . . . . . 12 July, „

The submission did not satisfy the French government and nation, and the demand for a guarantee against the repetition of such an acceptance irritated the Prussian government, and led to the termination of the negotiations, the king refusing to receive the count Benedetti, the French minister . . . . 13 July, „

Energetic but fruitless efforts to avert the war were made by earl Granville, the British foreign minister . . . . about 15 July, „

War was announced by the emperor, with the hearty consent of the great majority of the chambers. The left or republican party opposed the war; M. Thiers and a few others only protested against it as premature . . . . . . 15 July, „

[After his surrender on 2 Sept., the emperor told count Bismarck that he did not desire war, but was driven into it by public opinion. He appears to have been greatly deceived as to the numerical strength of his army, and its state of preparation.]

The greatest national crime that we have had the pain of recording since the days of the first French revolution has been consummated. War is declared—an unjust but premeditated war."—*Times*, 16 July, 1870.

(*For details of the battles see separate articles.*)

French Army, about 300,000:—
1st corps, under marshal MacMahon.
2nd corps, under general Frossard.
3rd corps, under marshal Bazaine.
4th corps, under general Ladmirault.
5th corps, under general De Failly.
6th corps, under marshal Canrobert.
Imperial guard, under general Bourbaki.
Commander-in-chief, the emperor; general Le Bœuf, second; succeeded by marshal Bazaine.

Prussian Army, about 640,000:—
1. Northern, under general Vögel von Falckenstein, about 220,000, defending the Elbe, Hanover, &c.
2. Right, under prince Frederick Charles, about 180,000.
3. Centre, under generals Von Bittenfeld and Von Steinmetz, about 80,000.
4. The left, under the crown prince of Prussia, about 166,000.

Commander-in-chief, king William; second, general Helmuth Karl Bernhard von Moltke (born 26 Oct., 1800; died 24 April, 1891).

The North German army, at the beginning of August, consisted, firstly, of 550,000 line, with 1,200 guns and 53,000 cavalry; secondly, of 187,000 reserve, with 234 guns and 18,000 cavalry; and, thirdly, of 205,000 landwehr or militia, with 10,000 cavalry, making a grand total of 944,000 men, with 1,680 mobilised guns and 103,000 horses.

To these must be added, firstly, the Bavarians, 69,000 line, with 192 guns and 14,800 horses—25,000 reserve with 2,400 horses, and 22,000 landwehr; secondly, the Würtembergers—22,000 line with 54 guns and 6,200 horses, 6,500 reserve, and 6,000 landwehr; and, thirdly, the Badenese—16,000 line with 54 guns, 4,000 reserve, and 9,600 landwehr.

All the German troops taken together as under arms at present, 1,124,000 men. Aug. 1870.

Four weeks previously, on the peace footing, they numbered only 360,000.

The French and Germans in this war were considered to be equally brave and efficient; but the French generals appear to have acted greatly upon impulse. The Germans seem to have been invariably guided by a well-matured plan, their tactics mainly consisting in bringing vast masses to bear on the point where they were anxious to prevail. From Saarbrück to Sedan, Moltke appears to have left nothing to chance; and all his arrangements were ably carried out.

The causes of the early ruin of the French army were: "1, the enormous superiority of the Germans in regard to numbers; 2, the absolute unity of their command and concert of operation; 3, their superior mechanism in equipment and supplies; 4, the superior intelligence, steadiness and discipline of the soldiers; 5, superior education of the officers, and the dash and intelligence of the cavalry."—*Quarterly Review*.

Estimated cost of the war to France, 395,400,000*l*., Jan. 1875.

War resolved on by the French government, 15 July; declaration delivered at Berlin . . . 19 July, 1870

The north German parliament meet at Berlin, and engage to support Prussia in the war 19 July, „

Würtemberg, Bavaria, Baden, and Hesse Darmstadt declare war against France, and send contingents to the army . . . . . 20 July, „

War proclamation of the emperor Napoleon, declaring that the national honour, violently excited . . . alone takes in hand the destinies of the country . . . . 23 July, „

Part of the bridge at Kehl blown up by the Prussians . . . . 23 July, „

Proclamation of the king that "love of the common fatherland, and the unanimous uprising of the German races, have conciliated all opinions, and dissipated all disagreements . . . . The war will procure for Germany a durable peace, and from this bloody seed will arise a harvest blessed by God—the liberty and unity of Germany," 25 July, „

Skirmish at Niederbronn; a Bavarian officer killed, 26 July, „

Day of general prayer observed in Prussia, 27 July, „

The emperor Napoleon joins the army; at Metz assumes the chief command, and issues a proclamation declaring that the war will be long and severe, 28, 29 July, „

Repulse of a French attack at Saarbrück, 30 July, „

20 Badenese enter France at Lauterburg; Mr. Winsloe killed; some captured; others escape with valuable information . . . 31 July, „

Proclamation of the king of Prussia to his people, granting an amnesty for political offences, and "resolving, like our forefathers, placing full trust in God, to accept the battle for the defence of the fatherland" . . . 31 July, „

He leaves Berlin for the army, 1 Aug., and announces that "all Germany stands united in arms" 3 Aug. „

The French government announce that "they make war, not against Germany, but against Prussia, or rather against the policy of count Bismarck" . . . . . 2 Aug. „

The French under Frossard bombard and take Saarbrück in the presence of the emperor and his son; the Prussians, dislodged, retire with little loss . . . . 2 Aug „

The duc de Grammont, French foreign minister, publishes a circular replying to Bismarck's charges against France . . . . 3 Aug. „

The crown prince crosses the Lauter, the boundary of France, and defeats the French under Frossard, storming the lines of Wissemburg and Geisberg; general Douay killed . . . . . . 4 Aug. „

Battle of Woerth: in a desperate, long-continued battle the crown prince defeats marshal MacMahon and the army of the Rhine; they retire to Saverne to cover Nancy . . . . . 6 Aug. „

Battle of Forbach: Saarbrück recaptured, and Forbach (in France) taken by generals Von Goeben and Von Steinmetz, after a fierce contest; all the French retreat . . . . 6 Aug. „

General Turr publishes, in a letter, statements of proposals by Bismarck for the annexation of Luxemburg and Belgium by France, in 1866 and 1867 . . . . 6 Aug. „

The emperor, reporting these defeats, says, "Tout peut se rétablir" . . . . . . 7 Aug. 1870
The Germans occupy Forbach, Haguenau, and Sarreguemines . . . . . . 7 Aug. ,,
Marshal Bazaine appointed to the chief command of the French army at Metz (about 130,000); MacMahon has about 50,000 near Saverne; Canrobert about 50,000 near Nancy . . 8 Aug. ,,
Nine French iron-clads pass Dover for the Baltic, 9 Aug. ,,
St. Avold occupied by the Germans . 9 Aug. ,,
Marshal Bazaine takes command of the army at Metz . . . . 9 Aug. ,,
Phalsburg invested . . . . . . 9 Aug. ,,
Treaty with Great Britain guaranteeing the neutrality of Belgium, signed on behalf of Prussia, 9 Aug.; of France . . . . . 11 Aug. ,,
Forced resignation of the Ollivier ministry 9 Aug. ,,
New ministry constituted under general Cousin Montauban; comte de Palikao, war minister, 10 Aug. ,,
Strasburg invested by the Germans . 10 Aug. ,,
The king of Prussia, at Saarbrück, proclaims that "he makes war against soldiers, not against French citizens" . . . . . 10 Aug. ,,
Lichtenburg capitulates to the Germans 10 Aug. ,,
MacMahon's army retreating upon the Moselle, 11 Aug. ,,
The little fortress, "La Petite Pierre," evacuated, 11 Aug. ,,
Communication with Strasburg cut off 11 Aug. ,,
Nancy occupied by the Germans without resistance, 12 Aug. ,,
The Bavarians pass the Vosges . . . 12 Aug. ,,
The king at St. Avold forbids conscription for the French army in territories held by Germans, 13 Aug. ,,
Marshal Bazaine made commander of the army of the Rhine . . . . 13 Aug. ,,
Bombardment of Strasburg begun . 14 Aug. ,,
The French government declare that "there can be, for a moment, no question of negotiation of peace" . . . . 14 Aug. ,,
Blockade of the German ports on the Baltic, from 15 Aug., announced by the French admiral, 14 Aug. ,,
Many French volunteer sharp-shooters (*francs-tireurs*) take the field (not recognised as soldiers by the Germans) . . . . about 14 Aug. ,,
Toul refuses to surrender . . . . 14 Aug. ,,
The emperor retires to Verdun . . . 14 Aug. ,,
Marshal Bazaine's army defeated in several long-continued sanguinary battles before Metz (see *Metz*):—
1. Battle of Courcelles (Pange or Longeville) gained by Von Steinmetz and the 1st army, 14 Aug. ,,
2. Battle of Vionville or Mars-la-Tour, gained by prince Frederick Charles and the 2nd army . . . . 16 Aug. ,,
3. Battles of Gravelotte and Rezonville, gained by the combined armies commanded by the king . . . . 18 Aug. ,,
French sortie from Strasburg repulsed; German attack on Phalsburg repulsed 16 Aug. ,,
MacMahon reaches Châlons, 16 Aug.; joined by the emperor; his army between 130,000 and 150,000, 20 Aug. ,,
The king appoints governors-general of Alsace and Lorraine . . . . 17 Aug. ,,
Energetic fortification of Paris by general Trochu, the governor, and the "defence committee" 18 Aug. ,,
Estimated German losses: killed, wounded, and missing, 2088 officers, 46,480 men; up to 18 Aug. ,,
Severe bombardment of Strasburg . 19 Aug. ,,
MacMahon's army of the Rhine retreats as the Prussians under the king and crown prince advance; prince Frederick Charles opposed to Bazaine at Metz; [German armies in France about 500,000; the French armies about 300,000; communications between marshals Bazaine and MacMahon very difficult] . . . about 20 Aug. ,,
Lieut. Harth, a Prussian spy, tried and shot at Maris . . . . 20 Aug. ,,
MacMahon raises his camp at Châlons 20 Aug. ,,
The troops extended along the line of the Marne, 21 Aug. 1870
Exportation of food prohibited . . . 21 Aug. ,,
Bazaine at Metz said to be completely isolated, 22 Aug. ,,
MacMahon at Rheims with his army, including the remains of the corps of Failly and Canrobert; he marches in hope of joining Bazaine, 23 Aug.; the crown-prince and prince of Saxony start in pursuit, 23 Aug.; march upon Châlons . 24 Aug. ,,
Prussian royal head-quarters removed from Pont à Mousson to Bar-le-Duc (125 miles from Paris) 24 Aug. ,,
The alleged violation of the neutrality of Belgium denied by its government . . . . 25 Aug. ,,
The Germans enter the arrondissement of Vassy, 25 Aug ,,
Germans repulsed in an attack on Verdun, 25 Aug. ,,
800 French national guards captured at St. Menehould . . . . 25 Aug. ,,
Châlons occupied by the Germans . . 25 Aug. ,,
Capitulation of Vitry, a small fortress . 25 Aug. ,,
Formation of three German armies of reserve in Germany, and a fourth army in the field, under the crown-prince of Saxony, to co-operate with the crown-prince of Prussia against Paris, 26 Aug. ,,
Strasburg suffering much by bombardment, 23-26 Aug.
Powerful sortie of Bazaine from Metz repulsed, 26 Aug. ,,
Phalsburg heroically resisting . . . 26 Aug. ,,
Thionville invested by the Germans . 27 Aug. ,,
Engagement at Busancy, between Vouziers and Stenay: a regiment of French chasseurs nearly annihilated . . . . 27 Aug. ,,
Two German armies (220,000) marching on Paris, 28 Aug. ,,
Continued retreat of MacMahon's army: severe fighting at Dun, Stenay, and Mouzon 28 Aug. ,,
Nicholas Schull, a German spy, shot at Metz 28 Aug. ,,
Vrizy, between Vouziers and Attigny, stormed by the Germans . . . . 29 Aug. ,,
Municipal meetings at Berlin, Königsberg, and other German cities, protest against foreign intervention for peace . . . . 30, 31 Aug. ,,
MacMahon's army, about 150,000, accompanied by the emperor, retreating northwards; part of it, under De Failly, surprised and defeated near Beaumont, between Mouzon and Moulins; several other engagements, unfavourable to the French, occurred during the day . . . . . 30 Aug. ,,
Count Bismarck-Bohlen installed governor of Alsace at Haguenau . . . . . 30 Aug. ,,
The Germans enter Carignan; attack the French in the plain of Douzy; the French, at first successful, are defeated, and retreat to Sedan 31 Aug. ,,
A French army of old soldiers, about 100,000, are said to be forming near Lyons . . 31 Aug. ,,
Bazaine defeated in his endeavour to escape from Metz; after a fierce struggle, retreats into Metz, 31 Aug. 1 Sept. ,,
Battle round Sedan: begun at 4 a.m. between Sedan and Douzy; the French at first successful; after a severe struggle and dreadful carnage, the Germans victorious; MacMahon wounded, 5.30 p.m.; general de Wimpffen refuses to accept the terms offered by the king of Prussia . 1 Sept. ,,
Capitulation of Sedan and the remainder of MacMahon's army; the emperor surrenders to the king (see *Sedan*) . . . . . . 2 Sept. ,,
Vigorous artillery action at Strasburg; a sortie repulsed . . . . 2 Sept. ,,
Revolution at Paris after the declaration of the capture of MacMahon's army; proclamation of a republic (see *France*) . . . . . 4 Sept. ,,
Rheims occupied by the Germans and the king, 5 Sept. ,,
Jules Favre, the French foreign minister, in a circular to the French diplomatic representatives, says, "We will not cede either an inch of our territories or a stone of our fortresses" 6 Sept. ,,
General Vinoy and a corps sent too late to aid MacMahon; retreat and arrive in Paris, 6, 7 Sept. ,,
St. Dizier occupied by the Germans . . 7 Sept. ,,
Strasburg invested by 60,000 men . . 8 Sept. ,,
Verdun vigorously resisting . . . . 8 Sept. ,,

The German army, in five corps, advancing on Paris, 9 Sept. 1870
Laon surrendered to save the town from destruction; by the accidental or treacherous explosion of a magazine some of the German staff and many French perish . . . . 9 Sept. „
Metz, Strasburg, Thionville, Phalsburg, Toul, Bitsche, and other fortified places holding out, 10 Sept. „
Messages between belligerents transmitted by lord Lyons (at Paris) and count Bernstorff (Prussian minister) in London . . . . 9-10 Sept. „
German attack on Toul repulsed . . 10 Sept. „
Bridge at Creil over the Oise blown up . 12 Sept. „
Seven German corps (about 300,000 men) approaching Paris, which is said to contain 300,000 combatants . . . . 13 Sept. „
M. Thiers arrives in London on a mission from the government . . . . . . 13 Sept. „
Colmar occupied by the Germans . . 14 Sept. „
General Trochu reviews the troops in Paris, 13 Sept.; delivers a stirring address; the daily guard ordered to be 70,000 . . . . 14 Sept. „
Estimated German loss: 60,000 killed and wounded; between 20,000 and 30,000 sick; about 1,000 prisoners . . . . . . 15 Sept. „
French prisoners in Germany: 62 generals, 4,800 officers, 140,000 privates, about . 15 Sept. „
Correspondence between count Bernstorff and earl Granville respecting neutrality, said to have been broken; denied by the earl 1-15 Sept. „
Siege of Paris begun; ingress and egress prohibited without a permit . . . . . 15 Sept. „
Blockade of the Elbe and Weser non-effective, 15 Sept. „
Important circular of M. Favre, condemning the war and recognising the obligations of the country, 17 Sept. „
Circular letters of count Bismarck, recounting the history of French aggressions on Germany, and asserting the necessity of obtaining material guarantees for the future safety of Germany, and removing the frontiers and point of attack further west . . . . 13, 16 Sept. „
Prussian head-quarters at Meux (20 miles from Paris) 18 Sept. „
32 German merchant ships reported to have been captured by the French fleet up to . 18 Sept. „
Vessels sunk in the Seine and Marne, and other vigorous defensive measures adopted, 18, 19 Sept. „
Paris said to be completely invested; the fortifications reconnoitred by the king, who has fixed his head-quarters at Baron Rothschild's château at Ferrières, near Lagny . . . 19 Sept.
Three French divisions under general Vinoy attack the Germans on the heights of Sceaux; repulsed with loss of 7 guns and 2500 prisoners: the defeat attributed to the disorder of the Zouaves; the national guard behave well . . . 19 Sept. „
Count Bismarck consents to receive Jules Favre (about 16 Sept.); they meet at Château de la Haute Maison, 19 Sept.; and at the king's head-quarters, Ferrières, near Lagny . 20 Sept. „
Jules Favre reports to the government the result of his interviews with count Bismarck: Prussia demands the cession of the departments of the Upper and Lower Rhine and part of that of Moselle, with Metz, Château Salins and Soissons, and would agree to an armistice in order that a French constituent assembly might meet; the French to surrender Strasburg, Toul and Verdun (or Phalsburg according to Favre), and Mont Valérien, if the assembly meet at Paris; these terms are positively rejected by the French government . . . . . . 21 Sept. „
Versailles and the troops there surrender, 19 Sept.; entered by the crown prince of Prussia 20 Sept. „
A lunette captured at Strasburg . . 20 Sept. „
General Von Steinmetz sent to Posen as governor-general; prince Frederick Charles sole commander before Metz . . . . . . 21 Sept. „
Sèvres surrenders . . . . . . 22 Sept. „
The blockade of German ports raised; officially announced in London . . . . 22 Sept. „
The French government issue a circular expressing readiness to consent to an equitable peace, but refusing "to cede an inch of our territory or a stone of our fortresses" . . . . 23 Sept. 1870
Three conflicts before Paris: at Drancy, Pierrefitte, and Villejuif; the two last reported favourable to the French . . . . 23 Sept. „
Toul surrenders after a most vigorous resistance, 23 Sept. „
Levée en masse of men under 25 ordered by the French government . . . . . 23 Sept. „
Germans repulsed in conflicts before Paris; said by them to be unimportant . . . 23 Sept. „
Verdun invested by the Germans . . 25 Sept. „
Desperate ineffective sallies from Metz, 23, 24, 27 Sept. „
All the departments of the Seine and Marne occupied by Germans . . . . . 26 Sept. „
The iron cross given by the crown prince of Prussia to above 30 soldiers beneath the statue of Louis XIV. at Versailles . . . . . 26 Sept. „
Circular of Von Thile, Prussian foreign minister, stating that as the ruling powers in France decline an armistice, and as no recognised government exists in Paris (the government *de facto* being removed to Tours), all communications with and from Paris can only be carried on so far as the military events may permit . 27 Sept. „
Clermont occupied by the Germans after a brief vigorous resistance, overcome by artillery, 27 Sept. „
Commencement of attack on Soissons . 28 Sept. „
Capitulation of Strasburg, 27 Sept.; formally surrendered . . . . 28 Sept. „
Sortie of general Vinoy's army (at Paris); repulsed, after two hours' fighting, crown prince present; above 200 prisoners taken; general Giulham killed . . . . 30 Sept. „
Above 375,000 national guards said to be in Paris, 30 Sept. „
Conflict near Rouen; at first favourable to the French; their loss 1,200 killed and wounded; 300 prisoners . . . . 30 Sept. „
Beauvais captured by the Germans . 30 Sept. „
Mantes occupied by the Germans . . 1 Oct. „
Circular from count Bismarck, disclaiming any intention of reducing France to a second-rate power, 1 Oct. „
The American general Burnside visits M. Favre, 1 Oct. „
Surgeon-major Wyatt writes that Paris is well-provisioned, and nearly inexpugnable . 1 Oct. „
M. Thiers' fruitless visit to Vienna, 23 Sept.; to St. Petersburg, 27 Sept.; dined with the czar, 2 Oct. „
The grand duke of Mecklenburg at Rheims appointed governor of the country conquered in addition to Alsace and Lorraine . . . 2 Oct. „
M. Favre, in the name of the diplomatic body, requests count Bismarck to give notice before bombarding Paris, and to allow a weekly courier; the count declines both requests, but permits the passage of open letters; reported . . 3 Oct. „
Count Bismarck in a circular corrects Favre's report of the negotiations, and accuses the French government of keeping up the difficulties opposed to a conclusion of peace; reported . . 3 Oct. „
Epernon and La Ferté occupied by the Germans after an engagement . . . . . 4 Oct. „
The king's head-quarters removed to Versailles; arrival of the king, Bismarck, Moltke, and others, 5 Oct. „
The Germans victors in several small engagements, 2-6 Oct. „
General Treskow, in command of a German army, to advance into Southern France . . 5 Oct. „
Colmar occupied by the Prussians for an hour, 5 Oct. „
Battle at Thoury; General Reyan, with the advanced guard of the army of the Loire under general La Motte Rouge, defeats the Germans between Chaussy and Thoury, and captures some prisoners and cattle . . . . . 5 Oct. „
Fictitious manifesto of the emperor Napoleon III., entitled "*Les Idées de l'Empereur,*" advocating peace on moderate terms, dated 26 Sept., published in the imperialist journal in London, *La Situation*, and in *Daily News*, 4 Oct.; disclaimed by the emperor . . . . . . 6 Oct. „

M. Thiers' mission to foreign courts reported to be quite abortive . . . . . . 6 Oct. 1870
Part of the army of Lyons, under general Dupré, defeated by the Badenese under general Von Gegenfeld, near St. Rémy; French loss, about 1,500, and 660 prisoners; German loss, about 430, 6 Oct. ,,
General Burnside leaves Paris in order to meet count Bismarck . . 7 Oct. ,,
Great sortie from Metz; the Germans surprised; 40,000 French engaged; repulsed after severe conflicts; French loss, about 2,000; German, about 600 . . . . 7 Oct. ,,
Estimated number of French prisoners in Germany, 3577 officers, and 123,700 men . . . 8 Oct. ,,
Neu Breisach bombarded . . . . . . 8 Oct. ,,
Breton volunteers organising by M. Cathelineau; volunteers in the west organising by general Charette (from Rome) . . . . 8 Oct. ,,
German attack on St. Quintin vigorously repulsed, 8 Oct. ,,
Long despatch from count Bernstorff to earl Granville, complaining of the British supplying arms to France . . . . . . 8 Oct. ,,
M. Thiers again at Vienna . . . . 8 Oct. ,,
Garibaldi arrives at Tours; enthusiastically received; reviews the national guard at Tours, 9 Oct. ,,
Direct mediation declined by Russia, Great Britain, and Spain . . . . 10 Oct. ,,
Prussian circular to the European powers, regretting the obstinate resistance of the French government to peace, and foretelling the consequences—social disorganisation and much starvation, 10 Oct. ,,
Ablis, near Paris, burnt for alleged treachery (killing sleeping soldiers) . . . . . 10 Oct. ,,
M. Gambetta escapes from Paris by a balloon, 7 Oct.; in his proclamation at Tours, states that Paris possesses 560,000 troops; that cannon are cast daily, and that women are making cartridges; he urges unanimous devoted co-operation in carrying on the war . . . . . 10 Oct. ,,
Part of the army of the Loire defeated at Arthenay, near Orleans, by Bavarians under Von der Tann; about 2,000 prisoners taken . . . 10 Oct. ,,
Prussian attack on Cherizy repulsed . 10 Oct. ,,
French reply to Bismarck's circular on the negotiations . . . . 10 Oct.
About 20 villages burnt, and 150 peasants shot for illicit warfare . . . . . up to 11 Oct. ,,
The French fleet appears off Heligoland . 11 Oct. ,,
3,000 national guard mobilised at Rouen . 11 Oct. ,,
Three first shots fired against Paris . . 11 Oct. ,,
Orleans captured by gen. Von der Tann after nine hours' fighting; the army of the Loire defeated retires behind the Loire . . . . 11 Oct. ,,
Stenay captured by a sortie from the French garrison of Montmédy . . . . . 11 Oct. ,,
Gen. Bourbaki accepts the command at Tours; gen. La Motte Rouge superseded in the command of the army of the Loire by gen. D'Aurelle de Paladines . . . . 12 Oct. ,,
Battalions of Amazons said to be forming in Paris, 12 Oct. ,,
Favourable intelligence from Paris by balloons received . . . . 12 Oct. ,,
Garibaldi appointed commander of the French irregulars . . . . 12 Oct. ,,
Epinal captured by the Germans . . . 12 Oct. ,,
M. Arlès Dufour of Lyons appeals to the people of Great Britain for active sympathy in endeavouring to obtain peace . . . . . . 12 Oct. ,,
Breteuil occupied by the Germans after a sharp resistance . . . . 12 Oct. ,,
Slight engagements (termed victories by the French) before Paris . . . . . . 13 Oct.
All the Vosges district in arms; no regular army; the defiles occupied by the francs-tireurs, 13 Oct. ,,
Reported successful sorties; Neu Breisach completely invested . . . . . . 13 Oct. ,,
Reported French success at Bagneux, near Paris—the Prussians surprised . . . . 13 Oct. ,,
St. Cloud fired on by the French and burnt, 13, 14 Oct. ,,
Frequent sorties from Metz . about 14 Oct. ,,

Sharp fight at Ecouis; the French escape from being surrounded . . . . . 14 Oct. 1870
Gambetta announces that the Germans are dislodged from their innermost belt round Paris, 14 Oct. ,,
M. Thiers arrives at Florence; Garibaldi at Besançon . . . . 14 Oct. ,,
Gen. Boyer, aide-de-camp to marshal Bazaine, arrives at Versailles and meets count Bismarck, 14 Oct. ,,
Gen. Trochu's letter to the mayors of Paris, on reorganising the national guard and repressing the ardent desire for immediate action . 15 Oct. ,,
Soissons surrenders after three weeks' investment and four days' bombardment . . . 16 Oct. ,,
French successes before Paris denied by the Prussians, who hold the same position as on 19 Sept., 16 Oct. ,,
M. Gambetta proceeds to the army of the Vosges; gen. Bourbaki appointed commander of the army of the north; gen. Mazière appointed to a command in the army of the Loire . . 17 Oct. ,,
Montdidier attacked by the Germans: 150 mobile guards captured . . . . . . 17 Oct. ,,
The emperor Napoleon declares that "there can be no prospect of peace, near or remote, on the basis of ceding to Prussia a single foot of French territory; and no government in France can attach its signature to such a treaty and remain in power a single day" . . . . 17 Oct. ,,
4,000 French attacked and defeated near Châteaudun after ten hours' fighting and the barricaded town stormed . . . . 18 Oct. ,,
Circular of Jules Favre, asserting that Prussia "coldly and systematically pursues her task of annihilating us. France has now no illusions left. For her it is now a question of existence. . . . We prefer our present sufferings, our perils, and our sacrifices to the consequences of the inflexible and cruel ambition of our enemy. France needed, perhaps, to pass through a supreme trial—she will issue from it transfigured," 18 Oct. ,,
Asserted repulse of the Germans at Fort Issy before Paris . . . . 18 Oct. ,,
Despatch from earl Granville to count Bismarck urging the negotiations for peace on terms lenient to the French . . . . . 20 Oct. ,,
Conclusive reply of earl Granville to count Bernstorff's charge of breach of neutrality . 21 Oct. ,,
Vigorous sortie from Mont Valérien against Versailles; an engagement at Malmaison; the French retire after three hours' fighting, losing about 400 killed and wounded and 100 prisoners; German loss about 230 killed and wounded, 21 Oct. ,,
Chartres occupied by the Germans under Wittich, 21 Oct. ,,
Intervention of the British government (supported by the neutral powers) to obtain an armistice for the election of a national assembly . 21 Oct. ,,
Vesoul occupied by the Germans . . 21 Oct. ,,
Many deserters from Metz . . 20—22 Oct. ,,
Schelestadt bombarded vigorously . 22 Oct. ,,
Engagement near Evreux . . . . 22 Oct. ,,
Fighting at Vouray, Cussey, &c., in the Vosges; French "army of the east" defeated . 22 Oct. ,,
German attack on Châtillon le Duc repulsed by gen. Cambriels . . . . 22 Oct. ,,
M. de Kératry assumes command of the army in Brittany . . . . 23 Oct. ,,
St. Quentin taken by the Germans after half-an-hour's cannonading, 21 Oct.; evacuated by them, 23 Oct. ,,
Reported failure of the suggestions concerning an armistice, through Prussia demanding that France should consent to a cession of territory, 24 Oct. ,,
Gambetta informs the mayors of towns that "resistance is more than ever the order of the day," 24 Oct. ,,
Reported negotiations for the surrender of Metz, 24 Oct. ,,
Thiers undertakes the mission to obtain an armistice, about 24 Oct. ,,
Capitulation of Schelestadt (2,400 prisoners and 120 guns taken) . . . . . . 24 Oct. ,,
A girl calling herself a successor of Jeanne d'Arc at Tours . . . . 24 Oct.

Marshal Bazaine surrenders Metz and his army, "conquered by famine" (see *Metz* and *France*, Oct.-Dec. 1873) . . . 27 Oct. 1870
The French defeated near Gray (Haute Saône) by Von Werder . . . 27 Oct. ,,
About 2000 sick and wounded of both nations in Versailles . . . 27 Oct. ,,
Le Bourget, near Paris, recaptured by the French, 28 Oct. ,,
A safe-conduct given to M. Thiers to enter Paris for negotiation . . . 28 Oct. ,,
Despatch from count Bismarck to earl Granville, expressing desire for the meeting of a French national assembly to consider terms of peace; but stating that overtures must come from the French, 28 Oct. ,,
Badenese troops defeated near Besançon; Prussian attack on Formerie on the Oise repulsed 28 Oct. ,,
Gen. Von Moltke created a count on his 70th birthday . . . 28 Oct. ,,
Vigorous proclamation of Bourbaki to the French army of the north . . . 29 Oct. ,,
The crown prince and prince Frederick Charles created field-marshals . . . 29 Oct. ,,
Dijon captured after bombardment . . 29 Oct. ,,
The francs-tireurs defeated by the Würtembergers between Montereau and Nangis . . 29 Oct. ,,
Estimated: 856,000 Germans in France; French prisoners in Germany, 223,000 . . 29 Oct. ,,
Le Bourget retaken by the Germans; heavy losses on both sides; about 1200 French prisoners, 30 Oct. ,,
Proclamation of Gambetta, accusing Bazaine of treason; the war to go on . . . 30 Oct. ,,
M. Thiers enters Paris . . . 30 Oct. ,,
Garibaldi defending Dôle (Jura) with about 7500 men . . . 31 Oct. ,,
M. Thiers receives powers from the French defence government to treat for an armistice, and has interviews with count Bismarck, 31 Oct. and 1 Nov. ,,
Gen. Bourbaki attempting to form an army of the north, near Lille . . . . Oct.—Nov. ,,
Thionville invested . . . 1 Nov. ,,
The francs-tireurs dispersed in several slight engagements between Colmar and Belfort, 2, 3 Nov. ,,
Letter from marshal Bazaine repelling the charge of treason . . . 2 Nov. ,,
Count Bismarck offers an armistice of 25 days for the election of a French national assembly, 3 Nov. ,,
Defeat of an attempted revolution in Paris: see *France* . . . 3 Nov. ,,
M. Favre declares to the national guard that the government has sworn not to yield an inch of territory, and will remain faithful to this engagement . . . 3 Nov. ,,
Proclamation of Garibaldi to the army of the Vosges, and appealing to other nations, about 3 Nov. ,,
"*Campagne de 1870: par un Officier attaché à l'état major-général*" (a pamphlet ascribed to the emperor), appears in the *Daily Telegraph*, Nov. ,,
Failure of the negotiation, as count Bismarck will not permit food to enter Paris during the armistice without any military equivalent; M. Thiers ordered to break off negotiation . . 6 Nov. ,,
Châteaudun recaptured by the French . . 6 Nov. ,,
The Prussian semi-official journal says, "The French government having refused to listen to reason the cannon will be resorted to for giving them a lesson" . . . 7 Nov. ,,
Bombardment of Thionville . . . 7 Nov. ,,
Circulars on the armistice negotiations—of M. Favre, 7 Nov.; of count Bismarck . 8 Nov. ,,
The king's permission for the election of a French national assembly declined by the French government . . . 7 Nov. ,,
Orders that no one shall enter or quit Paris, 7 Nov. ,,
A Prussian column repulsed in an attack on the army of the Loire at Marchenoir . 7 Nov. ,,
Capitulation of Verdun . . . 8 Nov. ,,
Seven persons, captured in balloons from Paris, sent to German fortresses to be tried by court martial, 8 Nov. ,,
The French fleet off Heligoland . . 8 Nov. ,,
German corps, under Manteuffel, advancing on Amiens and Rouen . . . 8 Nov. ,,

Firm circular from M. Favre to French diplomatic representatives, about . . . 8 Nov. 1870
The Germans enter Montbeliard (Doubs) 9 Nov. ,,
The Germans, under gen. Von der Tann, defeated between Coulmiers and Baccon, near Orleans, retire to Thoury . . . 9 Nov. ,,
M. Thiers' report of the unsuccessful negotiations for an armistice . . . dated 9 Nov. ,,
Reported naval victory of the Prussian steamer *Meteor* over the French steamer *Bouvet* off Havannah . . . 9 Nov. ,,
Continued fighting; Orleans retaken by general D'Aurelle de Paladines: French losses, 2000; Germans about 700, and 2000 prisoners . 10 Nov. ,,
Capitulation of Neu Breisach, 5000 prisoners and 100 guns taken . . . 10 Nov. ,,
The French repulsed near Montbeliard on the Swiss frontier . . . 10 Nov. ,,
Von der Tann's army reinforced by 30,000, now 70,000, the grand duke of Mecklenburg commander; the Loire army about 150,000, but only 12,000 regulars . . . 12 Nov. ,,
Bankers at Berlin and Frankfort arrested for dealing in French war loan . . . about 12 Nov. ,,
Dôle, near Dijon, occupied by the Germans, 12 Nov. ,,
Calm, truthful proclamation of gen. Trochu, at Paris . . . 14 Nov. ,,
The armies in central France have been placed under prince Frederick Charles and the grand duke of Mecklenburg . . . 14 Nov. ,,
Eleven French towns, 3653 guns, 155 mitrailleuses, nearly 500,000 chassepots, about 90 eagles and standards, and nearly 4,000,000*l.* in money, taken by the Germans . . . up to 14 Nov. ,,
Montmédy completely invested . . 15 Nov. ,,
French sorties from Mézières repulsed, 15 Nov.; from Belfort repulsed . . . 16 Nov. ,,
The grand duke of Mecklenburg repulses the army of the Loire near Dreux, which is captured by Von Treskow . . . 17 Nov. ,,
Successful French sortie from Mézières, 500 Germans said to be killed . . . 17 Nov. ,,
Germans victorious in an engagement near Châteaudun; French claim the success 18 Nov. ,,
Ricciotti Garibaldi said to have beaten 700 or 800 men at Châtillon . . . 19 Nov. ,,
The national guard at Evreux repulse a German attack . . . 19 Nov. ,,
The German army under prince Frederick Charles and the grand duke of Mecklenburg (135,000) said to be retreating towards Paris . 19 Nov. ,,
Paris engirdled with a second line of investment, 20 Nov. ,,
French attempt to release La Fère repulsed with heavy loss . . . 20 Nov. ,,
Several balloons from Paris captured about 20 Nov. ,,
French mobile guard defeated at Bretoncelles, 21 Nov. ,,
Bombardment of Thionville begun . . 22 Nov. ,,
Ham occupied by the Prussians . . 22 Nov. ,,
Prince Frederick Charles takes up a position near Orleans . . . 24 Nov. ,,
Thionville, in flames, capitulates, with about 2000 prisoners . . . 24 Nov. ,,
The Germans repulsed near Amiens and near Stagil, 24 Nov. ,,
La Fère surrenders, after two days' bombardment, with about 70 guns and 2000 men . 27 Nov. ,,
The Garibaldians defeated near Pasques (Côte d'Or) by Von Werder . . . 27 Nov. ,,
The French army of the north defeated by Manteuffel between Villers Bretonneux and Soleur, near Amiens . . . 27 Nov. ,,
Amiens occupied by Von Goeben after a severe engagement . . . 28 Nov. ,,
Severe engagement near Beaune la Rolande (Loiret) between part of the army of the Loire under D'Aurelle de Paladines and the Germans under Voigts Rhetz; prince Frederick Charles arrives and turns the day; the French retire; heavy loss on both sides . . . 28 Nov. ,,
M. de Kératry resigns his command, accusing M. Gambetta of misconduct, 28 Nov.; Bourbaki appointed to command an army corps . 29 Nov. ,,
Fruitless endeavours of the army in Paris and the army of the Loire to unite . 29 Nov.—4 Dec. ,,

Sorties from various parts of Paris repulsed with loss . . . . 29 Nov. 1870
Great sortie of 120,000, under generals Trochu and Ducrot, who cross the Marne; severest conflict between Champigny-sur-Marne, Brie-sur-Marne, and Villiers-sur-Marne; the French retain the taken possessions, but their advance is checked; great loss on both sides (chiefly Saxons and Würtembergers engaged) . . . . . 30 Nov. ,,
The contest resumed at Avron; the Germans retake Champigny and Brie; the French retreat 2 Dec. ,,
The army of the Loire: Chanzy defeated by the grand duke of Mecklenburg at Bazoche des Hautes, 2 Dec.; near Chevilly (the French report these engagements indecisive) . . 3 Dec. ,,
Prince Frederick Charles dislodges an encampment in the forest of Orleans. . . . 3 Dec. ,,
Ducrot bivouacks in the woods of Vincennes, 3 Dec.; he issues a final order of the day, referring to two days' glorious battles . 4 Dec. ,,
General D Aurelle de Paladines entrenched before Orleans; proposes to retreat; the government opposes him, but yields; he determines to await the attack; part of his army defeated by prince Frederick Charles, and the grand duke of Mecklenburg; he retreats with about 100,000 men; Orleans threatened with bombardment; surrenders at midnight . . . . 4 Dec. ,,
The Germans said to be in pursuit of D'Aurelle de Paladines (superseded) . . . . 5 Dec. ,,
10,000 prisoners, 77 guns, and 4 gun-boats captured at Orleans . . . . . 5 Dec. ,,
Rouen occupied by Manteuffel . . . 6 Dec. ,,
General order of the king of Prussia, "We enter on a new phase of the war . . Every attempt to break through the investment or relieve Paris has failed" . . . . 6 Dec. ,,
The grand duke of Mecklenburg attacks gen. Chanzy and the army of the Loire near Beaugency; indecisive, 7 Dec.; the Germans victorious, taking about 1100 prisoners and six guns, and occupying Beaugency (severe loss to Germans), 8 Dec. ,,
Gen. Manteuffel's army in two parts, one occupies Evreux, and marching to Cherbourg; the other marching to Havre . . . . 8 Dec ,,
Continued severe engagements between the Germans and the army of the Loire; the defeated French retreat (7 battles in 9 days) 9, 10 Dec. ,,
Vigorous siege of Belfort; obstinately defended, 9 Dec. ,,
Pamphlet (attributed to the emperor Napoleon) published under the name of his friend, the marquis de Gricourt, throwing the blame of the war upon the French nation . . . early in Dec. ,,
Fighting along the whole line of the army of the Loire, under general Chanzy and others; it retreats, but obstinately resists . 5—10 Dec. ,,
Brilliant action by De Chanzy . . . 11 Dec. ,,
The delegate government transferred from Tours to Bordeaux; Gambetta remains with the army of the Loire . . . . 11 Dec. ,,
Dieppe occupied by the Germans . 12 Dec. ,,
La Fère threatened by Faidherbe, commander of the army of the north . . . 12 Dec. ,,
Phalsburg surrenders, subdued by famine; commencement of bombardment of Montmédy, 12 Dec. ,,
Evreux and Blois occupied by the Germans, 13 Dec. ,,
Montmédy surrenders . . . 14 Dec. ,,
Sharp engagement at Fréteval; which is taken and abandoned by the Germans . . 14 Dec. ,,
Nuits near Dijon captured by the Badenese under Von Werder, after a severe conflict 18 Dec. ,,
The French government issue a circular against the propagation of false news. . . . 20 Dec. ,,
Conflict at Monnaie: about 6000 French gardes mobiles driven back to Tours . . 20 Dec. ,,
Vigorous sortie from Paris repulsed—an artillery action. . . . . 21 Dec. ,,
Tours partially shelled; submits, but not occupied by Germans . . . . . . 21 Dec. ,,
Chanzy and part of the army of the Loire said to have reached Le Mans and joined the Bretons, about 21 Dec. ,,
Seven hours' battle at Pont à Noyelles between Manteuffel and the army of the north under Faidherbe: both claim the victory; Faidherbe retreats . . . . 23 Dec. 1870
Six English colliers, said to have had Prussian permits, after delivering coal at Rouen, are sunk in the Seine at Duclair near Havre by the Prussians for strategic reasons . . . . 21 Dec. ,,
Explanation given by Bismarck and compensation promised . . . . 26 Dec. ,,
Chanzy, in a letter to the German commandant at Vendôme, accuses the Germans of cruelly pillaging St. Calais, and, denying his defeat, says, "We have fought you and held you in check since 4 Dec." 26 Dec. ,,
Trochu said to be making Mont Valérien a vast citadel . . . . 27 Dec. ,,
Mont Avron, an outlying fort near Paris, after a day's bombardment, abandoned and occupied by the Germans . . . . . . 29 Dec. ,,
Alleged defeat of the Germans by detachment of Chanzy's army near Montoire . . 27 Dec. ,,
Several small engagements in Normandy—reported successful to the French . . 28—31 Dec. ,,
Capitulation of Mézières with 2000 men and 106 guns . . . . 1, 2 Jan. 1871
Severe battles near Bapaume between the army of the North under Faidherbe and the Germans under Manteuffel and Von Goeben; victory claimed by both, the French retreat . . . 2, 3 Jan. ,,
Indecisive conflict near Dijon le Mans: between general Chanzy and prince Frederick Charles, 6 Jan. ,,
Daujoutin, S. of Belfort, stormed by Germans, 6 Jan. ,,
Bombardment of eastern front of Paris, and of the southern forts, 4 Jan.; forts of Issy and Vanvres silenced . . . . 6 Jan. ,,
Fortress of Rocroy taken by the Germans, 5, 6 Jan. ,,
General Roy defeated near Jumiéges . 7 Jan. ,,
Von Goeben in the north, Manteuffel sent to the east about 7 Jan. ,,
Conflicts (in the east) between Von Werder and Bourbaki at Villarais, south of Vesoul 9, 10 Jan. ,,
Bombardment of Paris, many buildings injured, and people killed: the French government appeal to foreign powers . . . . . 9, 10 Jan. ,,
Capitulation of Péronne with garrison . 9 Jan. ,,
Chanzy retreating; defeated near Le Mans by prince Frederick Charles and the grand duke of Mecklenburg . . . . 11 Jan. ,,
Prince Frederick Charles enters Le Mans; after 6 days' fighting, (about 20,000 French prisoners made; German loss about 3400) . 12 Jan. ,,
Vigorous sorties from Paris repulsed . 13 Jan. ,,
Chanzy retreating, 14 Jan.; defeated near Vosges, 15, 16 Jan. ,,
Indecisive conflicts between Bourbaki and Von Werder, near Belfort . . . . 15, 16 Jan. ,,
St. Quentin recaptured by Isnard under Faidherbe, 16 Jan. ,,
Bourbaki defeated near Belfort after three days' fighting, 15—17 Jan.; retreats south 18 Jan. ,,
The grand duke of Mecklenburg enters Alençon, 17 Jan. ,,
Bombardment of Longwy begun . . 17 Jan. ,,
Faidherbe defeated near St. Quentin; after seven hours' fighting; by Von Goeben, 4000 prisoners taken . . . . 19 Jan. ,,
Great sortie from Paris of Trochu and 100,000 men repulsed with loss of about 1000 dead and 5000 wounded . . . . 19 Jan. ,,
Bourbaki hard pressed by Von Werder 19 Jan. ,,
Armistice for two days at Paris refused 22 Jan. ,,
Bombardment of St Denis and Cambrai 22 Jan. ,,
Faidherbe asserts that the German successes are exaggerated . . . . . . 22 Jan. ,,
Resignation of Trochu; Vinoy, governor of Paris, 23, 24 Jan. ,,
Favre opens negotiations with Bismarck 24 Jan. ,,
Longwy capitulates; 4000 prisoners, 200 guns, 25 Jan. ,,
Letter from M. Guizot to Mr. Gladstone proposing the demolition of fortresses on both sides of the Rhine; and the maintenance of the balance of power by congresses; published 26 Jan. ,,
Capitulation of Paris; armistice for 21 days signed by count Bismarck and Jules Favre 28 Jan. ,,

The forts round Paris occupied by the Germans, 29 Jan. 1871
Advance of German troops into France suspended, 30 Jan. „
Bourbaki and his army, about 80,000, driven by Manteuffel into Switzerland near Pontarlier, about 6000 having been captured . 30 Jan.. 1 Feb. „
French loss about 350,000 men, 800 guns up to Jan. „
Dijon occupied by the Germans . 1 Feb. „
Belfort capitulates with military honours 13 Feb. „
Negotiations for peace between Thiers and Bismarck 22—24 Feb. „
Preliminaries of a treaty accepted by Thiers, Favre, and 15 delegates from the national assembly; it includes cession of parts of Lorraine, including Metz and Thionville and Alsace less Belfort; and payment of 5 milliards of francs, 200,000,000*l.*, 25 Feb., signed 26 Feb., accepted by the national assembly . . . . 1 March, „
German loss in battles throughout the war; killed or died soon after, 17,570; died of wounds eventually 10,707; total killed and wounded 127,867.
German troops enter Paris and remain 48 hours, 1—3 March, „
They quit Versailles . . . . . 12 March, „
Conference for peace open at Brussels, 28 March „
Treaty of peace signed at Frankfort, 10 May; ratified by the French national assembly . 18 May, „

FRANCO-SCOTTISH SOCIETY. The establishment of this society with a Scottish branch was proposed at a meeting in Edinburgh by lord Reay, lord Lothian, the duke of Fife, and others, to promote historical research in relation to the two countries and to assist students in their universities. The purchase and endowment of the disused "College des Escossois" in Paris, proposed 29 Oct. 1895. Inaugural meeting at Paris; lord Reay, sir Archibald Geikie, and others, received by M. Jules Simon: M. Berthelot, and others present, at the Sorbonne, 16-18 April, 1896; first annual meeting in Edinburgh, 11 Nov. Annual meetings held.

FRANCS-TIREURS, free shooters, took an active part in the Franco-Prussian war from about 14 Aug. 1870; and more especially after the surrender of MacMahon's army at Sedan, 2 Sept. Their conduct was much censured.

FRANKENHAUSEN, N. Germany: near this place Philip, landgrave of Hesse, and his allies defeated the insurgent peasantry headed by Munzer the anabaptist, 15 May, 1525.

FRANKFORT-ON-THE-MAINE, central Germany, founded in the 5th century; was the residence of Charlemagne in 794; walled by Louis I. 838; a capital city, 843; an mperial city, 1245. Population in 1885, 154,513; in 1890, 179,850; 1900, 288,489. See *Germany*.

Union of Frankfort: treaty between France, Sweden, Prussia, and other German states led to war with Austria . . . . 22 May, 1744
Frankfort captured by the French by a surprise, 2 Jan. 1759
Captured by Custine, 28 Oct.; retaken by the Prussians . . . . . . 2 Dec. 1792
Bombarded by the French; surrendered to Kleber, 16 July, 1796
Made part of the confederation of the Rhine . 1806
A grand duchy under Carl von Dalberg . 1810
Republic restored; appointed capital of the Germanic confederation 1815
Vain attempts at insurrection by students, April, 1833 . . . . May, 1834
The Frankfort diet publish a federative constitution, 30 March, 1848
The plenipotentiaries of Austria, Bavaria, Saxony, Hanover, Würtemberg, Mecklenburg, &c., here constitute themselves the council of the Germanic diet . . . . 1 Sept. 1850
The German sovereigns (excepting the king of Prussia) met at Frankfort (at the invitation of the emperor of Austria), to consider a plan of federal reform, 17 Aug.; the plan was not accepted by Prussia . . . . 22 Sept. 1863
Meeting of diet of Germanic confederation; condemn the treaty of Gastein . . . 1 Oct. 1865
The diet adopts the Austrian motion, that Prussia has broken the treaty; the Prussian representative declares the confederation at an end, and proposes a new confederation . . . . . 14 June, 1866
Entered by the Prussians, who exact heavy supplies, 16 July, „
Annexed to Prussia by law of 20 Sept.; promulgated at Frankfort; (the legislative corps and 15,000 citizens protest against it) . . . 8 Oct. „
Visited by the king of Prussia; an ancient cathedral, St. Bartholomew (founded 1315, completed 1512), destroyed by fire . . . . . 14, 15 Aug. 1867
Frankfort supported Prussia in the war . July, 1870
Treaty of peace between France and Germany, signed here . . . . 10 May, 1871
Riots through rise in price of beer; suppressed by N. German soldiers: 37 of the people killed; about 100 wounded . . . 21, 22 April, 1873
International Electro-Technical congress opened 8 Sept. *et seq.*, 1891
Goethe celebrations; the empress Frederick and other royalties present . . . 27, 28 Aug. 1899
Fire in an explosives factory at Griesheim; over 15 deaths, many injured . . 25 April, 1901

FRANKFORT-ON-THE-ODER (N. Germany); a member of the Hanseatic league; suffered much from marauders in the middle ages, and in the thirty years' war. The university was founded in 1506, and incorporated with that of Breslau in 1811. Near Frankfort, 12 Aug. 1759, Frederick of Prussia was defeated by the Russians and Austrians, see *Cunnersdorf*. Population, 1890, 55,724; 1900, 61,835.

FRANKING LETTERS, passing letters free of postage, was claimed by parliament about 1660. The privilege was restricted in 1839, and abolished after the introduction of the uniform penny postage, 10 Jan. 1840. The queen was amongst the first to relinquish her privilege.

FRANKLIN, the English freeholder in the middle ages; see "the Franklin's Tale," in Chaucer's Canterbury Tales (written about 1364).

FRANKLIN, SEARCH FOR. Sir John Franklin, with captains Crozier and Fitzjames, in H. M. ships *Erebus* and *Terror* (carrying in all 138 persons), sailed on his third arctic expedition of discovery and survey, from Greenhithe, on 19 May, 1845; see *North-west Passage*. Their last despatches were from the Whalefish islands, dated 12 July, 1845. Their protracted absence caused intense anxiety, and several expeditions were sent from England and elsewhere in search of them, and coals, provisions, clothing, and other necessaries, were deposited in various places in the Arctic seas by our own and by the American government, by lady Franklin, and numerous private persons. The *Truelove*, captain Parker, which arrived at Hull, 4 Oct. 1849, from Davis's Straits, brought intelligence (not afterwards confirmed) that the natives had seen sir John Franklin's ships in the previous March, frozen up by the ice in Prince Regent's inlet. Other accounts were equally illusory. Her majesty's government, on 7 March, 1850, offered a reward of 20,000*l.* to any party of any country, that should render efficient assistance to the crews of the missing ships. Sir John's first winter quarters were found at Beechy island by captains Ommanney and Penny.

1. H.M.S. *Plover*, capt. Moore (afterwards under capt. Maguire), sailed from Sheerness to Behring's Straits, in search . . . . . 1 Jan. 1848

2. Land expedition under sir John Richardson and Dr. John Rae, of the Hudson's Bay Company, left England . . . . 25 March, 1848
[Sir John Richardson returned to England in 1849, and Dr. Rae continued his search till 1851.]
3. Sir James Ross, with the *Enterprise* and *Investigator* (12 June, 1848), having also sailed in search to Barrow's Straits, returned to England (Scarborough) . . . . 3 Nov. 1849
4. The *Enterprise*, capt. Collinson, and *Investigator*, commander M'Clure, sailed from Plymouth for Behring's Straits . . . . 20 Jan. 1850
[Both ships proceeded through to the eastward.]
5. Capt. Austin's expedition, viz.: *Resolute*, capt. Austin, C.B.; *Assistance*, capt. Ommanney; *Intrepid*, lieut. Bertie Cator; and *Pioneer*, lieut. Sherard Osborn, sailed from England for Barrow's Straits . . . . 25 April, „
[Returned Sept. 1851.]
6. The *Lady Franklin*, capt. Penny; and *Sophia*, capt. Stewart, sailed from Aberdeen for Barrow's Straits . . . . 13 April, „
[Returned home Sept. 1851.]
7. The AMERICAN expedition in the *Advance* and *Rescue*, under lieut. De Haven and Dr. Kane (son of the judge), towards which Mr. Grinnell subscribed 30,000 dollars, sailed for Lancaster Sound and Barrow Straits; after drifting in the pack down Baffin's Bay, the ships were released in 1851 uninjured . . . . 25 May, „
8. The *Felix*, sir John Ross, fitted out chiefly by the Hudson Bay Company, sailed to the same locality, 22 May, „
[Returned in 1851.]
9. H.M.S. *North Star*, commander Saunders, which had sailed from England in 1849, wintered in Wolstenholme Sound, and returned to Spithead, 28 Sept „
10. H.M.S. *Herald*, captain Kellett, C.B., which had sailed in 1848, made three voyages to Behring's Straits, and returned in . . . 1851
Lieut Pim went to St. Petersburg with the intention of travelling through Siberia to the mouth of the river Kolyma; but was dissuaded from proceeding by the Russian government . . 18 Nov. „
[The *Enterprise* and *Investigator* (*see* No. 4 *above*) not having been heard of for two years.]
11. Sir Edward Belcher's expedition, consisting of —*Assistance*, sir Edward Belcher, C.B.; *Resolute*, captain Kellett, C.B.; *North Star*, capt. Pullen; *Intrepid*, capt. M'Clintock; and *Pioneer*, capt. Sherard Osborn, sailed from Woolwich 15 April, 1852
[This expedition arrived at Beechy Island 14 Aug. 1852. The *Assistance* and *Pioneer* proceeded through Wellington Channel, and the *Resolute* and *Intrepid* to Melville Island; the *North Star* remaining at Beechy Island.]

LADY FRANKLIN'S EQUIPMENTS.

Lady Franklin, aided by a few friends (and by the "Tasmanian Tribute" of 1500*l.*), equipped four expeditions (Nos. 12, 13, 14, 16).
12. *Prince Albert*, capt. Forsyth, sailed from Aberdeen to Barrow Straits . . . . 5 June, 1850
[Returned 1 Oct. 1850.]
13. The *Prince Albert*, Mr. Kennedy, accompanied by lieut. Bellot, of the French navy, and John Hepburn, sailed from Stromness to Prince Regent's Inlet . . . . . 4 June, 1851
[Returned Oct. 1852.]
14. The *Isabel*, commander Inglefield, sailed for the head of Baffin's Bay, Jones's Sound, and the Wellington Channel, 6 July; and returned Nov. 1852
15. Mr. Kennedy sailed again in the *Isabel*, on a renewed search to Behring's Straits 1853
16. H.M.S. *Rattlesnake*, commander Trollope, despatched to assist the *Plover*, capt. Maguire (who succeeded capt. Moore), at Point Barrow in April; met with it . . . . Aug. „
17. The second AMERICAN expedition, the *Advance*, under Dr. Kane . . . early in June, „
18. The *Phœnix* (with the *Breadalbane* transport), commander Inglefield, accompanied by lieut. Bellot, sailed in May; he returned, bringing despatches from Sir E. Belcher, &c. . . Oct. „
The *Investigator* and sir E. Belcher's squadron were safe; but no traces of Franklin's party had been met with. Lieut. Bellot was unfortunately drowned in August while voluntarily conveying despatches for sir E. Belcher. Capt. M'Clure had left the *Herald* (10) at Cape Lisburne, 31 July, 1850. On 8 Oct. the ship was frozen in, and so continued for nine months. On 26 Oct. 1850, while on an excursion party, the captain discovered an entrance into Barrow's Straits, and thus established the existence of a N.E.—N.W. *passage*. In Sept. 1851, the ship was again fixed in ice, and so remained till lieut. Pim and a party from capt. Kellett's ship, the *Resolute* (11), fell in with them in April, 1853. The position of the *Enterprise* (4) was still unknown.
A monument to Bellot's memory was erected at Greenwich. His "Journal" was published in 1854
Dr. Rae, in the spring of 1853, again proceeded towards the magnetic pole; and in July, 1854, he reported to the Admiralty that he had purchased from a party of Esquimaux a number of articles which had belonged to sir J. Franklin and his party—namely, sir John's star or order, part of a watch, silver spoons, and forks with crests, &c. He also reported the statement of the natives, that they had met with a party of white men about four winters previous, and had sold them a seal; and that four months later, in the same season, they had found the bodies of thirty men (some buried), who had evidently perished by starvation; the place appears, from the description, to have been in the neighbourhood of the Great Fish river of Back. Dr. Rae arrived in England on 22 Oct. 1854, with the relics, which have since been deposited in Greenwich hospital. He and his companions were awarded 10,000*l.* for their discovery. Dr. Rae, aged 80, died . . . . . . 22 July, 1893
19. The *Phœnix*, *North Star*, and *Talbot*, under the command of capt. Inglefield, sailed in May, and returned in . . . . . . Oct. 1854
Sir E. Belcher (No. 11), after mature deliberation, in April, 1854, determined to abandon his ships, and gave orders to that effect to all the captains under his command; and capt. Kellett gave similar orders to capt. M'Clure, of the *Investigator*. The vessels had been abandoned 15 May* when the crews of the *Phœnix* and *Talbot* (under capt. Inglefield) arrived (19). On their return to England all the captains were tried by court martial and honourably acquitted 17-19 Oct. „
Capt. Collinson's fate was long uncertain, and another expedition was in contemplation, when intelligence came, in Feb. 1855, that he had met the *Rattlesnake* (16) at Fort Clarence on 21 Aug. 1854, and had sailed immediately, in hopes of getting up with capt. Maguire in the *Plover* (1), which had sailed two days previously. Capt. Collinson having failed in getting through the ice in 1850 with capt. M'Clure, returned to Hong-Kong to winter. In 1851 he passed through Prince of Wales's Straits, and remained in the Arctic regions without obtaining any intelligence of Franklin till July, 1854, when, being once more released from the ice, he sailed for Fort Clarence, where he arrived as above mentioned. Captains Collinson and Maguire arrived in England in . . . . May, 1855
20. The third AMERICAN expedition in search of Dr Kane, in the *Advance*, consisted of the *Release* and the steamer *Arctic*, the barque *Eringo*, and another vessel under the command of lieut. H. J. Hartstene, accompanied by a brother of Dr. Kane as surgeon . . . 31 May, „
[On 17 May, 1855, Dr. Kane and his party quitted the *Advance*, and journeyed over the ice, 1300

* Capt. Kellett's ship, the *Resolute*, was found adrift 1000 miles distant from where she was left, by a Mr. George Henry, commanding an American whaler, who brought her to New York. The British government having abandoned their claim on the vessel, it was bought by order of the American congress, thoroughly repaired and equipped, and entrusted to capt. H. J. Hartstene, to be presented to queen Victoria. It arrived at Southampton, 12 Dec. 1856; was visited by her majesty on the 16th; and formally surrendered on the 30th. When the ship was broken up a desk was made of the wood, and presented by queen Victoria to the president of the United States, 29 Nov. 1880.

miles, to the Danish settlement; on their way home in a Danish vessel, they fell in with lieut. Hartstene, 18 Sept.; and arrived with him at New York, 11 Oct. 1855. Dr. Kane visited England in 1856; he died in 1857.]

The Hudson's Bay Company, under advice of Dr. Rae and sir G. Back, sent out an overland expedition, June 1855, which returned Sept. following. Some more remains of Franklin's party were discovered 1855

21. The 18th British expedition (equipped by lady Franklin and her friends, the government having declined to fit out another)—the *Fox*, screw steamer, under capt. (since sir) F. L. M'Clintock, R.N. (*see* No. 11)—sailed from Aberdeen 1 July, 1857; returned . . . . . 22 Sept. 1859

On 6 May, 1859, lieut. Hobson found at Point Victory, near Cape Victoria, besides a cairn, a tin case, containing a paper, signed 25 April, 1848, by capt. Fitzjames, which certified that the ships *Erebus* and *Terror*, on 12 Sept. 1846, were beset in lat. 70° 50′ N., and long. 98° 23′ W.; that sir John Franklin died 11 June, 1847; and that the ships were deserted 22 April, 1848. Captain M'Clintock continued the search, and discovered skeletons and other relics. His Journal was published in Dec. 1859; and on 28 May, 1860, gold medals were given to him and to lady Franklin by the Royal Geographical Society.

Mr. Hall, the arctic explorer, reported, in Aug. 1865, circumstances that led him to hope that capt. Crozier and others were surviving.

A national monument by Noble, set up in Waterloo-place, was inaugurated, 15 Nov. 1866. It is inscribed to "FRANKLIN the great navigator and his brave companions who sacrificed their lives in completing the discovery of the north-west passage, A.D. 1847-8."

Sir John Franklin discovered the *north-west passage* by sailing down Peel and Victoria Straits, now named Franklin Straits.

"Franklin search expedition," under lieut. Schwatka, of U.S. navy, in an overland expedition in summer and autumn of 1879, discovers some human remains of the crews of the ships and other things; he set up memorials, and brought away the remains of lieut. John Irving, of the *Terror*; and returned to Massachusetts about 23 Sept. 1880

Remains of lieut. John Irving buried at Edinburgh, 7 Jan. 1881

Lady Franklin, aged 83, died . . . 18 July, 1875

50th anniversary of the departure of sir John Franklin's expedition, celebrated by the Royal Geographical society . . . . 20 May, 1895

Mr. H. D. Traill's "Life of sir John Franklin," published . . . . March, 1896

FRANKS (or freemen), a name given to a combination of the North-western German tribes about 240, which invaded Gaul and other parts of the empire with various success in the 5th century; see *Gaul* and *France*; see *Franking*.

FRANZ JOSEF LAND, see *N.-E. and W. Passages*, 1871 and 1894. "A Thousand Days in the Arctic," 2 vols., by Fred. G. Jackson; explorations and scientific work described, published, 1899. Queen Victoria sea discovered, 1895.

FRASER'S MAGAZINE, first appeared, Feb. 1830; discontinued Oct. 1882.

FRATRICELLI (Little Brethren), a sect of the middle ages, originally strict Franciscan monks. Their numbers increased, and they were condemned by a papal bull in 1317; and suffered persecution; but were not extinct till the 16th century. They resembled the "Brethren of the Free Spirit."

FRAUDS, STATUTE OF. 29 Charles II., c. 3, 1677. "An act for prevention of frauds and perjuryes."

FRAUDULENT TRUSTEES ACT, 20 & 21 Vict. c. 54, passed Aug. 1857, in consequence of the delinquencies of sir John D. Paul, the British Bank frauds, &c. It was brought in by sir R. Bethell, then attorney-general (afterwards lord Westbury), and is very stringent.

FRAUNHOFER'S LINES, see *Spectrum*.

FREDERICKSBURG (Virginia, N. America). On 10 Dec. 1862, general Burnside and the federal army of the Potomac crossed the small deep river Rappahannock. On 11 Dec. Fredericksburg was bombarded by the federals and destroyed. On the 13th commenced a series of desperate unsuccessful attacks on the confederate works, defended by generals Lee, Jackson, Longstreet, and others. General Hooker crossed the river with the reserves, and joined in the conflict, in vain. On 15 and 16 Dec. the federal army recrossed the Rappahannock. The battle was one of the most severe in the war.

FREDERICKSHALD (Norway). Charles XII. of Sweden was killed by a cannon-shot before its walls, while examining the works. His hand was on his sword, and a prayer-book in his pocket, 11 Dec. 1718.

FREDERICTON, the capital of the province of New Brunswick, Canada, and the centre of a large lumber trade. Population 6,502.

FREE CHURCH COUNCIL, see *National Free Church Council*.

FREE CHURCH OF ENGLAND (Evangelical). An Episcopal Church founded in 1844, and enrolled in her majesty's High Court of Chancery in 1863. See *Catechism*, 1899.

This church grew out of the Oxford tractarian movement of 1830. The first church was planted at Bridgetown, Devon, by the rev. James Shore, M.A., curate of the parish; it was built by the duke of Somerset, and opened in 1844. Two other churches were established in the same year—one at Exeter, and the other at Ilfracombe. But it was not till 1849 that much progress was made, when an impetus was given to the movement by the late bishop of Exeter's (Philpott) prosecution of Mr. Shore, for preaching in his diocese without his licence. The work spread, and the organization was enrolled under a deed poll as an "Episcopal Church." But as "Consecration" could not be obtained a bishop president was elected till 1876, when the secession of the right rev. bishop Cummins from the "Protestant Episcopal Church of America" (the first bishops of which church were consecrated by the archbishop of Canterbury at Lambeth Palace chapel, in 1787), afforded an opportunity, which was embraced, of obtaining episcopal consecration for the bishops of the Free Church of England in the Canterbury line of episcopal succession.

The services of the F. C. E. are conducted exactly as those of the evangelical section of the national church, excepting the omission of some words in the offices which the F. C. E. consider express doctrines opposed to the Protestant Reformation.

A Free Church congress met at Manchester, 10 Nov. 1892; at Birmingham, 26 March, 1895; Nottingham, 10 March, 1896; Bristol, 8 March, 1898. Nonconformists, with the exception of Unitarians, are admitted to the congress. Annual meetings.

National council of the Evangelical Free Church, 1st annual session, president, rev. Hugh Price Hughes, 1896; 2nd annual session, president, rev. Monro Gibson, London . . . . . 9 March, 1897

FREE CHURCH OF SCOTLAND was formed by an act of secession of nearly half the body from the national church of Scotland, headed by Dr. Thos. Chalmers and other eminent ministers, 18 May, 1843. The difference arose on the question of the right of patrons to nominate to livings; see *Patronage*. The Free Church claims for the parishioners the right of a veto. Much distress was endured the first year by the ministers of the new church, although 366,719*l.* 14*s.* 3*d.* had been subscribed. In 1853 there were 850 congregations; in 1873, 954. A large college was founded in 1846. In 1856 the sustentation fund amounted to 108,638*l.* from which was paid the sum of 138*l.* each to 700 ministers.

The Rev. Mr. Knight, censured for opinions respecting prayer, seceded . . . . 22 Oct. 1873
The Reformed Presbyterian Church (see *Cameronians*), joined the Free Church . . 25 May, 1876
Professor Robertson Smith, generally censured for his article "Bible, &c.," in the "Encyclopædia Britannica," 1875, after long consideration by the assembly, admonished only . . 27 May, 1880
Professor Robertson Smith expelled from his professorship, but to retain salary, by the general assembly (394—231) . . . . . 26 May, 1881
Jubilee celebrated . . . . . . 18 May, 1893
Union of the Free and United Churches effected, under the title of the United Free Church of Scotland, at Edinburgh . . . 31 Oct. 1900
Mission of the United "Free Churches;" large meetings held in London . . end of Jan. 1901

FREE CHURCH SOCIETY, or National Association for Freedom of Public Worship, established in 1857, to abolish the pew-rent system and revive the weekly offertory to defray the expenses of public worship. The Free and Open Church Association was formed in 1866.

FREE COMPANIES AND LANCES, see *Condottieri*.

FREEDMEN'S BUREAUS, established in the Southern States of North America in March, 1865, to protect the freed negroes. Having the support of martial law, these bureaus became very oppressive, and the act of congress making them permanent was vetoed by president Johnson in Feb. 1866.

FREE EDUCATION ACT. See under *Education*, 1891.

FREE FOOD LEAGUE, see *Preferential Tariffs*.

FREEHOLDERS. Those *under* forty shillings per annum were not qualified to vote for members of parliament by 8 Hen. VI. c. 7, 1429. Various acts have been passed for the regulation of the franchise at different periods. The more recent were, the act to regulate polling, 9 Geo. IV., 1828; act for the disqualification of freeholders in Ireland, which deprived those of forty shillings of this privilege, passed 13 April, 1829; Reform acts, 1832, 1867, 1868. County elections act, 7 Will. IV., 1836. See *Chandos Clause*.

FREE HOSPITAL, ROYAL, Gray's Inn-road, founded in 1828 by Dr. William Marsden (born Aug. 1796), who actively superintended it till his death, 16 Jan. 1867. In 1851, he founded the Cancer Hospital (Brompton), *which see.* Patients admitted without letters. In 1878 Mr. Wm. Birks Rhodes, "the Hounslow miser," bequeathed to the hospital about 39,000*l.*

FREE LABOUR REGISTRATION SOCIETY, established for the benefit of employers and non-unionist workmen, in opposition to trades' unions, July, 1867. The struggle of free labour and the unions was very severe 1890 *et seq.* See under *Shipping, Strikes, &c.* 1st congress of the national *free labour association* met in Clerkenwell, 31 Oct. 1893; again, 30 Oct. 1894; at Newcastle-on-Tyne, 7 Oct. 1895; Manchester (150,000 members), 5 Oct. 1896; London, 11 Oct. 1897; Manchester, 10 Oct. 1898; London, 9 Oct. 1899; London, 14 Oct. 1901; Leeds, 20 Oct. 1902.

FREE LAND LEAGUE, see *Land*.

FREE LIBRARIES, see *Libraries*.

FREEMASONRY. Writers on masonry, themselves masons, affirm that it has had a being "ever since symmetry began, and harmony displayed her charms." It is traced by some to the building of Solomon's temple; and it is said the architects from the African coast, Mahometans, brought it into Spain, about the 9th century. A modern speculative cosmopolitan freemasonry with some analogies has essential differences from some early secret societies, and is not earlier than the seventeenth century. In 1717, the grand lodge of England was established; that of Ireland in 1730; and that of Scotland in 1736. Freemasons were excommunicated by the pope in 1738; again condemned, 30 Sept. 1865. Freemasons' Hall, Great Queen-street, London, built 1771; rebuilt, and consecrated 14 April, 1869. Partly burnt, 3 May, 1883. A portrait of George Washington, gift of Mr. Wellcome, unveiled here by Mr. Choate, U.S. ambassador, 8 Aug. 1902. The charity instituted, 1788. The duke of Sussex and the earl of Zetland were each twenty-five years grand-master of England. Earl de Grey, afterwards marquis of Ripon, was installed grand-master of the English freemasons in room of the earl of Zetland, 14 May, 1870. The marquis (on becoming a Romanist) resigned 1 Sept. 1874. He was succeeded by the prince of Wales; installed in the Royal Albert Hall, 28 April, 1875. The duke of Leinster, grand-master for Ireland for 60 years, died 10 Oct. 1874; succeeded by the duke of Abercorn. The prince of Wales was installed at Edinburgh as patron of the freemasons of Scotland, 12 Oct. 1870. As grand-master past and present of the mark masons, London, 8 Dec. 1883. Installed as Grand Master of the Grand Lodge, 1 July, 1886; re-elected, March 2, 1898; again 25 April, 1900; resigns, entitled Protector of English Freemasons. The duke of Connaught grand-master, 17 July, 1901; installed grand-master of mark masons, 3 June, 1902. Prince Leopold installed as master of the "lodge of antiquity" (at one time held by sir Christopher Wren), 25 June, 1879.

Royal Masonic Institutions: for girls (Battersea), founded 1788; for boys (Wood Green), 1798; for the aged and widows 1842
Gould's "History of Freemasonry" 1886
Large representative gathering at the Albert hall, the prince of Wales present; an address to the queen voted . . . . . 14 June, 1897
Mr. Henry Maudslay, an old and active member and philanthropist, dies . . . . 17 July, 1899

FREE PORTS, see *Hanse Towns*.

FREETHINKERS, professors of natural religion; see *Deists*. Mr. John M. Robertson, in his "Short History of Freethought," published 1899, defines "Freethought" "*as a revision or rejection of current religious doctrines by more or less practical people.*"

FREE TRADE principles, advocated by Adam Smith in his "Wealth of Nations" (1776), triumphed in England when the corn laws were abolished in 1846, and the commercial treaty with France was adopted in 1860. Richard Cobden, who was very instrumental in passing these measures, and termed "Apostle of Free Trade," died 2 April, 1865. Since 1830 the exports have been tripled. See *French Treaty*. An agitation for free trade has begun in the United States. A reform league was formed at Boston, 20 April, 1869; and the movement became active in New York in Nov., and has since continued. A free-trade budget was brought in by the ministry in Sydney in 1873. A new free-trade league was inaugurated in London in Dec. 1873; and one at Melbourne, Australia, Sept. 1876.

Free trade warmly advocated in New South Wales, supported in New Zealand; opposed in Canada and in Victoria, Australia, 1877-80. Much agitation against free-trade in 1880-2 and in 1903. See *Anti-Corn Law League, Fair Trade,* and *Preferential Tariffs.* American Free Trade League formed at Detroit, June, 1883. Protection, *which see*, dominant in Europe, Feb. 1885 *et seq.*

President Cleveland's message strongly urges fiscal reform, large reduction of protective duties and other taxation 6 Dec. 1887.

Reform club at New York to support tariff reform; first banquet 21 Jan. 1888.

Powerful speech of M. Léon Say on behalf of free trade in the chamber of deputies, pointing out the dangers of retrogression 9 and 11 May, 1891.

The marquis of Salisbury, in a speech at Hastings, advocates duties on foreign luxuries, 18 May, 1892.

Mr. Grover Cleveland, a free-trader, re-elected president of the United States, N.A., 8 Nov. 1892; he condemned protection, 4 March, 1893. See *United States*, Aug. 1894.

Important speech of Mr. Chamberlain at Birmingham on trade preference and reciprocity with the colonies, holding that the fiscal relations of the country had wholly changed since the days of Cobden and Bright, and advocating retaliation with foreign nations, if necessary, when the interests of England and her colonies were threatened, and proposes a tax on imported corn, 15 May, 1903

Mr. Chamberlain's proposals much discussed in England, the Colonies, the United States, and on the Continent . . . . . mid May, *et seq.* ,,

Lord Rosebery on Mr. Chamberlain's proposed fiscal changes . . . . . 19 May, ,,

Debate in the commons on Mr. Chamberlain's new policy . . . . 28 May, ,,

Tariff Reform league formed to promote Mr. Chamberlain's fiscal policy, and Free Trade union to resist that policy . . . . . mid July, ,,

Great issue of fiscal literature, *pro* and *con*, Aug. ,,

Mr. Balfour's pamphlet, "Insular Free Trade," issued . . . . 15 Sept. ,,

Resignation of Mr. Chamberlain, Mr. Ritchie, and lord George Hamilton, announced . 18 Sept. ,,

Mr. Balfour addresses a great meeting at Sheffield; a tax on food was not within practical politics, but the country ought to have the power of negotiating . . . . 1 Oct. ,,

Duke of Devonshire resigns (for Cabinet changes see *Balfour Administration* in *Addenda*) . 6 Oct. ,,

Mr. Chamberlain opens his fiscal campaign at Glasgow . . . . 6 Oct. ,,

Speech of lord Rosebery at Sheffield in defence of free trade . . . . 13 Oct. ,,

Sir H. Campbell-Bannerman speaks at Bolton in favour of free trade . . . . . 16 Oct. ,,

Mr. John Morley upholds the doctrine of Cobden and Bright in opposition to Mr. Chamberlain's scheme, Manchester . . . . . 18 Oct. ,,

Mr. Chamberlain speaks at Newcastle . 20 Oct. ,,

National conference of miners' delegates at Westminster palace hotel pass a resolution in favour of free trade . . . . 22 Oct. ,,

Mr. Asquith speaks at Newcastle and opposes Mr. Chamberlain's policy . . . . . 24 Oct. ,,

Mr. Chamberlain addresses a great meeting, at which some 4,000 working men are present, at the Hippodrome, Liverpool . . . 27 Oct. ,,

[See further in *Addenda*.]

FREEZING, see *Congelation* and *Ice*.

"FREIHEIT," German newspaper. See *Trials*, 1881.

FRENCH ASIA, see *Indo-China*.

FRENCH ASSOCIATION FOR THE ADVANCEMENT OF THE SCIENCES was established by the general assembly, 22 April, 1872, its chief founders being MM. Balard, Claude Bernard, Delaunay, Dumas, Pasteur, Berthelot, Würtz, and others. It held its first meeting at Bordeaux, 5 Sept. 1872, when many foreign scientific men were present, M. De Quatrefages, president; second, Lyons, 21 Aug. 1873; third, Lille, 20 Aug. 1874; fourth, Nantes, 19 Aug. 1875; fifth, Clermont Ferrand, 19 Aug. 1876; sixth, Havre, 30 Aug. 1877; seventh, Paris, 22 Aug. 1878; eighth, Montpellier, 28 Aug. 1879; ninth, Rheims, 11 Aug. 1880; tenth, Algiers, 14 April, 1881; La Rochelle, 23 Aug. 1882; Rouen, 17 Aug. 1883; Blois, 3 Sept. 1884; Grenoble, 12 Aug. 1885; Nancy, 12 Aug. 1886; Toulouse, 22 Sept. 1887; Oran, Algeria, 29 March, 1888; Paris, 8-14 Aug. 1889; Limoges, 7-14 Aug. 1890; Marseilles, 17 Sept. 1891; Pau, 1892; Besançon, 3 Aug. 1893; Caen, 9 Aug. 1894; Bordeaux, 4-9 Aug. 1895; Tunis, 1 April, 1896; St. Etienne, 5-15 Aug. 1897; Nantes, 4 Aug. 1898; Boulogne, mid Sept. 1899; Paris, 2-9 Aug. 1900; Montauban, 4-9 Aug. 1902; Angiers, early Aug. 1903.

FRENCH CHURCH, see *Church of France*.

FRENCH CONGO, see *French West Africa*.

FRENCH EXHIBITION, at Earl's Court, West Brompton, London, W., was opened by the lord mayor Isaacs, 17 May, closed 1 Nov. 1890.

The exhibition principally consisted of objects which appeared in the Universal Exhibition at Paris, 1889. It included works of art, manufactures, books, panoramas of parts of Paris, and a hippodrome. In the "Wild East grounds" appeared Algerian Arabs, with their families and steeds; a chariot drawn by three African lions was driven round the arena.

FRENCH GUINEA constituted a colony, March, 1893. M. Ballay, governor. Successful fighting with the natives reported, 29 March, 1894.

FRENCH LANGUAGE is mainly based on the rude Latin of the western nations subjugated by the Romans. German was introduced by the Franks in the 8th century. In the 9th the Gallo-Romanic dialect became divided into the *Langue d'oc* of the south and the *Langue d'oil* of the north. The dialect of the Isle of France became predominant in the 12th century. The French language as written by Froissart assimilates more to the modern French, and its development was almost completed when the Académie Française (established by Richelieu in 1634) published a dictionary of the language in 1674. The French language, laws, and customs were introduced into England by William I., 1066. Law pleadings were changed from French to English in the reign of Edward III., 1362. *Stow.* See *Drama*.

PRINCIPAL FRENCH AUTHORS.

	Born	Died		Born	Died
Chanson de Roland	11th century.		La Rochefoucauld . .	1613	1680
Roman d' Alexandre	12th century.		Corneille . .	1606	1684
R. Wace Roman de Brut	12th century.		La Fontaine .	1621	1695
Roman de la Rose	12th century.		Mad. de Sevigné	1626	1696
Villehardouin .	1160	1213	La Bruyère .	1645	1696
Joinville . .	1223	1319	Racine . . .	1639	1699
Froissart . .	1333	1410	Bossuet . .	1627	1704
Monstrelet about	1390	1453	Bourdaloue . .	1632	1704
Comines . .	1445	1509	Bayle . . .	1647	1706
Marot . . .	1495	1544	Flechier . .	1632	1710
Rabelais . .	1483	1553	Boileau . .	1636	1711
Ronsard . .	1524	1585	Fénélon . .	1651	1715
Montaigne .	1533	1592	Vertot . .	1655	1735
Beza . . .	1519	1605	Rollin . . .	1661	1741
Malherbe . .	1555	1628	Massillon . .	1663	1742
Des Cartes . .	1596	1650	Le Sage . .	1668	1747
Paul Scarron	1610	1660	Montesquieu .	1689	1755
Pascal . .	1623	1662	Voltaire . .	1694	1778
Molière . .	1622	1673	J. J. Rousseau .	1712	1778
			D'Alembert .	1717	1783
			Diderot . .	1713	1784
			Buffon . . .	1707	1788

	Born	Died
Beaumarchais	1732	1799
Marmontel	1723	1799
Mad. Cottin	1773	1807
Delille	1738	1813
St. Pierre	1737	1814
De Staël	1766	1817
De Genlis	1746	1830
Sismondi	1773	1842
C. Delavigne	1793	1843
Châteaubriand	1768	1848
Balzac	1799	1850
D. F. Arago	1786	1853
Augustin Thierry	1795	1856
Béranger	1780	1857
Eugène Sue	1804	1857
Alfred de Musset	1810	1857
A. Eugène Scribe	1791	1861
A. de Vigny	1797	1863
A. G. De Barante	1782	1866
A. F. Villemain	1790	1867
Victor Cousin	1792	1867
A De la Martine	1790	1869
Sainte Beuve	1804	1869
Alexandre Dumas	1803	1870
Hégésippe Moreau	1810	1838
C. F. Montalembert	1810	1870
P. Mérimée	1803	1870
Théophile Gautier	1811	1872
Amédée Thierry	1797	1873
F. Guizot	1787	1874
Jules Michelet	1798	1874
E. Quinet	1803	1875
L. A. Thiers	1797	1877
Lanfrey	1828	1877
Louis Blanc	1811	1882
L. H. Martin, hist.	1810	1883
Victor Hugo	1802	1885
George Sand	1804	1876
E. About	1828	1885
E. Renan	1823	1892
H. A. Taine	1828	1893
Erckmann	1822	1899
Chatrian	1826	1890
Alphonse Karr	1808	1890
Octave Feuillet	1812	1891
Henry Guy de Maupassant	1850	1893
Alexandre Dumas *fils*	1824	1895
Victor Cherbuliez	1829	1899
Emile Zola	1840	1902
Alphonse Daudet	1840	1897

FRENCH NATIONAL SOCIETY, for social, commercial, and artistic purposes, founded in London 15 Jan. 1881.

FRENCH NAVY, see *Navy* and *Fleets*.

FRENCH PROTESTANT HOSPITAL, founded in 1708 to maintain poor descendants of French protestant refugees, 40 females, 20 males.

FRENCH RELIEF FUND, see *Mansion-house Fund*. The French peasant relief fund, originated by the *Daily News*, in Sept. 1870, was closed April, 1871.

FRENCH REVOLUTIONARY CALENDAR. In 1792, the French nation adopted a calendar professedly founded on philosophical principles. The first year of the era of the republic began at midnight, between 21 and 22 Sept. 1792; but its establishment was not decreed until the 4th Frimaire of the year II., 24 Nov. 1793. The calendar existed until the 10th Nivose, year of the republic XIV., 31 Dec. 1805, when the Gregorian mode of calculation was restored by Napoleon I. 1800 was not a leap year.

	AUTUMN.	
Vendémiaire	Vintage month,	22 Sept. to 21 Oct.
Brumaire	Fog month	22 Oct. to 20 Nov.
Frimaire	Sleet month	21 Nov. to 20 Dec.
	WINTER.	
Nivôse	Snow month	21 Dec. to 19 Jan.
Pluviôse	Rain month	20 Jan. to 18 Feb.
Ventôse	Wind month	19 Feb. to 20 Mar.
	SPRING.	
Germinal	Sprouts' month,	21 Mar. to 19 April.
Floréal	Flowers' month,	20 April to 19 May.
Prairial	Pasture month,	20 May to 18 June.
	SUMMER.	
Messidor	Harvest month,	19 June to 18 July.
Fervidor, or Thermidor	Hot month	19 July to 17 Aug.
Fructidor	Fruit month	18 Aug. to 16 Sept.

SANSCULOTIDES, OR FEASTS DEDICATED TO

Les Vertus	The Virtues	17 Sept.
Le Génie	Genius	18 Sept.
Le Travail	Labour	19 Sept.
L'Opinion	Opinion	20 Sept.
Les Récompenses	Rewards	21 Sept.

FRENCH REVOLUTIONS, see *France*.

FRENCHTOWN (Canada), was taken from the British by the American general Winchester, 22 Jan. 1813, during the second war with the United States of America. It was retaken by the British forces under general Proctor, 24 Jan., and the American commander and his troops were made prisoners.

FRENCH TREATY, the term given to the treaty of commerce between Great Britain and France, signed 23 Jan. 1860, at Paris, by lord Cowley and Richard Cobden and by the ministers MM. Baroche and Rouher. The beneficial results of this treaty compensated for the depression of trade occasioned by the civil war in North America (1861-5). The French assembly determined that on 15 March, 1871, this treaty should cease in 12 months from that date. A fresh treaty was signed at Paris 29 Jan. 1873. Free trade was somewhat restricted, but the new French navigation law was relaxed. Negotiations for a new treaty began in London, 26 May, 1881. See *France*, 1881-2; see also *Anglo-French Treaty* under *France* in *Addenda*.

FRENCH WEST AFRICA includes Senegal, the Soudan, French Guinea, French Congo, Ivory Coast, and Dahomey; M. Chaudie appointed gov.-gen., and col. Boileve commander of the troops, 16 June, 1895; M. Roume appointed gov.-gen., Jan. 1902. See *French Africa* under *Africa*.

Lieut. Voulet concludes treaties with the chiefs of the Nabas, Gurunsi, and Sati; reported, 15 Jan. 1897

Lieut. Hourst and members of the expedition from Timbuktu down the Niger (in 1896), received in Paris . . . . 15 Jan. ,,

Successful operations of two missions: the "Guma" district placed under French protection, contact established between Dahomey and the French Sudan; announced . 25 March, ,,

Franco-German convention, settling the Niger frontier . . . . 23 July, ,,

A French column takes possession of Say, on the Middle Niger; reported . . . . . 4 Aug. ,,

Treacherous attack on a detachment, by Samory's bands; 2 officers and others killed . 21 Aug. ,,

Bontuku occupied by the French, by arrangement with the British . . . . . 5 Dec. ,,

Neutral territory of Salaza and Yendi occupied by the British; reported . . . . Jan. 1898

French punitive expedition from Bammako captures Sikasso, the capital of Kenedugu, king Babemba and many of his men killed, May; lieut. Woelfel totally defeats the Sofas at Cavally . . . . 9 Sept. ,,

Samory captured with all his Sofas by capt. Gourand, reported . . . . 13 Oct. ,,

M. Legeal, geologist of the Trentinig mission, killed in a fight with the Tuaregs, in the French Sudan, 7 March, 1899

Rising in the Cavally region, Blidura captured, reported . . . . 7 April, ,,

An expedition to Lake Chad, under capts. Voulet and Chanoine, leaves Say, Jan. 1899; col. Klobb, sent to inquire into reported cruelty to the natives, overtakes capt. Voulet near Sinder, on the Niger, who deliberately fires on the party approaching; col. Klobb and 6 men killed, the rest, some mortally wounded, fled, 14 July; Voulet and Chanoine were afterwards themselves killed by their black troops . . . . Oct. ,,

The French Sudan divided between Senegal, Guinea, Ivory coast, and Dahomey, by decree signed . . . . 17 Oct.

Lieut. Bretonnet's mission to lake Chad, to extend French interests into Wadai, end of 1898; massacred near the Bagirmi by Rabah, the usurper, of Bornou's men, July; M. Béhagle, the explorer, also killed by Rabah, reported, 3 Nov.

The Foureau-Lamy's mission to cross the Sahara to lake Chad left Biskra Sept. 1898, reached Air mid Aug. 1899; Sinder, 2 Nov.; joins the Gentil and other expeditions at Kusuri, on the Shari,

and together defeat and kill Rabah at Kusli, major Lamy and 19 French killed, 22 April, 1900; the rest of Rabah's bands routed, 2, 7 May, 1900; M. Foureau reached Brazzaville . 11 July, 1899
MM. Fourneau and Foudère's expedition left France Sept. 1898; explored the Sangha river in French Congo to Wesso and the Ogowé valley, &c., to the Gabun; reported successful . autumn, 1900
Col. Peroz appointed commander of the new territory between the Niger and lake Chad . Dec. ,,
Capt. Robillot defeats Rabah's sons S.W. of Tonjba, reported . . . . 10 Feb. 1901
Tuaregs repulsed at Bir Alabi, near lake Chad, 1 June, 1902
Fighting in Ngoumè, French Congo, 17 towns and plantations destroyed by the French, reported, 30 Aug.; expedition against the Fan tribe, reported unsuccessful . . . 30 Oct. ,,

FRESCO PAINTINGS are executed on plaster while fresh. Very ancient ones exist in Egypt, Italy, and England, and modern ones in the British houses of parliament, at Berlin, and other places. The fresco paintings by Giotto and others at the Campo Santo, a cemetery at Pisa, executed in the 13th century, are justly celebrated. See *Stereochromy*.

FRESHWATER FISH, see *Fish*.

FRÈTEVAL (Central France). Here Richard I. of England defeated Philip II. of France, and captured his royal seal, archives, &c., 15 July, 1194. Frèteval was taken by the Germans, 14 Dec., 1870, and soon abandoned.

FRIARS (from the French *frère*, a brother); see *Minorites, Carmelites, Dominicans, Franciscans, Crutched Friars*, and other orders.

FRIDAY, the sixth day of the week; so called from Friga, or Frea, the Scandinavian Venus, the wife of Thor, and goddess of peace, fertility, and riches, who with Thor and Odin composed the supreme council of the gods. See *Good Friday* and *Black Friday*.

FRIEDLAND (Prussia). Here the allied Russians and Prussians were beaten by the French, commanded by Napoleon, on 14 June, 1807. The allies lost eighty pieces of cannon and about 18,000 men; the French about 10,000 men. The peace of Tilsit followed, by which Prussia was obliged to surrender nearly half her dominions.

FRIENDLY ISLES, in the Southern Pacific, consist of a group of more than 180 islands, the largest of which is Tonga-taboo, the sacred isle, 130 sq. m. These islands were discovered by Tasman, in 1643; visited by Wallis, who called them Keppel Isles, 1767; and by captain Cook, who named them on account of the then friendly disposition of the natives, 1777. Pop. 1901, 20,672.

The isles were visited by missionaries in 1797; of whom the Wesleyans were most successful in conversions, 1820, *et seq.*
Many chiefs submitted to king George I. in 1845. He set up a constitution and summoned a parliament of 40 members in 1862. He concluded a treaty with Germany, 1 Nov. 1876; and with Great Britain, 29 Nov. 1879. His chief adviser, the rev. Shirley Baker, who had, it is stated, usurped and abused much power, was expelled by sir John B. Thurston, the British high commissioner of Fiji, and replaced by Mr. Basil Thomson, who published an account of the affair in 1895.
King George I. died, aged upwards of 90, 19 Feb. 1893; and was succeeded by his great-grandson, Jioaji Tubou II., born 18 June, 1874.
The declining population, reported under 20,000 in 1894.
German claims renounced, reported, 8 Nov. 1899.
British protectorate proclaimed at Tonga, 19 May, 1900.
Death of the queen of the Tonga islands, 30 April, 1902.

FRIENDLY SOCIETIES, which originated in the clubs of the industrious classes, were subjected to slight control in 1793, and have been regulated by various enactments. Other acts were passed in 1855, 1858 and 1860; important ones, 1875, 1876, 1882, 1887, 1893 and 1895. Law consolidated in 1896. In London, the Defoe Friendly Society dates from 1687; the Norman, 1703; the Lintot, 1708.

An example of fraud, credulity, and mismanagement was given on investigation by the registrar-general into the affairs of the "Independent Mutual Brethren Friendly Society," founded in 1873, and broken up in 1886. Members, 2,225,000; capital, about 16,000,000*l.*; return, July, 1891; 3,587,513 members, capital over 20,000,000*l.*, in Sept. 1901.
Report on friendly societies in England and Wales published as a blue book (1856–80), Nov. 1896.
Conference of 30 friendly societies, capital, over 20,000,000*l.*, 19 March, 1897.
Conference on the subject of old-age pensions; committee appointed to prepare a scheme, 2 Oct. 1901.

FRIENDS, see *Quakers*, and under *Clergy*.

FRIENDS OF THE PEOPLE, an association formed in London to obtain parliamentary reform, 1792.

FRIESLAND: EAST (N. Germany), the ancient Frisia, formerly governed by its own counts. On the death of its prince Charles Edward, in 1744, it became subject to the king of Prussia; Hanover disputed its possession, but Prussia prevailed. It was annexed to Holland by Bonaparte, in 1806, to the French empire, 1810; and awarded to Hanover in 1815. The English language is said to be mainly derived from the old Frisian dialect.—FRIESLAND, WEST, in Holland, was part of Charlemagne's empire in 800. It passed under the counts of Holland about 936, and was one of the seven provinces which renounced the Spanish yoke in 1580. The term *Chevaux de Frise* (or *Cheval de Frise*, a *Friesland Horse*) is derived from Friesland, where it was invented.

FRIULI (Venetia), made a duchy by Alboin the Lombard, when he established his kingdom about 570. It was conquered by Charlemagne. Henri, a Frenchman, made duke, was assassinated in 799, which was the fate of duke Berengarius king of Italy and emperor, in 924. The emperor Conrad gave the duchy to his chancellor Poppo, patriarch of Aquileia, in the 11th century; it was conquered by Venice in 1420; annexed to Austria, 1797; France, 1805; Austria, 1814; Italy, 1866.

FROBISHER'S STRAITS, discovered by sir Martin Frobisher, who tried to find a north-west passage to China, and after exploring the coast of New Greenland, entered this strait, 11 Aug. 1576. He returned to England, bringing with him a quantity of black ore, supposed to contain gold, which induced queen Elizabeth to patronise a second voyage. This led to a third fruitless expedition. He was mortally wounded at Brest, Nov. 1594.

FRŒBEL SOCIETY, see under *Kindergarten*.

FROGMORE, near Windsor, Berks. A house here, built by Nash, was purchased by queen Charlotte 1800, and afterwards became a residence of the duchess of Kent. Here is situated the mausoleum of the late prince consort whose remains were transferred to it 1862. See *Albert*. Queen Victoria was buried here 4 Feb. 1901.

FROHSDORF, a village 30 miles south of Vienna on the river Leitha, with a magnificent castle, which from 1844 to 1883 was the head-quarters of the elder Bourbon party. The late comte de Chambord, who chiefly resided here, improved and beautified the interior of the castle.

FROISSART'S CHRONICLE, a history of the period between 1326 and 1400, treating chiefly of contemporary events in France, England, Scotland and Flanders, which are described in a vivid and interesting manner, with valuable information also on Spain, Italy and Germany. The first part of the Chronicle, the period 1326-56, is based on the writings of Jean le Bel, canon of Liège. Froissart (1327-1410), whose life was one of travel and adventure, was educated for and took orders in the church, but his inclination for poetry and gallantry led him to a roving life. He visited England in 1360, where his reputation of being a gay poet and narrator of chivalric deeds had preceded him, and became secretary to queen Philippa of Hainault, wife of Edward III., a post he held for some years; he revisited England in 1395, and spent some time at the court of Richard II. Among his various patrons was Wencelas duke of Brabant, whose poems, with certain pieces of his own, Froissart collected under the title of "Méliador, or the Knight of the Golden Sun;" this work was discovered in 1894. On the death of his patron, he entered the service of Guy, count of Blois, who presented him with the canonry of Chimay. About 1388 Froissart visited the comte de Foix, of whose court he gives a delightful description. He died at Chimay 1410. The earliest translation of the Chronicle is that of sir John Bourchier, lord Berners, 1525; Buchon edited the Chronicle, 1824-26; Johnes, 1803-5; and Luce 1869-88.

FRONDE, CIVIL WARS OF THE, in France, in the minority of Louis XIV. (1648-52), during the government of queen Anne of Austria and cardinal Mazarin, between the followers of the court and the nobility, and the parliament and the citizens. The latter were called *Frondeurs* (*slingers*), it is said, from an incident in a street quarrel. In a riot on 27 Aug. 1648, barricades were erected in Paris.

FROSTS. The following are some of the most remarkable recorded: (see *Cold*.)

The Euxine Sea frozen over for 20 days 401
A frost at Constantinople, when the two seas there were frozen a hundred miles from the shore, Oct. 763—Feb. 760
A frost in England on Midsummer-day is said to have destroyed the fruits of the earth . . . 1035
Thames frozen for 14 weeks 1063
Dreadful frosts in England from Nov. to April . 1076
The Cattegat entirely frozen 1294
Baltic passable to travellers for six weeks . . 1323
The Baltic frozen from Pomerania to Denmark . 1402
In England, when all the small birds perished . 1407-8
The ice bore riding upon it from Lübeck to Prussia, 1426
Severe frost, when large fowl of the air sought shelter in the towns of Germany 1433
The river frozen below London-bridge to Gravesend, from 24 Nov. to Feb. 10 1434
The Baltic frozen, and horse passengers crossed from Denmark to Sweden 1460
The winter so severe in Flanders that the wine distributed was cut by hatchets 1468
Carriages passed over from Lambeth to Westminster 1515
Wine in Flanders frozen into solid lumps . . . 1544
Sledges drawn by oxen travelled on the sea from Rostock to Denmark 1548
Diversions on the Thames . . . . 21 Dec. &c. 1564
The Scheldt frozen so hard as to sustain loaded waggons 1565
The Rhine, Scheldt, and sea at Venice frozen . . 1594
Fires and diversions on the Thames 1607-8
The rivers of Europe and the Zuyder Zee frozen; ice covers the Hellespont 1622
Charles X. of Sweden crossed the Little-Belt over the ice from Holstein to Denmark, with his whole army 1658
The forest trees, and even the oaks in England split by the frost; most of the hollies were killed; the Thames covered with ice eleven inches thick; and nearly all the birds perished, Dec. 1683—Feb. 1684
"The people kept trades on the Thames as in a fair, till 4 Feb. 1684. About forty coaches daily plied on the Thames as on drye land. Bought this book at a shop upon the ice in the middle of the Thames." *Entry in the memoranda of a Citizen.*
The wolves, driven by the cold, entered Vienna, and attacked cattle and men 1691
Three months' frost, with heavy snow, from Dec. to March 1709
A fair held on the Thames, and oxen roasted; frost continued . . . . . 24 Nov. to 9 Feb. 1716
One lasted 9 weeks, when coaches plied upon the Thames, and festivities and diversions of all kinds were enjoyed upon the ice. (The "hard winter") 1740
From 25 Dec. to 16 Jan. and from 18 to 22 Jan.: most terrible 1766
One general throughout Europe; the Thames passable opposite the Custom House Nov. to Jan. . 1789
One from 24 Dec. 1794, to 14 Feb. 1795, with the intermission of one day's thaw . . . 23 Jan. 1795
Intense frosts . . . . all Dec. 1796
Severe frost in Russia 1812
Very destructive to the French army in its retreat from Moscow. Napoleon commenced his retreat on the 9th Nov. The men perished in battalions, and the horses fell by hundreds on the roads. France lost in the campaign of this year more than 400,000 men.
Booths erected on the Thames; the winter very severe in Ireland 1813-14
Severe frost (Thames blocked) . 7 Jan.–Feb., 1838
The frosts so intense in parts of Norway, that quicksilver freezes, and persons exposed to the atmosphere lose their breath . . . 2 Jan. 1849
Very severe frost in London, 14 Jan. to 24 Feb.; and very cold weather up to 26 June . . . 1855
On 22 Feb. fires were made on the Serpentine, Hyde Park. A traffic on the ice of 35 miles long, was established in Lincolnshire . . . ,,
Very severe frost, 20 Dec. 1860; to . . 5 Jan. 1861
Very severe frosts . . . . Dec. 1874
Long frost with thaws . . 22 Nov. 1879–2 Feb. 1880
Very severe frost in Britain, begun 18 Jan. lasted about 14 days 1881
Fairs on the Thames recorded, 1564, 1607–8, 1620, 1683-4 (special), 1688–9, 1715–16, 1739-40, 1788–9, 1813–14.
A frost in Britain began 25 Nov. 1890, and continued with intermissions till . . . 22 Jan. 1891
A trap with a tandem team driven across the Serpentine . . . . 16 Jan. ,,
Frost, 24 Dec. 1892—8 Jan. 1893: severe frost in Britain and the Continent, many deaths reported; 1–8 Jan. 1894
Severe frost in Britain and on the Continent; cold began, 30 Dec. 1894 (*mild*, 14–21 Jan.)—5 March, 1895, many deaths. (Loughboro', 1° F.; London, 13° F., 9 Feb.), see *Thames* 1895
Severe 3 weeks' frost in Britain; Braemar, 0° F.; London, 15·8°; Greenwich, 14·3° . 14–16 Feb. 1902

FROST'S INSURRECTION, see *Newport*.

FRUCTIDOR CONSTITUTION; that promulgated in France on the 5th Fructidor, year 3, or 22 Aug. 1795. See *Directory* for changes.

FRUITS. Several varieties introduced into Italy, 70 B.C. *et seq.* Many exotic fruits and flowers, previously unknown in England, were brought thither between 1500 and 1578, and very many in the present century See *Gardening*, and *Flowers*. A conference of British fruit-growers was held at the Crystal Palace, London, 7 Sept.; association formed 11 Oct. 1888. Many donations were made to the fund for the encouragement of fruit-culture, founded by the lord mayor and the Fruiterers' Company, autumn, 1889. Successful fruit-growing reported, Dec. 1890. Experimental fruit farm at Woburn, founded by the duke of Bedford and Mr. Spencer Pickering, F.R.S., was inspected by a scientific party, and reported very successful; 12 June, 1895. Many of the following dates are uncertain:—

Almond-tree, Barbary, about	1548
Apples, Syria	1522
Apple, custard, N. America	1736
Apple, osage, ditto	1818
Apricots, Epirus	1540
Cherry-trees, Pontus	100
Cherries, Flanders	1540
Cornelian cherry, Austria	1596
Currant, the hawthorn, Canada	1705
Fig-tree, S. Europe, before	1548
Gooseberries, Flanders, before	1540
Grapes, Portugal	1528
Lemons, Spain	1554
Limes, Portugal, about	1554
Limes, American, before	1752
Melons, before	1540
Mulberry, Italy	1520
Mulberry, white, China, about	1596
Mulberry, the red, N. America, before	1629
Mulberry, paper, Japan, before	1754
Nectarine, Persia	1652
Olive, Cape	1730
Olive, the sweet-scented China	1771
Oranges	1595
Peaches, Persia	1562
Pears, uncertain	* *
Pine-apple, Brazils	1568
Pippins, Netherlands	1525
Plums, Italy	1522
Pomegranate, Spain, before	1548
Quince, Austria	1573
Quince, Japan	1796
Raspberry, the Virginian, before	1696
Strawberry, Flanders	1530
Strawberry, the Oriental, Levant	1724
Walnut, the black, N. America, before	1629

FUCHSIA, an American plant named after the German botanist Leonard Fuchs, about 1542. The Fuchsia fulgens, the most beautiful variety, was introduced from Mexico, about 1830. In S. America a black dye is obtained from the wood of some species.

FUEL, see *Coal*, *Bogs*. In the autumn of 1873, it was announced that Louis Rayneckers, a French peasant, had discovered that earth mixed with coal and a little soda made good fuel.

FUENTES DE ONORO (central Spain). On 2 May, 1811, Massena crossed the Agueda with 40,000 infantry, 5000 horse, and about 30 pieces of artillery, to relieve Almeida. He expected every day to be superseded in his command, and wished to make a last effort for his own military character. Wellington could muster no more than 32,000 men, of which only 1200 were cavalry. He however determined to fight rather than give up the blockade of Almeida. After much fighting, on 3 May, night came on and stopped the conflict. Next day Massena was joined by Bessières with a body of the Imperial guard; and on 5 May, made his grand attack. In all the war there was not a more dangerous hour for England. The fight lasted until evening, when the lower part of the town was abandoned by both parties—the British maintaining the chapel and crags, and the French retiring a cannon-shot from the stream. *Napier.*

FÜESSEN, Bavaria. By a treaty signed here, 22 April, 1745, peace was made between Maria Theresa, queen of Hungary, and the elector of Bavaria, the latter renouncing his claim to the imperial crown and recovering his lost territories.

FUGGER, an illustrious German family (the present head, prince Leopold Fugger Babenhausen, since 28 May, 1836), derives its origin from John Fugger, a master weaver in Augsburg in 1370; and its wealth by trade, and by money-lending to monarchs, especially the emperors.

FUGITIVE OFFENDERS ACT passed, 27 Aug. 1881.

FUGITIVE SLAVE BILL passed by the American legislature in 1850. It imposed a fine of 1000 dollars and six months' imprisonment on any person harbouring fugitive slaves or aiding in their escape. This law was declared to be unconstitutional by the judges of the superior court on 3 Feb. 1855, was carried into effect with great difficulty, and was not received by Massachusetts. It was repealed 13 June, 1864; see *Slavery in America.*

FUGITIVE SLAVE CIRCULARS, see *Slavery.*

FUGUE in Music (in which one part seems to chase another), is described in Morley's "Introduction to Practicall Musicke," 1597. Sebastian Bach and Handel were eminent fugue-writers.

FULDA (W. Germany), the seat of an abbey, founded by St. Boniface, the apostle of Germany, in 744. It was made a bishopric in 1752, and a principality in 1803. Napoleon incorporated it with Frankfort in 1810; but in 1815 it was ceded to Hesse-Cassel.

FULFORD, Yorkshire. Here Harold Hardrada of Norway, and Tostig, brother of Harold of England, defeated the earls Edwin and Morcar, 20 Sept. 1066; and the people near York submitted to them; see *Stamford-bridge.*

FULHAM PALACE, the official residence of the bishops of London since 1141. The present building is comparatively modern. Many of the bishops are interred in the church.

FULLER CASE, see *India*, 1876.

FUMIGATION. Acron, a physician of Agrigentum, is said to have first caused great fires to be lighted and aromatics to be thrown into them to purify the air, and thus to have stopped the plague at Athens and other places in Greece, about 473 B.C.

FUNDS, see *Stocks*, and *Sinking Fund* and *Foreign Bondholders.*

FUNERALS. David lamented over Saul and Jonathan, 1056 B.C., and over Abner, 1048 B.C. 2 *Sam.* i. and iii. In Greece, Solon was the first who pronounced a funeral oration, according to Herodotus, 580 B.C. The Romans pronounced harangues over their illustrious dead. Theopompus obtained a prize for the best *Funeral Oration* in praise of Mausolus, 353 B.C. Popilia was the first Roman lady who had an oration pronounced at her funeral, which was done by her son, Crassus; and it is observed by Cicero that Julius Cæsar did the like for his aunt Julia and his wife Cornelia.—*Funeral Games*, among the Greeks and Romans included horse-races, dramatic representations, processions, and mortal combats of gladiators. These games were abolished by the emperor Claudius,

A.D. 47. A tax was laid on funerals in England, 1793.

Cremation society founded 1874
Church of England Funeral and Mourning Reform Association, founded at Sheffield, by earl Nelson and others . . . . . . 5 Oct. 1878
Foundation-stone of first crematorium within a cemetery in the United Kingdom laid at Ilford, 14 Oct. 1903

See *Burials* and *Windsor*.

PUBLIC FUNERALS voted by parliament :—

Duke of Rutland, in Ireland	17 Nov.	1787
Lord Nelson (see *Nelson*)	9 Jan.	1806
Wm. Pitt	22 Feb.	,,
Chas. Jas. Fox	10 Oct.	,,
Richard Brinsley Sheridan	13 July,	1816
George Canning	16 Aug.	1827
Duke of Wellington	18 Nov.	1852
Viscount Palmerston (at her majesty's request),	27 Oct.	1865
Lord Napier of Magdala (by order)	21 Jan.	1890
Queen Victoria	4 Feb.	1901

FURNACE, see *Blowing-machines*, *Iron*.

FURNITURE. Specimens of Egyptian furniture, represented on the interior walls of the pyramids, appear in Rosellini's "*Monumenti dell' Egitto*," 1832-44, Vol. II. Mr. J. G. Pollen's "Ancient and Modern Furniture and Woodwork" in the South Kensington museum, 1874, illustrated by photographs and engravings, was published, July, 1874. Many interesting examples will be found in Fosbroke's "*Encyclopædia of Antiquities*," Vol. I. 1825.

FURRUCKABAD (N. India), a province acquired by the East India company, in June, 1802. Near the capital of the same name, 17 Nov. 1804, lord Lake defeated the Mahratta chief Holkar, and about 60,000 cavalry, himself losing 2 killed and about 20 wounded.

FURS were worn by Henry I. about 1125. Edward III. enacted that all persons who could not spend 100*l.* a year should be prohibited this species of finery, 28 March, 1336-7. Furs of various kinds are now extensively worn. The chief supplies come from Siberia and N. America, chinchillas (the finest and most delicate of all furs) from S. America, opossum and kangaroo from Australia, and leopard skins from Africa. Europe produces large quantities of common furs, as those of the fox, hare, and rabbit. The principal fur companies are the Hudson Bay co., founded 1670, and the N. America Fur-sealing co., established 1890. Formerly the Skinners' company, one of the city guilds, possessed many privileges and rights connected with the trade in fur. These ancient rights are now in abeyance. Great fur sales are held periodically at Leipsig, and at Nijni Novgorod.

FUSILIERS. Foot soldiers, formerly armed with fusees with slings to sling them. The 7th regiment (or Royal English Fusiliers) was raised, 11 June, 1685; the 21st (or Royal North British), 23 Sept. 1679; the 23rd (or Royal Welsh), 17 March, 1688. *Grose.*

FUSION of the French legitimists and Orleanists into one monarchical party, 5 Aug. 1873. See *France*.

FUTTEHGHUR (India). Here Nana Sahib massacred both the English defenders of the fort and their Sepoy assailants, July, 1857; and here the Sepoy rebels were defeated by sir Colin Campbell, 2 Jan. 1858.

G.

GABELLE (from *Gabe*, a gift), a term applied to various taxes, but afterwards restricted to the duty upon salt, first imposed by Philip the Fair on the French in 1286. *Duruy*. Our Edward III. termed Philip of Valois, who exacted the tax rigorously, the author of the *Salic* law (from *sal*, salt), 1340. The assessments were unequal, being very heavy in some provinces and light in others; owing to exemptions purchased from the sovereigns. The tax produced 38 millions of francs in the reign of Louis XVI. It was a grievous burden, and tended to hasten the revolution, during which it was abolished (1790).

GADES, S.W. Spain, an ancient town successively subjected by the Phœnicians, Carthaginians, and Romans; see *Cadiz*.

GAELIC, the northern branch of the Celtic languages, Irish, Erse or Highland Scottish, and Manx. The "Dean of Lismore's book" (written 1511-51) contains Gaelic poetry; specimens were published, with translations, in 1862, by rev. T. M'Lachlan. See *Celts*, *Clan-na-gael*.

Gaelic Society of London, founded 1777.
Gaelic speaking population of Scotland, 1881, 231,602.
The Gaelic Union, organised in Ireland, proposed the publication of a monthly journal, to be devoted to Irish literature, 1 Nov. 1882.
A Gaelic athletic association existing in Ireland; said to be infected with fenianism . . Dec. 1887

GAETA (the ancient Cajeta), a fortified Neapolitan seaport, has undergone several remarkable sieges. It was taken by the French, 4 Jan. 1799; by the English, 31 Oct. 1799; by the French, 18 July, 1806; and by the Austrians in 1815 and 1821. Here pope Pius IX. took refuge, 24 Nov. 1848, and resided more than a year. Here also Francis II. of Naples, with his queen and court, fled, when Garibaldi entered Naples, 7 Sept. 1860; and here he remained till the city was taken by the Sardinian general Cialdini, 13 Feb. 1861, after a severe siege, uselessly prolonged by a French fleet remaining in the harbour. Cialdini was created duke of Gaeta.

GAGGING ACT, properly so called, meant to protect the king and government from the harangues of seditious meetings, was enacted 8 Dec. 1795, when the popular mind was much excited. In Dec. 1819, soon after the Manchester affray, an act was passed for restraining public meetings and cheap periodical publications; it was popularly called "gagging bill." See *Six Acts*. Statutes coercing popular assemblies, particularly in Ireland, have been also so designated. See *Germany*, 1879. The terms "gagging" and "guillotining" were applied to Mr. Gladstone's resolutions for restricting (by the closure) the discussion on the Irish Home Rule bill, 30 June, 21 Aug. 1893. Mr. W. H. Smith, leader of the house, 1887-91, was said to "pounce" whenever he moved the closure.

GAIETY THEATRE, Strand, opened 21 Dec. 1868, Mr. John Hollingshead, manager, closed, last performance, "The Linkman," 4 July, 1903; new Gaiety Theatre opened 24 Oct. 1903, with "The Orchid."

GAIKAS AND GALEKAS, see *Kaffraria*.

GALAPAGOS, islands ceded to the United States by Ecuador, 3 Nov. 1854, the British, French, and other powers protesting against it.

GALATIA, a province of Asia Minor. In the 3rd century B.C. the Gauls under Brennus invaded Greece, crossed the Hellespont, and conquered the Troas, 278; were checked by Attalus I. in a battle about 241; and then settled in what was called afterwards Gallogræcia and Galatia. The country was ravaged by Cneius Manlius, 189 B.C., and was finally annexed to the Roman empire, 25 B.C., on the death of the king Amyntas. St. Paul's Epistle to the Galatians was probably written A.D. 58.

GALATZ (Moravia). The preliminaries of peace between Russia and Turkey signed here, 11 Aug. 1791, led to the treaty of Jassy, 9 Jan. 1792. The site of several conflicts, in which the Russians defeated the Turks, Nov. 1769; 10 May, 1828.

GALAXY, see *Milky Way*.

GALICIA, a province, N.W. *Spain*, was conquered by D. Junius Brutus, 136 B.C. and by the Vandals A.D. 419; and was subdued by successive invaders. In 1065, on the death of Ferdinand I. king of Castile and Leon, when his dominions were divided, his son Garcia became king of Galicia. Ruling tyrannically, he was expelled by his brother Sancho; returned at his death in 1072; was again expelled by his brother Alfonso, 1073; and died in prison in 1091. Alfonso, son of Urraca, queen of Castile, was made king of Galicia by her in 1109. He defended his mother, a dissolute woman, against her husband, Alfonso VII., and at her death in 1126, acquired Castile, and once more re-united the kingdoms.

GALICIA, *Poland*. East Galicia was acquired by the emperor of Germany at the partition in 1772; and West Galicia at that of 1795. The latter was ceded to the grand duchy of Warsaw in 1809; but recovered by Austria in 1815. The appointment of count Goluchowski, a Pole, as governor, in Oct. 1866, gave much satisfaction to the Poles, about 2,000,000 in this province; see *Poland*, note. Pop., 1900, 7,295,538.

Stry, a prosperous town, destroyed by fire; great privation; over 100 deaths, 18-22 April, 1886.
Lisko (about 7,000 inhabitants) burnt, 27-28 April, 1886.
For emigration frauds, see *Austria*, March, 1890.
Great fires in the petroleum works at Boryslaw, 35 houses burnt, some deaths, 24 Nov. 1902; and at Kuty, 370 houses and other buildings burnt, 8 Feb. 1903.

GALIGNANI'S WEEKLY MESSENGER, English newspaper, published in Paris; began in 1814, at the restoration. William Galignani died Dec. 1882, aged 84. Galignani home, for decayed printers and booksellers, founded at Neuilly, 1889.

GALILEE, one of the four Roman divisions of Palestine, including in the time of Christ the northern district of Palestine from the Mediterranean to the Jordan, and divided into upper and lower Galilee. Its chief towns were Tiberias and Sepphoris; Nazareth, Capernaum, Cana, and Nain are mentioned in the Gospels. It now is part of the pashalic of Damascus, under Turkish rule.

GALILEE, the porch or small chapel annexed to a church, in which public penitents stood, dead bodies were placed preparatory to interment, and religious processions formed. Here, in certain religious houses, the women were only allowed to worship, or, if relatives of the monks, to converse with them, a practice based on the words of St. Matt. xxviii. 7, "He goeth before you into Galilee; there shall ye see Him." Galilees are attached to Durham, Ely, and Lincoln cathedrals.

GALL, ST. (in Switzerland). The abbey, founded in the 7th century, was surrounded by a town in the 10th. St. Gall became a canton of the confederation in 1815.

GALLERIES, see *National*, *Louvre*, and *Versailles*.

GALLEYS, long boats, sometimes with sails, with seats for rowers, varying in number, much employed by the Venetians and Genoese till the 16th century. "Galley slaves" were condemned criminals employed in navigation. In France they had a general of galleys, of whom the baron de la Garde was the first, 1544. The punishment of the galleys (*galères*) was superseded by the "*travaux forcés*," forced labour, regulated by a law of 1854, the men being called "*forçats*."

GALLICAN CHURCH, see *Church of France*.

A building for the Catholic Gallican church was opened by father Hyacinthe Loyson, 9 Feb. 1879.

GALLIPOLI, the ancient Callipolis, a seaport in Turkey in Europe, 128 miles west of Constantinople. It was taken by the Turks in 1357, and fortified by Bajazet I. The first division of the French and English armies proceeding against the Russians landed here in March and April, 1854.

GALLIUM, an elementary metal, discovered by Lecoq de Boisbaudran, by means of the spectroscope: reported to French academy of sciences, 20 Sept., and 6 Dec. 1875.

GALOCHES, *French* for overshoes, formerly of leather; but since 1843 made of vulcanised India rubber. The importation of *Galoshes* was prohibited by 3 Edw. IV. c. 4 (1463).

GALVANISM AND GALVANO-PLASTICS, see under *Electricity*.

GALWAY (W. Ireland). The ancient settlers here were divided into thirteen tribes, a distinction not yet forgotten. It was conquered by Richard de Burgh in 1232. In 1690 Galway city declared for king James, but was taken by general Ginckel soon after the decisive battle of Aughrim, 12 July, 1691. It is the seat of a R.C. see. Queen's college was endowed by government, pursuant to act 8 & 9 Vict. c. 66 (1845), inaugurated, 30 Oct. 1849; see *Colleges* and *Ireland*, 1872-3. Pop., 1901, 13,414.

In 1858 the sailing of mail steam packets from Galway to America began; but the subsidy ceased in May, 1861, through the company's breach of contract, which occasioned much discussion in parliament. In July, 1863, the contract for the conveyance of mails from Galway to America was renewed, and 75,000*l.* voted for the purpose. The scheme was not successful. On 9 Nov. the steamer *Anglia* struck on the Black rock, and the mails were taken to Dublin. The last packet sailed in Feb. 1864.

The Duke of Edinburgh warmly received here, middle of Aug. 1884.

Visit of the king and queen, 30 July, 1903.

GAMBIA, West Africa. The proposed cession of Gambia to France in exchange for other territories was opposed in Jan. 1876, and eventually given up. Administrator, Sir Robert Llewelyn, 1891; Sir G. Denton, Jan. 1901.

Gambia separated from Sierra Leone and made an independent colony, 22 Dec. 1888.

Chief town, Bathurst. Some villages of a marauding chief punished for aggressions, about 7 Jan. 1892.

Toniataba destroyed after a battle; capt. A. S. Roberts killed, 28 April; successful British expedition, reported 11 May, 1892.

An expedition of 200 men of the naval brigade under capt. Gamble, from H.M.S. *Raleigh* and others, against Fodi-Silah, a slave-raiding chief, destroy 2 villages, a division is surprised by an ambush while returning to their boats, and 15 men, including lieuts. W. H. Arnold, Francis W. Hervey, sub-lieut. Francis W. Meister are killed at Medina Creek, 23 Feb. 1894.

An attack of about 2,000 natives repulsed by lieut.-col. Corbet and about 100 men of the West India regiment, on the British Combo river, 26 Feb. 1894.

Reinforcements arrive at Bathurst, commanded by major S. G. Fairtlough, 1 March; (he died at Sierra Leone, May, 1894).

Busamballa occupied by the West India column under major Madden, an attack of the natives repulsed, 3 March; continued fighting, enemy's loss reported heavy, 6 March; Birkama taken after a hot fight, 7 March; Gonjur bombarded by rear-admiral Bedford, 7 March; Fodi-Silah's force broken, reported 10 March; he surrendered to the French in Senegal, 11 March; died 19 Sept. 1894; peace restored, reported, 21 March, 1894.

Messrs. Sitwell and Silva and 6 constables killed at Sankandi, June, 1900; Anglo-French punitive operations; col. Brake captures Dumbutu, 6 chiefs and 200 men, 11 Jan. 1901.

Sallikeni burnt; 6 ringleaders captured, 16, 17 Jan. 1901.

Medina taken by the French; the hostile chief Fodi Kabba and 150 others killed, 23 March, 1901.

Successful punitive expedition against the Yolahs, May, 1902.

Population: colony, 13,456; protectorate, about 90,000, 1901.

GAMBOGE, a medicine and pigment, brought from India by the Dutch, about 1600. Hermann in 1677 announced that it was derived from two trees of Ceylon, since ascertained to belong to the order Guttifera.

GAME LAWS are a remnant of the forest laws imposed by William the Conqueror, who, to preserve his game, made it forfeiture of property to disable a wild beast, and loss of eyes, for a stag, buck, or boar. The clergy protested against ameliorations of these laws, under Henry III. The first game act passed in 1496. Game certificates were first granted with a duty in 1784. The Game act (1 & 2 Will. IV. c. 32), greatly modifying all previous laws, was passed in 1831. By it the sale of game is legalised at certain seasons. By the Game Poaching Preventive act, passed in 1862, greatly increased powers were given to the county police. Licences to kill game (3*l.* a year) granted for the year 1856-7, 28,950; for 1865-6 43,231; for 1869, 54,203; 1902, 76,807; received for licences, 1877-8, 196,352*l.*; 1883-4, 177,834*l.*; 1887-8, 179,143*l.*; 1902, 209,680*l.*

Motions for abolition made annually in commons by Mr. P. Taylor, lost (160-87) . . 2 March, 1880

The Ground Game act, to protect farmers from injury to crops, 43 & 44 Vict. c. 47, passed 7 Sept. „

Proposed reduction of licence to shoot game to 1*l.* for short periods . . . . . April, 1883

A game act relating to hares was passed in . . 1892

Internat. conference for the perservation of big game in Africa meets in London, 24 April; report issued, with recommendations . 30 May, 1900
See *Africa*, 1900.

GAMES. Candidates for athletic games in Greece were dieted on new cheese, dried figs, and boiled grain, with warm water, and no meat. The sports were leaping, foot-races, quoits, wrestling, and boxing; see *Capitoline, Isthmian, Olympic, Pythian, Secular Games, American Baseball*, &c.

GAMING was introduced into England by the Saxons; the loser was often made a slave to the winner, and sold in traffic like other merchandise. *Camden.*
Act prohibiting gaming to all gentlemen (and interdicting tennis, cards, dice, bowls, &c., to inferior people, except at Christmas time) . . . 1541
Gaming-houses licensed in London 1620
Any person losing, by betting or playing, more than 100*l.* at any one time, not compellable to pay the same, 16 Chas. II. 1663
Bonds or other securities given for money won at play not recoverable; and any person losing more than 10*l.* may sue the winner to recover it back, 9 Anne, c. 14 1710
Act to prevent excessive and fraudulent gaming, when all private lotteries and the games of faro, basset, and hazard were suppressed . . . 1739
The profits of a gaming-house in London for one season have been estimated at 150,000*l.* In one night a million of money is said to have changed hands at this place. *Leigh.* A bankrupt was refused his certificate because he had lost 5*l.* at one time in gaming . . . . 17 July, 1788
Three ladies of quality convicted in penalties of 50*l.* each for playing at faro . . March 11, 1797
Gaming-houses were licensed in Paris until . . 1838
Amended laws respecting games and wagers, 8 & 9 Vict. c. 109 (1845); by 3 Geo. IV. c. 114 (1822), a gaming-house keeper is to be imprisoned with hard labour; and by 2 & 3 Vict. c. 47, gaming-houses may be entered by the police, and all persons present taken into custody 1839
Betting-houses suppressed 1853
Public gaming-tables totally suppressed at Wiesbaden, Homburg, &c. See *Monaco* . 31 Dec. 1872
Mr. Jenks, proprietor of the Park Club house, and others, heavily fined for gambling, 7 Feb.; sentence confirmed . . . . . 24 June, 1884
The clock tower club and institute, Newington Butts, a bad gambling house suppressed; John James Hunt, the proprietor, sentenced to six years' penal servitude . . . 23 Sept. 1887
The proprietors of the Field Club (Mr. Seaton) and of the Adelphi Club (Mr. S. C. Cohen) fined each 500*l.* for keeping a gambling house, London, W., the subordinates fined; the players discharged 20 & 23 May, 1889
Similar prosecutions and penalties . . . 1889–1903
National anti-gambling league begins work in Glasgow, April, 1891; a large meeting in London. See *Sports* . . . . . . 12 June, 1894
New gaming act passed . . . . 20 May, 1892
"The History of Gambling in England," by John Ashton, *Athenæum* . . . . 26 Nov. 1898
Parl. committee appointed 1901, on the initiative of the bp. of Hereford, "to inquire into the increase of betting among all classes, and whether any legislative measures are possible and expedient for checking the abuses occasioned thereby," issued its report 1902
Lord Davey's Betting bill rejected in the house of lords, 48—39 . . . . . . 18 May, 1903

GAMUT. The scale of musical intervals (commonly termed *do* or *ut, re, mi, fa, sol, la*, to which *si* was added afterwards), for which the first seven letters of the alphabet are now employed, is mentioned by Guido Aretino, a Tuscan monk, about 1025.

GANDAMAK (or **GUNDAMUK**), N. India. A treaty with Yakoob Khan, ameer of Afghanistan, was signed here by major Cavagnari, 26 May, 1879, principal articles, British to hold Khyber Pass, &c. a British Resident to be at Cabul, annual subsidy of 60,000*l.* to the ameer, &c. The treaty was not carried out, see *Afghanistan*, Sept. 1879.

GANESA, the special deity of Prudence, in the worship of the Hindus, whose favour is invoked at the beginning of any enterprise; every book is inscribed with the name *Ganeçâya*, "honour to Ganesa." The god is represented with the head of an elephant, and riding upon a rat.

GANGES, the great sacred river of N. India, which rises in the S. Himalayas, receives several great rivers, divides into several branches, ending in the Bay of Bengal. The Ganges Canal, for irrigating the country between the Ganges and the Jumna. The main line (525 miles long) was opened 8 April, 1854. The immense difficulties in its execution were overcome by the skill and perseverance of its engineer, sir Proby Cautley. The lower Ganges canal, an extension of the above, commenced 1873.

GANGS, see *Agricultural Gangs* and *Hooliganism.*

GANJA, a preparation of the leaves, flowers and stem of the hemp plant (cultivated in Lower Bengal), largely consumed like opium; reported autumn, 1892.

GAOL DISTEMPER, see *Old Bailey.*

GAOLS, see *Prisons.*

GARDENERS' CHRONICLE, a weekly paper, long edited by Dr. John Lindley, first appeared, 2 Jan. 1841.

GARDENING. The first garden, Eden, planted by God. *Gen.* ii. The Scriptures abound with allusions to gardens, particularly the Song of Solomon and the prophets; and Christ's agony took place in a garden. Xenophon describes the gardens at Sardis; and Epicurus and Plato taught in gardens. Theophrastus's History of Plants was written about 322 B.C. Horace, Virgil, and Ovid derive many images from the garden (50 B.C. to A.D. 50); and Pliny's Tusculan villa is circumstantially described (about A.D. 100). The Romans introduced gardening into Britain, the religious orders maintained it, and its cultivation increased in the 16th century, when many Flemings came here to escape the persecutions of Philip II. Miller's dictionary was published in 1724; the Horticultural Society (*which see*) was established in 1804; Loudon's Encyclopædia of Gardening was first published in 1822, and his Encyclopædia of Plants in 1829; an act for the protection of gardens and ornamental grounds in cities was passed in 1863. See *Botany, Flowers, Fruits.* Gardeners' Royal Benevolent Institution, founded 1838. Schools of practical gardening for women are in successful operation at Swanley, Kent, and elsewhere. Exhibition of Gardening and Forestry at Earl's-court, Kensington, opened by the Duke of York, 13 May, closed, 14 Oct. 1893. School of practical gardening for boys established by the Technical Education board at the Royal Botanic Society, Regent's Park, early 1901.

GARENGANZE. See *Katanga.*

GARIGLIANO, a river (S. W. Italy). After long waiting and refusing to recede a step, the great captain Gonsalvo de Cordova made a bridge over this river, 27 Dec. 1503, and surprised and totally defeated the French army. Gaëta surrendered a few days after.

GAROTTE, a machine for strangling criminals, used in Spain. After five years' interval, a young woman, her lover, and an accomplice thus executed in Madrid for murder, 11 April, 1888. Many attempts to strangle made by thieves (termed "garotters") in the winter of 1862-3, led to the passing of an act in July, 1863, termed the "Garotting Act," to punish these acts by flogging.

GARTER, Order of the. Edward III., when at war with France and eager to draw the best soldiers of Europe into his interest, projected the revival of king Arthur's round table, and proclaimed a solemn tilting On New Year's day 1343-4, he published letters of protection for the safe coming and returning of such foreign knights as would venture their reputation at the jousts and tournaments about to be held. These took place 23rd April, 1344. A table was erected in Windsor castle of 200 feet diameter, and the knights were entertained at the king's expense. In 1346 Edward gave his garter for the signal of a battle that had been crowned with success (supposed to be Cressy), and being victorious on sea and land, and having David, king of Scotland, a prisoner, he, in memory of these exploits, is said to have instituted this order, 23 April, 1349. *See below.*

Edward III. gave the garter pre-eminence among the ensigns of the order; it is of blue velvet bordered with gold, with the inscription in old French—"*Honi soit qui mal y pense*" (Evil be to him who evil thinks). The knights are installed at Windsor, and styled *Equites aureæ Periscelidis*, knights of the golden garter. *Beatson.*

The order until king Edward VI.'s time was called the order of St. George, the patron saint of England. His figure on horseback, presented as holding a spear, and killing the dragon, was first worn by the knights of the institution. It is suspended by a blue ribbon across the body from the shoulder.

Instituted, according to Selden, 23 April, 1344; according to Nicolas, 1347; to Ashmole . . . 1349
The office of "*Garter king of arms of Englishmen*" instituted . . between May and July, 1417
Additions to the statutes decreed . . . 1421, 1423
Order of the Garter in Ireland instituted by Edward IV., 1466; abolished . . . 1494
Collar and George of the order instituted by Henry VII. . . . about 1497
The statutes reformed by order, 28 May, 1519; issued . . . 23 April, 1522
The ceremonies altered in consequence of the reformation . . . 20 April, 1548
Revision of the statutes . . . 1560
The annual feast of St. George discontinued . . 1567
The escocheon converted into a star . . . 1629
The number of knights increased by seven . . 1786
The order reconstituted; to consist of the sovereign, the prince of Wales, 25 knights companions, and lineal descendants of George III., when elected, 17 Jan. 1805
Several European sovereigns elected . . 1813-14
Abdul Aziz, sultan of Turkey, invested with the garter by the queen on board her yacht at the naval review. . . . 17 July, 1867
The shah of Persia invested by the queen at Windsor . . . 20 June, 1873
Alphonso XII. of Spain invested with the order at Madrid . . . 11 Oct. 1881
There were 54 knights in . . . Jan. 1895
William, crown prince of Germany, invested with the order at Osborne by Edward VII. . 28 Jan. 1901
Special statute issued by the king for conferring on the queen the title of a Lady of the order, 12 Feb. ,,
Alphonso XIII. of Spain invested with the order at Madrid . . . 16 May, 1902
Six royal princes invested with the order, June, July ,,
Dukes of Wellington and Sutherland . 26 June ,,

ORIGINAL KNIGHTS.

King Edward III., sovereign.
Edward, prince of Wales (called the Black Prince).
Henry, duke of Lancaster.
Thomas, earl of Warwick.
John, captal de Buch.
Ralph, earl of Stafford.
William, earl of Salisbury.
Roger, earl of Mortimer.
Sir John Lisle.
Bartholomew, lord Burghershe.
John, lord Beauchamp.
John, lord Mohun, of Dunster.
Sir Hugh Courtenay.
Thomas, earl of Kent.
John, lord Grey, of Rotherfield.
Sir Richard Fitz-Simon.
Sir Miles Stapleton.
Sir Thomas Wale.
Sir Hugh Wrottesley.
Sir Nele Loryng.
Sir John Chandos.
Sir James Audeley.
Sir Otho Holand.
Sir Henry Eam.
Sir Sanchet d'Abrichecourt.
Sir Walter Paveley.

GAS, in chemistry, a permanently elastic aëriform fluid; see *Oxygen, Hydrogen, Nitrogen, Chlorine, Argon, Crypton,* &c.

It is stated that Monge and Clouet condensed sulphurous acid before 1800, and Northmore liquefied chlorine 1805
Faraday determined a gas to be the vapour of a volatile liquid existing at a temperature considerably above the boiling point of the liquid; and that the condensing points of different gases are merely the boiling points of the liquids producing them; he by pressure condensed chlorine gas into a liquid 1823
Other gases liquefied by intense cold and great pressure (as indicated by Faraday); oxygen by Cailletet, at Paris, 2 Dec., and independently by Raoul Pictet at Geneva . . . 22 Dec. 1877
Nitrogen and atmospheric air, liquefied by Cailletet, soon after 1877-8
The process exhibited at the Royal Institution, London, by prof. James Dewar . 14 June, 1878
Ozone liquefied by Hautefeuille and Chappuis, Oct. 1880
Liquefied gases used by Krupp in casting guns, &c. 1884
The researches of the Polish profs. Wroblewski and Olszewski on the liquefaction of gases much aided by their production of extreme cold, 1884 *et seq.*; for prof. Dewar's liquefaction and solidification of gases at low temperatures in 1884 *et seq.*, see *Cold* and *Air*, footnote, *Hydrogen* and *Fluorine*.
See Giffard's gun, in article *Cannon*.
Prof. Thos. Graham's paper on the law of the diffusion of gases appeared, 1834; he showed that platinum and other metals can absorb gases . . 1866
Furnaces in which gases are used as fuel invented by C. W. Siemens, and employed in glass works, &c. 1861
Gas engines. Barnett patented a plan for employing heated gas as a motive power . . . 1838
Lenoir's gas-engine, in which the motive power is obtained by the ignition of combined gases by electricity 1861
143 of these engines had been working in Paris; and introduced into England . . . Dec. 1864
Pierre Hugon's gas-engine (said to be superior to Lenoir's, 1871) exhibited 1867
The Otto-Langen gas engine, exhibited in 1876, has been superseded by the Otto Silent Gas Engine.
Gas engines have been greatly improved by Messrs. Crossley Bros., and are now so largely employed that sir F. Bramwell foretold their eventually superseding steam engines . . . 5 Sept. 1888
Mr. Purnell's gas engine, of simple construction, driven by a mixture of gas and air, exhibited at Webber Street, S.E. . . . . . Jan. 1890
Natural gas rising from the ground largely employed as fuel at Pittsburg, U.S. &c., 1884 *et seq.*, long known to the Persians, Chinese, and others.
Natural gas, from the Kimmeridge clay, discovered at Heathfield, Sussex, while boring for water in 1895; candle-power of 12 to 14 candles, used for lighting; boring, &c., rapidly proceeding . Sept. 1902

See *Tram-roads*, 1894.

GASCONY (S. W. France), a duchy, part of Aquitaine (*which see*).

GAS INSTITUTE. The name assumed, 16 June, 1881, by the British Association of Gas Managers, founded in 1863 for the advancing of gas engineering.

GAS-LIGHTS; the inflammable aëriform fluid, carburetted hydrogen, evolved by the combustion of coal, was described by Dr. Clayton in 1739.

Application of coal gas to the purposes of illumination tried by Mr. Murdoch, in Cornwall . . . 1792
Gaslight introduced at Boulton and Watt's foundry in Birmingham 1798
Lyceum Theatre lit with gas as an experiment by Mr. Winsor 1803
Permanently used at the cotton-mills of Phillips and Lee, Manchester (1000 burners lighted) . 1805
Introduced in London, at Golden-lane, 16 Aug. 1807; Pall Mall, 1809; generally through London 1814-20
Mr. David Pollock, father of the late chief baron, was governor of the first "chartered" gas company which began in 1810 (called "the gas light and coke company") 1812
Westminster bridge lighted with gas 1813
Gas first used in Dublin, 1818; the streets generally lighted . . . . . Oct. 1825
Gas engine, by Lenoir, by explosive mixture of gas and air, 1860; Otto's gas engine 1876
Later improvements: Robson's, Andrew's, the Griffin engines, etc., also in use.
Gas-lighting introduced in Paris, 1819; ten gas companies in Paris . . . . July, 1865
Sydney, in Australia, was lit with gas 25 May, 1841
The *sale of gas* is regulated by acts passed in . 1860
The gas-pipes in and round London extend upwards of 2000 miles, and are daily increasing. It was said in 1860, that of the gas supply of London a leakage of 9 per cent. took place through the faulty joints of the pipes.
Processes to obtain illuminating *gas from water* have been patented by Cruickshanks (1839), White (1849), and others. *Water-gas* made by Ruck's process mixed with ordinary gas tried and reported successful at Chichester, Aug. 1873; at Harrogate (it is extensively used in United States) . . . . . . Aug. 1890
Water-gas employed in metallurgy by Mr. Samson Fox at Leeds, reported . . . . Sept. 1890
A combination of various processes set up by Mr. Samson Fox at the Leeds forge works 29 Sept. 1887, and reported successful . . . Jan. 1889
Gas-meters patented by John Malam (1820), sir W. Congreve (1824), Samuel Clegg (1830), Nathan Defries (1838), and others.
Explosion of a large gasometer at the London Gas-light Company's works at Nine-elms; 10 persons killed, and many injured (first accident of the kind) . . . . 31 Oct. 1865
Moscow first lit with gas . . . . 27 Dec. 1866
An economical gas produced from bitumen at Woolwich arsenal . . . . . Jan. 1868
Central Gas Company, London, established . . 1849
Gas successfully tried as fuel for the generation of steam by Jackson's patent . . . April, 1868
The Central Gas company robbed of about 70,000*l.* by Benjamin Higgs, a clerk; discovered, April, 1869
Gas-light tried at Howth lighthouse, near Dublin, July, „
Gasworks clauses act passed . . . . 13 July, 1871
By the London gas act, passed 13 July, 1868, ordinary gas charged 3*s.* 9*d.* the 1000 cubic feet, after 1 Jan. 1870. The charges raised on account of dearness of coal and labour, Jan. 1874.
Strike of London gas-stokers, 2400 out, 2 Dec.; the inconvenience met by great exertion, 2-6 Dec.; several tried and imprisoned . . . Dec. 1872
Gas supply of London: receipts 1872, 2,133,000*l.*; 1873, 2,544,000*l.*
Street gas lit by electricity, by Mr. St. G. Lane Fox's method; a trial, partially successful, Pall Mall, &c. . . . . 13 April, 1878
Capital of metropolitan companies, 12,681,818*l.* ("Chartered Company," 9,096,771*l.*); total annual income, 3,926,769*l.* (average profit, 9*l.* 3*s.* 5*d.* per cent.) 1879
Depression in gas companies through prospects of electric light, Oct. 1878; recovery . . . 1879-80
Explosions of gas-mains near Bedford-street, Tottenham-court-road, London; 2 killed; others injured; much property destroyed . . 5 July, 1880
"Koh-i-noor Gas," produced from shale oil by Messrs. Rogers, of Watford, (said to be pure and cheap) 1881-3
Mr. West's and Mr. Cooper's inventions for the economical production of pure coal gas, with reduction of human labour, at Tunbridge wells gas works . . . . . . Jan. *et seq.* 1884
The Bower-lamp, a combination of the Grimstone patents on the regenerative principle, (the products of combustion being burned), invented by Messrs. G. Bower and son, St. Neots, Hunts . 1884
Mr. Lawrence's gas economizer, stated to increase light and diminish expense, exhibited by a company . . . . . 29 Nov. 1888
Strikes of gas-stokers in Southwark and Manchester successfully resisted . . . . . 12 Dec. 1889
See *Strikes*, Feb. 1890.
The London Gas Light and Coke Company (which illuminates the metropolis the north of the Thames) makes great preparations against a possible strike. A conference with the Union; no strike or lockout ensues . . . . . 3 Oct. 1890
Acetylene Gas (*which see*) produced by Wohler, 1862; made on a commercial scale as an illuminant . 1895
Water-gas committee appointed 9 Feb. 1898; report issued, with recommendations . mid Feb. 1899
A conference on the present increase in the price of gas at the Guildhall, Mr. A. C. Morton in the chair; resolutions carried against the giant monopoly created by the Gas acts of 1847 and 1860, &c., 31 Oct. 1900
Great advance in the development of light by incandescent gas burners since sir Edw. Frankland's double-chimney argand, 1852; regenerative burners perfected by Siemens, 1879 *et seq.*
New gas invented by Dr. Ludwig Mond furnishes power and heat at about 2*d.* per 1,000 cubic feet; reported . . . . May, 1901
Mond gas bill passed . . . . . . 1 Aug. „

GAS MUSIC, see *Pyrophone*.

GASTEIN (Salzburg, Austria). The long discussion between Austria and Prussia respecting the disposal of the duchies conquered from Denmark, was closed by a provisional convention signed here by their ministers (Blum for Austria and Bismarck for Prussia) 14 Aug. 1865. This convention was severely censured by the other powers and abrogated in 1866.

Austria was to have the temporary government of Holstein, and Prussia that of Sleswig; the establishment of a German fleet was proposed, with Kiel as a Federal harbour, held by Prussia; Lauenburg was absolutely ceded to Prussia, and the king was to pay Austria as a compensation 2,500,000 Danish dollars.
Emperors of Austria and Germany met at Gastein Aug. 1886

GATE-MEETINGS, see *Races*.

GATES, see *Tolls*.

GATESHEAD, a borough in Durham, on the Tyne, opposite Newcastle. At Gateshead-fell, William I. defeated Edgar Atheling and his Scotch auxiliaries in 1068. Gateshead was made a parliamentary borough by the reform act in 1832. Returns one member (1885). Population, 1881, 65,803; 1891, 85,709; 1901, 109,887.

Between twelve and one o'clock, 5, 6 Oct. 1854, a fire broke out in a worsted manufactory here, which set fire to a bond warehouse containing a great quantity of nitre, sulphur, &c., causing a terrific explosion, felt at nearly twenty miles' distance, and totally destroying many buildings, and burying many persons in the ruins. At the moment of the explosion, large masses of blazing materials flew over the Tyne and set fire to many warehouses in Newcastle. About fifty lives were lost, and very many persons were seriously wounded. The damage was estimated at about a million pounds.

Collapse of chemical condensers through fire at the Friar Goose chemical works, on the Tyne, near Gateshead; seven men killed, 26 July, 1891. Estimated loss about 10,000*l.*

At the Theatre Royal, by a panic caused by an alarm of fire, 11 persons, chiefly young, are crushed to death; the exit from the gallery was insufficient, 26 Dec. 1891.

GATLING GUN OR BATTERY. Invented by Mr. R. J. Gatling, an American, in 1862 (he died 26 Feb. 1903). It was intended to discharge at once a number of projectiles smaller than the shells of field guns, and it had as many locks as barrels. Tried at Shoeburyness and rejected as inferior to a field gun firing shrapnel. A powder to be used in the Gatling, invented by M. Pertuiset, was tried in London, Aug. 1870.

GAUGAMELA, see *Arbela*.

GAUGES (in railways). Much discussion (termed "the battle of the gauges") began among engineers about 1833. Mr. I. M. Brunel approved of the broad gauge, adopted on the Great Western Railway; and Mr. R. Stephenson, Joseph Locke, and others, chose the narrow. A 2 foot gauge was recommended in Feb. 1870, having been successful on the Festiniog railway, Wales; with Robt. Fairlie's "bogie" engine was much adopted at home and abroad. About 200 miles of the S.W. lines of the Great Western were altered from the broad to the narrow gauge in a few days, June, 1874, and on 20-23 May, 1892, the broad gauge was totally superseded on the Great Western.

GAUGING, measuring the contents of any vessel of capacity, with respect to wine and other liquids, was established by a law, 27 Edw. III. 1352.

GAUL AND GAULS. Gallia, the ancient name of France and Belgium. The Gauls termed by the Greeks Galatæ, by the Romans, Galli or Celtæ, came originally from Asia, and invading Eastern Europe, were driven westward, and settled in Spain (in Galicia), North Italy (Gallia Cisalpina), France and Belgium (Gallia Transalpina), and the British isles (the lands of the Cymry or Gaels).

	B.C.
The Phocæans found Massilia, now Marseilles	600
The Galli Senones under Brennus defeat the Romans at the river Allia, and sack Rome, but are repulsed from the Capitol, accept a ransom and retire; a fabulous legend asserts that they were defeated and expelled by Camillus	390
Defeated	360
The Gauls defeated by the Romans at Sentinum	295
The Senones defeat the Romans at Arretium; nearly exterminated by Dolabella	283
The Gauls overrun Northern Greece, 280 B.C.; are beaten at Delphi, 279; and by Antigonus, king of Macedon	273
The Gauls defeated with great slaughter near Pisa	225
The Insubres totally overthrown by Marcellus, and their king Viridomarus slain	222
They assist Hannibal	218, &c.
The Romans conquer Gallia Cisalpina, 220; invade Gallia Transalpina, with varied success	121-58
They colonise Aix, 123 B.C.; and Narbonne	118
Julius Cæsar subdues Gaul in 8 campaigns	58-50
Lyons (Lugdunum) founded	41
	A.D.
Druids' religion proscribed by Claudius	43
Adrian visits and favours Gaul, hence called Restorer of the Gauls	120
Introduction of Christianity	160
Christians persecuted . . 177, 202, 257, 286,	288
The Franks and others defeated by Aurelian	241
And by Probus, 275, 277; who introduces the culture of the vine	280
Maximian defeats the Franks	281
Constantine proclaimed emperor of Gaul	306
Julian arrives to relieve Gaul, desolated by barbarians; defeats the Alemanni at Strasburg	357
Julian proclaimed emperor at Paris, 360; dies	363
Gaul harassed by the Alemanni	365-377
Invasion and settlement of the Burgundians, Franks, Visigoths, &c.	378-450
Clodion, chief of the Salian Franks, invades Gaul; is defeated by Aëtius	447
The Huns under Attila defeated by Aëtius near Chalons	451
Ægidius, the Roman commander, murdered	464
Childeric the Frank takes Paris	"
All Gaul, west of the Rhone, ceded to the Visigoths	475
End of the Roman empire of the West, and establishment of the kingdom of the Franks	476

(See *France*.)

GAUNTLET, an iron glove, first introduced in the 13th century, perhaps about 1225. It was commonly thrown down as a challenge to an adversary.

GAUZE, a fabric much prized among the Roman people. "Brocades and damasks and tabbies and gauzes have been lately brought over" (to Ireland). *Dean Swift*, in 1698. The manufacture of gauze and articles of a light fabric at Paisley, in Scotland, began about 1759.

GAVEL-KIND (derived from the Saxon *gif eal cyn*, "give all suitably;" or from *gafolcynd*, and yielding rent), the custom in Kent of dividing paternal estates in land, the wives to have half, the rest equally among male children, without any distinction, 550. By the Irish law of gavel-kind, even bastards inherited. *Davies.* Not only the lands of the father were equally divided among all his sons, but the lands of the brother also among all his brethren, if he had no issue of his own. *Law Dict.*

GAZA, a city of the Philistines, of which Samson carried off the gates about 1120 B.C. (*Judges* xvi.) It was taken by Alexander after a long siege, 332; and near to it Ptolemy defeated Demetrius Poliorcetes, 312 B.C. It was taken by Saladin A.D. 1170; by Bonaparte, March, 1799; and by the Egyptians under Ibrahim Pacha in 1831.

GAZETTES, see *Newspapers*.

GELHEIM, near Worms, central Germany. Here the emperor Adolphus of Nassau was defeated and slain by his rival Albert I. of Austria, 2 July, 1298.

GEMARA OR GHEMARA, see *Talmud*.

GEMS. The Greeks excelled in cutting precious stones, and many ancient specimens remain. The art was revived in Italy in the 15th century. In Feb. 1860, Herz's collection of gems was sold for 10,000*l.* Rev. C. King's "Antique Gems" appeared in 1860, and his "Natural History of Precious Stones and Gems" in 1865. Dr. A. Billing's "Science of Gems," 1868. Artificial gems have been produced by chemists (Ebelmen, Deville, Wöhler, and others), 1858-65.

The duke of Marlborough's collection, valued at 60,000*l.*, sold by auction for 36,750*l.*, 28 June, 1875; again sold for 34,827*l.* 7*s.* 6*d.*	29 June, 1899
A pearl necklace (Gordon-Lennox jewels), realized 22,500*l.*	1 May, 1903

GENEALOGY, from the Greek *genea*, birth, descent. The earliest pedigrees are contained in the 5th, 10th, and 11th chapters of Genesis. The first book of Chronicles contains many genealogies. The pedigree of Christ is given in *Matt.* i. and *Luke* iii. Many books on the subject have been published in all European countries; one at Magdeburg, Theatrum Genealogicum, by Henninges, in 1598. Anderson, Royal Genealogies, London, 1732.

Sims' Manual for the Genealogist, &c., 1888, will be found a useful guide. The works of Collins (1756 *et seq.*), Edmondson (1764-84), Nicolas (1825 and 1857), Debrett, and Burke, on the British peerage, are highly esteemed. The Genealogical society, London, established in 1853. "The Genealogist," published quarterly, began 1875. "The Genealogist's Guide to Printed Pedigrees," by George W. Marshall, published in 1879.

GENERAL ASSEMBLY, see *Church of Scotland.*

GENERAL COUNCILS, WARRANTS, see *Councils, Warrants.*

GENERALS. Matthew de Montmorency was the first general of the French armies, 1203. *Hénault.* Balzac states that cardinal Richelieu coined the word *Generalissimo*, upon his taking the supreme command of the French armies in Italy, in 1629. Ulysses Grant was the first general of the army of the United States of America, so styled in 1866; see *Commanders-in-Chief.*

GENERATION (in Chronology), the interval of time between the birth of a father and the birth of his child: 33 years are allowed for the average length of a generation. Harvey's thesis "*Omne vivum ex ovo*" (Every living being springs from an egg), has been disproved by the researches of Von Sebold and others. See *Spontaneous.*

GENEVA, a town of the Allobroges, a Gallic tribe, 58 B.C.; became part of the empire of Charlemagne, about A.D. 800; and capital of the kingdom of Burgundy, 426.

The Republic founded in 1512
Emancipated from Savoy 1526
Calvin settled here, and obtaining much influence, Geneva was termed the "Rome of Calvinism" about 1536
Through him Servetus burnt for heresy, 27 Oct. 1553
Geneva allied to the Swiss Cantons 1584
Insurrection, Feb. 1781; about 1000 Genevese, in consequence, applied, in 1782, to earl Temple, lord-lieutenant of Ireland, for permission to settle in that country: the Irish parliament voted 50,000*l.* to defray the expenses of their journey, and to purchase them lands near Waterford. Many of the fugitives came to Ireland in July, 1783; but they soon after abandoned it; many Genevese settled in England 1784
A revolution; executions and imprisonments, July, 1794
Geneva incorporated with France . 26 April, 1798
Admitted into the Swiss Confederation, 30 Dec. 1813
The constitution made more democratic . . . 1846
Revolution, through an endeavour of the Catholic cantons to introduce Jesuits as teachers; a provisional government set up . . 7 Oct. 1848
[The scheme was withdrawn.]
About 50 persons from Geneva land at Thonon and Evian, to set up the Swiss flag; but are brought back by Swiss troops . . . . 30 Mar. 1860
Election riots, with loss of life, through the indiscretion of M. Fazy . . . . . 22 Aug. 1864
49th annual meeting of the Helvetic Society of National Sciences held . . . 21-23 Aug. 1865
Violent peace congress — Garibaldi present, 12 Sept. 1867
The Alabama arbitration commission met; received the cases and adjourned to 15 June, 1872, 18 Dec. 1871
Formal meeting of the commission (see *Alabama*), 15 June, 1872
Monsignor Mermillod, nominated bishop of Geneva (in the diocese of the bishop of Lausanne), and vicar apostolic; his arrest proposed, 2 Feb.; ordered to quit, if he will not submit to the civil government by 15 Feb. he is expelled 17 Feb. ,,
Geneva visited by the shah . . . July, 1873
The ex-duke of Brunswick dies here and bequeaths his vast property (above 764,000*l.*) to the city 18 Aug. ,,
Violent hail storm; great destruction of glass and crops . . . . 7, 8 July, 1875
Rousseau centenary celebrated . . 2 July, 1878
The duke of Brunswick's remains placed in the grand mausoleum . . . . . 7 Sept. 1879
Riots through Salvation army . Jan.-Sept. 1883
Collision of steam boats on the lake, 20 persons drowned . . . . 23 Nov. ,,
Explosion of a boiler on the steamer *Mont Blanc* on the lake; 26 persons perish . . 9 July, 1892
Swiss national exhibition opened . . 1 May, 1896
Bomb outrage at the entrance to the cathedral, windows in the square shattered . . 24 Dec. 1902
Population, 1888: Canton, 105,509; City, &c., 71,807; 1901, 105,139.

GENEVA CONVENTION, for the succour of the wounded in time of active warfare. Having been a witness of the horrors of the battle-field of Solferino, 24 June, 1859, M. Henri Dunant, a Swiss, published his experiences, which induced the *Société Genévoise d'Utilité Publique* in Feb. 1863 to discuss the question whether relief societies might not be formed in time of peace to help the wounded in time of war by means of qualified volunteers. At an international conference held 26 Oct. 1863, fourteen governments, including Great Britain, France, Austria, Prussia, Italy, and Russia, were represented by delegates. The propositions then drawn up were accepted as an international code by a congress which met at Geneva, 8 Aug. 1864, and on 22 Aug. a convention was signed by twelve of the delegates, and it was eventually adopted by all civilised powers except the United States. International conferences were held at Paris in 1867 and at Berlin in 1869 for further developing in a practical manner the objects of the Geneva conference. The International Society (termed "the Red Cross Society"), established in consequence of these proceedings was very energetic in relieving the wounded and sick during the Franco-Prussian war in 1870, its flag being recognised as neutral. See *Aid to Sick and Wounded.* Above 13,000 volunteers said to be employed in attending the sick and wounded, Sept.—Dec., 1870. Additional articles applying to naval warfare adopted during the Spanish-American war, 1898.

GENOA, the ancient Genua (N. Italy). Its inhabitants were the Ligures, who submitted to the Romans, 115 B.C. It partook of the revolutions of the Roman empire. Population, 1890, 206,485; 1901, 234,800.

Genoa becomes a free commercial state . about 1000
Frequent wars with Pisa 1070-1284
Frederick II. captures 22 galleys, and vainly besieges Genoa 1242
The families of Doria and Spinola obtain ascendency, about 1270
The Genoese destroy the naval power of Pisa at Melora (*which see*) . . . . . 6 Aug. 1284
Frequent wars with Venice . . 1218-32; 1293-99
Rafaele Doria and Galeotto Spinola appointed captains 1335
Simon Boccanegra made the first doge, 1339: set aside by the nobles, 1344; re-appointed . . 1356
Great discord; many doges appointed . . . 1394
Genoa successively under protection of France, 1396; of Naples, 1410; of Milan, 1419; losing and regaining freedom 1421-1512
Sacked by the Spaniards and Italians under Prosper Colonna 1522
Andrew Doria deserts the French service, and restores the independence of his country . 1528
Genoa bombarded by the French . . May, 1684
By the British . . . . . . Sept. 1745
Taken by the imperialists, who are soon after expelled . . . . Sept. 1746
Another siege raised . . . . 10 June, 1747
The celebrated bank failed 1750
Genoa made the Ligurian republic . . May, 1797

The city, blockaded by a British fleet and Austrian army, until literally starved, evacuated by capitulation, 5 June; it was surrendered to the French soon after their victory at Marengo . 14 June, 1800
Genoa annexed to the French empire . 4 June, 1805
Surrenders to the English and Sicilians 18 April, 1814
United to the kingdom of Sardinia . . . Dec. „
The city seized by insurgents, who, after a murderous struggle, drove out the garrison and proclaimed the Ligurian republic, 3 April; but surrendered to general La Marmora. . 11 April, 1849
Columbus's first voyage, 1492, celebrated, the king and queen present, and many foreign warships 8 Sept. *et seq.* 1892

GENS-D'ARMES were anciently the king's horse-guards only, but afterwards the king's *gardes-du-corps;* the musqueteers and light horse were reckoned among them. There was also a company of gentlemen (whose number was about 250) bearing this name. Scots guards were about the persons of the kings of France from the time of St. Louis, who reigned in 1226. They were organised as a royal corps by Charles VII. about 1441; the younger sons of Scottish nobles being usually the captains. The name gens-d'armes was afterwards given to the police; but becoming obnoxious, was changed to "municipal guard" in 1830.

GENTLEMAN (from *gentilis*, of a *gens*, a race or clan). The Gauls observing that during the empire of the Romans, the *scutarii* and *gentiles* had the best appointments of all the soldiers, applied to them the terms *écuyers* and *gentilshommes.* This distinction of gentlemen was much in use in England, and was given to the well-descended about 1430. *Sidney.* Gentlemen by blood were those who could show four descents from a gentleman who had been created by the king by letters patent.

GENTLEMEN-AT-ARMS (formerly styled the Band of Gentlemen Pensioners) is the oldest corps in England, with the exception of the Yeomen of the Guard. The band was instituted by Henry VIII. in 1509, and was originally composed entirely of gentlemen of noble blood, whom he named his pensioners or spears. William IV. commanded that it should be called his majesty's honourable corps of gentlemen-at-arms, 7 March, 1834.

GENTLEWOMEN'S SELF-HELP INSTITUTION, London, established by the earl of Shaftesbury, duchess of Sutherland, and others, May, 1870.

GEODESY (from *daiö*, I divide), the art of measuring the surface and determining the figure of the earth, &c. Col. A. Clarke's "Geodesy," published 1880. See *Latitude.*

The 7th international Geodetic congress met at Rome 15–24 Oct. 1883. It recommended the international unification of the hour, and longitude with Greenwich. An international conference of 40 delegates met at Washington, 1 Oct., president Adm. Rogers, agree to recommend Greenwich as prime meridian; France and Brazil abstain, 13 Oct. 1884; the terms of a universal day also agreed to, 1 Nov. 1884; at Berlin, 27 Oct. 1886; at Salzburg, 17 Sept. 1888; at Paris, 3 Oct. 1889; at Berlin, 30 Sept. 1895; Stuttgart, 3 Oct. 1898; Copenhagen, 4 Aug. 1903.
The internat. geographical congress at London declare for Greenwich as prime meridian . July, 1895
Dr. Rubin leaves Cape Town to measure an arc of meridian . . . . . . 28 April, 1903

GEOGRAPHY. The first geographical records are in the Pentateuch, and in the book of Joshua. Homer describes the shield of Achilles as representing the earth surrounded by the sea, and also the countries of Greece, islands of the Archipelago, and site of Troy. *Iliad.* The priests taught that the temple of Apollo at Delphos was the centre of the world. Anaximander of Miletus was the inventor of geographical maps, about 568 B.C. Hipparchus attempted to reduce geography to a mathematical basis, about 135 B.C. Strabo, the great Greek geographer, lived 71-14 B.C. Ptolemy flourished about 139 A.D. The science was brought to Europe by the Moors of Barbary and Spain, about 1240. *Lenglet.* Maps and charts were introduced into England by Bartholomew Columbus to illustrate his brother's theory respecting a western continent, 1489. Geography is now divided into mathematical, physical, and political, and its study has been greatly promoted during the present century by expeditions at the expense of various governments and societies. The *Royal Geographical Society* of London was established in 1830; that of Paris in 1821. The Geographical Society's exhibition opened by the marquis of Lorne, 9 Dec. 1885. The society issued a circular for promoting a more uniform spelling of geographical names, Dec. 1891. The society instituted courses of lectures, Nov. 1892. Proposal that ladies be admitted as fellows; approved by letter-votes, 30 June; rejected by special meeting (172–158), 3 July, 1893. See *Africa, North-East and West Passage, &c.*

Major James Rennell, an eminent geographer, born 3 Dec. 1742; died . . . . . . 29 March, 1830
An international congress of geographers held at Antwerp in 1871; 2. at Paris, 3 Aug. 1875; 3. at Venice, 15 Sept. 1881; 4. Paris, 6–11 Aug. 1889; 5. Berne, 10–14 Aug. 1891; Imperial institute, London, opened by the duke of York; president, Mr. (aft. sir) Clements Markham, May, 1896; 7. Berlin . . . . 28 Sept.–4 Oct. 1899
Dr. August Heinrich Petermann, founder and editor of the celebrated "Mittheilungen über wichtige neue Erforschungen auf der Gesammtgebiete der Geographie" in 1855, and an eminent cartographer, died . . . . 26 Sept. 1878
Congress on *commercial* geography at Brussels, Oct. 1879
Mr. (aft. sir) E. H. Bunbury's "History of Ancient Geography among the Greeks and Romans," published 1879. (He died, 5 March, 1895.) He refers especially to Hecatæus, Herodotus, Hanno, Pytheas (discoverer of Britain); Eratosthenes (born B.C. 276) made a map; and to Ptolemy, about A.D. 139.
E. A. Freeman's "Historical Geography of Europe," 1881
65 geographical societies in the world . . Jan. „
British Commercial Geographical Society; founded at the mansion house, London, 15 July, met 27 Oct. 1884
Scottish Geographical Society, Edinburgh, inaugurated . . . . 3 Dec. „
Manchester Geographical Society established Jan. 1885
Sudden death of the great Russian explorer, gen. Prjevalsky at Vernoje in Asia, announced 2 Nov. 1888
Death of Henry Seebohm, naturalist, etc. 26 Nov. 1895
Prof. Kiepert, a distinguished geographer and cartographer (born 1818), died . . 21 April, 1899
"The International Geography," by 70 authors, edited by Dr. H. R. Mill, published . Sept. „
Elizabethan tercentenary celebrated by Royal Geographical Society . . . . 23 March 1903
Discovery of two early maps in the library of Waldburg, at Wolfegg, Wurtemberg, drawn by the German geographer, Waldseemüller; the earlier, probable date *cir.* 1507, gives the name of America to the New World. Another map, probably by the same cartographer, discovered by Mr. H. N. Stevens, and considered by him to be of still earlier date than the map mentioned above, is thought to be the first map on which the name America appears. *Whitaker* . . „
Visit of French geographers to London . 9 Aug. „

GEOK TEPE, a strong Turkoman fortress; see *Russia*, 1879-81.

GEOLOGY, the science of the earth, is said to have been cultivated in China before the

Christian era, and occupied the attention of Aristotle, Theophrastus, Pliny, Avicenna, and the Arabian writers.

In 1574 Mercati wrote concerning the fossils in the pope's museum: Cesalpino Majoli, and others (1597), Steno (1669), Scilla (1670), Quirini (1676), Plot and Lister (1678), Leibnitz (1680) recorded observations, and put forth theories on the various changes in the crust of the earth.

Hooke (1668), in his work on Earthquakes, said that fossils, "as monuments of nature, were more certain tokens of antiquity than coins or medals, and though difficult, it would not be impossible *to raise a chronology out of them.*"

Burnet's "Theory of the Earth" appeared 1690, Whiston's 1696; Hutton's "Theory of the Earth" 1795.

Buffon's geological views (1749) were censured by the Sorbonne in 1751, and recanted in consequence. The principle he renounced was that the present condition of the earth is due to secondary causes, and that these same causes will produce further changes. His more eminent fellow-labourers and successors were Gesner (1758), Michell (1760), Raspe (1762-73), Pallas and Horace B. de Saussure (1793-1800).

Werner (1775) ascribed all rocks to an *aqueous* origin, and even denied the existence of volcanoes in primitive geological times, and had many followers, Kirwan, De Luc, &c.—James Hutton (1788) supported by Playfair (1801) warmly opposed Werner's views, and asserted that the principal changes in the earth's crust are due to the energy of *fire*. The rival parties were hence termed Neptunists and Vulcanists.

Mr. (aft. sir) A. Geikie and other eminent modern geologists, ascribed the origin of the landscape features of the earth chiefly to denudation by the action of water 1865 *et seq*, Sir A. Geikie's "Founders of Geology" [Jean Étienne Guettard, Desmaret, and others in the 18th century], published 1897.

William Smith, the father of British geology (who had walked over a large part of England) drew up a Tabular View of British Strata, in 1799, and published it and his Geological Map of England and Wales, 1812-15; died 28 Aug. 1839. The Rev. Adam Sedgwick, another father, died 27 Jan. 1873, aged 87. Sir Charles Lyell, died 22 Feb. 1875.

The rev. Wm. Buckland, D.D., born 1784. Reader in geology, Oxford, 1818; published "Reliquiæ Diluvanæ," the results of his examination of the fossil bones of large mammals, elephants, tigers, hyenas, &c., discovered in the Kirkdale cave, Pickering, Yorkshire, in 1821. "Geology and Mineralogy," in relation to natural Theology (Bridgewater Treatise), 1836. Dean of Westminster, 1846; died Aug. 1856.

In 1803 the Royal Institution possessed the best geological collection in London, collected by H. Davy, C. Hatchett, and others; the proposal of sir John St. Aubyn, sir Abraham Hume, and the right hon. C. F. Greville, to aid the government in establishing a school of mines there in 1804-7, was declined, 13 Nov. 1807.

In 1807 the *Geological Society of London* was established. By collecting a great mass of new facts, it greatly tended to check the disposition to theorise, and led to the introduction of views midway between those of Werner and Hutton.

The Geological Society of Dublin, 1832; of Edinburgh, 1834; of France, 1830; of Germany, 1848.

In 1835 Mr. (afterwards sir Henry) De la Beche suggested the establishment of the present *Museum of Geology*, which began at Craig's-court, and which was removed to its present position in Jermyn-street. To him are also due the valuable geological maps formed on the ordnance survey. The building was erected by Mr. Pennethorne, and formally opened by the prince consort, 14 May, 1851. Attached to the Museum are the Mining Records office, a lecture theatre, laboratories, &c. Sir H. De la Beche, the first director, died 13 April, 1855; succeeded by sir Roderick Murchison, who died 22 Oct. 1871; succeeded by professor (afterwards sir) A. C. Ramsay, March, 1872, died 9 Dec. 1891; by Archibald Geikie, 1881, knt., 1891. A similar institution founded at Calcutta in 1840.

A great many maps have been published, with memoirs. The survey of England on the scale of an inch to a mile, was completed in Jan. 1884. Some maps have been made on a scale of six inches to a mile. The surveys of Scotland and Ireland are in progress.

New geological map of England and Wales, 4 miles to the inch, published by government, 1898.

International geological congress originated at the Buffalo meeting of the American association for the advancement of science in 1876; met at Paris 1878; Bologna, 26 Sept. 1881; Berlin, 29 Sept. 1885; London, 17 Sept. 1888; Washington, 1891; Zurich, 29 Aug. 1894; St. Petersburg, 1897; Paris, Aug. 1900; Vienna, 20 Aug. 1903.

The English standard works on geology at the present time are those of Lyell, Murchison, Phillips, De la Beche, Mantell, Ansted, Geikie, and Nicholson.

Cuvier and Brongniart's work on Geology of Paris, 1808 *et seq.*

Sir Wm. Dawson, eminent geologist, born 1820, died 19 Nov. 1899.

L. Agassiz, "Poissons Fossiles," 1833-45.

The strata composing the earth's crust may be divided into two great classes:

I. Those generally attributed to the agency of water;

II. To the action of fire: which may be subdivided as follows:—

Aqueous formations, stratified, rarely crystalline:—
- Sedimentary or fossiliferous rocks.
- Metamorphic or unfossiliferous.

Igneous formations, unstratified, crystalline:—
- Volcanic, as basalt, &c.
- Plutonic, as granite, &c.

Fossiliferous, or Sedimentary, rocks are divided into three great series:—
- The Palæozoic (most ancient forms of life) or Primary.
- The Mesozoic (middle life period), or Secondary.
- The Neozoic or Cainozoic (more recent forms of life), or Tertiary.

TABLE OF STRATA (*chiefly from Lyell*).

NEOZOIC:

I. POST-TERTIARY:

A. *Post-Pliocene:*

1. *Recent:* Marine strata; with ***human remains;*** Danish peat; kitchen middens; bronze and stone implements; Swiss lake-dwellings; temple of Serapis at Puzzuoli.

2. *Post-Pliocene:* Brixham cave, with flint knives, and bones of living and extinct quadrupeds; ancient valley gravels; glacia drift; ancient Nile mud; post-glacial N. American deposits: remains of ***mastodon;*** Australian breccias.

II. TERTIARY OR CAINOZOIC SERIES:

B. *Pliocene:*

3. *Newer Pliocene* (or Pleistocene) Mammalian beds, Norwich Crag. [***Marine Shells.***]

4. *Older Pliocene:* Red and Coralline Crag (Suffolk, Antwerp).

C. 5, 6. *Miocene:* Upper and Lower; Bordeaux; Virginia sands and Touraine beds; Pikermé deposits near Athens; volcanic tuff and limestone of the Azores, &c.; brown coal of Germany, &c. [***Mastodon, Gigantic Elk, Salamander,*** &c.]

D. 7, 8, 9. *Eocene:* Upper, Middle, and Lower; Freshwater and Marine beds; Barton Clays; Bracklesham Sands; Paris Gypsum; London Plastic, and Thanet Clays. [***Palms, Birds,*** &c.]

III. SECONDARY OR MESOZOIC SERIES:

E. 10. *Cretaceous:* Upper; British Chalk; Maestricht beds. — Chalk with and without Flints, Chalk Marl, Upper Green Sand, Gault, Lower Green Sand. [***Mesosaurus; Fish, Mollusks,*** &c.]

11. Lower (or *Neocomian* or *Wealden*); Kentish rag; Weald Clay; Hastings Sand. [***Iguanodon, Hylæosaurus,*** &c.]

F. 12. *Oolite:* Upper; Purbeck beds, Portland Stone and Sand, Kimmeridge Clay; Lithographic Stone of Solenhofen with ***Archæopteryx.*** [***Fish.***]

13. Middle: Calcareous Grit, Coral Rag, Oxford Clay, Kelloway Rock. [*Belemnites* and *Ammonites*.]
14. Lower: Cornbrash, Forest Marble, Bradford Clay, Great Oolite, Stonesfield Slate, Fuller's Earth, Inferior Oolite. [*Ichthyosaurus*, *Plesiosaurus*, *Pterodactyl*.]

G. 15. *Lias*: Lias Clay and Marl Stone. [*Ammonites*, *Equisetum*, *Amphibia*, *Labyrinthodon*.]

H. 16. *Trias*: Upper; White Lias, Red Clay, with Salt in Cheshire, Coal Fields in Virginia, N.A. [*Fish*, *Dromatherium*.]
17. Middle or Muschelkalk (wanting in England). [*Encrinus*; *Placodus gigas*.]
18. Lower: New Red Sandstone of Lancashire and Cheshire. [*Labyrinthodon*, *Footprints of Birds and Reptiles*.]

IV. Primary or Palæozoic Series:

I. 19. *Permian*: Magnesian Limestone, Marl Slates, Red Sandstone and Shale, Dolomite: Kupferschiefer. [*Firs*, *Fishes*, *Amphibia*.]

K. 20, 21. *Carboniferous*, Upper and Lower: Coal Measures, Millstone Grit, Mountain Limestone. [*Ferns*, *Calamites*, *Coal*.]

L. 22, 23, 24. *Devonian*, Upper, Middle, and Lower: Tilestones, Cornstones, and Marls, Quartzose, Conglomerates. [*Shells*, *Fish*, *Trilobites*.]

M. 25, 26, 27. *Silurian*, Upper, Middle, and Lower: Ludlow Shales, Aymestry Limestone, Wenlock Limestone, Wenlock Shale, Caradoc Sandstone, Llandeilo Flags; Niagara Limestone. [*Sponges*, *Corals*, *Trilobites*, *Shells*.]

N. 28, 29. *Cambrian*, Upper and Lower: Bala Limestone, Festiniog Slates, Bangor Slates and Grits, Wicklow Rock, Hasleets Grits, Huronian Series of Canada. [*Zoophytes*, *Lingula*, *Ferns*. *Sigillaria*, *Stigmaria*, *Calamites*, and *Cryptogamia*.]

O. 30. **Laurentian*, Upper Gneiss of the Hebrides (?): Labradorite Series, N. of the St. Lawrence; Adirondack Mountains, New York.
31. *Lower: Gneiss and Quartzites, with Interstratified Limestones, in one of which, 1000 feet thick, occurs a foraminifer, *Eozoön Canadense*, the oldest known fossil, according to Dr. Dawson and others; by some geologists regarded as ophicalcite, a mineral structure.

GEOMETRY, so termed from its original application to measuring the earth, is ascribed to the Egyptians; the annual inundations of the Nile having given rise to it by carrying away the landmarks and boundaries.

Thales introduced geometry into Greece, about 600 B.C.
Pythagoras cultivated the science about 580.
The doctrine of curves originally attracted the attention of geometricians from the conic sections, which were introduced by Plato, about 390 B.C.
Euclid's *Elements* compiled about 300 B.C.
Archimedes, a discoverer in geometry, 287-212 B.C.
The conchoid curve invented by Nicomedes, 220 B.C.
Ptolemy, the astronomer, 2nd century A.D.
Geometry taught in Europe in the 13th century.
Books on geometry and astronomy were destroyed in England as infected with magic, 7 Edw. VI., 1552. *Stow.*
Descartes published his *Analytical Geometry*, 1627.
Sir Isaac Newton (*Arithmetica Universalis*, &c.), 1642-1727.
Simson's edition of Euclid, first appeared, 1756.
La Place's *Mécanique Céleste*, 1799-1805.

GEORGE. A gold coin current at 6*s*. 8*d*. in the reign of Henry VIII. *Leake.*

GEORGE, ST., the tutelary saint of England, and adopted as patron of the order of the garter by Edward III. His day is 23 April. Special celebration in honour of the English soldiers in London and other parts of England, 1900. See *Garter*, and *Knighthood*.

St. George was a tribune in the reign of Diocletian, and being a man of great courage, was a favourite; but complaining to the emperor of his severities towards the Christians, and arguing in their defence, he was put in prison, and beheaded, 23 April, 290.—On that day, in 1192, Richard I. defeated Saladin.
St. George's, Hanover-square, returns one M.P., by act passed 1885. Population (parl. constit.), 1891, 78,364; 1901, 76,734; see *Fires*, 18 Nov. 1896.
St. George's in the East returns 1 member by the act of 1885. Population, 1891, 47,918; 1901, 51,193; see *Trials*, April, 1896.
The *Order of the Sons of St. George*, established at Philadelphia as a society to succour emigrants (see under *Emigration*). It gradually acquired political influence, and many branches were formed in order to counteract the dominant aggressive policy of the Irish party. It works in unison with the "British American association," which was formed to promote naturalization—its organ being the *British American*, a weekly newspaper, Dec. 1887.

GEORGES' CONSPIRACY, in France. General Moreau, general Pichegru, Georges Cadoudal, who was commonly known by the name of Georges, and others, were arrested at Paris, charged with a conspiracy against the life of Bonaparte, and for the restoration of Louis XVIII., Feb. 1804. Pichegru was found strangled in prison, 6 April. Twelve of the conspirators, including Georges, were executed 25 June, and others imprisoned. Moreau was exiled, and went to America. In 1813 he was killed before Dresden (*which see*).

GEORGIA, the ancient Iberia, now a province of S. Russia, near the Caucasus, submitted to Alexander about 331 B.C., but threw off the yoke of his successors. It was subjugated to Rome by Pompey, 65 B.C., but retained its own sovereigns. Christianity was introduced into it in the 3rd century. In the 8th century, after a severe struggle, Georgia was subdued by the Arab caliphs; by the Turkish sultan Alp-Arslan, 1068; and by the Tartar hordes, 1235. From the 14th to the 18th centuries, Georgia was successively held by the Persian and Turkish monarchs. In 1740 Nadir Shah established part of Georgia as a principality, of which the last ruler Heraclius, surrendered his territories to the czar in 1799; and in 1802 Georgia was declared to be a Russian province.—Georgia, in North America, was settled by gen. Oglethorpe, in 1732. Separating from the congress of America, it surrendered to the British, Dec. 1778; and its possession was of vast importance to the royalists in the war. Count d'Estaing joined the American general Lincoln, and made a desperate attack on Georgia, which failed, and the French fleet returned home; the colony was given up to the Union by the British in 1783 It seceded from the Union, by ordinance, 18 Jan 1861, and was conquered by Sherman in 1864-5, and readmitted as a state Jan. 1868. A ridiculous negro insurrection suppressed Aug. 1875. Fatal fight with negroes at Pittsburg, 7 deaths and a block of buildings burnt, 17 May, 1902. Population in 1880, 1,542,180; 1890, 1,837,353; 1900, 2,216,331; Atlanta, 65,533; Savannah, 43,189. See *United States*.

Riots at Jessop: fight between whites and negroes; 22 negroes killed and 2 whites . . 25, 26 Dec. 1889
Destructive cyclone with loss of life in many places, 6 Jan. 1892; 4 March, 1893; and on 28-29 Aug. 1893, when Savannah was nearly destroyed, and above 50 persons killed.
Sanguinary disputes between the whites and blacks . . . . Dec. 1894

* Included in the *Archæan system*, the basement division of the stratified rocks.

Tornado at Gainesville; 64 deaths, 1,000 people destitute, loss of property 300,000 dols. 1 June, 1903
GEORGIA, in the Pacific, was visited by capt. Cook in 1775

GEORGIUM SIDUS, the first name of the planet Uranus (*which see*), discovered 13 March, 1781.

GERBEROI (Normandy, N. France). Here William the Conqueror was wounded in battle by his son Robert, who had joined the French king Philip I., 1078.

GERM THEORY OF DISEASE supposes "that many diseases are due to the presence and propagation in the animal system of minute organisms [termed *microbes*] having no part or share in its normal economy." *Maclagan*, 1876. See *Animalcules* and *Bacteria*. Dr. Cohn, of Breslau, whose work was published in 1872, classifies bacteria as—I. Sphœro or micrococci; II. Micro-bacteria, or bacteria proper (rod-shaped); III. Desmo-bacteria, the same but longer; IV. Spiro-bacteria, spiral-shaped or curly. Translation of his work, 1881. See *Cholera*.

The doctrine of *contagium animatum* was held in the middle ages and put forth in the 16th century, but contagious organisms were not discovered till the 19th by professors Pasteur, Tyndall, Dr. Wm. Budd, and others, 1875 *et seq.* At the British Association, 14 Sept. 1870, professor Huxley expressed his concurrence with the "germ theory." See under *Dust* and *Vivisection*, 1882.

Dr. Robert Koch is said to have identified the microscopical germs of cattle disease, of consumption, of cholera, and other diseases, 1879 *et seq.*, discredited in England, May, June, 1885. See *Tuberculosis*.

Dr. E. Klein, Feb. 1885, reported his investigations on the relation of bacteria to cholera. At the Royal Institution, May 27, 1887, he demonstrated the propagation of scarlet fever by microbes in cow's milk.

Numerous specimens of these germs were exhibited at the Royal Institution in illustration of professor Tyndall's discourse on "Living contagia," 16 Jan. 1885.

By taking means to exclude these germs from wounds, &c., sir Joseph Lister (baron 1897) introduced antiseptic surgery with great success, in which carbolic acid is largely used, 1864 *et seq.*; the protection of wounds from air is not now considered necessary.

"Louis Pasteur," by M. Radot, his son-in-law, gives an account of Pasteur's success in mitigating the virulence of some diseases by inoculation. A translation by lady Claud Hamilton was published in Feb. 1885. M. Pasteur's 70th birthday celebrated in Paris, &c. 27 Dec. 1892. He died, 28 Sept. 1895; see *Hydrophobia*.

M. Engelmann demonstrated the action of microbes in the development of vegetable cells from carbonic acid and moisture in the atmosphere.

Profs. Behring and Kisasato of Berlin announce their method of treating tetanus and diphtheria, Jan. 1891.

Discovery of the influenza bacillus by Dr. Richard Pfeiffer, announced Jan. 1892; yellow fever bacillus, by prof. G. Sanarelli, Jan. 1897.

Maj. R. Ross's paper at the Royal Colonial Institute on "Malaria and its treatment," with special reference to the microbe *Anopheles*, a genus of mosquito, 10 Nov. 1903.

Other bacilli under investigation, 1903.

GERMAIN, ST., near Paris. The palace here was begun by Louis the Fat, 1124, and enlarged and embellished by his successors, especially by Francis I., Henry IV., and Louis XIV. Here James II. of England resided in state after his abdication, in 1689, and here he died, 16 Sept. 1701; See *Treaties*.

GERMAN ASSOCIATION, see *German Union*.

GERMAN COLONIZATION SOCIETY, constituted at Frankfort, 6 Dec. 1882. A Charter was granted by the emperor to Dr. Carl Peters and others, whereby this society was authorised to acquire Usagara, N'Gury, and other territories west of Zanzibar, 27 Feb. 1885. Increase of members, less than 18,000 in 1896, over 30,000 28 May, 1899.

GERMAN CONFEDERATION, NORTH, established in room of the Germanic Confederation (*which see*): population 1867, estimated 29,906,092. The confederation ceased on the re-establishment of the German empire, 1 Jan. 1871.

The king of Prussia invites the states of North Germany to form a new confederation 16 July, 1866
Treaty of alliance, offensive and defensive, between Prussia and the following states:—Saxe-Weimar, Oldenburg, Brunswick, Saxe-Altenburg, Saxe-Coburg-Gotha, Anhalt, two Schwarzburgs, Waldeck, the younger Reuss, two Lippes, Lübeck, Bremen, and Hamburg, signed . . 18 Aug. „
And two Mecklenburgs . . . . . 21 Aug. „
And Hesse (for country north of the Maine), 3 Sept. „
And the elder Reuss . . . . . 26 Sept. „
And Saxe-Meiningen . . . . . . 8 Oct. „
And Saxony . . . . 21 Oct. „
Meeting of North German Parliament (295 deputies from the 22 states) at Berlin . . . 24 Feb. 1867
See *Germany*.

GERMAN EAST AFRICA, see under *Africa*.

GERMAN EXHIBITION at Earl's Court, West Brompton, London, W. Hon. president, duke of Saxe-Coburg-Gotha; hon. president of committee in Germany, prince Blucher von Wahlstatt; director-general, John J. R. Whitley, assisted by lieut. F. Jaffé. Opened by the lord mayor, Mr. Joseph Savory, in the presence of the marquis of Lorne, and many eminent persons, 9 May; closed 10 Oct. 1891. Total number of visitors, 1,377,908. The galleries contained specimens of arts classified in nine groups; 300 artists were represented by 700 pictures, and a gigantic trophy of Germania and many interesting models.

GERMAN HOSPITAL, Dalston, founded 1845, for Germans, and English in cases of accident. German Society of Benevolence and Concord, established 1817.

GERMAN LANGUAGE has two great branches: *hoch* and *platt Deutsch*, high and low German. The former became the literary language, principally through its use by Luther in his translation of the Bible and in other works, 1522-34. The latter is that spoken by the lower classes. There are many dialects: the satirical epic in low German, "Reineke Fuchs," appeared in 1498; see *Reynard*, and *Drama*.

PRINCIPAL GERMAN AUTHORS.

	Born.	*Died.*
Ulfilas (Gothic Bible) about A.D. 360		
Martin Luther (German Bible, &c. 1522-34)	1483	1546
Hans Sachs	1494	1578
Godf. Leibnitz	1646	1716
G. F. Gellert	1715	1769
G. E. Lessing	1729	1781
G. A. Bürger	1748	1794
J. G. von Herder	1744	1802
Fred. T. Klopstock	1724	1803
Im. Kant	1724	1804
J. C. Fred. von Schiller	1759	1805
Ch. M. Wieland	1733	1813
C. T. Körner	1791	1813
Jean Paul Richter	1763	1825
J. H. Voss	1751	1826
F. Schlegel	1772	1829
G. W. F. Hegel	1770	1831
B. G. Niebuhr	1776	1831
J. W. von Goethe	1749	1832
Wm. von Humboldt	1767	1835
A. Wm. Schlegel	1767	1845
L. Tieck	1773	1853

	Born	Died
H. Heine	1797	1856
Alex. von Humboldt	1769	1859
Ernst M. Arndt	1769	1860
Chr. Carl J. Bunsen	1791	1860
F. C. Schlosser	1776	1861
J. Hillebrand	1788	1862
G. G. Gervinus	1805	1871
E. H. Fichte	1797	1879
Leopold Ranke	1795	1886
Theod. Mommsen	1817	1903
Leopold von Sacher-Masoch	1836	1895
Gustav Freytag	1816	1895
Heinrich von Sybel	1817	1895
Heinrich von Treitschke	1834	1896
Ernst Curtius	1814	1896
Friedrich Emil Rittershaus	1885	1897

GERMAN NAVY LEAGUE, founded by 44 gentlemen in Berlin on the invitation of the prince of Wied, May, 1898. 47 branch societies; total members, 114,345, reported 9 May, 1899; 599,141 members, 1010 branches, 24 Jan. 1901.

GERMAN OCEAN, see *North Sea.*

GERMAN SILVER, an alloy of nickel, copper, and zinc, first made at Hildburghausen in Germany. There are many patents; Cutler's, 1838, Parkes', 1844, &c.

GERMAN UNION OF NATURAL PHILOSOPHERS, the forerunner of the British Association, was founded by Oken, at Leipsic, in 1822; partly to promote political unity in Germany. It has met annually, except in troubled years, such as 1848, 1866, and 1870; 50th time, 17 Sept. 1877; at Dantzic, 18 Sept. 1880; Salzburg, 18 Sept. 1881; Eisenach, 18 Sept. 1882; Freiburg, 17 Sept. 1883; Magdeburg, 18 Oct. 1884; Strasburg, 17 Sept. 1885; Berlin, 16 Sept. 1886; Wiesbaden, 18 Sept. 1887; Cologne, 18 Sept. 1888; Heidelberg, 1889; Bremen, Sept. 1890; Halle, Sept. 1891; Vienna, 24 Sept. 1894; Lübeck, 16 Sept. 1895; Frankfort-on-the-Main, 21 Sept. 1896; Brunswick, 20 Sept. 1897; Düsseldorf, 19 Sept. 1898; Munich, 17 Sept. 1899; Aachen, 17 Sept. 1900; Hamburg, 22 Sept. 1901; Carlsbad, 21 Sept. 1902. The Union is now termed the "German Association of Naturalists."

GERMANIA, colossal statue, see *Germany*, Sept. 1883.

GERMANIC CONFEDERATION, superseding the confederation of the Rhine (*which see*), was constituted 8 June, 1815; held its first diet at Frankfort, 16 Nov. 1816, and its last, 24 Aug. 1866. See *next article.* It comprised—

1 Austria; 2. Prussia; 3. Bavaria; 4. Saxony; 5. Hanover; 6. Würtemberg;
7. Baden; 8, 9. Hesse (electorate and grand duchy);
10. Denmark (for Holstein and Lauenburg);
11. Netherlands (for Luxemburg);
12. Saxe-Weimar, Saxe-Coburg, Saxe-Meiningen, and Saxe-Altenburg;
13. Brunswick and Nassau;
14. Mecklenburg-Schwerin, and Mecklenburg-Strelitz;
15. Oldenburg, three Anhalts, and two Schwarzburgs;
16. Two Hohenzollerns, Liechtenstein, two Reuss, Schaumburg-Lippe, Lippe, and Waldeck;
17. Free cities:—Lübeck, Frankfort, Bremen, and Hamburg.

The diet declares for a constituent assembly, 30 March, which met	18 May,	1848
The diet remits its functions to the archduke John, vicar of the empire (see *Germany*)	12 July,	,,
The diet re-established, meets	30 May,	1851
The emperor of Austria proposes a reform of the confederation, 17 Aug.; accepted by the diet, 1 Sept.; rejected by Prussia	22 Sept.	1863
The diet celebrates the fiftieth anniversary of its establishment	8 June,	1865
Vote of the majority of the diet supports Austria in the dispute respecting Schleswig and Holstein; Prussia announces her withdrawal from the confederation, and its dissolution; the diet declares itself indissoluble, continues its functions, and protests	14 June,	1866
The diet removes to Augsburg during the war,	14 July,	,,
The confederation renounced by Austria at Nikolsburg	26 July,	,,
The diet holds its last sitting	24 Aug.	,,

GERMANITES, a name given to a sect, of which members appeared in the British Mediterranean fleet in 1867. They called themselves "non-fighting men," and hold no communion with other religious bodies.

GERMANIUM, a metal discovered by Dr. Winkler early in 1886.

GERMANS, ST., was made the seat of the bishopric of Cornwall for a short time, about 905.

GERMANY (*Germania, Alemania*), anciently, as now, divided into independent states. The Germans long withstood the attempts of the Romans to subdue them; and although that people conquered some parts of the country, they were expelled before the close of the 3rd century. In the 5th century the Huns and other tribes prevailed over the greater portion of Germany. In the latter part of the 8th century, Charlemagne subdued the Saxons and other tribes, and was crowned emperor at Rome, 25 Dec. 800. A list of his successors is given in another page. At the extinction of his family, the empire became elective, 911, and was subsequently obtained by members of the house of Hapsburg (from 1437 till 1804). Germany was divided into circles, 1501-12. The confederation of the Rhine was formed 12 July, 1806; the Germanic confederation, 8 June, 1815; and the North German confederation, 18 Aug. 1866; the treaty ratified, 8 Sept. 1866. The present German empire was established in 1871. The emperor is styled "German emperor." (*See that date below.*) See *Franco-Prussian War*, 1870-71. Population of the German empire 1880, 45,234,061; in 1885, 46,855,704; 1890, 49,421,803; 1 Dec. 1900, 56,367,178; total fighting strength about 8,000,000 men in 1901.

The empire of Germany was established Jan. 1, 1871, founded upon treaties concluded between the North German confederation (*which see*) and, 1. the grand duchies of Baden and Hesse, 15 Nov. 1870; 2. the kingdom of Bavaria, 23 Nov. 1870; 3. the kingdom of Würtemberg, 25 Nov. 1870; ratified, 29 Jan. 1871. William I., king of Prussia, was proclaimed German emperor at Versailles, 18 Jan. 1871.

Population in 1871 (including Alsace-Lorraine, conquered, 1870), 41,069,846. The parliament (reichstag) is elected by manhood suffrage and ballot.

The first chancellor of the empire, prince Otho von Bismarck, May, 1871; resigned 18 March, 1890.

The Teutones, united with the Cymry, defeat the Romans at Noreia	B.C.	113
After varying success are defeated by Marius		102
Drusus invaded Germany		12-3
Battle of Teutoburg; Hermann or Arminius destroys the Romans under Varus	A.D.	9
Hermann assassinated		19
The Franks invade Gaul		238
Great irruption of Germanic tribes into Gaul		450 *et seq.*
Charlemagne after a long contest subdues the Saxons, who become Christians		772-785
He is crowned emperor of the West at Rome by the pope	25 Dec.	800
He adds a second head to the eagle, to denote that the empires of Rome and Germany are united		802

Louis (*le Débonnaire*) separates Germany from France 839-840
The Germans under Arnold take Rome . . . 896
The German princes assert their independence, and Conrad I. of Franconia reigns . . . 8 Nov. 911
[The electorate began about this time. See *Electors*.]
Reign of Henry I. [king], surnamed the Fowler; he vanquishes the Huns, Danes, Vandals, and Bohemians 918-934
Otho I. extends his dominions, and is crowned emperor by the pope 962
Otho II. conquers Lorraine 978
Henry III. conquers Bohemia 1042
Contest between Henry IV. and Gregory VII. (Hildebrand) 1075
Henry's humiliation at Canossa (*which see*) . . 1077
He takes Rome 1084; and Gregory dies in exile at Salerno 1085
Disputes with the pope relating to ecclesiastical investitures 1073-1123
The Guelph and the Ghibeline feuds begin . . 1140
Conrad III. leads an army to the holy wars; it was destroyed by Greek treachery 1147
Frederick Barbarossa emperor, 1152; wars in Italy, 1154-77
He destroys Milan 1162
Ruins Henry the Lion (see *Bavaria*) . . . 1180
Is drowned during the crusade in Syria, 10 June, 1190
Teutonic order of knighthood . . . . . ,,
Hanseatic league established . . . . about 1245
Reign of Rodolph, count of Hapsburg, chosen by the electors 1273
The edict, called the Golden Bull, by Charles IV. . 1356
The Tyrol acquired 1363
Sigismund, king of Bohemia, elected emperor. He betrays John Huss and Jerome of Prague, who are burned alive (see *Bohemia*) . . . 1414-16
Sigismund driven from the throne, Albert II., duke of Austria, succeeds 1437
The pragmatic sanction confining the empire to the house of Austria 1439
Peasants' wars 1502, 1514, 1524
Era of the Reformation (see *Lutheranism*) . . 1517
German Bible and liturgy published by Luther, 1522-46
Luther excommunicated by the diet at Worms, 17 April, 1521
War with the pope—the Germans storm Rome . 1527
Diet at Spires; Protestants condemned, 13 March, 1529
Confession of Augsburg published . . 25 Jan. 1530
Protestant League of Smalcalde . . . 31 Dec. 1531
The anabaptists seize Munster, 24 June, 1535; defeated, and John of Leyden slain 1536
Death of Luther . . . . . . 18 Feb. 1546
War with the protestants . . . . 26 June, ,,
Who are helped by Henry II. of France—Peace of religion at Passau . . . . . 31 July, 1552
Abdication of Charles V. announced . 25 Oct. 1555
Hungary joined to the empire 1570
The Thirty years' war begins between the evangelic union under the elector palatine, and the catholic league under the duke of Bavaria 1618
Battle of Prague, which ruined the elector palatine, 8 Nov. 1620
Gustavus-Adolphus of Sweden invades Germany, June, 1630
Gustavus-Adolphus, victor, killed at Lutzen, 16 Nov. 1632
Treason of Wallenstein; he is assassinated, 25 Feb. 1634
End of the Thirty years' war: treaty of Westphalia, establishing religious toleration . . 24 Oct. 1648
War with France 1674
John Sobieski, king of Poland, after defeating the Turks, obliges them to raise the siege of Vienna, 12 Sept. 1683
Peace of Ryswick (with France) . . 20 Sept. 1697
The peace of Carlowitz (with the Turks) 26 Jan. 1699
War with France, &c., 6 Oct. 1702; Marlborough's victory at Blenheim . . . . . 13 Aug. 1704
Peace of Utrecht . . . . . . 11 April, 1713
The pragmatic sanction (*which see*) 1722
Francis I., duke of Lorraine, marries the heiress of Austria, Maria-Theresa (1736); she succeeds her father, and becomes queen of Hungary, 20 Oct. 1740
The elector of Bavaria elected emperor as Charles VII. . . . . 22 Jan. 1742
He dies Jan. 20; Francis I., duke of Lorraine, elected emperor . . . . 15 Sept. 1745
The Seven years' war between Austria and Prussia and their respective allies begins Aug. 1756; ends with the peace of Hubertsburg . . 15 Feb. 1763
Lorraine ceded to France 1766
Joseph II. extends his dominions by the dismemberment of Poland, 1772; many civil reforms and liberal changes 1782
War with Turkey 1788
Victory of the Austrians and Russians at Rimnik, 22 Sept. 1789
J. G. Basedow, educational reformer, dies 25 July, 1790
The Rhenish provinces revolt 1793
Francis I. joins in the second partition of Poland, 1795
In the ruinous wars between Germany and France, the emperor loses the Netherlands, all his territories west of the Rhine, and his states in Italy, 1793-1803
Cessions of territory to France by the treaty of Luneville . . . . 9 Feb. 1801
Francis II. assumes the title of Francis I., emperor of Austria . . . . 11 Aug. 1804
Napoleon establishes the kingdoms of Bavaria and Würtemberg, 1805; and of Westphalia, 1807; dissolution of the German empire; formation of the confederation of the Rhine . . 12 July, 1806
North Germany annexed to France . 13 Dec. 1810-1
Commencement of the war of independence: the order of the *iron cross* instituted . . March, 1813
Final defeat of the French at Leipsic 16-19 Oct. ,,
Congress of Vienna . . 1 Nov. 1814 & 25 May, 1815
The Germanic confederation (*which see*) formed 8 June, 1818
The Zollverein (*which see*) formed . . . . ,,
"Society for promoting the knowledge of ancient German history," founded by Stein . . . 1819
A German scientific association formed, "Naturforscher Vereine" (see *German Union*) . . Sept. 1822
General depression in trade 1824
Death of J. H. Voss, poet, &c . . . 29 March, 1826
Revolution at Brunswick (flight of the duke) 7 Sept. 1830
In Saxony (abdication of the king) . . 13 Sept. ,,
Death of Goethe, poet, novelist, and philosopher, 22 March, 1832
Becker's song about the free German Rhine; and Alfred de Musset's song in reply, "Le Rhin Allemand" (see *Rhine*) appear 1841
Excitement about Ronge, the catholic reformer, and the holy coat of Treves 1844
Insurrection at Vienna and throughout Germany (see *Austria, Hungary, &c.*) 1848
Revolt in Schleswig and Holstein (see *Denmark*) March, ,,
The king of Prussia takes the lead as an agitator, to promote the reconsolidation of the German empire, by a proclamation . . 27 March, ,,
German national assembly meet at Frankfort (see *Germanic confederation*) . . . . 18 May, ,,
Archduke John of Austria elected vicar of the empire . . . . 12 July, ,,
The national assembly elects the king of Prussia emperor, 28 March; he declines . 3 April, 1849
He recalls the Prussian members of the assembly, 14 May, ,,
The Frankfort assembly transfers its sittings to Stuttgardt . . . . 30 May, ,,
Treaty of Vienna between Austria and Prussia for the formation of a new central power for a limited time; appeal to be made to the governments of Germany . . . . . 30 Sept. ,,
Protest of Austria against the alliance of Prussia with the smaller German states . . 12 Nov. ,,
Treaty of Munich between Bavaria, Saxony, and Würtemberg, for a revision of the German confederation . . . . 27 Feb. 1850
Parliament meets at Erfurt . . . . March, ,,
The king of Würtemberg denounces the insidious ambition of the king of Prussia . 15 March, ,,
German diet meets at Frankfort . . . 10 May, ,,
Hesse-Cassel sends no representative to Erfurt, 7 June; Hesse-Darmstadt withdraws from the Prussian league . . . . . . 20 June, ,,
Austria calls an assembly of the German confederation, 19 July; which meets at Frankfort, 2 Sept. ,,
Austrian, Bavarian, and Prussian forces enter Hesse-Cassel (see *Hesse-Cassel*) . . 12 Nov. ,,
Conferences on German affairs at Dresden, 23 Dec. 1850, to 15 May, 1851

Max Schneckenburger, author of the song "Die Wacht am Rhein," died 1851
Re-establishment of the diet of the Germanic confederation at Frankfort . . . . 30 May, ,,
Conference at Nuremberg relative to a general code of commerce . . . . 15 Jan. 1857
Great excitement in Germany at the French successes in Lombardy: warlike preparations in Bavaria, &c. . . . . . May and June, 1859
Meetings of new liberal party in Eisenach, Saxe Weimar, 17 July; seven resolutions put forth recommending that the imperfect federal constitution be changed; that the German diet be replaced by a strong central government; that a national assembly be summoned; and that Prussia be invited to take the initiative 14 Aug. ,,
This proposal not accepted by Prussia, and warmly opposed by Hanover . . . . . Sept. ,,
The Austrian minister, Rechberg, severely censuring the duke of Saxe-Gotha, for a liberal speech, 4 Sept.; and accusing the Prussian government of favouring the liberals, meets with cutting retorts . . . . Sept. ,,
Death of Ernst Moritz Arndt, patriot and poet, 29 Jan. 1860
The federal diet maintains the Hesse-Cassel constitution of 1852 against Prussia . 24 March, ,,
Meeting of the French emperor and the German sovereigns at Baden, 16, 17 June; and of the czar and the emperor of Austria and the regent of Prussia at Toplitz . . . . . 26 July, &c. ,,
Meeting at Coburg in favour of German unity against French aggression . . . 5 Sept. ,,
Dispute with Denmark respecting the rights of Holstein and Schleswig . . . . Nov. ,,
First meeting of a German national shooting match at Gotha . . . . 8-11 July, 1861
Meeting of German national association at Heidelberg; decides to form a fleet . . 23 Aug. ,,
Subscriptions received for fleet . Sept. and Oct. ,,
The national association meet at Berlin; they recommend the formation of a united federal government with a central executive, under the leadership of Prussia . . . . . 13 March, 1862
Meetings of plenipotentiaries from German states on federal reform . . . 8 July—10 Aug. ,,
Deputies from German states meet at Weimar, and declare that Germany wants formation into one federal state . . . . 28, 29 Sept. ,,
Congress of deputies from German states declare in favour of unity . . . . . 21 Aug. 1863
The emperor of Austria invites the German sovereigns to a congress at Frankfort, 31 July; king of Prussia declines, 4 Aug.; nearly all the sovereigns meet, 16, 17 Aug.; they approve the Austrian plan of federal reform, 1 Sept.; which is rejected by Prussia . . . . . 22 Sept. ,,
The diet determines to have recourse to federal execution in Holstein if Denmark does not fulfil her obligations . . . . 1 Oct. ,,
50th anniversary of the battle of Leipsic celebrated 18 Oct. ,,
Death of Frederick VII. of Denmark . 15 Nov. ,,
German troops enter Holstein for "federal execution" (see *Denmark* for events) . . 23 Dec. ,,
Death of Maximilian II. of Bavaria . 10 March, 1864
Prussia retains the duchies; discussion between Austria and Prussia; the diet adopt the resolution of Bavaria and Saxony, requesting Austria and Prussia to give up Holstein to the duke of Augustenburg; rejected . . . . 6 April, 1865
50th anniversary of the establishment of the Germanic confederation . . . . . 8 June, ,,
The Gastein convention (*which see*) . . 14 Aug. ,,
Condemned by the diet at Frankfort . . 1 Oct. ,,
The diet calls on Austria and Prussia to disarm, 19 May, 1866
Meeting of deputies from smaller German states condemn the impending war . . . 20 May, ,,
Austria declares that Prussia has broken the treaty by invading Holstein, 11 June; the diet adopts this by 9 votes; the Prussian representative declares the Germanic confederation at an end, and invites the members to form a new one, excluding Austria . . . . 14 June, ,,
The Prussians enter Saxony, and the war begins, 15 June, ,,
The diet determines for war, 16 June; proclaims prince Charles of Bavaria general of the confederation troops . . . . 27 June, 1866
[For the war and its consequences, see *Prussia*, and *German Confederation, North.*]
Treaty of alliance between Prussia and the northern states; ratified . . . . . . 8 Sept. ,,
Continued disputes between the diet and Austria and Prussia respecting Schleswig-Holstein, Oct. and Nov. ,,
Draft of new constitution for North Germany settled . . . . 9 Feb. 1867
Elections commence . . . . . . 12 Feb. ,,
North German parliament opened at Berlin by the king of Prussia, 24 Feb.; Dr. Simson elected president . . . . 2 March, ,,
The federal constitution adopted (printed in *Almanach de Gotha*, 1868); the parliament closed, 17 April ,,
The constitution put in action . . . . 1 July, ,,
Meeting of 50 deputies from parliaments of Bavaria, Würtemberg, Baden, and Hesse-Darmstadt, declare necessity of union with North Germany, Aug. ,,
Luxemburg evacuated by the Prussian garrison, 9 Sept. ,,
New North German parliament meets, 10 Sept.; closed . . . . 26 Oct. ,,
Opened by king of Prussia, 23 March; closed, 20 June, 1868
Delegates from the Zollverein meet, April; close 23 May, ,,
Inauguration of the Luther monument at Worms by the king of Prussia . . . . . 25 June, ,,
German rifle association meeting at Vienna, 26 July; addressed by Von Beust at the close, giving as toast, "Peace and Reconciliation" . 6 Aug. ,,
After negotiations between Bavaria, Würtemberg, and Baden, July, a South German military commission appointed . . . . Oct. ,,
Wilhelmshafen, at Hippens, bay of Jahde, Oldenburg, the first German military port, inaugurated by the king of Prussia . . . . . 17 June, 1869
Centenary of the birth of Alexander von Humboldt celebrated . . . . 14 Sept. ,,
Count Arnim, German representative at Rome, protests against the doctrine of papal infallibility May, 1870
German parliament opened by the king, 14 Feb.; closed . . . . 26 May, ,,
Count Bismarck announces the declaration of war by France, and terms it groundless and presumptuous . . . . 19 July, ,,
Bavaria, Würtemberg, Hesse-Darmstadt, and Baden, support Prussia in the war declared by France. (See *Franco-Prussian War*). 15 July, ,,
Munich, Stuttgart, and other cities, declare for union with North Germany . . about 6 Sept. ,,
Socialists declare against annexation of Alsace, &c. Sept.-Nov. ,,
Baden and Hesse-Darmstadt join the North German Confederation by treaty, about 15 Nov; also Würtemberg, 25 Nov.; and Bavaria, 23 Nov.; retaining certain powers in military and diplomatic affairs . . . . Nov. ,,
The North German parliament opened at Berlin by Dr. Simson on behalf of the king . . 24 Nov. ,,
The parliament vote 100,000,000 thalers to continue the war . . . . 28 Nov. ,,
The king of Bavaria, in a letter to the king of Saxony, proposes the king of Prussia to be nominated emperor of Germany about 4 Dec. ,,
The parliament in an address request the king to become emperor (votes for, 188; against, 6), 10 Dec. ,,
The address solemnly presented to the king in an assembly of princes by Dr. Simson . . 18 Dec. ,,
Re-establishment of the German empire, 1 Jan.; William I. of Prussia proclaimed emperor at Versailles . . . . 18 Jan. 1871
Mr. Odo Russell (aft. ld. Ampthill) appointed ambassador at Berlin . . . . ,,
Several German bankers condemned to imprisonment for subscribing to the French loan 3 Jan. ,,
Preliminaries of peace with France signed at Versailles . . . . 26 Feb. ,,

The emperor reviews part of his army at Longchamps, near Paris . . . . . 1 Mar. 1871
First reichstag or imperial parliament opened at Berlin by the emperor, 397 members . 21 Mar. „
The new constitution of the empire comes into force . . . . 4 May. „
Chancery of the empire: prince Bismarck, chancellor . . . . . . 12 May, „
The treaty of peace ratified . . . . . 16 May, „
Dr. Döllinger, of Munich, excommunicated for opposing the dogma of papal infallibility, 18 April; made D.C.L. of Oxford . . June, „
Triumphal entry of the German armies into Berlin; statue of Frederick William IV. inaugurated, 16 June, „
Dr. Döllinger elected rector of the university at Munich . . . . 29 June, „
The emperors of Austria and Germany meet at Salzburg, Bismarck and Beust present 6-8 Sept. „
The Bavarian minister of public worship declares against the dogma of papal infallibility in a letter to the archbishop of Munich . 27 Sept. „
The German parliament opened by the emperor; who expresses his conviction "that the new German empire will be a reliable shield of peace," 16 Oct. „
Reform in the coinage: introduction of a gold coin approved by the federal council about 6 Nov. „
Law forbidding the clergy to meddle with politics in the pulpit . . . . about 26 Nov. „
Triennial war-budget voted . . . . 1 Dec. „
Sharp despatch from count Bismarck to the German ambassador at Paris respecting the acquittal of murderers of Germans at Melun and Paris, 7 Dec. „
Ultramontane agitation against the government; excitement amongst the Polish Romanists; count Bismarck carries his school inspection bill against the Roman catholic clergy . . . Mar. 1872
The empress-queen visits England . . . May, „
Bismarck reports to the parliament the pope's refusal to receive cardinal Hohenlohe as ambassador . . . . 14 May, „
Bill for the expulsion of the Jesuits passed in the German parliament (131–93); end of session, 19 June; the law published . . . 5 July, „
Inauguration of a memorial to Von Stein, the patriotic statesman at Nassau, by the emperor 9 July, „
Imperial congress: the czar arrives at Berlin, 5 Sept.; the emperor of Austria, 6 Sept.; both leave; prince Bismarck declares the meeting to be merely an act of friendship; "prince Gortschakoff thankful that nothing was written," about 6 Sept. „
Great emigration of young men to America to avoid the conscription; forbidden by government. Sept. „
The German parliament opened . . 12 Mar. 1873
Treaty with France settling the total evacuation of the departments held by German troops on payment of the indemnity in Sept. signed 15 Mar. „
The emperor William warmly received at St. Petersburg . . . . . . 27 April—11 May, „
The monetary reform law passed, 23 June; the parliament closed . . . . . . 25 June, „
Last payment of French war indemnity . 5 Sept. „
The emperor's visit to Vienna . . . 17 Oct. „
Elections for the parliament—(397 members; about two-thirds nationalist liberals; about 100 ultramontanists) . . . . 10 Jan. 1874
Parliament opened . . . . . . 5 Feb. „
Letter from earl Russell to the emperor, expressing sympathy of himself and others with the struggle against the pope, 28 Jan.; the emperor replies 18 Feb. „
Bismarck confined by illness . March, April, „
Constitutional struggle in the parliament respecting the army bill . . . March, „
The government require 401,659 men (instead of 360,000) permanently:—compromise; the army to be settled for seven years . about 10 April, „
The parliament session closed by the emperor with a pacific speech . . . . . . 26 April „
German liberal association, formed against particularists and ultramontanists . about June, „
Count Harry Arnim, formerly ambassador at Rome and Paris, suddenly arrested and imprisoned in Berlin: ostensibly for refusing to give up official papers, 4 Oct.; released on bail . . 28 Oct. 1874
Parliament opened by the emperor; declaration of firm legislative and defensive policy . 29 Oct. „
Bismarck resigns the chancellorship after an adverse vote in the parliament, 16 Dec., on a vote of confidence (199–71) retains it . . 18 Dec. „
Important registration law for births, deaths, and marriages passed . . . . . . Jan. 1875
Civil marriage bill passed . . . . 25 Jan. „
International rifle meeting at Stuttgart . 1 Aug. „
Statue of Hermann (or Arminius), by Von Bandel, at Detmold, uncovered by the emperor William 16 Aug. „
Parliament meets; pacific speech of the emperor read . . . . 27 Oct. „
The imperial bank of Germany opens . 1 Jan. 1876
Proposal for purchase of all the railways by the imperial government (opposed in the south) 20 March, „
The czar at Berlin . . . . . . 11 May, „
Parliament opened with a royal pacific speech, 30 Oct. „
Elections: liberal majority; socialist democrats elected for Berlin . . . . . 10, 11 Jan. 1877
Parliament opened by the emperor: he hopes for peace in the east . . . . . . 22 Feb. „
Supreme court for Germany settled to be at Leipsic by parliament . . . . . . 21 March, „
New code of laws enacted . . . . . „
Resignation of Bismarck as chancellor, 3 April; withdrawn . . . . 8 April, „
Exportation of horses forbidden . . 7 July, „
Parliament re-opened . . . . . 6 Feb. 1878
In consequence of the attempted assassination of the emperor by Hödel, 11 May, a stringent bill to repress socialism is brought into the parliament, and rejected (251—57) . . 24, 25 May, „
Grosser Kurfürst, ironclad, sunk by collision with *König Wilhelm* off Folkestone, about 300 lost 31 May, „
The emperor fired at and wounded by Dr. Karl Edouard Nobiling, a professor of philology and socialist, at Berlin . . . . . . 2 June, „
The crown-prince authorised to direct public affairs, 4, 5 June, „
Parliament dissolved . . . . . 12 June, „
Death of king George of Hanover . . 12 June, „
Emil Heinrich Max Hödel condemned 10 July, „
Elections held (severe struggle) . . 30 July, „
The Berlin conference (*which see*) 13 June—13 July, „
Hödel executed at Berlin . . . . 16 Aug. „
New parliament opened: national liberals, 123; 119 imperialists and conservatives; 105 centre (Roman catholics, &c.) . . . . . 9 Sept. „
Dr. Nobiling dies of self-inflicted wounds, 10 Sept. „
The emperor quite recovered; announced 14 Sept. „
The repressive socialist bill passed (72 majority) 19 Oct. „
Decree for expulsion of socialists and others, issued Nov. „
The emperor returns to Berlin and resumes government . . . . 5 Dec. „
174 clubs, 44 newspapers, and 157 other papers suppressed by injunctions up to . . Dec. „
Parliamentary discipline bill (to "muzzle" speakers); a "gagging bill" introduced about 9 Jan. 1879
Bismarck's negotiations with the Roman curia respecting the Falk laws (*Culturkampf*) fruitless Jan. „
"gagging" bill rejected by the parliament 7 March, „
Prince Bismarck's protectionist tariff bill virtually passed, about . . . . . . 9 May, „
Resignation of Von Forckenbeck (liberal), president of the parliament, 20 May; election of an ultramontane, about . . . . . 22 May, „
The emperor's golden wedding kept . 11 June, „
Resignation of Falk and other ministers; announced . . . . 30 June, „
Bismarck in the parliament disclaims connection with the liberal party . . . . 9 July, „
The customs bill finally passed (217-117); session closed . . . . 12 July, „
Ministry reconstituted about . . . . 14 July, „

Adm. Batsch tried and sentenced to 6 months' imprisonment for loss of *Grosser Kurfürst* (see 31 May, 1878) . . . . July, 1879
Grand military manœuvres at Königsberg 5-9 Sept. „
Meeting of Bismarck and Jacobini, papal nuncio, at Gastein, about . . . . . 16 Sept. „
Bismarck visits Vienna; renews friendship with Andrassy, 21-24 Sept.; supreme court for all Germany, opened at Leipsic . . . . 1 Oct. „
New code of laws made in 1877 come into operation, Nov. „
Bill for enlargement of the army (by 27,000 men), proposed . . . . Jan. 1880
German parliament opened; pacific speech from the emperor . . . . 12 Feb. „
In the federal council 22 small states out-vote Prussia, Saxony, and Bavaria, respecting new stamp duties . . . . . 3 April, „
Bismarck's resignation not accepted by the emperor; the states give in . . . . . April, „
The new army bill passed (186-96) . . . 9 April, „
The parliament prorogued . . . . 10 May, „
"New liberal" party formed by secession from the reactionary "national liberals" . . . Aug. „
Grand army manœuvres in a plain 10 miles south of Berlin . . . . . . 10 Sept. *et seq.* „
German parliament opened . . . 16 Feb. 1881
German army manœuvres near Hanover 30 Aug. and Sept. „
General elections; large liberal majority . 28 Oct. „
The parliament opened by Prince Bismarck with pacific message from the emperor . 17 Nov. „
Bismarck says Germany is not to be ruled after English fashion . . . . 29 Nov. „
He is defeated in a financial question 169-83 1 Dec. „
Imperial rescript against parliamentary government published . . . . 7 Jan. 1882
Violent debates in the parliament . 24 Jan. *et seq.* „
Bismarck's tobacco tax bill rejected by his economic council 21 March; rejected by Parliament 276-43 14 June, „
Important autumn manœuvres near Breslau 6 Sept. „
German Colonization society constituted at Frankfort . . . . 6 Dec. „
The budget rejected by the chambers . 11 Dec. „
Death of Prince Charles, brother of the Emperor 21 Jan. 1883
Enthusiastic commemoration of Luther's birth (see *Lutheranism*) . . . . . . Aug.-Sept.
Autumn manœuvres at Merseburg, 15 Sept., at Homburg . . . . 20 Sept. „
Germania, a colossal statue, &c., by Prof. Schilling, a national memorial of German unity and victories of 1870-1 set up in the Niederwald at Rudesheim on the Rhine, uncovered by the emperor William in the presence of German sovereigns and 5,000 spectators; Von Moltke there but not Bismarck 28 Sept. „
[Plot to blow up the monument by dynamite and destroy the royal and eminent persons present this day, frustrated by bad weather; discovered in 1884].
The fourth centenary of Luther's birth (10 Nov. 1483) celebrated at Erfurt, Halle, &c. 31 Oct. *et seq.* „
Successful visit of the Crown Prince to Spain and Italy . . . . . . 23 Nov.—22 Dec. „
Prince Bismarck refuses to present to the chamber a letter of condolence from the United States on the death of the eloquent Dr. Lasker, formerly his supporter, afterwards his opponent . Feb. 1884
German parliament opened; disputes respecting the Lasker affair . . . . . 6, 7 Mar. „
Mr. Sargent, the obnoxious U.S. minister, settled to be removed to St. Petersburg, 26 Mar.; declined . . . . 27 Mar. „
Anti-socialist law prolonged for two years (189-157), 10 May; trial of Kraszewski, Polish poet and novelist, and captain Hentsch, ex-telegraph official at Leipsic, for high treason in military communications to Austrian, French, and other governments in 1866-71; Kraszewski sentenced to 3½ years' imprisonment [released on bail Nov. 1885]; Hentsch to 9 years' penal servitude . 12-19 May, „
Foundation of the new German parliament-house at Berlin laid by the emperor . . . 8 June „
Autumn manœuvres at Düsseldorf, 15 Sept. *et seq.* „
German colony founded at Cameroons, and Bimbia, west coast of Africa, by Herr Nachtigall; Aug. 1884
Death of Lord Ampthill, British ambassador, Aug.; succeeded by Sir Edward Malet . . Sept. „
Elections for the parliament; number of liberals diminished, social democrats increased 28 Oct. „
Parliament opened by the emperor . 20 Nov. „
Bismarck defeated; votes for payment of members, 180-99, 26 Nov.; parts of May ecclesiastical laws repealed (217-93) . . . . . 3 Dec. „
Eight dynamitards, Friedrich A. Reinsdorf and others, for attempting to kill the emperor, 28 Sept. 1883 (*see above*): tried at Leipsic; F. A. Reinsdorf, Rupsch, and Küchler sentenced to death; two to imprisonment; three acquitted 15-22 Dec. „
German flag said to be hoisted on N. coast of New Guinea, New Britain, and other islands, Dec. „
Great increase of emigration (fivefold) . . 1879-1884
"Germany does not want colonies"—Bismarck, 1871—180,000 marks voted for protection of colonies . . . . 10 Jan. 1885
Speech of Prince Bismarck attacking the Gladstone cabinet . . . . 2 Mar. „
Dispute said to be settled . . . 9 Mar. „
Lieske convicted of murder of Rumpff at Frankfort 1 July, „
Parliament opened . . . . . 19 Nov, „
Prince Bismarck's "Schnapps" (dram of spirits) monopoly bill introduced 11 Jan.; rejected by committee 12 March 1886
Sarauw sentenced to 12 years' penal servitude for high treason (giving information respecting fortresses to the French government) . 11 Feb. „
Prince Bismarck reproves parliament for opposing government bills . . . . 26 March, „
The "Schnapps" bill rejected (181-3) 27 March, „
Socialist law prolonged for two years 31 March, „
Leopold von Ranke, the historian, died (aged 90) 23 May, „
Autumn manœuvres at Strasburg; the army reported to be perfect . . . about 15 Sept. „
Parliament opened . . . . . . 25 Nov. „
Bill for increase of the army (41,000) for seven years brought in 3 Dec.; much opposed by clericals, socialists, and others; adjourned to Jan. 1887, 17 Dec. 1886; amendment limiting increase to three years carried (183-154); parliament immediately dissolved . . . 4 Jan. 1887
Elections: (efforts to make the army parliamentary instead of imperial); majority for the government . . . . 21 Feb. „
Parliament opened . . . . . 3 March, „
Army bill passed (227-31) . . . . 11 March, „
Treaty of alliance with Austria and Italy signed 13 March, „
The emperor's 90th birthday royally celebrated at Berlin . . . . 22 March, „
Arrest of M. Schnæbell (see under *France*) 20-22 April, „
Foundation stone of opening lock of a canal from the Baltic to the North Sea, 61 miles long, laid at Holtenau near Kiel by the emperor; (estimated cost 7,800,000*l.*) . . . . 3 June, „
Eight Alsatians, members of the "Ligue des Patriotes" formed for the reunion of Alsace-Lorraine to France (advocated by M. Déroulède, a fiery poet of "La Revanche"), tried at Leipsic for high treason, 13 June; four sentenced to one to two years' imprisonment; four acquitted 18 June; Klein and Grebert sentenced to six and five years' respectively . . . . . 8 July, „
Parliament closed . . . . . 18 June, „
The emperor present at military manœuvres at Stettin . . . . 12 Sept. „
Celebration of 25th anniversary of Prince Bismarck's premiership of Prussia . 23 Sept. „
Border disputes (see *France*) . . . . „
Signor Crispi, Italian premier, visits prince Bismarck . . . . 2, 3 Oct. „
The czar formally received in Berlin . 18 Nov. „
Meeting of the parliament . . . . 24 Nov. „
Statement in the *Cologne Gazette* of the existence of letters, &c., purporting to come from prince Bismarck sent to the czar tending to create disaffection; asserted to be forged; attributed to Orleanists, especially princess Clementine of Coburg, daughter of king Louis Philippe . Nov. „

Cabannes sentenced to ten years' penal servitude for selling military secrets to the French government 19 Dec. 1887

Indisposition of the crown prince (since termed *perichondritis*), winters in Italy and S. France under the care of sir Morell Mackenzie, 1887; stated to be malignant growth in the larynx; tracheotomy performed (the German doctors and sir Morell Mackenzie differ) . . . . Feb. 1888

Herr von Puttkamer's more stringent anti-socialist bill opposed by all parties; revelations of government detectives inciting socialists to violence in Zurich: the bill committed 30 Jan. 1888; passed 17 Feb. ,,

Defensive treaty with Austria against Russian or other aggression, 7 Oct. 1879; first published 3 Feb. ,,

Powerful speech of prince Bismarck, alike for peace and preparation for war . . . 6 Feb. ,,

Serious illness of the emperor; prince William (grandson) entrusted with official powers, 17 Nov. 1887; this publicly announced . 8 March, ,,

"The great emperor who founded Germany's unity is dead."—*Prince Bismarck* . . 9 March, ,,

The emperor Frederick III. arrives at Berlin 11 March, ,,

Solemn German national funeral of the emperor at Berlin; present the kings of Belgium, Saxony, and Roumania, the prince of Wales and the duke of Cambridge, the crown princes of Austria, Russia, Denmark, and other princes and nobles (not the emperor Frederick, prince Bismarck, and count Moltke) . . . . . 16 March, ,,

Parliament prorogued . . . 20 March, ,,

Rescript empowering the crown prince to act for the emperor in state affairs when required 21 March, ,,

Visit of the queen of England. . 24–26 April, ,,

Continued improvement of the emperor's health 15 May, ,,

The emperor becomes much worse 11, 12 June; dies (of cancer of the larynx) 15 June, ,,

Simple, impressive funeral at Potsdam 18 June, ,,

The imperial parliament opened by the emperor with much pomp; many princes present; in his speech the emperor said "I will follow the same path by which my deceased grandfather won the confidence of his allies, the love of the German people, and the goodwill of foreign countries," 25 June. The house adjourns after voting a cordial address . . . . . 26 June, ,,

Herr Dietz, a former railway official in Alsace-Lorraine, his wife, and Appel convicted of treason and giving railway information to the French government, 5 July; Dietz sentenced to ten years' penal servitude, his wife to four years, and Appel to ten years' confinement . 9 July, ,,

The emperor's visit to the czar at Peterhof, 19-23 July; visited Stockholm and Copenhagen July, ,,

The emperor arrives at Vienna, 3 Oct.; at Rome, 11 Oct.; at Naples 16 Oct. ,,

Sir Morell Mackenzie publishes "The Fatal Illness of Frederick the Noble"; its sale temporarily prohibited in Germany; he stops the sale in England of the German surgeon's report of the case; statements differ . about 15 Oct. ,,

Opening of parliament by the emperor . 22 Nov. ,,

The East African bill passed, granting money for the defence of German interests and the suppression of the slave trade, 30 Jan.; adopted by the federal council (see *Africa*, *German East Africa*), 1 Feb. 1889

The empress Frederick and her daughters visit England . . . . 19 Nov. 1888—26 Feb. ,,

Three German war vessels lost; nine officers and 87 men drowned, in a storm off Samoa (*which see*) . . . . . 16 March, ,,

Great strike of coal miners in Westphalia (*which see*) . . . . . May, ,,

The king of Italy, his son, and Signor Crispi warmly received at Berlin . 21-26 May, ,,

33 Silesian miners engaged in the strikes; sentenced to various terms of penal servitude (Enkel, the ringleader, to 7 years for riotous conduct). . . . . 24 July, ,,

Prince Bismarck's bill to compel the working class, with the assistance of the state and their employés, to provide for sickness (passed 1883), for accidents (passed 1884), for old age and infirmity, passed . . . . 24 May, 1889

The emperor with a fleet arrives at Spithead, 1 Aug., and proceeds to the queen at Osborne, 2 Aug.; created a British admiral; present at the grand naval review, 5 Aug., and at a sham fight at Aldershot, 7 Aug.; queen Victoria made colonel of a German regiment to be called "the Queen of England's own,' about 3 Aug.; the emperor leaves England . . . 8 Aug. ,,

The emperor of Austria and his heir at Berlin, 12–15 Aug. ,,

The emperor visits Strasburg, well received, 20 Aug.; at Metz. . . . 24 Aug. ,,

The emperor present at the autumn army manœuvres near Hanover . . . Sept. ,,

Prince Bismarck declines to give state support to the German colonial company in S.W. Africa, Sept. ,,

The czar visits Berlin . . . . 11–13 Oct. ,,

The imperial parliament opened with a pacific speech . . . . . 22 Oct. ,,

Bill for amending the socialist law of 1878, prolonging it indefinitely, introduced . . Oct. ,,

The emperor and empress present at the marriage of his sister to the duke of Sparta, 27 Oct.; warmly received by sultan at Constantinople . 2–6 Nov. ,,

Visit Venice . . . . . . 12 Nov. ,,

The Austrian and German emperors meet at Innsbruck . . . . . 14 Nov. ,,

91 socialists, members of a secret society, tried at Elberfeld for illegally promoting socialism, 20 Nov. *et seq.*; 47 acquitted, the rest sentenced to imprisonment (terms 18 months to 14 days) 30 Dec. ,,

The stringent anti-socialist bill rejected (169–98), the parliament closed with a moderate speech by the emperor . . . . . . 25 Jan. 1890

Two rescripts issued by the emperor, urgently recommending action for the improvement of the condition of the working classes, and suggesting the co-operation of France, England, Belgium, and Switzerland. See *Berlin* . . 4 Feb. ,,

Elections for the new parliament, increased number of socialists elected. See *Cartel*. 20 Feb. *et seq.* ,,

Resignation of prince Bismarck, chancellor of the empire [his political maxim was said to be *Do ut des* (Grotius ?)—I give that thou mayest give] 18 March, ,,

He declines being created duke of Lauenburg, about 23 March, ,,

He is succeeded by gen. George von Caprivi de Caprera de Montecuculi . . about 20 March, ,,

Count Herbert Bismarck, secretary for foreign affairs, resigns, succeeded by baron Marschall von Biederstein . . . . . about 1 April, ,,

New colonial department formed, reported 16 April, ,,

About 25,000 workmen on strike in Germany reported . . . . . . 30 April, ,,

The demonstration in favour of an eight hours' working day passes off tranquilly . 1 May, ,,

The new parliament opened by the emperor; in his speech, while professing ardent desire for peace, he required supplies for the increase of the army (18,000,000 marks) . . . . 6 May, ,,

Vote of 4,500,000 marks, and an annual subsidy of 350,000 marks, for the suppression of slavery, and protection of German interests in East Africa, proposed by gen. von Caprivi . 12 May, ,,

First German national horse show (at Berlin) 12 June *et seq.* ,,

The new army bill passed by the parliament 28 June, ,,

Anglo-German convention (*which see*) respecting East Africa, signed at Berlin . . 1 July, ,,

Newly created colonial department subjected to the chancellor in . . . . . July, ,,

The emperor visits queen Victoria at Osborne 4–8 Aug.; visits Heligoland (*which see*) 10 Aug. ,,

The emperor visits Russia; met by the czar at Nawa, 17 Aug.; at Peterhof; left 23 Aug. ,,

Naval review at Kiel . . . . . 3 Sept. ,,

Military manœuvres in Silesia . . . Sept. ,,

Cordial meeting of the German emperor and the emperor of Austria at Rhonstock in Silesia 17–20 Sept.; at Vienna, &c. . . 1–8 Oct. ,,

The socialist (or "muzzling") law of 1878 expires; great demonstration . . . 30 Sept. ,,

International socialist congress at Halle, Prussian Saxony . . . . 12–18 Oct. 1890
Establishment of a colonial council decreed 15 Oct. ,,
Birthday of field-marshal count Hellmuth Moltke (born 26 Oct., 1800) celebrated at Berlin; the emperor, the king of Saxony, and other German sovereigns and the count himself present 26 Oct. ,,
Marriage of the princess Victoria, daughter of the empress Frederick II., to prince Adolphus of Schaumburg-Lippe, at Berlin . . . 19 Nov. ,,
The parliament (adjourned in July) meets 2 Dec. ,,
The emperor, at a conference in Berlin, strongly advocates reform in public education 4–17 Dec. ,,
Sudden death of field-marshal von Moltke, aged 90, 24 April; grand military funeral, accompanied by the emperor, German sovereigns, state officers, ambassadors and a great multitude, Berlin 28 April; quiet interment at Kreisau in Silesia 29 April, 1891
Prince Bismarck elected deputy for the parliament at Geestemünde . . . . . . 1 May, ,,
The parliament adjourns (the important Trades law amendment act passed) . . . 9 May, ,,
The triple alliance renewed . . . 28 June, ,,
Tour of the emperor and empress; they land at Heligoland, 30 June; arrive at Amsterdam (in the *Hohenzollern*); warmly received by the queens, 1 July; at the Hague and Rotterdam, 3 July; received at Port Victoria by a British squadron; arrive at Windsor (*which see*), 4 July; at Buckingham palace; receptions and opera at Covent Garden, 8 July; garden party at Marlborough house; state concert at Albert hall, 9 July; visit the naval exhibition; state entry into the city; banquet at Guildhall; speech of the emperor ("My aim is above all the maintenance of peace") 10 July; he reviews about 25,000 volunteers at Wimbledon; at Crystal palace; review of National fire brigade; concerts; dinner by the prince of Wales; grand fireworks, 11 July; at St. Paul's; visit to Hatfield (marquis of Salisbury), 12 July; banquet at Hatfield; farewell to the queen at Windsor; the empress goes to her five sons at Felixstowe, Suffolk, 13 July; the emperor proceeds from London to Leith; embarks on the *Hohenzollern*, sails up the Forth to view the bridge, and then proceeds to the coast of Norway, 13, 14 July; lands at various places, 18 July *et seq.*; at North Cape, 21 July; leaves Bergen, 4 Aug.; arrives at Kiel, 8 Aug.; the empress and the princes leave Felixstowe . . . . 6 Aug. ,,
Great rise in the price of grain, especially rye, through the prohibition of exportation by the czar . . . . Aug. ,,
Socialist congress at Erfurt closed . . 21 Oct. ,,
Strike of journeymen printers throughout Germany for a 9 hours' day begun at Berlin about 2 Nov. ,,
The *Weissenburg*, ironclad named by the emperor at Stettin . . . . 14 Dec. ,,
New commercial treaty with Austria, Italy, and Belgium, adopted by the parliament . Dec. ,,
Gen. von Caprivi made a count . . 18 Dec. ,,
The printers' strike supported by above 3,000*l.* sent by English trade unions, 2 Jan.; collapse of the strike reported . . . . . . 15 Jan. 1892
The emperor's speech at Brandenburg, in which he severely censures the opponents of his political policy, styling them "grumblers," causes great sensation among all parties . 24 Feb. *et seq.* ,,
Several newspapers at Berlin confiscated for reprinting the *Times* leader on the emperor's speech 3 March, ,,
Rioting at Berlin, Hanover, Dantzig, and other places through distress . 25 Feb. *et seq.* ,,
Ministerial crisis in Prussia (*which see*) 22 March, ,,
The government defeated in the parliament; the vote for an imperial corvette negatived 29 March, ,,
The parliament prorogued . . . 31 March, ,,
The government warns its representatives abroad against prince Bismarck's strictures on its policy May–July, ,,
Prince Bismarck visits Jena; makes defensive speeches . . . . . . 30, 31 July, ,,
The emperor visits England . . . . 1–8 Aug. ,,
The armour-clad *Hildebrand*, and the iron-clad *Wörth*, launched at Kiel . . . . 7 Aug. ,,
"Long-distance ride" of Germans and Austrians, see *Riding* . . . . 7 Oct. ,,
The emperor, the duke of York, with representatives of the protestant sovereigns of Europe and Germany, present at the dedication of the restored Castle-church of Wittenberg, *which see* 31 Oct. 1892
The parliament opened by the emperor 22 Nov. ,,
The army bills introduced by count von Caprivi 23 Nov. ,,
German conservative congress in Berlin opened 8 Dec. ,,
Herr Ahlwardt, a member of the chamber, anti-semitic agitator, sentenced to five months' imprisonment for libels against Löwe & Co., Jewish rifle manufacturers . . . . 9 Dec. ,,
A new "National party" advocating bi-metallism, anti-semitism, colonization, &c., reported, 22 Dec. ,,
Very severe winter, Dec. 1892 . . . . Jan. 1893
Meeting at Berlin to establish a German agrarian league to oppose the importation of foreign grain, 18 Feb.; agitation throughout the empire Feb. ,,
Navy estimates: increase of the navy, &c. stopped by parliament . . . . . . 8 March, ,,
The emperor and empress present at the silver wedding of the king and queen of Italy, Rome, 22 April; they visit the pope, 23 April; received at Naples, 27 April; at Lucerne, 2 May; at Berlin . . . . 4 May, ,,
Official examination into Ahlwardt's anti-semitic charges, 27 April; declared unfounded, 29 April; he withdraws them, and is censured by vote of the committee . . . . . . 2 May, ,,
The parliament finally rejects the army bills (210–162) and is dissolved . . . . 6 May, ,,
Monument to the memory of William I. at Görlitz, unveiled by the emperor . . . 18 May, ,,
General election, small majority for the Government . . . . June, ,,
The parliament opened by the emperor with a conciliatory speech . . . . . 4 July, ,,
The army bills read a first time, 8 July; passed (201–185); the session closed . 15 July, ,,
Seven weeks' drought closed by a violent storm 11 July, ,,
The emperor visits the queen at Osborne 29 July—7 Aug. ,,
Russian duty on German imports raised 50 per cent.; German reprisals . . . . 2 Aug. *et seq* ,,
Explosion on the *Baden* warship in the Baltic; 9 men killed . . . . 2 Aug. ,,
Army banquet at Coblentz; speech by the emperor; crown prince of Italy present . . . 1 Sept. ,,
Manœuvres begin . . . . 4 Sept. ,,
The emperor and empress entertained by the king of Würtemberg at Stuttgart . . . 15 Sept. ,,
The army bill comes into force . . . . 1 Oct. ,,
Two years' service substituted for three; the peace footing of the army is fixed at 479,229 men, from 1 October to 31 March, 1899, being an increase of 70,000.
50th anniversary of the doctorate of prof. Mommsen, the historian of Rome, &c., archæologist, and jurist, celebrated . . . . . 8 Nov. ,,
The parliament opened by the emperor . 16 Nov. ,,
Anti-Jesuit law of 4 July, 1872; bill for its repeal introduced; passed (173–136) . . . 1 Dec. ,,
Degony and Delguey-Malvas arrested as French spies at Kiel, 28 Aug.; Degony sentenced to 6 years', Delguey-Malvas to 4 years' imprisonment 16 Dec. ,,
Reconciliation between the emperor and prince Bismarck: the prince warmly and honourably received by the emperor; popular demonstrations on the road and in Berlin . . . 26 Jan. ,,
Commercial treaty with Russia for 10 years, signed 10 Feb.; comes into force . . . 20 March, 1894
By the bursting of several steam-pipes on board the *Brandenburg*, 1st class battleship, 42 men were killed . . . . 16 Feb. ,,
The parliament closed . . . . . 19 April, ,,
A deputation of British officers of the 1st royal dragoons received by the emperor (their newly appointed colonel-in-chief) at Berlin . 7 June, ,,
Two French officers, *see above*, Aug. 1893, released by the emperor . . . . . 1 July, ,,
The emperor visits the queen at Osborne, &c. 6–14 Aug. ,,
Death of Hermann von Helmholtz, eminent physiologist and physicist, aged 73 . . 8 Sept. ,,

Dedication of 132 new standards presented to the new fourth battalions by the emperor . 18 Oct. 1894

Resignation of the chancellor, count von Caprivi, 26 Oct.; received the order of the black eagle, with brilliants . . . . 29 Oct. ,,

Prince Clovis von Hohenlohe appointed chancellor and president of the Prussian ministry 29 Oct. ,,

Death of princess Bismarck, aged 70; a devoted wife . . . . 27 Nov. ,,

The new parliament-house opened by the emperor, at Berlin . . . . 5 Dec. ,,

Imperial finance (reform) bill introduced 27 Jan. 1895

Heavy snowfall throughout the country; railways and roads blocked . . 30 Jan.—1 Feb. ,,

Agrarian congress meets; an address presented to the emperor, well received . . . 18 Feb. ,,

The emperor presents to prince Bismarck a sword of honour for his 80th birthday (1 April) at Friedrichsruh . . . . 26 March, ,,

The day celebrated in Germany, in London, and other places . . . . . . 1 April, ,,

Aegir, new ironclad launched by the emperor at Kiel . . . . 3 April, ,,

An association formed at Berlin to maintain the existing gold currency . . . 3 April, ,,

Gustav Freytag, author of "Soll und Haben," &c., born, 1816; died . . . . 30 April, ,,

The anti-revolutionary bills rejected by the parliament . . . . 11 May, ,,

Tobacco-taxation bill rejected . . . . 13 May, ,,

Session of parliament closed . . . 24 May, ,,

Herr Mellage acquitted of libelling the catholic private asylum at Mariaberg, near Aix-la-Chapelle, his accusations of cruelty having been proved, 9 June; the asylum closed by order . June ,,

Prince Bismarck presented with a silver shield by the German agrarian league . . . 9 June, ,,

The North sea and Baltic canal opened by the emperor William II., see *Kiel* . . . 20 June, ,,

Prof. Rudolf von Gneist, jurist and statesman, born 13 Aug. 1816; died . . . . 21 July, ,,

Christian Bernhard Tauchnitz, eminent publisher, born 25 Aug. 1816; died . . . . 13 Aug. ,,

See *Prussia*.

Sir Frank Lascelles (G.C.B. Jan. 1897) appointed British ambassador in Berlin . . . 11 Sept. ,,

Collapse of a factory at Bocholt, near Wesel, with great loss of life . . . . . . 9 Oct. ,,

Several editors of the social democratic press imprisoned for lèse-majesté . . . . Oct.–Dec. ,,

Parliament opened . . . . 3 Dec. ,,

The emperor intervenes in the Transvaal difficulty (*which see*) . . . . 2 Jan. 1896

Celebration of the 25th anniversary of the foundation of the German empire, which the emperor terms a "world empire" . . . . 18 Jan. ,,

New civil code for the empire, based on the report of commissions in 1874 and 1890, submitted to parliament . . . . Jan. ,,

The emperor and empress visit Venice, 11 April; Vienna, 14 April; return to Berlin . 29 April, ,,

Baron von Schrader killed in a duel with Herr von Kotze, much scandal; semi-public funeral, 15 April; Herr von Kotze sentenced to 2 years' imprisonment . . . . 18 May, ,,

The reichstag request the government to endeavour to suppress duelling, 20, 21 April; again with little effect . . . . Nov. ,,

Heinrich von Treitschke, historian and poet, born 15 Sept. 1834; died . . . . . 28 April, ,,

Prosecution of 47 social democrats at Berlin; 32 acquitted and the rest fined . 15–18 May, ,,

Mr. Stern, an American, heavily fined for resenting regulations and scale of fees on foreign visitors; United States government protests, but the German government justifies the sentence: reported . . . . 21 May, ,,

Monumental statue of the emperor William I., a memorial of united Germany, set up on the Kyffhäuser hill in Thuringia; unveiled by William II. . . . . 18 June, ,,

The new civil code (to come into force 1 Jan. 1900) passed . . . . 1 July, ,,

The *Kaiser Friedrich III.* launched by the emperor 1 July, ,,

The imperial diet prorogued till 10 Nov. . 2 July, ,,

Iltis, gunboat, foundered off the Shan-tung promontory, 57 deaths . . . . 23 July, 1896

Army manœuvres in Silesia . . . 8–12 Sept. ,,

Resignation of Dr. Kayser, colonial secretary, announced . . . . 15 Oct. ,,

Baron Ehrhardt and 6 others sentenced at Dusseldorf to various terms of imprisonment for insulting a court of honour respecting duels . 20 Oct. ,,

Discussion in the reichsrath respecting the so-called Bismarckian "revelations" on a Russo-German treaty of William I. and the Triple alliance; affair closed . . . . 11–16 Nov. ,,

Herr Leckert and Herr von Lützow, journalists, sentenced to 18 months' imprisonment for libel against baron Marschall, foreign minister, and count von Eulenburg, court marshal, in connection with the report of the czar's speech at Breslau, others fined . . . . . . 7 Dec. ,,

New stock and produce regulations come into force, 1 Jan.; much opposed; business transacted under the auspices of the new "Free commercial union" . . . . . . 2 Jan. 1897

Imperial cabinet order restricting duelling in the army, announced . . . . . . 5 Jan ,,

Centenary of the birth of the emperor William I.; the national monument to him at Berlin unveiled by William II. with great pomp and rejoicing . . . . 22 March, ,,

New commercial code passed . . . . 7 April, ,,

Koschemann, a young anarchist, sentenced to 10 years' imprisonment for sending an infernal machine through the post . . . 15 April, ,,

The *Kaiser Wilhelm der Grosse*, of the N. German Lloyd steamship company, launched, the emperor present, at Stettin . . . . 4 May, ,,

Emergency bill declaring that associations of every kind may enter into union, and repealing all provisions to the contrary in the laws of the other states, passed in the reichstag (207–53) . 20 May, ,,

Von Tausch, political detective, acquitted of perjury (about 14 days' trial) . . . . 4 June, ,,

Denunciation of the Anglo-German treaty of commerce (30 May, 1865) by the British government, 30 July, ,,

Autumn manœuvres begin at Coblenz, the emperor present, 30 Aug.; collapse of a bridge at Weimar, many soldiers killed . . . . . 3 Sept. ,,

Visit of the king and queen of Italy; received by the emperor at Hamburg . . 3 Sept. *et seq.* ,,

Kaiser Wilhelm II. launched at Stettin . 14 Sept. ,,

Prince Bismarck, cruiser, launched at Kiel 25 Sept. ,,

Parliament opened by the emperor . . 30 Nov. ,,

Squadron, under the command of prince Henry, leaves Kiel for the east . . . . 16 Dec. ,,

New coinage completed . . . . . . Dec. ,,

Budget presented by Dr. von Miquel . . 12 Jan. 1898

Herr Johannes Trojan, editor of the comic paper, *Kladderadatsch*, sentenced to 2 months' imprisonment in a fortress for lèse-majesté . 25 Jan. ,,

Kiao-chau treaty with China (*which see*) ratified, 6 March; capt. Rosendahl appointed governor at Kiao-chau, 7 March; prince Henry arrives there, 1 June, ,,

Bill for the reform of military judicial procedure, civil code and navy act passed, 28 March; reichstag closed by the emperor . . . . 6 May, ,,

General elections . . . . . 16–29 June, ,,

Outrage at the German embassy, London (see *Trial*) June, ,,

Death of prince Bismarck (b. 1 April, 1815), 30 July, his connection with Dr. Moritz Busch, editor of his diary; his "Autobiography" published, see *Times* . . . . 1 Oct., 29 Nov. ,,

The emperor and empress leave Berlin for a tour in the east, 11 Oct.; received by king Humbert at Venice, 13 Oct.; by the sultan at Constantinople, 18 Oct.; present at a review of troops, 21 Oct.; they leave, with gifts, 22 Oct.; land at Haifa, Palestine, 25 Oct.; Jaffa, 27 Oct.; Jerusalem (*which see*), 29 Oct.; Beirut, 5 Nov.: Damascus, 7 Nov.; monument erected by the sultan unveiled by the emperor at Baalbek, 10 Nov.; leave Beirut to visit harbours, 12 Nov.; return to Potsdam . . . . 26 Nov. ,,

See *Lippe-Detmold* and *Bavaria*, 1898.

State entry of the emperor and empress into Berlin, 1 Dec. ,,

Reichstag opened by the emperor . . . 6 Dec. 1898
Imperial bank-notes forged by Gränenthal, manager of the Imperial Printing Office (who committed suicide in prison); 483,000 marks loss made up, reported . . . . . 19 Jan. 1899
Gen. count von Caprivi, chancellor 1890–94, born 24 Feb. 1831, died . . . . . 6 Feb. ,,
New German imperial 3 per cent. loan, and the new Prussian 3 per cent. consols, well taken up, Feb. ,,
Mr. Cecil Rhodes received by the emperor; successful negotiations respecting the Trans-African telegraph . . . . 11–16 March, ,,
Ludwig Bamberger, political author (born 1823), and Prof. Heymann Steinthal, philologist and author (born 1823), died . . 14 March, ,,
Army bill, amended by the budget committee, adopted . . . . . 16 March, ,,
Prof. Hans Delbrück fined 500 marks for censuring the government for the expulsion of Danes from Schleswig-Holstein . . 25 March, ,,
Imperial penny postage (letters) to colonies and protectorates started . . . 1 May, ,,
Dr. Martin Eduard von Simson, ex-president of the reichstag, and of the supreme court of the empire, &c., died, aged 88 . . . . 2 May, ,,
Nat. male choirs' competition at Kassel, the emperor present, his prize won by Cologne, 26 May, ,,
Kaiser Wilhelm der Grosse, battleship, 393 ft. long, 68 ft. broad, launched, at Kiel, by the emperor, 1 June, ,,
Death of prof. Klaus Groth (*Plattdeutsch*), poet, about 2 June, ,,
Bill prolonging the most-favoured-nation treatment to the commerce of the British empire (except Canada), and one ratifying treaty with Spain, *which see*, for the acquisition of the Caroline islands, passed; penal servitude (labour strikes) bill rejected by a large majority in the diet, 21, 22 June, ,,
Dr. Quarck, socialist editor, sentenced to 4 months' imprisonment for lèse-majesté . mid June, ,,
Strike-riot of colliers at Herne, near Bochum, 5 deaths; troops called out . . 27–29 June, ,,
The emperor visits the French training ship *Iphigénie* at Bergen; cordial messages exchanged between his majesty and pres. Loubet . 6 July, ,,
Great meeting of the union of German co-operative associations, Berlin; statue of Schulze-Delitzsch, founder of the Nat. Union, 1859, unveiled in Berlin . . . . . . 1, 4 Aug. ,,
Count Münster, ambassador in Paris, made a prince for his services at the peace conference . 8 Aug. ,,
The Dortmund–Ems canal opened by the emperor at Dortmund . . . . . 11 Aug. ,,
Demonstrations in the provinces in honour of the deposed Landräthe; see *Prussia* . . Sept. ,,
Army manœuvres, Black Forest district, early Sept. ,,
Queen of Holland and her mother visit Potsdam, 7–11 Oct. ,,
Kaiser Karl der Grosse battleship launched at Hamburg by the emperor . . . . 18 Oct. ,,
The czar and czarina visit Potsdam . 8 Nov. ,,
Reichstag meets, 14 Nov.; labour (penal servitude) bill again rejected . . . . 20 Nov. ,,
The emperor and empress visit the queen, 20 Nov.; return to Potsdam . . . . 30 Nov. ,,
Debate in the reichstag on the proposed increase of the navy; able speech of Herr Richter, leader of the opposition . . . . . 11, 14 Dec. ,,
Herzog and *Bundesrath*, German vessels, seized by English cruisers on suspicion of carrying contraband of war, end of 1899; some controversy ensued.
The emperor's speech in favour of the navy bill, Berlin . . . . 7 Jan. 1900
Diet opened, see *Prussia* . . . . . 9 Jan. ,,
Death of the duchess Frederick of Augustenburg, mother of the empress . . . 25 Jan. ,,
Navy (increase) bill introduced . . . 8 Feb. ,,
Prince Henry of Prussia warmly received in Berlin after 2 years' naval duty in the Far East, 13 Feb. ,,
Reichstag meets . . . . . . 24 April, ,,
The coming of age of the crown prince celebrated in Berlin, the emperor Francis Joseph, duke of York, and other royal guests present . 4–6 May, ,,
Anti-semitic riot in Konitz, W. Prussia; "state of siege" proclaimed . . . . 10 June, 1900
Navy bill passed, 201–103; the reichstag adjourns, 12 June, ,,
North German Lloyd disaster; see *New York*, 30 June, ,,
Circular note on the Chinese crisis to the federated States issued, reported . . . 12 July, ,,
Treasury bonds (80,000,000 mks.) placed in the United States, announced . . . 14 Sept. ,,
Max Harden, writer and editor, sentenced to 6 months' imprisonment for lèse-majesté; 4 other trials . . . . 8 Oct. ,,
Foundation-stone of the Imperial "Limes" museum, in the Saalburg, near Homburg, laid by the emperor . . . . . . 11 Oct. ,,
Prince Hohenlohe, imperial chancellor, aged 81, resigns, 16 Oct.; succeeded by count von Bülow, 18 Oct. ,,
Baron von Richthofen appointed foreign secretary, 24 Oct. ,,
Reichstag opened with a firm speech by the emperor . . . . 14 Nov. ,,
Debate on the Chinese estimates . . 19 Nov. ,,
The emperor declines to receive Mr. Kruger, ex-president of the Transvaal, 1 Dec.; see *Holland*, 6 Dec. ,,
Imperial edict granting reforms in secondary schools, issued . . . . . 2 Dec. ,,
Count von Bülow announces German intervention in S. Africa to be impossible . . 10 Dec. ,,
Sternberg, a banker in Berlin, sentenced to 2½ years' imprisonment for offences against the law for the protection of girls (corruption in the police force revealed during the trial) . 21 Dec. ,,
Failure of the "Spielhagen banks," 4 directors arrested, reported . . . . 21 Dec. ,,
Imperial loan, 15,000,000*l.*, at 3 per cent., successful, reported . . . . . 4 April ,,
Field-marshal count von Blumenthal dies, aged 90, 21 Dec. ,,
Count von Bülow presented with the order of the Black Eagle . . . . . mid Dec. ,,
Grand duke of Saxe-Weimar-Eisenach, wise and beneficent patron of art and literature, dies, aged 86 . . . . 5 Jan. 1901
Reichstag opened by count von Bulow, 8 Jan.; interpellation on duelling, gen. von Gossler's statement unsatisfactory . . . 15 Jan. ,,
The emperor present at the queen's death, see *England*, 22 Jan.; made field-marshal, the crown prince K.G., 27, 28 Jan.; returns about 7 Feb. ,,
Police-commissary Thiel sentenced to 3 years' imprisonment for taking bribes, &c., in the Sternberg case . . . . . . 15 Feb. ,,
King Edward visits the empress Frederick at Kronberg . . . . 25 Feb.—2 March, ,,
Tariff bill, introduced by count von Bulow, early Dec.; first reading carried . . . 26 Feb. ,,
The emperor wounded in the face, while driving in Bremen, by Wieland, an epileptic . 6 March, ,,
Baron von Stumm, ironmaster and a leader of the free conservatives, died . . . 8 March, ,,
The reichstag adjourns till 26 Nov. . 15 May, ,,
The queen of Holland and her consort visit Berlin, 30 May—1 June, ,,
Warships: *Wettin*, launched at Danzig; *Zähringen*, at Kiel . . . . . . 6, 12 June, ,,
Stoppage of banks at Leipzig and Dresden, 25 June, ,,
Industrial crisis through speculation and overproduction . . . . . early July, ,,
Death of prince Hohenlohe, ex-chancellor, aged 82, 6 July, ,,
Declaration against duelling signed by 104 German nobles, issued . . . . . 12 July, ,,
Death of the empress Frederick (the princess Royal of Great Britain and Ireland), a noble and gifted woman, aged 60, 5 Aug.; funeral at Potsdam, 13 Aug. ,,
Marten, a non-commissioned officer, sentenced to death by court-martial for the murder of capt. von Krosigk; evidence inconclusive; great indignation at the sentence . . . . 20 Aug. ,,
Prince Chun, Chinese envoy, presents a letter to the emperor from the Chinese emperor, and expresses regret for the revolutionary events of 1900, and particularly for the death of baron von Ketteler . . . . 4 Sept. ,,

The czar and emperor meet at Danzig; view the German naval manœuvres . . 11, 12 Sept. 1901
Prince Henry of Prussia made full admiral of the fleet . . . . . . mid Sept. „
Celebrations in honour of prof. Virchow's 80th birthday; he receives the gold medal for science from the emperor, and gifts from the king of Italy; lord Lister and many foreign scientists present . . . . 12 Oct. „
Dr. Georg von Siemens, eminent business man and promoter of railways in Asia Minor, died, aged 62, 23 Oct. „
The emperor receives Dr. Benzler, the R.C. bp. of Metz, in state . . . . . 24 Oct. „
Lieut. Blaskowitz killed by lieut. Hildebrand in a duel at Insterburg, forced on him by a court of honour, Nov. 4; col. von Reisswitz, who could have prevented the disaster, suspended by imperial order and cashiered; lieut. Hildebrand sentenced to 2 years' imprisonment (but released May, 1902) . . . . Nov. „
Mecklenburg battleship launched at Stettin, 9 Nov. „
Dr. Leyds, Transvaal envoy, arrives in Berlin, 11 Nov. „
Anti-British agitation; Mr. Chamberlain's speech at Edinburgh (*which see*, 25 Oct.) misinterpreted and denounced; meetings held . mid Nov.
Count Hatzfeldt, 16 years ambassador in London, dies, aged 70 . . . . . . 22 Nov. „
The reichstag re-opens: an interpellation on the Insterburg duel . . . 26, 27 Nov. „
Visit of the marquis Ito from Japan . 5 Dec. „
New customs tariff bill debated . 2-12 Dec. „
Visit of the grand duke Michael, heir-presumptive of Russia; he receives the order of the Black Eagle . . . . 15 Dec. „
The reichstag meets: economic depression, reported . . . . 8 Jan. 1902
Adverse speeches by count von Bülow and others in the reichstag on England and the war, 10 Jan. „
Mr. Chamberlain's firm British speech at Birmingham *effective* on the continent . 11 Jan. „
Socialist interpellation in the reichstag on the industrial crisis and the unemployed . 17 Jan. „
Imperial and Prussian 3 per cent. loans (115 and 185 million marks) subscribed 61 and 43 times over . . . . 23 Jan. „
The prince of Wales visits the emperor; made colonel of a Cuirassier regiment . . 25-29 Jan. „
Navy estimates adopted . . . 7 Feb. „
Agrarian league meets in Berlin; protests against the tariff bill . . . . . . 10 Feb. „
Navy league; annual congress held at Berlin, 20 Feb. „
Prince Henry of Prussia visits America, 23 Feb.—11 March, „
Prince Münster, formerly ambassador in London and Paris, dies, aged 81 . . . 28 March, „
Sergeants Marten and Hickel charged with being concerned in the murder of capt. von Krosigk, in custody since early 1901, tried for the third time and acquitted, 30 April; see *above*, 20 Aug. 1901.
Commercial losses in consequence of German Anglophobia, reported . . . 7 May, „
Mass meeting against the tariff bill, Berlin, 12 May, „
Visit of the shah and crown prince of Siam, 29 May, „
Sugar bill passed; reichstag adjourns . 11 June, „
Jubilee of the Germanic museum at Nuremberg, the emperor present . . . . . 16 June, „
King Albert of Saxony, eminent commander in the war of 1870, died, aged 74 . . 19 June, „
Torpedo-boat sunk in collision with the ss. *Firsby*, off Cuxhaven, 6 deaths, sir Edw. Birkbeck and 3 other Englishmen saved, 24 June; message of sympathy from king Edward . . 28 June, „
The triple alliance renewed . . 28 June, „
Budget: deficit for 1901, 40,000,000 mks. . 29 June, „
Bank trial (8 weeks) in connection with the Spielhagen failure, Dec. 1900; Eduard Sanden and 3 other directors sentenced to various terms of imprisonment and fines, 18 July; Leipzig bank trial, *re failure*, June, 1901; Exner and Gentsch, managers, sentenced to 5 and 3 years' imprisonment; 6 members of the board fined . 23 July, „
Rudolph von Bennigsen, statesman, died, aged 80, about 8 Aug. „

The emperor and the czar meet at Reval, 6 8 Aug. 1902
101st sitting of the reichstag tariff committee, tariff bill, 946 clauses, read first time . 11 Aug. „
The emperor's telegram to the prince-regent of Bavaria, criticising the diet's rejection of a vote for art, severely commented on . . 13 Aug. „
Revenue deficit 48,000,000 marks for 1901, reported, 19 Aug. „
The emperor unveils a statue of the late empress Frederick at Homburg . . . 19 Aug. „
Visit of the king of Italy . . . . 27-31 Aug. „
Prof. Rudolf Virchow, the great scientist and politician (published his "Cellular Pathology" 1856), died, aged 81, 5 Sept.; public funeral, Berlin, 9 Sept. „
Mr. Brodrick (war sec.), lord Roberts, gens. Kelly-Kenny, French, Ian Hamilton, and other foreign guests of the emperor, present at the army parade near Frankfort, 6 Sept.; state dinner, Potsdam, 8 Sept.; and army manœuvres at Frankfort, 9-12 Sept. „
Visit of the king of Saxony . . . . 13 Sept. „
Congress of German bankers, Frankfort; resolutions against existing Bourse laws and increased taxation, passed . . . . 19, 20 Sept. „
New articles of war promulgated by the emperor, Sept. „
Congress on German colonial enterprise, Berlin, 10 Oct. „
Konitz murder case (that of a schoolboy, Ernst Winter) ends, after many trials and sentences for perjury, in the acquittal of Levy and his son from complicity . . . . . . 11 Oct. „
Reichstag meets, 14 Oct.; deadlock on the tariff bill . . . . 20 Oct. „
Visit of the crown prince of Denmark . 27 Oct. „
Four Italians sentenced from 8 to 3 years' imprisonment, &c., for betrayal of military secrets to France . . . . 8 Nov. „
The emperor visits England . . . 8-10 Nov. „
New rule of procedure in the reichstag; vote by ballot instead of roll-call, adopted . 14 Nov. „
Death of Friedrich Alfred Krupp (see *Cannon, Steel, Essen*), aged 48, 22 Nov.; funeral at Essen, the emperor present (Frau Krupp gives 150,000*l.* to workmen's benefit funds) . . 26 Nov. „
Parliamentary crisis: indignation at an attempt to pass the new tariff *en bloc*, angry scenes, 27-29 Nov., 1, 3 Dec.; Herr Singer suspended, sitting adjourns, 4, 5 Dec.; changes in the rule of procedure passed, 206-92, 9 Dec.; tariff bill read 2nd time *en bloc*, 183-136, 11 Dec.; passed 14 Dec. „
Count von Bülow and others decorated . 15 Dec. „
Braunschweig battleship, launched at Kiel, 20 Dec. „
Estimated total deficit for 1903, 5,937,500*l.*, 10 Jan. 1903
Reichstag meets . . . . 12 Jan. „
Budget introduced . . . . . . 19 Jan. „
Adverse criticism on the emperor's political speeches stopped by the president of the reichstag, count Ballestrem, 20 Jan.; resigns, 23 Jan.; re-elected . . . . 29 Jan. „
Dr. Rudolph von Delbrück, eminent statesman, died, aged 85 . . . . . . 1 Feb. „
Agrarian league meets in Berlin, protests against the new tariff . . . . 9 Feb. „
Hugo Wolf, musician and songwriter, dies, aged 43, 22 Feb. „
Herr Bebel, the social democratic leader, calls attention to duelling in the army, and the ill-treatment of soldiers by non-commissioned officers . . . . 9 March, „
Large reductions made in the budget . 10 March, „
General order on subject of the maltreatment of private soldiers by their superiors issued, early April, „
New 3 per cent. loan of 14,500,000*l.* issued, 17 April,
The emperor visits Rome . . . . 2-6 May,
Naval ensign Hüssner degraded and sentenced to 4 years' imprisonment for fatally stabbing Hartmann, a marine . . . . . 26 May, „
Elsass, battleship, launched at Danzig . 26 May, „
General elections . . . . . 16-27 June, „
Emperor present at the unveiling of a memorial to emperor William I. at Hamburg; in a speech he said, "In future centuries the venerable form of his grandfather would occupy the same prominent position in the imagination of the German people as the figure of Frederick Barbarossa" 20 June

Second ballots show the composition of the new reichstag to be: clericals 99, social democrats 83, national liberals 47, conservatives 67, radical left 25, moderate radicals 10, other groups 37 . . . . . . 25 June, 1903
Court at Leipzig decides that Tolstoy's pamphlet, "Thou shalt not kill," amounts to *lèse-majesté*; all unsold copies to be destroyed . 12 Aug. ,,
Memorial tablet to late empress Frederick in English church at Hamburg, unveiled 15 Aug. ,,
Railway accident between Rothenkirchen and Oberkrinitz, 3 killed, 20 seriously injured, about 14 Aug. ,,
Trust of sugar refiners formed with reference to the situation created by the Brussels convention, mid Aug. ,,
Final accounts for the financial year 1902 show a deficit of about 1,536,120*l*. . . . end Aug. ,,
Socialist congress opened at Dresden . 13 Sept. ,,
Emperor unveils a monument to memory of William I. at Danzig . . . . 21 Sept. ,,
Launch of battleship *Hesse*, 19 Sept., and cruiser *Berlin* . . . . . 21 Sept. ,,
Trial at Berlin of Karl Leid and Julius Kaliski, social democrat journalists, for *lèse-majesté* and libel . . . . 25 Sept. ,,

[For later events see *Addenda*.]

EMPERORS OF ROME AND KINGS OF GERMANY.

CARLOVINGIAN RACE.

800. Charles I., the Great, or Charlemagne.
814. Louis I., *le Débonnaire*, king of France.
840. Lothaire I., or Lother, son of Louis; died in a monastery at Treves, Sept. 855.
855. Louis II., son of Lothaire.
875. Charles II., the Bald, king of France; died 877
881. Charles III., the Fat, crowned king of Italy; deposed; succeeded by
887. Arnulf or Arnoul; crowned emperor at Rome, 896.
899. Louis III., the Blind.
,, Louis IV., the Child, son of Arnulf; the last of the Carlovingian race in Germany.

SAXON DYNASTY.

911. Otho, duke of Saxony; refuses the dignity on account of his age.
,, Conrad I., duke of Franconia, *king*.
918. Henry I., the Fowler, son of Otho, duke of Saxony, *king*.
936. Otho I., the Great, son of Henry, crowned by pope John XII., 2 Feb. 962, the beginning of the holy Roman empire.
973. Otho II., the Bloody; massacred his chief nobility at an entertainment, 981; wounded by a poisoned arrow.
983. Otho III., the Red, his son, yet in his minority, poisoned.
1002. Henry II., duke of Bavaria, surnamed the Holy and the Lame.

HOUSE OF FRANCONIA.

1024. Conrad II., surnamed the Salique.
1039. Henry III., the Black, son.
1056. Henry IV., son; a minor; Agnes, regent; deposed by his son and successor; Rudolph (1077) and Herman (1082) nominated by the pope; and Conrad (1087).
1106. Henry V.; married Maud or Matilda, daughter of Henry I. of England.
1125. Lothaire II., surnamed the Saxon.

HOUSE OF HOHENSTAUFEN, OR OF SUABIA.

1138. Conrad III., duke of Franconia.
1152. Frederick I., Barbarossa; drowned by his horse throwing him into river Saleph, 10 June, 1190.
1190. Henry VI., son, surnamed Asper, or Sharp; detained Richard I. of England a prisoner; died 1197.
[Interregnum and contest for the throne between Philip of Suabia and Otho of Brunswick.]
1198. Philip, brother to Henry; assassinated at Bamberg by Otto of Wittelsbach.
1208. Otho IV., surnamed the Superb; excommunicated and deposed; died 1218.
1215. Frederick II., king of Sicily, son of Henry VI.; deposed by his subjects, who elected Henry, landgrave of Thuringia, 1246; Frederick died in 1250, naming his son Conrad his successor; but the pope gave the imperial title to
1247. William, earl of Holland (nominal).
1250. Conrad IV., son of Frederick.
[His son Conradin was proclaimed king of Sicily, which was, however, surrendered to his uncle Manfred, 1254, on whose death it was given by the pope to Charles of Anjou in 1263. Conradin, on the invitation of the Ghibeline party, entered Italy with a large army, was defeated at Tagliacozzo, 23 Aug. 1268, and beheaded at Naples 29 Oct., thus ending the Hohenstaufen family.]
1256. [Interregnum.]
1257. Richard, earl of Cornwall, and Alphonso, of Castile, merely nominated.

HOUSES OF HAPSBURG, LUXEMBURG, BAVARIA, ETC.

1273. Rudolph, count of Hapsburg.
1291. [Interregnum.]
1292. Adolphus, count of Nassau, to the exclusion of Albert, son of Rodolph: deposed; slain at the battle of Gelheim, 2 July, 1298, by
1298. Albert I., duke of Austria, Rodolph's son; killed by his nephew at Rheinfels, 1 May, 1308.
1308. Henry VII. of *Luxemburg*.
1313. [Interregnum.]
1314. Louis IV. of *Bavaria*, and Frederick III. of Austria, son of Albert, rival emperors; Frederick died in 1330.
1330. Louis reigns alone.
1347. Charles IV. of Luxemburg. (At Nuremberg, in 1356, the *Golden Bull* became the fundamental law of the German empire.)
1378. Wenceslas, king of Bohemia, son, twice imprisoned; forced to resign; but continued to reign in Bohemia.
1400. Frederick III., duke of Brunswick; assassinated immediately after his election, and seldom placed in the list of emperors.
1400. Rupert, count palatine of the Rhine; crowned at Cologne; died 1410.
1410. Jossus, marquess of Moravia; chosen by a party of the electors; died next year.
,, Sigismund, king of Hungary; elected by another party, on the death of Jossus recognised by all; king of Bohemia in 1419.

HOUSE OF AUSTRIA.

1438. Albert II., the Great, duke of Austria, and king of Hungary and Bohemia; died 27 Oct. 1439.
1439. [Interregnum.]
1440. Frederick IV. (or III.), surnamed the Pacific; elected emperor 2 Feb., but not crowned unti June, 1442.
1493. Maximilian I., son; died in 1519. In 1477. married Mary of Burgundy.
Francis I. of France and Charles I. of Spain became competitors for the empire.
1519. Charles V. (I. of Spain) son of Joan of Castile and Philip of Austria, elected; resigned both crowns, 1556; retired to a monastery, where he died 21 Sept. 1558.
1556. Ferdinand I., brother; succeeded by his son
1564. Maximilian II., king of Hungary and Bohemia.
1576. Rodolph II., son.
1612. Matthias, brother.
1619. Ferdinand II., cousin, king of Hungary.
1637. Ferdinand III., son.
1658. Leopold I., son.
1705. Joseph I., son.
1711. Charles VI., brother.
1740. Maria-Theresa, daughter, queen of Hungary and Bohemia; her right sustained by England.
1742. Charles VII., *elector of Bavaria*, rival emperor, whose claim was supported by France.
[This competition gave rise to a general war. Charles VII. died Jan. 1745.]
1745. Francis I. of *Lorraine*, grand-duke of Tuscany, consort of Maria-Theresa.
1765. Joseph II., son.
1790. Leopold II., brother.
1792. Francis II., son, became emperor of *Austria* only, as Francis I., 1804.

See *Austria*.

HOUSE OF HOHENZOLLERN (see *Prussia*).

1871. William I. king of Prussia, 18 Jan. (born 22 March, 1797; died 9 March, 1888; empress, Augusta, born 30 Sept. 1811, died 7 Jan. 1890).

1888. Frederick (William) III. "the Noble," son; born 18 Oct. 1831; died 15 June, 1888 (married princess Victoria, princess royal of England (born 21 Nov. 1840) 25 Jan. 1858, died 5 Aug. 1901).
„ William II., son, born 27 Jan. 1859 (married princess Auguste Victoria (born 22 Oct. 1858), 27 Feb. 1881.
Heir: William, born 6 May, 1882; other children. Princess Victoria Louise, born 13 Sept. 1892.
See *Prussia*.

GERMINAL INSURRECTION, in the faubourgs of Paris, suppressed on 12th Germinal, year III. (1 April, 1795).

GERONA (N.E. Spain), an ancient city, frequently besieged and taken. In June, 1808, it successfully resisted the French; but after suffering much by famine, surrendered 12 Dec. 1809.

GERRYMANDERING, an American slang term, signifying the arranging the political divisions of a state, so that the minority may get the advantage over the majority. The name is derived from the action of Elbridge Gerry, governor of Massachusetts, in 1811. The Irish Party causelessly applied the term to earl Spencer, lord-lieutenant of Ireland, in regard to electoral boundaries in 1885.

GERSAU, a Swiss valley, near the Rigi, about 4 miles by 3, the site of a miniature republic, which bought its independence in 1359, maintained it till 1798, and still, every May, elects government officers.

GESTA ROMANORUM; a collection of popular tales derived from Oriental and classical sources, written in Latin by an unknown author, about the middle of the 14th century, and one of the first books printed in the 15th. These tales have been largely used by our early poets and dramatists, including Shakspeare. The English translation, by the Rev. C. Swan (from an edition printed at Hagenau, 1508), appeared 1824.

GETTYSBURG (Pennsylvania). Here severe fighting took place 1-3 July, 1863, between the invading confederate army under generals Lee, Longstreet, and Ewell, and the federals under general George Meade. The confederates were long successful, but eventually were compelled to retire from Pennsylvania and Maryland. The killed and wounded on each side estimated at about 15,000.

Grand national and military demonstration held here, 1–3 July, 1888.

GHEMARA, see *Talmud*.

GHENT (Belgium), an ancient city, built about the 7th century, during the middle-ages became very rich. John, third son of Edward III. of England, is said to have been born here in 1340 (hence named *John of Gaunt*) during the revolt under Jacob Van Artevelde, a brewer, whose son Philip revived the insurrection against Louis, count of Flanders, 1379-82. Population in 1887, 147,912; in 1890, 153,740; 1900, 160,949.

Ghent rebelled against Philip of Burgundy, 1451; against the emperor Charles V., 1539; severely punished, 1540.
"*Pacification of Ghent*" (when the north and south provinces of the Netherlands united against Spain) proclaimed 8 Nov. 1576, broken up 1579. The 300th anniversary celebrated 3-10 Sept. 1876.
Ghent taken by Louis XIV. of France, 9 March, 1678; and by the duke of Marlborough, 1706.
Ghent seized by the French, 1793; annexed to the Netherlands, 1814; made part of Belgium, 1830.
Peace of Ghent, between Great Britain and America, signed 24 Dec. 1814.
New docks opened at Ghent by the king, Sept. 1881.

GHIBELINES, see *Guelphs*.

GHIZNEE, or **GHUZNEE** (East Persia), the seat of the Gaznevides, who founded the city, 969. They were expelled by the Seljuk Tartars in 1038. The British under sir John Keane attacked the strong citadel of Ghiznee at 2 A.M. 23 July, 1839. At 3 o'clock the gates were blown in by the artillery, and under cover of a heavy fire the infantry forced their way into the place, and at 5 fixed the British colours on its towers.—It capitulated to the Afghans, 1 March, 1842, who were defeated 6 Sept. and general Nott re-entered Ghiznee 7 Sept. same year. Seized for Musa Khan by Mahomed Jan in Jan., retaken after a conflict, 19-20 April, 1880.

GHOORKAS, see *Goorkhas*.

GHOSTS, produced by optical science. Mr. Dircks described his method at the British Association meeting in 1858. Dr. John Taylor produced ghosts scientifically in March; and Mr. Pepper exhibited the ghost illusion at the Royal Polytechnic institution, July, 1863. See *Cock-lane Ghost*.

Many letters appeared in the *Times*, June *et seq.* 1897, respecting mysterious sounds heard at Ballechin, a country house in Perthshire, attributed by scientists to slight earthquake shocks. See *Times*, 2 Nov. 1897.

GIANTS are mentioned in *Gen.* vi. 4. The bones of reputed giants, 17, 18, 20, and 30 feet high, have been proved to be remains of animals.—The battle of Marignano (1515) has been termed the "battle of the *Giants*." See *Dwarfs*.

Og, king of Bashan, of the remnant of the giants: his bedstead was 9 cubits long (about 16½ feet), 1451 B.C. (*Deut.* iii. 11.)
Goliath of Gath's "height was 6 cubits and a span." Killed by David about 1063 B.C. (1 *Sam.* xvii. 4.)
Four giants, sons of Goliath, killed (2 *Sam.* xxi. 15–22) about 1018.
The emperor Maximin (A.D. 235) was 8½ feet in height, and of great bulk. Some say between 7 and 8 feet; others above 8.
"The tallest man that hath been seen in our age was one named Gabara, who in the days of Claudius, the late emperor, was brought out of Arabia. He was 9 feet 9 inches high." *Pliny.*
John Middleton (born 1578), commonly called the child of Hale (Lancashire), whose hand, from the carpus to the end of his middle finger, was 17 inches long; his palm 8½ inches broad; his whole height 9 feet 3 inches. *Plot, Nat. Hist. of Staffordshire*, p. 295.
Patrick Cotter, Irish giant, born in 1761, was 8 feet 7 inches in height; his hand, from the commencement of the palm to the extremity of the middle finger, measured 12 inches, and his shoe was 17 inches long; died Sept. 1806.
Charles Byrne, called O'Brien, 8 feet 4 inches high; died 1783; his skeleton is in the museum, Royal College of Surgeons.
Big Sam, porter of the prince of Wales, at Carlton-palace, near 8 feet high, performed as a giant in "Cymon," at the Opera-house, 1809.
M. Brice, a native of the Vosges, 7 feet 6 inches high. He exhibited himself in London, Sept. 1862, and Nov. 1863.
Robert Hales, the Norfolk giant, died at Great Yarmouth, 22 Nov. 1863 (aged 43). He was 7 feet 6 inches high, and weighed 452 lbs.
Chang-Woo-Gow, a Chinese, aged 19, 7 feet 8 inches high, exhibited himself in London in Sept., &c., 1865. Grown to 8 feet, exhibited at Westminster Aquarium; with him Brustav, a Norwegian, 7 feet 9 inches, aged 35, 11 June, 1880.
Capt. Martin Van Buren Bates, of Kentucky, and Miss Ann Hanen Swann, of Nova Scotia, both about 7 feet high; exhibited themselves in London, in May; and married at St. Martin's-in-the-fields, 17 June, 1871.
Marian, the amazon queen, 8 feet 2 inches high; born at Benkendorf, Thuringia, 21 Jan. 1866; exhibited in London, July, 1882.

Josef Winkelmaier, an Austrian, 8 ft. 9 in. (born, 1865), healthy, exhibited in London, 10 Jan. 1887; died at Lengau, 24 Aug. 1887.

Elizabeth Lyska, Russian, aged 12, height 6 ft. 8 in., exhibited at the Royal Aquarium, London, Nov. 1889; again, 30 Jan. 1893.

GIAOUR, Turkish for infidel, a term applied to all who do not believe in Mahomedanism.—Byron's poem, "The Giaour," was published in 1813.

GIBBON COMMEMORATION, proposed by Mr. Frederic Harrison and carried out by the Royal Historical society, included an exhibition of MSS., portraits and relics, chiefly lent by lord Sheffield, at the British museum, 12 Nov. *et seq*., and a discourse by Mr. Harrison at the Museum of Geology, 15 Nov. 1894.

Edward Gibbon (born 27 April, 1737; died 16 Jan. 1794), resolved at Rome to write the "History of the Decline and Fall of the Roman Empire," 15 Oct. 1764; completed, 27 June, 1787; published in 6 vols., 4to, 1776–88: the edition by Dr. Wm. Smith, including the notes of dean Milman and M. Guizot, published, 1854–5.

GIBRALTAR. The ancient Calpe (which, with Abyla, on the opposite shore of Africa, obtained the name of the Pillars of Hercules), a town on a rock in South Spain, on which is placed a British fortress, considered impregnable. The height of the rock, according to Cuvier, is 1437 English feet. It was taken by the Saracens under Tarik, whence its present name (derived from *Gibel-el-Tarik*), in 711. Population, 1891, civilians, 19,100; troops, 5,896; 1901, civilians, 20,355; troops, 6,475; port, 630.

Taken from the Moors, 1309; surrendered to them, 1333; finally taken from them by Henry IV., of Castile, 1462; strengthened by Charles V. . . 1552
Attacked by the British under sir George Rooke, the prince of Hesse-Darmstadt, sir John Leake, and admiral Byng, 21 July; taken . 24 July, 1704
Besieged by the Spanish and French; they lose 10,000 men; the victorious English but 400, 11 Oct. ,,
Sir John Leake captured several ships, and raised the siege . . . . . 10 March, 1705
Ceded to England by treaty of Utrecht 11 April, 1713
The Spaniards in an attack repulsed with great loss 1720
They again attack it with a force of 20,000 men, and lose 5000; English loss, 300 . 22 Feb. 1727
Siege by the Spaniards and French, whose armaments (the greatest brought against a fortress) wholly overthrown . . . . 16 July, 1779
In one night their floating batteries were destroyed with red-hot balls, and their whole line of works annihilated by a sortie commanded by general Eliott; the enemy's loss in munitions of war, on this night, was estimated at upwards of 2,000,000*l*. sterling; the army amounted to 40,000 men, 27 Nov. 1781
Grand defeat by a garrison of only 7000 British, 13 Sept. 1782
The duke of Crillon commanded 12,000 of the best troops of France. 1000 pieces of artillery were brought to bear against the fortress, besides which there were 47 sail of the line, all three-deckers; 10 great floating batteries, esteemed invincible, carrying 212 guns; innumerable frigates, xebeques, bomb-ketches, cutters, and gun and mortar-boats; while small craft for disembarking the forces covered the bay. For weeks together 6000 shells were daily thrown into the town.
Blockade ceased . . . . . . 5 Feb. 1783
Royal battery destroyed by fire . . . . Nov. 1800
Engagement between the French and English fleets in the bay; H.M.S. *Hannibal*, 74 guns, lost, 6 July, 1801
The *Royal Carlos* and *St. Hermenigildo*, Spanish ships, each of 112 guns, blew up, with their crews, at night-time, in the straits here, and all on board perished . . . . 12 July, ,,
A malignant disease caused great mortality Sept. 1804
A dreadful plague raged 1805
A malignant fever raged . . . . . Aug. 1814
Again: courts of justice and places of worship closed by proclamation . . . . 5 Sept. 1828
The fatal epidemic ceased . . . . . 12 Jan. 1829
Destructive storm . . . . . . 17 Nov. 1834
Bishopric of Gibraltar established 1842
Gen. sir Richard Airey appointed governor Sept. 1865
Popular discussion respecting its exchange for Ceuta . . . . . . Dec. 1868—Jan. 1869
Destructive fire . . . . . . 28 June, 1874
Gen. sir Fenwick Williams of Kars, governor, Aug. 1870—Nov. 1875
Destructive storm and floods . . . 23-24 Nov. ,,
Lord Napier of Magdala, governor . . . . Jan. 1876
Visit of prince of Wales . . . . 15 April, ,,
Sir John Miller Adye, governor . . . 1 Jan. 1883
General sir Arthur Hardinge, governor . . Nov. 1886
Gen. hon. sir Leicester Smyth, Aug. 1890; died 27 Jan. 1891
Gen. sir Lothian Nicholson, April, 1891; died 27 June, 1893
For the loss of *Utopia* steamer (see *Wrecks*) 17 March, 1891
Gen. sir Robt. Biddulph appointed governor, July, 1893; leaves . . . . . . 12 July, 1900
Inspecting visit of the duke of Cambridge, early March, 1894
Tourmaline case, see *Morocco*, 1898–99.
Mass meeting held in the theatre to raise a volunteer battalion for local defence (700 offered to serve) . . . . 30 Jan. 1900
Sir George White, governor, arrives . mid July, ,,
The duke and duchess of Cornwall on tour, welcomed . . . . 20–22 March, 1901
Labour troubles, shipping coal supplies stopped, 19 May; employers' terms accepted . 16 July, 1902
Fatal riot at the Spanish lines, martial law, 9–10 Oct. ,,
Visit of king Edward VII. . . . 8–13 April, 1903

GIBSON GALLERY, see *Royal Academy*.

GIFFORD LECTURESHIPS, on Natural Theology in its widest sense without reference to creeds, founded in the universities of Edinburgh, Glasgow, Aberdeen, and St. Andrews, by bequest of 80,000*l*., by Adam Lord Gifford, a Scotch judge, 21 Aug. 1885.

GILBERT CLUB was established 28 Nov. 1889, by sir Wm. Thomson (lord Kelvin in Feb. 1892), president, sir F. Bramwell, professors D. E. Hughes, G. Forbes, Silvanus Thompson, and other physicists, to celebrate the tercentenary of William Gilbert and his work, and to publish translations of his "De Magnete," and other works connected with magnetism and electricity.

GILBERTINES, an order of canons and nuns established at Sempringham, Lincolnshire, by Gilbert of that place, 1131-1148. At the dissolution there were 25 houses of the order in England and Wales.

GILBERT ISLANDS, one of the Pacific groups, annexed by the British in 1822. Placed under the jurisdiction of the high commissioner for the Western Pacific, 1893, with a deputy commissioner for the Gilbert and Ellice Islands. Pop. of these groups, about 35,000.

GILCHRIST TRUST. A fund of between 3000*l*. and 4000*l*., left by Dr. John Gilchrist in 1841 to promote education. The interest is applied to the support of scholarships for young men and women after a competitive examination. Scientific lectures are delivered under the auspices of the trust. Office, 1, Plowden-bldgs., Temple.

GILDING on wood formed part of the decorations of the Jewish tabernacle, 1490 B.C. (*Exod.*

xxv. 11); was practised at Rome, about 145 B.C. The capitol was the first building on which this enrichment was bestowed. *Pliny.* Of gold leaf for gilding the Romans made but 750 leaves, four fingers square, out of a whole ounce. *Pliny.* Gilding with leaf gold on *bole ammoniac* was first introduced by Margaritone in 1273. See *Electrotype.*

GIN, ardent spirit, flavoured with the essential oil of the juniper berry. The "gin act," 1735, laying an excise of 5*s.* per gallon upon it, passed 14 July, 1736. In London alone 7044 houses sold gin by retail; and a man could intoxicate himself for one penny. *Salmon.* About 1700 gin-shops were suppressed in London in 1750. *Clarke.*

GIN (contracted from engine), a machine for separating cotton wool from the seed; see under *Cotton.*

GINGER, the root of the *Amomum Zinziber*, a native of the East Indies and China, now cultivated in the West Indies. In 1842 the duty was reduced from 53*s.* to 10*s.* per cwt. of foreign ginger, and from 11*s.* to 5*s.* per cwt. of that from British colonies.

GIPSIES, see *Gypsies.*

GIRAFFE or **CAMELOPARD**, a native of the interior of Africa, was well known to the ancients. In 1827 one was brought to England for the first time as a present to George IV. It died in 1829. On 25 May, 1835, four giraffes, obtained by M. Thibaut, were introduced into the Zoological gardens, Regent's-park, where a young one was born in 1839. The last giraffe living at the Zoological gardens died 28 March, 1892. A young female was purchased by the society in 1895; a male, 18ft. high, presented to the queen, arrived 19 Sept., died soon after, Sept. 1897. Another male died Aug. 1898. A young male arrived from the Cape, 9 April, 1899. Specimens of a five-horned giraffe, N.E. Uganda, discovered by Sir H. H. Johnson, Messrs. Karl Ericsson and Doggett, May, 1901.

GIRLS, charities for.

Girls' Industrial Home, Stockwell, established . . 1857

Girls' Home, 22, Charlotte-street, Portland-place, established 1867

Girls' Friendly Society, to provide homes, &c., for working girls, supported by the archbishops and bishops, founded 1878

In 1902 the G.F.S. in the dioceses of England and Wales numbered 1,359 branches in 6,670 parishes, with 17,321 working associates, 14,887 hon. associates, 149,939 members and 61,486 candidates. Branches exist in Scotland, Ireland, the colonies, and India. In the United States the G.F.S. numbers 25,399.

GIRONDISTS, an important party during the French revolution, principally composed of deputies from the Gironde. They were ardent republicans, but after the cruelties of Aug. and Sept. 1792, laboured in vain to restrain the cruelties of Robespierre and the Mountain party, and their leaders, Brissot, Vergniand, and many others, were guillotined 31 Oct. 1793. Lamartine's "Histoire des Girondins," published in 1847, tended to hasten the revolution of 1848.

GIRTON COLLEGE, Cambridge, for the higher education of women. It began at Hitchin, 1869; removed here, and was opened Oct. 1873. Newnham college, Cambridge, in connection with it, was opened 18 Oct. 1875. Miss Anne Clough, who ably managed the little hall from which the college rose in 1871, died 27 Feb. 1892; succeeded by Mrs. Henry Sidgwick. Prof. Henry Sidgwick, a great promoter of the college and women's education, died, Sept. 1900.

Miss Charlotte Angas Scott, aged about 22, attained the position of "wrangler" (for mathematics), Jan. 1880.

Lady Margaret and Somerville halls, similar institutions, established at Oxford, 1884.

Miss Agneta Frances Ramsay, of Girton, and Miss B. M. Hervey, of Newnham, obtained the highest honours. See *Cambridge*, 18 June, 1887.

GISORS, BATTLE OF (France), on 20 Sept. or 10 Oct. 1198, when Richard I. of England defeated the French. His parole for the day, "*Dieu et mon droit*"—"God and my right"—afterwards became the motto to the arms of England.

GITSCHIN (Bohemia), was captured by the Prussians after a severe conflict with the Austrians, 29 June, 1866. Near Gitschin, the same evening, the crown prince of Prussia was victor in another engagement.

GIURGEVO (Wallachia). Here the Russians were defeated by the Turks, aided by some English officers, 7 July, and repulsed in an attack, 23 July, 1854.

GLACIARIUM, at King's-road, Chelsea; containing a surface of artificially made ice for rinking, constructed by Dr. John Gamgee, and opened March, 1876. The freezing was accomplished by Raoul Pictet's process, and W. E. Ludlow's rotary engine and pump were employed. Dr. M'Leod's newly invented skating surface, successfully tried at Lillie Bridge, 10 May, 1884.

GLADIATORS were originally malefactors, who fought for their lives, or captives who fought for freedom. They were first exhibited at the funeral ceremonies of the Romans, 263 B.C., and afterwards at festivals, about 215 B.C. Their revolt under Spartacus, 73 B.C., was quelled by Crassus, 71. When Dacia was reduced by Trajan, 1000 gladiators fought at Rome in celebration of his triumph, for 123 days, A.D. 103. These combats were suppressed in the East by Constantine the Great, 325, and in the West by Theodoric in 500.

GLADSMUIR, see *Preston Pans.*

GLADSTONE ADMINISTRATIONS.* Mr. Disraeli resigned 2 Dec. and was succeeded by Mr. Gladstone, whose ministry received the seals 9 Dec. 1868. In consequence of a majority of three against the Irish University bill, early on 12 March, 1873, Mr. Gladstone tendered his resignation, but withdrew it a few days after, as Mr. Disraeli declined office with the existing house of commons.

* William Ewart Gladstone, born 29 Dec. 1809; master of the mint, Sept. 1841; president of the board of trade, May, 1843—Feb. 1845; secretary for colonies, Dec. 1845—July, 1846; chancellor of the exchequer, Jan. 1853—Feb. 1855, June, 1859—June, 1866; lord high commissioner extraordinary to the Ionian Isles, Nov. 1858; M.P. for Newark, 13 Dec. 1832–46; for Oxford, 1847–65; for South Lancashire, 1865–8; for Greenwich, Nov. 1868; announced the dissolution of parliament, 23 Jan. 1874; resigned, 17 Feb. 1874; temporarily resigned leadership of liberal party, 13 Jan. 1875; elected M.P. for Mid-Lothian (1579–1368), 5 April, 1880; his ministry resigned on account of minority on the budget bill (264–252) 9 June, 1885; he declines an earldom, 16 June, 1885.

Among the measures carried by the Gladstone ministries are:—The Irish church act, the Irish land act of 1870, the education act, the ballot act, the Irish land law act

Changes were made Aug.-Sept. 1873; the ministry resigned 17 Feb. 1874.

FIRST ADMINISTRATION (1868-74).

First lord of the treasury, Wm. Ewart Gladstone (and chancellor of exchequer, Aug. 1873).

Lord chancellor, sir Wm. Page Wood, baron Hatherley, *resigned;* sir Roundell Palmer, baron Selborne, Oct. 1872.

Lord president of the council, Geo. Fred. Samuel Robinson, earl de Grey and Ripon (marquis of Ripon, 1871); succeeded by Mr. Austin Bruce, made lord Aberdare, Aug. 1873.

Lord privy seal, John Wodehouse, earl of Kimberley; succeeded by viscount Halifax, July, 1870.

Chancellor of the exchequer, Robert Lowe; succeeded by Mr. Gladstone, Aug. 1873.

Secretaries—home, Henry Austin Bruce; succeeded by Mr. Lowe, Aug. 1873; *foreign*, Geo. Wm. Fred. Villiers, earl of Clarendon (died 27 June, 1870); succeeded by earl Granville; *colonies*, Granville Geo. Leveson-Gower, earl Granville; succeeded by earl of Kimberley, July, 1870; *war*, Edward Cardwell; *India*, George Douglas Campbell, duke of Argyll.

Chancellor of duchy of Lancaster, Frederick, lord Dufferin, appointed governor-general of Canada; succeeded by H. E. Childers, Aug. 1872; by John Bright, Sept. 1873.

First lord of admiralty, Hugh Culling Eardley Childers; succeeded by G. Joachim Goschen, 9 March, 1871.

Chief secretary for Ireland, Chichester S. Fortescue; succeeded by the marquis of Hartington, 1 Jan. 1871.

President of board of trade, John Bright; succeeded by Chichester S. Fortescue, Dec. 1870.

President of poor law (now local government) board, George Joachim Goschen; succeeded by James Stansfeld, 9 March, 1871.

Wm. Edward Forster, vice-president of the committee of council on education; admitted to the cabinet, July, 1870.

The above formed the cabinet.

Lord-lieutenant of Ireland, John Poyntz, earl Spencer.

Office of works, Austen Layard; succeeded by Acton S. Ayrton, Nov. 1869; by Wm. Patrick Adam, Aug. 1873.

Postmaster-general, Spencer C. Cavendish, marquis of Hartington; succeeded by Wm. Monsell (*not in the cabinet*), Jan. 1871; by Dr. Lyon Playfair, Nov. 1873.

This ministry carried—the disestablishment of the Irish church in 1869; the Irish tenant act in 1870; was censured in the house of lords for advising the royal warrant abolishing purchase in the army (162—82), 1 Aug. 1871; carried the ballot in 1872. See letter in note, *Disraeli Administration*.

SECOND ADMINISTRATION (28 April, 1880—9 June, 1885).

See under *England* and *Parliament*.

First lord of the treasury (and chancellor of the exchequer till 16 Dec. 1882), Wm. Ewart Gladstone.

Lord chancellor, Roundell Palmer, baron Selborne.

Lord president of the council, John Poyntz, earl Spencer; succeeded by Chichester S. Fortescue, lord Carlingford, 9 March, 1883.

Lord privy seal, George Douglas Campbell, duke of Argyll; *resigned;* succeeded by lord Carlingford, April, 1881; Archibald Philip Primrose, earl of Rosebery, 11 Feb. 1885.

Secretaries—home, sir Wm. Harcourt; *foreign affairs*, George Leveson-Gower, earl Granville; *the colonies*, John Wodehouse, earl of Kimberley, succeeded by Edward, earl of Derby, 16 Dec. 1882; *India*, Spencer C. Cavendish, marquis of Hartington, succeeded by John Wodehouse, earl of Kimberley, 16 Dec. 1882; *war*, Hugh C. E. Childers, succeeded by marquis of Hartington, 16 Dec. 1882.

First lord of the admiralty, Thos. Geo. Baring, earl of Northbrook.

Chancellor of the exchequer, Hugh C. E. Childers, 16 Dec. 1882.

Lord-lieutenant of Ireland, John Poyntz, earl Spencer May, 1882.

Chancellor of duchy of Lancaster, John Bright; *resigns* about 15 July, 1882; earl of Kimberley, 25 July; John George Dodson (afterwards lord Monk Bretton), 28 Dec. 1882; George O. Trevelyan, about 20 Oct. 1884.

President of local government board, John George Dodson, succeeded by sir Charles Wentworth Dilke, 28 Dec. 1882.

President of board of trade, Joseph Chamberlain.

Postmaster-general, George Shaw Lefevre, entered the cabinet, 11 Feb. 1885.

The above formed the cabinet.

Lord-lieutenant of Ireland, Francis Thomas de Grey, earl Cowper; *resigned*, May, 1882; earl Spencer (*see above*).

Postmaster-general, Henry Fawcett, died 6 Nov. 1884; George Shaw Lefevre, 18 Nov. 1884.

Chief secretary for Ireland, W. E. Forster; *resigned* about 2 May, 1882; lord Frederick Cavendish, 4 May; assassinated, 6 May; G. O. Trevelyan, 9 May, 1882; Henry Campbell Bannerman about 20 Oct. 1884.

Chief commissioner of works, W. P. Adam, succeeded by G. Shaw Lefevre till Nov. 1884.

Attorney-general, sir Henry James.

Solicitor-general, sir Farrer Herschell.

Governor-general of India, Geo. Fred. Samuel Robinson, marquis of Ripon; succeeded by Frederick Temple Hamilton-Blackwood, earl of Dufferin, Nov. 1884.

Chairman of ways and means, Dr. Lyon Playfair.

THIRD ADMINISTRATION (2-6 Feb. resigned 20 July, 1886).

See under *England* and *Parliament*.

First lord of the treasury, Wm. Ewart Gladstone.

Lord chancellor, sir Farrer Herschell (lord Herschell).

Lord president of the council, John Poyntz, earl Spencer.

---

of 1881, the employers' liability act, the agricultural holdings act, the burials act, the ground game act, the franchise act.

He introduces his Irish bill, see *Ireland*, 8 April; rejected (343-313), 7-8 June; minority in general election; resigns 20 July, 1886; opposes the government crimes bill unsuccessfully Feb.-July, 1887; receives silver trophy from Americans, 9 July, 1887.

The term "grand old man" is said to have been first applied to Mr. Gladstone by Mr. Henry Labouchere, M.P., about April, 1881; he turned the first sod of the Wirral railway connecting Wales and Lancashire, 21 Oct., and delivered the first Romanes lecture at Oxford, 24 Oct.; received the freedom of Liverpool, 3 Dec. 1892; his second home rule bill, see *Ireland*, Sept. 1893; great speech at Edinburgh, 28 Sept.; his declaration in the commons against the house of lords, 1 March, 1894; resignation as premier, 3 March, 1894; letter to sir John Cowan, farewell to his party and constituents, 17 March; successful operation for cataract, 24 May; he declines re-election for Mid-Lothian or elsewhere, June; at Hamburg, Copenhagen, and Kiel, June, 1895; much excited by the Armenian massacres; great speech at Liverpool, 24 Sept., 1896; pamphlet published in favour of Greece, 13 March, 1897; he died at Hawarden, 19 May; universally lamented and honoured; laid in state, 23-25 May, at Westminster, 26, 27 May; buried in the Abbey, the lords and commons present, 28 May, 1898. Mr. John Morley's "*Life of Gladstone*," published, 8 Oct. 1903.

GLADSTONE NATIONAL MEMORIAL.—Meeting at Grosvenor house, executive committee formed, 21 June; another meeting, the prince of Wales president, the duke of Westminster chairman, the earl of Crewe hon. treasurer, and captain John Sinclair hon. sec. of the general committee, 1 July, 1898: Monuments to be erected in London, Edinburgh, Dublin, and a new library at Hawarden, an appeal to the public decided on, 21 July; total 13,633*l.* 10*s.*, end of Aug. 1898; foundation stone of a new church in the Hawarden district, to which Mr. Gladstone had subscribed 1,000*l.*, laid by Mrs. Gladstone, 14 Sept. 1898; a bust of Mr. Gladstone in the National Wallace monument unveiled by lord Aberdeen, 22 Aug. 1900; Gladstone memorial meeting at Grosvenor house, prince of Wales present, 16 Feb. 1899; 1,000*l.* from Mr. Andrew Carnegie, total 32,000*l.*, July, 1899; death of Mrs Gladstone, aged 88, 14 June, 1900; Gladstone park, Dollis-hill, Willesden, bought for the public and laid out, total cost, 56,683*l.*; opened by lord Aberdeen, 25 May, 1901.

Gladstone Day commemorated in Edinburgh, 17 May, 1902.

St. Deiniol's library, at Hawarden (Gladstone memorial. cost 10,000*l.*, (first stone laid by the late duke of Westminster, 5 Oct. 1899); opened by lord Spencer, 14 Oct. 1902.

Secretaries—home, Hugh C. E. Childers; *foreign*, Archibald Philip Primrose, earl of Rosebery; *colonial*, George Leveson-Gower, earl Granville; *India*, John Wodehouse, earl of Kimberley; *war*, Henry Campbell-Bannerman.
Chancellor of the exchequer, sir William George Granville Vernon-Harcourt.
First lord of the admiralty, George Frederick Samuel Robinson, marquis of Ripon.
President of the local government board, Joseph Chamberlain, succeeded by James Stansfeld, 27 March, 1886.
Secretary for Scotland, George Otto Trevelyan; succeeded by John William Ramsay, earl of Dalhousie; (not in the cabinet), 27 March, 1886.
President of the board of trade, Anthony John Mundella.
Chief secretary for Ireland, John Morley.
The above formed the cabinet.
Lord-lieutenant of Ireland, John Campbell Hamilton-Gordon, earl of Aberdeen.
Postmaster-general, George Grenfell Glyn, lord Wolverton.
First commissioner of works, Albert Edmund Parker, earl of Morley; succeeded by Victor Alexander Bruce, earl of Elgin, 13 April.
Attorney-general, sir Charles Russell, Q.C.
Solicitor-general, sir Horace Davey, Q.C.
Chancellor of duchy of Lancaster, Edward Heneage; succeeded by sir U. Kay-Shuttleworth, 10 April, 1886.

FOURTH ADMINISTRATION.
(Succeeded the second Salisbury Administration, *which see*, 18 Aug. *et seq.*, 1892).

First lord of the treasury and lord privy seal, Wm. Ewart Gladstone.
Lord high chancellor, Lord Herschell.
Lord president of the council and secretary of state for India, Earl of Kimberley.
Secretaries—home, Herbert Henry Asquith; *foreign*, Archibald Philip Primrose, earl of Rosebery; *colonial*, George Frederick Samuel Robinson, marquis of Ripon; *War*, Henry Campbell-Bannerman.
First lord of the admiralty, John Poyntz, earl Spencer.
Chancellor of the exchequer, sir William George Granville Vernon-Harcourt.
Chief secretary for Ireland, John Morley.
Secretary for Scotland, sir George Trevelyan.
President of the board of trade, Anthony John Mundella.
President of the local government board, Henry H. Fowler.
First commissioner of works, George John Shaw-Lefevre.
Chancellor of duchy of Lancaster, James Bryce.
Postmaster-general, Arnold Morley.
Vice-president of the committee of council on education, Arthur Acland.
The above form the cabinet.
Lord-lieutenant of Ireland, Robert O. A. Milnes, baron Houghton.
Financial secretary to the treasury, Mr. Hibbert (after. sir).
Attorney-general, sir Charles Russell.
Solicitor-general, John Rigby (after. sir).
Lord advocate for Scotland, J. B. Balfour.
Attorney-general for Ireland, The MacDermot.
Lord chancellor of Ireland, Samuel Walker.
President of the board of agriculture, Herbert Gardner.
Secretary to the admiralty, sir Ughtred Kay-Shuttleworth.
Secretary to the local government board, sir W. Foster.

GLADSTONIANS. A name given to the adherents of Mr. Gladstone in his Irish policy; they included earl Granville, earl Spencer, marquis of Ripon, earl of Rosebery, sir W. Vernon Harcourt, Mr. John Morley, and other liberals, 1886; see *Liberals*. The supporters of the earl of Rosebery's cabinet were termed "Ministerialists," March, 1894.

GLASGOW (Lanarkshire), the largest city in Scotland. Its prosperity greatly increased after the union in 1707, in consequence of its obtaining some of the American trade. Glasgow returns seven M.P.s by Act passed 25 June, 1885. See *Population*.

The cathedral or high church, dedicated to St. Kentigern or Mungo, began about 1136
Erected into a burgh 1190
Charter was obtained from James II. 1451
University founded by Pope Nicholas V. and bishop Turnbull 1450
Made a royal burgh by James VI. 1611
Town wasted by a great fire 1652
Charter of William and Mary 1690
Glasgow Courant, the first newspaper published . 1715
First vessel sailed to America for its still great import, tobacco 1718
Great Shawfield riot 1725
Calico printing begun, about 1742
Plundered by rebels 1745
Theatre opened 1764
Power-loom introduced 1773
Theatre burnt; *Glasgow Herald* published . . 1782
Chamber of commerce formed 1783
Trades' hall built 1791
Walter Stirling's public library founded, by will . ,,
Spinning machinery by steam introduced . . 1795
Anderson's university founded . . . 7 May, ,,
New College buildings erected 1811
Great popular commotion . . . April, ,,
Trials for treason followed . . . July, ,,
Theatre again burnt . . . . Jan. 1829
The royal exchange opened . . . 3 Sept. ,,
Great fire, loss 150,000*l*. . . . 14 Jan. 1832
The Glasgow lotteries, the last drawn in Britain, were granted by licence of parliament to the commissioners for the improvement of Glasgow. The third and final Glasgow lottery was drawn in London, at Coopers' Hall, 28 Aug. 1834. Their repetition was forbidden by 4 Will. IV., c. 37 . 1834
British Association meet here . . . 24 Sept. 1840
Wellington's statue erected . . . 8 Oct. 1844
False alarm of fire at the theatre, when 70 persons are crushed to death . . . 17 Feb. 1849
Visit of the queen and prince Albert . . 14 Aug. ,,
British Association meet (2nd time) . 12 Sept. 1855
Failure of Western Bank of Scotland, and City of Glasgow bank, and other firms . . Nov. 1857
In which great frauds were discovered . Oct. 1858
New water-works at Loch Katrine opened by the queen . . . . 14 Oct. 1859
[Supplies 25,000,000 gallons daily, can supply 50,000,000; engineer, J. F. Bateman; cost about 918,000*l*. independent of price paid for old works.]
Self-supporting cooking establishments for working classes begun by Mr. Thos. Corbett, 21 Sept. 1860
Glasgow visited by the empress of the French, 27 Nov. ,,
Theatre burnt again . . . . 31 Jan. 1863
Visited by lord Palmerston; installed lord rector, 29 March, ,,
Industrial exhibition opened . . . 12 Dec. 1865
Fine stained glass windows, by German artists, put up in the cathedral by private munificence . 1859-66
Site of the old university sold to railway company; new buildings to be erected near Western-park . 1866
Great reform demonstration; visit of John Bright, 16 Oct. ,,
The duke of Edinburgh inaugurates the statue of the prince consort, in George's-square 18 Oct. ,,
Glasgow and Aberdeen universities to elect one M.P., and Glasgow to elect three instead of two M.P.'s, by the Scotch reform act, passed 13 July, 1868
Foundation of the new university buildings laid by the prince of Wales . . . 8 Oct. ,,
Foundation of Albert bridge laid . . 3 June, 1870
The new university buildings opened . 7 Nov. ,,
[The spire completed 14 Oct. 1887.]
Technical college established about . . . ,,
Scott centenary celebrated . . . 9 Aug. 1871
Fraser and Maclaren's warehouse, Buchanan-street, burnt; about 100,000*l*. lost . . 27 March, 1872
Explosion at Tradeston flour mills; about 14 killed; loss 70,000*l*. . . . 9 July, ,,
Mr. Disraeli installed lord rector . . 19 Nov. 1873
Mr. Stephen Mitchell bequeaths 70,000*l*. to found a free library, &c. . . . spring, 1874
Great fire in Buchanan-street . . 22 April, 1876
British Association meeting (3rd) . . . ,,
Rt. hon. R. A. Cross receives freedom of the city 2 Oct. ,,
Foundation of new post-office laid by the prince of Wales . . . . 17 Oct. ,,
Statue of Burns in George's square uncovered by lord Houghton . . . 25 Jan. 1877
New stock exchange opened . . . 3 April, ,,
Weaving school opened . . . . 3 Sept. ,,
Freedom of city presented to gen. U. Grant, ex-president, U.S. . . . . 13 Sept. ,,
New Queen's dock opened . . . . 18 Sept. ,,

Freedom of city presented to the marquis of Hartington . . . . . 5 Nov. 1877
Statue of Thos. Campbell, in George's square, uncovered . . . . . . 28 Dec. ,,
Apothecaries' hall burnt, loss about 30,000*l*. 9 June, 1878
Stoppage of "City of Glasgow" bank, with many branches, total ruin to many, see *Banks* 2 Oct. ,,
National fund formed to relieve sufferers, 9 Nov.; amount received, about 118,000*l*. . . 12 Nov. ,,
Glasgow relief bank founded, 321,423*l*. received, 13 Dec. ,,
"City of Glasgow" bank: Stronach and some directors sentenced to 18 months' imprisonment, others to 8 months, see *Trials* . . . . 1 Feb. 1879
Theatre Royal burnt . . . . . 2 Feb. ,,
Boiler explosion, Glasgow ironworks, 23 killed, 5 March, ,,
Statue of Livingstone, George's-square, unveiled, 19 March, ,,
Sir Wm. Harcourt, home secretary, receives freedom of the city . . . . 25 Oct. 1881
Mr. Macdonald, M.P., bequeaths a mining library and 1000*l*. to the university . . . Nov. ,,
Black and Wingate's weaving mills burnt 3 Dec. ,,
Great fires: Anchor line engine works on the Clyde and Parker's soap works; damage, about 50,000*l*. 1882
Destructive fire in the Trongate, 15,000*l*. estimated damage . . . . . . 17 Aug. ,,
The duke of Albany receives the freedom of the city 14 Oct. ,,
Galbraith's spinning mill burnt . . 14 Oct. ,,
Rt. hon. W. E. Forster receives the freedom of the city . . . . 18 Dec. ,,
Mr. Bright installed as lord rector . 22 March, 1883
The *Daphne* steamer, during launch in the Clyde, heels over; 124 perish . . . . 3 July, ,,
Wylie and Lochhead's premises, near Buchanan-street, burnt; loss about 200,000*l*. . 3 Nov. ,,
"John Elder" professorship of naval architecture at the university endowed by Mrs. Elder, 12,500*l*. announced Nov. ,,
Mr. Fawcett, M.P., elected lord rector . 15 Nov. ,,
Trial of Terence M'Dermott and nine other ribbonmen at Edinburgh for conspiracy to blow up buildings in Glasgow; M'Dermott and four sentenced to penal servitude for life, five others to seven years . . . . . . 17-21 Dec. ,,
Through Glasgow Improvement Act, great numbers of horrible rookeries removed, 1866, and wholesome houses erected . . . . announced ,,
Great popular demonstration in favour of the government and the Franchise bill; Mr. Trevelyan there . . . . 6 Sept. ,,
Visit of the marquis of Salisbury; great conservative demonstration . . . 30 Sept. *et seq.* ,,
Star theatre; 15 persons killed through false panic of fire . . . . 1 Nov. 1884
The Elderslie rock in the Clyde near Renfrew removed by dynamite; cost about 40,000*l*. . 1880–6
Templeton's carpet manufactory burnt, about 30,000*l*. damages . . . . . 28 Jan. 1886
Underground railway opened . . 15 March, ,,
Bailie Young, Councillor Duncan and five other persons killed and many injured by poisonous gases of ignited gunpowder rushing into the vacancy occasioned by the blasting of an enormous mass of rock near Loch Fyne 25 Sept. ,,
Glasgow blind asylum burned down . 3 Dec. ,,
Jubilee fête of 30,000 school children . 10 Sept. 1887
Great international exhibition, the largest in the empire since that in London in 1862; patron, the queen; the buildings in the west end park occupied about 16 acres, cost about 70,000*l*.; opened by the prince and princess of Wales; the route of the procession was five miles (fine day) 8 May; visit of the queen, magnificent reception, new municipal buildings, George's-square, inaugurated; the exhibition publicly visited 22 Aug.; she visited Paisley 23 Aug., privately, the exhibition, the university, and queen Margaret's college, 24 Aug. The queen was the guest of sir Archibald Campbell of Blytheswood 22–24 Aug.; exhibition closed, 10 Nov. 1888; reported number of visitors, 5,748,379, surplus 40,000*l*.
Destructive thunderstorm with loss of life 19 May, 1888
Fire in Buchanan-street, 155,000*l*. damages 14 Oct. ,,
Destructive storm, the exhibition and other buildings much injured, and loss of life 16 Nov. 1888
Mr. Wm. Stirling bequeaths 20,000*l*. to Glasgow charities; he died . . . . . Sept. 1889
The magnificent municipal buildings in George's-square, architect Mr. Wm. Young; cost about 550,000*l*., opened by the lord provost, sir James King . . . . 7 Oct. ,,
Mr. R. Ramsay's hide and wool mart burnt; estimated loss, 30,000*l*. . . . . 27 Oct. ,,
Messrs. Templeton's carpet-weaving mill, in the course of erection at Greenhead, during a gale falls on the sheds where about 140 girls were at work, about 29 killed . . . . 1 Nov. ,,
Co-operative societies of the United Kingdom 22nd annual congress (the earl of Rosebery president), 26 May *et seq.* 1890
The freedom of the city given to Mr. H. M. Stanley, 12 June, ,,
Meeting of miners' delegates from all parts of Scotland demanding increase of wages, &c., 15 Sept. *et seq.* ,,
Strike and lock-out in the iron-works, respecting wages . . . . 4 Oct. ,,
The earl of Rosebery receives the freedom of the city . . . . 10 Oct. ,,
Great meeting of Scotch railway men; a general strike resolved on; see under *Railways* 21 Dec. ,,
Eastern-end Industrial Exhibition opened by the marquis of Lothian . . . . . 23 Dec. ,,
Freedom of the city presented to the marquis of Salisbury . . . . . . 20 May, 1891
Great strike of shipwrights on the Clyde, 5 July; ended . . . . 20 Aug. ,,
Visit of the lord mayor of London and sheriffs, 17–22 Aug. ,,
Mr. A. J. Balfour, lord rector of the university, delivers his address on "Progress" 26 Nov. ,,
Messrs. Wm. Primrose's flour mills burnt; loss about 10,000*l*. . . . . . . 27 Feb. 1892
Erection of a new fine art gallery at the west-end proposed by a committee . . . 13 April, ,,
Proposed reduction of wages of seamen and firemen; great meeting of the men, 28 April; strike begins . . . . 4 May, ,,
Queen Margaret college, incorporated with the university . . . . Nov. ,,
The trustees of the Bellahouston fund (500,000*l*.), the bequest of the Misses Steven, of Bellahouston, to Glasgow, decide to commence distribution in May, 1893, about . . . . 21 Dec. ,,
William M'Keown executed for the murder and mutilation of Elizabeth O'Connor at Pollokshields (11 Oct.) . . . . . . 18 Jan. 1893
Visit of Mr. Goschen; speech against Irish home rule bill . . . . 4 April, ,,
Sir J. Gorst elected lord rector of the university, 15 Nov. 1893; installed . . . . 2 Nov. 1894
Theatre Royal, Hope-street, burnt . 1 March, 1895
Disastrous fire at Messrs. Samuel Higginbotham & Co., calico printers, South-side, several deaths, 11 Oct. ,,
Eastern portion of the Central railway opened, 1 Nov. ,,
Jubilee celebration of lord Kelvin as professor of Nat. Phil. in the university; banquet by the corporation, many foreign delegates present, 15, 16 June, 1896
Burns exhibition opened (centenary of death), 15 July; celebration at Dumfries, and throughout the country . . . . 21 July, ,,
Visit of Li Hung-Chang; grand secretary 18 Aug. ,,
Mr. Joseph Chamberlain, elected lord rector of the university . . . . 31 Oct. ,,
Indian famine fund, large sums remitted 2 Feb. 1897
Destructive fire at the Fairfield Shipbuilding yard, estimated damage 50,000*l*. . . . . 4 Feb. ,,
Royal Glasgow Art institute, annual exhibitions opened . . . . 8 Feb. ,,
Passengers from the Glasgow steamer *Victoria*, force a landing at Dunoon; barriers broken: Sundays . . . . . . 18 & 25 July, ,,
Destructive fire and explosion at Broxburn Oil works; 1 death . . . . . 19 Aug. ,,
Visit of the duke and duchess of York 10 Sept. ,,
Mr. Chamberlain installed lord rector of the university: address on "Patriotism," 3 Nov.; received the freedom of the city . . 8 Nov. ,,

Fire at Messrs. W. & R. Hatrick & Co., wholesale chemists, Renfield-street; 4 firemen killed by an explosion . . . . 7 Jan. 1898
People's Palace and Winter garden, erected on Glasgow-green (public subscription); opened by the earl of Rosebery . . . . . 22 Jan. ,,
Mr. Wm. Houldsworth gives 5,600*l.* for scientific research to the university . . . 1 April, ,,
Mr. Adam Teacher bequeaths 50,000*l.* to charities, and all his pictures, etc., to the city of Glasgow, April, ,,
Explosion at the Scottish Cold Storage and Ice Co., 3 deaths . . . . 17 Sept. ,,
Mr. James Orr bequeaths over 50,000*l.* and Mr. James Brown Thomson, 80,000*l.*, to Glasgow educational and benevolent institutions, March and Aug. 1899
Dr. James Colquhoun, solicitor and ex-treasurer of the city, charged with embezzling over 50,000*l.*, pleaded guilty, and was sentenced to 5 years' penal servitude by lord Trayner at Edinburgh, 4 Oct. ,,
Lord Rosebery elected lord rector . 28 Oct. ,,
Socialist and labour conference, many city improvements, reported . . . . mid April, 1900
Messrs. Hopkins & Co.'s offices, &c., Robertson-st., burnt down, estimated damage, 65,000*l.*, 2 June, ,,
Princess Christian opens the new Ruchill hospital; 13 June, ,,
Slight outbreak of plague, about 7 deaths, inoculation successful . . . 27 Aug.–14 Nov. ,,
Lord Rosebery, lord rector, delivers his address on "Imperialism" . . . . 16 Nov. ,,
Epidemic of smallpox, 228 deaths, April, 1900; city free . . . . . . 30 April, 1901
Grand internat. exhibition in the Kelvingrove park opened by the duke and duchess of Fife (they were afterwards presented with the freedom of the city), 2 May; fire in the tea-rooms, over 3,000*l.* damage, 8 July; state visit of the lord mayor and sheriffs of London, 9 Aug.; exhibition closed, total attendance, 11,496,220; estimated profit, 80,000*l.* . . . . 9 Nov. ,,
Mr. Andrew Carnegie provides 100,000*l.* for libraries, May, ,,
Jubilee (9th) of the university celebrated, 12 June, ,,
New supply tunnel opened at Loch Katrine waterworks, doubling city water supply . 21 June, ,,
Mr. R. W. Hanbury, M.P., who promoted municipal telephones in the city, presented with the freedom, 29 Aug.; also lord Balfour of Burleigh and Mr. Andrew Carnegie . . . . . 10 Sept. ,,
The British Association meets; address by the president, prof. Rücker, 11 Sept.; closed, 18 Sept. ,,
Lord Rosebery opens an exhibition, &c., to do with the Scottish Home Industries association, 22 Oct. ,,
Mr. James Dick, benefactor, dies, leaving 100,000*l.* to his employés and the bulk of his fortune to charities . . . . 7 March, 1902
Lord Rosebery addresses a large liberal meeting, 10 March, ,,
Disaster at a football match through the collapse of a terraced stand, 25 deaths, over 500 injured, 5 April, ,,
Visit of the colonial premiers . . 28 July, ,,
Rt. rev. Dr. Maguire appointed R.C. archbp. . Aug. ,,
Statue of Mr. Gladstone in George-square unveiled by lord Rosebery . . . . . 11 Oct. ,,
Mr. George Wyndham (see *Ireland*) elected lord rector of the university . . . . 25 Oct. ,,
Glasgow art galleries and museum, Kelvin-grove, cost 180,000*l.*, opened . . . . . 25 Oct. ,,
Dr. J. Stevenson bequeaths 50,000*l.* to the United Free church and 11,400*l.* to charities, etc. . Jan. 1903
Carnegie trustees make a grant of 55,000*l.* to Glasgow university . . . . . . Mar. ,,
Visit of the king and queen, stone laid for Technical college . . . . 14 May, ,,
First Atlantic turbine-driven liner (for the Liverpool-Canada service) to be constructed by a Glasgow firm, announced . . . . 3 Oct. ,,
Mr. Chamberlain opens his "fiscal campaign" with a great speech at St. Andrew's-hall . 6 Oct. ,,

GLASGOW, Bishopric of. Kennet, in his *Antiquities*, says it was founded by St. Kentigern, *alias* Mungo, in 560; Dr. Heylin, speaking of the see of St. Asaph, in Wales, says that *that* see was founded by St. Kentigern, a Scot, then bishop of Glasgow, in 583. This prelacy became archiepiscopal in 1491, ceased at the Revolution, and is now a post-revolution bishopric. The cathedral, commenced in 1121, has a noble crypt; see *Bishops*.

GLASITES (in Scotland) and **Sandemanians** (in England). In 1727, John Glas, a minister of the church of Scotland, published "The Testimony of the King of Martyrs, concerning his Kingdom (*John* xviii. 36)," in which he opposed national churches, and described the original constitution of the Christian church, its doctrines, ordinances, officers, and discipline, as given in the New Testament. Having been deposed in 1728, he and others established several churches formed upon the primitive models. The publication of a series of letters on Hervey's "Theron and Aspasio," by Robert Sandeman, in 1757, led to the establishment of churches in London and other places in England, and also in North America.

GLASS. The Egyptians are said to have known the art of making glass 1150 B.C. The discovery of glass took place in Syria. *Pliny.* Glass-houses were erected in Tyre. It was in use in the time of Tiberius; glass windows were used in Pompeii, Gregory of Tours speaks of church windows of coloured glass.

Glass is said to have been brought to England by Benedict Biscop, abbot of Wearmouth, in . . 674
The glass manufacture established in England at Crutched-friars, and in the Savoy (*Stow*) . . 1557
Great improvements have been made in the manufacture, through the immense increase of chemical knowledge in the present century. Professor Faraday published his researches on the manufacture of glass for optical purposes in . . 1830
The duties on glass, first imposed 1695; repealed, 1698; re-enacted, 1745; finally remitted, 24 April, 1845
Glass-Painting was known to the ancient Egyptians. It was revived about the 10th century, and is described in the treatise by the monk Theophilus; was practised at Marseilles in a beautiful style, about 1500, and attained great perfection about 1530. Specimens of the 13th century exist in England; C. Winston's work is the best on the subject, 1846, new edition . . 1868
"Stained Glass Windows," by Lewis F. Day, published . . . . Nov. 1897
Glass-Plate, for coach-windows, mirrors, &c., made at Lambeth by Venetian artists, under the patronage of Villiers, duke of Buckingham . . 1673
The manufacture was improved by the French, who made very large plates; and further improvements in it were made in Lancashire, when the British Plate Glass company was established 1773
Manufacture of British sheet glass introduced by Messrs. Chance, of Birmingham, about . . . 1832
Tempered or Toughened glass: M. De la Bastie's process (plunging heated glass into a hot bath of oleaginous or alkaline compounds) announced, April, 1875; largely manufactured in France, and sold cheap in London 1876
Mr. Frederick Siemens described his process for producing strong homogeneous tempered glass at the Society of Arts . . . . 26 Feb. 1885
The application of glass for rails proposed by Mr. H. Lindsay-Bucknall and for railway sleepers proposed by Mr. F. Siemens, 1885–6. This glass asserted to be much stronger than iron.
The manufacture of Venetian glass probably introduced from Constantinople and perfected in the 15th and following centuries. Venetian glass is now manufactured at Venice and in England (1892) by Dr. Salviati; he presented a splendid glass vase to the queen on the anniversary of her coronation day, 28 June, 1892, see *Mosaics*.
Depression of English glass manufacture through the action of the trade union and foreign competition; reported, *Times* . . . . 31 Aug. 1896
Long-continued strike of glassmakers in the Stourbridge district 1902–03

GLASTONBURY (Somerset), traditionally said to have been the residence of Joseph of Arimathea, and the site of the first Christian church in Britain, about 60. A church was built here by Ina about 708. The town and abbey were burnt, 1184, and an earthquake did great damage in 1275. Richard Whiting, the last abbot, who had 100 monks and 400 domestics, was hanged on Tor-hill in his pontificals for refusing to take the oath of supremacy to Henry VIII., 14 Nov. 1539. The monastery was suppressed 1540. Visit of pan-anglican bishops, 3 Aug. 1897. See *Lake Dwellings*, 1892.

GLEBE (*gleba*, a clod), the land belonging to a parish church, or ecclesiastical benefice.

An act to facilitate the sale of glebe land was passed in 1888.

GLEE, a piece of unaccompanied vocal music, in at least three parts. Their composition began early in the 18th century. Eminent composers, Samuel Webbe (1740-1816), Stevens, Callcott, Horsley, Danby, Paxton, Lord Mornington, Spofforth, &c. The *Glee Club*, founded by Dr. J. W. Callcott, Dr. Arnold, and others, 1787.

GLENALMOND, Perthshire. Trinity College here, projected in 1841, was opened in 1847. It was founded principally by the exertions of Mr. W. E. Gladstone and Mr. Hope Scott, aided by dean Ramsay, the duke of Buccleuch, the marquis of Lothian, and other gentlemen, to support the Scottish episcopal church. The site was given by Mr. George Patton, afterwards lord Glenalmond, 1846. The foundation-stone of a new wing was laid by Mr. W. E. Gladstone, 1 Oct. 1891.

Trinity college much injured by fire; damage about 5,000*l.*, 10, again 18 Oct. 1894; Alan W. J. Fergusson, a pupil (mentally weak), charged with arson 27 Oct; confessed; sentence of 12 months' imprisonment . . . . 24 Nov. 1894

GLENCOE MASSACRE of the Macdonalds, a Jacobite clan, for not surrendering before 1 Jan. 1692, the time stated in king William's proclamation. Sir John Dalrymple, master (afterwards earl) of Stair, their enemy, obtained a decree "to extirpate that set of thieves," which the king is said to have signed without perusing. Every man under 70 was to be slain. This mandate was treacherously executed by 120 soldiers of a Campbell regiment, hospitably received by the Highlanders, 13 Feb. 1692. About 60 men were slain; and many women and children, turned out naked in a freezing night, perished. This excited great indignation; and an inquiry was set on foot, May, 1695, but no capital punishment followed.

GLENDALOUGH, or "Seven Churches," an ancient Irish bishopric, said to have been founded by St. Keven in 498; united with Dublin, 1214.

GLOBE. The globular form of the earth, the five zones, some of the principal circles of the sphere, the opacity of the moon, and the true causes of lunar eclipses, were taught, and an eclipse predicted, by Thales of Miletus, about 640 B.C. Pythagoras demonstrated, from the varying altitudes of the stars by change of place, that the earth must be round; that there might be antipodes on the opposite part of the globe; that Venus was the morning and evening star; that the universe consisted of twelve spheres—the sphere of the earth, the sphere of the water, the sphere of the air, the sphere of fire, the spheres of the moon, the sun; Venus, Mercury, Mars, Jupiter, Saturn, and the spheres of the stars; about 506 B.C.—Aristarchus of Samos maintained that the earth turned on its own axis, and revolved about the sun, which doctrine was held by his contemporaries as so absurd that the philosopher nearly lost his life, 280 B.C.; see *Circumnavigators*.

To determine the figure of the earth, a degree of latitude has been measured in different parts of the world; by Bouguer and La Condamine in Peru, and by Maupertuis and others in Lapland, 1735.

Estimated density 5·6 that of water; weight, 6,000,000 000,000,000,000,000 tons.—*Proctor*, 1875.

France and Spain measured by Mechain, Delambre, Biot, and Arago, between 1792 and 1821.

Measurements made in India by col. (afterwards sir George) Everest, published in 1830.

Experiments made by pendulums to demonstrate the rotation of the earth by Foucault in 1851; and to determine its density by Maskelyne, Bailly, and others; and in 1826, 1828, and 1854, by Mr. (aft. sir) G. B. Airy, the astronomer-royal.

ARTIFICIAL GLOBES. It is said that a celestial globe was brought to Greece from Egypt, 368 B.C., and that Archimedes constructed a planetarium about 212 B.C.

The globe of Gottorp, a concave sphere, eleven feet in diameter, containing a table and seats for twelve persons, and the inside representing the visible surface of the heavens, the stars and constellations, all distinguished according to their respective magnitudes, and being turned by means of curious mechanism, their true position, rising and setting, are shown. The outside is a terrestrial globe. The machine, called the globe of Gottorp, from the original one of that name, which, at the expense of Frederick II. duke of Holstein, was erected at Gottorp, under the direction of Adam Olearius, and was planned after a design found among the papers of the celebrated Tycho Brahe. Frederick IV. of Denmark presented it to Peter the Great in 1713. It was nearly destroyed by fire in 1757; but it was afterwards reconstructed. *Coxe.*

The globe at Pembroke-hall, Cambridge, erected by Dr. Long (master, 1733), eighteen feet in diameter.

In 1851 Mr. Abrahams erected in Leicester-square, for Mr. Wyld, a globe 60 feet 4 inches in diameter, lit from the centre by day, and by gas at night. It was closed in July, 1861; the models were sold, and the building eventually taken down.

Mr. James Wyld, geographer to the queen, died 17 April, 1887.

GLOBE THEATRE, BANKSIDE (London), was built by agreement dated 22nd Nov. 1593, and licensed to Shakespeare and others; see *Theatres*, and *Shakespeare's Theatre*.—The Globe "Theatre," erected on the site of Lyon's-inn, Strand, was opened 28 Nov. 1868, Mr. Sefton Parry, manager; closed 1903.—The *Globe* evening newspaper; formerly whig, now conservative; established 1803. Special centenary number issued 8 Jan. 1903.

GLOIRE, French steam frigate, see *Navy, French.*

GLORY, the nimbus drawn by painters round the heads of saints, angels, and holy men, and the circle of rays on images, adopted from the Cæsars and their flatterers, were used in the 1st century. The doxology, "*Gloria Patri*," is very ancient, and originally without the clause "as it was in the beginning," &c. In the Greek it began with "*doxa*," *glory*.

GLOUCESTER (Roman *Glevum*), submitted to the Romans about 45, and to the Saxons 577. The statutes of Gloucester, passed at a parliament held by Edward I. 1278, relate to actions at law. This city was incorporated by Henry III.; and was fortified by a strong wall, which was demolished after the Restoration, in 1660, by order of Charles II., as a punishment for the successful resistance of the city to Charles I., under col. Massey, Aug., Sept. 1643. The Gloucester and Berkeley canal was completed in April, 1827.

Gross bribery took place here at the election for the parliament in 1859.—The BISHOPRIC was one of the six erected by Henry VIII. in 1541, and was formerly part of Worcester. It was united to Bristol in 1836, but in 1884 an act was passed to provide for their again becoming separate bishoprics. The bishopric of Bristol reconstituted 7 July, 1897. The church, which belonged to the abbey, and its revenues, were appropriated to the maintenance of the see. The abbey, which was founded by king Wulphere about 700, was burnt in 1102, and again in 1122. In it are the tombs of Robert, duke of Normandy, and Edward II. In the king's books, this bishopric is valued at 315*l.* 17*s.* 2*d.* per annum. Present income, 5000*l.* An act was passed in 1884 to provide for the disunion of the sees of Gloucester and Bristol. Restoration of the cathedral proceeding, 1893-7; the lady chapel reopened 29 Sept. 1897. Population, 1881, 36,542; 1891, 39,444; 1901, 47,944.

Epidemic of smallpox Jan.–July, 1896 (434 deaths), stamped out by the vaccination committee, 27 April, *et seq.* 1806–07.

Public library opened (7,000 books) by lord Avebury, 31 May, 1900.

Mr. John Bellows, philanthropist and archæologist, died, aged 72, 5 May, 1902.

RECENT BISHOPS OF GLOUCESTER AND BRISTOL.

1802. George Isaac Huntingford, translated to Hereford, June, 1815.
1815. Hon. Hen. Ryder, translated to Lichfield, 1824.
1824. Christopher Bethell, translated to Exeter, 1830.
1830. James Henry Monk, died.
1856. Charles Baring, translated to Durham, Sept. 1861.
1861. Wm. Thomson, translated to York, 1862.
1862. Charles John Ellicott (present bishop).

GLOVES. Woodstock and Worcester leather gloves are of ancient celebrity. In the middle ages, the giving a glove was a ceremony of investiture in bestowing lands and dignities; and two bishops were put in possession of their sees by each receiving a glove, 1002. In England, in the reign of Edward II. the deprivation of gloves was a ceremony of degradation. The Glovers' company of London was incorporated in 1556. Embroidered gloves are presented to judges at maiden assizes. The importation of foreign gloves was not permitted till 1825. "Gloves and their Annals," by S. W. Beck, published in 1883.

GLUCINUM (from *glukus*, sweet). In 1798 Vauquelin discovered the earth *glucina* (so termed from the sweet taste of its salts). It is found in the beryl and other crystals. From glucina Wöhler and Bussy obtained the rare metal glucinum in 1828. *Gmelin.*

GLUCOSE, see *Sugar*.

GLUTEN, an ingredient of grain, particularly wheat, termed the vegeto-animal principle (containing nitrogen). Its discovery is attributed to Beccaria in the 18th century.

GLYCERINE, discovered by Scheele, about 1779, and termed by him the "sweet principle of fats," and further studied by Chevreul, termed the "father of the fatty acids." It is obtained pure by saponifying olive oil or animal fat with oxide of lead, or litharge. Glycerine is much employed in medicine and the arts, and in the manufacture of nitro-glycerine *(which see)*, and other explosives.

GLYOXYLINE (invented by Mr. (aft. sir) F. A. Abel, the chemist of the war department, in 1867), an explosive mixture of gun-cotton, pulp and saltpetre saturated with nitro-glycerine. It was abandoned for compressed gun-cotton.

GNEISENAU, German training-ship, wrecked off Malaga, 38 deaths, 16 Dec. 1900.

GNOMIUM, a new element discovered by Gerhard, Kruss, and F. W. Schmidt in 1889.

GNOSTICS (from the Greek *gnosis*, knowledge), a sect who, soon after the preaching of Christianity, endeavoured to combine its principles with the Greek philosophy. Among their teachers were Saturnius, 111; Basilides, 134; and Valentine, 140. Priscillian, a Spaniard, was burnt at Treves as a heretic, in 384, for endeavouring to revive Gnosticism.

GOA (S.W. Hindostan), was taken by the Portuguese under Albuquerque in 1510, and made their Indian capital. It was visited by the prince of Wales, 27 Nov. 1875. New harbour and railway works inaugurated, 31 Oct. 1882.

Election riots, conflict with the police and military, 17 persons shot dead, accounts conflicting, 22, 23 Sept. 1890
Order restored . . . . 26 Sept. ,,
Treaty with Great Britain (1878) respecting customs duty, and an annual payment to Portugal of 2 lakhs of rupees, suffered to expire through disagreement . . . . 14 Jan. 1892
Mutiny of Portuguese troops ordered to Africa, regarding their pay, etc. . . 14 Sept.–1 Dec. 1895
A detachment of soldiers made prisoners by rebels after a sharp fight, reported . . 13 Oct. ,,
Alphonso, duke of Oporto, appointed commander of the expedition against the rebels, arrives 12 Nov. ,,
Rebels defeated at Satary, reported . . 17 Dec. ,,
Insurrection attributed to maladministration; prince Alphonso appointed gov-gen.; amnesty promised without effect, 23 March, 1896; the prince leaves, reported . . . . . June 1896
Renewed disturbances, the Ranes attack Pernem and burn the treasury; rebels dispersed, reported . . . . 17 Dec. ,,
Lord Curzon, viceroy of India, received by the governor-general . . . . 13 Nov. 1900

GOAT SHOW at Alexandra palace, 16-22 Sept. 1880, supported by the British Goat Society, recently established. A goat farm for the supply of milk established near Dorking, 1882.

Annual shows of the British goat society have been held; one opened 8 June, 1886.

GOBELIN-TAPESTRY, so called from a house at Paris, formerly possessed by wool-dyers, whereof the chief (Jehan Gobelin), in the reign of Francis I., is said to have found the secret of dyeing scarlet. This house was purchased by Louis XIV. about 1662, for a manufactory of works for adorning palaces (under the direction of Colbert), especially tapestry, designs for which were drawn by Le Brun, about 1666. Establishment (1878) cost about 8000*l.* a year.

"GOD SAVE THE KING." This melody is said to have been composed by John Bull, Mus.D., in 1606, for a dinner given to James I. at Merchant Taylors' Hall; others ascribe it to Henry Carey, author of "Sally in our alley," who died, 4 Oct. 1743. It was much sung 1745-6. It has been claimed by the French. The controversy on the subject is summed up in Chappell's "Popular Music of the Olden Times" (1859). The melody has been adopted for the German national anthem ("Heil dir im Siegerkranz!"), and also for the Danish. "God save the king," revised version, 1902.

The words translated in 15 East Indian dialects . 1882
Meeting at the Mansion-house to promote their adoption . . . . 2 Nov. ,,

GODERICH ADMINISTRATION. Viscount Goderich * (afterwards earl of Ripon) became first minister on the death of Mr. Canning, 8 Aug. 1827; he resigned 8 Jan. 1828.

Viscount Goderich, *first lord of the treasury.*
Duke of Portland, *president of the council.*
Lord Lyndhurst, *lord chancellor.*
Earl of Carlisle, *lord privy seal.*
Viscount Dudley, Mr. Huskisson, and the marquis of Lansdowne, *foreign, colonial, and home secretaries.*
Lord Palmerston, *secretary-at-war.*
Mr. C. W. Wynn, *president of the India board.*
Mr. Charles Grant (afterwards lord Glenelg), *board of trade.*
Mr. Herries, *chancellor of the exchequer.*
Mr. Tierney, *master of the mint, &c.*

GODFATHERS AND GODMOTHERS, or *sponsors.* The Jews are said to have had them at circumcision; but there is no mention of them in scripture. Tradition says that sponsors were first appointed by Hyginus, a Roman bishop, about 154, during a time of persecution. In Roman Catholic countries bells have godfathers and godmothers at their baptism.

GODOLPHIN ADMINISTRATIONS (see *Administrations*), 1684 and 1690. Lord Godolphin became prime minister to queen Anne, 8 May, 1702. The cabinet was notified in 1704. The earl resigned 8 Aug. 1710, and died 1712.

Sidney, lord (afterwards earl) Godolphin, *treasury.*
Sir Nathan Wright, *lord keeper.*
Thomas, earl of Pembroke and Montgomery, *lord president.*
John Sheffield, marquis of Normanby (afterwards duke of Normanby and Buckingham), *privy seal.*
Hon. Henry Boyle, *chancellor of the exchequer.*
Sir Charles Hedges and the earl of Nottingham (the latter succeeded by Robert Harley, created earl of Oxford in 1704), *secretaries of state.*

GODS, Greek and Roman; see under *Mythology.*

GODWIN SANDS, sand-banks off the east coast of Kent, occupy land which belonged to Godwin, earl of Kent, the father of king Harold II. Earl Godwin is said to have died suddenly, 15 April, 1053. This ground was afterwards given to the monastery of St. Augustine at Canterbury; but the abbot neglecting to keep in repair the wall that defended it from the sea, the tract was submerged about 1100, leaving these sands, upon which many ships have been wrecked. *Salmon.*

GOETHE SOCIETY (ENGLISH), founded in February, 1886, for making known and illustrating German literature. Professor Max Müller, president. Inaugural meeting, 28 May.

GOG AND MAGOG, see *Guildhall.*

GOLD (mentioned *Gen.* ii. 11), the purest, and most ductile of all the metals, for which reason it has been considered by almost all nations as the most valuable. It is too soft to be used pure, and to harden it it is alloyed with copper or silver: our coin consists of twenty-two carats of pure gold, and two of copper. By 17 & 18 Vict. c. 96 (1854), gold wares are allowed to be manufactured at a lower standard than formerly;—wedding rings excepted, by 18 & 19 Vict. c. 60 (1855). The present stated price is 3*l.* 17*s.* 10½*d.* per oz.; see *Coin of England,* and *Guineas.* In 1816, it was enacted by 56 Geo. III. c. 68, that "gold coins only should be legal tender in all payments of more than 40s.," the tender of silver being previously unlimited.

* Born 1782; held various inferior appointments from 1809 to 1818, when he became president of the board of trade; was chancellor of the exchequer from 1818 to April, 1827, when he became colonial secretary, which office he held in the Grey cabinet, Nov. 1830; created earl of Ripon, 1833: died 28 Jan. 1859.

Estimated amount of gold in the world; value, 1848, 550,000,000*l.*; 1875, 1,000,000,000*l.*
The value of gold compared with silver is said to have been estimated in the time of Herodotus, B.C. 450, about 10 to 1; of Plato, B.C. 38, 12 to 1; A.D. 1876, more than 15 to 1. See *Silver.*
The weight of the maharajah of Travancore in gold given in charity (an old custom), May, 1885.
The Amalgamation of Gold is described by Pliny (about 77) and Vitruvius (about 27 B.C.). The alchemist Basil Valentine (in the 15th century) was acquainted with the solution of the chloride of gold and fulminating gold. Andreas Cassius, in 1685, described the preparation of *gold purple,* which was then adapted by Kunkel to make *red glass,* and to other purposes. *Gmelin.* Gold has been subjected to the researches of eminent chemists, such as Berzelius and Faraday.
Mr. Rowland Jordan, of London devised a new and successful method of preventing waste, in separating gold from its ore, announced Oct. 1884.
H. R. Cassel's process for extraction of chlorine used in London, 1885.
Mr. B. C. Molloy's hydrogen-amalgam process for extracting gold from the ores exhibited by Messrs. Johnson of Finsbury, London, Aug. 1887.
Mr. T. Rowland Jordan's method of extracting gold, exhibited in George Street, London, E.C., Oct. 1889.
GOLD MINES. Gold was found most abundantly in Africa, Japan, and South America. In the last it was discovered by the Spaniards in 1492, from which time to 1731 they imported into Europe 6000 millions of pieces of eight, in register gold and silver, exclusively of what were unregistered.

Peter the Great re-opened ancient gold mines in Russia, 1699.

The Ural or Oural mountains of Russia long produced gold in large quantity.

A piece of gold weighing ninety marks, equal to sixty pounds troy (the mark being eight ounces), was found near La Paz, a town of Peru, 1730.

Gold discovered in Malacca in 1731; in New Andalusia in 1785; in Ceylon, 1800; 2887 oz. of gold, value 9991*l.*, obtained from mines in Britain and Ireland in 1864; it has been found in Cornwall, and in the county of Wicklow in Ireland (1797).

Gold discovered in California, Sept. 1847; and in Australia, 1851. On 28 April, 1858, a nugget, said to weigh 146 pounds, was shown to the queen. It is estimated that between 1851 and 1859 gold to the value of 88,889,435*l.* was exported from Victoria alone (see *California* and *Australia* severally).

Gold discovered in what is now termed New Columbia in 1856: much emigration there in 1858.

Gold discovered in New Zealand, and in Nova Scotia in 1861.

Gold discovered in South Africa (Transvaal republic, &c.), discovered in Sutherlandshire; much excitement, Oct. 1868; in West Australia, reported Sept. 1870; in the Bendigo fields, Victoria, Nov. 1871; in Land of Midian, by capt. R. Burton, announced, May, 1877.

The district of Witwatersrand, S. Africa, declared a public goldfield 20 Sept. 1886.

The prosperous town of Johannesburg erected, March 1887.

Productive gold fields discovered in the valley of the Djolgute river, opposite Ignachino on the Amoor, May, 1884; a Russian colony with foreign adventurers formed, January, 1885.

Great discovery of auriferous quartz, E. of the Transvaal, 1886.

Discovery of alluvial gold at Waukaranga, South Australia, Oct. 1886.

Alleged discovery of gold at mount Lyell in Tasmania, July, 1886.

"Midas" gold nugget named "lady Loch," weight 617 ozs.; value 2,537*l.*; found in the Midas gold company's claim, 3 Aug. 1887; exhibited with other nuggets by Miss Alice Cornwall at Queen Victoria-street, London, 28 Oct. 1887.

Discovery of gold in large quantities in Mr. Pritchard Morgan's Gwynfynydd mines, Mawddach valley, Merionethshire, Wales, announced, *Times,* 7 Dec. 1887; great success reported; the crown claims heavy royalties, April, but makes concessions, May, 1888; work going on, April, 1889-90. Yield of gold valued at

50,000l., royalty paid to the state, reported March, 1890; legal decision by Mr. Justice North that the mine is royal property; working restrained till the royalties are paid to the state, 6 Aug. 1890; the mine transferred to a company, which obtained a licence, and paid royalties.

Mr. Morgan's appeal against the decision of Aug. 6, disallowed, 21 Jan. 1891; his estate seized by the government for the royalties due, 22 March; the bailiffs withdrawn, pending an arrangement; work resumed, early April, 1892.

Important gold discoveries in Queensland, *which see* 1882–9.

In Malay Peninsula, announced Aug. 1889.

Gold mining greatly developed in the Transvaal district, especially at Leydenberg, 1872 *et seq.;* also in Utah, U.S.A., Dec. 1892.

Gold found in Western Australia, July, 1891; in New South Wales, March, 1894. Total output of gold from the 7 Australian colonies, 2,899,650 oz. in 1897; 4,462,488 oz. in 1899.

Gold discovered in E. Siberia, reported, 17 Sept. 1896; and in Canada on the Yukon, reported, 4 April, 1897; and on the Klondyke, N.W. Canada, and British Columbia, 1896–97; again, on the Stewart river and the Yukon, Nov. 1898.

Gold mining successfully carried on in Nova Scotia; gold found in large quantities at Whycocomagh; reported, 15 Feb. 1898.

Gold obtained in United Kingdom; value in 1861, 10,816l.; in 1862, 20,390l.; in 1863, 1747l.; in 1864, 9991l.; in 1865, 5894l.; in 1868, 3522l.; in 1876, 1138l.; in 1878, 2848l.; in 1880, 38l.; in 1882, 863l.; in 1887, 210l.; in 1888, 29,982l.; in 1889, 13,227l.; in 1890, 675l; 1891, 13,700l.; 1892, 10,511l.; 1893, 8691l.; 1894, 14,811l.; 1895, 18,520l.; 1896, 5,035l.

Estimated value of annual production of gold throughout the world, 1887, 21,765,000l.; 1892, 30,207,000l.; 1897, 49,061,000l.; 1901, 54,428,000l.

The Transvaal output of gold valued at 16,273,000l. in 1899.

Gold discovered in S. Australia, early 1903.

Gold Wire was first made in Italy about 1350. An ounce of gold is sufficient to gild a silver wire above 1300 miles in length; and such is its tenacity that a wire the one-eighteenth part of an inch will bear the weight of 500 lb. without breaking. *Fourcroy.*

Gold Leaf. A single grain of gold may be extended into *a leaf* of fifty-six square inches, and gold leaf can be reduced to the 300,000th part of an inch, and gilding to the ten-millionth part. *Kelly's Cambist.*

Gold Robbery. Three boxes, hooped and sealed, containing gold in bars and coin to the value of between 18,000l. and 20,000l. were sent from London, 15 May, 1855. On their arrival in Paris, it was found that ingots to the value of 12,000l. had been abstracted, and shot substituted, although the boxes bore no marks of violence. Many persons were apprehended on suspicion; but the police obtained no trace till Nov. 1856. Three men named Pierce, Burgess, and Tester, were tried and convicted 13-15 Jan. 1857, on the evidence of Edward Agar, an accomplice. They had been preparing for the robbery for eighteen months previous to its perpetration.

GOLD COAST, West Africa, see *Guinea*; settlements made by the Dutch; transferred to Great Britain by treaty, signed 2 Feb. 1872; joined with Lagos to form the "Gold Coast Colony," governor, capt. Geo. Cumine Strahan, appointed 1874; Lagos separated in 1886; Sandford Freeling, 1876; Herbert Taylor Ussher, 1879; sir Samuel Rowe, 25 Jan. 1881; William A. G. Young, died 25 April, 1885; sir W. Brandford Griffith, 1886; sir W. E. Maxwell, Jan. 1895; dies at sea, Dec. 1897; Mr. (aft. sir) F. M. Hodgson, March, 1898; major Matthew Nathan (aft. sir), Oct. 1900; Mr. J. P. Rodger, Oct. 1903. Population of the colony and protectorate, estimated at 2,000,000, 1902. Chief towns, Accra, Cape Coast Castle, and Elmina.

British mission (42), under lieut. Henderson, attacked at Dawkita by Sofas, 28 March; fought its way to Wa, 3 April; Mr. George Fergusson, British native commissioner, killed, in the fighting . . . . . . 31 March, 1897

Lieut. Henderson goes alone to arrange peace with Samory, and is kept a prisoner, April; but released . . . . 4 May, 1897

Settlement of peace with Samory made by sir Wm. Maxwell . . . . Aug. ,,

Bontuku in the *Hinterland* occupied by a British force, under capt. Mitchell; the Sofas retired, 20 Sept. 1897; Bontuku included in the French sphere . . . . Feb. 1899

Buna and Wa occupied by a British force, Jan.; French force also established there; announced, Feb. 1898

Punitive expedition, under lieut.-col. Northcott, made C.B. July, 1898, and others; enemy driven off, and their town occupied . . 19 April, ,,

Appeal to government against the house-tax at Accra . . . . 25 April, ,,

See *French West Africa*, Oct. 1898.

Mr. P. A. McCann takes 1,200 photographs during a 4 years' expedition in the *Hinterland*, visits unexplored country about the Gaboon and Elobey rivers, and collects valuable *data*, returns . . . . Feb. 1899

Col. H. P. Northcott's Gambaga expedition very successful, British post established, order restored, March; col. Northcott appointed administrator of the Northern Territories, Aug. (killed at Modder river, see *S. African War*) . 28 Nov. ,,

Frontier in the Hinterland of German Togoland, agreed to, announced . . . . . 8 Nov. ,,

Sir Fred. Hodgson entertains the loyal kings and chiefs of Ashanti who escaped with him from Kumassi (see *Ashantees*, 1900), at Accra, 6 Aug. 1900

Anglo-French boundary-line completed, Jan. 1901–1902

Col. Morris, chief commissioner of the Northern Territories; British post established at Salaga, great progress and loyalty, reported, mid Aug. ,,

Railway completed from Sekondi to Akropong, 9 Oct. ,,

GOLD FISH (the golden carp, *cyprinus auratus*), brought to England from China in 1691; but not common till about 1723.

GOLDEN BULLS, ROSE, see *Bulls, Rose*, note.

GOLDEN FLEECE (see *Argonauts*). Philip the Good, duke of Burgundy, in 1429, at his marriage, instituted the military order of "*Toison d'or*" or "golden fleece;" it was said on account of the profit he made by wool. The number of knights was thirty-one. The king of Spain, as duke of Burgundy, afterwards became grand master of the order. The knights wore a scarlet cloak lined with ermine, with a collar opened, and the duke's cipher, in the form of a B, to signify Burgundy, together with flints striking fire, with the motto "*Ante ferit, quam flamma micat.*" At the end of the collar hung a golden fleece, with this device, "*Pretium non vile laborum.*" The order afterwards became common to all the princes of the house of Austria, as descendants of Mary, daughter of Charles the Bold, last duke of Burgundy, who married Maximilian of Austria in 1477, and now belongs to both Austria and Spain, in conformity with a treaty made 30 April, 1725. The prince of Wales, the duke of York and other royal princes are knights (1895); president Faure, 1898; the duke of Connaught, 16 May, 1902; the shah of Persia, 6 Sept. 1902. For the legend of the Golden Fleece, see *Argonauts.*

GOLDEN HORDE, a name given to the Mongolian Tartars, who established an empire in Kaptchak (or Kibzak), now S.E. Russia, about 1224, their ruler being Batou, grandson of Gengis Khan. They invaded Russia, and made Alexander Newski grand-duke, 1252. At the battle of Bielawisch, in 1481, they were crushed by Ivan III. and the Nogai Tartars.

GOLDEN LEGEND, "Legenda Aurea." A name given to a collection of the lives of our Lord, the Old Testament worthies, and many Christian saints, with mnch Bible narrative, compiled by Giacomo Varragio, or Jacobus de Voragine, a Dominican monk, archbishop of Genoa, 1292–8. The work, which is of a very varied character, has afforded many subjects for poets and painters. A translation of "The Golden Legend," by William Caxton was printed by him in 1483, and became very popular. Of this, an edition in 3 vols., 4to, edited by William Morris and F. E. Ellis, was published by Bernard Quaritch early in 1893.

GOLDEN NUMBER, the cycle of nineteen years, or the number that shows the years of the moon's cycle; its invention is ascribed to Meton, of Athens, about 432 B.C. *Pliny.* To find the golden number or year of the lunar cycle, add one to the date, and divide by 19; the quotient is the number of cycles since Christ, and the remainder the golden number. The golden number for 1893, 13; 1894, 14; 1895, 15; 1896, 16; 1897, 17; 1898, 18; 1899, 19; 1900, 1; 1901, 2; 1902, 3; 1903, 4; 1904, 5; 1905, 6.

GOLDEN WEDDING, see *Wedding.*

GOLDSMID FAMILY. Aaron Goldsmid, a native of Holland, settled in London in 1763, and brought with him wealth and important commercial influence. His son Asher joined in establishing the firm of Mocatta and Goldsmid, bullion brokers to the Bank of England. The Goldsmids became at the end of the 18th and the beginning of the 19th century most distinguished financiers of the realm.

Isaac Lyon, the son of Asher Goldsmid, was conspicuous in the formation of the London Institution, the building of the London Docks, the earliest attempts in the introduction of railways, the improvement of prisons, the establishment of the Society for the Diffusion of Useful Knowledge, and the founding of the London University (afterwards called University College). In his numerous national and philanthropic works he was aided by his sons, Francis Henry, and Frederick David. In 1844 the queen of Portugal conferred on him the title of Baron da Palmeira, in recognition of his services in regulating the debt due by Brazil to Portugal. Regarding him and his son Francis, see also "*Jews.*"

GOLDSMITHS' COMPANY (London) began about 1327, and incorporated 16 Rich. II., 1392. The old hall was taken down in 1829, and the present magnificent edifice by Philip Hardwick, was opened 15 July, 1835; see *Assay,* and *Standard.* The first bankers were goldsmiths.

Goldsmiths' hall marks on gold and silver plate are five:—1. The sovereign's head (after 1784); 2, lion passant (the standard mark), probably introduced between 1538 and 1558; 3, the standard mark, fixed 8 & 9 Will. III. 1696-7; 4, leopard's head, the hall mark; 5, the maker's mark (an old custom).

[The *date-letter* is one of an alphabet of 20 letters; A to U or V, J being omitted. The letter is changed on 30 May annually, and the shape of the letter every 20 years; thus 1716, A, &c.; 1736, a, &c.; 1756, 𝔄, &c.; 1776, a, &c.; 1796-1816, A, &c.; 1816-36, a, &c.; 1836-56, 𝔄, &c.; 1856-76, a, &c.; 1876-1896, A, &c. The earliest known alphabetical series began 1438-9.]

A parliamentary commission on hall marking reported in favour of its continuance with modifications, May, 1879.

The company offer about 85,000*l.* for the establishment of the goldsmiths company's polytechnic institute, New Cross, Surrey, Oct. 1888; accepted by the Charity Commissioners, 1889. See *Polytechnic Institutions.*

Goldsmiths' exhibition at Vienna opened, 22 April, 1889.

Mr. Chaffer's "Hall-marks on gold and silver plate," published 1863, 8th edition, with essay by C. A. Markham, illustrated, 1897.

GOLF or **GOFF,** an ancient Scottish game in which the rival players drive hard white balls with clubs into holes placed at certain distances in the turf, according to rules laid down by the St. Andrews golf club, established 1754. The game was checked by the Scottish parliament, 1457 and 1491, but it continued and was played at Leith in 1516–75. The existing English golf club at Blackheath was founded by James I., 1608, but the game did not become popular till recent years. Golf clubs have been formed in the United Kingdom, colonies and abroad, 1893 *et seq.* Works on golf have been published by Mr. Robert Clark, 1876; Messrs. W. & R. Chambers, 1887, and others.

Winners of the Open Championship: 1896, H. Vardon, *score,* 316; 1897, H. H. Hilton, 314; 1898, H. Vardon, 307; 1899, H. Vardon, 310; 1900, J. H. Taylor, 309; 1901, J. Braid, 309; 1902, A. Herd, 307; 1903, H. Vardon, 300.

Mr. N. J. Travis, at Gordon city links, N. York, drove his ball 382 yds.; claimed to be a world's record . . . . 22 Jan. 1903

GOLIATH, training-ship, burnt, 22 Dec. 1875; see under *Wrecks.*

GOMARISTS, see *Arminians.*

GOMEL, Russia, anti-Semitic outrages on Jews, 11 Sept. 1903. See *Russia.*

GONFALONIER, or **STANDARD BEARER OF JUSTICE,** originally a subordinate officer in Florence; instituted 1292; became paramount in the 15th century, and was suppressed, 27 April, 1532, when the constitution was changed and Alexander de Medicis made duke.

GONIOMETER. An instrument for measuring solid angles, used in crystallography. The contact goniometer of Carangeau is generally employed. By the reflecting goniometer of Dr. Wm. Hyde Wollaston (who died in 1828) very minute crystals may be measured. Modifications of this instrument are now employed.

GOOD FRIDAY (probably God's Friday), the Friday before Easter day, on which a solemn fast has long been held, in remembrance of the crucifixion of Christ on Friday, 3 April, 33, or 15 April, 29. Its appellation of *good* appears to be peculiar to the church of England; our Saxon forefathers denominated it *Long Friday,* on account of the length of the offices and fastings enjoined on this day. See *Easter.*

GOODMAN'S FIELDS THEATRE, London, opened 1729. Here David Garrick made his *début* as Richard III., 19 Oct. 1741. The new theatre erected about 1746, was burnt down, June, 1802. The Garrick Theatre here was opened in 1830; burnt, 4 Nov. 1846; and since rebuilt.

GOOD TEMPLARS (first lodges formed in America, 1851), pledge themselves not to make, buy, sell, furnish, or cause to be furnished, intoxicating liquors to others as a beverage. The first English lodge was formed by Joseph Malins at Birmingham in May, 1868. Grand lodge of England instituted by him, 1870. There were 1,400 lodges, and 111,000 members of the Grand lodge in 1902. Annual sessions of the Grand lodge of England are held. Triennial congress held at Stockholm, mid July, 1902. The Grand lodge of Scotland has 1,171 lodges, and 96,000 members. 500 lodges in Ireland and Wales.

GOODWIN, see *Godwin.*

GOODWOOD RACES, see *Races.*

GOOJERAT (N. India), see *Guzerat*.

GOORKHAS, a warlike tribe of Nepaul, became prominent in the 17th century. Their invasions were defeated about 1791 by the Chinese, whose vassals they became. In a war with the British in 1814 they were at first successful, but were eventually subdued, and a treaty of peace was signed in Feb. 1816. Since 1841 the native regiments have been largely recruited by Goorkhas, who have rendered valuable service in nearly all our Indian wars, and in Afghanistan, 1878-9.

GOOSE, see *Michaelmas*.

GORDIAN KNOT, is said to have been made of the thongs that served as harness to the waggon of Gordius, a husbandman, afterwards king of Phrygia. Whosoever loosed this knot, the ends of which were not discoverable, the oracle declared should be ruler of Persia. Alexander the Great cut away the knot with his sword until he found the ends of it, and thus, in a military sense at least, interpreted the oracle, 330 B.C.

GORDON MEMORIAL; proposed by lady Burdett-Coutts in the *Times*, 24 Feb. 1885. See *Khartoum* and *Mansion House*.

Committee formed: the prince of Wales, duke of Cambridge, archbishop of Canterbury, Mr. Gladstone, marquis of Salisbury, cardinal Manning, Chinese minister, marquis of Lorne, earl Granville and other persons, 24 Feb. *et seq.* 1885.
Proposed grant of 20,000*l.* to the Gordon family, March, 1885.
Gordon Memorial Hospital at Port Said proposed at Mansion House, London, 14 March, 1885.
Subscriptions 20,320*l.* 19 Oct. 1885; given to trustees of Gordon boys' home. Port Said hospital scheme given up, 30 May, 1885.
Opening of penny subscription to establish a Gordon camp at Aldershot for the military training of destitute boys; originated by Mr. Hallam Tennyson, May, 1885.
Gordon league to provide entertainment for the very poor, instituted by the princess Louise and others, 19 May, 1885; first meeting 18 Oct. 1885.
A *Gordon memorial boys' home* proposed 1 July, united with memorial fund, 20 July, opened at Fareham near Portsmouth, 1 Oct. 1885. *Woking*: 239 boys in the home, 31 Dec. 1902. Of 98 who left 32 joined the army and 3 the navy, making a total of 499 who have joined these two services direct from the home since 1885. Enlisted after leaving the home, 80. Income, 1902, 9,185*l.*
A statue proposed by government, about 14 July, 1885. Statue by Mr. Hamo Thornycroft set up in Trafalgar-square, 25 Sept.; uncovered by Mr. D. R. Plunket, 16 Oct. 1888.
Another statue, by Mr. Onslow Ford, at the school of military engineering, Chatham, uncovered by the prince of Wales, 19 May, 1890; and one at Gravesend, unveiled by the mayor, Mr. G. M. Arnold, 4 Oct. 1893.
Gordon memorial college at Khartoum, proposed by lord Kitchener, supported by the marquis of Salisbury, 23 Nov. 1898. Opened . 7 Nov. 1902

GORDON'S "NO POPERY" RIOTS, occasioned by the zeal of lord George Gordon, June 2-9, 1780.

On 4 Jan. 1780, he tendered the petition of the Protestant Association to lord North.
On Friday, 2 June, he headed the mob of 40,000 persons who assembled in St. George's Fields, under the name of the Protestant Association, to carry up a petition to parliament for the repeal of the act which granted certain indulgences to the Roman Catholics. The mob proceeded to pillage, burn, and pull down the chapels and houses of the Roman Catholics first, but afterwards of other persons, for nearly six days. The Bank was attempted, the gaols opened (the King's Bench, Newgate, Fleet, and Bridewell prisons). On the 7th, thirty-six fires were seen blazing at one time. At length by the aid of armed associations of the citizens, the horse and foot guards, and the militia of several counties, then embodied and marched to London, the riot was quelled on the 8th.
210 rioters were killed and 248 wounded, of whom 75 died afterwards in the hospitals, and many were tried, convicted and executed.
The loss of property was estimated at 180,000*l.*
Lord George was tried for high treason and acquitted, 5 Feb. 1781. He died a prisoner for libel, 1 Nov. 1793.
Alderman Kennett was found guilty of a dereliction of duty, 10 March, 1781.

GOREE, a station near Cape Verd, W. coast of Africa, planted by the Dutch, 1617. It was taken by the English admiral Holmes in 1663; seized by the French, 1677; and ceded to them by the treaty of Nimeguen in 1678; taken by the British in 1758, 1779, 1800, and 1804; ceded to France, 1814. Governor Wall was hanged in London, 28 Jan. 1802, for the murder of sergeant Armstrong, committed while governor at Goree in 1782.

GOREY (S.E. Ireland). Near here the king's troops under colonel Walpole were defeated, and their leader slain, by the Irish rebels, 4 June, 1798.

GORGET, the ancient breast-plate, was very large, varying in size and weight. The present diminutive breast-plate came into use about 1660, see *Armour*.

GORHAM CASE, see *Trials*, 1849-50.

GORILLA, a powerful ape of W. Africa, about 5 feet 7 inches high. It is a match for the lion, and attacks the elephant with a club. It is considered to be identical with the hairy people called *Gorullai* by the navigator Hanno, in his *Periplus*, about 400 B.C. In 1847 a sketch of a gorilla's cranium was sent to professor Owen by Dr. Savage, then at the Gaboon river, and preserved specimens have been brought to Europe, and a living one died on its voyage to France. In 1851 professor Owen described specimens to the Zoological Society; in 1859 he gave a summary of our knowledge of this creature at the Royal Institution, London; and in 1861 several skins and skulls were there exhibited by M. Du Chaillu (died 29 April, 1903), who stated that he killed 21 of them in his travels in Central Africa. The gorilla was not known to Cuvier.

A young gorilla landed at Liverpool, 21 June, 1876; went to Berlin; was exhibited at Westminster aquarium, 23 July; died at Berlin, 13 Nov. 1877; another brought to the Crystal palace, England, soon died, Aug. 1879.
An African gorilla landed at Liverpool, Sept. 1881.
Another Sept. 1885.
One placed in the zoological gardens, London, Oct.; died 9 Dec. 1887.
A large one brought from the French Congo to the gardens, 6 March, 1896.
Johanna, the "educated" gorilla, performs at Olympia, 27 Dec. 1897.

GOSPELLERS, a name given to the followers of Wickliffe, who attacked the errors of popery, about 1377. Wickliffe opposed the authority of the pope, the temporal jurisdiction of bishops, &c., and is called the father of the Reformation.

GOSPELS (Saxon *god-spell*, good story). Mathew's and Mark's are conjectured to have been written between A.D. 38 and 65; Luke's 55 or 65; John's, about 97. Irenæus in the 2nd century refers to each of the gospels by name. Dr. Robert Bray was one of the authors of the Society for the Propagation of the Gospel in Foreign Countries, incorporated in 1701. A body termed "Bray's Associates," still exists; its object being to assist in forming and supporting clerical parochial libraries.

GOSPORT (Hampshire), contains the Royal Clarence victualling yard. The great Haslar hospital, near Gosport, was built in 1762.

GOTHA, capital of the duchy of Saxe Coburg-Gotha. Here is published the celebrated *Almanach de Gotha*, which first appeared in 1764, in German. Population, 1890, 29,134; 1900, 34,651.

GOTHARD, see *Gotthard* and *Alps*.

GOTHENBURG SYSTEM (in Sweden and Norway, about 1871). By this alcoholic drinks are dispensed by persons deriving no profit from the sale. It was advocated in England by Mr. Chamberlain, M.P., and much discussed, 1876–7. The bishop of Chester introduced a bill for establishing the system, read first time, 2 March, 1893; rejected by the lords, 6 June, 1893. The system advocated at a meeting at the Duke of Westminster's, 6 July, 1894. Much controversy ensued, 1894–95. See the bishop's letter, in *Times*, 15 Jan. 1895, and "Sober by Act of Parliament," by E. Goadby.

GOTHIC ARCHITECTURE began about the 9th century after Christ, and spread over Europe. Its great feature is the pointed arch; hence it ha been suggested to call it the *pointed style*. "Gothic" was originally a term of reproach given to this style by the renaissance architects of the 16th century. Its invention has been claimed for several nations, particularly for the Saracens. The following list is from Godwin's Chronological Table of English Architecture :—

ANGLO-ROMAN—B.C. 55 to about A.D. 250—St. Martin's church, Canterbury.

ANGLO-SAXON—A.D. 800 to 1066—Earl's Barton church; St. Peter's, Lincolnshire.

GOTHIC ANGLO-ROMAN—A.D. 1066 to 1135—Rochester cathedral nave; St. Bartholomew's, Smithfield; St. Cross, Hants, &c.

EARLY ENGLISH, OR POINTED—A.D. 1135 to 1272—Temple church, London; parts of Winchester, Wells, Salisbury, and Durham cathedrals, and Westminster Abbey.

POINTED, called Pure Gothic—A.D. 1272 to 1377—Exeter cathedral, Waltham Cross, &c., St. Stephen's, Westminster.

FLORID POINTED—A.D. 1377 to 1509—Westminster Hall; King's College, Cambridge; St. George's Chapel, Windsor; Henry VII.'s Chapel, Westminster.

ELIZABETHAN—A.D. 1509 to 1625—Northumberland House, Strand, pulled down 1874; part of Windsor Castle; Hatfield House, Schools at Oxford.

Revival of Grecian architecture about 1625. Banqueting House, Whitehall, &c.

The revival of Gothic architecture commenced about 1825, mainly through the exertions of A. W. Pugin. The controversy as to its expediency was rife in 1860–1.

GOTHLAND, an isle in the Baltic sea, was conquered by the Teutonic knights, 1397–8; given up to the Danes, 1524; to Sweden, 1645; conquered by the Danes, 1677, and restored to Sweden, 1679. Mariestad almost entirely destroyed by fire, 5 Dec. 1895.

GOTHS, a warlike nation that inhabited the country between the Caspian, Pontus, Euxine, and Baltic seas. They entered Mœsia, took Philippopolis, massacring thousands of its inhabitants; defeated and killed the emperor Decius, 251; but were defeated at Naissus by Claudius, hence surnamed Gothicus, 320,000 being slain, 269. Aurelian ceded Dacia to them in 272; but they long troubled the empire. After the destruction of the Roman western empire by the Heruli, the *Ostrogoths*, under Theodoric, became masters of the greater part of Italy, where they retained their dominion till 553, when they were finally conquered by Narses, Justinian's general. The *Visigoths* settled in Spain, and founded a kingdom, which continued until the country was subdued by the Saracens.

GOTTHARD, ST., near the river Raab, Hungary. Here the Turks, under the grand vizier Kupriuli, were totally defeated by the Imperialists and their allies, commanded by Montecuculi, 1 Aug. 1664. Peace followed this great victory. St. Gotthard tunnel, opened 1882. See *Alps*.

GÖTTINGEN (Hanover), a member of the Hanseatic league about 1360. The university "Georgia Augusta," founded by George II. of England in 1734, was opened 1737. It was seized by the French, 1760, and held till 1762. In 1837 several of the most able professors were dismissed for their political opinions. Population, 1890, 23,693; 1900, 30,234.

GOVERNESSES' BENEVOLENT INSTITUTION, was established in 1843, and incorporated in 1848. It affords to aged governesses annuities and an asylum; and to governesses in distress a temporary home and assistance.

GOVERNMENT ANNUITIES ACT, see *Annuities*. The building of the new GOVERNMENT OFFICES began in 1861.

GOVERNMENT CONTRACTS, select committee (fair wages resolution of 13 Feb. 1891), appointed 1896–7; report issued 21 July, 1897. See *Sweating*.

GOVERNMENT OF IRELAND BILLS, see *Ireland*, 1886, 1893.

"**GOVERNOUR**, THE," a moral and educational work, full of anecdotes, by sir Thomas Elyot, first published in 1531; an annotated edition with a glossary by Mr. H. H. S. Croft was published in 1880.

GOWRIE CONSPIRACY. John Ruthven, earl of Gowrie, in 1600, reckoning on the support of the burghs and the kirk, conspired to dethrone James VI. of Scotland, and seize the government. For this purpose the king was decoyed into Gowrie's house in Perth, on 5 Aug. 1600. The plot was frustrated, and the earl and his brother, Alexander, were slain on the spot. At the time, many persons believed that the young men were rather the victims than the authors of a plot. Their father, William, was treacherously executed in 1584 for his share in the raid of Ruthven, in 1582; and he and his father, Patrick, were among the assassins of Rizzio, 9 March, 1566.

GRAAL, HOLY (Sangreal). The publication of Tennyson's poem "Holy Grail," Dec. 1869, led to much discussion. Tennyson treats it as the cup in which Christ drank at the Last Supper. The mediæval romances treat it as the dish which held the paschal-lamb. The word is probably old French, *gréal*, from the old Latin *gradalis*, a dish.

GRACE, a title assumed by Henry IV. of England, on his accession, in 1399. *Excellent Grace* was assumed by Henry VI. about 1425. Till the time of James I. 1603, the king was addressed by that title, but afterwards by the title of *Majesty* only. "Your Grace" is the manner of addressing an archbishop and a duke in this realm.—The term "*Grace of God*" is said to have been taken by bishops at Ephesus, 431 (probably from 1 *Cor.* xv. 10), by the Carlovingian princes in the 9th century, by popes in the 13th century; and about 1440 it was assumed by kings as signifying their divine right. "*Dei gratia*" was put on his great seal by

William II. of England, and on his gold coin by Edward III. The king of Prussia's saying, that he would reign "by the grace of God," gave much offence, 18 Oct. 1861.

GRACE AT MEAT. The ancient Greeks would not partake of any meat until they had first offered part of it, as the firstfruits, to their gods. The short prayer said before, and by some persons after, meat in Christian countries is in conformity with Christ's example, *John* vi. 11, &c.

GRÆCIA MAGNA, colonies planted by the Greeks, 974-748 B.C.; see *Italy*.

GRAFFITI, a term given to the scribblings found on the walls of Pompeii and other Roman ruins; selections were published by Wordsworth in 1837, and by Garrucci in 1856.

GRAFTON ADMINISTRATION, succeeded that of lord Chatham, Dec. 1767. The duke resigned, and lord North became prime minister, Jan. 1770; see *North's Administration*.

Augustus Henry, duke of Grafton, *first lord of the treasury* [born, 1735; died 1811].
Frederick, lord North, *chancellor of the exchequer*.
Earl Gower, *lord president*.
Earl of Chatham, *lord privy seal*.
Earl of Shelburne and Viscount Weymouth, *secretaries of state*.
Sir Edward Hawke, *first lord of the admiralty*.
Marquis of Granby, *master-general of the ordnance*.
Lords Sandwich and Le Despencer, *joint postmasters-general*.
Lords Hertford, duke of Ancaster, Thomas Townshend, &c.
Lord Camden, *lord chancellor*, succeeded by Charles Yorke (created lord Morden), died (it is said by his own hand) 20 Jan. 1770.

GRAHAM'S DIKE (Scotland), a wall built in 209 by Severus Septimus, the Roman emperor, or, as others say, by Antoninus Pius. It reached from the Firth of Forth to the Clyde. Buchanan relates that there were considerable remains of this wall in his time, and vestiges of it are still to be seen.

GRAIN. Henry III. is said to have ordered a grain of wheat gathered from the middle of the ear to be the original standard of weight: 12 grains to be a pennyweight; 12 pennyweights one ounce, and 12 ounces a pound Troy. *Lawson*.

An act for the safe carriage of grain (43 & 44 Vict. c. 43), passed 7 Sept. 1880.

GRAMMARIANS. A society of grammarians was formed at Rome so early as 276 B.C. *Blair*. Apollodorus of Athens, Varro, Cicero, Messala, Julius Cæsar, Nicias, Ælius Donatus, Remmius, Palemon, Tyrannion of Pontus, Athenæus, and other distinguished men, were of this class. A Greek grammar was printed at Milan in 1476; Lily's Latin grammar (Brevis Institutio), 1513; Lindley Murray's English Grammar, 1795; Cobbett's English Grammar, 1818.—Harris's Hermes was published in 1750, Horne Tooke's "Epea Pteroenta," or the "Diversions of Purley," in 1786, treatises on the philosophy of language and grammar. Cobbett declared Mr. Canning to have been the only purely grammatical orator of his time; and Dr. Parr, speaking of a speech of Mr. Pitt's, said, "We threw our whole grammatical mind upon it, and could not discover one error." The science of grammar has been recently much studied with excellent results.

GRAMMAR SCHOOLS, see *Education*.

GRAMME, see *Metrical System*. *Gramme* machine, see under *Electricity*.

GRAMMOPHONE AND GRAPHOPHONE, see under *Phonograph*.

GRAMPIAN HILLS (central Scotland). At Ardoch, near *Mons Grampius* of Tacitus, the Scots and Picts under Galgacus were defeated by the Romans under Agricola, 84 or 85.

GRAMPOUND (Cornwall) was disfranchised in 1821, for bribery and corrupt practices in 1819. Sir Manasseh Lopez was sentenced by the court of king's bench to a fine of 10,000*l*. and two years' imprisonment.

GRAN (Hungary). Here the Hungarians defeated the Austrians, 27 Feb. 1849.

GRANADA, a city, S. Spain, was founded by the Moors in the 8th century, and formed at first part of the kingdom of Cordova. In 1236, Mohammed-al-Hamar made it the capital of his new kingdom of Granada, which was highly prosperous till its subjugation by the "great captain," Gonsalvo de Cordova, 2 Jan. 1492, who is interred in the monastery of St. Geronimo. In 1609 and 1610 the industrious Moors were expelled from Spain, by the bigoted Philip III., to the lasting injury of his country. Granada was taken by marshal Soult in 1810, and held till 1812. See *New Granada*. Granada is the seat of an archbishopric. The cathedral, begun in 1529, contains the tombs of Ferdinand and Isabella, and of Philip I. and his consort Juana. The university was founded 1531. Population, 1887: province, 484,638; city, 73,006; 1897, province, 477,768; city, 75,054.

In the *province* of Granada, five towns were destroyed, 914 persons killed, with an immense loss of property, through the earthquakes of 25 Dec. *et seq.* 1884.

GRANARIES were formed by Joseph in Egypt, 1715 B.C. (*Genesis* xli. 48.) There were three hundred and twenty-seven granaries in Rome. *Univ. Hist.* Twelve new granaries were built at Bridewell to hold 6000 quarters of corn, and two store houses for sea-coal to hold 4000 loads, thereby to prevent the sudden dearness of these articles by great increase of inhabitants, 7 James I. 1610. *Stow*.

GRAND ALLIANCE between the emperor and the Dutch States-General (principally to prevent the union of the French and Spanish monarchies in one person), signed at Vienna, 12 May, 1689, to which England, Spain, and the duke of Savoy afterwards acceded.

GRAND COMMITTEES, see *Committees*.

GRAND-DUKE, see *Duke*.

GRANDEES, see *Spanish Grandees*.

GRAND JUNCTION CANAL (central England), joins several others, and forms a water communication between London, Liverpool, Bristol, and Hull. The canal commences at Braunston, on the west borders of Northamptonshire, and enters the Thames near London. Executed 1793-1805.

GRAND JURIES, see *Juries*.

GRANDMONTINES, a monastic order established in Limousin, in France, by Stephen, a gentleman of Auvergne, about 1076. They came to England in the reign of Henry I. (1100-35). *Tanner*.

GRAND PENSIONARY, a chief state functionary in Holland, in the 16th century. In the Constitution given by France to the Batavian republic, previously to the erection of the kingdom of Holland, the title was revived and given to the head of the government, 29 April, 1805, Rutger Jan Schimmelpenninck being made the grand pensionary; see *Holland*.

GRAND REMONSTRANCE, see *Remonstrance*.

GRANICUS (a river N.W. Asia Minor), near which, on 22 May, 334 B.C., Alexander the Great signally defeated the Persians. The Macedonian troops (30,000 foot and 5000 horse) crossed the Granicus in the face of the Persian army (600,000 foot and 20,000 horse). *Justin*. The victors lost fifty-five foot soldiers and sixty horse. Sardis capitulated, Miletus and Halicarnassus were taken by storm, and other great towns submitted to the conqueror.

GRANSON, near the lake of Neufchatel, Switzerland, where Charles the Bold, duke of Burgundy, was defeated by the Swiss, 3 March, 1476.

GRANTON PIER, breakwater, &c. forming a harbour, on the Forth, three miles from Edinburgh, were constructed by Messrs. Stevenson, at the cost of about 500,000*l*., given by Walter, duke of Buccleuch, 1835-44.

GRAPES. Previously to the reign of Edward VI. grapes were brought to England in large quantities from Flanders, where they were first cultivated about 1276. The vine was introduced into England in 1552; being first planted at Bloxhall, in Suffolk. In the gardens of Hampton-court palace is a vine, stated to surpass any in Europe; it is 72 feet by 20, and has in one season produced 2272 bunches of grapes, weighing 18 cwt.; the stem is 13 inches in girth; it was planted in 1769. *Leigh*.

GRAPHIC, illustrated weekly journal, established 4 Dec. 1869. The *Daily Graphic* first appeared 4 Jan. 1890.

GRAPHITE (from the Greek *graphein*, to write), a peculiar form of mineral carbon, with a trace of iron, improperly termed black lead and plumbago. In 1809 sir Humphry Davy investigated into the relations of three forms of carbon, the diamond, graphite, and charcoal. A rude kind of black-lead pencil is mentioned by Gesner in 1565. Interesting results of sir B. C. Brodie's researches on graphite appeared in the International Exhibition of 1862. Fresh discoveries were made in the nearly exhausted Borrowdale mines, Cumberland, in 1875.

GRAPHOSCOPE, an optical apparatus for magnifying and giving fine effects to engravings, photographs, &c., invented by C. J. Rowsell; exhibited in 1871.

GRAPHOTYPE, a new process for obtaining blocks for surface-printing, the invention of Mr. De Witt Clinton Hitchcock in 1860. It was described by Mr. Fitz-Cook at the Society of Arts, 6 Dec. 1865. Drawings were made on blocks of chalk with a silicious ink; when dried, the soft parts were brushed away, and the drawing remained in relief; stereotypes were then taken from the block. Now superseded by the zinco-type and other processes.

GRATES. The Anglo-Saxons had arched hearths, and chafing-dishes were in use until the introduction of chimneys about 1200; see *Chimneys*, and *Stoves*.

GRATTAN'S PARLIAMENT, a name popularly given to the Irish parliament, after it had been declared independent, mainly by the exertions of Henry Grattan, by an act passed in England, May, 1782. It came to an end by the passing of the Act of Union, 2 July, 1800. In 1806, Grattan said of his parliament "I have a parental recollection. I sat by her cradle; I followed her hearse." Grattan strongly urged the passing of an act for Catholic emancipation till his death 4 June, 1820.

GRAVELINES (N. France). Here the Spaniards, aided by an English fleet, defeated the French on 13 July, 1558.

GRAVELOTTE, BATTLE OF, 18 Aug. 1870. See *Metz*.

GRAVESEND, Kent (Domesday *Graveshaf*), on the Thames; burned by the French, 1380; chartered by Elizabeth, 1562; fortified, 1588; destructive fire, 24 Aug. 1727; another in 1850; has one M.P. by act of 1867. Population, 1881, 23,302; 1891, 24,067; 1901, 27,175.

GRAVITATION, as a supposed innate power, was noticed by the Greeks, and also by Seneca, who speaks of the moon attracting the waters, about 38. Kepler investigated the subject about 1615, and Hooke devised a system of gravitation about 1674. The principles of gravity were demonstrated by Galileo at Florence, about 1633; but the great law on this subject, laid down by Newton in his "Principia," in 1687, is said to have been proved by him in 1670. The fall of an apple from a tree in 1666 is said to have directed his attention to the subject.

Newton says, "I do not anywhere take on me to define the kind or manner of any action, the causes or physical reasons thereof, or attribute forces in a true and physical sense to certain centres, when I speak of them as attracting, or endued with attractive powers."

On 15 July, 1867, M. Chasles laid before the Paris Academy of Sciences some letters alleged to be from Newton to Pascal and others tending to show that to Pascal was due the theory of gravitation. The authenticity of these letters was authoritatively denied, and their forgery and his own delusion were acknowledged by M. Chasles before the academy 13 Sept. 1869.

GREAT BETHEL, see *Big Bethel*.

GREAT BRITAIN, the name given in 1604 to *England*, *Wales*, and *Scotland* (*which see*). King James I. styled himself king of Great Britain, 1604. See *Population*. "Greater Britain," the title of sir Charles Dilke's book, describing his travels in the British colonies, published in 1868; 8th edition, June 1885. See *British Empire*.

"Greater Britain" exhibition at Earl's court, Kensington, opened by the duke of Cambridge, 8 May, 1899.

GREAT BRITAIN, EASTERN, &c., see under *Steam*.—The Eastern Counties Railway assumed the name of GREAT EASTERN in 1862, when it was incorporated. The GREAT NORTHERN RAILWAY Company, an amalgamation, was incorporated in 1846. Their station at King's-cross, London, was opened in Oct. 1852. Grinling's "History" published, March, 1898.—The GREAT WESTERN RAILWAY opened as far as Maidenhead, 4 June, 1838; as Twyford, 1 July, 1839; between London and Bristol, 30 June, 1841; was re-modelled by acts of 1867 and 1869.—GREAT CENTRAL name given to the Manchester, Sheffield and Lincolnshire railway in 1897 on its extension to London terminus, Marylebone-road.

GREAT EXHIBITION, see *Exhibition*.

GREAT PAUL, see *Bells*.

GREAT SEAL OF ENGLAND. The first seal used by Edward the Confessor was called the broad seal, and affixed to the grants of the crown, 1048. *Baker's Chron.* The most ancient seal with arms on it is that of Richard I. James II., when fleeing from London in 1688, dropped the great seal in the Thames. The great seal of England was stolen from the house of lord chancellor Thurlow, in Great Ormond-street, and carried away, with other property, 24 March, 1784, a day before the dissolution of parliament; it was never recovered, and was replaced the next day. A new seal was brought into use on the union with Ireland, 1 Jan. 1801. A new seal for Ireland was brought into use and the old one defaced, 21 Jan. 1832. The Great Seal Offices Act, passed 7 Aug. 1874, abolished certain offices, transferred duties, &c. The Great Seal Act passed, 2 Aug. 1880, relates to appointment of judges, patents, &c. A new great seal for the United Kingdon, designed by Mr. De Saulles, to replace that of 1878, reported, 19 July, 1900.

GRECO-TURKISH WAR.

Bands of Greek irregulars of the "Ethnike Hetairia," a national society, cross the frontier at Krania; 12 hours fighting near Kalambaka, 9 April; Bettino and Bozovo taken by the Greeks, 10 April, 1897

Frontier raids by Greeks repulsed, 12 April; severe conflict at Analipsis, Turks repulsed and their outposts captured, 16–18 April; Turkish forts in the Ambracian gulf destroyed; Prevesa bombarded, 18–20 April; desperate battle in the Maluna pass, Hafiz pasha (80), a hero in the Russo-Turkish war, killed; Greek blockhouses carried by assault, 17–19 April; severe fighting near Arta in Epirus, Bonghazi and Fort Vigla captured by the Greeks, 19 April; Filippiada and Strevina burnt and abandoned by the Turks, 21 April, "

Greek fleet bombards Platamona and other places in the gulf of Salonika, 2 Turkish ships captured . . . . 21–23 April, "

Severe battle at Mati on the road to Larissa, crown prince and prince Nicholas present; Greeks defeated . . . . 22, 23 April, "

Greeks severely defeated at Reveni and Turnavo, on the plain of Larissa . . . 20–23 April, "

Larissa, Turnova, and Reveni abandoned by the Greeks; panic and stampede of men, women, and children, about 500 or 600 killed; retreat of the Greeks to Phersala (Pharsalia), the crown prince the last to leave Larissa . 23–25 April "

Gen. Ricciotti Garibaldi arrives at Athens with volunteers . . . . 24 April, "

Nicopolis and other places bombarded by the Greeks, 23, 24 April; the Turks recapture fort Pentepigadia, after severe fighting . 24 April, "

Fight (7 hours) at Kumutzades; Greek flight 25 April, "

Greek army (30,000) at Phersala, col. Smolenski appointed chief commander, 29 April; Turks repulsed with loss by col. Smolenski's brigade at Velestino . . . . 30 April, "

Battle of Pentepigadia, 28, 29 April; panic and flight of the Greeks . . . 30 April, 1 May, "

Phersala and Velestino attacked simultaneously by the Turks; Greeks outnumbered and overpowered after desperate fighting and much slaughter; retreat to Domoko . . . 5 May, "

Volo occupied by Hakki pasha, 8 May; Greek force routed and Kamerina occupied by the Turks, 8 May, "

Col. Vassos and the Greek army recalled from Crete . . . . 9 May, "

Mediation of the powers accepted; armistice proposed; Cretan autonomy agreed to by Greece, 11 May; submitted to Turkey 12 May; Turkish conditions: 10,000,000*l*. T. indemnity, annexation of Thessaly, revision of treaties affording exterritorial privileges; a cartel of extradition, to precede an armistice, presented . 15 May, "

Severe fighting on the Imaret Heights 12–14 May, 1897

Nicopolis and Prevesa besieged by the Greeks, 13–15 May, "

Fierce battle near Gribovo, much slaughter, 14 May, "

The powers intervene, 16 May; by request of the czar, the sultan orders suspension of hostilities, 17 May, "

Desperate battle at Domoko, nearly 3,000 Turks killed; Greeks retreat; capt. Baratassi, in command of foreign legion, killed, 17 May; Domoko occupied, and the Phourka pass taken by the Turks, 18 May; the Greeks fall back on Thermopylæ, 19 May; armistice: end of the war; negotiations between the ambassadors and the porte, at Constantinople; announced . . 20 May, "

Collective note of the powers to the porte on the conditions of peace . . . . . 25 May, "

The "Ethnike Hetairia" volunteers, disarmed; ordered . . . . 26 May, "

Greece entrusts her cause to the powers 1 June, "

Peace negotiations at Constantinople: the powers resist the demands of the porte as to the annexation of Thessaly, the capitulations, and the war indemnity . . . . . . 3 June *et seq.* "

Armistice till the close of the negotiations, signed at Lamia . . . . 3 June, "

Greece protests to the powers of the infraction of the armistice by the Turks . . . . 18 June, "

The sultan refuses to accept the views of the powers on the boundary question . 7 July, "

The powers demand the cessation of obstruction to peace negotiations . . . . 3, 8 July, "

Turkish atrocities in Epirus and Thessaly; reported . . . . July, "

Draft treaty of peace presented by the porte, 18 July; not accepted by the ambassadors, 19 July; an iradé promulgated accepting the frontier, with reservations, 21 July. See *Greece*, 18 Sept. 1897; *Turkey*, 4 Dec. 1897.

Full report of the war by the crown prince, issued, 14 Jan. 1899

GREECE, anciently termed Hellas. The name of Græcia first occurs in the writings of Aristotle (B.C. 384–322). Greece was so called from an ancient king, Græcus, and Hellas from another king, Hellen, the son of Deucalion. From Hellen's sons, Dorus and Æolus, came the Dorians and Æolians; another son Xuthus was father of Achæus and Ion, the progenitors of the Achæans and Ionians. Homer calls the inhabitants indifferently Myrmidons, Hellenes, and Achaians. They were also termed Danai, from Danaus, king of Argos, 1474 B.C. Greece anciently consisted of the peninsula of the Peloponnesus, Greece outside of the Peloponnesus, Thessaly, and the islands. The principal states of Greece were Athens, Sparta, Corinth, Thebes, Arcadia, and afterwards Macedon (*all which see*). The limits of Modern Greece are much more confined. Greece became subject to the Turkish empire in the 15th century. The population of the kingdom, established in 1829, 96,810; in 1861, 1,096,810, with the Ionian isles (added in 1864), about 1,348,522 in 1870, 1,457,894; in 1879, 1,979,147; in 1889, 2,187,208; 1896 2,433,806. The early history is mythic, and the dates *purely conjectural*.

Sicyon founded (*Eusebius*) . . . . . B.C. 2089

Uranus arrives in Greece (*Lenglet*) 2042

Revolt of the Titans; War of the Giants . . . * *

Inachus king of the Argives 1910

Kingdom of Argos begun by Inachus (*Eusebius*) . 1856

Reign of Ogyges in Bœotia (*Eusebius*) 1796

Sacrifices to the gods introduced by Phoroneus . 1773

Sicyon now begun (*Lenglet*)

Deluge of Ogyges (*which see*) 1764

A colony of Arcadians emigrate to Italy under Œnotrus: the country first called *Œnotria*, afterwards *Magna Græcia* (*Eusebius*) . . . 1710

The Pelasgi hold the Peloponnesus 1700–1550; succeeded by the Hellenes 1550–1300

Chronology of the Arundelian marbles commences (*Eusebius*) 1582

Cecrops arrives from Egypt . . . . . about 1550

The Areopagus established 1504
Deluge of Deucalion (*Eusebius*) . . . 1503
Panathenæan games instituted 1495
Cadmus with the Phœnician letters settles in Bœotia, and founds Thebes . . . . about 1493
Lelex, first king of Laconia, afterwards called Sparta 1490
Danaus said to have brought the first ship into Greece, and to have introduced pumps (see *Argos*) 1485
Reign of Hellen (*Eusebius*) 1459
First Olympic games at Elis, by the *Idæi Dactyli* . 1453
Who are said to have discovered iron . . . 1406
Corinth re-built and so named 1384
Eleusinian mysteries instituted by Eumolpus (1356) and Isthmian games 1326
Kingdom of Mycenæ created out of Argos . . . 1313
Pelops, from Lydia, settles in south Greece, (Peloponnesus) . . . . about 1283
Argonautic expedition (*which see*) 1263
The Pythian games begun by Adrastus . . . „
War of the seven Greek captains against Thebes . 1225
The Amazonian war 1213
Rape of Helen by Theseus . . . . . . „
Rape of Helen by Paris 1198
Commencement of the Trojan war 1193
Troy taken on the night of the 7th of the month Thargelion (27th of May, or 11th June) (see *Troy*) 1184
Æneas said to arrive in Italy . . . about 1182
Migration of Æolians who build Smyrna, &c. . . 1123
Return of the Heraclidæ . . . . about 1103
Settlement of the Ionians in Asia Minor . . . 1044
The Rhodians begin navigation laws 916
Lycurgus flourishes 884
Olympic games revived at Elis, 884; the first Olympiad 776
The Messenian wars 743-669
Sea-fight, the first on record, between the Corinthians and the inhabitants of Corcyra . . . 664
Byzantium built 657
Seven sages of Greece (Solon, Periander, Pittacus, Chilo, Thales, Cleobulus, and Bias) flourish, about 590
Persian conquests in Ionia 544
Sybaris in Magna Græcia destroyed: 100,000 Crotonians under Milo defeat 300,000 Sybarites . . 508
Sardis burnt by the Greeks, which occasions the Persian invasion, 504; Thrace and Macedonia conquered 496
Athens and Sparta resist the demands of the king of Persia 491
The Persians defeated at Marathon . . 28 Sept. 490
Xerxes invades Greece, but is checked at Thermopylæ by Leonidas . . . . . Aug. 480
Battle of Salamis (*which see*) . . . 20 Oct. „
Mardonius defeated and slain at Platæa; Persian fleet destroyed at Mycale . . . 22 Sept. 479
Battle of Eurymedon (end of Persian war) . . . 469
Athens begins to tyrannise over Greece . . . 459
The sacred war begun 448
War between Corinth and its colony Corcyra . . 435
Leads to the Peloponnesian war 431-404
Disastrous Athenian expedition to Syracuse 415-413
Retreat of the 10,000 under Xenophon . . . 400
Death of Socrates 399
The sea-fight at Cnidus 394
The peace of Antalcidas 387
Rise and fall of the Theban power in Greece . 370-360
Battle of Mantinea; death of Epaminondas . . 362
Ambitious designs of Philip of Macedon . . . 353
Sacred wars ended by Philip, who takes all the cities of the Phoceans 346
Athens and allies declare war against Philip, 340; who totally defeats them at Chæronea (*which see*) 338
Philip assassinated by Pausanias 336
Alexander, his son, subdues the Athenians, and destroys Thebes . . . . „
Alexander conquers the Persian empire, 334-331; dies 323
Greece harassed by his successors; the Ætolian and Achaian leagues revived 284-280
Greece invaded by the Gauls, 280; they are defeated at Delphi, 279; and expelled 277
Dissensions lead to Roman intervention . . . 200
Macedon made a Roman province, after the defeat of the last king, Perseus, at Pydna 168
Greece conquered by Mummius and made a Roman province 147-146

* * * * * * * *

Greece visited and favoured by Augustus, 21 B.C.; and by Hadrian . . . . . . A.D. 122-133
Invaded by Alaric 396
Plundered by the Normans of Sicily 1146
Conquered by the Latins, and subdivided into small governments 1204
The Turks under Mahomet II. conquer Athens and part of Greece 1456
The Venetians hold Athens and the Morea . . . 1466
Greece mainly subject to the Turks . . . 1540
The Morea held by Venice, 1687; till taken by the Turks 1715
Great struggle for independence with Russian help; 1770 *et seq.*, fruitless insurrection of the Suliotes 1803
Secret Society, the Hetairia, established . . . 1815
Insurrection in Moldavia and Wallachia, in which the Greeks join, suppressed 1821
Proclamation of prince Alexander to shake off the Turkish yoke, March, 1821; he raised the standard of the cross against the crescent and the war of independence began . . 6 April, „
The Greek patriarch put to death at Constantinople 23 April, „
The Morea gained by the Greeks . . . June, „
Missolonghi taken by Greeks . . . . Nov. „
Independence of Greece proclaimed . 27 Jan. 1822
Siege of Corinth by the Turks . . . Jan. „
Bombardment of Scio; its capture; most horrible massacre recorded in modern history (see *Chios*) 11 April, „
The Greeks victors at Thermopylæ, &c. 13 July, „
Massacre at Cyprus . . . . . . July, „
Corinth taken . . . . 16 Sept. „
National congress at Argos . . . 10 April, 1823
Victories of Marco Botzaris, June; killed 10 Aug. „
Lord Byron lands in Greece to devote himself to its cause . . . . Aug. „
First Greek loan . . . . Feb. 1824
Death of lord Byron at Missolonghi . . 19 April, „
Defeat of the capitan pacha, at Samos . 16 Aug. „
Provisional government of Greece set up 12 Oct. „
Ibrahim Pacha lands, 25 Feb.; takes Navarino, 23 May; Tripolitza . . . . . 30 June, 1825
The Greek fleet defeats the capitan pacha June, „
The provisional government invite the protection of England . . . . July, „
Ibrahim Pacha takes Missolonghi by assault, after a long and heroic defence . . . 23 April, 1826
70,000*l.* raised in Europe for the Greeks . . „
Reschid Pacha takes Athens . . . 2 June, 1827
Egypto-Turkish fleet destroyed at Navarino, 20 Oct. „
Treaty of London, between Great Britain, Russia, and France, on behalf of Greece, signed 6 July, „
Count Capo d'Istria president of Greece 18 Jan. 1828
The Panhellenion or Grand Council of State established . . . . 2 Feb. „
National bank founded . . . . . 14 Feb. „
Convention of the viceroy of Egypt with sir Edward Codrington, for the evacuation of the Morea, and delivery of captives . . . . . 6 Aug. „
Patras, Navarino, and Modon surrender to the French . . . . 6 Oct. „
The Turks evacuate the Morea . . . . Oct. „
Missolonghi surrendered to Greece . . 16 May, 1829
Greek National Assembly commences its sittings at Argos . . . . 23 July, „
The Porte acknowledges the independence of Greece by the treaty of Adrianople . 14 Sept. „
Prince Leopold declines the sovereignty 21 May, 1830
Count Capo d'Istria, president of Greece, assassinated by the brother and son of Mavromichaelis, a Mainote chief whom he had imprisoned, 9 Oct. 1831
The assassins immured within close brick walls, built around them up to their chins, and supplied with food until they died . . 29 Oct. „
Otho of Bavaria made king of Greece by a convention signed . . . . 7 May, 1832
Colocotroni's conspiracy . . . . . Sept. „
He is condemned but spared . . . 7 June, 1834
Otho I. assumes the government . . 1 June, 1835
University at Athens established, 1837; building commenced 1839
A bloodless revolution at Athens is consummated, establishing a new constitution, enforcing ministerial responsibility and national representation, 14 Sept. 1843
The king accepts the new constitution 16 March, 1844

Admiral Parker, in command of the British Mediterranean fleet, blockades the harbour of the Piræus, the Greek government having refused the payment of moneys due to British subjects, and to surrender the islands of Sapienza and Caprera, 18 Jan. 1850
France interposes her good offices, and the blockade is discontinued . . . . . 1 March, „
Negotiations terminate, and the blockade of Athens is renewed . . . . 25 April, „
Dispute with France accommodated . 21 June, „
Insurrections against Turkey in Thessaly and Epirus, favoured by the Greek court, Jan. and Feb.; lead to a rupture between Greece and Turkey, 28 March, 1854
After many remonstrances, the English and French governments send troops which arrive at the Piræus; change of ministry ensues, and the king promises to observe a strict neutrality, 25, 26 May, „
A newspaper in the modern Greek language printed in London, beginning . . . . 9 July, 1860
Great Britain, France, and Russia remonstrate with the Greek government respecting its debts, 18 Oct. „
Agitation in the Ionian isles for annexation to Greece; the parliament prorogued . . March, 1861
The king retires to Bavaria . . . . July, „
Attempted assassination of the queen by Darios, an insane student . . . . . . 18 Sept. „
Great earthquake in the Peloponnesus . 26 Dec. „
Leopold of Bavaria proposed as heir to the throne, Jan. 1862
Military revolt begins at Nauplia . . 13 Feb. „
Blockade of the coast decreed . . . 9 March, „
The insurgents demand reforms and a new succession to the throne . . . . . . April, „
The royal troops enter the citadel of Nauplia; insurgents removed . . . . . 25 April, „
Change of ministry: Colocotroni becomes premier, 7 June, „
Insurrection begins at Patras and Missolonghi, 17 Oct.; a provisional government, established at Athens, deposes the king, 23 Oct.; he and the queen flee; arrive at Corfu, 27 Oct.; the European powers neutral; general submission to provisional government . . . . . . 31 Oct. „
Great demonstrations in favour of prince Alfred of Great Britain, who is proclaimed king at Lamia in Phthiotis, 22 Nov.; great excitement in his favour at Athens . . . . 23 Nov. „
The provisional government establish universal suffrage . . . . 4 Dec. „
The national assembly meets at Athens . 22 Dec. „
The national assembly elects M. Balbis president, 29 Jan.; and declares prince Alfred king of Greece by 230,016 out of 241,202 votes . 3 Feb. 1863
Military revolt of lieut. Canaris against Bulgaris and others, who resign, 20 Feb.; a new ministry appointed under Balbis . . . . . . 23 Feb. „
The assembly decides to offer the crown to prince William of Schleswig-Holstein, 18 March; proclaim him as king George I. . . . 30 March, „
Protocol between the three protecting powers, France, England, and Russia, signed at London, consenting to the offer of the crown on condition of the annexation of the Ionian isles to Greece, 5 June, „
The king of Denmark accepts from the aged admiral Canaris the Greek crown for prince William, whom he advises to adhere to the constitution and gain the love of his people . . 6 June, „
Military revolt at Athens, suppressed 30 June—9 July, „
The king arrives at Athens, 30 Oct.; takes the oath to the constitution . . . . . . 31 Oct. „
The Balbis ministry formed . . . 28 April, 1864
Protocol annexing the Ionian isles to Greece, signed by M. Zaïmis and sir H. Storks, 28 May; the Greek troops occupy Corfu, 2 June; the king arrives there . . . . 6 June, „
New ministry under Canaris formed . 7 Aug. „
The assembly recognises the debt of 1824 5 Sept. „
After much delay, and a remonstrance from the king, 19 Oct. a new constitution (with no upper-house) is passed by the assembly, 1 Nov.; and accepted by the king . . . . 28 Nov. „
New ministry under Coumoundouros 29 March, 1864
The anniversary of the beginning of the war of independence (6 April, 1821) kept with enthusiasm, 6 April, „
The king visits the eastern provinces; general tranquillity . . . . 20 April, „
The king opens chamber of deputies . 9 June, „
Death of Alexander Mavrocordato, one of the early patriots . . . . 18 Aug. „
The king gives up one-third of his civil list to relieve the treasury . . . . . 25 Sept. „
An economical financial policy proposed; a new ministry formed . . . . Nov. „
Brigandage prevails; frequent ministerial changes under Deligeorges, Coumoundouros, Bulgaris, and Roufos . . . . . . Oct. 1865—June, 1866
New ministry under Bulgaris and Roufos, 23 Jan. „
Chambers vote payments to themselves; suddenly dissolved by the king . . . . . . 3 Feb. „
Great agitation in favour of the Cretan insurrection (see *Candia*) . . . . . . Aug.-Dec. „
New ministry headed by Coumoundouros . Jan. 1867
Manifesto of the so-named "Greek nation," issued at Paris . . . . 19 April, „
Great sympathy with the insurrection in Candia; the blockade run by Greek vessels with volunteers, arms, and provisions . . April *et seq.* „
Marriage of the king with the grandduchess Olga of Russia . . . . 27 Oct. „
Their cordial reception at Athens . 24 Nov. „
New ministry under Moraïtinis, 1 Jan.; under Bulgaris . . . . Feb. 1868
Constantine, duke of Sparta, heir to the crown, born . . . . 2 Aug. „
Greek vessel *Enosis* fires on Turkish vessels and enters port of Syra . . . . . 14 Dec. „
Rupture between Turkey and Greece in consequence of Greek armed intervention in Candia (*which see*) . . . . Dec. „
After a conference of representatives of the Western powers at Paris, Jan., their requisitions were accepted, and diplomatic relations between Turkey and Greece resumed . . 26 Feb. 1869
Prince and princess of Wales visit Athens, 19 April, „
Law authorising the cutting the isthmus of Corinth passed . . . . 7 Nov. „
New ministry under M. Zaïmis . . . 9 Jan. 1870
Concession to cut a canal through the isthmus of Corinth granted to a French company . April, „
Lord and lady Muncaster and a party of English travellers seized by brigands at Oropos, near Marathon; lord Muncaster and the ladies sent to treat; 25,000*l.* demanded as ransom, with free pardon . . . . 11 April, „
The brigands retreating, and surrounded by troops, kill Mr. Vyner, Mr. Lloyd, Mr. Herbert, and the count de Boyl . . . . 21 April, „
Great excitement; the king shows great liberality; but many influential persons are charged with connivance at brigandage . . May, June, „
Several brigands killed; seven captured, tried and condemned, 23 May; five executed . 20 June, „
A new ministry under M. Deligeorges . 19 July, „
Greek college opened at Bayswater, London, W. 1 Oct. „
Decree for suppression of brigandage issued Oct. „
Two gentlemen carried off . . . . 11 Oct. „
A new ministry under M. Coumoundouros 22 Dec. „
Coumoundouros ministry resigns . . 6 Nov. 1871
Succeeded by Zaïmis . . . . . 8 Nov. „
Bulgaris minister, 7 Jan.; resigns; Deligeorges again minister . . . . . . 26 July, 1872
The Laurium mines of lead, zinc, &c., were purchased by MM. Roux and Serpieri and a company, 1863; and worked profitably; roads being made and a village built. The mines having been heavily taxed and scoriæ claimed by the government, loss ensued; the company's offer to sell the mines to the government was accepted, but payment evaded by the legislature. Hence arose disputes with France and Italy, and ministerial changes in Greece . . . . autumn, „
Speech of the king to the legislature, announcing formation of roads and other improvements. [The Laurium mines had been purchased by M. Syngros, a Greek capitalist, supported by the banks] . . . . 25 Feb. 1873

52nd anniversary of Greek independence kept in London . . . . 5 April, 1873
The university at Athens closed, through insubordination of the students. . . . Dec. ,,
New cabinet under Bulgaris, 22 Feb.; resigns, 27 April; resumes office . . . 7 May, 1874
Tricoupi minister, 8 May; dissolves chambers, 31 May; meet . . . . Aug. 1875
Greece neutral in regard to insurrection in the Herzegovina . . . . July—Sept. ,,
The prince of Wales warmly received at Athens, 18 Oct. ,,
New ministry under Coumoundouros, about 27 Oct. ,,
Several ex-ministers fined for extortion from bishops and others on appointment . . April, 1876
The king and queen travelling in England in July; at the Crystal palace . . . 19 July, ,,
Greece neutral in the Servian war . . July, ,,
Deligeorges forms a ministry, 8 Dec.; replaced by Zaimis and Coumoundouros . . 10 Dec. ,,
Deligeorges prime minister, 10 March—28 May; succeeded by a coalition ministry, 29 May; reformed under the aged Canaris . . 3 June, 1877
National excitement for war allayed by the king, 29 May, ,,
Discovery of relics at Spata near Athens; tombs containing bones, precious metal ornaments, &c. (removed to Athens by M. Stamataki) about 1 July, ,,
Revival of the Theban "sacred band," instituted by Epaminondas (to be 1000 instead of 300) about July, ,,
Death of the aged Canaris, 14 Sept.; the king takes his place as president . . . 14 Sept. ,,
British and Turkish governments remonstrate with Greece for apparently arming against Turkey, Sept., Oct. ,,
Death of Bulgaris, statesman, about . 10 Jan. 1878
New ministry under Coumoundouros . . 23 Jan. ,,
Insurrection in Thessaly against Turks, 28 Jan.; 10,000 Greeks enter the country, retire at the armistice . . . . . early in Feb. ,,
Insurrection struggling; battles at Macrinitza, 28, 29 March; Mr. C. Ogle, *Times* correspondent, killed by Turks (investigation led to no result) 29 March, ,,
Insurrection closed through British intervention; announced . . . . . 6 May, ,,
Greece disappointed by the Berlin treaty, 13 July: rectification of the frontiers by the sultan, proposed about . . . . . 24 July, ,,
Safvet Pacha's despatch resisting the claims for Greece . . . . . . 8 Aug. ,,
New ministry under Tricoupi . . . 31 Oct. ,,
Defeated in assembly, 4 Nov.; Coumoundouros forms a ministry . . . . 7-10 Nov. ,,
Recruiting law for the army (all men between 21 and 40 liable) . . . . . Nov. ,,
Death of Deligeorges, late minister . 26 May, 1879
Monument of Mr. Ogle set up at Athens . Aug. ,,
Recruiting law came into force . . . 1 Jan. 1880
Crisis; Coumoundouros remains . 28 Jan. ,,
Tricoupis ministry formed . . 22 March, ,,
Berlin conference to propose settlement of the Turkish and Greek frontiers, meets . 16 June, ,,
The king visits England; receives freedom of London, 16 June; leaves . . . 5 July, ,,
Order for mobilisation of the army signed, 5 Aug. ,,
The king and queen arrive at Athens after a long European tour; national feeling warlike; Thessaly and Epirus demanded . . 17 Oct. ,,
King's speech opening parliament; moderate and firm . . . . 21 Oct. ,,
Tricoupis ministry defeated; resigns . 22 Oct. ,,
Coumoundouros forms a ministry . . 25 Oct. ,,
Much discussion with negotiations respecting Greek and Turkish frontiers, (see *Turkey*), Oct. 1880—May, 1881
Convention between Turkey and Greece agreed to at Constantinople; Thessaly ceded to Greece, 24 May; signed . . . . . 2 July, ,,
Carried into effect; Greek flag raised in Arta, 6 July, ,,
The parliament dissolved by the king . 4 Nov. ,,
New ministry under Tricoupi . . 15 March, 1882
Cutting of the Isthmus of Corinth begun (see *Corinth*) . . . . 5 May, ,,
Frontier disputes in Thessaly, between Greeks and Turks, at Navantyk, near Derbend, Bosnia, about 26 Aug ,,
Settlement . . . . 9 Nov. 1882
Death of the statesman Coumoundouros, much lamented . . . . . 9 March, 1883
Improved finances; good budget, announced March, 1884
Tricoupis ministry resigns, 17 Feb.; M. Delyannis unsuccessful; M. Tricoupi resumes office 21 Feb. 1885
Chamber dissolved . . . . . 23 Feb. ,,
Railway between Athens and Corinth opened 15 April, ,,
Tricoupis ministry resigns through minority in elections about 20 April; Delyannis ministry formed . . . . 1 May, ,,
Enthusiastic military movements consequent upon the *coup d'état* in Roumelia . . . Oct. ,,
Vote for loan of 1,200,000*l*. . . . 7 Nov. ,,
Increased warlike demonstration; British intervention supported by the great powers, about 23 Jan.; foreign ironclads sent to Suda bay, Crete . . . . . . 30 Jan. *et seq.* ,,
Great discovery of statuary, &c., near the Acropolis, Athens . . . . ,,
National fête to commemorate declaration of independence in 1821, 6 April, 1884, and . 6 April, 1886
Proposed loan of about 800,000*l*. to raise the army from 85,000 to 110,000, about 14 April; and calling out of reserves . . . . . 19 April, ,,
Ultimatum of the powers calling upon Greece to disarm, delivered 26 April; special intervention of the French minister, about 26 April; inadequate reply of Greece . . . . . . 30 April, ,,
The British, Austrian, German, and Italian ambassadors leave Athens . . . 7 May, ,,
Greek troops sent to the front . 7, 8 May, ,,
Blockade of Greek ports notified and enforced, 8 May, ,,
Resignation of M. Delyannis, 9 May; M. Tricoupis declines to form a ministry, 10 May; M. Papamichalopoulos also declines, 11 May; provisional one formed by M. Valvis, 12 May; succeeded by M. Tricoupi . . 20 May, ,,
The king signs a decree for disarmament, 24 May, announced to the powers . . . 1 June ,,
Fighting at the outposts near Nezeres; the origin uncertain; 20, 21 May; about 200 killed and wounded; armistice agreed on, 24 May; formal declaration of the raising of the blockade, 7 June, ,,
Great electoral reform bill passed . 17 June, ,,
New chamber opened . . . . 3 Feb. 1887
The 100th anniversary of the birth of Lord Byron, celebrated at the Greek church, Bayswater, London, W. . . . . . . 22 Jan. 1888
The king returns to Athens after a foreign tour 8 Oct. ,,
Celebration of the 25th anniversary of the king's accession . . . . . . 31 Oct. ,,
National industrial exhibition at Athens opened by the king . . . . 1 Nov. ,,
Marriage of the princess Alexandra and the archduke Paul of Russia . . . . . 17 June, 1889
The king visits Paris . . . . 22 July, ,,
Marriage of the duke of Sparta and the princess Sophie of Prussia, at Athens, in the presence of the empress Frederick (her mother), the king and queen of Greece (his parents); the king and queen of Denmark, the German emperor and empress, the prince and princess of Wales, the czarewitch of Russia, and other relatives, 27 Oct. ,,
Prince Albert Victor of Wales at Athens, 17 April *et seq.* 1890
Formation of a "Young Greek party" at Athens, leader M. Ralli . . . . . Aug. ,,
Statues, &c., supposed to be the work of Phidias, at Rhamnus in Attica; discovered during excavations made for the Archæological school of Athens; reported . . . . . Oct. ,,
Elections; great majority for the opposition, 26 Oct. ,,
M. Tricoupi resigns, 28 Oct.; M. Delyannis forms a ministry, 3 Nov.; the new chamber opened by the king . . . . 10 Nov. ,,
Loan from C. J. Hambro & Son . . . ,,
By an avalanche near Trikkala, 25 persons are killed . . . . . . 29 Jan. 1891
Seventieth anniversary of Greek independence, celebrated . . . . . 6 April, ,,
Death of the grandduchess Paul (*see above*, 1889), 25 Sept. ,,

A commission exonerates M. Tricoupi from charges against him, about . . . . . 27 Dec. 1891
Mr. Egerton, appointed British minister at Athens, in succession to the hon. sir Edmund J. Monson, about 21 Jan. 1892
A fanatical mob attack and destroy the new Protestant church at the Piræus and ill-use the ministers and congregation; the riots suppressed by the military . . . . . . 14 Feb. ,,
The proposed impeachment of M. Tricoupi dropped by the government . . . 22 Feb. ,,
The king, for financial reasons, dismisses M. Delyannis; a new ministry formed by M. Constantopoulo, 1 March; the king is supported by the parliament, large retrenchments to be made, 5 March, ,,
Dissolution of the chamber, 25 March; new chamber elected; majority for M. Tricoupi, 15 May; he forms a new ministry . 22 June, ,,
Dispute respecting Greek schools in Bulgaria (*which see*) . . . . 1 Oct. *et seq.* ,,
Dispute with Roumania respecting a legacy to support Greek institutions, from Constantine Zappa and his brother, residents, declared illegal by Roumania; ineffectual negotiations; diplomatic rupture, ... about 15 Oct. ,,
[The Roumanian courts adjudge the property to the heirs, 16 March, 1893. Diplomatic relations renewed, July, 1896.]
Parliament opened, 10 Nov.; budget introduced; improved financial prospects, 30 Nov. 1892; report by major Fitzgerald Law, a British agent March, 1893
Visit of the princess of Wales, the duke of York, and her daughters . . . 10 April—2 May, ,,
Dr. C. Waldstein conducts explorations at the Heræum or temple of Hera, between Argos and Mycenæ . . . . April, ,,
Failure of attempts to procure a loan; the ministry resigns, 10 May; new ministry under M. Sotiropoulos . . . . 14 May, ,,
Convention for a loan of 4,000,000*l.* at 5 per cent. from Messrs. Hambro, of London, &c., signed, 11 June, ,,
Explosion of powder and dynamite magazines at Scaramanga, near Salamis; 16 deaths . 16 June, ,,
The Corinth canal opened (see *Corinth*, 1882 *et seq.*) 6 Aug. ,,
The chamber opened by the king; the convention for a loan from London reported unsuccessful, 8 Nov. ,,
Resignation of M. Sotiropoulos; succeeded by M. Tricoupi . . . . 11 Nov. ,,
Great financial embarrassment . . . . Nov. ,,
Bill annulling the funding loan and authorizing reduction of interest on foreign loans, passed 16 Dec. ,,
Bill for the readjustment of the Greek debt signed by the king, reported. . . . . 24 Dec. ,,
Introduction of budget; sanguine promises 2 Jan. 1894
The Russian fleet in the Piræus; left . 21 Jan. ,,
The government financial measures passed after much discussion, 20 March; the chamber prorogued . . . . 1 April, ,,
Destructive earthquakes at Thebes (*which see*), Livadia, Atalanti, Chalcis, and many villages; slight shocks at Athens; 207 deaths reported, 20 April—7 May; royal decree for a grant to relieve the sufferers, 29 April; much assistance given by Russian and British ships (see *Mansion House fund*) . . . . May, ,,
A military commission appointed to reconstruct villages, &c., May; 400 deaths reported up to 1 May, ,,
Negotiations between the government and foreign bondholders . . . . June, ,,
M. Tricoupi's proposals accepted by the French only . . . . 23 July, ,,
Increase of brigandage; a judge and officer killed; a band of brigands exterminated after a fight with the military, near Lamia, reported . 20 Sept. ,,
Meeting of the chamber . . . . . 8 Nov. ,,
Much opposition to proposed taxation; military called out to suppress rioting . 17 Jan. 1895
Resignation of the ministry (owing to the crown prince's interference to stop a conflict between the military and the people on 20 Jan.) 22 Jan. ,,
New ministry formed by M. Nikolaos Delyanni, 24 Jan. 1895
Elections; government majority . 29 April, ,,
A pension awarded to M. Tricoupi . . May, ,,
A large capture of brigands at Kravasara and Tsuka . . . . 4, 21 June, ,,
M. Zaimis elected president of the chamber; ministry resigns; a cabinet formed by M. Theodore Delyanni . . . . 11 June, ,,
Great distress; opposition to the currant tax, July, ,,
Budget passed, and parliament prorogued 1 Aug. ,,
Statue of lord Byron, the poet, with the inscription, "Hellas to Byron," at Athens, unveiled by the king . . . . 2 March, 1896
Budget passed by the chamber, 28 hours' debate 28 March, ,,
Revival of the Olympic games (*which see*) 6 April ,,
Death of M. Charilaos Tricoupi (born, 1832) at Cannes, 11 April; funeral at Athens, the king and royal family and about 50,000 persons present . . . . 23 April, ,,
Cretan refugees (9000) arrive at the Piræus, 2 Aug. ,,
Public meeting at Athens expressing gratitude to the powers for their intervention in Crete, 5 Sept. ,,
15 brigands and others executed at Athens, 11 Sept. ,,
The chamber opened . . . . . 5 Nov. ,,
The king issues a rescript for the increase and maintenance of the army; reported . 6 Dec. ,,
See *Inundations*, 23 Dec. 1896.
The queen lays the foundation stone for a new hostelry for students at Athens . . 14 Jan. 1897
Flotilla under prince George, sanctioned by parliament, sails for Crete . . . . 10 Feb. ,,
The government appeals to the powers . 11 Feb. ,,
Departure of troops for Crete from the Piræus, 14 Feb. ,,
Collective identical note from the powers received by the government, see *Crete* 23 Feb., 2 March.
Col. Smolenitz, war minister, resigns, succeeded by col. Metaxas . . . . . 3 March, ,,
Concentration of troops in Thessaly . 7 March, ,,
All night sitting of the cabinet 7, 8, March, ,,
Greek army estimated (80,000, with reserves), 10 March; mobilized . . . . 15 March, ,,
The crown prince arrives and takes the command at Larissa . . . . . 29 March, ,,
Turkish army under Edhem pasha (estimated at 150,000 men).
The powers declare that the aggressor on the Greek frontier in case of conflict shall be held responsible and derive no benefit . . . . 5 April, ,,
Independence day celebrated at Athens and by the army at Larissa . . . . 6 April, ,,
The porte protests to the powers against Greek aggression . . . . . . 10 April, ,,
Memorial of 100 liberal British M.P.'s expressing sympathy with Greece . . . . . April ,,
War declared by Turkey, with immediate action, 17 April; see *Greco-Turkish war*.
Great excitement and disorder at Athens, 27 April, ,,
The Delyanni ministry dismissed . . 28 April, ,,
M. Ralli forms a cabinet; chiefly followers of the late M. Tricoupi, M. Skouloudi, foreign minister, 29, 30 April, ,,
Great distress, destitution, and mortality amongst the refugees throughout Greece; much relief afforded by sir Edwin and lady Egerton, Mr. Noel, and others . . . . . June, July *et seq.* ,,
Patriotic fund for the payment of the war indemnity started, the bp. of Zante gives his jewelled mitre and 150*l.*, many others subscribe; announced . . . . 30 July, ,,
Peace negotiations: difficulties; lord Salisbury's proposals, Aug.; accepted . . 6 Sept. ,,
Peace preliminaries signed at Constantinople, 18 Sept.; presented to the government . 27 Sept. ,,
Vote of confidence in the government rejected 30 Sept.; ministry resigns, 1 Oct.; M. Zaimis, president of the chamber, forms a cabinet 3 Oct. ,,
Sir Edgar Vincent arrives, with financial proposals, Athens . . . . 7 Oct. ,,
Chamber opened, 11 Nov.; M. Roma elected president . . . . 16 Nov. ,,
Great distress and destitution amongst the refugees in Eubœa and elsewhere; much relief sent from England; reported . . . . Nov. ,,

Committee appointed to investigate the conduct of officers during the war, and the origin of the war, 24 Nov.; officers suspended . Dec. 1897
Treaty of peace signed at Constantinople, 4 Dec.; passed by the Greek chamber, 17 Dec.; ratified, 19 Dec. ,,
Draft of the law respecting the indemnity loan, 6,850,000*l.*, &c., signed by the foreign minister and the delegates of the three powers, England, France, and Russia, 12 Jan.; negotiations closed satisfactorily, 24 Feb.: bill passed 2 April; final payment of the war indemnity . . 10 July, 1898
Rifaat Bey, Turkish minister, received by the king, 3 Feb. ,,
Deaths from exposure, &c., of about 20,000 peasants in Thessaly during the last 6 months . 3 Feb. ,,
King George fired at by 2 men while driving near Athens with his daughter, princess Marie, 26 Feb. ,,
Karditzi, aged 35, member of an anti-dynastic society, formerly a soldier, gave himself up, and confessed his guilt, 28 Feb.; John Kyriakos, accomplice (22), arrested, 1 March; both executed, 9 May, ,,
International control (finances) bill, passed, 7 March; royal assent . . . . . 9 March, ,,
Famine and disease among the Cretan refugees in the Piræus; many deaths reported . 11 March, ,,
Withdrawal of Turkish troops from Thessaly, 14 May—6 June, ,,
International finance commission of control, Mr. (afterwards sir Edward) Law, chairman, meets, 15 May; succeeded by Mr. Vincent Corbett, 30 Dec. ,,
Tour of the king and queen in the Peloponnesus; warmly received at Patras, open an industrial exhibition, 21 May; return to Athens . 5 June, ,,
The forest of Zoria, between Patras and Œgium, burnt, enormous damage . . . . 23 July ,,
The cabinet resigns; reconstructed; the chamber dissolved . . . . . . 7–10 Nov. ,,
Settlement of Crete: see *Candia* . . 26 Nov. ,,
General election, 19 Feb.; the chamber opened by the king . . . . . . 16 March, 1899
Death of M. Andreas Syngros, philanthropist; bequeaths the bulk of his fortune to national objects, 25 Feb.; see *Athens* . . March, ,,
M. Tsamados (Tricoupist) elected president of the chamber; the Zainsis' ministry resigns, 12 April, ,,
M. Theotokis' cabinet formed; M. Simopoulos (finance), 14 April; chamber meets . 24 May, ,,
The government scheme of reforms in internal administration opposed in Thebes and elsewhere . . . . June, ,,
Suppression of the military police and other important reforms voted; session ends, 27 July, ,,
The king visits Paris . . . . 26 Oct. ,,
The chamber meets; budget (1900) and other measures passed . . . . . 11 Dec. ,,
Sympathy towards England, relating to Africa; stirring speeches of MM. Theotokis and Delyanni in the chamber, reported . . . . 12 Jan. 1900
The queen's thanks expressed by sir E. Egerton, British minister . . . . . . 5 Feb. ,,
Army reorganisation (by foreign officers) bill passed by the chamber . . . 24 March, ,,
The crown prince appointed commander-in-chief, 21 Sept. ,,
Navy increase bill passed by the chamber, 22 Dec. ,,
Commercial convention with Roumania concluded, early . . . . Jan. 1901
Budget passed after some days' and two nights' debate . . . . 13 Jan. ,,
Greek bronze statues discovered by divers near Cerigo (Cythera) . . . . . . Jan. ,,
Failure of currant and olive crops, great distress in W. Greece . . . . . . April, ,,
Stormy debate in the chamber; cabinet vote, 109–87; the ministry resigns, see *Athens*; M. Zaimis forms a cabinet, 24 Nov.; the chamber adjourns . . . . 26 Nov. ,,
Vote of confidence in the ministry carried 7 Feb. 1902
International financial commission's 4th annual report, issued . . . . about 14 April, ,,
Budget passed, after an all-night sitting; session closed . . . . . . 18, 21 April, ,,
M. Karapanos presents his collection of antiquities to the nation, reported . . . . 1 July, ,,
Revival of brigandage, popular sympathy with the outlaws, reported . . . . 23 July, 1902
Excavations near Andritizænas, a small temple of Pan discovered, reported . . . 11 Aug. ,,
Currant crop injured by storms and rains . Aug. ,,
Exportation of arms forbidden by decree, 11 Sept. ,,
Chamber dissolved by royal decree . . 3 Oct. ,,
Forest fires, suspected incendiarism, early Sept.; again at Pikermi, great damage . 9, 10 Oct. ,,
The king received by M. Loubet in Paris . 16 Oct. ,,
General election, ministry defeated . 30 Nov. ,,
New cabinet; M. Delyanni, premier and finance minister, justice *ad interim* . . . 6 Dec. ,,
The king opens the chamber . . . 22 Dec. ,,
Prince Mavrocordato, ex-minister, dies . 13 Feb. 1903
M. Ralli elected president of the chamber . 18 Feb. ,,
Budget: reduction of 9,000,000 drachmas in expenditure proposed by economies in departments of the public service . . . . . . 20 Feb. ,,
Conflict between the ministry and the court by introduction of army bills . . . mid March, ,,
Ministerial crisis, col. Lambritis resigns, 3 April, ,,
Convention granting monopoly of the currant trade for 20 years to an English syndicate, signed 25 May, ,,
International exhibition opened at Athens 3 June, ,,
Agitation over the subject of the currant monopoly, June *et seq.* ,,
The ministry defeated on a vote of confidence, 114–95, resigns . . . . . 25 June, ,,
M. Theotokis forms a cabinet . . 27 June, ,,
Delyannist cabinet formed with M. Ralli as prime minister; vote of confidence passed by the chamber; bill reducing the number of deputies from 234 to 198 passed . . . . 13 July, ,,
Earthquake shocks in Athens and throughout Greece . . . . 11 Aug. ,,
Popular excitement over municipal elections; riotous demonstration and fighting at Athens, 14 persons killed and wounded . . . 13 Sept. ,,
The old British cemetery at Corfu, by arrangements between the British and Greek governments in 1900, to come under the municipality of Corfu in . . . . Oct. ,,
Prince Andrew of Greece married to princess Alice of Battenberg, at Darmstadt, by rites of both the Lutheran and Greek churches . . 7 Oct. ,,

KINGS OF GREECE.

1832. Otho I., prince of Bavaria; born, 1 June, 1815; elected king, 7 May, 1832; under a regency till 1 June, 1835; married, 22 Nov. 1836, to Maria Frederica, daughter of the grand-duke of Oldenburg; deposed, 23 Oct. 1862; died in Bavaria, 26 July, 1867.

1863. George I. (son of Christian IX. of Denmark), king of the Hellenes; born 24 Dec. 1845; made king 5 June, takes the oath 31 Oct. 1863; declared of age, 27 June, 1863; married grand-duchess Olga of Russia, 27 Oct. 1867.

Heir: Constantine, duke of Sparta, born 2 Aug. 1868; married to the princess Sophie of Prussia, 27 Oct., 1889. *Issue*, George, born 19 July, 1890; Alexander, 1 Aug. 1893.

George, born 24 June, 1869; Nicolas, born 21 Jan. 1872; married the grand duchess Hélène Vladimirovna, 29 Aug. 1902; Marie-Madeleine, born 3 March, 1876; André, born 1 Feb. 1882; Christophe, born 10 Aug. 1888.

GREEK ARCHITECTURE, see *Architecture.*

GREEK CHURCH, or Eastern church, established in Russia and Greece, disowns the supremacy of the pope, and is strongly opposed to many of the doctrines and practices of the Roman church. The Greek orthodox confession of faith appeared in 1643; see *Fathers of the Church*. This church, in 1876, had 279 dignitaries, under the patriarch of Constantinople; 136 bishops, 66 in Russia, 24 in Greece, 15 in Jerusalem, 11 in Austria, &c. Russian church, 1895; 61 bishops, including metropolitans (St. Petersburg, Moscow, and Kieff), 15 archbishops, 38 vicar and 5 monastery bishops. In Russia, 73,000,000 Greek Catholics (1903).

Catechetical school at Alexandria (Origen, Clemens, &c.) 180-254
Rise of monachism . . . . . about 300
Foundation of the churches of Armenia, about 300; of Georgia or Iberia 318
First council of Nice (see *Councils*) 325
Rivalry between Rome and Constantinople begins about 340
Ulphilas preaches to the Goths . . . . about 376
Nestorius condemned at the council of Ephesus . 431
Monophysite controversy; churches of Egypt, Syria, and Armenia separate from the church of Constantinople 461
Close of the school of Athens; extinction of the Platonic theology 529
The Jacobite sect established in Syria by Jacobus Baradæus 541
The struggle with the Mahometans begins . . 634
The Maronite sect begins to prevail . about 676
The Paulicians severely persecuted . . . 690
Iconoclastic controversy begins . . . about 726
Pope Gregory II. excommunicates the emperor Leo, which leads to the separation of the Eastern (Greek) and Western (Roman) churches . . . 729
Image worship condemned 734
Foundation of the church in Russia: conversion of princess Olga, 955; of Vladimir 988
The Maronites join the Roman church . . . 1182
Re-union of Eastern and Western churches at the council of Lyons, 1274; again separated . . . 1277
Proposed union with the Church of England . . 1723
The patriarchate of Moscow established, 1582; suppressed in 1762
Successful drainage of lake Topolias (the ancient Cephissis and Copais), much land reclaimed and disease prevented . . . . . . 1881 *et seq.*
The archimandrite Nilos, representing Constantinople and 4 patriarchates, visits London on behalf of the Greek clergy in the Danubian principalities 1863
The pope's invitation to an œcumenical council, 8 Dec. 1869, firmly declined by the patriarch of Constantinople . . . . . . about 3 Oct. 1868
Letter from the patriarch Gregory to the archbishop of Canterbury acknowledging receipt of English prayer-book, and objecting to some of "39 Articles" . . . . . . dated 8 Oct. 1869
Greek church at Liverpool consecrated by an archbishop . . . . 16 Jan. 1870
A new church of S. Sophia consecrated by the archbishop of Corfu . . . . 5 Feb. 1882
Political reforms in Turkey affect privileges of the Greek church; see *Turkey*, 1883; new patriarch, Joachim IV. (archbishop of Dercos), not elected till 13 Oct.; ratified by the Porte 18 Oct. 1884; resigns . . . . Nov. 1886
Dionysius, bishop of Adrianople, elected patriarch 4 Feb. 1887
He resigns through disapproval of the appointment of Bulgarian bishops in Macedonia by the Turkish government, about 5 Aug.; after fruitless negotiations, the Œcumenical synod orders the closure of all the orthodox churches in Turkey, 15 Oct.; the sultan renews and defines former rights and privileges granted to the church, about 25 Oct.; this not accepted by the synod, 27 Oct.; churches generally continued closed . . . . Nov. 1890
Decision of the Turkish government respecting various disputed points, issued 2 Dec. 1890; the disputes ended; the patriarch remains, the churches re-opened . . . . . 6 Jan. 1891
Neophytos, archbishop of Nikopolis, elected patriarch in succession to Dionysius V. 8 Nov. ,,
See article *Pope*, 1894.
Dissensions between the Œcumenical patriarch and the holy synod . . . Jan.-Feb. 1897
Mgr. Constantine V. elected Œcumenical patriarch, head of the church . . . about 15 April, ,,
Count Leo Tolstoi, see *Socialism*, excommunicated; see *Times*, 19 March . . . . 9 April, 1901
Father Seraphim of the Saroff monastery (died 1833), canonised by the holy synod as a new saint . . . . March, 1903

GREEK EMPIRE, see *Eastern Empire*.

GREEK FIRE, a combustible composition (now unknown, but thought to have been principally naphtha), thrown from engines, said to have been invented by Callinicus, an engineer of Heliopolis, in Syria, in the 7th century, to destroy the Saracens' ships, which was effected by the general of the fleet of Constantine Pogonatus, and 30,000 men were killed. A so-called "Greek fire," probably a solution of phosphorus in bi-sulphide of carbon, was employed at the siege of Charleston, U.S., in Sept. 1863.

GREEK LANGUAGE. The study was revived in western Europe about 1450; in France, 1473; William Grocyn, or Grokeyn, an English professor of this language, introduced it at Oxford, about 1491, where he taught Erasmus, who himself taught it at Cambridge in 1510. *Wood's Athen. Oxon.* England has produced many eminent Greek scholars, of whom may be mentioned Richard Bentley, died 1742; professor Richard Porson, died 1808; Dr. Samuel Parr, died 1825; and Dr. Charles Burney, died 1817. "Society for promoting Hellenic Studies," formed 16 June, 1879. Modern Greek literature is now cultivated. See *Aristotelian* and *Egyptian Exploration.*

Homer flourished . . . . about B.C. 962-927
Hesiod . . . . about 850
Æsop 572
Anacreon . . . . . . about 559
Æschylus 525-456
Herodotus . . . . . . about 443
Pindar 522-439
Bacchylides . . . . about B.C. 470
Aristophanes 427
Euripides 480-406
Sophocles 495-405
Thucydides 470-404
Xenophon 443-359
Plato 429-347
Isocrates 436-338
Aristotle 384-322
Demosthenes 382-322
Menander . . . . . . about 321
Æschines 389-314
Theocritus . . . . . . about 272
Epicurus 342-270
Theophrastus 287
Archimedes 287-212
Polybius 207-122
Diodorus . . . . . B.C. 50—A.D. 13
Strabo 10
Dionysius Halicarnassus . . . about 30
Plutarch . . . . . . about 96
Epictetus . . . . . . about 118
Appian . . . . . . about 147
Arrian . . . . . . about 148
Athenæus . . . . . . about 194
Lucian . . . . . . about 120-200
Herodian . . . . . . about 204
Longinus . . . . . . dies 273
Julian, emperor 331-363

(See *Fathers*, and *Philosophy*.)

GREENBACKS, a name given, from the predominating colour of the ink, to notes, for a dollar and upwards, first issued by the United States government, in 1862. Notes for lower sums (even 3 cents) were termed "fractional currency." For *Greenbackers* see *United States*, 1878.

GREEN-BAG INQUIRY took its name from a *Green Bag*, full of documents of alleged seditions, laid before parliament by lord Sidmouth, 3 Feb. 1817. Secret committees presented their reports, 19 Feb.; and bills were brought in on the 21st to suspend the Habeas Corpus act, and prohibit seditious meetings, then frequent.

GREEN CLOTH, BOARD OF, in the department of the lord-steward of the household, included an ancient court (abolished in 1849), with jurisdiction of all offences committed in the verge of the court.

GREENLAND, an extensive Danish colony in North America, discovered by Icelanders, under Eric Raude, about 980, and named from its verdure. It was visited by Frobisher in 1576, and by John Davis, 1585. The first ship from England to Greenland was sent for the whale-fishery by the Muscovy company, 2 James I. 1604. In a voyage performed in 1630, eight men were left behind by accident, who suffered incredible hardships till the following year, when the company's ships brought them home. *Tindal*. The Greenland Fishing company was incorporated in 1693.—Hans Egede, a Danish missionary, founded a new colony, called *Godhaab*, or Good Hope, in 1720-3; and other missionary stations have been since established. Scoresby surveyed Greenland in 1821; and captain Graah, by order of the king of Denmark, in 1829-30. Population in 1878, about 9408; in 1888, 10,221; 1901, 10,516. Nordenskjöld and others advanced into the interior, and found nothing but mountainous ice and snow, July-Sept. 1883.

Dr. Fridtjof Nansen, Mr. Sverdrup, and two other Norwegians and two Lapps wearing snow shoes crossed Greenland from E. to W., amid great hardships, 17 July *et seq.* 1888, and arrived at Copenhagen, 21 May, 1889.

Dr. Nansen described his journey across Greenland at a meeting of the Royal Geographical soc. 24 June, 1889.

His first crossing of Greenland published Dec. 1890.

Lieut. Peary reports at Philadelphia the results of his exploration of N. Greenland, 1 Nov. 1892; his book published, Nov. 1893; other explorations and discoveries in 1893, 1895, and 1896.

Lieut. Amdrup explores the east coast up to 67° 22′ N.; new islets discovered; traces of extinct Eskimo tribes found and scientific collections made, &c.; expedition returns to Copenhagen, 12 Sept. 1899; explores and maps out hitherto unknown land from Cape Dalton, 69° 28′, to Aggas island, 67° 22′, 18 July—2 Sept. 1900; returns to Copenhagen, 4 Oct. 1900.

Paper, "Four years Arctic Exploration, 1898–1902," read by com. Peary before the Royal Geographical soc. 10 Nov. 1903.

GREENOCK (W. Scotland). Charters were granted in 1635 to John Shaw, and 1670 to his son sir John, of the barony of Greenock. It was a fishing station till 1697, when the Scottish Indian and African company resolved to erect salt-works in the Firth, and thus drew the attention of sir John Shaw, its superior, to its maritime advantages. It was made a burgh of barony in 1757, and a parliamentary burgh in 1832. The erection of the new quay was entrusted, about 1773, to James Watt, who was born here in 1736. The East India harbour was built 1805-19, and Victoria harbour 1846-50. James Watt docks opened by provost Shankland, 5 Aug. 1886. End of strike of iron shipbuilders (8 weeks), 24 Aug. 1891. The Globe sugar refinery burnt, damage about 25,000*l*., 14 Oct. 1896. Mr. Chamberlain speaks at town hall, 7 Oct. 1903. Population, 1891, 63,498; 1901, 67,645.

Dock fire, estimated damage 20,000*l*. . . 1 June, 1903

GREEN PARK (near Buckingham palace, London) forms a part of the ground enclosed by Henry VIII. in 1530, and is united to St. James's and Hyde-parks by the road named Constitution-hill. Over the arch at the entrance, the Wellington statue was placed in 1846. On the north side was a reservoir of the Chelsea water-works, filled up in 1856.

GREENWICH (Kent), anciently Grenawic, an ancient manor, near which the Danes murdered the archbishop Elphege, 1012. The *Hospital* stands on the site of a royal residence erected in the reign of Edward I. and much enlarged by his successors. Here were born Henry VIII., Mary and Elizabeth, and here Edward VI. died. Charles II. intended to build a new palace here, but erected one wing only. Returns one M.P. by act of 1885. Made a municipal borough by the act of 1899 (5 aldermen, 30 councillors). Pop. 1901, 185,149.

William III. and Mary converted the palace into a Royal hospital for seamen, 1694, and added new buildings, erected by Wren . . . . .

100 disabled seamen admitted 1750

The estates of the attainted earl of Derwentwater (beheaded in 1716) bestowed upon it . . . 1735

A charter granted to the commissioners 6 Dec. 1775

The chapel, the great dining-hall, and a large portion of the buildings appropriated to the pensioners, destroyed by fire . . . . . . 2 Jan. 1779

The chapel rebuilt 1789

Sixpence per month to be contributed by every seaman; the payment advanced to 1s. from . June, 1797

The payment abolished in 1829, and that of "the merchant seamen's" sixpence also in . . . 1834

The hospital had lodging for 2710 seamen and a revenue of about 150,000*l*. per annum . . . 1853

(*Greenwich Fair* was discontinued . . April, 1857)

The office of the commissioners was abolished . . 1865

Reported annual income, 155,532*l*., 1867; income, 168,305*l*., 1887-8; 199,000*l*., 1901; estimated 197,140*l*., 1902.

By an act of parliament, about 900 indoor pensioners received additions to their pensions, quitted the hospital, 1 Oct. 1865; henceforth to be used as an infirmary. All the remaining inmates, except 31 bedridden persons, had left the place . 1 Oct. 1869

The patients of the *Dreadnought* seamen's hospital removed here . . . . . . 13 April, 1870

Acts for the application of the revenues were passed in 1869-1872; amended by act passed . . . 1883

A part of the buildings appropriated for a naval college, opened . . . . . 1 Feb. 1873

Greenwich Royal Hospital Schools (on the industrial plan), opened under the auspices of Mr. Childers, 1870

Construction of great steamship ferry (on the American system) over the Thames, authorised by the commons; formally opened, 13 Feb. 1888; soon closed; re-opened middle of . . . 1892

Stone monument in memory of about 20,000 officers and men of the navy and marines, formerly inmates of the hospital, interred in the old burial ground, 1749–1869; unveiled by earl Spencer, 17 Feb. 1893

Bi-centenary of the hospital; 1,000 boys of the hospital schools reviewed by queen Victoria at Windsor . . . . 3 July, 1894

Choleraic epidemic in the workhouse; 8 deaths, 16 Oct. ,,

Martial Bourdin, a Frenchman, killed by an explosive in his pocket through falling, near the Observatory, 15 Feb.; funeral at Finchley; anarchists protected from the mob . 23 Feb. ,,

Greenwich hospital act passed, 25 July, 1890; amended. 1898

Remains of a Roman villa, &c., discovered in the park, reported . . . . . 19 March, 1902

GREENWICH OBSERVATORY, built at the solicitation of sir Jonas Moore and sir Christopher Wren, by Charles II., on the summit of Flamsteed-hill, so called from the first astronomer-royal. The building was founded, 10 Aug. 1675, and Flamsteed commenced his residence, 10 July, 1676. In 1852, an electric telegraph signal ball in the Strand was completed, and put in connection with Greenwich observatory. Greenwich recommended as the universal meridian by the Geodetic congress at Rome, Oct. 1883, and at an international conference at Washington, 13 Oct. 1884. Telegraphic communication completed between Greenwich and M'Gill college observatory, Montreal, 1890.

A new refracting telescope, 28 in. in aperture and 28 ft. long, erected, and enlargement of the new physical observatory 1893–94

Sir Henry Thompson offers 5000*l.* to provide a large photographic telescope, 26 in. in aperture and 22½ ft. focal length, March, 1894; the telescope, or, rather, a combination of telescopes, the largest hitherto possessed, erected . April, 1897
New observatory building, completed March, opened officially . . . . 3 June, 1899

ASTRONOMERS-ROYAL.

John Flamsteed 1675
Edmund Halley 1719
James Bradley 1742
Nathaniel Bliss 1762
Nevil Maskelyne 1765
John Pond 1811
George Biddell Airy (knt. 1872) 1835
(Under whose superintendence the apparatus was greatly increased and improved; he died, 2 Jan. 1892.)
Wm. Henry Mahoney Christie (K.C.B. 1897) Aug. 1881

GREGORIAN CALENDAR, see *Calendar*, and *New Style*.—Gregorian Chant received its name from pope Gregory I., who is said to have improved the Ambrosian chant, about 590. See *Chanting*.

Gregorian Modes, musical scales as set in order by pope Gregory the Great about 590. On these the ritual music of the western churches is founded.

GRENADA, a West India island, discovered by Columbus in 1498; settled by the French, 1650; captured by the British, 5 April, 1762; re-taken by the French, July, 1779; given up by them by treaty of Versailles, 3 Sept. 1783. Population in 1891, 53,209; 1901, 63,438; revenue 1901-02 70,009*l.* expenditure 65,490*l.* See *Granada, New Granada*, and *Windward Isles*.

GRENADE, an explosive missile, so named from *granada*, Spanish, invented in 1594. It is a small hollow globe, or ball, of iron, about two inches in diameter, which is filled with fine powder, and set on fire by a fusee at a touchhole.

GRENADIERS. The Grenadier corps was a company armed with a pouch of hand-grenades, established in France in 1667; and in England in 1685. *Brown.* See *Guards* and *Army*, 1890.

GRENELLE, see *Artesian Wells*.

GRENOBLE (the Roman Gratianopolis), S.E. France. Here Napoleon was received on his return from Elba, 8 March, 1815, and here he issued three decrees. Population in 1901, 68,052.

GRENVILLE ADMINISTRATIONS. The first succeeded the Bute administration, 8 April, 1763; and resigned in July, 1765.

George Grenville (born 1712, died 1770), *first lord of the treasury and chancellor of the exchequer*.
Earl Granville (succeeded by the duke of Bedford), *lord president*.
Duke of Marlborough, *privy seal*.
Earls of Halifax and Sandwich, *secretaries of state*.
Earl Gower, *lord chamberlain*.
Earl of Egmont, *admiralty*.
Marquis of Granby, *ordnance*.
Lord Holland (late Mr. Fox), *paymaster*.
Welbore Ellis, *secretary-at-war*.
Viscount Barrington, *treasurer of the navy*.
Lord Hillsborough, *first lord of trade*.
Lord Henley (afterwards earl of Northington), *lord chancellor*.
Duke of Rutland, lords North, Trevor, Hyde, &c.

Second Grenville administration, formed after the death of Mr. Pitt, on 23 Jan. 1806. From the ability of many of its members, their friends said it contained "*all the talents, wisdom, and ability of the country*," a term applied to it derisively by its opponents. The death of Mr. Fox, 13 Sept. 1806, led to changes, and eventually the cabinet resigned, 25 March, 1807:—

Lord Grenville, *first lord of the treasury*.
Lord Henry Petty (afterwards marquis of Lansdowne), *chancellor of the exchequer*.
Earl Fitzwilliam, *lord president*.
Viscount Sidmouth (late Mr. Addington), *privy seal*.
Charles James Fox, *foreign secretary*.
Earl Spencer, *home secretary*.
William Windham, *colonial secretary*.
Lord Erskine, *lord chancellor*.
Sir Charles Grey (afterwards viscount Howick and earl Grey), *admiralty*.
Lord Minto, *board of control*.
Lord Auckland, *board of trade*.
Lord Moira, *master general of the ordnance*.
R. B. Sheridan, *treasurer of the navy*.
Richard Fitzpatrick, &c.
Lord Ellenborough (*lord chief justice*) had a seat in the cabinet.

GRESHAM COLLEGE (London), established by sir Thomas Gresham in 1575, founder of the Royal Exchange. He left a portion of his property in trust to the city and the Mercers' company to endow this college for lectures in divinity, astronomy, music, geometry, civil law, physic, and rhetoric; he died 21 Nov. 1579. The lectures commenced in Gresham's house, near Broad-street, June, 1597 (where the founders of the Royal Society first met in 1645). The buildings were pulled down in 1768, and the Excise office erected on its site, the property having been acquired by the crown for an annuity of 500*l.* The lectures were then read in a room over the Royal Exchange for many years. On the rebuilding of the exchange, the Gresham committee erected the present building in Basinghall-street, which was designed by G. Smith, and opened for lectures, 2 Nov. 1843. It cost above 7000*l.* In 1871 the college acquired a valuable collection of books and pictures, bequeathed by Mrs. Hollier. Changes respecting the lectures were advocated in 1875, and some made in 1876.

The amalgamation of the university teaching extension society advocated by Mr. Goschen, 15 Oct. 1888
The proposal to make the college a teaching university for London was referred to a royal commission, March. Earl Cowper, chairman; first meeting, see *London University*, 1894 . 30 June, 1892

GRETNA GREEN (Dumfries, S. Scotland, near the border). Here runaway marriages were contracted for many years, as Scotch law ruled that an acknowledgment before witnesses made a legal marriage. John Paisley, a tobacconist, and termed a blacksmith, who officiated from 1760, died in 1814. His first residence was at Megg's hill, on the common or green betwixt Gretna and Springfield, to the last of which villages he removed in 1782. A man named Elliot was afterwards the principal officiating person. The general assembly, in 1826, in vain attempted to suppress this system; but an act of parliament, passed in 1856, made these marriages illegal after that year, unless one of the persons married had lived in Scotland 21 days.

GREY ADMINISTRATION succeeded the Wellington administration, which resigned 16 Nov. 1830. It carried the Parliamentary and Corporation Reform acts (*which see*), and terminated 9 July, 1834.

Earl Grey,* *first lord of the treasury*.
Lord Brougham, *lord chancellor*.
Viscount Althorpe, *chancellor of the exchequer*.
Marquis of Lansdowne, *president of the council*.
Earl of Durham, *privy seal*.
Viscounts Melbourne, Palmerston, and Goderich, *home, foreign, and colonial secretaries*.

* Born 13 March, 1764; M.P., as Charles Grey, in 1786; first lord of the admiralty and afterwards foreign secretary in 1806; resigned in 1806 on account of his favouring Roman catholic emancipation; died 17 July, 1845.

Sir James Graham, *admiralty*.
Lord Auckland and Mr. Charles Grant (afterwards, 1830, lord Glenelg), *boards of trade and control*.
Lord Holland, *chancellor of duchy of Lancaster*.
Lord John Russell, *paymaster of the forces*.
Duke of Richmond, earl of Carlisle, Mr. Wynne, &c.
E. G. Stanley (afterwards earl of Derby), *chief secretary for Ireland*, became *colonial secretary*, March, 1833.

GREY COAT HOSPITAL, Westminster, founded (for girls) 1698; reconstituted 1873.

GREY FRIARS, see *Christ's Hospital*.

GREYLADIES, a sisterhood, so named from the distinctive colour of their costume. Its members are self-supporting, pay their living expenses, and give their services to the diocese of Rochester, working chiefly in the parishes of the south of London. The "Greyladies" are not attached to any party in the English church. The bishop of Southwark founded the sisterhood, and their first house was dedicated by Dr. Randall Davidson, then bishop of Rochester, 2 Feb. 1893. At the present time (1903) the "Greyladies" have 5 houses with 41 members.

GREYTOWN, see *Mosquito Coast*.

GRIFFITH'S VALUATION of land in Ireland; that calculated by Mr. afterwards sir Richard Griffith (appointed commissioner in 1828) and published about 1850; 4th edition, 1855; much discussed, 1880-1.

GRIMM'S LAW of the transmutation of consonants in the Aryan family of languages; propounded by Jacob L. Grimm in his "History of the German Languages," in 1848.

	Labials.			Dentals.			Gutturals		
Greek, Latin, Sanskrit	*p*	*b*	*f*	*t*	*d*	*th*	*k*	*g*	*ch*
Gothic	*f*	*p*	*b*	*th*	*t*	*d*		*k*	
Old High German . .	*b* (*v*)	*f*	*p*	*d*	*z*	*t*	*g*	*ch*	*k*

EXAMPLES: Sanskrit, *pitri*; Greek and Latin, *pater*; Italian, *padre*; Spanish, *padre*; French, *père*; Gothic, *fadrein* (*pl.*); Old High German, *vatar*; English, *father*.

GRIMSBY or **GREAT GRIMSBY**, a seaport of Lincolnshire, on the Humber, the largest fishing port in the kingdom. The docks (about 350 acres) were constructed by the Manchester, Sheffield and Lincolnshire Railway Co., 1849-58. The church, in the Early English style, was restored in 1859. Population, 1851, 12,263; 1881, 45,351; 1901, 63,138.

A statue of the prince consort unveiled, 1879, and a public park opened in 1883
Trawlers' dispute *re* the employers' proposals to introduce a profit-sharing system with a guaranteed *minimum* rate of wage, opposed by the men, 1 July *et seq.* 1901
Riot at the docks; the offices of the Fishing Owners' federation sacked and set fire to by a mob of about 5000 men, 18 Sept. 1901; further rioting, troops called in, 19 Sept.; lord Yarborough's intervention partially successful, 27 Sept.; joint committee appointed, resumption of work on the owners' terms, pending the result of arbitration, agreed to, 2 Oct.; the ships go to sea, 7 Oct.; sir Edw. Fry's award issued, see *Times*, 24 Dec. 1901; further disputes, Sept.–Dec. 1902; officially closed . . . . . 12 Jan. 1903

GRIQUALAND, WEST and **EAST**, two districts in British South Africa, containing diamond fields. The first diamond was discovered in West Griqualand in March, 1867, and caused a great influx of immigrants from all nations, and the formation of many settlements. Diamonds value 12,000,000*l.* found there between 1871 and 1880; about 15,000,000*l.* between 1883 and 1887; 3,365,994*l.* in 1902. The district annexed to Cape Colony 27 Oct. 1871, incorporated with it in 1880. Kimberley, the capital, was founded and named after lord Kimberley (then col. sec., died 8 April, 1902) in 1871; for its fine defence against the Boers, 15 Oct. 1899-15 Feb. 1900, see *South African War*. Population in 1890, about 6,000 Europeans and 10,000 natives. GRIQUALAND EAST, between the Kaffir border and Southern Natal, was annexed to Cape Colony in 1875; population in 1888, 98,000.

By a tremendous explosion of stored dynamite near Kimberley, only two men were killed . . Jan. 1884
Kimberley was the site of the South African and International exhibition, opened by sir H. B. Loch, 8 Sept., not financially successful; closed 8 Dec. 1892
Col. Kekewich, the defender of Kimberley, 15 Oct. 1899-15 Feb. 1900, presented with a sword of honour, &c., 10 July, 1902; visit of Mr. Chamberlain . . . . 29-31 Jan. 1903

GRISONS, a Swiss canton; see *Caddee*. It was overrun by the French in 1798 and 1799. The ancient league was abolished, and the Grisons became a member of the Helvetic confederation, 19 Feb. 1803.

GRISSELL CASE, see *Parliament*, 1879-80.

GRIST-TAX (*imposta sul macinato*). Principle of the tax adopted by the Italian parliament, 1 April, 1868.

GROAT, from the Dutch *groat*, value of fourpence, was the largest silver coin in England until after 1351. Fourpenny pieces were coined in 1836 to the value of 70,884*l.*; in 1837, 16,038*l.*; discontinued since 1856.

GROCERS anciently meant "ingrossers or monopolisers," as appears by a statute 37 Edw. III. 1363: "Les marchauntz nomez engrossent totes maners de merchandises vendables." The Grocers' company, one of the twelve chief companies of London, was established in 1345, and incorporated in 1429.

The Grocers' and Shopkeepers' Licensing acts, passed in 1860 and 1861, authorise the sale by them of wine, spirits, and beer, in bottles; (No. 2 Ireland) act passed, 30 July, 1900.

GROCHOW, near Praga, a suburb of Warsaw. Here took place a desperate conflict between the Poles and Russians, 19, 20 Feb. 1831, the Poles remaining masters of the field of battle. The Russians shortly after retreated, having been foiled in their attempt to take Warsaw. They are said to have lost 7000 men, and the Poles 2000; see also *Poland*, 1861.

GROG, sea term for rum and water, derived its name from admiral Edw. Vernon, who wore grogram breeches, and was hence called "Old Grog." About 1745, he ordered his sailors to dilute their rum with water.*

GROSSER KURFÜRST, see *Wrecks*, 1878.

GROSVENOR GALLERY, &c., Bond-street, London, W., for the exhibition of modern pictures, erected by sir Coutts Lindsay, at a cost of about 100,000*l.*, supported by eminent artists, Aug. 1876; opened 1 May, 1877. The last regular exhibition in the Grosvenor gallery was that of the society of British Pastellists, opened 18 Oct. 1890; the building was afterwards solely occupied by the

* He did great service in the West Indies, by taking Portobello, Chagre, &c.; but by his disagreement with the commander of the land forces, the expedition against Carthagena, in 1741, is said to have failed. He was dismissed the service for writing two pamphlets attacking the admiralty; he died 30 Oct. 1757.

Grosvenor club, by whom pictures for sale were from time to time exhibited.

Differences in regard to management having arisen, a secession of subscribers ensued, who, headed by Messrs. Hallé and Comyns Carr, opened "the New Gallery," (*which see*) Regent Street 9 May, 1888

GROSVENOR GALLERY LIBRARY, opened 25 March, 1880.

GROUND GAME, see *Game*.

GUADALOUPE, a West India Island, discovered by Columbus in 1493. The French took possession of it in 1635, and colonised it in 1664. Taken by the English in 1759, and restored in 1763. Again taken by the English in 1779, 1794, and 1810. The allies, in order to allure the Swedes into the coalition against France, gave them this island. It was, however, by the consent of Sweden, restored to France at the peace in 1814. It was again taken by the British, 10 Aug. 1815, and restored to the French, July, 1816. Hundreds of houses burnt down, no loss of life, at Point-à-Pitre, 18 April, 1899 (attributed to incendiarism). Heavy fall of ashes here; see *Martinique*, 30, 31 Aug. 1902.

GUAD-EL-RAS (N. W. Africa). Here the Spaniards signally defeated the Moors, 23 March, 1860, after a severe conflict: general Prim manifested great bravery, for which he was ennobled. The preliminaries of peace were signed on the 25th.

GUANO or **HUANO** (the Peruvian term for manure), the excrement of sea-birds that swarm on the coasts of Peru and Bolivia, and of Africa and Australia. It is mentioned by Herrera in 1601, and Garcilasso stated that the birds were protected by the incas. Humboldt was one of the first by whom it was brought to Europe, in order to ascertain its value in agriculture. The importation of guano into the United Kingdom appears to have commenced in 1839. 283,000 tons were imported in 1845 (of which 207,679 tons came from the western coast of Africa); 243,016 tons in 1851 (of which 6522 tons came from Western Australia); 131,358 tons in 1864; 237,393 tons in 1865; 135,697 tons in 1866; 280,311 in 1870; 114,454 in 1875; 152,989 in 1877; 177,793 in 1878; 74,221 in 1883; 21,175 in 1887; 1888, 24,432; 1889, 28,604; 1890, 27,095; 1893, 18,311; 1896, 20,214; 1900, 33,636; 1901, 22,830.

GUARANTEES. The "Guarantee by Companies act," relating to the security by means of sureties required for persons employed in the public service, was passed 20 Aug. 1867 (30 & 31 Vict. c. 108).

GUARDIAN, a moderate high-church weekly journal, first published 21 Jan. 1846.

GUARDS. The custom of having guards is said to have been introduced by Saul, 1093 B.C.

Body guards were appointed to attend the kings of England, 1 Henry VII. 1485.

Horse Guards were raised 4 Edw. VI. 1550.

The *royal regiment of guards* was first raised by Charles II. in Flanders in 1656, colonel, lord Wentworth; another regiment was raised by colonel John Russell, 1660, under whom they were combined in 1665. The *Coldstream Guards*, raised by general Monk, were constituted the 2nd regiment in 1661; see *Coldstream*. These guards were the beginning of our standing army.

Gen. sir F. Wm. Hamilton's "History of the Grenadier Guards," an elaborate work, appeared 1874.

The Horse Grenadier guards first troop, raised in 1693, was commanded by general Cholmondeley; the second troop was raised in 1702, and was commanded by lord Forbes his corps was reduced in 1783, the officers retiring full pay. See *Army*, 1890.

GUARDS' INSTITUTE, Francis-street, Vauxhall-bridge road; reading and lecture rooms, &c., for all officers and soldiers in the metropolis; inaugurated by the duke of Cambridge, 11 July, 1867.

See *Horse Guards*, *Yeomen*, *National*, and *Imperial Guards*.

GUASTALLA, N. Italy, a city, near which the imperial army, commanded by the king of Sardinia, was defeated by the French, 19 Sept. 1734. The ancient duchy, long held by the dukes of Mantua, was seized by the emperor of Germany, 1746, and ceded to Parma, 1748. After having been comprised in the Italian republic, 1796, and subjected to other changes, it was annexed to Parma, 1815, and to Modena, 1847.

GUATEMALA. A republic in Central America, revolted from Spain, 1821, and declared independent, 21 March, 1847. Constitution settled, 2 Oct. 1859. President (1862), general Raphael Carrera, elected 1851; appointed for life, 1854; died 14 April, 1865; succeeded by Vincent Cerna, 3 May, 1865-9. Manuel Garcia Granedos, Dec. 1872; R. Barrios, 9 May, 1873; General Barillas, Jan. 1886. A war between Guatemala and San Salvador broke out in Jan. 1863; and on 16 June the troops of the latter were totally defeated. An insurrection became formidable, July, 1871. Alliance with Honduras against San Salvador, March, 1872. Population, 1887, 1,394,233; 1892, 1,510,000; 1900, 1,574,338. Capital, New Guatemala.

Col. Gonzales, commandant of San José de Guatemala, imprisoned, flogged, and nearly killed Mr. John Magee, the British consul, who was rescued by capt. Morse, of the Pacific Mail Company's steamer, *Arizona*, about 24 April, 1874.

Announced, that Gonzales had been sentenced to five years' imprisonment, and that Mr. Magee had received 10,000*l*. as compensation, Oct. 1874.

Plot to kill the president and his ministry; conspirators shot, 7 Nov. 1877.

General Barrios's proposal to re-unite the States of Central America under himself, as dictator, March; resisted; defeated and killed in a severe battle at Chalchuapa, 2 April, 1885; succeeded by Barillas; peace signed 16 April, 1885. M. L. Barillas, president, 15 March, 1886.

War with San Salvador, *which see*, July—27 Aug. 1890.

Revolt against president Barillas, suppressed, July–Aug. 1890.

The insurgent general and ex-minister Bunundia shot while resisting arrest on board the U.S. steamer *Acapulco*, 28 Aug.; his young daughter fails in her attempt to shoot the U.S. minister, Mizner, 1 Sept. 1890.

Peace with San Salvador signed . . . 17 Nov. 1890

Gen. Reina Barrios assumes office as president, 16 March, 1892; re-elected . . . Sept. 1897

Revolution in the west; insurgents in possession of Plaza San Marcos, reported . . . 10 Sept. „

Government victories in various places, reported 6 Oct.; order restored . . . . . 19 Oct. „

Pres. R. Barrios assassinated by Oscar Solinger, who is afterwards killed . . . . 8 Feb. 1898

Señor Morales, vice-president, succeeds, 9 Feb. 1898; his death reported . . . . Aug. „

New ministry formed, reported . . 12 Feb. „

Don Manuel Estrada Cabrera proclaimed president for the term 1899–1905 . . . . 25 Sept. „

Fearful earthquake, Quezaltenango and 8 towns destroyed; great loss of life . . . 18 April, 1902

Nat. relief fund started, pres. Cabrera, 20,000 dol. reported . . . . 27 May, „

Volcanic eruptions near Quezaltenango, 24, 25 Oct. „

Dispute with San Salvador settled . 30 March, 1903

GUEBRES (from the Arabic Kafir, unbeliever), a name given to the descendants of the fire-worshippers of Persia by their Arab conquerors, in the 7th century. They are now represented by the Parsees of Bombay, whither they migrated, see *Parsees*.

GUELPHIC ORDER of knighthood was instituted for Hanover by the prince regent, afterwards George IV., 12 Aug. 1815.

GUELPHS AND GHIBELINES, names given to the papal and imperial factions who destroyed the peace of Italy from the 12th to the end of the 15th century (the invasion of Charles VIII. of France in 1495). The origin of the names is ascribed to the contest for the imperial crown between Conrad of Hohenstaufen, duke of Swabia, lord of Wiblingen (hence *Ghibelin*), and Henry, nephew of Welf, or Guelf, duke of Bavaria, in 1138. The former was successful; but the popes and several Italian cities took the side of his rival. *Hie Guelf* and *Hie Gibelin* are said to have been used as war-cries in 1140, at a battle before Weinsberg, in Würtemberg, when Guelf of Bavaria was defeated by the emperor Conrad IV., who came to help the rival duke Leopold.* The Ghibelines were almost totally expelled from Italy in 1267, when Conradin, the last of the Hohenstaufens, was beheaded by Charles of Anjou. Guelph (of uncertain origin) is the popular name of the present royal family of England; see *Brunswick*.

The GUELPH EXHIBITION of pictures and objects of interest connected with the Royal House of Guelph, was opened in the New Gallery, Regent street, 31 Dec. 1890; closed, 9 April, 1891. The queen contributed greatly to the exhibition, and gave it its name.

Guelph Fund, see under *Cumberland*.

GUERNSEY, see *Jersey*. Major-gen. sir Edward Bulwer appointed lieut.-governor of Guernsey in succession to lt.-gen. Elkington, 1889; lt.-gen. N. Stevenson, 1894; maj.-gen. Saward, 1900; maj.-gen. B. Campbell, 1903.

Mrs. Neve, the king's oldest subject in the islands, died, aged 111 years . . . . . 4 April, 1903

GUERRILLA, Spanish, "a little war"; a term applied to the armed peasants who worried the French armies during the Peninsular war, 1808-14. The resistance of the dacoits to the British in Burmah was of guerrilla character.

GUEUX (beggars), a name given by the comte de Barlaimont to the 300 protestant deputies from the Low Countries, headed by Henri of Brederode and Louis of Nassau, who petitioned Margaret, governess of the Low Countries, to abolish the inquisition, 5 April, 1566. The deputies at once assumed the name as honourable, and immediately organised armed resistance to the government; see *Holland*.

GUIANA (N.E. coast of South America), discovered by Columbus in 1498, visited by the Spaniards in the 16th century; and explored by sir Walter Raleigh in 1596 and 1617. The French settlements here were formed in 1626-43; (protected posts established under officers, 1895;) and the Dutch, 1627-67. Demerara, Essequibo, and Berbice were ceded to Great Britain in 1814; see *Demerara*. Governor of British Guiana, John Scott, 1868; James Robert Longden, 1874; C. H. Kortright, 1876; sir Henry T. Irving, 1882; Viscount Gormanstown, Dec. 1887; sir C. Cameron Lees, April, 1893; sir Augustus W. L. Hemming, Dec. 1895; sir Walter J. Sendall, Nov. 1897; sir J. A. Swettenham, Sept. 1901. See *Venezuela*, 1895; *Brazil*, 1899.

Mr. Kaufmann discovered in the goldfields 633 valuable diamonds early in 1891.

Revolt in Dutch Guiana of the lower against the upper classes; much alarm, 13 May, 1891.

Goldfields industry increasingly prosperous; revenue of the colony, 555,774*l.*; expenditure, 599,616*l.*; imports, 1,341,709*l.*; exports, 1,899,457*l.*; population (estimated), 1900, 294,943.

Centenary of capture of colony from the Dutch, celebrated, Sept. 1903.

GUIDE-BOOKS for travellers are an English invention. Paterson's "British Itinerary," appeared in 1776; the last edition in 1840; when it was superseded by railway guides. Galignani's "Picture of Paris," 1814. Murray's "Handbook for Travellers on the Continent," the parent of the series, appeared in 1836. The publication of Carl and Fritz Baedeker's foreign guide-books began in 1828 with a handbook for the Rhine in German-French. This was followed by German handbooks for other parts of the continent, which owed much to Murray's handbooks, and included much original matter. The first English editions appeared in 1860. New editions of the illustrated guide-books, price 1*s.* each, published by Messrs. Ward, Lock, and Co., were issued 1894 *et seq.* See *Murray*.

GUIDES, a corps in the French army, especially charged with the protection of the person of the general, was formed by Bessières, under the direction of Bonaparte, who had been nearly carried off by the enemy, 30 May, 1796. Several squadrons of "guides" were formed in 1848, to guard the ministers. They formed a portion of the imperial guard till Sept. 1870.

GUIENNE, a French province, was part of the dominions of Henry II. in right of his wife Eleanor, 1152. Philip of France seized it in 1293, which led to war. It was alternately held by England and France till 1453, when John Talbot, earl of Shrewsbury, in vain attempted to retake it from the latter.

GUILDHALL (London) was built in 1411. When it was rebuilt (in 1669), after the great fire of 1666, no part of the ancient building remained, except the interior of the porch and the walls of the hall. The front was erected in 1789; and a new roof built, 1864-5. Beneath the west window are the colossal figures of Gog and Magog, said to represent a Saxon and an ancient Briton; replaced older ones, 1708; renewed, 1837. The hall can contain 7000 persons. Here were entertained the allied sovereigns in 1814, and Napoleon III., 19 April, 1855; and here the city industrial exhibition was held, 6 March, 1866, and the International Botanical banquet, 22 May, 1866. A memorial window, the gift of the cotton workers of Lancashire, to commemorate the munificence of the metropolis towards them in the famine of 1862-4, was uncovered, 15 July, 1868. The prince consort memorial window was unveiled in the presence of prince Arthur, 3 Nov. 1870. A library existed in the Guildhall in 1426, from which books were taken by the protector Somerset in the reign of Edward VI. A new library was founded, 2 June, 1824. This library is open to the public. The new handsome building by Horace Jones was opened by the lord chancellor Selborne, 5 Nov. 1872; see *London*. The law sittings which had been removed to the Royal law courts, were resumed in the Guildhall, 28 Oct. 1891, when the lord chief justice was received by the lord mayor; discontinued, Dec. 1894.

Art gallery opened 24 June, 1886.

Magnificent memorials by J. E. Price published, 1886.

Guildhall School of Music founded (62 pupils) 1880; 3600 pupils, 1893; new building on the Thames Embankment, 9 Dec. 1886; theatre, &c., opened by the lord mayor, 11 July, 1898.

---

* It is stated, traditionally, that the emperor condemned all the men to death, but permitted the women to bring out whatever they most valued; on which they carried out their husbands on their shoulders.

Visit of the German emperor and empress, 10 July, 1891.
Exhibition of pictures by British artists of the Victorian era, 1837 *et seq.*, opened 6 April, 1897; loan exhibition of French pictures, opened 4 June, 1898; Turner exhibition and his contemporaries, opened by the lord mayor, 10 April, 1899.
Over 1200 poor children entertained at dinner, 4000 hampers, &c., distributed, 3 Jan. 1899.
A picture of the Queen's visit to St. Paul's, 22 June, 1897, by A. C. Gow, R.A., gift of Mr. H. Clarke, unveiled by the lord mayor, 18 Oct. 1899.
Exhibition of pictures for the Artist's war fund, opened by the marchioness of Lorne, 22 Jan. 1900. Another of works of living British artists, 9 April—14 July; Spanish collection, 29 April—28 Aug. 1901; French and English, 18th century, 21 April—26 July, 1902; Dutch, 27 April, 1903.
Ex-pres. Kruger's state ox-wagon and a Boer "Long Tom" gun, from lord Kitchener, accepted, 2 Oct. 1902.
Mr. Chas. Gassiot's bequest of 112 English pictures, exhibition opened by the lord mayor, 1 Dec. 1902.

GUILDS. Associations of men of the same class or trade, formed for mutual aid and protection; in England, of Saxon origin, about the 8th century. In the middle ages there were religious, social, mercantile, and craft guilds. Some of the London livery companies were formed out of the merchant and craft guilds in the 13th century. See *Companies*.

The guild of Corpus Christi, York, had 14,800 members when a return respecting these guilds was ordered to be made, 1388.
The Early English Text society published the "Ordinances" of more than 100 guilds, 1870.
"The Gild Merchant," by Charles Gross, Ph.D., published in 1891, is a valuable work.
The "Guild of Literature and Art" (including sir E. B. Lytton, C. Dickens, and others) founded an institution (on ground given by sir E. B. Lytton, at Stevenage, consisting of thirteen dwellings, retreats for artists scholars, and men of letters, which were completed and inaugurated, 29 July, 1865.
The revival of religious guilds began in 1851, with that of St. Alban, which held its 21st anniversary 20 June, 1872.
Guilds Inquiry Commission, see Companies.

GUILLOTINE, an instrument for causing immediate and painless death, named after its supposed inventor, a physician named Joseph Ignatius Guillotin. In 1866 M. Dubois, of Amiens, stated that the idea only was due to Guillotin, who at a meeting of the legislative assembly in 1789 expressed an opinion that capital punishment should be the same for all classes. Accordingly, at the request of the assembly, M. Louis, secretary of the "Académie de Chirurgie," submitted to it on 20 March, 1792, a mode of capital punishment, "sure, quick, and uniform," which he had invented. The first person executed by it was a highway robber named Pelletier, on 25 April; and Dangremont was its first political victim, 21 Aug. following. Guillotin died in 1814. The guillotine at Paris was burnt by the communist insurgents, 7 April, 1871. A similar instrument (called the *Mannaia*) is said to have been used in Italy, at Halifax in England (see *Halifax*), and in Scotland, there called the Maiden and the Widow. See *Gagging*.

GUINEA (S. W. coast of Africa), said to have been visited by the Genoese about 1291, and by the French in 1364.

Portuguese settlements founded by prince Henry of Portugal; much gold found, 1481 *et seq.*
Other European traders arrive; successfully repelled, with cruelty, by the Portuguese till the arrival of the Dutch, 1595.
Sir John Hawkins, with adventurers, visits Guinea, carries off 300 negroes, whom he sells at Hispaniola, and returns home with a profitable cargo, 1503
Cape Coast Castle (*which see*) settled, 1610.
Slave trade with America carried on by English companies, 1618, *et seq.*
The Portuguese expelled by the Dutch, 1640.
Cape Coast Castle seized by the Dutch; recovered by adm. Holmes, who takes the Dutch settlements, which are retaken by Ruyter, who captures all the English settlements except Cape Coast Castle, 1663–5.
The Dutch settlements declined during the war with Napoleon; all ceded to Great Britain; signed by treaty, Feb. 1872.
War with Ashantees (*which see*), 1824 *et seq.*
Gold Coast colony (*which see*), formed 1874.
French Guinea constituted a colony, 17 March, 1893.

GUINEAS, English gold coin, so named from having been first coined of gold brought by the African company from the coast of Guinea in 1663, valued then at 20*s.*; but worth 30*s.* in 1695. Reduced at various times; in 1717 to 21*s.* In 1810 guineas were sold for 22*s.* 6*d.*; in 1816, for 27*s.* In 1811 an act was passed forbidding their exportation, and their sale at a price above the current value, 21*s.* The first guineas bore the impression of an elephant, having been coined of this African gold. Since the issue of sovereigns, 1 July, 1817, guineas have not been coined.

GUINEGATE, BATTLES OF, 11 July, 1302, and 16 Aug. 1513. See *Spurs*.

GUINNESS TRUST, see *Artisans*.

GUISE, a French ducal family:—

Claude of Lorraine, first duke, a brave warrior, favoured by Francis I.; died . . . . April, 1550
Francis, the great general, born, 1519; assassinated, 24 Feb. 1563
Henry, head of the Catholic league; born 1550; revenged his father's death; assassinated by order of Henry III. . . . . . . 23 Dec. 1588
Charles, first opposed, and then submitted to, Henry IV.; died 1640
Henry died without issue 1664

GULLIVER'S TRAVELS, by Dean Swift, first published 1726-7.

GUN, see *Artillery, Cannon, Fire-arms.*—GUN-CLUB, for pigeon-shooting, founded by sir Gilbert East, in 1862, had 200 members, noblemen and gentlemen, in July, 1867.

GUN-COTTON, a highly explosive substance, invented by professor Schönbein, of Basel, and made known in 1846. It is purified cotton, steeped in a mixture of equal parts of nitric acid and sulphuric acid, and afterwards dried, retaining the appearance of cotton wool. See *Collodion*. Its nature was known to Braconnot and Pelouze.

The diet of Frankfort voted, 3 Oct. 1846, a recompense of 100,000 florins to professor Schönbein and Dr. Bœttger, as the inventors of the cotton powder, provided the authorities of Mayence, after seeing it tried, pronounced it superior to gunpowder as an explosive.
Improvements were made in the manufacture of gun-cotton by an Austrian officer, Baron von Lenk, about 1852, and it was tried by a part of the Austrian army in 1855, but did not obtain favour.
In 1862 details of the manufacture were communicated by the Austrian government to our own government, and Mr. (late sir Frederick) Abel, our war-office chemist, was directed to experiment on the constitution and desirability of gun-cotton. The British Association also appointed a scientific committee to consider its merits. A complete decision was not arrived at.
The first trial of English-made gun-cotton was made in the spring of 1864, at the manufactory at Stowmarket, Suffolk, by Messrs. Prentice.
There was manufactured, by a company, the "patent safety gun-cotton," according to Mr. Abel's patent (including the pulping, compressing, and wet processes), based on researches commenced in 1866. The cotton was said to be explosive by detonation, and not by ignition. A great explosion took place at Stowmarket;

24 persons were killed (including A. E. H. and W. R. Prentice, managers); about 60 were dreadfully wounded, and nearly the whole town was destroyed as if by a bombardment, 11 Aug. 1871.

The verdict at the inquest attributed the explosion to the culpable "addition of sulphuric acid to the gun-cotton subsequent to its passing the tests required by government," 6 Sept. 1871.

A government commission, appointed in Sept. to consider the manufacture and use of gun-cotton, reported in favour of both, with special regard to compressed gun-cotton, 13 Dec. 1871.

Another report recommended this gun-cotton to be stored wet, with drying apparatus near; and to be kept in slighter boxes, 25 July, 1872.

Mr. E. O. Brown, of the war department, Woolwich, discovers that wet gun-cotton can be exploded by concussion by a detonating fuse, about Nov. 1872.

It is used as an explosive agent in mining, &c.

GUN-CLOTH, made on a similar principle, was patented by Mr. W. A. Dixon, about 1866.

COTTON-GUNPOWDER, patented by Mr. R. Punshon, 1871. A modified form was tried and reported successful, near Faversham, 3 Feb. 1875. See *Ivory*.

Fire at the Cotton powder works near Faversham; estimated damage, 6000*l.* 1 March, 1896.

GUNDAMUK, see *Gandamuk*.

GUN LICENCE ACT, passed 9 Aug. 1870;

annual licence, 10*s*. Licences issued: year 1876-7, 77,068; 1877-8, 75,571; 1880-1, 72,834; 1901-2, 76,807. See under *Game Laws*, 1883.

GUNPOWDER.

The invention of gunpowder is generally ascribed to Bertholdus or Michael Schwartz, a Cordelier monk of Goslar, south of Brunswick, in Germany, about 1320. But many writers maintain that it was known much earlier in various parts of the world. Some say that the Chinese and Hindoos possessed it centuries before. Its composition, moreover, is expressly mentioned by Roger Bacon, in his treatise *De Nullitate Magiæ*. He died in 1292 or 1294. Various substitutes for gunpowder have been recently invented, such as the white gunpowder of Mr. Horsley and Dr. Ehrhardt, and gun-paper by Mr. Hochstödten. A new gunpowder by M. Newmayer, of Toya, near Leipsic, was discussed in Nov. 1866. "Pellet gunpowder" was ordered to be used in gun-charges in the army, March, 1868. An act to amend the law concerning the making, keeping, and carriage of gunpowder, &c. was passed 28 Aug. 1860, and other acts since. See *Birmingham*, 1870. In May, 1872, a company was formed to manufacture Mr. R. Punshon's patent cotton-gunpowder, asserted to be very safe and controllable. The manufacture of the German "brown" or "cocoa" powder was set up at Chilworth in Surrey, 1886. See *Chronoscope*.

The use of gunpowder was denounced by Ariosto, 1516; by Jean Marot, 1532; by Cervantes, 1604; termed "villanous salt-petre" by Shakspeare, about 1598.

ENGLISH WAR GUNPOWDER: 75 parts nitrate of potash (saltpetre); 10 sulphur; 15 carbon. These proportions may be slightly varied.

W. Hunter, after a careful examination of the question, in 1847, thus states the result:—"July and August, 1346, may be safely assumed to be the time when the explosive force of gunpowder was first brought to bear on the military operations of the English nation."

Above 11 tons of gunpowder on board the Lottie Sleigh, in the Mersey, exploded; much damage done in Liverpool and Birkenhead, but no lives lost, 16 Jan. 1864.

About 104,000 lbs. of gunpowder exploded at the Belvedere powder magazines of Messrs. Hall & Co., at Plumstead, near Woolwich; 13 persons perished, and the shock was felt at 50 miles' distance, 1 Oct. 1864. Searching inquiries were made into the circumstances, and new regulations for the keeping and transmission of powder issued in November; see *Dartford*.

Mr. Gale, a blind gentleman of Plymouth, on 22 June, 1865, patented his method of rendering *gunpowder uninflammable* by combining with it finely powdered glass, which can be readily separated by a sieve when the powder is required for use. Successful public experiments were made.

Mr. Gale exhibited his process before the queen at Windsor, 10 Nov. 1865, and it was severely tested at a martello tower, near Hastings, 20 June, 1866. The attainment of perfect security was still doubtful. Gale's Protected Gunpowder company was formed, Oct. 1865, and wound up, March, 1867.

Great explosion at Messrs. Hall's powder-mills, near Faversham; 11 men killed, much damage done; shock felt at Canterbury, 10 miles off, 28 Dec. 1867. Another explosion about 21 Dec. 1868.

Dixon & Beck's works blown up; 9 lives lost, 25 July, 1868.

Explosion at Hounslow mills, 3 lives lost, 6 Sept. 1872; again one life lost and great destruction of property, 3 May, 1887.

Milner's powder-magazines placed in fire at Woolwich arsenal and found secure, 8, 9 Oct. 1872.

About 5 tons of gunpowder in barrels exploded in the barge *Tilbury*, on the Regent's canal, near the North Bridge-gate, Regent's-park, nearly 5 A.M. 2 Oct. 1874. Three men on the barge killed; shock felt about 30 miles off; destruction extended over about a square mile; some houses thrown down; very many windows blown in; the house of Mr. Alma-Tadema, the artist, much injured.

The powder was sent by Pigou and Wilks to Derbyshire for blasting purposes;—order of the barges: *Ready*, tug steamer; *Jane*, *Dee*, *Tilbury*, *Limehouse*, and *Hawkesbury*.

6333*l.* had been subscribed for the sufferers up to 1 May, 1875.

Verdict of Inquest—Explosion caused by ignition of vapour from benzoline by a fire or light in the cabin of the *Tilbury*. The Junction Canal company guilty of gross negligence, and the present laws inadequate for public safety, 19 Oct. 1874.

The company declared responsible on trial (by Capt. Jackson), 14 May, 1875.

One thousand and fifty-four claims had been settled for 63,660*l.*, June, 1876.

Recently smokeless gunpowder has been produced; the Duttenhofer, the Stein, the Pallina, the Schultz and Hengst, Chilworth and Lebel powders give very little smoke, 1888-9.

The smokeless gunpowder of Herr Falkenstein tried at Berlin, reported efficient, Aug. 1889.

Sir F. A. Abel, in a discourse at the Royal Institution, 31 Jan. 1890 (*Proceedings*, vol. XIII.), explained and illustrated the merits and demerits of "smokeless explosives." Smokeless gunpowder much used in the autumn manœuvres, 1890.

See *Rome*, 23 April, 1891.

M. St. Marc's smokeless gunpowder tried at the Armstrong artillery range, Silloth, Cumberland; reported successful, about 14 Dec. 1892.

Explosion at Waltham abbey; 9 men killed and others injured, 13 Dec. 1893; inquest, open verdict, 11 Jan. 1894; a committee of inquiry censured some of the arrangements, and recommended additional precautions, 25 April; further changes recommended by a committee, reported 10 Sept. 1894; 4 men killed by an explosion in the nitro-glycerine factory for cordite, 7 May, 1894; 3 men killed there, and 2 killed in the cordite factory at Cliffe, Kent, 15 Dec. 1902.

Gunpowder exported: 1876, 14,268,672 lbs.; 1880, 14,927,500 lbs.; 1890, 10,330,400 lbs.; 1896, 8,089,000 lbs.; 1900, 7,047,200 lbs.; 1901, 6,865,712 lbs.

GUNPOWDER PLOT,

for springing a mine under the houses of parliament, and destroying the king, lords, and commons there assembled, was discovered on 4 Nov. 1605. It was projected by Robert Catesby early in 1604, and several Roman catholics of rank were in the plot. Guy Faux was detected in the vaults under the house of lords, hired for the purpose, preparing the train for being fired on the next day. Catesby and Percy (of the family of Northumberland) were killed at Holbeach house, whither they had fled, 8 Nov.; and Guy Faux, sir Everard Digby, Rookwood, Winter, and others, were executed, 30, 31 Jan. 1606. Henry Garnet, a Jesuit, suffered as an accomplice, 3 May following. An anonymous letter sent to lord Monteagle led to the discovery. It contained the following words, "Though there be no appearance of any stir, yet I say they shall receive a terrible blow this parliament, and yet they shall not see who hurts them." The vault called Guy Faux cellar, in which the conspirators lodged the barrels of gunpowder, remained till 1825, when it was converted into offices. "What Gunpowder plot really was," an answer to Father Gerard (who expressed his belief that the story of the plot was fabricated by lord Salisbury, the minister of James I., for his own purposes), by prof. S. K. Gardiner, published, July, 1897.

GUNTER'S CHAIN, used in measuring land, invented by Edmund Gunter, in 1606.

GURNEY'S ACT, 31 & 32 Vict., c. 116 (1868), amends the law relating to larceny and embezzlement.

GUTTA PERCHA is procured from the sap of the Isonandra Gutta, a large forest tree, growing in the Malayan peninsula and on the islands near it. It was made known in England by Drs. De Almeida and Montgomery, at the Society of Arts, in 1843. As a non-conductor of electricity it is invaluable in constructing submarine telegraphs, an application suggested by Faraday and Werner Siemens independently, 1847. 70,176 cwts. were imported into the United Kingdom in 1890; 40,490 cwts. 1893; 126,059 cwts. 1900; 1901, 88,438 cwts.

GUY'S HOSPITAL (London). Thomas Guy, a wealthy bookseller, after bestowing large sums on St. Thomas's, determined to found a new hospital. At the age of seventy-six, in 1721, he commenced the present building, and lived to see it nearly completed. It cost him 18,793*l.*, and, in addition, he endowed it with 219,499*l.* In 1829, 196,115*l.* were bequeathed to this hospital by Mr. Hunt, to provide accommodation for 100 additional patients.

Income much reduced by agricultural depression; 100,000*l.* proposed to be raised; Mansion House, 17,000*l.* received 20 Dec. 1886 *et seq.*

New laboratories and dental school buildings opened by sir John Lubbock, 17 July, 1893.

Reduced income; 1000*l.* donation from Mr. A. L. Cohen, Nov. 1895; 151,000*l.* received up to June, 1896; 1000*l.* from the baroness de Hirsch, April, 1897; other donations; see *Hospitals, Prince of Wales' Fund.*

Mr. H. L. Raphael gives 20,000*l.* to build a "Nurses' Home," Jan. 1898 (he died 11 May, 1899).

Special appeal for 180,000*l.*, 12 Nov. 1901; meeting at the mansion house (64,000*l.* received), 15 Jan. 1902; Mr. G. A. King bequeaths 30,000*l.*, 28 Feb. 1902; 100,000*l.* received (2,000*l.* from His Majesty's theatre), 8 June, 1903.

S. African war memorial unveiled, and the Wills' library (the gift of sir F. Wills) opened, 3 July, 1903.

GUZERAT, a state in India, founded by Mahmoud the Gaznevide, about 1020, conquered by Akbar in 1572; became subject to the Mahrattas 1732 or 1752. At the battle of Guzerat, near the Chenab, in the Punjab, 21 Feb. 1849, lord Gough totally defeated the Sikhs and captured the town of Guzerat.

GWALIOR, an ancient state in Central India, occupied by the Mahrattas; since 1803, under British protection. Scindiah, the maharajah, remained faithful during the revolt of 1857; visit of the prince of Wales, 31 Jan. 1876. His present of carved stone work of a gate, arrived in London in the autumn of 1884. Population, 1881, 1,115,857; 1891, 3,378,774; 1901, 2,933,000.

The ancient citadel was taken by major Popham in the Mahratta war in 1780; seized by the rebels during the Indian mutiny, 13 June; and retaken by sir Hugh Rose, 19 June, 1858. Surrendered to the maharajah by lord Dufferin, the viceroy, 2 Dec. 1885, for 15 lakhs of rupees; actually surrendered, 10 March, 1886. The maharajah Bhajeerut Rao Scindiah, aged 51, died 21 June, 1886. Succeeded by his son, a boy, with a regency. Investiture of the young maharajah with full powers, 15 Dec. 1894.

Gwalior visited by the marquis of Lansdowne, warmly received, 18 Nov. 1891.

Visit of the duke and duchess of Connaught, Jan. 1903.

GYMNASIUM, a place where the Greeks performed public exercises, and where philosophers, poets, and rhetoricians repeated their compositions. In wrestling and boxing the athletes were often naked (*gymnos*), whence the name. A London gymnastic society, formed in 1826, did not flourish. In 1862, M. Ravenstein set up another gymnastic association. The German Gymnastic Institution, in St. Pancras-road, London, was opened on 29 Jan. 1865, and a large and perfect gymnasium at Liverpool was inaugurated by lord Stanley, 6 Nov. 1865. A London athletic club existed in Nov. 1866. Since then gymnastics have been much cultivated. An international athletic congress opened in Paris, 16 June, 1894.

GYMNOSOPHISTÆ, a set of naked philosophers in India. Alexander (about 324 B.C.) was astonished at the sight of men who seemed to despise bodily pain, and endured tortures without a groan. *Pliny.*

GYPSIES, GIPSIES, or EGYPTIANS (French, *Bohémiens;* Italian, *Zingari;* Spanish, *Gitanos;* German, *Zigeuner*); vagrants, supposed to be descendants of low-caste Hindoos expelled by Timour, about 1399. They appeared in Germany and Italy early in the 15th century, and at Paris in 1427. In England an act was made against their itinerancy, in 1530; and in the reign of Charles I. thirteen persons were executed at one assizes for having associated with gypsies for about a month. The gypsy settlement at Norwood was broken up, and they were treated as vagrants, May, 1797. There were in Spain alone, previously to 1800, more than 120,000 gypsies, and many communities of them yet exist in England. Notwithstanding their intercourse with other nations, their manners, customs, visage, and appearance are almost wholly unchanged, and their pretended knowledge of futurity gives them power over the superstitious. Esther Faa was crowned queen of the gypsies at Blyth, on 18 Nov. 1860. The Bible has been translated into gypsy dialects. Gypsy parliaments are occasionally held. George Smith, king of the gypsies, Falcoln hall, Edinburgh, protested against the Movable Dwellings bill, 10 Jan. 1891. The Gypsy Lore society, founded in 1888, had 70 members in 1891, and published a journal.

GEORGE BORROW fraternised with the gypsies, and wrote several works describing his adventures, especially "The Zincali" (1841); "The Bible in Spain" (1842); "Lavengro" (1850); and a "Dictionary of the Gypsy Language" (1874). He was born in 1803, and died in Aug. 1881.

A band of 89 gypsies from Corfu, with 500*l.* bound for America, landed at Millwall docks, July; passage refused them at Liverpool; connection disclaimed by the Greek government; some remain at Liverpool and others at Hull, Aug.-Sept. 1886. Wandering in England, Oct. 1886; at Sunderland, April, 1887. Some of them conveyed to King's Cross station, London, 16 April, 1887; at Chester, April, 1887.

Matilda II. crowned queen of the American gypsies near Dayton, Ohio, Nov. 1888.

GYROSCOPE (from *gyrere*, to revolve), the name of a rotatory apparatus invented by Fessel of Cologne (1852), and improved by professor Wheatstone and M. Foucault of Paris. It is similar in principle to the rotatory apparatus of Bohnenberger of Tübingen (born 1765, died 1831).—The gyroscope, by exhibiting the combined effects of the centrifugal and centripetal forces, and of the cessation of either, illustrates the great law of gravitation.

H.

HAARLEM, an ancient town in Holland, once the residence of the counts, was taken by the duke of Alva, in July, 1573, after a siege of seven months. He violated the capitulation by butchering half the inhabitants. The lake was drained, 1839-51. Population, 1890, 51,626; 1900, 65,189.

HABEAS CORPUS. The subjects' *Writ of Right*, passed "for the better securing the liberty of the subject," 31 Charles II. c. 2, 27 May, 1679. If any person be imprisoned by the order of any court, or of the queen herself, he may have a writ of habeas corpus, to bring him before the court of queen's bench or common pleas, which shall determine whether his committal be just. This act (founded on the old common law) is next in importance to *Magna Charta*. The *Habeas Corpus* act can be suspended by parliament for a specified time when the emergency is extreme. In such a case the nation parts with a portion of its liberty to secure its own permanent welfare, and suspected persons may then be arrested without cause or purpose being assigned. *Blackstone.*

Act suspended for a short time in . 1689, 1696, 1708
Suspended for Scots' rebellion 1715-6
Suspended for twelve months 1722
Suspended for Scots' rebellion in 1745-6
Suspended for American war 1777-9
Again by Mr. Pitt, owing to French revolution . 1794
Suspended in Ireland, on account of the great rebellion 1798
Suspended in England, 28 Aug. 1799; and 14 April, 1801
Again, on account of Irish insurrection . . . 1803
Again, owing to alleged secret meetings (see *Green Bag*) . . . . 21 Feb. 1817
Bill to restore the *Habeas Corpus* brought into parliament . . . . 28 Jan. 1818
Suspended in Ireland (insurrection) . 24 July, 1848
Restored there . . . . . . 1 March, 1849
Suspended again (see *Fenians*), 17 Feb. 1866; 26 Feb. and 31 May, 1867; and 28 Feb. 1868 till 25 March, 1869, and virtually in 1881
The constitution of the United States provides that "the privilege of habeas corpus shall not be suspended, unless when, in cases of rebellion or invasion, the public safety may require it;" but does not specify the department of the government having the power of suspension. A series of contests on this subject between the legal and military authorities began in Maryland, May, 1861
In consequence of the affair of John Anderson (see *Slavery in England*, note), an act was passed in 1862, enacting that no writ of *Habeas Corpus* should issue out of England into any colony, &c., having a court with authority to grant such writ.

HABITUAL CRIMINALS ACT, for the more effectual prevention of crime, giving powers for the apprehension of habitual criminals on suspicion, passed 11 Aug. 1869; 117,568 reported in the metropolis, 1873.

A *black book*, printed at Brixton prison, contained the names and aliases of 12,164 criminals, selected from 179,601 entered on the register, 1869-76.

HABITUAL DRUNKARDS, see *Drunkards.*

HABSBURG, see *Hapsburg.*

HACKNEY, a parish N.E. of London; by the division of the Tower Hamlets, was made a metropolitan borough by the Reform act, 15 Aug., 1867. Two members were elected. The election 4 Feb. 1876, void, through neglect of officers. Returns three members by the act of 1885. Constituted a municipal borough of London government act 1899 (10 aldermen, 60 councillors). Population, 1881, 186,462; 1891, 229,531; 1901, 220,000.

HACKNEY COACHES, probably from the French *coche-à-haquenée*, a vehicle with a hired horse, *haquenée*. Their supposed origin in Hackney, near London, is a vulgar error; see *Cabriolets*, and *Omnibuses.*

Four were set up in London by a capt. Bailey; their number soon increased 1625
They were limited by the star-chamber in 1635; restricted in 1637 and in 1652
The number was raised to 400, in 1662; to 700, in 1694; to 800, in 1715; to 1000, in 1771; to 1100, in 1814; and finally, to 1300, in 1815
One-horse hackney carriages (afterwards cabriolets) permitted to be licensed . . . . . "
All restriction as to number ceased, by 2 Will. IV. (the original fare was 1s. a mile) 1831
Two hundred *hackney chairs* were licensed . . 1711
Office removed to Somerset-house 1782
Coach-makers made subject to a licence . . . 1785
Lost and found office for the recovery of property left in hackney coaches, established by act 55 Geo. III. 1815
All public vehicles to be regulated by the act 16 & 17 Vict. cc. 33, 127, by which they are placed under the control of the commissioners of police, June and Aug. 1853
By the Metropolitan Carriages act, passed 12 Aug. 1869, various restrictions respecting the amount of fare, &c., were removed, commencing 1 Jan. 1870
Further regulations for cabs issued by the home secretary . . . . 10 March, 1871
"Hackney carriages, tables of distances,' published 1901

HAFSFIORD (Norway). Here Harold Hårfager, in a sea-fight, finally defeated his enemies; and consolidated his kingdom, 872. A millenary festival was held throughout Norway, and a monument to his memory at Hangesund, inaugurated by prince Oscar of Sweden, 18 July, 1872.

HAGUE, capital of the kingdom of Holland, once called the finest *village* in Europe; the place of meeting of the states-general, and residence of the former earls of Holland since 1250, when William II. built the palace here. Population in 1887, 149,447; in 1890, 160,531; in 1897, 191,530; 1900, 212,211.

Here the states abjured the authority of Philip II. of Spain 1580
A conference upon the five articles of the remonstrants, which occasioned the synod of Dort . 1610
Treaty of the Hague (to preserve the equilibrium of the North), signed by England, France, and Holland . . . . 21 May, 1659
The De Witts torn in pieces here . . . . 4 Aug. 1672
The French, favoured by a hard frost, took possession of the Hague; the inhabitants and troops declared in their favour; general revolution ensued, and the stadtholder and his family fled to England . . . . 19 Jan. 1795
The Hague evacuated by the French . . . Nov. 1813
The stadtholder returned . . . . Dec. "

Peace conference (*which see*) met, 18 May, 1899;
Hague arbitration court constituted early April, 1901; first case settled (see *Mexico*) . . Oct. 1902

HAILEYBURY COLLEGE (Herts), wherein students were prepared for service in India; it was founded by the East India company in 1806 in Hertford castle; the new building opened in 1809; was closed in 1858. The present college founded 1862; royal charter, 1864.

In the case of "Hutt and another *v.* the Governors of the college and others," Mr. Robertson, the head-master, and Mr. Fenning, assistant, were exonerated from the charges of unlawfully expelling Henry Hutt, aged 15, on suspicion of stealing money; and the boy was declared innocent by the Queen's Bench division, 19 June; 100*l.* awarded to the plaintiffs, 27 June, 1888.
"Memorials of Old Haileybury College," published 1894.

HAINAULT, a province in Belgium, anciently governed by counts, hereditary after Regnier I., who died in 916. The count John d'Arsenes became count of Holland in 1299. Hainault henceforth partook of the fortunes of Flanders.

HAINAULT FOREST (Essex), disafforested in 1851. Here stood the Fairlop oak (*which see*).

HAIR. In Gaul, hair was much esteemed, hence the appellation *Gallia comata;* cutting off the hair was a punishment. The royal family of France held it as a privilege to wear long hair artfully dressed and curled. "The clerical tonsure is of apostolic institution!" *Isidorus Hispalensis.* Pope Anicetus forbade the clergy to wear long hair, 155. Long hair was out of fashion during the protectorate of Cromwell, and hence the term *Roundheads;* in 1795; and also 1801.—*Hair-powder* came into use in 1590; and in 1795 a tax of a guinea was laid upon persons using it, which yielded at one time 20,000*l.* per annum. The tax was repealed 24 June, 1869, when it yielded about 1000*l.* a year. See *Beard.*

Some members of a Burmese family totally covered with hair were exhibited in London in July, 1886.

HAITI, see *Hayti.*

HAKLUYT SOCIETY, established for the publication of rare voyages and travels, 15 Dec. 1846, was named after Richard Hakluyt, who published his "Principal Navigations, Voyages, and Discoveries made by the English Nation," in 1589; and died 23 Nov. 1616. Mr. Wm. Foster's "Embassy of sir Thos. Roe," published 1899.

HALF CROWNS, see under *Coinage* and *Crowns.*

HALIARTUS, a town in Bœotia, near which Lysander the Spartan general was killed in battle with the Thebans, 395 B.C.

HALICARNASSUS, Caria (Asia Minor); the reputed birth-place of Herodotus, 484 B.C.; the site of the tomb of Mausolus, erected 352; was taken by Alexander, 334; see *Mausoleum.*

HALIDON HILL, near Berwick, where, on 19 July, 1333, the English defeated the Scots, the latter losing upwards of 14,000 slain, among whom were the regent Douglas and a large number of the nobility; a comparatively small number of the English suffered. Edward Balliol thus became king of Scotland for a short time.

HALIFAX (Yorkshire). The woollen manufactory was successfully established here in the 15th century. The power of the town to punish capitally (by a peculiar engine resembling the guillotine) any criminal convicted of stealing to the value of upwards of thirteen pence halfpenny, was used as late as 1650. In 1857, Mr. J. Crossley announced his intention of founding a college here, and Mr. F. Crossley presented the town with a beautiful park. Boiler explosion at Batme and Pritchard's; Mr. Pritchard and 5 men killed, 9 Oct. 1879. Public demonstration for the franchise bill, 9 Sept. 1884. Population, 1881, 73,630; 1891, 82,864; 1901, 104,933.

HALIFAX, the capital of Nova Scotia, was founded in 1749 by the hon. Edwd. Cornwallis, and named after the earl of Halifax. Population, 1881, 36,100; 1891, 38,556. About 31 were burnt to death in an almshouse hospital here . . . . Nov. 1882
Large graving dock opened . . . . 20 Sept. 1889
Great fire, 10 wharves and 35 warehouses destroyed 1 Oct. 1891
Tablet in honour of Sebastian Cabot unveiled by the earl of Aberdeen . . . . . 24 June, 1897
Visit of the duke and duchess of Cornwall and York, 19 Oct. 1901
Memorial to soldiers who fell in the S. African war, unveiled . . . . 26 June, 1902

HALIFAX ADMINISTRATION. Charles, earl of Halifax, was appointed first lord of the treasury, 5 Oct. 1714. He died 19 May, 1715, and was succeeded by Charles, earl of Carlisle, on 10 Oct. following; and Robert Walpole became premier.

Charles, earl of Halifax, *first lord of the treasury.*
William, lord Cowper, aft. earl, *lord chancellor.*
Daniel, earl of Nottingham, *lord president.*
Thomas, earl of Wharton, *privy seal.*
Edward, earl of Oxford, *admiralty.*
James Stanhope, afterwards earl Stanhope, and Charles, viscount Townshend, *secretaries of state.*
Sir Richard Onslow, *chancellor of the exchequer.*
Dukes of Montrose and Marlborough, lord Berkeley, Robt. Walpole, Mr. Pulteney, &c.

HALIFAX AWARD, see *Canada*, 1877.

HALL, principal apartment in mediæval mansions. Westminster and Eltham halls are fine examples; see *Westminster Hall.*

HALL MARK, see *Goldsmiths* and *Standard.*

HALLE (Saxony, N. Germany), first mentioned in 801, was made a city by the emperor Otho II. in 981. The orphan-house here was established by August Francke, 1698-9. Halle suffered much by the Thirty years' and Seven years' wars. It was stormed by the French, 17 Oct. 1806, and added to the kingdom of Westphalia; but given up to Prussia in 1814. Population, 1891, 101,401; 1900, 156,611.

HALLELUJAH AND AMEN (*Praise the Lord*, and *So be it*), expressions used in the Hebrew hymns; said to have been introduced by Haggai, the prophet, about 520 B.C. Their introduction into Christian worship is ascribed to St. Jerome, about A.D. 390.

HALLS in London, see *Agricultural, Egyptian, Exeter, Floral, Freemasons', Independents, James's (St.), Music* and *Westminster.*

HALYS, a river (Asia Minor), near which a battle was fought between the Lydians and Medes. It was interrupted by an almost total eclipse of the sun, which led to peace, 28 May, 585 B.C. (the fourth year of the 48th Olympiad). *Plin. Nat. Hist.* ii. Others give as the date 584, 603, and 610 B.C. This eclipse is said to have been predicted many years before by Thales of Miletus. *Herodotus*, i. 75.

HAM, on the Somme, N. France. The castle was built in 1470 by the constable Louis of Luxembourg, comte de St. Pol, beheaded by Louis XI. 19 Dec. 1475. Here were imprisoned the ex-ministers of Charles X., 1830; and Louis Napoleon Bonaparte after his attempt at Boulogne, from Oct. 1840 till 25 May, 1846, when he escaped.

HAMBURG, formerly a free city, N.W. Germany, founded by Charlemagne, about 809. It joined the Hanseatic league in the 13th century, and became a flourishing commercial city. Population, 1875, 388,618; in 1880, 453,869; in 1885, 518,620; 1890, 622,530; 1894, 647,479; 1900, 768,349. *Hamburg Massacre*; see *Massacres*, 1876.

A free imperial city by permission of the dukes of Holstein, 1296; subject to them till 1618; purchased its total exemption from their claims . 1768
French declared war upon Hamburg for its treachery in giving up Napper Tandy; see *Tandy*, Oct. 1799
British property sequestrated . . March, 1801
Hamburg taken by the French after the battle of Jena, in 1806
Incorporated with France 1810
Evacuated by the French on the advance of the Russians into Germany 1813
Restored to independence by the allies . May, 1814
Awful fire here, which destroyed numerous churches and public buildings, and 2000 houses; it continued for three days . . . . 4 May, 1842
Half the city inundated by the Elbe . 1 Jan. 1855
New constitution granted by the senate, July, 1860; the new assembly (of 191 members) first met, 6 Dec 1890
The constitution began . . . . 1 Jan. 1860
Hamburg joined the N. German confederation, 1861 21 Aug. 1866
Joined the German empire, Jan.; its privileges as a free port confirmed 16 April, 1871; these were given up, and Hamburg joined the Zollverein, being the last of the German free ports . 15 Oct. 1888
The emperor William II. with a hammer completes the new great harbour works . . . 29 Oct. ,,
Exhibition of Trade and Industry . 15 May—7 Oct. 1889
Strike of gas-workers, city some time in darkness; violent rioting, checked by armed police, with bloodshed . . . . . about 13–15 May, 1890
Visitation of cholera (*which see*) . . Aug.–Nov. 1892
Arrival of the emperor and other distinguished persons, *en route* for the opening of the North sea canal; grand banquet in the new town hall, 19 June, 1895
Strike of dockers and others . . . . 20 Nov. 1896
Mr. Tom Mann expelled . . . 26 Nov. ,,
Foreign labour engaged; general strike of workers in the harbour . . . . . 4 Dec. ,,
Destructive rioting in the docks, reported 16 Dec. ,,
Strike organised and maintained by the social democrats; ends by the surrender of the men; some disturbances between strikers and blacklegs, 50 arrests . . . . . . 6 Feb. 1897
Cabdrivers' strike, motor-cars much used . Aug. 1902

HAMILTON, Ontario, founded in 1813. Population in 1861, 19,096; 1891, 48,959; 1901, 52,634.

HAMILTON PALACE SALE. The total sum realised by the sale of the vast collection of pictures and other works of art, cabinets, crystals, &c. amounted to 397,562*l.* 20 July, 1882. Wm. Alexander, the 12th duke of Hamilton, born 12 March, 1845; died, 16 May, 1895.

The MSS. purchased by the German government; reported price about 70,000*l.*, Oct. 1882. Part resold to the British Museum, soon after. The greater part returned to London for sale; the British Museum bought the most valuable part for 15,189*l.* 15*s.* 6*d.* . . . . . . May, 1889
Sale of the united Beckford and Hamilton libraries realised 86,444*l.* 1883-4

HAMMERSMITH, a parish in S. Middlesex, made a parliamentary borough in 1885, returning one member. A suspension bridge was erected 1825-7; a new one was opened by Prince Albert Victor, 18 June, 1887; population, 1901, 112,233.

HAMPDEN CLUBS, see *Radicals*, and *Chalgrove*.

HAMPSTEAD, N.W. of London; originally a chapelry of Hendon, was made a parish after the Reformation. The ancient chapel was taken down 1745; and a church was consecrated, 8 Oct. 1747. An act authorising the Metropolitan Board of Works to purchase the heath from sir John Maryon Wilson, bart., passed 29 June, 1871, and the heath was formally taken possession of by the Metropolitan Board of Works, 13 Jan. 1872, 45,000*l.* being paid. Hampstead made a municipal borough (7 aldermen, 42 councillors) by London government act, 1899. Hampstead returns one M.P. by act of 1885. Population, 1881, 45,452; 1891, 68,425; 1901, 81,942.

Temporary small-pox hospital established . . 1871
Charges of mismanagement against the officers; official inquiry (33 meetings, from 23 Sept. to 3 Nov.); inquiry respecting disappearance of a child, Elizabeth Bellue; medical officers exonerated from blame. . . . . . . Dec. ,,
A small-pox hospital erected here by Metropolitan District Asylum Board was much opposed, and led to litigation, see *Trials*, 1878; the house of lords on appeal decided against the inhabitants 7 March, 1881
Finally the board agreed to buy the property affected for 20,000*l.* . . . . . . Dec. 1883
The Board of Works voted 152,500*l.* towards the purchase of "Parliament Hill" fields, about 261 acres, as an addition to the heath; the parishes of Hampstead and St. Pancras having voted 50,000*l.* 14 Oct. 1887
50,000*l.* given by the Charity Commissioners and above 46,000*l.* subscribed by the public; final meeting of the Hampstead Heath Extension committee, 23 March, 1889. The duke of Westminster, chairman, and Mr. Shaw Lefevre, vice-chairman.
For Hampstead, or rather Kentish town murder, see *Trials* . . . . Dec. 1890
On Easter Monday, above 100,000 persons were on the heath; 2 women and 6 boys were suffocated by the dense crowd descending the stairs at the railway station, 6 p.m. . . . . 18 April, 1892
The mound on Parliament hill examined; reported probably ancient burial place . . . Nov. 1894
Public library founded by Mr. Henry Harben and sir Spencer Wilson . . . . . 10 Nov. 1896
The late sir Thos. Spencer Wells' Golders'-hill estate opened to the public (total cost, 42,000*l.*), 1 Dec. 1898
The baroness de Hirsch gave 70,000*l.* to endow Tudor house as a convalescent home; she died 2 April, 1899
Princess Christian lays the first stone of new hospital buildings . . . . . 21 Oct. 1902

HAMPTON COURT PALACE (Middlesex), built by cardinal Wolsey on the site of the manor-house of the knights-hospitallers, and in 1525 presented to Henry VIII.; perhaps the most splendid offering ever made by a subject to a sovereign. Here Edward VI. was born, 12 Oct. 1537; here his mother, Jane Seymour, died, 24 Oct. following; and here Mary, Elizabeth, Charles, and others of our sovereigns resided. Much was pulled down, and the grand inner court built by William III. in 1694, when the gardens, occupying 40 acres, were laid out. The vine was planted 1769. Here was held, 14, 16, 18 Jan. 1604, the CONFERENCE between the Puritans and the Established church clergy, which led to a new translation of the Bible; see *Conference*. An alarming fire in apartments over the picture gallery extinguished; one woman suffocated, 14 Dec. 1882.

By another fire many apartments destroyed and injured, 19 Nov. 1886; estimated damage, 20,000*l.*
Alterations and changes in the palace; pictures removed to Kensington palace; Queen Anne's drawing-room opened to the public, 15 July, 1899; Indian troops encamped here, summer, left 15 Aug. 1902.

HANAPER OFFICE (of the court of chancery), where writs relating to the business of the subject, and their returns, were anciently kept *in hanaperio* (in a wicker hamper); and those relating to the crown, *in parva baga* (a little bag). Hence the names *Hanaper* and *Petty Bag Office*. The office was abolished in 1842.

HANAU (Hesse-Cassel), incorporated 1303. Here a division of the combined armies of Austria and Bavaria, of 30,000 men, under general Wrede, encountered the French, 70,000 strong, under Napoleon I., on their retreat from Leipsic, 30 Oct. 1813. Both armies suffered severely, but the allies most, and were compelled to retire. The county of Hanau was made a principality in 1803; seized by the French in 1806; incorporated with the duchy of Frankfort in 1809; restored to Hesse in 1813; which was annexed to Prussia in 1866.

HANDEL'S COMMEMORATIONS. The *first* was held in Westminster abbey, 26 May, 1784; king George III. and queen Charlotte, and above 3000 persons being present. The band contained 268 vocal and 245 instrumental performers, and the receipts of three successive days were 12,746*l*. These concerts were repeated in 1785, 1786, 1787, and 1791.

Second great commemoration, in the presence of king William IV. and queen Adelaide, when there were 644 performers, 24, 26, 28 June, and 1 July, 1834.

Great Handel festival (at the Crystal Palace) on the centenary of his death, projected by the Sacred Harmonic Society. Grand Rehearsal at the Crystal Palace, 15, 17, 19 June, 1857, and 2 July, 1858.

Performances: Messiah, 20 June; Selections, 22 June; Israel in Egypt, 24 June, 1859, when the prince consort, the king of the Belgians, and 26,827 persons were present.

There were 2765 vocal and 393 instrumental performers, and the performance was highly successful. The receipts amounted to about 33,000*l*., from which there were deducted 18,000*l*. for expenses; of the residue (15,000*l*.), two parts accrued to the Crystal Palace Company, and one part to the Sacred Harmonic Society. Handel's harpsichord, original scores of his oratorios, and other interesting relics, were exhibited.

Handel festivals (at the Crystal Palace): 4000 performers; highly successful; 23, 25, 27 June, 1862; again, 26, 28, 30 June, 1865; again, 15, 17, 19 June, 1868 (about 25,000 present); also, 19, 21, 23 June, 1871 (about 84,000 persons subscribed); also, 22, 24, 26 June, 1874 (total present, 78,839); also, 25, 27, 29 June, 1877 (present, 74,124); 18, 21, 23, 25 June, 1880 (present, 79,643); 15, 18, 20, 22 June, 1883 (present, 87,769); (centenary) 22, 24, 26 June, 1885 (present, 85,437); 25, 27, 29 June, 1888, chorus above 3,000 (present 86,337); 19, 22, 24, 26 June, 1891; 25, 27, 29 June, 1894; 11, 14, 16, 18 June, 1897; 19, 21, 23 June, 1900; 20, 23, 25, 27 June, 1903.

HANDEL SOCIETIES; for publication of Handel's works:—

Founded in London, 1843; first volume issued, 1843-4; society dissolved, 1848; work continued by Cramer & Co. completed, 1855.

Founded at Leipsic, in 1856; publications began, 1858.

Handel and Haydn Society, Boston, U.S. for performances only; founded 1815.

HANDKERCHIEFS, wrought and edged with gold, used to be worn in England by gentlemen in their hats, as favours from young ladies, the value of them being from five to twelve pence for each in the reign of Elizabeth, 1558. *Stow's Chron.* Paisley handkerchiefs were first made in 1743.

HANDS, imposition of, was performed by Moses in setting apart his successor Joshua (*Num.* xxvii. 23); in reception into the church, and in ordination, by the apostles (*Acts* viii. 17; 1 *Tim.* iv. 14).

HANGING, DRAWING, AND QUARTERING, said to have been first inflicted upon William Marise, a pirate, a nobleman's son, 25 Hen. III., 1241. Five gentlemen attached to the duke of Gloucester were arraigned and condemned for treason, and at the place of execution were hanged, cut down alive instantly, stripped naked, and their bodies marked for quartering, and then pardoned, 25 Hen. IV. 1447. *Stow*. The Cato-street conspirators (*which see*) were beheaded after death by hanging, 1 May, 1820. Hanging in chains (pirates, murderers, and others), an old custom, was abolished in 1834; see *Death*.

HANGO BAY (Finland). On 5 June, 1855, a boat commanded by lieut. Geneste left the British steamer *Cossack* with a flag of truce to land some Russian prisoners. They were fired on by a body of riflemen, and five were killed, several wounded, and the rest made prisoners. The Russian account, asserting the irregularity to have been on the side of the English, was not substantiated.

HANOVER (N. W. Germany), successively an electorate, and a kingdom, chiefly composed of territories which once belonged to the dukes of Brunswick (*which see*). Population of the province in 1859, 1,850,000; in 1875, 2,017,393; in 1885, 2,172,702; 1890, 2,230,491; 1900, 2,590,939; of the city, 1885, 139,731; 1890, 165,499; 1900, 235,666. It was annexed to Prussia, *which see*, at the close of the war, 20 Sept. 1866; see *Guelph*.

Hanover became the *ninth electorate* . . 19 Dec. 1692
Suffered much during the seven years' war . 1756-63
Seized by Prussia . . . . . . 3 April, 1801
Occupied and hardly used by the French, 5 June, 1803
Delivered to Prussia in 1805
Retaken by the French 1807
Part of it annexed to Westphalia 1810
Regained for England by Bernadotte . 6 Nov. 1813
Erected into a kingdom . . . . . 12 Oct. 1814
The duke of Cambridge appointed viceroy, and a representative government established, Nov. 1816
Visited by George IV. . . . . . . Oct. 1821
Ernest, duke of Cumberland, king . 20 June, 1837
He granted a constitution with electoral rights, 1848; which was annulled in obedience to the decree of the federal diet . . . 12 April, 1855
The king claims from England crown jewels, which belonged to George III. (value about 120,000*l*.), 1857; by arbitration, the jewels given up . Jan. 1858
Stade dues given up for compensation, 12 June, 1861
In the war the king takes the side of Austria; and the Prussians enter and occupy Hanover, 13 June, *et seq.* 1866
The Hanoverians defeat the Prussians at Langensalza, 27 June; but are compelled to surrender, 29 June, ,,
Hanover annexed to Prussia by law, 20 Sept.: promulgated . . . . 6 Oct. ,,
Protest of the king of Hanover addressed to Europe 23 Sept. ,,
Arrangement with Prussia by a treaty ratified 18 Oct. 1867
The king celebrates his "silver wedding" at Hietzing, near Vienna, expressing hopes of recovering his kingdom, &c. . . . . . 18 Feb. 1868
Part of his property sequestrated by Prussia, March, ,,
Still further, in consequence of his maintaining a Hanoverian legion (the king protested against it), Feb. 1869
The emperor William II. warmly received at Hanover, during the autumn manœuvres, 11 Sept. 1889; again reviews the garrison, 24 Jan. 1899; cordially welcomed . . . . . . 16 June ,,

ELECTORS.

1692. Ernest-Augustus, youngest son of George, that son of William, duke of Brunswick-Luneburg, who obtained by lot the right to marry (see *Brunswick*). He became bishop of Osnaburg in 1662, and in 1679 inherited the possessions of his uncle John, duke of Calenberg; created ELECTOR of Hanover in 1692.

[He married, in 1659, the princess Sophia, daughter of Frederick, elector palatine, and of Elizabeth, the daughter of James I. of England. In 1701, Sophia was declared next *heir to the British crown*, after William III., Anne, and their descendants.]

1698. George-Lewis, son of the preceding; married his cousin Sophia, the heiress of the duke of Brunswick-Zell; became *king of Great Britain*, 1 Aug. 1714, as GEORGE I.

1727. George-Augustus, his son (GEORGE II. of England), 11 June.

1760. George-William-Frederick, his grandson (GEORGE III. of England), 25 Oct.

KINGS.

1814. George-William-Frederick (the preceding sovereign), first king of Hanover, 12 Oct.

1820. George-Augustus-Frederick, his son (GEORGE IV. of England), 29 Jan.

1830. William-Henry, his brother (WILLIAM IV. of England), 26 June; died, 20 June, 1837.

[Hanover separated from the crown of Great Britain.]

1837. Ernest-Augustus, duke of Cumberland, brother to William IV. of England, on whose death he succeeded (as a distinct inheritance) to the throne of Hanover, 20 June.

1851. George V. (born 27 May, 1819), son of Ernest; ascended the throne on the death of his father, 18 Nov. *His states annexed to Prussia*, 20 Sept. 1866; visited England, May, June, 1876; died, 12 June, 1878.

1878. Ernest-Augustus II., son, born 21 Sept. 1845; maintained his claims in a circular to the sovereigns of Europe, dated 11 July, 1878; married princess Thyra of Denmark, 21 Dec. 1878. See *Cumberland*.

HANOVER SQUARE, built about 1718; the concert rooms opened by John Gallini, 1 Feb. 1775; the house taken for a club, Dec. 1874; rebuilt, 1875.

HANSARD'S DEBATES and UNION, see *Reporting*.

HANSE TOWNS. The Hanseatic league (from *hansa*, association), formed by port towns in Germany against the piracies of the Swedes and Danes: began about 1140; the league signed 1241. At first it consisted only of towns situate on the coasts of the Baltic sea, but in 1370 it was composed of sixty-six cities and forty-four confederates. The league proclaimed war against Waldemar, king of Denmark, about the year 1348, and against Eric in 1428, with forty ships and 12,000 regular troops, besides seamen. On this several princes ordered the merchants of their respective kingdoms to withdraw their effects. The Thirty Years' War in Germany (1618-48) broke up the strength of the association, and in 1630 the only towns retaining the name were Lübeck, Hamburg, and Bremen. The league suffered also by the rise of the commerce of the Low Countries in the 15th century. Their privileges by treaty in England were abolished by Elizabeth in 1578.

HANSOM, see *Cabriolets*.

HANWELL LUNATIC ASYLUM, for Middlesex, established 1831.

HAPSBURG (HABSBURG or HABICHTSBURG), HOUSE OF, the family from which the imperial house of Austria sprang in the 11th century, Werner being the first named count of Habsburg, 1096. Hapsburg was an ancient castle of Switzerland, on a lofty eminence near Schintznach. Rodolph, count of Hapsburg, became archduke of Austria, and emperor of Germany, 1273; see *Austria*, and *Germany*.

HARBOURS. England has many fine natural harbours; the Thames (harbour, dock, and depôt), Portsmouth, Plymouth, &c. Acts for the improvement of harbours, &c., were passed in 1847, 1861, and 1862. Harbours, docks and piers association, 12th annual meeting, 5 June, 1894.

HARES AND RABBITS ACT. See *Game*.

HARFLEUR, seaport, N.W. France, taken by Henry V., 22 Sept. 1415.

HARLAW (Aberdeenshire), the site of a desperate indecisive battle between the earl of Mar, with the royal army, and Donald, the lord of the Isles, who aimed at independence, 24 July, 1411. This conflict was very disastrous to the nobility, some houses losing all their males.

HARLEIAN LIBRARY, containing 7000 manuscripts, besides rare printed books, collected by Robert Harley, afterwards earl of Oxford and Mortimer, 1705, *et seq.*, is now in the British Museum. A large portion of his life and wealth was spent on the collection. He died 21 May, 1724. The Harleian Miscellany, a selection from the MSS. and Tracts of his library, was published in 1744 and 1808.

HARLEIAN SOCIETY, founded in 1869 for the publication of heraldic visitations, &c.

HARLEY ADMINISTRATION, see *Oxford*.

HARLEY STREET, London, W. At No. 139, the house inhabited by Mr. Henriques, the decomposed body of a woman, stabbed in the breast and covered with chloride of lime, was found 3 June; verdict of coroner's inquest, wilful murder by person unknown, 14 June, 1880.

HARMONICA, or musical glasses (tuned by regulating the amount of water, and played by a moistened finger on the rim), were played on by Gluck in London, 23 April, 1746; "arranged" by Puckeridge and Delaval, and improved by Dr. Franklin in 1760; Mozart, Beethoven, and others composed for this instrument; see *Copophone*. "HARMONICON," an excellent musical periodical, edited by W. Ayrton, Jan. 1823—Sept. 1833.

HARMONICHORD, a keyed instrument, in which sounds are produced by friction, invented by Th. Kauffmann in 1810.

HARMONISTS, a sect, founded in Würtemberg by George and Frederick Rapp, about 1780. Not much is known of their tenets, but they held their property in common, and considered marriage a civil contract. They emigrated to America, and built New Harmony in Indiana in 1815. Robert Owen purchased this town about 1823; but failed in his scheme at establishing a "social" community and returned to England: see *Socialists*. The Harmonists removed to Pittsburg in Pennsylvania in 1822.

HARMONIUM, a keyed instrument, resembling the accordion, the tones being generated by the action of wind upon metallic reeds. The Chinese were well acquainted with the effects produced by vibrating tongues of metal. M. Biot stated, in 1810, that they were used musically by M. Grenié; and in 1827-29, free reed stops were employed in organs at Beauvais and Paris. The best known harmoniums in England are those of Alexandre and Debain, the latter claiming to be the original maker of the French instrument. In 1841, Mr. W. E. Evans, of Cheltenham, produced his English harmonium, then termed the Organ-Harmonica, and by successive improvements he produced a fine instrument, with diapason quality, and great rapidity of speech, without loss of power. Dawes' melody attachment patented 1864.

HARMONY, the combination of musical notes of different pitch, appears not to have been practised by the Greeks.

Hucbald, a Flemish monk, published combinations in his "Enchiridion Musicæ," 9th century.
Harmony greatly promoted by Palestrina, and especially by Monteverde.
Jean de Muris wrote "Ars Contrapuncti" in 14th century.
Francis of Cologne described "descant," 1600.
Beethoven greatly enlarged the range of harmonic bases.

HARNESS, chariots and the leathern dressings used for horses to draw them, are said to have been the invention of Erichthonius of Athens, who was made a constellation after his death, under the name of *Boötes* (Greek for ploughman), about 1487 B.C.

HARO, CRY OF (*Clameur de Haro*), traditionally derived from Raoul, or Rollo, of Normandy, ancestor of our Norman princes of England. Rollo administered justice so well, that injured persons uttered the cry "*Ha Rou! Ha Rou! A mon aide, mon prince, on me fait tort.*" The cry was raised in a church in Jersey in 1859.

HARP. Invented by Jubal, 3875 B.C. (*Gen.* iv. 21). David played the harp before Saul, 1063 B.C. (1 *Sam.* xvi. 23.) The Cimbri, or English Saxons, had this instrument. The celebrated Welsh harp was strung with gut; and the Irish harp, like the more ancient harps, with wire. Erard's improved harps were first patented in 1795.

One of the most ancient harps existing is that of Brian Boroimhe, monarch of Ireland: it was given by his son Donagh to pope John XVIII., together with the crown and other regalia of his father, in order to obtain absolution for the murder of his brother Teig. Adrian IV. alleged this as being one of his principal titles to the kingdom of Ireland in his bull transferring it to Henry II. This harp was given by Leo X. to Henry VIII., who presented it to the first earl of Clanricarde: it then came into possession of the family of De Burgh; next into that of MacMahon of Clenagh, county of Clare; afterwards into that of MacNamara of Limerick; and was at length deposited by the right hon. William Conyngham in the College Museum, Dublin, in 1782.

The *claviharp*, fitted like the pianoforte with a keyboard, and played like the pianoforte, was introduced into Brussels and Antwerp by Mdlle. Dratz, and played on by her at Prince's Hall, London, 13 March, 1888.

HARPER'S FERRY (Virginia), see *United States*, 1859-62.

HARPSICHORD, see *Pianoforte*, note.

HARRISON'S TIME-PIECE, made by John Harrison, of Foulby, near Pontefract. In 1714, the government offered rewards for methods of determining the longitude at sea; to obviate the irregularities in the rate of clocks by variations of temperature, Harrison invented the method of compensation, before 1720. He came to London, and produced his first time-piece in 1735; his second in 1739; his third in 1758; and his fourth, which procured him the reward of 20,000*l.* offered by the Board of longitude, a few years after. He obtained 10,000*l.* of his reward in 1764, and other sums, more than 24,000*l.* in all, for further improvements in following years. He was born, May, 1693, and died in 1776.

In the patent museum at South Kensington is an eight-day clock made by Harrison in 1715. It strikes the hour, indicates the day of the month, and with one exception (the escapement) its wheels are entirely made of wood. The clock was going in 1871.

HARROGATE (Yorkshire). The first or old spa in Knaresborough forest was discovered by capt. Slingsby in 1571: a dome was erected over the well by lord Rosslyn in 1786. Two other chalybeate springs are the Alum well and the Towit spa. Sulphureous well discovered 1783. Theatre was erected 1788. Bath hospital erected by subscription 1825. Kursaal (cost 40,000*l.*) opened 27 May, 1903. Pop., 1901, 28,423.

HARROW-ON-THE-HILL SCHOOL (Middlesex), founded and endowed by John Lyon in 1571. To encourage archery, the founder instituted a prize of a silver arrow to be shot for annually on the 4th of August; but the custom has been abolished. Lord Palmerston, sir R. Peel, the statesman, and lord Byron, the poet, were educated here. The school building suffered by fire, 22 Oct. 1838. The school arrangements were modified by the public schools act, 1868. Visit of the prince and princess of Wales, speech day, 7 July, 1894. Charles II. called Harrow church "the visible church." Fire, 8, 9 Feb. 1896.

HARTLEPOOL, E. Durham, an ancient seaport, said to have been burnt by the Danes, 800, fortified by the Bruces and others, and chartered by John. The foundation of West Hartlepool, with its harbour, docks, churches, &c., is due to the sagacity, skill, and energy of Mr. Ralph Ward Jackson. The work began in 1844, and the harbour was opened 1 June, 1847. The population, about 400 in 1840, was 16,998 in 1881; and 21,521 in 1891; 1901, 22,723. West Hartlepool, 1881, 29,448; 1891, 42,492; 1901, 62,614. Mr. R. W. Jackson, first M.P. for "The Hartlepools" in 1868-74, died 6 Aug. 1880, much honoured at home and abroad.

HARTLEY COAL MINE (Northumberland). On 16 Jan. 1862, one of the iron beams, about 20 tons weight, at the mouth of the ventilating shaft, broke and fell, destroyed the brattice, divided the shaft, and carried down sufficient timber to kill five men who were ascending the shaft, and buried alive 202 persons, men and boys. Several days elapsed before the bodies could be removed. Much sympathy was shown by the queen and the public, and about 70,000*l.* were collected for the bereaved families. The coroner's verdict asserted the necessity of two shafts to coal mines, and recommended that the beams of colliery engines should be of malleable instead of cast iron.

HARTWELL (Buckinghamshire), the retreat of Louis XVIII., king of France, 1807-14. He landed in England at Yarmouth, 6 Oct. 1807, took up his residence at Gosfield-hall, in Essex, and afterwards came to Hartwell, as the count de Lille. His consort died here in 1810. On his restoration, he embarked at Dover for France, 24 April, 1814. See *France*.

HARUSPICES, priests or soothsayers, of Etruscan origin, who foretold events from observing entrails of animals. They were introduced to Rome by Romulus (about 750 B.C.), and abolished by Constantine, A.D. 337, at which time they were seventy in number.

HARVARD COLLEGE, Cambridge (Massachusetts, North America), was founded by the general court at Boston, on 28 Oct. 1636. It derived its name from John Harvard, of Emmanuel College, Cambridge, who bequeathed to it his library and 779*l.* in 1638. Present annual income now (1903) over $1,000,000, chiefly under the management of the state until 1865, when the government was vested in a board of 30 overseers. Among the university buildings are the Agassiz museum of comparative zoology, the Peabody museum of

American archæology, the memorial hall erected in honour of the alumni who fell in the Civil war, and the theatre. 250th anniversary of its foundation kept 6-8 Nov. 1886. $50,000 given for the foundation of a museum of Semitic antiquities, 1900.

HARVEIAN ORATION. William Harvey bequeathed his property to the Royal College of Physicians. The annual delivery of the oration began in 1656. See under *Blood.*

HARWICH, a sea-port, Essex, a Roman station, and the Saxon Harewic; chartered by Edwd. 2nd; absorbed into Essex, 1885.

Near here Alfred defeated the Danish fleet.
Parkeston, the new port near Harwich, was constructed in 1882.

HASTINGS, a cinque-port, Sussex; said to owe its name to the Danish pirate Hastinge, who built forts here, about 893; but Mr. Kemble thinks it was the seat of a Saxon tribe named Hastingas. At Senlac, now Battle, near Hastings, more than 30,000 were slain in the conflict between Harold II. of England and William duke of Normandy, the former losing his life and kingdom, 14 Oct. 1066, his birthday. He and his two brothers were interred at Waltham abbey, Essex. The new town, St. Leonard's-on-sea, was begun in 1828. A new pier here was inaugurated by earl Granville, 5 Aug. 1872. New town-hall opened by the mayor, 7 Sept. 1881. Convalescent home and Alexandra Park opened by the prince of Wales, 26 June, 1882. Marine parade much damaged by high tide, 24 Nov. 1882. Great conservative meeting, powerful speech of the marquis of Salisbury, 18 May, 1892. Foundation of a new harbour, laid by the marquis of Dufferin, 16 June, 1897. Population, 1881, 42,258; 1891, 52,340; 1901, 65,528.

HASTINGS' TRIAL. Warren Hastings, governor-general of India, was tried by the peers of Great Britain for high crimes and misdemeanours. Among other charges was his acceptance of a present of 100,000*l.* from the nabob of Oude; see *Chunar, Treaty of.* The trial occupied 145 days, and lasted seven years and three months; commencing 13 Feb. 1788, terminating in his acquittal, 23 April, 1795. Mr. Sheridan's speech on the impeachment excited great admiration.

Hastings was born in 1732; went to India as a writer in 1750; became governor-general of Bengal in 1772; of India, 1773; governed ably, but, it is said, unscrupulously and tyrannically, till he resigned in 1785. The expenses of his trial (70,000*l.*) were paid by the East India Company; and a pension was granted to him. He died a privy-councillor in 1818.

HATELEY FIELD, see *Shrewsbury.*

HATFIELD'S ATTEMPT. On 15 May, 1800, during a review in Hyde-park, a shot from an undiscovered hand was fired, which wounded a young gentleman who stood near king Geo. III. In the evening, when his majesty was at Drury-lane theatre, Hatfield fired a pistol at him. Hatfield was confined as a lunatic till his death, 23 Jan. 1841, aged 69 years.

HATHERLEY'S ACT, see *Bankrupt.*

HATS, first made by a Swiss at Paris, 1404. When Charles VII. made his triumphal entry into Rouen, in 1449, he wore a hat lined with red velvet, and surmounted with a rich plume of feathers. Henceforward, hats and caps, at least in France, began to take the place of chaperons and hoods. *Henault.* Hats were first manufactured in England by Spaniards in 1510. *Stow.* Very high-crowned hats were worn by queen Elizabeth's courtiers; and high crowns were again introduced in 1783. A stamp-duty laid upon hats in 1784, and in 1796, was repealed in 1811. Silk hats began to supersede beaver about 1820.

None allowed to sell any hat for above 20*d.* nor cap for above 2*s.* 8*d.*, 5 Henry VII. 1489. Every person above seven years of age to wear on Sundays and holidays, a cap of wool, knit, made, thickened, and dressed in England by some of the trade of cappers, under the forfeiture of three farthings for every day's neglect, 1571. Excepted: maids, ladies, and gentlewomen, and every lord, knight, and gentleman, of twenty marks of land, and their heirs, and such as had borne office of worship, in any city, town, or place, and the wardens of London companies, 1571.

HATTERAS EXPEDITION, see *United States,* Aug. 1861.

HATTON GARDEN, now covered by a mass of houses, was formerly the garden of a palace of the bishop of Ely, demised to the crown and given by queen Elizabeth to sir Christopher Hatton, the lord keeper, who died 20 Nov. 1591. See *Jewel Robberies.*

HAU-HAU FANATICS, see *New Zealand,* 1865.

HAUSA ASSOCIATION, established to improve the condition of the Hausas, a people dwelling near the basin of the Niger. The study of their language and translations, advocated by the abp. of Canterbury, lord Aberdare, prof. Max Muller, and others in 1892. The work was begun by the late rev. J. A. Robinson, member of the Church Missionary Society. Annual meetings held. "Hausaland, or fifteen hundred miles through the central Soudan," by C. H. Robinson, published Feb. 1896.

HAVANA, capital of Cuba, West Indies, founded by Velasquez, 1511–19; taken by lord Albemarle, 14 Aug. 1762; restored, 1763; the remains of Columbus were brought from St. Domingo and deposited in the Cathedral here, 1795; exhumed, in the presence of gen. Blanco and others, 26 Sept.; taken to Seville, mid Dec. 1898; deposited in a special mausoleum, 17 Nov. 1902. By an explosion of gunpowder here, 34 persons were killed, and about 100 injured, 17 May, 1890. American cruiser *Maine* (*which see*) blown up, 15 Feb. 1898.

HAVRE-DE-GRÂCE (N. W. France) was defended for the Huguenots by the English in 1562; who, however, were expelled in 1563. It was bombarded by Rodney, 6 to 9 July, 1759; by sir Richard Strachan, 25 May, 1798; and blockaded, 6 Sept. 1803. The attempts of the British to burn the shipping here failed, 7 Aug. 1804. The International Maritime Exhibition here opened, 1 June, 1868 another exhibition, 7 May, 1887. The volunteers visited Havre: began to shoot, 26 May; 50 British received prizes, 29 June, 1874. The French Association for Science met here, 30 Aug. 1877. Population, 1891, 109,541; 1901, 129,044.

HAWAII, see *Owhyhee,* and *Sandwich Isles.*

HAWKERS AND PEDLARS were first licensed in 1698. Licensing commissioners were appointed in 1810. The expense of licensing was reduced in 1861, and regulated by the Pedlars' Act, 1871. Exemptions from charges on licences granted by the Hawkers Act, 1888.

HAWKING, see *Falconry.*

HAY, average value of the produce of the United Kingdom in 1874, 48,000,000*l*. Hay-making machinery exhibited at Taunton, July, 1875. Mr. Wm. A. Gibbs's apparatus, with artificial heat for drying hay, corn, &c.: tried at Gilwell Park, Chingford, Essex, reported successful, 3 July, 1875; at other places in July, 1880. His drying machines used for other purposes, such as gunpowder works (1885). See *Ensilage*.

HAYMAN CASE, see *Rugby*.

HAYMARKET (Westminster), opened in 1664, was removed to Cumberland-market, 1 Jan. 1831. The Haymarket theatre was opened in 1702; see *Theatres*.

History of the Haymarket theatre, by Mr. Cyril Maude, published . . . . . . Oct. 1903

HAYTI or **HAITI**, Indian name of a West Indian island, discovered by Columbus in Dec. 1492, and named Hispaniola, and afterwards St. Domingo. Before the Spaniards fully conquered it, they are said to have destroyed, in battle or cold blood, three million of its inhabitants, including women and children, 1495. The island now comprises the Dominican republic (*which see*) in the east, and the republic of Hayti in the west. The population of Hayti in 1887 was about 550,000; 1894, about 1,000,000; capital, Port-au-Prince, 1894, about 34,000.

Hayti seized by the filibusters and French buccaneers 1630
The French government took possession of the whole colony 1677
The negroes revolt against France . . 23 Aug. 1791
And massacre nearly all the whites 21–23 June, 1793
The French directory recognise Toussaint l'Ouverture as general-in-chief 1794
The eastern part of the island ceded to France by Spain 1795
Toussaint establishes an independent republic in St. Domingo . . . . . . 9 May, 1801
He surrenders to the French . . . 7 May, 1802
Is conducted to France, where he dies . . . 1803
A new insurrection, under the command of Dessalines; the French quit the island . Nov. ,,
Dessalines proclaims the massacre of all the whites, 29 March; crowned emperor of Hayti, as Jacques I., Oct. 1804
He is assassinated, and the isle divided 17 Oct. 1806
Henry Christophe, a man of colour, president in Feb. 1807; crowned emperor by the title of Henry I., while Pethion rules as president at Port-au-Prince . . . . March, 1811
Numerous black nobility and prelates created . ,,
Pethion dies: Boyer elected president . May, 1818
Christophe commits suicide, Oct. 1820; the two states united under Boyer as regent for life, Nov. 1820; who is recognised by France 1825
Revolution: Boyer deposed 1843
St. Domingo and the eastern part of Hayti proclaim the "*Dominican republic*," Feb. 1844; recognised by France, 1848; Buenoventura Baez, president 1849–53
Hayti proclaimed an empire under its late president Solouque, who takes the title of Faustin I., 26 Aug. 1849; crowned . . . 18 April, 1852
Santana, president of the Dominican republic, 1853-6; succeeded by B. Baez 1856–8
Faustin attacking the republic of St. Domingo, repulsed . . . . 1 Feb. 1856
José Valverde elected president of the republic of St. Domingo, or Dominican republic . March, 1858
Revolution in Hayti: general Fabre Geffrard proclaims the republic of Hayti . . 22 Dec. ,,
Faustin abdicates . . . . . 15 Jan. 1859
Geffrard takes oath as president of Hayti 23 Jan. ,,
Sixteen persons executed for a conspiracy against Geffrard . . . . Oct. ,,
Spanish emigrants land: a declaration for reunion with Spain signed 18 March, decreed by the queen . . . . 20 May, 1861
Insurrection against Spain in St. Domingo, 18 Aug. 1863
A Spanish force sent; the insurgents generally defeated 1864
Great fire at Port-au-Prince; 600 houses destroyed, 23 Feb. 1865
St. Domingo renounced by Spain . . 5 May, ,,
Military insurrection under Salnave against Geffrard, 7 May; Cape Hayti seized . . 9 May, ,,
Cabral provisional president of St. Domingo, Sept. 1865; B. Baez proclaimed president . 14 Nov. ,,
Valdrogue, a rebel vessel, fires into British Jamaica packet, near Acul, St. Domingo, 22 Oct.; Capt. Wake, H. M. S. *Bulldog*, threatens *Valdrogue*; Salnave orders the removal of refugees from British consulate at Cape Hayti, shoots them, and destroys the building. The *Bulldog*, failing to obtain satisfaction, shells the fort, sinks the *Valdrogue*, but gets on a reef; the crew is taken out, and she is blown up. H.M.S. *Galatea* and *Lily* take the other forts and give them up to Geffrard; the rebels flee inland . . 9 Nov. ,,
Capt. Wake censured by court-martial for losing his ship . . . . Jan. 1866
Hayti—another revolt against Geffrard suppressed, 5–11 July, ,,
Revolution; Geffrard flies; banished for ever; Salnave president of Hayti . . . 27 March, 1867
New constitution . . . . . . June, ,,
Revolution caused by Pimentel; Baez flies; Cabral becomes president of St. Domingo . . June, ,,
Revolt against Salnave . . . . . Sept. ,,
The ex-emperor Faustin (born a slave, 1791), died Aug. ,,
City of San Domingo nearly destroyed by the hurricane . . . . 30 Oct. ,,
B. Baez, president of Dominican republic, March, 1868
Insurrection against Salnave, 10 May; said to be successful, 26 May; English consul protecting foreigners . . . . June, ,,
Salnave defeats insurgents, and kills his prisoners, 2 June, ,,
Salnave proclaims himself emperor, Aug.; offers an amnesty . . . . Oct. ,,
Civil war continued: Saget and Dominguez proclaimed president by their respective followers, Oct. ,,
Salnave, finally defeated, flies to the woods. 18 Dec. 1868; captured, tried, and shot . . 15 Jan. 1870
Sale of Samana bay to the United States discussed, Jan. ,,
Gen. Nissage Saget elected president of Hayti for four years (from 15 May) . . . 19 March, ,,
Baez supports an insurrection against Hayti Aug. 1871
Tranquillity of Hayti reported by Saget . 9 May, 1872
Gen. Ganier d'Aton, president of St. Domingo, Oct. 1873
Michel Dominguez elected president of Hayti (from 15 May). . . . . . . 14 June, 1874
Insurrection in St. Domingo in favour of Baez, 30 Aug. 1875
Insurrection headed by Louis Tanis about 7 March, 1876
Cruel executions of suspected persons by president Domingue . . . . . 20 March ,,
Insurrection successful, Dominguez flies to St. Thomas's . . . . . middle of April ,,
Election of Boisrond Canal as president of *Hayti*, 19 July, ,,
Peaceful revolution in St. Domingo; president Espaillat replaced by Gonzales . . . Oct. ,,
Insurrection in St. Domingo; city surrounded by Guillermo and Bellini: Baez almost powerless, about 22 Feb. 1877
Guillermo declared president . . . March, ,,
Revolution; hard fighting: Boisrond Canal resigns; about 17 July, 1879
Gen. Salomon elected president of *Hayti* 22 Oct. ,, [re-elected 14 July, 1886]
Hayti reported tranquil . . . . . 1 Jan. 1880
Don Fernando Arturo de Mariño, a priest, president of *San Domingo*, Oct. 1880; said to become dictator . . . . June, 1881
Revolution broke out March 25, and government troops defeated . . . . . 31 March, 1883
Bridge exploded by rebels, about 2000 killed May, ,,
Insurrection nearly quelled; amnesty proclaimed end of June . . . . ,,
Fresh insurrection; battle at Jacmel indecisive 3 Aug. ,,

Negro insurrection at Port-au-Prince, suppressed after damage to persons and property 22 Sept. 1883
Alp, British steamer, fired on by the government Oct. ,,
Death of the rebel leader Bazelais; surrender of rebel town Jeremie, announced 26 Dec.; collapse of the insurrection . . . about 10 Jan. 1884
Gen. F. Bellini proclaimed president of San Domingo 11 Aug. ,,
Sir Spencer St. John in his *Black Republic* describes the degraded, profligate, cruelly savage condition of Hayti ,,
General Ulises Heureaux elected president of *San Domingo* for 1886–8 . . . 28 June, 1886
Insurrection; rebels defeated: reported 14 Aug. ,,
National bank of Hayti; mysterious disappearance of bonds and cheques; M. Vouillon, the director, charges Mr. D'Almena (American), sub-manager, and Mr. Coles (British), accountant, with theft, and others with receiving, summer 1884; prisoners tried, at first acquitted, afterwards illegally convicted and imprisoned; the American, French, and British governments protest; British squadron at Port-au-Prince; prisoners released 1885–6
Revolution in Hayti; gen. Salomon deposed; arrives in Cuba 16 Aug.; dies at Paris . . 19 Oct. 1888
Insurrection of gen. Télémaque; in an attack on the Palais National at Port-au-Prince killed with 300 of his followers 29 Sept. civil war between north and south Hayti. . . . . Oct. ,,
Gen. Légitime elected president . . 22 Oct. ,,
Cape Haytien bombarded . . . 7 Dec. ,,
Indecisive conflict between gens Hippolyte and Légitime . . . . . . 21 Dec. ,,
Gen. Hippolyte installed president at Haytien; announced . . . . . . 1 Jan. 1889
General Légitime recognised as president by Great Britain and France . . . . . Feb. ,,
President Légitime defeated by gen. Hippolyte; reported . . . . . . 29 Jan. ,,
Gen. Hippolyte defeated about 20 Feb. ,,
Dessalines captured; announced . 16 April, ,,
Reported advance of Gen. Hippolyte on Port-au-Prince 28 May ,,
The blockade of Haytian ports, of November last declared to be non-effective, and he ports to be open; *London Gazette* . . . 12 July, ,,
Unsuccessful attacks of gen. Hippolyte on Port-au-Prince . . . 11, 12, and about 25 July ,,
Port-au-Prince surrendered to gen Hippolyte by gen. Légitime (who goes to France) . 24 Aug. ,,
Gen. Hippolyte elected president . 16 Oct. ,,
Gen. Hippolyte confirmed as president . 15 May, 1890
Attempted revolution at Port-au-Prince suppressed with bloodshed, about 30 killed . 28 May, 1891
M. Rigaud, French citizen, shot; 80,000 francs paid to his widow by the Haytian government . . reported 20 July, ,,
The ministry censured by the chamber, then resigns . . . . 15 Aug. ,,
New cabinet formed . . . . 17 Aug. ,,
By an overflow of the river St. Marc, about 80 lives lost . . . . 14 Aug. ,,
An amnesty proclaimed . . . . 10 Dec. ,,
Gen. Ulises Heureaux re-elected president of San Domingo . . . . . . 16 Dec. 1892
Rupture between France and San Domingo in relation to a petty bank dispute . . 18 April, 1893
San Domingo, plot against the government discovered; gen. Bobadilla ordered to be shot, 27 July, 1894
Dispute with France settled; indemnities to be paid, reported . . . . 10 March, 1895
Three French war-ships warmly received in San Domingo . . . . 19 April, ,,
Death of gen. Hippolyte, president, announced 25 March 1896
Gen. Theresias Augustin Simon Sam elected 31 March ,,
Diplomatic rupture relating to the short imprisonment of Herr Lüders in Oct.; indemnity refused, Nov. 1897; 2 German cruisers arrive at Port-au-Prince; ultimatum, payment in 8 hours demanded, and sum paid 6 Dec. 1897
Martial law; new ministry formed . . 13 Dec. ,,
Great fire at Port-au-Prince, 800 buildings burnt, 3000 persons homeless, 28 Dec., and earthquake shocks . . . . . . 29 Dec. ,,
Gen. Heureaux, ex-president, assassinated at Moca, and an old man standing beside him also killed, by Ramon Caceres . . . 26 July, 1899
(2 other assassins captured and shot, reported 2 Aug.)
Gen. Figuereo, vice-pres., accepts the presidency of *San Domingo* . . . . . . 30 July, ,,
Revolutionary movement successful; government forces defeated with loss near Monte Christo, 12–24 Aug.; Puerto Plato and other towns occupied by the revolutionists; the president resigns; provisional government formed; Monte Christo surrenders, reported . . . 5 Sept. ,,
Sen. Jimenez, president . . . . . Nov. ,,
Barahona captured by revolutionists, but bombarded and retaken by a government gunboat; martial law proclaimed, reported, 31 March, 1902; rebellion reported crushed . . . 10 April, 1902
Gen. Tiresias Simon Sam, president, resigns, reported . . . . . . 9 May, ,,
Provisional government formed, M. B. Canal president, about . . . . 27 May, ,,
Revolutionary outbreak in favour of M. Firmin, much fighting . . . . 27–29 June, ,,
M. Firmin proclaimed president in Artabonite, reported . . . . . . 21 July, ,,
Civil war declared; provisional government dissolved, reported . . . . 26 July, ,,
Petit Goare burnt down, many deaths, 4000 homeless, reported, 11 Aug.; severe fighting near Cap Haitien, 28 Aug.; troops defeated near Limbe, 3, 4 Sept.; Haytian gunboat sunk for piracy by a German gunboat, adm. Killick and 3 others perished, reported 7 Sept.; gen. Nord defeated at Limbe, 17 Sept.; troops again severely defeated at Montrouis, 11 Oct.; insurrection suppressed, flight of gen. Firmin, reported . . . . 17 Oct. ,,
Gen. Nord declared president by the troops, 17 Dec.; elected . . . . 22 Dec. ,,
Port de Paix destroyed by fire, loss of shipping 26 Feb. 1903
Alleged fraudulent issue of government securities, the ministers resign, war minister excepted, reported . . . . 26 May, ,,
State of siege proclaimed at Port au Prince and national guard summoned to arms, reported mid July, ,,

HEAD ACT, see *Ireland*, 1465.

HEAD MASTERS, incorporated association of, founded 1891. Annual meeting, Guildhall, 9 Jan. 1901.

HEALTH, General Board of, was appointed by the act for the promotion of the public health, passed in 1848. This board was reconstructed in Aug. 1854, and sir Benjamin Hall was placed at its head, with a salary of 2000*l.*; succeeded by W. F. Cowper, Aug. 1855, and by Ch. B. Adderley in 1858. In 1858 this board was incorporated into the privy council establishment; Dr. Simon being retained as medical officer. See *Hygiene*, *Hygeiopolis*, *Sanitation*, *Exhibitions*, *Public Health*, &c.

HEARTH, or Chimney, Tax, on every fire-place or hearth in England, was imposed by Charles II. in 1662, when it produced about 200,000*l.* a year. It was abolished by William and Mary at the Revolution in 1689; imposed again, and again abolished.

HEAT (called by French chemists Caloric). Little progress had been made in the study of the phenomena of heat till about 1757, when Joseph Black put forward his theory of latent heat (heat, he said, being absorbed by melting ice), and of specific heat. Cavendish, Lavoisier, and others, continued Black's researches. Sir John Leslie put forth his views on radiant heat in 1804. Count Rumford put forth the theory that heat consists in motion among the particles of matter, which view he supported by experiments on friction (recorded in 1802). This theory (now called the dynamical or mechanical theory of heat, and used to explain all the phenomena of physics and chemistry) has been further substantiated by the independent researches of Dr. J. Meyer of Heilbronn and of Mr. James P. Joule of Manchester, who assert that heat is the equivalent of work done. Mr. Joule, in his papers published 1841–2, laid the foundation of the science of thermo-dynamics, on which he worked till his death, 11 Oct. 1889. The Joule Memorial fund proposed, 30 Nov. 1889, was instituted by the Royal Society, Jan. 1890. In 1854, Sir William Thomson (aft. lord Kelvin), of Glasgow, published his researches on the dynamical power of the sun's rays. Thermo-electricity, produced by heating pieces of copper and bismuth soldered together, was discovered by Seebeck in 1823. A powerful thermo-electric battery was constructed by Marcus of Vienna, in 1865. Professor Tyndall's "Heat, a Mode of Motion," first published Feb. 1863; third edition, 1868, sixth edition, 1880. The researches of philosophers are still devoted to this subject; see *Boiling* and *Calorescence*. Greatest heat in the hot summer of 1868: at Nottingham, in sun, 122·4; in shade, 92·2, 22 July, 1 p.m.: 14 Aug. 1876, 95·7 in the shade; 147 in sun; 26 June, 1878, 95 in the shade.

Sir George Cayley invented a heated-air engine in 1807, and Mr. Stirling applied it to raising water in Ayrshire in 1818. One invented by Mr. Wenham was described in 1873. Improvements have been made by C. Wm. Siemens. Coal gas is generally employed.—See *Gas Engines*.

Captain John Ericsson constructed a ship, in which caloric, or heat, was the motive power. On 4 Jan. 1853, it sailed down the bay of New York, at the rate of 14 miles an hour, it is said at a cost of 80 per cent. less than steam. Although caloric engines were not successful, capt. Ericsson continued his experiments, and patented an improved engine in 1856. In 1868 he proposed condensation of the sun's rays, and their employment as a motive power; in March, 1889, he exhibited his apparatus in New York shortly before his death, aged 86.

A portable heat radiator, a small vessel containing burnt charcoal, used by the peasantry of Kashmir; adopted by lord Dundonald in his "Instra," and recommended by him for the troops (*Times*), and developed, 13 Dec. 1897.

Dr. Hans Goldschmidt's process of producing high temperatures by the combustion of aluminium and oxide of iron (the mixture termed "thermite") shown in London, 1 May, 1901.

Mr. C. Prince states that on 14 July, 1847, the temperature was 98° in the shade at Uckfield, Sussex. In London, 94°·1 in the shade, 15 July, 1881. In London, W. 11 Aug. 1884, in the shade, 92·6. In Princetown, Dartmoor, 94° in the shade, 24 July, 1885. London, 91° in the shade, 31 Aug. 1885. See *United States*, 1892.

A wave of intense heat passed over Europe, causing many deaths, 19–22 Aug. 1892. Temperature in the shade, Paris, 96·8°, 19 Aug.; Trieste, 110°, 21 Aug.; Vienna, 107°, 18 Aug.; 102°, 21 Aug.; Berlin, 95°, 20 Aug.; Madrid, 106°, 17 Aug.; Seville, 120°, 15 Aug.

MAXIMUM TEMPERATURES OF 90° OR UPWARDS, IN SHADE, AT CAMDEN-SQUARE, LONDON.

		Deg.			Deg.
1858.	June 16	92·6	1876.	Aug. 13	92·3
1859.	July 12	91·9	,,	Aug. 14	92·1
,,	July 13	90·1	1881.	July 5	92·7
,,	July 18	90·4	,,	July 15	94·6
1868.	July 16	91·0	1884.	Aug. 11	92·0
,,	July 21	93·3	1885.	July 26	90·4
,,	July 22	93·2	1893.	June 19	90·4
,,	July 27	90·4	,,	Aug. 16	90·7
,,	Sept. 7	91·0	,,	Aug. 17	92·7
1869.	July 22	91·0	,,	Aug. 18	93·6
1870.	June 22	91·2	,,	Aug. 21	72·
,,	July 22	90·8	,,	Aug. 23	60·
1871	Aug. 13	90·0	1898.	Aug. 22	89·
1872.	July 25	92·3	1900.	July 16	95·2
1873.	July 22	90·1	1901.	May 29	88
1874.	July 9	90·4	1902.	July 14	86·1
1874.	July 20	90·8			
1876.	July 15	92·6			

G. J. Symons, F.R.S. (he died 10 March, 1900).

Madrid, 15 Aug., 112°, 1893.

Heat wave in U.S.N.A., New York, 105°, 31 July, 1894; London, 86·2, 30 May, 1895. High temperature in Sept., London, 86°, 24, 25 Sept. 1895. London, 87°, 14 July, 1896; New York, 97° F., 11 Aug 1896 (many deaths); Chicago, 51 deaths, 10 Aug. 1896. See *New South Wales*, Jan. 1896.

Heat wave averaging 107° in the shade in S. Australia, Victoria, and New South Wales, 26 Dec. *et seq.* 1897.

London, 92·1°, 8 Sept. 1898. Heat wave in England, 22 Aug., London, 90°, 25 Aug. 1899. Adelaide, 112·2°, 1 Jan. 1900. Heat wave in U.S.N.A.; many deaths, New York, 106° F., 28 June, 1901.

HEBREWS; see *Jews*. The Epistle to the Hebrews ascribed to St. Paul is dated 64. The chief classic authors of all nations, except Greece, have been translated into Hebrew.

HEBRIDES (the *Ebudæ* of Ptolemy and the *Hebudes* of Pliny), western isles of Scotland, long subject to Norway; ceded to Scotland in 1264; and annexed to the Scottish crown in 1540 by James V. The heritable jurisdictions were abolished in 1747.

HEBRON (in Palestine). Here Abraham resided, 1860 B.C.; and here David was made king of Judah, 1048 B.C. On 7 April, 1862, the prince of Wales visited the reputed cave of Machpelah, near Hebron, said to contain the remains of Abraham and his descendants.

HECATOMB, an ancient sacrifice of a hundred oxen, particularly observed by the Lacedæmonians when they possessed a hundred cities. The sacrifice was subsequently reduced to twenty-three oxen, and goats and lambs were substituted.

HECLA, MOUNT (Iceland). Its first recorded eruption is 1004. About twenty-two eruptions have taken place, according to Olasson and Paulson. Great convulsions of this mountain occurred in 1766, since when a visit to the top in summer is not attended with great difficulty. Perhaps the most awful volcanic eruption on record took place in 1784–5, when rivers were dried up, and many villages overwhelmed or destroyed. The mount was in a state of violent eruption from 2 Sept. 1845, to April, 1846. Three new craters were formed, from which pillars of fire rose to the height of 14,000 English feet. The lava formed several hills, and pieces of pumice stone and scoriæ of 2 cwt. were thrown to a distance of a league and a half; the ice and snow which had covered the mountain for centuries melted into prodigious floods.

HEGIRA, ERA OF THE, dates from the flight (Arabic *hejra*) of Mahomet, from Mecca to Medina, on the night of Thursday, 15 July, 622. The era commences on the 16th. Some compute this era from the 15th, but Cantemir proves that the 16th was the first day. 33 of its lunar years are equal to 32 of those of the vulgar era.

HEIDELBERG (Germany) was the capital of the Palatinate, 1362–1719. The protestant electoral house becoming extinct in 1693, a war ensued, in which the castle was ruined, and the elector removed his residence to Mannheim. It was annexed to Baden in 1802. Here was the celebrated tun, constructed in 1343, when it contained twenty-one pipes of wine. Another was made in 1664, which held 600 hogsheads. It was destroyed by the French in 1688; but a larger one, fabricated in 1751, which held 800 hogsheads, and was formerly kept full of the best Rhenish wine, is said to be mouldering in a damp vault, empty, since 1769. Population, 1890, 31,737; 1900, 40,119.

The anniversary of the foundation of the university in 1386 was enthusiastically celebrated early in August, 1886.

HELDER POINT (Holland). The fort and the Dutch fleet lying in the Texel surrendered to the British under the duke of York and sir Ralph Abercromby, for the prince of Orange, after a conflict. 540 British were killed, 30 Aug. 1799. The place was left in Oct.; see *Bergen*.

HELENA, ST., an island in the South Atlantic Ocean, discovered by the Portuguese under Juan de Nova Castilla, on St. Helena's day, 21 May, 1502. The Dutch afterwards held it until 1600, when they were expelled by the English. The British East India Company settled here in 1651; and the island was alternately possessed by the English and Dutch until 1673, when Charles II., on 12 Dec., assigned it to the company once more. St. Helena was the place of Napoleon's captivity, 16 Oct. 1815; and here he died, 5 May, 1821. His remains were removed in 1840, and interred at the Hôtel des Invalides, Paris; see *France*, 1840. The house and tomb have been purchased by the French government. The bishopric was founded in 1859. Governor, adm. sir Chas. Elliot, 1863–9; adm. Charles George Edward Patey, 1869; Hudson Ralph Janisch, 1873, died April, 1884; col. Grant Blunt; hon. Wm. Grey Wilson, 1889; K. A. Sterndale, March, 1897, died 3 Oct. 1902; col. H. L. Gallwey, Nov. 1902. Population, 1871, 6241; in 1883, 5,085; 1891, 4,116; 1901, 3,342. Revenue, 1900, 15,391*l.*; expenditure, 12,603*l.*

No crime, debt or disease reported by the governor, spring, 1890

By the fall of a rock near Jamestown, 9 persons killed . . . . 1 May, „

Gen. Cronje and other Boer prisoners arrive here, 14 April, 1900. Gen. Ben Viljoen and 38 others arrive, 25 Feb. 1902. See *South African War*.

"St. Helena," by E. L. Jackson, pub. June, 1903.

HELENS, ST., Lancashire, originally a village, now the centre of a large manufacturing district; constituted a municipal borough, 1868, a parliamentary borough, one member, 1885. The town-hall with a public library was opened 1876. Col. Gamble lays foundation stone of a public library, technical school, &c. He gives the site, and 30,000*l.* for the building, 2 Oct. 1894; the institute opened by the earl of Derby, 5 Nov. 1896. The Theatre Royal (built 1890) burnt down, 13 Oct. 1899. Mr. J. Seddon, premier of New Zealand, receives the freedom, 5 July, 1902. Population, 1871, 45,134; 1891, 71,288; 1901, 84,410.

HELIGOLAND, an island in the North Sea, formerly a dependence of the duchy of Holstein, subject to Denmark, was taken from the Danes by the British, 5 Sept. 1807; made a depôt for British merchandise; confirmed to England by the treaty of Kiel, 14 Jan. 1814. In a naval engagement off Heligoland, between the Danes and the Austrians and Prussians, the allies were compelled to retire, 9 May, 1864. A fashionable bathing place for Germans. Governor, col. Henry F. B. Maxse, 1863; lt.-col. J. T. N. O'Brien, 1881; Mr. A. C. S. Barkley, Nov. 1888. Heligoland was ceded to Germany by the Anglo-German agreement, 18 June; given up by Mr. Barkley to the new German governor, 9 Aug.; visited by the emperor William II., and proclaimed part of the empire, 10 Aug. 1890. Populatiou, 1881, about 2000.

HELIOGRAPHY (from *helios*, the sun).

A system of telegraphing by mirrors flashing the rays of the sun, said to have been employed by the ancients in the time of Alexander, about 333 B.C.

A portable heliograph, invented by Mr. H. Mance, of the Persian telegraph department, was announced in 1875. It was employed in India, 1877–78; in the Afghan and Zulu campaigns, 1879–80, and S. African war, 1899–1902. See also *Photography*.

HELIOMETER, an instrument for measuring the diameters of the sun, moon, planets, and stars, invented by Savary, in 1743; applied by M. Bouguer, in 1744. A fine heliometer, by Repsold of Hamburg, was set up at the Radcliffe observatory, Oct. 1849.

HELIOPOLIS; see *Baalbec* (in Syria). The name was also given to a city in Lower Egypt (the biblical On or Bethshemesh) in the earliest known times, a chief seat of the worship of the sun. It suffered much by the Persian invasion, 525 B.C., and was in ruins in the time of Strabo, who died about A.D. 24.

HELIOSCOPE (a peculiar sort of telescope, prepared for observing the sun so as not to affect the eye), was invented by Christopher Scheiner in 1625.

HELIOSTAT, an instrument invented to make a sunbeam stationary, or apparently stationary, invented by s'Gravesande about 1719, and greatly improved by Malus and others. One constructed by MM. Foucault and Duboscq was exhibited at Paris in Oct. 1862.

HELIUM, a gas discovered by prof. Ramsay with argon in the mineral cleveite, 1895. See *Hydrogen*, 1898.

HELLAS, in Thessaly, the home of the Hellenes and the Greek race, which supplanted the Pelasgians from the 15th to the 11th century B.C., derived its name from Hellen, king of Phthiotis, about 1600 B.C. The Hellenes separated into the Dorians, Æolians, Ionians, and Achaians. The present king of Greece is called "king of the *Hellenes*:" see *Greece*.

HELLENIC SOCIETY, to promote Hellenic studies, formed at a meeting, 16 June, 1879, by Mr. C. T. Newton and others. Journal published 1881, *et seq.*

HELLESPONT (now the Strait of the Dardanelles) was named after Helle, daughter of Athamas, king of Thebes, who was drowned here. According to the legendary story of the loves of Hero of Sestus, and Leander of Abydos, Leander was drowned in a tempestuous night as he was swimming across the Hellespont (about one mile), and Hero, in despair, threw herself into the sea, dated seventh century B.C. Lord Byron and lieut. Ekenhead also swam across, 3 May, 1810. See *Xerxes*.

HELL-FIRE CLUBS. Three of these associations were suppressed, 1721. They met at Somerset-house, and at houses in Westminster and in Conduit-street.

HELLHOFFITE, a new, powerful and safe explosive, composed of nitrates, &c., invented by Hellhoff and Gruson of St. Petersburg, announced August, 1885.

HELMETS, among the Romans, were provided with a vizor of grated bars, to raise above the eyes, and beaver to lower for eating; the Greek helmet was round, the Roman square. Richard I. of England wore a plain round helmet; but most of the English kings had crowns above their helmets. Alexander III. of Scotland, 1249, had a flat helmet, with a square grated vizor, and the helmet of Robert I. was surmounted by a crown, 1306. *Guillim.*

HELOTS, *captives*, derived by some from the Greek *helein*, to take; by others from Helos, a city which the Spartans hated for refusing to pay tribute. The Spartans, it is said, ruined the city, reduced the Helots to slavery, and called all their slaves and prisoners of war *Helotæ*, 700 B.C. The number of the Helots was much enlarged by the conquest of Messenia, 668 B.C.; and is considered to have formed four-fifths of the inhabitants of Sparta. In the Peloponnesian war the Helots behaved with uncommon bravery, and were rewarded with liberty, 431 B.C.; but the sudden disappearance of 2000 manumitted slaves was attributed to Lacedæmonian treachery. *Herodotus*. The connection between the Helots and Helos, is now considered mythical.

HELVETIAN REPUBLIC. Switzerland having been conquered by the French in 1797, a republic was established April, 1798, with this title; see *Switzerland*.

HELVETII, a Celto-Germanic people, who inhabited part of what is now called Switzerland. They joined the Cimbri, were with them when the Romans were defeated near Geneva, and the consul Longinus killed, 107 B.C., and when they themselves were defeated by Marius and Catulus, 101. Invading Gaul, 61 B.C., they were defeated and massacred by Julius Cæsar, 58 B.C., near Geneva.

HEMEL HEMPSTEAD, Hertfordshire. The office of high bailiff dates from Henry VIII. Charter of incorporation granted, Dec. 1897. Population, 1891, 9,064; 1901, 11,244.

HEMP AND FLAX. Flax was first planted in England, when it was directed to be sown for fishing-nets, 1532-3. "Bounties were paid to encourage its cultivation in 1783; and every exertion should be made by the government and legislature to accomplish such a national good. In 1785 there were imported from Russia, in British ships, 17,695 tons of hemp and flax." *Sir John Sinclair*. The importation of hemp and flax in 1870, was 3,510,178 cwt.; 1879, 2,943,738 cwt.; 1883, 3,082,109 cwt.; 1887, 3,105,169 cwt.; 1890, 3,777,364 cwt.; 1900, 3,302,280 cwt.; 1901, 3,887,140 cwt. The cultivation of flax was revived at the dearth of cotton during the American civil war, 1861-4.

HENGESTDOWN (Cornwall). Here Egbert is said to have defeated the Danes and West Britons, 835.

HENOTICON (from the Greek *henotes*, unity), an edict of union for reconciling the Eutychians with the church, issued by the emperor Zeno at the instance of Acacius, patriarch of Constantinople, 482. It was zealously opposed by the popes of Rome, and was annulled by Justin I. in 518. The orthodox party triumphed, and many heretic bishops were expelled from their sees.

HEPTARCHY (or government of seven rulers) in England was gradually formed from 455, when Hengist became king of Kent. It terminated in 828, when Egbert became sole monarch of England. There were at first nine or ten Saxon kingdoms, but Middlesex soon ceased to exist, and Bernicia and Deira were generally governed by one ruler, as Northumbria: see *Britain*.

HERACLEA, see *Pandosia*.

HERACLIDÆ, descendants of Hercules, who were expelled from the Peloponnesus about 1200 B.C., but reconquered it in 1048, 1103-4 or 1109 B.C., a noted epoch in chronology, all the history preceding being accounted fabulous.

HERALDRY. Marks of honour were used in the first ages. *Nisbet*. The Phrygians had a sow; the Thracians, Mars; the Romans, an eagle; the Goths, a bear; the Flemings, a bull; the Saxons, a horse; and the ancient French a lion, and afterwards the fleur-de-lis (*which see*). Heraldry, as an art, is ascribed first to Charlemagne, about 800; and next to Frederick Barbarossa, about 1152; it began and grew with the feudal law. *Mackenzie*. The great English works on Heraldry are those of Barcham or Barkham, published by Gwillim (1610), Edmondson (1780), and Burke's "Armory" (1842; new ed. 1883, contains a history and the arms of above 66,000 British families, &c.). See *Blazonry*, *Crests*, and *Armorial Bearings*.

Edward III. appointed two heraldic kings-at-arms for the south and north (Surroy, Norroy) . . 1340
Richard III. incorporated and endowed the HERALDS' COLLEGE 1483-4
Philip and Mary enlarged its privileges, and confirmed them by letters patent . . 15 July, 1554
Formerly, in many ceremonies, the herald represented the king's person, and therefore wore a crown, and was always a knight.
The college has an earl marshal, 3 kings of arms (Garter, Clarencieux, and Norroy), 6 heralds (Richmond, Lancaster, Chester, Windsor, Somerset, and York), 4 pursuivants, and 2 extra heralds; see *Earl Marshal*, and *Kings-of-Arms*.
The building in Doctors' Commons, London, was erected by sir Christopher Wren (after the great fire in 1666), 1683; buildings now in Queen Victoria Street, E.C.
HERALDS' VISITATIONS were occasionally held in former times, at which the landed gentry were required to attend to prove their pedigrees, which were then entered in a book. The last is said to have been held in 1687. Some of the records have been printed.
A heraldic exhibition to which the queen contributed was opened in Edinburgh, July—August, 1891. The Treatise by the Rev. J. Woodward and the late G. Burnett was completed in two vols. . 1892
Committee appointed by the treasury to inquire into the constitution, duties, and administration of the Heralds college, the courts of Lyon and Ulster kings at arms, and the chanceries of the various orders of knighthood . . . Jan. 1903

HERAT, on the confines of Khorasân, a strong city, called the key of Afghanistan. It was conquered by Persia, early in the 16th century; by the Afghans, in 1715; by Nadir Shah, 1731; recovered by the Afghans, 1749. The Persians, baffled in an attempt in 1838; took it 25 Oct. 1856, in violation of the treaty of 1853; and war ensued between Great Britain and Persia. Peace was made in April, 1857; and Herat was restored 27 July following. It was seized again by Dost Mahommed, 26 May, 1863; taken by Yakoob Khan, rebelling against his father, 6 May, 1871. Yakoob, reconciled to his father, was made governor, 16 Sept. 1871.

Ayoub governor for his brother Yakoob, ameer at Cabul . . . . May, 1879
Mutiny, many officials killed . . . . 5 Sept. ,,
Ayoub invades Candahar (*which see*); defeated, 1 Sept.; returns to Herat . . . . . Sept. 1880
His troops defeated in several conflicts; Ayoub flees to Persia; and the Ameer's general enters Herat . . . . Oct. 1881
For following events, see *Afghanistan*.

HERBERT HOSPITAL for Soldiers, Woolwich, erected 1866.

HERCULANEUM, an ancient city of Campania, overwhelmed, together with Pompeii, by an eruption of lava from Vesuvius, 23 or 24 Aug. 79.

Successive eruptions laid them still deeper under the surface, and all traces of them were lost until excavations began in 1711; and in 1713 many antiquities were found. In 1738 excavations were resumed, and works of art, monuments, and memorials of civilized life were discovered. 150 rolls of MSS. papyri were found in a chest, in 1754; and many antiquities were purchased by sir William Hamilton, and sold to the British Museum, where they are deposited; but the principal relics are preserved in the museum of Portici. The "Antichità di Ercolano," 8 vols. folio, were published by the Neapolitan government, 1757-92.

HEREDITY. The transmission of qualities of like kind of those of the parents has been specially studied by Mr. Francis Galton, F.R.S. who published "Hereditary Genius," 1869, and "Records of Family Faculties," containing tabular forms to be filled up, in order to obtain authentic data for his new science of "Eugenics." Money prizes, 5*l.* and upwards, were offered for the best records. His "Inquiries into Human Faculty" was published in 1883, and "Natural Inheritance" in 1889. Works also by Haeckel, Hertwig, Nägeli, Herbert Spencer, Virchow, Guyau, and others.

Dr. August Weismann, in his "Studies in the Theory of Descent," English translation, 1882, and in his "Essays on Heredity," &c., 1889, set forth his reasons for opposing the theory, and referred to his researches on the lowest forms of animal life, *protozoa*, &c., and to Darwin's principle of natural selection, which he considers as the only possible theory for explaining the difficulties connected with metamorphoses of species. Much controversy ensued, in which the late prof. G. J. Romanes took a leading part.

HEREFORD was made the seat of a bishopric about 676, Putta being first bishop. The cathedral was founded by a nobleman named Milfride, in honour of Ethelbert king of the East Saxons, who was treacherously slain by his intended mother-in-law, the queen of Mercia. The tower fell in 1786, and was rebuilt by Mr. Wyatt. The cathedral was re-opened after very extensive repairs, on 30 June, 1863. The see is valued in the king's books at 768*l.* per annum. Present income, 4,200*l.* St. Nicholas's church, the cathedral, and other buildings damaged by earthquake, 5 a.m. 17 Dec. 1896. St. James's church, built about 1871, burnt 23 Dec. 1901. Princess Henry of Battenberg unveils a memorial window in the cathedral and lays the first stone of new municipal buildings, 13 May, 1902. Population, 1881, 19,821; 1891, 20,267; 1901, 21,832.

BISHOPS.

1803. Folliott H. W. Cornwall, translated to Worcester, 1808.
1808. John Luxmoore, translated to St. Asaph, 1815.
1815. George Isaac Huntingford, died 29 April, 1832.
1832. Hon. Edward Grey, died 24 June, 1837.
1837. Thomas Musgrave, trans. to York, Dec. 1847.
1847. Renn D. Hampden (election much opposed on account of his opinions), died 23 April, 1868.
1868. James Atlay; consecrated 24 June; died 24 Dec. 1894, aged 77.
1895. John Percival; consecrated 25 March.

HERETICS (from the Greek *hairesis*, choice). Paul says, "After the way they call *heresy*, so worship I the God of my fathers," 60 (*Acts* xxiv. 14). Heresy was unknown to the Greek and Roman religions. Simon Magus is said to have broached the Gnostic heresy about 41. This was followed by the Manichees, Nestorians, Arians, &c.; see *Inquisition*. It is stated that the promulgation of laws for prosecuting heretics was begun by the emperor Frederick II. in 1220; and immediately adopted by pope Honorius III.

Epiphanius chosen bishop of Constantius in Cyprus, 367, wrote "Panarium," a discourse against heresies, died 402
Thirty heretics came from Germany to England to propagate their opinions, and were branded in the forehead, whipped, and thrust naked into the streets in the depth of winter, where, none daring to relieve them, they died of hunger and cold (*Speed*) 1160
Laws against heretics repealed, 25 Henry VIII. 1534-5
The last person executed for heresy in Britain was Thomas Aikenhead, at Edinburgh . . . 1696
[The orthodox Mahommedans are Sonnites; the *heretics*—Shiites, Druses, &c.]

HERITABLE JURISDICTIONS (*i. e.*, feudal rights) in Scotland, valued at 164,232*l.*, were abolished by the act 20 Geo. II. c. 43 (1747), and restored to the crown for money compensation after 25 March, 1748. *Heritable and Movable Rights*, in the Scottish law, denote what in England is meant by real and personal property: *real* property in England answering nearly to heritable rights in Scotland, and *personal* property to the movable rights.

HERMANDAD, SANTA (Spanish for holy brotherhood), associations of cities of Castile and Arragon to defend their liberties, began about the middle of the 13th century. The brotherhood was disorganised in 1498, order having been firmly established. It is said to have been continued as a species of voluntary police.

HERMAS, author of "the Shepherd," a Christian apocryphal book, supposed to have been written about 131. Some believe Hermas to be mentioned in *Romans* xvi. 14.

HERMETIC BOOKS, the name of forty-two books forming the sacred canon of the ancient Egyptians, and constituting a synopsis of Egyptian wisdom. The name is derived from Hermes Trismegistus, the Greek name of Thoth, the Egyptian god of wisdom.

HERMETIC SOCIETY, a mystical, spiritual philanthropic association, based upon Christianity, founded by Dr. Anna Kingsford, early in 1884, presumed author of "The Perfect Way" (lectures delivered in 1881, and since published).

Mrs. Anna Kingsford died 22 Feb. 1888. See under *Theosophists*.

HERMITS, see *Monachism*.

HERNE BAY, Kent, a watering-place, begun 1830; the pier, five-eighths of a mile long, having decayed, a new one was opened, 27 Aug. 1873, by lord mayor Waterlow; pier lengthened in 1898. The Passmore Edwards convalescent home (railway men) opened 8 June, 1901. Population, 1881, 2,816; 1891, 3,829; 1901, 6,688.

HERO, BRITISH MAN-OF-WAR, see *Wrecks*, 1811.

HERRERA (Arragon). Here don Carlos, of Spain, in his struggle for his hereditary right to the throne, at the head of 12,000 men, encountered and defeated general Buerens, who had not much above half that number of the queen of Spain's troops. Buerens lost about 1000 in killed and wounded, 24 Aug. 1837.

HERRING-FISHERY was largely encouraged by the English and Scotch in very early times. The "statute of herrings," passed in 1357, placed the trade under government control. The mode of preserving herrings by pickling was discovered about 1397. *Anderson*. The British Herring-Fishery company was instituted 2 Sept.

1750. A scientific commission in relation to the fishery was appointed in 1862.

HERRINGS, Battle of the, fought 12 Feb. 1429, obtained its name from the duc de Bourbon being defeated while attempting to intercept a convoy of salt fish, on the road to the English besieging Orleans.

HERRNHUTERS, see *Moravians*.

HERSCHEL TELESCOPE, see *Telescopes*.

HERTFORD, Hertfordshire, a Saxon town. Castles were erected here by Alfred and by Edward the Elder. Charters were granted in 1588 and 1680. All Saints' church burnt, 21 Dec. 1891. Lord Cranborne receives the freedom, 4 July, 1902. Population, 1881, 7,747; 1891, 7,232; 1901, 9,322.

HERTFORD COLLEGE, Oxford; founded in 1312; dissolved, 1805; revived, and Magdalen hall incorporated with it, 1874.

HERULI, a German tribe, which ravaged Greece and Asia Minor in the 3rd century after Christ. Odoacer, their leader, overwhelmed the western empire and became king of Italy, 476. He was defeated and put to death by Theodoric the Ostrogoth, 491–3.

HERVEY ISLANDS (Pacific Ocean), Rarotonga, &c. British protectorate proclaimed, 20 Sept. 1888.

HERZEGOVINA or **Hertsek** (European Turkey), originally a part of Croatia, was united with Bosnia in 1326, and made the duchy of St. Saba by the emperor Frederic III. in the following century. It was ceded to Turkey in 1699 at the peace of Carlowitz. In Dec. 1861 an insurrection against the Turks broke out, fostered by the prince of Montenegro. It was subdued; and on 23 Sept. 1862, Vucatovitch, chief of the insurgents, surrendered on behalf of his countrymen to Kurschid Pasha, and an amnesty was granted.

Insurrection against the Turks; conflicts with varying results . . . . . . 1 July, 1875
The European Powers counsel to send a commission to redress grievances . . . 22 Aug. ,,
Server Pacha unsuccessful; Turkish victories Aug. ,,
The insurgents in a document describe their sufferings, as Christians; demand full and real freedom, and declare that they will not be subject to the Turks again . . . . . 12 Sept. ,,
Futile intervention of foreign consuls . Sept. ,,
Sanguinary engagements; various results; 29 Sept., 13 Oct. 11–14 Nov. ,,
Insurgents defeated near Trebinje; Bacevics, a leader, killed . . . . . . 18–20 Jan. 1876
Negotiations of the Austrian gen. Rodich fail; the insurgents ask too much . . . April ,,
Mukhtar Pasha said to have defeated insurgents, and revictualled Niksichs besieged . 29 April ,,
Other engagements reported . . May, June, ,,
The new Sultan, Murad, grants an armistice for negotiation . . . . . . June ,,
All intelligence very uncertain. July, 1875–July, ,, See *Turkey*.
Herzegovina was occupied by the Austrians in Aug. 1878, in conformity with the treaty of Berlin . . . . 13 July, 1878
Fighting at Mostar, the capital . . . . 4 Aug. ,,
Novi-Bazar quietly occupied by Austrians, 8 Sept. 1879
Insurrection (see *Austria*) . . . . . Jan. 1882
Civilisation and prosperity, reported 1898
Baron S. Burian appointed administrator of Bosnia and Herzegovina . . . . . . July, 1903

HESSE (W. Germany), the seat of the Catti, formed part of the empire of Charlemagne; from the rulers of it in his time, the present are descended. It was joined to Thuringia till about 1263, when Henry I. (son of a duke of Brabant and Sophia, daughter of the landgrave of Thuringia) became landgrave of Hesse. The most remarkable of his successors was Philip the Magnanimous (1509), an eminent warrior and energetic supporter of the Reformation, who signed the Augsburg Confession in 1530 and the League of Smalcald in 1531. At his death, in 1567, Hesse was divided into Hesse-Cassel and Hesse-Darmstadt, under his sons William and George, and their descendants played an eminent part in the convulsions of Germany during the 17th and 18th centuries.* In 1803 Hesse-Cassel became an electorate, and in 1806 Hesse-Darmstadt a grand duchy; which titles were retained in 1814. In 1807 Hesse-Cassel was incorporated with the kingdom of Westphalia, but in 1813 the electorate was re-established. Capital, Darmstadt. Population (1875), grand duchy, 884,218; (1885), 956,611; (1890), 993,659; 1900, 1,120,135.

Hesse-Cassel (made an electorate, 1803; incorporated with Westphalia, 1807; restored, 1813).

ELECTORS.

1803. William I.; born 3 June, 1743; succeeded as landgrave, 1785; made elector, 1803; deprived of his states, 1806; restored, 1813; died 27 Feb. 1821.
1821. William II.; born 28 July, 1777; died 20 Nov. 1847
1847. Frederic William; born 20 Aug. 1802.

The elector, in 1850, remodelled the constitution given in 1831 (by which the chamber had the exclusive right of voting the taxes), and did not convene the chamber until the usual time for closing the session had arrived, when his demand for money for 1851 was laid before it. The chamber called for a regular budget, that it might discuss its items. The elector dissolved the chamber, and declared his dominions in a state of siege, 7 Sept. 1850.
He fled to Hanover, and subsequently to Frankfort; and on 14 Oct. he formally applied to the Frankfort diet for assistance to re-establish his authority in Hesse. On 6 Nov. an Austro-Bavarian force of 10,000 men entered Hesse-Cassel, under the command of Prince Thurn-und-Taxis, who fixed his head-quarters in Hanau; and on the next day a Prussian force entered Cassel. The elector returned to his capital, the taxes having been collected under threats of imprisonment, 27 Dec. 1850.
The constitution of 1831 was abolished, and a new one established, 1852.
The conflict was soon resumed, and continued till, by law of 20 Sept. 1866, Hesse-Cassel was annexed to Prussia, 8 Oct. 1866.
The ex-elector's property sequestrated for intriguing against Prussia, 2 Nov. 1868 and Feb. 1869. He died 6 Jan. 1875.
The landgrave of Hesse mysteriously drowned near Batavia, 14 Oct. 1888.

Hesse-Darmstadt. (Population, 1900, 1,119,093.)
Visit of queen Victoria, 23–29 April, 1895.
The town of Brotterode almost destroyed by fire, 2 deaths, 10 July, 1895.
Visit of the czar and czarina to Darmstadt, 10 Oct. 1896.
Death of prince Henry of Hesse, eminent in the army, aged 62, 16 Sept. 1900.

GRAND-DUKES.

1806. Louis I.; born 14 June, 1753; died 6 April, 1830.
1830. Louis II.; born 26 Dec. 1777; died 16 June, 1848.

* Six thousand Hessian troops arrived in England, in consequence of an invasion being expected in 1756. The sum of 471,000*l.* three per cent. stock was transferred to the landgrave of Hesse, for Hessian auxiliaries lost in the American war, at 30*l.* per man, Nov. 1786. The Hessian soldiers were again brought to this realm at the close of the last century, and served in Ireland during the rebellion in 1798.

1848. Louis III.; born 9 June, 1806. By treaty with Prussia, 15 Sept. 1866, he ceded the northern part of Hesse-Darmstadt, and paid a war contribution; supported Prussia in the Franco-Prussian war, Aug. 1870; died 13 June, 1877.

1877. Louis IV., nephew, born 12 Sept. 1837; married princess Alice of Great Britain (born 25 April, 1843), 1 July, 1862; died of diphtheria after nursing her husband and children, 14 Dec. 1878. The grand-duke died 13 March, 1892.

Issue: Ernest Louis; Frederick-William, 2nd son, killed by a fall, 29 May, 1873; and 5 other children.

[Sisters married: Victoria to prince Louis of Battenberg, 30 April; Elizabeth to Grand duke Sergius of Russia, 15 June, 1884; Irene, married to prince Henry of Prussia, 24 May, 1888; Alix, born 6 June, 1872; married Nicholas II., czar of Russia, 26 Nov. 1894.]

1892. Ernest Louis; born 25 Nov. 1868; married at Coburg to his cousin, princess Victoria Melita, daughter of the duke of Coburg, in the presence of their grandmother, queen Victoria, the emperor William, the prince of Wales, the cesarewitch, and other royal persons; 19 April, 1894. The marriage dissolved by mutual consent, 21 Dec. 1901.

Issue: Elizabeth, born 11 March, 1895.

HESSE-HOMBURG, a landgraviate, established by Frederic, son of George of Hesse-Darmstadt, in 1596. His descendant, Augustus-Frederic, married 7 May, 1818, Elizabeth, daughter of George III. of England, who had no issue.

The landgraviate was absorbed into the grand duchy of Hesse in 1806, but re-established in 1815 with additional territories. The landgrave Ferdinand succeeded his brother, 8 Sept. 1848, and died 24 March, 1866.

Hesse-Homburg annexed to Prussia, 8 Oct. 1866.

HESSIAN FLY (Cecidomyia destructor), the American wheat midge, very destructive to the corn in the United States in 1786, whither it is said to have been brought by the Hessian soldiers in British pay—hence its name.

The crops suffered severely in New York state in 1846 and 1886. It appeared in England in 1788, and was described by sir Joseph Banks. Its appearance here in 1887 occasioned much alarm throughout the country.

Its action said to be checked by a parasite—Saw-fly (*Ceraphron destructor*)—*W. Freum*, Aug. 1887. Very prevalent in eastern coast of Britain, not much inland. *Ormerod*, Aug. 1887.

In twenty English and ten Scotch counties; the alarm considered to be exaggerated. *Parl. Rep.* Sept. 1887.

Presence of the insect reported in Lincoln, Suffolk, Herts, Perthshire . . . . . . 28 July, 1890

HETEROGENY, see *Spontaneous Generation.*

HEWLEY'S CHARITY, see *Unitarians.*

HEXAMETER, the most ancient form of Greek verse, six measures or feet, each containing two long syllables (a spondee), or a long one and two short (a dactyl), the form of verse in which Homer wrote his Iliad and Odyssey, and Virgil the Æneid.

HEXHAM or **HAGULSTAD**, Northumberland. The see of Hexham was founded about 678; it had ten bishops successively, but by reason of the rapine of the Danes it was discontinued; the last prelate appointed 810. At the BATTLE OF HEXHAM the Yorkist army of Edward IV. obtained a complete victory over the Lancastrian army of Henry VI., 15 May, 1464. Population, 1881, 5,919; 1891, 5,945; 1901, 7,071.

HEXTHORPE, Yorkshire, see *Railway Accidents*, 16 Sept. 1887.

HIBBERT FUND. Robert Hibbert on 19 July, 1847, established a trust fund "for the promotion of comprehensive learning and thorough research in relation to religion as it appears to the eye of the scholar and philosopher, and wholly apart from the interest of any particular church or system."

Hibbert lectures; first course of, seven by prof. Max Müller (given at Westminster) "on the Origin and Growth of Religion, as illustrated by the Religions of India" . 25 April—30 May, 1878

Since given by M. Renouf, in 1879; M. Ernest Renan, 6–14 April, 1880; by Mr. T. W. Rhys Davids, 26 April–24 May, 1881; by professor Kuenen, 25 April–May, 1882; by Mr. C. Beard, 1883; by professor Albert Reville, 21 April *et seq.* 1884; by Professor O. Pfleiderer, 1885; Mr. J. Rhys, 1886; by professor A. Sayce . . . . . April, 1887

HIBERNIA, Ibernia, Ivernia, and Ierne, a name given to Ireland by ancient writers (Aristotle, Ptolemy, &c.); see *Ireland*, and *Wrecks*, 1833.

HICKS'S HALL, Clerkenwell, London. The sessions-house of the justices of Middlesex was long so named on account of its having been erected for them by sir Baptist Hicks, at his own expense, 1611-12.

HIEROGLYPHICS, literally sacred sculptures or engravings, the representation of objects to express language, used by the ancient Egyptians, Mexicans, and other nations. The Egyptians used about 1700 hieroglyphs, engraved on stone, painted on wood, and written on papyri. They were either phonetic or ideographic. Their invention is mythically ascribed to Athotes. See "Book of the Dead," in article *Death*. Young, Champollion, Rosellini, Lepsius, Brugsch, Mariette, Chabas, Birch, and others (in the present century) have much elucidated Egyptian hieroglyphics; see *Rosetta Stone*. A. Erman's "Egyptian Grammar," English translation by J. H. Breasted, published about July, 1894.

HIGH AND LOW CHURCH, sections in the Church of England became prominent in the reign of Elizabeth. High church principles were maintained by Abp. Whitgift, and set forth by Richard Hooker "the judicious" in his Ecclesiastical Polity, 1593-7. They were opposed by the Puritans. The contest, hot in the reign of Anne, has continued since. Dr. Sacheverell, preacher at St. Saviour's, Southwark, was prosecuted for two seditious sermons preached (14 Aug. and 9 Nov. 1709) to create apprehension for the safety of the church, and to excite hostility against dissenters. His friends were called High Church and his opponents Low Church, or moderate men, 1720. The queen favoured Sacheverell, and presented him with the rectory of St. Andrew's, Holborn. He died in 1724.

HIGH COMMISSION, COURT OF, an ecclesiastical court, erected by 1 Eliz. c. 1, 1559, by which all spiritual jurisdiction was vested in the crown. It originally had no power to fine or imprison; but under Charles I. and archbishop Laud it assumed illegal powers, was complained of by the parliament, and abolished in 1641.

HIGH CONSTABLE, see *Constable.*

HIGH COURT OF JUSTICE, see *Supreme Court.*

HIGH COURT OF JUSTICIARY, see *Supreme Court* and *Law.*

HIGHER CRITICISM, see *Rationalism.*

HIGHGATE ARCHWAY, over a road made to avoid the hill; first stone laid by Edward Smith, 31 Oct. 1812; toll through ceased, 1 May, 1876. Rebuilding proposed, 1893; completed, 1900. See *London, Nov.* 1889.

HIGHGATE COLLEGE, founded by sir Roger Cholmeley, 1565.

HIGHLANDS (of Scotland), long held by semi-barbarous clans, were greatly improved by the construction of military roads by general Wade, about 1725–6; by the abolition of heritable jurisdiction of feudal rights in 1747, and by the establishment of the Highland and Agricultural Society in 1784; centenary celebrated at Edinburgh, July, 1884. See *Regiments, Crofters.*

Highland Society of London, founded 28 May, 1778. *Highland Land League* held fifth annual conference at Oban, 15 Sept. 1887; Glasgow, Sept. 1893.

HIGHNESS. The title of *Highness* was given to Henry VII.; and this, and sometimes *Your Grace*, was the manner of addressing Henry VIII.; but about the close of the reign of the latter, the titles of "Highness" and "Your Grace" were absorbed in that of "Majesty." Louis XIII. of France gave the title of Highness to the prince of Orange, in 1644; this prince had previously only the distinction of Excellency. Louis XIV. gave the princes of Orange the title of High and Mighty Lords, 1644. *Hénault.*

HIGH PRIEST, see *Priest.*

HIGH TREASON. To regulate the trials for this crime the statute, so favourable to liberty, the 25th of Edward III., 1352, was enacted, by which two living witnesses are required. By an act passed 19 April, 1821, this provision was extended to Ireland, parliament having refused to sanction the sentence of death against the duke of Somerset. In 1800 it was enacted that when the overt act was a direct attempt on the life of the sovereign, the trial should be conducted in the same manner as in the case of an indictment for murder. The trial of John Horne Tooke and others for constructive high treason failed, see *Horne Tooke*, Nov., Dec. 1794. See *Treason.*

The last two cases of execution for high treason :—

I. William Cundell *alias* Connell, and John Smith; tried on a special commission, 6 Feb. 1812, being two of fourteen British subjects taken in the enemy's service in the isles of France and Bourbon. Mr. Abbot, afterwards lord Tenterden and chief justice, and sir Vicary Gibbs, attorney-general, conducted the prosecution, and Mr. Brougham, aft. lord Brougham, defended the prisoners. The defence was, that they had assumed the French uniform to aid their escape to England. They were hanged and beheaded on the lodge of Horsemonger-lane gaol on 16 March, 1812.

All the other convicts were pardoned, upon condition of serving in colonies beyond the seas.

II. The *Cato-street Conspirators* (*which see*), executed 1 May, 1820.

"Colonel" Lynch, member-elect for Galway, who fought on the side of the Boers in the S. African war, prosecuted by the crown on the charge of high treason, and tried at the king's bench before the lord chief justice, Mr. justice Wills, and Mr. justice Channell, and sentenced to death 23 Jan. 1903. The lord chief justice laid down, "that if a subject, in time of war, joined the king's enemies, for whatever purpose, that was an act of treason." Sentence afterwards commuted to penal servitude for life.

HIGHWAYS, see *Roads.*

HILL, ROWLAND, MEMORIAL FUND, see *Mansion House.*

HILLSBOROUGH (Down, N.E. Ireland), founded by sir A. Hill, in the reign of Charles I. Here were held two great protestant meetings in favour of the Irish church: (1.) on 30 Oct. 1834, to protest against the "appropriation clause;" (2.) 30 Oct. 1867, in consequence of a commission of inquiry into the Irish church establishment, and the agitation consequent thereon.

HIMALAYA, a range of mountains between India and Tibet. Its loftiest peak is Mount Everest, height 29,002 ft., the highest known in the world.

Mr. W. W. Graham, with two Swiss guides, ascended Mount Kabru (height 24,000 feet) and three other mountains over 19,000 feet in the Sikkim group with much difficulty, Nov. 1883.

Dr. Karl Diener explores the Central Himalayas to the height of 19,000 ft., April–July, 1892.

Mr. (aft. sir) Wm. Martin Conway's "Climbing in the Karakoram-Himalayas," published 1894; he ascended great glacier heights.

On 6 Sept. 1893, near Gohna, in the district of Garhwal, Bengal, nearly the whole of the hill Maithána fell into the river Birahi Ganga, a tributary of the Alaknanda, damming it up and forming a long deep lake, which gradually increased in size, and eventually overflowed and burst its banks, causing great destruction of buildings, bridges, &c., at Gohna and Hardwar, &c., 26–27 Aug. 1894. This event was anticipated by geologists, and through scientific precautions no loss of life ensued.

Whilst exploring the Nanga Parbat region, Mr. A. F. Mummery and 2 Gurkhas were killed by an avalanche, mid. Aug. 1895.

An international expedition begins to ascend Broad Peak, 30 June, 1902.

HIMERA (Sicily). Here (in 480 B.C.) Gelon of Syracuse and Theron of Agrigentum defeated the Carthaginians; and at Ecnomus, near here, the latter defeated Agathocles of Syracuse, 310 B.C.

HINDOO ERA (see *Cali-yuga*) began 3101 B.C., or 756 before the Deluge, in 2348. The Hindoos count their months by the progress of the sun through the zodiac. The Samoat era begins 56 B.C.; the Saca era A.D. 79.

HINDOSTAN, see *India.*

HIPPODROME, a circus for horse-riding. One opened by Mr. John Whyte, near Notting-hill, London, on 29 May, 1837, was closed in 1841 by the Kensington vestry. See under *Agricultural Hall.*

LONDON HIPPODROME, Leicester-square, originally styled "The Royal Hippodrome," was opened by Moss' Empires, Ltd., 15 Jan. 1900, with a spectacular aquatic carnival "Giddy Ostend," by H. Chance, with music composed by M. G. Jacobi; "Little Tich," and Herr Julius Seth, the lion-tamer, with 21 forest-bred lions, took part in the performances. Among the artistes who have appeared at the Hippodrome, are R. Cottrell and the Misses Powell, equestrians, and Herr Sawade, with his wild-beast show. Sensational water dramas have been a feature, and include "Siberia," "Tally Ho," and "The Redskins;" the pantomimes "Cinderella," "Aladdin," and "Dick Whittington" have also been produced at the Hippodrome. Two performances are given daily.

HIPPOPHAGY, see *Horse.*

HIPPOPOTAMUS (Greek, *river-horse*), a native of Africa, known to, but incorrectly described by, ancient writers. Hippopotami were exhibited at Rome by Antoninus, Commodus, and others, about 138, 180, and 218. The first brought to England arrived 25 May, 1850, and was placed in the Zoological Gardens, Regent's-park, London; (died, 11 March, 1878;) another, a female, four months old, was placed there in 1854 (died, Dec. 1882). One born here, 21 Feb. 1871, and another born 1 Jan. 1872, lived a few days only; another born

5 Nov. 1872. Two young ones born at Paris in May, 1858, and June, 1859, were killed by their mother. One born at Amsterdam, 29 July, 1865.

HISPANIA, Latin name of Spain.

HISPANIOLA, see *Hayti*.

HISTOLOGY (from *histos*, a web), the science which treats of the tissues which enter into the formation of animals and vegetables; mainly prosecuted by the aid of the microscope. Schwann, Valentin, Kölliker, Quekett, and Robin are celebrated for their researches. Professor Quekett's "Lectures on Histology" were published in 1852 and 1854. Important "Atlas of Histology," by Drs. E. Klein and E. N. Smith, published in 1880; "Elements of Histology," by Dr. E. Klein, third edition published in 1884.

HISTORY. The Bible, the Parian Chronicle, the histories of Herodotus, "the father of history," and Ctesias, and the poems of Homer, are the foundations of early *ancient* history. Later ancient history is considered as ending with the destruction of the Roman empire in Italy, 476. *Modern* history dates from the age of Charlemagne, about 800. There was not a professorship of modern history in either of our universities until the years 1724 and 1736, when Regius professorships were established by George I. and George II. At Oxford professor E. A. Freeman, appointed 1884, died 16 March, 1892, succeeded by Mr. J. A. Froude, April, 1892; died, 20 Oct. 1894; succeeded by Mr. F. York Powell, Dec. 1894. At Cambridge professor sir J. R. Seeley, 1869-95; lord Acton, R. C., Feb. 1895. —*Royal Historical Society*, London, established 1868, Earl Russell president, 1872, incorporated by charter, Aug. 1889; amalgamated with the Camden society 30 Oct. 1897. *Historical MSS. Commission*, a commission was appointed 31 Aug. 1869, to examine historical MSS. in the possession of institutions and private families, and to publish any considered desirable. It has issued several reports, 1870, *et seq*. New commission appointed, 18 June, 1883; many volumes of calendars since issued. New commission appointed, 20 Dec. 1897; the Stuart papers, vol. i., issued, 1902.

HITTITES, descendants of Heth, second son of Canaan, a commercial tribe, from whom Abraham bought a grave for his wife 1860 B.C. *Gen.* xxiii. They opposed Joshua, B.C. 1451; and the Egyptians, about 1340 B.C.

The castle of Jerablus, a mound and ruins, 20 miles below Beredjik on the Euphrates; was visited by Henry Maundrell, 1699; by Dr. Pococke, 1745; and by J. H. Skene and Mr. Geo. Smith (died 1876), who agreed in considering the remains to be those of Carchemish, the ancient capital of the Hittites, captured and annexed by Sargon, king of Assyria (about 721 B.C.) when the nation was thoroughly subdued. The site had been held successively by Hittites, Assyrians, Babylonians, Greeks, Romans, and Arabs.

A rich harvest may be expected from its exploration.

Captain C. R. Conder's discovery of a key to the language of Hittite inscriptions on bas-reliefs, gems, &c., some of which were discovered by Burckhardt, 1808, and re-discovered by Mr. Palmer in 1870, announced 26 Feb. 1887; they consist of invocations, hymns, &c. to the sun, &c. His "Altaic Hieroglyphs and Hittite Inscriptions" published 1887.

Prof. A. Sayce, in 1879, considered the Hittites to have been in very early times the predominant power in Asia Minor and N. Syria. The investigations of Messrs. Ramsay, Hogarth and Headlam, in 1890, supported by the English Asia Minor Exploration Fund, led to many discoveries which are described in the *Times* of 25 July, 1891. Investigations proceeding, 1903. New discoveries by the French expedition of 1893-94, and by M. E. Chantre, in Cappadocia, in 1898; *see* capt. Conder's letter, *Times*, 10 Oct. 1899. 3rd and enlarged edition of "The Hittites," by prof. Sayce, 1903, describes his partially successful efforts in interpreting the cuneiform Hittite inscriptions.

HOBART TOWN or **HOBART,** a sea-port and capital of Van Diemen's Land, was founded in 1804 by col. Collins, the first lieutenant-governor, who died here in 1810. Population in 1881, 21,118; in 1891, 24,905; 1894, 35,073; 1901, 34,604.

HOBHOUSE'S ACT, 1 & 2 Will. IV. c. 60, 1831, relates to vestries and charities.

HOCHKIRCHEN (Saxony). Here, on 14 Oct. 1758, the Prussian army, commanded by Frederick II., was surprised and defeated by the Austrians commanded by count Daun. Marshal Keith, a Scotsman in the Prussian service, was killed. The Austrian generals shed tears, and ordered his interment with military honours. A conflict between the Russians and Prussians and the French, in which the last were victorious, took place 21 May, 1813.

HOCHSTADT, a city on the Danube, in Bavaria, near which several important battles have been fought: (1.) 20 Sept. 1703, when the Imperialists were defeated by the French and Bavarians, under marshal Villars and the elector of Bavaria. (2.) 2 (N. S. 13) Aug. 1704, called the battle of Blenheim (*which see*). (3.) 19 June, 1800, when Moreau totally defeated the Austrians, and avenged the defeat of the French at Blenheim.

HOFWYL, see *Pestalozzian System*.

HOGARTH CLUB, 36 Dover-st., closed; sale, 20 Jan. 1897. Hogarth's house at Chiswick sold to lieut.-col. Shipway for 1,500*l*., 25 Nov. 1901.

HOGUE, see *La Hogue*.

HOHENLINDEN (Bavaria). Here the Austrians, commanded by archduke John, were beaten by the French and Bavarians, commanded by Moreau, 3 Dec. 1800. The peace of Luneville followed.

HOHENSTAUFEN, see *Germany*, and *Guelphs*.

HOHENZOLLERN, the reigning family in Prussia. Its origin is referred to Thassilo, about 800, who built the castle of Hohenzollern. In 1417, Frederick of Nuremburg, his descendant, was made elector of Brandenburg. The princes of Hohenzollern-Hechingen and Hohenzollern-Sigmaringen abdicated in favour of the king of Prussia, 7 Dec. 1849. Charles, son of Charles Anthony, the prince of Hohenzollern-Sigmaringen, was elected prince of Roumania, 20 April, 1866 (see *Danubian Principalities*). His brother Leopold, nominated candidate for the throne of Spain, withdrew July, 1870; their father Charles Anthony died 2 June, 1885. See *Brandenburg*, and *Prussia*.

HOLBEIN SOCIETY, for obtaining photolithographic representations of ancient wood engravings, established in 1868, sir William Stirling Maxwell president.

HOLBORN (Holeborne, in Doomsday book), said to be identical with the river Fleet. Holborn-hill, in the time of Stow, 1600, was termed "heavy-hill." Gerard, the herbalist, speaks of his "house in Holborne," 1597. The *Holborn-theatre* was opened by Mr. Sefton Parry, 6 Oct. 1866, with "Flying Scud," a new piece, by Mr. Dion

Boucicault. The *Holborn amphitheatre* was opened 25 May, 1867. The Holborn valley viaduct, founded by Mr. F. H. Fry, 3 June, 1867 (Mr. William Haywood, chief engineer), was opened for foot-passengers 14 Oct., and inaugurated by the queen, 6 Nov. 1869. "Middle-row" was pulled down in 1867. Western Approach-street opened 25 June, 1868. The statue of prince Albert uncovered by the prince of Wales, 9 Jan. 1874. Holborn town-hall opened by the lord mayor, 18 Dec. 1879. Constituted a municipal borough by London Government act, 1899 (7 aldermen, 42 councillors). New roadway (Kingsway and Aldwych) connecting Holborn with the Strand in progress 1903.

HOLIDAYS, see *Bank Holidays*.

HOLLAND (*Hollow land*, or, some say, *Wooded land*), a kingdom, N.W. Europe, the chief part of the northern Netherlands, composed of land rescued from the sea, and defended by immense dykes. It was inhabited by the Batavi in the time of Cæsar, who made a league with them. It became part of Gallia Belgica, and afterwards of the kingdom of Austrasia. From the 10th to the 15th century it was governed by counts under the German emperors. In 1861, the population of the kingdom in Europe was 3,521,416; of the colonies, 18,175,910; of both in 1863, 21,805,607; 1876, 3,865,456; colonies, about 25,110,000; 1879, kingdom, 4,012,693; 1887, 4,450,870; 31 Dec. 1893, 4,732,912; 31 Dec. 1900, 5,179,138 (colonies about 35,194,200). Revenue, 1889, 10,184,158*l*.; 1893, 10,562,366*l*.; expenditure, 1889, 11,256,249*l*.; 1893, 10,862,475*l*.; revenue, 1901-02, 12,833,520*l*.; expenditure, 13,935,265*l*.

The parties termed *Hooks*, (followers of Margaret, countess of Holland,) and *Cod-fish*, (supporters of her son William, who endeavoured to supplant her,) create a civil war, which lasts many years . 1347
Holland united to Hainault, 1299; and Brabant . 1416
Annexed to Burgundy by duke Philip, who wrests it from his niece Jaqueline, of Holland, daughter of the last count 1436
Annexed to Austria through marriage of Mary of Burgundy with archduke Maximilian 1477
Government of Philip of Austria 1495
Of Margaret of Austria and Charles V. . . . 1506
Of Philip II. 1555
Philip II. establishes the Inquisition; the Hollanders having zealously embraced the reformed doctrines; severe persecution; about 100,000 persons said to have perished 1555 *et seq.*; the Confederacy of Gueux (Beggars) formed by the nobles 1566
Compromise of Breda presented . . . Jan. ,,
Commencement of the revolt under William, prince of Orange 1572
Elizabeth of England declines the offered sovereignty, but promises help 1575
The pacification of Ghent—union of the North and south provinces 1576
The seven northern provinces contract the league of Utrecht 1579
And declare their independence . . 25 July, 1581
Assassination of William of Orange . 10 July, 1584
The ten southern provinces conquered by the prince of Parma 1585
The provinces solicit help from England and France; expedition of the earl of Leicester; English and Dutch disagree 1585-7
Battle of Zutphen—sir Philip Sidney mortally wounded . . . . . 22 Sept. 1586
Prince Maurice appointed stadtholder . . . 1587
Death of Philip II. His son Philip III. cedes the Netherlands to Albert of Austria, and the infanta, Isabella 1598
Campaigns of Maurice and Spinola . . . 1599-1604
Maurice defeats the archduke at Nieuport 2 July, 1600
The independence of the United Provinces recognised; truce of Antwerp for twelve years, 9 April (30 March), 1609
Batavia in Java built 1610
Fierce religious dissensions between the Arminians and Gomarists 1610-19
Maurice favours the latter and intrigues for royal power 1616
Synod of Dort; persecution of the Arminians 1618-19
Execution of the illustrious Barneveldt 14 May, 1619
Renewal of the war; Maurice saves Bergen-op-Zoom 1622
His tyrannical government: plot against him, and sixteen persons executed 1623
His death; his brother Frederick succeeds him, and annuls the persecution 1625
Manhattan, now New York, North America, founded; massacre of English at Amboyna, East Indies 1624
Victories of Van Tromp, who takes two Spanish fleets off the downs . . 16 Sept. and 21 Oct. 1639
Peace of Westphalia, the republic recognised by Europe 1648
War with England—naval actions—Blake defeats De Ruyter, 22 Oct.; but is surprised by Van Tromp, who takes some English ships, and sails through the channel with a broom at his masthead . . . . . . 29 Nov. 1652
Indecisive sea-fights, 12-14 June; death of Van Tromp, 31 July; peace follows . . . 1653
Victorious war with Sweden 1659
Another war with England 1665
Indecisive sea-fights, 1-4 June; victory of Monk over De Ruyter . . . . 25 July, 1666
Triple alliance of England, Holland, and Sweden against France 1668
Charles II. deserts Holland; joins France . . 1670
The French overrun Holland 1671
Desperate condition of the States—the populace massacre the De Witts—William III. made stadtholder 1672
The French repelled by the sluices being opened ,,
Indecisive campaigns 1673-7
William marries princess Mary of England . 1677
Peace with France (Nimeguen) 1678
William becomes king of England . . . 1689
Sanguinary war with France 1689-96
Peace of Ryswick signed . . . 20 Sept. 1697
Death of William . . . . . 8 March, 1702
No stadtholder appointed—administration of Heinsius . . . . ,,
War against France and Spain; campaigns of Marlborough 1702-13
Peace of Utrecht . . . . . 11 April, 1713
Holland supports the empress Maria-Theresa . 1743-8
William Henry hereditary stadtholder . . . 1747
Peace of Aix-la-Chapelle . . . 18 Oct. 1748
War with England for naval supremacy—Holland loses colonies 1781-3
Civil wars in the Low Countries . . . 1787-9
The French republicans march into Holland; the people declare in their favour . . . 1793
Unsuccessful campaign of the duke of York . 1794
The *Batavian republic* established in alliance with France 1795
Battle of Camperdown, Duncan signally defeats the Dutch . . . . . . 11 Oct. 1797
The Texel fleet, of twelve ships of the line, with thirteen Indiamen, surrenders to the British admiral, without firing a gun . 30 Aug. 1799
A new constitution is given to the Batavian republic; the chief officer (R. J. Schimmelpenninck) takes the title of grand pensionary . 26 April, 1805
Holland erected into a *kingdom*, and Louis Bonaparte, father of Napoleon III., declared king . 5 June, 1806
The ill-fated Walcheren expedition . July, Sept. 1809
Louis abdicates . . . . . . 1 July, 1810
Holland united to France . . . . 9 July, ,,
Restored to the house of Orange, and Belgium annexed to its dominions . . . 17 Nov. 1813
The prince of Orange proclaimed sovereign prince of the united Netherlands . . . 6 Dec. ,,
Religious discord between Holland and the southern provinces . . . . 1817, &c.
The revolution in Belgium . . . 25 Aug. 1830
Belgium separated from Holland . . 12 July, 1831
Holland makes war against Belgium . . 3 Aug. ,,
Treaty between Holland and Belgium, signed in London . . . . . . 19 April, 1839
Abdication of William I. . . . 7-10 Oct. 1840
Death of the ex-king William I. . . 12 Dec. 1843
Louis Bonaparte, count de St. Leu, ex-king of Holland, dies of apoplexy at Leghorn . 25 July, 1846

The king agrees to political reform, March; a new constitution granted . . . . 17 April, 1848
Death of William II. 17 March, 1849
Re-establishment of a Roman Catholic hierarchy announced . . . . . 12 March, 1853
General van den Bosch's scheme carried out by the society of beneficence of home colonization in east Holland for destitute persons of all sorts, started about 1815, having failed is modified; free and penal colonies constituted; (generally successful) 1859
Inundations: 40,000 acres submerged; nearly 30,000 villagers made destitute Jan. and Feb. 1861
Great fire at Endschedé, the Manchester of Holland, loss about a million pounds . . 7 May, 1862
The states-general pass a law for the abolition of slavery in the Dutch West Indies [after 1 July, 1863] . . . . 6 Aug. ,,
Treaty for capitalising Scheldt dues signed 12 May, 1863
Slavery ceases in the Dutch West Indies 1 July, ,,
50th anniversary of deliverance from France, 17 Nov. ,,
Commencement of canal to connect Amsterdam with the North sea . . . . . 8 March, 1865
The government undertake a canal to connect Rotterdam with the sea . . . March, ,,
Commercial treaty with France . . . 7 July, ,,
New ministry (protectionist) . . . . 1 June, 1866
Correspondence with Prussia respecting the Prussian garrison in Luxemburg . July–Aug. ,,
The lower chamber barely passes a vote of censure on the ministry respecting government of Java, &c.; the king dissolves the chamber . 10 Oct. ,,
Alleged treaty with France respecting cession of Luxemburg (*which see*) . . 22 March, 1867
The fortifications of Luxemburg razed . May, 1868
Long struggle between the ministry and the chambers, Nov. 1867–May, 1868, the ministry resign; a new ministry formed by M. de Thorbecke, June, ,,
International exhibition opened at Amsterdam by prince Henry . . . . 15 July, 1869
Meeting of the chambers; strict neutrality in the Franco-Prussian war to be maintained 19 Sept. 1870
Cession of Dutch possessions in Guinea to Great Britain, voted . . . . . . 7 July, 1871
Tercentenary celebration of the commencement of Dutch independence by the capture of Briel, 1 April, 1872
Death of de Thorbecke, a great statesman 4 June, ,,
A new ministry formed by Devries . . 29 June, ,,
Discussions respecting the war against the Sultan of Achin in Sumatra (*which see*) April, 1873
New port at Flushing opened by the king . 8 Sept. ,,
Expedition against the Achinese (see *Sumatra*) embarks . . . . . Dec. ,,
New ministry, under Dr. Heemskirk . 28 July, 1874
New penal code issued . . . . . Aug. 1875
Tercentenary of Pacification of Ghent celebrated, Sept. 1876
Canal between North sea and Amsterdam, passed by a monitor (*see* 1865) 4 Oct.; inaugurated by the king . . . . . . 1 Nov. ,,
New ministry; president, baron Kappeijne van de Coppello . . . . . 3 Nov. 1877
Marriage of prince Henry, the king's brother, to princess Marie Elizabeth of Prussia . 24 Aug. 1878
Death of prince Henry, the king's brother, aged 58: 13 Jan. 1879
New cabinet, under M. Van Lynden . 19 Aug. ,,
The king and queen visit England . . 26 April, 1882
Commercial treaty with France rejected by the chamber; the ministry resign . 9 May, ,,
Resignation of baron van Lynden and his cabinet 1 March, 1883
New ministry under Dr. Heemskerk (interior) 22 April, ,,
International exhibition at Amsterdam opened by the king . . . . 1 May, ,,
Committee for revision of the constitution appointed 12 May, ,,
The king and queen of Belgium warmly received at Amsterdam, &c. . . . . 18 Oct. *et seq.* ,,
The king and queen warmly received at Brussels 20–22 May, 1884
Death of the prince of Orange . . 21 June, ,,
The queen appointed by a congress to be regent if necessary . . . . 1 Aug. ,,

Resignation of the ministry, 13 April; declined by the king . . . . . . 22 April, 1886
The king's assent given to bill for revision of constitution, 8 Nov.; the revised constitution promulgated . . . . . . 30 Nov. 1887
New ministry; interior baron Mackay 17 April, 1888
Continued illness of the king; the queen nominated regent, and the duke of Nassau regent of Luxemburg, April; the king suddenly recovers; regency deferred, April; the king resumes government May, 1889
Celebration of the 40th anniversary of the king's accession . . . . . . 12 May, ,,
The parliament declares the king incapable of ruling; the council of state to govern for a month 29 Oct. 1890
The queen appointed regent at a sitting of the two chambers, 13 Nov.; takes the oath 20 Nov. ,,
Death of King William III., a real constitutional ruler; accession of his daughter Wilhelmina, 23 Nov.; grand public funeral . . . 4 Dec. ,,
See *Luxemburg*.
Visit of the German emperor and empress, see *Germany* . . . . . . 1–3 July, ,,
Resignation of the ministry, 8 July; new ministry formed by M. Vantienhoven, 5 Aug.; he becomes foreign minister, and M. Tak van Poortvliet premier . . . . 11 Aug. 1891
New Parliament opened by the queen-regent . 15 Sept. ,,
A section of the Merwede canal, from Amsterdam to the north of the Leck, opened in presence of the queen and queen-regent . . 4 Aug. 1892
The new ironclad, *Koningin Wilhelmina*, launched at Amsterdam; the queen present . 22 Oct. ,,
Labour riots in various parts, about . 31 Dec. ,,
The budget for 1894 shows a deficit of 3 million florins . . . . . . 22 Sept. 1893
An electoral reform bill withdrawn on an amendment being carried in the 2nd chamber 9 March, 1894
The parliament dissolved . . . 20 March, ,,
Elections; majority for the opposition . 26 April, ,,
J. P. R. Tak Van Poortvliet and his ministry resign . . . . 28 April, ,,
New ministry formed under Jonkheer Roell, premier . . . . 9 May, ,,
The parliament opened . . . . . 16 May, ,,
Insurrection in the Dutch East Indies; the Dutch are surprised by an ambush at Tjakra-Negara, near Mataram, in the island of Lombok; defeated with heavy loss; gen. Van Ham, 8 officers, and 200 men killed . . . 25–27 Aug. ,,
The Dutch men-of-war bombard Mataram, Kampong and Tanabat, reported . . 30 Aug. ,,
Reinforcements arrive . . . . . 4 Sept. ,,
Arveng captured . . . . . . 6 Sept. ,,
Mataram taken after severe fighting 29 Sept. ,,
Tjakra-Negara attacked . . . . 18 Nov. ,,
The rajah surrenders . . . . . 21 Nov. ,,
General submission, reported . . 26 Nov. ,,
The parliament re-opened . . . . 18 Sept. ,,
The queen and queen-regent visit England; received by the prince of Wales, 27 April; by the queen, 3 May; left . . . . 9 May, 1895
Parliament opened by the queen-regent 17 Sept. ,,
Strike of diamond-cutters in Amsterdam; riotous demonstrations . . . . . 5 Oct. ,,
Conversion of the national debt from 3½ to 3 per cent., bill submitted . . . . 2 Dec. ,,
RISING IN THE E. INDIES: desultory fighting in Sumatra, headed by the Achinese chief Toekoe Djohan; 2 forts relieved, and rebel intrenchments captured by the Dutch, 8, 12 April, 1896; 4 Achinese forts evacuated by the Dutch, after heavy fighting, 18 April; Tokoe Omar's capital Lampisang taken, May; Dutch successes, and flight of rebels; Loempong bombarded, 14 June; enemy routed at Blang-Bitang; Tokoe Baid rebel chief surrenders; gen. Moulin dies, while trying to cross a morass in Atjeh, Aug.; desultory fighting, Sept.; lieut.-col. Van Vliet appointed governor of Atjeh, 20 Oct.; the sultan of Pazir overthrown, and banished, Oct.; Tokoe Omar captured after a hot fight, near Poeding, much slaughter, Jan. 1897; rebels defeated with heavy loss, reported, 26 Jan.; Indrapaori occupied by the Dutch, 15 Feb.; Dutch successes, March,

June; Kampong taken by the Dutch; deadly fight near Indrapura, Aug.; desultory fighting, Sept. 1897; expedition to Pedir attacked by Achinese, enemy repulsed, and 110 killed; 30 June, 1898, the Achinese again defeated, 80 killed, near Edi; quiet restored, flight of the enemy, 18 July, 1895; further resistance in Matangkoli, Oct. 1898; Tokoe Oemar surprised by an ambuscade and mortally wounded; his troops dispersed, 10 Feb. 1899; sharp fighting, many Achinese killed, early March and mid April, 1901; Dutch punitive expedition in Djambi repulsed, 7 killed, reported 23 Nov.; Dutch bivouac surprised, 12 killed, enemy 24, reported, 19 July, the sultan surrendered end, Dec. 1902.

Suffrage extension bill passed . . . . 6 Sept. 1896

States-general opened by the queen-regent, 15 Sept. ,,

Budget for 1897, deficit, 3,330,000*fl*. . 17 Sept. ,,

Mr. Henry Howard appointed British minister at the Hague; announced . . . 21 Sept. ,,

Sugar (bounties) bill passed . . . 23 Dec. ,,

Claim of capt. J. C. Carpenter, of the *Costa Rica* (Australian whaler), for compensation for ill-usage and imprisonment by the Dutch authorities in the Moluccas (Nov. 1891), referred to Russian arbitration, Sept. 1895; 8,550*l*. awarded him . . . . . . 1 March, 1897

New liberal cabinet: Dr. Pierson premier and minister of finance . . . . . 20 July, ,,

States-general opened by the queen-regent, the queen present . . . . . . 21 Sept. ,,

Budget for 1898: deficit, 6,300,000*fl*. . 24 Sept. ,,

C. W. M. Van de Velde, distinguished traveller, artist, and cartographer, born, 1818; died, 20 March, 1898

The queen and her mother visit Paris . April, ,,

East Indian loan of 55,000,000*fl*. agreed to, 16 June, ,,

Obligatory personal military service, bill passed 4 July, ,,

Coronation of the queen at Amsterdam, great rejoicings . . . . 6 Sept. ,,

Coronation festivities, grand historical procession, illuminations, &c., 7 Sept.; Rembrandt exhibition opened by the queen, 8 Sept.; royal entry into The Hague, 9 Sept.; states-general opened by the queen with a speech from the throne, 20 Sept. ,,

Imperial penny postage started . . 1 Jan. 1899

Dutch physical and medical congress (7th) held at Haarlem . . . . 7 Aug. ,,

Riots at Hilversum, martial law proclaimed, 1 death . . . . . . 22, 23 Aug. ,,

Parliament opened by the queen . . 19 Sept. ,,

The queen and her mother visit the German emperor . . . . 7 Oct. ,,

The queen reviews the Dutch fishing fleet (about 2000) on the Zuyder Zee . . . . 3 Aug. ,,

The states-general opened by the queen . 18 Sept. ,,

Budget for 1901: deficit, 5,250,000fl. . 20 Sept. ,,

Mr. Kruger, ex-president of the Transvaal, warmly received at the Hague, 6 Dec.; by the queen for a few minutes, 8 Dec.; at Amsterdam . 19 Dec. ,,

Marriage of queen Wilhelmina to duke Henry of Mecklenburg-Schwerin at the Hague, 7 Feb.; state entry into Amsterdam, 5 March, 1901; they visit Berlin . . . . . 30 May–1 June, 1901

Elections: Catholic majority, mid June; the cabinet resigns . . . . 28 June, ,,

M. de Kuyper forms a ministry (3 R.C. members out of 8) . . . . 27 July, ,,

Parliament opened by the queen . . . 17 Sept. ,,

Death of prof. C. P. Tiele, theologian and historian, aged 70 . . . . . . 11 Jan. 1902

Illness of the queen from typhoid fever, announced, 18 April; recovery reported, 31 May; her letter of thanks to the nation for sympathy, published . . . . 10 June, ,,

Conventions regarding European marriage and divorce laws drawn up at the Hague, 1900; signed . . . . 12 June, ,,

Mr. Kruger visits Mr. Steyn at Scheveningen, 6 Aug. ,,

The Boer generals visit Mr. Kruger at Utrecht, 20 Aug.; conference held with Dr. Leyds and others at the Hague . . . . . 21 Aug. ,,

Increase of nat. debt 1890–1900 owing to costly railway and canal construction; new elementary education and military laws, budget, 1902; actual deficit, about 83,000*l*., reported . . 9 Sept. 1902

States-general opened by the queen . 16 Sept. ,,

Boer generals appeal for relief funds . 22 Sept. ,,

Brussels sugar convention ratified . . 2 Dec. ,,

Strikes in Amsterdam . . . . . . Feb. 1903

Railway and dock strikes . . . 6–13 April, ,,

Anti-strike bills passed . . . . 11 April, ,,

Gift of $1,500,000 by Mr. A. Carnegie for a temple of peace for the Permanent Court of Arbitration at the Hague, reported . . . 25 April, ,,

Queen opens parliament, refers in her speech to the labour troubles in the spring, announces various legislative measures of social reform, 15 Sept. ,,

Budget for 1904 presented, estimated revenues, 164,000,000*fl*.; expenditure, 176,000,000*fl*.; cost of military operations during the strike in April stated to be 1,100,000*fl*. . . . . 22 Sept. ,,

PRINCES OF ORANGE (see *Orange*), STADTHOLDERS.

1502. Philibert de Chalons.

1530. Réné de Nassau, his nephew.

1544. William of Nassau, styled the Great, cousin to Réné, recovers the principality of Orange in 1559. Nominated STADTHOLDER, 1579; killed by an assassin hired by Philip II. of Spain, 10 July, 1584.

1584. Philip William, his son; stolen away from the university of Louvain; the Dutch would never suffer him to reside in their provinces: died 1618.

1618. Maurice, the renowned general; became STADTHOLDER in 1584; he was a younger son of William by a second marriage.

1625. Frederick Henry (brother) STADTHOLDER.

1647. William II., STADTHOLDER: married Mary, daughter of Charles I. of England, by whom he had a son, who succeeded in 1672.

1650–72. John De Witt, grand pensioner; no stadtholder.

1660. William-Henry: STADTHOLDER in 1672; married Mary, eldest daughter of James II. of England, 1677.

1702–47. NO STADTHOLDER.

1702. John-William, nephew of William III., loses the principality of Orange, which is annexed to France.

1747. William-Henry becomes HEREDITARY STADTHOLDER; married princess Anne of England: succeeded by his son.

1751. William IV.; retired on the invasion of the French in 1795; died in 1806.

1795. [Holland and Belgium united to the French republic.]

KINGS AND QUEEN.

1806. Louis Bonaparte made king of HOLLAND by his brother Napoleon, 5 June, 1806; abdicated, 31 July, 1810.

1810. [Holland again united to France.]

1813. *House of Orange* restored. William-Frederick, prince of Orange (born 1772), proclaimed 6 Dec. 1813; took the oath of fidelity as sovereign prince, 30 March, 1814; assumed the style of king of the NETHERLANDS, 16 March, 1815; formally abdicated in favour of his son, 7 Oct. 1840: died 12 Dec. 1843.

1840. William II. born 6 Dec. 1792; succeeded on his father's abdication; died 17 March, 1849, succeeded by

1849. William III., son; born 19 Feb. 1817; married Sophia of Würtemberg, 18 June, 1839. (She died, 3 June 1877.) *Issue:* William, prince of Orange, born 4 Sept. 1840; died 11 June, 1879; Alexander (philosopher), born 25 Aug. 1851; died 21 June, 1884. Married Emma of Waldeck-Pyrmont, 7 Jan. 1879; *issue:* Wilhelmina, born 31 Aug. 1880. The king died 23 Nov. 1890.

1890. Wilhelmina (the queen-mother regent), daughter; crowned, 6 Sept., 1898; married duke Henry of Mecklenburg-Schwerin, 7 Feb. 1901.

LANGUAGE AND LITERATURE.—Dutch is an essential link in the chain of Teutonic languages. Old English has been said to be Dutch. A knowledge of Dutch is necessary to understand the historical development of English.—*Chambers*. The principal Dutch writers were Hooft, *p.* and *d.*, 1581–1647; Vondel, a great poet, 1587–1679; Jacob Cats, *p.* and comedian, 1577–1660; Vander Goes, *p.*, 1647–84; Oudaen, *p.* and *d.*, 1628–92; C. Huyghens, *ph.*, 1629–1693; Erasmus, *theo.* and *sat.*, 1467–1536; Boerhaave, physician, 1668–1738; Grotius, *hist.* and *theo.*, 1583–1645; Spinoza, *ph.*, 1632–1677; wrote in Latin]; Feith, *p.*, 1753–1824; Bilderdijk, *p.*, 1756–1831; Tollens, *p.*, 1780–1856; Beets, styled the Charles Dickens of the Dutch, born 1814–1903; Hofdijk, *p.* and *hist.*, died 1888; R. Fruin, *hist.*, 1824–99; many others of high excellence.

HOLLAND, NEW, see *Australia* and *Australasia*.

HOLLOWAY HOSPITALS and COLLEGE. Thos. Holloway, proprietor of the popular ointment, &c., offered the government 250,000*l.* to erect, for the use of the middle classes, a Sanatorium or asylum for the insane, and hospitals for incurables and convalescents. The asylum was erected at St. Anne's Hill, Egham, near Virginia Water, 1873 *et seq.* Opened by the prince of Wales 16 June, 1885.

Royal Holloway College for the Higher Education of Women, Egham. First brick laid, 12 Sept. 1879. Opened by the queen, 30 June, 1886. It includes library, reading-room, museum, and picture gallery. The princely buildings are in the French renaissance style, *temp.* Francis I. (1515–1547); architect, W. Crossland. There is good accommodation for 250 students. The session opened 4 Oct. 1887. Mr. Holloway gave 250,000*l.*, and promised 100,000*l.* additional for endowment. He died 26 Dec., 1883, aged 83, leaving an immense fortune, although he was exceedingly generous during his lifetime; he is said to have expended 45,000*l.* a year in advertisements.

HOLMFIRTH FLOOD. On 5 Feb. 1852, the Bilberry reservoir above Holmfirth, near Huddersfield, Yorkshire, burst its banks, and levelled four mills and many ranges of other buildings, killing more than 90 persons, and devastating property estimated at above half a million.

HOLOPHOTE, a form of lamp in which the light is converged and directed to a particular spot to prevent collisions at sea, &c. Different kinds have been invented by Stevenson, Macdonald, Preece and others.

HOLSTEIN AND SCHLESWIG (N.W. Germany), duchies once belonging to Denmark. The country, inhabited by Saxons, was subdued by Charlemagne in the beginning of the 9th century, and afterwards formed part of the duchy of Saxony. In 1106 or 1110, Adolphus of Schauenberg became count of Holstein: his descendants ruled till 1459, when Adolphus VII. died without issue, and the states of Holstein and Schleswig elected Christian, king of Denmark, his nephew, as their duke, through fear of his arms. In 1544, his grandson, Christian II., divided his states amongst his brothers, with the condition that the duchies should remain subject to Denmark. The eldest branch of the family reigned in Denmark till the decease of Frederick VII., 15 Nov., 1863. From a younger branch (the dukes of Holstein-Gottorp) descended through marriage, the kings of Sweden from 1751–1818, and the reigning family in Russia since 1762, when the duke, as the husband of Anne, became czar. In 1773, Catherine II. of Russia ceded Holstein-Gottorp to Denmark in exchange for Oldenburg, &c. The duchies were occupied by the Swedes in 1813, but restored to Denmark in 1814, and on 28 May, 1831, constituent assemblies were granted to them. Since 1844 disputes have been rife between the duchies and Denmark, and in 1848 the states-general of the duchies voted their annexation to the German confederacy, in which they were supported by Prussia; war ensued, which lasted till 1850, when they submitted to Denmark. The agitation in the duchies, encouraged by Prussia, revived in 1857. The Germans in Schleswig desired it to be made a member of the German confederation, like Holstein; but both duchies demanded a local government more independent of Denmark, which changes were resisted by that power. For the events of the war of 1864, see *Denmark*. By the convention signed at Gastein (*which see*), 14 Aug. 1865, the government of Holstein was left with Austria, and that of Schleswig with Prussia. The whole of Holstein and part of Schleswig were ceded to Prussia by the treaty of Prague, signed 23 Aug. 1866. Population in 1860, 1,004,473. The 5th clause, directing North Schleswig to be given to Denmark if the people voted for it, was not acted on, although claimed; and was abrogated, Feb. 1879. Expulsion of Danes, see *Prussia*, Oct. 1898.

HOLY ALLIANCE was ratified at Paris, 26 Sept. 1815, between the emperors of Russia (its originator) and Austria, and the king of Prussia, by which they ostensibly bound themselves, among other things, to be governed by Christian principles in all their political transactions, with a view to perpetuating the peace they had achieved. The compact was severely censured in this country as opposed to rational liberty.

HOLY BROTHERHOOD, see *Hermandad*.

HOLY CROSS, Society of, formed in 1855, by several clergymen of the Church of England, "for deepening spiritual life in their brethren;" president, the Rev. A. H. Mackonochie. It favours auricular confession and other Romanist practices. One of its books "The Priest in Absolution," was censured by the bishops in convocation, 6 July, 1877, and caused much public excitement. See under *Winchester*.

HOLYDAYS ACT, see *Bank Holidays*.

HOLY GHOST, see *Esprit*.

HOLYHEAD, W. Anglesea. A college was established here in the 12th century. The harbour was improved by Rennie, and Holyhead was made the chief packet station for Ireland. The breakwater, erected by Rendel and Hawkshaw (1846 *et seq.*) was inaugurated by the prince of Wales, 19 Aug. 1873; and a new harbour and railway extension inaugurated by the prince, 17 June, 1880. Population, 1881, 8,680; 1891, 8,726.

HOLY ISLAND, see *Lindisfarne*.

HOLY LEAGUE, see *Leagues*.

HOLY MAID OF KENT. Elizabeth Barton was incited by the Roman Catholic party to oppose the Reformation by pretending to inspirations from heaven. She foretold the speedy and violent death of Henry VIII. if he divorced Catherine of Spain, and married Anne Boleyn, and direful calamities to the nation. She and her confederates were executed at Tyburn, 5 May, 1534.

HOLYOKE, Massachusetts, U.S. A Roman Catholic church here took fire; a panic ensued; and about 80 were burnt or trampled to death, 26, 27 May, 1875.

HOLY PLACES IN PALESTINE. These places have been a source of contention between the Greek and Latin churches for several centuries. In the reign of Francis I. they were placed under Latin monks, protected by the French government; but the Greeks from time to time obtained firmans from the Porte invalidating the rights of the Latins, who were at last (in 1757) expelled from the sacred buildings, which were committed to the care of the Greeks by a hatti-scheriff, or imperial ordinance.

The holy sepulchre partially destroyed by fire and rebuilt by the Greeks, who claim additional privileges, and cause fresh dissensions 1808
The Russian and French governments sent envoys (M. Daslikoff and M. Marcellus) to adjust the dispute; an arrangement prevented by the Greek revolution 1821
The subject again agitated, and the Porte proposed that a mixed commission should adjudicate on the rival claims. M. Titoff, the Russian envoy, acting on behalf of the Greeks, and M. Lavalette, the French envoy, on that of the Latins, took up the question very warmly 1850
A firman issued by the Porte, confirming and consolidating the rights previously granted to the Greek Christians, and declaring that the Latins had no right to claim exclusive possession of certain holy places specified, but permitting them to possess a key of the church at Bethlehem, &c., as in former times . . . . . 9 March, 1852
The French government acquiesced with much dissatisfaction; but the Russian envoy still desired the key to be withheld from the Latin monks. M. D'Ozeroff made a formal declaration of the right of Russia to protect the orthodox in virtue of the treaty of Kainardji in 1774, and demanded that the firman of 9 March, 1852, should be read at Jerusalem, although it militated against his pretensions, which was accordingly done. The dispute still continued, the Porte being exposed to the attacks of both the Russian and French governments . . . . . . March, 1853
Prince Menschikoff arrives at Constantinople as envoy extraordinary, and in addition to the claims respecting the holy places, made demands respecting the protection of the Greek Christians in Turkey which led to the war of 1854-6. (See *Russo-Turkish War*) . . . . 28 Feb. ,,

HOLY ROMAN EMPIRE. The German empire received this title under the emperor Otho I. the great, crowned at Rome by pope John XII., 2 Feb. 962. See *Rome*, and *Germany*.

HOLY ROOD or CROSS. A festival instituted on account of the recovery of a large piece of the cross by the emperor Heraclius, after it had been taken away, on the plundering of Jerusalem, about 615. The feast of the invention (or finding) of the Cross is on 3 May; that of the exaltation of the Cross, 14 Sept. At Boxley abbey, in Kent, was a crucifix, called the *Rood of Grace;* at the dissolution it was broken in pieces as an imposture by Hilsey, bishop of Rochester, at St. Paul's cross, London, 1536.

HOLYROOD PALACE (Edinburgh), formerly an abbey, was for several centuries the residence of the monarchs of Scotland. The abbey, of which some vestiges remain, was founded by David I. in 1128, and in the burial-place within its walls are interred several of his successors. The palace is a large quadrangular edifice of hewn stone, with a court within surrounded by piazzas. In the north-west tower is the bed-chamber which was occupied by queen Mary; and from an adjoining cabinet to it David Rizzio, her favourite, was dragged forth and murdered, 9 March, 1566. The north-west towers were built by James V., and the remaining part of the palace was added during the reign of Charles II. The palace was burnt in 1650, and rebuilt in 1659. Great improvements were made in 1857. Queen Victoria held a court here, 30 Aug. 1850; King Edward VII., 12 May, 1903.

HOLY SEPULCHRE, a Byzantine church in modern Jerusalem. Fergusson, Robinson, and others, consider the true site of the holy sepulchre to be the mosque of Omar, the "dome of the Rock." The question is still undecided. The order of the Holy Sepulchre was founded by Godfrey of Bouillon, 1099; revived by pope Alexander VI. 1496; re-organised, 1847 and 1868.

HOLY WARS, see *Crusades.*

HOLY WATER is said to have been used in churches as early as A.D. 120. *Ashe.*

HOLY WEEK, or the "Week of Indulgences," is the week before Easter. "Holy Year," 1900, inaugurated at Rome, see *Pope*, 24 Dec. 1899. See *Passion Week.*

HOME AND COLONIAL SCHOOL SOCIETY, Gray's Inn Road; founded 1836. Governesses and teachers are trained.

HOME HOSPITALS' ASSOCIATION FOR PAYING PATIENTS, founded in July, 1877. The first home hospital, in Fitzroy-square, London, was opened 28 June, 1880. Supported by queen Victoria 1884.

HOME MISSIONARY SOCIETY, founded 1819. In 1878 it had 192 stations, and employed 187 agents and 243 lay preachers.

HOME-READING UNION, see *National Home-Reading Union.*

HOME RULE. The Home Government Association (for *Home Rule*), established in Dublin in 1870; held its first anniversary meeting, 26 June, 1871. It includes both catholics and protestants amongst its members.

Mr. Isaac Butt, a leader of the movement, elected M.P. for Limerick . . . . 20 Sept. 1871
Home-rule advocated by archbishop McHale and others of the Romanist clergy in Ireland . . 1873
The programme of the party requiring an Irish parliament of queen, lords, and commons, and other powers, published . . . . 25 Oct. ,,
A conference at the Rotondo, Dublin, reported a failure . . . . 18—21 Nov. ,,
A motion in the commons in favour of home rule defeated (314 to 52) . . . . . 20 March, 1874
Mr. I. Butt's motion for a committee on the subject, 30 June; was negatived (458 to 61), 2, 3 July, 1875
again (291 to 61), 30 June, 1 July, 1876; again (417 to 67) . . . . 24 April, 1877
Stormy convention at Dublin, Mr. Butt, chairman, 21, 22 Aug. ,,
The home rule party in the house of commons very obstructive (see *Parliament*) ,,
Meeting of home rule M.P.'s at Dublin; Mr. Butt still leader . . . . 9 Oct. ,,
He virtually gives in to the obstructionists, Jan.; resigns . . . . April, 1878
Meeting at Dublin, 14 Oct.; continued dissensions between moderate party (Mr. Butt and others) and obstructives (Mr. Charles Stewart Parnell and others) . . . . . . Oct.—Nov. ,,
Death of Mr. Butt, 5 May; succeeded as leader by Mr. Wm. Shaw 1879
Mr. Parnell proposes election of a convention to meet at Dublin, 11 Sept.: this is opposed by Mr. W. Shaw, Mitchell Henry, and others Sept. ,,
Meeting at Dublin; pronounced opposition to British government . . . . 20, 21 Jan. 1880
About 65 home rulers in the new parliament, under Mr. Shaw and Mr. Parnell . . . . April, ,,
Mr. Parnell chosen by 45 as parliamentary chairman . . . . 17 May, ,,
31 home rulers voted with the government; 16 with Mr. Parnell . . . . 13 July, ,,
Home rule convention at Newcastle-on-Tyne, 9 Aug. ,,
Meeting at Dublin; Mr. Justin McCarthy appointed vice-president; resolution to resist coercion in Ireland adopted . . . . . . 27 Dec. ,,

Trial of Mr. Parnell and others at Dublin (see *Trials*) . . . . 28 Dec. 1880–25 Jan. 1881
Strong manifesto of Mr. Parnell; a counter one by Mr. Shaw . . . . Feb. ,,
Home rule agitation revived; meeting at Dublin 8 Nov. ,,
Mr. Shaw, opposed to the separatists, secedes from the party . . . . about 3 Dec. ,,
Home rule movement in Scotland; first annual meeting of the burgh convention at Edinburgh propose a representative assembly to legislate on Scotch affairs, subject to the approval of parliament . . . . 4 April, 1882
Proposal for Scotch home rule rejected by the commons . . . . 20 Feb. 1890
Again (no house) . . . . 6 March, 1891
Home rule conference at Dundee, 25 Sept. 1880; at Edinburgh, 24 Sept. 1890; again at Edinburgh, 12 March, 1892
The home rule league (closing meeting, 24 Nov. 1882) merged into Irish national league; first meeting . . . . 7 Feb. 1883
Mr. A. M. Sullivan, an eminent nationalist died 17 Oct. 1884
Mr. Parnell and 85 followers elected for parliament Dec. 1885, again, July 1886; and . 13 Feb 1893
For Mr. Gladstone's Irish government (Home Rule) bill see *Ireland* . . . . . 8 April, 1886
British home rule association started in London, 10 Feb.; United kingdom home rule league formed 23 July; these two combined as the home rule union . . . . about 1 Dec. ,,
Annual meetings held 1891
It publishes a new Home Rule bill differing from Mr. Gladstone's . . . . Aug. ,,
Dr. Clark's resolution for giving home rule separately to England, Scotland, Ireland, Wales, rejected by the commons, 29 April, 1892; 23 June, 1893
Irish home rule bill in parliament, see *Ireland*, Feb.–Sept. ,,
Mr. Dalziel's resolution for establishing local legislative assemblies (home rule) throughout the United Kingdom adopted by the commons (128–102) . . . . 29 March, 1895

(See *Ireland*, *Parliament*, and *Parnellites*.)

HOME SECRETARY, see *Secretaries*, and all the administrations under the name of their premier. New Home Office, Westminster, occupied 6 Aug. 1875.

"HOME, SWEET HOME." The words are attributed to John Howard Payne, an American actor, who died in 1852; the music is said to be Sicilian, but it is probably by sir Henry Bishop, who introduced the song into Clari, or the Maid of Milan, in 1823.

HOMER'S ILIAD AND ODYSSEY, the earliest and most perfect epic poems in the world. The first begins with the wrath of Achilles, and ends with the funeral of Hector; the second recounts the voyages and adventures of Odusses or Ulysses, after the destruction of Troy. Various dates are assigned to these works, from 962 to 915 B.C.

F. A. Wolf, in his Prolegomena, in 1795, argued that the Homeric poems were composed of independent epic songs, collected and arranged by Peisistratus about 550 B.C. This theory occasioned much controversy between scholars and poets; Mr. Andrew Lang, in "Homer and the Epic," vigorously defends "the one author theory," March, 1893.

The first English version of the Iliad, by Arthur Hall, appeared in 1581. The present text is attributed to the time of Pericles, who died B.C. 429. The most celebrated versions of Homer's works are Chapman's, 1616; Hobbes', 1675; Pope's, 1715-25; Cowper's, 1791. The translation of the Iliad by the earl of Derby (1864) is much commended.

HOMICIDE is said to have been tried at Athens by the Areopagites. Among the Jews, wilful murder was capital; but for chance-medley the offender was to flee to one of the cities of refuge, and there continue till the death of the high-priest, 1451 B.C. (*Num.* xxxv.). 9 Geo. IV. c. 31 (1828), distinguishes between justifiable homicide and homicide in its various degrees of guilt, and circumstances of provocation and wilfulness; see *Murder*.

Animals have been tried and punished for killing human beings. A bull was hanged for homicide near the abbey of Beauprès . . . . May, 1499

HOMILDON HILL (Northumberland), where the Scots, headed by the earl of Douglas, were defeated by the Percies (among them Hotspur), 14 Sept. 1402. Douglas and the earls of Angus, Murray, Orkney, and the earl of Fife, son of the duke of Albany, and nephew of the Scottish king, with many of the nobility and gentry, were taken prisoners.

HOMILIES in early Christian times were discourses delivered by the bishop or presbyter, in a homely manner, for the common people. Charlemagne's "Homilarium" was issued 809. The Book of Homilies drawn up by abp. Cranmer, and published 1547, and another prepared by an order of convocation, 1563, were ordered to be read in those churches that had not a minister able to compose proper discourses.

HOMŒOPATHY, a hypothesis promulgated in his "Organon of Medicine," 1810, and in other works, by Dr. Samuel Hahnemann, of Leipsic (died 2 July, 1843), according to which every medicine has a specific power of inducing a certain diseased state of the system (*similia similibus curantur*, likes are cured by likes); and if such medicine be given to a person suffering under the disease which it has a tendency to induce, such disease disappears, because two similar diseased actions cannot simultaneously subsist in the same organ. *Brande.* Infinitesimal doses of medicine, such as the millionth of a grain of aloes, have been employed, it is said, with efficacy. The system requires the patient to regulate his diet and habits carefully. It has led to a more accurate study of the materia medica. Introduced into England, 1827. The Hahnemann hospital was opened in Bloomsbury-square, 16 Sept. 1850. "The World's Convention of Homœopathic Physicians" opened at Philadelphia, 26 June, 1876, London School of Homœopathy, founded 15 Dec. 1876. Congress, Liverpool, 14 Sept. 1877; Southport, 22 Sept. 1892; London, 3 June, 1898; London, 11 July, 1902. Fifth quinquennial international congress at Queen's hall London, 4 Aug, 1896. Under the heading *Odium Medicum*, many controversial letters from allopaths and homœopaths appeared in the *Times*, Jan. 1888.

HOMOUSION AND HOMOIOUSION (*Greek*, same essence, and similar essence or being), terms employed with respect to the nature of the Father and the Son in the Trinity. The orthodox party adopted the former term as a party cry at the council of Nice, 325; the Arians adopted the latter at Seleucia, 359.

HOMS, Syria. Here Ibrahim Pacha and the Egyptians severely defeated the Turks, 8 July, 1832.

HONDURAS, discovered by Columbus in 1502, and conquered by the Spaniards 1523, is one of the republics of Central America; see *America*. Great Britain ceded the Bay Islands to Honduras, 28 Nov. 1859. President, general J. M. Medina, elected 1 Feb. 1864, and in 1869. Provisional president, C. Arias (Dec. 1872). P. Leiva, 1875; M. A. Soto, 29 May, 1877; general Louis

Bogran, 27 Nov. 1883; re-elected, 1887. Gen. Pariano Leista elected 10 Nov. 1891. War with San Salvador, May, 1871, and May, 1872. The town of Omoa, Spanish Honduras, was bombarded by H.M.S. *Niobe*, to obtain redress for injuries to British subjects, 19 Aug. 1873. Population, 1889, 431,917; 1900, 587,500; capital, Tegucigalpa, population, 1894, 15,000; 1900, 12,600.

Insurrection; Tegucigalpa besieged; the president, gen. Bogran, surrounded; reported 11 Nov.; he escapes, gen. Sanchez holds the capital, 12 Nov.; gen. Bogran recovers the capital; gen. Sanchez commits suicide . . . . 15 Nov. 1890
Insurrection, headed by sen. L. Sierra, reported 12 Dec.; sen. Policarpo Bonilla proclaimed president . . . . . . 12 Dec. 1891
Civil war begins, May, 1892; severe defeat to rebel forces at El Corpus, 12 Sept.; gen. Nucilla, insurgent leader, tried and shot at Truxillo; reported . . . . 18 Sept. 1892
Insurrection in S. Honduras, headed by gen. Matute, about 5 March; reported successful; gen. Bogran and president Leiva escape to British Honduras; reported . . . . 18 April, 1893
Gen. Vasquez elected president . . . 20 Sept. ,,
War with Nicaragua, Honduras insurgents, assisted by Nicaragua, invade Honduras and take Corpus Yuscoran; reported 30 Dec. 1893; many conflicts . . . . 1 Jan. *et seq.* 1894
Gen. Bonilla, leader of the Honduras insurgents, assumes the presidency and forms a cabinet, 5 Jan. ,,
Indecisive engagement at Tegucigalpa with heavy loss, 23 Jan.; continued fighting . 27 Jan. ,,
Gen. Vasquez repulses the insurgents . 10 Feb. ,,
End of the war; reported . . . . 25 Feb. ,,
Martial law proclaimed . . . . 12 March, 1896
Insurrection again breaks out . . April-May, 1897
Gen. Sierra elected president . . . 1 Feb. 1899
Dr. Bonilla elected president . . . . Jan. 1903
Dr. Bonilla defeats gen. Sierra, 22 Feb.; captures Santa Barbara, reported 19 Mar.; occupies Tegucigalpa . . . . 13 April, ,,
Dr. Arias, appointed president by gen. Sierra, surrenders to president-elect, Dr. Bonilla, 14 April, ,,

BRITISH HONDURAS, Central America, was settled by English from Jamaica soon after a treaty with Spain in 1667. They were often disturbed by the Spaniards, and sometimes expelled, till 1783. Balize or Belize, the capital, is a great seat of the mahogany trade. In 1861, the population was 25,635; in 1881, 27,452; 1891, 31,471; 1901, 37,479. Governor, James R. Longden, 1867; Wm. W. Cairns, 1870; major Robert Miller Mundy, 1874; F. P. Barlee, 1877; Roger Tuckfield Goldsworthy, 1884; sir Cornelius Alfred Moloney, Feb. 1891; col. (aft. sir) D. Wilson, Jan. 1897.

HONG-KONG, an island off the coast of China, was taken by capt. Elliott, 23 Aug. 1839, and ceded to Great Britain, 20 Jan. 1841. Its chief town is Victoria, built in 1842, and erected into a bishopric in 1849. Sir John Bowring, governor from 1854 to 1859, was succeeded by sir Hercules Robinson: Governors, sir Rich. G. MacDonnell, 1865; sir Arthur Edward Kennedy, 1872; John Pope Hennessy, Nov. 1876; sir G. F. Bowen, Dec. 1882; sir G. C. Strahan, appointed Jan. 1887; died 17 Feb. 1887; sir George William des Vœux, 1887; sir Wm. Robinson, July, 1891; sir Henry A. Blake, Nov. 1898; sir M. Nathan, Oct. 1903. Population 200,990 (1886); 238,724 (1893); 254,500 (1898).

The queen's jubilee warmly celebrated by the British and Chinese, 9, 10 Nov. 1887.
The governor, sir Geo. W. des Vœux, reports the flourishing state of the colony, Nov. 1889.
Visit of the duke and duchess of Connaught, 1–4 April, 1890.
Attack of bubonic plague; great mortality of Chinese, 5 May, 1894, *et seq.*; general exodus of the natives; 2,442 deaths; reported 19 July; total mortality, 2,560; reported 29 Aug.; the port declared free, 3 Sept. 1894; reappears, Feb. (many deaths) 1896; subdued, led to great improvements, in 1897; reappears, April, subsides, July, 1898.
Petition of the colony to parliament for a change in their constitution presented, 21 March, 1895.
The value of the trade, small before the cession, had risen to 133,217,855 taels (tael, nominal value, 6s. 6¾d., really much less), 1894; reported, 1896.
Territories and the island of Lan-tao opposite Hong-kong leased to England for 99 years by convention, signed 9 June, 1898.
Lord Charles Beresford arrives, 25 Dec. 1898.
Large Chinese meeting in favour of the "open door" and reorganisation of the army and navy under British officers, 22 Jan. 1899.
Delimitation of the Kau-lung extension, March; British troops attacked, Chinese driven off, 14, 15 April, 1899.
British flag hoisted at Kau-lung, 17 April, 1899.
Rebels driven out of the extension, order restored, 21–28 April, 1899.
Sam-chun occupied 6 months without resistance, 16 May, 1899.
Sir H. Blake receives 300 elders at Taipo-hui, who vow allegiance, 2 Aug. 1899.
Territory divided into districts under native committeemen; good report issued 20 Nov. 1900.
Stone laid of the naval yard extension, 15 Jan. 1902.
Duke of Connaught's statue unveiled, 5 July, 1902.

HONI SOIT QUI MAL Y PENSE, "Evil be to him who evil thinks." It is mythically said that the countess of Salisbury, at a ball at court, happening to drop her garter, the king, Edward III., took it up, and presented it to her, with these words, which afterwards became the motto of the order of the garter; see *Garter*.

HONOUR. Temples were erected to Honour by Scipio Africanus, about 197 B.C.; and by C. Marius, about 102 B.C.—The *Legion of Honour* was created by Bonaparte in 1802.

HONVEDS, the militia of Hungary. They supported the rebellion against the emperor in 1849, but on the completion of the changes whereby the independence of Hungary was secured, in 1868, they offered a loyal address to the emperor-king.

HOOKS AND CODFISH, party names, see *Holland*, 1347.

HOOLIGANISM, a termed derived from Hooley gang, used in 1900 *et seq.* for street ruffianism and rowdyism, chiefly in the East-end of London. Conferences held at sir Henry Burdett's, mid Oct., and at the Hotel Métropole; junior clubs, lads' brigades, and cadet corps to be founded and encouraged; a committee formed, Mr. W. H. Dickinson, L.C.C., chairman, Mr. Chas. Booth, sir Samuel Hoare, the lord mayor, and others, 30 Oct. 1900. See *Trials*, 5 Feb. 1901; 3 July, 1902.

HOOP-PETTICOAT, see *Crinoline*.

HOPS are said to have been introduced into England from Flanders in the early part of the 16th century, and to have been much cultivated in Kent by Reginald Scot in the 16th century. In the year ending 5 Jan. 1853, there were 46,157⅜ acres under hops in England and Wales, chiefly in Herefordshire, Kent, and Worcestershire, which paid 447,144*l.* duty; the quantity yielded was 51,102,494 lbs., whereof 955,855 lbs. were exported; average acreage in England, 59,833, 1885–96; 48,024 in 1902. The duty on hops was repealed in 1862, after many applications. An act for preventing fraud in the trade was passed in June, 1866.—The hop and malt exchange, Southwark, was opened in Oct. 1867.

HORATII AND CURIATII, see *Rome*, 669 B.C.

HORN BOOKS used in education in England from early times to the 18th century, were tablets on which were inscribed the alphabet, the nine digits, etc., protected by a thin plate of transparent horn. Great variety of forms, now very rare. Four were exhibited at the Caxton exhibition, 1877, and nine at the loan exhibition of the Horner's company, 1882. Mr. Andrew Tuer's handsome and exhaustive "History of the Horn book," dedicated to queen Victoria by command, was published, May, 1896.

HORN; HORNPIPE. The horn is thought to be, next to the reed, the earliest wind instrument, and has been found among most savage nations. It was first made of horn, hence the name; afterwards of brass, with keys, for the semi-tones, in the last century.—The dance called the Hornpipe is supposed to be so named from its having been performed to the Welsh *pib-corn*, that is hornpipe, about 1300. *Spencer*. Many hornpipes were composed in the 18th century. The "College hornpipe" was very popular.

HORNE TOOKE, &c. The trial of Messrs. Hardy, Tooke, Joyce, Thelwall, and others, on a charge of constructive high treason, caused a great sensation. They were taken into custody on 20 May, 1794. Mr. Hardy was tried 29 Oct., and, after a trial of eight days, was honourably acquitted. John Horne Tooke was tried and acquitted, 20 Nov.; and Mr. Thelwall was acquitted, 5 Dec.; the others were discharged. Acts were passed to prohibit Mr. Thelwall's political lectures in 1795.

HORNIMAN MUSEUM, library and gardens, at Forest-hill, London, the gift of Mr. F. J. Horniman (cost over 40,000*l*.), opened by the duke of Fife, 29 June, 1901.

HOROLOGY, see *Clocks*. The British Horological institute, Clerkenwell, London, established in 1858, for the benefit of watchmakers, publishes a monthly journal.

HORSE. The people of Thessaly were excellent equestrians, and probably first among the Greeks who broke them in for service in war; whence probably arose the fable that Thessaly was originally inhabited by centaurs. "Solomon had 40,000 stalls of horses for his chariots, and 12,000 horsemen," 1014 B.C. 1 *Kings* iv. 26. The Greeks and Romans had some covering to secure their horses' hoofs from injury. "The Horse," by W. Youatt, new edition, 1880. See *Races and Carriages*, 1896.

British horses. Their great strength is described by Julius Cæsar about 54 B.C. Henry VIII. established a royal stud, and enacted laws to promote the breed of strong horses in certain shires, hence the term *shire horses*; these afterwards became draught or cart horses.

The horse-tax was imposed in 1784. Its operation was extended, and its amount increased, in 1796; and again in 1808. The existing duty upon "horses for riding" only, in England, amounts to about 350,000*l*. per year 1862

Annual licence duty on horses and mules, 10*s*. 6*d*. each; horse-dealers' licence, 12*l*. 10*s*. (act passed 1869) 1870

Mr. J. S. Rarey, an American, made a great sensation in London by taming vicious and wild horses, and even a zebra from the Zoological Gardens. His system is founded on a profound study of the disposition of the animal, and on kindness. He initiated many illustrious persons in his method (on 20 March, lord Palmerston and twenty others) binding them to secrecy; from which they were released in June, when his book was reprinted in England without his consent . . 1858, 1859

He was engaged to instruct cavalry officers and riding masters of the army . . . July, 1859

He gave a lecture to the London cabmen, 12 Jan. 1860; and in the same year he received a present of 20 guineas from the Society for the Prevention of Cruelty to Animals . . . . . May, 1860

Mr. Sydney Galvayne, Australian horse-trainer, exhibited and taught his method of training at the Wellington Riding School, London, June, 1890; his patrons included the queen with many peers and military officers.

Great annual *horse-shows* held at the Agricultural Hall, Islington, began . . . . July, 1864

Horse-flesh. An establishment for the sale of it as human food was opened at Paris on 9 July, 1866, with success, and its use as food strongly advocated. About 150 persons (including sir Henry Thompson and sir John Lubbock) dined on horse-flesh at the Langham hotel, London . 6 Feb. 1868

A great Franco-Anglo-American horse, mule, and donkey banquet was held at Paris . . 3 April, 1875

The sale of horse-flesh, &c., regulation act, passed 24 June, 1889

Subscriptions (of 100*l*. each person for five years) to improve the breed of horses, proposed by earl Calthorpe, headed by the prince of Wales, many nobles and gentlemen, the London General Omnibus Company, and others . . . June, 1875

Horse-shoeing is very ancient. It is represented on a coin of Tarentum, S. Italy, probably about 300 B.C. Iron and bronze horse shoes have been found in ancient tumuli in France, Germany, Belgium and Britain. "The smith of the court" was an officer under the early princes of Wales, and the farrier's art was much honoured in mediæval times.—*G. Fleming*.

Goodenough's American horse-shoes, made by machinery, put on cold (patented 1860), were used by the London General Omnibus Company, Oct.-Dec. 1868. The international horse-shoe company for adopting the patent was established early in 1870

Horse epidemic ("epizoötic"), from Canada, at New York, Boston, &c., caused much inconvenience, Oct. 1872

Scarcity of horses in Britain; a commission of inquiry appointed, Feb., reported (no result) Aug. 1873

[Another commission issued its report Dec. 1887. The queen's plate for races in Great Britain abolished, and the money to be devoted to the improvement of the breed of horses.]

Stud Company, to improve the breed of horses, held first annual meeting . . . . 20 Sept. ,,

Horse duty taken off 1874

British Empire Horse-supply Association, established . . . . Spring 1878

English Cart-horse Society (since named the Shire Horse Society), established, earl of Ellesmere, president, 3 June, 1878. Annual shows are held at the Agricultural hall; and annual cart horse parades in Regent's-park, 819 horses and 666 drivers were entered, 30 May. 1898.

The queen and some of the royal family, present at the show of the Hunter and Hackney Horse Show at the Agricultural hall . . . . 5 March, 1892

The English Horse Society's first show at Olympia, W. Kensington, 15 May, 1889; at Islington, 29 May, ,,

Royal commission on horse-breeding met in London, May, 1893 *et seq.*, recommendations approved, reported . . . . . . 1 Jan. 1897

Strike of London farriers for increase of wages, 24 May, 1897; ended by compromise . 28 May, ,,

Horse show at the Crystal palace, opened 5 June, ,,

Home of rest for horses, Friar's-place, Acton; New year's dinner given to the animals . . 1 Jan. 1898

Export of infirm horses prohibited . mid Nov. ,,

Horse show at Wembly park, opened, 7 June, 1899; annual horse and hound show at Peterborough, 4 July,

International horse show at the Paris exhibition, total 1718; closed . . . . . 10 Sept. 1900

Horses imported 1862–1872, 79,000; 1873–1882, 197,000; in 1900, 51,786. Horses exported, 1890, 12,192; 1900, 30,038; 1901, 27,612; 1902, 30,085.

Mr. T. Jennings, senior, famous trainer, died, aged 77, 12 Dec. 1900; and Mr. J. Dawson, aged 74, died . . . . 13 May, 1903
24th annual Shire horse show at the Agricultural hall . . . . 24 Feb. „

HORSE GUARDS. The regiment is said to have been instituted in the reign of Edward VI. 1550, and revived by Charles II. 1661. The first troop of Horse Grenadier Guards was raised in 1693, and was commanded by general Cholmondeley; and the second troop, commanded by lord Forbes, was raised in 1702. There was a reduction of the Horse and Grenadier Guards, and Life Guards, as now established, were raised in their room, 26 May, 1788. *Philips.* The present edifice called the Horse Guards was erected about 1758. In the front are two small arches, where horse-soldiers, in full uniform, daily mount guard. In the building was formerly the office of the commander-in-chief, now in Pall Mall.

HORSE-RACING, see *Races*.

HORTENSIAN LAW, passed by Q. Hortensius, dictator, 286 B.C., after the secession of the plebeians to the Janiculum, affirmed the legislative power granted them by previous laws in 446 and 336 B.C.

HORTICULTURE (from *hortus* and *cultura*), the art of cultivating gardens; see *Gardening*.

Horticultural societies established at Edinburgh, 1809; at Dublin 1817
The (now royal) Horticultural society of London founded by sir Joseph Banks and others in 1804: incorporated, 17 April, 1809; transactions first published 1812
Planting the garden at Chiswick begun . . . 1822
Annual exhibitions 1831
The library sold 1859
Proposal for laying out a garden for the society on the Brompton estate, belonging to the Crystal Palace Commissioners, July, 1859; received the support of the queen, nobility, &c., and Mr. Nesfield's design was adopted, May, 1860; the new gardens opened by the prince consort, who planted a *Wellingtonia gigantea* (*which see*) 5 June. The queen planted one . . . . 24 July, 1861
The Albert memorial uncovered in the presence of the prince and princess of Wales . . 10 June, 1863
Dr. John Lindley (who "raised horticulture from an empirical art to a developed science") secretary, 1822-62. . . . . . died 1 Nov. 1865
An international horticultural exhibition was opened in the gardens. . . . 23-31 May, 1866
International horticultural exhibition opened 24 Aug. 1881
The society compelled to quit South Kensington, the greater part of the ground being required for the imperial institute. The council of the society proposes important alterations and appeals for support, 9 Dec. 1887. At the annual meeting, 14 Feb. 1888, arrangements were made for the maintenance of the society. Shows to be held at the drill hall of the London Scottish volunteers, James-street, Westminster; first opened 27 March, 1888. The revival of the society reported at the meeting . . . 12 Feb. 1889
International horticultural exhibition at Earl's court, Kensington, with extra attractions (including "the Wild West," by col. Cody), opened by the duke of Connaught, 7 May; closed 15 Oct. 1892
International horticultural congress opened at Paris, 24 May, 1895; at Dresden . . 2 May 1896
Dr. Robt. Hogg, eminent horticulturist, born, 1818, died . . . . 14 March, 1897
The king gives 100gs. towards a new hall for the Roy. Horticultural soc., . . . 30 Sept. 1902
Sir Thos. Hanbury presents the fine garden and estate of the late G. F. Wilson, F.R.S., Wisley, near Woking, to the society, announced, 10 Aug. 1903

HOSIERY, see *Stockings*, and *Cotton*.

HOSPITALLERS, see *Malta*.

HOSPITAL SUNDAYS are said to have begun at Birmingham, 13 Nov. 1859. Glasgow began hospital Sundays about 1844. It is said the present system of hospital Sunday began at Manchester in 1870. Near the end of 1872, it was proposed that collections for the benefit of hospitals and dispensaries in London should be annually made on one Sunday in the year at all places of worship. A committee for effecting this met at the Mansion-house, 31 Jan. 1873; and soon after, 15 June was appointed as the day for the collection.

HOSPITAL SUNDAYS IN LONDON:

1873. 15 June. About 25,511*l*., received on the day from about 1200 places of worship, including Jews; 1859*l*. received afterwards (July). 24,571*l*. awarded to 54 hospitals; 2185*l*. to 53 dispensaries.
1874. 14 June. About 29,817*l*. received.
1875. 13 June. About 26,703*l* received.
1876. 18 June. About 27,042*l* received. (23,943*l*. awarded to 73 hospitals; 2,336*l*. to 45 dispensaries, 9 Aug. 1876.)
1877. 17 June. 26,083*l*. received; 25,870*l*. distributed.
1878. 30 June. About 24,904*l*. received, 25 July.
1879. 15 June. 26,501*l*. received; 24,961*l*. distributed.
1880. 13 June. 12,000*l*. received, 16 June; 29,000*l*., 5 July; 30,000*l*., 12 July; 30,411*l*., 31 Oct.; 30,423*l*., Nov.
1881. 19 June; received up to 29 June, 25,000*l*.; Nov. 31,855*l*.
1882. 11 June; total receipts (9 Dec.) 34,146*l*.
1883. 10 June; 26,000*l*.; 19 June; total, 33,935*l*.; 1 Dec. 39,329*l*.
1884. 15 June; 11 July; 32,000*l*.
1885. 14 June; total receipts, 34,320*l*.; Dec.
1886. 27 June; total receipts, 40,399*l*.; 30 Nov.
1887. 19 June; total receipts, 40,607*l*.; 30 Nov.
1888. 10 June; total receipts, 40,379*l*.; 10 Dec.
1889. 23 June; amount received up to 29 July, 41,107*l*.; up to 31 Oct. 41,744*l*.
1890. 8 June; amount received up to 11 June, about 15,000*l*.; 28 Nov. 42,814*l*.
1891. 7 June; amount received up to 2 July, 39,000*l*.; 24 Nov. 45,330*l*. (5,000*l*. from the duke of Cleveland and 1,000*l*. from sir Savile Crossley).
1892. 19 June; received, 29 July (sir Savile Crossley, 1,000*l*., 24 June; Miss Anderdon, 100*l*.), 41,512*l*., 25 Nov.
1893. 11 June; 39,200*l*. up to 31 Oct.
1894. 10 June; 43,600*l*., 17 Dec.
1895. 16 June; 25,000*l*.; 44,410*l*. 29 July; 3,400*l*. from Stock Exchange; 904*l*. bequest of Mr. W. A. Guesdon; total, 60,360*l*., 25 Nov.
1896. 14 June; 41,600*l*., 9 July; total, 46,035*l*., 15 Dec.
1897. 20 June; total, 43,485*l*. up to Dec.
1898. 12 June; 40,397*l*. 2*s*. 10*d*., Nov.
1899. 11 June; 53,504*l*.
1900. 24 June; 51,993*l*.
1901. 16 June (4,000*l*. from sir F. Cook), total 54,731*l*; 16 Dec.
1902. 15 June; Mr. George Herring gives over 40,000*l*. in 4 years (10,000*l*. from Mr. Lucas Tooth, of Australia, to the king, presented by him to the fund, July); 62,669*l*. received in the year ending 31 Oct.
1903. 14 June; collected St. Paul's cathedral, King and royal family present, 5,000*l*., 7 June; 60,700*l*. up to 31 Oct. (12,312*l*. from Mr. Herring).

HOSPITAL SATURDAYS IN LONDON for workmen, began 17 Oct. 1874, the movement being greatly promoted by capt. Charles Mercier and lord Brabazon; 6,141*l*. collected:

1875.	31 July . .	5,343*l*.	1880.	4 Sept. . .	6,604*l*.
1876.	2 Sept. . .	5,525*l*.	1881.	3 Sept. . .	8,372*l*.
1877.	1 Sept. . .	4,500*l*.	1882.	2 Sept. . .	8,861*l*.
1878.	7 Sept. . .	6,528*l*.	1883.	1 Sept. . .	9,497*l*.
1879.	6 Sept. . .	6,152*l*.	1884.	6 Sept. . .	10,173*l*.

1885. 18 July; total receipts, 11,192*l*. 8*s*. 10½*d*.; 31 Dec.
1886. 17 July; total receipts, 12,213*l*.; 31 Dec.
1887. 11 June; total receipts, 11,300*l*.; Dec.
1888. 14 July; receipts, 9,069*l*.; 11,426*l*. Dec

1889. 13 July; outdoor receipts, 4,644*l.*; workshop collections, 8,800*l.*; total, 14,090*l.*
1890. 12 July; outdoor receipts, 5,096*l.*; workshop collections, nearly 15,000*l.*; total receipts, Jan. 1891, 20,333*l.*
1891. 18 July; receipts up to 4 Jan. 1892, 19,646*l.*
1892. 16 July; receipts up to Feb. 1893, 20,309*l.*
1893. 15 July; 19,544*l.*
1894. 7 July; over 20,000*l.*; Dec.
1895. 13 July; 11,000*l.*; Aug.
1896. July, 20,000*l.*, reported 16 Jan. 1897.
1897. (Street collection abolished) July, 19,945*l.*, reported, Dec.
1898. July; total receipts, 19,338*l.* 8*s.* 4*d.*, reported, 21 Jan. 1899.
1899. Total receipts, 20,023*l.*, reported, 27 Jan. 1900.
1900. 13 Oct.; 20,187*l.*, reported, Jan. 1901.
1901. 12 Oct.; 21,547*l.*, reported, April, 1902.
1902. 11 Oct.; 22,964*l.*, reported, 4 April, 1903.

HOSPITALS, originally *Hospitia* for the reception of travellers. That at Jerusalem, built by the knights of St. John, 1112, was capable of receiving 2000 guests, and included an infirmary for the sick. The "five royal hospitals" under "the pious care of the lord-mayor of London," are St. Bartholomew's, St. Thomas's, Bridewell, Bethlehem, and Christ's; see *Infirmaries*, and *Dispensaries*. Benjamin Attwood, who gave anonymously about 250,000*l.* in cheques of 1000*l.* to hospitals, &c., died in 1874. In April, 1890, the house of lords appointed a select committee to enquire into the management of metropolitan hospitals and similar institutions, first sitting 5 May. Reports issued, 1890, 1891, 1892. The *Hospital*, a weekly periodical, first appeared, 1886.

In 1888 there were in the metropolis 24 general and 110 special hospitals; described in Low's hand-book to the charities of London.

Royal Commission respecting hospitals for infectious diseases (lord Blachford, sir James Paget, and others) appointed . . . Nov. 1881

The Hospitals Association for the consideration and discussion of hospital management, &c., originated in the National Social Science Association, 1881 *et seq.*; founded 1884

About 7,100*l.* was given to London hospitals by baron Hirsch . . . . . Jan. 1893

Mr. Henry C. Burdett's "Hospitals and Asylums of the World," 4 vols., with plans, &c., completed . . . . . . Jan. ,,

Act for establishing isolation hospitals, passed . ,,

Central hospital board proposed by the Charity Organisation Society; committee appointed 25 Jan. 1897

Sir J. Blundell Maple gives 100,000*l.* to rebuild the University hospital, announced . 25 Feb. ,,

Mr. James Toleman, London, bequeaths 1,000*l.* each to 8 hospitals, announced . 22 April, ,,

Foundation stone of the new University College Hospital, to be erected at the cost of sir J. Blundell Maple, laid by the prince of Wales, 21 June, 1898

"The prince of Wales's hospital fund for London," to commemorate the 60th anniversary of the queen's reign, inviting subscriptions of 1*s.* per annum or more, lord Rothschild treasurer, the prince of Wales president of the general council, announced (he subscribes annually 105*l.*), 5 Feb. 1897

Fund largely responded to during the year; meeting at Marlborough house; total in hand, 187,000*l.*: 22,050*l.* annual subscriptions; 99,000*l.* invested; 122,000*l.* divisible, 20 Dec.; 60,000*l.* to be distributed, *e.g.*, Middlesex hospital, received 2,925*l.*; University college, 2,581*l.* 5*s.*, 30 Dec.; London, 3,937*l.* 10*s.* and 5,000*l.* per ann., 3 Jan.; Guy's, 7,912*l.* 10*s.*, Jan. 1898; 1st annual meeting at Marlborough house, 3 Feb.; total paid to fund during 11 months ending 31 Dec. 1897, 227,553*l.* 12*s.* 5*d.*; receipts for 1898, 39,270*l.*, Feb. 1899; receipts for 1899, 47,808*l.*, Dec. 1899; receipts for 1900, 43,468*l.*, and 6,000*l.* from the League of Mercy, Dec. 1900, styled "King Edward's Hospital Fund," the prince of Wales president, 1 Jan. 1902 154*l.* from the prince of Wales and family, 5 Jan. 1902; Mr. E. Speyer, 25,000*l.*, Jan. 1902; Mrs. S. Lewis, 10,000*l.* (annually); coronation gift, 115,000*l.* from all classes, presented to the king, 11 Aug. 1902; liberal gift from the maharajah of Jaipur, and 10,000*l.* from the maharajah Sindhia of Gwalior, presented by the king, Aug.; an endowment producing 16,000*l.* per ann. from lords Mount-Stephen and Strathcona, 2 Sept.; receipts in 1902, 604,803*l.* reported 14 Feb. 1903.

Alexandra (children's), new buildings, Queen's-sq., Bloomsbury, opened by the prince and princess of Wales . . . . . . 20 July, 1899

Mr. Wm. Vokins bequeaths 49,000*l.* to London hospitals . . . . Jan. ,,

Miss E. Flemming bequeaths over 28,000 to London hospitals . . . . . . April, ,,

Prof. David Hughes, the eminent electrician (see *Microphone*), bequeaths over 300,000*l.* as a trust fund to London hospitals . . . 22 Jan. 1900

The N. London Consumptive hospital receives over 100,000*l.* . . . . . July, 1901

Isolation hospitals (No. 2) act passed . 26 July, ,,

The Portland hospital, equipped by the duke of Portland and family, did good work at the front, in the S. African war, see *Athenæum* . 24 Aug. ,,

Mr. M. Whiting bequeaths 120,000*l.* to London hospitals, reported . . . . 6 Nov. ,,

Mr. A. O. Crooke bequeaths 20,000*l.* in trust for London and Surrey hospitals; 15,000*l.* from capt. Turnor . . . . . . Jan. 1902

Mr. W. W. Astor gives 50,000*l.* to the Children's hospital, Great Ormond-street, for new out-patient department, announced . 25 Dec. ,,

Mr. Robt. Storks bequeathed in all about 60,000*l.* to King's College hospital, reported . 29 Jan. 1903

Stock Exchange collection for the London hospital realized 13,800*l.*, reported . . early Feb. ,,

Annual meeting of the council of King Edward's Hospital fund for London, report total receipts, 1902, 604,803*l.*; 101,000*l.* distributed to hospitals, 14 Feb. ,,

Metropolitan Asylums board reported cost of small-pox epidemic to the board, 491,159*l.*, 21 Feb. ,,

King and queen open the new wing of the London hospital . . . . . . 11 June, ,,

Princess Louise, duchess of Argyll, opens the new buildings for the Hospital for Epilepsy and Paralysis, Maida-vale . . . . 13 June, ,,

Report of the Mansion-house committee, pronounces strongly in favour of the maintenance of St. Bartholomew's hospital on its present site, issued . . . . 27 July ,,

Mr. W. W. Astor gives 20,000*l.* to the Cancer Research fund; announced . . mid Sept. ,,

Decision of the council of King's College hospital to remove the hospital to a site in S. London, announced . . . . Oct. ,,

Bethlehem (oldest lunatic asylum in Europe except one at Granada) founded 1547

Cancer, Brompton 1841

Charing-cross, founded 1818; new hospital built, 1831; duke of Connaught lays the stone for the new building . . . . . . 20 June, 1902

Consumption, Brompton 1841

Dental (new buildings, Leicester-square, 1902) . . 1858

Dreadnought ship (seaman's) 1821

Evelina (baron Rothschild's) 1869

Fever 1802

Free, Royal, Gray's Inn-road 1828

Friedenheim (home of peace for the dying, founded by Miss F. M. Davidson, at Mildmay, 1885), Upper Avenue-road, S. Hampstead; opened by the duchess of Teck . . . . . 7 Nov. 1892

German, Dalston 1845

Great Northern, 1856; New Central at Holloway . 1888

Guy's (see *Guy's*) 1721

Hahnemann (homœopathic) 1850

Idiots' 1847

Incurables 1850

Jews' 1747

King's College 1839

Lock 1746

London 1740

London Ophthalmic, Royal, Finsbury, 1804; new buildings opened by the duke of York, 27 June, 1899

London Ophthalmic, Central, Gray's Inn-road . . 1843

Lying-in, British 1749
,, City of London 1750
,, General, Lambeth 1765
,, Queen Charlotte's 1752
,, Queen Adelaide's 1824
Middlesex (see *Middlesex*) 1745
National Dental, Gt. Portland-street 1861
North-west London hospital, Kentish-town-road . 1878
City Orthopædic, founded in 1851; rebuilt in Hatton-garden, opened by the duke of Cambridge . . . . . . 5 July, 1899
Paddington Green (children's) 1883
Samaritan Free, for women and children . 1847 and 1889
Small Pox 1746
St. Bartholomew's (see *Bartholomew, St.*) . 1102, 1546
St. George's 1733
St. John's, Leicester Square (skin) 1863
St. Luke's (lunatics) 1751
St. Mark's 1835
St. Mary-le-bone 1871
St. Mary's, Paddington 1843
St. Thomas's (removed 1862 and 1871) 1553
Sick Children, 1852; new building opened . Nov. 1875
Temperance Hospital, opened . . . Oct. 1873
Throat, Golden-square, founded by Dr. (after sir) Morell Mackenzie, 1863; memorial wing . June, 1899
Throat and Ear diseases, Gray's Inn-road March, 1874
University College 1833
Victoria, Kingston-on-Thames (memorial of the queen's reign), opened . . . 12 Dec. 1898
Westminster 1719
Westminster Ophthalmic, Royal 1816
Women's, Soho-square 1842
Women and Children (superintended by women), Crawford-street 1866
Women's hospital in Marylebone, 1871; Euston-road (superintended by women) . . 7 May, 1889

HOSPITAL SHOPPING DAY. A scheme organised, Sept. 1903, by a committee, with lord Dunraven as chairman, to augment King Edward's Hospital fund; the king and the prince of Wales as patron and president signifying their approval. Shopkeepers of all classes, to the number of 33,000, were invited to give a certain percentage, according to individual choice, of their takings on a specified day to the fund, and a special appeal was made to the public to make extra purchases to aid the object in view. A large number of firms in the West-end and in other parts of London responded favourably to the proposal. The first "Hospital Shopping Day" took place, 3 Nov. 1903. Receipts to 17 Nov. 1,027*l*.

HOST, ELEVATION OF THE, introduced into Roman Catholic worship, and prostration, said to have been enjoined about 1201. Pope Gregory IX. was the first pontiff who decreed a bell to be rung as a signal for the people to adore the host, 1228. *Rees.*

HOT BLAST, see *Blowing Machine.*

HÔTEL DE VILLE, Paris, the residence of the chief magistrate, the prefect of the Seine, was begun in 1533, and completed, after his own design, by Dominico da Cortona, 1628. Here La Fayette introduced Louis-Philippe, the citizen-king, to the people, Aug. 1830; and here the republic was proclaimed, 26 Feb. 1848. The communists, who had established themselves here, set fire to the building, 24 May, 1871, after their total defeat. The Hôtel was reopened 13 July, 1882.

HÔTEL DIEU, see *Paris,* 656, 1877.

HOTEL METROPOLE, Northumberland Avenue, London, an enormous building with highly decorated suites of rooms, designed by F. & H. Francis, F. F. Sanders and others, completed May, 1885.

HOUR. The early Egyptians divided the day and night each into twelve hours, a custom adopted by Jews or Greeks probably from the Babylonians. The day is said to have been first divided into hours from 293 B.C. when L. Papirius Cursor erected a sun-dial in the temple of Quirinus at Rome. Previously to the invention of water-clocks (*which see*) 158 B.C., the time was called at Rome by public criers. In England, the measurement of time was, in early days, uncertain; one expedient was by wax candles, three inches burning an hour, and six wax candles burning twenty-four hours, said to have been invented by Alfred, A.D 886; see *Day.* For *Hours of Prayer, Horæ,* see *Breviary.* The *Hour,* daily conservative newspaper, first appeared, 24 March, 1873; last time, 11 Aug. 1876.

HOUSE DUTY was imposed in 1695. Its rate was frequently changed till its repeal. It was re-imposed as a substitute for the window-tax, in 1851. The duty was reduced for houses rented at from 20*l.* to 40*l.* to 2*d.*, and for those rented at from 40*l.* to 60*l.* to 4*d.* and 6*d.*, 17 April, 1890. In the year 1872-3 it produced 1,243,818*l.*; in 1875-6, 1,421,052*l.*; 1880, 1,623,000*l.*; 1885, 1,885,000*l.*; 1891, 1,570,000*l.*; 1893-4, 1,425,000*l.*; 1898-9, 1,570,000*l.*; 1899 - 1900, 1,670,000*l.*; 1900 - 1, 1,720,000*l.*; 1901-2, 1,775,000*l.* See *Taxes. House League,* see *Ireland,* 1886.

HOUSEHOLD SUFFRAGE, after one year's residence, was introduced into parliamentary elections for boroughs, by the reform act passed 15 Aug. 1867. Attempts have been frequently made to extend household suffrage to counties, and have failed; Mr. (afterwards sir) G. O. Trevelyan's proposal lost in the commons (287 to 173), 13 May, 1874; (268 to 166), 7 July, 1875; (264 to 165), 30 May, 1876; (276 to 220), 29 June, 1877; (271 to 219), 22-23 Feb. 1878; (291 to 226), 4 March, 1879. The object was effected by the act of 1884-5.

HOUSELESS POOR ACT (Metropolitan) passed, 1864; made perpetual, 1865. See *Poor* and *Artisans.*

HOUSE OF COMMONS, LORDS, &c., see *Parliament, Lords,* and *Commons.*

HOUSING OF THE POOR ACT, passed 14 Aug. 1885; another important act passed, 18 Aug. 1890; see under *Artisans.* Small houses (acquisition of ownership) act passed, 9 Aug. 1899; report of joint select parliamentary committee on housing, issued, Aug. 1902.

HOVAS, see *Madagascar.*

HOWARD ASSOCIATION, instituted in 1866, under the patronage of the late lord Brougham, for the improvement of prison discipline and prevention of crime. See *Prisons, Bedford.* Mr. H. Gurney, chairman of the committee, visited the sultan of Morocco, early in 1902, with reference to the carrying out of reforms in prison administration in that country (see *Times,* 27 Sept. 1902). Mr. Tallack, secretary of the society for many years, retired in 1902, succeeded by Mr. E. Grubb. Office: Devonshire-chambers, Bishopsgate-street.

HOWARD FAMILY. John Howard, son of Margaret, the heiress of the Mowbrays, was created earl marshal and the 7th duke of Norfolk in 1483. He was slain with his master, Richard III., at Bosworth, 22 Aug. 1485. His son was restored to the earldom of Surrey in 1489; in reward for having gained the victory of Flodden, 9 Sept. 1513, he was created the 8th duke of Norfolk, in 1514. Thomas, the 10th duke, was beheaded for conspiracy against queen Elizabeth on behalf of Mary, queen of Scots, in 1572. Henry Fitzalan Howard, now the 21st duke of Norfolk, and the 15th of the Howard family, premier duke and earl of England and hereditary earl marshal, was born in 1847.

HOWARD MEDAL. One was awarded by the Statistical Society to the best essay "On the Improvements in Education during the 18th and 19th centuries," in Nov. 1879.

HOWE DISASTER, see *Navy of England*, 1892–3.

HOWITZER, a German piece of ordnance, ranking between a cannon and a mortar, came into use early in the 18th century.

HUASCAR, see *Peru*, 1877 and 1879.

HUBERTSBURG (Saxony). The treaty between the empress, the king of Prussia, and the elector of Bavaria, signed here, 15 Feb. 1763, ended the Seven Years' War, whereby Prussia gained Silesia.

HUDDERSFIELD, a manufacturing town, W. R. Yorkshire, chiefly the property of the Ramsden family. Sir John Ramsden built the town-hall, 1765. The theatre was burnt, 15th Feb. 1880; the new market hall opened, 31 March, 1880. Population, 1881, 86,502; 1891, 95,422; 1901, 95,008.

First Musical Festival . . . . 20–22 Oct. 1881
Fine art and industrial exhibition opened 1 July, 1883
Beaumont park opened by the duke of Albany 13 Oct. ,,

HUDIBRAS. The first three cantos of this political satire, by Samuel Butler, appeared in 1663; the other parts in 1664 and 1678.

HUDSON'S BAY, discovered by Sebastian Cabot, 1512, and re-discovered by captain Henry Hudson, when in search of a north-west passage to the Pacific Ocean, 1610, had been visited by Frobisher. The "governor and company of adventurers of England trading to Hudson's Bay," obtained a charter from Charles II. in 1670. The "fertile belt" was settled by lord Selkirk in 1812. For these territories the bishopric of Rupert's Land was founded, 1849. The charter having expired, the chief part of the company's territories, on the proposition of earl Granville, the colonial secretary (9 March, 1869), were transferred to the Dominion of Canada for 300,000*l.*, and a right to claim a certain portion of land within fifty years, and other privileges; the company having consented to this, 9 April, 1869. A portion of the people resisted the annexation, and gen. Louis Riel proclaimed independence and seized the company's treasury, Jan. 1870. On 3 or 4 March he tried and shot Thomas Scott, a Canadian, who had escaped from his custody. Col. (afterwards lord) Wolseley conducted a Canadian expedition to the territories (now named Manitoba), and issued a proclamation to the loyal inhabitants, 23 July, saying "our mission is one of peace." Riel was unsupported and offered no resistance. The lieut.-governor, Adams George Archibald, arrived 3 Sept. The Company had a large sale of furs in 1888. Annual meetings are held (1893). Extensive explorations by Mr. Tyrell, Dr. Bell, and Mr. Henry O'Sullivan, 1893 *et seq.* See *Manitoba* and *Western Territories.*

HUÉ, see *Tonquin*, 1883.

HUE AND CRY, the old common-law process of pursuing "with horn and with voice," from hundred to hundred, and county to county, all robbers and felons. Formerly, the *hundred* was bound to make good all loss occasioned by the robberies therein committed, unless the felon were taken; but by subsequent laws it is made answerable only for damage committed by riotous assemblies. The pursuit of a felon was aided by a description of him in the *Hue and Cry*, a gazette established for advertising felons in 1710. *Ashe.*

HUGSTETTEN, Baden; see *Railway Accidents*, 1882.

HUGUENOT SOCIETY of London, established by sir H. Austen Layard and other descendants of Huguenots, about 15 April, 1885. The society publishes historical works, 1888.

HUGUENOTS, a term (derived by some from the German *Eidgenossen*, confederates; by others from Hugues, a Genevese Calvinist) applied to the Reformed party in France, followers of Calvin. They took up arms against their persecutors in 1561. After a delusive edict of toleration, a great number were massacred at Vassy, 1 March, 1562, when the civil wars began, which lasted with some intermission till the edict of Nantes in 1598 (revoked in 1685). The massacre of St. Bartholomew's day, 24 Aug. 1572, occurred during a truce; see *Calvinists*, *Protestants*, *Bartholomew*, *Edict*, and *Camisard*. S. Smiles's "History of the Huguenots," appeared in 1867. The crypt in Canterbury cathedral, assigned to French protestants in 1550, is still used by them for divine worship.

HULL (E. Yorkshire), a rising commercial place in 1200, was named Kingston-upon-Hull in 1296 by Edward I., who purchased the town, formed the port, and granted a charter. Great fire; damage about 100,000*l.*, 15 Aug. 1864. Royal Albert dock opened by the prince of Wales, 21 July, 1869. Inauguration of the Alexandra dock, and the Hull and Barnsley railway, 23 Jan. 1885. Fire at Messrs. Stead's crushing mills, about 80,000*l.* damage, 16 March, 1885. Hull returns three M.P.s by act passed 25 June, 1885; made a city, June, 1897. See under *Population*. Serious dispute between the Shipping Federation and the Dockers' Union closed 31 Dec. 1890.

Serious disputes between Messrs. Thomas Wilson & Co. (who had left the *Federation*) and the local *Dockers' Union*; opposition to free labour, early April; ships blocked and work stopped; work resumed by free labour, much resisted, 11 April *et seq.*; rioting checked by police and military; end of the strike by compromises . . 19 May, 1893
[Intervention of the union leaders in London, &c., May.]
Great fires (incendiarism suspected) at Messrs. Wade's timber-yards, 30 April *et seq.*; at Messrs. Simpson's saw-mills, &c. . . . 2–3 May, ,,
Opening of the Hymer's college (founded by the gift (50,000*l.*) of Mr. Robt. Hymer) by lord Herschell . . . . 30 Oct. ,,
One hundred and six Hull fishermen lost in the gales . . . . . . Dec. 1894, and Jan. 1895
Explosion at Messrs. Major and Co.'s distillery, 5 deaths . . . . 21 Dec. 1897
Great fire, grain warehouse, &c., destroyed, estimated damage, 90,000*l.* . . . 29 July, 1899
Mr. Walter Long, M.P., opens a new street and is presented with the freedom . . 15 Oct. 1901
Lord Avebury opens the new Central Free library, cost about 20,000*l.* . . . . 6 Nov ,,
Visit of the prince and princess of Wales, 12 May, 1903

HULSE'S FOUNDATIONS. The rev. John Hulse, who died in 1790, bequeathed his estates in Cheshire to the university of Cambridge for the advancement of religious learning:—by the maintenance of two scholars; the payment of a prize of 40*l.* annually for a theological dissertation; the establishment of the office of Christian advocate (made a professorship of divinity, 1 Aug. 1860); and the payment of a lecturer, to be chosen annually. The first Hulsean lectures were given by the rev. Christopher Benson, in 1820.

HUMAITÁ, a strong post on the river Paraguay, fortified at a great cost with a battery of 300 cannon, by Lopez, the president of Paraguay, and believed to be impregnable, was passed by the Brazilian ironclads, 17 Feb. 1868. On the 19th, Caxias, the Brazilian general, stormed a work to the north of Humaitá, and captured many stores. Humaitá itself, after a severe siege, was abandoned, 24 July, 1868.

HUMAN LEOPARD SOCIETY, see *Sierra Leone*, 1895.

HUMANE SOCIETY, ROYAL (London), for the recovery of persons apparently drowned, was founded in 1774, by Drs. Goldsmith, Heberden, Towers, Lettsom, Hawes, and Cogan, but principally by the last three. The society has above 280 depôts supplied with apparatus. The principal one was erected in 1794, on a spot of ground given by George III. on the north side of the Serpentine river, Hyde-park. The motto of this society is appropriate—"*Lateat scintillula forsan*"—"a small spark may perhaps lie hid." Nearly 500 persons were relieved in 1887; 544 in 1890; 536 persons rewarded for bravery. 580 lives saved in 1894; 527 rewards; 812 lives saved in 1895, 800 rewards; 650 lives saved, 716 rewards in 1897. Leonard H. Webber, aged 5 years, received the society's award for saving his baby-brother from drowning at Walthamstow, 31 Aug. 1899; 715 lives saved, 791 rewards in 1901; 708 saved, 782 rewards in 1902. See *Drowning*, and *Lisbon*, Dec. 1890.

HUMANISM, a name given to the philosophical study of man's personality as distinguished from a class, especially advanced by Petrarch and other energetic advocates of the revival of the study of ancient classic literature, termed the "new learning," and ("*literæ humaniores*") the age of the *renaissance*, in the 14th, 15th, and 16th centuries, whereby freedom of thought and language was greatly promoted.

HUMANITARIANS, a small sect in London, founded by Mr. Kaspary, a German Jew. Their moral principles are set forth in "The Fifteen Doctrines of the Religion of God," written in 1866. These include pantheism and transmigration of souls. Meetings of the Humanitarian league held in London, 1895 *et seq.* Their monthly organ is termed "Humanity." See *Positive Philosophy*.

HUMANITY, RELIGION OF, see *Positive Philosophy*, and *Secularism*.

HUMBERT TRIAL, see *France*, 1903.

HUMILIATI, a congregation of monks, said to have been formed by some Milanese nobles, who had been imprisoned by Frederick I. 1162. The order had more than ninety monasteries; but was abolished for luxury and cruelty by pope Pius V., and the houses were given to the Dominicans, Cordeliers, and other communities in 1570.

HUMMING BIRDS. Mr. Gould's beautiful collection of the skins of these birds exhibited at the Zoological Gardens, London, in 1851, was bought with other birds for the British museum for 3000*l.*, April, 1881. His elaborate work on them in five folio volumes, with richly coloured plates, was completed in 1862.

HUNDRED, a Danish institution, was a part of a shire, so called, as is supposed, from its having been composed of a hundred families, at the time the counties were originally divided, about 897. The hundred-court is a court-baron held for all the inhabitants of a hundred instead of a manor.

HUNDRED DAYS; a term given to Napoleon's restoration, dating from his arrival in Paris, 20 March, to his departure on . . . . . 29 June, 1815.

HUNDRED YEARS' WAR, in French history, commenced with the English invasion in 1337.

HUNGARY, part of the ancient Pannonia and Dacia, was subjected to the Romans about 106, and retained by them till the 3rd century, when it was seized by the Goths, who were expelled about 376 by the Huns. See *Huns*, and *Attila*. After Attila's death, in 453, the Gepidæ, and in 500 the Lombards held the country. It was acquired by the Avars about 568, and retained by them till their destruction by Charlemagne in 799. About 890 the country was settled by a Scythian tribe, named Vingours or Ungri (whence the German name *Ungarn*) and the Magyars of Finnish origin. The chief of the latter, Arpad (889), was the ancestor of a line of kings (*see below*). The progress of the Magyars westward was checked by their defeat by the emperor Henry the Fowler, 934. Population of the kingdom, including Transylvania, Fiume, Croatia, and Slavonia, 31 Dec. 1887, 16,901,023; in 1890, 17,463,791: 1900, 19,203.531; Revenue, 1890, 355,307,000 florins; expenditure 355,815,000 florins. 1893, income, 36,395,166*l.*: expenditure, 34,802,833*l.* 1895, income, 42,640,226*l.*; expenditure, 41,261,224*l.*; 1900, revenue, 49,876,500*l.*; expenditure, 45,146,708*l.*; 1901, revenue, 43,810,833*l.*; expenditure, 45,909,708*l.* See *Austria*.

Stephen, founder of the monarchy of Hungary, embraces and establishes Christianity and subdues the Slaves, &c., receives the title of the *Apostolic king* from the pope 996

The Poles overrun Hungary 1061

Bela III. introduces the Greek civilisation 1174, &c.

Golden Bull of Andrew II. granting personal rights 1222

Ravages of the Tartars under the sons of Genghis Khan, throughout Hungary, Bohemia, and Russia, 1241 *et seq.*

Death of Andrew III., end of the *Arpad dynasty* . 1301

Victories of Louis the Great in Bulgaria, Servia, and Dalmatia 1344-82

He marches into Italy and avenges the murder of his brother, Andrew, king of Naples . . 1348

Sanguinary anarchy: Elizabeth, queen of Louis, is drowned: and *King* Mary, the daughter, marries Sigismond, of Brandenburg; they govern with great severity 1382

[The Hungarians had an aversion to the name of *queen*; and whenever a female succeeded to the throne, she was termed *king*.]

Sigismond's atrocious cruelties compel his subjects to invite the assistance of the Turks . . 1393

Battle of Nicopolis: Bajazet vanquishes Sigismond and a large army . . . . . 28 Sept. 1396

Sigismond obtains the crown of Bohemia, and is elected emperor of Germany 1410

Albert of Austria succeeds to the throne of Hungary 1437

Victories of the great John Hunniades (reputed illegitimate son of Sigismond) over the Turks 1442-4

Who obtain a truce of ten years 1444

Broken by Ladislas, king of Hungary (at the pope's instigation); he is defeated and slain, with the papal legate, at Varna . . . . 10 Nov. ,,

John Hunniades escapes; becomes regent . 1444-53

Raises siege of Belgrade, 14 July; dies 10 Sept. . 1456

Hungarians insult Turkish ambassadors; war ensues: Solyman II. takes Buda 1526
Disastrous battle of Mohatz (*which see*) 29 Aug. ,,
Hungary subject to Austria . . . ,,
Peace of Vienna, granting toleration to Protestants, 23 June, 1606
John Sobieski defeats the Turks in several battles, and raises the siege of Vienna . . 12 Nov. 1683
The duke of Lorraine retakes Buda (*which see*) 2 Sept. 1686
Prince Louis of Baden defeats the Turks at Salenckemen . . . . 19 Aug. 1691
Prince Eugene defeats them at Zenta 11 Sept. 1697
Peace of Carlowitz . . . . 26 Jan. 1699
Pragmatic sanction, authorising female succession to the throne 1722-3
Servia and Wallachia ceded to Turkey at the peace of Belgrade 1739
The Hungarians enthusiastically support Maria-Theresa against France and Bavaria 1740
The protestants permitted to have churches . 1784
Independence of Hungary guaranteed . . . 1790
The diet meets; Hungarian academy established . 1825
The people, long discontented with the Austrian rule, break out into rebellion . . 11 Sept. 1848
Murder of the military governor, count Lamberg, by a mob at Pesth; the Hungarian diet appoint a provisional government under Kossuth and Louis Batthyany, 28 Sept.; Hungarians defeat the ban of Croatia . . . . 29 Sept. ,,
The diet denounces as traitors all who acknowledge the emperor of Austria as king of Hungary, 8 Dec. ,,
The insurgents defeated by the Austrians at Szaikszo, 21 Dec.; at Mohr by the ban Jellachich, 29 Dec. ,,
Buda-Pesth taken by Windischgrätz . 5 Jan. 1849
Bem defeats the Austrians at Hermannstadt, 21 Jan. ,,
Hungary declares itself a free state, Kossuth supreme governor . . . . . 14 April, ,,
The Hungarians defeat the Imperialists before Gran, 18 April, ,,
March of the Russian army through Gallicia to assist the Austrians . . . . . . 1 May, ,,
The Austro-Russian troops defeat the Hungarians at Pered . . . . 20 June, ,,
Battles of Acs between the Hungarians and Austrians; former retire . . . . 2, 10 July, ,,
Hungarians defeat Jellachich . . . 14 July, ,,
The Hungarians defeated by the Russians: Görgey retreats after three days' battle . 15 July, ,,
Battle before Komorn, between the insurgents and the Austro-Russian army . . . 16 July, ,,
Insurgents under Bem enter Moldavia, 23 July; defeated by the Russians at Schässberg 31 July, ,,
Utter defeat of the Hungarian army before Temeswar, by gen. Haynau . . . 10 Aug. ,,
Görgey and his army surrender to the Russians, 13 Aug. ,,
Kossuth, Andrassy, Bem, &c., escape to the Turkish frontiers, and are placed under protection at New Orsova (see *Turkey*) . . . 21 Aug. ,,
Komorn surrenders to the Austrians; close of the war. . . . . 27 Sept. ,,
Louis Batthyany tried at Pesth, and shot; many other insurgent chiefs put to death at Arad 6 Oct. ,,
Amnesty granted to the Hungarian insurgents, who return home . . . . . . 16 Oct. ,,
Bem dies at Aleppo . . . . 10 Dec. 1850
Count Julius Andrassy, in exile, sentenced to death, as traitor; announced . . . 23 Feb. 1851
The country remains in an unsettled state; many executions 1853-5
Crown of St. Stephen and royal insignia discovered and sent to Vienna . . . 8 Sept. 1853
Amnesty for political offenders of 1848-9 12 July, 1856
The emperor and empress visit Buda 4 May, 1857
During the Italian war in 1859, an insurrection in Hungary was in contemplation, and communications took place between Louis Napoleon and Kossuth; which circumstances it is said led the emperor of Austria to accede to the peace of Villafranca so suddenly, and shortly afterwards to promise many reforms and to grant more liberty to the protestants in Hungary . Aug.-Oct. 1859
Recall of archduke Albert; general Benedek appointed governor . . . . . . April, 1860
Demand for restoration of the old constitution; reunion of the Banat and Voivodina with Hungary, &c. . . . . Oct. 1860
Restoration of old constitution promised 20 Oct. ,,
Schmerling appointed minister . . 13 Dec. ,,
National conference at Gran . . . Dec. ,,
Demand for the constitution of 1848 . Jan. 1861
The emperor promulgates a new liberal constitution for the empire . . . . 26 Feb. ,,
Which does not satisfy the Hungarians March, ,,
Hungarian diet opened . . . 6 April, ,,
Meeting of the Reichsrath at Vienna: no deputies present from Hungary or Croatia . 29 April, ,,
Count Teleki (see *Austria*, 1860) found dead in his bed at Pesth: intense excitement . 8 May, ,,
The diet votes an address to the emperor, desiring restoration of the old constitution . . 5 July, ,,
The military begin to levy the taxes . . July, ,,
Imperial rescript refusing the entire independence of Hungary, 21 July: the diet protests, 20 Aug.; and is dissolved . . . . . . 21 Aug. ,,
The archbishop of Gran, the primate, indignantly protests against the act of the imperial government . . . . Sept.-Oct. ,,
Summoned to Vienna; he stands firm . 25 Oct. ,,
The magistrates in the comitat of Pesth resign; military government established; passive resistance of the nobility . . . . . Dec. ,,
Amnesty declared for political offences, and cessation of prosecutions . . . . . 18 Nov. 1862
Newspapers confiscated for publishing seditious speeches . . . . . . 29 March, 1863
The emperor visits Buda-Pesth; well received; inauguration of a new policy; the rights of Hungary to be restored . . . . . 6-9 June, 1865
Imperial rescript, abolishing the representative constitution of the empire, with the view of restoring independence of Hungary, &c. . . 21 Sept. ,,
The Deak or moderate party demand restoration of the monarchy, with a responsible government, 11 Nov. ,,
The emperor visits Pesth; the diet opened, 14 Dec.; Carl Szentivanyi elected president . 20 Dec. ,,
Emperor and empress arrive at Pesth . 29 Jan. 1866
Hungarian legions join the Prussian army, June: (after the peace, they were allowed to return to their allegiance) . . . . Oct. ,,
Prolonged political negotiations for autonomy; Deak and national party wearied, threaten to break off . . . . Oct. ,,
Hungarian diet opened by a conciliatory rescript, 19 Nov. ,,
Deak's address in reply, demanding the restoration of the constitution, adopted by the diet with a large majority . . . . . . 15 Dec. ,,
Much opposition to the convocation of the Reichsrath . . . . Jan. 1867
Restoration of the constitution of 1848; an independent ministry appointed, headed by count Julius Andrassy . . . . . . 17 Feb. ,,
[Andrassy carries freedom of the press, removal of Jewish disabilities and promotes railways, &c., 1867 *et seq.*]
The Croats protest against incorporation with Hungary . . . . 25 May, ,,
The emperor and empress crowned at Buda with the ancient ceremonies . . . 8 June, ,,
Amnesty granted for all political offences 9 June, ,,
The coronation gift to the emperor of 50,000 ducats bestowed on orphans and invalids . 10 June, ,,
Discussion between the Austrians and Hungarians respecting the division of the liability for the national debt . . . . . Aug.-Sept. ,,
A financial convention signed by deputations, 23 Sept. ,,
Kossuth's letter to his constituents at Waitzen, censuring Deak and the moderate party . Oct. ,,
Deak joined by Klapka and other liberals . Nov. ,,
The "Nazarenes," a sect resembling Quakers, become prominent . . . . . . Nov. ,,
Bills for financial arrangement with Austria, and for Jewish emancipation, received royal assent, 29 Dec. ,,
First trial by jury of press offences; (fine and imprisonment inflicted for publishing a letter of Kossuth) . . . . 27 Feb. 1868

Kossuth (elected a member of the legislature) resigns by letter . . . . 14 April, 1868
A Croatian deputation accepts union with Hungary, 27 May, ,,
Prince Napoleon Jerome's visit; warmly received, June, ,,
Dispute respecting the apportionment of the army settled . . . . . 5 Dec. ,,
The diet of 1865 closed with an address from the emperor . . . . . . 10 Dec. ,,
Congress of Hungarian Jews opened; Joseph Eötvos minister . . . . . 14 Dec. ,,
Powerful counter-addresses from Andrassy and Kossuth published . . . . Jan. 1869
Royal Hungarian guard organised . . . 9 Feb. ,,
Chamber of deputies meet . . . 22 April, ,,
Remains of Louis Batthyany (executed and privately buried, Oct. 1849), re-interred solemnly in the public cemetery, Pesth . . 9 June, 1870
Count Andrassy promotes the neutrality of Austria in the Franco-German war . . . July, ,,
Joseph Eötvos, author, patriot, and minister, died, deeply lamented, aged 58 . . 3 Feb. 1871
Autumn military manœuvres, near Waitzen, 22 Sept. *et seq.* ,,
Andrassy succeeds count von Beust as foreign minister at Vienna; count Lonyay, Hungarian premier, 14 Nov. ,,
The diet, after sitting three years, dissolved, 16 April, 1872
Elections; increased majority of the Deak or constitutional party, July; diet opened 4 Sept. ,,
Resignation of the count Lonyay ministry, 2 Dec.; Szlavy forms a ministry . . . . Dec. ,,
The Fiume railway partly opened . 24 June, 1873
Buda-Pesth formally constituted the capital, Nov. ,,
Ministry resigns; crisis; Bitto forms a cabinet, 20 March, 1874
Parliament closes . . . . 14 Aug. ,,
Ministry resigns, 11 Feb.; coalition ministry under baron von Wenckheim formed, 26 Feb.—1 March, 1875
Elections; greatly in favour of government July, ,,
Koloman Tisza, chief of the ministry . 20 Oct. ,,
Death of the constitutional patriot, Francis Deak, 28 Jan., state funeral . . . . 3 Feb. 1876
Ministerial crisis; Tisza resigns; remains in office Feb. 1877
Projected raid into Roumania to favour the Turks checked; censured by Klapka . end of Sept. ,,
Miskolcz nearly destroyed by a waterspout, 30 Aug. 1878
Resignation of Szell, finance minister, 26 Sept.; followed by that of the Tisza ministry . 4 Oct. ,,
Tisza ministry retained modified . . 5 Dec. ,,
Distressing inundation at Szegedin; great loss of life and much property (see *Inundations*), 12, 13, March, and 12 Dec. 1879
Murder of lord chief justice George von Majlath von Szekhely, about . . . 29 Mar. 1883
Joseph Scharf and nine other Jews tried at Nyireghyhaza for alleged murder of a Christian maid, Esther Solymosi (on 1 April, 1882) . June, ,,
Acquitted . . . . . . 3 Aug. ,,
Violent anti-jewish riots Pesth, Zala, Egersseg, &c. July, Aug.; martial law proclaimed 29-30 Aug. ,,
Three men convicted of the murder of the chief justice . . . . . . 6 Oct. ,,
Thirty-six Socialists arrested at Pesth; many expelled about . . . . 13 Mar. 1884
Liberal majority in the elections, about 13 June, ,,
National exhibition at Buda-Pesth opened by the emperor 2 May; closed . 4 Nov. 1885
Bi-centenary of the recapture of Buda from the Turks celebrated . . . 2 Sept 1886
Panic in the Franciscan church in Radna through ignition of the altar cloth; 15 persons crushed to death . . . . . 12 Sept. ,,
M. Tisza declares for maintenance of the treaty of Berlin and Bulgarian independence . 30 Sept. ,,
Increased army estimates voted . . 5 March, 1887
Accident through explosion of dynamite at Jasz Bereny near Pesth; 27 persons killed 5 July, ,,
Bronze statue of Francis Deak unveiled by the emperor . . . . . 29 Sept. ,,
Great opposition to M. Tisza's army bill; demonstration in Buda-Pesth . . . Feb. 1889
The small town of Paks totally destroyed by fire 20 July, ,,
The army ordered to be styled "Imperial and Royal" by desire of the Hungarian ministry . 19 Oct. 1889
Count Julius Andrassy dies in Istria, 18 Feb.; funeral service at Buda-Pesth; the emperor and ministry present, 21 Feb.; buried in family vault at Terebes . . . . . . 22 Feb. 1890
M. Tisza, the premier, an earnest liberal, resigns, through opposition of his colleagues, 7 March, succeeded by count Julius Szapáry 13 March, ,,
The town of Moar burnt, estimated damage 2,000,000 florins . . . . . 7 Aug. ,,
Unveiling at Arad of the national monument of the 13 generals executed 6 Oct. 1849 . . 6 Oct. ,,
At Bistritz on the Waag, about 30 persons were drowned by the upsetting of a ferry-boat, 10 Nov. ,,
Death of cardinal John Simor, archbishop of Gran, primate of Hungary, who crowned the king and queen in 1867, 23 Jan.; succeeded by arch-abbot Claude Vaszara . . . . 1 Nov. 1891
Currency reform bills (gold to be the basis) introduced into the diet . . 14 May, 1892
Death of gen. Klapka, the hero of Komorn [buried at Buda-Pesth] . . . about 17 May, ,,
The 25th anniversary of the coronation of the emperor as king celebrated . . 8 June, ,,
Destructive inundations near Komorn, &c., about 15 June, ,,
Celebration of the 90th birthday of L. Kossuth (*see above*, 1849); present to him of a sum of money, 19 Sept. ,,
The currency reform bill passed, 19 July; first new gold coin presented to the emperor . 19 Oct. ,,
Resignation of count Szapary, 9 Nov.; a new cabinet formed by Dr. Wekerle . 16 Nov. ,,
Conference of the bishops, supported by the pope, opposing obligatory civil marriages, &c., as proposed by the government, 15 Dec. 1892—5 March, 1893
Disastrous floods in various parts through overflowing of the Danube, reported . 28 Feb. ,,
Riot at Szoboszlo, near Debreczin, against market tolls; suppressed with bloodshed . 1 March, ,,
The Ultramontane minority in the chamber active in opposition; the government policy supported by the municipalities . . . . . March, ,,
Coolness between the government and the Vatican in relation to Italy . . . March—April, ,,
Attempt on the life of cardinal Vaszary, the primate, by a former servant; the defending secretary seriously wounded . . . 10 April, ,,
The author and publisher of the pamphlet "Replica," for attacking the government, fined and imprisoned . . . . . . 31 Aug. ,,
A Pan-Roumanian agitation for a formation of a Roumanian state denounced by the Hungarian minister . . . . 7 Oct. ,,
A royal ordinance, superseding the Austrian court functionaries by Hungarians at Budapest, issued 26 Nov. ,,
Jubilee of the literary career of Moritz Jokai, eminent writer; 100 vols.; born in 1825, 6–8 Jan. 1894
Banquet of Hungarians in London . 9 Jan. ,,
"Louis Kossuth's Library," purchased by a committee, to be kept intact in the national museum at Budapest . . . . . March, ,,
Louis Kossuth born 16 Sept. 1802, in Monok, co. Zemplin; died at Turin . . 20 March, ,,
Funeral service at Turin; public demonstrations of respect . . . . . 28 March, ,,
Public funeral at Budapest, after lying-in-state; immense concourse of people; oration by M. Moritz Jokai . . . . . 1 April, ,,
Trial of the Pan-Roumanian party (20 members) for illegality, 7 May; sentenced to terms of imprisonment, varying from 8 months to 5 years, 25 May, ,,
The civil marriage bill rejected by the magnates, 10 May, ,,
Resignation of the Wekerle ministry, about 1 June; re-constructed . . . . . 10 June, ,,
The civil marriage bill passed by the magnates, 21 June, ,,
Messrs. Wolfner & Co.'s tanning works burnt, at Neupest, near Budapest, with loss of life; 1,000,000 fl. damage . . . . 1 July, ,,
The magnates and lower house pass 3 bills granting freedom of religious worship, and recognizing the Jewish religion . . . . . . 29 Oct. ,,
Royal assent . . . . 10 Dec. ,,

M. Francis Kossuth takes the oath of allegiance to the king . . . . 26 Nov. 1894
Resignation of Dr. Wekerle's (liberal) ministry, 21 Dec. ,,
Ministry formed by baron Banffy; gazetted, 16 Jan. 1895
The Ultramontane party styled the "people's party," issue a programme demanding reforms, preservation of the R. C. faith, free education, &c. . . . . Jan. ,,
General opposition and rejection of the clause for the reception of the Jewish faith in the freedom of worship bill due to the papal allocution, March; operation of the law delayed, April; the house again sends the bill unchanged to the magnates, 28 April; the mutilated bill returned to the lower house . . . . . 15 May, ,,
A protest respecting the conduct of the papal nuncio, Mgr. Agliardi, prepared by baron Banffy for transmission to Rome is delayed by count Kalnoky, 3 May; the two ministers agree to the transmission of the remonstrance to the Vatican, 5 May; resignation of count Kalnoky, 16 May; differences with the Vatican amicably settled, May, ,,
Royal assent to the new ecclesiastical bills, 1 July, ,,
Special act of parliament in commemoration of the foundation of the monarchy, passed . 21 April, 1896
Millennial exhibition at Budapest, opened by the emperor-king; address by M. Daniel, minister of commerce, 2 May; closed . . . 3 Nov. ,,
Grand *Te Deum* at the cathedral . . . 3 May, ,,
Congratulations to the emperor-king from queen Victoria and the other powers . . . May, ,,
The Hungarian parliament occupies its new house, speech by the emperor-king . . . . 8 June, ,,
Fire, causing explosion at the town-hall, Fünfkirchen; many persons killed . . 30 July, ,,
Parliament dissolved, with a cheerful speech; reported . . . . 5 Oct. ,,
Elections, 28 Oct; great liberal majority 30 Oct. ,,
Stephen von Papay, eminent statesman, court councillor, born 1827, died . . . 6 Jan. 1897
Conflict between the police and miners at Temesvar, 9 persons killed; mines held by the troops; reported . . . . 21 Jan. ,,
Election riots, at Bosnyaizi, 14 persons killed by the troops; reported . . . . . 23 May, ,,
Long conflict in the diet respecting the jury bill; ended by compromise . . . . 30 July, ,,
M. Francis Pulszky, eminent patriot and scholar, friend of Kossuth, died, aged 83 . 9 Sept. ,,
German Emperor present at the army manœuvres at Totis, 15 Sept.; at Budapest . . 20 Sept. ,,
The erection of 10 historical monuments at Budapest, ordered by the emperor-king at his own cost; much popular enthusiasm . 26 Sept. ,,
Bill for the provisional extension of the *Ausgleich* (customs and commercial treaty) with Austria, introduced by the diet, 21 Oct.; great speech of count Albert Apponyi in favour of the bill, 17 Dec.; passed by the lower house, 4 Jan. 1898; passed by the diet . . . . . . 8 Jan. 1898
Discontent at recent special legislation ignoring the just claims of the peasantry . . Feb. ,,
Agrarian socialist rioting, in the Szabolcs district; 2 deaths, 13 Feb.; again 4 deaths . 31 March, ,,
Loyal address to the emperor king on the 50th anniversary of the constitution of 1848 . 11 April, ,,
Conference respecting the Ausgleich . 24–30 Aug. ,,
Plot against the emperor, 3 men sentenced to various terms of imprisonment at Budapest, 30 Sept.; and 32 socialists likewise . 4 Nov. ,,
Increasing revolt, mainly agrarian, against clerical interference in secular affairs . . Nov. ,,
Stormy scenes in parliament respecting the removal of the Hentzi monument, some arrests, 21, 23 Nov. ,,
Organised obstruction in the chamber; parliament prorogued, 10 Dec.; see *Austria*, 31 Dec. 1898 *et seq.*
Great tumult in the chamber of deputies, 30 Dec. 1898; prolonged crisis . . . . . Jan. 1899
Duel between baron Banffy and M. Horansky, leader of the national party, neither hurt, 3 Jan. ,,
Riot in Arad district over the election of a judge, 4 deaths . . . . mid. Jan. ,,
Banffy cabinet resigns; M. Koloman Szell forms a coalition ministry, 24 Feb.; Ausgleich prolonged provisionally, 10 March; conference of pr miers respecting it at Budapest successful, due to the emperor, 9 May; bills embodying the Ausgleich compromise passed by the reichsrath, 14 June; reichsrath prorogued . . . . . 12 July, 1899
The Hentzi memorial inaugurated on its new site at Budapest, the archduke Joseph present, 12 Aug. ,,
M. Szilagyi, eminent statesman, died 31 July 1901
Parliament dissolved, 9 Sept.; elections . 2 Oct. ,,
Diet opened by the emperor-king . . . 28 Oct. ,,
Agrarian riot at Also-Idecs, 10 deaths, many wounded, reported . . . . . 19 Jan. 1902
M. Koloman Tisza, eminent statesman, born 10 Dec. 1830, died 23 March, ,,
Centenary of Louis Kossuth, patriot 19 Sept. ,,
British arts and crafts exhibition in Budapest, opened . . . . 28 Sept. ,,
Count Apponyi, pres. of the reichstag, issues a manifesto against the nationality agitation, 3 Nov. ,,
The Ausgleich renewed on revised terms, 31 Dec. ,,
Parliament opened, Jan. 9; army bills opposed, 17 Feb. 1903
Demonstration against the bills, Budapest, 7 Mar.; deadlock continues . . . . April, May, ,,
Popular excitement among peasants in Croatia; demand for financial separation for Hungary; count Hedervary, the Banus of Croatia, restores order with troops . . . . . . 12 May, ,,
Violent disturbances between soldiers and peasantry in Agram; incidents provocative of discord between Austria and Italy occur at Innsbruck and Trieste . . . . 20 May, ,,
Renewed disturbances at Agram . 31 May–1 June, ,,
Resignation of the Szell ministry . . 16 June, ,,
Violent earthquake at Erlau, causes much damage 26 June ,,
Count Stephen Tirza failing to construct a cabinet, count Khuen Hedervary forms a new ministry, with himself as premier and minister of the interior . . . . 28 June, ,,
Count Pejacsevich appointed Banus of Croatia in succession to count Hedervary . . mid July, ,,
Continued disorder in Croatia, 2 dynamite explosions in Agram, reported . . . 14 July, ,,
Strained relations between Hungary and Austria on the subject of the sugar allotment system, about 30 July, ,,
Resignation of count Hedervary and cabinet, 10 Aug. ,,
Croatian riots at Zapresic in connection with the celebration of the emperor's 73rd birthday, 3 persons killed and many wounded by gendarmes, 18 Aug. ,,
Count Hedervary formally reinstated as premier; an order of the day, issued by the emperor, declaring that he will hold fast to the existing common and military organisation of the army, and never relinquish his rights and privileges as its head; hostile attitude of the Hungarian and the Magyar press; manifesto of conciliation to the Hungarian nation issued by the emperor and countersigned by count Hedervary; it is favourably received by the liberal party mid Sept. ,,
Resignation of count Hedervary, 30 Sept.; new cabinet formed by count Stephen Tisza 26 Oct. ,,

SOVEREIGNS.

997. St. Stephen, duke of Hungary (son of Geisa); established the Roman catholic religion (1000), and received from the pope the title of Apostolic King, still borne by the emperor of Austria, as king of Hungary.
1038. Peter, the German; deposed.
1041. Aba or Owen.
1044. Peter, again: deposed; and his eyes put out.
1047. Andrew I.: deposed.
1061. Bela I.: killed by the fall of a ruinous tower.
1064. Salamon, son of Andrew.
1075. Geisa I. son of Bela.
1077. Ladislas I. the Pious.
1095. Coloman, son of Geisa.
1114. Stephen II. named Thunder.
1131. Bela II.: had his eyes put out.
1141. Geisa II.: succeeded by his son,
1161. Stephen III.: and Stephen IV. (anarchy)

1173. Bela III.: succeeded by his son,
1196. Emeric: succeeded by his son,
1204. Ladislas II.; reigned six months only.
1205. Andrew II. son of Bela III.
1235. Bela IV.
1270. Stephen IV. (or V.) his son.
1272. Ladislas III.: killed.
1290. Andrew III. surnamed the Venetian, son-in-law of Rodolph of Hapsburg, emperor of Germany (last of the house of Arpad), died 1301.
1301. Wenceslas of Bohemia, and (1305) Otho of Bavaria, who gave way to
1309. Charobert, or Charles Robert of Anjou.
1342. Louis I. the Great; elected king of Poland, 1370.
1382. Mary, called *King* Mary, daughter of Louis.
1385-6. Charles Durazzo.
1387. Mary and her consort Sigismond: the latter became king of Bohemia, and was elected emperor in 1410.
1392. Sigismond alone (on the death of Mary).
1437. Albert, duke of Austria, married Elizabeth, daughter of Sigismond, and obtains the thrones of Hungary, Bohemia, and Germany; dies suddenly.
1439. Elizabeth alone: she marries
1440. Ladislas IV. king of Poland, of which kingdom he was Ladislas VI.: slain at Varna.
1444. [Interregnum.]
1445. John Hunniades, regent.
1458. Ladislas V. posthumous son of Albert: poisoned.
,, Matthias-Corvinus, son of Hunniades.
1490. Ladislas VI. king of Bohemia: the emperor Maximilian laid claim to both kingdoms.
1516. Louis II. of Hungary (I. of Bohemia): loses his life at the battle of Mohatz.
1526. { John Zapolski, waivode of Transylvania, elected by the Hungarians, and supported by the sultan Solyman: by treaty with Ferdinand, he founds the principality of Transylvania, 1536. Ferdinand I. king of Bohemia, brother to the emperor Charles V.; rival kings.
1540. Ferdinand alone: elected emperor, 1558.
1563. Maximilian, son; emperor in 1564.
1572. Rodolph, son; emperor in 1576.
1608. Matthias II. brother; emperor in 1612.
1618. Ferdinand II. cousin, emperor.
1625. Ferdinand III. son; emperor, 1637.
1647. Ferdinand IV. son; died in 1654, three years before his father.
1655. Leopold I. brother: emperor, 1657.
1687. Joseph I. son: emperor in 1705.
1712. Charles VI. (of Germany), brother, and nominal king of Spain.
1741. Maria-Theresa, daughter; empress; survived her consort, emperor Francis I., from 1765 until 1780; see *Germany*.
1780. Joseph II. son, emperor in 1765: succeeded to Hungary on the death of his mother.
1790. Leopold II. brother; emperor; succeeded by his son,
1792. Francis I. son (Francis II. as emperor of Germany): in 1804 he became emperor of *Austria* only.
1835. Ferdinand V. son: Ferdinand I. as emperor of Austria.
1848. Francis-Joseph, emperor of Austria, nephew; succeeded on the abdication of his uncle, 2 Dec. 1848; crowned king of Hungary, 8 June, 1867. See *Austria*.

PRINCIPAL HUNGARIAN AUTHORS.—Alexander Kisfaludy, *p.*, 1772–1844; Charles Kisfaludy, *d.*, 1788–1830; Sandor Petöfi, *p.*, 1823–49; Vörösmarty, *p.*, 1800–55; János Arany, *p.*, 1817–82; Baron Nicholas Josika, *n.*, 1794–65; Baron Joseph Eötvös, *n.*, 1813–71; Maurice Jókai, *n.*, born 1825; Alex. Szilagyi, *hist.*, 1828–99.

HUNGERFORD BRIDGE, over the Thames from Hungerford-stairs to the Belvedere-road, Lambeth, opened 1 May, 1845, was taken down in July, 1862, to make way for the Charing-cross railway-bridge, and transferred to Clifton (*which see*). The market (opened in July, 1833), was removed at the same time.

HUNS, a race of warlike Asiatics, said to have conquered China, about 210 B.C., and to have been expelled therefrom about A.D. 90. They invaded Hungary, about 376, and drove out the Goths. Marching westward, under Attila, they were thoroughly beaten at Chalons by the consul Aëtius, 451; see *Attila*.

HUNTERIAN ORATION, annually at the Royal College of Surgeons, London, founded 1813.

HUNTERIAN SOCIETY (surgical) established Feb. 1819; first president, sir Wm. Blizard. See *Surgeons, College of*.

HUNTING: an ancient pastime. The "Bokys of Hawking and Huntyng," by Dame Julyana Barnes, was printed at St. Alban's, 1486. "The Kings of the Hunting Field," by Thormanby, published 1899.

HUNTINGDON, Huntingdonshire; a Saxon town; a royal castle was erected here by Edward the Elder, 917, the town was incorporated in 1189. Oliver Cromwell, the protector, was born here 25 April, 1599; his statue unveiled at St. Ives, 23 Oct. 1901. Population, 1881, 4,228; 1891, 4,349; 1,901, 4,346.

HUNTINGDON CONNECTION, see *Whitefieldites*.

HURRICANES, see *Cyclones* and *Storms*.

HUSSARS, Hungarian militia, provided by the landholders; instituted by Matthias Corvinus, about 1359. (Hussar is derived from *husz*, 20; and *ar*, price) The British Hussars were enrolled in 1759.

HUSSITES. After the death of Huss,* many of his followers took up arms, in 1419, and formed a political party under John Ziska, and built the city of Tabor. He defeated the emperor Sigismond, 11 July, 1420, and a short truce followed. Ziska, blinded at the siege of Rabi, beat all the armies sent against him. He died of the plague, 18 Oct. 1424, and is said to have ordered a drum to be made of his skin to terrify his enemies even after death. Two Hussite generals, named Procopius, defeated the imperialists in 1431; and a temporary peace ensued. Divisions took place among the Hussites, and on 30 May, 1434, they were defeated, and Procopius the elder slain at Bömischbrod or Lippau. Toleration was granted by the treaty of Iglau, and Sigismond entered Prague 23 Aug. 1436. The Hussites opposed his successor, Albert of Austria, and called Casimir of Poland to the throne; but were defeated in 1438. A portion of the Hussites existed in the time of Luther, and were called "Bohemian brethren."

HUSTINGS (said to be derived from *house court*, an assembly among the Anglo-Saxons), an ancient court of London, being its supreme court of judicature, as the court of common council is of legislature. The court of *hustyngs* was granted to the city of London, to be holden and kept weekly,

* The clergy having instigated the pope to issue a bull against heretics, John Huss (born in Bohemia in 1373), a zealous preacher of the Reformation, was cited to appear before a council of divines at Constance, the emperor Sigismond sending him a safe-conduct. He presented himself accordingly, but was thrown into prison, and after some months' confinement was adjudged to be burned alive, which he endured with resignation, 6 or 7 July, 1415. Jerome of Prague, his intimate friend, who came to this council to support and second him, also suffered death by fire, 30 May, 1416, although he also had a safe-conduct.

by Edward the Confessor. 1052. One was held to outlaw defaulters, Guildhall, London, 6 Dec. 1870; others in 1882 and 7 July, 1896. Above 4,000 wills are on the roll of the court, commencing with the 43rd year of king Henry III. Winchester, Lincoln, York, &c., were also granted hustings courts.

HUTCHINSONIANS included many eminent clergy, who did not form any sect, but held the opinions of John Hutchinson, of Yorkshire (1674-1737); they rejected the Newtonian system, and contended that the scriptures contain a complete system of natural philosophy. His work, "*Moses' Principia*," was published in 1724. He derived all things from the air, whence, he said, proceeded fire, light, and spirit, types of the Trinity. In 1712 he invented a time-piece for finding the longitude. He died in 1737.

HUXLEY MEMORIAL. Great meeting of general committee at Jermyn street, London. Resolved that a statue by Mr. Onslow Ford be set up in the Natural History Museum, S. Kensington, medals, &c., 27 Nov. 1895.

First Huxley lecture in London by prof. Michael Foster, 5 Oct. 1896; 2nd by prof. Rudolf Virchow, 3 Oct. 1898; 3rd by prof. Cunningham, F.R.S., 21 Oct. 1902. His "Scientific Memoirs," vol. i., edited by profs. M. Foster and E. Ray Lankester, published Oct. 1898; his "Life," by his son Leonard Huxley, published 1900.

HYDASPES, a river in India, where Alexander the Great defeated Porus, after a severely contested engagement; 327 B.C.

HYDE-PARK (London, W., 352 acres), the ancient manor of Hyde, belonging to the abbey of Westminster, became crown property at the dissolution, 1535. It was sold by parliament in 1652; but was resumed by the king at the restoration in 1660. The Serpentine was formed 1730-33. "Hyde Park," by John Ashton, published 1896.

Colossal statue of Achilles, cast from cannon taken in the battles of Salamanca, Vittoria, Toulouse, and Waterloo, and inscribed to "Arthur, Duke of Wellington, and his brave companions in arms, by their countrywomen," erected on . . 18 June, 1822
Hyde Park corner entrance erected 1828
Marble arch from Buckingham Palace set up at Cumberland Gate . . . . . 29 March, 1850
Crystal palace erected for the great exhibition. . 1851
Disturbances in consequence of a Sunday bill having been brought before parliament by lord Robert Grosvenor, which was eventually withdrawn, Sundays, 24 June, and 1 and 8 July, 1855
Riotous meetings held here, on account of the high price of bread . . Sundays 14, 21, 28 Oct. ,,
Democratic meetings on the reform question, March, 1859
The queen reviewed 18,450 volunteers . 23 June, 1860
Great meeting of admirers of Garibaldi, 28 Sept.; who are violently attacked by the Irish; many persons wounded . . . . . . 5 Oct. 1862
Public meetings in the park prohibited . 9 Oct. ,,
20,000 volunteers reviewed by the prince of Wales, 28 May, 1864
Proposed reform meeting in the park opposed; great rioting; the palings broken down, and much damage done; fierce conflicts with the police, and many hurt . . . . . 23, 24 July, 1866
See *Times* leader, 4 June, 1898.
Peaceful reform demonstrations in the park, 6 May and 5 Aug. 1867
Regulations with restrictions on public meeting in the parks issued (afterwards modified) . Oct. 1872
Meeting of Fenian sympathisers in Hyde park contrary to the regulations . . . . 3 Nov. ,,
Odger and others prosecuted and fined . . Nov. ,,
The convictions confirmed by the judges on appeal 22 Jan. 1873
Great meeting on behalf of the Tichborne claimant, Dr. Kenealy and Mr. Guildford Onslow present, Easter Monday, 29 March, 1875
Great meetings for and against government policy on the eastern question Sundays 24 Feb. and 10 March, 1878
Great orderly meeting to protest against arrest of Irish agitators (Killen, Daly, and Davitt) 30 Nov. 1879
About 40,000 persons meet to protest against arrest of Mr. Parnell and others; Mr. O'Donnell chief speaker; little sympathy . 23 Oct. 1881
Mass meeting to support the London government bill . . . . 13 July, 1884
Great demonstration; seven meetings of trade delegates, political clubs, &c., about 40,000, to protest against the peers' rejection of the franchise bill and to support the Gladstone Ministry 21 July, ,,
Demonstration for abolition of house of lords; nine meetings, Sunday . . . . . 26 Oct. ,,
Great meeting of the social democratic federation, Sunday . . . . . . 21 Feb. 1886
Great demonstration against the Irish coercion bill . . . . 11 April, 1887
Jubilee entertainment of about 30,000 children of elementary schools, see *Jubilee* . 22 June ,,
Meeting of the unemployed; dispersed by the police after a fight, 18-19 Oct. 1887; orderly meetings . . 23 Oct., and 15, 20, 27 Nov. ,,
Orderly demonstration to meet the released Irish M.P.'s, Mr. T. D. Sullivan and Mr. E. Harrington, 13 Feb. 1888
Demonstration against proposed compensation to publicans dispossessed by local government bill, 2 June, ,,
Meetings to protest against the treatment of Mr. W. O'Brien, M.P., and others in prison (see *Ireland*); . . . . . . 10 Feb. 1889
See *Strikes*, 1889.
Meeting of Postmen's union . . . 20 Oct. ,,
Demonstrations in relation to the proposed bakers' strike and the Silverton strike . . 10 Nov. ,,
Great meeting of men employed on railways 15 Dec. ,,
Meeting of trades unions to support the gas-stokers' union . . . . . . 19 Jan. 1890
"Labour Day" demonstrations, see *Working-men* 1, 4 May, ,,
Great meeting of railway workers and others, 11 May, ,,
Demonstration against government proposal to compensate publicans and others for loss of drink licences . . . . . 7 June, ,,
'Labour Day" demonstrations, orderly; foreign anarchists, 1 May; building trade unions, 2 May; combined trades unions, in favour of an eight hours working day; present, Mr. Cunninghame Graham, M.P., Messrs. John Burns, Ben Tillet, Tom Mann, and Dr. Aveling . . 3 May, 1891
Mass meeting to support the omnibus strike, 7 June, ,,
Great demonstration of the building trades in favour of an eight hours' day . 27 Sept. ,,
Great meeting of the Salvation Army to welcome gen. Booth on his return from his long tour in Europe, Africa, Asia, and Australia . 13 Feb. 1892
Mass meeting of London anarchists . 10 April, ,,
Mass meeting of members of the National Union of Clerks . . . . 24 April ,,
"Labour Day;" great orderly meeting to support and promote an international 8 hours working day . . . . 1 May, ,,
Labour demonstration for eight hours day, 7 May, 1893
Irish home rule demonstration . . 21 May, ,,
Demonstration in favour of the direct veto bill; sir Wilfrid Lawson present . . . 10 June, ,,
Labour demonstration for the fund for the collier strikers . . . . 15 Oct. ,,
Demonstration in favour of an eight hours' working day; John Burns, M.P., present, 6 May, 1894, and 5 May, 1895
Cab strike demonstrations . . . 20, 27 May, 1894
International peace demonstration and socialist congress, etc.; proceedings stopped by a thunderstorm . . . . . . 26 July, 1896
Demonstration in favour of Cretans and sympathy with Greece . . . . 7 March, 1897
Farriers (London) strike for increase of wages; demonstrations, 16, 23 May, see *Horse* . . . ,,

May-day demonstrations, 1897, 1898, 1899.
Memorial service to Mr. Gladstone, large assemblage 5 June, 1897
Labour demonstration in favour of a national old-age pension scheme and the better housing of the working classes . . . . . 20 Aug. 1899
Demonstration in favour of and in sympathy with capt. and madame Dreyfus . . . 16 Sept. ,,
Demonstration in sympathy with gen. Buller, "the saviour of Natal" . . . . . . 1 Dec. 1901
National democratic league convenes a meeting against the corn duty . . . 11 May, 1902
Demonstration, protesting against recent House of Lords' decisions in trade union cases, demanding a bill for protection against legal persecution, &c., 31 Aug. ,,
Demonstration of reserve and time-expired men to protest against their treatment by the War Office, 19 Oct. ,,
Demonstration against the London Education Bill, 23 May, 1903

HYDERABAD (S. India), the territory of the Nizam (the greatest mahometan potentate in India), who derives his authority from Azof Jah, a chief under Aurungzebe, who made him viceroy as Nizam-ool-Moolk, regulator of the state. He died in 1748. Pop. 1881, 9,845,594; 1891, 11,537,000; 1901, 11,141,142; city and suburbs, 448,466.

Civil war between his descendants ensues . 1748-65
Nizam Ali dethroned his brother, 1761; ravaged the Carnatic, 1765; made a treaty with the East India Company, 1766; he joined Hyder Ali: left him, 1768; acquired part of Tippoo Sultan's territories; and became feudatory of the British empire, 1799 *et seq.*; died 1802
One of his successors, Secunder Jah, ruled feebly; died, succeeded by an illegitimate son . . 1829
The nizam died, leaving his young son in charge of Salar Jung (or Jang); enjoining him to support the British during the mutiny, which he did faithfully 1857-8
Sir Salar Jung made K.C.S.I.; visits Europe; presented to the Queen, 29 June; returned to Bombay, 24 Aug. 1876; died . . . . 8 Feb. 1883
The young nizam Mir Mahbub Ali (aged 18) installed at Hyderabad by the viceroy of India, the marquis of Ripon . . . . 5 Feb. 1884
The nizam in a letter to lord Dufferin, the viceroy, makes an offer to present 20 lakhs of rupees for three years, total 600,000*l.*, for the defence of the N.W. Indian territories, Sept.; acknowledged with thanks by the viceroy, announced 10 Oct.; and by the queen, about 26 Oct. 1887; the offer with others declined (see *India*) . 18 Nov. 1888
The long-standing disputes between the Nizam's government and the Deccan company, settled on terms approved by the India office, signed at Hyderabad . . . . 2 Jan. 1890
See *Chloroform*, 1889-90.
For the "imperial diamond" case, see *Trials*, Dec. 1891.
Visit of the viceroy, lord Lansdowne, 3 Nov. *et seq.* 1892

HYDRAULIC PRESS, see under *Hydrostatics.*

HYDROCHLORIC ACID or CHLORHYDRIC ACID, the only known compound of chlorine and hydrogen, was discovered by Dr. Priestley, 1772; its constitution determined by Davy, 1810. It is also called muriatic acid and spirit of salt; see under *Alkalies.*

HYDROGEN (from *hydōr*, water). Paracelsus observed a gas rise from a solution of iron in oil of vitriol, about 1500; Turquet de Mayerne discovered its inflammability, 1656; as did Boyle, 1672; Lemery noticed its detonating power, 1700. In 1766 Cavendish proved it to be an elementary body; and in 1781, he and Watt first showed that in the combination of this gas with oxygen, which takes place when it is burnt, water is produced; subsequently Lavoisier decomposed water into its elements, and gave hydrogen its present name instead of "inflammable air." One volume of oxygen combines with two volumes of hydrogen to form water. Hydrogen is never found in the free state.

In 1877, Cailletet and Wroblewski obtained by rapid expansion of the compressed gas, a condensation or mist, which was supposed to be produced by the liquefaction of hydrogen. Olszewski had seen a few drops of an unknown liquid falling in a glass tube and remaining for a few instants unevaporated, subsequently proved to be due to impurities. Prof. Dewar's paper on "The Density of Hydrogen in Palladium," was published in 1873; "The Absorption of Hydrogen by Palladium at high temperatures, pressures, etc.," was published in 1897. On 10 May, 1898, at the Royal Institution, he produced half a wine-glassful of liquefied hydrogen at 240 deg. centigrade (below zero) in 5 min., and on the 12th he doubled the quantity. On the 12th he reported it to the Royal Society, and on the 16th to the French Academy. By means of this liquid he also, on the 10th, liquefied a mixture of helium and other gas or gases.
Lecture on liquid hydrogen at the Royal Institution, 20 Jan. 1899; further researches; boiling point by exhaustion, 15° of absolute temperature; liquid hydrogen exhibited boiling in a vacuum tube immersed in liquid air, 21° absolute temperature; and experiments with liquid hydrogen and the vitality of seeds; see *Athenæum*, 16 Dec. 1899; hydrogen obtained in the solid state by prof Dewar, 16° absolute scale, reported, Jan. 1900.

HYDROGENIUM, a hypothetical metal. In a paper read before the Royal Society, 7 Jan. 1869, Mr. Thomas Graham, master of the Mint, suggested that a piece of the metal palladium, into which hydrogen had been pressed, became an "alloy of the volatile metal hydrogenium."

HYDROGRAPH, an apparatus invented by capt. Neale, for transmitting sound by water, for the purpose of signalling between ships, lighthouses, &c.; it consists of a transmitter, a receiver, and electric recorder; experiments were made on the Solent under the auspices of the Trinity Board.—*Times*, 19 Oct. 1893.

HYDROGRAPHY is the description of the surface waters of the earth. The first sea-chart is attributed to Henry the Navigator, in the 16th century. There is a hydrographic department in the British admiralty, by which a series of charts has been issued. International Hydrographic and Biological congress meets at Stockholm, 15 June, 1899. See *China*, May, 1903.

HYDROMETER, the instrument by which is measured the gravity, density, and other properties of liquids. The oldest mention of the hydrometer occurs in the 5th century, and may be found in the letters of Synesius to Hypatia; but it is not improbable that Archimedes was the inventor of it, though no proofs of it are to be found. *Beckmann.* Archimedes was killed in 212 B.C., and Hypatia was torn to pieces at Alexandria, A.D. 415. "Hypatia," by the rev. Charles Kingsley, appeared in 1853. Robert Boyle described a hydrometer in 1675: Baumé's (1762) and Sykes', about 1818, have been much employed. Modifications of the apparatus have been invented.

HYDROPATHY, a term applied to the treatment of diseases by cold water, practised by Hippocrates in the 4th century B.C., by the Arabs in the 10th century A.D., and revived by Dr. Currie in 1797. A system was suggested in 1825 by Vincenz Priessnitz, of Grafenberg, in Austrian Silesia. The rational part of the doctrine was understood and maintained by Dr. Sydenham, before 1689. Priessnitz died 26 Nov. 1851.

A grand hydropathic establishment at Bushey, Herts, opened, 13 Feb. 1883. Many others exist throughout the kingdom.

HYDROPHOBIA, in man, rabies in animals, M. Pasteur announced his discovery of a method of checking this disease, analogous to vaccination, the system afterwards applied to various diseases.

He operates on monkeys and other animals successfully, May, on dogs, Aug. 1884; on 40 persons 14 Dec. 1885. An international hospital, afterwards termed the Pasteur institute, founded (40,000*l.* subscribed) May, 1886; opened by president Carnot, 14 Nov. 1888. Out of 726 cases treated, 4 deaths reported 12 April, 1886; 1673 persons treated, 1 May, 1888, to 1 May, 1889. The principle much opposed 1886–7. A British commission for inquiry (sir James Paget, Dr. Burdon Sanderson, and others) appointed 12 April, 1886; visits Paris, and reports confidence in M. Pasteur's treatment, 27 June, 1887. M. Pasteur proposes and verifies other applications of his principles, 1887–8. The book, "M. Pasteur, Histoire d'un Savant," was published in 1883; and an English translation by lady Claud Hamilton in . 1885

Reported number of patients by M. Pasteur (he died 28 Sept. 1895) since 1885, 6,950, to 28 June, 1889; 1,830 patients, 7 deaths in 1889; 1,520 patients, 5 deaths, in 1895; 1,308 patients, 4 deaths in 1896; 1,521 patients, 6 deaths in 1897; 1,614 patients, 4 deaths in 1899; 1,321 patients, 8 deaths in 1901; 1,105 patients, 2 deaths in . . 1902

The 8th institute in France opened at Lyons, 1 Jan. 1900; many in other countries; one at Kasauli, India, opened 1900, reported very successful, 9 Aug. ,,

50,000 rupees and 10,000 rupees from sir Chas. Rivas to the Indian Pasteur institute at Kasauli; also Drumbar house from the Punjaub government, and other grants, reported . . Sept. ,,

Meeting at the mansion house, London, to support the Pasteur institute, 1 July; above 2,000*l.* subscribed, 2 Oct. 1889; Mdme. Hirsch presents 2,000,000 francs, Jan. 1897 (died 2 April, 1899).

Rabies stamped out by isolation and quarantine of dogs from abroad. Preventive measures, 1895 *et seq.* Hydrophobia microbe discovered by prof. Sormani . . . . Jan. 1903

See *Mansion House Funds.*

HYDROPHONE, an electrical, telephonic apparatus for coast defence by secret communication between ships and the shore, of the approach of a torpedo-boat, invented by capt. M'Evoy; announced, Nov. 1892.

HYDROSTATICS, &c., were probably first studied in the Alexandrian school about 300 B.C.

Pressure of fluids discovered by Archimedes, about B.C. 250

The forcing pump and air fountain invented by Hero about 120

Water mills were known . . . . about A.D. 1

The science revived by Galileo, Castellio, Torricelli, and Pascal (who suggested the principle of the hydraulic press) . . . . . 17th century

The theory of rivers scientifically understood in . 1697

The correct theory of fluids and oscillation of waves explained by Newton 1714

A scientific form was given to hydro-dynamics, by Bernouilli 1738

Joseph Bramah's *hydrostatic or hydraulic press* patented first in 1785

Sir Wm. Armstrong's *hydraulic crane* patented . 1846

John Crowther's 1825

Dr. Emil Fleischer's *Hydromotor* successfully applied to the propulsion of ships on the Elbe, near Dresden . . . . . 11 Oct. 1883

HYGEIOPOLIS (city of health), planned by Dr. B. Ward Richardson, in 1875. A company was proposed for its erection, Jan. 1877. No result.

HYGIENE (Hygeia, goddess of health), see *Sanitation.*

International congresses on Hygiene and Demography: 1. Brussels, 27 Sept. 1876; 2. Paris, 1 Aug. 1878; 3. Turin, Aug. 1880; 4. Geneva, 4 Sept. 1882; 5. Hague, 21 Aug. 1884; 6. Vienna, 26 Sept. 1887; 7. London, the queen patron, the prince of Wales president, 10–17 Aug. 1891; 8. Budapest, 2 Sept. 1894; 9. Paris, 27 June, 1895; Madrid, 10 April, 1898; 10 Aug. 1900; Brussels . . . . 2 Sept. 1903

HYGROMETER, an instrument for measuring the moisture in the atmosphere. That by Saussure (who died in 1799) is most employed. It consists of a human hair boiled in caustic lye, and acts on the principle of absorption. *Brande.* Daniell's hygrometer (1820) is much esteemed. M. Crova's new hygrometer, said to be very accurate, described, June, 1882.

HYKSOS, a race, probably of Tatar origin, who overthrew the dynasty of lower Egypt, captured Memphis, and made Avaris (Tanis) the seat of their kingdom. Joseph is supposed to have been vizier to Apepi, one of the Hyksos, or "Shepherd Kings," as they are also called. They were overthrown by Aahmes I. of the 18th dynasty, *cir.* 1700 B.C. See *Egypt.* XV. Dynasty, *et seq.*

HYMNS. The song of Moses is the most ancient, 1491 B.C. (*Exod.* xv.) The Psalms date from about 1060 B.C. to about 444 B.C. (from David to Ezra). The hymns of the Jews were frequently accompanied by instrumental music. Paul (A.D. 64) speaks of Christians admonishing one another "in psalms and hymns and spiritual songs" (*Col.* iii. 16.) The composition of hymns for the Christian church is very ancient. The hymns of Dr. Watts (died 1784), of John Wesley (died 1791), and of his brother Charles (died 1788), are used by English churchmen and dissenters. "Hymns, Ancient and Modern," edited by rev. sir Henry Baker, first appeared in 1860. "A Dictionary of Hymnology," edited by the rev. John Julian, D.D., was published Jan. 1892.

HYPNOTISM (Greek *hypnos, sleep*) or nervous sleep, terms given by Mr. Braid (in 1843) to a sleep-like condition, produced in a person by steadily fixing his mind on one particular object. Minor surgical operations have, it is said, been performed without pain on persons in this state. The lecture by R. Heidenhain, at Breslau 19 Jan. 1880, on "Hypnotism or Animal Magnetism" was translated by L. C. Wooldridge; and published in 1888. See also "Suggestive Therapeutics," by Bernheim, translated by Herter, 1889; Björnström, on Hypnotism, 1889, and "Psycho-therapeutics," by Tuckey, 1891. See *Mesmerism—Trials* (Addenda) 1898.

"The use of hypnotical suggestion" (the entire concentration of the mind on one subject caused by the suggestion of another person) in medical practice, has been advocated by Bernheim, Beaunis and other foreign physicians, Oct. 1889; but strongly opposed by other eminent physiologists, especially Du Bois Reymond . Oct. 1890

The first meeting of the International Congress on Hypnotism took place at Paris, Aug. 1889; 2nd, 12–16 Aug. 1900

Prof. Germane's experiments were exhibited at the Aquarium, Westminster . . . . . Nov. 1891

HYPOSCOPE, an instrument for aiming guns under cover, by means of mirrors, invented by Mr. W. Youlten; tried at Bisley, July, 1902.

HYPOTHEC, LAW OF, in Scotland gives landlords a preferential right to levy for rent and follow and seize crops and cattle. A bill for its abolition was brought in annually since 1874. One was read a second time 19 March, 1879, but did not pass till 24 March, 1880 (43 Vict. c. 12); which came into operation 11 Nov. 1881.

HYPSOMETER, a thermometrical barometer for measuring altitudes, invented by F. J. Wollaston in 1817, much improved by Regnault, about 1847.

HYRCANIA, Asia, near the Caspian, a province subject to Persia, B.C. 334; held by Parthians, 244. It is now Mazenderan, a Persian province.

HYTHE, Kent, a cinque-port. The haven has been choked up with sand since the end of the 16th century. A school of musketry was established here in 1854, under the charge of major-gen. Charles Crawford Hay. He resigned in 1867. Railway to Sandgate opened, 9 Oct. 1874. Population, 1881, 4,173; 1891, 4,351; 1901, 5,557.

I.

IAMBIC VERSE, mythically named from the poetical effusions of Iambe, an attendant of Metanira, wife of Celeus, king of Sparta. Archilochus is said to have been the first who wrote satirical iambic verses B.C. 700.

IBERIA, see *Georgia*, and *Spain*.

IBERUS, a river in N.E. Spain, now called Ebro, *which see*. It was very important during the second Punic war, 218—201 B.C.

ICE. Galileo observed ice to be lighter than water, about 1597. See *Congelation*, where is a notice of the ice-making machines of Harrison and of Siebe. In 1841 there were sixteen companies in Boston, U.S., engaged in exporting ice, brought from Wenham lake and Fresh and Spy Ponds, about 18 miles from that city. The trade was begun by Mr. Tudor in 1806. 156,540 tons were sent from Boston alone in 1854. In New York, in 1855, 305,000 tons were stored up, of which 20,000 were for exportation. The Wenham lake company import ice largely from their ponds near Christiania, Norway, from whence 43,359 tons were shipped to Great Britain in 1865.

Regelation and other properties, exhibited by professor Faraday, in 1850, became the subject of investigation by eminent physicists of the day, especially J. D. Forbes, Dr. Tyndall, and sir William Thomson.

"Icy night" or "silver thaw" in London, 22 Jan. 1867. After a severe frost came rain freezing as it fell. Many accidents occurred in consequence of the glassy pavements and roads.

Powerful boat icebreakers employed in the Baltic and Russian ports; reported, 1897; one built by Messrs. Armstrong & Co., launched on the Tyne, 29 Oct. 1898; and another, the *Yermak*, used successfully in the Finnish Gulf, March–April, 1899.

ICELAND (North Sea), discovered by Norwegian chiefs, about 861; according to some accounts, it had been previously visited by a Scandinavian pirate. Population, 1888, 69,224; 1898, about 76,237.

Colonised by Norwegians 874
Christianity introduced . . . . . . about 1000
The annual general assembly was termed Althing: there were four great schools, like universities, founded in the 11th century; and education was general . . . .
The great warrior, statesman, and poet, Snorri Sturluson, was murdered . . . . . 22 Sept. 1241
Had a republican government, and a flourishing literature, till it was subjected to Hakon, king of Norway 1264
Protestantism introduced about 1551
Thousands perished by famine through failure of the crops 1753-4
Cleasby's great Icelandic-English Dictionary, published in England 1869-73
A new constitution signed by the king, 5 Jan., came into operation 1 Aug., when king Christian of Denmark visited Iceland, and the thousandth anniversary of the colonisation was celebrated at the capital, Reykjavik . . . . 1 Aug. 1874
Iceland has suffered much by volcanic eruptions, especially in 1783; and on 29 March, 1875, whole districts of pasture land were devastated.
A reported severe famine (see *Mansion House funds*). Summer, 1882
Relief was given by prof. Magnusson to many sufferers . . . . Oct. ,,
A large emigration of Icelanders to west Canada, 1872 *et seq*.
Agitation for home-rule; resisted by Denmark, Nov. 1885; demanded by the diet . July–Aug. 1886
Death of Dr. Vigfusson, great Icelandic scholar, Feb. 1889
Exhibition of Icelandic handicraft at Kensington May, ,,
Mr. Frederick W. W. Howell ascended the Oræfa Jökull (about 6,550 feet) . . . . 17 Aug. 1892
See *Eddas* and *Hecla*.
Helgi Hálfdánorson, the Icelandic poet, born 18 Aug. 1826; dies at Reykjavik . . Jan. 1894
The hot springs, Geysir and Strokkur, bought by Mr. James Craig, of Belfast . . . May, ,,
Destructive earthquake: churches, farms, etc., destroyed . . . . . . 26, 27 Aug. 1896
Fresh shocks in the south-west, 3 deaths, 5, 6 Sept. ,,
Coal discovered at Nordfjord, on the east coast, April, 1902
Boating disaster near Westman islands, 27 deaths, 21 May, ,,
Constitutional (by which an independent and responsible minister shall reside in Reykjavik) and other bills adopted; session closed . 26 Aug. 1902
The Althing accepts the bill of the Danish government amending the constitution of the island, reported . . . . mid Aug. 1903

ICENI, a British tribe which inhabited chiefly Suffolk and Norfolk. In 61, while Suetonius Paulinus was reducing Mona (Anglesey) they marched southwards and destroyed Verulam, London, and other places, with great slaughter of the Romans; but were defeated by Suetonius near London, and their heroic queen Boadicea or Boudicca died or committed suicide.

"ICH DIEN," *I serve*, the motto under the plume of ostrich feathers found in the helmet of the king of Bohemia slain at the battle of Cressy, at which he served as a volunteer in the French army, 26 Aug. 1346. Edward the Black Prince, in respect to his father, Edward III., who commanded that day, though the prince won the battle, adopted the motto, which has since been borne with the feathers, by the heirs to the crown of England.

ICHNOLOGY, the science of footprints, treats of the impression made in mud or sand by the animals of former ages. Dr. Duncan discovered the footprints of a tortoise in the sandstone of Annandale, in 1828; since then numerous discoveries have been made by Owen, Lyell, Huxley, and others.

ICHTHYOLOGY, the science of fish. Eminent authors are Aristotle (384—322 B.C.), Willoughby, Ray, Valenciennes, Cuvier, Owen, Agassiz, &c. Yarrell's "British Fishes" (1836-59) is a classical work; see *Fish*.

ICONIUM (Syria). Here Paul and Barnabas preached, 38. Soliman the Seljuk founded a kingdom here in 1074, which lasted till 1307, when it was conquered by the Turks. It had been subdued by the Crusaders in 1097 and 1190; see *Konieh*.

ICONOCLASTS (image-breakers). The controversy respecting images (which had been introduced into churches for popular instruction about 300) was begun about 726, and occasioned much disturbance and loss of life in the Eastern Empire. Leo Isauricus published two edicts for demolishing images in churches in that year, and enforced them with great rigour in 736. The defenders of images were again persecuted in 752 and 761, when Constantine forbade his subjects becoming monks. The worship of images was restored by Irene in 780. This schism was the occasion of the second council of Nice, 787. Theophilus banished all the painters and statuaries from the Eastern Empire, 832. The Iconoclasts were finally excommunicated at the 8th general council at Constantinople, 869-870. This controversy led to the separation of the Greek and Latin churches. Many images in churches were destroyed in Scotland and the Netherlands in the 16th century, and in England during the Reformation and the civil war, 1641-8.

IDAHO, a northern "territory" of the United States of North America, was organised in 1863; as a state, 1890. Capital Boisée. Conflicts among the miners at Cœur d'Alene; 4 non-union men killed, 11 July; union men victors, state of rebellion declared; several soldiers and unionists killed; martial law; railway bridges blown up to stop troops coming, 14, 15 July; insurrection suppressed by president Harrison's proclamation, 15-18 July, 1892. Great fire at Wardner; hundreds homeless, 21 April, 1893. Population in 1880, 32,610; 1890, 84,385; 1900, 161,772.

IDEALISM, see *Philosophy* No. of "Nature," 29 Sept. 1898.

IDENTISCOPE, an optical apparatus for combining two photograph portraits into one, sold in 1884. See *Composite Portraits*.

IDES (Latin *Idus*), were eight days in the Roman and church calendar, following the Nones. They were reckoned backward. In March, May, July, and October, the 8th Idus was on the 8th of the month, the 7th on the 9th, &c., the first, or Ide, being the 15th. In the other months the 8th Ide fell on the 6th, and the first on the 13th. On the Idus of March (the 15th) 44 B.C., Julius Cæsar was assassinated.

IDIOTS. About 1855 there were in England, exclusive of lunatics, pauper idiots, or idiots protected in national institutions, males, 3372; females, 3893; total, 7265; see *Lunacy*. The Idiot Asylum at Earlswood, near Reigate, Surrey, began in 1847; was chartered, 1862; additional buildings were founded by the prince of Wales, 28 June, 1869. The foundation of the Imbecile Asylum, Caterham, was laid by Dr. Brewer, M.P., 17 April, 1869. Idiots Act passed, 1886.

IDOLS. Images are mentioned in *Gen*. xxxi. 19, 30, 1739 B.C. The Jews frequently deserted the worship of God for idols till their captivity, 588 B.C. Edict of Theodosius for the suppression of idolatry, 392. Idolatry was revived in Britain by the Saxons about 473, but it gave way in Britain, after the coming of Augustin, about 597. See *Iconoclasts*, *Week*.

IDSTEDT (N. Germany). Here the insurgent army of Holstein and Schleswig, commanded by Willisen, was defeated by the Danes, 25 July, 1850.

IDUMÆA, the country of the Edomites, the descendants of Esau, the brother of Jacob: see *Gen*. xxxvi., *Josh*. xxiv. 4.

The Edomites prevent the Israelites from passing through their country . . . . B.C. 1453
They are subjugated by David 1040
They revolt against Ahaziah, 892; and are severely defeated by Amaziah 827
They join the Chaldæans against Judah, and are anathematised in *Psalm* cxxxvii. . about 570
John Hyrcanus, the Maccabee, subjugates and endeavours to incorporate them with the Jews . . 125
Herod the Great, son of Antipater an Idumæan, king of Judæa 40

IERNE, see *Ireland*.

IGLAU, see *Hussites*.

ILBERT BILL, see *India*, 1883.

ILDEFONSO, ST., Spain. Here was signed a treaty between France and Spain, 19 Aug. 1796; and another by which France regained Louisiana, 1 Oct. 1800.

ILIUM (Asia Minor), see *Troy*.

ILLINOIS, a western state of North America, was settled by the French in 1749; acquired by the British, 1763; made a territory, 1809; and admitted into the Union as a state, 3 Dec. 1818. Capital, Springfield. Population, 1880, 3,077,871; 1890, 3,826,351; 1900, 4,821,550. See *Railway Accidents*, 11 Aug. 1887.

By flooding of a coal mine 75 men drowned 16 Feb. 1883
Convent and school at Belleville burnt, about 27 young persons perish . . . 5-6 Jan. 1884
Cyclone; two churches and other buildings destroyed at Redbud . . . . . 17 Nov. 1892
Great fire at Kehlor's flour mills at Litchfield, estimated loss, 1,000,000 dollars . 21 March, 1893
Riotous strike at Lamont, in the drainage works; checked by police and military . . 9 June, ,,
Shawneetown destroyed by a flood, 100 deaths 3 April, 1898
Fatal strike, riot at Virden, troops sent, 12 Oct. ,,
Sudden death of ex-governor Altgeld at Joliet, at end of a violent anti-British speech, 12 March, 1902

ILLUMINATED BOOKS. The practice of adopting ornaments, drawings, and emblematical figures, and even portraits, to enrich MSS., is of great antiquity. Varro wrote the lives of 700 illustrious Romans, which he embellished with their portraits, about 70 B.C. *Plin. Nat. Hist.* Some beautiful missals and other works were printed in the 15th and 16th centuries *et seq.*, and fine imitations have lately appeared.

ILLUMINATI, heretics who sprang up in Spain, where they were called Alombrados, about 1575. After their suppression in Spain, they appeared in France. One of their leaders was friar Anthony Buchet. They professed to obtain grace and perfection by their sublime manner of prayer. A secret society bearing this name, opposed to tyranny and priestcraft, was founded at Ingoldstadt, Bavaria, by Dr. Adam Weishaupt, in May, 1776, and was suppressed in 1784-5.

ILLUSTRATED LONDON NEWS, the earliest publication of the kind, established by Mr. Herbert Ingram, M.P., first appeared on 14 May, 1842. Jubilee number published, 14 May, 1892; Coronation number issued, 7 June, 1902.

He purchased the *Illustrated Times*, first published 9 June, 1855, and incorporated it with the *Penny Illustrated Paper*, established by the Ingram family; first number . . . . . 12 Oct. 1861
Mr. Ingram and his eldest son were accidentally drowned in the *Lady Elgin* in Lake Michigan, (see *Wrecks*) 8 Sept. 1860
Illustrated Sporting and Dramatic News, begun . 1874
English Illustrated Magazine begun by Macmillan Oct. 1883
Illustrated Scientific News, monthly, begun . Oct. 1902

ILLYRIA (now Dalmatia, Croatia, and Bosnia), after several wars (from 230 B.C.) was made a Roman province, 167 B.C. In 1809 Napoleon I. gave the name of Illyrian provinces to Carniola, Dalmatia, and other provinces, then part of the French empire, now Carinthia, Carniola, &c.

ILMENIUM, a metal of the tantalum group, discovered by R. Herrmann, about 1847, but rejected by chemists; its claims were reasserted by him in 1867.

IMAGE WORSHIP, see *Iconoclasts*.

"IMITATION OF JESUS CHRIST" (De Imitatione Christi). The author of this devotional work is unknown. It has been attributed to an abbot Gersen (whose very existence is doubtful); to Jean Gerson, the celebrated chancellor of Paris, who died in 1429; and to Thomas à Kempis, said to have been merely a compiler and editor, who died 25 July, 1471.

IMMACULATE CONCEPTION, see *Conception*.

IMMIGRATION into the United Kingdom first estimated in the Emigration Report for 1875. In 1870, 49,157; in 1874, 118,129; in 1877, 81,848; 1879, 53,973; 1881, 77,105; 1883, 100,503; 1884, 123,466; 1885, 113,549; 1886, 108,879; 1887, 119,013 (33,538 foreigners); 1888, 128,879; 1889, 147,398; 1890, 155,910; 1891, 151,369; 1892, 143,747; 1893, 141,054; 1894, 185,799; 1895, 175,674; 1896, 159,913; 1897, 155,114; 1898, 139,346; 1899, 162,111; 1900, 175,747; 1901, 165,018; 1902, 170,874. See also *Emigration*.

IMMORTALS (Greek, *athanatoi*), the flower of the Persian army, limited to 10,000 in number, and recruited from the nobility alone, about 500 B.C. The name was also given to the body-guard of the emperors at Constantinople in the 4th and 5th centuries.

IMPEACHMENT. The first impeachment by the commons house of parliament, and the first of a lord chancellor, Michael de la Pole, earl of Suffolk, was in 1386. By statute 12 & 13 Will. & Mary, 1700, it was enacted that no pardon under the great seal shall be pleaded to an impeachment by the commons in parliament.

Impeachment of Warren Hastings, 13 Feb. 1788, to 25 April, 1795; acquittal.
Impeachment of lord Melville, 9 April; acquittal, 12 June, 1806.
Inquiry into the charges of colonel Wardle against the duke of York, 27 Jan. to 20 March, 1809; acquittal.
Trial of Caroline, queen of George IV., by bill of pains and penalties, before the house of lords, commenced 16 Aug.; Mr. Brougham entered on her majesty's defence, 3 Oct.; and the last debate on the bill took place 10 Nov. 1820; see *Queen Caroline*.
Impeachment of the president; see *United States*, 1868.

IMPERIAL CHAMBER, see *Aulic Council*.

IMPERIAL DEFENCE: an act for defraying the expenses of carrying into effect an agreement for naval defence with the Australasian colonies, and providing for the defence of certain ports and coaling stations, and for making further provision for imperial defence, passed 13 Aug. 1888. Changes made by the Finance Act of July, 1894. See *Colonies*.

IMPERIAL FEDERATION of Great Britain and her colonies (for defence, &c.), the principle was affirmed, and a provisional committee of an association constituted at a great meeting of eminent politicians of all parties, and representatives of the colonies, held at Westminster Palace hotel, Mr. W. E. Forster, M.P. in the chair, 29 July; a league constituted 18 Nov. 1884. The electric telegraph has now brought the colonies into closer communication than Exeter and Newcastle were formerly. In 1885 many of the colonies offered military assistance in the Soudan, and gave assistance, 1899–1902, during the war in S. Africa.

Conference at the Colonial and Indian Exhibition, London; earl Rosebery, president, 1 July, 1886; rt. hon. Edward Stanhope, Sept. 1892. The report of sir Rawson Rawson discloses great difficulties through opposing tariffs, March, 1888.
Fourth annual meeting of the League held in London 23 May, 1889; meeting at the Mansion House 15 Nov. 1889; meeting at Edinburgh 12 Feb.; at People's Palace, E. London, duke of Cambridge in the chair, 28 April, 1890; at Westminster, 18 June, 1891.
Funds much wanted; reported July, 1893; the league, having become defunct, was succeeded by the British empire league (*which see*), and by the Imperial federation (defence) committee, about 1893.
Queen's proclamation of the Commonwealth of Australia as from 1 Jan. 1901; issued . 18 Sept. 1900
Commonwealth inaugurated at Sydney by lord Hopetoun, who reads a message from the queen, 1 Jan. 1901
First parliament of the Commonwealth opened by the duke of Cornwall and York at Melbourne, 9 May, „
See *Australia*.
Conferences held between colonial premiers and Mr. Chamberlain at colonial office, various points agreed upon for the strengthening and defence of the empire . . . . . June, July, Aug. 1902

IMPERIAL GUARD of France, was created by Napoleon from the guard of the convention, the directory, and the consulate, when he became emperor in 1804. It consisted at first of 9775 men, but was afterwards enlarged. It was subdivided in 1809 into the old and young guard. In Jan. 1814, it numbered 102,706. It was dissolved by Louis XVIII. in 1815; revived by Napoleon III. in 1854. It surrendered with Metz to the Germans 27 Oct. 1870; and was abolished by government soon after. It took part in the Crimean war in 1855.

IMPERIAL INSTITUTE OF THE COLONIES AND INDIA, to represent arts, manufactures, and commerce: established as a memorial of the queen's jubilee, proposed by the prince of Wales in a letter to the lord mayor of London, 13 Sept. 1886.

Preliminary meeting at the Mansion House, 27 Sept. prince of Wales's committee meet 10 Nov. 1886. sir Frederick Abel (died 6 Sept. 1902), organizing secretary . . . . Nov. 1886
Issue of report recommending the constitution of the Institute at South Kensington, consisting of two sections; I. to illustrate the commercial and natural resources of the Colonies and India; II. the condition of the natural products and manufactures of the United Kingdom; with suitable accompaniments . . . . . 23–24 Dec. „
Meetings at St. James's Palace and Mansion House 12 Jan. 1887
Sir F. Abel expounded the objects of the Institute at the Royal Institution with the approbation of the prince of Wales, who was in the chair 22 April, „
25,000*l.* awarded to the Institute out of the surplus of the Colonial Exhibition of 1886, 30 April, „
Architect, Mr. T. E. Colcutt; contractors, John Mowlem and Co.
Munificent donations from Indian princes; the maharajah of Jodhpore gave 10,000*l.* June, 1887; maharajah Holkar of Indore, 100,000 rupees, Feb. 1889; the maharajah of Jeypore, 20,000*l.* Nov. 1890; the Indian government grant 1,000*l.* annually for the museum . . beginning Nov. 1891
Foundation stone laid by the queen (ode by Mr. Lewis Morris, music by sir Arthur Sullivan, sung; addresses) . . . . . . 4 July, 1887
20,000*l.* received from Canada . . . 24 Aug. „
Amount received or definitely promised, 400,000*l.* Oct. „

Receipt of 310,000*l.* exclusive of the Indian contribution, reported . . . . . 2 July, 1888
See *Oriental studies*, 1890.

The premiers of the Australasian colonies, announce their hearty co-operation in the work of the Institute, June, 1890; the constitution of the Imperial Institute, published in the *London Gazette*, 28 April, 1891; the prince of Wales nominated first president; governing body 18 governors, 12 nominated by the queen, 6 by the president, and 8 ex-officio officers, abp. of Canterbury, lord chancellor, and others. First meeting of the permanent governing body, Lord Herschell (died 1 March, 1899) elected chairman, and the executive council constituted . . . . 23 July, 1891

The Institute was partly opened to the Fellows and public . . . . 22 June, 1892

Imperial institute year-book published . summer, ,,

First annual meeting; the prince of Wales in the chair; above 3,500 members, reported . 26 Nov. ,,

A peal of 10 bells, the "Alexandra," set up in the "Queen's" tower; ordered by Elizabeth Millar, an aged Australian lady, to be made by Messrs. John Taylor & Co., of Loughborough, as a gift to the prince of Wales, reported 19 Oct. 1892; first rung . . . . 10 May, 1893

London jubilee fund (5,700*l.*) transferred to the institute . . . . May, ,,

The institute was inaugurated by the queen.

After an address to the queen from the executive body, read by the prince of Wales, describing the objects of the institute, the queen in her reply declared the institute to be now open, and concluded with an earnest prayer "that it may never cease to flourish as a lasting emblem of the unity and loyalty of her empire." The ceremony was closed by a benediction from the archbishop of Canterbury.

The royal procession proceeded from Buckingham palace to the institute, both sides of the route being lined by military and a vast concourse of people of all ranks. Among the military engaged during the day were contingents from Canada, Australia and India.

The beautiful key used by the queen in opening the institute was composed of gold and other metals brought from the colonies, and was made by Messrs. Chubb . . . 10 May, ,,

Grand reception by the prince of Wales, of the royal family, the ministry, eminent officials, foreign princes, and others; about 20,000 persons, 17 May, ,,

The institute opened to the public, under regulations . . . . 18 May *et seq.* ,,

Lectures on the relations between the United Kingdom and her colonies; opening address by Mr. W. H. Lecky . . . . . . 20 Nov. ,,

Donation of 1,000*l.* from the Goldsmiths company, April, 1894

Imperial Institute Journal; monthly; No. 1 . Jan. 1895

International railway congress; opened by the prince of Wales . . . . . . 26 June, ,,

International geographical congress; opened by the duke of York . . . . 26 July, ,,

Scientific department completed, reported . Oct. 1896

Yachting and fisheries exhibition opened by the prince and princess of Wales . . . 17 May, 1897

"Dominion-day" celebrated at the institute, an "at home" by sir Donald Smith . . 1 July ,,

Exhibition of the City and Guilds institute (by candidates at the examinations) opened by the duke of Devonshire . . . . . 9 June, 1899

Ecclesiastical art exhibition opened . . 7 Oct. ,,

English education exhibition opened by the prince of Wales (about 180 delegates) . . 5 Jan. 1900

Exhibition of gifts, &c., to the prince and princess of Wales on their colonial tour, opened, 15 May, 1902

Lord Northbrook receives princes . . 24 June, ,,

Imperial institute (placed under the Board of Trade) act, royal assent . . . 22 July, ,,

Prof. Wyndham Dunston appointed director, Jan. 1903

Prince of Wales visits Exhibition of Irish minerals and building stones . . . . . 27 Feb. ,,

IMPERIAL PARLIAMENT, see *Commons*, *Lords*, *Parliament*, and *Reform*.

IMPERIAL SERVICE ORDER, THE, instituted by the king 26 June, 1902, as a decoration for members of the Imperial Civil Service, and conferred for long and meritorious service. The order consists of the sovereign, the prince of Wales, and companions appointed by the sovereign. It is limited to members of the administrative or clerical branches of the service, the number of which must not exceed 425, the home civil service 250, the civil services of the colonies and protectorates 175. Appointments are made on the recommendation of the secretary of state or for "eminently meritorious service."

IMPERIAL WAR FUND, THE, was founded in 1882.

IMPERIALISM. The term introduced by lord Beaconsfield in 1878, to signify that which related to the welfare of the British empire as a whole, in contradistinction to that of Great Britain itself or any other separate part of the empire.

IMPI, or Imbizo, see *Mashonaland*.

IMPORTS OF MERCHANDISE. The vast progressive increase of our commercial intercourse with other countries is shown by our imports and exports (*which see*):—

VALUE OF IMPORTS INTO GREAT BRITAIN, FROM ALL PARTS OF THE WORLD.

Year	Value	Year	Value
In 1710	£4,753,777	In 1876	£375,154,703
1750	7,289,582	1877	394,419,682
1775	14,815,855	1878	368,770,742
1800	30,570,605	1879	362,991,875
1810	41,136,135	1880	411,229,565
1820	36,514,564	1881	397,022,489
1830	46,245,241	1882	413,019,608
1840	62,004,000	1883	426,891,579
1845	85,281,958	1884	390,018,569
1850	95,252,084	1885	370,967,955
1851	103,579,582	1886	349,863,472
1856	172,544,154	1887	362,227,564
1857	187,844,441	1888	387,635,743
1859	179,182,355	1889	427,637,595
1861	217,485,024	1890	420,691,997
1864	274,952,172	1891	435,441,264
1865	271,072,285	1892	423,793,882
1866	295,290,274	1893	404,688,178
1867	275,183,137	1894	408,344,810
1868	294,693,608	1895	416,689,658
1869	295,460,214	1896	441,808,904
1870	303,257,493	1897	451,238,683
1871	331,015,480	1901	521,990,198
1875	373,939,577	1902	797,000,000

	From foreign countries.		Exports to.
1871	1875	1877	1877
£258,071,062	£289,515,606	£304,865,684	£176,593,870
From British possessions.			
£72,944,418	84,423,971	89,553,998	75,752,150

IMPOSTORS. The following are among the most extraordinary:—

Aldebert, a Gaul, in 743, pretended he had a letter from the Redeemer, which fell from heaven at Jerusalem; he seduced multitudes to follow him into woods and forests, and to live in imitation of John the Baptist. He was condemned by a council at Rome in 745.

Gonzalvo Martin, a Spaniard, pretended to be the angel Michael in 1359: he was burnt by the inquisition in Spain in 1360.

George David, son of a waterman at Ghent, styled himself the son of God, sent into the world to adopt children worthy of heaven: he denied the resurrection, preached in favour of a community of women, and taught that the body only could be defiled by sin; he had many followers; died at Basle, 1556, promising to rise again in three years.

Otrefief, a monk, pretended to be Demetrius the son of Ivan, czar of Muscovy, whom the usurper Boris had put to death; he maintained that another child had been substituted in his place: he was supported by Poland; his success led the Russians to invite him to the throne, and deliver into his hands, Feodor, the reigning czar, and all his family: his imposition discovered he was assassinated in his palace, 1606.

Sabbata Levi, a Jew of Smyrna, amused the Jews and Turks a long time at Constantinople and other places, by personating our Saviour, 1666.

Joseph Smith, see *Mormonites*.

Apparition of our Lady of Salette; the imposture exposed and several persons prosecuted, April, 1846. The superstition revived and flourishing, Aug. 1872.

Pilgrimage of about 20,000 persons to Lourdes, in the Pyrenees, on account of alleged miracles (the virgin was said to have appeared to two girls, 11 Feb. 1858), 6 Oct. 1872; see *France*.

Insurrection of the Mahdi, see *Soudan* 1881 *et seq.*

An adventurer, who named himself "Comte Blanco," and "prince Louis Marie César of Bourbon, grandson of Ferdinand VII. of Spain," was recognised at Paris in 1869 by queen Isabella and others. Detected by a photographer as his son-in-law. Supported by a rich English widow. Kept a small court at Jurangon near Pau, as a king. Deposed and expelled by the police, he went to Holland and England, and died in London.

John Smith Piggott, leader of the Agapemone (*which see*), claimed to be the Messiah; riotous scenes at Clapton . . . . . . Sept. 1902

Dr. Dowie, head of the Zionists (*which see*), professes to be the "Second Elijah," see *Zion Restoration Host*, conducts campaign in New York, Oct. 1903

[See *Abstinence* and *Sugar*.]

IN BRITISH HISTORY.

A man pretending to be the Messiah, and a woman assuming to be the Virgin Mary, were burnt, 1222.

Jack Cade assumed the name of Mortimer; see *Cade*, 1450.

In 1487, Lambert Simnel, tutored by Richard Simon, a priest, supported by the duke of Burgundy, personated the earl of Warwick. Simnel's army was defeated by Henry VII., and he was made a scullion in the king's kitchen.

For Warbeck's imposture in 1492, see *Warbeck*.

Elizabeth Barton, styled the Holy Maid of Kent, spirited up to hinder the Reformation by pretending to inspirations from heaven, foretelling that the king would have an early and violent death if he divorced Catherine of Spain and married Anne Boleyn. She and her confederates were executed at Tyburn, 21 April, 1534.

In 1553 (first year of Mary's reign, after her marriage with Philip of Spain), Elizabeth Croft, a girl 18 years of age, was secreted in a wall, and with a whistle made for the purpose, uttered many seditious speeches against the queen and the prince, and also against the mass and confession, for which she did penance.

William Hacket, a fanatic, personated our Saviour, and was executed for blasphemy, 1591.

Valentine Greatrix, an Irish impostor, who pretended to cure all diseases by stroking the patient: his imposture deceived the credulous, and occasioned very warm disputes in Ireland and England about 1666. Boyle and Flamsteed believed in him.

Dr. Titus Oates, see *Oates*.

Robert Young, a prisoner in Newgate, forged the hands of the earls of Marlborough, Salisbury, and other nobility, to a pretended association for restoring king James: the lords were imprisoned, but the imposture being detected, Young was fined 1000*l.*, and put in the pillory, 1692. He was afterwards hanged for coining.

Three French refugees pretend to be prophets, and raise tumults; convicted as impostors, Nov. 1707.

Mary Tofts of Godalming, by pretending she bred rabbits within her, so imposed upon many persons (among others, Mr. St. Andre, surgeon to the king), that they espoused her cause, 1726.

The Cock-lane ghost impostures by William Parsons, his wife, and daughter, 1762; see *Cock-lane Ghost*.

Johanna Southcote, who proclaimed her conception of the Messiah, and had a multitude of followers; she died 27 Dec. 1814.

W. Thom, see *Thomites*.

Louis XVII., see *France*, list of sovereigns.

IMPRESSIONISTES, a name given to artists who aim at producing rapid unstudied effects independent of the canons of art, such as Manet, Duez, and others in France. In England Mr. Whistler exhibited such pictures in 1877, including moonlight scenes, &c., painted in two days, showing great sense of colour. For Mr. Ruskin's criticisms see *Trials*, 1878. The Impressionistes are also characterized as illustrators of their own times by pure art; MM. Manet, Durand, Ruel, Degas, and Renoir, are French examples; they exhibited in London in June, 1882 and since, especially in April, 1889.

IMPRESSMENT OF SEAMEN, affirmed by sir M. Foster to be of ancient practice. The stat. 2 Rich. II. speaks of impressment as a matter well known, 1378. The first commission for it was issued 29 Edw. III. 1355. Pressing, either for the sea or land service, declared to be illegal by the parliament, Dec. 1641, but practised till present times. Impressment was not resorted to in the Russian war, 1854-5.

IMPRISONMENT FOR DEBT, see *Arrests*, *Debtors*, and *Ferrars' Arrest*.

IMPROPRIATION (applying ecclesiastical property to lay purposes). On the suppression of abbeys in 1539, their incomes from the great tithes were distributed among his courtiers by Henry VIII.; and their successors constitute 7597 lay impropriators.

INCAS, see *Peru*.

INCENDIARIES. See *Arson*.

INCEST. Marriage with very near relations, almost universally forbidden, took place in Egypt, Persia, and Greece. For recent cases see *Portugal*, 1760, 1777, and 1826; *Italy*, 1888. The table of kindred in the book of common prayer was set forth in 1563. For the Hebrew law see Leviticus, chap. xviii. 1490 B.C.

INCH. It was defined in 1824 by act of parliament, that 39·13929 inches is the length of a seconds pendulum in the latitude of London, vibrating in vacuo at the sea level, at the temperature of 62° Fahrenheit; see *Candle*, and *Standard*.

INCHCAPE BELL, see *Bell Rock*.

INCLOSURE ACT, to facilitate the inclosure and improvement of commons, appointing commissioners, etc., 8 & 9 Vict. c. 118, passed 8 Aug. 1845; another act passed in 1876; see *Commons*.

INCOME TAX. In 1512, parliament granted a subsidy of two-fifteenths from the commons, and two-tenths from the clergy, to enable the king to enter on a war with France. In Dec. 1798, Mr. Pitt proposed and carried, amid great opposition, resolutions for increased taxes "as an aid for the prosecution of the war" with France.

Graduated duties on income imposed, beginning with 60*l.* per annum, by the act passed 9 Jan. 1799.

The "property tax" passed which levied a rate of 5 per cent. on all incomes above 150*l.* and lower rates on smaller incomes, 11 Aug. 1803.

Increased to 6¼ per cent. 1805; 10 per cent., embracing the dividends at the bank, 1806.

In 1800 the tax produced 5,716,572*l.*; in 1804, 4,650,000*l.*; in 1806, 11,500,000*l.*; in 1808, 16,548,985*l.*; in 1815, 14,978,557*l*; 1900, 18,750,000.

The tax produced from lands, houses, rentages, &c., 8,657,937*l.*; from funded and stock properties, 2,885,505*l.*; the profits and gains of trade, 3,831,088*l.*; and salaries and pensions, 1,174,456*l.* Repealed 18 March, 1816, on motion of H. Brougham.

Sir Robert Peel's bill imposing a tax at a rate of 7*d.* in the pound (2*l.* 18*s.* 4*d. per cent.*) on annual incomes of 150*l.* and upwards (for three years) passed 22 June, 1842.

It produced about 5,350,000*l.* a-year; and led to repeal of about 12,000,000*l.* indirect taxes.

Renewed for three years, 1845; and 1848.

Large meetings assembled in Trafalgar-square, London (for the ostensible purpose of opposing the income tax); rioting ensued, which was soon quelled, 6, 7 March, 1848.

Tax continued for one year in 1851 and 1852.

The tax of 7*d.* limited to seven years (till 1860); to be gradually reduced in amount; but all incomes from 100*l.* to 150*l.* made liable to 5*d.* in the pound for all that period: the tax also extended to Ireland, June, 1853.

Crimean war: rates doubled, 14*d.*, 1854.

2*d.* (making 16*d.*) added to the tax on incomes above 150*l.*, and 1½*d* on those between 100*l.* and 150*l.*; the former being 1*s.* 4*d.*, the latter 11½*d.* in the pound, 1855.

The former assessment reduced to 7*d.*, the latter to 5*d.*, 1857. Both became 5*d.*, 1858.

The former raised to 9*d.*, the latter to 6½*d.*; and the tax on incomes, derived from lands, tenements, &c., raised from 3½*d.* to 5¼*d.* for England, and from 2½*d.* to 4*d.* for Scotland and Ireland, July, 1859.

The assessment on incomes raised—on those above 100*l.* to 7*d.*; on those above 150*l.* to 10*d.*

[The object of the increase was to provide for a deficiency occasioned by extra expenditure for defending the country, April, 1860.]

A committee to inquire into the working of the income tax appointed, 14 Feb. 1861.

Reduction of the last assessment from 7*d.* to 6*d.*, and from 10*d.* to 9*d.* for three-quarters of the financial year 1861-62.

The rates of 6*d.* and 9*d.* to continue, April, 1862.

The rate of 7*d.* on all chargeable incomes; 3½*d.* on farms, &c., in England; and 2½*d.* in Scotland and Ireland. Incomes under 100*l.* a-year exempted; those above 100*l.* and under 200*l.* allowed an abatement on 60*l.*, 8 June, 1863.

The rate of 6*d.* on chargeable incomes, with some exemptions and abatement, 13 May, 1864.

The rate of 4*d.* on chargeable incomes, with same exemptions and abatement, May, 1865–7.

Raised to 5*d.* (for year ending 1 April, 1868), to provide for Abyssinian war, Nov. 1867.

Raised to 6*d.* (for 1868–9), May, 1868.

Reduced to 5*d.* in the pound, April, 1869; to 4*d.*, April, 1870. Raised to 6*d.* on account of re-organisation of army, abolishing purchase, 1871. Reduced to 4*d.*, April, 1872.

Renewed agitation against the tax; conference at Birmingham, 22 May; at the Mansion-house, London, proposed formation of a National Anti-Income Tax League, 13 Dec. 1872.

Reduced to 3*d.* from 6 April, 1873; to 2*d.*, 23 April, 1874.

Mr. C. Lewis's motion for reducing or abolishing the tax defeated (139–38), 3 July, 1874.

Raised to 3*d.*; incomes under 150*l.* to be exempt; 120*l.* of incomes under 400*l.* exempt, April, 1876.

Raised to 5*d.* (through preparations for war), April, 1878.

Raised to 6*d.* by Mr. Gladstone, June; act passed, 12 Aug. 1880.

Reduced to 5*d.* by Mr. Gladstone; budget 4 April, 1881.

Raised to 6½*d.* for the year (in consequence of the Egyptian expedition), Aug. 1882; reduced to 5*d.* April, 1883; raised to 6*d.* 1 Dec. 1884; to 8*d.* 30 April, 1885; continued, April, 1886; reduced to 7*d.* April, 1887; land, &c., England 3½*d.*; Scotland and Ireland, 2½*d.* (act 23 May, 1887); reduced to 6*d.* 16 May, 1888; continued April, 1889–92; raised to 7*d.*, 12 May, 1893; to 8*d.*, 31 July, 1894; to 1*s.* 9 April, 1900; to 14*d.* 26 July, 1901; to 15*d.* 4 July, 1902; reduced to 11*d.* 23 April, 1903.

Mr. Bartley's motion for a committee to enquire into the working and incidence of the income-tax negatived by the commons (161–106), 24 Feb. 1891.

The house of lords decides on appeal that religious and charitable societies are exempt from income-tax 20 July, 1891.

In 1898, incomes up to 160*l.* exempt; 160*l.* to 400*l.*, 160*l.* abatement; 400*l.* to 500*l.*, 150*l.* abatement; 500*l.* to 600*l.*, 120*l.* abatement; 600*l.* to 700*l.*, 70*l.* abatement; above 700*l.*, no abatement.

PRODUCE OF THE INCOME TAX.

Year		£	Year		£
1842	. . .	£571,055	1877	(31 March)	£5,284,091
1844	. . .	5,191,597	1878	,,	5,820,000
1846	. . .	5,395,391	1879	,,	8,710,000
1852	. . .	5,509,637	1880	,,	9,230,000
1855	(31 March)	10,642,621	1881	,,	10,650,000
1856	,,	15,070,958	1882	,,	9,945,000
1857	,,	16,089,933	1883	,,	11,900,000
1858	,,	11,586,115	1884	,,	10,718,000
1859	,,	6,683,587	1885	,,	12,000,000
1860	,,	9,596,106	1886	,,	15,160,000
1861	,,	10,923,186	1887	,,	15,900,000
1862	,,	10,365,000	1888	,,	14,440,000
1863	,,	10,567,000	1889	,,	12,700,000
1864	,,	9,084,000	1890	,,	12,770,000
1865	,,	7,958,000	1891	,,	13,250,000
1866	,,	6,390,000	1892	,,	13,431,000
1867	,,	5,700,000	1893	,,	13,417,000
1868	,,	6,177,000	1894	,,	15,600,000
1869	,,	8,618,000	1895	,,	15,600,000
1870	,,	10,044,000	1896	,,	16,100,000
1871	,,	6,350,000	1897	,,	16,650,000
1872	,,	9,084,000	1898-9	,,	17,250,000
1873	,,	7,403,736	1899	,,	18,000,000
1874	,,	5,641,791	1900	,,	18,750,000
1875	,,	4,315,132	1901	,,	26,920,000
1876	,,	4,109,000	1902	,,	34,800,000

(Estimated that 1*d.* in the pound yields 772,000*l.* a-year, 1842; 1,727,000*l.* 1876; 1,900,000*l.*, 1878; 1,980,000, 1885; 1899–1900, 2,364,000.)

TOTAL ANNUAL VALUE OF PROPERTY AND PROFITS ASSESSED, UNITED KINGDOM.

1868	£430,368,976
1873	513,807,284
1878	578,294,971
1882	601,450,977
1887	629,397,962
1888	636,154,693
1889	645,158,689
1890	669,358,613
1891	698,407,549
1892	710,752,684
1893	712,181,099
1896	709,651,556
1898	729,328,295
1899	758,571,709
1900	788,023,603

ESTIMATED ANNUAL INCOME.

	England and Wales.		Scotland.		Ireland.	
	1814	1893	1814	1893	1854	1891
Real property, land, &c.	53,495,000	169,107,193	6,643,000	19,991,006	11,892,000	13,612,019
Professions, trades, &c.	34,288,000	313,407,425	2,771,000	35,435,412	4,780,000	11,461,198
	87,783,000	482,514,618	9,414,000	55,426,418	16,672,000	25,073,217

INCORPORATED, see *Authors, Law.*

INCUMBENTS' RESIGNATION ACT, with provision for pensions, passed 13 July, 1871, amended 1887.

INCUMBERED ESTATES, see *Encumbered Estates.*

INCURABLES. The royal hospital for incurables, founded by Dr. Andrew Reed, at Carshalton in Surrey, in 1850, has since been removed to Putney.

British Home for Incurables, Clapham-rise, established 1861
National Hospital for Incurables, Oxford . . . 1874
Home for Incurable Children, Maida-vale . . 1875

INDEMNITY BILL, by which the minister of the crown or the government is relieved from the responsibility of measures adopted in extreme and urgent cases, without the previous sanction of parliament. One was passed 19 April, 1801; another to indemnify ministers against their acts during the suspension of the *Habeas Corpus* act, was carried in the commons (principal divisions, 190 to 64); and in the lords (93 to 27), 10 March, 1818. In 1848 and 1857, bills of indemnity were passed for the suspension of the Bank Charter act by the ministry; see *Oblivion.* An *indemnity bill* is passed at the end of every session of parliament for persons who transgress through ignorance of the law. The practice began in 1715.

INDEPENDENCE, DECLARATION OF, by United States of North America, 4 July, 1776, is annually celebrated on *Independence Day.*

"**INDEPENDENT THEATRE**," a name assumed by a society conducted by Mr. J. T. Grein at the Royalty Theatre, providing entertainments resembling those of the *Théâtre-Libre* of M. Antoine, to include the plays of Ibsen and Tolstoi which could not be licensed in this country. As the theatre is supported by subscription, and no money taken at the doors, it is considered independent of the lord chamberlain's censorship in regard to the plays performed. Ibsen's "Romersholm" was performed 23 Feb., and his "Ghosts" 13 March, 1891. Other performances were given at the private theatre in the club-house erected on the site of Evans' hotel, Covent Garden, 22 May, 1891 *et seq.* An English version of Zola's "Thérèse Raquin" given at the Royalty, 9 Oct. 1891. Other pieces licensed by the lord chamberlain, 4 March, 1892. The censorship accepted, July, 1892.

The "Duchess of Malfi," at the Opera Comique 21 Oct. 1892
Mr. Bernard Shaw's "Widower's Houses" at the Royalty . . . . 9 Dec. "
Ibsen's strange new play, "The Master Builder," performed at the Trafalgar-square theatre 20 Feb. 1893
Mr. George Moore's "Strike at Arlingford" performed at the Opera Comique . . . 21 Feb. "
Other pieces performed at different theatres, 1893–1903

INDEPENDENTS or **CONGREGATIONALISTS**, hold that each church or congregation is independent of all others in religious matters; that there is no absolute occasion for synods or councils, whose resolutions may be taken for advice, but not as decisions to be peremptorily obeyed; and that one church may advise or reprove another, but has no authority to excommunicate. Robert Brown preached these doctrines about 1585, but, after 32 imprisonments, he eventually conformed to the established church. A church was formed in London in 1593, when there were 20,000 independents They were driven by persecution to Holland, where they formed several churches; that at Leyden was under Mr. Robinson, often regarded as the author of Independency. In 1616 Henry Jacobs returned to England and founded a meeting-house. Cromwell, himself an independent, obtained them toleration, in opposition to the Presbyterians. The independents published an epitome of their faith, drawn up at a conference at the Savoy, in 1658; and the congregational union of England and Wales formed in 1831, published their "declaration of faith, order, and discipline," in 1833. In 1851 they had 3244 chapels for 1,067,760 persons in England and Wales; in 1902 United Kingdom, 4,873 churches; 3,121 ministers; 1,743,583 sittings, 431,517 church members, 1902. Annual meetings of the union are held; see *Worship.* The first independents in Scotland were the Glasites (*which see*). The first independent church in America was founded by the followers of John Robinson, at Plymouth, New England, in 1620.

Congregational Fund Board to assist poor ministers, established 1695
Congregational Board of Education, Homerton . 1843
Nonconformist Bicentenary fund begun . . 1862
The Congregationalist Memorial-hall, Farringdon-street, London, erected in memory of the ministers ejected in 1662, as a home for religious societies, was subscribed for and opened 19 Jan. 1875
An important congregationalist synod, held in London . . . . early in Oct. "
Rev. John Waddington's "Congregational History, 1200–1854," published 1869–78
Samuel Morley, a wealthy London merchant, a liberal supporter of the independent churches, and general philanthropist, died . . 5 Sept. 1886
James Spicer, a man of similar character, died 23 Jan. 1888
The first International Council of Congregationalists held at Memorial-hall, London, rev. R. W. Dale, of Birmingham, presiding . 13–24 July, 1891
Rev. John Stoughton, D.D., eminent scholar, active minister, born 18 Nov. 1807; died 24 Oct. 1897
Rev. Chas. A. Berry, D.D., eminent minister, born 1852, died suddenly in the pulpit, 31 Jan. 1899; principal Cave, eminent scholar and minister, d., aged 53, 19 Dec. 1900; rev. dr. Newman Hall, eminent Nonconformist, d., aged 85, 18 Feb. 1902; dr. Joseph Parker, d., aged 72 . 28 Nov. 1902
Report of general committee on Congregational Union appointed May, 1902, "to prepare a scheme which may serve to unite Congregational Churches more closely for common purposes," published . . . . April, 1903

INDEXES OF PROHIBITED BOOKS. The Index by which the reading of the Scriptures was forbidden (with certain exceptions) to the laity, was confirmed by a bull of pope Clement VIII. in 1595.

The council of Nice (325) forbade magical books.
Pope Paul IV., 1555, began the "Index" published by Pius IV., 1559. The Talmud and heretical books were especially prohibited, causing much dissatisfaction. The Inquisition was engaged in the work, which was organized by the Council of Trent. The Congregation of the Index was instituted and rules laid down.
The Indexes are—1. *Prohibitorius*, of books absolutely forbidden to be read; 2. *Expurgatorius*, of books not to be licensed till purged from error.
Many of the works of the great authors of France, Spain, Germany, and England, are thus prohibited. On 25 June, 1864, Hugo's "Les Misérables" and other books were added to the number, and many others since.

INDEX SOCIETY, established by the librarians of various London scientific and literary institutions and societies, and literary men, to form a library of indexes, and to make indexes to rare serial works, important books, &c. 17 Dec. 1877.

INDIA or **HINDOSTAN**. The Hindoo histories ascribe their origin to a period ages before the ordinary chronologies. The Tyrians, Egyptians, and Romans carried on commerce with India.

The expansion, consolidation, and conciliation of India were greatly effected during the reign of queen Victoria, 1837 *et seq.* 117 native states 1888.* "The Golden Book of India," by sir Roper Lethbridge, first published Feb. 1893; sir Wm. Hunter's "History of British India," vol. I., published, March, 1899.

Religions: the pre-historic Hindu or Vedic system was reformed and superseded by Buddhism about B.C. 500. The reformed and modified Vedic system, since termed Brahmanism, was restored about A.D. 500, and prevailed till the introduction of Mahometanism, early in the 11th century; see *Population* in foot-note, below.

Provinces, Bengal, Bombay, Madras, Punjaub, N.W. and Central provinces, Assam, and Burmah.

Northern India is said to have been invaded and conquered by an Arian race from central Asia, between B.C. 1500 and 1000.

Invasion of Alexander the great; king Porus is defeated, submits and retains his kingdom . . . 327

Irruptions of the Mahometans, under Mahmud Ghuzni, 1001–24. He captured Somnath . . A.D. 1024

Extinction of the house of Ghuzni, 1186; rule of the slave-kings of Delhi, 1206–1288; of the Kilghis and house of Toghlak, 1288–1412; of the Syuds, 1412–50; of the house of Lodi 1450–1526

Pathan, or Afghan empire, founded 1205

Mogul invasion under Genghis Khan, 1219; he died, 1227

The Mogul Tartars, under the conduct of Timour, or Tamerlane, invade Hindostan, and take Delhi; defeat the Indian army, 1397; conquer Hindostan, and butcher 100,000 of its people . . . 1398–9

The Cape route to India discovered by Vasco da Gama; he left Lisbon, 8 July, 1497, arrived at Calicut, 20 May, 1498, and returned to Lisbon, Aug. or Sept. 1499

The first European settlement (Portuguese) established by him at Cochin (S. Coast) 1502

Albuquerque governor-general, 1508; dies at Goa, 1514

Conquest of India completed by the sultan Baber, founder of the Mogul empire 1519–26

Reign of his son Humayun 1531–56

Reign of Akbar, greatest sovereign of Hindostan 1556–1605

The Portuguese introduce tobacco 1600

The Dutch first visit India, 1601; establish a United East India Company 1602

Tranquebar granted to the Danes 1619

Reign of Jehanghir 1605–27

Reign of Shah Jehan; golden age of the Moguls, 1627–58

Aurungzebe dethrones his father and murders his brothers, 1658; reigns 1658–1707

French East India Company established . . . 1664

Rise of the Mahratta power under Sevajee, 1659; he assumes royalty, 1674; dies 1680

Aurungzebe conquers Golconda, &c. 1687

His prosperity wanes, 1702; dies . . . 22 Feb. 1707

Bahadoor Shah succeeds, 1707; dies 1712

Jehander Shah, 1713; dethroned and killed . . 1718

Accession of Mahomed Shah 1719

Independence of the Nizam of the Deccan . . 1723

Rise of the Mahratta families, Holkar and Scindiah 1730

Invasion of the Persian Nadir Shah or Kouli Khan: at Delhi he orders a general massacre, and 150,000 persons perish; carries away treasure amounting to 125,000,000*l.* sterling 1739

Mahomed Shah dies 1748

[The Mogul empire now became merely nominal, independent sovereignties being formed by petty princes. In 1761, Shah Alum II. attacking the English was defeated at Patna, 15 Jan. In 1764, after the battle of Buxar, he was thrown upon the protection of the English, who established him at Allahabad. After the victory at Delhi in 1803, gen. Lake restored the aged monarch to a nominal sovereignty, which descended at his death to his son, Akbar Shah. Akbar died in 1837, and was succeeded by the last king of Delhi (his son), who received a pension of about 125,000*l.* per annum. [He joined the mutiny in 1857; was tried in 1858, and transported to Rangoon; died there, 11 Nov. 1862.]

BRITISH POWER IN INDIA.

Attempt made to reach India by the north-east and north-west passages 1528

Sir Francis Drake's expedition 1579

Levant company's land expedition 1589

First commercial adventure from England . . . 1591

First charter to the London company of merchants (see *India Company*) 1600

Factories established at Surat, &c. 1612

Sir Thos. Roe, first English ambassador . . . 1615

Madras founded, 1640; made a presidency . . . 1652

Bombay ceded to England as part of dowry of Catherine, queen of Charles II. 1662

French company established 1664

They settle at Pondicherry 1668

Calcutta purchased 1698

War between the English and French in India 1746–9

English besiege Pondicherry, the seat of the French government, without success . . . 1748

Clive takes Arcot 1751

Peace made 1754

Severndroog and other strongholds of the pirate Angria taken . . . 11 Feb. 1755–6

Capture of Calcutta by Surajah Dowla; suffocation of English in the Black hole (*which see*) 20 June, ,,

Calcutta retaken by Clive, 2 Jan.; he defeats the Soubah at Plassey . . . 23 June, 1757

Fort William, the strongest fort in India, built . ,,

French successful under Lally 1758

But lose nearly all their power 1759

The French under Lally defeated by sir Eyre Coote near Wandewash . . . 2 July, 1760

Hyder Ali usurps the sovereignty of Mysore . 1763–4

Conquest of Patna . . . . 6 Nov. 1763

Battle of Buxar (*which see*) . . . 23 Oct. 1764

The nabob becomes subject to the English . . 1765

* British India extends from 8° to 34° N. lat. and from 70° to 90° E. long. (exclusive of the Burmese additions), about 1,500,000 square miles. The population in all India, 1881, 252,541,210; 1891, 289,187,316; British India, 221,356,187; Native States, 66,803,485. (Hindoos, 207,654,407; Mussulmans, 57,365,204; Christians, 2,284,191; Jains, 1,416,109; Sikhs, 1,907,836; Buddhists, 7,101,057; Parsees, 89,887; Jews, 17,180; forest tribes, animal worshippers, 9,302,083). 1901 (revised) 294,266,701; British India, 231,085,000; Native States, 63,181,000 (Hindoos, 207,075,000; Mussulmans, 62,458,000; Christians, 2,923,000; Jains, 1,334,000; Sikhs, 2,195,000; Buddhists, 9,184,000; Parsees, 94,200; Jews, 18,228; animal worshippers, 8,584,000). Cotton was planted in 1839, and the tea-plant in 1834. Railways (8545 miles in 1879) and the electric telegraph are being rapidly constructed, and canals for irrigation; see *Ganges Canal*; railways in 1890–1, 16,996 miles open; 1902, 26,561 miles open. The Indian revenue in 1854–5 was 20,371,450*l.* The expenditure, 22,915,160*l.* In 1858-9: revenue, 36,060,788*l.*; expenditure, 49,642,350*l.* In 1869–70: revenue, 52,942,482*l.*; expenditure, 56,184,489*l.* In 1875–6, revenue, 52,515,788*l.*; expenditure, 55,117,536*l.* In 1877–8, revenue, 58,969,301*l.*; expenditure, 66,917,000*l.*; 1881–2, revenue, 73,606,000*l.*; expenditure, 71,113,000*l.*; 1883–4, revenue, 67,274,000*l.*; expenditure, 66,617,000*l.*; 1886–7, revenue, 77,337,134Rx. *(ten rupees)*; expenditure, 77,158,707Rx.; 1889–90, revenue, 85,085,203Rx.; expenditure, 82,473,170Rx.; 1891, revenue, 85,741,649Rx.; expenditure, 82,053,478Rx.; 1892, revenue, 89,143,283Rx.; expenditure, 88,675,748Rx.; 1893–4, rev., 90,005,700Rx.; expenditure, 91,600,800Rx.; 1894–5, rev., 95,187,429Rx.; expenditure, 94,494,319Rx. (additional expenditure, 4,446,231Rx.); 1896–7 (deficit owing to famine and plague); 1900–03, surplus, 8,300,000*l.*, 10 Nov. 1902. Exports and imports, 1837, about 21,000,000*l.*; 1856, 53,000,000*l.*; 1885–6, 156,000,000*l.*; 1888–9, about 80,000,000Rx.; 1890–1, 196,260,382Rx. Exports, 1897–98, 104,671,442Rx.; imports, 89,896,406Rx., trade increased by 5,050,100*l.*, 1902-03.

Lord Clive obtains the Dewanny by an imperial grant, which constitutes the company the receivers of the revenue of Bengal, Bahar, and Orissa, and gives the British the virtual sovereignty of these countries . . . . 12 Aug 1765

Treaty with Nizam Ali: the English obtain the Northern Circars . . . . . 12 Nov. 1766

Hyder Ali ravages the Carnatic . . . Jan. 1769

Frightful famine in Bengal 1770–1

Warren Hastings governor of Bengal . 13 April, 1772

India Bill; supreme court established (see *India Bills*) 1773

Treaty with Bhootan 1774

Death of Clive; ungratefully treated . . . . ,,

Accusations commence against Warren Hastings; accused of taking a bribe from a concubine of Meer Jaffier (see *Hastings*) . . 30 May, 1775

Nuncomar, a Brahmin, accuses Warren Hastings of receiving bribes . . . . 11 March, 1776

Is hanged for forgery . . . . . 5 Aug. ,,

[Sir Elijah Impey, the judge, was censured at the time, but afterwards vindicated]

Pondicherry taken . . . . . 11 Oct. 1778

Fortress of Gwalior taken by Popham . 4 Aug. ,,

Hyder Ali overruns the Carnatic, and defeats the British, 10 Sept.; takes Arcot . . 31 Oct. 1780

Hyder Ali defeated by sir Eyre Coote . 1 July, 1781

Warren Hastings accused of taking more bribes (see *Chunar*) . . . . . . 19 Sept. ,,

Bussy lands with a French detachment March, 1782

War with Hyder Ali aided by the French . . ,,

Hyder Ali overthrown by Coote . . 2 June, ,,

Death of Hyder, and accession of his son, Tippoo Sahib . . . . Dec. ,,

Tippoo, who had taken Cuddalore, now takes Bednore . . . . April, 1783

Pondicherry restored to the French, and Trincomalee to the Dutch . . . . . ,,

Fox's India bill thrown out . . . . . ,,

Pitt's India bill establishing the board of control (*which see*) 1784

Ignoble peace with Tippoo . . . 11 March, ,,

Charges against Warren Hastings 1786

His trial begun . . . . . 13 Feb. 1788

War with Tippoo renewed 1790

Bangalore taken (see *Bangalore*) . . 21 March, 1791

Cornwallis defeats Tippoo at Arikera . 15 May, ,,

Fortress of Savandroog taken . . . 21 Dec. ,,

Definitive treaty with Tippoo; his two sons hostages . . . . 19 March, 1792

Civil and criminal courts erected 1793

Pondicherry again taken . . . . . ,,

Tippoo's sons restored . . . . 29 March, 1794

First dispute with the Burmese; adjusted by general Erskine 1795

Warren Hastings acquitted . . . 23 April, ,,

Death of Christian F. Schwartz, 50 years missionary and philanthropist, "the apostle of India," aged 71 . . . . 13 Feb. 1798

Government of lord Mornington, afterwards marquis Wellesley . . . . . 17 May, ,,

Seringapatam stormed by gen. Baird; Tippoo Sahib killed, 4 May; Mysore divided . 22 June, 1799

Victories of the British; the Carnatic conquered 1800

The nabob of Furruckabad cedes his territories to the English for a pension . . . 4 June, 1802

Important treaty of Bassein (with Mahrattas) 31 Dec. ,,

Mahratta war. Victories of sir Arthur Wellesley and general Lake 1803

Wellesley's great victory at Assaye . . 23 Sept. ,,

Pondicherry (restored 1801) retaken . . Dec. ,,

War with Holkar 1804–5

Capture of Bhurtpore . . . . 2 April, 1805

Lord Wellesley superseded by the marquis Cornwallis, who dies . . . . . . 5 Oct. ,,

The Mahratta chief, Scindiah, defeated by the British; treaty of peace . . . 23 Nov. ,,

Treaty of peace with Holkar . . . 24 Dec. ,,

Sepoy mutiny at Vellore; 800 executed . July, 1806

Cunoona surrenders . . . . . 21 Nov. 1807

Mutiny at Seringapatam quelled . . 23 Aug. 1809

Act opening the trade to India . . . July, 1813

War with Nepaul 1814–15

Holkar defeated by sir T. Hislop . . 21 Dec. 1817

Pindaree war. English successful . . . 1817–18

Peace with Holkar . . . . . . 6 Jan. 1818

Burmese war. The British take Rangoon 5 May, 1824

Lord Combermere commands in India . . . ,,

Malacca ceded, and Singapore purchased . . ,,

Barrackpore mutiny, many sepoys killed . Nov. ,,

General Campbell defeats the Burmese near Prome, 25 Dec. 1825

Bhurtpore stormed by Combermere . . 18 Jan. 1826

Peace with the Burmese . . . . 24 Feb. ,,

[They pay 1,000,000*l.* sterling, and cede a great extent of territory.]

Abolition of suttees, or the burning of widows (see *Suttee*) . . . . 7 Dec. 1829

Act opening the trade to India, and tea trade, &c., to China, forming a new era in British commerce . . . . 28 Aug. 1833

Coorg annexed; Rajah deposed . . 10 April, 1834

The natives admitted to the magistracy . 1 May, ,,

The Nawab Shumsoodden put to death for the murder of Mr. Frazer, British resident 8 Oct. 1835

Severe famine 1837–8

Postal service begun 1837

Slavery abolished . . . . . . 1 Aug. 1838

Afghan war. Proclamation against Dost Mahomed 1 Oct. ,,

The British occupy Candahar . . 21 April, 1839

Battle of Ghiznee; victory of sir John (afterwards lord) Keane (see *Ghiznee*) . . . 23 July, ,,

Wade forces the Khyber pass . . . 26 July, ,,

English defeat Dost Mahomed . . . 18 Oct. 1840

Kurrock Singh, king of Lahore, dies; at his funeral his successor is killed by accident, and Dost Mahomed, next heir, surrenders to England 5 Nov. ,,

Rising against the British at Cabul; sir Alex. Burnes and others murdered . . . 2 Nov. 1841

Sir Wm. Macnaghten assassinated . . 23 Dec ,,

Jellalabad held by sir R. Sale 1841–2

The British under a convention evacuate Cabul, placing lady Sale, &c., as hostages with Akbar Khan; a massacre ensues of about 16,000 men, women, and children . . . 6–13 Jan. 1842

The British evacuate Ghiznee . . . 1 March, ,,

Sortie from Jellalabad; general Pollock forces the Khyber pass . . . . . . 5 April, ,,

Ghiznee retaken by general Nott . . 6 Sept. ,,

General Pollock enters Cabul . . . 16 Sept. ,,

Lady Sale and other prisoners rescued by sir R. Shakspeare; arrive at gen. Pollock's camp 21 Sept. ,,

Cabul evacuated after destroying the fortifications 12 Oct. ,,

Scinde war. Ameers defeated by sir Charles Napier at Meanee . . . . 17 Feb. 1843

Scinde annexed to the British empire; sir Charles Napier governor . . . . . June, ,,

Gwalior war. Battles of Maharajpoor and Punniar: the strong fort of Gwalior, the "Gibraltar of the East," taken . . . . . . 29 Dec. ,,

Danish possessions in India purchased . . 1845

*Sikh war.** The Sikhs cross the Sutlej river and attack the British at Ferozepore . 14 Dec. 1845

Sir H. Hardinge, after a long rapid march, reaches Moodkee; the Sikhs (20,000) make an attack; after a hard contest they retire, abandoning their guns (see *Moodkee*) . . . . . . 18 Dec. ,,

Battle of Ferozeshah (*which see*) . . 21, 22 Dec. ,,

Battle of Aliwal; the Sikhs defeated (see *Aliwal* and *Sutlej*) . . . . 28 Jan. 1846

Great battle of Sobraon; the enemy defeated with immense loss (see *Sobraon*) . . 10 Feb. ,,

Citadel of Lahore occupied by sir Hugh Gough, and the war terminates . . . . 20 Feb. ,,

Sir R. Sale dies of his wounds received at Moodkee (18 Dec. 1845) . . . . . . 23 Feb. ,,

The governor-general and sir Hugh Gough raised to the peerage, as viscount Hardinge and baron Gough; receive the thanks of parliament and of the E.I. company . . . . 2, 6 March, ,,

---

* Runjeet Singh, long the ruler of the Sikhs and the Punjab, lived in amity with the British. After his death, 27 June, 1839, several of his successors (children and grandchildren) were in turn assassinated. During the minority of his son Dhuleep Singh, the favourite of the Maharanee, Lall Singh, ruled; and finding the army ungovernable, sanctioned the unprovoked attack on the British, as given above.

Treat of Lahore signed . . . . . 9 March, 1846
Vizier Lall Singh deposed . . . . 13 Jan. 1847
Mr. Vans Agnew and lieut. Anderson killed by the troops of the dewan Moolraj . 21 April, 1848
Lieut. Edwardes joins general Courtland, and most gallantly engages the army of Moolraj, which he defeats after a sanguinary battle of nine hours, at Kennyree . . . . 18 June, „
General Whish raises the siege of Mooltan through the desertion of Shere Singh . . . 22 Sept. „
Cavalry skirmish at Ramnuggur . . . 22 Nov. „
Shere Singh, entrenched on the right bank of the Chenab, with 40,000 men and 28 pieces of artillery; gen. Thackwell crosses the river with 8 infantry regiments, with cavalry and cannon, 1 Dec., and attacks his left flank at Sadoolapore, 3 Dec. „
Lord Gough attacks the enemy's advanced position: victory of Chillianwallah (*which see*) . 13 Jan. 1849
Unconditional surrender of the citadel of Mooltan by Moolraj (see *Mooltan*) . . . . 22 Jan. „
Victory of Guzerat (*which see*) . . . 21 Feb. „
Sir Chas. Napier appointed comm.-in-chief, 7 March, „
The Sikhs surrender unconditionally 14 March, „
Formal annexation of the Punjab to the British dominions; Dhuleep Singh obtains a pension of 40,000*l*. . . . . . . 29 March, „
Moolraj sentenced to death for the murder of Mr. Agnew and lieut. Anderson, Aug.; commuted to transportation for life . . . . Sept. „
Sir Charles Napier disbands the 66th Bengal native infantry, for mutiny . . . . 27 Feb. 1850
Dr. Healy, of the Bengal army, and his attendants, murdered by the Affreedis . . . 20 March, „
Embassy from the king of Nepaul to the queen of Great Britain arrives in England (see *Nepaul*) 25 May, „
Resignation of his command in India by sir Charles Napier . . . . 2 July, „
His farewell address to the Indian army 15 Dec. „
Burmese war. Death of Bajee Rao, ex-peishwa of the Mahrattas. [His nephew Nana Sahib's claim for continuance of the pension (80,000*l*.) refused.] 28 Jan. 1851
A British naval force arrives before Rangoon, in the Burman empire, and commodore Lambert allows the viceroy thirty-five days to obtain instructions from Ava . . . . . 29 Oct. „
The viceroy of Rangoon interdicts communication between the shore and the British ships of war: and erects batteries to prevent their departure, 4 Jan. 1852
[Commodore Lambert blockades the Irawaddy; the Fox, Hermes, &c., attacked by the batteries, destroy the fortifications, and kill nearly 300 of the enemy.]
Martaban (5 April), Rangoon (14 April), and Bassein stormed by the British . . . . 19 May, „
Pegu captured, afterwards abandoned . 4 June, „
Prome captured by general Godwin . . 9 July, „
Pegu recaptured by general Godwin . 21 Nov. „
Pegu annexed to our Indian empire by proclamation of the governor-general . . 20 Dec. „
Revolution at Ava; the king of Ava deposed by his younger brother . . . . . Jan. 1853
Rangoon devastated by fire . . . . . 14 Feb. „
Capt. Lock and many men killed in an attack on the stronghold of a robber chief, 3 Feb.; which is taken by sir J. Cheape . . . 19 March, „
First Indian railway opened (from Bombay to Tannah) . . . . 16 April, „
Termination of the war . . . . June, „
New India bill passed . . . . . 20 Aug. „
Death of general Godwin . . . . 26 Oct. „
Assassination of capt. Latter . . . 8 Dec. „
Rajah of Nagpoor dies, and his territories fall to the E. I. Company . . . . 11 Dec. „
Opening of Ganges canal 1854
First Indian postage stamp struck in . . . „
Opening of the Calcutta railway . . 3 Feb. 1855
Treaty of friendship with Dost Mahomed of Cabul 30 March, „
Insurrection of the Sonthals (*which see*) . July, „
Which is only finally suppressed . . . May, 1856
Oude annexed (see *Oude*) . . . . . 7 Feb. „

MUTINY OF THE NATIVE ARMY.

Mutinies in the Bengal army: at Barrackpore, &c., several regiments disbanded . . . March, 1857
"India is quiet throughout."—*Bombay Gazette.* 1 May, „
Mutiny at Meerut* (near Delhi) 10 May. The mutineers seize Delhi, commit dreadful outrages, and proclaim the king of Delhi emperor, 11–12 May, &c. „
Three native regiments disbanded at Lahore by the energy of Mr. Montgomery and brigadier Corbett, who save the Punjab . . . 12 May, „
Martial law proclaimed by the British lieut.-governor, J. R. Colvin . . . . May, „
British troops under general Anson advance on Delhi: his death . . . . . . 27 May, „
Mutineers often defeated . . . 30 May–23 June, „
Mutiny at Lucknow . . . . . . 30 May, „
Neill suppresses the mutiny at Benares, 3 June; and recovers Allahabad . . . . 4 June, „
Mutiny spreads throughout Bengal: fearful atrocities committed † . . . . „
Native troops disbanded at Mooltan, which is saved . . . . 11 June, „
Ex-king of Oude arrested . . . . 14 June, „
Siege of the residency at Lucknow by the rebels, commences . . . . 1 July, „
Sir H. Lawrence dies of his wounds at Lucknow, 4 July, „
The liberty of the press restricted . . 4 July, „
Sir H. Barnard, commanding before Delhi, dies of cholera, succeeded by general Reed . 5 July, „
General Nicholson destroys a large body of rebels at Sealcote . . . . 12 July, „
Cawnpore surrenders to Nana Sahib, who kills the garrison, &c., 28 June; he is defeated by general Havelock, 16 July: who re-captures Cawnpore (see *Cawnpore*) . . . . . . 17 July, „
Mutinies suppressed at Hyderabad, 18 July; and at Lahore . . . . 20 July, „
General Reed retires, and sir Archdale Wilson takes the command before Delhi . . . 22 July, „
Revolt at Dinapore: the British repulsed with severe loss at Arrah . . . . . 25 July, „
Heroic exertions and numerous victories of general Havelock and his army, although suffering from disease . . . . . 29 July—16 Aug. „
Lord Canning's so-called "clemency" proclamation . . . . 31 July, „
Victory of Neill at Pandoo Nuddee . . 15 Aug. „
General Nicholson's victory at Nujuffghur [he dies 23 Sept.] . . . . 25 Aug. „

* On the introduction of the improved (Enfield) musket in the Indian army, greased cartridges had been brought from England. These were objected to by the native soldiers, and the issue of them was immediately discontinued by orders in Jan. 1857. A mutinous spirit however gradually arose in the Bengal native army. In March several regiments were disbanded, followed by others, till in June the army had lost by disbandment and desertion, about 30,000 men. On 5 April, a sepoy, and on 20 April, a jemadar, or native lieutenant, were executed. At the end of May 34 regiments were lost. In April, 85 of the 3rd Bengal native cavalry at Meerut refused to use their cartridges. On 9 May they were committed to gaol. On Sunday, the 10th, a mutiny in the native troops broke out; they fired on their officers, killing col. Finnis and others. They then released their comrades, massacred many Europeans, and fired the public buildings. The European troops rallied and drove them from their cantonments. The mutineers then fled to Delhi (*which see*).

† At the end of June the native troops at the following places were in open mutiny: *Meerut*, *Delhi*, Ferozepore, Allyghur, Roorkee, Murdaun, Lucknow, *Cawnpore*, *Nusseerabad*, *Neemuch*, *Hansi*, *Hissar*, *Jhansi*, Mehidpore, Jallundur, Azimghur, Futtehghur, Jaunpore, *Bareilly*, Shahjehanpore, *Allahabad*. At the stations printed in italics, European women and children were massacred.—The *Relief Fund* for the sufferers in India was commenced 25 Aug. 1857. The Queen, the emperor Napoleon, and the Sultan, gave each 1000*l*. In Nov. 1857, 280,749*l*. had been collected; in Nov. 1858, 433,620*l*. In Dec. 1861, 140,000*l*. had been distributed to sufferers in India; and 100,000*l*. to those at home; 246,069*l*. remained for the benefit of widows and orphans. A fast was observed on 7 Oct.

Assault of Delhi, 14 Sept.; taken, 20 Sept.; the king captured, 21 Sept.; his son and grandson slain by colonel Hodson . . . 22 Sept. 1857
Sir James Outram joins Havelock and serves under him . . . . 16 Sept. ,,
Havelock marches to Lucknow and relieves the besieged residency; retires and leaves Outram in command; Neill killed . . . 25, 26 Sept. ,,
Colonel Greathed defeats the rebels at Bolundshohur, 27 Sept.; destroys a fort at Molaghur, 29 Sept.; takes Allyghur, 5 Oct.; and defeats rebels at Agra . . . . 10 Oct. ,,
Sir Colin Campbell (afters. lord Clyde) appointed commander-in-chief, 11 July; arrives at Cawnpore 3 Nov. ,,
Marches to Alumbagh, near Lucknow, 9 Nov.; and takes Secunderabagh . . . 16 Nov. ,,
Joined by Havelock, he attacks the rebels and rescues the besieged in the residency, 18–25 Nov. ,,
Havelock * dies of dysentery at Alumbagh, 24 Nov. ,,
General Windham (at Cawnpore) repulsed with loss in an attack on the Gwalior contingent, who take part of Cawnpore . . . 27 Nov. ,,
Sir C. Campbell arrives at Cawnpore, which he retakes, 28 Nov.; and defeats the Gwalior rebels, 6 Dec. ,,
The rebels defeated by Seaton, 14, 17, and 27 Dec.; at Goruckpore by Rowcroft, 27 Dec.; and at Futtehghur by sir C. Campbell . . . 2 Jan. 1858
Lucknow strongly fortified by the rebels . Jan. ,,
Generals Rose, Roberts, Inglis, and Grant, victorious in many encounters . . Jan. and Feb. ,,
Trial of king of Delhi; sentenced to transportation 27 Jan. to 9 March, ,,
Sir C. Campbell marches to Lucknow, 11 Feb.; the siege commences, 8 March; taken by successive assaults; the enemy retreat; Hodson killed, 14–19 March, ,,
Severe proclamation of the governor-general in Oude † . . . . 14 March, ,,
General Roberts takes Kotah . . 30 March, ,,
Sir Hugh Rose beats the enemy severely, and takes Jhansi . . . . 4 April, ,,
General Whitelock takes Budaon . . 19 April, ,,
Death of capt. sir W. Peel, of small-pox, at Cawnpore . . . . 27 April, ,,
General Penny killed in Rohilcund . . 4 May, ,,
Bareilly recaptured . . . . . 7 May, ,,
Sir Hugh Rose defeats the rebels several times—at Kooneh, May 11, and near Calpee, which he retakes . . . . 23 May, ,,
Victory of sir E. Lugard at Jugdespore 29 May, ,,
The rebels seize Gwalior, the capital of Scindiah, who escapes to Agra . . . 13 June, ,,
The rebels defeated by sir H. Rose (the heroic Ranee of Jhansi killed), 17 June; Gwalior retaken and Scindiah reinstated . . . 19 June, ,,
Tantia Topee heads a division of the rebels . ,,
Rajahs of Jeypore, &c., surrender; Rohilcund and other provinces tranquillised . . . July, ,,
General Roberts destroys the remains of the Gwalior rebels . . . . . . 14 Aug. ,,
Many Oude chiefs surrender . . . Aug. ,,
An attempt of disbanded regiments to retake their arms at Mooltan, suppressed by major Hamilton (300 killed on the spot, and 800 slain or captured afterwards) . . . . . . 31 Aug. ,,
The government of the East India Company ceases, 1 Sept. ,,
General Mitchell defeats Tantia Topee, near Rajghur . . . . 15 Sept. ,,
The queen proclaimed throughout India—lord Canning to be the first viceroy . . . 1 Nov. ,,
Campaign in Oude begins; several chiefs submit, others subdued . . . . . 1–30 Nov. ,,
At Dhooden Khera lord Clyde (formerly sir C. Campbell) defeats Beni Mahdo . . . 24 Nov. ,,

* Born 5 April, 1795; educated at the Charterhouse, London, where he was called "*old Phlos;*" went to India, 1823: served in the Burmese war, 1824; and in the Sikh war, 1845. He was a Baptist.

† Lord Ellenborough, the minister for India, sent, unknown to his colleagues, a despatch severely censuring this proclamation. This despatch became public and led to his resignation and very nearly to the defeat of the ministry, a vote of censure being moved for in both houses of parliament, but not carried.

Flight of Tantia Topee—he is beaten in Guzerat by major Sutherland . . . . 25 Nov. 1858
The ex-king of Delhi sails for the Cape of Good Hope, 4–11 Dec.; the colonists refuse to receive him; he is sent to Rangoon . . . . ,,
Brigadier John Jacob dies at Jacobabad (greatly lamented) . . . . . . 6 Dec. ,,
Indecisive skirmishes with Ferozeshah . Dec. ,,
Who joins Tantia Topee: they are defeated in several small engagements . . . Jan. 1859
Enforcement of the Disarming Act in the north-west provinces . . . . . Jan. ,,
The Punjab made a distinct presidency . 1 Jan. ,,
Rebels completely expelled from Oude; enter Nepaul . . . . Jan. ,,
Guerilla warfare continues in Rohilcund . Feb. ,,
Tantia Topee hemmed in; deserted by his troops, about 25 Feb. ,,
Defeat of the Begum of Oude and Nana Sahib by general Horsford . . . . 10 Feb. ,,
The new Indian tariff creates much dissatisfaction, March, ,,
Maun Singh surrenders . . . . 2 April, ,,
Tantia Topee taken, 7 April; hanged . 18 April, ,,
Thanksgiving in England for pacification of India 1 May, ,,
Mutinous conduct of British troops lately in the company's service at Meerut and other places, on account of their transfer to the queen's service without bounty . . . . . . 5 May, ,,
Sir Hope Grant defeats Nana Sahib in the Jorwah pass . . . . 23 May, ,,
A court of inquiry appointed . . . June, ,,
Sir Chas. Wood becomes sec. for India . 22 June, ,,
Dissatisfaction among the troops at their transfer from the service of the company to that of the crown, without a bounty, settled by discharge offered to them, which about 10,000 accept July, ,,
Thanksgiving day observed in India . . 28 July, ,,
An income tax bill (called "the Trades' and Professions' Licensing Bill") passes the legislative council; great meetings at Calcutta and Madras protesting against it . . . . . Sept. ,,
Rajah Jey-loll Singh hanged . . . 1 Oct. ,,
Nana Sahib, in force, in Nepaul on the frontiers of Oude . . . . Oct. ,,
Insurgents in Nepaul dispersed . . 24 Dec. ,,
Important financial changes made by Mr. James Wilson, new finance secretary . . . Feb. 1860
Company formed to obtain cotton, flax, &c., from India . . . . March, ,,
Paper currency determined on . . . March, ,,
Bahadoor Khan, ex-king of Bareilly, hanged for murders caused by him . . . 2 March, ,,
Sir Chas. Trevelyan recalled from Madras, for publishing a government minute against Mr. Wilson's commercial scheme . . . . . . May, ,,
Sir Hugh Rose takes command of the Indian army, amalgamated with the British . . . July, ,,
Lord Clyde arrives in London . . . 18 July, ,,
Lord Canning's recommendation that the adopted successors of Indian princes should be recognised agreed to by the home government . 21 July, ,,
Death of sir H. Ward, new governor at Madras, 3 Aug.; and of Mr. James Wilson . . 11 Aug. ,,
Nana Sahib, supposed to have died of jungle fever in Aug. 1858, is said to be living in Tibet . Dec. ,,
Mutiny of 5th European regiment at Dinapore, suppressed; breaks out again, 5 Oct.; is again suppressed, Wm. Johnson shot, and the regiment disbanded . . . . 13 Nov. ,,
British troops repulsed in Sikkim . . Nov. ,,
Agitation against the income tax suppressed at Bombay and other places . . . . Dec. ,,
Excitement against sir Chas. Wood's grant of 520,000*l.* to descendants of Tippoo Sahib . Dec. ,,
Mr. Samuel Laing, successor to Mr. James Wilson, arrives . . . . 10 Jan. 1861
Awful famine in N.W. provinces through failure of the crops; immense exertions of the government and others to relieve the sufferers, Jan.–June, ,,
Expedition marches against Sikkim; natives retire Feb. ,,
Disturbances in the indigo districts . . March, ,,
Kootoob-ood-deen, grandson of Tippoo Sahib, murdered by his servants . . . . 31 March, ,,

British subscriptions for relief of the famine commence at the Mansion-house, London, with 4000*l.*, 28 March; 52,000*l.* subscribed 20 April; closes with 114,807*l.* . . . . Nov. 1861
Order of the "Star of India" (*which see*) constituted 25 June, ,,
Excitement through the printing and circulation of "Nil Darpan," a Hindu drama libelling the indigo planters . . . . June, ,,
The rev. James Long, the translator, sentenced to fine and imprisonment . . . . . . Aug. ,,
New Indian council and new high court of judicature established . . . . Aug. ,,
Mr. J. P. Grant, lieut.-governor of Bengal (who had authorised the translation of "Nil Darpan") and Mr. Seton Kerr, his secretary (who had, without authority, distributed copies) are censured and resign . . . . Sept. ,,
Law of property in India altered; sale of waste lands authorised . . . . . . Oct. ,,
Lords Harris and Clyde, sir J. Lawrence, Dhuleep Singh, and others invested with the Star of India by the queen . . . . 1 Nov. ,,
Reported prosperity of Indian finances; licence tax not to be reimposed . . . . . . 31 Dec. ,,
First meeting of new legislative council; includes several Indian princes . . . . . 18 Jan. 1862
Lord Elgin, new governor-general, installed at Calcutta . . . . 12 March, ,,
Lord Canning arrives at Southampton, 26 April; dies . . . . 17 June, ,,
Mr. S. Laing returns to England through ill health; censured by sir C. Wood; he justifies himself and resigns . . . . July, ,,
High court of judicature at Bengal inaugurated 12 July, ,,
Reported suspension of sale of waste lands Aug. ,,
Rao Sahib hanged for murders during the revolt 8 Sept. ,,
Great increase in the cultivation of cotton in India, reported . . . . Oct. ,,
Sir Charles Trevelyan, new finance minister, arrives 8 Jan. 1863
First agricultural exhibition at Calcutta 19–30 Jan. ,,
Rise of Ram Singh, a fanatic, in N.W. provinces Oct. ,,
War with warlike hill-tribes on the N.W. frontiers, Oct.; severe conflict, gen. Chamberlain wounded, 20 Nov.; command assumed by major-gen. John Garvock, who totally defeated the enemy (about 15,000) in Chamta pass, 15, 16 Dec.; war ended 29 Dec. ,,
The Hindu religion deprived of government support Dec. ,,
Death of the viceroy, lord Elgin . . . 20 Nov. ,,
Sir John Lawrence, his successor, assumes office 12 Jan. 1864
Excitement amongst the Hindoos on account of government suppressing funeral rites on sanitary grounds . . . . March. ,,
Prosperous financial statement of sir Charles Trevelyan . . . . April, ,,
Mr. Ashley Eden, envoy at Bhootan, seized and compelled to sign a treaty giving up Assam about April, ,,
Gold currency (a sovereign = 10 rupees) ordered to be introduced at Christmas . . . . July, ,,
Terrific cyclone—immense loss of life, property, and ships at Calcutta and elsewhere . . . 5 Oct. ,,
Grand durbar, held by sir John Lawrence, at Lahore; 604 native princes present . . 18 Oct. ,,
War with the Bhootanese—fortress of Dhalimcote taken . . . . 12 Dec. ,,
Much commercial speculation at Bombay Dec. ,,
The Bhootanese attack on Dewangiri repulsed with severe loss, 29 Jan., evacuated by the British Feb. 1865
Opening of the Indo-European telegraph—a telegram from Kurrachee received . . 1 March, ,,
W. Massey succeeds sir C. Trevelyan as finance minister; he arrives at Calcutta . . 31 March, ,,
Sir Charles Trevelyan declares a large deficit in the revenue . . . . 1 April, ,,
Dewangiri recaptured by gen. Tombs . 2 April, ,,
Sir Hugh Rose retires from command of the army; which is assumed by sir Wm. Mansfield, 23 April, ,,
Sir Charles Trevelyan's plans reversed by sir C. Wood . . . . May, ,,
Death of the able and beneficent hon. Juggonath Sunkersett, the recognised representative of the Hindoo community . . . . 31 July, 1865
Negotiation with the Bhootanese . . . July, ,,
Shipwreck of the *Eagle Speed* near Calcutta; 265 coolies perish through neglect . . . 24 Aug. ,,
Peace with the Bhootanese signed . . 13 Nov. ,,
Much dissatisfaction at mildewed cotton goods being received from England. . . July–Oct. ,,
Settlement of the question respecting marriage of Hindoo converts . . . . . . April, 1866
"*Simla Scandal.*" Trial of capt. E. Jervis; acquitted on charge of peculation of stores belonging to sir W. Mansfield, commander-in-chief, but condemned for insubordination; sentence (dismissal from the service) approved by sir W. Mansfield . . . . 17 Sept. ,,
Awful famine in Orissa, Bengal; about 1,500,000 perished . . . . Aug.–Nov. ,,
Relief by Government . . . . . . Oct. ,,
Dr. Cotton, bishop of Calcutta, accidentally drowned 6 Oct. ,,
Famine abating; official inquiry ordered . Nov. ,,
Great durbar held at Agra, by sir J. Lawrence 10–20 Nov. ,,
Simla case; sentence against capt. Jervis confirmed, and sir W. Mansfield censured by the duke of Cambridge, by letter dated . . . 17 Jan. 1867
Deficiencies in the revenue; Massey's proposed new licence tax much opposed . . April & May, ,,
False rumour of mutiny at Meerut . . . 20 May, ,,
Report on Orissa famine; authorities blamed, June, ,,
Deficiency in revenue for 1867, 2,400,000*l.* reported Aug. ,,
Massacre of Hindoo chiefs by the nawab of Tonk (for which he was deposed) . . . 1 Aug. ,,
Grand durbar at Lucknow . . . . 9–17 Nov. ,,
The fierce Wagheers of Kattywar, in a night attack, are nearly exterminated; capts. Hibbert and La Touche killed . . . . 29 Dec. ,,
Mr. Massey's budget; surplus of 800,000*l.*; licence tax abolished, tax on trades, &c., substituted; expenditure of 1,700,000*l.* on public works proposed 14 March, 1868
War on the N.W. frontier; the Bazotees, fanatical Mahometans, defeated by general Wilde; 30 killed and wounded; all dispersed, 4 Oct.; villages burnt as punishment for outrages . . . . Oct. ,,
Death of the begum of Bhopal, who helped the British during the mutiny . . . 30 Aug. ,,
The duke of Argyll secretary for India . 9 Dec. ,,
Arrival of the earl of Mayo, the new viceroy, at Calcutta . . . . 12 Jan. 1869
Severe famine 1868-9
Sir R. Temple's budget; deficiency of about 2,750,000*l.*; a 1 per cent. income tax put on (excessively opposed) . . . . . March, 1869
Meeting of the viceroy and Shere Ali, the Afghan sovereign, who receives a subsidy and presents 27 March, ,,
New divorce act in operation . . . 1 April, ,,
Rise of a body of Indian religious reformers termed the Brahmo Somaj (see *Deism*) . . . . Aug. ,,
Act for the better governing India and defining the governor-general's powers passed . . 11 Aug. ,,
India visited by the duke of Edinburgh, Dec. 1869–April, 1870
Railway between Calcutta and Bombay completed March, ,,
Announced deficiency in the revenue; increased taxation proposed; much opposition to the income tax . . . . May, ,,
Grand durbar at Bhurtpore . . . . 10 Oct. ,,
Indian coinage act passed . . . . . ,,
Lamented death of sir H. Durand, from fall from an elephant . . . . 1 Jan. 1871
Sir Proby Cautley, designed Ganges canal works, &c., died, aged 68 . . . . . . 25 Jan. ,,
Volunteer system proposed for India . . Jan. ,,
Indian finance committee appointed . . . Feb. ,,
Sir R. Temple's budget . . . . . 9 March, ,,
Moulvi Liakat Ali, a cruel rebel who in 1857 ruled as viceroy at Allahabad, apprehended . 5 July, ,,
Indian civil engineering college, Cooper's-hill, opened by the duke of Argyll, secretary for India, 5 Aug. ,,
Justice Norman stabbed at Calcutta, 20 Sept.; dies 21 Sept.; assassin convicted, 28 Sept.; executed 4 Nov. ,,

Much corrupt opposition to the income tax reported Nov. 1871

Lord Mayo visits Palumpore fair, and holds a rural durbar . . . . 6 Nov. ,,

Military expedition under generals Nutthall and Bourchier, aided by the rajah of Munnipore, against the Looshais, about 13 Nov.; skirmishes, 1 Dec. ,,

Death of the earl of Ellenborough, a late governor-general (see *Somnath*) . . . . . 22 Dec. ,,

Skirmishes with the Looshais, 21, 23 Dec.; they sue for peace . . . . . . 29 Dec. ,,

The king of Siam visits Calcutta . . 7–12 Jan. 1872

Outbreak of the Kookas, near Loodiana, severely suppressed by commissioners Cowan and Forsyth (see *Kookas*) . . . . . . 15–17 Jan. ,,

Camp at Delhi; military manœuvres, by sir H. Tombs and others . . . . 13–23 Jan. ,,

Looshais repulsed and strongholds taken 28 Jan. ,,

The viceroy arrives at Rangoon, 28 Jan.; on his return he visits the convict establishment in the Andaman Islands, and is assassinated at Port Blair by Shere Ali, a convict, while about to embark in the *Glasgow* . . . . 8 Feb. ,,

Lord Napier acts as viceroy . . . 23 Feb. ,,

Looshais surrender unconditionally; army returning 28 Feb. ,,

The Kamous tribe, while carrying off Looshai captives, defeated, and captives rescued; British returning to Calcutta . . . . 7 March, ,,

Shere Ali hanged, without confessing associates, 12 March, ,,

Annual pension from Indian government to lady Mayo, 1000*l.*; grant of 20,000*l.* for children, March, ,,

Sir Richard Temple's budget favourable; income tax to be reduced . . . . . . April, ,,

Lord Northbrook sworn in as viceroy . 3 May, ,,

Liakat Ali, on confession, condemned to transportation for life . . . . . 27 July ,,

Christian marriage bill passed . . . . July, ,,

The begum of Bhopal made a knight of the Star of India at Bombay . . . . . 16 Nov. ,,

Changes in criminal procedure; compromise in ,,

The income tax not renewed . . . . 21 March, 1873

Riots of the Moplahs, Mahometan fanatics, on coast of Malabar, suppressed by military; about 13, 14 Sept. ,,

New tax (road cess) reported successful . Oct. ,,

Messrs. Bernard, Geddes, and Robinson appointed commissioners in anticipation of famine in Bengal . . . . Nov. ,,

Sir R. Temple appointed superintendent of relief in Behar . . . . Jan. 1874

15 districts (25,000,000 inhabitants) much distressed; 11 districts (14,000,000) affected middle of Jan. ,,

Subscriptions at Mansion-house (*which see*), London begun 24 Jan. ,,

1,000*l.* given by the Queen . . . . . . 4 Feb. ,,

The marquis of Salisbury secretary for India, 21 Feb. ,,

Report from Calcutta: "people well employed on public works; no adult should die now from starvation" . . . . 25 March, ,,

A loan, not exceeding 10,000,000*l.* for India Government authorised by parliament . . 30 March, ,,

Sir R. Temple installed lieut.-gov. of Bengal in room of sir George Campbell: about 500 deaths from disease and hunger reported, about 8 April, ,,

The famine kept under; estimated net expenditure on relief, 6,500,000*l.* (see *Mansion-house*) May, ,,

Crisis of famine past; reported declining; much rain; good prospects . . . . . June, ,,

Only 24 deaths from famine alone; 125,000*l.* raised for relief in London . . . . . 27 July, ,,

Abundance of rain . . . . Sept. ,,

Sadun Khan, a cruel leader in the mutiny, sentenced to death . . . . Sept. ,,

A person said to be Nana Sahib captured at Gwalior by the Maharajah Scindia (identity since disproved) . . . . 21 Oct. ,,

Attempts to poison col. Phayre, resident at Baroda, Nov.; he is replaced by col. Pelly . . Dec. ,,

Outrages of Dufflatribes on N. W. frontier (troublesome, 1838–9; 1852; Feb. 1873); expedition against them . . . . Dec ,,

Mulhar Rao, gaekwar of Baroda, carried to Calcutta for trial for attempting to poison col. Phayre; his child recognised as his successor, provisionally . . . . 14 Jan. 1875

The Duffla tribes surrender and pay fine . 29 Jan. ,,

The gaekwar's trial begins, 3 native judges (Scindiah, the maharajah of Jeypore, and one other) and 3 British . . . . 23 Feb. ,,

Lieut. Holcombe and a surveying party (about 70) in Assam, massacred by Naga natives about 24 Feb. ,,

Close of inquiry into the conduct of the gaekwar of Baroda; verdict of 3 British judges, guilty; of 3 natives, not proved; 30 March; he is deposed for misgovernment by the viceroy, and ordered to live in British India with suitable provision; proclamation that a successor be appointed 23 April, ,,

Naga tribes chastised severely; the objects of the expedition accomplished . . 15–25 March, ,,

Eldest son of the gaekwar appointed successor 22 May, ,,

Difficulties with Burmah . . . . . May, ,,

Mission of sir Douglas Forsyth to Mandalay (see *Burmah*) . . . . June, ,,

New gaekwar of Baroda installed . . . 3 June, ,,

Establishment of a new Mahometan college for the N. W. provinces (chiefly by Ahmed Khan); announced . . . . July, ,,

Dispatch from marquis of Salisbury on repeal of cotton duties . . . . Sept. ,,

The Prince of Wales sails for India, 11 Oct., arrives at Bombay, 8 Nov.; warmly received at Baroda, 9 Nov.; at Goa, 27 Nov.; in Ceylon, 1-8 Dec.; at Madras, 13 Dec.; at Calcutta, 23 Dec.; grand reception of Indian potentates . . . 24 Dec. ,,

Unveiled statue of Lord Mayo at Calcutta . 1 Jan. 1876

At Benares, Lucknow, &c., 5 Jan. *et seq.*; in Nepaul, 12 Feb.; sails from Bombay . . . 13 March, ,,

Lord Lytton, new viceroy, takes oath at Calcutta. 12 April, ,,

The Queen proclaimed Empress of India in London 1 May, ,,

Indian finances: deficiency through depreciation of silver currency; loss about 2,300,000*l.*, proposed loan of 4,000,000*l.* . . . . 11 Aug. ,,

Vice-regal proclamation of the Queen's title, "Empress of India;" (to be proclaimed at Delhi, 1 Jan., 1877) . . . . 19 Aug. ,,

Sir John Strachey appointed financial minister, about 17 Oct.; governor of N.W. Provinces, Nov. ,,

At Agra Mr. Fuller slapped for neglect a native servant, 31 Oct. 1875, who died soon after; he was fined by a magistrate; sentence considered too light by the high court; the viceroy in a minute censured all; this caused much dissatisfaction (lord Salisbury supported the viceroy, 1877) . . . . July, ,,

Famine in Bombay, Madras, &c. . Nov., Dec. ,,

Proclamation of the queen as empress of India with much magnificence at Delhi, by the viceroy; also at Calcutta, Madras, and Bombay 1 Jan. 1877

Creation of the "Order of the Empire of India" announced . . . . 1 Jan. ,,

Sir R. Temple removed from Bengal to Bombay 19 Jan. ,,

Relief works organizing, favourable reports announced . . . . 29 April, ,,

The raids of the Affreedis on N.W. frontiers suppressed; announced . . . . end of April, ,,

Famine formidable, but energetically met June, ,,

Misery increasing; establishment of "Mansion-house relief fund" (*which see*) . 12 Aug. ,,

The secretary for India authorised by parliament to raise a loan for 5,000,000*l.* . . . 14 Aug. ,,

919,771 employed by government; 1,326,971 relieved gratuitously; reported . . . . 29 Aug. ,,

Disturbances on N.W. frontier; raids of the Jawakies, or Jowakies, an Affreedi tribe; chastised by expedition under sir Rd. Pollock, 29, 30 Aug.; again by gen. Keyes . . . . . . Nov. ,,

Copious rain in the south reported; greatly improved prospects . . . . Sept., Oct. ,,

Formation of a new N.W. government proposed Oct., Nov. ,,

Mansion-house Indian fund closed, by request of the duke of Buckingham (by telegram) . 5 Nov. ,,

Jummu, the Jawakies' stronghold, taken; they are defeated and dispersed . . . Nov., Dec. 1877

Sir John Strachey's budget; 1,500,000*l.* to be raised annually for famines (they cost 16,000,000*l.* in five years); taxation raised; trade licences, &c. . . . Dec. ,,

"Imperial Order of the Crown of India," for ladies; instituted . . . . 31 Dec. ,,

The Jawakies defeated by cavalry, 15 Feb.; surrender unconditionally; announced 22 Feb. 1878

Bill to restrain licence of the native press, passed by the council at Calcutta . . 14 March, ,,

The Indian press commission to help and control the press, established . . . . . . ,,

Budget; cost of famine about 3,450,000*l.* March, ,,

Native Indian troops sent to Malta, April; commended by the duke of Cambridge, June; removed to Cyprus . . . . . . Aug. ,,

War with Afghanistan (*which see*) . . . Sept. ,,

England now holds the passes through which India is accessible by land . . . . Feb. 1879

Revenue—Gross receipts, 65,207,694*l.* 1878-9
Expenditure, 67,545,201*l.* . . . . ,,

8545 miles of railways opened (expenditure about 120,000,000*l.*) up to . . . 31 March, 1879

Treaty of peace signed at Gandamuk (*which see*), 26 May, ,,

Indian railways guarantee act passed . 11 Aug. ,,

Loan of sum under 5,000,000*l.* for India; authorized by act . . . . 15 Aug. ,,

Disaffection and plundering of the Rumpa hill tribes, Aug.; subdued . . . . . . Oct. ,,

Mutiny and massacres at Cabul (see *Afghanistan*), Sept. ,,

Murder of Mr. Damant, commissioner, in Naga hills by natives, during an outbreak 14 Oct. ,,

New stringent rules for newspaper correspondents with army; issued . . . . . . Oct. ,,

Lord Lytton fired at by Busa, a half-mad, intoxicated East Indian; no injury . 12 Dec. ,,

Rumpa rebellion in Central India dying out; several defeats of rebels . . . . ,,

Naga raids and murders . . . . . . Jan. 1880

Indian budget, by sir John Strachey, surplus of 119,000*l.* reported . . . . . 24 Feb. ,,

Marquis of Ripon, new viceroy, arrives at Calcutta; col. Gordon, his secretary . . . . . . ,,

Errors in the budget, through mistakes in estimating Afghan war expenses; large deficiency; announced May; sir John Strachey resigns (succeeded by major Baring) . . . . June, ,,

Deficiency stated to be about 900,000*l.* by marquis of Hartington . . . . 5 July, ,,

By a landslip the hill station Nynee Tal or Naini Tal, in the Himalayas, destroyed; many lives lost (see *Landslips*) . . . . . 18 Sept. ,,

Sir Donald Stewart appointed commander-in-chief of the Indian army . . . . . Jan. 1881

Death of Gholam Hussein Khan, able and faithful friend to the British . . . . March, ,,

War declared against the Wazaris, 12 April; ends with their submission . . . about 8 May, ,,

Proposals for loan of 3,000,000*l.*, issued, 27 June, ,,

Budget introduced by the marquis of Hartington; revenue, 68,484,666*l.*; expenditure, 69,667,615*l.*; deficit, 1,182,949*l.* . . . . . 22 Aug. ,,

The budget for 1882–3—Revenue, 66,439,000*l.* 9 Mar. 1882
Expenditure, 66,174,000*l.* . ,,

The Indian contingent distinguished in Egyptian war . . . . Aug.—Sept. ,,

Officers visit London . . . . Nov. ,,

The Sirhind canal (502 miles, for irrigation) opened by the viceroy . . . . . . 24 Nov. ,,

Mr. Ilbert's Criminal Procedure Amendment bill strongly opposed by all the non-official Europeans and the army throughout India; very great meeting at Calcutta . . . . . 28 Feb. 1883

European and Anglo-Indian defence association, Calcutta, formed; first meeting . 29 March, ,,

An Anglo-Indian association for the natives formed in London . . . . April, ,,

Mr. Banerjee, editor of the *Bengalee*, sentenced to two months' imprisonment for gross libel against judge Norris; great excitement of Hindoos, monster meeting at Calcutta [appeal refused in England, July] . . . . . about 11 May, ,,

Dreadful inundation in Cachar, N.E. Calcutta, causing great distress; prompt British help 16 May, ,,

Major Baring succeeded by sir Auckland Colvin as finance minister . . . . . . July, 1883

High courts of Bombay and Madras favour, that of Calcutta opposes, the Ilbert bill . July—Aug. ,,

Abundant food supply and great prosperity Oct. ,,

Ilbert bill: compromise announced; Europeans allowed to claim a jury wholly or partly European 21 Dec. ,,

Akha raids into Assam; major Beresford's forces repulsed . . . . 24 Dec. ,,

Budget—revenue 71,727,000*l.* 1883–4
expenditure, 70,340,000*l.* . . . . ,,

The Akhas dispersed by gen. Hill . . . 8 Jan. 1884

He returns . . . . Jan. ,,

Ilbert bill amended and passed . . . 25 Jan. ,,

Great increase of cultivation and exports through railways since 1848.

Exports: 25,000,000*l.* raised to 147,837,920*l.* in 1883 announced ,,

Indian budget: finances sound and improving, 8 Aug. ,,

Expedition to the Zhob valley to punish the Kakar Pathans for their raids into British territory about 22 Sept. ,,

They are defeated by gen. Tanner; 56 killed 23 Oct. ,,

No resistance reported, 6 Nov.; troops return 22 Nov. ,,

Upwards of 1000 addresses from natives to the marquis of Ripon on his leaving India . Nov. ,,

Earl of Dufferin installed viceroy at Calcutta 13 Dec. ,,

Budget—revenue, 70,690,681*l.* 1884–5
expenditure, 71,077,127*l.* . . . . . ,,

Important Bengal tenancy bill passed 11 March, 1885

Sir A. Colvin's budget; combined surplus of 3 years (1882–5), 1,378,000*l.*; lessened by depreciation of silver currency; revenue for 1885–6, 73,508,100*l.*; expenditure, 1885-6, 76,488,960*l.* . . 17 March, ,,

Sir Donald Stewart, with 50,000 men, ordered to advance to Quetta . . . . . . March, ,,

Meeting of the Ameer of Afghanistan and the viceroy at Rawul Pindi conference and durbar 2–12 April, ,,

The nawab of Moorshedabad and other princes offer to sell their jewels, &c., to provide money to aid the British government in India against Russia April–May, ,,

Thorough defence of India determined on by the British government, declared . . . 12 May, ,,

Proposed loan of 10,000,000*l.* 21 May *et seq.*; act passed . . . . 22 July, ,,

The formation of native volunteer corps under the commander-in-chief . . . . . . May, ,,

Lord Randolph Churchill appointed secretary for India . . . . 24 June, ,,

Sir Frederick Roberts appointed commander-in-chief; announced . . . . . . 30 July, ,,

National congress of 71 delegates (principally lawyers, schoolmasters, and editors, not Mahometans) meet at Bombay, express great loyalty to the queen, and pass nine resolutions to endeavour to obtain a royal commission of inquiry and increased political power . . . end of Dec. ,,

Grand military review at Delhi held by the viceroy (35,000 troops, 709 officers, &c.) . . 19 Jan. 1886

Lady Dufferin's fund for providing female medical practitioners for the natives of India, highly successful 1885–6

Upper Burmah annexed by proclamation of the viceroy, lord Dufferin . . . . . 1 Jan. 1886

Powerful speech of lord Dufferin; deficit of about 2,000,000*l.* through war preparations, &c.; proposed increase of income-tax . . . 4 Jan. ,,

Income-tax bill passed . . . . . 29 Jan. ,,

Earl of Kimberley appointed secretary for India, about 6 Feb. ,,

Sir A. Colvin's budget, 1886–7; revenue, 75,798,700*l.*; expenditure 75,616,500*l.* . . . . 24 March, ,,

Sir Richard, aft. viscount Cross, appointed secretary for India . . . . July, ,,

National Indian congress at Calcutta, 400 delegates (Hindoos) to promote native advancement, 28 Dec. 1886; and again early in 1887

The queen's jubilee celebrated with great magnificence; honours distributed; 25,000 prisoners of good character released . . 16 Feb. *et seq.* ,,

Maharajah of Indore and many Indian princes present at the jubilee celebration in Westminster Abbey . . . . 21 June, ,,

13,390 miles of railway in India; reported . . . ,,

The nizam of Hyderabad in a letter to lord Dufferin the viceroy, offers to present 20 lakhs of rupees for three years, total 600,000*l.*, for the defence of the N.W territories, Sept.; acknowledged with thanks; announced . 10 Oct. 1887
The rajah of Kaparthala offers his army and five lakhs of rupees for the defence of India; announced . . . . 31 Oct. ,,
Four lakhs offered by rajah of Nabha . . Nov. ,,
Similar offers by other princes . . . Nov. ,,
Subscriptions to lady Dufferin's jubilee fund in support of the national association for supplying female medical aid amounts to 478,465 rupees in India, and 1,770*l.* in England 15 Oct.; amount received 50,000*l.* . . . . . 25 Oct. ,,
Districts in Beloochistan annexed (*which see*) announced . . . . Nov. ,,
India 4 per cent. stock converted into 3½ per cent. by act . . . . 23 May, ,,
The maharajah of Darbhanga in Bengal, establishes a female medical hospital in aid of lady Dufferin's fund . . . . autumn, ,,
Military demonstration against Sikkim (*which see*) ordered . . . . 24 Jan. 1888
Budget 1887–8; great deficit; tax on petroleum and increase of salt duty proposed Jan.; passed 10 Feb. ,,
Lord Dufferin, the viceroy, announces his intention of resigning, for private reasons . . 9 Feb. ,,
Moderate National Indian Congress at Madras recommends representative institutions, &c. Feb. ,,
Major L. R. Battye and captain H. B. Urmiston and five Sepoys killed by the Akozais during an exploration on British territory near Black Mountain, N.W. frontier . . 10 June, ,,
Black Mountain expedition, or "The Hazara Field Force" under general McQueen to avenge the outrage of 19 June; organised Sept.; advance, seizure of Manakadana 4 Oct.; the enemy defeated with the loss of 200 men by gen. Galbraith; guerrilla warfare; British success at Kotkai with slight loss 5 Oct.; villages burnt, enemy retiring; British casualties, 59 killed and wounded 9 Oct.; gen. McQueen advances 18 Oct.; more villages burnt; col. Crookshank dies of wounds 24 Oct.; the tribes submit and pay fines 21–30 Oct.; Gorapher peak of the Chaila mountains, 9,500 feet, taken by gen Channer 2 Nov.; return commenced 5 Nov.; final submission announced 18 Nov. ,,
Lord Dufferin at a durbar at Patiala announces the decision of the government to decline the acceptance of money from the princes; but recommends to raise the character of their armies and so to fit them to combine with the British for defence of India . . . . 18 Nov. ,,
Farewell address of 700 native ladies presented to lady Dufferin privately . . . . 4 Dec. ,,
Installation of the marquis of Lansdowne as viceroy; departure of lord Dufferin . 10 Dec. ,,
Raid of Lushais on the Chittagong border announced 23 Dec. ,,
Native Indian congress at Allahabad (moderate and illogical) opened . . . . . 26 Dec. ,,
Fortress of Quetta, a bulwark of India, finished Jan. 1889
Raid of Chittagong hill tribes on British territory near Tipperah, 24 villages destroyed, above 100 British subjects killed and 91 carried off prisoners, announced . . . . 28 Jan. ,,
Sukkur bridge opened . . . . . . 27 March, ,,
Mr. Arthur Travers Crawford, an able commissioner for 34 years in Bombay, after a long investigation, was acquitted of serious charges of financial misconduct, but was for indiscreet borrowing dismissed the service. After some correspondence the sentence was confirmed by lord Cross, secretary for India, in a despatch . . 29 March, ,,
Military expedition sent to chastise the hill tribes for their raids and the murder of lieut. Steward; object effected; reported . . . . April, ,,
Proposal for a new 4 per cent. loan (20,000,000 rupees) issued . . . . . . 1 July, ,,
Subscription list closed . . . . . 30 July, ,,
Lord Reay's condoning the native Bombay officials, who confessed themselves guilty of bribery and corruption in relation to the Crawford case, much censured, but eventually approved by the government . . . . Sept. 1889
Tantia Bheel, robber chief of the central provinces, a kind of Robin Hood, in the Holkar territory began his career about 1874; robbed the rich and helped the poor; lately suffered much, captured about 18 Aug., convicted of murder (in 1879), about 20 Oct., executed at Jubbulpore . 4 Dec. ,,
Tour of the viceroy in the N.W. provinces, Oct.; a durbar held at Quetta . . . . 19 Nov. ,,
5th native Indian Congress meets at Bombay (Mr. Bradlaugh present) . . . 26 Dec. *et seq.* ,,
Military expedition of sir R. G. Sandeman to promote commerce by opening a road through the Zhob districts, N.W. frontier, reported successful without bloodshed . . . . . 2 Feb. 1890
Treaty with China respecting Sikkim, *which see*, signed . . . . 17 March, ,,
Sir David Barbour's budget presented; a large surplus . . . . 21 March, ,,
Prince Albert Victor of Wales received at Bombay by the duke of Connaught and lord Reay; Hyderabad, 15 Nov.; Madras, 19 Nov.; Mysore, 23 Nov.; Rangoon, 20 Dec.; Mandalay, 24 Dec., 1889; Calcutta, received by the viceroy, 3 Jan. 1890; Benares, 14 Jan.; Lucknow, 18 Jan.; N.W. provinces, 20 Jan. *et seq.*; Lahore, 25 Jan.; Khyber pass, 31 Jan.; Delhi, 9 Feb.; Bombay, 22 March; embarked for home . 28 March, ,,
Expeditions (organised by gen. Gordon) to chastise the Chins and Lushais for their raids, and to form a road connecting Upper Burmah and Lower Bengal; gen. Symons proceeds from the east, gen. Tregear from the west, to form a junction, Jan.; the resistance generally feeble; the troops at times suffered much by disease; the Yokwa Chins submit to gen. Symons, 10 Jan.; peaceful surrender of Mongpunga or Lienpunga, a Lushai chief; construction of road proceeding; reconnaissances and skirmishes; 200 Hakas submit, two villages burnt; health of troops improved; junction of the two parties reported, Feb. ,,
Guerilla warfare; Haka chiefs submit . about 22 March, ,,
The Tashon chiefs submit to gen. Symons and pay fine and tribute . . reported 24 March,
Major Gordon-Cumming on convoy duty, shot dead, from an ambuscade . about 24 March, ,,
Ten days' reconnaissance of gen. Symons southward; col. Tregear at Haka . 13–16 April, ,,
The new road to Haka completed connecting Burmah and India; Haka and other posts garrisoned reported 20 April, ,,
Gen. Symons and the expedition return to India . 1 May *et seq.* ,,
Submission of Malliam-pai chiefs to gen. Tregear; raiding to cease, roads to be made, &c. 20 May, ,,
Increased agitation in India and England against Hindoo child marriages . . . . . Aug. ,,
Revolution at Manipur . . . . . . 21 Sept. ,,
Insurrection in Cambay with bloodshed, the nawab appeals to the British for help: they restore order . . . . . . reported 23 Sept. ,,
[Major Kennedy, a political officer, was authorised to redress grievances, reform the finances, &c., Jan. 1891.]
Insurrection in Manipur in N.E. state; the Maharajah abdicates in favour of his brother, who had seized the palace, &c. . . . 21–24 Sept. ,,
Eruption of the Lushais near Dalleswary river; capt. Herbert Browne killed, reinforcements sent reported 12 Sept. ,,
Lieut. Swinton killed in an attack . . 2 Oct. ,,
The Black Mountain Expedition under gen. sir J. M. M'Queen starts, 22 Oct.; returns . 3 Nov. ,,
The Zhob valley expedition under gen. White arrives at Fort Sandeman . . . . . 30 Oct. ,,
Ultimatum sent; skirmish . . . . 30 Oct. ,,
The tribes submit . . . reported 12 Nov. ,,
The Lushai party under capt. Shakespear and Mr. Pughe advance to Jadunas village, 34 miles W. of Fort White, 6 Nov.; returns successful . 20 Nov. ,,

Tour of the viceroy in the N.W., he visits Delhi, &c., Nov.; holds a durbar at Agra, 24 Nov.; Benares . . . . 4 Dec. 1890
Indian Factory commission; report with recommendations issued . . . early Dec. ,,
The principal Lushai chiefs surrender unconditionally . . . . 9 Dec. ,,
The 6th National Congress of mixed character, no government officials present, 26–30 Dec. 1890; sir A. Scoble introduces a bill into the legislative council to raise the age of consent to marriage by girls from 10 to 12 . . . . . 9 Jan. 1891
Capt. Rundall with 200 rifles marches to Lushailand about 22 Jan. ,,
A strong force marches against the marauding tribes of the Miranzai valley on the N.W. frontier about 30 Jan. ,,
Several tribes submit . about 16 Feb. *et seq.* ,,
Mukkmudin, principal chief of the Rubbia Kheyl tribe, surrenders, reported 19 Feb.; the force returns . . . . . . about 24 Feb. ,,
The important factory bill for the protection of women and children passed . . 19 March, ,,
After much public discussion, the "age of consent to marriage bill" is passed by the legislative council . . . . . . 19 March, ,,
Disastrous expedition to Manipur, *which see* March, ,,
Sir D. Barbour's financial statement; reported surplus, 20 March; he recommends a commission to consider the currency and the introduction of a gold standard, &c. . . . . . . March, ,,
Black Mountain Expedition, N.W., under gen. Elles, two columns under col. Williamson and col. Hammond, starts about 15 Jan., crosses the frontier . . . . . about 15 March, ,,
The Ghazis attack the Pioneers, slight loss, 19 March; successful movement forward 26 March, ,,
Sharp engagement, 9 soldiers killed . 5 April, ,,
Road-making party attacked, 14 sepoys killed reported 7 April, ,,
Bridge of boats over the Indus, broken up about 20 April, ,,
The party ascend the Machai peak, 9,800 feet high, a few shots exchanged, 18 April; difficult travelling, severe weather, April; huts to be constructed for the troops . . . . May, ,,
The country evacuated by the British . . Dec. ,,
Miranzai Valley Expedition.—Sir W. Lockhart with 7,000 men at Kohat preparing to resist the Orakzais and other tribes (Pathans and Afreedes); sudden attack of the tribes repulsed by the Punjaub infantry, reported 12 April; the Samana heights held by Syed Mir Basha, a fanatical priest; the Mollahs preaching a *jihad*, which see reported 12 April, ,,
Sir W. Lockhart with three columns captures some outposts, and clears the Samana ridge, col. Cramer and major Egerton severely wounded, 17, 18, April; successful fighting; the enemy dispersed and villages burnt, 19, 20 April; about 300 Orakzais killed, they disperse, and other tribes retreat . . . . 21 April *et seq.* ,,
Sir W. Lockhart advances against the very aggressive Akhel tribe; severe fighting, several villages destroyed . . . . . . 22 April, ,,
Samana range occupied; several tribes submit April, May, ,,
Sir W. Lockhart advances to punish the Shekhans, 29 April, their towers blown up; various tribes submit, accepting conditions . . . 3 May, ,,
The tribes restore stolen property, and seek for peace; all opposition ceases, reported 12 May; the troops ordered to return . . . 17 May, ,,

A representative meeting of delegates agrees to resolution to be sent to the viceroy condemning sir Joseph Pease's resolution respecting opium, adopted by the commons, 12 April (see *Opium*) 12 May, ,,
Alarming deficiency of rain, especially in Madras, Rajputana, the Punjaub, and the south, middle of July; supply of rain in north and north-west about 2 Aug. ,,
Trial of the Bangabasi newspaper for sedition concluded; jury disagree; no verdict, 24 Aug., the defendants submit and apologise . . 23 Sept. ,,
A good supply of rain in Malabar and other places about 27 Sept. 1891
The N.W. provinces relieved . . . Sept. ,,
The Hunza and Nagar tribes oppose British road-making; fighting ensues near Gilgil, N. of Cashmere; a fort of Nilt, taken by lieut.-col. Durand who is wounded; several sepoys killed . 2 Dec. ,,
Further successes of capt. Colin Mackenzie, lieut. Manners Smith and others near Nilt; about 70 natives killed; other places occupied; Jafar Khan of Nagar submits; end of the war 20–22 Dec. ,,
Seventh Indian National congress opened at Nagpur with strong professions of loyalty 28–30 Dec. ,,
Gen. sir Frederick Sleigh Roberts created a peer as Baron Roberts of Candahar . . . Feb. 1892
M. Clément Thomas, governor-general of French India, received by the viceroy at Calcutta 8 Jan. *et seq.* ,,
General mourning throughout India at the death of the duke of Clarence and Avondale . 14 Jan. ,,
Death of col. sir Robert Groves Sandeman, 29 Jan.; eulogised by the viceroy in council (see *Beloochistan*) . . . . Feb. ,,
Increased gloom in the districts threatened by famine through want of rain . Feb., March, ,,
Total employed on relief works, 32,855 . early March, ,,
Sir Juland Danvers, able government director of Indian guaranteed railway companies for fifty years, retires . . . . . 23 March, ,,
Famine relief works; persons employed; Madras, 48,000; Bombay 2,000; Bengal, 17,000; Burma, 28,000; Mysore, 13,000; Rajputana, 33,000 reported 2 April, ,,
The Hunza-Nagar rising suppressed, and order restored . . . . . reported 25 March, ,,
Desultory war with the Lushai tribes, the British under Mr. M'Cabe generally successful March, April, ,,
The Lushais attack the tea-estate at Boorooncherra and kill 52 coolies . . reported 4 April, ,,
Advance of capt. Shakespeare . . . . April, ,,
Death of gen. sir Lewis Pelly, M.P., an able official, aged 67 . . . . 22 April, ,,
Report of the Public service commission; important changes recommended . about 24 April, ,,
Extensive rising of the Lushai tribes; several conflicts, villages destroyed, about 24 April; several chiefs surrender to Mr. M'Cabe, about 26 April; tranquillity gradually restored . . 3–29 May, ,,
Rain in Bengal . . . . end of April, May, ,,
71,000 total on relief works . . . . 12 May, ,,
The maharajah of Ulwar, enlightened and loyal, dies 22 May, ,,
His heir 10 years old; his minister assassinated reported 26 May, ,,
Indian Currency Association formed to promote the abolition of silver as the sole standard in India . . . . May, ,,
The maharajah gaekwar of Baroda dines with the queen at Windsor (see above, 1874–5) . 4 July, ,,
Good monsoon; famine averted; relief works diminished . . . . July, ,,
Value of the rupee reduced to 1s. 3*d.*; great anxiety, Aug. ,,
Petition of the Currency Association to parliament respecting the depreciation of the rupee; largely signed at Calcutta, Bombay, Madras, &c., Aug. ,,
Earl of Kimberley appointed secretary for India, 18 Aug. ,,
Expedition of 5,000 men (the Isazai field force) against the Black Mountain tribes; organized under col. sir W. Lockhart marches . 1 Oct. ,,
Sir W. Lockhart occupies and destroys Baio, 5 Oct.; the force returns, reported . . . 8 Oct. ,,
The Indian Currency committee (lord chancellor Herschell, Mr. Leonard Courtney, sir Thomas Farrer, and others) meets . . . . 27 Oct. ,,
Opposition of natives in Bengal against restriction of the jury system; ordered . . 10 Nov. ,,
Tour of the viceroy; he visits Hyderabad, Mysore, Madras . . . . Nov. ,,
Fighting on the N. W. frontier; tribes repulsed, Nov. ,,

Major-general sir George Stewart White appointed commander-in-chief in succession to lord Roberts, Dec. 1892
Calcutta: visit of the maharajah of Mysore, 26 Dec. „
The jury question referred to the home government, about . . . . . 27 Dec. „
[A commission appointed, Feb. 1893.]
Eighth Indian National congress meets at Allahabad; claims increased representation, &c., 30, 31 Dec. „
Col. Turner occupies Bulandkhel on the Afghan borders . . . . . . 6 Jan. 1893
British intervention in Chitral (*which see*) . Jan. „
Farewell of gen. lord Roberts to deputations at Lahore . . . . 9 Jan. „
Deputation of officials, respecting the depreciation of the rupee, received by the viceroy . 31 Jan. „
Sir William Hunter, at the Society of Arts, describes the great progress of India since 1858 under the government by the crown, in relation to territory, army, credit, native government and law, commerce, morals, education and literature, 16 Feb. „
Farewell dinner to lord Roberts at Calcutta; large subscriptions for an equestrian statue, 11 March; leaves Bombay . . . . . . 8 April, „
The tribes defeated in an attack on Chilas, a N. W. fort, with above 150 killed; major Averell Daniell and 22 others killed, 4 March; major Twigg in command of the garrison . July, „
Sir David Barbour's budget, 1893–4; expected deficit, about 1,595,100 rupees; presented 23 March, „
The Bengal jury commission in their report approve of the old system, and recommend the removal of the restrictions, with some amendments (this is adopted by government) . . 28 March *et seq.* „
Gen. sir George White arrives at Bombay, 2 April, „
Disturbances at Keunjhar, in Orissa . 10 May, „
The sultan of Johore and other princes were present at the inauguration of the Imperial institute, 10 May; and at the duke of York's wedding, 6 July, „
The re-arming of the troops proceeding . July, „
Indian currency committee report received at Calcutta; sir D. Barbour introduces a bill adopting its recommendations, suspending free coinage of silver, to accept gold for silver at the rate of 16*d.* for the rupee; a gold standard to be established; bill passed, well received . . 26 June, „
Abdication of the khan of Khelat; succeeded by his son, Mir Mahmud, reported . . 15 Aug. „
Scheme for compensation to government servants for loss by the rate of exchange for the rupee, announced . . . . 20 Aug. „
Sir Henry Norman declines the appointment as viceroy in succession to lord Lansdowne . Sept. „
The earl of Elgin appointed viceroy, about 11 Oct. „
The East India loan bill (10,000,000*l.*) passed, 21 Dec. „
The 9th Indian national congress meets at Lahore; 1,000 delegates present; Mr. Naoroji, M.P., president . . . . 27 Dec. „
Skirmish with the Abor tribesmen on the border of Assam; 7 of the military police killed at Bamjur . . . . 2 Jan. 1894
Dumbak and Silluk captured by capt. Maxwell's force . . . . Jan. „
The earl of Elgin arrives at Calcutta . . 25 Jan. „
Departure of lord and lady Lansdowne (greatly regretted) from Calcutta . . . 27 Jan. „
James Fairbairn Finlay, finance minister . Jan. „
Nine of the Bengal infantry, 6 police, and 8 followers, killed by the Abors at Bordak, and 19 prisoners carried off from Duffla . . 27 Feb. „
Villages burnt by capt. Maxwell's force, reported 8 March, „
Safe arrival of capt. Maxwell's punitive expedition at Sadiya . . . . . . 16 March, „
Revenue, 1893–4: improvement in land and railways; loss in opium and salt, reported, 21 March, „
The Lansdowne hospital at Udaipur, constructed by the maharana of the Rajput states, opened, March, „
Failure of the wheat harvest in the N. central provinces, reported . . . . . 12 April, „
Destructive storm in N. W. India, with loss of life, and railways blocked, reported . . 23 July, „
See *Himalayas.*

The interest on loans, &c., converted from 4 to 3½ per cent.; above 91½ millions had been converted, Nov. 1894
An attack of 2,000 Mahsud Waziris on col. A. H. Turner's delimitation party (Afghan frontier) defeated at Wano; 350 killed; British loss, lieut. P. J. F. Macaulay and 44 men . . 3 Nov. „
Punitive expedition under sir Wm. Lockhart into Waziristan against the Mahsuds, and to carry out the demarcation . . . . . . 17 Dec. „
Makin destroyed; desultory fighting . 21, 22 Dec. „
First medical congress at Calcutta; opened by the viceroy; great improvement in public health through sanitation since 1868, reported, 24–29 Dec. „
Tenth Indian national congress opened at Madras; 1,150 delegates; Mr. Webb, M.P., president, 26 Dec. „
A customs duty of 5 per cent. (abolished in 1882) on imported cotton goods, and a countervailing excise duty of 5 per cent. on certain classes of cotton goods manufactured in India, imposed by the legislative council to increase the revenue suffering by the depreciation of the rupee; bills passed . . . . . . about 27 Dec. „
Public debt, 116,000,000*l.*; assets (railways, irrigation works, canals, &c.), 185,500,000*l.*; uncovered debt, 35,750,000*l.*; interest reduced from 4 to 3½ per cent.; deficit caused by depreciation of the rupee; *Mr. H. Fowler* . 29 Jan. 1895
Sir Henry James's motion in the commons against the cotton duty negatived, 304—109 . 21 Feb. „
A gathering of about 700 tribesmen (Waziristan) surrenders to col. Egerton . . . 8 Jan. „
Sir Wm. Lockhart issues an ultimatum to the Mahsud chiefs at Wano, 21 Jan.; his terms accepted . . . . 5 March, „
Delimitation concluded of the southern border, 12 Feb. „
Col. sir Henry Creswicke Rawlinson, diplomatist and Oriental scholar; born 11 April, 1810; died, 5 March, „
Gen. sir George T. Chesney, M.P., statesman and military expert; author of "Indian Polity," 1868, the source of many reforms; born 1830; died, 31 March, „
E. India railway, from Tarakeswar to Magra (the first constructed by native capital and engineers), opened by the lieut.-gov. of Bengal, sir Chas. Elliott . . . . 2 April, „
A royal commission appointed to inquire into the administration and expenditure of the Indian army; lord Welby, chairman . about 11 May, „
Secretary of state, lord George Hamilton, 25 June, „
Sir Jaswant Singh Bahadur, maharajah of Jodhpur, an able ruler, much lamented, died . . Oct. „
Punitive expedition against Kairuma, a hostile chief, in the N. Lushai hills . . . Dec. „
The 11th Indian national congress opened at Poona; 1,600 delegates, Surendra Nath Bannerji, president . . . . 27 Dec. „
Bills for the revision of the cotton duties introduced by sir James Westland, 23 Jan.; passed, 3 Feb. 1896
Death of the maharajah of Bhownugger, aged 38, a wise, enlightened ruler . . . 29 Jan. „
Great distress through want of winter rains in N. W. and Central provinces, Rajputana, etc.; 296,000 employed on relief works . . March–May, „
Sir James Westland's budget, improved revenue prospects; annual famine grant to be renewed, 18, 19 March, „
Royal commission appointed, 19 May; see *Indian Expenditure* . . . . . . 19 May, „
The home government decides that the Indian government shall partly support the Indian troops sent to Suakin, 30 June; India protests, *Times* . . . . 3 July, „
Death of lieut.-gen. sir W. K. Elles, an eminent officer, at Naini Tal, N.W.P. . . 5 Aug. „
Indian budget passed by the British parliament: prosperity and solvency; reported . Aug. „
Sanari station, Quetta railway, attacked by Marris, massacre of the staff and men on the line; troops called out; reported . . . . 17 Oct. „
Death of Mr. M. Ghose, first native barrister, 9 Nov. „

The legislative council pass a bill raising the paper currency from 8 to 10 crores of rupees 17 Dec. 1896
12th Indian national congress opened at Calcutta, 700 delegates . . . . 28 Dec. ,,
[INDIAN FAMINE:
Famine prospect through failure of rains, in Oudh, Punjab, N.W. and Central provinces, relief works, construction of wells, railways, etc., opened; 66,900 employed . . . . 8 Nov. ,,
Irrigation of the Punjab, reported, successful; some relief by storms and rains in Madras, Bombay, Bengal, and Behar . . . Nov., Dec. ,,
Appeal from the Indian government to Great Britain for aid . . . . . . 23 Dec. ,,
New relief works opened; energetic official action; total on relief, 404,200, 21 Dec.; 2,000,000, 29 Jan.; 4,500,000, June; 3,303,968, 13 July, 1897.
National fund opened at the Mansion house (*which see*), 8 Jan. *et seq.* 1897; relief committees founded in Russia, Canada, Glasgow, Singapore, and other places.
Famine relief fund organised at Calcutta, the queen-empress, patroness, the viceroy, president, 13 Jan. 1897
Great meeting at the Mansion house, London, duke of Connaught and lord George Hamilton, present; report; famine affected area, 164,000 sq. mi., population, 36,000,000; area of scarcity, 121,000 sq. mi.; population, 44,000,000; the government spending 100,000 rupees daily on relief 16 Jan. ,,
Blue book issued relating to famine . . 10 Jan. ,,
Energetic action of sir Anthony Macdonnell in N.W. Provinces and Oudh, one-and-a-half million on relief or public works (18 distressed districts), Feb. ,,
Many deaths in the central native states and Bundelkhand district; famine severe in S. Punjab, government works efficient . . . . Feb. ,,
Monsoon and general rains reported in all affected districts, 28 June; good crops expected; famine ceasing . . . . . . Aug., Sept. ,,
Total relief fund from all sources estimated, 1,500,000*l.*; 4,500,000 persons relieved in June: total cost to the Indian government, estimated 10,000,000*l.* sterling; reported at the Mansion house . . . . 7 Oct. ,,
A letter of thanks from sir Francis Maclean, chief justice of India, *Times*, 10 Nov. . . . . ,,
Contributions, including 773,000*l.* British, and 1,000*l.* from the queen, about 1,750,000*l.*, reported 30 Dec. [final report, and thanks from the viceroy, received 15th July, 1898] . . ,,
[Famine relief cost: 5,390,000 Rx.; against a budget estimate of 3,640,000 Rx.; for 1897–8; reported, 20 March, 1898.]
Death of Mr. James Talboys Wheeler, historian of India . . . . 13 Jan. ,,
Death of gen. sir Robt. Phayre, aged 77 28 Jan. ,,
Indian plague bill passed at Calcutta . 4 Feb. ,,
Epidemic diseases act, passed . . . . Feb. ,,
A loan authorised by the government for improving docks, etc., at Kidderpur . . . . 8 Feb. ,,
Plague localized in Bombay and Lower Scinde; decreasing, 9 March; see *Bombay* and *Plague*, 1896–7.
Thanks of native members in the legislative council, for liberal aid, from England and other countries, during the famine . . . . . 26 March, ,,
Irrigation of 3,000,000 acres by canals in N.W. Provinces, announced . . . . . April, ,,
Mahomed Afzul, Afghan by birth, eminent general and diplomatist in the British service; born, 1834, died . . . . April, ,,
General warm expression of loyalty to the queen-empress throughout India . . . . April, ,,
Treacherous attack of Waziris on Mr. Gee, political officer, and his escort, at Maizar, in the Tochi valley, N.W. frontier; lieut.-col. A. C. Bunny, capt. J. F. Browne, lieuts. H. A. Cruickshank and Higginson, and 22 others killed; escort retired under 4 hrs. sharp fighting to Dattakhel; 50 Waziris killed . . . . . . 10 June, ,,
Tochi punitive expedition: 6,000 men under major-gen. Corrie Bird, col. Egerton, and col. Symons; proclamation issued; 50 tribesmen captured, 3 July; British sentinels killed, 6 July; Maizar found deserted, 20 July; Sadda Khan and other chiefs, surrender conditionally, 1–14 Nov. . . ,,
Extensive shocks of earthquake: widespread ruin; Calcutta and Assam (*which see*), 1897; over 1,542 deaths . . . . 12–18 June, 1897
Diamond jubilee celebrated throughout India, release of prisoners, durbahs, etc. . . 22 June, ,,
Contagious diseases bill passed legislative council, 22 July, ,,
[FRONTIER WAR; Fanatical rising of the "mullah's followers" in the Swat valley, night attack on Malakand, repulsed; major Taylor, lieut.-col. John Lamb, lieut. Manley, and 13 men killed, 26 July; severe fighting, rapid march of the Guides from Maidan, 27 July; enemy repulsed with heavy loss . . . . 29 July, ,,
Field force (8,000) organised, under major-gen. sir Bindon Blood and others . . . 30 July, ,,
Rebels driven with great loss from the hills about Malakand . . . . 31 July, ,,
Chakdara fort besieged, 26 July, by Pathans, over 3,000 killed; gallant defence (7 men killed during the siege), relieved by gen. Meiklejohn 2 Aug. ,,
Shabkadr fort attacked by 6,000 Afghans and Mohmands, 7 Aug.; enemy routed, after a sharp fight, and brilliant cavalry charge, by gen. Elles: lieut.-col. Wood, and 3 British killed . 9 Aug. ,,
Government friendly remonstrance, heartily accepted by the ameer . . . . 16 Aug. ,,
Landikai occupied, after a desperate fight with 3,000 tribesmen; great heroism; lieuts. Greaves and Maclean killed . . . . . 17 Aug. ,,
Surrender of tribes in the Upper Swat valley, arms brought in . . . . Aug. ,,
Fort Maude and other outposts in the Khyber pass, captured by the Afridis, 23 Aug.; the Afridis shelled and dispersed by gen. Westmacott's force, 24, 25 Aug. ,,
Landi Kotal, and other small native forts, raided by Afridis, in the Khyber pass . . 25 Aug. ,,
Small police posts burnt by Orakzais, E. and W. of the Samana range, 26 Aug.; severe fighting in the Ublan pass, great heroism of medical officers and others . . . . 27 Aug. ,,
Four disturbed areas: Quetta, Kuram pass, the Orakzai, Afridi, and Mohmand hills, and the Swat valley; fines paid, and arms surrendered at Uch, and Swat valley . . . Aug.–1 Sept. ,,
Enemy repulsed by gen. Yeatman-Biggs, with heavy loss, in the Samana hills 2, 3, 11 Sept. ,,
Native states offer support to the government 5 Sept. ,,
Saraghari post on the Samana taken by the enemy (180 killed); the garrison, 21 Sikhs, died fighting to the last, 12 Sept.; post re-captured by gen. Yeatman-Biggs, forts Gulistan and Lockhart also relieved, large forces of the enemy driven back . . . . 14 Sept. ,,
Night attack on gen. Jeffrey's brigade in the Rambat pass; lieuts. Wm. E. Tompkins, A. W. Bailey, H. A. Harrington killed, 14 Sept; enemy (6,000) routed after a severe fight, lieuts. Hughes and A. T. Crawford killed; total loss, 144, 16 Sept. ,,
Gundab fort occupied, without opposition, by gen. Elles, after a trying march into the Mohmand country . . . . 15 Sept. ,,
Gen. sir Wm. Lockhart appointed commander in succession to sir George White . . 17 Sept. ,,
Gen. Jeffrey drives the enemy from Damodota; Umra Khan's fort blown up, towers, etc. destroyed . . . . 18 Sept. ,,
Message from the queen expressing sympathy with the troops . . . . 19 Sept. ,,
Attacks by about 4,000 of Hadda Mullah's force on sir B. Blood's camp at Nawagai, repulsed, 19, 20 Sept. ,,
Gen. Elles drives the Mohmands from the Badmanai pass and captures the heights . 23 Sept. ,,
The enemy completely dispersed, flight of the 2 Mullahs . . . . 24 Sept. ,,
Jarobi and forts, etc., destroyed by gen. Westmacott's brigade . . . . . 25 Sept. ,,
Submission of tribes in the Swat valley, 25 Sept.–2 Oct. ,,
The ameer refuses help asked by the Afridis and others . . . . Sept. ,,
Punitive operations: 15 towers, etc., destroyed, 29 Sept. ,,

Agrah and Gat taken after a severe fight; enemy 2,000 strong; lieut.-col. O'Bryen and lieut. Browne-Clayton and others, killed . 30 Sept. 1897

Badelai in the Mohmand valley stormed, all the fortifications, etc. destroyed . . 3 Oct. ,,

Mohmand campaign (3 weeks) ended; 72 towers, 40 forts destroyed, arms captured, and fines paid. Oct. ,,

Gen. sir Wm. Lockhart arrives at Samana to command the Tirah expedition against the Afridis and Orakzais for breaking the treaty of 1881 10 Oct. ,,

Capt. Fred. Newcome Jones and corporal John Walton killed on patrol . . . . 10 Oct. ,,

Settlement with the Mohmands completed, arms surrendered . . . . Oct. ,,

Sir A. Palmer drives the enemy (about 8,000) from Chagru defile and Dargai heights with severe loss; major Jennings-Bramly killed . 18 Oct. ,,

The enemy re-occupied Dargai and Chagru on the withdrawal of the troops, and were again driven from the ridge with great loss, after a desperate fight, great heroism shown, the heights won in 40 minutes by a gallant dash of the Gordon Highlanders under lieut.-col. Mathias, and others, through a murderous fire; major C. B. Judge, capts. J. G. Robinson and W. E. Smith, lieut. A.L. Lamont and 33 men killed . . 20 Oct. ,,

Re-opening of the Indian mint for silver recommended by U.S.A. and French governments, July; declined . . . . Oct. ,,

The difficult and strongly-defended Sampagha pass captured, capt. De Butts and 4 others killed, 29 Oct.; the Arhanga pass taken . 30 Oct. ,,

Guerilla fighting; Tirah, Maidan occupied, Afridis dispersed . . . . 5 Nov. ,,

Firing into camp, lieut. Giffard and capt. E. Y. Watson (entomologist) killed . . 6 Nov. ,,

Picket of one native officer and 35 Sikhs massacred in the Karmana defile, their retreat was cut off by a jungle fire . . . . . 7 Nov. ,,

Sixty hamlets and towers destroyed, severe loss inflicted on the enemy in the Arhanga pass, 8 Nov. ,,

Saran Sar occupied with slight resistance, but on retiring, sir Wm. Lockhart's and gen. Westmacott's brigades were fiercely attacked, the Northamptons and Sikhs bravely covering the withdrawal; lieuts. A. H. Macintire, J. T. Waddell and 18 men killed, enemy's loss severe, 9 Nov.; successful reconnoissance, villages destroyed . . . . 11 Nov. ,,

The Orakzai and Afridi jirgahs received by sir Wm. Lockhart at Maidan, terms of submission announced . . . 12 and 21 Nov. ,,

General Kempster's force attacked by Zakka-khels and Akakhels in the Tseri-Kandao pass, capt. N. A. Lewarne, lieuts. R. E. A. Hales, G. D. Crooke, G M. Wylie and 25 men killed . . 16 Nov. ,,

Northamptons, Dorsets, Sikhs and Gurkhas highly commended . . . . . 17 Nov. ,,

March of gen. Westmacott's force to Datoi, 3 days' fighting, etc., lieut. D. E. O. Jones killed 22–24 Nov. ,,

Lozaka pass cleared after a sharp fight by gen. Gaselee's brigade, 5 killed . . 26, 27 Nov. ,,

Col. Spurgin's rearguard encounters heavy fighting over the Kotal hills, 4 killed . . . 29 Nov. ,,

Chamkanni valley taken, villages burnt, lieut. R. M. Battye killed, enemy routed . . 1, 2 Dec. ,,

The Afridis' towers, etc. destroyed in the Waran and Rajgul valleys . . . . 8, 9. Dec. ,,

Gen. Lockhart's proclamation to the Afridis issued, 11 Dec. ,,

Severe attacks on gen. Kempster's rearguard, 9 killed; lieut. West killed at Mamani, 11, 13 Dec. ,,

Operations over in the Tirah district, forces withdrawn . . . . 19 Dec. ,,

The heights from Fort Maude to Ali Mesjid occupied by the British . . . . 23 Dec. ,,

Gen. Lockhart moves up the Khyber pass without opposition, 24 Dec.; defeats the Madda-khels in the Alachi pass; enemy repulsed with heavy loss in the Bazar valley; Landi Kotal fort destroyed by gen. Hammond's column . . 27 Dec. ,,

The 13th Indian national congress meets at Amrati; Mr. Sankaran Nayar president; frontier policy condemned; thanks for famine relief, etc. 27–29 Dec. ,,

Sir Henry Havelock-Allen, M.P., aged 67, son of gen. Havelock, left his escort near the Khyber pass, killed by Afridis . . . . . 30 Dec. 1897

Zakka-khel villages, etc. destroyed by gen. Hammond's force; hard fight in the Khyber pass, 3 men killed . . . . 30, 31 Dec. ,,

Major D. W. Hickman killed while out on convoy duty . . . . 3 Jan. 1898

Death, from exposure, of gen. Yeatman-Biggs, aged 54, at Peshawar . . . . . Jan. ,,

The enemy surprised and the Persai pass taken by col. Adams . . . . . . 6 Jan. ,,

The Tanga pass taken and 2 standards of the enemy, by gen. sir B. Blood . . . 7 Jan. ,,

Large investiture of honours, speech by the viceroy, at Calcutta . . . . . 13 Jan. ,,

Gen. Jeffreys receives the full submission of the Chamlawals at the Ambela pass . . 17 Jan. ,,

Guerilla warfare carried on by the Zakka-khels in the Khyber pass . . . . . . Jan. ,,

Government terms complied with by the Afridis and the Bonerwals; gen. Blood's force withdraws from Boner . . . . . 19 Jan. ,,

Sir J. Westland's currency bill (notes against gold), with a proviso, passed . . 21 Jan. ,,

Successful advance of 3 columns to clear the Kajurai plain; the 4th from Mamani, attacked by Afridis in the Shin Kamar pass, Bazar valley, lieut.-col. J. Haughton, lieuts. Turing, Dowdall, Hughes, Walker, 28 Yorkshires and 2 Sikhs killed; enemy's loss, 30 . . . . . 29 Jan. ,,

Sir Wm. Lockhart at Calcutta eulogises the conduct of the army during the late difficult campaign . . . . 31 Jan. ,,

Operations in Mekran; enemy completely routed, at Gok Parosh, by a small force under lieut.-col. Mayne . . . . mid-Feb. ,,

Tochi expedition: 3 British officers, over 100 soldiers, 50 natives, and others, died from sickness; troops highly commended for their endurance, etc. . . . . 11 Feb. ,,

[Losses on the frontier: 684 British, including 43 officers, killed: 90 wounded, 12 men missing, and 1,233 native troops killed, from 10 June, 1897–7 Feb. 1898.]

Sedition (press law) amendment act passed, 18 Feb. ,,

Indian postal system greatly extended in the late 12 years, reported . . . . . 25 Feb. ,,

Sir Wm. Lockhart's despatches on the Tirah campaign published . . . . . . 4 March, ,,

The Khyber pass reported peaceful; pass to be open from . . . . 11 March ,,

Sir W. Lockhart gives a jirgah of all sections of the tribes their final choice of peace or war, 12 March, ,,

Criminal procedure bill passed by the legislative council . . . . 12 March, ,,

The Ranjar dacoity gang (about 2 years' trial) finally convicted; 70 transported for life . . 16 March, ,,

Sir J. Westland's budget statement, 21 March; he declares a silver standard, or the re-opening of the mints impossible; the viceroy refers the question to London, and defends the Indian government and army, 28 March; a departmental committee of inquiry into the monetary system of India agreed to in the commons . 29 March, ,,

Payment of fines and surrender of rifles by the Afridis, completed . . . . . 1 April, ,,

Sir Wm. Lockhart's friendly farewell of the Afridis, 4 April, ,,

Sir Saiyid Ahmad, social reformer, eminent Mahometan friend of England, born 1817; K.C.S.I. 1888, died . . . . April, ,,

Indian currency committee appointed, sir Henry Fowler, chairman . . . . . 29 April, ,,

Great fire at Peshawar (25 hrs.), 4,000 houses burnt, 31 May, ,,

Act passed for a loan of 10,000,000*l.* to meet losses by famine, plague, earthquakes, and war . 1 July, ,,

Budget estimate, 1898–9, revenue, 99,085,400 Rx.; expenditure, 98,194,000 Rx.; Mr. F. S. Wilde, engineer, murdered by Pathans in the N. Cachar hills . . . . 12 July, ,,

Fighting between the tribal forces of the Nawab of Dir and the Bajauris in the Jhandol valley; 136 Bajauris and 31 of the Dir forces killed, 24 July; quiet reported . . . . . 16 Aug. ,,

Indian currency commission: evidence issued as a blue book . . . . 25 Aug. ,,

Inland postage to be reduced from . 1 Oct. 1898

Sir Wm. Lockhart appointed commander-in-chief, Oct. ,,

Outbreak of plague in Madras and Mysore, see *Seringapatam* . . . . 18 Nov. ,,

Indian plague commission, Dr. Thos. Fraser, F.R.S., president, arrives at Bombay . 26 Nov. ,,

The Hadda Mullah crosses the Swat river; serious fighting with native forces, losses on both sides, 25, 26 Nov.; British reinforcements sent to Chakdara and Malakand, 1 Dec.; the Mullah's force defeated by native forces, 1–7 Dec.; he is finally expelled from the Swat valley, and retreats into Kokistan . . . . 10 Dec. ,,

Royal Indian famine commission's report, with recommendations, issued . . early Dec. ,,

Maharajah of Darbhangah, loyal benefactor, born 1856, died . . . . 16 Dec. ,,

Jirgahs of all the Swat clans swear to major Deane at Thana not to assist the Mullah in any rising, 17 Dec. ,,

Indian national congress meets at Madras, 28 Dec. ,,

Mr. J. M. Tata offers property worth 200,000*l.* on trust, to found an Indian university of research, and also to endow it with an annual income of 125,000 rx.; other subscriptions promised, 31 Dec. 1878; bill drafted . . . . Jan. 1899

Lord Curzon appointed viceroy Aug. 1898; welcomed at Calcutta . . . . 3 Jan. ,,

Gomatti, a village, seized and 7 outlaws captured; 6 British killed; towers, &c., destroyed, 5, 8 Feb. ,,

Punitive expedition against the Chamkanni tribe for raids; 9 villages destroyed, 100 prisoners taken . . . . 1 March, ,,

Countervailing duties on imported bounty-fed sugar, passed by the council, comes into operation . . . . 20 March, ,,

Col. sir R. Warburton, born 1842, distinguished for his able management of the Afridis and security of the Khyber pass, 1879–97, served in the Tirah expedition 1897–8, died . . . 22 April, ,,

Dacoit raids frequent: conference at Agra . July, ,,

Indian currency commission, Aug. 1898; their report in favour of a gold standard, the sovereign to be legal tender, legal rate for the rupee to be 1s. 4*d.*, adopted by government . 25 July, ,,

New frontier policy, tribal militias substituted for regulars at frontier garrisons . . . Aug. ,,

Peaceful settlement arranged at a meeting between the khan of Nawagai and the Nawab of Dir, after some conflicts . . . . early Aug. ,,

Lord George Hamilton's financial statement; large surplus for 1898–99, 4,759,000 rx., due to reduced expenditure, &c. . . . . . 8 Aug. ,,

Currency conversion act (gold made a legal tender, the rupee fixed at 16d.) passed (made permanent 1900) . . . . 15 Sept. ,,

See *Landslips* . . . . Sept. ,,

Raid of Bhils near Khergaum, severe fighting, many killed, reported . . . . 29 Sept. ,,

Thanks from the home government for prompt dispatch of troops to S. Africa . early Oct. ,,

The viceroy holds a durbar at Lucknow . 13 Dec. ,,

15th Indian national congress opened at Lucknow, 27 Dec. ,,

The queen thanks her Indian subjects for their loyalty . . . . Dec. ,,

[*Indian famine* through drought (1899–1901): severe in Bombay, Central Provinces, Punjaub, and elsewhere, began Sept. 1899; the government and its officers prompt and energetic in relieving distress and saving life; total on relief works, &c., 3,563,000, Jan. 1900; famine area, 420,000 sq. mi.; population, 62,000,000; relief fund started; 465,000 rx. subscribed at a meeting in Calcutta, the viceroy presiding, 16 Feb.; see *Mansion house*, 1900; central relief committee received about 1,000,000*l.* sterling; liberal gifts from abroad, about 25,000*l.* raised on the emperor's initiative in Germany, May; total on relief, 6,356,000, 7 Aug.; declining, Sept.; 2,292,000, 16 Oct.; India subscribes 32 lakhs, reported, 19 Oct.]

Loyal meeting of Hindus and Mahometans at Calcutta; fine speech by the maharajah of Darbhanga, 63,000 rs. subscribed to the Transvaal war fund . . . . 27 Jan. 1900

Lumsden's Horse (volunteers) leaves Calcutta for S. Africa . . . . 26 Feb. ,,

Indian plague commission reports favourably on Mr. Haffkine's inoculation system, thousands inoculated, *Times* . . . 5 March, 1900

Death of sir Wm. Lockhart, able commander-in-chief, aged 59 . . . . . 18 March, ,,

The maharajah of Jaipur presents 15 lakhs, *in trust*, towards the famine fund, to be permanent, announced . . . . . . 19 March, ,,

Legislative council opened by the viceroy; Mr. Clinton Dawkins, able finance minister, reports increase of trade, &c.; budget for 1898–99, 2,641,000*l.* surplus . . . . 21 March, ,,

Report of the royal commission (1895) on Indian expenditure, proposed grant of 50,000*l.* a year to the India office, issued . . . . 9 April, ,,

Lord Curzon holds a durbar at Quetta; exhorts the chiefs to settle feuds and to stop murderous Ghazi raids, &c. . . . . . 12 April, ,,

Plague riots in Cawnpore, the segregation camp destroyed by the mob, 5 constables killed, troops called out, 10 deaths, 11 April; plague regulations modified . . . . . mid April, ,,

Famine expenditure by Indian government, 13,000,000*l.* ann. . . . . . 26 July, ,,

The viceroy visits the famine centres and relief works in Gujarat . . . . . 2–4 Aug. ,,

Government committee *re* the proposed sugar industry in Behar meets in Calcutta . 15 Oct. ,,

Punjab land alienation act, to prevent land passing into the hands of non-agriculturalists, passed, 19 Oct. ,,

Mahsud Wazari raids on N.W. frontier frequent; lieut. Hennessey killed . . . . 23 Oct. ,,

Death of the maharajah of Patiala . . . 7 Nov. ,,

The viceroy's tour round India, about 6,000 mi., very successful . . . mid Oct.–17 Dec. ,,

Blockade against the Mahsuds in Waziristan, 1 Dec. *et seq.* ,,

Universal mourning on the death of the queen-empress Victoria . . . 22 Jan.–2 Feb. 1901

The king-emperor thanks the princes and people of India for loyalty and assistance in the S. African war . . . . 4 Feb. ,,

Lord Curzon proposes a memorial to queen Victoria at a meeting in Calcutta, large donations received, 6 Feb. ,,

New North-west Frontier province, see *Punjaub*, Feb.–Nov. ,,

Budget: 1899–1900, surplus, 2,774,623*l.*; 1900–1901, surplus, 1,670,000*l.* . . . . 20 March, ,,

Gen. sir A. Palmer appointed commander-in-chief, March, ,,

The mines bill (1899), modified, passed . 22 March, ,,

Indian Famine 1899–1900: commission appointed, sir Anthony Macdonnell and others, Dec. 1900, report issued; great mortality in Gujarat and Bombay province, estimated deaths, 1,250,000; the great future problem being to relieve the pressure of the population on the soil; 509,559,000 gratuitously relieved; 625,794,000 on relief works, 8 May, ,,

Indian Famine Union, to investigate cause and means of prevention, meets in London, 7 June, ,,

Scheme for an imperial cadet corps of the sons of Indian princes and nobles; royal assent, reported . . . . . . 18 July, ,,

Kashmir Kar, British post in the Gomal Pass, raided by Mahsud Waziris, 7 men killed, 6 Aug. ,,

Lord G. Hamilton's financial statement; estimated loss in W. India by 3 years' drought, 50,000,000*l.*; relief expenditure, 15,000,000*l.*, met without additional taxation . . . . . 16 Aug. ,,

Cooper's Hill college controversy, compensation claimed by civil engineers; parliamentary paper published, see *Times* . . . . 7 Sept. ,,

Jhelam irrigation canal at Rasul opened, 29 Oct. ,,

Sepoys ambushed by Waziri Mahsuds near the Gomal Pass, 24 and 6 other persons killed, 3 Nov. ,,

Sir Antony Macdonnell retires from India after 36 years' eminent service . . . 14 Nov. ,,

Scientific plague commission commenced local investigation, 29 Nov. 1898; full report issued, with recommendations, *Times* . . 13 Nov. ,,

Punative operations against the Mahsuds in Waziristan, 192 prisoners taken, villages, &c. destroyed, 25–27 Nov.; further fighting, 7 villages and towers destroyed . . . 5, 6 Dec. ,,

The viceroy tours through the North-Eastern provinces, early Nov.; welcomed at Manipur, 15 Nov.; holds durbars at Mandalay, 27 Nov.; Rangoon . . . . 9 Dec. 1901

Nodiz fort in Mekran seized by Persian raiders, recaptured by the British; Mahomet Ali, the leader, and others, killed, 63 captured, the rest dispersed, 20 Dec. ,,

Indian National congress (over 5,000 present) held at Calcutta . . . . 26-28 Dec. ,,

Indian mines act (government inspection, &c.) passed . . . . ,,

Commission to report on the work of the universities and colleges, appointed . . . Jan. 1902

Mahsud Waziris submit, British lost 31 killed, blockade withdrawn . . . early March, ,,

Budget: surplus for 1901-02, 4,900,000*l*. . April, ,,

British force ambushed by outlaws on the Mahsud frontier, 8 killed, reported . . . 8 April, ,,

The Berar question settled, the nizam of Haidarabad cedes all territorial claims and receives 30 lakhs rupees annually, reported . . 17 April, ,,

The rajah of Panna deposed and imprisoned for inciting to poison his uncle, the late rajah (June, 1901), reported . . . . . . 22 April, ,,

Lord Curzon holds a durbar at Peshawar and explains the government policy towards the frontier tribes . . . . . 26 April, ,,

Sugar duties bill (German and Austrian) passed, 6 June, ,,

Reforms and progress in India; generous government grants, reported . . . . June, ,,

Swami Vivekananda, a religious reformer and denouncer of the caste system, died, aged 36, 4 July, ,,

Loan of 150 lakhs of rupees subscribed 3 times over, 9 July, ,,

Commission of inquiry into police reform, appointed . . . . . . about 6 July, ,,

Blue-book report of the famine and relief operations, 1900–1902; excess mortality during 12 months' drought, 750,000, including 230,000 deaths from cholera and smallpox, issued, 6 Aug. ,,

Indian princes received by the king and queen, London . . . . 12 Aug. ,,

Blue-book, loans to native rulers during famine 1899–1900, 2,333,000*l*., reported . . 23 Aug. ,,

The queen wrote to lady Curzon:—"The Indian coronation robes you so kindly designed are perfect, and make the most brilliant effect. I am so proud at wearing an Indian dress on this great occasion. I hope you will make this known in India"—*Times* . . . . 2 Sept. ,,

Good rains, 21 Aug.; crop reports favourable, Sept. ,,

Number on famine relief, 5,660,000, 29 Aug.; 58,000, 13 Nov. ,,

Mr. Nowrojee M. Wadia offers about a million sterling to a trust for the relief of those deprived of subsistence *by any sudden calamity*, reported, 23 Sep. ,,

The viceroy's tour in Central India ends; he visits Rajputana . . . . 7 Nov. ,,

Lord George Hamilton's good budget; estimated surplus for 1902–3, 1,700,000*l*. . . 10 Nov. ,,

Punitive Kabul-Khel Waziri expedition for raids, &c.; prisoners captured, Gumati fort stormed and destroyed; capt. White killed, col. Tonnochy mortally wounded, 4 Sepoys killed, 17, 18 Nov.; operations closed successfully, 59 towers, &c., destroyed . . . . . 29 Nov. ,,

Lord Kitchener, commander-in-chief, arrives; army manœuvres at Delhi, . 28 Nov.–Dec. ,,

Death of the rajah of Mandi . . . . 10 Dec. ,,

Decennial missionary conference for India, Ceylon, Burma and Arabia held at Madras . 11 Dec. ,,

Death of the Haddah Mullah, N.W. frontier 22 Dec. ,,

Indian national congress meets in Bombay 24 Dec. ,,

STATE ENTRY of the viceroy, the duke and duchess of Connaught into Delhi, 50 native princes and chiefs . . . . 29 Dec. ,,

Indian art exhibition opened by the viceroy, 30 Dec. ,,

CORONATION DURBAR, King Edward VII. proclaimed emperor at Delhi (and throughout India) with great splendour and rejoicings; over 100 Indian rulers, about 600 *Mutiny* veterans, and a vast and brilliant assemblage present; investiture of honours, the Nizam of Haidarabad made a G.C.B., lord Geo. Hamilton, and the rajah of Cochin, G.C.S.I., the rajahs of Travancore and Nabha, G.C.I.E., and 8 knighted; 16,188 prisoners released, and many others in native states 1 Jan. 1903

Durbar closed . . . . 9 Jan. ,,

The duke and duchess of Connaught visit Peshawar, Meerut, 11 Jan.; other places, 18-19 Jan.; Bombay . . . . 19-23 Jan. ,,

Increased military expenditure, 17,100,000*l*. reported 26 Feb. ,,

Surplus for 1902-03, 2,738,500*l*.; budget for 1903–4, surplus after reduction of the salt-tax, and income-tax exemptions, 948,700*l*. . . 25 March, ,,

Mr. Henry Phipps gives a total of 30,000*l*. for scientific research, agricultural education, and a Pasteur institute, reported . . early April ,,

The viceroy's tour ends in Gwalior . 23 April ,,

Order issued to army by lord Kitchener calling attention to assaults on natives by British soldiers and intimating his determination to punish severely such conduct . . . mid June ,,

Lord Curzon announces his decision to accept the offer of the home government for an extension of his term of office . . . . . . 4 Aug. ,,

Lord Curzon addresses strong protest to lord Geo. Hamilton against the government proposal to charge India with the cost of the increased garrison in S. Africa . . . . early Aug. ,,

The viceroy reports prospects of crops generally good . . . . 12 Aug. ,,

Annual review of the trade of India, 1902–3, by director general of statistics, gives total imports, Rs.104,04,36,358; exports, 1902–3, Rs.137,62,63,756, issued . . . . Aug. ,,

Report issued by the Irrigation commission proposing an outlay of 44 crores of rupees extending over 20 years on protective works . mid Aug. ,,

GOVERNORS-GENERAL OF INDIA, &c.*

Warren Hastings assumes the govt. . . 13 April, 1772

Sir John Macpherson . . . . . . 1 Feb. 1785

Lord Cornwallis . . . . . . 12 Sept. 1786

Sir John Shore (afterwards lord Teignmouth) 28 Oct. 1793

Lord (afterwards marquis) Cornwallis again: he relinquished the appointment.

Sir Alured Clarke . . . . . . 6 April, 1798

Lord Mornington (afterwards Marquis Wellesley) 17 May, ,,

Marquis Cornwallis again . . . . 30 July, 1805

Sir George Hilaro Barlow . . . . 10 Oct. ,,

Lord Minto . . . . 31 July, 1807

Earl of Moira, afterwards marquis of Hastings, 4 Oct. 1813

Hon. John Adam . . . . . . 13 Jan. 1823

George Canning, relinquished the appointment . ,,

William, Lord (afterwards earl) Amherst . 1 Aug. ,,

Hon. W. Butterworth Bayley . . . 13 March, 1828

Lord Wm. Cavendish Bentinck . . . 4 July, ,,

[This nobleman became the first governor-general of India, under the act 3 & 4 Will. IV. c. 85: Aug 28, 1833.]

Sir Charles Theophilus Metcalfe (afterwards lord Metcalfe) . . . . 20 March, 1835

William, lord Heytesbury; did not proceed . ,,

George, lord Auckland (afterwards earl of Auckland) 4 March, 1836

Edward, lord Ellenborough . . . 28 Feb. 1842

William Wilberforce Bird . . . 15 June, 1844

Sir Henry (afterwards viscount) Hardinge, 23 July, ,,

James-Andrew, earl (afterwards marquis) of Dalhousie . . . . 12 Jan. 1848

Charles John, viscount Canning, appointed, July, 1855

Proclaimed the first VICEROY throughout India, 1 Nov. 1858

James, earl of Elgin, appointed, Aug. 1861; died 20 Nov. 1863

Sir John Lawrence appointed . . . . Dec. ,,

Richard Southwell, earl of Mayo (see *Mayo*) appointed. [Assassinated 8 Feb. 1872.] Oct. 1868

Thomas George Baring, lord Northbrook . Feb. 1872

Edward Robert Bulwer Lytton, lord Lytton, took oath at Calcutta . . . . . . 12 April, 1876

* Several of these appointments were provisional, as, for instance, sir Alured Clarke, sir George Hilaro Barlow, hon. William Butterworth Bayley, William Wilberforce Bird, &c. The *appointments* of governors-general were, of course of earlier date than their assumption of office.

George Frederick Samuel Robinson, marquis of Ripon . . . . May, 1880
Frederick Temple Hamilton-Blackwood, earl of Dufferin, Sept. 1884; created marquis of Dufferin and Ava . . . . . . 12 Nov. 1888
Henry Charles Keith Fitz-maurice, marquis of Lansdowne, installed . . . . 10 Dec. „
Victor Alexander Bruce, earl of Elgin (K.G. Jan. 1899), appointed . . . about 10 Oct. 1893
George N. Curzon (baron, Sept. 1898), appointed, Aug. 1898

INDIA COMPANY, EAST. The first commercial intercourse of the English with the East Indies was a private adventure of three ships fitted out in 1591. Only one of them reached India; and, after a voyage of three years, the commander, captain Lancaster, was brought home in another ship, the sailors having seized his own; but his information gave rise to a mercantile voyage, and the establishment of a company, whose first charter, in Dec. 1600, was renewed in 1609, 1657, 1661, 1693, and 1744. Its stock in 1600 consisted of 72,000*l*., when it fitted out four ships. Meeting with success, it continued to trade, and India stock sold at 500*l*. for a share of 100*l*. in 1683. East India, Vols. I. and II. 1898.

A new company (the "English") was chartered 5 Sept. 1698, and the old (the "London") suspended from trading for three years; the two were united 1702
New East India company established 1708
Privileges of the company continued till 1783 . . 1744
Affairs of the company were brought before parliament, and a committee exposed a series of intrigues and crime . . . . . . Aug. 1772
As remedial measures two acts passed, (one authorised a loan of 1,000,000*l*. to the company; the other celebrated as the *India bill*) effected most important changes in the constitution of the company and its relations to India. A governor-general was appointed to reside in Bengal, to which the other presidencies were then made subordinate; a supreme court of judicature was instituted at Calcutta: the salary of the governor was fixed at 25,000*l*. per year; that of the council at 10,000*l*. each; and of the chief judge at 8000*l*.; the affairs of the company were controlled; all the departments were re-organised, and all the territorial correspondence was henceforth to be laid before the British ministry . . . June, 1773
Mr. Pitt's bill appointing the Board of Control (*which see*), passed . . . . . 18 May, 1784
The company's charter was renewed for 20 years . 1793
Trade with India thrown open 1813
Trade to China opened; Charter renewed till 1854 . 1833
The government of India was continued in the hands of the company till parliament should otherwise provide 1853
In consequence of the mutiny of 1857, and the disappearance of the company's army, the government of India was transferred to the crown, the Board of Control was abolished, and a Council of State for India instituted by the act 21 & 22 Vict. c. 106, which received the royal assent, 2 Aug.* 1858
The company's political power ceased on 1 Sept., and the queen was proclaimed as Queen of Great Britain and the Colonies, &c., in the principal places in India, amid much enthusiasm 1 Nov. „
The company to be dissolved, 1 June, 1874, and dividends redeemed, by the "East India Stock Dividend Redemption Act," passed 15 May, 1873
The EAST INDIA-HOUSE built 1726; enlarged and a new front erected, 1799; sold with the furniture, 1861; pulled down in Sept. and Oct. 1862

* Lord Palmerston brought in a bill for the purpose on 12 Feb., which was accepted by the house on 18 Feb. He resigned on the following day, and the bill dropped. A similar bill was introduced by Mr. Disraeli on 12 March; but many of its details being objected to, it was withdrawn. On lord John Russell's proposition, the house proceeded to consider the matter by way of resolutions; on 17 June, lord Stanley brought in the above mentioned bill, being the third on the subject introduced during the session.

INDIA, COUNCIL OF, established by act of parliament, 2 Aug. 1858, in the place of the board of control (*which see*). It consists of 15 members (salary 1200*l*. a year), eight of whom were appointed by the queen, and seven elected by the directors of the East India company. The members may not sit in parliament. The council met first on 3 Sept. 1858, when lord Stanley, secretary of state for India, presided. The members of the *first* council are recorded below. Members were added to the council by an act, passed 20 June, 1892.

ELECTED.

Charles Mills.	Sir J. Weir Hogg.
John Shepherd.	Elliot Macnaghten.
Ross D. Mangles.	Henry T. Prinsep.
William J. Eastwick.	

APPOINTED.

Sir Frederick Currie.	Sir John Lawrence.
Sir Henry Rawlinson.	Sir Henry Montgomery.
Sir R. Hussey Vivian.	Sir Proby Cautley, and
J. Pollard Willoughby.	Wm. Arbuthnot.

INDIA, EMPRESS OF; queen Victoria so proclaimed in London, 1 May, 1876, in India, 1 Jan. 1877; king Edward proclaimed *Emperor* 1 Jan. 1903. See *India*. Order of the Indian Empire instituted, 1 Jan. 1878. Enlarged, 15 Feb. 1887.

INDIA MUSEUM, THE, was proposed by sir Charles Wilkins and approved by the East India company in 1798. The valuable collections were removed from Leadenhall-street to Fife house, behind the chapel royal, Whitehall, and opened 24 July, 1861; removed to the East India museum, which was opened to the public May, 1869; removed to South Kensington, opened June, 1875; closed 25 Oct. 1879, and the collections removed to Kew Gardens Museum, there re-opened 17 May, 1880. *Indian Empire Exhibition* at Earl's Court, opened by the duke of Cambridge, 27 May, 1895.

INDIAN ASSOCIATION (Constitutional), to promote social progress and education in India, was established under the patronage of the princess of Wales in 1870. Annual meetings are held.

INDIANA, a western state of North America. It was included in Ohio till 1801; was constituted a territory in 1809, and admitted into the Union 11 Dec. 1816. Capital, Indianapolis; population, 1890, 105,436; 1900, 169,164. Population, 1880, 1,978,301; 1890. 2,192,404; 1900, 2,516,462.

Great fire at Indianapolis about 13 firemen were killed and 19 injured—loss 200,000 dols. 17 March, 1890
Burning of a hospital at Indianapolis, 19 persons perish . . . . 22 Jan. 1892
Collapse of the large span of the nearly completed bridge over the Ohio; 40 persons killed, 15 Dec. 1893
Lynching riot at Evansville, mob dispersed by troops, 10 killed . . . . early July, 1903

INDIAN CIVIL SERVICE COLLEGE, established at Cooper's hill, Surrey, 1870.

INDIAN EXPENDITURE. Royal commission of inquiry appointed, lord Welby chairman, sir Donald Stewart, sir William Wedderburn, and others, 19 May, 1896; meetings in 1896–7: report issued, proposed grant of 50,000*l*. a year to the India office, see *Times*, 10 April, 1900.

INDIAN HEROES' FUND approved by the prince of Wales and lord George Hamilton, the Indian secretary; lord Roberts, president of the committee. £5,564 13*s*. 7*d*. received, July, *et seq*. (452 gs. from the queen and royal family; £100 from lord Curzon, 24 Oct.) 1898; 78,962Rs. received, Nov. 1899. See *India*, 1897.

INDIAN INSTITUTE, Oxford; promoted by professor (afterwards sir) Monier Williams, 1875 *et seq.*; established 1878; first stone of the building laid, 2 May, 1883; opened, 14 Oct. 1884.

The Institute has received liberal donations from Indian princes; reported . . . . Dec. 1891
Additional buildings opened . . . 2 June, 1894
Rev. Solomon Cæsar Malan, who presented to the institute his valuable library and MSS., &c., died at Bournemouth, aged 82 . . . . 25 Nov. ,,
The completed buildings opened by lord George Hamilton, secretary for India, 1 July, 1896. The institute has been supported by liberal donations 1875–1903

INDIAN NATIONAL CONGRESS, advocating legislative and administrative changes in favour of the natives, met at Bombay, end of Dec. 1885, and annually since. Not favoured by Mahometans. See *India*, 1885 *et seq.*

INDIANS occupying the south-western parts of the United States, termed *Indian territory*, in direct connexion with the government, were numbered at 239,506 in 1861; 261,912 in 1881; 249,253 in 1900. The larger tribes are the Cherokees (22,000), the Choctaws (18,000), the Creeks (13,550), and the Chickasaws (5000); the Sioux (30,000). A large proportion are in comfortable circumstances, and have schools and churches; other tribes are the Delawares, Sacs, Foxes, Shawnees, Sioux, and Ioways. During the American civil war in 1861, the Choctaws joined the confederates, who permitted two Choctaw delegates to sit in congress; the first being Sampson Folsom and Eastman Loman; but the principal chief of the Cherokees, on 4 May, 1861, issued a proclamation of neutrality, which was maintained with great difficulty. In a war provoked by outrages general Sheridan defeated the Indians, and they surrendered unconditionally Dec. 1868. Negotiations undertaken by the Quakers had no effect, and the war was renewed June, 1869. As a chastisement for murders and other outrages major Baker killed 173 Indians, including women and children, Jan. 1870. In June following a deputation of eminent chiefs was received by the president at Washington, and promises and presents were made to them. On 1 Oct. 1869 prince Arthur visited the villages of the Canadian Indians, and was made a chief of the "Six Nations." A deputation of Indian chiefs were well received by the president at Washington, Jan. 1870. A meeting of delegates from various tribes met at Ocmulgee, 5–17 June, 1871, and agreed to a constitution for the common government by means of a senate and parliament representing 17 tribes of 60,000 people; see *Modoc*.

Professor Marsh reports to the president of the United States the corruption and fraudulent conduct of the "Indian Ring," the officials employed to pay compensation, and deal with the Indians (this said to cause war of 1876); corroborated by gen. Custer . . . . . July, 1875
[Bishop Butler, an American, said that if the Indians were treated as fairly as they are in Canada there would be no wars, 1878.]
Thirteen Iroquois and 14 Canadians performed the Canadian national game "La Crosse," before the Queen at Windsor . . . . 27 June, 1876
Gen. Geo. A. Custer, a brave, able officer, attacks about 2,500 Sioux Indians, led by Sitting Bull, an able chief, on Little Horn river, Montana, in a ravine; he and his family and nearly all his force destroyed (275 killed, 60 wounded) 25 June, ,,
Urgent measures taken by the United States government, Sheridan put in command . . July, ,,
Sheridan unsuccessful; commissioners arrange a treaty with the Sioux Indians to remove for self-sustentation . . . . 7–27 Oct. ,,
War going on; gen. Howard opposed to an able chief, Joseph . . . . July, 1877
The tribe "Nez Percés" defeat the U.S. troops in Idaho, and kill about 33, during and after the battle . . . . . about 14 Sept. ,,
Great conference of Indian chiefs with president Hayes, at Washington; they accept terms end of Sept. ,,
"Sitting Bull" and Sioux Indians defeated in a raid retire to Canada [when pardoned returned to his tribes] . . . . . . July, 1879
Fighting with Indians at Mill creek, near Rawlins, in Colorado; 17 whites and major Thornbury killed, 29 Sept.; gen. Merritt entrenched; said to be surrounded; reinforced; Indians retreat 14 Oct. ,,
200 Apache Indians turn and kill 32 of the pursuing whites . . . . 9 Nov. ,,
Indians in Canada. In 1883, 110,505; in 1892, 121,638; numbers increasing; condition improving and prosperous 1892
The Sioux sell to the United States 11,000,000 acres, part of their Dakota reservation, for 14,000,000 dollars; the Chippewa agree to sell 4,000,000 acres of their lands . . . . Aug. 1889
A rising of the Sioux Indians, about 25,000, in Badlands (the Mauvaises Terres of the French pioneers), in South Dakota, stated to be suffering by want, in consequence of the reduced government rations; they are incited by their fanatical medicine men, who predict the coming of a conquering Messiah, and begin their ghost war-dances; they attack the outlying white settlers and friendly Indians; marauding and outrages ensue, causing great alarm; troops and supplies of food sent to the Dakota frontier; the Sioux are soon joined by other tribes, Nov.; col. Wm. F. Cody, "Buffalo Bill" (see *American Exhibition*), sent to the front . . . . 23 Nov. 1890
Gen. Miles, chief, commanding in Dakota aided by gen. Brook; the troops in Missouri, Nebraska, Kansas, Dakota, Montana, and Wyoming, ordered for active service . . . . . . 25 Nov. ,,
Rapid advance of troops and cannon into the reservations; Little Wound and other Sioux chiefs tender submission . . . . . 26 Nov. ,,
Father Jule, a missionary, visits the Indian fortified camp, to dissuade them from war; the older chiefs inclined to yield, the younger determined; he returned . . . . . . 6 Dec. ,,
The hostile Indians said to be demoralised by a display of troops and cannon . . . . 12 Dec. ,,
The old Sioux chief Sitting Bull (see above, 1876–77) captured by the police, 14 Dec., and in an attempt to rescue him, his son Crow Foot and himself are killed with others, and his camp is occupied by the troops . . . . . 15 Dec. ,,
Gen. Miles' head-quarters at Rapid city . 18 Dec. ,,
Red Cloud, at a great council, recommends surrender, and warns resisters . . 19 Dec. ,,

Battle of Wounded Knee Creek.

Desiring to revenge Sitting Bull's death, the remains of his band join Big Foot's band on Cheyenne River; they start for Badlands, and are joined by other Indians, making about 160 warriors in all; they are met by the 7th cavalry under lieut. Hawthorne, and artillery under major Whiteside, and made to surrender, 28 Dec.; in the evening major Forsyth with other troops arrives. While pretending to surrender their arms, at the command of major Whiteside, the Indians suddenly attack the dismounted troopers, and a murderous hand-to-hand fight ensues; the Indians are joined by others, and additional troops arrive, the Indians flee to the ravines, are pursued by the artillery, much slaughter ensues; during the confused fight, Big Foot and his band were nearly exterminated, together with many women and children (about 200). Capt. Wallace, lieuts. Casey and Mann, and several non-commissioned officers and privates were killed . . . . 29 Dec. ,,
Vigorous attack on the Pine Ridge Agency, repulsed, 29 Dec. *et seq.*; sharp skirmish in which nearly 3,000 Indians are dispersed by major Forsyth . . . . . . 29, 30 Dec. ,,

The great body of 3,000 Indians near Pine Ridge Agency, gradually surrounded by the 2nd Infantry regiment under gen. Brook 2 Jan. *et seq.* 1891
A sharp Indian attack on supply waggons repulsed 5 Jan. ,,
Kansas and other states called on to supply troops 7 Jan. ,,
Gen. Miles receives the submission of the rebel chiefs of the Brules; provisions sent to the Indians . . . . . . 14 Jan. ,,
About 4,000 Indians, nearly surrounded by the troops, come in and surrender their arms 15 Jan. *et seq.* ,,
Gen. Miles, in an address, commends his troops, and declares the war at an end . . 19 Jan. ,,
He takes 40 Indians and also some friendly chiefs to Washington, Feb.; they have a conference with Mr. Noble, secretary of the Interior, 7 Feb., and president Harrison . . . . . 12 Feb. ,,
Proposed enlistment of about 2,000 young Indians, as separate companies in the army about 10 Feb. ,,
The delegates return to Pine Ridge from Washington, much dissatisfied with their reception; their loyal chief "American Horse," complains bitterly of the injustice and harshness of the government and the officials, but speaks well of gen. Miles 23 Feb. ,,
Revolt of the Chippewa and other Indians in Minnesota and Arizona, reported 12 July; defensive measures ordered by government . . July, ,,
Great mining explosion at Krebs, in the Indian territory; about 70 men killed . . 7 Jan. 1892
Rising of the Navajo Indians near S. Colorado, reported . . . . 30 April, 1893
Mr. G. B. Grinnell's "Pawnee Hero Stories" and "Blackfoot Lodge Tales" published . . . . ,,

INDIA RUBBER, see *Caoutchouc*.

INDICTION, a Roman term originally applied to a tribute of corn, paid every fifteen years, and to the time at which it was paid. The first examples in the Theodosian code are of the reign of Constantius II., who died 361.—In memory of the great victory obtained by Constantine over Maxentius, 8 Cal. Oct. 312, the council of Nice ordained that the accounts of years should be no longer kept by the Olympiads, but by the Indiction, which has its epocha 1 Jan. 313. It was first used by the Latin church in 342.

INDIGO, the dye obtained from the woad plant, *isatis tinctoria*, was used by the Egyptians, and other ancient nations; and the processes are described by Pliny. After the passage of the Cape of Good Hope, in 1497, it was gradually superseded by the eastern indigo, got from the *indigofera*. The mention of indigo occurs in English statutes in 1581. Its cultivation was begun in Carolina in 1747. The quantity imported into Great Britain in 1840 was 5,831,269 lbs.; in 1850, 70,482 cwt.; in 1861, 83,109 cwt.; in 1871, 106,307 cwt.; in 1881, 81,088 cwt.; in 1890, 81,854 cwt.; 1893, 66,981 cwt.; 1900, 33,877 cwt.; 1901, 51,359 cwt.

After long-continued experiments, especially by prof. A. Baeyer, the dye has been prepared artificially from its chemical elements in coal tar 1869-80
Professor H. E. Roscoe, at the Royal Institution, proved that the properties of the artificial and natural indigo were identical . . 27 May, 1881

INDIRECT CLAIMS, see *Alabama*, *Washington*.

INDIUM, a metal discovered in the arsenical pyrites of Freiberg by F. Reich and T. Richter in 1863. Its name is due to its giving an indigo blue ray in its spectrum.

INDIVIDUALISM, the principal maintained by Herbert Spenser and others in opposition to too much state control and socialism. "The coming individualism," by A. Egmont Hake and O. E. Wesslau, published Jan. 1896.

INDO-CHINA, a name given to central Asia. The countries under French government or protection are Annam, Cochin China, Cambodia, and Tonquin. Burmah is subject to Great Britain, and Siam is independent, 1893. M. de Lannessan appointed gov.-general (actively aggressive), superseded by M. Armand Rousseau, 29 Dec. 1894; he died, Dec. 1896; succeeded by M. Doumer, Dec. 1896; succeeded by M. Beau, July, 1902.

INDORE, a province of British India; the principal native rulers have been the Mahratta chiefs, named Holkar, rivals of the Scindiahs at Gwalior. Rao Holkar received a grant of territory from the British in 1733. After severe conflicts the Mahratta chiefs were finally quelled in 1818. The town of Indore, founded in 1767, was destroyed by Scindiah after a battle on 14 Oct. 1801. The maharajah Shivaja Rao Holkar died 17 June, 1886. Succeeded by his son, Tuckaji Rao Holkar, who was present at the queen's jubilee in London in 1887. Indore was visited by the viceroy, the marquis of Lansdowne, 24 Nov. 1891. The maharajah Shivaji Rao Holkar in ill-health, abdicated in favour of his son, Tukoji Rao, aged 12, 31 Jan. 1903. Population, 1881, 1,055,217; 1891, 1,091,689; 1901, 850,690.

INDUCTION of electric currents, discovered by Faraday, and announced in his "Experimental Researches," published in 1831-2. Ruhmkorff's magneto-electric induction coil was constructed in 1850. See under *Electricity*.

INDUCTIVE PHILOSOPHY, based on the results of observations and experiments, really *common sense*, is especially expounded by Bacon in the second book of his "*Novum Organon*," published 1620. Wm. Harvey (1578-1657) endeavoured "to search out the secrets of nature by the way of experiment." See *Blood*.

INDULGENCES in the early church were the moderation of ecclesiastical punishment. The papal system for the absolute pardon of sin, commenced by Leo. III. about 800, were granted in the 11th century by Gregory VII., and by Urban II., and by others, in the 12th century as rewards to the crusaders. Clement V. was the first pope who made public sale of indulgences, 1313. In 1517, Leo X. published general indulgences throughout Europe, and the resistance to them led to the Reformation.

INDUSTRIAL DWELLINGS, see *Artisans*.

INDUSTRIAL EXHIBITIONS, in Great Britain, are now frequent. One for South London was opened at Lambeth, 1 March, 1864; for North London, by earl Russell, at the Agricultural hall, Islington, 17 Oct. 1864; for West London, at the Floral hall, Covent-garden, 1 May, 1865; for the city of London, at Guildhall, 6 March, 1866; one was opened at York, 24 July, 1866; and several since. The Workmen's International Exhibition, Agricultural Hall, London, was opened 16 July; closed, 31 Oct. 1870; one by the Article club at the Crystal palace opened by the duke of Connaught, 30 May, 1899; others since.

INDUSTRIAL PROPERTY; an international conference for its protection was opened at Paris, 6 March, 1883; Rome, 30 April, 1886;

Madrid, 1890; London, 1 June, 1898; Turin, 16 Sept. 1902.

INDUSTRIAL REMUNERATION CONFERENCES, at Prince's Hall, Piccadilly, London, held 28-30 Jan. 1885. Papers read on the relation between Capital and Labour, &c. by lord Bramwell, sir Thomas Brassey, and others.

INDUSTRIAL AND PROVIDENT SOCIETIES ACTS, 1852 and 1862, were amended by acts passed 1867, 1871, and 1876. Acts consolidated in 1893; amended, 1895.

INDUSTRIAL SCHOOLS ACT, 21 & 22 Vict. c. 48 (1857) was enacted to make better provision for the care and education of vagrant, destitute, and disorderly children. Another act was passed, 1861. These acts were consolidated by an act passed in Aug. 1866; amended 1894. Forty-seven of these schools had been certified under these acts up to 29 Sept. 1864. The act was extended to Ireland, 1868. England and Wales, 1872, 71 schools (4870 boys, 1516 girls); in 1890, 133 schools; in 1892, 138 schools; 1901, 223 schools.

INDUSTRIAL SOCIETIES, see *Co-operative Societies*.

INDUSTRIAL VILLAGES, the formation of these by the removal of workmen from towns, was proposed at a meeting of the Society of Arts, 26 June, 1885. Annual meeting, 26 July, 1888.

INDUSTRY, see *Scientific*. A conference for the christian organisation of industry met in Holborn town hall, 29 Nov. 1893.

INEBRIATES, see *Drunkards*.

INFALLIBILITY OF THE POPE, in regard to faith and morals, was decreed by the Vatican Council, and promulgated, 18 July, 1870. The doctrine was much opposed in Germany, and led to the constitution of the church named "Old Catholics," *which see*. Mr. Gladstone's pamphlets, "The Vatican Decrees in their bearing on Civil Allegiance," published Nov. 1874, and "Vaticanism," in Feb. 1875.

INFANTICIDE, especially female, was very prevalent in barbarous countries. Lord Macartney stated that 20,000 infants were killed annually; it is now gradually decreasing in India. On 12 Nov. 1851, Mr. Raikes induced the Chohan chiefs to agree to resolutions against it, and a great meeting in the Punjab was held for the same purpose, 14 Nov. 1853. Much suspicion was caused in London in 1867 through the deaths of children farmed out to improper persons. The agitation revived, June, 1870. Margaret Waters was convicted of the murder of John Cowen, an illegitimate infant, by poison and neglect, 23 Sept. 1870. She had adopted about 40 children, receiving a few pounds as premium; in four years, many had died. John and Catherine Barns, of Tranmere, near Birkenhead, convicted of manslaughter (see *Trials*), 29 Oct. 1879. The Infant Life Protection act passed 25 July, 1872; amended, 1897. Female infanticide prohibited in China about June, 1873. Amelia E. Dyer, a baby farmer, convicted of the murder of infant children, the bodies having been thrown into the Thames at Reading, 22 May; executed, 10 June, 1896. Two women "baby-farmers" executed at Holloway, 3 Feb. 1903.

INFANTRY, foot soldiers; their organisation much improved during the wars of Charles V. and Francis I., in the 16th century. The British army comprised 99 regiments of regular infantry in 1858, when the Canadians raised a regiment termed the 100th. The number 109, beside the rifle brigade until 1881 included the nine regiments formerly in the pay of the East India company, and several colonial corps. In 1871 the principle of localisation, the linking of battalions, and short service, came into operation, in 1881 the existing 109 regiments and the rifle brigade were reorganised forming 71 territorial regiments of the line, each regiment comprising usually 2 battalions of its own and linked battalions of the militia and volunteers. The army scheme of reorganisation introduced by Mr. Brodrick, March 1901, increases the strength of the infantry and raises the number of militia. Marshal Soult (or marshal Bugeaud) said, "The British infantry is the finest in the world: happily there is not much of it." In 1902, 178,361. *Mounted infantry* were largely and successfully employed in the operations of the war in S. Africa, 1899-1902.

INFANTS' RELIEF ACT, passed 7 Aug. 1874, to amend the law relating to contracts made by persons under age.

The powers of wives and widows in respect to the care and training of their children, were somewhat enlarged in 1839, more so in 1873, and very much more by a bill brought in by Mr. James Bryce, read a second time 26 March, 1884.

Guardianship of Infants Act passed, 1886.

INFANT SCHOOLS began in New Lanark, Scotland, in 1815; in London in 1818.

INFECTIOUS DISEASES. By an act passed 30 Aug. 1889, notification of any person suffering from infectious disease is required to be given by the nearest relative or any person in charge, and also by the medical attendant to the medical officer of health of the district; extension of same act passed, 20 June, 1899. An act to prevent the spread of infectious disease was passed 4 Aug. 1890.

INFERNAL MACHINES, see *France*, 1800, 1835, and 1858; *Baltic*, note: *Dynamite*; *Russia*, 1880-1; *Liverpool*, 1881; *Explosives*.

INFIRMARIES. Ancient Rome had no houses for the cure of the sick; diseased persons were carried to the temple of Æsculapius for cure. Institutions for the accommodation of travellers, the indigent, and sick were founded by the emperor Julian about 362; and infirmaries or hospitals were frequently built to cathedrals and monasteries. The emperor Louis II. caused infirmaries situated on mountains to be visited, 855. In Jerusalem the knights and brothers attended on the sick. There were hospitals for the sick at Constantinople, in the 11th century. The oldest mention of physicians and surgeons established in infirmaries occurs in 1437. *Beckmann*; see *Hospitals*. Parish workhouse infirmaries established, 1867.

INFLUENZA, a name given in Italy about 1741 to an epidemic febrile catarrh with variations, probably known to the ancients.

It prevailed in Europe in 1510, and has since frequently appeared, generally commencing in Russia and thence spreading over the continent. It appeared in Britain in 1762 and frequently since, especially in 1830-1, 1833, 1836-7, and 1847. It appeared at Paris in 1866-7, and at Berlin, 1874-5. In Oct. 1889, it was severe in St. Petersburg, and thence spread over Europe, reaching Great Britain, Canada and the United States N.A., Jan. 1890, causing indirectly the deaths of several eminent persons. In the spring, the disease was severe in India and Australia. In 1891 the disease was severe in the west of the United States N.A., and in London and other parts of England, and also on the Continent. The disease reappeared in Jan. 1892, in much the same localities. In London the general mortality was much increased, all classes being attacked. The death of the duke of Clarence and Avondale, 14 Jan. 1892, was attributed to pneumonia following influenza. Reports of the epidemic of 1889–90, by Dr. Parsons, issued by government, 1891–3. Moderate outbreak in London, Feb. 1893, chiefly among the upper and middle classes, the marquis of Salisbury, duke of Abercorn, marquis of Londonderry and others, March; many cases autumn and winter, 1893–94; epidemic in London; prevalent in United Kingdom and on the continent, many deaths, Feb.-April, 1895. Epidemic in St. Petersburg and S. Russia, March, 1895. Epidemic in London and home counties, Jan., Feb. 1898; again rife in London and Paris, spring, 1899; again in London and other parts, Jan. 1900.

INFORMERS, upon penal statutes, compounding with defendants without leave of the court, were punishable with fine and pillory, by 18 Eliz. c. 5 (1576). Their share of a penalty was regulated by 2 & 3 Vict. c. 71 (1839).

INFUSORIA, see *Animalcules*.

INGESTRE HALL, Staffordshire, destroyed by fire 12 Oct. 1882. It was built in 1676. Many valuable portraits, &c. were destroyed.

INGOUR, a river rising in the Caucasus and falling into the Black Sea. Omar Pasha, marching to the relief of Kars, crossed this river on 6 Nov. 1855, with 10,000 men, and attacked the Russians, 12,000 strong, who, after a struggle, retreated with the loss of 400 men. The Turks had 68 killed and 242 wounded. Kars, however, was not saved.

INK. The ancient black inks were composed of soot and ivory black, and Vitruvius and Pliny mention lamp-black; but they had ink of various colours, as red, gold, silver, and purple. Red ink was made of vermilion and gum. INDIAN INK was brought from China, and must have been in use by the people of the east from the earliest ages. INVISIBLE, or SYMPATHETIC INKS, were known at early periods. Ovid (A.D. 2) teaches young women to write with new milk. Receipts for preparing invisible ink were given by Peter Borel, in 1653, and by Le Mort, in 1669. *Beckmann.*

INKERMANN (Crimea). The Russian army (about 40,000) having received reinforcements, and being encouraged by the presence of the grandukes Michael and Nicholas, attacked the British (8000) near the old fort of Inkermann, before daybreak, 5 Nov. 1854. They were kept at bay for six hours till the arrival of 6000 French. The Russians were then repulsed, leaving 9000 killed and wounded. The loss of the allies was 462 killed, 1952 wounded, and 191 missing. Sir George Cathcart, and generals Strangways, Goldie, and Torrens, were among the slain. On 15 Nov. 1855, an explosion of about 100,000 lbs. of gunpowder occurred near Inkermann, and caused great loss of life.

INLAND NAVIGATION, see *Canals*.

INLAND REVENUE BOARD was constituted in Feb. 1849. It comprises the boards of *Excise*, *Stamps*, and *Taxes* (*which see*). The law respecting the inland revenue amended 1871. Total inland revenue, 1896, 64,360,000*l.* up to 31 March; 1897, 64,720,000*l.*; 1900, 75,830,000*l.*; 1901, 83,300,000*l.*; 1902, 90,900,000*l.*

INNOCENTS' DAY, 28 Dec. in the western church; 29 Dec. in the Greek or eastern church; see *Childermas*.

INNS at Rome were regulated by laws; and Edward III. enacted that they should be subjected to inquiry, 1353. See *Taverns*, and *Victuallers*.

INNS OF COURT (London) were established at different periods, in some degree as colleges for teaching the law. Annual revenue in 1872 said to be about 25,000*l.* See *Barristers*.

The Temple founded, and the church built by Knights Templars	1185
The Inner and Middle Temple made inns of law about 1340; the Outer about (*Stow*)	1560
Barnard's Inn, an inn of Chancery (on sale, 49,400*l.* refused 20 June, 1888, let to Art Workers' Guild, Oct. 1888)	1445
Clement's Inn	before 1478
Clifford's Inn, 20 Edw. III.	1345
Furnival's Inn, 5 Eliz.	1563
Gray's Inn, 32 Edw. III.	1357
Lincoln's Inn, 4 Edw. II.	1310 or 1312
Lyon's Inn	1420
New Inn, 1 Hen. VII.	1485
Serjeants' Inn, Fleet Street	1429
Serjeants' Inn, Chancery-lane (sold for 57,000*l.* 23 Feb. 1877)	1666
Staples Inn, 4 Hen. V.	1415
Thavies' Inn, 10 Hen. VIII.	1519
Staple Inn sold, Dec. 1884; Clifford's Inn sold for 100,000*l.*	14 May, 1903

INNSBRUCK, capital of the Tyrol, captured by Maurice of Saxony in 1552; by the Bavarians in 1703; by the French and Bavarians, 1805. Much fighting took place in 1809, and Innsbrück changed masters several times, being finally taken by the Austrians, 12 Aug. The emperor Francis Joseph met queen Victoria here, 23 April, 1888.

INOCULATION, see *Small Pox*. Lady Mary Wortley Montagu introduced inoculation from small pox to England from Turkey. In 1718 she had her son inoculated at Adrianople with success. She was allowed to have it first tried in England on seven condemned criminals, 1721; and in 1722 two of the royal family were inoculated. The practice was preached against by many of the bishops and clergy until 1760. Dr. Mead practised inoculation very successfully up to 1754, and Dr. Dimsdale of London, inoculated Catherine II., empress of Russia, in 1768. Of 5964 who were inoculated in 1797–99, only three died. An inoculation hospital was established in 1746. *Vaccine* inoculation was introduced by Dr. Jenner, 21 Jan. 1799; he had discovered its virtue in 1796, and had been making experiments during the intermediate three years. Inoculation was forbidden by law in 1840. Dr. A. E. Wright's typhoid vaccine elaborated in 1896, introduced in the army, reported, June, 1899; satisfactory results obtained at Ladysmith, 1899–1900, reported, 5 Sept. 1902; M. Haffkine's system of inoculation against cholera and plague used successfully in India, see *Bombay*. Dr. Kitasato's method of treating dysentery by serum inoculation very successful, 1895–99. See *Vaccination*, *Sheep*, *Hydrophobia*, and *Diphtheria*.

INQUESTS, see *Coroner*.

INQUISITION or HOLY OFFICE. Previous to Constantine (306), heresy and spiritual offences were punished by excommunication only; but shortly after his death capital punishments were added, and inquisitors were appointed by Theodosius, 382. Priscillian was put to death in 384 by the emperor Maximus. Justinian decreed the doctrine of the four holy synods as to the holy scriptures and their canons to be observed as laws, 529; hence the penal code against heretics. About 800 the power of the western bishops was enlarged, and courts were established for trying and punishing spiritual offenders, even with death; the punishment being termed in Spain *auto-da-fé*, "an act of faith." In the 12th century many heresies arose, and during the crusades against the Albigenses, Gregory IX., in 1233, established by rules the inquisitorial missions sent out by Innocent III., 1210-15, and committed them to the Dominicans. Pietro da Verona (styled Peter Martyr), the first inquisitor who burnt heretics, assassinated by an accused gonfalonier, 6 April, 1252, was canonized.

Pierre de Castelnau sent against the Albigenses, 1210; St. Dominic made the first inquisitor-general 1215
The Inquisition constituted by Gregory IX., 1233; established in Aragon, 1233; Venice, 1249; France, 1255; Castile 1290
The Inquisition revived by a bull . . 1 Nov. 1478
The Holy Office was reinstituted in Spain by Ferdinand and Isabella; Torquemada inquisitor-general 1480
Nearly 3000 persons burnt in Andalusia, and 17,000 suffer other penalties 1481
"Instructions" of the new tribunal promulgated, 29 Nov. 1484
New articles were added . . . . 1488 & 1498
Established in Portugal 1526
The establishment resisted in Naples, and only introduced into other parts of Italy with jealous limitations by the temporal power . . . 1546-7
New ordinances in 81 articles compiled by the inquisitor-general Valdez 1561
Suppressed in France by edict of Nantes . . . 1598
Carnesecchi executed at Rome, 1567, and Galileo compelled to abjure his philosophical opinions . 1633
Louis XIV. revoked the edict of Nantes, but refused to introduce the Inquisition 1685
20 persons perish at an *auto-da-fé* at Goa . . 1717
Gabriel Malagrida, a jesuit, burnt at Lisbon . . 1761
A woman accused of making a contract with the devil burnt at Seville . . . . 7 Nov. 1781
The tribunal abolished in Tuscany and Lombardy . 1787
Suppressed in Spain by Napoleon, 4 Dec. 1808 and by the Cortes . . . . . 12 Feb. 1813
Restored by Ferdinand VII. . . . 21 July, 1814
Finally abolished by the Cortes 1820
[Llorente states that in 236 years the total number of persons put to death in Spain by the Inquisition was about 32,000; 291,000 were subjected to other punishments.]

INSANITY, see *Lunatics*.

INSECTS. About 200,000 species known, Jan. 1877. An exhibition of these creatures, illustrating their structure, food, and habits, was opened in the gardens of the Tuileries, at Paris, 7 Sept., 1874; at the Westminster Aquarium, 9 March, 1878; and in the Zoological gardens, Regent's park, 1881. About 8,000 new species of insects named annually; total *estimated* 10,000,000 forms, 1902. See *Entomology*.

INSOLVENCY. The first insolvent act was passed in 1649, but it was of limited operation; a number of acts of more extensive operation were passed at various periods, and particularly in the reign of George III. The benefit of the act known as the Great Insolvent Act, was taken in England by 50,733 insolvents from the time of its passing in 1814, to March, 1827, a period of thirteen years. Since then the acts relating to insolvency have been several times amended. Persons not traders, or being traders whose debts are less than 300*l*., might petition the court of bankruptcy, and propose compositions, and have *pro tem.* protection from all process against their persons and property, by 6 Vict. c. 116 (1842). In 1861, by a new bankruptcy act, the business of the insolvent debtors' court was transferred to the court of bankruptcy; and a number of imprisoned debtors were released in Nov. 1861. See *Bankrupts*.

INSTITUTE OF FRANCE, see *Académies* (Paris). On 22 Aug. and 25 Oct. 1795, all the Academies (formerly Royal), viz., the French academy, the academy of inscriptions and belles lettres, that of the mathematical and physical sciences, of the fine arts, and of the moral and political sciences, were combined in one body, under the title of "Institut National," afterwards *Royal*, *Imperial*, and again *National*. Centenary celebrated, 23 Oct. *et seq.* 1895.

INSTITUTES, see *Code*, *Actuaries*, *Agriculture*, *Architects*, *Chemical*, *Inventors*, &c.

INSTITUTION, see *Royal*; *London*, *Civil Engineers*, &c.

INSURANCE ON SHIPS AND MERCHANDISE. Suetonius conjectures that Claudius was the first contriver of the insurance of ships A.D. 43.

Insurance in general use in Italy, 1194, and in England 1560
Insurance policies first used in Florence . . . 1523
The first law relating to insurance was enacted . 1601
Insurance of houses and goods against FIRE, in London, began the year following the Great Fire of London 1667
An office set up for insuring houses and buildings, chiefly on the plan of Dr. Barton, one of the first and most considerable builders of London . . "
The first regular office set up in London was the *Hand-in-Hand*, 1696; bi-centenary celebrated, 12 Nov. 1896
First *Life* Insurance Office (the *Amicable*), established 1706
Sun fire-office established 1710
The *Sun* introduces the *double option system* (invented by Mr. Harris Saunders) combining two forms of assurance against death and old age, announced 1839
The first *Marine* Insurance was the Royal Exchange Insurance, and the London Insurance . . . 1721
Duty first laid on insurances of 1s. 6d. per 100*l*. insured, 1782; duty increased 1797
In 1857, 1,451,110*l*. were paid as duty for fire insurances on property amounting to 72,136,585*l*.
A new Commercial Union fire insurance, founded in consequence of the increased charges of the companies . . . . . . Sept. 1861
Rate of tax on insurance, reduced from 3s. to 1s. 6d. per cent. on stock in trade, from 13 May, 1864; on household goods 1865
Sea insurance duties reduced . . . 31 May, 1867
Policies of Assurance act (enabling assignees of assurances to sue in their own names for policy monies), passed . . . . 20 Aug. "
Fire insurance duties totally repealed . 24 June, 1869
Albert Assurance Company fail for about 8,000,000*l*. Aug. "
Acts amending the law respecting life assurance companies passed 1870-1-2
The "People's Provident Assurance Society," established 2 Sept. 1854; named *European Assurance Society*, 1869; said to have absorbed 44 other societies; brought into chancery, 1871; subjected to arbitration by act of parliament, 1872; first meeting before lord Westbury, 22 Oct. 1872; successive arbitrators, lord Romilly, sir Wm. James; Mr. Francis Reilly (last); final award signed 2 Sept. 1879. Immense loss to shareholders.
A scheme for the insurance of the lives of its sailors, and others, proposed by the Shipping Federation, see under *Shipping* . . April, 1891

AMOUNT INSURED.

1782	£130,000,000
1802	220,000,000
1822	399,000,000
1842	652,000,000
1862	1,007,000,000

Sum insured in 125 offices, about 338,000,000*l.*; accumulated life-funds, 94,000,000*l.*; premium income nearly 11,000,000*l.*—*Board of Trade Report*, 1874.

INSURRECTIONS, see *Conspiracies*, *Massacres*, *Rebellions*, *Riots*, &c.

INTELLIGENCE DEPARTMENTS, Military, see under *Army*, 1 April, 1873; Naval, see under *Navy*, 1 Feb. 1887.

INTENDMENT OF CRIMES. In cases of treason, wounding, burglary, &c., intention proved was made as punishable as crime completed, by 7 Geo. II. 1734. The rigour was modified by sir Robert Peel's revision of the statutes, 4-10 Geo. IV. 1823-29.

INTERDICT or **ECCLESIASTICAL CENSURE**, seldom decreed in Europe till the time of Gregory VII. 1073, but often afterwards. When a prince was excommunicated, all his subjects retaining their allegiance were excommunicated also, and the clergy were forbidden to perform any part of divine service, or any clerical duties, save the baptism of infants, and taking the confessions of dying penitents. In 1170, pope Alexander put all England under an interdict; and when king John was excommunicated in 1208, the kingdom lay under a papal interdict for six years. England was put under an interdict, on Henry VIII. shaking off the pope's supremacy, 1535; and pope Sixtus V. published a crusade against queen Elizabeth of England in 1588; see *Excommunication*.

INTEREST, see *Usury*. The word interest was first used in an act of parliament of the 21st James I. 1623, wherein it was made to signify a lawful increase by way of compensation for the use of money lent. The rate fixed by the act was 8*l.* for the use of 100*l.* for a year, in place of usury at 10*l.* before taken. The Commonwealth lowered the rate to 6*l.* in 1651; confirmed in 1660; and by an act of the 13th of queen Anne, 1713, it was reduced to 5*l.* The restraint being found prejudicial to commerce was somewhat relaxed in 1839, and was totally removed by 17 & 18 Vict. c. 90 (1854).

INTERIM OF AUGSBURG, a decree issued by the emperor Charles V. in 1548, with the view of attempting to reconcile the Catholics and Protestants, in which it entirely failed. It was revoked in 1552. The term *Interim* has been applied to other decrees and treaties.

INTERMEDIATE EDUCATION ACT for Ireland, passed 16 Aug. 1878; another act passed, 6 Aug. 1900.

INTERMEZZI, light dramatic entertainments, introduced between the acts of a tragedy, comedy, or grand opera; of very ancient origin. They became more important in the 16th century. Those connected with Bardi's "*Amico Fido*," 1589, were very fine.

INTERMITTENT FILTRATION of Sewage, a process much advocated by Professor E. Frankland and others, in 1875, and stated to have been successful at Merthyr Tydvil since 1872.

INTERNATIONAL AFRICAN ASSOCIATION, see *Congo*.

INTERNATIONAL ASSOCIATION OF ACADEMIES proposed at Göttingen in 1898; met in Paris 16–20 April, 1901; 18 constituent bodies represented (British delegates, Sir Michael Foster, Sir Archibald Geikie, sir Norman Lockyer, prof. Ray Lankester, and others); M. Darboux president (M. Berthelot, M. Gaston Bossier, sir Michael Foster, M. de Goeje, and Dr. Mommsen, hon. presidents). The association includes 2 divisions, letters and science, which meet separately, the general assembly afterwards sitting in congress to discuss and act on their decisions; the council met in London, June, 1903; the next triennial meeting to be in London, 1904.

INTERNATIONAL, see *Chess*, *Cholera*, *Copyright*, *Cosmopolis*, *Education*, *Electricity*, *Exhibitions*, *Geneva*, *Havre*, *Horticulture*, *Literary*, *Statistics*, *Scientific*, *Working-men*, *Game*, &c.

INTERNATIONAL LAW. See *Neutral Powers*.

The professorship of international law, at Cambridge, endowed by bequest of Dr. Wm. Whewell, master of Trinity College, 1867.

The Association for the Reform and Codification of the Law of Nations first met at Brussels, 10 Oct. 1873; Geneva, 2-5 Sept. 1874; The Hague, Sept. 1875; Bremen, 1876; Antwerp, 30 Aug.—3 Sept. 1877; Frankfort, about 20 Aug. 1878; London, 11 Aug. 1879; Berne, 24 Aug. 1880; Cologne, 16-19 Aug. 1881; Liverpool, about 15 Aug. 1882; Turin, 11 Sept. 1882; Milan, 11 Sept. 1883; London, July, 1887; Liverpool, Aug. 1890; London, Oct. 1893; Brussels, 1 Oct. 1895.

The Institute of International Law was organised at Ghent by Dr. Lieber, M. Jaquemyns, and M. Moynier, in 1873. It has since met at Geneva, 1874; the Hague, 1875; Zurich, 1876; Paris, 1878; Brussels, Sept. 1879; Oxford, 6-10 Sept. 1880; Turin, 1882; Munich, 4 Sept. 1883; Hamburg, 9 Aug. 1885; Heidelberg, 5 Sept. 1887; Lausanne, 8 Sept. 1888; Hamburg, 7 Sept. 1891; Geneva, 6 Sept. 1892; Paris, 27 March, 1894; Cambridge, 9 Aug. 1895; Venice, 24 Sept. 1896; Copenhagen, 26 Aug. 1897; The Hague, Aug. 1898; Buffalo, 31 Aug. 1899; Glasgow, 20 Aug. 1901; Brussels, 18 Sept. 1902.

See under *Peace*.

INTEROCEANIC CANAL between the Atlantic and Pacific. See *Panamá*.

INTER-PARLIAMENTARY CONFERENCES, held by members of different legislatures, when not in session, see under *Peace*.

INTERPRETATION ACT, "for consolidating enactments relating to the construction of acts of parliament and for further shortening the language used in acts of parliament" was passed 30 Aug. 1889.

INTERREGNUM, see *Commonwealth*.

INTESTATE. A person who dies without leaving a will. Intestates' Estates act passed, 25 July, 1890.

INTRANSIGENTES, or Irreconcileables, a party of extreme republicans in Spain, who withdrew from the Cortes and became very troublesome, 1 July, 1873; joined by communists they held Carthagena from August to 12 Jan. 1874.

INUNDATIONS. The following are among the most remarkable:—

	A.D.
An inundation of the sea in Lincolnshire laid under water many thousand acres. *Camden*	245
Another in Cheshire, by which 3000 persons and an innumerable quantity of cattle perished	353
An inundation at Glasgow, which drowned more than 400 families. *Fordun*	758
The Tweed overflowed its banks, and laid waste the country for 30 miles round	836
An inundation on the English coasts, demolished a number of sea-port towns	1014

Earl Godwin's lands, exceeding 4000 acres, overflowed by the sea, and an immense sand-bank formed on the coast of Kent, now known by the name of the Godwin sands. *Camden*. . . . 1100
Flanders inundated by the sea, and the town and harbour of Ostend totally immersed . . . 1108
More than 300 houses overwhelmed at Winchelsea by an inundation of the sea 1280
At the Texel, which first raised the commerce of Amsterdam 1400
The sea broke in at Dort, and drowned 72 villages, and 100,000 people (see *Dort*) . . 17 April, 1421
The Severn overflowed during ten days, and carried away men, women, and children, in their beds, and covered the tops of many hills; the waters settled upon the lands, and were called the Great Waters for 100 years after, 1 Richard III. *Hollinshed*. 1483
A general inundation by the failure of the dikes in Holland; the number of drowned said to have been 400,000 1530
The waters rose above the tops of the houses, and above 100 persons perished in Somersetshire and Gloucestershire 1607
At Catalonia, where 50,000 persons perished . . 1617
An inundation in Yorkshire, when a rock opened, and poured out water to the height of a church steeple. *Vide Phil. Trans.* 1686
Part of Zealand overflowed, 1300 inhabitants were drowned, and incredible damage was done at Hamburg 1717
At Madrid, several of the Spanish nobility and other persons of distinction perished . . . 1723
In Yorkshire, a dreadful inundation, called Ripon Flood. 1771
In Navarre, where 2000 persons lost their lives by the torrents from the mountains . . Sept. 1787
Inundation of the Liffey, which did immense damage in Dublin, 12 Nov. 1787; again, 2-3 Dec. 1802
Lorca, a city of Murcia, in Spain, destroyed by the bursting of a reservoir, which inundated more than 20 leagues, and killed 1000 persons, besides cattle . . . . 14 April, „
At Pesth, near Presburg, the overflow of the Danube, by which 24 villages and their inhabitants were swept away . . . . April, 1811
In the vicinity of Salop, by the bursting of a cloud during a storm, many persons and much stock perished . . . . May, „
Dreadful inundation in Hungary, Austria, and Poland, in the summer of 1813
Overflow of the Danube; a Turkish corps of 2000 men, on a small island near Widdin, surprised, and met instant death . . . . 14 Sept. „
In Silesia, 6000 inhabitants perished, and the ruin of the French army under Macdonald was accelerated by the floods; also in Poland 4000 lives were supposed to have been lost . . . . . „
At Strabane, Ireland, by the melting of the snow on the surrounding mountains, most destructive floods were occasioned . . . . . . 2 Jan. 1816
In Germany, the Vistula overflowed; many villages were laid under water, and great loss of life and property was sustained . . . 21 March, „
In England, 5000 acres were deluged in the Fen countries . . . . June, 1819
Inundation at Dantzic, occasioned by the Vistula breaking through some of its dikes, by which 10,000 head of cattle and 4000 houses were destroyed, and numerous lives lost . . 9 April, 1829
The "Moray Floods," caused by rainfall, when the Spey and Findhorn rose in some places 50 feet above their ordinary level, and caused great destruction of property. Many lives were lost, and whole families who took refuge on elevated places were with difficulty rescued. *Sir T. Dick Lauder*. 3, 4, 27 Aug. „
At Vienna, the dwellings of 50,000 of its inhabitants laid under water . . . . Feb. 1830
20,000 houses swept away, and about 1000 persons perished, at Canton, in China, in consequence of an inundation, occasioned by incessant rains. Equal or greater calamity was produced by the same cause in other ports of China . . Oct. 1833
Awful inundation in France: the Saone poured its waters into the Rhone, broke through its banks, and covered 60,000 acres; Lyons was inundated; in Avignon 100 houses were swept away; 218 houses were carried away at La Guillotière; and upwards of 300 at Vaise, Marseilles, and Nismes; the Saone had not attained such a height for 238 years . . . . . 31 Oct. to 4 Nov. 1840
Lamentable inundation at Brentford and the surrounding country; several lives lost, and immense property destroyed . . . . 16 Jan. 1841
Disastrous inundation in the centre, west, and south-west of France; numerous bridges, with the Orleans and Vierzon viaduct, swept away; the latter had cost 6,000,000 of francs. The damage done exceeded 4,000,000*l.* sterling. The Loire rose twenty feet in one night . . 22 Oct. 1846
Lamentable catastrophe at Holmfirth (see *Holmfirth Flood*) . . . . 4 Feb. 1852
Inundation of the valleys of the Severn and Teme after a violent thunderstorm . . . 5 Sept. „
Inundations of the basins of the Rhine and the Rhone, overflowing the country to a great extent, 19 Sept. „
Hamburg half-flooded by the Elbe . . 1 Jan. 1855
Inundations in south of France, with immense damage (see *France*) . . May and June, 1856
In Holland, nearly 40,000 acres submerged, Jan. 1861
Great inundation through the bursting of the outfall sluice at St. Germain's, near King's Lynn (see *Levels*) . . . . 4-15 May, 1862
Another marshland sluice bursts; many acres inundated . . . . 4 Oct. „
Bursting of the Bradfield reservoir (see *Sheffield*); about 250 persons drowned . . . 11 March, 1864
Great inundations in France . . . 26 Sept. *et seq.* 1866
Great floods in north of England, immense damage in Yorkshire, Lancashire, and Derbyshire; farms destroyed, mines flooded, mills thrown down, railways stopped; and much suffering at Leeds (about 20 drowned), Manchester, Preston, Wakefield, &c. . . . . 16-17 Nov. „
Inundations at Cork, Dublin, and other places, about 30 Jan. 1869
Inundation at Rome, causing great distress; relieved by the king . . . . 28, 29 Dec. „
Great inundations from the mountains in N. Italy; the Po and other rivers overflow; thousands of people unhoused; Mantua, Ferrara, &c., suffer much . . . . . latter part of Oct. 1872
Floods on banks of the Thames through very high tide . . . . 20 March, 1874
Mill River Valley, near Northampton, Massachusetts, U. S., several villages destroyed through the bursting of a reservoir, badly dammed; above 144 perished . . . . 16 May, „
Eureka, Nevada; through rain and a waterspout; between 20 and 30 persons perish . . 24 July „
Pittsburg and Alleghany, W. Pennsylvania; storm of rain; the rivers overflow; about 220 persons drowned . . . . 26 July, „
A large part of Toulouse destroyed by the rising of the Garonne; about 1000 lives lost and much property (St. Cyprien quarter, a sepulchre) June, 1875
Heavy rains cause inundations in West of England and Wales; destruction and loss of life at Newport and Monmouth, 15-16 July; in the midland and western counties, especially near Nottingham, about 17-23 Oct.; again . . 13-16 Nov. „
Great storms in India; Ahmedabad inundated; about 20,000 homeless . . . 22-24 Sept. „
Severe inundations in Holland and France . Mar. 1876
Severe floods in England through heavy rain, 25-31 Dec. „
Piers at Folkestone, Dover, and Hastings much injured . . . . 1 Jan. 1877
Much damage through floods on banks of the Thames, and throughout the country, middle of June, „
Inundations in London through heavy rain, 10, 11 April, 1878
Szegedin, Hungary; through storms and rain, the dams of the river Theiss gave way; the town was nearly destroyed; out of 6566 houses, only 331 stood; many persons drowned; thousands homeless, 12-13 March, 1879. [Another inundation here not quite so disastrous, about 3 June, 1887; again March, 1888].
North Italy; much damage through overflowing of the Po and Mincio . . . . June, „

Inundations in Murcia, Spain, through heavy rains; provinces of Andalusia, Alicante, Almeria, and Malaga; about 1000 lives lost; much damage to property; about 2000 houses destroyed, 16, 17 Oct. 1878

Again in Hungary . . . . about 10 Dec. ,,

Midland counties of England; much damage, about 8-11 Oct. 1880

Much rain; floods in Cheshire, Lancashire, &c. Aug. 1881

Great inundations in S.E. Europe through rains Oct. ,,

Inundations by the rising of the Lossie and Spey, N. Scotland; bridge is broken and other damage mid. Sept. 1882

Inundations in the Tyrol; much damage with loss of life in north Italy and Hungary, and south of France . . . . . . Sept. ,,

In Germany: great rise of the Rhine and Danube, Nov.—Dec.; destruction of five villages with above 250 houses, near Wiesbaden . . Dec. ,,

Great floods in the Thames valley and midland counties of England . . . . Dec. ,,

Much destruction near Worms; about 60 drowned early in Jan. 1883

Raab in Hungary partly submerged . . 10 Jan. ,,

In Pennsylvania, Ohio, and Cincinnati . . Feb. ,,

Cachar in India in great distress . . 16 May, ,,

In Silesia, the river Neisse rises; much damage about 21 June, ,,

In Thames valley, Ontario, Canada, much destruction of property, about 30 lives lost about 11-12 July, ,,

Overflow of the river Peneus, Thessaly, Greece; much damage . . . . announced 29 Oct. ,,

Great inundations in Ohio, Pennsylvania, &c.; about 15 deaths and 5000 homeless about 7 Feb. 1884

Disastrous floods in E. Spain . end of May, ,,

Floods in Galicia; new railway bridge over the Vistula destroyed; 20 lives lost about 23 June, ,,

Great inundation through heavy rains in eastern Spain; much distress in Alicante, Almeria and Valencia . . . . . . Nov. ,,

Great inundation of lower town of Montreal; about 500,000*l.* damage; much privation 17–18 April, 1886

Great inundation at Mandalay, Burmah . 18 Aug. ,,

Great floods in S. United States . . . . July, 1887

Great overflow of the Hoang-Ho or Yellow River (see *China*), Sept.-Oct. 1887, and Sept. 1889.

Overflow of the Elbe; about 100 villages submerged; loss of life and destruction of property, about 26 March; also of the Vistula, about 77 villages submerged . . about 27 March, 1888

Great flood in the Canton river; 3,000 people said to be drowned, announced . . . 8 May, ,,

Destructive freshet in the Mississippi; Illinois coast; Quincy, Hannibal, Alexandria and other towns overflowed . . . . . 17 May, ,,

Inundations in Mexico through heavy rains; great loss of life . . . . . . 17–20 June, ,,

Heavy rains caused the rising of rivers in Essex and Kent; form lakes navigable by boats; stop railways; sweep away the crops from the soil, creating much calamity 30–31 July, 1 Aug. ,,

Great floods also in Germany, July, Aug.; France and Switzerland . . . . . . Oct. ,,

Destructive floods in the midland and S.W. England; Leicester, Bristol, Taunton and other places suffer much . . . . 8, 9 March, 1889

Conemaugh Valley, &c. See *Pennsylvania* and *United States* . . . . May, ,,

Destructive floods in China and Japan (*which see*) July, Aug. 1889; and *China* . . . Aug. 1890

Disastrous floods on the upper Severn; much suffering . . . . . . early Feb. ,,

Destructive floods through heavy rains in the Mississippi valley and Southern States, U.S.A. (see *Mississippi*) . . . . about 13 March ,,

Destructive floods in Austria, Bohemia, central Europe and France See *New South Wales* Aug.—Sept. ,,

Overflow of the Orinoco and tributaries, S. America, causing great destruction . . 16, 17 Sept. 1890

Destructive inundations caused by violent gales throughout Europe, especially in Germany, Austria, Mecklenburg, Baltic coast, Belgium, and Denmark . . . . . 23-25 Nov. ,,

Serious floods in Kent, &c., through the thaw, after the long frost; also in many places on the Continent . . . . Jan. 1891

Destructive inundations in W. Virginia, Ohio, Alleghany, &c., about 17 Feb.; in Arizona (*which see*) reported 2 March; in Tennessee and Mississippi . . . . . about 8 March ,,

Destructive floods by the rising of the Yang-tse-Kiang; great loss of life at Foochoo about 21 July ,,

Great floods in Posen, loss of life and destruction of property . . . . about 26 July ,,

Heavy rains and destructive floods in E. Lancashire 13, 14 Aug. ,,

Heavy rains and destructive inundations in Spain (*which see*) . . . . . 13 Sept. *et seq.* ,,

Disastrous floods in Spain, France, Italy, and England (especially S. and W.) about 22 Oct. *et seq.*

Collapse of buildings through floods at Limoux, France; about 20 persons killed, about 25 Oct. ,,

Great floods in Somersetshire, with destruction of buildings and crops; travelling impeded, much distress . . . . Nov. ,,

Disastrous floods in Andalusia, Murcia, and Estremadura, about 12 March, *et seq.*, and in upper Italy; railway communications stop about 31 March, 1892

Rise of the rivers in Illinois; 15 towns flooded (see *Mississippi* and *Iowa*) . . . about 6 May, ,,

Great floods in Italy, near Genoa; bridges, &c., destroyed; several deaths; lake Como overflows, about 13 Oct.; railway communication between Rome and Genoa stopped . 15 Oct. *et seq.* ,,

Great floods through heavy rains in N. E. Yorkshire; much damage in York, Leeds, and other places; several persons, and cattle and sheep drowned . . . . . . 13–15 Oct. ,,

Destructive floods in Derbyshire and Wales, 13 Oct. *et seq.* ,,

Disastrous floods in Sardinia and Venezuela (*which see*) . . . . Oct. ,,

Destructive floods in Queensland, 5 Feb. *et seq.*; in Hungary, 28 Feb. *et seq.*; N. S. Wales, 9 March (*all which see*) 1893

Inundations in Roumania; railways stopped and villages destroyed . . . . . May, ,,

Destructive floods in upper Hungary; more than 30 lives lost, reported . . . 14 Aug. ,,

Destructive inundations in Spain (*which see*), about 15 Sept.; in Naples and in N. Italy, through heavy rains . . . . . . 1–2 Oct. ,,

Overflow of the river Noir, near Quebec, caused by a landslide; about 20 deaths, much live-stock and property destroyed . . . 28 April, 1894

Destructive floods in Wisconsin, U.S.A., and other places; bridges destroyed and railway traffic stopped, 15–17 May; receding . 22 May, ,,

Destructive floods in the Punjaub, May (*which see*), and in Hungary . . . . . . June, ,,

Floods at Lucknow; houses submerged, reported, 13 Sept. ,,

Floods in France and Belgium; about 100,000 hands out of work, reported . . . . 31 Oct. ,,

Heavy rains; overflow of the Avon at Bath; much damage . . . . . . 12–13 Nov. ,,

Overflow of the Thames from Windsor to Oxford; railway stopped and much damage . 15 Nov. ,,

Destructive floods in the Thames valley, S. W. counties and Wales . . 21 Jan. *et seq.* 1895

Floods on the lower Danube; villages submerged; much suffering; some deaths, reported, 21 April, ,,

Bursting of a reservoir in the Vosges, see *France*, 27 April, ,,

Great loss of life and destruction of property through the overflow of the Tigris, in Mesopotamia; reported . . . . . 2 March, 1896

Floods in many parts of Switzerland, through snow and heavy rains . . . . . . March, ,,

Great floods, accompanied by a heavy gale, in N. Wales, railway traffic suspended; houses flooded; much suffering at Llanelly, estimated damage over 100,000*l*. . . . . 6–8 Oct. 1896
Destructive floods through heavy rains in Italy and France . . . . 20 Oct. ,,
Destructive floods, with loss of life, in Sao Miguel, Azores . . . . 4 Nov. ,,
Great floods, with loss of life, in N. Greece, 23 Dec.; increasing, villages submerged 31 Dec. ,,
Floods in Spain through the rising of the Guadalquiver . . . . 9 Jan. 1897
Extensive floods through heavy rains and snow, in S. midlands and eastern counties early Feb. ,,
Destructive floods, with loss of life, in the Mississippi valley . . . . . 20 March, ,,
Destructive floods in Silesia and Saxony, great loss of life . . . . . . 30 July–1 Aug. ,,
Destructive floods and tidal wave, Kentish coast, estimated damage, 30,000*l*. . . . 28–30 Nov. ,,
Destructive floods in Shan-Tung . early Nov. 1898
Overflow of the Brazos, in Texas (over 100 deaths), *which see* . . . . . early July, 1899
Serious floods in Silicia, Galicia, and N.W. Hungary, crops destroyed, much damage, reported, 11 July, ,,
Destructive floods in Chubat, Argentina 10 Aug. ,,
Floods in Austria, 19 lives lost by the collapse of a bridge over the Traun . . . 15 Sept. ,,
Destructive floods, villages, &c., swept away, 40 deaths, in Salem, 7, 8 Oct. 1899 . April, 1900
Floods in various parts of Japan, 200 deaths reported . . . . 15 Aug. ,,
Floods in Calcutta and Delhi, with loss of life, reported . . . . 22 Sept. ,,
Heavy floods in the Midlands and W. of England, 30, 31 Dec. ,,
Fatal floods in Italy, at Padua, Veneta, and elsewhere . . . . 20 March, 1901
Destructive floods in Canada and Quebec, towns submerged . . . . . . early April, ,,
Floods on the Yang-tsze river, near Han-kan; great loss of life and property . . 15–24 July, ,,
Floods in Japan, many deaths . . mid July, ,,
Floods in Zaragoza, Spain, some deaths . 24 Aug. ,,
Floods in Scotland, Wales, and Derbyshire, 31 Dec. 1901–Jan. 1902
Floods in S. Bengal, 25 villages and 2 bridges swept away, 6,000 homeless, reported . 15 Sept. ,,
Destructive floods, Clydesdale, Glasgow 9 Feb. 1903
Floods in Canada and Pennsylvania 2–25 March, ,,
Destructive floods at St. Louis, U.S. end May, early June, ,,
Disastrous floods in the Thames and Lea valleys, Bucks, and elsewhere, caused by heavy rainfall: much damage to fruit and crops . 8–19 June, ,,
Torrential rainfall, the heaviest in records of Weather Bureau, and floods, N. York and middle Atlantic States, and eastern coastboard, cities under water, lives lost, thousands homeless, great damage to property, reported . 11 Oct. ,,

See *Mansion House Funds*.

INVALIDES, HÔTEL DES, Paris, founded in 1671 by Louis XIV. Its chapel contains the body of Napoleon I., deposited there 15 Dec. 1840.

INVASIONS OF THE BRITISH ISLANDS, see *Britain*, and *Danes*. From the death of Edward the Confessor, only the following invasions marked (*s*) have been successful:—

William of Normandy (*s*.) . . . . . 29 Sept. 1066
The Irish 1069
The Scots, 1091; king Malcolm killed 1091
Robert of Normandy 1103
The Scots 1136
The empress Maud 1139
Ireland, by Fitz-Stephen (*s*.) 1169
Ireland, by Edward Bruce 1315
Isabel, queen of Edward II. (*s*.) 1326
Duke of Lancaster (*s*.) 1399
Queen of Henry VI. 1462
Earl of Warwick (*s*.) 1470
Edward IV. (*s*.) 1471
Queen of Henry VI. 1471
Earl of Richmond (*s*.) 1485
Lambert Simnel 1487
Perkin Warbeck 1495
Spaniards and Italians, Ireland 1580
Ireland, Spaniards 1601
Duke of Monmouth 1685
William of Orange (*s*.) 1688
James II., Ireland 1689
Old Pretender 1708
Pretender again 1715
Young Pretender 1745
Ireland (see *Thurot*) 1760
Wales, the French 1797
Ireland: the French land at Killala (*which see*) . . 1798

INVENTION. See *Cross*, *Patents*, *Tools*. An international exhibition of inventions and music at South Kensington in 1885; proposed, Aug. 1884; opened by the prince of Wales, 4 May, 1885; chairman, sir F. J. Bramwell; closed 9 Nov. 1885; 3,760,581 persons admitted. The receipts were 214,403*l*. See *Colonies*.

INVENTORS' INSTITUTE, established in May, 1862; first president, sir David Brewster.

INVERARAY, Argyllshire, made a royal burgh, 1648. The duke of Argyll's castle, rebuilt by Adam, 1745-8, was greatly injured by fire, 12 Oct. 1877.

INVERNESS (N.W. Scotland), a city of the Picts up to 843. It was taken by Edward I.; retaken by Bruce, 1313; burnt by the lord of the isles, 1411; taken by Cromwell, 1649; and by prince Charles Edward in 1746. He was totally defeated at Culloden, about five miles from Inverness, 16 April, 1746. Population, 1881, 17,365; 1891, 19,214; 1901, 21,193.

INVESTIGATION. See *Delicate*.

INVESTITURE OF ECCLESIASTICS, was a cause of discord between the pope and temporal sovereigns in the middle ages; and led to actual war between Gregory VII. and the emperor Henry IV. 1075-1085. The pope endeavoured to deprive the sovereign of the right of nominating bishops and abbots, and of investing them with the cross and ring. Henry V. gave up the right, by treaty, Feb. 1111; but other sovereigns resolutely refused to concede it.

INVINCIBLE ARMADA or **SPANISH ARMADA,** see *Armada*.

INVINCIBLES, IRISH, see *Irish Invincibles*, *Fenians* and *Ireland*, 1882-3.

INVOCATION OF THE VIRGIN AND SAINTS to intercede with God. This practice of the Romish church has been traced to the time of Gregory the Great, 593. The Eastern church began (in the 5th century) by calling upon the dead, and demanding their suffrage as present in the divine offices.

IODINE (from the Greek *iōdēs*, violet-like), was discovered by M. De Courtois, a manufacturer of saltpetre at Paris in 1812, and investigated by M. Clement, 1813. On the application of heat it rises in the form of a dense violet-coloured vapour, easily evaporates, and melts at 220 degrees: it changes vegetable blues to yellow, and a seven-thousandth part converts water to a deep yellow colour, and starch into a purple.

IONA, ICOLMKILL, or **HII,** one of the Hebrides. About 565 St. Columba founded a monastery here, which flourished till the 8th and 9th centuries, when it was frequently ravaged by the Norsemen. Other religious bodies afterwards were formed here, and the isle was long esteemed sacred.

IONIA (Asia Minor). About 1040 B.C. the Iones, a Pelasgic race, emigrated from Greece, and settled here and on the adjoining islands. They built Ephesus, Smyrna, and other noble cities. They were conquered by the great Cyrus about 548 B.C.; revolted 504, but were again subdued. After the victories of Cimon, Ionia became independent and remained so till 387, when it was once more subjected to Persia. It formed part of the dominions of Alexander and his successors; was annexed to the Roman empire, 133, and conquered by the Turks.—Ionia was renowned for poets, historians, and philosophers. The "Antiquities of Ionia" were published by Chandler, Revett, and Pars, 1769-1840, and the Dilettanti Society, 1840-1881.

IONIAN ISLANDS (on W. coast of Greece). Corfu, the capital, Cephalonia, Zante, Ithaca, Santa Maura, Cerigo, and Paxo. They were colonised by the Iones, and partook of the fortunes of the Greek people; were subject to Naples in the 13th century, and in the 14th to Venice.

The islands ceded to France by the treaty of Campo Formio . . . . 17 Oct. 1797
Formed into the republic of the seven islands under Russia and Turkey . . . . 21 March, 1800
Restored to France by treaty of Tilsit . 7 July, 1807
Taken by the English . . . . . 3-12 Oct. 1809
Formed into an independent state under the protection of Great Britain (sir Thomas Maitland, lord high commissioner) . . . . . . 5 Nov. 1815
A constitution ratified . . . . . 11 July, 1817
A university established at Corfu 1823
The constitution liberalised during the government of lord Seaton 1848-9
In consequence of complaints, Mr. W. E. Gladstone went out on a commission of inquiry, &c. . Nov. 1858
Sir H. Storks, lord high commissioner . . Feb. 1859
The parliament declare for annexation to Greece, March, 1861, and April, 1862
The islands annexed to Greece, 28 May; the British troops retired, 2 June, and king George I. arrived at Corfu (see *Greece*) . . . . . . 6 June, 1864
Zante suffered greatly by earthquakes, beginning with a violent shock, 31 Jan., followed by other shocks in the town of Zante and the neighbourhood; several thousands were rendered homeless and endured many privations, which were much relieved by the officers of H.M.S. *Camperdown* and other foreign vessels. It is stated that only 6 persons were killed by the shocks. The island was visited by the king and queen of Greece, by whom means of relief were organized, 6-8 Feb.; estimated damage, over 600,000*l.* Subscriptions received in Greece, London, &c., Feb.; frequent shocks, Feb., March; violent shocks in the town of Zante, the church and other buildings destroyed; 17 deaths; shocks, with many deaths, in other parts of the island, 17 April; much help given by Greek and French ironclads and H.M.S. *Inflexible*, 17, 18 April; more shocks . 21 April, 1893

IONIC ORDER OF ARCHITECTURE, an improvement on the Doric, was invented by the Ionians about 1350 B.C. *Vitruvius.* Its distinguishing characters are the slenderness and flutings of its columns, and the volutes of rams' horns that adorn the capital.

IONIC SECT OF PHILOSOPHERS, founded by Thales of Miletus about 600 B.C., distinguished for its abstruse speculations under his successors and pupils, Anaximander, Anaximenes, Anaxagoras, and Archelaus, the master of Socrates. They held that the world is a living being, and that water is the origin of all things.

IOWA, a western state of North America, was organised as a territory 12 June, 1838; and admitted into the Union, 28 Dec. 1846. Capital, Des Moines. Population, 1880, 1,624,615; 1890, 1,911,896; 1900, 2,231,853.

Sioux City suffered much by inundations, causing great loss of life . . . . about 18 May, 1892
Hotel burnt at Cedar Rapids; 10 deaths 20 Feb. 1903
Inundations caused by heavy rains occasion great damage . . . . end of May, ,,

IPSUS (Phrygia), **BATTLE OF,** Aug. 301 B.C., when Seleucus was confirmed in his kingdom of Syria by the defeat and death of Antigonus, king of Asia. The latter led into the field an army of about 70,000 foot and 10,000 horse, with 75 elephants. The former had 64,000 infantry, besides 10,500 horse, 400 elephants, and 120 armed chariots. *Plutarch.*

IPSWICH (Suffolk), the Saxon Gippeswic, was ravaged by the Danes, 991 and 1000. Wolsey was born here, 1471; and founded a school in 1525. The port was greatly improved by the erection of wet docks, 1837-42. The railway to London was opened 25 June, 1846; and the new town-hall, 29 Jan. 1868. New corn exchange opened, 26 July, 1882. The British Association met here in 1851 and 1895. Lord Kitchener presented with the freedom, 22 Sept. 1902. Victoria Nursing Institute opened by Princess Christian 9 May, 1903. Pop. 1901, 66,622.

IQUIQUE, see *Chili*, 1879.

IRELAND, anciently named Eri or Erin, Ierne and Hibernia, is said to have been first colonised by Phœnicians. The early mythical history has many beautiful legends. The Irish language is a branch of the Gaelic. See *Church of Ireland*, and *Population*, 1891, 4,706,162; 1901, 4,456,546. "The Annals of the Four Masters," edited by O'Donovan, were published in Irish and English, 1848. J. T. Gilbert's "History of the Viceroys of Ireland," published 1865. Dr. Hyde's "Literary History of Ireland," published 1899; *Forus Feasa ar Eirinn*, "The History of Ireland," by Geoffrey Keating, edited, with translation and notes, by David Comyn; Vol. I. published 1902.

A.D.
Arrival of St. Patrick . . probably 4th or 5th century
Christianity established . . . . . about 448
The Danes and Normans, known by the name of Easterlings, or Ostmen, invade Ireland . . 795
They build Dublin and other cities . . . about 800
Brian Boroimhe totally defeats the Danes at Clontarf; and is killed . . . . 23 April, 1014
Magnus III., king of Norway, defeated and slain during an invasion 1103
[In the 12th century Ireland is divided into five kingdoms, viz.: Ulster, Leinster, Meath, Connaught, and Munster, besides a number of petty principalities, whose sovereigns continually warred with each other.]
Adrian IV. permitted Henry II. to invade Ireland, on condition that he compelled every Irish family to pay a carolus to the holy see, and held it as a fief of the Church 1155
Dermot MacMurrough, king of Leinster, driven from his throne for his oppression 1166

Flees to England, where he takes an oath of fidelity to Henry II. who promises to restore him . . 1168
Invasion of the English under Fitz-Stephen . . 1169
Landing of Strongbow at Waterford . . . . ,,
Dermot dies 1171
Henry II. lands near Waterford, and receives the submission of the princes of the country, settles the government, and makes his son John lord of Ireland . . . . May, 1177
Invasion of king John, English laws, &c., introduced 1210
Invasion of Edward Bruce, 1315; crowned king . 1316
Defeated and slain at Foughart, near Dundalk 1318
Lionel, duke of Clarence, third son of Edward III., marries Elizabeth de Burgh, heiress of Ulster . 1361
Statute of Kilkenny passed by him (*which see*) . 1367
Richard II. lands at Waterford with a train of nobles, 4000 men-at-arms, and 30,000 archers; gains the affection of the people by his munificence, and confers the honour of knighthood on their chiefs 1394
Richard again lands in Ireland 1399
The sanguinary Head act passed at Trim, by the earl of Desmond, deputy, to suppress robbery. Much slaughter is said to have ensued . . . 1465
Apparel and surname act (the Irish to dress like the English, and to adopt surnames) . . . . ,,
Sir Edward Poynings sent to punish the Anglo-Irish for supporting Perkin Warbeck; he enacts a law, subjecting the Irish parliament to the English council 1494
Great rebellion of the Fitzgeralds, or Geraldines subdued 1534
Henry VIII. assumes the title of *king*, instead of *lord* of Ireland 1542
The reformed religion embraced by some of the English settlers in the reign of Edward VI. . . 1547
Insurrection of Shan O'Neill, earl of Tyrone, 1561; pardoned and received in London, 1562; rebels and becomes dominant in Ulster, 1564; assassinated . . . . 2 June, 1567
Ireland finally divided into shires 1569
Printing in Irish characters introduced by N. Walsh, chancellor of St. Patrick's 1571
Great expedition of Walter Devereux, earl of Essex, to put down the O'Neills, sanguinary, but unsuccessful . . . . 1573 *et seq.*
700 Italians, headed by Fitzmaurice, land in Kerry; they are treacherously butchered by the earl of Ormond 1580
Hugh or Shan O'Neill, who had been brought up at the court of Elizabeth, returns to Ireland as earl of Tyrone; revolts, 1597; defeats the English at Blackwater (*which see*) . . 14 Aug. 1598
Unsuccessful expedition of Robert, earl of Essex 1599
O'Neill invites over the Spaniards, and settles them in Kinsale; defeated by the lord deputy Mountjoy 1601–2
Flight of the earls of Tyrone, Tyrconnel, and others, to join the Spaniards 1606
In consequence of repeated rebellions and forfeitures, 511,465 acres of land in the province of Ulster became vested in the crown, and James I. after removing the Irish from their hills and fastnesses, divides the land among such of his English and Scottish protestant subjects as choose to settle there. (See *Irish Society*) . . . 1609–12
Ulster civil war: More and Maguire's rebellion; the catholics said to conspire to expel the English, and massacre the protestant settlers in Ulster, commenced on St. Ignatius' day [some doubt the massacre] . . . . 23 Oct. 1641
O'Neill defeats the English under Monroe at Benburb . . . . 5 June, 1646
Massacre and capture of Drogheda by Cromwell 12 Sept. 1649
Cromwell and Ireton reduce the whole island and redivide it 1649–1659
Landing of James II. . . . 12 March, 1689
3000 protestants attainted . . . July, ,,
William III. lands at Carrickfergus . 14 June, 1690
Battle of the Boyne; James defeated . 1 July, ,,
Treaty of Limerick (see *Limerick*) . . 3 Oct. 1691
Linen manufacture encouraged 1696
Popery act passed 1704
Excitement against Wood's halfpence (*which see*) . 1724
Thurot's invasion (see *Thurot*) 1760
Indulgences granted to the catholics by the relief bill 1778
Ireland admitted to a free trade 1779
Henry Grattan claims independence for the Irish parliament in speeches delivered 19 April, 1780, and 16 April, 1782
The Irish parliament declared independent by an act passed in the English parliament, May 1782; confirmed by another act passed 1783
Genevese refugees received in Waterford . . . ,,
Order of St. Patrick established . . . . . ,,
Society of United Irishmen founded 1791
Orange clubs, &c., formed (see *Diamond*) . . . 1795
Irish rebellion commenced 4 May, 1798; cost 150,000 Irish lives, 20,000 English; gradually suppressed 1799
Legislative Union of Great Britain and Ireland 1 Jan. 1801
Emmett's insurrection . . . . . 23 July, 1803
English and Irish exchequers consolidated 5 Jan. 1817
Visit to Ireland of George IV. . 11 Aug.–16 Sept. 1821
The Catholic Association organised by Daniel O'Connell and others (see *Roman Catholics*) . 1823
The currency assimilated . . . . 1 Jan. 1826
Daniel O'Connell is elected M.P. for Clare, but does not sit . . . . 5 July, 1828
Roman catholic emancipation act passed 13 April, 1829
Customs consolidated . . . . . 6 Jan. 1830
Dr. Whately, supporter of Irish National School system, becomes abp. of Dublin 1831
Irish reform act passed . . . . 7 Aug. 1832
Poor laws introduced: act passed . . 31 July, 1838
"Young Ireland" (*which see*) party formed . . 1840
Population by census, 8,196,597 1841
Great Repeal movement, lead by O'Connell; meeting at Trim (see *Repeal*) . . 16 March, 1843
Molly Maguire, a secret society, formed . . . ,,
O'Connell's trial (for political conspiracy), found guilty (see *Trials*) . . . 15 Jan.–12 Feb. 1844
Appointment of new commissioners of charitable bequests (rank of the R. C. bishops recognised) 18 Dec. ,,
Irish National Education Board incorporated 23 Sept. 1845
Committal of William Smith O'Brien to the custody of the serjeant-at-arms, for contempt in not obeying an order of the house of commons to attend a committee . . . . 30 April, 1846
Failure of the potato crop throughout Ireland; sufferers relieved by parliament . . . . . ,,
William Smith O'Brien and the "Young Ireland," or physical force party, secede from the Repeal Association . . . . 29 July, ,,
O'Connell's last speech in the commons 8 Feb. 1847
Grants from Parliament amounting to 10,000,000*l.* to relieve the people suffering from famine and disease . . . . ,,
Death of O'Connell at Genoa, on his way to Rome, in his 73rd year; he bequeathed his heart to Rome 15 May, ,,
Deputation from the Irish people (?)—Smith O'Brien, Meagher, O'Gorman, &c.—to Lamartine and others, members of the provisional government at Paris . . . . 3 April, 1848
Great meeting of "Young Irelanders" at Dublin 4 April, ,,
Arrest of Mitchell, editor of the *United Irishman* 13th May, ,,
State trials in the Irish queen's bench 15–27 May, ,,
Mitchell found guilty and sentenced to transportation for 14 years . . . . . 26 May, ,,
Arrest of Gavan Duffy, Martin, Meagher, Doheny, &c., for felonious writings, speeches, &c. 8 July, ,,
Confederate clubs prohibited . . . 26 July, ,,
The Habeas Corpus act suspended . . 26 July, ,,
O'Brien's rebellion suppressed . . . 29 July, ,,

Arrest of Smith O'Brien at Thurles; he is conveyed to Kilmainham gaol, Dublin . . 5 Aug. 1848
Arrest of Meagher, O'Donoghue, &c. . . 12 Aug. ,,
Martin sentenced to transportation . 14 Aug. ,,
Encumbered estates act passed . . Sept. ,,
Smith O'Brien, Meagher, and the other confederates tried and sentenced to death . 9 Oct. ,,
The Irish court of queen's bench gives judgment on writs of error sued out by the prisoners convicted of high treason, and confirms the judgment of the court below 16 Jan. 1849
O'Brien, Meagher, McManus, and O'Donoghue transported . . 9 July, ,,
Orange and catholic affray at Dolly's Brae; several lives lost 12 July, ,,
Her majesty visits Ireland, and holds her court at Dublin castle . . 5 Aug. ,,
First court under the encumbered estates act (*which see*) held in Dublin 24 Oct. ,,
Queen's university in Ireland established 15 Aug. 1850
Synod of Thurles condemns queen's colleges 22 Aug. ,,
Census taken; population, 6,574,278 . 30 March, 1851
Roman catholic university originated, and large sums subscribed . . 5 May, ,,
Death of R. Lalor Sheil, at Florence . 25 May, ,,
McManus escapes from transportation, and arrives at San Francisco, in California . . 5 June, ,,
The Irish Tenant League hold a meeting on the site of the battle of the Boyne . 14 July ,,
First meeting of the "Catholic Defence Association" 17 Oct. ,,
Meagher escapes from Van Diemen's Land and arrives at New York . . 24 May, 1852
Cork National Exhibition opened 10 June, ,,
Irish Industrial Exhibition set on foot; Mr. Dargan, a railway contractor, contributes towards it 26,000*l.* 24 June, ,,
"Tenant Right" demonstration at Warrenstown dispersed by the magistrates . 3 July, ,,
Fierce religious riots at Belfast . 14 July, ,,
Fatal election riot at Six-Mile Bridge 22 July, ,,
Irish members of parliament found a "Religious Equality Association" . 10 Sept. ,,
Cork Industrial Exhibition closed . . 11 Sept. ,,
Income tax extended to Ireland . . June, 1853
Mitchell escapes from Hobart Town . 9 June, ,,
Dublin Exhibition opens . . . 12 May, ,,
Queen visits Ireland . . . 29 Aug. ,,
Tenant Right League conference . 4 Oct. ,,
Dreadful railway accident near Dublin . 5 Oct. ,,
Dublin Exhibition closed . 1 Nov. ,,
Train wilfully upset after an Orange demonstration at Londonderry, one person killed and many hurt 15 Sept. 1854
A pardon granted to O'Brien; he shortly after returned to Ireland . . 3 May, 1856
Religious riots at Belfast . Sept. 1857
Progress of cardinal Wiseman in Ireland Sept. 1858
A packet from Galway reaches N. America in six days . . Sept. ,,
Proclamation against secret societies . Nov. ,,
Arrests of members of Phœnix Society . Dec. ,,
Proposed demonstration of landlords (headed by marquis of Downshire) given up . . 27 Jan. 1859
National Gallery founded Feb. ,,
Agitation against the Irish National School system, Sept. ,,
Religious revival movement in the north, particularly at Belfast . Oct. ,,
Great emigration to America in the spring . . 1860
Many Irishmen enlist in the service of the pope, May, June; many return dissatisfied July, ,,
The remainder taken prisoners by the Sardinians are released, and return to Dublin, where they receive an ovation . Nov. ,,
Attempted revival of Repeal agitation . Dec. ,,
Agrarian outrages; alderman Sheehy murdered, 23 Oct. ,,
Census taken; population, 5,798,967 . 8 April, 1861
Suspension of packet service between Galway and America through the company's breach of contract, 23 May, ,,
Visit of the prince of Wales, 29 June; and the queen and prince consort . . 24-31 Aug. ,,
Irish Law Court commission appointed 13 Dec. ,,
Numerous agrarian murders; Gustav Thiebault, 28 April; Francis Fitzgerald, 16 May (and others); Michael Hayes shoots Mr. John Braddell, 30 July, 1862
The primate, J. G. Beresford, abp. of Armagh, dies, aged 89 . . . 19 July, ,,
Building for the catholic university founded, 20 July, ,,
An Orange demonstration at Belfast leads to destructive riots . . . 17 Sept. ,,
Great agricultural distress; many murders and outrages, end of 1862, beginning of . 1863
Galway packet service restored by subsidy of 70,000*l.* (see *Galway*) . . Aug. ,,
Insignificant "Nationalist" meeting . 15 Aug. ,,
Death of archbishop Whately . . 8 Oct. ,,
Great emigration of able-bodied labourers in . ,,
Appearance of the Fenians (*which see*) . Jan. 1864
Death of Smith O'Brien, descendant of king Brian Boroimhe . . 16 June, ,,
Address of the "National Association" to liberate tenant capital, recover the property of the Catholic church, &c. 12 Jan. 1865
Opening of the International Exhibition at Dublin by the prince of Wales . . 9 May, ,,
General election favourable to the government and liberal party . . July, ,,
Importation of cattle from England prohibited on account of the plague . 25 Aug. ,,
Seizure of the newspaper *Irish People* and 30 Fenians (see *Fenians*) 15-17 Sept., 14 Oct. ,,
International Exhibition closed . 9 Nov. ,,
Stephens escapes from gaol . . 24-25 Nov. ,,
Fenian trials began at Dublin, 27 Nov.; Thomas Clarke Luby convicted of treason felony; sentenced to 20 years' penal servitude 1 Dec. ,,
O'Leary and others convicted, Dec.; O'Donovan Rossa sentenced to imprisonment for life, 13 Dec. ,,
More Fenians arrested and convicted at Cork and Dublin . . Jan., Feb. 1866
Discovery of an arms manufactory at Dublin; the city and county proclaimed as put under the provisions of the Peace Preservation act, 11 Jan.
Habeas Corpus act suspended; many Fenians flee 17 Feb. ,,
Agitation respecting Irish church; debates in parliament . April, ,,
Lord Abercorn made lord-lieutenant . July, ,,
About 320 suspected Fenians remain in prison, 1 Sept. ,,
Great seizure of fire-arms . . 15 Dec. ,,
Clare and other counties proclaimed under Peace Preservation act . Dec. ,,
Election riots at Dungarvan; capt. Barthol-Kelly killed . . 28 Dec. ,,
Death of Wm. Dargan, promoter of Irish Exhibition, 7 Feb. 1867
Irish college of science established at Dublin early in ,,
Another Fenian outbreak (see *Fenians*), 5-13 March, ,,
Appointment of commission respecting church of Ireland agreed to . . 24 June, ,,
Chancery and Common-law Offices act passed, 20 Aug. ,,
Irish church commission appointed, earl Stanhope chairman . . 30 Oct. ,,
More trials of Fenians . Nov. ,,
Execution of Fenians (Allen, Gould, and Larkin) for murder of Brett, a policeman, at Manchester, 23 Nov. ,,
Funeral demonstrations for them at Cork, 24 Nov.; Dublin and Limerick . . 1 Dec. ,,
Party funeral processions prohibited . 12 Dec. ,,
Protest of Irish noblemen and gentlemen against Irish church establishment signed, about 12 Dec. ,,
Declaration of many Roman catholic clergy professing loyalty, but claiming self-government for Ireland . . . 23 Dec. ,,
Bp. Moriarty, of Kerry, publishes a circular censuring the funeral processions for Fenians 30 Dec. ,,
Prosecution of the *Irishman* newspaper for sedition . 10 Jan. 1868
Arrest of Geo. Francis Train on his arrival from America, on suspicion of Fenianism; soon discharged (claimed 10,000*l.*) . 18 Jan. ,,
Publication of facts proving the increased prosperity of the country . . 28 Jan. ,,
Great protestant defence meeting at Dublin, many peers present. . . . 6 Feb. ,,

Habeas Corpus act suspended till 1 March, 1869 (83 persons detained on suspicion) . . . Feb. 1868

Messrs. Sullivan and Pigott, convicted of seditious libels in their newspapers (the *Weekly News* and *Irishman*), sentenced to imprisonment and fine . . . . 18, 19 Feb. ,,

Mr. Johnston, grand master of an Orange lodge, imprisoned for infraction of Party Processions act, March,

Train arrested for debt . . . . . 3 March, ,,

Four nights' debate on Ireland in the Commons ended (Mr. Gladstone declared for disestablishment of the Irish protestant church) 16 March, ,,

Irish reform bill introduced into the Commons, 19 March, ,,

Debate on Mr. Gladstone's proposal for a committee on his resolutions for the disestablishment of the church (carried by 328 to 272), 30 March to early morning of . . . . . . 4 April, ,,

Mr. Featherstonehaugh, J.P., a deputy-lieut., shot dead while returning from Dublin (he had recently raised the rent of his tenants) . 15 April, ,,

Visit of prince and princess of Wales; arrive at Dublin; intense enthusiasm . . . 15 April, ,,

The prince and princess at Punchestown races, 16 April, ,,

The prince installed as a knight of St. Patrick, 18 April, ,,

The prince and princess at review in Phœnix-park, 20 April; leave Dublin . . . 24 April, ,,

Increased emigration to United States . . April, ,,

Mr. Gladstone's first resolution passed in the commons (by 330 to 265) early on 1 May; second and third resolutions passed . . . . 7 May, ,,

Irish archbishops and bishops present address to the queen at Windsor, on behalf of the Irish Church establishment . . . . 14 May, ,,

Irish Church commission recommend consolidation of dioceses and other reforms (1st report), 27 July, ,,

Earl Spencer lord lieutenant . . . . Dec. ,,

Visit of prince Arthur . . . . 5 April *et seq.* 1869

Many murders: Mr. Anketell, 3 March; Mr. Bradshaw, J.P., 24 April; Capt. Tarleton 28 April, ,,

Mayor of Cork, for a speech eulogizing Fenians, 27 April compelled to resign . . . . 11 May, ,,

Address of archbishop Leahy condemning agrarian murders . . . . 16 May, ,,

Irish Church bill introduced into the commons, 1 March; after much opposition passed, 26 July, ,,

Irish mixed schools denounced by abp. Cullen; support for a Catholic university demanded in a circular dated . . . . 18 Aug. ,,

Great agitation for amnesty to the Fenian convicts, Oct. ,,

Tenant-right agitation; a conference at Cork, 10 Sept.; county meeting at Kilkenny . 18 Oct. ,,

Jeremiah O'Donovan Rossa, a Fenian convict, elected M.P. for Tipperary . . 25 Nov. ,,

Many agrarian outrages . . . . Jan., Feb. 1870

O'Donovan Rossa's election annulled . 10 Feb. ,,

Irish Church convention met . about 21 Feb. ,,

Irish Land bill, read a second time in commons (442 against 11), 1 A.M., 12 March; read second time in the lords . . . . . . 17 June, ,,

New "Irish Peace Preservation act" passed, 4 April, ,,

Eight counties placed under this act . 29 April, ,,

Reported growth of a "Nationality" party among the Protestants . . . . . . July, ,,

Irish Land act passed . . . . . . 1 Aug. ,,

The "Home Government Association," to include all parties, meet at Dublin . . . 1 Sept. ,,

Aggressive outrages and murders . . Nov. ,,

Some Fenian convicts released from prison, Jan. 1871

John Martin, a nationalist, elected M.P., for Meath, 5 Jan. ,,

Census taken; population, 5,402,759 . 3 April, ,,

Bill for protection of life and property in Westmeath brought in (and passed 16 June) on account of ribandism . . . . 2 May, ,,

Chief constable Talbot shot, night of 11 July; died 15 July, ,,

Visit of the prince of Wales to open the Royal Agricultural exhibition . . . . . 1 Aug. ,,

Riot through attempted repression of Fenian sympathisers; several killed . . 7 Aug. ,,

French deputation (comte de Flavigny and others) to thank the Irish for the assistance of the Irish ambulance during the war; warmly received, with seditious demonstrations against England, 16-28 Aug 1871

Mr. Isaac Butt, leader of Home-rule movement, elected M.P. for Limerick . . . 20 Sept. ,,

The R. C. bishop of Derry, the O'Donoghue, and others, declare against the movement, Jan.; members in its favour elected for Galway and Kerry . . . . Feb. 1872

Peaceful state of the south; few prisoners for trial, March, ,,

Mrs. Neill murdered at her own door near Dublin, 27 May, ,,

Capt. Nolan, M.P. for Galway, unseated for intimidation by his agents; the R. C. bishops and clergy severely censured by justice Keogh in giving sentence . . . about 27 May, ,,

O'Byrne *v.* Marquis of Hartington, and others (police) for exceeding duty in suppressing a meeting in Phœnix-park, Dublin, in Aug. 1871; verdict for plaintiff, 25*l.* damages . 11 July, ,,

Fathers Loftus and Quain tried for undue interference in Galway election; jury disagreed, 10-14 Feb. 1874

Mr. Gladstone brings into the commons the Irish University bill (rejected and withdrawn) 13 Feb. ,,

The R. C. bishop of Clonfert, Dr. Duggan, tried and acquitted (see *Dublin*) . . 15-19 Feb. ,,

Trial: O'Keeffe *v.* Cardinal Cullen; begins (see *Trials*) 12 May, ,,

Home rule and amnesty associations active, Oct. ,,

Motions in favour of Home-rule (*which see*) defeated in parliament . . . 20 March & 3 July, ,,

Ireland reported very prosperous . . Aug. ,,

John Mitchell (*see above*, 1848, 1853), elected M.P. for Tipperary, 16 Feb.; election declared null by the Commons; he died 20 March; his friends, John Martin, M.P., died 29 March; and sir John Gray, M.P. died . . . . . . 9 April, 1875

Mitchell's election declared void . . 26 May, ,,

Peace Preservation Act renewed . . 28 May, ,,

Centenary of the birth of Daniel O'Connell celebrated at Dublin, many foreign R. C. dignitaries present; much dissension at the banquet between the Clerical and Home-rule parties . . 6 Aug. ,,

Mr. McSwiney, lord mayor of Dublin, endeavours to form a new party for "faith and fatherland," opposed to Home-rule . . . . Aug.-Sept. ,,

Catholic synod at Maynooth; mixed education censured . . . . Sept. ,,

Riots at Callan, Mr. O'Keeffe's chapel and house attacked (28 men committed for trial) . 11 Oct. ,,

Dissension between members of O'Connell centenary committee, which is dissolved . 26 Nov. ,,

Agrarian outrage, Mr. Bridges and party fired on in daylight, the coachman killed; several wounded at Mitchelstown, Cork (Crowe convicted of murder 25 July, executed 25 Aug.) . . 30 March, 1876

O'Keeffe (see above, *May*, 1874) submits to cardinal Cullen for compensation . . . . . May, ,,

An Irish university bill introduced by Mr. Butt (withdrawn) . . . . . . 16 May, ,,

County officers and courts act passed . 14 Aug. 1877

Supreme court of judicature act for Ireland, passed 14 Aug. ,,

Temporary strike of men on Great Southern and Western railway, about . . . 14-22 Sept. ,,

Dr. Moriarty, R. C. bp. of Kerry, patriotic, judicious . . . . died 1 Oct. ,,

Mr. Gladstone's private visit . 17 Oct. *et seq.* ,,

The judicature act comes into operation . 1 Jan. 1878

The earl of Leitrim (eccentric), his clerk, and driver shot dead near his lodge, Manor Vaughan, Donegal . . . . 2 April, ,,

Bill for reducing Irish borough suffrage to 1*l.* rejected in the commons (232-26) . . 15 May, ,,

Irish Sunday closing (public houses) bill, much opposed; passed . . . . . . 16 Aug. ,,

Irish intermediate education act passed . 16 Aug. ,,

Irish volunteer bill lost . . . . . 7 Aug. 1879

Bill to abolish the Queen's University, and to establish a new university (for Roman catholics), introduced by lord chancellor Cairns, 30 June; carried in commons (257-90), 25 July; passed 15 Aug. ,,

Prevention of crime act passed . . 15 Aug. ,,

An Irish national convention to meet at Dublin, proposed by Mr. Charles Stewart Parnell (see *Home Rule*). . . . . . . 11 Sept. 1879
Progresses of Mr. Parnell; much anti-rent agitation autumn, ,,
Appeal for the Irish national land league by Mr. Parnell, soliciting subscriptions to buy the land for the tenants . . . . 9 Oct. ,,
Exciting speeches of Mr. Parnell at Navan 11, 13 Oct. ,,
James Bryce Killen, barrister, J. W. Daly, proprietor of "Connaught Telegraph," and Michael Davitt (ex-Fenian, on ticket of leave) arrested at Dublin for sedition (at anti-rent meeting at Gurteen, Sligo, 2 Nov.); [prosecution lapsed,] 19 Nov. ,,
Great orderly meetings held at Dublin, Balla, &c. 21 Nov. *et seq.* ,,
Government arrangements for relieving distress published in Dublin . . . . . 22 Nov. ,,
Pastoral by abp. McCabe against the agitation; read . . . . 23 Nov. ,,
Thos. Brennan arrested for seditious speech (at Balla, on 22 Nov.) . . . . . . 5 Dec. ,,
The duchess of Marlborough (the viceroy's wife) appeals for help for distress in the west (*Times*). (See under *Mansion House*, 1879) 18 Dec. ,,
Mr. Parnell arrives at New York to agitate for help to relieve Ireland politically and pecuniarily 2 Jan. 1880
Riots at Carraroe, Connemara, and other places in Galway, in consequence of notices of eviction 2 Jan. *et seq.* ,,
Contributions to the famine funds arrive from Canada, Australia, India, United States, &c. Jan. Feb. ,,
Mr. Parnell's agitation said to be a dead failure Feb. ,,
20,000*l.* received from lord mayor of London; (Dublin co. returns, 82,422*l.*) . . . 28 Feb. ,,
Seed supply act passed . . . . 1 March, ,,
Relief of distress (Ireland) act passed 15 March, ,,
Relief fund: 129,000*l.* received up to 25 March; 141,562*l.* . . . . . . up to 17 April, ,,
Charter for new Irish university signed by the queen 19 April, ,,
Relief for Irish distress brought in the *Constellation* from United States; arrives at Cork 20 April, ,,
Received for Irish distress, 177,401*l.*; distributed, 170,357*l.* . . . . . . up to 23 July, ,,
Compensation for Disturbance bill (to check evictions, restrain landlords, and benefit tenants), 2nd reading in commons (295-217), 5-6 July; passed in commons (303-237), 27 July; rejected by the lords (282-51) . . . . . 3 Aug. ,,
Mr. Thos. Boyd, crown solicitor, and sons fired at and wounded, Charles killed, at Shanlough, near New Ross . . . . . . Sunday, Aug. 8, ,,
40 cases of arms (960 weapons), stolen from the *Juno*, a Norwegian vessel, in the docks at Cork, 11 Aug.; some found concealed . 13 Aug. ,,
Rioting at Dungannon, Belfast . 15-18 Aug. ,,
Violent speech of Mr. Dillon, M.P., at Kildare, in favour of the land league, 15 Aug.; termed "wicked and cowardly" by Mr. W. E. Forster, who justifies the terms in parliament 23 Aug. ,,
Mr. Parnell proposes that tenant should become owner of land after paying 35 years' just rent Sept. ,,
The duchess of Marlborough's relief fund; total received from all parts 135,245*l.*, and 119*l.* interest from the Bank of Ireland; reported 19 Sept. ,,
Lord Mountmorres shot at Rutheen near Clonbar, Galway, about 8 p.m. . . . . 25 Sept. ,,
Progress of agitation; exciting speeches of Messrs. Parnell, Redpath, Dillon, and others advocating the principle of "boycotting" . Sept., Oct. ,,
105 leading landowners with agents wait on the lord-lieutenant at Dublin, describing the terrorist state of the south and west of the country and need of protection. . . . . . 7 Oct. ,,
R. C. abp. McCabe's pastoral against agitation and murders; read in chapels . . . 10 Oct. ,,
Agrarian outrages; John Downing, a driver, killed by a shot aimed at his employer, Mr. Samuel Hutchins, near Drimoleague, Cork . 16 Oct. ,,
Arrest of Timothy M. Healy, Mr. Parnell's secretary, and Mr. Walsh, for intimidation of Mr. Manning (on 16 Oct.) . . . 26, 27 Oct. ,,
Messrs. Parnell and others arrested for conspiracy and intimidation to prevent tenants paying rent, &c. (19 counts); notices served 3 Nov. *et seq.* 1880
Mr. Boycott of Lough Mask farm, near Ballinrobe, Mayo, besieged; his labourers threatened; his tradesmen refuse to supply him;—his crops gathered by immigrant labourers, protected by military, &c. . . . . . 11, 12 Nov. ,,
Mr. Henry Wheeler, land agent, murdered 12 Nov. ,,
Mr. Forster, Irish Secretary, sends a circular to the magistrates reminding them of their statutory powers . . . . . . about 8 Dec. ,,
Mr. W. Bence Jones of Ballinascorthy, treated like Mr. Boycott . . . . . . Dec. ,,
Three judges (Fitzgerald, Barry, and Dowse), deliver alarming charges on state of country Dec. ,,
Trial of Mr. Parnell and others for conspiracy, begins (see *Trials*) . . . . . 28 Dec. ,,
Jury disagree; discharged . . . . 25 Jan. 1881
About 25,000 soldiers in Ireland . . Jan. ,,
Report of Agricultural Commission (for Ireland) issued; great distress, 1877-9; good harvest, 1880; it opposes the three F's.; recommends emigration in some districts . . . . Jan. ,,
Bill for protection of life and property (termed *coercion bill*) brought in by Mr. Forster, 24 Jan.; long debates; much obstruction (see *Parliament*); passed commons, (281-36), 25, 26 Feb.; passed lords, 1-3 March; royal assent . . 3 March, ,,
Peace preservation bill (arms bill); introduced 1 March; passed commons, 11, 12 March; passed lords, 18 March; royal assent . . 21 March, ,,
Many agitators arrested; 23 in Kilmainham gaol, 10 March, ,,
"Clan-Na-Gael" secret society to replace Fenians said to be formed . . . . . . March, ,,
Irish land bill ("legalized confiscation"—*Beaconsfield*) introduced into the commons by Mr. Gladstone . . . . 7 April, ,,
More arrests (total about 40) . up to 20 April, ,,
Cruel outrages in different places; Dublin city proclaimed under coercion act, 1 May; John Dillon, M.P. arrested [released Aug.] . . 2 May, ,,
Division in Irish parliamentary party; Mr. Parnell and others oppose the land bill, about . 5 May, ,,
Increase in amount of crime . April, May, ,,
Total arrests, 54; increase of evictions . May, ,,
Irish land bill read 2nd time (352-176); Mr. Parnell and about 20 retire, 19, 20 May; 3rd time (220-14) 29 July, ,,
Agrarian outrages, 439, Jan.; 170, Feb.; 146, March; 296, April; 238 in three weeks . May, ,,
Riots connected with evictions at Scareff, co. Clare; some persons killed; many injured . 2 June, ,,
Rioting at various places in co. Cork., &c., 5, 6, 7 June, ,,
Population diminished one-ninth in ten years (by census) . . . . June, ,,
First publication of *United Ireland* . . July, ,,
Land bill in house of lords; read 2nd time, 2, 3 Aug.; 3rd time (with amendments), 8 Aug.; the commons reject some of the amendments, 12 Aug.; the lords resist, 13 Aug.; the commons modify the amendments, 15 Aug.; the lords yield, 16 Aug.; royal assent . . 22 Aug. ,,
Increased boycotting of shop-keepers and others, and much cruelty . . . . . . Sept. ,,
Great meeting of delegates from the Land League, denouncing the land act as a sham; Mr. Parnell present . . . . 17-19 Sept. ,,
Mr. Parnell arrested on charge of inciting to intimidation and for urging non-payment of rent; put into Kilmainham gaol, Dublin (*which see*) 13 Oct. ,,
This arrest "legal, merited, and expedient," *Times* 15 Oct. ,,
Arrest of Messrs. Sexton, O'Kelly, J. P. Quinn, secretary of Land League, Dillon, O'Brien, and others . . . . 14-16 Oct. ,,
Violent rioting at Dublin and Limerick; about 2000*l.* damage; soon suppressed; more arrests 15-18 Oct. ,,
More troops sent to Ireland from Chatham, &c.; manifesto of the Land League denouncing the government, and ordering non-payment of rent 18 Oct. ,,
This manifesto censured by archbishop Croke 19 Oct. ,,

First meeting of the Irish Land Commission court; addressed by justice O'Hagan . . . 20 Oct. 1881
Great calm at Dublin and Limerick 20 Oct. *et seq.* „
The lord lieutenant on the responsibility of Mr. W. E. Forster proclaims the suppression of the Land League as an illegal and criminal organization, 20 Oct.; the leaders declare for passive resistance; archbishop M'Cabe's pastoral against the Land League manifesto read in R. C. churches in Dublin . . . . . 30 Oct. „
Important decisions in favour of tenants by sub-commissions at Belfast, &c. . . . . Nov. „
2448 persons in prison; more arrests; some released announced 5 Nov. „
Home rule meeting at Dublin . . 8 Nov. „
Death of Dr. M'Hale, archbishop of Tuam, "Lion of the fold of Judah" . . . . 8 Nov. „
Above 40,000 applications to the land courts 12 Nov. „
Continuance of agrarian murders and outrages Nov. „
Strike against payment of rent in Limerick; evictions ordered . . . . . . 30 Nov. „
Irish Property Defence association (formed Nov. 1880) active and successful (see *Mansion-house Fund*) . . . . Nov.—Dec. „
Great increase of crime in Munster announced Dec. „
An association formed to support the law about 20 Dec. „
Proclamation against possession of arms in Dublin, &c. . . . . 27 Dec. „
Appointment of five special magistrates, with extra powers, in disturbed districts; 4439 agrarian outrages in the year . . . about 30 Dec. „
Several lady land leaguers arrested 2 Jan. *et seq.* 1882
Day of humiliation for Protestants . . 13 Jan. „
About 40 suspects arrested . . . . 28 Jan. „
Frequent murders reported . . . . Feb. „
Committee to enquire into working of land act voted by lords (96—53, 17 Feb.), earl Cairns chairman . . . . 23 Feb. „
Michael Davitt, convict, elected M.P. for co. Meath, 22 Feb.; annulled by the commons (see *Fenians*) . . . . 28 Feb. „
Bailey, an informer against Land League, murdered at Dublin . . . . 25 Feb. „
Mr. Gladstone's resolution against the lords' committee, 27 Feb.; carried (303—235) 9-10 March, „
The lords' committee sit . . . . . March, „
Continuance of murderous outrages . . March, „
Archbishop M'Cabe created cardinal 27 March, „
Mr. Forster confesses failure of government policy through influence of secret societies 27 March, „
511 suspects in prison . . . . . 1 April, „
Mr. Parnell released *en parole* for ten days, 10 April „
New government policy; resignation of Mr. W. E. Forster [Mr. Forster narrowly escaped assassination several times]; release of Mr. Parnell and other suspects; earl Spencer appointed lord lieutenant about 2 May, 1882; release of Michael Davitt . . . . 6 May, „
Lord Frederick Cavendish, new chief secretary, and Mr. T. H. Burke, permanent under-secretary, assassinated by stabbing, by four men ("Invincibles") about 7 p.m., in Phœnix-park, Dublin, 6 May; manifesto expressing abhorrence of the deed signed by C. S. Parnell, J. Dillon, and M. Davitt . . . . 7 May, „
Government offers 10,000*l.* reward for discoveries of the murderers; Mr. G. O. Trevelyan appointed chief secretary . . . . 9 May, „
Bill for the prevention of crime in Ireland introduced by sir W. V. Harcourt (new tribunal of three judges without jury for special occasions; powers of police increased; alien act to be revived; supervision of newspapers and of assemblies, &c.), 11 May, 1882; second reading (383—45) . . . . 19-20 May, „
Many arrests . . . . 12 May *et seq.* „
Alleged agreement of the government with Mr. Parnell and party, early May, 1882, sarcastically termed the *treaty of Kilmainham*; arrears of rent bill, second reading (269—157) . . . 23-24 May, „
Mr. Walter Bourke and corporal Wallace, his escort, shot dead by five men near Gort, Galway 8 June, „
Mr. John Henry Blake, agent to the marquis of Clanricarde, and his steward, Mr. Kane, shot dead near Loughrea 29 June, „
A long discussion in the commons on the prevention of crime bill; 23 Irish members suspended, 30 June—1 July, 1882
Mr. Parnell and home rulers withdraw, July, 1882; 22 arrests at Loughrea, 4 July; government defeated in an amendment checking domiciliary visits of suspected persons at night, 207—194; prevention of crime bill read third time, 7-8 July; passed by the lords, 11 July; royal assent, 12 July, „
17 counties proclaimed . . . about 13 July, „
170 suspects in custody . . . . . 2 Aug. „
The Lords' committee on the land act adjourns, 15 Aug. „
Mr. Edmund Dwyer Gray, M.P., high sheriff of Dublin, ex-lord mayor, sentenced to three months' imprisonment and a fine of 500*l.* for contempt of court in articles in *Freeman's Journal* attacking the jury on trial of Francis Hynes . 16 Aug. „
Arrears bill passed in the commons (285—177), 21 July; by the lords, with injurious amendments (169—98), 31 July; which are modified or negatived by the commons, 8, 9 Aug.; the revision accepted by the lords, 10 Aug.; royal assent, 18 Aug. „
50 suspects released . . . . . about 18 Aug. „
John Joyce and his wife, son and daughter, shot dead by band of men near Maamtrasma, in Clonder district, Galway, for giving information to the police . . . . . . 17-18 Aug. „
John Leahy, aged farmer, of Scarteen, Killarney, murdered by a moonlight party . . 20 Aug. „
Discontent and insubordination of the constabulary at Dublin, Cork, and especially at Limerick, settled by firmness and judicious concessions end of Aug. „
Dismissal of some police for holding a public meeting in Dublin; all the police of the city resign; order maintained by the military, who charge on rioters in the evening, 1 Sept.; special constables sworn in 2 Sept.; resignation withdrawn penitently with respectful petition 3 Sept.; 208 reinstated . . . . 6-7 Sept. „
Execution of Francis Hynes (for murder of John Doloughty) at Limerick, 11 Sept.; of Patrick Walsh, for murder of Martin Lyden, at Galway, 22 Sept. „
Successful progress of the lord lieutenant, earl Spencer, in the west . . . middle Sept. „
Conviction of Michael Walsh, for murder of Kavanagh, a policeman, 29 Sept.; penal servitude for life . . . . 19 Oct. „
Mr. E. D. Gray released . . . . . 30 Sept. „
Expiration of coercion act; all suspects released 30 Sept. „
Land league fund in North America closed 6 Oct. „
Nationalistic conference at Dublin constitutes a new Irish National League (ultra) to obtain self-government and land-law reform, Mr. C. Parnell president . . . . 17 Oct. „
Diminution of agrarian crime . . April—Nov. „
Murderous assault on justice Lawson at Dublin by Patrick Delany, a returned convict . . 11 Nov. „
Irish land commission report issued about 13 Nov. „
The land corporation of Ireland dissolved Nov. „
Conviction of murderers of Joyce family; Patrick Joyce, 15 Nov.; Patrick Casey, 17 Nov.; Myles Joyce, 18 Nov. [all executed, 15 Dec.]; Michael Casey, Thomas Joyce, John Casey, and Martin Joyce, confess; sentence commuted; Thomas Casey and Philbyn, approvers . . . 21 Nov. „
Murderous assault on detectives in Dublin; Cox killed; his murderer, Dowling, severely wounded 25 Nov. „
Mr. Field, a juryman, stabbed, 27 Nov.; reward of 5000*l.* for assassin; Dublin proclaimed under martial law . . . . 28 Nov. „
Patrick and Thomas Higgins convicted of murder of Haddys at Lough Mask [executed 15-17 Jan. 1883] . . . . 13 and 16 Dec. „
Also Michael Flyn . . . . . . 20 Dec. „
Sylvester Poff, James Barrett, convicted of murder, at Cork . . . . 22 Dec. „
Emigration from Ireland, 89,566 in the year . . „
Great distress in Donegal in the north-west; 3433 agrarian outrages in the year . . Dec. 1882—1883
Arrest in Dublin of 21 persons, suspected of conspiracy to murder . . . 12, 13 Jan. „

Robert Farrell, approver, reveals plot for assassination of the government . . . . 19 Jan. 1883
The pope's letter to archbishop McCabe, exhorting the clergy against secret societies, &c. about 20 Jan. ,,
Execution of Sylvester Poff and James Barrett, at Tralee, for murder . . . . 23 Jan. ,,
M. Davitt, Thos. Healy, M.P., and P. Quinn bound over for seditious speeches, 24 Jan.; elect to be imprisoned, 6 Feb.; imprisoned . . 8 Feb. ,,
Eight men charged with complicity in murder of lord Frederick Cavendish and Mr. Burke 3 Feb. ,,
Irish national league, first meeting . . 7 Feb. ,,
Revelations of James Carey, approver, implicating the Land League (Thos. Brennan, sec., and P. J. Sheridan); statement respecting the Irish Invincibles; arrest of Mrs. F. Byrne, charged with transmitting arms, &c., 17 Feb.; discharged 20 Feb. ,,
Accused prisoners committed for trial . 20 Feb. ,,
Mr. W. E. Forster's defence in the commons, and charges against Mr. Parnell; Mr. O'Kelly suspended for a week, for giving him the lie 22-23 Feb. ,,
Mr. Parnell's unsatisfactory reply . 23 Feb. ,,
Arrest of Mr. Byrne at Paris, 27 Feb.; released, about 9 March, ,,
Flight of Patrick Egan, treasurer of the Land League, from Dublin, 1 March; in New York, 12 March, ,,
Many thousand young forest trees for planting given by English, Scotch, and Irish nurserymen spring, ,,
R. C. bishops advocate government relief for distress in Connaught, Jan.; refused, poor-law relief reckoned sufficient . . . March, ,,
Twelve members of the "Patriotic Brotherhood" (established at Crossmaglen, 1881) sentenced to penal servitude for conspiracy to murder landlords . . . . 28 March, ,,
Phœnix-park murders; Robt. Farrell, Jas. Carey, and others, approvers; trial of Joseph Brady, convicted, 11-13 April; Timothy Kelly, third trial, 7-9 May; Thomas Caffrey pleads guilty, 2 May; Patrick Delany and Daniel Curley, 16-18 April; Michael Fagan . . . 25-27 April, ,,
Irish convention at Philadelphia; Parnell's policy adopted; dynamiters defeated . 25-27 April, ,,
Detection of conspiracy of the "Vigilance" murder organization at Dublin; prisoners examined, May, ,,
Powerful circular from the pope, strictly enjoining the bishops to abstain from favouring disaffection to the government, not to subscribe to testimonials, &c. [archbishop Croke, of Cashel, had given 50*l.* to the Parnell testimonial, &c.] 11 May, ,,
James FitzHarris and others convicted of conspiracy to murder; sentenced to penal servitude 16 May *et seq.* ,,
Messrs. Davitt, Healy, and Quinn released 4 June, ,,
Executed: Joseph Brady (actual murderer), 14 May; Daniel Curley, 18 May; Michael Fagan, 28 May; Thomas Caffrey, 2 June; Timothy Kelly, 9 June, ,,
Irish lace exhibition at the Mansion-house, London 25 June—7 July, ,,
James Carey, the approver, shot dead by Patrick O'Donnell, 29 July, on board the *Melrose Castle*, near Port Elizabeth, South Africa . 29 July, ,,
Loans amounting to 4,600,000*l.* for public works authorised by parliament . . . 25 Aug. ,,
National League invade Ulster, strongly resisted by the Orangemen at Auchnacloy, Dungannon, and other places . . . end of Sept. ,,
Sir Stafford Northcote warmly received at Belfast, Londonderry, &c. . . . . 3 Oct. ,,
Meeting of National League at Ennis prohibited 5 Oct. ,,
Meetings of Orangemen and National Leaguers at Garrison, Fermanagh, prohibited . . 13 Nov. ,,
Patrick O'Donnell convicted . . . 1 Dec. ,,
Mr. Trevelyan reports great diminution in agrarian outrage . . . . Oct.—Dec. ,,
38,000*l.* presented to Mr. Parnell ("as a national tribute" from the Irish people) at a banquet at the Rotunda, Dublin . . . 11 Dec. ,,
Execution of Patrick O'Donnell (see 29 July), at Newgate, 17 Dec.; of James Poole, at Dublin, for murder of John Kenny, informer . 18 Dec. ,,

A Parnellite land law amendment bill rejected by the commons (as tending to confiscation), by 235—72 . . . . . 5 March, 1884
Earl Spencer warmly received at Belfast 18 June, ,,
Serious libellous charges against Mr. Bolton, crown solicitor; subornation of witnesses, &c. July, Aug. ,,
Charges disproved; letter from earl Spencer 23 Aug. ,,
Irish National League convention at Dublin, Mr. P. O'Connor in the chair; urges revival of agitation against the government . . 6 Sept. ,,
Death of Mr. A. M. Sullivan, eminent Nationalist 17 Oct. ,,
Mr. H. Campbell-Bannerman, chief secretary, sworn in . . . . . 24 Oct. ,,
Maamtrasma trial impugned; their verdict supported by the commons (219—48) . 28 Oct. ,,
Attempted explosion of Edinburn-house (Samuel Hussey, land agent) by dynamite, near Tralee, Kerry; no deaths . . . 28 Nov. ,,
Death of cardinal McCabe, pacific and loyal 11 Feb. 1885
Parnellite manifesto directing Nationalist corporations to maintain an attitude of reserve during the prince of Wales' visit in April, issued about 16 Mar. ,,
The prince of Wales arrives at Dublin, 8 April; sails from Larne . . . . 27 April, ,,
The Irish R. C. bishops summoned to Rome; arrive 21 April; rebuked by the pope for disloyalty, &c., in separate interviews, 27 April–15 May; bishop Nulty's pastoral, foretelling secession of Ireland from Rome, causes great displeasure; the bishops oppose projected reforms at Maynooth, but are said to submit, announced 19 May; dismissed about . . 25 May, ,,
The earl of Carnarvon, lord lieutenant, arrives in Dublin . . . . . 30 June, ,,
Sir William Hart-Dyke appointed chief Secretary June ,,
Stoppage of the Munster bank for about 70,000*l.*; fraud disclosed July–Aug. 1885; reconstituted; opened . . . . . 19 Oct. ,,
Lord Ashbourne's act, granting 5,000,000*l.* for the purchase of land by tenant to be paid by instalments, passed . . . . 14 Aug. ,,
Progress of the earl of Carnarvon, lord lieut. in the west; well received . . 17 Aug. *et seq.* ,,
Mr. Parnell's resolute declaration to the nationalists at Dublin . . . . 25 Aug. ,,
Prevention of crime act expires; revival of boycotting and outrages . . . Sept. ,,
The first county convention, for controlling elections, held at Wicklow under Mr. Parnell . 5 Oct. ,,
Cork defence union formed (the earl of Bandon president) against the tyranny of the national league . . . . . Oct. ,,
The Cork steam packet company threatened with boycotting by the league; the company determined on resistance . . . 10 Oct. ,,
Aghadoe house, Killarney (Mr. Hussey's), attacked by "moonlighters" and defended with fire-arms 11 Oct. ,,
Manifesto of Mr. Parnell claiming "home rule" &c., published . . . . 11 Nov. ,,
Castle farm, Molahiffe, in Kerry, attacked for arms by moonlighters; Mr. John O'Connell Curtain killed, while his sons and daughters bravely resist; one assailant killed . . 13 Nov. ,,
[S. Cassey and D. Daly convicted of burglary, &c. 21 Dec.]
Elections: home-rule manifesto issued 21 Nov. ,,
Irish defence union formed to support local defence unions . . . . . . ,,
Irish loyal and patriotic union (southern), afterwards Irish unionist association, formed . . ,,
Mr. W. H. Smith, M.P., chief secretary for a short time . . . . . . Jan. 1886
The earl of Aberdeen, as lord lieut., and John Morley, as chief secretary, sworn in . 10 Feb. ,,
Irish loyal union, report to Mr. Gladstone, the systematic cruel oppression of the national league . . . . 27 March, ,,
Mr. Gladstone in a long speech introduces a bill "to make better provision for the future government of Ireland"; it proposes to establish a legislative body to sit in Dublin, to consist of two orders each with a veto; I. twenty-eight representative peers and seventy-five members elected for ten years; II. the present 103 Irish

members, and 101 additional: the lord-lieutenant with a privy council to be independent of Great Britain; the new body empowered to enact laws and to impose and collect taxes, except the customs, but not to interfere with the army and navy, or foreign and colonial affairs, and not to enact any religious endowment; present legal and police arrangements to remain temporarily subject to the crown; no Irish members to sit at Westminster, 8–9 April; read first time, 13–14 April; second reading rejected (343 [250 conservatives, 93 liberals]–313) . . . 7–8 June, 1886

The loyal and patriotic union formed May, 1885; great meeting at H. M.'s theatre, London, earl Cowper in the chair, the marquises of Salisbury and Hartington, and many leading conservative and liberal leaders present. Resolutions condemning Mr. Gladstone's Irish government bill passed; petitions to be presented to parliament 14 April, ,,

Sale and purchase of land bill introduced by Mr. Gladstone; (proposed creation of 50,000,000*l.* 3 per cent. stock from 1887-90) read 1st time 16 April, ,,

944 agrarian offences in 1885, reported . April, ,,

Archbishop Croke and his clergy express warm gratitude to Mr. Gladstone . about 30 April, ,,

Important meetings of liberals and conservatives against Mr. Gladstone's policy . 14–15 May, ,,

Intimidation practised by the "house league" upon owners of houses in Kerry, &c., to procure reduction of rent . . . . . May, ,,

Riots at Belfast *(which see)* . 9, 10 June *et seq.*

Armagh and Tyrone proclaimed under peace preservation act . . . . . 18 June, ,,

Dissolution of parliament; Mr. Gladstone being in a minority, resigns 20 July; Marquis of Salisbury supported by unionists, resumes office 26 July, ,,

The marquis of Londonderry as lord-lieut., and sir Michael Hicks-Beach as chief secretary, appointed . . . . . 26 July, ,,

Convention of about 1,000 delegates of Irish national league of America meet at Chicago; John Fitzgerald elected president 19–22 Aug. ,,

Gen. sir Redvers Buller with civil plenary powers appointed to command in Kerry, Clare, and Cork; arrives at Killarney . . . . 30 Aug. ,,

Mr. Parnell's amendment on the address negatived (304–181) . . . . . . 27, 28 Aug. ,,

Mr. Parnell introduces tenants' relief bill, 11 Sept.; rejected (297-202) . . . . 21–22 Sept. ,,

Capture of moonlighters and arms at Castleisland, Kerry . . . . 26 Sept. ,,

Two women shot by moonlighters for refusing to give up arms at a farm near Williamstown, Cork, 4 Oct. ,,

Plans of organization (termed *plan of campaign*) of tenantry in each estate against the landlords with stringent measures proposed (probably by Mr. John Dillon, leader of the national party, and Mr. William O'Brien) in *United Ireland*, organ of the national league (the tenant was to pay his rent to the league, and be supported by it if evicted) . . . . . 21 Oct. ,,

Sir Robert Hamilton, under secretary (said to be home ruler) resigns; (sir Redvers Buller temporary successor); col. Turner acts in Kerry 30 Nov. ,,

Increased agrarian agitation . . . Nov. ,,

Offices opened for the receipt of rents at Charleston, Mayo (lord Dillon's estate), many deposits 2 Dec. ,,

Prosecution of Mr. Dillon; the attorney-general terms the "plan of campaign" a combination of debtors to coerce creditors 11 Dec.; court of queen's bench requires Mr. Dillon to find securities for good behaviour, or be imprisoned for six months . . . . 14 Dec. ,,

Messrs. Dillon, Wm. O'Brien, Matthew Harris, and Sheehy arrested whilst receiving rents on lord Clanricarde's estate, the books and money seized 16 Dec. ,,

Proclamation against "plan of campaign" 18 Dec. ,,

Rents still illegally received by several M.P.'s about 18 Dec. *et seq.* ,,

The seat of prosecution removed from Loughrea to Dublin . . . . 20 Dec. ,,

Mr. Parnell states that he defers his opinion on the plan of campaign . . . . about 18 Dec ,

Chief Baron Palles in sentencing 36 Irish rioters, censures the "dispensing power" of the executive and the abstention of the police during riots at evictions . . . . 5 Jan. 1887

Prosecution of Mr. Dillon, five other M.P.s, and Mr. O'Brien (editor of *United Ireland*) begun at Dublin, 23 Dec.; committed and bailed 11 Jan. ,,

Mr. Parnell's amendment on the address relating to Irish affairs negatived (352 [68 liberals]–246) 11, 12 Feb. ,,

Evictions resisted by armed men; an "emergency" man dies of wounds at Ballycar . 14, 15 Feb. ,,

Resignation of sir M. Hicks-Beach, chief secretary, for ill-health; succeeded by Mr. Arthur J. Balfour . . . . . . 5 March, ,,

Riots at Youghal with bloodshed . 8 March, ,,

Justice O'Brien at Kerry says: "Law is at an end. There is a state of war with authority." 10 March, ,,

"*Parnellism and crime*" (which see) published in the *Times* . . . . 7 March *et seq.* ,,

Arrest of father Keller (supported by abp. Walsh) for contempt of court in refusing to give evidence (as a confessor) in a bankruptcy case, 18 March; committed to prison 19 March; father Ryan committed for same cause . 29 March, ,,

Increase of crime and lawlessness in south and west . . . . March, ,,

Trial of Messrs. Dillon and others, 14 Feb.; jury disagreeing, discharged 24 Feb.; proceedings withdrawn . . . . . . 1 April, ,,

Fathers Keller and Ryan and others released 21–24 May, ,,

Liberal unionist organization begins in Ireland 24 May, ,,

New criminal law procedure bill introduced by Mr. Balfour, 28 March; much opposition, Irish members and others retire 17–30 June, read 3rd time 8–9 July, passed by the lords 18 July; royal assent * . . . . . 19 July, ,,

Evictions at Bodyke in Clare, on property of colonel O'Callaghan; violently resisted early June, ,,

Labourer shot by a gang near Killarney 13 June, ,,

Prince Albert Victor and George of Wales visit Ireland . . . . . . 27 June, ,,

Jubilee address of unionist Roman catholics to the queen . . . . . . 29 June, ,,

Great meeting at Cork to resist the operation of the crimes act . . . . . . 19 July, ,,

Eighteen counties proclaimed under the crimes act; twelve counties partly proclaimed, together with Dublin and nine other cities . . 23 July, ,,

Monsignor Persico visits Ireland on behalf of the pope . . . . July, ,,

New Irish land bill (favourable to the tenant) passed; royal assent . . . . 23 Aug. ,,

The national league proclaimed as a "dangerous association" 19 Aug.; Mr. Gladstone's motion for an address to the queen against the proclamation negatived (272–194) . . . 25–26 Aug. ,,

Nationalist meeting at Ballycoree in Clare proclaimed 31 Aug.; attempted meeting dispersed 4 Sept. ,,

Meeting in support of Mr. W. O'Brien, M.P., and Mr. Mandeville, who refuse to obey the magistrates' summons respecting speeches at Mitchelstown on 9, 10 Aug.; about 150 horsemen and crowd, about 3,000, armed with

* *Members of parliament sentenced to imprisonment under the new act.* 1887. Mr. W. O'Brien 31 Oct.; Mr. E. Harrington 1 Dec.; Mr. T. Harrington 19 Dec.; Mr. Hooper 19 Dec.; Mr. Sheehy 21 Dec.

1888. Mr. J. R. Cox 25 Jan.; Mr. P. O'Brien 8 Feb.; Mr. Pyne 15 Feb.; Mr. Flyn 25 Feb.; Mr. Gilhooly 5 March; Mr. W. O'Brien 3 May, 20 June; Mr. Condon 27 May; Mr. Dillon 20 June; Mr. James O'Kelly 10 Aug.; Mr. Redmond 26 Sept.

1889. Mr. John O'Connor 31 Jan.; Mr. D. Sheehy 1 Feb.; Mr. J. R. Cox 2 Feb.; Mr. T. Condon 7 Feb.; Mr. Kilbride 8 Feb.; Mr. W. O'Brien 19 Feb.; Mr. Carew 21 Feb.; Dr. Tanner 7 March; Mr. Condon, Mr Connor, and Dr. Tanner 1 May; Mr. Conybeare 3 May; Mr. W. O'Brien and Mr. Gilhooly 25 Aug.; Mr. Redmond 22 Sept.

1890. Messrs. Wm. and Patrick O'Brien and John Dillon 19 Nov.

1891. Mr W. O'Brien and J. Dillon, 13 Feb.—31 July.

bludgeons and stones; Messrs. Labouchere, Dillon, Brunner and other M.P's. present; the police with the government reporter (Conderon) attacked with stones and bludgeons, retreat to barracks; return reinforced; compelled to fire; Michael Lonergan and John Shinnery killed and many wounded; town quieted by military 9 Sept. 1887

Constable Whelehan killed and three others wounded in defending T. Sexton's house near Lisdoonvarna against moonlighters . 11 Sept. ,,

[Leary and four others sentenced to penal servitude 10 Dec.]

The national league in Clare and several baronies (200 branches) suppressed by proclamation 20 Sept. ,,

Mr. O'Brien and Mr. Mandeville sentenced to three months' imprisonment . . . . 24 Sept. ,,

The lord mayor of Dublin (Mr. T. D. Sullivan) charged with offence against the crimes act (see *Dublin*) . . . . 6 Oct. ,,

Many meetings of suppressed branches of the national league . . . . . 9 Oct. ,,

Mr. Joseph Chamberlain, M.P., warmly received at Belfast and other places in Ulster by the liberal unionists and others . . . 11 Oct. *et seq.* ,,

Verdict of coroner's jury on deaths at Mitchelstown; wilful murder against county inspector Brownrigg, sergeants Ryder and Kirwan, and constables Gavan, Brennan, and Doran . 12 Oct. ,,

[Verdict quashed by the queen's bench, Dublin, 10 Feb. 1888.]

Col. sir Joseph West Ridgeway succeeds sir Redvers Buller as under-secretary for Ireland about 15 Oct. ,,

Midnight meeting at Woodford; Mr. O'Brien present . . . . 16 Oct. ,,

Cork county and city placed under the crimes act 24 Oct. ,,

At a riotous meeting at Woodford which had been proclaimed, Mr. Wilfrid Blunt, the chairman, and others arrested, and the meeting dispersed, 23 Oct; Mr. Blunt sentenced to two months' imprisonment; appeals . . . . 27 Oct. ,,

[Sentence confirmed 7 Jan. 1888.]

Many evictions violently resisted, autumn . . ,,

Mr. W. O'Brien withdraws his appeal; after resistance sent to prison for three months; sentence confirmed against Mr. Mandeville, two months' imprisonment, 31 Oct.; removed from Cork to Tullamore gaol, King's county 2 Nov. ,,

Other arrests and imprisonments . . . Nov. ,,

Limerick city proclaimed . . about 14 Nov. ,,

The national league suppressed in Kerry 22 Nov. ,,

Serious riots at Limerick through attempted meeting to inaugurate a memorial of the so-called martyrs executed at Manchester *(which see)* in 1867 . . . . 27 Nov. ,,

Great unionist meeting at Leinster hall, Dublin, to receive lord Hartington and Mr. Göschen; the most eminent persons in professions, learning, commerce, &c. present . . . . 29 Nov. ,,

Death of Dr. Daniel M'Gettigan, R. C. archbishop of Armagh; judicious, tolerant, and amiable 3 Dec. ,,

Convention of Irish landlords in Dublin to consider their prospects and conduct, 15 Sept.; require legislation . . . . . 13–15 Dec. ,,

Father Matthew Ryan, R. C., sentenced to one month's imprisonment for sedition . 22 Dec. ,,

Large reductions of rents ordered by the land commission . . . . . . 27 Dec. ,,

Many arrests under the crimes act, and imprisonments . . . . . . Dec. 1887–Jan. 1888

Visit of the marquis of Ripon and Mr. John Morley, M.P., to Dublin . . . 1–3 Feb. ,,

Mr. Parnell's amendment on the address attacking the government Irish policy moved, 13 Feb.; negatived (317–229) . . . . . 17 Feb. ,,

Mr. Parnell's land law amendment bill dealing with arrears rejected (328–243) . . . 21 March, ,,

Attempted proclaimed meetings dispersed by the police and military at Loughrea, Ennis (by col. Turner), and other places . . . 8 April, ,,

The plan of campaign and boycotting condemned by the pope on moral grounds, 18 April; rescript issued . . . . 20 April, ,,

Mr. Carew's county government bill rejected (282–195) . . . . 25 April, ,,

Execution of Daniel Hayes and Daniel Moriarty for the murder of James Fitzmaurice, a farmer (on 31 Jan.) . . . . 28 April, 1888

Execution of James Kirby at Tralee gaol for the murder of Patrick Quirke at Liscahane, Kerry, (8 Nov. 1887) . . . . 7 May, ,,

The exchequer division affirms right of county court to increase sentences on appeal 17 May, ,,

Meeting of catholic M.P.s in Dublin, who resist the pope's interference in political affairs, 17 May; of others in Phœnix park . 20 May, ,,

The R. C. bishops accept the papal rescript May, ,,

Mr. John Morley's motion for vote of censure of the government for its Irish policy negatived (366–273) . . . . . . 25–27 June, ,,

The duke of Argyll's resolution in the lords warmly commending the government's Irish policy accepted *nem. con.* . . . . 12 July, ,,

Evictions on the Vandeleur estate violently but unsuccessfully resisted . . 19, 20, 24 July, ,,

Coroner's inquiry into the death of Mr. John Mandeville (imprisoned Nov. 1887); 19 July; [suicide of Dr. Ridley of Tullamore gaol, 20 July; 1888] verdict—disease caused by ill-usage in prison . . . . 28 July, ,,

Mr. Parnell in the house of commons asserts the letters attributed to him in *Parnellism and crime* to be forgeries, and the charges against him to be false, 6 July; Mr. Parnell's request for a select committee to investigate the charges in the *Times* refused by the government, 9 July; Mr. W. H. Smith proposes the appointment of a royal commission of judges to examine these charges, 12 July; bill read first time, 16–17 July; names mentioned, sir James Hannen, president, Mr. Justice Day, and Mr. Justice A. L. Smith; act passed . . . . 1–3 Aug. ,,

Great diminution of crime; boycotting reduced by three-fourths in twelve months . . . Aug. ,,

Mr. Parnell proceeds against the *Times* in the Scotch courts . . . . Aug. ,,

See *Parnellite commission.*

Nonconformist ministers of Ireland present an address to the marquises of Salisbury and Hartington, protesting against the separatist policy . . . . 14 Nov. ,,

Mr. E. Harrington fined 500*l.* for contempt of court in his paper, the *Kerry Sentinel* . Nov. ,,

Renewal of lord Ashbourne's act of 1885, granting 5,000,000*l.* proposed Nov.; Mr. Gladstone's amendment rejected (330–246), 20 Nov.; 2nd reading carried (299–224), 22 Nov.; passed 24 Dec. ,,

Verdict for Mr. Joyce against lord Clanricarde for libel on appeal . . . . Dec. ,,

Letter from pope to Irish people expressing sympathy and advice and gifts to the Irish churches . . . . 1 Jan. 1889

Mr. Wm. O'Brien, M.P., sentenced to four months' imprisonment, 25 Jan.; (escaped), arrested at a meeting at Manchester . . . . . 29 Jan. ,,

Deputy inspector Wm. Limerick Martin killed while attempting to arrest father McFadden, P.P., at Gweedore, Donegal . . . . . 3 Feb. ,,

The court of session, Edinburgh, dismisses Mr. Parnell's action against the *Times* with costs 5 Feb. ,,

Mr. Dillon, sir Thomas Esmonde, and Mr. Deasy, M.P.'s, Home Rule delegates to Australia, &c., arrive at Adelaide . . . . . 11 April, ,,

Mr. Parnell moves for a trial against the *Times* in the exchequer division, Dublin 11 Feb.; finally stopped . . . . April, ,,

Great decrease of agrarian outrages (1881, 4,439; 1888, 660) announced . . . . . 21 Feb. ,,

Liberal subscription to support Mr. Olphert of Gweedore, Donegal, in his conflict with the national league and the plan of campaign May, ,,

The negotiations between Mr. T. W. Russell and Mr. Shaw to settle the dispute fail . . . May, ,,

Resisted evictions on the Vandeleur, Lansdowne, Smith-Barry, Ponsonby, and other estates May–July, ,,

Mr. A. J. Balfour explains his bills for the improvement of Ireland (drainage of the Bann, Barrow, and Shannon, by grants of 383,000*l.*, and the construction of light railways was also proposed) 31 May, ,,

Mr. William O'Brien arrested for speech at Clonakilty . . . . 30 June, 1889

Mr. W. O'Brien and Mr. Parnell announce the formation of a New Tenants' Defence League, (*which see*) . . . . 10, 11 July, „

Dr. Tanner sentenced to one month's imprisonment for an assault, and to three months' for contempt of court . . . . 29 July, „

The light railways bill read scond time 19 July, „

The mission of Mr. Dillon and other delegates to Australia to obtain support for home rule, reported unsuccessful; meetings at Sydney, Melbourne, and Brisbane, protest against them . . July, „

The Suck drainage bill and the light railways bill passed . . . . 30 Aug. „

Mr. William O'Brien sentenced to two months' imprisonment and Mr. James Gilhooly to six weeks 25 Aug. „

Father O'Dwyer and 9 of his parishioners sentenced to 5 months and other terms of imprisonment for intimidation and conspiracy . . middle Sept. „

The earl of Zetland sworn in as lord-lieutenant 5 Oct. „

National league proclaimed in Dungarvan district 7 Oct., and in places in county Tipperary, 11 Oct. „

Mr. Justice Gibson at Maryborough tries persons implicated in the murder of deputy-inspector Martin at Gweedore (3 Feb.) 17 Oct. Sentences for manslaughter Wm. Coll, 10 years' penal servitude:—pleaded guilty, Patrick Roarty and Dominick Rogers, 7 years'; Connell M'Gee, 5 years': 3 others, 6 months' imprisonment with hard labour; father M'Fadden reprimanded . . . 30 Oct. „

Meeting of the Tenants' Defence Association at Thurles . . . . 28 Oct. „

The mission of Mr. Dillon and other M.P.'s to Australia, said to have received 27,000*l*.; proceeds to New Zealand . . . . about 31 Oct. „

The tenants on the Ponsonby estate, who have paid no rent and refused very liberal terms, appeal against ejectment . . . . . . 5 Nov. „

Failure of Plan of Campaign through combination of landlords; the tenants of the Olphert estate pay the rent due . . . . . . Nov. „

Mr. Parnell speaks at Nottingham 17, 18 Dec.; visits Mr. Gladstone at Hawarden, 18 Dec.; at Liverpool . . . . 19 Dec. „

First meeting of the Landlords' convention at Dublin . . . . 18 Dec. „

Proclamations relaxing the stringency of the Crimes act in some counties . . . 24 Jan., 16 Feb. 1890

The Irish Democratic Labour Association started at Cork by Michael Davitt . . . 21 Jan. „

Mr. Parnell's censure of the government policy in Ireland (negatived 307–240) . . 14–18 Feb. „

Mr. Joseph Gillis Biggar, M.P., eminent Parnellite, dies suddenly . . . . . . 19 Feb. „

New Land Purchase bill introduced by Mr. A. J. Balfour 24 March, read 2nd time, 348–286 1 May, „

The new Land Purchase bill re-introduced by Mr. A. J. Balfour . . . . . . 28 Nov. „

Ponsonby estate, Cork (237 tenants), plan of campaign adopted, Nov. 1886; evicted, 1887, 10; 1888, 3; 1889, 32; the remainder without resistances . . . . 17–30 April, „

Nationalist meeting at New Tipperary, held though proclaimed; Messrs. Dillon, W. O'Brien, J. O'Connor, and others present . . . 25 May, „

General Viscount Wolseley appointed commander-in-chief in Ireland (beginning Oct., succeeding prince Edward of Saxe-Weimar) . . July, „

Thomas Walsh and two others sentenced to seven years' penal servitude for moonlight outrages 26 July, „

The National League issues a circular to its branches urging exertions to obtain subscriptions, &c., announced 7 Aug. „

Strikes in Dublin, Belfast, and other places July, *et seq.* „

Tour of Messrs. John Dillon and William O'Brien in Tipperary, &c.; arrested with three M.P.'s and seven others, on charge of conspiring to induce Mr. Smith Barry's tenants not to pay rent, and to intimidate them; bailed, 18 Sept.; prosecution begun at Tipperary before Mr. J. B. Irwin and Mr. G. R. Shannon . . . 25 Sept. „

[Mr. W. O'Brien and Mr. Dillon do not appear, 10 Oct.; at Paris, 16 Oct.; sail for America, 25 Oct.; at New York, 2 Nov.]

Sentences: W. O'Brien, M.P., John Dillon, M.P., Patrick O'Brien, M.P., and John Cullinane, 6 months' imprisonment; Michael O'Brien, Dalton, Patrick Mockler, and Thos. Walsh, 4 months' 19 Nov. 1890

Mr. A. J. Balfour visits Mayo and other western districts threatened with famine; warmly received . . . . 24–30 Oct. „

Bridget Flanagan, daughter of Patrick, shot dead in her bed by moonlighters, probably in mistake for her father, who had taken a derelict farm about 28 Oct. „

Mr. Balfour visits Donegal, &c. . . . 4–7 Nov. „

Extensive evictions on the Olphert's estate at Falcarragh . . . . . 12 Nov. *et seq.* „

Intervention of the R. C. bishop of Raphoe, Dr. O'Donnell: Mr. Olphert requires the total abandonment of the "plan of campaign" on the estate; no agreement 12 Nov.; evictions proceed 15 Nov. „

The National League suppressed in townlands in Fermanagh, Monaghan and Waterford . 14 Nov. „

Mr. Balfour introduces new Land Purchase and Congested Districts bills, 27 Nov.; and a bill to relieve the congested districts by providing seed potatoes, and by the construction of railways, roads, &c., 4 Dec.; royal assent given to the bills 9 Dec. „

For the division in the Irish Home Rule party see *Parnellites* . . . . Dec. „

Mr. Parnell warmly received at Dublin, Cork, &c. 10 Dec. *et seq.* „

He forcibly occupies the office of *United Ireland* at Dublin, 9, 10 Dec.; two rival editions issued 12 Dec. „

Moonlighters of Clare and Leitrim, convicted of outrages, at Sligo: sentenced to penal servitude: Timothy Lalor for life; seven others for 20 years; four for two years, and two for 1 year . 19 Dec. „

North Kilkenny election; Mr. Vincent Scully, Parnellite, opposed by sir J. Pope Hennessy, anti-Parnellite; fierce conflicts; Hennessy elected. 23 Dec. „

The construction of the light railways begun at Valencia; road-making begun . . . Dec. „

The anti-Parnellite newspaper named *Insuppressible* about 24 Dec. „

The earl of Zetland, lord lieutenant, and Mr. A. J. Balfour appeal to the public for assistance in the relief of the distress in the congested districts of the western coast, 3 Jan. (see *Irish Distress Fund*), published . . . . . . 5 Jan. 1891

Relief works actively progressing; several thousands employed—men, women, and children Jan. „

The *Insuppressible* stopped . . . . 24 Jan. „

Mr. Shaw-Lefevre's resolution for the application of arbitration in disputes between landlord and tenant negatived (213–152) . . . . 30 Jan. „

Bartholomew Sullivan executed at Tralee for the murder of Patrick Flahive (30 Aug. 1886), who had taken an evicted farm . . . . 2 Feb. „

Men employed on light railways, 281; unskilled, 7,412 . . . . 2 Feb. „

Mr. Parnell refuses to resign his leadership; disruption of the party, 11 Feb.; Messrs. W. O'Brien and J. Dillon, after fruitless conferences with Mr. Parnell at Boulogne, come to Folkestone, are arrested and conveyed to Clonmel gaol, 13 Feb.; to Galway . . . . 19 Feb. „

Mr. John Morley's resolution, condemning the Tipperary prosecutions, negatived by the commons (320–245) . . . . . 16–17 Feb. „

Mr. Parnell commences a long series of public meetings on Sundays; at Roscommon and other places 22 Feb. „

The *National Press*, anti-Parnellite paper, first published . . . . 7 March, „

National Federation (*which see*), anti-Parnellite, inaugurated at Dublin . . . . 10 March, „

Mr. A. J. Balfour reports to the commons the successful results of the efforts made to relieve Irish distress; 55,831*l*. voted for relief works, &c.; 136,200*l*. for construction of light railways (7,392 persons employed on 28 Feb.) . . . 12 March, „

Great decrease of crime in the south, reported by justice Monroe . . . . . . 18 March, „

The countess of Zetland, Miss Balfour, and others

visit the relieved districts; warmly received 6–11 April, 1891
The lord lieutenant visits counties Cork, Kerry, Clare, and Galway; warmly received 5–14 May, ,,
Explosion of a powder magazine by dynamite at Donaghadee, co. Down . . . . 13 May, ,,
The crimes act suspended throughout Ireland, except in co. Clare and a few baronies . 13 June, ,,
Mr. A. J. Balfour in the commons reports the complete success of his remedial measures . 22 July, ,,
Mr. W. O'Brien and Mr. Dillon liberated from gaol; declare their opposition to Mr. Parnell . 31 July, ,,
Purchase of Land and Congested Districts act passed . . . . 5 Aug. ,,
The *Freeman's Journal* proprietors determine to support the anti-Parnellites . . . . 28 Aug. ,,
Visit of the duke of Cambridge to inspect the forces; arrives in Dublin . . . . . 26 Sept. ,,
National League convention at Limerick . Oct. ,,
Mr. Parnell delivers an address at Greggs, Galway, 27 Sept.; dies of rheumatic fever near Brighton, 6 Oct.; public Nationalist funeral at Dublin, orderly and impressive . . . . . 11 Oct. ,,
Mr. Wm. L. Jackson becomes chief secretary 9 Nov. ,,
Relief works closed as not required . . Nov. ,,
The *Independent*, new Parnellite journal, published 18 Dec. ,,
Mr. J. E. Redmond, Parnellite, elected M.P. for Waterford, in opposition to Mr. Michael Davitt, the clerical candidate . . . . . 23 Dec. ,,
The corporation of London, the Irish Society, and 43 London companies, summoned to appear in Dublin to answer charges respecting the management of their Irish estates . . . 2 Jan. 1892
Landowners' convention, annual meeting 3, 4 Feb. ,,
Mr. Justin M'Carthy elected by the anti-Parnellites sessional chairman . . . . . . 5 Feb. ,,
Above 150 tenants on the Ponsonby estate sign agreements to purchase their holdings under the Ashbourne act . . . . Feb. ,,
Irish Education bill introduced by Mr. Wm. L. Jackson, 22 Feb., much opposed by the R. C. clergy . . . . . . early March, ,,
Evicted Tenants' (relief) bill rejected by the commons (229–174) . . . . . . 2 March, ,,
The *National Press* amalgamated with the *Freeman's Journal* (litigation ensued) . about 25 March, ,,
Meeting of Ulster men at Belfast to form a convention to oppose Home Rule (to be on 17 June) 8 April, ,,
Meeting of Irish unionist alliance at Dublin 28 April, ,,
Local Government bill (*which see*) introduced by Mr. Balfour, 18 Feb., read 2nd time, 24 May; withdrawn . . . . 13 June, ,,
The education bill passed . . . . 27 June, ,,
Ulster convention (*which see*) at Belfast . 17 June, ,,
Great unionist meetings at Dublin . . 23 June, ,,
Elections: Parnellites, 9; anti-Parnellites, 72, July, ,,
Lord Houghton appointed lord-lieutenant, Mr. John Morley chief secretary . . . 18 Aug. ,,
Operation of the Crimes act in county Mayo and other formerly disturbed counties suspended, 12 Aug.; in all Ireland, and the National League declared legal . . . . . . 13 Sept. ,,
Outrages by "moonlighters" near Macroom, Cork. 16 Sept. ,,
Appointment of a commission to inquire into the position of evicted tenants; sir James C. Mathew, judge Queen's Bench, England, and others, about 14 Oct.; first sitting, 7 Nov.; the landlords decline to appear . . . . . . Nov. ,,
Savage assault on district-inspector Lilly, near Ballivor, Meath, 11 Oct.; 5 men arrested, 19 Oct. ,,
Dismissal of col. Turner, divisional commander and magistrate in Munster . . about 17 Oct. ,,
Proposal by abp. Croke respecting the Irish fund at Paris accepted by the Parnellites and anti-Parnellites . . . . 29 Oct. ,,
Eviction at a farm at Abbeyfeale, Limerick, effected with difficulty, 10 Nov.; another near Kanturk, Cork, 17 Nov. . . . . . . 17 Nov. ,,
Inundations in co. Cork, causing much damage, with loss of life . . . 20 Nov. *et seq.* ,,
Mr. Patrick Fullam, M.P. for S. Meath, unseated on account of illegal R. C. clerical influence; powerful address by Mr. justice O'Brien, 30 Nov. ,,

Moonlight outrage at Reomare, Kerry; John Greaney nearly killed . . . . 6 Dec. 1892
Mr. Michael Davitt, M.P. for N. Meath, unseated on account of R. C. priestly influence . 23 Dec. ,,
Explosions at Dublin castle (*which see*), 31 Dec. 1891, and . . . . . . 24 Dec. ,,
The Gweedore convicts (*see above*, Feb.–Oct. 1889) released . . . . 23 Dec. ,,
Meeting at Cork, held by the mayor, demanding the release of the dynamite prisoners . 15 Jan. 1893
Evictions on Bodyke, property of col. O'Callaghan; much resisted . . . . . middle Jan. ,,
Meetings in Ulster, opposing home rule; Belfast and Armagh, 17 Jan.; Dungannon, 20 Jan.; Omagh, 21 Jan.; Derry, 23 Jan.; Ballymena, 24 Jan.; Newry . . . . . . 25 Jan. ,,
Great Unionist meetings in Ulster (*which see*), Belfast, &c., 17 Jan. *et seq.*; Dublin . 26 Jan. ,,
Mr. Gladstone introduces a new Home Rule bill ("to amend the provision for the government of Ireland"); chief features, viceroy (non-political) for a fixed term; two chambers; legislative council, 48 members to be elected by 20*l.* voters; legislative assembly, 103 members, 80 members to sit at Westminster, as now . . 13 Feb. ,,
Bill read 1st time, 18 Feb.; 2nd time (347—304), 21–22 April; committee, 8 May—28 July; the bill much changed; many amendments not considered; 3rd reading, 30 Aug.—2 Sept. (301–267); lords: read 1st time, 1–2 Sept.; on 2nd reading rejected (419–41) . . . . 5, 8, 9 Sept. ,,
The Queen's Bench Division decide that the police authorities have no right to refuse protection to the sheriffs on duty in the night-time; appeal of the crown disallowed . . . . 16 Feb. ,,
Irish Agricultural Association, ostensibly for the benefit of landlords, tenants and labourers; inaugural meeting at Dublin . . . 21 Feb. ,,
Agrarian outrages: 1 July—30 Sept., 94 (63 in Munster); 1 Oct.—31 Dec., 80, reported, 24 Feb. ,,
The Irish National League of America condemns the new home rule bill in a manifesto . 25 Feb. ,,
Fall in bank and railway stocks . Feb.—March, ,,
Many meetings and petitions against the home rule bill . . . . . . Feb.—March, ,,
Mr. justice O'Brien's severe remarks at Ennis on the lawlessness of co. Clare, 27 Feb.; warmly discussed by the commons, 2 March; by the lords . . . . 3 March, ,,
Anti-Parnellite convention at Dublin adopts the home rule bill . . . . . 8 March, ,,
Report of the Evicted Tenants commission, with recommendations, presented to the commons, 9 March, ,,
A Parnellite convention at Dublin, Mr. John Redmond in the chair, declares for present neutrality respecting the home rule bill . . 9 March ,,
Deputation of above 50 Unionists (commercial, &c.) from Leinster, Munster and Connaught, received by the marquis of Salisbury, Mr. A. J. Balfour, Mr. Goschen, and lord Randolph Churchill; and by the duke of Devonshire, Mr. Chamberlain, and sir Henry James . . . . . . 10 March, ,,
Disagreement among directors of the *Freeman's Journal* company; opposition of abp. Walsh and Mr. T. Healy . . . about 13 March *et seq.* ,,
Manifesto of R. C. laity against the home rule bill, with petition to parliament . about 14 March, ,,
Synod of the Protestant church at Dublin; protests against the home rule bill . . . 14 March, ,,
Great Unionist meeting of all creeds and classes in Leinster hall, Dublin; lord Iveagh in the chair, 15 March, ,,
The General Assembly of the Presbyterian church of Ireland at Belfast protests against the home rule bill . . . . 15 March, ,,
The Irish Unionist Alliance appeals for funds, 18 March, ,,
Roman Catholic Unionist Association formed at Limerick . . . . 18 March, ,,
Protest of Society of Friends, N. Ireland, against the home rule bill . . . about 22 March, ,,
Mr. A. J. Balfour's resolution in the commons, censuring the Irish executive for releasing convicts, negatived (319—272) . . . 27 March, ,,
R. C. petition against the home rule bill . April, ,,
Great Unionist meeting at Albert hall, London; the duke of Abercorn in the chair about 10,000

persons present, including 1,200 delegates from Ireland . . . . 22 April, 1893
The Irish delegates entertained at St. James's hall and other places, 22 April; by the marquis of Salisbury at Hatfield; about 1,600 delegates present; addresses by the Unionist leaders, 24 April, „
Revival of moonlighting outrages in Kerry, Kilkenny, Limerick and Clare . . April, May, „
Visits to Ulster (*which see*); Mr. A. J. Balfour, 3, 4 April; the marquis of Salisbury . 23 May, „
A petition to the queen against home rule, signed by 103,000 Irish women of all classes and creeds; presented . . . . 12 Aug. „
James Donovan, caretaker of an evicted farm at Glenhara, owned by the earl of Cork, murdered, 21 April, 1894
By the upsetting of an overcrowded boat, near Westport quay, about 33 harvesters, chiefly women and girls, were drowned; about 75 lives saved by the crew of the *Elm*, under capt. Carswell (the people of Achill island were going to England and Scotland to earn money to repay the government loan incurred in 1891) . 14 June, „
Increase of outrages, cattle poisoning, &c., co. Limerick; moonlighting, &c., co. Cork, reported July, „
Mr. Gladstone and lord Tweedmouth each give 100*l.* to the Irish parliamentary fund (see *Parnellites*), Aug. „
Severe storm in co. Kerry and other parts, with loss of life . . . . . 24 Oct. „
Diminution of crime in 1894 reported in the queen's speech . . . . 5 Feb. 1895
John Twiss executed for murder of Jas. Donovan, a caretaker, at Cork . . . . 9 Feb. „
Inaugural banquet of the Irish Loyalist club in London; speech of the marquis of Salisbury, 16 Feb. „
Death of the earl of Bessborough, a popular landlord, aged 79 . . . . 12 March, „
Boards of guardians (Ireland) bill; 2nd reading, 13 March, „
Outrage on a tenant of an evicted farm at Abbeyfeal, Cork . . . . 13 March, „
The seed potatoes supply bill passed . 14 March, „
Land bill, commons read 2nd time . . 5 April, „
See *Witchcraft*, 1895.
Bill virtually repealing the Crimes act (1887) read 2nd time in commons . . . . 8 May, „
Irish Agricultural Organization society; first annual meeting at Dublin; the hon. Horace Plunkett, M.P., president . . . 8 May, „
Decrease of crime reported . . . . 10 June, „
New ministry: lord-lieut. earl Cadogan; lord chancellor, lord Ashbourne; chief secretary, Gerald Balfour . . . . . . 25 June *et seq.* „
Municipal franchise bill withdrawn, in the lords, 5 July, „
Dissension between Mr. Justin M'Carthy, Mr. Healy, and others . . . . Aug. „
Irish national convention at Chicago (see *United States*) . . . . . . Sept.–Oct. „
Field-marshal lord Roberts of Kandahar as commander-in-chief arrives in Dublin . . 1 Oct. „
Expulsion of Mr. T. M. Healy and 3 others from the Irish National Federation, 14 Nov.; Mr. John Dillon elected chairman, 7 Feb. 1896.
Death of James Hack Tuke, aged 76, philanthropist, active in relief of the famines, 1846–7 and 1880–86 . . . . 13 Jan. 1896
Mr. Harrington's amendment for the release of the Irish political prisoners (dynamiters), rejected; majority, 162 . . . . 17 Feb. „
Disputes on the Ponsonby estates, co. Cork, and the Smith-Barry estate, Tipperary, amicably settled . . . . March, „
Lord-lieut. earl Cadogan hospitable and popular; brilliant season in Dublin . . . March, „
Mr. Gerald Balfour's Land bill rather favourably received . . . . . . 14 April, „
271 agrarian offences in 1895; reported . May, „
Hybrid recess committee respecting Irish affairs, formed by Mr. H. Plunkett, M.P., autumn, 1895; report issued . . . . . . 4 Aug. „
Local taxation; act passed . . . 14 Aug. „
Land law act introduced by Mr. Gerald Balfour, 13 April, based on the act of 1881; passed 14 Aug. „

"Convention of the Irish race" (organized by Mr. Dillon), 2,000 delegates from all parts of the world; Dr. O'Donnell, R.C. bishop of Raphoe, president; message from the pope read, resolutions for unity, &c., passed; appeals for unity and money support . . . . . 1–3 Sept. 1896
Arrest of P. J. Tynan, "No. 1," accused of the Phœnix Park murders (*see above*, 6 May, 1882), at Boulogne, 13 Sept.; extradition refused by the French government on legal grounds, 14 Oct.; released . . . . 15 Oct. „
Mixed political meetings at Dublin; a resolution passed affirming the excessive imperial taxation of Ireland, 2,500,000*l.* too much, as disclosed by the report of the Financial Relations commission, and demanding restitution for the past and reduction in future (see *Finance*) . 14, 28 Dec. „
Irish landowners' convention meets at Dublin, the new land act (*see above*, 14 Aug. 1896), censured, 27, 28 Jan. 1897; also by tenants and landlords, March; a great meeting at Dublin, duke of Abercorn, lord Londonderry, lord Dufferin, and others present, compensation, &c., demanded, 30 April . . . . „
In the commons Mr. Blake moves a resolution, that the report of the royal commission proves the necessity for remedial legislation, 29, 30 March; negatived, 317—157 . . . . 31 March, 1897
An Independent Nationalist association (Parnellites), Mr. J. Redmond, president; inaugurated, 20 April, „
An Irish Financial reform league formed in Dublin, (annual meetings) . . . . 22 April, „
Mr. A. J. Balfour's statement of bills proposed for the benefit of Ireland . . . . 21 May, „
Royal commission on the Irish land acts, chairman, sir Edward Fry, Messrs. Robt. Vigers, George Gordon, Dr. Traill, and others, reported, 9 July; sat in Dublin, 22 Sept. 1897; last sitting at Belfast, 15 Oct.; Cork, 19 Oct.; report issued, Feb. 1898.
The Shannon route opened up for tourists 2 Aug. „
Judicature (Ireland) acts 1877 to 1888 (amendment), bill passed . . . . 6 Aug. „
Failure of the potato and other crops in Cork, Kerry, and Clare, reported . . . . 3 Sept. „
The duke and duchess of York arrive at Kingstown (see *Dublin*), 18 Aug.; visit Killarney, &c., 28 Aug.; Londonderry, 4 Sept.; Belfast, 8, 9 Sept. „
Thanks for reception from the queen and the duke, 8 Sept. „
Application to the High court by the earl of Gosford for a *mandamus* compelling the land commission to rehear applications made by his tenants for the fixing of fair rents; discharged without costs . . . . 29 Nov. „
Lord Clarina (Eyre Massey), popular landowner in Limerick (conservative); born, 1830, died 16 Dec. „
Lord Carlingford, chief secretary for Ireland, 1865, died . . . . 30 Jan. 1898
Mr. Gerald Balfour's Irish local government bill passed . . . . 12 Aug. „
Appeal from Dublin to the British empire for the relief of distress in the south and west of Ireland, 31 March; again . . . . 27 April, „
Sir John Gilbert, eminent Irish historian, born 1829, died . . . . 25 May, „
Resolution alleging Ireland to be unfairly treated in her financial relations rejected in the commons, 286–144 . . . . 5 July, „
Seed supply and Potato Spraying Act passed, 12 Aug. „
Annual Parnellite convention, Mr. J. Redmond, president, held in Dublin . . . . 10 Oct. „
Country tranquil and prosperous, reported, 9 Jan. 1899
Appeal commission, under the local government act, Sir John Colomb, chairman, meets . 10 Jan. „
Lord Cadogan appoints a commission of inquiry into the intermediate system of education; witnesses examined . . . . . . 11 Jan. „
Local government elections begin; many ladies vote, 16 Jan. 1899; victory of the labour party in Dublin, Cork, and Limerick.
The rt. hon. C. Talbot Redington, vice-chancellor of the Royal University, born 1847; died 5 Feb. (lord Harris elected . . . . . . July, „

The Irish landowners' convention, annual meeting, Dublin; resolution adopted to carry out the recommendations of the Fry commission, 22 Feb. 1899

Parliamentary grant for national education, 1,097,546*l.*, year ending . . . 31 March, „

Irish congested districts' board; good report of sea-fisheries and development of other industries in the west, issued for year ending . 31 March, „

A "unity conference" of Nationalist parties, except Parnellites, held in Dublin . . . . 4 April, „

County council elections: 546 Nationalists, 113 Unionists, announced . . . . 12 April, „

Lady Betty Balfour cuts the first sod of a "Balfour line" at Carndonagh, co. Donegal 23 May, „

Mr. Henniker Heaton and other M.P.'s visit Killarney and other places . . May, „

Field manœuvres at Curragh, duke and duchess of Connaught present . . . . 3–5 July, „

Military manœuvres, under lord Roberts, closed by a review, at Abbeyleix . . 9–16 Aug. „

Agriculture and technical instruction (Ireland) act passed . . . . . . 9 Aug. „

Primrose league *fête* at Clontarf, Dublin . 2 Sept. „

Mr. Wm. Talbot Crosbie, a beneficent landowner in Kerry, dies, aged 82 . . . 4 Sept. „

Mr. Michael Davitt, M.P. for S. Mayo, opposed to the government's policy in the Transvaal, &c.; resigns his seat . . . . 26 Oct. „

Lifeboat Saturday first held in Dublin . 28 Oct. „

Sir Thos. Deane, eminent architect, dies, aged 71, 8 Nov. „

Irish Nationalist conference to promote unity; committee appointed to confer with the Redmondites . . . . . . 23 Nov. „

Killarney (the Muckross estate) bought by lord Ardilaun for about 50,000*l.* . . . 27 Nov. „

Mr. Justice O'Brien, an eloquent, fearless and impartial judge (see *above*, 1887), dies, aged 66, 5 Dec. „

Mr. Chamberlain visits Dublin; made LL.D. of Trinity college, and warmly received, 16–18 Dec. „

Lord Roberts appointed commander-in-chief in South Africa (his only surviving son, lieut. F. Roberts, killed at Magersfontein, 11 Dec.); leaves Dublin . . . . . mid Dec. „

The duke of Connaught appointed commander-in-chief; welcomed in Dublin . . . 9 Jan. 1900

Mr. John Redmond, M.P., chairman of the re-united Irish party, issues a manifesto . 10 Feb. „

The queen, with princess Christian and princess Henry of Battenberg, warmly welcomed at Kingstown, 3 April; the lord mayor at Dublin presents her with the keys of the city and the civic sword, &c.; received by lord and lady Cadogan at the Viceregal lodge amid great rejoicings, 4 April; reviews about 52,000 children from all parts of Ireland in Phœnix park, and 1,000 more at the Viceregal lodge, 7, 12 April; visits Kilmainham hospital, 14 April; reviews 6,400 troops under the duke of Connaught, 21 April; receives many addresses and visits many institutions; expresses to her Irish people, in a letter to the lord-lieutenant, "how very much she has been gratified and how deeply touched by her reception; after the lapse of 39 years her reception has equalled that of previous visits, and she carries away with her a most pleasant and affectionate memory of the time she has spent in Ireland, having been received by all ranks and creeds with an enthusiasm and an affection which cannot be surpassed"; gives 1000*l.* to the poor of Dublin, and leaves, 25, 26 April; sent 25*l.* to the royal zoological society, 29 April, „

Sir Peter O'Brien, lord chief justice, made a peer, May, „

Education grant of 1,292,069*l.* voted . 20 July, „

Irish intermediate education bill and the Irish tithe-rent-charge amendment bill passed, 8 Aug. „

Sir Wm. Stokes, eminent surgeon, on hospital service, dies suddenly in Natal, aged 61, 18 Aug. „

Irish land commission's report, 1 April, 1899–31 March, 1900, issued as a blue-book, about 22 Aug. „

Nationalist demonstration in Phœnix park, Dublin; programme of the Irish National League adopted, 2 Sept. „

General election; great victory of Mr. W. M. O'Brien's *United Irish League* . . Nov. 1900

Nationalist convention at Dublin, president, Mr. J. Redmond; exclusion of Mr. T. Healy from the party, carried . . . . . 11 Dec. „

Mr. Vere Foster, a promoter of social and educational work and emigration, dies at Belfast, aged 81 . . . . 21 Dec. „

Mr. George Wyndham, chief secretary, 12 Nov.; tours through the western districts, Nov.; and through Connemara; receives many addresses, and returns to Dublin . . . . 8 Feb. 1901

"King *v.* M'Hugh," Mr. P. A. M'Hugh, M.P., proprietor of the *Sligo Champion*, sentenced to 6 months' imprisonment for threatening jurors, Dublin . . . . . . 22 April, „

Queen Victoria memorial fund started in Dublin, end April, „

The *Irish People*, Mr. Wm. O'Brien's Dublin weekly paper, seized for a gross libel on the king, 9 May, „

Mrs. Smyly, an eminent philanthropist, dies, aged 87 . . . . . . 16 May, „

Sir Robert Sexton, a prominent Dublin citizen, dies, aged 87 . . . . . 27 June, „

Dr. Walsh, R. C. abp. of Dublin, resigns his seat on the Board of nat. education . . 29 June, „

Education grant, 1,300,771*l.*, voted . 12 July, „

Congested districts board, satisfactory reports for year ending 31 March, issued. . . . Aug. „

Decrease of crime, reported . . . . Aug. „

Purchase of land (No. 2) bill, passed . 15 Aug. „

Local govmt. (Ireland) and Congested districts board (amendment) bills (grant of 66,182*l.*), passed . . . . . . 16 Aug. „

Military manœuvres, fruitful in tactical lessons, etc., closed . . . . . . 16 Aug. „

Pan-Celtic congress (*which see*) held in Dublin, 19–23 Aug. „

Mr. justice Murphy, eminent and popular judge, died, aged 74 . . . . . 5 Sept. „

Lord Morris and Killanin, late lord chief justice of Ireland, common pleas and appeal, died, aged 73, 8 Sept. „

Demonstration in support of the compulsory land sale movement held in Londonderry . 2 Oct. „

The United Irish league powerful in Leitrim and the west; much intimidation and boycotting, Nov. „

"No-rent" campaign on lord de Freyne's and other western estates . . . . . Dec. „

Four M.P.'s and other agitators for non-payment of rent, &c., sentenced to a few weeks' imprisonment, 18–24 Dec. „

United Irish league convention held in Dublin, Mr. J. Redmond, M.P., chairman; 1,230 branches in Ireland . . . . 8 Jan. 1902

Coercive measures of the league in the west increasing; boycotting in Sligo . Jan.-March, „

Roy. commission on university education in Ireland, lord Robertson chairman, appointed, June, 1901; first meeting, Belfast . . . 2 April, „

Irish unionist alliance meets in Dublin, strong protest against the United Irish league . 10 April, „

Mr. Jasper Tully, M.P., placed in gaol (14 days) for illegal assembly . . . . 14 April, „

Certain districts placed under sections 2, 3, 4, relating to boycotting, of the crimes act (1887), 16 April, „

Agrarian outrages co. Galway . . 16, 17 April, „

Prince Henry of Prussia, with German naval squadron, visits Dublin . . . 17–23 May, „

United Irish league's annual meeting held in Manchester . . . . 17 May, „

Mr. P. A. M'Hugh, M.P., sentenced to three months' for contempt of court . . 18 June, „

Agricultural and technical instruction act, royal assent, 23 June (No. 2 bill, royal assent, 18 Dec.); pauper children bill passed, 26 June, „

Mr. A. Smith-Barry, eminent Irish landlord, created baron Barrymore, co. Cork; Mr. A. M. Porter, master of the rolls, a baronet . 26 June, „

Evictions continue on lord de Freyne's estate, 8–23 July, „

Lord Roberts entertained in London, and presented with a silver cup by the graduates of the Dublin, Queen's and Royal universities . . 8 July, „

Debate in the commons on the case of ex-sergeant Sheridan (by whose false accusations men had been imprisoned, one of whom had died, Jan.); Mr. Dillon's motion to reduce the vote for the constabulary by 500,000*l.* rejected, 195–102, 10 July, 1902

Lord Cadogan, lord-lieut., resigns . . 17 July, ,,

Dr. Croke, abp. of Cashel, died, aged 78 . 22 July, ,,

Angry debates in the commons; reduction of the vote for the chief secretary, rejected, 196–135; motion to remove alleged overtaxation, rejected, 168–117 . . . . . . 23, 24, 25 July, ,,

Mr. W. R. Fenton, crown solicitor for Sligo, *v.* Mr. P. A. M'Hugh, M.P., proprietor of the *Sligo Champion*, for libel and conspiracy; verdict for plaintiff, 3,500*l.* damages . . . . 28 July, ,,

Public libraries (Ireland) act passed . 31 July, ,,

Great fire in Dunluce-street, Larne, co. Antrim, buildings gutted; estimated loss, 28,000*l.* 4 Aug. ,,

Blue-book, land commissioners' report, 1 April, 1901–31 March, 1902 . . . . . 4 Aug. ,,

Balfour ministry: lord-lieut., earl Dudley; lord chancellor, lord Ashbourne; chief secretary, George Wyndham . . . . . . 8 Aug. ,,

Meeting of the Irish parliamentary party, city hall, Dublin . . . . 9 Aug. ,,

Lord and lady Cadogan leave amid hearty demonstrations . . . . 12 Aug. ,,

Evictions resumed on lord de Freyne's Frenchpark estate . . . . 13, 14 Aug. ,,

The duke of Abercorn presides at the Irish landowners' convention; resolutions carried in favour of Mr. Wyndham's land bill; the newly-formed Irish land trust, and for a royal commission of inquiry into landlords' losses . . 29 Aug. ,,

Crimes act extended to Dublin, Limerick and seven counties, 31 Aug. *et seq.*

Several Irish M.P.'s imprisoned for intimidation, &c. . . . . 1 Sept.–Oct. ,,

Roy. commission on university education in Ireland (July, 1901), 3rd report issued . 9 Sept. ,,

Indignation meetings at the mansion house and city hall and Phœnix park, Dublin, 5, 12, 13 Sept. ,,

State entry of lord Dudley, lord-lieut., into Dublin, 25 Sept. ,,

Samuel Harris, secretary to the (E. Limerick) United Irish league, sentenced to nine months' imprisonment for *intimidation;* Mr. McCarthy, editor of the *Irish People*, sentenced to two months' imprisonment for *intimidation*, 27, 29 Sept. (confirmed on appeal, 20 Dec.) . . . ,,

Meeting at the mansion house, Dublin; "nat. defence fund" started to resist prosecutions under the crimes act; 300*l.* subscribed . . 3 Oct. ,,

Irish landowners' convention met, Dublin; motion for a conference between *representatives* of landlords and tenants, rejected, 77–14 . 10 Oct. ,,

Mr. P. A. M'Hugh, M.P., sentenced to two months' for conspiracy and intimidation . . 16 Oct. ,,

United Irish league accused of tyranny, &c. 17 Oct. ,,

Martin, Patrick and Thos. Joyce (see *above*, Nov. 1882) released . . . . . . 24 Oct. ,,

Large consignment of arms and ammunition from Birmingham, reported . . . . . 27 Oct. ,,

Mr. W. Redmond, M.P., arrested and taken to Kilmainham gaol . . . . . . 4 Nov. ,,

Tallow conspiracy case (5th trial) settled by chief baron Palles and special jury; verdict, 5,500*l.* damages for plaintiff, David O'Keeffe, small trader, who had been boycotted by the 10 defendants, members of the United Irish league, 13 Nov. ,,

Split between the R.C. hierarchy and the leaders of the United Irish league . . . . Nov. ,,

Lord and lady Dudley visit Connemara, 19 Oct.; Belfast and Coleraine . . . 24, 28 Nov. ,,

Munster assizes, Cork; the grand jury threw out the bills in the case against major Studdert and others charged with conspiracy in connection with the purchase of remounts . . 4 Dec. ,,

The earl of Meath appointed chancellor of the royal university . . . . . . Dec. ,,

Mr. Denis Kilbride, an ex-M.P., sentenced to eight months' imprisonment for inciting to murder (in a speech at a united Irish league meeting), 10 Dec. ,,

Local government bill (No. 2), royal assent, 18 Dec. 1902

Lord Dunraven's land conference (five hrs.), 22 Dec. ,,

Lord Dunraven's land conference (22 Dec., 1902) issues report, 3 Jan. 1903; formally received by the landlords' convention . . . . 7 Jan. 1903

Mr. T. Harrington, M.P., re-elected for the third time lord mayor of Dublin . . . . 23 Jan. ,,

Summary jurisdiction clauses of crimes act, 1887, revoked in Dublin and many other urban and rural districts, several prisoners released . 2 Feb. ,,

Sir Chas. Gavan Duffy, eminent Irishman (see *Ireland*, *Young*, and *Victoria*) died aged 87, 9 Feb. ,,

Mc Tierney, auctioneer *v.* the Clareman Newspaper co., libel action (the plaintiff's trade had suffered, his horses had been maimed, and his customers' houses fired at): verdict for plaintiff with 600*l.* damages . . . . 13 Feb. ,,

Irish University commission's report, scheme for a R.C. college in Dublin; issued . . 11 March ,,

Education estimates 1903–4, 1,347,101*l.*, issued 14 March, ,,

Andrew Moore sentenced to death for the murder of the rev. Wm. Bell, rector of Kilmeen, Cork (22 Nov. 1902) . . . . . 21 March, ,,

Bank holidays (Ireland) bill, constituting St. Patrick's day a bank holiday, passed . 23 March ,,

Irish land bill, first reading (commons) . 25 March, ,,

Conference held to promote the establishment of a commercial and industrial institute and an international exhibition in Dublin . . 15 April, ,,

Nationalist convention on the land bill held at Dublin; special resolution for Home rule, and amendment to the bill carried . 16–17 April, ,,

International motor-car race . . . 2 July ,,

Disorderly scenes at meeting of the Dublin corporation, on motion of moderate section of members to present the king with a municipal address on the occasion of his visit to Dublin; meeting broken up by disorderly crowd in the gallery of the hall . . . . . 3 July ,,

Royal visit to Ireland, the king and queen arrive at Kingstown and Dublin, 21 July; enthusiastically greeted by large crowds; they drive in state to Dublin castle; the queen presents badges to Jubilee nurses, and the king replies to various addresses presented; holds a levée and visits Trinity college, sends message of deep regret and condolence for news of the pope's death to the Sacred college by cardinal Logue, 22 July; presents colours to the Royal Hibernian military school; holds a review in Phœnix park, and attends race meeting, dines with the duke of Connaught, and holds a court at the castle, 23 July; visits various places of interest in Dublin, and Maynooth college; receives an address in the names of the bishops and college authorities, 24 July, at Mount Stewart, seat of Lord Londonderry, 25 July; visit to Belfast, where the king unveils a statue of Queen Victoria and opens the new Victoria hospital, 26 July; at Londonderry 27 July; motor car excursion through villages in Connemara, 29 July; at Kenmare and Derreen and visits lord Lansdowne, 31 July; visits Cork and presents colours to the 2nd batts. Royal Irish reg. and Royal Munster Fusiliers; and issues an address to "My Irish People," in which he says "he has been deeply touched by their kindness and goodwill. He eagerly awaits the fulfilment of the hope that a brighter day is dawning upon Ireland, its realization largely depending on the development of self-reliance and co-operation, better education, the growth of industrial and commercial enterprise, and the increase of mutual respect and toleration;" honours conferred: privy councillors in Ireland, sir John C. Colomb, K.C.M.G., M.P., Mr. Thos. Andrews; 6 baronetcies, including the lord mayor of Dublin, and the lord mayor of Cork; 9 knights bachelors; the rt. hon. H. Plunkett made a K.C.V.O., 1 Aug.; lord Iveagh gives 50,000*l.* to the king for distribution among the Dublin hospitals in commemoration of the royal visit to Ireland; king returns to Cowes . 2 Aug. ,,

Centenary of execution of Robt. Emmet observed by a memorial procession through the streets of Dublin . . . . 20 Sept. ,,

Irish Land Purchase bill; royal assent . 14 Aug. ,,

Conference of Ulster tenants at Belfast to consider

action to be taken in connection with the new Land act . . . . 9 Oct. 1903

For other events see *Addenda*.

KINGS AND GOVERNORS OF IRELAND.*

KINGS.

979 or 980. Maol Ceachlin II. (Malachi) deposed.
1001 or 1002. Brian Baromy or Boroimhe, king of Munster, slain after totally defeating the Danes at Clontarf, 23 April, 1014.
1014. Maol Ceachlin II. restored; dies 1022 or 1023. [Disputed succession.]
1058. Donough, or Denis, O'Brian, son.
1072. Tirloch, or Turlough, nephew; dies 1086.
1086-1132. The kingdom divided; fierce contests for it.
1132. Tordel Vach; killed in battle.
1166. Roderic, or Roger, O'Connor.
1172. Henry II. king of England.
[The English monarchs were styled "Lords of Ireland" until the reign of Henry VIII., who first styled himself *king*.]

GOVERNORS OF IRELAND (with various titles.) †

1172. Hugues de Lasci. 1173, Rich. Fitz-Gislebert, earl of Pembroke. 1176, Raymond le Gros. 1177, prince John (afterwards king), made lord of Ireland.
1184 *et seq.* Justiciars. *The changes were so frequent that the more important officers only are given.* See "Gilbert's History of the Viceroys," 1865.
1189, 1203, 1205. Hugues de Lasci.
1199, 1204. Meiller Fitz-Henri (son of Henry II.)
1215, 1226. Geoffrey de Marreis.
1229-32-33. Maurice Fitzgerald.
1308. Piers Gaveston, earl of Cornwall. 1312, Edmund le Botiller. 1316, Roger de Mortimer. 1320, Thomas Fitzgerald. 1321, John de Bermingham. 1327, earl of Kildare. 1328 and 1340, Prior Roger Utlagh. 1332, sir John d'Arcy. 1337, sir John de Cherlton. 1344, sir Raoul d'Ufford. 1346, sir Roger d'Arcy; sir John Moriz. 1348, Walter de Bermingham. 1355, Maurice, earl of Desmond. 1356, Thomas de Rokeby. 1357, Almeric de St. Amand. 1359, James, earl of Ormond. 1361, Lionel, duke of Clarence. 1367, Gerald, earl of Desmond. 1369 and 1374, William de Windsor. 1376, Maurice, earl of Kildare, and James, earl of Ormond. 1380, Edmund Mortimer, earl of March. 1385, Robert de Vere, earl of Oxford. 1389 and 1398, sir John Stanley. 1391, James, earl of Ormond. 1393, Thomas, duke of Gloucester. 1395, Roger de Mortimer, earl of March, killed. 1398, Reginald Grey and Thomas de Holland.
1401 and 1408, Thomas, earl of Lancaster. 1413, sir John Stanley and sir John Talbot. 1420, James, earl of Ormond. 1423, Edmund de Mortimer, earl of March. 1425, sir John Talbot. 1427, sir John de Grey. 1428, sir John Sutton, lord Dudley. 1431 and 1435, sir Thomas Stanley. 1438, Leon, lord de Welles. 1446, John, earl of Shrewsbury. 1449, Richard, duke of York. 1461, George, duke of Clarence. 1470, earl of Worcester. 1478, John de la Pole, earl of Suffolk. 1481, Richard, earl of Kildare. 1483, Gerald, earl of Kildare. 1484, John de la Pole, earl of Lincoln. 1485, Jasper, duke of Bedford. 1494, Henry, duke of York, afterwards Henry VIII. (his deputy, sir E. Poynings). 1496, Gerald, earl of Kildare, and in 1504, 1513. 1521, Thomas Howard, earl of Surrey. 1529, Henry, duke of Richmond. Gerald, his son, 1556-61. Thomas, earl of Sussex. [Among the lord deputies, 1560, &c., sir Wm. Fitzwilliam. 1584, sir John Perrot]. 1599, Robert, earl of Essex.
1603. Sir Charles Blount, lord Mountjoy, made earl of Devonshire. 1640, Thos., viscount Wentworth, earl of Strafford. 1643 and 1648, James, marquis of Ormond. 1647, Philip, lord Lisle. 1649, Oliver Cromwell. 1657, Henry Cromwell. 1662, James Butler, duke of Ormond. 1669, John Roberts, lord Roberts. 1670, John, lord Berkeley. 1672, Arthur Capel, earl of Essex. 1677, James Butler, duke of Ormond. 1685, Henry Hyde, earl of Clarendon. 1687, Richard Talbot, earl of Tyrconnel. 1690, Henry Sydney, lord Sydney. 1695, Henry Capel, lord Capel.
1700. Laurence Hyde, earl of Rochester. 1703, James Butler, duke of Ormond. 1707, Thomas, earl of Pembroke. 1709, Thomas, earl of Wharton. 1710, James, duke of Ormond, again. 1713, Charles, duke of Shrewsbury. 1717, Charles, duke of Bolton. 1721, Charles, duke of Grafton. 1724, John, lord Carteret. 1731, Lionel, duke of Dorset. 1737, William, duke of Devonshire. 1745, Philip, earl of Chesterfield. 1747, William, earl of Harrington. 1751, Lionel, duke of Dorset, again. 1755, William, duke of Devonshire. 1757, John, duke of Bedford. 1761, George, earl of Halifax. 1763, Hugh, earl of Northumberland. 1765, Francis, earl of Hertford.
1767. George, viscount Townshend, 14 Oct.
1772. Simon, earl of Harcourt, 30 Nov.
1777. John, earl of Buckinghamshire, 25 Jan.
1780. Fred., earl of Carlisle, 23 Dec.
1782. Wm. Henry, duke of Portland, 14 April.
,, George, earl Temple, 15 Sept.
1783. Robert, earl of Northington, 3 June.
1784. Charles, duke of Rutland, 24 Feb.; died 24 Oct. 1787.
1787. George, marquis of Buckingham (late earl Temple), again, 2 Nov.
1790. John, earl of Westmorland, 5 Jan.
1794. William, earl Fitzwilliam, 10 Dec.
,, John, earl Camden, 11 March.
1798. Charles, marquis Cornwallis, 13 June.
1801. Philip, earl of Hardwicke, 25 May.
1806. John, duke of Bedford, 18 March.
1807. Charles, duke of Richmond, 19 April.
1813. Charles, earl Whitworth, 26 Aug.
1817. Charles, earl Talbot, 9 Oct.
1821. Richard, marquis Wellesley, 29 Dec.
1828. Henry, marquis of Anglesey, 1 March.
1829. Hugh, duke of Northumberland, 6 March.
1830. Henry, marquis of Anglesey, again, 23 Dec.
1833. Marquis Wellesley, again, 26 Sept.
1834. Thomas, earl of Haddington, 29 Dec.
1835. Henry, marquis of Normanby, 23 April.
1839. Hugh, viscount Ebrington, afterwards earl Fortescue, 3 April.
1841. Thomas Philip, earl de Grey, 15 Sept.
1844. William, lord Heytesbury, 12 July.
1846. John William, earl of Bessborough, 9 July; died 16 May, 1847.
1847. George William Frederick, earl of Clarendon, 26 May.
1852. Archibald William, earl of Eglinton, 28 Feb.
1853. Edward Granville, earl of St. Germans, Jan.
1855. George, earl of Carlisle, March.
1858. Archibald, earl of Eglinton, again, Feb., resigned.
1859. George, earl of Carlisle, again, June; died 5 Dec. 1864.
1864. John, lord Wodehouse, aft. earl of Kimberley, 1 Nov.
1866. James, marquis of Abercorn, July; made duke, 6 Aug. 1868.
1868. John, earl Spencer, Dec.
1874. James, duke of Abercorn, Feb.; died 31 Oct. 1885.
1876. John, duke of Marlborough, 28 Nov.
1880. Francis T. de Grey, earl Cowper, 5 May. Resigned April, 1882.
1882. John Poyntz, earl Spencer, May.
1885. Henry Howard Molyneux Herbert, earl of Carnarvon, 24 June, resigned Jan. 1886.
1886. John Campbell Hamilton Gordon, earl of Aberdeen, about 5 Feb.
1886. Charles Stewart Vane-Tempest-Stewart, marquis of Londonderry, Aug.

* The list of Irish sovereigns, printed in previous editions, has been omitted. The Irish writers carry their succession of kings very high. The learned antiquary, Thomas Innes, of the Scots' College of Paris, expressed his wonder that "the learned men of the Irish nation have not, like those of other nations, yet published the valuable remains of their ancient history whole and entire, with just translations, in order to separate what is fabulous, and only grounded on the traditions of their poets and bards, from what is *certain* history." "O'Flaherty, Keating, Toland, Kennedy, and other modern Irish historians, have rendered all uncertain, by deducing their history from the Deluge with as much assurance as they deliver the transactions of Ireland from St. Patrick's time."—*Anderson*.

† Lords justices and deputies, and latterly LORDS LIEUTENANT. It has been several times proposed to abolish the viceroyalty of Ireland, but without success. The last time 25 March, 1858.

1889. Lawrence Dundas, Earl of Zetland, 29 May; marquis, Aug. 1892.
1892. Robert O. A. Milnes, baron Houghton, 18 Aug.
1895. George Henry, earl Cadogan, June.

IRELAND FORGERIES. In 1786 W. H. Ireland made public the Shakspeare manuscripts which he had forged, and deceived many critics. The play, "Vortigern," was performed at Drury-lane theatre on 2 April, 1796. He shortly after acknowledged the forgery, and published his "Confessions" in 1805. He died in 1835.

IRELAND, YOUNG, a party (or rather "school"), formed for the regeneration of the country, founded by Thos. Osborne, Charles Gavan Duffy (who established and conducted "The Nation" from 1842 to 1855), Smith O'Brien and others in 1840. Some of their proceedings led to the state trials of 1843 and 1848. Mr. Duffy (afterwards premier of Victoria, Australia, and K.C.M.G., died 9 Feb. 1903) published "Young Ireland, a Fragment of Irish History, 1840-50," in 1880. The formation of a "Young Ireland league," was proposed at a meeting in Dublin, 17 Sept. 1891.

IRIDIUM AND OSMIUM. In 1804 Tennant discovered these two rare metals in the ore of platinum, in which, in 1845, Claus discovered a third, Ruthenium. Iridium is said to be the heaviest known metal, 1878. See *Weights*.

IRISH CHURCH; see *Church of Ireland*. The Irish Presbyterian Church act, passed 16 June, 1871, regulates the management of certain trust properties for that church.

IRISH DISTRESS FUND, to relieve the sufferers by the failure of the potato crop in the western coasts of Ireland, was started in Dublin by the lord lieutenant, the earl of Zetland, and Mr. A. J. Balfour, the chief secretary, 3 Jan. 1891. Received, up to 26 Jan. 39,000*l.*; up to 9 April, 49,067*l.* The queen gave 200*l.*; the mayor of Belfast 2000*l.*; sir Edward C. Guinness (lord Iveagh) 2,000*l.* Large donations of clothing were also received.

IRISH EXHIBITION, in the Olympia, W. Kensington, opened by the Lord Mayors of London (De Keyser), and Dublin (Sexton), 4 June, 1888.

It included natural products, manufactures of all kinds, valuable antiquities, fine works of art, facsimiles of a castle, round towers, a village &c., horses and cows. The amusements comprised theatrical performances, concerts, races, &c. Lord Arthur Hill, honorary secretary; among the patrons were the duke of Westminster, lord Leitrim, lord Charles Beresford, sir John Lubbock, archbishop of Canterbury, cardinal Manning, lord Hartington. The exhibition was closed . . . . Oct. 1888

The exhibition was financially unsuccessful, and an indemnity fund was started in . . July, 1891

IRISH HOME RULE BILL. See *Ireland*, Feb.-Sept., 1893.

IRISH INVINCIBLES, a secret society established in Dublin Nov., 1881, said by James Carey, a member, to have been formed by one Walsh and others, from England, to "make history" by killing tyrants. Each member was bound to obey orders, under pain of death. By some of its members the life of judge Lawson was attempted, and lord Frederick Cavendish and Mr. Burke murdered, 6 May, 1882. Mr. W. E. Forster was frequently watched with a similar intention. See under *Fenians*, *Ireland*, 1882-3. In Feb. 1883 there were said to be 250 members in Great Britain and Ireland. "The general No. 1," was said to be a wealthy man. "Murder leagues," and "assassination circles" were mentioned.

IRISH LAND BILLS, see *Ireland*, 1870, 1880-81, 1887, 1890, 1903.

IRISH LAND LAW ACT (44 & 45 Vict. c. 49, passed 22 Aug. 1881. See *Ireland*, April-Aug. 1881). It settles the rights of landlords and tenants; establishes a court of commission, which first met, 20 Oct. 1881, to try differences between them, and determines the conditions by which tenants may become proprietors; it affirms the virtual ownership of tenants with the power of selling their rights, securing the payment of a just rent to the landlords to be settled by the court, and restricting evictions. First court of commission, sergeant O'Hagan, Edward Falconer Litton, and John Edward Vernon. Royal Assent, 22 Aug. 1881.

Important decisions in favour of tenants by the sub-commissions at Belfast, &c. . . Nov. 1881

Above 2500 applications to the land courts up to 11 Nov. ,,

Bill for amending purchase clauses of land act; means of purchase greatly facilitated: not above 5,000,000*l.* to be advanced by the state in one year, and not more than 20,000,000*l.* in all; bill introduced by Mr. Trevelyan, 27 May, withdrawn 10 July, 1884

Bill extending the powers of the act of 1881, introduced by Mr. Gerald Balfour, 13 April, 1896; royal assent . . . . . . 14 Aug. 1896

See also *Land Bill Ireland*, 1903.

IRISH LANGUAGE, a branch of the Celtic or Gaelic, of which much literature exists in books and MSS. of early date. The New Testament was published in Irish in 1603, and the Old in 1685. A society for the preservation of the Irish language has been formed; in its annual report for 1890, it was stated that Irish is taught in 45 national schools. At a meeting of the Irish literary society held at the Society of Arts, London, lord Russell of Killowen, president, in the chair, a lecture was delivered by Mr. Douglas Hyde, on "Gaelic literature," 31 Oct. 1894; 435 members in 1896. Irish Literary Theatre founded 1898, 3rd annual series of performances, *The Twisting of the Rope*, by Dr. Douglas Hyde, the first play in Irish produced in a Dublin theatre; and *Diarmid and Grania*, by W. B. Yeats and George Moore, 21 Oct. 1901.

IRISH LOYAL AND PATRIOTIC UNION, see *Ireland*, 1886. Annual meetings.

IRISH MOSS, see *Carrageen*.

IRISH NATIONAL LEAGUE. See *Ireland*, 17 Oct. 1882; annual meetings.

IRISH PROPERTY DEFENCE ASSOCIATION, formed by landlords, Nov. 1880.

IRISH REPUBLIC. Treasonable plans for its establishment dated 1869, were discovered in James F. Egan's garden in Birmingham, April, 1884.

IRISH SOCIETY, THE HONOURABLE, the name given to a committee of citizens of twelve London companies invited by king James I. to colonize the confiscated lands in the north of Ireland, termed the Ulster plantations, including Londonderry and Coleraine, 1609. The committee received a charter, 1613, which was taken away in 1637, and restored after various changes 1670. The affairs of this company and its methods of business were discussed in parliament in 1868 and 1869.

The sale of the companies' estates under lord Ashbourne's act began in 1887. Receipts from the estates in 1887, 9,061*l.* besides receipts for fisheries and other rents.

The select committee respecting the Irish Society (sir Wm. T. Marriott, Mr. John Morley, sir Richard Temple, and others), first met, 17 July, 1889; met again 9 June *et seq.*, 1890. Three reports adopted, 4 May, 1891; see *Ireland*, Jan. 1892

Income, 34,767*l.* in 1896.

IRISH UNIVERSITY BILL (to combine Trinity College and the Catholic College), introduced by Mr. I. Butt, 16 May, 1876; withdrawn.

IRISH UNIVERSITY COMMISSION, see *Education* and *Ireland*.

IRON. The Greeks ascribed the discovery of iron to themselves, and referred glass to the Phœnicians. Moses relates that iron was wrought by Tubal-Cain (Gen. iv. 22). Swedish iron is very celebrated, and Dannemora is the greatest mine of Sweden.—The weekly publication "*Iron*," which began 18 Jan. 1873, was a continuation of the "*Mechanics' Magazine*" (started 1823), and was combined with "*Industries*," in 1893. See *Steel*.

Belgium, an early seat of the iron manufacture; coal said to have been employed at Marche-les-dames, 1340.

British iron cast by Ralph Page and Peter Baude, in Sussex, 1543. *Rymer's Fœdera.*

Iron-mills used for slitting iron into bars for smiths, by Godfrey Bochs, 1590.

Tinning of iron introduced from Bohemia, 1681. Till about 1730 iron ores were smelted entirely with wood charcoal, which did not wholly give way to coal and coke till 1788.

The Carron iron works in Stirlingshire, where there is much ironstone and coal, were established mainly by the exertions of dr. John Roebuck, 1759–60; this was the beginning of the great Scotch iron-works.

The operation termed *puddling*, and other very great improvements in the manufacture, invented by Mr. Henry Cort, about 1781, who did not reap the due reward of his ingenuity. He died in 1800.

Mr. James B. Neilson, of Glasgow, patented his *hot air blast* in 1828; see under *blowing machines*.

Mr. (after sir) Henry Bessemer patented his method of manufacturing iron and steel, 17 Oct., 5 Dec., 1855; 12 Feb. 1856.

Strike of the puddlers and lock-out of the masters in Staffordshire, Northumberland, &c., lasted during March, April, and May, 1865.

Ironworkers of Great Britain determine to form one trades' union, with one executive, Oct. 1866.

Strike of ironworkers in the north over, 31 Dec. 1866.

Mr. Wm. Robinson announced a method of making wrought iron from cast iron by means of magnetism, July, 1867.

Mr. John Heaton's process for making steel announced about Nov. 1867, discussed Oct. 1868.

One of the finest, thickest, and heaviest armour-plates ever rolled in the world was pressed into the very perfection of a manufactured armour-plate at the great Atlas Ironworks of sir John Brown and Co., Sheffield. The size of it when in the furnace was a little over 20 feet long by about 4 feet broad and 21 inches thick. Its rough weight was over 21 tons. It was built up in the furnace before being rolled by five mould plates, each 3 inches thick, and one solid plate of 6 inches. This mass when reduced by intense heat to the consistency of dough, was withdrawn from the furnace, and in the course of less than a quarter of an hour was passed between the enormous rollers many times, was reduced to a compact slab of iron of a uniform thickness of 15 inches, and then passed on to its bed to cool till fit for having its rough edges planed down to the proper dimensions, 6 Sept. 1867. Armour-plate 24 inches thick rolled at same works, Oct. 1876.

Iron forts (cost about 1,000,000*l.* made by Whitworth & Co. at Manchester) put up at Spithead early in 1872.

Mr. Crampton's iron furnace, in which definite proportions of coal dust and air are introduced under pressure, was tried at Woolwich and was reported successful, May, 1873.

Ironstone miners in Yorkshire: great strike through reduction in wages, May, 1874.

Iron trades, see *Employers*.

Iron merchant vessels built in 1860, 181; in 1877, 545.

Alfred Newman, an eminent art iron-worker; of the "smithy," Haymarket, London, dies aged 35, Jan. 1887.

Iron Manufacture: between 1865-75 the capital invested rose from 7,000,000*l.* to 29,000,000*l.* Number of puddling furnaces rose from 3462 to 7159; also great increase in blast furnaces.

Great depression since 1876; due to excessive production and increased and cheap manufacture of steel; revival 1889 *et seq.*

Iron and Steel congress at New York . Sept.–Oct. 1890

Strike or lock-out in the Scotch iron trade respecting wages . . . . 4 Oct. ,,

The Bessemer medal for 1899 accepted by the queen in commemoration of the progress made in the iron and steel industries during her reign, 4 May, 1899

Great veins of iron discovered at Vadsö, Norway, reported . . . . . . 25 Aug. 1902

IRON PRODUCED IN GREAT BRITAIN.

Year	Furnaces		Tons
1740	59	furnaces	17,350 tons.
1788	77	,,	61,920 ,,
1796	121	,,	124,789 ,,
1802	168	,,	227,000 ,,
1806	227	,,	250,000 ,,
1820	260	,,	400,000 ,,
1825	374	,,	581,367 ,,
1840	402	,,	1,396,400 ,,
1848	623	,,	1,998,558 ,,
1852	655	,,	2,701,000 ,,

In 1855, 3,217,154 tons of pig iron were produced; in 1857, 3,659,447 tons; in 1865, 4,819,254 tons; in 1869, 5,445,757 tons; in 1873, 6,566,451 tons; in 1876, 6,555,997 tons; in 1879, 5,995,337 tons; in 1882, pig, 8,586,680 tons; in 1884, 7,811,727 tons; in 1886, 7,009,754 tons; in 1887, 7,559,518 tons; in 1888, 7,998,969 tons; in 1889, 8,322,824 tons; in 1890, 7,904,214 tons; 1893, 6,976,990 tons; 1896, 8,659,681 tons; 1897, 8,796,465 tons; 1899, 9,421,435 tons; 1900, 8,959,691 tons; 1901, 7,928,647 tons.

Exports of Iron and Steel, from United Kingdom. 1860, 1,502,500 tons; 1865, 1,687,071 tons; 1870, 2,825,575, tons; 1875, 2,457,306 tons; 1879, 2.883,484 tons; 1883, 4,043,308 tons; 1885, 3,130,682 tons; 1887, 4,143,028 tons; 1889, 4,186,182 tons; 1890, 4,001,430 tons; 1891, 3,240,146 tons; 1893, 2,856,574 tons; 1890, 3,550,398 tons; 1898, 3,244,350 tons; 1900, 3,540,689 tons; 1901, 2,897,719 tons.

IRON AND STEEL INSTITUTE, the duke of Devonshire, president, held its first meeting in London 22 June, 1869, first provincial meeting at Merthyr-Tydvil, 6 Sept. 1870; first foreign meeting at Liége, 18 Aug. 1873; second at Paris, 16 Sept. 1878. Frequently at other places (Vienna, 19 Sept. 1882); at New York, Sept., Oct., at Ottawa, Nov. 1890; London, 1893; Brussels, 21 Aug. 1894; Bilbao, 1 Sept. 1896; Stockholm, 26 Aug. 1898; Paris, 18 Sept. 1900 (Mr. Andrew Carnegie presents 13,000*l.* to the Institute, May, 1901); Düsseldorf, 3 Sept. 1902.

IRONCLADS, see *Circular*, *Navy*, and *United States*, 1862; *Germany*, 1878.

IRON CROSS, an order of knighthood established by Frederick William III. of Prussia, 10 March, 1813, to honour patriotic bravery in the war against France; was revived by William I. in the Franco-Prussian war, and awarded by him to his son for his victory at Wissembourg, 4 Aug. 1870. About 40,000 persons were decorated in 1870-71.

IRON CROWN (of Italy), of gold and precious stones, set in a thin ring of iron, said to have been forged from a nail of Christ's cross, was made by order of Theudelinde for her husband, Agilulf, king of the Longobards, 591. She presented it (to be kept) to the church at Monza. Charlemagne was crowned with this crown, and after him all the emperors who were kings of Lombardy; Napoleon I. at Milan, on 26 May, 1805, put it on his head, saying, "*Dieu me l'a donnée; gare à qui y touchera.*" (God has given it to me; woe to him who touches it.) The crown was removed from Monza to Mantua by the Austrians, on 23 April, 1859. After the peace of Vienna in 1866, the crown was given up to general Menabrea on 11 Oct., and presented to king Victor Emmanuel, at Turin, on 4 Nov. The order of the "Iron Crown of Italy," instituted by Napoleon 26 May, 1805, was abolished in 1814, but revived by the emperor of Austria 12 Feb. 1816; see *Gotha.* The order of the Crown of Italy was instituted by king Victor Emmanuel 20 Feb. 1868.

IRON-MASK, THE MAN WITH THE.* A mysterious prisoner in France, wearing a mask and closely confined under M. de St. Mars, at Pignerol (1679), Exilles (1681), Sainte Marguerite (1687), and at the Bastille (1698), where he died 19 Nov. 1703. He was of noble mien, and was treated with profound respect; but his keepers had orders to despatch him if he uncovered. M. de St. Mars himself always placed the dishes on his table, and stood in his presence.

IRON-PLATED SHIPS, see *Ironclads*.

IRREDENTISTS, see *Italia Irredenta*.

IRRIGATION, practised in the east and in Egypt from the most remote ages. It was strenuously advocated for India by sir A. Cotton and others at the Social Science Congress at Manchester, Oct. 1866. In 1865 acts were passed for utilising London sewage in the irrigation of grass land, and the results are said to be generally favourable. The subject was much discussed, Aug. 1873. A method of producing artificial rain from ponds by means of steam-power, patented by Isaac Brown, of Edinburgh, was tried by Mr. Coleman, at Stoke Park, and reported successful; see *Sewage*, and *Intermittent Filtration*, *Madras* (1895), *Egypt*, *Nile*.

IRUN (a frontier village of Spain). On 16 May, 1837, the British auxiliary legion under general Evans, marched from St. Sebastian to attack Irun (held by the Carlists), which after a desperate resistance was carried by assault, 17 May.

IRVINGITES, followers of Edward Irving,† now called the "Holy Catholic Apostolic Church." They use a liturgy (framed in 1842, and enlarged 1853), and have church officers named apostles, angels, prophets, &c. In 1852 lighted candles were placed on the magnificent altar, and burning of incense during prayers was prescribed. The Gothic church in Gordon-square was solemnly opened 1 Jan. 1854. It is said that all who join the church offer it a tenth of their income. They had 30 chapels in England in 1851.

ISANDULA, Isandlana, or Isandlwana, termed the "English Cremera"; see *Zululand*, 22 Jan. 1879.

ISAURIA (a province in Asia Minor), conquered by the Romans B.C. 78, by the Saracens A.D. 650; was retaken by the emperor Leo III., who founded the Isaurian dynasty, 718, which ended with Constantine VI. in 797. Isauria was incorporated with Turkey 1387.

ISCHIA, see *Earthquakes*, 1883.

ISERNIA (S. Italy). Here the Sardinian general Cialdini defeated the Neapolitans, 17 Oct. 1860.

ISLAM, or ESLÂM, submission to God, the name given to *Mahometanism* (*which see*).

ISLE OF FRANCE, MAN, &c., see *Mauritius*, *Man*, &c.

ISLES, BISHOPRIC OF. This see contained not only the Hebrides, or Western Isles, but the Isle of Man, which for nearly 400 years had been a separate bishopric. The first bishop of the Isles was Amphibalus, 360; see *Iona*. Since the revolution (when this bishopric was discontinued) the Isles have been joined to Moray and Ross, or to Ross alone. In 1847, however, Argyll and the Isles were made a seventh post-revolution and distinct bishopric; see *Bishops*.

ISLINGTON (anciently Isendone, Iseldone, and "Merrie"), a large suburban parish in N. London, still containing Roman and mediæval remains, and old buildings, all gradually disappearing. Four members returned by the Act of 1885. Made a municipal borough by the London Government Act, 1899 (10 aldermen, 60 councillors). Population, 1801, 10,121; 1881, 282,865; 1891, 319,433; 1901, 334,928.

The great northern central hospital, Holloway-road, opened by the prince of Wales . . 17 July, 1888

Union Chapel, Compton-terrace, erected in 1802 by a union of Episcopalians and Nonconformists; rebuilt, opened 5 Dec. 1877; completed and surmounted by a tower, Oct. 1889. The rev. dr. Henry Allon, at first co-pastor (1843) with the first minister, the rev. Thomas Lewis, and afterwards sole pastor, an accomplished writer and active administrator of schools, &c., died, aged 73 (colleague and successor, the rev. W. Harwood) 16 April, 1892

Public baths and wash-houses opened by lord mayor Evans . . . 21 May and 26 July, ,,

Public electric lighting inaugurated by lord mayor sir W. Wilkin, cost 80,000*l*. . . . 4 March, 1896

The rev. Chas. H. Turner made suffragan bishop of Islington . . . . 10 May, 1898

* The following conjectures have been made as to his identity:—An Armenian patriarch forcibly carried from Constantinople (who died ten years before the mask); the duc de Vermandois, son of Louis XIV., reported to have perished in the camp before Dixmude; the duc de Beaufort, whose head is reported to have been taken off before Candia; James, duke of Monmouth, executed on Tower-hill; a son of Anne of Austria, queen of Louis XIII., either by cardinal Mazarin, or by the duke of Buckingham; the twin brother of Louis XIV. (a conjecture received by Voltaire and others); Foucquet, an eminent statesman in the time of Louis XIV.; and a count Matthioli, secretary of state to Charles III., duke of Mantua. M. Delort and the right hon. Agar Ellis (afterwards lord Dover) endeavoured to prove Matthioli to have been the person. The mask, it seems, was not made of iron; but of black velvet, strengthened with whalebone, and fastened behind the head with a padlock.

† Edward Irving was born 15 Aug. 1792, and was engaged as assistant to Dr. Chalmers, at Glasgow, in 1819. In 1823 he attracted immense crowds of distinguished persons to his sermons at the Scotch church, Hatton-garden. A new church was built for him in Regent-square in 1827. Soon after, he propounded new doctrines on the human nature of Christ: and the "Utterances of Unknown Tongues," which began in his congregation with a Miss Hall and Mr. Taplin, 16 Oct. 1831, were countenanced by him, as of divine inspiration. He was expelled from the Scotch church, 15 March, 1833. His church, "reconstituted with the threefold cord of a sevenfold ministry," was removed to Newman-street. He died 8 Dec. 1834.

ISLY (N.W. Africa). Here Abd-el-Kader, the Arab chief, was totally defeated by the French, under Bugeaud, 14 Aug. 1844.

ISMAIL (Bessarabia) was taken by the Russians, 6 Aug. 1770, after a long siege, when the Russians lost 20,000 men; the town was taken by storm, 22 Dec. 1790; when Suwarrow, the most merciless warrior of modern times, put the brave Turkish garrison (30,000 men) to the sword and delivered up Ismail to pillage, and ordered the massacre of 6000 women. It was again captured by the Russians 26 Sept. 1809, and retained till the treaty of Paris in 1856, when it was ceded to Moldavia.

ISMAILIA, the half-way station on the Suez Canal. It is supposed to occupy nearly the site of Rameses. Sir Samuel Baker named it Ismailia instead of Gondokoro, May, 1869. The rebel Egyptian army was defeated near here by the British, 25 Aug. 1882. See *Egypt*.

ISPAHAN was made the capital of Persia by Abbas the Great, in 1590. It lost its supremacy in 1796, when Teheran became the capital.

ISRAEL, KINGDOM OF, see *Jews*.—Handel's oratorio, "Israel in Egypt," first performed 4 April, 1739.

ISSUS (Asia Minor), the site of Alexander's second great battle with Darius, whose queen and family were captured, Oct. 333 B.C. The Persian army, according to Justin, consisted of 400,000 foot and 100,000 horse; 61,000 of the former and 10,000 of the latter were left dead on the spot, and 40,000 were taken prisoners. Here the emperor Septimius defeated his rival Niger, A.D. 194.

ISTAMBOUL, see *Constantinople*.

ISTER, see *Danube*.

ISTHMIAN GAMES received their name from the isthmus of Corinth, where they were observed: their institution is mythically attributed to Sisyphus of Corinth, 1326 B.C., and to Theseus in honour of Neptune about 1234. The games, which were solemnly kept every third year, were discontinued at the destruction of Corinth by Lucius Mummius, 146 B.C. The games were revived by Julius Cæsar, 60 B.C.; and by the emperor Julian, A.D. 362, and ceased in 396, when Corinth was sacked by the Goths.

ISTRIA was finally subdued by the Romans, 177 B.C. After various changes it came under the rule of Venice in 1378, and was annexed 1420. It was obtained by Austria 1796; by France 1806; by Austria 1814. Population in 1890, 317,610; 1900, 344,173.

ITALIA IRREDENTA ("unredeemed Italy"), a secret society which first appeared in Italy Nov. 1877, and said to have 200 committees, the chief at Naples. Its professed object is to add to the Italian kingdom Trieste, the Tyrol, and other Austrian provinces on the Adriatic.

Cry for Italia Irredenta: meetings at Rome, &c. 21 July, 1878

In 1879, col. Haymerle, an Austrian military resident at Rome, published "*Res Italicæ*," freely discussing the subject. The Italians were much annoyed, and the publication was disavowed by the Austrian government.

Sig. Crispi, in a speech at Florence, strongly declares against the Irredentists . . . . 8 Oct. 1800

ITALIAN AFRICA, see *Massowah* and *Zanzibar*, 1893-5.

ITALIAN ASSOCIATION FOR THE ADVANCEMENT OF SCIENCE, first met at Pisa, under the patronage of the grand duke of Tuscany, in 1837. It met in Rome, 20 Oct. 1873, and at other places since.

ITALIAN BENEVOLENT SOCIETY, London, founded by the king of Italy and others, 1861.

ITALIAN CATHOLIC CHURCH (between two and three thousand persons); first bishop, Domenico Panelli; a synod met at Naples in 1875. Great progress reported Feb. 1888.

Its statute (of 62 articles) asserts that the Catholic church is nothing but the society of all believers in Jesus Christ, and that he only is its supreme head and pastor; rejects all miracles since the death of the Apostles; declares that the Catholic faith is only that revealed in the Holy Scriptures, &c. The congregation of St. Paul, of the Italian Catholic church headed by Mons. Savarese, declared heretical, Oct. 1884.

ITALIAN EXHIBITION, West Brompton, London, opened by the Lord Mayor, 12 May, 1888.

It comprised models of the Roman forum, coliseum &c., diorama of the bay of Naples, &c., paintings, sculpture, manufactures and natural products of Italy. The celebrated sculptor, signor Focardi, had a studio there and did work. Closed 31 Oct. 1888.

ITALIAN LANGUAGE, based on Latin, is said by Dante to be formed of a selection of the best portions of the different dialects. Pure, elegant poetry was written by Guido Cavalcanti, who died 1301; and good prose by Malespini, about 1250. See *Drama*.

PRINCIPAL ITALIAN AUTHORS.

	Born	*Died*		*Born*	*Died*
Dante . .	1265	1321	Monti . .	1754	1828
Petrarca . .	1304	1374	Leopardi .	1798	1837
Boccaccio .	1313	1375	Gioberti .	1801	1852
Boiardo .	1434	1494	Nicolini .	1782	1861
Machiavelli .	1469	1527	Manzoni .	1784	1873
Ariosto .	1474	1533	Amari . .	1806	1889
Guicciardini	1482	1540	Romagnosi .	1761	1835
Tasso . .	1544	1595	Massimo d'Azeglio	1798	1866 or 5
Galileo . .	1564	1642			
Metastasio .	1698	1782	Niccolo Tommaseo	1802	1874
Goldoni .	1707	1795			
Parini .	1729	1799	Guerazzi .	1804	1874
Alfieri . .	1749	1803	Mazzini . .	1805	1872
Volta . .	1745	1826	Carducci . .	1836	—

The following terms are often used with reference to certain periods in the history of Italian literature and art.

1. *Trecento* (three hundred), from the birth of Dante (1265) to the death of Boccaccio (1375), which two, with Petrarca, are styled "the triumvirate of the Trecento."
2. *Quattrocento* (four hundred), from 1375 to the revival of Italian literature by Lorenzo de' Medici in the 15th century. During this period Latin was revived, to the prejudice of Italian.
3. *Cinquecento* (five hundred), from about 1480 to 1590. A sensuous style of art, founded on the heathen mythology, began to prevail.
4. *Seicento* (six hundred), from 1590 to 1700. The bad taste which prevailed during this period is ascribed to the influence of the Spaniards and the Jesuits throughout Italy. *Seicentisti* is a term of reproach.

The *Trecento* and *Cinquecento* were the most flourishing periods.

ITALIAN REPUBLIC was the name given to the remodelled Cisalpine republic. Napoleon Bonaparte, president, Jan. 1802.

ITALY, a name mythically derived either from Italus, an early king, or *italus*, a bull calf. The invading Pelasgians from Greece, and the Aborigines (Umbrians, Oscans, and Etruscans), combined, form the Latin race, still possessing the southern part of Europe. The history of Italy is soon absorbed into that of Rome, founded 753 B.C. In the middle ages it was desolated by intestine wars and the interference of the German emperors; since then, Spain, France, and Germany struggled for the possession of the country, which has been divided among them several times. Spain, which predominated in Italy during the 16th and 17th centuries, yielded to the house of Austria at the beginning of the 18th. The victories of Bonaparte in 1797-8 changed the government of Italy; but the Austrian rule was re-established at the peace in 1814. In 1848 the Milanese and Venetians revolted and joined Piedmont, but were subdued by Radetzky; see *below*. The hostile feeling between Austria and Piedmont gradually increased till war broke out in April, 1859. The Austrians were defeated, and the kingdom of Italy, comprising Piedmont, Sardinia, Lombardy, Tuscany, Modena, Parma, the Romagna, Naples, and Sicily was re-established, 17 March, 1861, by the Italian parliament (consisting of 443 deputies from 59 provinces). On 29 Oct., 1861, the internal government was reorganized; the 59 provinces were placed under prefects, subject to four directors-general. War with Austria was declared 18 June, 1866; and on 3 Oct., peace was signed at Vienna, and Venetia was ceded to Italy; see *below* for the events. The settlement of the kingdom of Italy was consummated by the occupation of Rome as the capital, 1870. Estimated population of the kingdom, 1862, 25,003,635 (Rome was added in 1870). 1878, 28,209,620; Jan. 1882, 28,452,639; 9 Feb. 1901, 32,449,754. 1890-91, revenue, 78,129,383*l.*; 1893, 69,368,397*l.*; expenditure, 81,850,050*l.*; 1893, 71,699,867*l.*; imports, 71,905,383*l.*; exports, 51,171,079*l.*; 1901-2, revenue, 72,883,756*l.* expenditure, 71,927.780*l.*; imports, 70,228,758*l.*; exports, 56,651,951*l.* For other details see *Rome* and the various Italian cities throughout the volume.

Early history mythical; Italy (Saturnia) fabled to have been ruled by Saturn during the golden age . . . B.C. 2450
Arrival of Œnotrus from Arcadia, 1710; and of Evander; reign of Latinus . . . about 1240
Æneas the Trojan said to land in Italy, defeat and kill Turnus, marry Lavinia, daughter of king Latinus, and found Lavinium, in South Italy, 1182, &c.
Greek colonies (see *Magna Græcia*) founded . . 974-443
Romulus builds Rome 753

[For subsequent history, see *Rome*.]

Odoacer, leader of the Heruli, establishes the *kingdom* of Italy . . . . A.D. 449
The Ostrogoths invade Italy, 489, and retain it till 761
They are expelled by the Imperial generals Narses and Belisarius 525

[See Kings of Italy, and *Iron Crown*.]

Narses, governor of Italy, invites the Lombards from Germany, 568; who overrun Italy . . . 596
Invasion and defeat of Constans II. . . . 662
Venice first governed by a doge 697
Pepin gives Ravenna to the pope 754
Charlemagne invades Italy, 774; overcomes the Lombards; crowned emperor of the west at Rome by pope Leo III. . . . . . . 25 Dec. 800
The Saracens invade Italy and settle at Bari . 842
Invasion of Otho I. 951; crowned emperor, 2 Feb. 962
Genoa becomes important 1000
The Saracens expelled by the Normans . . 1016-17
The Normans acquire Naples from the pope . . 1051
Pope Gregory VII., Hildebrand, pretends to universal sovereignty, in which he is assisted by Matilda, countess of Tuscany, mistress of the greater part of Italy 1073-85

Disputes between the popes and emperors, relative to ecclesiastical investitures, begin (and long agitate Italy and Germany) . . . . about 1073
Rise of the Lombard cities . . . . . about 1120
Who war with each other 1144
The Venetians obtain many victories over the Eastern emperors 1125
Wars of the Guelphs and Ghibelines (*which see*) begin about 1161
Frederic I. (Barbarossa) interferes: his wars 1154-75
Lombard league formed 1167
His defeat at Legnano . . . . 29 May, 1176
Peace of Constance 1183
Civil wars again . . . . 1199, &c.
Rise of the Medici at Florence . . . about 1251
Wars of Frederick II. and the Lombard league, 1236-50
His natural son, Manfred, king of Sicily, defeated and killed at the battle of Benevento, by Charles of Anjou . . . . 26 Feb. 1266
Who defeats Conradin, at Tagliacozzo . 23 Aug. 1268
The Visconti rule at Milan 1277
The Sicilian vespers; massacre of the French, who are expelled from Sicily . . . 30 March, 1282
Clement V. (pope, 1305), fixes his residence at Avignon in France 1309
Louis Gonzaga makes himself master of Mantua, with the title of imperial vicar 1328
First doge of Genoa appointed 1339
Lucca independent 1370
Rome again the seat of the pope 1377
Charles VIII. of France invades Italy, 1494, and conquers Naples, 1495; loses it in . . . 1496
Louis XII. joins Venice and conquers Milan (soon lost) 1499
League of Cambray (1508) against Venice, which is despoiled of its Italian possessions . . . 1509
Leo X. pope, patron of literature and art . . 1513-22
Wars of Charles V. and Francis I. . . . 1515-21
Francis defeated and prisoner at Pavia 24 Feb. 1525
Parma and Placentia made a duchy for his family by pope Paul III. (Alexander Farnese) . . . 1545
Peace of Cateau-Cambresis 1559
War of the Mantuan succession 1627-31
Catinat and the French defeat the duke of Savoy at Marsaglia . . . . . . 4 Oct. 1693
War of Spanish succession commences in Italy . 1701
Battle of Turin . . . . 7 Sept. 1706
Division of Italy at the peace of Utrecht, 11 April, 1713
The duke of Savoy becomes king of Sardinia . . 1720
Successful French campaign in Italy 1745
Milan, &c., obtained by the house of Austria, 1706; confirmed by treaty of Aix-la-Chapelle . . . 1748
Italy overrun by the French . . . May—Dec. 1796
Division of the Venetian states by France and Austria by the treaty of Campo Formio; Cisalpine republic founded . . . . . 17 Oct. 1797
Pius VI. deposed by Bonaparte . . . . Feb. 1798
The Russians, under Suwarrow, defeat the French at Trebia, &c. 1799
Bonaparte crosses the Alps, 16-20 May; defeats the Austrians at Marengo . . . . 14 June, 1800
The *Cisalpine* becomes the *Italian* republic (Bonaparte, president) . . . . . . Jan. 1802
Napoleon crowned king of Italy . . . 26 May, 1805
Eugène Beauharnais made viceroy of Italy . . . ,,
Austria loses her Italian possessions by the treaty of Presburg; ratified . . . . . 1 Jan. 1806
The kingdom ceases on the overthrow of Napoleon, 1814; the Lombardo-Venetian kingdom established for Austria . . . . . . 7 April, 1815
Formation of the young Italy party by Mazzini; insurrections 1831-33
Italian Association for Science first met (at Pisa) . 1837
Insurrection in Lombardy and Venice, March; supported by the king of Sardinia and by the pope, April, 1848
The king defeated at Novara, abdicates, 23 March; and Lombardy reverts to Austria . . . May, 1849

[See *Sardinia* and *Austria*.]

"Napoléon III. et l'Italie" published . . . Feb. 1859
The Austrian ultimatum, rejected by Sardinia, 26 April, ,,
The Austrians cross the Ticino, 27 April; and the French enter Genoa . . . . . . 3 May, ,,
Peaceful revolution at Florence, 27 April; Parma, May 3; Modena . . . . . . 15 June, ,,

The Austrians defeated at Montebello, 20 May; Palestro, 30-31 May; Magenta, 4 June; Marignano, 8 June; Solferino (*which see*) . 24 June, 1859
Provisional governments established at Florence, 27 April; Parma, May; and Modena [the sovereigns retire] . . . . . . 15 June, ,,
Insurrection in the papal states; Bologna, Ferrara, &c. . . . . 13-15 June, ,,
Massacre of the insurgents at Perugia by the Swiss troops . . . . . . 20 June, ,,
The allies cross the Mincio . . . . 1 July, ,,
Armistice between Austria and France 8 July, ,,
Preliminaries of peace signed at Villafranca; Lombardy surrendered to Sardinia . 11 July, ,,
Italy dismayed at the peace; agitation at Milan, Florence, Modena, Parma, &c.; resignation of count Cavour as minister . . . . July, ,,
The pope appeals to Europe against the king of Sardinia . . . . . . 12 July, ,,
Garibaldi exhorts the Italians to arm . 19 July, ,,
Grand duke of Tuscany abdicates . 21 July, ,,
Constitutional assemblies meet at Florence, 11 Aug.; and at Modena . . . . . 16 Aug. ,,
Tuscany, Modena, Parma, and the Romagna enter into a defensive alliance, and declare for annexation to Piedmont, 20 Aug.-10 Sept.; fiscal restrictions between them and Piedmont abolished, 10 Oct. ,,
Assassination of col. Anviti at Parma . 5 Oct. ,,
Garibaldi appeals to the Neapolitans; subscriptions in Italy and elsewhere to supply arms for the Italians . . . . Oct. ,,
Tuscany, &c., choose the prince Eugène of Carignan-Savoy, as regent of central Italy, 5 Nov.; the king of Sardinia refusing his consent, the prince declines the office, but recommends the chevalier Buoncampagni . . . . . . 14 Nov. ,,
Treaty of Zurich (establishing Italian confederacy, &c.), signed . . . . 10 Nov. ,,
Garibaldi retires from Sardinian service . 18 Nov. ,,
New Sardinian constitution proclaimed 7 Dec. ,,
The pope condemns the pamphlet "*Le Pape et le Congrès*" . . . . 31 Dec. ,,
The emperor Napoleon recommends the pope to give up the legations . . . . . 31 Dec. ,,
The pope refuses and denounces the emperor, 8 Jan. 1860
Count Cavour charged with the formation of a ministry . . . . 16 Jan. ,,
Annexation to Sardinia voted for (by universal suffrage) in Parma, Modena, and the Romagna, 13 March; Tuscany, 16 March; accepted by the king, 18-22 March, ,,
Treaty ceding Savoy and Nice to France signed, 24 March; approved by the Sardinian parliament, 29 May, ,,
The French troops retire from Italy . . May, ,,
Vain insurrections in Sicily . 4 April; 2 May, ,,
Garibaldi lands at Marsala in Sicily, 11 May; assumes the office of dictator, 14 May; defeats the Neapolitans at Calatifimi, 15 May; and at Melazzo, 20 July; by a convention the Neapolitans agree to evacuate Sicily (see *Sicily*), 30 July, ,,
Garibaldi lands at Reggio in Calabria, 18 Aug.; enters Naples; king Francis retires . 7 Sept. ,,
Insurrection in Papal States, 8 Sept.; the Sardinians enter, 11 Sept.; defeat the papal troops at Castel-fidardo, 18 Sept.; take Ancona, 17-29 Sept. ,,
Victor-Emmanuel takes the command of his army, 4 Oct. ,,
The Sardinians enter kingdom of Naples, 15 Oct.; defeat Neapolitans at Isernia . . 17 Oct. ,,
Garibaldi defeats Neapolitans at the Volturno, 1 Oct. 1860: meets Victor-Emmanuel, and says, "King of Italy!" the latter replies, "I thank you!" 26 Oct. ,,
By universal suffrage (plebiscitum), Sicily and Naples vote for annexation to Sardinia 21 Oct. ,,
Capua bombarded; the Neapolitans retire, 2 Nov.; and are defeated at the Garigliano . 3 Nov. ,,
Victor-Emmanuel enters Naples as king, 7 Nov.; Garibaldi resigns the dictatorship and retires to Caprera . . . . 9 Nov. ,,
Victor-Emmanuel receives homage from the Neapolitan clergy, &c.; gives money to encourage education; appoints a ministry, including Poerio, &c., Nov. 1860
Siege of Gaëta commences; attack by sea prevented by the presence of the French fleet, 3 Nov. &c. ,,
Treaty of Zurich signed (see *Zurich*) . 10 Nov. ,,
Decree in honour of Garibaldi's army . 16 Nov. ,,
Reactionary movements suppressed . Nov.-Dec. ,,
Prince of Carignan-Savoy appointed lieutenant of Naples . . . . Jan. 1861
The French fleet retires from Gaëta, 19 Jan.; after severe bombardment it surrenders; Francis II. retires to Rome . . . . . 13 Feb. ,,
Monastic establishments in Naples abolished, with compensation to the inmates; schools established, Feb. ,,
Assembly of the first Italian parliament, 18 Feb., which decrees Victor-Emmanuel king of Italy, 26 Feb. and 14 March, ,,
Naples unsettled through reactionary intrigues of the papal party . . . March and April, ,,
Italy recognised by Great Britain . 31 March, ,,
Order for the levy of 70,000 soldiers . April, ,,
Cavour forms a new ministry, including members from all parts of Italy . . . . April, ,,
The pope protests against the kingdom, 15 April, ,,
Altercation in parliament between Cavour and Garibaldi, 18 April; reconciled . 25 April, ,,
Bourbonist bands defeated . . 7 May, &c. ,,
Prince of Carignan resigns; San Martino appointed lieutenant at Naples . . . . 13 May, ,,
Death of count Cavour, aged 52 . . 6 June, ,,
Ricasoli forms a ministry to continue Cavour's policy, 11 June, ,,
The kingdom recognised by France . 24 June, ,,
San Martino resigns the government of Naples; active measures taken against the insurgents and brigands by Cialdini, his successor, appointed, 16 July, ,,
The king opens the exhibition of Italian industry at Florence . . . . . . 14 Sept. ,,
The kingdom recognised by Portugal and Belgium, 1 Oct.; divided into fifty-nine prefectures, &c., 13 Oct. ,,
Skirmishes in the south with brigands and foreign emissaries in the cause of Francis II. . . Oct. ,,
Cialdini retires, and La Marmora becomes lieutenant-general of Naples . . . . 2 Nov. ,,
Brigandage still prevailing in the south, aided by the king of Naples; insurgents defeated; and many killed . . . . 19 Nov. ,,
José Borges, a Spaniard, lands in Calabria, 15 Sept.; calls on the people to rise for Francis II., Sept.; taken and shot . . . . . 8 Dec. ,,
The reactionist warfare continues; cruelties of the brigands lead to reprisals, Dec. 1861, Jan. and Feb. 1862
Ricasoli compelled to resign by court influence, 1 March; Rattazzi forms an administration, 3 March, ,,
The kingdom recognised by Prussia . 1 March, ,,
Surrender of Civatella del Tronto, the last Bourbon fortress in Sicily . . . . . 14 March, ,,
Triumphant progress of Garibaldi through Italy, establishing rifle clubs . March and April, ,,
Mr. J. F. Bishop, an active English Bourbonist propagandist, captured . . . . . 2 April, ,,
Conspiracy among the Neapolitan soldiers at Milan suppressed . . . . 19 April, ,,
The king received at Naples with great enthusiasm, 28 April, ,,
The French general Guyon aids in the suppression of the Bourbonist brigands . . . April, ,,
The kingdom recognised by Russia . . 3 July, ,,
Garibaldi proceeds to Sicily; at Marsala he calls for volunteers, giving as his watchword, "Rome or death!" . . . . 19 July, ,,
Calls on the Hungarians to rise . 26 July, ,,
The king issues a proclamation against his proceedings, as tending to rebellion . . 3 Aug. ,,
Garibaldi enters Catania, and organises a provisional government . . . . . . 19 Aug. ,,
Sicily proclaimed to be in a state of siege, 21 Aug.; and put under general Cialdini 22 Aug. ,,

Garibaldi issues his last proclamation; embarks at Catania; lands at Melito, in Calabria, and marches towards Reggio, 25 Aug.; La Marmora proclaims a state of siege, 26 Aug.; Garibaldi and his followers fall in with the royalists under Pallavicini, at Aspromonte, where, after a short skirmish, he is wounded and taken prisoner, 29 Aug.; removed to Varignano, near Spezzia . . . 1 Sept. 1862
Mr. J. F. Bishop sentenced to 10 years' imprisonment . . . 6 Sept. ,,
General Durando issues a diplomatic circular condemning Garibaldi's proceedings, yet asserting the necessity of the Italian government possessing Rome . . . 10 Sept. ,,
A subscription in England enables professor Partridge, of King's College, London, to go to Garibaldi, 19 Sept. ,,
Princess Maria Pia married by proxy to the king of Portugal . . . 27 Sept. ,,
Garibaldi issues a rhetorical appeal to the English nation, urging its intervention for the cause of liberty . . . 28 Sept. ,,
Inflammatory manifesto addressed to the people of Italy by Joseph Mazzini . . . Sept. ,,
Amnesty granted to Garibaldi and his followers, 5 Oct. ,,
Sharp reply of M. Drouyn de Lhuys to Durando's note . . . 8 Oct. ,,
End of state of siege in Naples and Sicily . 17 Oct. ,,
Disorderly encounter between Italians and Austrians on the banks of the Po . . . 1 Nov. ,,
Father Passaglia and 10,000 (out of 80,000) Italian priests sign a declaration against the temporal authority of the pope . . . Nov. ,,
Garibaldi removed to Pisa, 9 Nov.; ball extracted from his foot by Zanetti . . . 23 Nov. ,,
Meeting of parliament; determined opposition to Rattazzi, 18 Nov.; he resigns . . . 30 Nov. ,,
New ministry formed by Farina . . . 9 Dec. ,,
It declines further negotiations with France on the Roman question . . . 18 Dec. ,,
Commercial treaty with France signed . 17 Jan. 1863
Farina resigns; Minghetti succeeds . 24 March, ,,
Grand Cavour canal for irrigation of Piedmont opened . . . 1 June, ,,
Income tax bill passed . . . July, ,,
Tristany and other bandits captured . . . July, ,,
Commercial treaty with Great Britain signed, 6 Aug. ,,
Death of Farina . . . 5 Sept. ,,
Several bandits captured on board the French ship Aunis; given up to France, July; restored to Italy, 12 Sept. ,,
The army of Piedmont (50,000) consolidated by La Marmora and expanded into the "army of Italy" (250,000) . . . Oct. ,,
The king visits Naples; reviews National Guard, &c. 11-17 Nov. ,,
Mr. (after sir) James Hudson, British minister, greatly assisted Cavour in the unification of Italy . . . 1852-63
General election; triumph of the moderate party, Jan. 1864
Garibaldi's visit to England amidst much enthusiasm, April, ,,
Franco-Italian convention signed (French troops to quit Rome in two years [from 6 Feb. 1865], Florence to be the capital of Italy, &c.), 15 Sept. ,,
Riots at Turin in consequence; many persons killed by the military . . . 21-22 Sept. ,,
Minghetti and his colleagues blamed; resigned; a ministry formed by La Marmora . . 24 Sept. ,,
Garibaldi denounces the convention . . 10 Oct. ,,
Desperate state of the finances announced by Sella, the minister; he proposes stringent remedies, Nov. ,,
Railway from Turin to Florence opened . 4 Nov. ,,
The convention approved by the chamber of deputies, 19 Nov.; by the senate (after an able speech by Cialdini, 6 Dec.) . . . 9 Dec. ,,
Decree for transfer of the capital published, 11 Dec. ,,
Prince Humbert resides at Naples . . . Dec. ,,
Stated that 346 brigands had been killed in action; 453 taken in action, and 132 surrendered; about 300 remain to be tracked; many pretend to be subjects of the ex-king Francis II. of Naples, Dec. ,,
Demonstration against the king at Turin, 30 Jan.; he goes to Florence . . . 3 Feb. 1865
Amnesty for political offences published; brigandage in the Neapolitan and Roman states increasing, March, ,,
Fruitless negotiations with the pope by Vegezzi respecting the position of bishops, April to July, ,,
The king and court proceed to Florence, 13 May; he opens the Dante festival, the 600th anniversary of the poet's birth . . . 14 May, ,,
Mr. Moens, a British subject, seized and retained by brigands . . . 15 May, ,,
45 monks and others arrested at Salerno on charge of a Bourbonist conspiracy . . . 12 June, ,,
Inauguration of a national rifle meeting at Florence; the king fires the first shot . . . 18 June, ,,
Numerous atrocities committed by brigands; Giardullo and 8 brigands captured . . . 19 June, ,,
The kingdom recognised by Spain . . . June, ,,
Mr. Moens released after a ransom of 5000*l.* had been paid . . . 26 Aug. ,,
Bank of Italy established . . . 7 Nov. ,,
French troops leaving Italy; general election, the moderate party predominate . . . Nov. ,,
The new parliament meets at Florence . 18 Nov. ,,
Serious financial deficiency; heavy taxation proposed, 13 Dec.; much dissatisfaction; the ministers resign, 21 Dec.; a new ministry formed under La Marmora . . . 31 Dec. ,,
Death of the patriot and soldier, Massimo D'Azeglio, 15 Jan. 1866
Formation of the "Consorzio Nazionale," a public subscription for reducing the national debt, 27 Feb. ,,
Massacre of Protestants at Barletta, Naples; attributed to priests . . . 19 March, ,,
Alliance with Prussia . . . 12 May, ,,
Volunteers numerously enlisted . 7 June, *et seq.* ,,
War declared against Austria . . . 18 June, ,,
New ministry formed under Ricasoli . 20 June, ,,
Royal manifesto to the people . . . 20 June, ,,
The army, headed by the king, crosses the Mincio, 23 June; defeated at Custozza . . 24 June, ,,
Venetia ceded to France by the emperor of Austria, 3 July, ,,
Fruitless conflicts; the volunteers under Garibaldi defeated at Monte Suello . . 4 July, ,,
Bill for suppression of monasteries and confiscation of property passed . . . 7 July, ,,
Cialdini crosses the Po, and enters Venetia, 8 July, ,,
Naval battle near Lissa; Italians defeated by Austrians (*Rè d'Italia* and *Palestro* blown up), 20 July, ,,
The Italians beaten at Versa; the last conflict, 26 July, ,,
Armistice for four weeks signed . . 12 Aug. ,,
Volunteers disbanded; Garibaldi retires to Caprera, 15 Aug. ,,
Treaty of peace with Austria signed at Vienna, 3 Oct.; ratified . . . 12 Oct. ,,
Court constituted at Florence to try admiral Persano for neglect of duty at battle of Lissa . 11 Oct. ,,
The Austrians retire from Peschiera, 9 Oct.; Mantua, 10 Oct.; Verona, 16 Oct.; Venice, 17 Oct. ,,
General Menabrea pays to count Mensdorff a sum of money, and receives the iron crown of Italy, 11 Oct. ,,
National loan freely subscribed . . . Oct. ,,
Plebiscitum in Venetia; for annexation with Italy, 641,758; against, 69 . . . 21 Oct. ,,
This result reported, and the iron crown presented to the king at Turin . . . 4 Nov. ,,
The king enters Venice, 7 Nov.; visits Verona, Mantua, &c. . . . Nov. ,,
Circular of Ricasoli to the prefects, recommending industrial development and commerce, forbidding agitation, and enjoining neutrality regarding Rome, 15 Nov. ,,
Letter from Ricasoli to the clergy recommending a free church in a free state . . . 26 Nov. ,,
Persano committed for trial; examination begins, 1 Dec. ,,
Parliament opened by the king, who declares that "Italy is now restored to herself" . . 15 Dec. ,,
Sig. Tonello received by the pope, 15 Dec.; many bishops return to their dioceses . . . Dec. ,,
Persano acquitted of cowardice at Lissa . 30 Jan. 1867

Government proposal for investing part of the property of the religious bodies for support of clergy ("Free Church and Ecclesiastical Liquidation bill") brought forward . . . . Jan. 1867
Great reduction in the army (to 146,000) ordered, Jan. ,,
Defeat of the ministry on question of the right of public meetings in Venetia, 11 Feb.; parliament dissolved . . . . . . 13 Feb. ,,
Ricasoli reconstructs his ministry . . 17 Feb. ,,
The pope accepts Italian help to suppress brigandage, March, ,,
Elections give a majority for government March, ,,
Resignation of Ricasoli, 5 April; a ministry formed by Rattazzi . . . . . 8 April, ,,
Persano condemned; degraded and dismissed the service for disobedience, incapacity, and negligence . . . . . . 15 April, ,,
Treaty of commerce with Austria signed at Florence, 23 April, ,,
Public funeral of the patriot Carlo Poerio 1 May, ,,
Italy joins in the conference at London respecting the Luxemburg question . . . 7-11 May, ,,
National financial embarrassments; the king gives up part of his civil list; proposed sale of church lands, and reduction of expenditure, May, *et seq.* ,,
17,200,000*l.* advanced for church lands by Fould and others of Paris . . . . . May, ,,
Church property bill passed . . . Aug. ,,
Garibaldi, about to enter the Roman territory with volunteers, captured by Italian government at Sinalunga (or Asinalunga) and sent to Alessandria, 23 Sept. ,,
Sent to Caprera, 27 Sept.; escapes to Leghorn, and is sent back . . . . . 2 Oct. ,,
Bands of Garibaldians invade Roman territories, Sept.-Oct. ,,
Garibaldi escapes from Caprera . . 15 Oct. ,,
Embarkation of French troops at Toulon, suspended by the resignation of Rattazzi and his ministry, 20 Oct. ,,
Cialdini tries to form a ministry in vain, 21-25 Oct. ,,
Garibaldi at Florence announces an expedition against Rome . . . . . . 22 Oct. ,,
The French minister Moustier's circular against the invasion . . . . . . 25 Oct. ,,
Garibaldians defeated at Viterbo . . 25 Oct. ,,
Enter Roman territories; defeat papal troops, and take Monte Rotondo . . . . 26, 27 Oct. ,,
Menabrea's ministry formed; proclamation of Victor-Emmanuel against the Garibaldian invasion, 27 Oct. ,,
Riots at Naples, Turin, Pavia, and other places, suppressed . . . . 26-28 Oct. *et seq*
French army arrives at Cività Vecchia, 28 Oct.; two brigades enter Rome . . . . . 30 Oct ,,
Royal Italian troops enter papal territory; Menabrea's justificatory circular; suppression of insurrectional committees in Italy . . . 30 Oct. ,,
De Moustier's reply . . . . . 1 Nov. ,,
Garibaldi defeated at Mentana, 3 Nov.; retreats into Italy with his son; captured and sent to Varignano, gulf of Spezzia . . . . 4 Nov. ,,
Fiery manifesto of Mazzini . . . . 8 Nov. ,,
Garibaldi sent to Caprera . . . . 25 Nov. ,,
French proposal of a European conference on Roman question discussed . . 9 Nov.-Dec. ,,
French troops left Rome for Cività Vecchia, 3 Dec. ,,
Meeting of parliament; judicious firmness; an amnesty for Garibaldians proclaimed . . 5 Dec. ,,
Long army debate; vote against the ministry (201 to 199); Menabrea resigns . . . 22 Dec. ,,
His ministry reconstituted . . . . 5 Jan. 1868
M. Cambray Digny's financial statement: great deficit; a grist tax proposed . . . 21 Jan. ,,
Exculpatory letter of La Marmora issued . Feb. ,,
Government financial measures announced Feb. ,,
New order of knighthood, the "Crown of Italy," constituted . . . . . . 20 Feb. ,,
Grist tax adopted after 21 days' debate . 1 April, ,,
Enthusiastic reception of the crown prince of Prussia, 20, 21 April, ,,
Marriage of prince Humbert to his cousin Margherita at Turin . . . . 22 April, ,,

Frightful atrocities committed by brigands in south Italy . . . . April, May, 1868
Grist tax adopted by the senate . . June, ,,
Arrangement made for debt of the late papal provinces . . . . 30 July, ,,
Government tobacco monopoly ordered to be farmed; resignation of the ministers, Lanza and Sella, 8 Aug. ,,
Long-continued rain; dreadful inundations in the Alpine regions; great storm . . 27 Sept. ,,
Meeting of chamber of deputies; Garibaldi withdraws . . . . 24 Nov. ,,
Ministerial victory respecting the grist tax in the chambers . . . . . 26 Jan. 1869
Thomas, duke of Genoa, entered a pupil at Harrow (see *Spain*, 1870) . . . . April, ,,
Circular of Menabrea against the council at Rome, 5 Oct. ,,
Victor-Emmanuel Ferdinand, son of prince Humbert, born at Naples . . . . 11 Nov. ,,
Serious illness and recovery of the king, 6-20 Nov. ,,
Offered resignation of Menabrea, about 19 Nov.; Cialdini and Sella unable to form a ministry, 10 Dec.; Lanza and Sella succeed . 13 Dec. ,,
Œcumenical council at Rome (see *Rome, Councils*) opened . . . . 8 Dec. ,,
Republican risings in Pavia and other places quelled, about 24 March, 1870
Neutrality in the Franco-Prussian war announced, 18 July, additional armaments ordered . 4 Aug. ,,
Mazzini arrested at Palermo and sent to Gaëta, 14 Aug. ,,
Fruitless mission of prince Napoleon to obtain help for France . . . . . 21-25 Aug. ,,
Circular note from the government recounting the failure of all attempts to conciliate the pope since 1860; and proposing favourable terms 29 Aug. ,,
French vessel *Orénoque* placed at Cività Vecchia on behalf of the pope . . . . . Aug. ,,
Respectful letter from the king to the pope, announcing the occupation of Rome necessary to order . . . . 8 Sept. ,,
The Italian troops enter the papal territories (see *Rome*); occupy Viterbo and other places, 12 Sept. ,,
General Bixio marches towards Rome, 18, 19 Sept. ,,
After a short resistance, the Italians under General Cadorna enter Rome. [For details see *Rome*.] 20 Sept. ,,
Plébiscite in papal territories: for union with the kingdom of Italy (out of 167,548 voters) 133,681; against 1507 . . . . . . 2 Oct. ,,
The king receives the result of the *plébiscite*, 8 Oct. ,,
Rome incorporated with Italy by royal decree, general La Marmora governor . . . 9 Oct. ,,
Arrival of La Marmora at Rome as viceroy; reported agitation in Nice for reunion with Italy or autonomy . . . . Oct. ,,
Capture and death of Pilone, a great Bourbonist brigand chief . . . . . . 14 Oct. ,,
Mazzini arrives at Florence . . . 15 Oct. ,,
Amnesty to political offenders proclaimed, 10 Oct.; including Mazzini . . . . 16 Oct. ,,
Diplomatic circular announcing the occupation of Rome as the capital of Italy . . 18 Oct. ,,
Roman provinces united into one, with five subprefectures . . . . . . 19 Oct. ,,
Ministerial changes completed . . . 30 Oct. ,,
Ricasoli retires into private life; about 14 Nov. ,,
Amadeus, duke of Aosta, the king's second son, elected king by the Spanish cortes . 16 Nov. ,,
Elections favourable to the government; all the ministers elected . . . about 28 Nov. ,,
Parliament meets; the king declares Rome to be the capital of Italy . . . . . 5 Dec. ,,
Bills introduced for the transfer of the capital and the preservation of the pope's rights, about 10 Dec. ,,
The Cenis tunnel completed . . . 25 Dec. ,,
Great inundation; the king visits Rome 31 Dec. ,,
The senate vote the transfer of the capital from Florence to Rome (94—39) . . . 26 Jan. 1871
The king and ministers remove to Rome, 1, 2 July, which is inaugurated as the capital . 3 July, ,,
The parliament opened there by the king 27 Nov. ,,
Telegraphic conference at Rome . . 18 Dec. ,,
Joseph Mazzini dies at Pisa . . . 10 March, 1872
Elections favourable to the liberals . . Aug. ,,

Great inundations in the valley of the Po, &c., loss of life and of much property; much saved by the exertions of the military . . . Oct. 1872

Opposition to the income-tax in the assembly; majority for government (144—116) . . Dec. ,,

Great sorrow at the death of Napoleon III., 9 Jan. proposals for monument in Milan . . Jan. 1873

Bill dealing with the religious establishments at Rome introduced . . . . . . April, ,,

The Lanza-Sella ministry resign; but resume office at the request of the king . . about 4 May, ,,

Death of Alessandro Manzoni . . . 22 May, ,,

Death of Urbano Rattazzi . . . 5 June, ,,

Law for expulsion of Jesuits passed . 25 June, ,, See *Jesuits*.

Lanza and Sella resign, 26 June; a ministry formed by Minghetti . . . . . 10 July, ,,

The king's visit to Vienna, 17 Sept.; to Berlin, 22-26 Sept. ,,

Monuments to Cavour at Turin inaugurated by the king . . . . 8 Nov. ,,

The king opens parliament with congratulatory speech . . . . 15 Nov. ,,

Academy of San Luca replaced by a new academy, Jan. 1874

National festival on the 25th anniversary of the king's accession . . . . . 23 March, ,,

Minghetti ministry defeated on a finance bill; their resignation not accepted by the king . 24 May, ,,

Accoltellatori (secret assassinating societies) reported in Ravenna and other places, Sept.-Oct. ,,

About 80 secret extortioners (see *Camorra*) in Naples seized and transported . . Sept.-Oct. ,,

Teodali, a papal chamberlain, seized by brigands, ransomed for 2000*l.* . . . about 8, 9 Oct. ,,

The *Orénoque* (French) sails from Civitá Vecchia 13 Oct. ,,

Jesuits ordered to quit their establishments 15 Oct. ,,

Result of elections in support of government, Nov. ,,

The Camorra, Maffei, and Brigantaggio (terrorist secret societies) prevalent in south Italy . . ,,

Garibaldi declines a sum of money (3500*l.*) voted to him . . . . 31 Dec. ,,

He enters Rome amid great excitement, takes his seat in the chamber of deputies, and takes the oath to the king . . . . . . 24 Jan. 1875

Accepts the sum voted and devotes it to improvement of the Tiber, &c. . . . . . 12 Feb. ,,

The emperor of Austria and king of Italy meet at Venice . . . . 5-7 April, ,,

Treaty of commerce with Great Britain, to expire 26 June, 1876, announced . . . June, ,,

Synod of Italian Catholic church (*which see*) held at Naples . . . . Aug. ,,

Elections of parish priests declared valid in opposition to the bishops . . . . July-Aug. ,,

Michel-Angelo fête at Florence . . 12 Sept. ,,

Italian Catholic congress, blessed by the pope, meets at Florence; scanty attendance, 22-25 Sept. ,,

Visit of the emperor of Germany to Milan; warmly received by the king and people . . 18-23 Oct. ,,

Minghetti ministry defeated on the budget, 18 Mar.; resign . . . . 19 March, 1876

Agostino Depretis forms a cabinet . . March, ,,

The *Duilio*, great iron-clad, launched at Castellamare, in presence of the king . . . 8 May, ,,

Discovery of a "black book" in the home-office, recording misdeeds of many officials, &c.; gives much offence . . . . June, ,,

Italian geographical society's expedition in Africa; ill-treated at Zeila; the khedive informed July, ,,

Marchese Mantegazza tried for forging the signatures of the king and prince Humbert on bills and letters to obtain money; confessed, but refused to disclose name of associate or instigator, 18 Aug.; sentence, 8 years' penal servitude 31 Aug. ,,

Elections; great majority for Depretis ministry, about 6 Nov. ,,

Maria Vittoria, duchess of Aosta, ex-queen of Spain, aged 28, dies, greatly lamented . . 8 Nov. ,,

Parliament opened by the king . . 20 Nov. ,,

Discovery near Verona of above 50,000 coins of Gallienus and others, chiefly bronze . . Jan. 1877

Bill for repressing clerical abuses adopted by the deputies; the pope expresses great displeasure in his circular to foreign powers, 21 March; the bill rejected by the senate . . . . 7 May, 1877

Antonelli Case—Countess Loreta Lambertini claims property of her alleged father, cardinal Antonelli; resisted by his brothers, 30 June; trial; her case not proved . . . . 6 Dec. ,,

Ministerial changes . . . . about 12 Nov. ,,

Monument at Mentana (*which see*) inaugurated, 25 Nov. ,,

Resignation of the ministry, 15 Dec.; Depretis re-forms his ministry (Nicotera replaced by Crispi) . . . . 16-26 Dec. ,,

Father Curci (see *Jesuits*) publishes "Dissidio Moderno fra la Chiesa e l'Italia," against the pope's temporal power . . . . . . Dec. ,,

Death of La Marmora, aged 74, 5 Jan.; death of king Victor Emmanuel II., 9 Jan.; his funeral; procession 2 miles long; buried in the Pantheon, Rome . . . . 17 Jan. 1878

Death of pope Pius IX. 7 Feb.; election of Leo XIII. . . . . 20 Feb. ,,

Antonelli Case—the countess permitted to appear in court: the case deferred . . . . Feb. ,,

Resignation of the Depretis ministry . 10 March, ,,

Cairoli forms a liberal ministry, Corti foreign minister; new men . . . . 23 March, ,,

Seismet Doda, finance minister, announces probable surplus . . . . June, ,,

Dandolo, largest Italian ironclad, launched at Spezzia, in presence of the king . . . 10 July, ,,

Popular discontent at the Berlin treaty; desire for acquiring Trent and Trieste; cry of "Italia irredenta!" (*which see*) meetings at Rome, &c. about 21 July, ,,

Death of Giorgio Pallavicino, senator, patriot, friend of Cavour, aged 84 . . . . . 3 Aug. ,,

David Lazzaretti, "the saint," a peasant, aged 48, founder of a religious socialistic sect in 1868, with 12 apostles, &c., and creed somewhat protestant; proposed to erect seven hermitages; marched towards Arcidosso, in Tuscany, with between two and three thousand followers; David, clad in a half-regal, half-pontifical costume, proclaiming the Christian republic, resisted dispersion by the police, who, when fired on, fired and killed David and one of his followers; these retired, carrying off David's body . . . . . . 18 Aug. ,,

Ministerial crisis; resignation of Corti and others, 19 Oct.; of all the Cairoli ministry 22 Oct. ,,

Sig. Cairoli reconstitutes the ministry . 25 Oct. ,,

Attempted assassination of the king at Naples by Giovanni Passanante, an internationalist, aged 20; the king and Cairoli, the minister, slightly wounded . . . . 17 Nov. ,,

"Pietro Barsanti" Clubs (in memory of a sergeant executed for gross insubordination a few years ago) become prominent; oppose ministry, autumn, ,,

The Cairoli ministry defeated on vote of confidence (263-189), 11 Dec.; resign . . . 12 Dec. ,,

Sig. Depretis's ministry takes office . 19 Dec. ,,

Passanante condemned to death at Naples, 7 March; to perpetual imprisonment (by the king), 29 March, 1879

Antonelli Case—the countess Lambertini's appeal rejected . . . . 3 July, ,,

Government defeated on the grist bill (251-159); resigns . . . . 3 July, ,,

Sig. Cairoli forms a ministry . . 8-12 July, ,,

New clerical conservative party issues a manifesto, 12 Aug. ,,

"*Res Italicæ*" pamphlet (see *Italia Irredenta*), Aug. ,,

The followers of Lazzaretti tried and acquitted, 12 Nov. ,,

Cairoli ministry reconstructed . 18-24 Nov. ,,

First publication of "*Aurora*," a papal daily newspaper, at Rome . . . . . 1 Jan. 1880

Parliament opened by the king; relief of taxation promised . . . . 17 Feb. ,,

Majority in chamber against ministers, 17 Feb.; its resignation not accepted by the king, 29 April; dissolution of the chamber . . . 2 May, ,,

Elections: absolute majority for the Cairoli ministry; parliament meets . . . . 26 May, ,,

Cordigliani, a half-mad tailor, condemned to imprisonment for throwing paving-stones at a group of deputies (25 June) . . . . 26 Aug. ,,

Celebration of capture of Rome by Italians in 1870, 20 Sept. 1880

Italia, great ironclad, launched at Castellamare, 29 Sept. „

Garibaldi (and his son Menotti) resign as deputies on account of the imprisonment of his son-in-law, gen. Canzio, for republican manifestations, 27 Sept.; Garibaldi goes to Genoa, Oct.; Canzio released . . . 10 Oct. „

Col. John Whitehead, "Garibaldi's Englishman," dies, aged 69 . . . . . 21 Nov. „

Resignation of Cairoli and his cabinet, 3 April; return to office; censured on account of the Tunis affair . . . . . 18 April, 1881

The Cairoli ministry again resign . . 14 May, „

M. Depretis forms a ministry . . 28 May, „

Father Curci publishes "New Italy and Old Zealots," June, „

The king and queen warmly received at Vienna, 28-31 Oct. „

The government complain of Vatican intrigues about 28 Dec. „

Death of Lanza, General Medici patriot, died 9 Mar. „

Opening of St. Gothard railway from Lucerne to Milan . . . . . 20, 21 May, 1882

Death of Garibaldi at Caprera, deeply lamented 2 June, „

Buried there in the presence of thousands 8 June, „

Parliament dissolved . . . . 4 Oct. „

Destructive floods in North Italy . Sept., Oct. „

Elections in favour of the ministry about 28 Oct. „

First reform parliament opened by King Humbert 22 Nov. „

Death of the duke of Sermoneta . . . 12 Dec. „

Demonstrations against Austria on account of execution of Oberdank for threatening the mperor's life . . . . . 20–22 Dec. „

International fine art exhibition opened at Rome 21 Jan. 1883

Specie payments resumed . . . . 12 April, „

Lepanto, Italian built iron-clad launched at Leghorn; the king present . . . . 17 Mar. „

The four-hundredth anniversary of Raphael's birth celebrated at Rome . . . . 28 Mar. „

Confidence in the Depretis ministry voted (348-29); it resigns, and returns . . . 25, 26 May, „

New important treaty with Great Britain signed, 15 June, „

About 50 persons perish by fire in a theatre at Dervio, near Como . . . 24 June, „

King Victor Emmanuel's body removed to the Pantheon 5 Jan.; thousands of pilgrims visit his tomb up to . . . . . 21 Jan. 188[illegible]

Death of Sig. Sella, great financial minister, 14 Mar. „

Resignation of the Depretis ministry, 20 Mar.; reconstituted . . . 22 Mar.–10 April, „

Discussion respecting the sale of the Propaganda property at Rome . . . . April, „

National exhibition at Turin opened by the king, 26 April, closed . . . . 20 Nov. „

Fifth ironclad launched at Castellamare . . „

Twenty-one new members added to the Senate 28 Nov. „

Total number of soldiers in the army, 2,113,969 1 Jan. 1885

Navy consisted of 112 vessels afloat or building 1 Jan. „

Heavy snowstorms in Piedmont, near Mont Cenis; many avalanches; many villages destroyed; very great loss of life . . . . 16–28 Jan. „

Expedition to Assab to avenge the massacre of Guiletti and Bianchi.

Ironclad *Castelfidardo* arrived at Beilul . 25 Jan. „

The ministry determine to assist Great Britain in the Soudan . . . . . 6 Feb. „

Italian flag hoisted at Massowah (*which see*) 6 Feb. „

Resignation of the Depretis ministry on account of Mancini's foreign policy, 18 June; reconstituted about 24 June, „

Ironclad *Francisco Morosini* launched at Venice, 30 July, „

Elections: ministerial majority about 55, about 24 May, 1886

Death of Marco Minghetti (prime minister in 1864 *et seq.*), aged 70 . . . . . 10 Dec. „

Depretis ministry resigns . . . 8 Feb. 1887

Destructive earthquakes (*which see*) 23, 24 Feb. „

Several statesmen having declined office, the Depretis ministry resumes office . 5 March, 1887

Defensive treaty of alliance with Austria-Hungary and Germany signed . . . 13 March, „

Coalition cabinet formed, Depretis, foreign minister, premier . . . . . 3 April, „

Depretis dies, aged 74, 29 July; M. Crispi becomes premier . . . . . Aug. „

Francesco Crispi visits prince Bismarck . 2, 3 Oct. „

Signor Crispi at Turin declares his policy to be thorough peace . . . . 25 Oct. „

Parliament opened . . . . 16 Nov. „

Increased formation of workman, socialistic, and republican leagues 1882–87

Duke Torlonia, syndic of Rome, dismissed for congratulating the pope on his jubilee 2 Jan. 1888

The progress of the Italian catholic church opposed to the papacy, reported . . Feb. „

Fall of vast avalanches in north Italy; 23 persons killed at Valtorta, 23 Feb.; 30 persons killed at Sparone, 29 Feb. 1888; above 200 persons said to have perished in the Alps Feb.–March „

Italian exhibition (*which see*), London, 12 May,–31 Oct. „

The abolition of capital punishment passed by the chambers . . . . . June, „

Cheap popular edition of the Italian bible (with Cassell's illustrations) issued by signor Sonzogno, editor of the *Secolo*, Milan . . . July, „

For war with Abyssinia, *see Massowah*. . 1887–88

Marriage of the duke of Aosta, ex-king of Spain, with his niece princess Lœtitia, daughter of his sister Clotilde and prince Napoleon Jerome, 11 Sept. 1888

The emperor William II. warmly received at Rome, 11 Oct.; 32,000 troops reviewed at Centocelle, 13 Oct. at Naples; (launch of the great ironclad *Re Umberto* at Castellamare) 16 Oct. „

Landslip between Salandra and Graseano; destruction of an excursion train, about 22 persons killed . . . . . . 20 Oct. „

Marquis of Dufferin, British ambassador, received by the king . . . . . 7 Jan. „

Death of Father Gavazzi, church reformer, aged 80 9 Jan. „

Opening of parliament by the king . 28 Jan. „

Signor Crispi resigns 28 Feb. but reconstitutes his ministry . . . . . 7 March, „

The king, his son and Signor Crispi warmly received at Berlin . . . 21–26 Mar. 1889

Death of Benedetto Cairoli, aged 63, patriot and statesman, associated with Victor Emanuel, Cavour and Garibaldi, in the unification of Italy, deeply lamented . . . . 8 Aug. „

Sig. Crispi injured by a stone thrown at him during a carriage drive by Emilio Caporali, a silly youth 13 Sept. „

The king ratifies treaty of 2 May with Abyssinia . 2 Oct. „

Italian protectorate over Abyssinia announced . 14 Oct. „

The parliament opened with a cheerful speech by the king . . . . . 25 Nov. „

Death of the duke of Aosta, aged 44 18 Jan. 1890

Ministry defeated in the senate on a minor question, 5 May; the crisis passes over 9 May, *et seq.* „

Democratic congress at Rome, 470 associations represented . . . 11 May, *et seq.* „

Riots at Conselice, in the Romagna, 3 or 4 rioters killed by the military . . about 24 May „

Confidence in Signor Crispi's ministry voted (329-61) 31 May, „

The prince of Naples visits St. Petersburg, Berlin May, June, „

Major Gaetani Casati returns from his expedition to Emin pasha (see *Africa*); received at Rome, 14 July; by the king . . . . 17 July, „

Sig. Filonardi becomes director of the Italian East Africa company . . . announced 12 Aug. „

Anglo-Italian steamer line (Naples, Palermo, and London), inaugurated . . . 22 Aug. „

Destructive cyclone—San Marino, Turin, Como, Naples, Sardinia, &c. . . . 26 Aug. „

Great ironclad, *Sardegna*, launched at Spezzia . 20 Sept. „

Conference at Naples, of representatives of Great Britain and Italy, respecting the limits of the territories in East Africa; sig. Crispi and lord Dufferin present; disagreement respecting Kassala, &c.; the conference closes without result . . . . . . 4–10 Oct. 1890
The parliament dissolved . . . . 24 Oct. „
Parliamentary elections held, great majority for the government . . . . . 23 Nov. „
Ministerial changes . . . . . 8–9 Dec. „
Parliament opened 10 Dec.; confidence in the ministry voted . . . . . 19 Dec. „
Signor Crispi defeated on a financial question (186–123), and resigns . . . . . 31 Jan. 1891
New Ministry; marquis di Rudini (president and foreign minister), and others, 6 Feb. *et seq.*; they propose maintenance of peace, and reduced expenditure, &c. . . . . . . 11 Feb. „
Vote of confidence in the ministry adopted . . 21 March, „
Treaty for the delimitation of the British and Italian spheres of influence in East Africa, signed at Rome . . . . . . 15 April „
Financial difficulties; opposition to reduction of the army expenditure . . about 31 March „
Trial of 179 persons connected with the Mala Vita conspiracy at Bari, see *Camorra* . . April „
The triple alliance renewed . . . . 28 June, „
Tour of the prince of Naples; arrives in London, received by the prince of Wales, 22 July; dined with the queen at Osborne, 24 July; visited the marquis of Salisbury at Hatfield, 25 July; other visits; with lord Mayor, 28 July; made K.G. at Osborne, 3 Aug.; visits Edinburgh and other places in Scotland, 7 Aug. *et seq.*; at Newcastle, 14 Aug.; leaves for Bergen, &c. . . 15 Aug. „
The mail steamer *Taormina* sunk by collision with the Greek steamer *Thessalia*, off Cape Sunium, about 60 lives lost, 2 a.m. . . . . 12 Sept. „
The Russian foreign minister, M. de Giers, meets the Marquis di Rudini, the Italian premier, at Milan, 12 Oct.; they visit the king at Monza (no political results) . . . . 13 and 17 Oct. „
Trial of 60 anarchists . . . . 14 Oct. „
New commercial treaty with Austria and Germany signed at Rome . . . . . 16 Dec. „
Lord Vivian succeeds lord Dufferin as British minister . . . . . . about 22 Jan. 1892
Death of count de Launay, minister at Berlin successively for Sardinia and Italy for 37 years . 7 Feb. „
Signor Crispi retires from public affairs . Feb. „
Cipriani Palla and other anarchists sentenced to different terms of imprisonment . 24 March „
Resignation of the cabinet through differences respecting finance, 14 April; most of the resignations withdrawn . . . . . 21 April, „
Difficulty with the United States settled, see *New Orleans* . . . . . about 14 April, „
Anarchist leaders arrested in Rome and other places, 25 April, *et seq.*; 48 arrested up to 29 April; 42 arrests on . . . . 30 April, „
The Rudini ministry, defeated in the Chamber (193–185), resign . . . . . 5 May, „
A new ministry formed by sig. Giolitti 11–15 May, „
Resignation of the ministry not accepted by the king . . . . 27 May, „
Ministerial victory in the chambers (majority, 194), 11 June, „
The king and queen received at Potsdam by the German emperor . . . . . 20–24 June, „
Death of general Cialdini, duke of Gaëta, eminent patriot and soldier, aged 81 . . 8 Sept. „
Increase of brigandage; many arrests . . Oct. „
The chamber dissolved . . . . . 10 Oct. „
Destructive floods in the north (see *Inundations*), 13 Oct. *et seq.* „
General election; great government majority, 6 Nov. „
Parliament opened by the king . . . 23 Nov. „
Death of admiral Pacoret de Saint-Bon, chief of the navy . . . . 26 Nov. „
The chamber votes confidence in the ministry (296—82) . . . . . . 16 Dec. „
Arrest of signor Cuciniello, manager of the Rome branch of the bank of Naples, 22 Jan.; report of government committee presented . 20 March, 1893

The pope's jubilee at Rome (see *Pope*) . Feb. 1893
Bill to make civil marriage obligatory introduced, 8 March, „
Establishment of the "Bank of Italy" proposed, about 29 March „
Mr. Harry Ogilvie, engineer, murdered at Civitâ Vecchia . . . . 5 April, „
The silver wedding of the king and queen celebrated at Rome with great festivities; the German emperor and empress, and the duke of York present, 22 April; historical tournament, 25 April; celebrated at Naples . . . 28 April, „
Resignation of signor Giolitti and his ministry, 20 May; reconstituted . . . . 24 May, „
Signor Cuciniello sentenced to 10 years' imprisonment; signor Dalesandro, cashier, to 6 years' imprisonment, for embezzlement . . 13 June, „
New bank law passed by the senate . . 9 Aug. „
Conflicts, with bloodshed, between the French and Italian salt-workers at Aigues-Mortes, on the Mediterranean littoral, 16 Aug.; lead to demonstrations against the French at Rome, Naples, Turin, and Milan, &c.; many rioters arrested, 18–21 Aug.; rioters acquitted . . . 30 Dec. „
Visit of British squadron, under adm. sir Michael Culme-Seymour, at Taranto, 16 Oct.; warmly received at Spezzia . . . . . 23–29 Oct. „
Death of lord Vivian, British ambassador, aged 59, 21 Oct.; public funeral; the prince of Naples, adm. Seymour, the diplomatic corps, and many officials present; buried in the English cemetery at Testaccio . . . . Oct. „
Sir Clare Ford appointed British ambassador, Nov. „
Opening of the chambers . . . . 23 Nov. „
Investigations into the affairs of the banks; signor Giolitti censured; he and his ministry resign, 24 Nov. „
New ministry formed by signor Crispi . 11–15 Dec. „
Seizure of revolutionary manifestoes in Rome, 9 Jan. 1894
Riots in Carrara (*which see*) . . . . . „
Indemnity (420,000 f.) paid by France to the relatives of the Italians killed at Aigues-Mortes (*see above*, 16 *Aug.*, 1893) . . . . 25 Jan. „
Thirty thousand francs paid by the Italian government to France to compensate the sufferers by the riots, 16 Aug. 1893, in Rome, Naples, &c. 28 Jan. „
Budget introduced; deficit, 130,000,000 lire, 4 Feb. „
Signor Sonnino's financial scheme; new duties on corn, &c., and increased taxation . 21 Feb. „
Vote of confidence in signor Crispi . 3 March, „
Bomb explosion outside the Chamber of Deputies in Rome; 2 deaths . . . . . 8 March, „
Signor Crispi applies for extraordinary powers, executive and financial, for himself, aided by a committee . . . . . . 16 April, „
Trial of signor Talongo, ex-governor, and officials of the Banca Romana, 2 May; acquitted, 28 July, „
The military budget passed . . . . May, „
Resignation of signor Crispi and ministry 5 June „
The Crispi ministry re-constructed . 14 June, „
Signor Crispi shot at, whilst driving, by Carlo Lega, an Anarchist, 16 June; much sympathy expressed; Lega sentenced to 20 years' imprisonment . . . . 19 July, „
The government financial proposals adopted by the chamber (180—74) . . . . . 29 June, „
Signor Bandi, a newspaper director at Leghorn, who had published articles against the anarchists, assassinated, 1 July. (Rosolini Romiti, the murderer, sentenced to life imprisonment, and two others to 30 years, 22 May, 1895.)
Murders by anarchists at Pisa and Empoli, 4 July, „
Two hundred and fifty anarchists under arrest in Rome, and about 2,208 among the prisons in other towns, reported . . . . . 9 July, „
Anti-anarchist bill passed by the chamber, 11 July, „
Decree issued dissolving all revolutionary socialistic societies . . . . 22 Oct. „
Destructive earthquakes in Reggio, Calabria, and Sicily; many deaths . . . 16–21 Nov. „
Parliament opened by the king . . . 3 Dec. „
Baron Sonnino's financial statement; deficit reduced; additional taxation proposed; well received; announced . . . . . 10 Dec. „

The deputies, Giolitti (ex-premier), Mazzino and Martuscelli, charged with forgery of documents relating to the Banca Romana, damaging the character of signor Crispi and others; prosecution ordered and parliament adjourned . Dec. 1894

Sir Giacomo Filippo Lacaita, K.C.M.G., patriot and scholar, born at Manduria in Lecce, 1813; took part in the movement of 1848 (see *Naples*); sent by the temporary liberal government as secretary of legation to London; remains there, and is naturalised; lectured at the Royal institution on Italian Literature and History, 1855–8; accompanied Mr. W. E. Gladstone in his mission to the Ionian isles, Nov. 1858; returns to Italy after its liberation in 1860; elected a member of the chamber of deputies, and in 1876 made a senator; loved England, and visited it annually; died at Naples . . . . 5 Jan. 1895

Severe winter; increased state expenditure for the poor . . . . Feb. ,,

The proceedings against sig. Giolitti quashed by the court of cassation on his appeal . 24 April, ,,

Tri-centenary of the death of Tasso celebrated; an exhibition of MSS., pictures, and other relics, at Rome, opened by the king . . . 25 April, ,,

Chamber dissolved through opposition . 8 May, ,,

Shocks of earthquake (*which see*) in Central Italy, 18 May, ,,

Parliamentary elections; large majority for sig. Crispi . . . . 27 May, ,,

Attempted assassination of signor Ferrari, a deputy, at Rimini, 3 June; died . . . . 10 June, ,,

The king opens parliament, strongly recommending further financial reform . . . 10 June, ,,

Strong opposition to signor Villa, president of the chamber . . . . 13 June, ,,

Budget introduced; retrenchment and some additional taxation required . . . . 13 June, ,,

Defeat of the opposition; riotous scene in the chamber . . . . 17, 19 June, ,,

Marriage of the duke of Aosta and princess Hélène of Orleans at Kingston-on-Thames . 25 June, ,,

Visit of the fleet under adm. the duke of Genoa to Portsmouth, the duke and officers received by adm. sir Nowell Salmon, on Nelson's ship *Victory*; banquet, the duke of York, Mr. Goschen, and others present, 9 July; received by the queen at Windsor, 12 July; illumination of combined fleets, &c., left . . . . 18 July, ,,

Financial bills passed . . . . . . 7 Aug. ,,

National fêtes (see *Rome*) . . . . . 20 Sept. ,,

Budget, 1895–96; financial improvement reported 25 Nov. ,,

Documents relating to M. Giolitti presented to parliament, Nov.; case shelved by vote . 13 Dec. ,,

War in Abyssinia, see *Massowah*, 1895.

Debate in the chamber, government majority 19 Dec. ,,

Resignation of the Crispi ministry; European (except Russian) sympathy with Italy 4 March, 1896

Great excitement in the chamber and throughout the country; impeachment of the ministry proposed; gen Baratieri, by decree, placed on half-pay list; popular desire for the abandonment of Erythrea expressed at Milan and other places, 5 March, ,,

Socialist manifesto against the war . 7 March, ,,

New ministry formed by the marquis di Rudini; gen. Ricotti, war, duke of Sermoneta, foreign ministers . . . . 9, 10 March, ,,

Decree of amnesty to political offenders, 14 March, ,,

Declaration of the marquis di Rudini in the chamber expressing admiration of the army; negotiations for peace authorised . . . 17 March, ,,

The African credits adopted by the chamber, 20 March; and senate . . . . . 25 March, ,,

Budget for 1895–6, deficit, through the African war, 2,828,000 lire; for 1896–7, a deficit of 1,197,713 lire anticipated . . . . 5 May, ,,

The government policy adopted by the chamber (278–133) . . . . 9 May, ,,

Gen. Baratieri tried by court martial at Asmara for misconduct as general; acquitted 5–13 June ,,

The British squadron, under sir M. Culme-Seymour, visits Rome, the officers and men warmly received by the government and the pope, 14 June, ,,

Resignation of the ministry, 11 July; re-formed by the marquis di Rudini . . . . 14 July, 1896

The *Doelwyk*, Dutch steamer, containing arms, captured by the *Etna*, Italian cruiser, in Italian waters . . . . 8 Aug. ,,

Treaty between France and Italy respecting Tunis, signed . . . . 30 Sept. ,,

Montenegrin princely family visit Rome, 22–29 Oct. ,,

Marriage of the prince of Naples to princess Helen of Montenegro in the Quirinal; grand banquet, general amnesty decreed, 24 Oct.; review of 20,000 troops . . . . 27 Oct. ,,

Peace with Abyssinia signed, 26 Oct., ratified, 16 Nov. ,,

Debate in the chamber on the colony of Erythrea, 30 Nov.; victory of the government on the home policy, 9 Dec.; see *Somaliland*, 2 Dec. 1896.

General elections; the Crispi party much reduced, 21 March, 1897

Parliament opened by the king . . . 5 April, ,,

Attempt to stab the king while driving to the races by Pietro Acciarito, fanatic (sentenced to penal servitude for life, 29 May), at Rome 22 April, ,,

Vote of confidence in the government and its African policy, 148 majority . . . 22 May, ,,

Commercial treaty with Abyssinia and frontier, negotiated by major Nerazzini, accepted, 30 Aug. ,,

The count of Turin challenges prince Henry of Orleans, for libels against Italian officers, prince Henry wounded by him in a duel, near Paris, 15 Aug. ,,

Visit of the king and queen to Germany (*which see*), 3 Sept. *et seq.* ,,

Bank scandals, 20 persons convicted, at Como; appeals . . . . Sept. ,,

The *Garibaldi*, armoured cruiser, launched at Genoa, 27 Sept.; the *Emmanuele Filiberto*, 1st class battleship, launched at Castellmare, 30 Sept, ,,

A popular demonstration in Rome against the scheme of taxation on incomes and personal property came into conflict with the troops, 1 death, 11 Oct. ,,

Discontent allayed by a pacific circular . 15 Oct. ,,

All proceedings against signor Crispi stopped on his appeal . . . . 8 Nov. ,,

Dr. Giuseppe Bottero, 50 years editor of the *Gazette del Popolo*, born 1816; died . . . 16 Nov. ,,

Speech of sig. Crispi desiring an impartial inquiry with regard to his relations with the bank of Naples, 2 Dec.; neutral commission of inquiry appointed, 3 Dec. 1897; no ground for impeachment, but censured politically in its report, 19 March; 1898 adopted by the chamber (207—7), 23 March; sig. Crispi resigns as deputy, 24 March; re-elected, 17 April, ,,

Debate on the military promotion bill; gen. Pelloux, minister of war resigns, 3, 4 Dec.; the ministry resigns, 6 Dec.; re-formed by the marquis di Rudini, marquis Visconti Venosta, foreign, sig. Zanardelli, justice, 14 Dec.; vote of want of confidence rejected, 20 Dec. 1897; adjourns, 21 Dec. till . . . . . . 25 Jan. ,,

Jubilee of the anniversary of the Italian constitution (1848) celebrated at Rome (see *Turin*) 4 Mar. ,,

Sig. Felice Cavallotti, radical leader, killed in a duel by sig. F. Maccola, conservative deputy, 6 March (Maccola sentenced to 13 months' imprisonment, 21 Oct.; reduced to 7, March, 1899) ,,

Bread riots owing to rise in prices at Bari and Faenza, buildings sacked and burnt by the mob, 27, 28 April; council of ministers order remedies for the distressed, 30 April; further rioting, conflicts with troops at Milan, Florence, Leghorn, Pisa, Pavia, and other places, 82 killed, 3–8 May; price of bread reduced, 9 May; state of siege at Naples, 10 May; quiet restored, chambers prorogued . . . . 14 May, ,,

Army fund for the families of the poorer soldiers, 100,000 lire by the king and royal family, 18 May, ,,

Sig. Brin, minister of marine, eminent naval architect and politician, died . . . 24 May, ,,

The ministry resigns, 28 May; reconstructed by the marquis di Rudini . . . . 1 June, ,,

Sir Philip Currie (made a peer, Jan. 1899) appointed ambassador, arrives at Rome . . . 2 June,

The chamber of deputies meets, baron Sonnino, leader of the opposition, severely criticises the policy of the marquis di Rudini, a want of confidence in the new ministry voted, 16 June; the marquis resigned, and the house adjourned *sine die* . . . . 18 June, 1898

Gen. Pelloux forms a cabinet, a ministry of the left, foreign sec. adm. Canevaro, 29 June; the chamber meets, pacific policy announced, 4 July; vote of confidence in the government 11 July; bill passed for the preservation of public order, and the chamber adjourned . . 12 July, „

See *Columbia*, 1898.

Arbitration treaty between Italy and Argentina 23 July, „

Railway collision near Ponte Decimo, 11 killed, 11 Aug. „

Giovanni Battista Ortelli, Italian philanthropist, in London, died, aged 67 . . . . . 1 Nov. „

Parliament opened by the king . . . 16 Nov. „

New commercial treaty with France, signed, 21 Nov. „

Budget statement, large deficit . . . 3 Nov. „

Tax riot at Picerno, one death . . . 27 Nov. „

Anglo-Italian (commercial) convention, delimiting boundaries north of Erythrea, signed at Asmara, 7 Dec. „

Visit of the duke and duchess of Connaught; received by the pope, 28 Jan., and by the king, 29 Jan.; they leave . . . . . 31 Jan. 1899

Bill adopted, withdrawing the 1-lira and 2-lire notes, equivalent to the abolition of forced currency . . . . 31 Jan. „

Anti-fiscal demonstrations in N. Italy, and a meeting at Naples . . . . 5 Feb. „

The king and queen arrive at Cagliari, Sardinia (*which see*) . . . . 12 April, „

The chamber meets, 25 April; foreign policy of the government, China, etc., strongly opposed in the chamber, 1, 2 May; gen. Pelloux and his cabinet resign, 3 May; he forms a new (conservative) ministry; foreign minister, marqu. Visconti Venosta, 14 May; the chamber meets, government statement with regard to China; sig. Zanardelli resigns presidency of the deputies, 25 May; government majority 81–327; violent scenes . . . . 26, 27 May, „

Sig. Chinaglia elected president of the chamber, 30 May; fine speech on the public safety bill, Chinese policy, government majority 99, 31 May, „

Financial statement, surplus about 120,000*l*. 8 June, „

Festival of the Italian constitution . . 4 June, „

Vote of confidence in the cabinet, 203–85, 14 June, „

Stormy scenes and socialist obstruction to the public safety bill (relative to strikes, meetings, press offences), 20, 21 June; the bill promulgated by royal decree, 22 June; violent scene, free fight in the chamber; session closed by royal decree . . . . 30 June, „

Internat. (silk and industrial) and Volta centenary exhibition at Como opened by the king, 20 May; burnt down, estimated damage 500,000*l*., the Volta relics destroyed . . . . . . 8 July, „

Volta centenary conferences at Como and Milan, June; his statue unveiled, and a national electrical congress (opened by the king and queen) held, 18–23 Sept. „

See *Earthquakes*, July 1899; demonstrations in honour of sig. Crispi, aged 80; see *Sicily*, 4 Oct. „

Destructive floods with loss of life in the province of Salerno . . . . 7, 8 Oct. „

The king opens parliament, his speech well received . . . . 14 Nov. „

Sig. Boselli's budget, 15,000,000 lire surplus, 1898–99 . . . . 28 Nov. „

Amnesty to political offenders and others (see *above*, May, 1889), signed . . . . 31 Dec. „

Gen. Mirri, minister of war, resigns . . 4 Jan. 1900

Growth and progress of the politico-catholic movement 1870–1900

Protocol delimiting Italian and French possessions in the Red Sea littoral, signed . . 24 Jan. „

See *Turkey*, 30 Jan. 1900.

Sig. Visconti Venosta, in the chamber of deputies, avows Italy's sympathy with England in S. Africa; and gen. Ricciotti Garibaldi offers to raise volunteers for England. . about 10 Feb. 1900

Stormy debates on the public safety bill, 1–28 March; political crisis, reform of the standing orders and withdrawal of the public safety bill proposed; wild uproar in the chamber; sig. Colombo resigns with the entire bureau, 29, 30 March; is re-elected (265–158), and the government's proposals carried amid great tumult; the amendments to the standing orders to overcome obstruction adopted; the chamber adjourns, 2, 3 April, „

The chamber meets, the new rules carried by the majority; sitting closed amidst uproar, 15 May; parliament prorogued *sine die*, 16 May; dissolved, 18 May, „

General election: ministerialists, about 300; constitutional opposition, about 110; extreme left, 94 . . . . early June „

New parliament opened by the king; sig. Gallo elected president of the deputies; fruitless negotiations, the cabinet resigns, 16, 18 June; new one formed by sig. Saracco, the marqu. Visconti Venosta, foreign minister, 24 June; sig. Villa elected president of the chamber; new standing orders ratified, 28, 29 June; chamber adjourns, supplies granted, collapse of the deadlock, 10 July, „

King Humbert fatally shot by Gaetano Bresci, an anarchist, at Monza . . . . 29 July, „

Intense sorrow throughout Italy; general sympathy . . . . 30 July, „

Proclamation, moderate in tone, issued by king Victor Emmanuel III. . . . . . 3 Aug. „

Violent scene, due to the socialists, in the chamber, 6 Aug. „

Many anarchists arrested, 31 July; 50 arrested in Rome . . . . 7 Aug. „

The king's funeral, long procession to the Pantheon, 9 Aug. „

The king's speech, on taking the oath of fealty to the constitution, in the senate well received, 11 Aug. „

Bresci, the regicide, tried at Milan and sentenced to life imprisonment, 29 Aug. (committed suicide, 22 May, 1901); Padre Volponi, vicar of St. Sebastian, sentenced to 8 months' imprisonment for stating that regicide was sometimes justifiable . . . . 29 Aug. „

Baron F. de Renzis, ambassador to Gt. Britain, dies, aged 64 . . . . 28 Oct. „

Chamber grants an appanage of 40,000*l*. a year for queen Margherita, 218–42 . . . . 30 Nov. „

Sig. Rubini's budget: 200,000*l*. surplus, 1899–1900, 30 June; he resigns office, 21 Dec.; succeeded by sig. Finali . . . . 7 Jan. 1901

Sig. Verdi, the composer (see *Opera*), dies, aged 87 (bequeaths a large sum to the "Home for Indigent Musicians," founded recently by him, at Milan, at a cost of 20,000*l*.) . . . 27 Jan. „

The Saracco cabinet defeated for its vacillating policy on the labour question, 318–102, after confused debate, 6 Feb.; the ministry resigns, 7 Feb. „

Sig. Zanardelli forms a cabinet, sig. Giolitti (interior), sig. Prinetti (foreign) . . . 14 Feb. „

Dockers' strike at Palermo, spreads to other classes, riots suppressed by troops, 1, 2 March, „

Fatal floods at Padua, Mantua and elsewhere, 20 March, „

The chamber adopts the war estimates and adjourns . . . . 30 March, „

Budget adopted, 10 May; large surplus, year ending 30 June, „

National pilgrimage to the Pantheon, in memory of king Humbert . . . . . 29 July, „

Agrarian disorders in Lombardy, arson, &c., early Aug. „

Sig. Crispi, a great statesman, died, aged 81, 11 Aug.; an impressive funeral . . . 14 Aug. „

The king and queen open large electric works at Vizzola . . . . 9 Oct. „

Benedetto Brin battleship, launched at Castellamare . . . . 7 Nov. „

Parliament meets . . . . 27 Nov. „

Anglo-Italian agreement relating to the frontier between the Soudan and Erythrea, signed, 26 Nov. 1901

Government bills reducing local duties on bread and flour, &c., adopted by the senate, 20 Jan. 1902

Parliament opened by the king; government defeated in the election of a president to the chamber; cabinet resigns . 20, 21 Feb. ,,

General railway strike averted by prompt action of the government, armistice, 24 Feb.–10 March; concessions to the men granted . 8 March, ,,

Vote of confidence in the Zanardelli cabinet, majority, 92 . . . . . . 15 March, ,,

Diplomatic rupture with Switzerland, due to excesses of the anarchist press in 1901, 10 April; conciliatory tone of the Swiss nat. council, 22 April, ,,

New $3\frac{1}{2}$ per cent. loan, total amount, 100,000,000 lire, reported . . . . . . 16 June, ,,

The triple alliance renewed . . 28 June, ,,

Many bills passed, chamber adjourns . 1 July, ,,

The king visits Russia . . . 13–17 July, ,,

Dispute with Switzerland settled through Germany . . . . 30 July, ,,

Mafia (*which see*) murders trial at Bologna, Palizzolo, ex-deputy, Trapani and Fontona, sentenced to 30 years' imprisonment for the murder of signori Miceli (July, 1892) and Notobartolo (Feb. 1893), (10 months' trial) . . . . 30 July, ,,

Death of gen. Ferrero, Italian ambassador in London, 1895-8 . . . . . . 7 Aug. ,,

The king visits Germany . . . . 27–31 Aug. ,,

Anniversary of the entry of Italian troops into Rome, celebrated . . . . . 20 Sept. ,,

Distress in the south, reforms urged by baron Sonnino . . . . 9 Nov. ,,

Chambers meet . . . . 26 Nov. ,,

Severe earthquake shock at Syracuse . 28 Dec. ,,

Austrian ambassador officially denounces the commercial treaty between Austria-Hungary and Italy, which therefore lapses 31 Dec. 1903 29 Dec. ,,

Lord Currie, British ambassador, resigns from ill-health, Dec. 1902; succeeded by sir Francis Bertie . . . . Jan. 1903

Court of Cassation in Rome quashes sentence passed upon Palizzolo, for the murder of signor Miceli and Notobartolo, by the assize court of Bologna; orders a new trial in Florence . . end Jan. ,,

Budget, 1903–4, for Eritrea presented to Chamber of Deputies; revenue, 9,600,000 lire (7,000,000 lire subsidies from the state); expenditure, 9,000,000 lire . . . . early Feb. ,,

Papal jubilee, 25th anniversary of the elevation of pope Leo XIII. to the pontificate celebrated in the Vatican, 70,000 persons present, many gifts presented, including a papal tiara of gold offered by cardinal Respighi in the name of all catholics in the world . . . . 20 Feb. ,,

25th anniversary of pope's coronation held at St. Peter's, 70,000 people present . . . . 3 Mar. ,,

Imports for 1902, 1,774,240,561 lire; exports, 1,472,408,198 lire, increase over 1901 of 55,751,973 lire and 97,950,308 lire respectively, early March, ,,

Strike of students in secondary schools in all parts of Italy in consequence of circular issued by signor Nasi, minister of education, March 1, making new regulations for the final examinations . . . . mid March, ,,

Bill for construction of a powerful radiographic station on the Marconi system for communication between Italy and Argentina approved by the Senate . . . . end March, ,,

Historical congress established by king at Rome 5 April, ,,

International congress of agriculture opened at Rome, king and queen present . . 13 April, ,,

Centenary celebration of the French academy in the Villa Medici, attended by king and queen 18 April, ,,

Resignation of signor Prinetti, minister for foreign affairs; succeeded by admiral Morin 20–22 April, ,,

First stone of the new Campanile at Venice laid 25 April, 1903

Visit of king Edward VII. to Italy: Naples, 23 April; Rome, 27 April, enthusiastic greeting; visits Pantheon, the Coliseum and the Forum, 28 April; present at review of 21,000 troops; visits pope at the Vatican, 29 April; leaves Rome . . . . 30 April, ,,

German emperor visits Rome, meets with hearty reception . . . . 2 May, ,,

Freedom of Rome conferred on signor Marconi 7 May, ,,

Army estimates passed, 125–88 . . 23 May, ,,

Resignation of Zanardelli ministry, signor Zanardelli, premier, forms a new cabinet 13 June, ,,

Parliament reassembles, 25 June, the premier defends the ministry and the work of the session, vote of confidence carried, 257–71 . 26 June ,,

Illness of the pope reported . . . 3 July, ,,

Death of pope Leo XIII. . . . . 20 July, ,,

Cardinal Sarto elected pope; takes the title of Pius X. . . . . 4 Aug. ,,

Coronation of Pius X. in St. Peter's . . 9 Aug. ,,

Earthquake shocks at Naples, Catania, and Syracuse. . . . . 11 Aug. ,,

Violent hurricane over the Venetian provinces, much injury to crops, and great damage done at Vincenza . . . . 13 Sept. ,,

King and queen visit Paris . . 14–19 Oct. ,,

Resignation of sig. Zanardelli, 21 Oct.; new cabinet sig. Giolitti, premier . . . . . 1 Nov. ,,

Suicide of sig. Rosano, minister of finance, 9 Nov. ,,

Visit of king and queen to England . 17–21 Nov. ,,

KINGS OF ITALY.

476. Odoacer, king of the Heruli, invades Italy, and becomes king, conquered and slain by
493. Theodoric, king of the *Ostrogoths*, an able prince. He put to death the philosophers Boëthius and Symmachus, falsely accused, about 525.
526. Athalaric, his grandson, dies of the plague.
534. Theodatus elected; assassinated.
536. Vitiges elected.
540. Theodebald (Hildibald) elected; assassinated.
541. Totila, or Badiula, a great prince; killed in battle against the imperial army under Narses.
552. Theias falls in battle.
Italy subject to the eastern empire till
568. Alboin, king of the *Lombards*, with a huge mixed army, conquers Italy; poisoned by his wife Rosamond, for compelling her to drink wine out of a cup formed of her father's skull.
573. Cleoph; assassinated.
575. Autharis; poisoned.
591. Agilulph.
615. Adaloald; poisoned.
625. Arioald.
636. Rotharis; married the widow of Arioald published a code of laws.
652. Rodoald (son); assassinated.
653. Aribert I. (uncle)
661. Bertharit and Godebert (sons); dethroned by
662. Grimoald, duke of Benevento.
671. Bertharit re-established.
686. Cunibert (son).
700. Luitbert; dethroned by
701. Ragimbert.
,, Aribert II. (son).
712. Ansprand elected.
,, Luitprand (son), a great prince, and a favourite of the church.
744. Hildebrand (nephew); deposed.
,, Rachis, duke of Friuli, elected; became a monk.
749. Astolph (brother).
756. Desiderius (Didier), quarrelled with the pope Adrian, who invited Charlemagne into Italy, by whom Desiderius was deposed, and an end put to the Lombard kingdom.
781. Pepin or Carloman (son of Charlemagne).
812. Bernard.
820. Lothaire (son of Louis le Débonnaire).

EMPERORS.

875. Charles the Bald.
877. Carloman.
879. Charles the Fat.
888. Berenger I.
889. ,, and Guy.
894. ,, and Lambert.
921. ,, and Rudolph of Burgundy.
926. Hugh of Provence.
945. Lothaire II.
950. Berenger II. and Adalbert his son; deposed in 961 by the emperor Otho the Great, who added Italy to the German empire.

MODERN KINGS OF ITALY.

1805. Napoleon I. proclaimed king of Italy, 18 March; crowned at Milan, 26 May; abdicated, 1814.
1861. Victor-Emmanuel II. (of Sardinia, *which see*), born 14 March, 1820; declared king of Italy by the parliament, 17 March, 1861; died 9 Jan. 1878.
1878. Humbert (son), born 14 March, 1844; married his cousin Margherita (born 20 Nov. 1851), 22 April, 1858; assassinated, 29 July, 1900.
1900. Victor-Emmanuel (son), prince of Naples, born 11 Nov. 1869; married, Helen, princess of Montenegro, 24 Oct. 1896; Yolanda Margherita, born 1 June, 1901; Mafalda, born 19 Nov. 1902.

ITHACA, kingdom of Ulysses, see *Ionian Isles*. It was explored by Dr. Schliemann, in 1878; few discoveries being made.

ITINERARIES. The Roman Itinerarium was a table of the stages between important places. The "Itineraria Antonini," embracing the whole Roman empire, usually ascribed to the emperor Aurelius Antonius, and his successors, A.D. 138-180, was probably based upon the survey made by order of Julius Cæsar, 44 B.C. The "Itinerarium Hierosolymitanum" was drawn up for the use of the pilgrims about A.D. 333.

IVORY was brought to Solomon from Tarshish, about 992 B.C. (1 *Kings* x. 22). The colossal statues of Jupiter, Minerva, &c., by Phidias, were formed of ivory and gold, 444 B.C. Ivory tusk, 7 feet long, sent by the Zulu king Cetywayo to lord Chelmsford, as a token of peace, summer, 1879. Celluloid, an imitation of ivory, tortoiseshell, etc., composed of guncotton and camphor is used for the manufacture of buttons, billiard balls, and various ornaments; it is inflammable at low temperatures.

IVORY COAST, W. Africa, a French colony constituted 17 March, 1893. M. Binger, governor. Successful expedition to Indenia, hostile villages burnt, reported, 29 March, 1894.

Grand Bassam destroyed by an explosion of gunpowder caused by a fire at a factory, several persons injured . . . . . about 1 Feb. 1897
Massacre of a French force under major Caudrelier in the Lobi region by Samory's troops (Sofas) 20 Aug. ,,
Punitive expedition against the Bourbouris for the murder of Mr. Eade and M. Levras, Aug.; severe fighting, towns destroyed, French loss heavy, they retire to Dabon, Nov. 1898; epidemic of fever at Grand Bassam, May–Sept. 1899; severe fighting with the Tepos Marsh; Grabo occupied, natives submit . . . . . . June, 1899
The Hostains-d'Ollone mission left Bereby, 14 Feb. 1899; reached Beyla (route opened to the Sudan), 14 Dec. ,,
Yellow fever outbreak at Grand Bassam, July–mid Sept. 1902

IVRY (near Evreux, N.W. France). Here Henry IV. totally defeated the duc de Mayenne, and the League army, 14 March, 1590.

J.

J was distinguished from I by the Dutch scholars of the 16th century, and introduced into the alphabet by Giles Beys, printer, of Paris, 1550. *Dufresnoy.*

JACOBINS, a name given to the Dominicans in France, because their first convent was the hospital of the pilgrims of St. James (Jacobus), at Paris, at the request of pope Honorius III. (1216-27). The Jacobin club (first called "club Breton") consisted of about forty gentlemen and men of letters, who met in the hall of the Jacobin friars, at Paris, in Oct. 1789, to discuss political and other questions. Similar societies were instituted in all the principal towns of the kingdom. The club was closed 11 Nov. 1794.

JACOBITES, a Christian sect, so called from Jacob Baradæus, a Syrian, about 541; see *Eutychians*.—The partisans of James II. (Latin, Jacobus II.) were so named after his expulsion from England in 1688-9.

A sentimental revival of Jacobitism appeared in England in 1891, the "White Rose League" having been formed. The marquis de Ruvigny and other members of the "Legitimist Jacobite League" were stopped in their attempt to place a large floral wreath on the tomb of Mary, queen of Scots, in Westminster Abbey, 8 Feb. 1892.

JACOBUS, a gold coin, so called from king James I. of England, in whose reign it was struck, 1603-25.

JACQUARD LOOM, for figured fabrics, invented by Joseph Marie Jacquard, of Lyons, and patented 23 Dec. 1801.

JACQUERIE, a term applied to bands of revolted peasants (headed by one Caillot, called Jacques Bonhomme), who ravaged France during the captivity of king John in 1358, and were quelled with much bloodshed. Similar insurrections occurred in Germany. One was termed the *Bundschuh*, from the large shoe especially worn by peasants, in 1502; and another termed the Bund (or league) of the Poor Conrad, 1514 and 1524, which also cost about 100,000 lives, and led to the insurrection of the anabaptists.

JAFFA, a seaport of Syria, celebrated in scripture as Joppa, whence Jonah embarked (about 862 B.C.), and where Peter raised Tabitha from the dead (A.D. 38); in mythology the place whence Perseus delivered Andromeda. Jaffa was taken by the caliph Omar, in 636; by the Crusaders, 1099; by Saladin, 1193; by Louis IX., 1252; and by Bonaparte, 7 March, 1799; the French were driven out by the British in June the same year. Here, according to sir Robert Wilson, were massacred 3800 prisoners by Bonaparte; but this is doubted. Jaffa suffered by an earthquake in Jan. 1837, when it is said that 13,000 persons were killed.

JAGELLONS, a dynasty which at times reigned over Lithuania, Poland, Hungary, and Bohemia, beginning with Jagellon, duke of Lithuania (husband of Hedwig, daughter of Louis of Hungary, 1384), who became king of Poland as Ladislas III. or V. in 1399, and ending with Sigismund II., who died in 1572.

JAINS, see *Jeynes*.

JAMAICA, a W. India island, discovered by Columbus, 3 May, 1494, and named St. Jago. Its aboriginal name was Xaymaca, or "land of wood and water." It was conquered from the Spaniards by admiral Penn, with land forces commanded by Venables, 3 May, 1655, and settled soon after. Population in 1861, 13,816 whites; 81,074 coloured; 346,374 blacks; in 1871, 506,154; whites, 13,101; coloured, 100,346; blacks, 392,707; in 1881, 585,582; 1891, 639,491; 1901, 745,104. Revenue, 1890-1, 764,045*l.*; 1893-4, 863,644*l.*; expenditure, 1890-1, 510,058*l.*; 1893-4, 800,418*l.*; revenue, 1895-6, 646,103*l.*; expenditure, 626,934*l.*; revenue, 1900-1, 760,187*l.*; expenditure, 763,869*l.*; 1903, surplus 15,000*l.* The government of Jamaica includes Turk's and Caicos islands. Population, 1902 (estimated) 770,242.

An awful earthquake here . . . . 2 June, 1692
The Maroons (runaway slaves) permitted to settle in the north of the island 1738
Desolating hurricanes in . . . . 1722, 1734. & 1751
In June, 1795, the Maroons rose against the English, and were not quelled till . . . . March, 1796
Many transported to Sierra Leone 1800
Slave trade abolished . . . . 1 May, 1807
Tremendous hurricane, by which the whole island was deluged, hundreds of houses washed away, vessels wrecked, and 1000 persons drowned, Oct. 1815
Bishopric established 1824
Insurrection of the negro slaves; numerous plantations burnt; the governor, lord Belmore, declared martial law. . . . . 22 Dec. 1831
Emancipation of the slaves . . . . 1 Aug. 1834
About 50,000 die of cholera in 1850
In May, 1853, the dissension between the colonial legislature and sir Charles Grey, the governor, occasioned his recall; his successor, sir H. Barkly, arrived . . . . Oct. 1853
Bishopric of Kingston established 1856
Charles Henry Darling appointed governor . . . 1857
Edward John Eyre appointed governor . . July, 1864
Negro insurrection begins at Morant-bay, by resisting the capture of a negro criminal, 7 Oct.; the court-house fired on; baron Ketelholdt, rev. V. Herschell, and others cruelly murdered, and many wounded. . . . . 11 Oct. 1865
Rebellion spreads, and many atrocities are committed; it is suppressed by the energy of the governor, the military and naval officers, volunteers, the Maroons, and loyal negroes, 13-24 Oct. ,,
George Wm. Gordon, a coloured member of the legislature, convicted of encouraging the rebellion, 21 Oct.; executed . . . . 23 Oct. ,,
Paul Bogle executed . . . . 24 Oct. ,,
Numerous executions . . . . Oct. & Nov. ,,
Sir Henry Storks summoned from Malta, and sent to Jamaica, with Messrs. Russell Gurney and John B. Maule, as commissioners, to inquire respecting the disturbances, and the measures taken in suppressing them . . . . 11 Dec. *et seq.* ,,
Governor Eyre temporarily suspended; sir Henry Storks arrives in Jamaica . . . 6 Jan. 1866
The legislative assembly of Jamaica dissolves itself, and abrogates the constitution (which had existed 200 years) . . . . 17 Jan. ,,
1600*l.* subscribed at Jamaica for defence of gov. Eyre . . . . Feb. ,,
Commission opened 23 Jan.; closed . 21 March, ,,
They receive evidence of the existence of widely spread discontent during 1865; they reported that 439 persons had suffered by martial law; that about 1000 dwellings had been burnt; that about 600 (many women) had been flogged; that they considered the punishments inflicted excessive, the

executions unnecessarily frequent, the burning the houses wanton; and that they saw no proof of Gordon's complicity in the outbreak, or in an organised conspiracy against government, 9 April, 1866
The "Jamaica Government act" passed in England 23 March, ,,
Sir J. P. Grant gazetted governor in room of governor Eyre . . . . 16 July, ,,
A "Jamaica Committee," J. S. Mill, chairman, propose prosecution of governor Eyre . . 27 July, ,,
He arrives at Southampton, 12 Aug.; welcomed by a banquet . . . . 21 Aug. ,,
A committee for his defence formed . . . Sept. ,,
The governor, sir J. P. Grant, promulgates the new constitution; opening of the legislative council (consisting of the governor and six members), 16 Oct. ,,
G. D. Ramsay, accused of murder, discharged by grand jury . . . . 18 Oct. ,,
Warrants issued against gov. Eyre, col. Nelson, and lieut. Brand, Feb.; the grand jury discharges the bills against Eyre, 29 March, and the others, 11 April, 1867
A bill of indictment for misdemeanour against governor Eyre brought in, 15 May; discharged by grand jury . . . . 2 June, 1868
Chief-justice Cockburn disclaimed agreement with part of justice Blackburn's charge on the occasion; an almost unexampled case . . . 8 June, ,,
Trial of Phillips *v.* Eyre (for beating and imprisonment during the rebellion of 1866); Eyre pleaded act of indemnity; verdict for defendant 29 Jan. 1869
Episcopal church disestablished . . . 31 Dec. ,,
Appeals in England for its support . . . July, 1870
Legal expenses of Mr. Eyre ordered to be paid, after discussion in the commons . . . 8 July, 1872
Many estates in Jamaica offered for sale in the London papers . . . . . . July, ,,
Returning prosperity reported . . . . May, 1873
Sir Wm. Grey appointed governor . . . March, 1874
Sir Anthony Musgrave, appointed governor . Nov. 1876
Edward Everard Rushworth, governor, April, 1877; gen. sir Henry Wylie Norman . . . Oct. 1883
Destructive fire at Port Antonio . . . 18 Oct. ,,
Introduction of representative government proposed; Sir Henry W. Norman arrives 21 Dec. ,,
Great public dissatisfaction at the proposals, Feb. 1884
The legislature rejects proposed confederation with Canada . . . . 11 Nov. ,,
Sir Henry Arthur Blake appointed governor Dec. 1888
Rioting of the 1st West India regiment at the races at Kingston; severe conflict with the police, who are badly injured; the rioting quelled by pickets from the camp . . reported 28 Jan. 1891
The International exhibition at Kingston was suggested by Mr. Wm. Fawcett, director of public gardens, 9 July 1889; 15,000*l.* subscribed by the public, and 15,000*l.* given by the government; the exhibition was opened by prince George of Wales, who was in the harbour with a squadron, 27 Jan., and closed by the governor . . . 2 May, ,,
Jamaica made the head-quarters of the Imperial forces in the West Indies, announced March, ,,
Sir Augustus Hemming appointed governor, Nov. 1897; arrived at Kingston . . . 11 Feb. 1898
The council grants 7,000*l.* annually for increased militia force . . . . 18 May ,,
The railway taken over by the government, 23 Jan. 1899
Deadlock in the council, tariff bill passed by aid of additional members, 5 April; crisis, extra members withdrawn . . . . 11 April, ,,
Sir David Barbour's report, suggesting an income tax, increased land tax, stamp duties, and an imperial loan, issued . . . . . 26 July, ,,
Destructive storm and floods, with loss of life, 27–30 Oct. ,,
The subsidy of 49,000*l.* a year for the development of the fruit trade, granted 1900
The *Port Morant*, first ship of the imperial direct service from Bristol, arrives at Kingston, 1 March, 1901
Legislative council meets, decrease of revenue, reported . . . . 4 Feb. 1902
Rioting at Montego bay, suppressed . 5, 6 April, ,,
Beautiful sunsets due to volcanic dust in the air, see *St. Vincent* . . . . . . May, ,,
Surplus 115,000 dol. for year ended June, stated, 4 July, 1902
Large financial assistance granted to sugar estates, 4 Nov. ,,
Mr. Chamberlain's fruit trade policy very successful . . . . early Nov. ,,
Report on Jamaica 1901–02 issued by Colonial office: value of exports increasing 1,823,684*l.*, fruit representing 50 per cent. of total exports, 11,003,840 bunches of bananas valued at 825,288*l.* 3 Jan. 1903
Legislative council pass resolution to place 2,500*l.* at disposal of government to encourage steam communication between Jamaica and Canada; estimates show surplus of 15,000*l.* . . mid Feb. ,,
Great hurricane causing much damage to crops, 10 Aug. ,,
Port Antonio in ruins . . . . ,,
Government grant 50,000*l.* for the relief of the planters . . . . end Aug. ,,

JAMESON "RAID," see *Transvaal*, Dec. 1895–July, 1896, and *Rhodesia*, Aug. 1896, and 30 Jan. *et seq.* 1897. Dr. Jameson, in the Cape assembly, alluded to the "Raid" as a bad business, for which penance had been done, 28 Aug. 1902.

JAMES'S GAZETTE, ST., anti-radical evening paper, first appeared, 31 May, 1880. Price 2*d.*, reduced to 1*d.* 2 Jan. 1882.

JAMES'S HALL, ST., near Piccadilly, erected for public meetings, &c., was opened on 25 March, 1858, with a concert for the benefit of the Middlesex hospital. Mr. Owen Jones was the architect. The "Popular Monday Concerts" established by Mr. Thos. Chappell here began 14 Feb. 1859.

The Moore and Burgess ("Christy") Minstrels began regular performances here 1865.

JAMES'S PALACE, ST., &c., London, was built by Henry VIII. on the site of an hospital of the same name, 1530-6. It has been the official town-residence of the English court since the fire at Whitehall in 1698, and many royal births, deaths, and marriages have here taken place. "Memorials of the Palace," by the rev. Edgar Sheppard, published, April, 1895. Ancient relics found during excavations in the palace courtyard, Feb. 1902.

The PARK, 91 acres, a marsh till Henry VIII. enclosed and laid it out in walks 1530
Much improved by Charles II., who employed Le Nôtre to plant lime-trees, and to lay out "the mall," for the purpose of playing a game with a ball called a mall 1668
William III. granted a passage into it from Spring-gardens 1699
A grand display of fireworks took place here at the peace, when the pagoda bridge erected here by sir W. Congreve was burnt . . . . 1 Aug. 1814
The park improved by Geo. IV. . . . . 1827 *et seq.*
The enclosure first opened to the public in Jan. 1829: the opening by Carlton-steps in 1831
The marble arch at Buckingham-palace removed to Cumberland-gate, Hyde-park . 29 March, 1851
An iron bridge over the ornamental water constructed 1857

JAMES'S THEATRE, ST., erected by Beazley for John Braham, the singer; opened 14 Dec. 1835. See *Theatres*.

JANINA, see *Albania*.

JANISSARIES (Turkish *iéni tchéri*, new soldiers), an order of infantry in the Turkish army; originally, young prisoners trained to arms; were first organised by Orcan, about 1330, and remodelled by his son Amurath I. 1360; their numbers being increased by following sultans. In later days they degenerated from their strict discipline, and several times deposed and killed the sultans. During an insurrection, 14-15 June, 1826, when nearly 3000 of them were killed, the Ottoman army was re-organised by Mahmud II. and a firman was issued on 17 June, abolishing the Janissaries.

JANSENISTS, persons who embraced the doctrines of Cornelius Jansen, bishop of Ypres, who died in 1638. The publication of his "*Augustinus*," 1640, in which he maintained the doctrine of free grace, kindled a fierce controversy, and was condemned by a bull of pope Urban VIII. in 1642. Through the Jesuits Jansenism was condemned by Innocent X. in 1653, and by Clement XI., in 1713, by the bull Unigenitus. This bull the French church rejected. Jansenism still exists at Utrecht and Haarlem; see *Port Royalists*. Loos, abp. of Utrecht, died, June, 1873.

JANUARY derives its name from Janus, an early Roman divinity. January was added to the Roman calendar by Numa, 713 B.C. He placed it about the winter solstice, and made it the first month, because Janus was supposed to preside over the beginning of all business. In 1751 the legal year in England was ordered to begin on 1 Jan. instead of 25 March. Mild Januaries in England, 1804, mean temperature, 43·2; 1834, 44·4; 1846, 43·7; 1875, 43·4; 1884, 43·9; 1890, 43·5 (on 18 days above 50).

JANUS, TEMPLE OF, at Rome, was erected by C. Duilius in 3rd century B.C., kept open in time of war, and closed in time of peace. It was shut at the close of the first Punic war, 235 B.C.; and under Augustus, 29, 25, and 5 B.C.

JAPAN, an Asiatic empire, comprehends four large islands, Niphon or Nippon, Shikoku, Kyushu, and Yezo and about 3,850 small ones. In 1869 Tokio, previously called Jedo, was declared the eastern capital, the ancient Kyoto becoming the western. Population, 1892, 41,089,940; 1900, 43,759,577.

The early history is legendary till A.D. 500. Jimmu Tennō, the founder of the present dynasty, is said to have reigned B.C. 665.
The empress Jingo is said to have conquered Corea 201 A.D.
Corean civilization introduced 285.
Introduction of Buddhism from Corea about 552.
Its hierarchy established, 624.
Yoritomo, *Shogun* or generalissimo, since called by the Chinese *Tycoon*, usurps supreme power, the *Mikado* or emperor becoming the spiritual emperor, 1192 *et seq.*
Sanguinary wars among the chiefs during four centuries.
Japan visited by Marco Polo, a Venetian, about 1275-95.
[His "Maravigliose Cose" printed 1496.]
Weak rival dynasties in the north and south, 1333-92.
Japan visited by Mendez Pinto, a Portuguese, about 1537-58.
Tyeyasu, victorious over southern barons, establishes a strictly conservative government at Jedo, 1600.
[His dynasty lasted till 1868.]
The Portuguese establish trading settlements about 1543, and introduce Jesuit missionaries who make many converts; by a fierce persecution beginning 1590, the Portuguese and their missionaries are expelled, and their converts massacred, 1637-42.
The Dutch settlements under severe restrictions, suffered to remain for a time, 1600 *et seq.*
The learned Engelbert Kæmpfer visits Japan about 1690.
[All foreigners rigidly excluded from Japan till 1853.]
An American expedition, under commodore Parry, reaches Jedo, and is favourably received; but remains only a few days . . . 8 July, 1853
A treaty of commercial alliance concluded between the two countries . . . 31 March, 1854
A similar treaty with Great Britain . . 14 Oct. ,,
With Russia . . . . 26 Jan. 1855
Destructive earthquake; Anasaca and Simoda destroyed, Jedo much injured . . 23 Dec. 1854
Nagasaki and Hakodadi opened to European commerce 1856
Commercial treaty with Russia . . 19 Aug. 1858
Lord Elgin visits Japan, with a present of a steamer for the emperor, and is honourably received, July; obtains the treaty of Jedo, opening Japan to British commerce . . 26 Aug. ,,
The secular emperor dies (aged 36) . . 16 Sept. ,,
Mr. (afterwards sir) Rutherford Alcock appointed consul-general, Dec. 1858; envoy extraordinary, Nov. 1859
A Japanese embassy visits Washington, New York, &c., United States . . 14 May—30 June, 1860
Attack on the British embassy at Jedo; some persons wounded . . . 5 July, 1861
Embassy received at Paris, 13 April; London, June; in Holland, Prussia, &c. . . July—Sept. 1862
Foreign ministers transfer the residence from Jedo to Yokohama . . . 27 June, ,,
Mr. Richardson murdered and his companions cruelly assailed by a Japanese noble and his suite, 14 Sept. ,,
[Monument erected by Mr. Kurokawa, a Japanese gentleman, in honour of Mr. Richardson, 1884.]
The batteries and vessels of the prince of Nagato fire on an English and a French vessel at the entrance of the straits of Simonosaki, 15, 19 Nov. ,,
Some English, French, and American vessels bombard his forts and his vessels . . 15-19 July, 1863
Reparation demanded; 100,000*l.* paid by the government; the prince of Satsuma resists payment of 25,000*l.*, his portion; admiral Kuper enters the bay of Kagosima, and is fired upon; whereupon he bombards the town and burns the prince's steamers . . . 15 Aug. ,,
The Japanese minister announces that the ports opened by virtue of the treaties will be closed, 24 June, ,,
The prince of Satsuma pays the 25,000*l.* 11 Dec. ,,
The Japanese government refuse to abide by the treaties; a combined fleet enters the straits of Simonosaki, 4 Sept.; and attacks and destroys the Japanese batteries . . 5, 6 Sept. 1864
Major Baldwin and lieut. Bird murdered, 20 Nov.; two assassins executed . . . Dec. ,,
Sir Harry Parkes appointed to succeed sir R. Alcock as envoy . . . April, 1865
Treaties with England, France, &c., ratified, 25 Nov. ,,
Two more ports opened . . . Jan. 1866
Death of the tycoon: his successor said to be favourable to foreigners . . Sept. ,,
Town of Yokohama and third part of European settlement destroyed by fire . 26 Nov. ,,
Jedo and other places opened to trade, by the government . . . 25 April, 1867
Visit of sir Harry Parkes to the tycoon, Stots Bashi, 1 May, ,,
Prince Minbontaiyou, brother of the tycoon, arrives at Dover, 2 Dec.; presented to the queen, 4 Dec. ,,
Osaka and Niogo opened to European commerce, 1 Jan. 1868
Insurrection of the Daimios; rivalry between the mikado and tycoon, Dec.; foreigners neutral, 27 Jan.—Feb. ,,
Japanese outrages on French sailors; culprits executed, 16 March; further outrages punished, 23 March, ,,
The mikado's troops defeat the tycoon's, who flies, 26-30 Jan.; the mikado's defeated near Jeddo, 10-17 May, ,,
After long war and varying success the rebellion ends; the mikado re-established . . July, ,,
Majority of the mikado proclaimed . . Nov. ,,
His marriage, 9 Feb.; another rebellion of the tycoon's partisans . . . Feb. 1869
Visit of the duke of Edinburgh, 29 Aug.; received by the mikado . . . . 22 Sept. ,,
The tycoon submits to the mikado . . Dec. ,,
Great progress of internal improvements, and assimilation to European civilisation; proposed establishment of railways, telegraphs, &c. . 1870-71

Industrial exhibition opened at Kioto . . 10 April, 1872
Destructive fire at Jedo . . . . May, ,,
Embassy of distinguished Japanese arrives at Washington, 4 March: in London . . 17 Aug. ,,
Pacific mail screw steamer *America* burnt at Yokohama; about 40 killed . . . . 24 Aug. ,,
First railway (from Yokohama to Shinagawa) opened, 12 June, to Jedo: opened by the mikado, Oct. ,,
Japanese ambassadors received by queen Victoria, 5 Dec. ,,
English proposed as the national tongue . Dec. ,,
Public library at Tokio established . . . . ,,
Insurrection, through desire for war with Corea; soon suppressed . . . . Feb.–April, 1874
A successful expedition against Formosa to chastise savage tribes for massacring Japanese sailors, May; Chinese protest, Aug.; Japanese withdraw (see *Formosa*), announced . . . . Nov. ,,
Mr. L. Haber, German consul, murdered at Hakodadi, by a fanatic, 8 Aug.; executed . 26 Sept. ,,
The Japanese minister received by queen Victoria, 3 Mar. 1875
The mikado decrees a new constitution; 2 chambers, &c. . . . . 14 April, ,,
The mikado opens a parliament of officials, nominated by himself, in Jedo . . . . 20 June, ,,
Industrial exhibition 1876
Insurrection of Satsuma and other clans specially against the ministry, Feb.; suppression announced . . . . Sept. 1877
"*Foo Soo*," iron-clad man-of-war, launched at Poplar, London, Chinese ambassador present, 14 Apl. ,,
Insurrection suppressed; power of the Daimios virtually suppressed; principals only punished; announced . . . . 13 Oct. ,,
Progress in Japan: 3744 post-offices; 22,053,430 letters, and 7,372,566 domestic newspapers sent by post; 2 railways in operation; 34 lighthouses; ample religious freedom and virtual free trade . ,,
Okuto, able reforming minister of the interior, killed by six men (political motives) . 14 May, 1878
Scientific works in English, published by Tokio university 1879-80
Imperial decree convoking a national assembly in 1890 . . . . 12 Oct. 1881
Entirely new criminal code enforced . . . ,,
53,760 primary schools and compulsory education established . . . . . . autumn, 1882
The Japanese commander in chief with presents received by the queen at Windsor . 25 Nov. ,,
Rev. Arthur W. Poole, consecrated Anglican bishop of Japan . . . . 18 Oct. 1883
All Japan to be thrown open to foreign trade, with mixed tribunals . . . announced Nov. ,,
Death of the last tycoon . . . . . April, 1884
A new order of hereditary nobility instituted Sept. ,,
The national religion disestablished and freedom given to other religions . . . 11 Aug. ,,
A Japanese village exhibited in London, 1885; burnt 2 May; re-opened . . . 2 Dec. 1885
A Japanese dictionary printed in Roman characters, completed . . . . . . summer, ,,
Amicable correspondence between the mikado and the pope . . . . Oct. ,,
Bishop Poole died 9 July; succeeded by rev. E. Bickersteth . . . . Nov. ,,
Gradual adoption of alphabetical in place of ideographic writing by agency of the Roma-ji-Rai, or Roman Alphabet Association . . . . . ,,
Decree giving enlarged power to the prime minister solely responsible to the mikado . . 1 Dec. ,,
Prince Komatsu arrives in London to confer on the prince of Wales the order of the chrysanthemum 20 Nov.; received by the queen at Windsor 22 Nov. 1886
Japanese commission to examine the fine arts in Europe and America; reports in favour of Japan; "pure art is asleep in Japan, but dead in Europe" 1886–7
Count Ito, the prime minister, energetically introduces western dress and habits . . spring, 1887
Death of Shimadju Saburo, ex-prince of Satsuma 6 Dec. ,,
Japanese Fine Art Exhibitions opened in London 1887–8
Completion of the translation of the Bible into Japanese celebrated . . . . . 3 Feb. 1888
Volcanic eruption at Sho-Bandai-San; reported 400 persons killed . . . . . . 15–18 July, ,,
New constitution promulgated by the mikado at Tokio; the houses of lords and commons established; religious liberty and general freedom granted . . . . 11 Feb. 1889
The government desires new commercial treaties with the European powers; they hesitate; one with the United States promptly signed, Feb.; with Russia 8 Aug.; with Italy, with Germany, with France . . . . ,,
Destructive storms and inundations in Yezo, &c., April, ,,
On west coasts, 1,200 houses destroyed . June, ,,
Volcanic eruption on Ishima Island, 300 houses destroyed; 170 persons killed . 13, 14 April ,,
Earthquakes at Kumamoto, 19 persons perish 28 July–3 Aug. ,,
The southern island of Kiushiu, embankments, &c., destroyed, July; S.E. Japan the Chikugo river rose 28½ feet above its usual level twice, 73,694 persons made destitute . . . . . Aug. ,,
Japanese commission of enquiry respecting parliamentary procedure in Europe, arrives in London early in . . . . Oct. ,,
Japanese national banks reported highly prosperous, Oct. ,,
Nine non-treaty ports opened to commerce, early Oct. ,,
Several changes in the ministry . Oct.-Dec. ,,
N. Japan, destructive gales, 11 Sept., total loss 12 prefectures devastated; 2,419 persons killed, above 90,000 destitute, 50,000 houses swept away; 150,000 acres of crops destroyed, 6,000 bridges destroyed, reported . . . about 18 Nov. ,,
Volcanic eruption of the Zoo, Bingo district, Fukuyama buried, inhabitants escaped 16 Jan. 1890
Violent cyclone on the coast; 900 fishing boats wrecked, great loss of life . . . . 24 Jan. ,,
The pope proposes to appoint a metropolitan, and four bishops for Japan . . . . 12 March ,,
National Industrial and Fine Art Exhibition opened at Tokio by the mikado . . . . 27 March, ,,
New civil code promulgated . . . . 21 April, ,,
The duke and duchess of Connaught visit Yokohama . . . . 15–22 April, ,,
The mikado institutes a new order of knighthood, "the Golden Falcon," to commemorate the 2,555th anniversary of the coronation of Jimmu Tenno, the semi-mythical first sovereign of Japan, reported . . . . 12 May, ,,
First parliamentary election . . . . 1 July, ,,
The Japanese mail steamer, *Musha Maru*, founders in a gale off the Japanese coast, losing nearly all her crew, reported . . . . . . 18 Sept. ,,
The first Japanese parliament opened by the emperor, with great rejoicing . . 29 Nov. ,,
The parliament house (wood) burnt down 15 Jan. 1891
The Japanese commodore, Canaka, warmly received by the sultan at Constantinople, and thanked for help given to the wrecked *Ertogrul* (18 Sept. 1890) . . . . 8 Feb. ,,
Death of prince Sanjo, prime minister since 1868, highly honoured . . . . . . 18 Feb. ,,
The czarewitch travels in Japan; wounded by a fanatic at Otsa, 11 May, visited by the mikado, 13 May, ,,
Collision between the *Tamaye* and the *Miyoshi* (racing in Suirakami Bay, off the coast of Yezo), about 260 lives lost . . . . . . 12 July, ,,
Typhoon at Kobe, H.M.S. gunboat *Tweed* and many other vessels sunk with great loss of life 16 Aug. ,,
Very destructive earthquake on the Niphon islands; about 84,000 houses and railways, bridges, &c., destroyed; about 10,000 persons killed and 300,000 homeless; minor shocks follow; estimated loss 2,000,000*l*. . . . . . 28 Oct. ,,
The parliament, opposing the government, dissolved . . . . 25 Dec. ,,
Government ordinance to provide for the relief of the sufferers by the earthquake . . 29 Dec. ,,
Violent election riots with loss of 22 lives 15 Feb. 1892
The establishment of a Roman Catholic hierarchy authorized, reported . . . . . 15 March, ,,
The Japanese parliament opened by the mikado, 6 May, ,,

New cabinet formed by count Ito . . 29 Aug. 1892
Hurricane in Tokushima district; about 300 killed, reported . . . . 17 Sept. ,,
The *Chishima*, cruiser, sunk by collision with the Peninsular and Oriental company's steamship *Ravenna*, off Iyo; 75 lives lost; 20 saved, reported, 1 Dec. 1892; the P. & O. company agree to pay by compromise, 10,000*l*., announced, Dec. 1895. See *Wrecks* . . . . Dec. ,,
Parliament opened by the emperor, 29 Nov.; increase of national defences proposed . 1 Dec. ,,
Yoshino, large protected Japanese cruiser, launched at the Elswick works, Newcastle . 20 Dec. ,,
Great fire at Osaka; 275 buildings destroyed; 125 persons perish . . . . . . 20 Dec. ,,
Continued opposition to the ministry; parliament prorogued, 3 Feb.; deadlock closed by compromise, 17 Feb.; diet closed . . . March, 1893
Increase of the navy agreed on . about 3 March, ,,
Death of count Terashima, eminent statesman, aged 60 . . . . 6 June, ,,
Fire at Hachiogii; about 5,000 houses destroyed, reported . . . . 25 Aug. ,,
Destructive floods and a landslip in the Gifu district; great loss of life, reported . 15 Sept. ,,
The officers of the new Japanese ironclad *Yoshino* dined with the lord mayor of London . 7 Nov. ,,
Destructive floods, with great loss of life, reported . . . . 13 Nov. ,,
Parliament opened, 28 Nov.; great disorder; parliament dissolved, 30 Dec. 1893; general election; liberal victory . . . . . 1 March, 1894
Disastrous floods throughout the country . May, ,,
Death of Mr. Hugh Fraser, British minister, at Yokohama . . . . 4 June, ,,
Parliament dissolved, after much dissension, reported . . . . 4 June, ,,
Fire at Yamagata; over 1,200 houses destroyed; 13 deaths, reported . . . . 1 June, ,,
Destructive fire and earthquake at Yokohama, with loss of life . . . . 20 June, ,,
Mr. P. le Poer Trench appointed British minister at Tokio . . . . July, ,,
War with China (see *Corea*) . . . . July, ,,
Loan of 50,000,000 dollars authorized, 17 Aug.; the nobles subscribe 80,000,000 dollars, 22 Aug. ,,
Anglo-Japanese treaty signed, 16 July; ratified; the tariff modified and the foreign jurisdiction at the treaty ports to be abolished; British residents equalised with the Japanese; treaty to come into force in 5 years . . . . 25 Aug. ,,
General prosperity and loyalty; the government, aided by a military party, actively promote the war with China . . . . . . Aug. ,,
Parliament opened by the mikado with a firm speech against China; a large loan authorized, 17 Oct.; other bills passed by the parliament; with thanks to the army and navy; session closed . . . . 22 Oct. ,,
Earthquake in Yamagata and Akita; the town of Sakata nearly destroyed, with great loss of life, 22 Oct. ,,
Treaty with United States N. A. signed . 23 Nov. ,,
Parliament opened; cheerful speech from the throne; progress of parliamentary government, 24 Dec. ,,
Treaty of peace with China; concluded 17 April (see *Corea*); ratifications exchanged . 8 May, 1895
Sir Ernest Satow appointed minister at Tokio, 26 June, ,,
Train on a sea-wall wrecked during a gale, 140 soldiers killed . . . . 27 July, ,,
Counts Ito, Yamagata, Oyama created marquises; others raised to dignity . . . . Aug. ,,
Parliament opened by the emperor . . 28 Dec. ,,
Yashima, warship, launched on the Tyne at Elswick . . . . 28 Feb. 1896
Fuji, warship, launched on the Thames, 31 March, ,,
Treaty of commerce, etc., with Germany, signed at Berlin . . . . 4 April, ,,
Kamaishi, in N. Japan, almost completely destroyed by earthquakes, about 1,000 lives lost, 150 shocks in 20 hrs.; about 20,000 persons drowned by a seismic wave, and many towns destroyed, 15–17 June; *Times*, 3 Aug.; see *Mansion house*, Nov. 1896

Resignation of the marquis Ito and ministry, Aug. 1896
Earthquake in N.E. province, Rokugo destroyed, many deaths . . . . 31 Aug. ,,
Count Matsukata appointed premier and minister of finance; count Okuma, foreign minister; announced . . . . 18 Sept. ,,
Great development of trade, new lines of steamers, docks, etc., constructed; reported . 27 Nov. ,,
Parliament opened, 25 Dec.; closed 24 March, 1897
Typhoon at Yokohama, with loss of life . 9 Sept. ,,
Parliament opened, with a cheerful speech from the throne, 21 Dec.; the ministry resigns, 27 Dec.; an independent ministry formed by the marquis Ito, 12 Jan.; he resigns; succeeded by count Okuma . . . . . 28 June, 1898
The *Vara* transport vessel wrecked on her way to the Pescadores, 85 deaths; reported 16 Jan. ,,
Chinese war indemnity paid, 11,008,857*l*. . 7 May, ,,
Terrible gale on N.E. coast, 1,500 fishermen drowned . . . . 11 May, ,,
New commercial and civil code comes into operation . . . . 16 July, ,,
Catalogue of more than 5,000 Japanese books in the British Museum, by prof. Douglas, reported, Sept. ,,
Count Okuma's cabinet resigns, 31 Oct.; the marquis Yamagata forms one . . . 6 Nov. ,,
Shikishima battleship launched at Blackwall (Thames) . . . . 1 Nov. ,,
Parliament opened with an imperial message, 3 Dec. ,,
Lord Charles Beresford visits Yokohama; urges an alliance between Great Britain, Japan, Germany, and U.S.N.A., to prevent war in the Far East; leaves . . . . 25 Jan. 1899
Severe earthquake in Niphon, loss of life and property . . . . 7 March, ,,
Asaki battleship launched at Glasgow, 13 March, ,,
Increased expenditure on the army and navy, taxes raised, expansion of commerce, &c., reported . . . . April, ,,
Loan of 10,000,000*l*. issued in London . June, ,,
New press law (1897), free press restrictions removed . . . . 1 July, ,,
Imperial rescript issued, 30 June; foreign treaties revised; Japan open to Europeans; consular jurisdiction abolished, 17 July; ratified, 15 Aug. ,,
Chinese mission to treat for a treaty of alliance fails . . . . mid Aug. ,,
Copper mine flooded at Besshi Ihikoku, 600 deaths, reported . . . . 1 Sept. ,,
Vaccination made compulsory . . . summer, ,,
House-tax becomes due, foreigners protest as exempt by treaty . . . . . . Oct. ,,
Government earthquake investigation committee appointed, 1893; catalogue issued by prof. Oman, Jan. 1900
Grand naval review (30 warships) off Kobe, the emperor present . . . . . 30 April, ,,
Mobilisation of 20,000 troops ordered, owing to Chinese crisis . . . . . . 26 June, ,,
Eruption of Mount Adsuma, near Bandai San, 200 persons reported killed or injured . 17 July, ,,
Yamagata's ministry resigns, succeeded by the marquis Ito . . . . . . 29 Sept. ,,
Mikasa warship, largest afloat, launched at Barrow, 8 Nov. ,,
Dr. Kitasato's new method of treating dysentery by inoculation very successful . . 1895–Nov. ,,
Political crisis, early March; taxation bills passed by the peers . . . . . 16 March, 1901
Bill recognising the titles of foreign landholders, passed . . . . March, ,,
Budget passed . . . . . . 22 March, ,,
Financial panic, 20 banks suspend payment, reported . . . . 25 April, ,,
Crisis; cabinet resigns, 3 May; visct. Katsura forms a ministry . . . . . . 3 June, ,,
M. Hoshi Toru, liberal leader, assassinated by Iba Sotaro (sentenced to life-imprisonment, 10 Sept.) in the Tokio city council . . . 21 June, ,,
Baron Iwasaki buys and presents prof. Max Müller's library (about 13,000 vols. and 81 Sanscrit MSS.) to Tokio university . . . July, ,,
Surplus for 1900, 3,000,000 yen, reported, 10 Sept. ,,
The Chinese emperor's letter apologising for the murder of M. Sugiyama in Pekin (11 June, 1900)

and expressing his gratitude to the Japanese for their "beneficent influence" and moderation, accepted by the emperor, who hopes that reforms in China may soon be in progress by means of which "permanent peace in Asia" will be secured . . . . Sept. 1901
Sir Claude MacDonald, British minister, arrives, 22 Oct. ,,
The emperor opens parliament . . 10 Dec. ,,
Budget presented, 23 Dec.; withdrawn, 26 Dec. ,,
Marquis Ito leaves for U.S.N.A., mid Sept.; visits Paris, St. Petersburg, Berlin, Brussels, arrives in London, 24 Dec.; received by the king, 27 Dec.; entertained at the Mansion house, 3 Jan. 1902; made G.C.B.; in Paris, 9 Jan.; Rome (decorated by the king) . 15–20 Jan. 1902
Mikasa battleship launched at Barrow-in-Furness, satisfactorily tried . . . . . Jan. 1902
Infantry detachment (210) lost in the snow, only 13 survived . . . . . 23 Jan.–2 Feb. ,,
Anglo-Japanese treaty of alliance signed, London (well received by France and Russia, March), 30 Jan. ,,
Large financial improvement, reported . 6 Feb. ,,
Baron Hayashi, minister to Gt. Britain, created a viscount; others decorated . . . . Feb. ,,
Marquis Ito received by the emperor, reported, 9 March, ,,
Parliament (16th session) closed . . 10 March, ,,
Issues of bonds, over 7½ million yen, for railways and public works . . . . 29 March, ,,
Great fire at Fukui, reported . . 31 March, ,,
An association similar to Lloyds, formed, princes Arisugawa and Konoye pres. and vice-pres., reported . . . . 29 April, ,,
Herring fleet lost in a gale off Yezo, 250 deaths, 30 April, ,,
British naval squadron fêted at Tokio . 26 May, ,,
Prince Komatsu and visct. Hayashi entertained by the lord mayor, in London . . 23 June, ,,
Russian grand duke Boris visits Tokio, 2–12 July, ,,
Insurgents defeated in S. Formosa . 26 July, ,,
Tori Shima, a small island, overwhelmed by a volcanic eruption, the inhabitants (over 150) killed . . . . 13–15 Aug. ,,
General election; new system, reported satisfactory . . . . 22 Aug. ,,
House-tax (on foreigners) dispute, referred to arbitration . . . . 28 Aug. ,,
Typhoon at Yokohama, great loss of life, Odawara swept by a wave, about 200 drowned, 29 Sept. ,,
Japanese loan of 5,000,000*l.* issued London, 7 Oct. ,,
Naval expansion scheme, budget, 3,700,000*l.*, 1901–02, settled . . . . . . early Oct. ,,
Parliament opened by the emperor . 9 Dec. ,,
The government's financial proposals opposed; parliament dissolved on rejecting compromise, 16, 28 Dec.; general elections to be held, 1 March, 1903.
Visit of the crown prince of Siam . . mid Dec. ,,
Miniature of king Edward VII. set in diamonds, with autograph letter in terms of cordial friendship as a mark of goodwill, presented to the mikado by British minister . . . . . . early Feb. 1903
During fêtes celebrating accession of first Japanese emperor and promulgation of the constitution, British minister gives a banquet to 30 Japanese graduates of Oxford and Cambridge . . 11 Feb. ,,
Death of prince Komatsu, aged 61, the representative of Japan at the coronation of king Edward VII., chief of the Japanese guards in the Satsuma rebellion 1877, field-marshal of Japanese forces in the Chinese war of 1894-95, and distinguished statesman . . . . 18 Feb. ,,
General election . . . . 4 March, ,,
Consent of Corean government to grant to Japanese subjects equal whaling privileges on the eastern coast as have been granted to Russian government since 1899, including 3 stations on shore, early May, ,,
Emperor opens the diet, 12 May, financial measures passed; the Formosan camphor monopoly extended to the whole empire; diet closed 4 June, ,,
Increasing excitement over the Manchuria question in Japan, reported . . . . . June ,,
Dispute between Japan and Corea respecting the opening of Wi-ju, for which Japan presses and Corea refuses on ground of Russian objection, early July, 1903
Cabinet changes, the marquis Ito closes his connection with the Seiyu-Kai, and accepts office of president of privy council, which will in future assume great importance in state affairs; the marquis Yamagata and count Matsugata appointed privy councillors; the premier resumes office; end of crisis . . . . . 13 July, ,,
Pressure put upon Corea for the opening of Wi-ju, plea that Russia objects regarded by Japan as irrelevant . . . . . . about 10 July, ,,
Strained relations caused by rivalry of Russia and Japan in Corea in consequence of Russian activity having secured a position on the Corean side of the Ya-lu and Tuman rivers. Russia seeks for the right to assist in the construction of a railway through Wi-ju to Seoul; Japanese proposal for a *modus vivendi* regarding Russian policy in Corea and Manchuria presented at St. Petersburg . . . . 12 Aug. ,,
Trade increasing, total value of exports and imports, 54,107,552*l.* in 1902, reported . . 25 Aug. ,,
M. Hakano, baron Kioura, and M. Kaiboba, appointed respectively ministers of justice, agriculture and commerce, and education and communication . . . . . 23 Sept. ,,
Strained relations between Japan and Russia on the question of the non-evacuation of Manchuria by the latter by 8 Sept. according to the terms of the convention, and Japanese interests in Corea, Oct.–Nov. ,,

REIGNING EMPEROR OR MIKADO.

Mutsu Hito, born 3 Nov., 1852; succeeded his father, Komei Tenno, 1867. . . . 13 Jan. 1867
Heir apparent, prince Yoshi Hito, born 31 Aug. 1879, installed 3 Nov. 1889; married princess Sada, 10 May, 1900; son born . 29 April, 1901

JAPAN SOCIETY, London, was founded by lord de Saumarez, Mr. Arthur Diosy, professors W. Anderson, Church, and others, to promote the study of Japanese art, science, finance, commerce, language, literature, etc.; instituted Jan.; inaugural meeting, 29 April, 1892. The mikado of Japan presented 105*l.* to the society, Nov. 1892.

JARGONIUM, a new metal discovered by professor A. Church in combination with the zircon of Ceylon. The spectrum was shown by Mr. H. Sorby, 6 March, 1869.

JARNAC (W. France). On 13 March, 1569, the duke of Anjou, afterwards Henry III. of France, here defeated the Huguenots under Louis, prince of Condé, who was killed in cold blood by Montesquieu. The victor (seventeen years of age), on account of his success here and at Moncontour, was chosen king of Poland.

A Jarnac Stroke; a term of opprobrium, is derived from the Seigneur de Jarnac, who, in a duel with La Chataigneraye, for a great insult, disabled his antagonist by an unexpected wound in the ham 1547

JASMINE or **JESSAMINE** (*Jasminum officinale*), native of Persia, &c., was brought hither from Circassia, before 1548. The Catalonian jasmine came from the East Indies, in 1629, and the yellow Indian jasmine in 1656

JASSY, the capital of Moldavia, frequently occupied by the Russians; taken by them in 1739, 1769, and 1828. A treaty between them and the Turks was signed here, 9 Jan. 1792. Population, 1885, 90,000; 1899, 78,067.

JAVA, a large island in the Eastern Archipelago, is said to have been reached by the Portuguese in 1511, and by the Dutch in 1595. The latter, who now possess it, built Batavia, the capital, about 1619; see *Batavia*. The atrocious massacre of 20,000 of the unarmed natives by the Dutch, sparing neither women nor children, to possess their effects, took place in 1740. The island capitulated to the British, 18 Sept. 1811. The sultan was dethroned by the English, and the hereditary prince raised to the throne, in June, 1813. Java was restored to Holland by treaty in 1814, and given up in 1816. The English promoted free labour instead of forced; but the Dutch reverted to the old system, and in 1830 abolished free labour, introducing the "culture system," by which the government controls the cultivation of the land and buys the produce at its own price. In Aug. 1860, the Swiss soldiers here, aided by the natives, mutinied, but were soon reduced, and many suffered death. The diminished prosperity of Java led to warm discussions in the Dutch chamber in 1866.

The valuable "History of Java," by sir T. Stamford Raffles (successful governor 1811–16; his life by Mr. Demetrius Boulger, published 1898), was published 1817.

Java has a great many volcanoes, and has frequently been devastated by eruptions and earthquakes; those of 5 Jan. 1699, 31 Oct. 1876, and 10 June, 1877, were very destructive.

Java and neighbouring isles desolated by a series of violent eruptions from about two-thirds of its 46 volcanoes, beginning with Krakatoa, casting up immense quantities of lava, mud, ashes, and fragments of rocks, darkening the air for about 50 square miles. Mountains were split up, some disappeared, and many new craters were formed. Rumbling noises heard 25 Aug., violent eruptions of Krakatoa 26 Aug. There was much submarine disturbance, and an immense "tidal wave" destroyed Anjer and other places, 27 Aug. The lighthouses in the straits of Sunda were swallowed up, and new volcanic peaks appeared, rendering navigation highly dangerous. Loss of life estimated at 35,000, 25-28 Aug. Great atmospheric, oceanic, and electrical disturbances for thousands of square miles. See under *Sun*, 1883.

A committee of the Royal Society issued a report on the eruption, Oct. 1888.

Serious volcanic outbreaks; great destruction; about 500 persons perish, early May, 1885.

Insurrection of the natives at Anjer; some Europeans and natives killed; the revolt checked by the police and settled, 16 July, 1888.

By a great eruption of the volcano of Galoenggoen in 1822 114 villages were destroyed, and over 4,000 lives lost; several villages destroyed by another eruption, reported, 20 Oct. 1894.

Eruption of Keloet, 181 deaths, about 23 May, 1901.

JAWAKIES, see *India*, 1877–8.

JEAN DE LUZ, ST. (S. France, near the Pyrenees). Soult's strong position here was taken by general Hill and marshal Beresford. 10 Nov. 1813.

JEDDA, the port of Mecca, Arabia. On 15 June, 1858, the fanatic Mahometans massacred twenty-six of the Christian inhabitants, among them the English and French consuls and part of their families; but many fled to the shipping. On the delay of justice, commodore Pullen, with the *Cyclops*, bombarded the town, 25, 26 July. On 6 Aug. eleven of the assassins were executed; the ringleaders afterwards.

Murderous attack on foreign consuls, for their sanitary regulations, by Bedouin; 1 man killed, 30 May; immediate punishment ordered by the sultan, as demanded by the powers, 1 June, 1895 [indemnity paid, 20 May, 1896.]

Cholera hospital destroyed by the Bedouin, reported, 5 June, 1895

Order restored, reported . . . . 15 June, ,,

Outbreak of plague . . . . . Feb.–March, 1899

Great distress due to influx of pilgrims from Mecca, see *Cholera* . . . . March, 1902

JEDO or **YEDO** (the name was changed to Tokio about 1869), the eastern capital of Japan, on the island of Niphon. Here was signed the treaty with Great Britain, 26 Aug. 1858; see *Japan*. 5000 houses destroyed by fire, 8 Dec. 1873, and 2,547, March, 1890, see *Tokio*.

JEHAD, see *Jihad*.

JELLALABAD, Afghanistan, defended by sir Robert Sale from 8 Jan. to 5 April, 1842, when the siege was raised by general G. Pollock, who destroyed the fortifications.

JE MAINTIENDRAI, "I will maintain," the motto of the house of Nassau. When William III. came to the throne of England, he continued this, but added "the liberties of England and the Protestant religion," at the same time ordering that the old motto of the royal arms, "*Dieu et mon droit*," should be retained on the great seal, 1689.

JEMAPPES (N.W. Belgium), the site of the first pitched battle gained by the French republicans (under Dumouriez), in which 40,000 French troops drove out 19,000 Austrians, who were entrenched in woods and mountains, defended by redoubts and many cannon, 6 Nov. 1792. The number killed on each side was reckoned at 5000.

JENA and **AUERSTADT** (Central Germany), where two battles were fought, 14 Oct. 1806, between the French and Prussians. The French were commanded at Jena by Napoleon, and at Auerstadt by Davoust: the Prussians by prince Hohenlohe at the former place, and the king of Prussia at the latter. The Prussians were defeated, losing nearly 20,000 killed and wounded, and nearly as many prisoners, and 200 field pieces; the French lost 14,000 men. Napoleon advanced to Berlin, and issued the Berlin decree (*which see*).

JENKINS' EAR. In 1731, an English merchant-vessel was boarded by a Spanish guardship, and the captain, Robert Jenkins, cruelly used, his wounded ear being torn off. He obtained no redress by appeal to his government. He appeared before parliament in 1738, when the convention of the Pardo was severely discussed, and war ensued. Jenkins' story was verified by Admiralty Records in 1889

JENNERIAN INSTITUTION, founded 1803; Jenner society established at Gloucester (*which see*), 1896. Jenner celebration in Russia 6 Dec. 1896, see *Vaccination* and *Preventive Medicine*.

JEPHTHAH delivered Israel from the Ammonites B.C. 1143, *Judges* xi. "Jephthah," Handel's last oratorio; composed 21 Jan.—30 Aug. 1751; performed 26 Feb. 1752.

JERSEY. The chief island of the Channel archipelago (which includes Guernsey, Sark, Alderney, &c.), formerly held by the Romans in the 3rd and 4th centuries after Christ—Jersey being termed Cæsarea. The isles were captured by Rollo, and thus became an appanage of the duchy of Normandy, and were united to the crown of England by his descendant, William the Conqueror. The inhabitants of the Channel Islands preferred to remain subjects of king John, at the period of the conquest of Normandy by Philip Augustus, and while retaining the laws, customs, and (until lately) the language of their continental ancestors, have always remained firm in their allegiance to England. Almost every war with France has been characterised by an attack on Jersey, the most formidable of which, under the baron de Rullecour, was defeated by the English garrison and Jersey militia, commanded by major Pierson, 6 Jan. 1781. Mr. J. Bertrand Payne, in his "Armorial of Jersey," and his "Gossiping Guide," has exhaustively treated the general and family history of the island. Jersey became a place of refuge for MM. Rouher, Baroche, Drouyn de Lhuys, and other distinguished French imperialists, Sept. 1870. Some of the Trappists and other monks expelled from France, settle in Jersey, 1880-1. Philip Gosset, sentenced to 5 years' imprisonment for fraud against the state (£27,000), and a banking company, 8 May, 1886. Dissensions in regard to the exclusion of the English language in the legislative assemblies of the islands, etc. Feb. 1896. Lieut.-gov., gen. C. B. Ewart, 1887; lieut.-gen. Edward Markham, 1892; major-gen. Edw. Hopton 1895 (died 8 Aug. 1903); major-gen. H. R. Abadie, 1900. The population of the channel isles in 1861 was 90,978; in 1871, 90,563; in 1881, 87,702; 1891, 92,272; 1901, 95,841.

The Theatre Royal and 2 houses burnt, 29 March, 1899
Town militia arsenal burnt down; heavy loss, 23 Jan. 1900
Sir Wilfrid (Canadian premier) and lady Laurier warmly welcomed . . . . 13 Aug. 1902

JERSEY CITY, U.S.A., population 1880, 120,722; 1890, 163,003; 1900, 206,433. See *New Jersey*.

JERUSALEM, called also SALEM, 1913 B.C. (*Gen.* xiv. 18). Its king was slain by Joshua, 1451 B.C. It was taken by David, 1048 B.C., who dwelt in the fort, calling it the city of David; see *Jews*, and *Holy Places*. Population about 1887, 43,000.

The first temple founded by Solomon, 1012 B.C.; and solemnly dedicated on Friday . . . 30 Oct. 1004
Jerusalem taken by Chosroes the Persian, A.D. 614; retaken by the emperor Heraclius, 628; by the Saracens, 637; and by the Crusaders, when 70,000 infidels were put to the sword: a new kingdom founded . . . . . 15 July, 1099
The "assize of Jerusalem," a code of laws, established by Godfrey of Bouillon, king . . . 1100
King Guy defeated at Tiberias, and Jerusalem taken by Saladin . . . . . 2 Oct. 1187
By the Turks, who drive away the Saracens, 1217 & 1239
Surrendered to the emperor Frederick II. by treaty, 1228
Surrendered to the Crusaders 1243
Taken by Carizmians 1244
Taken from the Christians 1291
Taken by the Turks 1516
Held by the French under Bonaparte . Feb. 1799
Jerusalem visited by the prince of Wales, &c., 31 March, 1862
Convention for the preservation of the holy sepulchre, signed on behalf of Russia, France, and Turkey . . . . 5 Sept. ,,
Jerusalem and the neighbourhood surveyed by a party of royal engineers since . . . Sept. 1864
German colony founded at Haifa 1868
Visited by the prince of Prussia, 4 Nov.; by the emperor of Austria . . . . . 9 Nov. 1869
Greatly benefited by sir Moses Montefiore, who visited it for the seventh time, when aged 90 . 1875
Discovery of pavement attributed to Constantine Nov. 1887
Ibrahim Hakki pasha appointed governor, 10 Nov. 1890
Mr. Carl Frosch's cycloramic painting of Jerusalem, A.D. 33, was exhibited in York-street, Westminster Dec. ,,
A panorama of Jerusalem, &c., exhibited in Victoria-street, Westminster . . . 18 April, 1892
A railway from Jerusalem to Jaffa constructed by a French company; opened . . . 13 Sept. ,,
The purchase of the reputed garden tomb of Christ, outside the Damascus gate, proposed by Mr. Henry A. Campbell, Mr. John Murray, the abp. of Canterbury, the bishop of Cashel, Dr. Dyce Brown, and others; much discussed, Oct.; subscriptions were received, Nov., Dec. 1892; the purchase, with adjoining land, effected for 2,000*l*., about 1,300*l*. subscribed . . . . June, 1894
Tewfik bey appointed governor . . 26 Oct. 1897
Visit of the German emperor; dedication of the Church of the Redeemer; the site of the house of the Virgin Mary on Mt. Zion given by the emperor to German Catholics . . 31 Oct. 1898
Djevad Bey appointed governor . . 11 June, 1901
Conflict in the church of the Holy Sepulchre between Latins and Greeks . . 4 Nov. ,,
34 Greeks, including 12 priests, sentenced from 1 week to 9 months' imprisonment . 9 July, 1902

CHRISTIAN KINGS.

Godfrey of Bouillon (styled himself "baron of the holy sepulchre") 1099
Baldwin I. 1100
Baldwin II. 1118
Fulk of Anjou 1131
Baldwin III. 1144
Amauri (or Almeric) 1162
Baldwin IV., 1173, a leper, set aside; his sister Sybilla, his heiress, 1185, on the suspicious death of her child, Baldwin V., crowned her second husband, Guy de Lusignan, in 1186
Henry of Champagne 1192
Amauri de Lusignan 1197
Jeanne de Brienne 1210
Emperor Frederick II. 1229-39
Protestant Bishopric of Jerusalem erected by treaty 7 Sept. 1841, under the protection of Great Britain and Prussia:
S. M. S. Alexander consecrated bishop . 7 Nov. 1841
Samuel Gobat, bishop, 1846; died 11 May . . 1879
Joseph Barclay, LL.D., consecrated 25 July, 1879; died . . . . 22 Oct. 1881
[No successor appointed; the compact dissolved June, 1886; formally announced, 18 Aug. 1887. An exclusively Anglican bishop was proposed by the archbishop of Canterbury; subscriptions invited, Feb. 1887. Dean G. F. P. Blyth, April, 1887, was appointed bishop.]
The Jerusalem, Cowper's Court, Cornhill, originally a coffee-house, opened early in the 17th century; burnt in the great fire 1666, and again in 1748, last rebuilt in 1880. It is supported by a company and subscribers, and forms a rendezvous for ship-owners, brokers, and others closely connected with shipping and commerce with the East, Australasia and the Cape.

"JERUSALEM DELIVERED," the great Italian epic, by Tasso, was published in 1580.

JERVIS'S ACTS, 11 & 12 Vict., cc. 42, 43 (1848), relate to legal proceedings against criminals.

JESTER is described as "a witty and jocose person, kept by princes to inform them of their faults, and of those of others, under the disguise of a waggish story." Several of our kings, particularly the Tudors, kept jesters. Rahere, the founder of St. Bartholomew's priory, West Smithfield, London, 1133, is said to have been a court jester and minstrel. There was a jester at court in the reigns of James I. and Charles I., but we hear of no licensed jester afterwards.

JESUITS. The society or company of Jesus, was founded by Ignatius Loyola, a page to Ferdinand V. of Spain, subsequently an officer in his army, and afterwards canonised. Having been wounded in both legs at the siege of Pampeluna, in 1521, he devoted himself to theology, and renounced the military for the ecclesiastical profession. He dedicated his life to the Blessed Virgin as her knight; made a pilgrimage to the Holy Land, and on his return laid the foundation of his society at Paris, 16 Aug. 1534. He presented his institutes, in 1539, to pope Paul III., who made many objections; but Ignatius adding to the vows of chastity, poverty, and obedience, a fourth of implicit submission to the holy see, the institution was confirmed by a bull, 27 Sept. 1540. The number of members was not to exceed sixty, but that restriction was taken off by another bull, 14 March, 1543; and popes Julius III., Pius V., and Gregory XIII. granted many privileges. Loyola died 31 July, 1556. Francis Xavier, and other missionaries, the first brethren, carried the order to the extremities of the habitable globe, but it met with great opposition in Europe, particularly in Paris: see *Paraguay* and *Jansenists*. The order still exists in many European states contrary to the laws.

The society condemned by the Sorbonne, Paris, 1554; expelled from France, 1594; re-admitted, 1604; but after several decrees is totally suppressed in France and its property confiscated . 1764
Ordered by parliament to be expelled from England, 1579, 1581, 1586, 1602; and by the Catholic relief act in 1829
Expelled from—Venice, 1607; Holland, 1708; Portugal, 1759; Spain 1767
Abolished by Clement XIV. . . . . 21 July, 1773
Restored by Pius VI. . . . . . 7 Aug. 1814
Father Pierre J. Beckx, elected general 1853; active and successful; retired, 1883 [died 4 March, 1887].
Expelled from—Belgium, 1818; Russia, 1820; Spain, 1820, 1835; France, 1831, 1845; Portugal, 1834; Sardinia, Austria, and other states, 1848; Italy and Sicily 1860
The chief of the order appeals to the king of Sardinia for redress of grievances . . 24 Oct. ,,
Report of the order; total number of Jesuits, 8167: in France, 2422, in 1866; 12,947 reported Jan. 1892
In consequence of the activity of the order on behalf of the papal supremacy, a bill for its expulsion from Germany passed by the parliament at Berlin (181-93), 19 June; promulgated . 5 July, 1872
The head-quarters of the order proposed to be removed from Rome to Malta . . . . Oct. 1873
Expulsion of the Jesuits from Italy, decreed 25 June; carried into execution, 20 Oct.—2 Nov. . . ,,
Father Curci, orthodox and eloquent, resigned (virtually expelled) for recommending the pope to submit to loss of temporal power, Oct. 1877; publishes "Il Moderno Dissidio fra la Chiesa e l'Italia." . . . . Dec. 1877
Submits to the Pope in a humble letter; received into favour . . . . about 16 Oct. 1884
27 Jesuits' colleges in France; 848 teachers . . 1879
The order in France dissolved by decree, 30 March, 1880
Decree for expulsion of Jesuits and other orders from France, 30 March; carried out . 30 June, ,,
A large gathering of Jesuits of all countries at Rome; Father Anderledy appointed Vicar-General Sept. 1883; dies . . . . 20 Jan. 1892
Father Martin elected general of the Jesuits at the monastery of Loyola, in Guipuzcoa . 1 Oct. ,,
The Jesuits leave France owing to the new associations law . . . . . . July–Oct. 1901

JESUIT'S BARK, called by the Spaniards fever-wood, from the cinchona or chinchona tree, discovered, it is said, by a Jesuit, about 1535 (and used by the order). Its virtues were not generally known till 1633, or 1638, when it cured of fever the wife of the viceroy (Chinchona) at Peru, hence termed *pulvis comitissæ*. It was sold at one period for its weight in silver, and was introduced into France in 1649; and is said to have cured Louis XIV. of fever when he was dauphin. It came into general use in 1680, and sir Hans Sloane introduced it here about 1700. The cinchona plant, largely planted in the Neilgherry hills, India, in 1861, is said to be thriving greatly, and also in Ceylon; see *Quinine*.

JESUS CHRIST, the SAVIOUR OF THE WORLD. 1 Tim. iii. 16. The following dates given in the English bible have been much controverted, and others have been proposed by eminent chronologers, such as Hales and Clinton, see *Nativity* and *Crucifixion*. The birth of Christ is dated, 4 B.C.; his baptism and first ministry, 27 A.D.; his crucifixion, resurrection, and ascension, 33 A.D.

The divinity of Christ, denied by the Arians, was affirmed by the council of Nice 325
Drawings illustrating the life of Christ by M. Tissot (died 8 Aug. 1902) exhibited in Bond-street, London . . . . . . March, 1896

JEU DE PAUME (the tennis court). The king having closed the hall of the assembly at Versailles, the third estate (*tiers-état*) met here, and swore not to dissolve till a constitution was established, 20 June, 1789. (It is the subject of a painting by David.) Commemorated 20 June, 1883.

JEWELLERY was received by Rebekah as a marriage gift, 1857 B.C. (*Gen.* xxiv. 53). Pliny the elder says he saw Lollia Paulina (wife of Caius Cæsar, and afterwards Caligula) wearing ornaments valued at a sum equal to 322,916*l.* sterling. Jewels were worn in France by Agnes Sorel in 1434, and encouraged in England about 1685. The standard of gold for jewellery, except wedding rings, was lowered by parliament in 1854. See *Gems*.

JEWEL ROBBERIES, see *Trials*, 1871, 1873, Dec. 1891, and Nov. 1903.

The countess of Dudley's jewels (value 15,000*l.*) stolen at Great Western Railway Station 12 Dec. 1874
Messrs. Williams, of Hatton Garden, London, robbed of 25,000*l.* worth . . . 25 March, 1876
Duchess of Cleveland, at Battle Abbey, Sussex, robbed of between 5000*l.* and 10,000*l.* worth, early in Feb. 1877
Countess of Aberdeen's (value above 5000*l.*) stolen, Halstead Place, Sevenoaks, Kent . 19 Nov. ,,
Hatton Garden Post-Office, London; gas suddenly extinguished at 5 p.m., two mail bags stolen, one containing diamonds, and other jewels, watches, &c., in registered letters; value above 15,000*l.* 16 Nov. 1881
Lord Arthur Hill Trevor's house, Bryn-Kinalet, near Chirk, Wales, robbed of jewels valued 60,000*l.* Sunday, 4 Dec. ,,
Lady Miles's jewels (value 30,000*l.*), at Leigh court, near Bristol, stolen, Sunday . . 18 Dec. 1892
Baroness Schroeder's jewels (value 3,000*l.*), at Worleston, Cheshire . . . 16 March, 1893
Countess Wilton's jewels at the Hatch, near Maidenhead . . . . 1 Aug. ,,
Mr. Spyzer, of Antwerp, overpowered by chloroform at 70 Hatton garden, and robbed of diamonds, &c. (value 20,000*l.*) . . . . 13 Sept. 1894
Mrs. Langtry *v.* the Union bank, Sloane-street, to recover 35,000*l.*, the value of jewels deposited by her at the bank and delivered up to an unauthorised person bearing a forged order, 24 Aug. 1895; verdict for the defendants without costs, they agreeing to pay Mrs. Langtry 10,000*l.* . 5 May, 1896
At the Diamond Merchants' Alliance, Piccadilly, jewel robbery, estimated value, 15,000*l.* 30 or 31 Oct. 1897
The dowager-duchess of Sutherland's jewels (value about 25,000*l.*) stolen at the Nord railway station, Paris, 17 Oct. 1898; Wm. Johnson pleads guilty to the possession of about 5,000*l.* worth, sentenced to 7 years' imprisonment . 18 Jan. 1899
The princess Leiningen's jewels (many heirlooms), estimated value 6,000*l.*, stolen from an hotel at Liverpool . . . . . . 30 April, 1900
Lord Anglesea's jewels, valued over 30,000*l.*, stolen from an hotel in Piccadilly, 10 Sept. 1901; Julian Gault, 23, valet, pleads guilty, sentenced to 5 years' imprisonment . . . . 22 Oct. 1901
Lady Carnarvon's jewel-case extracted from a dressing case on journey from Paris to London (value considerable, amount not stated) . . . 1902
Lady Bowyer's valuables stolen from her railway compartment at the Gare de Lyon, Paris (value 3,000*l.*) . . . . 5 Oct. 1903

Messrs. Knight, Frank and Rutley, of Conduit-street, premises entered prior to sale (value 8,000*l.*) . . . . 15 Oct. 1903

JEWISH COLONIZATION ASSOCIATION, registered as a company by the Board of Trade, Sept. 1891. Nominal capital, 2,000,000*l.*; promoted by lord Rothschild, sir Julian Goldsmid, and other gentlemen to carry out baron Hirsch's scheme for the emigration of distressed Jews from Europe and Asia to N. or S. America. Baron Maurice de Hirsch, born 1831; died in Hungary, 21 April, 1896.

First general meeting; amount subscribed 39,826*l.* (Messrs. N. M. Rothschild, 10,000*l.*; Messrs. R. Raphael, 4,000*l.*; sir Julian Goldsmid, 3,000*l.*; Messrs. S. Montagu, Mrs. Nathaniel Montefiore, E. L. Raphael, and Messrs. Stern, 2,000*l.* each), 14 Oct. 1891; 89,463*l.* received up to . 29 Dec. 1891
Negotiations with the Argentine republic for settlements. The arrangements placed under the command of lieut.-col. Albert Goldsmid . . Dec. ,,
"Colony Hirsch" formed in N. W. Canada in . 1892
Early disorders composed; good report by lieut.-col. Goldsmid . . . . 11 June, 1893
The society's first annual report issued . . Jan. ,,
Four colonies in the Argentine republic . Jan. 1894
Council appointed for the direction of affairs, M. S. H. Goldschmidt president . . . May, 1896
Successful progress reported . . . . April, 1898

JEWISH DISABILITIES, see under *Jews*, 1269-1867.

JEWISH ERA AND CALENDAR. The Jews usually employed the era of the Seleucidæ until the 15th century, when a new mode of computing was adopted. They date from the creation, which they consider to have been 3760 years and 3 months before the commencement of our era. To reduce Jewish time to ours, subtract 3761 years. The Jewish year consists of either twelve or thirteen months, of 29 or 30 days. The civil year commences with the month Tisri, immediately after the new moon following the autumnal equinox; the ecclesiastical year begins with Nisan.

Civil year, 5662–63.

Sebat	9 Jan.	1902
Adar . . 8 Feb.; *Ve-Adar* or 2nd Adar*		,,
Nisan or Abib	8 April,	,,
Ijar	8 May,	,,
Sivan	6 June,	,,
Thammuz	6 July,	,,
Ab	4 Aug.	,,
Elul	3 Sept.	,,
Tisri (first day of new year, 5663)	2 Oct.	,,
Marchesvan	1 Nov.	,,
Chislev	1 Dec.	,,
Thebet	31 Dec.	,,

The Jewish calendar is given annually in the best almanacks.

JEWS, successively called Hebrews, Israelites, and Jews, the descendants of Abraham, with whom God made a covenant, 1898 B.C. *Gen.* xvii. See *Jerusalem*. Computed number of Jews in the world May 1889, 6,300,000 (Europe 5,400,000, Africa 350,000, America, 250,000; 360,000 in New York in 1902). The following dates are generally those by Usher given in the English Bible; differing dates are given by Hales, Clinton, and other chronologers.

Call of Abram to enter Canaan . . . B.C. 1921
Isaac born to Abraham 1896
Birth of Esau and Jacob 1837
Death of Abraham 1822
Joseph sold into Egypt 1729

* Intercalated every third year, to supply the deficiency of the Jewish year of 354 days.

The male children of the Israelites thrown into the Nile; Moses born 1571
The Passover instituted; the Israelites go out of Egypt, and cross the Red Sea 1491
The law promulgated from Mount Sinai . . . ,,
The Tabernacle set up 1490
Death of Moses; Joshua leads the Israelites into Canaan and conquers it 1451
The first bondage (Othniel, judge, 1405) . . . 1413
The second bondage (Ehud, 1325) 1343
The third bondage (Deborah and Barak, 1285) . 1305
The fourth bondage (Gideon, 1245) . . . 1252
The fifth bondage (Jephthah, 1187) . . . 1206
The sixth bondage 1157
Samson slays the Philistines 1136
Samuel governs as judge, about 1120
Samson pulls down the temple of Dagon . . . 1117
Saul made king 1095
David slays Goliath, about 1063
Death of Saul; David made king 1055
David besieges and takes Jerusalem, and makes it his capital 1048
Solomon king, 1015; lays the foundation of the temple, 1012; which is dedicated . . . 1004
Death of Solomon; the kingdom divided . . . 975

KINGDOM OF ISRAEL.

Jeroboam establishes idolatry 975
Bethel taken from Jeroboam: 500,000 Israelites slain 957
Israel afflicted with the famine predicted by Elijah 906
The Syrians besiege Samaria 901
Elijah translated to heaven 896
Miracles of Elisha the prophet 895
The Assyrian invasion under Phul . . . 771
Pekah besieges Jerusalem 741
Samaria taken by the king of Assyria: the ten tribes are carried into captivity, and an end is put to the kingdom of Israel 721

KINGDOM OF JUDAH.

Shishak, king of Egypt, takes Jerusalem, and pillages the temple 971
Abijah defeats the king of Israel, 500,000 men are slain in battle 957
Asa defeats the Ethiopians; abolishes idolatry . 941
Jehoshaphat orders the law to be taught 912; defeats the Ammonites, &c. 896
Usurpation and death of Athaliah 884
Hazael desolates Judah 857
Pekah, king of Israel, lays siege to Jerusalem; 120,000 of the men of Judah are slain in one day. 741
Hezekiah abolishes idolatry 726
Sennacherib invades Judea, but the destroying angel enters the camp of the Assyrians, and in one night destroys 185,000 of them 710
Holofernes said to have been killed at the siege of Bethulia by Judith 656
In repairing the temple, Hilkiah discovers the book of the law, and Josiah keeps a solemn Passover . 624
Nebuchadnezzar subjugates Judea 605
He takes Jerusalem after a long siege . . . 588
Jerusalem fired, the temple burnt, the walls razed to the ground 587

KINGS.		PROPHETS.
Saul began to reign	B.C. 1095	Samuel.
David, king of Judah, 1055; of all Israel,	1048	Nathan.
Solomon ,, ...	1015	

B.C.	Kings of Judah.	Kings of Israel.	
975.	Rehoboam .	Jeroboam I.	Ahijah.
958.	Abijah	,,	
955.	Asa	Nadab (954)	Azariah.
953.	,,	Baasha ,,	Hanani.
930.	,,	Elah ,,	Jehu.
929.	,,	Zimri	,,
925.	,,	Omri	,,
918.	,,	Ahab	Elijah.
914.	Jehoshaphat	,,	,,
897.		Ahaziah	Elisha.
896.		Jehoram or Joram	Jahaziel.
889	Jthoram	,,	,,
885.	Ahaziah	,,	,,
884	Athaliah	Jehu.	
878	Joash or Jehoahaz	,,	
857.	,, ,,	Jehoahaz	
839.	Amaziah	Jehoash (841)	

B.C.	*Kings of Judah.*	*Kings of Israel.*	PROPHETS,
825.	Amaziah	Jeroboam II.	Jonah.
810.	Uzziah or Azariah	,,	Hosea Amos.
784.	,, ,,	Anarchy	
773.	,, ,,	Zechariah	Joel
772.	,, ,,	Shallum. Menahem.	
761.	,, ,,	Pekahiah.	
759.	,, ,,	Pekah.	
758.	Jotham	,,	Isaiah & Micah.
742.	Ahaz	,,	
730.	,,	Hoshea.	
726.	Hezekiah	[Captivity, 721.]	Nahum.
698.	Manasseh.		
643.	Amon		Jeremiah.
641.	Josiah		Zephaniah
610.	Jehoahaz (Shallum). Jehoiakim.		Habakkuk
599.	Jehoiachin (Coniah), Zedekiah		Daniel. Ezekiel.

BABYLONISH CAPTIVITY.

Daniel prophesies at Babylon . . . . . B.C. 603
Shadrach, Meshach, and Abed-nego, refusing to worship the golden image, are cast into a fiery furnace, but are delivered by the angel . . . 587
Obadiah prophesies . . . . ,,
Daniel declares the meaning of the handwriting against Belshazzar; cast into the lions' den; prophesies the return from captivity, and the coming of the Messiah 538

RETURN FROM CAPTIVITY.

Cyrus, sovereign of all Asia, publishes an edict for the return of the Jews and rebuilding of the temple 536
Haggai and Zechariah prophets 520
The second temple finished . . 10 March, 515
The Jews delivered from Haman by Esther . . 510
Ezra, the priest, arrives in Jerusalem to reform abuses 458
Here begin the 70 weeks of years predicted by Daniel, being 490 years before the crucifixion of the Redeemer 457
The walls of Jerusalem built by Nehemiah . . 445
Malachi the prophet 415

[The Scripture history of the Jews ends, according to *Eusebius*, in 442 B.C.; and from this time Josephus and the Roman historians give the best account of the Jews.]

Alexander the Great marches against Jerusalem to besiege it, but, it is said, on seeing Jaddus, the high-priest, clad in his robes, he declares he had seen such a figure in Macedonia, inviting him to Asia, and promising to deliver the Persian empire into his hands; he goes to the temple, and offers sacrifices to the God of the Jews 332
Jerusalem taken by Ptolemy Soter 320
Ptolemy Philadelphus said to employ 72 Jews to translate the Scriptures . . . about 285
The Sadducee sect formed 250
Jews massacred at Alexandria 216
Antiochus takes Jerusalem, pillages the temple, and slays 40,000 of the inhabitants 170
Government of the Maccabees begins 166
Treaty with the Romans; the first on record with the Jews 161
Judas Hyrcanus Aristobulus assumes the title of "king of the Jews" 107
Alexander Jannæus suppresses a rebellion of Pharisees cruelly 86
Jerusalem taken by the Roman legions under Pompey 63
The temple plundered by Crassus 54
Antipater made intendant of Judæa by Julius Cæsar 49
Herod, son of Antipater, marries Mariamne, granddaughter of the high priest 42
Invasion of the Parthians 40
Herod employs the aid of the senate; they decree him to be the king . . . . . ,,
Jerusalem taken by Herod and the Roman general Sosius 37
Herod kills Mariamne, 29; rebuilds the temple 29-18
JESUS CHRIST born 4
Pontius Pilate is made procurator of Judea A.D. 26
John the Baptist begins to preach . . . . ,,
Christ's ministry and miracles, 27-33; his crucifixion and resurrection 33
The Jews persecuted for refusing to worship Caligula 38
Receive the right of Roman citizenship . . . 41
Claudius banishes Jews from Rome 50
Invasion of Vespasian 68
Jews settle at Merida, Spain 69
Titus takes Jerusalem; the city and temple sacked and burnt, and 1,100,000 of the Jews perish, 8 Sept. 70
Targum of Onkelos written about 100
Adrian rebuilds Jerusalem (calling it Ælia Capitolina), and erects a temple to Jupiter . . . 130
Rebellion of Bar-cochba; takes Jerusalem 132; killed in war with Julius Severus, 135; desolation of Judea 135-136
More than 580,000 of the Jews are slain by the Romans . . . . ,,
Jews favoured by Antoninus Pius; college of Jamnia opened 138
The Mischna (see *Talmud*) compiled by Rabbi Judah, the prince . . . . . . before 200
The Jews favoured by Severus, 196; by Constantine, 310; by Julian, 363; persecuted by Constans 353
Jews massacred at Alexandria 415
The Babylonian Talmud completed . . about 600
Jerusalem taken by Omar 653
Jews first mentioned in English chronicles . . 740
Formation of the sect termed Karaïtes (*which see*) by Anan, about 754
Jewish college founded at Cordova 948
Talmud translated into Arabic 1006
Jews said to be banished from England by Canute 1020
Polygamy in Christian countries prohibited by the Jewish synod at Worms 1030
Jews return to England 1066

[Chiefly settled in London and Lincoln.]

The Jews massacred in London, on the coronation day of Richard I., at the instigation of the priests 1189
500 Jews besieged in York castle by the mob, cut each other's throats to avoid their fury . . 1190
Jews of both sexes imprisoned; their eyes or teeth plucked out, and numbers inhumanly butchered, by king John 1204
The Rabbi Moses Maimonides died . . . . ,,
700 Jews are slain in London, a Jew having forced a Christian to pay him more than 2*s.* per week as interest on a loan of 20*s.* (*Stow.*) . . . 1262
Statute that no Jew should enjoy a freehold . . 1269
Every Jew lending money on interest compelled to wear a plate on his breast, signifying that he was a usurer, or to quit the realm. (*Stow.*) . . 1274
267 Jews hanged and quartered, accused of clipping coin 1278
All Jews (16,511) banished from England. (*Rapin.*) 1290
Much pillaged and persecuted in France during the 14th and 15th centuries.
A fatal distemper raging in Europe, they are suspected of having poisoned the springs, and numbers are massacred. (*Lenglet.*) . . . 1348
Several hundred thousand Jews banished from Spain, Portugal, and France . . . 1492-94
Edicts against Jews rescinded by pope Sixtus V. . 1585
Jews favoured in Holland 1603
After having been banished England 370 years, they are permitted to return by Cromwell . . 1650
Who grants a pension to Manasseh Ben Israel . 1655
First Portuguese synagogue, King-street, Duke's-place, erected 1656
Statute to compel them to maintain their protestant children enacted 1702
Jews acquire right to possess land in England . . 1723
Bill to naturalise the professors of the Jewish religion in Ireland (where 200 Jews then resided) refused the royal assent 1746
Statute to naturalise them in England passed . . 1753
Repealed on the petition of all the cities . . 1754
The Jews of Spain, Portugal, and Avignon are declared to be citizens of France 1790
The synagogue, Duke's-place, London, E., consecrated . . . . 26 March ,,
The Jews in France emancipated . . 27 Sept. 1791

The Denmark-court (Strand) synagogue constituted, 1797; centenary celebrated . 21 Nov. 1897
Sitting of the great Sanhedrim of Paris convened by the emperor Napoleon . . . . 18 Sept. 1806
Jews' hospital, London, founded . . . . . . ,,
London society for promoting Christianity among the Jews established 1808
Jews' free school, Spitalfields, London, established 1817
Alexander of Russia grants land on the sea of Azoph to converted Jews . . . . 1 Sept. 1820
The brothers Rothschild made barons of the Austrian empire 1822
Jews' orphan asylum founded 1831
Mr. (aft. sir) Francis H. Goldsmid, the first Jew called to the British bar. 1833
Mr. David Salomons elected sheriff of London (the first Jewish one); an act passed to enable him to act . . . . 24 June, 1835
Bill for Jewish emancipation in England lost on the second reading by a majority in the commons, 228 against 165 . . . . 17 May, 1836
Moses Montefiore, esq., elected sheriff of London, and knighted by the queen, being the first Jew on whom that honour has been conferred . 9 Nov. 1837
Ukase of the emperor of Russia, permitting the title of citizen of the first class to be held by any Jew who renders himself worthy of it 1839
Owing to the disappearance of a Greek priest, a persecution of the Jews began at Damascus (see *Damascus*) . . . . 1 Feb. 1840
Jewish mission to the East under sir Moses Montefiore . . . . ,,
Congregation of British Jews formed (*see below*) 1840-1
Sir F. H. Goldsmid founded the Jewish Infant school 1841
Sir Isaac Lyon Goldsmid, the first Jew made a Baronet . . . . ,,
Dr. Nathan M. Adler installed chief rabbi of the Jews in the empire, London . . 9 July, 1845
Act to relieve Jews elected to municipal offices from taking oaths, &c., 9 Vict. 1846
Baron Lionel de Rothschild returned to Parliament for the city of London by a majority of 6619 votes; his opponent, lord John Manners, polling only 3104 . . . . 3 July, 1849
Alderman Salomons elected member for Greenwich, 28 June, 1851
Neither permitted to sit . . . . . . ,,
The Jews' Oaths of Abjuration bill passed the house of commons . . . . . . 3 July, ,,
Baron Rothschild again returned for the city of London at the general elections, July, 1852; March, 1857; July, 1857; and July, 1865.
Violent outbreak against the Jews in Stockholm, 3 Sept. 1852
The Jewish Oath bill passed in commons, 15 April; thrown out in the lords . . . 29 April, 1853
Alderman Salomons the first Jewish lord mayor of London . . . . 9 Nov. 1855
The Jewish Oath bill several times passed in the commons and thrown out in the lords . . 1854-7
Edgar Mortara, a Jewish child, forcibly taken from his parents by order of the archbishop of Bologna, on the plea of having been baptized when an infant by a Roman Catholic maid-servant 24 June, 1858
Sir F. H. Goldsmid, the first Jew made Q.C. . . ,,
An act passed enabling Jews to sit in parliament by resolution of the house . . . . . July, ,,
Baron Lionel de Rothschild takes his seat as M.P. for London . . . . 26 July, ,,
To commemorate this event he endowed a scholarship in the City of London School . . . . ,,
The French government having in vain urged Mortara's restoration to his parents, sir Moses Montefiore proceeds to Rome (but obtains no redress), 22 Dec. ,,
Alderman Salomons elected M.P. for Greenwich (died 18 July, 1873); baron Meyer de Rothschild for Hythe . . . . 15 Feb. 1859
Protest respecting the seizure of the boy Mortara signed at London by the abp. of Canterbury, and bishops, noblemen, and gentlemen, sent to the French ambassador, Oct.; and presented by lord John Russell . . . . Nov. ,,
Board of guardians for the relief of the Jewish poor, one of the grand institutions of the Jews in London, founded in . . . . ,,

Oppressive laws against the Jews in the Austrian empire annulled . . . . 6, 10 Jan. 1860
Act passed permitting Jewish M.P.'s to omit from the oath the words "on the faith of a Christian," 6 Aug. ,,
Additional political privileges granted to the Jews in Russia, 26 Jan.; and in Poland . June 1862
Jews persecuted at Rome . . . . . . Dec. 1864
Alderman Benjamin Samuel Phillips, second Jewish lord mayor . . . . 9 Nov. 1865
Persecution of Jews at Bucharest reported, July, 1866
A synagogue at Berlin, said to be the largest and most beautiful in the world, consecrated, 5 Sept. ,,
Jewish emancipation bill, Hungary, received royal assent . . . . 29 Dec. 1867
Benjamin Disraeli, of Jewish extraction, premier of England . . . . 29 Feb. 1868
Jews' synagogue at Barnsbury, London, N., founded by baron F. Rothschild, 24 Dec. 1867, consecrated 29 March, ,,
Jews permitted to return to Spain . . . . Oct. ,,
Jewish congress at Pesth opened by the minister of public worship, Eötvös . . . . 14 Dec. ,,
It closes and presents the new statutes to the ministers . . . . 25 Feb. 1869
Jewish reform convention at Philadelphia, U.S., alterations in rituals, &c., resolved on . Oct. ,,
Alfred Davis, a Jew, a munificent benefactor of education, Jewish and Christian, died . 7 Jan. 1870
New central synagogue in Great Portland-st., W., founded by baron Rothschild, 18 March, 1869; consecrated . . . . 7 April, ,,
"Hebrew Literature Society" established in London 29 June, ,,
Anglo-Jewish Association constituted for the moral, social, and intellectual progress of Jews (in connection with the Universal Israelitish Alliance, in Paris). First president, the late Mr. Jacob Waley, M.A. . . . . 2 July, ,,
The emperor of Brazil attended worship at the West Central London synagogue . . 8 July, ,,
Jews permitted to work on Sundays by a Workshops Act . . . . ,,
Society formed at Birmingham to resist proselytism ,,
A Jew made M.A. at Oxford (after the abolition of tests) . . . . 22 June, 1871
Sir George Jessel, a Jew, solicitor-general, Nov. 1871; master of the rolls . . . 29 Aug. 1873
Estimated number of Jews in Great Britain, 51,520; in London, 39,833 1876
New synagogue founded at Bayswater . 7 June, 1877
Movement against the Jews in Berlin, &c., (*Judenhetze*); opposed by Mommsen, Virchow, and others; censured by the crown prince; debate in the chambers; no vote, 22 Nov. Many Jews leave Berlin, Dec. 1880
Anti-Semitic league formed; presents a petition to Bismarck to restrict the liberty of the Prussian Jews . . . . 13 April, 1881
Jews severely persecuted at Kieff and other places in South Russia . . . . May, ,,
About 60,000 Russian Jews request permission to return to Spain, granted . . . . June, ,,
Persecution going on in Prussia, the emperor interfering to stop it . . . . . Aug. ,,
Severe restrictive edict against the Jews in Russia issued, but not *fully* carried out, increasing civil disabilities . . . . May *et seq.* 1882
Committees formed at Berlin and London to receive money to help Jewish emigration, April; 108,759*l.* received in London . . . . . . 25 Oct. ,,
New synagogue at Abbey-road, London, N.W. consecrated . . . . 30 July, ,,
The Jews violently attacked at Presburg, Hungary; martial law proclaimed . . 29 Sept. ,,
Trial of Jews (see *Hungary*) 1883
Violent attacks on Jews at St. Petersburg, Pesth, Zala Egerszeg, &c. . . . . July, Aug. ,,
Death of Charlotte, Baroness de Rothschild, great benefactress . . . . . . 13 Mar. 1884
Jews still persecuted in Russia . Aug. *et seq.* ,,
Commission to enquire into the condition and rights of the Jews . . . . . . Oct. ,,
The Jews enjoy at present full citizenship in Europe (with the exception of Portugal, Roumania, Russia and Spain); also in the United States . 1884

Sir Moses Montefiore completes his 100th year, celebrated by Jews all over the world as a very great benefactor (27 Oct. Jewish Calendar) 25-26 Oct. 1884; died . . . 28 July, 1885
Sir Nathaniel de Rothschild, son of Lionel, created a peer; takes his seat 9 July, 1885; made lord-lieut. of Buckinghamshire . . . May, 1889
Estimated population of the Jews in the world, 6,377,602 1885
Exhibition of Anglo-Jewish antiquities at the Royal Albert Hall opened . . . 4 April, 1887
Expulsion of Jews from Odessa and Finland decreed . . . . . April, 1888
Henry Aaron Isaacs, 3rd Jewish lord mayor Nov. 1889
Dr. Nathan Adler, chief rabbi, London, dies 21 Jan. 1890
Enforcement of the severe edict of May, 1882, against the Jews in Russia, about 2,000,000 said to be ordered, July; officially contradicted at St. Petersburg, 6 Aug.; many Jews expelled from Russia . . . . . . Dec. ,,
At a great meeting in the Guildhall, London, an appeal to the Czar to mitigate the laws against the Jews agreed to (see under *London*, Feb. 1891 10 Dec. ,,
Dr. Hermann Adler chosen chief rabbi by delegates . . . . . 4 June, 1891
Expulsion of Jews from S. Russia ordered about 29 May ,,
Relaxation of the persecution; enforcement of the decree of expulsion from St. Petersburg adjourned . . . . about 18 July ,,
3,000 acres of land at Hulberton, Cumberland county, New Jersey, purchased by Mr. Leon Lait, a Russian, for a Hebrew colony . . about 20 July ,,
The Jewish Colonization Association, *which see*, founded . . . . about 11 Sept. ,,
Anti-Jewish riots at Starodoub and other districts in Russia, about 30 deaths; order restored by the military, 170 arrests . . 11 Oct. *et seq.* ,,
New synagogue at Dublin consecrated by the chief rabbi Adler . . . . . 4 Dec. 1892
Large expulsion of Jews from Russia ordered before 1 Nov., 10 Feb.; execution of the order suspended, reported . . . 4 March, 1893
Mr. Jacob Montefiore, philanthropist, died, aged 95 . . . . 3 Nov. 1895
Sir Julian Goldsmid, M.P., born 1838; died 7 Jan. 1896
Baron de Hirsch died; many bequests to Jewish and other charities . . . 21 April, ,,
Foreign Jews permitted to enter Russia . 28 June, ,,
Meeting of the Jewish historical society of England to commemorate the re-settlement of the Jews (*see above*), 1650; Dr. Adler presided, Maccabean rooms, Piccadilly . . . . 7 Feb. 1897
Death of the grand rabbi Lazare Wogue at Paris, reported . . . . . 15 April, ,,
Zionist congress (*which see*) . . . 29 Aug. ,,
New synagogue in Mare-street, S. Hackney, opened by the hon. Walter Rothschild . 19 Sept. ,,
Passport laws regarding Jews in the medical profession repealed by the czar . . . 8 Dec. ,,
Fifth annual "Hanuca" military service for Jewish marines and soldiers at the Hampstead synagogue . . . . . . 19 Dec. ,,
Baron Ferdinand de Rothschild, popular landlord, patron of art, born 1839, died (bequeaths over 127,000*l.* to charities) . . 17 Dec. 1898
Baroness de Hirsch, philanthropist, died, 2 April, 1899
Death of Dr. Israel Hildesheimer, an eminent rabbi, aged 79, reported . . . 17 June, ,,
Lady Simon (Miss Rachel Salaman), author of "Records and Reflections" and "By the Still Waters," born 1823, died . . 7 July ,,
Dr. David Kaufmann, a remarkable cosmopolitan writer, died, aged 47 . . . mid July, ,,
Large influx of foreign Jews during . . . 1900
Persecution of Jews in Russia, May, 1899; hundreds refused at the universities . . Sept. 1901
Conference of Jewish literary societies meets, Bloomsbury . . . . 29 June, 1902
Lord Meath issues a list of restrictive laws against the Jews in Roumania, Aug. 22; *which see* Sept. ,,
Sir Marcus Samuel, 4th Jewish lord mayor, Nov. 1902
Death of sir Joseph Sebag Montefiore, pres. of Board of Elders of the Ancient Congregation of Spanish and Portuguese Jews, generous benefactor to Jewish charities and institutions, 18 Jan. 1903
Jewish conference at Manchester on the Kishineff massacres . . . . . . 14 June, ,,
Jewish Colonization Association act, royal assent, 21 July, ,,
Zionist Congress at Basel opens, . . 23 Aug. ,,
See *Russia*, 19 April, 1903, *et seq.*

REFORMED OR BRITISH JEWS. In 1840 and 1841 a congregation was formed by Spanish and German Jews, for simplifying the ritual observances. Their West London Synagogue in Burton-street, opened 1 Jan. 1842; removed to Margaret-street, Regent-street, 1849; succeeded by a magnificent synagogue, in Upper Berkeley-street, consecrated 22 Sept. 1870

The Reformed Jews recognise the authority of the Old Testament or written law only, and reject the oral law embodied in the Talmud, which is accepted by the Orthodox or Rabbinical Jews.

JEWISH REFORM UNION, to provide services in English for Jews to whom the ordinary synagogue service does not appeal, formed 1901.

JEW'S HARP (probably Jaws' harp), an ancient instrument. Charles Eulenstein produced remarkable effects with Jews' harps at the Royal Institution, London, 15 Feb. 1828.

JEYNES or **JAINS**, a sect of Buddhists, in India, dating from the 9th century. They do not recognise a creator, but believe matter to be eternal, and refrain from destroying life, considering animals to be sacred.

Their discipline is very strict; a trial for defamation of character by a libel, accusing certain members of breaking the laws of caste, lasted 34 days at Moorshedabad, and cost above 100,000 rupees. The verdict was for the defendants March, 1891

JEYPOOR, one of the four principal Rajpoot states of India, tributary to the British. The new capital, Jeypoor, termed the Paris of India, was built in the last century. The Maharajah, friendly to the British, by whom he was supported, died in Sept. 1880; he nominated a successor, installed 30 Sept. 1880. Pop. 1901, 159,550.

JEZREELITES, New and Latter House of Israel, was founded by James Jershom Jezreel (James White), who died 1885. They asserted that the Gospel is sufficient for the salvation of the soul, but for the salvation of the body the Law must be added. Jezreel's widow, "Queen Esther," died in 1888; since then the sect has become almost extinct. Their headquarters were at Gillingham, near Chatham.

JIDDAH. See *Jedda*.

JIHAD, or religious warfare against unbelievers, although inculcated in the Mohammedan law, was prohibited by the Sheeahs, and only permitted by the Sonnites in some cases; certainly not with any nation with whom they had made a treaty of peace. The Jihad was preached by fanatics in India in 1871, and prohibited by government.

A jihad against the Russians was announced by the sheikh-ul-Islam, at Constantinople, about 28 May, 1877
A jihad against the British in Afghanistan, proposed by Shere Ali . . . . Oct. 1878
A jihad against the British was proclaimed by Arabi Pasha . . . . about 24 July, 1882
A copy of the Ameer's book on Jihad reported in England, *Times* . . . . 11 Sept. 1897

See *Egypt*.

JINGO PARTY, a name given (in 1878) to persons who preferred war with Russia to submission to her aggressive policy. A popular song said—

"We don't want to fight, but, by jingo if we do,
We've got the ships, we've got the men, and we've got the money too."

"By jingo" occurs in Jarvis's "Don Quixote," and the "Vicar of Wakefield."

JOAN OF ARC, the maid of Orleans, born at Domremy, imagined that she had a divine commission to expel the English, who under the earl of Salisbury were besieging Orleans. Charles VII. entrusted her with the command of some French troops, and she raised the siege, and entered Orleans with supplies, 29 April, 1429; and the English, who were before the place from 12 Oct. preceding, abandoned the enterprise 8 May following. She captured several towns in the possession of the English, whom she defeated in a battle near Patay, 18 June, 1429. She was wounded several times herself, but never shed any blood with her own hand. She was taken at the siege of Compiègne, 25 May, 1430; and, after a trial, burnt for a witch at Rouen, 30 May, 1431. A statue of Joan of Arc, the work of the late princess Marie of France, was inaugurated at Orleans, 13 Sept. 1851, and the 435th anniversary of the deliverance of the city was celebrated there on 14 May, 1865. The anniversary of her death celebrated, 30 May, 1878. See *Patay*. Her statue at Beaurevoir unveiled 9 Aug.; at Domremy 26 Aug. 1891; at Chinon, 14 Aug. 1893; at Rheims, 15 July, 1896; at St. Pierre-le-Moutier, 24 Aug. 1902. Her beatification approved by the pope, 27 Jan. 1894. Her canonization proposed, Feb. 1903.

JOCKEY CLUB. See *Races*.

JOHANNESBURG, see *Transvaal*, 1887 *et seq.* Population 80,000, reported, July, 1902.

JOHN BULL, a nickname given to Englishmen, is said to be derived from Dr. Arbuthnot's satire "John Bull," published 1712.—*Brewer*. "John Bull," a comedy, by George Colman the younger, was performed 1805. The "John Bull," a Tory newspaper, supported by Theodore Hook, was first published 1820. Its publication ceased in 1892.

"JOHN COMPANY," a name formerly given to the East India company, was sometimes given to the South Africa company, 1891. See *Zambesi*.

JOHN DOE AND RICHARD ROE, names well known, as standing pledges for the prosecution of suits. In early times real and substantial persons were required to pledge themselves to answer to the crown for an amercement or fine set upon the plaintiff, for raising a false accusation, if he brought an action without cause, or failed in it; and in 1285, 13 Edw. I. sheriffs and bailiffs were, before they made deliverance of the distress, to receive pledges for pursuing the suit, and for the return of the property, if return were awarded. But this becoming a matter of form, the fictitious names of Doe and Roe were used until the form was declared to be no longer necessary by the Common Law Procedure Act, 1852.

JOHN O'GROAT'S HOUSE, an ancient house formerly situated on Duncan's Bay Head, the most northerly point of Great Britain, deriving its name from John of Groat, or Groot, and his brothers, originally from Holland, said to have settled here about 1489. The house was of an octagon shape, being one room, with eight windows and eight doors, to admit eight members of the family, the heads of different branches of it, to prevent their quarrels for precedence at table. Each came in by this contrivance at his own door, and sat at an octagon table, at which, of course, there was no chief place or head.

JOHN, ST., see *Newfoundland*, *Cambridge*, *New Brunswick*, and *Oxford*.

St. John's Night, or Midsummer eve, 23 June: bonfires are still made in Ireland, and in some parts of England, and thought to be the relic of a pagan custom—resembling the Phœnician worship of Baal.

JOHN, ST., KNIGHTS OF, see *Malta*.

THE KNIGHTS OF ST. JOHN (*Johanniter Ritter*), a Lutheran order of high rank, formed by Frederick William III. of Prussia, 23 May, 1812, and reorganised 15 Oct. 1852. These knights co-operated with the knights of St. John of Malta and various other bodies in rendering energetic assistance to the wounded during the Franco-Prussian war, in 1870-1; the chief office being at the ancient gate of the priory of St. John, Clerkenwell, London, E.C.; the prince of Wales a prior of the order, 1892.

The Russian and English orders claim connection with the original institution at Malta as two of its *langues*.

The St. John Ambulance Association, founded and established by the Order of St. John of Jerusalem in 1877: its objects are—1. The dissemination of instruction in "first aid," *i.e.*, the preliminary treatment of the sick and injured *pending the doctor's arrival*; 2, lectures to women on home nursing and hygiene; 3, the deposit in appropriate localities of material (such as stretchers, hampers, splints, bandages, &c.) for use in case of accident; 4, the development of ambulance corps for the transport of the sick and injured. Upwards of 250 administrative "centres" and some thousands of "detached classes" have been formed in all parts of the United Kingdom, India, the colonies, and elsewhere abroad, and over 100,000 certificates of proficiency have been awarded. Sir Edmund A. H. Lechmere, bart., M.P., chairman; John Furley, esq., honorary director of stores and manager of transport department; major sir Herbert C. Perrott, bart., chief secretary. The prince of Wales installed at St. John's Gate as Grand Prior of the Order of the Hospital of St. John of Jerusalem in England incorporated by Royal Charter, 18 July, 1888. The prince of Wales (Grand Prior) unveils a memorial tablet in St. John's church to the members of the brigade who died on service in S. Africa, 11 June; presents medals, &c., 14 July, 1902. New hall and ambulance rooms at St. John's gate opened by prince of Wales, 9 July, 1903.

JOHN'S GATE, ST. (St. John's Square, Clerkenwell, London), a fine vestige of monastic building, was the gate of the priory of St. John of Jerusalem (suppressed in 1540), and was the place where the *Gentleman's Magazine* was first published, 6 March, 1731. The house was often visited by Dr. Johnson, Garrick, and their friends. The gate was purchased for the Order of the Knights of St. John, by Sir Edmund A. H. Lechmere, bart., secretary of the English league. The first meeting held here 24 June, 1874.

JOHNSON'S CLUB, see *Literary Club*. A society for the study of Dr. Johnson's works, &c. (was founded at Pembroke college (his own college) at Oxford) in 1871.

JOHNSTOWN INUNDATION, see under *Pennsylvania*, 1889.

JOHORE. A state and town in the Malay Peninsula. The sultan received by the queen, at Windsor, 21 Feb. 1891. During his visit, some territorial arrangements were made. He left England 15 March, 1891. In the case of Miss Jenny Mighell *v.* the sultan of Johore for breach of promise of marriage, made under an assumed name in England, queen's bench division, verdict for the defendant, as an independent sovereign, 4 Nov. 1893; he died in London, 4 June, 1895; succeeded by his son, Ibrahim, crowned 2 Nov. 1895.

JOINT STOCK COMPANIES (good and bad) were very numerous during the nineteenth century (especially in 1825, 1846, 1866, and 1872). Many acts have been passed for their regulation; the most important in 1844, 1855, 1857, and 1858. An important act for the incorporation, regulation, and winding-up of trading companies and other associations passed in 1862, was amended in 1867 and 1900; see *Companies*, and *Limited Liability*. 1,632 new companies were registered in 1881-2; in 1885, 1,482; 1888, 2,550; 1891, 2,686; 1896, 4,735; 1897, 5,229; 1898, 5,182; 1899, 4,975; 1900, 4,967.

JONATHAN, BROTHER. This national name for America is attributed to Washington's reliance for advice and support on Jonathan Trumbull, governor of Connecticut, whom he termed "the first of patriots" (Trumbull died 9 Aug. 1785).—*Brewer*.

JOPPA, see *Jaffa*.

JORDAN, a river of Palestine, crossed by the Israelites B.C. 1451, when they entered Canaan. A plan for forming a canal from the Mediterranean to the gulf of Akabah was discussed at the British Association, Sept. 1883.

JOSHUA, successor of Moses, led the Israelites into Canaan, B.C. 1451. (See *Bible*.) Handel's 14th oratorio "Joshua" was finished 19 Aug. 1747; produced 9 March, 1748. It contained "See the Conquering Hero comes," afterwards transferred to "Judas Maccabæus."

JOURNAL DES SAVANTS, see *Reviews*.

JOURNALISTS, NATIONAL ASSOCIATION OF, established at Birmingham, 1884.

The annual meeting at London was largely attended, 18 Dec. 1887; at Newcastle . . Feb. 1888
Institute of Journalists, London, inaugurated 9 Mar. 1889; incorporated . . . . 8 Feb. 1890
First annual conference held at Birmingham 27 Sept. 1890; in London, M. Zola present, supports anonymity, 21 Sept. 1893; at Plymouth, 2 Sept. 1895; Belfast. 1 Sept. 1896; Cardiff, 30 Aug. 1897; Leeds, 26 Aug. 1901; Birmingham, 1 Sept. 1902; Bristol . . . . 1 Sept. 1903

JOURNALS, see *Newspapers*.

JOURNALS OF THE HOUSE OF COMMONS, commenced in 1547, first ordered to be printed in 1752, when 5000*l*. were allowed to Mr. Hardinge for the execution of the work. The journals of the HOUSE OF PEERS (commencing 1509) were ordered to be printed in 1767.

JOWAKIES, see *India*, 1877–8.

JUAN FERNANDEZ, an island in the Pacific, named from its discoverer in 1567. Alexander Selkirk, a native of Scotland, left on shore here by his captain in Nov. 1704, and lived alone till he was discovered by captain Rogers in 1709. He died lieutenant of H.M.S. *Weymouth*, 1723. A monument to his memory was erected on the island in 1868, then colonised by Germans. From his narrative De Foe is said to have derived his *Adventures of Robinson Crusoe*, first published in 1719. The present governor, Rodt, a Swiss adventurer, settled on the island about 1874.

JUAN, SAN, a small island, near Vancouver's island. The possession of this island, on account of its commanding the straits between British Columbia and the United States territories, led to disputes between the two countries, owing to the doubtful interpretation of the treaty of Washington respecting the boundaries, 12 June, 1846. See *United States*, 1859 and 1860. The matter (by the treaty of Washington, 8 May, 1871) was referred for arbitration to the emperor of Germany, who decided in favour of the United States, Oct. 1872. The isle was evacuated by the British 22 Nov. following.

JUBILEES (Heb. *yôbêl*, the sound of a trumpet). The Jews were commanded to celebrate a jubilee every fifty years, 1491 B.C. (*Lev.* xxv. 8.) Among the Christians a jubilee every century was instituted by pope Boniface VIII. in the year 1300. It was ordered to be celebrated every fifty years by pope Clement VI.; and by Urban VI. every thirty-third year; and by Sixtus V. every twenty-fifth year. Leo XIII. celebrated his pontifical jubilee, Feb. 1903, see *Pope*.

National jubilee in England on account of George III. entering the 50th year of his reign 25 Oct. 1809
Jubilee in celebration of the general peace, and of the centenary of the accession of the Brunswick family . . . . 1 Aug. 1814
Shakspeare's Jubilee, projected by David Garrick, was celebrated at Shakspeare's birth-place, Stratford-on-Avon . . . . . 6, 7, 8, Sept. 1769
A Shakspeare festival at Stratford . . . 23 April, 1836
A Shakspeare festival at Stratford . . . 23 April, 1865
The Scott centenary celebrated (he was born 15 Aug. 1771) . . . . 9 Aug. 1871
International musical jubilee at Boston, U.S. (see *Boston*) . . . . 17 June—4 July, 1872
QUEEN VICTORIA'S JUBILEE, 1887 (accession 20 June, 1837). Grand procession witnessed by many thousands; solemn thanksgiving service in Westminster Abbey, in the presence of the queen, the royal family, the kings of Denmark, Belgium, Greece, and Saxony; the crown princes of Germany, Austria, Portugal, and Sweden; the grand duke Sergius of Russia, Amadeus, duke of Aosta, prince Ludwig of Bavaria, the maharajah Holkar and many Indian princes, the queen of Hawaii, also the dignitaries of the empire, and many persons eminent in science, art, and literature 21 June, 1887
By her majesty's command, a picture representing the scene, was painted by Mr. W. E. Lockhart, R.S.A., and by her permission was exhibited at Waterloo House, Pall Mall (engravings were sold by Messrs. Doig & Co.) . . . . . . ,,
Magnificent illuminations throughout the metropolis; two deaths recorded, and not many personal injuries . . . . . . 21 June, ,,
Jubilee beacon fires throughout England and Wales, started on the Malvern Hills 10 p.m., and seen from Cottington Hill, Hants; over 80 fires seen 21 June, ,,
About 26,000 elementary school children entertained in Hyde Park at the instance of Mr. Lawson of the *Daily Telegraph*. The queen presents a memorial cup to Florence Dunn, aged 12, of St. Mary's, Westminster; the prince of Wales and many of the nobility present . . . 22 June, ,,
Grand fête in Pontypool park, Monmouthshire, organized by captain Gus. Bevan (who was thanked by the queen); about 80,000 persons present; great Eisteddfod; a prize of 200*l*. awarded to Dowlais choir; fireworks, &c. . . . 11 April, ,,
Jubilee celebrated in India and all the colonies, and throughout the civilized world, June; envoys from the pope (Mons. Ruffo Scilla), Japan and Siam ,,
Citizens' thanksgiving service at St. Paul's, after formal procession from Guildhall . . 23 June, ,,
The queen issues a letter to the nation, expressing her profound gratitude for the very kind reception of the vast multitude during her progress to and return from Westminster Abbey, and her high admiration for the excellent order preserved 24 June, ,,

Jubilee yacht race round the island (see *Yachts*) 14–27 June, 1887
28,000 volunteers reviewed by the queen at Buckingham Palace, 2 July . . . . ,,
The queen lays foundation-stone of the Imperial Institute . . . . . 4 July, ,,
The queen reviews about 60,000 men at Aldershot 9 July, ,,
Grand naval review by the queen (see *Navy of England*) . . . . . 23 July, ,,
The presents given to the queen exhibited at St. James's Palace, rich, beautiful, and eccentric, 12 Sept. ,,
Medals presented to the metropolitan police for their conduct during the jubilee celebration ordered . . . . . 3 Sept. ,,
The queen expresses her thanks for jubilee addresses from all parts of the empire . . 14 Sept. ,,
Great number of addresses from municipal corporations, scientific societies, and other bodies 27 June, ,,
East India chiefs received and decorated at Windsor, 30 June, ,,
The queen thanks the mayors and municipal bodies for their presents; *London Gazette* . . 4 Nov. ,,
Long official account of the jubilee proceedings, *London Gazette* . . . . . 3 Jan. 1888
Jubilee offering of the women of the British Empire (from 1*d*. to 1*l*.); 75,000*l*. presented to the queen 22 June; her letter of thanks published 2 July, 1887; sum increased to 84,116*l*. in March, ,,
The queen approved the application of about 70,000*l*. for the sick poor, and the benefit of nurses and nursing institutions. About 10,000*l*. was set apart for a colossal statue of the prince consort, and about 4,116*l*. for a personal ornament to be worn by the queen; reported 20 April, ,,
Statue of the queen by sir J. E. Boehm, subscribed for by the graduates, unveiled by the prince of Wales at the University of London, Burlington-gardens, 8 May; one by L. J. Williamson, at the College of Physicians, Thames embankment unveiled . . . . . . 24 May, 1889
Picture of the emperor William I. and his family, painted by Anton von Werner, presented to the queen by the Germans residing in England . . 16 May, ,,
Royal Victoria [Jubilee] Hospital, Bournemouth, cost 8,000*l*., opened by the prince of Wales 16 Jan. 1890
The Jubilee offering of the officers of the British army.—A silver gilt centre piece, representing the greatness of the empire, designed by Mr. Alfred Gilbert, R.A., presented to the queen at Buckingham palace by the duke of Cambridge and a deputation . . . . 10 May ,,
The bronze equestrian statue, by sir J. E. Boehm, was set up near Virginia water, Windsor great park, and was uncovered by the queen . 12 May, ,,
Jubilee statue of the queen (as in 1837), by the princess Louise, in Kensington-gardens, unveiled by the queen . . . . . . 28 June, 1893
[*Queen's Commemoration Fund*, for the Jubilee institute for nurses: 12,500*l*. from lord Iveagh; total, 156,000*l*. in 1897; 45,000*l*. reported, 12 June, 1902.]

DIAMOND JUBILEE: March of colonial troops from Victoria park to the Mansion house 19 June, 1897
The queen's 60th regnal year completed. Solemn thanksgiving day (the bp. of Wakefield's hymn, music by sir A. Sullivan, sung by request of the queen) at St. Paul's, London, Westminster abbey, and all places of worship throughout the empire, *Sunday* . . . . . . 20 June, ,,
Diamond Jubilee odes by the poet-laureate, and others, *Times* . . . . . 21, 22 June, ,,
State banquet, foreign princes, envoys, and others received by the queen . . . . 21 June, ,,
Commemoration day: 22 June: route of procession: Buckingham palace, Constitution-hill, Piccadilly, St. James'-street, Pall-mall, Strand, Fleet-street, St. Paul's, Cheapside, Mansion house, King William-street, London bridge, Southwark, Westminster bridge, Whitehall, the Mall, and back again to the palace. The colonial, Asiatic, and African contingents led by lord Roberts, accompanied by the colonial premiers, left Buckingham palace, about 9 A.M. The royal procession started 11.15 A.M.; the queen on leaving the palace sent this telegram to *all* her subjects: "From my heart, I thank my beloved subjects: may God bless them."
The procession included the naval and military forces, foreign envoys, Indian imperial escort, British and foreign princes, the empress Frederick, the princesses and children; commander-in-chief lord Wolseley: the QUEEN, princess of Wales, and princess Christian, prince of Wales, dukes of Edinburgh, connaught, and Cambridge; troops, and the Royal Irish constabulary.
The queen on the site of Temple Bar, received the city sword from the lord mayor, and returned it.
At St. Paul's Cathedral, west front: Thanksgiving choral service, was held by the abps. of Canterbury and York, and other bishops.
Reception at the Mansion house; the queen returned to Buckingham palace at 1.45 P.M.
Jubilee honours, announced, *Times* . . 22 June, 1897
Illuminations and festivities throughout the British empire, and foreign states . . 19–26 June, ,,
Over 2,500 beacon fires from Cornwall to Caithness, 1,981 in England . . . . . 22 June, ,,
Colonial and foreign congratulatory addresses to the queen and the British nation . 22 June, ,,
The queen received the mayors and provosts of Great Britain and Ireland, and others; the house of lords and house of commons; reviews 10,000 school children in the Green park, who received medals and refreshments; she received addresses from their representatives, lord Londonderry, the bp. of London, card. Vaughan, and others; arrived at Windsor, reviews the Eton boys, and received addresses . . . . . 23 June, ,,
Lords of the admiralty and foreign admirals received by the queen at Windsor, the castle illuminated . . . . 24 June, ,,
State banquet by the prince of Wales at Buckingham palace, to foreign princes and envoys, 24 June, ,,
Jubilee dinners to 330,000 metropolitan poor, in 56 districts, initiated by the princess of Wales (see *Mansion house*), April; some dinners visited by the prince and princess of Wales 24 & 30 June, ,,
The queen inspects about 6,000 school children in Windsor park, and reviews the fire-brigades from all parts of the country, under the duke of Marlborough; sir Eyre Shaw, and others present; torchlight procession of the Eton boys, 25 June, ,,
Prince and princess of Wales, the royal family, foreign princes and envoys, and others entertained at the Mansion house . . . 25 June, ,,
Grand naval review at Spithead (see *Navy*), 26 June, ,,
The queen visits Kensington, receives addresses, and gives a state garden-party at Buckingham palace; about 6,000 present . . 28 June, ,,
Grand army review at Aldershot (*which see*), 1 July, ,,
Fancy-dress ball illustrating the court dress, &c., of the 16th, 17th, and 18th centuries, given by the duke and duchess of Devonshire at Devonshire house, the prince and princess of Wales and the royal family present . . . . 2 July, ,,
The house of commons and ladies received by the queen at a garden party at Windsor castle, 3 July, ,,
The queen decorates the Indian officers at Windsor, 5 July, ,,
400 soldiers and sailors who had fought in battle between 1837–97, inspected by the prince of Wales, lords Wolseley and Roberts, and others, 5 July, ,,
Letter of thanks from the queen to her people, 15 July; *Times*, 17 July; gazetted . 16 July, ,,
The Diamond jubilee presents exhibited at the Imperial institute . . . . 18 Oct. *et seq.* ,,
Princess Christian opens the (Diamond Jubilee) Victoria recreation ground, over 17 acres, 10 May, 1902
New (Diamond Jubilee) hospital at East Ham (5,000*l*. from Mr. Passmore Edwards) opened by the countess of Warwick . . . . 12 June, ,,

The Diamond jubilee described in the *London Gazette Extraordinary*, published 14 March, 1898, price 1s.

See *Church House, Imperial Institute, Nurses, and Hospitals.*

JUDAH, see *Jews*.

JUDAS MACCABÆUS, Handel's 12th oratorio, composed 9 July—11 Aug. 1746; produced 1 April, 1747. See *Maccabees*.

JUDGE ADVOCATE GENERAL, and judge martial of all the forces, an ancient office, held by patent from the crown. He is the legal adviser of the commander-in-chief in military cases, and by his authority all general courts martial are held. An advocate-general accompanied the army to France in 1625, and the office was constituted soon after the restoration. Dr. Samuel Barrowe was appointed 1666.

John R. Davison appointed Dec. 1870; died 15 Apr. 1871
Sir Robert Phillimore (admiralty judge) acted provisionally 1871-3
Acton S. Ayrton . . . . 21 Aug. 1873—Feb. 1874
Stephen Cave . . . . . Feb. 1874—Nov. 1875
Geo. A. F. Cavendish Bentinck, 25 Nov. 1875—May, 1880
George Osborne Morgan . . . . . May, ,,
William T. Marriott . . . . June, 1885
John Wm. Mellor . . . . 15 Feb. 1886
William T. Marriott, July, 1886-92; knighted April, 1888
Sir Francis H. Jeune . . . . about 24 Dec. 1892

JUDGES appointed by God, when the Israelites were in bondage, ruled from 1402 B.C. till the election of Saul as king, 1095; see *Jews, Chancellors, Justices, Circuits, Lords Justices, Vice-Chancellors, Privy Councils*, and *Supreme Court*.

Judges punished for bribery and Thomas de Weyland banished 1289
William de Thorp hanged for bribery 1351
John de Cavendish beheaded by the Suffolk rebels, 1381
Tresylian, chief justice, executed for favouring despotism, and other judges condemned . . . 1388
The prince of Wales said to have been committed by judge Gascoigne for assaulting him on the bench 1412
Sir Thos. More, late lord chancellor, beheaded, 6 July, 1535
Judges threatened with impeachment, and Berkeley taken off the bench and committed by the commons, on a charge of treason . . . 13 Feb. 1641
Three judges impeached for favouring the levying ship-money 1680
Judge Jefferies committed by the lord mayor to the Tower, where he died 1689
The judge's office made tenable for life (during good behaviour) instead of during the pleasure of the crown by 13 Will. III. c. 2 1702
Their commissions made permanent, notwithstanding the demise of the crown (by 1 Geo. III.) 1761
Three additional judges appointed, one to each law court, 1784; and again in 1830
A new judge took his seat as vice-chancellor, 5 May, 1813
Two new vice-chancellors appointed 1841
A third vice-chancellor and two new chancery judges (styled lords-justices) appointed . . . 1851
A council of judges, was by the judicature act of 1873, ordered to be held at least once every year, on such day as should be fixed by the lord chancellor and lord chief justice, to consider the operation of the act, and such councils were held 17, 21, 23 June, 1892. In their report issued 6 Aug., they propose many important legal reforms.
The report was referred to a committee of the bar for consideration (the Incorporated Law society and others . . . . . . Nov. *et seq* 1892
A bill adopting the recommendations of the committee read 2nd time in the lords . 26 June, 1893
New resolutions issued . . . . . 2 June, 1894
In the case of Mr. Buckley, attorney-general of New Zealand, *v.* Mr. Worley B. Edwards, a puisne judge, the judicial committee of the privy council decided that the appointment of a judge is not valid unless the payment of his salary is previously secured by statute . . . 21 May, 1894
An additional judge (chancery) appointed, 1899; including lords of appeal, there were 33 judges, total about 464 in the United Kingdom . . 1902

JUDICATURE, see *Law; Supreme Court*.

JUDICIAL COMMITTEE OF THE PRIVY COUNCIL, see *Privy Council*.

JUDICIAL SEPARATION of married persons may now be decreed by the Divorce Court, established by act of parliament in 1857. The persons separated may not marry again.

JUDICIAL STATISTICS FOR ENGLAND AND WALES began with the year (1856) in 1857. See under *Crime*. The new series beginning with the year 1893, included many changes, and criminal statistics of some foreign countries.

JUGGERNAUT, correctly *Jagannâth*, or "Lord of the World," one of the incarnations of Krishna, is an idol formed of an irregular pyramidal black stone, with two rich diamonds to represent eyes; the nose and mouth are painted vermilion. The number of pilgrims that visit the god is stated at 1,200,000 annually. Formerly some were crushed by the wheels of the car (so lately as Aug. 1864); a great many never returned, and, to the distance of fifty miles, the way was strewed with human bones. The temple of Juggernaut has existed about 800 years. The state allowance to the temple was suspended by the Indian government in June, 1851. The festival was kept, June, 1872. Twelve persons were said to be killed by accident, Aug. 1873. The festival of 1878 reported a failure.

JUGURTHINE WAR. Jugurtha murdered his cousin, Hiempsal, king of Numidia, and usurped his throne, 118 B.C. He gave Adherbal a share in the government, but killed him in 112. He then provoked the Romans to war. Cæcilius Metellus was first sent against him, and defeated him in two battles; and Marius brought him in chains to Rome to adorn his triumph, 106 B.C., where he was put to death in 104. This war has been celebrated by the pen of Sallust.

JULIAN ERA and **YEAR**, see *Calendar*. *Julian period* (by Joseph Scaliger, about 1583), a term of years produced by the multiplication of the lunar cycle 19, solar cycle 28, and Roman indiction 15. It consists of 7980 years, and began 4713 years before our era. It has been employed in computing time to avoid the ambiguity attendant on reckoning any period antecedent to our era, an advantage in common with the mundane eras used at different times. By subtracting 4713 from the Julian period, our era is found; if before Christ, subtract the Julian period from 4714.

JULIERS, a Prussian province; made a duchy in 1356; became the subject of contention on the extinction of the ruling family in 1609; was allotted to Neuburg in 1659; seized by the French in 1794; and ceded to Prussia in 1815.

JULY, the seventh, originally fifth, Roman month, named by Marc Antony from *Julius* Cæsar, the dictator of Rome, who was born in it.

The early part of July, 1888, was very cold; many thunderstorms, followed by destructive floods in the latter part. See *Inundations*.
July Revolution. See *France*, 1830.

JUNE, originally the fourth, now the sixth month, owes its name to *Junius*, which some derive from *Juno*, and others from *Juniores*, this being the month for the young, as May was for aged persons. Ovid, in his *Fasti*, introduces Juno as claiming this month. "Glorious 1st of June;" see *Ushant*.

JUNG RIVER, west Africa. Natives chastised for outrage on Mr. Laborde, envoy, and others, by gen. Havelock, governor of Sierra Leone, May, 1882.

JUNIUS'S LETTERS began in the *Public Advertiser*, 21 Jan. 1769.

They have been ascribed to Mr. Wm. Burke, Mr. William Gerard Hamilton, commonly called Single-speech Hamilton, John Wilkes, Mr. Dunning (afterwards lord Ashburton), serjeant Adair, the rev. J. Rosenhagen, John Roberts, Charles Lloyd, Samuel Dyer, general Lee, the duke of Portland, Hugh Boyd, lord George Sackville, earl Temple, and sir Philip Francis. The last-named is generally considered to have been the author. Junius said, "I am the depositary of my own secret, and it shall perish with me." The work of Mr. Chabot and hon. E. T. B. Twisleton was considered decisive of sir Philip Francis being Junius, May, 1871. "Junius is as much unknown as ever."—*Athenæum*, 8 Sept. 1888.

Sale of manuscript papers of sir Philip Francis, reported to be inconclusive respecting "Junius," June, 1892; the sir Philip Francis correspondence sold for 430*l*. 2*s*. . . . . . . 27 Nov. 1897

Mr. Charles Knight in his description of the letters in his "Popular History of England," 1860, asserts that they abound in gross exaggeration and venomous abuse. Mr. H. R. Francis, in his "Junius" *Revealed*, published March, 1894, maintains that his grandfather (Sir Philip) was Junius. The *Athenæum* (17, 24 March, 1894, and Mr. Fraser Rae, in 6 papers, 19 Feb. 1898) considers the book unsatisfactory. Mr. Fraser Rae's paper, "New Light on Junius," and facsimiles of handwriting, appeared, *Athenæum*, 8, 15 April, 6 May, 1899.

JUNKER PARTY (*Junker*, German for *young noble*), a term applied to the aristocratic party in Prussia, which came into power under Otho von Bismarck-Schönhausen, appointed prime minister, 9 Oct. 1862. Their political organ is the *Kreuz-Zeitung*.

JUNO, the planet discovered by M. Harding, of Lilienthal near Bremen, 1 Sept. 1804. Its distance from the sun is 254 millions of miles, and it accomplishes its revolution in four years and 128 days, at the rate of nearly 42,000 miles an hour.

JUNONIA, festivals in honour of Juno (the Greek Hēra, or Hērē) at Rome, and instituted 431 B.C.

JUNTA. The Spanish provincial juntas or councils declared against the French in 1808, and incited the people to insurrection.

JUNTO, a name given to the leaders of the whig party in the reigns of William III. and Anne (1689-1714); the chiefs were admiral Edward Russell, John Summers, Charles Montague, and Thomas Warton.

JUPITER, known as a planet to the Chaldeans. The discovery of the satellites, incorrectly attributed to Simon Mayr (Marius) in 1609, was made by Galileo on 8 Jan. 1610; see *Planets*. JUPITER'S moons were all invisible on 21 Aug. 1867; a very rare occurrence. A fifth very small satellite was discovered by Mr. Barnard at the Lick observatory, 9 Sept. 1892. Dark spots observed, 1901–2. —JUPITER AMMON'S temple in Libya was visited by Alexander, 332 B.C. Cambyses' army sent against it perished miserably, 525 B.C. The Greek Zeus was the Roman Jupiter, contracted from Diovis pater, the father of Heaven.

JURIDICAL SOCIETY was established in Feb. 1855, and opened with an address by sir R. Bethell on 12 May following.

JURIES. Trial by jury was introduced into England during the Saxon heptarchy, mention being made of six Welsh and six Anglo-Saxon freemen appointed to try causes between the English and Welsh men of property, and made responsible, with their whole estates real and personal, for false verdicts. *Lambard*. By most authorities their institution is ascribed to Alfred about 886, which is not historical. In *Magna Charta*, juries are insisted on as the great bulwark of the people's liberty. When either party is an alien born, the jury shall be one half denizens, and the other half aliens, stat. 28 Edw. III. 1353. By the common law a prisoner upon indictment or appeal might challenge peremptorily thirty-five, being under three juries; but a lord of parliament, and a peer of the realm, who is to be tried by his peers, cannot challenge any of his peers. An act for the trial by jury in civil cases in Scotland was passed in 1815. An act to consolidate and amend the laws relating to juries in Ireland was passed 4 Will. IV. 1833. A new act respecting juries, regulating their payment, &c., was passed 9 Aug. 1870. The clause respecting their payment was rescinded by act passed 28 Feb. 1871. Laws respecting juries in Ireland amended, 14 Aug. 1871. New Juries bill brought in by the attorney-general, sir John Coleridge, Feb. 1873. Special juries bill passed, May, 1898. Juries are summoned to assist the coroner in investigating the causes of sudden or violent death.—GRAND JURIES (of not less than 12 or more than 23 persons), decide whether sufficient evidence is adduced to put the accused on trial.—The constitution of 1791 established the trial by jury in France.—An imperial decree abolished trial by jury throughout the Austrian empire, 15 Jan. 1852.—Trial by jury began in Russia, 8 Aug. 1866; in Spain, 1889—A true bill for libel granted against alderman sir F. Truscott in his absence, who was honourably acquitted, 18 Sept. 1879.

COERCION OF JURIES.—It is said that in early times the suitors used to feed the jury empanelled in their action, and hence arose the common law of denying sustenance to a jury after the hearing of the evidence. A jury may be detained during the pleasure of the judge if they cannot agree upon a verdict; and may be confined without meat, drink, or fire, candle light excepted, till they are unanimous.—Some jurors have been fined for having fruit in their pockets, when they were withdrawn to consider of their verdict, though they did not eat it. *Leon Dyer*, 137. A jury at Sudbury not being able to agree, and having been some time under duress, forcibly broke from the court where they were locked up, and went home, 9 Oct. 1791. *Phillips*. In Scotland, Guernsey, Jersey, and France, juries decide by a majority; in France, since 1831, a majority of two-thirds is required.

"JUSTE MILIEU" (moderation and conciliation to parties), according to Louis-Philippe (in 1830), is the only principle of government which can secure the welfare of France.

JUSTICE GENERAL, Lord, Scotland, see *Court of Session*.

JUSTICES OF THE PEACE are unpaid local magistrates, invested with extensive powers in minor cases, but subject to supersession and punishment by the King's Bench for an abuse of their authority. They were first nominated by William I. in 1076. *Stow*. Persons termed conservators of the peace in each county were appointed by

1 Edw. III. c. 2, 1327; and their duties were defined in 1360. The form of a commission of the peace settled by the judges, 23 Eliz. 1580. *Hawkins*; see *Eyre*.

JUSTICES, LORDS, were appointed by English sovereigns to govern during their absence; especially by William III., George I. and George II. (1695-1760). George III. never left England. In Sept. 1821, when George IV. went to Hanover, lords justices were appointed, the duke of York being the first. No such appointment was made during the reign of queen Victoria, it having been decided by the law authorities in 1843 to be unnecessary when the queen went to France. Ireland is always ruled by lords justices when the lord-lieutenant is out of the country, or his office is vacant.—Two *lords justices of the court of appeal in chancery*, having rank next after the chief baron of the exchequer, were appointed from 1 Oct. 1851, salary 6000*l*. For recent changes see *Appeal* and *King's Bench*.

1851. Sir James L. Knight-Bruce, resigned Oct., died 7 Nov. 1866.
,, Robert lord Cranworth (afterwards lord chancellor).
1853. Sir George Jas. Turner, Jan., died, 9 July, 1867.
1866. Sir Hugh M. Cairns, 29 Oct., became lord-chancellor, 29 Feb. 1868.
1867. Sir John Rolt, July; resigned Feb. 1868.
1868. Sir Charles Jasper Selwyn, 8 Feb., died 11 Aug. 1869.
,, Sir William Page Wood, March; lord-chancellor, 2 Nov.
1869. Sir George M. Giffard, Dec., died 13 July, 1870.
1870. Sir George Mellish, July; died 15 June, 1877.
1875. Sir Richard Baggallay, resigned 1885.
1882. Sir Charles S. C. Bowen.
1883. Sir Edward Fry, 9 April, resigned 1892.
1893. Sir Horace Davey, Sept., lord of appeal, Aug. 1894.

Present Lords Justices.

1881. Sir Nathaniel Lindley, made master of the rolls, Oct. 1897; lord of appeal, May, 1900.
1885. Sir Henry Charles Lopes, Dec., made baron Ludlow 21 June, 1897, resigned 23 Oct. 1897; died, 25 Dec. 1899.
1890. Sir Edwd. E. Kay, Nov.; resigned, Jan. 1897; died, 16 March, 1897.
1892. Sir Archibald Levin Smith, June; made master of the rolls, Oct. 1900; resigned mid, died, 20 Oct. 1901.
1894. Sir John Rigby, Oct.; resigned, Oct. 1901; died 26 July, 1903.
1897. Sir Joseph Chitty, Jan.; died, 15 Feb. 1899.
,, Sir Richard Henn Collins, Oct.; made master of the rolls, Oct. 1901.
,, Sir Roland Vaughan Williams, Oct.
1899. Sir Robert Romer, Feb.
1900. Sir James Stirling, Oct.
1901. Sir James Charles Mathew, Oct.
,, Sir H. H. Cozens-Hardy, Oct.

JUSTICIARS. In ancient times the kings of England used to hear and determine causes; but it is declared by law that if the king cannot determine every controversy, he, to ease himself, may divide the labour among persons, men of wisdom and fearing God, and out of such to appoint judges. The Saxon kings of England appointed a judge after this manner, who was, in fact, the king's deputy. After the Norman conquest, the person invested with that power had the style of *Capitalis Justiciæ*, or *Justiciarius Angliæ*. These judges continued until the erection of the courts of king's bench and the common pleas. The first justiciars of England were Odo, bishop of Bayeux, and William Fitz-Osborne, in 1067; and the last was Philip Basset, in 1261, or Hugh le Despencer, 1263 (Henry III). Authorities vary.

JUSTICIARY, COURT OF, see *Court of Justiciary*.

JUSTINIAN CODE compiled by a commission appointed by the emperor Justinian I. Feb. 528, wherein was written what may be termed the statute law (scattered through 2000 volumes reduced to fifty). It was promulgated, April, 529. To this code Justinian added the Digest or Pandects, the Institutes, and Novels, promulgated 16 Nov. 534. These compilations have since been called, collectively, the body of civil law (*Corpus Juris Civilis*).

JUTE, the fibres of two plants, the chonch and isbund (*Corchorus olitorius* and *Corchorus capsularis*), since 1830 extensively cultivated in Bengal for making gunnycloth, &c. Jute has been much manufactured at Dundee as a substitute for flax, tow, &c., and in July, 1862, assertions were made that it could be employed as a substitute for cotton. In 1853, 275,578 cwt.; in 1861, 904,092 cwt.; in 1871, 3,454,120 cwt.; in 1874, 4,270,164 cwt.; in 1875, 3,416,617 cwt.; in 1877, 3,649,877 cwt.; in 1879, 4,759,363 cwt.; in 1881, 4,928,805 cwt.; in 1883, 7,385,028 cwt.; in 1885, 285,674 tons: in 1887, 327,221 tons, of undressed jute were imported into the United Kingdom; in 1888, 313,828 tons; in 1890, 369,958 tons; 1893, 278,634 tons; 1896, 340,649; 1900, 280,919 tons; 1901, 321,331.

JUTLAND (Denmark), the home of the Jutes who settled in our southern counties. South Jutland was taken by the allies in 1813, and restored in 1814. Great fire at Aarhuus, estimated loss 2,000,000 kroner, 18 Aug. 1899.

JUVENILE OFFENDERS. In 1838, an act was passed for instituting a prison for instructing and correcting juvenile offenders, and the military hospital at Parkhurst in the Isle of Wight was appropriated for this purpose. An act for their committal to reformatories was passed in 1854. Another act passed, 1901.

K.

KAABA, see *Caaba*.

KABBALA, see *Cabbala*.

KABYLES, see *Algiers*.

KADSEAH, see *Parsees*.

KAFFRARIA, a country in S. Africa, extending from the north of Cape Colony to the Orange river. Our war with the natives began in 1798.

The Kaffirs, headed by Mokanna, a prophet, attack Grahamstown; repulsed with much slaughter . 1819
Again defeated, 1828, 1831 1834
The Kaffirs rise; sir Harry Smith, the governor, proclaims martial law, and orders the inhabitants to rise *en masse* to defend the frontier 31 Dec. 1850
Disastrous operations against the Kaffirs in the Waterkloeff follow; colonel Fordyce and several officers and men of the 74th regiment killed 6 Nov. 1851
Wreck of the *Birkenhead* with reinforcements from England (see *Birkenhead*) . . . . 26 Feb. 1852
The hostilities of the Kaffirs having assumed all the features of regular warfare, the governor-general, Cathcart, attacked and defeated them, 20 Dec. „
The conditions offered by Cathcart accepted, and peace restored . . . . 9 March, 1853
Death of Makomo, an eminent chief . 11 Sept. 1873
Insurrection of Langalibalele, suppressed; see *Natal*
Kreli, a Galeka chief in the Transkei territory attacks the Fingoes and their British protectors; repulsed at Ibeka . . . 24 and 29 Sept. 1877
Sir Bartle Frere, the governor general, with officers and volunteers proceeds to the spot; Kreli defeated by commandant Griffith, his kraal burnt, 9 Oct.; deposed and his lands annexed . Oct. „
Galekas defeated and expelled from their territories 2 Dec. „
Rise of the Gaikas under Sandilli, an old chief (who after education relapsed into barbarism), about . . . . 30 Dec. „
Cetywayo, king of the Zulus, troublesome; sir B. Frere requests help; 90th regiment and a battery of artillery sent from England . . . . Jan. 1878
British advance; rebels defeated, 24, 26 Jan.; at Quintana, 7 Feb., by gen. Thesiger (about 400 Kaffirs killed; Sandilli escapes,) 18, 19 March; again (capt. Donovan, lieut. Ward, and capt. Shawe killed,) about 21 March; continued fighting, sometimes severe . . . . March—May, „
Sandilli and other chiefs reported dead; his sons captured; Kaffir refugees in dreadful condition June, „
Amnesty proclaimed to all surrendering rebels, about . . . . 2 July, „
Thanksgiving day for restoration of peace . 1 Aug. „
War still lingered on the borders during Aug. „
Tini Macomo and Gangubele condemned to death as traitors intercession for them in London; reprieved . . . . Sept. „
For the war, see also *Basuto Land, Transvaal, and Zululand.*

KAGOSIMA, see *Japan*, 1863.

KAINARDJI (Bulgaria). Here a treaty was signed, July, 1774, between the Turks and Russians, which opened the Black Sea, and gave the Crimea to the latter.

KALAFAT, on the Danube, opposite the fortress of Widden. This place was fortified by the Turks under Omar Pacha when they crossed the river, 28 Oct. 1853. In December, prince Gortschakoff, with the Russian army, determined to storm their intrenchments. The conflict lasted from 31 Dec. to 9 Jan. 1854, when the Russians were compelled to retire. Among these conflicts one occurred at Citate, 6 Jan.; see *Citate*. Kalafat was invested 28 Jan. and general Schilders attacked it vigorously on 19 April, without success, and the blockade was raised 21 April.

KALAKH, ancient capital of middle Assyria; where many discoveries have been made by Layard and others. See *Assyria*.

KALEIDOSCOPE, an optical instrument, which, by an arrangement of mirrors, produces a symmetrical reflection of various transparent substances placed between, was invented by Dr. (afterwards sir David) Brewster, of Edinburgh; it was suggested in 1814, and perfected in 1817; see *Debusscope*.

KALEVALA, epic poem, see *Finland*.

KALENDS, see *Calends*.

KALI YUGH, see *Cali Yugh*.

KALITSCH (Poland). Here the Russians defeated the Swedes, 19 Nov. 1706, and here the Saxons, under the French general, Reynier, were beaten by the Russians under Winzingerode, 13 Feb. 1813.

KALMAR, see *Calmar*.

KALMUCK, see *Tartar*.

KALUNGA FORT (E. Indies), attacked unsuccessfully by the British forces, and general Gillespie killed, 31 Oct. 1814; and again unsuccessfully, 25 Nov. It was evacuated by the Nepaulese, 30 Nov. same year.

KAMPTULICON, a substance used for flooring, patented by Elijah Galloway in 1843, and manufactured since 1851, by Messrs. Tayler, Harvey, and Co. It is composed of India-rubber and cork, combined by masticating machines.

KAMTSCHATKA, a peninsula, E. coast of Asia, was discovered by Morosco, a Cossack chief, 1690; taken possession of by Russia in 1697; and proved to be a peninsula by Behring in 1728. Four months, commencing at our midsummer, may be considered as the spring, summer, and autumn here, the rest of the year being winter. The amiable captain Clarke, a companion of captain Cook, died in sight of Kamtschatka, 22 Aug. 1779, and was buried in the town of St. Peter and Paul, in the peninsula. Eruption of the Avachinsky volcano, 20 July–4 Aug. 1901.

KANDAHAR, see *Candahar*.

KANDY, see *Candy*.

KANGAROOS, animals indigenous to Australia (first seen by captain Cook, 22 June, 1770), were bred at San Donato, the estate of prince Demidoff, in 1853, and since.

KANO EXPEDITION, see *Nigeria*.

KANSAS, a western state in N. America, organised as a territory, 30 May, 1854; admitted into the union, 29 Jan. 1861; and left open to slavery, contrary to the Missouri Compromise; see *Slavery in America*. During 1855-8 this state was a scene of anarchy and bloodshed through fruitless efforts to make it a slave state. Capital, Leavenworth; population, 1880, 996,096; 1890, 1,427,096; city, 132,716; 1900, 1,470,495; city, 163,752.

Uniontown destroyed by the bursting of a dam caused by heavy rains, several lives lost, reported . . . . 17 June 1889
Destructive cyclone at Wellington and other places with loss of life . . . . . . 27 May 1892
Violent disputes at Topeka between the republicans and populists in the lower house of the legislature; checked by the militia, about 15 Feb.; the populists subdued . . . . . . Feb. 1893
Destructive cyclone over Williamstown; about 20 deaths . . . . 21 June, ,,
Collision on the Santa Fé railway near Emporia, 12 deaths . . . . . . 8 Sept. 1897

KAPUNDA, see under *Wrecks*, 1887

KARACHI, a flourishing port in N. W. India, capital of Sind, was taken by the British, 3 Feb. 1839. Outbreak of bubonic plague, remedial measures adopted; deaths from Dec. 1896, up to July, 3,402; reappears, Sept. 1897-8, and in 1903.

KARAÏTES (or READERS), the protestants of Judaism, a remnant of the Sadducees, formed into a sect by Anan-ben-David, in the 8th century. They profess adherence to the Scriptures alone, and reject the Talmud and Rabbinical traditions. They still exist in Turkey, Poland, the Crimea, and other parts of the East. Their name is of uncertain origin.

KARRACK, see *Carrack*.

KARS, a town in Asiatic Turkey, captured by the Russians under Paskiewich, 15 July, 1828, after three days' conflict. In 1855 it was defended by general Fenwick Williams, with 15,000 men, and with three months' provisions and three days' ammunition, against the Russian general Mouravieff, with an army of 40,000 infantry and 10,000 cavalry. The siege lasted from 18 June to 28 Nov. 1855. The sufferings of the garrison were very great from cholera and want of food. The Russians made a grand assault on 29 Sept. but were repulsed with the loss of above 6000 men, and the garrison were overcome by famine alone. *Sandwith*. Kars was restored to Turkey, Aug. 1856.

On accepting general Williams' proposal for surrendering, general Mouravieff said:—"General Williams, you have made yourself a name in history; and posterity will stand amazed at the endurance, the courage, and the discipline which this siege has called forth in the remains of an army. Let us arrange a capitulation that will satisfy the demands of war, without disgracing humanity." In 1856 the general was made a baronet, with the title of sir William Fenwick Williams of Kars, and granted a pension; he died 26 July, 1883.
The Russians besieging Kars, compelled to retire by Mukhtar Pacha, ... about 13 July, 1877
Under the grand duke Michael and Loris Melikoff, defeated 2, 4 Oct.; defeat the Turks at Aladja Dagh (*which see*) . . . . . . 14, 15 Oct. ,,
Kars taken, after 12 hours' fighting, by surprise (it is said by treachery) . . . . 17, 18 Nov. ,,
[Killed and wounded: Russian, about 2500; Turkish, 5000; with loss of 10,000 prisoners, 100 guns, &c.]
Kars ceded to Russia by the Berlin treaty 13 July, 1878

KASHGARIA, eastern Turkestan, central Asia; subdued by China; annexed by Keen Lung, 1760; insurrections subdued, 1826 *et seq.* Mahomed Yakoob Beg, during an insurrection of the Tungani, made himself ruler of Kashgaria, 1866, and sent envoys to London, &c., 1867. He was at length attacked by the Chinese, totally defeated, and said to have been assassinated, 1 May, 1877. The capital, Kashgar, was taken, and the country regained by China, Nov.; and the war closed, Dec. 1877. Dr. Stein's excavations (1899, 1900) very successful, stucco sculptures, Buddhist shrines, MSS., &c., discovered, 1901. Severe earthquake, villages wrecked 3,000 deaths, 22 Aug. 1902.

KASHMIR, see *Cashmere*.

KASSALA, capital of the Egyptian province of Taka, near Abyssinia, captured by the Italians from the dervishes, see *Massowah*, 17 July, 1894, 1895-6.

Taken by Osman Digna, chief of the dervish army, after two years siege . . . . . July, 1885
Abandonment of Kassala by the Italians, announced . . . . . . 20 May, 1897
Col. Parsons, the governor, arrives, 18 Dec.; withdrawal of the Italian troops, fort occupied by Egyptian government force . . . 25 Dec. ,,
Col. Parsons, with 600 native levies, attacks and defeats the dervishes on the Atbara; El Fasher taken, 19 dervishes killed, 22 Dec.; fort Osobri taken after a desperate fight . . . 28 Dec. ,,
Reinforcements under capt. M'Kerrell and Sidi Ali, Morgani chief, arrive . . . . . 4 Jan. 1898
See *Egypt*.

KASSASSIN (4 battles); see *Egypt*, 28 Aug. and 9 Sept. 1882.

KATANGA or **GARENGANZE**, a native kingdom near the head stream of the Congo, in central Africa.

The Katanga company was constituted at Brussels to develop the country and promote free trade, 15 April, 1891
A settlement was formed subject to the Congo Free State; reported prosperous . . . . Feb. 1892
Capt. W. Grant Stairs, who conducted an expedition successfully for the company, died when returning . . . . 9 June, ,,
M. Hodister, an able officer of the company, and others, killed by the natives . . about 15 May, ,,
Capt. Cameron reported at a meeting of the company at Brussels that he had established a transport company in S. E. Africa . . . 12 Nov. ,,
See *Congo*.

KATHARINE'S HOSPITAL, ST., founded about 1148, by Matilda, queen of Stephen, and refounded by Eleanor, queen of Henry III., 1273. The hospital was removed to Regent's Park in 1827, the site having been bought for 163,000*l.* by the St. Katharine's docks company. The brethren are in orders, and not restricted from marriage; the sisters are unmarried or widows. A school, attached in 1829, was enlarged in 1849.

Order of St. Katharine for nurses instituted by the queen; annual payment 50*l.* for 3 years, badge for life; first investiture . . . . 4 June, 1879

KATSBACH (Prussia); near this river the Prussian general Blücher defeated the French under MacDonald 26 Aug. 1813. He received the title of prince of Wahlstatt, the name of a neighbouring village.

KEATING'S ACT, 18 & 19 Vict. c. 67 (1855) relates to bills of exchange.

KEBLE COLLEGE (Oxford), founded in memory of the rev. John Keble, author of the "Christian Year," born 25 April, 1792, died 29 March, 1866. The first stone of the building was laid by the archbishop of Canterbury, 25 April, 1868; the building was dedicated, 23 June, 1870; the chapel, the gift of William Gibbs, was dedicated, and the library opened, 25 April, 1876.

KEEPER OF THE KING'S CONSCIENCE. The early chancellors were priests, and out of their supposed moral control of the king's mind grew the idea of an equity court in contradistinction to the law courts. A bill in chancery is a petition through the lord chancellor to the king's conscience for remedy in matters for which the king's common law courts afford no redress. The keeper of the king's conscience is therefore now the officer who presides in the court of chancery; see *Chancellor* and *Lord Keeper*.

KEEPER (LORD) OF THE GREAT SEAL OF ENGLAND differed only from the lord chancellor in that the latter had letters patent, whereas the lord keeper had none. Richard, a chaplain, is said to have been the first keeper under Ranulph, in 1116. Foss says that the distinction between the two offices was made 1232. The two offices were made one by 5 Eliz. 1563. *Cowell*; see *Chancellor*. The office of lord keeper of the great seal of SCOTLAND was established in 1708, after the union.

KELTS, see *Celts* and *Gauls*.

KENILWORTH CASTLE (Warwickshire), was built about 1120, by Geoffrey de Clinton, whose grandson sold it to Henry III. It was enlarged and fortified by Simon de Montfort, to whom Henry gave it as a marriage portion with his sister Eleanor. Queen Elizabeth conferred it on her favourite, Dudley, earl of Leicester. His entertainment of the queen commenced 19 July, 1575, and cost the earl daily 1000*l*.

After the battle of Evesham and defeat and death of Simon de Montfort, by Prince Edward (afterwards Edward I.) 1265, Montfort's younger son, Simon, shut himself up in Kenilworth castle, which sustained a siege for six months against the royal forces of Henry III., to whom it at length surrendered. Upon this occasion was issued the "*Dictum de Kenilworth*," or "ban of Kenilworth," enacting that all who had borne arms against the king should pay him the value of their lands for periods varying from 7 years to 6 months.

KENNINGTON COMMON (Surrey). The Chartist demonstration, 10 April, 1848, took place on the common. It was directed to be laid out as a public pleasure-ground in 1852.

KENSAL GREEN, see *Cemeteries*.

KENSINGTON: the palace was purchased by William III., from lord chancellor Finch, who made the road through its park. The gardens were improved by queens Mary, Anne, and Caroline, who died here. Here died George, prince of Denmark, and George II.; and here queen Victoria was born, 24 May, 1819. The state rooms restored at national expense; visited by queen Victoria, 15 May; opened to the public, 24 May, 1899. Kensington returns two M.P.'s by Act of 1885; a royal borough, 18 Nov. 1901 (10 aldermen, 60 councillors).

By permission of the government, a military band played in Kensington gardens on Sundays, Aug. . 1855
Objected to; discontinued 1856
New parish church erected by sir Gilbert G. Scott was consecrated . . . . . 14 May, 1872
New town-hall by R. Walker opened by the duchess of Teck . . . . . . 7 Aug. 1880
Free central public library opened by the princess Louise . . . . . . 29 Nov. 1889
Queen Victoria unveils the statue of herself (as in 1837), by the princess Louise, near the palace (subscribed for) . . . . . 28 June, 1893
Population, 1881, 163,151; 1891, 166,321; 1901, 176,623.
See *South Kensington*.

KENT, see *Britain* and *Holy Maid*. Odo, bishop of Bayeux, brother of William the Conqueror, was made earl of Kent, 1067; and Henry Grey was made duke of Kent in 1710; he died without male heirs in 1740. Edward, son of George III., was created duke of Kent in 1799, was father of queen Victoria, and died 23 Jan. 1820; see *England*.

KENT, an East Indiaman, of 1350 tons burthen, left the Downs, 19 Feb. 1825, bound for Bombay. In the Bay of Biscay she encountered a dreadful storm, 28 Feb. On the next day she accidentally took fire, and all were in expectation of perishing, either by the tempest or the flames. The *Cambria*, captain Cook, bound to Vera Cruz, providentially hove in sight, and nearly all on board were saved. The *Kent* blew up, 2 March.

KENTISH FIRE, a term given to the continuous cheering common at the protestant meetings held in Kent, 1828 and 1829, with the view of preventing the passing of the Catholic Relief bill.—KENTISH PETITION to the house of commons, censuring its proceedings, was signed at Maidstone, 29 April, 1701. It gave much offence.

KENTISH TOWN, N.W. London, an old manor, church property, originally formed part of the great forest of Middlesex. Since 1855 building has very greatly increased. New baths and washhouses in Prince of Wales-rd. (total cost, 93,000*l*.) opened by sir J. Blundell Maple, 9 Oct. 1901.

KENTUCKY, a western state of N. America, admitted into the union 1792. It declared for strict neutrality in the conflict between the North and South in April, 1861, but was invaded by the Southern troops in August. On their refusal to retire, after much correspondence, the legislature of Kentucky gave in its adhesion to the union, 27 Nov. 1861. In the campaign that ensued sharp skirmishes took place, and on 19 Jan. 1862, the confederates under Zollicoffer were defeated and himself killed at Mill Spring, and in March no confederate soldiers remained in Kentucky; capital, Frankfort. Population, 1880, 1,648,690; 1890, 1,858,635; 1900, 2,147,174. See *United States*.

Murderous ten years' feud or vendetta at Morehead, Rowan county, chiefly between Holbrooks and Underwoods, beginning with a charge of horse-stealing against John Martin, sometimes rising to actual war. Closed by the sheriff killing Craig Tolliver and his gang . . 22 June, 1887
By the fall of a new bridge between Covington and Newport, about 30 workmen perished 15 June, 1892

KERBEKAN, BATTLE OF, see *Soudan*, 10 Feb. 1885.

KERMADEC ISLANDS, north of New Zealand, annexed by the British Government, May, 1886.

KEROSELENE, an anæsthetic, derived from the distillation of coal-tar by Mr. W. B. Merrill, of Boston, U.S., was made known early in 1861.

KERTCH, formerly Panticapæum, capital of the ancient kingdom of Bosporus, late a flourishing town on the straits of Yenikale, sea of Azof. It was entered by the allies (English and French) 24 May, 1855; the Russians retired after destroying stores, &c. The place was dismantled by the allies, and most of the inhabitants removed.

KET'S REBELLION: a revolt in July, 1549, instigated by William Ket, a tanner, of Wymondham, Norfolk. He demanded the abolition of inclosures and the dismissal of evil counsellors. The insurgents amounted to 20,000 men, but were quickly defeated by the earl of Warwick. More than 2000 fell; Ket and others were tried 26 Nov., and hanged soon after.

KEW (Surrey). The palace was successively occupied by the Capel family and Mr. Molyneux; by Frederick, prince of Wales, 1730, and George III. Queen Charlotte died here, 4 Nov. 1818. The old palace ordered by the queen to be opened as a

public museum, the grounds being annexed to Kew gardens, Jan., opened 21 May, 1898. A new palace erected by George III., under the direction of Mr. Wyatt, was pulled down in 1827. The gardens contained a fine collection of plants, and were decorated with ornamental buildings, most of them erected by sir William Chambers, about 1760.

BOTANIC GARDENS.

Mr. Aiton retired from his office of director, after fifty years' service 1841
Succeeded by sir William Hooker, 1 April, 1841, at whose recommendation the gardens were opened to the public daily. The royal kitchen and forcing gardens incorporated with the botanic gardens . 1847
Collections in the museum of Economic Botany began with the private collection of sir William Hooker, given by him in . . . . . . ,,
Under his charge the gardens were greatly improved, and magnificent conservatories erected.
He died 12 Aug. 1865, and was succeeded by his son, Dr. (now sir Joseph) D. Hooker, 1865, who resigned (succeeded by Mr. W. T. Thiselton Dyer, K.C.M.G. 30 Jan. 1899) . . . . 30 Nov. 1885
687,972 (great increase) visitors in 1877
The Meteorological Observatory presented to the British Association, 1842; purchased by J. P. Gassiot for 10,000*l.*, and presented to the Royal Society 1871
Great damage done to conservatories and plants by storm (cost about 2000*l.*) . . . . 23 Aug. 1879
Miss Marianne North's present of a collection of pictures of fruit and flowers of all nations, painted by herself, and placed in a building erected at her expense, opened to the public . . . summer, 1882
[She died, Sept. 1890. Her "Recollections of a Happy Life," were published early in 1892.]
Gardens first opened at noon . . . . 1 April, 1883
The valuable bulletins first issued 1887
"Index Kewensis plantarum phanerogamarum nomina et synonyma" (the Kew index of plant-names), 2 vols. 1893–4. This work, suggested by Mr. C. R. Darwin, who bequeathed money for its publication, was executed, under sir Joseph Hooker, by Mr. Daydon Jackson and the staff of the gardens.
The gardens enlarged by a gift from the queen, April, 1895, and May, 1898
New bridge over the Thames opened by the king, 20 May, 1903

KEYS. See *Locks*, *Man, Isle of*.

KHARTOUM, capital of Nubia, at the confluence of the Blue and White Nile, built by Mohamed Ali, 1820. Its prosperity was destroyed by the rapacity of the governors. Population in 1877 only about 15,000.

After successful administration col. Charles George Gordon compelled to leave Khartoum, and returned to England 1877
In his defence of Khartoum against the Mahdi (from Feb. 1884) he was greatly aided by colonel Hamill Stewart and Mr. Frank Power, correspondent of the *Times* (who were both massacred during an expedition, near Berber, Sept. 1884). He manifested much military skill, political sagacity, tender humanity, and marvellous power in inducing his followers to overcome serious difficulties and patiently endure great sufferings and privations.
Khartoum was surrendered, and Gordon and his faithful followers killed, early on 26 Jan. 1885. See under *Soudan*.
The British and Egyptian flags hoisted on Sunday, 4 Sept. 1898
GORDON MEMORIAL COLLEGE (undenominational) at Khartoum (proposed by lord Kitchener), patrons the queen and prince of Wales, warmly supported by lord Salisbury and others, 30 Nov. 1898. Meeting at the Mansion house, lord Kitchener present, 50,000*l.* received for the "Sirdar's Fund," 1 Dec.; see *Mansion House*, Dec. 1898; 100*l.* from the khedive, 15 Dec.; 100 gs. from the Aga Khan, 2 Jan. 1899. Foundation stone laid by lord Cromer, 5 Jan.; a "Hamill Stewart" scholarship started by him, Jan.; the general council meets at the Bank of England, lord Salisbury present, liberal subscriptions, 18 Jan.; over 1040*l.* from Canada, June, 1899; total, 123,015*l.*, 31 Dec. 1901. Many gifts presented, Mr. H. S. Wellcome a scientific laboratory; education steadily progressing, 4 schools started . . 1900–01
The khedive visits Khartoum, 3 Dec.; holds a review and opens the new mosque . . 5, 6 Dec. 1901
First stone of the new markets laid . 17 March, 1902
Lord Kitchener, warmly welcomed, opens the GORDON COLLEGE . . . . 7 Nov. ,,

KHEDIVE, or Kedervi, king or lord, a title given to the viceroy of Egypt, instead of vali or viceroy, 14 May, 1867.

KHELAT, see *Beloochistan*.

KHERSON, an ancient Dorian colony (deriving its name from Chersoneseus, a peninsula), came under the sway of the great Mithridates about 120 B.C.; and afterwards under that of Rome, A.D. 30. It continued important, and its possession was long disputed by the Russians and Greeks. Justinian II. cruelly treated it. It was taken by Vladimir, grand-duke of Russia in 988, when he and his army received Christian baptism, and he married the emperor's sister Anne, who obtained Kherson as her dowry. The city was destroyed by the Lithuanians; and the Turks found it deserted when they took possession of the Crimea in 1475. What ancient remains the Turks and Tartars had spared, the Russians conveyed away for the construction of Sebastopol.

KHERSON, a Russian city on the Dnieper, founded 1778. Potemkin, the favourite of Catherine, who died at Jassy in 1791, is buried here, and John Howard, the English philanthropist, who died here, 20 Jan. 1790, is buried about three miles from the town, where an obelisk has been erected to his memory, by the czar Alexander I. New port opened here, 27 July, 1901.

KHIVA (formerly Carasmia), in Turkestan, Asia, successively formed part of the territories of the Seleucidæ, Bactria, Parthia, Persia, and the Califate, till about 1092, when it was subjugated by the Seljuk Tartars, by the Moguls in 1221, and by Timour the Tartar in 1370, whose descendants ruled till 1511, when they were expelled by the Uzbegs, a Turkish tribe who still inhabit the country. An expedition sent against it by the emperor Nicholas of Russia in 1839 perished through the rigour of the climate in 1840. In 1875, colonel F. A. Burnaby reached Khiva, after a perilous ride, when his progress was stopped by Russian jealousy. Population, about 700,000 (1894).

To obtain redress for many outrages, a Russian expedition sent to Khiva . . . . . Feb. 1873
After several defeats the town, Khiva, surrendered unconditionally . . . . . . 10 June, ,,
The khan fled, but returned, and became a vassal of the czar . . . . 5 July, ,,
An insurrection against the Russians repressed Aug.; part of Khiva annexed . . 15 Oct. ,,
The country disturbed by revolts 1873-4
The khan, Syed Mohamed Rahim, received at St. Petersburg . . . . Jan. 1893

KHOKAND, a khanate in central Asia, subject to China about 1760; rebelled and became tributary only, 1812. A rebellion, which broke out in Sept. was suppressed Oct. 1874.

War with Russia; gen. Kaufmann defeats about 30,000 men, 4 Sept.; entered Khokand without resistance, and the khanate subdued . 16 Sept. 1875
He defeats 5000 more . . . . . 21 Sept. ,,
The people expel the new khan . . . 21 Oct. ,,
Part of Khokand annexed by Russia . . . Oct. ,,
Russian garrison massacred by natives . . Nov. ,,
Rebels totally defeated at Assake . . 30 Jan. 1876
Khokand formally annexed as Ferghana . 29 Feb. ,

Fanatical rising, Russian force (300) surprised, and 22 killed at Andijan; rebels finally repulsed, 11 killed and their leader captured, 1 June; officials dismissed, 3—9 June, 1898; 24 rebels hanged, 362 banished to Siberia, announced . Oct. 1898

KHUSCHK-I-NAKHUD, see *Maiwand*.

KHYBER PASS (the principal northern entrance into Afghanistan from India). It is ten miles west of Peshawur, extending about thirty-three miles towards Jellalabad; lying between lofty slate cliffs, varying from 600 to 1000 feet in height; held by Afridis and other warlike tribes, to whom Dost Mahomed formerly paid subsidies, which were discontinued by his son Shere Ali, ameer of Afghanistan.

The pass forced by col. Wade, 26 July, and gen. sir John Keane retired through it after his victorious campaign 1839
Again forced by general (aft. sir George) Pollock, on his way to chastise Cabul for the massacres in the previous winter . . . 5-14 April, 1842
At Ali Musjid, a fort in the pass, the further advance of sir Neville Chamberlain on a mission from the viceroy to the ameer was forbidden, with threats of violence . . . 22 Sept. 1878
The pass held by the British . . . till March, 1881
The viceroy, the marquis of Lansdowne, rode through the pass . . . . 30 Oct. 1889
The pass opened to trade under the Indian government, Landi Kotal to be fortified, terms accepted by the Afridis . . . . 28 Oct.-4 Nov. 1899
The regular troops withdrawn . . . 20 Dec. „
Visit of the duke and duchess of Connaught, 13 Jan. 1903

See *Afghanistan, India*, 1897-8.

KIDDERMINSTER (Worcestershire), renowned for its carpet manufactures, established about 1735. It was made a parliamentary borough again in 1832. The statue of Richard Baxter, the nonconformist, was unveiled by Mrs. Philpotts, wife of the bishop of Worcester, 28 July, 1875; an address was delivered by dean Stanley. Fierce rioting through carpet trade disputes quelled, 4-8 April, 1884. Typhoid fever prevalent, Sept. to Oct. 1884, 87 deaths. Population, 1881, 24,270; 1891, 24,803; 1901, 24,692.

KIDNAPPING ACTS (1872 and 1875). passed to prevent and punish criminal outrages upon natives of the islands in the Pacific Ocean; see *Slavery*, *Queensland*, and *Melanesia*.

KIEFF (Kiov or Kiow), chief town of a province of the same name in European Russia, made a principality 1137, annexed to Poland 1386, and after several changes was ceded to Russia 1686. Population of the province, 1886, 3,026,036.

The cathedral of St. Sophia was founded in 1037, the Greek academy 1588, the university in . . 1834
Visit of the czar; consecration of a new cathedral of St. Vladimir; statue of the emperor Nicholas I. unveiled . . . . 2 Sept. 1896
Student troubles, see *Russia* . . . . April, 1899
Jewish synagogues and schools ordered to be closed in Berditcheff . . . . . . Sept. „
Destructive hurricane and rainstorm, 23 deaths, 20 July, 1902
Strikes and serious riots . . . . 5-7 Aug. 1903

KIEL, a seaport of Schleswig-Holstein, and a member of the Hanseatic league in 1300. The university was founded in 1665. By a treaty between Great Britain, Sweden, and Denmark, signed here 14 Jan. 1814, Norway was ceded to Sweden; see *Norway*. An extraordinary assembly of the revolted provinces, Schleswig and Holstein, met here 9 Sept. 1850. By the convention of Gastein between Austria and Prussia, 14 Aug. 1865, the former was to govern Holstein, but Kiel to be held by Prussia as a German federal port. This was annulled in 1866 by the issue of the war. Population, 1890, 69,214; 1900, 121,790.

Foundation stone of opening lock of the canal from the Baltic to the North Sea laid by the emperor William I. . . . . . 3 June, 1887
The canal was opened with great ceremony, 20 June, 1895. The emperor William II., with his sons, in the imperial yacht *Hohenzollern*, followed by 23 other vessels, German and foreign, passed the huge water-gates and entered the canal at Brunsbüttel on the North sea at 4 a.m., and arrived at Holtenau, on the Baltic, a distance of 61 miles, at 12.45 p.m., being received with many salutes and other demonstrations from the foreign war-ships assembled in Kiel harbour.*
The emperor dined on board lord Walter Kerr's flagship, the *Royal Sovereign*, 24 June; on adm. Kirkland's flagship, the *New York* . 26 June, 1895
Explosion on board a German pinnace, 5 deaths, 28 July, „
Braunschweig, battleship, launched . . 20 Dec. 1902
Visit of American squadron, emperor visits adm. Cotton on board the U.S. battleship *Kearsage*, 25 June; banquet and speech by emperor, 26 June, 1903

KILCULLEN (Kildare). Here a large body of the insurgent Irish defeated the British forces commanded by general Dundas, 23 May, 1798. The general in a subsequent engagement overthrew the rebels near Kilcullen-bridge, when 300 were slain.

KILDA, ST. An island in the Atlantic, 52 m. W. of Harris, one of the Hebrides. Population, 76, 31 March, 1901.

KILDARE (E. Ireland). The Curragh or race-course here was once a forest of oaks. Here was the nunnery of St. Bridget, said to have been founded by her in the 5th century, and here was a building called the fire-house, where, it is supposed, the nuns kept the inextinguishable fire which existed till the reformation. The see was one of the earliest episcopal foundations in Ireland; St. Conlæth, who died 519, the first prelate. The first Protestant bishop was Thomas Lancaster, in 1550. The see is valued, by an extent returned 39 Hen. VIII., at 69*l.* 11*s.* 4*d.* Irish per year. Kildare was united to Dublin in 1846; see *Dublin*. The insurrection in Kildare, which swelled into the rebellion, commenced, 23 May, 1798. On that night, lieut. Gifford of Dublin and a number of other gentlemen were murdered by insurgents. This rebellion was quelled in 1799. The Curragh is now a military camp. St. Brigid's cathedral reopened, the archbishops of Canterbury, Armagh, and Dublin present, 22 Sept. 1896.

KILFENORA (Clare), a bishopric, said to have been founded by St. Fachnan. Cardinal Paparo, in 1152, rendered it a suffragan see to Cashel; but in 1660 it was annexed to Tuam, and to Killaloe in 1752.

KILIMA-NJARO, a lofty volcanic mountain in E. Equatorial Africa, discovered by Rebmann in 1848.

Mr. H. H. Johnston ascended 16,200 feet from the summit of Kibö . . . . Nov. 1884

* The key-stone of the works at Holtenau was solemnly laid by the emperor William, and the canal was named by him, in memory of his grandfather, the *Kaiser-Wilhelm* canal. Kiel was for several days the scene of great festivities. The flags of 14 nations were floating in the harbour on upwards of 80 sea-going men-of-war, and over 300 yachts and steamers of various nationalities were present. Dr. von Boetticher, president of the committee of commerce, received much honour from the emperor for his great services in relation to this national work.

Dr. Hans Meyer (unsuccessful 1887 and 1888), with Herr Purtscheller and one native, climbed up the icy steeps to the highest pinnacle of the ridges of the volcanic crater about 19,700 feet high, which he named "Kaiser Wilhelm's Peak," after having planted on it the German flag, 6 Oct.; they left the mountain . . . . 30 Oct. 1889
Dr. Meyer gave an account of his travels to the Royal Geographical Society, London . 14 April, 1890
Major von Wissmann establishes a fortified station at Kilima-Njaro, in charge of lieutenant Witzleben 15 Feb. 1891; Germans defeated; fort abandoned 10 June; re-occupied without fighting, 29 July, 1892; limits defined by convention . . July, 1893
Dr. Lent, botanist, and Dr. Kretzschmar, zoologist, and several of their followers, killed, reported, 26 Oct. 1894

KILKENNY (S. E. Ireland), an English settlement about 1170. The castle was built 1195, by Wm. Marshall, earl of Pembroke. At the parliament held here by Lionel duke of Clarence 1367, the statute of Kilkenny was passed.* After a siege the town surrendered to Cromwell, 28 March, 1650, on honourable terms. The duke and duchess of York well received, 19 April *et seq.*, 1899. Population, 1901, 12,000.

KILLALA (Mayo) was invaded by a French force landing from three frigates, under general Humbert, 22 Aug. 1798. The invaders were joined by the Irish insurgents, and the battles of Castlebar and Colooney followed; and the French were defeated at Ballynamuck, 8 Sept. same year.

KILLALA (Sligo), an early see. The author of the Tripartite life of St. Patrick, says, "that in 434 he came to a pleasant place where the river Muadas (Moy) empties itself into the ocean; and on the south banks of the said river he built a noble church called Kil-Aladh, of which he made one of his disciples, Muredach, the first bishop." The see of Achonry was united to Killala in the 17th century; and both were united to Tuam in 1839; see *Tuam* and *Bishops*.

KILLALOE (Clare), a see supposed to have been founded by St. Molua, whose disciple, St. Flannan, son to king Theodoric, consecrated at Rome by John IV. in 639, was also bishop. At the close of the 12th century, Roscrea was annexed to Killaloe, and Kilfenora has been held with it. Clonfert and Kilmacduach were added in 1836.

KILLIECRANKIE (a defile in Perthshire). Here the forces of William III. commanded by general Mackay were defeated by the adherents of James II. under Graham of Claverhouse, viscount Dundee, who fell in the moment of victory, 17 or 27 July, 1689.

KILMACDUACH (Galway). This see was held with Clonfert, from 1602. St. Coleman was its first bishop, in the 7th century. It was valued, 29 Eliz. 1586, at 13*l.* 6*s.* 8*d.* per annum. It is united to Killaloe.

KILMAINHAM HOSPITAL (Dublin), the noble asylum of aged and disabled soldiers in Ireland, built by Wren, was founded by Arthur, earl of Granard, marshal-general of the army in Ireland, 1675; and the duke of Ormond perfected the plan in 1679.

The term *Treaty of Kilmainham* was applied to an alleged agreement between Mr. Gladstone's government and Mr. Parnell and other land-leaguers imprisoned in the Kilmainham gaol on 13 Oct. 1881. The government is said to have entered into a negotiation with them while there, May, 1882. See Mr. J. Morley's "Life of Gladstone," 1903.

KILMALLOCK (Limerick). An abbey was founded here by St. Mochoallog or Molach about 645, and an abbey of Dominicans was built in the 13th century. *Ware.* A charter was granted to Kilmallock by Edward VI., and another by Elizabeth in 1584. The town was invested by the Irish forces in 1598, but the siege was raised by the earl of Ormond. There was much fighting here in 1641 and 1642; see *Fenians*, March, 1867.

KILMORE (Armagh), an ancient town, whose bishops were sometimes called Brefinienses, from Brefney, and sometimes Triburnenses, from Triburna, a village; but in 1454, the bishop of Triburna, by assent of pope Nicholas V., erected the parish church of St. Fedlemid into a cathedral. Florence O'Connacty, the first bishop, died in 1231. Valued, 15 Jas. I. with Ardagh, at 100*l.* per annum. The joint see of Elphin and Ardagh was united to it in 1841.

KILSYTH (central Scotland). Here Montrose defeated the Covenanters, 15 Aug. 1645, and threatened Glasgow.

KIMBERLEY, see under *Griqualand*. *Kimberley's Act*, see under *Crime*.

KIMMERIDGE CLAY: Rev. H. Moule announced his successful use of this clay for fuel and gas-making, March, 1874; practicability doubted.

KINBURN, a fort, at the confluence of the rivers Bug and Dnieper. Here Suwarrow defeated the Turks, 28 June, 1788. Kinburn was taken by the English and French, 17 Oct. 1855. Three floating French batteries, said to be the invention of the emperor, on the principle of horizontal shell-firing, was very effective. On the 18th the Russians blew up Oczakoff, a fort opposite.

KINDER-GARTEN (children's garden), a system of education devised by Frœbel, but practically carried out by Mr. and Mrs. Ronge, in Germany, in 1849, and in England in 1851. The system, founded mainly on self-tuition, and enlivened by toys, games, and singing, is set forth in Ronge's "Kinder-garten," published in 1858; and has been largely adopted in English schools. The Frœbel Society established 1874.

KINDRED TABLE OF, in the Book of Common Prayer, was set forth in 1563, see *Leviticus*, chap. xviii., B.C. 1490.

KINEMATICS (Greek *kineo*, I move), the science of motion. Reuleaux's "Kinematics of Machinery," translated by A. B. W. Kennedy; published, June, 1876. "Kinematism" is a method of treating certain diseases by movement. Prof. Rankine's "Machinery and Millwork" first appeared, 1809; new ed. 1876; see *Motion*.

KINEMATOGRAPH or **CINEMATOGRAPH**, a machine invented by Mr. Thomas A. Edison, combining electricity with photography, by means of which the movements of the actors in a scene at the theatre (accompanied by their voices

* It enacted among other things, "that the alliance of the English by marriage with any Irish, the nurture of infantes, and gossipred with the Irish, be deemed high treason." And again, "if anie man of English race use an Irish name, Irish apparell, or anie other guize or fashion of the Irish, his lands shall be seized, and his body imprisoned, till he shall conform to English modes and customs." Said never to have been enforced. It abolished the Brehon laws.

and the music) are reproduced upon a screen. The kinematograph was described by Mr. Edison at New York 28 May, and in the *Times*, 29 May, 1891; see *Paris*, 4 May, 1897.

M. M. A. and L. Lumière's Cinematograph (living photos) exhibited in London . . March, 1896
Cinematograph pictures of the Jubilee procession, 22 June (exhibited before the queen at Windsor, 23 Nov. 1897), much in vogue, 1903.

KINETOSCOPE. An apparatus invented by Mr. Edison, for the continuous photography of objects in motion, the first series of photographs were of the strong man Sandow, reported, New York, 7 March, 1894.

Various scenes exhibited in London: blacksmiths at work, dancers, &c. . . 17 Oct. *et seq.* 1894
By the theatrograph, invented by Mr. Robt. W. Paul, kinetoscopic pictures projected on a full-sized lantern screen, were exhibited at the Royal Institution, 28 Feb. 1896. A ship in motion, with spectators walking on the shore, and other scenes were represented.

KING: German *König*, equivalent in meaning to the Latin *Rex*, Scythian *Reis*, Spanish *Rey*, Italian *Rè*, French *Roy*: Hebrew *Rosch*. *Rex* is thought to be connected with the Hindu rajah, derived from the Sanscrit *ragan*, the root of which is *arg*, *argami*, to possess. *Rex* therefore means possessor. Nimrod was the first founder of a kingdom, about 2245 B.C. The "manner of the king" is set forth in 1 *Samuel* viii., 1112 B.C. Saul was the first king of Israel, 1095 B.C. Most of the Grecian states were originally governed by kings; and kings were the first rulers in Rome.

King of England.—The style was used by Egbert, 828; but the title *Rex gentis Anglorum*, king of the English nation, existed during the Heptarchy; see *Britain*.
The plural phraseology, *we*, *us*, *our*, was first adopted among English kings by John 1199
Pope Leo X. conferred the title of "Defender of the Faith" on Henry VIII. . . . 11 Oct. 1521
Henry VIII. changed *lord* of Ireland into king. . 1542
The style "Great Britain" was adopted at the union of England and Scotland, 6 Anne 1707
That of the "United Kingdom of Great Britain and Ireland" at the union, when the royal style and title was appointed to run thus:—"*Georgius Tertius, Dei Gratia, Britanniarum Rex, Fidei Defensor*," "George the Third, by the grace of God, of the United Kingdom of Great Britain and Ireland, king, Defender of the Faith" (France being omitted) . . . . 1 Jan. 1801
Hanover omitted in the queen's style 21 June, 1837
The queen was proclaimed in all the important places in India, as "Victoria, by the Grace of God, of the United Kingdom of Great Britain and Ireland, and the colonies and dependencies thereof in Europe, Asia, Africa, America, and Australia, queen," &c. (see *Empress*). 1 Nov. 1858
The national assembly decreed that the title of Louis XVI. "*king of France*," should be changed to "*king of the French*" . . . 16 Oct. 1789
The royal title in France abolished 1792
Louis XVIII. styled "by the grace of God king of France and Navarre" 1814
Louis-Philippe I. was invited to the monarchy under the style of the "king of the French" . 9 Aug. 1830
The emperors of Germany, in order that their eldest sons might be chosen their successors in their own life-time, politically obtained them the title of "*king of the Romans.*" The first emperor so elected was Henry IV. 1055
Richard, brother of Henry III. of England, was induced to go to Germany, where he disbursed vast sums under the promise of being elected next emperor; he was elected "king of the Romans" (but failed in succeeding to the imperial crown) 1256
The title of "king of France" assumed, and the French arms quartered, by Edward III., in right of his mother, 1340; discontinued by Geo. III. 1802
The style "king of Rome" was revived by Napoleon I. for his son, born . . 20 March, 1811
The title "king of Italy" conferred on Victor Emmanuel II. of Sardinia by Italian parliament 17 March, 1861
Edward VII., by the Grace of God of the United Kingdom of Great Britain and Ireland and of the British dominions beyond the seas, king, defender of the Faith, emperor of India, proclaimed . . . . 4 Nov. 1901

KING-OF-ARMS: three for England,—Garter, Clarencieux, and Norroy; Lyon king-at-arms for Scotland, and Ulster for Ireland. These offices are very ancient: Clarencieux is so named from Lionel, third son of Edward III., the sovereign who founded the order of the Garter; see *Garter*. Lionel having by his wife the honour of Clare, was made duke of Clarence; which dukedom afterwards escheating to Edward IV., he revived the office of Clarence king-at-arms. The office of Bath king-of-arms, created in 1725, was changed to Gloucester king-of-arms, 14 June, 1726. Ulster was substituted, it is said, in lieu of Ireland king-of-arms, by Edward VI., 1553; but the monarch himself named it as a new institution.

KING'S ADVOCATE, a title of the Lord Advocate for Scotland. First appointed by James III. about 1480. King's Advocate was first entitled *Lord Advocate* in 1598. See under *Advocate*.

KING'S BENCH, or QUEEN'S BENCH, COURT OF, obtained its name from the king sometimes sitting here on a high bench, and the judges, to whom the judicature belongs in his absence, on a low bench at his feet. This court in ancient times was called *Curia Domini Regis*. The court of queen's bench sat for the last time, July, 1875, (see *Supreme Court*). Chief justice Cockburn received the freedom of London, 9 March, 1876; said to be the first case of the kind. The Queen's Bench Division of the high court of justice till 1881 consisted of the chief justice of England and four judges. The chief justice of the king's bench division is now chief justice of England; the exchequer and common pleas division were abolished in 1881.

CHIEF JUSTICES IN ENGLAND FROM HENRY VIII.

1509. John Fineux.
1526. John Fitz James.
1539. Sir Edward Montagu.
1546. Sir Richard Lyster.
1552. Sir Roger Cholmely.
1553. Sir Thomas Bromley.
1554. Sir William Portman.
1556. Sir Edward Saunders.
1559. Sir Robert Catlyn.
1573. Sir Christopher Wray.
1591. Sir John Popham.
1607 Sir Thomas Fleming.
1613. Sir Edward Coke.
1616. Sir Henry Montagu.
1620. Sir James Ley.
1624. Sir Ranulph Crewe.
1626. Sir Nicholas Hyde.
1631. Sir Thomas Richardson
1635. Sir John Brampston.
1643. Sir Robert Heath.
1648. Henry Rolle.
1655. John Glyn.
1659. Sir Rd. Newdigate.
,, Robert Nicholas.
1660. Sir Robert Foster.
1663. Sir Robert Hyde.
1665. Sir John Kelyng.
1671. Sir Matthew Hale.
1676. Sir Richard Raynsford.
1678. Sir William Scroggs.
1681. Sir Francis Pemberton
1683. Sir Edmd. Saunders.
1683. Sir George Jefferies, aft. lord Jefferies and lord chanc.
1685. Sir Edward Herbert.
1687. Sir Robert Wright.
1689. Sir John Holt.
1709. Sir Thomas Parker, aft. lord Parker, earl of Macclesfield, and lord chanc.
1718. Sir John Pratt.
1725. Sir Robert Raymond, aft. lord Raymond.
1733. Sir Philip Yorke, aft. ld. Hardwicke and lord chanc.
1737. Sir William Lee.
1754. Sir Dudley Ryder.
1756. Wm. Murray, lord, aft. earl of Mansfield.
1788. Lloyd, lord Kenyon, 9 June.
1802. Sir Edward Law, 12 April; aft. lord Ellenborough.
1818. Sir Charles Abbott, 4 Nov.; aft. lord Tenterden.
1832. Sir Thomas Denman, 7 Nov.; aft. lord Denman: resigned.
1850. John, lord Campbell, March; aft. lord chancellor.

1859.	Sir Alexander Cockburn, June; (died 20 Nov. 1880).	1894.	Charles, lord Russell of Killowen, 30 June; died, aged 68, 10 Aug. 1900.
1880.	John Duke, lord Coleridge, 26 Nov.; (died 14 June, 1894).	1900.	Sir Richard E. Webster, lord Alverstone, July.

CHIEF JUSTICES IN IRELAND (see *Supreme Court*).

1690.	Sir Richard Reynell, 6 Dec.	1803.	William Downes, 12 Sept.: aft. lord Downes.
1695.	Sir Richard Pyne, 7 June.	1822.	Chas. Kendal Bushe, 14 February.
1709.	Allan Brodrick, 24 Dec.	1841.	Edward Pennefather, 10 November.
1711.	Sir Richard Cox, 5 July.	1846.	Francis Blackburne, 23 Jan.
1714.	W. Whitshed, 14 Oct.	1852.	Thos. Lefroy, March.
1727.	John Rogerson, 3 Apr.	1866.	James Whiteside, July; died 25 Nov. 1876.
1741.	Thomas Marlay, 29 Dec.	1877.	George Augustus Chichester May, 9 Feb.
1751.	St. George Caulfield, 27 Aug.	1887.	Sir Michael Morris, Jan.; made lord of appeal as lord Morris, Dec. 1889; died, 8 Sept. 1901.
1760.	Warden Flood, 31 July.	1889.	Sir Peter O'Brien, Dec.; made a peer, May, 1900.
1764.	John Gore, 24 Aug.; aft. earl Annaly.		
1784.	John Scott, 29 April; aft. earl of Clonmel.		
1798.	Arthur Wolfe, 13 June; aft. lord Kilwarden (killed in Emmet's insurrection, 23 July, 1803).		

KING'S BENCH PRISON (Southwark), near the site of one of the oldest prisons of London, long used for the confinement of debtors. Here, it is said, prince Henry (afterwards Henry V.) was committed by Justice Gascoigne. The prison was burnt down by the London rioters, 7 June, 1780; see *Gordon's No-Popery Riots*. It was rebuilt in 1781, and contained about 230 rooms. Formerly, the debtors were allowed to purchase the liberties, to enable them to have houses or lodgings without the walls, or to purchase day-rules, to go out of the prison under certain regulations. The rules included St. George's Fields, &c. A consequence of the bankruptcy act, 1861, was the release of many insolvent debtors; and an act was passed in 1862 "for discontinuing the queen's prison and removal of the prisoners to Whitecross-street prison." The buildings, used as a military prison, were pulled down and the site sold, 1879-80.

KING'S BOOK, or "Valor Ecclesiasticus temp. Henrici VIII." the return of the commissioners appointed in 1534 to value the first fruits and tenths granted to the king. An edition by John Bacon ("Liber Regis") was published in 1780, and it was printed for the Record Commission, 1810-25.

KING'S BOUNTY, an annual grant of 1000*l.* for the Maunday royal alms distributed by the lord high almoner, began early in the reign of George III. and continued till 10 George IV. 1829. See *Maunday*.

KING'S COLLEGES, see *Aberdeen* and *Cambridge*. King's College, London, incorporated 14 Aug. 1829, and opened 8 Oct. 1831. It was incorporated with the university of London in 1837. The hospital was founded in 1839. The dining-hall and kitchen fell in, through drainage, 8 a.m., 6 Dec. 1869; no lives were lost. In consequence of the withdrawal of the government grant, on account of denominational tests, the council of the college issues an appeal to the public for additional funds (50,000*l.*), 24 Jan. 1891: new buildings of the school at Wimbledon opened by the duke of Cambridge, 6 July, 1899. The Christian Knowledge Society votes 5,000*l.*, payable in instalments, 4 Dec. 1894. The government annual grant of 1,700*l.* was restored irrespective of tests, 1 April, 1896. New laboratories opened by lord Lister, 30 Oct. 1900. The council passes a resolution (22-2) abolishing religious tests, theology excepted, 13 June, 1902; an appeal for endowment issued at a meeting. 19 Nov. 1902. Rev. A. C. Headlam, principal (April 1903), in succession to Dr. Robertson, consecrated bp. of Exeter.

KING'S COUNSEL, the first under the degree of serjeant was sir Francis Bacon, made so, *honoris causâ*, without patent or fee, in 1604, by James I. The first modern king's counsel was sir Francis North, afterwards lord keeper, in 1663.

KING'S COUNTY (Ireland), formed out of confiscated property, and so named from Philip, king of Spain, the husband of queen Mary of England, in 1556.

KING'S CROSS MARKET, N. London, opened 7 Aug. 1868; did not succeed.

KINGSDOWN'S ACT, 24 & 25 Vict. c. 114 (1861) relates to wills.

KING'S EVIL (scrofula), formerly supposed to be cured by the king's touch; the first being Edward the Confessor, in 1058. In the reign of Charles II. 92,107 persons were touched; and, according to Wiseman, the king's physician, they were nearly all cured! Queen Anne officially announced in the *London Gazette*, 12 March, 1712, her intention to touch publicly. The custom was dropped by George I., 1714.

KING'S LYNN, see *Lynn Regis*.

KING'S PROCTOR, the name formerly given to a class of practitioners in the Admiralty and Ecclesiastical courts. The king's proctor is the official, now the solicitor to the treasury, who intervenes to oppose a petition for divorce if collusion or fraud are suspected.

KING'S REMEMBRANCER, see *Exchequer, Court of*.

KING'S SPEECH. The first from the throne is said to have been by Henry I., 1107.

KING'S THEATRE, see *Opera-house*.

KINGSTON, see *Hull*.—KINGSTON, Jamaica, was founded in 1693, after the great earthquake in 1692 which destroyed Port Royal; it was constituted a city, 1802. An awful fire here ravaged a vast portion of the town, and consumed 500,000*l.* of property, 8 Feb. 1782; another fire in 1843; another great fire; town nearly destroyed; estimated loss about 3,000,000*l.*, 5 deaths announced, 11 Dec. 1882. See *Mansion House*. The bishopric was established in 1856; see *Jamaica*.

KINGSTON TRIAL. The duchess of Kingston was arraigned before the lords in Westminster-hall, on a charge of bigamy, having married first, capt. Hervey, earl of Bristol, and next, during his lifetime, Eveyln Pierrepont, duke of Kingston, 15-22 April, 1776. She was found guilty, but, on pleading the privilege of peerage, the punishment of burning in the hand was remitted, and she was discharged on paying the fees.

KINGSTOWN (Dublin). The harbour here was commenced in June, 1817. The name was changed from Dunleary in compliment to George IV., who here embarked for England at the close of his visit to Ireland, 3 Sept. 1821. Kingstown railway from Dublin opened 17 Dec. 1834.

KIOTO, see *Kyōto*.

KIRBEKAN, BATTLE OF, see *Soudan*, 10 Feb. 1885.

KIRKDALE CAVE, see *Geology* (Buckland).

KISHINEFF MASSACRES, see *Russia*, 19, 20 April, 1903.

KISSING the hands of great men was a Grecian custom. Kissing was a mode of salutation among the Jews, 1 *Samuel* x. 1, &c. The "kiss of charity," or "holy kiss," commanded in the Scriptures (*Romans* xvi. 16, &c.), was observed by the early Christians, and is still recognised by the Greek church and some others. Kissing the pope's foot (or the cross on his slipper) began with Adrian I. or Leo III. at the close of the 8th century.

KIT-KAT CLUB, of above thirty noblemen and gentlemen, instituted in 1703, to promote the Protestant succession. The duke of Marlborough, sir R. Walpole, Addison, Steele, and Dr. Garth were members. It took its name from its dining at the house of Christopher Kat, a pastry-cook in King-street, Westminster.

KITT'S, see *Christopher's, St.*

KLADDERADATSCH, the German "*Punch*," first published in Berlin, by Albert Hoffmann, the proprietor, originally a bookseller's assistant. He amassed a fortune, and died 10 Aug. 1880, aged 62.

KLONDIKE GOLDFIELDS, see *Canada*, 1897 *et seq*. Dawson City, the *business centre*, population, 1901, 4,500.

KNEELING. The knee was ordered to be bent at the name of Jesus (see *Philippians* ii. 10), about the year 1275, by the order of the pope. The ceremony of a vassal kneeling to his lord is said to have begun in the 8th century.

KNIGHTS. The word knight is derived from the Saxon *Cniht*, a servant (*i.e.*, servant to the king, &c.). The institution of the Roman knights (*Equites* or horsemen, from *equus*, a horse), is ascribed to Romulus, about 750 B.C., when the curiæ elected 300. Knighthood was conferred in England by the priest at the altar, after confession and consecration of the sword, during the Saxon heptarchy. The first knight made by the sovereign with the sword of state was Athelstane, by Alfred, A.D. 900. *Spelman*. The custom of ecclesiastics conferring the honour of knighthood was suppressed in a synod held at Westminster in 1100. *Ashmole's Institutes. Salmon*. On the decline of the empire of Charlemagne, all Europe being reduced to a state of anarchy, the proprietor of every manor became a petty sovereign; his mansion was fortified by a moat, and defended by a guard, and called a castle. Excursions were made by one petty lord against another, and the women and treasure were carried off by the conqueror. At length the owners of rich fiefs associated to repress these marauders, to make property secure, and to protect the ladies; binding themselves to these duties by a solemn vow, and the sanction of a religious ceremony. Cervantes' "Don Quixote," a satire on knight-errantry, was published in 1605; see *Banneret*, *Chivalry*, *Tournaments*, *Holy Sepulchre*, *John*, and *Michael*.

PRINCIPAL MILITARY, RELIGIOUS, AND HONORARY ORDERS OF KNIGHTHOOD.*

African star, Congo state	1888
Albert the Bear, Anhalt	1836
Albert, Saxony	1850
Alcantara, instituted about	1156
Alexander Nevskoi, St., Russia	1722
Amaranta, Sweden (*female*)	1645
Andrew, St., Russia	1698
Andrew, St., Scotland (see *Thistle*)	787, 1540, 1687
Angelic Knights, Greece	337, 1191
Anne, St., Holstein, now Russia	1735
Annonciada, Savoy, about	1360
Annunciada, Mantua	1618
Anthony, St., Hainault	1382
Anthony, St., Bavaria	1382
Avis, Portugal, about	1162
Bannerets. See *Bannerets*.	
Bath, England, 1399. Revived (see *Bath*)	1725
Bear, Switzerland	1213
Bee, France (*female*)	1703
Bento d'Avis, St., Portugal	1162
Black Eagle, Prussia	1701
Blaise, St., Armenia, 12th century.	
Blood of Christ, Mantua	1608
Bridget, St., Sweden	1366
Broomflowers, France	1234
Brotherly (or Neighbourly) Love, Austria (*female*)	1708
Calatrava, Castile, instituted by Sancho III.	1158
Catherine, St., Palestine	1063
Catherine, St., Russia (*female*)	1714
Charles, St., Würtemberg	1759
Charles III. (or the Immaculate Conception), Spain	1771
Charles XIII., Sweden	1811
Chase, Würtemberg	1702
Christ, Livonia	1203
Christ, Portugal and Rome	1317
Christian Charity, France	1558
Cincinnati, America (soon dissolved)	1783
Compostello (see *St. James*).	
Conception of the Virgin	1618
Concord, Prussia	1660
Constantine, St., Constantinople, about 313; by emperor Isaac, 1190; Parma, 1699; since removed to Naples.	
Crescent, Naples, 1268. Revived	1464
Crescent, Turkey	1801
Cross of Christ	1217
Cross of the South, Brazil	1822
Crown of Italy	1868
Crown of India (*female*)	31 Dec. 1877
Crown of Oak, Netherlands	1841
Crown, Prussia	1861
Crown Royal, France (Friesland)	802
Crown, Würtemberg	1818
Danebrog, Denmark, instituted by Waldemar II., 1219; revived by Christian V.	1671
Death's Head (*female*), by the widow Louisa Elizabeth of Saxe Masburg	1709
Denis, St., France	1267
Distinguished service, British army	1886
Dog and Cock, France	500
Dove of Castile	1379
Dragon, Hungary	1439
Dragon Overthrown, German	1418
Eagle (see *Black*, *Mexican*, *Red*, *White*).	
Ear of Corn and Ermine, Brittany, about	1442
Elephant, Denmark (about 1190), by Christian I.	1462
Elizabeth, St., Portugal and Brazil (*female*)	1801
Elizabeth Theresa, Austria (*female*)	1750
Empire of India	1877
Esprit, St., France	1579
Ferdinand, St., Naples	1800
Ferdinand, St., Spain	1811
Fidelity, Baden	1715
Fidelity, Denmark	1732
Fools, Cleves	1380
Francis I., Two Sicilies	1829
Francis Joseph, Austria	1849
Frederick, Würtemberg	1830

* Enlarged and corrected from Edmondson, Carlisle, and the "Almanach de Gotha;" the early dates are doubtful. Many orders were instituted after the settlement of Europe in 1815.

Friesland (or Crown Royal), France 802
Garter (*which see*), England 1349
Generosity, Brandenburg 1685
Genet, France 726
George, St., and the Reunion, Naples 1800 and 1819
George, St., Angelic Knights 1191
George, St., Austria 1470, 1494
George, St., Defender of the Immaculate Conception, Bavaria 1729
George, St., England (see *Garter*) . . . 1349
George, St., Genoa 1472
George, St., Hanover 1839
George, St., Ionian Isles 1818
George, St., Rome 1492
George, St., Russia 1769
George, St., Spain 1317
George, St., Venice 1200
Gerion, St., Germany 1190
Glaive, Sweden 1522
Glory, Turkey 1831
Golden Angel (afterwards St. George), about 312
Golden Falcon, Japan (*which see*) . . . 1890
Golden Fleece, instituted at Bruges by Philip the Good, Austria and Spain . . 10 Jan. 1429
Golden Lion, Hesse Cassel 1770
Golden Lion, Nassau, and Holland . . . 1858
Golden Shield and Thistle, France . . . 1370
Golden Spur, by Pius IV. 1559
Golden Stole, Venice, before 737
Gregory, St., Rome 1831
Guelphic, Hanover 1815
Henry, St., Saxony 1736
Henry the Lion, Brunswick 1834
Hermengilde, St., Spain 1814
Hohenzollern, Prussia 1851
Holy Ghost, France 1579
Holy Sepulchre (*which see*) 1099, 1496
Holy Vial (St. Remi), France 499
Hospitallers (*which see*), 1099; of Rhodes, 1308; of Malta 1521
Hubert, St., Germany (by the duke of Juliers and Cleves), Bavaria 1444
Imperial Service, British Empire . 26 June, 1902
Imtiaz (Turkey) . . . . . . Nov. 1879
Iron Cross, Prussia 1813
Iron Crown, Lombardy, 1805; revived . . 1816
Iron Helmet, Hesse Cassel 1814
Isabella, St., Spain, 1804; Portugal (*female*) . 1801
Isabella the Catholic, Spain 1815
James, St., Holland 1290
James, St., Portugal 1310
James, St., of the Sword, Santiago, 1175; Spain and Portugal 1177
Januarius, St., Naples 1738
Jerusalem (see *Malta*) 1048
Jesus Christ, Rome. instituted by John XXII., 1320. Reformed as Jesus and Mary, by Paul V. . 1615
Joachim, St., Germany 1755
John of Acon, St., after 1377
John of Jerusalem, St. (see *Hospitallers*), Rome 1048
John, St., Prussia 1812
Joseph, St., Tuscany 1807
Julian of Alcantara, St. 1156
Katherine, St., England (female nurses) . . 1879
Knot. Naples 1352
La Calza, Venice, about 737
Lamb of God, Sweden 1564
Lazarus, St., France, before 1154; united with that of St. Maurice, Savoy 1572
Legion of Honour, France 1802
Leopold, Austria 1808
Leopold, Belgium 1862
Lily of Aragon 1410
Lily of Navarre, about 1043
Lion, Holland 1815
Lion (see *Sun*) 1808
Lion of Zähringen, Baden 1812
Lioness, Naples, about 1399
Loretto, Lady of 1587
Louis, Bavaria 1827
Louis, Hesse Darmstadt 1807
Louis, St., France 1693
Louisa Prussia (*female*) 1814
Malta (see *Hospitallers*).
Maria de Merced, St., Spain 1218
Maria Louisa, Spain (*female*) 1792
Maria Theresa, Austria 1757
Mark, St., Venice, about 828. Renewed . . 1562
Martyrs, Palestine 1014
Maurice, St., Savoy 1434
Maximilian Joseph, Bavaria 1806
Medjidié, Turkey 1852
Merit, Bavaria 1808, 1866
Merit, Belgium 1867
Merit, Hesse Cassel 1769
Merit, Oldenburg 1838
Merit, Prussia 1740
Merit, Saxony 1815
Merit, Würtemberg 1859
Merit, Military, Baden 1807
Merit, England . . . . . . 26 June, 1902
Mexican Eagle 1865
Michael, St., Bavaria 1693
Michael, St., France 1469
Michaël, St., Germany 1618
Michael and George, Sts., 1818; re-organised, March, 1869
Montjoie, Jerusalem, before 1180
Neighbourly Love, Austria (*female*) . . . 1708
Nicholas, St. (Argonauts of), Naples . . . 1382
Noble Passion, Saxony 1704
Oak of Navarre, Spain 722
Olaf, St., Sweden 1847
Osmanié, Turkey 1861
Our Lady of Montesa 1316
Our Lady of the Conception of Villa Viçosa . 1818
Our Lady of the Lily, Navarre 1043
Palatine Lion 1768
Palm and Alligator, Africa, granted to Gov. Campbell in 1837
Passion of Jesus Christ, France 1384
Patrick, St., Ireland 1783
Paul, St., Rome 1540
Pedro I., Brazil 1826
Peter, Frederick Lewis, Oldenburg . . . 1838
Peter, St., Rome 1530
Philip, Hesse Darmstadt 1840
Pius, founded by Pius IV. 1559
Pius IX., Rome 1847
Polar Star, Sweden. Revived 1748
Porcupine, France 1393
Reale, Naples, about 1399
Red Eagle, Prussia, 1705, 1712, 1734. Revived . 1792
Redeemer (or Saviour), Greece 1833
Remi, St. (or Holy Vial), about 499
Rosary, Spain 1212
Rose, Brazil 1829
Round Table, England, by Alfred (see *Garter*), 516 or 528
Royal Red Cross (*female*) . . . . 23 April, 1883
Royal Victorian, England . . . . 23 April, 1896
Rue Crown, Saxony 1807
Rupert, St., Germany 1701
Saviour, Aragon 1118
Saviour, or Redeemer, Greece 1833
Saviour of the World, Sweden 1561
Savoy, Italy 1815
Scale, Castile, about 1316
Scarf, Castile, 1330. Revived 1700
Sepulchre, Holy, Palestine 1099
Seraphim, Sweden . . . . . 1260 or 1265
Ship and Crescent, France 1269
Slaves of Virtue, Germany (*female*) . . . 1662
Stanislas, St.. Poland 1765
Star, France 1022
Star, Sicily 1351
Star of India, British 1861
Star of the Cross (*female*), Austria . . . 1668
Star of the North, Sweden 1748
Stephen, St., Hungary 1764
Stephen, St., Tuscany 1561
Sun and Lion, Persia 1808
Swan, Flanders, about 500
Swan, Prussia (*female*) 1440, 1843
Sword (or Silence), Cyprus, ... 1195
Sword, Sweden, 1525. Revived 1748
Templars (see *Templars*) 1119
Teste Morte (Death's Head), Würtemberg (*female*) . 1652
Teutonic, Austria, about 1190; abolished, 1809; 1522; re-organised 1840, 1865
Thistle of Bourbon 1370
Thistle, Scotland, 809. Revived . . . 1540. 1687
Thomas of Acon, St., after 1377
Toison d'Or (Golden Fleece) 1429
Tower and Sword, Portugal, 1459. Revived . 1808
Tusin, or Hungarian Knights, about . . . 1562
Two Sicilies 1808
Vasa, Sweden 1772

Victoria and Albert, India (*female*) 1862
Vigilance, or White Falcon, Saxe-Weimar 1732
Virgin Mary, Italy 1233
Virgin of Mount Carmel, France 1607
Wends, Mecklenburg 1864
White Cross, Tuscany 1814
White Eagle, Poland, about 1325. Revived . . 1705
White Falcon, Saxe-Weimar 1732
Wilhelm, Holland 1815
Wing of St. Michael, Portugal 1172
Wladimir, St., Russia 1782

FEMALE KNIGHTS. It is said that the first were the women who preserved Tortosa from the Moors in 1149, by their stout resistance. Large immunities were granted to the women and their descendants. Several female orders appear in the preceding list. Ladies have been admitted to several male orders.

KNIGHTS OF GLYN and KERRY IN IRELAND. The heads of two branches of the family of Fitzgerald, who still enjoy the distinctions bestowed on their ancestors by sovereigns in the 13th century. The 19th knight of Kerry died 6th Aug. 1880.

KNIGHTS OF THE SHIRE, OR OF PARLIAMENT; summoned by the king's writ and chosen by the freeholders, first summoned by Simon de Montfort, in 1258, and in a more formal manner, 20 Jan. 1265. There are writs extant as far back as 11 Edward I., 1283. The knights are still girded with a sword when elected, as the writ prescribes.

KNIGHTS OF LABOUR. A large secret trade union in the United States, said to have been originated by a man named Uriah Stevens in Philadelphia in 1869, for protection of workmen against capitalists. They were energetic in the promotion of railway and other strikes, especially in Missouri in March, 1886. Head quarters at Philadelphia, number about 400,000, May, 1886. The society is condemned by the pope. Decline of the order reported Aug. 1888; active in Aug. 1890. *Knights of Industry* active in regard to strikes, 1893.

KNIVES. In England, Hallamshire (the country round Sheffield) has been renowned for its cutlery for five centuries; Chaucer speaks of the "Sheffield thwytel." Stow says that Richard Mathews on the Fleet-bridge was the first Englishman who made *fine* knives, &c.; and that he obtained a prohibition of foreign ones, 1563. Clasp or spring knives became common about 1650; coming originally from Flanders.—*Knife-cleaning machines* were patented by Mr. George Kent in 1844 and 1852; others have been invented, by Masters, Price, &c.; see *Forks*.

KNOW-NOTHINGS, a society which arose in 1853, in the United States of N. America. Their principles were embodied in the following propositions (at New York, 1855). They possessed several newspapers and had much political influence:—

1. The Americans shall rule America.
2. The Union of these States.
3. No North, no South, no East, no West.
4. The United States of America—as they are—one and inseparable.
5. No sectarian interferences in our legislation or in the administration of American law.
6. Hostility to the assumption of the pope, through the bishops, &c., in a republic sanctified by Protestant blood.
7. Thorough reform in the naturalisation laws.
8. Free and liberal educational institutions for all sects and classes, with the Bible, God's holy word, as a universal text-book.

A society was formed in 1855 in opposition to the above, called *Know-Somethings*. Both bodies were absorbed into the two parties, Democrats and Republicans, at the presidential election in Nov. 1856.

KNUTSFORD, Cheshire. The foundation stone of St. Paul's college for the northern counties here was laid, 24 Sept. 1873.

KOH-I-NOOR, or "Mountain of Light," the East India diamond; see *Diamonds*.

KOLA, a West African nut, from which is obtained, by grinding, a stimulating and sustaining drug, much used by the natives in long journeys, enabling them to endure thirst and hunger, 1892.

KOLIN or KOLLIN (Bohemia). Here the Austrian general Daun gained a signal victory over Frederick the Great of Prussia, 18 June, 1757. In commemoration, the military order of Maria Theresa was instituted by the empress-queen.

KÖLN, see *Cologne*.

KOMORN or COMORN (Hungary), an ancient fortress town, often taken and retaken during the wars with Turkey. Near it the Hungarians, under gen. Klapka, defeated the Austrians, 11 July, 1849, but surrendered the town 1 Oct.

KONIEH (formerly Iconium). Here the Turkish army was defeated by the pasha of Egypt, after a long sanguinary fight, 21 Dec. 1832. The grand vizier was taken prisoner.

KÖNIGGRÄTZ (Bohemia). Near here was fought the decisive battle between the Austrians commanded by marshal Benedek, and the Prussians commanded by their king William I., 3 July, 1866. Prince Frederick Charles halted at Kammeniz on Monday, 2 July, his troops commenced their march at midnight, and the first shot was fired about 7.30 a.m. 3 July. The attack began at Sadowa (after which the battle is also named) about 10 o'clock, and a desperate struggle ensued, the result appearing uncertain, till the army of the crown prince of Prussia arrived about 12.30. When Chlum, which had been taken and lost seven times by the Prussians, was taken for the eighth time, the fate of the day was decided; and the retreat of the Austrians, at first orderly, became a hasty disastrous flight. About 400,000 men were engaged in this battle, one of the greatest in modern times. The Austrians are said to have lost 174 guns, about 40,000 killed and wounded, and 20,000 prisoners. The Prussians lost about 10,000 men. The victory gave the supremacy in Germany to Prussia, unity to North Germany, and Venetia to Italy; and led to the legislative independence of Hungary.

KÖNIGSBERG, the capital of east Prussia, was founded by the Teutonic knights in 1255, and became the residence of the grand master in 1457. It joined the Hanseatic league in 1365. University founded, 1544. It was ceded to the elector of Brandenburg in 1657, and here Frederick III. was crowned the first king of Prussia in 1701. It was held by the Russians 1758-64, and by the French in 1807. Here king William I. and his queen were crowned, 18 Oct., 1861; his monument unveiled by the emperor, 4 Sept.; the emperor at a banquet censures the nobles for opposing his plans, promises additional grants to the province, and declares that he reigns by Divine right, 6 Sept. 1894. Population, in 1885, 151,151; 1890, 161,528; 1900, 187,897.

KÖNIGSTEIN TUN (Nassau, Germany), most capacious, was built by Frederick Augustus, king of Poland, in 1725. It was made to hold 233,667 gallons of wine; and on the top, which was railed in, was accommodation for twenty persons to regale themselves. The famous tun of St. Bernard's was said to hold 800 tons; see *Heidelberg Tun*.

KOOKAS, a warlike reforming sect in N. W. India, founded by Baluk Ram about 1845, and after his death, about 1855, headed by Ram Singh, who preached the restoration of the old Sikh religion, which venerated cattle and punished their slaughterer. After several outrages against the Mahometans, an outbreak of the Kookas took place near Loodiana, which was vigorously suppressed, 15 Jan. 1872, by commissioner Cowan, who ordered 49 prisoners to be blown from cannon, 17 Jan. Several others were tried and executed by commissioner Forsyth soon after. For this severity Mr. Cowan was ordered to be dismissed, and Mr. Forsyth removed to another station, April, 1872. The Kooka leaders claim 800,000 followers; but the probable number is about one-tenth.

KORAN or **ALCORAN (AL KURAN)**, the sacred book of the Mahometans, was written about 610, by Mahomet (who asserted that it had been revealed to him by the angel Gabriel in twenty-three years), and published by Abu-bekr about 635. Its general aim was to unite the professors of idolatry and the Jews and Christians in the worship of one God (whose unity was the chief point inculcated), under certain laws and ceremonies, exacting obedience to Mahomet as the prophet. The leading article of faith preached is compounded of an eternal truth and a necessary fiction, namely, that there is only one God, and that Mahomet is the apostle of God. *Gibbon.* The Koran was translated into Latin in 1143; into French, 1647; into English by Sale, 1734; and into other European languages, 1763 *et seq.* It is a rhapsody of 6000 verses, divided into 114 sections; see *Mahometanism*, &c.

KOREA, see *Corea.*

KOREISH, an Arab tribe which had the charge of the Caaba, or shrine of the sacred stone of Mecca, and strenuously opposed the pretensions of Mahomet. It was defeated by him and his adherents, 623-30.

KOSSOVA, see *Cossova.*

KOSZTA AFFAIR. Martin Koszta, a Hungarian refugee, when in the United States in 1850, declared his intention of becoming an American citizen, and went through the preliminary forms. In 1853 he visited Smyrna, and on 21 June was seized by a boat's crew of the Austrian brig *Huzzar.* By direction of the American minister at Constantinople, captain Ingraham, of the American sloop *St. Louis*, demanded his release; but having heard that the prisoner was to be clandestinely transported to Trieste, he demanded his surrender by a certain time, and prepared to attack the Austrian vessel on 2 July; Koszta was then given up. On 1 Aug., the Austrian government protested against these proceedings in a circular addressed to the European courts, but eventually a compromise was effected, and Koszta returned to the United States.

KOYUNJIK, the site of the ancient Nineveh (*which see*).

KRAAL, a Dutch name for a South African village. See *Zululand.* Women visitors excluded from the Kaffir kraal in the Savage South African exhibition, Earl's Court (opened May, 1899), 28 Aug.; the action upheld by Mr. Justice Cozens-Hardy, 8 Sept. 1899.

KRAKATOA, see *Java*, 1883.

KRAO. A hairy female Burmese child exhibited at the Westminster Aquarium, Jan. 1883; thought incorrectly by some to be a specimen of the missing link between man and the anthropoid apes.

KRASNOI (central Russia). Here the French defeated the Russians, 15 Aug. 1812; and here they were themselves defeated after a series of conflicts, 14-18 Nov. following.

KREASOTE, see *Creasote.*

KREMLIN, a palace at Moscow, built by Demetri, grand-duke of Russia, about 1376. It was burnt down in Sept. 1812, and rebuilt in 1816; partly burnt about 23 July, 1879.

KRIEGSPIEL, see *War Game.*

KROMSCHRÖDER GAS, a new hydrocarbon (air saturated with petroleum spirit), was tried in May, 1873, at Great Marlow, for street lighting, and reported successful. The gas was said to be cheap and quickly generated, the combustion giving a brilliant white smokeless light.

KROUMIRS, see *Tunis.*

KRUPP'S CAST STEEL Factory, see *Essen.*

KRYPTOGRAPH, see *Cryptograph.*

KRYPTON, a new gas discovered by prof. Ramsay by means of the spectroscope, reported 6 June, and exhibited at the Royal society, 8 June, 1898.

KU KUX KLAN, the name of a secret society in the southern states of the Union, principally in Tennessee in North America, bitterly opposed to the ruling men. Early in 1868, this society issued lists of proscribed persons, who, if they did not quit the country after warning, became liable to assassination. General Grant endeavoured to suppress this society in April. Its repression by the militia in Arkansas was ordered, Nov. 1868, and it became the subject of legislation at Washington, June, 1871.

KULDJA, a revolted province of China; was seized by Russia in 1871, and restored by treaty in 1879.

KULTUR-KAMPF, the conflict in Prussia respecting worship, see Prussia, 1873, *et seq.*

KUNNERSDORF, BATTLE OF, see *Cunnersdorf.*

KUNOBITZA, in the Balkan. Here John Hunniades, the Hungarian, defeated the Turks, 24 Dec. 1443.

KURDISTAN, Western Asia (the ancient Assyria), subject partly to Turkey and Persia. In Oct. 1880, the Kurds, warlike and agricultural tribes, nominal Mahometans, invaded and ravaged Persia, and were subdued after fierce conflicts with their chief, Obeid-ullah, a Turkish sheikh, Nov.–Dec. 1880. In 1881 he went to Constantinople and was well received, but kept in a kind of honourable restraint, Sept. 1881. In Sept. 1882 he escaped to Kurdistan and incited the Kurds to revolt against Persia; captured by the Turks; rescued by his son, Nov. 1882; said to have died at Mecca in 1883. See *Armenia*, 1892, *et seq.*

KUSHK-I-NAKHUD, see *Maiwand.*

KUSTRIN or **CUSTRIN** (Prussia), a fortified town, besieged and burnt by the Russians, 22 Aug. 1758; taken by the French in 1806; given up, 1814.

KYŌTO or **MIAKO**, for over 1,000 years the capital of Japan, with many fine Buddhist temples, lies about 26 miles inland from Ozaka. The singing girls of this city are famed for their graceful dances; and the pottery, porcelain, brocades, enamels, bronze work, &c., are greatly admired. *Chambers.*

KYRLE SOCIETY (named after John Kyrle, who died 1724, extolled by Pope as the Man of Ross), started by Misses Miranda and Octavia Hill in 1875, and founded in 1877 by prince Leopold, princess Louise, the duke of Westminster, and others, with the object of "bringing beauty home to the people," by means of decorative art, gardening, music, &c. First public meeting held 27 Jan. 1881.

L.

L. *s. d.* see *Coin*.

LABARUM, see *Standards*.

LABORATORY. The Royal Institution laboratory, the first of any importance in London, was established in 1800, and rebuilt, 1872. In it were made the discoveries of Davy, Faraday, Tyndall, Frankland, Dewar, and Rayleigh; see *Royal Institution*. The Royal Laboratory, Woolwich Arsenal, was re-organised in 1855. First state laboratory to detect adulteration in commerce, etc., near King's college hospital, 38 rooms, erected under sir John Taylor, of the office of works, reported 5 Oct. 1897; see *Chemical*. Blue-book issued, report of the government laboratory, *Times*, 25 Aug. 1902 and 13 Aug. 1903.

LABOUR COMMISSION. The relations between capital and labour having been greatly disturbed in recent years, especially since 1888, leading to many strikes, the government were induced to appoint a royal commission "to inquire into the relations between employers and employed, and to report whether legislation can with advantage be directed to remedy any evils that may be disclosed," &c.

Among the persons nominated, 10 April, 1891, were the following: the marquis of Hartington (duke of Devonshire, 21 Dec. 1891) chairman, the earl of Derby, sir M. Hicks-Beach, Mr. Mundella, Mr. Courtney, Mr. Jesse Collings, Mr. Burt, sir F. Pollock, Mr. Tom Mann, Mr. Plimsoll, with several chairmen of public companies and employers of labour. Secretaries, Mr. John Burnett and Mr. Geoffrey Drage. Miss Orme, Miss Abrahams, Miss Collett and Miss Irwin were appointed lady sub-commissioners . . . . . March 1892

First meeting, the marquis of Hartington in the chair . . . . 1 May 1891

The first report laid before parliament . 1 April 1892

Meetings continued, 1892. Evidence closed, 2 Feb. 1893. Adjournment, *sine die*, 14 Feb. 1894. The cautious report, issued 20 April, 1894, is the result of profound study of the abundant evidence; the recommendations are negative or neutral in regard to legislature respecting the time of labour and the settlement of disputes by conciliation or arbitration. Various remedial proposals were dismissed.

LABOUR QUESTION. The relations between capital and labour have been much discussed in recent years. See *Germany*, 1889-90; *Berlin, Strikes, Trades Union, Shipping, Gas Light, Working-men* (Labour Day), 1 May, 1890-3, *United States*, 1 Sept. 1890-3, *Unemployed*.

The "Independent Labour party" held their first annual conference at Bradford; 115 delegates of various opinions; Mr. J. Keir Hardie, M.P., elected president, 13 Jan.; a revolutionary programme adopted, 14 Jan. 1893; at Manchester, 3 Feb. 1894; Newcastle, Mr. Keir Hardie, M.P., president, 15 April, 1895; Nottingham, 6 April, 1896; London, 19 April, 1897; Birmingham, 11 April, 1898; Leeds, 3 April, 1899; Leicester, 8 April, 1901; Liverpool, 31 March, 1902; York, 3 April, 1903

LABOUR DEPARTMENT (under the Board of Trade), constituted under Mr. Robert Giffen; Mr. Llewellyn Smith, commissioner for labour, and 25 correspondents . . . . . . Jan. 1893

"Labour Statistics," a blue-book by Mr. Burnett, (published annually) . . . . . May, 1893

The "Labour Gazette," No. 1, published . 15 May, „

The Labour Disputes bill introduced by government; withdrawn . . Sept. „

Mr. Chas. Booth's "Life and Labour of the People in London"; 9 vols.; (5 vols., completion, 1903), June, 1897

Mr. Tom Mann, about to attend a labour meeting, expelled from Paris . . . . . 14 May, „

Report of the Mosely Industrial Commission to the United States issued . . . . 18 April, 1903

LABOURERS, STATUTE OF, regulating wages, enacted 1349, 1357. A conference of philanthropists on the condition of agricultural labourers was held at Willis's rooms, Westminster, 28 March, 1868. LABOURING CLASSES Dwelling House Acts, passed, 1855, May, 1866, Aug. 1903. Labourers' (Ireland) Act passed 1886. See *Agriculture, Artisans*, and *Working-men*.

A *labourers' league* was established to assist the labourers in the exercise of the rights given them by the Local Government Act . May, 1888

LABRADOR (North America), a dependency of Newfoundland, discovered by Sebastian Cabot, 1497; visited by Corte Real in 1500; made a Moravian missionary station in 1771. Much distress through famine reported Sept. 1884. Failure of the fisheries, reported 2 Oct. 1896; and again Sept. 1897.

LABUAN, an Asiatic island, N. W. Borneo; ceded to the British in 1846, and given up to sir James Brooke in 1848. The bishopric was founded 1855. Governor, John Pope Hennessy, 1867, sir H. E. Bulwer, 1871; Herbert Taylor Usher, 1875; Chas. Cameron Lees, 1879; P. Leys, 1884; C. Vandeleur Creagh, Nov. 1889; L. Paul Beaufort, 1895; Hugh C. Clifford, Dec. 1899; E. W. Birch, 1901. Labuan was given up to the North Borneo company in 1889. Successful progress reported Nov. 1890; see *Borneo*.

LABURNUM, *Cytisus Laburnum*, called also the golden chain, was brought to these countries from Hungary, Austria, &c., about 1576. *Ashe*.

LABYRINTHS. Four are mentioned: the first, said to have been built by Dædalus, in the island of Crete, to secure the Minotaur; the second, of Arsinoe, in Egypt, in the isle of Mœris, by Psammeticus, king of that place, about 665 B.C.; the third, at Lemnos, remarkable for its sumptuous pillars, which seems to have been a stalactite grotto; and the fourth, at Clusium, in Italy, erected by Porsenna, king of Etruria, about 520 B.C. *Pliny*. The labyrinth of Woodstock is connected with the story of Fair Rosamond; see *Rosamond*. The Maze at Hampton Court was formed by William III. in the 17th century.

LACE is said to have been made in the 14th century in France and Flanders. Its importation into England was prohibited in 1483; but it was used in the court costume of Elizabeth's reign. Dresden, Valenciennes, Mechlin, and Brussels, have long been famous for their fine lace. An ounce weight of Flanders thread has been frequently sold for four pounds in London; and its value, when manufactured, has been increased to forty pounds, ten times the price of standard gold. A framework knitter of Nottingham, named Hammond, is said to have invented a mode of applying his stocking-frame to the manufacture of lace from studying the lace on his wife's cap, about 1768. *Macculloch*. So many improvements have been made in this manufacture, particularly by Heathcote (1809, 1817, &c.), Morley and Leaver (1811, &c.), that a piece of lace which about 1809 cost 17*l.* may now be had for 7*s.* (1853). *Ure.* The process of "gassing" by which cotton lace is said to be made equal to fine linen lace, was invented by Samuel Hall of Basford, near Nottingham. He died in Nov. 1862. Seguin's "La Dentelle; Histoire," &c., published, 1874. Irish lace exhibition at the Mansion House, London, 25 June–7 July, 1883. Scheme for encouraging the Irish lace manufacture supported by the government, June, 1884. Mrs. Bury Palliser's "History of Lace," 3rd edition, 1875.

LACEDÆMON or LACONIA (*Tzakonia*), see *Sparta*.

LA CROSSE. A game of ball, with running, among the Red Indians of Canada; adopted successively by the French and English settlers, and transmitted to the United States and to the United Kingdom. Its rules were systematised by Dr. Beers in 1860. Many clubs have been formed. Canadians beat the duke of Argyll's team, 11 goals to 3, at Lords; the king and other royalties present, 26 April, 1902.

LACTEALS (absorbent vessels connected with digestion), were discovered in a dog by Jasper Asellius of Cremona, 1622, and their termination in the thoracic duct by Pecquet, 1651; see *Lymphatics*.

LADIES' COLLEGES, see under GIRTON COLLEGE.

LADIES' NATIONAL AID ASSOCIATION, formed to contribute to the relief of the sick and wounded in the Soudan and Egypt. Originated by the duchesses of Buccleuch, St. Albans, and Marlborough, the marchioness of Salisbury and others, Feb. 1885. See *Aid*.

LADOCEA, in Arcadia. Here Cleomenes III. king of Sparta, defeated the Achæan league, 226 B.C.

LADRONE ISLES (N. Pacific), belonging to Spain, discovered by Magellan in 1520. He first touched at the island of Guam. The natives having stolen some of his goods, he named the islands the *Ladrones*, or Thieves. In the 17th century they obtained the name of Marianna islands from the queen of Spain. See *Spanish-American War*.

LADY. The masters and mistresses of manor-houses, in former times, served out bread to the poor weekly; and were therefore called *Lafords* and *Lefdays*—signifying *bread givers* (from *hlaf*, a loaf): hence Lords and Ladies. Wedgewood considers this fanciful, and derives the words from the Anglo-Saxon, *laford*, lord, and *hlæfdig*, lady.—LADY DAY (March 25), a festival instituted about 350, according to some authorities, and not before the 7th century according to others; see *Annunciation*. The year, which previously began on this day, was ordered to begin on Jan. 1, in France in 1564; and in Scotland, by proclamation, on 17 Dec. 1599; but not in England till 3 Sept. 1752, when the style was altered.

LADY-BIRDS. About 18th August, 1869, great flights of these insects alighted on the S.E. coasts of England, and arrived as far as London; a similar event occurred in 1867.

LADYSMITH, a town in Natal, about 90 miles by rail N.W. Pietermaritzburg. It derives its name from the wife of a former governor. It came into prominent notice 1899–1900, during the South African war, when Ladysmith was isolated and besieged by the Boers (2 Nov. 1899). Gen. sir George White and his forces, and the naval brigade under capt. (now rear-adm.) Lambton, whose naval guns rendered great service, were shut up (but making gallant sorties during the interval) until relieved, 28 Feb. 1900, by the Natal Carbineers and Imperial horse, under lord Dundonald, see *South African War*. Visited by Mr. Chamberlain during his tour in S. Africa, 1 Jan. 1903.

LAFFELDT, Holland. Here marshal Saxe defeated the English, Dutch, and Austrians, 2 July, 1747.

LAGOS, an island in the Bight of Benin (Africa), was assaulted and taken by the boats of a British squadron, under commodore Bruce, 26, 27 Dec. 1851. This affair arose out of breaches of a treaty for the suppression of the slave-trade. In 1861, the place was ceded to the British government, and created a settlement: Henry Stanhope Freeman, first governor. Lagos was constituted a distinct colony in 1886, see *Gold Coast Colony*.

Governor, sir Cornelius A. Moloney in 1889; Gilbert T. Carter (aft. sir), in Feb. 1891; resigns, succeeded by major H. E. M'Callum, Jan. 1897; Sir Wm. MacGregor . . . . . . Jan. 1899

Treaty with the king of Jebu securing freedom of roads, signed at Lagos by delegates . 21 Jan. 1892

The Jebus and Egbas threaten Lagos and the Gold Coast; checked by the arrival of troops under major Madden and col. Scott, April; the Jebus repulsed in their attack on Col. Scott's expedition and their villages taken . . 12 May *et seq.* ,,

Total defeat of the Jebus, surrender of the king, Jebu Ode occupied, army dispersed . 17–20 May ,,

Opposition again subdued . . Sept., Oct. ,,

Abeokuta, the Egba capital, visited by sir G. T. Carter, reported . . . . . . 12 Jan. 1893

Informal treaty with the Egbas, about 3 Feb.; confirmed . . . . 15 Aug. ,,

Treaty of the governor with the chiefs at Jebu Remo to abolish human sacrifice, slave dealing, &c. . . . . 4 Aug. 1894

Further annexations, reported . . . Nov. ,,

Destructive effects of the increased importation of cheap spirituous liquors, reported . . June, 1895

Native rising in the Hinterland, capt. Bower defeats the king of Yoruba, and bombards Oyo, 12 Nov. 1895; the king murdered, about 20 Nov.; 2,000 Ilorins attack the British, and are repulsed, 31 March, 1896; defeated again with loss at Odo Otin, April; totally defeated, their chief Adamu killed . . . . early March, 1897

Great loyal meeting of chiefs and natives 21 Aug. ,,

Various posts on the N.W. frontier occupied by the British; the French retire to Boussa: a British force mistaken for French is attacked by Baribas, who are repulsed (about 300 killed) by capt. Homfrey, reported . . . . . 15 Oct. ,,

French encroachments: Saki and Hassi in Yoruba occupied by them, Nov.; they retire on the arrival of a British force; Ilesha and Bere occupied by the British . . . . . 29 Dec. ,,

The French advance to Borea, and order the Haussa officer to haul down the British flag, demand refused; the French retired 9 Feb. 1898

Lt.-col. M'Callum (made K.C.M.G. July, 1898), receives the envoys of the kings of Borgu and Yoruba at Saki; settlement of the feud; treaties made, 28 Feb.; he is well received at Ilesha by the king and chiefs of Bariba; Wori Yaro made king of Borgu, 9 March; arrives at Okuma 11 March (see *Newfoundland*, 1899) . . . . . ,,

Col. Allan holds a palaver with the king and chiefs and hoists the British flag at Bode, treaties signed; reported . . . . . March, 1898
Kishi (*Hinterland*) evacuated by the French, occupied by the British . . . . . May, „
The French evacuate Boussa and occupy Bona and Lobi, reported . . . . . 10 Oct. „
Capt. Denton opens the railway from Lagos to Abbeokuta; a durbah held, etc. . 21, 22 April, 1899
Sir Wm. MacGregor opens the Lagos-Ibadan railway, amid great rejoicings, 5 March, 1901; a branch from Aro to Abbeokuta . . 14 Dec. 1901

LAGOS BAY (Portugal). Here was fought a battle between admiral Boscawen and the French admiral De la Clue, who lost both his legs in the engagement, and died next day, 17, 18 Aug. 1759. The *Centaur* and *Modeste* were taken, and the *Rédoubtable* and *Ocean* run on shore and burnt: the scattered remains of the French fleet got into Cadiz.

LA HOGUE (correctly Hague) (N. W. France), BATTLE OF, 19 May, 1692, when the English and Dutch fleets under admirals Russell and Rooke, defeated the French fleet commanded by admiral Tourville. The English burnt thirteen of the enemy's ships, and destroyed eight more, thus preventing a descent upon England.

LAHORE (N. W. India), was taken by Baber about 1520, and was long the capital of the Mongol empire. It fell into the power of the Sikhs in 1798. It was occupied by sir Hugh Gough, 22 Feb. 1846, who in March concluded a treaty of peace. See *Durbar*. Visit of the prince of Wales, 18 Jan. 1876, and of his son prince Albert Victor, who laid the foundation stone of the "Jubilee Museum and Technical Institute of the Punjab," 2-5 Feb. 1890. a statue of queen Victoria erected by public subscription, unveiled, 1 Jan. 1902. Population in 1891, 176,854; 1901, 120,058.

LAING'S NEK, see *Transvaal*, 1881.

LAKE DWELLINGS contain relics of the stone, iron, and bronze ages. Herodotus (about 450 B.C.) described the Pæonians as living on platforms in Lake Prasias. In 1855, Dr. Keller discovered the remains of lake habitations which had been supported on piles in several Swiss lakes ages ago. His book was published in England in 1866. Similar relics discovered in lake Constance, March, 1882; they have also been discovered in Britain and various parts of Europe, Africa, and South America; they are now considered to be evidence of a stage in human progress. The artificial fortified islands termed "Crannoges" discovered in some Irish lakes are attributed to the 9th and 10th centuries. They have been frequently used as places of refuge. *Artificial lake*, see under *Liverpool*, 1881 *et seq*.

Mr. Arthur Bulleid, in the spring of 1892, discovered, by excavation, near Glastonbury, in Somersetshire, remains of a pre-historic lake-village, in about 60 low mounds, enclosing wooden structures, many of which had been probably workshops. The many interesting relics of bronze, iron, bone, &c., with fragments of pottery, were deposited in the Glastonbury museum; R. Munro, M.D., "Lake Dwellings of Europe," Sept. 1892; excavations continued . 1897

LAKE POETS, a term applied to Wordsworth (1770-1850), Coleridge (1772-1834), and Southey (1774-1843), from their residence in the neighbourhood of the lakes of Westmoreland.

LAKE REGILLUS (Italy), where, tradition states, the Romans defeated the Latin auxiliaries of the expelled Tarquins, about 498 B.C.

LAKES CHAMPLAIN, ERIE, AND ONTARIO were the scenes of many actions between the British and Americans in the war of independence (about 1776 and 1777), and in the war of 1813-14.

LAMAISM, the religion of Mongolia and Thibet dating about 1357), is a corrupt form of Buddhism *which see*).

LAMBETH, parish, N. E. Surrey, became the seat of the abps. of Canterbury, 1197. Lambeth returns four members by act of 1885; municipal borough by London government act, 1899 (10 aldermen, 60 councillors). Population, 1891, 279,202; 1901, 301,895.

Lambeth public library, at Brixton-oval (cost 15,000*l*.); the gift of Mr. Henry Tate (bart. 1898); was opened by the prince of Wales, 4 Mar., 1893

Lambeth Palace. A considerable portion was built in the 13th century, by Hubert Walter, archbishop of Canterbury. The tower of the church was erected about 1375; and other parts of the edifice in the 15th century. Simon of Sudbury, archbishop of Canterbury, was killed here by the followers of Wat Tyler, who attacked the palace, burnt the furniture and books, and destroyed the registers and public papers, 14 June, 1381. The domestic portion of the palace was greatly enlarged for archbishop Howley (who died 1848), by Mr. Blore, at an expense of 52,000*l*. The palace was reopened after restoration, Oct. 1873; see *Canterbury, Articles*. For Lambeth Conferences see *Pan-Anglican Synods*. Lambeth bridge was freed from toll 24 May, 1879.

Lambeth degrees are those conferred by the archbishop of Canterbury by virtue of 25 Henry VIII., c. 21., 1533-4.
Archbishop's park (over 9 acres), given to the public by the abp. of Canterbury (laid out by the London County Council at cost 4,600*l*.), opened by the abp. 24 Oct. 1901; a drinking fountain presented by Miss Du Bois, end Oct. 1901.

LAMIAN WAR, 323 B.C. (excited by Demosthenes, the orator), between Athens and her allies and Antipater, governor of Macedon. Antipater fled to Lamia, in Thessaly, and was there besieged. He escaped thence and defeated his adversaries at Cranon, 322 B.C.

LAMMAS-DAY, the 1st of August, one of our four cross quarter-days of the year. Whitsuntide was the first, Lammas the second, Martinmas the third, and Candlemas the last; and such partition of the year was once equally common with the present divisions of Ladyday, Midsummer, Michaelmas, and Christmas. Some rents are yet payable at each of these quarterly days in England, and very generally in Scotland. *Lammas* probably comes from the Saxon *hlammæsse*, loaf mass, because formerly upon that day our ancestors offered bread made of new wheat. Anciently, those tenants that held lands of the cathedral church of York were by tenure to bring a lamb alive into church at high mass.

LAMPETER COLLEGE (Cardiganshire), was founded by bishop Burgess in 1822, and incorporated 1828. Henry James Prince, founder of the Agapemone (*which see*), was one of the revivalist Lampeter brotherhood, instituted among the students here about 1836.

LAMPS. The earthen lamp of Epictetus the philosopher sold after his death for 3000 drachmas. Lamps with horn sides said to be the invention of Alfred. London streets were first lighted with oil-lamps in 1681, and with gas-lamps in 1814. A lamp "constructed to produce neither smoke nor smell, and to give considerably more light than any lamp hitherto known," was patented by M. Aimé Argand in 1784, and was brought into general use in England early in the nineteenth century. On his principle are founded the lamps invented by Carcel about 1803, and since 1825, the moderator lamps of Levavasseur, Hadrot, and Neuburger. See *Safety Lamp*. Paraffin oil and naphtha spirit are now much used in lamps. The Water Safety Lamp invented by Mr. Devoll, was tried and approved 2 June, 1890. The flame is extinguished by the water if the lamp is overturned. The Kitson oil lamp, in which petroleum is burnt as gas, used successfully in Portland-place, May, 1901. See *Petroleum*.

LANARK (W. Scotland), was a Roman station, and made a royal burgh 1103.

LANCASHIRE was created a county palatine by Edward III. for his son John of Gaunt, who had married the daughter of Henry first duke of Lancaster, in 1359, and succeeded him in 1362. The court of the duchy chamber of Lancaster was instituted in 1376. On the accession of Henry IV. in 1399 the duchy merged into the crown. Net revenue to the queen in 1888, 50,000*l*.; total receipts, 86,284*l*.; total receipts in 1893, 81,747*l*., net revenue, 13,080*l*. For chancellors, see *Grey* and other administrations. See *Cotton*.

LANCASTER, supposed to have been the *Ad Alaunam* of the Romans. Lancaster was granted by William I. or II. to Roger de Poitou, who erected a castle upon its hill. It was taken by the Jacobites, Nov. 1715 and Nov. 1745. It was disfranchised for bribery by the Reform act of 1867. The public park, value about 23,000*l*., was presented by Mr. Jas. Williamson, of Rylands, 21 Nov. 1881. The Storey Institute (technical), founded by sir Thomas Storey (died, aged 73, 13 Dec. 1898), by a gift of 20,000*l*., in memory of the queen's jubilee in 1887, when he was mayor, opened by the marquis of Hartington, 23 Oct. 1891. A new infirmary opened by the duke and duchess of York, 24 March, 1896. Population, 1881, 24,239; 1891, 31,038; 1901, 40,329.

LANCASTERIAN SCHOOLS, based on a system of education by means of mutual instruction, devised by Joseph Lancaster about 1796, were not much patronised till about 1808. The system led to the formation of the British and Foreign School society, in 1805, whose schools are unsectarian, and use the Bible as the only means of religious instruction. Lancaster was accidentally killed at New York in 1838.

LANCASTRIANS, see *Roses*.

LANCERS, see *Regiments*.

LANCET, a weekly medical journal, established and edited by Thomas Wakley, surgeon (afterwards coroner for Middlesex and M.P. for Finsbury), first published 3 Oct. 1823. An injunction obtained by Mr. Abernethy against the publication of his lectures in the "*Lancet*," was dissolved by the lord chancellor in 1825. Mr. Wakley, born 1795, died 16 May, 1862. The proprietors of the "Lancet" have at various times employed medical men as commissioners of enquiry. The reports of the Analytical Sanitary Commission of the "Lancet" in 1851-54, were published by Dr. A. H. Hassall, as "Food and its Adulterations," in 1855. The "Lancet" commissioners (three physicians) enquired into the state of workhouse infirmaries in London, 1865, and in the country, 1867.

LAND is said to have been let generally in England for 1*s*. per acre, 36 Hen. VIII. 1544. The whole rental of the kingdom was about 6,000,000*l*. in 1600; about 14,000,000*l*. in 1688. In 1798 Mr. Pitt proposed his income tax of 10 per cent. on an estimate of 100 millions, taking the rent of land at 50 millions, that of houses at 10 millions, and the profits of trade at 40 millions; but in his estimate were exempted much land, and the inferior class of houses. The rental of the United Kingdom was estimated at 59,500,000*l*. in 1851. The rateable value of land in England was 39,835,000*l*. in 1870; 33,654,000*l*. in 1894. An act for rendering the transfer of land more easy was passed in 1862; see *Agriculture, Domesday*, old and new.

A species of *Land-tax* was exacted in England in the 10th century, which produced 82,000*l*. (see *Danegelt*) in 1018

Land Banks were proposed by Yarranton in . . 1648

The *Land-tax* grew out of a subsidy scheme of 4*s*. in the pound (which produced 500,000*l*. in 1692), imposed 1699

Ministers were left in a minority in the house of commons on the *land-tax bill* in 1767; it being the first instance of the kind on a money bill since the revolution. Its rate varied in different years from 1*s*. to 4*s*. in the pound.

Mr. Pitt made the tax perpetual at 4*s*. in the pound, but introduced his plan for its redemption, 2 April, 1798

The tax in 1810 produced 1,418,337*l*.; in 1820, 1,338,420*l*.; in 1830, 1,423,618*l*.; in 1840, 1,298,622*l*.; in 1852, 1,151,613*l*.; in year 1872-3, 1,108 225*l*. in 1875-6, 1,090,177*l*.; 1880, 1,047,000*l*.; 1885, 1,065,000*l*.; 1891, 1,030,000*l*. From the revolution to the year 1800, the land-tax had yielded 227,000,000*l*.

Land-tax and house-duty (to 31 March), in 1875, 2,440,000*l*.; 1876, 2,496,000*l*.; 1877, 2,532 000*l*.; 1878, 2,670,000*l*.; 1879, 1,075,511*l*. (land tax only). Changes made in the land-tax by the Finance Act, 1896. 1897, land-tax, 920,000*l*.; house duty, 1,510,000*l*.; *land tax and house duty*, 1900, 2,460,000*l*.; 1901, 2,475,000*l*.; 1902, 2,500,000*l*.; 1903, 2,550,000*l*.

Land Allotments. Lord Braybrooke's successful experiment in Essex, of allotting small portions of land to poor families, to assist them and relieve the parish poor-rates 1819

[The little colony was first called *Pauper Gardens*, but afterwards *New Village*, and it is calculated that 200*l*. *per annum* were saved to the parish.]

Landed Estates Court, established to "facilitate the sale and transfer of land in Ireland" (see *Encumbered Estates Act*) 1858

The *Land Registry office* for transfer of land opened in 1862; reported to be a failure by a commission, March, 1870

LAND TENURE REFORM LEAGUE held its first meeting, John Stuart Mill in the chair, 15 May, 1871

Bill to facilitate sale and transfer of land by means of registration brought in by lord chancellor Selborne, 29 April, 1873; by lord chancellor Cairns, 26 March, 1874

The transfer of land in Scotland facilitated by the conveyancing act passed . . . 7 Aug. "

Agricultural holding act and land transfer act for England passed . . . . 13 Aug. 1875

4 bills respecting land introduced by lord chancellor Cairns . . . . 23 Feb. 1880

Owners of Land in England and Wales (exclusive of the metropolis), of less than one acre, 703,289; one acre and more, 269,547. Estimated value, 124,000,000*l*.; tithes—estimated, 5,000,000*l*.

Important land act passed (see *Ireland*) 22 Aug. 1881

Settled Land Act passed 1882

[Tenants for life acquire power to sell or lease and use the proceeds.]

A new land commission unites in one body the Enclosure, Copyhold, and Tithes commissions . . "

New Agricultural Holdings Act passed . . . . "

Nationalization of the land advocated by the Trade Union Congress, 1882; negatived by the same at Nottingham (90-34) . . . . . 14 Sept. 1883

The National Land Company founded by the dukes of Argyll and Westminster, the earl of Ripon, and others, for the object of buying land to be sold in small portions to be farmed, 24 April, 1885
Purchase of land (Ireland) act passed, 14 Aug. 1885; said to have worked well; another act passed, see *Ireland* . . . . . 24 Dec. 1888
Allotments and small holdings association founded to carry out the allotments act of 1882, 1883–4; second annual meeting . . . . 11 Jan. 1886
The political cry "Three acres and a cow" much used during the elections of Nov.–Dec. 1885 (said to have originated in a handbill printed at Birmingham), and to have been acted upon by lord Tollemache in regard to his labourers. He died 9 Dec. 1890, aged 85.
Free land league formed, supported by Mr. Arthur Arnold and others; it proposes nationalization of the land and changes in tenure and transfer 1885–93
Irish land commission; earl Cowper, lord Miltown, sir J. Caird and others, announced 21 Sept. 1886; report presented . . . . . 24 Feb. 1887
Land transfer bill (England) read second time in the lords, 25 April, 1887 [dropped].
New Irish land bill passed . . . . 23 Aug. 1886
Allotments in England and Wales, 643,315 existing in ,,
Allotments act enabling sanitary authorities to acquire land, make arrangements, &c., passed 16 Sept. 1887
Welsh land league formed (see under *Wales*) . ,,
Large reduction of rents ordered by the land commission . . . . 27 Oct. ,,
Lord Ashbourne's purchase of land act passed (see *Ireland*) 14 Aug. 1885; another act passed 24 Dec. 1888; great success reported Nov. 1889. Land had been sold amounting in value to 3,792,532*l.* up to . . . . . . 31 Dec. 1888
The lord chancellor's land transfer bill dropped, 5 July, 1889; passed by the lords, 1893; again by the lords, 3 April, 1895; land transfer bill (tentative) passed . . . . . . 6 Aug. 1897
New allotment act passed 1890
New purchase of land bill introduced by Mr. A. J. Balfour (see *Ireland*), 24 March, 1890; dropped, 14 July, 1890; re-introduced in two parts, 27 Nov.; 2nd reading, 3 Dec. 1890; passed . . 5 Aug. 1891
[This act provides further funds for the purchase of land in Ireland, and makes permanent the Land Commission, it also creates a Congested Districts Board.]
Select committee on the Irish land acts, &c., appointed, 16 April; report issued . . . Aug. 1894
Mr. J. Morley's Irish land bill read 2nd time, 5 April, 1895
Land law (Ireland) act passed . . 14 Aug. 1896
Land Charges act passed . . . . 30 July, 1900
Lands Valuation Amendment act (Scotland) passed, 13 June, 1902
Land Purchase (Ireland) Act, royal assent 14 Aug. 1903

LAND CREDIT COMPANY (for Silesia), established by Frederick the Great; see *Crédits Fonciers*, 1763.

LAND LAW ACT, see *Irish Land Law Act*.

LANDED INTEREST, a term given by sir James Caird, agriculturist, born 1816, died 1892, to all persons deriving profits from land, much depressed in the latter half of the 19th century.

LANDEN or NEERWINDEN (Belgium). Near here the French under marshal Luxembourg defeated the allies, commanded by William III. of England, chiefly through the cowardice of the Dutch, 19 July (N.S. 29), 1693. The duke of Berwick, illegitimate son of James II., fighting on the side of France, was taken prisoner.

LANDGRAVE (from *land* and *graf*, a count), a German title, which commenced in 1130 with Louis III. of Thuringia, and became the title of the house of Hesse about 1263.

LAND LEAGUE, see under *Leagues* and *Ireland*, 1879.

LANDLORD, see *Rent* and *Ireland*, 1887, *et seq.*

LANDLORD AND TENANT ACT (Ireland), passed 1 Aug. 1870.

LAND NATIONALIZATION SOCIETY, formed at Westminster 16 Jan. 1882. The object has been warmly advocated by Mr. Henry George in his "Progress and Poverty," published Feb. 1881, and since. He condemns compensation. He met about 2,000 men at the Royal Exchange, London, 17 Jan. 1885. Annual meetings held.

LANDSHUT (Silesia), where the Prussians were defeated by the Austrians under marshal Laudohn, 23 June, 1760.

LANDSLIPS. Landslips are due to decay of the rocks or excessive saturation of the soil by rain.

Rossberg mountain behind the Rigi slipped down, burying villages and hamlets with above 800 inhabitants 1806
Lyme Regis, Dorset, a strip of chalk cliff three-fourths of a mile long, between 100 and 150 feet high, undermined by rain, slid forward on the beach, carrying fields, houses, and trees 24–27 Dec. 1839
Naini or Nynee Tal, a sanitary hill-station in the Himalayas, India, was destroyed by the descent of the mountain; about 30 valuable British lives (including major Martin Morphy, col. Fred. Sherwood Taylor, and capts. F. T. Goodeve, H. S. F. Haynes, and A. Balderston) and 200 natives perished . . . . 18 Sept. 1880
Near Northwich, Cheshire, salt works stopped 6 Dec. *et seq.* ,,
Elm, Glarus Canton; fall of about 30 houses; above 150 persons perished . . . . . 11 Sept. 1881
Subsidence on the Furness railway, near Lindal; an engine buried; no deaths . . 22 Sept. 1892
By subsidences in the western part of Sandgate (3 miles) many houses were shattered and families rendered homeless; damage to property, about 5000*l.*; much assistance was given by the military at Shorncliffe, the coastguard and police, and relief was promptly sent from Folkestone and Hythe, 4–5 March; the subsidences were attributed to the subsoil being saturated by heavy rains, or by the scouring action of the sea; liberal subscriptions in London and throughout the country (about 6,000*l.*) . . . . 20 March, 1893
Landslip at Vaerdalen, in N. Trondhjem; over 30 buildings destroyed; about 113 deaths, 18 May, ,,
A train of railway workmen buried by a landslip, about 48 persons perish, between Maçon and Aix-les-Bains . . . . . . 17 Oct. 1896
Serious landslip in the "Warren," between Folkestone and Dover . . . . early Nov ,,
Destructive landslip near Bantry, co. Cork, reported . . . . 31 Dec. ,,
Landslip from the Sasso Rosso, at Airolo; houses destroyed, 3 deaths . . . . 27 Dec. 1898
Landslips at Darjeeling, India, owing to a storm and other causes; 10 European children and about 300 other lives lost, 23, 24 Sept. 1899; the queen sends her deep sympathy . . . . 28 Sept. 1899
Amalfi, Italy, a mass of rocks above the town swept down towards the sea, hotels and other houses buried; much damage in the harbour; 10 deaths . . . . 22 Dec. ,,
Whitby, landslip owing to heavy rains; 2 houses destroyed and 3 lives lost . . . 10 Jan. 1900
Great landslip in Barbados, plantations wrecked and 85 houses swept into the sea, reported, 19 Oct. 1901
Landslips and floods; several hundred deaths reported . . . . 19 Aug. 1902
Landslip at Frank, Canada, estimated deaths 95, 25 April, 1903

See *Quebec*, 1889, *Himalaya*, 1894, *Bogs*, 1896.

LANDWEHR (German, *land-defence*). A force so named was raised in Austria in 1805, and in

Prussia in 1813, against the French. This force, the militia of Germany, especially of Prussia, was very effective in the war with Austria in 1866, and in that with France in 1870. No ranks in life are exempt from this service, and many persons in foreign countries returned to serve in 1870.

LANGDALE'S ACT, LORD, 7 Will. IV. & 1 Vict. c. 26 (1837), relates to copyholds, &c.

LANGENSALZA (N. Germany). Here the Hanoverian army on its way to join the Bavarians was attacked by the Prussians, who were defeated with the loss of about a thousand killed and wounded, and 912 prisoners, 27 June, 1866. The victory was of little avail, for the Hanoverians were soon surrounded by Falckenstein, and compelled to capitulate on honourable terms on 29 June.

LANGOBARDI, see *Lombards.*

LANGSIDE (S. Scotland), where the forces of the regent of Scotland, the earl of Murray, defeated the army of Mary queen of Scots, 13 May, 1568. Mary fled to England and crossed the Solway Frith, landing at Workington, in Cumberland, 16 May. Soon afterwards she was imprisoned by Elizabeth.

LANGUAGE must either have been revealed originally from heaven, or the fruit of human invention. The latter opinion is embraced by Horace, Lucretius, Cicero, and most of the Greek and Roman writers; the former by the Jews and Christians, and many modern philosophers. Some suppose Hebrew to have been the language spoken by Adam; others say that the Hebrew, Chaldee, and Arabic are only dialects of the original tongue. "And the whole earth was of one language and of one speech" (*Genesis* xi. 1).* George I. in 1724, and George II. in 1736, appointed regius professors of modern languages and of history to each of the universities of England.

The original European languages were thirteen, viz.: Greek, Latin, German, Sclavonian, spoken in the east; Welsh; Biscayan, spoken in Spain; Irish; Albanian, in the mountains of Epirus; Tartarian; the old Illyrian; the Jazygian, remaining yet in Liburnia; the Chaucin, in the north of Hungary; and the Finnic, in east Friesland.

From the Latin sprang the Italian, French, Spanish, and Portuguese.

The Turkish is a mixed dialect of the Tartarian.

From the Teutonic sprang the present German, Danish, Swedish, Norwegian, English, Scotch, &c.

There are 3424 known languages, or rather dialects, in the world. Of these, 937 are Asiatic; 587 European; 276 African; and 1624 American languages and dialects. *Adelung.*

In 1861 and 1862 professor Max Müller lectured on the "Science of Language" at the Royal Institution, London. He divides languages into three families:—

I. ARYAN (in Sanskrit, *noble*).

Southern Division. India (Prakrit, and Pali; Sanskrit; dialects of India; Gipsy).

Iranic (Parsi; Armenian, &c.).

Northern Division. Celtic (Cymric: Cornish, Welsh, Manx, Gaelic, Breton, &c.).

Italic (Oscan; Latin; Umbrian;—Italian, Spanish, Portuguese, French, &c.).

Illyric (Albanian).

Hellenic (Greek, and its dialects).

Wendic (Lettic: Old Prussian; *Slavonic dialects,*—Bohemian, Russian, Polish, Lithuanian, &c.).

Teutonic (*High* German: Modern German; *Low* German: Gothic; Anglo-Saxon; Dutch; Frisian; English. *Scandinavian:* Old Norse, Danish, Swedish, Norwegian, Icelandic).

II. SEMITIC: *Southern.* Arabic (including Ethiopic and Amharic). *Middle.* Hebraic (Hebrew, Samaritan, Phœnician inscriptions). *Northern.* Aramaic (Chaldee, Syriac, Cuneiform inscriptions of Babylon and Nineveh).

III. TURANIAN (from *Tura*, swiftness).

Northern Division. Tungusic (Chinese, &c.); Mongolic; Turkic; Samoyedic, and Finnic.

Southern Division. Taic (Siamese, &c.); (Himalayas); Malayic (Polynesia, &c.); Gangetic; Lonitic (Burmese, &c.); Munda; Tamulic.

"The Speech of Monkeys," by R. L. Garner, Sept. 1892.

Modern Language Association, founded in 1890; first president, prof. Max Müller; annual meetings held.

* *Eminent Linguists.*—Anas Montanus, editor of the Antwerp Polyglott Bible (1527-98); sir Wm. Jones (1746-94); Cardinal Giuseppe Mezzofanti (1774-1849) is said to have known 114 languages or dialects, and 50 well; and Niebuhr (1776-1831) knew 20 languages in 1807, and more afterwards; Hans Conon von der Gabelentz knew many languages critically: he died 3 Sept. 1874, aged nearly 67. Solomon Cæsar Malan (1812–94), eminent in Oriental languages, see *Indian Institute.*

LANGUE D'OC, see *Troubadours.*

LANGUEDOC (a province, S. France), formed part of the Roman Gallia Narbonensis; was named Gothia, as having been held by the Visigoths 409, who were expelled by the Saracens, in turn driven out by Charles Martel in the 8th century. In the dark ages the country was named Septimania (probably from its containing seven important towns): afterwards Languedoc (from its dialect, see *Troubadours*), about 1270, when annexed to the monarchy. It suffered during the persecutions of the Albigenses and Huguenots.

LANSDOWN, near Bath (Somersetshire). The parliamentary army under sir Wm. Waller was here defeated, 5 July, 1643.

LANTERNS of scraped horn were invented in England, it is said, by Alfred; and it is supposed that horn was used for window lights also, as glass was not generally known, 872-901. *Stow.* London was lighted by suspended lanterns with glass sides, 1415.

LANTHANUM, a rare metal discovered in the oxide of cerium, by Mosander in 1839.

LAOCOÖN, an exquisite work of Grecian art, in marble, modelled by Agesander, Athenodorus, and Polydorus, all of Rhodes, and other eminent statuaries (about A.D. 70); it represents the death of the Trojan hero, Laocoön, priest of Neptune, and his two sons, as described by Virgil. *Æneis,* ii. 200. It was discovered in 1506 in the Sette Salle near Rome, and purchased by pope Julius II. It is now in the Vatican.

LAODICEA, see *Seven Churches.*

LAON (N. France). A succession of actions between the allies (chiefly the Prussians) and the French, was fought under the walls of the town, which ended in the defeat of the latter with great loss, 9-10 March, 1814. Laon surrendered to the Germans 9 Sept. 1870. As the last man of the garde mobile left the citadel, a French soldier, in contravention of the capitulation, blew up the powder magazine, causing great destruction to the town and fortress. The grand-duke William of Mecklenburg-Schwerin was bruised, and 95 German riflemen and 300 French gardes mobiles were killed or wounded; general Theremin Du Hame, the commander, was wounded. The French attributed the explosion to accident.

LA PEROUSE'S VOYAGE. In 1785 La Perouse sailed from France for the Pacific, with the *Boussole* and *Astrolabe* under his command, and was last heard of from Botany Bay, in March, 1788. Several expeditions were subsequently despatched in search of Perouse; but no certain information was obtained until captain Dillon, of the East India ship *Research*, ascertained that the French ships had been cast away on the New Hebrides, authenticated by articles which he brought to Calcutta, 9 April, 1828.

LAPLAND or **SAMELAND** (N. Europe), nominally subject to Norway in the 13th century, and now to Sweden and Russia. Several Laplanders were exhibited at the Westminster Aquarium, Nov. 1877.

LA PLATA, the capital of the Argentine province of Buenos Ayres, *which see*, was founded in 1882. Population in 1888, 65,000, 1895, 45,410. See *Wrecks*, 1874.

LARCENY, French, *larcen;* Latin, *latrocinium;* see *Theft*.

LARENTALIA, see *Laurentalia*.

LARGS (Ayrshire, S. Scotland). Here the great expedition of Haco of Norway was finally defeated by Alexander III. after a succession of skirmishes, 3 Oct. 1263.

LA ROTHIÈRE (France). Here the French, commanded by Napoleon, defeated the Prussian and Russian armies, with great loss, after a desperate engagement, 1 Feb. 1814. This was one of Napoleon's last victories.

LARYNGOSCOPE, an instrument consisting of a concave mirror, by which light is thrown upon a small plane mirror placed in the posterior part of the cavity of the mouth. By its means the vocal chords of the interior of the larynx, &c., are exhibited, and have been photographed. It was invented by Mr. Manuel Garcia, and reported to the Royal Society 24 May, 1855. One constructed by Dr. Türck was greatly modified, in 1857, by Dr. Czermak, who exhibited its successful action in London in 1862. A similar apparatus is said to have been constructed by Mr. John Avery, a surgeon in London, in 1846. The British Laryngological and Rhinological Association was founded in 1888.

LA SALETTE, see *Pilgrimages*.

LATERAN, a church at Rome, dedicated to St. John, "the mother of *all* the churches," was originally a palace of the Laterani, a Roman family, and was given to the bishops of Rome by Constantine, and inhabited by them till their removal to the Vatican in 1377. Eleven councils have been held there.

LATHE. The invention is ascribed to Talus, a grandson of Dædalus, about 1240 B.C. Pliny ascribes it to Theodore of Samos, about 600 B.C. Great improvements have been made in recent times.

LATHOM-HOUSE (Lancashire), was heroically defended for three months against the parliamentarians, by Charlotte, countess of Derby. She was relieved by prince Rupert, 27 May, 1644. The house was, however, surrendered 4 Dec. 1645, and dismantled.

LATIN KINGDOM, EMPIRE, &c., see *Latium, Eastern Empire* 1204, and *Jerusalem*.

LATIN LANGUAGE, a member of the Aryan family, and one of the original languages of Europe, from which sprang the Italian, French, and Spanish; see *Latium*. A large portion of our language is derived from the Latin. It ceased to be spoken in Italy about 581; and was first taught in England by Adelmus, brother of Ina, in the 7th century. The use of Latin in law deeds in England gave way to the common tongue about 1000; was revived in the reign of Henry II.; and again was replaced by English in the reign of Henry III. It was finally discontinued in religious worship in 1558, and in conveyancing and in courts of law in 1731 (by 4 Geo. II. c. 25). A corrupt Latin is still spoken in Roumelia. The foreign pronunciation of Latin (*a*, ah; *e*, a; *i*, e, &c.) was adopted in English universities and many schools about 1875-6. For "Latin name," see *Latium*.

PRINCIPAL LATIN WRITERS.

	Died		Died
Plautus . . . B.C.	184	Lucan	65
Ennius	169	Seneca	65
Terence . (*flourished*)	166	Pliny the Elder . .	79
Cato the Elder . .	149	Quintilian (*flourished*)	80
Lucilius	103	Valerius Flaccus ,, .	81
Lucretius	52	Pliny the Younger ,, .	100
Julius Cæsar . . .	44	Statius . . (*about*)	100
Cicero	43	Tacitus . (*flourished*)	100
Catullus	40	Silius Italicus . .	101
Sallust	34	Martial . (*flourished*)	104
Vitruvius (*flourished*)	27	Suetonius . (*about*)	120
Propertius . . .	26	Juvenal	128
Virgil	19	Aulus Gellius (*flourished*)	169
Tibullus	18	Apuleius	174
Horace	8	Ammianus Marcellinus	390
Celsus (*flourished*) A.D.	17	Claudian	408
Livy	18	Macrobius	415
Ovid	18	Boethius	524
Paterculus . . .	31		
Persius	62		

(See *Fathers of the Church*.)

LATIN UNION (Monetary), that of France, Italy, Belgium, and Switzerland, to maintain the use of the same coinage, from 1865 *et seq.*; re-constituted in 1885; arranged to be continued from year to year, autumn 1889; renewed till 31 Dec. 1893, Oct. 1891; conference at Paris, 9 Oct. 1893.

LATITAT, an ancient writ, directing the sheriff to apprehend persons to be brought before the king's bench court, had its name from its being supposed that the person was lying hid, and could not be found in the county to be taken by bill. The writ was abolished by the Uniformity of Process act, 23 May, 1832.

LATITUDE. First determined by Hipparchus of Nice, about 162 B.C. It is the extent of the earth or the heavens, reckoned from the equator to either pole. Maupertuis, in 1737, in latitude 66·20 measured a degree of latitude, and made it 69·493 miles. Swanberg, in 1803, made it 69·292. At the equator, in 1744, four astronomers made it 68·732; and Lambton, in latitude 12, made it 68·743. Mudge, in England, made it 69·148. Cassini, in France, in 1718 and 1740, made it 69·12; and Biot, 68·769; while a recent measurement in Spain makes it but 68·63—less than at the equator, and contradicts all others, proving the earth to be an oblate spheroid (which was the opinion of Cassini, Bernouilli, Euler, and others), instead of a prolate spheroid; see *Longitude*.

LATITUDINARIANS, a name given to certain theologians who endeavoured to reconcile the church and nonconformists in the 17th century, such as Hales, Chillingworth, Tillotson, and Burnet.

LATIUM, now **CAMPANIA** (Italy), the country of the Latini and their mythical king, Latinus, popular date, 1240 B.C. Laurentum was the capital of the country in the reign of Latinus, Lavinium in that of Æneas, and Alba in that of Ascanius; see *Italy*, and *Rome*.

The Latins ally with Rome . . . . (*about*) B.C. 520
Join Porsenna to restore Tarquin II. 508
Defeated by Romans near Lake Regillus . 498 or 496
League with the Romans, 463; desert them in trouble, 388; union restored 359
Defeated in war; (before the great victory, near mount Vesuvius, the consul, P. Decius Mus, devoted himself to death, 340), 339; subdued and incorporated with Rome 338
Obtain Roman citizenship 90
The "*Latin name*" in the 3rd century, B.C., included the colonies in Italy founded by the Romans in their conquered territories, as well as those founded by the Latins.

LA TRAPPE, see *Trappists*.

LATTER-DAY SAINTS, see *Mormonites*.

LAUDANUM, see *Opium*.

LAUDERDALE EARLDOM, &c. (dated from 1590). Major Frederick Henry Maitland's claim to it established before the House of Lords, 22 July, 1885. A romantic story.

LAUENBURG, a duchy, N. Germany; was conquered from the Wends by Henry the Lion of Saxony, about 1152; ceded to Hanover, 1689; incorporated with the French empire, 1810; ceded to Denmark, 1815; annexed by Prussia, 14 Aug. 1865; possession taken 15 Sept. following; see *Gastein*.

LAUFACH, Bavaria (S. W. Germany), was taken by the Prussians under Wrangel, on 13 July, 1866, after a sharp action, in which the Hessians were defeated, the Prussian needle-gun being very efficacious.

LAUNCESTON, Cornwall. The granite church was erected in 1511; the new town-hall in 1887. Population, 1881, 3,808; 1891, 4,345.

LAUNCESTON, Tasmania, was founded 1804; incorporated 1858; made a city 1889. Population, 1881, 12,753; 1891, 8,937; 1901, 7,798.

LAUNDRY, London and Provincial Steam Laundry, Battersea, erected by a company; opened in 1880; and others since.

LAUREATE, see *Poet Laureate*.

LAUREL was sacred to Apollo, god of poetry; and from the earliest times the poets, and generals of armies, when victors, were crowned with laurel. Petrarch was crowned with laurel, 8 April, 1341.—The *Prunus laurocerasus* was brought to Britain from the Levant, before 1629; the Portugal laurel, *Prunus lusitanica*, before 1648; the royal bay, *Laurus indica*, from Madeira, 1665; the Alexandrian laurel, *Ruscus racemosus*, from Spain, before 1713; the glaucous laurel, *Laurus aggregata*, from China, 1806 or 1821.

LAURENTALIA were festivals celebrated at Rome in honour of Acca Laurentia, or Larentia, said to have been either the nurse of Romulus and Remus, or a rich dissolute woman, who bequeathed her property to the Roman people. The festival commenced about 621 B.C., and was held on he last day of April and the 23rd of December.

LAURIUM MINES, see *Greece*, 1872.

LAURUSTINUS, *Viburnum Tinus*, an evergreen shrub, was brought to England from he south of Europe, before 1596.

LAUSANNE, capital of the canton of Vaud, Switzerland, originally a Roman station. The cathedral was consecrated in 1275, and the university founded 1535. Here Gibbon completed his "Decline and Fall," 27 June, 1787. The International Workmen's congress assembled here Sept. 1867. Population, 1888, 33,340; 1901, 47,039.

LA VALETTA, see *Malta*.

LAVALETTE'S ESCAPE. Count Lavalette, for joining the emperor Napoleon on his return in 1815, was condemned to death, but escaped from prison in the clothes of his wife, 20 Dec. 1815. Sir Robert Wilson, Mr. Michael Bruce, and captain J. H. Hutchinson, aiding the escape, were sentenced to three months' imprisonment in the French capital, 24 April, 1816. Lavalette was permitted to return to France in 1820, and died in retirement in 1830.

LA VENDÉE (W. France). The French royalists of La Vendée took arms in March, 1793, and were successful in a number of hard-fought battles with the republicans, between 12 July, 1793, and 1 Jan. 1794, when they experienced a severe reverse. Their leader, Henri comte de Larochejaquelin, was killed, 4 March, 1794. A short peace was made at La Jaunay, 17 Feb. 1795. The war was terminated by gen. Hoche in 1796, and a treaty of peace was signed at Luçon, 17 Jan. 1800; see *Chouans*.

LAVENDER, *Lavandula spica*, brought from the south of Europe, before 1568.

LAW, see *Canons*, *Codes*, *Common Law*, *Civil Law*, *Crime*, *Digest*, *Supreme Court*. The Jewish law was given by God, and promulgated by Moses, 1491 B.C.

The laws attributed to Phoroneus, in the kingdom of Argos were reduced to a system by Draco, for the Athenians, 623 B.C.; whose code was superseded by that of Solon, 594 B.C.

The Spartan laws of Lycurgus were made about 844 B.C.; they remained in full force for about 700 years, and formed a race totally different from all others living in civilised society.

The Roman laws of Servius Tullius 566 B.C. were amended by the Twelve Tables published in 449 B.C., and remained in force till Justinian, nearly a thousand years.

BRITISH LAWS.

The British laws of earliest date were translated into the Saxon in . . . . A.D. 590
Saxon laws of Ina published about 690
Alfred's code of laws, the foundation of the common law of England, is said to have been arranged about 886
Edward the Confessor collected the laws . 1050-1065
Stephen's charter of general liberties . . . 1136
Henry II.'s confirmation of it . . . 1154 and 1175
The maritime laws of Richard I. (see *Oleron*) . . 1195
Magna Charta, by king John, 1215; confirmed by Henry III. 1216 *et seq.* (see *Magna Charta*, and *Forests Charter*).

Lord Mansfield, lord chief justice of the king's bench, declared, "That no fiction of law shall ever so far prevail against the real truth of the fact, as to prevent the execution of justice," 21 May, 1784

Many legal technicalities were got rid of by 14 & 15 Vict. c. 100. The act for the improvement of the administration of criminal justice, passed 7 Aug. 1851

LAWYERS.

Pleaders of the bar, or barristers, are said to have been first appointed by Edward I. 1291

"No man of the law" to sit in parliament, by stat. of 46 Edward III. and 6 Hen. IV. 1372

This prohibition was declared to be invalid by Coke and unconstitutional by Blackstone; attention was drawn to it in July, 1871; and the statutes were repealed 1871

Serjeants, the highest members of the bar, were alone permitted to plead in the court of common pleas. The first king's counsel under the degree of serjeant was sir Francis Bacon, in 1604

Law Association charity for widows founded in . . 1817

Incorporated Law Society of solicitors formed in 1823; plan enlarged, 1825: a charter obtained, 1831; renewed, 1845; new charter, 1872. The building in Chancery-lane, from the designs of Vulliamy, was commenced in 1829; provincial meetings are held, Manchester, Oct. 1893; controversy respecting the malpractices of certain solicitors: report of the committee; see *Times* leader, 25 June, 1900; *Trials*, Jan. 1901; 31 solicitors struck off the rolls in 1900

Juridical Society established in 1855

Law Times, established . . . . . 8 April, 1843

Law Journal . . . . Jan. 1866

The establishment of a legal university strongly advocated by the lord chancellor and others, Jan. 1871

The council of legal education put forth a scheme involving many changes, Nov. 1872; another scheme, Dec. 1891.

Legal Practitioners' Society, established . Nov. 1873

See *Barrister*, *Counsel*.

LAW REFORM.

LAW AMENDMENT SOCIETY, founded in 1843. It holds meetings during the session of parliament, and publishes a journal and reports. Its first chairman was lord Brougham, who introduced the subject of Law Reform by a most eloquent speech in the house of commons, on 7 Feb. 1828. Many acts for Law Reform have been passed since, and vigorous measures proposed.

Royal commission to inquire into the operation and constitution of the English courts of law, &c., issued 18 Sept. 1867.

The Judicature Commission (appointed 1867) recommended the consolidation of all the superior courts into one supreme court divided into chambers, April, 1869. It issued its fifth and last report, Sept. 1874.

The High Court of Justice Bill introduced into the house of lords, 18 March, 1870, was dropped near the end of the session.

Royal Commission on the administrative departments of Courts of Justice (Lord Lisgar and others) appointed, 4 Oct., 1873.

Supreme Court of Judicature Bill introduced by lord chancellor Selborne for establishing a High Court of Justice, and a High Court of Appeal 13 Feb., passed 5 Aug. 1873.

Its operation deferred from 2 Nov., 1874 to 1 Nov., 1875

The abolition of the house of lords as an Appeal Court rescinded 1875

Commission on Legal Procedure; report, recommending simplifying changes, published 8 Oct. 1881

New rules issued . . . . July, 1883

International commission on judicial reform recommends the establishment of an international tribunal for dealing with foreigners, except in capital cases . . . . May, 1884

See *Supreme Court* for details.

Scheme of law reform issued by the bar council, Aug. 1897

LAW-COURTS.—Commissioners appointed in 1859 reported in favour of the concentration of the law-courts in London, on a site near Carey-street, Chancery-lane, about 7 acres, on which stood about 400 houses. The estimated expense was about 1,500,000*l.*, which it was recommended to take from the accumulated Chancery fund, termed "Suitors' fund." Acts of parliament to carry out the plan were passed in 1865 and 1866.

Competitive designs were invited, and after much discussion (public and professional), Mr. Street's design was selected, 30 May, 1868; much attacked, but approved by the commission, Aug. 1870; contracts signed 17 Feb. 1874, and the works were begun immediately by Bull and Son, to be finished in 1881.

There were to be 18 courts, varying in size; a central hall, 231 feet long, 48 feet wide, 30 feet high; principal entrance in the Strand.

Offices in Eastern Block occupied 21 April, 1879.

Buildings completed, Oct. 1882.

Opened by the queen, 4 Dec. 1882.

All the buildings constitute by statute the *Palace of Justice*.

The Courts occupied Hilary sittings, 11 Jan. 1883

LAW REPORTS: A new and more economical plan of preparing and publishing law reports was finally adopted by a committee of barristers on 11 March, 1865 (see *Year-books*).

LAW TERMS, see *Terms*, abolished by Supreme Court of Judicature Act, 5 Aug. 1873.

International Law, see *Neutral Powers* and *International Law*.

Expenditure for law and justice from the public purse exclusive of county rates, in the year 1865-6, 2,344,540*l.*

Courts of Justice: salaries, &c., one year (to 31 March, 1877), 631,791*l.*

Encyclopædia of the laws of England, edited by Mr. Wood-Renton, vol. i. 1897

Cyclopædia of Scotch law 1895–6

LAW'S BUBBLE. John Law, of Edinburgh (born 1681), was made comptroller-general of the finances of France, upon the strength of a scheme for establishing a bank, and an East India and a Mississippi company, by the profits of which the national debt of France was to be paid off. See *Mississippi*. He first offered his plan to Victor Amadeus, king of Sardinia, who told him he was not powerful enough to ruin himself. The French ministry accepted it; and in 1716, he opened a bank in his own name, under the protection of the duke of Orleans, regent of France, and the deluded rich subscribed for shares both in the bank and the companies. In 1718 Law's was declared a royal bank, and the shares rose to upwards of twenty-fold the original value; so that, in 1719, they were worth more than eighty times the amount of all the current specie in France. In 1720 this fabric of false credit fell to the ground, spreading ruin throughout the country. Law died in poverty at Venice in 1729.—The South Sea Bubble in England occurred in 1720; see *South Sea*.

LAWN TENNIS, see *Tennis*.

LAYAMON'S BRUT, or Chronicle of Britain, a poetical semi-Saxon paraphrase of the Brut of Wace, made between 1100 and 1230, was published with a literal translation by sir Frederick Madden, in 1847.

LAYBACH (near Trieste, in Illyria). A congress met here in Jan. 1821, and was attended by the sovereigns of Austria, Russia, Prussia, and Naples. It broke up in May, after having issued two circulars, stating it to be their resolution to occupy Naples with Austrian troops, and put down popular insurrections.

The town suffered much by an earthquake, with loss of life, 14, 15 April; relief sent by the emperor . . . . 18 April, 1895

LAYER'S CONSPIRACY. Christopher Layer, a barrister, conspired with other persons to seize George I., the prince of Wales, lord Cadogan, and the principal officers of state, to seize the tower, to plunder the bank, and bring in the Pretender. Layer was hanged, 17 May, 1723. He was hanged for enlisting soldiers for the Pretender. Bishop Atterbury was accused of complicity and attainted, but permitted to quit the country.

LAY BROTHERHOOD OF ST. PAUL, for the diocese of London, was formed by the bishop of Marlborough, with the sanction of the bishop of London in 1891.

LAY HELPERS, to hold a position between the clergy and laity, proposed by the archbishop of Canterbury, and others, Oct. 1881. The association of Lay Helpers for London began in 1865.

LAYMEN, HOUSE OF, composed of 102 members elected in the dioceses, as a purely consultative body to assist the Convocation of the clergy, its main object being the promotion of church reform. It first met with Convocation at Westminster, 16 Feb. 1886. Lord Selborne, chairman; Mr. G. A. Spottiswoode, vice-chairman. They met in the Church house, 12 Feb. 1890.

LAZARISTS (the Priests of the Mission), a congregation devoted to education, founded by St. Vincent de Paul, 1625, were so named from their first establishment in a house which once belonged to the military order of St. Lazarus. They are also called *Vincentines*. See *France*, Oct. 1902.

LAZARO, ST. (N. Italy). Here the king of Sardinia and the Imperialists defeated the French and Spaniards after a long and severe conflict, 4 June, 1746.

LAZISTAN, a Turkish province in the pachalik of Trebizond, on the Black sea. Batoum, its seaport, was ceded to Russia by the treaty of Berlin, 13 July, 1878. The inhabitants at first resisted the change, but submitted on persuasion, many emigrating.

LAZZARITES, see *Italy*, 1878.

LAZZARONI (from *lazzdro*, Spanish for a pauper or leper), a term applied by the Spanish viceroys to the degraded beings in Naples, half-clothed and houseless. No man was born a lazzáro; and he who turned to a trade ceased to be one. The viceroy permitted the lazzaroni to elect a chief with whom he conferred respecting the imposts on the goods brought to the markets. In 1647, Masaniello held the office, and made an insurrection; see *Naples*. In 1793, Ferdinand IV. enrolled several thousands of lazzaroni as pikemen (spontoneers), who generally favoured the court party; on 15 May, 1848, they were permitted, on the king's behalf, to commit fearful ravages on the ill-fated city.—*Colletta*.

LEAD is found in various countries, and is abundant in various parts of Britain, and in some places richly mixed with silver ore. The famous Clydesdale mines were discovered in 1513. Pattinson's valuable method for extracting the silver was made known in 1829. The lead-mines of Cumberland and Derbyshire yield about 15,000 tons per annum. British mines produced 65,529 tons of lead in 1855; 69,266 in 1857; 67,181 in 1865; 73,420 in 1870; 58,777 in 1875; 58,667 in 1876; 51,635 in 1879; 50,328 in 1882; 40,075 in 1884; 37,890 in 1887; in 1888, 37,578; 1889, 35,604; 1890, 33,590; 1893, 29,698; 1896, 30,818; 1898, 25,355; 1899, 23,552; 1900, 24,364; 1901, 20,034.

Leaden pipes for the conveyance of water were brought into use in 1236

In 1859, 23,696 tons of pig and sheet lead were imported, and 18,414 tons exported; in 1866, 36,946 tons imported; 27,388 tons exported; in 1875, 79,825 tons imported, 35,398 tons exported; in 1883, 101,715 tons imported, 39,315 tons exported; in 1887, 114,493 tons imported, 44,301 tons exported; in 1888, 132,880 tons imported, 48,616 tons exported; in 1889, 145,203 tons imported, 52,040 tons exported; in 1890, 158,649 tons imported, 55,557 tons exported; 1901, 218,060 tons imported, 37,575 tons exported.

By an explosion caused through ignited gas at the Mill Close lead mine, Derbyshire, five men were killed, 3 Nov. 1887. Explosions in lead mines are very rare.

The deadly manufacture of white lead greatly ameliorated by the sublimation process invented in America and adopted by John Hall & Sons of Bristol in 1886

Professor Mac Ivor's new process was reported cheap, quick and safe; works, Clapham, London, S.W. . . . . . . July, 1890

Mr. J. B. Hannay's process of manufacturing sulphate of lead reported innocuous . . Jan. 1893

In a lead mine at Mazarron, Murcia, 27 men were suffocated, reported . . . . . 17 Feb. „

The report of a committee of experts referred to the serious dangers connected with the use of white lead in various manufactures, Dec. 1893; further investigations, 1898; report issued, with recommendations and restrictions . . . March, 1899

Seven men killed while descending a lead mine, near Shrewsbury, by the breaking of a rope, 6 March, 1895

LEAD, BLACK, see *Graphite*.

LEADENHALL MARKET, London, founded by sir Richard Whittington, in 1408, and presented to the city. A granary was added by Simon Eyre, 1419. The demolition of the old market began in Sept. 1880; first stone of new one laid 28 June; opened by the lord mayor, 15 Dec. 1881; cost 47,500*l*.

LEADVILLE. A high mining district in Colorado; highly successful results of excavations for the precious metals, 1878 *et seq*.

LEAGUES. Four kings combined to make war against five, about 1913 B.C. (*Gen.* xiv.) The kings of Canaan combined against the invasion of the Israelites, 1451 B.C. The more eminent Greek leagues were the Ætolian, powerful about 320 B.C., which lasted till 189 B.C., and the Achæan, revived 280 B.C., which was broken up by the conquest of Greece by the Romans, 146 B.C. The fall of these leagues was hastened by dissension.

Hanseatic league 1140

Lombard leagues against the emperors (see *Lombardy*). . . . . . . 1167 and 1226

Caddee league (*which see*) about 1396 *et seq*.

League of the Public Good was formed in Dec. 1464, by the dukes of Calabria, Brittany, and Bourbon, and other princes against Louis XI. of France, under pretext of reforming abuses; an indecisive battle was fought at Monthléri, 16 July; and a treaty was signed . . . . . 25 Oct. 1465

League of Cambray against Venice 1508

Holy League (the pope, Venice, &c.), against Louis XII. 1510

League of Smalcald 1530

League of the Beggars (*Gueux*); the protestants so called (though Roman Catholics joined the league) to oppose the institution of the Inquisition in Flanders 1566

The HOLY LEAGUE, to prevent the accession of Henry IV. of France, who was then of the reformed religion, was formed at Peronne and lasted till Henry embraced Romanism . . . 1576-93

League of Wurtzburg, by Catholics; of Halle, by Protestants 1610

League against the emperor 1626

Solemn League and Covenant in Scotland, against the episcopal government of the Church (see *Covenant*) 1638

League of Augsburg against France 1686

League of St. Sebastian instituted to promote the restoration of his temporal dominions to the pope, about 1870; held 9th annual meeting in London . . . . 20 Jan. 1879

League in aid of Christians in Turkey formed; earl of Shaftesbury, chairman, . . . 27 July, 1876
National Irish Land League *ostensibly* formed to buy up farms for the tenants; supported by Mr. Parnell and others, 1879; its enforcement stringent rules against landlords and loyal tenants created a reign of terror; led to legislation. See *Ireland* 1880-1
Charged with complicity and outrages; dissolved by government . . . . . . 20 Oct. 1881
New Irish National league formed (see *Ireland*, 1882 *et seq.*) (Organ *United Ireland*, 1886). 17 Oct. 1882
See *Home Rule*, 1890, and *National Federation*.
Free land league, see *Land*.
Annual convention of the Irish National League of Great Britain met at Cardiff, 29 Oct. 1887, at Birmingham, 29 Sept. 1888; Manchester, Sept. 1889; Edinburgh, 27 Sept. 1890; London 12 Dec. 1891; at other places since, Liverpool, 12 May, 1894; Leeds 1895
Several other leagues formed to obtain home rule 1879 *et seq.*
"National Land League of Great Britain" formed; Mr. Justin McCarthy, president, 26 March; met at Newcastle-on-Tyne, 29 Aug. 1881, and at other places since.
National league for the unification and consolidation of the empire, met at Westminster; strongly opposed to unfair free trade . . 8 Sept. *et seq.* ,,
League of Mercy, to help the London hospitals; preliminary meeting at Marlborough house, the prince and princess of Wales present, report adopted, 18 Dec. 1899. See *Mercy*.
Twentieth Century league, to promote healthy amusement for boys and girls in and about London, by means of clubs and institutes; first meeting at London house, St. James's-sq., 21 Nov. 1901; Victoria league to promote closer union throughout the empire, 1901; annual meeting . . . . 2 July, 1903

LEAP-YEAR or **BISSEXTILE**, originated with the astronomers of Julius Cæsar, 46 B.C. They fixed the solar year at 365 days, 6 hours, comprising, as they thought, the period from one vernal equinox to another; the six hours were set aside, and at the end of four years, forming a day, the fourth year was made to consist of 366 days. The day thus added was called intercalary, and was placed a day before the 24th of February, the sixth of the calends, which was reckoned *twice*, hence called *bissextile* or *twice sixth*. This added day with us is Feb. 29th; see *Calendar*. This arrangement makes the year nearly three minutes longer than the astronomical year: to obviate this, 1700, 1800, and 1900 were not leap-years, but 2000 will be one; see *Calendar* and *Year*.

LEARNING AND THE ARTS flourished among the Greeks, under Pisistratus, 537 B.C., and especially under Pericles, 444 B.C.; and with the Romans at the commencement of the Christian era, under Augustus. The Greek refugees caused their revival in Italy, particularly after the taking of Constantinople by the Turks in 1453, and the invention of printing shortly before,—the period of the *Renaissance*. Leo X. and his family (the *Medici*) greatly promoted learning in Italy, in the 16th century; when literature revived in France, Germany, and England; see *Literature*, and authors under *Greek*, *Latin*, *English*, and other *languages*.

LEASE (from the French *laisser*, to let), a kind of conveyance invented by serjeant Moore, soon after the statute of uses, 27 Henry VIII. 1535. Acts relating to leases were passed in 1856 and 1858. *Forged Leases case*, see *Trials*, Jan. 1878.

LEATHER was very early known in Egypt and Greece, and the thongs of manufactured hides were used for ropes, harness, &c., by all ancient nations. The Gordian knot was made of leather thongs, 330 B.C. A leather cannon was proved at Edinburgh, fired three times, and found to answer, 23 Oct. 1778. *Phillips*. The duty on leather imposed 1697, produced annually in England, 450,000*l*. and in Ireland about 50,000*l*. It was abolished, 29 May, 1830. Many bankruptcies were declared in the leather trade, in the autumn of 1860 in England. In the case of Lawrence, Mortimore, and Co., enormous fraudulent dealings in bills were disclosed. A plan for making artificial leather out of cuttings, &c., was made known in 1860.—*Leather cloth* (invented by Messrs. J. R. & C. P. Crockett, of Newark, U.S., and patented in 1849) is unbleached cotton coated with a mixture of boiled linseed oil and turpentine, and coloured. The Leather-cloth company, London, successors to Messrs. Crockett, was established, 1859. An exhibition of leather manufactures at Northampton in 1873; at the Agricultural Hall, London, 15-23 Sept. 1880; 26 Sept. 1881; and 15 Sept. 1882. Internat. assoc. of leather trade chemists, 6th annual conference, Leeds, 3 Sept. 1902.

LEBANON (*white mountain*), the mountain range between Syria and North Palestine, assigned to Israel, but never conquered, and long attached to Syria. Special ordinance for preservation of the ancient cedar forest, Sept. 1881. The governor-general since 1861 has been appointed by Turkey, subject to the assent of the great powers. Governors, 1873, Rustem Pasha; 1883, Wassa Pasha, died 29 June, 1892; successor Naoum Effendi; Muzaffer Pasha, 27 Sept. 1902; see *Assassins*, *Druses*, *Maronites*, and *Syria*.

LECH, a river, S. Germany, near which at a village named Rain the cruel imperialist general Tilly was defeated by the Swedes, under Gustavus Adolphus, 5 April, 1632, and died of his wounds.

LECTIONARY, the name given to the Anglican table of scripture lessons; changes in calendar of lessons, made 1871, by sanction of parliament; see *Common Prayer*.

LECTURES. Those on Physic were instituted by Dr. Thomas Linacre, of the College of Physicians (founded by Henry VIII.) about 1502. *Clinical* lectures, at the bed-side of the patients in hospitals are said to have been given (by Dr. John Rutherford) in Edinburgh, about 1748; in Dublin, about 1785; in London, by sir B. C. Brodie (1813-17). Mr. G. Macilwain, about 1824, gave surgical clinical lectures in connection with a dispensary. The political lectures of Thelwall, commenced in Jan. 1795, were interdicted by an act of parliament. In the autumn of 1857 and since, many distinguished noblemen and gentlemen lectured at mechanics' institutes. An act passed in 1835 prohibited the publication of lectures without the consent of the lecturers. See *Gresham College*, *Boyle's Lectures*, *Royal* and *London Institutions*, *Trials*, 1887, &c.

LEEDS (Yorkshire), the Saxon *Loidis*, once a Roman station, received a charter in 1627. See *Population*.

Leeds bridge built 1327
Shenfield's grammar school founded . . . 1552
Coloured Cloth hall built 1758; White Cloth hall . 1775
Literary and Philosophical society established . 1820
Enfranchised by the Reform act (2 members) . . 1832
Magnificent new town-hall opened by the queen, the mayor, Peter Fairbairn, knighted 7 Sept. 1858
Musical festivals begun . . . 7-10 Sept. ,,
British Association met here Sept. ,,
Great Reform meeting; Mr. Bright there 8 Oct. 1866
An additional M.P. given to Leeds by Reform act, 15 Aug. 1867

Exhibition of art treasures, opened by the prince of Wales, 19 May, closed . . . . 31 Oct. 1868
Roundhay-park inaugurated as a public park by prince Arthur, and new exchange founded, 19, 20 Sept. 1872
Church congress met . . . . . . 8-11 Oct. ,,
New bridge opened . . . . . . 9 July, 1873
Musical festival . . . . . . 14-17 Oct. 1874
Yorkshire college of science opened 26 Oct. 1874; new buildings opened by the prince of Wales 15 July, 1885
Yorkshire exhibition of arts and manufactures opened by the duke of Edinburgh . . 13 May, 1875
Theatre Royal burnt . . . . . . 28 May, ,,
New exchange opened . . . . . . 31 Aug. ,,
Great amphitheatre burnt; loss, about 30,000*l*. 2 March, 1876
Musical festival . . . . . . 19-22 Sept. 1877
New municipal offices and public free library opened 17 April, 1884
Leeds returns five M.P.'s by act passed 25 June, 1885
Fine art gallery and museum cost 10,000*l*. opened 3 Oct. 1888
Col. J. T. North presents Kirkstall Abbey and grounds to the corporation . . . . Jan. 1889
Sir Edward Baines, chief proprietor of the *Leeds Mercury*, M.P. for Leeds 1859–74; knighted 1880, liberal nonconformist; died, aged 89 2 March, 1890
Strike of gas-stokers; the town in darkness; above 15,000 rioters attacking the gasworks, repulsed after fighting; many persons severely injured, police reinforced from neighbouring towns, and by the military, 30 June; strike ends by concession to strikers . . . . . 3 July, ,,
Meeting of British association . . . . 2 Sept. ,,
At a church bazaar, Oldfield, Wortley, 11 out of 15 children dressed in cotton wool, with Chinese lanterns, perished through fire . 31 Dec. *et seq.* ,,
The dispute between the corporation and the gas-stokers amicably settled . . . 26 Feb. ,,
Great fire in the stores under the railway arches; estimated loss, about 200,000*l*. . . 13 Jan. 1892
Leeds constituted a city, the mayor to be styled lord 1893
The electric lighting works opened by alderman Ward, the lord mayor . . . . 10 May, ,,
Great fire in the central market; reported loss, 80,000*l*. . . . . . . 21 Sept. ,,
Visit of the duke and duchess of York; new school of medicine, &c., opened . . . 5 Oct. 1894
Destructive fire at Messrs. Hepworth & Co., Claypit-lane; about 1000 out of work . 28 Dec. 1895
Death of col. J. T. North, benefactor, the "nitrate king" . . . . 5 May, 1896
Strike in the building trade begins May; ends (½d. per hour conceded to the men) . 19 Sept. ,,
Mr. Robt. Arthington gives over 50,000*l*. to charities . . . . . May *et seq.* 1900
New park of Potter Newton opened by the lord mayor . . . . . . 12 Sept. 1901
Demonstration against the Education bill, as supporting sectarian dogmas, clerical management, &c. . . . . 20 Sept. 1902
Lieut.-gen. sir J. French receives the freedom, 6 Nov. ,,
Col. Harding, ex-lord mayor, presents city with handsome statuary for city square; and receives freedom of city . . . . . 16 Sept. 1903

LEEK, the Welsh emblem, worn on St. David's day, 1 March. The custom is traditionally assigned to a command from Dewi or David, afterwards archbishop of St. David's, in 519. The Britons are said to have worn a leek in their caps when Cadwallader defeated the Saxons, 540.

LEESBURG HEIGHTS, see *Ball's Bluff*.

LEEWARD ISLES, West Indies: Antigua (made a crown colony, 1898), Barbuda, Montserrat, St. Christopher's, Nevis, Anguilla, Virgin Isles, and Dominica (*which see*). An act for their federation passed 21 Aug. 1871. Governor-general of the British Isles, col. Stephen John Hill, 1863; sir B. C. C. Pine, 1869; sir H. Turner Irving, 1873; hon. Geo. Berkeley, 1874; sir J. H. Glover, Dec. 1881; sir Chas. Cameron Lees, 1883; Viscount Gormanston, Aug. 1885; sir Charles Bullen Hugh Mitchell, Dec. 1887; sir W. F. H. Smith, Nov. 1888; sir Francis Fleming, Jan. 1895; sir Henry M. Jackson, June, 1901; sir Gerald Strickland, April, 1902. Total population of the isles in 1891, 127,723. Disastrous floods, with loss of life, at Montserrat, reported 13 Jan. 1897.

Terrific hurricane, Montserrat devastated, great loss of life, see *West Indies*, 7 Aug. 1899; relief works opened, Aug.

LEGACIES. In 1780 receipts for legacies were subjected to a stamp duty, and in 1796 the legacy duty was imposed. The impost was increased several times subsequently, particularly in 1805, 1808, and 1845. In 1853 the legacy duty was extended to landed or real property. Further changes were made in 1881, 1888, 1889; the duty was replaced in 1894 by the "Estate duty," *which see*, also *Succession Duty Act*, and *Wills*. John Camden Neild, an eccentric miser, died 30 Aug. 1852, bequeathing about 250,000*l*. to the queen.

Received for legacy and succession duty in years ending 31 March: 1880, 3,700,606*l*.; 1881, 3,592,777*l*.; 1882, 3,540,585*l*.; 1883, 3,536,538*l*.; 1884, 3,335,817*l*.; 1885, 3,741,609..; 1886, 3,332,963*l*.; 1887, 3,375,488*l*.; 1888, 3,645,062*l*.; 1889, 3,736,847*l*.; 1890, 3,789,055*l*.; 1891, 3,835,243*l*.; 1892, 4,028,509*l*.; 1893, 4,697,897*l*.; 1894, 3,983,509*l*.

LEGAL PRACTITIONERS' SOCIETY, for reforming abuses, &c., established Nov. 1873.

LEGATES (*legatus*). Roman ambassadors; and also governors of the provinces into which Augustus divided the empire, 27 B.C. Legates are also ambassadors from the pope. The legate's court in England, erected in 1516 by cardinal Wolsey, to prove wills, and for the trial of offences against the spiritual laws, was soon discontinued.

LEGATIONS were the twenty administrative divisions in the states of the church, governed by legates. They rebelled in 1859-60, and are now included in the kingdom of Italy; see *Rome*.

LEGHORN, *Livorno*, Tuscany, a mere village in the 15th century, owes its prosperity to the Medici family. It suffered dreadfully by an earthquake in 1741; and was entered by the French army, 27 July, 1796, but the British property had been removed. It was held by the French 1796-9 and retaken, 1800. It was unsuccessfully attacked by the British and Italian forces in Dec. 1813. The Austrians took this city from the insurgents, 12, 13 May, 1849, and quelled a slight insurrection, July 6, 1857. In June, 1857, above 60 persons were killed at the theatre, through an alarm of fire; see *Tuscany* and *Italy*. Population, 1890, 104,960; 1901, 98,505.

LEGION, a corps of soldiers in the Roman armies, said to have been formed by Romulus, when it consisted of 3000 foot and 300 horse, about 720 B.C. When Hannibal was in Italy, 216 B.C., the legion consisted of 5200 soldiers; and under Marius, in 88 B.C., it was 6200 soldiers besides 700 horse. There were ten, and sometimes as many as eighteen, legions kept at Rome. Augustus had a standing army of 45 legions, together with 25,000 horse and 37,000 light-armed troops, about 5 B.C.; and the peace establishment of Adrian was thirty of these formidable brigades. A legion was divided into ten cohorts, and every cohort into six centuries, with a vexillum, or standard, guarded by ten men. The peace of Britain was protected by three legions. See *Thundering Legion*.

LEGION OF HONOUR, a French order embracing the army, civil officers, and other individuals distinguished for services to the state; instituted by Napoleon Bonaparte, when first consul, 19 May, 1802, to replace the old suppressed orders of knighthood, &c. The order was confirmed by Louis XVIII. in 1815, and its constitution modified in 1816 and 1851. The honour was conferred on many British subjects who distinguished themselves in the Russian war, 1854-6, and in the Paris exhibitions of 1855, 1867, 1878 and 1889. The palace and offices were burnt by the communalists, 23 May, 1871. The Legion comprised upwards of 54,000 members in 1887. The alleged traffic in decorations caused much excitement, Oct. 1887; council censured by the chamber, resigns, 16 July; plans for re-organisation proposed, Oct.; gen. Davout made grand chancellor of the reconstituted council, Dec. 1895; great outcry on his removal and the appointment of gen. Florentin, end Nov. 1901. See *France*.

LEGITIMISTS, a term (since 1814) applied to those who support the claims of the elder branch of the Bourbon family to the throne of France, whose representative, Henry, duc de Bordeaux, called comte de Chambord, born 29 Sept. 1820, died 24 Aug. 1883. They held a congress at Lucerne on 24-29 June, 1862, and agreed to continue a pacific policy. The party was active in Feb 1871-5. Their efforts to recover power have proved ineffectual; see *France*.

LEGNAGO, a fortress on the Adige, N. Italy, one of the Quadrilateral. It was captured by the French in 1796; but reverted to the Austrians in 1815. It was surrendered to the Italians in Oct. 1866.

LEGNANO, Lombardy. Here the emperor Frederick Barbarossa was defeated by the Milanese and their allies, 29 May, 1176, and the treaty of Constance ensued in 1183.

LEICESTER (central England), a bishopric for a short time in the 8th century, returned two members to parliament in the reign of Edward I. Here Richard III. was buried, 25 Aug. 1485; and here cardinal Wolsey died, 29 Nov. 1530. During the civil war, Leicester was taken by Charles I. 31 May, and by Fairfax, 17 June, 1645. The stocking manufacture was introduced in 1680. New town-hall opened, 8 Aug. 1876. New Abbey park opened by the prince of Wales, 29 May, 1882. Population, 1881, 122,376; 1891, 142,051; 1901, 211,581.

Riot occasioned by a strike, quelled by the police, 11-12 Feb.; end of strike . . . . 19 Feb. 1886
Great opposition to vaccination 1883 *et seq.*; sanitary precautions strictly enforced, see *Vaccination*, 1885-1887
Messrs. Bradshaw & Payne's shoe factory burnt, loss above 15,000*l*. . . . . 29 Oct. 1889
Water famine through long drought, Sept., Oct.; relieved by great exertions and heavy rains, Nov. 1894
Royal agricultural society's show held here in 1868; again . . . . 23 Jan. 1896
New reservoir and waterworks opened at Charnwood Forest . . . . 10 Sept. ,,
New art and technical schools opened by the bishop of London . . . . 5 Oct. 1897
"Records of the Borough of Leicester, 1103-1327," by Mary Bateson, published 1899
Fine speech of Mr. Chamberlain on the S. African war . . . . 29 Nov. ,,
The late Miss Emily Dalton leaves about 18,000*l*. to Leicester charities and 23,000*l*. to other charities, reported . . . . . . 9 July, 1900
Mr. Andrew Carnegie's gift of 12,000*l*. for a public library, accepted . . . . . 30 June, 1902
New wing (memorial to queen Victoria) to the infirmary, opened . . . . . 24 July, ,,
Canon Clayton appointed bp. suffragan of Leicester, Jan. 1903
Trade union congress held here 1877; again 7 Sept. ,,

LEICESTER SQUARE, London. See *Globe*. The square, after remaining some time in a disreputable state, was renovated by Mr Albert Grant (died, aged 68, 30 Aug. 1898), who bought up the enclosure, and presented it to the Metropolitan Board of Works, 2 July, 1874.

LEIGHLIN (W. Carlow), a see founded by St. Laserian, about 628. Burchard, the Norwegian, the son of Garmond, founded or endowed the priory of St. Stephen of Leighlin. Bishop Doran, appointed in 1523, was murdered by his archdeacon, Maurice Cavenagh, who was hanged on the spot where the crime was committed. *Beatson*. In 1600 Leighlin was united to Ferns; the combined see united to Ossory in 1835; see *Ferns* and *Bishops*.

LEININGEN (or LINANGE), a principality partly in Bavaria, Baden, and Hesse, mediatised in 1806. The present prince Ernest, born 9 Nov. 1830, a captain in the British navy, is the son of prince Charles, the half-brother of queen Victoria. Feodore, dowager princess of Hohenlohe Langenburg, the queen's half-sister, died 23 Sept. 1872, aged nearly 65. Her son, count Gleichen, afterwards prince Victor of Hohenlohe, born 1833, died 31 Dec. 1891. He entered the British navy in Sept. 1848, and was long in active service, especially in the Crimean war. He was also an eminent sculptor. The first husband of the duchess of Kent, prince Emich of Leiningen, died 4 July, 1814.

LEINSTER, a kingdom in 1167, now one of the four provinces of Ireland. The abduction of Devorgilla, wife of O'Ruare, a lord of Connaught, by Dermot king of Leinster in 1152, is asserted to have led to the landing of the English and the subsequent conquest. The province of Leinster gave the title of duke to Schomberg's son in 1690. The title became extinct in 1719, and was conferred on the family of Fitzgerald in 1766.

LEIPSIC (Saxony), an ancient city, famous for its university (founded 1409) and its fair (1458). At Breitenfeld, near here, Gustavus Adolphus, king of Sweden, defeated the Imperialists, under Tilly, 7 Sept. 1631; and the Imperialists were again defeated here by the Swedes, under Torstensen, 23 Oct. 1642. Here took place, on 16, 18. 19 Oct. 1813, "*the battle of the nations*," between the French army and its allies, commanded by Napoleon (160,000), and the Austrian, Russian, and Prussian armies (240,000 strong). The French were beaten chiefly owing to 17 Saxon battalions, their allies, turning upon them in the heat of the engagement. 80,000 men perished on the field, of whom more than 40,000 were French, who also lost 65 pieces of artillery, and many standards. The victory was followed by the capture of Leipsic, of the rear guard of the French army, and of the king of Saxony and his family. The 50th anniversary was celebrated 18 Oct. 1863. The *Leipsic book fair* began 1545. The new Supreme Court for all Germany, opened here 1 Sept. 1879. Population in 1885, 170,340; in 1890, 353,272; 1900, 455,120.

LEITH, the port of Edinburgh, was burnt by the earl of Hertford in 1544. It was fortified by the French partisans of queen Mary in 1560, and surrendered to the English. The "Agreement of Leith" between the superintendents and ministers was made, Jan. 1572. The docks were begun 1720. Leith was made a burgh in 1833. Population, 1891, 69,696; 1901, 76,667.

LEITHA, a river dividing the Austrian territories; see *Austria*.

LEITH HILL, near Dorking, Surrey, said to have been a Roman station, and has a view of eleven counties, being about 1000 feet above the sea level. The lofty tower on its summit was erected in 1766 by Mr. Richard Hull the then owner of Leith Hill Place, he died 18 Jan. 1772 and was buried within the tower.

LELEGES, a Pelasgic tribe which inhabited Laconia about 1490 B.C., and after many contests merged into the Hellenes, see *Hellas*.

LE MANS, a French city, department of the Sarthe. Here the retreating French general Chanzy was overtaken and defeated by the Germans under prince Frederick Charles and the grand-duke of Mecklenburg, after some conflicts: 10, 11 Jan. 1871. Le Mans was entered 12 Jan. In six days' fighting about 22,000 French made prisoners.

LEMURES. The ancients supposed that the soul, after death, wandered over the world, and disturbed the peace of the living. The happy spirits were called *Lares familiares*, and the unhappy, *Lemures*. The Roman festival, *Lemuralia*, kept on 9, 11, 13 May, is mythically said to have been instituted by Romulus about 747 B.C., to propitiate the spirit of the slaughtered Remus.

LENNIE MUTINY. See *Mutinies*, 1875.

LENT (from the Saxon, *lencten*, spring). The forty days' fast observed in the Greek, Roman catholic, English, and other churches from Ash-Wednesday to Easter-day. The commencement of Lent varied, but in the 8th or 9th century Ash Wednesday became the first day. Lent was first observed in England by command of Ercombert, king of Kent, in 640 or 641. *Baker's Chron*. Flesh was prohibited during Lent; but Henry VIII. permitted the use of *white meats* by a proclamation in 1543, which continued in force until, by proclamation of James I., in 1619 and 1625, and by Charles I., in 1627 and 1631, flesh was again wholly forbidden; see *Ash-Wednesday*, *Quadragesima*.

LEON, Kingdom of, see under *Spain*.

LEONARDS' ACTS, Lord St., 22 & 23 Vict. c. 35; 23 & 24 Vict. c. 38 (1859-60), relate to legal proceedings.

LEONINE CITY (*Città Leonina* or *Borgo*), formerly a suburb, now included in the city of Rome, was founded by Leo IV., pope 847-55, and named Leopolis. It comprehends the castle of St. Angelo, the hospital of San Spirito, the Vatican palace and gardens, and St. Peter's. Its possession was allotted to pope Pius IX. when the Italian royal troops entered Rome, 20 Sept. 1870. About 1500 inhabitants of the Leonine city voted for union with the kingdom of Italy, 2 Oct. 1870.

LEONINES, hexameter and pentameter verses, rhyming at the middle and the end, are said to have been first made by Leoninus, a canon, about the middle of the 12th century, or by pope Leo II. about 682.

LEOPOLD'S, PRINCE, ANNUITY ACT (passed 7 Aug. 1874), provided for him 15,000*l*. a year, from 7 April, 1874, when he came of age.

LEPANTO (near Corinth), Battle of, 7 Oct. 1571: when the combined fleets of Spain, Venice, Genoa, Malta, and Pius V., commanded by don John of Austria, defeated the whole maritime force of the Turks, and completely checked their progress.

LEPROSY, a skin disease described in *Leviticus* xiii. (B.C. 1490), which prevailed in ancient times throughout Asia. It has now almost disappeared from Europe. It chiefly affected the lower classes, yet occasionally proved fatal to the very highest personages. Robert Bruce of Scotland died of leprosy in 1329. A hospital for lepers was founded at Granada, by queen Isabella of Castile, about 1504, and a large number of leper houses were founded in Britain. Dr. Edmondson met with a case in Edinburgh in 1809.

The great increase of leprosy in the Sandwich Islands compelled the government to isolate the lepers, and large numbers were transported to Molokai, where they endured much suffering. Since 1873 Father Joseph Damien (de Venster), R. C. Belgian missionary, devoted his whole life most successfully to their general relief, and finally died of their disease, aged 49, 10 April, 1889 (succeeded by Father Wendolin). Other missionaries, male and female, are continuing his labours.

The *Father Damien Memorial Fund*, under the auspices of the prince of Wales, was founded about 18 June, 1889; and on 29 June it was determined to set up a memorial statue of Father Damien at Kalawao, and to establish a fund for the medical treatment of the disease in the United Kingdom, and for the promotion of the study of it at home and abroad especially in India.

Sir Henry B. Loch founds a hospital at Robben island, Cape Colony . . . . . 8 April, 1890

National Leprosy Fund; subscription dinner at the Hôtel Métropole, the prince of Wales in the chair, 13 Jan. ,,

The Albert Victor leprosy hospital at Calcutta founded . . . . Jan. ,,

The hon. sir Dinshaw Manockjee Petit presents 100,000 rupees to found a leper hospital at Bombay, announced . . . . 7 Feb. ,,

The British leprosy commission arrived at Calcutta, Nov. 1890; they report that there are about 110,000 lepers in India and Burmah; that leprosy is not increasing, and may probably be reduced by sanitation; that it is not generally hereditary or contagious, and originates chiefly in dirt; they recommend judicious isolation . . . April, 1893

Miss Kate Marsden honoured by the queen for her exertions among the Siberian lepers, about 24 Oct. 1892; her book published . . . . Jan. ,,

International congress at Berlin, prof. Virchow, discoverer of the leprous cells, president, 11 Oct.; commission appointed . . . 14 Oct. 1897

Segregation of lepers reported successful in India, April, 1899

Dr. Armaner Hanson, the discoverer of the bacillus of leprosy, his bust unveiled at Bergen, 10 Aug. 1901

Mr. J. Hutchinson reports, from investigation, the primary cause of the disease in S. Africa the eating of badly-cured salt fish . . March, 1902

Dr. Razlag's cure successful in the Philippines, reported . . . . . . 6 Oct. ,,

LERIDA, the ancient Ilerda, E. Spain, founded by the Carthaginians. Near it Julius Cæsar defeated Pompey's lieutenants, 49 B.C. It was made the residence of the kings of Aragon, 1149. It was captured for Philip V. by the French under the duke of Orleans, 13 Oct. 1707, and by Suchet, 13 May, 1810.

LÈSE-MAJESTÉ, or leze-majesty, any crime committed against sovereign power, see *Germany*.

LESSONS, see *Common Prayer*.

LETTERS, see *Alphabet*, *Anonymous*, *Belles Lettres*, *Copying Machine*, *Epistles*, *Literature*, *Marque*, and *Privateers*.

LETTRES DE CACHET, sealed letters issued by the kings of France since about 1670, by virtue of which those persons against whom they were directed were thrown into prison or exiled. The National Assembly decreed their abolition, 1 Nov. 1789.

LETTUCE, introduced into England from Flanders about 1520. It is said that when queen Catherine wished for a salad, she had to send to Holland or Flanders for lettuce.

LEUCTRA, in Bœotia, N. Greece, where the Thebans under Epaminondas defeated the superior force of Cleombrotus, king of Sparta, 8 July, 371 B.C. 4000 Spartans, with their king, were slain. The Spartans gradually lost their preponderance in Greece.

LEUDES, from the German, *Leute*, people. Native feudal vassals, faithful to the German and French sovereigns in the 6th and 7th centuries.

LEUTHEN (S. Prussia); see *Lissa*.

LEVANT (the East), a term applied to Greece, Turkey, Asia Minor, &c. Levant companies, in London, were established in 1581, 1593, and 1605.

LEVELLERS, a fanatical party in Germany, headed by Muncer and Storck in the 16th century. who taught that all distinctions of rank were usurpations on the rights of mankind. At the head of 40,000 men, Muncer commanded the sovereign princes of Germany and the magistrates of cities to resign their authority; and on his march his followers ravaged the country. The landgrave of Hesse at length defeated him at Frankenhausen, 15 May, 1525; 7000 of the enthusiasts fell in the battle, and the rest fled; their leader was taken and beheaded at Mulhausen. The English "Levellers," powerful in parliament in 1647, were put down by Cromwell in 1649, and their leader Lilburn was tried and acquitted. At the period of the French revolution some Levellers appeared in England. A "Loyal Association" was formed against them by John Reeves, Nov. 1792.

LEVELS. The great Level of the Fens is a low-lying district of about 2000 square miles, in Lincolnshire, Huntingdonshire, Cambridgeshire, and Norfolk, said to have been overflown by the sea during an earthquake, 368. It was long afterwards an inland sea in winter, and a noxious swamp in summer, and was gradually drained—by the Romans, the Saxons, and especially by the monks during the reigns of the Plantagenet kings. One of the first works on a large scale was carried out by Morton, bishop of Ely, in the reign of Henry VII. A general drainage act was passed by the advice of lord Burghley, in 1601, but little work was done till the reign of James I., who, in 1621, invited over the great Dutch engineer, Cornelius Vermuyden, to assist in the general drainage of the country. After completing several great works, Vermuyden agreed (in 1629) to drain the "Great Level." He was at first prevented from proceeding with his undertaking through a popular outcry against foreigners; but eventually, aided by Francis, earl of Bedford, in spite of the great opposition of the people, for whose benefit he was labouring, he declared his great work complete in 1652. He also reclaimed much valuable land at Axholme, in Lincolnshire, 1626-30, and many Dutch and French protestants settled here about 1634; and a few of their descendants still remain.—There are the Middle, Bedford, South, and North Levels.

The drainage of the Great Level employed the talents of Rennie (about 1807), and of Telford (1822), and of other eminent engineers.

The Middle Level commission cut through certain barrier banks, and replaced them by other works 1844

These were reported unsound in March, and the outfall sluice at St. Germains, near King's Lynn, gave way . . . . 4 May, 1862

High tides ensuing, about 6000 acres of fertile land were inundated, causing a loss of about 25,000*l*. After unwearied, and, for a while, unsuccessful efforts, a new coffer dam was constructed under the superintendence of Mr. Hawkshaw, which was reported sound . . . . . . July, "

Another inundation, begun through the bursting of a marshland sluice, near Lynn, was checked 4 Oct. "

New outfall sluice opened . . . . 26 Nov. 1877

LEVERIAN MUSEUM, formed by sir Ashton Lever, exhibited to the public at Leicester-house, London; it was offered to the public, in 1785, by the chance of a guinea lottery, and won by Mr. Parkinson, in 1785, who sold it by auction, in lots, May-July, 1806.

LEVIATHAN, see *Steam Navigation*.

LEWES (Sussex), where Henry III., king of England, was defeated by Montfort, earl of Leicester, and the barons, 14 May, 1264. *Blaauw*. The king, his brother Richard, king of the Romans, and his son Edward, afterwards Edward I., were taken prisoners. One division of Montfort's army, a body of Londoners, gave way to the furious attack of prince Edward, who, pursuing the fugitives too far, caused the battle to be lost; see *Evesham*. Population, 1881, 11,199; 1891, 10,997; 1901, 11,249.

LEXICON, see *Dictionaries*.

LEXINGTON (Massachusetts), Battle of, at the beginning of the war of independence. The British obtained the advantage, and destroyed the stores of the revolted colonists, but lost in the battle 273 men, killed and wounded, 19 April, 1775. The hostilities thus commenced continued to 1783.—LEXINGTON, a town in Missouri, U.S., fortified by the Federals, was attacked by the confederate general Price, on 29 Aug., and after a gallant resistance by colonel Mulligan, surrendered on 21 Sept. 1861.

LEYDEN (Holland), *Lugdunum Batavorum*, important in the 13th century. Between 31 Oct. 1573, and 3 Oct. 1574, when it was relieved, it endured two sieges by the armies of Spain, during which 6000 of the inhabitants died of famine and pestilence. In commemoration the university was founded, 1575. In 1699 two-thirds of the population perished by a fever, which, it was said, was aggravated by its improper treatment by professor De la Boe. The university was almost destroyed by a vessel laden with 10,000 lbs. weight of gunpowder blowing up and demolishing a large part of the town, and killing numbers of people, 12 Jan. 1807. The *Leyden* jar was invented about 1745, by Kleist, Muschenbroek, and others; see *Electricity*. Population, 1890, 43,510; 1900, 54,421.

The third centenary of the foundation of the university celebrated joyfully . . . . . 8 Feb. 1875

The Spinoza museum opened at Rhynsburg, 24 March, 1899

LIBEL. By the Roman laws of the Twelve Tables, libels which affected the reputation of another were made capital offences. In the British law, whatever renders a man ridiculous, or lowers a man in the opinion and esteem of the world, is deemed a libel. "The greater the truth the greater the libel," the well-known law maxim of a high authority, is now disputed; see *Trials*, 1788, 1790, 1792, 1803, 1808 *et seq.*, 1863, 1882 *et seq.*; and (note) *Patents* and *Times*.

Dispersing slanderous libels made felony . 1545
Wm. Prynne, a puritan lawyer, fined 5000*l.*, placed in the pillory, where his ears were cut off, and imprisoned, for writing "Histriomastix," a condemnation of stage plays; which was considered to be a libel on the queen, who favoured them, 1633; he was tried and further punished for his satirical writings in 1637
Fox's libel bill, which enlarged the discretionary power of juries in cases of libel, thrown out by the lords in 1791; passed in 1792
Blasphemous and seditious libels, on the second offence, made punishable with transportation . 1819
An action for libel was brought in the court of King's Bench by a bookseller named Stockdale, against Messrs. Hansard, the printers to the house of commons; this action related to an opinion expressed in a parliamentary report of a book published by Stockdale, 7 Nov. 1836. Lord Denman, in giving judgment, said he was not aware that the authority of the house of commons could justify the publication of a libel—an opinion which led to some proceedings on the part of the house, and to other actions by Stockdale . 1837-39
Verdicts were given in his favour, and in Nov. 1839, the sheriffs took possession of Hansard's premises. This caused much excitement in parliament, and they were ordered to appear at the bar of the house of commons, and were formally committed to the custody of the serjeant-at-arms, 21 Jan., but immediately discharged: the conflict was maintained by the law officers and the commons till . . . . . . May, 1840
A law was passed giving summary protection to persons employed by parliament in the publication of its reports and papers . . . 14 April, „
The severity of the law in respect to newspapers relaxed by lord Campbell's act, 6 & 7 Vict. c. 96 . 1843
A bill relieving newspapers from actions for libel in reporting speeches at lawful public meetings, read third time in the commons, Aug. 1867, but dropped; read 2nd time 1 April; and withdrawn, 1 July, 1868
Wason *v.* Walter ("Times"); parliamentary reports and fair comments, declared no libel . 25 Nov. „
Newspaper Libel Act passed . . . 27 Aug. 1881
New Libel Law passed . . . . 24 Dec. 1888

LIBERALS, a name given to the more advanced Whigs and reformers since 1828. The party held office under Earl Grey, Viscount Melbourne, Earl Russell, Viscount Palmerston, Mr. W. E. Gladstone, and the earl of Rosebery. See *Administrations*.

The *Liberal*, a paper begun by Byron, Shelley and Leigh Hunt, 4 numbers only published . 1822
New city liberal club; earl Granville, president; organised . . . . . . May, 1874
New liberal club for west end, founded . June, „
A new liberal cry proposed "Free church, schools, and land" (Mr. Chamberlain) . autumn. „
Mr. Gladstone resigned the leadership of the party in the commons, 13 Jan.; his successor, the marquis of Hartington . . . . 13 Jan. 1875
Associations composed of elected delegates to organise liberal voters, have been formed in Birmingham, Southwark, Bradford, and other boroughs . . . . . . 1876 *et seq.*
Mr. W. E. Forster refused to submit to the dictation of the committee of the Bradford association in respect to his voting . . . Aug. 1878
See *Caucus*.
National Liberal Federation; constituted at Birmingham, 31 May, 1877; first annual meeting (at Leeds), 22 Jan. 1879. Great liberal conference at Leeds, 17 Oct. 1883. At the meeting at Nottingham, 18 Oct. 1887, Mr. Gladstone severely condemned the government Irish policy and action; also at Birmingham, 5 Nov. 1888. Meetings held, 1889 *et seq.*; Liverpool, Jan. 1893; Leeds, May, 1894; Cardiff, earl of Rosebery declares his programme, 18 Jan. 1895; Huddersfield, 26 March, 1896; Norwich, 17 March, 1897; Leicester, 22 March, 1898; Hull, 7 March, 1899; Nottingham, 27 March, 1900; Bradford, 14 May, 1901; Bristol, 13, 14 May, 1902; Scarborough, 14 May, 1903.

National liberal club, Westminster, founded Nov. 1882; inaugural banquet, 2 May, 1883; foundation of house at Whitehall laid by Mr. Gladstone, 4 Nov. 1884
The liberal majority in 1885, 82 (exclusive of 86 Parnellites)
Many secessions (lord Hartington, lord Selborne, earl Derby, Mr. John Bright, Mr. Goschen, Mr. Chamberlain, sir John Lubbock, sir H. James, and others) against Mr. Gladstone's Irish policy (termed unionist or dissentient liberals), Jan.–May; at a conference they resolve to support the Salisbury government . . . . 7 Dec. 1886
Inaugural meeting of the London Liberal and Radical Union . . . . 11 Jan. 1887
"Round Table" conference at sir Wm. Harcourt's, for re-union of unionists and Gladstonians; reported unsuccessful . . . 13 Jan. *et seq.* „
The *Liberal Unionist*, a new review published 30 March, „
Lord Hartington and a great many liberal unionists retire from the National Liberal Club . . Dec. 1888
The National *Radical* Union becomes the National *Liberal* (see *Radical*) . . . . 24 April, 1889
The Women's Liberal Confederation (Gladstonian) consists of 33,500 members . . . May, „
A great Liberal *Unionist* banquet at the Crystal palace, in honour of the marquis of Hartington, 13 May, 1890
National Liberal *Unionist* conference at Manchester; sir Henry James chairman, the marquis of Hartington (duke of Devonshire in 1891) and the duke of Argyll present . . . . . 10 Nov. 1891
Mr. W. E. Gladstone premier, Aug. 1892; succeeded by the earl of Rosebery, March, 1894–June, 1895
Great majority for conservatives and unionists in the elections . . . . . July, „
New Radical committee, 19 M.P.'s (Mr. Labouchere, sir Wm. Wedderburn, Mr. Dalziel, and others) propose to form a "distinctive advanced radical section" in parliament, and to carry on an active campaign in the country in favour of democracy, *Times* . . . . 20 May, 1896
The earl of Rosebery resigns the leadership; see *Rosebery*, 6 Oct. 1896; lord Kimberley leader in the lords, sir Wm. Vernon Harcourt leader in the commons, Jan. 1897.
The "Liberal Forward" party formed by the "Armenian Cave" in the liberal party, Mr. George Russell's committee, reported . 7 Dec. „
Protest against coercion of Greece in Crete, meetings held . . . . . 5, 27 March, 1897
Strong speech of sir Wm. V. Harcourt in W. Monmouth, 27 April, 1897, and 27 July, 1898; letter (8 Dec.) to Mr. John Morley resigning the leadership, *Times* . . . . . . 14 Dec. 1898
Nat. liberal association, meeting at Derby, new programme proposed . . . . . 7 Dec. „
Sir H. Campbell-Bannerman accepts the leadership, 6 Feb. 1899; many divisions on the S. African war, great disorganisation, 1900–1901.
Mr. Thomas E. Ellis, the liberal whip and leader of the "Young Wales" party, born 1859, died, 5 April, 1899
Imperial liberal council formed to advance imperialism, &c., lord Brassey, president, meetings held in London . . . . 31 Jan.–12 Feb. 1901
The League of Liberals against aggression and militarism; first annual meeting held in London, 24 April, „
Inaugural meeting of the London Liberal federation in St. James's hall, sir H. Campbell-Bannerman chairman . . . . 13 Jan. 1902
Lord Rosebery's stirring speech at Chesterfield, 16 Dec. 1901; issued under the title of "National Policy," 1 Jan. 1902; at Liverpool he exhorts the liberals to *clean their slate* of the Irish question &c., and start afresh, 14 Feb.; sir H. Campbell-Bannerman adheres to Home Rule, &c., 19 Feb.; lord Rosebery's letter announcing his definite separation from the party, *Times*, 21 Feb. and 13 Oct. „
Liberal league of imperialists and unionists formed by lord Rosebery, Mr. Asquith, sir H. Fowler, sir Edw. Grey, and others . . . . Feb. „
Sir Wm. V. Harcourt declined a peerage . June, „

LIBERATION OF RELIGION FROM STATE PATRONAGE AND CONTROL, Society for, was established by eminent political dissenters, May, 1844. 16th triennial conference opened, 3 May, 1892. Jubilee celebrated, 30 April, 1894. Conferences, 1 May, 1895; 2 May, 1898; 3 May, 1899; 30 April, 1901.

"LIBERATOR," a name popularly given to Mr. Daniel O'Connell, for his successful exertions relating to Roman Catholic emancipation, completed by Parliament in 1829. "Liberator" was the name of an American anti-slavery journal founded by Wm. Lloyd Garrison, Jan. 1831, and edited by him till 1866. He was aided by Mr. John G. Whittier. See *Building Societies*, 1892.

LIBERIA, the republic of freed and indigenous negroes on the coast of Upper Guinea, West Africa, was founded in 1820 by the American Colonisation Society, which was established by Henry Clay in 1816: capital, Monrovia. The independence of Liberia was proclaimed, 24 Aug. 1847; recognised by Europe in 1848, by America, in 1862. Presidents: J. J. Roberts, an able statesman, 1847; Daniel B. Warner, elected 1864; James Spriggs Payne, installed 6 Jan. 1868; E. J. Roy, president, Jan. 1870, was deposed, Oct. 1871; escaped from prison; drowned, Feb. 1872. J. J. Roberts re-elected Jan. 1872 and 1874; died 25 Feb.; J. Spriggs Payne, elected 3 June, 1876; A. W. Gardner, 1878; A. J. Russell, 1883; H. R. W. Johnson, 7 Jan. 1884; J. J. Cheesman, 4 Jan. 1892; died 11 Nov. Wm. David Coleman, 13 Nov. 1896 (resigns 11 Dec.); G. W. Gibson, 20 Dec. 1900. Population, about 30,000 Liberians and 1,500,000 natives, 1902.

The territories largely increased by annexations, 1847 *et seq.*, and by the adhesion of Maryland, a negro republic (founded 1821–54) 1857
The president Roberts, visits London 1862
The aborigines defeated at Cape Palmas . 17 Sept. 1875
Peace concluded . . . . March, 1876
Kingdom of Medina (*which see*) annexed . Feb. 1880
Martha Anna Ricks, a freed negress, aged 76, from Liberia, received by the queen at Windsor 16 July, 1892
War with cape Palmas native chiefs at Rock Town; the Liberians defeated about . . 23 Feb. 1893
Limitation convention respecting the French territories, signed at Paris, 8 Dec. 1892, ratified at Monrovia, reported . . . . . 21 Jan. 1894
French encroachments on the territory . Feb. ,,
Limitation treaty signed . . . . . 10 Aug. ,,
Several ports blockaded for tribal disturbances, Oct. 1895
Col. Cardew, governor of Sierra Leone, in H.M.S. *Alecto*, arrives at Monrovia, to protect British subjects, 28 Oct.; indemnity paid, at Grand Bassa . . . . early Nov. 1896
Native towns burnt by Liberian troops . Feb. 1897
Treaty of extradition with France, signed at Paris, 5 July, ,,
Sub-lieut. Baily Forelière and M. Pauly, French explorers, murdered at Zoulon, N. Liberia, reported . . . . 5 June, 1898
Chief Kafra invades British territory, is defeated, and 4 towns captured by capts. Atkins and Blakeney, reported . . . . . 2 Feb. 1899
Electioneering riots, houses and churches burnt, reported . . . . 4 June, ,,
Big town raided by the Gebroes, reported, 23 Aug. ,,

LIBERTINES (signifying freedmen and their sons), was a sect headed by Quintin and Corin, about 1525, who held monstrous opinions.

LIBERTY, see *Press* and *Trees*. A colossal statue of Liberty, 150 feet high by M. Bartholdi, French sculptor, presented to the United States of N. America, was set up at New York Harbour and was publicly dedicated 28 Oct. 1886.

LIBERTY AND PROPERTY DEFENCE LEAGUE, formed by lords Elcho (since earl of Wemyss), Bramwell, and others, to obviate the effects of legislation since 1871. First meeting 5 July; first general meeting 29 Nov. 1882; annual meetings are held. The league has many affiliated societies. At the general meeting on 1 July, 1886, M. Léon Say was president.

LIBRARIES.* Accadian or Chaldean libraries are said to have been formed 1700 B.C. The remains of those formed by Assyrian monarchs (744 *et seq.*) at Nineveh, &c., consisting of tablets of baked clay, were discovered by Botta, Layard, and others, 1843 *et seq.*; see *Nineveh*. Diodorus Siculus describes a library in the tomb of Osymandyas, king of Egypt. A *public* library was founded at Athens by Pisistratus, about 540 B.C. Another was founded by Ptolemy Philadelphus, 284 B.C. It was partially destroyed when Julius Cæsar set fire to Alexandria 47 B.C. 400,000 valuable books in MS. are said to have been lost by this catastrophe. *Blair.*

The first *private* library was Aristotle's. *Strabo.* B.C. 334
The first library at Rome brought from Macedonia 167
According to Plutarch, the library at Pergamos contained 200,000 books. It came into the possession of the Romans at the death of Attalus III., who bequeathed his kingdom to the Roman people 133
The library of Appellicon, sent to Rome from Athens, by Sylla 86
Library founded at Constantinople by Constantine, A.D. about 355
Library at St. Mark's, Venice, begun, by gifts from Petrarch, 1352; enlarged by cardinal Bessarion . 1468
Matthias Corvinus, king of Hungary, collected a library of nearly 500,000 volumes at Buda; died . 1490
The first public library in Italy founded at Florence by Niccolo Niccoli, one of the great restorers of learning. At his death he left his library to the public, 1436. Cosmo de' Medici enriched it with the invaluable Greek and Hebrew MSS. about 1560
The Vatican Library at Rome, founded by pope Nicholas V. in 1447, and improved by Sixtus V., (contained about 150,000 volumes and 40,000 MSS., 1868). 1588
Imperial Library of Vienna, founded by Frederick III. in 1440, and by Maximilian I. . . . 1500
Royal Library of Paris, founded by John 1350, enlarged by Charles V., 1364; said to contain 815,000 volumes and 84,000 MSS. in 1860; 1,700,000 vols. in 1876. A new reading-room has been built.
Royal Libraries founded at Copenhagen by Christian III. about 1533: at Stockholm, by Gustavus Vasa, about 1540; at Munich, by Albert III. . about 1550
Escurial at Madrid, commenced with the foundation of the palace, by Philip II. 1557
Harvard University Library (see *Harvard*), Massachusetts, U.S., founded 1632, endowed . . 1638
Imperial Library at St. Petersburg (principally the spoils of Poland), founded 1714
Astor Free Public Library, New York, founded by John Jacob Astor, by gift of 80,000*l.*, 1839; he died in 1848, and the library has since been warmly supported by his wealthy son, Wm. Blackhouse Astor (died 1875), and his grandson, John Jacob Astor (died 1890).
Sen. Canovas bequeathed 3,000 books to the National library . . . . . . 8 Aug. 1897

LIBRARIES IN GREAT BRITAIN.

Richard de Bury, chancellor and high treasurer of England, purchased thirty or forty volumes of the abbot of St. Alban's for fifty pounds' weight of silver 1341
University Library, St. Andrews, founded . . 1411
Glasgow University Library, founded about . 1473
Lambeth palace Library founded by abp. Bancroft, about 1610
Sion College Library, founded 1630

* A *Conference of British and foreign librarians* met at the London Institution, 2 Oct. 1877; again at the Guildhall, sir John Lubbock president, 13 July, 1897. It founded the Library Association of the United Kingdom.

Royal Society Library, founded 1667
Harleian Library (*which see*) begun 1705
University Library, Cambridge, founded 1475; Geo. I. gave 6000 guineas to purchase Dr. Moore's collection 1715
Bodleian Library at Oxford, founded 1598; opened 8 Nov. 1602. See *Bodleian*.
Cottonian Library, founded by Sir Robert Cotton about 1588; appropriated to the public, 1701; partly destroyed by fire, 1731; removed to the British Museum (*which see*) 1755
Dr. Daniel Williams's Public Library. He died 1716; bequeathed his library and money for a building, which was opened at 49, Redcross-street, City, in 1729; it was successively removed to Queen's-square, Bloomsbury, 1864, and to Grafton-street East, and opened Sept. 1873; to Gordon-square, Gower-street 1890
Radcliffe Library at Oxford, founded by the will of Dr. Radcliffe, 1714; opened 1749
The Libraries of the Royal Institution (founded 1803), the London Institution (1805), and the Royal College of Surgeons (1786), have *classified catalogues*.
Library of the University of Dublin (1601), and the Advocates' Library in Edinburgh (1680), are extensive and valuable.
Library of East India Company, founded . . . 1800
Royal Libraries in England: that of Edward IV., mentioned 1480, increased in the reigns of Edw. VI. and James I.; much enlarged by Richard Bentley, while librarian, 1694–1735; added to the British Museum by Geo. II., 1759; rich library of Geo. III., presented to the nation, 1823; deposited in the British Museum 1829
In 1609 the Stationers' Company agreed to give a copy of every book published to the Bodleian Library, Oxford. By 14 Charles II. c. 33 (1662), three copies were required to be given to certain public libraries; by 8 Anne, c. 19 (1709), the number was increased to nine; by 41 Geo. III. c. 107, to eleven; which number was reduced to five by 5 & 6 Will. IV. c. 110 (1835): the British Museum, the Bodleian, Oxford, the Public Library, Cambridge, the Advocates' Library, Edinburgh, and Trinity College, Dublin.
FREE LIBRARIES successfully established, since 1850, at Manchester, Liverpool, Birmingham, &c. Many others formed under acts passed in 1845, 1850 *et seq.*
Notting-hill free library, maintained by Mr. Jas. Haywood, died . . . . Oct. 1897
On 5 Nov. 1855, a proposal to establish a Free Library in the city of London was negatived, and in 1857 that in Marylebone was closed for want of support, but was re-opened 1 May, 1890.
The new city library, Guildhall (free) was opened 5 Nov. 1872
Metropolitan Free Library Association formed, 4 April, 1879
The great library collected by Charles Spencer, 3rd earl of Sunderland, the property of the duke of Marlborough, partly sold by auction (under the Blenheim Settled Estates Act of 1880) 1-12 Dec. 1881
Library of sir Francis Drake and family sold, Mar. 1883
United Hamilton and Beckford libraries sold for 86,444*l*. 1883–4
The Syston Park library (sir John Hayford Thorold), including a Mazarin bible, early printed classics, &c., sold for about 28,000*l*. . . . 12–20 Dec. 1884
The library of Michael Wodhull, collected in the last century, realized by 10 days' sale 11,973*l*. 4*s*. 6*d*. 21 Jan. 1886
133 free libraries established up to 1887. [Many since founded and presented by Mr. Passmore Edwards.]
Lord Aylesford's library realised, 10,754*l*. March, 1888
The magnificent Althorp library, collected by George John, earl Spencer, was described and illustrated by Dr. T. F. Dibdin in his "Bibliotheca Spenceriana," 7 vols., published 1814–23. It was privately sold by the present earl to Mrs. Rylands, widow of John Rylands, a cotton manufacturer, and added to a public library, founded by her in Manchester as a memorial of her husband, Aug. 1892; opened . . . . . 6 Oct. 1899
The library of lord Orford realized 2,609*l*. 11 June, 1895
The library of the late sir Thomas Phillipps, bart., an eminent collector, was sold by Messrs. Sotheby & Co., for a large sum. Selections from the MSS. (many transcripts) realized, 33,873*l*., 1895–1898; a further sale (6 days) realized 3,784*l*. 19*s*. 6*d*., 10 June, 1899
Ashburnham library, 20 days' sale, 62,712*l*. 7*s*. 6*d*., closed, 14 May, 1898; MSS. "Appendix" realised 8,595*l*., 1 May, 1899; the splendid MS. of the "Evangelia Quatuor" sold for 10,000*l*., by private treaty, mid Jan. 1901; the "Barrois" MSS., including a 14th-century MS. of "San Graal et Lancelot du Lac," 1,800*l*. . . . . 14 June, 1901
Libraries Offences act passed . . . . 12 Aug. 1898
The library of Mr. Augustin Daly realised 34,500*l*., mid March, 1900
Prof. Foxwell's library of Economic Literature, 30,000 vols., bought by the Goldsmiths' Company for 10,000*l*. . . . . end June, 1901
Lord Crawford's collection of illuminated and other MSS. sold to Mrs. Rylands, of Manchester, reported . . . . 3 Sept. ,,
Monument to Edward Edwards, born 14 Dec. 1812, died 7 Feb. 1886, pioneer of the public library movement, inaugurated at Niton, Isle of Wight, 7 Feb. 1902
Mr. Andrew Carnegie makes large grants to aid and found free libraries, 13,000*l*. to Finsbury, reported, 17 July 1902; he purchases the late lord Acton's library (about 70,000 vols.), and presents it to Mr. John Morley, announced, 31 July, Mr. Morley presented it afterwards to Cambridge, 20 Oct. ,,
Viscount Goschen presides at a conference on free libraries and higher education, Oxford . 12 Aug. 1903
See *Breviary*, *Caxton's*, in article *Printing*, and *Circulating Library*.

LIBRARY ASSOCIATION OF THE UNITED KINGDOM, founded at a conference of librarians at the London Institution, 2 Oct. 1877. It met at Oxford, 1–3 Oct. 1878; at Manchester, 23 Sept. 1879; Edinburgh, 5 Oct. 1880; London, 1881; Cambridge, 5 Sept. 1882; Liverpool, 11 Sept. 1883; Dublin, 30 Sept. 1884; Plymouth, 15 Sept. 1885; London, 28 Sept. 1886; Birmingham, 20 Sept. 1887; Glasgow, 4 Sept. 1888; London (Gray's Inn), 2 Oct. 1889; Reading, 16 Sept. 1890; Nottingham, 16 Sept. 1891; Paris, 12 Sept. 1892; Aberdeen, 5 Sept. 1893; Belfast, 4 Sept. 1894; Cardiff, 10 Sept. 1895; Buxton, 3 Sept. 1896; London, 20 Oct. 1897; Southport, 23 Aug. 1898; Manchester, 4 Sept. 1899; Bristol, 25 Sept. 1900; Plymouth, 27 Aug. 1901; Birmingham, 23 Sept. 1902; Leeds, 8 Sept. 1903.

LIBRO D'ORO (Book of Gold). The title of an ancient register of 24 ruling Venetian families before 813; and also of another book, dated 1506, recording the genealogies of the noble houses who ruled Venice till the fall of the republic in 1797.

LIBYA, Greek name for all Africa, but specially for the interior as distinguished from the north; it is mentioned by Homer and described by Herodotus. It was temporarily subdued by Cambyses, king of Persia, about 525 B.C. The country was explored for trade purposes by Ptolemy II., III., and IV.

LICENCES. This mode of levying money was introduced by Richard I. about 1190; but was then confined to such of the nobility as desired to enter the lists at tournaments. See *Press* and *Liquor*.

Games and gaming-houses licensed in London . 1620
Licence system for excisable articles enforced in various reigns, from the 12th Charles II. . . 1660
Lottery office-keepers to take out licences, and pay 50*l*. for each. This reduced the number from 400 to 51 . . . . Aug. 1778
General licensing act, 9 Geo. IV. c. 61 1828
Licences for public-houses granted in 1551, and for refreshment-houses, with wine licences . . 1860

In the case of *Sharp* v. *Wakefield*, the house of lords, on appeal, decided that the licensing justices have the power of refusing to renew a licence to publicans, when they think fit . 20 March, 1891
The licensing system was applied to India as a kind of income-tax, 1859; ceased in 1861
Licences for the sale of tea, coffee, chocolate, and pepper were abolished and other licences modified by acts passed in 1869-70
Licensing Reform Agitation 1870-71
Acts for licensing plays and playhouses by the lord chamberlain, were passed in 1736 (10 Geo. II. c. 28); and in 1843 (6 & 7 Vict. c. 68); and for music and dancing in public-houses, in 1752 (25 Geo. II. c. 36).
New licensing act, regulating the sale of intoxicating liquors; very much opposed; passed and came into operation. . . . . . . 10 Aug. 1872
Another *licensing act* passed . . . 30 July, 1874
The licensing clauses of the local taxation bill (much opposed), dropped by the government, 24 June, 1890
A meeting on licensing reform on the lines of lord Peel's report, resolution carried, Queen's hall, 21 Nov. 1899
Three bills on liquor law reform drafted by a committee of abps. and bps. approved at a conference of magistrates and others, text published, *Times*, 16 Aug. 1900
216 liquor licences refused renewal in England and Wales in . . . . ,,
National temperance conference held at Manchester; recommendations of lord Peel's licensing report carried . . . . . . 12 Feb. 1901
A stringent *licensing* act passed . . 31 July, 1902
Superfluous licences refused at Farnham, Surrey; 6 appeals dismissed; 2 licences renewed under conditions; *Times* . . . . 4 Oct. ,,
Meeting on the licensing question, see *Liverpool* . 1903
Amount received for licences for the sale of spirits, in 1893-94 15,189,345*l.*; beer, 9,536,948*l.*

LICHFIELD (Staffordshire). The see of Mercia (at Lichfield) was founded about 656; removed to Chester, 1075; to Coventry, 1102. In 1121 Robert Peche was consecrated bishop of Lichfield and Coventry. By an order in council, Jan. 1837, the archdeaconry of Coventry was added to the see of Worcester, and Dr. Samuel Butler became bishop of Lichfield. This see has given three saints to the Romish church; and to the British nation one lord chancellor and three lord treasurers. It is valued in the king's books at 559*l.* 18*s.* 2*d.* Present income, 4,200*l.* Population, 1881, 8,349; 1891, 7,864; 1901, ~,902.

Lichfield cathedral was first built about 656; the present structure was founded by Roger de Clinton, the 37th bishop, in 1148. Walter de Langton (bishop in 1296), built the chapel of St. Mary, now taken into the choir, and under bishop Heyworth (1420) the cathedral was perfected. The building was despoiled at the Reformation, and was scandalously injured in the parliamentary war (when its monuments, its fine sculptures, and beautifully painted windows, were demolished). It was repaired at the restoration, 1660; in 1788; and by Gilbert G. Scott, 1860-63 and 1884.
In Lichfield castle, king Richard II. kept his Christmas festival, 1397, when 200 tuns of wine and 2000 oxen were consumed. A charter was granted to Lichfield, constituting it a city, by Edward VI., 1549. It was absorbed into the county in 1885.
Visit of the prince of Wales, 29 May, 1894.

BISHOPS OF LICHFIELD AND COVENTRY.

1781. James, earl of Cornwallis, died 1824.
1824. Hon. Henry Ryder, died 31 March, 1836.

BISHOPS OF LICHFIELD.

1836. Samuel Butler, died 4 Dec. 1839.
1839. James Bowstead, died 11 Oct. 1843.
1843. John Lonsdale, died 19 Oct. 1867.
1867. Geo. Aug. Selwyn, late bishop of New Zealand, died 11 April, 1878.
1878. William Dalrymple Maclagan, consecrated 24 June, translated to York, May, 1891.
1891. Hon. Augustus Legge, June.

LICHFIELD HOUSE COMPACT, said to have been made between the Whig government and Daniel O'Connell in 1835 at Lichfield-house, 13, St. James's-square.

LICINIAN LAWS. In 375 B.C., C. Licinius Stolo and L. Sextius, tribunes of the people, promulgated various rogationes or laws to weaken the power of the patricians and benefit the plebeians: one was to relieve the plebeians from their debts; another enacted that no person should possess more than 500 jugera of the public land, or more than 100 head of large cattle, or 500 of small, in the Roman states; and the third, that one of the consuls should be a plebeian. After much opposition these were carried, and L. Sextius became the first plebeian consul, 366. Another law, 56 B.C., of this name, imposed a severe penalty on party clubs, or societies assembled for election purposes; and another, about 103 B.C. (brought forward by P. Licinius Crassus), limited the expenses of the table.

LICK OBSERVATORY, see *Observatory*.

LIEBENAU (Bohemia). Here was fought the first action of the seven weeks' war, 26 June, 1866; when the Austrians were compelled to retreat by the Prussians under general Von Horn.

LIEBIG, an extract of beef, named after the inventor of the process; *Lemco*, a name given to it 1902, the initials of the Liebig Extract of Meat Co.

LIECHTENSTEIN, a principality, S. Germany. Population, in 1880, 9,124; 1891, 9,434. Constitutional charter, 26 Sept. 1862. Prince John II., born 5 Oct. 1840, succeeded his father Alois-Joseph, 12 Nov. 1858.

LIÉGE (Belgium), a bishopric, under the German empire, from the 8th century till 1795. Liége frequently revolted against its prince-bishops. After a severe contest, the citizens were beaten at Brusthem, 28 Oct. 1467, and Liége taken by Charles the Bold, duke of Burgundy, who treated them with great severity. In 1482 Liége fell into the power of De la Marck, the Boar of Ardennes, who killed the bishop, Louis of Bourbon, and was himself defeated and killed. Liége was taken by the duke of Marlborough, 23 Oct. 1702; and by the French and others, at various times, up to 1796, when it was annexed to France. It was incorporated with the Netherlands in 1814, and with Belgium in 1830. Iron-works were established at Liége in the 16th century, and have been greatly enlarged by the Cockerills in the 19th, see *Seraing*. An international volunteer shooting contest held here, Sept. 1869. The Iron and Steel Institute met here 18 Aug. 1873. Dynamite explosions; the church of St. Martin much injured, 1, 2 May; nine anarchists convicted; sentences, penal servitude, one, 25 years; two, 20 years; four, 15 years; one, 10 years; one, 3 years; trial, 18-26 July, 1892. Population, in 1890, 149,789; 1900, 173,706.

LIEGNITZ, see *Pfaffendorf*.

LIEUTENANTS, LORD, for counties, were instituted in England, 3 Edw. VI., 1549, and in Ireland in 1831. Their military jurisdiction abolished by Army Regulation Act, 1871. For the lords lieutenant of Ireland, see *Ireland*.

LIFE ASSURANCE COMPANIES ACT, passed 9 Aug. 1870, requires the companies to publish annual returns of receipts, expenditure, &c.

LIFE-BOAT, &c., see *Wrecks*.

Patent granted to Mr. Lionel Lukin for a life-boat . 1785

A reward, offered by a committee in South Shields for a life-boat, 1788, obtained by Mr. Henry Greathead, of that town (he received 1200*l.* from parliament), 1789; it first put to sea . . 30 Jan. 1790

Another life-boat was invented by William Wouldhave. His name was inscribed on a memorial erected in honour of Henry Greathead on the pier at South Shields, uncovered . 25 June, 1890

31 life-boats built, and 300 lives saved up to . . 1804

The duke of Northumberland offered a reward of 105*l.* for a life-boat, 1850; obtained by Mr. James Beeching, of Yarmouth 1851

The tubular life-boat of Mr. H. Richardson, the *Challenger*, patented in Jan.; a cruise was made by him from Liverpool to London in it . . 1852

The *National Life-boat Institution*, founded in 1824; made *Royal* 1808; its journal first published, 1852; the duke of Northumberland president from 1866, died 2 Jan. 1899. In 1856 it received a bequest of 10,000*l.* from Hamilton Fitzgerald, esq., and of 39,000*l.* from Mr. Wm. Birks Rhodes, "the Hounslow miser," in 1878.

185 life-boats in the United Kingdom, 1865; 284, 1884; 293, 1888; 303, 1891; 304, 1892; 303, 1893; 308, 1894; 303, 1895; 296, 1896; 295, 1897; 296, 1898; 287, 1901; 288, 1902.

Lives saved by the Institution's life-boats, &c., 1824–1902, 40,474:—

Year	Lives	Year	Lives	Year	Lives
1824	124	1881	1121	1892	1,056
1834	214	1882	884	1893	598
1844	193	1883	955	1894	790
1854	355	1884	792	1895	709
1864	698	1885	555	1896	461
1874	743	1886	761	1897	659
1875	921	1887	572	1898	756
1876	600	1888	617	1899	676
1877	1048	1889	627	1900	865
1878	616	1890	555	1901	490
1879	855	1891	736	1902	455
1880	697				

Hans Busk Life-ship Institute founded . Oct. 1869

The *American Life-raft*, composed of cylinders lashed together, sailed from New York, 4 June, 1867, navigated by three men, capt John Mikes and Messrs. Miller and Mullane, and arrived at Southampton, 25 July following.

LIFE-PRESERVER, the apparatus of capt. Manby (brought into use in Feb. 1808), effects a communication with the distressed vessel by a rope, thrown by a shot from a mortar, with a line attached to it. For the night, a night-ball is provided with a hollow case of thick pasteboard, and a fuse and quick match, and charged with fifty balls, and a sufficiency of powder to inflame them. The fuse is so graduated that the shell shall explode at the height of 300 yards. The balls spread a brilliant light for nearly a minute, and give a clear view of every surrounding object. In 20 years, 58 vessels and 410 of their crews and passengers had been saved. Capt. Manby died 18 Nov. 1854, aged 89. See *Rockets*.

The BOAT-LOWERING APPARATUS, in consequence of many being lost when boats were lowered from the *Amazon* in 1852, invented by Mr. Charles Clifford, of London, in 1856, has been much approved of, and has been generally adopted in the royal navy.

Capt. Kynaston's hooks were approved by admiral sir Baldwin Walker in 1862, and by a committee on the subject in 1872.

Exhibition of life-boats, life-rafts, &c., at the London Tavern opened 15 April, 1873.

Hicks' Life-raft, reported good on trial in East India docks . . . . 1 Oct. 1874

Capt. Boyton's Life preserving dress (of india-rubber), with means for signalling at sea, tried by him on the Thames successfully, 23 Jan. and 6 March, at Cowes, before the queen, while in the water he fired rockets, caught fish, &c., 5 April; nearly crossed the channel from Dover (paddled two miles an hour); stopped by the French pilot April, 1875

Captain Boyton crossed the Channel from Grisnez to the South Foreland in 23½ hours . 28-29 May, ,,

Christie's Life-saving raft tried on the Thames, could not be sunk . . . . 17 March, ,,

Edmund Thompson's Life-raft, partially successful off Poplar . . . . 22 April, ,,

Boyton race on the Thames by six young men, three prizes awarded by the duchess of Teck . 10 Aug. ,,

Rev. E. L. Berthon's Collapsible Life-boat taken out by the *Essequibo*, and proved to be successful Sept. 1882

Gold medal given to vice-admiral Ward, chief inspector of life-boats for 32 years . . . Aug. 1883

Much assistance rendered by life-boats during a severe gale . . 14–16 Oct. and 8, 9 Dec. 1886

The *Mexico* wrecked near Southport; the Lytham lifeboat saves 12 lives; the Southport and St. Anne's lifeboats capsized without righting themselves; 27 of the crews perish . . . 9 Dec. ,,

Adequate subscriptions for their wives and families and nucleus of a permanent fund formed Dec. ,,

The *Storm King* patent life-boat 30 feet long, with its inventor, capt. Joergensen and a man named Nelsen, left London 12 Sept. 1889, encountered heavy gales; arrived at Cape Town . 2 March, 1890

Death of Joaquin Lopez, boatman, aged 92, who had saved many lives from drowning and received foreign honours . . . . 22 Dec. ,,

The *Duke of Northumberland*, a new fast steel hydraulic steam life-boat, with 15 water-tight compartments, designed by Messrs. R. and H. Green, to be stationed at Harwich, tried on the Thames near Blackwall, 24 July, and since brought into service . . . . ,,

About 714 lives saved by lifeboats, during the great gale . . . . 6, 7 Nov. ,,

The queen presents the Albert medal to Laurence Hennessy, seaman, for having saved the lives of 31 men during ship-wrecks . . . 18 Feb. 1892

Life-boat Saturday in about 90 principal towns of Great Britain set apart to collect funds for the institution, 1891 *et seq.*; the first in London, a demonstration in the grounds of the Imperial institute, 16 May, 1896; again, 15 May, 1897; 16,206*l.* collected in 1896; 25,890*l.* 18*s.* in 1901; London, 10 May, 1902.

44 life-boats launched, 99 lives saved, during the great gale of . . . . . 22, 23 Dec. 1894

54 lives saved by lifeboats in the gale . 2, 3 Oct. 1895

24 lives saved by lifeboats, 25 Sept., and 24 in a gale . . . . 8 Oct. 1896

Select committee of the commons appointed to inquire into the Lifeboat institution, 17 March, 1897; report favourable . . . 14 July, 1897

The Margate lifeboat, *Friend of all Nations*, upset in a gale, 9 men drowned (over 8,000*l.* subscribed for the widows and children), 2 Dec. 1897; again wrecked, but the crew saved . 1 Dec. 1898

Mr. Fred. Cruden Baines bequeaths 10,000*l.* to the Roy. Nat. Lifeboat institution, and 2,048*l.* 14*s.* 11*d.* received from the Civil Service lifeboat fund during 1898, announced Jan. 1899 (1,000*l.* from Mr. J. Busk); Mr. F. Freeman bequeaths 2,000*l.* 3 Feb. 1902; Mrs. Moore bequeaths 1,050*l.* Dec. 1902; Miss A. Miles gives 1,200*l.* March, 1903.

Total amount (including the Lifeboat Saturday fund, founded 1891), received in 1900, 69,693*l.*; in 1902, 72,138*l.*

The Aldeburgh lifeboat capsized in a gale, 6 deaths, 7 Dec. ,,

Steam lifeboat, the *James Stevens*, capsized in a gale off Padstow, Cornwall; 7 deaths and 4 fishermen drowned also . . . . . . 11 April, 1900

New lifeboat or raft for merchant ships invented by M. Von Andrep; successfully used at Copenhagen . . . . Sept. ,,

The Caister lifeboat *Beauchamp*, near Yarmouth, capsized in a gale, 9 deaths . . . 14 Nov. 1901

German emperor sends 45*l.* to the West Hartlepool crew (who rescued the crew of a German vessel, Dec. 1901) . . . . 12 July, 1902

65 lives saved by lifeboats in the gale 15, 17 Oct. 1902
Capt. Doenvig's life-saving globe successfully tried in Norway, 15 Sept.; again in the English Channel . . . . . . 18 Nov. „
Electrical communication between stations, lighthouses, &c., started 1893, see *Wireless Telegraphy*, 1903.
Mumbles life-boat capsized . . . 1 Feb. 1903
New lifeboats; one at Aldeburgh from Winchester, and one at Caistor from Mr. W. H. Lucy, 23 July, „

LIFE-GUARDS, see *Guards*.

LIFE INSURANCE, see *Insurance* and *Annuities*.

LIFE-PEERAGES. A bill for creating them was read a second time in the lords, 27 April, 1869, but afterwards rejected. Two peers for life created to act as appeal judges, 5 Oct. 1876. See *Lords*.

LIFE, PRESERVATION OF. See *Sanitation*. The Life Saving society was founded in 1891, for the promotion of technical education in swimming, life-saving, and the resuscitation of the apparently drowned, etc.; 400 organizations, at home and abroad, in 1896. International congress at Nantes, ends, 2 Aug. 1902.

LIFE-SHIPS. To promote the construction and use of these the Hans Busk Life-Ship Institute was founded, Oct. 1869. The life-ship, *Peronelle*, was launched at Southampton, 25 Aug. 1873.

LIGHT. The law of refraction discovered by Snellius, about 1624. The motion and velocity of light discovered by Reaumur, and after him by Cassini, and calculated by Rœmer (1676) and Bradley (1720). Its velocity ascertained to be about 190,000,000 of miles in sixteen minutes, or nearly 200,000 miles in a second, which is a million of times swifter than the velocity of a cannon ball, about 1667. The light of the sun takes eight minutes and eight seconds for its transmission through space to the earth. See *Emission Theory*. The undulatory theory of light, its polarisation, and its chemical action, were all made known in the nineteenth century by Dr. Thos. Young, Weber, Fresnel, Malus, Arago, Biot, Brewster, Wheatstone, Ritter, Niepce, Daguerre, Talbot, Stokes, Tyndall, Rayleigh, Dewar, Crookes, &c.; see *Optics*, *Photography*, *Calorescence*, *Fluorescence*, *Röntgen Rays*, *Radium*.

Velocity of Light. Direct determination by the toothed-wheel method by Fizeau agreed with the astronomical result 1849
Foucault, with the revolving mirror, gave 298,000 kilometres in a second of mean time 1865
Cornu's improved tooth-wheel apparatus gave 300,400 kilometres in a second of mean time . . 1874
Professor Simon Newcomb, of Washington, with his "phototachometer" (completed in May, 1880) gave 299,860 kilometres in a second of mean time, 1886
Mr. aft. sir Wm. Crookes, F.R.S., considered that he had demonstrated the mechanical action of light by experiments with delicate balances in the highest procurable vacuum, and calculated the force of the sun's rays upon the earth to be 2·3 tons to the square mile, 1873-6. His apparatus was termed *Radiometer* (*which see*). After much investigation, Mr. Crookes admitted that the action was not due to radiation, but to difference of heat-absorption and the reaction of residual air.
Mr. Crookes at the Royal Society announces experiments respecting an ultra-gaseous state of matter, supporting the emission theory . . . . 5 Dec. 1878
Dr. C. Wm. Siemens reported to the Royal Society that the electric light acts on vegetation like solar light . . . . 4 Dec. 1880

LIGHT BRIGADE. See *Balaklava*.

LIGHTHOUSE, called Pharos (now *phare*, French; *faro*, Italian), from one erected at Pharos, (*which see*) near Alexandria, Egypt, 550 feet high, said to have been visible forty-two miles, about 283 B.C. There was one at Messina, at Rhodes, &c. The light was obtained by fires. A coal-fire light was exhibited at Tynemouth castle, Northumberland, about 1638. The first true lighthouse erected in England was the Eddystone lighthouse (*which see*) in 1758-60. Lights were exhibited in various places by the corporation of the Trinity-house early in the 16th century. 2814 lighthouses in the world (1867).

BRITISH LIGHTHOUSES.

The lighthouse (40 years old, height 80 feet, weight 300 tons) on the pier at Sunderland, Durham, was moved forward 500 feet without stopping the illumination, under the superintendence of Mr. John Murray, October, 1841.
The Commissioners on Lights, &c. (1861), report 171 shorelights in England, 113 in Scotland, and 73 in Ireland (total, 357); and 47 floating-lights.
6 lighthouses building, April, 1867.
The French have 224 lighthouses on shore.
The source of light in our lighthouses is principally oil; but in harbour lights gas has been successfully used. Glass reflectors were used in 1780, and copper ones in 1807. A common coal-fire light was discontinued at St. Bees so recently as 1822. Fresnel's Dioptric system (*which see*), devised about 1819, was adopted for the first time in England by Messrs. Wilkins, at the direction of the corporation of the Trinity-house, 1 July, 1836.
The most brilliant artificial light ever produced—derived from magneto-electricity by a machine devised by professor Holmes—was first employed at the South Foreland lighthouse, near Dover, on 8 Dec. 1858; and at Dengeness (or Dungeness) in 1862. Mr. Holmes' arrangement, and a similar one constructed by M. Serin, were shown at the International exhibition, London, in 1862.
Mr. H. Wilde's apparatus for producing a most powerful magneto-electric light, on trial in northern lighthouses, Oct. 1866.
Lime-light (*which see*) employed at the S. Foreland lighthouse in 1861.
Gas light tried successfully at Howth Bailey lighthouse, Dublin Bay, July, 1869.
Mr. Wigham's triform light: glass belt round the gaslight, prisms below the belt, and prisms forming a cupola: tried near Dublin; approved by Dr. Tyndall, July, 1873; further improvements by Mr. J. R. Wigham, shown, Dec. 1894.
C. Wm. Siemens' magneto-electric light used at the Lizards, 29 March, 1878.
The cost of erecting the three great British lighthouses —viz., the Skerry-Vore (west coast), 158 feet high, 83,126*l*.; the Bishop Rock, Scilly Isles, 145 feet high, 36,559*l*.; and the Bell Rock, Scotland, 117 feet high, 61,331*l*.
Return to inquiries respecting officials, their duties, salaries, &c. issued early in Dec. 1883.
Important experiments at South Foreland on electricity, gas, and oil as illuminants, June, 1884. Report adopted by Trinity House; electric light brightest, but most expensive; gas and oil nearly equal; oil recommended for practical purposes; electricity for special use on headlands, &c., about 25 Aug. 1885.
Royal commission respecting telegraph communication between lighthouses met, 18 June, 1892. First report issued recommending electric communication between 25 lighthouses (adopted), 1 Feb. 1893; final report issued, 15 Oct. 1897.
Retirement of sir James Douglass, born, 16 Oct., 1826; constructor of the present Eddystone, Wolf Rock, and other lighthouses, Nov. 1892; died, 10 June, 1898.
Telegraphic and telephonic communication established between life-boat stations in Liverpool bay, lighthouses, &c.; also between other stations on the Welsh coast, reported, Jan. 1895.
New lighthouse on the Admiralty pier, Dover, completed, announced 25 Dec. 1895.
New lighthouse on Lundy island, Devon, opened 18 Nov. 1897.
Little Crosby lighthouse on the Mersey destroyed by fire during a gale, 3 deaths, 2 Feb. 1898.

New lighthouse at Cape Grisnez, N. France, opened, 15 Feb. 1899.
Donaghadee lighthouse burnt down, 12 May, 1900.
New lighthouse at Pendeen, Cornwall, opened 26 Sept. 1900; and another on the Foreland, Bristol channel, 28 Sept. 1900; new one on Beachy Head, 142 feet high, opened, 2 Oct. 1902.
Lizard lighthouse illuminated with a single electric light, said to be the most powerful in the world, Oct., 1903.

LIGHTING UP (Towns, &c.), see *London*, 1684, 1694; *Gas* and *Electric Light*.

LIGHTNING-CONDUCTORS were first set up for the protection of buildings by Franklin shortly after 1752, when he brought down electricity from a thunder-cloud. Richmann, of St. Petersburg, was killed while repeating these experiments, Aug. 1752. The first conductor in England was set up at Payne's Hill, by Dr. Watson. In 1766 one was placed on the tower of St. Mark, at Venice, which has since escaped injury, although frequently injured by lightning previously. A powder magazine at Glogau, in Silesia, was saved by a conductor in 1782; and, from the want of one, a quantity of gunpowder was ignited at Brescia in 1767, and above 3000 persons perished. In 1762, Dr. Watson recommended conductors to be used in the navy; and they were employed for a short time, but soon fell into disuse from want of skill and attention. Mr. (afterwards sir William) Snow Harris devoted his attention to the subject from 1820 to 1854, and published a work, in 1843, detailing his experiments. In 1830, above thirty ships were fitted up with his conductors, and in 1842 his plans were adopted, and his conductors are now manufactured in the royal dockyards. In 1854 parliament granted him 5000*l*. A lightning research committee formed, Jan. 1901, with a view to the better protection of buildings, 200 observers in the United Kingdom, and others abroad. 713 deaths by lightning in the United States in 1900 (291 in the open, 57 under trees, 158 in houses).

LIGHT RAILWAYS, see *Railways*, 1894, *et seq.*

LIGNY (near Fleurus, Belgium), where Napoleon defeated the Prussian army under Blucher, 16 June, 1815; see *Waterloo*.

LIGUORIANS, or REDEMPTORISTS, a Roman catholic order, established in 1732 by Alfonso de Liguori, approved by pope Benedict XIV., 1749.

LIGURIANS, a Celtic tribe, N. Italy, invaded the Roman territory, and were defeated 238 B.C. They were not subjugated till 172 B.C.—The LIGURIAN REPUBLIC, founded in May, 1797, on the ruin of Genoa, was incorporated with France in 1805, and then merged into the kingdom of Italy.

LILAC TREE, *Syringa*. The Persian lilac from Persia was cultivated in England about 1638; the common lilac by Mr. John Gerard about 1597.

LILLE, see *Lisle*.

LILLI-BURLERO, part of the refrain of a popular song ridiculing the Irish papists, 1688. The words are attributed to lord Wharton, the music to Henry Purcell.

LILY, a native of Persia, Syria, and Italy, was brought to England before 1460; the martagon from Germany, 1596.

LILYBÆUM, a strong maritime fortress of Sicily, besieged by Pyrrhus, king of Epirus, 276 B.C., and relieved by the Carthaginians 275 B.C. It was taken by the Romans, 241 B.C., after a siege of nine years, which led to the end of the second Punic war.

LIMA (Peru). In 1534, Pizarro, marching through Peru, was struck with the beauty of the valley of Rimac, and there he founded this city, and gave it the name of *Ciudad de los Reyes*, or city of the kings, 1535. Here he was assassinated, 26 June, 1541. Awful earthquakes occurred here, 1586, 1630, 1687, and 28 Oct. 1746. In 1854-5, thousands perished by yellow fever. Mr. Sullivan, the British consul, was assassinated at Lima, 11 Aug. 1857; see *Peru*, 1872, 1881-3. Buildings injured by an earthquake, 20 Sept. 1897. The church of San Francisco, founded by Pizarro, 1535, burnt, 20 Sept. 1899. Population, 1900, 105,000.

LIMBURG (Netherlands), a duchy in the 10th century; acquired by the dukes of Brabant about 1288; added to Burgundy about 1429; passed to the house of Austria in 1477; became one of the United Provinces, 1609; conquered and annexed to the French republic, 1795; restored to the Netherlands, 1814; divided between Holland and Belgium, 1830; completely separated from the German confederation by treaty, 11 May, 1867.

LIME or LINDEN TREE, probably introduced in the 16th century. The limes in St. James's park are said to have been planted at the suggestion of Evelyn, who recommended multiplying odoriferous trees, in his "Fumifugium" (1661). A lime-tree planted in Switzerland in 1410, existed in 1720, the trunk being thirty-six feet in circumference.

LIME-LIGHT, produced by the combustion of oxygen and hydrogen or carburetted hydrogen on a surface of lime. This light evolves little heat and does not vitiate the air. It is also called Drummond Light, after its inventor, lieut. Thomas Drummond, who successfully produced it as a first-class light in 1826, and employed it on the ordnance survey. It is said to have been seen at a distance of 112 miles. It was tried at the South Foreland lighthouse in 1861. Lieut. Drummond was born, 1797, died 15 April, 1840. To him is attributed the maxim that "property has its duties as well as its rights."

LIMERICK, anciently Lumneach (S. W. Ireland). About 550, St. Munchin is said to have founded a bishopric and built a church here, which latter was destroyed by the Danes in 853. Donald O'Brien, king of Limerick, founded the cathedral about 1200. Limerick obtained its charter in 1195, when John Stafford was made first provost; and its first mayor was Adam Servant, in 1198. It was taken by Ireton after six months' siege in 1650. In Aug. 1690 it was invested by the English and Dutch, and surrendered on most honourable terms, 3 Oct. 1691.* An awful explosion of 218 barrels of gunpowder greatly shattered the town, killing 100 persons, 1 Feb. 1694. Another explosion of gunpowder here killed many persons, 2 Jan. 1837. Awful and destructive tempest, 6-7 Jan. 1839. A

* By the treaty it was agreed that all arms, property and estates should be restored; all attainders annulled, and all outlawries reversed; and that no oath but that of allegiance should be required of high or low; the freedom of the Catholic religion was secured; relief from pecuniary claims incurred by hostilities was guaranteed; permission to leave the kingdom was extended to all who desired it; and a general pardon proclaimed to all then in arms. *Burns.* This treaty was annulled by the Irish parliament, 1695. Limerick is still called "the city of the broken treaty."

new graving-dock was opened by the lord-lieutenant, earl Spencer, 13 May, 1873. A new R. C. cathedral, St. John's, consecrated, 21 June, 1894. Mr. Michael Hogan, "The bard of Thomond," died, aged 66, 19 April, 1899. The right rev. Dr. Graves, bp. of Limerick, an antiquarian, dies, 17 July, 1899, succeeded by Dr. T. Bunbury, 6 Oct. Population, 1881, 38,555; 1891, 37,072; 1901, 38,085.

LIMITATIONS, STATUTE OF, 21 James I. c. 16, 1623. By it actions for trespass or debt, or simple contract, must be commenced within six years after the cause of action, and actions for assault, menace, or imprisonment within four years. The Real Actions Limitation act, 1874, came into operation 1 Jan. 1879.

LIMITED LIABILITY. An act for limiting the liability of joint stock companies, 18 & 19 Vict. c. 133 (passed 1855), was several times amended 1856-7-8. On 31 May, 1864, "3830 joint stock companies had been formed and registered on the limited liability principle, and 938 had ceased to exist." Much calamity in 1866 was occasioned by the abuse of the system. The Companies act of 1862 was amended in 1867. 1241 registered in 1874; 1,791 registered in 1886; total 1862-86, 25,042. The principle adopted by some joint stock banks in 1879-80. New companies act passed, 8 Aug. 1900. See under *Banks*.

LIMOGES AFFAIR, see *France*, Dec. 1877.

LIMOURS MURDERS, N.-central France. Several barbarous murders, especially of aged people, took place here, Jan., Sept., Nov., 1873, and Jan. 1874; several persons denounced, proved innocence. In June, 1874, one Poirier confessed to similar murders at Nogent and other places, in Nov. 1873 and Jan. 1874. Executed at Chartres, 29 Sept. 1874.

LINCELLES (N. France), where the allied English and Dutch armies defeated the French, 18 Aug. 1793. General Lake commanded three battalions of foot-guards.

LINCOLN, the Roman *Lindum Colonia*, and at the period of the conquest rich and populous. It was taken several times by Saxons and Danes. The castle was built by William I. in 1086. Without Newport-gate upon Lincoln plain was fought the battle between the partisans of the empress Maud, commanded by the earl of Gloucester, and the army of Stephen, in which the king was defeated and taken prisoner, 2 Feb. 1141. Louis, dauphin of France, invited over by the discontented barons in the last year of king John's reign, was acknowledged by them as king of England here; but the nobility, summoned by the earl of Pembroke to Gloucester to crown Henry III., marched against Louis and the barons, and defeated them in a most sanguinary fight (called the Fair of Lincoln), 20 May, 1217; and Louis withdrew. Theatre Royal burnt, 26 Nov. 1892. Population, 1881, 37,313; 1891, 41,491; 1901, 48,783.

LINCOLN, BISHOPRIC OF. Sidnacester or Lindisse and Dorchester, two distinct sees in Mercia, were united about 1078, and the see was removed to Lincoln by bishop Remigius de Feschamp, who built a cathedral (1086), afterwards destroyed by fire, but rebuilt by bishop Alexander (1127) and bishop Hugh of Burgundy. The diocese is very large, although the dioceses of Ely (1109), Oxford, and Peterborough (1541) were formed from it, and were further enlarged in 1837. The see was valued at the dissolution of monasteries at 2065*l.* per annum; and after many of its manors had been seized upon, it was rated in the king's books at 894*l.* 10*s.* 1*d.* Present income, 4500*l.* It has given three saints to the church of Rome, and to the civil state of England six lord chancellors. The great bell of the cathedral, called *Great Tom of Lincoln*, weighs four tons eight pounds.

RECENT BISHOPS.

1787. George Pretyman (afterwards Tomline), translated to Winchester, 1820.
1820. Hon. George Pelham, died 1 Feb. 1827.
1827. John Kaye, died 19 Feb. 1852.
1852. John Jackson, translated to London, 1869.
1869. Christopher Wordsworth, consecrated 24 Feb.; resigns Dec. 1884; died 21 March, 1885.
1885. Edward King, Feb. For his trial for ritualistic practices, see under *Canterbury*.

LINCOLN'S-INN (London), derives its name from Henry de Lacy, earl of Lincoln, who erected a mansion on this spot in the reign of Edward I., which had been the bishop of Chichester's palace. It became an inn of court, 1310. The gardens of Lincoln's-inn-fields were laid out by Inigo Jones, about 1620, and erroneously said to occupy the same space as the largest pyramid of Egypt, which is 764 feet square; Lincoln's-inn square being 821 feet by 625 feet 6 inches. William lord Russell was beheaded in Lincoln's-inn-fields, 21 July, 1683. The square (formed in 1618) was enclosed with iron railings about 1737. The new hall and other buildings were opened, 30 Oct. 1845, and the square planted. The *theatre* in Lincoln's-inn-fields was built in 1695; rebuilt in 1714; made a barrack in 1756, and pulled down in 1848. The fields (enclosed in 1735) opened to the public (cost 12,000*l.*) by sir John Hutton, L.C.C., 23 Feb. 1895.

LINCOLN TOWER, Westminster Bridge Road, was erected, by the united subscriptions of Britons and Americans, as a memorial of the abolition of slavery, and of Abraham Lincoln, president. The foundation-stone was laid by general Schenk, then American minister here, 9 July, 1874; and the head stone was placed by the Rev. Newman Hall, minister of Surrey chapel, 28 Sept. 1875. The tower, which is 220 feet high, cost about 7000*l.* The church, named Christ church (to replace Surrey chapel), and schools adjoining (cost about 60,000*l.*), were dedicated, 4 July, *et seq.* 1876. The rev. Rowland Hill's body was removed from Surrey chapel and placed here, 14 April, 1881.

LINDISFARNE, or HOLY ISLAND, on the coast of Northumberland, became a bishop's see, 635. It was ravaged by the Danes under Regnar Lodbrok in 793, and the monastery destroyed by them in 875. The bones of the bishop, St. Cuthbert, who died in 687, were conveyed, among other places, to Chester-le-street, 883, and to Ripon, 995, and finally to Durham, *which see*.

LINEN. Pharaoh arrayed Joseph in vestures of fine linen, 1716 B.C. (*Gen.* xli. 42.)

First manufactured in England by Flemish weavers, under the protection of Henry III. 1253
A company of linen weavers established in London 1368
The art of staining linen known . . . about 1579
A colony of Scots in the reign of James I., and other Presbyterians who fled from persecution in succeeding reigns, planted themselves in the north-east part of Ireland, and there established the linen manufacture, which was liberally encouraged by the lord deputy Wentworth in 1634; by William III. 1698
Hemp, flax, linen, thread, and yarn, from Ireland, permitted to be exported duty free 1696

Irish linen board established in 1711; the Linen-hall, Dublin, opened 1728; the board abolished . 1828
A board of trustees to superintend the Scotch linen manufacture established 1727
Duty on linen taken off 1860
An "all pure" linen ball to stimulate and increase the demand for pure linen, held under distinguished patronage at the Ulster-hall, Belfast, 27 March, 1903
Dunfermline in Fifeshire, Dundee in Forfarshire, Leeds and Barnsley in Yorkshire and Belfast in Ireland are chief seats of our linen manufacture.

LINGAM, an ancient Hindoo god (much worshipped by women), who had many temples in Delhi, before the Mahometan conquest. One of his idols set in gold, diamonds, and other precious stones, was sold by Messrs. Phillips of Bond Street, London, for 2,450*l*., 5 Dec. 1888.

LINLITHGOW-BRIDGE (near Edinburgh), near which the forces of the earl of Angus, who held James V. in their power, defeated the forces of the earl of Lennox, who, after receiving promise of quarter, was killed by sir James Hamilton, 1526. Mary, queen of Scots, was born in the palace of Linlithgow, 8 Dec. 1542, James V., her father, dying of a broken heart, 14 Dec., in consequence of his defeat by the English at Solway Moss, 25 Nov. previous.

LINNÆAN SYSTEM of botany, arranged by Linné or Linnæus, a Swede, 1725-30. He classed the plants according to the number and situation of the sexual parts, and made the flower and fruit the test of his various genera. Linnæus lived from 1707 to 1778. His library and herbarium were purchased by sir James E. (then Dr.) Smith, and given to the *Linnean Society* in London, which was instituted in 1788, and incorporated 26 March, 1802; at Milan, about 20 Sept. 1892.

The centenary of the foundation of the Linnean Society celebrated; gold medals were presented to sir Joseph Hooker, and sir Richard Owen, 24 May, 1888.

LINOTYPE. See under *Printing*.

LION AND UNICORN, the former English, the latter Scottish, became the supporters of the royal arms on the accession of James I. in 1603. The lions in Trafalgar-square, designed by sir Edwin Landseer, were uncovered, 31 Jan. 1867.

LION. True lions belong to the old world exclusively. They existed in Europe, Egypt, and Palestine, but have long disappeared from those countries; their present country being Africa. A lion named Pompey died in the Tower of London in 1760, after 70 years' confinement.
Mr. Gordon Cumming, the lion-slayer, published his "Sporting Adventures in South Africa" in . 1850
Van Amburgh was very successful in taming lions; but many have perished through rashness. The Lion-queen was killed at Chatham, 1850; and Massarti (John McCarthy) was killed by a lion, 3 Jan. 1872
Lion Sermon preached annually on 16 Oct. at St. Katherine Cree church, London, in memory of the escape of sir John Gayer from a lion in Arabia 16 Oct. 1630

LIPPAU, see *Hussites*.

LIPPE, a constitutional principality (N.W. Germany). Population, 1885, 123,212; 1900, 140,000. Prince Leopold, born 1 Sept. 1821; succeeded his father, Leopold, 1 Jan. 1851; died 8 Dec. 1875—his brother Waldemar, born 18 April, 1824, succeeded; died 20 March, 1895; Alexander (deranged), brother, succeeded; disputed succession; count Ernst nominated regent and successor by a tribunal, July, 1897. Lippe became a member of the North German confederation, 18 Aug. 1866. The federal princes memorialised by the count regent on a difference with the emperor regarding a point of military etiquette, see *Bavaria*, 1898, *Times*, 12 Nov. 1898. Settlement of the controversy, disputed succession, &c. postponed, 5 Jan. 1899.

LIPPSTADT, see *Lützen*.

LIQUEFACTION. See *Gases*, *Cold*, *Air*, *Hydrogen* and *Fluorine*.

LIQUOR TRAFFIC, royal commission, lord Peel chairman, sir Charles Cameron, the earl of Jersey, the bishop of London, sir William Houldsworth, and 19 others; hon. Sidney (aft. lord) Peel, sec., 31 March; first meeting, 19 May, 1896. Two reports, one by lord Peel, chairman; he resigned to sir Algernon West, 1899; much contradictory evidence, *Times*, 1 May, 1899; final report issued, 4 July, 1899. See *Licences*. Internat. conference on West African liquor traffic, duty increased, convention signed at Brussels, June, 1899. Sale of intoxicating liquors to children acts passed, 1886, 6 Aug. 1900 and 1901.

LISBON (Olisippo, and Felicitas Julia, of the ancients) was taken by the Arabs about 716, and became important under the Moorish kings, from whom it was captured by Alfonso I. of Portugal in 1147. It was made the capital of Portugal by Emanuel, 1506. Lisbon has suffered much by earthquakes, and was almost destroyed by one, 1 Nov. 1755; in Great Britain about 100,000*l*. was subscribed for the sufferers; see *Earthquakes*. The court fled to the Brazils, 10 Nov. 1807, and on 30 Nov. the French, under Junot, entered Lisbon, and held it until the battle of Vimeira, in which they were defeated by the British, under sir Arthur Wellesley, 21 Aug. 1808. A military insurrection at Lisbon, 21 Aug. 1831, was soon suppressed, and many soldiers were executed; see *Portugal*. Population in 1885, 243,010: 1900, 357,000.

A pleasure boat on the Tagus upset, about 60 drowned . . . . . 26 May, 1875
Lisbon Steam Tramway Company, favoured by duke of Saldanha, ambassador in London; company promoted by baron Albert Grant and others; tramway could not be made; see *Trials* . July, 1876
Great fire at the dockyard . . . 17–18 Dec. 1883
Great excitement through the British ultimatum respecting East Africa (see *Portugal*) . Jan. 1890
Strike of bakers; 6,000 encamped outside the city, soldiers employed as bakers . . 19 June, 1894
The chamber of deputies destroyed by fire, 17 June, 1895
Explosion at a house next the Opera-house, 4 Feb.; arrest of 60 anarchists . . . . 5 Feb. 1896
Repressive legislation introduced . . . 9 Feb. ,,
Sen. Domingor killed by dynamite at Alhandra, 18 April, ,,
Strike of gas workers against employment of foreigners; city in darkness; ended by concession . . . . 1–11 Aug. ,,
The 400th anniversary of Vasco da Gama's first arrival in India, celebrated . . 15–21 May, 1898
Dr. Pestana, director of the Bacteriological institute, dies of plague contracted during his researches at Oporto . . . . 15 Nov. 1899
Excavations, chapel and tombs, &c., dating before 755, discovered . . . . end Aug. 1902

LISLE (now Lille), N. France, has a strong citadel by Vauban. It was besieged by the duke of Marlborough and the allies; and, though deemed impregnable, was taken after a three months' siege in 1708. It was restored by the treaty of Utrecht, in 1713, in consideration of the demolition of the fortifications of Dunkirk. Lisle sustained a severe bombardment from the Austrians, who were obliged to raise the siege, 7 Oct. 1792. Population, 1886, 188,272; 1891, 200,935; 1901, 215,431.

The French Association for the Advancement of Science met here . . . . . . 20 Aug. 1874
Industrial exhibition here visited by sir Wilfrid Laurier and other colonial premiers . 27 Aug. 1902

LISMORE (S. Ireland.) St. Carthagh, first bishop, 636, says: "Lismore is a famous and holy city, of which nearly one-half is an asylum where no woman dare enter." The castle (built by king John when earl of Moreton, 1185), burnt in 1645, was rebuilt with great magnificence by the duke of Devonshire. The cathedral, built 636, was repaired by Cormac, son of Muretus, king of Munster, about 1130. The bishopric was united to that of Waterford, about 1363; and both to Cashel in 1839.

LISSA (or Leuthen, Silesia). Here the king of Prussia vanquished Charles of Lorraine; 6000 Austrians were slain, 5 Dec. 1757.—LISSA, in Poland, was laid in ruins by the Russian army in the campaign of 1707.—LISSA, an island in the Adriatic. Near here the Italian fleet, commanded by Persano, was defeated with severe loss by the Austrian fleet, commanded by Tegethoff, 20 July, 1866.

The Italians had 23 vessels, 11 of which were ironclads, and the Austrians had 23 vessels, 7 only being ironclads.

Persano, when in sight of the enemy, quitted his ship, the *Rè d'Italia*, and hoisted his flag on the *Affondatore*. His ironclads did not keep well together.

During the action, the ironclad *Palestro* took fire and exploded, and all on board perished (except 19 out of 200 men), exclaiming, *Viva il Rè! Viva Italia!* The *Rè d'Italia* was surrounded and sunk by the Austrians. The *Rè di Portobello* disabled the Austrian line-of-battle ship *Kaiser*, and compelled her to run ashore. Both parties soon after retired from the conflict, which had lasted four hours.

Admiral Persano was tried for misconduct and dismissed the service (see *Italy*) . 15 April, 1867

Battle off Lissa.

Capt. Wm. Hoste in the *Amphion*, with two other frigates; the *Active*, Capt. J. A. Gordon; the *Cerberus*, Capt. H. Whitby; and the *Volage*, 22-gun ship, Capt. P. Hornby, defeated a Franco-Venetian squadron which attacked him; he captured two vessels, the *Corona* and *Bellona*; he was badly wounded . . . . 13 March, 1811

LITANIES (Greek *litaneia*, supplication), were first used in processions, it is said, about 469; others say about 400. Litanies to the Virgin Mary were first introduced by pope Gregory I. about 595. The first English litany was commanded to be used in the Reformed churches by Henry VIII. in 1544.

LITERARY CLUB (at first called "The Club" and "Johnson's Club"), founded by Dr. Johnson and sir Joshua Reynolds, in 1764. Hawkins, Topham Beauclerk, Goldsmith, Burke, and Bennet Langton, were among the first members. The opinion formed of a new work by the club was speedily known all over London, and had great influence. Many eminent men have been members of the Club, including Hallam, Macaulay, the marquis of Lansdowne, and bishop Blomfield; Dr. Milman, dean of St. Paul's, was in the chair at the centenary dinner, on 7 June, 1864.

LITERARY AND ARTISTIC CONGRESS, International, met at Paris (Victor Hugo, president), 17 June; and founded "International Literary Association," 28 June, 1878; met in London, 9-14 June, 1879; at Lisbon, 20 Sept. 1880; at Vienna, 20-29 Sept. 1881; at Berne, 10 Sept. 1883; at Brussels, 27 Sept. 1884; at Berne, 7 Sept. 1885; at Madrid, 8 Oct. 1887; at Venice, 19 Sept. 1888; at Paris, 20 June, 1889; at Berne, 5 Oct. 1889; in London, 4 Oct. 1890; at Neufchâtel, 26 Sept. 1891; at Milan, about 20 Sept. 1892. Literary conference at Chicago, 10–15 July, 1893.

LITERARY FUND, ROYAL, was founded in 1790, to relieve literary men of all nations, by David Williams,* the friend of Benjamin Franklin, and incorporated in 1818. The king of the Belgians presided at the annual dinner, 8 May, 1872; the prince of Wales at the centenary dinner, 14 May, 1890; the duke of York, when chairman, 8 May, 1895, stated that among his predecessors were his great-grandfather, the duke of Kent, 1815, and his grandfather, the prince consort. The permanent fund in 1897 was 15,091*l.* 19*s.* 3*d.*; 15,591*l.*, 1898; 57,769*l.*, 1902; 56,410*l.*

LITERARY PROPERTY, SOCIETIES, &c., see *Authors, Copyright, Societies*, &c.

"*Literary Production Committee*" of authors; proposed formation, with the object of obtaining a good price for their works, July, 1878.

LITERATURE, see *Letters, English, French, German, Greek, Italian, Latin, and Spanish Language;* comprehends eloquence, poetry, history, language, and their subdivisions. *Literature*, a weekly critical journal, edited by H. D. Traill (died, aged 58, 21 Feb. 1900), issued at the *Times* office, but independent, price sixpence, 23 Oct. 1897. "Short histories of the literatures of the world," Japan, by W. G. Aston, May, 1899.

LITHIUM, the lightest metal known (specific gravity 0·59: atomic weight 7), is obtained from an alkaline substance termed *lithia;* discovered by M. Arfwedson, a Swede, in 1817.

LITHOFRACTEUR, or "STONE-BREAKER," an explosive material, a modification of dynamite (composed of gun-cotton, nitro-glycerine, with the constituents of gunpowder, and other substances), invented by professor Engels of Cologne, and made by Krebs, in 1869. It was occasionally used by the Germans in the war 1870-1, and was tried and well reported of for power and safety at Nant Mawy quarries, near Shrewsbury, 9, 10 May, 1871, and again on 20 Feb. 1872, before the government explosive committee, with similar results.

LITHOGRAPHY (drawing on stone). The invention is ascribed to Alois Senefelder, about 1796; and shortly afterwards the art was announced in Germany, and was known as polyautography. It became partially known in England in 1801 *et seq.*, but its general introduction is referred to Mr. Ackermann, of London, about 1817. Senefelder died in 1841. Improvements have been made by

* Floyer Sydenham, an eminent Greek scholar, of Wadham college, Oxford, and translator of some of the works of Plato, was arrested and thrown into prison for a trifling debt due for his frugal meals, and there, in 1788, died of a broken heart in want and misery, when nearly eighty years of age. The sympathy excited gave rise to this institution, since well supported. Williams was in early life a dissenting minister, and wrote on education. He was consulted by the early revolutionary party in France as to the form of a constitution for that country; he, Dr. Priestley, sir James Mackintosh, and other distinguished Englishmen, having been previously declared French citizens. He died 29 June, 1816.

Engelmann and many others; see *Printing in Colours*. Exhibition of lithographs (2000) at S. Kensington, opened, 21 Nov. 1898. "Wharf-litho," Mr. G. R. Hildyard's new process, 1899.

LITHOSCOPE. An instrument for distinguishing precious stones, invented by sir David Brewster; described by him Jan. 1864.

LITHOTOMY. The surgical operation of cutting for the stone, it is said, was performed by Ammonius, about 240 B.C. The "small apparatus," so called from the few instruments used in the operation, was practised by Celsus, about A.D. 17. The "high apparatus" was practised (on a criminal at Paris) by Colot, 1475; by Franco, on a child, about 1566; and in England, by Dr. Douglass, about 1519. The "lateral operation," invented by Franco, much performed in Paris by Frère Jacques, in 1697, has been greatly improved. The "great apparatus" was invented by John de Romanis, and described by his pupil Marianus Sanctus, 1524.

LITHOTRITY (or bruising the stone). The apparatus produced by M. Leroy d'Etiolles in 1822 has since been improved.

Prizes of 6000 and 10,000 francs were awarded M. Jean Civiale for his method of operation, 1827 & 1829.

LITHUANIA, formerly a grand-duchy, N. E. of Prussia. The natives (belonging to the Slavonic race) long maintained their independence against the Russians and Poles. In 1386, their grand-duke Jagellon became king of Poland and was baptized: Lithuania was not incorporated with Poland till 1501, when another duke Casimir, became king of that country. The countries were formally united in 1569. The larger part of Lithuania now belongs to Russia, the remainder to Prussia. Great fire at Grodno, buildings destroyed, reported, 3 Aug. 1899.

LITTLE ENGLANDISM, a term defined by sir Edward Grey as an *aimless antipathy to the British Empire*, *Times*, 18 July, 1901.

LITURGIES (from the Greek *leitos*, public, and *ergon*, work). The Greek and Roman liturgies are very ancient, having been committed to writing about the 4th and 5th centuries. The Romish church recognises four: the Roman or Gregorian, the Ambrosian, the Gallican, and the Spanish or Mosarabic. The Greek church has two principal liturgies: St. Chrysostom's and St. Basil's, and several smaller ones. Parts of these liturgies are attributed to the Apostles, to St. Ignatius, 250, to St. Ambrose (died 397), and to St. Jerome (died 420).

The present English Liturgy was first composed, and was approved and confirmed by parliament, in 1547-8. The offices for morning and evening prayer were then put into nearly the same form in which we now have them, and published 1549 and 1552.

At the solicitation of Calvin and others, the liturgy was reviewed and altered 1551

It was first read in Ireland, in the English language, in 1550, and in Scotland, where it occasioned a tumult, in 1637, and was withdrawn . 1638

The liturgy was revised by Whitehead, formerly chaplain to Anne Boleyn, and by bishops Parker, Grindall, Cox, and Pilkington, dean May, and secretary Smith.

John Knox is said to have used a liturgy for several years. The rev. Robert Lee, of Edinburgh, introduced a form of prayer in public worship, but gave it up when ordered to discontinue it in May, 1859; he soon after resumed it, and the discussion on the subject ceased only at his death, 14 March, 1868

See *Common Prayer*.

LIVERIES OF THE CITY OF LONDON. The term is derived from the custom of the retainers of the lord mayor and sheriffs wearing clothes of the form and colour displayed by those functionaries. Liveries were regulated by statute in 1392, and frequently since. The nobility gave liveries to their retainers. See *Companies*.

LIVERPOOL (W. Lancashire), is supposed to be noticed in Domesday-book under the name *Esmedune*, or *Smedune*.* Soon after the conquest, William granted that part of the country situated between the rivers Mersey and Ribble to Roger of Poitiers, who, according to Camden, built a castle here, about the year 1089. It afterwards was held by the earls of Chester and dukes of Lancaster. Liverpool is the second city of the Empire. The income of the estates of the Corporation 13*l.* in 1672, now about 12,500,000*l.* (1888), from renewal fines, &c. Changes in the leases, &c., proposed by the Corporation postponed, Jan. 1888. Garston, 1649 acres and 17,288 inhabitants, included within the city boundaries, Oct. 1901. See under *Population*.

Liverpool made a free borough by Henry III. . 1225
Made an independent port 1338
Liverpool "a paved town" (*Leland*) . . . 1559
"The people of her majesty's decayed town of Liverpool" petition Elizabeth to be relieved from a subsidy 1571
Separated from the duchy of Lancaster . . . 1628
Town rated for ship-money in only 26*l.* by Charles I. 1634
Besieged and taken by prince Rupert 26 June, 1644
Made a separate parish 1698
The old dock constructed, 1699; the first ship, the *Marlborough*, entered . . . . 8 June, 1700
Blue-coat hospital founded 1709
The town vigorously opposes the Young Pretender 1745
Town-hall commenced 1749
Infirmary established . . . . . . ,,
Seamen's hospital founded 1752
Salthouse dock opened 1753
Liverpool library founded 1757
A most destructive fire 1762
House of industry founded 1770
Theatre licensed, 1771; opened 1772
Liverpool equips, at the commencement of the war against France, 120 privateers, carrying 1986 guns, and 8754 seamen 1787
First musical festival 1785
King's dock constructed 1784
[The Queen's dock was also constructed about the same time.]
Memorable storm raged 1789
The exchange burnt 1795
The town-hall destroyed by fire . . . . ,,
The Athenæum opened . . . . 1 Jan. 1799
Union news-room erected 1800
The Lyceum erected 1802
Awful fire; loss exceeded 1,000,000*l.* . 14 Sept. ,,
Corn exchange opened . . . . 4 Aug. 1808
Royal Exchange completed 1809
Statue of George III. commenced . . 25 Oct. ,,
Fall of St. Nicholas' tower, 28 killed . 11 Feb. 1810
Royal Institution founded 1814
Wellington-rooms built 1815
Royal Institution opened by Mr. Roscoe 2 Nov. 1818
American seamen's hospital 1820
Prince's dock opened . . . . 19 July, 1821
St. John's market-place . . . . . Feb. 1822
Royal Institution incorporated . . . . ,,
Marine Humane Society formed 1823
New house of industry erected 1824
Liver theatre opened 1825

* In other ancient records its appellations are *Litherpul* and *Lyrpul*, signifying probably in the ancient dialect, the lower pool; though some have deduced its etymology from a pool frequented by an aquatic fowl, called the "Liver," or from a sea-weed of that name: and others, from its having belonged to a family of the name of Lever, whose antiquity is not sufficiently established to justify their conclusion.

Old dock closed 1826
Foundation of new custom-house laid . 12 Aug. 1828
Blackrock lighthouse built, and light first shown, 1 March, 1830
Lunatic asylum founded, 1792; new buildings erected . . . . ,,
Clarence dock completed . . . . Sept. ,,
Liverpool and Manchester railway opened* 15 Sept. ,,
Zoological gardens opened 1833
Great fire; 300,000*l.* property destroyed . 1 Jan. ,,
Lock hospital and Waterloo dock opened . . 1834
Victoria and Trafalgar docks opened . 8 Sept. 1836
British Association meet here, 1st time . Sept. 1837
Mechanics' institute opened . . . . ,,
New fish-market opened . . . . 8 Feb. ,,
Apothecaries' company formed . . . . ,,
Liverpool and Birmingham (Grand Junction) railway opened . . . . . . 4 July, ,,
Railway to London (now the North-Western) opened its entire length . . . . . 17 Sept. 1838
Statistical society and Polytechnic society founded ,,
The *Liverpool* steamer, of 461-horse power, sails for New York . . . . . . 28 Oct. ,,
Awful storm raged . . . . . . 6 Jan. 1839
Foundation of the collegiate institution laid by lord Stanley 1840
Liverpool Philharmonic society founded . . ,,
Foundation of St. George's hall and courts laid . . 1841
Immense fire; property worth more than half-a-million sterling destroyed . . . . 25 Sept 1842
Mr. Huskisson's statue erected . . . . Oct. 1847
Procession of Orangemen; fatal riot . 14 July, 1851
The queen visits Liverpool . . . 9 Oct. ,,
British Association meet here, 2nd time . Sept. 1854
St. George's hall opened . . . . 18 Sept. ,,
Bread riots (150,000 persons out of employ through the frost) . . . . . . 19 Feb. 1855
Great landing stage for large steamers opened, 1 Sept. 1857
Many commercial failures . . Sept. to Nov. ,,
Association for Social Science meets . . Oct. 1858
Sailors' home (cost 30,000*l.*) burnt . 29 April, 1860
Free library, &c., founded by Mr. (afterwards sir) W. Brown, M.P. for S. Lancashire, 15 April, 1857; free library, &c. opened . . . . . 11 Oct. ,,
Free Museum opened . . . . . . 17 Oct. 1861
Brownlow Hill church and workhouse school burnt, and 23 lives lost (20 children) . 8 Sept. 1862
Explosion of $11\frac{1}{2}$ tons of gunpowder in the *Lottie Sleigh*, in the Mersey, great damage . 16 Jan. 1864
Death of sir Wm. Brown, a great benefactor to Liverpool . . . . 3 March, ,,
Additional M.P. (now 3) by Reform act, 15 Aug. 1867
Royal bank of Liverpool stopped . . 21 Oct. ,,
Greek steamer (*Bubulina*) in the Mersey exploded; about 19 lives lost . . . . . 29 Nov. ,,
Reverdy Johnson, the United States' minister warmly received . . . . . . 22 Oct. 1868
A Greek church consecrated by the Greek archbishop of Syra . . . . 16 Jan. 1869
Panic through false alarm of fire at St. Joseph's Catholic chapel, 15 lives lost . . . 23 Jan. 1870
Stanley park, 100 acres (cost 42,000*l.*) opened 7 May, ,,
Stanley hospital; foundation laid by the earl of Derby . . . . 6 June, ,,
British Association meets here third time 14 Sept. ,,
Equestrian statue of the queen unveiled 3 Nov. ,,
Seamen's Orphan Institution founded . 11 Sept. 1871
Sefton park opened by prince Arthur 20 May, 1872
Great landing-stage burnt; loss abt. 150,000*l.* 28 July, 1874
Duke of Edinburgh lays foundation of the Art Gallery, 29 Sept.; and opens the Seamen's Orphanage . . . . 30 Sept. ,,
About 325,000*l.* bequeathed to charities by R. L. Jones, a timber merchant . . . . . Jan. 1875

* The first grand work of the kind, about 31 miles long. The first shaft was commenced in Oct. 1826, and the excavation of the tunnel, one mile and a quarter long, Jan. 1827; the tunnel was completed in Sept. 1828, and opened 30 July, 1829. At the opening of the railroad, the duke of Wellington and other illustrious persons were present; and Mr. Huskisson who alighted during a stoppage of the engines, was knocked down by one of them, which went over his thigh and caused his death, 15 Sept. 1830.

Visit of M. Michel Chevalier, free-trader 21 April, 1875
Statue of Wm. Rathbone, eminent merchant, unveiled . . . . 1 Jan. 1877
Rotunda theatre burnt . . . . . 9 July, ,,
Walker Art Gallery (gift of the mayor, Andrew Walker), cost above 30,000*l.*, opened by the earl of Derby . . . . 6 Sept. ,,
Bishoprics Act, permitting the erection of a see at Liverpool, passed . . . . 16 Aug. 1878
Panic through false alarm of fire at Colosseum theatre; 37 persons crushed to death 11 Oct. ,,
Strike of dock labourers and sailors; riots suppressed, 7 Feb.; strike ends . about 25 Feb. 1879
Mysterious disappearance of Miss Edwards, 3 Sept.; found in London . . . . . 21 Oct. ,,
Bishopric established . . . . . 24 March, 1880
Liverpool nominated a city . . . April, ,,
Foundation of University college; about 88,000*l.* subscribed . . . . Oct. ,,
New water works in the valley of the river Vyrnwy, 25 miles from Oswestry, begun, 14 July, 1881; inaugurated by the duke of Connaught starting a fountain at Liverpool . . . . . 14 July, 1892
[Lake 4 miles long formed, $\frac{1}{2}$ mile to 200 yds. wide, Llanwddyn village covered, 68 miles of aqueducts, tunnels, pipes, &c. The undertaking was projected in 1879 by Mr. G. F. Deacon, aided by Mr. C. Hawksley and Mr. J. Bateman, and carried out by Mr. Deacon as chief engineer.]
Discovery of infernal machines in steamers *Malta* and *Bavarian* announced . . . 24 July, 1880
Plot to blow up the town-hall discovered; bag of explosives found at door; 2 Fenians apprehended 10 June; convicted, sentenced to penal servitude, James McGrath for life; James McKnivett, 15 years . . . . 2 Aug. 1881
Dock space in 1810, 26 acres for ships, 704,000 tons; in 1857, 209 acres, tonnage, 4,320,000.
New Langton dock opened by the prince and princess of Wales, and named Alexandra. . 8 Oct. ,,
University College inaugurated by the earl of Derby, 14 Jan. 1882
New court-house founded . . . 1 June, ,,
Home for ancient mariners opened by the duke of Edinburgh . . . . 16 Dec. ,,
Lancelot's hay warehouse burnt (damage about 100,000*l.*) . . . . . . 21 April, 1883
Mersey tunnel, opened (see under *Tunnels*) 13 Feb. 1885
Liverpool returns nine M.P.'s by act passed 25 June, ,,
International Exhibition of Navigation, Commerce, &c.; proposed by alderman David Radcliffe; adopted by the earl of Derby; 60,000*l.* subscribed; site granted by the corporation 1885; opened by the queen; alderman Radcliffe, the mayor, knighted 11 May; the queen leaves 13 May; 2,468,098 visitors; reported receipts 131,032*l.*; expenditure 150,167*l.*; closed . . 8 Nov. 1886
Riots; socialist, orangemen, &c. . . 19 Sept. ,,
Messrs. Lewis's premises with a clock-tower burnt; estimated loss 250,000*l.* . . . . 24 Dec. ,,
Royal Jubilee Exhibition opened by the princess Louise . . . . 16 May, 1887
First meeting of the National Association for the Advancement of Art . . . . 3–7 Dec. 1888
Strike of sailors and firemen end of May; ended 12 July, 1889
Frequent dock strikes, met by a supply of men, Feb., March, 1890
About 20,000 men on strike, reported 7 March; soldiers from Preston arrive, 18 March; dispute settled . . . . 31 March, ,,
The duke of Clarence and Avondale opens the new Royal Infirmary . . . . . 29 Oct. ,,
Mr. George Holt presents 10,000*l.* to endow a chair of physiology in University College . 3 June, 1891
Naval exhibition opened by lord George Hamilton, 1 Feb. 1892
Great cotton fire at Bramley Moor Dock; estimated loss, about 100,000*l.* . . . . . 15 Feb. ,,
Mr. John Hartnup killed by falling from the top of the Liverpool observatory, Birkenhead, of which he was director . . . . . 21 April, ,,
Mr. W. B. Levy and Mr. G. J. Cohen, resident legatees of Mr. David Lewis, merchant, in accordance with his wishes, present about 350,000*l.* to the working classes of Liverpool and Manchester; announced . . . . June, ,,

St. Peter's hall burnt . . . . . 27 Nov. 1892
Mr. W. E. Gladstone receives the freedom of the city . . . . . 3 Dec. ,,
New Victoria buildings of the university college, to which the queen had given 4,000*l.*, opened by earl Spencer . . . . . 13 Dec. ,,
Great fire in Juniper-street, 2 firemen killed; estimated loss, 150,000*l.* . . . 5, 6 Jan. 1893
The overhead electrical railway at the docks, about 7 miles long, begun in 1889, inaugurated by the marquis of Salisbury . . . 4 Feb. ,,
Death of the earl of Derby; he bequeaths 2,000*l.* for the purchase of pictures, his cabinet of antiquities, to the city, and 2,000*l.* to found a scholarship or prize . . . . . 21 April, ,,
The title of "lord" granted to the mayor 15 June, ,,
Fire at Hornby dock; damage about 30,000*l.*, 24 July; fire at Canada dock, estimated damage 100,000*l.* . . . . . 5 Aug. ,,
Death of Mr. Charles Edward Horsfall, who bequeaths 14,700*l.* to charities . . . 21 Aug. ,,
Mr. George Holt presents 10,000*l.* to endow a chair of pathology at the University college and 5,000*l.* for the laboratory and staff . . . April, 1894
Visit of the duke and duchess of York; foundation stone of new post office laid and wedding gift received . . . . . 10 Sept. ,,
Death of Mr. George Holt . . . 3 April, 1896
British association meets here fourth time, 16–23 Sept. ,,
The foundation of the "David Lewis" northern hospital laid by the countess of Derby (lady mayoress) . . . . . 19 Oct. ,,
The earl of Derby elected lord mayor, Nov. 1895; returns his allowance of 2000*l.* . . 22 Oct. ,,
Rt. hon. sir Arthur B. Forwood, M.P., active mayor in 1877, bart. 1895, died . . 28 Sept. 1898
New laboratories, the gift of the rev. S. A. Thompson-Yates to the university college, opened by Lord Lister (15,000*l.* subscribed to them by Mrs. G. Holt and daughter, reported 14 Oct. 1899) 8 Oct. ,,
The earl of Derby and Mr. Sutton Timms subscribe 1,000*l.* each to the Liverpool church house, Jan. 1899; foundation stone laid by the countess of Derby . . . . . 1 Aug. 1899
School of tropical diseases (University college and Roy. Southern hospital), suggested 12 Nov. 1898; Mr. A. L. Jones subscribes annually 350*l.*; a ward opened at the Roy. Southern hospital by lord Lister, 22 April; see *Sierra Leone*.
The duke of York opens the new general post-office and visits the *Conway* training ship . 19 July, ,,
Mr. T. H. Ismay, shipowner and great organiser (White star co.), donor of 20,000*l.* towards a pension fund for Liverpool sailors (1887), dies, aged 61, 23 Nov. ,,
Sir Henry Tate, a liberal benefactor to the city (see *National Gallery*), dies, aged 80 (gave 42,000*l.* to University college) . . . 5 Dec. ,,
Church house (total cost 65,000*l.*), first section opened by abp. of York . . . 18 May, 1901
The duke of Devonshire opens a new central technical school . . . . . 26 Oct. ,,
Fire at the exchange, estimated damage 10,000*l.* 6 Dec. ,,
Fire at Dingle station (see *Railways*), six deaths, 23 Dec. ,,
Lord Derby's motion in favour of a university for the city, adopted; 80,000*l.* promised at a meeting held . . . . . 27 Jan. 1902
Lord Rosebery exhorts the liberals to wipe their slate clean and make a fresh start . . 14 Feb. ,,
Liverpool bank frauds; see *Trials* . . 17, 22 Feb. ,,
Mr. Wm. Rathbone, philanthropist, 12 yrs. M.P. for Liverpool, dies, aged 83 . . . 6 March, ,,
Mr. Wm. Johnston gives 25,000*l.* for medical research in the new university, announced, 7 March, ,,
Princess Louise, duchess of Argyll, opens a navy league exhibition, a church pupil teachers' college, and the David Lewis northern hospital, 12, 13 March, ,,
New botanical laboratories presented by Mr. W. P. Hartley, opened by sir Wm. Thiselton Dyer, 10 May, 1902
Sir W. Laurier, Canadian premier, opens the new produce exchange . . . . . 7 Oct. ,,
Lords Roberts and Kitchener presented with the freedom . . . . . 11 Oct. ,,
Mr. A. Carnegie opens a new library (cost 12,000*l.*), 15 Oct. ,,
Mr. Chamberlain speaks at the Hippodrome on Preferential tariffs . . . . . 27 Oct. 1903

LIVERPOOL ADMINISTRATION. Shortly after the assassination of Mr. Perceval (11 May, 1812), the earl of Liverpool became first minister.* His administration terminated when he was attacked by apoplexy, 17 Feb. 1827, and Mr. Canning succeeded as prime minister, 10 April.

Earl of Liverpool, *first lord of the treasury.*
Earl of Eldon, *lord chancellor.*
Earl of Harrowby, *lord president of the council.*
Earl of Westmorland, *lord privy seal.*
N. Vansittart, *chancellor of the exchequer* (succeeded by F. J. Robinson, 1823).
Viscount Sidmouth, *home secretary* (succeeded by Robert Peel, 1822).
Viscount Castlereagh, aft. marquis of Londonderry, *foreign secretary* (succeeded by George Canning, 1822).
Earl Bathurst, *colonial secretary.*
Viscount Melville, *first lord of admiralty.*
Earl of Buckinghamshire, *board of control* (succeeded by G. Canning, 1816; C. Bathurst, 1820; C. Wynne, 1822).
Charles Bathurst (1813), *chancellor of duchy of Lancaster* (succeeded by N. Vansittart, lord Bexley, 1823).
Wellesley Pole, afterwards lord Maryborough, 1815, *master of the mint.*
F. J. Robinson, 1818; W. Huskisson, 1823, *board of trade.*
Earl of Mulgrave, *ordnance* (succeeded by duke of Wellington, 1819).

LIVERPOOL BISHOPRIC established by order of the privy council, 24 March, 1880; St. Peter's church to be the cathedral; first bishop, John Charles Ryle, D.D. (died 10 June, 1900); Fras. Jas. Chavasse, consecrated 25 April, 1900.

LIVINGSTONE, see under *Africa*, 1856 *et seq.* LIVINGSTONE COLLEGE, Leyton, incorporated 1900, to train missionaries in the elements of medicine and surgery; also a medical mission dispensary, a travellers' health bureau, and *Climate*, an illustrated quarterly journal of health and travel, published by the bureau. Knott's-green house, Leyton, acquired by the college to form a memorial to Dr. Livingstone, total fund, 4,500*l.*, reported at a meeting in Whitehall, 4 Dec. 1900. King Lewanika of Barotseland received here, 11 July, 1902. Livingstone exhibition opened at Westminster, 18 June, 1901.

LIVONIA, a Russian province on the Baltic sea, first visited by some Bremen merchants about 1158. It has belonged successively to Denmark, Sweden, Poland, and Russia. It was finally ceded to Peter the Great in 1721. Population in 1886, 1,239,728; 1897, 1,300,640.

LIVRET D'OUVRIER, a species of workman's passport, introduced into France by Turgot about 1781; abolished 23 March, 1869.

LLANDAFF (S. Wales). The first known bishop was St. Dubritius, said to have died in 612.

* Robert Jenkinson, born 7 Jan. 1770, entered the house of commons under Mr. Pitt; opposed the abolition of the slave trade in 1792; became lord Hawkesbury in 1796; became foreign minister under Mr. Addington in 1801; succeeded his father as earl of Liverpool in 1808: died 4 Dec. 1828.

The see is valued in the king's books at 154*l.* 14*s.* 1*d.* per annum. Present income 4,200*l.*

RECENT BISHOPS.

782. Richard Watson; died 4 July, 1816.
1816. Herbert Marsh; trans. to Peterborough, 1819.
1819. Wm. Van Mildert; translated to Durham, 1826.
1826. Charles Richard Sumner; translated to Winchester, 1827.
1827. Edward Copleston; died 14 Oct. 1849.
1849. Alfred Ollivant, died 16 Dec. 1882.
1883. Richard Lewis, consecrated 25 April, 1883.

LLERENA, see *Villa Franca.*

"LLEWELLYN GIFT," over 20,000*l.*, bequeathed by Mr. Evan Llewellyn as a fund in trust to the magistrates of the metropolitan police courts for the poor, announced, 25 Jan. 1899.

LLOYD'S (London), at the Royal Exchange about 1692. A coffee-house, kept by Edwd. Lloyd, Abchurch-lane, became a place of meeting of merchants. After several removals it was established finally at the Royal Exchange in 1774, and remained there till the fire in 1838, when it was removed till the present building was completed in 1844. Here resort eminent merchants and shipowners, and here are effected insurances on ships and merchandise. A Register of ships began about 1764; and the terms A1, &c. were used about 1775. Two societies (underwriters and merchants) were united, and one register issued, Oct. 1834. Jubilee celebrated, 31 Oct. 1884. Lloyd's is supported by subscribers who now pay annually 5*l.* 5*s.*, formerly 4*l.* 4*s.* The books kept here contain an account of the arrival and sailing of vessels, and are remarkable for their early intelligence of maritime affairs. Many new signalling stations established, 1882-3. First annual issue of the "Universal Shipping Register," published here, May, 1886. In 1803, the subscribers instituted the *Patriotic Fund* (*which see*). The *Austrian Lloyd's*, an association for general, commercial, and industrial purposes, was founded at Trieste, by Baron Bruck, in 1833. It has established regular communication between Trieste and the Levant, by means of a fleet of steamers carrying the mails, and publishes a journal. Colonial premiers entertained at the new premises, Fenchurch-st., 14 July, 1902.

LOADSTONE, see *Magnetism.*

LOAN EXHIBITIONS, see *Exhibitions, National Portraits, Scientific Apparatus, &c.*

LOANO, Piedmont (N. Italy). Here the Austrians and Sardinians were defeated by the French, under Massena, 23, 24 Nov. 1795.

LOANS for the public service were raised by Wolsey in 1522 and 1525. In 1559 Elizabeth borrowed 200,000*l.* of the city of Antwerp, to enable her to reform her own coin, and sir Thomas Gresham and the city of London joined in the security. *Rapin.* The amount of some of the English and other loans, during memorable periods, viz.:—

Seven years' war	1755 to 1763	£52,100,000
American war	1776 to 1784	75,500,000
French revolutionary war	1793 to 1802	168,500,000
War against Bonaparte	1803 to 1814	206,300,000
2 loans, 1813	£21,000,000 and	22,000,000
War against Russia	1855 to 1856	16,000,000
For deficiency in revenue	1856	10,000,000
[Both taken by the Rothschilds alone.]		
By East India Company	1858	8,000,000

A subscription loan (18,000,000*l.*) to carry on the war, against France, filled up in London in 15 hours and 20 minutes (see *Loyalty Loans*), 5 Dec. 1796.

War loan, 29,550,000*l.*, April, 1900.

French loan on 9 July, 1855, on account of the war with Russia. The French legislature passed a bill for raising by loan 750 million francs (30,000,000*l.* sterling). On the 30th the total subscribed in France amounted to 3,652,591,985 francs (about 146,103,679*l.*), nearly five times the amount required; 2,533,888,450 francs were from Paris; from the departments, 1,118,703,535 francs. The number of subscribers was 316.864. No less than 231,920,155 francs were made up by subscription of 50 francs and under. About 600 millions came from foreign countries. The English subscription of 150,000,000 francs was returned, as double the amount required had been proffered.

The French government raised a loan of 20,000,000*l.* for the Italian war from its own people without difficulty, May, 1859.

A *Turkish* loan, in 1854, at 7½ per cent., recommended by lord Palmerston; a loan of 5,000,000*l.*, at 4 per cent., on the security of England and France, was taken up by Rothschild in Aug. 1855, and was well received: the stock rose to a small premium.

French loan for 17,600,000*l.* announced 29 Jan. 1868.

French loan 2,000,000,000 francs for 80,000,000*l.*: nearly twice the amount subscribed in France alone, 28 June, 1871; another loan (of 120,000,000*l.* at 6¼ per cent.), for speedy payment of the indemnity and evacuation of the provinces held by the Germans; announced 26 July, 1872; above twice the amount subscribed. See *France.*

Foreign Loans Committee: appointed to inquire concerning certain loans to Honduras, Costa Rica, and Paraguay, in their report comment on the exaggerated statements respecting the revenues and resources of the states in the prospectuses, the efforts of the contractors to make fictitious markets; the proceedings on the stock exchange to maintain their prestige; the secrecy adopted in the proceedings; "the best security against the recurrence of such evils will be found, not so much in legislative enactments as in the enlightenment of the public as to their real nature and origin, thus rendering it more difficult for unscrupulous persons to carry out schemes .... which have ended in so much discredit and disaster," July, 1875.

Loan bill (S. African war), 60,000,000*l.* passed, 9 Aug. 1901.

LOAN SOCIETIES. The laws relating to them were amended by the act 3 & 4 Vict. c. 110; passed Aug. 1840.

LOBSTERS and CRABS. The size at which they are to be sold is regulated by the Fisheries act, 1877.

LOCAL GOVERNMENT ACT, passed in 1858, was amended in 1861. Scotch local government bill introduced by the lord advocate, J. P. B. Robertson, 8 April, passed 26 Aug. 1889.

Mr. Ritchie's Local Government Bill (England & Wales) read first time 19 March; second time *nem. con.* 20 April; royal assent 13 Aug. 1888; 51 & 52 Vict. c. 41.

I. Establishes County Councils in every administrative county as defined by the act. Council to consist of councillors and aldermen, with a chairman; electors to be parliamentary voters, and male and female ratepayers.

II. 61 boroughs constituted county boroughs; the metropolis constituted the county of London, superseding the Metropolitan Board of Works.

III. Boundaries.

IV. Finance.

V. Supplemental.

VI. Transitory provisions; first election (for three years) in Jan., and duties entered on 1 April, 1889.

Local Government (Boundaries) Act. See under *Boundary Acts,* 1887.

Local Government (Electors) Act passed 16 May, 1888. (Elections) bill passed, 6 March, 1896.

Irish Local Government Bill introduced by Mr. A. J. Balfour (due provision made for the rights of minorities); read first time 18 Feb.; second reading (339–247) 24 May; withdrawn, 13 June, 1892; Mr. Gerald Balfour's bill passed, 12 Aug. 1898; bill (No. 2) royal assent, 18 Dec. 1902. See *Ireland*.

Bill for the establishment of parish councils (*which see*) read first time, 21 March, 1893; passed, 5 March, 1894.

Scotch Local Government Act passed, 25 Aug. 1894; amended March, 1895. See *Scotland*.

Parish councils (*which see*), guardians and district councils established, 1894. See *London Govmt. Act*, 13 July, 1899.

LOCAL GOVERNMENT BOARD (a new department of the government, comprising the supervision of the public health, and local government together with the powers and duties of the Poor Law board, including education, police, highways, &c.), was established in pursuance of an act passed 14 Aug. 1871. First president, Mr. James Stansfeld, appointed president of the poor law board, March, 1871. Mr. (aft. sir John) Lambert, C.B., first secretary, appointed Sept. 1871. Reports issued annually. See *Gladstone* and other *Administrations*, and *Children*, Jan. 1897.

LOCAL LOANS ACT, passed 13 Aug. 1875. By the National Debt and Local Loans Act passed 12 July, 1887, the local loans stock was created.

In May, 1891, the local indebtedness was stated to be about 195,400,000*l*., which is still increasing, being the result of expenditure by local authorities on important public works, frequently reproductive, and also sanitary improvements. The debtors include nearly all the great towns in the kingdom. See *National Debt*, 1895.

"LOCAL OPTION," see *Permissive Bill* and *Liquor Traffic*.

LOCAL PARLIAMENTS. The first of these mimic parliaments was opened in Liverpool, about 1864; a conference of about 150 delegates from 146 of these assemblies, with 20,000 members, in Great Britain, met at the Crystal Palace, 20-23 May, 1883.

LOCAL RATES in England, come from 26 sources.

Local self-government is a chaos of authorities, of rates, and areas. *G. J. Goschen.*

See *Probate Duty*, 1888.

The London Ratepayers' Defence League formed (the duke of Westminster president) 18 Nov. 1891.

Rating Act, 37 & 38 Vict. c. 54, passed, 7 Aug. 1874; abolishes exemption from the Poor Law Act, 43rd of Elizabeth, and provides for the rating of woods, mines, rights of fowling, fishing, &c. A bill for the rating of machinery was read a second time in 1890, 1892, 1893 and 1895.

Report on local taxation by Mr. Henry H. Fowler (president of the Local Government board), April, 1893.

[Expenditure, 1868, 24,740,000*l*.; 1891, 50,662,000, principally raised by rates. England and Wales, 1894, 32,223,972*l*.; Scotland, 3,355,022*l*.; Ireland, 2,867,770*l*.

He introduces a bill for the equalization of rates (London); read first time, 1 May; withdrawn, Sept. 1893; act passed, 25 Aug. 1894.

Royal commission on local taxation appointed; lord Balfour of Burleigh, lord Emlyn, Mr. J. B. Balfour, and others, met, 6 May, 1897; reports issued, 1 Feb. 1901; blue-book published, *Times*, 1 Sept. 1902.

LOCHLEVEN CASTLE (Kinross), built on an isle in Loch Leven, it is said by the Picts, was the royal residence of Alexander III. and his queen when taken from it to Stirling. It was besieged by the English in 1301, and in 1334. Patrick Graham, first archbishop of St. Andrews, imprisoned for attempting to reform the church, died here about 1478. The earl of Northumberland was confined in it, 1569. It was the place of queen Mary's imprisonment in 1567, and of her escape on Sunday, 2 May, 1568.

LOCKE'S ACT, 23 & 24 Vict. c. 127 (1860), relates to legal proceedings.

LOCKE KING'S ACTS; 17 & 18 Vict. c. 113 (1854), and 30 & 31 Vict. c. 69 (1867), relate to mortgages.

LOCK HOSPITAL, established 1747; the asylum, 1787.

LOCK-OUTS, see *Strikes*.

LOCKS, early used by the Egyptians, Greeks, Romans, and the Chinese. Denon has engraved an Egyptian lock of wood. Du Cange mentions locks and padlocks as early as 1381.

Barron's locks (on the many-tumbler principle) were patented in 1778; Bramah's, in 1788; and Chubb's "detector" locks in 1818.

Mr. E. Beckett Denison (now lord Grimthorpe) invented a lock asserted to be secure against picking in 1852.

New locks have been produced by Messrs. Day and Newell, Yale, Andrews, and others, especially in America.

Mr. Hobbs, an American, exhibited his own locks in the Crystal palace, in 1851, and showed great skill in picking others.

A "Key Bureau" to aid in the recovery of lost keys (charge 1*s*. per annum) established in London in 1885.

Chubb's "panic door lock" for easy opening of doors in theatres announced Oct. 1887.

Mr. F. J. Biggs's tubular lock, said to be cheaper and better than mortice locks, manufactured by a syndicate in London, May, 1890.

A beautiful key composed of gold and other metals brought from various colonies was made by Messrs. Chubb and used by the queen in opening the Imperial Institute, 10 May, 1893.

LOCOMOTIVES, see *Railways*. The use of steam locomotives on ordinary roads is regulated by acts passed in 1861, 1865, 1878 and 1898. See *Carriages*, 1896.

LOCRIANS, an ancient people of Northern Greece. They resisted Philip of Macedon, were aided by the Athenians and Thebans, and defeated by him at Chæronea, 6 or 7 Aug. 338 B.C.

LOCUSTS, one of the plagues of Egypt, 1491 B.C. (*Exod*. x.) The ravages of locusts in Cyprus have been greatly checked by the skill and energy of Mr. Richard Mattei and Mr. Samuel Brown, 1881 *et seq*. A swarm of locusts settled upon the ground about London, and consumed the vegetables; great numbers fell in the streets; they resembled grasshoppers, but were three times the size, and their colours more variegated, 4 Aug. 1748. They infested Germany in 1749, Poland in 1750, S. Africa 1797, 1877, and Warsaw in June, 1816. They are said to have been seen in London in 1857. Russia was infested by them in July, 1860; Algeria, severely, in 1866, 1874, 1889, and 1891-2; Sardinia in 1868; and Minnesota, U.S., 1873-74; S. Russia, June, 1884; Cyprus, 1884 *et seq*.; N. India, June, July, 1891; Morocco, Dec. 1891, June, 1892; Gibraltar, Algeria and Morocco, 26 April, 1893; Tokar, Soudan, Nov. 1896; Orange River colony, Dec. 1902. Poisoning with arsenic said to be successful in Natal, announced Sept. 1897.

LODGERS paying 10*l*. a year for a whole year for apartments without furniture, acquired the suffrage, by Reform act passed 15 Aug. 1867. Act to protect their goods from distraint, passed 16 Aug.

1871. The lodger franchise much increased by the Parliamentary and Municipal Registration act of 1878; and by the new Reform Bill, 6 Dec. 1884.

The assembled judges decide that with a non-resident landlord the lodger is a householder; with a resident landlord he must qualify as a compound householder.

LODGING-HOUSES. An act placing common lodging-houses under the watch of the police was passed in 1851. In that year a model lodging-house erected by prince Albert appeared at the Great Exhibition. Since then, blocks of lodging-houses for the poor have been erected by Baroness Burdett-Coutts and others. Mr. Peabody's donation of 12 March, 1862, has been appropriated for a similar purpose; see *Peabody* and *Rowton*. On 19 Nov. 1863, the city of London voted 20,000*l.* and a piece of land in Victoria-street (now Farringdon-road) for the purpose. See *London*, 1845.

LODI (N. Italy). Napoleon Bonaparte, commanding the French army, totally defeated the Austrians, under Beaulieu, after a bloody engagement, at the bridge of Lodi, 10 May, 1796. The republican flag floated in Milan a few days after. Monument to Victor Emmanuel inaugurated, 16 Sept. 1883.

LOGARITHMS, the indexes of the ratio of numbers one to another, were invented by John Napier, baron of Merchiston, who published his canon, or table, in 1614. The invention was completed by Mr. Henry Briggs, at Oxford, who published tables, 1616-18. The method of computing by means of marked pieces of ivory was discovered about the same time, and hence called *Napier's bones*.

"The Construction of Logarithms," 1619, by John Napier, baron of Merchiston, translated, with notes and a catalogue of Napier's works, by Wm. Rae Macdonald, published in 1889.

"LOGIA" (sayings or oracles) of our Lord, deciphered from a leaf of papyrus found at Oxyrynchus (Behnesa) by Messrs. Grenfell and Hunt, winter of 1896–97; fresh discoveries 1902-3.

LOGIC, "the science of reasoning." Eminent works on it are by Aristotle; Bacon, Novum Organon; Locke on the Understanding; and the modern treatises on Logic, by archbishop Whately, sir William Hamilton, and Mr. John Stuart Mill.

Earl Stanhope's Demonstrator, or Logical Machine, invented in the latter part of the 18th century, was described by rev. Robert Harley to the British Association, 19 Aug. 1878.
In his "Principles of Science," 1874, Mr. Wm. Stanley Jevons describes his "Logical Abecedarium" and "Logical Slate."
G. Boole on "Laws of Thought," 1854.
J. Venn's "Symbolic Logic," July, 1881.

LOGIERIAN SYSTEM of musical education, commenced by J. B. Logier, in Jan. 1815, and introduced into the chief towns of the United Kingdom, Prussia, &c. He died in 1846.

LOG-LINE, used in navigation, about 1570; first mentioned by Bourne in 1577. It is divided into spaces of 50 feet, and the way which the ship makes is measured by a half-minute sand-glass, which bears nearly the same proportion to an hour that 50 feet bear to a mile: the line used in the royal navy is 48 feet.

LOGOGRAPH, apparatus invented by Mr. W. H. Barlow, about 1874, to give graphic representation of the vibratory motions of the air-waves of speech, somewhat resembling a telegraphic message.

LOGOGRAPHIC PRINTING, in which the commoner words were cast in one mass, was patented by Henry Johnson and Mr. John Walter of the *Times* in 1783. Anderson's "History of Commerce," vol. iv., was printed by these types in 1789.

LOGRONO, see *Najara*.

LOI DES SUSPECTS, enacted by the French convention, 17 Sept. 1793, during the reign of terror, filled the prisons of Paris. The Public Safety bill, of a similar character, was passed, 18 Feb. 1858, shortly after Orsini's attempt on the life of the emperor, Napoleon III.

LOLLARDS (by some derived from the German *lollen*, to sing in a low tone, by others derived from the English verb to loll or lounge), the name given to the first reformers of the Roman catholic religion in England, the followers of Wykliffe. The sect is also said to have been founded in 1315 by Walter Lollard, who was burnt for heresy at Cologne in 1322. The Lollards are said to have devoted themselves to acts of mercy. The first Lollard martyr in England was William Sawtree, parish priest of St. Osith, London, 12 Feb. 1401, when the Lollards were proscribed by parliament, and numbers of them were burnt alive. Sir John Cobham, lord Oldcastle, a follower of Wykliffe, was accused of treason and condemned, Sept. 1413. He escaped to Wales, where he was captured, and brought to London and burnt, 25 Dec. 1418. Lollards' tower, part of the bishop's prison, was near St. Paul's, not Lambeth palace. *Dr. Maitland.*

LOMBARDISTS, disciples of Peter Lombard, the schoolman, bishop of Paris, author of the "Book of Sentences," who died in 1164.

LOMBARD MERCHANTS, in England, were understood to be composed of natives of some one of the four republics of Genoa, Lucca, Florence, or Venice. *Anderson.* Lombard usurers were sent to England by pope Gregory IX. to lend money to convents, communities, and private persons who were not able to pay down the tenths which were collected throughout the kingdom with great rigour that year, 13 Hen. III. 1299. They had offices in the street named after them to this day. Their usurious transactions caused their expulsion from the kingdom in the reign of Elizabeth.

LOMBARDY (N. Italy) derived its name from the Longobardi, a German tribe from Brandenburg, said (doubtfully) to have been invited into Italy by Justinian to serve against the Goths. Their chief, Alboin, established a kingdom which lasted from 568 to 774. The last king, Desiderius, was dethroned by Charlemagne. (For a list of the Lombard kings, see *Italy*.) About the end of the 9th century the chief towns of Lombardy fortified themselves, and became republics. The first *Lombard league*, consisting of Milan, Venice, Pavia, Modena, &c., was formed to restrain the power of the German emperors, in 1167. On 29 May, 1176, they defeated the emperor Frederick Barbarossa at Legnano, and eventually compelled him to sign the peace of Constance in 1183. In 1226 another *league* was formed against Frederick II., which was also successful. After this, petty tyrants rose in most of the cities, and foreign influence quickly followed. The Guelf and Ghibelline factions greatly distracted Lombardy; and from the 15th century to the present time, it has been contended for by the German and French sovereigns. The house of Austria obtained it in 1748, and held it till 1797, when it was conquered by the French, who incorporated it with the Cisalpine republic, and in 1805 with the kingdom of Italy. On the breaking up of the French empire in 1815, the LOMBARDO-VENETIAN KINGDOM was established by the allied sovereigns and given to Austria, who had lost her Flemish possessions. Lombardy and Venice revolted, and joined the king of Sardinia in March, 1848; but they did not support him well, and were again subjected to Austria after his defeat at Novara, 23 March, 1849. An amnesty for political offences was granted in 1856. Great jealousy of Sardinia was felt by Austria after 1849. In 1857 diplomatic relations were suspended; and in April, 1859, war broke out; the Austrians crossing the Ticino and entering Piedmont. The French emperor declared war against Austria, and immediately sent troops into Italy. The Austrians were defeated at Montebello, 20 May; Palestro, 30, 31 May; Magenta, 4 June; and Solferino, 24 June. By the peace of Villafranca (11 July), the largest part of Lombardy was ceded to Louis Napoleon, who transferred it to the king of Sardinia. It now forms part of the new kingdom of Italy, to which Venetia was also surrendered by the treaty of Vienna, 3 Oct. 1867. Population, 1890, 3,906,958; 1901, 4,278,188.

LOMBOK, an island in the Indian Archipelago, subject to the Dutch since 1863. See *Holland*, 1894 *et seq.*

LONATO (Brescia, N. Italy). Here Napoleon Bonaparte defeated Wurmser and the Austrians, 3 Aug. 1796.

LONDON, the capital of the British empire. The earliest history is traditional. The Celtic name is said to have been Lyn-din, lake-fort; Tacitus in the first century, calls it Londinium, and describes it as a flourishing trading city; it was afterwards called Augusta, an appellation frequently given to great cities; several other forms of the name appear in documents, such as Lundenbyrig, Lundonia, and London-wic. In 1860, London and the suburbs were estimated to cover 121 square miles (11 miles each way, being three times as large as in 1800; in 1880, 122 square miles. London was constituted an "administrative" county by the local government act, 1888, including as rateable value seven-eighths of Middlesex, about two-thirds of Surrey, and nearly one-third of Kent. The population of the "city" in 1801, 156,859; in 1811, 120,909; in 1821, 125,434; in 1831, 125,574; in 1841, 125,008; in 1851, 122,440; in 1861, 112,063; in 1871, 74,897; in 1881, 50,652. Day census, 25-30 April, 261,061; 1891, 5 April, 37,694 (day census, 27 April, 301,384). For London and suburbs, 1801 *et seq.* see table in article *Population* (5 April, 1891, 4,231,431). *Inner London*, 4,392,346; *Outer Ring*, 1,656,209; total, 6,048,555, June, 1895. Census of 29 boroughs in the county of London, 4,536,541 (total, with *Outer Ring*, 6,578,784), 31 March, 1901. Revenue of corporation, 1862, 437,341*l.*; 1875, 655,391*l.*: expenditure, 592,244*l.*; in 1877, revenue 634,734*l.*: expenditure, 667,812*l.*; in 1892, revenue, 788,398*l.*: expenditure, 770,118*l.*; in 1893, revenue, 729,709*l.*: expenditure, 717,029*l.* The city is said to have expended 11,223,277*l.* in the last 50 years for the benefit of the metropolis (1895). Annual rateable value (metropolitan district), April, 1881, 27,405,488*l.*; the "city," 3,537,561*l.* Jan. 1888, 34,346,596*l.*; gross value, 43,961,653*l.*; rateable value, 36,437,810*l.*, 31 March, 1898. Municipal debt of London (county), 37,941,704*l.*, March, published Nov. 1896; total debt, 38,681,661*l.* for year ending March, 1897, announced 21 Dec. 1897. The "port" of London extends from London Bridge to the North Foreland. Tonnage entering and leaving the port, 1871, 7,600,000; 1885, 12,000,000 (dues paid over 41,000*l.*). The "city" returns 2 instead of 4 members to parliament by Act of 1885. "*London Statistics*," published by London County Council, 1893–94. See *Docks*, *Mayors*, *Metropolitan Board of Works*, *London County Council*, and *Treaties*.

The town appears to have prospered under British, Roman, and Saxon rules, and to have been much indebted to Alfred and his successors, but suffered greatly by the Danes; it was not attacked by William I., by whom the citizens were conciliated, and its corporate government was recognized by his son Henry I. The city received many favours from the Plantagenet kings, but frequently resisted their exactions. London is governed by the lord mayor, the court of aldermen, the common council, and other offices. London was not included in the municipal corporations Act, 1835. The London county council was constituted by the local government Act passed in 1888.

LONDON (metropolitan district), contains 6612 miles of streets; 528,794 inhabited houses; population, 4,025,659 . . . . June, 1873
Income of the city estates, 538,651*l.* . . . ,,
Aulus Plautius invades Britain and erects a fort on the Thames . . . 41 or 43
Boadicea, queen of the Iceni, defeats the Romans and burns London; she is defeated by Suetonius and dies by suicide . . . 61
London held by the rebel emperors, Carausius and Allectus . . . 286
Conjectured date of the building of the wall . 350–369
800 vessels said to be employed in the port of London for the export of corn . . . 359
St. Paul's church founded by Ethelbert, about . 597
London termed the ecclesiastical capital of the East Saxons . . . 604
Mellitus, first bishop (soon expelled) . . . 604
A plague ravages London . . . 644
Great fire which nearly consumed the city . . 798
London pillaged by the Danes, 839; these expelled; Alfred repairs and strengthens London . . . 884
Easterlings settle in London before . . . 978
Another great fire . . . 982
Tower built by William I. . . . 1078
First charter granted to the city by the same king* 1079
Another great fire, St. Paul's burnt . . . 1086
606 houses thrown down by a tempest . . . 1090
Important Charter granted by Henry I. . . . 1101
St. Bartholomew's priory founded by Rahere, about ,,
London-bridge built, 1014; burnt with part of the city . . . 1136
Charter granted by Henry II . . . 1154
Old London-bridge begun . . . 1176
Henry Fitz-Ailwin, the first mayor (served twenty-four years) see *below*, 1889 . . . 1189 or 1191
Massacre of Jews . . . ,,
First stone bridge finished . . . 1209
Charter of king John: mayor and common council to be elected annually . . . 1214
Foreign merchants invited, settle here . . 1199-1220
Charter of Henry III. . . . 1233
Watch in London, 38 Henry III. . . . 1253
Privileges granted to the Hanse merchants (*which see*) . . . 1259
The liberties and privileges of the city maintained and enlarged by Walter Harvey, mayor . . . 1272
Tax called murage, to keep the walls and ditches in repair . . . about 1282
Henry le Waleys and 5 others first M.P.'s for London 1284

* It is still preserved in the city archives. This charter is written in beautiful Saxon characters, on a slip of parchment six inches long, and one broad, and is in English as follows:—"William the king greeteth William the bishop, and Gosfrith the portreeve, and all the burgesses within London, French and English, friendly. And I acquaint you, that I will that ye be all law-worthy as ye were in king Edward's days. And I will that every child be his father's heir, after his father's days. And I will not suffer that any man do you any wrong. God preserve you."

Water brought from Tyburn to West Cheap . . 1285
Expulsion of the Jews by Edward I. (16,511) . . 1290
The manor of Southwark conveyed to the citizens 1327
Charter granted by Edward III. . . 1328
Terrible pestilence, in which 50,000 (?) citizens perish * 1348
London sends 4 members to parliament 1355
William of Walworth lord mayor 1380
Wat Tyler's rebellion (see *Tyler*) 1381
Aldermen elected for life 1394
Great plague, 30,000 (?) died 1406
City first lighted at night by lanterns . . . 1415
Guildhall commenced 1411, finished . . . 1416
Whittington thrice lord mayor, viz., 1397, 1406, 1419
Jack Cade's rebellion ; see *Cade* . . . 1450
First civic procession on the water ; sir John Norman lord mayor 1453
Falconbridge attempts the city . . . 1471
Printing-press set up by Caxton . . . . ,,
Sweating sickness rages 1485
Fleet ditch navigable 1502
St. Paul's school founded by dean Colet . . 1509
The fatal sweat, *Sudor Anglicus* . . . 1517
Evil May-day (*which see*) . . . . ,,
Streets first paved (*Viner's Stat.*) . . . 1533
"Bills of Mortality" ordered to be kept . . 1538
Dissolution of religious houses . . . 1539
St. Bartholomew's monastery changed to an hospital ,,
Forty taverns and public houses allowed in the city, and three in Westminster, act 7 Edw. VI. . 1553
Christ's hospital founded by king Edw. VI. . . ,,
Russian trading company established . . . ,,
Coaches introduced about 1563
Royal Exchange built (see *Exchange*) . . . 1566
New buildings in London forbidden "where no former hath been known to have been," to prevent the increasing size† 1580
Thames water conveyed into the city by leaden pipes 1580-94
Stow publishes his survey 1598
Nearly all London yet built of wood . . . 1600
30,578 persons said to perish by the plague . . 1603
Thomas Sutton founds Charterhouse school, &c. . 1611
New river water brought to London . . . 1613
Principal streets paved 1616
Hackney coaches first plied 1625
A great plague . . . . . . ,,
Building of the western parishes, St. Giles's, &c. begun 1640
The city held for the parliament . . . 1642
London fortified 1643
Jews allowed to return to London by Cromwell . 1650
Banking begun by Francis Child about 1660
Royal Society of London chartered . . . 1662
The great plague (see *Plagues*) 1665
"Oxford" afterwards "London Gazette" published 7 Nov. ,,
Great fire of London (see *Fires*) . . 2-6 Sept. 1666
Act for a "new model of building" in the city . ,,
Monument erected by Wren (see *Monument*) . 1671-7
St. Paul's founded . . . . 21 June, 1675
A London directory published 1679
Charter granted by Charles II. 1680

* This terrible pestilence broke out in India, and spreading itself westward through every country on the globe, reached England. Its ravages in London were so great that the common cemeteries were not sufficient for the interment of the dead, and various pieces of ground without the walls were assigned for burial-places. Amongst these was the waste land now forming the precincts of the Charter-house, where upwards of 50,000 bodies were then deposited. This disorder did not subside till 1357. *Leigh.*

† This proclamation or decree was dated from Nonesuch, 7 July, 1580, and it was forbidden to erect new buildings where none had before existed in the memory of man. The extension of the metropolis was deemed calculated to encourage the increase of the plague; create a trouble in governing such multitudes ; a dearth of victuals ; multiplying of beggars, and inability to relieve them ; an increase of artisans more than could live together ; impoverishing other cities for lack of inhabitants. The decree stated that lack of air, lack of room to walk and shoot, &c., arose out of too crowded a city. A proclamation to the same effect was also issued by James I.

Penny post established 1683
London partly lit at night by Edward Heming's patent 1684-5
Settlement of French protestants 1685
Charter declared forfeited, 1682 ; but restored . . 1689
Bank of England established 1694
St. Paul's opened . . . . . 2 Dec. 1697
Awful storm . . . 26 Nov.-1 Dec. 1703
Sacheverel's sermon and mob (see *Riots*) . . 1709
Act for the erection of fifty new churches . . 1711
South Sea bubble commenced, 1710 ; exploded (see *South Sea Company*) 1720
Chelsea water works formed 1722
The Election act passed 1724
Bank of England built 1732-4
Glass lamps in the street . between 1694 & 1736
Fleet ditch covered, and Fleet market opened . 1737
"Great Frost," 25 Dec. 1739 to 8 Feb. . . 1740
London Hospital instituted . . . . ,,
New Mansion-house founded, 1739 ; completed . 1753
British Museum established . . . . ,,
Society of Arts established . . . . ,,
The New road, 1755-6 ; City road projected about 1760
Eight gates removed 1760-1
Shop signs removed 1762
Westminster paving-act passed . . . ,,
Blackfriars-bridge opened . . . 19 Nov. 1769
The lord mayor (Brass Crosby) committed to the Tower by the House of Commons for a breach of privilege . . . . . 27 March, 1771
Lord George Gordon's No-popery mob (see *Gordon's mob*) . . . . . . June, 1780
Thanksgiving of George III. at St. Paul's Cathedral 23 April, 1789
Building of Camden town, begun . . . 1791
Royal Institution of Gt. Britain founded . . 1799
London docks opened . . . 20 Jan. 1805
London Institution founded . . . . ,,
Lord Nelson's funeral . . . . 9 Jan. 1806
Gas first exhibited in Pall Mall . . . 1807
Riots on the committal of sir F. Burdett to the Tower . . . . . 6 April, 1810
The Mint finished 1811
Regent-street begun 1813
Civic banquet to the allied sovereigns at Guildhall, 18 June, 1814
Custom-house burnt . . . . 12 Feb. ,,
The city generally lighted with gas . . . ,,
Waterloo-bridge opened . . . 18 June, 1817
New Custom-house opened . . . . ,,
Southwark-bridge opened . . . 24 March, 1819
The great increase in building commences . . 1820
Bank of England completed by sir John Soane . 1821
Tumults at queen Caroline's funeral 14 Aug. ,,
Cabs introduced 1823
London Mechanics' Institution founded . . . ,,
Bubble companies' panic 1825
London University chartered . . 11 Feb. 1826
27 turnpikes removed by act of parliament . . 1827
New Post-office completed 1829
Farringdon-market opened . . . . ,,
Omnibuses introduced . . . . . ,,
New metropolitan police began . . 29 Sept. ,,
Covent-garden market rebuilt 1830
Memorable political panic, 5 Nov. ; and no lord mayor's show . . . . . 9 Nov. ,,
New London-bridge opened . . . 1 Aug. 1831
General Fast on account of the cholera in England, 6 Feb. 1832
Hungerford-market opened . . . 3 July, 1833
Houses of parliament burnt . . . 16 Oct. 1834
City of London school founded . . . ,,
The queen dines at Guildhall . . . 9 Nov. 1837
Royal Exchange burnt . . . . 10 Jan. 1838
Railway opened from London to Birmingham, 17 Sept. ; to Greenwich . . . 28 Dec. ,,
Penny-postage begun . . . . 10 Jan. 1840
Railway to Southampton opened . . 11 May, ,,
Wood pavement tried ; fails . . . . ,,
London library established 1841
Railway to Bristol opened . . . 30 June, ,,
Blackwall railway opened . . . 2 Aug. ,,
Railway to Brighton opened . . . 21 Sept. ,,
Thames Tunnel opened . . . 25 March, 1843
Royal Exchange opened by the queen 28 Oct. 1844
Erection of baths and wash-houses begins . . ,,
Fleet prison taken down . . . . . ,,
New building act begins operation . . 1 Jan. 1845

Penny steamboats begun 1845
Model lodging houses built . . . . ,,
Railway mania . . . . ,,
Twopenny omnibuses begun 1846
Great Chartist demonstration in London (see *Chartists*) . . . . 10 April, 1848
Re-appearance of the cholera . . . . Sept. 1849
Coal Exchange opened . . . . . 30 Oct. ,,
Lord mayor's great banquet (of mayors)—(see *Lord Mayors*) . . . . . . 21 March, 1850
Attack upon general Haynau . . . . 4 Sept. ,,
Great Exhibition *opened*, 1 May; *closed*, 11 Oct. 1851
Duke of Wellington dies, 14 Sept.; his funeral at St. Paul's (see *Wellington*) 18 Nov. 1852
Cab-strike . . . . 27-29 July, 1853
Visit of king of Portugal . . . . . 19 May, 1854
Attack of cholera . . . . . Aug. & Sept. ,,
Meeting for Patriotic fund . . . . . 2 Nov. ,,
Visit of emperor and empress of the French to the lord mayor . . . . . . 19 April, 1855
The queen distributes Crimean medals . 18 May, ,,
Failure of Paul, Strahan, & Co. (see *Trials*) 5 June, ,,
Metropolitan Local Management act passed 14 Aug. ,,
Visit of the king of Sardinia . . . 30 Nov. ,,
Metropolitan Board of Works, first meeting 22 Dec. ,,
Peace proclaimed, 29 April; illuminations and fireworks in the parks . . . . 29 May, 1856
Royal British Bank stops payment (see *British Bank*) 4 Sept. ,,
Meetings of unemployed operatives in Smithfield, Feb. 1857
Many commercial failures; Bank charter act suspended . . . . 12 Nov. ,,
James Morison (originally a poor boy), who mainly introduced the system of quick returns and small profits, dies exceedingly rich . . . 30 Oct. ,,
Metropolis divided into 10 postal districts 1 Jan. 1858
Great Eastern launched (began 3 Nov. 1857) 31 Jan. ,,
Complaints of the state of the Thames; act for its purification passed . . . . . 2 Aug. ,,
Panic on stock exchange (40 or 50 failures at reported French and Russian alliance against Austria . . . . April, 1859
A strike among the building trades, and a lock-out by the masters, 8 Aug.; the latter require the men to sign a *document*, declaring that they will not belong to any society which interferes with the freedom of the workman; the strike was dying out in . . . . Nov. ,,
Disgraceful riots at the church of St. George's in the East, through the indiscretion of the Tractarian clergyman, the rev. Bryan King, Sept. and Oct. The church (closed for a time) re-opened: fresh disturbances on 6, 13, 20 Nov.; the agitation continued till Mr. King retired; a compromise was effected . . . . . . 29 July, 1860
Metropolitan railway (underground) commenced in spring of . . . . ,,
Great distress through the severe winter; thousands relieved at the police offices . Dec. 1860, & Jan. 1861
Another strike in the building trades commences, 22 March, ,,
A street railway in the metropolis opened near Bayswater (temporary) . . . . 23 March, ,,
Great fire near Tooley-street (see *Fires*) 22 June, ,,
Sale of the East India house . . . 23 June, ,,
Meeting to establish the "City of London College," bishop of London in the chair . . . 2 Oct. ,,
Mr. George Peabody, the American merchant, gives 150,000*l.* to ameliorate the condition of the poor and needy of London . . . 12 March, 1862
The International Exhibition opens . . 1 May, ,,
Thames embankment bill passed, after much discussion . . . . Aug. ,,
Fights in Hyde-park between the Garibaldians and Irish . . . . . . 28 Sept. & 5 Oct. ,,
Public meetings there prohibited . . 9 Oct. ,,
Comtesse de Silly leaves 4000*l.* to poor of London ,,
The Metropolitan railway opened . . 10 Jan. 1863
Pneumatic despatch company begins to convey post-office bags . . . . . . 21 Feb. ,,
Princess Alexandra of Denmark enters London, 7 March, ,,
Prince and princess of Wales present at the city ball at Guildhall . . . . 8 June, ,,
Appeal of the bishop of London on account of the spiritual destitution of the metropolis (see *Church of England*) . . . . June, ,,
The common council vote 20,000*l.* and a site in Victoria-street, E.C. (now Farringdon-road), for a lodging-house for the poor . . 19 Nov. 1863
New street between Blackfriars and London-bridge opened . . . . 1 Jan. 1864
Charing Cross railway opened . . . . 11 Jan. ,,
First block of Peabody's dwellings in Spitalfields opened . . . . 29 Feb. ,,
Garibaldi enters London, 11 April; receives the freedom of the city . . . . . 21 April, ,,
Many turnpikes in the N. suburbs abolished, 1 July, ,,
Great excitement through the murder of Mr. Briggs in a carriage of the N. London railway . 9 July, ,,
The first railway train enters the city of London near Blackfriars-bridge . . . . 6 Oct. ,,
North London industrial exhibition, Islington, opened by earl Russell . . . . 17 Oct. ,,
Excitement through the performance of the Davenport brothers . . . . . Oct.-Dec. ,,
Great bullion robbery in Lombard-street, 3 or 4 Dec. ,,
Many burglaries in London; great robbery at Walker's, the jewellers, Cornhill . . 4, 5 Feb. 1865
South London industrial exhibition opened by earl of Shaftesbury . . . . . 1 March, ,,
The prince of Wales present at the opening of the main drainage works, at the southern outfall near Erith . . . . 4 April, ,,
Prince of Wales opens the international reformatory exhibition at Islington . . . 10 May, ,,
Cattle plague breaks out in cow houses near Barnsbury, about . . . . . . 27 June, ,,
Investigation into the state of the workhouse infirmaries from several paupers dying through neglect . . . . Aug. ,,
Many turnpikes in the S. suburbs abolished, 31 Oct. ,,
Mr. Peabody adds 100,000*l.* to his gift of 1862, 29 Jan. 1866
City industrial exhibition opened by lord mayor, 6 March, ,,
Horrible murder of Sarah Millson in Cannon-street (culprit undiscovered) . . . 11 April, ,,
Black-Friday; commercial panic; failure of Overend, Gurney, & Co., Discount Company (see *Bank*, 11 May) . . . . 10 May, ,,
Agra and Masterman's bank stops; great excitement, 6 June, ,,
Shocking revelations in London workhouse infirmaries . . . . . . June, *et seq.* ,,
Cholera prevails in east London (see *Cholera*), July-Sept. ,,
Riots in Hyde-park . . . . . 23, 24 July, ,,
Cannon-street railway station opened . 1 Sept. ,,
Lord mayor honourably entertained at Brussels by the king of the Belgians . . . . . Oct. ,,
Working classes industrial exhibition at Islington closed . . . . 12 Nov. ,,
Report of committee at common council recommending enlargement of constituency voting for municipal questions (from about 6700 to 15,000) 12 Nov. ,,
Reform demonstration by trades unions; procession of about 25,000 to Beaufort-house grounds, Brompton . . . . 3 Dec. ,,
Estimated population of the "*City*" by day, 283,520; by night, about 100,000 . . Dec. ,,
Severe frost: 40 lives lost by breaking in of ice on ornamental waters in Regent's park . 15 Jan. 1867
"Icy night"; many accidents through fall of rain and immediate frost . . . . . 22 Jan. ,,
London Street Reform Association organised, Jan. ,,
Great distress in east London; large subscriptions: Mansion-house Metropolitan Relief Fund established . . . . 26 Jan. ,,
Metropolitan poor act passed . . . 29 March, ,,
London conference on Luxemburg question 7-11 May, ,,
First stone laid of Holborn viaduct, 3 June; of new meat market . . . . 5 June, ,,
The lord mayor entertained the viceroy of Egypt 11 June; the Belgians, 12 July; the Sultan, 18 July, ,,
The Sultan gives 2500*l.* to the poor of London, 22 July, ,,
Electors for M.P.'s to have 3 votes only, by Reform act passed . . . . 15 Aug. ,,
County Court for the city established by act of parliament . . . . 20 Aug. ,,

Edw. M'Donnell shot by supposed Fenian, 28 Sept., died . . . . 5 Oct. 1867

Tailors' strike, began 22 April; over . . Oct. ,,

Lord mayor's state coach not used . 9 Nov. ,,

Common Council undertake erection of another cattle market (for foreign cattle) . . 6 Dec. ,,

Premeditated explosion outside Clerkenwell house of detention to release Fenians (7 persons killed and about 50 wounded) . . . . . 13 Dec. ,,

Much excitement through other attempted explosions; about 30,000 special constables sworn in, 17-24 Dec. ,,

Mysterious disappearance of the rev. B. Speke in Westminster . . . . . . 8 Jan. 1868

Great distress in the east of London through want of employment; meeting of employer and employed; work offered to the iron shipwrights at lower wages declined . . . . . 25 Jan. ,,

52,974 special constables in the metropolis up to 28 Jan. ,,

Mr. Speke (partially insane) found in Cornwall, 24 Feb. ,,

(East) London Museum Site act passed . 28 Feb. ,,

The queen lays foundation-stone of the new St. Thomas's hospital . . . . 13 May, ,,

Western approach street, Holborn Valley, opened, 25 June, ,,

Part of the Albert (southern) embankment of the Thames opened . . . . . 30 July, ,,

King's Cross market opened . . . . 7 Aug. ,,

Midland Counties railway station opened 1 Oct. ,,

Great meeting to relieve sufferers by South American earthquake (11,000*l.*) collected . 13 Oct. ,,

New meat market, Smithfield, inaugurated by the lord mayor, 24 Nov.; opened to the public, 1 Dec. ,,

Mr. Peabody gives another 100,000*l.* to the poor of London . . . . 5 Dec. ,,

London Association for prevention of poverty and crime founded . . . . . 17 Dec. ,,

S. London industrial exhibition opened 1 March, 1869

Columbia market, Bethnal-green, erected by Miss Burdett-Coutts; opened by her . . 28 April, ,,

Statue of Mr. Peabody uncovered, prince of Wales present . . . . 23 July, ,,

Inauguration of the Holborn viaduct and the new Blackfriars bridge by the queen . 6 Nov. ,,

Inauguration of the Victoria (northern) Thames embankment by the prince of Wales . 13 July, 1870

International workmen's exhibition at Islington opened by the prince of Wales . 16 July, ,,

London ratepayers' school-board association established . . . . 8 Oct. ,,

New city library and museum founded near Guildhall . . . . 27 Oct. ,,

London education board elected . . 29 Nov. ,,

Foundation-stone laid of new general post-office, 16 Dec. ,,

Mansion-house Relief Fund established for the French (24,000*l.* raised in 4 days) 18 Jan. 1871

Addresses of the corporation presented . 28 Feb. ,,

Royal Albert hall, Kensington, opened by the queen, 29 March, ,,

First annual International Exhibition at South Kensington opened by the prince of Wales (closed 30 Oct.) . . . . 1 May, ,,

St. Thomas's hospital opened by the queen, 21 June, ,,

Hampstead heath purchased by Metropolitan board of works for 45,000*l.*; act passed 29 June, ,,

The freedom of the city presented to prince Arthur, 13 July, ,,

Tolls on the Commercial roads, London, E., ceased, 5 Aug. ,,

Queen Victoria-street opened, 4 Nov.; St. Andrew's street, &c., opened. . . . 20 Nov. ,,

New lieutenancy appointed, 1 Nov. . . 8 Dec. ,,

National thanksgiving for the recovery of the prince of Wales; the queen and prince go to St. Paul's, 27 Feb. 1872

Strike of building trades begun, 1 June (see *Strikes*); lock-out by the masters begun . . 19 June, ,,

East London Museum at Bethnal-green opened by the prince and princess of Wales . 24 June, ,,

Murder of Mrs. Squires and daughter in Hoxton (undiscovered) . . . . noon 10 July, ,,

Failure of Gledstanes and Co. (East India firm) for nearly 2,000,000*l.*; announced . 22 Aug. ,,

Builders' strike and lock-out ends by agreement, about . . . . 27 Aug. ,,

Epidemic smallpox . . . . . July-Sept. 1872

Second annual International Exhibition opened 1 May; closed . . . . . . 19 Oct. ,,

New City Library and Museum at Guildhall opened by the lord chancellor . . . . 5 Nov. ,,

Brutal murder of Harriet Buswell, a gay woman, in Great Coram-street (undiscovered) 25 Dec. ,,

Forgery on the Bank of England to amount of 80,000*l.* detected . . . . . March, 1873

Banquet to mayors of corporate towns at the Mansion-house . . . . . . 26 March, ,,

Victoria-park visited by the queen; she went through Islington and returned through the city, 2 April, ,,

The City temple (to replace the Poultry chapel) founded near Holborn Viaduct . . 19 May, ,,

First *Hospital Sunday* (*which see*) . . 15 June, ,,

The Shah of Persia at a banquet at Guildhall, 20 June, ,,

The common council vote 10,000*l.* to buy Upton park, West Ham . . . . . . Nov. ,,

Bank-rate, 9 per cent., panic on stock exchange 7 Nov. ,,

Continued fog, much sickness, and many accidents 8-13 Dec. ,,

National training school for music, South Kensington; foundation laid by the duke of Edinburgh . . . . 18 Dec. ,,

Tichborne case closed (see *Trials*) . . 28 Feb. 1874

Duke and Duchess of Edinburgh enter London 12 March, ,,

Fourth International Exhibition, opened 6 April, ,,

City liberal club, earl Granville, president, organized . . . . May, ,,

The czar entertained at Guildhall . . 18 May, ,,

City Temple, Holborn Viaduct, opened . 19 ,, ,,

Banquet to provincial mayors at Mansion-house 3 June, ,,

Second Hospital Sunday . . . . 14 June, ,,

The czar presents 1000*l.*, to the bishop and the lord mayor for the poor of London . . . 2 July, ,,

First Hospital Saturday (*which see*) . . 17 Oct. ,,

Freedom given to sir Garnet J. Wolseley . 22 Oct. ,,

International exhibition closed . . . 31 Oct. ,,

Lord mayor Stone and the sheriffs at the opening of the new opera-house, Paris . . . 5 Jan. 1875

Congregational Memorial hall, Farringdon-street, opened . . . . 19 Jan. ,,

Arrival of Moody and Sankey (see *Revivals*), first meeting . . . . 9 March, ,,

Lord Elcho's bill for municipal government withdrawn . . . . May, ,,

Great *Failures* in the iron trade . . . 31 ,, ,,

Arrival of the Sultan of Zanzibar . . 9 June, ,,

Failure of Alex. Collie & Co. led to others (Collie absconded 9 Aug.) . . . . June, July, ,,

British and foreign mayors, burgomasters, prefets, &c., entertained by the lord mayor . . 29 July, ,,

Discussion on widening London Bridge Sept.-Oct. ,,

First pile of steam-ferry landing-place from Wapping to Rotherhithe struck by lord-mayor Stone 11 Oct. ,,

Prince Leopold takes up his freedom . . 25 Oct. ,,

Grocers' company wing, London hospital, opened by the queen . . . . 7 March, 1876

Freedom of the city given to chief-justice Cockburn (said to be first case of the kind) . 9 March, ,,

Banquet and ball to the prince of Wales on his return from India (11 May) . . . 19 May, ,,

Lord Elcho's resolution for reforming the corporation and establishing a metropolitan government withdrawn from the Commons . . . 13 June, ,,

Stock exchange very dull; new 3 per cent. consols, 97½ . . . . 24 July, ,,

Public meeting at Mansion-house respecting atrocities in Bulgaria (see *Turkey*) . 18 Sept. ,,

"Great Eastern-street" (from Shoreditch to Old-street), opened . . . . . . 12 Oct. ,,

Visit of municipal officers of Paris, to inspect railways, &c. . . . . . 30 April—8 May, 1877

Sir John Bennett thrice elected alderman, rejected by court of aldermen, third time, 16 Oct.; Edgar Breffitt elected by court of aldermen . 23 Oct. ,,

Temple Bar removed . . . . . 2—14 Jan. 1878

Revival of trade; bank discount 4 per cent. 1 Aug. ,,

Banquet to the ministers after the treaty of Berlin; freedom of city given to the earl of Beaconsfield and the marquis of Salisbury . . . 3 Aug. ,,

The Parochial Charities commission appointed (the

duke of Northumberland, canon R. Gregory, prebendary Wm. Rogers, and others) . 9 Aug. 1878
Bank discount raised to 5 per cent. . 12 Aug. ,,
Great Eastern-street completed and opened Aug. ,,
Foundering of the *Princess Alice* (*which see*) through collision with the *Bywell Castle* in Thames (see *Mansion House Fund*) . . . . . 3 Sept. ,,
Waterloo-bridge opened toll-free . 3 Oct. ,,
"City and Guilds of London Institute for the advancement of Technical Education," formally constituted . . . . 11 Nov. ,,
City Church and Churchyard Protection Society formed . . . . Feb. 1879
New-formed street between Shoreditch and Bethnal-green opened (it completes direct road from Oxford-street to Old-ford) . . . . 29 March, ,,
Holborn Town-hall opened by the lord mayor, 18 Dec. ,,
The king of Greece receives freedom of the city, 16 June, 1880
Municipality of London bill introduced by Mr. Firth and others . . . . 25 June, ,,
Explosion of gas main near Tottenham-court-road; 2 deaths; much property destroyed . 5 July, ,,
City Livery Companies' Commission appointed (earl of Derby, duke of Bedford, lord Sherbrooke, lord Coleridge, sir R. A. Cross, &c.) . . . July, ,,
Topographical Society of London founded, 28 Oct. ,,
Temple Bar Memorial uncovered (see *Temple*), 8 Nov. ,,
Mansion-house (*which see*); attempt to blow it up detected . . . . 16 March, 1881
Elcho shield placed in Guildhall, 10th time 29 Oct. ,,
Mr. W. Ward bequeaths 20,000*l.*, and other property to the Corporation, announced . 17 Nov. ,,
City of London College near Moorgate-st.; foundation laid . . . . 31 March, 1882
The lord Mayor takes freedom of the city to the King of the Netherlands at the Hague . 20 Sept. ,,
New city of London schools, Victoria Embankment, opened by the prince of Wales . . 12 Dec. ,,
Freedom given to lord Alcester . . 11 April, 1883
City of London Parochial Charities act, 46 & 47 Vict. c. 56, passed . . . . . 20 Aug. ,,
Much excitement about the dwellings of "Out-cast London" through Mr. G. R. Sims, "How the poor live," &c. . . . . . . Autumn ,,
Meeting at the Mansion House to raise 50,000*l.*, to aid the Beaumont legacy, in establishing a great institution for the instruction and recreation of the people of the East end . . 14 Dec. ,,
New street from King William street to the Tower opened . . . . 25 Jan. 1884
1,000*l.* offered by government, and 1,000*l.* by railway companies, for discovery of dynamite conspirators about . . . . . 3 March, ,,
See *Dynamite*, and *Explosions*, 1883-4.
Freedom of the city given to the earl of Shaftesbury, a life-long social philanthropist . 5 March, ,,
Proposed settlement of Oxford and Cambridge university men in E. London to improve social life . . . . May, ,,
Remains of Roman architecture, &c. discovered during excavations in Bevis Marks, E.C. . Aug. ,,
The common council meet in their new chamber at Guildhall . . . . 2 Oct. ,,
The common council agree to the construction of a low-level bridge between the Tower and Horsely-down, with lifting sections for the passage of ships, cost about 750,000*l.* . . . . 24 Oct. ,,
Great meeting of unemployed social democratic federation on Thames embankment; proceed to local government board; dissatisfied and riotous 16 Feb. 1885
Freedom of the city presented to prince Albert Victor of Wales . . . . . . 29 June ,,
Tower bridge act passed . . . 14 Aug ,,
Meeting of citizens at Guildhall; sir John Lubbock's resolution against an Irish parliament carried . . . . 2 April, 1886
Foundation-stone of the Tower bridge laid by the prince of Wales . . . . . 21 June, ,,
Fire panic in Hebrew dramatic club, Spitalfields, 17 killed . . . . 18 Jan. 1887
Parliamentary committee to enquire into charges of spending corporation funds to oppose municipal reform bill report the charge to be partially sustained in getting up metropolitan ratepayers' protection association; bogus meetings and much agitation (19,550*l.* spent in 1882-5), about 21 May, 1887; charge declared not proved by the common council . . . . . 9 Feb.
The queen receives the lord mayor and others with their jubilee address . . . . . 9 May, 1887
The queen proceeds from Paddington to Mile End to open the "People's Palace"; visits the Mansion-house; the houses in the route splendidly decorated; the line kept by the military, volunteers, and police; no disorder, 14 May, ,,
Death of sir Horace Jones, city architect, aged 68, 21 May. See *Jubilee*, June, 1887.
Terrific storm, destructive of life and property began 5.30 p.m., lasting about 4 hours 17 Aug. ,,
Increased spread of scarlet and other fever Sept.–Oct. ,,
Torchlight meeting of liberal and radical clubs at Rotherhithe, about 12,000 present condemning the Irish policy of the government . 24 Oct. ,,
Special constables sworn in (see *Riots*) 17–19 Nov. ,,
Freedom of the city of London conferred on the marquis of Hartington . . . . 18 April, 1888
The new city of London court opened by the lord mayor . . . . 6 Dec. ,,
The great free steam ferry between north and south Woolwich opened by lord Rosebery 23 March, 1889
The lord mayor Whitehead visits the exhibition at Paris, and is honourably entertained 6 May *et seq.* ,,
Freedom of the city given to the marquis of Dufferin (with banquet) . . . . 29 May, ,,
Freedom of the city presented to prince George of Wales . . . . 1 June, ,,
Strike of dock labourers (see *Strikes*) . Aug.–Sept. ,,
Ball at the Mansion-house to celebrate the 700th anniversary of the mayoralty . . 29 Oct ,,
Grand lord mayor's show arranged by Hon. Lewis Wingfield . . . . 9 Nov. ,,
Sir Sydney H. Waterlow presents a park at South Hampstead (see *Waterlow Park*) . . 12 Nov. ,,
Lord Napier of Magdala dies 14 Jan.; grand military funeral, St. Paul's . . . 21 Jan. 1890
The freedom of the city given to Mr. H. M. Stanley (see *Soudan*, 1887 *et seq.*) . . . 13 May ,,
New art gallery of the corporation opened by the lord mayor . . . . 10 June ,,
Temporary strikes of the postmen and police (*which see*) . . . . July ,,
Excavations near the post-office, St. Martin's-le-Grand; discoveries of Roman remains, the town ditch, &c. . . . . Sept. ,,
City and S. London Electric Railway opened by the prince of Wales . . . . . 4 Nov. ,,
The Corporation medal commemorating the foundation of the mayoralty in 1189, completed by Messrs. Kirkwood of Edinburgh . . Nov. ,,
Financial crisis through the serious difficulties of Messrs. Baring (liabilities, 21,000,000*l.*), who are promptly and judiciously assisted by the Bank of England, William Lidderdale, governor, aided by the Bank of France, and other establishments; Mr Bertram W. Currie very instrumental; panic hardly averted . . . 8–15 Nov. *et seq.* ,,
Baring Brothers constituted a limited liability company, principally by Mr. T. C. Baring and the family; registered . . . . . . 24 Nov. ,,
Great meeting in the Guildhall, London, appealing to the czar on behalf of the Jews, 10 Dec. 1890; memorial and the lord mayor's letter, returned to him, through the foreign office, by the Russian ambassador without comment . . . 7 Feb. 1891
The telephone system between London and Paris inaugurated (see *Telephone*) . . 18 March ,,
Freedom of the city presented to Mr. William Lidderdale, governor of the bank of England 6 May ,,
Omnibus strike (*which see*) . . . . 7–13 June, ,,
State visit of the German emperor and empress (see *Germany*) . . . . 10 July ,,
The prince of Naples dines with the lord mayor 28 July ,,
The London Ratepayers' Defence League formed at a meeting at the Guildhall . . . 18 Nov. ,,
Death of Mr. Benjamin Scott, aged 78, chamberlain since 1858, died, 17 Jan.; succeeded by alderman Wm. J. R. Cotton . . . . 5 Feb. 1892
Sir Charles Hall, Q.C., elected recorder . 8 Feb. ,,

The discovery of America by Columbus in 1492 celebrated by a banquet at the Hôtel Métropole 12 Oct. 1892
London chamber of arbitration first sitting at Guildhall . . . . 23 Nov. ,,
London Reform Union inaugurated . . 15 Dec. ,,
Royal commission respecting the unification of the administration of London appointed, Mr. L. H. Courtney, chairman, sir Thomas H. Farrer, and others, March, 1893; preliminary meeting, 4 May, 1893
Banquet at the Mansion House to M. Waddington, the retiring French ambassador . . 4 March, ,,
Sir John Gilbert, having presented pictures to the city, the hon. freedom is voted to him by the common council . . . . 27 April, ,,
Great meeting at the Guildhall, protesting against the Irish home rule bill . . . 3 May, ,,
The duke and duchess of York, after their wedding at St. James's palace (see *England*) drive through London to Liverpool St. station, and arrive at Sandringham . . . . 6 July, ,,
The king and queen of Denmark, the prince and princess of Wales and daughters, the cesarevitch, and other eminent persons, entertained by lord mayor Knill at the Guildhall . . . 8 July, ,,
Corporation gifts to the duke and duchess of York presented at York House, St. James's . 7 Oct. ,,
An industrial and loan exhibition in Westminster opened by the bp. of Wakefield . . 4 Dec. ,,
Meeting of merchants and others urging the government to increase the navy, and offering financial help . . . . 12 Dec. ,,
The corporation declines to give further evidence to the unification commission, 16 Feb.; report of a committee published, *Times* . . 17 Feb. 1894
The Autonomie club-rooms, Windmill-street, Tottenham-court-road, adroitly taken by the police, anarchist documents found, many persons temporarily arrested; other houses searched and explosives discovered, evidences of a conspiracy, 16 Feb. ,,
Proposals for the unification of London presented to the royal commission by the London county council (a lord mayor, 19 aldermen, 118 councillors, &c.), reported . . . . 27 Feb. ,,
Report adopted . . . . . . 16 March, ,,
Col. Wm. Haywood, engineer, constructor of the Holborn viaduct and other works, aged 72, died 13 April, ,,
Cab strike, *which see* . . . 16 May–11 June, ,,
Tower bridge, *which see*, opened by the prince of Wales . . . . 30 June, ,,
Equalization of rates (London) bill passed, 25 Aug. ,,
Report of the royal commission appointed in March, 1893; important changes recommended, viz., one governing body, with various independent local elected bodies; the whole area of London to be called the "City of London," a county in itself; the present "city" to be termed the "old city." The new governing body to consist of the "mayor, and commonalty, and citizens of London," to succeed the present corporation and London county council, issued, 29 Sept. ,,
Liquidation of the Baring estate practically ended, *see above*, Nov. 1890; reported . . . Nov. ,,
The earl of Rosebery at the Mansion-house, on behalf of friends, presents to the rev. Wm. Rogers, rector of Bishopsgate, a portrait of Mr. Rogers, by Mr. A. S. Cope, and a piece of plate in recognition of his eminent services to the poor; the earl also opened the Bishopsgate institute, established by means of ancient "dole" money . . . . 24 Nov. ,,
Thunderstorm with snow; churches slightly damaged by lightning, St. Bride's, St. Clement Danes, and St. Stephen's, Westminster, 23 Jan. 1895
Destructive gale, 4 deaths . . . 24 March, ,,
Visit of the Afghan prince, Nasrulla Khan, to the Guildhall . . . . . 6 June, ,,
Visct. Peel receives the freedom . . . 11 July, ,,
Visit of the king of Portugal . . . 12 Nov. ,,
Close of several weeks' excitement on the Stock exchange, chiefly relating to African mines, a few failures, reported . . . 18 Nov. ,,
The incorporation of Southwark with the city, approved by the common council . 15 April, 1896
Statue of the queen on the Victoria embankment, presented to London by sir A. Seale Haslam, unveiled by the duke of Cambridge . 21 July, 1896
Meeting at the Mansion house in aid of the Indian famine relief fund; see *India* . . 16 Jan. 1897
Bill for a vote for 96,000*l.* for fortifications (London), read 1st time . . . . . 1 Feb. ,,
Dr. and Mrs. Nansen and others arrive (see *North E. & W. Passage*), 3 Feb.; he lectures to the R. Geog. society at the Albert hall, receives a special medal from the prince of Wales; lieut. Scott-Hansen, scientific head of the expedition, also receives a medal; photographs exhibited 8 Feb. ,,
Thanksgiving day, 20 June; see *Jubilees*, 1897.
Edw. Charles Baring, lord Revelstoke, formerly head of the firm of Baring Bros. (see *above*), born 1828, died . . . . 17 July, ,,
Mr. Walter Burns, philanthropist, born 9 Sept. 1838, of the Anglo-American house of J. S. Morgan and Co., died . . . 22 Nov. ,,
Meeting at the Mansion house, proposing a national commemoration in 1901, of the death of king Alfred . . . . 18 March, 1898
Exhibition of Australian art at the Grafton galleries . . . . . 4 April–July, ,,
Lord Kitchener receives the freedom . 4 Nov. ,,
The queen warmly welcomed, 15 May (see *Kensington Palace* and *S. Kensington*); her 80th birthday celebrated; thanksgiving services at St. Paul's and the Abbey (see *Windsor*) . . 24 May, 1899
Mr. Henniker Heaton (see *Post-office*) receives the freedom . . . . 20 July, ,,
Meeting at the Guildhall in support of the government's S. African policy . . . 16 Oct. ,,
Lloyd's-avenue, site and 6000*l.* provided by Mr. J. Dixon, between Fenchurch-st. and Crutched-friars, opened by the lord mayor . . 11 Nov. ,,
See *Volunteers* and *England* . . . 19 Dec. ,,
City imperial volunteers, the "lord mayor's own," to serve in S. Africa, received at the Guildhall, 1 Jan. 1900; they receive the freedom; a service held at St. Paul's and banquet at the Inner Temple, 12 Jan., and leave 13 Jan.; 2nd and 3rd detachments, after receiving similar honours, leave . . . . . . 20 and 27 Jan. 1900
City subway between the Mansion-house, Bank of England and the Royal Exchange, partially opened . . . . 8 Jan. ,,
Great rejoicings at the relief of Ladysmith (see *S. African War*, 28 Feb.) . . . . 1 March, ,,
The queen drives through the city, presented with its sword by the lord mayor, and, returning it, said, "I wish to thank you for all that my city has done"; great demonstrations outside Buckingham palace, 8, 9 March; queen returns to Windsor . . . . 10 March, ,,
Death of sir Chas. Hall, recorder since 1892; died, 9 March; succeeded by sir Forest Fulton, 20 March, ,,
Carnivals in aid of the Transvaal war funds, held in St. Pancras and other parishes, 24 May *et seq.* ,,
Return of the volunteers from S. Africa, service at St. Paul's, the queen's message read at the banquet in Finsbury by lord Wolseley, expressing the pride and satisfaction with which she had heard of their gallant and soldierlike conduct during the dangers and hardships of the campaign, and alluding in pathetic terms to her sympathy with the relatives of those who have fallen (61), and to her own loss of a dear and most gallant grandson (prince Christian Victor of Schleswig-Holstein, died at Pretoria, 29 Oct.) . . . . . 29 Oct. ,,
The lord mayor opens a new street, FitzGeorge-avenue, W. Kensington . . . . 16 Jan. 1901
Death of Mandell Creighton, bp. of London, historian and lecturer, aged 57, 14 Jan., much lamented, buried in St. Paul's . . 17 Jan. ,,
The Horniman museum, *which see*, opened at Forest-hill . . . . . . 29 June, ,,
Great overflow meeting at the Guildhall in favour of the government's S. African policy 10 July, ,,
Sir James Willcocks (see *Ashantee*) receives the freedom and a sword of honour . . 11 July, ,,
Lord Milner receives the freedom, lords Goschen, Cromer and Mr. Chamberlain present . 23 July, ,,
Russian delegates (agriculturists, &c.) visit the markets, lunch at the Guildhall . 30 Sept. ,,

The lord mayor opens new buildings to the Queen's Jubilee hospital, Earl's-court . . 22 Oct. 1901
The duke and duchess of Cornwall welcomed home from colonial tour . . . . . . 2 Nov. ,,
The prince and princess of Wales entertained at the Guildhall; the prince speaks warmly of the loyalty and attachment to the old country displayed by the colonies during his tour, and that Gt. Britain, if she is to hold her own, "must wake up" . . . . 5 Dec. ,,
Electric explosions in the city, some damage and several persons injured. . . . 4, 5 Jan. 1902
Death of marquis of Dufferin and Ava, ambassador at Paris, former viceroy of India and gov.-gen. of Canada, aged 75 . . . . . . 12 Feb. ,,
Mr. Chamberlain enthusiastically received in the City; presented with an address at the Guildhall, expressing high appreciation of his ability as colonial secretary in welding together the "British dominions beyond the seas," 13 Feb. ,,
Mansion-house meeting; lord mayor, borough mayors, chairman of the county council, sir Thos. Lipton (bart. 26 June), to organise the king's dinner to the poor; committee formed, 18 March, ,,
The lord mayor opens the Colonial Products exhibition, Royal Exchange, 10 March; the "Paris in London" exhibition at Earl's court . 7 May, ,,
Prince and princess of Wales visit the Austrian exhibition at Knightsbridge . . . 31 May, ,,
Peace rejoicings, illuminations and fireworks, &c.; special service at St. Paul's; state visit of the lord mayor to the City of London school, 2 June, ,,
Death of sir Richmond Cotton, city chamberlain, aged 80 . . . . 4 June, ,,
Peace thanksgivings: the king and queen receive the sword of the city at Temple Bar, on their way to St. Paul's . . . . . . 8 June, ,,
Mansion-house meeting in aid of a coronation gift for "King Edward's Hospital Fund" . 9 June, ,,
Prince Komatsu of Japan decorates the lord mayor with the "Order of the Rising Sun" . 23 June, ,,
Royal and other distinguished foreign and colonial guests arrive for the coronation . 23 June, ,,
The king and queen warmly welcomed . 23 June, ,,
The king dangerously ill; coronation and most of the festivities postponed; see *England*, 24 June, ,,
Royal port and docks commission, lord Revelstoke, hon. Alf. Lyttelton, sir Robt. Giffen, sir John Wolfe-Barry, and others, appointed, 1900; report, proposing a central authority to organise and administer the whole 7,000,000*l*. for expenditure required, issued, *Times* . . . . 1 July, ,,
Prince of Wales presents the colours to the new battalion of the Roy. Fusiliers, the "Old Seventh" . . . . 4 July, ,,
Grand reception of the Indian princes, at the India office, by the prince and princess of Wales, 4 July, ,,
The king's dinner (cost 30,000*l*.) to about 600,000 poor; his message sent to the lord mayor and all the boroughs, expressing regret at not being present, and hoping his guests were enjoying themselves and passing a happy day; the prince and princess of Wales and other members of the royal family visited different districts; the news that the king was *out of danger* greatly applauded . . . . 5 July, ,,
The lord mayor entertains the abps. and bps. at the Mansion-house . . . . . 9 July, ,,
Children's fêtes at Kensington gardens, 25,000 in Battersea park; the duchess of Argyll present, 29 June, 9, 11 July, ,,
Empire coronation banquet at the Guildhall, 11 July, ,,
Coronation bazaar at the Roy. Botanic gardens in aid of the Children's hospital, Great Ormond-street, opened by the queen . 18–12 July, ,,
The king's dinner to the blind of London at Chelsea town-hall, the duchess of Argyll present, 12 July, ,,
Grand welcome to lord Kitchener; addresses presented by the mayors of Paddington and Westminster; entertained by the prince of Wales at St. James's palace; afterwards greeted by the king and queen and presented with the new order of merit . . . . . . 12 July, ,,
Queen's teas to 10,000 maid-servants in various districts . . . . . . 7 July *et seq.* 1902
Mr. Chamberlain and lord Kitchener receive the freedom of the Grocers' company . 1 Aug. ,,
Lords Roberts and Kitchener presented with addresses and plate at the Guildhall . 6 Aug. ,,
Coronation of the king and queen at the Abbey; great rejoicings . . . . . 9 Aug. ,,
Illuminations, &c.; the fine Canadian arch in Whitehall much admired . . . 9-11 Aug. ,,
The Metropolitan Mounted Rifles from S. Africa attend a thanksgiving service at St. Paul's; afterwards entertained by the lord mayor at the Mansion-house . . . . . . 24 Sept. ,,
Meeting against the Education bill, St. James's-hall . . . . 14 Oct. ,,
Lord mayor's banquet to Mr. Balfour . 15 Oct. ,,
The Cuming museum (founded 1782) and 8,000*l*. bequeathed by the late Mr. H. S. Cuming to Walworth-rd. public library, announced, 16 Oct. ,,
Royal procession to S. London; the king and queen entertained at Guildhall . . 25 Oct. ,,
Mansion-house committee on the Port of London, meets first . . . . 12 Nov. ,,
Sir Joseph Dimsdale, M.P., elected city chamberlain . . . . 12 Nov. ,,
Great meeting in support of the education bill, the bps. of London and Rochester present, 14 Nov. ,,
Death of Mr. R. M. Kerr, 42 years judge of city of London court, aged 81 . . . 21 Nov. ,,
The queen's Christmas dinner to 629 widows and 836 children of soldiers killed in the S. African war, at the Alexandria Trust, City-rd. 27 Dec. ,,
Mr. W. W. Astor gives 50,000*l*. to the hospital for sick children . . . . Jan. 1903
Marriage of Mr. Brodrick, secretary of state for war, with Miss Madeleine Stanley, St. George's, Hanover-square, Mr. Balfour "best man," 5 Jan. ,,
Mr. Quintin Hogg, philanthropist and founder of the Polytechnic, Regent-street, died from accidental suffocation, aged 57 . . . . 17 Jan. ,,
Fatal fire at Colney Hatch (see *Fires*) . . 27 Jan. ,,
London traffic commission appointed . . . Feb. ,,
Sale of fittings and relics of Newgate prison, 4 Feb. ,,
Demonstration of the unemployed in Trafalgar-square . . . . 14 Feb. ,,
King and queen visit Woolwich, and open a new nursing department at the Herbert hospital and present medals to a number of nurses, 16 Feb. ,,
Mr. Adrian Pollock elected city remembrancer in succession to sir Prior Goldney, retired, end Feb. ,,
Appointment of Mr. E. R. Henry as commissioner of the metropolitan police, on retirement of Col. sir Edward Bradford . . . . . 4 March, ,,
Sir Chas. Wyndham's new theatre, St. Martin's-lane, opened . . . . . . 12 March, ,,
First court of the season held by the king and queen . . . . 13 March, ,,
Death of Dr. Bradley, ex-dean of Westminster, aged 84 . . . . 13 March, ,,
Mr. Chamberlain enthusiastically received in the City on his return from S. Africa; presented with an address at the Guildhall, . . 20 March ,,
Demonstration of the properties of radium given by sir Wm. Crookes, at Royal society . March, ,,
Tercentenary of Queen Elizabeth's death celebrated by the Royal Geographical society . 23 March, ,,
The king starts on his foreign journey . 31 March ,,
University boat race won by Cambridge by 6 lengths . . . . 1 April, ,,
London water board holds its first meeting, 2 April, ,,
Marriage of Miss Nellie Samuel, daughter of the lord mayor, to Mr. Walter H. Levy, by the chief rabbi, in the Egyptian hall, Mansion-house, 7 April, ,,
Dr. Robertson, principal of King's college, elected bishop of Exeter . . . . . 13 April, ,,
Royal commission on food supply in time of war, appointed . . . . mid April, ,,
Mr. Chas. Booth's "Life and Labour of the People in London," third series, "Religious Influences," published . . . . mid April ,,
Stockbrokers' walk to Brighton . . . 1 May, ,,
Sale of jewels at Messrs. Christies' realised 58,293*l*. 1 May, ,,

Gambart collection of pictures sold for 31,014*l*. 2–4 May, 1903

Arrival of the king in London from his foreign journey . . . . 5 May, ,,

Death of Mr. Hanbury, president of the board of agriculture, 28 April; memorial service at St. Margaret's, Westminster . . . 6 May, ,,

Annual meeting of the navy league . . 13 May, ,,

Visit of the lord mayor and sheriffs to Brussels where they are fêted, 6 May; honours conferred by the king of the Belgians . . 7 May, ,,

South London electric tramway opened by the prince of Wales . . . . 15 May, ,,

Deputation from the committee of the queen's nurses' endowment fund received by the king and queen, to whom they present 66,050*l*. collected in England and Wales, and 5,864*l*. collected in Ireland, as a women's memorial to the late queen Victoria . . . . . 21 May, ,,

Demonstration in Hyde-park against the London education bill . . . . 23 May, ,,

The Derby won by sir J. Miller's "Rocksand"; king and queen present . . 27 May, ,,

The Oaks' stakes won by Mr. J. B. Joel's "Our Lassie" . . . . . 29 May, ,,

Marble hill-park, Twickenham, acquired for the public (72,000*l*.); opened by lord Monkswell, chairman London county council . 29 May, ,,

Violent thunderstorms in London, several deaths by lightning . . . . 29–30 May, ,,

The king and queen attend service at St. Paul's cathedral, special appeal on behalf of London hospitals; 4,300*l*. collected . . 7 June, ,,

Drama, *Flodden Field*, by the poet laureate, and *The Man who Was*, by Mr. Rudyard Kipling, performed at His Majesty's theatre; the king and queen present; proceeds devoted to Guy's hospital, 8 June, ,,

The king, queen and princess Victoria present at the marriage of lady Juliet Lowther to Mr. Duff, 2nd Life Guards, at St. Peter's, Eaton-square, 9 June, ,,

The Stationers' company celebrate the 500th anniversary of their foundation; archbp. of Canterbury present . . . . 10 June, ,,

The king and queen open a new wing of the London hospital . . . . . 11 June, ,,

Members of the international telegraphic convention received at the Mansion house . 15 June, ,,

Bicentenary of John Wesley's birth celebrated at the City road chapel . . . 17 June, ,,

Death of cardinal Vaughan, archbp. of Westminster, aged 69 . . . . . 19 June, ,,

Prof. Curie, of Paris, lectures on "Radium," at the royal institution . . . 19 June, ,,

Royal agricultural show opened at Park Royal, 23 June, ,,

Visit of the Khedive . . . . . 24 June, ,,

King's birthday officially celebrated in London and elsewhere honours announced, prince of Wales promoted to vice-adm., peerages conferred on Mr. Michael Biddulph, sir E. Lawson, Mr. G. T. Sotheran-Estcourt, and Mr. W. H. Watson-Armstrong, P.C.'s, baronetages, and knighthoods also conferred . . . 26 June, ,,

Mr. Chamberlain entertained at the Constitutional club, speaks on preferential tariffs . 26 June, ,,

First meeting of the British academy, lord Reay, the president, delivers an address . . 26 June, ,,

Letter from Lord Rosebery to lord Monkswell, offering on behalf of Messrs. Wernher, Beit & Co. 100,000*l*. to provide technical education, if the London County Council endow the new technical high school with 20,000*l*. per annum . 29 June, ,,

Death of viscount Colville of Culross, lord chamberlain to the queen, aged 84 . . . 1 July, ,,

Mr. Asquith speaks at an "emergency meeting" of the National Liberal federation, against Mr. Chamberlain's proposals; meeting of unionist members opposed to protective tax on British food imports at the house of commons . 1 July, ,,

President Loubet arrives in London, visits the French embassy, and dines with the king at Buckingham palace, 8 July; reception at the guildhall, presentation of an address and luncheon with the lord mayor, the prince and princess of Wales and a distinguished company; entertains the king, the prince of Wales and the duke of Connaught at a banquet at the French embassy; royal performances at the opera in Covent-garden, 9 July, 1903

Rear-adm. Cotton and officers of the United States warship at Portsmouth received by the king at Buckingham palace, 8 July; entertained at luncheon by the "Pilgrims," and dinner by the king, who sent a cordial message to president Roosevelt, 9 July; luncheon at the Mansion-house . . . . 10 July, ,,

Irish Land bill read the third time in the commons, 317 to 20 . . . . . 21 July, ,,

French senators and deputies received at the Mansion house . . . . . 23 July, ,,

Tariff Reform league inaugurated, the duke of Sutherland president . . 21 July, ,,

Capt. J. de Courcy Hamilton, R.N., appointed chief officer of the Fire brigade, in succession to Capt. Wells, R.N. . . . . 28 July, ,,

Death of sir John Rigby, formerly a lord justice of appeal, aged 69 . . . . 26 July, ,,

Royal assent given to London education bill, 14 Aug. ,,

Severe gale in London . . . . 15 Aug. ,,

Death of lord Salisbury, aged 73 (see *Times*, 24 Aug.) 22 Aug. ,,

Memorial service for lord Salisbury held in Westminster abbey; representatives of the king, queen, and other members of the royal family, the diplomatic service, peers and members of the house of commons, and many distinguished persons present . . . . . 31 Aug. ,,

Death of count Deym, Austrian ambassador at St. James' since 1888 . . . . 3 Sept. ,,

Excessive rainfall in London, June, July and August, 15·87 in. registered at Camden-square, 9·62 in. above the average.

St. Leger won by sir J. Miller's "Rock Sand," 9 Sept. ,,

Mr. Balfour's pamphlet on "Insular Free Trade" published . . . . . 15 Sept. ,,

Resignation of Mr. Chamberlain, lord Geo. Hamilton, and Mr. Ritchie, announced . 18 Sept. ,,

(For other changes see *Balfour Administration*).

Death of the rev. Borrett White, rector of St. Mary, Aldermary . . . . . 27 Sept. ,,

Earl Howe appointed chamberlain to the queen, Oct. ,,

New cabinet appointments announced . 6 Oct. ,,

Col. sir Wm. J. Colville, master of the ceremonies, died . . . . . . 16 Oct. ,,

Portion of old Roman wall discovered during demolition of Newgate prison, reported, early Oct.

Death of Mr. J. C. Horsley, R.A., aged 86, 18 Oct. ,,

Body of Miss Hickman, a lady doctor, who disappeared mysteriously 15 Aug., found in a plantation at Richmond park . . . 18 Oct. ,,

The king and queen attend the opening of the new Gaiety theatre and witness the performance of *The Orchid* . . . . . 26 Oct. ,,

London municipal elections, Progressive and Labour majority . . . . . 2 Nov. ,,

Visit of the king and queen of Italy to the Guildhall, enthusiastic reception . . 19 Nov. ,,

Total valuation of rateable administrative county of London (6 Apr. 1903), gross, 49,184,021*l*.; rateable, 40,610,415*l*.; assessable, 40,599,379*l*.

[See *England*; and the occurrences not noticed here, under their respective heads.

LONDON, BISHOPRIC OF, is said traditionally to have been founded in the reign of Lucius, about 179. Restitutus, bishop, is said to have been present at the council of Arles, 314. Augustin made Canterbury the metropolitan see of England. Mellitus was first bishop in 604; expelled 616; first successor, Cedd, 656. The see has given to the church of Rome five saints, and to the realm sixteen lord chancellors and lord treasurers; it was valued in the king's books, at 119*l*. 8*s*. 4*d*. per annum. Present income, 10,000*l*. In 1845 Hertford and part of Essex were taken from the see of London and added to that of Rochester.

RECENT BISHOPS.

1787. Beilby Porteus, died 14 May, 1809
1809. John Randolph, died 28 July, 1813.
1813. W. Howley, trans. to Canterbury, Aug. 1828.
1828. Charles James Blomfield; resigned Oct. 1856 (died 5 Aug. 1857).
1856. Archibald Campbell Tait, translated to Canterbury, Dec. 1868.
1869. John Jackson, from Lincoln, elected 14 Jan. (had consecrated 84 new churches, 1869-79), died 6 Jan. 1885.
1885. Fred. Temple, translated from Exeter; Canterbury, Oct. 1896.
1896. Mandell Creighton, translated from Peterborough, Nov.; elected, 5 Jan. 1897; died, aged 57, 14 Jan. 1901.
1901. Arthur F. Winnington-Ingram, bp. suffragan of Stepney, elected 25 March; confirmed, after some protests, 17 April, 1901.

LONDON BRIDGE. The first bridge said to have been built 994, was much injured by the Danes 1008 and destroyed by a flood 1091. Another bridge erected by command of William II., was burnt in 1136. The late old bridge was commenced about 1176, by Peter of Colechurch, and completed in 1209, with houses on each side, connected together by large arches of timber which crossed the street.

A fire at the Southwark end brought crowds on the bridge; the houses at the north end caught fire likewise, and prevented their escape: and upwards of 3000 persons lost their lives, being either killed, burned, or drowned . . July, 1212
The bridge restored in 1300, again destroyed by fire in 1471; 13 Feb. 1632, and . . . Sept. 1725
All the houses pulled down 1756
Waterworks begun, 1582; destroyed by fire . . 1774
The toll discontinued . . . . 27 March, 1782
In 1822 the corporation advertised for designs for a new bridge: that by John Rennie was approved, and the works were executed by his sons John and George. The first pile was driven 200 feet to the west of the old bridge, 15 March, 1824; the first stone was laid by the lord mayor, alderman Garratt . . . . 15 June, 1825
The bridge opened by William IV. and his queen, 1 Aug. 1831
The cost was 506,000*l.*
Plans for widening the bridge rejected . . . 1875
It was computed that on 17 March, 1859, there passed over London-bridge 20,498 vehicles (of which 4483 were cabs and 4286 omnibuses), and 167,910 persons (107,074 on foot, and 60,836 in vehicles). In April 1881 in one day (24 hours) passed over 78,943 passengers in 10,733 vehicles.
Attempt to explode S.W. end, damage to property, not life; near 6 p.m., 500*l.* reward offered, 13 Dec. 1884
Widening of the bridge; roadway increased in width from 34 ft. 6 in. to 37 ft.; footways from 9 ft. to 14 ft. 1901–3

LONDON CHAMBER OF ARBITRATION, see *London*, Nov. 1892. Instituted to decide on commercial disputes, and to avoid the cost and delay of legal proceedings, held its first sitting at Guildhall, the lord mayor president, 23 Nov. 1892. The scheme was widely supported by the citizens. The first case was decided by sir Albert Rollit, sole arbitrator, after 10 days' deliberation, 16 Dec. 1892.

LONDON CONFERENCE, of representatives of the chief European powers to reconcile Austria, Prussia, and Denmark, met 25 April to 25 June, 1864, without effect. A conference in London respecting the treaty of Paris, 1856, led to a treaty signed 13 March, 1871; see *Black Sea*.

Conference respecting Egyptian affairs; earl Granville, foreign secretary, &c., H. C. E. Childers, chancellor of the exchequer, met the following ambassadors: Count Karolyi (Austria), M. Waddington (France), count Münster (Germany), count Nigra (Italy), count De Staal (Russia), and Musurus Pasha (Turkey), 28 June, 1884; adjourned without result *sine die* . . 2 Aug. 1884

LONDON COUNCIL for the promotion of public morality, founded 1899; meeting at St. Martin's town-hall, bp. of London in the chair, the R. C. bp. of Southwark, the chief Rabbi, and others present, 1 Feb. 1900.

LONDON, COUNTY OF, constituted by the Local government act of 1888. It contains 24 parishes, total acres, 75,442 (29 boroughs, 1901). First lord-lieutenant the duke of Westminster, announced, 24 Oct. 1888.

LONDON COUNTY COUNCIL was constituted by the Local Government Act of 1888, and to it was transferred the powers, duties, property, and debts and liabilities, of the Metropolitan Board of Works (*which see*). The council consists of 118 members, elected by the ratepayers of the parishes, and 19 aldermen, including a chairman. The old "city" retains most of its ancient privileges.

First council elected; the earl of Rosebery, sir John Lubbock, Mr. Benjamin Cohen, and Mr. Henry Clarke returned for the city (lady Sandhurst and Miss Cobden elected councillors) 7 Jan. 1889
First provisional meeting, sir John Lubbock chairman, 31 Jan.; 19 aldermen elected, including lord Lingen, lord Hobhouse, and the earl of Meath, the majority progressive radicals, 5 Feb.; the earl of Rosebery appointed chairman, sir John Lubbock vice-chairman (both unpaid), Mr. J. F. Bottomley Firth deputy-chairman (salary 2000*l.*) 12 Feb. 1889. Mr. Firth died suddenly about 4 Sept.; succeeded by Mr. Alfred H. Haggis (salary 1000*l.*), 7 Nov. 1889; he died suddenly . . . . 24 Nov. 1891
The council entered on its duties by order of the local government board . . . 21 March, 1889
The queen's bench decides on appeal of lady Sandhurst that women are disqualified for election as councillors, 16 May, 1889; see *Women* . 1889–90
Sir John Lubbock elected chairman to succeed the earl of Rosebery (resigned), 22 July; sir Thomas H. Farrer, vice-chairman, 29 July; the three officers re-elected . . . . . 7 Nov. 1890
The council was authorised to raise money by acts passed 1889–90; acts passed 1892–1895.
Second council elected (progressives, 83; moderates, 35), 5 March; the earl of Rosebery elected chairman; Mr. John Hutton, vice-chairman; Mr. W. H. Dickinson, deputy-chairman, 15 March; the earl of Rosebery resigns 22 June; succeeded by Mr. John Hutton (knt. 24 May, 1894); Mr. Charles Harrison, vice-chairman . . 12 July, ,,
For the unification of London, see *London* March *et seq.* 1893
Proposals presented by the council to the royal commission, reported . . . . . 27 Feb. 1894
Third council elected (moderates, 59; progressives, 59), 2 March (afterwards 60 moderates, 58 progressives); Mr. Arthur Arnold (knt. 1895) elected chairman; Mr. J. W. Benn, M.P., vice-chairman; Mr. Dickinson re-elected deputy-chairman; resigned, July; all progressives; 19 aldermen (progressive majority), 12 March, 1895; Dr. Collins elected chairman, 61–59 . 9 March, 1897
Report of the Works committee, disclosing falsification of accounts and jobbery, dismissal of Mr. Holloway, manager, and Mr. Ruddle, agreed to, 17 Nov. 1896; special committee appointed, 24 Nov., 4 officials dismissed, 1 Dec.; Mr. W. Adams appointed manager, 2 Feb. 1897; report of special committee, fabricated accounts proved but no misappropriation of moneys, changes in management recommended, 6 April; new standing orders adopted, 20 July, 1897.
Buildings (Trafalgar-square) bill rejected by the commons . . . . 18 Feb. ,,
Fourth council elected (69 progressives, 48 moderates); Mr. T. M'Kinnon Wood, chairman; lord Welby, vice-chairman; and Mr. H. P. Harris, deputy-chairman (10 aldermen for 6 yrs.), elected,

15 March, 1898; annual meeting; lord Welby elected chairman . . . . . 14 March, 1899
Heavy expenditure, 11,000,000*l.* in 1899, reported, 9 Oct. 1900; over 10,000,000*l.*; 1901, 4,310,217*l.* 1902
Fifth council elected: 84 Progressives, 32 Conservatives and Unionists and 2 Independents, 2 March, 1901; Mr. A. Torrance, chairman; Mr. McDougall (knt. 1902), vice-chairman; lieut.-col. Rotton, deputy-chairman; 6 Progressive, and 3 Moderates aldermen, elected . . . 12 March, „
Lord Monkswell elected chairman; Mr. E. A. Cornwall, vice-chairman, and Mr. R. A. Robinson, deputy-chairman for 1903–4; 208,800*l.* to be expended on tramway under the new thoroughfares from Holborn to the Strand . . . 10 Mar. 1902
Tunnel under the Thames between Rotherhithe and Shadwell, to cost 1,340,000*l.*, approved 13 Oct. „

LONDONDERRY or **DERRY** (N. Ireland), mentioned 546. An abbey here was burned by the Danes in 783. A charter was granted to the London companies in 1615. The town was surprised, and sir George Powlett, the governor, and the entire garrison were put to the sword by rebels, in 1606. It was besieged by O'Neill in 1641. A grant was made of Derry, with 210,000 acres of land, to various companies in London, in 1619, when it took its present name. The siege of Derry by James II.'s army commenced 20 April, 1689. The garrison and inhabitants were driven to the extremity of famine; but under the rev. George Walker, they defended it until the siege was raised by gen. Kirke, on 30 July. James's army, under the French general Rosen, retired with the loss of about 9000 men. Foyle College act passed, 1874. A grand iron bridge over the Foyle, opened 1 Jan. 1878. Riots through orange opposition to the mayor of Dublin's visit, 31 Oct. 1883. Population 1881, 29,162; 1891, 32,893; 1901, 39,873.

The earl of Zetland, opened new Guildhall 31 July, 1890
Visit of the marquis of Salisbury, demonstrations against home rule . . . . . 26, 27 May, 1893
Disorderly scenes in connection with Nationalist processions in the city; riot act read, 13, 14 Aug. 1899
Visit of the king and queen . . . . 28 July, 1903

LONDON DIALECTICAL SOCIETY, see *Dialectical.*

LONDON EDUCATION ACT, similar to Education Act of 1902; royal assent, 14 Aug. 1903.

LONDON GAZETTE, see *Newspapers.*

LONDON GOVERNMENT ACT divides London, exclusive of the City, into 28 boroughs, with council scomposed of mayors, aldermen, and councillors (see *Women*, 1899); royal assent, 13 July, 1899. Commission appointed, July, 1899; 1362 councillors elected, 1 Nov. 1900; again 2 Nov. 1903.

LONDON HOSPITAL, Whitechapel, instituted Nov. 1740; for seamen, labourers, &c.

Foundation of present building laid by adm. sir Peter Warren, 15 Oct. 1752; had 130 beds . . 1760
The queen opened the Grocers' company's wing (raising number of beds to 790) . . 7 March, 1876
12,000*l.*, proceeds of a bazaar, handed in, 18 July, 1898
60,000*l.* bequeathed by the late baroness de Stern; 10,000*l.* from Mr. E. Raphael, reported. 6 Sept. 1899
Appeal for 170,000*l.*, issued by the hospital authorities (queen gives 1,000*l.*) . . . . 6 March, 1903
New wing for treatment of lupus, opened by the king . . . . 11 June „

LONDON INSTITUTION, "for the advancement of literature and the diffusion of useful knowledge," in imitation of the Royal Institution, was founded in 1805 by sir Francis Baring, bart., and others, at 8, Old Jewry, Cheapside, and incorporated 30 April, 1815. Prof. Porson, the first librarian, died 25 Sept. 1808. The present building in Finsbury-circus was opened on 21 April, 1819; the first lecture was delivered by Mr. W. T. Brande, on 5 May following. Mr. W. R. Grove, Q.C. (afterwards justice) (the inventor of the Voltaic battery which bears his name), was the first professor of experimental philosophy, 1840-6. The institution possesses an excellent library, lecture-room, and laboratory. Thomas Baring, M.P., long president, died 18 Nov. 1873; succeeded by Dr. Warren de la Rue; by Mr. Henry Hucks Gibbs, 2 March, 1886; sir John Lubbock, 1894; lord Avebury, 1900.

LONDON LIBRARY (circulating), at first in Pall-mall, now in St. James's-square, was founded by lord Eliot, Thos. Carlyle, W. E. Gladstone, T. B. Macaulay, and others, 24 June, 1840, and opened 1 May, 1841. Catalogues were printed in 1875-88, and 1903; 24,000 books in 1845. Death of Mr. Robt. Harrison, librarian 1857–93, 4 Jan. 1897. New buildings opened by Mr. Leslie Stephen, the president (K.C.B. June, 1902), 5 Dec. 1898; about 220,000 books in 1903. Annual meetings.

LONDON MISSIONARY SOCIETY, established 1795. In 1878 there were 151 European, and 543 ordained native missionaries: receipts in 1887, 105,382*l*; 1894, income, 139,835*l.*; 1897, 117,073; centenary celebrated, 15 Jan. 1895; centenary fund, 108,451*l.*: deficit, 8,416*l.* "History of the L.M.S. 1795–1895," 2 vols., by rev. R. Lovett, pub. 1899. The rev. Robt. Lang bequeaths 23,000*l.* to the society, 1900; income, 170,623*l.*; deficit, 1,657*l.* for 1902.

LONDON MUNICIPAL BILL, introduced by sir W. Harcourt, 8 April; withdrawn, 10 July, 1884.

The corporation of London was to be so extended as to comprehend the whole Metropolitan area; common council, (240 members) elected triennally by burgesses of 39 districts, to be sole governing body, and to combine functions of existing corporation, Metropolitan Board of Works, and other local authorities; and to elect annually a Lord Mayor and Deputy Mayor; and to control all local affairs except Poor Law Administration, Education, and Police.
Common council adopt a scheme for creation of nine municipal corporations in addition to that of London, 5 Nov.; published in *Times*, 6 Nov. 1885.
For opposition to the London municipal bill, see *London*, 21 May, 1887.

LONDON MUNICIPAL REFORM, a league was founded 10 March, 1881, to promote one representative municipal government for the metropolis; meetings were held in Oct. 1881; chairman of council, Mr. J. F. B. Firth, M.P. for Chelsea.

The *London Reform Union* inaugurated by the earl of Rosebery, Mr. Asquith, home secretary, Mr. Acland, Mr. Childers, Mr. Hutton, chairman of the county council, and others, at Exeter-hall, 15 Dec. 1892. The union absorbs the Municipal Reform League, and recommends the amalgamation of the city government with the county council with enlarged powers. Annual meetings held.
Citizen Sunday, when sermons are annually preached in the London churches on the duties of citizenship, was instituted by the London Reform union; also, *Citizens' Visits* to places of interest in and around London.
London Municipal Society founded by unionists and conservatives for the reform of London government, and promotion of its well-being. First general meeting, lord George Hamilton in the chair, 20 July, 1894. Annual meetings.

LONDON PARKS AND WORKS ACT, placed Battersea Park, Kennington Park, Bethnal Green Museum Gardens, Chelsea Embankment, and Victoria Park, under the direction of the

Metropolitan Board of Works, 1887. Col. Sexby's "London Parks and Gardens" (249) published, April, 1899.

LONDON PHILANTHROPIC SOCIETY was founded in 1841.

LONDON RAILWAYS, principal extensions and branches incorporated.

London and Blackwall, 1836; London, Brighton, and South Coast, 1846; London, Chatham and Dover, 1853; London and Greenwich opened 1838; London and North-Western (formed out of the London and Birmingham, Grand Junction and Manchester and Birmingham), 1847; see *North-Western*; London and South-Western (and Southampton till 1839), opened 1840; acts consolidated, 1855; Metropolitan, 1854; Metropolitan District, 1864; Midland, 1844; North London, 1846; South Eastern, 1836. See *Railways*.

LONDON SACRED HARMONIC SOCIETY, formed after the dismissal of Mr. Surman, conductor of the Sacred Harmonic Society, 6 March, 1848; gave last concert, 22 Dec. 1856.

LONDON SALVAGE CORPS, maintained by the Fire Insurance Companies, established 1866, when the London fire establishment was transferred to the Metropolitan Board of Works, and the Metropolitan Fire Brigade was organised.

LONDON SHIPPING EXCHANGE, see under *Exchange*.

LONDON SCHOOL BOARD, see *Metropolitan School Board*, and *Education*, 1870, *et seq.*

LONDON STEAMER, see *Wrecks*, &c., 11 Jan. 1866.

LONDON STONE. A stone said to have been placed by the Romans in Cannon-street, then the centre of the city, 15 B.C. London stone was known before the time of William I. It was removed from the opposite side of the way in 1742; and again moved to its present position in the wall of St. Swithin's church, 1798. It was against this stone that Jack Cade is traditionally said to have struck his sword, exclaiming "Now is Mortimer lord of this city!" 1450.

LONDON, UNIVERSITY OF. The "London university" was founded by the exertions of lord Brougham, Thomas Campbell, sir Isaac L. Goldsmid, and others; the deed of settlement dated 11 Feb. 1826. The building was commenced 30 April, 1827 (when the first stone was laid by the duke of Sussex); and was opened by an inaugural lecture from professor Bell, 1 Oct. 1828. On 28 Nov. 1836, two charters were granted: by one the "London university" was changed to "University college," and by the other the University of London was established, with a chancellor and other officers. New charters were granted to the latter on 5 Dec. 1837 and 21 April, 1858. It has power to grant degrees to students of the universities of the united kingdom, and of many collegiate establishments; and to women, by a supplemental charter, 1878. Its offices were long in Burlington-house, Piccadilly, London. The university was enfranchised by the Reform act of 1867, and Robert Lowe was elected the first M.P. 17 Nov. 1868; succeeded by sir John Lubbock (made a peer, Jan. 1900), June, 1880; sir Michael Foster, 8 Feb. 1900. The new buildings in Burlington-gardens, erected by Mr. Pennethorne, were inaugurated by the queen 11 May, 1870. Chancellors: earl of Burlington (aft. duke of) Devonshire, 1836; earl Granville, 1856 (died 31 March, 1891); earl of Derby, April, 1891 (died 21 April, 1893); Farrer, lord Herschell, June, 1893 (died 1 March, 1899); earl of Kimberley, March, 1899 (died 8 April, 1902); lord Rosebery, May, 1902; vice-chancellor, sir H. E. Roscoe, Feb. 1896. *University Hall*, Gordon-square, was founded in 1847. *University College*, new buildings opened, Oct. 1880. A scheme for establishing a teaching university of London, with four faculties (arts, laws, science and medicine), set forth at the Society of Arts, by lord Reay, and others, 15 Dec. 1884, and 5 Feb. 1885.

Report of the royal commission appointed 1888—Lord Selborne, sir George Stokes, sir Wm. Thomson (lord Kelvin 1902), sir James Hannen—recommends that a teaching university for London should be provided by the extension of the university of London . . . . May, 1889

Another scheme propounded by the senate of the university of London, Feb.; not approved by the colleges, March; rejected by the convocation (461–197) . . . . 12 May, 1891

University college issues an appeal to the public for additional funds (50,000*l.*) to enable it to carry on its work . . . . . . 24 Jan. 1892

Royal commission to consider the charter of the proposed teaching university in and for London, nominated: earl Cowper, chairman, lord Reay, Dr. J. S. Burdon Sanderson, and 10 others, 25 April; met . . . . . . 2 June, ,,

The establishment of a "Professorial university" for London was proposed in June, 1892, by sir H. E. Roscoe, professors Rücker, E. Ray Lancaster, and others.

A scheme set before the University commissioners, April, 1893

The new engineering and electrical laboratories for University College opened by the duke of Connaught . . . . . . 29 May, ,,

Scheme published by the Gresham commission, recommending the establishment of a teaching university for London, with a visitor, chancellor, senate, council, convocation, schools, &c., to replace the present university of London, whose convocation utterly opposes the scheme, 5 April, 1894; meeting of convocation; the Gresham scheme approved by a majority of 31 . 22 Jan. 1895

University of London bill read 1st time in the lords, 9 May, 1895; important memorial presented to the duke of Devonshire, *Times*, 30 Dec.; he introduces a bill into the lords, 6 July; withdrawn, 11 Aug. 1896; read 2nd time, lords, 23 July; withdrawn, 2 Aug. 1897; passed (royal assent) . . . . 9 Aug. 1899

Establishment of a "University of Westminster" proposed by a committee including sir Hugh R. Beevor, dean of King's college, *Times* . 23 Nov. ,,

London university commission bill passed by the standing committee of the lords; commissioners, lord Davey, the bishop of London, sir William Roberts, and others; passed, 12 Aug. 1898; final report issued, 1 March, 1900; the university to occupy part of the Imperial institute at S. Kensington, 5 July, 1899; the prince of Wales distributes the prizes in the new buildings S. Kensington . . . . 9 May, 1900

Mr. W. W. Astor gives 20,000*l.* to endow professorships at University college . . mid April, 1902

Mansion-house meeting: the duke of Devonshire speaks earnestly in support of the fund for higher education and research, and the incorporation of university and other colleges in the London university; the lord mayor presided; resolutions carried, 9 May; 92,000*l.* received, Oct. ,,

Schools of modern languages organised; chair of music established . . . . . autumn, ,,

Honorary degrees (first ever conferred by the university) on the prince and princess of Wales, lords Kelvin and Lister . . . . 24 June ,,

LONDON WATER SUPPLY, see *Water*.

LONE STAR, a secret society formed in 1848, in Alabama and other southern states of the North American Union, for the "extension of the institutions, power, influence, and commerce of the United States over the whole of the western hemisphere, and the islands of the Atlantic and Pacific oceans." The first acquisitions to be made by the order were Cuba and the Sandwich Islands. The knowledge of the existence of this society reached England in Aug. 1852.

LONG ISLAND or **FLATBUSH** (N. America), Battle of, 27 Aug. 1776, between the British troops under sir William Howe, and the revolted Americans, who suffered a severe defeat, after a well-fought action, losing 2000 men killed and wounded and 1000 prisoners.

LONGEVITY. Methuselah died, aged 969 2349 B.C. (*Gen.* v. 27). Golour M'Crain of the Isle of Jura, one of the Hebrides, is mythically said to have kept 180 Christmases in his own house, and died in the reign of Charles I. "In 1014 died Johannes de Temporibus, who lived 361 years (!)" *Stow.* Thomas Parr, a labouring man of Shropshire, was brought to London by the earl of Arundel, in 1635, and said to be in his 153rd year and in perfect health; he died 15 Nov. in the same year. Henry Jenkins, of Yorkshire, died in 1670, and was buried in Bolton churchyard, 6 Dec. aged 169 years (?) The researches of sir G. Cornewall Lewis, professor Owen, Mr. Wm. J. Thoms (in his "Human Longevity," May, 1873) and others, have disproved many alleged cases of longevity; and few statements of lives extending much beyond a century can be relied on. There were no records of baptism till the 16th century. In last decade about 800 alleged centenarians registered; 204 men. Deaths of 25 men and 66 women aged above 100 registered in 1881. See *Abstinence.*

Alleged instances (most of them *evidently false*).

Died.		Aged.
1656.	James Bowles, Killingworth	153
1691.	Lady Eccleston, Ireland	143
1759.	James Sheil, Irish yeoman	136
1766.	Colonel Thomas Winslow, Ireland	146
1772.	Mrs. Clum, Lichfield	138
1774.	William Beeby, Dungarvan (an ensign who served at the battles of the Boyne and Aughrim)	130
1780.	Robert Mac Bride, Herries	130
,,	Mr. William Ellis, Liverpool	130
1785.	Cardinal de Solis	110
1797.	Charles Macklin, actor, London	107
1806.	Mr. Creeke, of Thurlow	125
,,	Catherine Lopez, of Jamaica	134
1813.	Mrs. Meighan, Donoughmore	130
1814.	Mary Innes, Isle of Skye	127
1816.	Jane Lewson, Coldbath-fields, Clerkenwell	116
1840.	Mrs. Martha Rorke, of Dromore, county of Kildare, 27 Aug.	133
1853.	Mrs. Mary Power (aunt of Rd. Lalor Shiel), Ursuline convent, Cork, 20 March	116
1858.	James Nolan, Knockardrane, Carlow	116
1874.	Anthony Beresford (born 8 Feb. 1772) died at Alstonfield, 3 March, *authentic*	101
1875.	Count Jean Fred. Waldeck, painter; born at Prague, 16 March, 1766; died at Paris, 29 April, 1875	109
,,	Jacob Wm. Lüning, at Morden college	103
1876.	Madame Hulsenstein, said to have been maid of honour to the empress Maria Theresa	119
,,	Elizabeth Abbott, Ipswich, said to be	105
1877.	Pleasance, widow of sir James E. Smith, botanist, (*b.* 11 May, 1773; *d.* 3 Feb. 1877)	103
,,	Eunice Bagster, wife of Samuel, Bible bookseller, London, 22 Aug.	100
1878.	Thomas Budgen, Spitalfields, London 4 Aug.	104
1879.	Jane Hooper, St. Pancras, London	102
,,	Rev. Canon Beadon, Stoneham	102
,,	Margaret Crook, Durham	112
1880.	Sarah Way, Bristol	104½
,,	Johannette Polack (born Genth); Wiesbaden	101 and 5 months
1881.	Martha Gardner, Liverpool, 10 March	104 and 5 months
,,	Fanny Bailey, Worthing, 6 April	103½
,,	Annie Webb, sister of Sir Joseph Maxwell, Aug.	102
,,	Jane Pinkerton, of Lower Crumpsall, Manchester, (born 10 June, 1774) died 5 Oct.	107
,,	Archibald M'Arthur, Dunoon, born 1777	104
1882.	James Smith, St. Mary Cray, born 1777 died 27 Nov. aged nearly	105
,,	Thomas Bramley, Ilkeston, Derby, born 29 Dec. 1777, died Dec.	105
1883.	Betty Morgan, Garth in Wales, died 26 Feb.	107
,,	Stephen Lewes, Southampton, died May	106
1884.	Rhoda Dunn, Hunstanton, Norfolk	103
1885.	Sir Moses Montefiore, Ramsgate, died 28 July,	100½
,,	Mrs. Townsend, Faringdon, Berkshire, died 29 May	102
1886.	Miss Joanna Hastings (aunt of G. W. Hastings, M.P.), Great Malvern (born 14 March, 1782), died 12 March	103
,,	Richard Holmes, Heathfield, Sussex, died 5 May	107
,,	Sarah Marshall, Nantyglo, Wales, died 6 Aug.	107
,,	W. Nicholson, Wenden, Essex, died 15 Dec.	103
1887.	Miss Jane Gibson, Glasgow, died Dec.	102½
,,	The death of 31 alleged centenarians reported in 1887.	
1888.	M. Dimitrios Antippa, died Jan.	115 (?)
,,	Caroline Heathorne, died 3 Feb.	104
,,	Pattison Jolly, Dublin, died 5 Feb.	104
,,	Thomas Eggleston, West Virginia, U. S., died 3 May	111½
1889.	Mrs. R. Chapman, Lewes, died March	105
,,	Eugene Chevreul, Paris, 9 April	102
,,	Mrs. Catherine Voss, Shortlands, died 17 July	104
,,	Madame Poulaillon, or Roux, at Toulouse, died Nov.	106
1890.	Mr. Edward Grubb, Bristol, died about 1 July	109
1891.	Ann Telford, at Maryport, died 3 March	111
,,	Mrs. Ann Starling, Birmingham, died 30 Sept.	103
1892.	Magdalen Ponsa, at Vienna, died 4 Feb.	117
1895.	Mrs. Maryanne Parminster Glasse, Bournemouth, died early June	102
1896.	Mary Ann Peverell, born 17 July, 1792, died 6 Jan.	103
,,	Dr. William Salmon, of Penlynn court, Glamorganshie, born 1790, died 10 May	106
,,	AntoinerMountsoy, naval veteran, born at Bordeaux, 1787, died near Lichfield, 22 April	
,,	Mrs. Major, Sutton Veney, Wilts, died 2 Aug.	105
1897.	Mrs. Sarah Thomas, Burryport, died 29 (?) Jan.	108
,,	Mrs. Garland, Dublin, died mid March	105
1898.	Mr. Thomas Young, Watford, died 15 Dec.	105
1900.	M. Alonzo Péan, writer, died mid Oct.	100
1901.	Mrs. Ann Smith, Worcester, died 5 Jan.	109
,,	John Rose, Olney, Bucks, buried 9 April,	102
,,	Mrs. Elizabeth Hanbury, philanthropist, Richmond, Surrey, 31 Oct.	108
,,	John O'Brien, Illinois, died 31 Oct.	108
1902.	Mrs. (Margaretta Green) Miéville, Salop, died 16 June	102
,,	Mrs. Mary Morgan, Marylebone, died 14 Aug.	102
,,	Mrs. Betsy Moore, Bishop's Teignton, died 14 Sept.	102
1903.	Mrs. Elizabeth Alsop, Gosden, Guildford, died mid Jan.	102
,,	Mrs. Neve, Guernsey, died, 4 April	110
,,	Viscountess Glentworth, died, 28 Aug.	

EXAMPLES FURNISHED BY DR. J. WEBSTER, F.R.S.

(*unauthenticated.*)

Died.	Buried at	Aged.
1652.	Dr. W. Meade, Ware, Herts	148¾
1711.	Mrs. Scrimshaw, Rosemary-lane	127
1739.	Margaret Patten, Christchurch, Westminster	136
1741.	John Rovin, Temeswar, Hungary	172
1757.	Alexander M'Culloch, Aberdeen	132
1759.	Donald Cameron, Rannach, Aberdeenshire	130
1763.	Mrs. Taylor, Piccadilly	131

Died.		Aged.
1766.	John Mount, Langham, Dumfries	136
,,	John Hill, Leadhills, near Edinburgh	130
1771.	Mr. Whalley, Rotherhithe	121
1775.	Widow Jones, Campbell	125
1780.	Mr. Evans, Spitalfields	139
1784.	Mary Cameron, Braemar, Aberdeen	129
1791.	Archbd. Cameron, Keith, Aberdeenshire	122
1851.	Jean Golembeski, Hôtel des Invalides, Paris	126

LONGITUDE, determined by Hipparchus, at Nice, who fixed the first degree in the Canaries, 162 B.C. Harrison made a time-keeper, in A.D. 1759, which in two voyages was found to correct the longitude within the limits required by the act of parliament 12 Anne, 1714; and obtained the reward; see *Harrison's Timepiece*. The chronometers of Arnold, Earnshaw, and Bréguet, are highly esteemed. Chronometers are now received on trial at Greenwich Observatory. The act relating to the discovery of the longitude at sea was repealed in 1828. The Bureau des Longitudes at Paris was established in 1795.

LONGMAN'S MAGAZINE first published (to replace "Frazer's"), Nov. 1882.

LONGOBARDI, see *Lombardy*.

LONG PARLIAMENT met 3 Nov. 1640; was forcibly dissolved by Cromwell 20 April, 1653.

LONGWOOD, in St. Helena (S. Atlantic Ocean), the residence of the emperor Napoleon from 10 Dec. 1815 till his death, 5 May, 1821.

LONGWY (N.E. France), a frontier town, was taken by the allied army of Austrians and Prussians, 23 Aug. 1792, the beginning of the great war. It was again taken 18 Sept. 1815. After a bombardment it surrendered to the Germans, 25 Jan. 1871.

LOOCHOO ISLES; N. Pacific; long nominally subject to Japan; with a nearly independent king. Disputes between China and Japan respecting them, 1879; the isles annexed by Japan, 1879.

LOOKING-GLASSES, see *Mirrors*.

LOOM: was used by the Egyptians. The weaver's otherwise called the Dutch loom, was brought into use in London from Holland, about 1676. There were, in 1825, about 250,000 hand-looms in Great Britain, and 75,000 power-looms, each being equal to three hand-looms, making twenty-two yards each per day. The steam-loom was introduced in 1807; see *Cotton*, *Electric-loom*, *Jacquard*, *Pneumatic-loom*.

The needle-loom, invented by a German family in the United States, substituting needles for shuttles, successful in weaving ribbons, &c., exhibited in London . . . . . Nov. 1901

LOOSHAIS, a predatory nomadic Indian tribe, about 300 miles east of Calcutta. They frequently robbed the British tea plantations, killing the planters and carrying off their children. An expedition to chastise them was successful, Dec. 1871.

LORD, see *Lady*. When printed in the English Bible in small capitals LORD stands for Jehovah, the self-existing God, the name first revealed to Moses, 1491 B.C. *Exod.* vi. 3. When Lord is in ordinary type, it represents *Adonai*, lord or master.

LORD ADVOCATE, CHAMBERLAIN, CHANCELLOR, &c., see *Advocate*, *Chamberlain*, *Chancellor*, &c.

LORD MAYOR, see *Mayors*.

LORD'S DAY ACT, 29 Chas. II. c. 7, see *Sabbath*.

LORD'S SUPPER, instituted by Jesus Christ (*Matt.* xxvi. 17), 33, see *Sacrament* and *Transubstantiation*.

LORDS.* The nobility of England date their creation from 1066, when William Fitz-Osborn is said to have been made earl of Hereford by William I.; and afterwards Walter d'Evreux, earl of Salisbury; Copsi, earl of Northumberland; Henry de Ferrers, earl of Derby; and Gherbod (a Fleming) earl of Chester. Twenty-two other peers were made in this sovereign's reign. The first peer created by patent was lord Beauchamp of Holt Castle, by Richard II. in 1387. In Scotland, Gilchrist was created earl of Angus by Malcolm III. 1037. In Ireland, sir John de Courcy was created baron of Kingsale, &c., in 1181; the first peer after the obtaining of that kingdom by Henry II.

LORDS, HOUSE OF. The peers of England were summoned *ad consulendum*, to consult, in early reigns, and by writ, 6 & 7 John, 1205; but the earliest writ extant is 49 Hen. III. 1265. The commons did not form a part of the great council of the nation until some ages after the conquest; see *Parliament*. The house of lords includes the spiritual as well as temporal peers of Great Britain. The bishops are supposed to hold certain ancient baronies under the king, in right whereof they have seats in this house. Some of the temporal lords sit by descent, and some by creation: others by election, since the union with Scotland in 1707, and with Ireland, 1801. In 1719, with the king's consent, a bill for limiting the power of the sovereign of creating peers, was introduced into the lords and twice passed, but twice rejected by the commons.—Scotland elects 16 representative peers, and Ireland, 28 temporal peers for life. The house of lords in Jan. 1902, consisted of 4 princes of the blood, 2 archbishops, 22 dukes, 22 marquises, 144 earls, 37 viscounts, 336 barons, and 24 bishops; in all, 592. The valuable "Constitutional History of House of Lords," by L. O. Pike, was published in 1894. Sir Wm. Charles' "Crusade against the Constitution: a vindication of the House of Lords," published 1896.

House of lords at death of		Charles II. 1685	176 peers.
,,	,,	Will. III. 1702	192
,,	,,	Anne, 1714	209
,,	,,	Geo. I. 1727	216
,,	,,	Geo. II. 1760	229
,,	,,	Geo. III. 1820	339
,,	,,	Geo. IV. 1830	396
,,	,,	Will. IV. 1837	456
,,	in the	18th Vict. 1855	448
,,	,,	24th Vict. 1860	462
,,	,,	32nd Vict. 1868	464
,,	,,	39th Vict. 1876	494
,,	,,	41st Vict. 1878	501
,,	,,	61st Vict. 1898	519
,,	,,	64th Vict. 1900	523

The king, barons, and clergy enact the constitutions of Clarendon in 1164
Obtain Magna Charta in 1215

* Peers of England are free from all arrests of debts, as being the king's hereditary counsellors; therefore a peer cannot be outlawed in any civil action, and no attachment lies against his person; but execution may be taken upon his lands and goods. For the same reason, they are free from all attendance at courts leet or sheriffs' turns; or, in case of a riot, from attending the *posse comitatus*. He can act as a justice of the peace in any part of the kingdom. See *Baron*, *Earl*, &c.

Held the government 1264-5
House of lords abolished by the commons, 6 Feb. 1649
" " met again, ... 25 April, "
Unite with the commons in making William and Mary king and queen 1689
Reject the great reform bill, 7 Oct. 1831; pass it, 4 June, 1832
The parliament house destroyed by fire . 16 Oct. 1834
Take possession of their new house . 15 April, 1847
Oppose successfully the creation of life peerages,* 7 Feb. 1856
Voting by proxy abolished by standing order, 31 March, 1868
New regulations respecting committees 2 April, "
Six new peers were gazetted . . 17 April, "
Bankrupt peers not to sit or vote, decided 10 Feb.; settled by act . . . . 13 July, 1871
That peers cannot vote for M.P.'s affirmed by court of common pleas on appeal . . 15 Nov. 1872
Two peers for life may be created by her majesty as lords of appeal in ordinary, to aid the house of lords; as a court of ultimate appeal (see *Supreme Court*).
Lords Blackburn and Gordon created peers for life 5 Oct. 1876
Entitled to sit and vote in parliament while appeal judges; first sitting . . . 21 Nov. "
Lord Rayleigh (said to be) the first peer elected a professor of physics (at Cambridge) 12 Dec. 1879; Royal Institution, London 1887
Proposed abolition of the hereditary principle negatived (202–166) in the commons, 5 March, 1886; (223–162) 9 March, 1888; (201–160) 17, 18 May, 1889; (201–139) . . . . 21 March 1890
Lord Blackburn having resigned, permitted to sit by appellate jurisdiction act 1887
The earl of Rosebery's motion for a committee to consider reform of the house of lords rejected (97–50) . . . . 19 March, 1888
Lord Dunraven's bill for reforming the constitution of the house of lords withdrawn on the promise of the government dealing with the question 26 April, "
Marquis of Salisbury's bill for creation of life peers and exclusion of those whom he termed "black sheep" read first time 18 June; second time 10 July; dropped . . . . . . July, "
The lords of appeal are peers for life (see under *Appeals*).
Lord Salisbury resigns, the duke of Devonshire leader . . . . 14 July, 1902
Death of lord Colville of Culross, 1 July; the marquis of Salisbury, 22 Aug.; and the duke of Richmond and Gordon . . . . 27 Sept. 1903

LORDS JUSTICES, see *Justices*, *Appeal*, and *King's Bench*.

LORDS LIEUTENANTS, see *Lieutenants* and *Ireland*.

LORDS OF THE PALE, see *Pale*.

LORENZO MARQUEZ, see *Lourenço*.

LORETTO, near Ancona, Italy. Here is the *Casa Santa*, or Holy House, in which it is pretended the Virgin Mary lived at Nazareth, and said to have been carried by angels into Dalmatia from Galilee in 1291, and brought here a few years after. The lady of Loretto, gaudily dressed, stands upon an altar holding the infant Jesus in her arms, surrounded with gold lamps. Loretto was taken by the French in 1797; the holy image, which had been carried to France, was brought back with pomp, 5 Jan. 1803.

* *Peerage for life* only, with the title of lord Wensleydale of Wensleydale, was granted to baron sir James Parke, 10 Jan. 1856; the house of lords opposed his sitting and voting as a peer for life, and on 25 July, 1856, he was created a peer in the usual way, with the title of lord Wensleydale of Walton. He died in 1868. A bill for creating life peerages was read a second time in the lords, 27 April, 1869, but afterwards rejected.

L'ORIENT (W. France). Lord Bridport off this port defeated the French fleet, 23 June, 1795. The loss of the French was severe: that of the British inconsiderable. — The French flag-ship, L'Orient, blew up during the battle of the Nile, 1 Aug. 1798. Admiral Brueys and about 900 men perished. Strike and riot, 4, 5 Aug. 1903.

LORRAINE (Lotharingia), formerly a French now a German province, became a kingdom under Lothaire (son of the emperor Lothaire I.) about 855; and was divided at his death, in 869, part of it being made a duchy. From the first hereditary duke, Gerard, nominated by the emperor Henry III. in 1048, descended the house of Lorraine, represented now by the emperor of Austria, whose ancestor, the empress Maria Theresa, married in 1736 Francis formerly duke of Lorraine, then of Tuscany. Lorraine, given to the dethroned king of Poland, Stanislaus I., for life, was, at his death in 1766, united to France; see *Nancy*. Lorraine was the seat of war in Aug. 1870, and about the fifth part, including Metz and Thionville, was annexed to Germany at the peace, 26 Feb. 1871.

Visit of the German emperor and empress, 15 Oct.; the statue of emperor Frederick (William) III. at Worth unveiled . . . . . 18 Oct. 1895

LOTS. Casting lots, as an appeal to God, was sacred among the Jews, *Proverbs* xvi. 33. It was employed in the division of the land of Canaan, about 1444 B.C., by Joshua (xiv.), and in the election of Matthias the apostle, A.D. 33, *Acts* i.—Lots for life or death have been frequently cast. For an instance, see *Wales*, 1649, note.

LOTTERIES are said to have originated in Florence about 1530, and to have been legalised in France in 1539, and soon became common. They were prohibited by pope Benedict XIII. (1724-30), and sanctioned by Clement XII. (1730-40). See *Art Union* under *Arts* and *Paris* (exhibition 1889).

The first mentioned in English history took place, day and night, at the western door of St. Paul's cathedral. It contained 40,000 "*lots*" at 10s. each lot, the profits were for repairing the harbours, and the prizes were pieces of plate, 11 Jan.-6 May, 1569
A lottery, granted by the king, in favour of the colony of Virginia (prizes, pieces of plate), drawn near St. Paul's . . . . 29 June-20 July, 1612
First lottery for sums of money took place in . . 1630
Lotteries established (for more than 130 years yielded a large annual revenue to the crown) . . 1693
Lottery for the British Museum 1753
Cox's museum, containing many rare specimens of art, disposed of by lottery 1773
An act passed for the sale of the buildings of the Adelphi by lottery . . . . . 16 June, "
Irish state lottery drawn 1780
Lottery for the Leverian Museum . . . 1784-5
For the Pigott diamond, permitted, Jan. 2, 1801: it was afterwards sold at Christie's auction for 9500 guineas . . . . 10 May, 1802
For the collection of pictures of alderman Boydell, by act 1804-5
Lotteries abolished by 6 Geo. IV. c. 60, Oct.; the last drawn . . . . . 18 Oct. 1826
Act passed declaring that the then pending Glasgow lottery should be the last 1834
An act passed imposing a penalty of 50*l*. for advertising lotteries in the newspapers 1836
Lotteries suppressed in France . . 1793 and 1836
Mr. Dethiers' twelfth-cake lottery, Argyll-rooms, Hanover-square, suppressed . . 27 Dec. 1860
Twelve million national lottery tickets of one franc each, sold at Paris to pay for prizes to exhibitors, and expenses of working men visitors, 1878; 1st prize worth 5,000*l*., 2nd, 4,000*l*., 3rd and 4th 2,000*l*.; *total* 230,000 *rewards*. Drawing began 26 Jan. 1879

Missing Word Competition. In 1892, some weekly periodicals occasionally printed a sentence in which one word was omitted, and offered a money prize to the person who correctly supplied the deficiency; 1s. coupons being issued. This was condemned by sir John Bridge at Bow-street as a species of lottery, and several persons were fined. This sentence was confirmed by Mr. Justice Stirling in the Chancery division, in the case of Barclay and others *v.* Pearson (in relation to *Pearson's Weekly*), and he decided that the 23,628*l.* which had been paid into court, should be returned to Mr. Pearson, to be distributed by him to the claimants, to whom the court could give no help, as the affair was illegal, 9 Feb. 1893. This was done. See *Trials* . . June, 1899

LOUDOUN-HILL, or **DRUMCLOG**; see *Drumclog*.

LOUIS-D'OR, a French gold coin of 24 francs, struck by Louis XIII. in 1640; it was not legal, 1795-1814; superseded by the Napoleon, 1810.

LOUISIANA (N. America), one of the United States; discovered by Ferdinand de Soto, 1541; traversed by M. de Salle, 1682; settled by Louis XIV. (from whom it derived its name), about 1698. It formed the basis of Law's Mississippi scheme, 1717. Ceded to Spain when all east of the Mississippi was given to England, 1763. Capital, Baton Rouge; commercial capital, New Orleans. Pop., 1880, 939,946; 1890, 1,118,587; 1900, 1,381,625.

Restored to France 1801
Sold to the Americans, 1803; and made a state . 1812
Gen. Jackson defeated the British at New Orleans, 8 Jan. 1815
Seceded from the Union by ordinance . 25 Jan. 1861
Adm. Farragut takes New Orleans . 28 April, 1862
Louisiana restored to the Union 1865
The state disturbed by factions and civil war: at Grant parish many negroes massacred 11 April, 1873
Lockport destroyed by a cyclone; 6 deaths, 7 Sept. 1893
See *New Orleans* and *Mississippi*.

LOUIS, ST., commercial capital of the Mississippi valley. Founded by the French in 1764. Population, 1880, 350,518; 1900, 623,000.

Terrible cyclones, preceded by utter darkness, bridges, buildings, and much shipping destroyed, followed by fires . . . . . 27 May, 1896
Strike riots, 7 deaths . . . . . 9 June, 1900
Great floods, many deaths . . . . 6–10 June ,,
St. Louis international exhibition to be opened, 30 April, 1904; buildings and grounds dedicated by president Roosevelt . . . . 30 April, 1903

LOUISVILLE, chief commercial town in Kentucky, U.S., founded 1773; named after Louis XVI., France, 1780. The town suffered greatly by a tornado, 27 March, 1890, when about 93 persons perished; see *Storms*. Great fires and explosion, about 25 persons perished, 8, 9 Dec. 1891. Population, 1880, 123,758; 1890, 161,129; 1900, 204,731.

LOURDES, Hautes Pyrénées, S. France, see *France*, 1872, *et seq.*, and *Pilgrimages*.

LOURENÇO MARQUES, a Portuguese settlement, E. coast of Africa. In May, 1879, a treaty was agreed to permitting a railway to be made to the Transvaal territory. Its ratification was opposed in the chambers at Lisbon in 1881, and led to a change of ministry. See *Portugal*, 1881, and *Delagoa Bay*.

Kaffir rising against the hut-tax; raids by the natives, reported . . . . 9 Oct. 1894
State of siege reported . . . . . 12 Oct. ,,
Hostilities between the Portuguese and natives, Oct. 1894–Jan. 1895
Treacherous attack on the Portuguese camp at Maraqueen; lieut. Antonio and many others killed . . . . . . 2 Feb. 1895
The rebels routed and kraals destroyed on the Incomati river, reported . . . . 6 Feb. ,,
Kaffirs defeated with heavy loss near Maraqueen, 21 March, ,,
About 400 Portuguese soldiers arrive at Maraqueen, 19 April, ,,
Defeat of the rebels; end of the revolt, reported, 24 May, ,,
Natives defeated at Mague (300 killed) . 8 Sept. ,,
Gungunhana's army defeated with great slaughter, by col. Galhardo, near lake Coolera . 5 Nov. ,,
Manjacaze taken, submission of tribes . 11 Nov. ,,
Gungunhana, and his son Godide, captured by capt. Mousinho, at Chaimite, reported . . 4 Jan. 1896
Portugal maintains strict neutrality in the Transvaal difficulty . . . . . Jan. ,,
Two German warships in Delagoa bay, 9 Jan. 1896, withdrawn . . . . Feb. ,,
The Portuguese government grant 450*l.* to the English at Catembe, for losses during the native rising, announced . . . . . 25 Feb. ,,
Gungunhana, his son Godide, 2 indunas, etc., arrive as prisoners in Lisbon . . 13 March, ,,
Expedition against the Namarallos, reaches Monte Pao, reported successful, 8 March, 1897; chiefs submit, reported . . . . . . 29 May, 1897
Rising in Gazaland, against the hut-tax, rebels defeated, 29 May; rebellion crushed . 3 Aug. ,,
Major M. D'Albuquerque, governor-gen.; trouble with the natives on the Limpopo, soldiers captured, reported . . . . . 19 Jan. 1898
Thousands of refugees from the Transvaal arrive, reported . . . . . . 6 Oct. 1899
Portuguese troops return, after suppressing a rising on the Sabi river . . . . . 24 Nov. ,,
Law revived enforcing passports on all leaving Portuguese territory, reported . . . 8 Jan. 1900
Fire at the government offices, some destroyed, 19 May, 1901
Modus vivendi settled between Portugal and Great Britain, *re* the harbour . . . . . Dec. ,,
British military stores, estimated value 500,000*l.*, burnt down . . . . . . 3, 4 July, 1902
Lord Milner warmly received . . 11–14 Aug. ,,

LOUVRE, in Paris, is said to have been a royal residence in the reign of Dagobert, 628. It was a prison-tower constructed by Philippe Augustus in 1204. It afterwards became a library, and Charles VI. made it his palace (about 1364). The new buildings, begun by Francis I. in 1528, were enlarged and adorned by successive kings, particularly Louis XIV.—Napoleon I. turned it into a museum, and deposited in it the finest collection of paintings, statues, and treasures of art known in the world. The chief of those brought from Italy have since been restored to the rightful possessors. The magnificent buildings of the new Louvre, begun by Napoleon I. and completed by Napoleon III., were inaugurated by the latter in great state, 14 Aug. 1857. The library was destroyed and other buildings much injured by the communists, May, 1871. Baroness Nathaniel de Rothschild bequeaths Greuze's "Laitière," a fine collection of Botticellis and others to the Louvre, 1899. Five new rooms opened, 20 May, 1901; 111 pictures, 140 bronzes, given, Jan. 1902.

LOVE FEASTS, see *Agapæ*.

LOW COUNTRIES, the Pays Bas, now Holland and Belgium (*which see*).

LOWER EMPIRE. Some historians make it begin with the reign of Valerian, 253; others with that of Constantine, 323.

LOWERING BOAT APPARATUS, see *Life-boats.*

LOW SUNDAY, the first Sunday after Easter, said to derive its name from the inferiority of its solemnities to those of Easter Sunday; see *Easter.*

LOYAL AND PATRIOTIC UNION, see *Ireland*, 1886.

LOYALISTS, a term applied to the Royalist party during the American war of 1775-83, and to the supporters of the Union in Ireland in 1883.

LOYALTY LOANS were raised during the revolutionary wars. The term was applied to one opened in London 5 Dec. 1796; in fifteen hours and twenty minutes the sum of eighteen millions sterling was subscribed; see *National Association.*

LUBBOCK'S ACT, Sir John, see *Bank Holidays' Act.*

LÜBECK, a city in N. Germany, one of the four republics of the German confederation, was built in the 12th century, and was chief founder of the Hanseatic league about 1240, which lasted till 1630. Lübeck was declared a free imperial city about 1226; but was frequently attacked by the Danes. The French took it by assault, 6 Nov. 1806, and Napoleon incorporated it with his empire in 1810. On his fall in 1814 it became once more a free imperial city. It joined the North German confederation 18 Aug. 1866. The Elbe and Trave canal, connecting the North Sea and Baltic, opened by the emperor, 16 June, 1900. Population in 1871, 52,158; in 1880, 63,571; in 1885, 67,658; 1890, 76,485; 1900, 82,098.

LUCANIANS, a warlike people of S. Italy, defeated Alexander of Epirus at Pandosia, 332 B.C.; were subdued by the Romans, 272; revolted after the battle of Cannæ, 216; were reduced by Scipio, 201; again revolted, 90; admitted as Roman citizens, 88.

LUCCA (central Italy), a Roman colony, 177 B.C.; a Lombard duchy, A.D. 1327; a free city about 1370; took an active part in the civil wars of the Italian republics. It was united with Tuscany, and given as a principality to Eliza Bonaparte by her brother Napoleon I., 1805. Lucca, as a duchy, was given to Maria Louisa, widow of Louis, king of Etruria, in 1814. It was exchanged by her son Charles-Louis for Parma and Placentia in 1847; was annexed to Tuscany, and with it became part of the kingdom of Italy, in 1860.

LUCERNE (Switzerland) became independent in 1332, and joined the confederation. The city Lucerne is said to derive its name from a light (*lucerna*) set up to guide travellers. It dates from the 8th century, and was subject to the abbots of Murbach, who surrendered it to the house of Hapsburg. It was taken by the French in March, 1798, and was for a short time capital of the Helvetic republic; which, as the focus of insurrection against the French, was suppressed Oct. 1802. As a catholic canton, Lucerne was very active on behalf of education by the Jesuits, 1844; see *Switzerland.* Population, 1888: canton, 135,360; city, 20,314; 1901: canton, 146,474; city, 29,633.

LUCIA, ST. (West Indies), first settled by the English, 1639; expelled by the natives; settled by French in 1650; taken by the British several times in the subsequent wars. Insurrection of the French negroes, April, 1795. St. Lucia was restored to France at the peace of 1802; but was seized by England, 1803, and confirmed to her in 1814. Population in 1871, 31,811; 710 whites. In 1880, 38,265; 1891, 41,713; 1899, 48,650. See *Windward Isles.*

LUCIFER MATCHES came into use about 1834. Fri tion matches were invented by Walker of Stockton-on-Tees, 1829. In March, 1842, Mr. Reuben Partridge patented machinery for manufacturing the splints. In 1845, Schrötter of Vienna produced his amorphous phosphorus (by heating ordinary phosphorus in a gas which it cannot absorb), by the use of which lucifers are rendered less dangerous, and the manufacture less unhealthy. *Phosphoros* (Greek) and *lucifer* (Latin), both signify *light-bearer.*

Mr. Lowe's proposed tax on lucifers (with "*ex luce lucellum*" on the box) was much opposed, and withdrawn, April, 1871. For their exertions, a drinking fountain at Bow was inaugurated as a memorial to Bryant and May, 5 Oct. 1872. The match manufacture was made a monopoly in France in Oct. 1872, for 750,000*l.*

Strike of women and girls at Bryant and May's, assisted by socialists, 5-17 July, 1888.

The Swedish match company formed in 1888 reported unsuccessful, 6 March, 1889.

The manufacture in France became a state monopoly, 1 Jan. 1890. See *Phosphorus.*

LUCIGEN, a strong light for open-air work, produced by apparatus invented by Lyle and Hannay. The fuel is hydro-carbon oil and compressed air. It was tried at the King's Cross Station, Dec. 1885, and has been employed on the Forth Bridge Works. Exhibited at the Crystal Palace, 14 Sept. 1887.

Messrs. F. Braby & Co. patent a light created by a combination of heated oil, water and compressed air. The light said to be equal to 2,500 candles. It is intended to light public works and large areas, Oct. 1888.

LUCKNOW, the capital of Oude, since 1675; see *Oude*, and *India*, 1857. Visit of prince of Wales, Jan. 1876. Lucknow nearly submerged by an inundation, reported 13 Sept. 1894. A monument, recording the services of the 32nd Foot during the siege (1857), unveiled by lady Inglis, 5 April, 1899. Population in 1901, 263,951.

LUDDITES. Large parties of men under this designation, derived from Ned Lud, an idiot, who once broke some frames in a passion, commenced depredations at Nottingham, breaking frames and machinery, Nov. 1811. Skirmish with the military there, 29 Jan. 1812. Serious riots occurred again in 1814; and numerous bodies of unemployed artisans committed great excesses in 1816 *et seq.* Several of these Luddites were tried and executed, 1813 and 1818; see *Derby.*

LUGDUNUM, see *Leyden* and *Lyons.*

LUMINOUS PAINT, invented by Mr. W. H. Balmain, of University College, London; patented by Ihlee and Horne, of London.

Phosphorescent materials; lime and sulphur mixed with oil or water; clock-faces, statues, &c., painted with this mixture, exposed to light, remain luminous for some time. Besides domestic uses, it is applied to military purposes.

LUNAR SOCIETY, Birmingham, about 1780. The members, Joseph Priestley, James Watt, Erasmus Darwin, Dr. Withering, and others, met near the full of the moon, to discuss philosophy and politics.

LUNATICS. Insanity (defined by sir Wm. Hamilton as "the paralysis of the regulating or legislating faculties of the mind").

"The king shall have the custody of the lands of natural fools," &c., 17 Edw. II. 1324
Marriages with lunatics declared void, 15 Geo. II. c. 30 1742
Others were made in . . . . . 1774 and 1828
Act regarding criminal lunatics passed . Aug. 1840
Lunacy act, 8 & 9 Vict. c. 100, passed . . . 1845
The numerous laws respecting lunatics were consolidated and amended by 16 & 17 Vict. cc. 70, 96, 97 1853
A new lunacy act for Scotland passed . . . 1858
An act to amend the law relating to commissions of lunacy passed (said to be in consequence of the Wyndham case; see *Trials*, 1862) . . . 1862
A parliamentary committee reports favourably of the present system of custody of lunatics . . 1878
Lunacy Regulation act amended 1882
A trial of Lunatics act passed . . . 25 Aug. 1883
A stringent Lunacy bill introduced by lord chancellor Selborne, 26 March, 1885; re-introduced by lord-chancellor Herschell, 1 March, 1886; passed by the lords, 1 April, 1887; another bill introduced; dropped . . . . 10 July, 1888
11,954 lunatics in charge in Scotland . . 1 Jan. 1889
Lunacy acts amendment bill passed 26 Aug., 1889, and a consolidating act in 1890; amended . . 1891
The Cathcart case (see *Trials*) . . . . July, ,,

TREATMENT OF THE INSANE.

Till the end of the last century lunatics were treated with cruel severity; see Conolly "On the Treatment of the Insane," 1856.
The insane were exhibited at Bethlem as a show, for 1*d*. or 2*d*. till 1770
Enlightened principles of treatment were introduced by Wm. Tuke, at the Society of Friends' "Retreat," at York, and by Pinel, at the Bicêtre, Paris, with very great success 1792
Esquirol succeeds Pinel, and strongly recommends instruction in the management of mental disorders 1810
Exposure of enormous cruelties in the Bethlem hospital 1815
This led to gradual improvements, and at last to the total abolition of mechanical restraints at Lincoln, 1837; and at Hanwell Asylum (under the superintendence of Dr. John Conolly) and at other places 1839
Psychological Journal first published by Dr. Forbes Winslow 1848
Journal of Mental Science, by Dr. J. C. Bucknill . 1852
International congress on lunacy reforms opened at Antwerp . . . . . . 1 Sept. 1902

See *Hospitals*.

Lunatics in charge in England and Wales, 1 Jan. 1855.

	Private.		Pauper.		
	Male.	Female.	Male.	Female.	Total.
County Asylums .	132	123	6008	7316	13,579
Hospitals . .	895	723	91	94	1,803
Licensed houses .	1448	1350	1034	1279	5,111
	2475	2196	7133	8689	20,493

Lunatics, Idiots, and Persons of Unsound Mind in England and Wales:

1 *Jan.*	Registered.	1 *Jan.*	Registered.
1859	36,672	1881	73,113
1860	38,058	1882	74,842
1861	39,647	1883	76,765
1862	41,129	1884	78,528
1863	43,118	1885	79,704
1864	44,795	1886	80,156
1865	45,950	1887	80,891
1866	47,648	1888	82,643
1867	49,086	1889	84,340
1868	51,000	1890	86,067
1869	53,177	1892	87,848
1870	54,713	1893	89,822
1871	56,755	1894	92,067
1872	58,640	1895	94,081
1873	60,296	1896	96,446
1874	62,027	1897	99,365
1875	63,793	1898	101,972
1876	64,916	1899	105,086
1877	66,636	1900	106,611
1878	68,538	1901	107,944
1879	69,885	1902	110,713
1880	71,191	1903	113,964

Criminal lunatics in charge, Oct. 1890, 926; 1891, 900; 1892, 915; 1893, 728; 1895, 757; 1896, 769; 31 Dec. 1898, 781; 1899, 766; 1900, 770; 1901, 791.

1878. Male lunatics, 31,024; female, 37,514; ratio, 27.5 per 10,000.

Ratio per 1000 to the population: 1859, 1.86; 1865, 2.18; 1870, 2.47; 1874, 2.62.

In 1851, there were in Ireland nearly 15,000 lunatics of all classes; in Scotland in 1851, 3362 in charge; in 1855, 7403; of which only 3328 were under the protection of the law; 14,500 insane in Scotland; 18,966 in Ireland, 1 Jan. 1897; Scotland, 16,658, 1 Jan., 1903.

LUND-HILL, near Barnsley, in South Yorkshire. While the miners were dining in the pit, 19 Feb. 1857, the inflammable gas took fire and exploded. About 189 miners perished. In April and May bodies were still being extricated. There had been great laxity of discipline in the pit. 7000*l*. were subscribed for the bereaved.

LUNEBURG, see *Brunswick*.

LUNEVILLE (France), **Peace of**, concluded between the French republic and the emperor of Germany, confirmed the cessions made by the treaty of Campo Formio, stipulated that the Rhine, as far as the Dutch territories, should form the boundary of France, and recognised the Batavian, Helvetic, Ligurian, and Cisalpine republics, 9 Feb. 1801.

LUPERCALIA, a yearly festival observed at Rome on 15 Feb. instituted in memory of Romulus and Remus, according to Plutarch; but according to Livy, brought by Evander into Italy. These feasts are said to have been abolished in 496, by pope Gelasius, on account of their great disorders.

LUPUS, a disease of the skin produced by the bacillus tuberculosis. Treated by the Finsen light, and also by X (Röntgen) rays.

LUSATIA, a marquisate in N. Germany, given to John of Bohemia, 1319; obtained by Matthias of Hungary, 1478; ceded to Saxony in 1635.

LUSHAIS, see *Chins*.

LUSIAD, the great epic poem of the Portuguese, written in honour of their discoveries in India, by Luis de Camoëns, and published by him at Lisbon, 1572. The English translations are by sir Richard Fanshawe, 1655; by Wm. Julius Mickle, 1775; and others; the latest and best by J. J. Aubertin, 1884.

LUSITANIA, see *Portugal*.

LUSTRUM, an ancient expiatory sacrifice made for the Roman people, at the end of every five years, after the census had been taken. Every fifth year was called a *lustrum;* and ten, fifteen, or twenty years, were commonly expressed by two, three, or four *lustra*. The last lustrum took place, 74 A.D.

LUTE, an ancient instrument of oriental origin, (Arabic, *al'ud*); said to have been brought to Mecca, in the 6th century A.D., and thence to Europe. J. S. Bach and others composed for the Western lute in the 18th century.

LUTHERANISM,* the form of Christianity

* Martin Luther was born at Eisleben, 10 Nov. 1483; studied at Erfurt, 1501; was professor of philosophy at Wittenberg, 1508; resisted the sale of indulgences, affixing his theses against them on the door of the Castle church at Wittenberg (*which see*), 31 Oct. 1517; defended himself at Augsburg, 1518; at Worms, 1520; was excommunicated, 16 June, 1520; began his German bible, 1521; married Katherine de Bora, 1525; published his German bible complete, 1534; died 18 Feb. 1546.

professed by the majority of the people of the north of Germany, Prussia, Denmark, and Sweden. The doctrines are mainly embodied in Luther's catechisms, in the Augsburg Confession, and in the *Formula Concordiæ* of the Lutherans, published in 1580. Their first university was founded at Marburg, in 1527, by Philip, landgrave of Hesse. The Luther memorial at Worms was unveiled in presence of the king of Prussia and other sovereigns, 25 June, 1868. Fourth centenary of Luther's birth celebrated at Halle, Eisleben (where he was born), Berlin, and throughout Germany; also at London, Edinburgh, Dublin, and other places in the united kingdom; at Paris, and other places on the continent, 31 Oct.—17 Nov. 1883.

LUTINE, see *Wrecks*, 1799.

LUTZEN, or LUTZENGEN (N. Germany). Here Gustavus Adolphus, king of Sweden, defeated the imperialists under Wallenstein, 16 Nov. 1632, but was himself killed; and here the French army, commanded by Napoleon, defeated the combined armies of Russia and Prussia, commanded by general Wittgenstein, 2 May, 1813. The battles of Bautzen and Wurschen immediately followed (19-21 May), both in favour of Napoleon. The allies were compelled to pass the Oder, and an armistice was agreed to, afterwards prolonged; but, unfortunately for the French emperor, this did not produce peace.

LUXEMBURG, a grand duchy held by the king of Holland till Nov. 1890. Luxemburg, the capital, once considered the strongest fortified city in the world, has been many times besieged and taken: by the French in 984, 1443, 1479, 1542-3; by the Spaniards in 1544; by the French in 1684; restored to Spain in 1697; taken by the French in 1701; given to the Dutch as a barrier town, but ceded to the emperor at the peace in 1713. It withstood several sieges in the last century. It surrendered to the French after a siege, from Nov. 1794 to July, 1795; and was retaken by the allies in May, 1814. Population of the grand duchy, 1867, 199,958; 1875, 205,158; 1885, 213,283; 1890, 211,088; city, 18,187; 1900, 236,543; city, 42,308.

The grand duchy was annexed to the Netherlands, still remaining a member of the Germanic confederation, the capital having a Prussian garrison 1815
A portion given to the new kingdom of Belgium . 1830
After the dissolution of the Germanic confederation, the emperor Napoleon objected to the Prussian garrison, and offered to buy the grand duchy from the king of Holland . . . . March, 1867
In consequence of the opposition of Prussia, a conference of representatives of the great powers met in London, 7-11 May, who agreed upon a treaty guaranteeing the neutrality of the province, the retirement of the Prussian garrison, and the dismantling the fortress of Luxemburg . 7-11 May, ,,
The Prussian soldiers retired . . . . Nov. ,,
The fortifications dismantled . . . . Aug 1870
The people protest against absorption into Germany, 21 Oct. ,,
They are accused of violating neutrality, and the abrogation of the treaty is mooted by Prussia, early in Dec. ,,
The king of Holland, their sovereign, declared that he would maintain the treaty, 15 Dec.; and the government protested against the charge, 19 Dec. ,,
New treaty with Prussia; indemnity to be paid for breaches of neutrality; fortresses to be garrisoned by Germans . . . . Feb. 1871
Fortifications transformed to civil purposes . . 1874
The duke of Nassau, on the severe illness of the king of Holland, assumed the regency of Luxemburg . . . . 10 April, 1889
The king recovers and resumes the government, 3 May, ,,
The duke reassumes the government as regent, 6 Nov.; becomes grand duke on the death of the king, 23 Nov.; takes the oath and opens the parliament . . . . 9 Dec. 1890
M. de Xivry, the governor, assassinated at Arlon by a lunatic who afterwards shot himself, 26 Jan. 1901
Grand Duke, 1890, Adolphus William Charles, (titular duke of Nassau), born 24 July 1817. *Heir*, William Alexander, born 22 April, 1852.

LUXOR, or EL-UKSUR, Egypt, see *Thebes*.

LUXURY. Lucullus (died 49 B.C.), at Rome, was distinguished for inordinate luxury; see *Sumptuary Laws*.

LYCEUM (originally a temple of Apollo Lyceus, or a portico, or gallery, built by Lyceus, son of Apollo) was a spot near the Ilissus, in Attica, where Aristotle taught philosophy; and as he generally taught as he walked, his pupils were called *peripatetics*, *walkers-about*, and his philosophy that of the Lyceum, 342 B.C. *Stanley*; see *Theatres*.

LYCIA (Asia Minor), subject successively to Crœsus (about 560 B.C.), to the Persians (546 B.C.), to Alexander the Great (333 B.C.), and to his successors the Seleucidæ. The Romans gave Lycia to the Rhodians (188 B.C.). It became nominally free under the Romans, and was annexed to the empire by Claudius. The marbles brought from Lycia by sir Charles Fellows were deposited in the British Museum, 1840-46.

LYCURGUS, see *Laws*.

LYDIA, or Mæonia, an ancient kingdom in Asia Minor; the early history wholly mythical. Of a long dynasty of kings, the last was Crœsus, "the richest of mankind." The coinage of gold and silver money, and other useful inventions, are ascribed to the Lydians. Æsop, the fabulist, Alcman, the early lyric poet, Thales of Miletus, Anaximenes, Xenophanes, Anacreon of Teos, Heraclitus of Ephesus, &c., flourished in Lydia and Greece, from the 7th century B.C.

Agron, a descendant of Hercules, reigns in Lydia, *Herod.* . . . . about B.C. 1223
The kingdom, properly so called, begins under Ardys I. *Blair* 797
Alyattes I. reigns 761
Myrsus commences his rule. 747
Reign of Candaules (or Myrsilus) 735
Gyges, first of the race Mermnadæ, kills Candaules, marries his queen, usurps the throne about 690, and makes great conquests . . . . about 716
Ardys II. reigns, 678; the Cimbri besiege Sardis, the capital of Lydia 635
The Milesian war, commenced under Gyges, is continued by Sadyattes, who reigns 628
Reign of Alyattes II. 617
Battle upon the river Halys, between the Lydians and Medes, interrupted by an almost total eclipse of the sun. This eclipse had been predicted many years before by Thales of Milêtus. *Blair*. 28 May, B.C. 585
Crœsus, son of Alyattes, succeeds to the throne, and conquers Asia Minor 560-50
Crœsus, dreading Cyrus, whose conquests had reached to the borders of Lydia, crosses the Halys to attack the Medes, with 420,000 men and 60,000 horse 548
He is defeated, pursued, and besieged in his capital by Cyrus, who orders him to be burned alive: the pile is already on fire, when Crœsus calls aloud *Solon!* and Cyrus hearing him, spares his life. Lydia made a province of the Persian empire 546
Sardis burnt by the Ionians 499
Lydia conquered by Alexander 332
Becomes part of the kingdom of Pergamus . . 283
Conquered by the Turks . . . . A.D. 1326

LYING-IN HOSPITALS. The first, established in Dublin by Dr. Bartholomew Mosse, a physician, amid strong opposition, was opened March, 1745; see *Hospitals*.

LYMPHATICS (absorbent vessels connected with digestion), discovered about 1650 by Rudbek in Sweden, Bartbolin in Denmark, and Jolyffe in England. Asellius discovered the lacteals in 1622. In 1654, Glisson ascribed to these vessels the function of absorption; and their properties were studied by Wm. and John Hunter, Monro, Hewson, and other great anatomists.

LYNCH LAW, punishment inflicted by private individuals, independently of the legal authorities. The origin of the term is doubtful; the practice has been attributed to James Lynch Fitz-Stephen, warden of Galway, about 1526, to Lynch, a farmer in Virginia, and to Lynch, a person sent to America to suppress piracy, 1687-8. "Judge Lynch" is thought by some to be a mythical person. This mode of administering justice still exists in the outlying districts of the United States. Four robbers were taken from prison and hanged by a vigilance committee at New Albany, on the Ohio, 11 Dec. 1868.

Cases occurred at Savannah, Georgia, and near Bessemer, Alabama, and Como, Mississippi, Nov. 1890
At Salina village, Boulder county, Colorado . 21 Feb. 1891
New Orleans (*which see*) . . . . . . 14 March ,,
Numerous cases in 1891–94
Eight men killed and many wounded in attempting to lynch a prisoner at Roanoke, Virginia, 20 Sept. 1893
An anti-lynching committee existing in London, the duke of Argyll, sir J. E. Gorst, Mr. Justin M'Carthy, and others . . . . . . Oct. 1894
Five men lynched at Versailles, Indiana, 14 Sept. 1897
Five Italians lynched at Tallulah, Louisiana; the U.S. government express sincere regret to count Vinci, Italian chargé d'affaires . . 23 July, 1899
A negro burnt at the stake for murder at Corinth, Mississippi . . . . 28 Sept. ,,
Barbarous lynchings frequent in the south, reported, Sept. 1902 *et seq.*; lynching riot at Evansville, Indiana, mob dispersed by troops, 10 whites killed . . . . early July, 1903
President Roosevelt, in a letter to Mr. Durbin, governor of Indiana, strongly reprobates the system of lynching as "simply one form of anarchy, and anarchy is now, as it has always been, the handmaiden and forerunner of tyranny," early Aug. 1903

LYNDHURST'S ACT (5 & 6 Will. IV. c. 54), introduced by lord Lyndhurst, rendered valid certain marriages within the forbidden degrees (with deceased wife's sister) up to that time, but prohibited them for the future; passed 31 Aug. 1835.

LYNN REGIS, or King's Lynn, seaport of Norfolk, population, 1881, 18,454; 1901, 20,108. Chartered by king John in 1204; taken by the parliamentarians (3 weeks' siege), 1643. Outbreaks of typhoid fever, attributed to bad water, 1892 *et seq.* New supply of water to be ready in 1898. Thirteen business and other houses burnt down in the High-st., 27 Dec. 1897. The duke and duchess of York open a new wing to the hospital, 27 May, 1899.

LYONS (S. France), the Roman Lugdunum, founded by M. Plancus, 43 B.C. The city was reduced to ashes in a single night by lightning, A.D. 59, and was rebuilt in the reign of Nero. It was a free city till its union with France in 1307. Population in 1886, 367,822; in 1891, 401,930; 1901, 453,000.

Battle near Lyons; Clodius Albinus defeated and slain by Septimius Severus . . 19 Feb. 197
Two general councils held here (13th and 14th), 1245, 1274
Silk manufacture commenced 1515
Lyons taken by the republicans after 70 days' siege, 9 Oct.; awful pillage and slaughter follow; the Convention decreed the demolition of the city, 12 Oct. 1793
Capitulated to the Austrians . . . . March, 1814
Entry of Napoleon . . . . . 8 March, 1815
An insurrection among the artisans, which led to great popular excesses; quelled by an army, 21 Nov.-31 Dec. 1831
Dreadful riots, put down by military . 15 April, 1834
Railway to Paris opened . . . 7 April, 1839
A dreadful inundation at Lyons (see *Inundations*), 4 Nov. 1840
Another insurrection quelled, with much loss of life, 15 June, 1849
Grand banquet to Louis Napoleon . 15 Aug. 1850
A committee of public safety appointed here and the red flag raised soon after the revolution in Paris. M. Saigne, calling himself president, gen. Cluseret (expelled from Paris), and other extreme republicans, defeated in their endeavours to depose M. Challemel Lacour, the prefect of the Rhône, who was well supported by the national guard; gen. Mazure, the military commander, accused of treacherous inaction, was arrested . . . . 28 Sept. 1870
Arnaud, commandant of the national guard, murdered by the mob, after a mock trial, for resisting them . . . . 20 Dec. ,,
Visited by marshal MacMahon . . . . Sept. 1876
Rioting, see *France* . . . . . . Oct. 1882
Assassination of president Carnot, see *France*, 24 June, 1894
Anti-Italian riots . . . . 25 June *et seq.* ,,
About 3,000 ruined Italians quit Lyons, reported, 29 June, ,,
Pres. Loubet unveils a monument to pres. Carnot, 4 Nov. 1900

LYRE. Its invention is ascribed to the Grecian Hermes (in Latin Mercury), who, according to Homer, gave it to Apollo, the first that played upon it with method, and accompanied it with poetry. The invention of the primitive lyre, with three strings, is ascribed to the first Egyptian Hermes. It is said that Terpander added several strings to the lyre, making the number seven, 673 B.C., and that Phrynis, a musician of Mitylene, added two more, making nine, 438 B.C.

M.

MACADAMISING, a system of road-making invented by Mr. John Macadam, and published by him in an essay, in 1819, having practised it in Ayrshire. He prescribed stones to be broken to six ounces weight, and the use of clean flints and granite clippings. He received 10,000*l*. from parliament; was appointed surveyor-general of the metropolitan roads in 1827, and died in 1836; see *Roads*.

MACAO (in Quang-tong, S. China) was given to the Portuguese as a commercial station in 1586 (in return for their assistance against pirates), subject to an annual tribute, which was remitted in 1886. Here Camoens composed part of the "Lusiad." The abuses of the Coolie trade by the Portuguese led to its abolition here by the British and Chinese governments in 1873. Outbreak of plague reported, 23 April, 1895.

MACARONI. This name, given to a poem by Theophilus Folengo, 1509, continues to designate trifling performances, as buffoonery, puns, anagrams, "wit without wisdom, and humour without sense." His poem was so called from a nutritious preparation of wheat-flour in tubes and threads. These poems, in Italy and France, gave rise to *Macaroni academies*, and in England to *Macaroni clubs* (about 1772), when everything ridiculous in dress and manners was called "Macaroni." William's macaroni manufactory in London, only one in England, Dec. 1897.

MACCABEES, a name of the Asmonæans, who commenced their career during the persecution of Antiochus Epiphanes, 167 B.C. Mattathias, a priest, resisted the tyranny; and his son, Judas Maccabæus, defeated the Syrians in three battles, 166, 165 B.C.; but fell in an ambush, 161 B.C. His brother Jonathan made a league with the Romans and Lacedæmonians, and after an able administration was treacherously killed at Ptolemais by Tryphon, 143 B.C. His brother and successor, Simon, was also murdered, 135 B.C. John Hyrcanus, son of Simon, succeeded. His son Judas, called also Aristobulus, took the title of king, 107 B.C. The history of the Maccabees is contained in five books of that name, two of which are included in our Apocrypha. Four are accounted canonical by the Roman Catholic church; none by Protestant communions.

The magnificent Maccabees chapel at Geneva, founded in 1415, by the cardinal Jean de Broguier, president of the council of Constance and the place of his sepulchre. The building, much injured and desecrated at the time of the Reformation, was finely renovated in 1881 and fitted up as a museum.

McCARTHYITES, a name given to the Anti-Parnellites, see *Parnellites*, Dec. 1890.

MACCLESFIELD, Cheshire, was incorporated in 1260, disenfranchised in 1885. The church of St. Michael was founded by queen Eleanor in 1278; the grammar-school in 1502. Population, 1881, 37,514; 1891, 36,009; 1901, 34,634.

MACDONALD AFFAIR, see *Prussia*, 1861.

MACE, a weapon anciently used by the cavalry of most nations, was originally a spiked club, hung at the saddle-bow, and usually of metal. Maces were also early ensigns of authority borne before officers of state, the top being made in the form of an open crown, and commonly of silver gilt. The lord chancellor and speaker of the house of commons have maces borne before them. Edward III. granted to London the privilege of having gold or silver maces carried before the lord mayor, sheriffs, aldermen, and corporation, 1354. It was with the mace usually carried before the lord mayor on state occasions, that Walworth, lord mayor of London, is said to have knocked the rebel Wat Tyler off his horse, for rudely approaching Richard II., a courtier afterwards despatching him with his dagger, 15 June, 1381. Cromwell, entering the house of commons to disperse its members and dissolve the parliament, ordered one of his soldiers to "take away that bauble," the mace, which was done, and the doors of the house locked, 20 April, 1653.

MACEDON (N. Greece). The first kingdom is said to have been founded by Caranus, about 761 B.C. It was successively under the protection of Athens, of Thebes, and Sparta, until the reign of Philip, the father of Alexander the Great, who by his political wisdom and warlike exploits made it a powerful kingdom, and paved the way for his son's greatness.

Reigns of Caranus, about 761; Perdiccas I., 729; Argæus I., 684; Philip I., 640 or 609.
Reign of Amyntas, 540; of Alexander I. . B.C. 500
Macedon conquered by the Persians, 513; delivered by the victory of Platæa 479
Reign of Perdiccas II. 454
Potidæa, revolting, 433; re-taken by the Athenians 429
Archelaus, natural son of Perdiccas, murders the legitimate heirs; seizes the throne, and improves the country, 413; murdered by a favourite, to whom he promised his daughter in marriage . 399
Pausanias reigns 394
Reign of Amyntas II., after killing Pausanias . 393
The Illyrians enter Macedonia, expel Amyntas, and make Argæus, brother of Pausanias, king . . 392
Amyntas again recovers his kingdom . . . 390
Reign of Alexander II., 369; assassinated . . 367
Reign of Perdiccas III., 364; killed in battle . . 360
Reign of Philip II., and institution of the Macedonian phalanx 359
He defeats the Athenians and Illyrians . . 360, ,,
He takes Amphipolis 358
He conquers Thrace, Illyria, and Thessaly . 356-352
Birth of Alexander III. the Great 356
Close of the first sacred war 346
Illyricum overrun by the army of Philip . . . 344
Thrace made tributary to Macedon 343
Aristotle appointed tutor to Alexander . . . . ,,
War against the Athenians 341
Philip besieged Byzantium unsuccessfully . . 340
Battle of Chæronea; Philip victor . . . 338
Philip is assassinated by Pausanias at Ægæ during the celebration of games in honour of his daughter's nuptials; Alexander III., the Great, succeeds 336
The Greeks appoint him general of their armies against the Persians 335
The Thebans revolt; he levels Thebes to the ground; the house of Pindar alone left . . ,,
He passes into Asia, and gains his first battle over Darius at the Granicus . . . . 22 May, 334
Sardis surrenders, Halicarnassus taken, and cities in Asia Minor . . . . ,,
Memnon ravages the Cyclades; Darius takes the field with 460,000 infantry, and 100,000 cavalry 333
Darius defeated at Issus (*which see*) . . Nov. ,,
Alexander on his way to Egypt, lays siege to Tyre, which is destroyed after seven months . . 332

Damascus is taken; Gaza surrenders 332
Alexander enters Jerusalem; Egypt conquered; Alexandria founded ,,
The Persians totally defeated at Arbela 1 Oct. 331
Alexander master of Asia; enters Babylon ,,
Sits on the throne of Darius at Susa 330
Parthia, Media, &c., overrun by him B.C. 329
Thalestris, queen of the Amazons, visits him ,,
He puts his friend Parmenio to death, on a charge of conspiracy supposed to be false ,,
His expedition to India; Porus, king of India, is defeated and taken; and the country as far as the Ganges, is overrun 327
Callisthenes is put to the torture for refusing to render divine homage to Alexander 328
Voyage of his admiral Nearchus from the Indus to the Euphrates 328-325
Returns to Babylon, 324; dies 323
Philip III. (Aridæus) king 323
Alexander's conquests are divided among his generals, 323; his remains are transported to Alexandria, and buried by Ptolemy 322
The Greeks defeated by Antipater and the Macedonians, near Cranon (*which see*) ,,
Cassander reigns, 316; rebuilds Thebes 315
Seleucus recovers Babylon 312
Cassander kills Roxana and her son (the last of Alexander's family), and usurps the throne 311
Battle of Ipsus (*which see*); Antigonus killed 301
New division of the empire ,,
Death of Cassander 298
Reign of Alexander V. and Antipater, his sons ,,
Demetrius I., Poliorcetes, son of Antigonus, murders Alexander, and seizes the crown of Macedon 294
Achæan league formed against Macedon 281-243
Governments of Pyrrhus, 287; Lysimachus, 286; Ptolemy Ceraunus 281
Irruption of the Gauls; Ptolemy killed 279
Sosthenes governs 278
Reign of Antigonus Gonatas, son of Demetrius 277
Pyrrhus invades Macedon, defeats Antigonus, and is proclaimed king 273
Pyrrhus slain; Antigonus restored 278
Antigonus takes Athens 262
The Gauls again invade Macedon ,,
Revolt of the Parthians 250
Reign of Demetrius II. 239
Philip, his son, 232; set aside by Antigonus Doson 229
Philip V., 220; allies with Hannibal, 211; wars unsuccessfully against the Rhodians 202
Philip defeated by the Romans at Cynoscephalæ 197
Reign of Perseus, his son, 178; war with Rome 171
Perseus defeated at Pydna; Macedon made a Roman province 168
Perseus and his sons walk in chains before the chariot of Æmilius in his triumph for the conquest of Macedon 167
Insurrection of Andriscus, calling himself Philip, son of Perseus, quelled 148
Macedonia plundered by Theodoric the Ostrogoth A.D. 482
Conquered by the Bulgarians 978
Recovered by the emperor Basil 1001
Formed into the Latin kingdom of Thessalonica, by Boniface, of Montferrat 1204
After various changes, conquered by Amurath II., and annexed to Turkey 1430
A Macedonian Society formed to urge the execution of the Treaty of Berlin (1878) was active in 1885-95.
Macedonian congress at Sofia; petitions to prince Ferdinand and the czar April, 1895
The country greatly disturbed; conflicts between the people and the Turkish troops, reported, 23 June; many arrests June–Aug. ,,
The village of Dospat attacked and destroyed by a band of Macedonians, Aug. 1895. See *Times*, 7, 15 Jan. 1896
The Macedonian committee met at Sofia, demanding reforms from Turkey 21 June, ,,
Conflicts between Turks and Greeks, reported July, Aug. ,,
A Turkish consul assassinated by Albanians in Vrania; a band of insurgents routed by Turks, reported 24 Aug. ,,
Greek bands dispersed; further conflicts, 4–29 Sept. ,,
Tranquillity reported 2 Nov. ,,
Takis, Macedonian chief, captures Krania, a strong Turkish position 6 March, 1897
Frequent conflicts between Servians and Bulgarians Oct. ,,
Search for arms; torture and atrocities on Bulgarians in Uskub, Kossovo and elsewhere by Turkish officials Feb. 1898
Commission of inquiry sent by the porte; 127 Bulgarians released at Uskub, and 151 at Isteb, Feb. March; 6 Bulgarians sentenced to life imprisonment 27 March, ,,
Agitation for autonomy and reforms, and art. 23 of the Berlin treaty to be kept, by the Macedonian committee Dec. ,,
Military posts strengthened, but reforms evaded, Dec. ,,
Macedonian mainfesto issued 21 Jan. 1899
Agitation continues in Bulgaria and Roumania (*which see*); 700 political murders during 1900, reported 24 Jan. 1901
Repressive measures, many arrests, conflicts with Turkish troops, reported 17 Feb. ,,
Daily arrests of persons accused of complicity in the designs of the Macedonian committee; 7 Bulgarians sentenced to death, others imprisoned or banished 12, 13 May, ,,
Further disturbances, conflicts with troops, reported 29 March, 1902
Bulgarian outrages suppressed by Turkish troops, April; another fight at Patili early June, ,,
Mgr. Firmillian consecrated Servian bishop of Uskub 28 June, ,,
Commission of inquiry as to the disturbed districts recommends certain administrative reforms and reorganisation of gendarmerie 24 July, ,,
Macedonian congress at Sofia, 10 Aug.; open-air meeting against the government policy, 11 Sept. ,,
Bulgarian rising in Monastir and Salonika; severe fight at Vodena, 52 killed, 23 Sept.; reserves called out 29 Sept. ,,
150 Greeks murdered by Bulgarians, Aug.–Sep., reported. 30 Sept. ,,
Conflicts reported 11, 15, 18, 20 Oct. ,,
Zontcheff's band defeated near Nevrokop, reported, 25 Oct.; again at Fakire Tepe 1, 2 Nov. ,,
Fatal skirmishes on the frontier, Turkish barbarities, reported, 10–17 Nov.; again Dec. ,,
Turkish scheme of reforms published, 3 Dec.; reported unsatisfactory 8 Dec. ,,
Count Lamsdorff, Russian foreign minister, negotiates at Belgrade, Sofia, and Vienna, on the Balkan difficulties 24 Dec. ,,
Encounter between strong band of Macedonians and Turkish troops near lake Okhrida, the former defeated, reported early Feb. 1903
Bulgarian bands causing trouble in the Monastir district mid Feb. ,,
Austro-Russian programme of reforms presented to the other great powers 17 Feb. ,,
Austro-Russian programme, consented to by the great powers, includes the appointment of an inspector-general with extended powers, the organisation of the gendarmerie by European officers, an amnesty for political offences, and financial reforms, presented to the porte, 21 Feb. ,,
Blue book on the Macedonian question, 1900—Jan. 1903, issued 23 Feb. ,,
Fighting between Turkish troops and revolutionary bands at Brondo and in the district of Malesh, and other places, reported 28 Feb. ,,
Further fighting near lake Presba 3 March, ,,
2,000 Redifs and large supplies of ammunition sent from Asia to Monastir 7–8 March, ,,
Increasing disquiet and conflicts in the Malesh district between Turks and revolutionary bands; revolt in N. Albania against the reform scheme, and conflict with Turkish troops; attack on M. Stcherbina, the Russian consul at Mitrovitza, who is mortally wounded 31 March (died 10 April): the sultan tenders his regret to Russian ambassador at Constantinople 1 April ,,
Fight in the Istib district, alleged barbarities of the Turks; massacre of Christians by Albanians at Okrida 5 April, ,,
Conflict at Saparevo, Melnik district; capt. Saieff, a brave and prominent leader of the insurgents, killed o April, ,,

Engagement between Turkish troops and Bulgarians near Radovitch . . . 19 April, 1903
Further conflicts between Turks and insurgents, reported . . . . 22 April, „
Bomb explosion at Salonika by Bulgarian agitators; Ottoman bank destroyed, many lives lost, 28 April, „
Severe conflict between troops and Bulgarian bands, between Velet and Gradsko . 30 April, „
Turkish troops mobilized in Macedonia, 156 battalions, each of 700 men, 37 squadrons of cavalry, and 78 batteries . . early May, „
Attack of the Turkish populace upon Bulgarians at Monastir; many Bulgarians killed; persecution of Bulgarians in Macedonia, 6 May; panic, Turkish excesses reported . . 11, 12 May, „
More or less disquiet and conflicts between Turkish troops and insurrectionary party mid May-June, „
Turks occupy strategic positions in the Kossovo, Monastir, and Adrianople districts; protest of Bulgaria to the great powers about . 1 July, „
The Austrian, Russian, and British consuls report terrible outrages in the vilayet of Uskub by the Turks upon Bulgarians of both sexes; 3,043 Bulgarian peasants, men, women, and children, up to 23 June had taken refuge in Bulgaria; the Redif regiment replaced in consequence of its excesses, mid July, „
Famous Bulgarian brigand Alexis and others killed in conflict with Turkish troops near Petrich . . . . 10 July, „
Revolution proclaimed in the vilayet of Monastir in conformity with the decision of the central revolutionary committee, reported . 2 Aug. „
Dynamite outrages by insurgents on the railway between Salonika and Monastir . . 3 Aug. „
General rising in Macedonia, spread of the insurrection to the vilayet of Adrianople; murder of M. Rostkowsky, Russian consul at Monastir, by Turkish gendarme Halim . . . mid Aug. „
Port of Vasiliko on coast of the Black sea captured by insurgents; principal government buildings blown up with dynamite; fearful atrocities stated to be perpetrated by Turkish troops in vilayet of Monastir, reported . 12 Aug. *et seq.* „
Krustevo captured by the Turkish troops, reported, 15 Aug. „
Severe fighting reported near Monastir . 18 Aug. „
Spread of the rising in vilayet of Adrianople, train between Adrianople and Constantinople blown up, six persons killed, 15 injured . . . 28 Aug. „
Strained relations between Bulgaria and Turkey; European correspondents ordered by the porte to leave Macedonia; shocking reports of outrages by Turks and Albanians, reported 31 Aug. *et seq.* „
Frightful cruelties perpetrated on inhabitants of Smilievo, Armensko, Krustevo, and other places, reported . . . . . early Sept. „
Severe fight near Couklite, Perim district 17 Sept.; also at Batchevo and Mehonia; Turks commit many atrocities; fight at Kotchani, 18 Sept. and 23 Sept. „
Consular reports describe the devastation in the Adrianople vilayet, "too terrible for words," about 24 Sept. „
Identical note sent by Austria and Russia to Bulgaria and Turkey, stating their intention to institute a "more efficacious mode of control" in connection with the Macedonian reforms, 5 Oct. „

See *Turkey* and *Addenda*.

MACEDONIANS, a semi-Arian sect, followers of Macedonius, made bishop of Constantinople about 341. His appointment was greatly opposed and led to much bloodshed. He was expelled by the decree of a council held 360.

MACHIAVELLIAN PRINCIPLES, those of Nicolo Machiavelli of Florence (born 1469, died 1527), in his "Practice of Politics" and "The Prince." By some they are styled "the most pernicious maxims of government, founded on the vilest policy;" by others as "sound doctrines, notwithstanding the prejudice erroneously raised against them." The author said that if he taught princes to be tyrants, he also taught the people to destroy tyrants. "The Prince" appeared at Rome in 1532, and was translated into English in 1761.

MACIEJOVICE (near Warsaw, Poland). Here the Poles were totally defeated by the Russians, and their general, Kosciusko, taken prisoner, 10 Oct. 1794, after a murderous action. He strenuously endeavoured to prevent the junction of the Russian and Austrian armies. The statement that he said "Finis Poloniæ!" is contradicted.

MACKENZIE BASIN, see *Canada*, 1888.

MADAGASCAR (S. E. coast of Africa), a large island (capital, Antananarivo), said to have been discovered by Lorenzo Almeida, 1506. The people are called Hovas. Population, about 6,000,000 (1900).

Portuguese settlement, 1548; destroyed by the French one, 1642, on arrival of a French governor 1669
The French attempted to settle at Antongel-bay in 1774
Count Benyowski supreme in the island, Oct. 1775 killed in an encounter with the French 23 May, 1786
Their establishment at Fort Dauphin fell into the hands of the English with Bourbon and Mauritius in 1810-11
The settlements ceded to king Radàma, on his giving up the slave trade 1818
Radàma I. king 1810, who favoured Europeans and encouraged Christianity, died 1828
A reactionary policy under his energetic queen Rànavàlona, 1828. The English missionaries who came in 1820 obliged to depart 1835
The application of the native laws to the European settlers occasioned an unsuccessful attack on the town of Tamatave, by a united expedition from the English at the Mauritius, and the French from the isle of Bourbon . . . . June, 1845
All amicable intercourse ceases, the native Christians suffer persecution . . . . . 1846 *et seq.*
The French defeated in an attack on the island, 19 Oct. 1855
Conspiracy against the queen frustrated . June, 1857
The rev. W. Ellis published accounts of his three visits to the island, on behalf of the London Missionary Society, in 1854-5-6. 1858
The queen dies; succeeded by her son Radàma II., a Christian . . . . . . 23 Aug. 1861
Treaty with Great Britain and France signed, 12 Sept. 1862
A revolution; the king and his ministers assassinated; the queen Rasohérina proclaimed sovereign, May, 1863
Embassy from Madagascar arrives at Southampton, Feb. 1864
Disputes with the French . . . . Nov. „
Treaty with Great Britain; Christians to be tolerated, &c., 27 June, 1865; ratified . . 5 July, 1866
Rev. Wm. Ellis's "Madagascar Revisited," published . . . . 1 Feb. 1867
The queen died in March; her cousin, Rànavàlona II., succeeded as queen, 1 April, 1868; baptized, Feb 1869
Dr. Henry Rowley was consecrated bishop of Madagascar, Dec. 1872; Dr. R. Kestell-Cornish 1874
African slavery prohibited, 1873; solemnly June, 1877
Disputes with the French begin respecting land given to Laborde, a missionary, reclaimed by the Hovas; aggressive insolent conduct of French consuls, Cassas, Meyer, and Baudais . 1879 *et seq.*
The French claim protectorate of part of N.W. Madagascar, by virtue of a treaty made with rebel chiefs, 1840-1; on appeal the British government correspond with the French ministry July, Aug. 1882
Native embassy to France objecting to French protectorate, &c. . . . . . . Oct. „
The French government unyielding Nov.; the envoys come to London; received by earl Granville, 2 Dec., by the queen . . 12 Dec. „
Friendly modification of the treaty of 1868 with England . . . . Feb. 1883
Arrival of French war vessels in Madagascar 23 Feb. „
Treaty with the United States ratified about 14 March, „
H.M.S. *Dryad* at Tamatave . . . . 14 April, „

Treaty with Germany . . . . . . 15 May, 1883
Admiral Pierre bombards and seizes the custom-house at Majunga 24 May; Adm. Pierre bombards Tamatave, unresisting 11 June, captures it, 13 June, „
French ultimatum, offered and rejected, announced 13 June, „
The queen Rànavàlona II. dies about 13 July; succeeded by her niece Rànavàlona III. July, „
Tenoarivo destroyed; state of siege at Tamatave; adm. Pierre orders the British consul, T. C. Pakenham (ill) to quit within 24 hours, who dies, 22 June. Mr. Shaw, missionary, arrested; capt. Johnson of the *Dryad* insulted; the British government demands explanations 12 July, satisfaction ordered to be given . . . . . Aug. „
Adm. Pierre reports repulse of two night-attacks on . . . . . . 22 June and 5 July, „
Release of Mr. Shaw about . . . . . 7 Aug. „
Adm. Pierre dies . . . . . . 10 Sept. „
The Hovas retake French posts, except Majunga, announced . . . . . . 6 Sept. „
Mr. Shaw at Exeter Hall, describes his arrest, false charges against him, cruel usage and abrupt release . . . . 27 Sept. „
Great mortality among French troops . . Sept. „
1000*l.* awarded to Mr. Shaw, and apology made to the British government by the French, announced about 29 Oct. „
Much British property destroyed . . . . Nov. „
French demand raised, by M. Baudais . . Jan. 1884
The French chambers vote to support French honour in Madagascar (450—32) . . 27 March, „
French attack on the Hova camp repulsed 27 June, „
Two blue-books published by the Hova government giving the history of the disputes with the French, 1879-84 . . . . . . Aug. „
Desultory warfare and negotiations reported, French settlements in progress at Majunga, &c.; the Hovas prepare for war . . . . Aug. „
The French bombard Mahanoro . . . . 22 Sep. „
Mr. T. Wilkinson, missionary and trader, expelled from Antananarivo for newspaper correspondence Nov. „
The Hovas severely defeated . . . 2 Dec. „
The French take forts after sharp conflict 6-11 Dec. „
Seven French ships of war at Tamatave, the Hovas retreating inland . . . . . . Jan. 1885
French chambers vote for maintaining of *status quo*, July-Aug. „
Unsuccessful French attack on the Malagasy position near Tamatave . . . . 10 Sept. „
Another conflict (undecisive) announced 28 Sept. „
Negotiations for peace fail; French protectorate rejected . . . . . . 13 June–17 Aug. „
Treaty signed conceding partial French control on foreign affairs; 400,000*l.* as compensation for local injuries &c., by the agency of adm. Miot. 20 Dec. 1885; ratified by French senate 13 March, „
M. le Myre de Vilers, first French resident April, „
Tamatave evacuated by the French, re-occupied by the natives . . . . 25 Jan. 1887
Prosperity of the island reported . . . Oct. 1889
French protectorate recognised by Great Britain 5 Aug. 1890
Massacre of about 200 complaining natives, by the governor of Belanona, reported . . 9 Jan. 1891
The governor and his brother tried and executed, reported . . . . 24 March, „
Dr. Catat, at Paris, reports the results of an exploring scientific expedition in Madagascar sent out in 1888, by the government 23 March, „
Insurrection in the Comoro Islands (near Madagascar), ruled by Arab chiefs under French protection; massacres and exactions. Prince Salim refuses to negotiate with Dr. Ormières, the French resident, reported . . . . 28 March, „
The residents take refuge in the ships; slaves hold the town in Johanna Island, reported 3 April, „
Murder of Dr. Beziat, chief of the French medical staff, reported . . . . . . 30 Oct. „
M. Georges Muller, French explorer, shot by brigands near Mandritsara . . . . Aug. 1893
Conflicts between the French and the Hovas, reported . . . . 24 Dec. „
A cyclone at Diego Suarez; great destruction of property . . . . Feb. 5, 1894
Exploring expedition of prince Henri d'Orleans and M. de Grandmaison . . . July, Aug. „
Partial blockade of the ports by the French, reported . . . . 3 Oct. 1894
Arrival of M. le Myre de Vilers at Tamatave, 2 Nov.; his ultimatum rejected by the Hova government, reported 5 Nov.; diplomatic rupture 10 Nov.; Tamatave deserted by the Hovas, 14 Nov. „
The queen's manifesto exhorting to resistance, 28 Nov. „
Tamative occupied by the French . . . 10 Dec. „
The queen accepts the conditions of the French, 10 Dec. „
Defeat of the Hovas at Farafatra . . . 28 Dec. „
Murder of Mr. Sornay, a British subject, reported, 25 Dec. „
Majunga bombarded and occupied by the French, 16 Jan. 1895
M. le Myre de Vilers, dissatisfied with the queen's concessions, leaves, 27 Dec. 1894; arrives at Marseilles . . . . 20 Jan. „
Nossi-Vey, island, S.W. coast, taken by the French, 14 Feb. „
Mr. Waller, formerly U.S. consul at Tamatave, imprisoned by French for aiding the Hovas; U.S. government protests; he arrives at Marseilles, 20 April (released 19 March, 1896) . . „
The French occupy Ambommarine after severe fighting, reported . . . . . . 21 April, „
Gen. Metzinger storms Miadane, the Hovas fled, 3 April, „
Murder of M. Grève, naturalist, by the Hovas, reported . . . . 25 April, „
Marovoay stormed by gen. Metzinger; much slaughter; flight of the Hovas . . . 2 May, „
Gen. Duchesne, commander-in-chief, arrives at Majunga . . . . 6 May, „
Defeat of the Hovas; successful advance of the French, reported . . . . 19 May, *et seq.*
Great mortality amongst the French from fever, reported . . . . 21 May, „
Withdrawal of Col. Shervinton and English officers from Madagascar . . . . . . May, „
Repulse of the French advance, reported 15 May, „
Mevatanana occupied without resistance 12 July, „
Bridge over the Betsiboka completed; 300 ft. long, 22 July, „
Capture of Andriba by gen. Duchesne, 22 Aug.; slow advance of the French; the Hova government apparently incapable of preparing for defence or surrender; many French soldiers invalided and dying . . . . . Aug.–Sept. „
The Hovas defeated with great loss at Tsinainondry, by gen. Duchesne . . . . . . 15 Sept. „
Antananarivo, the capital, bombarded and captured by gen. Duchesne; flight of the queen and court, 30 Sept.; treaty of peace ratified by the queen, 1 Oct.; she accepts the French protectorate, and is reinstated; the prime minister arrested, 4 Oct.; gen. Metzinger appointed governor . . . . 10 Oct. „
Hova works at Farafatra captured . . 10 Oct. „
The queen holds an assembly, announcing the peace . . . . 6 Nov. „
Mr. and Mrs. Johnson and child murdered at a mission at Arivonimamo . . . . 22 Nov. „
Rebels defeated with much loss . . . 23 Nov. „
Estimated French loss during the campaign by disease, 3,500 . . . . Nov. „
M. Laroche appointed resident-general . . 1 Dec. „
Tribal risings against the Hovas . . . Jan. 1896
Skirmishes with the French . . . . April, „
Several pioneer explorers murdered by brigands, May, „
Antsirabo burnt by rebels, 3 days' siege of the Norwegian mission raised by M. Allez, rebel loss 200 . . . . about 4 June, „
Murders, looting, and burning of villages, etc., Aug., Sept. „
Scientific expedition under Dr. Forsyth-Major lands at Mananzara in 1894; returns with collections, Sept. „
M. Laroche recalled; gen. Gallieni appointed governor-gen. and commander-in-chief, arrives, 28 Sept. „
Prince Ratsimananga (the queen's uncle) and the ex-governor of Tamatave, tried and executed for rebellion at Antananarivo . . . 30 Oct. „

Insurrection over, improved conditions . Jan. 1897
The queen leaves for Réunion . . . 7 March, ,,
Two French protestant missionaries massacred in Ankaratra . . . abt. 10 June, ,,
Skirmish on the Tsiribihina, 3 officers and others killed . . . . Oct. ,,
Siege raised at Imerina and Betsiloe . mid Jan. 1898
Natives repulsed with loss by the French at Ambiky . . . . 22 Feb. ,,
Lord Salisbury protests against the abolition of the rights of British commerce, 9 July, 1898. (*Times*, 7 Jan. 1899.)
Mutiny of soldiers, Andjia plundered; they are disarmed and sent back to Diego Suares, Nov. ,,
Concessions demanded by Mr. Waller (see *above*), Feb. 1895; refused by the French . . Nov. ,,
Outbreak of plague at Tamatave, 108 deaths, Dec. 1898; decreasing . . . Jan. 1899
Rising at Ikongo, rebel position captured, 24, 25 June, 1899
Successful operations against rebels in the south, Oct.–mid Nov. 1901
The ex-queen allowed to visit St. Malo . Aug. 1902
Good financial report, trade progressing, 1900–Sept. ,,

MADDER, the root of the *Rubia tinctoria*, highly valued for dyeing properties. See *Alizarine*.

MADEIRA, an island, N. W. coast of Africa, discovered, it is said, in 1344, by Mr. Macham, an English gentleman, or mariner, who fled from France for an illicit amour. He was driven here by a storm, and his mistress, a French lady, dying, he made a canoe, and carried the news of his discovery to Pedro, king of Aragon, which occasioned the report that the island was discovered by a Portuguese, 1345. It is asserted that the Portuguese did not visit this island until 1419 or 1420, or colonise it until 1431. It was taken by the British in July, 1801; and again by admiral Hood and general Beresford, 24 Dec. 1807, and retained in trust for the royal family of Portugal, who had emigrated to the Brazils. It was restored to the Portuguese in 1814. Since 1852 the renowned vintages here have been almost totally ruined by the vine disease (oïdium). Population, 1882, 133,955; 1900, 150,528.

Opposition of the peasantry to new taxation; fighting with bloodshed announced . 16 Jan. 1888

MADIAI PERSECUTION, see *Tuscany*.

MADRAS (S. E. Hindostan), called by the natives Chennapatam, colonised by the English, 1640. Population of the province, 1881, 30,812,745; 1891, 35,588,850; 1901, 38,208,609; of the city, 1881, 405,848; 1891, 449,950; 1901, 509,397.

Fort St. George built, 1641; made a presidency . 1653
Bengal placed under Madras 1658
Calcutta, hitherto subordinate to Madras, made a presidency 1701
Madras taken by the French . 14 Sept. 1746
Restored to the English 1749
Vainly besieged by the French under Lally, 12 Dec. 1758
Hyder marches to Madras and obtains a favourable treaty . . . . April, 1769
Sir John Lindsay arrives . . . . July, 1770
He is succeeded by sir R. Hartland . . Sept. 1771
Lord Pigot, governor, imprisoned by his own council, 24 Aug. 1776; dies in confinement, 17 April, 1777; his enemies convicted and fined 1000*l.* each, 11 Feb. 1780
Sir Eyre Coote arrives . . . . . 5 Nov. ,,
He defeats Hyder . . . . . . 1 July, 1781
Lord Macartney arrives as governor . . 22 June, ,,
The Madras government arrest gen. Stuart for disobedience, and send him to England. . June, 1783
Lord Cornwallis arrives here . . . 12 Dec. 1790
Sir C. Oakley succeeds gen. Wm. Meadows as governor . . . . 1 Aug. 1792
Madras system of education introduced (see *Monitorial*). 1795
Lord Mornington (afterwards the marquis Wellesley) visits here . . . . Dec. 1798
General Harris with the Madras army enters Mysore, 5 March; and arrives at Seringapatam, 5 April, which is stormed by the British under major-general Baird, and Tippoo Sahib killed . 4 May, 1799
Appointment of sir Thomas Strange, first judge of Madras under the charter . . . 26 Dec. 1800
More than 1000 houses in Madras burnt . . Feb. 1803
The Madras army under general Arthur Wellesley (afterwards duke of Wellington) marches for Poonah (see *India*) . . . . . March, ,,
Mutiny among the native forces at Vellore; 600 sepoys killed; 200 executed. . . 10 July, 1806
Mutiny of the sepoy troops at Madras. . . . 1809
Arrival of lord Minto at Madras, who publishes a general amnesty . . . . . 29 Sept. ,,
Awful hurricane, by which the ships at anchor were driven into the town and seventy sail sunk, many with their crews . . . . . May, 1811
Madras attacked by the Pindarees . . . 1817
Appointment of the rev. Dr. Corrie, first bishop of Madras . . . . 14 Feb. 1835
Sir Charles Trevelyan, governor, Jan. 1859; recalled for publishing a minute in opposition to Mr. Jas. Wilson's financial schemes . . . 10 May, 1860
[Appointed financial secretary and a member of the Indian council at Calcutta, Oct. 1862.]
His successor, sir H. Ward, dies at Madras, 2 Aug. ,,
Sir Wm. Dennison appointed governor, Nov. 1860; arrives . . . . 18 Feb. 1861
Lord Napier appointed governor . . 31 Jan. 1866
Arrival of the duke of Edinburgh . . 22 March, 1870
Lord Hobart appointed governor, Feb. 1872; died, 27 April; the duke of Buckingham appointed, May, 1875
Visit of the prince of Wales . . . 13 Dec. ,,
The Rt. Hon. W. P. Adam appointed governor, Aug. 1880; died 24 May; the Rt. Hon. M. E. Grant Duff appointed governor . . June, 1881
He reports "a deep peace broods over the land," natives advancing in civilization . . Jan. 1884
The right hon. Robert Bourke (created lord Connemara) appointed governor . . . Aug. 1886
Great accidental fire began in booths at a fair in the people's park; great panic, about 405 persons said to have perished . . 31 Dec. ,,
25 persons killed by an explosion of gunpowder at a village festival . . . . . 14 Oct. 1888
A severe famine in Ganjam, the last crops having failed through deficiency of rain; high prices and much destitution; about 15,000 persons employed on relief works; deaths from cholera; about 1,400 weekly middle of May *et seq.* 1889.
Lord Connemara visits the district . June, 1889
Government relief aided by native princes; 9,429 persons employed on public works; 865 deaths from cholera in one week; reported . 18 June ,,
Lord Connemara reports improvement in the condition of Ganjam; employed on works, 15,425; deaths from cholera in a week, 602; reported 9 July, ,,
Lord Connemara resigns, much regretted . Nov. 1890
Beilby Lawley, lord Wenlock, appointed governor about 1 Dec. 1890; arrives . . . 19 Jan. 1891
A famine commissioner appointed . 19 Jan. 1892
Tour of lord Wenlock . . . April, May, ,,
Heavy rains, improved prospects . May, June, July, ,,
Employed on relief works, 15,728, Sept. 1889; 19,655, 10 Nov. 1891; 29,319, 16 Feb. 1892; 64,000, 5 May; 53,000, 22 July; under 9,000 . 3 Sept., ,,
Works stopped, reported . . . . 22 Sept. ,,
Great East Coast railway bridge at Bezwada, over the Kistna, opened by lord Wenlock. 17 March, 1893
Death of lieut.-gen. sir James Dormer, commander-in-chief, from wounds by a tiger . . 3 May, ,,
Madras and Bombay armies act passed . 5 Dec. ,,
The great Periyar Irrigation works executed by col. John Pennycuick, 1887–95 (the course of the river diverted from west to east, a great dam, tunnel and reservoir constructed, eastern drought supplied from western floods, cost about 500,000*l.*), opened by lord Wenlock . . 12 Oct. 1895
Rising of the Moplah fanatics, who are defeated in a conflict by capts. Cosens and Chad, 1 March, 1896

Riot at Negapatam through the lock-out by the railway company of 3,000 workmen; mob fired on by the police, 2 rioters killed, reported 24 Oct. 1896
Lord Ampthill appointed governor . . Sept. 1900
Statue of the king-emperor unveiled . 8 April, 1903

[For other events, see *India*.]

MADRID (New Castile), mentioned in history as Majerit, a Moorish castle. Population in 1887, 470,283; 1897, 512,150.

Sacked by the Moors 1190
Fortified by Henry III. about 1400
Humiliating treaty of Madrid between Charles V. and Francis I., his prisoner . . . 14 Jan. 1526
Made the seat of the Spanish court by Philip II. . 1560
The Escurial built . . . . . . 1563 *et seq.*
Taken by lord Galway . . . . . 24 June, 1706
The old palace burnt down 1734
Madrid taken by the French . . . . March, 1808
The citizens attempt to expel the French; defeated with much slaughter . . . . . 2 May, ,,
Joseph Bonaparte enters Madrid as king of Spain (but soon retires) . . . . . 20 July, ,,
Madrid retaken by the French . . . . 2 Dec. ,,
Retained till it is entered by Wellington . 12 Aug. 1812
Ferdinand VII. restored . . . . . 14 May, 1814
Madrid pronounces for provisional government against Isabella II. . . . . 29 Sept. 1868
English protestant church authorised . 9 Nov. ,,
Madrid (with Alcala de Henares) made a bishopric early in 1885
The bishop Martinez Izquierdo shot on the steps of the pro-cathedral by Cayetano Galeote, a priest suspended by him, 18 April; dies . 19 April, 1886
Destructive hurricane, about 32 persons killed and about 320 wounded, 12 May; sufferers visited by the queen . . . . 13 May, ,,
Grand Columbus celebration; historical exhibition opened . . . . . . 30 Oct. *et seq.* 1892
Much damage caused by the explosion of an aerolite, see *Meteorites*. . . . . 10 Feb. 1896
5 bombs exploded near the royal palace, no injury, several arrests . . . . . 19 Feb. ,,
A statue of Velasquez unveiled by the queen-regent . . . . . . mid June, 1899
The king lays the first stone of a free school, 13 May, 1902
Fêtes on the king's accession (see *Spain*), 17–21 May, ,,
First sod of a new railway direct to Bilbao turned, 20 Oct. ,,

See *Spain*, 1892–4.
Population, in 1857, 271,254; in 1870, 332,024; 1884, 391,829; 1897, 513,000 (including suburbs).

See *Spain*, 1840 *et seq.*

MADRIGAL, an unaccompanied song for three or more voices, of which fine examples are by English composers. Madrigals, invented in the Netherlands, were adopted in Italy, where fine specimens were produced. Many were published by Morley, 1594; Weelkes, 1597; Wilbye, 1598; and Bennet, 1599. The Madrigal Society in London began in 1741. English Glee and Madrigal Union founded in 1851. Rimbault's "Bibliotheca Madrigalium" published 1847. The madrigal, "Summer is i cumen in" is attributed to the 13th or 14th century.

MAESTRICHT (Holland), the ancient *Trajectum ad Mosam*, the capital of Limburg. It revolted from Spain, and was taken by the prince of Parma in 1579, when a dreadful massacre took place. In 1632, the prince of Orange reduced it after a memorable siege, and it was confirmed to the Dutch in 1648; Louis XIV. took it in 1673; William, prince of Orange, invested it in vain in 1676; but in 1678 it was restored to the Dutch. In 1748 it was besieged by the French, who were permitted to take possession of the city on condition of its being restored at the peace then negotiating. In Feb. 1793, Maestricht was unsuccessfully attacked by the French, but they became masters of it, Nov. 1794. In 1814 it was made part of the kingdom of the Netherlands, and now belongs to Holland. Population, 1891, 32,225; 1900, 34,182.

MAFIA, a secret terrorist murderous society in Sicily, comprising all classes; became prominent in 1860. It is opposed to the Camorra. Efforts for the suppression of both were made by the government in 1874-5. Murder trials (see *Italy*), Oct. 1901–July, 1902. See *New Orleans*, 1890–95.

MAFEKING, Siege of. See *S. African War*, 15, 16 Oct. 1899–17, 18 May, 1900. Maj.-gen. Baden-Powell (who with the little garrison and townspeople bravely held out against great odds) presented with a casket, by the mayor, 16 Sept. 1902.

MAGAZINE, at first a miscellaneous periodical publication. There are now magazines devoted to nearly every department of knowledge. The following are the dates of the first publication of the principal magazines, some of which are extinct. Jan. 1865, 544 magazines; Jan. 1872, 639; Jan. 1889 (including reviews), 1,593; Jan. 1892, 1,901; Feb. 1901, 2,446; 1902, 2,486; 1903, 2,531 were in course of publication in Great Britain and Ireland; see *Reviews* and *Newspapers*.

Gentleman's	1731
London	1732
Scots	1739
Royal	1759
Court	1760
Gospel	1768
Lady's	1772
European	1782
Methodist	1784
Evangelical	1792
Monthly	1796
Philosophical	1798
Blackwood's	1817
New Monthly	1814
Fraser's	1830
Metropolitan	1831
Penny	1832
Tait's	1833
Cassell's Family	1853
Cornhill	1859
Macmillan's	,,
Good Words	1860
Temple Bar	1861
Quiver	1861
St. Paul's	1868
Nineteenth Century	1877
Magazine of Art	1878
Antiquary	1880
Century	1880
Harper's	1881
Longman's	1882
Merry England	1883
English Illustrated	,,
Murray's	1887
Scribner's	1887
Strand	1891
Geographical Journal	1893
Pall Mall 1 May,	,,
Illustrated Archæologist June,	,,
The Minster (illustd.)	1894
Windsor	1895
The Englishwoman (illustrated)	,,
Badminton (illus.) Aug.	,,
Savoy (illustd. quarterly), Dec. (1895) Nov.	1896
Lady's Realm	,,
Pearson's	,,
Cosmopolis (international review, Jan.	,,
Architecture (illustd.)	,,
Royal	1898
The Wide World Mar.	,,
The Windmill (illustd. quarterly) Oct.	,,
London Magazine	,,
The International Monthly Jan.	1900
Smart Set	1901
The Tiger (monthly), March,	1902
Animal Life (monthly), July,	,,
Page's (monthly), June,	,,
Hibbert Journal, Oct.	,,

MAGAZINE RIFLES, see under *Firearms*.

MAGDALA, a very strong place in Abyssinia (*which see*). On Good Friday, 10 April, 1868, the troops of the emperor Theodore attacked the first brigade of the British army under sir Robert Napier, and were repulsed with great slaughter. On the next day all the European prisoners were given up, but Theodore himself refused to surrender; and on Easter Monday, 13 April, Magdala was stormed, and Theodore himself killed—it is said by his own hand.—British loss, 2 killed; 20 wounded: Abyssinian loss, about 500 killed and wounded out of about 5000. Magdala was burnt to the ground by the British, 17 April, 1868.

MAGDALENS AND MAGDALENETTES, communities of nuns, consisting chiefly of penitent courtesans. The order of penitents of St. Magdalen was founded 1272, at Marseilles. The convent of Naples was endowed by queen Sancha, 1324. That at Metz was instituted in 1452. At Paris, 1492. The Magdalen at Rome was endowed by pope Leo X., in 1515, and favoured by Clement VIII. in 1594. The Magdalen hospital, London, was founded in 1758, under the direction of Dr. Dodd. The asylum in Dublin was opened in June, 1766.

MAGDEBURG (Prussia). The archbishopric was founded about 967. The city suffered much during the religious wars in Germany. It was besieged and taken by the elector Maurice, Nov. 1550, and Nov. 1551; blockaded for seven months by the imperialists, under Wallenstein, in 1629; and barbarously sacked by Tilly on 10 May, 1631. It was given to Brandenburg in 1648; was taken by the French, 8 Nov. 1806; annexed to the kingdom of Westphalia, 9 July, 1807; restored to Prussia, May, 1813. Valuable fine art collection burnt 6 April, 1891. Population, 1890, 202,325; 1900, 229,663.

The *Magdeburg Experiment* is shown by means of a hollow sphere, composed of two hemispheres, fitting air-tight. When the air is exhausted by the air-pump, the hemispheres are held together by the pressure of the atmosphere, and require great force to separate them. The apparatus was suggested by Otto von Guericke, the inventor of the air-pump. He died in 1686. *Brande.*

MAGELLAN, STRAITS OF (connecting the Atlantic and Pacific oceans), was passed by Fernando de Magelhaêns (Magellan), a Portuguese, on 27 Nov. 1520. He gave the latter ocean its name on account of its calmness. Magellan completed the first voyage round the world, with a fleet of discovery fitted out by the emperor Charles V., but was killed in 1521. The Spaniards had a fort here, called Cape Famine, because the garrison perished from want.

MAGENTA, a small town in Lombardy, near which the French and Sardinians defeated the Austrians, 4 June, 1859. The emperor Louis Napoleon commanded, and he and the king of Sardinia were in the thickest of the fight. It is said that 55,000 French and Sardinians, and 75,000 Austrians were engaged. The former are asserted to have lost 4000 killed and wounded, and the Austrians 10,000, besides 7000 prisoners. The French generals Espinasse and Clerc were killed. The arrival of general MacMahon during a deadly struggle between the Austrians and the French, greatly contributed to the victory. The contest near the bridge of Buffalora was very severe. The Austrians fought well, but were badly commanded. The emperor and king entered Milan on 8 June following; MacMahon and Regnault d'Angely were created marshals of France. A monument erected here in memory of the slain was solemnly inaugurated 4 June, 1872.—The red dye, rosaniline, obtained by chemists from gas-tar, is termed *magenta;* see *Aniline.*

MAGI, an order of priests and teachers among the ancient Medes and Persians, with much political power. One of them who on the death of Cambyses asserted that he was Smerdis, a son of Cyrus, and claimed the throne of Persia, was deposed by Darius Hystaspes, 521 B.C., and a massacre of the Magi followed. They retained their religious position till the later Roman empire. The constitution of the order is traditionally assigned to Zoroaster, the Zarathustra of the Zendavesta, whose time and very existence are uncertain, the 6th century B.C. being mentioned. He is said to have taught the knowledge of Ormuzt, the supreme good principle, to the Magi, whom he classified as learners, masters, and perfect scholars, the possessors of all spiritual power, and the science of the age, see *Parsees.* The name Magi has been applied to the "wise men" of *Matt. ii.*, and the Parsees at Bombay are descendants of the Guebres or fire-worshippers.

MAGIC, see *Alchemy, Witchcraft,* &c. The invention of the MAGIC LANTERN is ascribed to Roger Bacon, about 1260, but more correctly to Athanasius Kircher, who died 1680. Sir David Salomons, in a discourse at the Royal Institution on "Optical Projection," exhibited an arrangement of the magic lantern, in which by the use of lenses magnifying up to 4,500 diameters, he stated that he was enabled to magnify a postage stamp to the size of 2½ acres, 26 Feb. 1892. See Godwin's "Lives of the Necromancers," 1834, and Ennemoser's "History of Magic," translated by W. Howitt, 1854.

MAGISTRATES, see *Justices.* Stipendiary borough magistrates may be appointed by 5 & 6 Will. IV. c. 76, 1853; and by 26 & 27 Vict. c. 97, 1863. The present arrangement of metropolitan magistrates (the chief sitting at Bow-street) was made by acts of parliament in 1792 and 1839. Eleven courts were appointed in 1840. Their salaries raised from 25 March, 1875. Henry Fielding, the novelist, was acting magistrate for Westminster and at Bow-street. He was succeeded by his half-brother, sir John Fielding, in 1761; by

Sir William Addington	1780
Sir Richard Ford	1800
Mr. Read	1806
Sir Nathaniel Conant	1813
Sir Robert Baker	1820
Sir Richard Birnie	1821
Sir Frederick Roe	1823
Mr. T. J. Hall	1839
Sir Thomas Henry (died suddenly, 16 June, 1876) .	1864

Sir James Taylor Ingham, July, 1876; died 5 March, 1890; sir John Bridge, March, 1890 (35 yrs. magistrate); resigns, July, 1899; died 26 April, 1900; sir Franklin Lushington, 1899; died, 10 Nov. 1901; Mr. Albert de Rutzen, Nov., knt., Dec. 1901

The new offices, Bow-street, opened . . 4 April 1881

MAGNA CHARTA. Its fundamental parts were derived from Saxon charters, continued by Henry I. and his successors. On 20 Nov. 1214, the archbishop of Canterbury and the barons met at St. Edmondsbury. On 6 Jan. 1215, they presented their demands to king John, who deferred his answer. On 19 May they were censured by the pope. On 24 May they marched to London, and the king was compelled to yield. The charter was sealed by John at Runnymede, near Windsor, 15 June, 1215. It was many times confirmed, by Henry III. and his successors. This last king's grand charter was granted in 1224, and was assured by Edward I.; see *Forests.* The original MS. charter is lost. The finest MS. copy, which is at Lincoln, was reproduced by photographs in the "National MSS." published by government, 1865.

MAGNA GRÆCIA, the independent states founded by Greek colonists in South Italy, Sicily, &c. Cumæ, in Campania, is said to have been founded in 1034 B.C., Pandosia and Metapontum in 774 B.C. These states were ruined through siding with Hannibal when he invaded Italy, 216 B.C.

Syracuse founded about . . . . B.C. 734
Leontinum and Catana 730
Sybaris 721
Crotona 710
Tarentum 708
Locri Epizephyrii 673
Lipara 627
Agrigentum 582
Thurium 432

MAGNANO (N. Italy). Here Scherer and a French army were defeated by the Austrians under Kray, 5 April, 1799.

MAGNESIA (Asia Minor). Here Antiochus the great, king of Syria, was defeated by the Scipios, 190 B.C.—*Magnesia alba*, the white alkaline earth used in medicine, was in use in the beginning of the 18th century. Its properties were developed by Dr. Black in 1755.

MAGNESIUM, a metal first obtained from magnesia by sir Humphry Davy in 1808, and since produced in larger quantities by Bussy, Deville, and especially by Mr. E. Sonstadt, in 1862-4. Its light when burnt is very brilliant, and is so rich in chemical rays that it may be used in photography. Lamps made for burning magnesium wire, were employed by the excavators of the tunnel through Mount Cenis. By its light photographs of the interior of the Pyramids were taken in 1865. Larkin's magnesium lamp (in which the metal is burnt in the form of a powder) was exhibited at the Royal Institution on 1 June, 1866, and before the British Association at Nottingham in Aug. 1866.

MAGNETISM. The attractive power of the loadstone or magnet was early known, and is referred to by Homer, Aristotle, and Pliny; it was also known to the Chinese and Arabians. The Greeks are said to have obtained the loadstone from Magnesia in Asia, 1000 B.C. Roger Bacon is said to have been acquainted with its property of pointing to the north (1294). The invention of the mariner's compass is ascribed to Flavio Gioia, a Neapolitan, about 1310; but it was known in Norway previous to 1266; and is mentioned in a French poem, 1150. See under *Electricity*.

Robert Norman, of London, discovered the dip of the needle . . . . about 1576
Gilbert's treatise "De Magnete," published . . 1600
Halley's theory of magnetic variations published . 1683
Marcel observed that a suspended bar of iron becomes temporarily magnetic by position . . 1722
Artificial magnets made by Dr. Gowan Knight . . 1746
The variation of the compass was observed by Bond, about 1668; the diurnal variation by Graham, 1722; on which latter Canton made 4000 observations previous to 1756
Coulomb constructed a torsion balance for determining the laws of attraction and repulsion, 1786; also investigated by Michell, Euler, Lambert, Robison, and others 1750-1800
The deflection of the magnetic needle by the voltaic current was discovered by Œrsted . . . 1820
Mr. Abraham invents a magnetic guard for persons engaged in grinding cutlery 1821
The magnetic effects of the violet rays of light exhibited by Morichini, 1814; polarity of a sewing needle so magnetised shown by Mrs. Somerville . 1825
Mr. Christie proves that heat diminishes magnetic force . . . . about ,,
Sir W. Snow Harris invents various forms of the compass 1831
Magnetic north pole discovered by commander (aft. sir) James Clark Ross (during sir John Ross's second voyage) . . . . . . 1 June, ,,
Electricity produced by the rotation of a magnet by professor Faraday, 1831; his researches on the action of the magnet on light, on the magnetic properties of flame, air, and gases (published 1845), on dia-magnetism (1845), on magno-crystallic action (1848), on atmospheric magnetism (1850), on the magnetic force. 1851-2
Magnetic observations established in the British colonies under the superintendence of col. Edward Sabine . . . . 1840 *et seq.*
Prof. Tyndall proves the existence of dia-magnetic polarity 1856
Mr. Archibald Smith described the results of his investigations respecting the deviation of the compass in iron ships at the Royal Institution, 9 Feb. 1866
Wm. Robinson patented a method of making wrought iron from cast iron by the help of magnetism, announced, July, 1867
Wilde's magneto-electric machine exhibited (see under *Electricity*) . . . . ,,
In the present century our knowledge of the phenomena of magnetism has also been greatly increased by the labours of Arago, Ampère, Hansteen, Gauss, Weber, Poggendorff, Sabine, Lamont, Du Moncel, Archibald Smith, sir Wm. Thomson (lord Kelvin), &c. (see *Animal Magnetism*).
In the Royal Institution, London, is a magnet by Logeman, of Haarlem, constructed on the principles of Dr. Elias, which weighs 100 lb, and can sustain 430 lb. Hæcker, of Nuremberg, constructed a magnet weighing 36 grains, capable of sustaining 146 times its own weight. This was exhibited in 1851, also at the Royal Institution.
sir Wm. Thomson's mariner's compass produced, 1872
Sir E. Sabine, eminent for life-long researches in magnetism, died (aged 94), 26 June, 1883.

MAGNETO-ELECTRICITY, the discovery of professor Faraday; see under *Electricity*. Magneto-electricity has been recently applied to telegraphic and to lighthouse purposes. The South Foreland lighthouse, near Dover, was illuminated by the magneto-electric light in the winter of 1858-9 and 1859-60 (the light removed to Dungeness in 1861), the Lizards, by Dr. C. William Siemens' magneto-electric light, 1878. See *Faradisation*.

MAGNOLIA. *Magnolia glauca* was brought here from N. America, 1688. The laurel-leaved Magnolia, *Magnolia grandiflora*, from N. America, about 1734. The dwarf Magnolia, *Magnolia pumila*, from China, in 1789; and (also from China), the brown stalked, 1789; the purple, 1790; and the slender, 1804.

MAGUIRE, see *Molly*.

MAGYARS, see *Hungary*.

MAHARAJPOOR (India). Here sir Hugh Gough severely defeated the Mahratta army of Gwalior, 29 Dec. 1843. Lord Ellenborough was present.

MAHDI (Guided by God), a name assumed by several Mahometan fanatics claiming to be divinely sent reformers and liberators. An eminent example is found in Ibn Tumert, the Almohade Mahdi in the 12th century. See *Babysm*, and for the latest Mahdis see *Soudan*, 1881, *et seq.* A Mahdi has risen in Bokhara, named Mahomed Abdallah Ben Oman, May, 1884. See *Dervishes*. "Ten Years' Captivity in the Mahdi's Camp" by Father Ohrwalder, published Autumn, 1892. Total defeat of the Khalifa at Omdurman, 2 Sept. 1898; again at Omdebrikat, when he and his chief emirs were killed (see *Soudan*, 24 Nov. 1899), and consequent end of Mahdism.

MAHEDPORE, see *Mehedpore*.

MAHOGANY is said to have been brought to England by Raleigh, in 1595; but not to have come into general use till 1720.

MAHOMETANISM embodied in the Koran, includes—the unity of God, the immortality of the soul, predestination, a last judgment, and a sensual paradise. Mahomet asserted that the Koran was revealed to him by the angel Gabriel during a period of twenty-three years. He enjoined on his disciples circumcision, prayer, alms, frequent ablution, and fasting, and permitted polygamy and concubinage.

The *Mahometan year*, 1319-1320. Months; Shawall (begins 11 Jan. 1902); Dulkaada (9 Feb.); Dulheggia (11 March); Muharram (10 April); Saphar (10 May); Rabia I. (8 June); Rabia II. (8 July); Jomada I. (6 Aug.); Jomada II. (4 Sept.); Rajab (2 Oct.); Shaaban (5 Nov.); Ramadán (2 Dec.).

(The dates are given in the best almanacks.)

Mahomet, Mohammed (the name is spelt many ways), born at Mecca . . . . 569 or 570

Announced himself as a prophet . . . . about 611

Fled from his enemies to Medina (his flight is called the Hégira) . . . . . . 15 July, 622

Defeats his enemies (the Koreish, the Jews, &c.) . 623-5

Defeats the Christians at Muta 629

Is acknowledged as a sovereign 630

Dies, it is said, of slow poison, administered by a Jewess to test his divine character . . 8 June, 632

The Mahometans are divided into several sects, the two chief being the *Sonnites*, or the Orthodox (who recognised as caliph Abubeker, the father-in-law of Mahomet, in preference to Omar and Ali), and the *Shiites* (Sectaries), or *Fatimites*, the followers of Ali, who married Fatima, the prophet's daughter.

The former (also called Sunnites) recognise the "Sunna" (traditions) sayings of Mahomet (supplementary to the Koran) which the Shiites reject. Husan and other sons of Ali were murdered A.D. 680, and a miracle play and a festival in their honour are still observed.

The Ottoman empire is the chief seat of the Sonnites, the sultan being considered the representative of the caliphs; Persia has been for centuries the stronghold of the Shiites.

Their progress in France was stopped by their defeat at Tours by Charles Martel, in 732

The Mahometan Arabs termed Saracens, conquered Arabia, North Africa, and part of Asia, in the 7th century; in the 8th they invaded Europe, conquering Spain, where they founded the califat of Cordova, which lasted from 756 to 1031, when it was broken up into smaller governments, the last of which, the kingdom of Grenada, endured till its subjugation by Ferdinand in 1492; but the Moorish Mahometans were not finally expelled from Spain till 1609

After a long contest, the Turks under Mahomet II. took Constantinople; he made it his capital and the chief seat of his religion 1453

Though considered to be declining, Mahometanism is calculated as including 100 millions amongst its votaries.

Coomroodeen Tyabjee, a Mahometan, admitted to practise as an attorney in England, having taken the oaths upon the Koran . . . . Nov. 1858

Budroodeen Tyabjee, a Mahometan, called to the bar . . . . 30 April, 1867

The first Mahometan mosque in England erected at Maybury, Woking, Surrey, to be completed by the exertions of Dr. G. W. Leitner (not a Mahometan), Aug. 1889; the ameer of Afghanistan, by his son, presents 500*l.* to the mosque, 4 June, 1895

The representation of a play called *Mahomed* on the English stage, was stopped by request, aided by the intervention of the sultan . . . Dec. 1890

A Mahometan marriage at the Moslem Institute, Liverpool, the first in England . . 18 April, 1891

"The Life and Teachings of Mohammed, or, The Spirit of Islâm," by Syed Ameer Ali, M.A., a judge in Bengal, published in 1873 and 1891.

A conference of Moslems protesting against attacks on their religion, &c., Sir E. Ashmead-Bartlett present, London . . . . . 15 May, 1895

Loyal declaration of the Moslem patriotic league at the Oriental academy, London . 13 Aug. 1897

Mr. Theodore Beck, the successful principal of the Mahomedan college at Aligarh since 1883, dies, aged 40 . . . . early Sept. 1899

MAHRATTAS, a people of Hindostan, who originally dwelt north-west of the Deccan, which they overran about 1676. They endeavoured to overcome the Mogul, but were restrained by the Afghans. They entered into alliance with the East India company in 1767, made war against it in 1774, again made peace in 1782, and were finally subdued in 1818. See *India* 1803, *et seq.*, *Gwalior* and *Indore*.

MAID, see *Holy Maid*, Elizabeth Barton, and *Joan of Arc*, maid of Orleans.

MAIDA (Calabria) where the French, commanded by general Regnier, were signally defeated by the British under major-general sir John Stuart, 4 July, 1806.

MAIDEN, see *Guillotine*.

MAIDS OF HONOUR. Anne, daughter of Francis II. duke of Brittany, and queen of Charles VIII. and Louis XII. of France (1483-98), had young and beautiful ladies about her person, called maids of honour. The queen of Edward I. of England is said to have had four maids of honour (1272-1307); queen Victoria had eight; queen Alexandra has 4.

MAIDSTONE, Kent, a British town, anciently termed the city of the Medway (Caer Meguaid), a possession of the archbishops of Canterbury in 1086-7. It was chartered by several kings, from Edward VI. to George II. The royalist Kentish men were here defeated by Faixfax, 1648. The archbishop's palace was built in 1348. Maidstone, which previously sent two members to parliament, since 1885 sends one. Typhoid epidemic attributed to bad water; Farleigh water supply cut off, 2 Oct. 1897 (see *Mansion-house Fund*). The lord mayor presented with the freedom, 21 Aug. 1903. Population, 1881, 29,263; 1891, 32,150; 1901, 34,000.

MAIL-COACHES, for the conveyance of letters, were first set up at Bristol by Mr. John Palmer, of Bath, 2 Aug. 1784. They were employed for other routes in 1785, and soon became general in England. The mails first sent by *rail* in 1838.

MAILLOTINS (small mallets), a name given to certain citizens of Paris, who, in March, 1382, violently opposed the collection of new taxes imposed by the duke of Anjou, the regent. They armed themselves with small iron mallets (taken from the arsenal), and killed the collectors; for which they were severely punished in Jan. 1383.

MAIMING AND WOUNDING, see *Coventry Act*.

MAINTENANCE, see *Barratry*.

MAIN PLOT, a name given to a conspiracy to make Arabella Stuart sovereign of England in place of James I. in 1603. Lord Cobham, sir Walter Raleigh, and lord Grey, were condemned to death for implication in it, but reprieved; others were executed. Raleigh was executed, 29 Oct. 1618.

MAINE, 1, a province, N.W. of France, seized by William I. of England in 1069. It acknowledged prince Arthur, 1199; was taken from John of England by Philip of France, 1204; was recovered by Edward III. in 1357; but given up, 1360. After various changes it was finally united to France by Louis XI. in 1481.—2. MAINE (N. America), was discovered by Cabot, 1497; and colonised by the English 1630 *et seq.*; it became a state of the union in 1820. Capital, Augusta. Population, 1880, 648,936; 1890, 661,086; 1900, 694,466. The boundary line between the British and the United States territories in Maine was settled by the Ashburton treaty, concluded 9 Aug. 1842. The *Maine liquor law*, prohibiting the manufacture, sale, and use of intoxicating drinks, with certain exceptions, was enacted in 1851. In 1872, it was officially reported to have greatly decreased drunkenness and rendered the trade disreputable.

Great fire at Camden; 80 warehouses and 50 houses destroyed . . . . 10 Nov. 1892

The Opera house and other buildings at Bath burnt, 30 March, 1893

Maine, United States cruiser, burnt by explosion in Havana harbour, 2 officers and 270 men killed, 9.40 P.M. . . . . 15 Feb. 1898

Court of inquiry finds no evidence to fix the responsibility, but attributes the explosion to a mine underneath the vessel, reported to congress, with a dignified message from the president, 28 March; the Spanish commission consider the explosion was from within, report received at Washington . . . . . . 29 March, „

At Mt. Desert, 20 deaths by the breaking of a ferry-slip . . . . 5 Aug. 1899

Maine, an American ship lent by Mr. Bernard Baker, turned into a hospital ship by lady Randolph Churchill and other Americans in London, leaves for S. Africa . . . . . mid Dec. „

MAIWAND, Afghanistan, about 50 miles from Candahar. On 27 July, 1880, gen. J. Burrows marched from Kushk-i-Nakhud, and attacked the army of Ayoob Khan, about 20,000 men, entrenched here on the river Helmund, and after four hours' severe conflict was compelled to retreat. About 300 of the British with many officers fell (including lieut.-col. Galbraith, major G. F. Blackwood, captains Garratt, McMath, Cullen, Roberts, and others), especially officers of the 66th regiment; with about 700 of the native troops killed or missing. The British commanders were censured. Ayoob Khan did not improve his victory, and was totally defeated by gen. sir F. Roberts, 1 Sept. 1880. See *Mazra*.

MAJESTY. Among the Romans, the emperor and imperial family were thus addressed, and also the popes and the emperors of Germany. The style was given to Louis XI. of France in 1461. *Voltaire.* Upon Charles V. being chosen emperor of Germany in 1519, the kings of Spain took the style. Francis I. of France, at the interview with Henry VIII. of England, on the Field of the Cloth of Gold, addressed the latter as Your Majesty, 1520. James I. used the style "Sacred," and "Most Excellent Majesty."

MAJOLICA WARE, see *Pottery*.

MAJORCA, see *Balearic Isles*, and *Minorca*. Majorca opposed Philip V. of Spain in 1714; but submitted, 14 July, 1715. Its first railway, from Palma, capital of the Balearic isles, to Inca, 18 miles, opened, 24 Feb. 1875.

MAJUBA HILL (see *Transvaal*). On Saturday night, 26 Feb. 1881, above 600 men under sir George P. Colley marching from the camp at Mount Prospect, ascended Majuba hill overlooking Laing's Nek, where the Boers were encamped, to surprise them. The attack of the Boers began 10.30 a.m. of the 27th. Fierce conflicts ensued; eventually overwhelmed by numbers and deadly fire, the British were routed and fled. Sir George Colley fell with his face to the enemy. Boer loss unknown, some say only one man. About 350 British engaged. Loss: killed, 3 officers and about 82 men; many wounded, 122 prisoners, and some missing.

MAKALAKA, see *Mashona*.

MALABAR (S.W. coast of Hindostan). The Portuguese established factories here in 1505; the English did the same in 1601. A murderous attack on the Hindus by the Moplah Mussulmans, punished by the British, 8 April, 1894.

MALACCA, on the Malay peninsula, E. Indies, was made a Portuguese settlement in 1511. The Dutch factories were established in 1640. The Dutch government exchanged it for Bencoolen in Sumatra in 1824, when it was placed under the Bengal presidency. It is now part of the *Straits Settlements* (which see).

MALAGA (S. Spain), a Phœnician town, taken by the Arabs, 714; retaken by the Spaniards, after a long siege, 1487; see *Naval Battles*, 1704. An insurrection against the provisional government was put down with much slaughter, 31 Dec. 1868. Population in 1887, 134,106; 1897, 126,000.

MALAKHOFF, a hill near Sebastopol, on which was situated an old tower, strongly fortified by the Russians during the siege of 1854-55. The allied French and English attacked it on 17, 18 June, 1855, and after a conflict of forty-eight hours were repulsed with severe loss; that of the English being 175 killed and 1126 wounded; that of the French 3338 killed and wounded. On 8 Sept. the French again attacked the Malakhoff; at eight o'clock the first mine was sprung, and at noon the French flag floated over the conquered redoubt; see *Sebastopol*. In the Malakhoff and Redan were found 3000 pieces of cannon of every calibre, and 120,000 lbs. of gunpowder.

MALARIA. The parasite of malaria—*i.e.*, ague and yellow fever—discovered by Laveran in 1880. The theory that mosquitoes conveyed the disease held also by King, Bignami and Manson. Major Ronald Ross (K.C.B. 1902) began his researches on sir Patrick Manson's theory in India in 1895, and proved deductively and experimentally that mosquitoes of the genus called *Anopheles Claviger* conveyed the disease, 1897–98; confirmed by profs. Koch and Grassi and Drs. Bignami and Bastianelli, Dec. 1898. See *Sierra Leone*, Aug. 1899.

Elephantiasis, a tropical disease, also conveyed by the mosquito, reported . . . 12 Aug. 1900

Major Ronald Ross proves that the prime source of mosquito infection is the native children, whose blood contains the parasites, Sept. 1900 (he received the Nobel prize, Dec. 1902).

Drs. Sambon and Low live perfectly free from fever in the worst malarial part of the Roman Campagna, near Ostia, without taking quinine or any other drug, by merely keeping within a mosquito-proof hut from an hour before sunset to an hour after sunrise, Aug.–Sept. 1900; successful experiments carried on with similar results by prof. Grassi and others.

Committee appointed jointly by Mr. Chamberlain, M.P., and the Royal Soc. in 1898 for the investigation of malaria and mosquitoes and allied insects in tropical countries; 3,000 specimens sent to the Nat. Hist. museum, Cromwell-rd., reported Sept. 1900 (researches continued 1903)

The prophylactic use of quinine, surface drainage, destruction of larvæ and the employment of mosquito nets, &c., advocated by major Ross in malarious places . . . . . 29 Nov. „

Campaign against the *anopheles* species carried also on in Gambia, Gold Coast (Ismailia, 1902–3), and elsewhere, 1901 *et seq.*

Navy-blue, a favourite colour with mosquitoes, proved very successful by Dr. Nuttall and Mr. Shipley's experiment, in 1901

The king of Italy gives 10,000 lire to the Italian Red Cross Soc. . . . . July, 1902
Drs. Stephens and Christopher report malaria to be an infectious fever present in nearly every native hut, and its suppression doubtful, *Times*, 4 Aug. 1903

MALA VITA (evil life), the name of a secret society in south Italy; the highest of its three grades is the Camorristi. At Lucera, in Foggia, 68 men were sentenced to various terms of imprisonment (from 5 to 10 years), reported 2 Oct. 1894; see *Camorra*.

MALAY ARCHIPELAGO. Great improvement in the country through British protection, slavery abolished, railways constructed, &c., since 1875. Lieut.-col. sir Charles B. H. Mitchell appointed high commissioner, 8 July, 1896; sir Frank A. Swettenham, 1901. Population, 1901, 676,138. Messrs. Annandale and Robinson's expedition completed, good results reported, July, 1902; excellent progress and prosperity reported, 9 Sept. 1902, and 20 July, 1903. See *Moluccas*, *Philippines*, *Straits*, &c.

MALDON (Essex), built 28 B.C., is supposed to have been the first Roman colony in Britain. It was burnt by queen Boadicea, and rebuilt by the Romans; burnt by the Danes, A.D. 991, and rebuilt by the Saxons. Maldon was incorporated by Philip and Mary. Absorbed into the county, 1885. The singular custom of Borough-English is kept up here, by which the youngest son, and not the eldest, succeeds to the burgage tenure on his father's death; see *Borough-English*.

MALICIOUS DAMAGES. The law respecting them was consolidated and amended by 24 & 25 Vict. c. 97. This act protects works of art, electric telegraphs, &c., 1861.

MALINES, see *Mechlin*.

MALINS' ACT, 20 & 21 Vict. c. 57, relating to the powers of women in regard to property, was passed in 1857.

MALMESBURY, Wiltshire, an old market-town. The abbey, founded about 670, was several times destroyed by the Danes and restored. Its chief was made a mitred abbot by Edward III. Athelstan was buried in the abbey. Thomas Hobbes, the philosopher, was born here, 5 April, 1588. By the act of 1885, Malmesbury was disenfranchised and absorbed into the county. Population, 1881, 3,176; 1891, 2,964; 1901, 2,854.

MALO, ST. (N.-W. France). This port, as a great resort of privateers, sustained a tremendous bombardment by the English under admiral Benbow in 1693, and under lord Berkeley in July, 1695. In June, 1758, the British landed in considerable force in Cancale bay, and went up to the harbour, where they burnt upwards of a hundred ships, and did great damage to the town, making a number of prisoners. It is now defended by a very strong castle, and the harbour is very difficult of access.

MALO-JAROSLAVITZ, near Moscow, central Russia: the site of severe encounters between the Russians and the retreating French army, 24 Oct. 1812. The latter were victorious, but with great loss.

MALPLAQUET (N. France). Here the allies under the duke of Marlborough and prince Eugene defeated the French, commanded by marshal Villars, 11 Sept. 1709. Each army consisted of nearly 120,000 choice soldiers. There was great slaughter on both sides, the allies losing 18,000 men, but captured Mons.

MALT, barley prepared for brewing and distillation. A duty was laid upon malt in 1667; repealed but reimposed 1697, *et seq.* Important acts for the regulation of malt duties were passed in 1830 and 1837. In March, 1858, there were 6157 licensed maltsters in the United Kingdom. The duty on malt in 1863 amounted to 6,273,727*l.* In 1864 the duty was remitted on malt used for cattle feeding; and in 1865, an act was passed allowing the excise duty to be charged according to the weight of the grain used. A parliamentary committee to consider repeal of malt tax was agreed to, 14 May, 1867, without success; a motion to repeal the tax was negatived (244–17), 23 April, 1874. Tax abolished, 1880 (when it was 2*s.* 8½*d.* a bushel). It ceased 1 Oct. 1880.

Revenue from the malt duties: in the year ending 31 March, 1850, 5,391,322*l.*;—1854, 5,418,418*l.*;—1856, 6,676,849*l.*;—1857 (tax reduced), 5,690,950*l.*;—1860, 6,648,881*l.*;—1862, 6,208,813*l.*; 1867, 6,816,385*l.*;—1871, 6,978,371*l.*;—1872, 6,910,366*l.*;—1873, 7,544,175*l.*;—1877, 8,040,378*l.*;—1878, 7,721,548*l.*

Malt made and retained in the United Kingdom: in 1825, 36,205,451 bushels; in 1835, 42,892,012; in 1847, 35,307,815; in 1857, 44,545,649; in 1861, 46,650,100; in 1870, 56,775,614; in 1875, 63,015,676.

MALTA (formerly Melita), an island in the Mediterranean, held successively by the Phœnicians, Carthaginians, and Romans, which last conquered it, 259 B.C. The apostle Paul was wrecked here, A.D. 62. (*Acts* xxvii., xxviii.) Malta was taken by the Vandals, 534; by the Arabs, 870; and by the Normans from Sicily, 1090. With Sicily it became successively part of the possessions of the houses of Hohenstaufen, of Anjou (1266), and of Aragon (1260). In 1530 Charles V. gave it to the Knights Hospitallers, who defended it most courageously and successfully, in 1551 and 1565, against the Turks, who were obliged to abandon the enterprise after the loss of 30,000 men. The island was taken by Bonaparte in the outset of his expedition to Egypt, 12 June, 1798. He found in it 1200 pieces of cannon, 200,000 lbs. of powder, two ships of the line, a frigate, four galleys, and 40,000 muskets, besides an immense treasure collected by superstition; and 4500 Turkish prisoners, whom he set at liberty. Malta surrendered to the British under Pigot, 5 Sept. 1800. At the peace of Amiens it was stipulated that it should be restored to the knights. The British, however, retained possession, and the war recommenced between the two nations; but by the treaty of Paris, in 1814, the island was guaranteed to Great Britain. A legislative constitution was established in 1849; and after various changes was replaced by a more popular one proclaimed 22 Dec. 1887. *La Valetta*, the capital, was founded in 1557 by the grand master La Valetta, and completed and occupied by the knights, 18 Aug. 1571. The Protestant college was founded in 1846. A grand new naval dry dock was opened, May, 1871. Governor of Malta and Gozo, sir Patrick Grant, March, 1867; sir C. T. Van Straubenzee, 1872; sir Arthur Borton, 1878; gen. sir John Lintorn A. Simmons, 1884; lt.-gen. sir Henry D'Oyly Torrens, March, 1888, died 1 Dec. 1889; gen. sir H. A. Smyth, Dec. 1889; lieut.-gen. A. J. Lyon Fremantle, Dec. 1893; sir Francis Grenfell, 15 Nov. 1898 (made a peer, June, 1902); lt.-gen. sir C. Mansfield Clarke, bt., 1 April, 1903.—The visit of prince of Wales, 6 April, 1876. Great immigration of destitute Europeans from Alexandria (see *Egypt*) middle June, 1882; about 2200, 6 July, 1882. See *Cholera*. Population of

Malta and adjacent isles 1890, 165,662; 1901, 186,491.

Negotiations respecting the Roman Catholics and marriage laws concluded by sir J. L. Simmons; see under *Pope*, Leo XIII. . . . 7 April, 1890
Jubilee statue of the queen unveiled, 6 Aug. 1891, by lady Smyth.
Naval and military manœuvres . . . April, 1899
Visit of the duke and duchess of Cornwall; exhibition of arts and crafts opened . 25–27 March, 1901
Mass meeting protesting against the language and fiscal questions . . . . . . 11 Aug. ,,
Proclamation issued withdrawing the announcement of 1899, that English was to become the official language of the law courts . 8 Feb. 1902
Visit of the duke and duchess of Connaught, 16 March, 1903
Visit of king Edward VII., 16–21 April, 1903; lays first stone of new breakwater at entrance to the Grand Harbour; great water carnival, 20 April, ,,
Education vote for current financial year thrown out by Council of Government after heated debate on the language question . 24 April, ,,
Governor reads new letters patent from Imperial government amending the constitution of Malta; elected members of the Council of Government reduced from 13 to 8, and official members increased from 6 to 9 . . . . . 22 June, ,,

MALTA, KNIGHTS OF. A military religious order, called also Hospitallers of St. John of Jerusalem, Knights of St. John, and Knights of Rhodes. Some merchants of Malfi, trading to the Levant, obtained leave of the caliph of Egypt to build a house for those who came on pilgrimage to Jerusalem, and whom they received with zeal and charity, 1048. They afterwards founded a hospital for the reception of pilgrims, from whence they were called Hospitallers (Latin, *hospes*, a guest). The military order was founded about 1099; confirmed by the pope, 1113. In 1119 the knights defeated the Turks at Antioch. After the Christians had lost their interest in the East, and Jerusalem was taken, the knights retired to Acre, which they defended valiantly in 1290. John, king of Cyprus, gave them Limisso in his dominions, where they stayed till 1310, in which year they took Rhodes, under their grand master De Vallaret, and the next year defended it under the duke of Savoy against an army of Saracens. The story that his successors have used F. E. R. T. (*Fortitudo ejus Rhodum tenuit*, or his valour kept Rhodes) for their device is much doubted. From this they were also called *knights of Rhodes;* but Rhodes being taken by Solyman in 1522, they retired into Candia, thence into Sicily. Pope Adrian VI. granted them the city of Viterbo for their retreat; and in 1530 the emperor Charles V. gave them the isle of Malta. The order was suppressed in England in 1540; restored in 1557; and again suppressed in 1559. St. John's Gate, Clerkenwell, a relic of their possessions, still exists. The emperor Paul of Russia declared himself grand master of the order in June, 1799. After the death of the grand master, Tommasi di Contara, in 1805, the order was governed by a lieutenant and a college at Rome, till Pope Leo XIII. made count Ceschi à Santa Cisce (lieutenant since 14 Feb. 1871) grand master, 28 March, 1879. The knights sent a hospital establishment into Bohemia during the war in 1866, which afforded great relief to the wounded and sick.

MAMELON, a hill, one of the defences of Sebastopol, captured by the French, 7 June, 1855.

MAMELUKES, originally Turkish and Circassian slaves, established by the sultan of Egypt as a body-guard, about 1260. They advanced one of their own corps to the throne of Egypt, May, 1260, and continued to do so until it became a Turkish province, in 1517, when the beys took them into pay, and filled up their ranks with renegades from various countries. On the conquest of Egypt by Bonaparte, in 1798, they retreated into Nubia; but, assisted by the Arnauts, reconquered Egypt from the Turkish government. In 1804, Napoleon embodied some of them in his guard. On 1 March. 1811, they were decoyed into the power of the Turkish pacha, Mehemet Ali, and slain at Cairo.

MAMERTINI, sons of Mamers or Mars, were Campanian soldiers of Agathocles. They seized Messina in Sicily, in 281, B.C., and when closely besieged by the Carthaginians, and Hiero of Syracuse, in 264, they implored the help of the Romans, which led to the first Punic war.

MAMMOTH, an extinct species of elephant. An entire mammoth, flesh and bones, was discovered in Siberia, in 1799. Remains of this animal have since been found at Harwich, in 1803, and at places in Europe, Asia, and America. Mammoth is also termed Mastodon.

MAN, ANTIQUITY OF. In 1836, M. Boucher de Perthes found some rude flint implements, which he believed to be of human manufacture, mingled with bones of extinct animals, in the old alluvium near Abbeville in Picardy, France, and also in 1847, near Amiens. Similar flints have since been found in Sicily by Dr. Falconer, at Brixham by Mr. Pengelly, and lately in various parts of the world. Hence many geologists infer that man existed on the earth many ages earlier than has been hitherto believed.

Some burnt bricks found in the Nile are considered to be 20,000 years old, and some bones found in lacustrine deposits in Florida, 30,000 years old.
The "Engis skull" found by Schmerling in the valley of the Meuse . . . . . . about 1834
Fossil human remains found in extinct volcanos of St. Denis, near Puy en Velay 1844
A human jaw said to have been found in the drift at Moulin Quignon, near Abbeville . March, 1863
Sir Charles Lyell's "Antiquity of Man" was published in 1863 (4th edition, 1873), and sir John Lubbock's "Prehistoric Times," 1865 (4th ed. 1878).
The skeleton of a man supposed to have been a contemporary of the mammoth and cave-bear was found with polished flint implements by M. Rivière in the Cavillin cavern, near Mentone, 26 March, 1872. Mr. W. Pengelly went to examine these remains.
"The Ancient Stone Implements, Weapons, and Ornaments of Great Britain," by John Evans, F.R.S., published, July, 1872; and his "Ancient Bronze Implements, Weapons, &c." published . May, 1881
"In our day the quaternary man is a fact universally accepted; but the tertiary man is a problem under discussion."—*Virchow* 1877
Flint implements found in Egypt, probable date 3000 B.C. (termed the "palæolithic age") reported 1895

MAN, ISLE OF, was subdued by Edwin, king of Northumberland, about 620; by Magnus of Norway, 1098; by the Scots, 1266; occupied by Edward at the wish of the inhabitants 1290; recovered by the Scots in 1313; but taken from them by Montacute, afterwards earl of Salisbury, to whom Edward III. gave the title of king of Man, in 1343. It was afterwards subjected to the earl of Northumberland, on whose attainder Henry IV. granted it in fee to sir John Stanley, 1406. It was taken from this family by Elizabeth, but was restored in 1610 to the earl of Derby, through whom it fell by inheritance to the duke of Athol, 1735. He received 70,000*l*. from parliament for all his rights in 1765; and the nation was charged with the further sum of 132,944*l*. for the purchase of his remaining interest in the revenues of the island in Jan. 1829. The countess of Derby held the isle against the parliament forces for a time in 1651. The new queen's landing pier (cost 46,400*l.*) inaugurated by the lieut. governor, H. B. Loch, 1 July, 1872. Act relating to the harbours and coasts, passed June, 1872. The first railway (from Douglas to Peel) opened, 1 July, 1873. Population, 1871, 54,042; in 1881, 53,558; 1891, 55,598; 1901, 54,758. Revenue, 1889-90, 63,824*l.*; expenditure, 57,947*l.*: 1894-5, estimated revenue, 72,000*l.*: expenditure, 67,000*l.* The BISHOPRIC is said to have been presided over by Amphibalus about 360. Some assert that St. Patrick was the founder of the see, and that Germanus was the first bishop, about 447. It was united to Sodor in 1113. The bishop has no seat in the house of lords; but lord Auckland (bishop, 1847-54) sat by right of his barony. Present income 2,000*l.*

The Tynwald, an independent legislative body, consists of two branches—1. The governor and council; 2. The house of Keys; their acts receiving the royal assent. The house of Keys was formerly self-elective; election by the people every seventh year was established by act of parliament, 1866; the property qualification for members abolished; household suffrage was granted in towns and suffrage conferred on women by royal assent in 1881. New Customs Act passed in 1887

The foundation stone of the Eiffel tower at Douglas laid by the earl of Lathom . . 23 Oct. 1890

According to custom, five bills, which had received the royal assent, one for the re-distribution of seats in the house of Keys, were promulgated to the legislature, in the open air on the Tynwald hill, by the lieut.-governor, Spencer Walpole, 30 March, 1891; ceremony shortened by bill passed 7 Nov. 1895

The bishop's palace near Ramsey partially burnt, 16 May, 1893

An electric tramway from Douglas to Laxey, opened . . . . Aug. 1894

Outburst of poisonous fumes at the Snaefell lead mines, Laxey, 20 deaths . . . 10 May, 1897

The house of Keys meets at Douglas . . 25 Feb. 1898

Portrait of the queen presented by herself to the island 12 April; Sir Wm. Drinkwater, 50 years Deemster (resigned, Oct. 1897); presented with an address, &c. . . . . 5 July, „

21,000 trees purchased by the landowners, reported . . . . 1 Nov. „

Sir John Goldie-Taubman, speaker of the house of Keys, an active public official, died . 9 Nov. „

Suspension of Dumbell's bank . . . . 3 Feb. 1900

Charles B. Nelson, director (see *Trials*, Feb. 1902), John Shimmon, manager; Wm. and Harold Aldred and Joseph Rogers, auditors of Dumbell's bank, convicted of issuing false balance-sheets, 14 Nov. 1900; Chas. B. Nelson and John Shimmon also found guilty of misappropriating the moneys of the bank, sentenced to 5 years' penal servitude, the rest to several months' imprisonment . . . . 19 Nov. „

Extensive damage by floods . . . . 18 Oct. 1901

Sir James Gell, acting governor, promulgates 3 new laws on the Tynwald hill . . . . 5 July, 1902

Isle of Man customs act, royal assent . 8 Aug. „

Visit of the king and queen . . . . 25 Aug. „

Mr. H. B. Noble bequeathed 31,350*l.* to charities, 2 May, 1903

RECENT BISHOPS OF SODOR AND MAN.

1784. Claudius Crigan: died in 1813.
1813. George Murray, trans. to Rochester, 1827
1828. William Ward; died in 1838.
1838. James Bowstead, trans. to Lichfield, Dec. 1839.
1840. Henry Pepys, trans. to Worcester, 1841.
1841. Thos. Vowler Short, trans. to St. Asaph, 1846.
1846. Walter Augustus Shirley; died in 1847.
1847. John Eden (lord Auckland), trans. to Bath, 1854.
1854. Hon. Horatio Powys; died 31 May, 1877.
1877. Rowley Hill, consecrated 24 Aug.; died 27 May, 1887.
1887. John Wareing Bardsley; translated to Carlisle, Dec. 1891.
1891. Norman D. J. Straton, Dec.

Recent lieut.-governors: H. B. Loch, 1863; Spencer Walpole, 1882; Sir Joseph West Ridgeway, Nov. 1893, till Sept. 1895; John M. lord Henniker, installed 24 Jan. 1896 (died, 27 June, 1902); lord Raglan, installed, 21 Oct. 1902.

MANASSAS JUNCTION (Virginia, United States), an important military position, where the Alexandria and Manassas Gap railways meet, near a creek named BULL RUN. 1. It was held by the confederates in 1861, when they were attacked by the federal general Irwin McDowell. He began his march from Washington on 16 July, and gained some advantage on the 18th at Centreville. On the 21st was fought the *first* battle of Bull Run. The federals, who began the fight, had the advantage till about three o'clock p.m., when the confederate general Johnston brought up reinforcements, which at first the federals took for their own troops. After a brief resistance, the latter were seized with sudden panic, and, in spite of the utmost efforts of their officers, fled, abandoning a large quantity of arms, ammunition, and baggage. The confederate generals Johnston and Beauregard did not think it prudent to pursue the fugitives, who did not halt till they arrived at Washington. The federal army is said to have had 481 killed, 1011 wounded, 1216 missing. The loss of the confederates was stated to be about 1500.—In March, 1862, when the army of the Potomac, under general McClellan, marched into Virginia, they found that the confederates had quietly retreated from the camp at Manassas. 2. On 30 Aug. 1862, this place was the site of another great battle between the northern and southern armies. In August, general "Stonewall" Jackson, after compelling the federal general Pope to retreat, defeated him at Cedar mountain on the 9th, turned his flank on the 22nd, and arriving at Manassas repulsed his attacks on the 29th. On the 30th general R. E. Lee (who had defeated general McClellan and the invading northern army before Richmond, 26 June to 1 July) joined Jackson with his army, and Pope received reinforcements from Washington. A desperate conflict ensued, which ended in the confederates gaining a decisive victory, compelling the federals to a hasty retreat to Centreville, where they were once more routed, 1 Sept. The remains of their army took refuge behind the lines of Washington on 2 Sept. Pope was at once superseded, and McClellan resumed the command to march against the confederates, who had crossed the Potomac and entered Maryland; see *United States*.

MANCHESTER (Lancashire), in the time of the Druids, was one of their most principal stations, and had the privilege of sanctuary attached to its altar, in the British language *Meyne*, a stone. It was one of the seats of the Brigantes, who had a castle, or stronghold, called *Mancenion*, or the place of tents, near the confluence of the rivers Medlock and Irwell. The site of this, still called the "Castle Field," was, about 79, selected by the Romans as the station of the *Cohors Prima Frisiorum*, and called by them *Mancunium*; hence its Saxon name *Manceastre*, from which its modern appellation is derived. *Lewis*. Manchester constituted a harbour and port, 22 Dec. 1893. See under *Population*.

Mancenion taken from the Britons 488
Captured by Edwin of Northumbria 620
The inhabitants become Christians . . about 627
The town taken by the Danes, 870; retaken . . 923

The charter (*Magna Charta* of Manchester), 14 May, 1301
"Manchester cottons" introduced 1352
The church made collegiate 1421
Free grammar-school founded 1516
Privilege of sanctuary moved to Chester . about 1541
An aulnager (measurer) stationed here . . . 1565
Sir Thomas Fairfax takes the town 1643
The walls and fortifications razed 1652
Cheetham college, or Blue-coat hospital, founded 1653
Tumult raised by "Syddall, the barber," afterwards hanged 1715
Prince Charles Edward, the Young Pretender, makes it his quarters . . 28 Nov. 1745
Queen's theatre first built 1753
The Infirmary instituted, 1752; built . . . 1755
The inhabitants discharged from their obligation to grind their corn at Irk-mill 1759
Cotton goods first exported 1760
Manchester navigation opened, by Bridgewater canal 1761
Lunatic asylum founded 1765
Agricultural society instituted 1767
Christian, king of Denmark, visits Manchester, and puts up at the Bull-inn 1768
The Queen's theatre rebuilt 1775
Subscription concerts established 1777
Riots against machinery . . . . 9 Oct. 1779
Manufacture of muslin attempted here . about 1780
Philosophical society established 1781
New Bailey bridge completed 1785
Queen's theatre burnt down, 19 June, 1789; re-erected 1790
New Bailey built . . . . ,,
Assembly-rooms, Mosley-street, built . . . 1792
Philological Society instituted 1803
Fever hospital erected, 1805; Theatre-royal . . 1806
The portico erected . . . . ,,
The weavers' riot . . . . . 24 May, 1808
Exchange and Commercial buildings erected, Jan. 1809
Manchester and Salford water-works established . ,,
Blanketeers' meeting . . . . . 4 Nov. 1817
Lock-hospital established 1819

Manchester reform meeting (called *Peterloo*) of from 60,000 to 100,000 persons, men, women, and children. Mr. Hunt, who took the chair, had spoken a few words, when the meeting was suddenly assailed by a charge of cavalry, assisted by a Cheshire regiment of yeomanry, the outlets being occupied by other military detachments. The unarmed multitude were driven upon each other; many were ridden over by the horses, or cut down by their riders. The deaths were 11, men, women, and children, and the wounded about 600 16 Aug. ,,

New Brunswick-bridge built 1820
Chamber of commerce established . . . . ,,
Law library founded . . . . ,,
Natural History society projected 1821
New Quay company founded 1822
Deaf and Dumb school instituted 1823
Royal Institution formed . . . . . . ,,
Floral and Horticultural society established . . ,,
Mechanics' institution founded 1824
Musical festival first held 1828
At the launch of a vessel which keeled and upset, upwards of 200 persons precipitated into the river; 51 perished . . . . 29 Feb. 1828
In a tumult, a factory burnt, and much machinery destroyed . . . . . . 3 May, 1829
New concert-room established . . . . . ,,
The races established 1830
Manchester and Liverpool railway opened—Mr. Huskisson killed (see *Liverpool*) 15 Sept. ,,
Manchester made a parliamentary borough (2 members) by Reform act . . . 7 June, 1832
Choral society established 1833
Statistical society formed (the first in England), 2 Sept. ,,
Church-rate refused . . . . . 3 Sept. 1834
Manchester incorporated, by Municipal Reform act 1835
Manchester and Leeds railway act passed . . . 1836
Geological Society instituted 1838
Charter of incorporation . . . . 23 Oct. ,,
Manchester police act . . . . 26 Aug. 1839
Great disorders in the midland counties among artisans: they extend to this town . . Aug. 1842
British Association meet here . . . 23 June, ,,
Great free-trade meetings held here (see *Corn Laws*) 14 Nov. 1843
Important meeting held at the Athenæum (see *Athenæum*) . . . . . . 3 Oct. 1844
Great anti-corn law meeting, at which 64,984*l.* were subscribed in four hours . . 23 Dec. 1845
The Queen's-park, Peel-park, and Philip's-park, opened . . . . Aug. 1846
Manchester made a bishopric . . . 10 Aug. 1847
Opening of Owens collegiate institution, to which John Owens bequeathed 100,000*l.* . 12 March, 1851
The Queen's visit to Manchester . . . 7 Oct. ,,
Great meeting in the Free-trade hall, to greet M. Kossuth . . . . . . 11 Nov. ,,
The engineers' strike . . . 3 Jan.-26 April, 1852
The Guild of Literature entertained at a banquet by the citizens . . . . . . 31 Aug. ,,
Opening of the Free library . . . . 2 Sept. ,,
Great Free-trade banquet . . . . . 2 Nov. ,,
Manchester declared to be a CITY, and formally so gazetted . . . . . . 16 April, 1853
Great strike of minders and piecers . . 7 Nov. 1855
EXHIBITION OF ART TREASURES determined on, 20 May, 1856: 1115 old paintings, 689 new paintings, 969 water-colours, 388 British portraits, &c. collected; opened by prince Albert, 5 May; visited by the Queen, 29, 30 June; visited by 1,335,915 persons; expenses, 99,500*l.*, receipts, 98,500*l.*; closed . . . . 17 Oct. 1857
Sir John Potter, a benefactor to the town, died 25 Oct. 1858
British Association meet here (2nd time), 4 Sept. 1861
Great county meeting: 130,000*l.* subscribed to the Lancashire Relief fund . . . . 2 Dec. 1862
Meeting of the Church Congress . . 13-15 Oct. 1863
Great Reform meeting; Mr. Bright there, 24 Sept. 1866
Manchester Education bill committee appointed . ,,
Additional M.P. granted by Reform act 15 Aug. 1867
Meeting of Manchester and Liverpool agricultural society . . . . 27 Aug. ,,
Trades' Unions commission opened; evidence obtained of gross outrages . . . 3-24 Sept. ,,
Two Fenians, Kelly and Deasy, forcibly taken from a police-van, near Manchester, and Brett, a policeman killed . . . . . 18 Sept. ,,
23 persons committed for trial; trial, 29 Oct.-12 Nov.; five condemned to death for murder, 1 Nov.; others to imprisonment; Allen, Gould, and Larkin executed . . . . 23 Nov. ,,
Jacob Bright elected M.P. (Lily Maxwell, a widow, voted for him) . . . . . 26 Nov. ,,
False alarm of fire at Lang's music-hall, 23 killed, 31 July, 1868
New town-hall founded . . . . . 26 Oct. ,,
Manchester Reciprocity Association founded, Sept. 1869
National Education Union meet . . 3, 4 Nov. ,,
Bishop James Prince Lee died, 24 Dec. 1869; succeeded by James Fraser . . . . Jan. 1870
Alexandra-park (provided by the corporation) opened . . . . 6 Aug. ,,
Owens college new buildings founded . 23 Sept. ,,
Grammar school: additional building opened by earl of Derby . . . . . 25 Oct. 1871
Visit of Mr. Disraeli; enthusiastically received, 2-5 April, 1872
The library at the Athenæum burnt 24 Sept. 1873
Proposal to rebuild the cathedral by subscription, spring, 1874
Athenæum lecture-rooms opened by lord chief just. Cockburn, the marquis of Salisbury, &c. 22 Jan. 1875
Humphry Nichols, who had given about 100,000*l.* to public charities, died . . . 31 Oct. ,,
Statue of Cromwell (by M. Noble) gift of Mrs. Abel Heywood, uncovered . . . . 1 Dec. ,,
Rev. Thos. Middleton bequeaths 14,000*l.* to Royal Infirmary . . . . May, 1876
Proposal to make Owens college a university, July, ,,
Death of sir Elkanah Armitage, a great benefactor 26 Nov. ,,
New town-hall opened, by Mr. Abel Heywood, the mayor . . . . 13 Sept. 1877
Owens college made the nucleus of Victoria University (*which see*) . . . . . July, 1880
New school of art opened by the earl of Derby, 27 April, 1881
Visit of the dukes of Edinburgh and Albany 12 Dec. ,,

Formation of a ship canal by junction of the Mersey and Irwell; Mr. Williams's plan approved about 26 Sept. 1882
Fine art and industrial exhibition opened . 20 Oct. „
Fire at Messrs. Wilkinson and Hodgkinson's, about 100,000*l.* damage . . . . . 17 Nov. „
New fine art gallery opened . . . 31 Aug 1883
Edmund Potter, manufacturer and benefactor of the city, died aged 81 . . . . 26 Oct. „
Three great meetings to support the government and the franchise bill . . . 26 July, 1884
Great conservative demonstration, present the marquis of Salisbury, sir R. Cross, lord Randolph Churchill, and others . . . . 9 Aug. „
Manchester Geographical Society established Jan. 1885
Manchester returns six M.P.'s by act passed 25 June, „
Royal Jubilee Exhibition of manufactures, science, and art opened by the prince and princess of Wales, 3 May; closed . . . 10 Nov. 1887
[4,765,137 persons admitted; receipts about 250,000*l.* The surplus over 43,000*l.* given to the Manchester Whitworth Institute, Dec. 1889.]
Sir Joseph Whitworth's trustees propose the establishment of the Whitworth Institute of Art and Industry . . . . . . May, 1888
Prince Albert Victor opens Birchfield recreation grounds and lads' club . . . 20 Oct. „
Manchester new college, Oxford, opened . 25 Oct. 1889
The Manchester Whitworth Institute chartered, Nov. 1889; inaugurated by the marquis of Hartington . . . . . 17 July, 1890
The Queen's theatre burnt . . . 17 Aug. „
Messrs. Holland's cotton mill burnt, estimated loss, 120,000*l.* . . . . 17 Aug. „
Statue of Mr. John Bright unveiled by the earl of Derby . . . . 10 Oct. 1891
Earl Spencer installed chancellor of the Victoria university . . . . 25 May, 1892
Rylands Free Library (see *Libraries*) (Althorp) . „
For Mr. David Lewis' bequest (see *Liverpool*) . . „
The title of "lord" granted to the mayor, 15 June, 1893
Death of Mr. Abel Heywood, aged 82, twice mayor, eminent bookseller and energetic opposer of the Stamp Act, 1832, *et seq.* . . . . . 19 Aug. „
The new Royal College of Music opened, 7 Oct. „
Statue of Dr. Joule, natural philosopher, unveiled by lord Kelvin (see *Heat*) . . . 8 Dec. „
Textile Workers' international congress opened, 24 July, 1894
The Waterworks at Thirlmere (cost 4,500,000*l.*); opened; a fountain in Manchester started by sir John Harwood . . . . . 13 Oct. „
Mr. Henry Wilde endows the Literary and Philosophical society with 8,000*l.* . . . Feb. 1895
Mr. Sam Weston bequeathed 177,000*l.* to charities in and about Manchester, and 50,000*l.* to the church, payment begun . . . Sept. 1896
Death of Mr. Francis Wm. Crossley, philanthropist, aged 57, founder of Star Hall, Ancoats 25 March, 1897
Royal agricultural show buildings etc., much injured by the gale, 16 June; opened 23 June, the duke of York (president) present . 28 June, „
Mr. J. Heywood's premises burnt, estimated damage, 20,000*l.* . . . . . 14 Feb. 1899
Mr. W. Roberts, architect, bequeaths 19,350*l.* for public purposes, reported . . . 23 Feb. „
Mr. Richard Johnson, philanthropist, born, 1827, died . . . . . . early March, „
Victoria theatre, foundation-stone laid by sir Henry Irving . . . . 4 Oct. „
The *John Rylands memorial library* erected by his widow (see *above*, 1892), opened; Mrs. Rylands presented with the freedom of the city, 6 Oct. „
Messrs. Ferguson's and 2 other factories burnt down, houses buried . . . 23 Nov. „
Mr. Balfour addresses large meetings in E. Manchester on the war in S. Africa; deprecates criticism of the commanders and upholds the War Office . . . . . 8, 10 Jan. 1900
Fire at the central post-office, telegraphic communication, &c., stopped . . . 19 Sept. „
Epidemic of peripheral neuritis, or arsenical poisoning, attributed to adulteration in beer; 36 deaths between 25 Nov. and 10 Jan. 1901. (Royal commission appointed, see *Arsenic.*)
Explosion at a hat factory, 13 deaths . 15 Jan. 1901
Lord Roberts opens a royal military tournament and presents war medals; unveils a statue of queen Victoria . . . . 9, 10 Oct. 1901
Mr. John Morley unveils a statue of Mr. Gladstone . . . . 23 Oct. „
Mr. J. H. Gartside endows Owens college with 10,000*l.* for scholarships of commerce and industries, announced . . . . . 3 March, 1902
The prince and princess of Wales open the new Whitworth-hall, cost 50,000*l.*, gift of the late Dr. Christie; statue of queen Victoria by the duchess of Argyll unveiled in the cathedral . 12 March, „
Sir Geo. White opens the royal military tournament . . . . 18 Sept.
Stone laid in Delamere forest for a sanatorium (at a cost of 70,000*l.* from Mr. W. J. Crossley), 7 Oct. „
Nat. union of Conservative assocs. meets; lord Derby elected president for 1903; Mr. Balfour's firm speech in favour of the education bill well received; he opens a new school of technology, 14, 15 Oct. „
Jubilee of the free library celebrated; message from the king . . . . . . 3 April, 1903
Celebration of publication by Dr. John Dalton of his discovery of the atomic theory . 19 May, „
Meeting held and committee appointed to arrange for holding an international exhibition in 1905, mid July, „

MANCHESTER SHIP CANAL act (with conditions) passed July, 1885; company formed, Mr. Daniel Adamson, active promoter, proposed capital 8,000,000*l.* Oct. 1885. To hold property of Bridgewater Navigation Company; to occupy about 7,500 square miles. Contract for work taken by Lucas and Aird for 5,750,000*l.* July; execution of the scheme suspended through non-subscription of capital announced 24 July, 1886; first sod cut at Eastham by lord Egerton of Tatton 11 Nov. 1887; satisfactory progress in the work reported, about one third done . . . . June, 1889
Mr. J. A. Walker, the contractor, dies 25 Nov.; progress retarded by the bursting of the Mersey bank at Statham . . . . . 7 Nov. 1890
Water of the Mersey first admitted into the Eastham section of the canal, 18, 19 June, 1891. Collapse of part of the embankment near the Eastham section; new embankment quickly constructed, 12 July; the first flotilla of traffic from Ellesmere port passed down the ship canal into the Mersey . . . . . 16 July, 1891
Through the error of a pointsman, George Pratt, aged 16, a train of carriages conveying rock débris and soil was precipitated down an embankment 60 feet deep, killing 10 men at supper below; 6 men on the train leaped from it and thus escaped, about 1 A.M. . . . . . 18 July, „
Amount expended, 10,359,597*l.* up to . 1 Aug. „
The Manchester Corporation lent 3,000,000*l.*, 1891; 1,500,000*l.* more required . . . Aug. 1892
Money loans: Manchester corporation, 2,000,000*l.* (additional); Salford, 1,000,000*l.* . 20–27 Oct. „
The *Lodore*, from Saltport, on the canal, arrives at the Regent's Canal dock, London . . 8 Dec. „
Oldham agrees to lend 250,000*l.* . about 17 Jan. 1893
The company authorizes the directors to borrow 2,000,000*l.* . . . . . 16 June, „
The canal completed; length, 35½ miles; width, 172 ft.; depth, from 26 to 28 ft.; total outlay, 1885–93, 13,470,221*l.*; inspection trips by the directors, &c., 16 Dec. 1893; public opening of the canal, a procession of steamers, &c. . 1 Jan. 1894
The canal inaugurated by the queen, after driving through Manchester and receiving addresses, 21 May, „
Mr. Williams, chief engineer, knighted . June, „
Unfavourable report respecting traffic . Nov. „
Revenue from all sources gradually increasing, 1895–1901
Manchester ship canal directors publish scheme for the readjustment of company's capital and its relations with the corporation . end of May. „

MANCHESTER, BISHOPRIC OF. An order in council in Oct. 1838, declared that the sees of St. Asaph and Bangor should be united on the next vacancy in either, and that the bishopric of Manchester should be immediately created within the jurisdiction of the archiepiscopal see of York; the county of Lancaster for that purpose to be detached from Chester. By act 10 Vict. (1847) the sees of St. Asaph and Bangor were to exist undisturbed, and that of Manchester was to be created.

BISHOPS.

1847. James Prince Lee; died 24 Dec. 1869.
1870. James Fraser, Jan. 1870; died 22 Oct. 1885.
1886. James Moorhouse, D.D. (bishop of Melbourne), Jan., retired 31 Oct. 1903.
1903. Edmund Arbuthnott Knox (bishop suffragan of Coventry).

MANCHURIA. N.E. division of the Chinese empire. Capital, Mukden; treaty port, Nin-Chuang. The Manchus conquered China in 1644, and founded the present Chin dynasty. The French (1838) and British (1861) have missionary stations there. Population estimated over a million. The Japanese invaded Manchuria during the war of 1894–5. Capt. Frank E. Younghusband's "Travels in Manchuria," published, March, 1896. Prosperity increased by Russian immigration, 1897–8. See *Corea*. For the massacres here, see *China*, 14 Aug. 1901. Great mortality from cholera, July *et seq.* 1902. The province is virtually occupied by Russia, causing strained relations with Japan (30 Nov. 1903), see *Russia*.

MANDALAY, capital of Upper Burmah; population, 1891, 188,815; 1901, 182,498. See *Burmah*.

MANERU, near Puente de la Reyna Navarre. Here took place a conflict between the republicans, under Moriones, and the Carlists, under Otto; both claimed a victory; 6 Oct. 1873.

MANGANESE. Black oxide of manganese, long used to decolorise glass, and called *Magnesia nigra*, was formerly included among the ores of iron. Its distinctive character was proved by the researches of Pott (1740), Kaim and Winterl (1770), and Scheele and Bergmann (1774); it was first eliminated by Gahn. Manganese combined with potassium is called mineral chameleon, from its rapid change of colour under certain circumstances. Forchammer employed it as a test for the presence of organic matter in water; and Dr. Angus Smith, successfully applied this test to air in 1858. The oxide is the important ingredient in Condy's "disinfecting fluid." Manganese bronze, is a metal produced by Mr. P. M. Parsons, inventor of white brass, 1876. Manganese steel produced by Messrs. Pfeil & Co. 1887.

MANICA, a territory in S. Africa in Mashonaland, near Mozambique, which on account of its mines, the Portuguese vainly endeavoured to acquire in the 16th century. See *Zambesi*.

The territory was acknowledged to be under the influence of Portugal by the convention of Aug. 1890.

Dispute with Great Britain; delimitation referred to arbitration of Italy, March, 1894; boundary settled, 30 Jan. 1897; further concessions, reported, 22 Feb. 1899.

MANICHEANS, a sect founded by Manes, in Persia, about 261. It spread into Egypt, Arabia, and Africa. A rich widow, whose servant Manes had been, left him much wealth, after which he assumed the title of Apostle, or envoy of Jesus Christ, and announced that he was the paraclete or comforter that Christ had promised to send. He maintained two principles, the one good he called light, the other bad he called darkness. He rejected the Old Testament, and composed a system of doctrine from Christianity and the dogmas of the ancient fire-worshippers. Sapor, king of Persia, believed in him at one time; but afterwards banished him. He was burnt alive by Bahram or Varanes, king of Persia, in 277. His followers dispersed, and several sects sprang from them.

MANILLA (or MANILA) (built about 1573), capital of the Philippine isles, a great mart of Spanish commerce. Manilla was taken by the English, 6 Oct. 1762, when the archbishop engaged to ransom it for about a million sterling; never wholly paid. Manilla has suffered greatly by earthquakes. It is stated that nearly 3000 persons perished by one in 1645. In Sept. 1852, the city was nearly destroyed, and on 3 July, 1863, about a thousand lives were lost. The duke of Edinburgh was hospitably entertained here, 19 Nov. 1869. See *Earthquakes* 1852, 1863, 1880. Destructive typhoon, 20, 21 Oct. 1882. Great fire; 4,000 houses burnt, many deaths, 1 April, 1893. Great fire, 30,000 persons homeless, reported 5 April, 1896; another, public buildings destroyed, several deaths, 28 Sept. 1897; another fire, 200 houses burnt, reported, 7 Feb. 1898. See *Spanish-American War*.

MANIPUR (Manipore), a small native state, N.E. India, adjoining Assam and Burmah; population, 1881, 221,070; army about 5,000.

The state has long been protected by the British from the attacks of the Burmese. In 1834, Gumbheer Singh, the restored rajah, died, and was succeeded by his son, Chandra Kirti Singh, two years old. The regent, Nar Singh, a relative, usurped the government, and ruled till his death in 1850, when the young rajah was restored; a British resident being afterwards placed in the capital, with good effect. Much trouble was given by rival members of his family till 1866; he died in 1885 or 1886. He left eight sons, who formed opposing parties. The eldest, Sura Chandra Singh, became maharajah, and appointed his eldest brother, Kula Chandra Dhuya Singh, jubraj, or heir-apparent, afterwards termed regent, a weak, incapable man. In Sept. 1890, his brother, Takendrajil Singh, the senaputti, or commander-in-chief, dethroned the maharajah and set up the jubraj in his place. The maharajah retired to Calcutta.

On 21 Feb. 1891, Mr. James W. Quinton, chief commissioner of Assam, was directed to proceed with a sufficient force to Manipur, to recognise the regent, and to remove the senaputti. He entered Manipur 22 March, with 470 men and officers, civil and military, and was well received by the regent and the senaputti, but could not succeed in getting the latter to attend a durbar or court. Mr. Quinton as an ultimatum required the surrender of the senaputti, the letter being taken by Mr. F. St. C. Grimwood, political agent, without any result, 23 March. On the 24th, colonel Skene proceeded with 250 men to arrest the senaputti at his house within the fort inclosure, of which they obtained possession after a sharp struggle, during which lieut. Brackenbury was mortally wounded. The senaputti had escaped. About 10 A.M., the Manipuris opened fire on the residency in front, and about noon on the rear, and shelled it. About 4 P.M. the troops were withdrawn from the senaputti's house, and all the force was posted in the residency, which was seriously damaged by artillery about 5 P.M., and the ammunition began to fall short. About 7 P.M. negotiations were re-opened by letter from Mr. Quinton, and the firing ceased, but the conditions offered by the regent could not be accepted. Having been invited by the senaputti halfway between the residency and the palace, Mr. Quinton took with him colonel Skene, Mr. F. St. C. Grimwood, Mr. H. Cossins, and lieut. Simpson, unarmed, and without escort. After a long parley, the party entered the fort and were seen no more, and it was afterwards discovered that they were all killed (beheaded or otherwise). The firing re-commenced about midnight. The ammunition having been greatly reduced, it was decided to retire from the residency, and to march across the country to meet captain Cowley's advancing party. This was done about 2 A.M. on the 25th, the party taking with them 17 wounded, and Mrs. Grimwood, who displayed much judgment, courage, and humanity. There was no serious resistance during the march, but a few skirmishes occurred. About 10 A.M. they met captain Cowley's party, who supplied them with food and other assistance. They continued their march, arriving, on 30 March, at Lakhipur on the Cachar frontier.

Lieut. C. J. W. Grant hearing, on 27 March, of the disaster at Manipur, volunteered to attempt the relief of the British captives, and marched with 80 native soldiers from Tamu in Burmah, 28 March; entrenched himself near Thobal, 31 March; held out against the attacks of the Manipuri army (about 3,000) till 7 April; and resisted negotiations judiciously; only 1 killed.

[Lieut. Grant was made major and otherwise honoured.]

About 2,000 Manipuris, entrenched near Tamu, attacked and dispersed by general Graham's party, captain Drury being especially successful, 25 April; three columns under gen. Graham, and others from different directions converge at Manipur, which they find totally deserted, the regent, senaputti, and other princes having fled, 26 April; the palace had been blown up; the heads of Mr. Quinton and his companions were found in the enclosure.

Funeral ceremony was held over the exhumed bodies of Mr. Quinton and his companions, 30 April; general Collett was left in command at Manipur, some of the troops left. The Manipuris returned to their homes, May; the regent and his minister were captured, 8 May, and the senaputti, about 23 May, 1891

The regent, the senaputti, and prince Angao Sena, a younger brother, were tried for rebellion and abetting to murder, and sentenced to death (all appealed) . . . . 9–20 June, „

The sentences of death on the senaputti and the Tongal general, as implicated in the murders, were confirmed. The sentences on the regent and his younger brother commuted to transportation for life to the Andaman Islands; forfeiture of property, announced 10 Aug. The senaputti and the Tongal general hanged at Manipur, 13 Aug. „

It was decided that Manipur should still be ruled by a native prince, 23 Aug.; and Chura Chand, aged 5, great grandson of Nar Singh, was appointed rajah, 13 Sept.; dignity to be hereditary, subject to the government of India; an annual tribute to be paid; declaration communicated . . Oct. „

The young prince was invested with a dignity, 29 April, 1892

Heavy rain, causing destructive floods and loss of life . . . . May, 1893

Lord Curzon held a durbar (of about 3,000) here, 16 Nov. 1901

MANITOBA, see *Rupert's Land* and *Hudson's Bay* (N. America). Manitoba was made a part of the confederation in 1870. Capital, Winnipeg. Population, 1886, 108,640; 1891, 154,442; 1901, 254,947. Lieut.-gov., John C. Schultz; succeeded by J. C. Patterson, June, 1895; D. H. McMillan, 1900. A Fenian attack on the colony was suppressed by American troops about 12 Oct. 1871. For insurrection in the neighbouring provinces in March, 1885, see *Canada*. For the Red River Railway disputes see *Canada*, Oct. 1888. Disputes with the Dominion government respecting the privileges of the Catholic schools, March *et seq.* 1895; negotiations closed, the difficulty settled by compromise, 17 Oct. 1896; bill passed, 25 March, 1897. Catholic schools of Winnipeg taken over by the school board by agreement, Sept. 1901. Prairie fires, villages burnt, 7 deaths, reported, 4 Oct. 1897.

MANNHEIM (S. Germany), founded in 1606, became the court residence of the palatine of the Rhine in 1719; but his becoming elector of Bavaria in 1777 caused the removal of the court to Munich. Mannheim surrendered to the French, under command of general Pichegru, 20 Sept. 1795. On 31 Oct. the Austrians under general Wurmser defeated the French near the city. Several battles were fought with various success in the neighbourhood during the wars of Napoleon I. Kotzebue, the popular dramatist, was assassinated at Mannheim, by Sand, a student of Wurtzburg, 2 April, 1819. Population, 1890, 79,044; 1900, 140,384.

MANOMETER (Greek, *manos*, thin), an instrument for measuring the rarity of the atmosphere, gases, and vapours. One is said to have been made by Otto von Guericke about 1660, and the "statical barometer" of Robert Boyle was a simple manometer. Various forms of the apparatus were devised by Ramsden (about 1773), by Roy (1777), by Cazalet (1789), and by Bourdon and others. A manometer was constructed for the investigation respecting the elasticity of steam conducted by Prony, Arago, Dulong, and Girard, 1830.

MANORS are as ancient as the Saxon times, and imply a territorial district with its jurisdiction, rights, and perquisites. They were formerly called baronies, and still are lordships. Each lord was empowered to hold a court called the court-baron for redressing misdemeanours, and settling disputes between the tenants. *Cabinet Lawyer*.

MANSFIELD COLLEGE, Oxford, for the study of Nonconformist theology opened in temporary rooms 19 Oct. 1886. The new college solemnly opened, 14 Oct. 1889. A settlement connected with the college, called *Mansfield house*, at Canning town, E. London.

MANSION-HOUSE, London. The residence of the lord mayor. It is situate at the east end of the Poultry on the site of the ancient Stocks-market. It was built of Portland stone by George Dance the elder, 1739-53; repaired and redecorated, 1867-68; see *Mayor* and *Hospitals*.

Attempt to blow up part of Mansion-House; a box of gunpowder (40 lbs.) discovered in a window, east side, about 11 p.m. 16 March, 1881; again, 12 May, 1882

Visited by the queen, after opening the People's Palace . . . . 14 May, 1887

Exhibition and sale of Irish work organised by the Irish industries association, opened by the prince and princess of Wales 16 March, 1900

Large national meeting for the organisation of the S. African war relief funds, lord Derby elected chairman of the central council; committees, appointed . . . . 19 Oct. „

Meeting of lords-lieutenant, mayors, and others, lord mayor president, for the organisation of war relief funds, lord Derby elected chairman of the central council, executive and sub-committees appointed . . . . 19 Oct. „

Public meeting in support of the Queen Victoria national memorial, the lord mayor presiding; 16,000*l.* subscribed (1,000*l.* from the king), 26 March, 1901

Meetings in support of a royal naval volunteer reserve, 10 Jan.; and for a coronation gift, see *Hospitals* . . . . 9 June, 1902

Mansion-House Funds:—

French Relief Fund for the sufferers by the siege of Paris, was established at a meeting . 18 Jan. 1871

In four days about 24,000*l.* had been received; up to 4 March, 113,599*l.*; finally, 126,609*l.* Col. H. Stuart Wortley and Mr. George Moore went to Paris on 3 Feb. with 68 tons of provisions, and personally superintended their distribution by the clergy, foreign consuls, and others. An official report issued by the lord mayor, dated 7 Nov. 1871, showed a balance of 4679*l.* in hand.

Bengal Relief Fund, begun 24 Jan 1874; prince of Wales became patron, 24 Feb.; public meeting, 14 April; above 55,000*l.* subscribed, 19 March; 125,000*l.*, 27 July, when the fund was closed.

EASTERN WAR SUFFERERS' FUND; 940*ol.* received up to 6 Oct. 1876; 18 Oct. 13,000*l.*; 27 Oct. 14,200*l.*

INUNDATIONS RELIEF FUND; 1877, received, 11 Jan. 3600*l.*; 20 Jan. 8100*l.*; closed, 14 Feb., 8792*l.*

INDIAN FAMINE RELIEF FUND, 1877-8; announced, 15 Aug.; received up to 20 Aug. 12,000*l.*; 11 Sept. 135,000*l.*; 23 Oct. 415,000*l.*; 5 Nov. 446,100*l.*; (fund declared closed by request of the duke of Buckingham, governor of Madras); since received, 22 Dec. 493,000*l.*; 15 Jan. 1878, 503,000*l.*; total received, 689,466*l.* 17*s.* . . . . 20 May, 1878

"EURYDICE" FUND (see *Wrecks*, 24 March, 1878); received for families of the men, 5496*l.*; transmitted . . . . 25 Sept. ,,

"PRINCESS ALICE" RELIEF FUND; opened 5 Sept. 1878; received, 21st Sept. 25,000*l.*; 1 Oct. 31,400*l.* See *Princess Alice*.

ABERCARN COLLIERY EXPLOSION FUND; opened 14 Sept. 1878; received, 21 Sept. 11,500*l.*; 21 Oct. 29,300*l.*: above 18,000*l.* received in the country.

DINAS COLLIERY EXPLOSION FUND (for 180 widows and children); opened in . . . . Feb. 1879

HUNGARIAN FLOODS FUND; opened 14 March; received 18 March, about 4,200*l.*; May 1, 11,248*l.* ,,

ZULU WAR FUND; opened, 31 March; received 2 April, 3,400*l.*; 25 April, 10,300*l.* . . . ,,

ROWLAND HILL MEMORIAL proposed 9 Sept. 1879; the lord mayor, Whetham, announced that as about 100*l.* only had been subscribed; the money would be returned; another committee was then formed, and lord mayor Truscott assumed charge of the fund, 11 Nov.; 6,300*l.* received 12 Dec. 1879; about 16,000*l.* 26 Feb. 1880; 17,286*l.* 5 Jan. 1881

DUCHESS OF MARLBOROUGH'S IRISH RELIEF FUND; opened on appeal by her grace, 22 Dec. 1879; about 2,300*l.* received 29 Dec.; total sent to Dublin, 34,164*l.* 6*s.* 6*d.*; fund closed . 10 Aug. 1880

"ATALANTA" FUND; to relieve sufferers by loss of the *Atalanta* (*which see*); opened . . 15 June, ,,

TRURO CATHEDRAL FUND opened 14 July; received, 1,085*l.* . . . . 9 Nov. ,,

RISCA COLLIERY EXPLOSION FUND, opened 16 July; received 7,317*l.* . . . . . . 9 Nov. ,,

NAINI TAL LANDSLIP FUND; opened . 22 Oct. ,,

AGRAM EARTHQUAKE FUND; opened . 17 Nov. ,,

PENYGRAIG COLLIERY EXPLOSION FUND; opened, 13 Dec. ,,

CHIOS OR SCIO EARTHQUAKE FUND; opened 7 April, 1881

DEFENCE OF PROPERTY IN IRELAND FUND, ("to uphold the rights of property against organized combination, to defend and to sustain freedom of contract and liberty of action,") begun, 13 Dec.; 1881; 18,226*l.* applied, balance of 1,268*l.* transferred to Irish Defence Union . 18 Dec. 1885

EGYPTIAN REFUGEES FUND: 2,100*l.*, 30 June, 1882; 2,700*l.*, 6 July; 7,800*l.*, 11 Aug.; 8,000*l.*, 10 Sept.; 21,308*l.* . . . . 10 April, 1883

RELIEF OF PERSECUTED RUSSIAN JEWS FUND, begun 1 Feb. 1882; 46,000*l.*, received, 13 Feb.; 50,365*l.* 20 Feb.; about 72,000*l.*, 19 May. Fund closed 108,759*l.*, received (over 110,000*l.* received, finally closed 9 July, 1886) . . . . . . 25 Oct. 1882

FUND FOR EMIGRATION OF THE UNEMPLOYED, established 13 April; unsuccessful, closed 25 April, ,,

ICELAND FAMINE FUND, formed 29 Aug. 1882; 1,500*l.* received 6 Sept.; 2,800*l.* 14 Sept.; 3,700*l.* 21 Sept.; 5,505*l.*, closed . . . . . April, 1883

CLAY CROSS COLLIERY EXPLOSION FUND, about 14 Nov.; 496*l.* 10*s.* 6*d.* remitted; fund closed, 26 Jan. ,,

JAMAICA FIRE RELIEF FUND, established, 22 Jan. received 4,400*l.*; 21 Feb. 7,620*l.*; closed, received 7,850*l.* . . . . 9 April, ,,

WEST COAST OF SCOTLAND FUND, 2,200*l.* received 3 April; 3,964*l.* 12 April; 4,861*l.* 8 May; 5,159*l.* fund closed . . . . 23 July, ,,

FUND FOR SUFFERERS BY NORTH SEA GALE, (6 March) . . . . 12 April, ,,

ISCHIA EARTHQUAKE FUND, opened 14 Aug.; 1,200*l.* 22 Aug.; about 29,000*l.* 12 Oct.; closed 31 Oct. ,,

EGYPTIAN CHOLERA FUND, opened 31 Aug. about 2,731*l.* received; closed . . . . . 9 Nov. ,,

EASTERN COUNTIES EARTHQUAKE FUND, begun 26 April, 1884; 2,000*l.* received, 2 May; 3,000*l.* 5 May; 6,000*l.* 15 May; 9,900*l.* 10 June; 10,413*l.* 31 July, 1884

NISERO FUND (see *Nisero*), established 17 July; 405*l.* received from earl of Derby and others; 600*l.* received from Rotterdam, Aug.; 1,237*l.* received, fund closed . . . . 1 Dec. ,,

NEAPOLITAN CHOLERA FUND, 1,000*l.* sent off, Oct. 1 final remittance, 323*l.* . . . . . . Nov. ,,

GORDON NATIONAL MEMORIAL FUND, (see *Gordon Memorial*) begun 25 Feb.; 13,500*l.* received up to 8 April; king of Belgium gives 100*l.* 8 April, 1885

SPANISH CHOLERA FUND begun 11 Sept.; 4191*l.* received; closed . . . . . . 4 Nov. ,,

UNEMPLOYED RELIEF FUND begun about 5 Feb.; over 3,300*l.* received; 76,225*l.* 26 March; 76,819*l.* 31 March; 77,910*l.* (1,200*l.* collected in the streets 3 April) 7 April; closed 19 April; total received 78,629*l.* 1886

ST. PAUL'S CATHEDRAL APPROACH FUND, begun about 5 Feb. ,,

EARTHQUAKE FUND for sufferers in Greece and Charleston, U.S. 7 Sept.; 5,000*l.* 17 Sept.; 6,500*l.* 24 Sept.; closed . . . . . 26 Oct. ,,

COLONIAL AND INDIAN INSTITUTE FUND proposed as a memorial of the queen's jubilee by the prince of Wales 13 Sept. 1886; 27,500*l.* received 27 Oct. 1887

EXETER THEATRE FIRE RELIEF FUND 8 Sept.; the queen gives 100*l.*; announced 12 Sept.; 1,300*l.* to 16 Sept. ,,

PRUSSIAN INUNDATION FUND, 9 April; 3,000*l.* received . . . . 13 April, 1888

CHINESE FAMINE FUND proposed 22 Jan.; 5,300*l.* received 30 Jan.; 18,250*l.* 4 March; 21,706*l.* 26 March; fund closed, over 32,654*l.* received May, 1889

The fund in aid of the Royal Agricultural Jubilee Show (see *Windsor*) amounted to 5,516*l.* 1 Aug. ,,

PASTEUR INSTITUTE FUND established (see *Hydrophobia*), 1 July, 1889; received from the prince of Wales 105*l.*, the duke of Westminster 200*l.*, the duke of Northumberland 100*l.*, and many others; amount received, 2,839*l.* . . . . . Dec. ,,

FRUIT CULTURE FUND begun by the lord mayor; the duke of Westminster gave 50*l.*, baroness Burdett-Coutts 50*l.*, and others . . . . 14 Oct. ,,

LLANERCH COLLIERY EXPLOSION FUND. Contributions received, 11 Feb., 363*l.*; 1 March, 5,000*l.*; 7,333*l.* remitted . . . . . 23 May, 1890

MORFA COLLIERY EXPLOSION FUND, 15 March. Contributions received, 22 March, about 1,300*l.*; 2 June, 2,800*l.* . . . . ,,

LORD STRATHNAIRN (sir Hugh Rose) MEMORIAL FUND. Amount received, 17 June, 1,500*l.* 2,700*l.* 6 Nov. Liberal contributions received from Indian princes . . . . ,,

SALONICA FIRE RELIEF FUND, 19 Sept. 3,373*l.* received, 7 Nov.; fund closed . . 8 Nov. ,,

LORD NAPIER OF MAGDALA MEMORIAL FUND. Received from city companies and others 2,000*l.*, 8 Feb. 1890; total received, 5,446*l.* . . 10 Nov. 1891

SERPENT WRECK RELIEF FUND (see *Navy*, 10 Nov. 1890, *et seq.*) started by request about 20 Nov.; 2,750*l.* received . . . . 8 Jan. ,,

MAURITIUS HURRICANE FUND, opened 30 April, 1892; received about 1,300*l.*, 24 May; (closed) 12,083*l.* . . . . 20 Sept. 1892

ST. JOHN'S, NEWFOUNDLAND, FIRE, RELIEF FUND for the sufferers started 12 July; received up to 15 July, 6,000*l.* (the queen 50*l.*, the prince of Wales 26*l.* 5*s.*, city of London corporation 210*l.*, Goldsmiths' company 500*l.*, and other companies; sir Donald A. Smith 1,000*l.*); 21,000*l.*, 20 Aug.; 24,502*l.*, Nov. ,,

PARK SLIP COLLIERY RELIEF FUND opened, 29 Aug.; the queen, 100*l.*; the marquis of Bute, 500*l.*; the lord mayor, D. Evans, 500*l.*; received up to 14 Sept. 3,300*l.*; 4,639*l.* . . . . 4 Nov ,,

VICTORIA DISASTER relief fund opened 23 June [see *Navy of England*, 22 June]; the queen, 200*l.*; prince and princess of Wales, 157*l.* 10*s.*; the duke of Edinburgh, 150*l.*; the duchess of York (reported surplus of wedding present fund, 800*l.*), and other eminent persons; total received up to 1894, 73,265*l.*, reported . . . . 29 May, 1895

THORNHILL COLLIERY explosion fund opened, 10 July; the queen, 50*l.*; 12 July, 6,661*l.*, reported . . . . 3 Aug. 1893

GREEK EARTHQUAKES relief fund opened, 30 April; princess of Wales, 50*l.*, 7 July; total, 5,288*l.*; closed . . . . 16 July, 1894

ALBION COLLIERY, Pontypridd, explosion fund opened, 26 June; prince and princess of Wales, 52*l.*, 9 July; the queen 50*l.*, 17 July; 5,000*l.*, 9 Aug.; 7,000*l.* received at Cardiff . . . ,,

CONSTANTINOPLE EARTHQUAKE fund opened, 17 July; Ottoman bank, credit of 5,000*l.*, 19 July; Messrs. Rothschild, 1,000*l.* . . . . . 23 July, ,,

AUDLEY COLLIERY disaster (14 Jan.) fund opened, 25 Jan. (local fund relief, 4,600*l.*, reported 28 Jan.); 50*l.* from the queen; total, 2,121*l.* 11*s.* 10*d.*, April, 1895

BECHUANALAND relief fund opened, 29 June, 1896; total received, 1,432*l.* 12*s.* 5*d.*

JAPAN EARTHQUAKE relief fund opened, 21 July; total, 3,895*l.* . . . . Nov. 1896

INDIAN FAMINE fund opened, 8 Jan. 1897; the queen 500*l.* 10 Jan.; again 500*l.* 10 Mar.; the prince and princess of Wales 250gs.; duke and duchess of Connaught 105*l.*; duke of York 105*l.*, 13 Jan.; 1,050*l.* London corporation; 1,000*l.* Bank of England; marquis of Salisbury, 250*l.*; other large sums: total, 550,000*l.*, Nov.; see *India* . . 1897

MONTSERRAT inundation relief fund opened, 16 Jan. 1897; total, 2,000*l.*; closed . . . . 1 April, ,,

ESSEX storm relief fund, 6 July, 1897; 100*l.* from the queen, 11 July; total, 28,000*l.* . . . Nov. ,,

Lady Mayoress's branch of the prince of Wales's Hospital fund, 5,000*l.* . . . . . . Nov. ,,

POOREST OF THE POOR London Jubilee dinner fund, initiated by the princess of Wales; large subscriptions; 29 April; 25,000*l.* from Mr. Lipton (knt. 1 Jan. 1898); reported total, 60,000*l.*; fund closed, May. [20,000 sheep sent from Australia.] See *Jubilees*. Surplus distributed to various funds, Jan. 1898.

CITY FIRE relief fund: for the workpeople; 4,000*l.*, 2 Dec. ,,

MAIDSTONE epidemic fund opened, 9 Oct. 1897; total, including local relief fund, 27,916*l.* 18*s.* 8*d.*, announced . . . . 16 July, 1898

THE DUCHESS OF TECK MEMORIAL (home of rest for poor women from London), 10,856*l* 7*s.* 4*d.* . ,,

HURRICANE, WEST INDIES RELIEF FUND; opened 17th Sept.; the queen 250*l.*, the prince of Wales 105*l.*, the duke of York 25 gs., city corporation 1,000 gs.; total, 46,121*l.* 3*s.* 5*d.*; closed . April, 1899

GORDON MEMORIAL COLLEGE, KHARTOUM, fund opened 1 Dec. 1898; 250*l.* from the queen, 100 gs. from the prince of Wales; total, 22,738*l.* 5*s.* 10*d.*; closed . . . . 17 April, ,,

NEWLYN AND LOWESTOFT fishery disaster, 7 April; fund opened 17 April; 7,000*l.* . . . 16 June, ,,

HURRICANE, WEST INDIES; Montserrat, St. Kitts, Nevis (Leeward group); relief fund opened, 15 Aug.; 7,200*l.* . . . . 23 Nov. ,,

TRANSVAAL WAR REFUGEES FUND; opened 12 Oct. 1899; 500 gs. from the prince and princess of Wales, 14 Oct.; 500 gs. from the queen, 16 Oct.; 50 gs. from the duke and duchess of York, 17 Oct.; total, 170,000*l.* . . . . Aug. 1900

TRANSVAAL WAR FUND; opened 21 Oct. 1899; 1,000*l.* from the queen, 6 Nov.; 1,001,000*l.* 21 Aug. 1900; 1,131,860*l.* . . . . 5 March, 1902 (Other funds also raised in London and provinces, 2,600,000*l.* end of 1900).

CITY IMPERIAL VOLUNTEER FUND; total, 117,000*l.* 21 Aug. 1900

BISHOP CREIGHTON MEMORIAL FUND; opened Jan.; total, 3,300*l.* . . . . 7 Nov. 1901

INDIAN FAMINE FUND; opened 16 Feb. 1900; the queen 1,000*l.*, the prince and princess of Wales 350 gs., and 100*l.* from the duke and duchess of York, 19 Feb.; total, 394,000*l.*; closed . March, ,,

OTTAWA FIRE FUND; opened 28 April; the queen 500 gs., the prince of Wales 250 gs., 4 May; duke of York 105*l.*, 5 May; proceeds of matinees, 1,019*l.* 1*s.* 2*d.*; total, 53,405*l.* 16*s.* 10*d.* . July, ,,

JOHANNESBURG REFUGEES FUND; 1,000*l.* Messrs. N. M. Rothschild . . . . . . 8 April, 1902

ST. VINCENT (volcanic eruption), W. Indies relief fund; opened 14 May; the pope 20,000 f. about 14 May; the king gives 400*l.*, the queen 500*l.*, prince and princess of Wales 250*l.*, 15, 16, 17 May; Canada, 25,000 dol.; the queen of Holland and her mother, 1,250 fl.; king of Denmark, over 100*l.* 31 May; 65,200*l.* 8 Oct.; 1,348*l.* 18*s.* 9*d.* from Belgium, reported . . . . 2 Sept. ,,

QUEEN VICTORIA NATIONAL MEMORIAL FUND; opened 26 March, 1901; (5,000*l.* from the New York chamber of commerce, 1,000*l.* from the hon. W. C. Whitney, nearly 15,000*l.* from U.S.N.A. reported, 13 Nov. 1902); Natal, 10,000*l.*; Cape Colony, 20,000*l.*; Ceylon, 5,000*l.*; Canada, 30,000*l.*; New Zealand, 15,000*l.*; total, 230,000*l.*; Nov. 1902, 250,000*l.* . . . . 30 Nov. 1903

MANSOURAH (Lower Egypt). Here Louis IX. was defeated by the Saracens and taken prisoner, 5 April, 1250. He gave Damietta and 400,000 livres for his ransom. Mansourah suffered much by cholera, summer, 1883.

MANTES, a town in the department of Seine-et-Oise, France, is situated on the river Seine, about 36 miles from Paris. It possesses a handsome Gothic church, and contains other objects of antiquarian interest. Here, while besieging the town, William the Conqueror received the fatal wound that caused his death, 1089.

MANTINEA (Arcadia, Greece). Here—(1) Athenians and Argives were defeated by Agis II. of Sparta, 418 B.C. (2) And here Epaminondas and the Thebans defeated the combined forces of Lacedæmon, Achaia, Elis, Athens, and Arcadia, 362 B.C. Epaminondas was killed in the engagement, and Thebes lost its power among the Grecian states. The emperor Adrian built a temple at Mantinea in honour of his favourite Alcinoüs. The town was also called Antigonia. Other battles were fought near it.

MANTIS, a genus of remarkable insects, whose forms and colours of their bodies and wings imitate the leaves and twigs that environ them. The praying mantis (*mantis religiosa*) derives its name from the peculiar position of its anterior pair of legs.

MANTUA (N. Italy), an Etruscan city, near which Virgil was born, 70 B.C. Mantua was ruled by the Gonzagas, lords of Mantua, from 1328 to 1708, when it was seized by the emperor Joseph I. It surrendered to the French, 2 Feb. 1797, after a siege of eight months; retaken by the Austrians and Russians, 30 July, 1799, after a short siege. After the battle of Marengo (14 June, 1800), the French again obtained possession of it. It was included in the kingdom of Italy till 1814, when it was restored to the Austrians, who surrendered it to the Italians, 11 Oct. 1866, after the peace.

MANU, see *Menu*.

MAORIS, see *New Zealand*.

MAPLE-TREE. The *Acer rubrum*, or scarlet maple, was brought here from N. America, before 1656. The *Acer Negundo*, or ash-leaved maple, before 1688. From the *Acer saccharinum* (introduced here in 1735) the Americans make good sugar.

MAPS, see *Charts*, and *Mercator*.

MARANON, see *Amazon*.

MARATHON (in Attica). Here, on 28 or 29 Sept. 490 B.C., the Greeks, only 11,000 strong, defeated the Persian army amounting to about 110,000. The former were commanded by Miltiades, Aristides, and Themistocles. Among the slain (about 6400) is said to have been Hippias, who had been expelled from Athens, and was the instigator of the war. The Persian army was forced to retreat to Asia; see *Greece*.

Investigations in 1890 on the presumed site of this battle led to the discovery of vases, and the probable grave of the 192 Athenians who fell.

MARBLE. Dipœnus and Scyllis, statuaries of Crete, were the first artists who sculptured marble, and polished their works; all statues previously being of wood, about 568 B.C. *Pliny*. The edifices or monuments of Rome were constructed of, or ornamented with, fine marble. The ruins of Palmyra are chiefly of white marble. The marble arch, London, erected at Buckingham palace, 1830, was removed to Hyde-park, March, 1851.

MARBURG (W. Germany). The cathedral was founded, 1231; and the first Protestant university in 1527. It suffered much during the Seven years' war, 1753-60.

MARCH, the first month of the Roman year, until Numa added January and February, 713 B.C. It is said that Romulus gave to this month the name of his supposed father, Mars; though Ovid observes, that the people of Italy had the month of March before the time of Romulus, but placed it differently in the calendar. The year commenced on the 25th of this month till 1753; see *Year*. The March of 1845 and 1886 had much frost and skating

MARCHES. The old boundaries between England and Wales, and England and Scotland. The Lords Marchers of the Welsh borders had vice-regal authority; the wardens of the Scotch marches were subordinate officers. These powers were abolished, 1536, and 1689.

MARCHFELD (Austria). Here Ottocar II. of Bohemia was defeated and slain by his rival, the emperor Rodolph of Hapsburg, 26 Aug. 1278; see *Bohemia*.

MARCIONITES, followers of Marcion, a heretic, about 150, who preceded the Manichees, and taught similar doctrines. *Cave*.

MARCOMANNI, a people of Southern Germany, expelled the Boii from Bohemia, and, united with other tribes, invaded Italy about 167, but were repelled by the emperors Antoninus and Verus. They were defeated by the legion called, from a fabled miracle, the Thundering Legion, 179; and finally driven beyond the Danube by Aurelian, 271.

MARENGO (N. Italy). Here the French army, commanded by Bonaparte, after crossing the Alps into Piedmont, attacked the Austrians, 14 June, 1800; his army was retreating, when the arrival of general Dessaix turned the fortunes of the day. The slaughter on both sides was dreadful. By a treaty between the Austrian general Melas and Bonaparte, signed 15 June, the latter obtained twelve strong fortresses, and became master of Italy.

MARESCHALS or MARSHALS, in France, were the esquires of the king, and originally had the command of the vanguard to observe the enemy and to choose proper places for its encampment. Till the time of Francis I., in 1515, there were but two marshals, who had 500 livres per annum in war, but no stipend in time of peace. The number was afterwards greatly increased. Napoleon's marshals were renowned for skill and courage; see *Marshal*.

MARGARINE, see under *Butter*.

MARGATE, Kent, Royal sea-bathing infirmary founded 1792, enlarged 1882. The town-hall was erected in 1820. Population, 1881, 16,030; 1891, 18,419; 1901, 23,057. New park, presented by Mr. J. Woodward, opened by the lord mayor, 1 June, 1898.

MARIAN PERSECUTION, see *Protestants*.

MARIGNANO (now MALEGNANO), N. Italy, near Milan. Three battles have been fought near here—1. Francis I. of France defeated the duke of Milan and the Swiss, 13, 14 Sept. 1515; above 20,000 men were slain. This conflict has been called the Battle of the Giants.—2. Near here was fought the battle of Pavia (*which see*), 24 February, 1525.—3. After the battle of Magenta, 4 June, 1859, the Austrians entrenched themselves at Malegnano. The emperor sent marshal Baraguay d'Hilliers with 16,000 men to dislodge them, which he did with a loss of about 850 killed and wounded, on 8 June. The Austrians are said to have lost 1400 killed and wounded, and 900 prisoners, out of 18,000 engaged.

MARINE BIOLOGICAL ASSOCIATION. See *Biology*.

MARINER'S COMPASS, see *Compass*, and *Magnetism*.

MARINES, soldiers serving on ship-board, were first established with the object of forming a nursery to man the fleet. An order in council, dated 16 Oct. 1664, authorised 1200 soldiers to be raised and formed into one regiment. In 1684, the third regiment of the line was called the Marine Regiment; but the system of having soldiers exclusively for sea service was not carried into effect until 1698, when two marine regiments were formed. More regiments were embodied in subsequent years; and in 1741 the corps consisted of ten regiments, each 1000 strong. In 1759 they numbered 18,000 men. In the latter years of the French war, ending in 1815, they amounted to 31,400, but there were frequently more than 3000 supernumeraries. The *jollies*, as they are called, frequently distinguished themselves. The "Royal Marine Forces" (so named 1 May, 1802), now comprehend artillery and light infantry. The vote for 1857 was for 16,000 marines, inclusive of 1500 artillery. *P. H. Nicolas*. Marine Engineers' Institution, founded in 1872. Officers of the marines made equal in rank with those in the army and navy, Dec. 1882. The Historical Records of the Royal Marines, edited by major L. Edye, published 1893, *et seq*.

MARINE SOCIETY (for the maintenance and instruction of boys for the navy), was founded by Jonas Hanway, 1756, and incorporated, 1772. It instituted the first training ship on the Thames, 1786. H.M.S. *Warspite* burnt, no deaths, 3 Jan. 1876; and the boys were removed to the *Conqueror*.

MARINO, SAN, a republic in central Italy. Its origin is ascribed to St. Marinus, a hermit, who resided here in the 5th century. Its independence lost for a short time, to Cæsar Borgia, 1503, and to the pope, 1739; was confirmed by pope Pius VII. in 1817. A convention with Italy, 27 March, 1872. New extradition treaty with Gt. Britain ratified, 1 Oct. 1900. Population, in 1858, about 8000; in 1869, 7303; in 1874, 7816; in 1891, about 8,000; 11,000 in 1900.

MARIOLATRY, worship of the virgin Mary, began in the 4th century, greatly increased in the 10th.

MARIONETTES, puppet plays. The *fantoccini*, popular in Italy in the 15th century; in the 18th in England, and Germany. See *Punch*.

MARITIME EXHIBITION at Havre opened by representatives of the government 1 June, 1868: (another at Havre, 7 May, 1887); a similar exhibition was opened at Naples by the prince of Piedmont, 17 April, 1871; at Paris, 10 July, 1875; at Liverpool, 11 May, 1886.

MARITIME LAWS, see *Navigation Laws*.

New international code of signals based on the English, introduced 1 Jan. 1901

MARK, a silver coin of the northern nations, and the name *mark-lubs* is still retained in Denmark. In England, the mark was two-thirds of 1*l.* sterling or 13*s.* 4*d.* The German mark is nearly equivalent to 1*s.* in English.

MARKET, see *Smithfield, Metropolitan Cattle Market, Billingsgate, Leadenhall, Farringdon, Columbia*, and *Covent Garden Markets*. There are also the Borough and Spitalfields markets (vegetables), Cumberland market, Hampstead-road (hay), and Shadwell (fish). New market constructed by Great Eastern Railway Co. at Bishopsgate street; opened, 1 July, 1882. Wholesale fish and poultry market opened, 19 Oct. 1882.

Royal Commission on Market Rights and Tolls appointed in 1888; issued first report March, . . . 1889
The Market and Fairs act, 1887, amended . . . 1891
Final report Jan. 1891, recommending reforms.

MARK'S, ST. (Venice). The church was erected between 977 and 1043. The Campanile (bell tower), 323 ft. high, 42 ft. wide at base, fell to the ground, 14 July, 1902; some art treasures damaged, but the church saved.

The restorations of the Palace of the Doges were completed and exposed to view . . Nov. 1889

MARLBOROUGH, a town in Wiltshire; a royal manor mentioned in Domesday book. King Henry III. passed the "*Statutes of Malbridge*" in the ancient castle in 1267. Marlborough returned two members to parliament since Edward I. Absorbed into the county, 1885. The grammar school was founded by Edward VI.—MARLBOROUGH HOUSE, Pall Mall, London, was built by Wren for the duke of Marlborough, 1709-10; was let to the princess Charlotte and prince Leopold in 1824; held by queen Adelaide, 1837-49, and became the residence of the prince of Wales, 1863. "Marlborough House," by Arthur H. Beavan, published 1896. See *Gems*. Population, 1881, 3,343; 1891, 3,012; 1901, 4,000.

MARLOWE MEMORIAL, a committee determine to erect a memorial to Christopher Marlowe, the dramatist (1564-93), in Canterbury, Dec. 1888. The statue unveiled by Mr. H. Irving, 16 Sept. 1891.

MAROCCO, see *Morocco*.

MARONITES, Christians in the East, followers of one Maron in the 5th century; they are said to have embraced the errors of the Jacobites, Nestorians, and Monothelites. About 1180 they numbered 40,000, living in the neighbourhood of mount Libanus, and were of service to the Christian kings of Jerusalem. They were reconciled to the church of Rome soon after. For an account of the massacres of the Maronites in 1860, see *Druses*.

MAROONS, a name given in Jamaica to runaway negroes. When the island was conquered from the Spaniards, a number of their negroes fled to the hills and became very troublesome to the colonists. A war of eight years' duration ensued, when the Maroons capitulated on being permitted to retain their free settlements, about 1730. In 1795 they again took arms, but were speedily put down and many were transported. *Brande*.

MARPINGER, village, near Saarbruck. The Virgin and Satan said to have been seen by children; and miracles wrought, 3 July, 1876. The priest, Neureuter, acquitted of the charge of imposture, April, 1879.

MAR-PRELATE TRACTS, virulently attacking episcopacy, were mostly written, it is believed, by John Penry, who was cruelly executed, 29 May, 1593, for writing seditious words against the queen (found about his person when seized). The tracts appeared about 1586. Some had very singular titles: such as "An Almand for a Parrat," "Hay any Worke for Cooper?" &c. They were collected and reprinted in 1843.

MARQUE, LETTERS OF, see *Privateer*.

MARQUESAS ISLANDS (Polynesia) were discovered in 1595 by Mendana, who named them after the viceroy of Peru, Marquesa de Mendoça. They were visited by Cook in 1774, and were taken possession of by the French admiral Dupetit Thouars, 1 May, 1842.

MARQUIS, a dignity, called by the Saxons markin-reve, by the Germans markgrave, took its original from mark or March, a limit or bound (see *Marches*); the office being to guard or govern the frontiers of a province. Marquis is next in honour to a duke. The first Englishman on whom the title was conferred was the favourite of king Richard II., Robert de Vere, earl of Oxford, created marquis of Dublin, and placed in parliament between the dukes and earls, 1385. James Stewart, second son of James III. of Scotland, was made marquis of Ormond, in 1476, without territories, afterwards earl of Ross.

MARRIAGE was instituted by God (*Gen.* ii.), and confirmed by Christ (*Mark* x.), who performed a miracle at the celebration of one (*John* ii.). Matrimonial ceremonies among the Greeks are ascribed to Cecrops, king of Athens, 1554 B.C. See *Age, Affinity*.

Law favouring marriage passed at Rome . . B.C. 18
Priests forbidden to marry after ordination . A.D. 325
Marriage in Lent forbidden 366
It was forbidden to bishops in 692, and to priests in 1015; and these latter were obliged to take the vow of celibacy 1073
Statute prohibiting marriages between certain persons within prohibited degrees 25 Hen. VIII. 1533-4
The celebration of marriage, as a sacrament, in churches ordained by pope Innocent III. about 1199; and so affirmed by the council of Trent . . 1547
Marriages solemnised by justices of the peace under an act of the commons 1653
A tax laid on marriages, viz.: marriage of a duke, 50*l.*; of a common person, 2*s.* 6*d.* 1695
Irregular marriages prohibited (see *Fleet Marriages*) 1753
Marriages again taxed 1784
New marriage act, 1822; partially repealed . . . 1823
Acts prohibiting marriages by Roman Catholic priests in Scotland, or other ministers not belonging to the church of Scotland, repealed . . . 1834
Act to render the children of certain marriages within forbidden degrees (*with deceased wife's sister*) legitimate; such marriages in future prohibited (Lyndhurst's act, *which see*); (efforts made to legalise marriage with deceased wife's sister ever since) 1835

The present marriage act for England, authorising marriages without religious ceremony, by registrar's certificate, or in a dissenting chapel, passed 1836 [amended in 1837 and 1856].

Marriage Registration act 1837

Amendment acts passed in . . . . 1840 and 1856

A bill to suppress irregular marriages in Scotland (see *Gretna*) passed in . . . . ,,

A court established for Divorce and Matrimonial Causes, which has the power of giving sentence of judicial separation for adultery, cruelty, or desertion without cause for two years and upward (see *Divorce*) 1857

In the case of Brook *v.* Brook, it was decided that such a marriage celebrated in a foreign country was not valid . . . . . . 17 April, 1858

This decision confirmed on appeal to the house of lords, on . . . . 18 March, 1861

A commission appointed to inquire into the working of the marriage laws of Scotland, 22 March, 1865, reported strongly in favour of changes being made to insure uniformity, simplicity, and certainty . . . . July, 1868

Consular Marriage Act, enabling acting British consuls abroad to solemnize marriages, passed, 16 July, 1868; amendment act passed, 1890.

Married Women's property act passed . 9 Aug. 1870

Marriage Law of Ireland amended by an act passed 10 Aug. 1870; amended . . . . . July, 1871

Matrimonial Causes Act (*which see*), passed . . . 1878

A bill for the recognition in Great Britain of such colonial marriages was read a 2nd time in the commons, 28 Feb. 1877; (21 majority) . 27 Feb. ,,

An act to encourage regular marriages in Scotland; passed . . . . 8 Aug. ,,

These marriages made legal by the legislature at Melbourne, Nov. 1872; at Sydney, 1875; in New Zealand, 1880; Canada 1882

The Marriage Law Reform association instituted (to legalise a marriage with a *deceased wife's sister*), 15 Jan. 1851. A bill for this purpose passed the commons, 2 July; was rejected by the lords, 23 July, 1858; again rejected, 1862; and again by the commons, 2 May, 1866; and 30 April, 1870, rejected by the lords (77-73) 19 May, 1870; passed by commons, 9 March, rejected by the lords (97-71), 27 March, 1871; passed by commons in 1872, 1873; and rejected by the lords (49-74), 14 March, 1873; rejected by commons (171-142), 17 Feb. 1875; by the lords (101-81); (the prince of Wales and duke of Edinburgh voted for it), 6 May, 1879; (101-90), 25 June, 1880; (132-128), 12 June, 1882; read second time by commons, (165-148) 11 June; rejected by the lords (145-140) . . . 28 June, 1883

Resolution for it adopted by the commons (238-127) 6 May, 1884; rejected by the lords (149–127) 24 May, 1886; read 2nd time by commons (239–182) 18 April, 1888; again for Scotland 3 April; rejected by the lords (147–120) . . . 9 May, 1889

Read 2nd time by the commons (222—155), 30 April, 1890; (202—155) 11 Feb.; withdrawn, 17 June, 1891; rejected by the lords (129-120), 15 June, 1894; passed by the lords, 10 July, 1896; stopped in the commons . . . . . Aug. 1896

Commander Christopher Bethell's marriage with Teepoo, a Baralong woman, in Bechuanaland, according to native rites, declared invalid in England ("Bethell *v.* Hildyard") . . 15 Feb. 1888

Marriage Act passed 1886 extends hour of marriage from 12 to 3 p.m. in England and Wales.

Marriages Abroad act passed . . . 27 June, 1892

The "World's Great Marriage Association" (to provide men with rich wives), Daniel Mortimer, J. C. Skates, and John Abrahams convicted of conspiring to defraud Alfred Jordan and others; Skates sentenced to 5, and the others to 3 years' penal servitude . . . . . . 5 March, 1896

Marriages Validity Act (Irish banns made valid), passed 1899

Marriage Act Amendment, passed, 6 Aug. 1900; marriages legalization act, passed. 1901

REGISTERED MARRIAGES IN ENGLAND AND WALES.

Year	Marriages	Year	Marriages
1750	40,300	1815	91,946
1800	73,228	1820	96,883
1810	84,473	1825	98,378

Registered Marriages in England Wales—*continued.*

Year	Marriages	Year	Marriages
1830	102,437	1857	159,097
1840	121,083	1858	156,070
1845	143,743	1859	167,723
1848	138,230	1860	170,156
1850*	152,744	1861 (*Cotton famine*)	163,706
1853	164,520	1862	164,030
1854	159,727	1863	173,510
1855 (*Crimean War*)	152,113	1864	180,387
1856	159,337		

MARRIAGES IN THE UNITED KINGDOM.

	England and Wales.	Scotland.	Ireland.†
1866	187,776	23,629	30,151
1867	179,154	22,521	29,796
1870	181,655	23,788	28,835
1871	190,112	23,966	28,060
1872	201,267	25,580	27,114
1873	205,615	26,730	26,270
1874	202,010	26,247	24,481
1875	201,212	25,921	24,037
1876	201,874	26,563	26,388
1877	194,352	25,790	24,722
1878	190,054	24,333	25,284
1879	182,082	23,462	23,254
1880	191,965	24,489	20,363
1881	197,290	25,948	21,826
1882	204,405	26,574	22,029
1883	206,384	26,855	21,368
1884	204,301	26,061	22,585
1885	197,745	25,256	21,177
1886	196,071	24,469	20,594
1887	200,518	24,876	20,945
1888	203,821	25,305	20,060
1889	213,865	26,318	21,521
1890	223,028	27,441	20,990
1891	226,526	27,969	21,475
1892	227,135	28,637	21,530
1893	218,251	27,090	21,710
1894	226,449	27,604	21,602
1895	227,865	28,380	23,120
1896	242,445	30,256	22,856
1897	249,145	31,050	22,891
1898	255,379	32,112	22,580
1899	262,334	32,935	22,311
1900	257,139	32,444	21,182

ROYAL MARRIAGE ACT, 12 Geo. III. c. 11, was passed in 1772, in consequence of the marriage of the duke of Gloucester, the king's brother, with the widow of the earl Waldegrave, and of the duke of Cumberland with the widow of colonel Horton and daughter of lord Irnham. [By this act, none of the descendants of George II., unless of foreign birth, can marry under the age of 25, without the consent of the king; at and after that age, after twelve months' notice given to the privy council, they may contract such marriage, which shall be good unless both houses of parliament disapprove. The marriage of the duke of Sussex with the lady Augusta Murray, solemnised in 1793, was pronounced illegal, 1794, and the claims of their son, sir Augustus d'Este, declared invalid, by the house of lords, 9 July, 1844. He married lady Cecilia Underwood (afterwards duchess of Inverness), 1831.

H. R. H. the princess Louise was married to the marquis of Lorne by the queen's consent, 21 March, 1871.

HALF MARRIAGE. *Semi-Matrimonium.* Among the Romans concubinage was a legitimate union, not merely tolerated but authorised. The concubine had the name of *semi-conjux.* Men might have either a wife or a concubine, provided they had not both together. Constantine the Great checked concubinage, but did not abolish it. This ancient custom of the Romans was preserved, not only among the Lombards, but by the French when they held dominion in that country. Cujas assures us that the Gascons and other people bordering on the Pyrenean mountains had not

* Of these marriages, it is stated in the registrar's returns that 47,570 men and 70,601 women could not write, and that they signed the marriage register with their marks.—In France, the marriages were 208,893 in 1820; 243,674 in 1825; and 259,177 in 1830. As respects Paris, 7754 marriages were, bachelors and maids, 6456; bachelors and widows, 368; widowers and maids, 708; widowers and widows, 222.

† Approximative, through doubtful returns.

relinquished this custom in his time, 1590. The women bore the name of "wives of the second order." *Hénault.* See *Morganatic Marriages.*

DOUBLE MARRIAGES. There are some instances of a husband and two wives (but they are very rare) in countries where polygamy was interdicted by the state. The first Lacedæmonian who had two wives was Anaxandrides, the son of Leon, about 510 B.C. Dionysius of Syracuse married two wives, viz.: Doris, the daughter of Xenetus, and Aristomache, sister of Dion, 398 B.C. It is said that the count Gleichen, a German nobleman, was permitted, under peculiar circumstances, by Gregory IX., in A.D. 1237, to marry and live with two wives. The Mormonites practise and encourage polygamy.

FORCED MARRIAGES. The stat. 3 Henry VII. (1487) made the principal and abettors in marriages with heiresses, &c., contrary to their will, equally guilty as felons. By 39 Eliz. (1596) such felons were denied the benefit of clergy. This offence was made punishable by transportation, 1 Geo. IV. (1820). The remarkable case of Miss Wharton, heiress of the house of Wharton, whom captain Campbell married by force, occurred in William III.'s reign. Sir John Johnston was hanged for seizing the young lady, and the marriage was annulled by parliament, 1690.—Edward Gibbon Wakefield was tried at Lancaster, and found guilty of the felonious abduction of Miss Turner, 24 March, 1827; and his marriage with her was immediately dissolved by act of parliament.

MARRIAGES BY SALE. Among the Babylonians, at a certain time every year, the marriageable females were assembled, and disposed of to the best bidder. This custom is said to have originated with Atossa, daughter of Belochos, about 1433 B.C.

FLEET MARRIAGES. See *Fleet.*

MARRIED WOMEN, see *Wives.*

MARRS MURDERS, see *Ratcliffe Highway.*

MAR'S INSURRECTION. John, earl of Mar, proclaimed James III. at Braemar, Aberdeenshire, 6 September, 1715. He was defeated at Sheriffmuir, 13 Nov., and escaped from Montrose with the Pretender, 4 Feb. 1716.

MARS, a planet, next to the earth in order of distance from the sun; the spots on its surface were first observed by Fontana, in 1636. Two satellites named Phobos and Deimos, were discovered by professor Asaph Hall, at Washington, U.S., 11 Aug. 1877.

M. Dubois of Paris suggests that these satellites may be planetoids attracted by Mars, Aethra and another of these bodies having disappeared about the time of the discovery.

M. Schiaparelli, of Milan, describes configurations like canals, 1882, and M. Perrotin since has mapped them and asserts that Mars has an atmosphere and clouds (1887)

"They have likewise discovered two lesser stars or satellites which revolve about Mars." — *Swift,* Gulliver's Travels—Voyage to Laputa, about 1726.

MARSAGLIA (Piedmont, N. Italy). Here the imperialists under prince Eugene and the duke of Savoy were defeated by the French under Catinat, 4 Oct. 1693.

MARSEILLAISE HYMN. The words and music are ascribed to Rouget de Lille, or L'Isle, a French engineer officer, who, it is said, composed it by request, 1792, to cheer the conscripts at Strasburg. It derived its name from a body of troops from Marseilles marching into Paris in 1792 playing the tune. This account is doubted by some (1879). The author was pensioned by Louis Philippe, 1830, and died in 1836.

MARSEILLES. The ancient *Massilia* (S. France), a maritime city, founded by the Phocæans about 600 B.C.; an ally of Rome, 218 B.C. Cicero styled it the Athens of Gaul, on account of its excellent schools. Population, 1881, 360,099; 1891, 375,378; 1901, 422,378.

Taken by Julius Cæsar after a long siege . . B.C. 49
By Euric the Visigoth . . . . A.D. 470
Sacked by the Saracens 839
Marseilles a republic 1214
Subjected to the counts of Provence 1251
United to the crown of France 1482
The plague rages 1649
It carried off 50,000 of the inhabitants. The bishop Belsunce devotedly exerted himself to relieve the sufferers 1720-1
Revolutionary commotions here . . 30 April, 1789
Marseilles opposes the revolutionary government, and is reduced . . . . . . 23 Aug. 1793
Dissensions and conflicts between the French and Italians; much stabbing; several deaths; about 200 arrests, 19, 20 June city quiet . 22 June 1881
Pharo Château and Park presented to the city, by the ex-empress Eugénie, Dec. 1882; finally accepted. . . . . July, 1883
Inauguration of great drainage works; M. Freycinet, the premier, and 4 other ministers present, 8 Oct. 1891
New cathedral, begun in 1852 by M. Leon Vaudoyer, consecrated . . . . . . 30 Nov. 1893
Dock strike, 28 Feb. 1901; some rioting, 20, 22 March; strike ends . . . . 9 April, 1901
Large deficits in the city finances, reported . 1900-1902
Strike of sailors, heavy losses . 25 Nov., 18 Dec. 1902

See *Cholera.*

MARSHALS. Two were appointed in London to clear the streets of vagrants, and to send the sick, blind, and lame to asylums and hospitals for relief, 1567. *Northouck.*

MARSHALS, BRITISH FIELD. This rank was first conferred upon John, duke of Argyll, and George, earl of Orkney, by George II. in 1736. The duke of Cambridge was made field-marshal, 9 Nov. 1862; the prince of Wales, 29 May, 1875; lord Napier of Magdala, 1 Jan. 1883, died 14 Jan. 1890; sir Patrick Grant, 24 June, 1883, died 28 March, 1895; lord William Paulet, 1886; sir Donald Stewart (died 1900) and viscount Wolseley, 24 May, 1894; gen. Fred. Sleigh, Lord Roberts, 24 May, 1895; prince Edward of Saxe-Weimar, June, 1897; Sir Neville Chamberlain, 24 April, 1900, died 17 Feb. 1902; the German Emperor, 27 Jan. 1901; the duke of Connaught and Sir Henry Wylie Norman, 26 June, 1902; sir H. Evelyn Wood and sir George S. White, April, 1903; the emperor of Austria, 3 Sept. 1903. See *Mareschal.*

MARSHALS OF FRANCE, appointed by the kings and revived by Napoleon I. during his wars, 1804-14.

Augereau, duke of Castiglione; died 12 June, 1816.
Bernadotte, prince of Ponte Corvo, king of Sweden, 1818; died 8 March, 1844.
Berthier, prince of Neufchatel and Wagram, killed or committed suicide at Bamberg, 1 June, 1815.
Bessières, duke of Istria; killed at Lützen, 1 May, 1813.
Brune, Guillaume M. A., murdered at Avignon, 2 Aug. 1815.
Davoust, or Davout, prince of Eckmühl and duke of Auerstadt; died 1 June, 1823.
Gouvion Saint-Cyr, Laurent; died 17 March, 1830.
Grouchy, Emmanuel de, died 29 May, 1847.
Jourdan, peer of France; died 23 Nov. 1833.
Kellermann, duke of Valmy; died 12 Sept. 1820.
Lannes, duke of Montebello, wounded at Aspern; died 31 May, 1809.
Lefebvre, duke of Dantzic; died 14 Sept. 1820.
Macdonald, duke of Tarento; died 24 Sept. 1840.
Marmont, duke of Ragusa; died 2 March, 1852.
Massena, prince of Essling and duke of Rivoli; died 4 April, 1817.
Molitor, Gabriel Jean Joseph; died 28 July, 1849 (doubtful).
Moncey, duke of Conegliano; died 20 April, 1842.
Mortier, duke of Treviso, killed by Fieschi, 28 July, 1835.
Murat, king of Naples, executed 13 Oct. 1815.

Ney, prince of Moskwa, duke of Elchingen, executed 7 Dec. 1815.
Oudinot, duke of Reggio; died 13 Sept. 1847.
Perignon, Dominique C.; died 25 Dec. 1818.
Poniatowski, prince Josef Anton, wounded at Leipsic, and drowned 19 Oct. 1813.
Serrurier, Jean Mathieu Philibert, comte; died 21 Dec. 1819.
Soult, duke of Dalmatia; died 26 Nov. 1851.
Suchet, duke of Albufera; died 3 Jan. 1826.
Victor, duke of Belluno; died 1 March, 1841
It is asserted that Arrighi, duc de Padoue (died 21 March, 1853), H. J. W. Clarke, duc de Feltre (died 28 Oct. 1818), and Andoche Junot, duc d'Abrantes (suicide 29 July, 1813), were only titular marshals, and that G. Christophe Michel Duroc (killed at the battle of Mackersdorff, 23 April, 1813), was only marshal of the palace.

Appointed since 1814: Bertrand, comte de Clausel (died 21 April, 1842); J. Baptiste Drouet, comte d'Erlon (died 25 Jan. 1844); Etienne Maurice Gerard (died 17 April, 1852); Jacques A. B. L. Lauriston (died 12 June, 1828); Nicolas J. Maison (died 13 Feb. 1840); François A. Bazaine (died 23 Sept., 1888), and Marie E. P. M. MacMahon, duc de Magenta (died 17 Oct. 1893).

François Canrobert, the last surviving marshal, died 28 Jan. 1895.

MARSHALSEA COURT, having jurisdiction in the royal palace, was very ancient, of high dignity, and coeval with the common law. Since the decision of the case of the Marshalsea (see *lord Coke's* 10 *Rep.* 68) no business has been done in this court; but it was regularly opened and adjourned at the same time with the Palace court, the judges and other officers being the same. These courts were removed from Southwark to Scotland-yard in 1801, were abolished by parliament, and discontinued 31 Dec. 1849; see *Prisons*.

MARSI, a brave people of Southern Italy, who, after several contests, yielded to the Romans, about 301 B.C. During the civil wars they and their allies rebelled, having demanded and been refused the rights of Roman citizenship, 91 B.C. After many successes and reverses, they sued for and obtained peace and the rights they required, 87 B.C. The Marsi being *Socii* of the Romans, this was called the *Social war*.

MARSTON-MOOR (near York). The Scots and parliamentary army were besieging York, when prince Rupert, joined by the marquis of Newcastle, determined to raise the siege. Both sides drew up on Marston-moor, on 2 July, 1644, and the contest was long undecided. Rupert, commanding the right wing of the royalists, was opposed by Oliver Cromwell, at the head of troops disciplined by himself. Cromwell was victorious; he drove his opponents off the field, followed the vanquished, returned to a second engagement and a second victory. The prince's artillery was taken, and the royalists never recovered the blow.

MARTELLO TOWERS, said to have been erected by Charles V. on the coasts of Italy. Similar circular buildings were erected in the beginning of the present century, on the southern coast of England, and other parts of the empire, as defences against invasion. The towers were said by some to be named from Cape Martello, or Mortella in Corsica. They are now being destroyed as obsolete.

MARTIAL LAW, see *Courts-Martial*, and *Military Law*.

MARTINESTI, see *Rimnik*.

MARTINIQUE (French West Indies), discovered in 1493 or 1502; settled by France, 1635. This and the adjacent isles of St. Lucia and St. Vincent, and the Grenadines, were taken by the British from the French in Feb. 1762. They were restored to France at the peace of the following year. They were again taken, 16 March, 1794; restored at the peace of Amiens in 1802; again captured 23 Feb. 1809. A revolution in this island in favour of Napoleon was finally suppressed by the British, 1 June, 1815, and Martinique reverted to its French masters. Severe earthquakes occurred here in 1766 and 1839; at other times 200 shocks in 1843.

Great destruction of life and property was caused by a cyclone and earthquake about 18 Aug. 1891; estimated deaths 378, besides losses by shipwrecks. Estimated loss 2,000,000*l.*

Strike riots, incendiary fires in La François, troops fire on the mob, 9 men killed, 5-13 Feb.; dispute referred so arbitration . . . . . 14 Feb. 1900

DESSTRUCTION OF ST. PIERRE, about 35,000 persons perished . . . . 8 May, 1902

Mont Pelee, a volcano 4,428 ft. high, about 4½ miles behind the town, caused some loss of life and property in 1760 and 1851, and began again to show signs of activity at the end of April, 1902; masses of steam were thrown out, and St. Pierre was covered with ashes, 3, 4 May; a stream of lava (20 ft. high) swept everything away before it to the sea, the Guérin factory and over 150 lives destroyed; the sea receded 300 ft., and, returning, flooded St. Pierre, 5 May; reassuring reports were issued by the Government, 6 May, but the eruptions increased in force, and finally, a little before 8 a.m., "with a terrific roar a huge column of white-hot sand, burning cinders and stones was shot up, and poured down a terrible volcanic torrent (spreading out for miles, round even as far as Fort de France), and within ten minutes St. Pierre became a city of the dead," and the whole (about 50 sq. m.) district a desolation, 8 May; *Times* . . . . 24 May, ,,

The governor, M. Mouttet (who had tried to allay the panic, and persuaded the people to remain), his wife, the British and American consuls and their families, and about 40,000 were killed. The *Grappler*, a cable ship, with a fine set of engineers and men, and about 18 other vessels were totally lost; the *Suchet*, French gun-boat, picked up in the afternoon eight men belonging to the British s.s. *Roraima*, and 10 others drifting about on wreckage; the British s.s. *Roddam* was saved by the pluck and fortitude of capt. Ed. Wm. Freeman, who, though burnt in the face and disabled, managed to steer it to a place of safety; but out of 44 on board only 18 survived, and most of these were injured; many reports issued; estimated damage, 200,000,000f., reported, 20 July, ,,

Seven craters active, 15 May; the work of search parties interrupted, 19 and 20 May; a torrent of ashes and mud destroyed what remained of Basse Pointe, 24 May; new crater active, 27-31 May, ,,

Active aid and general sympathy (king Edward, 1,000*l.*); total fund, 1,400,000*l.*, 27 May; 8,107,167f. 3 Sept. ,,

Special American, British and French expeditions were sent to Martinique and St. Vincent to investigate the volcanic conditions of the West Indies, May; one sent by the roy. soc. returned about . . . . 2 Aug. ,,

The destruction of St. Pierre attributed to a rush of gas at very high temperature; Le Prêchure and Ste Philomène to torrents of mud, which overwhelmed them—*Nature* . . . . 3 June, ,,

Fresh outbreaks, June, and 9, 12 July; again, 15 Aug. *et. seq.*; two of great violence, 25 and 28 Aug.; finally a terrible outburst destroyed Morne Rouge and Ajoupa Bouillon, Morne Boudon and three villages; 800 killed and about 200 hopelessly injured (a wave swept Carbet and about 200 were drowned). On the east, a portion of land over a mile long sunk into the sea, and the interior of the island laid waste; about 1,500 killed and more injured . . . 30, 31 Aug. ,,

Two French cruisers active, bringing the inhabitants from the northern districts to Fort de France, early Sept.; fresh eruption reported, 27 Dec. 1902

MARTINMAS, 11 Nov., the feast of St. Martin, bishop of Tours, in the 4th century, is quarter day in parts of the north of England and in Scotland. The high sheriffs of England and Wales are nominated on the morrow of St. Martin, 12 Nov.

MARTIN'S HALL, ST. (Long Acre, London), was opened as a concert-room for Mr. John Hullah, on 11 Feb. 1850; burnt down 26 Aug. 1860; rebuilt, 1861, opened as the New Queen's Theatre, by Mr. Alfred Wigan, 24 Oct. 1867. See *Westminster*, 1890.

MARTYRS. Stephen, the first Christian martyr, was stoned, 33. The festivals of the martyrs, of very ancient date, took their rise about the time of Polycarp, who suffered martyrdom about 169. St. Alban is the English protomartyr, 286; see *Persecutions*, *Protestants*, and *Diocletian Era*. The Martyrs' Memorial, Smithfield, erected by the Protestant Alliance, was inaugurated 11 March, 1870. The Martyrs' memorial church, St John's-street, Clerkenwell, was consecrated 2 June, 1871.

MARY-ANNE. Secret republican associations, especially in France. The name was given to the republic of 1792, to the guillotine, and to little statuettes of Liberty.

MARYLAND, named after queen Henrietta Maria, one of the first thirteen United States of North America, was granted in 1632 to lord Baltimore, and settled by a company of English Romanists in 1634. It contains the district of Columbia, in which Washington is situate. It continued in the Union when the other slave states seceded in 1860 and 1861. The confederate army, under general Lee, after their victory at Bull Run, 30 Aug. 1862, crossed the Potomac and entered Maryland. They were followed by the federal army under McClellan. Severe conflicts ensued, especially on 17 Sept., at Antietam Creek, with great loss on both sides, each claiming the victory. The confederates retired into Virginia in good order, and it is said with much booty. Capital, Annapolis; population, 1880, 934,943; 1890, 1,042,390; 1900, 1,188,044.

MARY-LE-BONE, a large parish, N.-W. London. The name is corrupted from St. Mary at the Bourne, or brook,—Tyebourne. It was chiefly pasture land in 1760. The manor was acquired by the duke of Portland in 1813. The hunting-grounds now form Regent's park (*which see*). The parishes of Marylebone, St. Pancras, and Paddington were made a parliamentary borough in 1832. By act of 1885 Marylebone alone returns two M.P.'s. Constituted a municipal borough by act of 1899 (10 aldermen, 60 councillors). St. Marylebone Churches Bill passed, 1898. Population, 1881, 154,910; 1891, 142,381; 1901, 133,301.

New higher grade and technical schools presented by ladies Howard de Walden and Ossington opened 30 July, 1890.

Mary-le-bone gardens—attached to the "Rose of Normandy"—a place of public entertainment, opened in the middle of the 17th century; mentioned by Pepys; closed 23 Sept. 1776; a music hall erected here, 1855.

The *Marylebone Murder*.—Miss Lucy Clark, dressmaker, aged 49, living at 86, George St., Portman Sq., found murdered 23 Jan. 1888.

New baths and washhouses opened by the duke of York, 6 March, 1897.

MASANIELLO, see *Naples*, 1647. Auber's opera, "La Muette de Portici" (1828), was produced in London as "Masaniello," 4 May, 1829.

MASCAT, see *Muscat*.

MASHONA, Makalakaland and Matabele lands, territories in south Africa, ruled by Lobengula. The country is rich in minerals, the Mashonas generally peaceful, the Matabeles described as warlike, aggressive and cruel. Lobengula entered into agreement with the British government, 11 Feb. 1888.

A deputation of two head men from him was received by queen Victoria, 2 March, 1889, requesting protection against a syndicate, to which he had inconsiderately conceded lands. The concession was afterwards legally withdrawn. See *Zambesi*, 1889.

The Imperial Mission conveying queen Victoria's letter to Lobengula, recommending the British South Africa chartered company, favourably received by him at Buluwayo, the Matabele capital, 29 Jan. 1890.

Successful progress of colonization, reported May, 1892.

Explorations of Mr. J. Theodore Bent; he discovers at Zimbabwe, an ancient fortress (probably Phœnician), a temple with ornamented walls, monoliths, specimens of good pottery, relics of gold-mining, etc., June–Aug. 1891. Mr. Bent gave an account of his exploration at a meeting of the Royal Geographical Society, 22 Feb. 1892.

About 400 oz. of Mashona gold exhibited at Cape Town, about 18 Nov. 1892.

Dr. Knight Bruce, first bishop, 1892.

Murderous raids of Matabeles on the Mashonas; invasion on British settlement near fort Victoria, unauthorised by Lobengula; repulsed with slaughter, 9 July, *et seq.* 1893; Dr. Jameson, administrator at fort Victoria, and Mr. C. J. Rhodes, prepare for war; angry message from Lobengula, reported 1 Aug.; intervention of sir H. B. Loch, Aug.; the chartered company directed to avoid aggression, 7 Sept.; reinforcements and volunteers from Cape Colony sent by the company to fort Victoria, against which 2 impis (native contingents) are advancing, 21 Sept.; capt. White's defensive force fired at by a Matabele impi, about 1 Oct.; the company's troops well armed, 500 men at forts Salisbury, Victoria, and Charter, 3 Oct.; an attack on the Bechuanaland border police (major Goold Adams, commander) by the Matabele on the Shasi river, near Macloutsie, 5 Oct.; the company's forces advancing to Matabele border; a free hand given to Dr. Jameson, 7 Oct.; junction of all the forces, joined by volunteers from Cape Town regiments, 16 Oct.; major Forbes commander; skirmish at Intaba Zimbi (the iron mountain), 15 Oct.; 22 Matabele killed; capt. Campbell wounded, died 16 Oct.; two envoys from Lobengula shot by mistake at Tati, about 23 Oct.; Lobengula's army (about 5,000 strong) severely repulsed, with heavy loss, near the Shangani river, 24–26 Oct. [British loss, Walters, Burnett, capt. Gwinydd Williams, and others]. British advance on Buluwayo attacked by Lobengula's picked regiments; the enemy defeated, with heavy loss, by deadly fire of Maxim guns, near the M'Bembezu river; British loss, 3, 1 Nov. 1893.

Major Forbes and Dr. Jameson occupy Buluwayo, 4 Nov. 1893.

Lobengula retreats towards Zambesi; ultimatum sent to Lobengula, 9 Nov. 1893.

Major Forbes starts in pursuit of Lobengula, 14 Nov.; sends forward capt. Wilson, 3 Dec., who is encountered by an ambush and cut off from the main force, 4 Dec. 1893.

Major Forbes' advance attacked by the Matabele, and checked by the rising of the Shangani river, retreats; arrives at Inyati, 15 Dec. 1893.

Major Allan Wilson and all his party killed, after severe fighting, 4 Dec. 1893; capts. Fitzgerald, Judd, H. Greenfield, Kirton, H. J. Borrow; lieuts. G. Hughes and Hofmeyer, and 22 others, reported, 3, 6 Jan. 1894.

Submission of the Matabele; end of the campaign; success attributed to the energy and foresight of Dr. Jameson and Mr. Cecil Rhodes.

Mr. A. R. Colquhoun 1st administrator of Mashonaland, Jan. 1894.

Conference regarding the Matabeleland settlement between sir Henry Loch, Mr. Cecil Rhodes, and Mr. Hofmeyer, at Cape Town, 10 Jan. 1894.
Submission of Matabele chiefs, 14 Jan. 1894.
Death of Lobengula by fever, 23 Jan., 40 m. S. of the Zambesi; most of his army surrenders, reported 9 Feb. 1894.
Quiet settlement of the country proceeding, 27 Feb. 1894.
The officers and men of the Bechuanaland police exonerated from blame by the government respecting the shooting of Lobengula's envoys at Tati in Oct. 1893, reported 5 March, 1894.
Some anonymous charges of cruelty made against the officers and men of the company's forces engaged in the war, which appeared in *Truth*, 15 Feb. 1894, a paper published in London by Mr. Labouchere, M.P., and which he justified in the *Times*, 21 Feb. and 2 March, were repelled, especially by the African explorer, Mr. F. C. Selous, in the *Times*, 19 Feb., and in a lecture at the Royal colonial institute, 13 March, 1894.
Dr. Jameson and the company's officers exonerated by a government commission of inquiry, July, 1894.
Temporary government; the administrator, a council of three, and a judge nominated by the company, with the assent of the secretary for the colonies, March, 1894.
Col. Rhodes at Buluwayo, 6 April, 1894
Daniels and Wilson, of the Bechuanaland police, having suppressed a message of submission from Lobengula to major Forbes and appropriated a present of 1,000*l*., thereby causing the deaths of major Wilson and his party, were tried at Buluwayo, and sentenced to 14 years' penal servitude, 29 May, 1894.
Settlements in Matabeleland (named Rhodesia, *which see*) open to claimants, 25 April; building proceeding, June—Aug. 1894.
Dr. Jameson, C.B., appointed administrator for the British S. Africa company, 16 Oct. 1894; superseded, 5 Jan. 1896, see *Transvaal*, 1895.
Three of Lobengula's sons arrive at Cape Town, to be educated at Mr. Cecil Rhodes expense, 13 Nov. 1894.
Native revolt during 1896; suppressed 1897; natives display great loyalty during the S. African war, 1899–1902.

MASKS. Masks of painted papyrus are said to have been occasionally worn by kings and priests of ancient Egypt. Horace attributes them to Æschylus; yet Aristotle says the inventor and time of their introduction were unknown.—Modern masks, and muffs, fans, and false hair for the women, were devised in Italy, and brought to England from France in 1572. *Stow*: see *Iron Mask*.

MASONIC INSTITUTIONS, see *Freemasonry*.

MASORAH (Hebrew, *tradition*), a collection of conjectural readings (Keris) of the Hebrew text of the Old Testament, with critical, grammatical, and exegetical remarks by various Jewish doctors, written between the 6th and 10th centuries, who also furnished the *Masoretic vowel points*.

The first Rabbinical Hebrew Bible, containing the Masorah, Targums, and comments, printed by Bomberg at Venice, 1518. The "Book of the Masorah, the Hedge of the Law," first printed at Florence, 1750.

MASQUERADES were in fashion in the court of Edward III., 1340; and in the reign of Charles II. 1660, masquerades were frequent among the citizens. The bishops preached against them, and made such representations as occasioned their suppression, 9 Geo. I. 1724. They were revived and carried to a shameful excess in violation of the laws, and tickets of admission to a masquerade at Ranelagh were on some occasions subscribed for at twenty-five guineas each, 1776. *Mortimer*. At the close of a bal masqué, given by Anderson the Wizard, 5 March, 1856, Covent-garden theatre was destroyed by fire.

MASQUES, precursors of the opera, introduced into England in the latter part of the 16th century; many were written by Ben Jonson, Beaumont and others; Inigo Jones designed the costumes, &c.; Wm. and H. Lawes, Banister, Locke and others composed the music. A very costly one was held at the Middle Temple on the marriage of princess Elizabeth, Feb. 1613. Milton's "Comus," the music by Henry Lawes, was represented at Ludlow castle in 1634. "Beauty's Awakening," arranged by Mr. Walter Crane and Mr. C. R. Ashbee, presented by the members of the Art Workers' Guild at the Guildhall, 27 June, 1899.

MASS, in the Roman church, is the office or prayers used at the celebration of the Eucharist, in memory of the passion of Christ, and to this every part of the service alludes. The general division consists in high and low; the first is that sung by choristers, and celebrated with the assistance of a deacon and sub-deacon; low masses are those in which the prayers are rehearsed without singing. Mass was first celebrated in Latin about 394; it was introduced into England in the 7th century. Prostration was enjoined at the elevation of the host in 1201. Dr. Daniel Rock, in "The Church of our Fathers" (1849), describes an ancient MS. of "The Service of the Mass, called the Rite of Salisbury," compiled for that cathedral, by St. Osmund and others, during the 12th century. The English communion service was adopted in 1549; see *Missal*, and *Ritualism*.

MASSACHUSETTS, the mother state of New England, North America, founded by the English puritans at Plymouth-rock, 1620. It abolished slavery 1783, and adopted the constitution of the United States, 1788. Capital, Boston. Population, 1880, 1,783,085; 1890, 2,238,943; 1900, 2,805,346. See *Pilgrim Fathers* and *Boston*.

Great fire at Lynn, a large shoe-making town. 296 buildings destroyed, and about 8,000 persons destitute, estimated loss 5,000,000 dollars, 26 Nov. 1889.

MASSACRES. The following are among the most remarkable, probably exaggerated:—

BEFORE CHRIST.

Of all the Carthaginians in Sicily, 397.
2000 Tyrians crucified and 8000 put to the sword for not surrendering Tyre to Alexander, 331.
Of 2000 Capuans, friends of Hannibal, by Gracchus, 211.
A dreadful slaughter of the Teutones and Ambrones, near Aix, by Marius, the Roman general, 200,000 being left dead on the spot, 102.
The Romans throughout Asia, women and children not excepted, massacred in one day, by order of Mithridates, king of Pontus, 88.
A great number of Roman senators massacred by Cinna, Marius, and Sertorius, 87.
Again, under Sylla and Catiline, his minister of vengeance, 82.
At Perusia, Octavianus Cæsar ordered 300 Roman senators and other persons of distinction to be sacrificed to the manes of Julius Cæsar, 40.

AFTER CHRIST.

At the destruction of Jerusalem, 1,100,000 Jews are said to have been put to the sword, 70.
The Jews, headed by one Andræ, put to death many Greeks and Romans, in and near Cyrene, 115.
Cassius, a Roman general, under the emperor M. Aurelius, put to death 300,000 of the inhabitants of Seleucia, 165.
At Alexandria, many thousands of citizens were massacred by order of Antoninus, 215.
The emperor Probus is said to have put to death 400,000 of the barbarian invaders of Gaul, 277.
Of the Gothic hostages by Valens, 378.
Of Thessalonica, when 7000 persons invited into the circus were put to the sword, by order of Theodosius, 390.

Of the circus factions at Constantinople, 532.
Massacre of the Latins at Constantinople, by order of Andronicus, 1184.
Of the Albigenses and Waldenses, commenced at Toulouse, 1208. Thousands perished by the sword and gibbet.
Of the French in Sicily, 1282; see *Sicilian Vespers*.
At Paris, of the Armagnacs, at the instance of John, duke of Burgundy, 1418.
Of the Swedish nobility, at a feast, by order of Christian II., 1520.
Of Protestants at Vassy, 1 March, 1562.
Of 70,000 Huguenots, or French Protestants, in France (see *St. Bartholomew*), 24 Aug. 1572.
Of the Christians in Croatia by the Turks, when 65,000 were slain, 1592.
Of the pretender Demetrius, and his Polish adherents, at Moscow, 27 May, 1606.
Of Protestants in the Valteline, N. Italy July, 1620.
Of Protestants at Thorn, put to death under a pretended legal sentence of the chancellor of Poland, for being concerned in a tumult occasioned by a Roman Catholic procession, 1724. All the Protestant powers in Europe interceded to have this unjust sentence revoked, but unavailingly.
At Batavia, 12,000 Chinese were massacred by the natives, Oct. 1740, under the pretext of an intended insurrection.
At the taking of Ismail by the Russians, 30,000 old and young were slain, Dec. 1790; see *Ismail*.
Of French Royalists (see *Septembrizers*), 2 Sept. 1792.
Of Poles, at Praga, 1794.
In St. Domingo, where Dessalines made proclamation for the massacre of all the whites, 29 March, 1804, and many thousands perished.
Insurrection at Madrid, and massacre of the French, 2 May, 1808.
Massacre of the Mamelukes, in the citadel of Cairo, 1 March, 1811.
Massacre of Protestants at Nismes, perpetrated by the Catholics, May, 1815.
Massacre at Scio, 22 April, 1822; see *Chios*.
Of the Janissaries at Constantinople, 14 June, 1826; at Cabul (see *Afghanistan*), 1841.
600 Kabyles suffocated in a cave Algeria, 18 June, 1845; see *Dahra*.
Massacre of Christians at Aleppo, 16 Oct. 1850.
Of 136 emigrants at Mountain Meadows, Utah (said to be by Mormons whom they had offended); a few children spared; 18 Sept. 1857.
[Bishops Ph. K. Smith and Lee accused; Brigham Young exonerated, 1875. Bp. Lee sentenced to death, Oct. 1876; shot, 23 March, 1877.]
Of Maronites, by Druses, in Lebanon, June, 1860; and of Christians, by Mahometans, at Damascus, 9-11 July, 1860; see *Druses* and *Damascus*.
Of 173 N.-W. Indians (including women and children) (as a chastisement for murders, outrages, and robberies), by major Baker, of U.S. army, Jan. 1870.
Of French missionaries and others, at Tien-tsin, 22 persons (see *China*), 21 June, 1870.
Of foreigners, by the native Gauchos in the Tandel district, Buenos Ayres, S. America, 1 Jan. 1872.
Of about 90 French colonists and others in New Caledonia, by natives, during a revolt, June, 1878.
Of about 6 negro militiamen, who had made a patriotic demonstration on 4 July, by whites, at Hamburg, South Carolina, 9 July, 1876.
Of Mehemet Ali Pacha, and others, at Ipek, near Scutari, by Albanians, 6 Sept. 1878.
At Cabul (see *Afghanistan*), 1879.
Alexandria (see *Egypt*), 11 June, 1882.
Of Christians in Cochin-China; 24,000 reported to be massacred, summer, 1885; and about 22,000 in Annam by rebels, July–Dec. 1885.
See *Indians*, *Minnesota*, *Modoc Indians*, and *Turkey*, 1876, and 25–29 Aug. 1896, *Armenia*, 1894–96, *Macedonia*, 1903, *Somaliland*, Nov. 1896, *Candia*, 1896–8, *Russia*, 1903.
Of missionaries and converts in China, *which see*, May, June, 1900.

MASSACRES IN BRITISH HISTORY.

Of 300 British nobles, on Salisbury Plain, by Hengist, about 450.
Of the monks of Bangor, to the number of 1200, by Ethelfrid, king of Bernicia, 607 or 612.
Of the Danes in the southern counties of England, in the night of 13 Nov. 1002, by order of Ethelred II. At London it was most bloody, the churches being no sanctuary. Amongst the rest was Gunilda, sister of Swein, king of Denmark, left in hostage for the performance of a treaty but newly concluded. *Baker*.
Of the Jews, in England. Some few pressing into Westminster hall at Richard I.'s coronation, were put to death by the people; and a false alarm being given that the king had ordered a general massacre of them, the people in many parts of England slew all they met. In York 500, who had taken shelter in a castle, killed themselves, rather than fall into the hands of the multitude, 1189.
Of the Bristol colonists, at Cullen's Wood, Ireland (see *Cullen's Wood*), 1209.
Of the English factory at Amboyna, in order to dispossess its members of the Spice Islands, Feb. 1624.
Massacre of the Protestants in Ireland, in O'Neill's rebellion, which began 23 Oct. 1641. Upwards of 30,000 British were killed in the commencement of this rebellion. *Sir William Petty*. In the first three or four days of it, forty or fifty thousand of the Protestants were destroyed. *Lord Clarendon*. Before the rebellion was entirely suppressed, 154,000 Protestants were massacred. *Sir W. Temple*.
Of the Macdonalds of Glencoe (see *Glencoe*), 13 Feb. 1692.
Of 184 men, women, and children, chiefly Protestants, burnt, shot, or pierced to death by pikes; perpetrated by the insurgent Irish, at the barn of Scullabogue, Ireland, in 1798. *Musgrave*.
Of Europeans at Meerut, Delhi, &c., by mutineers of the native Indian army (see *India*), May and June, 1857.
Of Europeans at Kalangan, on the south coast of Borneo, 1 May, 1859.
Of the Europeans at Morant bay, Jamaica, by the infuriated negroes, 11-12 Oct. 1865; see *Jamaica*.
Of lieut. Holcombe and surveying party (about 70) in Assam on Naga hills; about 24 Feb. 1875.
Of Mr. Margary and servants (with col. Browne's expedition into Western China) at Manwyne, by Chinese, 21 Feb. 1875.
Of commodore Goodenough, of the *Pearl*, and 2 seamen, by natives of Santa Cruz island, South Pacific ocean; attacked 12 Aug., died 20 Aug. 1875.
Of prof. Palmer and others; see *Egypt*, 1882.
Of gen. Gordon; see *Khartoum*, 1885.
Of Mr. Quinton and others, in Manipur (*which see*), about 24 March, 1891.

MASSAGETÆ, an ancient Scythian people (probably the ancestors of the Goths), who invaded Asia about 635. In a conflict with them Cyrus the Great was killed, 529 B.C.

MASSILIA, see *Marseilles*.

MASSORAH, see *Masorah*.

MASSOWAH, a port on the Red Sea, subject to Egypt. Certain commercial rights secured to Abyssinia by treaty with England and Egypt, May, 1884.

The Italian flag hoisted beside the Egyptian,	6 Feb.	1885
The Abyssinians under Ras Aloula severely defeat the Arabs at Kufeit near Amadib	23 Sept.	,,
Government of Massowah assumed by the Italians	2 Dec.	,,
Abyssinians attack Massowah and Italian outposts but suffer loss and retire	18 Jan. *et seq.*	1887
About 500 Italians proceeding with supplies to Sahati cut off by Abyssinians under Ras Aloula at Dagoli, near Massowah	25–26 Jan.	,,
Negotiations with Ras Aloula with respect to release of prisoners	11 March,	,,
Skirmishes between Italians and Deber tribe	27–28 March,	,,
Major Savoiroux made a prisoner, still kept by the Abyssinians, April; released	Sept.	,,
Proclamation issued declaring that a state of war exists in Massowah and its dependencies, with blockade of ports	2 May,	,,
The chief Kantibay submits to Italy	18 Oct.	,,
Declared to be in a state of siege	10 Nov.	,,
Italy notifies to the powers that it has annexed Massowah	July,	1888
Protectorate proclaimed at Zulla	3 Aug.	,,
Severe defeat of Italians at Sanganeiti on the borders through native treachery; four Italian officers killed	Aug.	,,
Keren occupied and annexed by the Italians	2 June,	1889

Gen. Baldissera occupies Asmara . . . 4 Aug. 1889
About 1,000 dervishes severely defeated after their incursion into Italian-protected country; captives and booty rescued, reported . . 29 June, 1890
Gen. Gandolfi, new governor, announces the termination of military rule, in the Italian possessions on the Red Sea (named Eritrea, 1 Feb.) 1 July „
Severe defeat of about 10,000 dervishes by the Italian troops under col. Arimondi at fort Agordat; about 4,000 dervishes killed, also Ghen Daref and 4 emirs, reported . . . . 20 Dec. 1893
The dervishes, after a murderous raid, pursued by Italians under col. Baratieri, gov.-gen., who captures Kassala by assault 17 July, 1894
Batagos, an Abyssinian chief, defeated and killed at Halai by Italians under major Toselli, reported, 20 Dec. „
Gen. Baratieri defeats the Abyssinians under Ras Mangascia at Coatit. . . . 13, 14 Jan. 1895
Another victory at Senafa, reported . . 17 Jan. „
Adigrat occupied by the Italians 25 March, „
The heights of Debra carried by assault, and Antalo occupied by gen. Baratieri, after a rapid march, 9 Oct. „
Major Toselli's column (about 2,450) surprised and defeated by 15,000 Shoans at Amba Alagi, major Toselli and 3 lieuts. killed, after a heroic defence, great slaughter on both sides; capts. Botrero and Pagella with the scattered troops retreat to Adera, and join gen. Arimondi . . 8 Dec. „
Shoans repulsed with heavy loss at Makaleh, by lieut.-col. Galliano . . . . 7–11 Jan. 1896
The Italians largely outnumbered, after a gallant resistance and great suffering, vacuate the fort with honours of war, 23 Jan.; and arrive at Adigrat . . . . . 30 Jan. „
Fruitless negotiations for peace with Menelik, 26 Jan., 15 Feb. „
Shoans defeated, and the Pass of Seeta captured, 16 Feb.; again defeated by col. Stevani at Maimara 26 Feb. „
The battle of Adowa: Italians under gen. Baratieri severely defeated by the Shoans; gen. Dabormida and prince Chigi killed at the head of their men (the brigade fought heroically all day); gen. Baratieri, incapable through weakness, retired; gen. Arimondi (fate unknown) and 150 officers killed; estimated Italian loss, 7,000, and 2,000 natives; gen. Albertoni, cols. Nava and Galliano (mortally wounded), 48 officers, and 1,500 men prisoners; Shoan loss, 4,000 . 29 Feb., 1 March, „
Fort Adigrat, provisioned for a month under major Prestinari, surrounded by Shoans, 2 March; the garrison relieved, 5 May; evacuated by the Italians, reported . . . 18 May, „
Gen. Baldissera assumes the command in Massowah, 4 March; gen. Baratieri arrives there greatly prostrated . . 11 March, „
Negotiations for peace opened . . 13 March, „
Dervishes repulsed with heavy loss near Kassala, 8 and 18 March; again by col. Stevani at Mt. Mocram; forts captured at Tucruf, 2 April; enemy's camp burnt, lieut. Partini and 3 others killed . . . . . 3 April, „
Dervish retreat from Kassala . . . 7 April, „
The Italians strongly entrenched at Dongollo and other places, the Abyssinians retreating, 26 May, „
Negotiations between gen. Baldissera and Ras Mangascia and other chiefs for release of prisoners, 8 May; many released 13 May *et seq.* „
Ambra Debra captured in a night attack by lieut. Sapelli, flight of enemy . . . 18 May, „
Gen. Baratieri tried by court martial at Asmara, and acquitted . . . . 5–13 June, „
1,300 Italian prisoners reported in Abyssinia, 6 Nov. „
Treaty of peace signed (see *Abyssinia*), 26 Oct. „
Advance of (5,000 or 6,000) dervishes on Agordat, Tucular occupied . . . . Jan. 1897
Gen. Vigano arrives at Agordat, concentration of troops, and defence organized . . 22 Jan. „
Retreat of the dervishes, to Amdarab . 1 Feb. „

MASTER OF THE CEREMONIES, see *Ceremonies*.

MASTER AND SERVANT ACT (amending the statute respecting them) was passed 20 Aug. 1867; another act repealing parts of preceding acts was passed 26 July, 1889. See *Servants*.

Royal commission to examine into its working, reported 31 July; published evidence . Oct. 1874

MASTER OF THE GREAT WARDROBE, an ancient office abolished in 1782; duties transferred to the lord chamberlain.

MASTER OF THE REVELS, an officer of the court. Solomon Dayrolle was the last appointed. Part of the duties were transferred to the licenser of plays, 1737.

MASTER OF THE ROLLS, an equity judge, derives his title from having the custody of all charters, patents, commissions, deeds, and recognizances, entered upon rolls of parchment; his decrees are appealable to the court of chancery. The repository of public papers, called the Rolls, was in Chancery-lane. The rolls were formerly kept in a chapel founded for the converted Jews; but after the Jews were expelled the kingdom in 1290 it was annexed for ever afterwards to the office of the mastership of the rolls. Here were kept all the records since the beginning of the reign of king Richard III., 1483; all prior to that period being kept in the Tower of London; see *Records*. The first recorded master of the rolls was either John de Langton, appointed 1286, or Adam de Osgodeby, appointed 1 Oct. 1295; but it is clear that the office was in existence long before. *Hardy*. The duties were defined in 1833; the salary regulated in 1837. Changes by the judicature act of 1881. By the supreme court of judicature act, the master of the rolls was made a judge of appeal only.

RECENT MASTERS OF THE ROLLS.

Sir Wm. Grant appointed . . . . 27 May, 1801
Sir Thomas Plumer . . . . . 6 Jan. 1818
Robert, lord Gifford . . . . 5 April, 1824
Sir J. S. Copley (*aft.* lord Lyndhurst) . 14 Sept. 1826
Sir John Leach . . . . . 3 May, 1827
Sir C. Pepys (*aft.* lord Cottenham) . 29 Sept. 1834
Henry Bickersteth (*aft.* lord Langdale) . 19 Jan. 1836
Sir John (baron 1865) Romilly . . 28 March, 1851
Sir George Jessel (a Jew), 29 Aug. 1873; died, 21 March, 1883
Sir Wm. Baliol Brett (lord Esher, 1885, visct. 1897), 3 April, 1883; resigned, 13 Oct. 1897, died 24 May, 1899
Sir Nathaniel Lindley, 20 Oct. 1897; resigned, May, 1900
Sir Richard Webster (lord Alverstone), May; lord chief justice . . . . . Oct. „
Sir A. L. Smith, Oct. 1900; resigned, mid Oct.; died . . . . . . 20 Oct. 1901
Sir Richard Henn Collins . . . . Oct. „

MASTERS IN CHANCERY, chosen from the equity bar, were first appointed, it is said, to assist the ignorance of sir Christopher Hatton, lord chancellor of England, in 1587. The office was abolished in 1852. The offices of the masters in the queen's bench, common pleas, and exchequer divisions of the high court of justice were amalgamated into one central office in the high court of justice in 1879.

MASTODON, see *Mammoth*.

MATABELE LAND. See *Mashona*.

MATACÃO, a small island near Sierra Leone; secured to the British by treaty, 18 April, 1826. It was occupied by the French, March, 1879; and after some discussion was left by them June following.

MATCHES, see *Lucifers*.

MATERIALISM, the doctrine held by those who maintain that the soul of man is not a spiritual substance distinct from matter, but is the result of a particular organisation of matter in the body. The term is rather loosely applied to the system of Epicurus, about 310 B.C.; Hobbes, about A.D. 1642; Priestley, about 1772; and many eminent men in the present day. It is not necessarily identical with atheism, see *Animism*.

MATERNITY CHARITY, ROYAL, Finsbury; founded 1757.

MATHEMATICS formerly signified all kinds of learning; but the term is now applied to the sciences relating to numbers and quantity; see *Arithmetic*. Among the most eminent mathematicians were Euclid, 300 B.C.; Archimedes, 287 B.C.; Descartes, died 1650 A.D.; Barrow, died 1677; Leibnitz, died 1716; sir Isaac Newton, died 1727; Euler, died 1783; Lagrange, died 1813; Laplace, died 1827; and Dr. Peacock, died 1858; sir G. B. Airy, Bartholomew Price (died, aged 79, 29 Dec. 1898); J. J. Sylvester (died 15 March, 1897), I. Todhunter (died 1884), and prof. Arthur Cayley, born 16 Aug. 1821, barrister, 1849–63; wrote above 800 papers, 1852–94; much honoured abroad (died 26 Jan. 1895); prof. Sophus Lie (born 12 Dec. 1842, died, 18 Feb. 1899), are eminent mathematicians. Mary Somerville, born 1790, author of the "Mechanism of the Heavens," died 1873.

The London Mathematical Society was founded, 16 Jan. 1865; professor Aug. De Morgan, president.

John Thomas Crossley, author of the popular "Intellectual Calculator," died 29 April, 1889, aged 89.

Mathematical congress at Zurich, mid. Aug. 1897, one at Paris in 1900.

MATHURINS, see under *Trinity*.

MATINS. The service or prayers first performed in the morning or beginning of the day in the Roman Catholic church. The *French Matins* were the massacre of St. Bartholomew, 24 Aug. 1572. The *Matins of Moscow* were the massacre of prince Demetrius, and the Poles his adherents, in the morning of 27 May, 1606.

MATRIMONIAL CAUSES ACT, passed 1859. By the act passed 27 May, 1878, a magistrate may grant judicial separation with maintenance to a wife suffering from a husband's violent usage. The act was amended in 1884.

MATTER is held to exist in three states: gaseous, liquid, and solid. Mr. William Crookes considers that there is a fourth state, "radiant matter," subtler than any of these, 1879-80. See *Light*.

MATTERHORN, a part of the main ridge of the Alps, about 14,836 feet high, S. Switzerland. After various fruitless attempts by professor Tyndall and other eminent climbers, in 1860, the summit was reached on 14 July, 1865, by Mr. Edward Whymper and others. During their descent, four of the party were killed. Mr. Hadow fell; the connecting rope broke, and he himself, lord Francis Douglas, the rev. Mr. Hudson, and Michael Croz, a guide, slipped down, and fell from a precipice nearly 4000 feet high. Miss Walker, with her father, ascended the Matterhorn, 22 July, 1871. Three gentlemen ascended without a guide, 21 July, 1876. Dr. W. O. Moseley, an American, was killed here, 14 Aug. 1879. Three persons attempting the ascent perished 12 Sept. 1890; Dr. Black and a Miss Bell killed here, 23 July, 1901.

MAUNDY-THURSDAY (derived by Spelman from *mande*, a hand-basket, in which the king was accustomed to give alms to the poor; by others from *dies mandati*, the day on which Christ gave his grand *mandate*, that we should love one another), the Thursday before Good Friday. *Wheatly.* On this day it was the custom of our sovereigns or their almoners to give alms, food, and clothing to as many poor persons as they were years old. It was begun by Edward III., when he was fifty years of age, 1363, and is still continued.

MAUR, ST., see *Benedictions*.

MAURITANIA (N. Africa), with Numidia, became a Roman province, 33 B.C. Augustus created (30 B.C.) a kingdom formed of Mauritania and part of Getulia, for Juba II., a descendant of the ancient African princes. Suetonius Paulinus suppressed a revolt here, A.D. 42, when it was made a province, divided into parts. The country was subjugated by the Vandals, 429, and Greeks, 533, and fell into the hands of the Arabs, about 680. See *Morocco*, and *Moors*.

MAURITIUS, or ISLE OF FRANCE (in the Indian Ocean), was discovered by the Portuguese, 1505; but the Dutch were the first settlers in 1598. They called it after prince Maurice, their stadtholder, but on the acquisition of the Cape of Good Hope, they deserted it; and it continued unsettled until the French landed, and gave it the name of one of the finest provinces in France, 1715. This island was taken by the British, 2 Dec. 1810, and confirmed to them by the treaty of Paris in 1814. The bishopric was founded 1854. Sir Henry Barkly, governor, in 1863, succeeded by sir Arthur H. Gordon, 1870; sir Arthur Purves Phayre, 1874; sir George F. Bowen, 1879; sir J. Pope Hennessy, Dec. 1882; sir Charles Cameron Lees, Sept. 1889; Sir Herbert E. H. Jerningham, April, 1893; sir C. Bruce, Jan. 1897. Population in 1861, 313,462; in 1875, 344,602; in 1890, 377,986; in 1901, 380,040. In 1866 two railways were in progress; both now opened. By an awful hurricane, on 11 March, 1868, great damage was done to shipping and buildings, with much loss of life.

A responsible government granted with a legislative assembly . . . . . . July–Sept. 1885

Dissensions between sir J. Pope Hennessy and Mr. Clifford Lloyd and the council, April; Mr. Lloyd removed (made governor of the Seychelles); sir Hercules Robinson as royal commissioner investigates the affairs, and suspends the governor from action, announced 28 Dec. 1886. Sir J. Pope Hennessy reinstated with admonition July, 1887; arrives at Mauritius . . . . 22 Dec. 1888

Violent hurricane, great destruction of buildings, shipping and crops; one-third of port Louis destroyed, with about 600 deaths, 29 April; total number of deaths reported, 1,230 . . 14 July, 1892

Relief committees organised (see *Mansion-house*); the queen 50*l.*; loan of 600,000*l.* to the colony guaranteed by the British government, about June, "

Great fire at St. Louis; great damage . . 23 July, 1893

Destructive cyclone, with loss of life . . 23 Feb. 1894

Statue of the queen unveiled at St. Louis, Jubilee day . . . . 22 June, 1897

Sir Célicourt Auguste Antelme, able financier, born 1818, died . . . . . 6 June, 1899

Outbreak of bubonic plague . . . July, 1899–1903

Visit of the duke and duchess of Cornwall foundation stone of the Queen Victoria memorial at Port Louis, laid . . . . . . 5 Aug. 1901

The Seychelles, hitherto a dependency of Mauritius, constituted a separate colony . 7 Nov. 1903

MAUSOLEUM. Artemisia married her own brother, Mausolus, king of Caria, Asia Minor, 377 B.C. At his death, 353, it is said she drank in liquor his ashes after his body had been burned, and erected to his memory at Halicarnassus a monument, one of the seven wonders of the world (350 B.C.), termed *Mausoleum*. She invited all the literary men of her age, and proposed rewards to him who composed the best elegiac panegyric upon her husband. The prize was adjudged to Theopompus, 357 B.C. She died 352 B.C. The statue of Mausolus is among the antiquities brought from Halicarnassus by Mr. (aft. sir) C. T. Newton in 1857, and placed in the British Museum. A mausoleum for the royal family of England was founded by the queen at Frogmore, 15 March, 1862.

MAUVE (French for *malva*, mallow), a dye produced by Dr. Stenhouse from lichens in 1848; now produced from *Aniline* (*which see*).

MAY, the fifth month of the year, received its name, some say, from Romulus, who gave it this appellation in respect to the senators and nobles of his city, who were denominated *majores;* others supposed it was so called from Maia, the mother of Mercury, to whom they offered sacrifices on the first day. The ancient Romans used to go in procession to the grotto of Egeria on May-day; see *Evil May-day*.

Mrs. Elizabeth Montague (who died in 1800) gave for many years, on May day, an entertainment at her house in Portman square, to the chimney-sweepers of London.

The annual festival of "Jack in the Green," and his companion sweeps, has gradually ceased, 1876.

See under *Working Men*, May 1890, 1891, 1892, 1893, 1894.

MAYENCE, see *Mentz*.

MAY-FLOWER, see *Pilgrim Fathers*.

"MAY LAWS," see *Prussia*, May, 1873.

MAYNOOTH COLLEGE (Ireland), founded by parliament, 1795, and endowed by a yearly grant voted for the education of students designed for the Roman Catholic priesthood in Ireland. An act for its government was passed in 1800. It contains about 500 students. Permanent endowment of this college (30,000*l*. for the enlargement of the buildings and 26,000*l*. annually) was granted by parliament, June, 1845. This occasioned much controversy in England, a motion being made for its abolition almost every session. The college was repaired and enlarged in 1860. By the Irish Church act, passed 26 July, 1869, the annual parliamentary grant was to cease after 1 Jan. 1871; a compensation being made. A synod held here, Sept. 1875, condemned mixed education. The buildings were much injured by fire, 31 Oct. 1878; damage estimated at 10,000*l*. The pictures and books were saved. The centenary celebrated, an international assembly of ecclesiastics present, 25-27 June, 1895. The king and queen visit the college (see *Ireland*, 1903), Mgr. Gargan, president since 1894, died, aged 84, 27 Aug. 1903.

MAYO ASSASSINATION. Richard Southwell Bourke, earl of Mayo, was born 21 Feb. 1822. As lord Naas he was chief secretary for Ireland, in the Derby and Disraeli administrations, 1852, 1858-9, 1866-8. In Sept. 1868, he was appointed viceroy of India, and energetically fulfilled the duties. He was assassinated at Port Blair in the Andaman islands, on a visit of inspection, by Shere Ali, a convict, 8 Feb. 1872. The Indian government granted an annual pension of 1000*l*. to the countess, and 20,000*l*. for the children; and 1000*l*. a year was added to lady Mayo's pension by parliament, voted unanimously, 22 July, 1872.

MAYORS OF THE PALACE, high officers in France, who had great influence during the later Merovingian kings, termed "*fainéants*," do-nothings:—Pepin the Old (or de Landen), 622 *et seq.;* Pepin Héristal, 687-714; Charles Martel, despotic, 714-741; Pepin le Bref, 741, who shut up Childeric III. in a monastery, and himself took the kingdom, 752.

MAYORS OF CORPORATIONS. At the time of the Norman conquest, 1066, the chief officer of London was called *port-grave*, afterwards softened into *port-reeve*, from Saxon words signifying chief governor of a harbour. He was afterwards called provost; but in Henry II.'s reign the Norman title of *maire* (soon after *mayor*) was brought into use. At first the mayor was chosen for life, but afterwards for periods of irregular duration; now he is chosen annually, but is eligible for re-election. He must be an alderman, and have been sheriff. His duties commence on 9 Nov. In early times the mayor was always an M.P. for the city. The prefix LORD is peculiar to the mayors of London, Dublin, York, Belfast, Liverpool, Manchester, Leeds, Birmingham, Sheffield, Bristol (1899), Cork (1900) Sydney and Melbourne (1902), and to the provosts of Edinburgh, Glasgow, Dundee, Aberdeen and Perth. The dukes of Norfolk and Sutherland, the marquis of Ripon, and the earls of Derby and Lonsdale, and 6 other peers were elected mayors, Nov. 1895.

The first mayor of London, Henry Fitz-Ailwin, held office for 24 years, appointed . 1189 or 1191

(Some say Thomas Legge, created lord mayor by Edw. III., 1354).

Sir Henry Pickard, who had been lord mayor of London in 1357, sumptuously entertained in one day four monarchs: Edward, king of England; John, king of France; the king of Cyprus; and David, king of Scotland; the Black Prince and many of the nobility being present. *Stow*. . 1363

Sir John Norman, lord mayor, went by water to be sworn at Westminster, and it is said instituted lord mayor's show 1453

The more costly pageants of the show laid aside . 1685

The lord mayor entertained the prince regent of England, the emperor of Russia, king of Prussia, and numerous foreigners of high rank 18 June, 1814

The lord mayor, Farncombe, gave a banquet to prince Albert and the mayors of most of the boroughs of the United Kingdom, in furtherance of the project of the great International Industrial Exhibition, 1851 . . 21 March, 1850

The lord mayor, sir F. Moon, entertained the emperor and empress of the French . 19 April, 1855

The lord mayor, B. S. Phillips, entertained the king and queen of the Belgians, July; entertained by them at Brussels . . . . . . Oct. 1866

The lord mayor entertained the viceroy of Egypt, 11 June; the sultan, 18 July, 1867; the shah of Persia, 20 June, 1873; the czar (others since), 18 May, 1874

Lord Mayor Nottage died while in office (the first since William Beckford, who died 21 June, 1770), 11 April, 1885

LORD MAYORS OF LONDON.

1800-1. Sir William Staines, bart.
1801-2. Sir John Eamer, bart.
1802-3. Charles Price.
1803-4. John Perring.
1804-5. Peter Perchard.
1805-6. Sir James Shaw.
1806-7. Sir William Leighton, bart.
1807-8. John Ainsley.
1808-9. Sir Charles Flower, bart.
1809-10. Thomas Smith.
1810-11. Joshua Jonathan Smith.
1811-12. Sir Claudius S. Hunter, bart.
1812-13. George Scholey.
1813-14. Sir William Domville, bart.
1814-15. Samuel Birch.
1815-16. Matthew Wood

1816-17. Matthew Wood again.
1817-18. Christopher Smith.
1818-19. John Atkins.
1819-20. George Brydges.
1820-1. John T. Thorpe.
1821-2. Christopher Magnay.
1822-3. William Heygate.
1823-4. Robert Waithman.
1824-5. John Garratt.
1825-6. William Venables.
1826-7. Anthony Browne.
1827-8. Matthias Prime Lucas.
1828-9. William Thompson.
1829-30. John Crowder.
1830-1 and 1831-2. Sir John Key, bart.
1832-3. Sir Peter Laurie.
1833-4. Charles Farebrother.
1834-5. Henry Winchester.
1835-6. William Taylor Copeland.
1836-7. Thomas Kelly.
1837-8. Sir John Cowan, bart.
1838-9. Samuel Wilson.
1839-40. Sir Chapman Marshall, bart.
1840-1. Thomas Johnson.
1841-2. John Pirie.
1842-3. J. Humphrey.
1843-4. Sir W. Magnay, bart.
1844-5. Michael Gibbs.
1845-6. John Johnson.
1846-7. Sir George Carroll.
1847-8. John Kinnersley Hooper.
1848-9. Sir James Duke, bart., M.P.
1849-50. Thomas Farncombe.
1850-1. Sir John Musgrove.
1851-2. William Hunter.
1852-3. Thomas Challis, M.P.
1853-4. Thomas Sidney.
1854-5. Sir Fras. G. Moon, bart.
1855-6. David Salomons, *Jew*.
1856-7. Thomas Quested Finnis.
1857-8. Sir Robert W. Carden (bart., May, 1887), (died 20 Jan. 1888).
1858-9. David W. Wire.
1859-60. James Carter.
1860-1. William Cubitt, M.P.
1861-2. William Cubitt, again.
1862-3. W. A. Rose.
1863-4. Wm. Lawrence.
1864-5. Warren S. Hale.
1865-6. Benj. Sam. Phillips, *Jew*.
1866-7. Thos. Gabriel.
1867-8. Wm. Ferneley Allen.
1868-9. James Lawrence.
1869-70. Robert Besley.
1870-1. Thomas Dakin.
1871-2. Sills John Gibbons.
1872-3. Sir Sidney Hedley Waterlow.
1873-4. Andrew Lusk, M.P.
1874-5. David Henry Stone.
1875-6. Wm. James Richmond Cotton.
1876-7. Sir Thomas White.
1877-8. Thomas Scambler Owden.
1878-9. Sir Charles Whetham.
1879-80. Sir Francis Wyatt Truscott.
1880-1. Wm. McArthur.
1881-2. John Whittaker Ellis (bart. May).
1882-3. Henry Edmond Knight.
1883-4. R. N. Fowler, M.P.
1884-5. George Swan Nottage; died 11 April, 1885.
1885. Sir R. N. Fowler, bart., M.P., re-elected 14 April.
1885-6. John Staples.
1886-7. Sir Reginald Hanson (bart., May, 1887).
1887-8. Polydore de Keyser (Belgian R.C.) (knt. Oct. 1888).
1888-9. James Whitehead (bart., Nov. 1889).
1889-90. Sir Henry Aaron Isaacs, *Jew*.
1890-1. Joseph Savory (bart., July, 1891.)
1891-2. David Evans (knt., July, 1892).
1892-3. Stuart Knill, R.C. (bart., July, 1893, died 19 Nov. 1898).
1893-4. George Robert Tyler (bart., 30 June, 1894).
1894-5. Sir Joseph Renals (bart., June, 1895).
1895-6. Sir Walter Henry Wilkin.
1896-7. George F. Faudel-Phillips, *Jew* (bart., June, 1897).
1897-8. Col. Horatio David Davies, M.P. (K.C.M.G. 1898).
1898-9. Sir John Voce Moore.
1899-1900. Alfred James Newton (bart., 1900).
1900-1. Frank Green (bart., 9 Nov. 1901, died 3 Dec., 1902).
1901-2. Sir Joseph Cockfield Dimsdale, M.P. (bart., 26 June, 1902).
1902-3. Sir Marcus Samuel, *Jew*.
1903-4. Sir James Thomson Ritchie.

LORD MAYORS OF DUBLIN.

John le Decer was appointed first provost in 1308; a gilded sword was granted to be borne before the provost by Henry IV. 1407
Thomas Cusack appointed first mayor 1409
The collar of SS. and a foot company granted by Charles II. to the mayors 1660
Sir Daniel Bellingham, the first mayor honoured with the title of lord, by Charles II., who granted 500*l*. per annum, in lieu of the company of foot . 1665
The new collar of SS. granted by William III. to the mayor, value 1000*l*., the former having been lost in James II.'s time 1697

MAZARIN BIBLE, see *Printing*, 1450-5.

MAZRA (or Baba Wali), near Candahar, Afghanistan. Here gen. sir Frederick Sleigh Roberts totally defeated Sirdar Mahomed Ayoob Khan, and captured his camp and all his cannon, 1 Sept. 1880. Amongst the killed were colonel F. Brownlow, capt. St. John F. Frome, and capt. E. Straton; lieut. Hector Maclaine (made prisoner 27 July) was found recently murdered. Ayoob Khan with some followers fled towards Herat.

MAZURKA, a Polish dance of the 16th century, introduced into England about 1845; Chopin's music for the mazurka is much admired.

MEAL TUB PLOT, against the duke of York, afterwards James II., contrived by one Dangerfield, who secreted a bundle of seditious letters in the lodgings of colonel Maunsell, and then gave information to the custom-house officers to search for smuggled goods, 23 Oct. 1679. After Dangerfield's apprehension, on suspicion of forging these letters, papers were found concealed in a *meal-tub* at the house of a woman with whom he cohabited, which contained the scheme to be sworn to, accusing the most eminent persons in the Protestant interest, who were against the duke of York's succession, of treason,—particularly the earls of Shaftesbury, Essex, and Halifax. On Dangerfield being whipped the last time, as part of his punishment, 1 June, 1685, one of his eyes was struck out by a barrister named Robert Francis. This caused his death, for which his assailant was hanged.

MEASURES, see *Weights*, and *Micrometer*. "Not men, but measures," a phrase used in parliament by Brougham, 2 Nov. 1830.

MEAT, see *Provisions*.

MEAT-BISCUIT, said to have been invented by Cecil Borden, 1850. See *Milk*.

MEATH (Ireland). Many episcopal sees in Meath (as Clonard, Duleek, and others of less note) were fixed at Clonard, before 1151-2, when the division of the bishoprics in Ireland was made by John Paparo, then legate from Pope Eugene III. Eugene was the first styled bishop of Meath, about 1174. Meath was valued, 30 Henry VIII., at 373*l*. 12*s*. per annum.

MECCA (in Arabia), the birth-place of Mahomet, about 571, whence he was compelled to flee, 15 July, 622 (the Hégira). On one of the neighbouring hills is a cave, where it is asserted he retired to perform his devotions, and where the greatest part of the Koran was brought to him by the angel Gabriel, 604. Mecca, after being vainly besieged by Hosein for the caliph Yezid, 682, was taken by Abdelmelek, 692. In 1803 it fell into the hands of the Wahabees, a Mahometan sect. They were expelled by the pacha of Egypt in 1818, who retired in 1841. It is said that 160,000 pilgrims visited Mecca in 1858, and only 50,000 in 1859. The grand shereef was assassinated by a fanatic, 21 March, 1880. Pilgrimage to Mecca still continues; annual average, 93,350 (1887); about 300,000 in 1893.

MECHANICAL ENGINEERS' INSTITUTION. See under *Engineers*, 1847.

MECHANICS. The simple mechanical powers have been ascribed to heathen deities; the axe, wedge, wimble, &c., to Dædalus; see *Steam Engine*, *Motion*.

Aristotle writes on mechanics about . . . B.C. 320
The properties of the lever, &c., demonstrated by Archimedes, who died 212
[He laid the foundations of nearly all those inventions, the further prosecution of which is the boast of our age. *Wallis* (1695).]
The hand-mill, or quern, was very early in use; the Romans found one in Yorkshire.
Cattle-mills, *molæ jumentariæ*, were also in use by the Romans.
The water-mill was probably invented in Asia; the first that was described was near one of the dwellings of Mithridates 70
A water-mill is said to have been erected on the river Tiber, at Rome 50
Pappus wrote on mechanics . . . about A.D. 350
Floating-mills on the Tiber 536
Tide-mills were, many of them, in use in Venice about 1078
Wind-mills were in very general use in the 12th century.
Saw-mills are said to have been in use at Augsburg 1332
Theory of the inclined plane investigated by Cardan about 1540
Work on Statics, by Stevinus 1586
Galileo's "Scienza Mecanica" 1634
Theory of falling bodies, Galileo 1638
Laws of percussion, Huyghens, Wallis, Wren, about 1660
Theory of oscillation, Huyghens 1670
Epicycloidal form of the teeth of wheels, Roemer . 1675
Percussion and animal mechanics, Borelli; he died 1679
Application of mechanics to astronomy, parallelism of forces, laws of motion, &c., Newton, Hooke, &c. 1666-1700
Problem of the catenary with the analysis, Dr. Gregory 1697
Spirit level (and many other inventions) by Dr. Hooke from 1660 to 1702
D'Alembert's researches on dynamics . . about 1743
Lagrange's "Mécanique Analytique" published . 1788
Laplace's "Mécanique Céleste" published 1799-1805
Borgnis' "Dictionnaire de Mécanique appliquée aux Arts," 10 vols. 1818-23
Edward H. Knight's excellent "Practical Dictionary of Mechanics," published . . . 1877-84
[Among the best modern writers on the science of mechanics are Poncelet, Whewell, Barlow, Moseley, Delaunay, Rankine, Bartholomew Price, Ball and Willis.]

MECHANICS' INSTITUTIONS. One was founded by Dr. Birkbeck in London, and another in Glasgow, in 1823; and many others since. They have revived since 1857, many noblemen and gentlemen giving lectures in them.

MECHANICS' MAGAZINE, weekly; established 30 Aug. 1823; was incorporated with a new paper termed *Iron*, Jan. 1873.

MECHLIN or **MALINES** (Belgium), renowned for its lace manufacture, was founded in the 6th century; destroyed by the Normans in 884; sacked by the Spaniards, 1572; taken by the prince of Orange, 1578, and by the English, 1580; and frequently captured in the 17th and 18th centuries, partaking in the evil fortunes of the country. A Roman Catholic congress was held here Sept. 1867. Population 1890, 50,962; 1900, 56,013.

MECKLENBURG (N. Germany), formerly a principality in Lower Saxony, now independent as the two grand duchies of Mecklenburg-Schwerin (population in 1885, 575,152; 1890, 578,565; 1900, 607,835); and Mecklenburg-Strelitz (population in 1885, 98,371; 1890, 97,978; 1900, 102,628). The house of Mecklenburg claims to be descended from Genseric the Vandal, who ravaged the western empire in the 5th century, and died 477. During the Thirty years' war Mecklenburg was conquered by Wallenstein, who became its duke, 1628; it was restored to its own duke, 1630. After several changes the government was settled in 1701 as it now exists in the two branches of Schwerin and Strelitz. In 1815 the dukes were made grand dukes. The dukes joined the new North German confederation by treaty, 21 Aug. 1866.

GRAND-DUKES OF MECKLENBURG-SCHWERIN.

1815. Frederic-Francis I.; died 7 March, 1842.
1842. Frederic-Francis II.; born 28 Feb. 1823; died 15 April, 1883.
1883. Frederic-Francis III. son, born 19 March, 1851; died 10 April, 1897; his brother, duke Johann Albrecht, regent during the minority of the heir; duke Frederic Wilhelm, half-brother to the regent, accidentally drowned, 22 Sept. 1897.
1901. Fred. Francis IV., born 9 April, 1882.

GRAND-DUKES OF MECKLENBURG-STRELITZ.

1815. Charles; died 6 Nov. 1816.
1816. George, born 12 Aug. 1779; died 6 Sept. 1860.
1860. Frederic William, born 17 Oct. 1819; married princess Augusta of Cambridge, 28 June, 1843.
Heir: his son, Adolphus-Frederic, born 22 July, 1848.
The royal family of England is intimately allied with the house of *Mecklenburg-Strelitz*. King George III. married Charlotte, a daughter of the duke, in 1761; their son, the duke of Cumberland (afterwards king of Hanover) married princess Frederica Caroline, a daughter of the duke, in 1815.

MEDALS, see *Numismatics*. The ancient medals resembled medallions. Modern medals began about 1453 in the 15th century with the works of Vittore Pisano, of Verona, who died 1456, and his followers. Charles I. authorized the presentation of a badge or medal for "forlorn hopes" soldiers, May, 1643. The house of commons resolved to grant rewards and medals to the fleet whose officers (Blake, Monk, Penn and Lawson) and men gained a glorious victory over the Dutch fleet, off the Texel, in 1653. Blake's medal of 1653 was bought by his majesty, William IV. for 150 guineas. In 1692 an act was passed for applying the tenth part of the proceeds of prizes for medals and other rewards for officers, seamen, and marines. Subsequent to Lord Howe's victory, 1 June, 1794, it was thought expedient to institute a naval medal. Medals were struck for the victory of Waterloo; a general war medal (for the war 1793-1814) was ordered in 1847; and special medals were given after the Caffre and Chinese wars. Medals were presented by the queen to persons distinguished in the war in the Crimea, 18 May, 1855. Medals were given to arctic voyagers of 1875-6, in 1877; after Egyptian war, 1882, distributed by the queen at Windsor, 21 Nov. 1882; medals for the Soudan war, 1885; a Burmah medal was given for the war, 1885-7; for the South African war, 1902. Col. Eaton exhibited 1000 medals in New Bond-street, May, 1880. See *Victoria Cross*.

Society of Medallists formed in the spring of 1885 by the hon. C. W. Fremantle, deputy-master of the Mint, president, sir Frederick Leighton and others.
Jubilee medal designed by sir Frederick Leighton, P.R.A., issued.
A list of military and naval medals is given in *Whitaker's Almanack* in 1888.
General Fred. Brine possesses a fine collection of war medals which he has exhibited.
New military medal for troops employed in W. Africa, 1887–92, reported 3 Nov. 1892.
"Numismata Londinensia," edited by Charles Welch, with photographs, 1895.
Diamond jubilee medals in gold, silver, and bronze issued by the Mint, June, 1897.
The Kaisar-i-Hind medal for public service in India, ordered, 11 May, 1900.
"British Empire," to commemorate the accession of Edward VII., struck, Dec. 1901.
The China medal, 1900, in Jan. 1902.
Coronation medal for lord mayors and mayors, lord provosts and provosts, 26 June, 1902.
278,648 war medals manufactured in 1901.
"King's S. Africa," "Africa General Service," and "Transport Service" medals, granted in 1902.

MEDIA, a province of the Assyrian empire, revolted, 711 B.C. Its chronology is doubtful.

Arbaces, reputed founder of the monarchy about B.C. 842
Succeeded by eight kings (*Ctesias*), or by four (*Herodotus*).
Deioces, founder of Ecbatana, reigns 709
Phraortes, or Arphaxad, reigns (he conquers Persia, Armenia, and other countries) 656
Warlike reign of Cyaxares 632–594
War with the Lydians (see *Halys*) 603
Astyages reigns 594
Astyages deposed by Cyrus, who established the empire of Persia (*which see*) 560

MEDIÆVAL, see *Dark Ages*.

MEDICAL ACT, see *Medical Council* and *Royal Army Medical Corps*.

MEDICAL ASSOCIATION, British, founded in 1832 for the promotion of medical science and the maintenance of the honour of the medical profession. It holds annual meetings at different places in the United Kingdom, and publishes the *British Medical Journal* weekly. Meetings in London, 1873, 1,500 members; July, 1895; Montreal, 30 Aug. 1897; Edinburgh, 26 July, 1898; Portsmouth, 1 Aug. 1899; Cheltenham, 30 July, 1901; Manchester, 29 July, 1902.

MEDICAL BENEVOLENT COLLEGE, Royal (Epsom), opened in 1855 by the prince consort. It provides an asylum for 20 pensioners male and female; and 40 foundation scholars (sons of medical men) are fed, clothed, and educated.

MEDICAL CONGRESSES, International, have been held at Paris, 1867; Florence, 1869; Vienna, 1873; Brussels, 1875; Geneva, 1877; Amsterdam, 1879; London, 2-9 August, 1881; Copenhagen, 10 Aug. 1884; Washington, 5-10 Sept. 1887; Berlin, 4-9 Aug. 1890; Rome, 29 March, 1894; Moscow, 19 Aug. 1897; Paris, Aug. 1900; to be at Madrid, 23 April, 1903.

MEDICAL COUNCIL. The Medical Act, 1858, "to regulate the qualifications of practitioners in medicine and surgery;" was amended in 1860, and an important amendment act, withdrawn 25 July, 1884, passed 1886. It established "the General Council of Medical Education and Registration of the United Kingdom." The Royal Colleges of Physicians and Surgeons form a conjoint examining board. The first meeting of this council took place on 23 Nov. 1858, when sir B. C. Brodie was elected first president (who on 30 Nov. was elected president of the Royal Society). He was succeeded by Mr. J. H. Green in June, 1860; by Dr. George Burrows, Jan. 1864; by Dr. George Edward Paget in 1870; and by Dr. Henry Wentworth Acland in 1874; Mr. John Marshall in 1887, and by sir Richard Quain, bart., in 1891 (died, 1898); Sir W. Turner, 1898. The first Medical Register was issued in July, 1859. In 1862 the council was incorporated by parliament, and authorised to prepare and sell a new Pharmacopœia, which was published as the "British Pharmacopœia," in 1864. New editions have appeared since.

MEDICAL SOCIETY OF LONDON, founded 1773. Royal Medical and Chirurgical Society, founded 1805.

MEDICI FAMILY, the restorers of literature and the fine arts in Italy, were chiefs or *signori* of the republic of Florence from 1434, in which year Cosmo de' Medici, who had been banished from the republic, was recalled and made its chief; he ruled for thirty years. Lorenzo de' Medici, styled "the Magnificent," and the "Father of Letters," ruled Florence from 1469 to 1492. Giovanni de' Medici (pope Leo X.) was the son of Lorenzo. *Roscoe*. From 1569 to 1737 the Medici family were hereditary grand dukes of Tuscany (*which see*). Cattarina de' Medici became queen of France in 1547, and regent in 1550. She plotted with the duke of Alva to destroy the Protestants in 1565.

MEDICINE, see *Physic*, and *Physicians*.

MEDINA (Arabia Deserta), famous for the tomb of Mahomet, in a large mosque, lighted by rich lamps. Medina was called the City of the Prophet, because here Mahomet was protected when he fled from Mecca, 15 July, 622; see *Hégira*. Medina was taken by the Wahabees in 1804; retaken by the pacha of Egypt, 1818.

MEDINA, Bopora country, Africa, a kingdom annexed to Liberia by consent, announced Feb. 1880. It is rich in forests and African products, with gold, iron, and other minerals.

MEDINA DE RIO SECO (Valladolid, Spain). Here Bessières defeated the Spaniards, 15 July, 1808.

MEDIOLANUM, see *Milan*.

MEDIUM, see *Spiritualism*.

MEDUN, near Podgoritza, European Turkey. In a ravine here, the Turks, under Mahmud Pacha, were severely defeated by the Montenegrins, 14 Aug. 1876.

MEEANEE. The Beloochees, amounting to 30,000 infantry, with 15 guns and 5000 cavalry, posted in a formidable position at Meeanee, were defeated with great loss on 17 Feb. 1843, by lieut.-gen. sir Charles Napier, with 2600 men of all arms.

MEERUT (near Delhi). Here the Indian mutiny began, 10 May, 1857; see *India*.

MEGÆRA, see *Wrecks*, 1871.

MEGALOPOLIS, a city of Arcadia, founded by the advice of Epaminondas, 371 B.C., long subject to the Macedonians. Having joined the

Achæan League, 234 B.C., it was taken and plundered by Cleomenes of Sparta, 222 B.C. It was partly restored 221, but gradually decayed.

During the excavations carried on for the British school of Archæology of Athens, many discoveries were made, including the site of a great theatre, a tumulus with bones, ornaments, etc., reported April, 1890. An account of the excavations was published by Mr. Ernest A. Gardner, 1893.

MEGAPHONE, a form of telephone (*which see*), invented by Mr. T. A. Edison, for the use of the deaf; announced 1878.

MEGARA, a city of ancient Greece, was subdued by the Athenians in the 8th century B.C. Pericles suppressed a revolt, 445 B.C. The Megarians founded Byzantium 657 B.C. Megara became a free city 307, and joined the Achæan League, 242, and sent a second colony, 628 B.C. The Megarian (Eristic or disputatious) school of philosophy was founded by Euclid and Stilpo, natives of Megara.

MEHADPORE or **MAHEDPORE** (W. India). Here sir Thomas Hislop and sir John Malcolm defeated the Mahrattas under Holkar, 21 Dec. 1817.

MEININGEN COURT COMPANY. See under *Theatres: Drury-lane.*

MEISTERSINGERS, see *Minnesingers.*

MELANESIA, South-west Pacific Isles. The rev. J. C. Patteson (son of sir John), born 1827, was consecrated missionary bishop of Melanesia. He and the rev. J. Atkin were murdered at the isle of Santa Cruz, one of the Queen Charlotte group, by the natives, Sept. 1871, it is supposed in revenge for the kidnapping natives for slaves for Queensland and the Fiji isles, a measure which the bishop himself strenuously opposed.

MELAZZO (W. Sicily). Here Garibaldi, on 20, 21 July, 1860, defeated the Neapolitans under general Bosco, who lost about 600 men; Garibaldi's loss being 167. The latter entered Messina; and on 30 July a convention was signed, by which it was settled that the Neapolitan troops were to quit Sicily. They held the citadel of Messina till 13 March, 1861.

MELBOURNE (Australia), capital of Victoria (*which see*). It was founded by J. P. Fawkener, 29 Aug. 1835; and laid out as a town by order of sir R. Bourke, in April, 1837. The first land sale took place in June, and speculation continued till it caused wide-spread insolvency, in 1841-2. Population in 1851, 23,000; 1891, 491,378; 1901, 493,956.

Made a municipal corporation, 1842; a bishopric . 1847
First legislative assembly of Victoria meets . . 1852
Gold found in great abundance about 80 miles from Melbourne in the autumn of 1851, and immense numbers of emigrants flocked there in consequence, causing an enormous rise in the prices of provisions and clothing . . . . . . ,,
The city greatly improved with public buildings, handsome shops, &c. 1853
The Victoria bank, Ballarat, broken open, and 14,300*l.* in money and 200 ounces in gold dust carried off [one of the robbers was taken in England, sent back to Melbourne, and there tried and hanged] . . . . . . 8 Oct. 1854
University founded 1855
Monster meeting held at Ballarat respecting the collection of the gold licences, followed by riots, during which the Southern Cross flag was raised; intervention of the military; 26 rioters and three soldiers killed, and many wounded . 30 Nov. ,,
The mayor comes to London to congratulate the queen on the marriage of the princess royal . 1858
Intercolonial exhibition opened . . . 25 Oct. 1866
Arrival of the duke of Edinburgh . . 23 Nov. 1867
Great telescope set up at the Observatory early in 1869
Theatre-royal burnt . . . . . 19 March, 1872
International exhibition opened by the marquis of Normanby . . . . 1 Oct. 1880
Direct railway to Sydney completed . . June, 1883
Centenary exhibition to celebrate the foundation of New South Wales colony opened by sir Henry Brougham Loch, the governor, 1 Aug. 1888–31 Jan. 1889
Great meeting to support Imperial Institute 9 May, ,,
Great fire in Collins street, 3 firemen killed, loss about 200,000*l.* . . . . . . 13 Sept. ,,
Meeting of Australian delegates respecting the federation (see *Australasia*) . . 6–14 Feb. 1890
Great strike of officers and men employed in shipping connected with the marine association, about 15 Aug. ,,
A union of employers formed, 4 Sept.; plenty of free labour . . . . 11 Sept. ,,
Gradual resumption of work; end of the strikes announced at a mass meeting . . 14 Nov. ,,
The new Anglican cathedral consecrated 22 Jan. 1891
Destructive overflow of the Yarra-Yarra owing to heavy rains about 11 July, *et seq.*; floods subside; 12,000*l.* subscribed for sufferers 21 July, ,,
The Standard Bank of Australia stops payment; temporary panic . . . . . . 4 Dec. ,,
The new great Western dock opened by lord Hopetoun . . . . 22 March, 1892
Melbourne murder: Frederick Bailey Deeming (alias Albert Oliver Williams), tried for the murder of Emily Mather whom he married at Liverpool 17 Oct., and brought to Australia 15 Dec., and murdered at Windsor, near Melbourne, about 25 Dec. 1891; convicted 28 April–2 May; executed 23 May, ,,

[It was stated that in Feb. 1881, he married Marie James, went with her to Sydney, and was there convicted of fraud in 1882; that he took Dinham Villa, Rainhill, near Widnes, Lancashire, England, 23 July, 1891; and there murdered his wife and four children about 26, 27 July, 1891; he was charged with the murders, by the verdict of the coroner's jury, 28 March, 1892.]

Destructive storm, 1 death . . . 15 March, 1896
St. Patrick's R. C. cathedral consecrated 31 Oct. 1897
Great fire, 20 buildings gutted, Elizabeth-st., Flinder's-lane, estimated loss, 1,000,000*l.* . 21 Nov.
Extreme heat, many deaths, bush fires, reported Feb. 1898
Great rejoicings on the arrival of the duke and duchess of Cornwall . . . . 6 May, 1901
See *Australasia.*
The prefix *lord* conferred on the mayor . 23 Nov. 1902
See *Victoria.*

MELBOURNE ADMINISTRATIONS. On the retirement of earl Grey, 9 July, 1834, viscount Melbourne* became first minister of the crown, 16 July. When viscount Althorp became earl Spencer, on his father's decease, Nov. same year, lord Melbourne waited on the king to receive his majesty's command as to the appointment of a new chancellor of the Exchequer, when his majesty said he considered the administration at an end. Sir Robert Peel succeeded, but was compelled to resign in 1835, and lord Melbourne returned to office. His administration finally terminated, 30 Aug. 1841, sir Robert Peel again coming into power; see *Administrations.*

FIRST ADMINISTRATION, July, 1834; resigned Nov. 1834.

Viscount Melbourne, *first lord of the treasury.*
Marquis of Lansdowne, *lord president.*
Earl Mulgrave, *privy seal.*
Viscount Althorp, *chancellor of the exchequer.*
Viscount Duncannon, viscount Palmerston, and T. Spring-Rice (afterwards lord Monteagle), *home, foreign, and colonial secretaries.*

* Wm. Lamb, born in 1779; became M.P. for Westminster, 1812; secretary for Ireland, 1827; succeeded his father as viscount Melbourne, 1828; died 24 Nov. 1848.

Lord Auckland, *admiralty.*
Mr. Charles Grant (afterwards lord Glenelg), and Mr. C. P. Thomson (afterwards lord Sydenham), *boards of control and trade.*
Lord John Russell, *paymaster of the forces.*
Lord Brougham, *lord chancellor.*
Sir John Hobhouse, Mr. Ellice, marquis of Conyngham, Mr. Littleton, &c.

SECOND ADMINISTRATION, April, 1835.

Viscount Melbourne, *first lord of the treasury.*
Marquis of Lansdowne, *lord president.*
Viscount Duncannon, *privy seal, and woods and forests* (succeeded by earl of Clarendon, Jan. 1840).
T Spring Rice, *chancellor of the exchequer* (succeeded by Francis T. Baring, Aug. 1840).
Lord John Russell, *home secretary* (succeeded by marquis of Normanby, Aug. 1839).
Viscount Palmerston, *foreign secretary.*
Lord Glenelg, *colonial secretary* (succeeded by marquis of Normanby, Feb. 1839; lord John Russell, Aug. 1839).
Viscount Howick, *secretary-at-war* (succeeded by T. B. Macaulay, Sept. 1839).
Lord Auckland, *admiralty* (succeeded by earl of Minto, Sept. 1835).
Sir John C. Hobhouse, *board of control.*
C. Poulett Thomson, *board of trade* (succeeded by Henry Labouchere, Aug. 1839).
Lord Holland, *chancellor of duchy of Lancaster* (succeeded by earl of Clarendon, Oct. 1840).
The chancellorship in commission; sir C. Pepys (afterwards lord Cottenham), became *lord chancellor,* Jan. 1836.

MELEGNANO, see *Marignano.*

MELÉNITE, a new explosive invented by M. Turpin, a French chemist; approved by the French War Minister, Dec. 1886. Several persons killed by an explosion of this material at Belfort.

By an explosion of melénite at Bourges four workmen were killed . . . . . . 10 Oct. 1890
The *mélinite scandal,* notice by the chamber of deputies, May, June, 1891. M. Turpin and captain Triponé sentenced to imprisonment, exile and fines for receiving money for communications respecting mélinite to foreigners, 17 June, 1891

MELFI (Apulia, S. Italy) was nearly destroyed by an earthquake, 14 Aug. 1851: about 600 persons perished.

MELODISTS' CLUB, founded in 1825 by admirers of Dibdin; prizes were offered.

MELODRAMA, in which dialogue is interspersed with music, began in Germany in the 18th century, and was introduced here by Thomas Holcroft.

MELORA or **MELORIA,** a small isle in the Mediterranean, near which the Pisan fleet defeated the Genoese, in 1241, capturing many bishops going with much treasure to a council. The total destruction of the Pisan fleet on 6 Aug. 1284, by the Genoese near the same place, after a most sanguinary conflict, was considered to be the just punishment of their impiety.

MELOS (now Milo), one of the Cyclades in the Ægean sea, early colonised by the Spartans. During the Peloponnesian war the Melians adhered to Sparta, till the island was captured, after seven months' siege, by the Athenians, who massacred all the men and sold the women and children as slaves, 416 B.C. A statue of Venus, found here in 1820, was placed in the Louvre, 1834.

Many statues, etc., discovered by excavations, reported . . . . May, 1896

MEMBERS OF PARLIAMENT (CHARGES AND ALLEGATIONS) ACT, passed 13 Aug., 1888. See under *Ireland* and *Parnellites.*

MEMEL, an important commercial port in Prussia, built about 1252 by the Livonian order. It was fortified by the Teutonic knights, 1404. It was almost totally destroyed by fire, 4 Oct. 1854.

MEMNONEIUM or **RAMESEION** (Thebes, Egypt), the first Egyptian monarch—4455, *Brugsch,* the tomb of Osymandyas, according to Diodorus, now considered to be that of Rameses III., about 1200, *Brugsch.*

MEMORIAL HALL, see *Independents.*

MEMORY, see *Mnemonics.*

MEMPHIS, an ancient city of Egypt ("of which the very ruins are stupendous"), is said to have been built by Menes. It included several grand temples with the tombs of the kings. The invasion of Cambyses, 525 B.C., began the ruin of Memphis, and the founding of Alexandria, 332, completed it. It was restored by Septimius Severus, A.D. 202. In the 7th century, under the dominion of the Saracens, it fell into decay.—MEMPHIS, Tennessee, U. S., on the Mississippi, was taken from the confederates by the federals after a severe conflict, 6 June, 1862.

The cyclorama of Memphis as it might have appeared at the departure of the Israelites from Egypt 1491 B.C., painted by Herr Edmund Beringer, was exhibited at Niagara-hall, Westminster, Jan. 1892.

"MEN OF THE REIGN," by T. Humphry Ward, published 1885. "Celebrities of the Century," by L. C. Sanders, 1887.

MEN OF THE TIME, a Dictionary of Contemporaries, first published 1852; 12th edition, by T. Humphry Ward, 1887. 13th edition "Men and *Women* of the Time," edited by G. W. Moon, 1891. 14th edition by Victor G. Plarr, April, 1895, combined with "Who's Who."—"Men of Mark," printed photographs, with biographical sketches, by Mr. T. Cooper, first appeared Jan. 1876.

MENAGERIE, see *Zoology, Tower.*

Mr. Phineas Taylor Barnum's great menagerie at Bridgport, Connecticut, burnt; a great many animals perish; loss about 140,000*l.* 20 Nov. 1887. Mr. Barnum stated to have purchased the old Wombwell's collection Jan. 1888. See *Barnum.*

MENAI STRAIT (between the Welsh coast, and the isle of Anglesey). Suetonius Paulinus, when he invaded Anglesey, transported his troops across this strait in flat-bottomed boats, 59. In crossing this strait, a ferry-boat was lost, and fifty persons, chiefly Irish, 4 Dec. 1785. The road from London to Holyhead has long been regarded as the highway from the British metropolis to Dublin; Mr. Telford was applied to by the government to perfect this route by the London and Holyhead mail-coach road, which he did by erecting beautiful suspension bridges over the river Conway and the Menai Strait, commenced in July, 1818, finished in July, 1825, opened 30 Jan. 1826. The Britannia tubular bridge over the Menai was constructed by Stephenson and Fairbairn in 1849-50; see *Tubular Bridges.*

MENDICANT FRIARS. Several religious orders commenced alms-begging in the 13th century, in the pontificate of Innocent III. They spread over Europe, and formed many communities; but at length by a general council, held by Gregory X. at Lyons, in 1272, were reduced to four orders—Dominicans, Franciscans, Carmelites, and Augustines. The Capuchins and others branched off. See *Franciscans,* &c.

MENDICITY SOCIETY (Red Lion-square, London), was established in 1818 for the suppression of public begging, and other impositions. Tickets received from the society are given by subscribers to beggars, who obtain relief at the society's house, if deserving. In 1857, 54,074 meals; in 1860, 42,912; in 1865, 52,137; in 1872, 26,330; in 1878, 55,180 were distributed. In 1878, 1700 begging letters were investigated; in 1891, 1358; in 1896, 1,516; in 1897, 1,611. 1,400*l.* were expended in relief in 1894; 1,244*l.* in 1897; and 1,182 vagrants apprehended; 1,146*l.* in 1901; 1,504 vagrants taken up; 889 begging letters received. (See *Poor.*) The society has been much aided by the action of the Charity Organization society, established in 1870; they agree to co-operate together, June, 1897.

MENDOZA, in the Argentine republic, nearly destroyed by an earthquake, one of the most awful recorded, 20 March, 1861: above 7000 persons perished.

MENIPPÉE, see *Satire.*

MENNONITES, four sects of Dutch, Flemish and German baptists; derive their name from Menno Symonis (1505-61), formerly a catholic priest, who became a teacher and leader of the anabaptists, about 1537, and published his "True Christian Belief" in 1556; subsequently divisions and changes ensued. The Mennonites, objecting to war, emigrated from Prussia to Odessa, to escape military service, and went thence to America, 1878.

MENSURATION. The properties of conic sections were discovered by Archimedes, to whom the chief advancement in mensuration may be attributed. He also determined the ratio of spheres, spheroids, &c., about 218 B.C.; see *Arithmetic.* The *Mensurator*, a new machine for the solution of triangles, was explained by Mr. W. Marsham Adams, at the British Association Meeting at Brighton, Aug. 1872.

MENTANA (near Monte Rotondo, in the old papal states). Here Garibaldi and his volunteers, after having intrenched his positions at Monte Rotondo and Mentana on their march towards Tivoli, on Sunday, 3 Nov. 1867, were totally defeated by the pontifical and French troops under generals Kanzlar and Polhès, after a severe conflict, in which general Failly said "the Chassepot rifles did wonders." There were about 5000 men on each side, but the Garibaldians were very badly armed. The loss of the papal and French troops was about 200 killed and wounded; that of Garibaldi about 800. Garibaldi crossed the Italian frontier, and was arrested at Corr・se, and eventually sent to Caprera (about 25 Nov.). See *Rome.* A monument to the Garibaldians who fell here was inaugurated 25 Nov. 1877.

MENTZ or **MAYENCE** (S.W. Germany), the Roman *Moguntiacum*, built about 13 B.C. The archbishopric was founded by Boniface, 745. Many diets have been held here; and here John Faust established a printing press, about 1440. A festival in honour of John Gutenberg was celebrated here in 1837, another June, 1890. See *Printing.* Mentz was given up to the Prussians, 26 Aug. 1866. 500th anniversary of the birth of Gutenberg, typographical exhibition opened by the grand duke of Hesse, 23 June, 1900. Population 1890, 72,934; 1900, 84,251.

MENU, INSTITUTES OF, the very ancient code of India. Sir Wm. Jones, who translated them into English (1794), considers their date should be placed between Homer (about 962 B.C.) and the Roman Twelve Tables (about 449 B.C.).

MERCANTILE MARINE ACT was passed in Aug. 1850, and amended Aug. 1851.

MERCATOR'S CHARTS, said to have been constructed by Gerard Mercator or Kauffmann and published 1556, and applied to navigation by Edward Wright about 1599.

MERCHANDISE MARKS ACT, passed in 1862 to punish forgeries of trade-marks. Another act passed in 1887; reported effectual, 1890; amended 1891—94; reported partially effectual by a committee, July, 1897.

At an International Conference on the subject of fraudulent trade-marks, held at Madrid 7-14 April, 1890, an important convention was agreed to.

MERCHANT ADVENTURERS' COMPANY, established by the duke of Brabant in 1296, was extended to England in Edward III.'s reign, and was formed into a corporation in 1564.—The MERCHANT-TAYLORS, a rich company of the city of London, of which many kings have been members, were so called after the admission of Henry VII. into their company, 1501, but were incorporated in 1466. Their school was founded in 1561. *Stow.*

MERCHANT SHIPPING ACT of 1854 was amended by acts passed in 1862, 1867, 1871, 1872, and 1873. The Act suddenly passed 13 Aug. 1875, gave further power to the Board of Trade for stopping unseaworthy ships. Other Acts passed 1876, 1880, 1882, 1883, 1889, 1892, consolidated 1894; amended, 1897 and 1898; merchant shipping (liability of shipowners and others) act passed, 6 Aug. 1900; see *Courts of Survey*, and *Seamen.*

Loss of life at sea having greatly increased, a new bill brought in by Mr. Joseph Chamberlain, president of the Board of Trade, to prevent overloading, under-manning, and over-insurance, 19 May; withdrawn . . . . . 3 July, 1884

Royal commission to inquire into merchant shipping (earl of Aberdeen, the duke of Edinburgh, Mr. J. Chamberlain, Mr. Burt, Mr. H. Green, Mr. T. C. Baring and eight others), gazetted 28 Oct. 1884; last meeting . . . . . 31 July, 1885

First report issued . . . . . . 15 Nov. „

Royal commission on loss of life at sea appointed 4 March, 1886

Issue report recommending such alteration of law of marine insurance as would prevent owners from making profit by the loss of their ships and other changes . . . . 27 Aug. 1887

MERCHANTS were protected by Magna Charta, 1215, and by many statutes. See *Acton Burnel.* An attempt made by queen Anne's ministry to exclude merchants from sitting in the house of commons in 1711, failed.

MERCIA, see under *Britain.*

MERCURY, the planet nearest the sun, and the smallest known to the ancients. Schiaparelli asserts his rotation to be as long as his revolution in his orbit. The transit of Mercury over the sun's disk, of rare occurrence and first observed by Gassendi, 1631, was well observed 5 Nov. 1868; at Athens, 10 May, 1891, well observed by Prof. Barnard at Lick Observatory, California, 10 Nov. 1894. See *Calomel* and *Quicksilver.* The Greek god Hermes was the Roman Mercury.

MERCY, ORDER OF (in France), was established with the object of accomplishing the redemption of Christian captives among the Saracens, by John de Matha in 1198. *Hénault.* Another order was formed by Pierre Nolasque in Spain, 1223. A League of Mercy (based on the plan of the guild founded by the late duchess of Teck), organized to further the objects of the prince of Wales's hospital fund for London; an "Order of Mercy," established in connection with the league, as a reward for free service to the sick and poor; meeting held at Marlborough house; the prince and princess of Wales, presidents, 1 March, 1899; succeeded by the present prince and princess of Wales, Nov. 1901.

MERIDA (Spain), a town in Estremadura (built by the Romans), was taken by the French, Jan. 1811. Near this town, at Arroy dos Molinos, the British army under general (afterwards lord) Hill defeated the French under general Girard, after a severe engagement, 28 Oct. 1811. The British took Merida from the French in 1812, general Hill leading the combined forces of English and Spanish troops.

MERIDIAN, see under *Geodesy*.

MERINO SHEEP, imported into England from Spain, 1788, are thought to be descendants of English sheep taken to Spain as part of the dowry of John of Gaunt's daughter Katherine, 1390.

MERIT, ORDER OF (British), created by king Edward VII. for those who have won distinction in the army, navy, literature, art and science, 26 June, 1902. First members: earl Roberts, viscount Wolseley, viscount Kitchener, adm. H. Keppel, adm. sir E. H. Seymour, lord Kelvin, lord Lister, lord Rayleigh, sir W. Huggins, rt. hon. John Morley, Mr. G. F. Watts, R.A., the rt. hon. W. E. H. Lecky (died 23 Oct. 1903).

MEROE, an ancient city and country of Africa, near the sources of the Nile, said to have flourished under sacerdotal government in the time of Herodotus, about 450 B.C.

The priest-king Ergamenes massacred the priests and became absolute, about 300 B.C.

The ruins of the ancient capital were discovered by Caillaud between 1819 and 1822.

MEROVINGIANS, the first race of French kings, 418-752; see *France* and *Mayors*.

MERRIMAC, see *United States*, 1862.

MERRY-ANDREW. The name is said to have been first given to Andrew Borde, a physician, who lived in the reign of Henry VIII., and who, on some occasions, on account of his facetious manners, appeared at court, 1547.

MERSEY TUNNEL, see *Tunnel*.

MERTHYR-TYDVIL (Glamorganshire). Riots commenced here, 3 June, 1831, and continued for several days; many persons were killed and wounded; see *Coal (Accidents)*.

MERTON (Surrey). At an abbey here, the barons under Henry III., 23 Jan. 1236, held a parliament which enacted the Provisions of Merton, the most ancient body of laws next after Magna Charta. They were repealed in 1863; see *Bastards*. The statute of Merton also provides for the inclosure of common lands.

MERV, or Meru (the ancient *Antiochia Margiana*), a town of independent Turkestan, Central Asia. It flourished under the Seljuk Turks, especially under Sultan Alp Arslan; it was sacked by the Monguls in 1221; it became subject to Persia in 1510; to the emir of Bokhara in 1787; to the Turkomans in 1856, and to Russia 1883-4. Nearly 10,000 Turcomans die of malignant fever, March-Oct. 1896. See *Russia* and *Turkestan*.

MESMERISM. Frederick Anthony Mesmer, a German physician, of Merseburg, published his doctrines in 1766, contending, in a thesis on planetary influence, that the heavenly bodies diffused through the universe a subtle fluid which acts on the nervous system of animated beings. Quitting Vienna for Paris, in 1778, he gained numerous proselytes and much money by experiments with and without metallic plates, producing effects termed then "animal magnetism," now "hypnotism." A committee of physicians and philosophers investigated his pretensions, and Bailly, in a paper drawn up in 1784, exposed the futility of animal magnetism. Mesmerism excited attention again about 1848, when Miss Harriet Martineau and others announced their belief in it. In 1859, the Mesmeric Infirmary issued its tenth annual report, archbishop Whately being president, and the earl of Carlisle and Mr. Monckton Milnes (since lord Houghton) among the vice-presidents. See *Animal Magnetism* and *Hypnotism*.

The "New Mesmerism" exhibited in Paris by Dr. Luys and others, which included the alleged externalization of sensations and transference of sensibility to inanimate objects, such as dolls, was well described in the *Times*, 28 Dec. 1892, and 5, 11 Jan. 1893, and by Mr. Ernest Hart in the *British Medical Journal* . . . . . Jan. 1893

MESOPOTAMIA, the district between the rivers Tigris and Euphrates (*which see* and *Aram*), successively held by Assyrians, Babylonians, Persians, Greeks, Romans, Arabs and Turks. Mesopotamia is mentioned in Gen. xxiv. 10; Acts ii. 9, and other places.

MESSALIANS, a sect professing to adhere to the letter of the gospel, about 310, refused to work, quoting this passage, "Labour not for the food that perisheth."

MESSENIA (now *Maura-Matra*), in the Peloponnesus, an ancient kingdom. It had long sanguinary wars with Sparta. It was at first governed by kings; after its restoration to power in the Peloponnesus it formed an inferior republic, under the protection first of the Thebans, and afterwards of the Macedonians.

The *first* Messenian war began 743 B.C.; was occasioned by violence offered to some Spartan women in a temple of devotion common to both nations; the king of Sparta being killed in his efforts to defend the females. Eventually, Ithome was taken, and the Messenians became slaves to the conquerors . . . . B.C. 724

The *second* war, to throw off the Spartan yoke, commenced about 685, ending in the defeat of the Messenians, who fled to Sicily 668

The *third* war (the Messenians emigrate) . 464-455

MESSIAH, synonymous with Christ "the anointed," foretold by *Daniel* ix. 25, about 538 B.C. "We have found the Messias, which is, being interpreted, the Christ." *John* i. 41. "The Messiah," Handel's greatest oratorio, composed by him in twenty-three days (22 Aug.-14 Sept. 1741), was first performed at Dublin, 13 April, 1742, the receipts being given by him to the charities of that city.

MESSINA (Sicily), so named by the Samians, who seized this city, then called Zancle, 671 B.C. It was seized by the Mamertini (*which see*), about 281 B.C. It belonged for many ages to the Roman empire; was taken by the Saracens, about A.D. 829. *Priestley*. Roger the Norman took it from them by surprise, about 1072.

Revolts against Charles of Anjou, and is succoured by Peter of Aragon 1282

Revolts in favour of Louis XIV. of France, 1676; the Spaniards punish it severely 1678
Almost ruined by an earthquake and eruption of Etna 1693
Nearly depopulated by a plague 1740
Half destroyed by an earthquake 1783
Head-quarters of the British forces in Sicily, prior to 1814
An insurrection here subdued . . . . 7 Feb. 1848
Garibaldi enters Messina after his victory at Melazzo 20-21 July, 1860
The citadel surrenders to Cialdini . . 13 March, 1861
Population 1890, 142,000.

METALS. Tubal-Cain is mentioned as an "instructor of every artificer in brass and iron." (*Gen.* iv.) The Phœnicians had great skill in working metals. Bunsen and Kirchhoff's method of chemical analysis by means of the spectrum has added cæsium, rubidium, thallium, indium, gallium, and others to the known metals. See *Elements, Mines, Iron*, and the other metals. "Metallurgy," published by Dr. John Percy, 1861-80; he died 19 June, 1889. "Electro-Metallurgy," translated from the German of Dr. W. Borchers, with additions by Walter G. McMillan, published, 1897.

METAMORPHISTS in the 15th century affirmed that Christ's natural body, with which he ascended into heaven, was wholly deified.

METAPHYSICS, the science of abstract reasoning, or that which contemplates the existence of things without relation to matter. The term, literally denoting "after physics," originated from these words having been put at the head of certain essays of Aristotle, which follow his treatise on Physics. *Mackintosh.* Modern metaphysics arose in the 15th century—the period when an extraordinary impulse was given to the study of the human mind in Europe, commonly called the "revival of learning." Hobbes, Cudworth, S. T. Coleridge, Dugald Stuart, and sir W. Hamilton, were eminent British metaphysicians, and Descartes, Pascal, Kant, Schelling, and Fichte, foreign ones. See *Philosophy*.

METAURUS, a river in central Italy, where Hasdrubal, the brother of Hannibal, was defeated and slain, 207 B.C., when marching with abundant reinforcements. The Romans were led by Livius and Claudius Nero, the consuls. The latter commanded the head of Hasdrubal to be thrown into his brother's camp. The victory saved Rome.

METEMPSYCHOSIS, a doctrine attributed to Pythagoras, about 528 B.C., asserts the transmigration of the soul from one body to another. It is also ascribed to the Egyptians, who would eat no animal food lest they should devour the body into which the soul of a deceased friend had passed. They had also an idea that so long as the body of the deceased was kept entire, the soul would not transmigrate; and therefore embalmed the dead. See *Buddhism*.

METEOROGRAPH, an apparatus for the invention of which father Secchi of Rome received a prize at the Paris International Exhibition, July, 1867. It is self-acting, and registers the various changes of the atmosphere in the form of a diagram.

METEOROLOGY (from the Greek *meteōros*, aërial), the science which treats of the phenomena which have their origin in the air, such as rain, lightning, meteors, fogs, &c. The writings of Theophrastus, on meteorology, 3rd century B.C. were translated by Jas. G. Wood, edited by G. J. Symons, published 1894. Aristotle, Bacon, Boyle, and Franklin wrote on the subject.

Meteorological Society of the Palatinate, established 1780.
Meteorological Society of London, first met, 15 Oct. 1823.
John Dalton's essay on meteorology appeared in 1793.
Luke Howard's work on the clouds appeared in 1802, and his "Barometrographia" in 1848. See *Clouds*.
Sir W. Reed published his work on the "law of storms" in 1838. The works of Daniell (1845), Kæmtz (1845), Müller (1847), and Buchan (1867) are esteemed.
The "British" Meteorological Society, established in 1850, chartered in 1866, became Royal, Oct. 1883; Mr. Henry Perigal, the treasurer, a scientist, died, aged 97, 6 June, 1898. By the exertions of Mr. James Glaisher, long the secretary, the apparatus at Greenwich was erected; and meteorology has appeared in the "Greenwich Observations" since 1848. See *Balloon—Scientific Ascents.*
The Royal Meteorological Society's annual exhibitions began in 1880.
Meteorological observatories have been erected in all parts of the globe.
The Meteorological department of the Board of Trade, established in 1855, under admiral Fitzroy, commenced the publication of reports in 1857. The admiral published his "Weather-Book" in 1863. His exertions are said to have overworked his brain; and on 30 April, 1865, he died by his own hand. The Meteorological office was soon after placed under the direction of Mr. Robert H. Scott. It has issued apparatus and instruction books to captains of ships and established observatories in many places in the empire. It was handed over to the Royal Society in 1871, and endowed by Mr. J. P. Gassiot. Annual reports on ocean-meteorology, weather telegraphy and climatology issued.
The Kew meteorological observatory given to the British Association in April, 1860. It was placed under the Meteorological council nominated by the Royal Society, but appointed by the treasury. R. H. Scott, secretary, July, 1877.
At the recommendation of M. Le Verrier and admiral Fitzroy, meteorological information, obtained by the telegraph from the principal places in the United Kingdom, has been transmitted daily to Paris, and thence to other parts of Europe since 1 Sept. 1860.
Storm-warnings first issued in Holland through M. Buys Ballot, 1860. His "law of the winds" points out the relation between the direction of the wind, and the atmospheric pressure.
Storm-warnings first sent to the coast by the Board of Trade, 6 Feb.; and first published 31 July, 1861; suspended, 7 Dec. 1866; restoration proposed, Nov. 1867; reissued at Christmas 1867, and have been since continued.
Daily international bulletin of the imperial observatory at Paris, under the direction of M. Le Verrier, first published in MS. 1 Jan. 1858, first issued to subscribers, 4 Nov. 1863. (This was the first chart with united maps.)
"*Daily weather charts*" first issued by the Meteorological Office, 1 Oct. (first prepared in MS. 3 Sept. 1860), 1872; "*Weekly Weather Report*" first published, 11 Feb. 1878.
International Meteorological congress at Vienna, 2-16 Sept. 1873; at Rome 14-22 April, 1879; and at Berne, 9-12 Aug. 1880.
"Weather Charts and Storm Warnings," by R. H. Scott, published, 1876 *et seq.*
Wrecks diminished in consequence, June 1876-7, 1805; 1879-81, 891.
Circular issued relating to a new plan for obtaining information from ships at sea, &c., 14 April, 1882.
Observatory erected on Ben Nevis; Mr. R. T. Omond appointed director, 6 Sept.; opened 17 Oct. 1883. New tower erected, 1884.
A French academy of meteorology organised a successful balloon ascent, 9 Aug. 1879.
An observatory on Sonnblick Salzburg (10,177 feet high), opened about 1 Sept. 1886.
Daily forecasts for midland counties, 1886, 310. Absolute successes 247, absolute failures 26, and partial successes 36, announced *Times*, 7 Feb. 1887.
Weather plant (Abrus precatorius) exhibited by professor Nowack at Vienna; changes in the weather said to be foretold by alteration in the leaves attributed to electro-magnetism in 24 to 48 hours previously, Aug.–Sept. 1888. The plant is grown in the Botanical society's gardens, London. Many other plants possess this

property (*W. Sowerby*), Sept. 1888. During the experiments made at the Jodrell laboratory, Kew, by Dr Oliver and Herr Joseph Nowack in October, 1889, when many weather changes occurred, only one forecast was given by the weather plant, which therefore cannot be relied upon for meteorological purposes. Mr. J. F. Nowack maintains the success of his new system of forecasting atmospheric, etc., disturbances, by it, *Times*, 13 Dec. 1897.

International Meteorological Congress at Munich 26 Aug. *et seq.* 1891; at Paris, Sept. 1896; St. Petersburg, 2–7 Sept. 1899.

The 13th annual exhibition of meteorological apparatus, London, opened 15 March, 1892.

State observatory established by prof. Assmann of Berlin on the Brocken, 1 Oct. 1895.

Observatory on Mt. Wellington, Tasmania, begun May, 1895.

Mr. G. J. Symons, eminent meteorologist (see *Rainfall*), dies 10 March, 1900.

Sir Cuthbert Peek, scientist and meteorologist, died, aged 46, 5 July, 1901.

Mr. Jas. Glaisher, eminent meteorologist and aëronaut, died, aged 93, 7 Feb. 1903.

See *Barometer*, *Thermometer*, &c.

METEORS, LUMINOUS, include shooting stars, fire-balls, and falling stones or aërolites. They were described by Halley, Wallis, and others early in the 17th century. The periodicity of the star showers about the 10th of August (termed in the middle ages St. Lawrence's tears) was discovered separately by Quetelet, 1836, and by Herrick in 1837. The following are remarkable epochs for their annual return:—2 Jan.; 29 July; 3 and 9-12 Aug.; 8-14 Nov.; 11 Dec. *R. P. Greg.* See *August.*

The magnificent continuous star-shower of 14 Nov. 1866, had been predicted by professor Newton some time previously. A fine display occurred on the night of 13 Nov. 1868, in the United States. A similar phenomenon had been witnessed by Humboldt at Cumana (S.A.), 12 Nov. 1799; and by Dr. D. Olmsted, at Newhaven (U.S.), 13 Nov. 1833. They were well observed in Britain and Europe, 27 Nov. 1872; and in Southern and Western Europe, 27 Nov. 1885.

AËROLITES, falling-stones, accompanying meteors, are found in our museums. They contain iron, nickel, and other minerals.

Explosion of an aërolite above Madrid, windows shattered, houses damaged, etc., 9.29 A.M. 10 Feb. 1896; another exploded, S. of Cyprus, 18 April, 1896.

Mr. Norman Lockyer announces his theory, based on spectrum experiments that all self-luminous bodies in the celestial spaces are composed of meteorites or masses of vapour produced by heat brought about by condensation of meteor swarms due to gravity; Royal Society, 17 Nov. 1887. A great meteor or fireball seen in England, 25 Jan. 1894.

Dr. G. Johnstone Stoney reported his studies of the November meteors, at the Royal Institution, London, 14 Feb. 1879, and 18 Feb. 1897.

The Leonid meteors well seen at Yerkes observatory, Wisconsin, U.S.N.A., 15 Nov. 1898.

Fall of meteorites at Mt. Zomba, 25 Jan. 1899.

The non-appearance of the November Leonids attributed to a change of orbit.—*Times*, 14 Nov. 1899; a fine meteor or fire-ball seen in the S. of England, 13 July, 1902.

A meteorite, about 10lb. in weight, fell at Crumlin, co. Antrim, 13 Sept. 1902.

METHOD (Greek, a way of transit), that which gives to knowledge its character. S. T. Coleridge's treatise on the science of method is prefixed to the first volume of the "Encyclopædia Metropolitana," 1845.

The most recent work on this subject is Professor Stanley Jevons' "Principles of Science: a Treatise on Logic and Scientific Method," 1874. "The powers of mind concerned in creation of science are discrimination, detection of identity, and retention."

METHODISTS, see *Wesleyans.*

METHUEN TREATY, a treaty for regulating the commerce between Great Britain and Portugal, made 27 Dec. 1703, concluded by Paul Methuen, our ambassador at Lisbon. It greatly favoured the importation of port wine into this country by lowering the duty, to the discouragement of French wines. It was abrogated in 1834.

METHYL, a colourless inodorous gas, a compound of hydrogen and carbon, obtained in the free state first by Frankland and Kolbe separately, in 1849.

METHYLATED SPIRITS. By an act passed in 1855 a mixture of spirits of wine with 10 per cent. of its bulk of wood-naphtha, or methylic alcohol, is allowed to be made duty free for use in the arts and manufactures, not less than 450 gallons being made at one time. In 1861 an act was passed permitting the methylated spirits to be retailed by licence.

METONIC CYCLE, a period of 19 years, or 6940 days, at the end of which the changes of the moon fall on the same days; see *Calippic Period*, *Golden Number*.

METRIC SYSTEM. Before the revolution there was no uniformity in French weights and measures. On 8 May, 1790, the constituent assembly charged the Academy of Sciences with the organisation of a better system. The committee named for the purpose by the academy included the names of Berthollet, Borda, Delambre, Lagrange, Laplace, Méchain, and Prony. Delambre and Méchain were charged with the measurement of an arc of the meridian between Dunkirk and Barcelona, and from their calculations the *mètre*, which is equal to a ten-millionth part of the distance between the poles and the equator (3·2808 English feet) was made the unit of length and the base of the system by law on 7 April, 1795. The system was completed in 1799, and made by law the only legal one on 2 Nov. 1801. A decree on 12 Feb. accommodated the old measures to the new system; but on 4 July, 1837, it was decreed that after 1 Jan. 1840, the metric and decimal system in its primitive simplicity should be used in all business transactions. The example of France has been followed by the greater part of Europe, and will probably in time be adopted in the British empire.

Unit of SURFACE, *centiare*=a square mètre=1·1960 English yard (a square décamètre or *are*=100 square mètres).

Unit of VOLUME OR SOLIDITY, *stère*=a cubit mètre.

Unit of CAPACITY, *litre*=a cubic décimètre (or 10th of a mètre)=1·76077 English pint.

Unit of WEIGHT, *gramme*=weight of a cubic centimètre (the 100th part of a mètre) of distilled water=0·56438 English drachm.

Unit of MONEY, the *franc*, a piece of silver weighing 5 grammes.

The multiples of these units are expressed by Greek numerals (*deca-*, 10; *hekato-*, 100; *kilo-*, 1000; *myria-*, 10,000). The divisors are expressed by Latin numerals (*deci-*, 10; *centi-*, 100; *milli-*, 1000).

Sir John Wrottesley brought the subject before parliament . . . . 25 Feb. 1824

A commission of inquiry appointed at the instance of the chancellor of the exchequer, Mr. Spring-Rice (since lord Monteagle) . . . May, 1838

Another commission was appointed (both consisted of eminent scientific men, and reported strongly in favour of the change) . . . . 20 June, 1843

A committee of the house of commons reported to the same effect . . . . 1 Aug. 1853

Mr. Gladstone, admitting the advantages of the system, thought its introduction premature.

Decimal Association formed for the purpose of obtaining the adoption of the system . June, 1854

Another commission for inquiry was appointed, consisting of lords Monteagle and Overstone, and Mr. J. G. Hubbard, who published a preliminary report (with evidence), but expressed no opinion, Nov. 1855

An International Decimal Association formed in . „

The decimal currency adopted in Canada 1 Jan. 1858

The new weights and measures bill (an approximation to the decimal system) was passed . . 1862

An act passed "to render permissive the use of the metric system of weights and measures," 29 July, 1864 (repealed by weights and measures act, 1878).

A bill for the compulsory adoption of the metric system rejected by the commons . . 26 July, 1871

Meeting at the Mansion-house, London, advocating its adoption . . . . 17 Jan. 1872

International Congress to promote the universal adoption of the metric system . . 24 Sept. „

International convention for adopting metric system, signed at Paris, by representatives of Austria, Germany, Russia, Italy, Spain, Portugal, Turkey, Switzerland, Belgium, Sweden, Denmark, United States of America, Argentine Republic, Brazil, and Peru, 20 May, 1875, England . 1884

The system (to come into force in 1889) adopted by Sweden . . . . May, 1876

International congress on weights and measures met at Paris . . . . 4 Sept. 1878

Adoption of decimal system; negatived (108-28); in the commons . . . . . 29 March, 1881

Delegates from the New Decimal association, chambers of commerce, and other bodies, received by sir W. V. Harcourt, chancellor of the exchequer; he declines taking up the question, 25 Jan. 1893

Metric system adopted by Turkey; 1 March, 1896; by Russia 1897

Report on the working of the system in various European countries, *Times* . . . 7 Aug. 1900

METRONOME, to regulate time in the performance of music, one patented 1816.

METROPOLIS OF GREAT BRITAIN includes the cities of London and Westminster, and the old boroughs of Southwark, Finsbury, Marylebone, Tower-Hamlets, Hackney, Lambeth, and Chelsea; great changes made by the re-distribution of seats act, 1885, 59 constituencies in all. The Metropolis Management Act, 18 & 19 Vict. c. 122, was passed in 1855; amended (by-laws) act passed, 1 Aug. 1899; estimated gross value of property, 6 April, 1903, 49,184,021*l.*; ratable, 40,610,415*l.*; see *London*, and *London, County of*.

METROPOLIS ROADS ACT (passed in 1863) transferred the management of certain roads north of the Thames from the commissioners to the parishes, and abolished certain turnpikes and toll-bars.

METROPOLIS WATER ACT, 1852, amended, 1871; another, royal assent 18 Dec. 1902, establishes the *Metropolitan Water Board* to acquire, manage, and carry on the undertakings of the Metropolitan water companies.

METROPOLITAN (from the Greek *metropolis*), a title given at the council of Nice, 325, to certain bishops who had jurisdiction over others in a province.

METROPOLITAN ASSOCIATION FOR IMPROVING THE DWELLINGS OF THE INDUSTRIOUS CLASSES. Founded 15 Sept. 1841; incorporated 16 Oct. 1845.

Capital originally 100,000*l.*; increased to 200,000*l.* (1884). Dividend not to exceed 5 per cent. Secretary, and chief originator, Mr. Charles Gatliff; offices, 118, Finsbury-circus. The late rt. hon. lord Claud Hamilton member 1845-84; chairman for 13 years.

METROPOLITAN BOARD OF WORKS was established by 18 & 19 Vict. c. 120 (1855),* amended in 1862. It held its first meeting and elected Mr. (aftds. sir) John Thwaites as chairman, 22 Dec. 1855. The office was in Spring-gardens. In 1858, its powers were extended in order to effect the purification of the Thames by constructing a new main drainage for the metropolis. The board was authorised to raise a loan and levy 3*d.* in the pound on the property in the metropolis. It was also authorised to construct the Thames Embankment. In 1861 the board received nearly a million pounds, and expended 900,000*l.*; see *Sewage*, and *Thames*. Sir John Thwaites, the chairman, died 8 Aug. 1870, aged 55. Much discussion ensued respecting the appointment of his successor; Mr. Bruce, the home secretary, having intimated the probability of the office being abolished by parliament, with other changes, 11 Aug., Col. (aftds. sir) James Macnaghten McGarel Hogg (created baron Magheramorne, June, 1887), a member of the board, was elected chairman for one year, 18 Nov. 1870; annually till 1889 (he died 27 June, 1890). The board was empowered to borrow money by acts passed 1869-87. Its powers extended over 117 square miles, and 3,266,287 persons in 1873. It was composed of delegates from various local boards, &c.

Royal commission of inquiry into the working of the board appointed by parliament, 1888. Lord Herschell chairman; charges against Messrs. Robertson, Goddard, and others; many dismissed June–July, 1888

The commissioners' "interim" report discloses cases of negligence, inefficiency, irregularities, errors in judgment, and some evidence of corruption . . . . Nov. „

The eminent engineer of the Board, sir Joseph Bazalgette, appointed 1856; resigns Feb. 1889; he died . . . . 15 March, 1891

The board was abolished by the local government act of 1888, and its powers, duties, property, debts and liabilities transferred to the London county council, beginning 21 April, 1889; carried into effect by the local government board, 21 March, „

The board accepted a tender for the construction of a tunnel from Blackwall to Greenwich for 318,840*l.* from Messrs. S. Pearson & Sons, 15 March, „

Final report of the commission issued . 4 May „

METROPOLITAN BUILDING ACTS, see *Building*.

METROPOLITAN CATTLE MARKET, inaugurated by the lord mayor and corporation on Wednesday, 13 July, 1855, in presence of the prince consort. It is situated in Copenhagen-fields, an elevated site north of London, occupying an area of about fifteen acres, larger by nine acres than Smithfield, and capable of containing 30,000 sheep, 6400 bullocks, 1400 calves, and 900 pigs. In the centre is a circular building, let to bankers and others having business connected with graziers and cattle-agents. Within and around the market are erected several large taverns. A place is set apart for slaughtering animals, with approved appliances for purposes of health, by ventilation, sewerage, &c.; there is also a place for haystands. Sales commenced on Friday, 15 June, 1855.—An act for establishing a meat and poultry market in Smithfield (*which see*) was passed in 1860.

METROPOLITAN COMMONS. Acts respecting them passed 1866, 1869, and 1878. See *Commons*.

* "For the management of public works in which the metropolis has a common interest."

METROPOLITAN CONVALESCENT INSTITUTION, FIRE BRIGADE, and HOUSELESS POOR. See *Convalescent*, *Fire Brigade*, and *Houseless Poor*.

METROPOLITAN DISTRICT ASYLUMS BOARD, instituted by parliament in 1867, proceeded to erect hospitals at Haverstock-hill, Caterham, &c., 1868, causing much discontent in several parishes. The asylum for idiots at Leavesden, near Watford, Herts, inaugurated 27 Sept. 1870. An act respecting the board passed in 1884.

The epidemic of fevers, especially scarlet, caused greatly increased demand for accommodation for patients, well met Sept. 1887–Jan. 1888. The spread of small-pox greatly checked.

Cases of infectious diseases notified to the managers.

Epidemic of small-pox, Aug. 1901, 945 cases, in London hospitals; 28 Jan., 1,554; 1 April, 1,362, 579 . . . . 12 July, 1902

See *Scarlet Fever*.

Cost to board of small-pox epidemic, 1901–2, 491,159*l*., reported . . . . . 21 Feb. 1903

METROPOLITAN DRAINAGE, see *Sewers*.

METROPOLITAN DRINKING FOUNTAIN AND CATTLE TROUGH ASSOCIATION; founded 1859. See *Drinking Fountains*.

METROPOLITAN MEAT MARKET, Smithfield, erected in accordance with an act passed in 1860, was inaugurated by the lord mayor, James Lawrence, 24 Nov. 1868, and opened for business, 1 Dec.

METROPOLITAN MUNICIPAL ASSOCIATION met 11 Dec. 1866.

METROPOLITAN POLICE ACTS, 1829 *et seq*., consolidated in 1887; amended 1898.

METROPOLITAN POLICE MAGISTRATES, see *Magistrates* and *Police*.

METROPOLITAN POOR ACT, "for the establishment in the metropolis of asylums for the sick, insane, and other classes of the poor," passed 29 March, 1867; was amended in 1869; see *Poor*.

METROPOLITAN RAILWAY (*Underground*), at first between Paddington and Victoria-street, near Holborn. The act for it passed in 1853; the construction began in the spring of 1860; and it was opened for traffic, 10 Jan. 1863. Many serious difficulties were overcome with great skill and energy by the engineer, John Fowler (knt. 1885; died, 20 Nov. 1898), and the contractors, Jay, Smith, and Knight. In the first six months of 1865 there were 7,462,823 passengers. It has been continued, and there is now an Inner and Outer Circle, and it has been supplemented by the Metropolitan District Railway.

METROPOLITAN SCHOOL BOARD, instituted by the Elementary Education act, 1870, was elected 29 Nov. 1870 (for three years). It included lord Lawrence, lord Sandon, professor Huxley, Miss Garrett, M.D., and Miss Davies. At its first meeting, 15 Dec., lord Lawrence was elected chairman, and Mr. C. Reed, M.P., vice-chairman; On 27 Nov. 1873, 30 Nov. 1876, and 27 Nov. 1879, Mr. (afterwards sir) Charles Reed was elected chairman. He died 25 March, 1881, succeeded by Mr. Edwd. North Buxton. Rev. J. R. Diggle elected chairman, 3 Dec. 1885; re-elected 4 Dec. 1888, and 3 Dec. 1891; lord George Hamilton elected chairman, 6 Dec. 1894; lord Reay elected chairman, 2 Dec. 1897. For history, &c., see *Education*, 1870 *et seq*. Its powers transferred to the London County Council by London Education Act, 1903.

METROPOLITAN STREETS ACT (30 & 31 Vict. c. 134) "for regulating the traffic in the metropolis, and for making provision for the greater security of persons passing through the streets," passed 20 Aug. 1867. A short act, modifying the clauses relating to costermongers and cabs, was passed 7 Dec. 1867.

METTRAY, see *Reformatory Schools*.

METZ, a fortified city in Lorraine, annexed to the empire of Germany, 10 May, 1871. It was the Roman Divodunum or Meti, capital of the Mediomatrici, a powerful Gaulish tribe, and afterwards of the kingdom of Austrasia, or Metz, in the 6th century. It was made a free imperial city, 985. It was besieged by Charles VII. of France for seven months in 1444, and was ransomed for 100,000 florins; was captured by Henry II., 10 April, 1552, and successfully defended by the duke of Guise against the emperor Charles V. with an army of 100,000 men, 31 Oct. 1552 to 15 Jan. 1553. Metz was ceded to France by the peace of Westphalia, 24 Oct. 1648, and was fortified by Vauban and Belleisle. On 28 July, 1870, the emperor Napoleon III. arrived at Metz and assumed the chief command. After the disastrous defeats at Woerth and Forbach, on 6 Aug. the whole French army (except the corps of MacMahon, De Failly, and Douay) was concentrated here, 10, 11 Aug., and by delay was hemmed in by the Germans. Marshal Bazaine assumed the chief command, 8 Aug. The emperor departed with the vanguard, which crossed the Moselle early on 14 Aug. Population, 1890, 60,194; 1900, 58,424.

1. Battle of Pange or Courcelles, gained by the first army under Von Steinmetz, after several hours' fighting, with great German loss, 14 Aug. 1870

Bazaine was censured for not advancing on 15 Aug. ,,

2. Battle of Vionville or Mars-la-Tour, gained by the 2nd army under prince Frederick Charles, after twelve hours' fighting. By the unexpected unmasking of a mitrailleuse battery, Henry, prince of Reuss, and many German nobles were killed in a few moments. The victory was at first claimed by the French. (This battle, the most sanguinary in the war hitherto, included a Balaclava charge of a German regiment of cavalry upon a French battery, by which it was decimated, but to which the victory was greatly due. Twice as many Germans were killed as at Königgratz, the killed and wounded being estimated at 17,000. The French loss was said to have been equally great) . . . 16 Aug. ,,

Bazaine masses his troops for a decisive conflict, 17 Aug. ,,

3. Battle of Rézonville or Gravelotte, gained by the combined 1st and 2nd armies, commanded by the king in person, after twelve hours' fighting. "The most desperate struggle took place on the slopes over Gravelotte, which the Germans gained by nightfall, after repeated fatal charges; the fortune of the day being long in suspense. But the right of the French had been outflanked, they fell back fighting to the last, and retired under cover of Metz. The French are said to have lost 19,000; and the Germans, 25,000." (The king, on the 19th, had not undressed for thirty hours. The carnage is considered to have been unexampled; a large number of French prisoners were made; and enormous loss was experienced by the imperial guard. The German army included Saxons and Hessians), 18 Aug. ,,

Bazaine repulsed in a sortie at Courcelles, near Metz (he claimed a victory) . . . 26 Aug. ,,

His whole army defeated by gen. Manteuffel of the army of prince Frederick Charles, in a battle lasting from the morning of 31 Aug. to noon, 1 Sept. ,,

Von Steinmetz sent to govern Posen; prince Frederick Charles sole commander before Metz, 21 Sept. 1870

Three vigorous but ineffective sallies, 23, 24, 27 Sept. ,,

About 100,000 soldiers estimated in Metz, 30 Sept. ,,

Great sortie; the Germans surprised; about 40,000 French engaged; they are repulsed after a severe engagement from 3 p.m. till dark; loss about 2000 French and 600 Germans . . . . . 7 Oct. ,,

About 600 oxen and 500 sheep captured during a sortie . . . . 8 Oct. ,,

General Boyer arrives at Versailles to treat for terms of capitulation . . . . . 14 Oct. ,,

Metz surrenders with the army, including marshals Bazaine, Canrobert, and Le Bœuf; 66 generals; about 6000 officers; 173,000 men, including the imperial guard; 400 pieces of artillery; 100 mitrailleuses; and 53 eagles or standards, 27 Oct. ,,

The capitulation was signed at Frescati by generals Jarras and Stiehle on behalf of the French and German commanders . . . . . 27 Oct. ,,

General order to the army issued by marshal Bazaine, saying that they were "conquered by famine," 27 Oct. ,,

Order to the army issued by prince Frederick Charles, recognising their bravery, great obedience, calmness, cheerfulness, and devotion, 27 Oct. ,,

The Germans enter Metz . . . . . 29 Oct. ,,

One cause of the fall of Metz was the great army it contained; it might have been successfully defended by 20,000 men.

Marshal Bazaine was tried and condemned to death for surrendering Metz and the army, 6 Oct.-10 Dec.; punishment commuted to 20 years' imprisonment, 12 Dec.; he escaped from Isle St. Marguerite . . . . . 9 Aug. 1874

The German emperor and empress were well received at Metz, 23 Aug. 1889; the emperor holds a military review . . . . . 18 May, 1901

See *France*.

MEXICO, anciently Anahuac, N. America, is said to have been conquered by the Aztecs, who founded the city of Mexico about 1325. It was discovered in 1517, and conquered by Fernando Cortez, 1519-21; explored by Alexander von Humboldt, 1799-1804. It consists of 27 confederate states. It is stated that there have been above 260 insurrections in Mexico since 1821. Population, 1874, about 9,276,079; 10,447,974 in 1882; 1895, 12,588,497: the city, Mexico, 44,377, 1895; 1900, about 13,545,462: city, about 400,000, 1901.

Montezuma emperor 1503

Cortes lands, 1519; captures the city of Mexico . 1521

Mexico constituted a kingdom. Cortes, governor . 1522

Mendoza, first viceroy of New Spain, 1530; establishes a mint 1535

Unsuccessful insurrections of Miguel Hidalgo, 1810; of Morelos, 1815; of Mina 1817

Mexico declared independent by the treaty of Aquala . . . . 23 Aug. 1821

Augustin Iturbide, president of a provisional junto, Feb.; Mexico formed into an empire; the crown declined by Spain; Iturbide made emperor, May, 1822

Compelled to abdicate . . . . . 26 March, 1823

Mexican federal republic proclaimed . . 4 Oct. ,,

Iturbide went to England; returns and endeavours to recover his dignity; shot . . . 19 July, 1824

Federal constitution established . . . . Oct. ,,

Treaty of commerce with Great Britain . April, 1825

Expulsion of the Spaniards decreed . . March, 1829

Spanish expedition against Mexico surrendered, 26 Sept. ,,

Mexican revolution: the president Guerrero deposed . . . . 23 Dec. ,,

Santa Anna president . . . . . 11 May, 1833

Independence of Mexico recognised by Brazil, June, 1830; by Spain . . . . 28 Dec. 1836

Declaration of war against France . . 30 Nov. 1838

This war terminated . . . . . 9 March, 1839

War with the United States . . . . 4 June, 1845

The Mexicans defeated at Palo Alto, and at Matamoras . . . . 8 May, 1846

Santa Fè captured, 22 Aug.; and Monterey, 24 Sept. ,,

Battle of Buena Vista; the Mexicans defeated by general Taylor, with great loss, after two days' fighting . . . . 22 Feb 1847

The Americans, under general Scott, defeat the Mexicans at Cerro Gorda . . . . 18 April, ,,

The Mexicans beaten in several actions; Mexico taken by assault by general Scott . 15 Sept. ,,

Treaty of peace ratified . . . . . 19 May, 1848

Political convulsions . . . . . . Sept. 1852

President Arista resigns, 6 Jan.; and Santa Anna returns, Feb.; dictator . . . . 16 Dec. 1853

He abdicates; Carera elected president . Jan. 1855

Who also abdicates; succeeded first by Alvarez, and afterwards by general Comonfort . Dec. ,,

Property of the clergy sequestrated . 31 March, 1856

New constitution established . . . 5 Feb. 1857

Beginning of a reformed Church by Aguilar and others . . . . ,,

Comonfort chosen president . . . . July, ,,

Coup d'état; constitution annulled by the church party; Comonfort compelled to retire, 11 Jan.; general Zuloaga takes the government, 21-26 Jan. 1858

Benito Juarez declared constitutional president at Vera Cruz . . . . 11 Feb. ,,

Civil war: several engagements . Aug. to Nov. ,,

General Miguel Miramon nominated president at Mexico by the Junta . . . . . 6 Jan. 1859

Zuloaga abdicates . . . . 2 Feb. ,,

In consequence of injury to British subjects, ships of war sent to Mexico . . . . . Feb. ,,

Miramon forces the lines of the liberal generals, enters the capital, assumes his functions as governor, and governs without respect to the laws of life and property . . . 10 April, ,,

Juarez confiscates the church property . 13 July, ,,

Miramon and the clerical party defeat the liberals under Colima . . . . . . 21 Dec. ,,

He besieges Vera Cruz, 5 March; bombards it; compelled to raise the siege . . 21 March, 1860

General Zuloaga deposes Miramon, and assumes the presidency . . . . . . 1 May, ,,

Miramon arrests Zuloaga, 9 May; the diplomatic bodies suspend official relations with the former, 10 May, ,,

Miramon defeated by Degollado . . . . 10 Aug. ,,

He governs Mexico with great tyranny; seizes 152,000*l.* belonging to English bondholders, Sept.; the foreign ministers quit the city . . Oct. ,,

He is defeated; compelled to retire; Juarez enters Mexico, 11 Jan.; re-elected president . . 19 Jan. 1861

Juarez made dictator by the congress . . 30 June, ,,

The Mexican congress decides to suspend payments to foreigners for two years . . . 17 July, ,,

Which leads to the breaking off diplomatic relations with England and France . . . 27 July, ,,

In consequence of many gross outrages on foreigners, the British, French, and Spanish governments, after much vain negotiation, claiming efficient protection of foreigners, and the payment of arrears due to fundholders, sign a convention engaging to combined hostile operations against Mexico . . . . 31 Oct. ,,

The Mexican congress dissolves, after conferring full powers on the president . . . 15 Dec. ,,

Spanish troops land at Vera Cruz, 8 Dec.; it surrenders . . . . 17 Dec. ,,

A British naval and French military expedition arrives . . . . 7, 8 Jan. 1862

The Mexicans resist, and invest Vera Cruz; their taxes raised 25 per cent. . . . . . Jan. ,,

Miramon arrives, but is sent back to Spain by the British admiral . . . . . Feb. ,,

Project of establishing a Mexican monarchy, for archduke Maximilian of Austria, disapproved of by British and Spanish governments . Feb. ,,

Negotiation ensues between the Spanish and Mexicans; convention between the commissaries of the allies and the Mexican general Doblado, at Soledad . . . . 19 Feb. ,,

The Mexican general Marquez takes up arms against Juarez; and general Almonte joins the French general Lorencez; Juarez demands a compulsory loan, and puts Mexico in a state of siege, March, ,,

Conference between plenipotentiaries of the allies at Orizaba; the English and Spanish declare for peace, which is not agreed to by the French, 9 April; who declare war against Juarez, 16 April, 1862
The Spanish and British forces retire; the French government sends reinforcements to Lorencez, May, „
The French, induced by Marquez, advance into the interior; severely repulsed by Zaragoza, at Fort Guadaloupe, near Puebla . . 5 May, „
Juarez quits the capital . . 31 May, „
The French defeat the Mexicans at Cerro de Borgo, near Orizaba . . . 13, 14 June, „
The Mexican liberals said to be desirous of negotiation . . . Aug. „
Gen. Forey and 2500 French soldiers land 28 Aug. „
Letter from the emperor Napoleon to Lorencez disclaiming any intention of imposing a government on Mexico; announced . . Sept. „
Death of Zaragoza, a great loss to the Mexicans, 8 Sept. „
Gen. Forey deprives Almonte of the presidency at Vera Cruz, and appropriates the civil and military power to himself . . Oct. „
Ortega takes command of the Mexicans 19 Oct. „
The Mexican congress assembles, and protests against the French invasion . . . 27 Oct. „
The French evacuate Tampico 13 Jan. 1863
Forey marches towards Mexico . . . 24 Feb. „
Siege of Puebla; bravely defended, 29 March; severe assault, 31 March to 3 April; it is surrendered at discretion by Ortega . 18 May, „
Juarez and the republican government remove to San Luis de Potosi . . . . 31 May, „
Mexico occupied by the French, under Bazaine, 5 June; Forey and his army enter, 10 June; provisional government „
Assembly of notables at Mexico decide on the establishment of a limited hereditary monarchy, with a Roman Catholic prince as emperor; and offer the crown to the archduke Maximilian of Austria: a regency established . . 6-10 July, „
The French re-occupy Tampico . . 11 Aug. „
Marshal Forey resigns his command to Bazaine, and returns to France . . . 1 Oct. „
The archduke Maximilian will accept the crown if it be the will of the people . . 3 Oct. „
The Mexican general Comonfort surprised and shot by partisans . . . . 12 Nov. „
Successful advance of the imperialists; Juarez retires from San Luis de Potosi, 18 Dec.; it is entered by the imperialists . . 24 Dec. „
The French occupy various places Jan. & Feb. 1864
The ex-president, general Santa Anna, lands at Vera Cruz, professing adhesion to the empire, 27 Feb.; dismissed by Bazaine 12 March, „
Juarez enters Monterey, which becomes the seat of the republican government . . 3 April, „
The archduke Maximilian definitively accepts the crown from the Mexican deputation at Miramar, 10 April, „
The emperor and empress land at Vera Cruz, 29 May; enter the city of Mexico . . 12 June, „
The emperor visits the interior; grants a free press, Aug. „
The republicans defeat the imperialists at San Pedro, 27 Dec. „
Juarez, at Chihuahua, exhorts the Mexicans to maintain their independence . 1 Jan. 1865
The emperor institutes the order of the Mexican eagle . . . . . „
Surrender of Oaxaca to marshal Bazaine 9 Feb. „
A constitution promulgated . . . 10 April, „
Ortega, at New York, enlists recruits for the republican army, May; discountenanced by the U.S. government . . . . June, „
Anniversary of Mexican independence; descendants of Iturbide made princesses, &c. 16 Sept. „
The emperor proclaims the end of the war, and martial law against all armed bands of men; much indignation excited . . 2 Oct. „
Juarist generals taken prisoners; shot . 16 Oct. „
The American government protests against the French occupation . . . Nov.-Dec. „
Presidency of Juarez expires; he determines to continue to act, 30 Nov.; he flies to Texas, 20 Dec. „

Bagdad, on the Rio Grande, seized by American Juarists, 4, 5 Jan.; occupied by the American general Weitzel, 5 Jan.; his conduct disavowed; and Bagdad re-occupied by imperialists, 20 Jan. 1866
Ministerial changes . . . March-April, „
Emperor Napoleon agrees to withdraw all his soldiers from Mexico between Nov. 1866 and Nov. 1867 April, „
Guerilla warfare going on, numerous conflicts, with varying success . . . March-May, „
Matamoras captured by the liberals, under Escobedo, 23, 24 June, „
The empress Charlotte departs for France, 13 July; conspiracy against the government suppressed, 15-17 July, „
Convention between Maximilian and the French; transfer of the receipts of the customs to France, 30 July, „
Juarez and his party take Tampico . . 1 Aug. „
The Americans disallow Maximilian's blockade of Matamoras . . . . 17 Aug. „
Dissension among the liberals; three rival presidents, Juarez, Ortega, and Santa Anna, Sept.-Oct „
The empress solicits help from France, in vain, Sept.; she falls ill . . . . Oct. „
Firm speech of emperor Maximilian . . 19 Sept. „
Emperor leaves Mexico for Orizaba; giving authority to Bazaine . . . . Oct. „
The French evacuate several places . . Nov. „
Imperial council at Orizaba determine to maintain the empire . . . . . 24 Nov. „
Death of Augustin Iturbide . . . 11 Dec. „
Maximilian, at the head of the army, arrives at Queretaro . . . . . 19 Feb. 1867
Departure of the French, 13 Jan., 5 Feb., 14 March, „
Contest for supremacy between Juarez, Diaz, and Ortega . . . . . April. „
Queretaro, after many conflicts, captured by treachery; Mendez shot . . . 15 May, „
Emperor Maximilian, Miramon, and Mejia, after trial, shot . . . . 19 June, „
Mexico city taken after 67 days' siege; republic re-established . . . . . 21 June, „
Surrender of Vera Cruz . . 25 June, „
Santa Anna captured; detained a prisoner July, „
Juarez enters Mexico; convokes the assembly to elect a president . . . 14, 15 July, „
Marquez and others said to be organising resistance to Juarez . . . . Aug. „
Numerous executions; reign of terror, Aug. *et seq.* „
Porfirio Diaz said to be nominated for the presidency, Sept. „
Santa Anna sentenced to eight years' banishment, Oct. „
Maximilian's body given up to the Austrian admiral Tegethoff . . . . 26 Nov. „
Mexican congress opened; Juarez acting as provisional president; foreign consuls said to be leaving, 8 Dec. „
Juarez re-elected president . . Dec. „
Juarez inaugurated as president . about 25 Dec. „
Maximilian's body buried at Vienna . 18 Jan. 1868
Rebellion against Juarez in Yucatan and other provinces . . . . Jan.-Feb. „
Hasty blockade of Mazatlan by capt. Bridge of H.M.S. *Chanticleer*, for an outrage 20 June; raised by admiral Hastings . . . July, „
Treaty with United States adopted . . Dec. „
Insurrection at Puebla suppressed . . Feb. 1869
General Almonte dies at Paris . . March, „
Encounter between Mexicans and United States troops who had pursued some Indian depredators; about 40 Americans killed; reported, 12 April, 1871
Election for president; Diaz, 1982 votes; Juarez, 1963; Lerdo, 1366; Juarez retains the power, 27 July, „
Insurrections arise . . . . . Aug. „
Insurrection headed by Negrete, Riveras, and others, suppressed with much slaughter 12 Oct. „
Juarez re-elected president . . . Oct. „
Insurgents under Porfirio Diaz twice defeated; announced . . . . . Jan. 1872
Civil war going on with varying success, April-June, „
Rebels nearly subdued . . . 1 July, „
Death of Benito Juarez (aged about 68) by apoplexy 18 July, „

The country tranquil; Diaz accepts the amnesty; announced . . . . 14 Aug. 1872
Lerdo de Tejado (of good character) elected president, Oct.; Diaz submits . . . . Nov. ,,
Railway from Mexico city to Vera Cruz completed; runs . . . . 23 Jan. 1873
Customs' tariffs liberalised . . . . . July, 1874
A senate voted by the Congress . . . . Aug. ,,
Religious orders suppressed . . . . . Dec. ,,
Religious disturbances: Catholic outrages on Protestants . . . . Jan. 1875
Insurrection by Porfirio Diaz, March; he takes Matamoras . . . . 1 April, 1876
Progress of reformed church; union with episcopal church of United States proposed . . April, ,,
Insurgents defeated at Oaxaca, 29 May; at Queretaro . . . . June, ,,
Death of Santa Anna, ex-president . . 20 June, ,,
Diaz defeats the government troops at Tekoar, 12 Nov.; enters Mexico, assumes power as provisional president . . . . Nov. 20 ,,
President Lerdo de Tejado retires: Iglesias takes arms as president . . . . . . Dec. ,,
Diaz defeats Iglesias, who retreats: Diaz elected president, 18 Feb.: proclaimed . . 5 May, 1877
Brief rebellion; about 80 hanged; announced, 28 Dec. 1878
Insurrection of Negrete; Diaz marches against him; becomes president . . . . 16 June, 1879
Manuel Gonzalez elected, 11 July; succeeds 1 Dec. 1880
About 200 lives lost through precipitation of train on San Morelos railway into the river near Cuartla, through fall of bridge, night of 24 June, 1881
Increase of railways constructed by Americans . ,,
British envoy re-appointed (sir Spencer St. John), June; received . . . . 17 July, 1883
Remains of an ancient city discovered in Sonora, near Magdalena, including a great pyramid, rooms cut in a stony mountain, implements, &c. and hieroglyphic inscriptions . . . . . ,,
Diplomatic relations with Great Britain resumed, announced, Aug. 1884
Concession obtained from the Mexican government by Mr. James B. Eades for 99 years for the construction of a railway for the conveyance of ships across the isthmus; estimated cost, 15,000,000*l.*; model exhibited at Long Acre, London . Aug. ,,
Riots in Mexico city on account of conversion of English debt; bloodshed . . . . 18 Nov. ,,
Porfirio Diaz inaugurated president . . . 1 Dec. ,,
Impending state insolvency through public works speculations; funding debts and loan proposed; much dissatisfaction . . . . . June, 1885
Insurrection at Nuevo Leon suppressed, Dec. 1885; another insurrection, Guerro captured, insurgents signally defeated; disturbances between the people of El Paso and the Texans; interference of the United States and Mexican governments, July, 1886
Mr. Cutting, an American journalist in Texas, imprisoned for libel; the U.S. government intervenes, July–Aug.; Mr. Cutting released 23 Aug. ,,
Inundations through heavy rains; great loss of life, especially at Leon and Silas 17–20 June, 1888
Wreck of an excursion steamer on Lake Chapala; loss of 50 lives . . . . . . March, 1889
Two companies of soldiers, while bathing, massacred by Yaqui Indians from Sonora; the government send 4,000 men to punish the Indians, announced . . . . . . 12 Oct. ,,
Famine in the agricultural districts, government assistance given, reported . . . 10 Dec. 1891
Insurrection; gen. Lorenzo Garcia killed by his troops, who join the rebels under Garza in Texas; he captures 45 soldiers and kills 4 officers, reported 31 Dec. 1891; Garza's band dispersed, reported 4 Jan. 1892; Diaz re-elected president 11 July, 1892
Indian rising suppressed, with slaughter, reported, 25 Oct. ,,
Conflicts on the frontier, with varying success, about 28 Dec. ,,
Gen. Urez shot as a rebel . . . . . 6 Feb. 1893
Renewed war with the Yaqui Indians, reported 18 June, ,,
Destructive storm in the gulf of Mexico; about 1,000 lives lost . . . . 2 Oct. ,,
Between Temamatla and Tenango (inter-oceanic railway) a train goes over a precipice; 140 lives lost . . . . 28 Feb. 1895
Boundary dispute between Mexico and Guatemala settled, reported . . . . . . 2 April, ,,
Pres. Diaz re-elected . . . . . . 1 Dec. 1896
Boundary dispute with Gt. Britain settled, April, 1897
Joaquin Arroyo, for attempting the life of the president, 16 Sept.; assassinated by the police, 17 Sept. ,,
Ten police officials sentenced to death, one to imprisonment, reported . . . . . 23 Nov. ,,
The Banco Central Mexicano, with a share capital of 6,000,000 dols., constituted . . 6 Feb. 1899
New 5 per cent. Mexican Loan successful, reported, 14 July, ,,
Hostilities against the Indians in Yucatan, mid Sept. ,,
The Yaqui Indians defeated in 2 fierce battles; much slaughter, reported . . . . 25 Sept. ,,
President Diaz re-elected, announced . 3 Oct. 1900
Diplomatic relations with Austria resumed . April, 1901
Great progress, peace and order, reported . Aug. ,,
Californian pious fund case settled by the Hague arbitration court; 1,420,682 dollars awarded to the United States; Mexico also to pay 43,051 dollars per annum . . . . . 14 Oct. 1902
Sir W. Pearson & Son procure a concession to establish an electric generator at a cost of 12,000,000 dols. in the mountains of Puebla, to transmit electricity, 80,000 horse-power, to the city, reported . . . . 27 Dec. ,,

EMPERORS.

1822. Aug. Augustin Iturbide, Feb.; abdicated 23 March, 1823; shot for attempting to recover his authority, 19 July, 1824.

1864. Maximilian (brother to the emperor of Austria), born 6 July, 1832; accepted the crown, 10 April, 1864; married 27 July, 1857, to princess Charlotte, daughter of Leopold I., king of the Belgians; adopted Augustin Iturbide as his *heir*, Sept. 1865; shot (after a trial), 19 June, 1867.

MEZZOTINTO, see *Engraving*.

MHOW COURT-MARTIAL, see *Trials*, Nov. 1863.

MICHAEL, ST., AND GEORGE, ST. This order of knighthood, founded for the Ionian Isles and Malta, 27 April, 1818, was reorganised in March, 1869, in order to admit servants of the crown connected with the colonies. Among the first of the new knights were the earl of Derby, earl Russell, and earl Grey. Order enlarged 30 Oct. 1902. Knights grand cross increased to 100, knights commanders to 300, companions to 600. See *Knights*.

MICHAELMAS, 29 Sept., the feast of St. Michael, the reputed guardian of the Roman Catholic church, under the title of "St. Michael and All Angels." Instituted, according to Butler, 487.

The custom of eating goose at Michaelmas has been erroneously attributed to Queen Elizabeth's eating of the bird at dinner on 29 Sept. 1588, at the house of sir Neville Umfreyville, at the time she heard of the destruction of the Spanish Armada. The custom is of much older date, and is observed on the continent. *Clavis Calendaria.*

MICHAEL'S MOUNT, ST. (Cornwall), is considered by some to be the Iktis of Diodorus Siculus, and an ancient resort of the tin merchants. St. Michael was said to have appeared on the mount, 495 or 710; and the place, thus reputed holy, became the seat of a body of monks, who received a charter from Edward the Confessor, 1044, and many privileges from pope Gregory VII., 1079.

MICHIGAN, a north-west state of N. America, settled by the French, 1670; admitted into the union, 26 Jan. 1837. Capital, Lansing. Lumber trade and manufacture of furniture the leading industries. At Grand Rapids half-year fairs are held. Buyers come from all parts of the world. Population, 1880, 1,636,937; 1900, 2,420,982.

About 500 persons perish and 10,000 made homeless by destructive forest fires on . . 5 Sept. 1881
Great fire at Grandhaven, 41 buildings destroyed, about 30 Sept. 1889
Explosion at Messrs. Farriwold's dynamite factory at White Pigeon, 16 men killed . . 3 Sept. 1891
Subsidence in a mine near Crystal Falls; about 40 deaths . . . . 28 Sept. 1893
Ontonagon destroyed by fire, great loss, 1,800 inhabitants destitute . . . . 25 Aug. 1896
University founded 1837. Library contains 133,000 vols. 3,441 students 1900

MICROBES, see *Germ*.

MICROMETER, an astronomical instrument used to measure any small distances and the minuter objects in the heavens, such as the apparent diameters of the planets, &c., was invented by Wm. Gascoigne, who was killed at the battle of Marston-moor, 2 July, 1644. It was improved by Huyghens about 1652. Sir Joseph Whitworth made a machine to measure the millionth of an inch, about 1858; the measurement of the 30,000th of an inch is now common. Dr. Carpenter measured a filament, the breadth being the 200,000th part of an inch, 1879.

MICROPHONE (Greek, *mikros*, little; *phōnē*, sound), a name given by Wheatstone, in 1827, to an instrument for rendering weak sounds audible by means of solid rods. The name was also given to an arrangement invented (in Dec. 1877) by professor D. E. Hughes (inventor of the type-writing telegraph, born in London 16 May, 1831, died 22 Jan. 1900), and shown to the Royal Society, 9 May, 1878.

MICROPHITE, a microscopic plant, especially parasitic; some physiologists consider bacteria and bacilli to be microphites, 1890.

MICROSCOPES, said to have been invented by Jansen, in Holland, about 1590; by Galileo, about 1610; by Fontana, in Italy, and by Drebbel, in Holland, about 1621. Those with double glasses were made at the period when the law of refraction was discovered, about 1624. Solar microscopes were invented by Dr. Hooke. In England great improvements were made in the microscope by Benjamin Martin (who invented and sold pocket microscopes about 1740), by Henry Baker, F.R.S., about 1763, and still greater during the present century by Wollaston, Ross, Jackson, Varley, Hugh Powell, and others. *Diamond microscopes* were made by Andrew Pritchard in 1824; and the properties of "test objects" to prove the qualities of microscopes, discovered by him and Goring in 1824-40. A *binocular microscope* (*i.e.*, for two eyes) was constructed by professor Riddell in 1851, and Wenham's binocular prism was made known in 1861. Nachet's *stereoscopic microscope*, 1867; Abbe's *orthoscopic* and *pseudoscopic*, 1881. Treatises on the microscope by J. Quekett (1848), by Dr. W. B. Carpenter (1856-1902), and Griffith and Henfrey's "Micrographic Dictionary" (1856, 1875, and 1883), are valuable. The Microscopical Society of London was established 20 Dec. 1839, and the Quekett Microscopical Club, 1865. In 1865 Mr. H. Sorby exhibited his *spectrum microscope*, by which the millionth of a grain of blood was detected.

MICROTOME, an instrument for cutting minute sections of organic tissue for the microscope, invented, 1885, by prof. Wm. Rutherford (who died, 21 Feb. 1899); improved by Dr. Paul Meyer and others.

MIDDLE AGES, see *Dark Ages*.

MIDDLE-CLASS EXAMINATION AND SCHOOLS, see *Education* (1858, and 1865-8).

Middle-Class Education Corporation, established in 1866, for education of children of clerks and others in similar ranks of life. Building in Cowper-street London.

MIDDLE-LEVELS, see *Levels*.

MIDDLESBROUGH, N. Riding of Yorkshire, on the Tees, a coal port and a chief seat of the iron manufacture, the first house erected by George Chapman, April, 1830. New dock, and literary and scientific institution opened, Oct. 1875. Mr. Henry W. F. Bolckow and John Vaughan, heads of great iron-works (Mr. Bolckow, the first mayor and M.P., died 18 June, 1878). The prosperity of the Cleveland district, which had greatly declined since 1874, began to revive in the autumn of 1879. At the jubilee celebration, 6 Oct. 1881, a bust of Mr. Bolckow was unveiled; and one of Mr. Vaughan was unveiled 2 June, 1884. See under *Steel*. Population, 1861, 18,992; 1881, 55,934; 1891, 75,516; 1901, 91,317.

South Gare breakwater, nearly 2¼ miles long, begun in 1864, opened by the right hon. W. H. Smith . . . . 25 Oct. 1888
A town hall &c. opened by the prince and princess of Wales . . . . . . 23 Jan. 1889
Stoppage of the firm of Messrs. Downey & Co., iron manufacturers . . . . . 28 March, 1892
Great distress in the district through the Durham miners' strike, April *et seq.*; relieved by subscriptions in London, &c. . . . May, June, "
Boiler explosion at Warrenby; nine deaths; estimated damage, 50,000*l.*; 400 persons thrown out of employment . . . . . 14 June, 1895

MIDDLESEX, the metropolitan county of England, was the seat of the Trinobantes in the Roman province, Flavia Cæsariensis, and the Middel-Sexe, or Middle Saxons, in the kingdom of East-Sexne, or Essex. Lionel Cranfield was created earl of Middlesex, 16 Sept. 1622; succeeded by his sons, James, 1645-51; Lionel, 1651-74, when the title became extinct. Charles Sackville was made earl in 1675; and his son became duke of Dorset in 1720. Area of the county formerly 181,301 acres; population, 1901, 3,585,139. By the Local Government Act, 1888, which came into force in 1902, 31,484 acres (including South Hornsey) were given over to London, and 771 to Hertfordshire. Middlesex now has an area of 178,754 acres; population, 1901, 810,213.

Middlesex returns forty-eight M.P's. by act passed 25 June, 1885
The Middlesex county record society was established in 1884. It has issued four volumes containing session rolls, &c. (1549 *et seq.*) 1888, 1892.
The earl of Strafford, lord lieutenant, president 1888
The Middlesex sessions now held at the Guildhall, Westminster; the county of London sessions held at Clerkenwell since . . . . "

MIDDLESEX HOSPITAL, London, founded, 1745; incorporated, 1836; cancer ward endowed, 1791. Cancer research laboratories opened, Nov. 1900.

MIDIAN, now ARZ MADIAN, N.W. Arabia; anciently held by the descendants of Midian, a son of Abraham. Having enticed the Israelites to idolatry, they were severely chastised, 1452 B.C. They invaded Canaan about 1249 B.C., and were thoroughly defeated by Gideon.

Capt. Richard F. Burton explored the ruined cities of Midian in 1877, and found the remains of ancient mines, many relics, and gold. An expedition, equipped by the khedive of Egypt, and placed under his command, started from Suez, 10 Dec. 1877, and returned 20 April, 1878. He brought home 25 tons of geological specimens, specimens of silver and copper ore, many coins and other antiquities, and photographs of the remains of ruined cities, &c.

MIDLAND INSTITUTE, BIRMINGHAM, incorporated 1854.

MIDLAND RAILWAY STATION, St. Pancras, N. London, possessing the largest known roof in the world (245 feet 6 inches wide, and 698 feet long), was opened for traffic 1 Oct. 1868. The engineer was Mr. H. W. Barlow. The architect of the magnificent Gothic hotel was sir G. Gilbert Scott.

MIDWIFERY. Women were the only practitioners among the Hebrews and Egyptians. Hippocrates, in Greece, 460 B.C., is styled the father of midwifery, as well as of physic. It advanced under Celsus, who flourished A.D. 37, and of Galen, who lived 131. In England midwifery became a science about the period of the institution of the college of physicians, 10 Hen. VII. 1518. Dr. Harvey engaged in the practice of it, about 1603; Astruc affirms that madame de la Vallière, mistress of Louis XIV., in 1663, employed Julian Clement, a surgeon, with great secrecy. Midwives Act, royal assent, 31 July, 1902.

MILAN, Mediolanum, capital of the ancient Liguria, now Lombardy, is reputed to have been built by the Gauls, about 408 B.C. The cathedral, termed *duomo*, was built about 1385. Population, 1890, 414,551; 1900, 498,681.

Conquered by the Roman consul Marcellus . B.C. 222
Seat of government of the western empire . A.D. 286
Council of Milan . . . 346
St. Ambrose, bishop of Milan . . . 375
Milan plundered by Attila . . . 452
Included in the Ostrogothic kingdom, 489; in the Lombard kingdom . . . 569
Becomes an independent republic . . . 1101
The emperor Frederic I. takes Milan, and appoints a podestà . . . 1158
It rebels; is taken by Frederic and its fortifications destroyed . . . 1162
Rebuilt and fortified . . . 1169
The Milanese defeated by the emp. Frederic II. . 1237
The Visconti become paramount in Milan . . 1277
John Galeazzo Visconti takes the title of duke . 1395
Francesco Sforza, son-in-law of the last of the Visconti, subdues Milan and becomes duke . . . 1450
Milan conquered by Louis XII. of France . . 1499
The French expelled by the Spaniards . . 1525
Milan annexed to the crown of Spain . . 1540
Great plague alleviated by the archbishop Borromeo . . . 1576
Milan ceded to Austria . . . 1714
Conquered by the French and Spaniards . . 1743
Reverts to Austria, upon Naples and Sicily being ceded to Spain . . . 1748
Seized by the French . . . 30 June, 1796
Retaken by the Austrians . . . 1799
Regained by the French . . . 31 May, 1800
Made the capital of the kingdom of Italy, and Napoleon Bonaparte crowned with the iron crown here, 26 May, 1805
The *Milan decree* of Napoleon against all continental intercourse with England . . 17 Dec. 1807
Insurrection against the Austrians; flight of the viceroy . . . 18 March, 1848
Surrenders to the Austrians . . . 5 Aug. ,,
Treaty of peace between Austria and Sardinia, 6 Aug. 1849
Another revolt promptly suppressed and rigorously punished . . . 6 Feb. *et seq.* 1853
Milan visited by the emperor of Austria . Nov. 1856
Amnesty for political offences granted . Dec. 1857
After the defeat of the Austrians at Magenta, 4 June, Napoleon III. and the king of Sardinia enter Milan, 8 June, 1859
Peace of Villafranca; a large part of Lombardy transferred to Sardinia . . . 12 July, ,,
Victor-Emmanuel enters Milan as king . 8 Aug. 1860
Reactionary plots of Neapolitan soldiery suppressed, 29, 30 April, 1861
The Victor-Emmanuel gallery opened by the king, 15 Sept. 1867
The arts exhibition opened by the king 26 Aug. 1872
Visit of the emperor of Germany . 18-23 Oct. 1875
The Mentana Memorial inaugurated by Garibaldi, 4 Nov. 1880
National exhibition, opened by the king 5 May, 1881
St. Gothard line to Milan, opened . . . 1882
Visit of the emperor William II. . . 19 Oct. 1889
First performance of Verdi's operas: *Otello*, 6 Feb. 1887; *Falstaff* . . . 9 Feb. 1893
United exhibitions opened by the king and queen, 6 May, 1894
Monument to Victor Emmanuel unveiled by the king . . . 24 June, 1896
Electric tramways, 1893; 80 miles held by the corporation . . . 1900
Great fire, several persons injured, much damage to property . . . 2 Sept. 1903

See *Italy*.

MILETUS, a Greek city of Ionia, Asia Minor, founded about 1043 B.C. The Milesians defended themselves successfully, 623-612 B.C. During the war with Persia it was taken, 494, but restored, 449. Here Paul delivered his celebrated charge to the elders of the church of Ephesus, A.D. 60 (*Acts* xx.).

MILFORD HAVEN (S.W. Pembroke). The finest natural harbour in the kingdom. Milford is a parliamentary borough, has extensive docks, is competing for the trade with America. Here the earl of Richmond, afterwards Henry VII., landed on his way to encounter Richard III., whom he defeated at Bosworth, 1485. The packets from this port to Ireland, sailing to Waterford, were established in 1787. The dock-yard, established here in 1790, was removed higher up the haven to Pembroke in 1814. Sham naval fights here 16 Aug. *et seq.* 1886.

Milford Haven adopted as an Atlantic terminus by the Anchor line company; their steamer, the *City of Rome*, arrives . . . 24 Oct. 1889

MILITARY ASYLUM, ROYAL, at Chelsea, "for the children of the soldiers of the regular army." The first stone was laid by the duke of York, 19 June, 1801.

MILITARY EDUCATION, see *Army*, June, 1868.

MILITARY EXHIBITION, ROYAL, Chelsea, president the duke of Cambridge, was opened by the prince of Wales, with the princess, the duke of Edinburgh, and other distinguished persons, 7 May, 1890; visited by the queen, 4 July. The exhibition consisted of the industrial work of the soldiers, articles of military equipment, pictures lent, and other objects of interest; military sports, drills, &c. Mr. Spencer's strong war balloon ascended 10 May, *et seq.* The exhibition was intended to promote the increase of soldiers' institutes in towns.

The exhibition closed . . . 1 Nov. 1890
The profits were reported to be 9,744*l.* . 9 May, 1891
Exhibition at Earl's-court opened by the duke of Cambridge . . . 4 May, 1901
A military tournament is annually held at the Agricultural Hall in May. See *Riding*, and *Tournaments*.

MILITARY KNIGHTS OF WINDSOR, see *Poor Knights of Windsor*.

MILITARY LANDS ACT, passed 27 June, 1892; amended, 1897. See *Commons*.

MILITARY or MARTIAL LAW is built on no settled principle, but is entirely arbitrary, and, in truth, no law; but sometimes indulged, rather than allowed, as law. *Sir Matthew Hale.* It has been several times proclaimed in parts of these kingdoms, and in 1798 was almost general in Ireland, where it was also proclaimed in 1803. Military manœuvres act passed, 1897. Military works act passed, 1897; another, 1899. The king's regulations and orders promulgated, 1901.

MILITIA, the standing national force of these realms, is traced to king Alfred, who made all his subjects soldiers, 872-901. See *Army Defence.*

Commission of array to raise a militia . . . 1122
Revived by Henry II. 1176
Again revived 1557
Said to amount to 160,000 men 1623
The militia statutes . . . . . . 1661 to 1663
Supplemental militia act passed 1796
Irish militia offered its services in England, 28 March, 1804
General militia act for England and Scotland, 1802; for Ireland 1809
Enactment authorising courts-martial to inflict imprisonment instead of flogging passed . . 1814
Acts to consolidate the militia laws . 1852*-54, 1882
Militia embodied on account of the Russian war, 1854; on account of the Indian mutiny, 1857; and on account of the war in the Soudan . 18 Feb. 1885
Militia reserve act passed 1867
Militia in 1872, 139,018; 1875, 149,330; 1877, 134,500; in 1884, 82,525; in 1886, 108,196; in 1887, 110,488; 1888, 141,593; 1890, 113,163; 1893, 124,692; 1899, 124,273.
Militia (volunteers) Enlistment Act, consolidating and amending the laws passed . . 11 Aug. 1875
A committee on the state of the militia reported, Feb. 1890, greatly increased efficiency since 1850.
Militia embodied on account of the S. African war, May, 1900; 99,000 were under arms; 22,000 were sent abroad; Militia and Yeomanry bill passed, 16 Dec. 1902

MILITIA OF JESUS, a society of Roman Catholic youth of France and Italy, formed to support the papal cause by moral agencies, became known in 1877.

MILK. The type of food as containing all things needful for the development of the animal body. A process for its condensation was invented by Mr. Gail Borden, near New York, in 1849, for which he was awarded a medal at the Great Exhibition in 1851, when he erected factories. He invented meat biscuit, 1850. The Anglo-Swiss condensed milk company was established in 1866; and since then the Aylesbury and other companies.

Typhoid fever is held to be propagated by milk; epidemics in various parts of the country have been traced to infected dairies. The first instance was in London . . . Aug., Sept. 1873

MILKY WAY (Galaxy) in the heavens. Juno is said by the Greek poets to have spilt her milk in the heavens after suckling Mercury or Hercules. Democritus (about 428 B.C.) taught that the *via lactea* consisted of stars, which Galileo (1610-42) proved by the telescope. See *Stars*, 1892.

MILLBANK PENITENTIARY, Westminster. The very unhealthy site was purchased of the Grosvenor family. The building, a modification of Jeremy Bentham's Panopticon (*which see*), first received convicts 27 June, 1816.

In consequence of many deaths during a great epidemic the convicts were placed in Woolwich hulks, 1822-3. On 16 June, 1843, a committee reported the penitentiary a failure. The system was abolished in parliament, and the building styled Millbank prison; made a military prison, 1870.
The buildings ordered to be pulled down and site sold, 1888.
It was finally closed 6 Nov. 1890.'
Management of the site transferred to the board of works, by act passed in 1892.
Building taken down and blocks of artizans' dwellings erected by the London County Council, 1893.
The National Gallery of British Art, the Tate Gallery, built and presented to the nation by Sir Henry Tate (died 1899), 1897; enlarged 1899.

MILLENARIANS (or Chiliasts) suppose that the world will end at the expiration of the seven thousandth year from the creation; and that during a thousand years (millennium) Christ and the saints will reign upon the earth; see *Rev.* xx. The doctrine was very generally inculcated in the 2nd and 3rd centuries, by Papias, Justin Martyr and others.

MILLENARY PETITION, presented to king James on his accession, 1603, on behalf of nearly a thousand Puritan ministers against the "human rites and ceremonies" of the church of England.

MILLS. Moses forbade mill-stones to be taken in pawn, because it would be like taking a man's life to pledge. *Deut.* xxiv. 6. The hand-mill was in use among the Britons previously to the conquest by the Romans. The Romans introduced the water-mill. Cotton mills moved by water were erected by sir Richard Arkwright, at Cromford, Derbyshire. He died in 1792. See *Mechanics.* Mill-work exhibition at the Agricultural Hall, London, N. 10-18 May, 1881.

MILWAUKEE. A town in Wisconsin, North America, founded 1835. The New Hall hotel was burnt 4 A.M. 10 Jan. 1883, when about 109 persons perished. George Scheller, lessee of the bar-room, arrested for arson about 17 Jan. 1883. Population, 1890, 204,486; 1900, 285,315. Great fire at the Union oil works; 600 buildings destroyed; estimated loss about 5,826,000 dollars, 28 Oct. 1892.

MINCIO, a river of Lombardy. Here the Austrians were repulsed by the French under Brune, 25-27 Dec. 1800; and by Eugène Beauharnais, 8 Feb. 1814, near Valeggio.

MIND-CURE. A sect termed Christian Scientists in Boston, U.S., led by Mrs. M. B. G. Eddy, professes to cure bodily diseases by acting on the mind through the body, &c., 1866, *et seq.* See *Trials*, Dec. 1898. The sect increasing in Germany; 1,000,000 cases said to be cured in the United States within 25 years, reported, 6 May, 1902.

MINDEN (Prussia), **BATTLE OF,** 1 Aug. 1759, between the English, Hessians, and Hanoverians (under prince Ferdinand of Brunswick), and the French (under marshal De Contades), who were beaten and driven to the ramparts of Minden. Lord George Sackville (afterwards lord George Germain) who commanded the British and Hanoverian horse, for some disobedience of orders was tried by a court-martial on his return to England, found guilty, and dismissed, 22 April, 1760. He was afterwards restored to favour, and became secretary of state, 1776.

* This militia act was consequent upon the then prevailing opinion of the necessity of strengthening our national defences against the possibility of French invasion. The act empowered her majesty to raise a force not exceeding 80,000 men, of which number 50,000 were to be raised in 1852, and 30,000 in 1855; the quotas for each county or riding to be fixed by an order in council.

MINERALOGY, the science of minerals, is a branch of geology; see *Geology*, *Mines*, and *Crystallography*. It was not much studied by the ancients. George Agricola in the 16th century made the first attempt to treat it scientifically.

The study of mineralogy was advanced by Becker, Kircher, and Woodward in the 17th century.
A British Mineralogical Society established in . . 1800
Haüy's "Traité de Minéralogie" appeared in . . 1801
Mineralogical society of Great Britain held first meeting in London, 3 Feb. 1876, and others since.
Another society termed itself *h, k, l*, Miller's symbol for the face of a crystal . . . 1876
James D. Dana's "System of Mineralogy," 6th edition, extended by E. S. Dana 1899

MINERVA, see *Parthenon* and *Athens*.

MINES. Strabo and Tacitus enumerate gold and silver as among the products of Britain. The earliest instance of a claim to a mine royal being enforced occurs 47 Hen. III. 1262. It related to mines containing gold, together with copper, in Devonshire. In Edward I.'s reign, according to Mr. Ruding, the mines in Ireland, which produced silver, were supposed to be so rich that the king directed a writ for working them to Robert de Ufford, lord justice, 1276. The lead mines of Cardiganshire, from which silver has ever since been extracted, were discovered by sir Hugh Middleton in the reign of James I.; see *Coal*, and the various metals. Average depth of mines (1891) 400 yards. Deep mines: Ashton Moss colliery, near Manchester, 2,850 ft.; part 3,000 ft.; copper mine, Calumet, near lake Superior, U.S., 3,900 ft. (1890); silver-lead mine, Przibram in Bohemia, 3,432 ft. *Chambers' Encyclopædia*, 1891.

Mining Journal established . . . 29 Aug. 1835
The Royal School of Mines, &c., Jermyn-street, St. James's, opened in . . . . Nov. 1851
An act for the regulation of mines passed in . . 1860
A Miners' Protection Association proposed by Mr. William Gurney and others in . . March, 1862
Value of the total mineral produce of the United Kingdom estimated at 29,155,701*l*. in 1854; 31,680,581*l*., 1859; 41,521,705*l*., 1868; 46,094,600*l*., 1870; 69,041,158*l*., 1873; 63,737,881*l*., 1879; 88,042,457*l*., 1881; 58,653,689*l*., 1887; 100,802,657*l*., 1890; 80,900,825*l*., 1894; 78,738,947*l*., 1896; 87,701,975*l*., 1898; 117,309,892*l*., 1899; 160,604,800*l*., 1900.
Miners' conference, for amelioration of their condition, held at Merthyr Tydvil; well conducted; Mr. Halliday president . . . . Oct. 1871
Lord Aberdare's Metalliferous Mines Regulation act passed . . . . . 10 Aug. 1872
The Amalgamated Association of Miners begun in Lancashire about 1869, held a conference at Newport, 1872; at Bristol . . . . 8 Oct. 1873
Royal commission on mines (see under *Coal*) appointed, Feb. 1879. Report issued . Nov. 1881
A miners' national conference on wages, &c.; opened at Birmingham, 20 April, 1881; at Manchester, 29 Aug. 1882, and frequently at other places.
Miners' association of Northumberland vote against continuance of payments to their M.P's, Messrs Burt and Fenwick, 19 Sept.; vote rescinded, Nov. 1887; further agitation on the subject; again rescinded . . . . . April, 1888
National Miners' Federation annual conferences, 1889; Birmingham, 22 Jan. *et seq.* 1890; Birmingham, 7 Jan. 1891; Stoke-on-Trent, 12 Jan. 1892; Birmingham, 11 Jan. 1893; Leicester, 16 Jan. 1894; Birmingham, 8 Jan. 1895; Leicester, 5 Jan. 1897; Bristol, 4 Jan. 1898; Edinburgh, 10 Jan. 1899; Cardiff, 9 Jan. 1900; Birmingham, 1 Oct. 1901; Southport . . . . . . 7 Oct. 1902
International exhibition of mining and metallurgy, Crystal palace . . . 28 July—11 Oct. 1890
Institute of Mining Engineers met at Nottingham, 24 Sept. 1890; at other places since.
International congress of miners at Jolimont, Belgium, 20–24 May, 1890; at Paris, 31 March–4 April, 1891; at Westminster, 7–10 June, 1892; at Brussels, 22 May, 1893; at Berlin, 14–19 May, 25 1894; at Paris, 3–7 June, 1895; Aix-la-Chapelle, May, 1896; London, 7 June, 1897; Vienna, 1 Aug. 1898; Brussels, 22 May, 1899; Paris, 25 June, 1900; London, 27 May, 1901; Düsseldof, 19 May, 1902
See *Coal* 1889 *et seq.*
Persons employed in mines in the United Kingdom, 1888, 592,696; 1891, 707,411; 1900, 814,517; 1901, 839,178; 1902, 855,603.
By the flooding of Wheal Owles, a Cornish tin mine, 20 men were drowned . . . 10 Jan. 1893
Royal commission on mining royalties, earl Northbrook, chairman, appointed, 1889; final report and evidence relating to the act of 1872, &c., signed . . . . . 24 March, 1893
The first annual report on the mineral industry of the United Kingdom (1894) by Dr. C. Le Neve Foster, published, Jan. 1896; second part, Aug. 1898
Miners' conciliation board, 1st meeting, London, advance of 5 per cent. on the standard of 1888, conceded . . . . 27 Jan. 1899
The mines (prohibition of child labour underground) act passed . . . . . 30 July, 1900
Committee appointed to inquire into the use of electricity in mines . . . . . Oct. 1902
Accidents in mines, see under *Coal*.

MINGRELIA, the ancient Colchis, mentioned in the legend of "Jason, the Argonauts, and the Golden Fleece." A province of Asiatic Russia, prince Nicolas having ceded his rights to the Czar in 1867. In 1887 the prince was spoken of as a candidate for the Bulgarian throne.

MINIATURE PAINTING was practised in England by Holbein, Isaac, and Peter Oliver, and others in the 16th century; by other eminent artists since. The new Society of Miniature Painters, president, Mr. Alyn-Williams, opened its first exhibition at 175, New Bond-street, London, 23 Sept. 1896. "The Society of Miniaturists," president, lord Ronald Gower, 1st exhibition, at the Grafton Galleries, London, 14 Nov. 1896. Sir Wm. Ross, 1794–1860, may be said to be the last miniaturist.

MINIE RIFLE, invented at Vincennes, about 1833, by M. Minié (born 1810). From a common soldier he raised himself to the rank of chef d'escadron. His rifle, considered to surpass all made previous to it, was adopted by the French, and, with modifications, by the British, 1852.

MINIMIZERS. A name given to certain writers who advocate the limitation of the sovereign power of the state as much as possible to the protection of life and property, which is styled by professor Huxley "administrative nihilism." They include W. von Humboldt, J. S. Mill (in his "Essay on Liberty"), and Mr. Herbert Spencer (in his "Political Institutions"), 1882.

MINIMS (from *minimi*, the least), an order of monks, founded by S. Francisco di Paolo (1416—1507), in Calabria, received their name, as professing themselves inferior to the Minorites (from *minor*, less); see *Franciscans*. St. Francis died in France in 1507; where he had established houses of his order.

MINISTERS, see *Administrations*.

MINISTERS in Scotland: church patronage was abolished in 1874.

MINNESINGERS, lyric German poets, of the 12th and 13th centuries, who sang of love and war to entertain knights and barons of the time. The *Meistersingers*, their successors, an incorporated fraternity in the 14th century, composed satirical ballads for the amusement of the citizens and lower classes. Hans Sachs, a shoemaker (1494-1576), a poet of the reformation, was for a time their dean. His works were published at Nuremberg, 1560. "Owleglass" and "Reynard the Fox," are attributed to the Meistersingers.

MINNESOTA, a western state of N. America, was organised as a territory, 3 March, 1849, and admitted into the union in 1858. On 17 Aug. 1862, the Sioux Indians commenced a series of outrages at Acton in Messler county, desolating the country and massacring above 500 persons, of both sexes, and of all ages. General Sibley beat the Indians in two battles and rescued many captives. Thirty-eight Indians were executed as assassins. Capital, St. Paul.

The great Tribune buildings at Minneapolis were burnt, about 20 persons perished, 30 Nov. 1889; another fire, 3 deaths; estimated loss, 2,000,000 dollars . . . . 13 Aug. 1893
Tornado, much destruction and loss of life in St. Paul and the neighbourhood; the *Sea-King*, steamer, on lake Pekin upset, about 100 persons drowned, and many others in small boats; total loss about 250 . . . . . . 13 July, 1890
Destructive tornado with loss of life 15, 16 June, 1892
Destructive forest fires; see *United States*, 31 Aug.–3 Sept. 1894.
Bill passed forbidding the marriage of insane, epileptic and idiotic persons, and requiring a medical certificate of applicants for marriage licences . . . . April, 1901
Dr. Whipple, bp. of Minnesota, friend and champion to the Indians, died, aged 79 . about 3 Oct. ,,
Population, 1880, 780,773; 1890, 1,301,826; 1900, 1,751,394.

MINORCA AND MAJORCA, the Balearic Isles (*which see*). Port Mahon in Minorca was captured by lieutenant-general Stanhope and sir John Leake in 1708, and was ceded to the British by the treaty of Utrecht in 1713. It was retaken by the Spanish and French in July, 1756, and admiral Byng fell a victim to public indignation for not relieving it; see *Byng*. It was restored to the British at the peace in 1763; taken 5 Feb. 1782; again captured by the British under general Stuart, without the loss of a man, 15 Nov. 1798; given up at the peace of Amiens, 25 March, 1802.

MINORITIES. In the new reform bill, passed 15 Aug. 1867, provision was made for the representation of minorities in constituencies with three members by limiting each elector to two votes. It was introduced as an amendment by lord Cairns in the lords, 30 July, and accepted by the commons, Aug. 1867. The principle was adopted in a new constitution by the state of Illinois, U.S., July, 1870. See *Proportional Representation*.

MINSTER, or **MONASTERIUM**, a place occupied by monks; see *Westminster* and *York*. "The Minster," an illustrated monthly magazine, supported by the archbishop of Canterbury, sir Benjamin Baker, and other eminent persons; No. 1, Jan. 1895.

MINSTRELS, originally pipers appointed by lords of manors to divert their copyholders while at work, owed their origin to the glee men or harpers of the Saxons, and continued till about 1560. John of Gaunt erected a court of minstrels at Tutbury in 1380. So late as the reign of Henry VIII. they intruded without ceremony into all companies, even at the houses of the nobility; but in Elizabeth's reign they were adjudged rogues and vagabonds (1597).

MINT. Athelstan enacted regulations for the government of the mint about 928. There were several provincial mints under the control of that of London. Henry I. is said to have instituted a mint at Winchester, 1125. Stow says the mint was kept by Italians, the English being ignorant of the art of coining, 7 Edw. I. 1278. The operators were formed into a corporation by the charter of king Edward III., in which condition it consisted of the warden, master, comptroller, assay-master, workers, coiners, and subordinates. The first entry of gold brought to the mint for coinage occurs in 18 Edw. III. 1343. Tin was coined by Charles II. 1684; and gun-metal and pewter by his successor James after his abdication. Sir Isaac Newton was warden, 1699-1727, during which time the debased coin was called in, and new issued at the loss of the government. Between 1806 and 1810, grants amounting to 262,000*l.* were made by parliament for the erection of the present mint, which was completed in 1810; it was injured by fire, 31 Oct. 1815. The new constitution of the mint, founded on the report of the hon. Wellesley Pole, took effect in 1817. Professor Thomas Graham, the master of the mint, died 16 Sept. 1869. By the Coinage Act, passed 4 April, 1870, the office was combined with that of the chancellor of the exchequer, the duties being transferred to the deputy-master (Sir C. W. Fremantle), K.C.B., 1 Jan. 1890; resigned, Sept. 1894; succeeded by Mr. Horace Seymour, made K.C.B. June, and died 25 June, 1902; Mr. W. E. Macartney appointed Jan. 1903. (Sir Wm. Roberts-Austen, chemist and assayer since 1870, died 22 Nov. 1902.) After reorganisation, the work was resumed, 8 Dec. 1882. See *Coin*.

MASTERS OF THE MINT.

1817. Wellesley Pole.
1823. Thomas Wallace.
1827. George Tierney.
1828. J. C. Herries.
1830. Lord Auckland.
1834. James Abercrombie.
1835. Alexander Baring.
,, Henry Labouchere.
1841. William E. Gladstone.
1845. Sir George Clerk.
1846. Richard L. Sheil.
1850. Sir John F. Herschel, F.R.S.
1855. Thomas Graham, F.R.S.

MINUET, a French dance, said to have been first danced by Louis XIV., 1653.

MINUS, see *Plus*.

MIRACLE PLAYS, see under *Drama*.

MIRIDITES, or **MIRDITES**, see *Turkey*, 1877.

MIRRORS. In ancient times mirrors were made of metal; those of the Jewish women of brass. Mirrors of silver were introduced by Praxiteles 4th *century* B.C. Mirrors or looking-glasses were made at Venice, A.D. 1300; and in England, at Lambeth, near London, in 1673. The improvements in manufacturing plate-glass, and that of very large size, have cheapened looking-glasses very much. Various methods of coating glass by a solution of silver, thus avoiding the use of mercury, so injurious to the health of the workmen, have been made known; by M. Petitjean in 1851; by M. Cimeg in 1861, and by Liebig and others.

MISCHNA, see *Talmud*.

MISERERE (*Psalm* li.) sung at Rome in the "*Tenebræ*," the service in Holy or Passion Week, in a peculiarly effective manner, to old music. One arrangement is by Costanzo Festa, dated 1517.

MISSAL, or **MASS BOOK**, the Romanist ritual compiled by pope Gelasius I. 492-6; revised by Gregory I. 590-604. Various missals were in use till the Roman missal was adopted by the council of Trent, 1545-63. The missal was superseded in England by the book of common prayer, 1549.

MISSING WORD COMPETITION. See *Lotteries*, 1893, and *Trials*, 1899.

MISSIONARY BISHOPS, see under *Bishops*.

MISSIONS,* see *Mark* xvi. 15. Among the Romanists, the religious orders of St. Dominic, St. Francis, St. Augustin, &c., have missions to the Levant and to America. Marco Polo is said to have introduced missionaries into China, 1275. The Jesuits have missions to China (*which see*) and to most other parts of the world. Among the Protestants, an early undertaking of this kind was a Danish mission, planned by Frederick IV. in 1706. The Society for the Propagation of the Gospel in foreign parts was established 1701, and the Moravian Brethren encouraged missions about 1732. The London Missionary Society held their first meeting, 4 Nov. 1794 (1st mission sent to the South Sea Islands in the *Duff*, 1796); centenary celebrated, 15 Jan. 1895. Most Christian sects now support missions. *British Contributions to Foreign Missions*: 1871, 855,742*l*. (in 1871-7, 6,977,586*l*.). Nearly 3,000,000*l*. spent in the world on missions in 1900.

Great congress of protestant missions in London; a large number of societies represented; the earl of Aberdeen president, 9-19 June, 1888.

Commander Allan Gardner, R.N., who left England in the *Ocean Queen* in Sept. 1850, on the Patagonian mission, with Mr. Williams, surgeon, Mr. Maidment, catechist, and four others, died on Picton Island, at the mouth of the Beagle Channel, to the south of Tierra del Fuego, having been starved to death; all his companions having previously perished, 6 Sept. 1851.

M. Schoffler, a missionary to Cochin-China, was publicly executed at Son-Tay, by order of the grand mandarin, for preaching Christianity, such preaching being prohibited by the law of that country, 4 May, 1851.

MISSISSIPPI, a great river, N. America, explored by De Soto about 1541. Captain Glazier discovered its source, 1884. Its length is now stated to be 2,960 miles. The Mississippi trade was begun in England, in Nov. 1716. Law's Mississippi scheme in France, commenced about the same period, exploded in 1720; at which time the nominal capital is said to have amounted to 100,000,000*l*. The ruin of thousands soon followed. See *Law's Bubble*.

Population, 1880, 1,131,597; 1890, 1,289,600; 1900, 1,551,270.

The great Eads bridge at St. Louis opened, 4 July, 1874

By the explosion of the boiler of the *Corona* at Port Hudson on the Mississippi, 43 persons perished . . . . 3 Oct. 1889

The North American state, MISSISSIPPI, was settled in 1716; admitted as a state of the union, 1817; seceded from it by ordinance, 8 Jan. 1861; submitted, 1865. Capital, Jackson.

About 85,000 persons made homeless through floods in the lower Mississippi valley early in March, 1882

The Mississippi valley suffers much by frequent inundations; one was very disastrous in March, April, 1890, when thousands of square miles were submerged, many towns isolated, and communications cut off. Louisiana suffered much in April following. 150,000 dollars voted by congress to relieve the sufferers . . . . . 25 April, 1890

Grenada nearly destroyed by fire . . 14 Jan. 1891

The great cantilever bridge, 3 miles long, at Memphis, joining Tennessee and Arkansas, completed; cost, 600,000*l*., announced . . 11 April, 1892

Destructive floods; about 250 lives lost, about 13 April *et seq.*; about 1,500 sq. miles covered near St. Louis; 11 million dollars estimated loss; great loss of life; floods abating . . 25 May, ,,

Great rising of the river . . . . May, 1893

Destructive floods in central and southern Mississippi; towns isolated and many lives lost, reported, 21 April, 1900; great rising of the river and loss of life . . . . June, 1903

MISSOLONGHI, a town in Greece, taken from the Turks, 1 Nov. 1821, and heroically and successfully defended against the Turks by Marco Botzaris, Oct. 1822—27 Jan. 1823. It was taken 22 April, 1826, after a long siege. Here Lord Byron died, 19 April, 1824. A statue of Byron was unveiled here, 6 Nov. 1881. It was surrendered to the Greeks in 1829.

MISSOURI, a south-western state in N. America, was settled in 1763, and admitted into the union, 10 Aug. 1821. It decided on neutrality in the conflict of 1861, but was invaded by both the confederate and federal forces in June of that year, and became one of the seats of war. Capital, Jefferson city; population, 1880, 2,168,380; 1890, 2,679,184; 1900, 3,106,665; see *United States*, 1861 *et seq.*—Great railway strike March, 1886. The university library, Columbia, burnt, 9 Jan. 1892. —For the MISSOURI COMPROMISE, see *Slavery in America*. The Missouri river is 3,047 miles long. See *Storms*, 28 April, 1899.

MITCHELSTOWN, Cork, see *Ireland*, 9 Sept. 1887.

MITHRIDATE, a medical preparation in the form of an electuary, supposed to be an antidote to poison and the oldest compound known, is said to have been invented by Mithridates, king of Pontus, about 70 B.C.

MITHRIDATIC WAR, caused by the massacre of 80,000 Romans, by Mithridates VI., king of Pontus, 88 B.C., and remarkable for its duration, its many sanguinary battles, and the cruelties of its commanders. Mithridates having taken the consul Aquilius, made him ride on an ass through a great part of Asia, crying out as he rode, "I am Aquilius, consul of the Romans." He is said to have killed him by causing melted gold to be poured down his throat, in derision of his avarice, 85 B.C. Mithridates was defeated by Pompey, 66 B.C.; and committed suicide, 63 B.C.

MITRAILLEUSE, or **MITRAILLEUR,** a machine-gun in which 37 or more large-bored rifles are combined with breech-action, by means of which a shower of bullets may be rapidly projected by one man. It was invented in Belgium, and adopted by the French emperor soon after the Prusso-Austrian war in 1866, and was much used in the Franco-Prussian war in 1870. Its peculiar "dry, shrieking, terrible sound" was described in the bombardment of Saarbrück, 2 Aug. 1870. Modifications of the mitrailleuse have been made by Montigny and others. The Fosbery mitrailleuse was tried and approved at Shoeburyness, 11 Aug. 1870.—It is mentioned in *Grose's Military Antiquities* (1801) that in England, in 1625, a patent was granted to William Drummond for a machine composed of a number of muskets joined together, by the help of which two soldiers can oppose a hundred, and named, on account of its effect, "thunder carriage," or more usually, "fire carriage." An English

* MISSIONS, "a series of sermons, generally by a 'missioner,' or special preacher, often followed by confessions and communions" (a species of revivalism), were authorised in the metropolis by the bishops of London, Winchester, and Rochester, held 1869 and since.

mitrailleuse, a modification of the American gatling, containing 50 cartridges, was tried at Woolwich, 18 Jan. 1872; fifty of them were ordered to be made by Armstrong.

MITRE. The cleft cap or mitre was worn by the Jewish high-priest, 1491 B.C. It had on it a golden plate inscribed "HOLINESS TO THE LORD." *Exodus* xxxix. 28. The most ancient mitre that has the nearest resemblance to the present one is that upon the seal of the bishop of Laon, in the 10th century. *Fosbroke.* Anciently the cardinals wore mitres, but at the council of Lyons, in 1245, they were directed to wear hats.

MITYLENE, or **LESBOS**, Ægean Sea. Near here the Greeks defeated and nearly destroyed the Turkish fleet, 7 Oct. 1824.

MNEMONICS, artificial memory, was introduced by Simonides the younger, 477 B.C. *Arund. Marbles.* "Mnemonica" was published by John Willis in 1618; and the "Memoria Technica" of Dr. Grey first appeared in 1730. A system of mnemonics was announced in Germany in 1806-7.

MOABITES, descendants of Lot, a people living to the south-east of Judæa. They were frequently at war with the Israelites, and were subdued with divine help by Ehud about 1336, by David about 1040, and by Jehoshaphat, 895 B.C., but often harassed the Jews in the decay of their monarchy. The discovery of a stone with inscription in Phœnician characters, relating to Mesha, king of Moab, referred to in 2 *Kings*, iii., was announced in Jan. 1870, and impressions were exhibited soon after.

MÖCKERN (Prussia). Here the French army under Eugène Beauharnais were defeated by the Prussians under Yorck, 5 April, 1813; and here Blücher defeated the French, 16 Oct. 1813.

MODELS. The first were figures of living persons, and Dibutades, the Corinthian, is the reputed inventor of those in clay. His daughter, being about to be separated from her lover, traced his profile by his shadow on the wall; her father filled up the outline with clay, which he afterwards baked, and thus produced a figure of the object of her affection, giving rise to an art till then unknown, about 985 B.C.

A beautiful model of the new town of Edinburgh, before the building began, was formed in wood.

A model was made of a bridge over the Neva, of uncommon strength as well as elegance; and of the mountains of Switzerland, by general Pfiffer (1766-85).

M. Choffin's model of Paris also was remarkable for its precision.

Fine models of Gibraltar, Quebec, and other fortified places, are deposited in the Rotunda at Woolwich. See *Waxwork* and *Lodging-houses*.

MODENA (formerly Mutina), capital of the late duchy in Central Italy; was governed by the house of Este, from 1288 till 1796, when the last male of that house, the reigning duke Hercules III., was expelled by the French. By the treaty of Campo Formio, the Modenese possessions were incorporated with the Cisalpine republic, 1797, and with the kingdom of Italy, 1805. The archduke Francis of Este, son of the archduke Ferdinand of Austria, and of Mary, the heiress of the last duke, was restored in 1814. Modena, in accordance with the voting by universal suffrage, was annexed to Sardinia on 18 March, 1860. Population of the city, 1881, 31,053; 1901, 64,941; of the province, 1881, 279,254; 1889, 303,541; 1901, 322,617.

GRAND DUKES.

1814. Francis IV. An invasion of his states by Murat was defeated, 11 April, 1815. He was expelled by his subjects in 1831, but was restored by the Austrians.

1846. Francis V. (born 1 June, 1819) succeeded 21 Jan. His subjects rose against him soon after the Italian war broke out, in April, 1859. He fled to Verona, establishing a regency, 11 June; which was abolished, 13 June; Farina was appointed dictator, 27 July; a constituent assembly was immediately elected, which offered the duchy to the king of Sardinia, 15 Sept., who incorporated it with his dominions, 18 March, 1860. Francis died, 20 Nov. 1875.

MODERADOS. A political party in Spain, long headed by Ramon Maria Narvaez, duke of Valencia (who died 23 April, 1868), who opposed the Progresistas headed by Espartero and Prim. The party was reinforced by the favourers of Don Carlos, after his total defeat in 1876.

MODERATES, opponents of the Progressives (*which see*).

MODOC INDIANS (a few hundreds), dwelling in lands south of Oregon, were removed to other lands by the United States government. Not obtaining subsistence, they returned to their old possessions, and their able leader captain Jack defeated the troops sent to expel them, 17 Jan. 1873. During negotiations for a peaceful settlement, they decoyed the United States commissioners into an ambush (11 April), and massacred general Canby and about 40 others. Fighting took place, 15, 16 April, and the Indians retreated to almost impregnable positions. The troops were fired on, and suffered much loss, 27 April. The Indians were gradually surrounded. Jack and about twenty warriors held out desperately. Some surrendered, and he himself was captured, 1 June; tried, July, and executed 3 Oct., 1873.

MŒSIA (now Bosnia, Servia, and Bulgaria), was finally subdued by Augustus, 29 B.C. It was successfully invaded by the Goths, A.D. 250, who eventually settled here; see *Goths*.

MOGULS, see *Tartary*.

MOHACZ (Lower Hungary). Here Louis king of Hungary, defeated by the Turks under Solyman II. with the loss of 22,000 men, was suffocated by the fall of his horse in a muddy brook, 29 Aug. 1526. Here also prince Charles of Lorraine defeated the Turks, 12 Aug. 1687.

MOHAMMEDAN, see *Mahometanism*.

MOHAMMERAH, a Persian town near the Euphrates, captured, after two hours' cannonading, by sir James Outram, during the Persian war, 26 March, 1857. News of the peace arrived 4 April.

MOHILEV, or **MOHILEF** (Russia). Here the Russian army, under prince Bagration, was signally defeated by the French under marshal Davoust, prince of Eckmühl, 23 July, 1812.

MOHOCKS, ruffians, who went about London at night, wounding and disfiguring the men, and indecently exposing the women. One hundred pounds were offered by royal proclamation in 1712, for apprehending any one of them. *Northouck.*

The "scourers" of the seventeenth century resemble the Mohocks.

MOHURRUM, a Mahometan festival in honour of the prophet's nephews: at its celebration in Bombay, Feb. 1874, the Mahometans fiercely attacked the Parsees, and were quelled by the military.

MOKANNA (Hakim ben Allah), "The Veiled," prophet, founder of a sect in Khorassan in the eighth century. He pretended to be an incarnation of God, and therefore veiled his face, but really to conceal the loss of an eye. He rebelled against the calif Almahdi, was for a time successful, but was subdued in 780, when he and the remains of his followers took poison. He is the subject of a poem by Thos. Moore in "Lalla Rookh," 1817.

MOLDAVIA, see *Danubian Principalities*.

MOLINISTS, a Roman Catholic sect, followers of Louis Molina, a Jesuit, born 1535. He maintained the reconcilability of the doctrines of predestination and free will, 1588.

MOLLY MAGUIRE, the name of a secret society in Ireland in 1843, and of another society (originally Buckshot, about 1853) in mining districts, United States (*which see*), 1877. It ceased about March, 1879.

MOLOKANI, a sect in West Russia, said to date from the 16th century, who maintain primitive Christian doctrines and practices; well described by Mr. D. Mackenzie Wallace in his "Russia," published 1877. Dassajeff, a peasant woman, one of the sect, received by the empress dowager for her kind assistance rendered to her son, the Cesarevitch, at his death at Abbas Tuman, 10 July, reported, 31 July, 1899.

MOLUCCAS, an archipelago in the Indian Ocean (the chief island, Amboyna), discovered by the Portuguese, about 1511, and held by them secretly until the arrival of the Spaniards, who claimed them, till 1529, when Charles V. yielded them to John III. for a large sum of money. The Dutch conquered them in 1607, and have held them ever since,—except from 1810 to 1814, when they were subject to the English. Earthquake at Amboina, the capital almost destroyed and 50 persons killed, 5 Jan. 1898.

MOLWITZ (in Prussian Silesia). Here the Prussians, commanded by Frederick II., obtained a great victory over the Imperialists, 10 April (O. S. 30 March), 1741.

MOLYBDENUM, a whitish, brittle, almost infusible metal. Scheele, in 1778, discovered molybdic acid in a mineral hitherto confounded with graphite. Hjelm, 1782, prepared the metal from molybdic acid; and in 1825 Berzelius described most of its chemical characters. *Gmelin*.

MOMBASA, chief town of the British East Africa territories; increasing prosperity reported, July, 1890. Kisawir, or Frere Town, is a thriving station of the Church Missionary society. See *Africa* (*British East*).

MONACHISM (from the Greek *monos*, alone). Catholic writers refer to the prophet Elijah, and the Nazarites mentioned in *Numbers*, ch. vi., as early examples. The first Christian ascetics appear to be derived from the Jewish sect of the Essenes, whose life was very austere, practising celibacy, &c. About the time of Constantine (306-22) numbers of these ascetics withdrew into the deserts, and were called *hermits*, *monks*, and *anchorets*;* of whom Paul, Anthony, and Pachomius were most celebrated. Simeon, the founder of the Stylitæ (or pillar saints), died 451. He is said to have lived on a pillar thirty years. St. Benedict, the great reformer of western monachism, published his rules and established his monastery at Monte Casino, about 529. The Carthusians, Cistercians, &c., are varieties of Benedictines. In 964, by decree of king Edgar, all married priests were ineffectually ordered to be replaced by monks. Religious orders expelled from France, by decree, 29 March, 1880. Relieved of their vows by the Pope, 1881. See *Abbeys*, and *Benedictines*.

* The anchorites of the 12th, 13th, and 14th centuries must not be confounded with the anachorets and anchorets, or hermits. The former were confined to solitary cells; the latter permitted to go where they pleased.

MONACO, a principality, N. Italy, held by the Genoese family Grimaldi since 968. By treaty on 2 Feb. 1861, the prince ceded the communes of Roquebrune and Mentone, the chief part of his dominions, to France, for 4,000,000 francs. The prince, Charles III., born 8 Dec. 1818, succeeded his father Florestan, 20 June 1856; died 10 Sept. 1889, was succeeded by Albert, born 13 Nov. 1848. A commercial convention between the prince and France, signed 9 Nov. 1865, was much discussed as tending towards the abolition of the French navigation laws. Petitions against Monte Carlo, the great gaming establishment, 1880-4; a 50 years' concession granted, reported, March, 1896. International sporting club opened, autumn 1903. Population, 1888, 13,304; 1901, 15,180.

MONARCHY. Historians reckon various grand monarchies—the Chaldæan, Assyrian, Babylonian, Median, Persian, Grecian, Parthian, and Roman (*which see*).

MONASTERIES, see *Abbeys*.

MONCONTOUR (near Poitiers, France). Here the admiral Coligny and the French Protestants were defeated with great loss by the duke of Anjou (afterwards Henry III.), 3 Oct. 1569.

MONCRIEFF SYSTEM, see *Cannon*.

MONDAY CONCERTS, see under *Music*.

MONDOVI (Piedmont). Here the Sardinian army, commanded by Colli, was defeated by Napoleon Bonaparte, 22 April, 1796.

MONETARY CONFERENCES, International, opened at Paris, 16 Aug. 1878; and 19 April, 1881; Cologne, 11-13 Oct. 1882; Paris, 21 July, adjourned, 5 Aug. 1885; the union continued till 1 Jan. 1887: conventions signed, 6 Nov., and 8 Dec. 1885. A congress was held at Paris 11 Sept. *et seq.*, 1889. See *Latin Union*. International monetary conference at Brussels, respecting bimetallism (*which see*), proposed by the United States, N.A.; 18 nations represented (sir Charles Fremantle, sir Wm. H. Houldsworth, M.P., Mr. Bertram Currie, Mr. Alfred Rothschild, and others, for Great Britain); opened by M. Beernaert, Belgian minister of finance, 22 Nov. 1892; conference adjourned to 13 May, 1893, 17 Dec. 1892. "International Monetary Conferences," by H. B. Russell, Aug. 1898.

MONEY is mentioned as a medium of commerce in *Genesis* xxiii., 1860 B.C., when Abraham purchased a field as a sepulchre for Sarah. The coinage of money is ascribed to the Lydians. Moneta was the name given to their silver by the Romans, it having been coined in the temple of Juno-Moneta, 269 B.C. Money was made of different metals, and even of leather and other articles, both in ancient and modern times. It was made of pasteboard by the Hollanders so late as 1574. The czar Nicholas struck coins in platinum. Parliamentary committee on money lending, meetings, T. W. Russell, chairman, July, 1897; Mr. John Kirkwood refused to answer certain questions, admonished at the bar of the commons, 16 July.

Money-lending act (regulating the business of money-lenders) passed 8 Aug. 1900. See *Coin; Gold; Copper; Mint; Banks, Latin Union,* &c. For *Money Orders*, see *Post Office*.

MONEYERS travelled with our early kings, and coined money as required; see *Mint*.

MONGOLS, see *Tartary*.

MONITEUR UNIVERSEL, a newspaper, established in Paris by C. J. Panckoucke, 5 May, 1789; daily paper, 24 Nov. 1789; the organ of the government, 28 Dec. 1799. It was superseded by the *Journal Officiel*, 1 Jan. 1869; resumed its official position about 23 Sept. 1870; and was again superseded by the *Journal Officiel*, Feb. 1871. It became the organ of MacMahon's government in 1875.

MONITORIAL SYSTEM (in education), in which pupils are employed as teachers, was used by Dr. Bell in the Orphan Asylum at Madras in 1795, and was also adopted by Joseph Lancaster, in London; see *Education*.

MONITOR SHIPS, see *United States*. The American monitor, *Miantonomah*, arrived at Plymouth in June, 1866, and excited much attention.

MONK, see *Monachism*.

MONMOUTH, Monmouthshire, was a Roman station, afterwards a Saxon fortress. The ancient castle rebuilt by John, lord of Monmouth, 1257, became the property of John of Gaunt, and in it his grandson, Henry V., was born, 9 Aug., 1388. Monmouth was first incorporated in 1550. Visit of the duke and duchess of York, 29 Oct. 1900. Population, 1881, 6,111; 1891, 5,470; 1901, 5,095.

MONMOUTH'S REBELLION. James, duke of Monmouth (born at Rotterdam, 9 April, 1649), a natural son of Charles II. by Lucy Waters, was banished England for his connection with the Rye-house plot, in 1683. He invaded England at Lyme, 11 June, 1685; was proclaimed king at Taunton, 20 June; was defeated at Sedgmoor, near Bridgewater, 6 July; and beheaded on Tower-hill, 15 July.

MONOCHORD, a box of thin wood, with a bridge, over which is stretched a wire or chord, said to have been invented by Pythagoras, about 600 B.C.

MONOLITH, Greek for single stone; see *Obelisk*.

MONOPHYSITES, see *Eutychians*.

MONOPOLIES were formerly so numerous in England that parliament petitioned against them, and many were abolished, about 1601-2. They were further suppressed by 21 Jas. I., 1624. Sir Giles Mompesson and sir Francis Mitchell were punished for their abuse of monopolies, 1621. In 1630, Charles I. established monopolies of soap, salt, leather, and other common things, to supply a revenue without the help of parliament. It was decreed that none should be in future created by royal patent, 16 Chas. I. 1640.

MONO-RAIL SYSTEM, see under *Railways*.

MONOTHELITES, heretics who affirmed that Jesus Christ had but one will, were favoured by the emperor Heraclius, 630; they merged into the Eutychians (*which see*).

MONROE DOCTRINE, a term applied to the determination expressed by James Monroe, president of the United States, in his message to the congress, 2 Dec. 1823, not to permit any European power to interfere with the concerns of any independent states of North or South America. This doctrine was referred to in 1859, 1865, 1895-96. A resolution strongly affirming the doctrine proposed by senator Davis to the senate, 20 Jan. 1896. The action of Great Britain and Germany in their dispute with Venezuela 1902-3 (see *Venezuela*) aroused considerable excitement in the United States as being contrary to the Monroe doctrine. See Capt. Mahan's article on the Monroe doctrine, *National Review*, Feb. 1903, and *Times*, 30 Jan. 1903.

MONTANA, a territory of the United States, north America, formed out of Idaho; became a territory in 1864, and a state in 1889. Capital, Helena. Population in 1880, 39,159; 1890, 132,159; 1900, 243,329.

Explosions of dynamite, &c., through a fire at Butte; 75 or 100 deaths; estimated loss, 1,000,000 dollars . . . . . 15 Jan. 1895

MONTANISTS, followers of Montanus, of Ardaba, in Mysia, about 171, who was reputed to have the gift of prophecy, and proclaimed himself the Comforter promised by Christ. He condemned second marriages as fornication, permitted the dissolution of marriage, forbade avoiding martyrdom, and ordered a severe fast of three lents. The eloquent father, Tertullian, joined the sect, 204.

MONT BLANC, in the French Alps, is the highest mountain in Europe, being 15,781 feet above the level of the sea. The summit was first reached by Jacques Balmat in June, 1786, and afterwards by H. B. Saussure, aided by Balmat, on 2 Aug. 1787. The summit was attained by Dr. Hamel (when three of his guides perished) in 1820, and by many other persons before and since. Accounts of the ascents of Mr. John Auldjo, Charles Fellows (1827), and of professor Tyndall (1857-8) have been published; see *Alps*. 57 ascents reported in 1873; 64 in 1881.

Herr Rothe and a guide killed by an avalanche, 20 Aug. 1891. Accidents frequent.

Erection of an observatory on the summit proposed; work proceeding, July; stopped about 28 Aug.; 3 deaths. Favourable report by M. Janssen to the Academy of Sciences, 2 Nov. 1891. Preparations for a renewal of the work, with precautions . . . . June, 1892

An association was formed, and by its means, a wooden observatory was constructed at Meudon and sent to Chamounix to be conveyed to the summit of the mountain . . . . Sept. ,,

The observatory on Mont Blanc erected, (to be transferred to a rocky point of the same altitude summer of 1898); observations on the spectrum of the solar rays by prof. Janssen, Sept., reported to the French Academy . . Oct. 1893

Clockwork registration apparatus set up by M. Janssen 1894

By the torrents consequent on the fall of a glacier, the "Etablissement des Bains" at St. Gervais and two villages were destroyed, and about 130 persons perished . . . . . 11, 12 July, 1892

Mr. C. E. Mathews' "Annals of Mont Blanc" published 1898-99

MONT CENIS, see *Alps*.

MONTEBELLO, in Piedmont, where Lannes defeated the Austrians, 9 June, 1800, and acquired his title of duke of Montebello; and where, after a contest of six hours, the French and Sardinians defeated the Austrians, who lost about 1000 killed and wounded, and 200 prisoners, 20 May, 1859. The French lost about 670 men, including general Beuret.

MONTE CARLO, see *Monaco*.

MONTE CASINO (Central Italy). Here Benedict formed his first monastery, 529. After affording a refuge for many eminent persons, its monastic character was abolished by the Italian government in 1866, care being taken for the preservation of its historical and literary monuments.

MONTEM, see *Eton*.

MONTENEGRO (Black Mountain), inhabited by a race of hardy mountaineers, inveterate enemies of the Turk; an independent principality in European Turkey, was conquered by Solyman II. in 1526. It rebelled in the 17th century, and in 1696 established a hereditary hierarchical government in the family of Petrovitsch Njeguch,—permitted, but not recognised by the Porte. Population, in 1891, 200,000. Capital, Céttingé.

The nephew and successor of the Vladika, Peter II., declined to assume the ecclesiastical function, and declared himself a temporal prince, with the title of Daniel I., 1851; and began war with Turkey 1852
Montenegro put in a state of blockade . 14 Dec. ,,
After indecisive encounters, tranquillity restored by the influence of the arms and negotiations of Omar Pacha, the general of the Turkish army; he left the province . . . . . . 25 Feb. 1853
Blockade raised . . . . . . 10 April, ,,
War again broke out; the Turks defeated at Grahovo, June; peace restored . . . . . Nov. 1858
The country much disturbed through the tyrannical conduct of prince Daniel, who was assassinated (aged 35) . . . . 14 Aug. 1860
Succeeded by his nephew Nicolas, or Nikita, (married) . . . . . . 8 Nov. ,,
An insurrection in Herzegovina the blockade of Montenegro . . . . . . 4 April, 1861
Omar Pacha invaded the province with an army of 32,000 men in . . . . . . Aug. ,,
Many conflicts with various success, but latterly in favour of the Turks; peace made, Turkish supremacy recognised . . . . . . 8-9 Sept. 1862
Conflicts between Christians and Mussulmen at Podgoritza; 21 Montenegrins said to be killed by Turks . . . . . . 20 Oct. 1874
Threatened war prevented by intervention of the great powers . . . . Jan. 1875
Some rioters executed . . . . 15 May, ,,
Montenegro with difficulty restrained from intervention in Herzegovina . Autumn and Winter, ,,
The prince declared war and joined the Servians 2 July, 1876
See *Turkey* and *Russo-Turkish war* . . . 1876-7-8
Declared independent of Turkey by treaty of San Stefano, 3 March; (with new boundaries, and Antivari for a seaport) by the Berlin treaty 13 July, 1878
Podgoritza surrendered by Turkey . . . 7 Feb. 1879
After much resistance by the Albanians, and negotiation with Turkey, Gussinge surrendered, April, 1880
Frontier disputes with Turkey settled, Nov. 1882; the prince well received at Constantinople, Sept. 1883
Building to contain state library, museum, and theatre, at Céttingé founded . . . . 12 May, 1884
A constitution promised . . . . . May, ,,
Temporary fighting between Turks and Montenegrins at Céttingé . . . . . 3, 4 July, 1886
The prince visits the czar at St. Petersburg May, 1889
Severe famine relieved by the great exertions of the prince, Sept.; aided by Russia, Hungary, and Turkey . . . . Oct. ,,
About 6,360 persons emigrate to Servia, Oct., Nov. 1889; famine continues . . . . . March, 1890
Colonel Bosko Martinovitch, cousin of the prince, murdered; the assassin lynched . . 7 July, ,,
Albanian raids checked by Turks . July, Aug. ,,
Agitation for more liberal government Jan. *et seq.* 1893
Frequent raids by the Albanians, appeal to the Porte; redress promised . . . March, April, 1894
Continued emigration into Austria-Hungary of nobles opposed to the new system of government, introduced by prince Nicolas, rep. . July, ,,
Formation of a standing army above 36,000 men, with Russian weapons 1895
Visit of the prince of Naples, Aug.; leaves 2 Sept. 1896
Princess Helen, the prince of Naples, and the duke of Genoa arrive at Bari, where she professes the R.C. faith, 21 Oct. (see *Italy*, Oct, 1896) . . ,,
Celebration of the bicentenary of the present dynasty; removal of the remains of Petrovitch Niegueh, the founder, from the cathedral to the mausoleum, designed by the princess of Naples; addresses by prince Nicholas and others, *O.S.* 14 Jan. 1897
Marriage of prince Francis Joseph of Battenberg and princess Anna of Montenegro, celebrated at Céttingé . . . . 18 May ,,
Successful European tour of prince Nicholas, returns to Céttingé . . . . 4 June, 1898
Conflicts on the frontier between Mahometans and Christians, many killed, including women and children; over 700 houses burnt . 16 June, ,,
National guard, under prince Mirko, organised, March, 1899
Marriage of the crown prince and the duchess Militza at Céttingé, 27 July; received by the sultan at Constantinople . . 2–6 Sept. ,,
Prince Nicholas assumes the title "Royal Highness" by request of his people . . 19 Dec. ,,
Conflicts with Turkish troops on the frontier, Feb. *et seq.* 1902
Existing treaty of commerce between Gt. Britain and Montenegro prolonged until 1 Jan. 1904, reported . . . . 6 Jan. 1903

PRINCES.

1851. Daniel, born 25 May, 1826; assassinated, 13 Aug. 1860.
1860. Nicolas, or Nikita (nephew), born 7 Oct. 1841; like his predecessors, a poet, and promoter of national education; married princess Milena, 8 Nov. 1860. *Issue:* (Helen, daughter, born 8 Jan. 1873; married the prince of Naples, at Rome, 24 Oct. 1896.)
Heir, Danilo Alexander, born 29 June, 1871; married the duchess Jutta (Militza) of Mecklenburg-Strelitz, 27 July, 1899.

MONTENOTTE, a village in Piedmont, memorable as being the site of the first victory gained over the Austrians by Napoleon Bonaparte, 12 April, 1796.

MONTEREAU (near Paris). On the bridge of Montereau, at his meeting with the dauphin, John the Fearless, duke of Burgundy, was killed by Tanneguy de Châtel in 1419. This event led to our Henry V. subduing France, the young duke Philip joining the English. Here the allied armies were defeated by the French, commanded by Napoleon, with great loss in killed and wounded; but it was one of his last triumphs, 18 Feb. 1814.

MONTEREY (Mexico), was taken by general Taylor after a three days' conflict with the Mexicans, 21-23 Sept. 1846.

MONTE-VIDEO (S. America), was taken by storm by the British forces under sir Samuel Auchmuty, but with the loss of nearly one-third of our brave troops, 3 Feb. 1807. It was evacuated 7 July the same year, in consequence of the severe repulse the British met with at Buenos-Ayres; see *Buenos-Ayres*. Monte-Video, a subject of dispute between Brazil and Buenos-Ayres, was given up to Uruguay, 1828. For recent war, etc., see *Brazil* and *Uruguay*. Fire at celebration service for Garibaldi, about 20 killed, 11 June, 1882. Latin-American scientific congress held here, 29-31 March, 1901. Stone laid for the new harbour works here, 18 July, 1901. The Victoria (memorial) hall, erected by British, opened, 14 Nov. 1902.

MONTFERRAT (Lombardy), HOUSE OF, celebrated in the history of the Crusades, began with Alderan, who was made marquis of Montferrat, by Otho, about 967. Conrad of Montferrat became lord of Tyre, and reigned from 1187 till 1191, when he was assassinated. William IV. died in a cage at Alexandria, having been thus imprisoned nineteen months, 1292. Violante, daughter of John II., married Andronicus Palæologus, emperor of the East. Their descendants ruled in Italy amid perpetual contests till 1533, when John

George Palæologus died without issue. His estates passed after much contention to Frederic II. Gonzaga, marquis of Mantua, in 1536, and next to the duke of Savoy.

MONTGOMERY, capital of Alabama, United States, founded 1817. Here the state convention passed the ordinance of secession from the union on 11 Jan. 1861; here the confederate congress met on 4 Feb. and elected Jefferson Davis president, and Alexander Stephens vice-president, of the confederate states of North America; and here they were inaugurated on 18 Feb. On 21 May the congress adjourned to meet on 20 July at Richmond, in Virginia, that state having joined the confederates and become the seat of war.

MONTH (from *mona*, Anglo-Saxon *moon*), the twelfth part of the calendar year. See *Year, Calendar, January* and other months, *French Revolutionary Calendar* and *Jewish Era*.

Lunar Month.—The period of one revolution of the moon (synodical); mean length, 29*d.* 12*h.* 44*m.* 2.87*s.*
Sidereal Month.—Time of moon's revolution from a star to the same again, 27*d.* 7*h.* 43*m.* 11.5*s.*
Solar Month.—The time the sun passes through one sign of the zodiac, 30*d.* 10*h.* 29*m.* 4.1*s.*
Information respecting the months of the Egyptians, Jews, Greeks, Romans, Persians, and other nations will be found in sir H. Nicolas's "Chronology of History." See under *Jewish era* and *Mahometanism.*

MONTI DI PIETÀ, charitable institutions for advancing money on pledges, were first established at Perugia, Florence, Mantua, and other Italian cities, 1462, *et seq.* The Franciscans, in 1493, began to receive interest, which was permitted by the pope, in 1515. *Monts de Piété*, established in France 1777, were suppressed by the Revolution, but restored, 1804; regulated by law, 1851-2; see *Pawnbroking*. The *Mont de Piété* started in England, failed, Aug. 1894.

MONTIEL (Spain), BATTLE OF, 14 March, 1369, between Peter the Cruel, king of Castile, and his brother Henry of Trastamare, aided by the French warrior, Bertrand du Guesclin. Peter was totally defeated, and afterwards treacherously slain.

MONTIGNY, see under *Firearms*.

MONTLHERY (Seine-et-Oise, France), site of an indecisive battle between Louis XI. and a party of his nobles, termed "The League of the Public Good," 16 July, 1465.

MONTMARTRE, HEIGHTS OF, near Paris, taken by Blücher, 30 March, 1814. They were fortified during the communist insurrection, March, 1871; and retaken by the army of Versailles, 28 May.

MONTMIRAIL (Marne, France). Here Napoleon defeated the allies, 11 Feb. 1814.

MONTPELLIER (S. France), built in the 8th century, prospered as the neighbouring city Maguelonne decreased. It was acquired by marriage by the king of Arragon, 1204; by the king of Majorca, 1276; was ceded to France, 1349; given to Charles the Bad, king of Navarre, in exchange for Mantes, &c., 1365; sequestered by France, 1378. It was seized by the Huguenots early in the reign of Henry III., and held by them till Sept. 1622, when it surrendered after a siege, followed by a treaty of peace, 20 Oct. Sexcentenary of the University celebrated, president Carnot present, 23 May, 1890. Mme. Bouisson, widow of a professor, bequeathed 1,500,000 f. to promote the study of medicine and theology, reported Nov. 1893. Valuable archives, pictures, etc. were destroyed by a fire at the exhibition, 18 Aug. 1896. Population in 1901, 76,364.

MONTREAL, the Birmingham of Canada, founded by the French, and named Ville Marie, 18 May, 1642. Population, 1881, 140,747; 1891, 216,650; 1901, 267,730 (with suburbs nearly 350,000).

Surrendered to the English . . . . . 8 Sept. 1760
Taken by the Americans . . . . . 12 Nov. 1775
Retaken by the British . . . . . 15 June, 1776
The church, Jesuits' college, prison, and many buildings burnt down . . . . . 6 June, 1803
Great military affray . . . . . 29 Sept. 1833
Bishopric founded 1836
Riots against the government . . . . . 6 Nov. 1837
The self-styled "loyalists" of Montreal assault the governor-general, lord Elgin; enter the parliament-house, drive out the members, and set fire to the building . . . . . 25 April, 1849
A bishopric established . . . . . „
A destructive fire . . . . . 23 Aug. 1850
Another, destroying 1200 houses; the loss estimated at a million sterling . . . . . 12 July, 1852
At an anti-papal lecture here by Gavazzi, riots ensued, and many lives were lost . . . . . 10 June, 1853
The cathedral destroyed by fire . . . . . 10 Dec. 1856
Victoria railway bridge (*which see*) formally opened by the prince of Wales . . . . . 25 Aug. 1860
Fierce riots at the attempt to bury Joseph Guibord, a Roman Catholic, while under censure, in the Roman Catholic cemetery . . . . . Sept. 1875
[He belonged to the "Institut Canadien," censured for possessing forbidden books; he died in 1869; after much litigation, the privy council judicial committee affirmed his right to burial against the clerical authorities.]
Riot at a memorial Romanist procession; 1 man killed . . . . . 26 Sept. „
Guibord buried with military and police escort, 16 Nov. „
Violent bread riots . . . . . 17 Dec. „
Fierce orange riots, with loss of life 12 July *et seq.* 1877
Ice palace erected and carnival held . . . . . 23 Jan. 1883
Prevalence of small pox; riots against compulsory vaccination suppressed, 29 Sept. 1,622 deaths in October 1885
Great inundation through ice gorge of the lower town; about 1,000,000*l.* damage; much privation 17–18 April, 1886
Great fires in 1887–8
The Longue Pointe Lunatic Asylum burnt, about 80 persons perish . . . . . 6 May, 1890
Visit of the duke and duchess of Connaught 2 June, „
Great fire at the Côte St. Antoine suburb; the loss about 50,000 dollars . . . . . 28 July, „
Visit of the comte de Paris, banquet . . . . . 25 Oct. „
Great labour demonstration . . . . . 7 Sept. 1891
Destructive earthquake, no deaths . . . . . 27 Nov. 1893
Attempted destruction of the Nelson monument, by dynamite, 3 militia officers arrested, 20 Nov. 1893; Mercier, Pelland and Demartigny plead guilty, fined 25 dollars each . . . . . 18 Jan. 1894
Statue of sir John Macdonald unveiled by the earl of Aberdeen . . . . . 6 June, 1895
The Lachine rapids, 20,000 to 25,000 horse power utilized for electric lighting; works opened, 25 Sept. 1896
Fire at a hospital in St. Hyacinthe, 13 deaths, 16 May, 1898
M'Gill university; 3 new buildings founded and endowed by sir Wm. C. McDonald, philanthropist (knt. Dec. 1898); opened by lord Minto, gov.-gen., 20 Dec. 1898; endowments by lord and lady Strathcona and others.
Great demonstration on the departure of the 2nd (French and English) Canadian contingent for South Africa . . . . . 4 Jan. 1900
A statue of the queen, by princess Louise, unveiled by the earl of Minto . . . . . 1 Nov. „
Great fire; important buildings burnt, 2 deaths; estimated damage over 4,000,000 dols. . . 23 Jan. 1901
Visit of the duke and duchess of Cornwall (see *Canada*) . . . . . 18, 19 Sept. „

Lord Strathcona presents the king in London with an address and a gold medal from the citizens of Montreal . . . . . . 14 April, 1902

MONTSERRAT, a W. India island, discovered by Columbus in 1493, and settled by the British in 1632. It has several times been taken by the French, but was secured to the British in 1783. Destructive floods, 75 deaths, reported, 4 Dec. 1896; see *Mansion house*, 1897. Terrific hurricane, 74 natives killed, see *West Indies*, 7 Aug.; great fire at Plymouth, reported, 23 Sept. 1899. Population, 1891, 11,762; 1901, 12,215. See *Leeward Isles*.

MONUMENT OF LONDON, built by sir Christopher Wren, 1671-7. The pedestal is forty feet high, and the edifice altogether 202 feet, that being the distance of its base from the spot where the fire which it commemorates commenced. It is the loftiest isolated column in the world. Its erection cost about 14,500*l*. The staircase is of black marble, consisting of 345 steps.* Fall of part of the stone coping, no one injured, 25 Sept. 1888; examined and repaired; re-opened 14 Jan. 1889. Of the four original inscriptions, three were Latin, and the following in English,—cut in 1681, obliterated by James II.; re-cut in the reign of William III.; and finally erased by order of the common council, 26 Jan. 1831. They produced Pope's indignant lines:—

> "Where London's column, pointing at the skies,
> Like a tall bully, lifts the head, and lies."

THIS PILLAR WAS SET VP IN PERPETVAL REMEMBRANCE OF THAT MOST DREADFUL BURNING OF THIS PROTESTANT CITY, BEGUN AND CARRYED ON BY Y[e] TREACHERY AND MALICE OF Y[e] POPISH FACTION, IN Y[e] BEGINNING OF SEPTEM. IN Y[e] YEAR OF OUR LORD 1666, IN ORDER TO Y[e] CARRYING ON THEIR HORRID PLOT FOR EXTIRPATING Y[e] PROTESTANT RELIGION AND OLD ENGLISH LIBERTY, AND Y[e] INTRODUCING POPERY AND SLAVERY.

MONUMENTS, see *Ancient*. An act passed 22 July, 1878, empowers the Metropolitan board of works to take care of Cleopatra's needle, and other monuments.

MONZA, or Monsa, formerly capital of the kingdom of Lombardy, frequently besieged. The cathedral was founded in the sixth century. The iron crown of Italy (*which see*) was kept here till 1859. See *Italy*, Oct. 1891.

MOODKEE (India). Here, on 18 Dec. 1845, the Sikhs attacked the advanced guard of the British, commanded by general Gough, and were repulsed three miles, losing many men and fifteen pieces of cannon. Sir Robert Sale was mortally wounded. The battle preceded that of Ferozeshah (*which see*).

MOOLTAN (N. W. India), an ancient city, was stormed by Runjeet Sing, 1818. Here his son, Moolraj Sing, ruler of the Sikhs, treacherously murdered Mr. Vans Agnew and lieutenant Anderson, 21 April, 1848. Several conflicts took place between the British and the Sikhs, in which the latter were beaten, and Mooltan taken after a protracted siege, 2-22 Jan. 1849.

* William Green, a weaver, fell from this monument, 25 June, 1750. A man named Thomas Craddock, a baker, precipitated himself from its summit, 7 July, 1780. Mr. Lyon Levy, a Jewish diamond merchant, of considerable respectability, threw himself from it, 18 Jan. 1810; as did more recently three other persons: in consequence of which a fence was placed round the railing of the gallery in 1839.

MOON. Opacity of the moon, and the true causes of lunar eclipses, taught by Thales, 640 B.C. Hipparchus made observations on the moon at Rhodes, 127 B.C. Posidonius accounted for the tides from the motion of the moon, and said that the moon borrows her light from the sun, 79 B.C. *Diog. Laert.*

Maps of the moon constructed by Hevelius, 1647. Cassini 1680
Beer and Mädler's map published 1834
Professor John Phillips invited the British Association to make arrangements to obtain a "systematic representation of the physical aspect of the moon" 1862
Photographs of the moon taken by Draper at New York, 1840; by Bond, 1850; by Mr. Warren de la Rue, 1857; by Rutherford 1871
Hansen's "Tables of the Moon," calculated at the expense of the British and Danish governments, published at the cost of the latter . . 1857
The British Association "lunar committee" publish two sections of a map of the moon, on a scale of 200 inches to her diameter . . . July, 1867
The earl of Rosse made experiments on the radiation of heat from the moon . . . 1868-99
Professor S. P. Langley, of Washington, U.S., published the results of experiments relative to the temperature of the moon . . . Nov. 1887
Professor J. F. Julius Schmidt, of Athens, completed his map of the moon after 34 years' work: diameter 2 metres 1874
Mr. James Nasmyth and Mr. J. Carpenter published the result of many years' observations, in "The Moon" . . . . 1874; new edition, 1885
Mr. Edmund Neison published "The Moon and the Conditions and Configurations of its Surface" July, 1876
Professor Schmidt's map published at Berlin . . 1878
Mr. C. V. Boys, of South Kensington, described at the Royal Institution how he obtained evidence of the heat of the moon by means of his very sensitive thermopile composed of quartz filaments, according to the anticipations of professor Piazzi Smyth . . . 17 April *et seq.* 1890
Prof. Pickering imputes many of the changes on the surface of the moon to the growth of lunar vegetation; other distinct changes noted in the canals, &c. . . . . . June, 1902.

See *Eclipses*.

"MOONLIGHTERS," a name given to the perpetrators of night outrages in 1880. See *Ireland*, 1885.

MOORS, formerly the natives of Mauritania (*which see*), but afterwards the name given to the Numidians and others, and now applied to the natives of Morocco and the neighbourhood. They frequently rebelled against the Roman emperors, and assisted Genseric and the Vandals in their invasion of Africa, 429. They resisted for a time the progress of the Saracens or Arab Mahometans, but were overcome in 707, and in 1019 were by them introduced into Spain, where their arms were long victorious. In 1063 they were defeated in Sicily by Roger Guiscard. The Moorish kingdom of Grenada was set up in 1237, and lasted till 1492, when it fell before Ferdinand V. of Castile, mainly owing to internal discord. The expulsion of the Moors from Spain was decreed by Charles V., but not fully carried into effect till 1609, when the bigotry of Philip III. inflicted this great injury to his country. About 1518 the Moors established the piratical states of Algiers and Tunis (*which see*). In the history of Spain, the Arabs and Moors must not be confounded.

MOPLAHS, industrious fanatical Mahometans in Malabar, E. Indies, gave trouble by their attacks on Hindoos and the British, especially in 1845; an outbreak was suppressed about 15 Sept. 1873.

MORAL PHILOSOPHY, the science of ethics, defined as the knowledge of our duty, and the art of being virtuous and happy. Socrates (about 430 B.C.) is regarded as the father of ancient, and Grotius (about 1623) the father of modern moral philosophy; see *Ethics* and *Philosophy*.

MORAT (Switzerland), where Charles the Bold of Burgundy was completely defeated by the Swiss, 22 June, 1476. A monument, constructed of the bones of the vanquished, was destroyed by the French in 1798, and a stone column erected. 400th anniversary kept, 1876.

MORAVIA, an Austrian province, occupied by the Slavonians about 548, and conquered by the Avars and Bohemians, who submitted to Charlemagne. About 1000 it was subdued by Boleslas of Poland, but recovered by Ulrich of Bohemia in 1030. After various changes, Moravia and Bohemia were amalgamated into the Austrian dominions in 1526. Moravia was invaded by the Prussians in 1866, and they established their head quarters at Brünn, the capital, 13 July. The demand of the Moravians for home rule was resisted Oct. 1871. Strike of 30,000 coal miners at Ostrau, and rioting suppressed by military, 16, 17 April, 1890. Population in 1890, 2,276,870; 1900, 2,435,081.

MORAVIANS, or UNITED BRETHREN, said to have been part of the Hussites, who withdrew into Moravia in the 15th century; but the brethren assert that their sect was derived from the Greek church in the 9th century. In 1722 they formed a settlement (called *Herrnhut*, the watch of the Lord) on the estate of count Zinzendorf. Their church consisted of 500 persons in 1727. They were introduced into England by count Zinzendorf about 1738; he died at Chelsea in June, 1760. In 1851 they had thirty-two chapels in England. They are zealous missionaries, and founded settlements in foreign parts, about 1732. London Association founded, 1817. Mr. Thos. Morton, a British merchant, who died 11 Sept. 1897, bequeathed a large sum, conditionally, to the Moravians.

MORAY FLOODS, see *Inundations*, 1829.

MORDAUNT, see *Administrations*, 1689.

MORDEN COLLEGE (Blackheath), almshouses for decayed merchants, with pensions, established by sir John Morden, 1695; opened, 1702.

MOREA, a name given to the Peloponnesus in the 13th century; see *Greece*.

MORETON BAY (New S. Wales). The colony founded here in 1859 has since been named *Queensland* (*which see*).

MORGANATIC* MARRIAGES, when the left hand is given instead of the right, between a man of superior and a woman of inferior rank, in which it is stipulated that the latter and her children shall not enjoy the rank or inherit the possessions of the former. The children are legitimate. Such marriages are frequently contracted in Germany by royalty and the higher nobility. It has been asserted that our George I. was thus married to the duchess of Kendal; the late duke of Sussex to lady Cecilia Underwood; Frederic VI. of Denmark to the countess of Danner, 7 Aug. 1850; and several Austrian princes, recently; the grand duke Paul of Russia with Mme. Pistolkors, reported, 2 Dec. 1902.

* Said to be derived from *Morgengabe*, the gift of a husband of a limited part of his property to such a bride on the morning after the marriage.

MORGARTEN (Switzerland). 1300 Swiss engaged 20,000 Austrians, commanded by the duke Leopold, whom they completely defeated, 15 Nov. 1315, upon the heights of Morgarten, overlooking the defile through which the enemy was to enter their territory from Zug.

MORICE DANCE, an ancient dance peculiar to some of the country parts of England, and, it is said, also to Scotland: it was performed before James I. in Herefordshire.

MORIER INCIDENT, see *Prussia*, 1889.

MORISONIANS, followers of the Rev. James Morison of Kilmarnock, suspended for heterodoxy, 1841.

MORLEY HALL and Welbeck Institute, Regent Street, London, for the Young Women's Christian Association, opened by princess Christian, 22 Nov. 1886.

MORMONS (calling themselves the Church of Jesus Christ of *the* LATTER-DAY SAINTS). This sect derives its origin from Joseph Smith, called the Prophet, who announced in 1823, at Palmyra, New York, that he had had a vision of the angel Moroni. In 1827 he said that he found the book of Mormon, written on gold plates in Egyptian characters. This book is said to have been written about 1812, by a clergyman named Solomon Spaulding (or by Martin Harris, who died Sept. 1875), as a religious romance in imitation of the scripture style. It was translated and published in America in 1830, in England in 1841. It fell into the hands of Rigdon and Smith, who determined to palm it off as a new revelation. The Mormons command the payment of tithes, permit polygamy, encourage labour, and believe in their leaders working miracles. Missionaries are propagating these doctrines in Europe with more success than would be expected.

The Mormonites organise a church at Kirkland, Ohio 1830
They found Zion, in Jackson county, Missouri 1831-2
From 1833 to 1839 the sect endured much persecution, and, driven from place to place, was compelled to travel westwards; till the city Nauvoo on the Mississippi was laid out and a temple was built 1840-1
Joseph and his brother Hyram, when in prison on a charge of treason, shot by an infuriated mob, and Brigham Young chosen seer . . . June, 1844
Much harassed by their neighbours; departure from Nauvoo determined on 1845
The Great Salt Lake chosen "for an everlasting abode," and taken possession of . . 24 July, 1847
The valley surveyed by order of the United States government 1849
The provisional government abolished and the Utah territory recognised by the United States; Brigham Young appointed the first governor; and the university of Deserét was founded . . . 1849-50
The population, 11,354 1851
The crops at the Utah settlement said to be destroyed by locusts . . . . . Aug. 1855
The United States judge at Utah resigned from inability to discharge his functions, in consequence of the violent and treasonable conduct of the Mormons, and their leader, Brigham Young 1857
A conference of Mormon elders, &c., was held in London; offensive speeches made and songs sung advocating polygamy . . . . . 1 Sept. ,,
The United States government sent an army to Utah: a compromise was entered into, and peace was established by governor Cummings in June, 1858

A Mormonite meeting at Southampton . 18 Feb. 1861
A French Mormonite priest preached at Paris in Oct. 1862
"Latter-day Saints'" meetings held in London . 1865
Utah settlement visited by Hepworth Dixon: he stated that it contained 200,000 persons, and an army of 20,000 rifles. ("New America," published in 1867) 1866
Reported schisms: through increasing opposition to polygamy . . . . . . June, 1867
Synod held in Store-street, London (London conference said to include 1172 members) 5 April, 1868
650 new Mormonites sailed from Liverpool for Utah, 6 June,
Bill depriving polygamists of civic rights passed U. S. house of representatives . . March, 1870
Brigham Young ordered to be tried for bigamy, flies; Hawkins, a Mormonite elder, sentenced to three years' imprisonment for adultery, end of Oct. 1871
Brigham Young surrenders for trial, 2 Jan.; proceedings annulled by the supreme court about May, 1872
Brigham Young resigns temporal powers, 10 April, 1873
The Mormonite conferences at the Holborn Amphitheatre . . . . 25 May, ,,
Nineteen missionaries for Britain arrive at Liverpool 12 Nov. ,,
Brigham Young again indicted for polygamy, about 15 Oct. 1874
Adjudged to support one of his wives while she sues for divorce, March; imprisoned in his own house, for non-compliance, Nov.; discharged . Dec. 1875
Bp. J. D. Lee shot for his share in Mountain Meadows massacre, (Brigham Young suspected,) (see *Massacres*) . . . . 23 March, 1877
Death of Brigham Young, aged 76 . 29 Aug. ,,
John Taylor, chief of 12 apostles, became president of the church . . . . . Sept. ,,
Conference in London opened . 30 Sept. ,,
Orson Pratt, a leader and colleague of Joseph Smith, died . . . . Nov. 1881
Six meeting-houses in London, March, 1882; estimated 85,000 English converts . . . 1837-82
Polygamy in the United States abolished by Act passed . . . . 23 March, 1882
Great meeting at Salt Lake; 57 missionaries sent out . . . . 6 Oct. 1883
Senator Edmund's bill for suppression of the Mormon church passed by the U.S. senate (38–7) 9 Jan. 1886
Meeting of Mormon elders and missionaries at St. George's Hall, Langham-place, London 12 Oct. ,,
John Taylor died . . . . 25 July, 1887
Decree for the suppression of the church; appealed against . . . . Oct. 1888
A new temple erected in Salt Lake City, capable of holding 14,000 persons, the granite walls 20 ft. thick at the base, taper upwards to 6 ft. reported Aug. 1889
Many Mormons disenfranchised for taking an illegal oath; the "Gentiles" obtain majority in elections . . . . Feb. 1890
President Woodruff and a conference of elders put forth a profession of faith, recognizing the Bible and the Book of Mormon as the Word of God, gifts of tongues, &c., and renouncing polygamy, about 25 Sept.; adopted by the church at a great meeting . . . . 6 Oct. ,,
144,352 Mormons in the United States, N. A.; census of 1890. Mr. Joseph Smith, jun., son of the founder of Mormonism, heads a party opposed to polygamy (about 30,000 members) Aug. 1891
New settlement on land granted by the Mexican government in N. Mexico; arrangements made by Mr. John Young, son of Brigham Young; a large number of Mormons ready to start from Utah, reported . . . . June, 1892
Amnesty granted for past polygamic marriages, future to be punished by law, about . 5 Jan. 1893
Dedication of the great temple at Salt Lake City, built in 40 years, stated cost, 5,000,000 dollars 6 April, *et seq.* ,,
Suppression of polygamy generally accepted July, 1894
Pardon granted to polygamists, by proclamation 27 Sept. ,,
Ten colonies in N. Mexico, reported prosperous, Jan. 1897
Mr Lorenzo Snow, 5th president of the church, died, aged 87, about 10 Oct.; succeeded by Mr. Joseph Smith . . . . 18 Oct. 1901

MORNING ADVERTISER first published, 8 Feb. 1794.

MORNING CHRONICLE, *Whig*, 1770, *extinct* 1762.

MORNING POST, fashionable daily paper, favourable to the Whigs and High Church party, first appeared, 2 Nov. 1772. Conservative, 1874. Price reduced to 1*d.*, 27 June, 1881.

MOROCCO, or **MAROCCO**, an empire in North Africa, formerly Mauritania (*which see*). In 1051 it was subdued for the Fatimite caliphs by the Almoravides, who eventually extended their dominion into Spain. These were succeeded by the Almohades (1121), the Merinites (1270), and in 1516 by the Scherifs, pretended descendants of Mahomet, the now reigning dynasty. The Moors have had frequent wars with the Spaniards and Portuguese, due to piracy. Population, 1891, about 8,000,000; Fez, the capital, 140, to 150,000.

Invasion of Sebastian of Portugal, who perishes with his army at the battle of Alcazar 4 Aug. 1578
Tangiers (*which see*) acquired by England, 1662; given up 1683
The Moors attack the French in Algeria at the instigation of Abd-el-Kader; the prince de Joinville bombards Tangiers, 6 Aug., and Mogador 16 Aug. 1844
Marshal Bugeaud defeats the Moors at the river Isly, and acquires the title of duke . 14 Aug. ,,
Peace between France and Morocco . 10 Sept. ,,
The Spaniards, who possess several places on the coast of Morocco (Ceuta, Penon de Velez, &c.), having suffered much annoyance by Moorish pirates, declare war . . . . . 22 Oct. 1859
Negotiations fruitless: the Spanish government increasing their demands as the sultan yielded; the English government interfered in vain. *For the war*, see *Spain* 1859-60
A Moorish ambassador (the first since the time of Charles II.) in London. (He gave 200*l.* to the lord mayor for the London charities) June-Aug. 1860
The British government gave a guarantee for a loan of 426,000*l.* to the sultan to meet his engagements with Spain . . . . 24 Oct. 1861
Insurrection of a pretender, Elkadin ben Abderahman, suppressed . . . . . Dec. 1873
Prince Sidi Shereef visits Britain . . Aug. 1877
The grand sherif of Wazan marries an English wife; liberates his slaves, &c.; persecuted, becomes a French subject . . . . Jan. 1884
The rebel tribes of Benin Guild district defeated after a severe engagement . . 25 June, 1888
The sultan's visit to Tangier delayed . Sept. ,,
An exploring expedition under Mr. Joseph Thomson and Mr. Harold Crichton Browne aided by the Royal and Geographical societies, spring and summer, ,,
Disputes among the foreign consuls; abuse of their powers and consequent Moorish resistance, autumn, ,,
The sultan visits Tetuan, 5 Sept.; Tangier, 22 Sept. 1889
Dispute with Spain respecting the seizure of a Spanish coasting vessel, *Miguel Texesa*, settled by due reparation . . . . . about 29 Sept. ,,
Affray between Moors and the Spanish cavalry of the fortress Melilla, several killed, 20 July; peace restored . . . . 25 July, 1890
The sultan defeats rebel tribes, and beheads 80 prisoners, reported 20 Aug.; further defeats of the rebels reported . . . . . 26 Sept. ,,
The Moorish government agrees to pay 50,000*l.* as indemnity for murder of persons connected with a British factory at Cape Juby in 1889 . Feb. 1891
Sir William Kirby Green, the able British minister to Morocco, died 25 Feb.; succeeded by sir Charles Euan Smith, from Zanzibar . . . ,,
Hostility of the Kabyles and other tribes to the governor; two British war-vessels arrive off Tangier, about 5 Jan.; 3 foreign vessels arrive, about 13 Jan. 1892

Tranquillity restored by the sultan dismissing the governor, and appointing a successor . 22 Jan. 1892
Sir C. Euan Smith received by the sultan at Fez, 14 May, ,,
A new commercial treaty considered . . May, ,,
Rebellion in Angera . . . . . . June, ,,
Sir C. Euan Smith's negotiations for a commercial treaty fail; the mission withdraws to Tangier 22 July *et seq.* ,,
Rebellion of 1,200 Angherites, or Anjerites, headed by Hmam, a desperate fanatic (chiefly against the governor), near Tangier, about 27 July; indecisive conflicts, July, Aug.; negotiations, 16, 17 Aug.; the Angherites defeated after severe fighting; they sue for peace, 4 Sept.; a new governor appointed, reported 13 Sept.; peace proclaimed, 16 Sept.; agreement signed . . . . 26 Oct. ,,
A French mission, under count d'Aubigny, arrives at Fez, 4 Oct.; departs, having obtained some concessions . . . . 5 Dec. 1892
Sir Charles Euan Smith absent on leave, 3 Oct.; Mr. Charles Eliot chargé d'affaires . 19 Oct. ,,
Juan Trinadad, a British subject, killed in a fracas at Tangier, 1 Dec. 1892; reparation demanded, 5 Jan.; an ultimatum sent to the sultan by Mr. Charles Eliot, requiring an answer within 48 hours . . . . 9 Jan. 1893
Three Moorish night-guards imprisoned for the murder of Juan Trinadad . . . 10 Jan. ,,
The sultan pays an indemnity of 1,000*l*. . 19 Jan. ,,
Reappearance of Ould Hmam in Anghera; fresh outrages, about 22 Jan., he is captured and taken to Tangier . . . . reported 24 Feb. ,,
Colonel sir J. West Ridgeway warmly received at Madrid, 25 Jan.; at Tangier, 31 Jan.; received by the commissioner for foreign affairs, 9 Feb.; returns to England . . . . 31 July, ,,
The mountaineers enter Wazan, and are subdued with much slaughter, reported . . 20 Feb. ,,
Renewed fighting; the tribes defeated with much slaughter, reported . . . . 9 July ,,
Mr. Ernest Satow, British minister, arrives, 29 Aug. ,,
About 7,000 Moors (Riff tribe) attack Fort Guaraich, near Ceuta, held by 300 Spanish troops, under general Margallo at Melilla, severe fighting all day, the Moors repulsed . . 2 Oct. ,,
The Moors driven from their entrenchments 21 Oct. ,,
The Spaniards repulsed, 27 Oct.; general Margallo killed, his body and cannon recovered, Spanish loss 22 killed and 81 wounded, 28 Oct.; general Macias appointed to the command, 29 Oct.; skirmishes, 3 Nov.; Melilla distressed, the Moors make strong entrenchments, 7 Nov.; the sultan condemns the action of the tribesmen and threatens punishment, reported . 9 Nov. ,,
Reinforcements sent from Spain . . . . Nov. ,,
Marshal Campos takes the command, 28 Nov.; reconstruction of Fort Sidi Guaraich begun, without opposition . . . . . . 30 Nov. ,,
Terms of peace proposed by marshal Campos to the tribes . . . . 7 Dec. ,,
Moorish concessions, two chiefs surrendered 27 Dec. ,,
Arrival of marshal Campos as Spanish ambassador in Morocco, 29 Jan.; received by the sultan 31 Jan 1894
Arrival of Moorish troops at Melilla, to punish the Riff tribes, etc. . . . . about 3 Feb. ,,
Spanish claims acceded to (792,000*l*.), 10 March, 1894; treaty completed . . . . Feb. 1895
Revolt of the Kabyles in the south, the government troops defeated, near Mazagan, reported 19 Aug. 1894
British and Spanish war-vessels sent to Mazagan 19, 20 Aug. ,,
Peace made with the Kabyles, reported . 13 Sept. ,,
British mission under Mr. Ernest Satow, warmly received at Fez by the sultan, 29 Oct. 1894; retires successful . . . . . 20 April, 1895
A British company's settlement at Cape Juby bought by Morocco; convention signed . April, ,,
French Mission received at Fez . . . 27 May, ,,
Sir Arthur Nicolson appointed minister . 26 June, ,,
Indemnity claimed for murder of a German subject; agreed to . . . . . . 11 Aug. 1895
Death of the shereef of Wazan, benevolent citizen, Oct. ,,
Sir Arthur Nicolson, British minister, arrives at Tangiers . . . . . . 3 Oct. ,,
Arab rebellion, Saffi attacked, severe fighting 7–11 Nov. ,,
Sir Arthur Nicolson cordially received by the sultan, 13 April, 1896; returns to Tangier, 22 May, 1896
Liberal grants from the sultan for works at Tangier, announced . . . . . . 27 May, ,,
The sultan marches with about 60,000 men to awe the Riffians and disaffected districts, 16 Sept.; rebels defeated at Tadla, Oct. 1897; rebels and prisoners treated with great cruelty, Jan. *et seq.* 1898
Trial of Mr. Gray and the crew of the British steamer Tourmaline for alleged attempt to smuggle arms into Sus, begins at Tangier, 14 June; all sentenced to short terms of imprisonment 2 July ,,
[Major Spilsbury tried and acquitted at Gibraltar, 19 April, 1899.]
Indemnity paid to the Portuguese and Italian governments for Riffian piracy (1898) . 3 Jan. 1899
Tribal fighting on the frontier, great slaughter, Dec. 1898–22 March, ,,
Compensation to Germany for losses in 1896, settled . . . . March, ,,
Kaid Gilooli's troops attack Sus and loot European property; estimated loss, 20,000*l*., reported, 28 April, ,,
Sid Ahmed Ben Musa, grand vizier and stern ruler, dies . . . . 13 May, 1900
The Moorish government protests against French encroachments upon Twat and Igli as a violation of the frontier treaty of 1845 (see *Algeria* 1900), and asks for arbitration . . . . 9 June, ,,
Great excitement at Fez owing to the French occupation of the Twat oases; M. Marcos Essagin murdered by the mob . . . . 28 June, ,,
The powers again appealed to . . . 20 Aug. ,,
Kaid Mehadi appointed grand vizier, May, 1901; received by the king in London, 10 June; visits France, Germany, and other powers; returns, about 29 July, 1901
A *modus vivendi* with France regarding the Algerian frontier settled . . . . . end July, ,,
Moorish mission visits Paris and St. Petersburg, July–Aug.; returns . . . . . 25 Aug. ,,
Village raided near Tangier, tribal disorders increasing . . . . 25 Sept. ,,
Free trade between the coast towns (due to lord Lansdowne) instituted . . . . . Sept. ,,
The government pays 30,000 dol. as indemnity to Spain for the abduction of 2 Spanish captives by the Kabyles, in May, and 1,600 dol. to the parents . . . . 31 Oct. ,,
Destructive floods and terrific cloud-burst at Saffi; about 100 deaths . . . . 29 Dec. ,,
Berber raids and rising, Aug.; their villages burnt and a tribe routed near Mekinez . 4 Sept. 1902
Death of the sultan's mother an enlightened lady, 6 Sept. ,,
Prison reforms started by the sultan, Nov. 1901; work progressing rapidly . . . . Sept. ,,
Submission of Berber tribes; armistice discussed, 25, 26 Sept. ,,
Algerian-Morocco frontier settled . . mid Oct. ,,
Mr. D. Cooper, missionary, shot near Fez by a fanatic, who was seized and executed (the sultan presents Mrs. Cooper with 1,000*l*., Nov.) 17 Oct. ,,
Rebels, under Omar Zarhuni "Bu Hamara," pretender to the throne, defeated near Tesa, 3 Nov. ,,
The Benider Kabyles defeated near Tetuan, 11, 14 Nov. ,,
Revolt increases: the sultan is defeated at Tesa, 29 Nov.; the pretender holds Tesa and surrounding districts . . . . 9 Dec. ,,
Rout of the sultan's army, 17 guns captured, near Tesa (see *Times*, 29 Dec.) . . . . 22 Dec. ,,
The sultan holds Fez, 23 Dec.; many tribes return and swear fealty, reported . . . 4 Jan. 1903
Villages near Tangier attacked by Fahsias, who are repulsed . . . . 13 Jan. ,,
French loan of 7,500,000 francs . . . 27 Jan. ,,

Skirmishing in the Fez district, many rebels killed and captured . . 19 Jan., 14, 15 Feb. 1903
The sultan's brother, Mulai Mohammed, proclaimed sultan by the Riff tribes . . . . 3 April, ,,
Fort Trajana captured by the rebels, reported, 13 April, ,,
Mekinez attacked and pillaged, reported, 22 April, ,,
Anarchy reported in Gharbia . . . 29 April, ,,
Arzila besieged in April, relieved . . 2 May, ,,
Defeat of the sultan's troops at Zelwan, reported, 7 May, ,,
Tetuan attacked, suburbs destroyed, 11 May; fort of Tesa captured, villages pillaged and burnt; Teutan relieved, reported . . . 16 May, ,,
Zimmuris desert the sultan, afterwards attacked, many killed, reported . . . 22 May, ,,
Heavy loss of sultan's troops near Rebat, reported, 26 May, ,,
Zenaga bombarded by the French . . 8 June, ,,
Village of Zinat burnt by the troops; Mr. Harris, correspondent of the *Times*, captured near there by the rebels, 16 June; released . . 6 July, ,,
Tesa recovered from the rebels by El Menebhi, 7 July, ,,
Continued fighting in the Teutan district, 20 July, ,,
Rebel villages near Tangier burnt by the sultan's troops . . . . . . 21 July, ,,
Severe fighting, 6, 7 Aug.; the rebel forces under Mulai Mohammed routed at Meknessa; other successes by sultan's troops, reported 13 Aug. ,,
Troops defeated with loss near Tesa, reported, 28 Aug. ,,
Native officials confer with commander of sultan's troops near Tangier respecting an armistice with the local rebel tribes; 1,200 Moorish soldiers sent to Ujda, return there after defeat by the pretenders at Sidi Mellouk, reported, early Sept. ,,
Kaid sir H. Maclean arrives at Tangier from Fez *en route* for London; expresses confidence the sultan will shortly crush the rebellion if a loan of 25,000,000 francs, preferably an Anglo-French loan, could be obtained . . 14 Sept. ,,
Sultan orders all Europeans except the consuls to leave Fez . . . . . . 18 Sept. ,,
Pourparlers between England and France respecting the guarantee of the *status quo* in Morocco, by agreement with the other powers, leaving the solution of affairs to France, interrupted by British ministerial crisis; no agreement arrived at by the powers . . reported early Oct. ,,
Troops commanded by the sultan in person, severely repulsed by the rebels . . . . . 12 Oct. ,,
Meeting of London shipowners and merchants connected with the Morocco trade; resolution passed to present a memorial to the government urging the adoption of a policy to maintain the equal trading conditions at present existing in Morocco . . . . 21 Oct. ,,
Sultan abandons his expedition against the rebels, which has proved a failure, sultan returning to Fez; the road to Fez blocked by the rebels; general state of anarchy, reported . 28 Oct. ,,

SULTANS.

1822. Muley Abderahman.
1859. Sidi Muley Mohammed, Sept., died Sept. 1873.
1873. Muley Hassan (son), proclaimed 25 Sept.; died 7 June, 1894.
1894. Muley Abdul Aziz (son, born 1879), proclaimed, 11 June.

MORPHIA, an alkaloid, discovered in opium by Sertürner, in 1803.

MORPHOLOGY (Greek, *morphe*, form), the science of form and structure, as distinguished from physiology, studied in the 19th century, by Goethe, Gegenbaur, Haeckel, and others.

MORRILL TARIFF, see *United States*, 1861.

MORRIS DANCE, see *Morice*.

MORTALITY TABLES have been frequently compiled. The Northampton tables (for 1735-80), by Dr. Price; the Carlisle tables (for 1780-87), by Dr. Hailsham; see *Annuities* and *Bills of Mortality*.

MORTARA ABDUCTION, see *Jews*, 1858.

MORTARS, a short gun with a large bore, and close chamber, for throwing bombs; said to have been used at Naples in 1435, and first made in England in 1543. The mortar left by Soult at Cadiz in Spain was fixed in St. James's-park in Aug. 1816. On 19 Oct. 1857, a colossal mortar, constructed by Mr. Robert Mallet, was tried at Woolwich; with a charge of 70 lbs. it threw a shell weighing 2550 lbs. $1\frac{1}{2}$ mile horizontally, and about $\frac{3}{4}$ mile in height.

MORTELLA TOWERS, see *Martello*.

MORTIMER'S CROSS (Herefordshire). The earl of Pembroke and the Lancastrians were here severely defeated by the young duke of York, afterwards Edward IV., 2 Feb. 1461. He assumed the throne as Edward IV. in March following.

MORTMAIN ACTS (*mort main*, dead hand). When the survey of all the land in England was made by William I., 1085-6, the whole was found to amount to 62,215 knights' fees, of which the church then possessed 28,015, to which additions were afterwards made, till the 7th of Edward I., 1279, when the statute of mortmain was passed, from a fear that the estates of the church might grow too bulky. By this act it was made unlawful to give any estates to the church without the king's leave; and this act, by a supplemental provision, was made to reach all lay-fraternities, or corporations, in the 15th of Richard II., 1391. Mortmain being such a state of possession as makes property inalienable, it is said to be in a dead hand. Several statutes have been passed on this subject; legacies by mortmain were especially restricted by the 9th Geo. II., c. 36 (1736). Law consolidated and amended 1888; 1891, 1892.

MOSAIC WORK (the Roman *opus tessellatum*), is of Asiatic origin, and is probably referred to in *Esther*, ch. i. 6, about 519 B.C. It had attained to great excellence in Greece, in the time of Alexander and his successors, when Sosos of Pergamus, the most renowned Mosaic artist of antiquity, flourished. He acquired great fame by his accurate representation of an "unswept floor after a feast." The Romans also excelled in Mosaic work, as evidenced by the innumerable specimens preserved. Byzantine Mosaics date from the 4th century after Christ. The art was revived in Italy by Tafi, Gaddi, Cimabue, and Giotto, who designed Mosaics, and introduced a higher style in the 13th century. In the 16th century Titian and Veronese also designed subjects for this art. The practice of copying paintings in Mosaics came into vogue in the 17th century; and there is now a workshop in the Vatican where chemical science is employed in the production of colours, and where 20,000 different tints are kept. In 1861, Dr. Salviati of Venice had established his manufacture of "Enamel-mosaics," and in July, 1864, he fixed a large enamel Mosaic picture in one of the spandrils under the dome of St. Paul's cathedral, London. He also executed commissions for queen Victoria and other persons. He died Feb. 1890, aged 74. See *Paul's, St.*, 1896.

MOSANDRIUM. See *Philippium*.

MOSCOW, the ancient capital of Russia, was founded, it is said, by Dolgorouki, about 1147. The occupation of the south of Russia by the Mongols, in 1235, led to Moscow becoming the capital, and beginning with Jaroslav II., 1238, its princes became the reigning dynasty. It is regarded as a holy city by the Russians. Population, 1886: province 2,204,930; city, 1885, 753,469; 9 Feb. 1897, 988,610; 1900, 1,023,817.

Cathedral of the Assumption built, 1326; of the Transfiguration 1328
The Kremlin founded 1367
Moscow plundered by Timour 1382
By the Tartars 1451, 1477
Massacre of Demetrius and his Polish adherents, the "Matins of Moscow" . . . 27 May, 1606
Moscow ravaged by Ladislas of Poland in . . . 1611
The university founded 1705
Entered by Napoleon I. and the French, 14 Sept.; the governor, Rostopchin, is said, doubtfully, to have ordered it to be set on fire (11,840 houses burnt, besides palaces and churches) . 15 Sept. 1812
The French evacuate Moscow . . . . Oct. ,,
Railway to St. Petersburg opened 1851
Industrial exhibition . . . . . . 16 July, 1865
Very great fire, about 50 houses burnt . 18 June, 1876
Zvartofsky's weaving-works burnt; about 24 persons perish . . . . . . 8 March, 1880
Exhibition of Russian arts and manufactures, summer, 1882
St. Saviour's cathedral (erected to commemorate the retreat of the French in 1812), founded by Nicholas I., 27 July, 1838; consecrated 7 June, 1883
The French exhibition of arts and manufactures solemnly opened, 11 May; visited by the czar and czarina . . . . . . 30 May, 1891
Admiral Gervais and the officers of the French fleet enthusiastically received . . . 7 Aug. ,,
Coronation of the czar, see *Russia* . . 26 May, 1896
The Panin hall, public library, burnt . 23 Aug. ,,
Student riots, 1,114 persons arrested, 662 found guilty, reported . . . . . . 17 Dec. ,,
Monument to Alexander II. unveiled by the czar, 28 Aug. 1898
Paul M. Tretiakoff, art collector, presented his splendid gallery of Russian pictures, &c., to the town in 1893; died, aged 66 . . . . 16 Dec. ,,
Restrictive measures against the Jews, adopted, April, 1899
Student agitation, see *Russia*, April, 1899–1902.
A million roubles bequeathed by W. J. Astrakoff to found a university for women, reported, April, ,,
Attempt on the life of Trepoff, chief of the police, by a governess . . . . . end March, 1902

MOSELY INDUSTRIAL COMMISSION, see *Labour Question*.

MÖSKIRCH (Baden). Here the Austrians were defeated by Moreau and the French, 5 May, 1800.

MOSKWA or BORODINO, BATTLE OF; see *Borodino*.

MOSQUE, a Mahometan house of prayer. Fine examples exist in Spain, India, and other countries. The dome and porticos are leading features. After the capture of Constantinople in 1453 by Mahomet II., the church of St. Sophia was transformed into a mosque, see *Sophia, St.* A mosque was erected in England in 1889; see under *Mahometanism*.

MOSQUITO COAST (Central America). The Indians inhabiting this coast were long under the protection of the British, who held Belize and a group of islands in the bay of Honduras. The jealousy of the United States long existed on this subject. In April, 1850, the two governments covenanted not "to occupy, or fortify, or colonise, or assume, or exercise any dominion over any part of Central America." In 1855 the United States charged the British government with an infraction of the treaty; on which the latter agreed to cede the disputed territory to the republic of Honduras, with some reservation.* The matter was finally settled in 1859.

H.M.S. *Cleopatra* landed 50 men for the protection of the chief, Robert Henry Clarence, president of the council, against the Nicaraguans, 27 Feb.; soon withdrawn, reported . 12 March, 1894
Conflicts between the British subjects and the Nicaraguans on Corn island; martial law proclaimed, reported . . . . 14 July, ,,
General Ortiz defeats the natives, reported, 7 Aug. ,,
Bluefields retaken by the Nicaraguans; British subjects and prince Clarence rescued by capt. Stewart of H.M.S. *Mohawk*, reported 12 Aug.; conveyed to Jamaica, reported . . 28 Aug. ,,
The British vice-consul, Mr. Hatch, and others, arrested and taken to Greytown by the Nicaraguans, 23 Aug.; released on parole, reported 28 Aug. ,,
Martial law revoked, Nicaragua supreme, reported 20 Sept.; recognized by U. S. N. A. but not by Great Britain . . . . . . 28 Nov. ,,
Ultimatum presented by Mr. Gosling, British minister, indemnity for injuries, 15,000*l*. 25 Feb. 1895

MOSQUITOS, see *Malaria*.

MOSS-TROOPERS, desperate plunderers, and lawless soldiers, secreting themselves in the mosses on the borders of Scotland. Many severe laws were enacted against them, but they were not extirpated till the 18th century.

MOTETTS, short pieces of church music, some of which are dated about the end of the 13th century. Good motetts were written between 1430 and 1480; and very fine ones in the 16th and 17th centuries. The "Motett Society," for the publication of these works, was founded in 1847, by Wm. Dyce.

MOTION. On 13 Nov. 1873, professor Sylvester described to the London Mathematical Society a machine for converting spherical into rectilinear, and other motions, and for producing perfectly parallel motion, the discovery of M. Peaucellier, a French engineer officer, about 1867. See *Kinematics*.

MOTOR CARRIAGES, see *Carriages*, 1896.

MOTTOES, ROYAL. *Dieu et mon Droit*, first used by Richard I., 1198. *Ich dien*, "I serve," adopted by Edward the Black Prince, at the battle of Cressy, 1346. *Honi soit qui mal y pense*, the motto of the Garter, 1349. *Je maintiendrai*, "I will maintain," adopted by William III., to which he added, in 1688, "the liberties of England and the Protestant religion." *Semper eadem*, was assumed by queen Elizabeth, 1558, and adopted by queen Anne, 1702. *See them severally*.

MOUNTAIN MEADOWS, see *Massacres*.

MOUNTAIN PARTY, see *Clubs, French*.

MOUNT EVEREST, 29,002 feet high, the highest point in the Himalayas and as yet known in the world, was named after the late sir George Everest, superintendent of the trigonometrical survey of India in Dec. 1843, by his successor, gen. sir Andrew Scott Waugh, R.E., F.R.S.

* St. Juan del Norte (Greytown) was held by the British on behalf of the Mosquitoes till the American adventurers, under col. Kinney, took possession of it in Sept. 1855. He joined Walker; and on 10 Feb. 1856, their associate, Rivas, the president, claimed and annexed the Mosquito territory to Nicaragua.

MOUNTS, see *Bernard*, *Calvary*, *Etna*, *Hecla*, *Himalaya*, *Olivet*, and *Vesuvius*.

Mr. W. M. Conway during his Karakoram expedition among the mountains bordering Cashmire, ascended a height of 20,000 ft. which he named Crystal Peak, and another peak about 23,000 ft. which he named Pioneer Peak. 31 July, 25 Aug. 1892; and reached the top of Yllimani, Cordilleras, with 2 guides, 9 Sept. 1898.

Mount St. Elias, in Alaska, highest peak in the Rockies, 18,000 feet, first ascended by the duke of Abruzzi and party . . . . . 30-31 July, 1897

MOURNING FOR THE DEAD. The Israelites neither washed nor anointed themselves during the time of mourning, which for a friend lasted seven days; upon extraordinary occasions a month or more. The Greeks and Romans fasted. White was used in mourning for the imperial family at Constantinople, 323. The ordinary colour for mourning in Europe is black; in China, white; in Turkey, violet; in Ethiopia, brown; it was white in Spain until 1498. Anne of Brittany, the queen of two successive kings of France, mourned in black, instead of the then practice of wearing white, on the death of her first husband, Charles VIII., 7 April, 1488. *Hénault*.

MOUSQUETAIRES or **MUSKETEERS**, horse-soldiers under the old French *régime*, raised by Louis XIII., 1622. This corps was considered a military school for the French nobility. It was disbanded in 1646, but was restored in 1657. A second company was created in 1660, and formed cardinal Mazarin's guard. *Hénault*. The Mousquetaires were abolished in 1775.

MOZAMBIQUE, chief of the Portuguese territories, E. Africa, was visited by Vasco da Gama, 1498; conquered by the Portuguese under Tristan da Cunha and Albuquerque, 1506; a settlement was established, 1508. Capital, Mozambique, on an islet.

Great rising of the natives against the Portuguese, who are said to have been severely defeated 23 Oct.; the rebellion quelled Dec. 1886; temporary revival 2-4 March, 1887.

Territorial disputes with the sultan of Zanzibar led to war. The Portuguese stormed Tungi 16 Feb.; the war ended early March, 1887. Fresh insurrection; Bonga defeated by the governor after a severe conflict, announced 12 Jan. 1889.

A company formed at Lisbon for the development of the resources of Mozambique, announced 12 Dec. 1889. For the disputes with England respecting East Africa, see under *Zambesi*.

Much hostility shown towards the English at Quilimane . . . . May, June, 1890

Col. Joaquim Jose Machado appointed governor-general of Mozambique . . . about 17 June, „

Lieut. Azevedo Continho, in the *Shiré* seizes the *James Stevenson*, belonging to the British African lakes company, at Chimoro, and sends the crew to Quilimane for trial, reported 31 July; he is censured by the government . . . 2 Aug. „

Mr. (aft. sir) H. H. Johnston, C.B., British consul at Mozambique, nominated consul-general for the Portuguese East Africa territories . . . Jan. 1891

A Portuguese royal charter granted to a company in Mozambique, 11 Feb.; modified . . 30 July „

Natives repulsed in an attack on Portuguese troops under major Mousinho Albuquerque, gov.-gen., 19 Oct. 1896; martial law, 5 Nov. 1896; campaign ended, commercial transit opened to Macuane in the interior, reported . . . . . 5 April, 1897

Sen. Ferreira appointed governor . . . July, 1898

A Portuguese expedition against Mataka; routes the natives . . . . mid Aug. 1899

Severe encounter with slave-dealers, 50 killed, 162 captured, 12 dhows seized, 700 slaves released, reported . . . . 18 March, 1902

MUCKER (*hypocrites*), a German sect; see *Ebelians* and *Brazil*, 1874.

MUGGLETONIANS, so called from Ludowic Muggleton, a tailor, known about 1641, prominent about 1650; convicted of blasphemy, Jan. 1676; died, 1697. He and John Reeve affirmed that God the Father, leaving the government of heaven to Elias, came down and suffered death in a human form. They asserted that they were the two last witnesses of God which should appear before the end of the world, *Rev.* xi. 3. This sect existed, 1850.

MÜHLBERG, on the Elbe, Prussia. Here the German protestants were defeated by the emperor Charles V., 24 April, 1547, and John Frederick, elector of Saxony, was taken prisoner.

MÜHLDORF (Bavaria). Near this place Frederick, duke of Austria, was defeated and taken prisoner by Louis of Bavaria, 28 Sept. 1322.

MULBERRY-TREES. The alleged first planted in England are in the gardens of Sion-house. Shakspeare is said to have planted a mulberry-tree with his own hands at Stratford-upon-Avon; and Garrick, Macklin, and others were entertained under it in 1742. Shakspeare's house was afterwards sold to a clergyman of the name of Gastrel, who cut down the mulberry-tree for fuel, 1765. A silversmith purchased the whole, and manufactured it into memorials.

MULE, a spinning machine invented in 1779, by Samuel Crompton, born at Bolton, Lancashire, in 1753; named, from Crompton's residence, *Hall-in-the-wood-wheel*; and *muslin-wheel*, from its giving birth to the British muslin and cambric manufacture; and *mule*, from its combining the advantages of Hargreave's spinning jenny, and Arkwright's adaptation. It is stated that Crompton at the time knew nothing of the latter. He did not patent his invention, but gave it up in 1780 to the public. It produced yarn treble the fineness and very much softer than any ever before produced in England. Parliament voted him 5000*l*. in 1812, now considered a most inadequate compensation. Mr. Roberts invented the *self-acting mule* in 1825.

MÜLHAUSEN (in Alsace-Lorraine), an imperial city, under Rodolph of Hapsburg; joined the Swiss confederation in 1515; annexed to France in 1798; conquered and annexed to Germany, 1870-1. The calico manufacture was introduced in 1746. Population, 1890, 76,968; 1900, 89,012.

MUMMIES (from the Coptic *mum*, bitumen, gum, resin); see *Embalming*. The mummies in the British Museum, with other Egyptian antiquities, were placed there about 1803 and since. Mr. Alex. Gordon, in 1737, published an essay on three Egyptian mummies, one of which was brought to England in 1722 by capt. Wm. Lethieullier; two others came in 1734, one of which was retained by Dr. Mead, the other was given to the College of Physicians. In 1834, Mr. T. J. Pettigrew published a "History of Egyptian Mummies." The discovery of about 39 mummies of kings, priests, and other eminent persons in sarcophagi at Renneh, near Thebes, Upper Egypt, was announced in Aug. 1881, supposed to be of the 21st dynasty, about 1100 B.C.

The mummies of Rameses II. (Sesostris) and III. were uncovered by MM. Gaston Maspero and E. Brugsch in the presence of the khedive of Egypt and others . . . . . 1 June, 1886

A mummy, dated about 800 B.C. unrolled by Mr. E. A. Wallis Budge at University college, London . . . . 18 Dec. 1889
Discovery of a large burial place of mummified cats, sacred animals, in central Egypt, sold as manure; 28 tons brought to Liverpool . Feb. 1890
Discovery by M. Grébaut, director-general of the excavations, of a vast tomb of the high priests of Amen, on the Libian mountains west of Thebes, near Deïr-el-Bahari, containing many sarcophagi, some dating from the 11th dynasty, statuettes, papyri, votive offerings, &c. Three galleries opened, one empty; the others contained 152 mummies intact, 149 of the 21st dynasty, about 1,100 B.C., and 2 of the 19th, the whole conveyed in barges to Cairo . . . . . . Feb. 1891
The high priests of Amen, at Thebes, were a line of powerful prelates, beginning under the kings of the 12th dynasty, between 3,000 and 2,000 B.C.
Four mummy coffins presented by the Khedive to the British Museum; reported . . . Nov. 1893
"The Mummy," by E. A. Wallis Budge, published, Nov. ,,
The British Museum now possesses about 44 human mummies, 80 coffins, well arranged, representing about 4000 years, commencing with Mycerinus III. (4th dynasty), builder of the third pyramid of Gizeh, about 3640 B.C., and ending with a lady and 3 children, about 400 A.D., see *Egypt* April, 1898

MÜNCHENGRATZ (Bohemia) was taken by the Prussians under prince Frederick Charles, after a severe action, 28 June, 1866. The Austrians lost about 300 killed and 1000 prisoners, and the prince gained about 12 miles of country.

MUNDA (now Monda, S. Spain). Here Cneius Scipio defeated the Carthaginians, B.C. 216; and here Julius Cæsar defeated the sons of Pompey, 17 March, 45, after a severe conflict.

MUNDANE ERAS. That of Alexandria fixed the creation at 5502 B.C. This computation continued till A.D. 284, Alex. era, 5786; but in A.D. 285 ten years were subtracted, and 5787 became 5777. This coincided with the Mundane era of Antioch (which dated the creation 5492 B.C.). *Nicolas.*

MUNICH, the capital of Bavaria, said to have been founded by duke Henry of Saxony, 962, on a site previously occupied by monks (*München*). It was taken by Gustavus Adolphus of Sweden in 1632; by the Austrians, in 1704, 1741, and 1743; and by the French under Moreau, 2 July, 1800. It abounds in schools, institutions, and manufactories. The university was founded by king Louis in 1826. A Bavarian art-exhibition was opened here by prince Adalbert, 20 July, 1869. A congress of "Old Catholics" (*which see*) met here, 23 Sept. 1871. International exhibition opened, 19 July, 1879. International art exhibition opened 1 July, 1883; others, 1 June, 1888, and 1892. Centenary of King Louis I., 30-31 July, 1888. Visit of the emperor William II., 7 Sept. 1801; again, 24 Nov. 1898. The new National museum opened by the prince-regent, 29 Sept. 1900. Population, Dec. 1871, 169,693; 1880, 230,023; 1885, 261,981; 1895, 407,307; 1900, 499,959.

MUNICIPAL CORPORATIONS, &c.; see *Corporations*, and *Socialism*.

MÜNSTER (W. Prussia). The bishopric, said to have been founded by Charlemagne, 780, was secularised in 1802; seized by the French, 1806; part of the duchy of Berg, 1809; annexed to France, 1810; ceded to Prussia, 1815. The Anabaptists, under John of Leyden, the king of Munster, held the city in 1534-5. Here were signed the preliminaries of the treaty of Westphalia (*which see*), or Munster, Jan. 1647; definitively signed 24 Oct. 1648. The academy of Münster raised to the *status* of a university, July, 1902. Population, 1890, 49,344.—MUNSTER, the southern province of Ireland, an ancient kingdom. See *Ireland*, 1014. In 1568 a commission was issued for its government by a president and council, and new colonies were founded in 1588.

MURADAL, see *Toloso*.

MURCIA, a province, formerly a kingdom, N. E. Spain, was subdued by the Moors, 713; by Ferdinand of Castile, 1240; and divided between Castile and Arragon, 1305. Population, 1887: province, 491,436; city, 98,538; city, 1897, 110,000.

Murcia, the capital, was sacked by the French under Sebastiani, 23 April, 1810. It was inundated by the Segura, after a violent storm, 15-17 Oct., 1879, when about 1000 persons perished.

MURDER, the highest offence against the law of God. (*Genesis* ix. 6, 2348 B.C.) A court of Ephetæ was established by Demophoön of Athens for the trial of murder, 1179 B.C. The Persians did not punish the first offence. In England, during a period of the heptarchy, murder was punished by fines only. So late as Henry VIII.'s time the crime was compounded for in Wales. Murderers were allowed benefit of clergy in 1503. Aggravated murder, or *petit treason* (a distinction now abolished), happened in three ways: by a servant killing his master, a wife her husband, and an ecclesiastical person his superior, stat. 25 Edw. III. 1350. The enactments relating to this crime are very numerous, and its wilful commission has been rarely pardoned by our sovereigns. The act whereby the murderer should be executed on the day next but one after his conviction, was repealed, 1836; see *Assassinations*, *Executions*, *Trials*; also *London*, 1872, *Bravo*, *Burton*, *Euston*, *Ratcliffe*, *Road*, *Richmond*, *Harley Street*, *Whitechapel*, *Poisoning*; *Railways*, 1864 and 1881; *Slough*, *Melbourne*. For St. Pancras murder, see *Trials*, 1898.

Murders in England and Wales (from Coroners' Inquests):—

1856 ..	205	1868 ..	261	1880 ..	157	1890–1	148
1857 ..	184	1869 ..	265	1881 ..	193	1891–2	155
1858 ..	183	1870 ..	222	(101 females)		1893 ..	170
1859 ..	204	1871 ..	226	1882 ..	176	1894 ..	157
1860 ..	268	1872 ..	257	1883 ..	177	1895 ..	152
1861 ..	210	1873 ..	223	1884 ..	192	1896 ..	183
1862 ..	221	1874 ..	223	1885 ..	158	1898 ..	169
1863 ..	270	1875 ..	200	1886 ..	177	1899 ..	142
1864 ..	246	1876 ..	207	1887 ..	196	1900 ..	145
1865 ..	226	1877 ..	199	1888 ..	190	1901 ..	208
1866 ..	272	1878 ..	176	1889 ..	167	1902 ..	113
1867 ..	255	1879 ..	153	1889–90	146		

MURET (S. France). Here the Albigenses, under the count of Thoulouse, were defeated by Simon de Montfort, and their ally Peter of Arragon killed, 12 Sept. 1213.

MURFREESBOROUGH (Tennessee, N. America) was the site of fierce conflicts between the federals under Rosencrans and the confederates under Bragg, from 31 Dec. 1862 to 3 Jan. 1863, when Bragg retired with great loss. This struggle is called also the battle of Stone River.

MURIATIC ACID, see *Alkalies*.

MURRAY'S HANDBOOKS FOR TRAVELLERS. The parent of the series, a "Handbook for Travellers on the Continent," which appeared in 1836, was the work of Mr. John Murray the publisher. Handbooks for France, Switzerland,

South Germany, &c., soon followed; one for Algeria appeared in Oct. 1873; one for Japan in 1884; New Zealand, 1893; Asia Minor, &c., 1896; and others since. Handbooks for all the counties in England completed, June, 1899.

Murray's Magazine first published by John Murray, of 50, Albemarle Street, London, W., Jan. 1887.

Mr. John Murray, aged nearly 84, died 2 April, 1892.

MUSCAT, or MASCAT, an Arab city on the gulf of Oman, was conquered by the Portuguese under Albuquerque in 1507, but recovered by the Arabs in 1648. Population, 1892, 60,000.

Ahmad bin Sa'id repelled a Persian invasion and founded present dynasty 1741
Sa'id, his son, succeeded 1775
Sa'id bin Sultan, his son 1803
Treaty with the British 1839
At his death his territories divided; after a conflict, his son Sa'id Thuwainy obtained Oman; and Majid, Zanzibar (*which see*) 1856
Syud Redin compelled to fly, and a chief, Azan bin Gheo, seized the government . . . . Oct. 1868
The imaum tried to regain his authority . Aug. 1870
The city was taken by Sa'id Toorkee, and the chief killed . . . . about 30 Jan. 1871
Grant of a subsidy, and new British treaty concluded by sir Bartle Frere, in 1873
Sa'id Abdool Aseer said to be deposed by his brother, Sa'id Toorkee, end of . . . . Dec. 1875
Rebellion against the sultan . . . . June, 1882
Muscat besieged by the sultan's brother, whose camp is shelled by the British ship *Philomel*; siege raised, announced . . . . 29-31 Oct. 1883
Rebels defeated and dispersed, announced 5 Nov. ,,
Five Arab horses presented by the sultan received by the queen at Windsor . . . 18 Nov. 1886
Death of the sultan; succeeded by Seyyid Feysal bin Turkee . . . . 4 June, 1888
British territorial treaty agreed to by the sultan, in 1891
Insurrection of Bedouins; the city plundered 24 Feb. 1895
Rebels retire on payment of 16,000 dollars . March, ,,
A British gun-boat sent there . . . 15 March, ,,
The sultan revokes the grant of a coaling station and naval base to the French under threat of bombardment by adm. Douglas; attends a durbah on the flagship *Eclipse* . . . 16 Feb. 1899
A coal dépôt ceded to France, with restrictions, March, ,,

MUSEUM, originally a quarter of the palace of Alexandria, like the Prytaneum of Athens, where eminent learned men were maintained by the public. The foundation is attributed to Ptolemy Philadelphus, who here placed his library about 280 B.C. Besides the British Museum, Soane's Museum, and the Museum of Geology (*which see*), there are very many others in London. The opening of public museums and galleries on Sunday was long advocated in parliament (see *Sunday*); agreed to by resolution for London (178—97), 10 March, 1896. Urban authorities authorised to provide museums and gymnasiums, by act passed 3 July, 1891.

Museum Sunday, 6 Nov. 1892, when by the agency of the Sunday Society, (*which see*), the Mansion house and various exhibitions and galleries in London were opened, and sermons were preached to support the movement at several churches; supporting meeting at the Mansion house, 8 March, 1893. Museum Sunday, 26 Nov. 1893; 2 Dec. 1894; annual.

MUSEUMS ASSOCIATION formed in 1890 to promote the efficacy of museums, first London meeting, sir W. H. Flower, president, many country delegates present, 3 July, 1893; at Dublin, 5 July, 1894.

"Essays on Museums, &c.," by sir W. H. Flower, published, June, 1898; he died, 1 July, 1899.

MUSIC.* "Jubal, the father of all such as handle the harp and the organ" (3875 B.C. *Gen.* iii. 21). The flute, and harmony, or concord in music, are said to have been invented by Hyagnis, 1506 B.C. *Arund. Marbles*. Vocal choruses of men are first mentioned 556 B.C., see *Athens. Dufresnoy*. See *Organ*, and other musical instruments. Prior to 1600, the chief music in England was masses, ballads, and madrigals, but dramatic music was much cultivated from that time. About the end of James I.'s reign, a music professorship was founded in the university of Oxford by Dr. Wm. Hychin; and the year 1710 was distinguished by the arrival in England of George Frederick Handel. Mozart came to England in 1763; Joseph Haydn in 1791; and Carl Maria von Weber in 1825. "The Oxford History of Music," Vol. IV., V., Feb. 1903. *The Polyphonic Period*, by prof. Wooldridge, published, 1902.

Dictionaries of Music, Rousseau's, published 1767; in "Encyclopédie Méthodique," 1791; Fétis, "Biographie Universelle des Musiciens," 1835-44, and 1860-65. The publication of the excellent "Dictionary of Music and Musicians," edited by Mr. (aft. Sir) George Grove, begun Jan. 1878, was completed in 1890; he died, 28 May, 1900.

Monthly Musical Record published, 1871 *et seq.*

MUSICAL NOTES, &c. See *Gamut*. The first six are said to have been invented by Guy Aretino, a Benedictine monk of Arezzo, about 1025. *Blair*. The notes at present used were perfected in 1338. Counterpoint was brought to perfection by Palestrina about 1555. Gafforio of Lodi read lectures on musical composition in the 15th century, and they effected great improvement in the science. The Italian style of composition was introduced into these countries about 1616.

The MUSICAL PITCH was settled in France in 1859. The middle A to be 870 simple or 435 double vibrations in a second; but through error of measurement the fork made gave (A) 439 double vibrations (C, 522). At a meeting on the subject, held at the Society of Arts, on 23 Nov. 1860, the concert pitch of C was recommended to be 528 vibrations in a second; but the fork made by Mr. J. H. Griesbach gives 539⅔ vibrations. Mr. Hullah adopted 512 vibrations.

A lower pitch was adopted at concerts in London in Jan. 1869. 528 vibrations for C adopted for performances at the international exhibition of 1872, at a meeting, 20 Jan. 1872.

[Handel's tuning-fork, 1740, was 495; the Philharmonic Society's, 1813-43, was 515.]

Mr. A. J. Ellis's elaborate "History of Musical Pitch" is published in "Journal of the Society of Arts," 5 March, 1880, and separately.

Sir G. Macfarren and a meeting agree to French normal diapason, 20 June; agreed to by international conference at Vienna, about 17 Nov. 1885; adopted by the Philharmonic society, Aug. 1895.

MUSICAL FESTIVALS IN ENGLAND. Dr. Bysse, chancellor of Hereford, about 1724, proposed to the members of the choirs a collection at the cathedral door after morning service, when forty guineas were collected and appropriated to charitable purposes. It was then agreed to hold festivals at Hereford, Gloucester, and Worcester, in rotation annually. Until the year 1753, the festival lasted only two days; it was then extended at Hereford to three evenings; and at Gloucester, in 1757, to three mornings, for the purpose of introducing Handel's "Messiah," which was warmly received, and has been performed annually ever since. Musical festivals on a great scale are now annually held at various cathedrals in England; Chester, 21 July, 1897; see *Handel* and *Crystal Palace*.

"*Sons of the Clergy*" annual musical performances at St. Paul's began 1709.

MUSICAL FESTIVALS. Several were held on the continent in the 18th century; for Haydn at Vienna, 1808-1811; others at Erfurt 1811, Cologne 1821, and frequently since.

* Pythagoras (about 555 B.C.) maintained that the motions of the twelve spheres must produce delightful sounds, inaudible to mortal ears, which he called "the music of the spheres." St. Cecilia, said to have enticed an angel from the celestial regions by her melody, is termed the patroness of music. She died in the second century.

Study of music greatly increased by the efforts and teaching of John Hullah since 1840 *et seq.*

The Tonic *sol-fa* system, in which the letters *d, r, m, f, s, l, t,* (for *do, re, mi, fa, so, la, ti,* or *si*) are used instead of notes, was invented by Miss Glover, of Norwich, and improved by rev. John Curwen, about 1841; he died 1880.

The Tonic Sol-fa Association founded 1853; the college established 1862; jubilee celebrated at St. Paul's, 7 July; Crystal Palace, 18 July, 1891.

MUSICAL INSTITUTIONS. The Ancient Academy of Music was instituted in 1710. It originated with numerous eminent performers and gentlemen wishing to promote the study of vocal harmony.

Madrigal Society was established in 1741, and other musical societies followed.

"Ancient concerts" began, 1776; ceased, 1848.

Royal Society of Music arose from the principal nobility and gentry uniting to promote the performance of operas composed by Handel, 1785.

Philharmonic Society's concerts began in 1813.

Royal Academy of Music, established 1822 (*which see*).

Melodists' Club, 1825.

New Philharmonic Society established 1852.

Sacred Harmonic Society, Exeter hall, established 1831. 500th performance, 13 Dec. 1867; performances at St. James's hall, 1880-1. It ceased to exist in 1882; final concert, 28 April (Handel's "Solomon"). The new society gave its first concert, 23 Feb. 1883.

British Orchestral Society, 1872.

Catch Club formed, 1761; centenary kept, July, 1861.

Glee Club formed, 1787.

Musical Union, founded by John Ella, 1844; he died 2 Oct. 1888.

Harmonic Union (for performances of ancient and modern music), 1852-4.

Musical Society of London, established 1858.

"Popular Monday Concerts" at St. James's hall, founded by Thos. and Arthur Chappell, commenced with a "Mendelssohn night," 14 Feb. 1859; Mr. Arthur Chappell retired from their direction, 18 Dec. 1901; Mr. Thos. Chappell died, June, 1902.

London Academy of Music founded in 1860.

Cæcilian Society, London, founded by Z. W. Vincent and others in 1785; ceased in 1861.

The People's Concert society founded, 1878.

The hon. Norman de L'Aigle Grosvenor, one of the founders, president, died, 21 Nov. 1898.

Folk Song society formed, inaugural address by sir Hubert Parry, 7 Feb. 1899.

"Musical Education Committee" of the Society of Arts, London, with the prince of Wales as chairman, held its first meeting 22 May, 1865. Its first report, dated 27 June, 1866, recommended the reconstitution of the Royal Academy.

National Training School for Music; building near the Albert hall, founded by the duke of Edinburgh, 18 Dec. 1873; opened by him 17 May, 1876; first public concert, 23 June, 1879. Premises given up to the prince of Wales as chairman of the proposed National College of Music, 6 April, 1882.

Guildhall School of Music founded 1880 (see under *Guildhall*).

Royal College of Music, Kensington; establishment proposed at a meeting at Marlborough-house, the prince of Wales in the chair, Aug. 1878, and 23 and 28 Feb. 1882. Charter granted; prince of Wales, president; sir George Grove, director; 21 April, 1883; Dr. Charles Hubert Parry, Nov. 1894 (knt. 1898); opened by the prince of Wales, 7 May; reported successful; first annual meeting 28 May, 1884; prince (George) of Wales, president, 27 May, 1902.

Mr. Samson Fox, civil engineer of Leeds, presented 30,000*l.* (increased to 45,000*l.*, 18 May, 1889), for the erection of buildings; personally accepted by the prince of Wales, Jan. 1888, who laid the foundation of new buildings, 8 July, 1890; state opening by the prince and princess of Wales; the Donaldson museum of ancient musical instruments, &c., also opened, 2 May, 1894.

"*Musical Association* for the Investigation and Discussion of subjects connected with the Art and Science of Music," founded 16 April, 1874, by Messrs. Spottiswoode, Wheatstone, Tyndall, G. A. Macfarren, J. Hullah, Sedley Taylor, Stone, Pole, Chappell, Barnby, and others. Publishes its "Proceedings."

Henry Leslie's musical choir formed about 1855; dissolved 1880; reorganised, Mr. Randegger conductor, July, 1882–87. Mr. Leslie died 4 Feb. 1896.

Church Choral Society, London, incorporated as Trinity College, 1875.

National Opera-house, N. Thames embankment, first brick laid by Mlle. Tietjens, 7 Sept.; first stone by the duke of Edinburgh, 16 Dec. 1875.

The Wagner Society in London gave concerts to introduce R. Wagner's so-called "Music of the Future" (the due combination of music and poetry), Feb. 1873.

Wagner's *Lohengrin*, performed at Covent-garden, 8 May, at Drury-lane, 13 June, 1875. *Tannhäuser* performed at Covent-garden, 29 April, 1876.

Three series of performances of Wagner's "Ring des Nibelungen," in four parts (*Rheingold, Walküre, Siegfried,* and *Götterdämmerung*), at Bayreuth, in presence of the emperors of Germany and Brazil, the king of Bavaria, and many other sovereigns and princes, 13 Aug. *et seq.*, 1876; at Berlin, May, 1881. In London, 5 May *et seq.* 1882.

Wagner Festival, Royal Albert hall, London (Wagner present), 7—19 May, 1877, and others since.

Richard Wagner died at Venice, 13 Feb. 1883.

National Society of Professional Musicians founded in 1882.

A fine collection of musical instruments at the Inventions Exhibition, South Kensington, opened 4 May, 1885.

Josef Hofman, aged about 10, plays brilliantly at St. James's hall long classical pieces from memory, summer and autumn; goes to America, where his performances are stopped by a philanthropist, 1887.

Otto Hegner, aged 11, plays in London, March, 1888; many other juvenile performers since.

Copyright of musical compositions, restricting their unauthorised performance, passed 5 July, 1888.

Mme. Patey, eminent contralto, died a few hours after singing an *encore* at Sheffield, 28 Feb. 1894.

Bi-centenary of the death of Henry Purcell celebrated in Westminster Abbey, 21 Nov. 1895.

The *Strand*, musical monthly magazine (illustrated), No. I. published, Jan. 1895.

First international music-trades exhibition at the Agricultural hall, London, 150 exhibitors, opened 13 June, prizes distributed 21 June, 1895.

Sir Charles Hallé, conductor and pianist, born 11 April, 1819, died 25 Oct. 1895.

Sir Joseph Barnby, conductor and composer, born 12 Aug. 1838, died 28 Jan. 1896.

Mdme. Clara Schumann (widow of Robert Schumann), pianist and composer, born 13 Sept. 1819, died 20 May, 1896.

The *Musician*, weekly paper, started mid May, 1897.

Musical festival at Dublin, a revival of the old Feis Ceoil, May, 1897; again, May, 1898.

National convention of choirmasters meets at Manchester, 16 Sept. 1897.

Incorporated Society of Musicians 13th annual meeting at the Mansion house, 4 Jan. 1898; Plymouth, 3 Jan. 1899.

London musical festival at the Queen's hall, 17 May, 1899.

Mdlle. Gabrielle Vaillant, eminent violinist, died, aged 46, 14 May, 1899.

The French diapason normal pitch of 1859 adopted by the Covent Garden opera in 1879; by the Queen's hall orchestra, under Mr. H. J. Wood, 1893; the Philharmonic, 1896, finally adopted for pianos by the leading firms, 1 Sept. 1899.

Death of M. Charles Lamoureux, the famous *chef d'orchestre* and upholder of Wagner, and others, 21 Dec. 1899.

Mr. Sims Reeves, the famous tenor, born, 26 Sept. 1818; died, 25 Oct. 1900.

Sir Arthur Seymour Sullivan died suddenly, much lamented, London, 22 Nov. 1900 (his bust, in front of the Savoy theatre, unveiled by the princess Louise, duchess of Argyll, 10 July, 1903).

Mr. Henry Russell, singer and writer of songs, "Cheer boys, cheer," and other stirring melodies, died, aged 88, 7 Dec. 1900.

Sir John Stainer, eminent organist and musician, born 1840; died, 31 March, 1901.

Sig. Piatti, eminent violoncellist, died, aged 79, 19 July, 1901.
Sig. Arditi, composer and conductor, died, aged 80; 1 May, 1903.
The *Monthly Magazine* first issued, 15 Nov. 1901.
Musical copyright act, royal assent, 22 July, 1902.
MUSICAL CHARITIES. Royal Society of Musicians, established 1738; incorporated 1790.
Royal Society of Female Musicians, established 1839; these two combined, 1866.
Choir Benevolent Fund, 1851.
Sacred Harmonic Benevolent Fund, 1855.

EMINENT MUSICAL COMPOSERS.

	Born	Died
Tallis	1529	1585
Palestrina	1524	1594
T. Morley	1550	1604
Orlando Gibbons	1583	1624
H. Lawes	1600	1662
Lully	1633	1672
Purcell	1658	1695
J. Seb. Bach*	1685	1750
G. F. Handel	1684	1759
T. A. Arne	1710	1778
C. Gluck	1714	1787
W. A. Mozart	1756	1791
Joseph Haydn	1732	1809
C. Dibdin	1748	1814
S. Webbe	1740	1817
J. W. Callcott	1766	1821
C. Weber	1786	1826
F. Schubert	1797	1828
L. Beethoven	1770	1827
M. Cherubini	1760	1842
F. Mendelssohn-Bartholdy	1809	1848
F. Chopin	1810	1849
H. Bishop	1787	1855
R. Schumann	1810	1856
L. Spohr	1783	1859
J. E. Halevy	1799	1862
J. Meyerbeer	1794	1864
J. Rossini	1792	1868
L. H. Berlioz	1803	1869
M. W. Balfe	1808	1870
D. T. Auber	1784	1871
W. Sterndale Bennett (knt. 1871)	1816	1875
J. Raff	1822	1882
R. Wagner	1813	1883
M. Costa	1810	1884
Julius Benedict (knt. 1871)	1804	1885
F. Liszt	1811	1886
G. A. Macfarren (knt. 1883)	1813	1887
Alfred Cellier	1844	1891
G. Verdi	1813	1901
R. Franz	1815	1892
George Job Elvey	1816	1893
C. F. Gounod	1818	1893
A. Rubinstein	1829	1894
J. Brahms	1833	1897
Chas. C. Saint-Saëns	1835	
J. Stainer (knt. 1888)	1840	1901
P. von Tschaikowsky	1840	1893
P. A. Dvorak	1841	
E. H. Greig	1843	
A. S. Sullivan (knt. 1883)	1842	1900
A. C. Mackenzie (knt. 1895)	1847	
Chas. H. H. Parry (bart. June, 1902)	1848	
C. V. Stanford (knt. June, 1902)	1852	
F. H. Cowen	1852	
Johann Strauss	1826	1899
Peter Benoit	1834	1901
Edward Elgar	1857	

MUSICAL GLASSES, see under *Harmonic*, and *Copophone*.

MUSICAL ARCS, invented by Mr. Duddell, by means of an arrangement of electric currents by which a musical note that can be altered to any pitch is obtained and a tune played—*Nature*, 20 Dec. 1900; 4 April, 1901.

MUSIC HALLS. In 1878, 347 of these were licensed in London: first class, 3; second class, 6; third class, 13; fourth class, 53; &c.

* He had eleven sons musicians; four distinguished.

MUSKETS, see *Firearms*.

MUSKETRY SCHOOLS at Hythe and Fleetwood were established in 1854 under major-general C. C. Hay. He resigned in 1867. The school at Fleetwood was closed the same year.

MUSLIN, a fine cotton cloth, so called, it is said, from having a downy nap on its surface, resembling moss (French, *mousse*); according to others, because it was first brought from Moussol, in India. Muslins were first worn in England in 1670. *Anderson.* By means of the *Mule* (*which see*), British much superseded India muslins.

MUSWELL HILL, N. London, see *Trials*, 1889.

MUTA (Syria). Here Mahomet and his followers defeated the Christians in his first conflict with them, 629.

MUTE. A prisoner is said to *stand mute*, when being arraigned for treason or felony, he either makes no answer, or answers foreign to the purpose. Until 1741, persons refusing to plead were subjected to torture by pressure.

Walter Calverly, esq., of Calverly in Yorkshire, having murdered two of his children, and stabbed his wife in a fit of jealousy, being arraigned for his crime at York assizes, stood mute, and was thereupon pressed to death in the castle, a large iron weight being placed upon his breast, 5 Aug. 1605. *Stow.*

Major Strangeway suffered death in a similar manner at Newgate for the murder of his brother-in-law, Mr. Fussell, 1657.

Judgment was awarded against mutes, as if they were convicted or had confessed, by 12 Geo. III. 1772.

A man refusing to plead was condemned and executed at the Old Bailey on a charge of murder, 1778, and another on a charge of burglary at Wells, 1792.

An act passed by which the court is directed to enter a plea of "not guilty" when the prisoner will not plead, 1827.

MUTINA (now Modena), N. Italy. Here Mark Antony, after defeating the consul Pansa, was himself beaten with great loss by Hirtius the other consul, and fled to Gaul, 27 April, 43 B.C.

MUTINIES, BRITISH. The mutiny throughout the fleet at Portsmouth for an advance of wages, April, 1797. It subsided on a promise from the Admiralty, which not being quickly fulfilled, occasioned a second mutiny on board the *London* man-of-war; admiral Colpoys and his captain were put into confinement for ordering the marines to fire, whereby some lives were lost. The mutiny subsided 10 May, 1797, when an act was passed to raise the wages, and the king pardoned the mutineers.

Mutiny of the Bounty, 28 April, 1789; see *Bounty*.

Mutiny at the Nore, which blocked up the trade of the Thames, broke out on 27 May, 1797, and subsided 13 June, 1797, when the principal mutineers were put in irons, and several executed (including the ringleader, who had assumed the name of rear-admiral Richard Parker), 30 June, at Sheerness.

Mutiny of the *Danaë* frigate; the crew carried the ship into Brest harbour, 27 March, 1800.

Mutiny on board admiral Mitchell's fleet at Bantry Bay, Dec. 1801, and January following (see *Bantry Bay*).

Mutiny at Malta, began 4 April, 1807, and ended on the 12th, when the mutineers (chiefly Greeks and Corsicans) blew themselves up by setting fire to a large magazine, consisting of between 400 and 500 barrels of gunpowder.

Mutiny on the *Flowery Land*, bound from London to Singapore; John Lyons and six foreign sailors murdered the captain and others, 10 Sept. 1863; Tiffin, a sailor, separated from the rest, gave information; seven were tried and five executed, 14–22 Feb. 1864.

Mutiny on the *Jefferson Borden*, U.S. schooner; two mates murdered; put down by the captain, 20 April; vessel arrived at Gravesend, May; 2 men condemned at Boston, U.S., 1 Oct., 1875.

Mutiny on the *Lennie*, British ship, bound for America, captain and two mates murdered by foreign seamen, 31 Oct. 1875. Van Hoydek, steward, managed to get the vessel to the Isle of Rhé; 11 men seized and conveyed to London, tried, 4 convicted, 4 May; executed, 23 May, 1876.

Mutiny on the *Caswell*, Glasgow barque, capt. G. Best, 4 Jan., on way home from Valparaiso; captain and 3 men killed; mutineers overcome by others, some killed; vessel brought to Queenstown, 13 May; Christos Baumbos sentenced to death, 31 July; executed at Cork, 25 Aug. 1876. Giuseppe Pistoria executed at Cork, 25 Aug. 1879.

Mutiny in 19th Hussars, Curragh camp, Dublin; through discontent with officers on account of extra duty, 8 Sept.; 75 arrested; court martial; sentenced to penal servitude, 2 for 5 years, 2 for 6 years, 1 for 7 years, 1 for 8 years, 14 Nov. 1877.

Mutiny on board the *Frank N. Thayer*, U.S. ship, 700 miles from St. Helena; two coolies from Manila wound the captain, cause panic, kill six men, imprison others, set fire to the ship; overpowered; leap overboard 2–3 Jan.; the captain and crew in boats reach St. Helena 10 Jan. 1886.

Mutiny of 3 American sailors on the *Leicester Castle*, British ship, 300 mi. off Pitcairn island, capt. Peattie wounded, and Mr. Nixon, mate, killed; the mutineers escaped on a raft, unheard of since, 2 Sept. 1902; 7 men murdered on the *Veronica*, 7 Dec. 1902; see *Trials*, May, 1903.

For *Indian Mutinies*, see *Madras*, 1806, and *India*, 1857.

MUTINY ACT (1 & 2 Will. and Mary, c. 5). for the discipline, regulation, and payment of the army, &c., was passed 12 April, 1689, and has since been re-enacted annually.

A parliamentary commission reported in favour of consolidating and simplifying military law, by combining the mutiny act and articles of war in a new act to be passed annually, &c., July, 1878, called the Army (Annual) Act. See under *Army*, 1879 and 1881.

MYCALE (Ionia, Asia Minor), BATTLE OF, fought between the Greeks (under Leotychides, the king of Sparta, and Xantippus the Athenian) and the Persians, 22 Sept. 479 B.C.; the day on which Mardonius was defeated and slain at Platæa by Pausanias. The Persians (about 100,000 men), who had just returned from the unsuccessful expedition of Xerxes in Greece, were completely defeated, thousands of them slaughtered, and their camp burnt. The Greeks sailed back to Samos with an immense booty.

MYCENÆ, a division of the kingdom of Argives, in the Peloponnesus. It stood about fifty stadia from Argos, and flourished till the invasion of the Heraclidæ. Early history mythical.

Perseus removes from Argos, and founds Mycenæ, B.C. 1431, 1313, or 1282
Reign of Eurystheus . . . 1289, 1274, or 1258
[Towards the close of his reign is placed the story of the labours surmounted by Hercules.]
Ægisthus assassinates Atreus; Agamemnon succeeds to the throne; becomes king of Sicyon, Corinth, and perhaps of Argos . . . 1201
He is chosen generalissimo of the Grecian forces going to the Trojan war . . . . about 1193
Ægisthus, in the absence of Agamemnon, lives in adultery with the queen Clytemnestra. On the return of the king they assassinate him; and Ægisthus mounts the throne . . . 1183
Orestes, son of Agamemnon, kills his mother and her paramour 1176
Orestes dies of the bite of a serpent . . . 1106
The Achaians are expelled . . . . . . ,,
Invasion of the Heraclidæ, and the conquerors divide the dominions 1103
Mycenæ destroyed by the Argives . . . A.D. 1468
Discoveries on the supposed site of Mycenæ made by Dr. Schliemann: reported March, 1874—Sept. 1876
Visited by the emperor of Brazil . 15 Oct. ,,
Discovery of tombs of Agamemnon and others, and of many treasures; announced by Dr. Schliemann . . . . 28 Nov. ,,
Dr. Schliemann reports his discoveries to the Society of Antiquaries, London, 22 March; publishes his "Mycenæ" . . . . . Dec. 1877
Renewed excavations with discoveries by Dr. Schliemann . . . . Sept. 1888
Dr. Schliemann died at Naples . . 26 Dec. 1890

MYLÆ, a bay of Sicily, where the Romans, under their consul Duilius, gained their first naval victory over the Carthaginians, and took fifty of their ships, 260 B.C. Here also Agrippa defeated the fleet of Sextus Pompeius, 36 B.C.

MYOGRAPHION, an apparatus for determining the velocity of the nervous current, invented by H. Helmholtz in 1850, and since improved by Du Bois Reymond and others.

MYSORE (S. India), was made a flourishing kingdom by Hyder Ali, who dethroned the reigning sovereign in 1761, and by his son, Tippoo Sahib, who considerably harassed the English. Tippoo was chastised by them in 1792, and on 4 May, 1799, his capital, Seringapatam, was taken by assault, and himself slain. Tippoo's last surviving son, Gholam Mahomet, a British pensioner, died at Calcutta, 11 Aug. 1872. The English established a prince of the old royal family as maharajah of part of Mysore in 1799; being without an heir he was permitted to adopt a child of four years of age, maharajah Chamarajendra Wodeyar Bahadur, in Aug. 1867; who succeeded him at his death, 27 Mar. 1868, and assumed the government in May, 1881; an able, beneficent ruler; died, 27 Dec. 1894; succeeded by his son, Krishnaraja Wadyar Bahadur, aged nine (his mother regent), 1 Feb. 1895; formally installed by lord Curzon, viceroy, 8 Aug. 1902. Visit of the viceroy, lord Lansdowne, 10 Nov. 1892. Population, in 1881, 4,186,188; in 1891, 4,859,760; 1901, 5,538,482. Agricultural banks formed in 1895.

Sir Sheshadri Iyer, an eminent and progressive statesman, who built up the gold and other industries, and whose "prudent and far-sighted measures" averted famine, &c., died, 13 Sept. 1901.

MYSTERIES, derived from the Greek *musterion*, a mystery or revealed secret. The *Sacred* mysteries is a term applied to the doctrines of Christianity, called the "mystery of godliness," 1 *Tim.* iii. 16, as opposed to the "mystery of iniquity," 2 *Thess.* ii. 7. The Holy Eucharist is also termed the sacred mysteries. The *Profane* mysteries were the secret ceremonies performed by a select few in honour of some deity. From the Egyptian mysteries of Isis and Osiris sprang those of Bacchus and Ceres among the Greeks. The Eleusinian mysteries were introduced at Athens by Eumolpus, 1356 B.C.—MYSTERY PLAYS; see *Drama*.

MYSTICS, a name given to those theologians who, in addition to the obvious meaning of the Holy Scriptures, assert that there are interpretations to be discovered by means of an emanation of the Divine Wisdom, by which the soul is enlightened and purified; for which purpose they advocate seclusion for contemplation and asceticism.

Mysticism taught at Alexandria by Clemens, Pantænus, Origen, and others, who mingled Christianity and Platonism, 2nd and 3rd centuries.

Much promoted by the works of the pseudo-Dionysius ("The Mystic Theology," &c), 6th century.

Introduced into the Western empire, 9th century.

Eminent mediæval mystics (opposed by the schoolmen), Master Eckhart (1251-1329); John Tauler of Strasburg, where he acted heroically during the plague, termed the "black death" (1290-1361); Henry Suso (1300-65). They aimed at a more spiritual religion than Romanism; but their followers were charged with immorality, pantheism, communism, and maintaining private inspiration.

Jacob Böhme or Behmen, the German mystic, published his "Aurora" (an alleged divine revelation) 1612; died, 18 Nov. 1624.

For modern mystics, see *Quakers, Quietists, Hutchinsonians*, and *Swedenborgians*.

MYTHOLOGY (Greek *mythos*, fable), the traditions respecting the gods and early history of any people. For the Egyptian mythology, see *Egypt*.

Greek Gods.	*Roman.*
Kronos, Rhea } parents of	Saturn, Cybele } parents of
Zeus	Jupiter (Diovis-pater).
Ploutōn (Aïdes, Hades)	Pluto.
Poseidōn	Neptune.
Hērē or Hēra	Juno.
Dēmētēr	Ceres.
Hestia	Vesta.
Persephone	Proserpine.
Dionysius	Bacchus.
Jupiter's Children.	
Apollōn	Apollo.
Ares	Mars.
Hermes	Mercury.
Hephaistos	Vulcan.
Athena or Athēnē	Minerva.
Aphroditē	Venus.
Artĕmis	Diana.

The chief Hindu gods are Brahma the creator, Vishnu, the preserver, and Siva the destroyer, but there have been many changes in the Hindu Pantheon.

N.

NAAS (E. Ireland). Here a desperate engagement took place between a body of royal forces and the insurgent Irish, 24 May, 1798, during the rebellion. The latter were defeated with the loss of 300 killed and many wounded.

NABONASSAR, ERA OF, received its name from the prince of Babylon, under whose reign astronomical studies were much advanced in Chaldæa. The years contain 365 days each, without intercalation. The first day of the era was Wednesday (said, in mistake, to be Thursday, in *L'Art de Vérifier les Dates*), 26 Feb. 747 B.C.—3967, Julian period. To find the Julian year on which the year of Nabonassar begins, subtract the year, if before Christ, from 748; if after Christ, add to it 747.

NACHOD (Bohemia). At this place the Prussians, under their crown prince, defeated the Austrians, after a severe conflict, 27 June, 1866. The Prussian Uhlans vanquished the Austrian cavalry.

NACOLEA (Phrygia). Near here the usurper Procopius was defeated, and soon afterwards slain by the emperor Valens, 366.

NAFELS (Switzerland). Here an Austrian army was defeated by a small body of Swiss, 1388.

NAGA HILLS MASSACRE, see *India*, 1875.

NAG'S HEAD STORY. Matthew Parker was consecrated archbishop of Canterbury at Lambeth, 17 Dec. 1559, by bishops Barlow, Coverdale, Scory, and Hodgkins. For forty-five years after, the Romish writers asserted that Parker and others had been ordained in an abnormal fashion by Scory at the Nag's Head Tavern, Cheapside. This fiction was refuted by Burnet, and is rejected by Roman Catholic authorities, such as Lingard.

NAHUM, FESTIVAL OF. Nahum, the seventh of the twelve minor prophets, about 713 B.C.; the festival is kept by the Eastern church on 1 December.

NAINI TAL, see *Landslips*, 18 Sept. 1880.

NAISSUS (Mœsia). The Goths were defeated near here with great slaughter by the emperor Claudius II., 269.

NAJARA or **NAVARRETE** (N. Spain). At Logroño, near these places, Edward the Black Prince defeated Henry de Trastamara, and re-established Peter the Cruel on the throne of Castile, 3 April, 1367.

NAMES. Adam and Eve named their sons. *Gen.* iv. 25, 26. A Roman citizen had generally three names; *prænomen*, denoting the individual; *nomen*, the gens or clan; *cognomen*, the branch of the clan: sometimes he had the *agnomen* (*e.g.*, Publius Cornelius Scipio Africanus). The popes change their names on their exaltation to the pontificate, "a custom introduced by pope Sergius, whose name till then was Swine-snout," 687. *Platina.* Onuphrius (followed by most of the modern authorities), refers it to John XII., 956; stating that it was done in imitation of SS. Peter and Paul, who were first called Simon and Saul. In France the name given at baptism was sometimes changed. The two sons of Henry II. of France were christened Alexander and Hercules; at their confirmation these names were changed to Henry and Francis. Monks and nuns, at their entrance into monasteries, assume new names. See *Surnames*. Miss Yonge's "History of Christian Names," published 1863 (new edition 1884). M. A. Lower's "Patronymica Britannica," 1860.

NAMUR, in Belgium, was made a county in 932; taken by the French, 1 July, 1692; by William of England, 4 Aug. 1695; ceded to the house of Austria by the peace of Utrecht, and garrisoned by the Dutch as a barrier town of the United Provinces in 1715. The city of Namur was ceded to Austria, 1713; taken by the French in 1746, but was restored in 1749. In 1782, the emperor Joseph expelled the Dutch garrison. In 1792 it was again taken by the French, who were compelled to evacuate it in 1793; regained 1794; delivered up to the allies, 1814; assigned to Belgium, 1831. It was a site of a severe conflict in June, 1815, between the Prussians and the French under Grouchy, when retreating after the battle of Waterloo. Population, 1890, 29,794; 1900, 32,223.

NANCY (N.E. France), an ancient city, capital of Lorraine, in the 13th century. After taking Nancy, 29 Nov. 1475, and losing it, 5 Oct. 1476, Charles the Bold of Burgundy was defeated beneath its walls, and slain by the duke of Lorraine and the Swiss, 5 Jan. 1477; see *Lorraine*. Nancy was embellished by Stanislas, ex-king of Poland, who resided and died here Feb. 1766. It was captured by Blücher, Jan. 1814, and on the retreat of MacMahon's army, and expecting the German army, surrendered to four Uhlans, 12 Aug. 1870. It was restored at the peace. Population in 1901, 102,463.

Prof. Bleicher, eminent scientist, murdered by M. Four, a chemist, who afterwards committed suicide, 8 June, 1901.

Grand fêtes; visits of president Carnot and the grand duke Constantine of Russia, 5–7 June, 1892.

NANKIN, said to have been made the central capital of China, 420. It was the court of the Ming dynasty from 1369 till Yung-lo removed it to Pekin in 1410. On 4 Aug. 1842, the British ships arrived at Nankin, and peace was made. The rebel Tae-pings took it on 19, 20 March, 1853. It was recaptured by the Imperialists, 19 July, 1864, and found to be in a very desolate condition. Estimated population, 1,000,000.

NANTES (W. France), formerly capital of the Namnetes. The edict in favour of the Protestants issued here by Henry IV., 13 April, 1598, was revoked by Louis XIV., 22 Oct. 1685 (bicentenary celebration, 22 Oct. 1885). Awful cruelties were committed here by the republican Carrier, Oct.-Nov. 1793; see *Drowning*. Population in 1886, 127,482; 1891, 121,054; 1901, 128,349.

NAPHTHA, a clear combustible rock oil, known to the Greeks, called "oil of Media," and thought to have been an ingredient in the Greek fire (*which see*). A rich spring struck near Berdiansk, Russia, Oct. 1899; wells found in cis-Caucasia, Aug. 1903. See *Petroleum*.

NAPIER'S BONES, see *Logarithms*.

NAPLES, formerly the continental division and seat of government of the kingdom of the Two Sicilies, began with a Greek colony named Parthenope (about 1000 B.C.), which was afterwards divided into Palæopolis (the *old*) and Neapolis (the *new* city); from the latter the present name is derived. The colony was conquered by the Romans in the Samnite war, 326 B.C. Naples, after resisting the power of the Lombards, Franks, and Germans, was subjugated by the Normans under Roger Guiscard, king of Sicily, A.D. 1131. Few countries have had so many political changes, and cruel and despotic rulers, or suffered so much by convulsions of nature, such as earthquakes, volcanic eruptions, &c. The eldest son of the king of Italy is styled prince of Naples. In 1856, the population of the kingdom of Naples was 6,886,030, of Sicily 2,231,020; total, 9,117,050. It now forms part of the revived kingdom of Italy. Population of the province in 1889, 1,060,032; 1901, 1,135,906; of the city in 1890, 530,872; 1901, 563,751.

Naples conquered by Theodoric the Goth . . . 493
The city retaken by Belisarius . . . 536
Taken again by Totila . . . 543
Retaken by Narses . . . 552
Becomes a duchy nominally subject to the Eastern empire . . . 568 or 572
Duchy of Naples greatly extended . . . 593
Robert Guiscard, the Norman, made duke of Apulia, founds the kingdom of Naples . . . 1059
Naples conquered, and the kingdom of the Two Sicilies founded by Roger Guiscard II. . . . 1131
The imperial house of Hohenstaufen (see *Germany*) obtains the kingdom by marriage, and rules 1194-1266
The pope appoints Charles of Anjou king, who defeats the regent Manfred (son of Frederick II. of Germany) at Benevento (Manfred slain) 26 Feb. 1266
Charles defeats Conradin (the last of the Hohenstaufens who had come to Naples by invitation of the Ghibellines), at Tagliacozzo, 23 Aug.: Conradin beheaded . . . 29 Oct. 1268
The massacre called the Sicilian vespers (*which see*) 30 March, 1282
Andrew of Hungary, husband of Joanna I., murdered 18 Sept. 1345
His brother Louis, king of Hungary, invades Naples 1349
Queen Joanna put to death . . . 22 May, 1382
Alphonso V. of Arragon (called the Wise and Magnanimous) on the death of Joanna II. seizes Naples 1435
Naples conquered by Charles VIII. of France . . . 1494
And by Louis XII. of France and Ferdinand of Spain, who divide it . . . 1501
Expulsion of the French . . . 1504
Naples and Sicily united to Spain . . . ,,
Insurrection of Masaniello, occasioned by the extortions of the Spanish viceroys. An impost was claimed on a basket of figs, and refused by the owner, with whom the populace took part, headed by Masaniello (Thomas Aniello), a fisherman; they obtained the command of Naples, many of the nobles were slain and their palaces burnt, and the viceroy was compelled to abolish the taxes and to restore the privileges granted by Charles V. to the city . . . June, 1647
Masaniello, intoxicated by his success, was slain by his own followers . . . 16 July, ,,
Another insurrection suppressed by don John of Austria . . . Oct. ,,
Henry II., duke of Guise, lands, and is proclaimed king, but in a few days is taken prisoner by the Spaniards . . . April, 1648
Naples conquered by prince Eugene of Savoy, for the emperor . . . 1706
Discovery of Herculaneum (*which see*) . . . 1711
The Spaniards by the victory at Bitonto (26 May) having made themselves masters of both kingdoms, Charles (of Bourbon), son of the king of Spain, ascends the throne, with the ancient title of king of the Two Sicilies . . . 1734
Order of St. Januarius instituted . . . 1738
Charles, becoming king of Spain, vacates the throne in favour of his third son, Ferdinand, agreeably to treaty . . . 1759
Expulsion of the Jesuits . . . 3 Nov. 1767
Dreadful earthquake in Calabria . . . 5 Feb. 1783
Enrolment of the lazzaroni (*which see*) as pikemen or spontoneers . . . 1793
The king flees on the approach of the French republicans, who establish the Parthenopean republic, 14 Jan. 1799
Nelson appears; Naples retaken; the restored king rules tyrannically . . . June, ,,
Prince Caracciolo tried and executed by order of Nelson . . . 29 June, ,,
The Neapolitans occupy Rome . . . 30 Sept. ,,
Dreadful earthquake; thousands perish . 26 July, 1805
Treaty of neutrality between France and Naples ratified . . . 9 Oct. ,,
Ferdinand, through perfidy, is compelled to flee to Sicily, 23 Jan.; the French enter Naples, and Joseph Bonaparte made king . . . Feb. 1806
The French defeated at Maida . . . 4 July, ,,
Joseph Bonaparte, after beginning many reforms, abdicates for the crown of Spain . . . June, 1808
Joachim Murat made king (rules well) . 15 July, ,,
His first quarrel with Napoleon . . . 1811
His alliance with Austria . . . Jan. 1814
Death of queen Caroline . . . 7 Sept. ,,
Joachim declares war against Austria . 15 March, 1815
Defeated at Tolentino . . . 3 May, ,,
He retires to France, 22 May, and Corsica: he madly attempts the recovery of his throne by landing at Pizzo: seized, tried, and shot . . . 13 Oct. ,,
Ferdinand, re-established, soon returns to tyrannical measures . . . June, ,,
A plague rages in Naples, Nov. 1815 to June . 1816
Establishment of the society of the Carbonari . 1819
Successful insurrection of the Carbonari under gen. Pépé; the king compelled to swear solemnly to a new constitution . . . 13 July, 1820
The Austrians invade the kingdom, at the king's instigation; general Pépé defeated . 7 March, 1821
Fall of the constitutional government . 23 March, ,,
Death of Ferdinand (reigned 66 years) . 4 Jan. 1825
[In 30 years, 100,000 Neapolitans perished by various kinds of death.]
Insurrection of the Carbonari suppressed . Aug. 1828
Accession of Ferdinand II., Bomba (as faithless and tyrannical as his predecessors) . . 8 Nov. 1830
Dispute with England respecting the sulphur trade, 1838; settled . . . May, 1840
Attilio and Emilio Bandiero, with eighteen others, attempting an insurrection in Calabria, are shot 17 Jan. 1844
[The statement that lord Aberdeen had given notice of this attempt was contradicted by his lordship.]
Prospect of an insurrection in Naples; the king grants a new constitution with liberal ministry, 29 Jan. 1848
Great fighting in Naples; the liberals and the national guard almost annihilated by the royal troops, aided by the lazzaroni . . . 15 May, ,,
A martial anarchy prevails; the chiefs of the liberal party arrested in . . . Dec. 1849
Settembrini, Poerio, Carafa, and others, after a mock trial, are condemned, and consigned to horrible dungeons for life . . . June, 1850
After remonstrances with the king on his tyrannical government (May), the English and French ambassadors are withdrawn . . . 28 Oct. 1856
Attempted assassination of the king by Milano 8 Dec. ,
The *Cagliari*, a Sardinian mail steamboat plying between Genoa and Tunis, sailed from the former port on 25 June, 1857, with thirty-three passengers, who, after a few hours' sail, took forcible possession of the vessel, and compelled the two English engineers (Watt and Park) to steer to Ponza . . . 25 June, 1857
[Here they landed, released some prisoners there, took them on board, and sailed to Sapri, where they again landed, and restored the vessel to its commander and crew. The latter steered immediately for Naples; but on the way the vessel was boarded by a Neapolitan cruiser, and all the crew were landed and consigned to dungeons, where they remained for nine months waiting for trial, suffering great privations and insults. This caused great excitement in England; and after much negotiation, the crew were released, the vessel given up to the British government, and 3000*l.* given as a compensation to the sufferers.]

Italian refugees, under count Pisaccane, land in Calabria, are defeated, and their leader killed, 27 June—2 July, 1857

Dreadful earthquake in the Apennines . 16 Dec. „

Amnesty granted to political offenders . 27 Dec. 1858

Poerio and sixty-six companions released and sent to N. America, Jan.; on their way, they seize the vessel, sail to Cork, 7 March; and proceed to London . . . . . 18 March, 1859

Death of Ferdinand II., after dreadful sufferings, 22 May, „

Diplomatic relations resumed with England and France . . . . June, „

A subscription for Poerio and his companions in England amounted to 10,000*l*. . . . July, „

Insubordination among the Swiss troops at Naples, many shot, July 7; major Latour sent to Naples by the Swiss confederation . . . 16 July, „

Army increased; defences strengthened . Oct. „

Many political imprisonments; the foreign ambassadors collectively address a note to the king stating the necessity for reform in his states, 26 March; the count of Syracuse recommends reform and alliance with England . . April, 1860

Garibaldi lands in Sicily, 11 May; defeats the Neapolitan army at Calatafimi . . . 15 May, „

Revolutionary committee at Naples . 15 June, „

Francis II. proclaims an amnesty; promises a liberal ministry; adopts a tricolor flag, &c. 26 June, „

Baron Brenier, French ambassador, wounded in his carriage by the mob . . . . 27 June, „

A liberal ministry formed; destruction of the commissariat of the police in 12 districts; state of siege proclaimed at Naples; the queen-mother flees to Gaeta . . . . . 28 June, „

Garibaldi defeats Neapolitans at Melazzo, 20 July; enters Messina, 21 July; the Neapolitans agree to evacuate Sicily . . . . . 30 July, „

The king of Sardinia in vain negotiates with Francis II. for alliance . . . . . . July, „

Francis II. proclaims the re-establishment of the constitution of 1848, 2 July; the army proclaim count de Trani king . . . . . 10 July, „

Garibaldi lands at Melito, 18 Aug.; takes Reggio, 21 Aug. „

Defection in army and navy; Francis II. retires to Gaeta, 6 Sept.; Garibaldi enters Naples without troops . . . . 7 Sept. „

Garibaldi assumes the dictatorship, 8 Sept.; gives up the Neapolitan fleet to the Sardinian admiral Persano, 11 Sept.; expels the Jesuits; establishes trial by jury; releases political prisoners Sept. „

He repulses the Neapolitans at Cajazzo, 19 Sept.; defeats them at the Volturno . . 1 Oct. 1860

The king of Sardinia enters the kingdom of Naples, and takes command of his army, which combines with Garibaldi's . . . . 11 Oct. „

Naples unsettled through intrigues . . Oct. „

Cialdini defeats the Neapolitans at Isernia, 17 Oct.; at Venafro . . . . 18 Oct. „

The plebiscite at Naples, &c.; almost unanimous vote for annexation to Piedmont (1,303,064 to 10,312) . . . . 21 Oct. „

Garibaldi meets Victor-Emmanuel, and salutes him as king of Italy . . . . . . 26 Oct. „

The first English protestant church built on ground given by Garibaldi; consecrated . 11 March, 1865

Cholera raged at Naples . . . autumn, 1866

Great eruption of Vesuvius began . 12 Nov. 1867

Land-slip at Naples; 20 persons engulfed 28 Jan. 1868

Victor-Emmanuel, prince of Naples (son of prince Humbert), born at Naples . . . 11 Nov. 1869

Maritime exhibition opened at Naples . 17 April, 1871

Great marine biological laboratory organised by Dr. Dohrn 1872

Manzo and his band of brigands (said to be the last), destroyed by soldiers . . . . 20 Aug. 1873

National exhibition of the fine arts opened at Naples by the king . . . . . . 8 April, 1877

Death of Sisto Riario Sforza, cardinal archbishop, a proposed successor to the pope . 6 Oct. „

Antonio Scialoia, statesman and financier, died, aged 61 . . . . about 17 Oct. „

Revival of brigandage, chiefly in the south, July, Aug. 1878

Asiatic cholera rages in Naples and Spezzia (see *Cholera*). The king energetic in relieving the sufferers, 7-14 Sept.; disease dying out . 6 Oct. 1884

Naples visited by the king Humbert and the emperor William II. . . . . . . 16 Oct. 1888

The king inaugurates new sanitary works 15 June, 1889

Trial of the two dukes of Vilarosa for the murder of lieut. Leone, a suitor for the hand of their sister, 30 Dec. 1888; one brother acquitted, the other sentenced to 5 years' imprisonment; much indignation . . . . 22 Dec. 1892

Panic through fire in a church at Torre dell' Annunziata, 13 deaths . . . . 23 April, 1893

Visit of the king and queen and the German emperor and empress . . . . . 27 April, „

Decree issued suspending the studies at the university for a year in consequence of disorders, Feb. 1895

Municipal elections, the Camorristi defeated, Nov. 1901

Naples visited by king Edward VII. . 23-27 April, 1903

Monte di Pietà burned down, damage, 2,000,000 lire, 2 June, „

[General history under *Italy*.]

Sovereigns of Naples and Sicily.

1131. Roger I. (of Sicily, 1130), *Norman*.
1154. William I. the Bad; son.
1166. William II. the Good; son.
1189. Tancred, natural son of Roger.
1194. William III. son, succeeded by Constance, married to Henry VI. of Germany.
1197. Frederick II. of Germany (*Hohenstaufen*).
1250. Conrad; son.
1254 Conradin, son; but his uncle,
1258. Manfred, natural son of Frederick II., seizes the government; killed at Benevento, in 1266.
1266. Chas. of *Anjou*, brother of St. Louis, king of France. [Conradin beheaded, 29 Oct. 1268.]
1282. Insurrection in Sicily.

(*Separation of the Kingdoms in* 1282.)

NAPLES.

1282. Charles I. of Anjou.
1285. Charles II.; son.
1309. Robert the Wise; brother.
1343. Joanna (reigns with her husband, Andrew of Hungary), 1343-45; with Louis of Tarento, 1349-62; Joanna put to death (22 May, 1382) by
1382. Charles III., grandson of Charles II.: he becomes king of Hungary; assassinated there, 1386.
„ Louis I., titular, crowned.
1385. Louis II., son of Louis I.
1386. Ladislas of Hungary.
1414. Joanna II., sister, dies in 1435, and bequeaths her dominions to Regnier of Anjou. They are acquired by

SICILY.

1282. Peter I. (III. of Arragon.)
1285. James I. (II. of Arragon.)
1295. Frederick II.
1337. Peter II.
1342. Louis.
1355. Frederick III.
1376. Maria and Martin (her husband).
1402. Martin I.
1409. Martin II.
1410. Ferdinand I.
1416. Alphonso I.

1435. Alphonso I. thus king of Naples and Sicily.

(*Separation of Naples and Sicily in* 1458.)

NAPLES.

1458. Ferdinand I.
1494. Alphonso II. abdicates.
1495. Ferdinand II.
1496. Frederic II. expelled by the French, 1501.

SICILY.

1458. John of Arragon.
1479. Ferdinand the Catholic of Spain.

The Crowns United.

1503. Ferdinand III. (king of Spain).
1516. Charles I. (V. of Germany).
1556. Philip I. (II. of Spain).
1598. Philip II. (III. of Spain).
1621. Philip III. (IV. of Spain).
1665. Charles II. (of Spain).
1700. Philip IV. (V. of Spain), Bourbons.
1707. Charles III. of Austria.

(*Separation in* 1713.)

NAPLES.	SICILY.
1713. Charles III. of Austria.	1713. Victor Amadeus of Savoy (exchanged Sicily for Sardinia, 1720.)

THE TWO SICILIES.

(*Part of the empire of Germany*, 1720-34.)

1735. Charles IV. (III. of Spain).	1759. Ferdinand IV., fled from Naples to Sicily, 1806.

(*Separation in* 1806.)

NAPLES.	SICILY.
1806. Joseph Napoleon Bonaparte.	1806-15. Ferdinand IV.
1808. Joachim Murat, shot 13 Oct. 1815.	

THE TWO SICILIES.

1815. Ferdinand I., formerly Ferdinand IV., of Naples and Sicily.	1859. Francis II., 22 May; born 16 Jan. 1836; last KING OF NAPLES; deposed; fled 6 Sept. 1860; died at Arco, 27 Dec. 1894.
1825. Francis I.	1861. Victor-Emmanuel II. of Sardinia, as KING OF ITALY, March; (see *Italy*, end).
1830. Ferdinand II., Nov. 8 (termed king Bomba).	

NAPOLEON CODE, see *Codes*.

NAPOLEON MEMORIAL: subscriptions from the Royal family and the three services for a statue of prince Louis Napoleon (killed in Zululand, 1 June, 1879), were closed about 15 July. 1879. The statue was placed in St. George's chapel, Windsor, May, 1881; placing it in Westminster Abbey having been much opposed.

NARBONNE (S.E. France), the Roman Narbo Martius, founded 118 B.C., made capital of a Visigothic kingdom, 462; captured by the Saracens, 720; re-taken by Pepin le Bref, 759. Gaston de Foix, the last vicomte (killed at Ravenna, 11 April, 1512), resigned it to the king in exchange for the duchy of Nemours. Many councils held here, 589-1374.

NARCEINE AND NARCOTINE, alkaloids obtained from *Opium* (*which see*). Narceine was discovered by Pelletier in 1832; and narcotine by Derosne in 1803.

Crystallized narceine was stated by M. Laborde at Paris to be an innocuous anæsthetic, June 1890.

NARVA (Esthonia, Russia). Here Peter the Great of Russia was totally defeated by Charles XII. of Sweden, then in his nineteenth year, 30 Nov. 1700. The army of Peter is said to have amounted to 60,000, some Swedes affirm 100,000 men, while the Swedes were about 20,000. Charles attacked the enemy in his intrenchments, and slew 18,000; 30,000 surrendered. He had several horses shot under him. He said, "These people seem disposed to give me exercise." Narva was taken by Peter in 1704.

NASEBY (Northamptonshire), the site of a decisive victory over Charles I. by the parliament army under Fairfax and Cromwell. The main body of the royal army was commanded by lord Astley; prince Rupert led the right wing, sir Marmaduke Langdale the left, and the king himself headed the body of reserve. The king fled, losing his cannon, baggage, and nearly 5000 prisoners, 14 June, 1645. Foundation of the Cromwell tercentenary library, proposed at the meeting here on the protector's birthday, 25 April, 1899; two rare records (illustrated) of the commonwealth secured, June, 1899.

NASHVILLE (Tennessee, N. America) was occupied by the confederates in 1861, and taken by the federals, 23 Feb. 1862. Near here the confederates under Hood were defeated by the federals under Thomas, 14-16 Dec. 1864. Population, 1890, 76,168; 1900, 80,865.

NASSAU, a German duchy, made a county by the emperor Frederic I. about 1180, for Wolfram, a descendant of Conrad I. of Germany; from whom are descended the royal house of Orange, now reigning in Holland (see *Orange* and *Holland*), and the present duke of Nassau. Wiesbaden was made the capital in 1839. On 25 April, 1860, the Nassau chamber strongly opposed the conclusion of a concordat with the pope, and claimed liberty of faith and conscience. The duke adopted the Austrian motion at the German diet, 14 June, and after the war the duchy was annexed to Prussia by decree, 20 Sept., and possession taken, 8 Oct. 1866. Population of the duchy in 1865, 468,311.

1788. Count Frederic William made DUKE in 1806.
1814. William-George, 20 Aug.
1839. Adolphus-William-Charles, born 24 July, 1817; assumed the regency of Luxemburg 10 April, 1889, became grand duke on the decease of the king of Holland, 23 Nov. 1890. See *Luxemburg*.

NATAL (Cape of Good Hope). Vasco de Gama landed here on 25 Dec. 1497, and hence named it Terra Natalis.

The Dutch attempted to colonise it about . . . 1721
The Zulu power established about . . . 1812
Lieut. Farewell, with some emigrants, settled . 1823
Capt. Allen Gardiner's treaty with the Zulus, 6 May, 1835
Dutch republic, Natalia, set up; put down by the British . . . 12 May, 1842
Natal annexed to the British possessions . 8 Aug. 1843
Made a bishopric (Dr. John Wm. Colenso, bishop), 1853; and an independent colony . . . 1856
Attempts to depose bishop Colenso for unsound doctrine having failed, the rev. W. R. Macrorie was sent out as bp. of Maritzburg, to act with the clergy opposed to their bishop Dec. 1868
See *Church of England*, 1863-8.
A bishop of Zululand appointed . . . 1871
Alleged insurrection of Caffres under Langalibalele, quickly suppressed . . Nov.-Dec. 1873
He and others were tried, it was said illegally, and punished with imprisonment; he is sent to Robben island . . . . . 4 Aug. 1874
Bishop Colenso came to England to advocate his case . . . . ,,
Sir Garnet Wolseley sent as temporary governor, Feb.; Langalibalele released, and placed under surveillance out of the colony; sir Garnet returns . . . . . Aug. 1875
Succeeded by Mr. Walter J. Sendall, appointed, Nov. 1882
Great dissatisfaction in the colony at this appointment . . . . . . Nov. ,,
Death of bishop Colenso . . 20 June, 1883
Governors of Natal: Robt. Wm. Keate, 1867; Anthony Musgrave, 1873; sir Benj. C. C. Pine, 1874; sir H. Ernest Bulwer, Sept. 1878; sir Garnet Wolseley, May, 1879; sir George Pomeroy Colley, May, 1880; killed at the battle of Majuba Hill, 27 Feb. 1881
Sir Henry E. G. Bulwer nominated governor, Dec. 1882; sir A. E. Havelock, Nov. 1885; sir Charles B. H. Mitchell, Aug. 1889; sir Walter F. Hely-Hutchinson, June; arrives . . 30 Sept. 1893
The legislative council offers to undertake the administration of Zululand at the cost of the colony to check the encroaching Boers about

22 Oct.; sanction refused by the British government announced . . . . 27 Oct. 1886
Slight military mutiny; two men killed in its suppression at Fort Napier . . 7 Aug. 1887
The council vote for a free and responsible government . . . . 26 June, 1890
At Pietermaritzburg (the capital) a statue of the queen by sir E. Boehm was unveiled by sir Charles Mitchell . . . . . . 8 July, „
The bill for a new constitution voted . 3 Feb. 1891
Parliament opened . . . . 30 April, „
Constitutional bill passed, parliament prorogued, 8 Aug. „
Conference of two Natal delegates, sir John Robinson and Mr. Sutton, with lord Knutsford May, 1892
Railway to Orange Free State opened . 13 July, „
Responsible government deferred by the legislative council, about 7 Oct. 1892; approved by the council, 1 March, 1893; bill passed by the council, 11 May; proclaimed . . . 4 July, 1893
A ministry formed, sir John Robinson, premier, 10 Oct.; parliament opened by the governor, 19 Oct.; prorogued . . . . . 27 Oct. „
The new parliament opened by the governor, 25 April, 1894
Mail train from Johannesburg wrecked near Durban, 35 deaths (mostly women and children) 30 Dec. 1895
Strong resistance to the immigration of Indians at Durban, reported . . . . . . Jan. 1897
Sir J. Robinson resigns; new ministry formed by the hon. H. Escombe, att.-gen. 13 Feb.; resigns, succeeded by Mr. Henry Binns (knt. 1898, died June, 1899) . . . . 5 Oct. „
British squadron, under rear-admiral Rawson, arrives at Durban, 16 April; leaves . . 20 April, „
Annexation of Zululand agreed to . 17 Dec. „
The monthly output of coal, 30,000 tons in Natal; the government offers to supply H.M. navy calling at Durban, 12,000 tons of coal annually, free of cost, 30 March; accepted gratefully 2 April, 1898
The town hall at Pietermaritzburg burnt down 12 July, „
Statue of the queen (by W. H. Thornycroft) at Durban, unveiled by the governor . 19 April, 1899
Parliament opened by the governor, increase of revenue reported . . . . . . 11 May, „
New ministry, col. Hime premier . . 10 June, „
Loyal meetings sympathising with the Uitlanders, see *Transvaal* . . . . 1 July, „
Preparations for war, reserves called out . Sept. „
Sir George White appointed commander of British forces in Natal; arrives . . . . 7 Oct. „
Boers concentrated on the frontier, Sept.; invade Natal; see *S. African War* . . . 10 Oct. „
Death of Mr. H. Escombe, ex-premier, aged 61, 27 Dec. „
The Natal ministry heartily supports the policy of the imperial government in S. Africa, 27 March, 1900
Lord Roberts warmly welcomed . . 30 Nov. „
Sir H. E. McCallum succeeds Sir W. F. Hely-Hutchinson as governor, Jan.; arrives, 13 May, 1901
Good budget; 3,000,000*l.* loan for railways, harbours, &c., proposed . . . . . 23 May, „
The duke and duchess of Cornwall visit Durban, 13 Aug.; the duke opens the new town hall at Pietermaritzburg, receives an address from 55 Zulu chiefs, reviews the troops and distributes medals, &c. . . . . 14 Aug. „
Parliament dissolved by proclamation . 30 Aug. „
Lord Milner is presented with an address at Pietermaritzburg, thanks Natal for its great services, and hopes for a peaceful, prosperous, progressive South Africa under the British flag, 25 Oct.; at Durban and Ladysmith . . . 25, 30 Oct. „
Parliament opened by sir H. McCallum . 27 Feb. 1902
Resolution passed in the legislative assembly repudiating the slanders on the British army and nation . . . . 3 March, „
Mr. Seddon, premier of New Zealand, warmly received at Durban . . . . . 17 May, „
Annexation (territory) bill (Vryheid reunited to Zululand; Utrecht and part of the Wakkerstroom district added to Natal) passed, 12 May, „
Martial law repealed, with certain restrictions, 4 Oct. „
Parliament opened by the governor, ministerial majority, one . . . . 13 Nov. 1902
Mr. and Mrs. Chamberlain enthusiastically received at Durban; he speaks warmly of his mission "to draw more closely together the people of the mother country and their kinsmen over seas," 26 Dec.; in a great speech at Pietermaritzburg, he urged the necessity of imperial as well as colonial union, and added that Natal, by renouncing claims for war losses, would contribute nearly 2,000,000*l.* to the war . . . 30 Dec. „
Visits Ladysmith, entertained at a banquet, 1 Jan.; visits Spion Kop . . . . 2 Jan. 1903
Parliament opened by sir H. McCallum . 30 April, „
New floating dock for Durban launched in England, 8 Aug. „
New ministry, Mr. Sutton, premier . 17 Aug. „
Population, 326,957 (20,490 whites), 1876; in 1886, 442,697; in 1891, 543,913; 1901, 925,118. See *Zululand.*

NATIONAL AGRICULTURAL HALL, see under *Agriculture.*

NATIONAL ANTHEM, see *God save the King.*

NATIONAL ASSEMBLY, French. Upon the proposition of the abbé Siéyès, the states-general of France constituted themselves the National Assembly, 17 June, 1789. On the 20th the hall of this new assembly was shut by order of the king; upon which the deputies of the *tiers état* repaired to the *Jeu de Paume*, or Tennis-court, and swore not to dissolve until they had digested a constitution for France. On the 22nd they met at the church at St. Louis. This assembly abolished the state religion, annulled monastic vows, divided France into departments, sold the national domains, established a national bank, issued assignats, and dissolved itself 21 Sept. 1792; see *National Convention.* In 1848 the legislature was again termed the National Assembly. It met 4 May, and a new constitution was proclaimed, 12 Nov. A new constitution was once more proclaimed by Louis Napoleon in Jan. 1852, after dissolving the National Assembly, 2 Dec. 1851. The present French National Assembly was elected 8 Feb., and met 12 Feb. 1871; new constitution adopted, 25 Feb. 1875; see *France.*

NATIONAL ASSEMBLY, German, see *Germany*, 1848.

NATIONAL ASSOCIATIONS. One was formed in 1584, headed by the earl of Leicester, to protect queen Elizabeth from assassination, in consequence of the discovery of various plots. Another was proposed in the house of commons, in Feb. 1696, by sir Rowland Gwyn, for the defence of the person and government of William III. soon after the discovery of the assassination plot (*which see*). The members of both houses of parliament and the majority of the male population joined it immediately; all persons holding office under government were required to be members; see *Aid to Sick and Wounded, Artillery, Arts, Colonies, Education, Employers, Farmers, Social Science, Tuberculosis,* and *Volunteers.*

NATIONAL BENEVOLENT INSTITUTION, established 1812, incorporated 1859. Pensions are granted to decayed gentry, and to professional people, teachers, and others in reduced circumstances.

NATIONAL CONVENTION of France, constituted in the hall of the Tuileries 17 Sept., and formally opened 21 Sept. 1792, when M. Grégoire, at the head of the National Assembly, announced that that assembly had ceased its functions. It was then decreed, "That the citizens named by the French people to form the National Convention, being met to the number of 371, after having verified their powers, declare that the National Convention is constituted." This convention continued until a new constitution was organised, and the executive directory was installed at the Little Luxembourg, 1 Nov. 1795; see *Directory*. The chartists (*which see*) in England formed a national convention in 1839.

NATIONAL COUNCIL OF THE EVANGELICAL FREE CHURCHES,

popularly known as "The Free Church Council," originated in an article by dr. Guinness Rogers to the *Methodist Times*, 20 Feb. 1890. The idea of the article, for the federation of the nonconformist bodies to promote their common interests, took practical shape, and the first free church congress was held at Manchester, 7 Nov. 1892. The second congress took place at Leeds, Mar. 1894, when it was determined that each congress should have an official president, dr. Berry being the first elected to hold that office. Since that date the congress has been held annually. The objects of the national council are "to facilitate intercourse and co-operation among the evangelical free churches; to assist in the organization of local councils; to encourage devotional fellowship and mutual counsel concerning the spiritual life and religious activities of the churches; to advocate the New Testament doctrine of the church, and to defend the rights of the associated churches; to promote the application of the law of Christ in every relation of human life." Among prominent past and present leaders of the movement have been and are dr. Clifford, rev. F. B. Meyers (president for 1903), dr. Guinness Rogers, the late rev. H. Price Hughes, dr. Munro Gibson, dr. Fairbairn, rev. T. Law (the secretary), the late dr. Dale, the late dr. Parker, the late dr. Berry, dr. Townsend, dr. A. Maclaren, Messrs. G. Cadbury, R. W. Perks, M.P., Evan Spicer, J. Rutherford, and other prominent nonconformists. In addition to social organizations, "free church lectures" on the history and principles of nonconformity are given. The free church council has taken a very active part in the nonconformist agitation against the education act of 1902, and that for London 1903, and also in the passive resistance movement (*which see*). Offices, Memorial hall, Farringdon-street, E.C.

NATIONAL DEBT. In 1693 an excise act was passed, granting duties for carrying on the war with France; the act also secured certain recompenses and advantages to such persons as should collectively advance 1,000,000*l*. for the same purpose; this sum was speedily subscribed. The permanent debt began by the establishment of the Bank of England in 1694, mainly through the exertions of Charles Montague, afterwards earl of Halifax, under the condition of its lending money to the government on interest, the repayment of the principal not to be demanded. The rapid growth of the debt was mainly caused by foreign wars, and its reduction was continually demanded. See *Stocks*, *Sinking Fund*, and *Local Loans*. Debts of the metropolitan authorities by loans, reported by Mr. Cosmo Rose-Innes (*Times*, 24 Oct. 1895), about 38,500,000*l*., yearly charge about 2,500,000*l*. Total debt of the English and Welsh local authorities 1885, 173,207,968*l*.; 1895, 202,742,864*l*.; 1900, 293,864,224*l*.

Amount of the National Debt, see *Wars*, 1689 *et seq.* 1691, 3,130,000*l*.; 1701, 12,552,486*l*.; 1714, 36,175,460*l*.; 1748, 75,812,132*l*.; 1763, 132,716,049*l*.; 1792, 239,663,421*l*.; 1815, 861,039,049*l*.; 1820, 834,900,960*l*.; 1830, 784,803,997*l*.; 1840, 789,578,720*l*.; 1850, 787,029,162*l*.; 1856, 807,981,788*l*.; 1901, 690,992,621*l*.; 1903, 770,779,000*l*.

(31 March)		*Debt.*
1861.	Funded debt	£785,119,609
	Unfunded	16,689,000
1866.	Funded debt	773,313,229
	Unfunded	8,187,700
1871.	Funded debt	732,043,270
	Unfunded	6,091,000
1876.	Funded debt	713,657,517
	Unfunded	*11,401,800
1881.	Funded debt	709,078,526
	Unfunded	22,077,500
1884.	Funded debt	640,631,095
	Unfunded	14,110,600
1885.	Funded debt	640,181,896
	Unfunded	14,033,100
1886.	Funded debt	638,849,694
	Unfunded	17,602,800
1887.	Funded debt	637,637,640
	Unfunded	17,517,900
1888.	Funded debt	609,740,743
	Unfunded	17,385,100
1889.	Funded debt	607,057,811
	Unfunded	16,093,322
1890.	Funded debt	585,959,852
	Unfunded	32,252,305
1891.	Funded debt	579,472,082
	Unfunded	36,140,079
1892.	Funded debt	577,944,665
	Unfunded	35,312,994
1893.	Funded debt	589,533,082
	Unfunded	20,748,270
1894.	Funded debt	587,631,096
	Unfunded	21,446,300
1895.	Funded debt	586,015,919
	Unfunded	17,400,300
1896.	Funded debt	589,146,878
	Unfunded	9,975,800
1897.	Funded debt	587,698,732
	Unfunded	8,133,000
1898.	Funded debt	585,788,000
	Unfunded	8,133,000
1899.	Funded debt	583,186,305
	Unfunded	8,133,000
1900.	Funded debt	552,606,898
	Unfunded	16,133,000
1901.	Funded debt	551,182,153
	Unfunded	78,133,000
1902.	Funded debt	609,587,248
	Unfunded	75,133,000

[Exclusive of terminable annuities, estimated, 1867, 27,521,513*l*.; 1872, 55,749,070*l*.; 1876, 51,911,227*l*.; 1878, 46,335,589*l*.]

The National Debt and Local Loans act passed 12 July, 1887, see *Local Loans*.

Mr. Matthew O'Reilly Dease, formerly M.P. for Louth, bequeaths about 40,000*l*. towards extinguishing the national debt; he died 17 Aug. 1887.

The National Debt Redemption act with suitable provisions was passed; royal assent, 11 April, 1889.

Sir Stafford Northcote's act provides the annual charge of 28,000,000*l*.; the surplus to be devoted to the reduction of the debt—1876.

The annual interest in 1850 was 23,862,257*l*.; and the total interest, including annuities, amounted to 27,699,740*l*. On 1 Jan. 1851, the total unredeemed debt of Great Britain and Ireland was 769,272,562*l*., the charge on which for interest and management was 27,620,449*l*. The total charge on the debt for interest and management, 1872, 26,839,601*l*.

Mr. Childers' plan for reducing national debt by terminable annuities, commencing 1885, April, 1883.

National Debt Conversion of Stock act passed 3 July, 1884; accepted, 17 Oct. 1884, 18,666,000*l*. for 2½ per cent.; 4,451,000*l*. for 2¾ per cent., by government, nearly 12,000,000*l*.

Annual charge reduced by 2,000,000*l*., April, 1887. Reduced to 25,000,000*l*. by new act passed, royal assent, 31 May, 1889.

* Including Suez Canal bonds, 1876, 4,000,000*l*.; 1877, 3,990,000*l*.; 1878, 3,929,200*l*.

Mr. Göschen's National Debt Conversion act; royal assent 27 March, 1888.

[3 per cent. stock reduced to 2¾ till 5 April, 1903, and afterwards to 2½, new stock not redeemable till 5 April, 1923.]

National debt redemption act passed, 1893.

See *Budget* 1899, 1900, 1901, 1902, 1903.

ESTIMATED FOREIGN NATIONAL DEBTS.

France (1902)	£1,157,687,553	Belgium (1901)	£111,122,054
Germany (1899)	117,283,000	Sweden (1901) .	19,396,240
Russia (1901) .	690,017,109	Norway (1900) .	12,695,879
Austria (1902) .	384,565,000	Denmark (1901).	12,071,901
Hungary (1902)	210,390,000	Switzerland (1900)	15,050,288
Italy (1902) .	512,040,000	Greece (1902) .	13,616,687
Spain (1901).	433,283,066	China (1899) .	54,500,000
Portugal (1901).	171,723,502	Japan (1902) .	52,957,264
Turkey (1902) .	123,729,595	United States	
Holland (1902).	95,032,537	(1901) . . .	275,935,067

NATIONAL DEFENCE, see *Colonial Defences Commission*, under *Colonies*, 1879, *Naval and Military Administration*, 1895.

Resolutions voted in the commons for supporting arrangements with the colonies in providing ships, &c., 850,000*l.*; and for defence of various ports and coaling stations, 2,600,000*l.* 15 May, 1888.

National Defence act passed 13 Aug. 1888; another act passed 31 May, 1889; see *Navy*, 1889.

NATIONAL DRAMATIC ACADEMY proposed by professor H. Morley and others in 1879.

NATIONAL FEDERATION (Irish) established in opposition to Mr. Parnell, by Mr. Justin M'Carthy and other M.P.'s, supported by the R. C. bishops and clergy; inaugural meeting at Dublin, 10 March, 1891. Its organ is the *National Press*, first published, 7 March, 1891. See *Ireland*, March, 1892.

NATIONAL GALLERY, London, began with the purchase, by the British government, of the Angerstein collection of 38 pictures, for 57,000*l.*, in 1824. The first exhibition of them took place in Pall-mall, on 10 May, 1824. Sir G. Beaumont (1826), Mr. Holwell Carr (1831), and many other gentlemen, as well as the British Institution, contributed many fine pictures; and the collection has been since greatly augmented by gifts and purchases. The present edifice in Trafalgar-square, designed by Mr. Wilkins, was completed and opened 9 April, 1838. In July, 1857, a commission appointed to consider the propriety of removing the pictures reported in favour of their remaining in their present locality; and in 1860, 15,000*l.* were voted to be expended in adapting the central part of the building to exhibition purposes. On 11 May, 1861, the National Gallery was reopened after having been closed eight months, during which time great improvements were made in the internal arrangements. On 19 June, 1865, the house of commons voted 20,000*l.* to buy land to enlarge the building, and an act for this purpose was passed 15 July, 1866. Visitors in 1866, 775,901; in 1871, 911,658; in 1883, 849,604; sum voted for year 1867-8, 15,895*l.*, for 1876, 20,098*l.* Legacy from Francis Wm. Clarke, about 24,000*l.*, fell in 1880; 1880, pictures 1040. The gallery opened to the public *free* Mon., Tues., Wed., Sat.; Student's days Thurs. and Fri., 6*d.*; Sun ay, Apr. to Oct. (inclusive) 2 to 5 or 6 p.m.

Sir Charles Eastlake, director, 1850; sir Fred. W. Burton, 1864; Mr. (afterwards sir) Edward J. Poynter, April, 1894; Mr. Hawes Harison Turner succeeds (Mr. Chas. L. Eastlake, 20 years keeper) . . March, 1898

A parliamentary return gives a list of pictures presented to or purchased for the National Gallery—284 presented, 256 bequeathed, and 313 purchased. The cost of the 313 purchases, which has been spread over 45 years, has been 254,527*l.* Up to 1871, 337,195*l.* had been expended. The Peel collection (70 pictures), bought for 75,000*l.*, spring, 1871. Two pictures of the Blenheim collection were bought for 83,520*l.*, March, 1885 (Raphael's "Ansidei Madonna" 70,000*l.*). The "Congress of Munster," a master-piece of Terburg (valued at 7280*l.* in 1868), presented by sir Richard Wallace, Oct. 1871.

Mr. Wynn Ellis (a silk merchant, born July, 1780; died 27 Nov. 1875) bequeathed about 800 pictures to the National Gallery on certain conditions. Re-opened; new galleries erected by E. Barry; pictures re-arranged, Aug., 1876.

About 1030 oil paintings in the gallery . March, 1882

Mr. Henry Tate presents 57 modern pictures (value nearly 90,000*l.*), announced 8 March; declined by the government for want of space; the government proposes placing his pictures in galleries at South Kensington, 26 June, 1890; sir John Millais' "Order of Release" bought by sir Henry Tate (5000 gs.) at the Renton sale, 30 April, presented by him to the gallery, May, 1898.

Three of the earl of Radnor's pictures purchased for the gallery for 55,000*l.* (Holbein's "Ambassadors," and two portraits by Velasquez and Moroni), reported July, 1890.

[The government gave 25,000*l.*, lord Rothschild, sir Edward Guinness (since lord Iveagh) and Mr. Charles Cotes, each 10,000*l.*]

Mr. (now sir) William Agnew offers to present 10,000*l.* towards the erection of a special National gallery of British art, near Kensington palace, 21 July, 1890.

An anonymous donor (Mr. Henry Tate) through Mr. Humphry Ward, offers to the government 80,000*l.* for the erection of a National gallery of British art, 12 March; accepted by Mr. Goschen, 19 March, 1891.

Mr. Tate, not approving of the site proposed by the government, withdraws his offer, 3 March, 1892.

The site of Millbank prison proposed by government, Nov.; accepted by Mr. Tate (bart. May, 1898; died, 5 Dec. 1899), Dec. 1892; the building, designed by Mr. Sidney Smith, erected by Messrs. Higgs and Hill, opened by the prince of Wales, 21 July, 1897; nine new rooms added, 27 Nov. 1899.

A collection of Gainsboroughs given to the nation by the Misses Lane, Dec. 1896.

Mr. Chas. Holroyd appointed keeper of the Gallery of British Art, July, 1897.

"Pictures in the National Gallery," with notes, &c., by C. L. Eastlake, illustrated, published 1899. "The National Gallery," edited by sir E. J. Poynter, vols. i. and ii., Dec. 1899.

"The Death of Chatterton," by Wallis, bequeathed to the nation by the late C. G. Clement, placed in the gallery, Dec. 1899.

Millais's "Boyhood of Raleigh" (realised 5,200 gs. 12 May), presented by lady Tate to the gallery, May, 1900.

National Gallery (purchase of adjacent land) act passed, 1901.

Lord Cheylesmore (died 10 July) bequeathed five pictures to the gallery, 1902.

Mr. G. F. Watts, R.A., completes his gift of ethical and allegorical pictures by his large picture, "The Court of Death" . . Feb. 1903

Cosmopolitan club present Mr. Watts' painting of "The Banquet of Anastasio degli Onesti" to the National Gallery . . . . Feb. "

"The Nation's Pictures" (Cassell & Co.), 48th part, completing the work . . published Aug. "

National Art Collections fund inaugurated, Sept. "

NATIONAL GUARD of France was instituted by the Committee of Safety at Paris on 13 July, 1789 (the day before the destruction of the Bastille), to maintain order and defend the public liberty. Its first colours were blue and red, to which white was added, when its formation was approved by the king. Its action was soon paralysed by the revolution, and it ceased altogether under the consulate and empire. It was revived by Napoleon in 1814, and maintained by Louis XVIII., but was broken up by Charles X., after a tumultuous review in 1827. It was revived in 1830, and helped to place Louis Philippe on the throne. In 1848 its reconstitution and its enlargement from 80,000 to 100,000 men led to the frightful conflict of

June, 1848. Its constitution was entirely changed in Jan. 1852, when it was subjected entirely to the control of the government. Formerly it had many privileges, such as choosing its own officers, &c. In consequence of the defection of part of the National Guard and the incompetency of the rest during the outbreak in Paris in 1871, its gradual abolition was decreed by the national assembly at Versailles (488-154), 24 Aug. 1871. The peaceful disarmament began in September. National guards established in Spain, Naples, and other countries, during the nineteenth century.

NATIONAL HEALTH SOCIETY, founded in 1873 for the collection and diffusion of sanitary knowledge, by lectures and otherwise.

NATIONALISTS. The name taken by the party in Ireland demanding legislative independence, &c., opposed by the Unionists. See *Ireland (Young)*, *Home Rule*, *Parnellites*, and *Separatists*.

NATIONALITY; a word much used since 1848. In Poland, Hungary, Italy, and Germany, the struggle for nationality has been long and severe. In 1866 agitation for this principle began in Bohemia, Slavonia, and other parts of the Austrian empire. The nationality of Ireland is the alleged basis of the Fenian agitation; see *Ireland*, 1870, and *Home Government*.

NATIONALIZATION, &c., see under *Land*.

NATIONAL LEAGUES, see *Leagues* and *Ireland*, 1882 *et seq*.

NATIONAL LIBERAL FEDERATION, see under *Liberals*.

NATIONAL OPERA HOUSE, N. Thames Embankment; Mr. Mapleson, proprietor; Mr. F. H. Fowler, architect; Mr. Wm. Webster, contractor. First *brick* laid by Mlle. Tietjens, 7 Sept.; first *stone* laid by the duke of Edinburgh, 16 Dec. 1875. Failure of the scheme reported, Nov. 1877. Materials sold, 24 June 1880, *et seq.*; estimated loss by the scheme about 100,000*l.*; the building was pulled down, May, 1888.

NATIONAL PHYSICAL LABORATORY, see *Physical*.

NATIONAL PORTRAIT EXHIBITIONS proposed by the earl of Derby, earl Granville, and others, at a meeting in London, 13 July, 1865. They were held in what had been the refreshment room of the Exhibition of 1862, at South Kensington. The 1st was opened 16 April; closed 18 Aug. 1866: 2nd, opened 3 May; closed 31 Aug. 1867: 3rd, opened 13 April; closed 22 Aug. 1868.

NATIONAL PORTRAIT GALLERY was determined on in Feb. 1857, in pursuance of votes from both houses of parliament. The sum of 2000*l.* was appropriated for the purchase of portraits of persons eminent in British history. Donations are received under certain restrictions. The gallery, Gt. George-street, Westminster, was opened 15 Jan. 1859. Director, &c., George Scharf, C.B.; K.C.B., 1895; literary artist; born, 1820; died, 19 April, 1895; succeeded by Mr. Lionel Cust, April, 1895. The collection was removed to South Kensington Dec. 1869, and reopened 28 March, 1870. The pictures removed to Bethnal Green museum for safety after the fire at the Indian museum, June, 1885. A valuable collection of national portraits appeared at the Manchester exhibition in 1857.

The marquis of Salisbury at the Royal Academy dinner, stated that the government had received an anonymous offer to erect a building for the National Portrait Gallery, if a site were provided, 4 May, 1889.

Mr. W. H. Alexander having given 100,000*l.*, the north extremity of the National Gallery chosen for the site of the new building, July; bill passed 26 July, 1889.

Mr. G. F. Watts presents 15 oil portraits and 2 drawings to the gallery, announced, 6 Dec. 1895.

The new gallery in St. Martin's-place, W.C., opened, 4 April, 1896.

Col. John Barrow, F.R.S., bequeathed a series of portraits by Mr. Stephen Pearce, relating to the search for Sir John Franklin (and arctic portraits bequeathed by Lady Franklin), received April, 1899; other gifts, June; the queen presents the portrait of herself by Sir George Hayter, Aug. 1899. Total bequests, &c., 1431 up to 1901.

National Portrait Gallery for Scotland.—30,000*l.* offered by a gentleman to form a collection and erect a building 1883–4. The building at Edinburgh was opened by the marquis of Lothian, 15 July, 1889.

NATIONAL REFORM UNION, see under *Reform Association*.

NATIONAL REVIEW, Conservative, first appeared March, 1883.

NATIONAL SCHOOLS, see *Education* and *Music*, 1873.

NATIONAL SERVICE LEAGUE, to advocate the adoption of drill as a compulsory subject in schools, and to urge that military and naval training be made compulsory by law; formed at a meeting at Apsley house, the duke of Wellington president, 26 Feb.; a meeting held at Oxford, 12 Nov. 1902. First annual meeting 26 May, 1903.

NATIONAL SOCIETY for promoting the Education of the Poor in the principles of the established church of England, founded 1811, incorporated 1817. In 1883 there were 2,385,374 children, and 28,000,000*l.* had been expended. Training colleges: St. Mark's, Chelsea, Whitelands, and Battersea. Annual meetings. National society for the employment of epileptics; colony started, 1895; four new houses at Chalfont St. Peter, Bucks, the gift of Mr. Passmore Edwards and others; opened by the duke of York, 23 June, 1899.

NATIONAL TESTIMONIALS (subscribed for) were presented to Rowland Hill (for his exertions in obtaining the penny postage), 17 June, 1846; and to Miss Florence Nightingale (for her beneficent exertions for the sufferers during the Crimean war), 29 Nov. 1855. See *Jubilee*, 1888, and *Nurses*.

NATIONAL THRIFT SOCIETY, formed at Oxford in 1878. Meetings have been held at the Mansion house, London, 1880 *et seq*. The erection of a Thrift hall proposed, 31 Dec. 1887.

NATIONAL TRADE SOCIETY formed in June, 1871, to watch over and secure the interests of traders, and promote amendments in the law affecting commercial interests. President, rt. hon. W. H. Smith, M.P. Civil Service trading, the income tax, and international exhibitions have been considered by the committee.

NATIONAL TRAINING SCHOOL for Music, South Kensington, founded by the duke of Edinburgh, 18 Dec. 1873; opened by him, 17 May, 1876.

NATIONAL TRUST, for places of historic interest or natural beauty; an association founded by the duke of Westminster, the marquis of Dufferin, the earl of Rosebery, and others; first meeting, 16 Nov. 1893; first annual meeting, London, 9 May, 1895.

NATIONAL UNION was formed in 1868 to combine a number of associations supporting the conservative party. Lecturers were employed and pamphlets circulated. The party was termed nationalist in Aug. 1871. Lord Randolph Churchill was chairman in 1884. Conference at Aberdeen, 16 Oct. 1884. The twentieth annual conference held at Oxford, 22 Nov. 1887, and at other places since.

NATIONAL UNION CONVENTION, see *United States*, 1866, and Dec. 1890.

NATIONAL VIGILANCE ASSOCIATION, for the promotion of social purity, and the protection of women and children, founded by Dr. G. Ridding (bishop of Southwell), Mr. Samuel Morley, and others, March, 1886.

Annual meetings are held; international congress, London, closed . . . . . . 1 June, 1899

NATIONAL WAIFS ASSOCIATION, see *Barnardo's Homes*.

NATIONAL WORKSHOPS, see *Ateliers Nationaux*.

NATIVITY. There are three festivals in the Roman and Greek churches, under this name. The Nativity of Christ, also observed by the protestants, on 25 Dec. (see *Christmas*); the Nativity of the Virgin Mary, not observed by the protestants at all. Pope Sergius I., about 690, established the latter, but it was not generally received in France and Germany till about 1000; nor by the eastern Christians till the 12th century. The festival of the nativity of St. John the Baptist, 24 June, Midsummer-day, is said to have been instituted in 488.

NATURAL HISTORY was studied by Solomon, 1014 B.C. (1 *Kings* iv. 33); Aristotle (384-322 B.C.); by Theophrastus (394-297 B.C.); and by Pliny (23-79 A.D.); see *Botany, Zoology, British Museum*, &c.

NATURAL PHILOSOPHY, see *Philosophy*.

NATURAL SELECTION, see *Species*.

NATURALIZATION is defined to be "the making a foreigner or alien a denizen or freeman of any kingdom or city, and so becoming, as it were, both a subject and a native of a king or country that by nature he did not belong to." The first act of naturalisation passed in 1437; and various similar enactments were made in most of the reigns from that time; several of them special acts relating to individuals. An act for the naturalisation of the Jews passed May, 1753, but was repealed in 1754, on the petition of all the cities in England; see *Jews*, for the privileges since granted them. The act for the naturalization of prince Albert passed 3 Vict., 7 Feb. 1840. A committee to inquire into the naturalization laws, appointed May, 1868, earl of Clarendon chairman, met 25 Oct. 1868; reported about Feb. 1869; and new acts for this purpose were passed 12 May, 1870, and 25 July, 1872. In 1870 there were about 9500 Americans in England, and about 2,500,000 British subjects in the United States of America. By the new act the latter were enabled to renounce their allegiance; and by the convention signed 3 Feb. 1871, the nationality of British subjects was made dependent on choice and not on birth. Naturalization (abroad) act passed, 6 July, 1895.

Committee on naturalization's report issued, with suggestions, see *Times* leader, 3 Oct. 1901.

NATURALISM, a realistic style in literature, mainly introduced by Balzac, 1829 *et seq.* "Naturalism" is now defined as the knowledge of phenomena, and the laws by which they are connected, but nothing more. Some writers combine with naturalism, agnosticism, positivism, and empiricism (*which see*).

Naturalism and Agnosticism," the Gifford lectures, 1896-8, 2 vols., by prof. James Ward, published 1899, in which he opposes the mechanical view of nature, viz. *naturalism*, and insists upon the recognition of mind as the animating principle.

Edmond and Jules de Goncourt published "Medical and Physiological Novels," 1846 *et seq.*

Emile Zola, in his "Rougon-Macquart" series, 1871 *et seq.*, portrayed deformed and diseased rather than true nature. A dramatised form of his "Assommoir," entitled "Drink," had a long run in London in 1879.

NATURE, a weekly illustrated journal of science, first appeared 4 Nov. 1869; editor, Mr. Joseph Norman Lockyer, F.R.S. Mr. Alex. Macmillan, one of the founders, born 1818, died, 25 Jan. 1896.

La Nature (founded and edited by M. Gaston Tissandier, died Sept. 1899; see *Balloons*) appeared in 1892.

NATURE PRINTING. This process consists in impressing objects, such as plants, mosses, feathers, &c., into plates of metal, causing these objects, as it were, to engrave themselves; and afterwards taking casts or copies fit for printing from. Kniphoff, of Erfurt, between 1728 and 1757, produced his *Herbarium vivum* by pressing the plants themselves (previously inked) on paper; the impressions being afterwards coloured by hand. In 1833, Peter Kyhl, of Copenhagen, made use of steel rollers and lead plates. In 1842 Mr. Taylor printed lace. In 1847 Mr. Twining printed ferns, grasses, and plants; and in the same year Dr. Branson suggested the application of electrotyping to the impressions. In 1849, professor Leydolt, of Vienna, by the able assistance of Mr. Andrew Worring, obtained impressions of agates and fossils. The first practical application of this process is in Von Heufler's work on the mosses of Arpasch, in Transylvania; the second (the *first* in this country) in "The Ferns of Great Britain and Ireland," edited by Dr. Lindley, the illustrations to which were prepared under the superintendence of Mr. Henry Bradbury in 1855-56, who also in 1859-60 printed "The British Sea-weeds," edited by W. G. Johnstone and Alex. Croall. The process was applied to butterflies by Joseph Merrin of Gloucester, in 1864.

NATURFORSCHER GESELLSCHAFT, see *German Union*.

NAUCRATIS, see under *Egypt Exploration Fund*.

NAUTICAL ALMANAC, first published in 1767, edited by Dr. Neville Maskelyne, astronomer royal; the new and improved series began in 1834. Dr. John Russell Hind (died 1895), for many years superintendent, was succeeded by Mr. A. M. W. Downing, Jan. 1892.

NAUVOO, Illinois, N. America, a city of the Mormonites (*which see*); founded 1840; left 1848.

NAVAL AND MILITARY ADMINISTRATION, royal commission appointed consisting of lord Hartington, lord R. Churchill, lord Revelstoke, Mr. Campbell Bannerman, Mr. Ismay, general Brackenbury, admiral sir F.

Richards, sir R. Temple, and Mr. W. H. Smith, 7 June, 1888.

First report, containing various recommendations with evidence, issued 20 March, 1890.

Mr. E. Stanhope, the war secretary, reports the proposal for the establishment of a council within the cabinet, for naval and military affairs, to decide on questions between the two departments, also to establish a war office council and a promotion board, 3 July, 1890.

The "Naval and military council," the duke of Devonshire president (cabinet ministers), established in 1895.

NAVAL AND MILITARY OFFICERS' ASSOCIATION, instituted to provide employment for retired officers, proposed spring 1885.

NAVAL ANNUAL, a valuable publication, begun by lord Brassey in 1886; continued by his son, Mr. T. A. Brassey, in 1896; Mr. John Leyland, 1900.

NAVAL ARCHITECTS' INSTITUTION was established in Jan. 1860. Annual international sessions are held; a meeting at Paris, lord Brassey, president, 11 June, 1895: at Hamburg, 9 June; Berlin, 10 June *et seq.* (the emperor present 11 June), 1896; London, 6 July, 1897; a German society, founded in 1898, met in Berlin, the emperor present; 18, 19 Nov. 1901.

NAVAL ARCHITECTURE. A scientific committee of fifteen appointed to consider the present state of naval architecture and the requirements of naval warfare; 6 naval officers, 9 scientific men; lord Dufferin chairman; about 19 Dec. 1870.

A royal school of naval architecture, established at South Kensington in 1864, merged into the Royal Naval College, Greenwich.

M. Raoul Pictet, of Geneva, announced his discovery of a new kind of keel to glide over water, Aug. 1881.

NAVAL ARTILLERY VOLUNTEER FORCE, ROYAL, established by act passed 5 Aug. 1873.

On March 22, 1889, a proposal to utilise these volunteers who are stationed at various ports was made in the house of lords.

NAVAL ASYLUM, ROYAL, begun at Paddington in 1801, was transferred to Greenwich in 1807. The interior of the central portion of the building was commenced in 1613 by Anne, queen of James I., and completed in 1635 by queen Henrietta-Maria, whose arms still adorn the ceiling of the room in which her son Charles II. was born, 1630.

NAVAL BATTLES. The first sea-fight on record is that between the Corinthians and Corcyreans, 665 B.C. The following are among the most celebrated naval engagements: for the details of which see *separate articles*.

B.C.

Battle of Salamis (Greek victory) . . . 20 Oct. 480
Battle of Eurymedon (ditto) . . . 469
Battle of Cyzicus; the Lacedemonian fleet taken by Alcibiades, the Athenian . . . 410
Battle of Arginusæ . . . 406
Battle of Ægospotamos (Spartans victors) . . . 405
The Persian fleet, under Conon, defeats the Spartan, at Cnidos; Pisander, the Athenian admiral, is killed; and the maritime power of the Lacedemonians destroyed . . . 394
Battle of Mylæ (Romans defeat Carthaginians) . . . 260
The Roman fleet, off Trepanum, destroyed by the Carthaginians . . . 249
The Carthaginian fleet destroyed by the consul Lutatius . . . 241
Battle of Actium . . . 31
The emperor Claudius II. defeats the Goths, and sinks 2000 of their ships . . . A.D. 269
Battle of Lepanto (Turks defeated) . . . 7 Oct. 1571
Bay of Gibraltar; Dutch and Spaniards (a bloody conflict and decisive victory, giving for a time the superiority to the Dutch) . . . 25 April, 1607
The Austrians defeat the Italians at Lissa (see *Lissa*) 20 July, 1866

NAVAL ENGAGEMENTS IN BRITISH HISTORY.

[Hallam considers that the naval glory of England can first be traced "in a continuous track of light" from the period of the Commonwealth.]

Alfred with 10 galleys, defeated 300 sail of Danish pirates on the Dorset and Hampshire coast. *Asser's Life of Alfred* . . . 897
Edward III. defeats the French near Sluys 24 June, 1340
Off Winchelsea; Edward III. defeated the Spanish fleet (*L'Espagnols sur mer*) of 40 large ships, and captured 26 . . . 29 Aug. 1350
The English and Flemings; the latter signally defeated . . . 1371
Earl of Arundel defeats a Flemish fleet of 100 sail, and captures 80 . . . 24 March, 1387
Near Milford Haven; the English take 8, and destroy 15 French ships . . . 1405
Off Harfleur; the duke of Bedford takes or destroys nearly 500 French ships . . . 15 Aug. 1416
In the Downs; a Spanish and Genoese fleet captured by the earl of Warwick . . . 1459
Bay of Biscay; English and French, indecisive, 10 Aug. 1512
Sir Edward Howard attacks the French under Prior John; repulsed and killed . . . 25 April, 1513
The *Spanish Armada* destroyed . . . 19 July, 1588
Dover straits; the Dutch admiral Van Tromp defeated by admiral Blake 28 Sept. The Dutch surprise the English in the Downs, 80 sail engaging 40 English, several of which are taken or destroyed, 28 Nov.; the Dutch admiral sails in triumph through the channel, with a broom at his masthead, to denote that he had swept the English from the seas . . . 29 Nov. 1652
The English gain a victory over the Dutch fleet off Portsmouth, taking and destroying 11 men-of-war and 30 merchantmen. Van Tromp was the Dutch, and Blake the English admiral . . . 18-20 Feb. 1653
Again, off the North Foreland. The Dutch and English fleets consisted of near 100 men-of-war each. Van Tromp commanded the Dutch; Blake, Monk, and Deane, the English. Six Dutch ships taken; 11 sunk, and the rest ran into Calais roads 2 June, ,,
Again, on the coast of Holland; the Dutch lose 30 men-of-war, and admiral Tromp was killed (the seventh and last battle) . . . 31 July, ,,
At Cadiz, when two galleons, worth 2,000,000 pieces of eight, were taken by Blake . . . Sept. 1656
Spanish fleet vanquished, and burnt in the harbour of Santa Cruz by Blake . . . 20 April, 1657
English and French: 130 of the Bordeaux fleet destroyed by the duke of York (afterwards James II.) 4 Dec. 1664
The duke of York defeats the Dutch fleet off Harwich; Opdam, the Dutch admiral, blown up, with all his crew; 18 capital ships taken, 14 destroyed 3 June, 1665
The earl of Sandwich took 12 men-of-war and 2 India ships . . . 4 Sept. ,,
A contest between the Dutch and English fleets for four days. The English lose 9, and the Dutch 15 ships . . . 1-4 June, 1666
Decisive engagement at the mouth of the Thames, the English gain a glorious victory. The Dutch lose 24 men-of-war, 4 admirals killed, and 4000 seamen . . . 25, 26 July, ,,
The Dutch admiral de Ruyter sails up the Thames and destroys some ships . . . 11 June, 1667
Twelve Algerine ships of war destroyed by sir Edward Spragg . . . 10 May, 1671
Battle of Southwold bay (see *Solebay*) . . . 28 May, 1672
Coast of Holland; by prince Rupert, 28 May, 4 June, and 11 Aug., sir E. Spragg killed; d'Etrees and Ruyter defeated . . . 1673
Off Beachy Head; the English and Dutch defeated by the French under Tourville . . . 30 June, 1690
Who is defeated by them near Cape La Hogue, 19 May, 1692
Off St. Vincent; the English and Dutch squadrons, under admiral Rooke, defeated by the French, 16 June, 1693

Off Carthagena, between admiral Benbow and the French fleet, commanded by admiral Du Casse. Fought . . . . 19 Aug. 1702

The other ships of the squadron falling astern, left Benbow alone to maintain the battle. A chain-shot shattered his leg, yet he would not be removed from the quarter-deck, but continued fighting till the morning, when the French sheered off. He died in Oct. following, of his wounds, at Jamaica, where, soon after his arrival, he received a letter from the French admiral, of which the following is a translation :—

"Carthagena, 22 Aug. 1702.

"SIR,—I had little hopes, on Monday last, but to have supped in your cabin ; yet it pleased God to order it otherwise. I am thankful for it. As for those cowardly captains who deserted you, hang them up, for by G—d they deserve it.

"DU CASSE."

Captains Kirby and Wade were shot on their arrival at Plymouth, having been previously tried by a court-martial.

Sir George Rooke defeats the French fleet off Vigo (*which see*) . . . . 12 Oct. 1702

Off Malaga ; bloody engagement between the French, under the count of Thoulouse, and the English, under sir George Rooke . . . . . 13 Aug. 1704

At Gibraltar ; French lose 5 men-of-war . 5 Nov. ,,

In the Mediterranean, admiral Leake took 60 French vessels, laden with provisions . . 22 May, 1708

Spanish fleet of 29 sail totally defeated by sir George Byng, in the Faro of Messina . 31 July, 1718

Bloody battle off Toulon ; Matthews and Lestock against the fleets of France and Spain. Here brave captain Cornewall fell with 42 men, including officers ; and the victory was lost by a misunderstanding between the English admirals 11 Feb. 1743-4

Off Cape Finisterre ; the French fleet of 38 sail taken by admiral Anson . . . . . 3 May, 1747

Off Finisterre ; when admiral Hawke took 7 men-of-war of the French . . . . . . 14 Oct.

Off Newfoundland ; when admiral Boscawen took 2 men-of-war . . . . 10 June, 1755

Off Cape Françoise ; 7 ships defeated by 3 English, 21 Oct. 1757

Admiral Pocock defeats the French fleet in the East Indies, in two actions, 1758, and again . 1759

Admiral Boscawen defeats the French under De la Clue, off Cape Lagos . . . . . 18 Aug. ,,

Admiral Hawke defeats the French fleet, commanded by Conflans, in Quiberon Bay, and thus prevents a projected invasion of England (see *Quiberon Bay*) . . . . . . 20 Nov. ,,

Keppel took 3 French frigates and a fleet of merchantmen . . . . 9 Oct. 1762

On Lake Champlain the provincial force totally destroyed by admiral Howe . . . 11 Oct. 1776

Capt. Sam. Marshall, of "the saucy *Arethusa*," 32 guns (part of Keppel's fleet), summoned *La Belle Poule* to surrender off Ushant, and fired across her bow ; after two hours' conflict, the French made sail and escaped . . . . 16 or 17 June, 1778

Off Ushant ; a drawn battle between Keppel and d'Orvilliers . . . . 27 July, ,,

In New England ; the American fleet totally destroyed . . . . 30 July, 1779

Near Cape St. Vincent ; admiral Rodney defeated a Spanish fleet under admiral don Langara (see *Rodney*) . . . . 16 Jan. 1780

At St. Jago ; Mons. Suffrein defeated by commodore Johnstone . . . . 16 April, 1781

Dogger-bank, between admiral Parker and the Dutch admiral Zoutman : 400 killed on each side, 5 Aug. ,,

Admiral Rodney defeated the French going to attack Jamaica ; took 5 ships of the line, and sent the French admiral, Comte de Grasse, prisoner to England . . . . 12 April, 1782

The British totally defeated the fleets of France and Spain in the Bay of Gibraltar . . 13 Sept. ,,

East Indies : a series of actions between sir Edward Hughes and Suffren, viz. : 17 Feb. 1782, the French had 11 ships to 9 ; 12 April they had 18 ships to 11, yet were completely beaten. Again, 6 July, off Trincomalee, they had 15 to 12, and were again beaten with loss of 1000 killed, 3 Sept. 1782 ; again . . . . . 20 June, 1783

Lord Howe defeated the French off Ushant; took 6 ships of war, and sunk one . . . 1 June, 1794

Sir Edward Pellew took 15 sail ; burnt 7, out of a fleet of 35 sail of transports . . . 8 March, 1795

French fleet defeated, and 2 ships of war taken by admiral Hotham. Fought . . 14 March, ,,

Admiral Cornwallis took 8 transports, convoyed by 3 French men-of-war. Fought . . 7 June, ,,

Eleven Dutch East Indiamen taken by the *Sceptre*, man-of-war, and some armed British Indiamen in company . . . . 19 June, ,,

L'Orient : the French fleet defeated by lord Bridport, and 3 ships of the line taken ; see *L'Orient*, 23 June, ,,

Dutch fleet, under admiral Lucas, in Saldanha Bay, surrenders to sir George Keith Elphinstone (see *Saldanha Bay*) . . . . 17 Aug. 1796

Victory off Cape St. Vincent (*which see*) . 14 Feb. 1797

Unsuccessful attempt on Santa Cruz ; admiral Nelson loses his right arm . . 24 July, ,,

Victory of Camperdown (*which see*) . 11 Oct. ,,

Of the Nile (*which see*) . . . . 1 Aug. 1798

Off the coast of Ireland ; a French fleet of 9 sail, full of troops, as succours to the Irish, engaged by sir John Borlase Warren, and 5 taken, 12 Oct. ,,

The Texel fleet of 12 ships and 13 Indiamen surrenders to admiral Mitchell . . . 30 Aug. 1799

Capture of the *Cerbère* (*which see*) . 29 July, 1800

Copenhagen bombarded (see *Copenhagen*), 2 April, 1801

Gibraltar bay ; engagement between the French and British fleets ; the *Hannibal*, of 74 guns, lost, 6 July, ,,

Off Cadiz ; sir James Saumarez obtains a victory over the French and Spanish fleets ; 1 ship captured. Fought . . . . . . 12 July, ,,

Sir Robert Calder, with 15 sail, takes 2 ships (both Spanish) out of 20 sail of the French and Spanish fleets, off Ferrol (Calder censured) . 22 July, 1805

Victory off Trafalgar (*which see*) . . 21 Oct. ,,

Sir R. Strachan, with 4 sail of British, captures 4 French ships, off Cape Ortegal . . 4 Nov. ,,

In the West Indies ; the French defeated by sir T. Duckworth ; 3 sail of the line taken, 2 driven on shore . . . . 6 Feb. 1806

Sir John Borlase Warren captures 2 French ships, 13 March, ,,

Admiral Duckworth effects the passage of the Dardanelles (see article *Dardanelles*) . 19 Feb. 1807

Copenhagen fleet captured . . . . 8 Sept. ,,

The Russian fleet of several sail, in the Tagus, surrenders to the British . . . . . 3 Sept. 1808

Aix or Basque Roads ; 4 sail of the line, &c., destroyed by lord Gambier . . . 11, 12 April, 1809

Two Russian flotillas of numerous vessels taken or destroyed by sir J. Saumarez . . . July, ,,

French ships of the line driven on shore by lord Collingwood (two of them burnt by the French next day) . . . . 25 Oct. ,,

Bay of Rosas, where lieut. Tailour, by direction of captain Hallowell, takes or destroys 11 war and other vessels (see *Rosas Bay*) . . . 1 Nov. ,,

Basseterre ; *La Loire* and *La Seine*, French frigates, destroyed by sir A. Cochrane . . . 18 Dec. ,,

The *Spartan* frigate gallantly engages a large French force in the bay of Naples . . . 3 May, 1810

Action between the *Tribune*, captain Reynolds, and 4 Danish brigs. Fought . . . . 12 May, ,,

Isle of Rhé ; 17 vessels taken or destroyed by the *Armide* and *Cadmus* . . . . . 17 July, ,,

Captain Barrett, in the merchant vessel *Cumberland*, with 26 men, defeats four privateers and takes 170 prisoners . . . . . 16 Jan. 1811

Twenty-two vessels from Otranto taken by the *Cerberus* and *Active* . . . . . 22 Feb. ,,

Off Lissa (*which see*); brilliant victory gained over a Franco-Venetian squadron by capt. Wm. Hoste, 13 March, ,,

Amazon French frigate destroyed off Cape Barfleur 25 March, ,,

Sagone Bay ; 2 French store-ships burnt by captain Barrie's ships . . . . . . 1 May, ,,

The British sloop *Little Belt*, and American ship *President* : their rencontre . . . 16 May, ,,

Off Madagascar ; 3 British frigates under captain Schomberg, engage 3 French larger-sized, with troops on board, and capture 2 . . . 20 May, ,,

The *Thames* and *Cephalus* capture 36 French vessels . July, 1811

The *Naiad* frigate attacked in presence of Bonaparte by 7 armed praams; they were gallantly repulsed 21 Sept. ,,

French frigates *Pauline* and *Pomone* captured by the British frigates *Alceste*, *Active*, and *Unité* 29 Nov. ,,

Rivoli, 84 guns, taken by *Victorious*, 74, 21 Feb. 1812

L'Orient: 2 French frigates, &c., destroyed by the *Northumberland*, capt. Hotham 22 May, ,,

Guerrière, British frigate, 46 small guns, captured by the American ship *Constitution*, 54 guns (an unequal contest) . 19 Aug. ,,

British brig *Frolic* captured by the American sloop *Wasp* . . . . 18 Oct. ,,

British frigate *Macedonian* taken by the American ship *United States*, large class . . 25 Oct. ,,

British frigate *Java* taken by the American ship *Constitution*, large class . . . . . 29 Dec. ,,

British frigate *Amelia* loses 46 men killed and 95 wounded, engaging a French frigate . 7 Feb. 1813

British sloop *Peacock* captured by the American ship *Hornet*; she was so disabled that she sunk with part of her crew . . . . 25 Feb. ,,

American frigate *Chesapeake* taken by the *Shannon*, captain Broke (see *Chesapeake*) 1 June, ,,

American ships *Growler* and *Eagle* taken by British gun-boats . . . . 3 June, ,,

American sloop *Argus* taken by the British sloop *Pelican* . . . . 14 Aug. ,,

French frigate *La Trave*, 44 guns, taken by the *Andromache*, of 38 guns . . . 23 Oct. ,,

French frigate *Ceres* taken by the British ship *Tagus* . . . . 6 Jan. 1814

French frigates *Alcmene* and *Iphigenia* taken by the *Venerable* . . . . 16 Jan. 1814

French frigate *Terpsichore* taken by the *Majestic* 3 Feb. ,,

French ship *Clorinde* taken by the *Dryad* and *Achates*, after an action with the *Eurotas*, 25 Feb. ,,

French frigate *L'Etoile* captured by the *Hebrus*, 27 March, ,,

American frigate *Essex* captured by the *Phœbe* and *Cherub* . . . . . . 29 March, ,,

British sloop *Avon* sunk by the American sloop *Wasp* . . . . 8 Sept. ,,

Lake Champlain: the British squadron captured by the American, after a severe conflict , 11 Sept. ,,

American ship *President* captured by the *Endymion* 15 Jan. 1815

Algiers bombarded by lord Exmouth; see *Algiers* 27 Aug. 1816

Navarino (*which see*) . . . . . . 20 Oct. 1827

Action between the British ships *Volage* and *Hyacinth* and 29 Chinese war-junks, which were defeated . . . . 3 Nov. 1839

Bombardment and fall of Acre. The British squadron under admiral Stopford achieved this triumph with trifling loss, while the Egyptians lost 2000 killed and wounded, and 3000 prisoners (see *Syria*) . . . . 3 Nov. 1840

Lagos attacked and taken by commodore Bruce, with a squadron consisting of the *Penelope*, *Bloodhound*, *Sampson*, and *Teazer*, war-steamers, and the *Philomel* brig of war . . 26-27 Dec. 1851

[For naval actions which cannot be called regular battles, see *China*, *Japan*, *Egypt*, 1882; *Manila*.]

SHIPS TAKEN OR DESTROYED BY THE NAVAL AND MARINE FORCES OF GREAT BRITAIN:—

	In the French War, ending 1802.					In the French War, ending 1814.					
Force.	French.	Dutch.	Spanish.	Other Nations.	Total.	French.	Spanish.	Danish.	Russian.	American.	Total.
Of the line	45	25	11	2	83	70	27	23	4	0	124
Fifties	2	1	0	0	3	7	0	1	0	1	9
Frigates	133	31	20	7	191	77	36	24	6	5	148
Sloops, &c.	161	32	55	16	264	188	64	16	7	13	288
Total	341	89	86	25	541	342	127	64	17	19	569

NAVAL COLLEGE, ROYAL, established at Greenwich Hospital, and opened 1 Feb. 1873. ROYAL NAVAL COLLEGE, *Osborne*, Isle of Wight, opened by the king, 4 Aug. 1903.

NAVAL CONSTRUCTION and Armaments Company, chairman, adm. H. Boys, registered 18 Feb. 1888.

NAVAL DEFENCE ACTS, see *Colonies*, 1865 and 1887. Act passed, 31 May, 1889; amended, 1893 and 1894.

NAVAL EXHIBITION, ROYAL, Chelsea embankment, was opened by the prince of Wales, 2 May; visited by the Queen, 7 May; by the German emperor, 10 July; by the prince of Naples, 28 July; closed 24 Oct. 1891.

Sir William Dowell was chairman of the executive committee.

The exhibition consisted of nine galleries, named Nelson, Benbow, &c., containing relics, pictures, ordnance, ancient and modern, models of the *Victory*, lighthouses, &c., and an arctic panorama. There was also a lake for nautical evolutions.

Total number of persons admitted 2,351,683; receipts, 155,447*l.*; by the surplus profit, 47,246*l.*, the ROYAL NAVAL FUND was founded, 29 June; first general meeting, 20 Dec. 1892; first annual meeting, the prince of Wales in the chair, 19 Feb. 1894.

NAVAL KNIGHTS OF WINDSOR, see *Poor Knights*.

NAVAL RECORDS, RESERVE, REVIEWS, SALUTE, AND VOLUNTEERS, see under *Navy*.

Naval volunteer home defence association, formed in 1885; decided in May, 1889, to break up in June following.

NAVAL WORKS ACT (at home and abroad), relating to docks, ports, passed 31 March, 1896; estimated cost, docks, 3,979,000*l.* 1896. Other acts passed 1897, 1899, and 1903.

NAVARINO (S. W. Greece), settled by the Arabs 6th century; taken by the Turks, 1500; by Venetians, 1686; by Turks, 1718; by Greeks, 1821; by Turks, 1825. Near here, on 20 Oct. 1827, the combined fleets of England, France, and Russia, under command of admiral Codrington, nearly destroyed the Turkish and Egyptian fleet. More than thirty ships, many of them four-deckers, were blown up or burnt, chiefly by the Turks themselves, to prevent their falling into the hands of their enemies. This destruction of the Turkish naval power was characterised by the duke of Wellington as an "untoward event." The port is also called Navarine.

NAVARRE, now a province of Spain, formed a part of the Roman dominions, and was conquered from the Saracens by Charlemagne, 778. His descendants appointed governors, one of whom, Garcias Ximenes, took the title of king in 857. In 1076, king Sancho IV. was poisoned, and Sancho Ramorez of Aragon seized Navarre. In 1134, Navarre became again independent under Garcias Ramorez IV. In 1234, Thibault, count of Champagne, nephew of Sancho VII., became sovereign of Navarre; and in 1284, by the marriage of the heiress Jane with Philip IV. le Bel, Navarre was united to France.

SOVEREIGNS OF NAVARRE.

1274. Jane I. and (1284) Philip-le-Bel of France.
1305. Louis X. Hutin of France.
1316. Philip V. the Long, of France.
1322. Charles I. the Fair, IV. of France.
1328. Jane II. (daughter of Jane I.), and her husband Philip d'Evreux.
1349. Charles II., the Bad.
1387. Charles III., the Noble.
1425. Blanche, his daughter, and her husband, John of Aragon.
1441. John II., alone, who became king of Aragon, in 1458. He endeavoured to obtain the crown of Castile also.
1479. Eleanor de Foix, his daughter.
,, Francis Phœbus de Foix, her son.
1483. Catherine (his sister) and her husband John d'Albret. Ferdinand of Aragon conquers and annexes all Navarre south of the Pyrenees, 1512.

LOWER NAVARRE (in France).

1516. Henry d'Albret.
1555. Jane d'Albret and her husband Anthony de Bourbon, who died 1562.
1572. Henry III. who became in 1589 king of France (Henry IV.), to which Lower Navarre was formally united in 1609.

NAVIES, see *Fleets*.

NAVIES (FOREIGN). Numerical strength of the navies of the foreign countries specified, as compared with the navy of Great Britain, compiled from the parliamentary paper issued 25 May, 1903:—

BATTLESHIPS—*1st class*, Great Britain, 42; France, 19; Russia, 13; Germany, 12; Italy, 12; United States, 10; Japan, 6. *2nd class*, Gt. Britain, 4; France, 8; Russia, 4; Germany, 4; Italy, 0; U. States, 1; Japan, 1. *3rd class*, Gt. Britain, 2; France, 1; Russia, 1; Germany, 12; Italy, 5; U. States, 0; Japan, 0.

COAST DEFENCE VESSELS—Gt. Britain, 2; France 1; Russia, 1; Germany, 11; Italy, 0; U. States, 15; Japan, 2.

CRUISERS, *Armoured*—Gt. Britain, 18; France, 9; Russia, 8; Germany, 2; Italy, 5; U. States, 2; Japan, 2. *Protected, 1st class*, Gt. Britain, 21; France, 7; Russia, 6; Germany, 1; Italy, 0; U. States, 3; Japan, 0. *2nd class*, Gt. Britain, 51 (including 3 partially protected); France, 16; Russia, 5; Germany, 8; Italy, 5; U. States, 11; Japan, 10. *3rd class*, Gt. Britain, 32 (including 1 partially protected); France, 17; Russia, 0; Germany, 10; Italy, 11; U. States, 2; Japan, 8. *Unprotected*, Gt. Britain, 10; France, 1; Russia, 3; Germany, 20; Italy, 0; U. States, 11; Japan, 9.

TORPEDO VESSELS—Gt. Britain, 34; France, 16; Russia, 9; Germany, 2; Italy, 14; U. States, 0; Japan, 1.

TORPEDO-BOAT DESTROYERS—Gt. Britain, 112; France, 14; Russia, 48; Germany, 28; Italy, 11; U. States, 14; Japan, 17.

TORPEDO-BOATS—Gt. Britain, 85; France, 247; Russia, 132; Germany, 93; Italy, 145; U. States, 27; Japan, 67.

SUBMARINE TORPEDO-BOATS—Gt. Britain, 5; France, 15; Italy, 1; U. States, 3.

In course of construction, 1903.

BATTLESHIPS—*1st class*, Gt. Britain, 12 (3 more to be laid down 1903–4); France, 7; Russia, 8; Germany, 8; Italy, 6; U. States, 9 (5 more to be laid down 1903–4). *2nd class*, France, 1.

COAST DEFENCE VESSELS—U. States, 1.

CRUISERS—*Armoured*, Gt. Britain, 9 (4 more to be laid down 1903–4); France, 13 (1 more to be laid down 1903–4); Germany, 3 (1 more to be laid down 1903–4); Italy, 1; U. States, 11. *Protected (1st class)*, Russia, 3. *2nd class*, Gt. Britain, 2; Russia, 2; U. States, 6; Japan, 2. *3rd class*, Gt. Britain, 4 (3 more to be laid down 1903–4); Germany, 5 (2 to be laid down 1903–4); Japan, 1.

SCOUTS—Gt. Britain, 4 (4 more to be laid down 1903–4).

TORPEDO-BOAT DESTROYERS—Gt. Britain, 19 (15 more to be laid down in 1903–4); France, 19 (4 more to be laid down in 1903–4); Russia, 6; Germany, 4 (6 more to be laid down 1903–4); Italy, 2; U. States, 6; Japan, 2.

TORPEDO-BOATS—Gt. Britain, 2; France, 18 (25 more to be laid down 1903–4); Russia, 7; Italy, 8; U. States, 4; Japan, 18.

SUBMARINE TORPEDO-BOATS—Gt. Britain, 4 (10 more to be laid down 1903–4); France, 25 (18 more to be laid down 1903–4); Russia, 2; Italy, 3; U. States, 5.

Note.—The first turbine-driven man-of-war (the third-class cruiser *Amethyst*) constructed (2 torpedo-boat destroyers, the *Velox* and *Eden*, had previously been built) for the British navy was launched at Elswick yard, Newcastle-on-Tyne, 5 Nov. 1903.

NAVIGATION began with the Egyptians and Phœnicians. The first laws of navigation originated with the Rhodians. The first account we have of any considerable voyage is that of the Phœnicians sailing round Africa.

Plane charts and mariner's compass used about . 1420
Variation of the compass observed by Columbus . 1492
That the oblique rhomb-lines are spiral, discovered by Nonius 1537
First treatise on navigation 1545
The log first mentioned by Bourne 1577
Mercator's chart 1599
Davis's quadrant, or backstaff, for measuring angles, about 1600
Logarithmic tables applied to navigation by Gunter 1620
Middle latitude sailing introduced 1623
Mensuration of a degree, Norwood 1631
Hedley's quadrant 1731
Harrison's time-keeper used 1764
Nautical Almanac first published 1767
Barlow's theory of the deviation of the compass . 1820
Quarterly Journal of Naval Science, edited by E. J. Reed, published . . . . . April, 1872-5

See *Compass, Latitude, Longitude, Steam, &c.*

NAVIGATION LAWS. A code of maritime laws is attributed to Richard I. of England, said to have been decreed at the isle of Oleron, 1194, and further enactments were made by Richard II. in 1381.—In Oct. 1651, the parliament passed an act entitled "Goods from foreign parts, by whom to be imported," the principles of which were affirmed by 12 Charles II. c. 18, "an act for the encouraging and increasing of shipping and navigation" (1660). The latter act restricts the importation and exportation of goods from or to Asia, Africa, or America, to English ships, of which the masters and three-fourths of the mariners are to be English. This was followed by many acts of similar tenor; which were consolidated by 3 & 4 Will. IV. c. 54 (1833). These acts were in the whole or in part repealed by the act "to amend the laws in force for the encouragement of British shipping and navigation" (passed 12 & 13 Vict. c. 29, 26 June, 1849, after much opposition), and which came into operation 1 Jan. 1850. The steam navigation act passed 14 & 15 Vict. c. 79, 1851, came into operation 1 Jan. 1852. The act regulating the navigation of the river Thames was passed in 1786.—In Feb. 1865 the emperor recommended the modification of the French navigation laws; in Feb. 1872, new restrictions were laid upon foreign ships, chiefly affecting British.

An *International Maritime conference*, at which 23 nations were represented by 50 delegates, Portugal not included, met at Washington, and were received by Mr. secretary Blaine and introduced to president Harrison. Adm. Franklin, U.S., elected president . . . . . . 16 Oct. 1889
Conference closed . . . . 31 Dec. ,,
[Subjects discussed by committees: lights, signalling, rules of the road, life-saving systems, seaworthiness, sailors, routes at sea.]
A government blue-book issued on the subject, Nov. 1890
A congress on international maritime law at Genoa, 26 Sept. *et seq.* 1892; Antwerp . . 29 Sept. 1898
International code of signal committee met at the Board of Trade office . . . . . 12 Jan. 1893
International maritime congress: 1st meeting at Paris, 1889; 2nd, London, 18 July, 1893; Brussels, 25 July, 1898; London, 14 July, 1899; Hamburg, For rule of the road, see *Seas*. 25 Sept. 1902

NAVIGATORS (or Navvies). These helpers in the construction of railways probably derived their name (about 1830) from formerly making the inland navigation in Lincolnshire, &c., and are doubtfully said to be descendants of the original Dutch canal labourers. Navvy Mission Society (new) met at Lambeth palace, 7 May, 1880. A "steam navvy" suitable for working in sand, gravel, or heavy clay, made by Messrs. Ruston, Proctor, & Co., of Lincoln, 1878.

NAVY OF ENGLAND, "whereon, under the good providence of God, the wealth, safety, and strength of the kingdom chiefly depends," *Act for the government of the Navy*. "The Royal Navy," 3 vols., by W. Laird Clowes, assisted by sir Clements Markham, capt. A. T. Mahan and others, published 1897-99. See *Naval Battles* and *Wrecks*.

A fleet of galleys built by Alfred 897
The number of galleys greatly increased under Edgar, who claimed to be lord of the ocean surrounding Britain . . . . . about 965
A formidable fleet equipped by the contribution of every town in England, in the reign of Ethelred II. when it rendezvoused at Sandwich, to be ready to oppose the Danes 1007
A fleet collected by Edward the Confessor to resist the Norwegians, 1042; and by Harold to resist the Normans 1066
Richard I. collected a fleet and enacted naval laws about 1191
[The Cinque ports and maritime towns frequently furnished fleets commanded by the king or his officers.]
Edward III.'s fleet defeat the French at the battle of Sluys, 24 June, 1340; and the Spanish off Winchelsea . . . . . . 29 Aug. 1350
Henry V. made efforts to increase the navy . 1415-1422
Henry VII. built the *Royal Harry*; considered to be the beginning of the Royal Navy 1488
The Trinity house established and the Navy office appointed (see *Admiralty* and *Trinity house*) . 1512
[The navy then consisted of *Great Harry*, 1200 tons, two ships, of 800 tons, and six or seven smaller.]
James I. and Charles I. improve the navy. The *Sovereign of the Seas* launched 1637
Frigates said to have been first built 1649
James II. systematises sea-signals and improves the navy 1685-8

Years.	Ships.	Tons.	Men.	Navy Estimates.
1546	58	12,455	8,546	no account.
1558	27	7,110	3,565	no account.
1578	24	10,506	6,700	no account.
1603	42	17,055	8,346	no account.
1658	157	57,000	21,910	no account.
1688	173	101,892	42,000	no account.
1702	272	159,020	40,000	1,056,915*l*.
1760	412	321,134	70,000	3,227,143
1793	498	433,226	45,000	5,525,331
1800	767	668,744	135,000	12,422,837
1808	869	892,800	143,800	17,496,047
1814	901	966,000	146,000	18,786,509

Reign of George III.; dimensions of ships increased; copper sheathing adopted for ships of every class; establishments of naval stores provided at all dockyards and naval stations; and various improvements made in shipbuilding 1760-1820
Great Britain had 901 ships; 177 of the line, in 1814; 621 ships, some of 140 guns each, and down to surveying vessels of two guns only; 148 sail employed on foreign and home service 1830
The screw propeller introduced in the Royal Navy, 1840
The total number of ships of all sizes in commission, 183 . . . . 1 Jan. 1841
The Navy consisted of 339 sailing and 161 steam vessels 1850
Naval Coast Volunteers' act passed . . Aug. 1853
Of 315 sailing vessels, 97 screw steamers, and 114 paddle steamers . . . . . . April, 1854
Review of the Baltic fleet at Spithead by the Queen, 10 March, 1854, and 23 April, 1856
Of 271 sailing vessels, carrying 9594 guns, and 258 steam vessels, carrying 6582 guns; together 573 vessels, carrying 16,176 guns; also 155 gunboats, and 111 vessels on harbour service, July, ,,
Proclamation for manning the navy . . 30 April, 1859
Naval Reserve Force authorised . . . . Aug. ,,
Flogging not to be inflicted on first-class seamen except after a trial . . . . . . Dec. ,,
Great excitement respecting the French Government building the plated frigate *Gloire* (see *Navy of France*) 1860
The *Warrior*, our first iron-plated steam frigate, the largest vessel then in the world except the *Great Eastern* (see *Steam*), length, 380 ft. breadth, 58 ft.; iron-plate, 4½ inches thick; 6170 tons burthen; cost about 400,000*l*.; launched [censured in 1864], 29 Dec. ,,
A royal commission recommends the abolition of the board of admiralty, and the appointment of a minister of the navy department . . March, 1861
Lord Clarence Paget, secretary of admiralty, states that England has 67 steam-ships of the line; while France has 37, Russia 9, Spain 3, and Italy 1 11 April, ,,
New act for the government of the navy (the Naval Discipline act) passes . . . . . 6 Aug. ,,
Four iron-plated vessels (400 ft. long; 59½ ft. wide; and cost about 600,000*l*. each) building . . Dec. ,,
Cupola or Turret ships. Capt. Cowper Coles' mode of constructing iron-plated vessels, with a cupola or turret for firing from, the other parts of the vessel being nearly submerged, made known in 1855, and recommended to the admiralty in 1861; adopted by Ericson in the *Monitor*, 1862; proposed to be adopted by the British government, 1862
Six different kinds of plated vessels said to be constructing; E. J. Reed authorised to build the *Enterprise* as a specimen of an iron-plated seagoing vessel . . . . . . April, ,,
Royal Oak, iron-clad steamer, launched at Chatham, 10 Sept. ,,
Twin or double screws for vessels of light draught introduced 1863
Mr. E. J. Reed appointed chief constructor of the Royal Navy . . . . Jan. ,,
Navy consists of 1014 vessels of all classes; 85 line-of-battle ships; 69 frigates; 30 screw corvettes, Jan. ,,
Steam ram *Valiant* launched . . . 14 Oct. ,,
Minotaur iron-steamer launched . . 12 Dec. ,,
Royal School of Naval Architecture, South Kensington, established 1864
The turret-ship *Sovereign*, constructed on Coles' principle, put out of commission, and placed among reserved ships; this blamed by some, Oct. ,,
Naval models from the time of Henry VIII. collected early in the present century by sir Robert Seppings, removed to South Kensington Museum, Dec. ,,
29 iron-clad vessels building "to be ready for sea this year" . . . . March, 1865
Bellerophon, iron-clad, by Mr. E. J. Reed; and the *Lord Warden*, iron-clad, launched . . . May, ,,
A British fleet entertained at Cherbourg, Brest, &c., 15 Aug., &c.; and a French fleet at Portsmouth, 29-31 Aug. ,,

Royal Navy "consists of 735 vessels and steamships of all classes" (30 iron-clads ready for sea), (see under *Cannon*) . . . . July, 1866
New Naval Discipline act, passed . . . Aug. ,,
Difficult launch of the *Northumberland* iron-clad, 17 March, *et seq.*; effected . . . 17 April, ,,
Experimental cruise of the iron-clad fleet in stormy weather; general performance satisfactory (*Times*) Sept.-Nov. ,,
150 wooden ships of all classes sold . . . 1859-67
[Of these were 7 line-of-battle ships and 6 frigates, cost above 1,000,000*l.*, sold for 87,543*l.*]
Acts for protection of naval stores passed, 1867 and 1869
Hercules, 12, armour-plated ship, 1200 horse-power, floated at Chatham . . . . . 10 Feb. 1868
The *Monarch*, our first armour-clad turret ship, launched at Chatham . . . . 25 May, ,,
47 armoured vessels afloat, with 598 guns; 66 efficient unarmoured vessels; and a large number of vessels of the old type, constitute the navy, April, ,,
Satisfactory trial trip of the Navy Reserve squadron, July, ,,
Explosion of the boiler of the *Thistle* gun-boat, on trial trip; 10 killed . . . . . . 3 Nov. 1869
Devastation, iron turret ship, first rivet of her keel clinched by Mr. Childers, the first lord, at Portsmouth . . . . 12 Nov. ,,
Resignation of Mr. E. J. Reed, chief constructor, July, 1870
Adm. sir T. M. C. Symonds reports on the *Monarch* and *Captain* turret ships (the latter said to be overmasted and unfit to cruise under sail alone) Aug. ,,
H.M.S. iron-clad frigate *Triumph* launched at Jarrow . . . . 27 Sept. ,,
The *Captain* founders near Finisterre about 12.15 A.M. . . . . 7 Sept. ,,
483 lives were lost, including the captain, Hugh Burgoyne, Captain Cowper Coles, the designer of the ship, Mr. Childers (a son of the first lord), and other officers, the *élite* of the service; 18 men of the crew were saved. "She capsized in a heavy squall shortly after midnight, and went down in three minutes."—*Gunner's report.* Her destruction was attributed to too low free-board, heavy top-weight, masts, and hurricane deck. She cost 440,000*l.* She was built by Messrs. Laird at Birkenhead.
A court-martial for the nominal trial of James May, the gunner, and 17 other survivors, was held 27 Sept. to 4 Oct.; Mr. E. J. Reed and other eminent authorities were examined; the verdict was, that the loss of the ship was due to instability from faulty construction: "a grave departure from her original design having been committed" Oct. ,,
Report on the *Monarch* that her reserve of energy to prevent upsetting by a squall, is 16 to 1 of that of the *Captain*.—*Times* . . . . 10 Nov. ,,
Navy.—55 armoured vessels afloat; 9 constructing; effective force afloat, 354 vessels; and a large number of others 1871
Megæra troopship lost near Amsterdam island (see *Wrecks*) . . . . 16 June, ,,
The *Agincourt*, capt. Hamilton Beamish, 6621 tons, struck on the Pearl Rock near Gibraltar, 11 A.M. 1 July; got off by great skill and management by the *Hercules*, capt. lord Guildford . 4 July, ,,
[After trial, admirals Wellesley and Wilmot ordered to strike flags; capts. Beamish and Well superseded; others censured; lord Guildford commended, Aug. 1871.]
Turret vessels of the *Monitor* type designed by E. J. Reed, launched: the *Glatton*, 6 March; *Devastation*, 12 July; *Cyclops* . . . 18 July, ,,
New rules respecting promotions, &c., published 9 Feb. 1872
The *Thunderer*, ocean-going turret ship, launched at Pembroke . . . . 25 March, ,,
Lord Clyde, iron-clad, stranded off Pantellaria, 15 March; capt. Bythesea and staff-commander May dismissed the service . . . . . May, ,,
A trial-trip of the *Devastation* reported successful, 15 April, 1873
Navy.—23 great iron-clads; 27 smaller . Aug. ,,

"We now carry 35-ton guns on board ships in turrets protected by 14-inch plates" (*Times*), 28 Aug. 1875
Royal Naval Artillery Volunteer force established by act passed . . . . 5 Aug. ,,
H.M.S. *Alexandra* launched at Chatham . 7 April, ,,
H.M.S. *Vanguard*, double-screw iron-clad (cost 350,000*l.*), sunk by collision with the *Iron Duke* during a fog off the Wicklow coast; crew (about 400) saved; 50 m. past noon . . . . 1 Sept. ,,
Court-Martial on capt. Dawkins; assigned as causes: 1. That the squadron (under admiral Tarleton), of which the *Vanguard* was one, was going at too great a speed for a fog; 2. That captain Dawkins had left the deck before an ordered evolution was performed; 3. That the speed of the *Vanguard* had been injudiciously reduced; 4, 5, 6. The increased speed of the *Iron Duke*, her improper navigation, and want of signals; captain Dawkins reprimanded and dismissed; others reprimanded, 29 Sept. ,,
The *Admiralty Minute* considered the speed of the squadron no cause of the accident; censured part of admiral Tarleton's evidence on responsibility of officers; and removed lieutenant Evans of the *Iron Duke* from his command . . 12 Oct. ,,
Iron Duke nearly lost through a valve left open, 28 Nov. ,,
The *Monarch*, iron-clad, injured by collision with Norwegian ship *Halden* in the Channel 28 Nov. ,,
The *Inflexible*, with 18-inch armour and four 81-ton guns, movable by hydraulic power, launched by princess Louise at Portsmouth . . 27 April, 1876
The *Téméraire*, smaller iron-clad, launched at Chatham . . . . 9 May, ,,
The *Thunderer* (see 1872 *above*): explosion of a boiler through sticking of safety valves; 45 deaths ensued; about 50 injured; during a trial trip in Stokes Bay, near Portsmouth; 14 July; inquest begun 27 July; (about 5,000*l.* subscribed for the sufferers); verdict, accidental deaths . 30 Aug. ,,
Bacchante, unarmoured war-ship, launched, 19 Oct. ,,
Launched at Glasgow, *Nelson*, iron-clad . 4 Nov. ,,
,, ,, *Northampton* . 18 Nov. ,,
Euryalus, unarmoured corvette, launched at Chatham . . . . 31 Jan. 1877
Commission of inquiry respecting the *Inflexible*, appointed about . . . . 14 July, ,,
4 new ironclads bought . . . . . March, 1878
Dreadnought, iron-clad; 10,886 tons; engines, 8000 horse-power; four 38-ton guns, &c.; most powerful fighting ship in the world; constructed . ,,
Eurydice, H.M.S. frigate; training ship, foundered in a gale off Dunose, Isle of Wight; about 300 perished with capt. Hare, 24 March; with much skill and labour raised and taken to Portsmouth 1 Sept., ordered to be broken up . . Sept. ,,
The *Thunderer* (see 1876), a 38-ton gun explodes while practising, near Ismid, in the Sea of Marmora, Turkey; 2 officers and 8 men killed, and between 30 and 40 wounded . . 2 Jan. 1879
On investigation the cause assigned was that the gun was charged and missed fire; re-charged and both charges were fired, when it exploded Feb. ,,
Agamemnon, iron-clad turret ship; 8492 tons; engines, 6000 horse-power; four 38-ton guns; launched at Chatham . . . . 17 Sept. ,,
Collision of the *Achilles* and *Alexandra*, off Larnaca, Mediterranean; boats injured, &c. . 2 Oct. ,,
Sham naval attack on Portsmouth; defended by torpedoes, &c. . . . . . . 16 Oct. ,,
Thunderer gun experiments at Woolwich (confirm decision of investigation committee of Feb. 1879), 9 Dec. 1879—3 Feb. 1880
Atalanta training ship lost in gale (see *Atalanta*), 12—16 Feb. ,,
Great naval demonstration at Portsmouth; attack on forts; electric light used at night . 10 Aug. ,,
Doterel, 6 guns; capt. Richard Evans; destroyed by explosion (attributed to *xerotine siccative*, 3 Sept.) in Straits of Magellan; out of 150 about 143 persons perished . . . . . 26 April, 1881
Polyphemus, huge double-screw steam armour-plated ram and torpedo boat; launched at Chatham (designed by sir G. Sartorius) . . 15 June, ,,
Launch of *Canada* corvette at Portsmouth, 26 Aug.; of *Conqueror*, steel-clad turret ship, at Chatham 8 Sept. ,,

Triumph, explosion of *xerotine siccative* (a patent drier for paint) near Coquimbo, coast of Chili, 23 Nov.; 3 men killed, 7 wounded . Jan. 1882
Ajax, new *armoured turret ship*, moved from Chatham . . . . 20 Feb. ,,
Two very large armour-plated war-ships launched; *Edinburgh*, at Pembroke, 18 March; *Colossus*, at Portsmouth . . . . . . 21 March, ,,
The *Phœnix* lost off Prince Edward's island, 12 Sept.; commander Greenfell dismissed . . . 1 Dec. ,,
The *Collingwood*, of "British Admiral class," launched at Pembroke . . . 22 Nov. ,,
Naval Intelligence Committee formed . . Dec. ,,
The duke of Edinburgh appointed to command the Channel fleet . . . about 26 Nov. 1883
Collision of the *Defence* and *Valiant* in Bantry Bay, 18 July; capt. Edwin John Pollard of the *Defence*, tried and dismissed from his ship for inefficiency . . . . . 30 July, 1884
Wasp, gun-boat (comm. Nicholls), wrecked off Tory island (attributed to bad navigation); about 52 perish . . . . 22 Sept. ,,
Rodney, great iron-clad, launched by the duchess of Edinburgh, at Chatham . . . . . 8 Oct. ,,
Navy Discipline act amended . . . . . . ,,
Great Britain has 46 iron-clads . . . . Dec. ,,
Large and important additions to the navy authorised . . . . Feb. 1885
Launch of *Mersey*, "protected corvette," at Chatham, 31 March, ,,
Benbow, ironclad battleship, launched at Blackwall, 15 June, ,,
Sham battle near Bantry Bay, 30 June; attempted attack on Greenock . . . . 14 July, ,,
Icarus, warship, launched at Devonport 27 July, ,,
Severn, fast sailing steel corvette launched at Chatham . . . . . . 29 Sept. ,,
Hero, steel built, armour-plated, turreted ram, launched at Chatham . . . . 27 Oct. ,,
Swallow, largest gun vessel launched at Sheerness 27 Oct. ,,
Camperdown, great ironclad war-ship launched at Portsmouth . . . . . . 24 Nov. ,,
The duke of Edinburgh takes command of the Mediterranean fleet . . . . . 22 Feb. 1886
Anson, twin-screw armour-plated barbette ship, launched at Pembroke dockyard . . 17 Feb. ,,
H.M.S. *Collingwood*, at Portsmouth, 43 ton gun burst; no casualty, 4 May; stated to be due to defective metal . . . . . . 6 Sept. ,,
Sham naval fights at Milford Haven 16 Aug. *et seq.* ,,
H.M.S. *Orlando*, first of the new class of belted cruisers, launched at Jarrow-on-Tyne . 23 Aug. ,,
The *Undaunted*, another belted cruiser, launched at Jarrow-on-Tyne . . . . . 25 Nov. ,,
Narcissus, new belted cruiser, launched at Hull, 15 Dec. ,,
The naval intelligence department formed as a committee, 10 April, 1884; as a department, 1 Feb. 1887
Report of commission on admiralty contracts censures system and recommends changes, about 10 March, ,,
Serpent, large torpedo cruiser launched at Devonport . . . . 10 March, ,,
Victoria (first called *Renown*), armour-clad warship, launched at Elswick yard, Newcastle, 9 April, ,,
Sans Pareil, iron-clad war-ship, launched at Blackwall . . . . 9 May, ,,
Serious collision between *Ajax* and *Devastation* on their way to Spithead . . . 18 July, ,,
Grand jubilee naval review by the queen at Spithead; 135 vessels, 20,200 men and about 500 guns, 23 July, ,,
Naval manœuvres and torpedo experiments on the coast . . . . Aug. ,,
Trafalgar, great steel twin-screw turret ram; 11,940 tons, 345 feet long, 73 feet broad, launched at Portsmouth . . . . . . 20 Sept. ,,
Wasp, gunboat, supposed to have foundered in a typhoon in the China seas . . 10 Oct. ,,
Nile, iron-clad, heaviest yet launched in England; 12,000 tons, 345 feet long, 73 feet broad; launched at Pembroke dock . . . . 27 March, 1888
H.M.S. *Magicienne*, twin-screw swift cruiser, launched at Govan . . . . . 12 May, ,,
H.M.S. *Medea*, twin-screw, second-class cruiser, launched at Chatham . . . . 9 June, 1888
H.M.S. *Marathon*, cruiser, launched by princess Beatrice in the Clyde . . . . 23 Aug. ,,
Naval manœuvres, sham capture of Liverpool and other ports . . . . Aug. ,,
Lord George Hamilton, first lord, at Glasgow, gives a favourable account of the state of the navy, 10 Oct. ,,
Navy afloat: 62 armoured vessels; 29 protected and partially protected; 282 unprotected; total, 373 ships; tonnage, 679,144; cost, 35,635,719*l.* 1 Jan. 1889
Lord George Hamilton proposes resolutions for the construction and equipment of 70 ships, including 10 battle ships (8 first and 2 second class), and 42 cruisers, 18 torpedo boats, &c., to be completed in 4½ years, cost 21,500,000*l.* (10,000,000*l.* from the consolidated fund in seven years; 11,500,000*l.* from five years' navy estimates), 7 March, ,,
The Northbrook programme of 1885 reported nearly complete . . . . 7 March, ,,
Lord George Hamilton's resolutions adopted by the commons . . . . . . 2–4 April, ,,
Sir A. Hoskins succeeds the duke of Edinburgh in command of the Mediterranean fleet 6 April, ,,
The *Sultan*, ironclad, run ashore on a rock at Comino channel, Maltese group, 6 March; abandoned; the crew saved; after strenuous attempts to save her, the vessel sank, 14 March; trial; captain Rice reprimanded for sailing too close to shore . . . . . . 8 April, ,,
[The admiralty appointed a court to enquire into all the circumstances, 29, 30 May, when the duke of Edinburgh, who had directed the salvage operations, was examined; the court reported its approbation of the steps taken for the recovery of the vessel.] . . 15 June, ,,
The *Sultan* was raised 20 Aug., sailed to Malta 26 Aug.; at Spithead . . . . . 23 Dec. ,,
H.M.S. *Vulcan*, swift cruiser, launched at Portsmouth . . . . 13 June, ,,
Naval Defence act passed (provision made for constructing 70 ships, including 10 battleships, 42 cruisers, 18 torpedo gunboats), royal assent, 31 May, ,,
The fleet assembled for the autumn manœuvres inspected by the emperor William II. (and his brother prince Henry), the prince of Wales, and members of both houses of parliament. The display consisted of 20 battle-ships (9 first-class, 9 second class and 2 third class), 38 first-class torpedo boats and other vessels, in all 106 vessels (the queen inspected the fleet later in the day), 5 Aug. ,,
The naval manœuvres begin; sham declaration of war, 15 Aug.; English fleet commanded by adm. Tryon, Achill or foreign fleet by adm. Baird; enemies' country, Ireland; Dublin, Belfast, Waterford captured by Tryon; Edinburgh captured, Aberdeen, Sunderland and other towns bombarded by Baird, invasion repelled 22–29 Aug. ,,
Barham, steel-plated cruiser, launched at Portsmouth . . . . 11 Sept. ,,
Lilly gun-boat struck on a rock, off Point Armour, Labrador coast, and sank, 7 lives lost; heroic conduct of the crew, 16 Sept.; commander Russell and lieut. Sharp censured and dismissed 4 Oct. ,,
Blake, protected cruiser, the largest yet constructed, length 375 ft., breadth 65 ft., launched at Chatham . . . . 23 Nov. ,,
Gossamer and *Gleaner*, gun-vessels, launched at Sheerness . . . . 9 Jan. 1890
Barracouta, cruiser (launched April, 1889), trial trip off Margate; explosion; Henry Ovendina and James Gould killed, 8 severely injured, 7 Feb.; inquest, 10 Feb.; verdict, accidental death; engineer censured . . . . . . 10 April, ,,
Latona, war cruiser, launched at Barrow 22 May, ,,
Pallas, second-class cruiser, the first of a set constructed under the Naval Defence act, launched at Portsmouth . . . . . . 30 June, ,,
Blenheim, large cruiser, launched at Blackwall 5 July, ,,

Naval manœuvres; defensive fleet under adm. sir George Tryon; enemy's fleet under adm. sir Michael Culme-Seymour; kept the seas but could not be met with; there was much practice and many evolutions but no conflict . 9–18 Aug. 1890

Launch of *Melampus*, steel protected cruiser, at Barrow . . . . 2 Aug. ,,

Andromache, cruiser, launched at Chatham, 14 Aug. ,,

Serpent, torpedo-cruiser, started from Plymouth 8 Nov.; during a gale struck on a rock at Penta del Buey, on the coast of Camariñas, 5 miles N. of cape Villano. Commander Harry L. Ross, lieuts. Guy A. J. Greville and Torquil Macleod, Mr. James W. Dixon, paymaster, and 169 others were drowned; three seamen, Edwin Burton, Frederick Joseph Gould and Oney Luxton were the only survivors . . . . . 10.30 p.m. 10 Nov. ,,

The bodies were honourably buried as they were washed ashore. Court-martial verdict, error in navigation . . . . . . 16, 17 Dec. ,,

A national fund for the relief of the families suffering by the wreck, was started at Devonport by the duke of Edinburgh, 18 Nov.; the duke gave 100*l*., the duchess 50*l*., the queen 50*l*., the prince of Wales 25*l*. (see *Mansion House Fund* and *Soldiers' and Sailors' Families Association*). Total sum collected 13,580*l*., reported . 15 Nov. 1891

Edgar, first-class cruiser, launched at Devonport 24 Nov. 1890

Pique, second-class twin-screw cruiser; launched at Howdon-on-Tyne . . . . . 13 Dec. ,,

Earnest appeal on behalf of the rank and file (warrant officers, &c.), for a system of promotion; circulated. . . . . . about 17 Jan. 1891

The queen, in the presence of her three sons and a large company at Portsmouth, names and launches the *Royal Arthur*, first-class protected cruiser; and also names, and causes the floating out of dock of the *Royal Sovereign*, the largest battleship in the Royal Navy (length 380 feet, breadth 75 feet); all very successful . 26 Feb. ,,

The *Empress of India*, great ironclad, 14,150 tons, 380 feet long, 75 feet broad, with 7 Whitehead torpedoes, launched at Pembroke docks by the duchess of Connaught . . . . 7 May, ,,

Cordelia, cruiser; 2 lieuts. and 4 men killed by the explosion of a gun while practising in the Pacific ocean . . . . 29 June, ,,

Naval manœuvres under admirals Seymour and Jones, tactical operations of all kinds 13 July–3 Aug. ,,

Endymion, armoured cruiser, launched at Hull, and named by the marchioness of Salisbury, 22 July, ,,

Hood, great turret ship, length 380 ft., breadth 75 ft., launched at Chatham, and named by Lady Hood . . . . 30 July, ,,

Victoria, flagship," runs aground near Platea, W. Greece, 29 Jan.; refloated, little injured, 5 Feb. *et seq.*; arrived at Malta for repairs, 12 Feb.; capt. Bourke reprimanded for negligence by a court-martial . . . 25 Feb. 1892

Grafton, swift cruiser, launched at the Thames Ironworks dockyard . . . . 30 Jan. ,,

Repulse, great turret ship, length 380 ft.; breadth 75 feet; launched at Pembroke, 27 Feb.; the *Ramillies*, a similar vessel, was launched on the Clyde . . . . 1 March, ,,

Gibraltar, first-class protected cruiser, launched at Govan, near Glasgow . . . . 27 April, ,,

Jason, torpedo gunboat, launched at Barrow-in-Furness . . . . 14 May, ,,

Resolution, first-class battleship, launched at Jarrow-on-Tyne . . . . . . 28 May, ,,

St. George, first-class battleship, launched at Hull 23 June, ,,

Naval manœuvres, 5–13 Aug.; 19 battleships and 17 other vessels engaged; red squadron, 2 divisions, under adm. H. Fairfax and rear-adm. R. O'B. Fitzroy; blue squadron under H. C. St. John; manœuvres in the St. George's channel and Irish sea; the two red divisions eventually unite and capture the blue squadron, the proposed object . . . . . . 11 Aug. ,,

Barfleur, ironclad, launched at Chatham . 10 Aug. ,,

Royal Naval Fund for the relief of widows and orphans, was founded by means of the surplus from the Naval exhibition of 1891 (*which see*), 29 June, ,,

The *Leda* and *Alarm*, gunboats, launched at Sheerness . . . . 13 Sept. 1892

The last 2 of the 8 great battleships ordered in 1889 launched: the *Revenge* in the Tyne, 3 Nov.; the *Royal Oak* in the Mersey . . . . 5 Nov. ,,

The *Bonaventure*, protected cruiser, launched at Devonport by the princess Marie of Edinburgh, 2 Dec. ,,

"*Discreditable project*," a term applied to a proposal in the *Army and Navy Gazette*, Nov. 1891, for the union of naval officers to bring their grievances before parliament; a circular, signed by comm. Chas. N. Robinson, was distributed through the fleet, Aug. 1892.—*Times* . 11 Oct. ,,

The *Howe*, battleship, runs aground on a reef off Ferrol; attributed to an incorrect chart, 2 Nov.; officers acquitted of blame, 30 Nov.; vice-adm. Henry Fairfax acquitted, 29 Dec. 1892—7 Jan. 1893; capt. Hastings and commander Dickson censured by the admiralty, 24 Feb.; the *Howe* floated, 29 March; arrives at Sheerness, 22 June, 1893

The *Victoria* (*see above*, 1887), flagship in the Mediterranean (vice-admiral sir George Tryon), sank by collision with the *Camperdown* (rear-admiral Markham) while manœuvring off Tripoli, on the coast of Syria, through an error of judgment of admiral Tryon; the vessels were 6 instead of 8 cables apart; he remained on the bridge till the vessel sank, taking all blame, 3.41 p.m. 22 June, ,,

[Besides admiral Tryon, 22 officers, 336 men, including lieut. Philip H. Munro, rev. S. S. Morris, chaplain, Felix Foreman, fleet-engineer, were drowned; much unselfish heroism was exhibited; 25 officers and 259 men landed at Malta, 30 June; liberal contributions for the relief of the families of the sufferers were received (see *Mansion House Fund*, June–Aug. *et seq.* 1893).]

A court-martial on board the *Hibernia*, admiral sir Michael Culme-Seymour president; the hon. Maurice Bourke, capt. of the *Victoria*, and other survivors, were acquitted. The court decided that the accident was due to the error of admiral Tryon, but regretted that admiral Markham did not act on his first intention to ask admiral Tryon for an explanation of his signal of 6 cables' distance . . . . 17–27 July, ,,

Naval manœuvres . . . . 27 July—4 Aug. ,,

Red squadron under vice-adm. H. Fairfax; blue squadron under R. O'B. Fitzroy, contend for the possession of the Irish sea; indecisive encounter off Calf of Man . . . . . . 29 July ,,

The Mediterranean squadron visit Taranto, &c. (see *Italy*) . . . . 16–29 Oct. ,,

H.M.S. *Resolution* much injured during a gale in the bay of Biscay; 1 man lost . . . Dec. ,,

Naval scare ended . . . . Dec. ,,

Launches: the *Cambrian*, protected cruiser, at Pembroke, 30 Jan.; *Astræa*, 2nd class cruiser, at Devonport, 17 March; *Speedy* (large torpedo gunboat), at Chiswick, 18 May; *Charybdis*, at Sheerness; *Fox*, at Portsmouth, 15 June; *Hermione*, 2nd class cruiser, at Devonport, 7 Nov.; *Flora*, 2nd class cruiser, at Pembroke, 21 Nov.; *Forte*, 2nd class cruiser, at Chatham, 9 Dec.; *Hornet*, at Poplar, 23 Dec. 1893; *Eclipse*, 2nd class cruiser, at Portsmouth . . . 19 July, 1894

Magnificent, 1st-class battleship, 390 ft. long, 75 ft. broad; launched at Chatham . . . 19 Dec. ,,

Mr. Wm. H. White, F.R.S., director of naval construction (K.C.B. 1895), in a discourse at the Royal Institution on the "Making of a Modern Fleet," reported that nearly all of the 70 ships ordered in 1889 were completed in the time specified in the act; cost, about 22¾ millions, 9 March, ,,

Navy estimates, 1894–5, net amount, 17,366,100*l*.; proposed construction of 7 first-class battleships, 6 cruisers, and others . . . . 15 March, ,,

Naval manœuvres . . . . . . 3–7 Aug. ,,

Red squadron under admirals Fitzroy and Dale; blue squadron under admirals Seymour and Drummond; engagement off Belfast Lough, 5 Aug.; victory awarded to the blue . 7 Aug. ,,

Majestic, battleship; 390 ft. long, 75 ft. broad; launched at Portsmouth by the princess Louise, 31 Jan. 1895

Renown, 1st class battleship, launched at Pembroke dock . . . . 8 May, ,,

Terrible, cruiser; 538 ft. long, 71 ft. wide; launched near Glasgow . . . . . 27 May, 1895
Powerful, 1st class cruiser, launched at Barrow by the duchess of Devonshire . . . 24 July, ,,
Prince George, 1st class cruiser, launched at Portsmouth by the duchess of York . 22nd Aug. ,,
Discussion on the proposed substitution of tubular for cylindrical boilers, hitherto tried in gunboats, April *et seq.* ,,
Manœuvres: tactical exercises, &c., by Channel fleet, reserve fleet and torpedo squadron, 24 July–7 Aug.; "hide and seek" . . . . 9–15 Aug. ,,
Victorious, battleship, 390 ft. long, 75 ft. broad; launched by Mrs. Goschen at Chatham 19 Oct. ,,
100 officers (taken from the naval reserve, &c., and 100 from the mercantile marine to the naval reserve), gazetted . . . . . Nov. ,,
H.M.S. *Edgar's* pinnace foundered off Chemulpho, 48 lives lost . . . . . . 13 Nov. ,,
Jupiter, 1st class battleship, 390 feet long, 75 ft. 9 in. broad; launched at Glasgow, by Miss Balfour . . . . . . 18 Nov. ,,
Flying squadron, rear-adm. A. T. Dale hoists his flag on the *Revenge* . . . . . 14 Jan. 1896
Great improvement of the navy in fighting power, 1886 *et seq.*, demonstrated . . . Jan. ,,
Mars, 1st class battleship, 390 ft. long, 75 ft. broad; launched at Birkenhead . . . . 30 March, ,,
Hannibal, 1st class battleship, launched at Pembroke Dock . . . . . 28 April, ,,
Naval manœuvres; mimic war, 4 fleets engaged, 24–30 July, ,,
28 vessels pass Osborne, and fire a final salute, 3 Aug.; inspected by the queen . 4 Aug. ,,
Cæsar, 1st class battleship, 390 ft. long, 75 ft. broad; launched at Portsmouth . . 2 Sept. ,,
Illustrious, 1st class battleship; launched at Chatham . . . . 17 Sept. ,,
Capt. H. B. Lang and 3 seamen of H.M.S. *Narcissus* China squadron, drowned at Fish river, 11 Sept. ,,
Lieut. Gerald A. Heyman and 7 others of H.M.S. *Satellite*, Pacific squadron, drowned through swamping of a boat at Unalaska . . 6 Sept. ,,
Lord Walter Kerr with the Channel squadron convoys the czar and czarina to meet the French fleet mid-channel . . . . . . 5 Oct. ,,
Gladiator, battleship; launched at Portsmouth, Dec. ,,
Niobe, cruiser; launched at Barrow . 20 Feb. 1897
Naval manœuvres: Channel fleet, 1st division, under adm. Stephenson, against 2nd division, under rear-adm. Fellowes, from N.W. Ireland, reserve fleet, under adm. Compton Domvile, in S. Ireland, technical evolutions, &c. 2–11 July, ,,
See *Cape of Good Hope*, 10 July, 1897.
Canopus, battleship; launched at Portsmouth, 13 Oct. 1897
Sir Harry Rawson, officers and men of the flagship *St. George* returned from the Cape, received by the queen at Osborne . . . . 2 Feb. 1898
Sub-lieut. Wm. Lowther and 5 men of the *Alarm* drowned by the capsizing of the gig, and 5 coastguardsmen drowned off Wells, Norfolk, 22, 23 Feb. ,,
Navy work much delayed by engineers' strike in 1897, reported . . . . . 9 March, ,,
Goliath, battleship, 390 ft. long, 74 ft. wide; launched at Chatham . . . . 23 March, ,,
Albion, battleship, launched at Blackwall; duke and duchess of York present; just as the launch took place a backwash of water swept about 200 people off a gangway; 37 deaths; many brave rescues; 21 June; fund raised, 50*l.* from the queen, 2,762*l.* . . . . . 18 July, ,,
Ocean, battleship; launched at Devonport by princess Louise . . . . . . 5 July, ,,
Usual manœuvres suspended in view South Wales coal strike; channel squadron to cruise as usual July, Aug. ,,
Aggregate strength of the Royal navy, 95,540 officers, men, and boys . . . . 11 July, ,,
Five men lost from H.M.S. *Cleopatra* by collision with *Livlig*, Norwegian barque, in the Kattegat, 29 Aug. ,,
Battleships launched: *Formidable*, at Portsmouth, *Irresistible*, at Chatham . . . 17 Nov. ,,
H.M.S. *Bruiser*; boat lost in a gale off Samos, 8 deaths . . . . 1 March, 1899

Battleships launched: *Implacable*, at Devonport; *Glory*, at Birkenhead . . . . 11 March, 1899
Explosion on *Bullfinch*, torpedo-boat destroyer, in the Solent; 13 deaths . . . . . 21 July, ,,
Vengeance, battleship, 12,950 tons displacement, launched at Barrow-in-Furness . . 25 July, ,,
Naval manœuvres: mimic war; wireless telegraphy of great service . . . 17 July—8 Aug. ,,
French trawler refusing to stop fishing in British waters, is fired on by the gunboat *Leda*, one man killed . . . . . . 8 Aug. ,,
The queen sends 400*l.* to his father . 16 Oct. ,,
Sir Fred. Richards (5 years), first naval lord of the admiralty board, resigns; succeeded by vice-admiral lord Walter Kerr . . . . 19 Aug. ,,
Committee (adm. Moore, sir Henry Norbury, Mr. Austen Chamberlain and surgeon Gipps) on the training of naval medical officers, issue report with important recommendations . . Sept. ,,
Training squadron established, 1885; reconstructed, the masted ships replaced by four modern warships . . . . 30 Oct. ,,
Battleships: *London*, 430 ft. long, 75 ft. wide (cost over 1,000,000*l.*), launched by Lady George Hamilton, 21 Sept.; *Venerable*, launched at Chatham by Mrs. Chamberlain . . 2 Nov. ,,
Total strength of navy, officers and men, 106,507, 1 April, 1900
The queen left Dublin, escorted by the channel squadron, and sent her "thanks to her escort, of which she was justly proud, and whose appearance she greatly admired" . 26 April, ,,
Capt. Lambton (rear-admiral, Oct. 1902) and the naval brigade thanked by the queen at Windsor for their fine services in the S. African war, 2 May, ,,
Experiments with lyddite, &c., on the *Belleisle* in the channel. . . . . . . May, ,,
Manœuvres: hostilities between two fleets of about equal strength, result indecisive, 24 July–4 Aug. ,,
Naval reserve (mobilization) act, passed . 8 Aug. ,,
Grand naval pageant on the funeral of the queen, see *England* . . . . . . 1 Feb. 1901
Battleships launched: *Russell*, at Jarrow-on-Tyne, 19 Feb.; *Montagu*, at Devonport; *Albemarle*, at Chatham; *Drake*, cruiser, at Pembroke; *Kent*, cruiser, at Portsmouth . . . 5, 6 March, ,,
Committee of inquiry *re* boilers (Sept. 1901) recommend the water-tube pattern in preference to the cylindrical (other reports issued, *Times*, 10 July, 1902, and 9 Jan. 1903) . . 13 March, ,,
Lieut. Vernon Maud, commander of H.M.S. *Leda*, and a seamen, drowned in Luce bay in a gale, 20 March, ,,
Battleships launched: *Duncan*, at Blackwall, 21 March; *Cornwallis*, at Blackwall . 17 July, ,,
The *Viper*, turbine torpedo-boat, lost near Alderney, all saved . . . . 3 Aug. ,,
Manœuvres: war declared, 9.30 a.m., 29 July; the B fleet, guarding the English Channel, totally defeated off the Lizard . . . . 6 Aug. ,,
Exmouth, battleship, launched at Birkenhead, 31 Aug. ,,
Cobra, turbine torpedo-boat destroyer, sank in a severe gale on the Outer Dowsing Shoal, Lincolnshire, lieut. Bosworth Smith, Messrs. M. Sandison, and Robt. Barnard, and 64 others, lost; 12 saved, 18 Sept.; funeral at Grimsby, attended by capt. Hugnet and crew of French gunboat, *Ibis*, 23 Sept.; the loss of the ship due to structural weakness, verdict of court-martial . 16 Oct. ,,
King Alfred, first-class cruiser, launched at Barrow, 28 Oct. ,,
Gun accident on board the *Royal Sovereign*; capt. Spurway and 5 men killed, 19 injured, 9 Nov. ,,
Active, coastguard cruiser, lost in a gale at Granton, 19 deaths, 11 Nov.; *Salmon*, torpedo-boat destroyer, run into by the *Cambridge* s.s., 2 deaths . . . . 2 Dec. ,,
Sir W. H. White, director of naval construction, resigns; succeeded (1 Feb. 1902) by Mr. Phillip Watts, designer of the Elswick cruisers, early Dec. ,,
Condor, sloop, foundered with all hands in a gale off Cape Fattery . . . . . . 3 Dec. ,,

Commander Clifton Sclater and 102 others lost, announced . . . . 28 March, 1902
Blue-book on the *Hyacinth* and *Minerva* boiler trials, issued . . . . . . 26 Feb. ,,
Queen, battleship, launched by queen Alexandra at Devonport . . . . . . 8 March, ,,
Prince of Wales, battleship, launched by the prince and princess of Wales at Chatham . 25 March, ,,
Explosion during gun practice on board the *Mars*, battleship, off Berehaven, lieuts. Bourne and Miller and nine men killed, 7 (one mortally), injured, 14 April; the German emperor sends his sympathy . . . . 21 April, ,,
Lieut. Arthur Pringle and two others killed by an accident on board the *Formidable* battleship off Maddalena, Mediterranean . . . . 28 April, ,,
Naval reserve volunteers act, royal assent, 22 July, ,,
Coronation naval review at Spithead, over 100 ships; four foreign cruisers, illuminations, &c. 16 Aug. ,,
Manœuvres in the Mediterranean 30 Sept.–5 Oct. ,,
Capt. prince Louis of Battenberg appointed director of naval intelligence . . . Oct. ,,
New admiralty scheme for naval and marine training, &c., issued (*Times*, 25 Dec.) 24 Dec. ,,
Collision between the *Pioneer* and the *Orwell* off Corfu, 15 deaths . . . . . 30 June, 1903
Reorganisation of the Home fleet and naval reserves to take complete effect in May, 1903; the command of the Home fleet to be separated from the command of the naval reserves, and from office work at the Admiralty, and the adm.-superintendent of naval reserves to cease to act as admiral in command of a sea-going squadron. As the commands fall vacant, vice-adm. sir A. K. Wilson to command the Home fleet, vice-adm. Lord Chas. Beresford to command the Channel squadron, vice-adm. Rice to command the naval reserves, announced . . end Feb. ,,
Navy estimates for 1903–4, 34,457,500*l.*, issued early March, ,,
Lord Chas. Beresford takes over the command of the Channel squadron . . . . 17 April, ,,
Commonwealth, battleship, launched by lady Linlithgow at Govan . . . . . . 13 May, ,,
Accident on board the *Good Hope* off Gibraltar, 2 died . . . . ,,
Adm. sir John Fisher, second sea lord, succeeds adm. sir Chas. Hotham as commander-in-chief at Portsmouth, and is succeeded at the Admiralty by rear-adm. sir Chas. Drury . . early June, ,,
Admiralty issues a circular on the selection, training, and advancement of navigating officers, June ,,
Report of committee on "berthing accommodation" for H.M.'s ships issued; new port at St. Margaret's Hope recommended . mid June, ,,
United States European squadron under adm. Cotton visit Portsmouth; illumination of British fleet and U.S. warships in the evening, 6 July; received by the king at Buckingham palace 8 July; adm. and officers entertained at the mansion house 10 July; at a banquet at Portsmouth 11th July; prince of Wales breakfasts on board the flagship *Kearsarge*; ball in new naval barracks in honour of the visitors 13 July; leaves 17 July, ,,
King Edward VII., battleship, launched by the princess of Wales at Devonport . 23 July, ,,
Cruiser *Melampus* runs down and sinks steam collier *Ruperra* near Scilly isles . 29 July, ,,
Torpedo manœuvres in the Irish sea and St. George's channel . . . . 3–8 Aug. ,,
Vice-adm. sir Robert H. Harris appointed president of the Royal Naval College, Greenwich, in succession to adm. sir R. H. M. Molyneux, 6 Aug. ,,
Boiler accident on the *Blake* at Funchal, 2 killed, 5 injured . . . . 7 Aug. ,,
Royal naval volunteer reserve, under the "Naval Forces act, 1902," raised . . . 10 Aug. ,,
Fleet manœuvres (65 ships) in the Atlantic; the B 2 fleet, under lord Chas. Beresford, though chased by the X fleet, succeeded in joining the B 1 fleet under sir A. Wilson, and the "Battle of the Azores" took place 9 Aug. (results referred to umpires), they all arrived at Lagos bay, Portugal . . . . 13 Aug. ,,
Dominion, battleship, launched by princess Louise (Argyll), at Barrow . . . . 25 Aug. 1903
Circular letter by Admiralty to all commanders embodying new scheme for organising and training of bands for the fleet; whole of naval band service to be transferred to the Royal Marines, issued . . . . 29 Aug. ,,
Adm. of the Fleet sir A. M. Lyons retires; succeeded by adm. sir C. F. Hotham, who hoists his flag on the *Victory* at Portsmouth . 30 Aug. ,,
Torpedo experiment at Portsmouth, to test the efficacy of corn pith cellulose, on the hulk *Belleisle*, which was sunk . . . . . 4 Sept. ,,
King Charles of Portugal appointed hon. adm. in British navy by the king . . . 8 Sept. ,,
Hampshire, cruiser, launched by lady Londonderry at Elswick . . . . 24 Sept. ,,
Controversy between rear-adm. Lambton and gen. sir A. Hunter, respecting evidence given by the latter before the War Commission relative to the practice of the naval guns at Ladysmith, Sept.-Oct. ,,
New dietary, in accordance with which the men have cocoa on waking and supper, thus giving each man 5 meals *per diem* instead of 3 as previously, came into force . . . . 1 Oct. ,,
Carnarvon, cruiser, launched by lady Penrhyn at Govan . . . . 7 Oct. ,,
Collision between the battleships *Prince George* and *Hannibal* while manœuvring off Ferrol; *Prince George* sustains serious damage . . 17 Oct. ,,
Accident to the *Victory*, her port side stove in, by the *Neptune* colliding with the flagship while being towed out of Portsmouth harbour; staff-captain Rawson subsequently decorated by the king with the Royal Victorian order, for smartness in docking the *Victory* after the collision, 23 Oct. ,,
Prince George of the Hellenes appointed by the king hon. adm. of British fleet, announced, 31 Oct. ,,
Vice-adm. H. L. Pearson selected as commander-in-chief at the Nore, announced . . 2 Nov. ,,
Orders issued by Admiralty for a number of the ships included in 1903–4 programme, announced in Feb. by earl of Selborne (which included 3 battleships, 4 armoured cruisers, and a number of smaller craft); orders issued comprise 3 armoured cruisers of 13,500 tons, 22½ knots speed (*Achilles*, *Cochrane*, and *Natal*, named after the colony); 4 scouts of 2,000 tons, 25 knots speed; and 6 torpedo-destroyers, 25½ knots speed, 4 Nov. ,,
Important experiments by capt. Egerton and staff of the *Vernon*, torpedo-school ship at Portsmouth, with submarine mines, carried out in Stokes Bay; simultaneous explosion of 40 mines charged with 2,000 lbs. of gun-cotton . 4 Nov. ,,

Annual Expenditure of the British Navy (estimates). —1850, 6,942,397*l.*;—1854, 6,640,596*l.*;—1855 (to 31 March, *Russian war*), 14,490,105*l.*;—1856, 19,654,585*l.*; —1859, 9,215,487*l.*; —1861, 13,331,668*l.*; —1862, 12,598,042*l.*;—1863, 11,370,588*l.*;—1864, 10,821,596*l.*; —1865, 10,898,253*l.*; —1866, 10,259,788*l.*; —1867, 10,676,101*l.*;—1868, 11,168,949*l.*;—1869, 11,366,545*l.*;—1870, 9,757,290*l.*;—1871, 9,456,641*l.*;—1872, 9,900,486*l.*; —1873, 9,543,000*l.*; —1874, 10,279,900*l.*; —1875, 10,680,404*l.*;—1876, 10,285,194*l.*;—1877, 11,288,872*l.*; —1878, 11,053,901*l.*; —1879, 10,586,894*l.*; —1880, 10,492,935*l.*;—1881, 10,725,919*l.*;—1882, 10,483,901*l.*; —1883, 10,899,500*l.*;—1884-5, 11,645,711*l.*;—1885-6 12,694,900*l.*;—1886-7, 12,993,100*l.*;—1887-8, 12,476,800*l.*; —1888-9, 13,082,800*l.*;—1889-90, 13,685,400*l.*;—1890-1, 14,557,856*l.*;—1891-2, 14,215,100*l.*;—1892-3, 14,302,000*l.*; —1893-4, 14,048,000*l.*; —1894-5, 16,366,100*l.*; —1895-6, 18,701,000*l.*;—1896-7, 21,823,000*l.*;—1897-8, 21,838,000*l.*; 500,000*l.* added (July); —1898-9, 26,669,021*l.*; —1899-1900, 26,594,500*l.*; —1900-1, 28,791,900*l.*; 1901-2, 30,875,500*l.*; 1902-3, 31,255,000*l.*; 1903-4, 34,457,500*l.*

Number of men voted for 1892-3, 74,100;—1893-4, 83,400; —1895-6, 88,850;—1896-7, 93,750;—1897-8, 100,050;—1898-9, 106,390 (6,340 increase);—1899-1900, 110,640; —1900-1, 114,880;—1901-2, 118,625;—1902-3, 122,500;—1903-4, 127,100 (officers and men).

Naval Salute to the British Flag began in Alfred's reign, and though sometimes disputed, may be said to have been continued ever since. The Dutch agreed to strike to the English colours in the British seas, in 1673. The honour of the flag salute at sea was also formally assented to by France in 1704, although it had been long previously exacted by England; see *Flag* and *Salutes at Sea*.

Naval Uniforms. The first notice of the establishment of a uniform in the British naval service, which we have met with, occurs in the *Jacobite's Journal* of 5 March, 1748, under the head of "Domestic News," in these terms:—"An order is said to be issued, requiring all his majesty's sea-officers, from the admiral down to the midshipman, to wear a uniformity of clothing, for which purpose pattern coats for dress suits and frocks for each rank of officers are lodged at the Navy-office, and at the several dockyards for their inspection." This is corroborated by the *Gazette* of 13 July, 1757, when the first alteration in the uniform took place, and in which a reference is made to the order of 1748, alluded to in the journal above mentioned, and which in fact is the year when a naval uniform was first established. James I. had indeed granted, by warrant of 6 April, 1609, to six of his principal masters of the navy, "liverie coats of fine red cloth." The warrant is stated to have been drawn *verbatim* from one signed by queen Elizabeth, but which had not been acted upon by reason of her death. This curious document is in the British Museum; but king James's limited red livery is supposed to have been soon discontinued.—*Quarterly Review*. An act respecting them was passed in 1894.

Navy Pay Office, organised in 1644, was abolished in 1836, when the army and navy pay departments were consolidated in the Paymaster General's office.

Navy List was first officially compiled by John Finlaison, the celebrated actuary, and published monthly in 1814 *et seq.*; Lean's "Royal Navy List" is published quarterly.

Naval Reviews. The queen reviewed the fleet at Spithead, near Portsmouth, 11 Aug. 1853; again, March, 1854, before it sailed to the Baltic, at the commencement of the Russian war; and again, at Portsmouth, on the conclusion of peace, in the presence of the parliament, &c. The fleet extended in an unbroken line of 5 miles, and consisted of upwards of 300 men-of-war, carrying 3800 guns, and manned by 40,000 seamen. There were about 100,000 spectators, 23 April, 1856.

A grand naval review (15 great wooden ships, 15 iron-plated, 16 gun-vessels and boats), was held at Spithead (the queen, the sultan, and the viceroy of Egypt present), 17 July, 1867; another at Spithead before the shah of Persia, 23 June, 1873: another at Spithead by the queen (10 broadside ships, 8 turret ships, &c.), 3 Aug. 1878; another at Portsmouth, the queen and colonial visitors present (at the expense of the officers), 23 July, 1886.

Grand unexampled naval review (jubilee) by the queen at Spithead, 23 July, 1887; 135 vessels of all kinds, including 26 ironclads, 20,200 officers and men; one man died through the bursting of a saluting gun. Diamond Jubilee review at Spithead; the prince of Wales, the royal family, and foreign visitors present: 165 British warships in 4 lines, 5 miles in length, between Portsmouth and the Isle of Wight; outside them, 2 lines of foreign warships, and special merchant vessels with guests; illuminations, &c. at night, 26 June, 1897.

Coronation Review, Spithead, 16 Aug. 1902. The fleet assembled on 28 June, but owing to the illness of the king the review was postponed. There were present 20 battle-ships, 24 cruisers, 15 torpedo-gunboats, 32 torpedo-destroyers, 5 training-ships, and 7 brigs, in all 103 vessels, exclusive of yachts, torpedo-boats, and special-service vessels. For the review on 28 June the following foreign men-of-war assembled:—Germany, 1 vessel; Russia, 1; France, 1; Spain, 1; Portugal, 1; Sweden and Norway, 2; Denmark, 1; Holland, 1; Greece, 1; Italy, 1; United States, 1; Japan, 2; Chili, 1; and the Argentine Republic, 1; only those belonging to Japan, Italy, and Portugal remained for the review on the 16 Aug. The review by the king passed off successfully, but a heavy thunderstorm in the evening marred the otherwise brilliant spectacle of the illuminated fleet.

Naval Volunteers (or *Reserve*). By 16 & 17 Vict. c. 73 (1853), the admiralty were empowered to raise a body of sea-faring men to be called the "Naval Coast Volunteers," not to exceed 10,000, for the defence of the coast, and for actual service if required. In 1859, acts were passed to enable the admiralty to raise a number of men, not exceeding 30,000, as a reserve force of seamen, to be called the "Royal Naval Volunteers." In November following, the admiralty issued a statement of the "qualifications, advantages, and obligations" of this reserve. The enrolment commenced on 1 Jan. 1860. The engagement is for five years, and the volunteers are entitled to a pension when incapacitated after the expiration of the term. At the prospect of war with the United States in Dec. 1861, a great number of seamen at Hartlepool, Dundee, London, Aberdeen, &c., offered their services. About 24,000 men, in 1896. Naval Reserve act passed, 14 Aug. 1896. Naval Volunteers Reserve act, 22 July, 1902.

First enrolled body of Royal Naval Volunteers inspected, about 18 Jan. 1873.

The Navy Records Society, established to promote the writing of a new adequate naval history of England, and the publication of books relating to the subject; first general meeting at the R. United Service Institution, 4 July, 1893; annual meetings.

The Navy League, established in 1894, to secure, as a primary object of the national policy, "the command of the sea," and to spread valuable information by means of publications, lectures, &c.; the late adm. sir Geoffrey Hornby, first president. No. 1 of the journal published July, 1895; appeal to the colonies for support responded to by the Cape, *Times* leader, 12 Oct. 1895; Mr. Wyatt, envoy, leaves for Canada, Sept. 1902; annual meetings.

NAVY of France. It is first mentioned in history, 728, when, like that of England at an early period, it consisted of galleys; in this year the French defeated the Frisian fleet. The French fleet was almost annihilated by Edward III. at the battle of Sluys, 24 June, 1340. It was considerably improved under Louis XIV. at the instance of his minister Colbert, about 1697. The French navy was in its splendour about 1781; became greatly reduced in the wars with England; see *Naval Battles*. It was greatly increased by the emperor Napoleon III., and in 1859 consisted of 51 ships of the line (14 sailing vessels and 37 steamers), and 398 other vessels, in all 449; including vessels building, converting, or ordered to be built. The new French iron-clad frigate *Gloire*, constructed by M. Dupuy de Lôme, launched in 1860, was generally considered as successful. The *Solferino* and *Magenta* were launched in June, 1861; other iron vessels since. The *Magenta* was destroyed by fire, 6 killed, 31 Aug. 1875. The *Devastation*, a great iron-clad, launched at Lorient, 19 Aug. 1879. France had 22 battle-ships, 11 armoured vessels for coast defence, besides gun-boats, cruisers and torpedo-boats; in all 256 vessels in 1888. The Supreme Navy Council was created by decree, 6 Dec. 1889. Navy league, founded 12 May, 1899. See *Navies (Foreign)*.

NAZARENE, a name given to Jesus Christ, and his disciples; but afterwards to a sect who rejected the doctrine of Christ's divinity in the first century. A sect named Nazarenes, resembling the Society of Friends in Britain, became prominent in Hungary in the autumn of 1867.

NEAPOLIS, see *Naples*.

NEBRASKA, a N.W. territory of North America (part of Louisiana), was organised 30 May, 1854. Capital, Lincoln; Omaha city, very important. Bradshaw destroyed by a tornado, 3 June, 1890. Great prairie fire above 15 miles in North Platt county; several villages destroyed; loss above 150,000 dollars, 30 March, *et seq.* 1893. Train wrecked at Lincoln, through suspected removal of rail on a trestle bridge; about 24 persons killed,

9 Aug. 1894. Population, 1880, 452,402; 1890, 1,058,910; 1900, 1,066,300.

NEBULÆ, the luminous cloudlike mist visible to the naked eye in some constellations, such as Orion, in others only by powerful telescope; much studied by astronomers, and formerly considered to be clusters of stars. Halley gave a list of 6 nebulæ, with a theory, in 1716. Messier, in 1784, gave 103. Sir Wm. Herschel discovered more than 2,500, and sir John Herschel more than 2,000; 7,840 known up to 1887; Dr. Dreyer's index catalogue gives 1,529, published total, 9,369, 1895.

The *Nebular Hypothesis* put forth by Laplace in his "Systeme du Monde," 1796, supposed that the solar system was evolved mechanically from a vast diffused revolving nebula, and that nebulæ were the early stages in the formation of planets and their satellites, by cooling, condensation, and contraction. This theory was adopted by sir William Herschel, and though at first opposed, is now generally accepted in a modified form. Mr. Lassell scrutinized the dumb-bell nebula in Orion, and reported that the bright parts did not appear to be stars, Oct. 1860. Dr. Wm. Huggins reported his analyses of certain nebulæ by their spectra, and believed them to be gaseous, 1865.

For sir Norman Lockyer's theory see under *Meteors*, 17 Nov. 1887.

Mr. Wm. Ford Stanley's "Notes on the Nebular Theory," a full work, published 1895.

Prof. Max Wolf, of Heidelberg, discovered a fine cluster in *Coma Berenices*, April, 1901.

NECROMANCERS, see *Magic*.

NECTARINE, the *Amygdalus Persica*, originally came from Persia about 1562. Previously, presents of nectarines were frequently sent to the court of England from the Netherlands; and Catherine, queen of Henry VIII., distributed them among her friends.

NEEDLES. "The making of Spanish needles was first taught in England by Elias Crowse, a German, about the eighth year of queen Elizabeth, and in Queen Mary's time there was a negro who made fine Spanish needles in Cheapside, but would never teach his art to any."—*Stow*. The manufacture was greatly improved at Whitechapel, London; Redditch, in Gloucestershire, and Hathersage, in Derbyshire. An exhibition of ancient needlework was formed at South Kensington Museum in 1873. Royal school of art (started 1872); new building erected at cost of 52,000*l*. (10,000*l*. from Mr. Edw. Stern). Opened by the princess of Wales, 29 April, 1903; princess Christian opens an embroidery exhibition, 30 April.

NEEDLE-GUN (*Zündnadelgewehr*), a musket invented by J. N. Dreyse of Sömmerda, about 1827, and made a breech-loader in 1836, which was adopted by the Prussian general Manteuffel about 1846. It was found to be a most effective weapon in the war with Denmark in 1864, and in that with Austria in 1866. The ignition of the charge is produced by a fine steel rod or needle being pressed through the cartridge. The principle is claimed for James Whitley, of Dublin, 1823; Abraham Mosar, 1831; and John Hanson, of Huddersfield, 1843.

NEERWINDEN, see *Landen*.

NEGRO TRADE, see *Slavery*.

NEGUS (wine and water), said to be named after col. Francis Negus, about 1714. The sovereign of Abyssinia is termed *negus*.

NELSON'S VICTORIES, &c., see *separate articles*.

Horatio Nelson, born at Burnham Thorpe, Norfolk 29 Sept. 1758
Sailed with captain Phipps to the North Pole . 1773
Distinguished himself in the West Indies . 1780
Lost an eye at the reduction of Calvi, Corsica . 1794
Captured Elba . . . . 9 Aug. 1796
With Jervis at the victory off St. Vincent, 14 Feb.; knighted and made rear-admiral 20 Feb. 1797
Lost his right arm at the unsuccessful attack on Santa Cruz . . . . . 25–26 July, „
Gained the battle of the Nile, 1 Aug.; created baron Nelson of the Nile 6 Nov. 1798
Attacks Copenhagen, 2 April; created viscount, 22 May; attacks Boulogne flotilla, and destroys several ships . . . . . . 15 Aug. 1801
Appointed to chief command in the Mediterranean, 20 May, 1803
Pursues the French and Spanish fleets, March to Aug.; returns to England, Aug.; re-appears at Cadiz, and defeats the fleets in Trafalgar Bay, where he is killed . . . . 21 Oct. 1805
The *Victory* man of war arrived off Portsmouth with his remains . . . . . . 4 Dec. „
The body lay in state in the Painted Hall, at Greenwich, 5 Jan.; removed to the Admiralty, 8 Jan.; funeral took place . . . 9 Jan. 1806
The prince of Wales (afterwards George IV.), the duke of Clarence (afterwards William IV.), and other royal dukes, almost all the peers of England, and the lord mayor and corporation of London, with thousands of military and naval officers and distinguished men, followed the funeral car to St. Paul's; the military amounted to near 10,000, independent of volunteers.
Nelson Column, Trafalgar-square, London, completed, and statue placed on it (see *Statues*), 4 Nov. 1843; repaired by Mr. Harrison, the Sheffield steeplejack . . . . 9 Nov. 1896
Relics, medals, &c., bought by government for 2,500*l*., July; transferred to Greenwich, Aug. 1895; stolen, 8 or 9 Dec. 1900; his bust at Windsor presented by the king to the royal united service museum . . . . 10 June, 1901

NEMEAN GAMES, celebrated at Nemea, in Achaia, said to have been instituted by the Argives, in honour of Archemorus, who died by the bite of a serpent; and revived by Hercules, who slew the Nemean lion. The conqueror was rewarded with a crown of olives, afterwards of green parsley. They were celebrated every third year, or, according to others, on the first and third year of every Olympiad.—*Herodotus*. They were revived by the emperor Julian, A.D. 362, but ceased in 396.

NEO-PLATONISM or **NEW PLATONISM**, see *Philosophy*.

NEPAUL (N. India) was conquered by the Ghoorkas, 1768, who made treaties with the British, 1791 and 1801; but frequently made incursions; and in consequence war with them commenced 1 Nov. 1814; terminated 27 April, 1815. A treaty of peace was signed between the parties, 2 Dec. 1815. War was renewed through an infraction of the treaty by the Nepaulese, Jan. 1816; and after several contests, unfavourable to the Nepaulese, the former treaty was ratified, 15 March, 1816. An extraordinary embassy from the king of Nepaul to the queen of Great Britain arrived in England, landing at Southampton, 25 May, and remained till Aug. 1850; it consisted of the Nepaulese prince, Jung Bahadoor, and his suite, to whom many honours were paid. He supported the English during the Indian mutiny in 1857. The prince of Wales was honourably received in Nepaul, 12 Feb. 1876.

War with Thibet on account of robbed merchants, May, 1884
Thibet submits . . . . June, „

Revolution: the prime minister and son murdered; 22 Nov. 1885

New ministry constituted: the maharajah, Pirthibi Bir Bikrum Sah (born 7 Aug. 1875; succeeded 17 May, 1881); prime minister, sir Bir Shamsher Rana Bahadur; appointed . . 22 Nov. „

Gen. lord Roberts' visit to Nepaul very satisfactory April, 1892

Bazaars destroyed by Tibetans and traders killed, 1895; ultimatum sent . . . . . April, 1896

Deb Shamshere, prime minister, dismissed for trying to introduce unacceptable reforms, reported, 2 July, 1901

Landslip and floods, many killed, reported, 29 Aug. 1902

NEPHALIA, sacrifices of sobriety among the Greeks, when they offered mead instead of wine to the sun and moon, to the nymphs, to Aurora, and to Venus; and burnt any wood but that of the vine, fig-tree, and mulberry-tree, esteemed symbols of drunkenness, 613 B.C.

NEPHOSCOPE (*nephos*, Greek, a cloud). An apparatus for measuring the velocity of clouds, invented by Karl Braun, and reported to the Academy of Sciences, Paris, 27 July, 1868.

NEPTUNE, a primary planet, first observed on 23 Sept. 1846, by Dr. Galle, at Berlin, in consequence of a letter from M. Le Verrier, who had conjectured from the anomalous movements of Uranus that a distant planet might exist nearly in the position where Neptune was situated. Calculations to the same effect had been previously made by Mr. J. Couch Adams, of Cambridge; but unfortunate delays occurred in their publication, and also of professor Challis's consequent discovery of the planet. The Royal Society of London awarded its gold medal to both astronomers as equals in the theoretical discovery. A satellite of Neptune was discovered by Mr. Lassell on 10 Oct. following. Neptune is said to have been seen by Lalande, and thought to be a fixed star. The Greek god Poseidon became the Roman Neptune. Prof. J. C. Adams died 21 Jan. 1892; his "Papers" published March, 1897.

NEPTUNIUM, a new metal discovered in tantalite, from Connecticut, by R. Herrmann in 1877; not generally admitted by chemists.

NERVES. Our knowledge of the nature and functions of the nervous system has been greatly enlarged by the researches and experiments of physiologists during the 19th century. Sir Charles Bell announced his discovery of the distinction between the nerves of motion and sensation, 1810. He published papers on the nervous system, 1821. See *Craniology*.

NERVII, a warlike tribe in Belgic Gaul, were defeated in a severe battle by Julius Cæsar 57, and subdued 53 B.C.

NERWINDEN, see *Landen*.

NESBIT, see *Nisbet*.

NESTORIANS, the followers of Nestorius, bishop of Constantinople (428-431), who is represented as a heretic. He was opposed by Eutyches; see *Eutychians*.

1. He rejected the error of those who said Christ was a mere man, as Ebion, Paul of Samosata Photinus. 2. He maintained that the Word was united to the humanity in Christ Jesus, and that this union was most intimate and strict. 3. He held that these two natures made one Christ, one Son, one Person; only made up of two natures. 4. And this one Person may have either divine or human properties attributed to Him.

Nestorian Christians in the Levant administer the sacrament with leavened bread and in both kinds, permit their priests to marry, and use neither confirmation nor auricular confession.—*Du Pin.*

A Nestorian priest and deacon were in London in July, 1862.

The Persian Nestorians (15,000) received into the Russian church at St. Petersburg . 6 April, 1898

NETHERLANDS. William Frederick, prince of Orange, assumed the title of King of the Netherlands 16 March, 1815, and his successors, kings of Holland, retain the title. See *Flanders*, *Holland*, and *Belgium*.

NETLEY HOSPITAL, near Southampton, for invalid soldiers. The foundation stone was laid by the queen, 19 May, 1856. Princess Henry of Battenberg visits the wounded from S. Africa, 25 Jan. 1900; and queen Victoria stays 3 hours there, 27 Feb.; again, 16 May.

NEUFCHATEL, a canton in Switzerland, formerly a lordship, afterwards a principality. The first known lord was Ulric de Fenis, about 1032, whose descendants ruled till 1373, after which by marriages it frequently changed governors. On the death of the duchesse de Nemours, the last of the Longuevilles, in 1707, there were many claimants; among them our William III. He and the allies however gave it to Frederick I. of Prussia with the title of prince. In 1806 the principality was ceded to France, and Napoleon bestowed it on his general Berthier, who held it till 1814, when it fell to the disposal of the allies. They restored the king of Prussia with the title of prince with certain rights and privileges; but constituted it a part of the Swiss confederation. Population: 1888, canton, 108,153; city, 16,261; 1901, canton, 125,804; city, 20,916.

After an unsuccessful attempt in 1831, the inhabitants repudiated their allegiance to Prussia, and proclaimed Neufchatel a free and independent member of the Swiss confederation 1848

The king of Prussia protested against this; and a protocol was signed between England, France, and Austria, recognising his claims 1852

Some of his adherents, headed by the count de Pourtalès, broke out into insurrection against the republican authorities, who, however, quickly subdued and imprisoned them, with the intention of bringing them to trial . . . . . Sept. 1856

War threatened by the king of Prussia, and great energy and determination manifested by the Swiss. On the intervention of the English and French governments, a treaty was signed by which the king of Prussia virtually renounced his claims, on receiving a pecuniary compensation, which he eventually gave up. He retains the title of prince of Neufchatel, without any political rights 11 June, 1857

The prisoners of Sept. 1856 were released without trial 18 Jan. „

NEUROLOGICAL SOCIETY OF LONDON, formed to promote the study of nerves from a psychological, physiological, anatomical, and pathological point of view, 1887. First president Dr. Samuel Wilks, F.R.S. Dr. Julius Althaus, eminent neurologist, dies, aged 67, 11 June, 1900.

NEUSTRIA or West France, a kingdom allotted to Clotaire by his father Clovis, at his death in 511. His descendant, Charlemagne, became sole king of France in 771. It was conquered by the Northmen and hence named Normandy (*which see*).

NEUTRALITY LAWS. A commission, in a report issued in May, 1868, recommended changes.

An act to make better provision for the preservation of neutrality was passed 9 Aug. 1870. John P. McDiarmid apprehended, for breach of neutrality laws, at Bow-street, 28 Oct. 1870.

NEUTRAL POWERS. By the treaty of Paris, signed by the representatives of Great Britain, France, Austria, Russia, Prussia, Turkey, and Sardinia, on 16 April, 1856, it was determined that privateering should be abolished; that neutrals might carry an enemy's goods not contraband of war; that neutral goods not contraband were free even under an enemy's flag; and that blockades to be binding must be effective. The president of the United States acceded to these provisions in 1861. Proclamation of neutrality in respect to the war between the United States and Spain by Great Britain, France and other powers, 26 April, *et seq.*, 1898.—See *International Law.*

NEVADA, a western territory of the United States of N. America, organised 2 March, 1861; admitted a state, 31 Oct. 1864. Capital, Carson city. Virginia city was nearly destroyed by fire, 26 Oct. 1875; several lives were lost; property about 2,000,000 dols.; 10,000 persons rendered homeless. Population of Nevada, 1880, 62,266; 1890, 45,761; 1900, 42,335.

NEVILLE'S CROSS or DURHAM, BATTLE OF, between the Scots under king David Bruce and the English it is said (probably incorrectly) under Philippa, consort of Edward III., and lord Percy, 12 or 17 Oct. 1346. More than 15,000 of the Scots were slain, and their king taken prisoner.

NEVIS (W. Indies), an island discovered by Columbus, planted by the English in 1628; taken by the French, 14 Feb. 1782; restored to the English in 1783. The capital is Charleston. See *Leeward Isles.*

NEWARK (Nottinghamshire). The church was erected by Henry IV. Here, in the midst of troubles, died king John, 19 Oct. 1216; here the royal army under prince Rupert repulsed the army of the parliament, besieging the town, 21 March, 1644; and here, 5 May, 1646, Charles I., after his defeat at Naseby, put himself into the hands of the Scotch army, who afterwards gave him up to his enemies. Newark was first incorporated by Edward VI., and afterwards by Charles II. Absorbed into the county, 1885. Population, 1881, 14,018; 1891, 14,457; 1901, 15,146.

NEWARK, a town in New Jersey, U.S.A., settled in 1666, and chartered in 1836. Population in 1890, 181,830; 1900, 246,070.

NEW BRUNSWICK was taken from Nova Scotia, and received its name as a separate colony in 1785. It was united with Canada by act passed 29 March, 1867. Population of New Brunswick in 1865, 272,780; in 1881, 321,233; 1891, 321,294. Capital, Fredericton. Lieut.-governor, Lemuel A. Wilmot, 1868; Samuel Leonard Tilley, 1874; Robert Duncan Wilmot, 1880; sir Samuel L. Tilley, 1886; John Boyd, 1893; John Jas. Fraser, 1894 (died Nov. 1896); succeeded by A. R. M'Clelan, 2 Dec. 1896; J. B. Snowball, Jan. 1902.

Great fire at St. John, 20-22 June, 1877; destruction of 12 churches, 25 public buildings; thousands houseless; about 20 killed, loss about 3,000,000*l.* Subscriptions in Britain.

Very destructive forest fires on both sides of the St. Lawrence, 10 June *et seq.* 1891.

The St. Lawrence lumber mills burnt, 24 Sept. 1891.

Great discovery of coal in Gloucester county reported, Feb. 1893.

Fire at Gibson, 80 houses and 2 churches destroyed, loss about 200,000 dollars, 20 June, 1893.

Great fire at St. John, 100 buildings burnt, 25 May, 1899.

Forest fires, Musquash destroyed, 4 June, 1903.

NEWBURY (Berkshire). Near here were fought two desperate battles—(1.) 20 Sept. 1643; between the army of Charles I. and that of the parliament under Essex; it terminated somewhat favourably for the king. Among the slain was the amiable Lucius Cary, viscount Falkland, deeply regretted. (2.) A second battle of dubious result was fought between the royalists and the parliamentarians under Waller, 27 Oct. 1644. Population, 1881, 14,018; 1891, 14,457; 1901, 11,002.

A memorial to lord Falkland and his companions, inaugurated by the earl of Carnarvon, 9 Sept. 1878.

Queen Victoria memorials, museum and art gallery, opened, 7 Nov. 1902; one presented by Mr. G. Sanger unveiled, 24 June, 1903.

NEW CALEDONIA (Pacific Ocean), discovered by Cook on 4 Sept. 1774, was seized by the French, 20 Sept. 1853, and colonised. The French government in Dec. 1864, redressed the outrages committed upon the British missionaries at a station established here in 1854.

In the latter part of June, 1878, some of the native tribes revolted, burnt some of the towns and villages, and killed about 90 of the European colonists, men, women, children and servants, including col. Gally-Passebose, the military commandant of the island. The insurrection was not subdued till the end of the year.

Now used as a French penal settlement; said to be very disorderly, 1884. See *Recidivists.*

Destructive hurricane, three ships wrecked, reported, 1 March, 1898.

NEWCASTLE - UPON - TYNE (Northumberland), the Roman Pons Ælia, the first coal port in the world,* and the commercial metropolis of the north of England. The coal-mines were discovered here about 1234. The first charter granted to the townsmen for digging coal was by Henry III. in 1239. See *Population.*

The castle built by Robert Courthose, son of William I. 1080

Taken by William II. 1095

St. Nicholas church built, about 1091; burnt in 1216; restored by Edward I., to whom John Baliol did homage here, 1292; rebuilt 1359

Newcastle surrenders to the Scotch 1640

Who here gave up Charles I. to the parliament 30 Jan. 1647

Occupied by general Wade in 1745

Antiquarian Society established 1813

Literary and Philosophical Society founded 1793; the foundation-stone of the building was laid by the duke of Sussex in 1822; liberally endowed by Robert Stephenson 1858-9

T. Bewick, the wood-engraver, dies 1828

The magnificent market erected by Richd. Grainger, who greatly improved the town 1835

British Association met here 1838

High-level bridge erected by Robert Stephenson; and grand central station built 1846-50

1538 persons die of cholera . 31 Aug. to 26 Oct. 1853

Great fire through the explosion at Gateshead (*which see*) . . . . 5, 6 Oct. 1854

Great distress through failure of Northumberland Joint-Stock Bank . . . . . Nov. 1857

Richard Grainger dies, aged 63 . . . . 4 July, 1861

* In 1306 the use of coal for fuel was prohibited in London, by royal proclamation, chiefly because it injured the sale of wood for fuel, great quantities of which were then growing about the city; but this interdiction did not long continue, and we may consider coal as having been dug and exported from this place for more than 500 years.

Enthusiastic reception of Mr. W. E. Gladstone, 7-9 Oct. 1862
British Association met here, second time 26 Aug. 1863
Great fire at Brown's flour mills, &c., near the new high-level bridge, which is injured; about 70,000*l.* loss 24 June, 1866
The Central Exchange destroyed by fire 11 Aug. 1867
Mr. Mawson, the sheriff, and Mr. Bryson, the town surveyor, and others, killed, while attempting to bury some nitro-glycerine in the town-moor, to get rid of it . . . . 18 Dec. ,,
Strike of about 9000 engineers, for day's work of nine hours; begun about . . . 16 May, 1871
College of Physical Science in connection with the Durham University, opened . . . Oct. ,,
Engineers' strike closed: terms, nine hours a day, to begin on 1 Jan. 1872; men to work overtime when needed; wages to remain the same; arranged by Mr. R. B. Philipson and Mr. Joseph Cowen . . . . . . 6 Oct. ,,
Elswick estate purchased by a committee for a public park, announced . . . . Aug. 1873
New R. C. church built by the Dominicans, opened 10 Sept. ,,
New swing-bridge over the Tyne (281 feet long; weight, 1450 tons, lifted by a hydraulic crane); begun 1868; completed . . . June, 1876
Bishoprics act; permitting the erection of a see at Newcastle, passed . . . 16 Aug. 1878
Technical college for north of England inaugurated 24 Sept. 1880
Centenary of birth of George Stephenson celebrated 9 June, 1881
Newcastle constituted a city; charter received 5 July, 1882
Public library opened 13 Sept. 1880; the new building was opened . . . . 1 Sept. ,,
Sanitary Institute of Great Britain and congress met here . . . . . . 26 Sept. ,,
Parks given by sir William Armstrong; addition Feb. 1883
Visit of prince and princess of Wales and family; enthusiastic reception; opening of Armstrong park, natural history museum, free library, Albert Edward dock, &c. . . 20, 21 Aug. 1884
Great distress through want of employment Oct. ,,
Royal mining, engineering, and industrial exhibition opened by the duke of Cambridge, 11 May; 2,092,273 admissions; reported successful; closed 29 Oct. ,,
Royal Agricultural Society's show opened 11 July; visited by the prince of Wales and sons 12 July, ,,
Newcastle and Durham college of physical science: foundation-stone laid by sir Wm. Armstrong (after lord), 15 June, 1887; opened by the princess Louise . . . . . . 5 Nov. 1888
Third meeting of the British Association 11 Sept. 1889
The new college of medicine (founded by the duke of Northumberland in 1887) opened by the mayor 2 Oct. ,,
Mr. John Fleming bequeaths above 100,000*l.* to local charities (Fleming Memorial Hospital for sick children, &c.), announced . . . Feb. 1890
Death of Mr. John Clayton, aged 98; 45 years town clerk (estate sworn at 728,746*l.*) . 14 July, ,,
Threatened strike of persons employed on the North-Eastern railway, averted by concessions . about 20 Dec. ,,
Newcastle programme, proposed at the meeting of the National Liberal Federation (by Mr. Gladstone). Re-constitution of the house of lords; one man, one vote; shorter parliaments; paid members; settlement of the Irish question; land laws, &c. . . . . 1 Oct. *et seq.* 1891
Great strike of the engineers on the Tyne and Wear respecting overtime, 2 Nov., ended . . 7 Nov. ,,
Strike and lock-out of ship-building engineers, and plumbers, on the Tyne, due to internal disputes, about 30 Jan.; about 20,000 out of work, 12 March; arbitration accepted; work resumed 27 April, 1892
The rev. Dr. John Collingwood Bruce, historian of "The Roman wall" dies, aged 86 . 5 April, ,,
End of the Durham miners' strike, see *Coal* . . 11 March–1 June, ,,
Centenary of the Literary and Philosophical Society warmly celebrated; lord Armstrong the president, dr. Wilberforce the bishop, the mayor and many eminent persons present, 7 Feb.; by a fire at 6–8 a.m. the premises and a large part of the valuable library (about 35,000 vols.) were destroyed or damaged . . . . 8 Feb. 1893
Freedom of the city presented to lord Roberts on his visit . . . . . . 20 March, 1894
Rutherford college opened by the duke of York 5 April, ,,
End of 18 weeks' strike of N.E. coast ironworkers 20 July, ,,
Strike of 1,500 moulders on the N.E. coast, consequent stoppage of nearly 20,000 workers, March; strike ended by ballot . . . 31 Aug. ,,
Annual meeting of the national union of conservative associations; Mr. A. J. Balfour warmly received; powerful speech . . 13 Nov. ,,
The old mansion house, near the quay, burnt 6 Oct. 1895

See *Strikes*, Feb. 1897.

Great fire at Messrs. Mawson and Clark's, oil refinery, Walker-gate, explosion of creosote, ten deaths, 110 injured . . . 29-31 Jan. 1898

See *Elswick*, 10 June, 1899.

Death of Mr. John Hall, shipowner, benefactor (bequeaths 130,000*l.* to local charities), 26 June, 1899
Lord Wolseley receives the freedom of the city and holds a review . . . . 15 July, ,,
Theatre Royal burnt down, estimated damage, 20,000*l.* . . . . 24 Nov. ,,
Central Exchange art gallery, the Vaudeville theatre, &c., burnt down . . . 23 Jan. 1900
Messrs. Robinson & Co.'s premises burnt down; estimated damage, 40,000*l.* . . . 7 March, ,,
The prince of Wales lays foundation-stone of a new infirmary . . . . . . 20 June, ,,
Lord Armstrong, founder of the Elswick works and inventor of modern artillery, dies aged 90, 27 Dec. ,,
Lord Kelvin opens the Electric Supply Co.'s new works . . . . . . 18 June, 1901
Mr. Watson Armstrong gives 100,000*l.* to the new infirmary; presented with the freedom of the city, 17 July, ,,
Foundation-stone of a new art gallery, the gift of Mr. Alex. Laing (20,000*l.*), laid by Mrs. Watson Armstrong . . . . 13 Aug. ,,
New bridge, cost 80,000*l.*, opened . . 13 Aug. ,,
Electric tramway, estimated cost 800,000*l.*, opened, 16 Dec. ,,
Destructive fires at Quayside . 15, 16 March, 1902
18,000*l.* subscribed for a sanatorium . 2 Oct. ,,
Princess Louise, duchess of Argyll, opens Temperance institute . . . . 14 Oct. ,,
Statue of queen Victoria, the gift of sir Wm. Stephenson, unveiled . . . . 24 April, 1903
Maj.-gen. sir Baden-Powell receives the freedom of the city . . . . . . 25 July, ,,
Exhibition in commemoration of the 150th anniversary of birth of Thos. Bewick, the engraver, opened . . . . . . 12 Sept. ,,
Scheme for quay extension and improvement, estimated cost 559,000*l.*, adopted by city council, end Sept. ,,

NEWCASTLE-UPON-TYNE, BISHOPRIC OF, founded by Order in Council 17 May, 1882.

BISHOPS.

1882. Ernest Roland Wilberforce consecrated at Durham, 25 July, 1882; translated to Chichester, Nov. 1895.
1895. Edgar Jacob, Nov. 1895; trans. to St. Albans Feb. 1903.
1903. A. T. Lloyd, Feb. 1903.

NEWCASTLE ADMINISTRATION, formed April, 1754; resigned Nov. 1756; when the duke of Devonshire became first lord of the treasury.

Thomas Holles Pelham, duke of Newcastle, *first lord of the treasury.*
Henry Bilson Legge, *chancellor of the exchequer.*
Earl of Holdernesse and sir Thomas Robinson (afterwards lord Grantham), *secretaries of state.* The latter succeeded by Henry Fox (afterwards lord Holland).

Lord Anson, *first lord of the admiralty.*
Earl Granville, *lord president.*
Lord Gower (succeeded by the duke of Marlborough 1755), *lord privy seal.*
Earl of Hardwicke, *lord chancellor.*
Duke of Grafton, earl of Halifax, George Grenville, &c.

NEWCASTLE AND PITT ADMINISTRATION (see *Chatham Administration*), formed June, 1757. After various changes it resigned May, 1762; lord Bute coming into power.

Thomas Holles Pelham, duke of Newcastle, *first lord of the treasury.*
William Pitt (afterwards lord Chatham), *secretary of state for the northern department, and leader of the house of commons.*
Earl of Holdernesse, *secretary of state for the southern department.*
Earl Granville, *lord president.*
Earl Temple, *privy seal.*
H. B. Legge, *chancellor of the exchequer.*
Duke of Devonshire, *lord chamberlain.*
Duke of Rutland, *lord steward.*
Lord Anson, *admiralty.*
Duke of Marlborough (succeeded by lord Ligonier), *ordnance.*
Sir Robert Henley, *lord keeper of the great seal.*
Henry Fox, George Grenville, viscount Barrington, lord Halifax, James Grenville, &c.

NEW CHURCH, see *Swedenborgians.*

NEW COLLEGE (St. John's Wood, London), erected by the Independent dissenters for the education of their ministers, 1850-1, was formed by the union of Homerton, Highbury, and Coward colleges. See *Oxford.*

NEW DEPARTURE DEMOCRATS, see *United States*, 1871.

NEW ENGLAND (N. America). The first settlement made in 1607, was named New England by captain Smith, in 1614. A band of 102 Puritans, now termed the "Pilgrim Fathers" (with 28 women), arrived here in the *May Flower*, and founded the settlement on Plymouth Rock, 25 Dec. 1620, which was named New Plymouth. This was the nucleus of Massachusetts, from whence were gradually developed New Hampshire, Vermont, Connecticut, and Rhode Island. In 1643 these settlements formed the first American confederation, a defensive union, with a constitution based on the Mosaic law, governed by a religious aristocracy, which lasted till 1693. Maine was made an independent state in 1820.

NEW FOREST (Hampshire), was made ("afforested") by William the Conqueror, 1079-85. It is said that the whole country, for thirty miles in compass, was laid waste. William Rufus was killed in this forest by an arrow shot by Walter Tyrrel, that accidentally glanced against a tree, 2 Aug. 1100, the site of which is now pointed out by a triangular stone. The New Forest Deer Removal act was passed 14 & 15 Vict. c. 76, 7 Aug. 1851. Agitation for the preservation of this forest, autumn, 1870. In accordance with an act passed in 1877, the forest is now managed by a court of Verderers as a public pleasure ground, and cattle farm. New Forest (sale of lands for public purposes) act passed, 24 July, 1902. See *Forests.*

NEWFOUNDLAND (N. America), said to have been discovered by John Cabot, who called it *Prima Vista*, 24 June, 1497. It was formally taken possession of by sir Humphry Gilbert, 1583. In the reign of Elizabeth other nations had the advantage of the English in the fishery. In 1577 there were 100 fishing vessels from Spain, 50 from Portugal, 150 from France, and only 15, but of larger size, from England.—*Hakluyt.* But the English fishery in some years afterwards (1625) had increased so much that the ports of Devonshire alone employed 150 ships, which sold their fish in Spain, Portugal, and Italy. The sovereignty of England was recognised in 1713, by the treaty of Utrecht, certain rights on the "French shores" being reserved for France. Newfoundland obtained the privilege of a colonial legislature in 1832; and the bishopric was established in 1839. Population, 1884, 197,335; 1901, 220,249. Appalling fire at St. John's, a great portion of the town destroyed, the loss estimated at 1,000,000*l.* sterling, 9 June, 1846. On 14 Jan. 1857, a convention was concluded between the English and French governments, confirming certain French privileges of fishery in exchange for others. The English colonists were dissatisfied with this convention. Newfoundland refused union with the dominion of Canada, March, 1869; a railway from St. John's to St. George's bay, proposed by the colonial government Aug. 1878. Capital, St. John's; population, 1884, 31,142. Governor, col. sir Stephen J. Hill, 1870; sir John H. Glover, Jan. 1876. Maxse died Sept. 1883; sir John Hawley Glover, Dec. 1883; died 30 Sept. 1885; sir G. Wm. des Vœux, Feb. 1886; sir J. Terence N. O'Brien, Nov. 1888; sir H. H. Murray, Sept. 1895; sir Henry McCallum, 1899; sir Cavendish Boyle, Jan. 1901. See *Canada*, Nov. 1877. "A History of Newfoundland," by Judge D. W. Prowse, published, May, 1895.

Fishery Dispute. At Fortune bay, U.S., fishers fixed nets on Sunday, 13 Jan. 1878; this being contrary to local regulations, they were forcibly removed; controversy ensued; Mr. Evarts on part of U.S. government sent despatch, 24 Aug.; correspondence, Sept.-Oct.; the marquis of Salisbury refused compensation; but earl Granville granted it; 15,000*l.* were awarded by arbitration 28 May, 1881
The French tri-colour flag set up at Cumberland Stage, near St. John's, by a French captain, 9 Sept. 1882
Conflicts between the Orangemen and Romanists at Harbour Grace; several killed . 26 Dec. 1883
Continued disputes through the British lobster factories on the French shore 1890
The people dissatisfied with the new arrangements begun after 1 July, 1889, termed *modus vivendi.* A great meeting at St. John's . . 26 March, „
Sir James Winter, ex-attorney-general, and other delegates, arrive in London . . . 13 May, „
Address to the queen voted by the Newfoundland legislature . . . . 14 May, „
A French war vessel requests the stoppage of British fishing in St. George's bay; indignation meeting at St. John's . . reported 24 May, „
The parliament votes an address to the queen and is prorogued . . . . 11 June, „
Fight between Newfoundlanders and French fishermen respecting lobsters, at Port-au-Port, with clubs, &c.; the latter beaten, about 19 June, „
Capt. Sir Baldwin Walker, of the *Emerald*, stops Mr. Baird's lobster factory at Sandy Point, about 26 June; Mr. Baird sues for damages . July, „
French war vessel at Port-au-Port drives off 30 British fishing vessels . . . . . 23 June, „
Sir William Whiteway, premier, and Mr. Harvey, delegates in London, 3 July *et seq.*; the colonists claim extinction of French rights, about 5 Aug.; Sir W. Whiteway returns to Newfoundland 12 Nov. *et seq.* „
The *modus vivendi* enforced by the *Emerald* and the *Forward* gunboat . . . Sept. *et seq.* „
Joseph Girardin, capt. of the French schooner *Minegard*, arrested for illegal acts; imprisoned till fines were paid; rescued from prison, regains his ship, puts off to sea; the ship runs aground, and is again seized . . . . . Oct. „

Great storm, destruction of shipping, buildings, &c. reported 8 Dec. 1890
Action of Mr. Baird against sir Baldwin Walker in the supreme court concluded; judgment reserved 10 Feb. 1891
Verdict for Mr. Baird, 18 March; appeal to the privy council, March, 1891; dismissed 4 Aug. 1892
Arbitration accepted by the British and French governments, the *modus vivendi* to continue, agreement signed in London, 11 March, at Paris, 13 March, and reported at St. John's 13 March, ,,
Bill brought into the house of lords to enforce the *modus vivendi*, early April; read second time 27 April, 1891
Sir William Whiteway and 4 other delegates appear at the house of lords, and make a statement . 23 April, ,,
The house of assembly adopts a petition to the queen, to ratify their convention with the United States . . . . 8 April, ,,
The British fishermen of Fortune's bay rise against the sale of bait to others, about 22 April; stockade raised, and bait seized . about 28 April, ,,
After some negotiation, the *modus vivendi* coercion act (to last till 1893) is passed by both branches of the Newfoundland legislature . 26 May, ,,
(The coercion bill in the British house of commons was withdrawn May.)
The French enforce the *modus vivendi*; difficulties; reported 18 June, ,,
Sixty British lobster factories closed by order under the *modus vivendi* . . reported 7 July, ,,
The Canadian government protests against the restrictions on the supply of herrings as bait for the fisheries and threatens reprisals, about 28 Nov.; and imposes import duties on fish 8 Dec. ,,
A sudden blizzard off the coast drove out 220 fishing boats, 27 men perished by frost, &c. 27 Feb. 1892
The *modus vivendi* respecting lobsters, renewed by the British and French governments 25 March, ,,
The French shore bill supported by the British government, for constituting a judicial commission court to settle the disputes submitted to the house of assembly, 30 April; rejected 14 May; a joint committee on the subject appointed 19 May ,,
The dispute with Canada settled; return to the *status* of 1889 . . . announced 21 May, ,,
The French fishermen break the *modus vivendi* by destroying 300 British lobster traps, about 13 June, ,,
Great fire at St. John's, from 5 p.m. 10 July till 8 p.m. 11 July, during a violent gale; about 11,000 homeless; the beautiful cathedral (by G.G. Scott), churches and chapels, colleges, and other public buildings, and the greater part of the city destroyed; shipping greatly damaged. Loss, about 2,500,000*l.*; 6 deaths and people missing. Relief largely supplied by the Dominion of Canada, the United States and the United Kingdom (see *Mansion House Funds*).
Meeting of the legislative assembly; energetic restoration of St. John's reported . 7 March, 1893
Destructive blizzard with loss of 5 lives 20 March, ,,
The operation of the Bait act suspended, 22 March, ,,
General election, the government of sir W. Whiteway returned to power . . . . 8 Nov. ,,
The ministry request dissolution of the legislature on account of charges of bribery at elections, 3 April; governor O'Brien refuses; the ministry resigns . . . . 12 April, 1894
New ministry formed by Mr. A. T. Goodridge 13 April, ,,
The Whiteway party retain possession of the chamber and demand a dissolution; the governor prorogues the legislature to 5 July . 15 April, ,,
Election trials, many members, including sir Wm. Whiteway, unseated for bribery, 5 May–30 July, ,,
Legislature prorogued . . . . . . 9 Aug. ,,
Elections, majority of the Whiteway party . Nov. ,,
Financial crisis; several banks and 6 firms stop payment through commercial embarrassment; application to the imperial government for help 10 Dec. ,,
Resignation of the ministry, 12 Dec.; new one formed by Mr. D. J. Green . . 13 Dec. ,,
Great distress at St. John's, 14 Dec.; parliament opened to consider the crisis . . 15 Dec. ,,
The Commercial bank charged with reckless mismanagement, &c.; the notes of the Union bank guaranteed by government . . . Dec. 1894
Mr. Cooke, manager, and 4 directors of the Commercial bank charged with fraud, arrested and bailed . . . . 27 Dec. ,,
The government much assisted by the bank of Montreal . . . . Jan. 1895
Gradual resumption of business, reported . 16 Jan. ,,
Bill passed removing the disqualification of unseated members . . . . . 22 Jan. ,,
Resignation of the ministry . . . . 31 Jan. ,,
Cabinet formed by sir Wm. Whiteway . 8 Feb. ,,
Much distress relieved by lady O'Brien's subscription fund . . . . . . 7 Feb. ,,
Negotiations for union with Canada; delegates sent to Ottawa, April; the scheme abandoned through differences respecting the terms . 16 May, ,,
Sir Herbert Murray, imperial commissioner, organizes relief works at St. John's . April, ,,
A loan of 2,500,000 dollars from London, floated in Montreal at (94) 4 per cent.; improved prospects reported, 31 May; the loan authorized by the chambers . . . . . . 13 June, ,,
French treaties bill passed (upper house) . 24 June ,,
House prorogued . . . . . . 4 July, ,,
Forest fires; railway settlement at Norris Arm burnt, reported . . . . . 10 July, ,,
Mr. James Gordon and Mr. John Gillard, official liquidators of the defunct Union bank, accuse the directors, sir Robt. Thorburn, ex-premier, hon. Augustus Harvey, Wm. Donnelly, Mr. Walter Grieve, and Mr. Pinsent, manager of the bank, of issuing a false statement of its affairs, and paying dividends which the bank had not earned, 19 July; warrants issued; bail accepted 20 July, ,,
Arrests in connexion with the smuggling scandals, Mr. M. Tobin and one of the governors of the savings bank . . . . . . 19 Oct. ,,
Sentenced to fine and imprisonment . 5 Nov. ,,
Discovery of coal towards the west coast Nov. ,,
Sir Herbert Murray arrives at St. John's as governor . . . . 29 Nov. ,,
Sir Robert Thorburn, bank director, and three others committed for trial, 15 Nov.; indictment ignored . . . . . . 21 April, 1896
Great destitution at St. John's, reported 15 Jan. ,,
Parliament opened; successful retrenchment, reported . . . . 11 June ,,
Oil struck at a depth of 1,000 feet on the W. coast by a company . . . . . . Dec. ,,
Legislature dissolved . . . . . 20 Sep. 1897
Elections: government defeated, 28 Oct.; new cabinet, sir James Winter premier, 9 Nov.; economical reforms effected . . . . Nov. ,,
Trial of the bank directors, 2 Nov.; acquitted and cases abandoned . . . . 17, 27 Dec. ,,
A government contract with Mr. Reid, taking up railways, docks, &c.; signed . . 3 March, 1898
Railway bill passed, 15 March; a *modus vivendi* passed both houses . . . 23 March, ,,
Sealers cut off from their ship, perish on the ice, 30 miles from Cape Bonavista, 55 deaths 21 March ,,
Seal fishery season, very successful . April ,,
Royal commission negotiates successfully with the ministry, and leaves . . . . 29 Oct. ,,
Sir Herbert Murray leaves St. John's . 25 Jan. 1899
Negotiations with France respecting the French shore question . . . . . . Jan. ,,
Imperial government declines to interfere in the legislation of the colony, and with the "Reid contract," see *Times* . . . . . 23 Jan. ,,
Legislature prorogued . . . . . . 7 Feb. ,,
Sir Henry McCallum appointed governor; arrives, 3 March, ,,
Sealing fleet inspected by sir H. McCallum, 8 March, ,,
French lobster factory near St. John's burnt, end of March (Ingram Taylor pleads guilty to arson, sentenced to 1 years' imprisonment and banishment, 8 Sept.).
Legislature opened by the governor, good report, economies effected, 11 May; closed . 19 July, ,,
British warships at St. John's, 1,000 men reviewed, 19 July, ,,
Severe storm; fishing settlements destroyed, 26 deaths, reported . . . 18 Sept. ,,

The Winter ministry defeated . . . 19 Feb. 1900
The *modus vivendi* re-enacted by bill passed, 20 Feb.; the ministry resigns, deadlock, 5 March; legislature prorogued, 14 March; Mr. Bond forms a ministry . . . 15 March, ,,
Legislature opened by the governor . 29 March, ,,
Seal fishery, value 600,000 dollars largest total since 1882 . . . . 24 April, ,,
Good revenue, large surplus, nearly 140,000 dollars for year ended . . . . . 30 June, ,,
Legislature dissolved . . . . . 23 July, ,,
Elections; great victory of the opponents of the "Reid contract" . . . . 7 Nov. ,,
The Bond ministry, 32–4, enlarged and reconstructed . . . . . . 7 Dec. ,,
Modus vivendi re the French shore, renewed, act passed . . . . 27 Feb. 1901
Legislature opened, good revenue, reported, 23 May, ,,
Sir Cavendish Boyle, arrives, . . . 17 June, ,,
Compromise with Mr. Reid effected; he surrenders ownership of the railway, but agrees to work it for 50 years . . . . . . mid July, ,,
Bill passed, 2 Aug.; Reid Newfoundland company formed . . . . 29 Aug. ,,
Mercantile stores in St. John's burnt, 2 deaths, estimated loss, 500,000 dollars . . 11 Sept. ,,
The duke and duchess of Cornwall welcomed at St. John's; Mr. Bond, premier, knighted, 24, 25 Oct. ,,
Chief justice Little, of St. John's, knighted, 9 Nov. ,,
French fishery on the Green Banks fails . June, 1902
Good surplus for year ending . . . 30 June, ,,
The Reid Newfoundland co. awarded 800,450 dollars, from the government, by arbitration, reported . . . . . . 8 Oct. ,,
Government and other buildings, the cathedral, schools, &c., burnt down at St. Pierre . 1 Nov. ,,
Bond-Hay reciprocity treaty *re* fish, signed at Washington . . . . 8 Nov. ,,
Modus vivendi bill passed, 12 March; again renewed, for 1903, 14 Dec. 1902, and for 1904, 23 March, 1903; revenue 2,200,000 dol. . . . 30 June, 1903
Seal fishery best for years, reported . 21 April, ,,
Decline of British imports 10 per cent. and increase of American 50 during 1902–03, reported . Oct. ,,
Codfish sales propuce 1,000,000 dols. more than in 1902, reported . . . . . end Nov. ,,

NEW FRANCE, see *Canada*.

"NEW" GALLERY, Regent Street, W., erected by seceders from the subscribers to the Grosvenor Gallery (*which see*), opened 9 May, 1888. In this building were held the Tudor, Stuart, Guelph, and Victorian exhibitions, *which see*, and Picture exhibitions.

NEWGATE, LONDON. The PRISON derives its name from the gate, to which was attached a small prison, gradually enlarged. One was erected in 1086 by the bishop of London. It was used as a prison for persons of rank as early as 1218; but was rebuilt about two centuries afterwards by the executors of sir Richard Whittington, whose statue with a cat stood in the niche till the time of its demolition by the great fire of London, in 1666. It was then reconstructed; but becoming an accumulation of misery and inconvenience, was pulled down and rebuilt between 1778 and 1780. During the riots in 1780, the interior was destroyed by fire, but shortly afterwards restored. In 1857 the interior was pulled down to be re-erected on a plan adapted to the reformatory system. Newgate was disused as an ordinary prison, 31 Dec. 1881. Building demolished 1902–3. Sale of fittings and relics 4 Feb. 1903. During the pulling down of the building, part of an old Roman wall was discovered. Major Arthur Griffiths' "Chronicles of Newgate," published Jan. 1884. See *Old Bailey*. Newgate MARKET, established in 1681, was ordered to be abolished by an act passed in 1861, which took effect when the meat and poultry market in Smithfield was opened, 1 Dec. 1868.

NEW GRENADA (S. America), discovered by Ojeda in 1499, and settled by the Spaniards in 1536. It formed part of the new republic of Bogota, established in 1811; and, combined with Caracas, formed the republic of Colombia, 17 Dec. 1819; see *Colombia*.

President M. Ospina entered on office . 1 April, 1857
After several reunions and dissolutions, the republic of New Grenada merged into the Grenadine Confederation, which includes Bolivar, Antioquia, Panama, and other small states . 15 June, 1858
Struggles between the conservatives, partisans of the old government, and the liberals . Jan. 1861
General Mosquera (liberal) deposes Ospina; and seizes the government . . . 18 July, ,,
A congress of the states determine on union, under the name of the United States of Colombia, 20 Sept. ,,
Arboleda, chief of the conservatives, assassinated (succeeded by Cassal) . . . . 1 Nov. 1862
New constitution established . . . 8 May, 1863
Mosquera invites Venezuela and Ecuador to join the confederation . . . . . Aug. ,,
Ecuador declines—war ensues . . . . 20 Nov. ,,
The troops of Ecuador defeated, 6 Dec.; peace ensues, and Ecuador remains independent 30 Dec. ,,
Coup d'état of Mosquera, who declares himself dictator . . . . 11 March, 1866
Mosquera deposed by Santos Acosta, who becomes provisional president . . . 23 May, 1867
Mosquera, the ex-president, exiled . . 1 Nov. ,,
General Santas Gutierrez Vergara, the president, deposed and imprisoned, and general Ponce made provisional president. Ponce compelled to abdicate; succeeded by Correoso, 29 Aug., who defeated his opponents . . . 12 Nov. 1868
The republic now named Colombia (*which see*).

NEW GUINEA or PAPUA, a large island, Pacific Ocean, discovered by the Portuguese after their settlement of the Moluccas between 1511 and 1530. It was visited by Saavedra, a Spaniard, in 1528. It is said to have been named New Guinea by Ortiz de Retes, a Portuguese, 1549. Torres Straits, which divide New Guinea and Australia, were discovered by Torres, a Spaniard, in 1606. It was frequently visited by the Dutch in the 17th century. They established a colony and erected a fortress, named Dubus, on the S.W. coast, in 1828, which was unsuccessful; and removed in 1835. A lofty range of mountains was named after capt. Owen Stanley, who first saw them from his vessel on sea about 1849. See *German New Guinea*.

On 9 Oct. the New Guinea Colonizing Association proposed to lord Carnarvon, the colonial secretary, to send to New Guinea an expedition of 200 men with 50 officers, in a ship of 1200 tons burden; he declined to sanction it, and referred to dangers, 30 Oct. 1875; part of the island annexed by the Queensland government, announced April, 1883, with the approval of an Australia; this act declared by the British government to be "null in point of law, and not to be admitted in point of policy," 2 July, 1883; signified by lord Derby's dispatch, also recommending a confederation of Australian states, 11 July, 1883.
Mr. MacIvor's proposed expedition to New Guinea prohibited by lord Derby, Oct. 1883.
Inter-colonial conference at Sydney recommend annexation, 6 Dec. 1883.
Protectorate of the southern part and adjacent islands under a high commissioner determined on, Aug. 1884; to be supported by the Australian colonies; Major-Gen. Peter H. Scratchley appointed, Oct. 1884; protectorate proclaimed in New Guinea, 6 Nov.
German flag hoisted on northern part and adjacent islands; Australian colonies protest, Dec. 1884.
The German colony named Kaiser Wilhelm's Land, March, 1885.
Agreement between England and Germany announced, 19 June, 1885.

Exploring expedition of geographical society of Australasia under captain Everill, in New Guinea, Sept. 1885.
Death of sir Peter Henry Scratchley announced, 3 Dec. 1885.
Bill regulating the government passed by legislature of Queensland, 4 Nov. 1887.
New Guinea constituted an independent colony by letters patent, 30 Oct. 1888. Seat of government, port Moresby; Mr. (aft. sir) W. Macgregor, lieut.-governor, March, 1895; succeeded by Mr. G. R. Le Hunte, Aug. 1898, resigns, April, 1903.
Sir Wm. Macgregor explores the Owen Stanley range of mountains and names one Victoria (13,121 feet high), another Albert Edward (12,500 feet), 40 miles inland from Port Moresby, . . May, June, 1889
Sir Wm. Macgregor lands at Demara with 22 men to search for murderers; repulses an attack of 250 natives and burns a village, announced 15 Oct. 1889; his explorations of the river systems, &c., reported, Oct. 1894; he is awarded the Royal Geographical Society's Founders' medal, 27 April, 1896; further explorations in the west division 8 Feb.—22 March, 1897
Murder of Mr. J. Hedley and the crew of the cutter *Isabel* (while pearl fishing) . reported 1 Oct. 1890
Massacre of 40 villagers by the Tugaree tribe . . reported 9 Jan. 1891
Five European miners killed by natives at Mambare 7–12 Jan. 1897
Mr. Green, government resident and eight constables murdered by natives at Tamata 14 Jan. ,,
Charter to a company for colonization, &c., applied for by three Dutchmen, reported, 3 Dec.; refused . . . . 10 Dec. ,,
The New Guinea company transfer rights to Germany over the protectorate, announced, 26 Oct. 1898; the German govnt. assumes the administration, 1 April, 1899; the Caroline, Pelew, and Marianne islands incorporated in German New Guinea . . . . Jan. 1900
Two white diggers killed and eaten, Feb. 1901; the rev. James Chalmers and 13 others massacred by natives on Coarabata island . . . 8 April, 1901
Expedition under Mr. Le Hunte attacked, 24 natives killed . . . . . 2 May, ,,
Mrs. Wolff murdered in the Bismarck archipelago; a tribe annihilated by a German punitive force, reported . . . . Aug. 1902
Messrs. Jeswick and Brackenbury murdered, 25 natives killed in a fight; drought and famine; some cannibalism, reported . . . 31 Dec. ,,
Intoxicating liquors prohibition, reported, 4 Aug. 1903
Medical expedition for ethnological investigation and collection of *data* for cancer research in New Guinea leaves London . . . . . Aug. ,,

NEW HAMPSHIRE, one of the early United States of N. America, was settled in 1623, placed under Massachusetts, 1641; separated, 1679. Capital, Concord. Population, 1880, 346,991; 1890, 376,530; 1900, 411,588.

A lunatic asylum near Dover burnt; over 50 inmates perish . . . . 9 Feb. 1893
Suicide of Isaac Abbott, city treasurer of Dover, and cashier of the National bank, after defalcation of 80,000 dollars . . . . . 14 Jan. 1895

NEW HARMONY, see *Harmonists*.

NEW HEBRIDES (S. Pacific Ocean), discovered by Quiros, who believing them to be a continent named them *Tierra Australia del Espiritu Santo*, in 1606. Bougainville in 1768 found them to be islands; and in 1774 Cook gave them their present name. On appeal, the British government promise protection to the natives against kidnapping, &c. 7 Feb. 1883.

In 1878 the British and French governments agreed not to occupy these islands, but French aggressions were protested against by the Australian colonies, 1887.
French vessels land troops here to protect their countrymen, 1 June, 1886.
Land dispute between French Hebrides company and native christian mission, reported 15 Sept. 1886.
Sir William Stawell appointed lieut-governor Jan. 1887; died, 1889.
The Anglo-French convention of 16 Nov. 1887, and the agreement of 26 June, 1888, placed the islands, for the protection of life and property, under a joint commission of French and English naval officers on the Pacific stations.

NEW HOLLAND, see *Australia, New South Wales*, &c.

NEW IRELAND, an island in the Pacific ocean, lat. 2° 3′ S., long. 152° E., 200 miles long, 25 miles average width. An attempt of the French marquis de Rays to colonise this island was reported a disastrous failure in August, 1880, and May, 1881. The island is now named New Mecklenburg.

NEW JERSEY, one of the early United States of N. America, was settled by the Dutch from New York, 1620; and by Swedes in 1627. Capital, Trenton. Population, 1880, 1,131,116; 1890, 1,444,933; 1900, 1,883,669.

The S. half of Seabright with fine buildings burnt, 17 June (see *Jews*) 1891
Great fires at Paterson, 26 blocks destroyed, 1 death, 20 injured, 9 Feb.; 3 blocks burnt down at Atlantic city, estimated loss over 2,000,000 dollars, 6 deaths, reported . . . 3 April, 1902

NEW JERUSALEM CHURCH, see *Swedenborgians*.

NEW LANARK (W. Scotland). A manufacturing village founded by David Dale, 1783. Here his son-in-law, Robert Owen, endeavoured to establish socialism in 1801; and here the first infant school was set up, 1815.

"NEW LEARNING," a term applied to the revival of the study of the Bible and the Greek and Latin classics, in their original tongues, in the 15th and 16th centuries, which conduced greatly to the Reformation. See *Humanism*.

NEWMARKET (Cambridgeshire), renowned for its horse-races. It is first mentioned in 1227; and probably derived its name from the market then recently established. James I. erected a hunting seat here, called the king's house, to which Charles I. was taken as a prisoner in 1647, when the parliament army was quartered in the neighbouring village of Kennet. Charles II., who was fond of racing, built a stand-house for the sake of the diversion, about 1667,* and from that period races have been annual to the present time; and many extraordinary races have been run; see *Races*. Population, 1881, 5,093; 1891, 6,213; 1901, 19,065.

NEW MEXICO (N. America), ceded to the United States in 1848, and organised as a territory, 9 Sept. 1850; admitted as a state by the house of representatives, 1892. Capital, Santa Fé. Precious metals are found in almost every part of the territory. Population, 1880, 119,565; 1890, 153,593; 1900, 195,310.

NEWNHAM COLLEGE, see *Girton*.

* During the races, on 22 March, 1683, Newmarket was nearly destroyed by an accidental fire, which occasioned the hasty departure of the company then assembled, including the king, the queen, the duke of York, the royal attendants, and many of the nobility; and to this disaster historians have ascribed the failure of the Rye house plot, the object of which was said to be the assassination of the king and his brother on the road from Newmarket to London, if the period of their journey had not been thus anticipated; see *Rye House Plot*.

NEW ORLEANS, capital of Louisiana, N. America (*which see*), founded in 1717, under the regency of the duke of Orleans. In 1788, seven-eighths of the city were destroyed by fire. The British attacked New Orleans in Dec. 1814, and were repulsed with great loss by the Americans under general Jackson, 8 Jan. 1815; the British general, sir Edward Pakenham, was killed. New Orleans was surrendered to the Federals in April, 1862. The strong feeling of the inhabitants in favour of the Confederates and against the Federals induced general B. Butler to rule them with military rigour, occasionally degenerating into brutal tyranny, especially towards females, May to October, 1862. He was replaced by general Banks, 16 Dec. 1862. Sanguinary riots; due to agitators, begun 30 July, 1866, only suppressed by martial law; about 40 persons, white and coloured, were killed, and about 160 wounded, similar riots occurred, 24 Oct. 1868, and often since. Population in 1880, 216,090; in 1890, 158,019; 1900, 300,000.

New Orleans.—John McEnery elected governor of Louisiana by the southern whites, 4 Nov. 1872; but W. P. Kellogg, elected by the coloured people and their white friends, was recognised by the Federal government. To defend themselves against tyranny, the southerns formed the "white league," and collected arms, which they refused to surrender on demand on 15 Sept. 1874. They deposed Kellogg at New Orleans after some resistance, and established McEnery as governor, but submitted to the president's proclamation; and Kellogg was restored 18 Sept.

The government troops eject members from the legislative assembly as unduly elected . 4 Jan. 1875
After much discussion, a peaceful compromise April, ,,
Much trouble, 2 governors at one time, Jan.; disputes settled in favour of Democrats by president Hayes; prospect of peace . . . 25 April, 1877
"World's Industrial and Cotton Centennial" Exposition . . . . . 16 Dec. 1884—30 May, 1885
Another exposition opened . . . 10 Nov. ,,
Mississippi steamer, *J. M. White*, burnt, 30 lives lost . . . . . . about 14 Dec. 1888
Mr. David Hennessy, chief of the police, assassinated by a party of the Sicilian vendetta society named *Mafia*, which see, 15 Oct.; 17 men arrested . . . . 19, 20 Oct. 1890
The committee of safety, aided by the Italian government, determine to clear the city from secret societies; meeting held. . . . 27 Oct. ,,
Indictment of 17 Sicilians for the murder of Mr. Hennessy, 22 Nov. 1890; 9 tried; 6 acquitted; no verdict on 3, 13 March, 1891; the mob, invited by Mr. Parkerson, lawyer, and other citizens, break into the gaol, and shoot or hang 11 prisoners (2 not American citizens). . 14 March, 1891
Strong protest of the Italian government 15 March, ,,
Secretary Blaine writes to Mr. Nicholls, governor of Louisiana, expressing the president's regret at the citizens' disparagement of the law; Baron di Fava, the Italian minister, recalled by his government . . . . 31 March, ,,
Correspondence between the Governments March, April, ,,
The United States government pays to the Italian, 25,000 dollars for the benefit of the heirs of the lynched Italians; diplomatic relations resumed . about 14 April, 1892
Destructive storm, about 1,200 deaths, buildings and works destroyed . . . . . 2 Oct. 1893
Severe drought, reported . . . . 23 Oct. 1894
Rioting between the whites and negroes, with bloodshed, reported . . . . 12 March, 1895
Order restored . . . . . . 13 March, ,,
Explosion in a saloon opposite the French market, attributed to the Mafia, *which see*, 15 persons killed . . . . 5 April, ,,

NEW PHILOSOPHY, a term applied in the 17th century to that of Bacon (*which see*).

NEW PLYMOUTH, see *New England*.

NEWPORT (Monmouthshire). Chartered by Edward III. and James I. Population, 1881, 38,469; 1891, 54,695; 1901, 67,290.

CHARTIST RIOTS.—About 10,000 chartists (*which see*), from the neighbouring mines, armed with guns, pikes, &c., arrived at Newport, 4 Nov. 1839. They divided themselves into two bodies—one, under the command of Mr. John Frost, an ex-magistrate, proceeded down the principal street; whilst the other, headed by his son, took the direction of Stow-hill. They met in front of the Westgate hotel, where the magistrates were assembled with about 30 soldiers of the 45th regiment, and several special constables. The rioters broke the windows and fired on the inmates, by which the mayor, Mr. (afterwards sir Thomas) Phillips, and several other persons, were wounded. The soldiers returned the fire, and dispersed the mob, which fled, leaving about 20 dead, and others wounded. A detachment of the 10th royal hussars arrived from Bristol, and the town became tranquil.

Frost was apprehended on the following day, together with his printer, and other influential persons among the chartists. He and others were tried and sentenced to death (afterwards commuted to transportation) . . . . . Jan. 1840
An amnesty was granted them, 3 May, and they returned to England . . . . Sept. 1856
Frost died, aged 96 . . . . . 29 July, 1877
Explosion on the *Tancarville* petroleum steamer in the dry dock; five men killed, many injured . 11 May, 1891
Mr. T. Cordes bequeaths 100,000*l.* to the Newport and Co. hospital, reported . . 17 Oct. 1901

NEW RIVER, for the supply of London with water, was begun 1609, and finished in 1613, when the projector, Hugh Myddelton, a London goldsmith, was knighted by James I.—*Strype*. This artificial river, which rises in Hertfordshire,* and which, with its windings, then forty-eight miles long, was brought to London, and opened 29 Sept. 1613. So little was the benefit of it understood, that for above thirty years the seventy-two shares (equally divided into *King's* and *Adventurers'*), netted only 5*l.* apiece. Charles I. sold his shares to Myddelton's representatives for an annuity of 500*l.* Each of these shares was sold originally for 100*l.* A part of a share sold at the rate of 94,050*l.* the share, 1 Nov. 1876; part of a king's share at rate of 90,000*l.*; of an adventurer's share at rate of 93,200*l.*, 15 May, 1878; king's share, rate 88,200*l.*; adventurer's, 91,000*l.*, Oct. 1878; king's share, rate 91,010*l.*; adventurer's, 94,500*l.*, Nov. 1880; king's share rate 85,800*l.*; adventurer's, 85,200*l.* Nov. 1887.

An entire freehold adventurer's share of the company was sold by auction for 122,800*l.* to the Prudential Assurance company . . 17 July, 1889
The annual income of the company from land and water was stated to be 511,356*l.* in 1888
An entire "king's share" sold for 95,100*l.* 21 May, 1890
A freehold adventurer's sold for 94,900*l.*, 15 Nov. 1893
An adventurer's share sold by auction for 122,500*l.*, 15 March, 1899; for 114,000*l.*, 1st week in July, 1899
See also under *Water*, 1902–3.

NEW ROAD, N. London (now Pentonville, Euston, and Marylebone roads), was cut through verdant meadows, 1756-7, after much opposition.

NEW ROSS (Wexford), S. E. Ireland. Here general Johnston totally defeated the rebels under Beauchamp D. Bagenal Harvey, 4 June, 1798.

(NEW) RUGBY, Tennessee, United States, N. America, a colony of British farmers and others, founded on English principles by Mr. Thomas Hughes, Q.C., formerly M.P., author of "Tom

* Myddelton turned the first sod at Chadwell, a spring rising at the foot of a hill near Ware, 19 April, 1609; the water issued out of a deep hole, and combined with another spring, Amwell; forming a river about 20 feet wide; he died poor, 10 Dec. 1631.

Brown's Schooldays," &c.; inaugurated 5 Oct. 1880. Reported failure of crops and prevalence of fever, Aug. 1881; more favourable reports, Sept. 1883.

NEWRY (N. Ireland). In the rebellion of 1641, Newry was reduced to a ruinous condition; it was surprised by sir Con. Magenis, but was retaken by lord Conway. After the Restoration the town was rebuilt. It was burnt by the duke of Berwick when fleeing from Schomberg and the English army, and only the castle and a few houses escaped, 1689. Serious rioting, 15 July, 1902. Population, 1901, 13,121.

NEWS-AGENTS' AND BOOKSELLERS' UNION first annual meeting, held at Stationers' hall, London, 18 Feb. 1897.

NEWS-LETTERS. News-writers in the reign of Charles II. collected from the coffee-houses information, which was printed weekly and sent into the country. The *London Gazette*, then the only authorised newspaper, contained little more than proclamations and advertisements.

NEW MODEL, see *Council of Officers*.

NEW SOUTH WALES, the principal colony of Australia on the eastern coast, was explored and taken possession of and named by captain Cook in 1770. At his recommendation a convict colony was first formed here. Captain Arthur Phillip, the first governor, arrived at Botany Bay with 800 convicts, 20 Jan. 1788; but he subsequently preferred Sydney, about seven miles distant from the head of Port Jackson, as a more eligible situation for the capital. Gold was discovered in 1851. A new constitution was granted in 1855 (18 & 19 Vict. c. 54). The Intercolonial Exhibition was opened at Sydney, by the governor-general lord Belmore, 30 Aug. 1870. It consisted of two departments, agricultural and non-agricultural. A conference of delegates from the Australian colonies met at Sydney in Jan. 1873, to deliberate on a customs' union, postal and railway arrangements, &c. The ministry introduced a free trade budget near the end of the year. Industrial exhibition opened by the governor, 11 April, 1874. Population, (1856), 269,722; (1862), 367,495; (1866), 411,388; (1871), 519,163; (1881), 750,000; (1891), 1,134,207; (1901), 1,366,408 (30 June). Imports 6,597,053*l.* in 1859; 20,960,157*l.* in 1883; 18,806,236*l.* in 1887; 22,954,015*l.* in 1890; 18,107,035*l.*, 1893; 21,744,350*l.*, 1897; 27,500,000*l.*, 1901; exports, 4,768,049*l.* in 1859; 19,886,018*l.* in 1883; 18,496,917*l.* in 1887; 13,266,222*l.* in 1890; 22,921,223*l.*, 1893; 23,602,991*l.*, 1897; over 28,000,000*l.*, 1901; revenue, 1889-90, 8,519,159*l.*; expenditure, 1889-90, 9,811,251*l.*; revenue, 1896-7, 9,729,117*l.*; expenditure, 1896-7, 10,698,167*l.*; revenue, 1898-99, 9,754,185*l.*; 1900-1, 10,794,233*l.*; 1900-3, debit balance, 484,355*l.* Governor, sir John Young, 1860; earl of Belmore, 1867; sir Hercules Robinson, April, 1872; lord Loftus, 1879; lord Carrington, 1885; the earl of Jersey, 1890; sir Robert Wm. Duff, 1893; visct. Hampden, June, 1895; resigns, succeeded by lord Beauchamp, Jan. 1899; sir F. M. Darley, 1901; adm. sir Harry Rawson, Jan. 1902. See *Australia*, *Sydney*, and *Rabbits*.

The bishopric of Australia was formed in 1836; New Zealand was detached in 1841, and Tasmania in 1842; the diocese of Australia was again divided in 1847, the sees of Sydney, Newcastle, Adelaide, and Melbourne being formed; the diocese of Perth was formed 1857; Goulburn, 1863; Bathurst, 1869; Grafton and Armidale, 1869; Ballarat, 1875; North Queensland, 1878; Riverina 1883

Town of Jerilderie seized and robbed by the Victorian thieves, "Kelly gang" . . 8-10 Feb. 1879
International Exhibition opened by Lord A. Loftus, 17 Sept. ,,
Building burnt down . . . . 22 Sept. 1882
The *Wolverene* was presented as a gift from the British government to the government of New South Wales . . . . . 16 Jan. ,,
Henry Parkes, originally farm labourer, came from Birmingham to Sydney in 1839; actively opposed convict immigration, 1849; member for Sydney in the legislative council, 1856, premier 1872-5, K.C.M.G., 1877, 1878-83.
New parliament; resignation of ministry; Mr. Alex. Stuart forms a new cabinet . 3 Jan. 1883
The legislature rejects the federal scheme by 1 vote about 1 Nov. 1884
Military contingent ordered to be sent to the Soudan; 30,000*l.* subscribed for the Patriotic Fund, at Sydney, 23 Feb.; amount raised to 45,000*l.* 3 March; contingent starts, 3 March; arrives at Suakim 29-30 March; left May, 1885
Resignation of ministry; new one formed by sir John Robertson, 17 Dec. 1885; coalition formed by sir J. Robertson and sir Patrick Jennings, 25 Feb. 1886
Explosion at Bulli colliery; 85 men perish, 23 March, 1887
Proposal to change the name of the colony to Australia . . . . 23 Nov. ,,
Reward of 25,000*l.* offered by government for the extermination of rabbits introduced from Europe.—M. Pasteur suggests the introduction of rabbits inoculated with microbes; professor Watson of Adelaide proposes a similar method, 1887; [reported unsuccessful, 1889-90.]
Sir Henry Parkes premier . . . 1887-8
Centenary of the landing of captain A. Phillip at Sydney . . . . . 24 Jan. *et seq.* 1888
Severe Chinese restriction bill (against the treaties of Nankin and Pekin) passed by the assembly 16-17 May, ,,
Conference of Australasian ministers on the Chinese question . . . . . . 12 June, ,,
Hon. G. R. Dibbs forms a new ministry, 15 Jan.; defeated 17 Jan.; dissolution of parliament; elections, 2 Feb. 1889; sir Henry Parkes forms a ministry . . . . . . 14 March, 1889
Great storm on the coast near Sydney with much loss of life and property . . 25 May *et seq.* ,,
Bill for the payment of legislature finally passed . 20 Sept. ,,
The town of Bourke temporarily submerged by the rising of the Upper Darling river, through heavy rain; much property damaged, no loss of life . 18-20 April, 1890
New parliament opened . . . 29 April, ,,
For the great strikes, see *Sydney* . . Aug. ,,
The Broken Hill (silver mines) proprietary company formed about 1883, prosperous till Sept. ,,
Death of sir John Robertson, eminent statesman, aged 75, premier 1860-63, 1868-70, 1875-77, 1885-6 announced 8 May, 1891
Parliament dissolved . . . . . 7 June, ,,
Elections; 48 ministerialists, 56 opposition, 31 labour candidates and others . . 30 June, ,,
Parliament opened 15 July; Mr. Dibbs' vote of want of confidence in sir Henry Parkes negatived (80 to 57) . . . . . . 23 July, ,,
The earl of Jersey's proclamation strictly forbidding all interference with free labour . 23 July, ,,
Settlement of the shearers' strike annd. 11 Aug. ,,
Resignation of sir H. Parkes and his ministry on account of the introduction of a bill limiting the hours of labour to 8 in coal-mines . . 19 Oct. ,,
New ministry formed by Hon. G. R. Dibbs 23 Oct. ,,
The Eight hours bill passed . . . 1 Dec. ,,
The new tariff bill voted by the legislative assembly by 50 votes against 3, 19 Dec. 1891; assent given . . . . . . 2 March, 1892
Great difficulty with the unemployed. . April, ,,
Railway accident near Bathurst, 9 deaths, 27 April, ,,
Seven months' drought relieved by rain . 26 May, ,,
The earl of Ancrum, aide-de-camp of the earl of Jersey, killed by a gun accident, about 17 June, ,,

The hon. G. R. Dibbs, premier, arrives in London, 8 June; knighted, 23 July; returned 12 Sept. 1892
Confidence in the ministry affirmed (68–64), 30 Sept. ,,
The funded stock bill (for 3,000,000*l.* at 4 per cent.) passed; the debt, about 50,000,000*l.* . 20 Oct. ,,
Mr. Francis Abigail, director, sentenced to 5 years' penal servitude, and Mr. Roderick M'Namara, manager, to 7 years', for fraud connected with the Australian Banking company . 3 Nov. ,,
Strike at the Broken Hill silver mines against reduction of wages, July; negotiations fail; the mines opened to free labour, 25 Aug.; order maintained by military, Sept.; 7 rioters sentenced to terms of imprisonment, with hard labour, 30 Oct.; strike ends . about 6 Nov. ,,
Vote of censure on the ministry rejected 22 Dec. ,,
Resignation of the earl of Jersey for personal reasons . . . . . . about 23 Jan. 1893
Sir H. Parkes's proposed vote of censure negatived (57–65); 32 hours' sitting . 3 Feb. ,,
The rt. hon. Robert Wm. Duff appointed governor, about 23 Feb.; arrives at Sydney 29 May, ,,
Floods, through rising of Hunter River; Newcastle and other places submerged . 9–11 March, ,,
Precautionary stoppage of the Australian joint stock bank, 20 April; and of the National bank of Australasia at Sydney, &c., 1 May; both reconstructed . . . . 4 May, ,,
New banking act passed . . . . . 3 May, ,,
Stoppage of the Commercial banking company of Sydney (started 1834), 15 May; proceedings in London, 29 May; re-opens . . . 19 June, ,,
Notes of various banks proclaimed legal tender in the colony . . . . 15 May, ,,
See *Australia*, May, 1893.
Case of the *Costa Rica* packet; the vessel wrongfully seized and the captain imprisoned by the Dutch in the Moluccas, Nov. 1891; lord Rosebery recommends the Dutch government to pay 2500*l.* as compensation, July; declared insufficient by sir George Dibbs . . 16 July, ,,
Parliament opened by sir Robert Duff 26 Sept. ,,
New bank note bill passed . . . . 28 Nov. ,,
Parliament prorogued . . . . . 8 Dec. ,,
Parliament opened . . . . . 17 Jan. 1894
Budget introduced, deficit about 1,200,000*l.* 1 Feb. ,,
Important discovery of gold at Wyalong, 33 m. S.W. of Sydney; a rush of miners to the spot, reported 16 March, ,,
A bill authorizing the issue of bank notes, except at Sydney, passed . . . . . 5 April, ,,
Parliament prorogued till 10 July . 11 June, ,,
Letter from sir George Dibbs to the hon. J. B. Patterson, premier of Victoria, proposing a scheme of Australian federation . 14 June, ,,
Parliament dissolved . . . . 25 June, ,,
Resignation of the Dibbs cabinet reported 30 July, ,,
New ministry formed by Mr. George H. Reid, 2 Aug.; parliament opened 28 Aug. ,,
Sir Alfred Stephen, G.C.M.G., statesman, chief justice, 1844–73; lieut.-governor, 1875–91; died 29 Oct. ,,
Railway collision at Redfern, 11 lives lost, many injured . . . . 31 Oct. ,,
Mr. George H. Reid proposes financial reform 7 Nov. ,,
Revenue for 1894, 9,476,000*l.* . . . . 31 Dec.
Death of sir Robt. W. Duff (born 1835), governor at Sydney, 15 March; state funeral . 17 March, 1895
Bill reducing the governor's salary from 7000*l.* to 5000*l.* passed by the house, 9 April; shelved by the legislative council . . . 18 April, ,,
Mr. G. H. Reid in his free-trade budget proposes a land-tax of one penny and an income-tax of sixpence in the pound to meet the deficit 9 May, ,,
Bill introduced to amend the constitution June, ,,
Parliament dissolved 5 July; government majority at the elections, 24 July; new parliament opened, speech by sir F. Darley, lieut.-gov. . 14 Aug. ,,
Land and income-tax assessment bill passed by the legislative assembly, 17 Sept. (land-tax exemption fixed at 200*l.*, income-tax exemption at 150*l.*) . . . . 18 Sept. ,,
Dean, convicted of poisoning his wife, reprieved by the action of his counsel, Messrs. Meagher and Crick, legislators: rearrested, 8 Oct.; Mr. Meagher arrested for perjury, 8 Oct. (acquitted 15 May, 1896); Dean committed for trial, 11 Oct.; sentenced to imprisonment for perjury, 25 Oct. 1895
Federal enabling bill passed, Nov. 1895; [amendment bill passed, Nov. 1897]; see *Australasia*, 1891 *et seq*; [votes for federation insufficient, June, 1898].
Visct. Hampden arrives at Sydney . 21 Nov. ,,
Great heat: average, 112° F., 35 deaths, Jan. 1896; 125°, 10 more deaths . . . . 22 Jan. 1896
Military conference of commandants from Australian colonies respecting federal defence, major-gen. Hutton president, at Sydney, 29 Jan.–5 Feb. ,,
See *Divorces*, 1895.
Sir Henry Parkes, born 1815, died . 27 April, ,,
Parliament opened by the governor, with a cheerful speech, 12 May; prorogued . 13 Nov. ,,
New S. Wales Defence guard established 26 May, ,,
Nevertire, destroyed by a cyclone, reported, 29 Dec. ,,
Long drought: (16 April) appointed as a day of humiliation and prayer . . . . 8 April, 1897
Parliament opened . . . . . 27 April, ,,
The "Australian Horse" new volunteer regiment, formed; about 1,000 men . . . Sept. ,,
Debate on the estimates (30 hrs.) . 10, 11 Nov. ,,
Successful irrigation by artesian wells, reported, 13 Nov. ,,
Colliery explosion, at Newcastle, 15 deaths, reported . . . . 21 March, 1898
Parliament opened, good revenue, &c., reported; 21 June; dissolved . . . . . 8 July, ,,
Special session on federation question opened, 21 Feb. 1899; Federal bill passed by the assembly, 2 March; amended by the council, 21 March; parliament prorogued, 2nd special session (12 new members in the council) opens . 11 April, 1899
Federal bill amended; passed by the assembly and by the council . . . . 13, 19 April, ,,
A squadron of New South Wales lancers, to be trained at Aldershot, arrives in London, 27 April, ,,
[Volunteer for service in South Africa, and leave England amid great enthusiasm, 10 Oct.]
Federal demonstration in Sydney . . 1 May, ,,
Earl Beauchamp, governor, welcomed at Sydney, 18 May, ,,
The *referendum* for the commonwealth bill, 107,274 for and 72,701 against the bill . . 20 June, ,,
Parliament opened by the governor; increased revenue, 147,000*l.* surplus . . . 18 July, ,,
Government defeated on a vote of censure, 78–41, 7 Sept.; Mr. Reid's ministry resigns, 11 Sept.; new cabinet; Mr. W. Lyne, premier (knt., May, 1900), ... 14 Sept. ,,
2nd New South Wales contingent leaves for South Africa . . . . 17 Jan. 1900
Parliament opened by the governor . . 12 June, ,,
Sir Saul Samuel, agent-general in England 18 years till 1898, dies, aged 80 . . . . . 29 Aug. ,,
Sir W. Lyne's budget statement: surplus for 1899, 169,230*l.* . . . . 4 Oct. ,,
Old age pensions bill passed by the council, 29 Nov. ,,
Lord Hopetoun, gov.-gen. of Australia, arrives at Sydney, 15 Dec.; asks sir W. Lyne to form a Federal ministry, 19 Dec.; he declines, after conferring with the premiers of Victoria and South Australia, 24 Dec. See *Australasia*, 1 Jan. 1901
Mr. John See forms a ministry, 10 April; elections; government majority . . . 3 July, ,,
Parliament opened . . . . . 23 July, ,,
Industrial arbitration bill passed by the legislative council . . . . 6 Dec. ,,
Land bill passed, both houses, reported . 17 Dec. ,,
Adm. sir H. Rawson, governor, arrives; opens parliament . . . . 27, 28 May, 1902
Women's franchise bill passed, both houses, 14 Aug. ,,
Drought ends in the northern districts, 22 Aug. ,,
Budget, surplus, 3000*l.*; existing deficit, 84,000*l.*, 24 Sept. ,,
Loan of 4,000,000*l.* against 4 per cent. treasury bills, London, passed by the assembly . 10 Dec. ,,
Parliament meets 16 June; estimated deficit (1904) 50,000*l.*, reported . . . . . 30 June, 1903
Strikes at the Hebburn colliery and elsewhere, 13 July, ,,

Defeat of the government in the assembly on vote of censure, 59–42 . . . . . . 16 July, 1903
Tumut (*which see*) proposed as the federal capital of Australia (rejected by senate Aug.) . 18 July, „
Water famine at Broken Hill, causing stoppage of mines, 27 June; water trains sent from S. Australia; relief works started by the government 17 July; general rain reported during Aug. and Sept. „

NEWSPAPER PROVINCIAL SOCIETY, established in 1836, became the Newspaper Society in 1889; see *Press Association*.

NEWSPAPERS. The Roman *Acta Diurna* were issued, it is said, 691 B.C. In modern times, a *Gazetta*, which derived its name from its price, a small coin, was published in Venice (about 1536). The *Gazette de France*, now existing, first appeared in April, 1631, edited by Renaudot, a physician. It was patronised by the king, Louis XIII., who wrote one article for it, and by Richelieu. The first real newspaper published in England* was established by sir Roger L'Estrange, in 1663: it was entitled the *Public Intelligencer*, and continued nearly three years, when it ceased, on the appearance of the *Gazette*. In the reign of James I., 1622, appeared the *London Weekly Courant;* and in the year 1642 (the period of the civil war) were printed a variety of publications, certainly in no respect entitled to the name of newspapers. See *Fourth Estate*. The following are the titles of some of them:—

England's Memorable Accidents.
The Kingdom's Intelligencer.
The Diurnal of Certain Passages in Parliament.
The Mercurius Aulicus.
The Scotch Intelligencer.
The Parliament's Scout.
The Parliament's Scout's Discovery, or certain Information.
The Mercurius Civicus, or London's Intelligencer.
The Country's Complaint, &c.
The Weekly Accounts.
Mercurius Britannicus.

A paper called the *London Gazette*,† published 22 Aug. 1642. The *London Gazette* of the existing series, published first at Oxford, the Court being there on account of the plague, 7 Nov. 1665, and afterwards at London, 5 Feb. 1666. A valuable index (1830–1883) compiled by Alex. Pulling for council of law reporting, published Nov. 1885.
Printing of newspapers and pamphlets prohibited, 31 Chas. II. 1680. *Salmon's Chron.*
The regular newspapers commenced on the abolition of the censorship of the press, in 1695.
Daily Courant said to have been first published in 1702.
The stamp duty imposed 1711
Sunday Newspapers began with *The British Gazette and Sunday Monitor*, 26 March, 1780; followed by the *Observer*, 1791; *Bell's Messenger*, 1796; *Weekly Dispatch*, 1801, &c. London ed. of *New York Herald*, 1889.
A penny charged for every sheet, and a halfpenny for every half sheet.
The duty made 1*d*. or 4*l*. 1*s*. 8*d*. the 1,000. . 1761
The duty raised to 1½*d*. in 1776; to 2*d*. in 1789; to 2½*d*. in 1794; to 3½*d*. in 1797; to 4*d*. in . . 1815

* Some copies of a publication are in existence called *The English Mercury*, professing to come out under the authority of queen Elizabeth, in 1588, the period of the Spanish Armada. The researches of Mr. T. Watts, of the British Museum proved these to be forgeries, executed about 1766. The full title of No. 50 is "*The English Mercurie*, published by authoritie, for the prevention of false reports, imprinted by Christopher Barker, her highness's printer, No. 50." It describes the Spanish Armada, giving "A journall of what passed since the 21st of this month, between her majestie's fleet and that of Spayne, transmitted by the Lord Highe Admiral, to the Lordes of council."

† On 22 May, 1787, a *London Gazette* Extraordinary was forged, with a view of affecting the funds.

Reduced to 1*d*., and ½*d*. for a supplement in . 1836
Abolished, the compulsory stamp being retained only for postal purposes 185
This also ceased . . . . . . 30 Sept. 1870
Newspapers first sent with a ½*d*. stamp affixed to the cover . . . . 1 Oct. „

NUMBER OF STAMPS ISSUED TO BRITISH NEWSPAPERS.

Year	Stamps	Year	Stamps
1753	7,411,757	1820	24,862,186
1760	9,404,790	1825	26,950,693
1774	12,300,000	1830	30,158,741
1790	14,035,639	1835	32,874,652
1800	16,084,905	1840	49,033,384
1810	20,172,837	1843	56,433,977

In the year ending 5 Jan. 1851, there were 159 London newspapers, in which appeared 891,650 advertisements; 222 English provincial newspapers, having 875,631 advertisements. In Scotland, same year, there were 110 newspapers, having 249,141 advertisements. In Ireland, there were 102 newspapers, having 236,128 advertisements.
The number of stamps issued was—in England, 65,741,271 at 1*d*., and 11,684,423 supplement stamps at ½*d*.; in Scotland, 7,643,045 stamps at 1*d*., and 241,264 at ½*d*.; in Ireland, 6,302,728 stamps at 1*d*., and 43,358 at ½*d*.
Reduction of newspaper duty from 4*d*. to 1*d*. took effect on 15 Sept. 1836.
The distinctive die came into use 1 Jan. 1837.
Duty on advertisements abolished, 1853.
By the act passed 15 June, 1855 (18 & 19 Vict. c. 27), the stamp on newspapers, as such, was totally abolished, and to be employed henceforth only for postal purposes. Many new papers were then started, which were but of short duration.
In 1857, 71 million newspapers passed through the post-office. In Jan. 1860, 1060 newspapers; in Jan. 1868, 1404 newspapers; in Jan. 1903, 2,431 newspapers were published in the United Kingdom.
On 1 Oct., 1861, when the paper duty came off, the *Times*, *Daily News*, and *Morning Post* reduced their price to 3*d*. each copy, unstamped.
"Penny a Week Country Daily Newspaper," single copy ½*d*.; No. 1, 25 June, 1873.
Petit Journal, ½*d*. daily, established by Marinoni, 1861; circulation about 840,000.
Sell's "Dictionary of the World's Press" for 1887, consists of 1,200 pages; increased considerably, 1892; published in 2 vols., 1899.
Newspaper libel and registration act passed 1881.
Law of libel relating to newspapers amended 1888.
Mitchell's annual newspaper press directory first published, 1845; jubilee number with essays by Mr. Wellsman, 37 years editor, Feb. 1895.
Estimated newspapers in the world, 41,000, Aug. 1890.
For copyright in newspaper articles, see *Trials*, June, 1892, and July, 1903.
"British and Irish Press Guide," issued by Mr. James Willing, 30th year, 1903.
"Anglo-Russian Trade Messenger," monthly, first published in Moscow, 13 Nov. 1897.
Daily Graphic, the only illustrated daily paper in Great Britain, first issued 1 Jan. 1890.
Daily Mail, the first halfpenny daily published in England, started 4 May, 1896.
A school of journalism proposed for New York; Mr. Pulitzer gives 2,000,000 dols. *Times*, 17 Aug. 1903.
Daily Mirror, the first daily newspaper published expressly for women in Great Britain, began 2 Nov. 1903.

IRISH NEWSPAPERS.

The first was the *Dublin News Letter*, by Joseph Ray, 1685; *Pue's Occurrences*, 1700 or 1703. *Faulkner's Journal* was established by George Faulkner, "a man celebrated for the goodness of his heart and the weakness of his head," 1728. The oldest of the existing Dublin newspapers is the *Freeman's Journal*, founded as the *Public Register*, by the patriot Dr. Lucas, about 1763. The *Limerick Chronicle*, the oldest of the provincial prints, 1766. Mr. Wm. O'Brien's *Irish People* first issue, 14 Sept. 1899; seized, 9 May, 1901.

PROVINCIAL NEWSPAPERS.

Norwich Postboy, 1702. *Worcester Postman*, 1709. *Newcastle-on-Tyne Courant*, 1711.

FOREIGN NEWSPAPERS.

Gazette de Vénise, early in the 17th century.

Gazette de France, started by Théophraste Renaudot (now publishing), 30 May, 1631.

Journal de Paris, alleged first French daily paper, 1 Jan. 1777.

Galignani's Weekly Messenger, Paris, begun 1814.

Moniteur, Paris, 1790–1901.

Chinese newspaper published in London, 1876.

Arabic newspaper ,, ,, ,,

The first published in America, the *Boston News Letter*, in 1704; the first at Philadelphia in 1719; and the first in Holland in 1732.

"America whose population is 23 millions and a half, supports 800 newspapers, 50 of these publishing daily), and their annual circulation is stated at 64,000,000. In Paris there exists 169 journals, literary, scientific, religious, and political."—*Westminster Review*, 1830. Nearly 3,000 in 1901. 2,000 dailies in 1903, United States.

REGISTERED NEWSPAPERS.	1850.	1865.	1876.	1881.	1885.	1895.	1903.
London daily	12	22	19	17	20	27	
London weekly	58	166	238	—	318	340	
London generally	—	—	320	378	405	456	454
Eng. prov.	222	750	956	1087	1202	1342	1443
Wales	—	—	—	—	—	—	107
Irish	102	132	138	154	161	168	175
Scotch	110	140	152	181	184	217	233
British isles	14	14	19	20	21	23	19

Total newspapers in the United Kingdom, Feb. 1898, 2418; Feb. 1901, 2488; 1902, 2532; 1903, 2431.

ESTABLISHMENT OF THE PRINCIPAL LONDON NEWSPAPERS, (*Mitchell*) DAILY (1903).

Lloyd's List (with Shipping and Mercantile Gazette) 1726
Public Ledger (*commercial*) . . . 1759
Morning Chronicle (*liberal*), 1770; *extinct* . . . 1862
Morning Herald (*conservative*), 1780, *extinct* 31 Dec. 1869
Morning Post (*whig*, latterly *conservative*) . . 1772
Times (*independent*) . . . 1 Jan. 1788
Sun (*liberal*) *extinct* . . . 1792
Morning Advertiser (*independent*) . . 8 Feb. 1794
Globe (*whig: 1866 conservative*) evening . . 1803
Standard (*conservative*) even. (morn. even. 29 June, 1857) . . . 1827
Shipping and Mercantile Gazette . . 4 Jan. 1836
Daily News (*liberal*) . . . 21 Jan. 1846
Daily Chronicle and Clerkenwell News (*liberal*) . 1855
Daily Telegraph* (*liberal*, latterly *conserv.*), 29 June, ,,
Sporting Life (and Bell's Life in London) . . 1859
Morning Star (*liberal*), 1856; *extinct* . . Oct. 1869
Pall Mall Gazette (*independent*), even. (morn. Jan.–April, 1870) . . . 1865
Sportsman . . . Aug. ,,
Glowworm (*liberal*), *extinct* . . . ,,
Echo ½d. (*independent*) . . . Dec. 1868
Financier (*neutral*) . . . 1870
Hour (*conservative*), 24 March, 1873; *extinct* 11 Aug. 1876
Continental Times (*neutral*) . . . 1878
St. James's Gazette (*anti-radical*) . . May, 1880
Argus (*independent*) . . . ,,
Financial News (*independent*) . . . 1884
Evening Post (*independent*) . . . 1887
Financial Times (*independent*) . . . 1888
Star, ½d. (*radical*) . . . ,,
Daily Graphic (*illustrated*) . . . 1890
Morning (*conservative*) . . . 1892
Morning Leader (*liberal*) . . . ,,
Sun (*independent*) . . . 1893
Westminster Gazette (*liberal*) . . . ,,
Jewish Express (*independent*) . . 21 Jan. 1895
Daily Mail (*imperialist*) . . . 4 May, 1896
Daily Express (*independent*) . . 24 April, 1900
Daily Mirror (*women's daily*) . . 2 Nov. 1903

* 144,000 copies sold on 16th Dec. 1861. The prince consort died on the 14th.

PRINCIPAL SUNDAY, WEEKLY, ETC. (1903).

Lond. Gazette, 7 Nov. 1665
St. James's Chronicle (*conser.*), *united with* 'Press' . . . 1763
County Chronicle . 1787
Mail 1789
Observer (*whig*) . . 1791
Bell's Messenger (*lib. conservative*) . . 1796
Weekly Dispatch (*lib.*) 1801
Examiner (*lib.*, *extinct*) 1808–81
Literary Gazette (*extinct*) . . 1817–62
John Bull (*conserv.*) 1820–92
Bell's Life in London (*sporting*), now with Sporting Life (daily) 1822
Sunday Times (*lib.con.*) ,,
Lancet (*medical*) . 1823
Mechanic's Magazine (*merged into* "Iron," 1873) . . . ,,
Atlas (*liberal*) *extinct* . 1826
Medical Gazette, 1827; Medical Times (*united*) 1850 (*extinct* 1885) 1828
Athenæum (*liter. and scientific*), 1 Jan. . . ,,
Spectator (*liberal*) . ,,
Record (*lib.conserv.*) . ,,
Law Magazine and Review (*new ser.* 1898) . ,,
Court Journal (*neut.*). 1829
Mark Lane Express . 1832
United Service Gazette 1833
Naval and Military Gazette (*extinct*) . ,,
Mining Journal . . 1835
Railway Times . . 1837
Era (*theatrical*) . . ,,
Publishers' Circular . ,,
Ecclesiastical Gazette 1838
Medical Press . . ,,
Tablet (*Rom. Catholic*) 1840
Gardeners' Chronicle . 1841
Nonconformist . . ,,
Punch . . . ,,
Jewish Chronicle . ,,
Pharmaceutical Journ. ,,
Illustrated London News (*neutral*) . 1842
Lloyd's Weekly London Newspaper (*rad.*) ,,
Builder . . . ,,
Inquirer (*lib.*) . . ,,
English Churchman & St. James's Chronicle (*High Church*) 1843
News of the World (*liberal*) . . ,,
Law Times . . . ,,
Economist (*liberal*) . ,,
Farmer (*agricultural*) ,,
Allen's Indian Mail (combined with Homeward Mail) . ,,
Musical Times . . 1844
Agricultural Gazette . ,,
Guardian (*HighChurch*) 1846
Educational Times . 1847
Notes and Queries (*lit. and antiquarian*) . 1849
Journal of Gaslighting ,,
Journal of Society of Arts . . . 1852
Press (*conserv.*), *united with* "St. James's Chronicle" (*extinct*) 1853
Field (*country gentlemen's*) . . . ,,
Civil Service Gazette . ,,
British Medical Journal . . . ,,
Building News . . 1854
Saturday Review (*lit.*) 1855
Overland Mail . ,,
Engineer . . . 1856
Court Circular . . ,,
City Press (*neutral*) . 1857
Homeward Mail . . ,,
Solicitors' Journal . ,,
Bookseller . . . 1858
Photographic News . ,,
Chemical News . . 1859
Christian World . ,,
Army and Navy Gaz. 1860
National Reformer . ,,
Catholic Times . . ,,
Fun (*comic*) . . 1861
Queen (*ladies'*) . . ,,
Church Review (*ritual*) ,,
Owl (*satirical*) *stopped* 1864
English Mechanic . 1865
Engineering . . 1866
Law Journal . . ,,
Land and Water (*nat. hist.*) . . . ,,
Bullionist . . . ,,
Rock (*Protestant*) . 1868
Pall Mall Budget . ,,
Vanity Fair . . ,,
Bazaar . . . ,,
Academy (*literary*) . 1869
Architect . . . ,,
Nature (*scientific*) . ,,
Graphic (*illustrated*) . ,,
Freemason . . . ,,
Journal of Education ,,
Garden . . . 1871
British Mail . . 1872
Metropolitan . . ,,
Iron (*manufactures and science*), 1873; *combined with* "Industries" . . . 1893
Money . . . 1872
Illustrated Sporting and Dramatic News 1874
Pictorial World . . ,,
World . . . ,,
Accountant . . ,,
British Architect . ,,
Sanitary Record . ,,
Whitehall Review . 1876
Bicycling News . . ,,
Truth . . . 1877
Referee . . . ,,
Statist . . . 1878
Electrician . . ,,
Citizen . . . ,,
Life . . . 1879
Lady's Pictorial . . 1880
St. James's Budget . ,,
War Cry . . . ,,
Knowledge . . . 1881
Stage . . . ,,
People . . . ,,
Industries and Iron . 1886
Stock Exchange . . 1887
National Observer . 1888
City Leader . . 1889
County Council Times ,,
Pelican (*society*) . . ,,
Law Gazette . . 1890
Speaker (*liberal*) . ,,
Woman (*for ladies*) . ,,
Black and White (*illustrated*) . . . 1891
Anti-Jacobin (*conservative*) . . . ,,
Express (*neutral*) . ,,
Trade Unionist . . ,,
Sketch (*illustrated*) . 1893
Engineering Review (*monthly*) . . . ,,
London . . . ,,
Westminster Budget . ,,
Commerce . . . ,,
"Lika Joko" (*comic*) 16 Oct. 1894
Realm (*unionist*) (*extinct*) . 16 Nov. ,,
Unicorn (*illus.*), 10 Sep. 1895

Literature (*critical, &c.*) . 23 Oct. 1897	Tatler (*illustrated*) 3 July, 1901
M.A.P. . . . 1898	T.P.'s Weekly, 14 Nov. 1902
Outlook (*conservative*) 5 Feb. ,,	King and his Navy, *amalgamation of the* King *and the* Army and Navy (*illustrated*) Mar. 1903
Review of the Week . 1899	
Sphere (*illustrated*) 26 Jan. 1900	
Military Mail (*independent*). 29 March, 1901	

ROYAL NEWSPAPER PRESS FUND, established 1864, chartered 1890. The king gives 25 guineas, April 1902.

NEW STYLE. Pope Gregory XIII., in order to rectify the errors of the current calendar, published a new one, in which ten days were omitted—5 Oct. 1582, becoming 15 Oct. The new style was adopted in France, Italy, Spain, Denmark, Holland, Flanders, Portugal, in 1582, in Germany in 1584, in Switzerland in 1583 and 1584, in Hungary in 1587; in Scotland in 1600, and in England in 1751. In 1752 eleven days were left out of the calendar—3 Sept. being reckoned as 14 Sept. The difference between the old and new style up to 1699 was 10 days; after 1700, 11 days; after 1800, 12 days. In Russia, Greece, and throughout the East, the old style is still retained. The czar, Alexander II., was born on the 17th April, 1818, old style, 29 April, new style; see *Calendar*.

NEW TESTAMENT, see *Bible*.

NEWTONIAN PHILOSOPHY, the doctrines respecting gravitation, &c., taught by sir Isaac Newton in his "Principia," published in 1687; see *Gravitation*. He was born 25 Dec., 1642; became master of the mint, 1699; president of the Royal Society, 1703; and died 20 March, 1727. A statue of him in marble by Roubiliac was set up at Trinity College, Cambridge, 14 July, 1755, and one in bronze by Theed, at Grantham, 21 Sept. 1858, when lord Brougham delivered a discourse on the life and works of Newton. The latter statue cost 1600*l*., a sum obtained by public subscription.

NEWTOWNBARRY RIOT (S.E. Ireland). At a seizure of stock for tithes, a conflict ensued here between the yeomanry and the people, when thirty-five persons were killed or wounded, 18 June, 1831. The jury at the inquest were unable to agree on a verdict.

NEWTOWN-BUTLER (N. Ireland). On 30 July, 1689, the Enniskilleners under Gustavus Hamilton thoroughly defeated the adherents of James II. commanded by general Maccarty, taking him prisoner with his artillery, arms, and baggage.

NEW YEAR'S DAY, &c. The beginning of the Jewish year was changed and the passover instituted, 1491 B.C. A feast is said to have been instituted by Numa, and dedicated to Janus (who presided over the new year), 1 Jan. 713 B.C.

On this day the Romans sacrificed to Janus a cake of new sifted meal, with salt, incense, and wine; and all the mechanics began something of their art of trade; the men of letters did the same, as to books, poems, &c.; and the consuls, though chosen before, took the chair and entered upon their office this day. Nonius Marcellus refers the origin of NEW-YEAR'S GIFTS among the Romans to Titus Tatius, king of the Sabines, who having considered as a good omen a present of some branches cut in a wood consecrated to Strenia, the goddess of strength, which he received on the first day of the new year, authorised the custom afterwards, and gave these gifts the name of Strenæ, 747 B.C.

NEW YORK, the "empire state" of the United States of N. America, is said to have been discovered by Verrazano, a Florentine in the French service, about 1524, and rediscovered by Hudson, an Englishman in the Dutch service, in 1609, and settled by the Dutch in 1614 the CITY being named Manhattan and New Amsterdam; but the English under colonel Nichols dispossessed them and the Swedes, 27 Aug. 1664, and changed its name, the king, Charles II., having given the territory to his brother, the duke of York. Population of the city, in 1860, 805,651; in 1870, 942,292; in 1880, 1,206,299; in 1890, 1,515,301; of the state in 1880, 5,082,871; in 1890, 5,997,853; 1900, 7,268,894; of Albany, the state capital, in 1880, 90,758; in 1890, 94,923; of Brooklyn, in 1880, 566,663; in 1890, 806,343; of Buffalo, in 1880, 155,134; in 1890, 255,664. Brooklyn with other towns consolidated with New York to form a single city under one government; bill passed 27 Feb. 1894. Population, greater New York, in 1900, 3,444,675.

The city confirmed to England by the peace of Breda . . . . 24 Aug. 1667
Taken by the Dutch, and named New Orange, 1673; surrendered 1674
The city a principal point of the struggle for independence. It surrendered to the British forces under general Howe . . . . 15 Sept. 1776
The city was evacuated by the British; "Evacuation day" made one of rejoicing ever since, 25 Nov. 1783
Academy of the fine arts, and a botanical garden, established in 1804
Fire here; 674 buildings destroyed, and property valued at nearly 20,000,000 dollars . 16 Dec. 1835
Astor library founded by John Jacob Astor I.; see under *Libraries* 1839
Fire; 302 houses burnt . . . . 19 July, 1845
The Park theatre destroyed by fire . 16 Dec. 1848
Serious riot (several lives lost) at the theatre, originating in a dispute between Mr. Macready (English) and Mr. Forrest (American), actors, 10 May, 1849
New York Times first appeared . . 18 Sept. 1851
The Crystal Palace, containing an exhibition of goods from all nations, was opened in the presence of the president of the United States and many other dignitaries . . . . 14 July, 1853
New York suffered severely by large commercial failures, and "hunger demonstrations" took place during the panic . . . . . Nov. 1857
The Crystal Palace destroyed by fire . . 5 Oct. 1858
A magnificent cathedral erected 1859
Great fire; about 50 lives lost . . . 2 Feb. 1860
During the civil war of 1861 New York strongly supported the government of president Lincoln (republican, or abolitionist); but during 1862 a reaction gradually took place, and the opposition (democrat) candidates for congress were elected by large majorities . . . . . Nov. 1862
Fierce riots against conscription; many persons killed and much property destroyed 13-17 July, 1863
Barnum's museum burnt; great loss, 13 July, 1865; again . . . . 2 March, 1868
Great loss and panic through James Fisk and others (the Erie Ring) buying up gold, 22-26 Sept. 1869
Riot through an Orange procession; about 30 killed, 12 July, 1871
Disclosure of great corruption in the municipal government (termed "Tammany frauds," from the council meeting in Tammany hall); public meeting to obtain prompt redress . . 4 Sept. ,,
The Tammany party excluded from office by the elections . . . . Nov. ,,
Demonstrations of the International Society of Workmen repressed . . . . . Dec. ,,
James Fisk, the railway and financial speculator, assassinated by Edw. Stokes, through jealousy, dies . . . . 7 Jan. 1872
Collapse of the Erie railway ring, ruled by Fisk and Jay Gould; new directors elected (including generals Dix and M'Clellan) . . . March, ,,
Much inconvenience by the horse disease . Oct. ,,
Legal proceedings against Gould suspended; he agrees to give up to the company 9,000,000 dollars, Dec. ,,

Stokes convicted of murder, 6 Jan.; new trial, sentenced to imprisonment . . . 30 Oct. 1873
Barnum's museum again burnt; menagerie destroyed; reported . . . . . . Jan. ,,
Financial excitement through the stoppage of Jay, Cooke & Co. . . . . about 18 Sept. ,,
The *hon.* Wm. M. Tweed, of the Tammany ring, convicted of embezzlement (sentenced to 12 years' imprisonment), 19 Nov. Tweed permitted to visit his own house, escapes . . 4 Dec. ,,
Death of W. B. Astor, very rich merchant 24 Nov. 1875
Great fire, with loss of life, 30 buildings destroyed 8 Feb. 1876
Death of Alex T. Stewart, very rich merchant 10 April, ,,
Tweed arrested at Vigo . . . . 8 Sept. ,,
Some of the rocks named "Hell Gate," blown up to improve entrance into the harbour 24 Sept. ,,
"Commodore" Vanderbilt, a "railway king" and great capitalist . . . . died Jan. 1877
Tweed discloses the system of the "Tammany frauds," incriminating many persons Sept. ,,
Abp. Bayley dies . . . . . . 3 Oct. ,,
Great fire at Greenfield's confectionery works, &c., 50 to 60 persons perished . about 20 Dec. ,,
Elevated street-railways in progress . . . 1877-8
Tweed dies in gaol . . . . 12 April, 1878
International exhibition here (in 1883) proposed . 1880
Fall of O'Kelly, the "boss" of New York; once very influential . . . . Dec. ,,
Abbey-park theatre burnt . . . . 30 Oct. 1882
Peter Cooper, philanthropist, founder of the Cooper Institute, died aged 92 . . . . 4 April, 1883
Bridge from New York to Brooklyn, 5989 feet long (constructed by the skill of Mr. and Mrs. Washington Rœbling), begun 3 Jan. 1870; opened 24 May; 12 persons killed in a panic 30 May, ,,
New Metropolitan opera-house opened . 22 Oct. ,,
Centenary of "Evacuation day" celebrated 26 Nov. ,,
The Standard theatre burnt . . . 14 Dec. ,,
Severe panic in the stock market, Wall-street, checked . . . . 12-14 May, 1884
Attempt to kill capt. Phelan, 9 Jan.; to kill O'Donovan Rossa (see *Fenians*) . 2 Feb. 1885
Great ironworkers' strike; compromise 1-16 June, ,,
General Grant's funeral (see *United States*) 8 Aug. ,,
About nine acres of rock (Flood rock) in Hell Gate channel exploded by dynamite . 10 Oct. ,,
Great strike on S.W. railway, early March, 1886; men submit . . . . about 31 March, 1886
Mr. Abram Hewitt elected mayor in opposition to Mr. Henry George . . . . 3 Nov. ,,
Alderman McQuade for bribery, &c., sentenced to seven years' imprisonment and fine . 20 Dec. ,,
Rev. Henry Ward Beecher, popular preacher, &c., of Plymouth church, Brooklyn, dies, aged 73, 8 March, 1887
Destructive blizzard, see *Storm* . 11-13 March, 1888
Messrs. Fairbank's lard refinery works and other establishments on the river side, about half a mile in extent, burnt; two persons killed, others missing; loss about $3,000,000 . 19, 20 April, 1889
Grand Washington celebration, see *United States*, 20-30 April, 1 May, ,,
John Jacob Astor, wealthy benefactor to charities, died . . . . 22 Feb. 1890
Western Union Telegraph building destroyed by explosion and fire; great loss . . 18 July, ,,
Great fire in central New York; estimated loss 1,000,000 dollars . . . . . 30 July, ,,
Strike of servants of the New York central railway, promoted by the Knights of labour, 8 Aug.; defeated, 11 Aug.; fresh strike. . . 15 Aug. ,,
Temporary financial panic connected with the crisis in London . . . about 15 Nov. ,,
Many commercial failures, about 10 Dec.; confidence restored . . . . 12 Dec. ,,
Clinton state prison nearly destroyed by fire, 3 Jan. 1891
Great snow-storm; electric light, telegraph, and telephone communication stopped . 24, 25 Jan. ,,
By a fire in Park-place above 60 persons perish 22 Aug. ,,
A man enters the office of Mr. Russel Sage, demands money, and causes a great explosion by dynamite by which he himself and 4 others are killed . . . . 4 Dec. ,,
The Hôtel Royal, Sixth-avenue, burnt; many perish . . . . 7 Feb. 1892
Mr. William Astor died . . . . . 25 April, ,,
Oswego lumber district nearly destroyed by fire about 21 May, ,,
Death of Mr. Jay Gould, a millionaire . 2 Dec. ,,
Great explosion in a tunnel near East River through the thawing of frozen dynamite; 9 persons killed, 28 Dec. ,,
The American Fine Arts society's buildings opened, Dec. ,,
Severe shock of earthquake in the city and Long Island . . . . 7 March, 1893
International naval review (see *United States*), 27 April, ,,
Death of gen. Wm. C. Young, constructor of canals and railways, aged 94 . . . . 22 Dec. ,,
Greater New York bill passed . . . 27 Feb. 1894
Dr. Talmage's tabernacle and many houses destroyed by fire . . . . . 13 May, ,,
Jones's woods and many buildings destroyed by fire; 50 horses burnt . . . . 15 May, ,,
Strike of 15,000 tailors in sweating establishments for increased wages . . . . 4 Sept. ,,
Great rejoicing at the arrival of the French Atlantic steamer *La Gascogne*, after 16 days' voyage from Havre; all well (part of the machinery broke down, 30 Jan.) . . . . . 12 Feb. 1895
The town of Hamilton (Utica) partly destroyed by fire . . . . 20 Feb. ,,
Max Grauer, an incendiary, sentenced to 30 years' imprisonment . . . . . 1 March, ,,
Death of Mr. Charles Lanman, artist and author; born 1819; reported . . . . 8 March, ,,
The Astor, Lenox, Tilden libraries consolidated (400,000 vols.) and endowed . . March, ,,
The Washington memorial arch inaugurated, 4 May, ,,
The construction of a railway suspension bridge over the Hudson, from New York to Jersey city, authorized . . . . June, ,,
Haarlem ship canal opened by a procession of vessels . . . . 17 June, ,,
Much official reform effected by the mayor, Mr. Strong . . . . . . Feb.—June, ,,
Grand marriage of the duke of Marlborough to Miss Consuelo Vanderbilt . . . 6 Nov. ,,
369 deaths from heat (97° F.) . . . 6-12 Aug. 1896
Mass meeting for the Armenians . . 26 Oct. ,,
National Grant monument inaugurated by pres. M'Kinley . . . . 27 April, 1897
Immigrant station at Ellis island burnt down, 15 June, ,,
Mr. Charles A. Dana, eminent journalist, died, aged 78 . . . . . . about 18 Oct. ,,
Express train falls over into the Hudson river, 28 deaths, near Garrisons . . . . . 24 Oct. ,,
Sudden death of Mr. Henry George, socialist, candidate for the mayoralty . . . 29 Oct. ,,
Judge van Wyck elected mayor, 235,181 votes; Mr. Low, 149,873 (Tammany victory) . 2 Nov. ,,
Disastrous fire in Lower Broadway; warehouses, &c., gutted . . . . . . 4 Dec. 1898
The Windor hotel, Fifth avenue, burnt; 45 deaths, many injured . . . . . 17 March, 1899
Fatal fire, 2 and 3 East Sixty-seventh-street; 12 deaths (Mr. and Mrs. Wallace Andrews and others) . . . . 7 April, ,,
"Idle Hour," Mr. Wm. K. Vanderbilt's house, Long island, burnt; estimated loss, 300,000 dollars . . . . 11 April, ,,
Hotels, &c., burnt down, Coney island . 26 May, ,,
Tramway strike at Brooklyn; serious rioting; dynamite outrage on the elevated railroad; 22 arrests . . . . 18-22 July, ,,
Adm. Dewey welcomed, see *United States*, 29, 30 Sept. ,,
Great fire at Hoboken; North German Lloyd's docks and piers destroyed, several liners greatly damaged; estimated deaths, 200; great heroism shown (189 deaths from the *Main Saale* and *Bremen*). . . . . . . 30 June, 1900
Explosion caused by a fire at Messrs. Tarrant & Co.'s.; many buildings destroyed, 38 persons reported killed or missing, and 104 injured, 29 Oct. ,,

The Carnegie Steel Co. and 6 other concerns purchased by a syndicate or trust headed by Mr. Pierpont Morgan, the capital of the new trust being over 200,000,000*l.* sterling . . Feb. 1901
Temporary panic on the New York stock market, 9 May, ,,
Many deaths from heat; 106° F., 28 June; 989 deaths week ending . . . . . 6 July, ,,
Mr. Low, the *Fusionist*, elected mayor, Tammany defeated by 30,000 . . . . 6 Nov. ,,
Conference between capital and labour *re* strikes, 16 Dec. ,,
Explosion of dynamite in an unfinished subway; 7 deaths, many injured, buildings damaged, 27 Jan. 1902
Fire at an armoury spreads to Park-avenue hotel; Mrs. Salome Foster, a philanthropist, and 16 others killed . . . . 22 Feb. ,,
Mr. O'Dell, republican, elected state governor, 4 Nov. ,,
Explosion of fireworks in Madison-square; 12 killed and 80 injured . . . . . . 4 Nov. ,,
New York chamber of commerce, new building dedicated by president Roosevelt . 11 Nov. ,,
Gen. Greene made police commissioner; initiates effective reforms . . . . . 1 Jan. 1903
Intense cold in New York, much inconvenience and distress caused by the coal famine, about 13 Jan. ,,
Explosion at fort Lafayette, 5 deaths . 19 Feb. ,,
Great mass meeting to protest against the Kishineff massacres and treatment of Jews in Russia (*which see*), April, 1903 . . . . . 7 June, ,,
Intense heat wave, 56 deaths, 182 cases of severe prostration . . . . . mid July, ,,
Members of the hon. artillery company land; entertained in New York while on their visit to the Boston artillery company of Massachusetts, 7 Oct. ,,
Magnetic storm, fine display of the *aurora borealis*; disorganization of telegraphic and telephonic services . . . . 31 Oct. ,,
Tammany victory (63,617 majority) at municipal elections, Mr. Geo. B. McClellan returned as mayor of New York . . . . . . 3 Nov. ,,

See under *United States*.

NEW ZEALAND (in the Pacific Ocean), discovered by Tasman in 1642. The country remained unknown, and was supposed to be part of a southern continent, till 1769-70, when it was circumnavigated by captain Cook. In 1773, he planted several spots of ground on this island with European garden seeds; and in 1777, he found some fine potatoes. European population in 1860, 84,294; Dec. 1865, 190,607; 1874, 310,895, natives (Maoris), 46,016; in 1881, 489,933; 1887, 603,340 Europeans; 1891, 626,830; about 42,000 natives; 1902, 851,063; 707,920 whites, 43,143 Maoris. 1859, imports, 1,551,030*l.*; exports, 551,484*l.*; 1874, imports, 6,464,687*l.*; exports, 5,610,371*l.*; 1887, imports, 6,245,515*l.*; exports, 6,865,169*l.*; 1890, imports, 6,260,505*l.*; exports, 9,811,720*l.*; 1896, imports, 7,035,379*l.*; exports, 9,321,105*l.* 1900-1901, imports, 10,646,096*l.*; exports, 13,246,161*l.*; 1902–1903, imports, 11,500,000*l.*, exports, 15,000,000*l.*; 1887-8, revenue, 3,521,490*l.*; expenditure, 4,082,634*l.*; 1890-91, revenue, 4,208,029*l.*; expenditure, 4,081,566*l.*; 1894-95, revenue, 4,406,515*l.*; expenditure, 4,266,722*l.*; 1896-97, revenue, 4,886,109*l.* 9*s.* 8*d.*; expenditure, 4,563,425*l.* 14*s.* 2*d.*; 1902-03, revenue, 6,447,435*l.*; expenditure, 6,214,019*l.* Public debt, 1888, 38,758,437*l.*; 1891, 38,830,350*l*; 31 March, 1897, 44,366,618*l.* Railways, miles working, in 1877, 860; in March, 1897, 2,018. Number of telegraph stations open in 1866, 13; in 1897, 780; in 1901, 7,469 mi. of telegraph lines.

The right of Great Britain to New Zealand recognised at the peace in 1814
No constitutional authority placed over it until a resident subordinate to New South Wales . 1833
New Zealand company established; Wellington founded 1839
Capt. Hobson, the first governor, landed, 29 Jan.; treaty of Waitangi signed, by which the chiefs cede a large amount of land . . . 5 Feb. 1840
New Zealand an independent colony and a bishop's see . . . . April, 1841
Capt. (aft. adm.) Fitzroy, governor, Dec. 1843 to Nov. 1845
Sir George Grey, governor . . . . Nov. ,,
A charter, founded upon an act passed in 1846, creating powers, municipal, legislative, and administrative . . . . . . 29 Dec. 1847
This charter was not acted on; a legislative council opened by the governor . . . 20 Dec. 1848
Foundation of Auckland, 1840; Nelson and Taranaki (or New Plymouth), 1841; Otago, 1848; Canterbury 1850
New Zealand company relinquish charter . . ,,
New constitution granted 1852
Settlement of Canterbury, South island, founded (capital Christchurch) 1850–3
Col. Wynyard, governor . . Jan. 1854—Sept. 1855
Governor Browne . . . . Oct. ,,
An earthquake; not much damage done, 23 Jan. ,,
Constitution modified 1857
New bishoprics established: Christ Church, 1856; Nelson and Wellington, 1858; Waiapu . 1859
Insurrection of the natives (Maoris) under a chief named William King (Wirrimu Kingi), arising out of disputes respecting the sale of land; the bishop Selwyn and others consider the natives unjustly treated . . . . March, 1860
Indecisive actions between the militia and volunteers and the Maoris . . . 14-28 March, ,,
War breaks out at Taranaki; the British repulsed with loss . . . . 30 June, ,,
Great excitement in Australia; troops sent to New Zealand, under gen. Pratt, land . . 3 Aug. ,,
Indecisive actions . . 10, 19 Sept., 9, 12 Oct. ,,
Gen. Pratt defeats the Maoris at Mahoetahi, and destroys their fortified places . . 6 Nov. ,,
New Zealand colonists in England justify the conduct of the governor . . . . 22 Nov. ,,
The Maoris defeated, 29 Dec. 1860; 23 Jan., 24 Feb. 16-18 March, 1861
The war ends: surrender of natives . 19 March, ,,
Sir George Grey re-appointed governor . . June, ,,
Gold discovered at Otago, &c. . . . . June, ,,
A native sovereignty proclaimed; 5000 British soldiers in the island . . . . . . July, ,,
Loyalty of the natives increasing . . . May, 1862
The Maori chiefs sign a poetical address of condolence to the queen on the death of the prince consort; received . . . . Nov. ,,
Natives attack a military escort and kill 8 persons, 4 May, 1863
Waikato tribe driven from a fort . . 17 July, ,,
War spreads; natives construct rifle pits . Aug. ,,
Proposed confiscation of Waikato lands . . Sept. ,,
Gen. Cameron severely defeats the Maoris at Rangariri . . . . 20 Nov. ,,
Continued success of gen. Cameron; capitulation of the Maori king . . . . . . 9 Dec. ,,
British attack on Galepa (the gate pah) repulsed with loss of officers and men . 29 April, 1864
Loan of 1,000,000*l.* to New Zealand; guaranteed by parliament . . . . July, ,,
Several tribes submit . . . . Aug. ,,
Maori prisoners escape and form the nucleus of a new insurrection . . . . . . Sept. ,,
Sir George Grey issues proposals of peace, 25 Oct.; the Aborigines Protection Society send religious, moral, and political advice to the Maoris (considered injudicious) . . . . . Nov. ,,
Change of ministry and policy; seat of government to be removed from Auckland to Wellington on Cook's Strait . . . . . . 24 Nov. ,,
Maoris' attack on Cameron severely defeated, 25 Jan.; again . . . . . . 25 Feb. 1865
Outbreak of the Pai Mariri or Hau-hau heresy, a compound of Judaism and paganism, amongst the Maoris; the rev. C. S. Volkner murdered and many outrages committed, 2 March; proclamation of governor sir George Grey against it; it is checked by the agency of a friendly native chief We-tako, April, ,,

William Thompson, an eminent chief, surrenders on behalf of the Maori king . . 25 May, 1865
New Zealand still unsettled . . . July, ,,
The Hau-haus beaten in several conflicts, Aug.; the governor proclaims peace, 2 Sept.; British troops about to leave . . . 15 Sept. ,,
The Maoris treacherously kill the envoys of peace; resignation of the Weld ministry; one formed by Mr. Stafford . . . . . Oct. ,,
Bishopric of Dunedin, Otago, founded . . ,,
General Chute subdues the Hau-haus . Jan. 1866
Progress of peace measures . . April, ,,
Murderers of Mr. Volkner executed . 17 May, ,,
Governor announces cessation of the war, 3 July, ,,
Death of Wm. Thompson, the Maori chief, 28 Dec. ,,
Sir George F. Bowen appointed to succeed sir George Grey; gazetted . . . 19 Nov. 1867
Act relating to the government of New Zealand passed in the British parliament . . . 1868
Geo. Samuel Evans (an eminent colonist, 1838-9) dies 23 Sept. ,,
Te Kooti, a chief, and about 150 Maori convicts, escape from Chatham island to the mainland, 4 July; they repulse troops sent against them, 7 Sept.; massacre the whites at Poverty bay, 10 Nov. ,,
Te Kooti and the rebels defeated by col. Whitmore; 130 Maoris killed . . . . 5 Jan. 1869
Massacre of settlers at Taranaki . . . 12 Feb. ,,
Change of ministry; hon. Mr. Fox's proposal to pay for British troops declined by the home government . . . . . Sept. ,,
Te Kooti, thrice defeated by the colonists and friendly natives, a fugitive . . . . Oct. ,,
Despatch from earl Granville, insisting on the withdrawal of the British troops (18th regiment) causes much dissatisfaction . . 7 Oct. ,,
Friendly interview between Mr. McLean and the Maori king's minister . . . 8 Nov. ,,
Increased demand for the New Zealand fibrous plant, *Phormium tenax* . . . 1869-70
Departure of the last British troops . 22 Jan. 1870
Te Kooti, refusing to surrender at discretion, 24 Jan., narrowly escapes . . 5 Feb. ,,
Te Kooti's party attacked and dispersed; his speedy capture anticipated . . 31 July, ,,
The duke of Edinburgh, in the *Galatea*, at Wellington . . . . . 27 Aug. ,,
Increase of prosperity reported; loan of 4,000,000*l.* proposed . . . . . Aug. ,,
Political union of the islands effected . . Aug. ,,
Murder of Mr. Todd, surveyor, by Maoris, 28 Dec. ,,
Te Kooti reported as living by plunder; acting as a fanatical potentate . . . . Nov. 1871
University with three colleges established in . ,,
Friendly meeting of Mr. McLean with Wirrimu Kingi and other chiefs, who submit to the British government . . . . . March, 1872
Mr. Stafford's ministry resigns, succeeded by one under Mr. Waterhouse (the Fox party) about Oct. ,,
Sir James Fergusson appointed governor, March, 1873
The marquis of Normanby governor . . Jan 1875
The Maori king (Tawhiao) submits to the British government . . . . . . Feb. ,,
The colony reported highly prosperous by sir Julius Vogel, ex-premier . . 31 Oct. 1877
Sir Hercules G. R. Robinson governor . April, 1879
Disputes with the Maoris; they expel British settlers near New Plymouth, Taranaki; and plough the land . . . . 25 May, ,,
The settlers recover their land by force 22 June, ,,
Great influence of Erueti, now Te Whiti, a fanatical Christian Maori, aged 45; he supports Maori claims, but checks bloodshed . . . ,,
Sir George Grey, energetic liberal premier, resigns; succeeded by hon. John Hall . . Oct. ,,
Sir Arthur Hamilton Gordon appointed governor . 1880
Apprehended outbreak at Parihaka under the Maori chief, Te Whiti; volunteers coming forward 31 Oct. 1881
Te Whiti arrested for sedition announced 6 Nov. ,,
He counsels passive resistance . . 8 Nov. ,,
124 arrests . . . . announced 17 Nov. ,,
Difficulty peaceably settled . announced 3 Dec. ,,
Resignation of the Hall ministry . about 10 April, 1882
Public debt, 31,400,000*l.* . . . 31 March, ,,
Several Maori chiefs in London; received by the prince of Wales, 17 Aug.; sail for home 7 Sept. ,,

Sir William Jervois, governor . . . Jan. 1883
Release of Te Whiti, John, and others 8 March, ,,
Mahuki and 20 others sentenced to imprisonment for outrages . . . . about 7 May, ,,
Communication between New Zealand and the Thames by steamers; time reduced to 40 days (14,000 carcases of sheep brought) . . Dec. ,,
Tawhaio, the Maori king, arrives in London, 2 June; visits theatres, &c., and receives visitors; received by the earl of Derby; appeals for redress, referring to the treaty of Waitangi (1840), 22 July; sails from Gravesend . . . 20 Aug. 1884
Mr. H. A. Atkinson forms a ministry, 28 Aug.; resigns 30 Aug. . . . . . ,,
Lieut. Bryce, colonial native minister, *v.* G. W. Rusden, for gross libel in "History of New Zealand," charging him with cruelty, &c., to the Maoris; damages awarded, 5000*l.* 12 March, 1886
Destructive volcanic eruption of Tarawera mountain; about 60 miles of beautiful fertile country desolated by showers of lava, hot cinders, and mud; about 100 persons killed; Wairoa destroyed . . . . . 9, 10 June, ,,
The Maori king reconciled, sits in the legislative council . . . . . . May, ,,
Maori incursions on European lands . . July, ,,
Ministry resign 30 Sept.; Mr. H. A. Atkinson forms a ministry . . . . 9 Oct. 1887
The earl of Onslow, governor . . . Nov. 1888
The debate on the Representation bill to increase the number of country members of parliament at Wellington lasted 76 hours, adjourned 27 July; amicable arrangement between town and country parties . . . . . . 29 July, 1889
International exhibition at Dunedin opened about 26 Nov. ,,
Rev. A. B. Suter, bishop of Nelson, declared primate . . . . . . Dec. ,,
A shipping strike begun at Wellington 5 Sept., ended . . . . . . 31 Oct. 1890
Resignation of ministry; new cabinet under hon. J. Ballance . . . . . 24 Jan. 1891
First visit to the Uriwera country, North island; the earl of Onslow well received by the Maoris, reported April; he resigns . . . Nov. ,,
Women authorized to serve in parliament and to vote at elections, 4 Sept.; the bill rejected by the legislative council . . . 10 Sept. ,,
Sir George Grey's 80th birthday enthusiastically celebrated . . . about 14 April, 1892
Tawhaio, the 2nd Maori king, accepts a pension, May, ,,
Buckley v. *Edwards*, see under *Judges* . 21 May, ,,
Two Americans, Messrs. Witham and Webster's old claim for compensation for seizure of land, purchased from native chiefs; the senate of U.S.A. recommend arbitration . . . 26 May, ,,
The earl of Glasgow governor . . . . 7 June, ,,
Arrival of the earl of Glasgow . . . 7 June, ,,
Disagreement between the earl of Glasgow, the governor, and the ministry, who desire the appointment of 12 additional members of the legislative council; the matter referred to the home government, about 23 Aug., which agrees with the ministry . . . . . 26 Sept. ,,
Twelve new members appointed . about 16 Oct. ,,
The Maoris' petition for a separate representative council declined . . . . Oct. ,,
Great fire at Hastings, Hawke's bay district; estimated damage 50,000*l.* . . . . 8 Feb. 1893
Death of Mr. J. Ballance, the premier; succeeded by Mr. Richard J. Seddon . . . 1 May, ,,
Act passed conferring the elective franchise on women . . . . 19 Sept. ,,
General election; victory of the government, reported . . . . . . 29 Nov. ,,
Financial surplus 200,000*l.*, reported . 13 April, 1894
The New Zealand loan and mercantile agency company, established 1865; misunderstandings about debentures; counsel consulted; advice not acted on, 1879-80; new debentures issued, 1892; petition to chancery for reconstruction of the company granted conditionally, 11 April, 1894; examination of the directors and officers before Mr. justice Vaughan Williams, chancery division, 13-27 April; his statement respecting the evidence; the directors collectively, including Mr. Mundella, sir John E. Gorst, and sir James

Fergusson, severely censured for reticence as to the unsecured condition of the early debenture-holders and the financial condition of the company, for misleading balance-sheets and reports, and for payments of dividends not justified, &c., 7 May, 1894
Death of Tawhiao, king of the Maoris . 27 Aug. ,,
Desire of the government to administer the Samoan isles, reported . . . . . . Oct. ,,
Parliament opened; cheerful prospects . 20 June, 1895
Death of Mr. justice Christopher Wm. Richmond, statesman, aged 74 . . . . . 3 Aug. ,,
Bill embodying the recommendations of the committee on the affairs of the New Zealand bank passed . . . . 3 Sept. ,,
An explosion of fire-damp at the Brunner mine, W. coast of South island, 67 deaths, 26 March . 1896
Mr. Watson, president of the bank of New Zealand, refusing to give evidence; pays 500*l*. fine, reported . . . . . . 20 July, ,,
Asiatics exclusion bill passed . . . 3 Sept. ,,
A committee of the legislative council issue their report on the banking legislation, 1894 and 1895, and exonerate the government from corruption, and declare the Bank of New Zealand to be in a stable condition, Sept.; reorganisation recommended . . . . Oct. ,,
The Banking bill abandoned by parliament, session closed, reported . . . . . 18 Oct. ,,
General election: government majority . 5 Dec. ,,
Sir James Prendergast, administrator . 8 Feb. 1897
Earl of Ranfurly appointed governor, April; arrives . . . . 10 Aug. ,,
Diamond Jubilee celebrations throughout the country . . . . . . 20 June *et seq.* ,,
Parliament opened, important measures proposed by the governor, 23 Sept.; eight hours day and labour bills passed . . . . 17 Nov. ,,
Death of prof. Kirk, eminent botanist, conservator of forests (1886) . . . abt. 12 March, 1898
The earl of Ranfurly, the governor, and rear-adm. Pearson visit Papanui; received with great loyalty by a large Maori gathering, about 26 May, ,,
Parliament opened by the governor . 24 June, ,,
Death of Sir George Grey . . . . Sept. ,,
Municipal franchise reform act passed . 15 Oct. ,,
Old-age pensions act passed (amended 1900–1901) 1 Nov. ,,
Difficulty with Austrian emigrants, great distress, Dec. ,,
The rev. Wm. Colenso, F.R.S., missionary and naturalist, died, aged 87 . . . 10 Feb. 1899
Sir Julius Vogel, ex-premier, great financier, born 1835, died . . . . . . 13 March, ,,
Divorce bill passed, 1898; royal assent 13 April, ,,
Victoria university college opened in Wellington, April, ,,
Sir James Prendergast, chief justice, resigns, 25 May; succeeded by sir Robert Stout, 22 June, ,,
Parliament opened by the governor with a cheerful speech . . . . 23 June, ,,
Vote of want of confidence rejected by a majority of 7, 6 July; session closed . . 24 Oct. ,,
Mr. Seddon's budget statement, 490,000*l*. surplus, 1 Aug. ,,
General election; government victory, reported, 6 Dec. ,,
Great enthusiasm on the departure of troops for S. Africa . . . . 20 Jan. 1900
Parliament opened by the governor. . 22 June, ,,
Mr. Seddon's budget statement; surplus, 605,000*l*. 17 Aug. ,,
Pacific islands visited by lord Ranfurly (Cook, Savage, and Suwarrow formally annexed, June, 1901) . . . . Oct. ,,
Fire at the Rochester orphan asylum, 28 deaths, 8 Jan. 1901
Lord Ranfurly returns from his tour in the Pacific . . . . 21 Jan. ,,
Universal mourning on the death of the queen, 22 Jan. ,,
British troops welcomed at Wellington . 9 Feb. ,,
Death of dean Jacobs, an influential churchman and writer . . . . . end March, ,,
Government 4-per-cent. loan of 500,000*l*., subscribed twice over, reported . . . . 23 April, ,,
Parliament opened . . . . . . 2 July, ,,
The duke and duchess of Cornwall land at Auckland, 11 June, 1902
Army and naval review, stone for a Maori girls' school laid, 12 June; the Maoris visited at Rotorna, 13 June; at Wellington, honours conferred on lord Ranfurly and others, 300 war medals distributed, 18, 19 June; grand military review at Christchurch, 24 June; first stone of a statue to Queen Victoria laid at Dunedin (see *Van Dieman's Land*) . . . . 27 June, ,,
Royal commission on federation, report unanimously against it . . . . . . Aug. ,,
Arbitration and conciliation bill read third time in the representatives . . . . 12 Oct. ,,
Patriotic mass meeting at Wellington; resolutions passed "approving the British conduct of the S. African war, and Mr. Chamberlain's refutation of foreign slanders" . . . . 17 Jan. ,,
Enthusiastic send-off of the 8th and 9th contingents (total sent during the war, 6,700 officers and men, 6,620 horses) . 8 Feb., 12 March, ,,
Loyal meeting of Maoris at Papawai, North Island, reported . . . . 7 April, ,,
Mr. Seddon, premier, presented with a warm address, 20,000 signatures (and a purse of about 5,000*l*.), at Christchurch . . . 8 April, ,,
Dr. Cowie, bishop of Auckland and primate, died, 27 June, ,,
Parliament opened, governor's speech . 1 July ,,
Maori councils (local self-government) act of 1901, reported successful . . . . . 8 July, ,,
Budget statement, surplus, 367,000*l*., public debt increased by 3,370,000*l*. in 1901; loan of 1,750,000*l*. proposed, 8 July; passed . . . . 7 Aug. ,,
Mr. Seddon welcomed at Johannesburg, Pretoria, and Cape Town, 21, 22, 26 May; London, the king's guest, 14 June; receives a testimonial, 21 July; in the provinces, Aug.; leaves 8 Sept. ,,
Parliament prorogued . . . . . . 4 Oct. ,,
Mr. Seddon welcomed home . . . . 25 Oct. ,,
General election, government majority, 49, 25 Nov. ,,
Mr. Seddon, in a speech at New Plymouth, refers to the continued prosperity of the colony; the prospect of a splendid harvest and the good prices obtained for products; there would be a surplus of 250,000*l*. in the revenue; considerable reduction had been made in the expenditure, and further economies would be made, especially on internal defence; the population of the colony was increasing at the rate of over 1,500 per month, mid Feb. 1903
Mahuta, the Maori king, appointed a member of the legislative and executive councils 22 May, ,,
Empire day, the governor opens the veterans' home in Auckland . . . . . . 24 May, ,,
Celebrations at Wellington in honour of Mr. Seddon (10 years premier); he reports progress and prosperity (surplus 303,905*l*.), 4 May; he unveils a war memorial at Hokitaka, speaks in favour of Mr. Chamberlain's fiscal scheme, resolution supporting it carried . . . . . . 3 June, ,,
Parliament opened; governor states that fiscal changes and amendment of the constitution of the privy council are necessary . . 30 June, ,,
Dispute between the judges and the executive respecting precedence, &c. . . Feb.–July, ,,
Budget revenue: increase 84,000*l*., credit balances 570,000*l*., reported . . . . . 11 Aug. ,,
Eruption of the Waimangu geyser, 4 persons killed, 29 Aug. ,,
Naval defence bill, providing for annual sum of 40,000*l*. towards the maintenance of the Australian squadron, introduced . . . mid Oct. ,,
1,000,000*l*. loan bill for public works passes the house of representatives, money to be raised in the colony; statement by Mr. Seddon, that notwithstanding the largely increased revenue of the colony economy would be practised by the government and the reduction in expenditure continued . . . . 16 Oct. ,,

NEY'S EXECUTION. Ney, duke of Elchingen, prince of the Moskwa, and one of the most valiant of the marshals of France, was shot as a traitor, 7 Dec. 1815. On 7 Dec. 1853, his statue was erected on the spot where he fell.

After the abdication of Napoleon I., 5 April, 1814, Ney took the oath of allegiance to the king, Louis XVIII. On Napoleon's return to France from Elba, he marched against him; but his troops deserting, he regarded the cause of the Bourbons as lost, and opened the invader's way to Paris, March, 1815. Ney led the attack of the French at Waterloo, where he fought in the midst of the slain, his clothes pierced with bullet-holes, five horses having been shot under him; night and defeat obliged him to flee. Though included in the decree of 24 July, 1815, which guaranteed the safety of all Frenchmen, he was sought out, and on 5 Aug. taken at the castle of a friend at Urillac, and brought to trial before the Chamber of Peers, 4 Dec. The 12th article of the capitulation of Paris, fixing a general amnesty, was quoted in his favour in vain.

NEZIB, Syria. Here Ibrahim and the Egyptians defeated the Turks, 24 June, 1839.

NIAGARA (N. America). At the head of this river, on the western shore, is Fort Erie, which was taken by the English, 24 July, 1759. It was abandoned in the war with the United States, 27 May, 1813, but was retaken, 19 Dec. following. A suspension bridge of a single span of 820 feet over the Niagara, connecting the railways of Canada and New York, was opened in March, 1855. It is elevated 18 feet on the Canadian, and 28 feet on the American side; superseded by a great new steel arch bridge, last panel fitted, 28, 29 March, 1897, a great engineering feat, constructed by the Pennsylvanian steel company for the Canadian and New York incorporations. There are at present four bridges crossing the river.

About eighteen miles below Fort Erie are the remarkable falls. The river is here 740 yards wide; the half-mile immediately above the cataracts is a rapid, in which the water falls 58 feet; it is then thrown, with astonishing grandeur, down a stupendous precipice of 150 feet perpendicular, in three distinct and collateral sheets; and, in a rapid that extends to the distance of nine miles below, falls nearly as much more. The river then flows in a deep channel till it enters lake Ontario, at Fort Niagara.

The falls visited by the prince of Wales, Sept. 1860.

Blondin crossed the falls on a tight rope, 30 June *et seq.* to 2 Sept. 1859; and again in 1860.

Professor Tyndall visited the falls, Nov., 1872, and lectured on them at the Royal Institution, 4 April, 1873.

Company formed to utilize its water power mechanically, 1877.

Capt. Matt Webb drowned while attempting to swim across the whirlpool rapids, 24 July, 1883.

Niagara international park purchased by the U.S. government, opened 15 July, 1885.

Mr. Carlisle D. Graham, an Englishman, passed through the rapids safely in a barrel shaped like a buoy, seven feet long, 11 July, 1886; again, 15 June, 1887.

Wm. J. Kendall in a cork vest swims through the rapids, 22 Aug. 1886.

The huge upper table rock fell, due to weight of accumulated ice, 13 Jan. 1887.

Mr. Hollingshead's grand "cyclorama" of Niagara, London, opened 12 March, 1888, closed 29 Nov. 1890.

Mr. Carlisle D. Graham after long preparation said to have "shot Niagara (rapids) in a barrel" 25 Aug. 1889.

Mr. Dixon crosses Niagara river below the falls on a wire rope, 6 Sept. 1890.

An international commission (president, sir Wm. Thomson, afterwards lord Kelvin) was appointed to consider the best method for utilizing 125,000 horse-power, of the force of the Niagara falls, which is computed to be about 4,500,000 horse-power. Prizes were given by the Cataract company to the authors of various projects 9 Feb. 1891.

In the *Times* of 8 June, 1892, professor George Forbes, who was engaged in the undertaking, reported that the engineering works were nearly completed, and that the electrical arrangements by which the vast force was to be transmitted, were begun.

The force is to be used in factories, in lighting Niagara Falls city, and in working railways. In 1892 the work was carried on by the Niagara Falls Power company.

The great power house completed, 5,000 horse-power dynamos constructed by the Westinghouse company, reported Dec., 1894.

Mr. T. C. Martin, of New York, gave an illustrated discourse on the "Utilisation of Niagara," at the Royal Institution, London, 19 June, 1896.

Receipt of 15,000 horse-power from the Niagara works at Buffalo, 26 miles distant, midnight, Sunday, 15 Nov. 1896.

Prof. Forbes introduces further developments with success, reported, 24 Aug. 1899; 100,000 horse power, in 1902.

Strike riot among workmen employed by the Canadian electrical power companies, resulting from a reduction of wages, 2 Nov. 1903.

NIBELUNGENOT or **Nibelungen-Lied**, a popular German epic of the 12th century, composed of various ancient mythical poems, termed sagas; which, according to the poet Wm. Morris, should be to our race what Homer was to the Greeks.

The first critical edition, by K. Lachmann, appeared 1826 and 1846. The best translation in modern German, by Simrock, 1827; a useful edition, with translation and glossary, by L. Braunfels, 1846; in English, by W. N. Lettsom, 2nd ed. 1874.

Richard Wagner's musical dramas, "The Ring of the Nibelungen," are based on this poem: the persons include the great Northern gods and goddesses, the giants, the dwarfs, and the daughters of the Rhine (see under *Music*).

NICÆA, see *Nice*.

NICARAGUA, a state in Central America (*which see*). The present constitution was established 19 Aug. 1858. At the commencement of 1855 it was greatly disturbed by two political parties: that of the president, Chamorro, who held Granada, the capital, and that of the democratic chief, Castellon, who held Leon. The latter invited Walker, the filibuster, to his assistance, who in a short time became sole dictator of the state.* By

* William Walker was born at Tennessee, in the United States, where he became successively doctor, lawyer, and journalist, and afterwards gold-seeker in California, whence he was invited to Nicaragua by Castellon, with the promise of 52,000 acres of land, on condition of bringing with him a band of adventurers to sustain the revolutionary cause. Walker accepted the terms, and on 28 June landed at Realejo with 68 men. He increased his forces at Leon, and soon after attacked the town of Rivas, where he was repulsed with loss. He then joined col. Kinney, who had occupied and governed Grey Town, 6 Sept. On 13 Oct. Walker captured Granada by surprise when in a defenceless state, shot Mayorga, one of the ministers, and established a rule of terror. By intervention of the American consul he made peace with the general of the state army, Corral, but shot him on 7 Nov., on finding him corresponding with fugitives at Costa Rica. Walker at first was only general-in-chief; but on Rivas, whom he had made president, deserting him, he became sole dictator. On 14 May, 1856, his envoy Vijil was recognised by the president of the United States, whence also he obtained reinforcements during his retention of power. Costa Rica declared war against him, 28 Feb. 1856; the other states of central America soon followed the example, and a sanguinary struggle ensued, lasting till May, 1857. On 25 Nov. 1856, Walker totally burnt Granada, being unable to defend it, and removed the seat of government to Rivas. This place he surrendered to gen. Mora on 1 May, 1857, on the intervention of capt. Davis, of the *St. Mary's*, U.S. Himself, his staff, and 260 men were conveyed in that vessel to New Orleans, where they were received with great enthusiasm. On 25 Nov., 1857, he again invaded Nicaragua, landing at Punta Arenas with 400 men; but on 8 Dec. was compelled to surrender to capt. Paulding, U.S., and was conveyed to New York. He escaped punishment by *nolle prosequi* (2 June, 1858): but capt. Paulding was tried for exceeding orders, and blamed—yet excused by president Buchanan. On 5 Aug. 1860,

the united efforts of the confederated states the filibusters were all expelled in May, 1857. On 1 May, 1858, Nicaragua and Costa Rica appealed to the great European powers for protection. Nicaragua railway, a transit route between the Pacific and Atlantic, proposed, and company formed Nov. 1866. President T. Martinez elected, 1859 and 1863; Fernando Guzman, elected 1 March, 1867; Vicente Quadra elected 1 Feb. 1871; Pedro Joaquin Chamorro, 1 Feb. 1875; Joaquin Zavala, 1 March, 1879; dr. Adam Cardenas, Jan. 1883; señor Carazo, 16 Dec. 1886. Population in 1897, 310,000.

Louis Napoleon, afterwards emperor, proposed the making a ship canal by the lake Nicaragua from the Atlantic to the Pacific, between 1842-4; the government of Nicaragua proposed it in 1846; colonel Childs made a survey in 1851; a company was chartered for 85 years, and conventions were signed, but the capitalists declined their support.

The scheme was revived in Feb. 1875. See *Panama* and *Loans*.

Treaty by which the United States may construct a canal (Menscall's plan) from San Juan (Grey Town) on the Caribbean sea to Brito, on the Pacific, with equal powers; contrary to the Bulwer Clayton treaty, *which see*, about 16 Dec. 1884; rejected by the United States legislature, 30 Jan. 1885.

The senate and house pass the Nicaragua canal bill, 7 Feb. 1889.

The construction of a breakwater at Grey Town begun June, 1889.

Death of sig. Carazo; Dr. Sacaza elected president; reported 2 Aug. 1889; re-elected about 9 Oct. 1890.

The construction of the Nicaragua canal begun 22 Oct. 1889; the bill for it abandoned by the U.S.A. senate, 27 Feb. 1891.

Insurrection in Granada suppressed with bloodshed (the leaders exiled), 23 Aug. 1891.

Convention of delegates respecting the canal meets at New Orleans, 30 Nov. 1892.

Insurrection; the rebels capture fort San Carlos and fort Castillo, 11 May, 1893; joined by ex-president Cardenaz and gen. Gutierrez; the insurgents defeated by president Sacaza, May; the government troops defeated at Masaya, 20 May; negotiations for peace; president Sacaza resigns; new government formed by compromise, 30 May; Salvador Machado, president, 1 June; the revolutionists enter the city, 6 June; take Corinto and Chinandega, reported July; gen. José Santos Zelaya, president, reported, 18 July; government overtures rejected by the insurgents; fighting continued, 21 July; Managua captured by the insurgents, reported 26 July; they occupy Masaya, 31 July; treaty of peace; the Leon party supreme; gen. Zelaya retires; amnesty reported, 3 Aug. 1893.

War with Honduras, *which see*, Jan. 1894.

Dispute with Mosquito territory (*which see*), 1894.

By an explosion at the military barracks at Granada, many lives lost, 9 Oct. 1894.

The canal bill passed by the U.S.A. senate; 70,000,000 dollars to be guaranteed; the secretary of the U.S. treasury to have the supervision of the work, ten of the directors to be appointed by the president, 26 Jan. 1895; unfavourable report of the commission of engineers, &c., on the scheme, announced, Dec. 1895; preliminary report, cost to be 115,000,000 dols., Dec. 1898; bill passed U.S.A. senate, 21 Jan. 1899; convention revising the Clayton-Bulwer treaty of 1850, signed by lord Pauncefote and Mr. Hay, 5 Feb. 1900; the concession to the Maritime Canal Co., reported, 26 April, 1900.

The new Hay-Pauncefote canal treaty, superseding the Clayton-Bulwer treaty, signed at Washington, 18 Nov. 1901. See *United States*.

The *Panama* canal bill passed by U.S. congress, 26 June; signed by pres. Roosevelt, 28 June, 1902.

Ultimatum: Great Britain demands 15,500*l.* as reparation for injuries to British subjects, &c., 19 March, 1895.

Nicaragua proposes that all questions should be referred to impartial arbitration, 15 April, 1895.

Arrival of 3 British war-ships at Corinto, 22 April, 1895.

Payment of indemnity demanded within 3 days, 24 April; refused, 26 April; the republic declared under martial law, 28 April, 1895.

Corinto occupied by the British unopposed, 27 April; capt. Trench installed governor, 28 April, 1895.

Pres. Zelaya protests against the British occupation, &c., 28 April, 1895.

Nicaragua agrees to pay 15,500*l.* within 15 days after the British evacuate Corinto, 30 April, 1895.

The minister of Salvador in London authorized to pay the indemnity: the British retire from Corinto, 4 May, 1895; a convention agreed to, announced, 18 March, 1896.

Revolt in the north-west; pres. Zelaya declares himself dictator, reported 25 Feb. 1897.

Severe defeat of the rebels at Matearis and Nargote, guns captured, reported, 2 March; Matapa and Mora taken by pres. Zelaya, reported, 18 March, 1897.

Serious disturbances by the Honduras soldiers at Corinto suppressed by the British and American marines, with the approbation of the president, 2-4 May, 1897.

Nicaraguan rebels (300) evacuate San Juan dal Sur, 7 Feb.; rebels defeated at Rivas, 8 Feb. 1898.

Country unsettled: Aguas Calientes captured by the troops, Feb. 1899; gen. Reyes, insurgent leader, surrenders to British and U.S. cruisers; marines landed at Blewfields, 28 Feb. 1899.

Gen. Torres, dictator, demands repayment of duties; martial law declared; reported, 25 March, 1899.

Gen. Zelaya inaugurated president on re-election, 2 Feb. 1902.

Concentration of troops on Pacific and Atlantic coasts, imposition of heavy war taxes, commerce suffering, reported, Dec. 1902.

NICE or **NICÆA**, a town in Bithynia, Asia Minor, N. W. Antigonus gave it the name Antigoneia, which Lysimachus changed to Nicæa, the name of his wife. It became the residence of the kings of Bithynia about 208 B.C. At the battle of Nice, A.D. 194, the emperor Severus defeated his rival, Pescennius Niger, who was again defeated at Issus, and soon after taken prisoner and put to death. The first general council was held here 19 June to 25 Aug. 325, which adopted the NICENE CREED and condemned the Arians. It was attended by 318 bishops from divers parts, who settled both the doctrine of the Trinity and the time for observing Easter. An addition was made to the creed, 381; was rejected, 431. See *Filioque*. When the Crusaders took Constantinople, and established a Latin empire there in 1204, the Greek emperors removed to Nice and reigned there till 1261, when they returned to Constantinople; see *Eastern Empire*. Nice was taken by the Ottoman Turks in 1330.

NICE (S.E. France) was the seat of a colony from Massilia, now Marseilles, and formed part of the Roman empire. In the middle ages it was subject to Genoa, and suffered from the frequent wars, being taken and retaken by the imperialists and French. It was taken by the Austrians under Melas, 1800; seized and annexed to France 1792; restored to Sardinia in 1814. Nice was again annexed to France in virtue of the treaty of 24 March, 1860; the people having voted nearly unanimously for this change by universal suffrage. The French troops entered 1 April, and definite possession was taken 14 June following. Garibaldi, a native, vehemently protested against this annexation. Population, 1901, 125,099.

Fire at the opera house, and panic, about 70 killed, 23 March, 1881

International exhibition . . . . 6 Jan. 1884

Walker landed near Truxillo, Honduras, and took the fort on the 6th. On the 7th he proclaimed that he made war on the government, not on the people of Honduras. On being summoned to surrender his booty by capt. Salmon, R.N., of the *Icarus*, he refused, and fled. He was pursued, caught, given up to the Honduras government, tried, and shot (12 Sept.). His followers were dismissed. Grey Town was surrendered to Nicaragua in 1860.

About 90 acres of forest destroyed by fire; three persons perish . . . . . 27 Feb. 1891
Statue of Garibaldi unveiled . . . 4 Oct. „
The queen visits Nice . March, April, 1896, 1897 1898; she opens a bridge over the Paillon, presents 4200f. to charities, &c., 27 April, 1899.

NICIAS, Peace of, between Athens and Sparta for 50 years, 421 B.C., negotiated by that unfortunate Athenian general, who with his colleague, Demosthenes, was put to death after the disastrous termination of the expedition against Syracuse, 413 B.C.

NICKEL, a white, ductile, malleable, magnetic metal, employed in the manufacture of German silver. Cronstedt in 1751 discovered nickel in the mineral copper-nickel. Nickel ordered to be substituted for bronze coinage in France, 1882.

The *nickel* heat engine of professor Stefan of Vienna in 1885 consisted of plates of nickel fixed on a wheel which rotated when the metal was heated, in the presence of a magnet. Similar machines have been constructed by E. Berliner, 1885, Edison, 1887, and F. J. Smith, 1892.

NICOBAR ISLES, Indian Ocean, S. of Bay of Bengal, given up by Denmark and occupied by Great Britain to suppress piracy; announced June, 1869. Combined with the Andaman Isles, *which see*.

NICOLAITANES, a sect mentioned in *Rev.* ii. 6, 15, said to have sprung from Nicolas, one of the first seven deacons (*Acts* vi.), and to have advocated a community of wives, and to have denied the divinity of Christ.

NICOMEDIA, the metropolis of Bithynia, Asia Minor, N.W., founded by king Nicomedes I., 264 B.C., on the remains of Astacus; destroyed by an earthquake, A.D. 115; and restored by the emperor Adrian, 124. The Roman emperors frequently resided here during their eastern wars. Here Diocletian resigned the purple, 305; and Constantine died at his villa in its neighbourhood, 337. It surrendered to the Seljukian Turks, 1078; and to Orchan and the Ottoman Turks in 1338.

NICOPOLIS, on the Danube, Bulgaria, founded by Trajan. Here was fought a battle between the allied Christian powers under Sigismund, king of Hungary, afterwards emperor, and the Turks under Bajazet; said to have been the first battle between the Turks and Christians; the latter were defeated, losing 20,000 slain, and as many wounded and prisoners, 28 Sept. 1396. Nicopolis was taken by the Russians after a severe conflict (2 pashas, about 6000 men, 2 monitors, and 40 guns were captured), 15, 16 July, 1877.

NIELLO-WORK, believed to have been produced by rubbing a mixture of silver, lead, copper, sulphur, and borax into engravings on silver, &c., an art known to the ancients, was practised in the middle ages, and said to have given to Maso Finiguerra the idea of engraving upon copper, about 1460.

NIEMEN, or Memel, a river flowing into the Baltic, and separating Prussia from Russia. On a raft on this river the emperor Napoleon met Alexander of Russia, 22 June, 1807, and made peace with him and Prussia. He crossed the Niemen to invade Russia, 24 June, 1812, and recrossed with the remains of his army, 28 Dec. Near it the Poles defeated the Russians 27 May, 1831.

NIGER. A great river of N.W. Africa. British settlements at the mouth established since 1841. Niger expedition, see *Africa*, 1841. British protectorate with free trade affirmed by the West African conference at Berlin, Dec. 1884; confirmed June, 1885. Capt. Binger successfully explored the area within the bend of the river, 1887–89.

NIGER COAST PROTECTORATE. NIGERIA, 1897, see *Oil Rivers*. Northern Nigeria and Southern Nigria, 1 Jan. 1900.

The National African company incorporated in 1882; chartered as the Royal Niger company in 1886; chairman, lord Aberdare. The company's territories were constituted by the combination of various settlements, 1879–85, and by treaties with petty chiefs and especially by the treaty of Nikki concluded by capt. Lugard, placing Kishi (13 Oct.) and Borgu (or Busah) under British protection, 10 Nov. 1894; Anglo-French treaty at Busah, 20 Jan. 1890; Royal Niger company act (transfer of Nigeria to the imperial government for 865,000*l.*) passed, 9 Aug. 1899.
Samuel Adjai Crowther, a native African, first bishop of the Niger territory, rescued when a child from a slave-ship by the British, and taken to Sierra Leone 1822; baptised and educated; became a missionary; consecrated at Canterbury cathedral, 1864; died 31 Dec. 1891.
Lieut. L. Mizon, leader of a French exploring expedition in the Niger country in 1891, on his return to Paris in June, 1892, accused the officers of the Niger company of opposition and ill-usage. The charges were firmly repelled by the company's chairman, lord Aberdare, 22, 25 July, 1892.
New expedition, 10 Aug.; his aggressive conduct towards the British, Germans and natives, reported Oct. *et seq.* 1892; his recall ordered.
M. Hoellé sent out; further complications, reported Sept.; proceedings of the company justified by lord Aberdare: *Times*, 19 Sept. 1893.
Lieut. Mizon sails for France, 12 Oct. 1893; dies, March, 1899.
Repressive measures of the company lead to native risings at Brass, 27 Jan. 1895.
Akassa looted, 28 Jan.; Mr. Wyse and other prisoners killed; sir Claude Macdonald holds Brass; reinforcements arriving, reported 15 Feb. 1895.
Adm. Bedford takes Sacrifice island, Nimbi, and Fish-town, defeats and punishes the Brass chiefs; lieut. Geo. J. Taylor and 2 seamen killed, 20–25 Feb. 1895.
Dispute ended; Brass reopened to trade, 25 April, 1895.
Sir George Taubman-Goldie, deputy-gov. under lord Aberdare (who died 25 Feb. 1895) since 1886, elected governor of the company; lord Scarborough deputy, March, 1895.
Reports of lieut. Baud's and capt. Decœur's mission; treaties signed, March–April, 1895.
The British and French Niger commission meet at Paris, 8 Feb.; the Boussa territory occupied by the company, Feb. 1896.
King Koko of Brass outlawed, reported, 18 April, 1896.
Terrible explosion at Bida, in the Nupé country, the emir Maleki's palace destroyed, 200 deaths, reported 16 May, 1896.
Successful repression of the slave trade, reported 11 June, 1896.
Katchella's stronghold on the Middle Binue river destroyed after a desperate fight and himself killed, many slaves rescued, 14 soldiers killed, Aug. 1896. See *Lagos*, Dec. 1896–7.
Successful expedition of major Leonard, Mr. James and 9 carriers, unarmed, to Bendi city, 180 miles inland; treaties with various kings and chiefs made, returns to Opobo, 19 Dec. 1896.
An expedition, under major Arnold and sir George Taubman Goldie, against the emir of Nupé and the Fulahs for tyranny and the breaking of treaties, 1885 and 1890, leaves Lokoja 6 Jan. 1897; reaches Sura, the enemy retreating on Bida, 11 Jan. 1897.
Mr. Wallace, agent-gen., with an armed flotilla, drives out the Fulahs and burns Shonga, their stronghold; the Nupés join the forces against the Fulahs, 14 Jan.; successful advance on Egbon; Ladi, the S. Fulah capital, destroyed, and 1200 slaves rescued, 22 Jan.; Bida taken by major Arnold after a desperate fight (1 a.m. to 4 p.m.), Fulahs (20,000) utterly routed; lieut. A. C. Thomson killed, 26, 27 Jan.; sir George Goldie enters Bida, deputations of Nupés received,

free farms granted S.W. of the Niger and protection proclaimed, 29 Jan; desultory fighting, prince Isa captured, 30 Jan. 1897.

Many surrenders, festivities, races, &c. 1 Feb.; treaty of peace with Mohammed, the new emir of Nupé, signed at Kosoji, 5 Feb.; treachery of the Ilorins, severe fighting near the Oyon river, 15 Feb.; the town of Ilorin bombarded and taken by major Arnold's column, 16 Feb.; the emir and 4 chiefs submit, treaty of Ilorin signed, giving power to the company and effecting a settlement of the Lagos frontier, 18 Feb. 1897.

French expedition from Dahomey descends the river Elo and occupies Busa, 13 Feb. (lieut. Bretonnet assumes the title of French resident of the Middle Niger, and M. Carron styled French resident at Busa, Mar.), 1897.

A treaty signed with the emir of Lafiagi, 23 Feb.; the troops return to Lokoja, 25 Feb.; other emirs send in their submission, March; prince Markum acknowledged emir of Bida; campaign entirely successful throughout the W. Soudan, March, 1897.

Submission of the Patanis at Abutshi, 5 March, 1897.

Lieut. Musters, who captured some Nupé horsemen singlehanded at Sheshi, dies at Forcados, 9 Mar. 1897.

Mr. Wallace's operations with the river tribes successful, Feb.–March, 1897.

French encroachments, reported, 11 Oct. 1897.

The Anglo-French Niger commission meets at Paris, 29 Oct, 1897; convention, signed, 14 June; *Times*, 16, 18 June, 1898.

Treaties negotiated by the Royal Niger company, *Times*, 12 Nov. 1897.

Major Arnold storms Kiffi, the stronghold of prince Arku, son of the king of Igara, rebel slave raider, the enemy routed, 17 Nov. 1897.

Niki occupied by the French, the Baribas routed, 30 Nov. 1897.

Successful expedition, under lieut. Festing, against the Ibouzas, between Asaba and Benin, Jan.; terms of peace: abolition of human sacrifices, one king, &c., settled by Mr. Wallace at a durbar, 17 Feb. 1898.

Death of the king of Niki; the king of Beri, whose territory is in British occupation, becomes king of all Borgu, Jan. 1898.

The sultan of Sokoto accepts the terms of the British alliance, Jan. 1898.

Hard fighting in the Ediba country against hostile tribes, lieut. Frank Fenton killed; tribes surrendering, Feb. 1898.

Bereguru and Bashoro, in Borgu, occupied by the British, Feb.; see *Lagos*, March, 1898.

Severe fighting on the Cross river; the Ekuris decline overtures of peace, their capital detroyed, 1 Feb.; district quiet, 15 Feb. 1898.

Niger coast protectorate expedition, under majors Searle, Cockburn, and others, leave Opobo, 2 April, to hold a palaver with the Nibo chief (who had been stopping trade, &c.), at Omukorosho; on his refusal to meet the British, his town was stormed and taken with some loss; the chief afterwards surrendered and agreed to terms, reported, 31 May, 1898.

Anglo-French convention to delimit frontier of N. Nigeria, signed, June, 1898.

Two expeditions by the Royal Niger company's forces against the emirs of Lapai and Argeyes for slave raiding very successful; Lapai captured and destroyed, 21 June; Argeyes occupied, enemy's loss heavy, no British killed, 24 June, 1898.

An expeditionary force from Lagos, under major Arnold, attacks and destroys Siama in Forcados to punish native piracy, &c., 28 Aug. 1898.

Busa (evacuated by the French) and Ilo occupied by the British, 4 Oct. 1898.

Borgu evacuated by the French, reported, 1 Sept. 1898.

Revolt in the Assaba hinterland against interference with sacrificial rites; severe fighting, many natives killed at Illah, Oct.–Nov. 1898.

Lieuts. Keating and Gale, with 14 natives, treacherously attacked, and all killed but 2 natives, Oct. 1898.

Assaba district subdued, the king of Ibo submits, 3–25 Dec. 1898.

Expedition under maj. Carter and capt. R. Gabbett to suppress fetishism in the Kwo Ibibio country, successful, 4 Feb.–15 March, 1899.

See *Oil Rivers*, 1899.

The chief of Suntai and his town captured by a punitive expedition, reported, 13 July, 1899.

Royal charter granted 1886, revoked, July; territory taken over by the imperial government by act passed, 9 Aug. 1899.

Company reconstituted, government terms adopted; lord Scarborough succeeds sir George Goldie as chairman, 23 Aug. 1899.

Testimonial presented to sir G. Goldie, 27 Oct. 1899.

Successful punitive expedition on the Binue; 8 towns destroyed after much fighting, reported, 13 Oct. 1899.

British protectorate: Upper and Lower Nigeria and Lagos; col. (aft. sir Frederick) Lugard proclaimed high commissioner in N. Nigeria; sir R. D. Moor high commissioner in S. Nigeria, 1 Jan. 1900.

Capt. Carroll, with a telegraph construction staff, under lieut. McClintock, N.E. of Lokoja, attacked by the Munshis tribes; enemy routed, 80 killed, 8, 10 Jan.; enemy again defeated and Ibi captured, 15 Jan. 1900.

Natives again routed by lieut. Monck-Mason and 150 men on the Gurara, N. of Lokoja, 21 Feb. 1900.

Punitive expedition under lieut.-col. Lowry-Cole against the Munshis; much fighting, 5 British killed, reported, 5 March, 1900.

Further fighting on the Gurara, enemy's camp destroyed reported, 23 March, 1900.

The Pagan stronghold at Lemo, N. Nigeria, stormed and burnt by col. Lowry-Cole; many natives killed, 9 May, 1900.

The hon. David Carnegie killed near Lokoja, 26 Nov. 1900.

Punitive expedition under col. Kemball; Kantagora and Bida, in N. Nigeria, captured, 19 Jan.–17 Feb. 1901.

Operations in S. Nigeria under maj. Heneker; towns captured, 20 March–May, 1901.

Capt. Keyes (26), in command of Ilo, on the French frontier, treacherously murdered in Argungu by 3 French traders; in some after fighting 2 of his party and 12 others were killed, 21 June, 1901.

Negotiations with Fadr-Allah Rabah's son, concluded, Aug.; he was afterwards attacked and killed by the French, at Godiba, Sept. 1901.

Punitive expedition under lieut.-col. Morland against the emir of Adamawa; Yola captured, the emir fled, 2 Sept.; his brother Bobo Amadu installed as emir by Mr. Wallace, C.M.G., 8 Sept. 1901.

The Aros attack Obagu and massacre the natives, about 15 Nov.; their position at Enyong creek, Cross river, shelled and occupied by the British under col. Montanaro, 28 Nov.; enemy again defeated, 30 Nov.; rapid progress, enemy's strong resistance successfully repulsed, 2, 5, 6, 8 Dec.; Bendi taken after 3 days' fighting, 16 Dec.; Oror taken, the Aros defeated, 6 chiefs surrender, 24-31 Dec.; col. Festing captures Oloks; 25 chiefs and others captured, 2, 11 Jan. 1902.

Stubborn resistance, enemy's loss severe, 25, 29, Jan.; a stronghold of the Igas captured; enemy defeated in Ngwa country, 12, 19 Feb.; many towns submit; campaign closed, 23 March, 1902.

Sir Fred. Lugard reports British occupation of 9 provinces, chiefly on the Niger and the Binue, Feb. 1902.

Gombe, Gujba, and Bautshi occupied by col. Morland without opposition; Mr. C. L. Temple installed as resident at Bautshi, Feb. 1902.

Col. Morland's expedition to lake Chad very successful; British posts established, reported, June, 1902.

Slave trade abolished in Long Ju-Ju; fetish destroyed, cash currency introduced in the Aro country, S. Nigeria, &c., reported, Sept. 1902.

Capt. Moloney, resident at Keffi, murdered by a native chief in N. Nigeria, 4 Oct. 1902.

Successful Ju-Ju expedition (to stop human sacrifices) against Oma Nabad, 7 natives rescued, 4 chiefs killed, 17 Nov. 1902.

The emir of Kano, N. Nigeria, makes hostile preparations against the British, reported, 5 Dec. 1902.

The Opobo chief, in S. Nigeria, surrenders; successful expedition, reported, 10 Dec. 1902.

Sir F. Lugard decides upon active operations against the emir of Kano, said to be the greatest military chief in Hausaland, in consequence of his increased hostility in affording protection to the murderer of capt. Moloney, British resident at Keffi, end Dec. 1902.

Emir of Kano flees to Sokoto, reported 2 Jan. 1903.

British force of 37 officers and 1050 men under the command of col. Morland concentrate at Zaria, the nearest port to Kano, 12 Jan. 1903.

Mixed British and German commission to demarcate at boundaries laid down by the Anglo-German agreement of 1893: frontier to be fixed from southern shore of lake Chad to Zola, reported mid Jan., 1903.

Two companies 600 strong of Lagos batt. of W. Africa frontier force leave Lagos for expedition against emir of Kano, 27 Jan. 1903.

Capture of Kano by col. Morland, 300 natives killed, 2 British officers, and 12 men wounded, 3 Feb. 1903.

Gen. Kemball leaves Kano for Sokoto, the great Fulah capital, 16 Feb. 1903.

Sokoto occupied after some fighting, the sultan and chief having fled, 15 March, 1903.

[British supremacy completed over 500,000 sq. mi., with a population of about 20,000,000.]

The ex-sultan of Sokoto, joined by a large number, who had fled N.E. of Bantshi, are pursued by capt. Sword's column to Burmi on the Dongola river; but want of guns causes failure of the attempt to capture the town; after severe fighting capt. Sword retreats with the loss of 4 killed and 60 wounded, enemy's loss much greater, 16 May, 1903.

Capt. Sword reaches Bantshi 23 May, the ex-sultan begins negotiations, but is only promised his life if he submits; Burmi again attacked by a force of 40 British and 500 native troops, and completely destroyed after desperate fighting, in which the ex-sultan Ataibihu, most of his emirs, and about 700 natives were killed, the British loss being maj. Marsh and 10 others killed, 3 officers and 69 men wounded, 27 July, 1903.

Anglo-German boundary commission under lt.-col. Jackson, completes survey of districts S. of lake Chad, reported 24 Aug. 1903.

NIGHTINGALE FUND. On 21 Oct. 1854, Miss Florence Nightingale left England with a staff of thirty-seven nurses, and arrived at Scutari, 5 Nov. She rendered invaluable services to the army; and returned to London, 8 Sept. 1856. In honour of this a meeting was held at Willis's rooms on 29 Nov. 1855, to raise funds to establish an institution for the training of nurses and other hospital attendants. Madame Jenny Lind-Goldschmidt sang at Exeter hall on 11 March, 1856, and gave the proceeds (1872*l.*) to the fund. The subscriptions closed 24 April, 1857, amounting to 44,039*l.* The queen gave Miss Nightingale a valuable jewel.

NIGRITIA, see *Soudan*.

NIHILISM, a popular name for the school of philosophy which believes nothing without physical evidence, renounces all forms of Divine revelation, and gives nothing in their place.

NIHILISTS, ultra-reformers in Russia, said to propose the destruction of all government, and to begin society afresh. They became known and spread in 1872; their alleged leader, Zychareff. The government began to suppress them, Sept. 1875. One of the leaders, Michael Bakounin, died at Lugano, 1 July, 1876. For recent events, see *Russia*, 1877-87 *et seq.* The term *Nihilist* was invented by the Russian novelist Turgénief, who died 3 Sept. 1883.

"The Nihilists ask concessions, which are the commonplaces of every free community."—*Times*, 16 April, 1881.

"Nihilism as it is" by Stepniak, edited by Dr. Spence Watson, Nov. 1894.

NIKA CONTESTS, see *Circus*.

NIKOLSBURG (Moravia). Here were signed, 26 July, 1866, the preliminaries of a peace between Austria and Prussia.

NIKSICH, a strong Turkish fortress in Montenegro, many times besieged. Having been left by the Turks with insufficient garrison, it was captured by Montenegrins, 7, 8 Sept. 1877, causing great rejoicings.

NIL DARPAN, see *India*, June, 1861.

NILE (Egypt). The longest river in Africa, formerly considered to have its rise in what were termed "the mountains of the moon." The travels of Bruce were undertaken to discover the source of the Nile. He set out from England in June, 1768; on the 14th of November, 1770, discovered the source of the Blue Nile in lake Tana, and returned home in 1773. The Nile overflows regularly every year, from about the 15th of June to the 17th of September, when, having given fertility to the land, it begins to decrease. The first Nilometer (a pillar) is said to have been set up by Osirtasen III., a king of the XII. dynasty, 2,300 B.C. One was set up by Solyman the Caliph, 715 A.D. In 1829, the inundations of the Nile rose to 26 instead of 22, by which 30,000 people were drowned and immense property lost. Mr. Petherick set out early in 1861 to explore the country at the source of the Nile. For recent discoveries, see *Africa* 1863. A bridge over the Nile (above 1300 feet) at Cairo, was completed by a French company, Aug. 1872. For the discoveries of Speke, Grant, and Baker, see *Victoria Nyanza, &c.*

Mr. H. M. Stanley, in his book, "Darkest Africa," published June, 1890, expressed his opinion that the newly-discovered lake Albert Edward Nyanza, at the head of the Semliki river which is fed by the snows of the mighty Ruivenzori range (possibly the mountains of the moon mentioned by Ptolemy the geographer in the 2nd century A.D.), is the real source of the Nile.

The *barrage* works of the Nile, consisting of two great dams or weirs for irrigation, and the conveyance of boats by means of locks, constructed under the direction of Mouget Bey, a Frenchman, 1843–61; were unsuccessful and eventually neglected.

In 1885 the great powers agreed to the expenditure of 1,000,000*l.* on irrigation works, and the renovation of the barrage was effected under the direction of sir Colin Scott Moncrieff, 1886–90; supplementary dams advised by sir W. E. Garstin in 1897.

Mouget Bey died at Paris, aged 82, Dec. 1890.

The White Nile cleared of *sudd* by major Peake; navigable from Khartum to fort Berkeley, end May, 1900

Survey of the Nile to determine its species of fish (organised by Dr. John Anderson, died Aug. 1900), by the Egyptian government, assisted by the British museum, began March, 1899; 2,500 fishes sent to Natural History museum, 14 new species . . . . Jan. 1901–June, 1903

Barrage completed at Assuan . . . 5 Feb. ,,

Lady Cromer lays the coping-stone . . . 15 Feb. 1902

14 boats passed through the locks, waterway through the first cataract to Wady Halfa, open, 3 Aug.; the great dam, 2185 yards wide, 130 ft. high, at Assuan formally opened by the khedive, the duchess of Connaught laying the last stone before the duke and distinguished company, 10 Dec. ,,

[The water stored behind the dam estimated by sir William Garstin at over a thousand millions of cubic metres; annual gain to the country, 2,608,000*l.*, to the state, 378,400*l.*, and over 1,000,000*l.* to be received for the sale of reclaimed lands. Sir Benjamin Baker made K.C.B., sir Wm. Garstin, G.C.M.G., Mr. Wm. Willcocks, major Hanbury Brown, and Fakry pasha, K.C.M.G.; other honours conferred; sir E. Cassel and sir John Aird decorated by the khedive, 10 Dec.]

Regions of the Upper Nile protected by the Anglo-Abyssinian treaty . . . . . 15 May, ,,

Zifteh barrage between Cairo and the sea, opened by the khedive . . . . . . 7 March, 1903

Expedition for the exploration of the Blue Nile under Mr. W. N. McMillan *en route* to Addis Abeba reported to be making good progress, 25 March, ,,

NILE, BATTLE OF THE (or Aboukir), 1 Aug. 1798, near Rosetta, between the French fleet under Brueys, and the British under sir Horatio Nelson. Nine of the French line-of-battle ships were taken, two were burnt, and two escaped. The French ship, *L'Orient*, with Brueys and 1000 men on board, blew up, and only 70 or 80 escaped. Nelson's exclamation upon commencing the battle was, "Victory or Westminster Abbey!"

NIMEGUEN (Holland). Here was signed the treaty of peace between France and the United Provinces, 1678. The French were successful against the British under the duke of York, before Nimeguen, 28 Oct. 1794; were defeated by them 3 Nov.; but gained the place 8 Nov. Population, 1890, 32,618, 1900, 44,043.

NINETEENTH CENTURY AND AFTER, a magazine open to writers of totally different opinions; first appeared, March, 1877; introductory sonnet written by lord Tennyson; editor, sir James Knowles (K.C.V.O., 6 Dec. 1903).

NINEVEH, the capital of the Assyrian empire (see *Assyria*), founded by Ashur about 2245 B.C. The empire fell when Nebuchadnezzar captured Nineveh 606 B.C. The discoveries of Layard and others since 1839, in the neighbourhood of Mosul, at Koyunjik, the site of the ancient Nineveh, and other places, have in a manner disinterred and re-peopled a city which for centuries had ceased to figure on the page of history. Botta commenced his explorations at Khorsabad in 1843, and published his great work "Monuments de Ninive," 1849-50. In 1848 Mr. (after sir, K.C.B.) Austen Henry Layard, published his "Nineveh and its Remains," and in 1853 his "Discoveries," in his second visit in 1849-50. He was born 5 March, 1817, and died 5 July, 1894. *See Gladstone*, 1868, ambassador at Constantinople, 1877-80. Mr. Hormusd Rassam, in 1854, discovered an ancient palace. Mr. George Smith described his excavations and their results in 1873-4, in "Assyrian Discoveries," 1875. He died at Aleppo, 19 Aug. 1876. See *Assyria*. Mr. Rassam, appointed his successor, among other valuable discoveries at Balawât, nine miles N.E. of Nimroud, and at Koyunjik, &c., found a bronze monument with inscriptions recording the names, title, genealogy, and exploits of king Assur-nazir-pal (B.C. 885-860), builder of the palaces and temples of Kalakh, the capital of the middle Assyrian empire. Mr. Rassam arrived in London with collections, Dec. 1882.

The forms, features, costume, religion, modes of warfare, and ceremonial customs of its inhabitants stand before us as distinct as those of a living people; and by help of the sculptures and their cuneiform inscriptions, the researches of the learned have increased the knowledge of Assyrian history. Among the sculptures that enrich the British Museum may be mentioned the winged bull and lion, and numerous hunting and battle pieces; and the bas-relief of the eagle-headed human figure, presumed to be a representation of the Assyrian god Nisroch (from *Nisr*, an *eagle* or *hawk*), whom Sennacherib was in the act of worshipping when he was assassinated by his two sons, about 710 B.C. 2 *Kings* xix. 37.

NIOBIUM, a rare metal, discovered by Hatchett in columbite, a black earth, and named columbium, 1801. It was pronounced to be identical with tantalum (or tantalium) by Wollaston; but was rediscovered by H. Rose in 1846, and named niobium.

NIRVANA, see *Buddhism*.

NISBET or **NESBET** (Northumberland). Here a battle was fought between the English and Scotch armies, the latter greatly disproportioned in strength to the former. Several thousands of the Scots were slain upon the field and in the pursuit, 7 May, 1402.

NISI PRIUS ("unless before"), words in a writ summoning a person to be tried at Westminster, *unless* the judges should come to hold their assizes in the place where he is. Judges sit in Middlesex by virtue of 18 Eliz. c. 12 (1576).

NISMES (Nîmes), S. France, was the flourishing Roman colony, Nemausus. Its noble amphitheatre was injured by the English in 1417. The inhabitants embraced Protestantism, and suffered much persecution in consequence, and Nismes has frequently been the scene of religious and political contests. The treaty termed the Pacification of Nismes (14 July, 1629) gave religious toleration for a time to the Huguenots.

NITRE, see *Saltpetre*.

NITRIC ACID, a compound of nitrogen and oxygen, formerly called *aqua fortis*, is said to have been first obtained in a separate state by Raymond Lully, an alchemist, about 1287; but we are indebted to Cavendish, Priestley, and Lavoisier for our present knowledge of its properties. H. Cavendish demonstrated the nature of this acid in 1785. *Nitrous acid* was discovered by Scheele about 1774. *Nitrous gas* was accidentally discovered by dr. Hales, *Nitrous oxide gas* (laughing gas) was discovered by dr. Priestley in 1776. The use of this gas as an anæsthetic, recommended by H. Davey in 1800, was begun in America (by Mr. Wells, a dentist), 1844; in Paris, 1866; in London, 31 March, 1868, ingenious apparatus having been invented for its application.

NITROGEN or **AZOTE** (from the Greek *a*, no, and *zaō* or *zō*, I live), an irrespirable elementary gas, and an important element in food, discovered by Rutherford about 1772. Before 1777, Scheele separated the oxygen of the air from the nitrogen, and almost simultaneously with Lavoisier discovered that the atmosphere is a mixture of these two gases. Nitrogen combined with hydrogen forms the volatile alkali ammonia, so freely given off by decomposing animal and vegetable bodies. See *Air*, 1894. Prof. Hermann Hellriegel (born 1831) demonstrated in 1886 the power of leguminous plants to fix free nitrogen through the agency of microbes in their root nodules whereby the soil is much enriched. Clover gives up to the soil that which wheat requires. He died 24 Sept. 1895.

NITRO-GLYCERINE (also called **NITROLEUM**), an intensely explosive amber-like fluid, discovered by Sobrero in 1847, is produced by adding glycerine (in successive small quantities) to a mixture of one part of nitric acid and two parts of sulphuric acid. Alfred Nobel, a Swede, first attempted its application as an explosive agent in 1864. It has caused several most disastrous accidents, with great loss of life. In attempting to bury some nitro-glycerine in the town moor at Newcastle-on-Tyne, 17 Dec. 1867, an explosion took place, and seven persons lost their lives, including Mr. Mawson, the sheriff, and Mr. Bryson, town surveyor; see *Dynamite*. Mr. Alfred Nobel's nitro-glycerine manufactory, near Stockholm, blown up; 15 persons killed, many injured, 10 June, 1868. An act prohibiting its importation for a time, and regulating its transmission, was passed in 1869, and repealed by the Explosives Act of 1875. Secret manufacture discovered, see *Birmingham*, 1883.

NIZAM, see *Hyderabad*.

NOBEL BEQUEST. Dr. Alfred Nobel, a Swede, died 1896 (see *Nitro-Glycerine*, *Blasting*

Gelatine, and *Dynamite*), left a large sum of which the interest was to be awarded annually by a board of control at Stockholm in prizes each of the value of about 8,000*l.* to those who in the previous year should have rendered the greatest service to mankind, in inventions or discoveries in physical sciences, chemistry, physiology or medicine, literary work, and the cause of international brotherhood, in the suppression or reduction of standing armies, or the founding of Peace congresses. Regulations for the competition issued, Oct. 1900. The Peace prize of 150,000 kronen divided between M. Henri Dunant (Swiss) and M. Frédéric Passy (French); 200,000f. each to M. Sully Prudhomme, French poet, for literature; to Dr. Behring, of Halle, for medicine; prof. van't Hoff of Berlin, for chemistry; and prof Röntgen of Munich, for physics. The distribution took place at Stockholm, the crown prince and others present, 10 Dec. 1901. The Peace prize awarded to Mr. William Randall Cremer, M.P., for his work on behalf of international arbitration; the four Nobel prizes were given to prof. Henri Becquerel of Paris, divided with M. and Mdme. Curie also of Paris, for physics; to prof. Arrhenius of Stockholm for chemistry; to prof. Finsen, of Copenhagen for medicine, and to M. Bjornstjerne Björnsen, of Christiana, for literature, 11 Dec. 1903. *Noebel Institutes* are in process of establishment to carry out scientific investigation on the lines of the above scheme of the founder.

The Nobel committee of the society of authors, formed for the purpose of recommending English candidates for the literature prize; first meeting held in London, Dr. Richard Garnett in the chair (lord Avebury elected permanent chairman), 14 Jan. 1902

NOBILITY. The Goths, after they had seized a part of Europe, rewarded their heroes with titles of honour, to distinguish them from the common people. The right of peerage seems to have been at first territorial. Patents to persons having no estate were first granted by Philip the Fair of France, 1095. George Neville, duke of Bedford (son of John, marquis of Montague), ennobled in 1470, was degraded from the peerage by parliament, on account of his utter want of property, 19 Edw. IV., 1478. Noblemen's privileges were restrained in June, 1773; see *Lords*, and the various orders of the nobility.

In 1845 a statistical writer said that there were 500,000 nobles in Russia, 239,000 in Austria; in Spain (in 1780), 470,000; in France (before 1790) 360,000 (of whom 4,120 were of the *ancienne noblesse*); in the United Kingdom, 1,631 with transmissible titles (dukes to baronets).

NOBILITY OF FRANCE preceded that of England. On 18 June, 1790, the National Assembly decreed that hereditary nobility could not exist in a free state; that the titles of dukes, counts, marquises, knights, barons, excellencies, abbots, and others be abolished; that all citizens take their family names; liveries and armorial bearings also to be abolished. The records of the nobility, 600 volumes, were burnt at the foot of the statue of Louis XIV., 25 June, 1792. A new nobility was created by the emperor Napoleon I., 1808. The hereditary peerage was abolished 27 Dec. 1831; re-instituted by Napoleon III., 1852.

NOBLE, an English gold coin (value 6*s.* 8*d.*), first struck in the reign of Edward III., 1343 or 1344, said to have derived its name from the excellence of the metal of which it was composed.

NOCTURNE, a name given by John Field (who died 1837) to a new and very pleasing musical composition. He was followed very successfully by Chopin, who died, 1849. The term was adopted by Mr. Whistler, the artist, for his night pieces, in which he began with line, form, and colour, 1877–8.

"NOLUMUS LEGES ANGLIÆ MUTARI," see *Bastards*, and *Merton*.

NOMINALISTS (or CONCEPTUALISTS), a scholastic sect, opposed to the Realists, maintain that general ideas have no existence outside our minds, and only exist by the names we give them. The founder of the sect, Jean Roscellin, a canon of Compiègne, was condemned by a council at Soissons, 1092, but the controversy was revived in the 12th century. Among the Nominalists are reckoned Abelard, St. Thomas Aquinas (partially), Occam, Hobbes, Locke, Berkeley, and Dugald Stewart. The Realists assert that general ideas are real things with positive existence.

NON-CONFORMISTS. The Protestants in England are divided into conformists and nonconformists; or, churchmen and dissenters. The first place of meeting of the latter, in England, was established at Wandsworth, near London, 20 Nov. 1572. The name of non-conformists was taken by the Puritans when the Act of Uniformity came into operation on 24 Aug. 1662 (termed "Black Bartholomew's day"), when 2000 ministers of the established religion resigned, not choosing to conform to the statute passed "for the uniformity of public prayers and administration of the sacraments;" see *Puritans*, and *Dissenters*. The laws against them were relaxed by the Toleration act, 24 May, 1689.—The *Nonconformist* newspaper (edited by Mr. Edward Miall, aft. M.P.) first appeared 14 April, 1841. He died 29 April, 1881.

The non-conformists presented to Mr. Miall 10,000 guineas for his exertions on behalf of religious equality . . . . 18 July, 1873
Meeting of bishops and dissenting ministers at Lambeth palace, to consider the alleged progress of irreligious thought . . . . . 24 July, 1876
Mansfield college, Oxford (*which see*) . opened, 1886
Three large bodies in England, Congregationalists (or Independents), Baptists, Wesleyan Methodists, 8 others of considerable importance, Presbyterians, Unitarians, Society of Friends (Quakers), Salvation Army and 4 Wesleyan bodies; Primitive Methodists, Methodist (New Connexion), United Methodist Free Churches, and Bible Christians in 1903.

NONES, in the Roman calendar, were the fifth day of each month, excepting March, May, July, and October, when the nones fell on the seventh day.

NON-JURORS considered James II. to have been unjustly deposed, and refused to swear allegiance to William III. in 1689. Among them were Sancroft, archbishop of Canterbury; Ken, bishop of Bath and Wells, and the bishops of Ely, Gloucester, Norwich, and Peterborough, and many of the clergy, who were deprived 1 Feb. 1691. Non-jurors were subjected to double taxation, and obliged to register their estates, May, 1723. They formed a separate communion, which existed till the beginning of the present century.

NON NOBIS, DOMINE! ("Not unto us, O Lord!" &c., *Psalm* cxv. 1), a musical canon, sung as a grace at public feasts, was composed by W. Birde in 1618.

NON-RESISTANCE OATH (containing a declaration that it is unlawful to take arms against the king upon any pretence whatever), enforced by the Corporation act, 1661, was repealed in 1719.

NOOTKA SOUND (Vancouver's Island), discovered by captain Cook in 1778, and settled by the British in 1786, when a few British merchants in the East Indies formed a settlement to supply the Chinese market with furs; but the Spaniards in 1789 captured two English vessels and took possession of the settlement. The British ministry demanded reparation, and the affair was amicably terminated by a convention, and a free commerce was confirmed to England in 1790.

"NO-POPERY RIOTS," see *Gordon*. The cry was revived against the Catholic emancipation bill, 1829. The Anti-popery association petitioned against the election of Mr. Alderman Knill, R. C., as lord mayor of London, Oct. 1892.

NORDLINGEN (Bavaria). Here the Swedes under count Horn were defeated by the Austrians, 27 Aug. 1634; and the Austrians and allies by Turenne in 1645.

NORE MUTINY, see *Mutinies*.

NORFOLK ISLAND (Pacific Ocean), discovered in 1774, by captain Cook, who found it uninhabited, except by birds. The settlement was made by a detachment from Port Jackson under governor Phillip, in 1788, in Sydney bay, on the south side of the island. This was at one time the severest penal colony of Great Britain. The island was abandoned in 1809, but re-occupied as a penal settlement in 1825, penal settlement removed in 1855. The descendants of the mutineers of the *Bounty* were removed to it in June, 1856, from *Pitcairn's Island* (*which see*). Visited by lord Hampden, transferred to New South Wales and endowed with a new constitution, col. Spalding installed resident magistrate, 14 Nov. 1896. Population, 1901, 827.

Excitement in the island and resignation of the "Council of Elders" as a protest against the absorption of the island into the Australian Commonwealth, reported . . . . June 1903

NORICUM, see *Austria*.

NORMAL SCHOOLS (from *norma*, a rule). One for the instruction of teachers, established at Paris by a law, 30 Oct. 1794, opened 20 Jan. 1795, under the direction of La Place, La Harpe, Haüy, and other eminent men, was soon closed. Another, established by Napoleon in 1808, was closed in 1822. The plan was revived in 1826, and has been developed in England and other countries. See *Science and Art*.

NORMANDY (N. France), part of Neustria, a kingdom founded by Clovis in 511 for his son Clotaire, which, after various changes, was united to France by Charles the Bald in 837. From the beginning of the 9th century it was continually devastated by the Scandinavians, termed Northmen or Normans, to purchase repose from whose irruptions Charles the Simple of France ceded the duchy to their leader Rollo, 905. Rollo, the first duke, held it as a fief of the crown of France, and several of his successors after him, until William, the seventh duke, acquired England, in 1066. It remained a province of England till the reign of king John, 1204, when it was conquered by Philip Augustus and reunited to France. It was re-conquered by Henry V., 1418, and held by England partially till 1450. The English still possess the islands on the coast, of which Jersey and Guernsey are the principal.

DUKES.

912. Rollo (or Raoul), baptized as Robert.
927. William I. Longsword.
943. Richard I. the Fearless.
996. Richard II. the Good.
1027. Richard III.
1028. Robert I. the Devil.
1035. William II. (I. of England).
1087. Robert II., Courthose (his son), after a contest despoiled by his brother.
1106. Henry I. (king of England).
1135. Stephen (king of England).
1144. Matilda and Geoffrey Plantagenet.
1151. Henry II. (king of England in 1154).
1189. Richard IV. (I. of England).
1199-1204. Arthur and John of England.

NORTH ADMINISTRATION, formed by lord North, Jan. 1770, who resigned March, 1782. (Lord North entered into a league with the Whigs; which led to the short-lived Coalition ministry, 1783. He succeeded to the earldom of Guildford in 1790, and died in 1792; see *Coalition*.)

Frederick, lord North, *first lord of the treasury*, and *chancellor of the exchequer*.
Earl Gower, *lord president*.
Earl of Halifax, *privy seal*.
Earl of Rochford, lord Weymouth (succeeded by lord Sandwich) and earl of Hillsborough, *secretaries of state*.
Sir Edward Hawke, *admiralty*.
Marquis of Granby, *ordnance*.
Sir Gilbert Elliot, lord Hertford, duke of Ancaster, lord Carteret, &c.

NORTHALLERTON (Yorkshire). Near here was fought the "battle of the Standard," where the English totally defeated the Scotch armies, 22 Aug. 1138. The archbishop of York brought forth a consecrated standard on a carriage at the moment when they were hotly pressed by the invaders, headed by king David.

NORTH AMERICA, see *America*, *United States*, *Indians*, *Canada*, &c.

NORTH AMERICAN REVIEW began at Boston, U.S., in 1815, as a rival of the Edinburgh and Quarterly Reviews. It was published at first every second month; in 1818, quarterly; in 1879, monthly, at New York.

NORTHAMPTON was burnt by the Danes in 1010. Here Henry III. proposed to found a university in 1260, and held a parliament in 1269. On 10 July, 1460, a conflict took place between the duke of York and Henry VI. of England, in which the king was defeated, and made prisoner (the second time) after a sanguinary fight which took place in the meadows below the town. Northampton was ravaged by the plague in 1637. It was seized and fortified by the parliamentary forces in 1642. A fire nearly destroyed the town, 3 Sept. 1675. Riots here because Mr. C. Bradlaugh was not elected M.P., 6 Oct. 1874, were suppressed by the military. Population, 1881, 51,881; 1891, 61,016; 1901, 87,021.

Statue of Mr. Charles Bradlaugh, M.P. for Northampton 1880-91, unveiled . . 25 June, 1894
Excavations at Castor; remains of a Roman temple, &c., discovered . . . . . . 13 Dec. 1902

NORTH BRITON, a newspaper, first published 29 May, 1762, supported by John Wilkes,

M.P. for Aylesbury, and a London alderman, and very bitter against the earl of Bute's administration, accusing him of unduly favouring the Scotch.

In No. 45 (termed "Wilkes's number"), the king was charged with uttering falsehood in his speech; published . . . . . 23 April, 1763
"General warrant" issued by lord Halifax against the authors, printers, and publishers 26 April, ,,
Wilkes and others arrested and committed to the Tower, and his house searched . . . 30 April, ,,
Brought by writ of habeas corpus before chief-justice Pratt, and discharged, his arrest being regarded as illegal . . . . 6 May, ,,
300*l*. damages granted to a printer for false imprisonment . . . . 6 July, ,,
No. 45 declared to be "a scandalous and seditious libel" by parliament, and ordered to be burnt by the hangman . . . . . . 15 Nov. ,,
Riot at the burning in Cheapside . . . 3 Dec. ,,
"General warrants" declared illegal by chief-justice Pratt; 1000*l*. damages awarded to Wilkes for seizure of his papers . . . . 6 Dec. ,,
4000*l*. damages obtained by Wilkes in an action against lord Halifax . . . . . 10 Nov. 1769
Wilkes elected lord mayor, 8 Oct.; elected fifth time M.P. for Middlesex . . . . . . Oct. 1774
Allowed to take his seat . . . . . Jan. 1775
Elected chamberlain of London, 1779; died, 26 Nov. 1797

NORTHBROOK CLUB. Originated in 1879 to promote comfort and social intercourse for young Indians of good families under education in England. New premises in Whitehall Gardens were inaugurated by the prince of Wales, 21 May, 1883. Lord Northbrook was an active promoter of the undertaking.

Northbrook Society, first annual meeting at the Imperial Institute, 23 March, 1893; grand reception . . . . 24 June, 1902

NORTH CAROLINA, NORTH GERMAN, see *Carolina*, *German*.

NORTH-EAST AND -WEST PASSAGES. The attempt to discover a north-west passage was made by a Portuguese named Corte Real, about 1500. In 1585, a company was formed in London called the "Fellowship for the discovery of the North-West Passage." From 1743 to 1818 parliament offered 20,000*l*. for this discovery. In 1818 the reward was modified by proposing that 5000*l*. should be paid when either 110°, 120°, or 130° W. long. should be passed; one of which payments was made to sir E. Parry. For their labours in the voyages enumerated in the *list below*, Parry, Franklin, Ross, Back, Richardson, M'Clure, Nares, and McClintock were knighted.

Sebastian Cabot's voyages to the arctic regions, 1498, 1517
Sir Hugh Willoughby's and Richard Chancellor's expedition to find a *north-east* passage to China, in the *Edward Bonaventura, Bona Esperanza*, and *Bona Confidentia*, sailed from the Thames. 20 May, 1553
Richard Chancellor, in the *Edward*, reached Archangel and afterwards Moscow; the rest perished off the coast of Lapland, about 1554
Sir Martin Frobisher's attempt to find a N.-W. passage to China 1576
Capt. Davis's expeditions to find a N.-W. passage, 1585, 1586, 1587
Barentz's Dutch expeditions (by N.-E.) . . . 1594-5
Waymouth and Knight's expedition 1602
Hudson's voyages (see *Hudson's Bay*) . . . 1607-10
Sir Thomas Button's 1612
Baffin's (see *Baffin's Bay*) 1616
Foxe's expedition 1631
[A number of enterprises, undertaken by various countries, followed.]
Behring's voyages 1728, 1729, 1741
Middleton's expedition 1742
Moore's and Smith's 1746
Hearne's land expedition 1769
Captain Phipps, afterwards lord Mulgrave, his expedition 1773
Capt. Cook, in the *Resolution* and *Discovery* July, 1776
Mackenzie's expedition 1789
Captain Duncan's voyage 1790
The *Discovery*, captain Vancouver, returned from a voyage of survey and discovery on the north-west coast of America . . . . . Sept. 1795
Lieut. Kotzebue's expedition . . . . Oct. 1815
Captain Ross and lieut. Parry in the *Isabella* and *Alexander* 1818
Captain Buchan's and lieut. Franklin's expedition in the *Dorothea* and *Trent* . . . . . ,,
Franklin's second expedition. 1819-22
Lieuts. Parry and Liddon, in the *Hecla* and *Griper*, 4 May, 1819
They return to Leith . . . . . 3 Nov. 1820
Capts. Parry and Lyon in *Fury* and *Hecla*, 8 May, 1821-23
Parry's third expedition with the *Hecla* . 8 May, 1824
Capts. Franklin* and Lyon, after having attempted a land expedition, again sail from Liverpool, 16 Feb. 1825
Capt. Parry* again in the *Hecla*, sails from Deptford, and reaches a spot 435 miles from the North Pole, 22 June; returns . . . . 6 Oct. 1827
Capt. Ross* arrived at Hull, on his return from his Arctic expedition, after an absence of four years, and when all hope of his return had been nearly abandoned † . . . . . . 18 Oct. 1833
Capt. Back and his companions arrived at Liverpool from their perilous Arctic land expedition (1833), after having visited the Great Fish River and examined its course to the Polar Seas 8 Sept. 1835
Capt. Back sailed from Chatham in command of his majesty's ship *Terror*, on an exploring adventure to Wager River . . . . . . 21 June, 1836
[The Geographical Society awarded the king's annual premium to capt. Back for his polar discoveries and enterprise, Dec. 1835.]
Sir John Franklin, and capts. Crozier and Fitzjames, in the ships *Erebus* and *Terror*, leave England, (see *Franklin*) . . . . . 24 May, 1845
[The NORTH-WEST PASSAGE was discovered by sir John Franklin and his companions, who sailed down Peel and Victoria Straits, since named Franklin Straits. On the monument in Waterloo-place is inscribed—"*To Franklin and his brave companions, who sacrificed their lives in completing the discovery of the north-west passage*, A.D. 1847-8." Lady Franklin received a medal from the Royal Geographical Society.]
Commanders Collinson and M'Clure, in the *Enterprise* and *Investigator*, sailed eastward in search of sir John Franklin ‡ . . . . . 20 Jan. 1850
A north-west passage discovered by capt. M'Clure, 26 Oct. ,,

* Sir John Franklin died 11 June, 1847 (see *Franklin*); Sir E. Parry died 8 July, 1855, aged 65; and sir John Ross died 30 Aug. 1856, aged 80.

† In 1830 he discovered Boothia Felix: on 1 June, 1831, his nephew, com. James Clark Ross, discovered the north magnetic pole, in 70° 5′ 17″ N. lat., and 96° 46′ 45″ W. long.

‡ Capt. M'Clure sailed in the *Investigator* in company with com. Collinson in the *Enterprise* in search of sir John Franklin, 20 Jan. 1850. On 6 Sept. he discovered high land, which he named Baring's land; on the 9th, other land, which he named after prince Albert; on the 30th the ship was frozen in. Entertaining a strong conviction that the waters in which the *Investigator* then lay communicated with Barrow's straits, he set out on 21 Oct., with a few men in his sledge, to test his views. On 26 Oct. he reached Point Russell (73° 31′ N. lat., 114° 14′ W. long.), where from an elevation of 600 feet he saw Parry or Melville Sound beneath them. The strait connecting the Atlantic and Pacific Oceans he named after the prince of Wales. The *Investigator* was the first ship which traversed the Polar sea from Behring's straits to Behring island. Intelligence of this discovery was brought to England by com. Inglefield, and the Admiralty chart was published 14 Oct. 1853. Capt. M'Clure returned to England, Sept. 1854. In 1855, 5000*l*. were paid to capt. (afterwards sir Robert) M'Clure, and 5000*l*. were distributed among the officers and crew. On 30 Jan. 1855, the Admiralty notified that the Arctic medal would be given to all persons engaged in the expeditions from 1818 to 1855.

A German arctic expedition (the *Germania* and the *Hansa*) sailed, 15 June; arrived at Pendulum bay, Greenland, 18 July, 1869; the vessels parted; the *Germania* arrived at Bremen, 11 Sept. 1870; the *Hansa* was frozen and sank, Oct. 1869; the crew escaped with provisions, and reached Copenhagen 1 Sept. 1870

Herr Julius von Payer after 2 years' exploration in the *Tegethoff*, discovers Franz-Josef land . . 1871

A Norwegian arctic expedition sailed in the spring 1872

A Swedish expedition, under professor Nordenskjöld, sailed from Trömso, 21 July, 1872; unsuccessful; returned summer 1873

Capt. Hall sailed from New York in the U.S. ship *Polaris*, 29 June, 1871; frozen in, Sept.; died, 8 Nov. After much suffering, the crew reached Newfoundland . . . . . 9 May, ,,

Mr. B. Leigh Smith sailed to lat. 81° 24′, and discovered land to the N.E. of Spitzbergen, 1871; in other voyages he discovered under-currents of warm water flowing into the polar basin; he relieved the Swedish expedition . . . 1872-73

An Austro-Hungarian expedition in the *Admiral Tegethoff*, and the *Isbörjnen*, under Weyprecht and Payer, sailed from Trömso, in Norway, 14 July, 1872; the ships parted company, and the *Tegethoff* sailed northward and discovered Franz-Josef Land, 31 Aug. 1873; frozen in, abandoned ship, May, 1874; reached Vardöe, Norway, by sledges, 3 Sept.; arrived at Vienna . 25 Sept. 1874

Mr. Disraeli consents to a new British arctic expedition, 17 Nov. 1874; 38,620*l.* voted for the expedition . . . . 5 March, 1875

Capt. G. S. Nares, of the *Challenger*, appointed to command the *Alert*, and capt. H. F. Stephenson to command the *Discovery*.

Telegram from the queen to capt. Nares before starting: "I earnestly wish you and your gallant companions every success, and I trust that you may safely accomplish the important duty you have so bravely undertaken."

In the reply, "Her majesty may depend on all doing their duty."

The ships sailed from Portsmouth 29 May, 1875; despatches received from Disco (all well) 15 July ,,

Alert (on return) arrived at Valentia, 27 Oct.; the *Discovery* at Queenstown, 29 Oct.; at Portsmouth . . . . 2 Nov. 1876

Results. Sledges reached 83° 20′ 26″, 12 May, 1876; passage to the pole declared to be impracticable; no signs of open polar sea; ships wintered, 82° 87′ lat.; sun absent 142 days; no Esquimaux beyond 81° 52′.

Out of 120 persons 4 deaths (1 frost bitten, 3 scurvy); greatest cold, 72°—zero; extremest N. point reached by Markham named Cape Colombia.

Cost of the expedition, 120,000*l.*

The "Voyage" published by Capt. Nares . . 1878

Expedition of capt. Allen Young in the *Pandora* (aided by lady Franklin), sailed 25 June; returned 19 Oct. 1875; sailed again, 2 June; returned 31 Oct. 1876

Dutch expedition sailed from Holland . April, 1878

Mr. James Gordon Bennett's expedition; lieut. de Long sailed in yacht *Jeannette* . . 8 July, 1879

Dutch exploring expedition in *Willem Barents*, sailed for Arctic Ocean, 6 May; successful; returned to Hammerfest, Norway . . 24 Sept. ,,

Another expedition in *Vega*, under prof. Nordenskjöld, started 4 July, 1878; at Port Dickson on the Yenisei, 6 Aug.; at the mouth of Lena, 27 Aug.; at Yakutsk, 22 Sept.; imprisoned in ice near Tschuctshe settlement, 28 Sept. 1878—18 July, 1879; passed East Cape, Behring's strait; entered St. Lawrence Bay, in Pacific Ocean, 20 July; reached Yokohama . . . . . 2 Sept. ,,

The NORTH-EAST PASSAGE from the Atlantic to the Pacific is thus accomplished; chiefly at the expense of Mr. (aft. baron) Oscar Dickson, a merchant of Gothenburg (died aged 73, 7 June, 1897) 1878-9

Mr. B. Leigh Smith's successful expedition in his yacht *Eira* from and to Peterhead, 22 June—12 Oct. 1880

Another expedition by him in the *Eira*, 14 June; *Eira* seen in Straits of Nova Zembla . 8 July, 1881

[The *Eira* injured by ice; at Cape Flora sank in deep water, 21 Aug.; stores saved, tent and house erected; the party live on seals, walrus, &c. during winter, 1881-2; return voyage began (boats hauled, &c.), 21 June; fell in with a Dutch vessel, *Willem Barents*, and soon after with the *Hope*, near Matotchkin Straits, Nova Zembla, 3 Aug.; sail for home, 6 Aug.; arrive at Aberdeen, 20 Aug.]

Search for him proposed; government to give 5000*l.* Geographical Society 1000*l.*; other sums offered . . . . March, 1882

The *Hope* (Capt. Sir Allen Young) sails in search of the *Eira* . . . . . 22 June, ,,

Expedition in the *Jeannette*, which is crushed by ice, 23 June; two boats with crew received by Russians at mouth of the Lena; one boat missing, Dec. 1881; bodies of capt. de Long and others found near the mouth of the Lena, 23 March, 1882; conveyed to Philadelphia, and buried 23 Feb. 1884

German arctic expedition, *Germania* sailed, summer, returned . . . . . . 23 Oct. 1882

British circumpolar expedition started . 11 May, ,,

Arrived at Fort Rae, 30 Aug.; good news 1 Dec. ,,

Austrian Polar expedition, *Polar* started 2 April, 1882; returned to Drontheim 11 Aug.; to Vienna 22 Aug. 1883

The British government presents the *Alert* to aid the expedition, under commander Winfield S. Schley, in search for the party under lieut. Greeley, 25 persons (which started for the Polar seas in the summer of 1881), Feb. 1884; the search expedition starts, 10 May, 1884; 5000*l.* reward offered by U. S. government for discovery of lieut. Greeley and party . . . May, 1884

Lieut. Greely's party reached Cape Sabine, Smith's Sound, 83 deg. 24′ N. lat.; 17 persons starved to death; 1 drowned, 6 survivors found by com. Schley with the *Thetis*, 22 June; arrive at St. John's, Newfoundland, 17 July; at Portsmouth, New Hampshire . . . . 1 Aug. ,,

[The *Alert* returned to the British government with thanks, Feb. 1885.]

Colonel Gilder's expedition starts from Winnipeg 2 Oct. 1886; returns . . . . 3 March, 1887

Bjorling and Kalstennius, young Swedish naturalists, and a small party, leave St. John's in the *Ripple* for Smith's Sound, 24 June, 1892; reach Disco island, Greenland, insufficiently equipped, 31 July; they crossed Baffins Bay, and arrived at Carey island, 16 Aug.; the vessel is driven on shore, 17 Aug.; in a desperate condition with shortness of provisions, embark for Clarence Head, Cape Faraday, Ellesmereland, in a small boat, 12 Oct.; not since heard of, reported Dec. 1893; traces of them found on Carey island, reported . 19 Oct. 1894

Dr. Fridtjof Nansen starts from Christiania in the *Fram* for Arctic regions, 24 June, 1893; Dr. Nansen with lieut. Johansen, left the *Fram* in charge of capt. Sverdrup and lieut. Scott-Hansen, 14 March, 1895; after having touched a point 4 degrees further north than any previous explorer. In their journey over the ice they reached 86° 14′ lat., 8 April; and arrived at Franz-Josef Land, 14 Aug., and there wintered: Dr. Nansen met Mr. Jackson there, 17 June, 1896; and they returned in the *Windward* to Vardöe, 3 Aug.; arrival of the *Fram* at Skjervöe, after reaching 85° 57′ N. lat., great rejoicing, 20 Aug.; Dr. Nansen and his companions received by the king at Christiania. 9 Sept.; arrived in London (*which see*), 3 Feb. 1897, Edinburgh, 12 Feb.; and other towns, Feb.; made D.Sc. at Cambridge. 16 March; farewell lecture, St. James's Hall, 24 March; Paris, 25 March; Berlin, received by the emperor, and granted medals, 3 April; received by the king at Copenhagen, 7 April.

"Farthest North," by Dr. Nansen and lieut. Johansen, published . . . . . Feb. 1897

The Norwegian parliament grants sums of money to the members of the expedition, March, 1897.

Lieutenant Peary starts from New York, with an expedition in two parties, 2 July, 1893; the expedition fails through bad weather and loss of dogs.

Peary relief expedition in the *Falcon* leaves St. John's, 7 July, 1894; returns there with the members of the expedition, including Mrs. Peary, all well, 15 Sept.; lieut. Peary, Mr. Hugh Lee, and Henson, a servant, remain in Greenland to continue their explorations; Peary relief expedition, in the *Kite*, leaves St. John's for Bowdoin bay, Inglefield gulf, July; returns with lieut. Peary, Mr. Lee, and Henson, who were nearly starved, 21 Sept. 1895. Lieut. Peary returns to Cape Breton with scientific collections, 26 Sept. 1896; returns to St. John's with the Cape York meteorite (45 tons), 20 Sept. 1897.

The *Falcon* wrecked off S. Greenland, Oct.; all perish [reported 27 Nov. 1894].

Mr. F. G. Jackson arrives at Hull after spending some months within the Arctic circle . 4 Feb. 1894

The Jackson-Harmsworth expedition (33 persons) in the *Windward*, Mr. A. C. Harmsworth defraying all expenses, about 25,000*l.* starts for Franz-Josef Land; London, 12 July; left Archangel, 5 Aug.; reached Franz-Josef Land, Sept. 1894, frozen in; exploration by Mr. Jackson; he and his party remain; the *Windward* leaves 3 July, and arrives at Gravesend . 22 Oct. 1895

Herr Andrée and M. Eckholm leave Tromsö in the *Virgo* for a balloon expedition to the N. Pole, 15 June, 1896; prevented, and return, 24 Aug.; he ascends in the *Eagle* with Drs. Strindberg and Fraenkel from Danes island (617 mls. from the N. Pole), 2.30 P.M. 11 July, 1897; relief expedition in the *Victoria* returns to Tromsö without news, 21 Nov. 1897

(Other expeditions unsuccessful, 1898–1900.)

Capt. Robertson, of the Dundee whaler *Balæna* discovers several islands on the S coast of Franz-Josef Land, reported . . . . 3 Sept. ,,

Arctic relief expedition to rescue whalers; arrived at Cape Vancouver . . . . . . 16 Dec. ,,

Herr Theodor Lerner's North Polar Expedition in the German steamship *Helgoland* leaves Berlin, 30 May, 1898

Capt. Sverdrup's polar expedition in the *Fram* leaves Christiania . . . . . 24 June, ,,

The Swedish expedition in the *Antarctic*, under Herr Nathorst, successfully explores King Charles Land, W. Spitzbergen, and North-East Land; returns to Tromsö . . . . . . 7 Sept. ,,

"Northward over the 'Great Ice,' 1886 and 1886–97," by lieut. R. Peary, 2 vols., published, autumn, ,,

Mr. Wellman's expedition to Franz-Josef Land; established an outpost, "Fort McKinley," 81° lat., autumn, 1898; Mr. Wellman pushed northward, mid Feb. 1899; unknown regions explored, and good scientific results, reported; they return to Tromsö . . . . . 17 Aug. 1899

Andrée search expedition, under Dr. Nathorst, discovers new inlets E. of Greenland, and arrives at Malmö . . . . . 12 Sept. ,,

Andrée's buoy No. 4 found at Skjervöe, containing message: N. 45° east, in excellent spirits, 11 July; M. Andrée reported by some to have been killed by natives. . . . . . . 31 Aug. 1900

Mr. Walter Wellman's (American) N. polar expedition in the *Frithyof* leaves Tromsö . 27 June, ,,

The duke of Abruzzi's expedition in the *Stella Polare* to Franz-Josef Land; left Christiania, 12 June, 1899, wintered on Rudolf Land; Capt. Cagni's party (the duke too severely frostbitten to go) started for the N. Pole, 11 March (lieut. Querini and two men lost since 22 March), reached 86° 33′ 49″ N., 25 April, 1900; returned, Sept. ,,

Baron Toll's expedition left Cape Wyssoki for Bennett land . . . . 13 July, 1902

The Baldwin-Ziegler expedition left Dundee, 28 June, 1901; visited Rudolph Land, Nansen's hut, Greely island; returned with new charts, &c., to Norway . . . . . . 31 July, ,,

Lieut. Peary, undaunted by previous suffering, advanced to extremity of Greenland, 83° 50′, spring, 1900; was stopped by the ice opening; again he started from Cape Hecla, Gruinnell Land, and reached 83° 15′, but had to fall back, spring, 1901; he started again, 1 April, 1902, with Henson and four Eskimos, &c., but failed to reach the Pole; all returned in the *Windward*, to Sydney, Cape Breton Island . . 18 Sept. ,,

Capt. Sverdrup, in the *Fram*, was blocked in the ice about 79° N. near Cape Sabine, Aug. 1898; in Aug. 1899, he rounded S. end of Ellesmere Land, through Jones Sound and Cardigan Strait; explored new lands, with important scientific results, to 81° 37′; returned to Norway, 19 Sept. 1902; honours and medals bestowed . 30 Sept. 1902

(Charts of the latest discoveries are published in Petermann's "Mittheilungen der Geographie.")

Scientific expedition to the region of the N. pole, under the patronage of, and subsidized by, the French Academy of Sciences, in process of organization by M. Jean Charcot. The expedition will include scientific investigations in Iceland, Spitzbergen, and Nova Zembla, with special reference to the biology of the codfish, and the northern currents of the Gulf stream, reported Jan. 1903

Ziegler expedition in the *America* leaves Trondhjem for Franz-Josef Land . . . 23 June, ,,

Canadian arctic expedition in the *Neptune* leaves Halifax for Hudson bay, and the Arctic seas, 22 Aug. ,,

NORTHMEN or NORSEMEN, see *Scandinavia*, and *Normandy*.

NORTH SEA, or GERMAN OCEAN, a canal connecting the sea with Amsterdam; opened by the king of Holland, 1 Nov. 1876. For the canal connecting the North sea with the Baltic, see *Baltic*, 1887-95, and *Kiel*.

NORTHUMBERLAND AVENUE, W. LONDON, opened 18 March, 1876.

NORTHUMBERLAND HOUSE, STRAND, LONDON, built on the site of a hospital, dedicated to the Virgin, by Henry Howard, earl of Northampton, was finished 1605; named Suffolk house by his nephew, Thomas, earl of Suffolk; and afterwards named Northumberland house from his descendant, Elizabeth, marrying Algernon, earl of Northumberland, by whom it was partially rebuilt.

The house was purchased by the Metropolitan Board of Works; 497,000*l.* being paid for it, June. The lion (set up 1749) taken down, 3 July, to be put up at Sion house; the house pulled down during the autumn 1874

NORTHUMBRIA, a Saxon kingdom, founded by Ida, 547; see under *Britain*.

NORTH-WEST TERRITORIES. See *Western territories*.

NORTH WESTERN PROVINCES of India, separated from Bengal in 1835 (Oude was annexed in 1856), and all were placed under one lieut.-governor in 1877. Capital, Allahabad. Population in 1881, 44,107,869; 1891, 46,905,085; 1901, 47,696,324. Lieut.-governors, Hon. sir Alfred Comyns Lyall, 1882; sir Auckland Colvin, autumn 1887; sir Charles Crosthwaite, Nov. 1892; sir Anthony Macdonnell, March, 1895; Sir James La Touche, 14 Nov. 1901.

Demarcation of the Perso-Baluchistan and Indo-Afghan frontier completed by col. Holdich and lieut. MacMahon, announced . . 27 April, 1896

Mr. W. Crooke's "North-Western Provinces," a valuable work, published 1897

See *Indian Famine*, 1897.

Agra municipality (native) censured by the lieut.-gov. for misgovernment, Jan. 1899; Mr. Morgan, joint magistrate, appointed official secretary to examine and re-organize every department, mid Jan. 1899

The Elgin bridge over the Gogra, opened by sir A. P. Macdonnell. . . . . . . 25 Jan. ,,

Tenancy bill, after long controversy, passed, 20 Oct. 1901

New north-west frontier province, see *Punjaub*, 9 Nov. 1901

NORTH-WESTERN RAILWAY, LONDON AND, constituted by the amalgamation of the London and Birmingham Grand Junction, and the Liverpool and Manchester railways, in 1847. Sir Richard Moon (director, 1848, chairman, 1862), on resigning, 20 Feb. 1891, reported the capital, Dec. 1890, to be about 110,077,934*l*., proprietors 34,000, persons employed, about 60,000, mileage, 1,900. See *Crewe*. Sir George Findlay, the able general manager for nearly 20 years, died 26 March, 1893, aged 63; succeeded by Mr. F. Harrison, April, 1893. Total receipts, 1895, 6,181,480*l*.; capital, 1895, 78,863,305*l*.; mileage, 1895, 21,866,967.

Dispute with the men settled by government intervention . . . . 11 Dec. 1896

NORWAY, until the 7th century, was governed by petty rulers. About 630, Olaf Trætelia, of the race of Odin termed Ynglings or youths, expelled from Sweden, established a colony in Vermeland, the nucleus of a monarchy, founded by his descendant, Halfdan III. the Black, a great warrior and legislator, whose memory was long revered. Population, 1887, 1,925,000; 1891, 1,988,997; 1900, 2,239,880.

Olaf Trætelia, 630; slain by his subjects 640
Halfdan I., 640; Eystein I., 700; Halfdan II., 730; Gudrod, 784; Olaf Geirstade and Halfdan III. . 824
Halfdan recovers his inheritance from his brother, whom he subdues, together with the neighbouring chiefs, 840; accidentally drowned 863
The chiefs regain their power during the youth of his son, Harold Härfager, or fair-haired, who vows neither to cut nor comb his hair till he recovers his dominion 865
He defeats his enemies at Hafsfiord, 872; dies . . 934
Eric I. (the bloody axe), his son, a tyrant, expelled, and succeeded by
Hako (the Good), 940; he endeavours in vain to establish Christianity; dies 963
Harold II., Graafeld, son of Eric, succeeds . . . ,,
Killed in battle with Harold of Denmark . . . 977
Hako Jarl, made governor of several provinces; becomes king, 977; his licentiousness leads to his ruin; deposed by Olaf I., Trygvæson; and slain by his slave 995
Olaf I., 995; establishes Christianity by force and cruelty 998
Defeated and slain, during an expedition against Pomerania, by the kings of Denmark and Sweden, who divide Norway between them 1000
Olaf II., the Saint (his son), lands in Norway . . 1012
Defeats his enemies and becomes king . . . 1015
Fiercely zealous in the diffusion of Christianity 1018-21
Successful invasion of Canute, who becomes king 1028-9
Olaf expelled; returns and is killed in battle . . 1030
Sweyn, at the death of Canute, succeeds as king of Norway, but is expelled in favour of Magnus I., bastard son of Olaf II. 1035
Magnus becomes king of Denmark, 1036; dies . . 1047
Harold Hardrada, king of Norway . . . . ,,
Invades England; defeated and slain by Harold II. at Stamford-bridge. . . . . . . 25 Sept. 1066
Olaf III. and Magnus II. (sons), kings, 25 Sept. 1066; Olaf alone (pacific) 1069-1093
Olaf III. founds Bergen 1070
Magnus III. (Barefoot), son of Olaf 1093
Invades the Orkneys and Scotland 1096
Killed in Ireland 1103
Sigurd I., Eystein II., and Olaf IV. (sons) . . ,,
Sigurd visits the Holy Land as a warrior pilgrim 1107-10
Becomes sole king, 1122; dies 1130
Magnus IV. (his son) and Harold IV. . . . ,,
Magnus dethroned 1134
Harold IV. murdered; succeeded by his sons, Sigurd II., &c.; civil war rages 1136
Nicolas Breakspear (afterwards pope Adrian IV.), the papal legate, arrives, reconciles the brothers, and founds the archbishopric of Drontheim . . 1152
Numerous competitors for the crown; civil war; Inge I., Eystein III., Hako III., Magnus V. . 1136-62
Magnus V. alone 1162
Rise of Swerro, an able adventurer, who becomes king; Magnus defeated; drowned 1186
Swerro rules vigorously; dies 1202
Hako, his son, king, 1202; Guthrum, 1204; Inge II. 1205
Hako IV., bastard son of Swerro 1207
Unsuccessfully invades Scotland, where he dies . 1263
Magnus VI., his son (the legislator), dies . . 1280
Eric II., the priest-hater, marries Margaret of Scotland; their daughter, the Maid of Norway, becomes heiress to the crown of Scotland . . . 1286
Hako V., his brother, king 1299-1319
Decline of Norwegian prosperity.
Magnus VII. (III. of Sweden), king . . . 1319-43
Hako VI. 1343-80
Olaf V. of Norway (II. of Denmark) . . . 1380-87
Norway united with Denmark and Sweden under Margaret 1389
At an assembly at Calmar the three states are formally united 1397
Sweden and Norway separated from Denmark, 1448; re-united 1450
Denmark and Norway separated from Sweden . . 1523
Christiania, the modern capital, built by Christian IV. 1624
Norway given to Sweden by the treaty of Kiel; Pomerania and Rugen annexed to Denmark 14 Jan. 1814
The Norwegians declare their independence, 17 May, ,,
The Swedish troops enter Norway . . 16 July, ,,
Charles Frederic, duke of Holstein, elected king of Norway; abdicates . . . . . 10 Oct. ,,
Charles XIII. of Sweden proclaimed king by the National Diet (Storthing) assembled at Christiania; he accepted the constitution which declares Norway a free, independent, indivisible, and inalienable state, united to Sweden . . . 4 Nov. ,,
Nobility abolished 1821
The national order of St. Olaf instituted by king Oscar I. 1847
Millennial festival of the establishment of the kingdom, kept . . . . 18 July, 1872
The king Oscar II. crowned at Drontheim, 17 July, 1873
Statue of Charles John XIV. unveiled at Christiania 7 Sept. 1875
Christian Selmer succeeds Fk. Stang as prime minister 1881
Disputes between the Storthing and the crown respecting constitutional changes . . . . ,,
Elections; liberal majority claiming Norwegian constitutional rights; many republicans Oct. 1882
Liberal leaders, Sorens Jaabœk (violent), Mr. Sverdrup (moderate) . . . . . . Jan. 1883
Opening of the Storthing, firm resistance of the crown ministers . . . . Feb. ,,
Who are threatened with impeachment, 9 March; which is adopted . . . . . . 23 April, ,,
Exhibition of art and industry opened at Christiania . . . . June, ,,
Impeachment of the minister, Christian Selmer, and his 10 colleagues, for advising the king to veto the bill for ministerial responsibility . . ,,
Trial of Selmer began . . . . . . 22 Oct. ,,
Selmer found guilty by the supreme council of Norway; sentenced to dismission from public service, and payment of expenses of prosecution, 27 Feb. 1884
M. Selmer resigns his post, the king accedes, but maintains his power of veto . . . 12 March, ,,
Trial and conviction of M. Kjerulf and other ministers . . . . . 20 March—1 April, ,,
The crown prince of Sweden appointed viceroy of Norway . . . . 19 March ,,
New ministry formed (councillor Schweigaard and M. Carl Lövenskjold, and others) . . 3 April, ,,
Resigns, 6 June; M. Johan Sverdrup forms a liberal ministry . . . . . . 26 June, 1884
Resignation of the Sverdrup ministry, 2 July; succeeded by Emil Stang . . . . . 12 July, 1889
Death of Christian A. Selmer . . . about 9 Sept. ,,
Visit of the German emperor at Christiania, grand reception . . . . . . 1 July *et seq.* 1890
Resignation of the Stang ministry, in consequence of a vote in the parliament demanding greater independence for Norway in political policy, tending to separation from Sweden . . . 23 Feb. 1891

M. Steen, the liberal leader, forms a cabinet 5 March, 1891
Norway desires autonomy in foreign affairs; opposed by Sweden, Feb.; adopted by the Storthing . . . . 10 June, 1892
Destructive fire at Christiansand; public buildings destroyed 8 July ,,
The Steen ministry resigns, 30 June; resumes office by compromise . . . . 27 July, ,,
A liberal-unionist party formed about . 28 Nov. ,,
Violent storm over the Lofoden islands, a fishing-fleet destroyed, about 123 lives lost . end of Jan. 1893
Continued demand for autonomy in foreign affairs, Feb.; the storthing ignores the conciliatory overtures of Sweden, March, and claims separate foreign consular establishment . 17 March, ,,
King Oscar visits Christiania, 17 April; on his refusal to consent to autonomy in foreign affairs the Steen ministry resigns and the storthing adjourns, 23, 24 April; new ministry formed by M. Emil Stang, 2 May; censured by vote (63–51) 6 May, ,,

See *Landslips*, May, 1893.

The storthing votes the partial substitution of the Norwegian flag for that of the Union . 21 June, ,,
Telephonic communication opened between Christiania and Stockholm . . . . . 2 Sept. ,,
Eightieth anniversary of the union of Norway and Sweden; king Oscar at a banquet speaks strongly in support of the union, specially in foreign affairs . . . . 4 Nov. ,,
Address of the storthing to the king, censuring the state of the army and navy . . 7 June, 1894
Parliamentary elections: left, 59; right and moderates, 55 . . . . . . 26 Nov. ,,
Resignation of the ministry, 31 Jan. 1895; negotiations between the king and the storthing, Feb.; no result, the old ministry retains office, 25 May, 1895
M. Bounvil declines to form a ministry . 19 June, ,,
Hardanger hotel, Odde, and several houses burnt (great loss to tourists) . . . . 9 Aug. ,,
A coalition ministry formed by M. Hagerup, premier . . . . 14 Oct. ,,
Storthing opened by the king . . 3 Feb. 1896
"The Fridtjof-Nansen Fund for scientific research," started to commemorate Dr. Nansen's Arctic expedition . . . . . . Oct. ,,
See *North-E.* and *W. Passage* 1896, and *London* 1897.
Harald Haarfagre, ironclad, launched at Walker, on the Tyne, 4 Jan.; *Tordenskjold*, sister ship, launched there . . . . 18 March, 1897
Namsos, in province of N. Trondhjem destroyed by fire . . . . 30 May, ,,
Storthing opened by the king . . 11 Feb. 1898
Resignation of the Hagerup ministry, 12 Feb.; new ministry formed by M. Steen . 17 Feb. ,,
Report of the Norwegian committee on the union with Sweden, presented to parliament, 7 March, ,,
International fisheries exhibition opened at Bergen, 16 May; and festival (1st) of Norwegian music, conducted by Dr. Edvard Grieg; 26 June–2 July, ,,
Storthing opened by the king . . 12 Oct. ,,
Joint commission to promote a *modus vivendi* with Sweden, fails . . . . . . Oct. ,,
New state loan of 20,000,000 kroner at 3½ per cent., redeemable in 20 years, announced . 12 Nov. ,,
The king refuses to sanction a purely *Norwegian* flag, Dec. ,,
Budget: revenue, 78,900,000 kroner; expenditure, 76,100,000 kroner; session closed. . 27 May, 1899
Inter-parliamentary peace conference at Christiania, M. Lund, president; opened by M. Steen, 2 Aug. ,,
New Norwegian national theatre in Christiania opened by the king; three days' dramatic festival ovations to Ibsen, Björnson and Grieg, 1–3 Sept. ,,
Elections: 77 members of the left, 37 of the right and moderates . . . . 10 Sept. 1899
Increasing prosperity and commerce in Norway; constitutional disagreements with Sweden continue, reported . . . . . . Oct. ,,
State loan, 30,000,000 kroner, authorized by the storthing . . . . . . 23 Oct. ,,
Illness of the king; the storthing opened by the crown prince, as regent, 24 Oct.; the king resumes his office . . . . . 21 Jan. 1901
Great fire in Farsund, over 1,200 persons homeless, 12 Aug. 1901
State loan of 35,000,000 kroner at 3½ per cent. for 60 years, concluded with a Scandinavian banking syndicate . . . . 11 Jan. 1902
M. Steen's ministry resigns, 16 April; one formed by M. Blehr . . . . . . 20 April, ,,
Henrik Niels Abel (mathematician), centenary celebrations (degrees conferred on lords Kelvin, Rayleigh, sir G. Stokes and 26 foreign scientists), 4–7 Sept. ,,
Capt. Sverdrup and the *Fram* N. Pole expedition welcomed in Christiania . . . . 28 Sept. ,,
Storthing opened, army reorganization proposed, 13 Oct. ,,
Storthing adopts, by 81 to 32, president's resolution for the establishment of a separate Norwegian consular system . . . . Jan. 1903
Blehr ministry resigns, prof. Hagerup forms new cabinet. . . . . 21 Oct. ,,

See *Denmark* and *Sweden*.

NORWEGIAN LITERATURE may be divided into two periods—ancient (comprising the Sagas and Eddas) and modern. Writers between the 13th and 19th centuries are included with the Danes, whose language they used.

Principal authors: Wergeland, *p.*, 1808–45; Welhaven, *p.*, 1807–73; Björnson, *n.* and *p.*, born 1832; Ibsen, *d.* and *p.*, born 1828; Kjelland, *n.* and *d.*, born 1849. Anna Thoresen, 1810–1903.

NORWICH (Norfolk), mentioned in history in the Saxon Chronicle at the period when Sweyn, king of Denmark, destroyed it by fire, 1004. See *Population*.

Artisans from the Low Countries establish here the manufacture of baizes, &c., about 1132
Cathedral first erected in 1088, by bishop Herbert Losinga; completed by bishop Middleton, about 1280; octo-centenary celebrated . July, 1896
A great plague 1348
Church of the Blackfriars, now St. Andrew's-hall, erected 1415
Norwich nearly consumed by fire 1505
Public library instituted, 1784; burnt 1 Aug. . 1898
John Stratford executed for poisoning John Burgess by arsenic . . . . . . 17 Aug. 1829
Norwich new canal and harbour were opened, 3 June, 1831
Church congress met . . . 3-7 Oct. 1865
The musical festival was attended by the prince of Wales . . . . 31 Oct. 1866
Norwich and Norfolk Industrial exhibition opened in St. Andrew's-hall . . . . Aug. 1867
British Association met here . . 20-26 Aug. 1868
Norfolk and Norwich Naturalists' Society founded 1869
Mutilated remains of a human body discovered near Norwich, 21-25 June, 1851; William Sherward, a publican of the place, confessed on 1 Jan. 1869, that they were the remains of his wife murdered by him; he recanted, but was tried and condemned, and executed . . . . . 20 April, ,,
Norwich Crown bank stopped; much distress occasioned; sir Robert H. J. Harvey, the chief partner, commits suicide: died . 19 July, 1870
Election commission; much corruption disclosed Aug.-Sept. 1875
Writ for election of M.P. suspended till dissolution of parliament, by act passed . . 15 Aug. 1876
National fisheries exhibition (opened by the prince of Wales) . . . . . 18-30 April, 1881
The castle, long used as a prison, proposed to be transformed into a museum, &c. . . . 1888
The choir of the cathedral re-opened after extensive restoration . . . . . . 2 May, 1894
Visit of the duke and duchess of York; the museum and fine art gallery at the castle opened, 23 Oct. ,,
Mr. Robert Fitch, F.S.A., F.G.S., chemist and druggist, gave his collections to the Norwich museum; died . . . . . 4 April, 1895
Musical festival, visit of the prince and princess of Wales, the duke and duchess of York, and others 7 Oct. 1896

Strike in the boot trade, with intimidation, March; closed . . . . . . 20 Oct. 1897
Mr. Wm. Cadge gives 10,000*l.* (20,000*l.* in all in recent years) to the Norwich hospital, announced . . . . 9 Jan. 1899
Mr. J. J. Colman bequeathed a selection of pictures by the Norwich School of Artists (1898), delivered at the Castle museum. . . . Feb. ,,
Visit of the prince and princess of Wales, the Jenny Lind infirmary for sick children opened 30 June, 1900
Lady Leicester opens a hospital and a nurses' home (15,000*l.* given by Leicester, 5,000*l.* promised) 16 July, 1903

NORWICH, BISHOPRIC OF, originally East Anglia; the first bishop was Felix, a Burgundian, sent to convert the East Anglians about 630. The see was divided into two distinct bishoprics—Elmham, in Norfolk, and Dunwich, in Suffolk, about 673. Both sees suffered extremely from the Danish invasions, insomuch that after the death of St. Humbert, they lay vacant for a hundred years. At last the see of Elmham was revived, and Dunwich was united to it; but Arfastus removed the seat to Thetford, where it continued till Herbert Losinga removed it to Norwich, 1094. This see has given to the church of Rome two saints; and to the nation five lord chancellors. It was valued in the king's books at 899*l.* 18*s.* 7½*d.* per annum. Present income, 4500*l.*; see *Bishoprics*.

RECENT BISHOPS OF NORWICH.

1790. George Horne; died 17 Jan. 1792.
1792. Charles Manners Sutton; translated to Canterbury, 1 Feb. 1805.
1805. Henry Bathurst; died 5 April, 1837. He was a strenuous supporter of catholic emancipation, and for a long time the only liberal bishop in the house of peers.
1837. Edward Stanley; died 6 Sept. 1849.
1849. Samuel Hinds; resigned 1857.
1857. Hon. John T. Pelham, May; resigned, March, 1893; died, 1 May, 1894.
1893. John Sheepshanks, March.

NOTABLES, French assemblies of nobles, bishops, knights, and lawyers. An assembly of the notables was convened by the duke of Guise, 20 Aug. 1560, and by other statesmen. Calonne, the minister of Louis XVI., summoned one which met on 22 Feb. 1787, on account of the deranged state of the king's finances, and again in 1788, when he opened his plan: but as any reform militated too much against private interest to be adopted, Calonne was dismissed, and soon after retired to England. Louis having lost his confidential minister, De Vergennes, by death, called De Brienne, an ecclesiastic, to his councils. The notables were re-assembled on 6 Nov. 1788. In the end, the states-general were convoked 5 Dec.; and from this assembly sprang the national assembly (*which see*). The notables were dismissed by the king, 12 Dec. 1788.—The *Spanish notables* assembled and met Napoleon (conformably with a decree issued by him commanding their attendance), at Bayonne, 25 May, 1808.

NOTARIES PUBLIC, said to have been appointed by the primitive fathers of the Christian church, to collect the acts or memoirs of the lives of the martyrs in the 1st century.—*Du Fresnoy.* This office was afterwards changed to a legal employment, to attest deeds and writings, so as to establish their authenticity in any other country. A statute to regulate public notaries was passed in 1801, and statutes on the subject have been enacted since.

"NOTES AND QUERIES," a medium of intercommunication for literary men and general readers, founded and edited by W. J. Thoms; first published on 3 Nov. 1849; bought by sir C. W. Dilke, about Aug. 1872.

NOTRE DAME, the cathedral at Paris, was founded in 1163, completed 1257. It narrowly escaped destruction by the communists, May, 1871. It has been beautifully and judiciously restored, at a cost of about 250,000*l.*, under the superintendence of Viollet-le-Duc, 1866 *et seq.*

NOTTINGHAM (Saxon, Snotingaham), created a city, June, 1897. The castle here was defended by the Danes against king Alfred, and his brother Ethelred, who retook it, 868. It was rebuilt by William I. 1068; and ultimately became a strong fortress. See *Population.*

Burnt in the civil wars 1140, 1153, 1173
Parliaments held . . . 1194, 1337, 1386, 1394, 1397
Here Charles I. raised his standard . 6 May, 1642
The riots at Nottingham, in which the rioters broke frames, &c. . . . . 14 Nov. 1811 to Jan. 1812
Much similar mischief . . . . . April, 1814
The Watch and Ward act was enforced . 2 Dec. 1816
Nottingham castle was burnt by rioters during the Reform excitement . . . . 10 Oct. 1831
Fierce election riots with "lambs" and others took place in . . . . July, 1865
The British Association met . . . 22 Aug. 1866
Suffragan bishop—Henry Mackenzie, D.D. . . 1870
The church congress met . . . . Oct. 1871
A gentleman gives 10,000*l.* to educate the working classes . . . . Jan. 1875
University college buildings founded 27 Sept. 1877
Midland Counties Art museum opened by the prince of Wales, 3 July, 1878; Mr. Henry Lammin bequeaths to it paintings, &c. value 4,000*l.* Aug. 1890
University free public library and free natural history museum opened by prince Leopold, duke of Albany . . . . 30 June, 1881
50th anniversary of the foundation of the Mechanics Institution celebrated; duke of St. Albans in the chair . . . . . . 1 Nov. *et seq.* 1887
The Royal Agricultural Society meet here, very successful . . . . . . 9 July, 1888
New guildhall opened by the mayor . 27 Sept. ,,
Settlement by conciliation of a great strike in the lace trade . . . . . . 9 Sept. 1889
Wilhelm E. H. Arnemann, dentist, sentenced to 20 years' penal servitude for shooting judge Bristowe at the railway station (19 Nov. 1889), 8 March, 1890
Adcock's factory burnt, estimated loss, 40,000*l.*, 5 June, 1891
The British Association met, 2nd time . 13 Sept. 1893
Great fire, lace manufactories destroyed; estimated damage about 140,000*l.* . . . 17 Nov. 1894
Messrs. Sampson's lace factory burnt; estimated loss, 200,000*l.* . . . . . 13 Jan. 1902
Sanatorium on Ratcher-hill opened by the duke of Portland . . . . 31 May, ,,

NOVARA (N.W. Italy). Near this town the Austrian marshal Radetzky totally defeated the king Charles Albert and the Sardinian army, 23 March, 1849. The contest began at 10 A.M. and lasted till late in the evening; the Austrians lost 396 killed, and had about 1850 wounded; the Sardinians lost between 3000 and 4000 men, 27 cannons, and 3000 prisoners. The king soon after abdicated in favour of his son Victor Emmanuel.

NOVA SCOTIA (N. America), was discovered by Cabot, 1497; visited by Verrazzani, 1524, and named Acadia; settled in 1622, by the Scotch under sir William Alexander, in the reign of James I. of England, from whom it received the name of Nova Scotia. Since its first settlement it has more than once changed proprietors, and was not confirmed to England till the peace of Utrecht, in 1713. It was taken in 1745 and 1758; but was again confirmed to England in 1763. Nova Scotia was divided into two provinces in 1784, and was erected into a bishopric in Aug. 1787. King's College, Windsor, was founded in 1788; see *Baronets*. Gold was found in Nova Scotia in 1861. By an act passed 29 March, 1867, Nova Scotia and New Brunswick were united with Canada for legislative purposes. On the agitation for secession Mr. John Bright presented a petition in the commons 15 May; his motion for a royal commission of inquiry negatived 16 June, 1868. The agitation soon subsided. Lieut.-governor, sir Charles H. Doyle, 1867; Joseph Howe died soon after his appointment, 1 June, 1873; Adams George Archibald, 1873; Matthew Henry Richey, 1883; A. M. McLelan, 1888 (died 26 June, 1890); M. B. Daly, 1890; re-appointed, 1895 (knt. 1900). Capital, Halifax. Population, in 1881, 440,572; 1891, 450,523; 1901, 459,116; Alfred Gilpin Jones, 1901.

The gaol and other buildings at Picton were burnt by the act of a prisoner, who perished, about 8 Nov.; estimated loss, 10,000*l*. 1890
The "Princess," a block of buildings at Yarmouth, burnt, loss about 10,000*l*. . reported 29 Dec. ,,
Explosion at Springhill coal mines; 122 deaths, 21 Feb.; subscriptions in England for sufferers; the queen gives 30*l*. . . . . . March, 1891
Construction of the Chignecto ship railway stopped, after the expenditure of 3,500,000*l*.; 1,500,000*l*. more required . . . . Dec. ,,
Destructive fire at Halifax, and hurricane, about 20 vessels wrecked, with loss of life . 21 Aug. 1893
Great fruit crop, large exportation of apples, 29 Jan. 1895
Clara Friend, American schooner, foundered near Liverpool harbour, during a snowstorm; crew (16) lost . . . . 11 Feb. ,,
Windsor, N.W. of Halifax, destroyed by fire, 17, 18 Oct. 1897; Pugwash, totally destroyed by fire . . . . 25 July, 1898
Thirty-second anniversary of the Canadian confederation; mobilization of the imperial forces under gen. lord Wm. Seymour . . 1 July, 1899
The legislature prorogued; revision of statutes and advancement of railway and mining enterprises, announced . . . . . . 30 March, 1900
Visit of the duke and duchess of Cornwall; see *Canada* . . . . 19 Oct. 1901
Great fire at Pugwash, 25 buildings burnt, 10 Nov. ,,
Disastrous forest fire, reported . . . 4 June, 1903

NOVATIANS, a sect which denied restoration to the church to those who had relapsed during persecution, began with Novatian, a Roman presbyter, in 250; see *Cathari*.

NOVELS (Novellæ), a part of Justinian's Code, published 535. See *Romances*. 1,743 new novels in 1902.

NOVEMBER (*novem*, nine), anciently the ninth month of the year. When Numa added January and February, in 713 B.C., it became the eleventh as now. The Roman senators wished to name this month in which Tiberius was born, by his name, in imitation of Julius Cæsar, and Augustus; but the emperor refused, saying, "What will you do, conscript fathers, if you have *thirteen* Cæsars?"

NOVEMBER METEORS, see *Meteors*.

NOVGOROD (Central Russia), made the seat of his government by Ruric, a Varangian chief, in 862, is held to be the foundation of the Russian empire. In memory of the event the czar inaugurated a national monument at Novgorod, on 20 Sept. 1862. Novgorod became a republic about 1150. Visited by the duke of Edinburgh, 20-27 Aug. 1875. Pan-Russian exhibition opened, 9 June; visited by the czar, 29 July, 1896. Population, 1886: province, 1,231,539; city, 66,585; 1897, province, 1,600,304; city, 95,124.

NOVI (N. Italy). Here the French, commanded by Joubert, were defeated by the Russians under Suwarrow, with immense loss, 15 Aug. 1799. Among the French slain was their leader, Joubert, and other distinguished officers.

NOVI-BAZAR, see *Herzegovina*.

NOVUM ORGANON, the great work of lord Bacon, containing his system of philosophy, was published 1620.

NOXIOUS VAPOURS, see *Alkalies and Chemical Works*.

NOYADES, see *Drowning*.

NUBIA, the ancient Æthiopia *supra Ægyptum*, said to have been the seat of the kingdom of the Meroë, received its name from a tribe named Nubes or Nubates. The Christian kingdom, with Dongola, the capital, lasted till the 14th century, when it was broken up into Mahometan principalities. It is now subject to the viceroy of Egypt, having been conquered by Ibrahim Pacha in 1822.

NUCLEUS THEORY IN CHEMISTRY, see *Compound Radicles*.

NUISANCES REMOVAL ACT; passed 1848; amended 1849; see *Sanitary Legislation*.

NUITS. A small fortified town, near Dijon, in Burgundy, N.E. France, chartered in 1212; frequently captured and ravaged, specially in 1569, 1576, and 1636. It was taken by the Badenese under Von Werder, 18 Dec. 1870, after five hours' conflict, in which above 1000 French are said to have been killed and wounded, and 700 prisoners taken. The German loss was also heavy. A depôt of arms and ammunition was gained by the victors.

NUMANTINE WAR. The war between the Romans and the Celtiberians (Celts who possessed the country near the Iber, now the Ebro) began, 143 B.C., on account of the latter having given refuge to their allies the Sigidians, who had been defeated by the Romans. Numantia, an unprotected city, withstood a long siege, in which the army of Scipio Africanus, 60,000 men, was opposed by no more than 4000 men able to bear arms. The Numantines fed upon horse-flesh, and their own dead, and then drew lots to kill one another. At length they set fire to their houses, and destroyed themselves, so that not one remained to adorn the triumph of the conqueror, 133 B.C.

NUMIDIA (N. Africa), the seat of the war of the Romans with Jugurtha, which began 111 B.C., and ended with his subjugation and captivity, 106. The last king, Juba, joined Cato and was killed at the battle of Thapsus, 46 B.C., when Numidia became a Roman province; see *Mauritania*.

NUMISMATICS, the science of coins and medals, an important adjunct to the study of history. In this country Evelyn (1697), Addison (1726), and Pinkerton (1789), published works on medals. Pellerin's "Recueil des Médailles," 9 vols. 4to (1762). Ruding's *Annals* is the great work on British coinage (new edition, 1840).—The Numismatic Society in London was founded by Dr. John Lee in 1836. It publishes the *Numismatic Chronicle*.—Mr. Yonge Akerman's Numismatic Manual (1840) is a useful introduction to the science. Foreign works are numerous.

NUNCIO, an envoy from the pope of Rome to catholic states. The pope deputed a nuncio to the Irish rebels in 1645. The arrival in London of a nuncio, and his admission to an audience by James II., July, 1687, is stated to have hastened the Revolution.

NUNNERY. The first founded is said to have been that to which the sister of St. Anthony retired at the close of the 3rd century. The first founded in France, near Poictiers, by St. Marcellina, sister to St. Martin, 360.—*Du Fresnoy.* The first in England was at Folkestone, in Kent, by Eadbald, or Edbald, king of Kent, 630.—*Dugdale;* see *Abbeys* and *Monachism.* The nuns were expelled from their convents in Germany, in July, 1785; in France, in Jan. 1790. In Feb. 1861, monastic establishments were abolished in Naples, compensation being made to the inmates. For memorable instances of the fortitude of nuns, see *Acre,* and *Coldingham.*

NUREMBERG, a free imperial German city in 1219. In 1522, the diet here demanded ecclesiastical reforms and a general council, and in 1532 secured religious liberty to the Protestants. It was annexed to Bavaria in 1805. Albert Dürer was born here in 1471. Population, 1890, 142,403; 1900, 261,022.

NURSES, their qualifications have been greatly raised during this century by the influence of Florence Nightingale and the viscountess Strangford, who died 24 March, 1887; both ladies rendered eminent services to the sick and wounded in the Russo-Turkish wars. Institution of Nursing Sisters founded 1840, and many others since. See *Nightingale Fund* and *John, St.*

Mr. (afterwards sir) Henry C. Burdett in Oct. 1887, proposed a scheme for the establishment of the National Pension Fund Royal 1890, for nurses and hospital officials. In Jan. 1888 Messrs. Gibbs, Hambro, J.S. Morgan and Rothschild presented 20,000*l.* towards its foundation; incorporated Feb. 1888; 22,500*l.* presented about 27 Oct. 1895; 5,000*l.* raised by subscription, presented 1 Jan. 1897. Total invested funds, over 372,000*l.* reported 17 March, 1898.

Certificates of membership of the fund presented by the princess of Wales at Marlborough House, 4 July, 1890, to about 650 nurses, who represented the first 1,000 investors in the fund; again to 1,200 nurses, 21 July, 1899.

The family of the late Junius S. Morgan presented 7,731*l.* 15*s.* 5*d.* to the fund named after him, 18 Dec., 1890. Total amount of the fund, 17,000*l.* March, 1898.

70,000*l.* of the Women's Jubilee Offering was devoted to the benefit of nurses and nursing institutions for the sick poor by direction of the queen, 1887; 5,000*l.* presented by Mr. (aft. sir) Henry Tate, Feb. 1896 (died 1899); total, 135,888*l.* 2*s.* 7*d.* subscribed in 1897-1899); (1,000*l.* from lady Tate, Dec. 1901.) See under *Jubilee.*

About 400 of the queen's Jubilee nurses received by the queen at Windsor, 2 July, 1896; 770 received by queen Alexandra, London, 3 July, 1901.

British Nurses' Association, founded 1887 Royal 1891; charter, 1893, princess Christian, president; the duchess of Connaught vice-president, 1899 Annual meetings. Club room and offices, 10, Orchard-street, W. Membership 1902, about 3,000.

"Burdett's Nursing Directory" first published, Nov. 1897.

The Victorian order of nurses founded by lady Aberdeen in Canada in 1897.

Queen Alexandra's Imperial Military Nursing Service (the queen president, lady Roberts vice-president), created, 27 March, 1902.

Women's memorial to queen Victoria; 66,050*l.* collected in England and Wales, total about 80,000*l.*, with subscriptions from Scotland and Ireland, for the queen's nurses endowment fund; presented 21 May, 1903; 1,000*l.* from queen Alexandra, reported, 26 May, 1903.

NYASALAND, the region S.W. and N.W. of Lake Nyasa, E. Africa, occupied by the African Lakes company of Glasgow since its foundation in 1878. It contains missionary stations at Blantyre and Bandawe. Active measures are taken to suppress the slave trade. Prosperity reported, May, 1896. See *Africa, British Central.*

Serious rising of the Southern Angoni in the Domwe district; lieut. Brogden's force encounters a large impi of Angoni, while reconnoitring, 1 Sikh killed, Angoni's loss severe; reported . . . . . 26 June, 1898

Rising ended, Domwe found deserted early July, ,,

British and Portuguese joint expedition against Mataka and other raiding chiefs; successful, Aug.-Oct. ,,

NYNEE TAL, see *Landslips,* 18 Sept. 1880.

NYSTADT, S.W. Finland. By a treaty, signed here 30 Aug. 1721, Sweden ceded Livonia, Esthonia, and other territories to Russia.

O.

OAK, styled the monarch of the woods, and an emblem of strength, virtue, constancy, and long life. That produced in England is considered to be the best calculated for ship-building. In June, 403, the "*Synod of the oak*," was held at Chalcedon. The constellation Robur Caroli, the oak of Charles, was named by Dr. Halley in 1676, in memory of the oak in which Charles II. saved himself from his pursuers, after the battle of Worcester, 3 Sept. 1651; see *Boscobel*, and *Races*.

The evergreen oak, *Quercus Ilex*, brought from the south of Europe before 1581
The scarlet oak, *Quercus coccinea*, brought from North America before 1691
The chestnut-leaved oak, *Quercus Prinus*, from North America before 1730
The Turkey Oak, *Quercus Cerris*, from the south of Europe 1735
The agaric of the oak was known as a styptic in . 1750
Herne's oak, Windsor Park, mentioned in Shakspeare's "Merry Wives of Windsor," finally destroyed by the wind . . . . . 31 Aug. 1863
Existing Oaks, 1879. Cowthorpe, Yorkshire; girth at the ground, 55 feet 6 inches. Newland, Gloucester (mentioned in Domesday Book), 46 feet.

OATES'S PLOT. Titus Oates, at one time chaplain of a ship of war, was dismissed for immoral conduct, and became a lecturer in London. In conjunction with Dr. Tongue, he invented a plot against the Roman Catholics, who he asserted had conspired to assassinate Charles II., and extirpate the Protestant religion. He made it known 12 Aug. 1678, and in consequence about eighteen Roman Catholics were accused, and upon false testimony convicted and executed; among them the aged viscount Stafford, 29 Dec. 1680. Oates was afterwards tried for perjury (in the reign of James II.), and being found guilty, was fined, put in the pillory, publicly whipped from Newgate to Tyburn, and sentenced to imprisonment for life, May, 1685. Pardoned on the accession of William and Mary, and a pension of 3*l*. a week granted to him, 1689.

OATHS were taken by Abraham, B.C. 1892 (*Gen.* xxi. 24), and authorised (B.C. 1491) *Exod.* xxii. 11. The administration of an oath in judicial proceedings was introduced by the Saxons into England, 600.—*Rapin*. That administered to a judge was settled 1344.

Icelandic Oath. "Name I to witness that I take oath by the ring, law-oath, so help me Frey and Niördh, and almighty Thor, as I shall this suit follow or defend, or witness bear, or verdict or doom, as I wit rightest and soothe stand most lawfully," &c. about 925
OF SUPREMACY, first administered to British subjects, and ratified by parliament, 26 Hen. VIII. (*Stow's Chron.*) 1535
Oaths were taken on the Gospels so early as 528; and the words "So help me God and all saints," concluded an oath until 1550
The ancient oath of allegiance, which contained a promise "to be true and faithful to the king and his heirs, and truth and faith to bear of life and limb and terrene honour; and not to know or hear of any ill or damage intended him without defending him therefrom," was modified by James I., a declaration against the pope's authority being added 1603: it was again altered 1689
The affirmation of a Quaker was made equivalent to an oath, by statute, in 1696, *et seq.*
OF ABJURATION, being an obligation to maintain the government of king, lords, and commons, the church of England, and toleration of Protestant dissenters, and abjuring all Roman Catholic pretenders to the crown, 13 Will. III. . . . 1701
The Test and Corporation oaths modified by stat. 9 Geo. IV. (see *Tests*) 1828
Act abolishing oaths in the customs and excise departments, and in certain other cases, and substituting declarations in lieu thereof, 1 & 2 Will. IV. 1831
Affirmation, instead of oath, was permitted to Quakers and other dissenters by acts passed in 1833, 1837, 1838, and 1863 (see *Affirmation*).
In 1858 and 1860, Jews elected M.P. were relieved from part of the oath of allegiance (see *Jews*).
By 24 & 25 Vict. c. 66, a solemn declaration may be substituted for an oath by persons conscientiously objecting to be sworn in criminal prosecutions . 1861
A bill for modifying the oath taken by Roman Catholics (passed by the commons), was rejected by the lords . . . . 26 June, 1865
The oath to be taken by members of parliament was modified by an act passed . . 30 April, 1866
New oath of allegiance provided by the 31st and 32nd Vict. c. 72 (1868), to be taken by the members of the new parliament:—"I do swear that I will be faithful and bear true allegiance to her majesty queen Victoria, her heirs and successors, according to law, so help me God."
Bradlaugh Case, see *Parliament*, 1880.
New parliamentary oaths bill brought in; discharged . . . . 5 July, 1881
Affirmations ordered to be accepted for oaths in France, 2 Feb.; in Spain . . . . April, 1883
Mr. Bradlaugh's Oaths Bill, substituting an affirmation for an oath, in all cases when required (by sec. 5 of this act the Scotch form of taking an oath is permitted when desired); royal assent, 24 Dec. 1888

OBELISK (Greek *obelos*, a spit, *monolithos*, a single stone). The Egyptian symbol of the supreme God. The first mentioned in history was that of Rameses II., king of Egypt, about 1322 B.C. The Arabians called them Pharaoh's needles, and the Egyptian priests the fingers of the sun. Several were erected at Rome; one was erected by the emperor Augustus in the Campus Martius, on the pavement of which was a horizontal dial that marked the hour, about 14 B.C. Of the obelisks brought to Rome by the emperors, several have been restored and set up by various popes. One was excavated and set up in the piazza of St. John Lateran, Rome, by Sixtus V. 1588.

Egyptian Obelisks.—42 are known, some broken: 12 at Rome; 1, from Luxor, set up in the Place de la Concorde, Paris, Oct. 1836; 5 in England (2 British museum; 1 Alnwick; 1 Soughton hall; 1 on Thames embankment).
The obelisks improperly named *Cleopatra's Needles* were erected by Thothmes III. at On (Heliopolis), about 1600 B.C. One was removed to Alexandria by Augustus, about 23 B.C. After being long imbedded in the shore, it was acquired for Great Britain by sir Ralph Abercromby, in 1801; but not removed. It was offered to the British government by Mehemet Ali, and again by the Khedive, 15 March, 1877.
Mr. James Erasmus Wilson (knt. Nov. 1881) having offered to pay all expenses, Mr. John Dixon, the engineer, undertook to convey it to England. The vessel, *Cleopatra*, containing it sailed with the *Olga* 21 Sept. During a violent gale, the vessels were separated, 14-15 Oct.; six lives were lost in a fruitless attempt to recover it. The *Cleopatra*, which was abandoned, was found by the *Fitzmaurice* (capt. Carter), and towed to Ferrol, whence it was towed by the *Anglia*, and arrived in London, 20 Jan. 1878.

The salvage awarded was 2000*l.*, 6 April, 1878.
After much discussion, the Thames embankment (between Charing cross and Waterloo bridges) was selected for its site; where, by much engineering skill, it was placed, 12 Sept. 1878.
The obelisk weighs 186 tons, 7 cwt., 2 stones, 11 lb. Height, from base to point, 68 feet 5½ inches.
It was placed under the care of the metropolitan board of works by act passed 22 July, 1878.
Sir J. Erasmus Wilson died 8 Aug. 1884.
In London are three English obelisks: first in Fleet-street, at the top of Bridge-street, erected to John Wilkes, lord mayor of London in 1775 (see *North Briton*); and immediately opposite to it at the south end of Farringdon-street, stands another of granite to the memory of Robert Waithman, lord mayor in 1824, erected 25 June, 1833; the third at the south end of the Blackfriars-road marks the distance of one mile and a fraction from Fleet-street. Controversy during 1903 respecting its removal and the substitution of an illuminated clock-tower on the site.
The *Washington Obelisk*, at Washington, U.S., 555 feet high, inaugurated, 21 Feb. 1885.

OBER-AMMERGAU PASSION PLAY, see *Drama*.

OBLIVION. In 1660 was passed an act of "free general pardon, indemnity, and oblivion for all treasons and state offences" committed between 1 Jan. 1637, and 24 June, 1660. The regicides and certain Irish popish priests were excepted. A similar act was passed 20 May, 1690. See *Amnesty*.

OBSERVANCE, FATHERS OF THE (or **OBSERVANTS**), a name given to certain members of the Franciscan order, about 1363, who voluntarily undertook the observance of their rule in its pristine rigour. This reformation was after a time enforced by the pope.

OBSERVATORIES, ASTRONOMICAL. The first is said to have been erected on the top of the temple of Belus at Babylon about 2247 B.C. The first in authentic history was at Alexandria, about 300 B.C., erected by Ptolemy Soter. "Observatory, a monthly review of astronomy," first appeared in 1877. Observatories of early date probably existed in Egypt, China, and India.

First modern meridional instrument by Copernicus 1540
First observatory at Cassel 1561
Tycho Brahe's, at Uranienburg 1576
Astronomical tower at Copenhagen . . . 1657
Royal (French) 1667
Royal observatory at Greenwich (*which see*) . . 1675
Observatory at Nuremberg 1678
At Utrecht 1690
Berlin, erected under Leibnitz's direction . . 1711
At Bologna 1714
At St. Petersburg 1725
At Pekin, about 1750
Oxford, *Dr. Radcliffe* 1772
Calton Hill, Edinburgh 1776
Dublin, *Dr. Andrews* 1783
Armagh, *Primate Robinson* 1793
Cambridge, England 1824
Pulkowa, Russia 1839
Cambridge, U.S. 1840
Washington, U.S. 1842
Liverpool, England 1844
Ben Nevis, Scotland 1883
Lick Observatory, on a peak of Mount Hamilton, California, U.S. (4,200 feet above sea-level), endowed by James Lick of San Francisco (who died 1 Oct. 1876); erected . . . . 1888 *et seq.*
The new observatory in the Vatican, completed Jan. 1890
New observatory at Abastrouman, Tiflis, opened 23 Aug. 1892
Mont Blanc, *which see*, 1891–3.
New observatory erected by prof. T. S. C. Lowe on the Sierra Madre mountains, 3,600 ft. above sea level, reported . . . . . 27 Oct. 1894
Blackford Hill, Edinburgh . . . 7 April, 1896
Yerkes observatory, 75 m. from Chicago, 1,200 feet above sea-level, opened . . . 21 Oct. 1897
An observatory established on the top of Mount Kosciusko, New Zealand, at a height of 7,000 feet, reported . . . . . . 11 Dec. 1897
Heidelberg, opened . . . . . 10 June, 1898
Mont Mounier, Maritime Alps, cost defrayed by M. Bischoffsheim, who also endowed the Nice observatory, announced . . . 24 Dec. ,,
Calcutta, at the Presidency college . . Jan. 1902
Regina Margherita, scientific observatory, with physiological laboratory, under prof. Mosso; good report, *Nature* . . . . 17 April, ,,

OBSERVER, Sunday paper (liberal), established 1791.

OC (for *hoc*, yes); *oil*, now *oui*, "yes." See *French Language*.

OCAÑA (central Spain), near which the Spaniards were defeated by the French, commanded by Mortier and Soult, 19 Nov. 1809.

OCCULT SCIENCES (from *occultus*, concealed); see *Astrology*, *Alchemy*, *Magic*, &c.

OCEANA, an imaginary republic, described in a book written by James Harrington, dedicated to Oliver Cromwell, and published in 1656.

OCEAN MONARCH, an American emigrant ship, left Liverpool, bound for Boston, 24 Aug. 1848, having nearly 400 persons on board. When within six miles of Great Orme's head, Carnarvonshire, N. Wales, she took fire, and in a few hours was burnt to the water's edge, and 178 persons perished.
The Brazilian steam-frigate, *Alfonzo*, happened to be out on a trial trip at the time, with the prince and princess de Joinville and the duke and duchess d'Aumale on board, who witnessed the catastrophe, and aided in rescuing and comforting the sufferers. The crews and passengers of the *Alfonzo* and the yacht *Queen of the Ocean* saved 156 persons, and 62 others escaped by various means.

OCTARCHY, see *Britain*.

OCTOBER, the eighth month in the year of Romulus, as its name imports, and the tenth in the year of Numa, 713 B.C. October still retained its first name, although the senate ordered it to be called *Faustinus*, in honour of Faustina, wife of Antoninus the emperor; Commodus called it *Invictus*, and *Domitianus*. October was sacred to Mars.
OCTOBER CLUB. A party of country gentlemen in the house of commons, about 1710, which professed high church principles, and favoured Bolingbroke and the Jacobite cause.

OCTROIS (from the low Latin *auctorium*, authority), a term applied to concessions from sovereigns, and to the taxes levied at the gates of towns in France on articles of food before entering the city. These octrois, of ancient origin, were suppressed in 1791; re-established, 1797, and reorganised in 1816, 1842, and 1852. In 1859, the octrois of Paris produced above 54 million francs. The Belgian government became very popular in July, 1860, by abolishing the *Octrois*. The Coal and Wine dues of London were of this nature.

ODDFELLOWS, Unity of, the name of a large friendly society, originally of a convivial character, which took its present name in 1812. It has numerous branches, but its headquarters are in Manchester. In 1886, there were 617,587 members; in 1892, 709,403 members, income, 1,361,314*l.*; capital, 7,630,228*l.*; 1895, 739,449 members, 8,420,452*l.* capital; 1901, 850,709 members, 10,750,954*l.* capital.

ODD VOLUMES, SETTE OF. A literary society established in London; dined at Freemasons' Tavern, London, Jan. 1884. The society prints for private distribution, small out-of-the-way works.

ODES are very ancient; amongst the Greeks they were extempore compositions sung in honour of the gods. Anacreon's odes were composed about 532; Pindar's, 498 to 446; and Horace's from 24 to 13, all B.C. Anciently odes were divided into strophe, antistrophe, and epode; see *Poets Laureate.*

ODESSA, a port on the Black Sea, built by the empress Catharine of Russia, 1784-1792, after the peace of Jassy. In 1817 it was made a free port, since when its prosperity has rapidly increased. It was partially bombarded by the British, 21 April, 1854, in consequence of the Russian batteries having fired on a flag of truce, 6 April. On 12 May the English frigate *Tiger* stranded here, and was destroyed by Russian artillery. The captain, Giffard, and many of his crew were killed, and the rest made prisoners. Population, 1885, 240,000; 9 Feb. 1897, 404,651.

Military and naval manœuvres begin; H.M.S. *Melita* most cordially received . 6-12 Sept. 1899
Great petroleum fire . . . . 18, 19 Nov. 1902

ODOMETER (from the Greek *hodos*, way, and *metron*, measure), see *Pedometer.*

ODONTOLOGY (from the Greek *odontes*, teeth), the science of the teeth, may be said to have really begun with the researches of professor Richard Owen, who in 1839 made the first definite announcement of the organic connection between the vascular and vital soft parts of the frame and the hard substance of a tooth. His comprehensive work, "Odontography" (illustrated with beautiful plates), was published 1840-45. The Odontological Society was established 1856.

ODRYSÆ, a people of Thrace. Their king Teres retained his independence of the Persians, 508 B.C. Sitalces, his son, enlarged his dominions, and in 429, aided Amyntas against Perdiccas II., of Macedon, with an army of 150,000 men. Sitalces, killed in battle with the Triballi, 424, was succeeded by Seuthes, who reigned prosperously; Cotys, another king (382-353), disputed the possession of the Thracian Chersonesus with Athens. After 9 or 10 years' warfare, Philip II. of Macedon reduced the Odrysæ to tributaries, and founded Philippopolis and other colonies, 343. The Romans, after their conquest of Macedon, favoured the Odrysæ, and in 42 their king Sadales bequeathed his territories to the Romans. The Odrysæ, turbulent subjects, and often chastised, were finally incorporated into the empire by Vespasian, about A.D. 70.

ODYL, the name given in 1845 by baron von Reichenbach to a so-called new "imponderable, or influence," said to be developed by magnets, crystals, the human body, heat, electricity, chemical action, and the whole material universe. The odylic force is said to give rise to luminous phenomena, visible to certain sensitive persons only. The baron's "Researches on Magnetism, &c., in relation to the Vital Force," translated by Dr. Gregory, were published in 1850. Emanuel Swedenborg (died 1772) described similar phenomena.

ŒCUMENICAL BISHOP (from the Greek *oikoumenē*, the habitable, *globe* understood), "universal bishop;" a title assumed by John, bishop of Constantinople, 587.

ŒNOPHYTA (Bœotia, N. Greece). Here Myronides and the Athenians severely defeated the Bœotians, 456 B.C.

OFEN, see *Buda.*

OFFA'S DYKE, the intrenchment from the Wye to the Dee, made by Offa, king of Mercia, to defend his country from the incursions of the Welsh, 779.

OFFICIAL SECRETS ACT, passed 26 Aug. 1889, punishes disclosures as a misdemeanour.

OFFICIAL INTELLIGENCE, see *Stocks.*

OGULNIAN LAW, carried by the tribunes Q. and Cn. Ogulnius, increased the number of the pontiffs and augurs, and made plebeians eligible to those offices, B.C. 300.

OGYGES, see *Deluge.*

OHIO, a western state of North America, settled by the French in 1673, was ceded to the British with Canada, in 1763; extensively settled in 1788, and admitted into the Union, 29 Nov. 1802. Capital, Columbus; see *Storms*, 1890. Explosion of 16 tons of gunpowder at King's powder mills, 20 miles from Cincinnati, 20 persons killed, 15 July, 1890. Population, 1880, 3,198,062; 1890, 3,672,316; 1900, 4,157,545.

Fire at lumber yards at Coalgrove, 3 deaths; estimated loss 750,000 dollars . . . . 7 April, 1893
Fire at Toledo, chamber of commerce, &c. destroyed, estimated loss 1,000,000 dollars . . 3 Jan. 1894
Destructive rioting at Cleveland, suppressed by the military . . . . 1 May, „
Lynching riot, suppressed by the military, 3 persons killed . . . . . . 16, 18 Oct. „
Anti-negro riot at Akron, city hall burnt, gaol attacked, 3 deaths and 18 wounded . 22 Aug. 1900

OHM'S LAW, for determining the quantity of the electro-motive force of the voltaic battery, was published in 1827. It is in conformity with the discovery that the earth may be employed as a conductor, thus saving the return wire in electric telegraphy.

OIL was used for burning in lamps as early as the epoch of Abraham, about 1921 B.C. It was the custom of the Jews to anoint with oil persons appointed to high offices, as the priests and kings, *Psalm* cxxxiii. 2; 1 *Sam.* x. 1; xvi. 13. The fact that oil, if passed through red-hot iron pipes, will be resolved into a combustible gas, was long known to chemists; and after the process of lighting by coal-gas was made apparent, Messrs. Taylor and Martineau contrived apparatus for producing oil-gas on a large scale, 1815.—OIL SPRINGS; see *Petroleum.* OIL FRESCOS; see under *Painting.*

To supply oil to calm the waves, pipes were laid down in the port of Aberdeen; experiments with Mr. Shield's apparatus, 26 Sept.; successful experiments reported . . . . . 4 Dec. 1882
Scotch fishing vessels provided with oil tanks, Nov. 1883
Mr. Shield's plans successful at Folkestone harbour, Jan. 1884
Capt. Chetwind reports oil to be ineffectual in regard to breakers and surf . . . . Oct. „
Mr. Gordon's oil-shells shot out at Montrose said to calm the sea . . . . . . 6 April, 1885
Crude petroleum tried as a dust layer near Farnborough . . . . . . 27 Sept. 1902

OIL PAINTING, see *Painting.* The Institute of Painters in Oil Colours established; first President Mr. J. H. Linton; 94 members elected, Feb.; first exhibition opened 17 Dec. 1883.

OIL RIVERS, now called "Niger Coast Protectorate" (1894), a territory on the W. coast of Africa, between Cameroons and Lagos, adjoining the territories of the Royal Niger company, see *Niger.* It contains six main rivers, which derive their general name from palm oil, the chief product, with a population reported above 12,000,000.

The country was visited first by missionaries early in the 19th century, and afterwards by traders, who by peaceful means have gradually established plantations and nearly 40 factories in the interior. The region was placed under British protection, with a consul, in 1884. The traders formed themselves into an association, Feb. 1890; major sir Claude Maxwell MacDonald appointed commissioner, with consular jurisdiction . . . Nov. 1890
Good report . . . . Jan. 1893
Conflicts with the chief Nana in Benin checked by H.M.S. *Alecto* and others, 25,29 Aug. 1894; captain Lalor died of his wounds, 3 Sept.; admiral Bedford, of the *Philomel*, captures Nana's stronghold on the Benin river, 25 Sept.; Nana surrenders at Lagos, reported 30 Oct.; sentenced to life imprisonment, 6 Dec. 1894; partially commuted, Nov. 1896

Consul-gen. Phillips, major Copland Crawford, capts. Boisragon and Maling, Dr. Elliott, Messrs. Campbell, Locke, Powis, and Gordon, with 250 native carriers, left Sapele, unarmed, on a peaceful mission to Benin city, 2 Jan. 1897; well received at Gwato, 4 Jan.; proceeded on their journey, intending to remonstrate with the king, who was carrying on an annual butchery of slaves; all shot dead from an ambuscade except capt. Boisragon, Mr. Ralph Locke, and about 15 carriers, who escaped into the bush (Mr. Campbell was captured and afterwards put to death), 5 Jan. 1897

Punitive expedition under lieut.-col. Bruce Hamilton, Mr. R. D. Moor, commissioner (K.C.M.G. June, 1897), and other officers, with a flotilla under rear-adm. Rawson, arrives at Siri, 6 Feb; adm. Rawson captures Gwato, Sapobo (lieut. Pritchard, of H.M.S. *Alecto*, and one man killed, 11 Feb.), and Ologbo . . . 12 Feb. ,,
Benin city taken by col. Bruce Hamilton's force after a running 8 hours' fight in the bush; Dr. C. J. Fyfe and 7 others killed, capt. G. Taylor Byrne mortally wounded; human sacrifices and corpses found everywhere . . . . . . 18 Feb. ,,
Fort erected at Benin city, lieut. A. H. Turner appointed resident, March (died of fever, Sept.) ,,
A patrol under lieuts. Carrol and Fitzgerald defeats the fugitive king of Benin, 9 June; and again in the Protectorate territory, lieut. Fitzgerald and 2 men killed, June; the king and about 3,000 men surrender at Benin city, 7 Aug.; removed to Old Calabar; 2 chiefs executed for the Benin massacre . . . . Oct. ,,
Capt. Roupell, resident, country peaceful . Sept. ,,
Further operations against rebellious tribes in the *Hinterland* of Benin; 2 towns captured, severe fighting, 150 natives killed, and 7 Hausas killed, 13–16 Nov. 1898

Capt. Parker killed in an attack by natives on his expedition . . . . . . early April, 1899
Punitive expedition under major Carter leaves Benin City 20 April; Ologbosheri's town and himself captured by capt. Gabbett after heavy fighting, lieut. Uniacke killed, 24 April; the chief charged with the massacre of Europeans and natives (Jan. 1897), is hanged, 28 June, 1899; his son Okoro given up by the natives . June, ,,

OKAPI, a new mammal (giraffe-like), first heard of by sir H. M. Stanley; discovered by sir Harry Johnston in the Semliki forest, Central Africa; *Times*, 7 May, 1901.

OKLAHOMA ("beautiful land"), a part of the "Indian Territory" situated between Texas, Kansas, and Arkansas, partly inhabited by Indians. The western part of the territory was ceded to the United States in 1866. It has been surveyed and divided into 85 townships. See *United States*, 1889.

Great distress caused through the destruction of the promising crops by a hot wind (15 June); about 30,000 destitute persons, government relief promised . . . . Dec. 1890
Destructive tornado, with loss of 100 lives, 25 April, 1893
Rioting and dynamite outrages, reported . 18 July, 1894
Towns: Guthrie, Oklahoma, Kingfisher, and others.
Additional lands opened, Sept. 1891. Population, 1890, 61,834; 1900, 398,331.

OLBERS, the asteroid, now termed *Pallas*, discovered by M. Olbers, in 1802.

OLD BAILEY SESSIONS COURT is held for the trial of criminals, and its jurisdiction comprehends the county of Middlesex as well as the city of London. It is held eight times in the year by the royal commission of *oyer* and *terminer*. The judges are, the lord mayor, those aldermen who have passed the chair, the recorder and the common-serjeant, who are attended by both the sheriffs, and one or more of the national judges. The court-house was built in 1773, and enlarged in 1808; the lord mayor lays the first stone of the new session house here, 20 Dec. 1902; see *Central Criminal Court*.

During some trials in the old court, the lord mayor, one alderman, two judges, the greater part of the jury, and numbers of spectators, caught the gaol distemper, and died . . . . . May, 1750
This disease was fatal to several 1772
Twenty-eight persons killed at the execution of Mr. Steele's murderers at the Old Bailey . 23 Feb. 1807

OLD BELIEVERS, a Russian sect, said to number about 12,000,000, originated in a revolt against the cruelties of the patriarch Nicon, whom they named Anti-Christ, 1654. They profess to adhere to the old reading of the Sclavonian sacred books, which have been superseded by the present Russian church. The czar Alexander II. granted liberty of worship to the sect in 1879.

OLD CATHOLICS, the name assumed in Germany by the members of the Roman Catholic church opposed to the dogma of papal infallibility, headed by professor Döllinger of Munich (see *Councils*, 18 July, 1870). After three days' conference at Munich, Sept. 1871, they decided to set up independent worship, first meeting in a church given them by the town council of Munich. The abbé Michaud began a similar movement in Paris in Feb. 1872. Dr. Döllinger preached in favour of union with the church of England, March, 1872. Père Hyacinthe (Charles Loyson), president of the party at Rome, issued a programme, respecting the Vatican decrees, recognising ecclesiastical authorities, demanding reform, yet opposing schism, about 5 May, 1872. The bishops of Lincoln (Wordsworth) and Ely (Browne) and the dean of Westminster (Dr. Stanley), by invitation, attended the conference at Cologne, and delivered addresses, 20-22 Sept. 1872. The Old Catholics elected their first bishop, Dr. Joseph Reinkens, 1 June, 1873, who was recognised by the emperor and other powers.

Congress of old Catholics held at Constance, 18 Sept. 1873; at Freiburg . . . . . 6 Sept. 1874
First synod held in Germany at Bonn, opened 27 May, ,,

Dr. Döllinger received delegates from eastern and western churches at Bonn, with a view for union with the old Catholics; and after much discussion certain preliminaries were agreed on; much result was not expected . . . 14 Sept. ,,
First old Catholic church in Berlin opened 30 Nov. ,,
In Prussia about 20,000 old Catholics (about 8,000,000 Romanists) 1875

Congress at Bonn: bishop of Winchester, canon Liddon, and several oriental clergy present, 12 Aug.; agreement respecting the *filioque* clause 16 Aug. ,,

Circular put forth by the old Catholics at Bonn asking for a church for their worship; (they declare opposition to the Vatican decrees of 18 July, 1870; they do not secede from the Catholic church, but desire Catholicism free from debasing doctrines; repudiate infallibility and supremacy of the pope; sanction reading of the Bible, and divine worship in the vulgar tongue; and marriage of priests) . . . . Dec. 1875
Congress at Bonn; strong opposition to celibacy of clergy; question deferred, early in . . June, 1876
Congress at Mentz opens . . . . . 28 Sept. 1877
Meeting at Berne: bishop Cotterill of Edinburgh and M. Hyacinthe Loyson there, 17 Aug. 1879; at Geneva, 23 May, 1880; at Baden-Baden 19-21 Sept. 1880; at Vienna, ... 8 Sept. 1886
Visits of the bishops of Lichfield (W. D. Maclagan) and Salisbury (J. Wordsworth), congresses at Bonn, &c., in Switzerland, and at Vienna, Oct. 1887; international congresses at Cologne, 12 Sept. 1890; at Lucerne, 12 Sept. 1892; at Rotterdam, Aug. 1894; at Vienna, 1 Sept. 1897; at Bonn . . . . 5 Aug. 1902
[The doctrines of the Old Catholics closely resemble those of the church of England.]
The progress of the Italian catholic church opposed to the papacy, reported . . . . . Feb. 1888
Dr. Döllinger's ninetieth birthday celebrated at Munich, 28 Feb. 1889; he died . 10 Jan. 1890
Dr. Weber, of Breslau, consecrated bishop in succession to dr. Reinkens, who died . . Jan. 1896

OLDENBURG, a grand duchy in North Germany, was annexed to Denmark in 1448; in 1773, Christian VII. ceded the country to Russia in exchange for Holstein Gottorp, and soon after the present dignity was established. The duke joined the North German confederation, 18 Aug. 1866, and obtained a slight increase of territory from Holstein, 27 Sept. following. The grand duchy comprises Oldenburg proper, the principality of Lübeck, and that of Birkenfeld. Population in 1864, 301,812; in 1871, 314,591; in 1880, 337,478; 1890, 354,968; 1900, 398,500.

DUKES.

1773. Frederick Augustus.
1785. Peter Frederick. The duchy was seized by Napoleon, and annexed to his empire in 1811; but restored in 1814.

GRAND-DUKES.

1829. May 21. Augustus.
1853. Feb. 27. Peter, son; born 8 July, 1827; died, 13 June, 1900.
1900. Frederick Augustus, son; born 16 Nov. 1852; married princess Elizabeth of Mecklenburg-Schwerin, 24 Oct. 1896. *Heir:* Nicholas, born 1897.

OLDHAM, Lancashire, a village in 1760, was incorporated in 1849, and has sent two members to parliament since 1832, when William Cobbett was elected one of the members. It has extensive cotton manufactories. The handsome town-hall was built in 1841, and enlarged in 1879. Alexandra park was opened in 1865. Population, 1881, 111,343; 1891, 131,463; 1901, 137,382.

OLD MAN OF THE MOUNTAIN, see *Assassins*.

OLD STYLE, see *New Style*.

OLEFIANT GAS, a combination of hydrogen and carbon, which burns with much brilliancy. In 1862, Berthelot formed it artificially by means of alcohol.

OLEOMETER, an instrument for determining the density of fixed oils at a standard temperature of 59° Fahr. The oleometers most in use are those of Gobby, Lefebre, Fisher and Brix. This instrument is also called the *Elaiometer*.

OLERON, see *Navigation Laws*.

OLIBANUM, a kind of gum obtained from various species of *Boswellia* found growing on the limestone rocks of Somaliland and in Southern Arabia. It is identical with the *thus* of the Romans, and is largely used as incense, and a considerable trade in this product is carried on at Aden. Large quantities of olibanum are used in India.

OLIVES are named in the earliest accounts of Egypt and Greece. They were first planted in Italy about 562 B.C. The olive has been cultivated in England since 1648 A.D.; the Cape olive since 1730. From the olive is obtained *oleic acid*, a colourless, oily fluid, and in its combined forms is used in medicine, and in soap manufacture.

MOUNT OF OLIVES, also named *Mount Olivet*, a ridge of rocks situated east of Jerusalem, from which it is separated by the valley of Jehoshaphat. Here Titus encamped when he besieged Jerusalem 70 A.D. The Mount is chiefly associated with the life of our Lord; here, according to tradition, the angels appeared to the disciples after the resurrection. Christ taught His disciples the Lord's prayer; and here he wept over Jerusalem. On the summit of the central peak is built the Church of the Ascension, the site of an earlier church erected by St. Helena.

OLMÜTZ, the ancient capital of Moravia. Here the emperor Ferdinand abdicated, on behalf of his nephew, Francis Joseph, 2 Dec. 1848; and here the latter promulgated a new constitution, 4 March, 1849. A conference was held here, 29 Nov. 1850, under the czar Nicholas, when the difficulties between Austria and Prussia respecting the affairs of Hesse-Cassel were arranged.

OLTENITZA. A Turkish force having crossed the Danube, under Omar Pacha, established themselves at Oltenitza, in spite of the vigorous attacks of the Russians, who were repulsed with loss, 2 and 3 Nov. 1853. On the 4th a desperate attempt to dislodge the Turks by general Danneberg with 9000 men, was defeated with great loss.

OLYMPIA, West Kensington, opened 27 Dec. 1886. See under *Agriculture*, and *Irish Exhibition*.

First great horse show of English Horse Society opened here . . . . 15 May, 1889
See under *Horse*.
The pictures not accepted by the Royal Academy for exhibition in 1889 were exhibited here 22 June, *et seq.*, ,,
See *Barnum's Show*.
Olympia opened as a skating rink for roller skates 21 April, 1890
Olympia taken by Mr. Augustus Harris and a syndicate . . . . Feb. 1891
Representations of ancient and modern Venice entirely designed and constructed by Mr. Imre Kiralfy, exhibiting the scenery, the life of the inhabitants, manufactures (including Dr. Salviati's glass manufacture), 100 gondolas, with gondoliers, a grand aquatic carnival, and other entertainments; opened, 26 Dec. 1891 . 7 Jan. 1893
Representation of Constantinople constructed by Mr. Bolossy Kiralfy, Mr. Wilson Bennington, Signor Joseph Goletti, and other artists; it included the bridge of boats across the Golden Horn, the Tower of Galata, &c., historic pageants, tableaux, &c. opened . . . . . 26 Dec. ,,
Visit of the prince and princess of Wales and family, 8 Feb.; closed . . . . 20 Oct. 1894
"The *Orient*," representing Turkey, Egypt, India, &c., opened . . . . . 26 Dec. ,,
A compulsory winding-up order granted, the company not having raised sufficient capital, 1 July, 1895; first meeting of creditors, 10 Aug. 1896.
New entertainments by sir Augustus Harris and others, 26 Dec. 1895; gardens and hall erected, opened . . . . May, 1896

The Barnum and Bailey show (about 1,600 men and women employed): spectacular military drama, "The Mahdi, or For the Victoria Cross," native dances, etc.; menagerie, Johanna, the educated gorilla, etc.; and human monstrosities, 27 Dec. 1897–2 April, 1898. 2nd exhibition opened . . . . 26 Dec. 1898–8 April, 1899
See *Barnum's Show.*

Buffalo's Bill's Wild West, 26 Dec. 1902 . 4 April, 1903
National sports exhibition, 26 Dec. 1903 to Easter 1904

OLYMPIADS, the era of the Greeks, from 1 July, 776 B.C., the year in which Corœbus was successful at the Olympic games. This era was reckoned by periods of four years, each period being called an Olympiad, and in marking a date the year and Olympiad were both mentioned. The computation of Olympiads ceased with the 305th, A.D. 440.

OLYMPIC GAMES, so famous among the Greeks, traditionally said to have been instituted in honour of Jupiter by the Idæi Dactyli, 1453 B.C., or by Pelops, 1307 B.C., revived by Iphitus, 884 B.C., were held at intervals of four years, on the banks of the Alpheus, near Olympia, in the Peloponnesus, now the Morea, to exercise the youth in five kinds of combats; the conquerors being highly honoured. The prize contended for was a crown made of a kind of wild olive, appropriated to this use. The festival was abolished by Theodosius, A.D. 394. In 1858 M. Zappas, a wealthy Peloponnesian, gave funds to re-establish these games, under the auspices of the queen of Greece.—OLYMPIC THEATRE, London, opened 1806; see *Theatres.*

The revival of the games every four years at some European capital was decided on at an international congress at Paris in 1894. First to be at Athens in 1896; second at Paris in 1900.
Preliminary contests to select champions held in the ancient stadium, capable of seating 50,000 persons, renovated by M. Averoff of Alexandria (died 27 July, 1899) (80,000*l.*), the king and family present (129 foreign athletes to compete), 21, 22 March, 1896
The statue of M. Averoff unveiled by the crown prince . . . . 5 April, ,,
The 75th anniversary of Greek independence, and inauguration of the Olympic games (ancient and modern) by the king and royal family, address by the crown prince, etc., 6 April; king Alexander of Servia present, 8 April *et seq.*; the race from Marathon won by Louis, a Greek peasant, 70,000 spectators, 10 April; end of the games, prizes distributed; Pindaric ode by Mr. G. S. Robertson, recited, several addresses presented, 15 April, ,,

OLYMPIEUM (near Peloponnesus), the great temple of Jupiter, erected by Libon, of Elis, about 450, at the charge of the Eleans, after their conquest of the country. For this temple Phidias made the colossal statue of the god, in gold and ivory, 437-433 B.C.

The German explorations by Messrs. Hirschfeld and Bötticher, planned by prof. Ernst Curtius, the historian, began in Oct. 1875. Torsos and other relics were found. Above 904 objects in marble, many coins, bronzes, inscriptions, &c., found, 1875-8. Explorations closed, Nov. 1880.

OLYNTHUS, a city, N. Greece. To resist the predominance of Sparta, it formed a league with other cities, which was subdued in war, 382-379 B.C. It resisted Philip of Macedon, 350 B.C., by whom it was destroyed, 347. Demosthenes delivered three orations on its behalf, 349.

OMAHA, the principal city of Nebraska, situated on the river Missouri, which is spanned by a bridge 2,750 ft. in length. Founded in 1854, the city has rapidly developed, and is now (1903) one of the most prosperous of the cities of the Eastern States. Omaha contains many handsome public buildings and churches. Manufactures and industries of various kinds are carried on, the most important being its large silver-smelting works, said to be the largest in the world, and its pork-packing business, third only in importance to that of Chicago. A large trade in grain is also carried on. Population 1860, 1,902; 1880, 30,518; 1890, 140,452.

OMAN, an independent Mahommetan state, S.E. Arabia, ruled by a sultan. Population 1,500,000 (about); capital Muscat, *which see.*

OMENS, see *Augury.* Alexander the Great and Mithridates the Great are said to have studied omens. At the birth of the latter, 131 B.C., there were seen for seventy days together, two splendid comets; and this omen, we are told, directed all the actions of Mithridates throughout his life.—*Justin.*

OMER, ST., N.E. France. At this town in 1592, the eminent Jesuit, father Parsons, founded a seminary for the education of English and Irish Roman Catholics, in which there were 50 pupils in 1594. The Seminary was suppressed in 1762, and the masters and pupils migrated successively to Bruges, Liége, and in 1794 to England, by invitation. The seminary of St. Omer was much referred to during the trials connected with Oates's plot in 1678. See *Stonyhurst.*

OMLADINA, an Austrian political society composed of Slav students, journalists, and working men; about 800 members, divided into groups, with officers, was formed at Vienna in 1890, to promote the federation of the empire, with equal rights for all classes. See *Austria,* 1894.

OMMIADES, a dynasty of Mahometan caliphs, beginning with Moawiyah, of whom fourteen reigned in Arabia, 661–750; and eighteen at Cordova, in Spain, 755-1031. Their favourite colour was green.

OMNIBUS (from *omnibus,* Latin "for all"). The idea of such conveyances is ascribed to Pascal, about 1662, when similar carriages were started, but soon discontinued. They were revived in Paris about 11 April, 1828; and introduced into London by a coach proprietor named Shillibeer. The first omnibus started from Paddington to the Bank of England on Saturday, 4 July, 1829. Regulations were made respecting omnibuses by 16 & 17 Vict. c. 33 (1853). See *Cabriolets* and *Hackney Coaches.* The London Omnibus Company was established in Jan. 1856. The saloon omnibuses ran in 1857-60. In Sept. 1865, it was stated that there were then running about 620 omnibuses belonging to the General Omnibus Company, and 450 belonging to private proprietors; in 1867, about 1050 omnibuses, with 13,000 drivers and conductors.—*Sir R. Mayne.* In 1873 about 1,400 omnibuses; 1891, 2,415; 1893, 2,366; 1896, 3,001; 1902, 4,200. Dividend, Aug. 1878, 12½ per cent.; 1903, 7 per cent. An *omnibus bill,* one which deals with many topics.

The London Road Car Company registered 1 Jan. 1883.
The number of omnibuses greatly increased, daily additions with cheap fares, some 1*d.* and ½*d.* 1889–92.
Strike of the men employed by the General Omnibus and Road Car Companies, claiming a twelve hours' day, 7 June; closed by concessions, 13 June, 1891.
The Workers' co-operative omnibus company formed; new omnibuses ordered, 30 Dec. 1891.

OMNIMETER, a new surveying apparatus (combining the theodolite and level, and comprising a telescope and microscope), invented by Eckhold, a German engineer, to supersede chain measuring; announced Sept. 1869.

ONE-POUND NOTES issued by the Bank of England, 4 March, 1797, withdrawn for England, 1823; re-issued for a short time, 16 Dec. 1825.

Mr. Goschen's proposal in 1891 to issue one pound notes to increase the reserve of gold at the Bank of England was much discussed, and at a meeting of the London chamber of commerce the consideration of the question was deferred (51 to 14), 21 Jan. 1892.

ONEIDA, collision with the *Bombay;* see *United States*, 1870.

ONTARIO, formerly Canada West, or Upper Canada; capital, Toronto. Bishopric founded 1861. Comber, 30 miles from Amherstburg, destroyed by fire, 27 April, 1891. Population, 1861, 1,396,091; 1881, 1,923,228; 1891, 2,112,989; 1901, 2,182,942. Lieut.-governor, hon. sir Alexander Campbell, 1887; hon. G. A. Kirkpatrick, 1892 (knt. 1897, died 13 Dec. 1899); sir Oliver Mowat, 1897 (died 19 April, 1903). W. Mortimer Clark, 21 April, 1903. During a meeting the flooring in the city hall, London, gave way, 22 persons were killed and over 100 injured, 3 Jan. 1898.

O. P. (old prices) RIOT began on the opening of the new Covent Garden Theatre, London, by J. P. Kemble, with increased prices of admission, 18 Sept., and lasted till 16 Dec. 1809, when the old charges were restored. Of the play, *Macbeth*, not one word was heard, and great injury was done to the theatre.

OPEN-AIR MISSION, founded 1853. Races, fairs, &c., are visited by preachers. Jubilee celebrated 21 April, 1903.

"OPEN DOOR," a term much used with regard to China, 1897 *et seq*, implying equality of treatment and absence of differential duties as between nation and nation; *Times*, 24 Nov. 1898.

Negotiations with the powers and Japan, maintaining the policy of holding China open to the world's commerce, successfully concluded by Mr. Hay, U.S. secretary of state, Washington, announced . . . . 2 Jan. 1900

OPEN SPACES ACT (METROPOLITAN), 40 & 41 Vict. c. 35 (1877), authorises the Metropolitan Board of Works and the corporation of London to acquire open spaces for the benefit of the public. Acts consolidated in 1887. Another act, 29 June, 1893, see *Commons*. About 220 open spaces, 1902.

OPERA, originated with the Greeks; the earliest librettos were by Sophocles and Æschylus, such as the *Agamemnon* and *Antigone*; a band of lyres and flutes constituted the orchestra; the dialogues were musically declaimed, and the choruses sung to the best music of the time. This was the germ of all later developments. *Grove.*

Adam de la Hale, a Trouvère, "le Bossu d'Arras," born 1240, composed the first comic opera, *Li Gieus* (Le Jeu) *de Robin et de Marion. Le Ballet comique de la Royne*, composed by Beaulieu and Salmon, was performed before Henri III. in 1581.

ITALIAN OPERA began with Cavaliere's *Il Satiro* (1590); Orazio Vecchi's *L'Amfiparnasso*, printed at Venice, 1594; Peri's *Dafne* (1597), libretto by Rinuccini; their *Euridice* was performed at Florence on the marriage of Henry IV. of France with Maria de' Medici in 1600. Monteverde's *Arianna* was produced in 1607; *Orfeo*, 1608; full score published at Venice in 1609. Perrin's *Pomone*, with music by Cambert, was performed in Paris in 1669; Lulli's *Atys*, 1676, etc.

Johann Theile's *Adam und Eva* was performed in German at Hamburg in 1678, and Reinhard Keiser, founder of the great German school, produced over 116 operas there: *Basilius*, 1693; *Circe*, 1734. Scarlatti composed 109 operas, followed by Stradella, Caldara, and others, 1680 *et seq.* N. Logroscino and Piccini developed the opera buffa, 1700–70. Handel wrote 42 operas: *Almira*, 1705; *Roderigo*, 1706; *Rinaldo*, brought out at the Haymarket, 1711; *Radamisto*, 1720, etc. J. A. Hasse produced many operas at Dresden. Gluck, a great reformer, composed *Orfeo ed Euridice*, 1762; *Alceste*, 1767; *Iphigénie en Aulide*, 1774; *Iphigénie en Tauride*, 1779. Mozart's *Die Entführung aus dem Serail* appeared, 1782; *Le Nozze di Figaro* and *Die Zauberflöte*, 1786; *Il Don Giovanni*, 1787; *La Clemenza di Tito*, 1791. Cimarosa's *Il Matrimonio segreto*, 1792. Cherubini's *Lodoiska*, 1791; *Les Deux Journées*, 1880; *Ali Baba*, 1833, etc. Beethoven's *Fidelio*, 1805; Spontini's *La Vestale*, and Mehul's *Joseph*, 1807. Rossini's *Il Tancredi*, 1813; *Barbiere di Seviglia* and *Otello*, 1816; *La Gazza Ladra*, 1817; *Semiramide*, 1823; *Guillaume Tell*, 1829. Spohr's *Jessonda*, 1823, etc. Weber's *Der Freischütz*, 1821; *Euryanthe*, 1823; *Oberon*, 1826. Marschner's *Der Vampyr*, 1828; *Templar und Judin*, 1829, etc. Auber's *Masaniello*, 1828, etc. Bellini's *La Sonnambula*, 1831; *Norma*, 1832, etc. Donizetti's *Lucia di Lammermoor*, 1835; *Lucrezia Borgia*, 1840, etc. Halévy's *La Juive*, 1835, etc. Meyerbeer's *Robert le Diable*, 1831; *Les Huguenots*, 1836; *Le Prophète*, 1843, etc. Berlioz's *Benvenuto Cellini*, 1838. Wagner, musician and poet, produced *Rienzi*, 1842; *Der fliegende Holländer*, 1843; *Tannhäuser*, 1845; *Lohengrin*, 1850; *Tristan und Isolde*, 1865; *Die Meistersinger*, 1868; *Der Ring des Nibelungen*, 1873–76; *Parsifal*, 1882, see *Music*, 1873–83. Gounod's *La Nonne sanglante*, 1854; *Faust*, 1859; *Philémon et Baucis*, 1861; *Roméo et Juliette*, 1867; *Polyeucte*, 1878, etc. Bizet's *Carmen*, 1875.

Verdi's *Oberto*, 1839; *Rigoletto*, 1851; *Il Trovatore* and *La Traviata*, 1853, etc.; *Aida*, 1871; *Otello*, 1887; *Falstaff*, 1891. (Verdi died, aged 87, 27 Jan. 1901.)

Ambroise Thomas's *La Double Echelle*, 1837; *Mignon*, 1866; *Hamlet*, 1868; *Françoise de Rimini*, 1882, etc.

Mascagni's *Cavalleria Rusticana*, 1892; Leoncavallo's *I Pagliacci*, 1892.

Humperdinck's fairy opera *Hänsel und Gretel*, 1893.

OPERA IN ENGLAND grew out of the *masque*. Henry Purcell was the first to change the masque into the opera. He wrote *Dido and Æneas* (1680), *King Arthur* (1691), *Bonduca* (1695), and many other complete operas, besides numerous dramatic compositions. By the exertions of Mr. Carl Rosa (Rosé) and the company formed by him, since 1875 (termed Royal, 1892) performances of English opera have been greatly promoted in England. The company was joined by Mr. (aft. sir) Augustus Harris in April, 1889, and obtained the command of Drury Lane in addition to Covent Garden and the Prince of Wales's.—Carl Rosa died, aged 46, 30 April, 1889, much lamented. See *Theatres*.

The Opera Company liquidating Jan. 1890; arrangements with Mr. A. Harris terminated . Nov. 1890

Sir Augustus Harris born 1852, died . 22 June 1896

The Carl Rosa Company held Daly's theatre, London, Jan.–15 Feb. 1896, and the Garrick, Jan.–6 Feb. 1897

The Royal English Opera House, Cambridge-circus, Shaftesbury-avenue, erected by Mr. D'Oyly Carte, opened, 31 Jan., 1891. See under *Theatres*.

Gay's *Beggar's Opera*, the music adapted by Dr. Pepusch, was first performed at the Lincoln's Inn theatre, 29 Jan. 1727. Dr. Arne's *Tom Thumb* was produced in 1733; *Artaxerxes*, 1762. Storace wrote 15 (1788–96), *Haunted Tower*, *Iron Chest*, etc. Dibdin, *The Waterman*, 1774; *The Quaker*, 1775, etc. Shield, *Rosina*, *Lock and Key*, etc. 1782–1807. Michael Kelly, *The Castle Spectre*, 1797; *Bluebeard*, 1798, etc. Sir Henry Bishop, *Guy Mannering*, 1816, etc. Michael Wm. Balfe, *Siege of Rochelle*, 1835; *Bohemian Girl*, 1843, etc. Sir Julius Benedict, *Lily of Killarney*, 1862.

Sir A. C. Mackenzie, *Colomba*, 1883.

A. Goring Thomas (died 1892), *Esmeralda*, 1883; *Nadeshda*, 1885.

C. Villiers Stanford, *The Veiled Prophet*, 1881; *Canterbury Pilgrims*, 1884, etc.; *Shamus O'Brien*, opera comique . . . . 2 March, 1896
Fred. H. Cowen, *Pauline*, 1876; *Signa*, 30 June, 1894; *Harold*, 1895.
Hamish MacCunn, *Diarmid*, book by the marquis of Lorne . . . . 23 Oct. 1897
Sir A. Sullivan's chief operas (librettos by W. S. Gilbert) performed at the Savoy, 1881 *et seq.* *H.M.S. Pinafore*, 1878; *Pirates of Penzance*, 1879; *Patience*, 1881; *Iolanthe*, 1882; *Princess Ida*, 1884; *The Mikado*, 1885; *Ruddygore*, 1887; *Yeoman of the Guard*, 1888. *The Gondoliers*, 7 Dec. 1889, performed before the queen at Windsor, 4 March, 1891; *Ivanhoe*, see *Royal English Opera*, *Theatres*, 1891; *Haddon Hall* (libretto by Sydney Grundy), 24 Sept. 1892; *Utopia (Limited)*, libretto by W. S. Gilbert, 7 Oct. 1893; *The Chieftain* (book by F. C. Burnand), 12 Dec. 1894; *The Grand Duke*, book by W. S. Gilbert, 7 March–10 July, 1896; *The Beauty Stone* (book by A. W. Pinero and J. Comyns Carr), 28 May, 1898; *The Rose of Persia*, book by Basil Hood, 29 Nov. 1899–28 June, 1900; sir Arthur died suddenly . . . . 22 Nov. 1900

OPERA COMIQUE, a new theatre, 299, Strand, opened 29 Oct. 1870, by Mdlle. Déjazet and a French company. The French *opéra comique* began 1715; destroyed by fire, about 131 persons perish, 25, 26 May, 1887, see *Paris*.

OPERA-HOUSE, THE ITALIAN, or **QUEEN'S**, or (since 1901) **HIS MAJESTY'S THEATRE.** The original building is generally supposed to have been constructed by sir John Vanbrugh, though Mr. Pennant attributes it to sir Christopher Wren. It was built as "the queen's (afterwards changed to king's) theatre," opened 9 April, 1705; and burnt down 17 June, 1789. The foundation of the new theatre was laid 3 April, 1790; and the house was opened 22 Sept. 1791, on an improved plan; a new exterior was erected in 1820, from designs by Mr. Nash, *relievo* by Mr. Budd, 1821. This theatre was totally destroyed by fire on the night of 6-7 Dec. 1867. The loss of the lessee, Mr. Mapleson, was about 12,000*l.*, and that of Mdlle. Titiens was valued at 2000*l.*; rebuilt, but internal arrangements not completed. Moody and Sankey's revival meetings were held here, 12 April, 31 May, 1875. The new house was opened for Italian opera by Mr. Mapleson, 28 April, 1877; see *Theatres*. The house was pulled down in 1892-3.—The ENGLISH OPERA (or Lyceum) was opened 15 June, 1816. It was entirely destroyed by fire 16 Feb. 1830. The new English Opera-house, or Lyceum, was erected from designs by Mr. S. Beazley, and opened in July, 1834; see *Theatres and National Opera-house*.

OPHICLEIDE, the keyed bassoon, said to have been invented by Frichot, a Frenchman, in London, between 1791 and 1800.

OPHTHALMIA, general term for disease of the eye.

Ophthalmic hospitals were founded in London, 1804, 1843, and since. The Ophthalmological Society of Great Britain was founded in 1880 mainly by sir W. Bowman, the first president. He died 29 March, 1892, having greatly advanced ophthalmic surgery.
Heere Shah and 3 Indian oculists acquitted of conspiracy to defraud, 30 Oct. 1893.
8th international ophthalmological congress (Edinburgh), 7 Aug. 1894; 9th at Utrecht, 14–18 Aug. 1899.

OPHTHALMOSCOPE, an apparatus for inspecting the interior of the eye, invented by professor H. Helmholtz, in 1851.

OPIUM, the juice of the white poppy, was known to the ancients, its cultivation being mentioned by Homer, and its medicinal use by Hippocrates. It is largely cultivated in British India, and was introduced into China by our merchants, which led eventually to the war of 1839, the importation being forbidden by the Chinese government. The revenue derived from opium by the Indian government in 1862 was about 7,850,000*l.*; in 1874, 8,000,000*l.*; in 1880, about 10,500,000*l.*, but it has since declined. Laudanum, a preparation of opium: was employed early in the 17th century. A number of alkaloids have been discovered in opium: narcotine by Derosne, and morphia by Sertürner, in 1803. A society for suppressing the opium trade held meeting in London, 17 Jan. 1881 and since, 8 Oct. 1902.

The Chinese government derives a large revenue from the duty on imported opium which was fixed by the treaty of 1858. The plant is now largely grown in China.
Sir Joseph Pease's resolution condemning the cultivation of opium in India, the traffic in the drug, and the revenue, was adopted by the house of commons (160–130), 10 April, 1891; this caused much excitement in India.
Mr. Webb's resolution for appointing a royal commission against the opium revenue negatived by the commons (184–105), 30 June, 1893.
Royal commission appointed, July; president, lord Brassey; first meeting, 7 Sept.; at Calcutta, 18 Nov. 1893; two sections sat at Indore, Bombay, and other places, Feb. 1894; in their report the commissioners do not recommend the prohibition of the growth and manufacture of opium, but suggest increased state supervision, April, 1895. The report accepted by the Imperial government.

OPOBO EXPEDITION, see under *Nigeria*.

OPORTO (W. Portugal), the ancient *Calle*, one of the most impregnable cities in Europe. After being held at various times by the Goths and Moors, Oporto was finally acquired by the christians 1092. Oporto is the mart of Portuguese wine known as "Port." A chartered company for the regulation of the port-wine trade was established in 1756. The French, under marshal Soult, were surprised here by lord Wellington, and defeated in an action fought 12 May, 1809. The Miguelites besieged Oporto, and were repulsed by the Pedroites, with considerable loss, 19 Sept. 1832. The Oporto wine company was abolished in 1834, but re-established by a royal decree, 7 April, 1838. An international exhibition was opened here by the king, 18 Sept. 1865. Population, 1890, 138,860; 1900, 172,421; see *Portugal*.

The Baquet theatre burnt; panic; about 100 lives lost; 20 March, 1888.
Business paralyzed by the strike of masters and men connected with the wine trade, through the government favouring speculators for a monopolizing company; riots quelled by the military about 30 May, *et seq.* 1889.
Revolt of about 600 of the garrison, led by captain Leitao, joined by citizens; suppressed by loyal troops; the rebels fortify themselves in the Hotel de Ville; they surrender after bombardment; about 50 killed and many wounded, 31 Jan.; many persons, civil and military, arrested, 1–4 Feb. 1891.
Trial by courts-martial of about 300 soldiers and 21 civilians, 27 Feb. *et seq.* Sentences: captain Leitao, 6 years' cell imprisonment, followed by 10 years' transportation; other officers and civilians various kinds and terms of imprisonment or transportation, the majority of the soldiers 18 months' imprisonment.
The Abbé of St. Nicholas, acquitted 23 March, 1891.
The rebels all pardoned by the king on his birthday 28 Sept. 1891.
Visit of the king and queen, 18 Nov. 1891.
Exhibition of National Manufactures opened by the king, 22 Nov.; review of troops, 25 Nov. 1891.
Several banks stop payment about 18 March, 1892.
Exhibition of national products opened, 18 Sept. 1897.

Several cases of plague, sanitary cordon round the town, 24 Aug. 1899; commission appointed by the king, 29 Aug., and repressive measures adopted, Sept.; theatres, &c. closed, 18 Oct.; total deaths, 108; epidemic declared over, 7 Feb. 1900.

Visit of the king and queen; foundation stone laid of a disinfecting station, 23 Oct. 1900.

OPPORTUNISTS, a name given to French politicians (especially the ultra-liberals,) who suspend agitation for their peculiar opinions till a suitable opportunity comes; among them Gambetta was prominent, 1876-82. See *France*. *Opportunism* in England is defined as the modification of political policy as the necessities of the time dictate, Oct. 1891. See *Trimmer*.

OPTICS, a science studied by the Greeks; and by the Arabians about the 12th century. See *Light*.

Burning lenses known at Athens . . . . . B.C. 424
A treatise on optics doubtfully attributed to Euclid, about 300
The magnifying power of convex glasses and concave mirrors, and the prismatic colours produced by angular glass, mentioned by Seneca, about A.D. 50
Treatise on optics by Ptolemy . . . . about 120
Two of the leading principles known to the Platonists 300
Greatly improved by Alhazen, who died 1038
Hints for spectacles and telescopes, given by Roger Bacon . . . . about 1280
Spectacles said to have been invented by Salvinus Armatus, of Pisa . . . . . . before 1300
Camera obscura said to have been invented by Baptista Porta 1560
Telescopes invented by Leonard Digges about 1571
Kepler publishes his "Dioptrice" 1611
Telescope made by Jansen (said also to have invented the microscope), about 1609, and independently, by Galileo . . . . . about 1630
Microscope, according to Huyghens, invented by Drebbel . . . . about 1621
Law of refraction discovered by Snellius about 1624
Inflection of light discovered, and the undulatory theory suggested by Grimaldi . . about 1665
Reflecting telescope, Jas. Gregory, 1663; Newton . 1666
Motion and velocity of light discovered by Roemer, and after him by Cassini 1667
[Its velocity demonstrated to be 190 millions of miles in sixteen minutes.]
Double refraction explained by Bartholinus . . 1669
Cassegrainian reflector 1672
Newton's discoveries in colours, &c. . . . 1674
Telescopes with a single lens by Tschirnhausen, about 1690
Polarisation of light and undulatory theory discovered by Huyghens . . . . . about 1692
Structure of the eye explained by Petit . about 1700
Newton's "Optics" and other treatises published . 1704
Aberration of light discovered by Bradley . . 1727
Achromatic telescope constructed by Mr. Hall (but not made public) in 1733
Constructed by Dollond, most likely without any knowledge of Hall's telescope 1757
Herschel's great reflecting telescope erected at Slough 1789
Dr. T. Young's discoveries (undulatory theory, &c.) 1800-3
Camera lucida (Dr. Wollaston) 1807
Malus (polarisation of light by reflection) about 1808
Fresnel's researches on double reflection, &c. . 1817
Optical discoveries of Wheatstone . . 1838 *et seq.*
Large telescope constructed by lord Rosse . . 1845
Arago (colours of polarised light, &c.) . . . 1811-53
Sir D. Brewster, optical researches (see *Kaleidoscope*, *Photography*) 1814-57
The spectroscope constructed and used by Kirchhoff and Bunsen 1861
Dr. Tyndall's Lectures on Light first illustrated by Duboscq's electric lamp, at the Royal Institution, London 1856
Researches of Mr. Wm. Spottiswoode on polarised light 1871-8
Mr. Shelford Bidwell's experiments in physiological optics, at the Royal society . . 13 June, 1894
See *Telescope*, *Microscope*, *Stereoscope*, *Pseudoscope*, *Spectrum*, *Photography*, *Magic*, *Ophthalmoscope*, &c.

OPTIC NERVES are said to have been discovered by N. Varoli, a surgeon and physician of Bologna, about 1538.—*Nouv. Dict.*

OPTIMISM (from *optimus*, the best), the doctrine that everything which happens is for the best, in opposition to Pessimism (from *pessimus*, the worst). The germ of optimism is to be found in Plato, and in St. Augustin, and other fathers; and has been especially propounded by Malebranche and Leibnitz, and adopted by Pope, Bolingbroke, Rousseau, and others. Optimism as expressed in the term, "the best of all possible worlds," is ridiculed by Voltaire (1694-1778) in his "Candide." The term *meliorism* (from *melior*, better) has been lately introduced. See *Pessimism*.

"**OPTION**," a term given at the time to the permission given to the inhabitants of Alsace and Lorraine by the German government to choose, before 30 Sept. 1872, whether they would quit their country or become German subjects. Great numbers emigrated into the French territories. The "option" of archbishops respecting their claims on a benefice becoming void on the creation or translation of a bishop, was abolished in 1845. A Stock Exchange term, meaning the liberty to sell or buy stock in a time bargain at a stated price.

ORACLES, a term applied to revelations made by God to man. They were given to the Jews at the Mercy-seat in the tabernacle; see *Exod.* xxv. 18-22. The Holy Scriptures are the Christian "oracles," *Rom.* iii. 2; 1 *Pet.* iv. 11. King Ahaziah sent to consult the oracle of Baalzebub at Ekron about 896 B.C. The Greeks consulted especially the oracles of Jupiter and Apollo (see *Dodona* and *Delphi*); and the Italians those of Faunus, Fortune, and Mars.

ORAN, Algeria (N. Africa), a Moorish city several times captured by the Spaniards; definitively occupied by the French in 1831, who have since added docks, &c.

ORANGE, a principality in S.E. France, formerly a lordship in the 9th or 10th century. It has been ruled by four houses successively: that of Giraud Adhemar (to 1174); of Baux (1182 to 1393); of Chalons (to 1530); and of Nassau (1530 to 1713); see *Nassau*. Philibert the Great, prince of Orange, the last of the house of Chalons, having been wronged by Francis I. of France, entered the service of the emperor Charles V., to whom he rendered great services by his military talents. He was killed at the siege of Florence, 3 Aug. 1530. He was succeeded by his nephew-in-law, René of Nassau; see *princes of Orange* under *Holland*. The eldest son of the king of Holland is styled the prince of Orange, although the principality was ceded to France in 1713. See *Arausio*.

ORANGE FREE STATE (annexed by Gt. Britain, and styled Orange River Colony, 28 May, 1900), a republic in South Africa, founded by Boers from Cape Colony in 1836. The British government proclaimed its authority over this territory on 3 Feb. 1848, but declared it independent 23 Feb. 1854. A constitution proclaimed, 10 April, 1854; revised, 1866 and 1879. The able president, sir John Henry Brand, first elected, 1863, died, 14 July, 1888. President Reitz elected, 11 Jan.

1889; re-elected, 27 Nov. 1893; resigns 17 Nov. 1895; Judge Steyn, the last president (see *S. African War*), elected, 21 Feb. 1896. Defensive treaty with the Transvaal, about 13 March, ratified 25 May, 1889. Concession granted to the Cape Government to construct a railway to Bloemfontein, the capital, May, 1889; railway opened at Bloemfontein, 17 Dec. 1890. Population, 1885, 133,518; 1900, 207,000 (78,000 whites).

The state earnestly supports the Transvaal government . . . . Dec. 1895 *et seq.*
Visit of pres. Kruger to Bloemfontein . 9 March, 1897
Committee appointed to revise the constitution, June; their report issued . . . . 19 Dec. ,,
The worst drought since 1862, signs of breaking up, great suffering in many districts . . Dec. ,,
Closer union with the Transvaal adopted . 5 Oct. 1898
Railway from Bloemfontein to Heilbron opened, 31 Jan. 1899
The raad opened; federation with the Transvaal rejected, until the abrogation of article iv. of the 1884 convention (*i.e.* British suzerainty) be obtained . . . . 4 April, ,,
Conference at Bloemfontein between Sir A. Milner and presidents Kruger and Steyn; negotiations fail . . . . 31 May–5 June, ,,
The raad votes 53,977*l.* for war purposes, 23 June, ,,
Conference between Messrs. Hofmeyr, Herholdt (Cape ministers), and pres. Steyn, Mr. Fischer, and others; proposals inadequate . 2–4 July, ,,
Raad opened with a defiant speech by pres. Steyn, 21 Sept. ,,
Military preparations carried on . . Sept.-Oct. ,,
Pres. Steyn espouses the cause of the Transvaal, 10 Oct.; British government denounced and martial law proclaimed . . . . 11, 12 Oct. ,,
Merchants and every available man commandeered, early Jan. *et seq.* 1900
See *S. African War.*
Raad opened at Kroonstadt by pres. Steyn, 2 April; adjourns *sine die* . . . . . . 4 April, ,,
Major-gen. Pretyman appointed military gov. of the Free State . . . . . . 20 April, ,,
The State formally annexed to the British Empire, under the name of "Orange River Colony," 28 May, ,,
Sir A. Milner, high commissioner of S. Africa, appointed governor (made a peer 24 May), and major Hamilton Goold-Adams, lieut.-gov. (made K.C.M.G., 26 June, 1902) . . . . . Jan. 1901
Land settlements begun; several returned yeomanry occupy government farms in Thaba Nchu district, reported . . . . 22 Nov. ,,
Civil administration appointed; industries and education re-established, country progressing, Jan.–Dec. ,,
Meetings held protesting against Continental slanders on the British Army . Feb.–March, 1902
Lord Milner (visct. 26 June) sworn in as governor of the colony at Bloemfontein) . . 23 June, ,,
Daily patrol of the colony by the S. African constabulary (formed 22 March), organized, early July, ,,
Vote of 8,000,000*l.* for the colony and the Transvaal, passed the commons . . . . 5 Nov. ,,
Martial law repealed . . . . . . 19 Nov. ,,
Lord Milner tours through the colony, 25 Nov.–16 Dec. ,,
Rapid repatriation of burghers . . . Dec. ,,
Rev. H. Duplessis, minister of the Dutch Reformed Church at Lindley, forced to resign owing to the systematic boycott of his congregation on account of his British sympathies, appointed by the government inspector of schools in the Transvaal 6 Jan. 1903
Legislative council (enlarged) opened . 14 Jan. ,,
Enthusiastic reception of Mr. Chamberlain at Bloemfontein, 3 Feb.; he receives a deputation headed by gen. Christian De Wet and Boer delegates who present a petition setting forth alleged grievances . . . . . 6 Feb. ,,
Intercolonial conference at Bloemfontein, lord Milner, president; Customs Union Convention, preferential treatment of British imports signed, 10–23 March, ,,
Estimated surplus, 1903–4, 102,000*l.*, reported 22 May, 1903
Intercolonial Council for the affairs of the Orange River Colony and the Transvaal established, 15 June, ,,

ORANGEMEN. The "Battle of the Diamond," 21 Sept. 1795 (see *Diamond*), and the treachery experienced by the Protestants on that occasion, convinced them they would become an easy prey to the Roman Catholics, from their small numbers, unless they associated for their defence, and consequently the Orange Society was formed in 1795. The first Orange lodge was formed in Armagh; but the name of Orangemen already existed. An Orange lodge was formed in Dublin; the members published a declaration of their principles (the maintenance of church and state under the house of Brunswick) in Jan. 1798. After 1813 Orangeism declined; but revived again in 1827, when the duke of Cumberland became grand-master; and it is stated that in 1836 there were 145,000 Orangemen in England, and 125,000 in Ireland. After a parliamentary inquiry Orange clubs were broken up in conformity with resolutions of the house of commons; but were revived in 1845—1889. In Oct. 1857, the lord chancellor of Ireland ordered that justices of the peace should not belong to Orange clubs. The Orangemen in Canada were greatly excited during the visit of the prince of Wales in Sept. 1860. Mr. Wm. Johnston, a grand-master, convicted of violating the Party Processions act, was elected M.P. for Belfast, Nov. 1869. See *Belfast*. The Orangemen vigorously oppose the home rule movement, see *Ulster*, 1892–3.

ORANGES. The sweet, or China orange, was first brought into Europe from China by the Portuguese, in 1547; and it is asserted that the identical tree, whence all the European orange-trees of this sort were produced, is still preserved at Lisbon, in the gardens of one of its nobility. Orange-trees were first brought to England, and planted, with little success, in 1595; they are said to have been planted at Beddington park, near Croydon, Surrey. The duty on imported oranges was repealed in 1860.

ORATOR HENLEY. An eccentric English gentleman of some talents, in 1726, opened his "oratory," a kind of chapel, in Newport-market, where he gave lectures on theological topics on Sundays, and on other subjects on Wednesdays, every week. Novelty procured him many hearers; but he was too imprudent to gain any permanent advantage. He removed his oratory to Clare-market, and sank into obscurity previously to his death, in 1756.

ORATORIANS (from the Latin *orare*, to pray), a regular order of priests established by St. Philip Neri, about 1564, and so called from the oratory of St. Jerome, at Rome, where they prayed. They had a foundation in France, commenced by Guillaume Gibieuf and Pierre de Berulle (afterwards cardinal), 1612, approved by pope Paul V. 1613.—The rev. Frederick Faber and others, as "Fathers of the Oratory," established themselves first in King William-street, Strand, in 1848, and afterwards at Brompton.

ORATORIO, a sacred musical composition, the subject of it being generally taken from the Scriptures. The origin of our oratorios (so named from having been first performed in an oratory) is ascribed to St. Philip Neri, about 1550. The first true oratorio, Emilio del Cavaliere's "Rappresentazione," was performed at Rome in 1600. He was followed by Giovanni Carissimi, Alessandro

Scarlatti, &c. Bach's "Passion Music," the "St. Matthew," was produced at Leipzig on Good Friday, 1729, see *Passion-Week*. Handel composed 17 English oratorios; his first, "Esther," was performed at the Haymarket theatre, 2 May, 1732. "Israel in Egypt" was produced in 1738, and the "Messiah" in 1741; Haydn's "Creation" in 1798; Beethoven's "Mount of Olives," 1803; Spohr's "Last Judgment" (properly "Last Things"), 1825; Mendelssohn's "St. Paul" in 1836, and "Elijah" in 1846; Costa's "Eli," 1865; "Naaman," 1864; S. Bennett's "Woman of Samaria," 1867; Macfarren's "John the Baptist," 1873, Sullivan's "Prodigal Son," 1869; "Light of the World," 1873; "Martyr of Antioch," 1880, &c. Latterly the name has been modified, e.g., *Dramatic Oratorio*, such as Mackenzie's "Rose of Sharon;" Hubert Parry's "Judith," "Job," "King Saul" (1894), &c. *Sacred Trilogy*, Gounod's "Redemption," Berlioz's "Childhood of Christ;" Elgar's "The Apostles," Pts. I. and II., 1903; or, again, as a form of *Dramatic Cantata*, as Schumann's "Paradise and the Peri," Sullivan's "Golden Legend," Mackenzie's "Dream of Jubal."

ORCHIDS, a natural order of plants of a very peculiar organization, recently much cultivated. In 1880 a great establishment for their cultivation was set up at St. Albans by Mr. Sander, "the orchid king," patronised by the Rothschilds, who introduced him to the queen at Waddesdon Manor, 14 May, 1890. The orchids at Blenheim sold for about 5,250*l.*, 19–23 Dec. 1892.

ORCHOMENUS, a small Greek state in Bœotia, was destroyed by the Thebans, 367 B.C.; restored by Philip II. of Macedon, 354; and given up by him to Thebes, 346.

ORDEAL was known among the Greeks and Jews (*Num.* v. 2). It was introduced into England by the Saxons. A prisoner who pleaded not guilty might choose whether he would put himself for trial upon God and his country, by twelve men, as at this day, or upon God only. The trial by ordeal was abolished in 1218.

ORDER OF THE CORPORATE REUNION, virtually a new episcopal church, said to arise out of the Christian Unity Association (*which see*). It proposed to form four stations, (Canterbury, York, Caerleon, and St. Andrews), with rectors and provincials; announced 11 Sept. 1877.

ORDERS, see *Knighthood*.

ORDERS IN COUNCIL were issued by the British government 7 Jan. and 11 Nov. 1807, prohibiting trade with the ports occupied by the French, being reprisals for Napoleon's *Berlin* and *Milan decrees* (see *Continental System*). They greatly checked the progress of manufactures in this country, and caused much distress and smuggling. They were repealed in regard to America, 18 June, 1812. The action under these orders led to the disastrous war with the United States in 1812–15.

ORDINANCES, see *Ordonnances, Self-Denying Ordinances*.

ORDINATION of ministers in the Christian church began with Christ and his apostles; see *Mark* iii. 14, and *Acts* vi. and xiv. 23. In England in 1549 a new form of ordination of ministers was ordered to be prepared by a committee of six prelates and six divines.

ORDNANCE OFFICE. Before the invention of guns, this office was supplied by officers under the following names: the bowyer, the crossbowyer, the galeater, or purveyor of helmets, the armourer, and the keeper of the tents. Henry VIII. placed it under the management of a master-general, a lieutenant, surveyor, &c. The master-general was chosen from among the first generals in the service of the sovereign. The appointment was formerly for life; but since the restoration, was held *durante bene placito*, and not infrequently by a cabinet minister.—*Beatson*. The letters patent for this office were revoked 25 May, 1855, and its duties vested in the minister of war, lord Panmure. The last master-general was lord Fitzroy-Somerset, afterwards lord Raglan. The revival of the office recommended by the Ordnance Commission (see under *Army*, 1886).

ORDNANCE SURVEY. The trigonometrical survey of England was commenced by gen. Roy, in 1784, continued by col. Colby, and completed by col. (aft. sir Henry) James in 1856. The publication of the maps (scale 7 inches to a mile), commenced in 1819, under the direction of col. Mudge, and was completed in 1862; a large part of these maps have been coloured geologically. The survey of Ireland (6 inches to a mile) has been completed and published; that of Scotland, completed Nov. 1882. By the Survey act, passed 12 May, 1870, the ordnance survey was transferred to the Board of Works, and by an act passed in 1889, to the Board of Agriculture, beginning 1 April, 1890. Directors, lieut.-gen. John Cameron, succeeded sir Henry James in 1875, died 30 June, 1878; col. A. C. Cooke; col. R. H. Stotherd, 1885; col. Farquharson (K.C.B. 1899); col. Duncan Johnston, 1901. In 1892 several sets of maps were in course of publication or preparation. The Ordnance Survey maps having been considered deficient, a departmental committee was appointed in April, 1892, and met during the year; sir John Dorington, M.P., chairman. Report, with recommendations, presented to the Board of Agriculture, 31 Dec. 1892; published, 6 March, 1893. New maps issued, May, 1902; survey sections sent to S. Africa, spring, 1902; 4-inch and 1-inch maps revised, issued, Aug. 1902; others issued 1903. Pocket maps of many of the sections, scale 1 in. and ½ in. to a mile, are published at a cheap rate.

ORDONNANCES, the laws enacted by the Capetian kings of France previous to 1789. They began with "in the name of the king," and ended with "such is our good pleasure." The first in French is dated 1287 (Philip IV.) The publication of these "ordonnances," ordered by Louis XIV., 1706, is still in progress. The "ordonnances" of Charles X., promulgated 26 July, 1830, led to the revolution.

OREGON TERRITORY (N. America), is said to have been visited by Drake in 1579. Lieut. Broughton took possession of part of it for Great Britain in 1792. In 1810 a settlement named Astoria, was founded by a New York Company. Oregon was occupied by the English in 1814, but was claimed by the United States government, to whom the greater part was ceded, after much negotiation, by the treaty of 12 June, 1846. Oregon was made a territory in 1848, and admitted as a state, Feb. 1859. Capital, Salem. Population, 1880, 174,768; 1890, 313,767; 1900, 413,536.

By the fall of a train through a broken bridge in Wascow county, 10 men were killed 4 Feb. 1890

Disastrous floods on the Willematte river, 6 Feb.; much distress at Salem and Portland . . about 7 Feb. 1890
The overland Pacific train wrecked on the long trestle bridge over lake Labish, 4 lives lost and many injured . . . . . . 12 Nov. ,,
Great fire at Portland; docks, &c., destroyed, 3 deaths . . . . . . 23 Sept. 1894
At Silverlake, by explosion of a lamp, 41 deaths, 24 Dec. ,,
Disastrous forest fires, loss of life, reported, 25 Sept. 1902
Cloud-burst wrecked the town of Heppner, over 300 lives lost. . . . . . . 15 June, 1903

ORGAN, a development of the pandean pipes; the "*organ*" in *Gen.* iv. 21 should be translated *pipe*. The invention is attributed to Ctesibius, a barber of Alexandria, about 250 B.C.; and to Archimedes, about 220 B.C. The organ was brought to Europe from the Greek empire, and was applied to religious devotions in churches, about A.D. 657.—*Bellarmine*. Organs were used in the western churches by pope Vitalianus, in 658.—*Ammonius*. It is affirmed that the organ was known in France in the time of Louis I., 815, when one was constructed by an Italian priest. The organ at Haarlem is one of the largest in Europe; it has 60 stops and 8000 pipes. At Seville is one with 110 stops and 5300 pipes. The organ at Amsterdam has a set of pipes that imitate a chorus of human voices. Of the organs in ENGLAND that at St. George's Hall, Liverpool, by Mr. Willis, was the largest; next in order that at York minster, and that in the music-hall, Birmingham. In London, the largest was, perhaps that of Spitalfields church; and that in Christ Church was nearly as extensive. The erection of the famous Temple organ was competed for by Schmidt and Harris; after long disputes, the question was referred to vote, and Mr. Jefferies, afterwards chief justice, gave the casting vote in favour of Schmidt (called Father Smith), about 1682. A monster organ was erected in the Crystal Palace, Sydenham, in June, 1857. The organ, by Willis, at the Royal Albert Hall, is now said to be the largest in the world; 1871. A larger proposed for a cathedral in Long Island, North America, 1880. A noble organ (by Bryceson), with many appliances, opened in the hall, Primrose-hill-road, London, N. Jan. 1876; see *Westminster Abbey*, 1895.

Barrel organs are said to have been first made early in the 18th century. The finest was the *Apollonicon* (*which see*).
William Thos. Best, born 1826, virtuoso player, died at Liverpool . . . . . 10 May, 1897
Mr. Henry Willis (Father Willis), the great organ-builder, died, aged 80 . . . . 11 Feb. 1901

ORGANIC SYNTHESIS, see *Chemistry*.

ORIEL COLLEGE (Oxford), founded, in 1326, by Adam de Brome, archdeacon of Stow, and almoner to king Edward II. This college derives its name from a tenement called *l'Oriole*, on the site of which the building stands.

ORIENTAL INSTITUTE, Woking, Surrey, founded by dr. G. W. Leitner, the distinguised Orientalist (died, aged 68, 22 March, 1899; see *Punjaub*), for the training of young Indians, about 1884. A mosque was erected here, Aug. 1889.

ORIENTALISTS. The first International Congress of these scholars was held at Paris, 1 Sept. 1873, M. Léon de Rosny, the founder, president; the second Congress met at the Royal Institution, in London, 14-19 Sept. 1874, dr. S. Birch president; the third Congress met at St. Petersburg, 1 Sept. 1876; the fourth at Florence, Sept. 1878; the fifth met at Berlin, 12-17 Sept. 1881, M. Dittman president; the sixth at Leyden, 10 Sept. 1883; the seventh, Vienna, 27 Sept. 1886; eighth, Stockholm, president king Oscar II., 2-7 Sept. 1889; independent, London, 1-10 Sept. 1891; ninth in London, 5-12 Sept. 1892; tenth, Geneva, 4 Sept. 1894; eleventh, Paris, 6 Sept. 1897; twelfth, Rome, 4-15 Oct. 1899; thirteenth, Hamburg, 5 Sept. 1902. See *Asiatic Societies*.

ORIENTAL STUDIES; Professor Max Müller, in the presence of the prince of Wales, at the Royal Institution, gave a discourse to inaugurate the establishment of a school for modern oriental studies by the Imperial Institute, in union with University College and King's College, London 11 Jan. 1890

ORIENTATION, the setting of the chancel of a church so that it points to the east. This custom is followed in the churches of England, and those of northern Europe, but is not strictly adhered to in Italy and the South. St. Peter's, at Rome, has its choir pointing to the west.

ORIFLAMME, see *Auriflamma*.

ORIGENISTS pretended to draw their opinions from the writings of Origen, who lived 185-253. They maintained that Christ was the son of God in no other way than by adoption and grace; that souls were created before the bodies; that the sun, moon, stars, and the waters that are under the firmament, have souls; that the torments of the damned shall have an end, and that the fallen angels shall, after a time, be restored to their first condition. They were condemned by councils, and the reading of Origen's work was forbidden.—*Burke*. These doctrines were condemned by the council of Constantinople in 553.

"ORIGIN OF SPECIES, BY MEANS OF NATURAL SELECTION," by Charles Robert Darwin, F.R.S., first published, 24 Nov. 1859. He was born 12 Feb. 1809, died 19 April, 1882. See *Species*.

ORION STEAM-SHIP. On 18 June, 1850, this splendid vessel, bound from Liverpool to Glasgow, struck on a sunken rock, northward of Portpatrick, within a stone's throw of land, and instantly filled. Of two hundred passengers more than fifty were drowned.

ORISSA, an ancient kingdom of India, now a province of N.W. Bengal, conquered by Clive in 1755, and nearly all acquired by the company in 1765. It suffered much by famine in 1770, and 1792-3, and more especially from the end of 1865 to Nov. 1866, when it is said about 750,000 persons perished. The government and officials were censured for neglect and want of forethought. It is also said that during a hurricane in Oct. 1836, 22,500 persons were drowned.

ORKNEY AND SHETLAND ISLES (North of Scotland), were conquered by Magnus III. of Norway, 1099, and were ceded to James III. as the dowry of his wife Margaret, in 1469. The Orkneys were the ancient Orcades; united with Shetland, they now form one of the Scotch counties. The bishopric of Orkney, founded by St. Servanus early in the 5th century, some affirm by St. Colm, ended with the abolition of episcopacy in Scotland, about 1689; see *Bishops in Scotland*. Orkney and Zetland small piers and harbours act passed, 14 Aug. 1896.

ORLEANS (a city in central France), formerly *Aurelianum;* gave title to a kingdom, 491, and afterwards to a duchy, usually held by one of the royal family. Attila the Hun, besieging it, was defeated by Aetius and his allies, 451. It was besieged by the English under earls of Salisbury and Suffolk, 12 Oct. 1428, bravely defended by Gaucour (as its fall would have ruined the cause of Charles VI. king of France), and relieved by the heroism of Joan of Arc, afterwards surnamed the Maid of Orleans, 29 April, 1429, and the siege was raised 8 May; see *Joan of Arc.* (The 439th anniversary was celebrated 10 May, 1868; the emperor and empress being present.) During the siege of Orleans, Feb. 1563, the duke of Guise was assassinated.

After nine hours' severe fighting, Orleans captured by the Germans, under general Von der Tann. More than 4000 prisoners were taken. The loss on both sides was heavy. About 35,000 on each side were engaged. The city was made to pay a war contribution of 60,000*l*. . . . 11 Oct. 1870

Von der Tann and the Bavarians defeated by generals D'Aurelle de Paladines and Pallières, and Orleans re-taken. The Germans acknowledged the loss of about 700 men and 1000 prisoners, chiefly wounded. The French asserted the numbers of both to be higher, and were much cheered with their victory. The French loss was heavy. The chief conflict took place between Coulmiers and Bacon or Baccon . . 9, 10 Nov. ,,

Severe conflicts at Bazoche and Chevilly, near Orleans, between a part of the army of the Loire and prince Frederick Charles and the grand-duke of Mecklenburg . . . . . 2-4 Dec. ,,

A battle, during which the suburbs were stormed, and about 10,000 unwounded prisoners, 77 guns, and four gunboats taken. The French retired; Orleans re-taken by the Germans . . 5 Dec. ,,

DUKES.

Louis contended for the regency with John the Fearless, duke of Burgundy, by whose instigation he was assassinated in 1407.

Charles taken prisoner at Agincourt, 1415; released, 1440; died, 1465.

Louis, became Louis XII. of France in 1498, when the duchy merged in the crown.

Bourbon Branch.—Philip, youngest son of Louis XIII., born, 1640; died, 1701.

Philip II., son, born, 1673; REGENT, 1715; died, 1723.

Louis, son, born, 1703; died, 1752.

Louis Philippe, son, born, 1725; died, 1785.

Louis Philippe Joseph, son, born, 1747; opposed the court in the French revolution; took the name *Egalité*, 11 Sept. 1792; voted for the death of Louis XVI.; was guillotined. 6 Nov. 1793.

Louis Philippe, son, born, 6 Nov. 1773; chosen king of the French, 9 Aug. 1830: abdicated, 24 Feb. 1848; died, 26 Aug. 1850. His queen, Marie Amélie, died, 24 March, 1866 (see *France*).

Ferdinand Philippe, son, duke of Orleans, born, 3 Sept. 1810; died, through a fall, 13 July, 1842.

Louis Philippe, son, count of Paris, born, 24 Aug. 1838, married Maria Isabella, daughter of the duke of Montpensier, 30 May, 1864; died at Stowe, Bucks, 8 Sept.; funeral at Weybridge, Surrey, the duke of York present, 12 Sept.; in his will he acknowledges his failure, but maintains his rights, and deplores French irreligion, 21 July, 1894. Their daughter, Hélène, married to the duke d'Aosta, 25 June, 1895. Son, Louis Philippe, duke of Orleans, born 7 Feb. 1869, see *France*, Feb. 1890; married the archduchess Maria Dorothea of Austria, . 5 Nov. 1896

Death, from shock, of Henri Eugène, duc d'Aumale (born 16 Jan. 1822, 4th son of Louis Philippe) 6 May, 1897

See *Paris*, 4 May, 1897.

The demand of the Orleans princes to return to France, 19 June, refused by the legislative assembly after discussion . . . . . 2 July. 1870

Their request to serve in the army after the fall of the empire declined . . . . . Sept. ,,

(The duc de Chartres served *incognito.*)

After discussion, the duc d'Aumale and the prince de Joinville permitted to take their seats as members of the national assembly . . 19 Dec. 1870

After much discussion, the comte de Paris at a personal interview recognized the comte de Chambord as the legitimate head of the Bourbon family and king of France . . . . 5 Aug. 1873

For consequent proceedings see *France* . 1873 *et seq*

The bodies of king Louis Philippe and others of his family removed from England and buried in the mausoleum at Dreux . . . . 9 June, 1876

Marriage of princess Marie, daughter of duc de Chartres, to prince Waldemar of Denmark 22 Oct. 1885

Marriage of princess Amelie, daughter of the comte de Paris, to the duke of Braganza . 22 May, 1886

Expulsion of the Orleans princes from France (see *France*) . . . . May–June, ,,

For acts of the comte de Paris see *France*, 1873 *et seq.*

The duc de Montpensier, born 1824 (see *Spain*, 1846 *et seq.*), died . . . . . 4 Feb. 1890

The prince de Joinville publishes "Vieux Souvenirs" . . . . . . April, 1894

Fêtes in honour of Joan of Arc . . 6–8 May, ,,

The duc de Nemours, 2nd son of king Louis Philippe, born 1814, died . . . . . 25 June, 1896

François Ferdinand, prince de Joinville, died, aged 81 . . . . 15 June, 1900

Prince Henry, elder son of the duc de Chartres, honoured for his explorations in the Far East, 11 March, 1896; dies, aged 34, at Sairgon 9 Aug. 1901

ORLEANS, NEW, see *New Orleans.*

ORMULUM, a metrical version of the Gospels and Acts, in early English, made by Orm, an ecclesiastic, in the 12th century, printed at Oxford in 1852, from a MS. in the Bodleian.

ORNITHOLOGY, see *Birds.*

ORNITHORHYNCHUS, the duck-billed platypus, or water-mole, a singular compound of the mammal and the bird, a native of Australia, was first described by Dr. Shaw, in 1819.

OROQUIETA, Navarre, N. Spain. Here don Carlos, calling himself king Carlos VII., grandson of don Carlos, brother of Ferdinand VII., commanding about 4000 men, was suddenly attacked by general Moriones with about 2000, and defeated after a short-conflict, 4 May, 1872. He fled, leaving 757 prisoners and 38 dead.

ORPHAN-HOUSES. The emperor Trajan first formed establishments for this purpose. Pliny relates in his Panegyric that he had caused 5000 free-born children to be sought out and educated, about A.D. 105. Orphan houses properly so called are mentioned for the first time in the laws of the emperor Justinian. At the court of Byzantium the office of inspector of orphans, *orphanotrophos*, was so honourable that it was held by the brother of the emperor Michael IV. in the 11th century; see *Foundling Hospitals.*

The Orphanotropheon at Halle, established by August Francke 1698-9

The Orphan Working Asylum for 20 boys was established at Hoxton in 1758. It is now situated at Haverstock-hill, and contains 350 boys and girls.

Asylum for Female Orphans, Lambeth; removed to Beddington, near Croydon; instituted . . 1758

London Orphan Asylum founded, 1813; removed to Clapton, 1823; new building at Watford, founded by the prince of Wales, 13 July, 1869; opened, 20 July, 1871

British Orphan Asylum, Clapham-rise, established 1827; removed to Slough, Bucks; re-opened, 25 June, 1863

The Infant Orphan Asylum at Wanstead (1827); and the Asylum for Fatherless Children (in 1844; settled at Reedham, Surrey), established mainly through the exertions of a congregational minister, the rev. Andrew Reed, D.D.

Orphan-houses, Ashley-down, Bristol, founded by George Müller, a Prussian (died, aged 92, 10 March, 1898), supported entirely by voluntary contributions, see *Scripture Knowledge*. (He began in a house in Bristol, 11 April, 1836.) 2,050 orphans were maintained, 1873; reported prosperous, 1895; 20,000*l*. bequeathed; see *Bristol*, Mar. 1899

Erdington Orphanage and Alms-houses, near Birmingham, erected and endowed (with 250,000*l*.) by Josiah Mason, a manufacturer of Birmingham, 1860-69

Royal Albert Orphan Asylum, at Bagshot, established, 1864; additional buildings founded by the queen, 29 June, 1867.

Alexandra Orphanage for Infants, Holloway, 1864; foundation of building laid, 6 July, 1867.

Stockwell Orphanage, Clapham-road, founded by Rev. C. Spurgeon, aided by legacy of Miss Hillyard 1867

Orphans' Homes:—Maida-hill, 1873; West-square, Southwark; and Gravesend . . . . ,,

Passmore-Edwards' Teachers' Orphanage, West-hill, Sydenham 1899

ORPHEONISTS, see *Crystal Palace*, 1860.

ORPHEUS, STEAMER, see *Wrecks*, 7 Feb. 1863.

ORRERY, a planetary machine to illustrate and explain the motions of the heavenly bodies, appears to have been coeval with the clepsydra. Ptolemy devised the circles and epicycles that distinguish his system about 130. The planetry-clock of Finée was begun 1553. The planetarium of De Rheita was formed about 1650. The planetarium, now termed the Orrery, it is said, was constructed by Rowley, after a pattern devised by the clock-maker, George Graham, at the expense of Charles Boyle, earl of Orrery, about 1715. A large "planetarium" was constructed by the rev. Wm. Pearson, for the Royal Institution, London, about 1803. An excellent planetarium, constructed in London by signor N. Perini, was exhibited in Dec. 1879.

ORSINI'S PLOT against the emperor Napoleon III.; see *France*, Jan. 1858.

ORTHES or **ORTHEZ** (S. France), once capital of the principality of Bearn. Near it the British and Spanish armies, commanded by Wellington, defeated the French, under Soult, 27 Feb. 1814. The battle of Toulouse soon followed.

ORTHOPÆDIC HOSPITALS, for the cure of club-foot, spinal curvatures, &c.: National, Great Portland street, founded, 1836; Royal, Hanover-square, 1838; City, 1851.

OSBORNE HOUSE (Isle of Wight), was purchased by the queen in 1845, and rebuilt by Mr. Cubitt. She died here, 22 Jan. 1901, and left the house and estate under her will to the king, who gave it to the nation, to be used as an army and navy convalescent home (for officers), 9 Aug. 1902; Osborne estate bill passed, 15 Dec. 1902. Royal Naval College, opened by king Edward VII., 4 Aug. 1903.

OSMIUM, one of the heaviest known metals, discovered in platinum ore by Tennant in 1803.

OSNABURG (N. Germany), made the seat of a bishopric, by Charlemagne, near the end of the 8th century. After the treaty of Westphalia in 1648, the bishop was a Roman Catholic and Protestant alternately, the latter being chosen from the house of Brunswick. Frederick, duke of York, the last bishop, resigned in 1803, when the lands were annexed to Hanover. He died 5 Jan. 1827

OSSORY (S.E. Ireland), **BISHOPRIC OF**, was first planted at Saiger, about 402; translated to Aghadoe, in Upper Ossory, in 1052; and to Kilkenny about the end of the reign of Henry II. It was united to Ferns and Leighlin in 1835.

OSTEND (Belgium). An important sea-port in the 11th century, was destroyed by the sea 1334, rebuilt and afterwards walled by Philip the Good, the duke of Burgundy, 1445; sustained a siege by the Spaniards, from July, 1601, to Sept. 1604, when it honourably capitulated. On the death of Charles II. of Spain, the French seized Ostend; but in 1706, after the battle of Ramillies, it was retaken by the allies. It was again taken by the French in 1745, but restored in 1748. In 1756, the French garrisoned this town for the empress-queen Maria Theresa. In 1792, the French once more took Ostend, which they evacuated in 1793, but regained in 1794. The English destroyed the works of the Bruges canal; but the wind shifting before they could re-embark, they surrendered to the French, 19 May, 1798. The Ostend East India company, established 1723, was dissolved 1731. Riotous attacks on British fishermen landing fish quelled with bloodshed; intervention of the king; peace restored 23-30 Aug. 1887. Population, 1890, 24,712; 1900, 39,541.

OSTIA, a Roman port, at the mouth of the Tiber, said to have been founded by Ancus Martius about 627 B.C.

OSTRACISM (from the Greek *ostrakon*, a potsherd or shell), a mode of proscription at Athens, is said to have been first introduced by the tyrant Hippias; others ascribe it to Cleisthenes, about 510 B.C. The people wrote the names of those whom they most suspected upon small shells; these they put in an urn or box and presented to the senate. Upon a scrutiny, he whose name was oftenest written was sentenced by the council to be banished from his altar and hearth. 6000 votes were required. Aristides, noted for his justice, and Miltiades, for his victories, were thus ostracized. The custom was abolished by ironically proscribing Hyperbolus, a mean person, about 338 B.C.

OSTRICH (the *struthios* of the ancients), a native of Africa (see *Job* xxxix. 14). Ostriches were hatched and reared at San Donato, near Florence, 1859-60; and at Tresco abbey, the seat of Augustus Smith, in the Scilly isles, 1866.

OSTROGOTHS, or **EASTERN GOTHS**, were distinguished from the Visigoths (Western Goths) about 330. After ravaging eastern Europe, Thrace, &c., their great leader, Theodoric, established a kingdom in Italy, which lasted from 493 to 553; see *Italy*.

OSTROLENKA (Poland). Near here the French defeated the Prussians, 16 Feb. 1807. In another battle here between the Poles and Russians the slaughter was immense, but the Poles remained masters of the field, 26 May, 1831.

OTAGO, see *New Zealand*, 1848, 1861, 1866.

OTAHEITE or **TAHITI**, an island in the S. Pacific Ocean, seen by Byron in 1765, and visited in 1767 by captain Wallis, who called it George the Third Island. Captain Cook came hither in 1768 to observe the transit of Venus; sailed round the whole island in a boat, and stayed three months; he visited it twice afterwards. See *Cook*. Omai, a native of this island, was brought to England by Cook, and carried back in his last voyage. In

1799, king Pomare ceded the district of Matavai to some English missionaries. Queen Pomare was compelled to put herself under the protection of France, 9 Sept. 1843. She retracted, and Otaheite and the neighbouring islands were taken possession of by admiral Dupetit-Thouars in the name of the French king, Nov. 1843. The French imprisoned Mr. Prichard, the English consul, 5 March, 1844, but the act was censured in France.

Queen Pomare IV., born, 23 Feb. 1813; succeeded her brother, Pomare III., in Jan. 1827; died 17 Sept. 1877, having reigned 50 years. By consent of her successor the island was formally annexed to France, 29 June, 1880. The queen arrived at Paris, 27 Feb. 1884.

Long rebellion in Raiatea and Huahine islands put down; the queen exiled by the French, reported, 10 April, 1897.

Rurutu and Tubuai islands annexed to France, 21 Aug. 1900.

OTHEOSCOPE (from *ōtheō*, I propel), apparatus invented by Mr. W. Crookes, for studying molecular motion, the effects of radiation; described by him, April, 1877.

OTOLOGY, the science of the ear. A congress of Otologists met at Brussels, Sept. 1888; another in London. 300 aurists present, 8 Aug. 1899.

OTTAWA (formerly **BYTOWN**), on the river Ottawa, was appointed to be the capital of Canada by the queen in August, 1858. The executive council met here 22 Nov. 1865, and the Canadian parliament was, for the first time, opened here by the governor-general, lord Monck, on 8 June, 1866. Mr. Darcy McGee, M.P. for Montreal (once an Irish agitator, but afterwards exceedingly loyal), was assassinated on his return from parliament, 7 April, 1868. Fenians were suspected, and the town was put in a state of siege. Whelan, convicted of the murder, 15 Sept. 1868, was executed Feb. 1869. A dominion exhibition was opened here 24 Sept. 1879. The duke and duchess of Connaught warmly received 4 June, 1890. National monument to sir John Macdonald unveiled, 1 July, 1895. Destructive fire in public offices, records burnt, 11 Feb. 1897. Population in 1861, 14,669; in 1871, 21,545; in 1881, 27,412; 1891, 44,154; 1901, 59,902.

Hull, a suburb and part of Ottawa, burnt down; see *Canada* . . . . . . 26, 27 Apl. 1900

Mr. Andrew Carnegie gives 20,000*l.* for a public library . . . . Mar. 1901

Visit of the duke and duchess of Cornwall; see *Canada* . . . . 20–24 Sept. „

Lord Dundonald unveils a soldiers' memorial, 6 Aug. 1902

Great fire . . . . 10 May, 1903

OTTERBURN (Northumberland). In 1388 the Scotch besieged Newcastle and were driven off by Henry Percy (Hotspur), son of the earl of Northumberland. Percy pursued them to Otterburn, where a battle was fought on 10 Aug., in which the earl of Douglas was killed and Percy taken prisoner. On this battle the ballad of *Chevy Chase* is founded.

OTTOMAN EMPIRE, see *Turkey*, 1299.

OUDE or **OUDH** (North India), formerly a vice-royalty held by the vizier of the great mogul. About 1760, it was seized by the vizier Sujah-ud-Dowlah, ancestor of the late king.

Battle of Buxar, where Sujah and his ally, Meer Cossim, are totally defeated, and the British become virtually masters of Oude . . 23 Oct. 1764

Reign of Asoph-ud-Dowlah, who cedes Benares, &c., to the East India Company, who place troops in Oude (see *Chunar*) 1775-81

[The annual subsidy to the company in 1787 was 500,000*l.*; in 1794, 760,000*l.*; in 1801, 1,352,347*l.*]

More territories ceded to the company . . . 1801

Ghazee-ud-deen becomes *king*, with the consent of the British 1819

Dreadful misgovernment of Nusser-ud-deen . 1827-37

[At his death, the British resident, Colonel Lowe, promptly suppresses an insurrection.]

Mahomed Ali governs well 1837-42

But his son, Umjeed Ali Shah 1842-7

And grandson, Waud Ali Shah, exceed all their predecessors in profligacy 1847-56

In consequence (by virtue of the treaty of 1801) Oude is annexed to the British territories, by decree, proclaimed . . . 7 Feb. 1856

The queen and prince of Oude, &c., arrive in London to appeal . . . . . . 20 Aug. „

Oude joins the Indian mutiny; ex-king of Oude imprisoned (on suspicion) . . . 14 June, 1857

The queen dies at Paris, 24 Jan.; and the prince at London . . . . . . 26 Feb. 1858

[For the war, see *India*, 1857-8.]

Triumphal entry of the governor-general into Lucknow; the Talookdars (landowners) receive a free grant of their estates . . . . 22 Oct. 1859

Grand durbar held at Lucknow by the viceroy, sir John Lawrence . . . . . . 12 Nov. 1867

Oude was annexed to the N.W. Provinces (*which see*) in 1856

OUDENARDE (Belgium). Here the English and allies under the duke of Marlborough and prince Eugène thoroughly defeated the French besiegers, 11 July, 1708.

OULART (S.E. Ireland). Here 5000 Irish insurgents attacked the king's troops, in small numbers, 27 May, 1798. The North Cork militia, after great feats of bravery, were cut to pieces, five men only escaping.—*Musgrave.*

OUNCE (from *uncia*), the sixteenth part of the pound avoirdupois, and twelfth of the pound troy. Its precise weight was fixed by Henry III., who decreed that an English ounce should be 640 dry grains of wheat; that twelve of these ounces should be a pound; and that eight pounds should be a gallon of wine, 1233.

OURIQUE (Portugal), where Alfonso, count or duke of Portugal, is said to have encountered five Saracen kings and a great army of Moors, 25 July, 1139, and signally defeated them; and then to have been hailed the first king Lisbon, the capital, was taken, and he soon after was crowned.

OUTLAW, one deprived of the benefit of the law, and out of the sovereign's protection; a punishment for such as being called in law do contemptuously refuse to appear. In the reign of Edward III. all the judges agreed that none but the sheriff only having lawful warrant therefor, should put to death any man outlawed.—*Cowel.* Outlawry in civil proceedings was abolished by 42 & 43 Vict. c. 59, 15 Aug. 1879.

OUZEL GALLEY SOCIETY. In 1700, the case of the *Ouzel Galley*, a ship in the port of Dublin, excited great legal perplexity, and was referred to an arbitration of merchants, whose prompt decision was highly approved. This led to the present society, founded in 1705.

OVATION, an inferior triumph which the Romans allowed those generals of their army whose victories were not considerable. Publius Posthumius Tubertus was the first who was decreed an ovation,

503 B.C. A sheep (*ovis*) was offered by the general instead of a bull.

OVERLAND MAIL, see *Waghorn*. The overland mail travelled first through the Cenis tunnel to Brindisi, saving 24 hours, 5 Jan. 1872.

Communication between the East and West has been greatly facilitated by the opening of the Suez Canal, 1869, and the railways between the Atlantic and Pacific oceans; by means of the Canadian Pacific railway the China and Japan mails were conveyed from Yokohama to London in 25 days, arriving in London . 13 May, 1891
Mr. H. de Windt travels 19,000 miles overland from Paris to New York . Dec. 1901–Sept. 1902
New overland route to China, *via* Siberian and Chinese Eastern railways, discussed in Paris, 8 Oct. ,,

OVERSEERS of the poor for parishes were appointed in 1601; see *Poor Laws*.

OWENS COLLEGE, Manchester, founded by means of a bequest of 100,000*l.* by John Owens, merchant, who died in 1846. A new constitution was obtained in 1870, and the duke of Devonshire, president, laid the first stone of the new building, 23 Sept. 1870; and opened it, 8 Oct. 1873. Mr. E. R. Langworthy bequeathed 10,000*l.* to develop the chair of experimental physics, 1874. In 1880 "Owens" became the first college of the new Victoria University, Manchester. The Beyer laboratories and natural history museums were erected 1887 at a cost of 80,000*l.* Mr. R. C. Christie, formerly professor, gives 50,000*l.*, 5 Oct. 1897. New physical (research) laboratory (cost 40,000*l.*) opened by lord Rayleigh, 29 June, 1900. See *Victoria University*. Connected with the college are the "Hulme" and the "Dalton" halls of residence for male students, and "Ashburne House" for female students.

OWEN'S SCHOOL, Islington, founded 1613, by Dame Alice Owen, in gratitude for her escape from death by an arrow; free education to 30 children and maintenance to 14 pensioners: the benefits of the charity since its foundation have been greatly increased; high-class education now given to 700 children at a nominal fee; new buildings erected by the Brewers' company under the trust, opened, 14 April, 1896. (Her statue unveiled, 21 Oct. 1897.)

OWHYHEE or **HAWAII**, the chief of the 12 islands which constitute the territory of Hawaii situated in the N. Pacific Ocean. The islands are said to have been discovered in 1542 by Gaetano, and were rediscovered by capt. Cook in 1778, who named them the Sandwich islands after lord Sandwich, then the first lord of the admiralty. Capt. Cook was killed at Owhyhee by the natives 1779. King Kamehameha I., who died 1819, united the 12 islands into one monarchy, and under his successor, Kamehameha II., idolatry was abolished, 1819–20; the king and his queen visited England, and died in London 1824. In 1840, Kamehameha III. established a constitution, which included an assembly of nobles, and a representative council. The independence of the kingdom was guaranteed by the English and French governments in 1843. A more popular constitution was granted in 1887, but in 1893 a revolution broke out, and the queen Liliuokalani was dethroned, and a republic was proclaimed in 1894. Hawaii was formally annexed to the United States 1898, and became one of its territories in 1900. Population, about 100,000. three-fourths of which are Japanese. Honolulu is the capital of the Hawaiian group; population about 30,000.

Eruption of the volcano Mauna Loa ceased, about 20 miles of lava, 8 Feb.; there have been frequent outbreaks of volcanoes on the island with occasional shocks of earthquake; earthquake shocks 5 May, 1887, *et seq.*; 167 persons killed; violent eruption of Mauna Loa and Kilcana, 4 July, 1899.

OWNERS OF LAND, see *Domesday*.

OXALIC ACID, which exists in several plants, especially in sorrel, is now abundantly obtained, for use in the arts, from sawdust acted upon by caustic potash or soda, according to dr. Dale's process, patented in 1862.

OXFORD, an ancient city, restored by king Alfred, who resided here and established a mint, &c., about 879. Returns one M.P. by Act of 1885. See *Population*.

Canute held a national council here 1017
Stormed by William I. 1068
Charter by Henry II., the city granted to the burgesses by John 1199
Henry III. holds the "mad" parliament here . . 1258
Bishops Ridley and Latimer burnt here, 16 Oct. 1555; and archbishop Cranmer . 21 March, 1556
Fatal (or Black) Oxford Assizes,—when the high sheriff and 300 other persons died suddenly of an infection from the prisoners 1557
Charles I. took Oxford, 1642, and held a parliament here 1644
Taken by the parliament . . . . 24 June, 1646
Charles II. held parliaments here . . . 1665 & 1681
Visit of the allied sovereigns 1814
British Association met here . 1832, 1847, 1860, 1894
Oxford Military College, Cowley, opened . 20 Sept. 1876
New high school opened . . . . 15 Sept. 1881
New theatre opened 13 Feb. 1886; greatly injured by fire . . . . . 10, 11 March, 1892
Statue of Thomas Sydenham unveiled by the marquis of Salisbury . . . . 9 Aug. 1894
New municipal buildings and the Sarah Acland Home opened by the prince of Wales 12 May, 1897
Ruskin hall, to promote the education of the working classes, founded by Mr. Vrooman and other Americans, opened . . 22 Feb. 1899
The new Radcliffe library, gift of the Drapers' co., London (cost 21,000*l.*), opened . 18 June, 1901
Conference on higher education . . 12 Aug. 1903

OXFORD ADMINISTRATION, formed 29 May, 1711.

Robert, earl of Oxford (previously right hon. Robert Harley), *lord treasurer*.
Sir Simon (afterwards lord) Harcourt, *lord keeper*.
John, duke of Normanby and Buckingham, *lord president*.
John, bishop of Bristol (aft. London), *privy seal*.
Henry St. John (afterwards viscount Bolingbroke), and William, lord Dartmouth, *secretaries of state*.
Robert Benson (afterwards lord Bingley), *chancellor of the exchequer*.
The duke of Shrewsbury succeeded lord Oxford, receiving the lord treasurer's staff on 30 July, 1714, three days before the death of queen Anne. From the reign of George I. the office of lord treasurer has been executed by commissioners.

OXFORD BISHOPRIC, established by Henry VIII., formed out of Lincoln, first placed at Osney in 1542; removed to Oxford cathedral (formerly St. Frideswide, now Christ Church), 1545. Present income, 5000*l.*

RECENT BISHOPS.

1807. Charles Moss; died, 16 Dec. 1811.
1812. William Jackson; died, 2 Dec. 1815.
1815. Edward Legge; died, 27 Jan. 1827.
1827. Charles Lloyd; died, 31 May, 1829.
1829. Richard Bagot; translated to Bath, Nov. 1845.
1845. Samuel Wilberforce; translated to Winchester, Nov. 1869; died, 22 April, 1901.
1869. John Fielder Mackarness; resigned about 21 June, 1888; died 16 Sept. 1889.
1888. William Stubbs; translated from Chester, July; died, 22 April, 1901.
1901. Francis Paget, appointed May, 1901.

OXFORD DECLARATION, see *Church of England*, 1864.

OXFORD MARBLES, see *Arundelian*.

OXFORD UNION SOCIETY, established as a debating club, in 1823; amongst its early members are or were Mr. Gladstone, bp. Wilberforce, lord Stanhope, abp. Manning, Sidney Herbert, abp. Tait, &c. It held a jubilee festival, 22 Oct. 1873, the lord chancellor Selborne in the chair.

OXFORD UNIVERSITY. The statement that king Alfred founded "the schools" is now discredited as legendary. See *Ashmolean*.

Charter granted by Henry III. 1248
Charter of Edward III. 1355; of Henry VIII. . . 1510
The university incorporated by Elizabeth . . 1570
Receives the elective franchise (to send two members to parliament) 1604
Bodleian Library opened, 8 Nov. 1602; building completed 1613
The botanic garden, &c., established by the earl of Danby 1622
Radcliffe Library opened, 13 April, 1749; the Radcliffe observatory completed 1786
A commission appointed (31 Aug. 1850) to inquire into its "state, studies, discipline, and revenues;" reported . . . . 27 April, 1852
Acts making alterations passed. . . . 1854, 1856
University Museum opened . . . . July, 1860
Examination statutes passed . 1801, 1807, 1850, 1862
Extension of the university proposed at a meeting held . . . . 16 Nov. 1865
University tests abolished by act passed 16 June, 1871
Royal commission to inquire respecting university property, &c., appointed . . . 6 Jan. 1872
Income in 1871, reported to be: university, 47,589*l*. 0*s*. 3*d*.; colleges and halls, 366,253*l*. 16*s*. 3*d*.; total, 413,842*l*. 16*s*. 6*d*. . . . . . Oct. 1874
Hebdomadal board reported that about 100,000*l*. was needed for education in science . June, 1875
Lord Ilchester's bequest to promote the study of Slavonian literature, especially Polish; first lectures given . . . . . . May, ,,
New commission appointed (lords Selborne and Redesdale, Montague Bernard, sir M. W. Ridley, dean Burgon, and Mr. Justice Grove); announced 27 March, 1876
Oxford University Bill withdrawn July, 1876; the Universities Act passed . . . 10 Aug. 1877
The commission publish a new scheme for professors, &c., very restrictive . . . 2 Nov. 1880
Statute passed admitting women to examination 29 April, 1884
Pusey memorial house, containing Pusey's library, &c., opened by bishop of Oxford . . 9 Oct. ,,
4 sets of rooms at Queen's College destroyed by fire 11 Dec. 1886
Museum for gen. Pitt-Rivers' collection of ancient weapons, &c., presented to the university, opened Feb. 1887
Combination of the municipal and academical civic powers in conformity with the local government act of 1888, consummated . . . 9 Nov. 1889
Catherine T. Riordon's attempt on the life of Dr. J. T. Bright, master of University College, 6 Nov.; sentenced to 6 years' penal servitude . 15 Nov. 1890
The first Romanes lecture, given by Mr. W. E. Gladstone on "University Life," 24 Oct. 1892; by T. H. Huxley, 18 May, 1893; by prof. Auguste Weismann, 2 May, 1894; Mr. Holman Hunt, 30 May, 1895; the bishop of Peterborough, "English National Character," 17 June, 1896; Mr. John Morley, "Machiavelli," 2 June, 1897; "Humanism," by prof. Jebb, June, 1899; by Mr. Bryce, M.P., 7 June, 1902; sir Oliver Lodge, "Modern Views of Matter" . . 12 June, 1903
Great meeting to support the Radcliffe infirmary; the marquis of Salisbury, chancellor, present, 1 March, 1819
Death of prof. Benjamin Jowett, influential master of Balliol . . . . 1 Oct. ,,
Prof. Romanes died suddenly at Oxford . 23 May, 1894
"School of English Language and Literature;" regulations issued . . . . . 4 Dec. ,,
Sir John Robt. Mowbray (father of the house of commons) sat since 1853, sen. member of the university; born 1815, died . . 22 April, 1899
Statue of Charles Darwin, by Mr. Hope Pinker, presented by prof. Poulton; unveiled by sir Joseph Hooker, at the museum . . 14 June, ,,
Mr. Cecil Rhodes bequeaths 100,000*l*. to Oriel, his old college, and 51,750*l*. per annum for 175 scholarships (60 colonial, 100 American, and 15 German) in the university. For his will, see *Rhodesia*. 1902
Bodleian tercentenary celebrated . . 8, 9 Oct. ,,
See *Women*, 3, 10 March, 1896.

COLLEGES.

University, founded by William, archdeacon of Durham, about 1249
Balliol; founded by John Baliol or Balliol, knt. (father to Baliol, king of the Scots), and Deborah, his wife 1263
Merton College, by Walter de Merton, bishop of Rochester 1264
Hertford College, 1312 (dissolved in 1805 and a Hertford scholarship appointed); revived, and Magdalen Hall incorporated with it . . . 1874
Exeter, by Walter Stapleton, bishop of Exeter . 1314
Oriel College, by king Edward II.; Adam de Brome, archdeacon of Stowe 1326
Queen's College, by Robert de Eglesfield, clerk, confessor to queen Philippa, consort of Edward III. 1340
New College, by William of Wykeham, bishop of Winchester; first called St. Mary of Winchester, founded 1379; occupied 1386 (500th anniversary celebrated 14 Oct. 1879).
All Souls' College, by Henry Chichely, archbishop of Canterbury 1437
Magdalen, by William of Waynflete, bishop of Winchester 1456
Lincoln College, by Richard Fleming, 1427; finished by Rotherham, bishop of Lincoln . . 1479
Brazenose, by William Smyth, bishop of Lincoln, and sir Richard Sutton 1509
Corpus Christi, by Richard Fox, bishop of Winchester 1516
Christ Church, by cardinal Wolsey, 1525; and afterwards by Henry VIII. 1532
Trinity, by sir Thomas Pope, on the basis of a previous institution, called Durham College . 1554
St. John's, by sir Thomas Whyte, lord mayor of London 1555
Jesus College, by dr. Hugh Price and queen Elizabeth 1571
Wadham, by Nicholas Wadham, and Dorothy, his wife 1613
Pembroke, by Thomas Teesdale and Richard Wightwick, clerk 1624
Worcester, by sir Thomas Cokes, of Bentley, in Worcestershire; it was originally called Gloucester College 1714
Keble College (see *Keble College*); first stone laid by archbishop of Canterbury 25 April, 1868; consecrated . . . . 23 June, 1870
Indian Institute, founded 1878 or 1879.
Somerville Hall, opened, 1879; Mansfield College, for Nonconformists 1886
Manchester New College 1889–93
Proposed establishment of Honour School of modern European languages . . . . . 3 May, 1887

HALLS (not incorporated).

St. Edmund's 1269
St. Mary's 1333
New Inn Hall 1392
St. Mary Magdalen (incorporated with Hertford college 1874) 1487
St. Alban's (united with Merton College, 1882) . 1547
[*Oxford University Calendar*.]

Hannington Hall, a memorial of the bishop (see *Uganda*, 1889 and 1892), opened . 26 Jan. 1897

First Professorships—Divinity (Margaret), 1502; Divinity, Law, Medicine, Hebrew, Greek, 1540, &c.

RECENT CHANCELLORS.

1809. William, baron Granville.
1834. Arthur, duke of Wellington.
1852. Edward, earl of Derby; *d*. 23 Nov. 1869.

1869. Robert, marquis of Salisbury, elected 12 Nov.; *d.* 22 Aug. 1903.
1903. George Joachim, viscount Goschen, 31 Oct.

OXFORD, PROVISIONS OF, for several political reforms; enacted by "the mad parliament," June 1258; several times annulled and confirmed during the "barons' war."

OXFORD'S ACT, BISHOP OF, see *District Churches.*

OXFORD'S ASSAULT ON THE QUEEN. Edward Oxford, a youth who had been a servant in a public-house, discharged two pistols at queen Victoria and prince Albert, as they were proceeding up Constitution-hill in an open phaeton from Buckingham palace, 10 June, 1840. He stood within a few yards of the carriage, but neither her majesty nor the prince was injured. Oxford was tried at the Old Bailey (10 July), and was adjudged to be insane, and sent first to Bethlehem hospital, next to Broadmoor; and set at liberty in 1868, on condition of going abroad.

OXFORD HOUSE, see *University Teaching.*

"OXFORD MOVEMENT, 1833-45," by R. W. Church," late dean of St. Paul's, published 10 March, 1891; see *Puseyism and Tractarianism.*

OXUS (the Persian and Turkish Djihoun, local name, Amou Daryá), a river of Central Asia; supposed to have changed its course before 1000 A.D., and to have resumed its ancient bed in 1878. The Oxus navigated as far as Faizabad Kali (Afghan frontier) by the Russians under adm. Baturin; reported, 11 Dec. 1894.

OXYGEN, a gas (named from the Greek *oxus*, sharp, as being generally found in acids), is the most abundant of all substances, constituting about one-third of the solid earth, and forming about nine-tenths of water and one-fifth of the atmosphere. It was first separated from red oxide of mercury by Priestley, 1 Aug. 1774, and by Scheele, who was ignorant of Priestley's discovery, in 1775. It is a supporter of animal life (in respiration), and of combustion. An oxygen gas company was announced in Dec. 1864; its object being the cheap manufacture of oxygen for its application to the production of perfect combustion in lamps, stoves, furnaces, &c. It is now largely produced with about 5 per cent. of inert nitrogen by the Brin method from atmospheric air (1893). Oxygen was liquefied by Raoul Pictet at Geneva (pressure, 320 atmospheres, temp. 140° below zero Cent.), 22 Dec. 1877. See *Ozone.*

Professor Dewar obtained 2 cubic centimètres ($\frac{1}{15}$ of a fluid oz.) of liquid oxygen by means of liquid ethylene (the illuminating part of coal gas), temp. 140° below zero Cent. (by Wroblewski and Olzewski's method), at the Royal Institution, London, in the presence of the prince and princess of Wales, 26 June, 1884. He exhibited for the first time some solid oxygen in the form of snow (temperature −200° Cent. −400° Fahr.), produced by placing liquid oxygen in a partial vacuum, at the Royal Institution 27 May, 1886.

Professor Dewar exhibited between 300 to 400 centimètres liquid oxygen at the Faraday Centenary, 26 June, 1891. The feeble magnetism of oxygen, demonstrated by Faraday, was shown by Professor Dewar to be greatly increased when reduced to the liquid state by a temperature of 180° below zero centigrade; announced 10 Dec. 1891. Some liquid oxygen placed in the magnetic field sprang to the poles and adhered to them till evaporated; this was publicly exhibited by the professor at the Royal Institution, 10 June, 1892. Several pints of liquid oxygen and liquid air were then produced in the presence of the audience.

At the Friday evening meeting of the Royal institution, 20 Jan. 1893, prof. Dewar exhibited some of the remarkable properties of liquid oxygen and air, and he showed how the liquid state could be maintained longer by surrounding it with a very high vacuum. These costly experiments had been aided by a gift of 1,000*l.* from the Goldsmiths' company. The lecture and experiments were repeated before the prince of Wales, the duke of York, and a distinguished company, 22 Feb. 1893. Prof. Dewar reported to the Royal society that he had obtained solid air in the form of ice, a mysterious body, 9 March, 1893. Further researches reported, 22 Jan. 1897.

Prof. Dewar was awarded the Rumford medal of the Royal society in 1894.

A statue of Priestley, by F. J. Williamson, at Birmingham, was unveiled by professor T. H. Huxley, 1 Aug. 1874, the centenary of the discovery of oxygen. This was also celebrated at Northumberland, Pennsylvania, where he was buried, Feb. 1804. The following telegram was sent 31 July: "The brethren at the grave to the brethren at the home of Priestley send greeting on this centennial anniversary of the birth of chemistry."

A method of obtaining oxygen from air, devised and patented by M. Margis, of Paris. The principle is that of dialysis, or diffusion under pressure, Sept. 1882. See *Gas* (liquefaction).

By the explosion of a cylinder of compressed oxygen, the carrier was killed, 15 March, 1895.

OXYGEN HOME, 2, Fitzroy square, London; founded for the treatment of ulcers and wounds by oxygen gas, about 1896; the oxygen is supposed to turn the toxins or poisons secreted by certain micro-organisms into oxy-toxins or antidotes; continued success reported, 10 May, 1899.

OYER AND TERMINER, a commission directed to the judges of the courts, by virtue whereof they have power to *hear and determine* treasons, felonies, &c., 1285.

O YES! A corruption of the French *oyez*, hear ye! The ancient term still used by a public crier and by the usher of courts of justice to enjoin silence and attention.

OYSTER (the Latin *Ostrea edulis*). British oysters are celebrated by the Roman satirist Juvenal (Sat. iv. 140) about 100. The robbery of oyster-beds is prohibited by 7 & 8 Geo. IV. c. 29 (1827). About 15,000 bushels of oysters were said to be produced from the Essex beds alone. In 1858 M. Coste commenced rearing oysters in great numbers on the coast of Brittany, and his plan has been found successful.

An act for promoting the cultivation of oysters in the United Kingdom, passed . . . Aug. 1866
One for the preservation of oyster fisheries 3 May, 1867
Certain restrictions of the Oyster Fisheries act, 1862, removed by the Fisheries act 1868
The fisheries (oyster, crab, and lobster) act forbids the sale of deep-sea oysters between 15 June and 4 August; and the sale of others, between 14 May and 4 August; passed . . . . 10 Aug. 1877
Professor Huxley at the Royal Institution asserts the uselessness of restrictions and a close time for oysters, and the present uncertainty of culture, 11 May, 1883
Artificial breeding greatly promoted by professor Brooks of Baltimore (who discovered non-hermaphrodite), lieutenant Winslow, U.S., and M. Bouchen-Brandely, announced . . . . June, 1884
Act for the cultivation of oysters in Ireland passed ,,
Dean of Winchester and other guests at a banquet poisoned by eating oysters, contaminated by sewage. The dean subsequently died . 22 Dec. 1902
Typhoid epidemic in Hampshire, occasioned by consumption of Emsworth oysters (see *Times*, 11 July, 1903) . . . . Dec. 1902–Jan. 1903
Committee representing the oyster trade to consider the contamination of oysters by sewage, pass various resolutions . . . . . 5 Jan. ,,

Oysters, about 1830 the commonest of food, are now becoming scarcer and scarcer, although their reproduction is about a million-fold. A committee recommend a close time for dredging, viz. 1 May to 1 Sept., deep-sea fishing to be restricted, as at present, from 15 June to 15 Aug.; no oyster to be sold under 2½ inches in diameter. The Whitstable beds in 1875 are said to have produced about 79,564,000 oysters; value about 55,140*l*.

American and Portuguese oysters are now largely imported.

Oysters successfully cultivated at Arcachon, near Bordeaux, 1889.

OZOKERIT, a mineral hydro-carbon found in Moldavia and Wallachia. From it is distilled a substance suitable for making candles, introduced in the autumn of 1871.

OZONE (from the Greek *ozein*, to yield an odour), was discovered by Schönbein, of Basel, in 1840, when experimenting with the then newly-invented battery of sir Wm. Grove, and was recognised by him successively as a minute constituent of the oxygen gas resulting from the electrolysis of water effected by a current of high tension; of air or oxygen through which electric discharges have taken place; and of air in which moist phosphorus has been undergoing slow oxidation.

Marignac determined the action of ozone on various substances to be due to their oxidation . . 1845

Ozonometers constructed 1858

M. Schönbein announced his discovery of another modification of oxygen, which he termed *antozone*, hitherto found only in the compound state (in peroxides of sodium, potassium, &c.) 1859

The French Academy of Sciences appointed a committee of eminent philosophers to inquire into the nature and relations of ozone . 4 Dec. 1865

Andrews and Tait demonstrated ozone to be a condensed form of oxygen . . . . . 1860, „

This further established by Soret and Brodie, by quantitative reactions. (Odling suggested and Brodie proved ozone to be 3 parts of oxygen compressed into the space of 2) 1872

Ozone, generated by a current produced by Wilde's magneto-electric machine, employed to bleach sugar, by Edward Beane's patent . . Aug. 1868

Liquefied by Hautefeuille and Chappuis . Oct. 1880

Other properties since discovered . . . 1881-4

The inhalation of ozone recommended as a remedy for phthisis; the institution at St. Raphael on the Mediterranean opened for the purpose; reported Dec. 1891

M. Emile Andreoli's system for the commercial production of ozone economically carried on by Messrs. Allen & Hanbury in London . July, 1893

M. Otto, in Paris, discovers the means of purifying water by ozone; reported . . . 6 Feb. 1902

Radium reported to possess the property of converting oxygen into ozone 1903

P.

PACIFICATION, EDICTS OF, the name usually given to the edicts of toleration granted by the French kings to the protestants; see *Ghent*.

First edict, by Charles IX., permitting the exercise of the reformed religion near all the cities and towns in the realm . . . . . Jan. 1562
The reformed worship permitted in the houses of lords justiciaries, and certain other persons, March, 1563
These edicts revoked, and all Protestant ministers ordered to quit France in fifteen days . . . 1568
Edict, allowing lords and others to have service in their houses, and granting public service in certain towns 1570
[In Aug. 1572, the same monarch authorised the massacre of St. Bartholomew (see *Bartholomew*).]
Edict of Pacification by Henry III., April; revoked, Dec. 1576; renewed for six years . Oct. 1577
[Several edicts were published against the protestants after the six years expired.]
Edict of Henry IV., renewing that of Oct. 1577 . 1591
Edict of Nantes (*which see*), by Henry IV., 13 April, 1598
Pacification of Nismes (*which see*) . . 14 July, 1629

PACIFIC ISLANDERS. See *Kidnapping Acts*.

PACIFIC OCEAN, the largest of the five oceans of the globe. It was first discovered in 1513 by Vasco Nûnez de Balboa, and received its name from Magellan in 1521. Sir Francis Drake was the first Englishman who sailed upon it in 1577. The Santa Cruz and Duff islands annexed by Gt. Britain, June, 1898; Wake island, by U.S.A., Dec. 1898; 14 others annexed by Gt. Britain, Dec. 1900; 3 more, May, 1903. See *Magellan; Steam*, 1851; *Wrecks*, 1856; *Kidnapping Acts; Panamá*.

PACIFIC CABLE. See *Electric city*. Bill passed 6 Aug. 1901; amended, 7 Aug. 1902.

PACIFIC RAILWAY, North America, from Omaha city, Missouri, to Sacramento, California, 1700 miles, opened 12 May, 1869. By a collision near San Francisco, about 15 persons were killed, 14 Nov. 1869. For new Pacific railway, see *Canada*, 1881 *et seq.* By means of this railway, the China and Japan mails were conveyed from Yokohama to London in 25 days; received 13 May, 1891.

PADLOCKS are said to have been invented by Beecher at Nuremberg, 1540, but are mentioned much earlier.

PADUA, the Roman Patavium, in Venetia, N. Italy, said to have been founded by Antenor, soon after the fall of Troy. It flourished under the Romans. Patavian Latin was considered very corrupt, and is traced in Livy, a native of Padua. After being an independent republic, and a member of the Lombard league, Padua was ruled by the Carrara family from 1318 with a short interruption till 1405, when it was seized by the Venetians. The university was founded about 1220. It was closed through disturbances, 1848-50.

PAGANS, the heathen, worshippers of idols, not agreeing in any set form or points of belief. See *Idols*. Constantine's nephew, Julian, attempted their restoration, 361; but Paganism was renounced by the Roman senate in 388, and finally overthrown in the reign of Theodosius the younger, about 391.

PAHANG, see *Straits Settlements*.

PAI MARIRE, a name given to the dogmas of the Hau-hau sect; see *New Zealand*, 1865.

PAINS AND PENALTIES, certain bills passed by the legislature to punish state offenders; see *Queen Caroline*.

PAINTING. This art was practised in Egypt and Greece in very early times; see under *Arts*.

Polygnotus, said to be the first portrait and historic painter, lived about . . . . B.C. 450
Zeuxis of Heraclea and Parrhasius of Ephesus, about 400
Apelles . . . . . . about 332
Pausias of Sicyon was the inventor of the encaustic, a method of burning the colours into wood or ivory . . . . . about 360-330
Antiphilus, an Egyptian, is said to have been the inventor of the grotesque. *Pliny*. . . B.C. 332
The art was introduced at Rome from Etruria, by Quintus Fabius, styled *Pictor*. *Livy*. . 291
Excellent pictures brought from Corinth by Mummius 146
After the death of Augustus, not a single painter of eminence appeared for several ages; Ludius, who was very celebrated, is supposed to have been the last . . . . . about A.D. 14
Painting on canvas seems to have been known at Rome in 66. Bede, the Saxon historian, knew something of the art, died 735
Giovanni Cimabue, of Florence, revived the art; he died 1300
John Van Eyck, of Bruges, and his brother, Hubert, are regarded as the founders of the Flemish school of painting in oil 1415
Uccello first studied perspective; died . . . 1432
Henry VIII. patronised Holbein, and invited Titian to his court . . . . . about 1523
In Aug. 1860, the sale of lord Northwick's pictures occupied eighteen days. It produced 95,725*l.* A Carlo Dolci fetched 2010*l.*, and a Murillo 1400*l.*
The Bicknell collection, sold in April, 1863, produced 25,600*l.*
Mr. Wm. Noy Wilkins invented a process of using oil with mineral colours for frescoes in 1853; published his "Durability in Art" 1875
Gainsborough's picture of Georgiana, duchess of Devonshire, bought by Messrs. Agnew for 10,605*l.*, stolen from their house in Bond-st. 24-25 May, 1876
Baron Albert Grant's collection said to have sold for 106,262*l.* . . . . . 28 April, 1877
Mr. Munro's Novar collection, sold for 64,975*l.* close of sale . . . . . 3 June, 1878
Leigh Court collection (sir P. W. Miles) sold for 44,296*l.* . . . . . 28 June, 1884
The collections of John Graham of Ayrshire: ancient masters sold for 69,168*l.* 12 April, 1886; modern masters, 62,297*l.* . . . 30 April, 1887
Mr. Bolckow's collection of about 70 modern pictures sold for 71,378*l.* . . . 5 May, 1888
Mr. Wells' (of Redleaf) collection of 104 pictures sold for 77,000*l.* . . . 10 May, 1890
Constable's "White Horse" sold for 6,200 guineas to Mr. Agnew . . . . 28 April, 1894
Gainsborough's "Market Cart" sold for 4,500*l.*, 26 May, ,,
Turner's "Ancient Italy" bought for the Louvre, price 8000*l.* . . . . . 5 June, ,,
Portrait of lady Betty Delmé and her children, by sir Joshua Reynolds, sold to Mr. C. Wertheimer for 11,000*l.* . . . . . 7 July, ,,
Collection of the late Mr. James Price, of Barcombe, S. Devon, sold for 87,143*l.* 15*s.*, 15 June, 1895
See under *Blenheim* and *Hamilton Palace*.
Picture by Romney of two ladies as Music and Painting, bought by Mr. C. Wertheimer for 10,500 guineas . . . . . 11 June 1896
The sale of sir Julian Goldsmid's pictures by Reynolds, Turner, and others realised 67,342*l.* 13 June, ,,
Sale of sir J. Millais' pictures, one by Holbein, realised 3,000 guineas . . . . 1 May, 1897
Sale of sir John Pender's pictures by Turner, Wilkie, Millais and others, realised 75,917*l.* 29 May, ,,

A fine collection of paintings by Millais, lord Leighton, Alma-Tadema, Rivière and others, destroyed at the fire at Eynsham hall, Oxfordshire . . . . 10 Jan. 1898
The Ruston collection sold for 44,995*l*. . 23 May, ,,
Two portraits by Romney realised 5,200 gs. and 3,000 gs. . . . . 25 June, ,,
The Burne-Jones sale realised nearly 29,475*l*. 8*s*.; "Love and the Pilgrim" sold for 5,500 gs., 18 July, ,,
Rembrandt exhibition at Burlington house . early 1899
The Miéville collection of ancient and modern pictures, sold for 41,751*l*. 3*s*. . . . 29 April, ,,
The late sir John Fowler's collection sold for 65,355*l*. 13*s*., a landscape by Hobbema realized 9,100 gs., and "a view of Venice" by Turner, 8,200 gs. . . . . 6 May, ,,
The late sir Cecil Miles' and other collections of pictures by old masters, realise about 35,000*l*., 13 May, ,,
The Bardini collection of pictures, &c., sold for 38,259*l*. . . . . 5–7 June, ,,
Sale of pictures by old masters realised about 20,000*l* . . . . 10 June, ,,
A portrait attributed to Reynolds sold for 2,800 gs.; a Watteau, 1,380*l*. . . . . . . 1 July, ,,
The Schubert sale (Munich) realised about 35,000*l*., a Hobbema, 4,300*l*. (bought for Dresden gallery), 23, 24 Oct. ,,
The Borghese collection bought by the Italian government for about 133,000*l*., reported . Feb. 1900
Peel heirlooms: 2 Van Dycks sold for 24,250*l*., 11 May, ,,
A portrait by Romney realised 7,000 gs., and landscape by Hobbema, 6,200 gs., 16 June; a Romney sold for 2,900 gs. . . . 7 July, ,,
Portraits (125) by Holbein, Van Dyck, Rubens, Velasquez, and others, destroyed by fire at the Château Belœil, near Tournay . . 14 Dec. ,,
The lost Gainsborough (stolen, 1876), recovered in Chicago, brought to London, 8 April, 1901, and sold to Mr. Pierpont Morgan for 30,000*l*., April, ,,
A Hobbema and a Romney realised 9,400 gs. and 5,600 gs. . . . . 27 April, 1901
A sketch by Rubens of his "Raising of the Cross," realised 3,200 gs. . . . . . . 4 May, ,,
A landscape by Hobbema realised 9,200 gs., a Raeburn, 6,500 gs., 3 May; a Rembrandt, 5,500 gs., 31 May; a portrait by Romney, 10,500 gs., 14 June; another, for which he received 25 gs., 4,100 gs. . . . . . . 5 July, ,,
M. Raffaelli's method of solidifying oil colours into cylindrical sticks, reported successful . 25 Nov. 1902
A portrait of his daughters, by Gainsborough, realised 5,600 gs. . . . . . . 6 Dec. ,,
A Paul Potter realised 2,835*l*. . 25 April, 1903
Sir L. Alma-Tadema's "Dedication to Bacchus" realised 5,600 gs.; one of Rosa Bonheur's 3,100 gs. 2 May, ,,
Portrait of sir John Sinclair, by Raeburn, realised 14,000 gs. . . . . 21 May, ,,
Mr. R. Vaile's collection realised 58,529*l*.; and other pictures reached a total of 105,845*l*. . 23 May, ,,

EMINENT PAINTERS.

	School.	Born or Flourished.	Died.
Guido da Siena		1220	—
Marghitone d'Arezzo	Florentine	1212	1289
Cimabue	Ditto	1240	1300
Giotto	Ditto	1276	1336
Simone Martino (Memmi)	Italian	1283	1344
Andrea Orcagna	Ditto	1329	1389
Hubert Van Eyck	Flemish	1366	1426
J. Van Eyck	Ditto	1266	1441
Fra Angelico da Fiesole.	Italian	1387	1455
Filippo Lippi	Ditto	1412	1469
Domenico Ghirlandajo	Ditto	1449	1498
Andrea Mantegna	Ditto	1431	1506
Giorgione	Venetian	1477	1511
Sandro Botticelli	Italian	1437	1515
Giovanni Bellini	Ditto	1426	1516
Leonardo da Vinci	Florentine	1452	1520
Raphael d'Urbino	Roman	1483	1520
Pietro Paolo Perugino	Italian	1446	1524
Albert Dürer	German	1470	1528
Quentin Matsys	Flemish	1460	1529
Andrea Vannuchi (del Sarto)	Florentine	1488	1530
Correggio	Lombardian	1494	1530
Parmegiano	Ditto	1503	1540
Hans Holbein	German	1495	1543
Giulio Romano	Roman	1492	1546
Sebastian del Piombo	Venetian	1485	1547
Lucas Cranach	German	1472	1553
Giovanni Razzi	Siennese	1479	1554
Michael Angelo Buonarotti	Florentine	1474	1564
Titian	Venetian	1477	1576
Paul Veronese	Ditto	1532	1588
Tintoretto	Ditto	1512	1594
Annibal Caracci	Lombardian	1568	1609
Breughel	Flemish	1565	1625
P. P. Rubens	Ditto	1577	1640
Domenichino	Bolognese	1581	1641
Vandyck	Flemish	1599	1641
Guido	Lombardian	1575	1642
Wm. Dobson	English	1610	1646
Both	Dutch	1600	1650
P. Potter	Ditto	1625	1654
Le Seur	French	1617	1655
Spagnoletto	Spanish	1589	1656
Snyders	Flemish	1579	1657
Velasquez	Spanish	1599	1660
Zurbaran	Ditto	1598	1662
N. Poussin	French	1594	1665
Guercino	Bolognese	1590	1666
Hobbema	Flemish	1611	1670
A. Cuyp	Dutch	1606	1672
Samuel Cooper	English	1609	1672
A. Vander Velde	Dutch	1638	1672
Salvator Rosa	Neapolitan	1615	1673
Rembrandt	Dutch	1606	1674
Gerard Douw	Ditto	1613	1680
Sir Peter Lely	German	1617	1680
Mieris	Dutch	1635	1681
Ruysdael	Ditto	1636	1681
Claude Lorraine	French	1600	1682
Ostade	Dutch	1610	1685
Murillo	Spanish	1618	1685
Berghem	Dutch	1624	1685
Carlo Dolci	Florentine	1616	1686
Wouvermans	Dutch	1620	1688
Le Brun	French	1619	1690
Teniers, junr.	Flemish	1610	1694
W. Vander Velde	Dutch	1633	1707
Watteau	French	1684	1721
Sir Godfrey Kneller	German	1648	1723
Sir J. Thornhill	English	1676	1732
Huysum	Dutch	1682	1749
Hogarth	English	1697	1764
Canaletti	Venetian	1697	1768
J. Mortimer	English	1739	1779
R. Wilson	Ditto	1714	1782
Gainsborough	Ditto	1727	1788
C. J. Vernet	French	1714	1789
Sir J. Reynolds	English	1723	1792
Romney	Ditto	1734	1802
George Morland	Ditto	1763	1804
Barry	Ditto	1741	1806
George Stubbs	Ditto	1724	1806
Opie	Ditto	1761	1807
Paul Sandby	Ditto	1725	1809
Bourgeois	Ditto	1756	1811
Copley	Ditto	1738	1815
West	Ditto	1738	1820
H. Raeburn	Ditto	1786	1823
Fuseli	Ditto	1741	1825
David	French	1748	1825
Lawrence	English	1769	1830
Northcote	Ditto	1746	1831
Thos. Stothard	Ditto	1755	1834
A. C. H. Vernet	French	1758	1836
Beechey	English	1753	1839
Wm. Hilton	Ditto	1786	1839
Wilkie	Ditto	1785	1841
Haydon	Ditto	1786	1846
Collins	Ditto	1788	1847
Etty	Ditto	1787	1849
Turner	Ditto	1775	1851
Martin	Ditto	1789	1854
C. R. Leslie	Ditto	1794	1859
Aug. Egg	Ditto	1816	1863
Wm. Mulready	Ditto	1786	1863
J. E. H. Vernet	French	1789	1863
F. V. E. De la Croix	Ditto	1798	1863
Wm. Hunt	English	1790	1864
D. Roberts	Ditto	1796	1864

	School.	Born or Flourished.	Died.
W. F. Witherington	English	1786	1865
Clarkson Stanfield	Ditto	1798	1867
P. Von Cornelius	German	1787	1867
J. D. A. Ingres	French	1781	1867
Thos. Creswick	English	1811	1869
F. Overbeck	German	1789	1869
D. Maclise	English	1811	1870
Sir George Hayter	Ditto	1792	1871
Sir E. Landseer	Ditto	1802	1873
W. Kaulbach	German	1805	1874
Jean B. C. Corot	French	1796	1875
P. F. Poole	English	1806	1879
E. M. Ward	Ditto	1816	1879
E W. Cooke	Ditto	1810	1880
Gustave Doré	French	1832	1883
Johannes Makart	German	1840	1884
Thos. Webster	English	1800	1886
Richd. Redgrave	Ditto	1804	1888
Frank Holl	Ditto	1846	1888
Arthur Stocks	Ditto	1846	1889
John R. Herbert	Ditto	1810	1890
J. C. Horsley	Ditto	1817	1903
C. W. Cope	Ditto	1811	1890
J. L. E. Meissonier	French	1815	1891
Edwin Long	English	1839	1891
W. P. Frith	Ditto	1819	
Fredk. Goodall	Ditto	1822	
Sir Wm. F. Douglas	Scottish	1829	1891
John Faed	Ditto	1820	1902
Thomas Faed	Ditto	1826	1900
Wm. Holman Hunt	English	1827	
Ford Madox Brown	Ditto	1821	1893
Sir Edw. Burne-Jones	Ditto	1833	1898
John Hayter	Ditto	1800	1895
John Evans Hodgson	Ditto	1831	1895
Henry Moore	Ditto	1831	1895
H. S. Marks	Ditto	1829	1898
Sir J. E. Millais	Ditto	1829	1896
Sir F. Leighton (lord 1896)	Ditto	1830	1896
G. Vicat Cole	Ditto	1833	1893
G. D. Leslie	Ditto	1835	
L. Alma-Tadema (knt. 1899)	Dutch	1836	
Peter Graham	Scottish	1836	
Thos. S. Cooper	English	1803	1902
Edw. Armitage	Ditto	1817	1896
Sir J. Gilbert	Ditto	1817	1897
J. C. Hook	Ditto	1819	
J. Sant	Ditto	1820	
George Fred. Watts	Ditto	1817	
Carl Haag	German	1820	
Phil. Calderon	Spanish	1833	1898
J. A. M. Whistler	American	1835	1903
W. O. Orchardson	English	1835	
E. J. Poynter (knt. 1896, bart. 1902)	Ditto	1836	
Marcus Stone	Ditto	1840	
Briton Rivière	Ditto	1840	
Jas. D. Linton	Ditto	1840	
Eliz. Thompson, since lady Butler	Ditto		
Sir John Pettie	Scottish	1839	1893
John MacWhirter	Ditto	1839	
Walter W. Ouless	English	1848	
Hubert Herkomer	German	1849	
George Richmond	English	1809	1896
Frederick Barnard	Ditto	1846	1896
Charles Parsons Knight	Ditto	1829	1897
François Louis Français	French	1814	1897
J. B. Burgess	English	1830(?)	1897
Wm. C. T. Dobson	Ditto	1817	1898
Pierre Puvis de Chavannes	French	1826	1898
Benjamin Constant	Ditto	1845	1902
Joseph Wolf (animal painter)	German	1820	1899
"Rosa" (Marie Rosalie) Bonheur	French	1822	1899
Aug. Baud-Bovy	Swiss	1848	1899
Wilhelm Amberg	German	1823	1899
Sir Fred. Wm. Burton	Irish	1816	1900
Fred. Edwin Church	American	1826	1900
Michel de Munkacsy	Hungarian	1844	1900
Vasili Verestchagin	Russian	1842	
Arnold Boecklin	Swiss	1827	1901
Eden Upton Eddis	English	1812	1901
Vasclav Brozik	Bohemian	1851	1901
Luis Alvarez	Spanish	1836	1901
Joseph Noel Paton	Scottish	1821	1901
John Brett	English	1832	1902
Ernest Waterlow (knt. June, 1902)	Ditto	1850	
Hendrik Willem Mesdag	Dutch	1831	
James Tissot	French	1836	1902
Henryk von Siemiradzki	Polish	1844	1902

PAISLEY, a borough, W. Scotland, the Roman Vanduara, and grew out of the priory of Passalet, founded 1160–4 by Walter Stewart, made an abbey about 1220; burnt by the English 1307, rebuilt 15th century. Made a burgh of barony 1488 and a Parliamentary borough 1832. Since 1805 Paisley silk and cotton shawls have been celebrated. Visited by the Queen, 23 Aug. 1888. Statue of Burns unveiled by the earl of Rosebery, 26 Sept. 1896. Serious fires, 55,000*l.* damage, 7 April, 1903. See *Population.*

PALACE COURT, see *Marshalsea*, and *Green Cloth.*

PALACE OF JUSTICE, or **Royal Courts of Justice**. The names given to the new Law Courts, London. See *Law Courts* under *Law.*

PALACES, see *Buckingham, St. James's, Parliament*, 1834-52, 1885, *Escurial, Tuileries, St. Cloud, Versailles*, &c. *Palace Theatre*, under *Theatres* (Royal English Opera-house).

PALÆOGRAPHY, ancient writing; see *Diplomatics, Writing.* Palæographical society founded 1873, dissolved, 1 July, 1895. M. Léon Gautier, eminent palæographer, born 1832, died Aug. 1897.

PALÆOLOGI, a family which reigned as emperors of the east from 1260 to 1453. George Palæologus raised Alexius Comnenus to the throne in 1081, and thereby founded his own family. Andrew, the last Palæologus, son of Thomas, ruler of the Morea, after the overthrow of his father, became a Mahometan at Constantinople about 1533. A person who called himself John Anthony Palæologus Lascaris died at Turin, Sept. 1874. His claims were doubted.

PALÆONTOLOGY (from the Greek *palaios*, ancient, and *onta*, beings), treats of the evidences of organic beings in the earth's strata. It combines biology and geology (*which see*). Wm. Buckland, Cuvier, Mantell, Agassiz, Owen, Edward Forbes, Cope, Marsh, and Blainville, all of the present century, may be reckoned as fathers of this science. The Palæontographical society, which publishes elaborate monographs of British organic remains, was founded in 1847. The journal "Palæontographica" (German) began 1851. Professor Owen's "Palæontology" was published in 1860. "Nearly 40,000 species of animals and plants have been added to the Systema Naturæ by palæontological research." *Huxley.* See *Man.*

PALÆOPOLIS, see *Naples.*

PALAIS ROYAL, Paris, originally Palais Cardinal, built for cardinal Richelieu by Lemercier, 1620-36, received its present name when occupied by Louis XIII., to whom the cardinal gave it shortly before his death in 1642. Louis XIV., in 1692, gave it to his nephew Philippe, duke of Orleans, and it became the residence of his successors. It was confiscated by the republic in 1793, after the execution of Philippe Egalité. Louis Philippe resided in it, 1814-31. It suffered much injury at the revolution in 1848. Under the second empire it became the residence of prince Jerome and his son Napoleon. The buildings were much injured by fire by the communists, 24 May, 1871.

PALATINATE OF THE RHINE, one of the seven ancient electorates of Germany. It was long united to Bavaria, but was separated in 1294.—Frederic V., the elector palatine in 1610, married in 1613 Elizabeth, the daughter of James I. of England, and thus was an ancestor of queen Victoria; see *Hanover*. In 1619 he was elected king of Bohemia, but lost all by his defeat by the Austrians at Prague in 1620. The Palatinate was horribly ravaged by Tilly in 1622, and by the French in 1688. Several thousands of the ruined peasantry were sent to America by the British government and people. The elector palatine, Charles Theodore, inherited Bavaria in 1778; since when the two electorates have been united; see *Bavaria*.

PALATINE. William the conqueror made his nephew, Hugh De Abrincis, count palatine of Chester with the title of earl, about 1070. Edward III. created the palatine of Lancaster, 1539; see *Lancaster, duchy of*. The bishopric of Durham also made county palatine. There is also mention made of the county palatine of Hexham, in 33 Henry VIII. c. 10, which then belonged to the archbishop of York, but by the 14th of Elizabeth it was dissolved, and made part of the county of Northumberland. The palatinate jurisdiction of Durham was separated from the diocese, and vested in the crown, 6 Will. IV. c. 19, 21 June, 1836.

PALE, the name given to the part of Ireland colonised by the English—viz., parts of the counties of Louth, Dublin, Meath, and Kildare. Anglo-Irish rulers were termed lords of the pale. Their arbitrary exactions led to a royal commission of inquiry in 1537. The defection of the lords of the pale in 1641 was followed by a general insurrection, and the royal cause was ruined in 1647. In 1652 Ireland was committed to the rule of four commissioners.

PALERMO (N. W. Sicily), the ancient Panormus. It has been held by the Carthaginians, 415 B.C.; taken by the Romans, 254 B.C.; by the Saracens, A.D. 832; and by the Normans, 1072. Here Roger II. was crowned king of Sicily, 1130. Palermo was the scene of the Sicilian Vespers (*which see*), 30 March, 1282. It suffered from earthquake in 1726 and 1740. The king Ferdinand resided at Palermo from 1806 to 1815, while Naples was ruled by Joseph Bonaparte and Joachim Murat. It revolted against the tyranny of Ferdinand II. 12 Jan. 1848. It was attacked by general Filangieri, 29 March, 1849, and surrendered on 14 May. It was taken by Garibaldi, 6 June, 1860. An insurrection against the abolition of the monastic establishments broke out in Palermo on 13 Sept. 1866, and was suppressed by the royal troops with much bloodshed; order was restored by 22 Sept. Population, 1890, 267,416; 1901, 310,352.

The Italian National Exhibition at Palermo opened in the presence of the king and the royal family, by signor Chimirri, minister of agriculture 15 Nov. 1891
The exhibition included manufactures, fine arts, Greek relics, an Abyssinian department, &c.,
New monument to Garibaldi uncovered; speech by sig. Crispi . . . . 27 May, 1892
Rioting suppressed by the military; 8 persons killed; the town clerk and his wife killed by the mob . . . . 10 Dec. 1893

See *Sicily*.

PALESTINE, the name given by Moses (*Exodus* xv., 14) and other ancient writers, to a broad strip of land on the east coast of the Mediterranean Sea, which originally included Philistia, but was afterwards limited to the part termed the land of Canaan or Israel, Judea, and the Holy Land; see *Jews*. After being several times conquered by the Saracens, and retaken from the 7th to the 10th century, and after being the scene of the wars of the Crusades (*which see*), and other conflicts, Palestine was united to the Ottoman empire by Selim I. in 1516. See *Bible* (note), *Holy Places*, and *Syria*.

Palestine visited by the prince of Wales, March and April, 1862
"The Palestine exploration fund" was founded in London by many eminent persons as a society "for the investigation of the archæology, topography, geology, and manners and customs of the Holy Land;" the archbishop of York (Dr. W. Thomson) was in the chair (annual meetings), 22 June, 1865
By its means captain (after sir Charles) Wilson and a party left England for Palestine in Nov. 1865; they arrived at Damascus Dec. 20; and in the following spring explored Jezreel, Nazareth, and many other parts of the Holy Land.
Excavations in Jerusalem carried on by captain (after sir Charles) Warren 1867-1870
The Moabite stone discovered 1868
The systematic trigonometrical survey of Palestine carried on by capt. Stewart, R.E., lieuts. Conder and Kitchener, R.E. 1872-7
A similar fund established at New York 1871
The ordnance survey of Sinai by capts. Wilson and Palmer, published 1872
The surveying party attacked by natives, rescued by soldiers, after much suffering . . 10 July, 1875
Survey of Western Palestine completed; announced Oct. 1877
Publication of map (1 inch to the mile) in 26 sheets May, 1880
Map and Memoirs of the Survey of Western Palestine published 1880-1
A raised map of Palestine completed by Mr. George Armstrong, assistant secretary to the fund, Sept. 1893
Survey of Eastern Palestine begun by lieuts. Conder and Kitchener 1881
The twenty-first anniversary of the foundation celebrated at the Royal Institution; the abp. of York in the chair . . . . . . 22 June, 1886
"Twenty-one Years' Work in the Holy Land," published . . . . June, ,,
For captain Conder's discovery of a key to the Hittite inscriptions see under *Hittites*, 26 Feb. 1887
Firman authorising excavations granted with conditions; the committee appoint Mr. Flinders Petrie, superintendent, announced . Feb. 1890
The archbishop of Canterbury (Dr. Benson) succeeds the archbishop of York, as president of the fund, April, 1891; died . . . . . 11 Oct. 1896
An association for the Colonization of Palestine by the Jews held an important meeting in east London, 7 Feb.; several colonies reported prosperous . . . . May, 1896
Palestine visited by the German emperor and empress . . . . . . Oct.–Nov. 1898
Excavations of Gezer, conducted by Mr. Stewart Macalister; important results . June–Sept. 1902

PALESTRO (N. Italy). Here the Sardinians defeated the Austrians, 30, 31 May, 1859.

PALIMPSEST (from the Greek, *palin*, again; and *psao*, I efface), parchments written on after the previous writing had been partially effaced. Cardinal Mai, by removing the second writing in some MSS., recovered the original. This was the case with Cicero's "De Republicâ," published by Mai in 1821. It had been covered by a treatise of Lactantius.

PALL, PALLIUM, in the Roman Church an ensign of dignity of a strictly personal character conferred by the pope upon archbishops. It consists of a narrow band of pure white wool, taken from two lambs, which annually, on the feast of

St. Agnes, are brought to the church of St. John Lateran, and after being blessed are presented to the pope; the wool is afterwards made up into pallia by a community of nuns. The pallium, which is worn around the shoulders, is ornamented with four purple crosses, and its form is indicated in the arms of the archbishop of Canterbury. By a decretal of pope Gregory XI. (about 1370), no archbishop could call a council, bless the chrism, consecrate churches, ordain a clerk, or consecrate a bishop, till he had received his pall from the see of Rome. The pall was first worn by an Irish archbishop in 1152, when Gelasius was recognised as primate of all Ireland. The late cardinal Vaughan was invested with the pallium in the pro-cathedral, Kensington—the first occasion of its investiture in England since the time of cardinal Pole. Archbishop Bourne, the new archbishop of Westminster, receives the pallium from pope Pius X. at Rome, 12 Nov. 1903.

PALLADIUM, the statue of Pallas, said to have fallen from heaven near the tent of Ilus, as he was building Ilium, which the oracle of Apollo declared should never be taken so long as the Palladium was found within its walls. The Greeks are said to have obtained it by craft during the Trojan war, 1184 B.C.; but some writers assert, another statue was taken, and that the real Palladium was conveyed from Troy to Italy by Æneas, 1183 B.C., and preserved by the Romans with the greatest secrecy in the temple of Vesta.—PALLADIUM is a rare metal, discovered in platinum ore by Dr. Wollaston, in 1803.

PALLAS, the planet, was discovered by Olbers, at Bremen, 28 March, 1802.

PALLISER'S CHILLED SHOT, see *Cannon*.

PALL MALL, a street near St. James's palace, London, is named from a French game at ball (*pale-mail*, being a wooden mallet), resembling the modern croquet, having been played there about 1600, and introduced into England about 1660. Among eminent inhabitants were Nell Gwyn and Dr. Thomas Sydenham. The PALL MALL GAZETTE, a daily independent political and literary journal, first appeared 7 Feb. 1865, and was edited by Mr. Frederick Greenwood till 1 May, 1880, when it became a liberal paper, edited by Mr. John Morley, who retired 25 Aug. 1883. Price *2d.* reduced to *1d.* 2 Jan. 1882. The paper became again conservative, Dec. 1892. Mr. H. J. C. Cust, M.P., editor, spring, 1893.

Nos. 6, 7, 8, 9 July, 1885, contained Mr. Stead's statements respecting offences against young women and children. Greatly disproved on investigation. See *Trials*, Oct.–Nov. 1885.

PALMERSTON ADMINISTRATION.* The resignation of the Aberdeen administration was announced 1 Feb. 1855, but nearly all its members returned to office soon after under lord Palmerston, lord Derby and lord John Russell having each in vain endeavoured to form an administration. On 22 Feb. Mr. Gladstone, sir James Graham, and Mr. Sidney Herbert resigned on account of the Sebastopol inquiry. Lord John Russell resigned 13 July. Lord Canning was appointed governor-general of India, 4 July, 1855. This cabinet resigned 20 Feb. 1858, in consequence of a vote of censure upon it for introducing the Foreign Conspiracy bill, and was succeeded by the Derby administration (*which see*).

First lord of the treasury, Henry viscount Palmerston.
Lord chancellor, lord Cranworth.
President of the council, earl Granville.
Lord privy seal, duke of Argyll; next, earl of Harrowby; afterwards the marquis of Clanricarde.
Secretaries—home, sir George Grey; *foreign*, earl of Clarendon; *colonial*, Sidney Herbert (resigned Feb. 22); afterwards lord J. Russell (resigned July 13); sir William Molesworth (died 22 Oct. 1855); next Henry Labouchere; *war*, lord Panmure.
Chancellor of the exchequer, W. E. Gladstone (resigned 22 Feb.); next, sir G. Cornewall Lewis.
First lord of the admiralty, sir James Graham (resigned 22 Feb.); next, sir Charles Wood.
Board of control, sir Charles Wood; next, R. Vernon Smith.
Public works, sir Wm. Molesworth; next, sir B. Hall (appointed 22 July, 1855).
Postmaster-general, viscount Canning (appointed governor-general of India, 4 July); next, duke of Argyll.
President of the board of trade, lord Stanley of Alderley.
Marquis of Lansdowne, without office.
Chancellor of the duchy of Lancaster, earl of Harrowby; next, M. T. Baines (appointed 24 Nov. 1855).

PALMERSTON-RUSSELL ADMINISTRATION. The second Derby administration (*which see*) resigned 11 June, 1859. Earl Granville was requested by the queen to form an administration, and obtained the support of lord Palmerston, but not of lord John Russell: the two last then agreed to form a cabinet, which came into office 18 June, 1859. On the decease of lord Palmerston, 18 Oct. 1865, earl Russell became premier; see *Russell*.

First lord of the treasury, Henry viscount Palmerston.
Lord high chancellor, John lord Campbell (died 23 June, 1861); succeeded by sir Richard Bethell, made Lord Westbury, who resigned 4 July, 1865; succeeded by lord Cranworth.
Lord president of the council, earl Granville.
Lord privy seal, duke of Argyll.
Secretaries—foreign affairs, lord John (afterwards earl) Russell; *colonies*, duke of Newcastle; succeeded by Edward Cardwell, 8 April, 1864; *home*, sir G. Cornewall Lewis; succeeded by sir George Grey; *war*, Sidney (afterwards lord) Herbert; succeeded by sir G. C. Lewis (died 13 April, 1863), and by earl de Grey (1 May); *India*, sir Charles Wood.
Chancellor of the exchequer, Wm. Ewart Gladstone.
First lord of the admiralty, duke of Somerset.
President of the board of trade, Thos. Milner Gibson.
[This office was offered to Mr. R. Cobden, and declined by him.]
Secretary of state for Ireland, Edward Cardwell; succeeded by sir R. Peel (not in the cabinet).
Chancellor of the duchy of Lancaster, sir George Grey, bart.; succeeded by Edward Cardwell; and by earl Clarendon, 8 April, 1864.
Postmaster-general, earl of Elgin (proceeded to China in April, 1860); succeeded by lord Stanley of Alderley, appointed Sept. 1860.
Poor-law board, T. Milner Gibson; succeeded by Charles P. Villiers (9 July, 1860).

PALMERSTON'S ACT for abatement of smoke nuisance (16 & 17 Vict. c. 128), 20 Aug. 1853.

PALMISTRY, or CHIROMANCY, the art of studying the lines in the palm, to discover the character and fortunes of a person, practised in ancient India and Greece. The subject was noticed by Aristotle, Pliny, Paracelsus, Albertus Magnus,

* Henry John Temple was born 20 Oct. 1784; was educated at Harrow, Edinburgh, and Cambridge; succeeded his father, viscount Palmerston, 1802; became M.P., and a junior lord of the admiralty, 1807; was secretary-at-war, 1809-28, and a secretary for foreign affairs, Nov. 1830-34, April, 1835 to Sept. 1841, and July, 1846 to Dec. 1851, and home secretary, Dec. 1852 to March, 1855, when he became first lord of the treasury. He was created lord warden of the cinque ports, 31 March, 1861; and master of the corporation of the Trinity house, 16 June, 1862. He sat for Tiverton, 1835-65. He died 18 Oct., and was buried in Westminster abbey, 27 Oct. 1865. His statue at Romsey, by M. Noble, was uncovered by earl Russell, 21 July, 1868. Lady Palmerston died 11 Sept. 1869, aged 82.

and Cardan. A work by Johann Hartlieb was published in Augsburg, 1475. M. le capitaine d'Arpentigny and M. Adrien Desbarrolles are chief modern authorities. A. R. Craig's "Book of the Hand" (1867), L. Cotton's "Palmistry" (1890). Dr. F. Galton published his study of "Finger Prints," 1893. See *Fortune Telling*. Sophia Robson, *alias* "Minerva," professor of palmistry, fined 25*l.* for pretending to tell fortunes, 15 Feb. 1895; Zuleika Cavalier, fined 25*l.*, 6 April, 1900; others fined, 8, 18 Jan. 1901.

PALM-SUNDAY. When Christ made his entry into Jerusalem, multitudes of the people who were come to the feast of the Passover, took branches of the palm-tree, and went forth to meet him, 33. It is usual, in some countries, to carry palms on the Sunday before Easter, hence called Palm-Sunday.

PALMYRA (Syria) was supposed to have been the Tadmor in the wilderness built by Solomon, but was manifestly Grecian. The brilliant part of the history of Palmyra was under Odenatus and his queen Zenobia. At the death of Odenatus, Zenobia assumed the title of queen of the East, in 267. Aurelian defeated her at Emesa, in 272, and made her captive, 273, and killed Longinus, the philosopher, her friend. Palmyra is now inhabited by a few Arab families. The ruins were visited in 1751, by Mr. Wood, who published an account of them in 1753. The rev. Dr. W. Wright published "Palmyra and Zenobia" in 1895.

PAMIRS, a lofty mountain ridge in Turkestan, Central Asia.

Col. Gromtchevski's Russian exploring expedition stopped by Afghan and British outposts in 1889.
Capt. Yonoff, with a military force, excludes capt. Younghusband and lieut. Davison, travellers, from the little Pamir, on the frontiers of Afghanistan, &c. The Russians afterwards retire on the advance of a party of Goorkhas Aug. 1891. The Russian government declares the action of capt. Yonoff to be illegal, and apologises, Feb. 1892.
Col. Yonoff, with a body of Russian troops, re-occupies the part which he quitted in 1891.
A collision ensued with the Afghans, attributed by col. Yonoff to their offensive conduct; 1 Russian and about 15 Afghans killed, about 24 July; col. Yonoff's letter transmitted to the viceroy, 23 Aug. 1892.
Russians evacuate the Pamirs and return to Russian territory, 14 Sept.—7 Oct. 1892.
China resists the claims of Russia, about 8 March, 1893.
A Russian expedition under col. Yonoff starts, 1 June, 1893.
"The Pamirs," by the earl of Dunmore, published, Dec. 1893.
The Russians (exploring) troops under col. Yonoff withdrawn, reported 13 Nov. 1894.
Agreement between Great Britain and Russia respecting their spheres of influence, March, 1895.
Anglo-Russian commission arrives to mark out the frontier, June; work completed, 18 Sept. 1895.
Roads rapidly made by Russians, 1897 *et seq.*

PAMPELUNA (N. E. Spain, taken by the French on their invasion of Spain), was invested by the British, between whom and the French obstinate conflicts took place, 27 and 29 July, 1813. It surrendered to the British, 31 Oct. in that year. Population, 1887, 26,663.

PAMPHLETS. Their first appearance amongst us is generally thought to have been in opposition to the church of Rome. Those who were first convinced of the reasonableness of the "new learning," as it was then called, propagated their opinions in small pieces, cheaply printed, and (what was then of great importance) easily concealed. Political pamphlets began in Edward VI.'s time, and were very numerous in the 17th and 18th centuries (by De Foe, Swift, Steele, and others).

Paul Louis Courier wrote "Simple Discours" and other pamphlets against the priests and nobles after the restoration of the Bourbons, 1815. His "Pamphlet des Pamphlets," defending the pamphleteer (published, 1824), probably led to his murder, 10 April, 1825.
Large collections are in the libraries of the British Museum and the Royal and London Institutions.
Certain enactments respecting pamphlets removed by an act passed July, 1869.
Political pamphlets, "Killing no Murder," &c., selected by Mr. A. F. Pollard, published, 1897.

PANAMÁ, the isthmus which joins the two Americas; see *Darien*. Across this a ship canal was proposed by the *Bulwer-Clayton treaty*, 19 April, 1850. A treaty for the construction of a ship canal through the isthmus by the United States was signed by representatives of that government and that of Colombia 26 Jan. 1870. A railway was opened in 1855. In that year a new state, New Granada, was divided into eight federal states, one of which is named PANAMÁ. A revolution took place in Panamá, on 9 March, 1865; the government was deposed, and don Jil Colunje became president; succeeded by Vincent Olarte, 1 Oct. 1866. Panamá is now subject to Colombia (*which see*). Aspinwall, a town at the extremity of the Panama railway, named after its originator, Mr. Aspinwall, a New York merchant, was officially named Colon in 1870. The government overthrown by Colombian troops without bloodshed, about 12 Oct. 1875. Civil war between dr. Damaso Cervera and gen. B. Ruiz; sharp fights; the *Morro* beats the *Alajuela*, 14 Oct. 1884. General Santo Domingo Vila installed as president, 8 Jan. 1884. Rebellion; government steamer *Ecuadouan* captures the rebel ship *Buacho*; much slaughter announced, 24 Dec. 1884. Insurrection in Panama; conflict with Colombian troops; about 20 people killed. Insurgents destroy Aspinwall railway terminus, &c.; the United States government intervenes with troops, &c. to protect colonists and restore buildings; rebels said to be totally defeated, 16 March-April. Railway reopened with protected trains, 13 April, 1885. Rebellion; severe fighting round Panama, much slaughter, 24 July; quiet restored, the liberals surrender, 26 July, 1900. Republic proclaimed, 3 Nov. 1903.

Gen. Türr and a committee propose a canal . . . Oct.	1876
Lieut. L. A. B. Wyse's survey (1875) published autumn	1877
Congress respecting a new canal meet at Paris; Ferdinand De Lesseps president . . . 1 May,	1879
Seven schemes proposed; canal from Gulf of Limon to Bay of Panamá recommended (by 74-8) 29 May,	,,
Scheme suspended for want of funds . . .	,,
Canal through Nicaragua proposed by Americans; favoured by gen. Grant . . . . . Sept.	,,
Lesseps' scheme opposed by the United States government . . . . . March,	1880
Lesseps at Liverpool describes his plan; canal to be 46 miles long . . . . . . 31 May,	,,
Engineers leave Paris to proceed to the work, 3 Jan.; at work . . . . . . 24 Feb.	1881
Mr. Blaine, the American secretary, issued a circular to the European powers protesting against joint international guarantees of the neutrality of the canal, asserting that the guarantee of the United States of 24 July, 1846, is sufficient 25 Oct.	,,
Railway and works partly destroyed by earthquakes 7, 9, 10 Sept.	1882
Colon and Aspinwall, with consulates, burnt by the rebels under gen. Aizpurn, announced . 1 April,	1885
United States marines defeat the rebels; destroy barricades and occupy Panamá, to protect property and railway transit . about 24 April,	,,
The Colombian government resume possession of Panamá; amnesty granted, with exceptions 30 April,	,,

Gen. Aizpurn arrested 4 May, 1885; martial law, about 12 June; quiet restored . . July, 1885
M. de Lesseps sails up about 3 miles . 20 Feb. 1886
Ten men killed by gunpowder explosion, announced 31 March, ,,
M. de Lesseps' proposal of a lottery loan opposed by the French premier, M. Tirard . . Jan. 1888
The lottery loan bill passed by the deputies 28 April; by the senate 5 June; progress of the scheme retarded . . . . . July *et seq.* ,,
M. de Lesseps asserts that the canal will be opened in July, 1890 . . . . . 21 Oct. ,,
The necessary amount of subscriptions to the loan not received; the company suspend payment 14 Dec.; the government bill permitting the company to suspend payments for three months rejected by the chambers (256–181) . 15 Dec. ,,
[about sixty million pounds already expended]
M. de Lesseps resigns and proposes liquidation 15 Dec. ,,
A great meeting of shareholders agree to the suspension of payments of coupons and annuities until the opening of the canal, and the raising of more capital, and profess continued confidence in M. de Lesseps . . . . 27 Dec. ,,
Report received that perfect order remains at the works, which are still carried on . . 8 Jan. 1889
The United States senate pass resolutions against any interference of foreign powers in regard to the canal . . . . 9 Jan. ,,
New company for the completion of the canal started (the old company dissolved) Jan.; sufficient shares not taken up; the company goes into liquidation . . . . Feb. ,,
Gradual suspension of the works . . . . Feb. ,,
The Panamá Canal Bill to promote the continuance of the work passed by the chamber of deputies 28 June, ,,
Canal bill passed by the French senate . 11 July, ,,
Report of Inquiry commission states that 900,000,000 francs will be required to complete the canal . . . . 5 May, 1890
Great fire at Colon (formerly Aspinwall), the Panamá railway buildings and a large part of the town destroyed, 23, 24 Sept. 1890; another great fire, 14 June, 1894.
Arrangement between the company and the republic of Colombia; the time for the completion of the canal extended by ten years; contract dated . . . . 10 Jan. 1891
After visitation of the works, total collapse of the scheme reported; legal investigation proposed Sept. ,,
Report of M. Monchicourt, the official liquidator, issued at Paris . . . . Nov. ,,
A committee of inquiry into the affairs of the company (M. Brisson and members of the chamber); painful disclosures; met . . 24 Nov. *et seq.* 1892
Prosecution of M. Ferdinand de Lesseps (age 87; ill), Charles de Lesseps, and other directors, for fraud, bribery, &c., opened 25 Nov. 1892; trial begun 10 Jan. 1893; 4 days' defence by M. Barboux; sentences: MM. Ferdinand and Charles de Lesseps, 5 years' imprisonment; MM. Fontane, Cottu and Eiffel, 2 years and fines, 9 Feb.; appeals presented, 11 Feb.; rejected . 24 Feb. 1893
Report of the committee by M. Brisson . 15 Feb. ,,
Trial of M. Charles de Lesseps and M. Fontane for giving bribes; MM. Baïhaut, Blondin, Sans Leroy, Béral, Dugué de la Fauconnerie, Gobron, Antonin Proust, Arton, for receiving bribes, 8 March *et seq.*; defensive statements by MM. Floquet, Clémenceau, and De Freycinet, 10 March; startling depositions of Madame Cottu leads to the temporary resignation of M. Bourgeois, minister of justice, 11 March; sentences: imprisonment, M. Charles de Lesseps, 1 year; M. Blondin, 2 years; M. Baïhaut, 5 years and fine of 750,000 francs; M. Cornelius Herz escapes to England; the others acquitted, 21 March; appeal; judgment set aside by the court; public surprise, 15 June, 1893; fresh trial, 18 Dec. 1897; all acquitted, 30 Dec.; M. Naquet, 3 March, 1898.
Difficulties respecting the concession of the Colombian government for renewal of the work; the contract of 1890 ignored, reported . 4 April, ,,
The committee of inquiry meets again . 23 June, ,,
M. Charles de Lesseps liberated . . 12 Sept. ,,
Proposed formation of a new company to complete the canal by M. Eiffel, M. Bartissol, and others; arrangements to be made with the old company, Feb. 1894
At a meeting of the shareholders, a resolution appointing a syndicate of 5 persons to form a new company adopted; capital to be 20,000,000 francs . . . . 4 April, ,,
Dr. Cornelius Herz arrested at Bournemouth, 19 Jan. 1893; ill; extradition not effected; in default, sentenced to 5 years' imprisonment with a fine of 3,000 francs, 3 Aug. 1894; his appeal to the court at Paris, 15 May, disallowed, 2 Aug.; 1895; sentence of imprisonment confirmed, 4 Nov.; legal proceedings begun against him at Bournemouth, 27 April, 1896; the charge dismissed at Bow-street, 2 May; another committee of inquiry appointed in 1897; he died 6 July, 1898.
M. Ferdinand de Lesseps; born 19 Nov. 1805; died, 7 Dec. 1894 (his statue unveiled by the Khedive at Port Said, 17 Nov. 1899).
Meeting of the new Panama canal company in Paris, M. de la Tournerie appointed chairman of the technical commission, 21 Dec. 1895; 2nd annual meeting, 15 Dec. 1896; other meetings in 1897; steady work reported on the canal, 3,500 labourers employed, reported . . 10 Jan. 1898
A company formed in New Jersey, U.S.A., purchase the canal. French interests acquired, 27 Dec.; the French directors resign, reported, 30 Dec. 1899
Panama canal bill (property of the Panama canal co., purchased for 8,000,000*l.*), &c., signed by pres. Roosevelt, 28 June, 1902; the new company meets, Paris, report adopted . 30 Dec. 1902
Panama canal treaty, between the U.S. and Colombia, signed at Washington 22 Jan.; ratified, 17 March, 1903
Treaty rejected by the Colombian senate, reported 17 Aug. ,,
[Under the terms of the Spooner Act the president is directed to proceed at once to negotiate with Nicaragua and Costa Rica, and then take the necessary steps for the construction of a canal by the Nicaraguan route.]
Revolution in Panama; independence of the Isthmus proclaimed; Colombian officials made prisoners, and Colombian warships captured, 3 Nov. ,,
Junta, pending the constitution of a republic, consisting of J. A. Arango, Fredk. Boyd, and Tomas Arias, reported . . . . 4 Nov. ,,
Colombian troops abandon Colon . . . 5 Nov. ,,
Important memorandum by Mr. Hay, U.S. secretary of state . . . . 7 Nov. ,,
Panama formally recognized as a republic by the United States . . . . . . 13 Nov. ,,

PAN-AMERICAN CONGRESS. 34 delegates from the states of North, South, and Central America, met at Washington 30 Sept. 1889. Mr. Secretary Blaine was appointed president 2 Oct. They visit Chicago and other cities, Oct., meet at Washington 18 Nov. *et seq.* Construction of connecting railways proposed Feb. 1890. Treaty adopting arbitration agreed on, &c. Banquet to president Harrison 16 April; the delegates depart for home 19 April, 1890. They meet at Mexico, 22 Oct. 1901.

PAN-ANGLICAN SYNOD, the popular name of a conference of 76 bishops, British, colonial, and American, who met at Lambeth-palace, 24-27 Sept. 1867. They issued an address, published their resolutions, of a very general character, and formally closed their conference on 10 Dec.

Another synod of about 100 bishops met . 2 July, 1878
Grand closing service at St. Paul's . 27 July, ,,
An encyclical letter issued proposing an episcopal board of reference for ecclesiastical questions, &c., 1878; another issued with practical moral recommendations, earnestly advocating unity and union with nonconformists 1888
The third conference of 145 bishops was held at Lambeth 7–28 July; the abp. of York preached at St. Paul's . . . . . . 27 July, ,,

The fourth conference of 199 bishops at Lambeth, 30 June; visit Canterbury, 3 July, 1897; cordial greeting from the general assembly of the church of Scotland received, 6 July; abps. and bishops received by the queen at Windsor, 13 July; closed, 2 Aug.; encyclical published, *Times*, 5 Aug.; 63 resolutions published, *Times* 11 Aug. 1897
See under *Presbyterians*.

PAN-ARMENIAN CONGRESS, over 2,000 members, in sympathy with the oppressed Armenians, met at Brussels, 17 July, 1902.

PAN-CELTIC CONGRESS held first in Dublin to promote the study of the ancient customs, languages, &c.; Irish, Scotch, Welsh, Manx, Cornish and Bréton represented; lord Castletown, president, 19–23 Aug. 1901.

PANDEAN PIPES (said to be the Greek syrinx, and the *ugab* or organ of the Bible, *Gen.* iv. 21 and *Psalm* cl.), usually seven tubes, popular in Britain early in the 19th century. A "Preceptor" for Davies' "new invented syrrynx" was published in 1807.

PANDECTS, a digest of the civil law, made by order of Justinian, 533. It is stated that a copy of these Pandects was discovered in the ruins of Amalfi, 1137; removed from Pisa in 1415, and preserved in the library of the Medici at Florence, as the *Pandectæ Florentinæ*.

PANDOSIA (Bruttium, S. Italy). Here Alexander, king of Epirus, was defeated and slain by the Bruttians, 326 B.C. Lævinus, the Roman consul, was defeated between Heraclea and Pandosia, in Lucania, by Pyrrhus, king of Epirus, 280 B.C.

PANEAS or **PANIUS** (Syria). Here Antiochus the Great defeated Scopas, the Egyptian general, and his Greek allies, 198 B.C.

PANICS, COMMERCIAL, generally the result of over-speculation; see *Bubbles*, *South Sea*, *Law's*.

Through French war: government issued 5,000,000*l.* exchequer bills	1793
Through Irish rebellion, &c. (3 per cents. at 44⅝)	1797
Through bubble companies, 770 banks stopped	winter, 1825-6
Through railway mania	Oct. 1847
Through American failures	Nov. 1857
Through fear of European war	April, 1859
Through over-speculation in limited liability companies	May, 1866
Through Franco-Prussian war	10 July, 1870
Through Russian attack on Afghans at Penjdeh (temporary)	9 April, 1885
War panics at Paris and London	3–4 Feb. 1887

See *London*, 24 Nov. 1890.

PANNONIA, part of Illyria, now Hungary. Was finally subdued by Tiberius, A.D. 7-9.

PANOPTICON OF SCIENCE AND ART, in Leicester-square, erected in 1852-3 for a chartered company, by Mr. T. H. Lewis, the architect; was opened in 1854 for lectures, musical performances, &c. It had a very large electrical machine, battery, &c. The speculation did not succeed; the building was sold in 1857, and in March, 1858, was opened for concerts and horsemanship, and called the Alhambra (*which see*).

Jeremy Bentham's book "Panopticon, or the Inspection House," an establishment in which persons may be kept under inspection, published 1791; see *Milbank*.

PANORAMAS, invented by Robert Barker, are bird's-eye views painted round the wall of a circular building. In 1788 he exhibited at Edinburgh a view of that city, the first picture of the kind. He then commenced similar exhibitions in London in 1789, having adopted the name "*Panorama*," and was ultimately enabled to build commodious premises in Leicester-square for that purpose. Panoramas were exhibited on the continent by himself and his associate, Robt. Fulton. M. Thuyer, having bought the invention from Fulton, exhibited panoramas in Paris about 1796. See *Colosseum*. (Barker died in April, 1806.) J. P. Loutherbourg, a painter, termed the panoramist, invented the "Eidophusikon," natural phenomena represented by moving pictures, exhibited at Lisle-street, Leicester-square, 3 April, 1781. "This was certainly not a panorama." *Dr. Rimbault*.

PANORMUS, see *Palermo*.

PANTAGRAPH (from the Greek *panta*, all things, and *graphein*, to write, and incorrectly termed *Pentagraph*), an instrument for copying, reducing, or enlarging plans, &c., invented by Christopher Scheiner, about 1603; improved by professor Wallace, and called "Eidograph," about 1821.

PANTALEON, a musical instrument (a drum with tuned strings), invented by Pantaleon Hebenstreit, about 1735.

PANTECHNICON, Motcombe-street, Knightsbridge, London, W., erected by Seth Smith, as a receptacle for paintings, jewellery, furniture, carriages, &c., 1830; was destroyed by fire 13—14 Feb. 1874, when much property was lost: re-built, 1874. See also *Fires*, 11 Sept. 1902.

PANTHAYS, Mahometans in the Chinese province, Yunan, became independent under a sultan, during the Tae-ping revolt, 1851-64. After its suppression, the Panthays, after a severe struggle, were also subdued. Their capital, Talifoo, was captured, and its inhabitants cruelly massacred in Feb. 1873. The Panthays sent an embassy to England in 1872, without effect. Sultan Suleiman committed suicide.

PANTHEISM, the formula of which is "everything is God, and God is one," was especially taught by Xenophanes, who died 500 B.C. The doctrine is attributed to Spinoza, Kant, Fichte, and other modern philosophers. Amalric of Chartres, censured for holding the doctrine, recanted 13th century. He is said to have asserted that "all is God, and God is all."

PANTHEON, at Rome, a circular temple built by Agrippa, the son-in-law of Augustus, 27 B.C. It had niches in the wall, where the image or representation of a particular god was set up; the gates brass, the beams covered with gilt brass, and the roof covered with silver. Pope Boniface III. dedicated it to the Virgin Mary and all the saints, by the name of S. Maria della Rotunda, or "ad Martyres," A.D. 608.*—The PANTHEON IN LONDON was erected by subscription, and opened 27 Jan. 1772; formed into an opera house; burned down 14 Jan. 1792; rebuilt for masquerades in 1795; opened as theatre, 1812; made a bazaar in 1834. The bazaar was closed in 1867, and the premises taken by Gilbey and Co., wine merchants, who lent the south part for a temporary church.

PANTHEON, Paris, a magnificent building founded by Louis XV. in pursuance of a vow, dedicated to Ste. Geneviève; built by Soufflot, 1757-90; named Pantheon, and decreed to be a mausoleum for eminent men, 1791; made a church, 1806; named Ste. Gene-

* Victor Emmanuel, first king of united Italy, was buried here, 17 Jan. 1878.

viève, 1821; re-named Pantheon, 1831; again a church, Nov. 1852; again secularised, 27 May, 1885; received the remains of Victor Hugo, 1 June, 1885. The remains of Voltaire and Rousseau found there by a commission, 18 Dec. 1897.

PANTOGEN, see *Atomic Theory*.

PANTOMIMES were representations by gestures and attitudes among the Greeks, and were introduced on the Roman stage by Pylades and Bathyllus, 22 B.C. Comic masques were introduced here from Italy about 1700. The first regular English pantomime is said to have been "Harlequin executed," produced by John Rich at the Lincoln's-inn-fields theatre, 26 Dec. 1717. Joseph Grimaldi (1779-1837) was a most eminent clown.

"PAPAL AGGRESSION." In a consistory holden in Rome, 30 Sept. 1850, the pope (Pius IX.) named fourteen new cardinals, of whom four only were Italians. Among them was Dr. Nicholas Wiseman, vicar-apostolic of the London district, who was at the same time nominated lord archbishop of Westminster.

Dr. Ullathorne enthroned as Roman Catholic bishop of Birmingham in St. Chad's cathedral 27 Oct. 1850
A pastoral letter from Dr. Wiseman read in all the Roman catholic chapels of his see (all England parcelled out into Romish dioceses) . 27 Oct. „
The answer of the bishop of London (Dr. Blomfield) to a memorial from the protestant clergy of Westminster, against a Romish hierarchy in this country, was followed by the "Durham" letter from lord John Russell, then chief minister of the crown, to the bishop of Durham, in which he severely censured, not only the papal aggression, but also the proceedings of the tractarian clergy of the Church of England . . . . 4 Nov. „
Immediately from every quarter of England addresses poured in to her majesty the queen, calling upon her and the government to resist the usurpation; 6700 addresses, it is said, had been voted from nearly as many influential meetings up to 31 Dec. „
Dr. Briggs, created Roman catholic bishop of Beverley, was enthroned in St. George's chapel at York, 13 Feb. 1851
Dr. Browne, created bishop of Clifton, and Dr. Burgess, bishop of Shrewsbury: both consecrated in St. George's cathedral, Southwark 27 July, „
The Ecclesiastical Titles act, 14 & 15 Vict. c. 60, prohibited the constitution of bishops of pretended provinces under a penalty of 100*l*. Aug. „
It was not acted upon, and was repealed 24 July, 1871

PAPAL INFALLIBILITY. This dogma, maintained by one party in the Roman church, tolerated by another, and utterly rejected by a third, was adopted and promulgated at the general council at Rome 18 July, 1870, a great many bishops having withdrawn. The dogma was inculcated by the false decretals of Isidore and others, but not adopted by the council of Trent; see *Councils XXI*. Professor Döllinger, the historian, was excommunicated at Munich for rejecting this dogma, 18 April, 1871: he was made a D.C.L. at Oxford about 16 June following; see *Old Catholics*. The doctrine was strenuously attacked by Mr. W. E. Gladstone, in his pamphlet, "The Vatican Decrees," Nov. 1874.

PAPAL STATES, see *Rome*, and *Popes*.

PAPER, see *Papyrus*. Paper was probably made in Egypt, and centuries before the Christian era. It was made of cotton about 600 A.D.; and of rags about 1300.* White coarse paper was made by sir John Speilman, a German, at Dartford, in England, 33 Eliz. 1580; and here paper mills were erected. *Stow*. Paper for writing and printing manufactured in England, and an act passed to encourage it, 2 Will. III. 1690; before this time we paid for these articles to France and Holland 100,000*l*. annually. The French refugees taught our people; we had made coarse brown paper almost exclusively, until they came among us; we made white paper first in 1690. *Anderson*. Paper-making by a machine was suggested by Louis Robert, who sold his model to Didot, the great printer, who brought it to England, and, conjointly with Fourdrinier, perfected the machinery. The latter obtained a patent for paper-making machinery in 1801; and for manufacturing paper of an indefinite length in 1807. The machinery was improved by Bryan Donkin. A sheet of paper, 13,800 feet long, and 4 feet wide, was made at Whitehall-mills, Derbyshire, in 1830; and one 21,000 feet long, and 6 feet 3 inches wide, was made at Colyton in Devon in 1860. Esparto, a Spanish grass, first imported in 1857, has been largely employed in the paper manufacture since 1864. In 1866 wood was largely manufactured into paper at Philadelphia; and at the Paris exhibition, 1867, fine specimens of wood-paper were shown; see *Parchment* (note). The paper duty, imposed in 1694 (producing about 1,400,000*l*. annually), after having been the subject of agitation for several years, was repealed in 1861. Hop-stalks said to be used for paper-making in France, 1873.

Paper-mills in Great Britain, 1877, about 385 (England, 300; Scotland, 65; Ireland, 20); annual produce about 360,000 tons; value, 16,090,000*l*. Great increase since.
Paper-exhibition at Berlin, Aug. 1878: contained not only great varieties of paper, but a paper house, tables, chairs, carpets, barrels, boats, &c.
Paper pianoforte exhibited, soft tone, July, 1885.
Bottles largely made of paper in America, 1887.
5th international paper and printing exhibition, Agricultural hall, London, opened, 23 June, 1897.
Causes of the deterioration of paper, investigated by a committee of the Soc. of Arts, Sept. *et seq.* 1897, report in their journal, 20 May, 1898.

PAPER-HANGINGS, &c. Stamped paper for this purpose was first made in Spain and Holland about 1555. Made of velvet and floss, for hanging apartments, about 1620. The manufacture of this kind of paper rapidly improved in this country during the present century. — PAPER BRICKS have been made in America; and paper tubing for water and gas, made by M. Jaloureau of Paris, was shown in 1860.

PAPER-MONEY, see *Banks* and *Greenbacks*.

PAPIER MACHÉ. This manufacture (of paper-pulp combined with gum and sometimes with china clay) has existed for above a century. Martin, a German snuff-box maker, is said to have learnt the art from one Lefevre about 1740. In 1745 it was taken up by Baskerville, the printer at Birmingham, and soon spread over that district. Papier maché is now largely employed in ornamenting the interior of buildings, &c. A large dome at Brussels ordered to be made of it, Dec. 1881.

* Mr. Joseph Hunter (in the *Archæologia*, xxxvii.) states that the earliest paper which he had seen was a MS. account-book, dated 1302, probably of Bordeaux manufacture. He gives engravings of manufacturers' marks, French and English, the dates of which range from 1330 to 1431. He also gives an extract from a work by Bartholus, a writer of the middle of the 14th century, in which mention is made of a paper manufactory in the Marches of Ancona. At the end of Wynkin de Worde's edition of Bartholomæus De Proprietatibus Rerum, 1494, its thin paper, *made by John Tate in England*, is commended.

PAPIN'S DIGESTER (see *Steam*), invented about 1681. Denis Papin, a French philosopher, assisted Boyle in his experiments about 1678.

PAPISTS, see *Roman Catholics*.

PAPUA, see *New Guinea*.

PAPYRUS, the reed from which was made the paper of Egypt and India, used for writings until the discovery of parchment, about 190 B.C. The earliest known specimens of papyri were found in the monuments attributed to the third dynasty, 3966 B.C. Many papyri were discovered at Herculaneum in 1754; and many were collected by the French in Egypt, 1798. A manuscript of the *Antiquities of Josephus* on papyrus, among the treasures seized by Bonaparte in Italy, and sent to the National Library at Paris, was restored in 1815.

Fac-similes of the largest known papyrus, found in 1855, behind Modinet Habu on the Nile, and now in the British Museum, were published with translations by the trustees in 1876.

A papyrus MS. of the poems of Bacchylides acquired by the British Museum, announced, Dec. 1896; a facsimile, edited by Frederick G. Kenyon, Vol. II. published, Dec. 1898.

Greek papyri, "Logia" of our Lord, &c., found at Behnesa during excavations by Mr. P. B. Grenfell and Mr. A. S. Hunt, reported, 29 May, 1897. Books published; see *Egyptian Exploration*, 1897.

PARABLE, see *Fable*.

PARACHUTE, see *Balloons*, 1785, 1802, 1837.

PARACLETE (Greek for comforter), a name given by Abélard to the convent which he founded in Champagne in 1122, of which Héloïse became the first abbess.

PARADISE LOST, the great English epic by John Milton, appeared first in ten books in 1667, in twelve books in 1674; the author received for the first three editions (1,500 copies) 5*l*. each. "Paradise Regained" was published in 1671.

PARADOX (Greek, *para*, beyond; and *doxa*, opinion), something contrary to common opinion. Professor De Morgan's "Budget of Paradoxes" (of all kinds) was published in 1872. John Paget's "Paradoxes and Puzzles, Historical, Judicial, and Literary," published 1874.

PARAFFIN (from *parum affinis*, from its having little affinity with anything), also called photogen, a solid substance, somewhat like spermaceti, produced by distillation of coal, and first obtained by Reichenbach in 1830, and by Dr. Christison about the same time. It was procured from mineral oil by Mr. James Young about 1848 at Alfreton in Derbyshire. Soon after it was largely obtained from Boghead coal. It is also obtained from Irish peat. It makes excellent candles. Much litigation ensued through interference with Mr. Young's patent-right. In 1882, 120,508 cwts. were imported into the United Kingdom; 1900, 984,571 cwts.; 1901, 839,437 cwts.

PARAGRAPH BIBLES, see under *Bibles*.

PARAGUAY, a republic in S. America, discovered by Juan Diaz de Solis in 1515, and by Sebastian Cabot in 1526; conquered by Alvarez Nuñez in 1535, and civilized by the Jesuits, who in 1608 commenced their missions there and held it till their expulsion in 1768. Paraguay rose against the Spanish yoke in 1811. In 1814, Dr. José G. R. Francia was elected dictator; he ruled vigorously but tyrannically; he was succeeded on his death in 1840 by Vibal. From 1814 to 1844 the country was rigidly closed against foreigners. The president, C. A. Lopez, elected in 1844, was succeeded by his son, Francis S. Lopez, Sept. 1862 (*see below*). Paraguay was recognised as an independent state by the Argentine Confederation, 14 July, 1852, and by Great Britain in 1853. Capital, Asuncion. Population in 1857, 1,337,439; in 1873, 221,079; in 1900 (estimated) 635,600.

Hostilities between Paraguay and Brazil began when a Brazilian steamer was captured as an intruder on the Paraguay . . . . . . 11 Nov. 1864

Brazil invaded in December . . . . . . ,,

Lopez invaded the territories of the Argentine republic, which immediately made alliance with Brazil . . . . . 14 April, 1865

The army of Lopez defeated . . . . . Sept. ,,

The allies captured Uruguayana and an army of Paraguayans . . . . 18 Sept. ,,

[For details of the war, see *Brazil*, 1865-9.]

A provisional government installed; Lopez totally defeated, proclaimed an outlaw . . 17 Aug. 1869

Lopez killed near the Aquidaban . . . 1 March, 1870

Peace signed with Brazil and Argentina republic, 20 June, ,,

President Salvador Jovellanos elected for three years . . . . 12 Dec. 1871

President Juan Bautista Gill . . . . 25 Nov. 1874

The president and his brother assassinated, April; Higinio Uriarte, president . . . 12 April, 1877

President Candido Bareiro (for 4 years) . 25 Nov. 1878

President gen. B. Caballero . . . . 25 Nov. 1882

President gen. Escobar . . . . . 25 Sept. 1886

President J. Gonzalez . . . . . 25 Sept. 1890

Revived prosperity of the country reported . Oct. ,,

Revolutionary attempt by major Vera and others suppressed with bloodshed, reported . 24 Oct. 1891

Establishment of a Socialist settlement by emigrants from Australia, to be named "New Australia" . . . . July, 1893

Coup d'état; señor Marinigo becomes president, reported . . . . 11 June, 1894

Señ. Egusguiza elected president . . . 26 Sept. ,,

Emilio Aceval elected president . . . 25 Nov. 1898

Revolution at Asuncion, pres. Aceval deposed; Hector Carvalho made president . . 9 Jan. 1902

High premium on gold, trade conditions unsatisfactory, reported . . . . . Sept. ,,

Señ. Escurra elected president, reported, 28 Sept. ,,

Sig. Boggiani, an explorer, murdered by Chamacoco Indians, his body found by a relief expedition under señ. Cancio, 1902; an attempt by two Englishmen to navigate lake Ipacary partially successful, end of 1902, reported . . Aug. 1903

PARALLEL MOTION, see *Motion*.

PARASOLS were used by the ancient Egyptians. A new form (said to have been devised by the duchess of Rutland) came into general use about 1820.

PARC AUX CERFS, a deer-park at Versailles, near Paris, made by Louis XII., and kept as such till 1694, when Louis XIV. took the land for building. The name was given to a house erected on it by madame Pompadour, popularly said to form a seraglio for Louis XV. in 1755. It was closed by madame Du Barry in 1771.

PARCEL POST (advised by Rowland Hill in 1842). Proposed in Parliament by Mr. H. Fawcett 27 March; act passed, 18 Aug. 1882; came into operation 1 Aug. 1883.

Maximum weight raised to 11 lbs. from 1 May, 1886.

Parcel Post extended to India, British Burmah, Aden, Gibraltar, and Egypt 1 July, 1885, and other countries since.

Coldbath fields prison was converted into offices for the Parcel Post, 1887.

Coaches started to convey parcels to various parts from London, 1892.

Parcels conveyed 1883-4, 21,000,000; 1891-2, 51,000,000.

Metropolis, Aug. 1883, 3,600,000; 1891-2, 9,000,000; 1902-3, 90,300,000.

PARCHMENT. Invented for writing books by Eumenes (some say by Attalus), of Pergamus, the founder of the celebrated library at Pergamus, formed on the model of the Alexandrian, about 190 B.C. Parchment-books from this time became those most used, and the most valuable as well as oldest in the world are written on the skins of goats. It should be mentioned that the Persians and others are said to have written all their records on skins long before Eumenes' time. Parchment superseded by paper of a special kind for grants of probate, Dec. 1900.

Parchment paper (or vegetable parchment) was invented and patented in 1857, by Mr. W. E. Gaine, C.E., who discovered, that when paper is exposed to a mixture of two parts of concentrated sulphuric acid and one part of water for no longer time than is required to draw it through the fluid, it is immediately converted into a strong tough skin-like material. It must be instantly washed with water. Its great strength points out many applications of this material, *e.g.*, maps, school and account-books, and drawing-paper. In 1859 it appeared that a similar invention had been made in Paris by Figuier and Poumarède in 1846.

PARDONS. General pardons were proclaimed at coronations: first by Edward III. in 1327. The king's power of pardoning is said to be derived *a lege suæ dignitatis;* and no other person has power to remit treason or felonies, stat. 27 Hen. VIII. 1535. *Blackstone.* A pardon cannot follow an impeachment of the house of commons: stat. Will. III. 1700.

PARENTS' NATIONAL EDUCATIONAL UNION, established to enlighten and assist parents in the discharge of their important duties in the training of their children, founded by Miss Mason; annual meetings, the earl of Meath, president, held in London, 27 June, 1895 *et seq.*

PARGA, a city in European Turkey: retained its civic independence under the protection of Venice till 1797, when that state was conquered by the French. It resisted various attempts to capture it; and in 1806 was garrisoned by Russians. It was given up to the French in 1807; taken by the English, 22 March, 1814; surrendered to the Turks, 1817; and abandoned by above 3000 of its inhabitants, who retired to the Ionian Isles, May, 1819.

PARIAN MARBLES, see *Arundelian Marbles.*

PARIS (formerly *Lutetia Parisiorum*), the capital of France, situated on the river Seine, which cuts it into two unequal parts, the strongest being towards the north, and in which are three isles, *la ville* (*the city*), the *île St. Louis*, and the *île Louviers.* In the time of Julius Cæsar, Lutetia comprised the *city* only. It was greatly improved by the emperor Julian, who made it his residence while he governed Gaul, 355 to 361. It became successively the capital of the kingdoms of Paris, Soissons, and Neustria, and eventually of all the kingdom. Many ecclesiastical councils were held at Paris, 360-1528. The representative of the house of Orleans is styled count of Paris. Population of Paris in 1856, 1,178,262; in 1872, estimated population, 1,851,792; in 1876, 1,988,806; in 1881, 2,269,023; in 1891, 2,424,705; 1896, 2,536,000; 1901, 2,714,068. See *France.*

Clovis makes Paris his residence . . . about 508
St. Denis founded 613
Hôtel Dieu hospital founded by bishop Landry about 656
Paris ravaged by the Normans (or Danes), 845, 855, 861: suffered from famine 845-940
Gallantly defended against the Danes by the count Eudes and the bishop Goslin 885
University founded, about 1200
Rebuilt 1231
Church of Notre Dame built 1160-1270
The parliament established 1302
Suffers by the factions of the Armagnacs and Burgundians 1411-1418
Taken by the English 1420
Retaken by the French 1436
Pont Notre Dâme built 1499
The Louvre commenced (see *Louvre*) 1522
Hôtel de Ville founded 1533
The Boulevards commenced 1536
Fountain of the Innocents erected 1551
The Tuileries begun (see *Tuileries*) 1564
Massacre of St. Bartholomew's . . . 24 Aug. 1572
The Pont Neuf begun 1578
Vainly besieged by Henry IV. 1589-90
Entered by him . . . . March, 1594
Hospital of Invalids 1595
Place Royale begun 1604
The Hôtel-Dieu founded 1606
Jardin des Plantes formed 1610
The Luxembourg, by Mary de Medicis . . . 1615
The Palais-Royal built 1629
The Val-de-Grâce 1645
Conflicts of the Fronde 1648-53
Royal palace at Versailles built: the court removed there 1661-72
The Academy of Sciences founded 1666
The Observatory established 1667
Champs Elysées planted 1670
Arch of St. Denis erected 1672
Palais d'Elysée Bourbon built 1718
The Palace of the Deputies 1722
The Military School 1751
The Pantheon (*which see*) St. Geneviève, founded 1764
The French revolution breaks out; the Bastile taken, 14 July, 1789
Pont de Louis XIV. finished 1790
Cemetery of Père la Chaise consecrated . . . 1804
Pont des Invalides, &c., erected 1806
Paris surrenders to the allies . . . 30 March, 1814
Paris lit with gas 1819
Revolution (see *France*) . . . . . July, 1830
Column of July founded . . . . 28 July, 1831
Fortifications of Paris (for which 140,000,000 francs were voted, 1833) commenced 15 Dec. 1840; completed . . . . March, 1846
Revolution (see *France*) . . . . . 22 Feb. 1848
Paris much improved by Louis Napoleon (probable cost 12,800,000*l.*) 1853-62
Industrial Exhibition opened by the emperor and empress, 15 May; visited by queen Victoria and prince Albert (the first visit of an English sovereign to Paris since 1422), 24 Aug.; exhibition closes, 15 Nov. 1855
Conference at Paris respecting the Danubian Principalities (*which see*); closes . . . Aug. 1858
Bois de Boulogne opened as a garden of acclimatisation . . . . 6 Oct. 1860
Remains of Napoleon I. deposited in the Invalides, 31 March, 1861
A building was erected for a permanent industrial exhibition by a company . . . . . Oct. 1862
The scheme failed . . . . Feb. 1864
Boulevard prince Eugène opened by the emperor, 7 Dec. 1862
Decree for an international exhibition of the products of agriculture, industry, and the fine arts, at Paris, in 1867; commissioners appointed, 21 Feb. 1864
Cab strike, 4 days 1865
Fine arts exhibition opened . . . . 1 May, 1866
The cathedral of Notre Dame and other buildings restored . . . . ,,
INTERNATIONAL EXHIBITION on the Champ de Mars (with a new park, comprising more than 100 acres); the oblong building designed by Leplay (enclosing 35 acres), 1245 feet wide, 1500 feet long, consisting of circles within circles; the external corridor was a belt of iron, 85 feet high and 115 feet wide; opened by the emperor and empress, 1 April, 1867

It was visited by the prince of Wales, the kings of Greece, Belgium, Prussia, and Sweden, the czar of Russia, the viceroy of Egypt, the sultan of Turkey, the emperor of Austria, and other inferior potentates . . . . May-Nov. 1867
Attempted assassination of the czar by Berezowski, a Pole . . . . 6 June, ,,
The czar and the king of Prussia entertained by M. Haussmann, prefect of Paris (cost 36,000*l.*), 8 June, ,,
Departure of the czar 11 June; of the king of Prussia . . . . 14 June, ,,
Distribution of prizes to exhibitors by the emperor in the presence of the prince of Wales, the sultan, &c. . . . . 1 July, ,,
Berezowski condemned to transportation for life, 15 July, ,,
Visit of the emperor of Austria . 23 Oct.-2 Nov.
Grand banquet to commissioners of international exhibition . . . . 26 Oct. ,,
Exhibition finally closed (instead of on 31 Oct.), Sunday, 3 Nov., gross receipts, 9,830,369 francs.
M. Haussmann, the prefect of the Seine, reported the budget of the city to exceed 9,200,000*l.* He resigned . . . . Jan. 1870
For the sieges and other recent events, see *France* and *Franco-German War* 1870-1
Versailles becomes the seat of government, March, 1871
Grand Opera-house burnt . . . 28-29 Oct. 1873
Great explosion with loss of life at Poirier's chemical works, near Paris . . . . . 19 Nov. 1874
Grand new opera-house; decreed 1860; designed by Garnier; opened in state . . . 5 Jan. 1875
Municipal officers visit London, to inspect railways, &c. . . . . 30 April, 1877
New Hôtel Dieu finished . . . . . Aug. ,,

INTERNATIONAL EXHIBITION: site, two unequal parts divided by the Seine. The main building in the Champ de Mars covers 263,593 square yards: (765 by 360 yards); the Trocadero (*which see*) palace is a stone structure, with a rotunda supported by columns, crowned by a dome, flanked by two lofty towers, the exterior gallery ornamented with statues.
The exhibition was opened by the president, marshal MacMahon ("in the name of the republic") in presence of the prince of Wales, the duc d'Aosta, and other distinguished persons, 1 May, 1878
111,955 persons visited exhibition (a fête day) 15 Aug. ,,
Grand distribution of medals by marshal MacMahon, with speech . . . . . 21 Oct. ,,
Closed Sunday . . . . 10 Nov. ,,
Total admissions, 16,032,725; daily average, 82,000; gross receipts, 12,653,746 francs.
International exhibition of applied science opened, 24 July, 1879
The senate and assembly meet again at Paris, 27 Nov. ,,
Electrical exhibition and congress (see under *Electricity*) . . . . Aug.-Oct. 1881
Statue of Alexandre Dumas, sen. by G. Doré uncovered. . . . . 4 Nov. 1883
International exhibition of manufactures and processes . . . . . . 23 July-23 Nov. 1885
Grand funeral of Victor Hugo . . . 1 June, ,,
International Workmen's Exhibition and Congress opened . . . . 2 June, 1886
Opera Comique destroyed by fire; panic; about 131 lives lost 25-26 May; M. Carvalho, the director, sentenced to three months' imprisonment and a fine of above 2,000*l.*; and the fireman André to one month's imprisonment . . . 15 Dec. 1887
Death of Mad. Boucicault, a great benefactress of the city, see *Bon Marché* . . . . . Dec. ,,
Strike of navvies, about 22 July . ends 16 Aug. 1888
Socialistic strikes of waiters and hairdressers Aug. ,,

UNIVERSAL EXHIBITION of Arts, Manufactures, &c. (proposed in 1884), opened by president Carnot (about 200,000 persons admitted), 6 May; officially closed, 6 Nov. 1889. The greatest of all the exhibitions hitherto held. The buildings were of colossal proportions, and with the charming gardens, occupied nearly the whole of the Champs de Mars. The chief galleries were surmounted by domes with a central one. Architect, M. Dutert; engineer, M. Contamin, decorations in excellent taste. The gigantic *Eiffel Tower*, 985 feet high, was constructed chiefly of iron by M. Eiffel and a company, it is said after the design of a young engineer Nonguier; probable removal, Aug. 1894. The building was inaugurated by M. Tirard, the premier, 31 March. The electric lighting by Messrs. Davey, Paxman and Co., the Société Gramme of Paris, very good . 1889
A grand nocturnal fête arranged by M. Alphand, manager . . . . 1 June, ,,
Total paying visitors about 22,277,000, 2,723,000 gratuitous; 402,065 admitted . . 13 Oct. ,,
Receipts, 41,000,000 francs (18,000,000 francs from the state; 7,000,000 francs from the city); expenses, 41,000,000 francs; surplus, 4,000,000 francs 14 Nov. ,,
Among the *distinguished visitors* were the prince and princess of Wales (9-15 June), the shah of Persia, the king of Greece, the duke of Braganza (since king of Portugal), the dukes of Cambridge and Edinburgh, prince Ferdinand of Bulgaria, the two sons of the khedive, and Milan, ex-king of Servia.
Awards of medals by international jurors; to British exhibitors, 910, out of 1,017.
The French honours granted to British subjects were distributed by M. Waddington, the French ambassador, at the Mansion-house, London, 25 Jan. 1890.
Many international congresses on social, moral, scientific, literary, and artistic subjects met at Paris during the exhibition.
The new commercial exchange was opened by M. Tirard, the premier . . . . 24 Sept. ,,
Death of sir Richard Wallace, benefactor to Paris, son of the marquis of Hertford . . 20 July, 1890
Baron Haussmann, who, supported by Napoleon III. and aided by M. Alphand, rebuilt Paris (1853 *et seq.*), dies, 11 Jan. 1891. Death of M. Alphand 7 Dec. 1891
The telephone system between London and Paris inaugurated (see *Telephone*) . . 18 March, ,,
Condemnation of certain artists and their models for improper dressing at a ball leads to a riot among the students of the Latin quarter, during which a man named Nuger is accidentally killed by a policeman, 1-2 July; students joined by the artisans; many persons injured and property destroyed; quiet restored by the police and military; about 200 arrests, followed by imprisonments . . . . 3-6 July, 1893
Izeyl, a sacred (Buddhist) drama by MM. Sylvestre and Morand, produced by Mdme. Sarah Bernhardt at the "Théâtre de la Renaissance," 24 Jan. 1894
A municipal loan of 200 million francs at 2½ per cent. fully taken up . . . . . 21 April, ,,
M. Ambroise Thomas, musical composer, invested with the grand cordon of the legion of honour by president Carnot, at a musical fête at the Opéra Comique; Verdi present . . . . 15 May, ,,
Military outfitting establishment and the Cité Petville destroyed by fire; 1 death . 1 July, 1895
Collision on the Ceinture railway near the Porte Maillot station through a fog, 2 deaths . 24 Jan. 1896
Tornado in Central Paris, about 1 min., 8 persons killed, much damage . . . . . 10 Sept. ,,
Visit of the czar and czarina (see *Russia*) . 6 Oct. ,,
Inauguration of the revived university of Paris at the new Sorbonne . . . . . 19 Nov. ,,
Fête in honour of Sarah Bernhardt, actress, 9 Dec. ,,
The Goncourt collection of drawings sold for 695,729 francs, announced . . . . . . 18 Feb. 1897
A grand charity bazaar, "Old Paris," in the rue Jean Goujon, on a site lent by Mdme. Henri Heine, supported by the leading ladies of the conservative and catholic parties, destroyed by fire through the ignition of ether in the lamp of a kinematograph, which was placed at the end of a hall built of old pinewood; 130 persons, mostly ladies, perished, including the duchesse d'Alençon, sister of the empress of Austria (who refused to escape), gen. Munier (died 6 May), and many other eminent persons, 4 May, 1897 (many died from injuries).
General mourning; theatres, &c. closed . 5 May, ,,
State requiem mass at Notre Dame . . 8 May, ,,

500 men and women rewarded for saving life, by M. Barthou, Eugène Georges, coachman, made chevalier of the legion of honour, 21 May (very liberal subscriptions) 1897
Bomb explosion in the Place de la Concorde, the Strassburg statue damaged . . . . 16 June ,,
Destructive cyclone at Asnières, about 20 persons killed . . . . 18 June, ,,
English diamond jubilee fund (30,121*l.*), devoted to charities . . . . . . 3 July, ,,
M. Armand Dreyfus (not related to capt. *Dreyfus*) and 4 others found dead in a room from the fumes of charcoal . . . . . . 8 Nov. ,,
INTERNATIONAL EXHIBITION (for 1900) proposed; buildings erecting, March, 1898; Royal commission for Gt. Britain, the prince of Wales, duke of Connaught, and others appointed, Feb., March, 1898
Paris metropolitan railway sanctioned by the senate . . . . 30 March, ,,
Dock strike, with rioting, order restored by the military, 5 Oct.; other bodies join, 45,000 men out, 9 Oct.; threatened railway strike, stations occupied by troops, 13 Oct.; strike subsides, 17 Oct. *et seq.* 1898
Destructive gale and heavy rain . . 2 Jan. 1899
Library (40,000 vols.) of the Paris chamber of commerce burnt . . . . . . 14 May, ,,
The Théâtre Française burnt down; mlle. Henriot, a young actress, killed (see *Comédie Française*), about noon, 8 March, 1900
INTERNAT. EXHIBITION opened by pres. Loubet, 14 April, ,,
Underground electric railway from Vincennes to the Porte Maillot, opened . . . 19 July, ,,
Many international congresses during the exhibition, one on colonial sociology, &c. . 6–11 Aug. ,,
Awards and honours distributed by M. Loubet to the president of groups of 75,000 exhibitors, over 40,000 people present in the Great-hall; Paris illuminated and a "nautical fête" at the exhibition . . . . 18 Aug. ,,
Free day, 449,000, 7 Aug.; closed, 12 Nov. (total admissions, 48,000,000).
Receipts, 114,000,000f. (40,000,000f. from the state and the city); expenses, 116,000,000f.
[The beautiful Avenue Nicolas II. and the Alexandre III. bridge remain as memorials of the exhibition of 1900].
Congress of learned societies; first meeting, 16 April, 1901
Explosion in a cartridge-factory at Issy, 17 deaths, 14 June, ,,
Paris Municipal debt, 95,480,000*l.*, reported, 16 Aug. ,,
Victor Hugo centenary monument unveiled in Place Victor Hugo . . . . 26 Feb. 1902
Great fire in the Rue Uzês and Rue Montmartre, 1 death . . . . 10, 11 March, ,,
Monument to Alphonse Daudet unveiled, 31 May, ,,
Demonstrations against the closing of unauthorised R.C. schools . . . . 22, 23, 26 July, ,,
The Dutuit bequest, fine art collection, accepted, 19 Aug. ,,
Death of M. de Blowitz, 30 years Paris correspondent of the *Times* . . . . 18 Jan. 1903
King Edward VII. visits Paris; enthusiastic reception; city *en fête* (see *France*) . . 1–4 May ,,
Violent encounters between Clericals and anti-Clericals, many injured . . . 23 May, ,,
Death of "Max O'Rell" (Paul Blouet), Paris correspondent of the *New York Journal* . 24 May, ,,
Socialist meeting, resolution passed denouncing the Russian government as the real authors of the Kishineff massacre (see *Russia*, 19, 20 April), 27 May; another meeting . . . . 26 June, ,,
Underground electric railway disaster, 84 deaths (see *France*) . . . . . . 10 Aug. ,,
Messages of sympathy from king Edward and president Loubet; public funeral, M. Combes and other ministers present . . . 13 Aug. ,,
Humbert trial begins 8 Aug.; sentence passed (see *France*) . . . . 22 Aug. ,,
The king and queen of Italy are enthusiastically welcomed by large crowds on their visit to Paris; state banquet given in honour of their majesties by pres. Loubet, the city brilliantly illuminated 14 Oct.; they visit Versailles; are present at a gala performance at the opera, Paris, 15 Oct.; visit the Invalides and tomb of Napoleon, lunch at the Italian embassy; present at state banquet given by M. Declassé at the foreign office, 16 Oct.; the king accompanies pres. Loubet on a shooting excursion to Rambouillet, 17 Oct.; king and queen leave Paris . . . . . 18 Oct. 1903
British commercial delegates in Paris received by the minister of commerce, the prefect of the Seine, and president of the municipal council, 29 Oct. ,,
Disturbance by a section of the working classes in Paris; collision with gendarmes and republican guards as the demonstrators after a meeting march through the streets . . . . 29 Oct. ,,
M. Lebaudy's balloon "Jaune" makes a successful journey from Moisson to the Champs de Mars, 12 Nov. ,,

IMPORTANT TREATIES OF PARIS.

Between England, France, Spain, and Portugal; cession of Canada to Great Britain by France, and Florida by Spain . . . . 10 Feb. 1763
Between France and Sardinia; the latter ceding Savoy, &c. . . . . . . 15 May, 1796
Between France and Sweden, whereby Swedish Pomerania and the island of Rugen were given up to the Swedes, who agreed to adopt the French prohibitory system against Great Britain 6 Jan. 1810
Capitulation of Paris: Napoleon renounces the sovereignty of France . . . . 11 April, 1814
Convention of Paris, between France and the allied powers; the boundaries of France to be the same as on the 1st of January, 1792 . . . 23 April, ,,
Peace of Paris ratified by France and all the allies, 14 May, 1814
Convention of St. Cloud, between marshal Davoust, and Wellington, and Blucher, for the surrender of Paris . . . . 3 July, 1815
[The allies entered it on the 6th.]
Treaty of Paris, between Great Britain, Austria, Russia, and Prussia, styling Napoleon the prisoner of those powers, and confiding his safeguard to England . . . . 2 Aug. ,,
Establishing the boundaries of France, and stipulating for the occupation of certain fortresses by foreign troops for three years . . 20 Nov. ,,
Treaty of Paris, confirming the treaties of Chaumont and Vienna, same day . . . . 20 Nov. ,,
Treaty of Paris, to fulfil the articles of the Congress of Vienna . . . . . . 10 June, 1817
Treaty of Paris between Russia and Turkey, England, France, and Sardinia (revised 13 March, 1871; see *Russia*) . . . . 30 March, 1856
Declaration of Paris, signed by European powers, not by United States, March, 1856: 1. Privateering abolished. 2. Neutral flags to exempt an enemy's goods from capture, except contraband of war. 3. Neutral goods under an enemy's flag not to be seized. 4. Blockade to be binding must be effective. This declaration was censured in parliament in 1871.
Treaty of Paris between England and Persia. 4 March, 1857
Treaty of Paris between the European powers, Prussia, and Switzerland, respecting Neufchâtel, 26 May, ,,
Important commercial treaty between France and England . . . . 23 Jan. 1860
Convention between France and Italy for withdrawal of French troops from Rome . 15 Sept. 1864

PARISHES. Their boundaries in England are said to have been fixed by Honorius, archbishop of Canterbury, 636, or by Alfred about 890. They were enlarged, and the number of parishes was consequently reduced in the 15th century, when there were 10,000. Parish registers were commenced in 1538. Acts were passed in 1844 and 1856 by which new parishes may be formed out of too extensive ones; acts amended in 1869. The appointment of parish constables was made unnecessary by an act passed Aug. 1872. See *Registers*, and *Benefices*. Number of ecclesiastical parishes or districts in 1893, 1,400. By the Local

Government act, passed 5 March, 1894, *Parish and District Councils* were appointed for rural parishes of 300 inhabitants or upwards, with suitable arrangements, to consist of from 5 to 15 members (women eligible) annually elected, on 15 April; 1st election in 7,142 parishes, 4 Dec. *et seq.* 1894. Parish councils were established in Scotland by the Local Government act of 1894. Parish registers of several counties are now published by the Parish Register Society, 1897. Parish councillors (tenure of office) act passed, 20 June, 1899.

PARISIENNE, LA, popular song by Casimir Delavigne, celebrating the defeat of the troops of Charles X. by the Parisians, 1 Aug. 1830; the music (an old air) was arranged by Auber.

PARKES MUSEUM, see *Sanitation.*

PARKESINE. A new substance, composed of gun-cotton, obtained from various vegetable bodies, and oil. It can be formed with the properties of ivory, tortoiseshell, wood, india-rubber, gutta-percha, &c. It is the invention of Mr. Alexander Parkes, of Birmingham, and was shown by him at the Exhibition in 1862. In Dec. 1865, at the Society of Arts, parkesine was proved to be an excellent electric insulator, and therefore likely to be suitable for telegraphic purposes.

PARK LANE MURDER, see *Trials,* 1872.

PARKS. The Romans attached parks to their villas. Fulvius Lupinus, Pompey, and Hortensius, among others, had large parks. In England, the first great park of which particular mention is made was that of Woodstock, formed by Henry I., 1125. Queen Caroline, consort of George II., inquired, it is said, of the first Mr. Pitt (afterwards earl of Chatham), how much it would cost to shut up the parks as private grounds. He replied, "Three crowns, your majesty." The design was never afterwards entertained. See *Finsbury, Southwark, Green, Hyde, James's, St., Regent's, Victoria, Alexandra, Battersea, West Ham,* and *People's Parks, Clissold, Waterlow,* and *Yellowstone Park, U.S.,* and *London Parks Act.*

The Parks Preservation Society, established by Mr. F. G. Heath and others 1871
The Parks' Regulation act, passed . 27 June, 1872
By new regulations, Hyde, Battersea, Regent's, and Victoria parks are the only metropolitan parks in which public addresses may be given, under certain restrictions . . . . . . Oct. ,,
These regulations (much objected to; broken, and offenders fined) were modified by the home secretary . . . . Feb. 1873
Acts for the establishment of public parks in England and Ireland were passed, 12 July, 1869; for Scotland . . . . 18 March, 1878
Parks railway bill (Hyde Park, &c.) rejected by commons committee . . . . 20 May, 1884
By the London Parks and Works Act, the charge of Battersea park, Bethnal Green museum and garden, Chelsea embankment and Victoria park were transferred to the Metropolitan Board of Works 1887
Clissold park, Stoke Newington, purchased for the public (price 96,045*l.*), 10 Jan. 1889.
Walpole park, Ealing (cost 40,000*l.*), opened by lord George Hamilton . . . . 1 May, 1901
Northbrook park, Lee, the gift of lord Northbrook and his son, opened . . . . 14 March, 1903
Avery hill, Eltham (cost 25,000*l.*), opened as a London park by lord Monkswell . 23 May, ,,

PARK'S TRAVELS. Mungo Park set sail on his first voyage to Africa, under the patronage of the African society, to trace the source of the river Niger, 22 May, 1795; and returned 22 Dec. 1797, after having fruitlessly encountered great danger. He again sailed from Portsmouth on his second voyage, 30 Jan. 1805, appointed to a new expedition by government. It is stated that his party fired on the natives when resisted, and that he was killed at Broussa on the Niger, Nov. 1805. His "Travels in Africa" were published in 1799.

PARLIAMENT (from the French *parlement,* discourse) derives its origin from the Saxon general assemblies, called *Wittenagemot.* The name was applied to the assemblies of the state under Louis VII. of France, about the middle of the 12th century, but it is said not to have appeared in our law till its mention in the statute of Westminster I., 3 Edw. I., 1272: and yet Coke declared in his *Institutes,* and spoke to the same effect, when speaker (1592), that this name was used even in the time of Edward the Confessor, 1041. The first clear account we have of the representatives of the people forming a house of commons, was in the 43rd Hen. III. 1258, when it was settled by the statutes of Oxford, that twelve persons should be chosen to represent the commons in the three parliaments, which, by the sixth statute, were to be held yearly. *Burton's Annals.* The general representation by knights, citizens, and burgesses, took place 49 Hen. III. 1265. *Dugdale's Summons to Parliament, edit.* 1685; see *Commons* and *Lords.* The power and jurisdiction of parliament are so transcendent and absolute, that it cannot be confined, either for causes or persons, within any bounds. It hath sovereign and uncontrollable authority in making and repealing laws. It can regulate or new-model the succession to the crown (as was done in the reigns of Henry VIII. and William III.). It can alter and establish the religion of the country, as was done in the reigns of Henry VIII., Edward VI., Mary, and Elizabeth. *Sir Edward Coke.** The ninth edition of May's "Practical Treatise on Parliament" was published in 1883; tenth edition, with many changes by sir Richard Palgrave, published Dec. 1893. Mr. G. Barnett Smith's elaborate "History of the English Parliament" was published Nov. 1892; see *Triennial* and *Septennial.* Return of the names of members of parliament from the earliest period to the present time, ordered by the house of commons, 4 May, 1876, and 9 March, 1877. Part I. (1213-1702), published 1879. See *Reform* and *Local Parliaments.*

First summons of barons by writ directed to the bishop of Salisbury, by John 1205
Parliament of Merton 1236
An assembly (the *mad* parliament) . 11 June, 1258
Simon de Montford, earl of Leicester, summons a parliament, including knights of the shire . . 1264
First assembly of the commons as a confirmed representation. *Dugdale* . . . . . 20 Jan. 1265
First regular parliament (according to many historians), 22 Edw. I. 1294
First a deliberative assembly; it becomes a legislative power, whose assent is essential to constitute a law 1308
The commons elect their first speaker, Peter De la Mare 1377
Parliament of only one day (Richard II. deposed) 29 Sept. 1399
"*Parliamentum Indoctum*" at Coventry (lawyers excluded) . . . . 6 Oct. 1404

* When the royal assent is given to a public bill, the clerk says "*Le roi* [or *la reine*] *le veut.*" If the bill be a private bill, he says "*Soit fait comme il est désiré.*" If the bill have subsidies for its object, he says, *Le roi* [or *la reine*] *remercie ses loyaux sujets, accepte leur bénévolence, et aussi le veut.*" If the king do not think proper to assent to the bill, the clerk says, "*Le roi* [or *la reine*] *s'avisera*" which is a mild way of giving a refusal. It is singular that the French language should still be used.

Members obliged to reside at the places they represented 1413
Forty-shilling freeholders only to elect knights . . 1430
"*Parliamentum diabolicum*" at Coventry: attainted the Yorkists 1459
Journals of the lords commenced 1509
Acts of Parliament printed in 1501, and consecutively from . . . . ,,
Members protected from arrest (see *Ferrars*) . . 1542
Journals of the commons begun 1547
Francis Russell, son of the earl of Bedford was the first peer's eldest son who sat in the house of commons 1549
The *Addled Parliament;* remonstrated with James I. respecting benevolences; dissolved by him in anger 5 April, 1614
The parliament in which were first formed the *Court* and *Country* parties, 1614, disputes with James I. June, 1620
Charles I. dissolves parliament, which does not meet for eleven years 1629
The *Long Parliament* (which voted the house of lords as useless) first assembled . . . . 3 Nov. 1640
The bishops excluded from voting on temporal matters . . . . ,,
The *Rump Parliament;* it voted the trial of Charles I. Jan. 1649
House of peers abolished . . . . . 6 Feb. ,,
A peer sat as a member of the commons . . . ,,
Cromwell roughly dissolves the *Long Parliament* 20 April, 1653
Barebone's parliament (*which see*) . . . 4 July, ,,
A convention parliament (see *Convention*) . . . 1660
Roman catholics excluded from parliament . . . 1678
The commons committed a secretary of state to the Tower . . . . Nov. ,,
The speaker of the commons refused by the king . 1679
A convention parliament (see *Convention*) . . . 1688
James II. convenes the Irish parliament at Dublin, which attaints 3000 protestants 1689
Act for triennial parliament (see *Triennial*) . . . 1694
First parliament of Great Britain met . 23 Oct. 1707
Members of the house of commons accepting any office of profit ordered to be re-elected by statute 6 Anne, cap. 7 . . . . ,,
The Triennial act repealed, and Septennial act voted (see *Septennial Parliament*) . . . 7 May, 1716
The journals ordered to be printed 1752
Privilege as to freedom from arrest of the servants of members relinquished by the commons . . . 1770
The lord mayor of London (Oliver) and alderman Crosby committed to the Tower by the commons in Wilkes's affair 1771
Reporting the debates permitted (see under *Reporting*) . . . . about ,,
Assembly of the first parliament of the United Kingdom of Great Britain and Ireland . . 2 Feb. 1801
Clergymen prohibited from becoming M.P.s . . ,,
Sir F. Burdett committed to the Tower . 6 April, 1810
Murder of Spencer Perceval, by Bellingham, at the house of commons . . . . . 11 May, 1812
Return for Clare county, Ireland, of Mr. O'Connell, the first Roman catholic commoner elected since the Revolution . . . . . 5 July, 1828
The duke of Norfolk took his seat in the lords, the first Roman catholic peer under the Relief bill (see *Roman Catholics*) . . . . 28 April, 1829
The Reformed Parliament meet . . . 7 Aug. 1832
Joseph Pease, the first Quaker admitted M.P. on his affirmation . . . . . . 15 Feb. 1833
Houses of Parliament destroyed by fire . 16 Oct. 1834
New houses of parliament commenced * . . . 1840
The members of the commons' and lords' houses relinquish the privilege of franking letters (see *Franking*) . . . . 10 Jan. ,,

Committal of Smith O'Brien by the commons for contempt (see *Ireland*) . . . . 30 April, 1846
The peers took possession of their house, that portion of the palace being ready . . 15 April, 1847
Reporters excluded by motion of John O'Connell for two hours . . . . 18 May, 1849
The commons assemble in their new house 4 Nov. 1852
The chairman of committees of the whole house appointed to act as a deputy-speaker of the house of commons . . . . Aug. 1853
The two houses began to communicate by letter . 1855
Baron L. Rothschild, the first Jew admitted 26 July, 1858
Court of referees to examine private bills established 1865
Henry Fawcett (blind), elected M.P. . . July, ,,
The parliamentary oaths modified and made uniform 30 April, 1866
Arthur M. Kavanagh (without arms and legs), elected Nov. ,,
Her Majesty authorised to proclaim prorogation of parliament during the recess, by act passed 12 Aug. 1867
New Reform bill received royal assent . 15 Aug. ,,
Great dissatisfaction in the commons at the smallness of their building; a committee's report (proposing changes or a new house) printed . Oct. ,,
Changes in mode of dealing with private bills in court of referees . . . . . March, 1868
Vote by proxy in the house of lords abolished by standing order . . . . . 31 March, ,,
Reform acts for Scotland and Ireland, and Parliamentary Boundaries act passed . . 13 July, ,,
Parliamentary Elections act passed . . 31 July, ,,
Parliament dissolved . . . . . . 11 Nov. ,,
New parliament met . . . . . . 10 Dec. ,,
Reporters excluded from the commons during debates on the Contagious Diseases act, 24 May and 20 July, 1870
The commons sat from 2 P.M. 15 July, to 5.30 A.M., 16 July, ,,
Meeting of parliament, in six days after proclamation, legalised by act passed . . . 9 Aug. ,,
Death of the earl of Onslow, father of the house of lords, aged 93 . . . . . . 24 Oct. ,,
Mr. Fawcett alone in the lobby (350-1, on grant of 30,000*l.* to princess Louise on her marriage), 16 Feb. 1871
Bankrupt peers disqualified from sitting or voting in parliament by act passed . . 13 July, ,,
Mr. Bonham Carter succeeds Mr. J. C. Dodson as deputy speaker and chairman of committees, 8 April, 1872
Mr. Biggar and others caused reporters and others to be excluded from the debates in the commons; much discussion ensued; Mr. Disraeli's resolution that strangers are not to withdraw without a vote of the house or order of the speaker, unanimously adopted . . . . 31 May, ,,
Only 89,938*l.* paid to members (commons) for salaries and pensions, civil, naval, and military July, ,,
The ballot act passed . . . . . 18 July ,,
Mr. Plimsoll, greatly excited, makes unparliamentary charges at the proposed withdrawal of the Merchant Shipping Bill, 22 July; apologises; motion for reprimand withdrawn . 29 July, 1875
The commons through Irish members (principally Messrs. Parnell, Biggar, O'Donnell, Power, Gray, Kirk, and Nolan) sat from 3.45 P.M. 2 July, to 7.15 A.M. 3 July; from about 4 P.M. 31 July, to 6.10 P.M. . . . . 1 Aug. 1877
Temporary resolution to check obstructiveness (by abuse of the power of moving the adjournment of the house) passed (282-32) . . . 27 July, ,,
Major O'Gorman, M.P. for Waterford, "*named*" by the speaker for refusing to submit to his authority, 6 Aug.; apologises . . . . 7 Aug. 1878
Much obstruction by home-rule party, June, July; Mr. Parnell's virtual vote of censure of the speaker (for directing notes to be taken, &c.) lost (29-421) . . . . . 11, 12 July, 1879
Breach of privilege; Mr. C. E. Grissell having stated that he could influence the committee on the "Tower high level bridge," is examined by a

---

* Termed the "Palace of Westminster." The first contract for the embankment of the river was taken in 1837, by Messrs. Lee; this embankment, faced with granite, is 886 feet in length, and projected into the river in a line with the inner side of the third pier of old Westminster-bridge. Sir Charles Barry (born 1795, died 1860) was the architect of the sumptuous pile of buildings raised since 1840. The whole stands on a bed of concrete twelve feet thick; to the east it has a front of about 1000 feet, and covers an area of nine statute acres. It contains 1100 apartments, 100 staircases, and two miles of passages or corridors. The great Victoria tower at the south-west extremity is 346 feet in height, and towers of less magnitude crown other portions of the building. In the recess of 1894-5 extensive alterations were made in the house and private rooms to promote the comfort of the members and public.

committee; he and Mr. John Sandilands Ward convicted, 16 July; Mr. Grissell went abroad; order for his apprehension issued; Mr. Ward appeared before the house; taken into custody, 23 July; released, 30 July; Mr. Grissell surrenders; sent to Newgate, 14 Aug.; released . 15 Aug. 1879
Motion for quinquennial parliaments negatived, (110-160) . . . . 24 Feb. 1880
Sir Stafford Northcote's resolutions against obstruction, 26 Feb.; adopted in the standing orders (160-20) . . . . 28 Feb. ,,
Mr. Grissell arrested, and committed to Newgate, 2, 3 March; discharged . . . . 24 March, ,,
Mr. Charles Bradlaugh, M.P. for Northampton (not believing in God) objects to take oath of allegiance; his affirmation refused, 3 May; his offer to take oath not permitted . . . . 21 May, ,,
A committee appointed; recommends that he be allowed to affirm, 16 June; much discussion ensues; resolution of Mr. Labouchere, M.P. for Northampton, that Mr. Bradlaugh be permitted to affirm, negatived (275-230) . . . 22 June, ,,
Mr. Bradlaugh's claim to take the oath, or affirm, denied by the house; he refuses to withdraw, and is taken into custody, and imprisoned in the clock tower (vote 326-38), 23 June; released by vote, 24 June, ,,
Resolution moved by Mr. Gladstone that affirmation be accepted instead of an oath in certain cases; opposed by sir Stafford Northcote as rescinding vote of 22 June; resolution accepted (303-249) 1, 2 July; Mr. Bradlaugh affirms, is admitted, and votes . . . . . 2 July, ,,
See *Trials*, 1881.
The commons sat continuously 21 hours (devoted to Irish affairs) . . . . . . 26, 27 Aug. ,,
Debate on Irish amendments to the address:
Mr. Parnell's lost (57-435) . . 6-14 Jan. 1881
Mr. Justin McCarthy's (37-201) . 17-19 Jan. ,,
Mr. Dawson (36-274) . . . . . 20 Jan. ,,
Mr. O'Kelly (34-178) . . . . . 20 Jan. ,,
House of Commons on Irish protection bill, sat from 4 p.m. 25 Jan. to 2 p.m. . . . 26 Jan. ,,
Mr. Gladstone's motion for urgency carried (251-33) . . . . ,,
On first reading of Mr. Forster's coercion bill, debate summarily closed by Mr. H. Brand, the speaker (termed *coup d'état*) 4 p.m. 31 Jan. to 9.30 p.m. . . . . 2 Feb. ,,
Thirty-six Irish members, Mr. Parnell, Mr. Justin McCarthy, and others, suspended for the sitting for disorderly conduct; Mr. Gladstone's resolutions; speaker invested with all the powers of the house to regulate business when voted urgent by three-fourths of the members (at least 200) (234-150) . . . . 3 Feb. ,,
New stringent rules to be enforced when business is declared urgent by a minister of the crown; laid on table by the speaker . . . . . 9 Feb. ,,
Supplemental rules, 17 Feb. modified; acted on 21 Feb.; new rules announced 11, 12 March, ,,
Mr. Gladstone's resolution for "urgency," with the supplies lost (212-296) . . . . 14 March, ,,
Mr. Bradlaugh re-elected for Northampton, 9 April, ,,
His offer to take the oath opposed (208-175); he is forcibly removed, 26 April; again ejected, 10 May, ,,
New parliamentary oaths bill discharged 5 July, ,,
Mr. Bradlaugh's attempt to enter the House of Commons, forcibly resisted by the police. Mr. Labouchere's motion to rescind the resolution of 10 May, 1881, negatived (191-7) . . . 3 Aug. ,,
Differences between the houses on the land bill settled by mutual concessions . . 12-15 Aug. ,,
Mr. Bradlaugh not permitted to sit; government motion negatived (286-228) . . . . 7 Feb. 1882
New rules of procedure including the clôture (the power of closing a debate) and delegation of business, proposed by Mr. Gladstone . 13 Feb. ,,
Proposal for writ for Northampton negatived (307-18); Mr. Bradlaugh repeats oath and takes a seat; withdraws when directed; 21 Feb. expelled (291-83); new writ to be issued . 22 Feb. ,,
Michael Davitt, convict, elected M.P. for co. Meath (see *Fenians*) . . . . 22 Feb. ,,
Mr. Bradlaugh re-elected for Northampton 2 Mar. ,,
Resolution of 7 Feb. re-affirmed (286-228) . 6 Mar. ,,
Mr. Marriott's amendment on Mr. Gladstone's new rule negatived (318-279) . 30-31 Mar. ,,
Discussion on the clôture deferred . . 1 May, 1882
Commons; sat 2 p.m.-8 p.m. 30 hours, committee on prevention of crime bill; 25 Irish members suspended for wilful obstruction 30 June and 1 July, ,,
Mr. O'Donnell suspended for 14 days (181-33) 3 July, ,,
Difference between the two houses; compromise (see *Ireland*) . . . . Aug. ,,
Mr. Bradlaugh publishes a determined manifesto, *Times* . . . . 23 Sept. ,,
Parliament meets 24 Oct.; discussion on procedure resumed . . . . 25 Oct. ,,
Mr. Gibbons' amendment (the clôture to be carried by two-thirds instead of bare majority) negatived 322-238 . . . . 1-2 Nov. ,,
The clôture adopted (304-260) . . . 10-11 Nov. ,,
The new rules made standing orders 27 Nov.-1 Dec. ,,
Affirmation bill introduced in the commons (184-53) 19-20 Feb. 1883
Mr. O'Kelly suspended for a week for giving Mr. Forster the lie . . . . 22 Feb. ,,
Grand committee's first meeting, Mr. Goschen chairman . . . . 9 April, ,,
Affirmation bill rejected by the commons (292-289) 3-4 May, ,,
Mr. Bradlaugh not permitted to take the oath 4 May, ,,
His exclusion voted (232-65) . . . . 9 July, ,,
Arrested by Mr. Gosset, the sergeant-at-arms, for attempting to enter the house, 3 Aug.; brings an action against the sergeant, 7 Dec.; verdict for defendant . . . . 9 Feb. 1884
Mr. Bradlaugh administers the oath to himself, sits, and votes; excluded by vote (228-120) 11 Feb.; re-elected for Northampton (4,032-3664) 19 Feb.; vote for his re-exclusion (226-173) . . 21 Feb. ,,
New Reform bill introduced by Mr. Gladstone 28 Feb. ,,
Commons: irregular debate on Egyptian policy; supplies; sat from 12.20 p.m. 15 March, to 5.45 a.m. (Sunday) . . . . 16 March, ,,
Queen *v.* Bradlaugh for voting without taking the oath, Queen's Bench . . . . . 13 June, ,,
Verdict for the crown . . . . 30 June, ,,
Conflict between the lords and commons, respecting the Franchise bill, (see *Reform*) . . . . . ,,
Explosion (dynamite) on the stair above the crypt in the house of commons; much damage done; two police constables, Wm. Cole and Thos. Cox, and Mr. Green seriously hurt. [Cole picked up a blazing parcel, to carry it out and saved the building; he and Cox commended by the queen, and rewarded for steady courage. Cole received the Albert medal, in Westminster Hall 26 March.]* Westminster Hall much injured by another explosion a few minutes past 2 p.m. 24 Jan. 1885
Mr. Bradlaugh's appeal disallowed by the lords justices . . . . 28 Jan. ,,
The new rules and the clôture first applied; Mr. O'Brien expelled . . . . . . 24 Feb. ,,
Mr. Bradlaugh not permitted to take the oath (263–219) . . . . 6 July, ,,
Retirement of Mr. Ralph A. Gosset; knighted after a long service and ten years sergeant-of-arms (died 27 Nov.) 30 Sept.; succeeded by H. D. Erskine ,,
Parliament dissolved . . . . 18 Nov. ,,
New parliament meets 12 Jan.; opened by the queen . . . . 21 Jan. 1886
Mr. Bradlaugh takes the oath, intervention stopped by the speaker . . . . 13 Jan. ,,

* The chief Commissioner of the Metropolitan Police, sir E. Y. W. Henderson, issued an order stating that the Prime Minister directed the payment of 50*l*., each to Cole and Cox from the Royal Bounty Fund, and further, that the Home Secretary has approved of the payment of 120*l*. to Cole and 70*l*. to Cox, while sir James Ingham granted them the sum of 30*l*. each from the Bow-street Reward Fund. Both were granted a pension of 78*l*. per annum each, April, 1886. Cole and Cox were each presented with a money testimonial from the members of both Houses (108*l*. 10*s*. each; Cole received a gold watch and chain). They both left the hospital at the end of March, 1885. On 5 Oct. 1885, John Colebrook, Esq., retired surgeon of the Indian army, a member of the Royal Institution of Great Britain, presented to both men a copy of this book at the institution.

Mr. Gladstone introduces his bill, "to make better provision for the future government of Ireland;" the House crammed, occupied by members from 6 A.M. . . . . 8 April, 1886

Sir T. Erskine May (author of the "Practice of Parliament," 1884 *et seq.*) assistant clerk to the commons 1856; clerk 1871; retires 15 April (created lord Farnborough 10 May; died 17 May); succeeded by Reginald Palgrave . . 1 May, ,,

Death of lord Redesdale, chairman of committees since 1851, 2 May; succeeded by the duke of Buckingham (122 against 103 for lord Morley), 10 May, ,,

New parliament meets (see *England*) . 5 Aug. ,,

Parliament prorogued . . . . . 25 Sept. ,,

New procedure rules with increased application of the closure, &c., introduced 21 Feb.; first and principal rule adopted (222–120) . 16 March, 1887

House of commons sat above 21 hours 21-22 March, ,,

The commons decide that an article in the *Times* of May 2 on Mr. Dillon is not a breach of privilege (Mr. Dillon rejects the offer of a public prosecution) 4, 5 May; Mr. Gladstone's motion for a committee rejected (317–233) . . 6, 7 May, ,,

Much obstruction of the opposition to the Criminal Law (Amendment) Ireland Bill in the commons; many amendments 28 March *et seq.* ,,

Mr. T. Healy suspended for 14 days . 29 July, ,,

Mr. C. Graham and Mr. E. Harrington suspended for speaking disrespectfully of the house of lords 13 Sept. ,,

New rules of procedure introduced; rule 1 (limiting the sittings of the commons on ordinary days from 3 P.M. to 1 A.M.) passed 24 Feb.; rule 2 (giving the power of closure to a majority in a house of 100), 3–8 (for repressing disorder and waste of time) passed 28 Feb.; 9–12 passed 29 Feb.; 13 (reviving grand committees, &c.) 7 March, 1888

Mr. C. A. V. Conybeare, M.P., suspended for a month (or to the end of the session) for libelling the speaker in the *Star* newspaper . 21 July, ,,

Illegal attempt by constable Jeremiah Sullivan to arrest Mr. Sheehy, M.P., in the precincts of the House; committee to consider breach of privilege appointed 26 Nov.; breach affirmed, but no action . . . . 7 Dec. ,,

Dr. Tanner suspended for insulting Mr. Balfour 21 Dec. ,,

The house of lords meets to pass the Appropriation Bill, 11.20 P.M. . . . . . 22 Dec. ,,

Parliament meets, 21 Feb.; prorogued . 30 Aug. 1889

Parliament meets . . . . . 11 Feb. 1890

Mr. Labouchere suspended from sitting for a week, for asserting his disbelief in lord Salisbury's denial of connection with a conspiracy for defeating the ends of justice in relation to a recent trial . . . . 28 Feb. ,,

A select committee on procedure in parliament nominated (Mr. Goschen (chairman), Mr. A. J. Balfour, Mr. J. Chamberlain, Mr. Gladstone, sir W. V. Harcourt, lord Hartington, and others), 27 June; first met, 30 June. Mr. Balfour's report not accepted; some of the members retire . . . . 14 July, ,,

[The committee recommended various means for saving the time of parliament in passing bills from one session to another, and for shortening the sessions, &c.]

The commons sat from 3 P.M. to 7 A.M. (obstruction to Irish light railways bill) . . 14, 15 Aug. ,,

The resolution against Mr. Bradlaugh, 22 June, 1880, ordered to be expunged from the journals of the commons, 27 Jan.; he died . 30 Jan. 1891

Sir William Whiteway, premier of Newfoundland, with other delegates, appears at the bar of the house of lords; he makes a statement in defence of the colony's claims . . . . 23 April, ,,

Mr. Cunninghame Graham, M.P., expelled from France for seditious speeches . . 11 May, ,,

Capt. Edmund Hope Verney expelled from the house of commons, having been sentenced to a year's imprisonment for a misdemeanour on his own confession . . . . . . 12 May, ,,

Mr. Atkinson, M.P., suspended for disrespect to the speaker . . . . . . 27 July, ,,

Parliament prorogued . . . . . 5 Aug. ,,

Mr. Edward S. W. De Cobain, M.P. for Belfast; fled from justice; commanded to attend the house on 23 July, 1891; expelled . 26 Feb. 1892

[See *Trials*, 17, 21 March *et seq.* 1893.]

Mr. George W. Hastings, M.P. for E. Worcestershire, sentenced to 5 years' penal servitude for fraud as a trustee (see *Trials*), 11 March; expelled from the house . . 21 March, 1892

Mr. Fenwick's resolution for the payment of members of parliament rejected by the commons (227—162) . . . . . . 25 March, ,,

Mr. James F. Buckley, Mr. John W. Maclure, M.P., Mr. William B. Hawkins, and Mr. John Conacher, directors of the Cambrian railway, were admonished by the speaker, by direction of the house of commons, for a breach of privilege in dismissing Mr. John Hood, a stationmaster, on account of his evidence given to the committee on the hours of railway servants . . . 7 April, ,,

Mr. Cunninghame Graham suspended for a week for disorderly conduct . . . . . 4 May, ,,

Parliament dissolved, 28 June; new parliament meets . . . . 4 Aug. ,,

The publication in the *Times* of Viscount Wolmer's words, asserting that some of the Irish members were paid by government, declared to be a breach of privilege; lord Wolmer withdrew his words . . . . . . 16 Feb. 1893

Mr. William Allen's resolution for the payment of members adopted by the commons (276–229) 24 March, ,,

Mr. Michael Davitt, in compliance with the Act of 1883, as a bankrupt, retires from parliament, about . . . . 12 May, ,,

The charge of breach of privilege against the *Daily News*, for burlesque in parliamentary reports, dropped . . . . 5 June, ,,

Mr. Gladstone's resolution (termed gagging) for restricting the discussion in committee on the Irish home-rule bill by means of the closure (*see above*, March, 1887), adopted (299–267), 30 June; the committee stage closed amid great excitement; order restored by calling in the speaker, see *Ireland*, 27 July; Mr. Sexton suspended for the night for refusing to withdraw his assertion that Mr. Brodrick's remark that the Irish were "an impecunious and garrulous race" was "grossly impertinent" . . . . 11 July, ,,

The closure much adopted in the debates on the Irish government bill, see *Gagging* and *Ireland*, July, Aug.; the bill passed by the commons (301—267), 2 Sept.; rejected by the lords (419—41), 8, 9 Sept.; parliament sits, 31 Jan.—22 Sept.; 2 Nov.—27 Dec.; prorogued, 5 March, 1894

Disagreement of the lords and commons, see *Employers' liability bill*, Dec. 1893, and *Local Government bill* (parish councils) . . . . . Feb. ,,

New session, 12 March . . . . . 25 Aug. ,,

New session . . . . 5 Feb. 1895

Mr. William Allen's resolution for the payment of members adopted by the commons (176—158) 22 March, ,,

Mr. Dalziel's resolution for a second ballot in certain cases in parliamentary elections, carried (132—72) . . . . 6 April, ,,

Resignation of Mr. Arthur Wellesley Peel, the speaker; hearty thanks of the house, 9 April; created viscount, with 4,000*l.* pension, receives freedom of the city of London . . April, ,

Mr. William Court Gully elected speaker (285—274) 10 April, ,,

The earl of Selborne's proposition to retain his seat in the commons as viscount Wolmer, after succeeding his father as a peer, set aside by the Vacation of Seats committee. . . . 20 May, ,,

Dissolution . . . . 8 July, ,,

Parliament meets (see *Commons*) 12 Aug., prorogued, 5 Sept.

Parliament meets, queen's speech, 11 Feb.; address voted, 18 Feb.; new sessional order respecting days reserved for supply (20 days) adopted, 27 Feb.; parliament prorogued . 14 Aug. 1896

Parliament re-assembles, queen's speech, 19 Jan.; address voted, 26 Jan.; the sessional order of 1896 renewed (commons) . . . 29 Jan. 1897

Mr. T. Redmond and 3 others suspended for disorder in the commons . . . . . 28 May, ,,

The house of lords attends worship at the Abbey and the house of commons at St. Margaret's, Westminster . . . . . . 20 June, ,,

Congratulatory addresses to the queen by the lords and commons (411–41), 21 June; presented at Buckingham palace . . . . . 23 June, 1897

Mr. John Kirkwood admonished by the commons for refusing to answer questions asked by a committee on money lending . . . . 16 July, „

Parliament prorogued . . . . . 6 Aug. „

Parliament meets, queen's speech, address voted in the lords, 8 Feb. 1898; the sessional orders renewed (commons), 8 Feb.; address voted, 18 Feb.; parliament prorogued . . 12 Aug. 1898

Parliament meets, queen's speech, address voted in the lords, 7 Feb. 1899; sessional orders renewed (commons), 7 Feb.; address voted, 21 Feb. 1899; adjourns . . . . . 28 March–10 April, „

Debates in both houses; sir A. Milner's *minimum* of reforms in the Transvaal warmly supported, 28 July, 1899

Parliament prorogued, 9 Aug.; *meets:* queen's speech on the S. African crisis, address voted (lords), 17 Oct.; (commons) Mr. Dillon's vote of censure rejected (322–54), 17 Oct.; Mr. Stanhope's negatived (362–135); address voted, 19 Oct.; parliament prorogued . . . . . 27 Oct. „

Parliament meets, address voted in the lords, 30 Jan. 1900; and in the commons, 9 Feb.; sessional order agreed to (303–62) . 15 Feb. 1900

Letters from Mr. Labouchere and other M.P.'s to Boer officials in S. Africa published as a parliamentary paper, much discussed . 23 Aug. „

Parliament prorogued, 8 Aug.; dissolved, 25 Sept. „

New Parliament meets; Mr. Wm. Court Gully re-elected speaker (see *Commons*) . . 3 Dec. „

Queen's speech: "I have watched with cordial satisfaction the development of my greater colonies into self-governing communities; I feel confident that the establishment of the great Federation of Australia will prove advantageous not only to the colonies immediately concerned, but to the empire at large"; address voted in the lords, 6 Dec.; sessional, orders renewed (commons), 6 Dec.; address voted (265–23), 10 Dec. „

Parliament meets (on the death of the queen, 22 Jan.) . . . . 23 Jan. 1901

R.C. peers formally protest against the terms of the Accession oath . . . . 14 Feb. „

Parliament opened by the king, speech from the throne; address voted in the lords, 14 Feb.; in the commons . . . . . . 26 Feb. „

Eleven Nationalists, Mr. Flavin and others, resisting the closure on the education vote of supply, refusing to go out on division, were suspended, and had to be forcibly removed by the police, 5 March, „

The standing order relating to disorderly conduct amended . . . . . . 7 March, „

The editor and publisher of the *Globe* newspaper reprimanded for breach of privilege . 16 Aug. „

New supply rule to hasten despatch passed, 7 Aug.; parliament prorogued . . 18 Aug. „

The closure of debate adopted 74 times during the session . . . . „

The king and queen open parliament; praise of the troops; *their cheerfulness amid the hardships of guerilla warfare, humanity in their treatment of the enemy, even to their own detriment,* strongly emphasized in the king's speech, 16 Jan.; address voted . . . . . 29 Jan. 1902

Some of the new rules of procedure adopted (289–98), issued 30 Jan.; came into force . 5 May, „

Mr. Archibald Milman, clerk of the house of commons, resigns; made K.C.B. mid Jan.; dies 14 Feb. „

Sir C. P. Ilbert appointed . . . . 7 Feb. „

Mr. Dillon suspended for a week . 20 March, „

Mr. Redmond, protesting against the enforcement of certain sections of the crimes act (1887) in Ireland, moves the adjournment of the commons; rejected (253–148) . . . . . 17 April, „

All-night debate on the new rules of procedure, closed 5.40 a.m. . . . . . . 30 April, „

Nationalists' motion against the speaker rejected (398–63) . . . . 7 May, „

"Col." Lynch (elected M.P. for Galway city, spring, 1902) arrested on a charge of treason 11 June, „

Mr. P. A. M'Hugh, M.P., arrested . . 15 June, „

Mr. Balfour warmly welcomed as prime minister (commons) . . . . 14 July, „

Parliament adjourns, 8 Aug.; meets, Mr. John O'Donnell suspended for disorder . . 16 Oct. 1902

Mr. Balfour's closure scheme (styled *guillotine* by some) for restricting discussion in committee and report stages of the Education bill, carried by 119 majority (*see above*, 1893) . . 11 Nov. „

New sessional orders relating to procedure converted into standing orders (155–61) . 1 Dec. „

Parliament prorogued . . . . . 18 Dec. „

Parliament opened by the king . . 17 Feb. 1903

Parliament opened by the king; king's speech; address voted in the lords, 17 Feb.; in the commons, after amendments (all negatived) [on housing of the working classes, provision of work for the unemployed; land forces' organisation; ministers of the crown and public companies, and other topics] . . . 26 Feb. „

Army estimates, 1903–4, considered in committee of supply . . . . . . 9, 10, 11 March, „

Unionist motion to reduce the number of men in army estimates by 27,000 defeated (245–154), 11 March, „

Church discipline bill (No. 1) passed second reading (190–139) . . . . . 12 March, „

Irish land bill introduced by Mr. Wyndham, well received by the Irish party . . 25 March, „

Navy estimates, 1903–4 . 16, 18, 30, 31 March, „

London education bill, first reading . . 7 April, „

Budget: reduction of income tax from 1*s.* 3*d.* to 11*d.*; abolition of the corn duty . 23 April, „

London education bill, second reading . 29 April, „

Resolution sanctioning Transvaal loan of 35,000,000*l.* agreed to without a division; Mr. Chamberlain's statement on the financial position of the Transvaal . . . . 6 May, „

Irish land bill debate, 4, 5 May; second reading (443–26) . . . . 7 May, „

Port of London bill read second time and referred to joint committee; resolution calling upon government to extend and amend workmen's compensation act, agreed to . . . 13 May, „

Resolution (lords) that parliament ought to meet earlier in the winter and rise early in July, carried . . . . 25 May, „

London education bill committee, carried with amendment (242–114), 19 May; reported 26 May, „

Motion that the lords' veto on any measure presented by the commons should be limited to one session, rejected (118–62) . . . 27 May, „

Sugar convention bill, first reading (commons) (142–82) . . . . 28 May, „

Sir Chas. Dilke called attention to Mr. Chamberlain's speeches on imperial fiscal reform; speeches by Mr. Balfour, Mr. Chamberlain and others . . . . 28 May, „

Bill to abolish the declaration made by the sovereign on accession (lords) rejected (109–62), 29 June, „

Irish land bill committee, 15 June; reported 17 July; third reading (317–20) . . 21 July, „

London education bill, third reading (228–118), 22 July, „

Debate (lords) on fiscal policy . . 23, 24 July, „

London education bill passes through committee (lords), 4 Aug.; third reading 11 Aug.; lords' amendments agreed to by commons . 12 Aug. „

Irish land bill passes through committee (lords), with slight alterations, 7 Aug.; third reading (lords), 11 Aug.; lords' amendments to commons' amendments agreed to . . . . 13 Aug. „

Indian budget . . . . 13 Aug. „

Royal assent to various measures; parliament prorogued 14 Aug. to 2 Nov.; further prorogued to 2 Feb. 1904.

Visit of British M.P.s to France duriug . Nov. „

NUMBER AND DURATION OF PARLIAMENTS, FROM 27 EDW. I. 1299, TO 59 VICT. 1895.

Edward I.	8 parl. in	8 yrs'.	reign
Edward II.	15 „	20	„
Edward III.	37 „	50	„
Richard II.	26 „	22	„
Henry IV.	10 „	14	„
Henry V.	11 „	9	„
Henry VI.	22 „	39	„
Edward IV.	5 „	22	„
Richard III.	1 „	2	„
Henry VII.	8 „	24	„

Reign.	Day of Meeting.*	When Dissolved.
HENRY VIII.	21 Jan. . 1510	23 Feb. . 1510
	4 Feb. . 1511	4 March . 1513
	5 Feb. . 1514	22 Dec. . 1515
	15 April . 1523	13 Aug. . 1523
	3 Nov. . 1529	4 April . 1536
	8 June . 1536	18 July ,,
	28 April . 1539	24 July . 1540
	16 Jan. . 1541	28 March . 1544
	30 Jan. . 1545	uncertain
	23 Nov. . ,,	31 Jan. . 1547
EDWARD VI.	4 Nov. . 1547	15 April . 1552
	1 March . 1553	31 March . 1553
MARY	5 Oct. . ,,	5 Dec. . ,,
	2 April . 1554	5 May . 1554
	12 Nov. . ,,	16 Jan. . 1555
	21 Oct. . 1555	9 Dec. . ,,
	20 Jan. . 1558	17 Nov. . 1558
ELIZABETH	23 Jan. . 1559	8 May . 1559
	11 Jan. . 1563	2 Jan. . 1567
	2 April . 1571	29 May . 1571
	8 May . 1572	19 April . 1583
	23 Nov. . 1584	14 Sept. . 1585
	29 Oct. . 1586	23 March . 1587
	12 Nov. . 1588	29 March . 1589
	19 Feb. . 1593	10 April . 1593
	24 Oct. . 1597	9 Feb. . 1598
	27 Oct. . 1601	19 Dec. . 1601
JAMES I.	19 March . 1604	9 Feb. . 1611
	5 April. . 1614	7 June . 1614
	16, 23, 30 Jan. . 1621	8 Feb. . 1622
	12 Feb. . 1624	27 March . 1625
CHARLES I.	17 May . 1625	12 Aug. . ,,
	6 Feb. . 1626	15 June . 1626
	17 March . 1628	10 March . 1629
	13 April . 1640	5 May . 1640
Long Parliament	3 Nov. . ,,	20 April . 1653
COMMONWEALTH	3 Sept. . 1654	22 Jan. . 1655
	17 Sept. . 1656	4 Feb. . 1658
	27 Jan. . 1659	22 April . 1659
	7 May . ,,	16 March . 1660
CHARLES II.	25 April . 1660	29 Dec. . ,,
Pensionary Parl.	8 May . 1661	24 Jan. . 1679
	6 March . 1679	12 July . ,,
Seven Prorogations.	17 Oct. . ,,	18 Jan. . 1681
JAMES II.	21 March . 1681	28 March . ,,
(Convention.)	19 May . 1685	2 July . 1687
WILLIAM III.	22 Jan. . 1689	6 Feb. . 1690
	20 March . 1690	11 Oct. . 1695
	22 Nov. . 1695	7 July . 1698
	24 Aug. . 1698	19 Dec. . 1700
ANNE	6 Feb. . 1701	11 Nov. . 1701
	30 Dec. . ,,	2 July . 1702
	20 Aug. . 1702	5 April . 1705
	25 Oct. . 1705	11 April . 1708
	18 Nov. . 1708	28 Sept. . 1710
	25 Nov. . 1710	8 Aug. . 1713
GEORGE I.	11 Nov. . 1713	15 Jan. . 1715
	21 March . 1715	10 March . 1722
GEORGE II.	9 Oct. . 1722	7 Aug. . 1727
	28 Jan. . 1728	18 April . 1734
	14 Jan. . 1735	28 April . 1741
	4 Dec. . 1741	18 June . 1747
	10 Nov. . 1747	8 April . 1754
GEORGE III.	14 Nov. . 1754	21 March . 1761
	3 Nov. . 1761	12 March . 1768
	10 May . 1768	30 Sept. . 1774
	29 Nov. . 1774	1 Sept. . 1780
	31 Oct. . 1780	25 March . 1784
	18 May . 1784	21 June . 1790
	26 Nov. . 1790	20 May . 1796
	27 Sept. . 1796	29 June . 1802
	16 Nov. . 1802	24 Oct. . 1806
	15 Dec. . 1806	29 April . 1807
	22 June . 1807	24 Sept. . 1812
	24 Nov. . 1812	10 June . 1818
GEORGE IV.	14 Jan. . 1819	29 Feb. . 1820
	23 April . 1820	2 June . 1826
	14 Nov. . 1826	24 July . 1830
WILLIAM IV.	26 Oct. . 1830	22 April . 1831
	14 June . 1831	3 Dec. . 1832
WILLIAM IV.	29 June . 1833	30 Dec. . 1834
	19 Feb. . 1835	17 July . 1837
VICTORIA	15 Nov. . 1837	23 June . 1841
	19 Aug. . 1841	23 July . 1847
	18 Nov. . 1847	1 July . 1852
	4 Nov. . 1852	21 March . 1857
	1 April . 1857	23 April . 1859
	31 May . 1859	6 July . 1865
	1 Feb. . 1866	11 Nov. . 1868
	10 Dec. . 1868	26 Jan. . 1874
	5 March . 1874	23 March . 1880
	29 April . 1880	18 Nov. . 1885
	12 Jan. . 1886	26 June . 1886
	5 Aug. . ,,	28 June . 1892
	4 Aug. . 1892	8 July . 1895
	12 Aug. . 1895	25 Sept. . 1900
	3 Dec. . 1900	
EDWARD VII.	14 Feb. . 1901	

* Corrected by the blue-book, "Parliaments of England," printed 1879.

* Corrected by the blue-book, "Parliaments of England," printed 1879

PARLIAMENT OF IRELAND, it is said, began with conferences of the English settlers on the hill of Tara, in 1173. Writs for knights of the shire were issued in 1295. The Irish parliament met last on 2 Aug. 1800; the bill for the union having passed.

PARLIAMENT OF SCOTLAND consisted of barons, prelates, and abbots, and occasionally of burgesses. A great national council was held at Scone by John Balliol, 9 Feb. 1292; and by Robert Bruce at Cambuskenneth, in 1326. A house of commons was never formed in Scotland. The parliament of Scotland sanctioned the act of union on 16 Jan. 1707, and met for the last time on 22 April, same year.

The parliament hall, Edinburgh castle, erected by James I., in 1434, was thoroughly and judiciously restored by M. Hippolyte Blanc, at the expense of the late Mr. Nelson and family. The hall was reopened, Feb. 1891. The undertaking was greatly promoted by the investigations of lords Napier and Ettrick, major Gore Booth, and Mr. R. Chambers.

PARLIAMENT OF PARIS was instituted by Philip Augustus II., 1190, and was made the chief court of justice in France by Philip IV.; at his suggestion it revoked a bull of pope Boniface VIII., 1302. It was suppressed by Louis XV., 1771; restored by Louis XVI., 1774; demanded a meeting of the states-general in 1787; and was suspended by the national assembly, 3 Nov. 1789; see *Commune*.

PARLIAMENTARY AND MUNICIPAL REGISTRATION ACTS (41 & 42 Vict. c. 26), passed 22 July, 1878.

PARMA (N. Italy), founded by the ancient Etrurians. It took part with the Lombard league in the wars with the German emperors. It was made a duchy (with Placentia), 1545. Population of Parma and Modena, 1890, 1,034,712; 1901, 616,929.

United to Spain by Philip V.'s marriage with Elizabeth Farnese 1714

Battle near Parma; the confederates, England, France, and Spain, against the emperor; both armies claimed the victory . . 29 June, 1734

Battle near the Trebbia; the French under Macdonald, defeated by Suwarrow, with the loss of 10,000 men and four generals . . . . 19 June, 1799

The duke of Parma made king of Etruria . Feb. 1801

Parma united to France: with Placentia and Guastalla conferred on Maria Louisa, ex-empress, by treaty of Fontainebleau . . . . 5 April, 1814

Parma occupied by the Austrians and Sardinians in the war of 1848

The Sardinians retire after the battle of Novara, 23 March, 1849

The duke Charles II. abdicates in favour of his son, Charles III. (died 17 April, 1883) . 14 March, ,,

Charles III. stabbed by an assassin,* 26 March, dies, 27 March, 1854

Robert I., a minor (born 9 July, 1848); whose mother becomes regent.

[See *Bulgaria*, 1893.]

War in Italy; the Parmesans establish a provisional government; the duchess-regent retires to Switzerland . . . . 1 May, 1859

Farina became dictator . . . . 18 Aug. ,,

Annexation to Sardinia voted . . . . 12 Sept. ,,

Col. Anviti, a former obnoxious police minister, having rashly returned, cruelly murdered by the mob . . . . 5 Oct. ,,

Parma is now part of the province of Æmilia in the kingdom of Italy, to which it was annexed by decree after a plebiscite . . . 18 March, 1860

Duchess-regent died . . . . . . 1 Feb. 1864

PARNELLITES, the followers of Mr. Charles Stewart Parnell, the principal leader of the more energetic section of the home-rule party, 1880 *et seq.* He was born 28 June, 1846, elected M.P. for co. Meath, 1875-80; for Cork, 1880-91; became Irish parliamentary leader, with great influence, which he lost greatly, Nov. 1890; he died suddenly near Brighton, 6 Oct. 1891; solemn funeral at Dublin, 11 Oct. 1891; his "Life," by R. Barry O'Brien, Nov. 1898; his mother, Mrs. Delia Parnell, died 27 March, 1898. Mr. John Howard Parnell, M.P., city marshal of Dublin in 1897 *et seq.* See *Home Rule* and *Ireland*, 1879 *et seq.*, *and below*.

The *Times* publishes a series of articles headed "PARNELLISM AND CRIME," 7, 10, 14 March, 1887 *et seq.*; the third series published June, 1887, related to the Clan-na-gael, based upon statements in *United Ireland* (Dublin), *Irish World* (New York), and other papers. The *Times* published the *facsimile* of a letter alleged to be signed by Mr. Parnell (dated 15 May, 1882), in which he is made to say "though I regret the accident of lord Cavendish's death, I cannot refuse to admit that Burke got no more than his deserts," 18 April, 1887. This letter Mr. Parnell in parliament termed an "anonymous fabrication" . . . . . 1 a.m., 19 April, 1887

Mr. Frank Hugh O'Donnell *v.* Mr. John Walter and others (for libel in the *Times*, "Parnellism and Crime"), damages claimed 50,000*l.*, Queen's Bench Division, no case; verdict for the defendants . . . . 2–5 July, 1888

Royal commission to examine into the authenticity of charges against certain Irish members of parliament . . . . 17 Sept. ,,

The court of session, Edinburgh, dismisses Mr. Parnell's action against the *Times* 23 Oct. 1888 and 5 Feb. 1889

Mr. Parnell moves for a trial in the exchequer division, Dublin (afterwards stopped) 11 Feb. ,,

Mr. Parnell's action against the *Times* in London deferred till Michaelmas sessions . . 18 June, ,,

PARNELLITE COMMISSION.

Sir James Hannen, president; Mr. justice Day and Mr. justice A. L. Smith, constituted by act passed 13 Aug. 1888. Preliminary meeting: sir C. Russell, Mr. Asquith, and others counsel for Mr. Parnell and other M.P.'s (65); attorney-general sir Richard Webster, Mr. W. Graham and others for the *Times*, 17 Sept. 1888; proceedings begin 22 Oct. 1888. Long examination of witnesses; examination of Mr. Parnell's alleged letters, 14 Feb. 1889; after the evidence and cross-examination of Mr. Soames, solicitor, and Mr. Macdonald, manager of the *Times*, and of Mr. Houston, from whom the alleged letters were obtained, Mr. Richard Pigott, Irish journalist, who had sold them to Mr. Houston, on cross-examination by sir Charles Russell, grossly prevaricated . . . . . 20–22 Feb. 1889

Mr. Pigott fled to Paris, and his confession that he forged some of the alleged letters, and had given false evidence, was read in the court, 27 Feb. (57th sitting); the attorney-general on behalf of the *Times* accepted the confession and expressed deep regret for the publication of the letters, 27 Feb., which was confirmed by the *Times* 28 Feb. ,,

Suicide of Richard Pigott at Madrid, 1 March; buried there . . . . . . 6 March, ,,

Long address of sir C. Russell ends . 12 April, ,,

Patrick Malloy sentenced to 6 months' hard labour for perjury before the commission . 15 April, ,,

On examination Mr. Parnell denies all complicity with crime . . . . . 30 April–8 May, ,,

Examination of archbishop Walsh and other priests 8 May *et seq.* ,,

91st to 100th sitting, Mr. T. Sexton and other M.P.'s examined . . . . . 18 June–4 July, ,,

101st sitting: Michael Davitt examined . 4 July, ,,

106th sitting: Mr. Houston, secretary of the "Loyal and Patriotic Union" (established in 1885), states that in 1885 he purchased the copyright of "Parnellism Unmasked" (by Richard Pigott). The court refuses to accede to the application of sir C. Russell to inspect the books of the "Loyal and Patriotic Union" . 12 July, ,,

107th sitting: Mr. Parnell and his friends with their counsel withdraw from the case . 15 July, ,,

112th sitting: examination of the Land League account books and documents [important books lost]: adjournment to 24 Oct. . . 25 July, ,,

113th sitting, 24 Oct.: speech by Mr. Biggar. Mr. M. Davitt began an address which was finished . . . . 31 Oct. ,,

118th to 128th sitting: Sir Henry James' address for the *Times* . . . . . 31 Oct.–22 Nov. ,,

The report of the commissioners was laid before parliament, 13 Feb. 1890. The following is an abridgment of their conclusions:—I. That the respondent members of parliament collectively were not guilty of conspiring for the absolute independence of Ireland as a separate nation, but that some of them (Messrs. M. Harris, Dillon, W. O'Brien, W. Redmond, O'Connor, J. Condon, and J. J. O'Kelly), together with Mr. Davitt, established the Land League mainly for that purpose. II. That the respondents [44] did conspire to promote agrarian agitation, the non-payment of rents, and the expulsion of the landlords (styled the English garrison). III. That they acquitted Mr. Parnell and others of the charge of insincerity in their denunciations of the Phœnix Park murders, and affirmed the fac-simile letter to be a forgery. IV. They found that the respondents did disseminate the *Irish World* and other newspapers, intending to incite to sedition and other crimes. V. That the charges of incitement to crime, except by intimidation, and of payments for that purpose, were not proved. VI. They found that the respondents did not denounce the system of intimidation, though they knew its effects; and VII. That they defended persons charged with agrarian crime, and supported their families, but it was not proved that they subscribed for testimonials for, or were intimately associated with, notorious criminals, or aided their escape by payments. VIII. That they found that the respondents made payments to compensate persons injured in the commission of crime. IX. That the respondents did invite and obtain the assurance and co-operation of the Physical Force Party in America, including the Clan-na-Gael, and did not repudiate the action of that party.

[Certain allegations against Mr. Parnell were declared not proved.]

The report adopted with thanks, by the commons, after 7 days' debate, 3–11 March; by the lords (without a division), 21 March, 1890. Mr. Gladstone's amendment rejected by 339 to 268.

Parnell *v.* Walter and another, for libel, Queen's bench division, justices Denman and Wills; damages claimed, 100,000*l.*; 40*s.* paid into court,

* Antonio Carra, in revenge of a private injury, and on behalf of the *Giovane Italiane*. He was acquitted through a flaw in the evidence, and died in Philadelphia Aug. 1887.

11 Jan. Verdict for the plaintiff, by consent, 5000*l.* damages . . . . . 3 Feb. 1890

[The publication voted not a breach of privilege by the commons (260—212), 11 Feb. 1890.]

In consequence of the issue of the divorce suit, capt. O'Shea, Mrs. O'Shea, and Mr. C. S. Parnell, 15–17 Nov. 1890, Mr. Parnell was requested by Mr. W. E. Gladstone and other English liberals to retire from the chairmanship of the Irish party. He declined, and issued a manifesto to the people of Ireland, giving an account of private conferences with Mr. Gladstone and Mr. John Morley, 29 Nov. The Irish R.C. bishops demanded Mr. Parnell's retirement, 3 Dec. After a week's angry discussion in the commons' committee-room No. 15, the Irish party divided; Mr. Justin M'Carthy, the vice-chairman, was elected chairman by 44 members; Mr. Parnell continuing chairman with 26 followers, 6 Dec. Manifestoes of the two parties issued . . . 9, 10 Dec. ,,

Collapse of negotiations (chiefly at Boulogne) of Mr. Parnell with Messrs. Wm. O'Brien, Dillon, Justin M'Carthy, Sexton, and others; Mr. Parnell refuses to resign the leadership, 11 Feb.; counter manifestoes issued . 12 Feb. *et seq.* 1891

Dispute between Mr. Parnell and Mr. M'Carthy respecting the disposal of the league funds (in Paris) . . . . Feb., March, ,,

Mr. Parnell in his campaign visits Roscommon, 22 Feb., Drogheda, and other places 1 March, *et seq.* ,,

The National Federation (*which see*) established by the Anti-Parnellites . . . . . 10 March, ,,

9 Parnellites (Mr. John Redmond, leader), 72 Anti-Parnellites (Mr. Justin M'Carthy, leader). elected M.P. . . . . July, 1892

Mr. Gladstone and lord Tweedmouth each give 100*l.* to "Irish Parliamentary Fund," in answer to an appeal, 22 Aug.; this leads to dissension in the Irish party . . . . . . Aug., Sept. 1894

Great meeting of Parnellites at Dublin, Mr. John Redmond, M.P., president . . . . 8 Oct. ,,

The Paris funds placed in the hands of Mr. Justin M'Carthy . . . . Oct. ,,

Disputes among the anti-Parnellites . . . Jan. 1895

Mr. Justin M'Carthy resigns the chairmanship of the party; succeeded by Mr. Dillon, Mr. Sexton declining . . . . . 18 Feb. 1896

The anti-Parnellites vote for the conservative education bill . . . . 12 May, ,,

PAROCHIAL CHARITIES COMMISSION, see *London*, 1878, and under *Charities*, 1883.

PARRICIDE. There was no law against it in Athens or Rome, such a crime not being supposed possible. About 172 B.C., L. Ostius having killed his father, the Romans scourged the parricide; sewed him up in a leathern sack made air-tight, with a live dog, a cock, a viper, and an ape, and thus cast him into the sea. Miss Blandy was executed at Oxford for the murder of her father, April, 1752; see *Trials*, March, 1890.

PARSEES or GUEBRES, the followers of Zaradusht, called by the Greeks Zoroaster, who is doubtfully said to have lived before sixth century B.C. (see *Magi*), dwelt in Persia till 638, when, at the battle of Kadseah, their army was decimated by the Arabs, and the monarchy annihilated at the battle of Náhávend in 641. Many submitted to the conquerors, but others fled to India, and their descendants still reside at Bombay (where they are termed Parsees). Sir Jamsetjee Jejeebhoy, the 3rd baronet, was elected president of the community there, July, 1877. Mr. Dadabhai Naoroji, a Parsee merchant, was for several years professor of Gujerati at University college, London. He was nominated as M.P. for the Holborn district, but not elected, 1886; elected 6 July, 1892, for Central Finsbury; visits Bombay, Dec. 1893. "History of the Parsis," by Dosabhai Framji Karaka, published, 1884. See *Bombay*. A Parsee fire temple at Bombay was consecrated, Nov. 1891.

Cowverbai, an eminent scholar, promoter of native female education, the mother of Mr. M. M. Bhownaggree, M.P. for N.E. Bethnal-green (1895), died, aged 65, at Bombay, 6 Feb. 1896.

Death of Bai Motlibai Wadia, great benefactress to Bombay, aged 87, 15 June, 1897.

Sir Dinshaw Manockjee Petit, a noble benefactor, died at Bombay, aged 78, 5 May, 1901.

"PARTANT POUR LA SYRIE," popular French song; words by comte Alexandre de Laborde; music by Hortense Beauharnais, wife of Louis Bonaparte, king of Holland, about 1809. The music became very popular after her son became emperor, in 1852, as Napoleon III.

PARTHENON (from Greek *parthenos*, virgin), a temple at Athens dedicated to Minerva, erected about 442 B.C. In it Phidias placed his renowned statue of that goddess, 438 B.C. The roof was destroyed by the Venetians in 1687. Ruinous state of the building through earthquakes, described *Times*, 14 Aug. 1897. "The Parthenon" published by Mr. James Fergusson in 1883. See *Elgin Marbles*.

PARTHENOPEAN REPUBLIC was established by the French at Naples (anciently called Parthenope), 23 Jan. 1799, and overthrown in June same year.

PARTHIA (Asia). The Parthians were originally a tribe of Scythians, who, being exiled, as their name implies, from their own country, settled near Hyrcania. Arsaces laid the foundation of an empire which ultimately extended over a large part of Asia, 250 B.C.; the Parthians were never wholly subdued by the Romans. The last king, Artabanus V., was killed, A.D. 226; and his territories were annexed to the new kingdom of Persia founded by Artaxerxes, who had revolted against Parthia.

PARTICULARISTS. The name given to those Germans who desire the maintenance of the independence of the German states, and oppose their absorption into the empire. M. Gasser, one of them, failed in an attempt to form a ministry in Bavaria, Sept. 1872. Particularism revived during the election in 1893.

PARTITION ACT, relative to the division of property sold by direction of the court of chancery, passed 25 June, 1688.

PARTITION TREATIES. The first treaty between England and Holland for regulating the Spanish succession (declaring the elector of Bavaria next heir, and ceding provinces to France) was signed 19 Aug. 1698; and the second (between France, England, and Holland, declaring the archduke Charles presumptive heir of the Spanish monarchy, Joseph Ferdinand having died in 1699), 13 March, 1700. Treaty for the partition of Poland; the first was a secret convention between Russia and Prussia, 17 Feb. 1772; the second between the same powers and Austria, 5 Aug. same year; the third was between Russia, Austria, and Prussia, 24 Oct. 1795.

PARTNERSHIP. The laws respecting it were amended in 1863 and 1890; see *Limited Liability*.

PARTY, see *Processions*.

PASIGRAPHY (from Greek, *pasi*, for all):

a system which professes to teach people to communicate with each other by means of numbers which convey the same ideas in all languages. A society for this purpose was established at Munich; and the president, Anton Bachmaier, published a dictionary and grammar for German, French, and English, 1868–71; 4334 mental conceptions may be thus communicated.

PASQUINADES. Small satirical poems obtained this name about 1533.

At the stall of a cobbler named Pasquin, at Rome, idle persons used to assemble to listen to his sallies, to relate anecdotes, and rail at the passers-by. After the cobbler's death, his name was given to a statue to which lampoons were affixed.

PASSAROWITZ TREATY, concluded 21 July, 1718, between Germany and Venice, and the Turks, by which the house of Austria ceded certain commercial rights, and obtained from Turkey the Temeswar, Belgrade, and part of Bosnia, Servia, and Wallachia. The Turks gained the Morea.

PASSAU (Germany), TREATY OF, whereby religious freedom was established, was ratified between the emperor Charles V. and the protestant princes of Germany, 31 July, 1552. In 1662 the cathedral and great part of Passau were consumed by fire.

PASSENGERS—by public vehicles, are protected by 1 & 2 Will. IV. c. 22 (1831), 1 & 2 Vict. c. 79 (1838), and 16 & 17 Vict. c. 33 (1853); another act was passed in 1889. Mr. Cleghorn, under whom the front seat on the near side of one of the general omnibus company's carriages had given way, recovered 400*l.* damages against the company, in a verdict by consent, in the Queen's bench, 10 Dec. 1856. The Ships' Passenger act, 18 & 19 Vict. c. 119, passed in 1855, was amended in 1863; see *Campbell's Act*, and under *Railways*.

PASSIONISTS, a congregation of clerks of the holy cross, founded by St. Paul of the Cross, who died 1775, and was canonized by the pope 1867. A home was set up in England in 1841, and others since. The monastery, Highgate, London, N., solemnly blessed by cardinal Manning, and opened, 16 July, 1876.

PASSION PLAY, see *Drama*.

PASSION-WEEK, the name given since the Reformation to the week preceding Easter, was formerly applied to the fortnight. Archbishop Laud says the two weeks were so called "for a thousand years together," and refers to an epistle, by Ignatius, in the 1st century, in which the practice is said to have been "observed by all." The week preceding Easter is now by some termed "Holy Week," the previous week "Passion Week."

PASSION-MUSIC: Gregory Nazianzen (A.D. 330-390) is said to have first set forth the history of the Passion in a dramatic form.

Guidetti, in 1586, published music for this subject, which has been treated since by many composers.

J. S. Bach's great "Passion Musik," first performed on Good Friday, 1729, has been revived with great success in this country, beginning with that "according to St. Matthew," 6 April, 1854; performed annually at St. Paul's on Tuesday in Holy Week.

PASSIVE RESISTANCE, the term used by the opponents of the Education act, 1902, in justification of their action in refusing to pay the rate levied for education on the alleged ground that the act gi es an unfair advantage to the schools of the established church, and to its doctrinal teaching in the supported schools. Early in the spring of 1903 many nonconformists in the neighbourhood of London and in the provinces refusing, as they stated, on conscientious grounds to pay the rate their goods were seized and sold. Much agitation has resulted and still (Nov. 1903) continues, see Education Acts 1902, 1903 in *Addenda*.

PASSMORE EDWARDS' SETTLEMENT, Tavistock-square, St. Pancras, founded by Mr. Passmore Edwards with a gift of 15,000*l.*, the duke of Bedford 1500*l.*, to promote education, &c., partially used since 9 Oct. 1897; opened by Mr. John Morley, lord Peel in the chair, 12 Feb. 1898. See *Li raries*.

The Passmore Edwards-hall, built for the London university school of economics (Mr. Passmore Edwards gave 11,000*l.*, lord Rothschild 5000*l.*; site granted by the London County Council) in Clare market, Strand; opened by Lord Rosebery . . . . 29 May, 1902

A summer vacation school started here by Mrs. Humphry Ward with great success; meeting held, Mr. Haldane, M.P., Mr. Buxton, M.P., lord Grey, the bishop of Hereford present . . 5 Aug. „

PASSOVER, the most solemn festival of the Jews, instituted 1491 B.C. (*Exodus* xii.) in commemoration of their coming out of Egypt; because the night before their departure, the destroying angel, who put to death the firstborn of the Egyptians, *passed over* the houses of the Hebrews without entering them; the door posts being marked with the blood of the Paschal Lamb killed the evening before. The passover was celebrated in the new temple, 18 April, 515 B.C. *Usher*.

PASSPORT SYSTEM forbids subjects to quit one country or enter another without the consent of the sovereign thereof. In 1858 the system was somewhat changed in this country, and the stamp duty on passports was reduced from 5*s.* to 6*d.* Passports were abolished in Norway in 1859; in Sweden in 1860; and (with regard to British subjects) in France, 16 Dec. 1860; in Italy, 26 June, 1862; in Portugal, 23 Jan. 1863; and are falling into disuse in other countries. The passport system was *established* in the United States on 19 Aug. 1861. The passport system, revived in France on account of the war, 1 Aug. 1870, was abolished by M. Thiers, 10 April, 1872, in compliance with the wish of the British government.

PASTEUR INSTITUTE, Paris, see under *Hydrophobia*. The remains of M. Pasteur (died 28 Sept. 1895) transferred from Notre Dame to a crypt in the institute, 26 Dec. 1896.

PASTEL, a roll of paste made of different colours ground with gum water, used as a crayon. Pastel painting has been recently much practised on the continent. The Society of British Pastellists, president sir Coutts Lindsay, first exhibited at the Grosvenor gallery, 18 Oct. 1890. Its members included Mr. Watts, Mr. Orchardson, and other eminent artists. Another started, exhibition at the Royal institute, Piccadilly, opened, 4 Feb. 1899.

PASTON LETTERS, the correspondence of a Norfolk family, 1422–83, giving a picture of social life in England, were edited by sir John Fenn, and published in five volumes, quarto, 1787–1823. Their authenticity was questioned Sept. 1865, but was satisfactorily vindicated by a committee of the Society cf Antiquaries in May, 1866.

Part of the MS. was soon after purchased by the trustees of the British Museum. The publication of a new edition, by James Gairdner, with additional letters, 1872–5. The MS. of the second series with other letters was found in 1875, by Mr. Frere, of Roydon Hall, near Diss, Norfolk. The MS. of the first series, long lost from the Royal Library, found in the library of col. Geo. Tomline at Orwell Park, who died 25 Aug. 1889; announced April, 1890.

311 MS. Paston letters put up for sale by Messrs. Christie, London, bought in at a high reserve, 31 July, 1888

PATAY (France), where Joan of Arc, the maid of Orleans, was present, when the earl of Richemonte signally defeated the English, 18 June, 1429. Talbot was taken prisoner, and the valiant Fastolfe was forced to flee. In consequence, Charles VII. of France entered Rheims in triumph, and was crowned 17 July, following year, Joan of Arc assisting in the ceremony in full armour, and holding the sword of state, see *Joan of Arc*.

PATENTS (from *pateo*, I lie open), licences and authorities granted by the king. Patents are said to have been granted for titles of nobility in 1344, by Edward III. They were first granted for the exclusive privilege of printing books, in 1591. The property and right of inventors in arts and manufactures were secured by letters patent by an act passed in 1623. The later laws regulating patents are very numerous; among them are 5 & 6 Will. IV. c. 83 (1835), and 15 & 16 Vict. c. 83 (1852). By the latter COMMISSIONERS OF PATENTS were appointed, viz., the lord chancellor, the master of the rolls, the attorney-general for England and Ireland, the lord advocate, and the solicitors-general for England, Scotland, and Ireland. In 1853, a journal was published under their authority, and indexes of patents, from March, 1617, to the present time. Specifications of patents may be consulted by the public at the Free Library and Reading-room, in Southampton-buildings, opened 5 March, 1854. A museum containing models, portraits, &c., was established in 1859 at South Kensington, mainly by the exertions of Mr. Bennet Woodcroft.

The "Illustrated Official Journal," combining six others published Jan. 1889.

An international congress for the protection of patents met at Vienna, Aug. 1873; at Paris, 6 March, 1883.

New patent bills introduced into parliament withdrawn, 1875, 1876, 1879; another read, 15 June, 1881.

Patent Design and Trade Marks Act, 46 & 47 Vict. c. 57, passed 25 Aug. 1883, began 1 Jan. 1884; amended 24 Dec. 1888. It greatly relieved patentees by lessening fees, &c.

In 1864, the alleged defalcations of Mr. Edmunds, a clerk in the patent office and an official of the house of lords, led to his retirement. He obtained a pension of 800*l*., which was taken from him by a vote of the house of lords on 9 May, 1865. Much litigation ensued. In an action against Mr. Gladstone, the prime minister, and others, for a libel, Mr. Edmunds was non-suited, 21, 22 June, 1872; and he failed in actions against several newspapers for printing a treasury minute. His appeal to the house of lords failed 16 June, 1873.

17,110 applications for patents in 1884; 16,101 in 1885; 17,162 in 1886; 18,051 in 1887; 19,103 in 1888; 21,008, 1889; 22,888, 1891; 24,169, 1892; 25,123, 1893; 25,386, 1894; 30,194, 1896; 30,958, 1897; 27,649, 1898; 25,800, 1899; 23,924, 1900; 26,777, 1901; 28,976, 1902.

Royal commission to enquire into the law relating to letters patent appointed 1862; Mr. Hindmarch's report issued 1864. In pursuance of recommendations for the formation of a roll of patent agents, the Institute of Patent Agents was registered 1882, chartered 1891. It has given much attention to legislation respecting patents.

New Patent Office facing Staple-inn, completed in 1897.

Patent Law Amendment bill passed, 1 Dec. 1902.

PATENT MEDICINES: received for stamps, year 1883-4, 159,238*l*.

PATHOLOGY, the science of disease, much studied with experiments in the present century, and said to be advanced by vivisection. Wilks and Moxon, Wagner, Cornil and Ranvier, Payne, Hamilton, Virchow ("Cellular Pathology," 1856; he died 5 Sept. 1902), Koch. Pasteur, Lister, and Paget are eminent pathologists. The Pathological society in London was founded, 1846.

Prof. D. J. Hamilton's *Text-book of Pathology* published, 1894.

Pathological institute at the London hospital, opened by sir H. Roscoe, 10 July, 1901.

PATHOMETER, an instrument to record automatically the distance travelled by a vehicle, also the various directions followed, and the hills ascended or descended; reported, Jan. 1899.

PATNA (N. India). Near here the English, under major Carnac, defeated the emperor Shah Alum on 15 Jan. 1761. The town was acquired by the British by their defeat of the sanguinary Meer Cassim, 23 Oct. 1764. Population, 1901, 135,172.

PATRIARCHS (a name given to Abraham, Isaac, Jacob, and his sons). The ecclesiastical historian Socrates gives this title to the chiefs of Christian dioceses, about 440. It was first conferred on the five grand sees of Rome, Constantinople, Alexandria, Antioch, and Jerusalem. The Latin church had no patriarchs till the 6th century. The first founders or heads of religious orders are called patriarchs.

Nectarius, bishop of Constantinople, as *ex-officio* chief of the Eastern bishops, was nominated patriarch of Constantinople at the second general council of Constantinople, 9 July, 381. This led the way to the schism between the Eastern and Western churches.

PATRICIANS, the highest citizens or aristocracy of Rome; their authority began with the city itself; see *Rome*.

PATRICK'S CATHEDRAL, ST. (Dublin), was founded in 1190 by archbishop Comyn, on the site of an old church. The cathedral was desecrated in 1546, and used as a law court; restored 1553. After renovation by the munificence of the late sir Benjamin Lee Guinness, it was re-opened 24 Feb. 1865. Several persons killed by the falling of a flying buttress, 14 Sept. 1882. See *Dublin*.

PATRICK, ST., KNIGHTS OF, an order instituted by king George III., 5 Feb., the statutes were signed 28 Feb. 1783. The number, originally fifteen, was increased in 1821, 1831, and 1833, and is now twenty-two. The prince of Wales was installed as knight, 18 April, 1868.—St. Patrick's Benevolent Society, London, instituted 1784. It sprang from the Irish Charitable Society, founded in 1704. See *Shamrock*.

PATRIOTIC ASSOCIATION, formed to aid in upholding the honour and interest of the British Empire. A meeting was held at St. James's hall, London, 27 March, 1880. "England," a weekly paper, was published same day. The duke of Abercorn, earl Stanhope, and others, were supporters.

PATRIOTIC BROTHERHOOD, see *Ireland*, 1883.

PATRIOTIC FUNDS, established to encourage the army and navy in times of war.

1. Founded by the subscribers to Lloyd's, "to animate the efforts of our defenders by sea and land" by providing a fund for the relief of themselves when wounded, and of their widows and orphans, and for granting pecuniary rewards and badges of distinction for valour and merit, 20 July, 1803: 24 Aug. 1809, 424,832*l.* had been received, and 331,611*l.* expended. From 1803 to 1826 the total sum received was 629,823*l.* 14*s.* 1*d.*

2. A commission (headed by prince Albert) was appointed to raise and distribute a fund bearing this name, for the relief of the families of those who might fall in the Russo-Turkish war, June; a great meeting held Nov. 1854.

Large sums were collected from this country and the colonies, amounting to 1,171,270*l.* in July, 1855; to 1,296,282*l.* on 16 Nov. 1855; finally to 1,460,861*l.* In Jan. 1874, 1,303,386*l.* expended.

200,000*l.* appropriated to founding an asylum for 300 orphan girls (the Royal Victoria Patriotic Asylum) on Wandsworth common, the first stone of which was laid by the queen, 11 July, 1857.

The royal family and many of the aristocracy contributed drawings, sold for high prices, in May, 1855.

3. A large fund contributed for the relief of the sufferers by the Indian mutiny, Aug. 1857, 434,729*l.* collected up to Nov. 1858. An act for its administration was passed, 12 Aug. 1867, amended 1886; see *India*, 1857.

The total of the funds administered was 755,102*l.*, 31 Dec. 1888; 764,211*l.*, 31 Dec. 1890; 774,606*l.* Dec. 1892.

The alleged mal-administration of the Patriotic Fund was brought before the house of commons by baron de Worms 9 Aug. 1880, and in Jan. 1881.

Liberal subscriptions to the fund from Australia, on account of the Soudan war; about 45,000*l.* at Sydney . . . . . . 2 March, 1885

Total capital of the fund, 881,167*l.*; expenditure, 41,877*l.*, 31 Dec. 1895; 892,068*l.* 6*s.* 7*d.*; expenditure, 42,141*l.* 17*s.* 3*d.*, 31 Dec. 1897; 1,263,208*l.* 4*s.* 9*d.*; expenditure, 84,272*l.* 16*s.* 6*d.*, 31 Dec. 1900; receipts of the Transvaal war fund, 479,377*l.*; expenditure, 1901, 93,862*l.*; total expenditure, 1854–1901, 2,921,139*l.*

Royal commission on the fund met in London, 6 Jan. 1898; 36th report, blue book issued, July, 1898; 40th report, for year ending July, 1902, issued, 12 Aug. 1902.

Scheme for merging all funds for the relief of soldiers, sailors, and their families into a new patriotic fund, proposed by the duke of Cambridge, 8 Jan. 1901.

3,399*l.* 18*s.* presented by the children of Canada to the queen; handed over by her wish to this fund, Jan. 1901.

Patriotic volunteer fund instituted by lord mayor Whitehead, see *Volunteers* 1889

Patriotic fund act, royal assent . . . 11 Aug. 1903

PATRONAGE of LIVINGS by Laymen in England is very ancient; in *Scotland* was opposed by the books of discipline 1560 and 1578, abolished 1649, restored 1660. The system led to the disruption of the established church, and the foundation of the free church, 18 May, 1843. The abolition of lay patronage was earnestly advocated by the authorities of the established church in March, 1870, and the duke of Argyll volunteered to resign his patronage in May. Of 1109 livings 319 belonged to the crown, and about 600 to private persons. An act (37 & 38 Vict. c. 82) for abolishing patronage in Scotland, brought in by the duke of Richmond, 18 May, passed, 7 Aug. 1874. In England a church patronage bill (to check sales and give rights to parishioners, &c.), introduced by the archbp. of Canterbury, 13 May, 1886; a bill passed by the lords, 1 April, 1887; another bill read third time, 2 May, 1893; another bill passed committee in the lords, 1895; dropped. See *Benefices*.

PAULIANISTS or PAULINIANS, followers of Paul bishop of Samosata, afterwards patriarch of Antioch, 260, who are said to have denied Christ's divinity and the trinity; he was excommunicated 269 by a council at Antioch.

PAULICIANS, a sect of Christian reformers, arose about 652. Although they were severely persecuted, they spread over Asia Minor, in the 9th century, and finally settled at Montford, in Italy, where they were attacked by the bishop of Milan in 1028. Severe decrees against them were made in 1163, and they gradually dispersed; very probably sowing the seeds of the great reformation of the 16th century.

PAUL JONES, a Scotchman, born 1742; died at Paris, 1792. He commanded an American privateer during the American war, and made daring depredations on British commerce. He pillaged the house of lord Selkirk, near Kirkcudbright, and at Whitehaven burnt shipping in the harbour, April 1778. The Dutch permitted Paul Jones to enter their ports with two British ships of war which he had taken, and which the stadtholder peremptorily refused to deliver up, 1779.

PAUL'S CATHEDRAL, ST. (London). For details of its history, see Dugdale's "History of St. Paul's," 1658 and 1716; Dean Milman's "Annals of St. Paul's," 1868; and Mr. Wm. Longman's "History of the Three Cathedrals, dedicated to St. Paul," 1873. Many royal pageants have taken place in the cathedral.

The first church, built on the site of a temple to Diana, supposed to have been destroyed during the Diocletian persecution (302), rebuilt in the reign of Constantine 223-337

Demolished by the pagan Saxons, and restored by Ethelbert and Sebert . . . . about 597-610

Injured by fire 962

Destroyed by the great conflagration, 1086, after which Mauritius, then bishop of London, commenced a magnificent edifice with the highest spire in the world about 1087; completed . . 1240

Nearly destroyed by fire 1444

The spire burnt 1561

A commission granted to Laud, then bishop of London, to restore the cathedral . 2 April, 1631

It was totally destroyed by the fire of . Sept. 1666

Clearing of the ground began . . . May, 1674

First stone of the present edifice laid . 21 June, 1675

The choir opened for divine worship . 2 Dec. 1697

The whole edifice completed under sir Christopher Wren (except some decorations, finished 1723) . . 1710

[The total cost (including 200 tons' weight of iron railing) was 1,511,202*l.*]

Lord Nelson buried . . . . . . 9 Jan. 1806

Ball and cross restored by Mr. Cockerell . . . 1822

Duke of Wellington buried . . . 18 Nov. 1852

Money having been subscribed to adapt St. Paul's for the purpose, evening services began, under the dome, when above 4000 persons were present, Sunday, 28 Nov. 1858

A national guinea subscription for completing the interior ornamentation, began . . . Feb. 1864

87th meeting of the charity school children 3 June, 1869

Great meeting held at the Mansion-house to complete the interior of the cathedral according to Wren's design, 13 July; 34,708*l.* collected by 4 Nov. 1870

Dr. Church, the new dean, gave 1000*l.* . . Nov. 1871

National thanksgiving for the recovery of the prince of Wales, see *Thanksgiving* . 27 Feb. 1872

"Thanksgiving fund" established . . . . ,,

The queen gave 1000*l.*, the prince 500*l.* . Feb. ,,

After an interval, annual meeting of the children resumed—[not held 1878] . . . 9 Oct. 1873

The iron railings (set up in 1710) sold, and soon after removed (the dean and chapter bought the enclosed space from the corporation), 8 Jan.; formally opened . . . . . . 26 Jan. 1874

Discussion respecting the ornamentation: Mr. Burges' plans censured, June; the engagement with him rescinded . . . . Nov. ,,

Meeting to endeavour to obtain a peal of bells, the lord mayor, the dean, &c., present, 2 Nov. 1875; arrangements being made . . . Sept. 1876

Grand concluding service of Lambeth episcopal synod; about 100 bishops present . 27 July, 1878
Peal of 12 bells (by Taylor, of Loughborough) given by the corporation and some of the companies, dedicated . . . . 1 Nov. ,,
The corporation authorised to deal with the churchyard as an open space, 1878; opened as a garden by the lord mayor . . . . 22 Sept. 1879
Great Paul (see under *Bells*) dedicated . 3 June, 1882
The clock by Langley Bradley, set up in 1708, was replaced by a new clock, designed by lord Grimthorpe, made by Messrs. Smith of Derby, dedicated by dean Gregory . . . . 21 Dec. 1893
Professor Palmer, capt. Gill, and lieut. Charrington buried in the crypt . . . . 6 April, 1883
The mutilated statue of queen Anne at the west front by Francis Bird, 1712; replaced by a new one by R. Belt and others; uncovered by the lord mayor . . . . . . 15 Dec. 1886
Citizen's jubilee service . . . . 23 June, 1887
Lord Napier of Magdala buried . . . 21 Jan. 1890
Memorial of Mr. William Bede Dalley, Australian statesman (the first colonial memorial) unveiled by the earl of Rosebery . . . . 17 July, ,,
"Reconciliation service," on account of the desecration of the cathedral by the suicide of Edward Easton on 28 Sept. . . . . . 13 Oct. ,,
Sir F. Edgar Boehm, sculptor, buried . 20 Dec. ,,
Bust of sir John Macdonald, premier of Canada, unveiled by the earl of Rosebery . 16 Nov. 1892
Continued progress of the decorative work of the dome, &c., by Mr. W. B. Richmond, Mr. Watts, sir Fred. Leighton, Mr. Poynter, Mr. A. Stevens, and Mr. Brittan 1862–95
Sir Frederick (lord) Leighton, died 25 Jan., buried in the crypt (his monument unveiled, 19 Feb. 1902) . . . . . . 3 Feb. 1896
The fine mosaics in the choir, designed by Mr. W. B. Richmond (K.C.B., 1897), and executed under his direction by English workmen, dedicated, 4 April, ,,
Sir John Everett Millais, died 13 Aug., buried in the crypt . . . . . . 20 Aug. ,,
Death of the rev. Wm. Sparrow Simpson, librarian and historian of St. Paul's, 1861 *et seq.* 28 March, 1897
George C. Martin, organist, knt. . . . June, ,,
Masonic commemoration of the opening of the new cathedral (1697) . . . . 2 Dec. ,,
Sir Arthur Sullivan, composer, died 22 Nov.; buried in the crypt . . . . . 27 Nov. 1900
Memorial services for soldiers and sailors of the empire killed in South Africa, 19 Dec. 1900; and 16 Dec. 1901
Mandell Creighton, bishop of London, buried here, 17 Jan. ,,
National memorial service on the death of queen Victoria . . . . . . 2 Feb. ,,
Memorial service for Mr. Cecil Rhodes (see *Rhodesia*), thousands unable to get in, as the church was full . . . . . . 10 April, 1902
The chancel, dome, nave and crypt lit by electricity (the gift of Mr. Pierpont Morgan, begun, 1899) . . . . . . 18 May, ,,
Thanksgiving for the conclusion of peace in South Africa; the king and queen present . 8 June, ,,
Illness of the king, 24 June; intercessory services, 26, 29 June; thanksgiving for his recovery, 10 Aug.; again the king and queen present, 26 Oct. ,,

See *Reredos*, 1891.

DIMENSIONS.

	feet.
Length of St. Paul's from the grand portico to east end	510
Breadth, north to south portico	282
Exterior diameter of the dome	145
Height from ground to top of cross	404
[Stated by surveyor to be 365 feet from the pavement.]	
Campaniles, or bell towers, at each corner, height	208
Breadth of western entrance	189
Circumference of dome	420
Entire circumference of the building	2292
Diameter of ball	6

PAUL'S CROSS, ST. (London), which stood at the north side of the cathedral, was a pulpit formed of wood, mounted upon steps of stone, and covered with lead, from which the most eminent divines were appointed to preach every Sunday in the forenoon. To this place the court, the mayor, the aldermen, and principal citizens used to resort. It was in use as early as 1259, and was appropriated not only to preaching, but to political and ecclesiastical discourses, &c. The cross was demolished in 1643, by order of the parliament.

PAUL'S SCHOOL, ST., was endowed in 1512 by John Colet, dean of St. Paul's, for 153 boys "of every nation, country, and class," in memory of the number of fishes taken by Peter (*John* xxi. 11). The first schoolhouse was burnt in 1666; the second, by Wren, was taken down in 1824, and another building erected by George Smith. William Lilly was the first master, and his grammar is still used by the school. *Timbs.* The claim of the Mercers' company to be owners instead of trustees of Colet's estate was set aside by the vice chancellor, 11 Feb. 1870. The school ordered to be removed to West Kensington; site bought, June, 1878. New building designed by Mr. Waterhouse opened by lord Selborne, 23 April, 1884. The number of scholars has been increased. New schemes for the management of the school were issued by the charity commissioners, 1876, 1879, and 1893; after much discussion and opposition a scheme was sent to the committee of council of education for approval, May, 1894; finally modified, July, 1894; new arrangement, Feb. 1899; further arrangement, 16 June, 1900, under which scheme it is now governed.

St. Paul's Industrial School, Mile End, ordered to be closed by the home secretary in consequence of serious charges against the managers; brought forward by Mrs. Surr, member of the metropolitan School Board, Nov.; she is warmly commended in the home secretary's letter, 15 Nov.; who remitted the case to the public prosecutor . Nov. 1881
Mr. T. Scrutton, manager, sued Miss Helen Taylor, and obtained 1000*l.* for damages; the charges were withdrawn . . . . 30 June, 1882

PAUPERS, see *Poor*.

PAVAN, Pavane, or Pavin, was a slow dance of the 16th and 17th centuries, sometimes accompanied by singing.

PAVEMENT. The Carthaginians are said to have been the first who paved their towns with stones. The Romans, in the time of Augustus, had pavement in many of their streets; the Appian way, a paved road, was constructed 312 B.C. In England there were few paved streets before Henry VII.'s reign. London was first paved about 1533. It was paved with flagstones between 1815 and 1825. Wood and asphalte paving were tried in 1839, and have been disused since 1847; see *Wood Pavement*. Asphalte has been much used since 1869. Wood reported to be the best for London, May, 1876.

Grano-metallic stone laid down in a plastic state in part of the Strand, London, and in other places, 1885
Tarred macadam, as a new and durable pavement at Hamilton, Ontario, reported successful, Nov. 1900

PAVIA (N. Italy), the ancient *Ticinum* or *Papia*. Its university, founded by Charlemagne, is said to be the oldest in Europe. Pavia was built by the Gauls, who were driven out by the Romans, and these in their turn were expelled by the Goths: in 568 it was taken by the Lombards, and became the capital of their kingdom. In the 12th century it was erected into a republic, but soon after was subjected to Milan and followed its fortunes. On 24 Feb. 1525, a battle was fought near here between the French and the Imperialists, when the former were defeated, and their king, Francis I., after fighting with heroic valour, and killing seven men with his own hand, was at last obliged to surrender himself a prisoner. It was long asserted that Francis wrote to his mother, Louisa of Savoy, regent of the kingdom during his absence, saying, *Tout est perdu, madame, fors l'honneur* (All is lost, madam, except honour). The words are now said to have been, *L'honneur et la vie qui est saulvé.*

PAWNBROKING. The Roman emperors lent money upon land. The origin of borrowing money by means of pledges deposited with lenders is referred to Perugia, in Italy, about 1462. The institutions were termed *monti di pietà* (*which see*). Soon afterwards it is said that the bishop of Winchester established a system of lending on pledges, but without interest. The business of pawnbrokers was regulated in 1756, and licences issued in 1783. The rate of interest on pledges was fixed in 1800. In London there were, in 1851, 334 pawnbrokers; and in England, exclusively of London, 1127; the number is increasing more than in proportion to the population. In 1860 an act was passed enabling pawnbrokers to charge a halfpenny for every ticket describing things pledged for a sum under 5*s*. The acts relating to pawnbrokers were amended in 1856, 1859, 1860. Pawnbrokers in Great Britain: 1851, 1873; in 1861, 2578; in 1871, 3540. The law was consolidated in the pawnbrokers' act passed 10 Aug. 1872.

PAX, a small tablet, generally silver, termed, *tabula pacis* or *osculatorium*, kissed by the Roman Catholic priests and laity; substituted for the primeval kiss of peace in the early church. The pax is said to have been introduced about the 12th century.

PAYMASTER-GENERAL. In 1836 the army and navy pay departments were consolidated into the paymaster-general's-office, sometimes held by a cabinet minister.

PAYMENT of M.P.'s, see *Parliament*, 1893, 1895. They are paid in the United States, N.A., and in some of our colonies.

PEABODY FUND. Mr. George Peabody, an American merchant (born 18 Feb. 1795, died 4 Nov. 1869), who had made his fortune in London, gave on 12 March, 1862, 150,000*l.*, on 21 Jan. 1866, 100,000*l.*, on 5 Dec. 1868, 100,000*l.*, and by his will directed his trustees to pay 150,000*l.*—in all 500,000*l.*—to ameliorate the condition of the London poor.

An autograph letter, promising her portrait in miniature, was sent him by the queen, 28 March, 1866

[Inscription on the miniature sent:—"V.R. presented by the Queen to G. Peabody, Esq., the benefactor of the poor of London."]

The first block of buildings for working classes, termed "Peabody dwellings," in Commercial street, Spitalfields, was opened 29 Feb. 1864; and others since, in Spitalfields, Islington, Shadwell, Westminster, Chelsea, Bermondsey, &c.; they have been found to be self-supporting, 1878. In 1879, net gain, 24,786*l.*; 1885, 23,691*l.*; 1887, 24,902*l.*; 1888, 29,611*l.*

Mr. Peabody's statue, at the east end of the Royal Exchange, was inaugurated by the prince of Wales . . . . 23 July, 1869

Funeral service at Westminster abbey . 12 Nov. ,,

Funeral at Portland, U.S., prince Arthur present 8 Feb. 1870

He also gave large sums, for educational purposes, in the United States.

39,763*l.* expended on land and buildings in 1885, making the total expenditure 1,210,550*l.*; 1,250,390*l.* in 1897; 1,285,107*l.* 2*s.* 7*d.* in 1899; 1902, 1,358,173*l.*

Net gains, rent and interest in 1890, 28,656*l.*; in 1894, 29,995*l.* 7*s.* 7*d.*; 1896, 28,787*l.*; 1897, 32,320*l*; 1899, 35,183*l.* 17*s.* 2*d.*; 1902, 32,673*l.*

Centenary of the birth of George Peabody, celebrated at Peabody, Mass., and other places, 18 Feb. 1895.

PEACE. A temple was dedicated to peace by Vespasian, 75; see *Fireworks*, *Treaties*, *Justices*, &c.—"PEACE OF RELIGION" (between catholics and protestants) was signed at Augsburg, 15 Sept. 1555.

A PEACE SOCIETY, founded 1816, for the promotion of universal peace; holds annual meetings; proposed amalgamation with the International Arbitration and Peace association (founded by Mr. Lewis Appleton in 1880), Dec. 1884. The association divided in May, 1886, when the British arbitration association was founded by Mr. Appleton. A congress of the friends of peace, from all parts of the world, commenced its sittings at Paris, 22 Aug. 1849. It met in London at Exeter hall, 30 Oct. following; and at Frankfort, in St. Paul's church, 22 Aug. 1850; at Birmingham, 28 Nov. 1850; and at Exeter hall, 22 July, 1851. A meeting was held at Manchester, 27 Jan. 1853; and at Edinburgh, 12 Oct. 1853; Glasgow, 10 Sept. 1901; London, 20 May, 1902, and . . . . . 20 May, 1903

Mr. Bright and Mr. Cobden were among the most conspicuous members of the society. A deputation from the Peace society, consisting of Messrs. J. Sturge, A. Pease, and another quaker friend, stated their views to the emperor of Russia at St. Petersburg, at an interview granted them in Feb. 1854

Stormy international arbitration and peace congress at Geneva; Garibaldi present . 9-12 Sept. 1867

A peace congress met at Berne . . . 24 Sept. 1868

At the peace congress held at Lausanne, the violence of the communists at Paris in May, was warmly reprobated . . . . 25 Sept. 1871

Congress held at Lugano, 23 Sept. 1872; at the Hague, 25 Sept. 1873; at Paris, 6 Sept. 1875; at Geneva, Oct. 1877; at Paris, 25 Sept. 1878; at Brussels, 17 Oct. 1882; at Berne . 4-9 Aug. 1884

Meeting at Crystal palace near London, 22 July, 1885; another meeting 16 July, 1886; at Geneva, 9 Sept. 1887; at Paris, 23 June, 1889; in London, 14 July, 1890; Rome 11 Nov. 1891; Berne, Aug. 1892; Antwerp, Aug. 1894; Budapest, 21 Sept. 1896

The principle of arbitration in place of war was adopted by the Pan-American congress at Washinton; a treaty was signed for several of the states . . . . 28 April, 1890

Inter-Parliamentary Conferences on International Arbitration (members of different legislatures): first meeting at Paris, M. Jules Simon president, June, 1889; London, lord Herschell president, 22 July, 1890; Rome 3-7 Nov. 1891; at Berne, 29-31 Aug. 1892; Brussels, 10 Oct. 1893; the Hague, 4 Sept. 1894; Brussels, 13 Aug. 1895; Brussels, 7 Aug. 1897; Christiania, 2 Aug. 1899; Paris, 31 July, 1900; Monaco . . 2 April, 1902

The International Arbitration society meets at Frankfort, 17 Sept. 1890; at Westminster, 1 July, 1891; 30 May, 1892; 30 June, 1893; 4 July, (annual meetings) 1894

The *British and foreign arbitration association* vote an address to the government respecting the Chinese and Japanese war . . . 15 Nov. 1894

Great international peace demonstration in Hyde park; delegates from 19 countries; proceedings checked by a thunderstorm . . . 26 July, 1896

"Peace day" celebrated throughout Europe and America . . . . 22 Feb. 1898

International peace congress meets at Turin, 26 Sept. ,,

Meeting at St. James's hall, in support of a peace conference, see *Russia*, Aug.-Sept. 1898; an international peace crusade favoured by lord Salisbury and others, 18 Dec.; the bishop of London chairman of executive committee, 27 Dec. ,,

Meetings held throughout the country, Jan. *et seq.* 1899

National convention at St. Martin's town-hall, lord Aberdeen and others present . 21 March, ,,

International peace bureau meets at Berne, mid May, 1900

International peace congress in Paris . 2 Oct. ,,

International Peace Conference (26 states represented) meets at the Hague, M. de Staal, Russian ambassador in London, elected president; British delegates: sir Julian Pauncefote (made a peer, July, 1899), sir Henry Howard, vice-adm. sir John Fisher, major-gen. sir John Ardagh, and others; M. de Beaufort (Netherlands foreign minister) delivers an address to the czar, the initiator of the conference, see *Russia*, Aug. 1898–11, Jan. 1899; 18 May, 1899; work divided into 3 sections—disarmament, laws of war, and arbitration; presidents and vice-presidents elected; sub-committee of 8, to discuss independent projects, 20–26 May; Great Britain and United States left in a minority concerning the prohibition of asphyxiating gases and expanding bullets of the "dum dum" type, 23 July; the Russian proposals for the limitation of armaments outvoted, 30 June; arbitration scheme (60 articles), permanent arbitration court, discussed, 7 July; signed by 16 powers; codification of the rules of war and the extension of the Geneva convention to naval warfare, signed by 15 powers; the disarmament proposals left unsettled; and the final act, including prof. Louis Renault's scheme, see *Times*, 1 Aug. 1899; protocol signed by all the 26 states represented, 29 July, 1899

The acts ratifying the treaties and declarations signed at the conference placed in the foreign office at the Hague, and a message sent to the czar . . . . . . 4 Sept. 1900

Permanent court of arbitration established at the Hague; lord Pauncefote (died 24 May, 1902, aged 74), sir E. Malet, sir Edw. Fry, prof. Westlake and other representatives appointed British members . . . . . Dec.–mid April, 1901

Boer appeal for arbitration signed by Dr. Leyds, Messrs. Fischer and Wolmarans, 10 Sept. 1901; rejected . . . . . . 20 Nov. „

Mr. Carnegie gives 1,500,000 dol. for a palace of peace reported . . . . . 25 April, 1903

See *Holland*; *Venezuela* . . . . „

PEACE PRESERVATION ACTS (IRELAND): one passed 4 April, 1870, was continued in 1876 to 31 June, 1880. A new act to last till 1 June, 1886, passed 21 March, 1881, continued till 31 Dec. 1887, 4 June, 1886. See *Arms Bills*.

PEACHES are said to have been introduced into this country from Persia about 1562.

PEARLS, mentioned *Job* xxviii. 18. M. Réaumur, in 1717, alleged that pearls are formed like other stones in animals. An ancient pearl was valued by Pliny at 80,000*l*. sterling. One which was brought in 1574 to Philip II., of the size of a pigeon's egg, was valued at 14,400 ducats. A pearl named the *Incomparable*, spoken of by De Boote, weighed thirty carats, equal to five pennyweights, and was about the size of a muscadine pear. The pearl mentioned by Tavernier, as being in possession of the emperor of Persia, was purchased of an Arab in 1633, and is valued at a sum equal to 110,400*l*. Value of pearls imported into Great Britain, 1856, 56,162*l*. Artificial mother of pearl is said to have been made at Berne by Mr. K. Gehmia.

PEASANTS' WAR, see *Jacquerie*.

PEAT, see *Bogs*. A peat coal and charcoal company, established in 1873, when coal was 41*s*. a ton.

"PECULIAR PEOPLE," a small sect founded in London by Wm. Bridges and Jas. Banyard in 1838; chief seat Essex. Two members, Thomas and Maryanne Wagstaffe, were tried and acquitted of manslaughter, 29 Jan. 1868. They had neglected getting medical assistance for their sick child, and depended on the efficacy of their elders' prayers and anointing it with oil (*James* v. 14). Many cases of healing by these means are asserted. On 8 May, 1872, a father was convicted for neglecting to get medical advice for his child who died of small pox; and the sect agreed to modify their practice. Establishments for healing diseases by prayer exist in Germany.

At another trial, Thomas Hines was acquitted, in accordance with the opinion of the court; Baron Pigott held that the case did not amount to criminal neglect because the prisoner had not called in a doctor to his sick child, 19 Aug. 1874; similar cases since; 1875-6.

John Robert Downes (for neglect respecting scarlet fever) sentenced to 3 months' imprisonment 21 Sept. 1876.

Thos. Senior sentenced to 4 months' imprisonment for manslaughter of his infant child, 15 Dec. 1898; similar cases since.

Disturbances at St. Martin's town-hall, London, at a lecture on "Faith Healing" by Dr. Dowie, 22 Oct. 1900.

PEDESTRIANISM. Euchidas, a citizen of Platæa, is said to have gone from thence to Delphi to bring the sacred fire. This he obtained, and returned with it the same day before sunset, having travelled 125 English miles. No sooner had he saluted his fellow citizens, and delivered the fire, than he fell dead at their feet. After the battle of Marathon, a soldier was sent from the field to announce the victory at Athens. Exhausted with fatigue, and bleeding from his wounds, he cried out, "Rejoice, we are conquerors!" and immediately expired.

Foster Powel, the English pedestrian, performed many astonishing journeys on foot. His expedition from London to York and back again, in 1788, is said to have been completed in 140 hours.

Captain Barclay, for a wager (on which many thousands of pounds depended), walked 1000 miles in 1000 successive hours, each mile in each hour, in forty-two days and nights (less 8 hours). His task was accomplished on 10 July, 1809.

Thomas Standen, aged 60, of Salehurst, walked 1100 miles in 1100 hours (1 mile in 1 hour), finished, July, 1811.

Richard Manks, a native of Warwickshire, undertook (in imitation of captain Barclay) to walk 1000 miles in 1000 hours: the place chosen was the Barrack-tavern cricket ground, in Sheffield; he commenced on Monday, 17 June, 1850, and completed the 1000 miles, 29 July following, winning a considerable sum.

On 7 Oct. 1861, a 12 miles foot-race was held, when Levett, the champion of England, ran 7 miles in 37 minutes 27 seconds; Deerfoot, a Seneca Indian, ran 12 miles in 65 minutes 5 seconds; and Mills ran 10 miles in 54 minutes 10 seconds; other races followed.

On 11 May, 1863, Deerfoot was beaten by White, who ran 10 miles in 52 minutes 14 seconds.

Miss Richards walked 1000 miles in 1000 hours 18 May–29 June, 1874

Edward Payson Weston (American), at Newark, U.S., walked 500 miles in 5 days 23 hours 34 min. 21-26 Dec. „

Wm. Perkins, at Lillie Bridge, London, S.W., walked 8 miles in less than one hour . 20 Sept. 1875

Match between Weston and Perkins at Agricultural Hall, London, N., began 9.25 p.m. 8 Feb. 1876; Perkins walked 50 miles in 9 h. 37 m. 41 s., rested 26 m., went on for 65 m., and stopped; Weston walked 50 miles in 9 h. 55 m. 52 s., went on for 16 h., stopped for 1 h., went on to 24 h. (walked 109 miles 758 yards) . . 8-9 Feb. 1876

Weston began to walk 500 miles in 6 days at Agricultural Hall, 12.5 a.m. 6 March, had walked 450 miles 11 March; he walked 111 miles in 24 consecutive hours at Manchester . . . April, „

Bella St. Clair walked 1000 miles in 950 hours 25 July *et seq.* „

Weston engaged to walk 505 miles in 6 days at Agricultural hall, London, walked 460 18-23 Dec. „

Match between Weston and O'Leary, for 1000 guineas; won by O'Leary, who walked 520 miles, Weston 510 miles . . . 2-7 April, 1877

Wm. Gale, aged 45, walked 1500 miles in 1000 consecutive hours, at Lillie bridge, London, S.W. 26 Aug.–6 Oct.; 4000 ¼-miles in 4000 consecutive 10 minutes, at Agricultural hall, London; completed . . . . 17 Nov. 1877
Match of 17 pedestrians at Agricultural hall; O'Leary won, walked 520 miles 18-23 March, 1878
Grand match (of 18 competitors) for championship and 500*l.*, Agricultural hall; 6 days and 6 nights; won by W. Corkey, who walked 521 miles 28 Oct.–2 Nov. ,,
E. P. Weston starts to walk over England 2000 miles in 1000 consecutive hours (except on Sundays), 18 Jan.; fails by 22½ hours . . . . . 28 Feb. 1879
Weston walked 550 miles at the Agricultural hall, and won sir John Astley's belt . 16-21 June, ,,
Blower Brown walked 553 miles in 6 days (won long distance championship of England, Astley's belt, &c.) . . . . 16-21 Feb. 1880
Belt, &c. won by Rowell . . . 1-6 Nov. ,,
Wm. Gale attempts to walk 2500 miles in 1000 hours; walks 2405½ miles. . . 20 Nov. 1880–1 Jan. 1881
Weston walks 5000 miles in 100 days (on teetotal principles) . . 21 Nov. 1883–15 March, 1884
Littlewood wins sir John Astley's belt at Westminster aquarium; 405 miles in six days . Nov. ,,
George Littlewood walks 623 miles 1320 yards in six days at New York; declared champion of the world; concluded . . . . . 1 Dec. 1888
H. Watkins, 10 miles champion runner, accomplished 11 miles 1286 yards in an hour, at Rochdale . . . . . . 16 Sept. 1899
Race won by L. Hurst, English champion, against Robt. Hallan, American champion, at Stamford-hill, London; Hurst ran nearly 13 miles in 1 hour 17 minutes 45 seconds at Stamford-hill. 23 Sept. 1901
J. Butler walked from Westminster clock to Brighton aquarium (52½ mi.) in 8 hrs. 43 min. 16 sec., 14 March, 1903; the same distance was competed for by 87 members of the Stock Exchange, and won by Mr. E. F. Broad in 9 hrs. 30 min. 1 sec. . . . . 1 May, 1903
A. Shrubb, at Ilford, ran 2 mi. in 9 min. 11 sec. 30 May, ,,
A "globe walk" from London to Brighton accomplished by Miss Florence, an American, 16-21 June, ,,
Leonard Hurst ran 25 mi. in 2 hrs. 33 mins. 42 sec. 27 Aug. ,,

Many annual matches.

PEDLARS, see *Hawkers*. The Pedlars act passed, Aug. 1871.

PEDOMETER AND ODOMETER, apparatus for measuring the distance traversed by a walker or carriage.

Odometers, or road-measurers, are said to have been known in the 15th century; and improvements in them were made in England by Butterfield, about 1678; and by Meynier, in France about 1724
Wm. Grayson's odometer, or road-measurer, to be attached to carriages, was patented . 1 Dec. 1851
Ralph Gouts' *pedometer* for indicating the steps taken by a walker, was patented . 4 Nov. 1799
Wm. Payne's pedometer for the waistcoat pocket, patented . . . . 15 Feb. 1831
Other improvements since.

PEEL ACTS. Among the most important were the Bank acts of 1819 and 1844; the acts amending the criminal laws, 1827; dividing parishes into districts, 1843, and the act repealing the corn-laws in 1846.

PEEL ADMINISTRATIONS.* The FIRST succeeded the Melbourne administration, which was broken up on the retirement of lord Althorp, the chancellor of the exchequer, in Nov. 1834. Sir R. Peel, then in Italy, was summoned home, the duke of Wellington holding the seals of office in the interim. They both resigned in April, 1835. In May, 1841, sir R. Peel carried a vote of want of confidence in the Melbourne cabinet, but did not take office; and in Sept. of that year, he became again premier. He lost the support of the conservative party by obtaining the repeal of the corn laws, and resigned 29 June, 1846.

FIRST ADMINISTRATION (Dec. 1834).

Sir Robert Peel, *first lord of the treasury* and *chancellor of the exchequer.*
Lord Lyndhurst, *lord chancellor.*
Earl of Rosslyn, *lord president.*
Lord Wharncliffe, *privy seal.*
Henry Goulburn, duke of Wellington, and earl of Aberdeen, *home, foreign,* and *colonial secretaries of state.*
Earl De Grey, *first lord of the admiralty.*
Lord Ellenborough and Alexander Baring, *board of control* and *trade.*
Sir Edward Knatchbull, *paymaster of the forces.*
J. C. Herries, *secretary of war.*
Sir George Murray, *master-general of the ordnance, &c.*

SECOND ADMINISTRATION (Sept. 1841).

Sir Robert Peel, *first minister.*
Duke of Wellington in the cabinet without office, *aft. commander-in-chief.*
Lord Lyndhurst, *lord chancellor.*
Lord Wharncliffe, *lord president.*
Duke of Buckingham, *lord privy seal* (succeeded by duke of Buccleuch).
Sir James Graham, earl of Aberdeen, and lord Stanley, *home, foreign,* and *colonial secretaries.*
Henry Goulburn, *chancellor of the exchequer.*
Earl of Haddington, *first lord of the admiralty.*
Earl of Ripon, *board of trade* (succeeded by W. E. Gladstone).
Lord Ellenborough, *India board* (succeeded by lord Fitzgerald; succeeded by earl of Ripon).
Sir Henry Hardinge, sir Edward Knatchbull, sir George Murray, &c.

[Terminated 29 June, 1846, by sir Robert's resignation.]

PEELITES, a name given to gentlemen, whigs and tories, who adhered to sir Robert Peel, after his defeat by the conservative party, on account of his free-trade measures carried in 1846. The principal were Henry Goulburn, W. E. Gladstone, Sidney (afterwards lord) Herbert, sir James Graham, Edward Cardwell, sir George Clerk, lord Lincoln (afterwards duke of Newcastle), and lords Canning and Elgin, and others. Several of them became members of the Palmerston and Aberdeen administrations (*which see*).

PEEL PICTURES. The family collection (70) were purchased for the National gallery for 75,000*l.* 1871.

PEEP-O'-DAY-BOYS, insurgents in Ireland, who visited the houses of their antagonists at break of day, in search of arms. They first appeared 4 July, 1784, and were long the terror of the country; see *Defenders.*

PEERESSES of the United Kingdom (*in their own right*): 7 in 1885, countess of Cromartie (duchess of Sutherland), baronesses Berkeley, Berners, Burdett-Coutts, Le Despencer, Willoughby D'Eresby, Bolsover. In 1903: viscountess Hambleden and baronesses Berkeley, Berners, Burdett-

* Sir Robert Peel was born 5 Feb. 1788; entered parliament in 1809; became under-secretary of the colonies in 1811, chief secretary for Ireland in 1812; M.P. for Oxford in 1818 (when he resigned his office); secretary for home department in 1822; resigned office and reappointed in 1827; resigned again in 1830; became premier in 1834 and 1841 (*see above*). He was thrown from his horse 29 June, and died 2 July, 1850. He greatly relaxed the severity of our criminal code in 1827 *et seq.*; established the new police, and carried the catholic emancipation bill in 1829, and the repeal of the corn laws in 1846. Statues have been erected to him—at Salford, in 1852; at Tamworth, Leeds, Bury, and Manchester, in 1853; and in London and Birmingham in 1855.

Coutts, Beaumont (a minor), Macdonald of Earnscliffe, Conyers (countess of Yarborough), Cromartie (countess); Dorchester; Clifton (a minor).

PEERS, see *Lords* and *Genealogy*.

PEGU, a province of the Burmese empire, discovered by the Portuguese in 1520. Pegu, the capital, was taken by major Cotton, with 300 men, in June, 1852, without loss; and afterwards abandoned. It was again occupied by the Burmese and strongly fortified, with a garrison of 4000 men. It was recaptured by general Godwin with 1200 men and two guns, in two hours, with the loss of six killed and thirty-two wounded. The province was annexed to our Indian possessions, by proclamation, 20 Dec. 1852, and has since prospered. In Feb. 1862, it was united with Arracan and Tenasserim as British Burmah.

PEIHO, see *China*, 1859, 1860.

PEISHWA, the prime minister of the Mahrattas, seized the sovereign power and settled at Poonah, 1749. The title was abolished in 1818.

PEIWAR PASS (Kotul), in the Khoorum valley, Afghanistan. Here general Roberts, with the 72nd highlanders and the Ghoorkas, defeated the Afghans, 2 Dec. 1878. Major Anderson and capt. Kelso were killed, and about 80 men were killed and wounded. The enemy's loss was very great.

PEKIN, the capital of China, was built by Kachilai-Khan, grandson of Genghis-Khan, about 1267. Here was held the court of the Mongol or Yuen dynasty, 1280 to 1368. In 1369, Hung-wu, of the Ming dynasty, removed to Nankin, which was the capital till Yung-lo removed his court to Pekin in 1410; and by him and his successors the city was enlarged, fortified, and beautified. It was visited by lord Macartney, Sept. 1793; surrendered to the allied English and French armies, 12 Oct. 1860; and evacuated by them 5 Nov., after peace had been signed 24 Oct. It was described as being in a very desolate state, and the inhabitants scattered and indigent. English and French representatives were settled at Pekin, March, 1861. Preliminary peace with France concluded here, 5 April, 1885. The famous temple or altar of heaven burnt 18 Sept. 1889. Population, estimated 1877, 1,650,000.

Russo-Chinese school opened . . . 21 July, 1899
Hong-kong and Sanghai bank, new building opened, early July, ,,

SIEGE AND HEROIC DEFENCE OF THE LEGATIONS: see *China*, 20 June–14 Aug. 1900; a memorial in front of the British legation unveiled . 14 Sept. 1901

PELAGIANS, followers of Pelagius, a Briton, appeared at Rome about 400. Their doctrines were condemned by councils at Jerusalem, Carthage, and other places, 415, 530. They maintained:—

1. That Adam was by nature mortal, and whether he had sinned or not would certainly have died. 2. That the consequences of Adam's sin were confined to his own person. 3. That new-born infants are in the same condition with Adam before the fall. 4. That the law qualified men for the kingdom of heaven, and was founded upon equal promises with the gospel. 5. That the general resurrection of the dead does not follow in virtue of Christ's resurrection.

PELASGI, the primitive inhabitants of Asia Minor, Greece, and Italy, appear to have belonged to the Indo-Germanic race. They were in Greece about 1900 B.C., and in Italy about 1600 B.C. They have been termed Tyrrheni, Sicani or Siculi, Apuli, &c. From the Pelasgi came the Dorians, Æolians, and Ionians; all three being Hellenes or Greeks. The Pelasgi appear not to have had the art of writing, but have left numerous architectural remains; they were probably a wealthy, powerful and intelligent people.

PELÉE, MONT, see *Earthquakes*.

PELEW ISLANDS (N. Pacific Ocean), discovered by the Spaniards in the 17th century. The East India company's packet *Antelope*, captain Wilson, was wrecked here in 1783. The king, Abba Thulle, allowed captain Wilson to bring prince Le Boo, his son, to England, where he arrived in 1784, and died of the small-pox soon after. The East India company erected a monument over his grave in Rotherhithe churchyard.

PELHAM ADMINISTRATION. Mr. H. Pelham replaced the earl of Wilmington as premier, 25 Aug. 1743; see *Wilmington*. In Nov. 1744, the following ministry was formed (termed "the broad bottom administration," because it comprehended a grand coalition of the parties). It was dissolved by the death of Mr. Pelham, 6 March, 1754.

Henry Pelham, *first lord of the treasury* and *chancellor of the exchequer*.
Lord Hardwicke, *lord chancellor*.
Duke of Dorset, *president of the council*.
Earl Gower, *lord privy seal*.
Duke of Newcastle and the earl of Harrington, *secretaries of state*.
Duke of Montagu, *master-general of the ordnance*.
Duke of Bedford, *first lord of the admiralty*.
Duke of Grafton, *lord chamberlain*.
Duke of Richmond, *master of the horse*.
Duke of Argyll, *keeper of the great seal of Scotland*.
Marquis of Tweeddale, *secretary of state for Scotland*.
All of the cabinet.
The duke of Devonshire and duke of Bolton were *not* of the cabinet.

PELLS (from *pellis*, skin), receipts on parchment rolls deposited in the court of exchequer. By an act passed in 1834, the office of clerk of the pells was abolished, and a comptroller-general appointed. "Pell records," or "issues of the exchequer," or payments made out of his revenue by James I., were published by the government in 1836.

PELOPIUM, see *Niobium*.

PELOPONNESUS (the island of Pelops), a peninsula, S. Greece, termed Morea in the 13th century, said to have been settled by Pelops about 1283 B.C. PELOPONNESIAN WAR continued for twenty-seven years between the Athenians and the people of the Peloponnesus, with their respective allies, and is the most famous of the wars of Greece. It began by an attempt of the Bœotians to surprise Platæa, 431 B.C., on 7 May, and ended 404 by the taking of Athens by the Lacedæmonians.

PELUSIUM (now *Tineh*), formerly Sin, the key of Egypt. Here, in 525 B.C., Psammeticus III. was defeated by Cambyses, the Persian, who thereby obtained possession of the kingdom. Pelusium surrendered to Alexander, 333; was taken by the Persians, 309; by Antiochus, 173; by Augustus, 30 B.C.; and after a protracted resistance by Amrou, the Saracen, A.D. 638.

PEMBROKE (S. Wales). A county palatine till 1536. The royal dockyard at Milford was moved to Pembroke in 1814. PEMBROKE COLLEGE and HALL, see under *Oxford* and *Cambridge*. Population, 1881, 14,156; 1891, 14,978; 1901, 15,853.

PENAL LAWS, see *Criminal Laws* and *Roman Catholics*. *Penal Servitude* was substituted for transportation by acts passed in 1853 and 1857, and amended in 1864. A penal servitude commission appointed, 22 Jan. 1878.

First session of the International Penal Law union opened at Brussels . . . . 7 Aug. 1889

The Penal Servitude acts, 1853 *et seq.* combined by act passed . . . . 5 Aug. 1891

PENANCE, a sacrament in the Roman church, arose out of the practice of auricular confession (*which see*). The council of Trent, in its 14th session (1551), decreed that every one is accursed who shall affirm that this sacrament was not instituted by Christ.

PENANG, or PRINCE OF WALES'S ISLAND, was given up to the East India company in 1786, by captain F. Light, who received it as a marriage portion with the daughter of the king of Keddah. After several changes it became one of the Straits Settlements (*which see*).

PENDULUMS. The isochronous property of the pendulum is said to have been applied to clocks by Galileo about 1639, and by Richard Harris about 1641. Christian Huyghens claimed this discovery, 1658. See *Clocks*. George Graham invented the compensating pendulum, 1715. Experiments were made to determine the density of the earth by pendulums by Mr. (aft. sir) G. B. Airy (aftds. astronomer royal), and others, in a mine in Cornwall, in 1826 and 1828; and at Horton colliery 1854. In 1851, M. Foucault demonstrated the rotation of the earth by the motion of a pendulum.

PENGE MYSTERY, Surrey, see *Trials*, Sept. 1877.

PENINSULAR COMPANY, see *Steam*, 1837–40.

PENINSULAR WAR, see under *Spain*, 1808-14.

Wellington computed that he lost 36,000 men in this war—killed, prisoners, deserters, &c. He took great care of his men (1836).

PENITENTIARIES. The London Female Penitentiary, Pentonville-road, was established in 1807; and the British Penitent Female Refuge at Cambridge heath, Hackney, in 1829. The Church Penitentiary association, founded 1851. International penitentiary congresses held, first in London, 1872, at other capitals since; at Paris, 30 June, 1895. See *Millbank*.

PENITENTS, see *Magdalens*. The Penitents of the name of Jesus in Spain were a congregation of persons who had led a licentious life, formed about 1550. The penitents of Orvieto were formed into an order of nuns about 1662.

PENNSYLVANIA (N. America), the first state in the Union in regard to mineral wealth. The settlement by the Swedes here in 1643, was taken by the Dutch in 1655, and acquired by the British in 1664. Pennsylvania was granted by Charles II. to the duke of York, 1664; and it was sold to the Penn family, 1681. Pennsylvania was afterwards purchased from the Indians by the celebrated William Penn (son of admiral Penn), who went out from England with a number of colonists; from which period the settlement gradually increased. Mr. Penn granted a charter in May, 1701, but the emigrants from the Low Countries refused it, and separated themselves from the province of Pennsylvania. They afterwards had their own assembly, in which the governor of Pennsylvania presided. This state adopted an independent constitution in 1787, and established the present in 1790. Capital, Harrisburg; principal city, Philadelphia. It was strongly unionist during the civil war, 1861-5; see *United States of America* and *Petroleum*. For strikes see *United States*, 1877, 1882. Population in 1860, 2,906,370; in 1880, 4,282,891; 1890, 5,258,014; 1900, 6,302,115.

Great destruction of property and life by a tornado, especially at Pittsburg and Reading, 9 Jan. 1889.

Several days' violent storms and heavy rain in the Alleghanies swelled the rivers, and caused the overflow of the lakes, May, 1889. At 5 p.m. 31 May, the South Fork reservoir, a lake about 4 miles square, burst the huge dam, and a mass of water rushed down the South Fork, four miles, by the deep circuitous Conemaugh valley, to its junction with the Conemaugh river, driving all before it. For a distance of about 12 miles round Johnstown the flood swept out towns and villages, destroying all the bridges, railways, and factories. South Fork, Johnstown, Cambria city, Morrelville, Sheridan, and other flourishing towns were completely blotted out. A great mass of floating wreckage, which was stopped by a stone railway bridge at Johnstown, took fire; above five hundred persons, who were hurled on the burning mass, perished.

The most energetic measures were taken by the government, by several states, and by the railway companies for the relief of the sufferers, and for averting imminent famine and pestilence. Robbers of the dead and living were lynched by a vigilance committee. Troops were sent to maintain order, liberal subscriptions were begun in London, Paris, and other places, June.

It is stated that the dam had previously given visible signs of its being in a very insecure condition, and had not been properly constructed. Several towns and villages submerged, June; many bridges swept away; above 150 deaths reported.

Latest statistics state the result of the Johnstown disaster to be about 6,000 deaths . . 26 July, 1889

Panic in a theatre at Johnstown, 10 persons killed, many injured . . . . 10 Dec. ,,

Destructive storms with loss of life at Pittsburg and neighbourhood . . . . . . 8 Feb. 1890

At Hartford coal-pit, Ashley, Wyoming valley, 28 men were entombed and 26 perished by a cave-in and explosion . . . . 15 May, ,,

A cyclone in the Wyoming valley and neighbourhood, about 54 killed . . . about 19 Aug. ,,

By an explosion in the Frick mine, ten miles from Mount Pleasant, 151 out of 160 men perished . 27 Jan. 1891

Johnstown again inundated through heavy rains about 16 Feb. ,,

Riotous strikes in the Pennsylvania coke district, much destruction of property, reported 30 March; desperate fight, 9 men killed, 2 April; 1000 soldiers maintaining order, 3 April; rioting renewed with desperate fights . . about 22 April, ,,

A train containing 75 men thrown off the line while rushing through a burning forest near Condersport, Potter county; 5 men killed, many injured . . . . about 12 May, ,,

After heavy rains, when the rivers had become torrents, early on 5 June, a cloud burst over the Pittsburg oil regions, causing great inundations. At Titusville the tanks of oil and distilled benzine were upset and were ignited by lightning and the city was fired. A flaming stream with floating wreckage carried all before it, destroying the bridges. Explosions followed, causing a panic, and the people fled to the hills, women and children being trampled on during the rush. The fiery river reached Oil city, 18 miles distant, and a large part of it was reduced to ashes or submerged. It was reported that 150 persons were either drowned or burnt at Titusville, and about 200 missing. The loss of property at the two cities was estimated at 3,000,000 dollars; large sums were immediately subscribed for the relief of the sufferers . . . . . 6 June *et seq.* 1892

Destructive forest fires in various parts, about 2 Nov. ,,

A cokers' strike and riots with bloodshed, chiefly Hungarians, S.W. Pennsylvania, 4 April *et seq.* 150 arrests . . . . . . April, May, 1894
Strike of about 50,000 colliers for an advance of 20 per cent. reported 20 April ; subsidence of the strike reported . . . . . . 10 June, ,,
Dynamite outrage at Salisbury, Mr A. J. Leim and wife killed . . . . 4 Oct. ,,
Forest fire in the North oilfields, several small towns destroyed, reported . . . 4 June, 1895
Railway collision near Atlantic city, on the Pennsylvania railway, 50 deaths . . . . 30 July, 1896
The Capitol at Harrisburg burnt down, reported, 2 Feb. 1897
A body of foreign miners on strike, refusing to disperse, fired on by order of sheriff Martin, 22 killed, near Hazleton, 10 Sept. ; strike over, men's terms agreed on, 12 Sept. ; further rioting, 16, 20 Sept. ,,
Sheriff Martin and 82 deputy-sheriffs tried for the deaths of 22 miners (10 Sept.), 1 Feb. 1898 ; all acquitted . . . . 9 March, 1898
Rioting at Shenandoah in connection with coal strike ; troops sent ; order restored, 30 July ; national guard ordered out in the strike region, 7 Oct. 1902
Part of the town Olyphant subsides 50 feet into mine workings ; 2 buildings burnt . . . 2 Jan. 1903

PENNY. The ancient silver penny was the first silver coin struck in England, and the only one current among the Anglo-Saxons. The penny until the reign of Edward I. was struck with a cross, so deeply indented that it might be easily parted into two for halfpence, and into four for farthings, and hence these names. Copper penny and two-penny pieces were coined by Boulton and Watt, at Soho, Birmingham, in 1797, and were accounted the finest of our copper currency; see *Coins*, &c.—PENNY-POST ; see *Post-office*. — THE PENNY MAGAZINE began in 1832; the PENNY CYCLOPÆDIA in 1833 (supplements in 1846 and 1858). The PENNY RECEIPT stamp was appointed in 1853 (postage stamps authorised to be used for receipts after 1 June, 1881), and in 1858 a penny stamp was directed to be placed on bankers' cheques.—PENNY BANKS (in 1861 about 200) were established about 1850. They have become numerous, and in 1878 were authorised to invest their funds.—PENNY READINGS, for the working classes, became general in 1859. Carpenter's "Penny Readings," published in 1865-7. "Penny Poets," &c. ; Mr. W. T. Stead began the series with Macaulay's "Lays of Ancient Rome," &c., price one penny, May, 1895.

The value of the Roman *penny* (mentioned *Matt.* xx. 2), or *denarius*, was estimated at 7½d. of our money.
Penny dinners for poor Board school children ; organization proposed at Society of Arts, 6 Dec. 1884 ; see *Destitute Children*. A similar self-supporting system existed in the provinces.

PENRHYN LIBEL SUIT, see *Trials*.

PENRUDDOCK'S REBELLION on behalf of Charles II. was suppressed, and colonel John Penruddock himself executed, 16 May, 1655.

PENSIONS. The crown's power of granting them, often much abused, was materially checked by statute 1 Anne, c. 1 (1702), see *Poor*, 1893–5.

English pension list fixed at 95,000*l*. 1781
Irish pension list said to amount to 489,000*l*. . . 1793
Provision made by parliament to reduce all the pension lists of the united kingdom from 145,000*l*. to a maximum of 75,000*l*. 1830
A committee appointed to define the proper persons to whom pensions should be granted : it reported in favour of servants of the crown and public, and also of those who "by their useful discoveries in science and attainments in literature and the arts, have merited the gracious consideration of their sovereign and the gratitude of their country" . 1834
The queen empowered to grant annually new pensions to the amount of 1200*l*. 1837
The political offices pension act passed . 9 Aug. 1869
The pensions commutation acts passed . 29 June, 1871 and 1882
Death of rev. Thos. Thurlow, nephew of the lord chancellor, whereby pensions for abolished offices, said to amount to 11,779*l*., ceased 26 Sept. 1874
Report of committee on such pensions published Sept. 1887
Perpetual pensions were granted to the dukes of Grafton, Richmond, Marlborough, and many others in the 17th and 18th centuries.
By virtue of an act passed in 1873, various perpetual pensions have been terminated by agreement for compensation 1890
The Old Age Pension scheme of Mr. Joseph Chamberlain, M.P., proposed the establishment of a state pension fund to be aided by annual parliamentary grants and contributions from local rates and annuitants, considered by a committee of the commons, 16 March ; adopted 17 May, 1892 ; total sum yearly, 611,464*l*. ; doles, 327,655*l*. ; reported, May ; report of committee, issued, 7 July, 1898 ; the committee report in favour of pensions of at least 5*s*. a week to needy persons over 65, half the cost to be paid from local rates and the other from the exchequer . . . . 26 July, 1899

PENTAMETER VERSE (five feet), first used about the 7th century B.C. ; see *Elegy*.

PENTATEUCH, the five books of Moses, probably written about 1452 B.C. See *Bible*.

PENTECOST signifies the fiftieth, and is the solemn festival of the Jews, called also "the feast of weeks," because it was celebrated fifty days, or seven weeks after the feast of the Passover, 1491 B.C. (*Lev.* xxiii. 15 ; *Exod.* xxxiv. 22) ; see *Whitsuntide*.

PENTLAND HILLS (near Edinburgh). Here the Scotch presbyterians, since called Cameronians (*which see*), who had risen against the government on account of the establishment of episcopacy, were defeated by the royal troops, 28 Nov. 1666.

PENZANCE, Cornwall. The town was burnt by the Spaniards, July, 1595. It was taken by Fairfax in 1646. Here sir Humphry Davy was born, 17 Dec. 1778, and here was inaugurated his memorial statue, 17 Oct. 1872. Visit of the king well received, 9 April, 1902. Population, 1881, 12,409 ; 1891, 12,448 ; 1901, 13,123.

PEONAGE SYSTEM, see *United States*, 1903.

PEOPLE. The duke of Norfolk and C. J. Fox, at a dinner in 1798, gave a toast "the majesty of the people," for which their names were struck off the list of privy councillors. A "people's petition" was presented to parliament by Mr. T. Duncombe, and rejected, 2 May, 1842. "PEOPLE'S PARKS," principally through private liberality, have been opened since 1846, at Manchester, Halifax, Birmingham, Sheffield, Dundee, Bradford, Hull, Bath, Bolton, Liverpool, Leeds, &c. (*which see*).

People's banks, based on co-operative principles, have been successfully introduced into Germany and Italy by Dr. Schulze-Delitzsch; they begin with a deposit of 2½*d*. and a monthly subscription of 5*d*. In 1887 there were 2200 of these banks in Germany and in that year, less than half of them dealt with more than 50,000,000*l*. sterling. Reported successful in Gt. Britain in 1896.
People's Café company established 1874, to give the working classes the advantages of club-houses, opened their first house in Upper Whitecross-street, London . . . . . . 16 April, 1875
A "People's Tribute" to the earl of Beaconsfield, a gold wreath, made by Hunt & Roskell, by subscription of 52,800 pennies ; collected by the agency of Mr. Tracy Turnerelli. Its presentation was declined by the earl . . . . 16 June, 1879
See *Entertainment*.

PEOPLE'S PALACE, see *Beaumont Trust.*

PEPPER was used by the Greeks; licences to sell pepper abolished, 1869. Pepper imported into the United Kingdom in 1863, 16,810,467 lbs.; 1883, 31,375,589 lbs.; 1890, 29,691,858 lbs.; 1893, 31,222,418 lbs.; 1896, 26,113,001 lbs.; 1900, 22,276,242 lbs.; 1901, 15,706,503 lbs.

PEPSIN, a peculiar organic substance found by Schwann in the gastric juice, and named by him from *pepsis*, digestion. It was experimented on by M. Blondlot in 1843, and has since been prescribed as a medicine.

PEPYS' DIARY. Samuel Pepys was born 23 Feb. 1632; became secretary to the admiralty about 1664; president of the Royal society, 1684; died 26 May, 1703. His "Diary," as published, begins 1 Jan. 1659-60; ends 31 May, 1669.

The MSS. at Magdalene College, Cambridge, was deciphered by the Rev. John Smith. The first edition (with a selection from his correspondence), by Richard, lord Braybrooke, appeared in 1825. The publication of a new edition, "deciphered with additional notes by the rev. Mynors Bright," 1875-9; a complete edition of this by H. B. Wheatley, 1893-6; vol. ix. *Index* . . June, 1899

PERA, a suburb of Constantinople, the residence of the British and other ambassadors; has frequently been destroyed by fire; see *Turkey*, 2 Aug. 1831, and 5 June, 1870.

PERAK, see *Straits Settlement.*

PERCEVAL ADMINISTRATION. It commenced on the dissolution of the duke of Portland's, through his death, 30 Oct. 1809. Mr. Perceval was assassinated in the lobby of the house of commons, by Bellingham, 11 May, 1812. The earl of Liverpool succeeded as premier.

Spencer Perceval [born 1762; *chancellor of exchequer*, 1807], *first lord of the treasury, chancellor of the exchequer*, and *chancellor of the duchy of Lancaster.*
Lord Eldon, *lord chancellor.*
Earl Camden, *lord president.*
Earl of Westmorland, *lord privy seal.*
Richard Ryder, marquis of Wellesley, and earl of Liverpool, *home, foreign*, and *colonial secretaries.*
Lord Mulgrave, *admiralty.*
Mr. Dumas and earl Bathurst, *boards of control* and *trade.*
Earl of Chatham, *ordnance.*
Viscount Palmerston, *secretary of war*, &c.

PERCUSSION CAPS, see *Fire-arms.*

PERCY FAMILY. William de Percy obtained lands in Yorkshire from William the Conqueror, and died at Antioch about 1096.

The heiress of the last baron Percy married Josceline de Louvaine, son of Godfrey, duke of Brabant, in the reign of Henry II. 1154-89
Henry de Percy, their descendant, created earl of Northumberland in 1377
Many of his descendants were slain during the wars of the Roses.
Lady Elizabeth Percy, the heiress of Josceline Percy, who died 1670, married Charles, duke of Somerset.
Lady Elizabeth Percy, heiress of their son Algernon Seymour, duke of Northumberland, married sir Hugh Smithson, created duke of Northumberland in 1766
Their descendant, duke Algernon, died without issue, 12 Feb. 1865, and was succeeded by his cousin, George Percy, earl of Beverley, who died 22 Aug. 1867; succeeded by George Algernon, the present duke.
The Percy Society, for the publication of ancient ballads, &c., named after Dr. Percy, bishop of Dromore (died 1811), who published ballads, was established in 1840, published 94 little volumes, and was dissolved 1852
Percy Anecdotes, classified, compiled by J. C. Robertson and Thomas Byerley, under the names of Sholto and Reuben Percy, 1820-3.

PERED (Hungary). Here the Hungarians under Görgey were defeated by Wohlgemuth and the Russians, 21 June, 1849.

PEREKOP, an isthmus, five miles broad, connecting the Crimea with the mainland. It was called by the Tartars Orkapou, "gate of the isthmus," which the Russians changed to its present name, which signifies a barren ditch. The lines across the isthmus were forced by the Russian marshal Munich, May, 1736, and the fortress was taken by Lacy, July, 1738. It was again strongly fortified by the khan, but was again taken by the Russians in 1771, who have since retained it.

PÈRE-LA-CHAISE, see *Cemeteries.*

PERFECTION, see *Illuminati.*

PERFUMERY. In *Exodus* xxx. (1490 B.C.), directions are given for making the holy incense. Philip Augustus of France granted a charter to the master perfumers in 1190. Perfumes became fashionable in England in the reign of Elizabeth. In 1860 there were about forty manufacturing perfumers in London; in Paris about eighty. No such trade as a perfumer was known in Scotland in 1763. *Creech.* A stamp-tax was laid on various articles of perfumery in England, and the vendor was obliged to take out a licence in 1786. At the corner of Beaufort-buildings, in the Strand, resided Lilly, the perfumer, mentioned in the *Spectator.*

PERGAMOS, see *Seven Churches, 3rd.*

PERIM, an island at the southern entrance of the Red Sea, held by the British, 1799-1800: and again in 1857; made a coaling station in 1883; under the government of Bombay. Population about 400.

PERIODICAL LITERATURE, see *Newspapers, Magazines*, and *Reviews.* "An Index to Periodical Literature," 1853 *et seq.*; by W. F. Poole. Published in two volumes, 1882-8.

PERIPATETIC PHILOSOPHY, see *Lyceum.*

PERIPLUS. The voyage of Hanno, the Carthaginian navigator, about the third century B.C. His account of his travels, written in the Punic language, was translated into Greek; an English translation, edited by Falconer, in London, 1797.

PERJURY. The early Romans threw the offender headlong from the Tarpeian precipice; and the Greeks set a mark of infamy upon him. After the empire became Christian, any one who swore falsely upon the Gospels, was to have his tongue cut out. The canons of the primitive church enjoined eleven years' penance; and in some states the false swearer became liable to the punishment he charged upon the innocent. In England perjury was punished with the pillory, fine, and imprisonment, 1562. By the Abolition of Oaths bill, persons making a false declaration are deemed guilty of a misdemeanor; Act 5 & 6 Will. IV. cc. 60 and 61, 9 Sept. 1835; a perjury bill was read a second time, 2 April, 1895. Perhaps the greatest perjurer in modern times was Titus Oates; see *Oates.* A woman named Alice Grey was convicted of many perjuries in 1856. See *Trials*, 1873.

PERKINS' METALLIC TRACTORS, see *Animal Magnetism.*

PERMANENT COMMITTEES. One was appointed, 15 Sept. 1871, by the French national assembly to watch over the proceedings of the government during a recess. It consisted of 25 persons of various parties. A similar committee of the Spanish cortes, appointed 22 March, 1873, was peremptorily dissolved by the government 22 April following.

PERMISSIVE PROHIBITORY BILL (which would give power to two-thirds of the ratepayers of a parish to refuse licences for the sale of intoxicating liquors), advocated by the United Kingdom Alliance party, was rejected by the house of commons, 8 June, 1864; 12 May, 1869 (193-87); 17 May, 1871 (206-124); 8 May, 1872 (369-15); 7 May, 1873 (321-81); 17 June, 1874 (301-75); 16 June, 1875 (371-86); 14 June, 1876 (299-81); withdrawn, 25 July, 1877; (278-84) 26 June, 1878. It is strongly advocated by sir Wilfrid Lawson, M.P.; resolution rejected (252-164) 11 March, 1879.

Resolution to give *local option* (that is, power to the inhabitants of any place to stop licensing public-houses) was rejected by the commons (248-134) 5 March, 1880; but adopted (229-203) 18-19 June, 1880; (196-154) 14 June, 1881; (228-141) 27 April, 1883; rejected 29 April, 1891.

A liquor traffic (local control or veto) bill introduced by sir W. V. Harcourt, 27 Feb. 1893; much opposed; withdrawn, 18 Sept. 1893.

A bill for Wales, read second time, 15 March, 1893; other bills relating to the sale of liquors introduced by the bishops of Chester and London and Mr. Bolitho, March, 1893; modified and re-introduced by him as local option bill, read first time in commons, 8 April, 1895.

"*Local Option,*" an Americanism, is said not to work satisfactorily in the United States.

See *Liquor Traffic.*

PERNAMBUCO, a province of Brazil, with a city of the same name, comprising Recife and other towns, founded in 1530; seized by the British, and retained for a month, 1594; insurrections here, 1661, 1710, 1817, 1821, and 1829. Population, 1890, 190,000.

PERONNE (N. France). Louis XI. of France, having placed himself in the power of the duke of Burgundy, here was forced to sign a treaty, confirming those of Arras and Conflans, and recognising the duke's independence; 14 Oct. 1468. The notables declared the treaty invalid and the duke a traitor, Nov. 1470.

PERPENDICULAR, see *Gothic Architecture.*

PERPETUAL EDICTS, see *Edicts.*

PERPETUAL MOTION. For this purpose machines have been constructed by the marquis of Worcester and many others, although the impossibility of attaining it was demonstrated by sir Isaac Newton and De la Hire, and affirmed by the academy of sciences at Paris, 1775. It is still the object of experiment by half-taught persons. See *Pensions.*

PERRANZABULOE, Perran in the sands (*in sabulo*), mid Cornwall, named from Perran, the patron of tinners. The remains of an ancient British oratory or church, resembling the arrangement of protestant churches, were discovered in the sand in 1835, with other interesting relics.

PERSECUTIONS. Historians usually reckon ten general persecutions of the Christians; see *Jews, Heretics, Inquisition, Huguenots, Protestants, Massacres, Bartholomew, St.,* &c.

I. Under Nero, who, having set fire to Rome, threw the odium upon the Christians; multitudes were massacred; wrapt up in the skins of wild beasts, and torn and devoured by dogs; crucified, burnt alive, &c. . . . . A.D. 64-68
II. Under Domitian 95
III. Under Trajan 106
IV. Under Marcus Aurelius 166-177
V. Under Septimus Severus 199-204
VI Under Maximus 235-8
VII. Under Decius, more bloody than any preceding 250-2
VIII. Under Valerian 258-60
IX. Under Aurelian 275
X. Under Diocletian, who prohibited divine worship; houses filled with Christians were set on fire, and many of them were bound together with ropes and cast into the sea 303-13

PERSEPOLIS, the ancient splendid capital of Persia. Alexander is accused of setting fire to it, while intoxicated, 331 B.C. Ruins of this city still exist.

During Mr. Cecil Smith's expedition, Nov. 1891 *et seq.*, supported by lord Savile and others, paper mouldings were taken of various sculptures by sig. Giuntini, including the historical frieze connected with the hall of Xerxes, a series of groups of animals, &c., and a cast of the monolithic monument of Cyrus. The casts presented to the British museum, to that at New York, and other collections, reported . . . . . Sept. 1892

PERSIA or IRAN, in the Bible called Elam,* W. Asia. The early history is mythical; see *Media, Xerxes' Campaign,* and *Magi.* Population of the present kingdom, about 6,500,000.

Cyrus revolts against the Medes, and becomes king of Persia, 559; overthrows the Medo-Babylonian monarchy, about 557; conquers Asia Minor about 548; becomes master of the east, 536; killed in a war with the Massagetæ . . . . B.C. 529
Cambyses, his son, king, 529; conquers Egypt (*which see*) 525
The false Smerdis killed; Darius Hystaspes king, 521; conquers Babylon 517
Conquest of Ionia; Miletus destroyed 498
Darius equips a fleet of 600 sail, with an army of 300,000 soldiers to invade the Peloponnesus, which is defeated at Marathon (*which see*) . . 490
Xerxes (king, 485); recovers Egypt, 484; enters Greece in the spring at the head of an immense force; battle of Thermopylæ 480
Xerxes enters Athens, after having lost 200,000 of his troops, and is defeated in a naval engagement of Salamis . . . . ,,
Persians defeated at Mycale and Platæa . 22 Sept. 479
Cimon, son of Miltiades, with a fleet of 250 vessels, takes several cities from the Persians, and destroys their navy, consisting of about 340 sail, near Cyprus 470
His victories at the Eurymedon 469
Xerxes is murdered in his bed by Artabanus . . 465
Artaxerxes I. Longimanus, king, 465; marries Esther, 458
Xerxes I. king, slain by Sogdianus, 425; who is deposed by Darius II., Nothus 424
Artaxerxes II. Mnemon, king, 405: battle of Cunaxa, Cyrus the younger killed 401
Retreat of the 10,000 Greeks (see *Retreat*) . . . ,,
War with Greece, 399; invasion of Persia . . . 396
Peace of Antalcidas (*which see*) 387
Artaxerxes III. (Ochus) kills all his relations at his accession 359
He is killed by his minister Bagoas, and his son, Arses, made king 338
Bagoas kills him and sets up Darius III., Codomanus, by whom he himself is killed 336
Alexander the Great enters Asia; defeats the Persians at the river Granicus, 334; near Issus, 333; at Arbela 331
Darius III. treacherously killed by Bessus . . . ,,
Alexander dies at Babylon, 323; when his empire was divided, Persia with Syria was allotted to Seleucus Nicator, whose successors, the Seleucidæ,

* Elamite antiquities presented to the British Museum by col. Ross, 1876.

ruled Persia, till it was conquered by the Parthians, led by Arsaces I., the founder of the dynasty of the Arsacidæ about 250; his successors ruled till the Persian revolt . . . A.D. 226
Artaxerxes I. founds the Sassanides dynasty; restores kingdom of Persia . . . ,,
Religion of Zoroaster restored and Christianity persecuted . . . 227
Artaxerxes murdered; succeeded by Sapor I.; Armenia becomes independent under Chosroes . 240
Sapor conquers Mesopotamia, 258; repels the Romans and slays the emperor Valerian . . 260
Sapor assassinated; succeeded by Hormisdas I.; who favours the Manichees . . . 272
Varanes I. (Baharam) persecutes them and the Christians . . . 273
Varanes II. defeated by the emperor Probus; makes peace . . . 277
Persia invaded by the emperor Carus, who conquers Seleucia and Ctesiphon . . . 283
Varanes III. king, 293; Narses . . . 294
The emperor Galerius conquers Mesopotamia, &c. . 298
Peace with Diocletian . . . ,,
Hormisdas II. king . . . 301 or 303
Ormuz built . . . about 303
Sapor II. king, 309; proscribes Christianity, 326; makes war successfully with Rome for the lost provinces . . . 337-360
The emperor Julian invades Persia; slain near the Tigris, 26 June; his successor Jovian purchases his retreat by surrendering provinces . . 363
Sapor annexes Armenia, 365; and Iberia, 366; makes peace with Rome . . . 372
Artaxerxes II. king, 380; Sapor III. . . 385
Armenia and Iberia independent . . . 386
Varanes IV., 390; Yezdejird I., 404; conquers Armenia . . . 412
Varanes V., 420, persecutes Christians; conquers Arabia Felix, 421; makes peace with the Eastern empire for 100 years . . . 422
Armenia again united to Persia . . . 428
Wars with Huns, Turks, &c. . . . 430-2
Yezdejird II. king, 440; Hormisdas III., 457; civil war, 458-86; Feroze king, 458; Pallas, 484; Kobad, 486; Jamaspes, 497; Kobad again . . 497
His son, Chosroes I. king; long wars with Justinian and his successors, with various fortune . . 531-79
Successful campaigns of Belisarius . . . 541-2
Hormisdas IV. continues the war; degrades his general, Baharam, who deposes him; but is eventually defeated . . . 590
Chosroes II. 591; renews the war with success, 603; Egypt and Asia Minor subdued . . . 614-6
Chosroes totally defeated by the emperor Heraclius, who advances on Persia . . . 627
Chosroes put to death by his son, Siroes, 628; Artaxerxes III. king, 629; Purandokt, daughter of Chosroes, reigns, 630; Shenendeh, her lover, 631; Arzemdokt, her sister, 631; Kesra, 631; Ferokhdad, 632; Yezdejird III. . . . 632
Persia invaded by the Arabs; the king flees, 641; is betrayed to them and is put to death, and his army exterminated . . . 642
Persia becomes the seat of the Shiite or Fatimite Mahometans . . . 661
The Taherite dynasty established, 813; the Sofferide, 872; the Samanide . . . 902
Persia subdued by Togrul Beg and the Seljukian Turks, 1038; who are expelled, 1194; subdued by Genghis Khan and the Mongols . . . 1223
Bagdad made the capital . . . 1345
The poet Hafiz died about . . . 1388
Persia invaded by Timour, 1380; ravaged by him . 1399
The poet Jami born . . . 1414
Persia conquered by the Turcomans, 1468, who are expelled by the Shiites, who establish the Sophi dynasty under Ismail I. . . . 1501
Ispahan made the capital . . . 1590
The Turks take Bagdad; great massacre . . 1638
Georgia revolts to Russia . . . 1783
Teheran made the capital . . . 1796
War with Russia . . . 1826-9
Rupture with England through the Persians taking Herat (*which see*), 25 Oct.; war declared 1 Nov. 1856
Persians defeated; Bushire taken . . 8-10 Dec. ,,
General Outram defeats the Persians at Kooshab, 8 Feb.; and at Mohammerah . . 26 March, 1857
Peace ratified at Teheran . . . 14 April, 1857
Commercial treaty with France, &c. . . June, ,,
Herat given up by the Persians . . . July, ,,
The shah re-organizes the government . 9 Sept. 1858
Railways in process of formation . . . 1865
Electric telegraph introduced . . . 1867
Great sufferings through three years' drought, accompanied by fever and cholera; about 16,000 persons perished at Ispahan, &c. July-Oct. 1871
Collection in London for relief; above 13,000*l.* subscribed . . . Oct. 1871—Feb. 1872
Concession to baron Julius de Reuter to make railways, waterworks, &c. for 70 years, with great power . . . 25 July, ,,
Prosperity restored through a good harvest, March, 1873
The shah starts to visit Europe, 19 April; arrives at St. Petersburg, 22 May; at Berlin, 31 May; at Brussels, 16 June; at London, 18 June; receives the garter at Windsor, 20 June; at Paris, 5 July; at Turin, 25 July; at Vienna, 30 July; at Constantinople, 19 Aug.; returned to Teheran 23 Sept. ,,
The shah visits Europe in summer; returned to Teheran . . . 9 Aug. 1878
Rebellious incursions of the Kurds suppressed after much bloodshed (see *Kurdistan*) . Oct.-Dec. 1880
Treaty with Russia signed . . . 22 Dec. 1881
The Russians attack the Shohsovan tribes going into winter quarters, killed about 80 . Jan. 1886
Sir H. D. Wolff, British minister . . 1 Dec. 1887
First railway constructed in Persia from Teheran to Shah-Abdul-Azim opened . . 25 June, 1888
The river Karun decreed open to all nations by the intervention of England . . 9 Sept. ,,
The shah visits Europe; at St. Petersburg, 23-26 May; Berlin, 9 June; Amsterdam, 16 June; Antwerp, 22 June; received by the prince of Wales at Gravesend, and sails to Westminster, 1 July; at Windsor, 2 July; at Guildhall, London, 3 July; visits Birmingham and other places 7-29 July; Paris, 30 July; Munich, 19 Aug.; Vienna, 23 Aug.; Budapesth, 26 Aug.; returns to Teheran . . . 20 Oct. 1889
Imperial bank of Persia established (concession to baron Julius de Reuter, 30 Jan.) . 23 Oct. ,,
Prince Malcolm khan, long minister in London, recalled to Persia . . . Dec. ,,
Mirza Mahomet Ali khan, new minister for England, received by the marquis of Salisbury . 4 March, 1890
Sir Frank C. Lascelles, British minister . July, 1891
Great opposition of the priests and people to the monopoly of the Imperial tobacco régie (corporation), 14 Dec.; the monopoly abolished in the interior, 19 Dec.; by a proclamation . 27 Dec. ,,
Complete abolition of the monopoly demanded, 4 Jan., granted 7 Jan.; compensation to the company to be paid . . . April, 1892
The Russian government offer to lend 500,000*l.* to pay the compensation to the tobacco corporation, reported 23 April; the offer declined; a loan from the Imperial bank of Persia, London, accepted . . . about 16 May, ,,
"Persia and the Persian Question," by the hon. George N. Curzon, M.P., published . May, ,,
Revolt of the Barharloos, suppressed . . Feb. 1893
Great earthquake at Kuchan, 12,000 deaths, reported . . . 17 Nov. ,,
Delimitation treaty with Russia ratified, 30 July; reported . . . 26 Nov. ,,
The coinage and importation of silver suspended, 2 March, 1894
Sir Mortimer Durand appointed British minister March, 1894; arrives at Teheran . 17 Nov. ,,
Kuchan rebuilt; again destroyed by earthquake; 11,000 lives lost . . . 17-22 Jan. 1895
Delimitation of the Russo-Persian frontier settled by commission . . . Feb. ,,
Zanjabad and several other villages partially destroyed by an earthquake, 300 deaths . 2 Jan. 1896
Goi completely destroyed, 800 deaths . 5 Jan. ,,
Assassination of the shah, 1 May (Mirza Reza, the murderer, executed at Teheran, 12 Aug.); succeeded by Muzaffer-ed-Deen, recognised by the powers . . . 2 May, ,,
Enthronement of the shah at Teheran . 8 June, ,,
Ministerial changes, the shah head of the cabinet of 12 ministers . . . Nov ,,

Earthquake with loss of life in the island of Kishim, 1,400 deaths . . . . . . 10, 11 Jan. 1897
Death of sir Joseph Tholozan, the shah's physician, Aug. ,,
Mr. Graves, of the telegraph department, murdered and his camp looted at Karwan; Indian troops sent to Jask, Dec.–Jan.; Shaki Mahomed, the murderer, executed at Jask, 31 May, 1898
The *Baluchistan*, steamship, of London, conveying arms, &c., seized by H.M.S. *Lapwing*, off Muscat, 24 Jan. ,,
Abdul Khan, Nasir-ul-Mulk, appointed finance minister . . . . 12 Feb. ,,
Serious fanatical riot at Hamadan, 27 deaths 22 Feb. ,,
The governor of Kirman takes Fanoch fort, held by rebels, who fly to the hills . . . March, ,,
Amin ed Dowleh, grand vizier, resigns 5 June, ,,
Lingah retaken from the Arabs . . 9 March, 1899
Great fire at Resht, damage, abt. 100,000*l.*, 15, 16 Nov. ,,
Financial agreement with Russia, 5 per cent. gold loan of 22,500,000 roubles issued by the Persian government to the Loan bank of Persia . 30 Jan. 1900
Sir Arthur Hardinge, British minister . Aug. ,,
The shah received by the czar at St. Petersburg, 17 July; at Paris, 28 July (shot at by Salsou, 2 Aug.); leaves, 11 Aug.; returns 27 Oct. ,,
New loan of 10,000,000 roubles, entitled 5 per cent. Persian gold loan, reported . . 8 April, 1902
The shah visits Europe—at Cracow, 12 May; present at a military review in Rome, 22 May; received by prince Arthur of Connaught at Dover, 17 Aug.; by the prince of Wales, London, 18 Aug.; by the king at Portsmouth, 20 Aug.; visits sir Hiram Maxim's engineering works, Westminster, and the Abbey, 21 Aug.; Woolwich, 22 Aug.; Windsor, Crystal palace, 23 Aug.; at Paris, 25 Aug.–14 Sept.; receives the Spanish order of the Golden Fleece, 6 Sept.; Berlin, 15 Sept.; with the czar at Kursk, 17, 18 Sept. ,,
Raiding dhows captured by H.M.S. *Lapwing* off Koweyt; enemy lost about 24, 1 British killed, 6 Sept. ,,
Scheme of financial reform with corporation of Belgian experts determined upon by Persian government, announced (*Cologne Gazette*), 27 Dec. ,,
Concession for construction of new road from Tabriz to Kazvin, granted to Russian bank at Teheran; detrimental to British trade in northern Persia . . . . 30 Dec. ,,
Order of the garter conferred by King Edw. VII. on Shah . . . . 1 Jan. 1903
Formal investiture by lord Downe, appointed as special envoy . . . . . . 2 Feb. ,,
Russo-Persian commercial agreement ratified by the Tsar. Provides *ad valorem* duties of treaty of 1828 shall be superseded by specific duties, the majority of export duties to be abolished; farming of taxes to be entirely abolished; customs stations to be established, and provisions relating to customs and traffic and toll dues; reported to come into operation, 14 Feb. ,,

A.D. SHAHS.

1502. Ismail or Ishmael: conquers Georgia, 1519.
1523. Tamasp or Thamas I.
1576. Ismail II. Meerza.
1577. Mahommed Meerza.
1585. Abbas I. the Great; made a treaty with the English, 1612; died in 1628.
1628. Shah Sophi.
1641. Abbas II.
1666. Shah Sophi II.
1694. Hussein; deposed.
1722. Mahmoud, chief of the Afghans.
1725. Ashraff the Usurper; slain in battle.
1730. Tamasp or Thamas II.; recovered the throne of his ancestors from the preceding.
[Thamas-Kouli-Khan, his general, obtained great successes in this and the subsequent reigns.]
1732. Abbas III., infant son of Tamasp, under the regency of Kouli-Khan, who afterwards caused himself to be proclaimed king as
1736. Nadir Shah (the victorious king); conquers India, 1739; assassinated at Khorassan by his nephew.
1747. Shah Rokh.
1751. [Interregnum.]
1759. Kureem Khan.
1779. Many competitors for the throne, and assassinations till—
1795. Aga-Mahommed Khan obtains the power, and founds the reigning (Turcoman) dynasty; assassinated, 1797.
1798. Futteh Ali-Shah.
1834. Mahommed-Shah, grandson of Futteh; died, 10 Sept. 1848.
1848. Nasr-ul-Deen, or Nasr-ed-Deen, son; born, 4 April, 1829; said to be an able prince and friendly to Britain, visited Europe, 1873, 1878 and 1889; shot in a mosque near Teheran by Mirza Reza, said to be a Babi fanatic, 1 May, 1896.
1896. Muzaffer-ed-Deen, son, born 25 March, 1853. *Heir*: son, Ali Mirza Itezad-es-Sultaneh, born 1872.

PERSON, Offences against. The statute laws respecting these were consolidated and amended in 1861. In the Reform bill, 1832, women were disfranchised by the insertion of the word (male) before *person*.

PERSPECTIVE in drawing was observed by the Van Eycks (1426-46) and treated scientifically by Michael Angelo, Leonardo da Vinci, and Albert Dürer, early in the 16th century. Guido Ubaldo published a treatise in 1608; Dubreuil's treatise (the "Jesuits' perspective") appeared in 1642, and the mathematical theory was demonstrated by Brook Taylor in 1731.

PERTH (the old capital of Scotland), said to have been founded by Agricola, about A.D. 70. It was besieged by the Regent Robert, 1339. On 20 Feb. 1437, James I. was murdered at the Black Friars' monastery here, by Robert Graham and the earl of Athol, for which they suffered condign punishment. Gowrie's conspiracy occurred here, 6 Aug. 1600. Perth was taken from the French garrison by the reformers, 26 June, 1559. The "Articles of Perth" relating to religious ceremonies, were agreed to by the General Assembly of Scotland, 25 Aug. 1618. Perth was taken by Cromwell in 1651; and by the earl of Mar after the battle of Dunblane, in 1715. The statue of the prince consort was inaugurated in the presence of the queen, 30 Aug. 1864. St. John's Cathedral much damaged by fire, 31 Dec. 1894. The Natural History museum opened by sir William Flower, 29 Nov. 1895. Population, 1881, 25,250; 1891, 30,760; 1901, 32,872.

Public library opened by lord Rosebery . 22 Oct. 1898
Mr. Andrew Carnegie receives the freedom, 8 Oct. 1902
Collapse of a stand at a cricket match, many injured . . . . 1 Aug. 1903

PERTH, capital of western Australia (*which see*), founded 1829. Population, 1891, 9,617; 1901, 36,199.

PERU (S. America), was long governed by incas, said to be descended from Manco Capac, who ruled in the 11th century. Population, 1876, 2,699,945; 1896, 4,559,550. Capital, Lima.

Peru explored and conquered by Francisco Pizarro and Almagro 1524-33
The last inca, Atahualpa, put to death . 29 Aug. 1533
Pizarro assassinated at Lima . . 26 June, 1541
Fruitless insurrection of the Peruvians under Tapac Amaru, an inca 1780
San Martin proclaims the independence of Peru, 28 July, 1821
War against Spain . . . . . . 14 Jan. 1824
Bolivar made dictator . . . . . . Feb. ,,
Mariano Prado president . . . 28 Nov. ,,
The Spaniards defeated at Ayacucho, and freedom of Peru and Chili achieved . . 9 Dec. ,,
The new Peruvian constitution signed by the president of the republic . . . . 21 March, 1828
War with Colombia; treaty of peace . 28 Feb. 1829

After a succession of fierce party conflicts, general Ramon Castilla becomes president; firm and politic 1845
Exportation of guano began 1846
President Echenique, deposed; Castilla again president 1855
New constitution, 1856; modified 1860
Population (without Indians) about 2½ millions . 1859
Marshal San Ramon president . . 24 Oct. 1862
General J. A. Pezet president . . . . 3 April, 1863
The Spanish admiral Pinzon took possession of the Chincha-isles (valuable for guano) belonging to Peru, stating that he would occupy them till the claims of his government on Peru were satisfied. 14 April, 1864
American congress at Lima; plenipotentiaries from Chili and other states meet to concert measures for defence against European powers . Nov. ,,
Negotiations followed by peace with Spain, 28 Jan.; Chincha islands restored . . . . 3 Feb. 1865
Revolt against president Pezet, 28 Feb.; several provinces soon lost . . . . . May, ,,
The insurgents declare war against Spain . Oct. ,,
They take Lima; Pezet flies, and Canseco becomes president . . . . Nov. ,,
Peru joins Chili, and declares war against Spain, Feb. 1866
The Spanish admiral Nuñez, in his attempt to bombard Callao, repulsed and wounded . 2 May, ,,
The Spaniards quit Peruvian waters . 10 May, ,,
Riots at Lima against religious toleration 15 April, 1867
Invasion of ex-president Castilla, May; dies of fever, 30 May, ,,
Mariano-Ignace Prado resigns dictatorship; made provisional president, 15 Feb.; proclaimed, 31 Aug. ,,
Insurrection against Prado; he resigns, 7 Jan.; succeeded by gen. La Puerta; Pezet's treaty with Spain confirmed . . . . 18 Jan. 1868
Col. J. Balta president . . . . 1 Aug. ,,
Several towns in Peru suffered by great earthquakes (see *Earthquakes*) . . . . . 13-15 Aug. ,,
Gold mines discovered at Huacho . . . Oct. 1871
Industrial exhibition opened at Lima . July, 1872
Military insurrection at Lima; Tomas Gutierrez, minister of war, makes himself dictator, and imprisons president Balta . . . . 22 July, ,,
Unsupported by the people, and not recognised by diplomatic representatives, he orders Balta to be shot; is himself compelled to fly; caught; killed by the people, and hanged to a lamp-post; col. Zavallos, vice-president, assumes the government; order restored; about 200 lives were lost during the *coup d'état* . . . . . . 26 July, ,,
Manuel Pardo elected president by the people, assumed office . . . . . . 2 Aug. ,,
Armed riots in Lima at the execution of cols. Ganrio and Zavallos as rebels . . . . . May, 1873
President Pardo escapes assassination . 22 Aug. 1874
Insurrection under Pierola; he is defeated at Sorota, near Tarata . . . . . 3 Dec. ,,
Talisman sailed from Cardiff for South America; consigned to Peruvian rebels; seized and condemned as a prize, and English sailors imprisoned, Nov. 1874-Nov. 1875; report on ill-usage, English government promise inquiry . March, 1876
President, Mariana I. Prado . . . . 2 Aug. ,,
Reported insurrection of Nicolas de Pierola, with about 6000 men, endeavouring to establish a southern confederacy . . . . . 6-10 Oct. ,,
He sails away with the *Huascar* ironclad, 29 May; this is attacked by adm. De Horsey, with H.M.S. *Shah* and *Amethyst*, as piratical, for attacking mail ships; it is compelled to go into Lima and surrender; the Peruvians resent British interference, and threaten reprisals . . June, 1877
Peruvian government issues a circular to the powers, 10 June; demands reparation 25 June, ,,
Sir John Holker, att.-general, in house of commons, said that the *Huascar* had committed acts which made her an enemy of Great Britain, and had no belligerent rights; and that De Horsey was justified in what he did . . 11 Aug. ,,
Pierolas and his adherents amnestied . Aug. ,,
Ex-president Pardo, president of the senate, assassinated at Lima . . . . . . 16 Nov. 1878
Peru and Bolivia declare war against Chili, announced . . . . 2 April, 1879

For the events of the war, see *Chili*, 1879—81.

Sanguinary revolution at Lima; Pierola proclaimed dictator; Prado flees . . 22 Dec. *et seq.* ,,
Lima occupied by the Chilians . . . 17 Jan. 1881
Señor F. G. Calderon provisional president at Magdalena . . . . March, ,,
Anarchy in Lima . . . . March, ,,
Pierolas, near Lima, declares for continual war, April, ,,
Pasco, a seaport, burnt by Peruvian soldiery; about 1000 inhabitants massacred, announced 20 Feb. 1882
Pierolas quits Peru, announced . . 10 April, ,,
President Montero opposed to truce with Chili; disaffection . . . . May, ,,
President Iglesias formed a ministry about 12 Sept.; he signs peace with Chili at Ancon 20 Oct. 1883
Important territories surrendered. . . . Oct. ,,
Lima evacuated by the Chilians . . . 23 Oct. ,,
Arequipa surrendered to the Chilians . 26 Oct. ,,
Gen. Iglesias' government confirmed by elections, about 29 Jan. 1884
Treaty with Chili ratified by the Notables, March; partial evacuation of Peruvian territory May, ,,
Gen. Caceres makes himself president in opposition to Iglesias; enters Lima with a rabble, and is quickly repulsed . . . . . . 27 Aug. ,,
Montero oscillates between the two parties; civil war continues; Truxillo captured for Iglesias; severe fighting announced . . . . 17 Oct. ,,
Gradual submission to the government . Dec. ,,
Insurrection; government troops defeated at Ayacucho, announced . . . . . 2 May, 1885
Gen. Caceres defeated by gen. Iglesias at Huancayo, about 28 May, ,,
Caceres' army disbanded, announced . 26 June, ,,
Renewed heavy fighting announced, 9 July; reported rebel victory . . . . . . 15 Aug. ,,
Government troops gain a victory over the forces of gen. Caceres, 16 Oct.; at Jania about 19 Nov.; Caceres attacks Lima; severe fighting; Iglesias surrenders 2 Dec.; Dr. Arenas elected president, 3 Dec.; Iglesias and Caceres retire from Lima through foreign intervention . . 4 Dec. ,,
Gen. Caceres president . . . . . 3 June, 1886
Col. Remigio Morales Bermudez, president, 10 Aug. 1890
Revolutionary attempt of Pierola's supporters near Lima defeated; about 40 killed . . 2 Dec. ,,
A new ministry formed by señor Justiniamo Borgono, 24 Aug. 1891; succeeded by sen. Carlos Elias. . . . . about 1 July, 1892
Great fire at Callao; buildings and much shipping destroyed . . . . 21 Aug. ,,
New ministry under gen. Velarde, 3 March; under sen. Jose Mariano Jimenez . . . 12 May, 1893
Crisis through the fall in price of silver (*which see*) end of June, ,,
Death of president Bermudez; vice-president col. Borgono assumes power . . . . 31 March, 1894
Gen. Caceres installed as president . 10 Aug. ,,
Insurrection in the south, reported, 11 Aug.; insurgents defeated near Mirave, reported, 29 Aug.; again defeated at Huarez, reported . 14 Oct. ,,
Bands of rebels defeated, reported . 12, 29 Nov. ,,
The rebels occupy Arequipa, reported . 31 Jan. 1895
Lima besieged by the insurgents under gen. Pierola, 18 Feb. ,,
Reported defeat of the government troops at Cabanillas . . . . 11 March, ,,
Gen. Pierola enters Lima, fighting with much slaughter; a truce obtained by the diplomatic corps . . . . 17-20 March, ,,
Gen. Pierola retires; president Caceres takes refuge on French man-of-war at Callao; a provisional government formed . 21, 22 March, ,,
Gen. Nicola Pierola elected president . 10 July, ,,
Señ. Barrinaja forms a cabinet . . . 1 Dec. ,,
Short rebellion of Seminario ends . . July, 1896
Congress opened by pres. Nicola Pierola, prosperity reported . . . . 28 July, ,,
Señ. Barrinaja resigns, succeeded by sen. Manuel Olacchea, announced . . . . . 8 Aug. ,,
Great fire at Guayaquil, churches and public buildings destroyed; estimated loss, 6,000,000*l.*, 6, 7 Oct. ,,

Congress opened, 12 Aug. 1897; the cabinet resigns, 29 Oct.; new one formed by señ. Romana, 26 Nov. 1897
The president in a secret message to congress owns to not having complied with several laws promulgated in 1896 . . . . . Nov. ,,
Bill passed providing for civil marriage, announced, 16 Dec. ,,
The president of the cabinet resigns . 24 Dec. ,,
Protocol regarding the *plébiscite* on the question of restoring land to Peru, signed at Santiago, 22 April, 1898
Congress opened by president Pierola; Washington postal convention accepted by Peru . 28 July, 1899
Señ. de Romaña installed president, 8 Sept.; new cabinet formed . . . . . mid Dec. ,,
Frequent changes of ministry . . . . Aug. 1900
Señ. Balaunde, ex-minister of finance, charged with appropriating 20,000*l*. from the national funds; great indignation mass meeting at Lima, troops called out, reported . . . . . 1 Oct. ,,
New coalition ministry formed, señ. Domingo Almenara, president and minister of finance, 3 Oct. ,,
Señ. Chacaltana forms a cabinet, reported, 12 Sept. 1901
Gold standard only, adopted by law passed 9 Dec. ,,
Señ. Alejandro de Ustua's ministry formed, 10 Aug. ,,
Argentina government appointed arbitrator between Bolivia and Peru respecting boundaries, 2 Jan. 1903
Señ. Manuel Candamo elected president . 30 May, ,,
Congress opened; pres. Romano states that the relations between Peru and other nations were friendly, and that the question between Peru and Bolivia had been submitted to arbitration; that a solution with Chili regarding the Tacna-Arica was impossible; no budget would be presented, 28 July, ,,
Senate passes a measure reducing the import duty on sugar to an equivalent of 6 francs, the maximum allowed by the Brussels convention, 8 Aug. ,,

PERUGIA, a city of central Italy; as Perousia, anciently one of the Etruscan confederation. It allied itself with the Samnites, but was ruined by two defeats by the Romans, 309 and 295 B.C. It was taken by Octavius Cæsar from the adherents of Antony; many of whom were immolated on altars by their victor, 41. Leo X. took Perugia from the rival families Oddi and Baglioni, in A.D. 1520. An insurrection here against the pope was put down by the Swiss with great cruelty, 20 June, 1859. Perugia was taken by the Sardinian general Fanti, in Sept. 1860, when the cruel papal general Schmidt and 1600 men were made prisoners.

PERUKE or **WIG**. The ancients used false hair, but the present peruke was first worn in France and Italy about 1620; and introduced into England about 1660, and prevailed more or less till about 1810.

It is said that bishop Blomfield (of London), in 1830, obtained permission for the bishops to discontinue wearing their wigs in parliament, of which they gradually availed themselves. On account of the heat, sir J. P. Wilde, and other judges and several counsel, appeared in court without wigs, 22, 23 July, 1868.

PERUVIAN BARK, see *Jesuits' Bark*.

PESCHIERA, a strong Austrian fortress, on an island in the Mincio, near the Lago di Garda, N. Italy. It has been frequently taken by siege:—by the French, 1796; by the Austrians and Russians, 1799; by the French again, 1801; given up by them, 1814; taken by the Sardinians, May, 1848; retaken by Radetsky, March, 1849. The Sardinians were preparing to besiege it in July, 1859, when peace was made. It was given up to the Italians, 9 Oct. 1866; see *Quadrilateral*.

PESSIMISM (from *pessimus*, the worst), the opposite doctrine to *optimism* (which see). Mr. James Sully's "Pessimism, a History and a Criticism," was published in 1877. Arthur Schopenhauer (1788-1860), an eminent pessimist, says, "All life is effort, all effort is painful, the pains of life must predominate."

PESTALOZZIAN SYSTEM of education was devised by John Henry Pestalozzi, born at Zurich in Switzerland, in 1746, died 17 Feb. 1827. In 1775 he turned his farm into a school for educating poor children in reading, writing, and working; but he did not succeed. In 1798 he established an orphan school where he began with the mutual instruction, or monitorial system, since adopted by Lancaster; but his school was soon after turned into a hospital for the Austrian army. In 1802, in conjunction with Fellenberg, he established his school at Hofwyl, which at first was successful, but eventually declined through mismanagement.

PESTH (Hungary), built about 889, on the east bank of the Danube, opposite Buda, was repeatedly taken and besieged in the wars of Hungary, particularly with the Turks. The great insurrection broke out here, and the minister, count Lamberg, was killed, 28 Sept. 1848. Buda-Pesth was taken by the imperialists, 5 Jan. 1849. The Hungarians afterwards defeated the Austrians, who were obliged to evacuate it 18 April, same year; see *Hungary*. Buda-Pesth formally constituted capital of Hungary, Nov. 1873.

Hungarian national exhibition opened 2 May, 1885.

PESTILENCE, see *Plague*.

PETALISM (from the Greek *petalon*, a leaf), a mode of deciding upon the guilt of citizens of Syracuse, similar to the Athenian ostracism, the name being written on a leaf (generally of an olive) instead of on a shell, about 460 B.C. If guilt were established the sentence was usually banishment.

PETARD, or **PETAR**, an invention ascribed to the Huguenots in 1579. Petards of metal, nearly in the shape of a hat, were employed to blow up gates or other barriers, and also in countermines to break through into the enemy's galleries. Cahors was taken by Henry IV. by means of petards, in 1580, when it is said they were first used. "Hoist with his own petar." *Shakspeare*, Hamlet iii. 4.

PETER THE GREAT'S WILL, see under *Wills*.

PETER THE WILD BOY, a savage creature found in the Harzwald, electorate of Hanover, when George I. and his friends were hunting. He was found walking on his hands and feet, climbing trees like a squirrel, and feeding on grass and moss, Nov. 1725. At this time he was supposed to be thirteen years old. He died, while under the care of an English farmer, Feb. 1785, unchanged in his habits.

PETERBOROUGH, anciently Medeshamstede (Northamptonshire); obtained its present name from a king of Mercia founding an abbey and dedicating it to St. Peter about 655. The church, destroyed by the Danes, was rebuilt with great beauty. The tower becoming dangerous, restoration resolved on, Dec. 1882. Foundation laid of new building, 7 May, 1884. Choir re-opened 11 July, 1889; Cathedral re-opened, 14 Oct. 1890; further restoration, May, 1894; completed (total cost about 80,000*l*.), July, 1902. The bishopric was erected by Henry VIII., out of the lands of dissolved monasteries in the diocese of Lincoln. The first bishop was John Chambers, the last abbot of Peterborough, 1541 The see was valued in the king's books at 419*l.* 19*s.* 11*d.* Present income 4500*l.* Population, 1881, 21,228; 1891, 25,172; 1901, 30,870.

Exhibition of relics of Mary queen of Scots opened 19 July, 1887.

RECENT BISHOPS.

1794. Spencer Madan; died, 8 Oct. 1813.
1813. John Parsons; died, 12 March, 1819.
1819. Herbert Marsh; died, 1 May, 1839.
1839. George Davys; died, 8 April, 1864.
1864. Francis Jeune, May; died 20 Aug. 1868.
1868. Wm. Connor Magee; elected 31 Oct.; translated to York, 1891.
1891. Mandell Creighton, elected 18 March; translated to London, Nov. 1896.
1896. Hon. Edward Carr-Glyn, Nov.; elected 6 Feb. 1897.

PETERLOO, see *Manchester Reform Meeting*, 16 Aug. 1819.

PETERSBURG, ST., the modern capital of Russia, founded by Peter the Great, 27 May, 1703. He built a small hut for himself, and some wooden hovels. In 1710, the count Golovkin built the first house of brick; and the next year, the emperor, with his own hands, laid the foundation of a house of the same material. The seat of empire was transferred from Moscow to this place in 1712. Here, in 1736, a fire consumed 2000 houses; and in 1780, another fire consumed 11,000 houses; this last fire was occasioned by lightning. Again, in June, 1796, a large magazine of naval stores and 100 vessels were destroyed. The winter palace was burnt to the ground, 29 Dec. 1837. The railway to Moscow was finished in 1851; to Berlin, opened 5 May, 1862. On 10 June, 1862, property to the amount of nearly a million sterling was destroyed by fire. Population, 1886: province, 1,660,859; city, 1885, 861,303; 9 Feb. 1897, 1,267,923 (with suburbs); 1900, 1,248,643. See *Russia*, 1862 *et seq.* —PETERSBURG, Virginia, see *United States*, 1864.

Peace of St. Petersburg, between Russia and Prussia, the former restoring all her conquests to the latter, signed . . . . 5 May,	1762
Treaty of St. Petersburg for the partition of Poland (see article, *Partition Treaties*) . . . 5 Aug.	1772
Treaty of St. Petersburg, led to a coalition against France . . . . 8 Sept.	1805
Treaty of Alliance, signed at St. Petersburg, between Bernadotte, prince royal of Sweden, and the emperor Alexander; the former agreeing to join in the campaign against France, in return for which Sweden was to receive Norway 24 March,	1812
Grand new Alexander II. bridge over the Neva opened . . . . 12 Oct.	1879
Ship canal to Cronstadt completed, Feb.; opened by the czar . . . . 27 May,	1885
War memorial uncovered by the czar . 26 Oct.	1886
Semi-centennial anniversary of the foundation of the British and American chapel; Russian dignitaries and foreign ambassadors present . 18 Dec.	1890
Exhibition of works of British artists visited by the czar and czarina . . . . . 22 Jan.	1898
Naval storehouses burnt, 10 June, 1900; and great dock fire, 13 June, 1901; 30 houses burnt down in the Narva quarter . . . . 10 July,	1901
Revolutionary demonstration, 17 March, 1901; again, many injured . . . . 16 March,	1902
Celebration of bi-centenary of the founding of St. Petersburg; new Troitski bridge formally opened in presence of the czar . . . 29, 30 May,	1903

PETER'S CHURCH, ST. (Rome), originally erected by Constantine, 306. About 1450, pope Nicholas V. commenced a new church. The present magnificent pile was designed by Bramante; the first stone laid by pope Julius II. in 1506. In 1514, Leo X. employed Raphael and two others to superintend the building. Paul III. committed the work to Michael Angelo, who devised the dome, in the construction of which 30,000 lbs. of iron were used. The church was consecrated 18 Nov. 1626. The front is 400 feet broad, rising to a height of 180 feet, and the majestic dome ascends from the centre of the church to a height of 324 feet; the length of the interior is 600 feet, forming one of the most spacious halls ever constructed. The length of the exterior is 669 feet; its greatest breadth within is 442 feet; and the entire height from the ground 432 feet. Renewal of the leaden envelope completed, July, 1884.

PETER'S PENCE, presented by Ina, king of the West Saxons, to the pope at Rome, for the endowment of an English college there, about 725; so called because agreed to be paid on Peter Mass, 1 Aug. The tax was levied on all families possessed of thirty pence yearly rent in land, out of which they paid one penny. It was confirmed by Offa, 777, and was afterwards claimed by the popes as a tribute from England, and regularly collected, till suppressed by Henry VIII. 1534. *Camden.* A public collection (on behalf of the pope) was forbidden in France in 1860.

A collection for the pope was proposed to be made in Hungary by the prince primate, reported, 16 Nov. 1892.

The Peter's pence presented at the pope's jubilee was said to amount to 263,960*l.*; Great Britain, 48,000*l.*; Ireland, 720*l.* Feb. 1893. See *Pope.*

PETERSWALDEN (Germany), CONVENTION OF, between Great Britain and Russia, by which a firm and decisive alliance between those powers was made against France, and the course of action against Napoleon Bonaparte was planned; signed 8 July, 1813. This alliance led to the overthrow of Bonaparte in the next year.

PETERWARDEIN (in Austria), was taken by the Turks, July, 1526. Here prince Eugene of Savoy gained a great victory over the Turks, 5 Aug. 1716.

PETITIONS. The right of petitioning the crown and parliament for redress of grievances is a fundamental principle of the constitution. Petitions are extant of the date of Edward I. In the reign of Henry IV. petitions began to be addressed to the house of commons in considerable numbers. In 1837 there were presented to parliament 10,831 petitions, signed by 2,905,905 persons; in 1859, 24,386, signed by 2,290,579; in 1867, 12,744, signed by 1,145,216; 1893-94, 33,742, signed by 5,010,056; 1901, 9,885, signed by 1,111,342. See *Abhorrers*, and *Rights.*

A petition from Boulogne for a consul was brought in, but not received by the commons . April-May, 1876

Evidence before a committee of the commons disclosed systems whereby vast numbers of fictitious and forged signatures were obtained, rendering the petitions for and against the continuance of the London coal and wine dues utterly valueless, May, 1887.

PETO'S ACT, 13 & 14 Vict. c. 28 (1850), renders more simple and effectual the titles by which religious bodies hold property.

PETRA, the ancient Sela, in mount Seir, near mount Hor, in the land of Edom. In the 4th century B.C. it was held by the Nabathæans, who successfully resisted Antigonus. About A.D. 70 it was the residence of the Arab princes named Aretas. It was conquered by Cornelius Palma, and annexed to the empire under Trajan, 105, to which period its remarkable monuments are ascribed. It was an important station for commercial traffic with Rome. It has been described by Burckhardt and other travellers.

PETRARCH AND LAURA; celebrated for the refined passion of the former for the latter, began in 1327, and the chief subject of his sonnets. He was born 1304, crowned with laurel, as a poet and writer, on Easter-day, 8 April, 1341; and died at Arqua, near Padua, 18 July, 1374. Laura died 6 April, 1348. A commemoration of his death at Avignon and other places, 18 July, 1874.

PETRO-BRUSIANS, followers of Pierre de Bruys, an early reformer, who was burnt at St. Gilles, Languedoc, as a heretic, in 1130.

PETROLEUM, rock oil or mineral oil similar to paraffin, has been found in many parts of the world, especially at Rangoon. In 1859 and since, a number of oil-springs were discovered in the bituminous coal regions of N. W. Pennsylvania, now termed "Petrolia," and others have been discovered in Ohio and other states, and also in Canada. Numerous artesian wells were sunk, manufactories erected, and an almost unlimited supply obtained; between 1859-77, 2,802,500,000 gallons; in 1863, 8,907,365 gallons. In consequence of the importation of this oil into this country, and many accidents having taken place through its inflammability at low temperature, acts for "the safe keeping of petroleum" were passed, 29 July, 1862; July, 1868, Aug. 1871, and 1879. Petroleum became an awful weapon in the hands of the insurgents in Paris, 23-27 May, 1871. About fifty killed by explosion at a petroleum manufactory near Rheims, 16 July, 1871. The Petroleum Association test petroleum, with the view of preventing the importation of that which is dangerous. Refined petroleum imported: 1872, 5,670,674 gallons; 1877, 33,474,955 gallons; 1881, 58,371,386 gallons. Unrefined and refined: 1882, 59,695,982 gallons; 1883, 70,526,996 gallons; 1886, 71,251,736 gallons; 1888, 94,401,285 gallons; 1890, 105,080,863 gallons; 1893, 155,125,667 gallons; 1900, 254,978,043 gallons; 1901, 253,784,741 gallons.

Petroleum oil found in Luneberger Haidee, Hanover; a colony formed named Œlheim . Aug. 1881
Petroleum fire at Bristol; fire floated through the drains into the river . . . . . 30 Nov. ,,
The great petroleum grounds near Baku, a Russian town on the Caspian, long monopolized, set free, 1872; greatly developed by Ludwig (died April 1888), and Robert Nobel, Swedes, since 1875; 34,000,000 gallons of oil produced in 1875; Russia supplied 200,000,000 in 1882; exportation begun and greatly increasing . . 1884-91
[Baku is the site of the ancient fire worship by the followers of Zoroaster.]
Petroleum largely discovered in Austrian Galicia, 1885
Mr. Edwin N. Henwood's invention for use of petroleum for the production of steam announced March, 1886; Spiel's petroleum engine announced . . . . April, 1886
Petroleum discovered in Egypt on the coast of the Red Sea, March, 1886; reported successful 22 Aug. 1887
Petroleum found in Burmah . . . . May, ,,
Destructive fire at the Markoff petroleum fountain near Baku . . . . 25 July, ,,
Large quantities of natural gas now used as fuel in ironworks &c. in Pittsburg, &c. . . . 1884 *et seq.*
Mr. Penn's system of lighting by petroleum lamps, was introduced at the Cuxton station, S.E. Railway . . . . Nov. 1890
Mr. Chenhall's process for solidifying petroleum to form cheap steam fuel reported successful 19 Nov. 1891
Oil is discovered in the waters of some wells on the Ashwick estates near Shepton Mallet, Somerset, reported *Times* . . . . . 31 Jan. 1894
Confirmed, on investigation, by prof. Redwood and Mr. Topley . . . . . . 10 March, ,,
A great petroleum fountain at Grozni, north of the Caucasus, takes fire; 17 workmen killed and much destruction, reported . . . 18 Oct. 1894
Mr. Boverton Redwood's "Petroleum," an exhaustive work, historical, geographical, scientific, and legal, 900 pages, with maps, etc., published, March, 1896
A number of wells discovered in Buzeo, Roumania, reported . . . . 31 Dec. ,,
Oil struck at a depth of 1,040 feet at St. Paul's inlet, Newfoundland . . . Dec. 1896–Jan. 1897
The petroleum committee's report recommends legislation . . . . . . 13 July, 1898
Ten factories and 5 depôts burnt at Baku, about 127 lives lost, many injured, early Feb. 1901; again 40 towers destroyed and 2 reservoirs burnt, 1 Oct. 1901
Strike at the Rothschild petroleum works at Batum, 17 March; fatal rioting . 21, 22 March, 1902
Petroleum discovered in Trinidad, reported, 11 July, ,,
Strike and rioting at Baku, oil wells set on fire, conflict between rioters and troops, 15-18 July, 1903

PETROLEUSES, a name given to women charged with throwing petroleum on the burning houses in Paris during the siege by the government, May, 1871.

PETROPAULOVSKI, a fortified town on the east coast of Kamtschatka, was attacked by an English and French squadron, 30 Aug. 1854. They destroyed the batteries, but failed in taking some Russian frigates, except the *Sitka*, a store-ship taken by the *President*, and a schooner taken by the *Pique*. Admiral Price was killed, it is supposed by the accidental discharge of his own pistol. A party of 700 sailors and marines landed to assault the place, but fell into an ambuscade; many were killed, including captain Parker and M. Bourasset, English and French officers. The objects of the attack were not attained, it is thought from want of stores. After this the Russians greatly strengthened their defences, but on 30 May, 1855, the allied squadron in the Pacific arriving here found the place deserted. The fortifications were destroyed, but the town was spared. The Russian ships escaped.

PETTY BAG, CLERK OF THE: power was given to the treasury, with consent of the lord chancellor and master of the rolls, to abolish this office, by the Great Seal Offices Act, 1874.

PEVENSEY (Sussex), said to be the site of the Roman Anderida, on which a Norman castle was erected. Here William of Normandy landed, 28 or 29 Sept. 1066. The duke of York, in the reign of Henry IV., was for some time confined within the walls of this castle; as was also queen Joan of Navarre, the last wife of Henry IV., who, with her confessor, friar Randal, was accused of a design to destroy Henry V., her step-son.

PEWS in churches. "In a London will we read of *sedile vocatum pew*" (a seat called pew), 1453. Pews were censured by Latimer and Bradford, 1553. *Walcot.* The church of Geddington St. Mary, Northamptonshire, long contained a pew dated 1602. The rev. W. M. H. Church (vicar 1844-6) restored and re-seated the church, and preserved the panel with the date in the door of the surplice press. Another pew in the chancel was dated 1604.

PFAFFENDORF AND LIEGNITZ (Silesia). Near these two places was fought a battle between the Imperialists and Prussians, 15 Aug. 1760. The Austrians were defeated by Frederick of Prussia, who thus prevented the junction of the Russian and Austrian armies.

PHALANSTERY, see *Fourierism.*

PHALANX, the Greek phalanx consisted of 8000 men in a square battalion, with shields joined, and spears crossing each other. The battalion of Philip of Macedon, called the Macedonian phalanx, was formed by him about 360 B.C.

PHALSBOURG (Pfalzburg, Palatine city), a strong town of Alsace, was founded in 1570, by the elector palatine George John. It was ceded to France in 1661, and its fortress erected by Vauban, 1679. It checked the progress of the victorious armies of the allies both in 1814 and 1815, and withstood the Germans from 16 Aug. to 12 Dec. 1870, when it capitulated unconditionally. It was retained at the peace in Feb. 1871.

PHARAOH, the general title of the kings of Egypt in the Old Testament, found only there and in the copyists. The Egyptian word, *pir-aa*, has been interpreted, *king* or *sun*. According to sir Erasmus Wilson, *Egypt of the Past* (1881), the hieroglyphs of *per*, a house, and *per-aa* a great house, are identical with that of Pharaoh, hence the signification, "royal ruler," "founder of a house."

PHARAOH'S SERPENTS, a dangerous chemical toy, composed of sulpho-cyanide of mercury, appeared in Paris in the summer of 1865.

PHARISEES, a sect among the Jews; so called from *pharash*, a Hebrew word for separated, because they pretended to a greater degree of holiness than the rest of the Jews. *Luke* xviii. 9-12. The Talmud enumerates seven classes of Pharisees.

PHARMACOPŒIA, a book of directions for the preparation of medicine, published by colleges of physicians, the earliest in England 1618. In 1862 the General Medical Council were empowered to prepare and sell a new pharmacopœia, to supersede those of the colleges of London, Edinburgh, and Dublin, which was published in June, 1864; succeeded by a new one in May, 1867; reprinted, 1890; another ordered, Dec. 1893; a new "Imperial" one, comprising the entire pharmacy of the empire, edited by prof. Attfield, reported, Dec. 1900.

PHARMACY: the knowledge of the chemical and medical properties of drugs and other things employed medicinally. The Pharmaceutical Society of Great Britain, founded 1 June, 1841, mainly by Mr. Jacob Bell, obtained its charter in 1843. Annual conferences. It publishes a weekly journal.—The pharmacy act, 1852, regulates the qualifications of pharmaceutical chemists. It was amended by the pharmacy act of 1868 which required all sellers of poisons to be registered after 31 Dec. 1868; act amended in 1869; amended 1898.

Sale of Food and Drugs Act passed . 11 Aug. 1875
Pharmaceutical Society of Ireland was instituted by the Irish Pharmacy Act, passed . 11 Aug. „
Pharmacy.—An international pharmaceutical congress (with an exhibition) was opened in London 1 Aug. 1881
International Pharmaceutical congress at Brussels, 31 Aug. 1885

PHAROS, an island on the coast of Egypt, on which was erected the celebrated lighthouse called the tower of Pharos, begun by Sostratus of Cnidus, 298, and completed by king Ptolemy Philadelphus about 283 B.C. On the top fires were constantly kept to direct sailors in the bay. See *Lighthouses.*

PHARSALIA, a strong city in Thessaly, N. Greece. Near it Julius Cæsar defeated his rival Pompey, 9 Aug. 48 B.C., and became virtually master of the known world. Pompey fled to Egypt, where he was treacherously slain, by order of Ptolemy the younger, then a minor, and his body left naked on the strand, till it was burnt by his faithful freedman, Philip. See *Greco-Turkish* war, 1897.

PHENOL, or phenic acid, names for carbolic acid (*which see*).

PHENOPHTHALMOSCOPE, an apparatus for investigating the movements of the eye-ball, invented by Donders, of Utrecht, and announced in 1870.

PHERÆ (Thessaly, N. Greece), see *Thessaly.*

PHIGALIAN MARBLES, in the British Museum, were purchased for it by the prince regent in 1815. They consist of portions of the frieze taken from the temple of Apollo Epicurus at Phigaleia in Arcadia, and are reputed to be works of the earlier school of Phidias, who died 432 B.C. The bas-reliefs represent the conflicts of the Greeks and Amazons, and of the Centaurs and Lapithæ.

PHILADELPHIA (Asia Minor), see *Seven Churches.*—PHILADELPHIA, Pennsylvania, was planned by William Penn 24 Oct. 1682, chartered by him as a city, 28 Oct. 1701. The William Penn charter school founded, 1689, and chartered by him, 1701-11 (first master, George Keith); it is still a flourishing school (1898). The first American congress assembled here in 1774, and promulgated the declaration of independence on 4 July, 1776. It was the capital of the Union till 1800, when Washington was selected in its place. The National Union Convention held its first meeting here 14 Aug. 1866; see *United States.* Population 1880, 847,170; 1890, 1,046,964; 1900, 1,293,697.

Beginning of centennial year celebrated with great demonstration . . . . 1 Jan. 1876
International exhibition opened by the president, the emperor and empress of Brazil present; very successful; about 130,000 persons present 10 May, „
Said to be the most extensive of all exhibitions hitherto; vista of three-eighths of a mile; main building 1900 feet long; 6 other large buildings, and 200 smaller.
Prizes awarded to exhibitors; out of 11,000, 488 given to Great Britain . . . . . 27 Sept. „
About 80,000 persons admitted by payment daily, Sept.; exhibition closed . . . . 10 Nov. „
[Total admitted, 9,789,392; daily average, 61,568; receipts, 3,813,749 dollars.]
International congress respecting education July, „
A permanent exhibition opened by president Hayes 10 May, 1877
Great storm: 384 dwellings, 31 churches, and many public buildings destroyed; 8 ships sunk; estimated loss, 2,000,000 dollars . . . 24 Oct. 1878
Grand festival to honour gen. Grant on return from his long tour . . . . . . 17-24 Dec. 1879
Foundation of city celebrated . . 24 Oct. 1882
Great Irish convention . . . 25-27 April, 1883
Fire at lunatic asylum, 28 perish . . 12 Feb. 1885
Celebration of the centenary of the adoption of the federal constitution (see *United States*) 15 Sept. 1887
Mr. John Bardsley, the defaulting city treasurer, sentenced to 15 years' solitary confinement and heavy fine . . . . 2 July, 1891
The Grand Central theatre, the *Times* offices and other buildings burnt, several persons perish . 27 April, 1892
Mr. George W. Childs, eminent publisher and benefactor; born 12 May, 1829; he set up many memorials in England to literary men and others; died . . . . 18 Jan. 1894
30 buildings burnt down . . . . 26 Jan. 1897

An equestrian statue of George Washington unveiled by the president . . . . 15 May, ,,
Peace jubilee, naval display, &c. . . . 25 Oct. 1898
National export exhibition opened . 14 Sept. 1899
Explosion in Locust-st., 5 buildings wrecked, 10 deaths and over 40 injured . . . . 5 Aug. 1901
Prince Henry of Prussia presented with the freedom of the city . . . . . 10 March, 1902
Panic in a cigar factory due to an alarm of fire, about 10 deaths, 20 injured . . . 30 April, ,,
Mr. C. Tower presents the library with 2,500 valuable Russian books, reported . . 24 Aug. ,,

PHILANTHROPIC SOCIETY, for the reformation of criminal boys, was established in 1788, and incorporated in 1806. It supports a farm-school at Redhill, Reigate, Surrey; see *Reformatory Schools*. Mr. George Smith, a brickmaker in childhood, who energetically promoted the civilization of brickmakers, the canal population and others, by acts of parliament, &c.; died, aged about 64, 21 June, 1895.

PHILHARMONIC SOCIETY (London), was established in 1813; first concert, 8 March. New Philharmonic Society began 1852.

PHILIPHAUGH, near Selkirk, S. Scotland, where the marquis of Montrose and the royalists were defeated by David Leslie and the Scotch covenanters, 13 Sept. 1645.

PHILIPPI (Macedonia), so named by Philip II. of Macedon. Here Octavius Cæsar and Marc Antony, in two battles, defeated the republican forces of Cassius and Brutus, who both committed suicide, Oct. 42 B.C. Paul preached here, A.D. 48, and wrote an epistle to the converts, 64.

PHILIPPICS, the term applied to the orations of Demosthenes against Philip II. of Macedon, 352-341 B.C., and also to the orations of Cicero against Marc Antony (one of which, called divine by Juvenal, cost Cicero his life), 44-43 B.C.

PHILIPPINE ISLES (in the Malay Archipelago), discovered by Magellan, in March, 1521, who here lost his life in a skirmish. They were taken possession of in 1565 by a fleet from Mexico, which first stopped at the island of Zeba, and subdued it. In 1570 a settlement was effected at the mouth of the Manila river, and Manila became the capital of the Spanish possessions in the Philippines; see *Manila* and *Earthquakes*. The Philippine commercial company was unsuccessful, 1785. A successful Philippine exhibition was opened in Madrid, autumn 1887. Population about 1885, reported, 5,636,000.

Rebels defeated in a fierce engagement at Lanas, reported 10 Sept. 1891
Mr. John Foreman's "Philippine Islands" was published in 1891.
Assault of the natives on the Spanish garrison at fort Mumungan; repulsed with great native loss, including their sultan, reported . . 26 June, 1893
Conflicts with the natives, reported March, *et seq.*; the natives defeated . . . . 24 July, 1894
Severe fighting in Mindanao; the Malay Mahomedans defeated; their sultan killed . 10 March, 1895
Insurgents defeated at Tatan . . . . Sept. ,,
Insurrection near Manila, state of siege proclaimed, rebels repulsed with loss . . . 30 Aug. 1896
Help from Hong Kong requested . . Sept. ,,
Rebels defeated in two engagements, many ringleaders killed, and others captured and shot, Sept. 1896
The insurgents masters of all the towns in Cavite; convents sacked; Spanish monks (40) murdered in the island of Luzon . . . 19, 20 Sept. ,,
Insurgents suffer heavy losses in 10 engagements near Manila; a plot discovered, and 100 conspirators arrested . . . . . . Sept. ,,
Insurgent attack on the Spanish post at Rechazada repulsed, their leader and 50 men killed, reported . . . . 25 Sept. 1896
Mutiny of native soldiers in Mindanao, officers killed . . . . Oct. ,,
Nasugdu captured by gen. Juramillo, rebels defeated with great loss . . . . . Oct. ,,
Insurgents signally defeated, Novaleta taken, early Nov.; again severely defeated at Santa Cruz and Angrat . . . . Nov. ,,
Gen. Polavieja succeeds gen. Blanco as governor-gen. . . . . Dec. ,,
Revolt of some of the troops, some soldiers shot at Mindanao; a European committee of Protection formed at Manila . . . Dec. ,,
Dr. Rizal shot for fomenting the rebellion 28 Dec. ,,
Insurgents defeated at Bulacan, with loss; Spanish loss, 23 . . . . Dec. ,,
13 persons, charged with conspiracy, shot 4 Jan. 1897
Insurgents surprised and routed at Agony, Almansas, and Noveleta . . . . . Jan. ,,
Sen. Rojas and 11 other insurgents shot, as instigators of the rebellion . . . . 11 Jan. ,,
Signal victory by the Spaniards, Silang stronghold captured; much slaughter . . . . Feb. ,,
Native rising in Manila city, suppressed with bloodshed . . . . . . 25 Feb. ,,
Salitran captured by the Spaniards, gen. Zaballa, 5 officers, 10 men, and 76 insurgents killed, March, ,,
Gen. Primo de Rivera appointed capt.-general, March, ,,
Imus and Cavite captured by the Spaniards, March; Naic, 500 rebels killed and 200 prisoners . May, ,,
Volcanic eruption and earthquake; a village destroyed in Mayon, 120 deaths, reported . 1 July, ,,
Rebels repulsed with loss at San Rafael, Aug.; see *Manila*, 1896–7.
Disastrous cyclone at Leyte . . . . 12 Oct. ,,
Complete submission of rebels in return for pardon, 25 Nov. *et seq.* ,,
Aguinaldo, rebel chief, exiled to Hong-kong, 27 Dec. ,,
Gen. Augustin appointed gov.-general . 26 Feb. 1898
A Spanish detachment surprised and 40 killed at Bolinao; other engagements . . . March, ,,
Battle of Manila, see *Spanish-American war*, 30 April–May, ,,
Rebel town in Panay island captured by the Spaniards and destroyed, great slaughter, 672 rebels killed, reported . . . . . 8 May, ,,
Assembly of 15 members of natives and others, instituted by the gov.-general, señ. Paterno, president . . . . 13 May, ,,
Aguinaldo returns from Hong-kong, supplied with arms, etc. from U. S. ships, captures Cavite province, after 3 days' severe fighting, Spanish outposts driven in, great slaughter; the whole archipelago in revolt, except Visayas isles, 31 May–2 June; Manila surrounded by insurgents; concessions offered to the natives by gen. Augustin; he appeals to Madrid for help . 8 June, ,,
Aguinaldo allies himself with the insurgents in the north, active operations against the Spaniards carried on everywhere north of Manila, 4 Sept.; insurgent conquest of Luzon, 9,000 Spanish prisoners, 9 Sept.; the insurgents evacuate Manila, trade active, 14 Sept.; the Filipino republic constituted at Malolos, gen. Aguinaldo president . . . . . . Nov. ,,
The Spaniards under gen. Rios evacuate Iloilo, 24 Dec. ,,
The government of the islands taken over by America; proclamation issued . . 5 Jan. 1899
Aguinaldo issues a manifesto calling on the Filipinos to declare their independence, 8 Jan.; again . . . . 22 Feb. ,,
Spanish governor and officers murdered by natives at Port Royalist, reported . . . 23 Jan. ,,
The insurgents are repulsed with heavy loss at Manila; 3 U.S. officers and 56 men killed, 4–5 Feb.; Caloocan captured after a desperate fight, 10 Feb. ,,
Iloilo and Jaro captured by gen. Miller, 11–12 Feb. ,,
Guerilla warfare; the U.S. flag raised by the natives on Negros island . . . Feb. ,,

Sharp fighting in and around Manila, incendiary fires, insurgents driven out with heavy loss, 21–24 Feb. 1899
Desultory fighting; insurgents driven out of Pasig, Paterno, &c., after 7 hours' fighting; many killed, 363 captured . . . . 15, 16 March, ,,
Insurgents repulsed with great loss at Caloocan, 25 March, ,,
Col. Egbert killed, and prince Loewenstein (while performing an act of heroism), near Polo, 26 March; Aguinaldo's main army routed near Malolos . . . . . 27 March, ,,
Malolos captured by gen. McArthur . 31 March, ,,
U.S. proclamation issued, announcing the cession of the islands by Spain to America . 4 April, ,,
Santa Cruz and gunboats, &c., seized by gen. Lawton; he returns to Manila after capturing 8 towns . . . . . . 11, 17 April, ,,
Yorktown, U.S. warship, rescues 85 Spaniards at Baler Luzon; lieut. Gilmore and 14 men captured . . . . . . 12 April, ,,
Continued skirmishing . . . 21–23 April, ,,
Rebel entrenchments carried by gens. McArthur and Hale's brigades after hard fighting; 75 rebels killed, 24 April; Calumpit captured; the Rio Grande river crossed (a daring feat) by U.S. troops under gen. Wheaton; entrenchments carried; Americans advance to Apalit, 26, 27 April, ,,
Negotiations between gen. Otis and the government fail . . . . . . 28, 29 April, ,,
Desultory fighting in Luzon; gen. Lawton occupies San Tomas and San Fernando . 4, 5 May, ,,
Gen. Lawton routs the enemy and captures San Isidro . . . . 17 May, ,,
U.S. civil commission receive Aguinaldo's peace commissioners; negotiations fail . 22 May, ,,
Enemy repulsed near San Fernando, 50 killed and 28 captured . . . . . 24 May, ,,
Gen. Luna (insurgent officer) assassinated at Cabanatuan . . . . . . 6 June, ,,
Guerilla warfare; gen. Lawton's brigades successfully engaged . . . . . 10 June, ,,
Gen. Lawton defeats the enemy on the Zapote river . . . . 13 June, ,,
Insurgent attack on San Fernando repulsed, 16 June, ,,
Robber bands in Negros defeated . . 19 July, ,,
Gen. McArthur drives the enemy north from San Fernando . . . . . . 9 Aug. ,,
Angeles occupied, and enemy routed . 16, 20 Aug. ,,
Chinese exclusion law applied to the islands by gen. Otis . . . . . . Aug. ,,
Further skirmishing, U.S. successes . early Sept. ,,
Col. Snyder defeats the enemy near Cebu, 22, 23 Sept. ,,
Porac carried by U.S. troops . . . 28 Sept. ,,
Severe fighting north and south . 30 Sept.–3 Oct. ,,
Novaleta captured, 200 insurgents killed; Rosario afterwards occupied . . . . 8, 9 Oct. ,,
Further skirmishing, Cabal occupied . 31 Oct. ,,
The U.S. commission advise the United States to keep possession of the isles, and force the insurgents to submit; agreed to by the U.S. government . . . . . . 3 Nov. ,,
Col. Bell captures Tarlac, the Filipino government seat . . . . 12 Nov. ,,
Insurgents routed near San Jacinto . 12 Nov. ,,
Enemy defeated in the hills S. of Lingayen, stock and guns captured, reported . 29 Nov. ,,
3,000 Spanish prisoners released during . Nov. ,,
Col. March destroys Aguinaldo's bodyguard, and liberates 575 Spaniards, reported . 13 Dec. ,,
Gen. Lawton killed while leading the attack on San Mateo, reported . . . . 19 Dec. ,,
Continued American successes . 5, 7, 9 Jan. 1900
Gen. Schwan captures San Diego, insurgents routed, 67 killed . . . . . 21 Jan. ,,
Gen. Otis retires; succeeded by gen. MacArthur, early April, ,,
Gen. Pio del Pilar, after a week's sharp fighting near San Miguel, captured . . 8 June, ,,
The American commission holds its first legislative session . . . . . . 12 Sept. ,,
Fresh outbreaks, desperate fight at Mavitac, American loss heavy, mid Sept.; many skirmishes, reported . . . . 26 Sept. ,,
Americans repulsed near Narvican . 24 Oct. ,,
Insurgents defeated N. of Manila . . mid Nov. 1900
U.S. military stations, 53, 1 Nov. 1899; 413, 1 Sept. ,,
3,227 insurgents killed, 694 wounded, 2,684 captured . . . . 1 Nov. 1899–1 Sept. ,,
Total American loss, 357 killed or mortally wounded, 1,085 died from disease, 1899–1900, reported . . . . Nov. 1900
Deportation of insurgent generals and others to Guam . . . . Jan. 1901
Gen. Trias, 9 officers and 199 men surrender, reported . . . . 16 March, ,,
Aguinaldo and some of his staff captured by a ruse of gen. Funston, at Palanan . 17 March, ,,
Aguinaldo declares allegiance to the U.S.; the Americans release 1,000 prisoners . 19 April, ,,
Gen. Chaffee appointed military governor . June, ,,
Continued surrenders . . 31 March, 24 June, ,,
Judge Taft appointed governor; civil government established . . . . 4 July, ,,
Gen. Bellarmino and 1,000 men surrender . 6 July, ,,
Maj. Alhambra, 3 officers and 28 men, the remnants of Aguinaldo's followers, captured at Casiguran, reported . . . . 22 Sept. ,,
American reverse at Balangiga, garrison surprised, and many killed . . . . . 28 Sept. ,,
Insurrection prevails in Samar, military and civil report unsatisfactory; San José, in Batangas, burnt by the insurgents, 24 Oct.; severe act against treason and sedition drafted by U.S. commission . . . . . . 1 Nov. ,,
Maj. Waller captures Sojotan, 26 insurgents killed; reported . . . . 9 Nov. ,,
Fighting at Dapday, Samar; enemy repulsed with loss, reported . . . . 27 Dec. ,,
Malvar, rebel leader, surrenders; resistance over in the north, mid April; further surrenders, 25 April, 1902
Gen. Davis captures the chief fort of the Daltos; reported . . . . 4 May, ,,
Seven American soldiers captured and murdered by natives near Manila . . . 30 May, ,,
Total American expenditure on the war, 170,326,586 dollars, reported . . . . . 20 June, ,,
Civil government bill signed by the president, Washington . . . . 2 July, ,,
American authority accepted; pacification complete, except in the Moro country; Aguinaldo and other political prisoners pardoned; general amnesty proclaimed . . . . . 1–4 July, ,,
Skirmishes near Manila and Cavite . 18 Aug. 1902
Governor Taft returns from conferences at Washington and Rome . . . . . . 22 Aug. ,,
Cholera epidemic, 19,640 deaths; agricultural depression, reported . . . . . 30 Aug. ,,
Rios, a fanatical leader, routed in Tayabas, 3 Sept.
American successes in the Macin country, 17–21 Sept.
Gen. Chaffee leaves, succeeded by gen. Davis, about 1 Oct. ,,
The Main Moros routed, 40 forts destroyed, reported . . . . 4 Oct. ,,
Brigandage suppressed, many killed, in Leyte and Bilaran, reported . . . . . 27 Nov. ,,
Outbreak of cholera reported . . . . Dec. ,,
Insurgents defeated near Mariquira . 8 Feb. 1903
Further fighting at Cus and Surigao in March; insurgents routed with loss near Mariquira, reported . . . . 27 March, ,,
A stronghold captured, 100 natives killed, reported, 10 April, ,,
Gen. Miles's report, confirming some American cruelties during the war, published . 27 April, ,,
Capture of 10 forts, heavy loss of the enemy, reported . . . . 7 May, ,,
Continued agricultural and commercial depression, reported . . . . 8 Aug. ,,

See *Spanish American war.*

PHILIPPIUM, a metal of the yttrium series, found in Samarskite earth (in Russia, North Carolina, &c.) by M. Marc Delafontaine, by means of the spectroscope; announced Oct. 1878. Also said to have been found by Mr. Lawrence Smith, and named Mosandrium, July, 1878.

PHILIPPOPOLIS, capital of (Eastern) Roumelia, *which see*. Population, 1888, 33,032; 1900, 42,849.

PHILISTINES, a people of Palestine, conquered Israel, 1156 B.C., and ruled it forty years. They were defeated by Samuel, 1120; and by Saul and Jonathan, 1087. They again invaded Israel about 1063, when David slew their champion, Goliath. After David became king he thoroughly subdued them, 1040. In common with Syria, their country was subjugated by the Romans, under Pompey, about 63.—In Germany, about 1830, Heine and the liberal party applied the term "Philistines" to the opponents of progress, or conservative party.

In England the term has been applied to the opponents of "culture" and refinement, chiefly among the upper middle classes by Mr. Matthew Arnold and others . . . . . . 1867 *et seq.*

PHILOBIBLION SOCIETY, was instituted in 1853 by Mr. R. Monckton Milnes (aft. lord Houghton), M. Sylvain Van de Weyer, the Belgian minister, and others. It publishes volumes of "Miscellanies," &c.

PHILOLOGY, the science of *language*, much studied during the present century.

John Horne-Tooke's "Diversions of Purley" published 1786
Philological society of London established 18 May, 1842
Lorenz Diefenbach's "Lexicon Comparativum" 1846-51
32nd congress of German philologists met at Wiesbaden, professor Curtius president, 26-29 Sept. 1877; the 42nd met at Vienna . 23 May, 1893
Hyde Clarke, D.C.L., an eminent philologist, born, 1815; died . . . . . 1 March, 1895
Prince Louis Lucien Bonaparte's philological library purchased by Mr. H. S. Nichols, announced . . . . . . Nov. 1896
Dr. John N. Valetta, D.C.L., a distinguished philologist, born 1818, died . . . . 2 Jan. 1900

[See *Language, Dictionaries,* and *Grammarians.*]

PHILOSOPHER'S STONE, see *Alchemy*.

PHILOSOPHICAL LAMP, constructed by Johann Wolfgang Döbereiner, who applied in it the property possessed by spongy platinum of causing the combination of oxygen and hydrogen, discovered by him in 1823.

PHILOSOPHY (love of wisdom), the knowledge of the reason of things (distinguished from history, the knowledge of facts, and from mathematics, the knowledge of the quantity of things)—the hypothesis or system upon which natural effects are explained. *Locke.* Pythagoras first adopted the name of philosopher (such men having been previously called sages) about 528 B.C. Philosophers were expelled from Rome, and their schools suppressed, by Domitian, A.D. 83. Philosophy is now divided into:—1. Moral or Ethical; 2. Intellectual; 3. Natural or Physical.

MORAL AND INTELLECTUAL PHILOSOPHY.

ANCIENT SCHOOLS.—The *Vedas* (*which see*) contain what is now considered to be the most ancient moral philosophy; the source of later systems, about the sixth or seventh century, B.C. (professor Max Müller, March, 1894.) *Pythagorean*, about 500 B.C.; *Platonic* (the academy), by Plato, 374; *Peripatetic* (the Lyceum), by Aristotle, 334; *Sceptic*, by Pyrrho, 334; *Cynic* by Diogenes, 330; *Epicurean* by Epicurus, 306; *Stoic*, by Zeno, 290; *Middle Academy*, by Arcesilaus, 278; *New Academy*, by Carneades, 160; *New Platonists* (who attempted to combine Platonism with Christianity): Ammonius Saccas, died A.D. 243; Plotinus, died about 270; Porphyry, died about 305; Jamblichus, died about 333; Julian the emperor, died 363.

MODERN SYSTEMS.—*Nominal*, Jean Roscellin, about 1092; Abelard, &c.; *Rational*, Bacon, about 1624; *Cartesian*, Descartes, about 1560: *Reflective* or *Perceptive*, Locke, 1690; *Idealistic*, Berkeley, 1710; *Elective*, Leibnitz, 1710; *Common Sense*, Reid, 1750-70; *Transcendental*, Kant, Hamilton, &c., 1770-1860; *Scientific*, Fichte, 1800-14; *Absolute Identity*, Schelling, 1800-20; *Absolute Idealism*, Hegel, 1810-30; *Utilitarian*, Bentham, Mill, &c. 1790-1873; *Positive*, Comte, 1830; *Realism* and *Evolutionary Materialism*, prevalent, Darwin, Herbert Spencer's, &c. 1873. "System of Synthetic Philosophy," 10 vols., 1860-96 (died 8 Dec. 1903). Mr. Howard Collin's "Epitome," 4th edition, published, autumn, 1897. [Prof. Wm. Wallace, of Oxford, died 19 Feb. 1897.] See *Ethics*.

NATURAL PHILOSOPHY.

Greek and Latin.—Thales, about 600 B.C.; Pythagoras, 590; Aristotle and Plato, 350; Euclid, 300; Archimedes, 287; Hipparchus, 150; Lucretius, about 100; Julius Cæsar, 50; Ptolemy, A.D. 150.

Middle Ages.—Arabians: Ben Musa, 800; Alhazen, &c., 1100. Gerbert, Decimals, 959. Roger Bacon, *Opus Majus*, 1266.

Inductive Philosophy:

Copernicus's system published 1543
Tycho Brahe 1546-1602
Gilbert's researches in electricity and magnetism 1600
Kepler's Laws 1609-18
Bacon's *Novum Organum* 1620
Galileo's *Dialogues* 1632
Royal Society begins (*which see*) 1645
Otto Guericke—air pump and electric machine . 1654
Huyghens on pendulums 1658
Newton—Fluxions, 1665; Analysis of Light, 1669; Theory of Gravitation, 1684; *Principia* published, 1687; death 1727
Bradley discovers aberration . . . . . „
Euler on Perturbation of the Planets . . . 1748
Black on Heat 1762
Laplace on Tides 1775
Lagrange, *Mécanique Analytique* 1788
Galvani and Volta's researches 1791
Laplace, *Mécanique Céleste*. 1799
Œrsted discovers electro-magnetism . . . 1819
Faraday, magneto-electricity 1831
I. Todhunter's "History of the Theory of Elasticity" published . . . . . . July, 1893
Herschell, Whewell, Tyndall, W. Thompson (lord Kelvin), Werner Siemens, C. W. Siemens, Helmholtz, Wildemann.

[See *Acoustics, Astronomy, Optics, Chemistry, Electricity, &c.*]

PHIPPS' EXPEDITION. The hon. captain Phipps (afterwards lord Mulgrave) sailed from England in command of the *Sea-Horse* and *Carcase* ships. to make discoveries, as near as possible to the North Pole. In August 1773, he was for nine days environed with barriers of ice, in the Frozen Ocean, north of Spitzbergen, 80° 48′ N. lat. A brisk wind in two or three days accomplished their deliverance. They returned to England without having made any discoveries, 20 Sept. 1773. Nelson was coxswain to the second in command.

PHLOGISTON, a term employed by Stahl to designate the hypothetical matter or principle of fire; "the inflammable principle" of bishop Watson, near the close of the 17th century. The chemical theory based upon it was refuted by Lavoisier, 1790, who substituted for it the theory of oxygenation.

PHOCIS, a state in Northern Greece. The Phocians seized Delphi 357 B.C., and commenced the second Sacred War. They were opposed by Thebes and other states, and were utterly subdued by Philip II. of Macedon in 346. By the excavations of the British school of archæology at Abæ the remains of two ancient temples of Apollo, with relics of bronzes, inscriptions, &c., and at Hyampolis, a shrine of Artemis (Diana), &c., were discovered, reported, 30 Aug. 1894.

PHŒNICIA, on the sea coast of Syria. The natives were the most eminent navigators and traders of antiquity, their cities or allied states being Tyre, Sidon, Berytus, Tripoli, Byblos, and Ptolemais, or Acre. From the 19th to the 13th centuries before Christ, they established colonies on the shores or isles of the Mediterranean—Carthage, Hippo, Utica, Gades, and Panormus, and they are said to have visited the British Isles. Phœnicia was conquered by Cyrus, 537 B.C.; by Alexander, 332; by the Romans, 47; and after partaking of the fortunes of Palestine, was added to the Ottoman empire, A.D. 1516. See *Sidon* and *Tyre*.

PHŒNIX CLUBS, of a treasonable character, were formed in Ireland in 1858. They met at night to drill. Several persons were arrested and tried in March, 1859, at Tralee; but the jury could not agree on their verdict. Daniel Sullivan was condemned to penal servitude for ten years, April, 1859. Eventually some of the prisoners pleaded guilty, and were discharged on being bound over to keep the peace.

PHŒNIX PARK. A beautiful park, 1,327 acres, in Dublin; for the murders here see *Ireland*, 1882-3, 1896.

PHONEIDOSCOPE, an instrument for observing the colour-figures of liquid films under the action of sonorous vibrations, being a visible demonstration of the vibratory and molecular motion of a telephone plate; invented by Mr. Sedley Taylor, 1877; manufactured by S. C. Tisley & Co., London, 1878.

PHONO-CINEMA, a combination of the phonograph and cinematograph, which preserves the face, voice and gestures of living beings, displayed at the Paris exhibition, June *et seq.* 1900.

PHONOGRAPH, a machine proposed to be attached to pianofortes and other keyed instruments, by which any music that is played may be written down on blank paper, since it rules and prints the notes simultaneously. It was patented by Mr. Fenby, 13 June, 1863. The motive-power is electro-magnetism. Machines with a similar object were projected by Mr. Creedd in 1847; Mr. J. F. Unger in 1774; and by Mr. Carreyre in 1827. See *Telephonograph*.

A new phonograph by Thomas Alva Edison, electrician of New Jersey, was announced . Dec. 1877

Linear indentations are made by means of a pin in a sheet of tinfoil by speaking or singing; and from these casts may be taken. When these are placed upon the diaphragm of a telephone connected with revolving apparatus, the sounds may be reproduced with a weirdlike effect. Improved by Mr. Shelford Bidwell, 1879. See *Telephone*.

A greatly improved instrument by Mr. Edison adapted for postal communication, announced, 21 Nov. 1887; successful experiments reported, 12 May, 1888

Professor Graham Bell's *graphophone*, a modification of Edison's phonograph, was announced . . Nov. 1887

Mr. Emile Berliner (of Washington) announced his *gramophone*, a modification of Leon Scott's *phonautograph* . . . . Nov. „

The *phonograph* and *graphophone* were both exhibited to the British Association at Bath . Sept. 1888

Exhibitions of Mr. Edison's greatly improved phonograph, considered perfect in the record, reproduction and preservation of sounds of all kinds (wax is used in place of tinfoil) Nov. 1888 *et seq.*

Mr. Edison receives phonograms from the duke of Cambridge, Mr. Gladstone, and others . Jan. 1889

Mr. Edison's talking dolls, which utter about 30 words, by means of a concealed phonograph and clockwork, were exhibited at the Savoy Hotel, Westminster, 25 July; Edison's phonographic toy company announced . . . . July, 1890

Mr. Edison adapts his phonograph to a water motor as well as electricity . reported Sept. 1890

The pope, by Mr. Moriarty, transmits a phonogram, containing a message, to the president of the United States N. A. . . . . 20 March, 1893

Many improvements made and others in progress, 1903

PHONOGRAPHY (from the Greek *phōnē*, sound), suggested by Franklin, 1768. The Phonetic society, whose object was to render our mode of writing and printing more consonant to sound, was established, 1 March, 1843; sir W. C. Trevelyan, president, and Mr. Isaac Pitman, secretary, the latter being the inventor of the system which was made known in 1837; knighted, May, 1894; died, aged 84, 22 Jan. 1897. Among other works published by the promoters of the system, was the "Phonetic News," in 1849. Phonography has been adopted for European and oriental languages, 1887, *et seq.* "Phonographic Quarterly Review," published, Nov. 1894; see *Visible Speech*.

"Pickwick Papers" in shorthand, first of a series, published by Mr. Pitman . . . . 1 May, 1883

Script Phonography, a simplified system of shorthand, combining the manual movement of longhand with the connection of vowels and consonants in their natural order, by Thos. Stratford Malone . . . . 2 Nov. 1885

Messrs. Pitman first publish in phonography the New Testament from engraved plates . 8 Oct. 1886

First *Phonographic* journal, published . 1 Jan. 1887

Sol-fa system in shorthand first published 5 Feb. „

The book of Common Prayer; and a National "Phonographic Library" begun in . April, „

PHONOPORE, an arrangement of telegraph wires to facilitate transmission of sound, by checking the influence of adjoining wires, the invention of Mr. C. Langdon Davies, announced, May, 1886. See *Telephones*. The system was stated to have worked successfully on the South Eastern railway between London and Folkestone, Feb. 1887, the Midland railway, and others, 1889-92.

PHONOSCOPE, an apparatus for testing the quality of musical strings, invented by Dr. Rudolph Kœnig, and exhibited at the International Exhibition in 1862. He died, aged 68, 2 Oct. 1901.

Mr. Edmunds' phonoscope, exhibited to the British Association, Aug. 1878, is an instrument for producing figures and light from the vibrations of sound.

The name phonoscope is given to apparatus used by M. M. G. Duneny in photographing the lips of a speaker and so combining the images thus produced that they may be understood by a deaf-mute, June, 1892. See *Photography*, 1891.

PHOSPHOR-BRONZE, an alloy of copper, tin, and phosphorus, invented by Messrs. Montefiore-Levi and Künzel, of Belgium, in 1867. It is very hard, ductile, and elastic, with a colour resembling gold.

PHOSPHORESCENCE. The property possessed by some bodies of retaining luminosity after exposure to light observed by the ancients; especially noticed by Vincenzo Cascariolo (1602), Boyle, Canton, Wilson, and others; and specially studied by Edmond Becquerel, and Balmain. See *Luminous Paint*, *Air* (footnote).

PHOSPHORUS was discovered in 1667, by Brandt, of Hamburg, who procured it from urine. The discovery was prosecuted by John Kunckel, a Saxon chemist, about 1670, and by the hon. R. Boyle about the same time. *Nouv. Dict.* Phosphoric acid is first mentioned in 1743, but is said to have been known earlier. Gahn pointed out its existence in bones in 1769, and Scheele devised a process for extracting it. Canton's phosphorus is so called from its discoverer, 1768. Phosphoretted hydrogen was discovered by Gengembre in 1812. The consumption of phosphorus has immensely increased since the manufacture of lucifer matches. In 1845, Schrötter, of Vienna, discovered allotropic or amorphous phosphorus, which ignites more slowly and is less unwholesome in working than ordinary phosphorus.

Mr. S. A. Rosenthal and dr. S. J. von Komocki succeed in preparing matches without yellow phosphorus, reported . . . . Sept. 1898

PHOTOGRAPHY. The action of light on chloride of silver was known as early as the 16th century. The phenomenon was studied by Scheele (1777), Senebier (1790), Ritter and Wollaston (1801). From the results of these investigations, experiments were made by Thos. Wedgwood and Humphry Davy, in the Royal Institution, London, which were published in its Journal, 1802. Wedgwood may be regarded as the first *photographer*. His paper was entitled "an account of a method of copying paintings upon glass, and of making profiles by the agency of light upon nitrate of silver."

Further discoveries were made by Niépce in 1814, and sir J. Herschel in 1819.

Louis J. M.-Daguerre commenced his experiments in 1824; and in 1826 joined Joseph Nicéphore Niépce, and worked with him till the death of the latter in 1833. The production of *Daguerreotype* plates was announced in Jan. 1839; and the French chamber of deputies granted a pension to Daguerre and to Niépce's son Isidore.

In 1839 Mr. Henry Fox Talbot first published his mode of multiplying photographic impressions by producing a *negative* photograph (*i. e.*, with the light and shades reversed) from which any number of positive copies may be obtained. His patent for producing the *Talbotype* or *Calotype* (on paper) is dated Feb. 1841.

In 1851, collodion (*which see*) was applied to photography by Mr. F. Archer.

Herr Franz Veress of Klausenburg, Transylvania, photographs colours on glass and paper; specimens are exhibited at the Photographic Institute at Vienna, March, 1890.

The Photographic Society of London was established in 1852 (royal, 1894). It publishes a journal. On 22 Dec. 1852, 774 specimens of photography were exhibited at the rooms of the Society of Arts, Adelphi. 42nd annual exhibition, very successful, 25 Sept. *et seq.* 1897; congress held, New gallery, Regent-street, 19 May, 1903.

Carte de visite portraits (*which see*) taken by M. Ferrier at Nice, 1857.

In 1861 Mr. Thompson, of Weymouth, photographed the bottom of the sea.

Photography was successfully applied to the transfer of works of art to wood blocks by Mr. John Leighton, in his illustrated edition of Lyra Germanica, 1861.

In 1861 professor O. M. Rood suggested the application of photography to the microscope.

The tannin process introduced by major Russell about 1861.

The *copyright* of photographs is secured by an act passed in 1862.

Dr. Henry Wright photographed objects of surgical interest in Jan. 1863.

The Wothlytype process, in which nitrate of silver and albumen are discarded and a double salt of uranium and collodion substituted, invented by Wothly, was announced in the autumn of 1864.

The light of ignited *magnesium* was employed for photographs by Mr. Brothers, of Manchester, in the spring of 1864.

Mr. H. Van der Weyde, an American artist, succeeded in making electric light very effectual in photography, 1876-8.

Photographs of the first page of the *Times*, containing many French advertisements ($1\frac{1}{2}$ inch long by 1 inch wide), sent to Paris from Bordeaux by balloons, Jan. 1871.

Criminals ordered to be photographed (by the act for prevention of crime), from 2 Nov. 1871.

Composite portraits (in which sometimes 9 components were used) formed by Mr. Francis Galton, by means of photography, 1877.

The *Autotype process* for transferring and printing reported successful, April, 1873.

Mr. E. J. Muybridge photographs, instantaneously, animals in rapid motion, 1881 *et seq.* See *Zoopraxiscope.*

Capt. Abney (K.C.B. 1900) photographs a disc in rapid motion by the electric spark, 17 March, 1882.

Celestial Photography began with professor Bond, the astronomer, of Cambridge, U.S., who exhibited a photograph of the moon in 1851. Since then, Mr. Warren de la Rue, of London, has produced excellent photographs of the moon, and other heavenly bodies, and on 18 July, 1860, photographed the solar eclipse.

By means of the gelatine dry plate, the results of the astronomical work of years is now obtained in hours. Delicate details are obtained not only of comets, nebulæ and faint stars, but also of stars invisible by the most powerful telescopes. Since 1876, Dr. W. Huggins and Mr. Andrew A. Common in England, and Mr. Draper in America, have been eminently successful in celestial photography. About 400 stars have been depicted in the space of two square inches.

The *Photochronograph*, an apparatus invented by father Fargis, Georgetown, U.S.A., for measuring star transits, reported Oct. 1892.

Photography successfully applied to the heavens by MM. Paul and Prosper Henry, 1885–8. Charts of the whole heavens expected in ten years.

Decision by justice North that a photographer has no right to sell or exhibit photographs of private sitters; "Pollard and wife *v.* The Photographic Company. Rochester" . . . . . 20 Dec. 1888

Mr. A. A. Common's excellent telescope specially adapted for photography, set up at Ealing, near London . . . . spring, 1890

Mr. W. E. Woodbury's "Encyclopædia of Photography," published . . . . . . .1890 *et seq.*

M. Marey's method of photographing the motions of living animals by his chrono-photograph applied by M. G. Demeny to the movements of the lips in speech, the results being readable by deaf-mutes; reported Aug. 1891

"Photographie des Couleurs par la Méthode interférentielle de M. Lippmann," by Alphonse Berget, published . . . . June, "

M. Gabriel Lippmann announced his method of photographing the spectrum in its natural colours by producing iridescence on the film, March, 1891–May, 1892

Mr. F. E. Ives at the Royal Institution, London, 10, 17 May, 1892, exhibited his patented method of photographing colours, by which he produced colour prints.

Mr. Van der Weyde lectures on his "photo-corrector" at the Society of Arts . . 26 April, 1893

Photographs of flowers, &c., exhibiting the natural colours, taken by M. Lumière (by an improvement on the original idea of M. Lippmann) on gelatino-bromide plates, were exhibited by the Photo club, Paris; the process is slow, 10 May, "

Congress of British photographic societies, opened in London; capt. Abney president . 10 Oct. "

Mr. Arthur Burchett's new process, by the combination of green and yellow screens, exhibited at the Camera club . . . . . . 25 Jan. 1894

Specimens of Dr. Joly's method of photography in natural colours on glass plates exhibited at the Royal society . . . . . . June, 1895

Mr. Vernon Heath, landscape photographer, born, 1820, died . . . . 25 Oct. "

The bottom of the Mediterranean photographed by M. Louis Bontan, in . . . . . . "

Mr. Campbell Swinton exhibited photographs (radiographs) of the interior of the hand, etc. at the Camera club; see *Röntgen Rays* . . 16 Jan. 1896

Mr. Friese-Greene's improvements in printing photographs (blocks dispensed with), exhibited at the Royal Institution . . . . 28 Feb. "

M. G. Lippmann at the Royal Institution described and illustrated his method of producing coloured photography, specimens included the spectrum, flowers, trees, etc. . . . . 17 April, "

M. Villedien Chassagne and dr. Adrien M. Dansac's invention of producing photographs showing the actual colours of the objects photographed, reported, *Times* . . . 30 Jan. 1897
Mr. Bennetto exhibits excellent specimens of his colour photography by the action of light on chemical substances at the Camera club, 8 March, 1897, and other places.
The National Photographic Record association, founded by sir Benjm. Stone, M.P. . 8 July, „
Royal Photographic Society's international exhibition at the Crystal Palace, opened by the prince of Wales . . . . . 25 April, 1898
M. Paul Boyer exhibits portraits taken by his new flash-light process, London . . . May, „
Mr. Francis Galton's new method of analytical photography, to isolate the differences between any two pictures, reported . . 27 Nov. 1900
See *Röntgen Rays*.

PHOTOHELIOGRAPH, an apparatus for registering the position of the sun's spots by means of clockwork and photography; erected at the suggestion of sir John Herschel at Kew observatory about 1857. It was used by Mr. Warren de la Rue to photograph the disc of the sun during the eclipse of 18 July, 1860.

PHOTOGALVANOGRAPHY, the art of producing engravings by the action of light and electricity. The earliest specimens were produced by Nicéphore Niépce, and presented by him in 1827 to the great botanist, Robert Brown. Great advances have since been made in this art by MM. Niépce de St. Victor (who published a treatise on it in 1856), Vitry, W. R. Grove, H. Fox Talbot, &c. In 1852, Paul Pretsch patented a process which he called "Photogalvanography."

PHOTOGLYPHIC ENGRAVING (a process by which the light actually etches a picture on a plate that may be and has been printed from) was patented by Mr. Fox Talbot in 1858, and is described and exemplified in the Photographic News, 9 and 16 Sept. 1859, a specimen being given in the latter number.

PHOTOZINCOGRAPHY (a process by which photographs are transferred to zinc plates which may be printed from) was devised by sir Henry James, chief of the Ordnance Survey, and made known in 1860. By it maps, charts, and engravings may be printed at a small cost.

PHOTO-SCULPTURE: M. Villème's employment of photographs in the formation of sculpture was announced in 1863.
Messrs. Goupil's process of *Photogravure*, rivalling mezzo-tint, reported highly successful; fine pictures reproduced, Feb. 1884.

PHOTOMETER (light measurer); one was constructed by Dr. W. Ritchie in 1825. Many improvements have been made recently in photometry. See under *Stars*.

Mr. A. Vernon Harcourt's new holophotometer highly approved June, 1888.
Stellar Photometry, the measurement of the light of the stars, has been much studied by astronomers, especially by sir John Herschel, prof. Argelander, prof. C. Pritchard and others. Mr. W. J. Dibdin, in his "Guide to the measurement of light," published in 1889, describes his application of terrestrial photometry to stellar light.

PHOTOPHONE. In this apparatus, constructed by professor Graham Bell and Mr. Sumner Tainter of Washington, in 1880, a thin plane mirror is thrown into vibration by the voice; a beam of light is reflected from this mirror and received at a distance by a cell of the metal selenium; when, by arrangement, this is connected with a telephone, the sounds are reproduced.

PHOTOSPHERE, see *Sun*, note.

PHOTOTACHOMETER, an instrument for measuring the velocity of light, invented by Professor Simon Newcomb of Washington, 1879-80.

PHOTOTHERAPY, the treatment of disease by light, successfully applied by prof. Finsen, of Copenhagen, in smallpox, 1893, and lupus, see *Tuberculosis*, 1901.

PHRENOLOGY, see *Craniology*.

PHRYGIA (now Karamania), a province in Asia Minor, became part of the Persian empire in 537 B.C., and partook of its changes. After their defeat of Antiochus the Great, king of Syria, 190 B.C., the Romans added Phrygia to the kingdom of Pergamus, which was bequeathed to them by Attalus III., the last king, 133 B.C.

PHYLLOXERA, see *Vine*.

PHYSIC appears to have been first practised by the Egyptian priests. Pythagoras endeavoured to explain the philosophy of disease and the action of medicine, about 529 B.C. Hippocrates, the father of medicine, flourished about 422 B.C., and Galen, born A.D. 131, was the oracle of medical science. About 980 Avicenna, an Arab, wrote a system of medicine. Dr. R. Quain's *Dictionary of Medicine*, published 1882. 3rd edition issued 1902. "The System of Medicine," consisting of contributions by eminent physicians and surgeons, edited by sir J. Russell Reynolds, in 5 vols., published 1866–75. A "System of medicine," by many writers, edited by dr. Clifford Allbutt, vol. I., June 1896; vol. III., 1898. See *Medical*.

The dogmatic age of medicine lasted till the Reformation, when it was attacked by Paracelsus (1493-1541), and Vesalius (1514-64). Since 1800 medical practice has been completely transformed by physiological and chemical research.
The discovery of the circulation of the blood, by Dr. Harvey, furnished an entirely new system of physiological and pathological speculation, 1628. See *Medical* and *Societies*.
PHYSICIAN TO THE KING.—John, the king's chaplain and physician (afterwards bishop of Bath and Wells), mentioned 1090.
The earliest mandate or warrant for the attendance of physician at court is dated 1454, and 33 Henry VI., a reign fertile in the patronage which was afforded to practitioners in medicine; but no appointment existed which can justly be called physician to the royal person. By this warrant the king, with the consent of his privy council, deputed to three physicians and two surgeons the regulation of his diet, and the administration of such medicines and remedies as might be sufficient for his cure, without any allusion to the previous existence or permanency of the office which they were authorised for a time to fill, or to a remuneration for their services.—*Life of Linacre*.
Miss Garrett (afterwards Mrs. Anderson) licensed at Apothecaries' hall, London, to practise medicine, 28 Sept. 1865.
At a meeting of the Royal Medical and Chirurgical Society, 3 May, 1869, it was resolved that the "Royal Society of Medicine" (including the various sections) be founded; the resolution was affirmed, 22 Feb. 1870; but in 1871 the project dropped.
School of Medicine for Women in London (council: Professors Burdon-Sanderson and Huxley, Mrs. Garrett-Anderson, M.D., Mrs. Blackwell, M.D., and others); opened, Oct. 1874.
Registration of medical women, permitted by Medical act, 39 & 40 Vict. c. 41, 11 Aug. 1876.
The queen lays the foundation of the Medical Examination hall on the Victoria embankment, 24 March, 1886.
The curriculum for medical students changed from 4 to 5 years; begins Oct. 1893.
London school of tropical medicine promoted by the liberality of Mr. Chamberlain, col. sec., Dec. 1898; established in the London Docks; good research work, reported, 3 Nov. 1902 *et seq.*
See *Anatomy*.

EMINENT MEDICAL MEN.

	Born	*Died*
Cornelius Celsus	14 A.D.	
Paulus Ægineta flourished	about 630	

EMINENT MEDICAL MEN.

	Born	Died
Averrhoes	12 Dec.	1198
Thomas Linacre	1460	1524
Paracelsus	1493	1541
Ambrose Paré, French surgeon	1509	1590
William Harvey	1578	1657
Thomas Sydenham	1624	1689
Malpighi	1628	1694
Hermann Boerhaave	1668	1738
R. Mead	1673	1754
Albert von Haller	1708	1777
William Hunter	1718	1783
John Hunter	1728	1793
R. T. Laennec	1781	1826
John Abernethy	1764	1831
Astley Cooper	1768	1841
Sir James Young Simpson (introducer of anæsthetics)	1811	1870
Sir Henry Holland	1788	1873
Henry Bence Jones	1813	1873
Sir Thomas Watson	1792	1882
Richard Quain	1803	1887
Sir Jas. Risdon Bennett	1809	
Sir Wm. W. Gull	1816	1890
Sir George Paget	1809	1892
Sir Jas. Paget	1814	1899
Sir Wm. Jenner	1815	1898
Sir Richard Quain	1816	1898
Sir Morell Mackenzie	1837	1892
Sir John Eric Erichsen	1818	1896
Sir Joseph Fayrer	1824	
Sir Andrew Clark	1826	1893
Sir Joseph Lister (made a peer 1897)	1827	
Sir George Johnson	1818	1896
Sir George Murray Humphry	1820	1896
George Harley	1829	1896
Sir B. Ward Richardson	1828	1896
Sir Thomas Spencer Wells	1818	1897
Sir William Roberts	1830	1899
Sir William Priestley	1829	1900
Sir William MacCormac	1836	1901
Sir Frederick Treves (bart. June, 1902)	1853	
William Smoult Playfair	1836	1903

PHYSIC GARDENS. The first cultivated in England was by John Gerard, surgeon of London, in 1567; that at Oxford was endowed by the earl of Danby, in 1652; that at Cambridge was commenced about the middle of the last century; and that at Chelsea, originated by sir Hans Sloane, was given to the Apothecaries' company in 1721; this last was very much admired by Linnæus. The trustees of the London parochial charities agree to dedicate 800*l*. per ann. to its maintenance, March, 1899. New laboratories and plant-houses opened by lord Cadogan, 25 July, 1902.

PHYSICAL EDUCATION, British College of, started in 1893; a meeting of the council was held at the earl of Meath's house, sir Benjamin Richardson in the chair, 20 Oct. 1894. Annual meetings. See *Scotland*. Royal Commission on PHYSICAL DETERIORATION appointed, 1903.

PHYSICAL SOCIETY, established 14 Feb. 1874; Dr. J. H. Gladstone, first president. NATIONAL PHYSICAL RECREATION SOCIETY founded, 1885-6; in full activity, Mr. Herbert J. Gladstone, president, Nov. 1896. NATIONAL PHYSICAL LABORATORY, committee appointed respecting its establishment, lord Rayleigh chairman, 3 Aug. 1897; favourable report issued, 4 Oct. 1898; government grants 14,000*l*. for erection and 4,000*l*. per ann. for maintenance, Mr. R. T. Glazebrook appointed director, Aug. 1899. Bushy-house, Teddington, granted by the queen to the Royal society for the laboratory, Dec. 1900; opened by the prince and princess of Wales, 19 March, 1902.

PHYSICIANS, ROYAL COLLEGE OF, of London (of England since 1858), was projected by Dr. Linacre, physician to Henry VIII., who, through his interest with cardinal Wolsey, obtained letters patent, constituting a corporate body of regular physicians in London, with peculiar privileges, 23 Sept. 1518. Linacre was elected the first president of the college. Dr. W. Harvey was a great benefactor to this institution, 1653. He built a library and public hall, which he granted for ever to the college, with his books and instruments. The college was afterwards held in a building in Warwick-lane, erected by sir C. Wren, where it continued till 1825, when the present elegant stone edifice in Trafalgar-square was erected from designs by sir R. Smirke. The college is composed of fellows and members, formerly called licenciates and extra-licenciates. The queen's bench division decided that the college was entitled by the medical act of 1886 to grant diplomas both of medicine and surgery, 8 March, 1893. The prince of Wales elected a fellow of the college, July, 1897.—The College of Physicians, Dublin, was founded by charter of Charles II. 1667, and was re-incorporated in 1692. The Royal College of Physicians, Edinburgh, 29 Nov. 1681.

RECENT PRESIDENTS OF ROYAL COLLEGE, LONDON.

1796.	Thomas Gisborne.
1804.	Sir Lucas Pepys.
1811.	Sir Francis Milman.
1813.	John Latham.
1820.	Sir Henry Halford.
1844.	John Ayrton Paris.
1857.	Thomas Mayo.
1862.	Sir Thomas Watson.
1867.	Sir James Alderson.
1871.	Sir George Burrows.
1876.	Sir James Risdon Bennett.
1881.	Sir Wm. Jenner; died 11 Dec. 1898.
1888.	Sir Andrew Clark; died 6 Nov. 1893.
1893.	J. Russell Reynolds, bart., 1895; died 29 May, 1896.
1896.	Samuel Wilks, bart., June, 1897.
1899.	Wm. Selby Church, bart., K.C.B. June, 1902.

PHYSICS, see under *Philosophy, Natural.*

PHYSIOGNOMY, a science which affirms that the dispositions of mankind may be discovered from the features of the face. The origin of the term is referred to Aristotle; and Cicero was attached to the science. It became a fashionable study from the beginning of the 16th century; and in the 18th century, the essays of Le Cat and Pernethy led to the modern system.

J. K. Lavater, who endeavoured to raise physiognomy to the rank of a science, published his celebrated work "Physiognomische Fragmente," 1775-78, of which an English translation by Holcroft was published in 1793. The subject was considered by C. R. Darwin in his work "Expression of the emotions in Man and Animals," 1873, and by Mantegazza in his "Physiognomy and Expression," 1890.

PHYSIOLOGY is that part of physics which treats of the inner constitution of animals and plants, and the several functions and operations of all their organs and tissues. The works of Müller, Milne-Edwards, Huxley, Carpenter, Virchow, Brown-Séquard, Helmholtz, Ludwig, Du Bois-Reymond, Salomon Stricker Rutherford and sir John Bucknill, are much celebrated, and Todd's "Cyclopædia of Physiology" (1836-59) is a library in itself. Physiological Society, in London, founded by Dr. Burdon-Sanderson (bart. 1899) and others, early in 1876; see *Anatomy, Biology, Morphology, Royal Institution*. International congresses of physiology: Basle, 1888; Liége, Aug. 1892; Berne, 9 Sept. 1895; Cambridge, 23-26 Aug. 1898; Turin, 17 Sept. 1901.

By means of the Röntgen rays the action of the heart and viscera in a living human body were made visible at a meeting in Munich . 6 Aug. 1896

PIACENZA, see *Placentia.*

PIANETTE, a small upright piano introduced by Bord of Paris in 1857.

PIANOFORTE.* The invention is attributed to Cristofalli (or Cristofori), an Italian, J. C. Schröter, a German, and Marius, a Frenchman, early in the 18th century. The strings are struck by small hammers, and not by quills, as in harpsichords. Schröter is said to have presented a model of his invention to the court of Saxony, in 1717; and G. Silberman manufactured pianofortes with considerable success in 1772. Pianofortes were made in London by M. Zumpie, a German, 1766, and have been since greatly improved by Clementi, Broadwood, Collard, Kirkman, Erard, Pleyel, and others.

Upright pianos, first made in this country, were suggested by Isaac Hawkins in 1800, and Thomas Lond, in 1802. Wm. Southwell patented "cabinet pianos" in 1807; superseded, from about 1840, by the cottage, piccolo, and other pianos.

A keyed instrument at Modena was named "piano e forte," 1598.

A "*stone pianoforte*," formed of a series of flints and other stones of various sizes, collected in France and arranged by M. Baudre, was played on by him at the Royal Institution, on 16 March, 1866.

The new *transposing* piano, invented by Mr. Henry Schallehn, was exhibited at the Savoy hotel, Westminster, 10 June, 1890.

The Janko pianoforte, with a new arrangement of keyboard, exhibited in the Portman rooms, London, W., 24 Nov. *et seq.* 1891, said to possess many advantages.

See Grove's "Dictionary of Music," article "*Pianoforte.*"

Mr. A. J. Hipkins' "History of the Pianoforte," published 1896.

A "double piano," a new harpsichord and harp, played on at Messrs. Pleyel's rooms, London, 12 April, 1897.

Among mechanical contrivances for pianoforte playing or "dumb pianists" are the *Pianola*, and the *Metzler Piano-player*, 1903.

PICARDY (N. France), was conquered by the English in 1346, and by the duke of Burgundy in 1417, to whom it was ceded by the treaty of Arras, 21 Sept. 1435, and annexed to France by Louis XI., 1463.

PICCADILLY, a fine street, W. London; the name, of uncertain origin, was Pickadilla and Pigudello, about 1660, when a house of entertainment existed near the Haymarket, termed Pickadilly hall, after which buildings were gradually extended westwards.

PICCOLO PIANO, a small pianoforte introduced by Robert Wornum in 1829.

PICENTINES, a Sabine tribe, subdued by the Romans, and their capital, Asculum, taken, 268 B.C. They began the Social war in 90, and were conquered in 89 B.C.

PICHEGRU'S CONSPIRACY, see *Georges*.

* The nucleus of the instrument was a little box over which was stretched strings: such was the citole, the dulcimer, and the psaltery. The clavitherium had keys; the clavichord (about 1500) had dampers; successive improvements were the virginals (on which queen Elizabeth played), the spinet (about 1700), and the harpsichord (with two rows of keys), said to have been used in the 15th century, for which Bach and Handel composed in the 17th century. A collection of harpsichords (one dated 1555) is in the South Kensington museum. A double-pianoforte (with two keyboards reversed), giving remarkable effects (patented by M. M. Mengeot), played on at Covent-garden theatre, 21 Oct. 1878.

PICKETING, see *Trials*, Aug. 1867 and 1897.

R. Read and four other cabinetmakers imprisoned for picketing . . . . May, 1875

Watching dwellings, &c., declared illegal, 20 Dec. 1898

PICQUET, a game with cards, invented, it is said, by Joquemin, for the amusement of Charles VI. of France, then in feeble health, 1390. *Mézéray*.

PICTS (possibly from *Picti*, painted), the name given to the earliest known inhabitants of the east of Scotland, by the Romans, who made expeditions into the country, 296 *et seq.*; see *Roman Wall*.

PICTURES, see *Painting*.

PIEDMONT (*Pedemontium*, Latin, foot of the mountains), a region in N. Italy, formerly the seat of government of the kingdom of Sardinia, *which see*, and *Savoy*. Population, 1890, 3,234,506.

PIE-POUDRE COURT, the Court of Dusty Foot, whose jurisdiction was established for cases arising at fairs and markets, to do justice to the buyer and seller immediately upon the spot. By stat. 17 Edw. IV., it had cognizance of all disputes in the precincts of the market to which it might belong, 1477.

PIER AND HARBOUR ACT, to facilitate the formation, management, and maintenance of piers and harbours in Great Britain and Ireland, was passed in 1862.

PIETISTS, a Lutheran sect, instituted in Leipsic, by Philip James Spener, a professor of theology, about 1689, with the view of reforming the popular religion. He established "colleges of pietists," with preachers resembling those of the society of friends and the methodists in Britain, about 1760. A body resembling the Pietists, named Chasidim, arose among the Jews in the Ukraine, and spread through Poland and European Turkey.

PIETRO BARSANTI CLUB, see *Italy*, 1878.

PIEZOMETER (Greek *piezo*, I compress), an apparatus for measuring the compressibility of liquids, invented by Œrsted (died 1851); improved by Despretz & Saigey.

PIGEONS were employed as carriers by the ancients. Hirtius and Brutus corresponded by means of pigeons at the siege of Modena. The pigeons of Aleppo served as couriers at Alexandretta and Bagdad. Thirty-two pigeons liberated from London at 7 o'clock in the morning, 22 Nov. 1819; at noon one of them arrived at Antwerp; a quarter of an hour afterwards a second arrived; the remainder on the following day. *Phillips*. At a pigeon race, 25 July, 1872, from Spalding to London, the speed allowed was 90 seconds a mile; see *Post Office*, 1870.

In a pigeon race from Dover to Plymouth, some pigeons attained the velocity of 1,233 yards, 1,218 yards and 1,008 yards per minute 22 July, 1886. About 300 pigeon-flying societies exist in France: the organization of carrier-pigeon stations ordered by the minister for war, Jan. 1888. About 350 similar societies exist in Germany, stated Jan. 1888.

National Peristeronic Society (originating from the Columbarian Society, founded in 1750), has annual shows.

A bill for prohibiting shooting pigeons rising from a trap attended with cruelties, passed by the commons with large majorities, in 1883 and 1884 (195—40), was rejected by the lords in 1883 (30—17), and on 9 May, 1884 (78—48).

The London Columbarian society opened its 15th annual exhibition of pigeons, at the Westminster Aquarium, 2 Dec. 1891.

Pigeon postal service successfully established between Auckland, New Zealand and Gt. Barrier island, summer, 1899.

National pigeon post for military and naval purposes, scheme inaugurated at the Crystal palace, 18 Dec. 1900.

PIGMIES, see *Dwarfs*.

PILCHARD FISHERY. Peculiar to Land's End, Cornwall, reverts to W. Ireland, after suspension of two centuries (stated July, 1883).

PILGRIMAGE OF GRACE, a name assumed by religious insurgents in the north of England, who opposed the dissolution of the monasteries. The movement, which commenced in Lincolnshire in Sept. 1536, was suppressed in Oct.; but soon after revived in Yorkshire; and an expedition, bearing the foregoing name, having banners on which were depicted the five wounds of Christ, was headed by Aske, and other gentlemen, and joined by priests and 40,000 men of York, Durham, Lancaster, and other counties. They took Hull and York, with smaller towns. The duke of Norfolk marched against them, and by making terms dispersed them. Early in 1537 they again took arms but were promptly suppressed, and the leaders, several abbots, and many others, were executed.

PILGRIMAGES began with the pilgrimage of the empress Helena to Jerusalem, 326. They became very frequent at the close of the 10th century. Robert II. of France made several pilgrimages; among others one to Rome about the year 1016, perhaps in 1020, when he refused the imperial dignity and the kingdom of Italy. The pilgrimage to Canterbury is described by Chaucer in his Canterbury Tales about 1383. The pilgrimage of Mahometans to Mecca, the birth-place of the prophet, is commanded in the Koran. This pilgrimage was very great from India, where it has been encouraged by the princes, but discouraged by the British as idolatrous. The great mortality due to want and disease compelled the government to intervene with strict sanitary regulations, and it is now stated that the number of deaths has diminished, and the number of pilgrims increased. The contract with Messrs. Cook and sons in 1886 to convey pilgrims from Bombay to Mecca is said to be a failure financially, reported, Jan. 1895. See *Cholera*. Pilgrimages to shrines of the Virgin Mary in France revived in 1873, and since, in consequence of miracles alleged to have taken place at La Salette in 1846 and at Lourdes, 11 Feb. 1858; those of La Salette discredited by Pope Leo X., 1879. See *Sacred Heart*.

100 American pilgrims received by the pope 9 June, 1874

About 100 agricultural labourers (locked out for being unionists) traversed England as pilgrims, receiving hospitality and money; beginning 30 June, *et seq.* ,,

English R.C. pilgrimage to shrine of St. Edmund, archbishop of Canterbury, at Pontigny . Sept. ,,

English pilgrimage to Lourdes directed by the "Catholic Union of Great Britain," start proposed; given up . . . . Aug. 1880

Many Irish pilgrims present at the pope's jubilee at Rome . . . . . 14 Feb. *et seq.* 1893

The duke of Norfolk and about 900 British pilgrims received by the pope (see *Pope*) . . 27 Feb. ,,

The count of Condé and 1,500 Belgians received by the pope . . . . . . 23 April, 1898

St. Winifred's well, in Flintshire, for centuries frequented by pilgrims; see *Trials* . June, 1899

Pilgrims (4 men and 36 women) killed by the partial collapse of a house in Porchov, Russia, many injured, reported . . 8 Oct. 1900

[See *Boulogne*.]

PILGRIM FATHERS, the name given in North America to a party of 74 English puritans and 28 women, members of John Robinson's church, who sailed in the *May Flower* from Leyden to North America, and landed on Plymouth Rock, where they founded a colony, 25 Dec. 1620.

The rev. A. E. Dunning, D.D., of Boston, U.S., with 46 American congregational ministers and others, following the track of the pilgrim fathers, arrive at Plymouth, 11 June; the party were received at Oxford, Bedford and other places; the visitors leave, much gratified, 2 July, 1896.

Memorial congregational church in memory of the "Pilgrim Father," John Robinson, founded at Gainsborough, 29 June, 1896.

The MS. log of the *Mayflower* presented to the President and citizens of the United States by the bishop of London, in compliance with the petition of Mr. T. F. Bayard, U.S. ambassador, 25 March, 1897; given up by him to governor Wolcott, of Massachusetts, 26 May, 1897.

"The Story of the Pilgrim Fathers," reprinted and edited by Mr. Edw. Arber, 1897.

"PILGRIM'S PROGRESS FROM THIS WORLD TO THAT WHICH IS TO COME," written by John Bunyan, in Bedford gaol, where he was imprisoned twelve years, 1660-72. The first part was published in 1678. A Hebrew version appeared in 1851; see *Bedford*. A first edition (1678) realised 1,475*l.*, 9 May, 1901.

PILLAR SAINTS, see *Monachism*.

PILLORY, a scaffold for persons to stand on, to render them publicly infamous. This punishment was awarded against persons convicted of forgery, perjury, libelling, &c. In some cases the head was put through a hole, the hands through two others, the nose slit, the face branded with one or more letters, and one or both ears were cut off. There is a statute of the pillory, 41 Hen. III. 1256. Many persons died in the pillory by being struck with stones by the mob, and pelted with rotten eggs and putrid offal. It was abolished as a punishment except for perjury, 1815, and totally abolished in 1837. The last who suffered at the Old Bailey was Peter Jas. Bossy, for perjury, 22 June, 1830.

PILNITZ (near Dresden, Saxony). The convention of Pilnitz took place between the emperor Leopold and the king of Prussia, 20 July, 1791. On 27 Aug. the treaty of Pilnitz, or, as some style it, the Partition treaty, was finally agreed upon at Pavia by the courts in concert. It was to the effect "that the emperor should retake all that Louis XIV. had conquered in the Austrian Netherlands, and uniting these provinces to the Netherlands, give them to his serene highness the elector palatine, to be added to the palatinate; Bavaria to be added to the Austrian possessions," &c.

PILOT. The act relating to pilots, 16 & 17 Vict. c. 129 (1853), with other acts, is embodied in the Merchant Shipping act; 15th annual conference of the United Kingdom Pilots' association at Carnarvon, 12 July, 1898; see *Trinity-House*.

PILPAY, see *Fables*.

PIMLICO, S.W. suburb of London, belonging to the Grosvenor family, who have built largely upon it since 1830.

On 20 Dec. 1881, Georgina Moore, 7½ years old, living with her parents in Winchester-street, disappeared; her body was found by bargemen in the Medway, near Yalding, 30 Jan. 1882. Esther Pay, with whom she was last seen, accused of her murder, was acquitted, 29 April, 1882.

Pimlico poisoning case. See *Trials*, April, 1886.

PINCHBECK, an alloy of 25 per cent. of zinc and 75 copper, used for watch-cases, &c.; named after either Christopher or Thomas Pinchbeck, London, mechanics; the former is said to have died in 1732, the latter in 1783.

PINDAREES, bands of freebooters, or mercenary soldiers in the central provinces of India, headquarters Malwa, who, after the fall of the Mogul empire, ravaged the native territories and the British settlements, 1804, *et seq.*, till finally crushed by two armies commanded by the marquis of Hastings in 1817.

PINE-TREES. The stone pine (*Pinus Pinea*), brought to these countries before 1548. The cluster pine (*Pinus Pinaster*), brought from the south of Europe before 1596. The Weymouth pine (*Pinus Strobus*), from North America, 1705. Frankincense pine (*Pinus Tæda*), from North America, before 1713. There are other varieties.

PING-PONG, *i.e.* Table Tennis, very popular, 1901 *et seq.*

PINKIE (near Edinburgh), where the English under the Earl of Hertford, protector, totally defeated the Scots under the regent Arran, 10 Sept. 1547. There fell not 200 of the English, but above 10,000 of the Scots. Above 1500 were taken prisoners.

PINS have been found in British barrows (*Fosbroke*); and are mentioned in a statute of 1483. Brass pins were brought from France in 1540, and first used in England, it is said, by Catherine Howard, queen of Henry VIII. Pins were made in England in 1543. *Stow.* They were first manufactured by machinery in England in 1824, under a patent of Lemuel Wellman Wright, of the United States.

PIOMBINO, a principality, Italy, previously ruled by the Appiani family, was acquired by the Spaniards, 1589. It was ceded to France, 1801, and given by Napoleon to his sister Elise, wife of prince Bacciochi, who held it from 1805 to 1815, when it was restored to the Buoncampagni family, subject to Tuscany. It became part of the kingdom of Italy, 1860.

PIPE ROLL SOCIETY, founded in 1884 for printing all extant public records prior to the year A.D. 1200.

PIRACY, Greek *pirati*, was severely suppressed by the Romans. Pompey destroyed the Cilician pirates, 67 B.C.; see *Buccaneers.* Many acts of parliament have been passed for the suppression of piracy; the latest in 1837.

PIRÆUS, the port of Athens, was united to the city by two long walls, one erected by Themistocles, and the other by Pericles, 456 B.C., which were destroyed by Lysander, 404 B.C. It was fortified by Conon, 393 B.C. The Piræus was able to contain 400 Greek vessels. It was occupied by the French during the Russian war in 1854.

PIRMASENS (Bavaria). Here Moreau and the French were defeated by the duke of Brunswick and the Prussians, 14 Sept. 1793.

PISA, an ancient city in Tuscany, was founded about six centuries before Christ, and was favoured by the early Roman emperors as a flourishing republic. The citizens took an active part in the Italian wars of the middle ages, but became subject to Florence, after a long siege, 1405-6. In 1494 Pisa became independent under the protection of Charles VIII. of France, but was retaken by the Florentines in 1509. The university was founded in 1343, and revived by the Medici in 1472 and 1542. The rival popes, Benedict XIII. and Gregory XII., were deposed at a council held at Pisa in 1409, and Alexander V. elected in their room. The Campanile or leaning tower was built about 1154,* and the Campo Santo about the same time. Fire panic in the cathedral, 9 persons crushed to death, 21 injured, 29 May, 1897.

PISCICULTURE, see *Fisheries.*

PISTOLS, the smallest fire-arms, said to have been invented at Pistoja in Italy; were first used by the cavalry of England about 1544. Of late years they have been made with a revolving cylindrical breech, in which are formed several chambers for receiving cartridges, and bringing them in succession into a line with the barrel ready for firing. The earliest model of this kind of arm is to be found in the museum of the United Service Institution, and is supposed to date from the reign of Charles I. An eight-chambered matchlock revolver of the 16th century is placed in the Royal Artillery Museum, Woolwich. The manufacture of pistols by machinery was first introduced into England from the United States, America, in the year 1853, by col. Colt, who invented the Colt revolving pistol, 1851. This system of manufacture induced the British government to establish the Enfield armoury, in 1855; see *Fire-Arms.*

A *pistols bill*, restricting the sale and carrying of pistols, read 2nd time (commons) . . 27 Feb. 1895

PIT BROW WOMEN, see *Coal*, 23 June, 1887.

PITCAIRN'S ISLAND, in the Pacific Ocean, said to have been discovered by Pitcairn in 1768, seen by Cook in 1773, and since colonised by ten mutineers from the ship *Bounty*, captain Bligh, in 1789; see *Bounty.*

The mutineers remained unknown to England until discovered accidentally in 1814. A ship nearing the island was hailed by a swarthy youth in the English language, when it appeared that the mutineers, soon after settling there, had married some black women from a neighbouring island, and had become a well-conducted community under the care of Adams, the principal mutineer. He died in 1829, when George Hunn Nobbs, an Englishman, who arrived a few years before, became chief. In Aug. 1852 admiral Moresby spent a few days on the island. By his means Nobbs was sent to England and obtained ordination. His death (aged 86) announced Jan. 1885. As their numbers increased, the island proved incapable of their support. The English government removed them, with all their property, in the ship *Morayshire*, on 3 May, 1856, and landed them, after a boisterous passage, on Norfolk Island, prepared previously for their reception, 8 June. The government stocked Norfolk Island with 2000 sheep, 450 head of cattle, and twenty horses, and gave them stores to last twelve months; their numbers were 96 males and 102 females.

The island visited by H.M.S. *Peterel* was found to be prosperous, Dec. 1875. Population, 15 Aug. 1879, 93; in 1890, 126.

Harry Christian sentenced to death for murdering a woman and her children (June, 1897), reported, 8 Nov. 1898; the *Sokota* s.s. visited the island, 30 Aug. 1902.

PITCH, see under *Music.*

* The Campanile was erected to contain bells, and stands in a square close to the cathedral. It is built entirely of white marble, and is a cylinder of eight stories, each adorned with a round of columns, rising one above another. It inclines so far on one side from the perpendicular, that in dropping a plummet from the top, which is 188 feet in height, it falls sixteen feet from the base. Some thought this was done purposely by the architect; others attributed it to an accidental subsidence of the foundation. From this tower Galileo made his observation on gravitation (about 1635).

PITT ADMINISTRATIONS.* The first administration was formed on the dismissal of the Portland ministry 18 Dec. 1783, and terminated by resignation in 1801. The second was formed 12 May, 1804; and terminated (after various changes) by Mr. Pitt's death, 23 Jan. 1806. A public funeral was decreed to him, and 40,000*l.* to pay his debts.

ADMINISTRATION OF 1783.

William Pitt, *first lord of the treasury* and *chancellor of the exchequer.*
Earl Gower, *lord president.*
Duke of Rutland, *privy seal.*
Marquis of Carmarthen and earl Temple (immediately succeeded by lord Sydney), *secretaries.*
Lord Thurlow, *lord chancellor.*
Viscount Howe, *admiralty.*
Duke of Richmond, *ordnance.*
William Wyndham Grenville, Henry Dundas, &c.
[Mr. Pitt was joined by the duke of Portland, earl Spencer, and other leading whigs in 1794; he continued minister until 1801. Many changes occurred in the ministry in the long period of seventeen years.]

ADMINISTRATION OF 1804.

William Pitt, *first lord of the treasury.*
Lord Eldon, *lord chancellor.*
Duke of Portland, succeeded by lord Sidmouth (late Mr. Addington), *lord president.*
Earl of Westmorland, *lord privy seal.*
Lord Hawkesbury, lord Harrowby (succeeded by lord Mulgrave), and earl Camden (succeeded by viscount Castlereagh), *home, foreign,* and *colonial secretaries.*
Viscount Melville (succeeded by lord Barham), *admiralty.*
Duke of Montrose, Mr. Dundas, &c.

PITTSBURG, the second city of Pennsylvania, founded on the site of Fort Duquesne (*which see*) in 1759, and named Fort Pitt, afterwards Pittsburg, in honour of the then British prime minister, William Pitt. See *United States*, July, 1877. The exhibition building burnt, 3 Oct. 1883. Population in 1880, 156,389; 1890, 238,617; 1900, 321,616.

Upwards of 100 persons perish by a mining explosion near here . . . about 11 Nov. 1888.
The use of coal as fuel gradually superseded in Pittsburg by inflammable gas rising from the ground . . . . 1884 *et seq.*
Strike of about 10,000 railway men and coal-miners begins 1 Oct. 1891
Strike and lock-out of about 3800 men at Messrs. Carnegie's steel works at Homestead, near Pittsburg, 29 June; rioting and conflicts with the police, with loss of life on both sides, 6–7 July; order at last restored at Homestead by the state militia and martial law, 26 July; work gradually resumed, Aug.—Nov.; strike quite over, reported . . . . 21 Nov. 1892
Plot to poison the non-unionists at Homestead discovered; many deaths, reported about 12 Dec.; several arrests; Patrick Gallagher, the cook, revealed the plot, 19 Dec. 1892; he is sentenced to 5 years', Dempsey and Beatty to 7 years', and Davidson to 3 years' imprisonment . 4 March, 1893
Legal proceedings respecting the Homestead riots closed . . . . 3 June, ,,
The Carnegie steel mills reopened . . 4 Sept. ,,
Mr. Andrew Carnegie presents 5000 dollars daily to the poor, and orders his mills to be kept running during Jan. and Feb. 1894 . . 28 Dec. ,,
Free library, museum, &c., cost about 1,000,000 dollars, presented by Mr. Andrew Carnegie, dedicated . . . . 5 Nov. 1895
Severe storm and floods, 17 persons drowned, reported . . . . 28 July, 1896
Mr. Andrew Carnegie gives 5,000,000 dollars to his workmen, &c., March, and 400,000*l.* to Pittsburg . . . . Nov. 1901
Steel strike, 35,000 men called out, 1 July; ends in defeat of the men . . . . . 14 Sept. 1901
Oil explosion at Sheraden in some naphtha cars, 20 deaths; the naphtha escaping caused another explosion at Esplenborough, wrecking 3 buildings, 12 May, 1902

PITTSBURG LANDING (near Corinth, Tennessee). On Sunday, 6 April, 1862, a great battle was fought between the American federals under Grant and Prentiss, and the confederates under Albert Sydney Johnston and Beauregard. The latter began the attack and were victorious, but lost their able general Johnston. The federals were reinforced the next day and renewed the attack; the confederates maintained their ground; but soon after retired in good order to Corinth. This engagement is also named the battle of Shiloh.

PITURINE, a new narcotic, said to have been discovered in 1882 in Australia. It resembles a mixture of opium and tobacco, and is extracted from the dried leaves of the *Duboisia pituri.*

PIUS IV., CREED OF, see *Confessions.*

PLACENTIA (now Piacenza), N. Italy, founded by the Romans about 220 B.C. It suffered in all the convulsions attending the fall of the empire and the wars of the middle ages. In 1254 it fell under the rule of the family of the Scotti. In 1302 Alberto Scotto was overcome, and Placentia was united to Milan, then ruled by the Visconti. On their extinction in 1447, Placentia revolted, but was taken by Sforza duke of Milan, and treated very cruelly. In 1513 it was given to pope Leo X. In 1545 Paul III. gave it with Parma as a duchy to his son Peter Louis Farnese. The French and Spaniards were defeated by the Austrians and Sardinians near Placentia, 16 June, 1746; see *Parma.*

PLACILLA, Chili (*which see*). The site of the decisive victory of the congressists over president Balmaceda, 28 Aug. 1891.

PLAGUE. The plagues of Egypt (1491 B.C.) are described in *Exodus* ix., &c. The first recorded general plague in all parts of the world occurred 767 B.C. *Petavius.* At Rome a desolating plague prevailed, 453 B.C. The devastating plague at Athens, which spread into Egypt and Ethiopia, 430 B.C., is admirably described by Thucydides. Another which raged in the Greek islands, Egypt, and Syria, destroyed 2000 persons every day, 187 B.C. *Pliny.* See *Cattle.*

At Rome, a most awful plague; 10,000 persons perished daily, A.D. 80.
Again ravaged the Roman empire, 167, 169, 189.
Another in the Roman empire. For some time 5000 persons died daily at Rome; many towns entirely depopulated, 250-265.
In Britain, a plague swept away such multitudes that the living were scarcely sufficient to bury the dead, 430.
A long-continued, dreadful one began in Europe in 558, extended all over Asia and Africa.
At Constantinople, when 200,000 of its inhabitants perished, and in Calabria, Sicily, and Greece, 746-749.
In London, 962.
At Chichester, in England, an epidemical disease carried off 34,000 persons, 772. *Will. Malms.*
In Scotland 40,000 persons perished, 954.
In London, great mortality, 1094; and Ireland, 1095.
Again, in London; it extended to cattle, fowls, and other domestic animals, 1111. *Holinshed.*
In Ireland; after Christmas this year Henry II. was forced to quit the country, 1172.
Again, in Ireland, when a prodigious number perished, 1204.
The "Black Death" in Italy, 1340

* William Pitt, second son of the great earl of Chatham, was born 28 March, 1759; became M.P. 23 Jan. 1782; moved for a reform in parliament, 7 May, 1782; became chancellor of the exchequer, July, 1782; died 23 Jan. 1806.

A plague raged throughout Europe, causing extensive mortality. Britain and Ireland suffered grievously. In London alone 200 persons were buried daily in the Charterhouse-yard, 1348-9. (That at Florence described by Boccaccio.)
["The Great Pestilence" (black death), by Francis Aidan Gasquet, D.D., an elaborate work, published in 1894.]
In London and Paris a dreadful mortality prevailed in 1361-2, 1367, 1369, and in Ireland in 1370.
A great pestilence in Ireland, called the *Fourth*, destroyed a great number of the people, 1383.
30,000 persons perished of a dreadful pestilence in London, 1407.
Again, in Ireland, superinduced by a famine; great numbers died, 1466; and Dublin was wasted by a plague, 1470.
An awful pestilence at Oxford, 1471; and throughout England, a plague which destroyed more people than the continual wars for the fifteen preceding years, 1478. *Rapin: Salmon.*
The *Sudor Anglicus*, or sweating sickness, very fatal in London, 1485. *Delaune.*
The plague in London so dreadful that Henry VII. and his court removed to Calais, 1499-1500 *Stow.*
The sweating sickness (mortal in three hours), in London, 1506; and in 1517. In most of the capital towns in England half the inhabitants died, and Oxford was depopulated, 9 Henry VIII. *Stow.*
Limerick was visited by a plague, when many thousands perished, 1522.
The sweating sickness again in England, 1528; and in North Germany in 1529; and for the fifth time in England, in 1551.
30,578 persons perished of the plague in London alone, 1603-1604. It was also fatal in Ireland.
200,000 perished of a pestilence at Constantinople in 1611.
In London a great mortality prevailed, and 35,417 persons perished, 1625.
In France a general mortality; at Lyons, 60,000 persons died, 1632.
The plague brought from Sardinia to Naples (being introduced by a transport with soldiers on board), raged with such violence as to carry off 400,000 of the inhabitants in six months, 1656.
THE GREAT PLAGUE OF LONDON, began Dec. 1664, which carried off 68,596 persons; some say 100,000. Fires were kept up night and day to purify the air for three days; and it was thought the infection was not totally destroyed till the great conflagration of Sept. 1666.
[Graphically described by De Foe in his partially imaginative *History of the Plague*.]
"Loimographia: an account of the Great Plague in 1665," by William Boghurst, apothecary, edited by Joseph Frank Payne, M.D., from the MS. in the British Museum, 1896.
60,000 persons perished of the plague at Marseilles and neighbourhood, brought in ship from the Levant, 1720.
One of the most awful plagues that ever raged, prevailed in Syria, 1760. *Abbé Mariti.*
In Persia, a fatal pestilence, which carried off 80,000 of the inhabitants of Bassora, 1773.
In Egypt, about 800,000 persons died of plague, 1792.
In Barbary, 3000 died daily; and at Fez 247,000 perished, 1799; in the east, 1800; 1840; 1873; many deaths in Bagdad, &c., April-May, 1876.
In Spain and at Gibraltar immense numbers were carried off by a pestilent disease in 1804 and 1805.
Again at Gibraltar, an epidemic fever much resembling the plague, caused great mortality, 1828.
The Asiatic cholera (see *Cholera*) made its first appearance in England, at Sunderland, 26 Oct. 1831; in Scotland, at Haddington, 23 Dec. same year; and in Ireland, at Belfast, 14 March, 1832.
The cholera again visited England, &c., 1848 and 1849 (see *Cholera*).
The cholera raged at Smyrna and Constantinople, and appeared in Paris, Marseilles, Naples; July-Dec. 1865.
A great cattle plague (*which see*) in England, resembling typhus, near London, begins June, 1865.
A new, and hitherto an incurable disease, named *black death*, on account of purple blotches coming out on the skin, appeared in Dublin; many persons of all ranks died a few hours after the seizure. March *et seq.* 1866.
Plague in Astracan, Jan.—April, 1879.
Plague in Hong-Kong (*which see*), June, July, 1894.
Plague in Bombay, Karachi (*which see*), and other parts of India, Oct. *et seq.* 1896-8.
Sanitary conference of the powers, 65 delegates, count Bonin elected president, 16 Feb. 1897; convention signed, 19 March, 1897.
The commission under prof. Koch issues a report, 20 July, 1897; official report issued, June, 1898.
Plague in Turkestan, Samarkand, great mortality, Oct.–Nov. 1898.
Plague severe in India, great mortality in Bombay (*which see*), 1898; estimated deaths, 600,000, Aug. 1901. (Punjaub, 530 deaths, 1899–1900; 6,399 deaths, 1900–1901; 200,000 deaths, 1901–02.)
Plague in Mauritius, 1899–1903; Oporto (*which see*).
Dr. Manson reports bubonic plague to be a rat-borne disease, and holds their extermination as a preventative, Oct. 1899 [disputed by dr. Bruce Low in his report of the spread of the disease in the world, 1898–1901; *Times*, 25 Oct. 1902].
Prof. Kitasato of Japan discovers the plague bacillus saprophytic, reported, ? 1900.
Prof. Haffkine's system of anti-plague inoculation successful; encouraged by government, Feb. 1900.
Plague at Sydney, spring *et seq.* 1900; total deaths, 103; town free, 8 Sept. 1900; 33 deaths up to 14 May, 1901.
Dr. Yersin's anti-plague serum obtained from horses, proved successful in Indo-China, Aug.–Oct. 1900.
Slight outbreak at Glasgow, 7 deaths, 27 Aug.–14 Nov. 1900; 4 cases, 1 death, 26 Oct. 1901.
Plague at Cape Town, 11 Feb. 1901.
Hong-kong: 113 deaths, week ending 18 May, 1901; total deaths, 1,509 (11 Europeans); subsiding, 24 July; 103 deaths, 7–21 June, 1902; subsides, reported clear, mid Sept. 1902; increasing Feb. 915 deaths, 18 April–Aug. 1903.
Oporto: 4 deaths, reported, 26 June, 1901.
Egypt: 173 cases, 83 deaths, 7 April–7 Oct. 1901; 147 deaths, April–19 July, 1902.
Plague in Liverpool: 6 deaths, 30 Oct.; 1 death, 7 Nov. 1901.
Plague in Madagascar: 4 deaths, 19–27 May, 1902.
Plague in Odessa: slight epidemic, Sept.–early Nov. 1902.
Plague in Durban: 27 deaths, reported, 26 Jan. 1903.
Plague in India, Bombay and elsewhere, 600,000 deaths, Jan.–Aug. 1903.

PLAIN-SONG, see *Chanting*.

PLAN OF CAMPAIGN (see *Ireland*), Oct. 1886. By this plan the tenant of a farm was to pay his rent to the National League instead of to the landlord, and was to be supported if evicted. It was condemned by the pope, 20 April, 1888; given up by many tenants throughout the country, and disavowed by Mr. Parnell and others, 1890-1. The plan given up by many on the Woodford estate, Galway, Oct. 1891.

Mr. Dillon stated before the Evicted Tenants commission that the total amount received from all sources for evicted tenants was 234,431*l*. 4 Jan. 1893

PLANE. A true plane, most successfully obtained by sir Joseph Whitworth. Fine specimens exhibited at the Royal Institution in 1873.

PLANETARIUM, see *Orrery*.

PLANETS. Jupiter was known as a planet to the Chinese and the Chaldeans, and inserted in a chart of the heavens, made about 600 B.C., and in which 1460 stars are accurately described; this chart is said to be in the national library at Paris. The four satellites of Jupiter discovered by Galileo, 7 Jan. 1601, see *Mars*, *Saturn*. We now know eight primary planets, termed major; *Mercury*, *Venus*, the *Earth*, *Mars*, *Jupiter*, *Saturn*, *Uranus*, *Neptune*; and secondary or minor, situated between the orbits of Mars and Jupiter. The numerical order differs in the lists of English, German, and French astronomers. In the French and German lists, *Aglaia* to *Pandora* are numbered 47 to 55; *Melete* is 56.

Uranus, formerly called *Georgium Sidus* and *Herschel*; discovered by W. Herschel (see *Georgium Sidus*) 13 March, 1781

Neptune, discovered by Galle (in consequence of the calculations of Le Verrier) (see *Neptune*), 23 Sept. 1846. It had been theoretically discovered by professor J. Couch Adams of Cambridge 1845

Vulcan (between Mercury and the Sun), said to be discovered by M. Lescarbault, a physician (not seen since), 26 March, 1859, and its discovery is now generally doubted; said to have been seen by Watson during the solar eclipse (doubted by Peters) . . . . . . 29, 30 July, 1878

A red star seen by M. Trouvelot during the solar eclipse, perhaps Vulcan . . . . . 6 May, 1883

MINOR PLANETS (*according to Mr. G. F. Chambers, the Royal Astronomical Society, and others*).

1. *Ceres*, discovered by Piazzi visible to the naked eye) . . . . . 1 Jan. 1801
2. *Pallas*, discovered at Bremen by Olbers (see *Pallas*) . . . . . 28 March, 1802
3. *Juno*, discovered by Harding . . 1 Sept. 1804
4. *Vesta*, discovered by Olbers . . 29 March, 1807
5. *Astræa*, by K. C. Hencke . . 8 Dec. 1845
6. *Hebe*, by the same . . 1 July, 1847
7. *Iris*, by J. R. Hind . . 13 Aug. ,,
8. *Flora*, by the same . . 18 Oct. ,,
9. *Metis*, by A. Graham . . 25 April, 1848
10. *Hygeia*, by A. de Gasparis . . 12 April, 1849
11. *Parthenope*, by the same . . 11 May, 1850
12. *Victoria*, by J. R. Hind . . 13 Sept. ,,
13. *Egeria*, by A. de Gasparis . . 2 Nov. ,,
14. *Irene*, by J. R. Hind . . 19 May, 1851
15. *Eunomia*, by A. de Gasparis . . 29 July, ,,
16. *Psyche*, by the same . . 17 March, 1852
17. *Thetis*, by R. Luther . . 17 April, ,,
18. *Melpomene*, by J. R. Hind . . 24 June, ,,
19. *Fortuna*, by the same . . 22 Aug. ,,
20. *Massilia*, by A. de Gasparis . . 19 Sept. ,,
21. *Lutetia*, by H. Goldschmidt . . 15 Nov. ,,
22. *Calliope*, by J. R. Hind . . 16 Nov. ,,
23. *Thalia*, by the same . . 15 Dec. ,,
24. *Themis*, by A. de Gasparis . . 5 April, 1853
25. *Phocæa*, by M. Chacornac . . 6 April, ,,
26. *Proserpine*, by R. Luther . . 5 May, ,,
27. *Euterpe*, by J. R. Hind . . 8 Nov. ,,
28. *Bellona*, by R. Luther . . 1 March, 1854
29. *Amphitrite*, by Mr. Marth . . 1 March, ,,
30. *Urania*, by J. R. Hind . . 22 July, ,,
31. *Euphrosyne*, by James Ferguson . . 1 Sept. ,,
32. *Pomona*, by H. Goldschmidt . . 26 Oct. ,,
33. *Polyhymnia*, by M. Chacornac . . 28 Oct. ,,
34. *Circe*, by the same . . 6 April, 1855
35. *Leucothea*, by R. Luther . . 19 April, ,,
36. *Atalanta*, by H. Goldschmidt . . 19 April, ,,
37. *Fides*, by R. Luther . . 5 Oct. ,,
38. *Leda*, by M. Chacornac . . 12 Jan. 1856
39. *Lætitia*, by the same . . 8 Feb. ,,
40. *Harmonia*, by R. Luther . . 31 March, ,,
41. *Daphne*, by H. Goldschmidt . . 22 May, ,,
42. *Isis*, by Norman Pogson . . 23 May, ,,
43. *Ariadne*, by the same . . 15 April, 1857
44. *Nysa*, by H. Goldschmidt . . 27 May, ,,
45. *Eugenia*, by the same . . 28 June, ,,
46. *Hestia*, by N. Pogson . . 16 Aug. ,,
47. **Melete*, by H. Goldschmidt . . 9 Sept. ,,
48. *Aglaia*, by R. Luther . . 15 Sept. ,,
49. *Doris*, by H. Goldschmidt . . 19 Sept. ,,
50. *Pales*, by the same . . 19 Sept. ,,
51. *Virginia*, by James Ferguson . . 4 Oct. ,,
52. *Nemausa*, by M. Laurent . . 22 Jan. 1858
53. *Europa*, by H. Goldschmidt . . 6 Feb. ,,
54. *Calypso*, by R. Luther . . 4 April, ,,
55. *Alexandra*, by H. Goldschmidt . . 10 Sept. ,,
56. *Pandora*, by Mr. Searle . . 10 Sept. ,,
57. *Mnemosyne*, by R. Luther . . 22 Sept. 1859
58. *Concordia*, by the same . . 24 March, 1860
59. *Danae*, by H. Goldschmidt . . 9 Sept. ,,
60. *Olympia*, by M. Chacornac . . 12 Sept. ,,
61. *Erato*, by MM. Förster and Lessing . . 14 Sept. ,,
62. *Echo* (orig. *Titania*), by J. Ferguson 15 Sept. 1860
63. *Ausonia*, by A. de Gasparis . . 10 Feb. 1861
64. *Angelina*, by M. Tempel . . 4 March, ,,
65. *Cybele* (orig. *Maximiliana*), by M. Tempel, 8 March, ,,
66. *Maia*, by H. P. Tuttle . . 9 April, ,,
67. *Asia*, by N. Pogson . . 17 April, ,,
68. *Leto*, by R. Luther . . 29 April, ,,
69. *Hesperia*, by M. Schiaparelli . . 29 April, ,,
70. *Panopæa*, by H. Goldschmidt . . 5 May, ,,
71. *Feronia*, by Peters and Safford . . 29 May, ,,
72. *Niobe*, by R. Luther . . 13 Aug. ,,
73. *Clytie*, by H. P. Tuttle . . 7 April, 1862
74. *Galatea*, by M. Tempel . . 29 Aug. ,,
75. *Eurydice*, by C. H. F. Peters . . 22 Sept. ,,
76. *Freia*, by M. d'Arrest . . 21 Oct. ,,
77. *Frigga*, by C. H. F. Peters . . 12 Nov. ,,
78. *Diana*, by R. Luther . . 15 March, 1863
79. *Eurynome*, by Jas. C. Watson . . 14 Sept. ,,
80. *Sappho*, by N. Pogson . . 2 May, 1864
81. *Terpsichore*, by M. Tempel . . 30 Sept. ,,
82. *Alcmene*, by R. Luther . . 27 Nov. ,,
83. *Beatrix*, by A. de Gasparis . . 26 April, 1865
84. *Clio*, by R. Luther . . 25 Aug. ,,
85. *Io*, by C. H. F. Peters . . 19 Sept. ,,
86. *Semele*, by F. Tietjen . . 4 Jan. 1866
87. *Sylvia*, by N. Pogson . . 16 May, ,,
88. *Thisbe*, by C. H. F. Peters . . 15 June, ,,
89. *Julia*, by M. Stephan . . 6 Aug. ,,
90. *Antiope*, by R. Luther . . 1 Oct. ,,
91. *Ægina*, by Alphonse Borelly . . 4 Nov. ,,
92. *Undina*, by C. H. F. Peters . . 7 July, 1867
93. *Minerva*, by J. C. Watson . . 24 Aug. ,,
94. *Aurora*, by the same . . 6 Sept. ,,
95. *Arethusa*, by R. Luther . . 23 Nov. ,,
96. *Ægle*, by M. Coggia . . 17 Feb. 1868
97. *Clotho*, by M. Tempel . . 17 Feb. ,,
98. *Ianthe*, by C. H. F. Peters . . 18 April, ,,
99. *Dikē*, by A. Borelly . . 28 May, ,,
100. *Hecate*, by J. C. Watson . . 11 July, ,,
101. *Helena*, by the same . . 15 Aug. ,,
102. *Miriam*, by C. H. F. Peters . . 22 Aug. ,,
103. *Hera*, by J. C. Watson . . 7 Sept. ,,
104. *Clymene*, by the same . . 13 Sept. ,,
105. *Artemis*, by J. C. Watson . . 16 Sept. ,,
106. *Dione*, by J. C. Watson . . 10 Oct. ,,
107. *Camilla*, by N. Pogson . . 17 Nov. ,,
108. *Hecuba*, by R. Luther † . . 2 April, 1869
109. *Felicitas*, by C. H. F. Peters . . 9 Oct. ,,
110. *Lydia*, by Alphonse Borelly . . 19 April, 1870
111. *Até*, by C. H. F. Peters . . 14 Aug. ,,
112. *Iphigenia*, by C. H. F. Peters . . 19 Sept. ,,
113. *Amalthæa*, by R. Luther . . 12 March, 1871
114. *Cassandra*, by C. H. F. Peters . . 23 July, ,,
115. *Thyra*, by J. C. Watson . . 6 Aug. ,,
116. *Sirona* (by R. Luther, 14 Sept.), by C. H. F. Peters . . 8 Sept. ,,
117. *Lomia*, by A. Borelly . . 12 Sept. ,,
118. *Peitho*, by R. Luther . . 15 March, 1872
119. *Althæa*, by J. C. Watson . . 3 April, ,,
120. *Lachesis*, by A. Borelly . . 10 April, ,,
121. *Hermione*, by J. C. Watson . . 12 May, ,,
122. *Gerda*, by C. H. F. Peters . . 31 July, ,,
123. *Brunhilda*, by C. H. F. Peters . . 31 July, ,,
124. *Alceste*, by C. H. F. Peters. . . 23 Aug. ,,
125. *Liberatrix*, by Prosper Henry . . 11 Sept. ,,
126. *Velleda*, by Paul Henry . . 5 Nov. ,,
127. *Johanna*, by Prosper Henry . . 5 Nov. ,,
128. *Nemesis*, by J. C. Watson . . 25 Nov. ,,
129. *Antigone*, by C. H. F. Peters . . 5 Feb. 1873
130. *Electra*, by C. H. F. Peters . . 17 Feb. ,,
131. *Vala*, by C. H. F. Peters . . 24 May, ,,
132. *Æthra*, by J. C. Watson . . 13 June, ,,
133. *Cyrene*, by J. C. Watson . . 16 Aug. ,,
134. *Sophrosyne*, by R. Luther . . 27 Sept. ,,
135. *Hertha*, by C. H. F. Peters . . 18 Feb. 1874
136. *Austria*, by J. Palisa . . 18 March, ,,
137. *Melibœa*, by J. Palisa . . 21 April, ,,
138. *Tolosa*, by M. Perrotin . . 19 May, ,,
139. *Juewa*, by J. C. Watson . . 10 Oct. ,,
140. *Siwa*, by J. Palisa . . 13 Oct. ,,
141. *Lumen*, by Paul Henry . . 13 Jan. 1875
142. *Polana*, by J. Palisa . . 28 Jan. ,,
143. *Adria*, by J. Palisa . . 23 Feb. ,,
144. *Vibilia*, by C. H. F. Peters . . 3 June, ,,

* It was believed at first to be *Daphne*, No. 41; and hence was called "*Pseudo-Daphne*," when E. Schubert proved it to be a new planet. It was not re-discovered by M. Goldschmidt till 1 Sept. 1862, when it received its present name, that of the Muse of Meditation.

† *Atropos* said to have been discovered by R Luther, 14 April, 1869. Not observed since.

No.	Planet	Date	Year
145.	*Adeona*, by C. H. F. Peters	3 June,	1875
146.	*Lucina*, by A. Borelly	8 June,	,,
147.	*Protogeneia*, by L. Schulhof	10 July,	,,
148.	*Gallia*, by Prosper Henry	7 Aug.	,,
149.	*Medusa*, by M. Perrotin	21 Sept.	,,
150.	*Nuwa*, by J. C. Watson	18 Oct.	,,
151.	*Abundantia*, by J. Palisa	1 Nov.	,,
152.	*Atala*, by Paul Henry	2 Nov.	,,
153.	*Hilda*, by J. Palisa	2 Nov.	,,
154.	*Bertha*, by Prosper Henry	4 Nov.	,,
155.	*Scylla*, by J. Palisa	8 Nov.	,,
156.	*Xanthippe*, by J. Palisa	22 Nov.	,,
157.	*Dejanira*, by A. Borelly	1 Dec.	,,
158.	*Koronis*, by V. Knorre	4 Jan.	1876
159.	*Aemilia*, by Paul Henry	26 Jan.	,,
160.	*Una*, by C. H. F. Peters	20 Feb.	,,
161.	*Athor*, by J. C. Watson	18 April,	,,
162.	*Laurentia*, by Prosper Henry	21 April,	,,
163.	*Erigone*, by M. Perrotin	26 April,	,,
164.	*Eva*, by Paul Henry	12 July,	,,
165.	*Loreley*, by C. H. F. Peters	10 Aug.	,,
166.	*Rhodope*, by C. H. F. Peters	17 Aug.	,,
167.	*Urda*, by C. H. F. Peters	29 Aug.	,,
168.	*Sibylla*, by J. C. Watson	27 Sept.	,,
169.	*Zelia*, by Prosper Henry	28 Sept.	,,
170.	*Maria*, or *Myrrha*, by M. Perrotin	10 Jan.	1877
171.	*Ophelia*, by Alphonse Borelly	13 Jan.	,,
172.	*Baucis*, by Alphonse Borelly	5 Feb.	,,
173.	*Ino*, by Alphonse Borelly	2 Aug.	,,
174.	*Phædra*, by J. C. Watson	3 Sept.	,,
175.	*Andromache*, by J. C. Watson	1 Oct.	,,
176.	*Idunna*, by C. H. F. Peters	14 Oct.	,,
177.	*Irma*, by Paul Henry	5 Nov.	,,
178.	*Belisana*, by J. Palisa	6 Nov.	,,
179.	*Clytemnestra*, by J. C. Watson	12 Nov.	,,
180.	*Garumna*, by M. Perrotin	29 Jan.	1878
181.	*Eucharis*, by Cottenot	2 Feb.	,,
182.	*Elsa*, by J. Palisa	7 Feb.	,,
183.	*Istria*, by J. Palisa	8 Feb.	,,
184.	*Deiopeia*, by J. Palisa	28 Feb.	,,
185.	*Eunike*, by C. H. F. Peters	1 March,	,,
186.	*Celuta*, by Prosper Henry	6 April,	,,
187.	*Lamberta*, by Coggia	11 April,	,,
188.	*Menippe*, by C. H. F. Peters	18 June,	,,
189.	*Phthia*, by C. H. F. Peters	9 Sept.	,,
190.	*Ismene*, by C. H. F. Peters	22 Sept.	,,
191.	*Kolga*, by C. H. F. Peters	30 Sept.	,,
192.	*Nausikaa*, by J. Palisa	17 Feb.	1879
193.	*Ambrosia*, by Coggia	28 Feb.	,,
194.	*Procne*, by C. H. F. Peters	21 March,	,,
195.	*Eurykleia*, by J. Palisa	22 April,	,,
196.	*Philomela*, by C. H. F. Peters	14 May,	,,
197.	*Arete*, by J. Palisa	21 May,	,,
198.	*Ampella*, by Borelly	13 June,	,,
199.	*Byblis*, by C. H. F. Peters	9 July,	,,
200.	*Dynamene*, by C. H. F. Peters	27 July,	,,
201.	*Penelope*, by J. Palisa	7 Aug.	,,
202.	*Chryseïs*, by C. H. F. Peters	11 Sept.	,,
203.	*Pompeia*, by C. H. F. Peters	25 Sept.	,,
204.	*Callisto*, by J. Palisa	8 Oct.	,,
205.	*Martha*, by J. Palisa	13 Oct.	,,
206.	*Hersilia*, by C. H. F. Peters	13 Oct.	,,
207.	*Hedda*, by J. Palisa	17 Oct.	,,
208.	*Lacrimosa*, by J. Palisa	21 Oct.	,,
209.	*Dido*, by C. H. F. Peters	22 Oct.	,,
210.	*Isabella*, by J. Palisa	12 Nov.	,,
211.	*Isolda*, by J. Palisa	10 Dec.	,,
212.	*Medea*, by J. Palisa	6 Feb.	1880
213.	*Lilæa*, by C. H. F. Peters	16 Feb.	,,
214.	*Aschera*, by J. Palisa.	1 March,	,,
215.	*Œnone*, by V. Knorre	7 April,	,,
216.	*Cleopatra*, by J. Palisa	10 April,	,,
217.	*Eudora*, by Coggia	30 Aug.	,,
218.	*Bianca*, by J. Palisa	4 Sept.	,,
219.	*Thusnelda*, by J. Palisa	30 Sept.	,,
220.	*Stephania*, by J. Palisa	19 May,	1881
221.	*Eos*, by J. Palisa	18 Jan.	1882
222.	*Lucia*, by J. Palisa	9 Feb.	,,
223.	*Rosa*, by J. Palisa	9 March,	,,
224.	*Oceana*, by J. Palisa	30 March,	,,
225.	*Henrietta*, by J. Palisa	19 April,	,,
226.	*Weringia*, by J. Palisa	19 July,	,,
227.	*Philosophia*, by Paul Henry	12 Aug.	,,
228.	*Agathe*, by J. Palisa	19 Aug.	,,
229.	*Adelinda*, by J. Palisa	22 Aug.	,,
230.	*Athamantis*, by L. De Ball	3 Sept.	,,
231.	*Vindobona*, by J. Palisa	10 Sept.	,,
232.	*Russia*, by J. Palisa	31 Jan.	1883
233.	*Asterope*, by Borelly	11 May,	1883
234.	*Barbara*, by C. H. F. Peters	12 Aug.	,,
235.	*Carolina*, by J. Palisa	28 Nov.	,,
236.	*Honoria*, by J. Palisa	26 April,	1884
237.	*Cœlestina*, by J. Palisa	27 June,	,,
238.	*Hypatia*, by V. Knorre.	1 July,	,,
239.	*Adrastea*, by J. Palisa	18 Aug.	,,
240.	*Vanadis*, by Borelly	27 Aug.	,,
241.	*Germania* by R. Luther	12 Sept.	,,
242.	*Kriemhild*, by J. Palisa	22 Sept.	,,
243.	*Ida*, by J. Palisa	29 Sept.	,,
244.	*Sita*, by J. Palisa	14 Oct.	,,
245.	*Vera*, by J. Palisa	6 Feb.	1885
246.	*Asporina*, by Borelly	6 March,	,,
247.	*Eukrate*, by Luther	14 March,	,,
248.	*Lameia*, by J. Palisa	5 June,	,,
249.	*Ilse*, by C. H. F. Peters	16 Aug.	,,
250.	*Bettina*, by J. Palisa	3 Sept.	,,
251.	*Sophia*, by J. Palisa	4 Oct.	,,
252.	*Clementina*, by Perrotin	27 Oct.	,,
253.	*Mathilde*, by J. Palisa	12 Nov.	,,
254.	*Augusta*, by J. Palisa	31 March,	1886
255.	*Oppavia*, by J. Palisa	31 March,	,,
256.	*Walpurga*, by J. Palisa	3 April,	,,
257.	*Silesia*, by J. Palisa	5 April,	,,
258.	*Tyche*, by Luther	4 May,	,,
259.	*Aletheia*, by C. H. F. Peters	28 June,	,,
260.	*Huberta*, by J. Palisa	3 Oct.	,,
261.	*Prymno*, by C. H. F. Peters	31 Oct.	,,
262.	*Valda*, by J. Palisa	3 Nov.	,,
263.	*Dresda*, by J. Palisa	3 Nov.	,,
264.	*Libussa*, by C. H. F. Peters	22 Dec.	,,
265.	*Anna*, by J. Palisa	27 Feb.	1887
266.	*Aline*, by J. Palisa	17 May,	,,
267.	*Tirza*, by Charlois	27 May,	,,
268.	*Adorea*, by A. Borelly	9 June,	,,
269.	*Justitia*, by J. Palisa	21 Sept.	,,
270.	*Anahita*, by C. H. F. Peters	8 Oct.	,,
271.	*Penthesilea*, by V. Knorre	16 Oct.	,,
272.	*Antonia*, by Charlois	4 Feb.	1888
273.	*Atropos*, by J. Palisa	8 March,	,,
274.	*Philagoria*, by J. Palisa	3 April,	,,
275.	*Sapientia*, by J. Palisa	15 April,	,,
276.	*Adelheid*, by J. Palisa	17 April,	,,
277.	*Elvira*, by Charlois	3 May,	,,
278.	*Paulina*, by J. Palisa	16 May,	,,
279.	*Thule*, by J. Palisa	25 Oct.	,,
280.	*Philia*, by J. Palisa	29 Oct.	,,
281.	*Lucretia*, by J. Palisa	31 Oct.	,,
282.	*Clorinde*, by J. Palisa	29 May	,,
283.	*Emma*, by Charlois	28 Jan.	1889
284.	*Amelia*, by Charlois	8 Feb.	,,
285.	*Regina*, by Charlois	3 Aug.	,,
286.	*Iclea*, by Charlois or J. Palisa	3 Aug.	,,
287.	*Nephthys*, by C. H. F. Peters	25 Aug.	,,
288.	*Glauke*, by R. Luther	20 Feb.	1890
289.	*Nenetta*, by M. Charlois	10 March,	,,
290.	*Bruna*, by J. Palisa	20 March,	,,
291.	*Alice*, by J. Palisa	25 April,	,,
292.	*Ludovica*, by J. Palisa	25 April,	,,
293.	*Brasilia*, by M. Charlois	20 May,	,,
294.	*Felicia*, by M. Charlois	15 July,	,,
295.	*Theresa*, by J. Palisa	17 Aug.	,,
296.	*Phaëtusa*, by M. Charlois	19 Aug.	,,
297.	*Cæcilia*, by M. Charlois	9 Sept.	,,
298.	*Baptistina*, by M. Charlois	9 Sept.	,,
299.	*Thora*, by J. Palisa	6 Oct.	,,
300.	*Geraldina*, by Charlois	3 Oct.	,,
301.	*Bavaria*, J. Palisa	16 Nov.	,,
302.	*Clarisa*, by Charlois	14 Nov.	,,
303.	*Josephine*, by prof. Millosevich	12 Feb.	1891
304.	*Olga*, by J. Palisa	14 Feb.	,,
305.	*Gordonia*, by Charlois	16 Feb.	,,
306.	*Unitas*, by prof. Millosevich	1 March,	,,
307.	*Nike*, by M. Charlois	5 March,	,,
308.	*Polyxo*, by M. Borelly	31 March,	,,
309.	*Fraternitas*, by J. Palisa	6 April,	,,
310.	*Margarita*, by Charlois	16 May,	,,
311.	*Claudia*, by Charlois	11 June,	,,
312.	*Pieretta*, by M. Charlois	28 Aug.	,,
313.	*Chaldaea*, by J. Palisa	30 Aug.	,,
314.	*Rosalia*, by Charlois	1 Sept.	,,
315.	*Constantia*, by Palisa	4 Sept.	,,
316.	*Goberta*, by Charlois	8 Sept.	,,
317.	*Roxana*, by Charlois,	11 Sept.	,,
318.	*Magdalena*, by Charlois	24 Sept.	,,
319.	*Leona*, by Charlois	8 Oct.	,,
320.	*Katharina*, by J. Palisa	12 Oct.	,,

321. *Florentina*, by J. Palisa . . . . 15 Oct. 1891
322. *Phæo*, by Borelly . . . . 27 Nov. ,,
323. *Brucia*, by Dr. Wolf . . . . 28 Nov. ,,
324. *Bamberga*, by Dr. Palisa . . . . 25 Feb. 1892
325. *Heidelberga*, by Dr. Wolf . . . 4 March, ,,
326. *Tamara*, by Dr. Palisa . . . 19 March, ,,
327. *Columbia*, by M. Charlois . . . 22 March, ,,
328. *Svea*, by Dr. Wolf . . . . 18 March, ,,
329. *Gudrun*, by Dr. Wolf . . . . 21 March, ,,
330. *Adalberta*, by Dr. Wolf (identical with 298) 19 March, ,,
331. *Etheridgea*, by Charlois . . . . 1 April, ,,
332. *Siri*, by Dr. Wolf . . . . 19 March, ,,
333. *Badenia*, by Dr. Wolf . . . . 22 Aug. ,,
334. *Chicago*, by Dr. Wolf . . . . . ,,
335. *Roberta*, by Staus . . . . . 1 Sept. ,,
336. *Lacadiera*, by Charlois . . . . 19 Sept. ,,
337. *Devosa*, by Charlois . . . . 22 Sept. ,,
338. *Boudrosa*, by Charlois . . . . 25 Sept. ,,
339. *Dorothea*, by Dr. Wolf . . . . 25 Sept. ,,
340. *Eduarda*, by Dr. Wolf . . . . 25 Sept. ,,
341. *California*, by Dr. Wolf . . . 25 Sept. ,,
342. *Endymion*, by Dr. Wolf . . . . 17 Oct. ,,
343. *Ostara*, by Dr. Wolf . . . . 15 Nov. ,,
344. *Desiderata*, by Charlois . . . . 20 Nov. ,,
345. *Tercidina*, by Charlois . . . . 23 Nov. ,,
346. *Hermentaria*, by Charlois . . . 27 Nov. ,,
347. *Pariana*, by Charlois . . . . 29 Nov. ,,
348. *May*, by Charlois . . . . . 29 Nov. ,,
349. *Dembowska*, by Charlois . . . . 9 Dec. ,,
350. *Ornamenta*, by Charlois . . . 14–15 Dec. ,,
351. *Yrsa*, by Dr. Wolf . . . . . 16 Dec. ,,
352. *Gisela*, by Dr. Wolf . . . . 12 Jan. 1893
353. *Ruperto-Carola*, by Dr. Wolf . . . 16 Jan. ,,
354. *Eleonora*, by Charlois . . . . 17 Jan. ,,
355. *Gabriella*, by Charlois . . . . 20 Jan. ,,
356. *Liguria*, by Charlois . . . . 21 Jan. ,,
357. *Ninina*, by Charlois . . . . 11 Feb. ,,
358. *Apollonia*, by Charlois . . . . 8 March, ,,
359. , by Charlois . . . . 10 March, ,,
360. *Georgia*, by Charlois . . . . 11 March, ,,
361. *Bonovia*, by Charlois . . . . 11 March, ,,
362. *Havnia*, by Charlois . . . . 12 March, ,,
363. *Padua*, by Charlois . . . . 17 March, ,,
364. *Isara*, by Charlois . . . . 19 March, ,,
365. *Cordoba*, by Charlois . . . . 21 March, ,,
366. *Vincentina*, by Charlois . . . . 21 March, ,,
367. *Amicitia*, by Charlois . . . . 19 May, ,,
368. *Haidea*, by Charlois . . . . 19 May, ,,
369. *Aeria*, by Borelly . . . . . 4 July, ,,
370. *Modestia*, by Charlois . . . . 14 July, ,,
371. *Bohemia*, by Charlois . . . . 16 July, ,,
372. *Palma*, by Charlois . . . . . 19 Aug. ,,
373. *Melusina*, by Charlois . . . . 15 Sept. ,,
374. *Burgundia*, by Charlois . . . . 18 Sept. ,,
375. *Ursula*, by Charlois . . . . 18 Sept. ,,
376. *Geometria*, by Charlois . . . . 18 Sept. ,,
377. *Campania*, by Charlois . . . . 20 Sept. ,,
378. *Holmia*, by Charlois . . . . 6 Dec. ,,
379. *Huenna*, by Charlois . . . . 8 Jan. 1894
380. *Fiducia*, by Charlois . . . . 8 Jan. ,,
381. *Myrrha*, by Charlois . . . . 10 Jan. ,,
382. *Dodona*, by Charlois . . . . 29 Jan. ,,
383. *Janina*, by Charlois . . . . 29 Jan. ,,
384. *Burdigala*, by Courty . . . . 11 Feb. ,,
... , by Dr. Wilson . . . . 30 Jan. ,,
385. *Ilmatar*, by Dr. Wolf . . . . 1 March, ,,
386. *Siegena*, by Dr. Wolf . . . . 1 March, ,,
387. *Aquitania*, by Courty . . . . 5 March, ,,
388. *Charybdis*, by Charlois . . . . 7 March, ,,
389. *Industria*, by Charlois . . . . 8 March, ,,
390. *Alma*, by Bigourdan . . . . 24 March, ,,
... , by Dr. Wolf . . . . 1 Nov. ,,
391. *Ingeborg*, by Dr. Wolf . . . . 1 Nov. ,,
392. *Wilhelmina*, by Dr. Wolf . . . . 7 Nov. ,,
393. *Lampetia*, by Dr. Wolf . . . . 7 Nov. ,,
394. , by Borelly . . . . 19 Nov. ,,
395. *Delia*, by Charlois . . . . 30 Nov. ,,
396. *Æolia*, by Charlois . . . . 1 Dec. ,,
397. *Vienna*, by Charlois . . . . 19 Dec. ,,
398. , by Charlois . . . . 28 Dec. ,,
399. *Persephone*, by Dr. Wolf . . . . 23 Feb. 1895
400. , by Charlois . . . . 15 March, ,,
401. *Ottilia*, by Dr. Wolf . . . . 16 March, ,,
402. *Chloe*, by Charlois . . . . 21 March, ,,
403. *Cyane*, by Charlois . . . . 18 May, ,,
404. *Arsinoe*, by Charlois . . . . 20 June, ,,
405. *Thia*, by Charlois . . . . . 23 July, ,,
406. , by Charlois . . . . 22 Aug. 1895
407. *Arachne*, by Dr. Wolf . . . . 13 Oct. ,,
408. *Fama*, by Dr. Wolf . . . . . 19 Oct. ,,
409. *Aspasia*, by Charlois . . . . 9 Dec. ,,
410. , by Charlois . . . . 7 Jan. 1896
411. , by Charlois . . . . 7 Jan. ,,
412. *Elisabetha*, by Dr. Wolf . . . . 7 Jan. ,,
413. *Edburga*, by Dr. Wolf . . . . 7 Jan. ,,
414. , by Charlois . . . . 16 Jan. ,,
415. *Palatia*, by Dr. Wolf . . . . 7 Feb. ,,
416. *Vaticana*, by Charlois . . . . 4 May, ,,
417. *Salvia*, by Dr. Wolf . . . . 6 May, ,,
418. *Alemannia*, by Dr. Wolf . . . . 3 Sept. ,,
419. *Aurelia*, by Dr. Wolf . . . . 7 Sept. ,,
420. *Bertholda*, by Dr. Wolf . . . . 7 Sept. ,,
421. *Zähringia*, by Dr. Wolf . . . . 7 Sept. ,,
422. *Berolina*, by Witt . . . . . 8 Oct. ,,
423. *Distima*, by Charlois . . . . 7 Dec. ,,
424. *Gratia*, by Charlois . . . . 31 Dec. ,,
425. *Cornelia*, by Charlois . . . . 28 Dec. ,,
426. (same as 188, *see above*), by Charlois 25 Aug. 1897
427. , by Charlois . . . . 27 Aug. ,,
428. *Monachia*, by Villiger . . . . 18 Nov. ,,
429. , by Charlois . . . . 23 Nov. ,,
430. , by Charlois . . . . 18 Dec. ,,
431. , by Charlois . . . . 18 Dec. ,,
432. *Pythia*, by Charlois . . . . 18 Dec. ,,
433. *Eros*, by Charlois . . . . 16 July, 1898
434. , by Witt . . . . . 13 Aug. ,,
434. *Hungaria*, by Dr. Wolf . . . . 11 Sept. ,,
435. *Ella*, by Drs. Wolf & Schwassmann 11 Sept. ,,
436. *Patricia*, by Drs. Wolf & Schwassmann, 13 Sept. ,,
439. *Ohio*, by Coddington . . . . 13 Oct. ,,
440. *Theodora*, by Coddington . . . . 13 Oct. ,,
437. , by Charlois . . . . 8 Nov. ,,
438. , by Drs. Wolf & Schwassmann, 6 Nov. ,,
441. , by Charlois . . . . 8 Dec. ,,
442. *Eichsfeldt*, by Drs. Wolf & Schwassmann, 15 Feb. 1899
443. *Photographica*, by Drs. Wolf & Schwassmann, 17 Feb. ,,
444. *Gyptis*, by Coggia . . . . 31 March, ,,
445. *Edna*, by Coddington . . . . 2 Oct. ,,
446. *Æternitas*, by Drs. Wolf & Schwassmann, 27 Oct. ,,
447. *Valentine*, by Drs. Wolf & Schwassmann, 27 Oct. ,,
448. *Natalie*, by Drs. Wolf & Schwassmann, 27 Oct. ,,
449. *Hamburga*, by Drs. Wolf & Schwassmann, 31 Oct. ,,
450. *Brigitta*, by
451. *Patientia*, by Charlois . . . . 4 Dec. ,,
454. *Mathesis*, by Dr. Schwassmann 28 March, 1900
455. *Bruchsalia*, by Drs. Wolf & Schwassmann, 22 May, ,,
456. , by Drs. Wolf & Schwassmann, 4 June, ,,
457. *Alleghenia*, by Dr. Wolf . . . . 15 Sept. ,,
458. *Hyrcynia*, by Wolf and Schwassmann, 21 Sept. ,,
470. *Kilia*, by Carnera . . . . 21 April, 1901
471. , by Dr. Wolf . . . . 7 June, ,,
472. *Roma*, by Carnera . . . . 12 July, ,,
475. *Ocllo*, by Stewart . . . . 14 Aug. ,,
476. *Hedwig*, by Dr. Wolf . . . . 17 Aug. ,,
477. *Italia*, by Dr. Wolf . . . . 23 Aug. ,,
478. *Tergeste*, by Carnera . . . . 21 Sept. ,,
479. , by Carnera . . . . 12 Nov. ,,
480. , by Dr. Wolf & Carnera . . 21 May, 1902
487. *Venetia*, by Carnera . . . . 9 July, ,,

During 1902 43 small planets were discovered. The minor planets are very small, being in general only a few miles in diameter. They are divided into three groups (Mars group, Chief group, and Jupiter group) according to their mean velocities.

The rapid discovery of planetoids by photography, especially by Wolf and Charlois, in recent years, has caused much confusion in records, 1892–1903.

Eight small planets during May and June discovered by Wolf and Dugan, reported 1 July, 1903, provisionally indicated by 1903

[Numbers unnamed are uncertain, not having been verified.]

PLANING-MACHINE. One for wood was constructed by Bramah, about 1802; and one for iron by Joseph Clement in 1825.

PLANTAGENET,* House of, to which

* Fulke Martel, earl of Anjou, having contrived the death of his nephew, the earl of Brittany, in order to

belonged fourteen English kings, from Henry II., 1154, to Richard III., 1485; see *England, Kings*.

PLANTATIONS, see *Trade*.

PLASSEY, in Bengal, India, the site of a battle fought between the British under Clive and the Hindoos under Surajah Dowlah, 23 June, 1757; 68,000 men were vanquished by 1000 British and about 2000 sepoys. The victory laid the foundation of our empire in India.

PLASTER OF PARIS. Gypsum, sulphate of lime, used for moulds, statuary, &c., first found at Montmartre, near Paris, whence its name. The method of taking likenesses by its use was first discovered by Andrea del Verrochio, about 1466.

PLATA, LA, see *Argentine Republic*.

PLATÆA (Bœotia, N. Greece), site of the battle between Mardonius, commander of the army of Xerxes of Persia, and Pausanias, commander of the Lacedæmonians and Athenians, 22 Sept. 479 B.C.; the same day as the battle of Mycale. Of 300,000 Persians scarce 3000 escaped with their lives. The Grecian army, about 110,000, lost but few men. The Greeks obtained immense plunder, and were henceforth delivered from the fear of Persian invasions. Platæa, as an ally of Athens, was destroyed by the Thebans, 372; and rebuilt by Philip II. after his victory at Chæronea, 338.

PLATE. In England, plate, with the exception of spoons, was prohibited in public-houses by statute 8 Will. III. (1696). The celebrated Plate act passed in May, 1756. This act was repealed in 1780. The act laying a stamp-duty upon plate passed in 1784; see *Goldsmiths' Company*. By 17 & 18 Vict. c. 96 (1854), gold wares were allowed to be manufactured at a lower standard; but a later act excepted marriage rings.—The art of covering baser metals with a thin plate of silver, either for use or for ornament (PLATING), said to have been invented by a Birmingham spur-maker, who began with making the branches of a pair of spurs hollow, and filling the hollow with a slender rod of steel. He continued to make the hollow larger and the iron thicker, till at last he merely coated the iron spur with silver; see *Electrotype*.

Mr. Wilfred Joseph Cripps' "Old English Plate," a valuable work, containing the researches of Mr. O. Morgan, published, 1878. His "Old French Plate," 1880.
Duty on silver plate to be reduced gradually till abolished, from 1 June, 1881; abolished 17 April, 1890.
"The Corporation Plate of England and Wales" (illustrated), by Mr. Jewitt and W. H. St. John Hope, published, 1895.
Elizabethan salt-cellar realised 3000*l*., at Christie's, 11 Dec. 1902.

PLATE-WAYS, on ordinary roads for waggons carrying goods, proposed at Liverpool about 1880, to supersede railways for cheapness; not adopted.

PLATFORM, see *Public Meetings*.

PLATINUM, the heaviest of all the metals, except iridium. The name originated with the Spaniards on account of its silvery colour; *Plata* signifying silver. It was found in the auriferous sand of the river Pinto, in South America, and was unknown in Europe until 1741, when don Antonio Ulloa announced its existence in the narrative of his voyage to Peru. *Greig*. In its ore have been found the metals palladium, rhodium, osmium, iridium, and ruthenium (*which see*). Platinum was rendered malleable and ductile by Dr. Wm. Hyde Wollaston, whose processes are described in the Royal Society's Bakerian lecture for 1829. He died in 1828, having, it is said, gained 30,000*l*. by his inventions. In 1859, M. H. Ste.-Claire Deville made known a new method of obtaining platinum from its ore, in great abundance and purity; and at the international exhibition of 1862 was shown a mass worth 3840*l*., weighing 266½ lb., of a metal hitherto considered infusible, obtained by his process, employing the oxy-hydrogen flame. See *Philosophical Lamp*.

Dodé's process for coating iron with platinum to prevent rust, shown at Johnson & Matthey's, 11 Jan. 1879.
Platinotypes, photographic reproductions of pictures, by a peculiar process by Mr. F. Hollyer, specimens exhibited in the Dudley Gallery, Oct. 1892.

PLATONIC PHILOSOPHY, the most popular of all systems (see *Philosophy*). Plato's dialogues have been termed "Philosophy backed by example." He was a disciple of Socrates, 409 B.C., and died 347. The leading feature of his mind was comprehensiveness. The Cambridge Platonists included Whichcote, Cudworth, John Smith, Henry More.

Professor Jowett's popular translation of "Plato's Dialogues" published in 1871; 3rd edition, 1893.

PLATONIC YEAR, the period of time which the equinoxes take to finish their revolution, at the end of which the stars and constellations have the same place with regard to the equinoxes that they had at first. Tycho Brahe says that this year or period requires 25,816 common years to complete it; Ricciolus computes it at 25,920; and Cassini at 24,800; at the end of which time some imagined that there would be a total and natural renovation of the whole creation.

PLATTSBURG. A British expedition against this place, a town of New York, on Lake Champlain, was designed under general sir George Prevost, but was abandoned after the naval force of England had suffered a defeat in an engagement with the Americans, 11 Sept. 1814, when the British squadron in Lake Champlain was captured; see *United States*.

PLAY-GROUNDS. In 1858 a society was established by the earl of Shaftesbury and other benevolent persons to provide play-grounds for the recreation of adults and the children of the humble classes. Ground was liberally offered by the government, and by the marquis of Westminster and others; and in 1859 an act of parliament was passed to facilitate grants of lands for this purpose, for which part of Smithfield was to be reserved. The scheme was not successful.

The Metropolitan Public Garden, Boulevard, and Playground association formed by lord Brabazon (aft. earl of Meath) and others in 1882 has done good service in the east of London.
The London Playing-fields association founded; very active in obtaining places, Feb. *et seq.* 1890–2.
Hackney marsh (337 acres), purchased by the London county council and others as a playground for east London, opened by sir John Hutton, 21 July, 1894.

PLAYS, see *Drama* and *Theatres*.

PLEADINGS. In the early courts of judicature in England, pleadings were made in the Saxon language; and in Norman-French from the period of the conquest in 1066 until 1362. Pleadings

succeed to the earldom, his confessor sent him, in atonement for the murder, to Jerusalem, attended by only two servants, one of whom was to lead him by a halter to the Holy Sepulchre, the other to strip and whip him there, like a common malefactor. Broom, in French *genet*, in Latin *genista*, being the only tough, pliant shrub in Palestine, the noble criminal was smartly scourged with it, and from this instrument of his chastisement he was called *Planta-genista*, or Plantagenet; other accounts are given. *Skinner* and *Mézeray*.

were ordered to be in English by 36 Edward III. 1362, and Cromwell extended the rule to all legal proceedings 1650. In English law the proceedings are the mutual statements of the plaintiff's cause of action and the defendant's ground of defence.

PLEBEIANS, Plebes, or Plebs, the commons of Rome, as distinguished from the Patricians; see *Rome*, 494-366 B.C.

PLEBISCITUM, a term given to a law passed by the *comitia tributa*, an assembly of the Roman people in their tribes, first established in 491 B.C. The term has been recently revived in France and Italy, and applied to *Universal Suffrage* (*which see*).

PLETHYSMOGRAPH, an apparatus for detecting the state of the mind by observing the relations of the circulation of the blood from the heart to the brain, invented by M. Mossol, of Turin, 1882.

PLEVNA, Bulgaria, 27 miles N.N.W. of Nicopolis; near the river Vid; the site of very fierce conflicts during the Russo-Turkish war, 1877.

Occupied by the Russians, 6 July, but retaken by Osman Pacha, 18 July, and held by him after severe combats, with Schildner-Schuldner, 19, 20 July; with Krudener . . . 29-31 July, 1877
The Russians lost about 2000 killed, 4000 wounded. The Russian attack was considered rash, like that at Balaclava, and a disastrous check.
Osman Pacha defeated in a desperate sortie, about 30 Aug. „
Gen. Scobeleff gained a great advantage by capturing Lovatz (or Loftcha) . . . 3 Sept. „
Siege began, 7 Sept., with an artillery duel lasting to . . . . 10 Sept. „
Fruitless sanguinary conflicts . . 11, 12 Sept. „
Chefket Pacha carried in reinforcements to Plevna, about . . . . . . 22 Sept. „
Todleben takes command of the staff . 28 Sept. „
Plevna completely invested; reported 8 Nov. „
Russian attacks repulsed . . . 12, 15 Nov. „
Osman Pacha, reduced by want of supplies, desperately endeavours to break out at night, 9 Dec.; surrounded and defeated with great slaughter; surrenders unconditionally (30,000 prisoners, 128 officers, 100 guns) . . . . . 10 Dec. „

PLOTS, see *Conspiracies* and *Rebellions*.

PLOUGH. "Thou shalt not plough with an ox and an ass together." *Deut.* xxii. 10 (1451 B.C.). The Roman plough is minutely described by Virgil, about 31 B.C. Engines to plough grounds, whether inland or upland, were patented by David Ramsay and Thomas Wildgoose, in 1618; and many improvements in ploughs have been patented since. The application of steam power to ploughing was patented by John Upton in 1837, and by others since, more especially by lord Willoughby D'Eresby, the marquis of Tweeddale, and the earl of Caithness, see *Steam-Plough*.

International trial of ploughs, &c., at Haarlem; prizes won by English makers (Howards, Ransomes, &c.), 17-19 Sept. 1879.

PLOUGH MONDAY, in January, the first Monday after the Epiphany. It received the appellation from its having been fixed upon by our forefathers as the day upon which they returned to the duties of agriculture after enjoying the festivities of Christmas. *Ashe*. On Plough Monday, too, the ploughmen of the north country used to draw a plough from door to door and beg plough money to drink. *Bailey*.

On Plough Monday, the lord mayor of London holds annually at Guildhall a grand court of wardmote, at which the election of the common council and other officers on St. Thomas' day, 21 Dec., is confirmed.

PLUM. We have two native plums; our finer kinds came from Italy and Flanders about 1522. The *Diospyros Lotus*, the date plum, was brought from Barbary, before 1596; the Pishamin plum, *Diospyros virginiana*, from America, before 1629. Formerly damsons, apricots, and peaches went by this name, as raisins do to this day.

PLUMBAGO, see *Graphite*.

PLUMBERS. The company is dated 1611. A bill for their registration introduced into the commons in 1894; withdrawn, 15 Aug. 1894; passed, 10 March, 1902.

PLURALITIES. Clergymen have been restrained from holding more than one benefice by several statutes; the first being 21 Henry VIII. 1529. In 1838 an act was passed prohibiting the holding of more than two benefices except they were at a distance less than ten miles; and the law on this subject was still further amended in 1850, 1855, and 1885, provisions being made for the amalgamation of neighbouring benefices. See *Electors*.

PLURAL NUMBER, see *We*.

PLUS (+) AND MINUS (—). Professor De Morgan attributes these signs to either Christopher Rudolf, who published a book on algebra about 1522, or Michael Stifelius, about 1544.

PLYMOUTH, a fortified seaport in Devonshire, originally Sutton, was incorporated as Plymouth in 1439. It was in 1588 the rendezvous of the English fleet of 120 sail under Howard, Drake, &c., which pursued the Spanish armada. The fine hotel and assembly-rooms were burnt 6 Jan. 1863; loss about 50,000*l*. The National Association for Social Science met here, Sept. 1872. See *Armada*, 1888, 1890, *Breakwater*, and *Population*.

Plymouth dock constructed, about 1689, named Devonport 1824, is now a great naval arsenal extending nearly 4 miles along the Hamoaze. It has two M.P.'s.
The new guildhall was opened by the prince of Wales . . . . 13 Aug. 1874
New wing to British female orphan asylum (established about 1834), founded by the duke of Edinburgh . . . . 7 Oct. „
Art and industrial exhibition opened . 23 May, 1881
Tercentenary of the birth of sir Francis Drake celebrated, statue unveiled . . . 14 Feb. 1884
Royal Agricultural shows, 1865 . 23-27 June, 1890
The duke of Edinburgh appointed commander-in-chief at Devonport, assumes command . 4 Aug. „
Two fishing-boats, *Sunbeam* and *Alonzo*, sunk by firing from the gunboat *Plucky*, one man drowned, 30 Oct. Court martial; lieut. Sydney R. Freemantle acquitted of negligence, 24-27 Nov. Compensation made to the sufferers . . Dec. 1891
Destructive fire at Devonport dockyard 16 June, 1894
Great fire at Messrs. Tuckett & Co.'s confectionery works, estimated loss 20,000*l*. . . 28 Nov. „
An official dinner given to the Austrian squadron by admiral sir Algernon Lyons . . 28 June, 1895
Visit of the Spanish fleet, see *Spain* 20 July, „
Palace theatre of varieties opened . 23 Dec. 1898
A system of electric lighting and tramway traction inaugurated . . . . . . 22 Sept. 1899
Sir Redvers Buller receives the freedom, 11 April, 1901
Visit of the king and queen, see *Navy*, 8, 10 March, 1902
Messrs. Spooner's and other buildings burnt down, 14 June, „
Lady Butler lays the first stone for a memorial to prince Christian Victor and others who fell in the South African war . . . . . 4 Aug. „
Fire in the Great Western docks; estimated damage, 20,000*l*. . . . 25, 26 Jan. 1903
Launch of battleship *King Edward VII*. at Devonport by the princess of Wales . . 23 July, „

PLYMOUTH BRETHREN, a body of Christians calling themselves "the Brethren," first appeared at Plymouth about 1830. In 1851 they had 132 places of worship in England and Wales. They object to national churches as too latitudinarian, and to other dissenters as too sectarian. They receive into communion all who confess Christ, and own the Holy Ghost as his vicar. Their doctrines agree with those of most evangelical protestant churches, but they recognise no order of ministers. Mr. Darby, regarded as their founder, afterwards separated from them with some adherents.

PNEUMATIC DESPATCH COMPANY, to convey letters and parcels through tubes by means of atmospheric pressure and a vacuum. The company's act was passed 13 Aug. 1859, and tubes were laid down in Threadneedle-street on 12 Sept. 1860; and on 20 Aug. 1861, successful experiments were performed at Battersea. In 1862 tubes were laid down from the Euston railway station to the N.W. post-office in Camden-town, and on 21 Feb. 1863, the conveyance of the mail-bags began. In Oct. 1865, tubes had been laid down between Euston railway and Holborn; and on 7 Nov. several persons travelled in them. Engineer, Mr. Rammell. The company stopped through insufficient support, 1876. A pneumatic tube by Siemens, employed to transmit telegraphic messages, began about Jan. 1871.

PNEUMATIC LOOM, in which compressed air is the motive power, invented by Mr. Harrison, was exhibited in London in Dec. 1864. A company was formed to bring it into general use. Pneumatic tyre company, see *Velocipede*, 1896.

PNEUMATICS, the science which treats of the mechanical properties of air and gases; see *Air* and *Atmospheric Railways*.

PODESTA (from *potestas*, power), an Italian governor, afterwards a judge; one with supreme authority was appointed at Milan by the emperor Frederick I., when he took the city in 1158.

PODOLL (Bohemia), the site of a severe conflict between the Austrians and a part of the army of prince Frederick Charles of Prussia, 26 June, 1866. The Prussians had the advantage.

PODOSCAPHE, see *Canoe*.

POET-LAUREATE. Selden could not trace the precise origin of this office.

Warton, in his *History of English Poetry*, states that in the reign of Henry III. there was a *Versificator Regis*, to whom an annual stipend was first paid of 100s.

Chaucer, on his return from abroad, assumed the title of poet-laureate; and in the twelfth year of Richard II., 1389, he obtained a grant of an annual allowance of wine.

In the reign of Edward IV., John Kay was laureate; Andrew Bernard was laureate, *temp.* Henry VII.; and John Skelton, *temp.* Henry VIII.

James I. in 1615 granted to his laureate a yearly pension of 100 marks; and in 1630, this stipend was augmented by letters patent of Charles I. to 100*l.* per annum, with an additional grant of one tierce of Canary Spanish wine to be taken out of the king's store of wine yearly. We believe that on Southey's appointment the tierce of Canary wine was commuted for 27*l.*

Laurence Eusden commenced a series of Birth-Day and New Year's Odes, which continued till the death of Pye, in 1813.

On the death of Warton its abolition was recommended by Gibbon, whose elegant compliment on the occasion still more forcibly applied on Wordsworth's death, in 1850—"This is the best time for not filling up the office, when the prince is a man of virtue, and the poet just departed was a man of genius."

POETS-LAUREATE.

Edmund Spenser, died 1599.
Samuel Daniel, died 1619.
Ben Jonson (born 1574), died 1637.
Sir William Davenant, 1637; died 1668.
John Dryden, 1670; deposed at the revolution, 1688.
Thomas Shadwell, 1688; died 1692.
Nahum Tate, 1692; died 1715.
Nicholas Rowe, died 1718.
Rev. Laurence Eusden, 1718; died 1730.
Colley Cibber, 1730; died 1757.
William Whitehead (on the refusal of Gray), 1757; died 1785.
Rev. Dr. Thomas Warton (on the refusal of Mason), 1785; died 1790.
Henry James Pye, 1790; died 1813.
Dr. Robert Southey (on the refusal of Scott), 1813; died 21 March, 1843.
William Wordsworth, 1843; died 23 April, 1850.
Alfred (aft. lord) Tennyson (born 1809), installed 1850; died, 6 Oct. 1892.
Alfred Austin, 1896.

POETRY. The song of Moses on the deliverance of the Israelites, and their passage through the Red Sea, 1491 B.C. (*Exodus* xv.). Ancient Egyptian poetry still extant. Orpheus of Thrace was deemed the inventor of poetry amongst the Greeks; see *Epics*, *Odes*, *Satire*, *Comedy*, *Tragedy*, *Sonnets*, *Ballads*, *Hymns*, and *Verse*. Mr. Courthope's "History of English Poetry," vol. I., published, May, 1895. Vol. II., June, 1897.

POICTIERS (W. France), near which was fought the battle between Edward the Black Prince and John, king of France, in which the English arms triumphed, 19 Sept. 1356. The standard of France was overthrown, many of her nobility slain, and her king was taken prisoner, and brought to London; see *Tours* and *Vouglé*.

POISONING. A number of Roman ladies formed a conspiracy and poisoned their husbands. A female slave denounced 170 of them to Fabius Maximus, who ordered them to be publicly executed, 331 B.C. It was said that this was the first public knowledge they had of poisoning at Rome. Poisoning was made petty treason in England, and was punished by boiling to death (of which there are some remarkable instances), 23 Henry VIII. 1531; see *Boiling to death*. The frequency of cases of poisoning by means of arsenic, in England, caused the British legislature to pass a law rendering the sale of arsenic difficult (14 Vict. c. 13, 6 June, 1851). The sale of poison is now regulated by the Pharmacy act of 1868. Additional restrictions by act passed in 1885. The *Poisoned Grain Prohibition Act* passed 28 July, 1863.

A deadly poison, freely administered by Italians in the seventeenth century, was called *aqua tofana*, from the name of the woman Tofania, who made and sold it in small flat vials. She carried on this traffic for half a century, and eluded the police; but, on being taken, confessed that she had been a party in poisoning 600 people. Numerous persons were implicated by her, and many of them were publicly executed. All Italy was thrown into a ferment, and many fled, and some persons of distinction, on conviction, were strangled in prison. It appeared to have been chiefly used by married women who were tired of their husbands. Four or six drops were a fatal dose; but the effect was not sudden, and therefore not suspected. It was as clear as water, but the chemists have not agreed about its real composition. A proclamation of the pope described it as aquafortis distilled into arsenic, and others considered it as a solution of crystallised arsenic.

Between 1666 and 1676, the marchioness de Brinvilliers poisoned her father and two brothers and many others. She was executed, 16 July, 1676.

W. Palmer was executed in 1856, and Miss M. Smith tried in 1857, for poisoning; see *Trials*. Catherine Wilson, a noted poisoner, was executed on 20 Oct. 1862. Edward William Pritchard, M.D., was executed at Glasgow, 28 July, 1865, for the slow murder of his wife and her mother by antimony.

Nov. 1858, 17 persons died at Bradford through eating sweetmeats in which arsenic had been mixed by

mistake. Mr. Hodgson, a chemist, was tried for homicide, and acquitted.
Weltmann, a bookbinder at Posen, poisoned 4 wives and 2 children, about 1859.
Christiana Edmunds, of Brighton, was convicted of murdering a child by poisoned sweetmeats; other persons barely escaped (sentence remitted on the ground of insanity), 16 Jan. 1872.
Mary Ann Cotton, imprisoned Oct. 1872, suspected of poisoning 16 persons, principally children; convicted of poisoning her child, 7 March; executed at Durham, 24 March, 1873.
About 25 wives convicted of poisoning their husbands at Gross Bedskereh in Hungary; Theckla Popav was said to be the head of the conspiracy, Aug. 1882.
Catharine Flanagan and Margaret Higgins (sisters) convicted of poisoning Thomas Higgins, to obtain insurance money, 9 Feb.; other charges not tried; they confessed, and were executed, 3 March, 1884.
Mad. Van Der Linden convicted of many poisonings at Leyden, 3 May, 1885.
Albert Pel poisoned mother, wife, mistress, and others, 1872 *et seq.*; convicted at Paris 13 June; penal servitude, 14 Aug. 1885.
Dr. Philip Cross convicted at Cork of poisoning his wife with arsenic and strychnine 17 Dec. 1887; executed 10 Jan. 1888.
Mrs. Maybrick charged with the murder of her husband James Maybrick by poisoning with arsenic, 6 June, 1889; she was tried before Mr. justice Stephen at Liverpool, and convicted 31 July—7 Aug.; sentence of death commuted to penal servitude for life, 22 Aug. 1889.
Ten women tried at Mitrowitz in Hungary for poisoning their husbands with arsenic, 30 June; four sentenced to death, four to penal servitude, and two acquitted . . . . . . 5 July, 1890
Poisoning at a wedding breakfast at Louisville, U.S.A.; 3 persons died . . . . 18 April, 1891
Thomas Neill, *alias* Cream, see *Trials* . Oct. 1892
Martha Needle, executed at Melbourne for poisoning her husband, children, and lodger 22 Oct. 1894
Mdme. Joniaux sentenced to death for poisoning 3 relatives, see *Belgium* . . . . . Feb. 1895
Hermann Springstein and his sister, Mdme. Bock, sentenced to death at Prenzlau for poisoning several relatives whose lives had been insured, 5 Nov. ,,
Four women sentenced to death for poisoning husbands and relatives, Budapest . 2 July, 1897
Walter Horsford executed (Cambridge gaol) for the murder of Annie Holmes by strychnine, at St. Neots . . . . 28 June, 1898
Valentine Lebeau (Mdme. Bianchini) sentenced to 5 years' imprisonment for attempting to poison her husband (10 May, 1898); (believed by him to be innocent) . . . . . . 7 March, 1899
Mary Ann Ansell, 21, executed at St. Albans for the murder of her sister by sending her poisoned cake . . . . 19 July, ,,
Edward Bell poisoned his wife by strychnine; executed . . . . 25 July, ,,
Severino Klosowski executed at Wandsworth for poisoning Maud Marsh by antimony . 7 April, 1903
See *Bravo case.*

POITOU, an ancient province, W. France, part of the dowry of Eleanor, queen of Henry II. of England, 1151. It partook of the fortunes of Aquitaine.

POLA (Illyria), a very ancient city, where Augustus founded the colony Pietas Julia, which flourished during the empire. Off Pola, the Genoese fleet, under Doria, defeated the Venetians under Pisani, 5 or 6 May, 1379, with great loss.

POLAND (N.E. Europe), part of ancient Sarmatia. It is said to have become a duchy under Lechus or Lesko I. 550; and a kingdom under Boleslaus, about 992. The natives belong to the great Sclavonic family. The word Pole, from Poliani, is not older than the 10th century. Population of the kingdom of Poland (Russian) in 1857 was 4,789,379; in 1867, 5,705,607; in 1872, 6,528,017; in 1885, 7,416,958; in 1890, 8,256,562. 9 Feb. 1897, 9,442,590.

Piastus, a peasant, is elected to the ducal dignity, about 842
[Piastus is said to have lived to the age of 120, and his reign to have been so prosperous that succeeding native sovereigns were called Piasts.]
Introduction of Christianity . . . . about 992
Boleslas II. murders St. Stanislaus, the bishop of Cracow, with his own hands, 1079; his kingdom laid under an interdict by the pope, and his subjects absolved of their allegiance 1080
He flies to Hungary for shelter; but is refused it by order of Gregory VII., and at length kills himself or dies in a monastery 1081
Tartar invasion 1241
Premislas assassinated 1296
Louis of Hungary elected king 1370
Ladislas VI. defeated and slain by the Turks at Varna 1444
War against the Teutonic knights . . . 1410; 1447
The Wallachian invaders carry off 100,000 Poles, and sell them to the Turks as slaves . . . 1498
The Wallachians defeated 1531
Splendid reign of Sigismund II. 1548
Lithuania incorporated with Poland 1569
Stephen forms a militia composed of Cossacks, on whom he bestows the Ukraine 1575
Poland conquered by the Swedes and Russians, 1654 *et seq.*
Recovered its independence 1660
Abdication of John Casimir 1668
Victories of John Sobieski over the Turks at Vienna 1683
Many protestants killed after an affray at Thorn . 1724
Stanislaus abolishes torture 1770
An awful pestilence destroys 250,000 persons . . ,,
Civil war so weakened the kingdom that it fell an easy prey to Russia, Austria, and Prussia . . 1772
The first partition treaty . . . 17 Feb. ,,
The public partition treaty, 5 Aug.; acted on, 18 Sept. ,,
A new constitution granted by the king 3 May, 1791
The Russians, &c., on various pretexts enter Poland 1792
Second partition treaty signed 1793
Insurrection under Kosciusko . . . March, 1794
After many successes he is defeated by the Russians at Maciejovice and taken prisoner . 10 Oct. ,,
Warsaw and Praga sacked by Suwarrow . 9 Nov. ,,
Courland is annexed to Russia 1795
Stanislaus resigns his crown at Grodno; final partition of his kingdom . . . 25 Nov. ,,
Kosciusko set at liberty . . . . . 25 Dec. 1796
He arrives in London . . . . . 30 May, 1797
The Poles enter the French army and greatly help to gain their victories . . . . 1797 *et seq.*
Stanislaus dies at St. Petersburg . . . 12 Feb. 1798
Napoleon I. enters Warsaw; his army wintered in Poland 1806-7
The Poles neglected by the treaty of Tilsit (*which see*) . . . . 7 July, 1807
General diet at Warsaw . . . . . June, 1812
The central provinces (the duchy at Warsaw, between 1807 and 1813) made the kingdom of Poland under Alexander of Russia . . . 30 April, 1815
New constitution granted and Cracow declared to be a free republic . . . . . 27 Nov. ,,
Polish diet opened . . . . . . Sept. 1820
A revolution at Warsaw; the army declare in favour of the people . . . . 29 Nov. 1830
The diet declares the throne vacant . . 25 Jan. 1831
Battle of Grochow, near Praga; the Russians lose 7000 men; the Poles, who keep the field, 2000, 19, 20 Feb. ,,
Battle of Wawz (*which see*) . . . . 31 March, ,,
Insurrection in Wilna and Volhynia . . 3 April, ,,
Russians defeated at Zelicho, 6 April; Seidlece, 10 April; at Ostrolenka . . . . 26 May, ,,
The Russian general Diebitsch dies . . 10 June, ,,
Battle of Wilna; Poles defeated . . . 19 June, ,,
Grand-duke Constantine dies . . . . 27 June, ,,
Battle of Minsk . . . . 14 July, ,,
Warsaw taken by Russians . . . . 8 Sept. ,,
The insurrection suppressed . . . . . 5 Oct. ,,
Ukase issued by the emperor Nicholas, decreeing that the kingdom of Poland shall henceforth form an integral part of the Russian empire, 26 Feb. 1832

Attempted revolution in Austrian Poland,* 22-27 Feb. 1846

The courts of Austria, Russia, and Prussia revoke the treaty of 1815, which constituted Cracow a free republic, and it is declared Austrian territory . . . . 16 Nov. „

[This annexation was protested against by England, France, Sweden, and Turkey.]

The kingdom of Poland declared a Russian province . . . . May, 1847

Great popular demonstration in commemoration of the battle of Cracow . . . . 25 Feb. 1861

Six members of the Royal Agricultural society killed by the military . . . . 27 Feb. „

Great excitement at their funeral; many citizens put on mourning; an address to the emperor Alexander signed by 60,000 persons; mild conduct of prince Gortschakoff, the governor 1-7 March, „

Mukhanoff, curator of Poland, who had written a circular exciting the peasantry against their lords, quits Warsaw, which is illuminated in consequence . . . . 17 March, „

The government promises reforms and the re-establishment of Poland as a separate kingdom; yet abolishes the Agricultural society . . 7 April, „

Great meeting in consequence; which is dispersed by the military (now 32,000 strong); above 100 are killed and wounded . . . . . . 8 April, „

Great agitation in the rural districts; the Russian officials quit Lublin; general Chruleff marches thither . . . . April, „

80,000 soldiers in Poland; reign of terror in Warsaw . . . . May, „

Death of prince Gortschakoff, lieut.-general of Poland . . . . 30 May, „

New administrative council appointed . June, „

Death of prince Adam Czartoryski at Paris, aged 91, 15 July, „

Oppressive regulations issued respecting dress . „

Fresh disturbances; Warsaw put in a state of siege, Oct. „

Military arrests in churches in Warsaw; they are closed by the priests . . . . . 17 Oct. „

The governor, count Lambert, leaves Warsaw, 23 Oct. „

General Gerstenzweig, the military governor, assassinated . . . . 25 Oct. „

Bialobzeski, catholic archbishop of Warsaw, arrested, 19 Nov.; tried and condemned to death as a rebel for closing the churches [he died shortly after] . . . . 18 Dec. „

The new archbishop Felinski exhorts the Poles to submission . . . . . . 15 Feb. 1862

Rigour of the government relaxed; amnesty granted to 89 convicted political prisoners . 29 April, „

Attempted assassination of Wielopolski, a liberal Pole, president of the council . . 7 Aug. „

The grand-duke Constantine appointed governor, 28 May; begins with lenient policy, but his life is attempted by Jaroszynsky, 3 July, who is executed, 21 Aug. „

Count Zamoyski, an eminent loyal Pole, exiled for presenting to the government the report of a meeting of nobles at Warsaw, for which he had been asked . . . . Sept. „

Telkner, the chief of the secret police, found murdered . . . . 9 Nov. 1862

Severe military conscription without notice, 14 Jan. 1863

Insurrection in the night; at Warsaw . 22 Jan. „

Many Russians murdered; Poland put in a state of siege . . . . 24 Jan. „

The Polish provisional government issues its first proclamation . . . . . . 2 Feb. „

Louis Mieroslawski announces himself as head of the Poles, 19 Feb.; his band defeated and dispersed . . . . 23 Feb. „

Marian Langiewicz declared dictator of Poland, 10 March; after several defeats he enters the Austrian territory, is detected and imprisoned, 19 March, „

The insurrection becomes general, and is supported by the landed proprietors, Feb.; successful guerilla warfare . . . March and April, „

The secret central committee assumes the supreme command . . . . March, „

The czar offers an amnesty to all who lay down arms before 13 May; rejected . . 12 April, „

European intervention on behalf of Poland, 17 April, &c.; firmly replied to by the Czar, 26 April, &c. „

The secret committee (as a provisional government) levies taxes, 3 May, and forbids payment of taxes to Russia . . . . 9 May, „

80,000*l.* taken from the Russian treasury at Warsaw for the provisional government, 12 June; the Poles claim the Poland of 1772 . 26 June, „

Fruitless intervention of European powers; sanguinary rule of Mouravieff at Wilna . June, „

General Berg replaces the marquis de Wiepolski, as lieut.-gen., and governs with great rigour, 7 July, „

Unsuccessful invasion of Volhynia by the Poles, under Wysocki and Horodycki, 1 July; Felinski, the R. C. archbishop of Warsaw, banished, July; frequent conflicts with varying results; many captured priests and nobles executed . . Aug. „

Lelewel, a brave Pole, after several victories, killed in battle . . . . 6 Sept. „

Earl Russell decides against armed intervention, Aug.: negotiation ceases . . . Sept. „

Gen. Berg fired at from the Zamoyski hotel, Warsaw, 19 Sept.; the hotel destroyed . . Sept. „

Many eminent Poles executed, Oct.; Wm. Alger, an Englishman, shot at Warsaw for making grenades; the Hotel de ville fired . 9 Oct. „

Mourning forbidden to be worn for the Poles at Warsaw, 27 Oct.: 41 ladies arrested at night, 3 Nov. „

The *Times* correspondent expelled from Warsaw, 27 Nov. „

The abbé Machiewicz, a warlike priest, venerated as a martyr, hanged . . . . . 28 Dec. „

Mouravieff rules Lithuania with great rigour, Dec. „

Numerous skirmishes, and many executions of prisoners captured by the Russians; the insurrection gradually dying out . . Jan.–April, 1864

The pope promulgates an arrogant encyclical letter to the Polish church . . . . . 30 July, „

Romuald Traugott, once a Russian colonel, head of the Polish provisional government, since Oct. 1863, and five others, hanged . . 5 Aug. „

Decree for reorganising education at Warsaw, founding a university, &c. . . . 11 Sept. „

The secret provisional government, after stating that 50,000 men had been slain, and 100,000 exiled to Siberia, still calls on the Poles to begin a "national war" . . . . . . 21 Sept. „

Many Roman Catholic convents closed for participating in the insurrection . . . Nov. „

Further measures for denationalising Poland adopted . . . . Dec. „

The ex-dictator Langiewicz released by the Austrians and sent to Switzerland [he died May, 1887] Feb. 1865

The abbé Stanislas Bizoski, and his lieutenant captured and executed . . . . . 23 May, „

Estates of suspected sympathisers with rebels ordered to be sold . . . . . 22 Dec. „

Church property appropriated by the government; the clergy to be paid by the state . . 9 Jan. 1866

Military government ceases, and state of siege partially raised . . . . . . 17 Feb. „

Count Goluchowski, a Pole, made governor of Gallicia . . . . Oct. „

* On 22 Feb. 1846, an Austrian force under general Collin, which had entered Cracow on the approach of armed bands of peasantry, was attacked and driven out of the town. A provisional government was then proclaimed by the insurgents, and two days afterwards they crossed the Vistula, expecting to be joined by the peasantry of Gallicia, who were solicited by the nobles and clergy to strike a blow in the cause of liberty. The Austrian government, in order to prevent this junction, excited in the peasantry a suspicion of the motives of the nobles, and offered a reward for every noble delivered up, alive or dead: a general massacre of the nobility and clergy in the circle of Tarnow followed: the insurgents from Cracow were defeated at Gdow, whence they retreated to Podgorze, a suburb of Cracow; here they were attacked by general Collin, and driven into Cracow on the 27th of February. The forces of the three powers then began to concentrate on Cracow; the people in the town opened negotiations with the Austrians about a surrender, and while these were going on a Russian corps entered the town without [r]esistance, and soon afterwards the revolution was [ended].

Insurrection of Polish exiles in Siberia, soon suppressed, July; many executed . . Nov. 1866
Decree abolishing all political distinctions of Poland as a kingdom . . . . 19 Dec. ,,
Promulgated . . . . 5 Jan. 1867
Amnesty to political offenders proclaimed, 31 May, ,,
Poland designated the "Vistula province" in a ukase . . . . . . Jan. 1868
Its separate internal government abolished, and complete union with the empire effected, 29 Feb. ,,
The distinct financial departments of Poland abolished . . . . . . April, ,,
The Polish language interdicted in public places, July, ,,
Conciliatory policy towards the Poles in Russia and Austria proposed . . . . . March, 1872
Count Berg, the last lieutenant-general for Poland, dies . . . . 18 Jan. 1873
Polish language prohibited in courts of law and public offices in Russian Poland . . June, 1876
The czar and czarina visit Warsaw (great precautions) . . . . . . 8–27 Sept. 1884
About 34,700 Poles expelled from Prussia Oct.–Nov. 1885
Movement for denationalising Poland (see *Prussia*) Feb. 1886
Count Ladislaw Platu, active in the revolutions of 1830 and 1863, dies in Switzerland (aged 83) 23 April, 1889
Conciliatory measures towards Polish landowners proposed . . . . May, ,,
The body of Adam Mickiewicz, the great Polish poet (1798–1855), brought from France, re-interred at Cracow . . . . 4 July, 1890
Second congress of Polish historians and archæologists opened at Leopol . . . . 17 July, ,,
Centenary of the Polish constitution of 1791, celebrated in Austrian Poland . . . 3 May, 1891
The emperor William II. appoints a Polish archbishop of Posen, 1891, and otherwise favours the Poles 1892
Brzeznica destroyed by fire, lives lost . 25 Sept. 1893
Political demonstration in Warsaw, many arrests 16 April, 1894
Polish deputation warmly received by the czar Nicholas II.; pardon granted to political prisoners of 1863, by manifesto . . 26 Nov. ,,
Increased toleration of the Roman catholics; gen. Gourko, the governor-general of Warsaw, resigns (died 24 Jan. 1891); succeeded by count Shuvaloff, 20 Dec. 1894; succeeded by prince Imeribinsky, 17 Jan. 1897
Adam Asnyk, eminent poet, born 1838, died 2 Aug ,,
The czar and czarina warmly received at Warsaw, 31 Aug.; grand review at Bielostok . 7 Sept. ,,
Panic in a synagogue at Lentschitz, 32 deaths reported . . . . 14 Sept. 1899
Petition for the instruction of Polish youth in their native language, history, &c., granted, mid Sept. ,,
R. C. archbishop of Vilna deprived of his office for opposing the government on the language question . . . . early April, 1902
The czar gives 200,000 roubles to sufferers from floods (July) in the Vistula district . Aug. 1903

See *Cracow*, *Warsaw*, and *Russia*.

DUKES AND KINGS OF POLAND.

842. Piastus, *duke*.
861. Ziemovitus, his son.
892. Lesko or Lescus IV.
913. Ziemomislas, son of Lesco.
964. Miecislas I. becomes Christian.
992. Boleslas I., surnamed the Lion-hearted; obtained the title of KING from the emperor Otho III.
Miecislas II.
1034. Richense or Richsa, his consort, regent: driven from the government.
1037. [Anarchy.]
1041. Casimir I., her son, surnamed the Pacific; he had retired to a monastery, but was invited to the throne.
1058. Boleslas II., styled the Intrepid.
1081. Ladislas I., called the Careless, *duke*.
1102. Boleslas III., surnamed Wry-mouth.
1138. Ladislas, son of the preceding.
1146. Boleslas IV., the Curled.
1173. Miecislas III., the Old; deposed.
1177. Casimir II., surnamed the Just.
1194. Lesko V., the White: abdicated.
1200. Miecislas III.; restored.
1202. Ladislas III.; retired.
1206. Lesko V.; restored; assassinated: succeeded by his son, an infant.
1227. Boleslas V., surnamed the Chaste.
1279. Lesko VI., surnamed the Black.
1289. [Horrid anarchy.]
1295. Premislas, styled king of Poland, governs wisely assassinated.
1296. Ladislas I. (IV.), the Short: deposed.
1300. Wenceslas, king of Bohemia, abandons Poland.
1304. Ladislas IV., the Short.
1333. Casimir III., the Great: encourages the arts, and amends the law: killed by a fall from his horse.
1370. Louis, king of Hungary, elected *king*.
1382. Maria; and 1384, Hedwige (daughters of Louis), and her consort, *Jagello*, duke of Lithuania, by the style of Ladislas V.
1399. Ladislas II. (V.), alone: annexed Lithuania.
1434. Ladislas III. (VI.), son: succeeded as king of Hungary, 1440.
1445. [Interregnum.]
,, Casimir IV.
1492. John (Albert) I., son.
1501. Alexander, prince of Livonia, his brother.
1506. Sigismund I., brother; obtained the surname of the Great.
1548. Sigismund II., Augustus, son (last of the Jagellon dynasty); a splendid reign: added Livonia to his kingdom: died 1572. Interregnum.

ELECTED MONARCHS.

1573. Henry de Valois, duke of Anjou, brother to the king of France; he afterwards succeeded to the French throne.
1575. Stephen Bathori, prince of Transylvania: established the Cossacks as a militia.
1586. [Interregnum.]
1587. Sigismund III., son of the king of Sweden, to the exclusion of Maximilian of Austria, elected by the nobles.
1632. Ladislas IV. (VII.), Vasa, son of Sigismund III.; succeeded by his brother.
1648. John II., or Casimir V.; abdicated 1668, and retired to France, where he died a monk, in 1672.
1668. [Interregnum.]
1669. Michael-Koributh-Wiesnowiski: in this reign the Cossacks join the Turks, and ravage Poland.
1674. John III., Sobieski; the last independent king: illustrious for victories over the Cossacks, Turks, and Tartars.
1697. [Interregnum.]
,, Frederick-Augustus I., son of John-George, elector of Saxony; and elector in 1694; deprived of his crown.
1704. Stanislas I. (Leczinski): forced to retire from his kingdom in 1709.
1709. Frederick-Augustus I. again.
1733. Frederick-Augustus II., son of the preceding sovereign.
1763. [Interregnum.]
1764. Stanislas II. Augustus Poniatowski, resigned his sovereignty, 25 Nov. 1795; died at St. Petersburg, a state prisoner, 12 Feb. 1798.

POLISH LANGUAGE, THE, is a widely-spread branch of the Slavonic family. Much of the early literature is in Latin. Casimir III. founded the University of Cracow, which continues to be the centre of intellectual life and culture in Poland. *Chambers.*

Principal Polish Authors:—Nicholas Rej, *p.*, 1505–69; Jan Kochanowski, *p.*, 1530–84; Boguslawski, *d.*, 1759–1829; Ignacy Krasicki, *m.*, 1735–1801; Karpinski, *p.*, 1745–1825; Woronicz, *p.*, 1757–1829; Kasimir Brodzinski, *p.*, 1791–1835; count Alex. Fredro, *d.*, 1793–1876; Adam Mickiewicz, *p.*, 1798–1855; Anton Malczewski, *p.*, 1792–1826; Sigismund Krasinski, *p.*, 1812–59; Julius Slowacki, *p.*, 1809–49; Ignacy Kraszewski, *n.*, 1812–87; Joachim Lelewel, *hist.*, 1786–1862; Gabriele Zmichowska, *p.*, 1825–78; Michel Balucki, popular *p.*, 1837–1901.

POLAR CLOCK. An optical apparatus invented by professor Wheatstone (about 1849), whereby the hour of the day is found by means of the polarisation of light.

POLAR CONFERENCES, INTERNATIONAL, to organize setting up stations round the polar area for continuous scientific investigation, met at Hamburg, 1879; at Berne in 1880; at St. Petersburg, 1-6 Aug. 1881, and at other places since.

POLARISATION OF LIGHT, see *Optics*.

POLAR REGIONS, see *North-East* and *-West Passage*, and *Southern Continent*.

POLE STAR or **POLAR STAR**, a star of the second magnitude, the last in the tail of the constellation called the *Little Bear*. As its nearness to the North Pole causes it never to set to those in the northern hemisphere, it is called the seaman's guide. Two stars in the constellation *Ursa Major*, or Great Bear, are called *pointers* to the Polar star. The discovery of the Pole star is ascribed by the Chinese to their emperor, Hong-ti, the grandson (they say) of Noah, who reigned and flourished 1970 B.C. *Univ. Hist.* Spectroscopic observations at Lick observatory prove the star to be a triple system, *i.e.*, a binary, with a revolution of about 4 days, moving round a third more distant star, Sept. 1899.

POLICE. The London police grew out of the London watch, instituted about 1253. Its jurisdiction was extended 27 Eliz. 1585, and 16 Chas. I. 1640; and the system improved by various acts in subsequent reigns. See *Magistrates*.

Police offices:—The jurisdiction of twenty-one magistrates, three to preside in each of the seven divisional offices, commenced . . . 1 Aug. 1792

The Thames police was established in . . . 1798

The *Police Gazette* (re-modelled by Mr. Howard Vincent in 1884) established 1828

The London police, remodelled by Mr. (afterwards sir Robert) Peel, by 10 Geo. IV. 19 June, commenced duty . . . . . . 29 Sept. 1829

The London police improvement acts passed 3 Vict. 1839, 4 Vict. 1840, which were amended by 19 & 20 Vict. c. 2. 1856

In 1857 the total expenditure was 445,212*l.* for the metropolitan police, consisting of 17 superintendents, 140 inspectors, 630 sergeants, and 5296 constables.

The total efficient police force in England and Wales, exclusive of the metropolis, in Sept. 1859, was 11,309, and in Sept. 1863, 14,661 (see *Constabulary*).

Division X was established to attend the International Exhibition in 1862

The whole police and constabulary in England and Wales amounted to 23,032 men; metropolitan police, 6590; city of London police, 743; dockyard police, &c., 743 . . . 29 Sept. 1863

Metropolitan police, 7493, 1 Jan. 1866; 7548, 1 Jan. 1867; great increase proposed in . . Dec. 1867

Col. Rowan and Richard Mayne, commissioners of metropolitan police, appointed, 1829; Mayne died 26 Dec. 1868

Colonel (after sir Edmund) Henderson appointed commissioner in room of sir R. Mayne . Feb. 1869

Resigns in consequence of the riots of 8 Feb. 1886 (see *Riots*), 22 Feb. 1886; succeeded by sir Charles Warren, 12 March, 1886, who resigned 8 Nov. 1888; succeeded by Mr. James Monro, 26 Nov. 1888; resigns 10 June, 1890; succeeded by sir Edward Ridley C. Bradford, 20 June, 1890.

The commissioner of the City of London police, sir James Frazer, appointed in 1863, resigned about 26 June; succeeded by col. Henry Smith, 28 July, 1890.

The first annual report of the commissioner issued, 1870

State: 8883 police constables for a radius of 15 miles from Charing Cross (exclusive of the city of London), including 3,563,410 inhabitants . Dec. 1869

The *detective* police, only 15 men in June, 1869, has been since raised to 266 men and a superintendent, with good effect . . . . . Oct. 1870

State: 9655 of all ranks, Dec. 1871; 9958 . Dec. 1874

Large meetings of police to agitate for an increase of pay . . . . . 17-24 Oct. 1872

Request granted; meeting of some constables through misapprehension . . . 16 Nov. „

Some constables prosecuted, 18 Nov.; 109 dismissed; 65 reduced in rank . . 20 Nov. „

Several policemen censured for misconduct and over-zeal, autumn 1873

Police detectives prosecution, see *Trials* . . 1877

Appointment of commission to investigate detective system in metropolitan police (sir H. Selwyn-Ibbetson, hon. col. Wm. Fielding, and others), about . . . . . . 13 Aug. „

Pay: first class constable, 30*s.* per week; reserve, 31*s.* 6*d.*; first class sergeant, 36*s.*; second class, 34*s.* 1878

Discontent among police respecting pay (crime said to have increased; apprehensions diminished).

Committee of inquiry (sir M. W. Ridley and Mr. J. B. Maule) appointed to inquire into the pay and organisation . . . . about 8 Aug. „

Various changes (with increase of pay in some cases) were ordered by the home secretary end of Aug. „

20,000 peculiarly made whistles, received for distribution among the police . . . March, 1884

Metropolitan police 13,319; cost 1,059,628*l.* in . 1885

Police arrangements north of Thames remodelled 1 April, 1886

Report of committee on the police, with vague recommendations, issued . . about 2 Oct. „

Police Disabilities Removal act, enabling police to vote at parliamentary elections, passed 23 May, 1887

Miss Cass arrested in mistake by police-constable Endacott in Regent-st. about 9.15 P.M. 28 June; inquiry refused by home secretary July; government defeated in commons (153–148) 5 July; Endacott acquitted of perjury . . . 1 Nov. „

Medals presented to the metropolitan police for their conduct during the jubilee celebrations in June, ordered . . . . 3 Sept. „

A testimonial to the police for their conduct at Trafalgar-square (see under *Riots*); combination of two funds Nov.; appropriated to their convalescent asylum at Dover . . . . Feb. 1888

Charges against the police of levying black mail made by Mr. W. S. Caine and others in July, 1887; investigated and declared not proved by sir Charles Warren, *Times* . . . . . 6 Feb. „

Agitation respecting pay, pension, &c. May, June, 1890

Bow-street station. Insubordination; 130 men for an hour refused to go on duty, 10 p.m.; some transferred to another district, 40 dismissed, 5 July; rioting of dismissed men and roughs quickly stopped by the foot-guards, 7 July; perfect order in the force reported . . 8 July, „

Increase of pay begun . . . . . 17 Dec. „

Col. sir Edward Ridley C. Bradford commissioner (G.C.B. June, 1897; bart. 26 June, 1902) . . „

Police Disabilities Removal acts passed . . . 1893

Police amendment act passed . . . . . „

Lieut.-col. Henry Smith commissioner for the city, 1895; K.C.B., June, 1897; resigns. . 2 Dec. 1901

Metropolitan police, 14,041, 31 Dec. 1887; 1891, 15,072; 1894, 15,216; 1896, 15,326; 1901, 15,977; 1902, 16,374.

Medals and clasps presented to the police and a grant of 4 days' pay for their conduct in the Diamond Jubilee week . . . 20–26 June, 1897

Increase of pay for metropolitan police . 31 Dec. 1900

International Christian Police association conference held at Birmingham . . 25–28 Sept. 1901

Capt. Nott Bower elected commissioner for the city . . . . 21 March, 1902

Police reservists act, royal assent . . 22 July, „

Mr. E. R. Henry, assistant-commissioner, appointed chief commissioner of metropolitan police, on resignation of sir E. Bradford . . 5 March, 1903

Police of England and Wales, year 1871-2, 27,999 men, cost 2,372,888*l.* (84*l.* 15*s.* a man); 1872-3, 28,550 men, cost 2,567,481*l.*; 1874-5, 29,460 men, cost 2,742,526*l.*; 1875-6, 29,719 men, cost 2,849,073*l.*; 1876-7, 30,016 men, cost 2,902,635*l.* (per man, 96*l.* 14*s.*); 1877-8, 30,673 men, cost 2,980,592*l.* (per man, 97*l.* 3*s.* 5*d.*); 1878-9, 31,407 men, cost 3,058,671*l.* (per man, 98*l.* 10*s.* 4*d.*); 1881-2, 33,173 men, cost 3,264,337*l.*; 1882-3, 34,488 men, cost

3,367,678*l.*; 1886-7, 36,912 men, cost 3,711,933*l.*; 1887-8, 37,296 men, cost 3,727,942*l.*; 1888-9, 37,957 men, cost 3,734,916*l.*; 1889-90, 39,221 men, cost 3,846,508; 1890-1, 39,673 men, cost 3,971,282*l.*; 1891-2, 40,596 men, cost 4,091,303*l.*; 1892-3, 41,164 men; 1896-7, 41,560; 1899, 43,450; 1900, 44,054. Scotland, 1890, 4103; 1893, 4488; 1899, 4867; 1901, 5278. Ireland, 1890, 13,921; 1893, 13,463; 1899, 12,351; 1900, 12,320.

System of identification by finger marks, to supersede anthropometry, authorized by the secretary of state justified by its practical working. New arrangements made from 1 July, 1902, whereby all persons convicted of certain offences in summary courts, and sentenced to more than one month's imprisonment, in addition to those convicted at all quarter sessions and assizes, are thus registered. During 1902 1,722 identifications made by this method, as against 462 in 1900 when anthropometry alone was used.

POLICIES OF ASSURANCE ACT, passed 20 Aug. 1867; see *Insurance.*

POLITICAL ECONOMY, the science which has for its object the improvement of the condition of mankind, and the promotion of civilisation, wealth, and happiness; was considered by Plato, Xenophon, and Aristotle. Its history in this country may be dated from the publication of sir Wm. Petty's "Treatise on Taxes," 1662, and "Political Arithmetic," 1691; Dr. Adam Smith's "Wealth of Nations," 1776. The works of J. S. Mill, M'Culloch, Malthus, Ricardo, Carey, Jevons, Sidgwick, Marshall, and Fawcett are celebrated. A professorship of political economy was established at Oxford by Mr. Henry Drummond, M.P., 1825; and at Cambridge, first by Mr. G. Pryme, in 1828; but regularly established by the university in 1863, Henry Fawcett (blind) being the first professor.

Archbishop Whately endowed a professorship at Trinity college, Dublin; Isaac Butt first professor 1832

The Political Economy club, London, founded in 1821, by Thos. Tooke and others, to propagate free trade principles, kept the hundredth anniversary of the publication of Smith's "Wealth of Nations" . . . . . . 31 May, 1876

Mr. R. H. Inglis Palgrave's "Dictionary of Political Economy," published 1891 *et seq.*

Imaginary systems: Plato's "Republic;" he died 347 B.C. Sir T. More's "Utopia" 1548; sir P. Sidney's "Arcadia," 1590; James Harrington's "Oceana," 1656; Wm. Morris's "News from Nowhere," 1891; and E. Bellamy's "Looking Backwards," 1888.

POLITICAL OFFICES PENSIONS ACT passed 9 Aug. 1869.

POLITICAL UNIONS were formed in England in 1831 to carry the Reform Bill; the most important was that of Birmingham.

POLITICIANS. A politician is described as a man well versed in policy, or the well regulating and governing of a state or kingdom; a wise and cunning man. A man of artifice; one of deep contrivance. *South.* The term was first used in France about 1569. A new faction appeared, known by the name of Politicians, headed by the duc d'Alençon and the Montmorencies, and strengthened by the accession of the Huguenots in 1574. The duke was arrested and the Montmorencies sent to the Bastille.

POLKA, a dance said to have been invented between 1830 and 1834 in Bohemia, and to have obtained its name in Prague in 1835. It became very popular, and was introduced into England about 1844.

POLL ACT passed in Ireland by the Junto of the Pale, putting a price upon the heads of certain Irish; the earl of Desmond being then deputy, 5 Edward IV. 1465. This act long endured, see *Ireland*, 1465.

POLLENTIA (Piedmont, N. Italy), the site of a great victory of Stilicho, the Imperial general, over Alaric the Goth, 29 March, 403.

POLL-TAX or CAPITATION TAX, existed among the ancient Romans. It was first levied in England in 1380; and occasioned the rebellion of Wat Tyler (see *Tyler*), 1381. It was again levied in 1513. By the 18th Charles II. every subject was assessed by the head, viz., a duke 100*l.*, a marquis 80*l.*, a baronet 30*l.*, a knight 20*l.*, an esquire 10*l.*, and every single private person 12*d.*, 1667. This grievous impost was abolished by William III. 1689.

POLLUTION OF RIVERS, see *Rivers.*

POLO, the game of ball termed hockey played on horseback, became popular in England in 1872, having been introduced from India. Games were played by lancers and life-guards at Woolwich, 16, 19 July, 1872. A polo club was formed, and international contests held; at Brighton one opened 3 Aug. 1878. Polo is said to have been an old Russian game, mentioned 1492 under the name of Chūgān, as brought from Persia. English beat the Americans, 3 games out of 4, June, 1902.

POLOTSK (Russia). The French under marshal Oudinot were here defeated by the Russians under general Wittgenstein, 30 and 31 July, 1812; the next day, the Russians were defeated. After several smaller actions with various results, Polotsk was stormed by the Russians, and retaken Oct. 1812.

POLTOWA, see *Pultowa.*

POLYGAMY, &c., was permitted among the early nations, and now by Mahometans. In Media, it was a reproach to a man to have less than seven wives. Among the Romans, Marc Antony is mentioned as the first who took two wives. The practice was forbidden by Arcadius, 394. The emperor Charles V. punished polygamy with death. In England, by stat. 1 James I. 1603, it was made felony, with benefit of clergy. It was formerly punished with transportation, but now by imprisonment or penal servitude; see *Marriages.* Polygamy exists among the Mormons (*which see*). Abolished in the United States, 23 March, 1882.—POLYANDRY (where one woman has several husbands) is permitted in some eastern countries, the children having equal rights.

POLYGLOT, from two Greek words denoting "many languages," is chiefly applied to editions of the Bible in several languages.

Giustiniani published a polyglot psalter, 1576.

1. The Complutensian Polyglot, in six vols. folio, was printed at Alcala (Complutensis), in Spain, 1502-14; the first edition published in 1522, at the expense of the celebrated cardinal Ximenes, costing 250,000 ducats. Six hundred copies of it were printed; three on vellum. Count MacCarthy, of Toulouse, paid 483*l.* for one of these copies at the Pinelli sale.
2. The Polyglot, printed at Antwerp, by Montanus, 8 vols. folio, in 1559-69, at the expense of Philip II. of Spain.
3. Printed at Paris, by Le Jay, in 10 vols. folio, 1628-45.
4. Edited by Bryan Walton, in 6 vols. folio, 1654-7.

Copies of all four are in the library of the British and Foreign Bible Society.

5. Edited by Dr. Samuel Lee, published by S. Bagster, 1 vol. folio, 1831.
6. Hexaglot bible: begun by Henry Cohn; completed by the rev. Edwd. R. De Levante and others, 6 vols. 4to, 1874.

POLYNESIA, a name recently given to the isles in the great Pacific Ocean, see *Owhyhee, Otaheite, Sandwich Islands, Fiji Isles*, &c. These islands have been classified as Micronesia, Melanesia, and East Polynesia. The Polynesian society, Wellington, New Zealand, was founded in 1892. The archipelago explored by Mr. Fred. W. Christian, 1890-98.

POLYOLBION, a poetical description of the tracts, rivers, mountains, forests, &c. of Great Britain, with historical details, by Michael Drayton, published 1606-22; a new edition, 3 vols., by the rev. Richard Hooper, was published 1876.

POLYPES, also named Hydræ (*many-footed* animals), on account of their property of reproducing themselves when cut in pieces, every part soon becoming a perfect animal; first discovered by Leeuwenhoek, and described by him in the *Philosophical Trans.* 1703. The polypes are of the order Zoophytes, and are partly animal and vegetable.

POLYTECHNIC INSTITUTION, ROYAL, Regent-street, London, was erected by Thompson in 1838, opened 6 Aug. 1839, and enlarged in 1848. It contained a hall of manufactures with machines worked by steam-power, lecture theatres, &c., diving-bell, electric machine, &c. *Timbs.* The institution did not prosper commercially, and its decline was hastened by the fall of a staircase on 3 Jan. 1859, when one person was killed and many injured. The institution was closed in May, 1859, but was re-opened by a new company on 12 Nov. 1860; see *Ecole Polytechnique.* Professor Pepper, the director for many years, resigned in 1872; returned, 1878. The classes were formed into a college, which was inaugurated by the earl of Shaftesbury, 7 Oct. 1872. Polytechnic institution announced to be closed on 27 Aug. 1881; affairs wound up. Plant sold for about 2000*l.* 23 March, 1882. In 1882 it was occupied by the Polytechnic young men's christian institute, principally by the instrumentality of Mr. Quintin Hogg (suffocated by fumes in a geyser bath, 17 Jan. 1903), for educational purposes, with about 2000 members; over 17,000, Jan. 1903.

Prof. John Pepper lectured here on Australia (from which he had just returned) . . . . 9 Nov. 1889
POLYTECHNIC INSTITUTIONS established in south London, promoted by the charity commissioners and liberally subscribed for 1888-9
Polytechnic Institute or People's palace for S.W. London, Westminster, Chelsea, Fulham, &c., proposed and liberally supported by the duke of Westminster, president, earl Cadogan, Mr. R. C. Antrobus, and others 1889-90
With reference to the City of London Parochial Charities act of 1883, the committee of Council on Education reports approval of schemes for the management of the following institutions:—1, the City Polytechnic, comprising the Northampton and Birkbeck Institutes, and the City of London college; 2, the Regent-street Polytechnic Institute; 3, the Battersea Polytechnic Institute; 4, the South-western Polytechnic Institute; 5, the Borough-road Polytechnic Institute, opened 30 Sept. 1902; 6, Northern Polytechnic Institute, Holloway, opened autumn, 1896; 7, Tottenham Polytechnic Institute, opened 10 Dec. 1897
Memorial stone of the Battersea Polytechnic, the first of the series, laid by the prince of Wales 20 July, 1891; opened by him . . . . 24 Feb. 1894
The Goldsmiths' Company's Technical and Recreative Institute at New-cross, Surrey, was opened by the prince and princess of Wales, 22 July, 1891; see *Goldsmiths' Company.*
Polytechnic at Chelsea; foundation stone laid by the prince and princess of Wales . 23 July, ,,
See *Beaumont Trust* and *Goldsmiths' Company.*
Memorial stone of the St. Bride Foundation Institute laid by the prince of Wales, 20 Nov. 1893; opened by the lord mayor . . . 20 Nov. 1894
Northampton Institute, St. John's-street-road, founded, 9 July, 1894; opened by the lord mayor, 18 March, 1898
Princess Louise, duchess of Argyll, distributes prizes at the Battersea Polytechnic . 5 Feb. 1902
Sir John Cass Technical Institute, Aldgate, cost over 40,000*l.*, opened by lord Avebury. 5 June, 1902
Passmore-Edwards Polytechnic, Camberwell, stone laid by lady Carrington . . . . 16 July, 1903

POMEGRANATE TREE (*Punica Granatum*) was brought to England from Spain before 1584.

POMERANIA, a Prussian province, N. Germany, was held by the Poles, 980, and by Denmark, 1210; made an independent duchy, 1479; and divided between Sweden and Brandenburg, 1648. The Swedish part, awarded to Denmark in 1814, was given up to Prussia for Lauenburg, 1815; see *Denmark; Wrecks*, 1878.

POMFRET or **PONTEFRACT** (S. York). At the castle (built 1080), Richard II. was confined and murdered, 10 Feb. 1400. Some writers assert that Richard escaped and died in Scotland. In this castle also, the earl Rivers, lord Grey, sir Thomas Vaughan, and sir Richard Haut or Hause, were put to death by order of the duke of Gloucester, then protector of England (afterwards Richard III.), about 26 June, 1483. The castle, which had stood four sieges, was dismantled in 1649. The first parliamentary election by ballot took place here, 15 Aug. 1872, very quietly. It lost one of its two members in 1885. Population, 1881, 8,798; 1891, 9,702; 1901, 13,398.

POMPEII (S. Italy), an ancient city of Campania, was partly demolished by an earthquake in A.D. 63. It was afterwards rebuilt, but was overwhelmed by an eruption of Vesuvius, accompanied by an earthquake, on the night of 24 Aug. 79. The principal citizens were then assembled in an amphitheatre where public spectacles were exhibited. The ashes buried the whole city and covered the surrounding country. After a lapse of fifteen centuries, a countryman, as he was turning up the ground, found a bronze figure; and this discovery led to further search, which brought numerous other objects to light, and at length the city was uncovered. The part first cleared was supposed to be the main street, 1750. The kings of Naples greatly aided in exploring Pompeii, and the present Italian government resumed the work in 1863.

A commemorative meeting of antiquaries and philosophers met at Pompeii, 25 Sept. 1879.
Further discoveries made, autumn 1882 *et seq.*
The remains of a handsome five-storied house were uncovered . . . . July, 1890

POMPEY'S PILLAR stands about three-quarters of a mile from Alexandria, between the city and the lake Mareotis. The shaft is fluted, and the capital ornamented with palm-leaves; the whole, which is highly polished, composed of three pieces, and of the Corinthian order. The column measures, according to some, 94 feet; to others 141, and even 160 feet; but of its origin, name, use, and age, nothing is certain.

It is generally believed that the column has no reference to Pompey, to whom a mark of honour was, nevertheless, set up somewhere about this part. One supposes the edifice was dedicated to Vespasian, another to Severus; and Mr. Clarke, from a half-effaced inscription on the base, considered that Adrian is the person honoured; while many assert, from the same inscription, that it is dedicated "to Diocletian Augustus, most adorable emperor, tutelar deity of Alexandria."

PONDICHERRY (S.E. India), the capital of French India, and first settled by the French in 1674. It was taken from them by the Dutch in 1693, restored 1697; besieged by the English, 1748; taken by them, Jan. 1761; restored, 1763; again taken, Oct. 1778; restored in 1783; taken 23 Aug. 1793, and in 1803; restored, 1815. Visited by the Viceroy of India (Earl Dufferin), Dec. 1886. Prosperous state of the colony reported Jan. 1889. Population in 1891, 282,923.

PONDOLAND, the coast between Cape Colony and Natal, S. Africa, the British protectorate was proclaimed and notified, 6 Jan. 1885.

Severe fighting among the natives reported, Feb.–March–April; the chief Umhlangaro surrenders to the Cape authorities . . . . . April, 1891
Renewed fighting; Sigcau defeated with great loss by the Umzizis, reported . . . . 15 Jan. 1894
Major Elliot's mission to the chiefs successful; they submit, and consent to annexation to Cape Colony, reported . . . . March, ,,
Deed signed by Sigcau and Nquiliso . 19 March, ,,
Sir Henry Loch proclaims the annexation to Cape Colony . . . . . . 20 March, ,,
Territory about 4000 square miles; population about 170,000 . . . . April, ,,

PONT-À-CHIN, see *Espierres*.

PONT-À-NOYELLES. At this place, near Amiens, took place a fierce indecisive conflict, lasting from 11 A.M. to 6 P.M., between the Germans under Manteuffel and the French army of the north under Faidherbe, 23 Dec. 1870. Both sides claimed a victory; the French general asserted that he remained master of the field.

PONTEFRACT, see *Pomfret*.

PONTIFFS (Latin *Pontifices*), the highest Roman sacerdotal order, established by Numa. The college first consisted of 4 patricians, with a chief (Pontifex Maximus); to these 4 plebeians were added, by the Ogulnian law, 300 B.C. Sylla increased the number to 15 (8 *majores*, 7 *minores*), (81), and Julius Cæsar to 16. T. Coruncanius, a plebeian, obtained this office, 254 B.C.

PONTUS, in Asia Minor, seems to have been a portion of Cappadocia, and received its name from its vicinity to the *Pontus Euxinus*. Artabazus was made king of Pontus by Darius Hystaspes in the 4th century B.C. His successors were mere satraps of the kings of Persia.

Reign of Mithridates I. . . . . B.C. 383
Ariobarzanes invades Pontus 363
Mithridates II. recovers it 336
Mithridates III. reigns 301
Ariobarzanes II. reigns 266
Mithridates IV. is besieged in his capital by the Gauls, &c. 252
Mithridates attacks Sinope, and is obliged to raise the siege by the Rhodians 219
Reign of Pharnaces, 190; he takes Sinope, and makes it the capital of his kingdom 183
Reign of Mithridates V. 157
He is murdered in the midst of his court . . 123
Mithridates VI., surnamed the Great, or Eupator, receives the diadem at 12 years of age . . . ,,
Marries Laodice, his own sister 115
She attempts to poison him; he puts her and accomplices to death 112
Mithridates conquers Scythia, Bosphorus, Colchis, and other countries 111
He enters Cappadocia 97
His war with Rome 89
Tigranes ravages Cappadocia 86
Mithridates enters Bithynia, and makes himself master of many Roman provinces, and puts 80,000 Romans to death . . . . ,,
Archelaus defeated by Sylla, at Chæronea; 100,000 Cappadocians slain . . . . ,,
Victories and conquests of Mithridates up to this time 74
The fleet of Mithridates defeats that under Lucullus in two battles 73
Mithridates defeated by Lucullus 69
Mithridates defeats Fabius 68
But is defeated by Pompey 66
Mithridates stabs himself, and dies 63
Reign of Pharnaces . . . . ,,
Battle of Zela (see *Zela*); Pharnaces defeated by Cæsar 47
Darius reigns 39
Polemon, son of Zeno, reigns 36
Polemon II. succeeds his father . . . . A.D. 33
Mithridates VII. reigns 40
Pontus afterwards became a Roman province.
Alexis Comnenus founded a new empire of the Greeks at Trebizond, in this country, 1204, which continued till the Turks destroyed it in 1459.

POONAH, a province, S.W. India, formerly the seat of the power of the peishwa of the Mahrattas, 1749. It was captured by Wellesley from Holkar, 19 April, 1803, for Bajee Rao, who had claimed British protection. Bajee resigned his office, 3 June, 1818, for a pension. Visited by the prince of Wales, 13 Nov. 1875, see *Bombay*, 1897.

POOR. The poor of England, till the time of Henry VIII., subsisted as the poor of Ireland until 1838, entirely upon private benevolence. By statute 23 Edw. III. 1349, it was enacted that none should give alms to a beggar able to work. By the common law, the poor were to be sustained by "parsons, rectors of the church, and parishioners, so that none should die for default of sustenance;" and by 15 Rich. II. impropriators were obliged to distribute a yearly sum to the poor; but no compulsory law was enacted till the 27th Hen. VIII. 1535. The origin of the present POOR LAW is referred to the 43rd of Elizabeth, 1601, by which overseers were appointed for parishes. See *Settlement, Act of*.

First Poor Law commission (E. Chadwick assistant commissioner), 1832–3.
New Poor Law board appointed (E. Chadwick, sec.), 1834; dissolved, 1846.
Additional workhouses ordered to be erected, 1819, 1834.
Poor Law Amendment bill passed 1834;* forming "*Unions*," &c., amended in 1836, 1838, 1846, and 1847.
Poor Law (Ireland) act passed 1838; amended 1839.
A Poor Law system established in Scotland, 1845.
Poor Law (Ireland) Rate in aid act passed in 1849.
In Scotland, in the year ending May, 1851, the number relieved was 141,870, at an average cost of 2*l.* 2*s.* 5*d.*, and the expenditure was 535,943*l.*
In Ireland, the poor's rate for the year ending Sept. 1851, was 1,101,878*l.*
Mr. Henry Mayhew publishes his "London Labour and the London Poor," 1851–2.
An agitation for the *equalisation of poor's rates* throughout the kingdom, began in 1857.
The *Times* drew attention to the condition of the *houseless* poor in London, which led to measures for their relief, Dec. 1858.
Society for relief of distress, St. James's, established 1860.
Laws respecting removal of the poor amended in 1861.

* "The principle of the poor law of 1834 (now in force):—(1) No one shall be allowed to perish through want of what is necessary for sustaining life and health; (2) every destitute parent is bound to demand and obtain from the guardians what is necessary for sustaining the health and life of his children; neglect of this duty is criminal; (3) it is obligatory on the guardians of the poor to afford sufficient relief to all persons unable to maintain themselves; refusal an indictable offence." (*F. Peek.*)

Union relief act passed to enable certain unions to obtain temporary aid (on account of the distress in Lancashire through suspension of cotton manufactures), 1862.

Metropolitan houseless poor act (authorising guardians to receive destitute persons into workhouses, and the metropolitan board to reimburse them) passed, 29 July, 1864.

Annual report of Poor Law board for 1864 shows great decrease of pauperism—issued Sept. 1865.

40 *refuges for houseless poor* established in London, 1864-5.

"Casual wards" in London workhouses receive 1000 per night, Jan. 1865.

Union chargeability act passed, 1865.

Field-lane Refuge: new building formally opened by earl of Shaftesbury, 6 June, 1866.

Metropolitan Poor act passed for establishment of asylums for the sick, insane, &c., 29 March, 1867.

Poor Law Amendment act makes Poor Law board permanent; passed, 20 Aug. 1867.

Much excitement respecting the bad condition of London workhouse infirmaries, June, 1866; of Farnham workhouse, Oct. 1867. Classification urgently needed.

Poor Law Amendment act passed . 31 July, 1868

Divided Parishes and Poor Law Amendment act passed . 15 Aug. 1876

Presidents of the Poor Law board: Gathorne Hardy, 9 July, 1866; earl of Devon, May, 1867; G. J. Goschen, 9 Dec. 1868, to March, 1871; see *Local Government Board*.

Minute of the poor law board defining limits of relief, and recommending organisation of metropolitan charitable institutions, 20 Nov., which is adopted by several parishes . . . Dec. 1869

General order for boarding-out pauper children, issued . . . . 25 Nov. 1870

Charity Organisation Society (see *Charitable Relief*), established, 1869; reported very successful Jan. 1878

The act for more equal distribution of charge for relief of in-door poor (passed 20 June) came into operation . . . . 29 Sept. ,,

Circular of poor law board respecting farming out pauper children . . . . . 25 Nov. ,,

New regulations for casual poor published in *Times* 27 Nov. ,,

Poor rate assessment acts amended . . . 1882

Poor law conference act passed . . 18 June, 1883

Commission to inquire into the state of the poor, appointed; abp. of Canterbury, earls Spencer, Onslow, and others . . . . March, 1888

New poor law act passed, 30 Aug. 1889; amended, 1899

Sir Edwin Chadwick, eminent poor law reformer, aged 90, died . . . . 5 July, 1890

Aged poor commission, lord Aberdare, chairman; the prince of Wales, lords Lingen, Brassey, Playfair, Mr. Joseph Chamberlain, Mr. C. T. Ritchie, Dr. W. A. Hunter, Mr. J. Arch, Mr. Henry Broadhurst, Mr. C. S. Loch, and others; Mr. E. Austin Browne, secretary, Jan.; first meeting, 1 Feb. 1893; many meetings; report issued; much difference of opinion, and various schemes propounded . . . . 30 March, 1895

Housing of the poor, see *Artisans*.

Circular of the local government board, respecting classification in workhouses, issued . Aug. 1896

See *Children*, 1896, *Diamond Jubilee*, 24 June, 1897, *Charitable Bequests*.

London Poor Law schools' exhibition of arts and crafts in Westminster town-hall, opened by the duke and duchess of York . . . 12 July, 1900

Poor Removal act passed . . . 30 July, ,,

Poor Relief (Ireland) act passed . . . 6 Aug. ,,

Efficient working of the Poor Laws, 1861 *et seq.*, reported . . . . 20 Sept. 1901

Received, for relief of the poor, in 1869, in England and Wales, 11,776,153*l.*; in Scotland, 892,712*l.*; in Ireland, 927,046*l.*; total, 13,595,911*l.*; receipts, 1900–1901, 27,638,433*l.*; expenditure, 27,673,677*l.*

Paupers receiving relief 1 Jan. 1878: England and Wales, 742,703; Ireland, 85,530; 14 May, 1877, Scotland, 96,404; total, 924,437; Feb. 1889, England and Wales, 762,853.

Paupers in the metropolis receiving relief:—Dec., 1869, 152,557; Dec., 1870, about 147,000; Dec., 1871, about 124,000; July, 1872, 104,280; April, 114,644; Aug., 104,578; Oct., 1873, 97,287; Sept., 1874, 104,983; June, 1875, 84,598 (indoor 32,661, out 51,937); Dec., 1875, 84,782 (indoor 35,673, out 49,109); July, 1876, 77,498 (indoor, 33,735, out 43,763); Jan. 1877, 82,950; June, 78,203 (indoor, 35,903); 8 Dec. 81,986 (indoor, 42,242); 27 March, 1878, 84,753 (indoor, 41,403); 27 July, 76,709 (indoor, 38,043); 31 Dec. 83,674; 8 Feb. 1879, 94,765 (indoor, 45,095); 19 April, 83,075; 28 June, 78,680; 27 Sept. 79,674; 717 vagrants; 27 Dec. 92,495. 1880, last week, March, 88,893; (indoor, 46,738); June, 84,137 (vagrants, 931); Sept. 82,188; Dec. 92,654 (vagrants, 697); 1881, last week March, 95,767; indoor, 52,012; vagrants, 780; June, 86,404 (indoor, 48,293); 1881, Oct., 89,740 (indoor, 50,792, vagrants, 932); Dec. 1st, 93,170; vagrants, 883; 1882, 1 April, 92,233 (indoor, 51,480, vagrants, 788); June, 86,417 (indoor, 48,363, vagrants, 643); Sept. 88,581 (indoor, 50,174, vagrants, 915); Dec. 96,687 (indoor, 54,373, vagrants, 696); 1883, March, 97,743 (indoor, 54,836, vagrants, 497); June, 85,555 (indoor, 49,713, vagrants, 386); Sept. 85,849 (indoor, 50,917, vagrants, 461); 1884, Jan. 94,540 (indoor, 55,965, vagrants, 471); April, 89,540 (indoor, 54,122, vagrants, 528); Aug. 85,069 (indoor, 51,849, vagrants, 482); Dec. 94,041 (indoor, 57,092, vagrants, 374); 1885, March, 94,047 (indoor 56,491, vagrants, 540); June, 85,555 (indoor, 49,713, vagrants, 592); Sept. 86,119 (indoor, 51,968, vagrants, 562); 26 Dec. 94,902 (indoor, 56,002, vagrants, 322); 1886, 27 March, 101,982 (indoor, 56,507, vagrants, 463); 26 June, 87,171 (indoor, 51,570, vagrants, 454); 25 Sept. 87,604 (indoor, 52,628, vagrants, 650); 25 Dec. 98,611 (indoor, 57,520, vagrants, 475); 1887, 26 March, 103,726 (indoor, 58,221, vagrants, 627); 27 Aug. 88,274 (indoor, 53,164, vagrants, 619); 26 Nov. 101,852 (indoor, 59,066, vagrants, 1,054); 1888, 28 Jan. 108,783 (indoor, 60,883, vagrants, 1,165); 28 April, 102,617 (indoor, 58,273, vagrants, 1,151); 28 July, 90,510 (indoor, 52,875, vagrants, 976); 27 Oct. 96,030 (indoor, 58,070, vagrants, 1,182); 1889, 26 Jan. 104,734 (indoor, 61,521, vagrants, 1,119); 27 April, 95,600 (indoor, 58,509, vagrants, 1,114); 29 June, 88,699 (indoor, 54,460; vagrants, 605); 28 Sept. 92,012 (indoor, 56,805; vagrants, 1,169); 28 Dec. 97,661 (indoor, 60,111; vagrants, 775); 1890, 5 April, 93,596 (indoor, 58,216; vagrants, 707); 28 June, 87,600 (indoor, 54,267; vagrants, 765); 27 Sept. 88,147 (indoor, 55,273; vagrants, 1,014); 27 Dec. 97,128 (indoor, 59,588; vagrants, 525); 1891, 28 March, 92,395 (indoor, 58,364; vagrants, 748); 27 June, 86,109 (indoor, 53,981; vagrants, 772); 26 Sept. 86,072 (indoor, 54,478; vagrants, 814); 31 Dec. 94,639 (indoor, 60,169; vagrants, 743); 1892, 26 March, 92,936 (indoor, 59,612; vagrants, 771); 26 June, 85,731 (indoor, 54,838; vagrants, 740); 24 Sept. 88,898 (indoor, 57,297; vagrants, 1,218); 24 Dec. 98,124 (indoor, 62,577; vagrants, 901); 1893, 25 March, 93,067 (indoor, 60,334; vagrants, 654); 30 June, 90,341 (indoor, 57,708; vagrants, 800); 30 Sept. 97,424 (indoor, 61,961); 31 Dec., total 104,823 (indoor, 65,937); 31 March, 1894, 99,885 (indoor, 63,854); 30 June, 93,697 (indoor, 59,679); 29 Sept. 96,055 (indoor, 61,015); 29 Dec. 104,242 (66,770), vagrants (men, women and children), 1,243; 31 Jan. 1895, 125,435; 30 March, 122,611 (indoor, 67,070; vagrants, 1070); 29 June, 96,905 (indoor, 60,982; vagrants, 1,059); 28 Sept. 99,477 (indoor, 63,154; vagrants, 1,309); 28 Dec. 106,186 (indoor, 67,193; vagrants, 1,079); 1896, 25 April, 101,059 (indoor, 63,845; vagrants, 1,024); 27 June, 96,989 (indoor, 60,807; vagrants, 936); 30 Sept. 98,619 (indoor, 62,316; vagrants, 1,178); 30 Dec. 104,327 (indoor, 66,633; vagrants, 883); 1897, 31 March, 103,118 (indoor, 65,660; vagrants, 959); 3 July, 96,143 (indoor, 60,565; vagrants, 716); 30 Sept. 99,468 (indoor, 63,509; vagrants, 1,122); 31 Dec. 104,487 (indoor, 67,337); 1898, 31 March, 104,615 (indoor, 67,278; vagrants, 1,260); 2 July (indoor, 62,696; vagrants, 959); 30 Sept. 99,309 (indoor, 63,825, vagrants, 1,024); 31 Dec. 104,286 (indoor, 67,542; vagrants, 881); 1899, 31 March, 106,114 (indoor, 68,676; vagrants, 1,065); 30 June, 97,117 (indoor, 62,360; vagrants, 959); 28 Oct. 100,884 (indoor, 65,618; vagrants, 1,090); 30 Dec. 104,806 (indoor, 68,294; vagrants, 1,071); 1900, 31 March, 103,255 (indoor, 66,466; vagrants, 874); 30 June, 96,384 (indoor, 61,476; vagrants, 725); 29 Sept. 97,425 (indoor, 62,420; vagrants, 975); 31 Dec. 103,034 (indoor, 66,507; vagrants, 1,107); 1901, 30 March, 106,045 (indoor, 67,705; vagrants, 982); 29 June, 98,479 (indoor, 62,153; vagrants, 737); Sept. 100,515 (indoor, 63,722; vagrants, 973); 28 Dec. 107,317 (indoor, 68,326; vagrants, 987); 1902, 29 March, 106,476 (indoor, 67,141; vagrants, 939); 28 June, 101,242 (indoor, 63,431; vagrants, 912); 27 Sept. 103,442 (indoor, 65,057; vagrants, 893); 20 Dec. 113,352 (indoor, 71,108; vagrants, 1,003).

The powers and duties of the Poor Law board merged into the *Local Government board* by act passed 14 Aug. 1871; president, James Stansfeld; G. Sclater-Booth . . . . . . Feb. 1874

A Poor Law act passed . . . . . 15 Aug. 1876

ENGLAND AND WALES.

Expended.	*Poor rates.*	*Expended.*	*Poor rates.*
In 1580 . . .	£188,811	In 1820 . . .	£7,329,594
1680 . . .	665,562	1830 . . .	8,111,422
1698 . . .	819,000	1835 . . .	6,356,345
1760 . . .	1,556,804	1840 . . .	5,468,699
1785 . . .	2,184,950	1845 . . .	5,543,650
1802 . . .	4,952,421	1853 . . .	6,522,412

PAUPERS RECEIVING RELIEF (NOT VAGRANTS)

	1849.	1858.	1862.	1870.	1875.	1883.	1889.	1890.	1900.	1901.
England & Wales, 1 Jan.	934,419	968,186	932,400	1,079,391	815,587	799,296	810,132	787,545	797,630	789,689
Scotland . about 14 May	82,357	69,217*	78,433†	126,187	105,895	92,618	90,918	88,606	96,929‡	100,819‡
Ireland . . 1 Jan.	620,747	50,582	59,541	73,921	80,993	115,684	109,957	107,774	103,866	101,090
Total . .	1,637,523	1,087,985	1,070,374	1,279,499	1,002,475	1,007,598	1,011,007	983,925	998,425	981,598

* 1857. † 1861. ‡ 14 Jan.

ENGLAND AND WALES.

Years ended Lady-day.	Average number of paupers. Indoor.	Outdoor.	Expenditure.
1858	122,613	786,263	£5,878,542
1859	121,232	744,214	5,558,689
1860	113,507	731,126	5,454,964
1861	125,866	758,055	5,778,943
1862	132,236	784,906	6,077,922
1863	136,907	942,475	6,527,036
1864	133,761	881,217	6,423,381
1865	131,313	820,586	6,264,966
1866	132,776	783,376	6,439,517
1867	137,310	794,236	6,959,840
1868 (1 Jan.) . . .	158,723	876,100	7,498,059
1869 ,, . .	163,071	876,478	7,673,100
1870 ,, . . .	165,324	914,067	7,644,307
1871 ,, . .	165,289	916,637	7,886,724
1872 ,, . . .	154,233	823,431	8,007,403
1873 ,, . .	154,171	736,201	7,692,169
1874 ,, . . .	149,558	679,723	7,664,957
1875 ,, . .	153,711	661,876	7,488,481
1876 ,, . . .	148,931	600,662	7,335,858
1877 ,, . .	157,191	571,159	7,400,034
1878 ,, . . .	166,875	575,828	7,688,650
1879 ,, . .	175,345	625,081	7,829,819
1880 (1 Jan.). . .	189,394	648,636	£8,015,010
1881 ,, . .	189,438	613,688	8,102,136
1882 ,, . . .	188,433	609,181	8,232,472
1883 ,, . .	190,386	608,910	8,353,292
1884 ,, . . .	187,593	586,717	8,402,550
1885 ,, . .	190,184	593,971	8,491,600
1886 ,, . . .	194,440	613,193	8,296,230
1887 ,, . .	196,853	620,436	8,176,768
1888 ,, . . .	200,666	624,843	8,440,821
1889 ,, . .	198,191	611,941	8,366,477
1890 ,, . . .	195,048	592,497	8,434,345
1891 ,, . .	192,942	581,963	8,643,318
1892 ,, . . .	192,460	562,025	8,847,678
1893 ,, . .	199,934	576,524	9,217,514
1894 ,, . . .	212,629	599,812	9,673,505
1895 ,, . .	215,548	601,883	9,866,605
1896 ,, . . .	216,872	610,345	10,215,974
1897 ,, . .	216,029	608,333	10,432,189
1898 ,, . . .	218,439	604,912	10,828,276
1899 ,, . .	217,833	590,039	11,286,973
1900 ,, . . .	217,148	580,606	11,567,649
1901 ,, . .	215,623	574,179	12,119,544

POOR CHILDREN'S AID SOCIETY, for providing food, clothing, &c., established 1887.

POOR KNIGHTS OF WINDSOR, or ALMS KNIGHTS. Soon after his institution of the order of the Garter, Edward III. founded this charity, for the provision of 24 (afterwards 26) poor persons eminent for military services. Edward IV. discharged the college from the support of the alms-knights, but Elizabeth re-established the charity for 13 knights, 1559. King William IV. changed the name to the "Military Knights of Windsor," in consequence of their all having held commissions in the army, Sept. 1833.—The "Naval Knights of Windsor" are maintained on a distinct foundation, under the bequest of Samuel Travers, 1724. The corporation was established in 1798. An act making lieutenants and widowers eligible was passed in 1867. Alterations made by act passed in 1885. An act to dissolve the corporation was passed in 1892.

POPE (from the Greek *Pappas* and *Papa*, a father or grandfather), considered by Romanists to be the visible chief of the church, the vicar of Jesus Christ, and the successor of St. Peter. He styles himself "servant of the servants of God." The title pope was formerly given to all bishops. It was first adopted by Hyginus, 139; and pope Boniface III. induced Phocas, emperor of the east, to confine it to the prelates of Rome, 606. By the connivance of Phocas also, the pope's supremacy over the Christian church was established; see *Italy*, *Reformation*, and *Rome*, *Modern*.

Wilfrid, abp. of York, expelled from his diocese, appeals to the pope 679

Custom of kissing the pope's toe introduced . . 708

Adrian I. caused money to be coined with his name 780

Sergius II. the first pope who changed his name on his election, 844; some contend that it was Sergius I. 687, and others John XII. . . . 956

Indulgences for the pardon of sin granted by pope Leo III. . . . . . . about 800

John XVIII., a layman, made pope 1024

The first pope who kept an army, Leo IX. . . 1054

Gregory VII. (Hildebrand) obliges Henry IV., emperor of Germany, to stand three days, in the depth of winter, barefooted at the gate of the castle of Canossa, to implore his pardon . . 1077

The pope's authority fixed in England . . . 1079

Appeals from English tribunals to the pope introduced (*Viner*), 19 Stephen 1154

Henry II. of England holds the stirrup for pope Alexander III. to mount his horse 1161

Celestine III. kicked the emperor Henry VI.'s crown off his head while kneeling, to show his prerogative of making and unmaking kings . . 1191

John, king of England, did homage to the pope's legate for his dominions, and bound himself and his successors to an annual payment to the pope, 15 May, 1213

The pope collected the tenths of the whole kingdom of England. 1226

The papal seat was removed for seventy years to Avignon in France. 1308

The pope's demands on England refused by parliament 1363

After the discovery of America, pope Alexander VI. granted to the Portuguese all the countries to the east, and to the Spanish all the countries to the west, of Cape Non, Africa, they might conquer . 1493

Pope Leo X. published the sale of general indulgences throughout Europe 1517

Appeals to Rome from England abolished (*Viner*) . 1533

The words "Lord Pope" struck out of all English books 1541

Kissing the pope's toe and other ceremonies abolished by Clement XIV. 1773

The pope's political influence greatly diminished by the French revolution 1789-1814

His temporal power lost, see *Rome* . . . Dec. 1870
See PIUS IX. under *Popes.*

BISHOPS AND POPES OF ROME
(*the names in italics were antipopes*):

42. ST. PETER: (said to have been the first bishop of Rome, and to have been crucified, head downwards, in 66.)
* * St. Clement (Clemens Romanus); according to Tertullian.
66. St. Linus:* martyred?
78. St. Cletus, or Anacletus? martyred
91. St. Clement II.: abdicated?
100. St. Evaristus: martyred; multiplied churches.
109. St. Alexander: martyred.
119. St. Sixtus I.: martyred?
127. St. Telesphorus: martyred.
139. St. Hyginus: condemns Gnostics; called himself *pope.*
142. St. Pius: martyred.
157. St. Anicetus.
168. St. Soterus: martyred under Marcus Antoninus.
177. St. Eleutherius: opposed the Valentinians.
193. St. Victor I.: martyred under Severus.
202. St. Zephyrinus: claimed to be Peter's successor.
219. St. Calixtus: martyred.
222. [The chair vacant.]
223. St. Urban I.: beheaded.
230. St. Pontianus: banished by the emperor Maximin.
235. St. Anterus: martyred.
236. St. Fabian: martyred under Decius, 250.
250. [The chair vacant.]
251. St. Cornelius: died.
252. St. Lucius: martyred 252. *Novatianus*: (denied restoration to the repentant lapsed).
53. St. Stephen I.: martyred in the persecution of Valerian.
257. St. Sixtus II. (his coadjutor): martyred three days before his disciple St. Laurence, in the persecution of Valerian, 258.
258. [The chair vacant.]
259. St. Dionysius: opposed the heresy of Sabellius.
269. St. Felix I. died in prison.
275. St. Eutychianus.
283. St. Caius: a relative of the emperor Diocletian.
296. St. Marcellinus: *said* to have lapsed under a severe persecution?; canonised.
304. [The chair vacant.]
308. St. Marcellus: banished from Rome by the emperor Maxentius.
310. St. Eusebius: died the same year.
311. St. Miltiades or Melchiades: coadjutor to Eusebius.
314 St. Silvester: commencement of temporal power by gifts of Constantine.
336. St. Marcus: died the next year.
337. St. Julius I.: of great piety and learning; maintained the cause of St. Athanasius.
352. Liberius: banished.
355. *Felix II.*, antipope: placed in the chair by Constans, during the exile of Liberius, on whose return he was driven from it with ignominy.

[The emperor would have the two popes reign together; but the people cried out, "*One God, one Christ, and one bishop!*"]

* St. Linus is frequently set down as the immediate successor of St. Peter; but Tertullian maintains that it was St. Clement. In the first century neither the dates nor order of succession of bishops are reconcilable by even the best authorities. Some assert that there were two or three bishops of Rome at the same time.

358. Liberius again: abdicated.
,, *Felix* became pope.
359. Liberius again: martyred 365.
366. St. Damasus: opposed the Arians: St. Jerome, his secretary, corrected Latin Bible.
367 *Ursinus*: expelled by Valentinian.
384. Siricius: combated heretics.
398. St. Anastasius: proscribed works of Origen.
402. St. Innocent I.: condemned Pelagians.
417. St. Zozimus: ditto.
418. St. Boniface I.: maintained by the emperor Honorius, against *Eulalius.*
422. St. Celestine I.: sent missions to Ireland.
432. Sixtus III.: opposed Nestorius and Eutyches.
440. St. Leo I. the Great: zealous; restrained Alaric; an able writer.
461. St. Hilary; rich, liberal.
468. St. Simplicius: wise, prudent.
483. St. Felix III.: opposed emperor Zeno respecting the Henoticon.
492. St. Gelasius: opposed heresy; fixed the canon of Scriptures; compiled the mass.
496. St. Anastasius II.: congratulated Clovis.
498. Symmachus: zealous against the Henoticon.
,, *Laurentius*: antipope.
514. Hormisdas: opposed Eutychians.
523. John I.: sent to Constantinople by Theodoric tolerant.
526. Felix IV.: introduced extreme unction as a sacrament.
530. Boniface II.—*Dioscorus.*
533. John II.: called Mercurius.
535. Agapetus: converted Justinian.
536. St. Silverius: son of pope Hormisdas, who had been married; the empress Theodora procured his banishment into Lycia (where he died of hunger), and made Vigilius pope.
537. Vigilius: banished, but restored.
555. Pelagius I.: an ecclesiastical reformer.
560. John III.: great ornamenter of churches.
573. [The see vacant.]
574. Benedict I., surnamed Bonosus.
578. Pelagius II.; died of the plague.
590. St. Gregory the Great: revised the liturgy; sent Augustin to convert the Anglo-Saxons.
604. Sabinianus: said to have introduced church bells.
606 or 607. Boniface III.: died in a few months.
607 or 608. Boniface IV.
614 or 615. St. Deusdedit.
617 or 618. Boniface V.
625. Honorius I.: interested in British churches.
639. [The see vacant.]
640. Severinus: } condemned Monothelites.
,, John IV.: }
642. Theodorus I.: }
649. Martin I.: }
654. Eugenius I.: liberal.
657. Vitalianus: favoured education in England.
672. Adeodatus, the gift of God.
676. Domnus I.: ornamented churches.
678. St. Agathon: tribute to the emperor ceased.
682. St. Leo II.: instituted holy water; favoured music.
683. [The see vacant.]
684. Benedict II.
685. John V.: learned and moderate.
686. Conon.—*Theodore* and *Pascal.*
687. Sergius: "governed wisely."
701. John VI.: redeemed captives; firm and wise.
705. John VII.: moderate.
708. Sisinnius: died 20 days after election.
,, Constantine: wise and gentle; visited Constantinople.
715. St. Gregory II.: sent Boniface to convert Germans.
731. Gregory III. independent; first sent nuncios to foreign powers.
741. St. Zacharias, a Greek.
752. Stephen II. elected: died before consecration.
,, Stephen II. or III.: temporal power of the church of Rome commenced.
757. Paul I.: moderate and pious.
767. *Constantine Theophylactus*: killed by Lombards.
768. Stephen III. or IV.: literary.
772. Adrian I.: sanctioned images.
795. Leo III.: crowned Charlemagne, 800.
816. Stephen IV. or V.

817. Pascal I. : ascetic, and built churches.
824. Eugenius II. : "father of the afflicted."—*Zosimus.*
827. Valentinus.
,, Gregory IV. ; pious and learned.
844. Sergius II.
847. Leo IV. : defeated the Saracens.
855. Pope Joan's election fabulous (*which see*).
,, Benedict III.—*Anastasius.*
858. Nicholas I., the Great : conversion of Bulgarians.
867. Adrian II. : eminent for sanctity.
872. John VIII. : crowned 3 emperors.
882. Marinus or Martin II. : condemned Photius.
884. Adrian III. ; ditto.
885. Stephen V. or VI. : very charitable.
891. Formosus ; political.—*Sergius.*
896. Boniface VI. : deposed.
897. Stephen VI. or VII. : vicious ; dishonoured the corpse of pope Formosus ; strangled by the people.
,, Romanus.—*Sergius.*
898. Theodorus II. : governed 22 days.
,, John IX.
900. Benedict IV. : "a great pope."
903. Leo V. : expelled : died in prison.
,, Christopher.
[Several popes made by the infamous Marozia.]
904. Sergius III. : disgraced by his vices.
911. Anastasius III.
913. Landonius, or Lando.
914. John X. : stifled by Guy, duke of Tuscany.
928. Leo VI. : considered an intruder.
929. Stephen VII. or VIII.
931. John XI. : son of Marozia ; imprisoned in the castle of St. Angelo, where he died.
936. Leo VII. : great for zeal and piety.
939. Stephen VIII. or IX. : "of ferocious character."
942. Marinus II. or Martin III. : charitable.
946. Agapetus II. : of holy life ; moderate.
956. John XII., the infamous : deposed for adultery and cruelty ; and murdered.
963. *Leo VIII.* : an honour to the chair.
964. Benedict V. : chosen on the death of John XII., but opposed by Leo VIII., who was supported by the emperor Otho : died at Hamburg.
965. John XIII., elected by the authority of the emperor against the popular will.
972. Benedict VI. : murdered in prison.
974. Domnus II.—*Boniface VII.*
975. Benedict VII.
984. John XIV. : imprisoned by *Boniface VII.*
,, John XV. : died before consecration.
985. John XVI. : loved gain.
996. Gregory V.—*John XVII.* : expelled by the emperor, and barbarously used.
999. Silvester II. (Gerbert) : learned and scientific ; said to have introduced the Arabic numerals, and invented clocks.
1003. John XVII. : legitimate pope, died same year.
,, John XVIII. abdicated.
1009. Sergius IV. (original name "Bocca di Porco," Pig's Snout).
1012. Benedict VIII. ; supported by the emperor against *Gregory.*
1024. John XIX. : elevated by bribery.
1033. Benedict IX. ; became pope, by purchase, at 12 years of age ; expelled for vices.
1044. *Sylvester III.* : 3 months.
,, Gregory VI. : deposed.—*Sylvester* ; and *John XX.* [The emperor very influential.]
1046. Clement II. died the next year (*Clemens Romanus*, the *first* Clement).
1047. *Benedict IX.* again : again deposed.
1048. Damasus II. : died soon after.
,, St. Leo IX. : a reformer of simony and incontinence.
1054. [The throne vacant one year.]
1055. Victor II. : a reformer.
1057. Stephen IX. or X.
1058. *Benedict X.* ; expelled.
,, Nicholas II. : increased the temporal power.
1061. Alexander II. : raised the papal power.—*Honorius II.*
1073. St. Gregory VII. (Hildebrand) : vigorous reformer ; opposed the emperor Henry IV. respecting investitures ; and excommunicated him, 1076 ; restored him at Canossa, 1077 ; died, in exile, 1085.
1080. *Clement III.* (Guibert).
1085. [The throne vacant one year.]
1086. Victor III. (Didier) : learned.
1088. Urban II. ; crusades commenced.
1099. Pascal II. (Ranieri) : Tuscany given to the papa by the countess Matilda.
1118. Gelasius II. : retired to a monastery.—*Gregor VIII.*
1119. Calixtus II. : settled investiture question.
1124. Honorius II.
1130. Innocent II. : condemned heresies : held an Lateran council.—*Anacletus II.*
1138. *Victor IV.*
1143. Celestine II. : ruled 5 months.
1144. Lucius II. : killed by accident in a popular commotion.
1145. Eugenius III. : ascetic.
1153. Anastasius IV.
1154. Adrian IV., or Nicholas Brakespeare, the only Englishman elected pope : born at Abbot's Langley, near St. Alban's ; Frederick I. prostrated himself before him, kissed his foot, held his stirrup, and led the white palfrey on which he rode.
1159. Alexander III. : learned ; canonised Thomas à Becket ; resisted Frederick I. ; 1159, *Victor V.* ; 1164, *Pascal III.* ; 1168, Calistus III. ; 1178, *Innocent III.*
1181. Lucius III.—The cardinals acquire power.
1185. Urban III. : opposed Frederick I.
1187. Gregory VIII. : ruled only 2 months.
,, Clement III. : proclaimed 3rd crusade.
1191. Celestine III.
1198. Innocent III. (Lothario Conti) : endeavoured to free Rome from foreign influence ; excommunicated John of England ; preached crusade against the Albigenses, 1204.
1216. Honorius III. : learned and pious.
1227. Gregory IX. : preached a new crusade ; collected decretals.
1241. Celestine IV. : died 18 days after his election. [The throne vacant 1 year and 7 months.]
1243. Innocent IV. : opposed Frederick II. : gave the red hat to cardinals.
1254. Alexander IV. : established inquisition in France.
1261. Urban IV. ; instituted feast of "Corpus Christi."
1265. Clement IV., an enlightened Frenchman, previously legate to England ; discouraged the crusades.
1268. [The throne vacant 2 years and 9 months.]
1271. Gregory X. : held a council at Lyons to reconcile the churches of the east and west.
1276. Innocent V. : died shortly after.
,, Adrian V. : legate to England in 1254 ; died 36 days after election.
,, Vicedominus : died the next day.
,, John XX. or XXI. : died in 8 months.
1277. Nicholas III. : died in 1280.
1281. Martin IV., French : supported Charles of Anjou.
1285. Honorius IV. : supported the French.
1288. Nicholas IV. : endeavoured to stir up a new crusade.
1292. [The throne vacant 2 years and 3 months.]
1294. St. Celestine V. : ascetic ; resigned.
,, Boniface VIII. : proclaimed that "God had set him over kings and kingdoms :" imprisoned his predecessor ; quarrelled with Philip of France ; laid France and Denmark under interdict.
1303. Benedict XI. : a pious and liberal pontiff : said to have been poisoned.
1304. [The throne vacant 11 months.]
1305. Clement V. (Bertrand de Got) : governed by Philip of France ; removed the papal seat from Rome to Avignon, 1309.
1314. [The throne vacant 2 years and 4 months.]
1316. John XXII.
1334. Benedict XII. (*Nicholas V.* at Rome.]
1342. Clement VI. : learned.
1352. Innocent VI. : favoured Rienzi.
1362. Urban V. : charitable : a patron of learning.
1370. Gregory XI. : protector of learning ; restored the papal chair to Rome ; proscribed Wickliffe's doctrines.

SCHISM—1378–1447.

1378. Urban VI. : so severe and cruel that the cardinals chose Robert of Geneva, as
,, *Clement VII.*

1389. Boniface IX.
1394. *Benedict* (called *XIII.*) at Avignon.
1404. Innocent VII.: died in 1406.
1406. *Gregory XII.*, Angelo Corario.
1409. Alexander V.: died, supposed by poison.
1410. John XXIII.: deposed.
1417. Martin V. Otho Colonna.
1424. *Clement VIII.*: resigned 1429.
1431. Eugenius IV. Gabriel Condolmera: deposed by the council of Basil, and Amadeus of Savoy chosen as *Felix V.*, in 1439, who resigned 1449.
1447. Nicholas V.: learned; proposed crusade against Turks.
1455. Calixtus III. Alfonso Borgia: courageous.
1458 Pius II. Æneas Silvius Piccolomini: learned.
1464. Paul II. Pietro Barbo: preached a crusade.
1471. Sixtus IV.: tried to rouse Europe against the Turks.
1484. Innocent VIII.
1492. Alexander VI. Roderic Borgia: poisoned at a feast by drinking of a bowl he had prepared for another.
1503. Pius III. Francisco Piccolomini: 21 days pope.
" Julius II. Julian della Rovere: martial; began St. Peter's.
1513. Leo X. Giovanni de' Medici: his grant of indulgences for crime led to the Reformation; patron of learning and art.
1522. Adrian VI.: just, learned, frugal.
1523. Clement VII. Giulio de' Medici: refused to divorce Catherine of Aragon, and denounced the marriage of Henry VIII. with Anne Boleyn.
1534. Paul III. Alexander Farnese: approved the Jesuits.
1550. Julius III. Giovanni M. Giocchi.
1555. Marcellus II.: died soon after his election.
" Paul IV. John Peter Caraffa. He would not acknowledge Elizabeth queen of England; instituted "the Index" (*which see*), and leagued with France against Spain.
1559. Pius IV. Cardinal de' Medici: founded Vatican press.
1566. St. Pius V. Michael Ghisleri: pious; energetic.
1572. Gregory XIII. Buoncampagno: great civilian and canonist: reformed the calendar.
1585. Sixtus V. Felix Peretti: an able governor; excom. Henry III. and Henry IV. of France.
1590. Urban VII.; died 12 days after election.
" Gregory XIV. Nicholas Sfrondrate.
1591. Innocent IX.: died in two months.
1592. Clement VIII. Hippolito Aldobrandini: learned and just: published the Vulgate.
1605. Leo XI.: died same month.
" Paul V. Camille Borghese; quarrelled with Venice.
1621. Gregory XV. Alexander Ludovisio: founded the Propaganda.
1623. Urban VIII. Maffei Barberini: condemned Jansenism.
1644. Innocent X. John Baptist Panfili: ditto.
1655. Alexander VII. Fabio Chigi: favoured literature.
1667. Clement IX. Giulio Rispogliosi: governed wisely.
1670. Clement X. Emilio Altieri.
1676. Innocent XI. Odescalchi: condemned Gallicanism and Quietism.
1689. Alexander VIII. Ottoboni, 6 Oct.; helped Leopold against Turks.
1691. Innocent XII. Antonio Pignatelli: 12 July; condemned Fénelon.
1700. Clement XI. John Francis Albani: 23 Nov.; issued the bull Unigenitus.
1721 Innocent XIII. Michael Angelo Conti: the eighth of his family; 8 May; pensioned Jas. Ed. Stuart.
1724. Benedict XIII. Orsini 29 May; favoured J. E. Stuart.
1730. Clement XII. Orsini: 12 July; restored San Marino (republic).
1740. Benedict XIV. Lambertini: 17 Aug.; learned, amiable.
1758. Clement XIII. Chas. Rezzonico: Avignon lost.
1769. Clement XIV. Ganganelli: 19 May; suppressed the Jesuits.
1775. Pius VI. Angelo Braschi, Feb. 15: dethroned by Bonaparte; expelled from Rome, and deposed in Feb. 1798; died at Valence, 29 Aug. 1799.
1800. Pius VII. Barnabo Chiaramonte: elected 13 March; agrees to a concordat with France, 15 July, 1801; crowns Napoleon, 2 Dec. 1804; excommunicates him, 10 June, 1809; imprisoned, 6 July, 1809; restored in 1814; died, 20 Aug. 1823. (He restored the Jesuits, 1814.)
1823. Leo XII. Annibale della Genga, 28 Sept.
1829. Pius VIII. Francis Xavier Castiglioni, 31 March.
1831. Gregory XVI. Mauro Capellari, 2 Feb.: died, 1 June, 1846.
1846. Pius IX. Giovanni Maria Mastaï-Ferretti (born 13 May, 1792): elected, 16 June. See *Rome*, 1846-71.
1848. His diplomatic relations with Great Britain authorised by parliament.
[Act repealed, 1875.]
1860–65. His powers in France greatly checked.
1869. The "Latæ Sententiæ," regarding excommunication and limiting absolution, signed, 12 Oct.; issued, Dec.
1870. The pope opens a general council (8 Dec. 1869), which propounds the doctrine of papal infallibility and list of anathemas (see *Councils*), Feb.; deprived of the remains of his temporal power (see *Rome*), Dec.
1871. Visited by the prince and princess of Wales, 27 March; celebrates a jubilee (25th anniversary of election), 16 June; nominates 14 Italian prelates, 24 Nov.
1872. Performs no Easter solemnities 31 March; in his allocution complains of the persecution of the church in Italy, Germany, and Spain, Dec. 23.
1873. Letter from the pope to the emperor of Germany complaining of his persecuting the bishops, and asserting his authority over all baptized persons, 7 Aug.; the emperor replies in justification, and asserts that there is no mediator between God and man but Jesus Christ, 3 Sept.; encyclical letter of the pope on wrongs of the church, 21 Nov.; he appoints 12 new cardinals, 22 Dec.
1874. The papal nuncio expelled from Switzerland; protests by letter, 17 Jan.; a bull (said to be forged), altering mode of electing a pope, &c., dated 28 May, 1873; appears, Jan.; 3600*l.* (from poor girls in Great Britain) presented to the pope by lady Herbert of Lea, 9 April; the pope receives 100 American pilgrims, 9 June; the English unofficial secretary of legation at the papal court withdrawn; leaves, 11 Nov.; in his allocution, the pope exhorts the faithful to patience, and forbids priests meddling with politics, 21 Dec.
1875. The pope re-appears at St. Peter's, after four years' seclusion, 9 Feb.; he dedicates the universal church to "the sacred heart," 16 June; his nuncio issues a circular against religious toleration in Spain, Sept.; allocution; new cardinals announced, 17 Sept.
1876. Announces an exhibition of sacred objects at the Vatican (in celebration of his jubilee) on 21 May, 1877, Aug.; performs a requiem for the souls of his enemies, 2 Nov.; death of his cardinal-secretary, Antonelli, 6 Nov.; succeeded by Simeoni, about 15 Nov.
1877. Creates 11 new cardinals, and issues a warm allocution against the Italian government, 12 March; and circular to foreign powers, on account of the bill to repress clerical abuses, 21 March; creates 3 cardinals, 22 June; 2 cardinals, &c., 28 Dec.
Died 7 Feb. 1878.
1878. Leo XIII. Gioachino Pecci (born 2 March, 1810); elected, 20 Feb. 1878.
Reduces his guards: holds a consistory, with an allocution; revives R. C. hierarchy in Scotland, 4 March.
Publishes encyclical endorsing policy of predecessor, but moderate, 25 April.
Makes his secretary of state cardinal Franchi, 5 March; cardinal Nina, Aug.
Issues an encyclical letter condemning communism, socialism, and nihilism, as results of the Reformation; dated 28 Dec.
1879. Appoints 10 cardinals (including J. H. Newman), 12 May.
Issues encyclical against modern false philosophy; recommends Thomas Aquinas, early in Aug.

1880. Issues encyclical on marriage, as a sacrament, and against divorce; published 18 Feb.

Delivers an allocution censuring the government of Belgium (*which see*), and praising the bishops, 20 Aug.

Cardinal Nina, secretary, resigns for bad health, 13 Oct.; cardinal Jacobini successor, 17 Nov.; he resigned Dec. 1886 (died 28 Feb. 1887).

1881. Proclaims an extra jubilee for the distressed Church, 15 May.

Issues an encyclical letter, asserting that all government is of divine origin, and that wars are consequences of the Reformation, July.

Canonizes De Rossi and three others, 8 Dec.

1882. Encyclical letter against heresy, socialism, &c., read in London churches, 5 Nov.

1883. Circular to Irish bishops enjoining abstinence from disaffection to the government, 11 May.

Letter to president Grévy censuring the republican warfare against religion, 23 June.

Courteous, firm answer delivered, 8 Aug.

Letter from the pope defending the papacy, and recommending the study of ecclesiastical history, Sept.

The pope addresses 20,000 pilgrims in St. Peter's, and recognises Italian unity, 7 Oct.

Visited by the crown prince of Germany, 18 Dec.

1884. Encyclical letter to French bishops, commending early French devotion to religion, and exhorting the bishops to redouble their vigilance in regard to heresy and infidelity, 11 Feb.

In a letter to cardinal Jacobini he offers 40,000*l.* to erect an hospital for cholera at Rome which he would visit, 10 Sept.

Allocution, 8 cardinals and many bishops created, 10 Nov.

1885. The pope's messenger, father Giulianelli, well received by the emperor of China, April.

Letter from the pope to the emperor of China, 1 Feb.; reply agreeing to receive a papal agent to protect R.C. missionaries, July.

Encyclical letter condemning liberalism, &c., 6 Nov.

1887. Monsignor Rampolla becomes pontifical secretary of state, March.

Allocution 23 May.

Letter from the pope asserting his territorial rights, 15 June.

The pope's jubilee (on being ordained priest, 31 Dec. 1837).

The duke of Norfolk, envoy extraordinary from queen Victoria, appointed, Dec.; received by the pope 17 Dec.; a massive basin and ewer of gold presented to the pope, 25 Dec.

1888. The pope's grand jubilee; masses at St. Peter's: present 48 cardinals, 238 archbishops and bishops, and about 30,000 persons, 1 and 5 Jan.; the pope's speech demanding the independence of the church, 3 Jan.; the pope condemns the plan of campaign and boycotting on moral grounds, announced 27 April.

The emperor William II. visits the pope 12 Oct.

Address of English R.C. bishops to the pope protesting against Italian repressive legislation respecting his temporal power, 10 Nov.

1889. The pope receives French pilgrims, 20 Oct.—Nov.

1890. The pope's encyclical letter on the moral duties of Catholics now much neglected, issued, 6 Jan.; published, 16 Jan.

Negotiations respecting the Roman catholics in Malta, between the British government and the pope, carried on by sir John Lintorn Simmons, concluded; he leaves Rome, 7 April.

1891. Encyclical concerning socialism and the Labour question issued 15 May.

1892. Encyclical to the French bishops enjoining on all good catholics entire submission to the government of the republic, 16 Feb.; obedience enforced by a brief, dated 3 May.

1893. The pope celebrates his episcopal jubilee, Feb.; about 50,000 pilgrims of various nations present in and about St. Peter's; mass celebrated by the pope amid great enthusiasm; many presents; St. Peter's illuminated, 19 Feb.; Peter's pence received, total, reported, 263,960*l.*; Great Britain 48,000*l.*, Ireland 720*l.*, Feb.; see *Phonograph*, 20 March; he receives the princess of Wales, the duke of York, and her daughters, and gives them his portraits, 23 March; receives the German emperor and empress, 23 April; letters from the pope to the French catholics, approving those who support him, but severely censuring malcontents, 3 Aug.; to the congress-general of German catholics at Wurzburg, reported 30 Aug.

1894. Encyclical to all princes and nations from the pope, praying that all Christian nations may be brought into the unity of the Roman church, 20 June; the pope presides at conferences with some Eastern patriarchs to consider the reunion of the dissident Eastern churches with the church of Rome, 24 Oct. *et seq.*; partial agreement at a final meeting, 8 Nov.

1895. Allocution against the Hungarian civil marriage law, reported, 21 March; "Apostolic letter to the English people," earnestly appealing for reunion with the catholic church, 14 April, *Times*, 20 April; pastoral letter from the abp. of Canterbury, 30 Aug.

Papal consistory: creation of 9 new cardinals, and 24 Italian bishops, 29 Nov.

1896. Encyclical advocating Christian unity, 30 June.

Apostolic letter confirming the decision of Paul IV. in 1555 and other popes against the validity of the Anglican orders, 13 Sept.

1897. Temperate reply of the archbishops of Canterbury and York, sustaining the validity of the Anglican orders, signed 19 Feb., *Times*, 9 March.

1898. "A vindication of the bull" by the R. C. cardinal, archbishops and bishops of Westminster, published, Feb.; the English archbishops' firm reply, 12 March. Encyclical to Italy, Aug.

1899. Encyclical to cardinal Gibbons and the American catholics, condemning "Americanism" and the doctrines of the Paulists, 22 Jan.

The bull, proclaiming the universal jubilee of 1900, read, 11 May.

The pope presides over the commission on the union of the churches, 20 May; see *France*, 15 June, 1899.

Papal encyclical *re* the Dreyfus case, vague and discursive, published 16 Sept.

Papal consistory and allocution, 14 Dec.

The holy year 1900 inaugurated by the opening of the "holy door" of St. Peter's, 24 Dec.

1900. Preconisation of bishops and allocution, 19 April.

Queen Margherita's prayer for the soul of her murdered husband, approved by the bishop of Cremona and recited in the churches; repudiated by the vatican, see *Times*, 24 Aug. 1900.

The pope gives his blessing to multitudes at St. Peter's, 29 Sept., 13 Oct., 15 Nov., 24 Dec.

Encyclical to the Roman prelates, stating that multitudes have flocked to the "threshold of the apostles," relying upon the indulgence offered by the church at the close of this century, 1 Nov.

Allocution against his continued loss of temporal power, 17 Dec.; closes the "holy door," 24 Dec.

1901. The pope receives about 800 British pilgrims; the duke of Norfolk reads an address from the catholic union, expressing their "indignation at the proselytising societies in Rome," and praying for the pope's restoration to temporal power. The pope in reply lamented the toleration to non-catholics in Rome, &c., 8 Jan.

The pope's Latin ode to the twentieth century, published 12 Jan.

Allocution bewailing the hostilities against the church in various parts of Europe, and the French religious associations bill; 12 cardinals created, 15 April.

1901. Commission of biblical exegesis appointed, Aug.

1902. The pope's pontifical jubilee, 3 March; special British mission; lord Denbigh presents an autograph letter from the king, 8 March.

Encyclical to the R. C. hierarchy "On the most holy eucharist," 28 May.

Papal consistory: creation of 3 new cardinals and several bishops; allocution deploring the attempt to dechristianize Rome and Italy by heresy, protestantism, &c., 9 June.

Dinner at the vatican to 1500 poor, and jubilee fête, 6 July.

The pope at his Christmas reception of the cardinals delivers a discourse in favour of the Christian democratic movement, and signifies his approval of clergy taking part in it, 25 Dec.

"Poems, charades, inscriptions of pope Leo XIII.," with English translation and notes by H. T. Henry, published, 1902.

1903. The pope receives king Edward VII. at the Vatican, 29 April; and the German emperor, 3 May.

Papal consistory: 7 new cardinals created, 22 June.

Death of pope Leo XIII., aged 93, 20 July; temporarily interred in St. Peter's, 25 July.

He bequeathed 50,000 lire to the poor of Rome, 30,000 lire to the poor of Perugia, 10,000 lire to the poor of Carpinets.

Pius X., Giuseppe Sarto (born 2 June, 1835), elected pope, 4 Aug.

Declares his intention to support the king of Spain, reported, 29 Aug.

Papal encyclical, dwelling on recent election, and declaring aim to be the restoration of all things in Jesus Christ, and to be in all things the minister of God, published 3 Oct.

Fire at the Vatican in rooms over the famous library, 1 Nov.

Papal consistory: Mgr. Callagari and mgr. Merry del Val (new papal secretary of state) created cardinals; allocution on the temporal power of the papacy, declaring continuance in the policy of his predecessors in protesting against the injury done to the pontificate by depriving it of its necessary liberty. He (the pope) would bear his part in politics whenever they were inseparable from catholic morality. The church opposed neither progress nor science, but was willing to assist both whenever they were derived from divine sources, 9 Nov.

Interview of M. Henri des Houx with the pope, who referring to old French catholics, expounded the doctrine that Christ, who ought to be the model for all Christians, had preferred a life of suffering and humiliation, reported in Paris *Matin*, 9 Nov.

1903. Papal consistory (public): 5 cardinals (3 created by Leo XIII.) invested with their hats; pallium conferred on Dr. Bourne, new abp. of Westminster, 12 Nov.

POPE, A., poet (1688—1744). His bi-centenary was celebrated by an exhibition of books, pictures, and other relics, and a lecture by professor H. Morley at Twickenham town-hall, 31 July, 1888.

POPE JOAN. It is falsely asserted that, in the 9th century, a female named Joan, having conceived a passion for Felda, a young monk, in order to be admitted into his monastery assumed the male habit, and that on the death of her lover she entered upon the duties of professor, and, being very learned, was elected pope, when Leo IV. died, in 855. Other scandalous particulars follow; "yet, until the reformation, the tale was repeated and believed without offence." *Gibbon.*

POPISH PLOTS, see *Gunpowder Plot* and *Oates's Plot*.

POPLAR TREES. The Tacamahac poplar (*Populus Balsamifera*) was brought hither from North America before 1692. The Lombardy poplar from Italy about 1758.

POPLIN (or Tabinet), an elegant rich fabric composed of silk and worsted, introduced by the Huguenot refugees from France about 1693; first manufactured in Dublin. Irish poplins are still deservedly esteemed.

POPULAR CONCERTS, see under *Music*.

POPULATION. The population of the world was estimated in 1869 at 1,228,000,000; (at Washington, 1874), 1,391,032,000; 1882, 1,433,887,500; 1890, 1,468,000,000 (Ravenstein); 1891, 1,480,000,000 (Behm and Wagner); 1902, 1,600,000,000. For the population of countries, see the table (after the preface) facing page 1.

	1869.	1878.*	1891.*
Europe	275,806,741	312,398,480	357,379,000
Asia	755,000,000	831,000,000	825,954,000
Africa	200,000,000	205,219,500	163,953,000
America	67,896,041	86,116,000	121,713,000
Australia	1,445,000 }	4,411,300 }	3,230,000
Polynesia	1,500,000 }		7,420,000

* Behm and Wagner.

ESTIMATED POPULATION OF ENGLAND AND WALES.

	Population.		Population.		Population.		Population.
1377	2,092,978	1710	5,240,000	1750	6,467,000	1790	8,675,000
1483	4,689,000	1720	5,565,000	1760	6,736,000		
1696	5,250,000	1730	5,796,000	1770	7,428,000		
1700	5,475,000	1740	6,064,000	1780	7,953,000		

Estimated population of SCOTLAND in 1751, 1,255,663.

Estimated population of IRELAND in 1652, 850,000; in 1712, 2,099,094; in 1754, 2,372,634; in 1805, 5,395,456.

POPULATION OF GREAT BRITAIN AND IRELAND BY CENSUS.

(The earlier returns given below are approximate, and have been corrected in subsequent Reports.)

Division.	1801.	1811.	1821.	1831.	1841.	1851.	1861.	1871.
England	8,331,434	9,551,888	11,261,437	13,089,338	14,995,138	16,854,142	18,949,130	21,487,688
Wales	541,546	611,788	717,438	805,236	916,619	1,060,626	1,111,705	1,216,420
Scotland	1,599,068	1,805,688	2,093,456	2,365,807	2,620,184	2,870,784	3,061,251	3,358,613
Army, Navy, &c.	470,598	640,500	319,300	277,017	312,493	142,916	162,021	207,198
Total	10,942,646	12,609,864	14,391,631	16,537,398	18,844,434	20,936,468	23,284,197	26,269,919
Ireland		5,937,856	8,175,124	7,784,934	8,175,124	6,515,794	5,764,543	5,402,759
Islands in British seas	. .	. .	. .	. .	. .	143,126	143,779	144,430
						27,595,388	29,192,419	31,817,108

Division.	Year.	Males.	Females.	Inhabited Houses.
England and Wales . .	1861	9,776,259	10,289,965	3,739,505
,, ,, ,, . .	1871	11,058,934	11,653,332	4,259,117
,, ,, ,, . .	1881	12,639,902	13,334,537	4,831,519
,, ,, ,, . .	1891	14,050,620	14,950,398	5,460,976
Scotland	1861	1,446,982	1,614,269	393,289
,, ...	1871	1,601,633	1,756,980	419,635
Ireland	1861	2,804,961	2,959,582	995,156
,, ...	1871	2,634,123	2,768,636	960,352

Abstract of the Census of 4 April, 1881; 5 April, 1891; and of 31 March, 1901: England and Wales, 1881, 25,974,439; 1891, 29,001,018; 1901, 32,527,843. Scotland, 1881, 3,734,370; 1891, 4,033,103; 1901, 4,472,103. Ireland, 1881, 5,159,839; 1891, 4,706,162; 1901, 4,458,775. [Wales, 1881, 1,360,505; 1891, 1,518,914; 1901, 1,455,680.] Channel Isles, 1881, 87,702; 1891, 92,272; 1901, 95,841. Isle of Man, 1881, 53,558; 1891, 55,598; 1901, 54,748. Total of the United Kingdom, 1881, 35,246,561; 1891, 37,888,153; 1901, 41,605,220.

Reports published Aug. 1892: Scotland, 1881, 3,735,573; 1891, 4,025,647. Ireland, 1881, 5,174,836; 1891, 4,704,750.

POPULATION OF THE PRINCIPAL TOWNS OF GREAT BRITAIN.

Towns.	1801.	1811.	1821.	1831.	1841.	1851.	1861.†	1871.†	1881.	1891.	1901.
London and suburbs .	864,845	1,009,546	1,225,694	1,474,069	1,873,676	2,362,236*	2,803.034	3,251,804	3,834,194	4,231,431	4,536,541
Manchester, &c. . .	94,876	115,874	161,635	237,832	242,583	404,465	357,979	383,843	462,303	505,303	543,969
Glasgow, &c.	77,385	100,749	147,043	202,426	274,533	340,653	394,857	477,144		792,728	761,665
Liverpool .	79,722	100,240	131,801	189,244	286,487	375,955	443,938	493,346	552,508	517,951	685,276
Edinburgh, &c. . .	82,560	102,987	138,235	162,403	168,182	193,929	168,098	196,500		261,261	316,479
Birmingham	73,670	85,753	106,721	142,251	182,922	232,841	296,076	343,696	400,774	429,171	522,182
Leeds, &c. .	* *	* *	83,796	123,393	152,054	172,270	207,165	259,201	309,119	367,506	428,953
Bristol, &c. .	63,645	76,433	87,779	103,886	122,296	137,328	154,093	182,524	206,874	221,665	328,842
Sheffield . .	* *	* *	69,479	91,692	111,091	135,310	185,172	239,947	284,508	324,243	380,717
Plymouth .	43,194	56,060	61,212	75,534	80,059	102,380	62,599	69,414	73,794	84,179	107,509
Portsmouth	43,461	52,769	56,620	63,026	63,032	72,096	94,799	112,954	127,989	159,255	189,160
Norwich .	36,832	37,256	50,288	61,116	72,344	68,195	74,891	80,390	87,842	100,964	111,728
Aberdeen .	27,608	35,370	44,796	58,019	63,288	71,945	73,794	88,125		121,905	153,108
Newcastle-on-Tyne .	36,963	36,369	46,948	57,937	70,860	87,784	109,108	128,160	145,359	186,345	214,803
Paisley . .	31,179	36,722	47,003	57,466	60,487	69,951	47,419	48,257		66,427	79,355
Nottingham	28,861	34,253	40,415	50,680	57,407	71,344	74,693	86,608	186,575	211,984	239,753
Hull . . .	34,964	32,467	41,874	49,461	71,629	84,690	97,661	123,111	86,502	95,422	240,618
Dundee . .	26,084	29,616	30,575	45,355	62,794	77,829	90,425	118,974		155,640	160,871
Brighton .	7,339	12,012	24,429	40,634	46,661	65,573	87,317	103,760	107,546	115,402	123,478
Bath . . .	30,113	32,214	36,811	38,063	38,304	54,240	52,528	53,714	51,814	51,843	49,821
York . . .	23,692	26,422	29,527	34,461	38,321	40,359	45,385	50,761	61,789	66,984	77,793
Preston . .	11,887	17,065	24,575	33,112	50,131	69,542	82,985	85,428	96,537	107,573	112,982
Cambridge .	13,360	13,802	14,142	20,917	24,453	27,815	26,361	34,029	35,363	36,983	38,393
Oxford . .	15,124	15,337	16,364	20,432	23,834	27,843	27,560	34,514	40,872	45,741	49,413

* In 1851, 1,106,558 males, and 1,255,678 females. † 1861 and 1871: parliamentary limits of the boroughs.

In Great Britain, Ireland, and islands, in 1901, 20,163,309 males, and 21,441,911 females; in London, 2,015,899 males and 2,520,641 females. Total in employment (over 10 years of age) in England and Wales, 1891, 22,053,857; 1901, 25,322,834.

[The returns for 1891 and 1901 are taken from the *Preliminary Report* of the census.]

Estimates of the population of the United Kingdom are given in the annual reports of the Registrars-general. London registration district, 4,411,271, 29 March, 1896.

IRELAND.

Dublin, 1881, 249,602; 1891, 254,709; 1901, 289,108. Belfast, 1881, 208,122; 1891, 255,896; 1901, 348,965. Cork, 1881, 80,124; 1891, 75,070; 1901, 75,978. Waterford, 1891, 21,693; 1901, 26,743. Londonderry, 1891, 32,893; 1901, 39,873. Limerick, 1891, 37,072; 1901, 38,085.

POPULATION OF THE CHIEF CITIES OF THE WORLD.

See separate Articles.

Cities.	*Inhabitants.*
Adelaide, 1901 . . .	160,691
Alexandria, Egypt, 1901 .	319,766
Amsterdam, 1901 . .	520,800
Antwerp, 1900 . . .	285,600
Athens, 1896 . . .	111,486
Baltimore, U.S., 1901 .	541,000
Barcelona, 1897 . .	509,589
Basle, 1901 . . .	111,009
Belgrade, 1901 . . .	72,000
Berlin, 1901 . . .	1,901,567
Berne, 1901 . . .	64,864
Bologna, 1901 . . .	152,009
Bombay, 1901 . . .	821,764
Bordeaux, 1901 . . .	257,471
Boston, U.S., 1900 . .	560,892
Bremen, 1900 . . .	163,297
Breslau, 1900 . . .	1,697,719
Brooklyn, 1890 . . .	806,343
Brussels, 1900 . . .	211,429
Buda-Pesth, 1900 . .	732,222
Buffalo, 1900 . . .	352,387
Cadiz, 1897 . . .	70,177
Cairo, 1900 . . .	570,062
Calcutta (including suburbs), 1901 . . .	1,121,664
Canton, 1890 . . about	1,600,000
Chicago, 1900 . . .	1,698,575
Christiania, 1900 . .	227,626
Cincinnati, 1900 . . .	405,000
Cleveland, 1900 . . .	381,768
Cologne, 1900 . . .	372,229
Constantinople, 1901 *estmd.*	1,125,000
Copenhagen, 1901 . .	378,235
Dresden, 1900 . . .	397,300
Florence, 1901 . . .	204,950
Frankfort-on-Main, 1900 .	288,489
Geneva, 1901 . . .	105,139
Genoa, 1901 . . .	234,800
Ghent, 1900 . . .	160,949
Hague, 1900 . . .	212,211
Hamburg, 1900 . . .	705,738
Hanover, 1900 . . .	235,666

Cities.		*Inhabitants.*
Königsberg, 1900		187,897
Leipsic, 1900		455,089
Liége, 1900		173,706
Lille, 1901		215,431
Lima, 1896		298,106
Lisbon, 1900		357,000
Lubeck, 1900		82,098
Lyons, 1901		453,155
Madras, 1901		509,397
Madrid, 1897		512,150
Malaga, 1897		125,559
Marseilles, 1901	*estimated*	494,769
Melbourne, 1901		493,956
Messina, 1901		149,823
Mexico, 1900		329,774
Milan, 1901		491,460
Montreal, 1901	*nearly*	350,000
Moscow, 1900		1,023,817
Munich, 1900		499,959
Nankin	*estimated*	1,000,000
Nantes, 1901		128,349
Naples, 1901		563,751
New Orleans, 1900		300,000
New York (including Brooklyn), 1900		3,444,675
Odessa, 1897		404,651
Oporto, 1900		172,421
Palermo, 1901		310,352
Paris, &c., 1901		2,660,550
Pekin, 1874		1.648,814
Philadelphia, 1900		1,293,697
Pittsburg, 1900		321,616
Prague, 1900		389,741
Quebec, 1901		1,620,974
Rio Janeiro, 1890		876,884
Rome, 1901		463,000
Rotterdam, 1900		332,185
Rouen, 1901		115,914
San Francisco, 1900		360,000
Santiago (Chili), 1899		320,638
Seville, 1897		146,205
Smyrna, 1901	*estimated*	201,016
Stockholm, 1900		300,624
St. Etienne, 1901		146,671
St. Louis, 1900		623,000
St. Petersburg, 1900		1,439,375
Stuttgart, 1900		176,705
Sydney, 1901		438,000
Teheran	*estimated*	210,000
Tien-tsin, 1887		950,000
Tokio, 1899		1,440,121
Toronto, 1681		207,971
Toulouse, 1901		147,696
Tunis	*estimated*	150,000
Turin, 1901		335,639
Upsal, 1900		22,855
Utrecht, 1900		104,194
Valencia, 1897		204,768
Valparaiso, 1899		143,022
Venice, 1901		151,841
Vienna, 1900		1,656,662
Warsaw, 1897		638,208
Washington, U.S., 1900		278,718

PORCELAIN, see *Pottery*.

PORPHYROGENITUS, "born in the purple," a term applied to emperors of the east, born while their fathers were reigning.

PORT ARTHUR, China. See *Corea*, Nov. 1894; *Russia*, 1898. Russian conference held here, July, 1903.

PORT BRETON, an isle near New Caledonia, South Pacific.

In 1877 the marquis Du Breil de Rays purchased of the king Maragano a quantity of land on which to found a colony. Glowing prospectuses were issued in France, a company was formed, and, the scheme being favoured by the legitimists, a large number of shares were purchased and much money received. Other speculating companies were formed, and colonial government officers nominated. In spite of warning and prohibition several vessels sailed in 1879 with emigrants to meet with misery, disease, and, to a large extent, with death. A few who had been landed in New Caledonia got back to France and published an account of their sufferings. The marquis and some of his associates were brought to trial 27 Nov. 1883; he was sentenced to four years' imprisonment and a fine of 3000 francs, his associates to shorter imprisonment, 2 Jan. 1884; on appeal, sentence confirmed, 14 March, 1884.

PORTE, or SUBLIME PORTE, official name of the court of the sultan of Turkey. Mostasem, the last of the Abbasside caliphs (1243-58), fixed in the threshold of the principal entrance to his palace at Bagdad a piece of the black stone adored at Mecca, and thus this entrance became the "porte" by eminence, and the title of his court. The sultans, successors of the caliphs, assumed the title. —*Bouillet*.

PORTEOUS MOB. Capt. Porteous, at Edinburgh, on 15 April, 1736, commanded the guard at the execution of Wilson, a smuggler, who had saved the life of a fellow criminal, by springing upon the soldiers around them, and by main force keeping them back, while his companion fled. This excited great commiseration, and the spectators pelted the guard with stones. Fearing a rescue, Porteous ordered his men to fire upon the mob, and seventeen persons were killed or wounded. He was found guilty of murder, 22 June, 1736; but the queen granted him a reprieve (the king being then in Hanover). The people, at night, broke open the prison, took out Porteous, and hanged him on a dyer's sign-post, in the Grass-market, 7 Sept. 1736. None of the rioters were ever detected.

PORTER. Dr. Ashe says that this malt liquor obtained its appellation on account of its having been drunk by porters in the city of London, about 1730. The number of licensed brewers in 1850, in England, was 2257; in Scotland, 154; and in Ireland, 96—total, 2507. On 17 Oct. 1814, at Meux's brewhouse two large vats of porter burst, destroying neighbouring houses. Several lives were lost; and the loss was between 8000 and 9000 barrels.

Chief Brewers.	*Barrels.*
In 1760.	
Calvert & Co. brewed	74,734
Whitbread	63,408
Truman	60,140
Sir William Calvert	52,785
Gifford & Co.	41,410
Lady Parsons	34,008
Thrale	30,740
Huck & Co.	29,615
Harman	28,017
Meux & Co.	10,012
In 1815.	
Barclay & Perkins	337,621
Meux, Reid & Co.	282,104
Truman, Hanbury & Co.	272,162
Whitbread & Co.	261,018
In 1840.	
Henry Meux & Co.	229,100
F. Calvert & Co.	219,333
Combe, Delafield & Co.	105,081
Barclay, Perkins & Co.	361,321
Truman, Hanbury & Co.	263,235
Whitbread & Co.	218,828
Reid and Co.	196,442
Combe, Delafield & Co.	177,542
Felix Calvert & Co.	136,387
Sir Henry Meux & Co.	116,547

PORTERAGE ACT, regulating the charge for porterage of small parcels, passed 1799.

The Fellowship of Free Porters established in London in the 13th century, with exclusive privileges, relating to grain, &c., much reduced by the act of parliament of 1872 and the construction of docks. The institution was gradually dying out. After urgent demands and much delay, the distribution of the accumulated funds and property amongst the members was ordered by the rulers, 12 Oct. 1893. The fellowship disbanded by the court of common council, June, 1894.

Final payment of assets, 10,379*l*. 4*s*. 7*d*., distributed to 495 members, 18 Dec. 1894.

PORT HAMILTON, see *Corea*.

PORT JACKSON (New South Wales), thirteen miles north of Botany Bay, was so named by capt. Cook in 1770; see *Sydney*. Here the duke of Edinburgh was shot by O'Farrell, a Fenian, 12 March, 1868, but soon recovered. The assassin was hanged, 21 April.

PORTLAND ADMINISTRATIONS. The first was the "coalition ministry," of which

William Henry Cavendish, duke of Portland,* as first lord of the treasury, was the head. It obtained the name of the "coalition" ministry, and included lord North with Mr. Fox, formerly inveterate opponents. Formed 5 April, 1783; dissolved by Mr. Pitt's coming into power, Dec. same year.

FIRST ADMINISTRATION.

Duke of Portland, *first lord of the treasury.*
Viscount Stormont, *president of the council.*
Earl of Carlisle, *privy seal.*
Frederick, lord North, and Charles James Fox, *home and foreign secretaries.*
Lord John Cavendish, *chancellor of the exchequer.*
Viscount Keppel, *admiralty.*
Viscount Townshend, *ordnance.*
Lord Loughborough, *chief commissioner of great seal.*
Charles Townshend, Edmund Burke, Richard Fitzpatrick, Richard B. Sheridan, &c.

SECOND ADMINISTRATION, 25 March, 1807.

Earl Camden, *lord president.*
Lord Eldon, *lord chancellor.*
Earl of Westmorland, *lord privy seal.*
Hon. Spencer Perceval, lord Hawkesbury (afterwards earl of Liverpool), Mr. Canning, and viscount Castlereagh (afterwards marquis of Londonderry), *home, foreign, and colonial secretaries.*
Earl Bathurst and Mr. Dundas, *boards of trade and control.*
Lord Mulgrave, *admiralty.*
Earl of Chatham, *ordnance.*

PORTLAND CEMENT, first mentioned in a patent granted to Joseph Aspden, a bricklayer of Leeds, 1824. His son made the true cement at Northfleet. Its value as a building material was established by Mr. John Grant's tests, 1859-71. Portland cement concrete was used by Mr. E. A. Bernay in 1867.

PORTLAND ISLE (off Dorset), the English Gibraltar. Fortified before 1142. Portland castle was built by Henry VIII. about 1536. Off this peninsula a naval engagement commenced between the English and Dutch, 18 Feb. 1653, which continued for three days. The English destroyed eleven Dutch men-of-war and thirty merchantmen. Van Tromp was admiral of the Dutch, and Blake of the English.—Here is found the noted freestone used for building our finest edifices. The Portland lights were erected 1716 and in 1789. The pier, with nearly half a mile square of land, was washed into the sea in Feb. 1792. Prince Albert laid the first stone of the Portland breakwater, 25 July, 1849, and the last stone was laid by the prince of Wales, 10 Aug. 1872. Mr. James Rendel, the first chief engineer, was succeeded on his death in 1856 by Mr. (aft. sir) John Coode. The breakwater and other harbour works cost 1,033,600*l*. exclusive of convict labour. The Portland prison was established in 1848. A mutiny among the convicts here in Sept. 1858, was promptly suppressed. The king visits the prison and Whitehead's torpedo works, 4 April, 1902.

PORTLAND (or BARBERINI) **VASE.** This beautiful specimen of Greek art (composed of a glass-like-substance, with figures and devices raised on it in white enamel; height 10 inches; diameter in the broadest part, 7; with a handle on each side) was discovered about the middle of the 16th century, in a marble sarcophagus in a sepulchre at a place called Monte del Grano, about 2½ miles from Rome. The sepulchre was supposed to have been that of the Roman emperor, Alexander Severus (222-235), and his mother Mammæa, and the vase is supposed to have been the cinerary urn of one of these royal personages. It was placed in the palace of the Barberini family, at Rome, where it remained till 1770, when it was purchased by sir William Hamilton, from whose possession it passed to that of the duchess of Portland, 1787; at the sale of her effects, it is said to have been bought by the then duke of Portland, who, in 1810, deposited it (on loan) in the British museum. On 27 Feb. 1845, this vase was smashed to pieces with a stone by a man named William Lloyd; it has been skilfully repaired, and is now shown to the public in a special room. Josiah Wedgwood made a mould of it, and took a number of casts.

* Born 1738; became lord chamberlain, 1765; lord lieutenant of Ireland, 1782; premier, 1783; home secretary, 1794; lord president, 1801; premier again, 1807; died 1809, when Mr. Spencer Perceval became premier.

PORT MAHON, see *Minorca.*

PORTO BELLO (S. America), discovered by Columbus, 2 Nov. 1502, was taken by Morgan the buccaneer in 1668; by the British under admiral Vernon, from the Spaniards, 21 Nov. 1739, and the fortifications destroyed. Before the abolition of the trade by the galleons, in 1748, it was the great mart for the rich commerce of Peru and Chili.

PORTO FERRAJO, capital of Elba (*which see*); built and fortified by Cosmo I., duke of Florence, in 1548. The fortifications were not finished till 1628, when Cosmo II. completed them with great magnificence; see *France.*

PORTO NOVO (S. India). Here sir Eyre Coote, with about 9500 men and 55 light field-pieces, skilfully defeated Hyder Ali, ruler of the Carnatic, with 80,000 men and some heavy cannon, 1 July, 1781. Hyder lost about 10,000, the British 587 killed and wounded. PORTO NOVO, W. Africa, a French settlement on the coast of Dahomey, *which see* (1890 *et seq.*).

PORTO RICO, a West India island, belonging to Spain; discovered by Columbus in 1493. Attacks on it by Drake and Hawkins repulsed, 1595. Revolt suppressed, 1823. Slavery abolished, 23 March, 1873. Ceded to United States, N.A., 10 Dec. 1898; see *Spanish American War.* Fearful hurricane, many deaths, 7 Aug. 1899; see *West Indies.* Mr. Wm. Hunt appointed governor, 30 Aug. 1901; fatal rioting *re* election registrations, reported, 29 Oct. 1902.

PORT PHILLIP (New S. Wales), original name of the colony of Victoria (*which see*).

PORTRAIT GALLERY, &c., see *National Portrait Gallery* and *Composite Portraits.*

The Society of Portrait Painters held its first exhibition at the Institute of Painters in Water Colours in Piccadilly, July, 1891. The society includes the most eminent artists. Annual autumn exhibitions.

The formation of a "British Museum of Portraits" (photographs) was proposed by Mr. James Glaisher in 1864, and partly begun. The undertaking resumed mainly by the exertions of Mr. Glaisher and the Amateur Photographic association, and a collection of portraits deposited in the art department at South Kensington museum, July, 1891

PORTREEVE (derived from Saxon words signifying the governor of a port or harbour). The chief magistrate of London was originally so styled; but Richard I. appointed two bailiffs, and afterwards London had mayors. *Camden;* see *Mayors.*

PORT ROYAL (Nova Scotia), capital of the French colony, Acadie, founded in 1604; after having been taken and restored several times, it was finally acquired by the British in 1710, and named Annapolis.

PORT ROYAL (Jamaica), once a considerable town, was destroyed by earthquakes in 1602 and 1692; laid in ashes by fire in 1702; reduced to ruins by an inundation of the sea in 1722; and destroyed by a hurricane in 1774. After these calamities, the custom-house and public offices were removed to Kingston. Port Royal was again greatly damaged by fire in 1750; by another awful storm in 1784; and by a devastating fire in July, 1815; in 1850 it suffered by cholera.

PORT ROYAL DES CHAMPS (near Paris) was a French Cistercian convent, founded by Odo, bishop of Paris, at the wish of king Philip Augustus, 1204. Having fallen into decay, it was revived and reformed in 1608 by Angelica Arnauld. In 1625 the increased community removed to Paris. The Port Royal des Champs, in 1656, became the retreat of the Arnaulds, Tillemont, Pascal, Lancelot, and other eminent Jansenists, who devoted themselves to education, and produced the Port Royal grammars, logic, and other works. This institution was condemned by the pope in 1709, and the buildings were pulled down, and tombs desecrated, by the order of Louis XIV., in 1710. The Port Royal at Paris was suppressed, with other monasteries, in 1790.

PORTSMOUTH (Hampshire), the most considerable haven for men-of-war, and most strongly fortified place in England. The dock, arsenal, and storehouses were established in the reign of Henry VIII. See *Population*.

The French under D'Annebaut attempted to destroy Portsmouth, but were defeated by viscount Lisle, in the then finest war-ship in the world, the *Great Harry* 1545
Here George Villiers, duke of Buckingham, was assassinated by Felton . . . . 23 Aug. 1628
Admiral Byng (see *Byng*) on a very dubious sentence was shot at Portsmouth . . 14 March, 1757
The dockyard was fired, the loss estimated at 400,000*l.* . . . . 3 July, 1760
Another fire occasioned loss of 100,000*l.* 27 July, 1770
[The French were suspected both times, but there was no actual proof.]
Fire caused by James Aitken (John the painter) 7 Dec. 1776; executed . . . . 10 March, 1777
Royal George (*which see*) sunk . . . 29 Aug. 1782
Grand naval mock engagement and parade of the fleet, the king being present, 22 to 25 June, 1773, and . . . . 30 June, 1794
Another great fire occurred . . . . . 7 Dec. 1776
The king of the French with a fleet arrives at Portsmouth, see *France* . . . . 6 Oct. 1844
A great naval review was held . . 25 April, 1856
Visited by a French fleet amid great rejoicings, 29 Aug.–1 Sept. 1865
Easter Monday volunteer review, &c., very successful 13 April, 1868
Naval review at Spithead before the shah of Persia. 23 June, 1873
Explosion at Priddy's hard; 5 killed . 5 May, 1883
See *Navy of England*, 1887, 1889, 1890, 1891.
The emperor William II. visited Portsmouth, 5 Aug. 1889, and . . . . 6 Aug. 1890
The prince of Wales opens the new town-hall 9 Aug. ,,
The Amphitheatre music-hall burnt (cost, 10,000*l.*) 25 Dec. ,,
The *Royal Arthur* and the *Royal Sovereign* launched by the queen, see *Navy* . . . 26 Feb. 1891
Visit of the French fleet, see *France* . 19–26 Aug. ,,
Visit of the Italian fleet, see *Italy* . . July, 1895
Visit of the czar and czarina . . . 4, 5 Oct. 1896
Lord Roberts presented with the freedom, 6 Dec. 1898 [and with that of the borough, 23 Oct. 1902].
The empress Frederick opens the Diamond Jubilee block of the Sailors' Rest . . . 30 Dec. 1898
The duke and duchess of York open 2 blocks of the new Portsmouth hospital . . 27 Feb. 1899
Messrs. Vosper & Co.'s engineering works, Broad-street, burnt . . . . . . 9 July, ,,
Demonstration and banquet in honour of capt. Lambton and the naval brigade of H.M.S. *Powerful* (see *South African War*) . . 24 April, 1900
Theatre Royal (3000 seats) opened . . 6 Aug. ,,
Lord Howe opens a naval and military exhibition, 16 June, 1902
Captain Percy Scott and officers and crew of the *Terrible* warmly welcomed on return from campaigns in S. Africa and China, 1899 *et seq.*, 19–23 Sept. ,,
Explosion at Priddy's yard, building damaged, 6 Nov. ,,
Statue of queen Victoria unveiled . . 8 July, 1903
United States squadron arrive under adm. Cotton, 7 July, 1903; banquet of 500 American and 300 British sailors and marines; statue of queen Victoria in the Town-hall-square unveiled; illumination of Channel squadron and U.S. ships at Spithead, 8 July (see *Navy*), leave . 17 July ,,
House in which Chas. Dickens was born, bought by corporation (1125*l.*) . . . . . 29 Sept. ,,
King and queen of Italy arrive here on their visit to king Edward VII. . . . . . 17 Nov. ,,

PORTUGAL, the ancient Lusitania. The present name is derived from Porto Callo, the original appellation of Oporto. After a nine years' struggle, under Viriathes, a brave able leader, the Lusitanians submitted to the Roman arms about 137 B.C. Portugal underwent the same changes as Spain on the fall of the Roman empire. There are in Portugal two universities, that of Coimbra, founded in 1308, and the smaller one of Evora, founded in 1533. Lisbon has also its royal academy, and the small town of Thomar has an academy of sciences; but, in general, literature is at a low ebb in Portugal. The poet Camoens, called the Virgil of his country, and author of the *Lusiad* (1569), translated into English by Mickle, was a native of Lisbon. Population of the kingdom and colonies, 31 Dec. 1863, 8,037,194; in 1872, kingdom on the continent, with Madeira and Azores, 4,390,589; colonies, 3,258,140; in 1878, kingdom and colonies, 8,031,831; 1881, kingdom, 4,708,178; 1 Dec. 1900, 5,428,800. Estimated revenue, 1890-1, 8,817,040*l.*; 1893-4, 9,146,674*l.*; expenditure, 1890-1, 9,574,150*l.*; 1893-4, 10,271,637*l.*; 1897-8, revenue, 52,865,478 reis; expenditure, 55,563,304 reis; 1901-02, revenue, 53,269,000 reis; expenditure, 55,239,000 reis. The constitution granted in 1826 was revised in 1852.

Settlement of the Alains and Visigoths here . . 472
Conquered by the Moors 713
The kings of Asturias subdue some Saracen chiefs, and Alfonso III. establishes bishops . . . 900
The Moors, conquered by Alfonso VI. the Valiant, of Castile, assisted by many other princes and volunteers; Henry of Besançon (a relative of the duke of Burgundy and king of France), very eminent; Alfonso bestowed upon him Theresa, his natural daughter, and Portugal as her marriage portion, which he was to hold of him as count . . . 1095
Alfonso Henriquez defeats five Moorish kings, and proclaimed king; see *Ourique* . . 25 July, 1139
Assisted by a fleet of Crusaders on their way to the Holy Land, he takes Lisbon from the Moors, 25 Oct. 1147
Part of Algarve taken from the Moors by Sancho I. 1189
Reign of Dionysius I. or Denis, father of his country, who builds 44 cities or towns in Portugal . 1279
University of Coimbra founded 1308
Military orders of Christ and St. James instituted, 1279 and 1325
Iñes de Castro murdered 1355
John I., surnamed the Great, carries his arms into Africa 1415
Maritime discoveries 1419–30
Madeira and the Canaries seized 1420

Code of laws digested 1425
Lisbon made the capital . . . . . about 1433
Prince Henry, the navigator, dies 1460
Passage to the East Indies by the Cape of Good Hope discovered by Vasco da Gama . 20 Nov. 1497
Discovery of the Brazils 1499
Brazil discovered by Cabral . . . . April, 1500
Camoens, author of the *Lusiad*, born . . about 1520
The Inquisition established 1526
University of Evora founded . . . . 1451 or 1533
African expedition; king Sebastian defeated and slain in the battle of Alcazar . . . Aug. 1578
The kingdom seized by Philip II. of Spain . . . 1580
The Dutch seize the Portuguese settlements in India, 1602-20
The Portuguese throw off the yoke, and place John, duke of Braganza, on the throne . . Dec. 1640
The Portuguese defeat the Spaniards at Villa Viciosa, 1665; war ended by the treaty of Lisbon . . 1668
Methuen treaty (*which see*) 1703
The great earthquake destroys Lisbon . 1 Nov. 1755
Joseph I. narrowly escapes death by assassins . 1758
[Some of the first families were tortured to death; their very names being forbidden to be mentioned; the innocence of many was soon afterwards made manifest; the Jesuits were also expelled.]
Joseph, having no son, obtains a dispensation from the pope to enable his daughter and brother to intermarry, which took place . . 6 June, 1760
The Spaniards and French invade Portugal, which is saved by the English . . . 1762 and 1763
John, prince of Brazil, marries his aunt, Maria Francesca 1777
Regency of John (afterwards king), owing to the lunacy of queen Maria 1792
War with Spain, 3 March; peace . . 6 June, 1801
Treaty between France and Spain for the partition of Portugal, Oct.; French invasion; Junot arrives at Lisbon, 27 Nov.; the court sail for Brazil, 29 Nov. 1807
Rise of the Portuguese; several times defeated, June and July; arrival of Wellington at Oporto, July; he defeats Junot at Vimiera, 21 Aug.; convention of Cintra confirmed . . 30 Aug. 1808
Oporto taken by Soult . . . 29 March, 1809
Almeida taken by Massena . . . 27 Aug. 1810
Massena defeated at Busaco . . . 27 Sept. ,,
Wellington secures the lines of Torres Vedras Oct. ,,
Massena defeated at Fuentes de Onoro; retreats, 5 May, 1811
The British parliament grants the sufferers by war in Portugal 100,000*l*. . . . . . ,,
Portugal cedes Guiana to France 1814
Union of Portugal and Brazil 1815
Revolution begins in Oporto . . . 29 Aug. 1820
Constitutional junta established . . . 1 Oct. ,,
Return of the court . . . . . 4 July, 1821
Independence of Brazil; the prince regent made emperor; see *Brazil* . . . . 12 Oct. 1822
The king modifies the constitution . . 5 June, 1823
Disturbances at Lisbon; Miguel departs . 1-9 May, 1824
Treaty with Brazil . . . . . 29 Aug. 1825
Death of John VI. . . . . . 10 March, 1826
Dom Pedro grants a constitutional charter, and confirms the regency . . . . 26 April, ,,
He relinquishes the throne in favour of his daughter, Donna Maria da Gloria . . . 2 May, ,,
Miguel takes oath of fealty at Vienna . . 4 Oct. ,,
Marquis of Chaves' insurrection at Lisbon in favour of Dom Miguel . . . . . 6 Oct. ,,
Dom Miguel and Donna Maria betrothed . 29 Oct. ,,
Portugal solicits the assistance of Great Britain, 3 Dec.; departure of the first British auxiliary troops for Portugal . . . . . 17 Dec. ,,
Bank of Lisbon stops payment . . . 7 Dec. 1827
Dom Miguel made regent; he arrives in London, 30 Dec. 1827; takes the oath at Lisbon 22 Feb. 1828
The British armament quits Portugal, 28 April; foreign ministers withdraw . . . 3 May, ,,
Sir John Doyle, a partisan of Donna Maria, arrested, 13 June, ,,
Dom Miguel assumes the title of king . 4 July, ,,
He dissolves the three estates . . . 12 July, ,,
His troops take Madeira . . . . 24 Aug. ,,
Release of sir John Doyle . . . . 7 Sept. ,,
The queen Donna Maria arrives in London 6 Oct. ,,
Miguel's expedition against Terceira defeated, 11 Aug. 1829
Duke of Palmella appointed regent . . March, 1830
Dom Pedro arrives in England . . . 16 June, 1831
Insurrection in Portugal in favour of the queen; more than 300 lives lost . . . 21 Aug. ,,
Dom Pedro's expedition sails from Belle-isle, 9 Feb.; at Terceira proclaims himself regent, 2 April; takes Oporto . . . . . . 8 July, 1832
The Miguelites attack Oporto, and are defeated with considerable loss on both sides . 19 Sept. ,,
Mount Cavello taken . . . . . 9 April, 1833
Admiral Napier takes Dom Miguel's squadron off Cape St. Vincent . . . . . 5 July, ,,
Lisbon evacuated by the duke of Cadaval; the queen proclaimed, 24 July; enters Lisbon, 22 Sept. ,,
After various conflicts Dom Miguel capitulates to the Pedroites, and Santarem surrenders, 26 May; Dom Miguel embarks at Evora for Genoa, 31 May, 1834
Massacres take place at Lisbon . . . 9 June, ,,
The cortes declare the queen of age . . 15 Sept. ,,
Dom Pedro dies . . . . . . 24 Sept. ,,
Oporto wine company abolished . . . . . ,,
Prince Augustus (duke of Leuchtenberg) prince consort; married, 1 Dec. 1834; dies . 28 March, 1835
The queen marries Ferdinand of Saxe-Coburg, 9 April, 1836
Revolution at Lisbon . . . . . 9 Aug. ,,
Another outbreak there . . . . . 8 Nov. ,,
The duke of Terceira attempts to restore Dom Pedro's charter . . . . . 18 Aug. 1837
He and Saldanha fail, and embark for England, 18 Sept. ,,
Oporto wine company re-established . 7 April, 1838
The northern province in a state of insurrection about this time . . . . . 20 April, 1846
The duke of Palmella resigns . . . . 31 Oct. ,,
Action at Evora, the queen's troops defeat the insurgent forces . . . . . 31 Oct. ,,
British squadron under admiral Parker arrives in the Tagus, at the queen's request . 31 Oct. ,,
Palmella banished . . . . . . 26 Nov. ,,
Marquis of Saldanha defeats count Bomfinn at Torres Vedras . . . . . . 22 Dec. ,,
The insurgents enter Oporto . . . 7 Jan. 1847
London conference: England, France, and Spain determine to assist the queen of Portugal to terminate the civil war . . . . 21 May, ,,
Submission of Sá da Bandeira . . . 11 June, ,,
A Spanish force enters Oporto, and the junta capitulates . . . . 26 June, ,,
An American squadron in the Tagus to enforce claims against the Portuguese . . 22 June, 1850
Military insurrection, headed by the duke of Saldanha, who, being outstripped in his march on Santarem by the king of Portugal, flees northward 10 April, 1851
Oporto declares for the duke, who had left the city for Vigo to embark for England; but is called back by the insurgents . . . 24 April, ,,
Saldanha's entry into Oporto . . . 29 April, ,,
The conde de Thomar, prime minister, resigns; arrives in England . . . . 16 May, ,,
Saldanha, prime minister . . . . 23 May, ,,
Dom Miguel marries the princess Adelaide of Lowenstein-Rosenberg . . . . 24 Sept. ,,
Revision of the charter by the cortes sanctioned by the queen; the prince royal takes the oath to the constitution . . . . . 18 July, 1852
Conversion of the public debt . . . 18 Dec. ,,
Death of the queen Maria II. . . . 15 Nov. 1853
King-consort recognised as regent . . 19 Dec. ,,
The young king visits England . . . June, 1854
The slaves on royal domains freed . . 30 Dec. ,,
The king visits France . . . . . May, 1855
Inauguration of the king . . . . 16 Sept. ,,
Resignation of Saldanha ministry . . 5 June, 1856
First Portuguese railway (from Lisbon to Santarem) opened . . . . 26 Oct. ,,
Fever rages in Lisbon; the king very active in relieving the sufferers . . Oct. and Nov. 1857
The French emigrant ship for negroes, *Charles-et-Georges*, seized . . . . . 29 Nov. ,,
Anger of the French government; its ultimatum sent, 13 Oct.; and ships of war to the Tagus; the vessel restored (see *Charles-et-Georges*) . 25 Oct. 1858
Death of the duke of Terceira, prime minister, April 26; succeeded by the senhor Aguiar, May 2, who resigns . . . . 2 July, 1860
Death of the king, Pedro V.; succeeded by his brother the duke of Oporto . . . 11 Nov. 1861

Death of John, the king's brother 29 Dec. 1861

The law of succession altered in favour of the king's sisters 3 Jan. 1862

The duc de Loulé becomes minister Feb. ,,

The king married to Princess Maria Pia of Savoy by proxy, at Lisbon 6 Oct. ,,

Elections: majority for the government Nov. ,,

Birth of Dom Carlos, heir to the throne 28 Sept. 1863

Ministerial changes Jan. 1864

Death of the celebrated statesman the duke of Palmella 2 April, ,,

Free-trade measures introduced 1 June, ,,

Frontier treaty with Spain concluded 29 Sept. ,,

U.S. vessels *Niagara* and *Sacramento* in the Tagus fired on, through suspicion of their sailing after the confederate vessel *Stonewall*, 27 March; the difficulty with the U.S. government arranged, 7 April, 1865

The premier, de Loulé, resigns; marquis Sá da Bandeira forms a ministry 17 April, ,,

Constitutional privileges granted to the colonies, May, ,,

Another prince born 31 July, ,,

New ministry formed; Aguiar premier 4 Sept. ,,

The international exhibition at Oporto opened by the king 18 Sept. ,,

The king visits England and France Dec. ,,

General Prim enters Portugal, 20 Jan.; ordered to depart 17 Feb. 1866

Death of Dom Miguel, the ex-king 14 Nov. ,,

The king and queen of Spain visit Lisbon 11 Dec. ,,

King and queen at the Paris exhibition, July–Aug. 1867

New ministry under count d'Avila 5 Jan. 1868

under Sá da Bandeira 21 July, ,,

under the duke de Saldanha 7 Jan. 1869

under the duke de Loulé 11 Aug ,,

Violent opposition of Saldanha; ordered back to Paris as ambassador there; he resigns Dec. ,,

Cortes dissolved Jan. 1870

Saldanha heads a military insurrection; seizes the royal palace; forms a new ministry 19 May, ,,

Neutrality in the French war proclaimed July, ,,

Manifestation against Saldanha in Lisbon and Oporto 2 Aug. ,,

The French republic recognized Sept. ,,

New ministry under the bishop of Vizeu, 30 Oct. ,,

New ministry under the marquis d'Avila, 30 Jan.; under Fontes Pereira de Mello 13 Sept. 1871

Great fire at Lisbon 13 June, 1872

Conspiracy against the government; officers in the army arrested about 26 Aug. ,,

Death of Joaquim A. Aguiar, statesman (see 1860, 1865) 26 May, 1874

The duke of Coimbra visits England Aug. 1875

The prince of Wales at Lisbon 1 May, 1876

Financial crisis: banks of Oporto and Portugal suspend payment; confidence soon returns, about 19-24 Aug. ,,

Death of the duke de Saldanha (buried in state at Lisbon) 21 Nov. ,,

Marquis d'Avila forms a new ministry 5 March, 1877

Resigns after vote of censure; new ministry formed under Fontes Pereira de Mello 29 Jan. 1878

Ministry resigns, 30 May, new one formed by sen. A. J. Braamcamp 1 July, 1879

Great demonstration in honour of Camoens and Vasco da Gama at Lisbon June, 1880

Discussion in the chambers respecting treaty with Great Britain, respecting Lourenço Marques (*which see*), E. coast of Africa; ministry resigns; succeeded by sen. Sampayo 21-26 March, 1881

Elections; majority in favour of ministry 21 Aug. ,,

The kings of Portugal and Spain open a new railway between Lisbon and Madrid 8 Oct. ,,

Visit of the king and queen of Spain 10 Jan. *et seq.* 1882

National art exhibition at Lisbon opened about 15 April, ,,

Reform bill introduced abolishing hereditary peerage end of Feb. 1883

The king and queen visit Madrid 22 May, ,,

Ministry reconstructed by Fontes Pereira de Mello 20 Oct. ,,

Circular affirming Portuguese rights over the Congo issued Oct. ,,

The crown prince returned from a visit to England 21 Dec. ,,

Government bill for reform of constitution adopted by the deputies 8 Feb. 1884

Mr. John Dixon's claims on the Guimarães railway company for compensation for their taking the Minho railway, constructed by him; complaint of judicial delays; British intervention; discussed May, 1884

Death of the king consort Ferdinand aged 69, 15 Dec. 1885

The de Mello ministry resigns, succeeded by that of senhor José de Castro 19 Feb. 1886

The king visits Great Britain, Denmark, and the continent (warmly received) Aug.–Sept. 1886; returns to Lisbon 26 Sept. ,,

Strike and riots at Oporto (*which see*), about 30 May, 1889

Dispute respecting the Delagoa railway (*which see*) June *et seq.* ,,

The wine trade much disturbed by bounties to wine-growers; granted by the chamber, 12 June, ,,

Death of king Luis I., 19 Oct.; funeral 26 Oct. ,,

British remonstrances on Portuguese encroachments in East Africa (see *Zambesi*) Nov., Dec. ,,

The king Carlos inaugurated 28 Dec. ,,

The king opens the cortes with a firm, temperate speech respecting E. Africa 2 Jan. 1890

Telegrams: lord Salisbury demands the immediate recall of the Portuguese forces from places in Africa under British protection or influence, 5 Jan. ,,

Sen. Barros Gomes accedes, under conditions; delays, 6—8 Jan. Ultimatum from lord Salisbury requiring immediate submission, threatening suspension of diplomatic relations; the council of state accede to all the British demands, under protest 11, 12 Jan. ,,

Excitement in Lisbon and the provinces against the British, promptly suppressed; about 63 arrests, 13–16 Jan.; the de Castro ministry resigns; sen. Serpa Pimental forms a cabinet; sen. Hintze Ribeiro, foreign minister 14 Jan. ,,

Sen. Serpa Pimental informs the chamber that he submits to England, who has might while Portugal has right 15 Jan. ,,

The Blue-book containing correspondence between lord Salisbury and sen. Barros Gomes, 22 June, 1887, to 20 Jan. 1890, published 12 Feb. ,,

Capt. Neves Ferreira resigns, about 18 Jan. ,,

Manifesto of the republican party about 19 Jan. ,,

The cortes dissolved 20 Jan. ,,

National defence fund started, 23 Jan.; 55,000*l.* received up to 4 March (nearly 33,000*l.* subscribed by the king and royal family), about 11 March, ,,

Decrees respecting public meetings, liberty of the press, judicial reforms, &c., issued 7 April, ,,

The new cortes opened by the king; friendly relations with Great Britain, reported 19 April, ,,

Major Serpa Pinto arrives at Lisbon, 20 April; made one of the king's adjutants 27 April, ,,

Anglo-Portuguese agreement respecting Africa, settled in London 20 Aug. ,,

Resignation of sen. Serpa Pimental ministry, 17 Sept. ,,

Gen. Chrysostomo d'Abreue-Sousa forms a ministry, 13 Oct., opposed to the proposed convention; cortes closed 15 Oct. ,,

A *modus vivendi* agreed on for six months; the agreement of 20 Aug. withdrawn; the *status quo ante* maintained, 10 Nov.; signed 14 Nov. ,,

East Africa: Capt. Paiva and the Bihé expedition resisted on the river Caquiema; fighting with the natives, with great loss 1 Nov. ,,

Celebration of the 250th anniversary of the re-establishment of the monarchy 1 Dec. ,,

For the disputes with the S. Africa company respecting the Manica company, see under *Zambesi* Sept.—Dec. ,,

Military expedition for the defence of Manica, sails from Lisbon 15 Jan. and 12 Feb. 1891

Arrival of col. Paiva d'Andrade, complaining of the conduct of the British in Manica (see *Zambesi*, Nov. 1890) 19 Jan. ,,

Military revolt at Oporto (*which see*) 31 Jan. ,,

The *Malange* steamer, with 700 men, arrives at Zanzibar 9 Feb. ,,

The cortes opened 4 March, ,,

The *Countess of Canarvon*, steamer, seized by the Portuguese, see under *Zambesi* March, ,,

Loan of 10,000,000*l.* on the tobacco monopoly voted 19 March, ,,

The cortes closed 20 March, ,,

Ministerial crisis ends, no change 17 April, ,,

Financial crisis; heavy fall in the funds, through increase of the national debt and great depression of trade; run upon the banks met by large coinage of silver, . . . about 8 May *et seq.* 1891

Decree authorising the suspension of payments by the banks; the Bank of Portugal suspends cash payments for 60 days . . . . 11 May, ,,

Treaty extending the *modus vivendi* for one month, signed . . . . 14 May, ,,

Financial improvement reported . . 14 May, ,,

New ministry formed by senhor Joao Chrysostomo, president and war general . . . 21 May, ,,

New Anglo-Portuguese convention signed (afterwards ratified) . . . . . . 11 June, ,,

Monetary crisis; sovereigns sold at a high price; traffic in silver coin . . 20 July—20 Aug. ,,

Meeting of the cortes; the king states that the treaty of June with England is being duly executed . . . . 2 Jan. 1892

Expiration of the treaty of Goa (*which see*) . 14 Jan. ,,

New cabinet formed by sen. Jose Dias Ferreira 15 Jan. ,,

The minister of finance reports great deficiency in the revenue and great increase of debt, and proposes large reductions in the expenditure and increase of taxation; accepted by the king, who proposes to largely reduce his civil list, and by the cortes . . . 20 Jan.—23 Feb. ,,

Violent cyclone at Lisbon, much damage; estimated loss, 45,000*l.*, 19 Feb. Great loss of life (105) and property on the coast by a violent gale 27 Feb. and 6 March, ,,

Revolts against the expedition to lake Nyassa in E. Africa, reported . . . 3 March *et seq.* ,,

The cortes closed by the king . . 2 April, ,,

Ministry reconstituted by sen. Ferreira . 27 May, ,,

Decree reducing the temporary payments to foreign bondholders, then due to one-third the amount; protest of the bondholders . . 14 June, ,,

General election; government majority . 23 Oct. ,,

The king and queen visit Madrid . 10–17 Nov. ,,

Retirement of sir George Petre, the able British minister; succeeded by sir H. MacDonell, Dec. ,,

The cortes opened by the king . . 2 Jan. 1893

The Dias Ferreira ministry resigns through disagreement with the king . . 20 Feb. ,,

Sen. Hintze Ribeiro forms a liberal ministry 22 Feb. ,,

The cortes closed . . . . . 15 July, ,,

Dissolution of the chamber of deputies . 7 Dec. ,,

Dispute between France and Portugal respecting railway arrangements; M. Bilhourd, French minister, leaves for Paris . . . . 17 Feb. 1894

Agreement arrived at . . . . 27 March ,,

Celebration of the 500th anniversary of the birth of prince Henry the navigator; foundation stone of a monument laid by the king; and an exhibition of colonial products opened at Oporto 1–4 March, ,,

Delimitation of Manicaland (*which see*) to be submitted to arbitration, reported 15 March, ,,

Large concession of territory on the West coast of Africa to a new company; reported, 16 March, ,,

Parliamentary elections; government majority 15 March, ,,

Great meeting of the progressist party at Oporto 8 June, ,,

Death of sen. Oliveira-Martins, historian, born 1845; minister of finance in 1892 . 24 Aug. ,,

Reconstruction of the ministry; premier, sen. Lobo d'Avila . . . . . . 3 Sept. ,,

The new cortes opened by the king . . 1 Oct. ,,

Sen. Hintze Ribeiro's budget; reduction of the deficit . . . . 29 Oct. ,,

The poet João de Deus decorated by the king, at Lisbon, with much honour . . 8 March, 1895

The chamber dissolved by decree; electoral reform; number of deputies reduced from 170—120 30 March ,,

Sen. Carlos Lobo d'Avila, able minister for foreign affairs, aged 34, died . . . . 9 Sept. ,,

Reform of the house of peers: 90 life members nominated by decree . . . . 26 Sept. ,,

The king starts to visit Spain and other countries 2 Oct. ,,

Met by the duke of Saxe-Coburg and Gotha at Charing-cross; received by the prince of Wales, at Sandringham, 6 Nov.; by the queen at Balmoral; made K.G., 9 Nov.: entertained by the lord mayor at the Mansion house, 12 Nov.; leaves England, 14 Nov.; returns to Lisbon . 16 Nov. 1895

Elections: government majority . . 18 Nov. ,,

The cortes opened by the king with a cheerful speech . . . . 2 Jan. 1896

João de Deus, popular poet, born 1830; died 11 Jan. ,,

At a club carnival ball, in Santarem, 42 women and 1 man perish by a fire occasioned by paper lanterns . . . . 18 Feb. ,,

The king confers honours on col. Galhardo and his officers, see *Lourenço Marques*, 1895, at Lisbon . . . . 25 April, ,,

New government loan for war vessels . 19 Nov. ,,

The king opens the cortes . . . . . 2 Jan. 1897

Resignation of the ministry, 4 Feb.; ministry formed by sen. José Luciano de Castro, 6 Feb.; amnesty to prisoners for press offences; the chamber of deputies dissolved . . . 8 Feb. ,,

Oceanographic exhibition, showing the results of the king's own scientific researches, opened by the king . . . . 12 April, ,,

Parliament opened by the king . . . 10 June, ,,

400th anniversary of the departure of Vasco da Gama to discover the sea route to the Indies; celebrated at Lisbon . . . . 8 July, ,,

Portuguese W. Africa, see *Africa* . . . . Dec. ,,

Parliament opened by the king, 2 Jan. . . . 1898

Bill for the conversion of the external debt passed, 29 April; cortes closed . . . 4 June, ,,

Dom Carlos I. cruiser launched at Elswick 5 May, ,,

New ministry, sen. Luciano de Castro, premier, 16 Aug. ,,

Death of sen. Henriques B. Gomes, ex-minister for foreign affairs . . . . . . 15 Nov. ,,

The cortes opened by the king . . . . 2 Jan. 1899

Adm. Rawson and British officers warmly received at Lisbon . . . . 13 May, ,,

Plague at Oporto (*which see*) . . . Aug.–Feb. 1900

Cortes opened . . . . 2 Jan. ,,

The ministry resigns, 21 June; one formed by sen. Hintze Ribeiro . . . . . 24 June, ,,

Adm. sir H. Rawson and British squadron much honoured, 6, 7 Dec.; queen Victoria thanks the king for his good wishes and the friendly alliance between the two countries . 9 Dec. ,,

Cortes opened by the king . . . . 2 Jan. 1901

The king visits England to attend the funeral of queen Victoria, 30 Jan.–4 Feb.; receives a deputation of the Evangelical alliance and promises toleration to all protestants in his dominions, 7 Feb. ,,

Some religious associations dissolved by government (decree published 20 April) . . March, ,,

Roman catholic protests received by the king, 11 April, ,,

Cortes dissolved . . . . 5 June, ,,

General election: government majority . 6 Oct. ,,

Cortes opened by the king . . . 2 Jan. 1902

Budget deficit 948 contos of reis, for 1902 14 Jan. ,,

Bill for the conversion of the external debt adopted by the chamber, 26 April; and the peers, 10 May, ,,

Sir Martin Gosselin, new British minister, arrives, 13 Oct. ,,

The king visits Paris, 18 Oct.; Windsor, 17 Nov.–8 Dec.; Madrid, 11 Dec.; returns . 16 Dec. ,,

Cortes opened by the king . . . . 2 Jan. 1903

Cabinet resigns, new one formed by sen. Ribeiro, 27, 28 Feb. ,,

King Edward VII. visits Lisbon; warmly welcomed, city decorated . . . . . . 2–7 April ,,

The king made an admiral of the English fleet by king Edward VII. . . . . . . 8 Aug. ,,

Earthquake shocks . . . . . . 9 Aug. ,,

British fleet salutes the king of Portugal at the close of the naval manœuvres at Lagos; adm. sir A. Wilson and officers entertained, they leave Lisbon . . . . 29 Aug. ,,

Severe storm over N.W. coast, destruction of many fishing boats and other vessels at Lavos and Torreir . . . . end Sept. ,,

SOVEREIGNS OF PORTUGAL.

1095. Henry, count or earl of Portugal.
1112. Alfonso, his son, and Theresa.
1128. Alfonso, count of Portugal, alone.
1139. Alfonso I. declared KING, having obtained a signal victory over a prodigious army of Moors on the plains of Ourique.
1185. Sancho I., son of Alfonso.
1212. Alfonso II., surnamed Crassus, or the Fat.
1223. Sancho II., or the Idle: deposed.
1248. Alfonso III.
1279. Denis or Dionysius, the father of his country.
1325. Alfonso IV., the Brave.
1357. Peter, the Severe.
1367. Ferdinand I., son.
1385. John I., the Bastard and the Great; natural brother; married Philippa, daughter of John of Gaunt, duke of Lancaster.
1433. Edward or Duarte.
1438. Alfonso V., the African.
1481. John II., the Great and the Perfect.
1495. Emmanuel, the Fortunate; cousin.
1521. John III., son; admitted the Inquisition, 1536, and the Jesuits, 1540.
1557. Sebastian; drowned after the great battle of Alcazarquivir, in Africa, 4 Aug. 1578.
1578. Henry, the cardinal, son of Emmanuel; great uncle.
1580. Anthony, prior of Crato, son of Emmanuel; deposed by Philip II. of Spain, who united Portugal to his other dominions.
,, Philip II. }
1598. Philip III. } kings of Spain.
1621. Philip IV. }
1640. John IV., duke of BRAGANZA; dispossessed the Spaniards in a bloodless revolution, and was proclaimed king, Dec. 1.
1656. Alfonso VI.; deposed in 1667, and his brother Peter made regent.
1683. Peter II., brother.
1706. John V., son.
1750. Joseph Emmanuel; son. The daughter and successor of this prince married his brother, by dispensation from the pope, and they ascended the throne, as
Maria I. and Peter III. jointly.
Maria I. alone: this princess afterwards falls into a state of melancholy and derangement; dies, 1816.
1792. Regency—John, son (afterwards king); declared regent, 1791.
1816. John VI., previously regent. He had withdrawn in 1807, owing to the French invasion of Portugal, to his Brazilian dominions; but the discontent of his subjects obliged him to return in 1821; died in 1826.
1826. Peter IV. (Dom Pedro), son; making his election of the empire of Brazil, abdicated the throne of Portugal in favour of
,, Maria II. (da Gloria); daughter; seven years of age.
1828. Dom Miguel, brother to Peter IV., usurped the crown, which he retained, amid civil contentions, until 1833.
1833. Maria II. restored; declared in Sept. 1834 to be of age; married Augustus, duke of Leuchtenberg, 1835; 2nd, Ferdinand of Saxe-Coburg, 9 April, 1836 (who died, 15 Dec. 1885); died, 15 Nov. 1853.
1853. Peter V. (Dom Pedro), son; born 16 Sept. 1837; died, 11 Nov. 1861.
1861. Luis I., brother; born 31 Oct. 1838; married Maria Pia, daughter of Victor Emmanuel, king of Italy (born 16 Oct. 1847), 6 Oct. 1862; a judicious reformer; died, 19 Oct. 1889.
1889. Dom Carlos (son), born 28 Sept. 1863; married Marie Amélie, daughter of the comte de Paris, 22 May, 1886.
Heir: Louis Philippe, born 21 March, 1887.

PORTUGUESE LANGUAGE AND LITERATURE. The earlier forms of Portuguese bore close affinity to Galician, and although it bears a strong resemblance to its sister language, the Castilian, it yet differs so widely in structure as almost to be regarded as an original tongue. *Chambers.* Principal Portuguese authors: King Diniz, *p.* in the 13th century; Gil Vicente, *d.*, 1470–1536; Sá de Miranda, *d.*, 1495–1558; Antonio de Ferreira, *d.*, *Ignez de Castro*, 1528–69; Camoens, *p.*, *The Lusiads*, 1524–80; de Barros, *hist.* 1496–1570, and many others.

PORT VICTORIA, on the Medway, Kent, a new port for London, established by the South-Eastern Railway company; communications opened, Sept. 1884. The German emperor gives 50*l.* to the restoration fund of Grayne church, March, 1901.

PORT, see *Wine*.

POSEN, a Polish province, annexed to Prussia 1772 and 1793; made part of the duchy of Warsaw, 1807; restored to Prussia, 1815. An insurrection here quelled, May, 1848.

About 2000 Austrian Poles expelled, Oct.–Nov. 1885.
Prince Bismarck's plan for Germanizing Posen, see *Prussia*, Feb. 1886.
Visit of the emperor; grand military parade; memorial to the emperor Frederick unveiled; conciliatory speech to the Poles, 3, 4 Sept. 1902.

POSITIVE PHILOSOPHY set forth by Auguste Comte, an eminent mathematician, born 19 Jan. 1798; died at Paris, 5 Sept. 1857, succeeded by M. Pierre Laffitte as director of positivism; died, aged 80, early Jan. 1903. M. P. Emile Littré, the great French philologist, ardently embraced the system, and published "De la Philosophie Positive," in 1845.—See *Calendar*.

Comte's "Cours de Philosophie Positive," published 1830–42; "Système de Politique Positive, ou Traité de Sociologie, instituant la Religion de l'Humanité (l'amour pour principe, l'ordre pour base, et le progrès pour but)," 1851–4.
It professes to base itself wholly on positive facts or observed phenomena, and rejects all metaphysical conceptions, which it considers negatives, having nothing real or true in them; and dispenses with the science of mind. It sets aside theology and metaphysics as two merely preliminary stages in life; and abandons all search after causes and essences of things, and restricts itself to the observation and classification of phenomena and the discovery of their laws. Comte asserted that Europe had now arrived at the third stage of its progress.
Positivism does not recognise the supernatural or the future state.
The Society of Positivists in London meet in Newton-hall, in Fleur-de-lys-court, near Gough-square, on Sunday evenings, when discourses on philosophy, morality, science, politics, &c., are delivered. Their professed object is to promote the perfection of man by means of education in its widest sense, aiming at the attaining of universal brotherhood independently of all professed religious sects; concerts are occasionally given; Frederick Harrison, president (*Pall Mall Gazette*, 29 Nov. 1883).
"The Church of Humanity" is a modified form of positivism, described by Mr. Richard Congreve, an ardent comtist (*Pall Mall Gazette*, 17 Jan. 1884); he died, aged 81, 5 July, 1899.
Commemorative meeting at Paris, address by Mr. Fred. Harrison, 5 Sept. 1896.

POSSIBILISTS. A section of the liberal party in Spain; aiming at reforms: Sen. Castelar, a chief, Oct. 1883.

The name is also given to the workmen's party in Paris, who aim at effecting social reforms by legal methods; they are said to have prevented a revolutionary outbreak of the violent Blanquists, or autonomists, at the presidential election, 3 Dec. 1887.

POSTAL UNION, GENERAL, was established by the Treaty of Berne, signed 9 Oct. 1874, and took effect from 1 July, 1875. From time to time conferences have been held at Berne, Jan. 1876; Paris, 1878 and 1880; Lisbon, 1885. At the congress at Vienna, 20 May—4 July, 1891, the British Australasian colonies were added to the union; Cape Colony added, 1 Jan. 1895; congress at Washington, 5 May, 1897.

POSTING. Post-chaises were invented by the French, and, according to Grainger, were introduced into this country by Mr. William Tell, son of the writer on husbandry. Posting was fixed by statute of Edward VI. at one penny per mile, 1548. By a statute, re-establishing the post-office, none but the postmaster or his deputies could furnish post-horses for travellers, 1660. The post-horse duty was imposed in 1779. Post-horse duty yielded, in 1852, in England, 128,501*l.*, and in Scotland, 16,933*l.*

POSTS, said to have originated in the regular couriers established by Cyrus, who erected post-houses throughout the kingdom of Persia, about 550 B.C. Augustus was the first who introduced this institution among the Romans, 31 B.C. This was imitated by Charlemagne about A.D. 800.—*Ashe.* Louis XI. first established post-houses in France owing to his eagerness for news, and they were the first institution of this nature in Europe, 1470.—*Hénault.* An international commission respecting postal arrangements met at Paris, 11 May, and broke up 9 June, 1863.

POST-OFFICE OF ENGLAND. In England, in the reign of Edward IV. 1481, riders on post-horses went stages of the distance of twenty miles from each other, in order to procure the king the earliest intelligence of the events that passed in the course of the war that had arisen with the Scots.—*Gale.* Richard III. improved the system of couriers in 1483. In 1543 similar arrangements existed in England.—*Sadler's Letters.* Post communications between London and most towns of England, Scotland, and Ireland, existed in 1635.—*Strype.*

The first chief postmaster of England, sir Thomas Randolph, appointed by queen Elizabeth . . 1581
James I. appointed Matthew de l'Equester as foreign postmaster, 1619; and Chas. I. appointed William Frizell and Thomas Witherings . . 1632
A proclamation of Chas. I., "whereas to this time there hath been no certain intercourse between the kingdoms of England and Scotland, the king now commands his postmaster of England for foreign parts to settle a running post or two to run night and day between Edinburgh and London, to go thither and come back again in six days," 1631
The king commanded his "postmaster of England for foreign parts," to open a regular communication by running posts between the metropolis and Edinburgh, West Chester, Holyhead, Ireland, Plymouth, Exeter, &c. (Rates of postage—1 letter carried under 80 miles 2*d.*; under 140 miles, 4*d.*; above that distance in England, 6*d.*; to any part of Scotland, 8*d.*).
An enlarged office erected by the parliament in 1643; and one more considerable in 1657, with a view "to benefit commerce, convey the public dispatches, and as the best means to discover and prevent many dangerous wicked designs against the commonwealth by the inspection of the correspondence" 1657
The post-office as at present constituted was founded 12 Chas. II. . . . . . 27 Dec. 1660
Farmed to John Manley, 1653; to Daniel O'Neil . 1663
Penny Post first set up in London and its suburbs by a Mr. Robert Murray, upholsterer . . . 1681
He assigned his interest in the undertaking to Mr. Dockwra, a merchant, 1683; but on a trial at the King's bench bar it was adjudged to belong to the duke of York, as a branch of the general post, and was thereupon afterwards annexed to the revenue of the crown 1690
This institution considerably improved and made a twopenny post, July, 1794, *et seq.*
Cross posts established by Ralph Allen . . . 1720
Between 1730 and 1740, the post was only transmitted three days a week between Edinburgh and London: and the metropolis, on one occasion, *sent a single letter*, which was for an Edinburgh banker, named Ramsay.

A penny post was first set up in Dublin . . . 1774
The mails conveyed by coaches; the first mail left London for Bristol (see *Mail Coaches*) . 2 Aug. ,,
The mails first conveyed by railway, 1830; by the overland route to India 1835
Post-office acts consolidated . . . 12 July, 1837
Early in 1837, Mr. Rowland Hill broached his plan of *penny postage*, which was adopted after a full investigation by a committee of the house of commons 1839
The new postage law, by which the uniform rate of 4*d.* per letter was tried as an experiment, came into operation . . . . 5 Dec. ,,
The uniform rate of 1*d.* per letter of half an ounce weight, &c., commenced . . . . 10 Jan. 1840
Stamped postage covers came into use 6 May, ,,
Adhesive stamps invented by Mr. James Chalmers of Dundee, 1834; they came into use, superseding Mulready's allegorical envelope (of 1 May, 1840) . 1842
Reduction in postage—to be 1*d.* instead of 2*d.* for every ounce above the first . . . April, 1865
Book Post.—A treasury warrant issued, providing for the carriage by post of *books, pamphlets*, &c., under certain restrictions—4 oz. for 1*d.*; 8 oz. for 2*d.*, &c. . . . . 5 June, 1855
Altered to under 2 oz., ½*d.*; every additional 2 oz., or part of 2 oz., ½*d.*; begun . . 7 Oct. 1870
A *Money-order Office*, set up in 1792, was little used on account of the expense, till 1840. In 1839, 188,291 money orders were issued for 313,124*l.*; in 1861, 7,580,455 orders for 14,616,348*l.*; in 1865, orders were issued for 17,829,290*l.*; in 1870, for 19,993,987*l.*
The *Postal Guide* first appeared in 1856; in which year London and the vicinity were divided into districts for postal purposes; viz., East, West, &c. The postmaster-general has issued Annual Reports since 1854
Postmaster empowered to purchase the electric telegraphs by act passed 31 July, 1868; work begun . . . . 5 Feb. 1869
Post-office money order system applied to France by virtue of a convention signed . . 5 Aug. 1870
Halfpenny stamped cards issued to the public, 1 Oct. ,,
By the post-office act (passed 9 Aug. 1870) the newspaper stamp for posting was abolished; registered newspapers and pamphlets or patterns under 2 oz. to be sent for ½*d.* on and after 1 Oct. ,,
Postage lowered: Letters sent at the rate of 1*d.* for 1 oz., 1½*d.* for 2 oz., &c., from . . 5 Oct. 1871
Short strike of telegraph clerks at Manchester, Liverpool, and Dublin . . . . . Dec. ,,
Pigeon post between London and Tours during the siege of Paris (48 day mails and 1186 night mails sent) . . . . 18 Nov. 1870—28 Jan. ,,
Post-office scandal, money spent from other funds on telegraph service without authority of parliament; censured by commons . . . . 29 July, 1873
Payment for *registered letters* reduced from 4*d.* to 2*d.*; charge for money orders raised; new postal wrappers issued . . . . . 1 Jan. 1878
Telegraph acts consolidated and amended by 41 & 42 Vict. c. 76 . . . . . 16 Aug. ,,
Messrs. Warren de la Rue & Co.'s tender for supply of postage-stamps accepted . . . 17 June, 1879
New postage stamps issued . . . 6 Jan. 1880
Returned letters, &c.: 1867, 3,618,838; year 1878-9, 4,286,648; 1883-4, 5,732,310; 1890-1, 5,750,527.
New system of receiving small sums for savings-banks by stamps tried in some counties; generally adopted . . . . ,,
New rates for money orders from 1*s.* . . 1 Jan. 1881
International postal congresses met at Paris, 7 April, 1878; and 9 Oct. 1880; at Lisbon, 16 March, 1885; (agreement signed 21 March).
POSTAGE STAMPS for 1*d.* authorised to be used for receipts after 1 June; and for telegrams after 1 Nov. ,,
Reduction of 6*d.* for 480 ½*d.* newspaper wrappers 1 Jan. 1882
Reply post-cards issued . . . . 2 Oct. ,,
Late letters received in the sorting carriage of mail trains at stations on and after . . 1 Nov. ,,

Parcel post comes into operation, *which see* 1 Aug. 1883
Post-office protection act passed . 14 Aug. 1884
Postal orders (like bankers' cheques) largely used (since 1880) 1885
Special postal trains established; letters received later and delivered earlier; beginning 1 July, „
Private posting boxes in London sanctioned April, 1886
After negotiation conveyance of American mails transferred from the Cunard and White Star companies to Inman, North German Lloyd, and others till 28 Feb. 1887, Dec. 1886; amicable settlement . . . . . . Feb. 1887
New sets of postage stamps issued; the penny stamp unchanged . . . . . . 1 Jan. „
"London Postmen's Rest," Dover, established by lord Wolverton, late postmaster . . Feb. „
Rented night letter-boxes authorised after 1 Aug. 1888
The government authorised to purchase the submarine electric telegraph with France 21 May, 1889
Post cards to be sold 10 for 6*d*. or 5½*d*. 1 July, „
Payment of money, 10*l*., at post-offices by telegraph authorised after 2 Sept., Aug. 1889; authorised for 1*l*. to 10*l*. from 1 March; announced about 18 Feb. 1890
Meeting of postmen's union in Hyde park to discuss grievances . . . . . . 20 Oct. 1889
Jubilee of the establishment of the penny post celebrated . . . . . . 10–15 Jan. 1890
Uniform colonial and India postage (2½*d*.), long advocated by Mr. J. Henniker Heaton, M.P., adopted by the government . . . . . . 17 April, „
Grand conversazione given by the lord mayor at the Guildhall; present, the prince of Wales, Mr. Raikes, the postmaster-general, and other officers, 16 May. There was an interesting exhibition of objects connected with the postal service 16–19 May, „
Exhibition of the Philatelic society's collection of postage stamps of all nations, at the Portman rooms, Baker-street, W., opened by the duke of Edinburgh, a zealous collector . . . 19 May, „
Jubilee fête for the Roland Hill benevolent fund at South Kensington museum; the queen patron, the duke of Edinburgh president. Exhibition of old and new postal operations and telegraphic communications in the United Kingdom, the colonies, and the United States, &c. Messrs. De la Rue's artistic Jubilee envelope, of which only a limited number were printed, was sold for 1*s*. each . . . . 2 July, „
Agitation among the London postmen respecting pay, pension, and hours May—July, „
Mass meeting of the postmen's union 7, 8 July, „
About 100 postmen at the parcel post depôt at Clerkenwell dismissed for attacking and expelling about 70 non-unionists, 10 July; about 130 men dismissed for insubordination in other districts about 10 July, „
[435, out of 6,000, dismissed up to 12 July, 1890.]
New general post-office, north, near St. Martin's-le-grand; memorial stone laid by Mr. H. C. Raikes, postmaster-general . . . . . . 20 Nov. „
Uniform colonial and India postage reduced to 2½*d*. for ½ oz., begins 1 Jan. 1891; to foreign countries, 1 July, 1892
About 240 clerks in the Savings-bank department suspended for refusing to work overtime, 2 Jan.; reinstated after apology . . . 8 Jan. 1891
"The Boy Messengers" and "District Messengers" companies, for the quicker conveyance of single letters for short distances, stopped by the post-office as illegal . . . . . . March, „
The post-office express delivery service, for the quicker delivery of letters and parcels, by boy messengers, begins, 25 March; at Edinburgh, Dublin, and other places, 26 March, *et seq.*; extended to the whole United Kingdom . 1 Aug. „
[The actions against the companies in the queen's bench division stopped by arrangement, the companies submit, and agree to take out licences from the post-office, 14 April, 1891.]
Automatic stamp distributors attached to the postal pillars, began . . . 29 April, „
International postal union congress, meeting at Vienna; sir A. Blackwood present; various improvements made . 20 May—4 July, 1891
Various improvements in the postal service begun 1 Jan. and 1 June, 1892
Post-office acts passed, 5 Aug. 1891; 1892; 1895; and 1988
Charge for embossed envelopes reduced . 1 July, 1893
Plain cards of proper size with ½*d*. stamp authorised, from . . . . . . 1 Sept. 1894
Free postal redirection of all letters, books, newspapers, &c. (except parcels), from . . 1 Jan. 1895
Gross receipts, 10,760,000*l*. 1894–5; 11,860,000*l*. 1896–7.
Transfer of the trunk telephone wires to the Post-office . . . . . . 4 April *et seq.*, 1896
New regulations respecting pensions, issued, 31 Dec. „
Reductions of payments and penalties, &c., after 1 Feb. 1897. See *Telephone* . . . 6 Feb. 1897
Postal changes (4 oz reduced to 1*d*., &c.) on and after . . . . 22 June, „
Philatelic exhibition in Piccadilly, opened by the duke of York . . . . . 22 July, „
Threatened strike of telegraphists and others, averted by concessions and reason . 13 Aug. „
Postman's Federation inaugurated at Nottingham, 22,000 members . . . . . . 2 Sept. „
Parcel postal convention with France for India and Australia, signed at Paris . . 1 Dec. „
Steam-motor (oil) mail service (parcels van), between London and Redhill, first started 16 Dec. „
Imperial penny postage established between Great Britain and every part of the British empire except Australia and N. Zealand, 25 Dec. 1898–Dec. 1899; silver pennies distributed by Mr. Henniker-Heaton, one accepted by the queen, as a memento of the occasion . . Christmas, 1898
Private posting boxes, two collections per day, &c., for moderate fees (1*l*. to 2*l*. per ann.), started, 1 Feb. 1899
Express Sunday morning delivery of letters, 3*d*. per mile additional pay, begins . . 11 Feb. „
International exhibition of postage stamps at Manchester . . . . . . June–5 July, „
Telephonic communication placed under the Post-office by act passed . . . . . 9 Aug. „
Forty-fifth annual report issued . . . 5 Sept. „
First annual congress of postal and telegraph officials opened at Derby . . . 29 Sept. „
Post-cards of larger size issued . . . 1 Nov. „
Parcel post from U.K. to Egypt agreed to, mid Feb. 1900
Postmen's park and cloister in Aldersgate opened by the lord mayor . . . . 30 July, „
Penny postage to the Orange River colony and the Transvaal from the U.K. on and after . 1 Dec. „
Penny postage from New Zealand starts . 1 Jan. 1901
Internat. postal and railway conference (England and France) opened at Dover . . 21 Feb. „
International Philatelic union's exhibition of postage stamps, London . . . 23 Feb. „
Official collection of postal packets gratis under regulations, announced . . . . 29 March, „
Telegraph money order system extended to Egypt, 1 Nov. „
New postage stamps with the king's portrait, issued . . . . 1 Jan. 1902
Money orders issued to and from 16 principal towns in the Transvaal, after . . . . 1 Jan. „
Imperial penny postage from Great Britain to Australia, announced, 27 April; also to Chinese ports, from . . . . . . 1 May, „
Post-office sites bill passed . . . . 29 July, „
Great increase of parcel post business, since 1897; over 86,800,000 in 1901–2.
Parcel post from U.K. to the United States, 1 Sept. „
Congress of *employés* in Holborn town-hall, 150 delegates; resolutions passed demanding reforms, &c. . . . . 13 Sept. „
Guinea postal order act, royal assent 21 July, 1903

NUMBER OF LETTERS, &C., DELIVERED IN THE UNITED KINGDOM.

1839 (including 6,563,024 franks)	82,470,596	1851-5 (average)	410,000,000
1840	168,768,344	1861-5 ,,	648,000,000
1851	360,651,187	1866-70 ,,	800,000,000
Scotland, 36,512,649. Ireland, 35,982,782.		Scotland, 76,000,000. Ireland, 60,000,000.	

	Letters.	Post Cards.	Books, Circulars, &c.	News-papers.	Money Orders.	Telegrams.	Net Revenue. Postal Service and Money Orders.	Net Revenue. Telegrams. Deficits*
1871 . . .	867,000,000	—	—	—	£22,573,547	12,473,796	£1,289,754	£303,457
1872 . . .	885,000,000	76,000,000	114,000,000	109,000,000	25,019,683	15,535,780	1,523,976	159,835
1879-80 . .	1,127,997,500	114,458,400	213,963,000	130,518,400	26,371,020	26,547,137	2,497,687	341,006
1880-1 . .	1,165,166,900	122,884,000	240,356,200	133,796,100	26,003,582	29,411,982	2,597,768	368,815
1883-4 . .	1,322,086,900	153,586,100	294,594,500	142,702,300	27,629,879	32,843,120	2,610,026	51,255
1887-8 . .	1,512,200,000	188,800,000	389,500,000	152,300,000	26,334,126	53,403,425	2,771,517	31,247
1889-90 . .	1,650,100,000	217,100,000	441,900,000	159,300,000	27,165,905	62,403,309	3,208,511	145,794
1890-91 . .	1,705,800,000	229,700,000	481,200,000	161,000,000	27,867,887	66,409,211	3,163,989	150,335
1893-4 . .	1,811,800,000	248,000,000	574,300,000	164,900,000	28,720,829	70,899,498	2,734,273	107,254
1894-5 . .	1,770,900,000	312,800,000	614,600,000	151,800,000	28,923,127	71,589,064	3,070,116	141,638
1896-7 . .	1,893,000,000	336,000,000	697,900,000	150,600,000	30,249,087	79,423,556	3,900,579	144,456
1897-8 . .	2,012,300,000	360,400,000	727,300,000	150,900,000	32,114,579	83,029,999	3,737,059	307,118
1898-9 . .	2,186,800,000	382,200,000	701,500,000	154,100,100	33,278,517	87,043,652	3,859,311	221,869
1899-1900 .	2,246,800,000	400,300,000	702,800,000	163,400,000	35,201,262	90,415,123	3,710,336	288,592
1900-1 . .	2,323,600,000	419,000,000	732,400,000	167,800,000	39,374,665	89,576,961	3,953,886	337,641
1901-2 . .	2,451,500,000	444,900,000	766,200,000	169,800,000	42,169,201	90,432,041	3,999,351	651,806
1902-3 . .	2,579,500,000	488,000,000	809,800,000	175,400,000	45,402,495	92,471,000		593,505

* Telegraph Receipts: 1898–9, 3,204,396*l.*; 1899–1900, 3,389,746*l.*; 1900–1, 3,380,589*l.*; 1901–2, 3,5700,46*l.*

REVENUE OF THE POST-OFFICE.

1643.	It yielded .	£5,000	1835.	U. Kingdom	£2,353,340
1653.	Farmed .	10,000	1839.	Ditto . .	2,522,495
1663.	Farmed .	21,500	1840.	New rate .	471,000
1674.	Farmed for	43,000	1845.	Netrevenue	761,982
1685.	It yielded .	65,000	1850.	Ditto . .	803,898
1707.	Ditto . .	111,461	1855.	Ditto . .	1,137,220
1714.	Ditto .	145,227	1859.	Ditto . .	1,150,960
1723.	Ditto . .	201,805	1860.	Ditto . .	1,102,479
1744.	Ditto . .	235,492	1861.	Ditto . .	1,161,985
1764.	Ditto . .	432,048	1862.	Ditto . .	1,236,941
1790.	Ditto . .	480,074	1863.	Ditto* . .	1,037,404
1800.	Ditto . .	745,313	1864.	Ditto . .	1,153,261
1805.	Gt. Britain	1,424,994	1865	Ditto . .	1,482,522
1810.	Ditto . .	1,709,065	1866.	Ditto . .	1,397,986
1815.	Ditto . .	1,755,898	1867.	Ditto . .	1,421,364
1820.	U. Kingdom	2,402,697	1868.	Ditto . .	1,416,922
1825.	Ditto . .	2,255,239	1870.	Ditto . .	1,493,610
1830.	Ditto . .	2,301,432	1903.	Ditto .	15,004,938

* After payment for foreign and colonial mails.

POST-OFFICES.

THE GENERAL POST-OFFICE of London was originally established in Cloak-lane, near Dowgate-hill, whence it was removed to the Black Swan, in Bishopsgate-street. After the great fire of 1666 it was removed to the Two Black Pillars, in Brydges-street, Covent-garden, and afterwards (about 1690) to sir Robert Viner's mansion in Lombard-street. It was transferred to the building in St. Martin's-le-Grand, erected on the site of an ancient college, from designs by R. Smirke, 23 Sept. 1829. Foundation of a new general post-office laid 16 Dec. 1870; occupied 1873; additional buildings completed, 1894.

The new post-office of Dublin opened, 6 Jan. 1818.

The foundation of a new post-office at Edinburgh was laid by the prince consort in Oct. 1861.

Public receptacles for letters before 1840, 4,028; in 1865, 16,246; in 1876, 24,171; in 1877, 25,082; Jan. 1879, 25,767; in 1884, 31,700; 1888, 36,750; 1891, 40,643.

In 1860, there were in the United Kingdom, 11,412 post-offices; 1862, 11,316; 1875, 13,226; 1877, 13,447; Jan. 1879, 13,881; 1884, 15,951; 1888, 17,587; 1891, 18,806; 1896, 20,398; 1899, 21,940.

The street *Letter-boxes* were erected in March, 1855. The first one was placed at the corner of Fleet-street and Farringdon-street. There were in 1860, 1,958; in 1875, 10,186; Jan. 1879, 11,880; 1891, 21,837; 1896, 27,622.

Staff employed: 1862, 25,285; in 1872, 28,959; 1874, 43,982; 1875, 44,644; 1879, 45,947; 1888, 56,460; 1891, 63,868; 1899, 167,070; 1900, 173,184; 1903, 183,595.

Revenue: post office, 1899, 12,710,000*l.*; 1900, 13,300,000*l.*; 1901, 13,800,000*l.*; 1902, 14,300,000*l.*; 1903, 15,004,938*l.* Telegraphs, 1899, 3,150,000*l.*; 1900, 3,350,000*l.*; 1901, 3,450,000*l.*; 1902, 3,490,000*l.*; 1903, 3,723,866*l.*

POST-OFFICE SAVINGS-BANKS established by parliament 1861 (began Sept. 16); interest 2½ per cent.; government responsible to depositors. The number of these banks and the amount of deposits received on 31 March, 1862, were—

	Banks.	*Deposits.*
England	1795	£668,879 10 2
Wales	129	28,392 2 10
Scotland	299	10,237 9 8
Ireland	300	26,064 18 8
The Islands . . .	9	1,679 15 0
	2532	£735,253 16 4
London district		267,329 13 8

1866. Computed total amount of capital held by these banks in the United Kingdom, 8,121,175*l.*

1901. 140,392,916*l.*

Foundation-stone of the new central offices at W. Kensington laid by the prince of Wales, 24 June, 1899. Headquarters of P.O. savings bank removed from Queen Victoria-street to W. Kensington, 14 April, 1903.

Dec. 1870, 1,183,153 depositors in United Kingdom; total sum held, 15,099,104*l.*; in 1883, 6,297,378 depositors; total sum held, 43,294,949*l.*; 31 Dec. 1887, 6,916,327; total sum held, 53,974,065*l.*; 31 Dec. 1890, 7,634,807*l.*; 8,776,566 depositors; 1893, 80,597,641*l.*; 9,838,198 depositors; 1896, 108,098,641*l.*; 6,862,035 depositors; 1899, 130,118,605*l.*; 8,046,680 depositors; 1900, 135,549,645*l.*; 8,439,983 depositors; 1901, 140,409,645*l.*; 8,787,675 depositors; 1902, 144,605,088*l.*; 9,000,000 depositors, April, 1903.

OTHER STATISTICS. 1902. Average number of letters to each person in the United Kingdom, 58·9; post-cards, 10·7; book packets (including circulars), 18·4; newspapers, 4·1; parcels, 2·1; *registered letters*, 18,800,313; undelivered postal packets, 10,183,866, value of property in them 668,529*l.*

POSTMASTERS.

The number of postmasters (2) reduced to 1, 1822.

The offices of postmaster-general of England and of Ireland united in one person, 1831.

Act passed permitting postmaster to sit in house of commons, July, 1866.

1823. Thomas, earl of Chichester.
1826. Lord Frederick Montague.
1827. William duke of Manchester.
1830. Charles duke of Richmond.
1834. Francis marquis of Conyngham
1835. William lord Maryborough.
1835. Francis marquis of Conyngham.
,, Thomas earl of Lichfield.
1841. William viscount Lowther.
1846. Edward earl of St. Germans.

1846. Ulick marquis of Clanricarde.
1852. Charles Philip earl of Hardwicke.
1853. Charles John earl Canning.
1855. George duke of Argyll.
1858. Charles lord Colchester.
1859. James earl of Elgin.
1860. Edward lord Stanley of Alderley.
1866. James duke of Montrose (July).
1868. Spencer marquis of Hartington (Dec.).
1871. Wm. Monsell (Jan.).
1873. Dr. Lyon Playfair (18 Nov.); died 29 May, 1898.
1874. Lord John Manners (21 Feb.).
1880. Henry Fawcett (3 May); died 6 Nov. 1884.
1884. Geo. Shaw-Lefevre (18 Nov.).
1885. Lord John Manners (24 June).
1886. George Grenfell Glyn, lord Wolverton (about 6 Feb.).
,, Henry Cecil Raikes, 26 July; died, 24 Aug. 1891.
1891. Sir James Fergusson, about 21 Sept.
1892. Arnold Morley, 18 Aug.
1895. Henry Howard, duke of Norfolk, July; resigned, March, 1900.
1900. Lord Londonderry, April.
1902. Austen Chamberlain, Aug.
1903. Lord Stanley, Oct.

CHIEF SECRETARIES.

1797. Francis Freeling.
1836. Wm. L. Maberley.
1854. Rowland Hill (sec. to postmaster-general, 30 Nov. 1846); received national testimonial, 17 June, 1846; resigned 29 Feb. 1864; made K.C.B. 1860, with a grant of 20,000*l.* and 2000*l.* pension; died 27 Aug.; buried in Westminster Abbey, 4 Sept. 1879 (see *Rowland Hill Memorial*).
1864. John Tilley, K.C.B. 1880; died 18 March, 1898.
1880. Sir Stevenson Arthur Blackwood; died 2 Oct. 1893.
1893. Spencer Walpole (Nov.), K.C.B., 1 Jan. 1898; retires, 14 Feb, 1899.
1899. George H. Murray (aft. sir); succeeded by H. Babington Smith, Sept. 1903.

POST-OFFICE ACT, passed 14 June, 1875, consolidates previous acts (1840, *et seq.*), and enacts some new regulations. The Post-office (Parcels) act was passed 18 Aug. 1882; other acts passed, 1891 and 1895.

POST-OFFICE DIRECTORY for London, published by Kelly & Co., since 1800. County directories and trade now published.

POST-OFFICE MONEY-ORDERS ACTS, 11 & 12 Vict. c. 88 (1848), 43 & 44 Vict. c. 33 (1880).

POSTMAN AND TUBMAN, ancient offices in the court of exchequer held by barristers with certain privileges.

POTASSIUM, a remarkable metal, discovered by Humphry Davy, who first succeeded in separating it from its oxide, potash, by means of a powerful voltaic battery, in the laboratory of the Royal Institution, London, about 19 Oct. 1807; and also the metals *Sodium* from soda, *Calcium* from lime, &c. The alkalies and earths had been previously regarded as simple substances. Potassium ignites on contact with moisture.

POTATOES, natives of Chili and Peru, generally considered to have been brought to England from Santa Fé, in America, by sir John Hawkins, 1565. Others ascribe their introduction to sir Francis Drake, in 1586; their general introduction, 1592. Their first culture in Ireland is referred to sir Walter Raleigh, who had large estates in that country, about Youghal, in the county of Cork. It is said that potatoes were not known in Flanders until 1620. A fine kind of potato was first brought from America by Mr. Howard, who cultivated it at Cardington, near Bedford, 1765; and its culture became general soon after. The *failure of the potato crop* in Ireland, several years, especially in 1846, caused famine, to which succeeded pestilent disease of which multitudes died; among them many priests and physicians. Parliament voted ten millions sterling; and several countries of Europe, and the United States of America, forwarded provisions and other succours; see *Ireland*. In 1868 it was reported that in England and Wales 500,000 acres, and in Ireland 1,000,000 acres, were under cultivation for potatoes. Potato disease prevailed greatly in England, autumn of 1872. In consequence the value of potatoes imported in 1872 was 1,654,240*l.*; in 1871, only 225,732*l.*; in 1877, 7,964,840 cwt., value, 2,348,749*l.*; in 1883, 5,149,509 cwt., value 1,585,260*l.*; in 1887, 2,763,357 cwt.; in 1889, 1,864,426 cwt.; in 1890, 1,940,100 cwt.; in 1900, 8,910,932 cwt.; in 1902., 5,699,090 cwt.; Temporary alarm respecting the American Colorado beetle or bug, autumn, 1876. Acres cultivated for potatoes in Great Britain in 1867, 492,217; 1871, 627,691; 1877, 512,471; 1883, 543,455; in 1887, 559,652; in 1890, 529,661; in 1902, 573,880; Ireland, 1902, 629,304.

[Mr. W. Carruthers considers that the disease did not appear in Britain before 1844; Mr. Thiselton-Dyer thinks that it did.]

International potato exhibition, Crystal Palace, 17-18 Sept. 1879; another 7-8 Oct. 1885.
Rain and want of sunshine greatly injured the crops in 1879.
Report of a select committee on the failure of the potato crop, Aug. 1880.
7th potato show (the 1st, 1874) at the Crystal Palace, very good, 23 Sept. 1880; 8th exhibition, 20 Sept. 1882.
Solanum maglia successfully cultivated in wet land by Mr. A. Sutton of Reading, 1884.
Tercentenary of the introduction of the potato into England celebrated at Westminster; exhibition and conference, about 500 varieties exhibited, 1–4 Dec. 1886.
Failure of the potato crop in Cork, &c., see *Ireland*, 1890.
The bouillie Bordelaise treatment of the disease by dressings of salts of copper recommended by Dr. Girard (1890), was tried by Messrs. Sutton, of Reading, with doubtful results, June, *et seq.* 1891. Favourable results reported by some persons.
Outbreak of disease in parts of Ireland, mid. July, 1893
Blight in co. Limerick and Clare, reported, 16 Aug. 1897
Heavy rains and floods of the summer and early autumn very deleterious to the potato crop in 1903
Local firm at Lincoln sells 7 lbs. of Eldorado potatoes for 700*l.*; purchaser resells part at 150*l.* per lb. . . . . 11 Dec. ,,

POTIDÆA, a town in Macedonia, a tributary of Athens, against which it revolted 432 B.C., but submitted in 429. It was taken from the Athenians after three years' siege, by Philip II. of Macedon in 356 B.C.

POTOMAC, see *United States*, Aug. 1861.

POTOSI (Peru). Silver mines here were discovered by the Spaniards in 1545; they are in a mountain in the form of a sugar-loaf.

POTSDAM (near Berlin), the Versailles of Prussia. It was made an arsenal in 1721. Here is situated the palace of *Sans Souci* (built, 1660-73), embellished by Frederick II., and occupied by Napoleon I. in Oct. 1806; and the new palace, erected by Frederick the Great, 1763-9, was the residence of the emperor Frederick III., when prince Frederick William of Prussia and his wife the princess royal of England, married 25 Jan. 1858. Population, 1890, 54,161; 1900, 59,814.

POTTERY AND PORCELAIN. The manufacture of earthenware (the ceramic art) existed among the Jews as an honourable occupation (see 1 *Chron.* iv. 23), and the power of the potter over the clay as a symbol of the power of God is described by Jeremiah, 605 B.C. (ch. xviii.) Earthenware was made by the ancient Egyptians, Assyrians, Greeks, Etruscans, and Romans.

The Majolica, Raffaelle, or Umbrian ware of the 15th century was probably introduced into Italy from the Moors from Majorca. Raffaelle and other artists made designs for this ware.

Pottery manufactured at Beauvais, in France, in the 12th century.

Enamelled pottery made at St. Cloud . . about 1688

Luca della Robbia (born about 1410) applied tin enamel to terra-cotta. Fayence ware was made in France by Bernard Palissy (died, 1589) and his family.

PORCELAIN, formed of earth *kaolin*, was made in China in the 2nd century after Christ. Chinese porcelain is mentioned in histories of the 16th century, when it was introduced into England, and eagerly sought after.

Porcelain made at Bow, near London, early in the 18th century, and at Chelsea, before 1698

Birch's "History of Ancient Pottery" (1858); Marryat's "History of Pottery and Porcelain, Mediæval and Modern" (1857); and Brongniart's "Arts Céramiques," are valuable works.

The first European porcelain was made at Dresden by Böttcher . . . . about 1700

[The manufacture was fostered by the king Augustus II.]

The Capo di Monte factory at Naples established 1736

Thomas Frye painted porcelain, 1749; and Dr. Wall established the manufacture at Worcester . . 1750

The St. Cloud China manufactory removed to Sèvres 1756

Josiah Wedgwood's patent ware was first made, 1762; his great works at Etruria in Staffordshire were established in 1771; his fine art works and ordinary crockery have been largely exported to all parts of the world.

The Royal Porcelain manufactory, at Copenhagen, started in 1775, was soon after taken up by the State and carried on till 1867, when it reverted into private hands. In 1882 it was purchased by the Aluminia company of Copenhagen.

The British manufacture greatly improved by Herbert Minton, who died 1858

The duty on earthenware taken off 1860

Lord Dudley's collection of china sold for 40,856*l.* 21 May, 1886

Great improvements in form and colour in decorative stoneware, glazed pipes, &c., were made in Messrs. Doulton's Lambeth pottery works, 1871, *et seq.*, in connection with the Lambeth School of Art. Lambeth faïence was introduced in 1873. Sir Henry Doulton, born, 1820; was knighted in 1887; died . . . . 17 Nov. 1897

The potter's wheel has greatly superseded moulding as producing more original work 1888

The sale of the collection of oriental porcelain, &c., of the late Mr. Wells, of Redleaf, realized 12,811*l.* 12*s.* 6*d.* . . . . . . 13, 14 May, 1890

Great lock-out in the pottery district, Staffordshire, respecting wages, 5 May; settled by compromise about 19 May, 1892

Sale of Mr. D. Macdonald's fine collection of old English porcelain . . . . . . 26-28 Nov. 1900

Lord Henry Thynne's old Chelsea porcelain realised 12,500*l.* . . . . 12 July, 1901

POTWALLOPERS (or boilers). Before the passing of the reform act of 1832, persons who had boiled a pot for six months claimed the right to vote for the election of members of Parliament.

POULTRY. An exhibition of poultry was held in London, Jan. 1853, when nearly 1000 cocks were exhibited; and similar exhibitions have been held at the Crystal palace since. A national poultry conference (first) opened at Reading by Mr. Walter Long, 11 July, 1899.

POULTRY COMPTER (London) was one of the most noted of the old city prisons. The compter of Wood-street belonged to the sheriff of London, and was made a prison-house in 1555. This latter and Broad-street compter were re-built in 1667. The Giltspur-street prison, built to supply the place of the old city compters, was pulled down in 1855. The Poultry chapel was erected on the site of the Poultry compter, in 1819.—*Leigh.*

POUND, from the Latin *Pondus*. The value of the Roman *pondo* is not precisely known, though some suppose it was equivalent to an Attic *mina*, or 3*l.* 4*s.* 7*d.* The pound sterling was in Saxon times, about 671, a pound troy of silver, and a shilling was its twentieth part; consequently the latter was three times as large as it is at present.—*Peacham.* Our avoirdupois pound weight came from the French, and contains sixteen ounces; it is in proportion to our troy weight as seventeen to fourteen; see under *Standard.*

POWDERING THE HAIR, see *Hair.*

POWER-LOOMS, see *Looms*, and *Cotton.*

POYNINGS' LAW, named after sir Edward Poynings, lord deputy of Ireland at the time of its passing, at Drogheda, 13 Sept. 1494. By this law all legislation in the Irish parliament was confined to matters first approved of by the king and the English council. The act was repealed, together with the English Declaratory act of the 6th of Geo. I. and other obnoxious Irish statutes, April, 1782.

PRÆMONSTRATENSIAN ORDER, or WHITE CANONS, founded in 1120 by Norbert, a monk, at Pré Montré, near Laon. Its first house in England was founded by Peter de Gousla or Gousel, at Newsham, in Lincolnshire, 1143—*Tanner*; according to others in 1146. The order spread widely through England soon after. The house at Newsham was dedicated to St. Mary and St. Martial.—*Lewis.*

PRÆMUNIRE, LAW OF. This law (which obtained its name from the first two words "*Præmoneri*," or "*Præmuniri facias*," "Cause to be forewarned," which is applied to any offence in the way of contempt of the sovereign or his government) derived its origin from the aggressive power of the pope in England. The offence introduced a foreign power into the land, and created an *imperium in imperio*. The first statute of Præmunire was enacted 35 Edward I. 1306.—*Coke.* The pope bestowed most of the bishoprics, abbeys, &c., before they were void, upon favourites, on pretence of providing the church with better qualified successors before the vacancies occurred. To put a stop to these encroachments, Edward III. enacted a statute in 1353. The statute commonly referred to as the statute of Præmunire is the 16th of Richard II. 1392. Several similar enactments followed. The assertion that parliament is independent of the sovereign was declared a *præmunire*, 1661.

PRÆTORIAN GUARDS, instituted by the emperor Augustus (13 B.C.); their numbers enlarged by Tiberius, Vitellius, and their successors. At first supporters of the imperial tyrants, they eventually became their masters, actually putting up the diadem for sale (as in March, 193 A.D., when it was bought by Didius Julianus). They committed many atrocities, and were finally disbanded by Constantine in 312.

PRÆTORS, Roman magistrates, afterwards termed consuls (*which see*), were elected at the establishment of the republic, 509 B.C. In 366 the *prætor urbanus* was appointed for the city, and the *prætor peregrinus* for foreigners, 246 B.C. Two prætors were appointed for the provinces, 227, and two more, 197. Sylla, the dictator, added two, and Julius Cæsar increased the number to 10, which afterwards became 16. After this, their number fluctuated, being sometimes 18, 16, or 12; till, in the decline of the empire, their dignity decreased, and their numbers were reduced to three.

PRAGA, a suburb of Warsaw, where a bloody battle was fought, 4 Nov. 1794; 30,000 Poles were killed by the Russian general Suwarrow. Near here, on 25 Feb. 1831, the Poles, commanded by Skrznecki, defeated the Russians, under general Giemsar, who lost 4000 killed and wounded, 6000 prisoners, and 12 pieces of cannon.

PRAGMATIC SANCTION, an ordinance relating to church and state affairs. The ordinances of the kings of France are thus called; in one the rights of the Gallican church were asserted against the usurpation of the pope in the choice of bishops, by Charles VII. in 1438. The Pragmatic Sanction for settling the empire of Germany in the house of Austria, 1439. The emperor Charles VI. published the Pragmatic Sanction, whereby, in default of male issue, his daughters should succeed in preference to the daughters of his brother Joseph I., 19 April, 1713; and he settled his dominions on his daughter Maria Theresa, in conformity thereto, 1723. She succeeded in Oct. 1740; but it gave rise to a war, in which most of the powers of Europe were engaged, and which lasted till 1748.

PRAGUE, the capital of Bohemia (*which see*). The old city was founded about 759; the new city rebuilt in 1348 by the emperor Charles IV., who made it his capital and erected a university. Prague has suffered much by war. Population, 1880, 162,323; 1890, 184,109; 1900, 389,741.

Victory of the Hussites under Ziska . 14 July, 1420
Frederick, the king, totally defeated by the Austrians near Prague . . . . . 8 Nov. 1620
Prague taken by the Swedes in 1648, and by the French in 1741; they left it 1742
Taken by the king of Prussia; obliged to abandon it, 1744
Great *battle of Prague* (the Austrians defeated by prince Henry of Prussia, and their whole camp taken; their commander, general Braun, mortally wounded, and the Prussian marshal Schwerin killed) . . . . . . 6 May, 1757
Insurrection in Prague; soon suppressed . June, 1848
A treaty of peace between Austria and Prussia signed at Prague (by its articles Austria consented to the breaking up of the Germanic confederation, and to Prussia's annexing Hanover, Hesse Cassel, Nassau, and Frankfort; and gave up Holstein, and her political influence in North Germany), and North Schleswig to Denmark if the people vote for it; (the last not carried out) 23 Aug. 1866; abrogated . . . . Feb. 1879
Riots of Czech and German students; Marshal Krause appointed governor about . 10 July, 1881
45 socialists sentenced to imprisonment . . Dec. 1882
Destructive floods; the ancient bridge over the Moldau greatly injured, 1—5 Sept., by the collapse of a wall of the bridge; 40 labourers were cast into the river and 23 drowned . 13 Oct. 1890
Bohemian Industrial exhibition opened, 15 May; closed . . . . 18 Oct. 1891
Visit of the emperor, warmly received . 26 Sept. ,,
Serious Czech rioting suppressed by the police, after fighting . . . . . 28 March, 1892
Demonstration of the Czechs against the Germans 30 Nov. 1897
Serious rioting against Germans and Jews, houses plundered and burnt; semi state of siege proclaimed by government, 4 persons killed, 150 wounded, troops concentrated . . 1–3 Dec. ,,
An aggressive manifesto issued by the young Czech party, newspapers confiscated . . 20 Dec. 1897

PRAGUERIE, WAR OF (so named from Prague, then celebrated for its civil disorders); the revolt of the dauphin, afterwards Louis XI., against his father Charles VII., aided by Alexander, the bastard of Bourbon, and other nobles. It was soon quelled; Louis was exiled, and Alexander put to death by drowning, July, 1440.

PRAIRIAL INSURRECTION at Paris. On 1, 2, 3 Prairial, year 3 (20, 21, 22 May, 1795), the fauxbourgs rose against the directory, and were quelled by the military.

PRAISE-GOD-BAREBONES' PARLIAMENT, see *Barebones*.

PRASLIN MURDER. The duchesse de Choiseul-Praslin was murdered by her husband, the duc de Praslin, at his own house, in Paris, 17 Aug. 1847. She was the only daughter of the celebrated marshal Sebastiani, the mother of nine children, and in her forty-first year. Circumstances were so managed by him as to give it the appearance of being the act of another. During the arrangements for the trial, the duke took poison.

PRAYER-BOOK, see *Common Prayer*. The Prayer-book and Homily Society, London, was founded in 1812.

Prayer-book Revision Society, established 1854, for promoting a revision of the book of common prayer, and such liturgical reforms in the church of England as in the opinion of the society would strengthen its Protestant and scriptural character.

PRAYERS. "Then began men to call upon the name of the Lord" (*Gen.* iv. 26), 3875 B.C. The mode of praying with the face to the east was instituted by pope Boniface II. A.D. 532. Prayers for the dead, first introduced into the Christian church about 190, are advocated by some ministers of the English church. Prayers addressed to the Virgin Mary and to the saints are said to have been introduced by pope Gregory, 593. See *Liturgies*.

PREBENDARY, a clergyman attached to a cathedral or collegiate church, who receives an income termed *prebenda* for officiating at stated times. The office slightly differs from that of a canon.

PRECEDENCE was established in very early ages, and was amongst the laws of Justinian. In England the order of precedency was regulated chiefly by two statutes, 31 Hen. VIII. 1539, and 1 Geo. I. 1714.

PRECEPTORS, COLLEGE OF, Bloomsbury, London, established in 1846, and incorporated by royal charter 28 March, 1849, for promoting sound learning, especially among the middle classes, by the instruction of teachers, and by the examination of pupils at stated times.

Professorship (the first in England) of the science and art of education, instituted, 1873.
New building in Bloomsbury Square opened by the prince of Wales, 30 March, 1887.

PREDESTINATION (*Ephes.* i.). The doctrine concerning this is defined in the seventeenth article of the Church of England (*Ephes.* i. and *Romans* ix.). It was maintained by St. Augustin, and opposed by Pelagius, in the early part of the 5th century. In later times it has been maintained by the Augustinians, Jansenists, the church of Scotland, and many dissenters (termed Calvinistic), and opposed by the Dominicans, Jesuits, and dissenters (termed Arminian), especially by the Wesleyan methodists.

PREHISTORIC ARCHÆOLOGY began in Sweden, and first systematised by Mr. Nillson. Daniel Wilson's "Archæology and Pre-historic Annals of Scotland," published 1851. An international congress for treating prehistorical subjects met at Neuchâtel in 1866, and at Paris in 1867. At the third meeting at Norwich, Aug. 1868, it assumed the name of "International Congress for Prehistoric Archæology," and published its transactions in 1869. A meeting was held at Stockholm 7-14 Aug. 1874. See *Barrows, Man, Ancient Monuments* and *Lake Dwellings*.

Sir John Lubbock divides prehistoric archæology into four great epochs: 1. The Drift or Palæolithic or old stone age; 2. The Neolithic or polished stone age; 3. The Bronze age; 4. The Iron age, when bronze was superseded.

PRE-RAPHAELITE SCHOOL, a name given about 1850, to J. E. Millais, Wm. Holman Hunt, D. G. Rossetti, and other artists, who opposed the routine conventionality of academic teaching, and resolved to study nature as it appeared to them, and not as it appeared in the antique. For a short time they published "The Germ, or Art and Poetry," beginning in 1850. Their works have been much criticised, but their influence has been beneficial. Their principles are much advocated by the great art-critic, John Ruskin.

PREROGATIVE COURT, in which formerly all wills were proved, and all administrations taken, which belonged to the archbishop of Canterbury by his prerogative, a judge being appointed by him to decide disputes.* Appeals from this court, previously to the pope, were commanded to be made to the king in chancery, 1533; to the privy council in 1830-2. This court was abolished, and the *Probate Court* established in 1857. Sir John Dodson, the last judge, died in 1858.

PREROGATIVE, ROYAL. In England the sovereign is the supreme magistrate, and it is a maxim that he *can do no wrong*. He is the head of the established church, of the army and navy and the fountain of office, honour, and privilege, but is subject to the laws, unless exempted by name. The royal prerogatives were greatly exceeded by several despotic sovereigns, such as Elizabeth, James I., and Charles I. Elizabeth used the phrase "We, of our Royal prerogative, which we will not have argued or brought in question" (1591). James I. told his parliament "that as it was blasphemy to question what the Almighty could do of His power, so it was sedition to inquire what a king could do by virtue of his prerogative." These extreme doctrines were nullified by the revolution of 1688, and the exercise of the prerogative is now virtually subject to parliament; see *Lords*.

PRESBURG, the ancient capital of Hungary, where the diets were held and the kings crowned. On 26 Dec. 1805, a treaty was signed between France and Austria, by which the ancient states of Venice were ceded to Italy; the principality of Eichstadt, part of the bishopric of Passau, the city of Augsburg, the Tyrol, all the possessions of Austria in Suabia, in Brisgau, and Ortenau, were transferred to the elector of Bavaria, and the duke of Würtemberg, who, as well as the duke of Baden, were then created kings by Napoleon. The independence of the Helvetic republic was also stipulated. A new iron and stone railway and passenger bridge over the Danube was inaugurated by the emperor, 30 Dec. 1890. Population, 1890, 52,444; 1900, 61,861.

PRESBYTERIANS are so called from their maintaining that the government of the church appointed in the New Testament was by presbyteries, or association of ministers and ruling elders, equal in power, office, and in order. "The elders (Greek, *presbyteros*) I exhort, who am also an elder (*sympresbyteros*)." 1 Peter v. 1. Presbyterianism was accepted by parliament in place of episcopacy in England in 1648, but set aside at the restoration in 1660. It became the established form of church government in Scotland in 1696. Its tenets were embodied in the formulary of faith said to have been composed by John Knox, in 1560, which was approved by the parliament, and ratified, 1567, and finally settled by an act of the Scottish senate, 1696, afterwards secured by the treaty of union with England in 1707. The first Presbyterian meeting-house in England was established at Wandsworth, Surrey, 20 Nov. 1572.

A pan-presbyterian congress held in London. Representatives of about fifty bodies, British, American, and foreign, agreed to form an "Alliance of Presbyterian churches" . . 19-22 July, 1875

The presbyterian church of England re-constituted at Liverpool (in union with the United Presbyterian Church of Scotland) . . . . 13 June, 1876

A pan-presbyterian congress, held at Edinburgh, 3 July, 1877; at Philadelphia, U.S.A., 23 Sept 1880

The delegates to the pan-presbyterian council assemble at Exeter Hall . . . . 4 July, 1888

Pan-presbyterian alliance met at Toronto, prof. Blackie president . . . . . 21 Sept. 1892

See *Church of Scotland, Cameronians, Burghers, Relief, Glasites, Free Church*, &c.

PRESCOTT (Upper Canada). On 17 Nov. 1838, the Canadian rebels were attacked by the British under major Young, and (on the 18th) by lieut.-colonel Dundas, who dispersed the insurgents, several of whom were killed, and many taken prisoners, and the remainder surrendered. The troops also suffered considerably.

PRESERVED MEAT, see *Provisions*.

PRESIDENT, see *Court of Session, Privy Council; United States*, 1789; *France*, 1848, 1871; *Wrecks*, 1841.—PRESIDENT OF THE COUNCIL, LORD, the fourth great officer of state, is appointed under the great seal, *durante beneplacito*, and, by his office, is to attend the sovereign's royal person, and to manage the debates in council, to propose matters from the sovereign at the council-table, and to report to his majesty the resolutions taken thereupon.

PRESS ASSOCIATION (a company "limited") was established by the newspaper proprietors of London and the provinces, at a meeting at Manchester, 29 June, 1868, to make arrangements to enable them to avail themselves of the increased facilities for the speedy transmission of news afforded by the post office, in consequence of the

* The records date from 1383; but the testamentary jurisdiction from that year to 1433 was exercised by the court of arches. Then abp. Stafford transferred it to a new court; president, the commissary of the prerogative court of Canterbury. There was also a prerogative court of the archbishop of York.

purchase of the rights of all the telegraph companies, authorised by the Telegraph Act of 1868. The organisation of the association was completed at a meeting in London, 3 March, 1869. The Provincial Newspaper Society, out of which it sprang, was founded in 1836, and became the Newspaper Society in 1889. Since 1868 the number of good daily provincial newspapers, containing the latest news of the world, has very greatly increased. Mr. John Hawkings, one of the founders of the central press, &c., died, aged 64, 19 Feb. 1899. Foreign press association registered as a society, March, 1898.

International press congress, Antwerp, 9 July, 1894; Bordeaux, 1895; Buda-pest, 1896; Stockholm, 1897; Lisbon, 1898; Rome, 1899; Leeds, 26 Aug. 1901; Berne, 21 July, 1902.

PRESS, LIBERTY OF THE. The *imprimatur* "let it be printed" was much used on the title-pages of books printed in the sixteenth and seventeenth centuries. The liberty of the press was severely restrained, and the number of master-printers in London and Westminster limited by the Star Chamber, 13 Charles I., July 1, 1637. John Milton published his noble work, "Areopagitica; or, a Speech for the Liberty of Unlicensed Printing," 1644. See *Fourth Estate*.

"Disorders in printing" were repressed by the parliament in 1643 and 1649, and by Charles II. . 1662
The censorship of the press (by a licence established in 1655 and 1693) abandoned 1695
The toast, "The liberty of the press; it is like the air we breathe—if we have it not we die," was first given at the Crown and Anchor tavern, at a Whig dinner 1795
Presses licensed, and the printer's name required to be placed on both the first and last pages of a book . . . . July, 1799
The severity of the restrictions on the French press relaxed by M. Persigny, minister of the interior, but soon restored . . . . . Dec. 1860
The liberty of the press in the United States greatly checked during the civil war 1861-1865
Certain restrictions on printers in the United Kingdom removed by act passed . . . . July, 1869
Bill greatly freeing the press in France introduced into the chamber . . . . . 24 Jan. 1881
Press (newspaper), a revolutionary journal, published in Dublin: commenced in Oct. 1797; Arthur O'Connor, Mr. Emmett, the barrister (whose brother was executed in 1803), and other conspicuous men, contributors to it; it inflamed the public mind in Ireland on the eve of the rebellion in 1798. The paper was suppressed by a military force . . . . . 6 March, 1798

PRESS-GANG for the royal navy was regulated by statute, 1378, and by 5 & 6 Will. IV. 1835; the compulsory service is limited to five years, see *Impressment*.

PRESSING TO DEATH, see *Mute*.

PRESTON (Lancashire). Near here Cromwell totally defeated the royalists under sir Marmaduke Langdale, 17 Aug. 1648. Preston was taken in 1715 by the Scotch insurgents, under Forster, who proclaimed king James VII. They were defeated in a battle on 12, 13 Nov. by generals Willes and Carpenter, who with the royal army invested Preston on all sides. The Scots laid down their arms, and their nobles and leaders were secured; some were shot as deserters, and others sent to London pinioned and bound together, to intimidate their party.—The stoppage of the cotton manufacture in 1861 and 1862, through the civil war in America, occasioned great suffering in Preston. See *Population*.

"*The Preston guild Merchant festival*," said to have been instituted in Saxon times, recorded as beginning 1328, and to have been kept once in 20 years regularly since 1562, was duly celebrated in Sept. 1862, Sept. 1882, and Sept. 1902
A fine art and industrial exhibition here opened 21 Sept. 1865
The new town hall opened by the duke of Cambridge 3 Oct. 1867
Statue of the late earl of Derby publicly inaugurated 3 June, 1873
Preston strikes.—In 1853, a great number of strikes took place among the workmen in the north of England. Those at Preston struck for an increase of 10 per cent. on their wages. On 15 Oct. the masters, in consequence, closed forty-nine mills, and 20,000 persons were thrown out of employment, who were mostly maintained for a long time by subscriptions from their fellows. In the week ending 17 Dec. 14,972 were relieved, at the cost of 2820*l*. 8*s*. The committee of workmen addressed lord Palmerston, 15 Nov., who gave them his advice . . . . . 24 Dec. 1853
After many attempts at reconciliation, the strike closed for want of funds . . . . 1 May, 1854
Another strike was closed in . . . . May, 1869
The executors of Mr. E. C. Harris, a solicitor, awarded 70,000*l*. for a free library, museum, &c., Sept. 1879; of which the foundation was laid by the earl of Lathom . . . . . 5 Sept. 1882
The foundation of the Lancashire county hall laid by the earl of Derby . . . . 14 Sept. ,,
Mr. Rich. Newsham bequeaths his pictures and art treasures, worth about 70,000*l*. to Preston announced Dec. 1883
Free library and museum, the gift of Mr. E. R. Harris, 300,000*l*., and others, opened by the earl of Derby; banquet . . . . . 26 Oct. 1893
Manchester cotton mill burnt, 2 men injured, 500 out of work . . . . . . 7 Aug. 1902
Earl of Derby presented with the freedom of the city . . . . 6 Aug. 1903

PRESTONPANS, near Edinburgh. At Gladsmuir, near this place, was fought a battle between the Young Pretender, prince Charles Edward Stuart, and his Scotch adherents, and the royal army under sir John Cope, 21 Sept. 1745. The latter was defeated with the loss of 500 men, and fled.

PRETENDERS. A name given to the son and grandsons of James II. of England.

The OLD PRETENDER, James Francis Edward Stuart, Chevalier de St. George, born 10 June, 1688, was acknowledged by Louis XIV. as James III. of England, in 1701.
Proclaimed, and his standard set up, at Braemar and Castletown, in Scotland . . . 3 Sept. 1715
Landed at Peterhead, in Aberdeenshire, from France, to encourage the rebellion that the earl of Mar and his other adherents had prompted, 25 Dec. ,,
This rebellion having been soon suppressed, the Pretender escaped to Montrose (from whence he proceeded to Gravelines) . . . . 4 Feb. 1716
Died at Rome . . . . . . 30 Dec. 1765
The YOUNG PRETENDER, Charles Edward, was born in 1720
Landed in Scotland, and proclaimed his father king 25 July, 1745
Gained the battle of Prestonpans, 21 Sept. 1745, and of Falkirk . . . . . . 17 Jan. 1746
Defeated at Culloden, and sought safety by flight, 16 April, ,,
He continued wandering among the wilds of Scotland for nearly six months; and as 30,000*l*. were offered for taking him, he was constantly pursued by the British troops, often hemmed round by his enemies, but still rescued by some lucky accident, and at length escaped from the isle of Uist to Morlaix in Sept. He died . 31 Jan. 1788
His natural daughter assumed the title of duchess of Albany; died in 1789

His brother, the cardinal York, calling himself Henry IX. of England, born March, 1725; died at Rome in . . . . Aug. 1807
His alleged grandson, Charles Edward Stuart comte d'Albanie, died . . . . . . 24 Dec. 1880
See *France*, Louis XVII.; and *Impostors*, 1606.

PRETORIA, capital of the Transvaal colony, in the neighbourhood of the goldfields of Lydenburg, situated 90 miles N.E. of Potchefstroom, and 980 miles from Cape Town. It derives its name from Andries Pretorius, who, during the Boer trek, by his military skill, waged war with the Zulus and defeated them on several occasions. Formerly the capital of the Transvaal or S. African republic. During the war in S. Africa 1899–1902 (*which see*) it was occupied by lord Roberts 5 June, 1900, and a new government under British authority instituted. Pretoria was visited (1903) by Mr. Chamberlain during his tour in S. Africa. The city has several handsome public buildings. Population (1899), 12,500.

PREVENTION OF CORRUPTION (Illicit commissions) Act passed, 6 Aug. 1900.

PREVENTION OF CRIME ACTS, 21 Aug. 1871, 15 Aug. 1879, and 12 July, 1882. See *Ireland*, May, 1882, 1887 *et seq.*

Criminal law and procedure (Ireland) act (1887) repeal bill (repealing the crimes act), read second time commons (222–208) . . 8 May, 1895

PREVENTIVE MEDICINE. The discoveries of Pasteur, Koch, and others, relative to the propagation of disease by minute germs (see *Germ Theory*), led to the gradual formation of a British (aft. Jenner) institute of Preventive Medicine by a committee of eminent physiologists and medical men, The institute was incorporated, sir Joseph Lister the first chairman, July, 1891; named the Lister institute, 7 Aug. 1903. 25,000*l.*, part of a legacy from Mr. Richard Berridge, awarded to the institute for the endowment of a laboratory at Chelsea, April, 1894. 250,000*l.* received from lord Iveagh, Dec. 1898. The Harben gold medal given to lord Lister, 1 Jan. 1899, and prof. Koch, 1901. See *Diphtheria*. Sir Geo. Buchanan, M.D., a government medical officer, 1871, an active promoter of preventive medicine, died 5 May, 1895; and sir Richard Thorne, his able successor, died 18 Dec. 1899.

PRICES, see *Corn*, *Bread*, and *Provisions*. Mr. T. Tooke, in 1838, published a "History of Prices from 1793 to 1856" He was latterly aided by Mr. W. Newmarch. "History of Agriculture and Prices" (1259-1702). By Mr. J. E. T. Rogers; six volumes published 1866-87; he died 13 Oct. 1890.

PRIDE'S PURGE. On the 6th Dec. 1648, colonel Pride, with two regiments, surrounded the house of parliament, and seizing in the passage forty-one members of the Presbyterian party, sent them to a low room, then called *hell*. Above 160 other members were excluded, and none admitted but the most furious of the Independents. The privileged members were named the *Rump parliament*, which was dismissed by Cromwell, 20 April, 1653.

PRIENE, one of the twelve cities of the Ionian league in Asia Minor. The temple of Minerva Polias, founded here by Alexander the Great, and the work of Pythios, was excavated by Mr. R. P. Pullan, for the Dilettanti Society, in 1868-9.

PRIEST (derived from *presbyteros*, elder), in the English church the minister who presides over the public worship. In *Gen* xiv. 18, Melchizedek king of Salem is termed "priest of the most high God." (1913 B.C.; see *Hebrews* vii.) The Greek *hiereus*, like the Jewish priest, had a sacrificial character, which idea of the priesthood is still maintained by the Romanists and those who favour their views. Among the Jews, the priests assumed their office at the age of thirty years. The dignity of high or chief priest was fixed in Aaron's family, 1491 B.C. After the captivity of Babylon, the civil government and the crown were superadded to the high priesthood; it was the peculiar privilege of the high priest, that he could be prosecuted in no court but that of the great Sanhedrim. The heathens had their arch-flamen or high priest, resembling the Christian archbishop. For "Priest in Absolution," see *Holy Cross*.

PRIMER. A book so named from the Romish book of devotions, and formerly set forth or published by authority, as the first book children should publicly learn or read in schools, containing prayers and portions of the scripture. Primers were printed 1535, 1539. Henry VIII. issued a prayer-book called a "primer" in 1545. The three were published by Dr. Burton in 1834.

PRIMITIVE CULTURE, see *Civilisation.*

PRIMOGENITURE, RIGHT OF. A usage brought down from the earliest times. The first-born in the patriarchal ages had a superiority over his brethren, and in the absence of his father was priest to the family. In some parts of England, by the ancient customs of gavel-kind and borough-English, primogeniture was superseded. It came in with the feudal law, 3 Will. I. 1068. The rights of primogeniture abolished in France, 1790. "Primogeniture," by Mr. Evelyn Cecil, published Feb. 1895.

PRIMROSE LEAGUE, formed in 1884 in memory of the late lord Beaconsfield (with whom the primrose is said to have been a favourite flower) and in support of conservative principles. He died 19 April, 1881, and the anniversary of that day is termed "Primrose Day," when the flower is generally worn by his admirers, and his statue in Parliament-square decorated. The marquis of Salisbury became grand master.

The league, which began with under a thousand members, was declared to consist of 810,228 knights, dames, and associates, with 1,992 "habitations" (2,414 in 1903), on . . 20 May, 1889
The league issues great number of political leaflets and songs. "Habitations" have been established in Scotland and Ireland.
Number of members reported, 1,002,097, April, 1891; 1,131,821, April, 1893; 1,617,983 . . April, 1903
Annual meetings: in Covent Garden theatre, the marquis of Salisbury in the chair, 6 May, 1892; 19 April, 1893; 19 April, 1894; 26 April, 1895; 29 April, 1896; 6 May, 1897; at the Albert hall, 4 May, 1898; 19 April, 1899; 9 May, 1900; 8 May, 1901; 7 May, 1902; 1 May, 1903, Mr. Balfour chairman.

PRINCE OF THE PEACE, a title conferred on Manuel Godoy by Charles IV. of Spain, for concluding the Treaty of Basle.

PRINCE EDWARD ISLAND (Dominion of Canada) was discovered by Cabot in 1497; was finally taken from the French by the British in 1758; united with Cape Breton as a colony in 1763; but separated in 1768. Population 1881, 108,894; 1891, 109,088; 1901, 103,259. Capital, Charlottetown. Lieut-governors: W. F. Robinson, Aug. 1870; sir Robert Hodgson, 1874; hon. Thomas Heath Haviland, 1879; hon A. A. Macdonald 1884;

J. S. Carvell, 1889, died 14 Feb. 1894; G. W. Howlan, 1894; Peter A. McIntyre, 1900.

PRINCE OF WALES'S ISLAND, see *Penang*.

PRINCE RUPERT'S LAND, see *Rupert's Land*, and *Hudson's Bay*.

PRINCESS ALICE, an iron saloon steamer, belonging to the London steamboat company, while carrying, it is supposed, above 900 persons, principally women and children, on their return from Sheerness, was immediately sunk by collision with the *Bywell Castle*, a large iron screw steamer, about 7.40 p.m. on Tuesday, 3 Sept. 1878, in the Thames, in Gallion's reach, about a mile below Woolwich arsenal. About 200 persons were saved, but of these about 16 died afterwards. About 640 bodies were recovered and buried; many at Woolwich.

The *Princess Alice* was 251 tons gross; 219 ft. 4 in. long; 20 ft. 2 in. broad; 8 ft. 4 in. deep. Engines, 140 horse power, by Caird, of Glasgow. Capt. Wm. Grinstead (lost), with (it is said) 6 sailors, 2 engineers, 3 firemen, 6 stewards, and 5 boys.

The *Bywell Castle*, 1376 tons gross; 254 ft. 3 in. long; 32 ft. 1 in. broad; 19 ft. 6 in. deep. Engines, 120 horse power. Owners, Hall Brothers, London. Captain Thomas Harrison.

Mansion House Relief Fund opened, 5 Sept. The queen sent 105*l.*; subscriptions came from royal family; 38,246*l.* 2*s.* 6*d.* received; final meeting, 30 Dec. 1878.

Board of Trade Inquiry.—Result: Officers of *Bywell Castle* and *Princess Alice* not considered responsible for the accident, but some were censured for carelessness, 28 Oct. The *Princess Alice* considered to be equal to her load; inquiry concluded, 31 Oct. Decision: "that the cause of the casualty was the breach of Rule 29 of the Thames Conservancy Regulations, by the *Princess Alice* not porting her helm when she came end on to the *Bywell Castle*, a vessel coming in the opposite direction." Report dated 6 Nov. 1878.

Coroner's Inquest.—Verdict: "*Bywell Castle* did not take necessary precautions in time, of easing, &c.; *Princess Alice* contributed to the collision by not stopping her engines and going astern, &c."; 14 Nov. 1878.

An action for damage against owners of *Bywell Castle* in Admiralty division began 27 Nov.; decision that both vessels were to blame, 11 Dec. 1878; decision on appeal that the *Princess Alice* was solely to blame, 15 July, 1879.

PRINCESS'S THEATRE, see under *Theatres*.

PRINCETON, New Jersey, N. America. Here Washington defeated the British, 3 Jan. 1777.

PRINTED GOODS, see *Calico*.

PRINTERS' PENSION SOCIETY, (now termed "Printers' Corporation"), founded 1827; chartered, 1865; almshouses instituted, 1841; orphan schools have been set up.

PRINTING. Block printing is said to have been invented by the Chinese about 593 A.D., movable types made in the 10th century. The honour of first printing with single types in Europe has been appropriated to Mentz, Strasburg, Haarlem, Venice, Rome, Florence, Basle, and Augsburg; but the names of the three first only are entitled to attention; the early history is very doubtful, and the subject of much controversy; see *Press*.

Adrian Junius awards the honour of the invention to Laurenzes John Koster, of Haarlem, "who printed with blocks, a book of images and letters, *Speculum Humanæ Salvationis*, and compounded an ink more viscous and tenacious than common ink, which blotted, about 1438."

[The leaves of this book, being printed on one side only, were afterwards pasted together.]

[In 1859, Mr. Samuel Leigh Sotheby issued an elaborate work compiled by his father and himself, entitled "*Principia Typographica*," containing fac-similes, &c., of the block-books of the 15th century; and Mr. J. Russell Smith published a fac-simile of the *Biblia Pauperum*, a very early block-book.]

John Fust established a printing-office at Mentz, and printed the *Tractatus Petri Hispani* . . 1442

John Gutenberg invented *cut* metal types, and used them in printing the earliest edition of the Latin bible (termed the Mazarin, from the discovery of a copy in the cardinal's library) at Mentz 1450-55

[At the sale of the Perkins library, 6 June, 1873, a copy of this bible on vellum sold for 3400*l.*, one on paper sold for 2690*l.*; a copy belonging to sir John Thorold, of Syston-park, sold for 3900*l.* 13 Dec. 1884; a copy belonging to the earl of Crawford sold for 2650*l.*, 15 June, 1887; lord Hopetoun's copy sold for 2000*l.*, 25 Feb. 1889.]

Book of Psalms, by Fust and Schœffer . 14 Aug. 1457

Sir John Thorold's copy on vellum sold for 4950*l.* [formerly sold for 136*l.*] 19 Dec. 1884.

The *Durandi Rationale*, first work printed with *cast* metal types 1459

[Printing was introduced into Oxford, about this time. *Collier*. Denied by Dibdin.]

A *Livy* printed. *Du Fresnoy* 1460

The first Latin bible with a date completed at Mentz by Fust and Schœffer 1462

Mentz taken and plundered, and the art of printing, in the general ruin, is spread to other towns . * *

The types were uniformly Gothic, or old German (whence our *old English* or *Black Letter*), until . 1465

Greek characters (quotations only) first used, same year . . . . "

Cicero de Officiis printed by Fust at Mentz . . "

Roman characters, first at Rome 1467

A *Chronicle*, said to have been found in the archbishop of Canterbury's palace (the fact disputed), bearing the date "*Oxford, anno* 1468."

Lactantius, by Sweynheym and Pannartz, near Rome, 1465; Livy by the same 1469

[To the west of the Sanctuary in Westminster Abbey, stood the Eleemosynary or Almonry, where the first printing press in England was erected about 1470–76, by William Caxton, encouraged by the learned Thomas Miling, then abbot.

He printed *Willyam Caxton's Recuyel of the Hystoryes of Troy, by Raoul le Feure*. *Phillips* . . . "

His early pieces were, *A Treatise on the Game of Chesse* and *Tully's Offices* (see below). *Dibdin* . 1474

"The Golden Legend," *which see* 1483

Æsop's Fables, printed by Caxton, is supposed to be the first book with its leaves numbered . . 1484

Aldus cast the Greek Alphabet, and a Greek book printed *ap. Aldi* 1476

He introduces the Italics . . . . . . * *

The *Pentateuch*, in Hebrew 1482

German Bible at Nuremberg 1483

Homer, *in folio*, beautifully done at Florence, eclipsing all former printing, by *Demetrius* . . 1488

Caxton prints the Boke of Eneydos 1490

Aldus Manutius begins printing at Venice . . 1494

Printing used in Scotland 1507

The first edition of the *whole* bible was, strictly speaking, the Complutensian Polyglot of cardinal Ximenes (see *Polyglot*) 1517

The *Liturgy*, the first book printed in Ireland, by Humphrey Powell 1550

Printing in Irish characters introduced by Nicholas Walsh, chancellor of St. Patrick's . . . 1571

The first newspaper said to be printed in England (see *Newspapers*) 1588

First patent granted for printing 1591

First printing press improved by William Blaeu, at Amsterdam 1601

First printing in America, in New England, when the *Freeman's Oath* and an almanack were printed 1639

"Bay Psalm-book" printed at Cambridge, Mass. . 1640

First bible printed in Ireland was at Belfast. *Hardy's Tour* 1704

First *types cast* in England by Caslon. *Phillips* . 1720

Stereotype printing practised by William Ged, of Edinburgh . . . . about 1730

[Specimen at Royal Institution, London.]

The present mode of stereotype invented by Mr. Tilloch . . . . about 1779

[Stereotype printing was in use in Holland in the last century. *Phillips.*]

Logographic printing in which words cast in one piece were employed: patented by H. Johnson and Mr. Walter of the *Times;* (soon disused) . 1783

Machine-printing (*which see*) first suggested by Nicholson 1790

The Stanhope press invented about 1800; in general use 1806

The Chiswick press, at which fine printing was produced by Chas. Whittingham, was established about 1811. He died in 1840. His nephew and successor, Charles Whittingham, who removed the work to Took's court, Chancery lane, in 1852, died in 1876. The work is now carried on at the same place by Messrs. Bell, of Covent garden.

Albion press introduced 1816

The roller, which was a suggestion of Nicholson, introduced . . . . ,,

Cowper's and Applegath's rollers 1817

Columbian press of Clymer patented . . . . ,,

Printing for the blind (by raised characters) begins 1827

Anastatic Printing, in which written or printed matter is transferred upon zinc plates, was invented by Baldermus of Berlin about 1841, and made known in London; lectured on by Faraday in 1845; and improved by Strickland and Delamotte in 1848

[A similar process was invented by Mr. Cocks of Falmouth in 1836.]

Printing-types electro-faced with copper about 1850

Engraved copper-plate electro-faced with iron and nickel 1858

Type-composing machines.—By James Young's several numbers of the "Family Herald" were set up, beginning 17 Dec. 1842; Hattersley's appeared at the Exhibition of 1862; Hart's was shown at the meeting of the British Association at Cambridge 6 Oct. 1862

W. H. Mitchel's composing machine was tried at Messrs. Spottiswoode's, 1861; these machines were said to be in use in America in . Jan. 1863

Kastenbein's composing and distributing machines (in use at the *Times* office) shown at the International exhibition 1872

The "Clowes" type-composing machine (Hooker's patent), in which electro-magnets are employed, was shown at the Caxton celebration exhibition, South Kensington . . . . July, 1877

[10,000 types per hour may be set up in page form.]

Alexander Mackie's type-composing machine in use at his office in Warrington, and at Messrs. Clay's, London, in 1871. It was said to be able to set up 4 columns of the *Times* in an hour.

Linotype.—An American composing and distributing machine, in which type matrices are employed instead of type. The manipulator brings letters, points, and spaces together in one line of the galley; this is passed into a casting-box, and a solid line of type is produced in stereo metal; this is repeated till the galley is full. The *New York Herald* uses 62 machines. An English company was formed in 1889, 2000 machines in use in Great Britain and about 5000 in America, reported, 1899.

Miss Emily Faithfull established the Victoria printing-office in Great Coram-street, London, in which female compositors are employed, 1860: the "Englishwoman's Journal" printed there Aug. 1861; appointed printer and publisher in ordinary to her Majesty, June, 1862; died . . June, 1895

Mr. William Blades, learned printer, printed facsimiles of several of Caxton's works, 1858, *et seq.* "Life of Caxton," 1861–3, and 1877; and other valuable works connected with printing; born, 1824; died . . . . 27 April, 1890

[See *Printing Machine, Stereotype,* and *Nature Printing.*]

TITLES OF THE EARLIEST BOOKS OF CAXTON AND WYNKYN DE WORDE.

THE GAME AND PLAYE OF THE CHESSE. *Translated out of the Frenche and emprynted by me* William Caxton. *Fynysshid the last day of Marche the yer of our Lord God a thousand foure hondred and lxxiiij.*

[A fac-simile of this book was printed by Mr. Vincent Figgins in 1859.]

The Recuyell of the Historyes of Troye; written in French by Raoul Lefevre; translated and printed by Wm. Caxton (about 1472–74); sold for 950*l.* at the Ashburnham sale, 9 Dec. 1897, and a French version of the same printed 1476, for 600*l.*; reprinted by H. Oskar Sommer, with index, glossary, and illustrations, 1895.

THE DICTES AND WISE SAYINGS OF THE PHILOSOPHERS, is stated to be the first book printed by Caxton in England, 1477. (Fac-simile published by Elliot Stock, 1877.)

Raoul Le Fevre's "Boke of the Hoole Lyf of Jason," translated and printed by Caxton at Westminster, about 1477; sold for 2100*l.* at the Ashburnham sale, 9 Dec. 1897.

THE BOKE OF TULLE OF OLDE AGE *Emprynted by me simple persone* William Caxton *into Englysshe as the playsir solace and reverence of men grouing in to old age the xij day of August the yere of our Lord* M. CCCC. *lxxxj.* HERBERT.

THE POLYCRONYCON *conteyning the Berynges and Dedes of many Tymes in eyght Bokes. Imprinted by* William Caxton *after having somewhat chaunged the rude and olde Englysshe, that is to wete* [to wit] *certayn Words which in these Dayes be neither vsyd ne understanden. Ended the second day of Juyll at Westmestre the xxij yere of the Regne of Kynge Edward the fourth, and of the Incarnacion of oure Lord a Thousand four hondred four Score and twcyne* [1482]. DIBDIN'S TYP. ANT.

THE CRONICLES OF ENGLOND *Empnted by me* Wyllyam Caxton *thabbey of Westmynstre by london the v day of Juyn the yere of thincarnacion of our lord god* M. CCCC. LXXX.

POLYCRONYCON. *Ended the thyrtenth daye of Apryll the tenth yere of the reyne of kinge Harry the seuenth And of the Jncarnacyon of our lord* MCCCCLXXXXV. *Empryn-ted by* Wynkyn The worde *at Wesmestre.*

THE HYLLE OF PERFECTION *emprynted at the instance of the reverend relygyous fader* Tho. Prior *of the hous of St. Ann, the order of the charterouse Accomplysshe*[d] *they fynysshe*[d] *att Westmynster the uiii day of Janeuer and yere of our lord Thousande* CCCC. LXXXXVII. *And in the xii yere of kynge Henry the vii by me* wynkyn de worde. AMES, HERBERT, DIBDIN.

THE DESCRIPCYON OF ENGLONDE *Walys Scotland and Irlond speaking of the Noblesse and Worthynesse of the same Fynyssked and emprynted in Flete strete in the syne of the Sonne by me* Wynkyn de Worde *the yere of our lord a* M CCCCC *and ij. mensis Mayiis* [mense Maii]. DIBDIN'S TYP. ANT.

The Festyvall or Sermons on sondays and holidais taken out of the golden legend enprynted at london in Flete-strete at yᵉ sygne of yᵉ Sonne by Wynkyn de worde. In the yere of our Lord M. CCCCC. VIII. *And ended the xi daye of Maye.* AMES.

"HELYAS, KNYGHT OF THE SWANNE," from Wynkyn de Worde's press, 1512, and undescribed by all bibliographers, sold for 410*l.*, 11 July, 1899.

CAXTON'S "RYAL BOOK" sold for 1,550*l.* 31 July, 1901; another copy, printed by him in 1487, realized 2,225*l.* 20 March, 1902.

THE LORD'S PRAYER [As printed by Caxton in 1483.] *Father our that art in heavens, hallowed be thy name: thy kingdome come to us; thy will be done in earth as is in heaven: our every day bread give us to day; and forgive us oure trespasses, as we forgive them that trespass against us; and lead us not in to temptation, but deliver us from all evil sin, amen.* LEWIS'S LIFE OF CAXTON.

A PLACARD. [As printed by William Caxton.] *If it plese ony man spirituel or temperel to bye ony pies of two or three comemoraciōs of Salisburi use* enprynted after the forme of this presēt lettre whiche ben wel and truly correct, late him come to westmonester in to the almonestye at the reed pale* [red pale] *and he shall have them good there.* DIBDIN'S TYP. ANT.

* Romish Service-books, used at Salisbury, by the devout called Pies (*Pica,* Latin), as is supposed from the different colour of the text and rubric. Our printing-type *Pica* is called *Cicero* by foreign printers.—*Wheatley.*

Caxton Celebration of 400th anniversary of discovery of printing: First meeting at Westminster abbey; dean Stanley in chair; Messrs. Spottiswoode, Rivington, Clowes, and others present, 17 Feb. 1877.

Exhibition (at South Kensington) of early printed books, bibles, and engravings; printing, paper-making, stereotyping, electrotyping, in operation; opened by Mr. W. E. Gladstone, 30 June; closed 1 Sept. 1877.

1116*l.* profit given to the Printers' Pension Corporation, 30 July, 1878.

The catalogue contains valuable information.

Printing-machines.—William Nicholson, editor of the *Philosophical Journal*, first projected (1790-1), but Mr. König first contrived and constructed a working printing machine, which began with producing the *Times* of 28 Nov. 1814, a memorable day in the annals of typography.

In 1818, Mr. E. Cowper patented improvements.*

König's machine printed 1800 an hour on one side; Cowper's improvements increased this number to 4200. This was raised to 15,000, by Mr. Applegath's machine, which printed the *Times*.

Hoe's American machine, introduced into London 1858, prints 20,000 an hour.

Marinoni's machine at Paris said to print 36,000 an hour; Dec. 1868.

Walter press, invented for the *Times* by J. C. Macdonald and Mr. Calverley, between 1862-9, prints about 17,000 an hour *perfected*; 1872.

American Campbell press said to print 50,000 sheets perfected in an hour, Feb. 1876.

Ingram web rotary machine, invented by Mr. (later sir) W. J. Ingram, M.P., for printing illustrated papers; first used to print *Illustrated London News*, 4 Oct. 1877.

Printing in Colours was first commenced by the employment of several blocks, to imitate the initial letters in MSS. (for instance, the Mentz Psalter of Fust, 1455, which has a letter in three colours). Imitations of chiaroscuro soon followed ("Repose in Egypt," engraving on wood after Louis Cranach, in 1519, in Germany; others by Ugo da Carpi, in Italy, 1518).

J. B. Jackson (1720-54) attempted, without success, to imitate water-colour drawings, and to print paper-hangings.

About 1783, John Skippe, an amateur, printed some chiaroscuros.

In 1819-22, Mr. William Savage produced his remarkable work, "Hints on Colour Printing," illustrated by imitations of chiaroscuro, and of coloured drawings, giving details of the processes employed.

In 1836, Mr. George Baxter produced beautiful specimens of Picture-Printing, and took out a patent, which expired in 1855. In some of the illustrations to the "Pictorial Album" (1836), he employed twenty different blocks.

It has been applied to Lithography (hence Chromolithography).

In 1849, Mr. G. C. Leighton produced imitations of water-colour drawings, by means of modifications and improvements of Savage's processes. In 1851 he commenced colour-printing by machinery, and has since availed himself of aqua-tinted plates, and also of electrotyped silver and copper surfaces to obtain purity of colour as well as durability; Mr. Leighton died, 8 May, 1895.

The large coloured prints of the *Illustrated London News* were first issued in Dec. 1856.

Mr. E. Meyerstein explained his process of printing many colours at one impression (stenochromy), Society of Arts, 13 Dec. 1876.

Mr. Ivan Orloff's colour-printing machine, multi-coloured designs produced by one operation; one set up in London, July, 1899.

Printing surfaces. Vulcanised india-rubber was first employed for this purpose by Mr. John Leighton, F.S.A., about 1862, and patented in the name of Alfred Leighton, 1864. The application is much used for hand-stamps for books, &c.

Mr. Fred Wicks' type-casting machine (cheap), reported *Times*, 19 Nov. 1896, adopted 1900.

* In 1817 was published Blumenbach's Physiology by Elliotson, the first book printed by machinery. The machine employed was König's, one which printed both sides in one operation at the rate of 900 sheets an hour (1816).

Printing Exhibition (of specimens, apparatus, materials, stationery, and machinery), at Agricultural Hall, London, include 5-17 July, 1880; 14 July *et seq.* 1881; and 30 July *et seq.* 1883.

International exhibition of printing at Stationers' hall, London, opened by the lord mayor, 14 Oct. 1889.

PRIORIES, at first dependent on the great abbeys, are mentioned in 722 in England; see *Abbeys*, and *Monasteries*. *Alien priories* were seized by the king (Edward I.) in 1285, and in succeeding reigns on the breaking out of war with France; but were usually restored on the conclusion of peace. These priories were dissolved, and their estates vested in the crown, 3 Henry V. 1414.—*Rymer's Fœdera.*

PRISCILLIANISTS, disciples of Priscillian, a Spanish bishop who propagated doctrines alleged to contain Gnosticism and Manicheism, 372. When condemned he appealed from the pope to the emperor, but was beheaded at Treves, 385.

PRISONERS of War, among the ancient nations, when spared, were usually enslaved. About the 13th century, civilized nations began to exchange their prisoners.

The Spanish, French, and American prisoners of war in England were 12,000 in number, 30 Sept. 1779

The number exchanged by cartel with France, from the commencement of the then war, was 44,000 June, 1781

The English prisoners in France estimated at 6000, and the French in England 27,000 . . Sept. 1798

The English in France amounted to 10,300, and the French, &c., in England to 47,600, in 1811

Great numbers made by the Germans in the war 1870-1

Boer prisoners made by the English, about 32,000 (24,996 deported oversea) in the war . . 1899-1902

PRISONERS' COUNSEL ACT, 6 & 7 Will. IV. c. 114 (1836), allows counsel to persons tried for felony; hitherto prohibited. Poor prisoners defence act, royal assent 14 Aug. 1903.

PRISONS of England and Wales. Annual cost: 1867-8, 482,414*l.*; 1869-70, 501,348*l.*; 1880-1, 421,686*l.*; 1883-4, 334,674*l.*; 1887-8, 340,483*l.*; 1890-1, 326,551*l.*; 1892-3, 348,689*l.*; 1902-3, 660,929*l.* (England and Colonies); Scotland, 91,131*l.*; Ireland, 113,641*l.*

Total of prisoners received in 1893, 183,143; in 1894, 186,225; 1899, 186,840; 1901-2, 185,643. Ireland, 1901, 32,086.

Number of persons (England and Wales) sentenced in 1901: death, 28; penal servitude for life, 1; for a term of years, 868; imprisonment on indictment, 6,804; on summary conviction or for want of sureties, 160,647. *Youthful Offenders*, 1901-2, under 12 years, male 17, female 2; 12 to 16 years, 1,235 males, 141 females; 16 to 21 years, 13,342 males, 2,200 females. *Soldiers and Sailors* (by courts-martial) 1901-2, 3,193; *debtors* (or on civil process) 14,039; in *default of sureties*, 1,415. Prisoners who could *read and write* in 1870, 33·8 per cent.; in 1900, 19·2 per cent. Value of *work* performed by prisoners at local and convict prisons and state inebriate reformatories 1901-2, 215,276*l.* 17*s.* 1*d.*, an average of 13*l.* 13*s.* 8*d.* per head.

PRISONS of London, see *Fleet*, *King's Bench*, *Newgate*, *Poultry*, *Clerkenwell*, *Millbank*.

Horsemonger-lane gaol was built in 1791; closed, 1878; opened as a playground . . 5 May, 1884

The state of prisons greatly improved after the exertions of Howard.* Cold-Bath Fields prison was built on his suggestion, 1794; converted into offices for the parcels post 1887-91

* John Howard was born 2 Sept. 1726; made sheriff of Bedford, 1773; investigated into the state of English prisons, 1773-5; and gave evidence thereon before the house of commons, which led to amendments by law, 1774; he visited prisons all over the continent, and died at Kherson, 20 Jan. 1790. Centenary celebrated 20 Jan. 1890.

The atrocities of governor Aris in this prison were exposed in parliament . . . . . 12 July, 1800
Sheriffs' fund society for assisting discharged prisoners established by aldermen C. Smith and sir R. Phillipps 1807
Whitecross-street prison for debtors erected . 1813-15
Millbank prison (see *Millbank*) received convicts as a *penitentiary* . . . . . 27 June, 1816
Borough compter mean and confined till visited by a parliamentary committee in 1817
Savoy prison, for the confinement of deserters from the Guards, formerly situated in the Strand, was pulled down to make room for Waterloo-bridge . 1819
New Bridewell prison was erected as a substitute for the City Bridewell, Blackfriars, in . . 1829
Tothill Fields Bridewell, built in 1618, rebuilt . 1836
The old Marshalsea prison, Southwark, built in the 13th century, taken down 1842
Pentonville Model prison completed . . . ,,
Millbank penitentiary reported a failure; changed to an ordinary prison 1843
Middlesex House of Detention, Clerkenwell, erected in 1847 (converted now into offices for the parcels post and Board School).
City prison, Holloway, opened . . . 6 Feb. 1852
Royal Discharged Prisoners' Aid society established 1858
Act passed for abolishing Queen's Bench prison . 1862
Prison Ministers' act passed 1863
Acts to consolidate and amend the law relating to prisons, passed . . 5 July, 1865; Aug. 1866
Howard Association (*which see*) instituted . . ,,
A National Prison Association was organized in New York . . . . . . 1869 or 1870
Millbank made a military prison, 1870; closed, 6 Nov. 1890
International prison congress met at the Middle Temple, London . . . . . 3 July, 1872
Prison Discipline Society, by the philanthropic labours of sir T. F. Buxton, M.P., was instituted in 1815, and held its first public meeting in 1820. Its objects were the amelioration of gaols, the classification and employment of the prisoners, and the prevention of crime.
Whitecross-street prison; ordered to be pulled down and materials sold . . . . . 11 Oct. 1870
The *Prison Acts*, for England, Ireland, and Scotland, passed 12 July and 14 Aug. 1877. They transfer management of prisons, after 1 April, 1878, from local authorities to the home secretary; provide for re-distribution and reduction of number of prisons, &c.
Other gaols closed 1878
An international *Prison Congress* met at Stockholm, 20–24 Aug. 1878; at Paris . . . July, 1895
Prisoners' aid societies, prison charities act passed 18 Aug. 1882
Discharged prisoners' aid societies are now attached to all prisons. The "metropolitan" society was established 1864
A receiving house for discharged prisoners was opened by gen. Booth at 30, Argyle-square, W.C. 30 Jan. 1891
The committee appointed to inquire respecting prison rules, reported in favour of their continuance in regard to dress and hair-cutting, for sanitary, disciplinary and general reasons . June, 1889
International congress respecting prisons at St. Petersburg, 550 delegates; president, prince of Oldenburg . . . . . 19 June, *et seq.* 1890
The departmental committee on prisons appointed, 5 June, 1894; Mr. H. J. Gladstone, chairman, issued its report, containing various recommendations, 23 April, 1895; the prisons board introduce a variety of fresh industrial occupations, Feb. 1896

[A continuation of the "Commission Pénitentiaire Internationale," founded in 1872, has met in London, Rome, and elsewhere.]

New prisons act, granting regulating powers to home secretary and other changes, passed 12 Aug. 1898
Report of the commissioners of prisons (decrease of crime) for year ended 31 March . . Sept. ,,
International prison congress (6th quinquennial) at Brussels . . . . . . 6–13 Aug. 1900
Commissioners' report, reforms instituted, classification of criminals, etc., decrease of crime and in the number of debtors, for year ended 31 March, Sept. ,,
Association of lady visitors of prisons, duchess of Bedford vice-president; first conference, London . . . . 18 June, 1901
The evils of Russian military imprisonment at Schlüsselburg "killing by inches," exposed *Times* . . . . 21 Aug. 1903.

PRIVATE BILLS, see *Acts of Parliament*.

PRIVATEER, a ship belonging to private individuals, sailing with a licence (termed a *Letter of Marque*), granted by a government in time of war, to seize and plunder the ships of the enemy. The practice, said to have been adopted by Edward I. against the Portuguese in 1295, was general during the war between Spain and the Netherlands in the 17th century, and during the last French war. Privateering was abolished by the great sovereigns of Europe by treaty, 30 March, 1856. The United States government refused to agree unless the right of blockade was also given up. The British government declined this, asserting "that the system of commercial blockade was essential to its naval supremacy." On 17 April, 1861, Jefferson Davis, president of the southern confederacy, announced his intention of issuing letters of marque, and on the 19th president Lincoln proclaimed that all southern privateers should be treated as pirates. This decree was not carried out: see *United States*. All the great powers forbade privateering during the American civil war (*which see*). By the treaty of Washington privateering was prohibited; and April, 1898, in relation to the Spanish-American war, a Spanish decree maintains liberty of action.

PRIVILEGED PLACES, see *Asylums*.

PRIVY COUNCIL. A council said to have been instituted by Alfred, 895. The number of the council was about twelve when it discharged the functions of state, now confined to the members of the cabinet; but it had become of unwieldy amount before 1679, in which year it was remodelled upon sir William Temple's plan, and reduced to thirty members: Anthony Ashley, earl of Shaftesbury, being president. The number is now unlimited. To attempt the life of a privy councillor in the execution of his office was made capital, occasioned by Guiscard's stabbing Mr. Harley while the latter was examining him on a charge of high treason, 9 Anne, 1711.

"The Proceedings and Ordinances of the Privy Council of England from 10 Richard II. to 33 Hen. VIII., edited by sir H. Nicolas, 7 vols," were published by the record commissioners, 1834-7.

The "Acts of the Privy Council," edited by Mr. J. R. Dasent, beginning with 1542, Vols. I.—IX., issued in 1890-4; Vol. XVI. 1897.

JUDICIAL COMMITTEE OF THE PRIVY COUNCIL.—In lieu of the Court of Delegates, for appeals from the lord chancellors of Great Britain and of Ireland in cases of lunacy—from the Ecclesiastical and Admiralty Courts of England, and the Vice-Admiralty courts abroad—from the Warden of the Stannaries, the courts of the Isle of Man, and other islands, and the Colonial courts, &c.,—fixed by statute 3 & 4 Will. IV., c. 41, 1833; amended by other acts in 1844, 1851, 1852.

JUDGES.—The lord president, lord chancellor, master of the rolls, vice-chancellor, lords justices in appeal, lord chief justice of the queen's bench and common pleas, lord chief baron, judges of the courts of bankruptcy, probate, and admiralty, and others appointed by the queen. In consequence of the increase of business, and consequent delay, the queen was empowered to appoint four new judicial members of the committee, by 34 & 35 Vict. c. 91 (21 Aug. 1871). The attorney-general, sir R. Collier, was made a judge of the Common Pleas, 7 Nov., and a member of the judicial committee 22 Nov. 1871.

These proceedings were considered contrary to the spirit of the act by several judges and the legal profession generally. A vote of censure on the Gladstone ministry was negatived in the house of lords (89-87), 15 Feb.; in the commons (268-241), 19 Feb. 1872.

Other changes were made by an act passed in 1876.

The addition of judges from the colonies authorized by an act passed 6 July, 1895.

PRIVY SEAL, THE LORD, the fifth great officer of state, has the custody of the privy seal, which he must not put to any grant, without good warrant under the king's signet. This seal is used by the king to all charters, grants, and pardons, signed by him before they come to the great seal. Richard Fox, bishop of Winchester, held this office in the reign of Henry VIII. previously to 1523, when Cuthbert Tunstall, bishop of London, was appointed. The privy seal has been on some occasions in commission.—*Beatson.* See under *Liverpool*, *Canning*, *Wellington*, and succeeding *Administrations*.

PRIZE-FIGHTING, see *Boxing*.

PRIZE MONEY, arising from captures made from the enemy, was decreed by government to be divided into eight equal parts, and distributed by order of ranks, 17 April, 1793. The distribution of army prize-money is regulated by an act passed in 1832. Naval prize-money is now regulated by royal proclamation; the last, 19 May, 1866.

PROBABILITY, THEORY OF (termed by Butler, "the guide of life"; by Laplace, "good sense reduced to calculation"), was originated by Pascal, and taken up by Fermat, in their correspondence in 1654.

Its object is "the determination of the number of ways in which an event may happen or fail, in order that we may judge whether the chances of its happening or failing are greater."—*Jevons.*

It has been treated upon by the most eminent mathematicians, viz., the Bernouillis, De Moivre, D'Alembert, Euler, Lagrange, Laplace, and Quetelet.

Isaac Todhunter's copious "History of Probability," published 1865.

PROBATE COURT, established in Aug. 1857 by 20 & 21 Vict. c. 77, which abolished all powers exercised by the ecclesiastical courts in the granting of probates of wills, &c.; see *Prerogative Court*. The first judge appointed, 5 Jan. 1858, was sir Cresswell Cresswell, who took his seat on 12 Jan. On his death, sir James P. Wilde (aft. lord Penzance) was appointed judge, 28 Aug. 1863; see *Supreme Court*. The president of the probate, divorce, and admiralty division, sir James Hannen (1872), succeeded by sir Charles P. Butt, Jan. 1891 (died 25 May, 1892); sir Francis Henry Jeune, 30 May, 1892. By the Judicature Act of 1873, the probate, divorce, and admiralty courts were constituted the 5th division of the Supreme Court. A probate and matrimonial division of the high court of justice of Ireland was established by Judicature act, 1877; present judge, rt. hon. Wm. Drennan Andrews. *Probate* is the exhibiting and proving a will before the proper authority. The probate registry is now at Somerset House.

Probate duties partly transferred to relieve local taxation by Local Government Act, 1888—amount received 1887-8, 4,596,620*l.* The duty was superseded in 1894 by the "estate duty," *which see.*

PROCEDURE RULES, see under *Parliament* 1882 and 1888, 1890.

PROCESSIONS ACT, 13 Vict. c. 2, passed 12 March, 1850, prohibited party processions, with banners, &c. It was repealed in 1872. Processions of workmen and others, for demonstrations in Hyde Park, prohibited in the great thoroughfares of London, by the police, 31 May, 1890.

PROCLAMATIONS, ROYAL, "have only a binding force when grounded upon and to enforce the laws of the realm."—*Coke.* Henry VIII., in 1539, declared that they were as valid as acts of parliament. This was annulled, 1547.

The lord-lieutenant of Ireland has power by proclamation to place districts under the provisions of the Criminal Law Procedure Acts, 1881 and 1887, which districts are then said to be *proclaimed*.

PROCONSUL, a Roman consul, whose tenure of office was extended beyond his legal term. Q. Publilius was the first proconsul appointed during the war with Parthenope, 327 B.C. The name was afterwards given to governors of provinces.

PROCTOR (from *procurator*), an office in ecclesiastical courts, corresponding to that of an attorney or solicitor in courts of common law. It was abolished by the Judicature act, 1873. The persons chosen to represent the clergy in convocation are termed proctors. The university proctors enforce discipline.

PROFILES. The first profile taken, as recorded, was that of Antigonus, who, having but one eye, his likeness was so taken, 330 B.C.—*Ashe.* "Until the end of the 3rd century, I have not seen a Roman emperor with a full face; they were always painted or appeared in profile, which gives us the view of a head in a very majestic manner."—*Addison.*

PROGRESISTAS, a political party in Spain, headed by Espartero, duke of Victory, and latterly by general Prim. Since 1865 they adopted a policy of inaction in public affairs; by uniting with the unionists and republicans in Sept. 1868, the government were overthrown, see *Spain*.

A party in Servia and also in Portugal are termed *Progressists*.

In England, since 1888 *et seq.*, the radical party in county councils, the school board, parish councils, and similar bodies have been termed PROGRESSIVES, and their opponents MODERATES.

"PROGRESS AND POVERTY," see *Land Nationalization*.

PROGRESSIONIST THEORY supposes that the existing species of animals and plants were not originally created, but were gradually developed from one simple form; see *Species*.

PROHIBITION OF EXPORTATION OF ARMS Act passed 6 Aug. 1900, and became law 7 Aug. 1900.

PROMISSORY NOTES were regulated and allowed to be made assignable in 1705. First taxed by a stamp in 1782; the tax was increased in 1804, and again in 1808, and subsequently; see *Bills of Exchange*.

"PRO NIHILO," a pamphlet, said to be by count Henry Arnim, attacking count Bismarck; published Nov. 1875. He was prosecuted for it in 1876; see *Prussia*.

PRONUNCIAMENTO, a revolution (in Spain or South America) effected by a military leader; in France, termed a *coup d'état*. See *France* and *Spain*.

PROPAGANDA FIDE, CONGREGATIO DE (congregation for the propagation of the faith of the Romish church), was constituted at Rome by Gregory XV. in 1622; the college, by Urban VIII., in 1627, for the education of missionaries to various countries, a special feature of the college being the education of some 200 natives at an early age for mission work in their own lands. It has a large and valuable library consisting of about 30,000 volumes, a museum, and a polyglot printing press. The Epiphany is celebrated as the great festival of the college.

PROPAGATION OF THE GOSPEL SOCIETY received its charter, 16 June, 1701. Its sphere, to minister to British subjects beyond the seas, much extended, see "Spiritual Expansion of the Empire," pub. 1899. Bicentenary celebrations, 16 June, 1900; great meeting in Exeter hall, abp. of Canterbury and lord Salisbury present, 19 June; S. London missionary and colonial exhibition opened by the lord mayor, 14 Nov. 1900. General income in 1867, 114,546*l.*; in 1879, 145,240*l.*; in 1884, 109,572*l.*; in 1894, 122,327*l.*; 1897, 317,512*l.*; 1898, 132,355*l.* 13*s.* 6*d.* (the queen gives 200*l.* to the bicentenary fund, May; the prince of Wales, 100 gs., June, 1900); bicentenary celebrated at the Guildhall, 12 Feb. 1901 (the king gives 105*l.* March); general fund, 88,585*l.*, 1902; total, 206,709*l.*, 1901; 152,529*l.*, 1902.

PROPERTY. The assessments on real property, under the property tax of 1815, were 51,898,423*l.*; of which Middlesex was 5,595,537*l.*; Lancashire, 3,087,774*l.*; and Yorkshire, 4,700,000*l.*; Wales, 2,153,801*l.* Estimated wealth of the country (1878), 8,500,000,000*l.* See *Land, Income Tax, Capital*.

PROPHESYING. About 1570 the puritanical part of the clergy, particularly at Northampton, held meetings (termed prophesyings) for prayer and exposition of the scriptures. These were forbidden by queen Elizabeth, 7 May, 1577, and immediately ceased.

The Prophecy Investigation society, formed about 1840, held a special meeting at the Mansion-house, London, 30 April, 1891.

PROPHETS, see under *Jews*.

PROPORTIONAL REPRESENTATION. The scheme propounded by Mr. Thomas Hare in 1857, in a pamphlet on "Representation," and perfected in his "Treatise on the Election of Representatives," published in 1859, which was well received by Mr. J. Stuart Mill. A society to introduce this principle was formed in Feb. 1884. It included sir John Lubbock (president), Mr. Leonard H. Courtney, and many other M.P.'s.

It proposed that "in all cases where an elector is entitled to one vote only, to enable the elector to nominate more than one candidate to whom, under certain circumstances, that vote might be transferred in the manner indicated by the elector." Negatived by the commons, 134—31, 3 March, 1885.

PROROGATION OF PARLIAMENT. By an act passed 12 Aug. 1867, her majesty was enabled to issue a proclamation for the prorogation of parliament during the recess.

PROSECUTOR. By the Prosecution of Offences Act, 42 & 43 Vict. c. 22 (3 July, 1879), the appointment of a director of public prosecutions with assistants was enacted, somewhat resembling officers in Scotland and Ireland. It came into operation 1 Jan. 1880. John Blossett Maule, appointed director of public prosecutions, Dec. 1879; succeeded by sir Augustus Stephenson, 1884; succeeded by the hon. Hamilton Cuffe, Oct. 1894.

A committee reported the plan to be a failure, and recommended changes, June; act amended, 1884. 551 prosecutions; 451 convictions in 1893; 449 in 1900.

A public prosecutor, "procureur du roi," in France, is mentioned in the 14th century; replaced by "accusateur publique" (elected), 1791; by "commissaire national," 1793; "procureur" restored by Napoleon I.

PROTECTION OF LIFE AND PROPERTY ACT (for part of Ireland), passed 16 June, 1871; another, 3 March, 1881. See *Ireland*.

PROTECTIONISTS, that section of the conservative party which opposed the repeal of the corn laws, and which separated from sir Robert Peel in 1846. The name was derived from a "Society for the *Protection* of Agriculture," of which the duke of Richmond was chairman, and which had been established to counteract the efforts of the Anti-Corn Law League, 17 Feb. 1844. Lord George Bentinck was the head of the party from 1846 till his death, 21 Sept. 1848. The Derby administration not proposing the restoration of the corn-laws, the above society was dissolved, 7 Feb. 1853.—The protection of native manufactures has been maintained in the United States since 1868, and in France, Germany, Italy, and other countries. See *France*, March, 1887; *England*, 1903; *United States*, Oct. 1890. President Cleveland condemned protection, 4 March 1893: Mr. McKinley, a protectionist, elected president of U.S.N.A. 3 Nov. 1896.

The revival of protection negatived by the house of commons without a division, 14 May, 1886. The national association for the preservation of agriculture and other industries held a meeting in London, 8 Dec. 1887. Other protection meetings, Mr. James Lowther, M.P., in the chair, in London, 13 Dec. 1895, and 10 Dec. 1896.

See *Fair Trade, Free Trade, Tariff Reform League*, and *Addenda*.

PROTECTIVE TARIFFS, see *Addenda*.

PROTECTORATES IN ENGLAND. That of the earl of Pembroke, 19 Oct. 1216, ended by his death, 1218. Of Humphry, duke of Gloucester, began 31 Aug. 1422; he was seized 11 Feb. 1447, and found dead a few days after. Of Richard, duke of Gloucester, began May, 1483, and ended by his assuming the royal dignity, 26 June the same year. Of Somerset began 28 Jan. 1547, and ended by his resignation in 1549. Of Oliver Cromwell began 16 Dec. 1653, and ended by his death, 3 Sept. 1658. [He firmly refused to be styled king, as solicited by the parliament, Feb.–May, 1657.] Of Richard Cromwell began 3 Sept. 1658, and ended by his resignation, 25 May, 1659; see *England*.

PROTEIN, from the Greek (*prōteion*, principal); a chemical term introduced by Mulder about 1844, for the basis of albumen, fibrin, and casein.

PROTESTANT REFORMATION SOCIETY, established 1820; it employs missionaries and readers.

PROTESTANTS. The emperor Charles V. called a diet at Spires in 1529, to request aid from the German princes against the Turks, and to devise means for allaying the religious disputes which then raged owing to Luther's opposition to the Roman catholic clergy. Against a decree of this diet, to support the doctrines of the church of Rome, six Lutheran princes, with the deputies of thirteen imperial towns, formally and solemnly *protested*, 19 April, 1529. Hence the term protestants was given to the followers of Luther; it afterwards included Calvinists, and other sects separated from the see of Rome. The six protesting princes were: John, elector of Saxony; George, margrave of Brandenburg; Ernest and Francis, the dukes of Lunenburg; the landgrave of Hesse; and the prince of Anhalt; these were joined by the citizens of Strasburg, Nuremberg, Ulm, Constance, Heilbron, and seven other cities; see *Lutheranism*, *Calvinism*, *Huguenots*, *Germany*, *Church of England*, &c.

Protestants persecuted in Scotland and Germany . 1546
Edward VI. established Protestantism in England . 1548
Mary re-establishes Romanism, and persecutes the Protestants: above 300 put to death . . 1553-8
Ridley, bishop of London, and Latimer, bishop of Worcester, were burnt at Oxford, 16 Oct. 1555: and Cranmer, abp. of Canterbury . 21 March, 1556
[During three years of Mary's reign, 277 persons were brought to the stake; besides those punished by imprisonment, fines, and confiscations. Among those who suffered by fire were 5 bishops, 21 clergymen, 8 lay gentlemen, 84 tradesmen, 100 husbandmen, servants, and labourers, 55 women, and 4 children. The principal agents of the queen were the bishops Gardiner and Bonner.]
Elizabeth restores Protestantism 1558
Protestant settlements formed in Ulster, N. Ireland 1608-11
The Protestant union of princes in Germany, 4 May, 1608; met last . . . . May, 1621
Thirty years' war between Romanists and Protestants in Germany 1618-48
Protestants persecuted at Thorn, in Poland . . 1724
Protestant Association (see *Gordon's "No-Popery" Mob*) 1780
A society for planting communities of the poorer Protestants on tracts of land, particularly in the northern counties of Ireland, established in Dublin in . . . . Dec. 1829
(London) Protestant Society, established 1827; Protestant Association, 1835; Protestant Alliance . 1849
Protestant Conservative Society established 9 Dec. 1831
Protestant Alliance formed at Armagh . 7 Nov. 1845
Pan-protestant conference held at Worms (about 1000 delegates) . . . . . 31 May, 1869
Meeting of a general synod of the Reformed Church of France (M. Guizot present), to propose return to early doctrine and discipline held at Paris, 7 June; the "liberal party" attack the doctrines of the authority of the Bible, the divinity and resurrection of Christ, &c.; an orthodox confession is carried amid strong opposition (61-45) 20 June, 1872
Protestant churchmen's alliance formed, see *Church of England* (annual meetings) . . 25 Feb. 1890
Death of M. Edmond de Pressensé, eminent free church pastor, at Paris, aged 67 . 8 April, 1891
National Protestant congress meets at Brighton 13 Oct. 1891; 7th, London, 12 Oct. 1896; Folkestone, 17 Oct., 1898.
United Protestant demonstration held at the Albert Hall, visc. Midleton in the chair, 4 Feb. 1902

PROTOPLASM, the material of the minute ultimate particles of all animal and vegetable tissues, formerly termed sarcode; by Von Mohl, protoplasm (1884), "the physical basis of life," by Huxley (1868). The protamœba, the lowest form of life, is a structureless mass of protoplasm; the amœba, a similar mass, contains a nucleus. Protoplasm is composed of hydrogen, oxygen, nitrogen, carbon, and sulphur.

PROTYLE, see *Elements*.

PROVENCE (the Roman *Provincia*), S. E. France, was made a kingdom by the emperor Lothaire for his son Charles. It afterwards became part of the kingdom of Arles as a feudal tief, and was re-united to the German empire in 1032 by Conrad II. On the fall of the Hohenstaufens it was acquired by Charles of Anjou, who married the heiress of the count in 1245, and became king of Naples, in 1268; and was held by his successors till its annexation to France by Charles VIII. in 1487.

PROVERBS. The book of Proverbs by Solomon is dated about 1000 B.C. The latter part was collected by order of Hezekiah, about 700 B.C. Ray's collection of English proverbs appeared in 1672, and Bohn's general collection in 1857. Martin F. Tupper's "Proverbial Philosophy" first appeared in 1839. Alfred Henderson's "Latin Proverbs," 1869. A society for the Revision of Proverbs existed in 1886.

PROVIDENCE, capital of Rhode Island, U.S. (*which see*), 1636. Population, 1890, 132,146; 1900, 175,597.

PROVIDENT KNOWLEDGE SOCIETY established in 1872, to forward the post-office financial schemes; by establishing penny banks, sending out lecturers, and publishing papers for the promotion of thrift among the lower classes. It held its first annual meeting, 9 May, 1873, the earl of Derby in the chair.

PROVISIONS OF OXFORD, see *Oxford*.

PROVISIONS—REMARKABLE STATEMENTS CONCERNING THEM. The high value of money at the time must be borne in mind.

Sale of Food and Drugs act passed 11 Aug. 1875 (see *Adulteration*).
Wheat for food for 100 men for one day worth only one shilling, and a sheep fourpence, Henry I. about 1130. The price of wine raised to sixpence per quart for red, and eightpence for white, that the sellers might be enabled to live by it, 2 John, 1200.—*Burton's Annals.*
When wheat was at 6*s.* per quarter, the farthing loaf was to be equal in weight to twenty-four ounces (made of the whole grain), and to sixteen the white. When wheat was 1*s.* 6*d.* per quarter, the farthing white loaf was to weigh sixty-four ounces, and the whole grain (the same as standard now) ninety-six, by the first assize, 1202.—*Mat. Paris.*
A remarkable plenty in all Europe, 1280.—*Dufresnoy.*
Wheat 1*s.* per quarter, 14 Edw. I., 1286.—*Stow.*
The price of provisions fixed by the common council of London as follows: two pullets, three half-pence; a partridge, or two woodcocks, three half-pence; a fat lamb, sixpence from Christmas to Shrovetide, the rest of the year fourpence, 29 Edw. I., 1299.—*Stow.*
Price of provisions fixed by parliament: at the rate of 2*l.* 8*s.* of our money for a fat ox, if fed with corn, 3*l.* 12*s.*; a shorn sheep, 5*s.*; two dozen of eggs, 3*d.*; other articles nearly the same as fixed by the common council above recited, 7 Edw. II., 1313.—*Rot. Parl.*
Wine the best sold for 20*s.* per tun, 10 Rich. II., 1387.
Wheat being at 1*s.* 1*d.* the bushel in 1390, this was deemed so high a price that it is called a dearth of corn by the historians of that era.
Beef and pork settled at a halfpenny the pound, and veal three farthings, by act of parliament, 24 Hen. VIII., 1533.—*Anderson.*
Document from a "*Book of the Joint Diet, Dinner and Supper, and the charge thereof, for Cranmer, Latimer, and Ridley*," kept by the bailiffs of Oxford, while they were in their custody:—

1 Oct. 1554. DINNER.

	£		
Bread and Ale	£0	0	2
Oysters	0	0	1
Butter	0	0	2
Eggs	0	0	2
Lyng	0	0	8
A piece of fresh salmon	0	0	10
Wine	0	0	3
Cheese and pears	0	0	2
The three dinners	0	2	6

Milk sold, three pints ale-measure for one halfpenny, 2 Eliz. 1560. *Stow's Chronicle.*

Liebig's discovery of his "Extractum Carnis," extract of meat, announced 1847.

Since the autumn of 1865, meat, milk, and butter greatly increased in price owing to the cattle-plague, &c.

The "Food Committee" of Society of Arts first met 21 Dec. 1866.

Meat very dear in England, 1868-73. Introduction of Australian preserved meat by Mr. John McCall in 1865; imported in 1866, 91 cwt.; in 1871, 237,160 cwt. Meat imported here in 1863, 3283 cwt.; in 1877, 599,181 cwt.

Carcases frozen by Harrison's method; cargo sent to England from Melbourne, Australia, 23 July; arrived, 18 Oct.; proved a failure, 2 Nov. 1873.

Good preserved American meat sold in London, 27 Dec. 1875. Great influx of meat preserved by cold, 1877.

Bell & Coleman's patent refrigerators reported successful in preserving meat, &c., Aug. Sept. 1878.

Meat to the amount of about 2,500,000*l.* imported annually, 1885.

Fresh meat brought from Australia, Feb. 1880.

5,000 frozen sheep arrived from New Zealand, 25 May, 1882; 1,879,961 in 1902; total carcases, 3,668,061, 1902.

Mr. Coleman explained his process at the Royal Institution, London, and showed that by these machines atmospheric air could be cooled down to 80° below zero Fahrenheit, whereby the vitality of microphytes was completely destroyed, 29 May, 1885.

Refrigerator railway car conveyed fresh herrings from Wick to London, 15 Aug. 1883.

10,000*l.* worth of fresh meat imported from Libau, Russia, during July, 1883.

The *Elderslie* with 25,000 frozen sheep from New Zealand, arrives in London, Dec. 1884.

Refrigerating barges for the distribution of imported frozen provisions, and constructed by the Pulsometer Engineering company, announced Jan. 1890.

A new system of refrigeration by cold air, published by the British and Foreign Refrigerating company, London.

For the price of *Bread* since 1735, see *Bread*.

From New Zealand and Australia, 2,514,541 carcases of frozen sheep, and 171,640 quarters of beef, received in 1893. Great increase in 1895–1903.

80 ships engaged in importing frozen meat; reported 13 March, 1895; 147, 31 Dec. 1902.

Royal commission to inquire into food imports during the time of war (see *Food Supply*), appointed April, 1903.

See *Milk*, *Cattle*.

PROVISORS, STATUTES OF, beginning 25 Edward III., 1351-2, prohibited the pope from appointing aliens and others to benefices before they were vacant.

PROVOST, the chief municipal magistrate of a city or burgh in Scotland, corresponding to the English *mayor*. The provosts of Edinburgh, Glasgow, Aberdeen, Perth, and in 1892 Dundee, are styled "lord provosts."

PROVVEDIMENTO SOCIETIES in Italy, formed to aid in acquiring Rome and Venice, elected Garibaldi as their chief, 10 March, 1862. They were tolerated by Ricasoli, and warned to be moderate by Rattazzi.

PROXIES. Voting by proxy, an ancient privilege of the house of peers, was very frequently abused. In the reign of Charles II., when the duke of Buckingham sometimes brought 20 proxies in his pocket, it was ordered that no peer should bring more than two proxies. From 1830 to 1867, both inclusive, proxies were only called 73 times. In conformity with the recommendation of a committee, a new "standing order" was adopted, 31 March, 1868, by which it was ordered "That the practice of calling for proxies on a division shall be discontinued."

PRUD'HOMMES, CONSEILS DE (from *prudens homo*, a prudent man), trade tribunals in France, composed of masters and workmen, were constituted to arbitrate on trade disputes in 1806. Similar bodies with this name existed as far back as 1452 at Marseilles, and at Lyons in 1464.

PRUSSIA. This country was anciently possessed by the Venedi. They were conquered by the Porussi, who inhabited the Riphæan mountains; and from these the country was called Borussia. The Porussi afterwards intermixed with the followers of the Teutonic knights, and latterly with the Poles. The constitution, established 31 Jan. 1850, was modified 30 April, 1851; 21 May, 5 June, 1852; 7 and 24 May, 1853; 10 June, 1854; 30 May, 1855; and 15 May, 1857. Population, with Lauenburg (annexed 14 Aug. 1865), 19,304,843; with Hanover, Hesse-Cassel, Nassau, and Frankfort Dec. 1867, 24,039,543; 1875, 25,742,204; 1880, 27,279,111; 1890, 29,959,388; Dec. 1900, 34,472,509. 1891-2, budget estimates, revenue, 79,580,650*l.*; expenditure, 79,580,650*l.*; revenue estimated 1894-5, 96,507,644*l.*; 1897-8, 102,301,566*l.*; revenue, 1900-01, 123,613,300*l.* *President of the ministry*, &c., prince Bismarck, Sept. 1862. *See below*, 1890, 1892.

St. Adalbert arrives in Prussia to preach Christianity, and is slain . . . . . about 997

Boleslas of Poland revenges his death by dreadful ravages 1018

The Prussians resist the Poles, and renounce Christianity . . . . . . about 1061

Berlin built by a colony from the Netherlands, in the reign of Albert the Bear 1163

The Teutonic knights returning from the holy wars, undertake the conquest and conversion of Prussia 1225

Thorn founded by them 1231

Prussia subjugated by the Teutonic knights . . 1283

Königsberg, lately built, made the capital . . 1286

Largely re-peopled by German colonists 12-13th century.

Frederick IV. of Nuremberg (the founder of the reigning family) obtains by purchase from Sigismund, emperor of Germany, the margraviate of Brandenburg 1415

Casimir IV. of Poland assists the natives against the oppression of the Teutonic knights . . 1446

Albert of Brandenburg, grand master of the Teutonic order, seizes its territories, renounces the Roman catholic religion, embraces Lutheranism, and is acknowledged duke of East Prussia, to be held as a fief of Poland 1525

Successful rebellion against the knights consummated by the treaty of Thorn 1466

University of Königsberg founded by duke Albert, 1544

John Sigismond created elector of Brandenburg and duke of Prussia 1608

The principality of Halberstadt and the bishopric of Minden transferred to the house of Brandenburg 1648

Poland obliged to acknowledge Prussia as an independent state, under Frederick William, surnamed the Great Elector 1657

Order of Concord instituted by Christian Ernest, elector of Brandenburg and duke of Prussia, to commemorate the part he had taken in restoring peace to Europe 1660

Frederick III. in an assembly of the states, puts a crown upon his own head and upon the head of his consort; is proclaimed king of Prussia by the name of Frederick I., and institutes the Order of the Black Eagle . . . . 18 Jan. 1701

Gueldres taken from the Dutch 1702

Frederick I. seizes Neufchâtel or Neunburg, and purchases Tecklenburg 1707

The principality of Meurs added to Prussia . . 1712
Frederick II. the Great, king, who made the Prussian monarchy rank among the first powers of Europe 1740
Breslau ceded to Prussia 1741
Silesia, Glatz, &c., ceded 1742
"Seven years' war" (see *Battles*) . . 1756-63
Frederick II. victor at Prague, 6 May; defeated at Kolin, 18 June; victor at Rosbach . 5 Nov. 1757
Gen. Lacy, with an Austrian and Russian army, marches to Berlin; the city is laid under contribution, &c.; magazines destroyed . . Oct. 1760
Peace of Hubertsburg (ends "seven years' war"); Silesia gained by Prussia . . . . 15 Feb. 1763
Prussia shares in the first partition of Poland . . 1772
Frederick the Great dies . . . . 17 Aug. 1786
Frederick William II. invades France 1792
Joins the coalition against France 1793
The Prussians seize Hanover . . 1801 and 1806
Prussia joins the allies of England against France, 6 Oct. ,,
Fatal battles of Jena and Auerstadt . . 14 Oct. ,,
[Nearly all the monarchy subdued.]
Berlin decree promulgated . . . . 20 Nov. ,,
Peace of Tilsit (*which see*) . . . . 9 July, 1807
Formation of the Tugendband (*which see*), a patriotic society (promoted by Von Stein) . . . . ,,
Convention of Berlin . . . . . . 5 Nov. 1808
Schaunhorst secretly restores the army by the system of reserves; forming a nation of soldiers 1809-13
The people rise to expel the French from Germany at the king's appeal, and form the "landwehr" or militia . . . . 17 March, 1813
Treaty of Paris . . . . . . 11 April, 1814
The king visits England . . . . . 6 June, ,,
Ministry of education established 1817
Congress of Carlsbad . . . . . 1 Aug. 1819
Blücher dies in Silesia, aged 77 . . 12 Sept. ,,
[From this time Prussia pursued a peaceful and undisturbed policy until 1848.]
Government disputes with R. C. clergy begin, through ultramontanism of the Radziwill family since 1830 1840
Serious attempt made on the life of the king, by an assassin named Tesch, who fired two shots at him 26 July, 1844
Insurrection in Berlin . . . . . 18 March, 1848
Berlin declared in a state of siege . . 12 Nov. ,,
The constituent assembly meets in Brandenburg castle . . . . 29 Nov. ,,
This assembly dissolved; the king issues a new constitution . . . . 5 Dec. ,,
The German National Assembly elect the king of Prussia "hereditary emperor of the Germans" 28 March, 1849
The king declines the imperial crown . 29 April, ,,
The kingdom put under martial law . . 10 May, ,,
The Prussians enter Carlsruhe . . 23 June, ,,
Armistice between Prussia and Denmark . 10 July, ,,
Bavaria declared for an imperial constitution with the king of Prussia at its head . . 8 Sept. ,,
Treaty between Prussia and Austria . 30 Sept. ,,
Austria protests against the alliance of Prussia with the minor states of Germany . . . 12 Nov. ,,
Prince Charles Anthony Hohenzollern-Sigmaringen, minister, resigns . . . . . . 6 Dec. ,,
New constitution, 31 Jan.; the king takes the oath required by it . . . . . . 6 Feb. 1850
Hanover withdraws from the Prussian alliance, 25 Feb. ,,
Treaty signed at Munich between Austria, Bavaria, Saxony, and Würtemberg to maintain the German union . . . . 27 Feb. ,,
Würtemberg denounces the insidious ambition of the king of Prussia, and announces a league between Würtemberg, Bavaria, and Saxony, under the sanction of Austria . . . . 15 March, ,,
Attempt to assassinate the king . . 22 May, ,,
Hesse-Darmstadt withdraws from the Prussian league . . . . 30 June, ,,
Treaty of peace between Prussia and Denmark, 2 July, ,,
A congress of deputies from the states included in the Prussian Zollverein opened at Cassel 12 July, 1850
Prussia refuses to join the restricted diet of Frankfort . . . . 25 Aug. ,,
The Prussian government addresses a despatch to the cabinet of Vienna, declaring its resolve to uphold the constitution in Hesse-Cassel, 21 Sept. ,,
Count Brandenburg, prime minister, dies, 6 Nov. ,,
Decree, calling out the whole Prussian army, 223,000 infantry, 38,000 cavalry, and 29,000 artillery, with 1080 field-pieces . . . . 7 Nov. ,,
The Prussian troops in Hesse occupy the military road in that electorate . . . . . 9 Nov. ,,
The Prussian forces withdraw from the grand duchy of Baden . . . . . . 14 Nov. ,,
General Radowitz, late foreign minister, visits queen Victoria at Windsor . . . . 26 Nov. ,,
Convention of Olmutz for the pacification of Germany . . . . 29 Nov. ,,
The Prussian troops commence their retreat from Hesse-Cassel . . . . 5 Dec. ,,
Prince Schwartzenberg visits the king . 28 Dec. ,,
The king celebrates the 150th anniversary of the Prussian monarchy . . . . . 18 Jan. 1851
The king visits the czar of Russia . . 18 May, ,,
Statue of Frederick the Great, by Rauch, inaugurated at Berlin . . . . . . 27 May, ,,
The king and czar leave Warsaw for Olmutz to meet the emperor of Austria . . . . 31 May, ,,
The king revives the council of state as it existed before the revolution of 1848 . . . 12 Jan. 1852
A Prussian industrial exhibition opened at Berlin, 28 May, ,,
Prussia repudiates a customs' union with Austria, 7 June, ,,
But agrees to a commercial treaty . . 19 Feb. 1853
Democratic plot at Berlin detected . . April, ,,
Death of Radowitz . . . . . . 25 Dec. ,,
Vacillation of the government upon the Eastern question . . . . . . March and April, 1854
Agrees to a protocol for preservation of the integrity of Turkey, which is signed at Vienna . 7 April, ,,
Declares neutrality in the war 6 Sept. and Oct. ,,
Excluded from the conferences at Vienna . Feb. 1855
Disputes with Switzerland (see *Neufchâtel*) Nov. 1856, to May, 1857
Alarming illness of the king, the prince of Prussia appointed regent . . . . . . 23 Oct. ,,
Chevalier Bunsen ennobled . . . . Jan. 1858
Prince Frederick William of Prussia married to the princess royal of England . . . 25 Jan. ,,
Queen Victoria visits them at Potsdam . 10 Aug. ,,
Prince of Prussia permanent regent . . 7 Oct. ,,
Resignation of Manteuffel ministry; succeeded by that of prince Hohenzollern-Sigmaringen (liberal): the elections end in favour of the new government Nov. ,,
Prince Frederick William, son of the princess royal of England, born . . . . . . 27 Jan. 1859
Italian war—Prussia declares its neutrality, but arms to protect Germany . May and June, ,,
The regent announces that "the Prussian army will be in future the Prussian nation in arms," 12 Jan. 1860
The regent and several German sovereigns meet the emperor of the French at Baden (see *Baden*), 15-17 June, ,,
Baron Bunsen dies (aged 70) . . . . 27 Nov. ,,
Disclosures respecting the oppressive system of Prussian police; Stieber, the director, prosecuted and censured, but not punished . . Nov. ,,
Death of Frederick William IV. Accession of William I. . . . . 2 Jan. 1861
Meeting of the chambers: on the motion for the address, M. von Vincke carries an amendment in favour of Italian Unity and "a firm alliance with England" . . . . 6 Feb. ,,
On 12 Sept. 1860, capt. Macdonald was committed to prison at Bonn, for resisting the railway authorities there; the English residents appealed and were censured; a correspondence ensued between the Prussian government and the British foreign

secretary; and strong language was uttered in the house of commons, 26 April, and in the Prussian chambers . . . . 6 May, 1861

The Macdonald affair settled by a firm yet conciliatory despatch from the Baron von Schleinitz, May, ,,

Attempted assassination of the king by Becker, a Leipsic student, 14 July; who is sentenced to 20 years' imprisonment . . . 23 Sept. ,,

The king meets the emperor Napoleon at Compiègne 6-8 Oct. ,,

The king and queen crowned at Königsberg; he declares that he will reign by the "Grace of God" . . . . 18 Oct. ,,

Bill for making the ministry responsible, passed 6 March, 1862

The chamber of representatives oppose the government in regard to the length of military service, 6 March: and resolve on discussing the items of the budget; the ministry resigns; the king will not accept the resignation, but dissolves the chambers . . . . 11 March, ,,

The ministry (liberal) resigns, and a reactionary cabinet formed under Van der Heydt, 18 March-12 April, ,,

Elections go against the government; only one minister elected . . . . May, ,,

Parliament opens; ministers appeal to the patriotism of the members . . . . 19 May, ,,

Severe discussion on military expenditure; the chamber reduces the vote for the maintenance of the army from 200,000 to 135,000 men 11-16 Sept. ,,

Van der Heydt resigns; succeeded as premier by the count Bismarck Schönhausen, 23 Sept.; who informs the chamber that the budget is deferred till 1863; the chamber protests against this as unconstitutional . . . . 30 Sept. ,,

The chamber of peers passes the budget without the amendments of the chamber of representatives; which (by 237 against 2) resolves that the act is contrary to the letter and spirit of the constitution . . . . 11 Oct. ,,

The king closes the session (65th) saying, "The budget for the year 1862, as decreed by the chamber of representatives, having been rejected by the chamber of peers on the ground of insufficiency, the government is under the necessity of controlling the public affairs outside the constitution" . . . . 13 Oct. ,,

Agitation in favour of the constitution proceeding; passive resistance adopted; several liberal papers suppressed . . . . Nov. ,,

The chambers reassemble; unconciliatory address from the king, 14 Jan.; bold reply of the deputies; adopted . . . . 23 Jan. 1863

They recommend neutrality in the Polish war 28 Feb. ,,

Violent dissension between the deputies and the ministry . . . . May ,,

The chamber of deputies address the king on their relation with the ministry, and the state of the country, 22 May; the king replies, that his ministers possess his confidence, and adjourns the session . . . . 27 May, ,,

The king resolves to govern without a parliament . ,,

The press severely restricted, 1 June; the crown prince in a speech disavows participation in the recent acts of the ministry, 5 June; and censures them in a letter to the king, 6 July; reconciled to the king . . . . 8 Sept. ,,

The liberal members fêted in the provinces 18, 19 July, ,,

The chamber of deputies dissolved, 2 Sept.; a liberal majority re-elected . . . . . Oct. ,,

A motion in favour of maintaining the rights of the duchies of Schleswig and Holstein, carried 2 Dec.; but the chamber obstinately refused its assent to it or to defray the expenses of war, Dec. ,,

Chambers dissolved . . . . Jan. 1864

[For the events of the war, see *Denmark*.]

Preliminaries for peace with Denmark . 1 Aug ,,

Peace with Denmark signed . . . . 30 Oct. ,,

The opening of the chambers, 14 Jan.; revival of the constitutional agitation for control over the army budget . . . . . . 16 Jan. 1865

International exhibition at Cologne opened by the crown prince . . . . 2 June, ,,

The deputies having rejected the budget, the bills for reorganizing the army and increasing the fleet, and meeting the expense of the war with Denmark, the chamber is prorogued; the government will rule without it . . . . . . 17 June, 1865

The king at Carlsbad issues a despotic decree appropriating and disposing of the revenue, 5 July, ,,

A political dinner of the liberal deputies prohibited at Cologne, and forcibly prevented at Oberlahnstein, in Nassau . . . . . 24 July, ,,

Convention of Gastein (see *Gastein*), signed 14 Aug. ,,

Navigation treaty with Great Britain concluded, 16 Aug. ,,

The king takes possession of Lauenburg, purchased from Austria with his own money . 15 Sept. ,,

Bismarck visits the emperor Napoleon at Biarritz, Nov. ,,

The chambers opened with a supercilious speech from M. Bismarck . . . . . . 15 Jan. 1866

The opposing chamber prorogued . . 22 Feb. ,,

Decree asserting Prussian jurisdiction over Holstein, 11 March, ,,

Prussian circular calling on German states to decide whether they will support Austria or Prussia (they profess neutrality) . . . 24 March, ,,

Prussia prepares for war . . . . 27 March, ,,

Treaty between Prussia and Italy, said to have been concluded . . . . 27 March, ,,

The French government professes neutrality, April, ,,

Austria demands the demobilisation of the Prussian army, 7 April: Bismarck proposes a German parliament . . . . 9 April, ,,

Great meeting at Berlin in favour of peace, 15 April, ,,

Blind's attempt to assassinate Bismarck fails, 7 May, ,,

Recriminatory correspondence between Mensdorff (Austrian) and Bismarck, calling for disarmament, April, May, ,,

Alliance with Italy . . . . May, ,,

The Prussians enter Holstein; Austrians retire, 7 June, ,,

Meeting of the Federal diet at Frankfort; the demobilisation of the Prussian army proposed by Austria; voted for by Bavaria, Saxony, Hanover, Hesse-Cassel, Nassau, and others; Prussia declares the Germanic confederation to be dissolved . . . . 14 June, ,,

Prince Alexander of Hesse appointed to command the Federal army . . . . . . June, ,,

The Prussians declare war against Hanover and Saxony . . . . 15 June, ,,

Justificatory manifestoes issued by Austria and Prussia . . . . 17 June, ,,

Prussia declares war; royal manifesto to the people 18 June, ,,

The Prussians occupy Hanover and Hesse-Cassel, Saxony and Nassau . . . . . 16-20 June, ,,

The Austrian northern army enters Silesia, 18 June; joined by the Saxons . . . . about 19 June, ,,

Nearly all the northern states join Prussia about 23 June, ,,

Prince Frederick Charles and the first army, and the army of the Elbe enter Bohemia, 23 June; victorious in severe engagements at Liebenau, Türnau, and Podoll, 26 June; Hühnewasser, 27 June; Münchengrätz, 28 June; Gitschin, 29 June, ,,

The crown prince and the second army (of Silesia) enter Bohemia, 22 June; repulsed at Trautenau, 27 June; victorious at Soor and Trautenau, 28 June; Königinhof . . . . . . 29 June, ,,

The left column of the crown prince's army defeat the Austrians at Nachod, 27 June; Skalicz, 28 June: Schweinschädel . . . . . 29 June ,,

Fruitless victory of the Hanoverians at Langensalza, 27 June; they capitulate to the Prussians, 29 June, ,,

Communications opened between the two armies, 30 June, ,,

The command assumed by the king . . . 1 July, ,,

Battle of Königgrätz, or Sadowa; total defeat of the Austrians under Benedek . . . . 3 July, ,,

Benedek superseded by the archduke Albrecht, 8 July, ,,

Campaign of the army under Vögel von Falkenstein against the army of the confederation, under princes Charles of Bavaria and Alexander of Hesse; Prussian victories at Wiesenthal and Dermbach, 4 July; Hammelburg and Kissingen, 10 July, ,,

Advance of the united armies under the king; cavalry skirmish at Saar; Austrians retire, 10 July, 1866
Prince Frederick Charles enters Brünn, capital of Moravia . . . . . . 12 July, ,,
Campaign on the Maine: Prussian victories at Laufach, 13 July, and Aschaffenburg 14 July, ,,
The members of the German diet retire from Frankfort to Augsburg . . . . . . 13 July, ,,
Austrians defeated at Tobitschau . . . 15 July, ,,
Frankfort occupied by Falkenstein . . 16 July, ,,
Severe fight at Blumenau stopped by the news of an armistice . . . . . . 22 July, ,,
Preliminaries of peace signed at Nikolsburg, 26 July, ,,
The Prussians occupy Wiesbaden, 18 July; victorious at Tauberbischofsheim, Hochhausen, Werbach, 24 July; Neubrunn, Helmstadt, Gerscheim, 25 July; Würzburg, 28 July; armistice granted, 30 July, ,,
The army reviewed by the king fifteen miles from Vienna, 31 July; begin their return home, 1 Aug. ,,
Franconia occupied by the Prussian army of reserve, under the grand-duke of Mecklenburg-Schwerin, 23 July-1 Aug.; armistices granted 1-3 Aug. ,,
The diet at Augsburg recognised the dissolution of the Germanic confederation . . . . 4 Aug. ,,
Bohemia and Moravia cleared by . . . 18 Aug. ,,
The treaty of peace signed at Prague . . 23 Aug. ,,
Meeting of special committee of the chamber of deputies; cost of the war stated, 88,000,000 dollars, 29 Aug. ,,
Peace with Würtemburg concluded, 13 Aug.; with Baden, 17 Aug.; with Bavaria, 22 Aug.; with Hesse-Darmstadt (ceding Hesse-Cassel, Hesse-Homburg, &c.) . . . . 3 Sept. ,,
Formation of the North German confederation (see *Germany*) . . . . Aug. ,,
Indemnity bill for the ministry passed . 8 Sept. ,,
Entry of the army into Berlin; *enthusiastic reception*, 20 Sept. ,,
Decree for the annexation of Hanover, Electoral Hesse, Nassau, and Frankfort . . . 20 Sept. ,,
Possession taken of Hanover, 6 Oct.: of Hesse, Nassau, and Frankfort . . . . 8 Oct. ,,
Treaty of peace with Saxony . . . 21 Oct. ,,
Electoral law for new German parliament promulgated at Berlin . . . . . . 23 Oct. ,,
Prussian chambers reassemble . . . 12 Nov. ,,
Schleswig and Holstein incorporated with Prussia by decree; promulgated . . . . 24 Jan. 1867
Chambers closed . . . . 9 Feb. ,,
North German parliament meet at Berlin, 24 Feb.; adopt a federal constitution; closed . 17 April, ,,
Prussian chambers opened by the king 29 April, ,,
They accept the North German constitution (sacrificing Prussian civil rights to German unity), 8 May, ,,
Luxembourg question settled by a conference at London (see *Luxembourg*) . . . 7-11 May, ,,
The king visits Paris; leaves it . . 14 June, ,,
The Prussian chambers approve North German constitution; closed by the king . . 24 June, ,,
The new Prussian parliament opened by the king, 15 Nov. ,,
Treaty with the United States respecting naturalisation of aliens signed at Berlin . . . 22 Feb. 1868
The parliament closed . . . . . . 29 Feb. ,,
Much of the king of Hanover's property sequestrated, on account of his maintaining a Hanoverian legion, &c. . . . . . . March, ,,
Prince Napoleon Jerome visits Berlin; left, March, ,,
North German parliament opened by the king, 23 March, ,,
Count Bismarck defeated in the North German parliament; his bill withdrawn . . . 22 April, ,,
König Wilhelm, a noble ironclad, originally constructed for the sultan by Mr. E. Reed, the chief constructor of the British admiralty, bought by Prussia, launched at Blackwall . . 25 April, ,,
Customs' parliament at Berlin . 27 April-23 May, ,,
21 Hanoverians convicted of incipient treason against Prussia . . . . . . 20 May, ,,
Count von Bismarck's temporary retirement through ill-health . . . . June, ,,
North German parliament closed by the king, 20 June, ,,
Workmen's congress at Berlin, to promote centralisation . . . . 26-29 Sept. 1868
Prussian chamber opened with a pacific speech from the king . . . . 4 Nov. ,,
Opposition in the chambers; violent speech of the minister, Leonhardt . . . . . 1 Dec. ,,
Bismarck, recovered, returns to Berlin . 8 Dec. ,,
The property of the king of Hanover sequestrated for his opposition . . . . . . 15 Feb. 1869
The parliament closed . . . . . 6 March, ,,
The Prussian army exercised in manœuvring at Stettin, Königsberg, &c. in presence of the king, Sept. ,,
The parliament meet, 6 Oct.; rejects the proposal for disarmament . . . . . . 21 Oct. ,,
The crown prince visits Vienna . . . 7 Oct. ,,
Prince Leopold, of Hohenzollern-Sigmaringen, consents to become candidate for the throne of Spain, about 5 July 1870
In consequence of the virulent opposition of the French government he, with the king's consent, relinquishes the candidature . . . 12 July, ,,
The French government requiring guarantees from the king against the future, the king repulses and declines to receive the French minister, Benedetti, 13 July; and issues a circular to his representatives at foreign courts . . 15 July, ,,
The emperor of the French declares for war, 15 July, ,,
The North German parliament meet, and vote to support Prussia . . . . . . 19 July, ,,
Proclamation of the king, granting "amnesty for political offences," and "accepting the battle for the defence of the fatherland," 31 July; and to the army, undertaking the command of the whole army . . . . 3 Aug. ,,
For the events of the war see *Franco-Prussian War.*
Order of the "Iron Cross" (distributed in the war of 1813) revived; given to the crown prince for his victory at Wissembourg on . . . 4 Aug. ,,
Prussian bishops protest against infallibility of the pope . . . . end of Aug. ,,
Great rejoicing at Berlin, &c., at the surrender of the emperor Napoleon . . . . 3 Sept. ,,
Munich, Stuttgardt, and other southern cities, demand union with North Germany . 6 Sept. ,,
M. Jacoby arrested at Königsberg by Von Falckenstein for speaking against the annexation of Alsace and Lorraine . . . . . early in Sept. ,,
Restriction on democratic meetings rescinded by gen. Von Falckenstein . . . . . 7 Oct. ,,
Herr Twesten, the liberal opponent of government in the chamber, dies . . . . 14 Oct. ,,
Jacoby and other liberals released by royal decree (Jacoby died 7 March, 1877) . about 26 Oct. ,,
Election of new parliament, Nov.; opened with speech promising internal reforms, 14 Dec.; aristocratic address from the peers congratulating the king as nominated emperor (see *Germany*), 21 Dec. ,,
The king proclaimed emperor of Germany at Versailles . . . . 18 Jan. 1871
The Prussian parliament closed . . . 17 Feb. ,,
The emperor arrives at Berlin . . . 17 March, ,,
The new imperial diet opened at Berlin 21 March, ,,
Bismarck created a prince . . . . 22 March, ,,
The czar arrives at Berlin . . . . 8 June, ,,
Triumphal entry of the German army into Berlin; inauguration of the statue of Frederick William III. . . . . 16 June, ,,
The bishop of Ermeland excommunicates Dr. Wollner for denying the pope's infallibility, 5 July; similar acts disapproved by the government, July, ,,
The imperial prince and princess arrive in London, 6 July, ,,
Convocation of the evangelical church at Berlin, 2 Aug. ,,
Meeting of the parliament . . . . 27 Nov. ,,
Von Mühler, minister of public instruction, ultra-conservative, forced to resign . . 17 Jan. 1872
Clerical interference with schools opposed in the parliament . . . . 8-10 Feb. ,,
Meeting of German princes at Berlin on the emperor's birthday . . . . . . 22 March, ,,
The new "national conservative party" formed about May, ,,

Law for expulsion of the Jesuits, published 5 July, 1872

Memorial to Von Stein, the statesman (see 1807), at Nassau, inaugurated . . . 9 July, ,,

Government disputes with the R. C. clergy supporting papal infallibility; the bishop of Ermeland's salary ordered to be suspended, from 1 Oct. ,,

The government defeated in the house of peers on the district administrations bill (145—18) (the bill would deprive the peers of power in the provinces by granting representatives to the peasants in the local assemblies) . . . . . 31 Oct. ,,

The parliamentary session closed, 1 Nov.; reopened, government firm . . . 12 Nov. ,,

24 new peers created . . . . . . 2 Dec. ,,

The principle of the reform bill passed by the peers (114—87) . . . . 7 Dec. ,,

Bismarck resigns the presidency; continues the foreign department; announced . . 18 Dec. ,,

Count Roon to be chairman of the ministry Dec. ,,

Great financial prosperity; surplus revenue said to be 187,000,000 thalers (3*s.* each) . . . . . ,,

Declaration of the R. C. archbishops of Cologne and Posen against proposed legislation on church affairs . . . . Feb. 1873

Subjection of the church to the state affirmed by the legislature . . . . 12 March, ,,

Laws introduced by M. Falk, minister of public worship, establishing a royal tribunal of ecclesiastical affairs, in opposition to the authority of the pope, 9 Jan.; passed . . . . . 11 May, ,,

The emperor recognises the "old Catholic" bishop, Reinkens . . . . about Aug. ,,

Letter from the pope to the emperor complaining of the ecclesiastical prosecutions, and asserting his authority over all baptized persons, 7 Aug.; the emperor replies justifying them, and asserting that there is no mediator between God and man but Jesus Christ . . . . . 3 Sept. ,,

Parliament dissolved, 11 Oct.; new parliament elected . . . . Nov. ,,

The emperor visits Vienna . . . 17 Oct. ,,

Archbishop Ledochowski of Posen fined for threatening to excommunicate a professor; and archbishop Melchers fined for instituting priests without government permission . . . Oct. ,,

The pope (by letter) encourages archbishop Ledochowski to resist . . . . 3 Nov. ,,

Parliament opened: (votes for government, 432; opposition, 121) . . . . . . 12 Nov. ,,

Government defeated in attempt to restrict the press; the ultramontanes join the opposition 3 Dec. ,,

A new oath of implicit obedience to the state proposed for the clergy; the civil marriage bill passed Dec. ,,

Several bishops fined for disobedience to the law Dec. ,,

Archbishop Ledochowski imprisoned, 3 Feb.; deprived . . . . 15 April, 1874

Serious illness of Bismarck, March; recovering June, ,,

New ecclesiastical laws, restraining authority of bishops, with punishment for disobedience, promulgated . . . . May, ,,

Van der Heydt, statesman (see 1862) dies 14 June, ,,

Martin, bishop of Paderborn, resists the ecclesiastical laws . . . . 10 July, ,,

Bismarck wounded by Kullmann, a fanatical cooper, near Kissingen . . . . . . 13 July, ,,

Catholic associations in Berlin closed . 21 July, ,,

Bishop of Paderborn, summoned to resign, refuses, 7 Sept.; sentenced to imprisonment for sedition 21 Sept. ,,

Launch of the iron-clad *Friedrich der Grosse* at Kiel, in the presence of the emperor . . 20 Sept. ,,

Arrest of count Harry Arnim and confinement in Berlin for refusing to give up documents sent to him as ambassador, 4 Oct.; for illness released on bail, 28 Oct.; again arrested . . 12 Nov. ,,

Kullmann sentenced to 14 years' imprisonment 30 Oct. ,,

Government defeated in parliament on a bank-note bill . . . . 16 Nov. ,,

Ultramontanes attack Bismarck in parliament; he replies . . . . 4 Dec. ,,

Bismarck's proffered resignation not accepted 17, 18 Dec. ,,

Arnim's trial, 9 Dec.; convicted of making away with ecclesio-political documents; acquitted of other charges; sentence, 3 months' imprisonment, 19 Dec. 1874

Catholic bishops and priests imprisoned for infraction of ecclesiastical laws . . . . Jan. 1875

Deprivation of the bishop of Paderborn 5 Jan. ,,

Parliament opened . . . . . . 16 Jan. ,,

Civil marriage adopted by the parliament 25 Jan. ,,

Encyclical of the pope to the bishops encouraging firmness, protested against by the R. C. deputies of parliament . . . . 5 Feb. ,,

Exportation of horses prohibited . . 4 March, ,,

Clerical control over parish funds taken away; bill for depriving the R. C. clergy of state aid brought in . . . . 16 March, ,,

Alarm of war with France arises . . April, ,,

Prussian bishops at Fulda appeal to the emperor against ecclesiastical legislation, 2 April; rebuked for not submitting to the law . . 9 April, ,,

Visit of the czar to Berlin; war panic in Europe, 10—13 May; diplomatic intervention of Great Britain leads to assurances of peace about 24 May, ,,

Bismarck abolishes the semi-official press about 26 May ,,

King and queen of Sweden arrive at Berlin 28 May, ,,

George von Vincke, an eminent constitutional statesman, dies . . . . June, ,,

Count Arnim's new trial, 15 June; verdict, confirming sentence . . . . 20 Oct. ,,

Partial submission of the bishops: announced Aug. ,,

Launch of the *Wilhelm*, iron-clad . . 17 Sept. ,,

Förster, prince-bishop of Breslau, sentenced to deprivation . . . . 6 Oct. ,,

The emperor warmly received by the king of Italy at Milan (prince Bismarck too ill to go) 18-23 Oct. ,,

Statue of Von Stein (see 1807 *above*) inaugurated by the crown prince . . . . 26 Oct. ,,

German parliament opened by the emperor; firm and pacific speech read . . . 27 Oct. ,,

Letter from count Arnim rebutting accusations in the *Times* of . . . . 19 Nov. ,,

He is to be prosecuted for treason in a pamphlet entitled "Pro Nihilo," published at Zurich Nov. ,,

Prussian diet opened . . . . . . 16 Jan. 1876

Asserted deficiency in revenue of about 2,500,000*l.* about 25 Jan. ,,

Archbishop Ledochowski released from prison (proceeds to Rome) . . . . . . 3 Feb. ,,

The empress visits England . . 3 May-June, ,,

Parliament dissolved, 14 Oct.; liberal majority in new parliament . . . . . . 27 Oct. ,,

The emperor celebrates his 70th military anniversary, 1 Jan.; eightieth anniversary birthday 22 Jan. 1877

Chambers opened . . . . . . 12 Jan. ,,

Berlin Conference on Eastern question (emperor of Russia, prince Gortschakoff, and count Andrassy). See *Berlin* . . . . 11, 12 May, ,,

Prince Bismarck's resignation not accepted; he retires temporarily for his health . . April, ,,

Count Eulenburg's policy as minister of interior displeases prince Bismarck; the count's resignation not accepted; he is granted six months' absence, Sept. ,,

Parliament opened; loan for military purposes proposed . . . . 21 Oct. ,,

Resolutions against government defeated in parliament through promised administrative changes, 27 Oct. ,,

Prince Bismarck resumes his active duties as chief of ministry, 15 Feb.; in the German parliament, asserts strict neutrality and non-interference with Russia in the Eastern question . 19 Feb. 1878

Ministerial crisis: resignation of Camphausen, finance minister . . . . . . 6 March, ,,

Ministry unsettled . . . . May, ,,

Hödel (called Lehman), a socialist, fires at the emperor and misses, at Berlin . . . 11 May, ,,

The emperor wounded by shots by Dr. Nobiling, 2 June; gradually recovered . . June—Sept. ,,

Hödel executed at Berlin . . . . 16 Aug. ,,

Statue of Frederick-William III. unveiled by the emperor at Cologne . . . . 26 Sept. ,,

Count Arnim publishes "Quid faciamus nos?" Jan. 1879

Marriage of princess Louise Margaret of Prussia to the duke of Connaught . . . . 13 March, ,,

The emperor's golden wedding kept . 11 June, 1879
New Parliament opened by the emperor (majority for Bismarck) . . . . . . 28 Oct. ,,
Letter from the pope to Melchers, abp. of Cologne, recommending submission of names of priests to the government, dated . . . . 24 Feb. 1880
Ecclesiastical laws (Falk) amendment bill, promoted by prince Bismarck; much discussed, May; passed (maimed; 206-202) . 28 June, ,,
Parliament opened . . . . 28 Oct. ,,
Discussion on the social movement against the Jews through jealousy; no vote . . 20-22 Nov. ,,
Anti-Semitic league very active; much opposed by the prince imperial and others . . Jan. 1881
The minister of the interior, count Eulenburg, resigns through offence of prince Bismarck, about 19 Feb. ,,
Prince William, grandson of the emperor and of queen Victoria, married to princess Augusta Victoria of Schleswig-Holstein . . 27 Feb. ,,
Death of count Arnim at Nice . . 19 May, ,,
Dr. Felix Korum nominated bishop of Treves, at Rome; approved by Bismarck . 14 Aug. *et seq.* ,,
Revenue surplus announced . . . 18 Jan. 1882
Bismarck's tobacco bill rejected by his economic council . . . . 21 March, ,,
Liberals rather weakened by elections about 29 Oct. ,,
Prospect of reconciliation with the Vatican; amendments of the ecclesiastical laws of May, 1873, introduced . . . . . . 5 June, 1883
Bill passed; diet closed . . . 2 July, ,,
Revival of the Prussian Council of State, the crown prince president, royal family members 18 June, 1884
Parliament opened . . . . 15 Jan. 1885
Death of prince Frederick Charles, the "Red Prince" aged 57 . . . . . . 15 Jan. ,,
Prince Charles Anthony Hohenzollern-Sigmaringen, dies aged 73 . . . . . . 2 June, ,,
General Manteuffel dies aged 76 . . 17 June, ,,
Prof. Graff acquitted of perjury, 9 days' trial, 8 Oct. ,,
Twenty-fifth anniversary of the king's accession celebrated . . . . . . 3 Jan. 1886
Prince Bismarck puts forth his plan for Germanizing Posen by purchasing Polish estates to be settled by Germans; 5,000,000*l.* to be raised for the purpose, Feb.; finally passed . . 7 April, ,,
Bill for greatly amending the ecclesiastical laws (see May, 1873) passed by the *upper house*, 13 April, ,,
Political meetings without permission prohibited by decree . . . . 14 May, ,,
Convention signed between Prussia and the Vatican about 11 Aug. ,,
The emperor's 90th birthday celebrated at Berlin, 22 March, 1887
Prince Bismarck introduces Church and State Bill, softening Falck laws . . . . . March, ,,
Death of emperor William I.; succeeded by his son Frederick III. . . . . 9 March, 1888
Amnesty for certain political offences proclaimed, 31 March, ,,
Prince Bismarck opposes the project of a marriage between prince Alexander of Battenberg and princess Victoria of Prussia; favoured by the emperor and empress; he withdraws his resignation and the project deferred . early April, ,,
Marriage of prince Henry of Prussia and princess Irene of Hesse, grandchildren of queen Victoria of England . . . . 24 May, ,,
Parliamentary quinquennial bill promulgated, 7 June, ,,
Death of emperor Frederick III; succeeded by his son William II. . . . . . . 15 June, ,,
Publication in the *Deutsche Rundschau* (Oct.) of alleged extracts from the diary of the emperor Frederick III., when crown prince asserting that it was he who suggested the unity of Germany and the empire, with other statements; said by prince Bismarck at first to be apocryphal and afterwards to be notes falsified and coloured; the work ordered to be prosecuted for publishing state secrets . . . . Sept. ,,
[The books were found locked up in the house at San Remo where the crown prince resided: the diary contains details of the war with France, 1870–1: it was stated that the books were given or shown by the prince to baron von Roggenbach, the Baden statesman.]

Dr. Geffcken arrested at Hamburg . . 29 Sept. 1888
A part of the prince's diary published in the *Kieler Zeitung* . . . . Sept. ,,
The *Kölnische Zeitung* 16 Dec. accuses the British ambassador at St. Petersburg (sir Robert B. D. Morier) when *chargé d'affaires* at Darmstadt, of giving information to marshal Bazaine of the movements of the Prussian army in 1870. Sir Robert writes to count Herbert Bismarck repelling the charge (and sends a letter from the marshal to himself to the same effect) 19 Dec. Sir Robert publishes the correspondence in the *Times*, 4 Jan.; much discussion ensues . Jan. 1889
Dr. Geffcken acquitted of criminal intents, 7 Jan. ,,
Prince Bismarck publishes the indictment and evidence . . . . 16 Jan. ,,
The king of Italy, his son, and signor Crispi at Berlin . . . . 21–26 May, ,,
Death of the empress Augusta, 7 Jan.; grand funeral . . . . 11 Jan. ,,
The emperor-king convokes the council of state respecting the working-classes, see *Germany* and *Berlin*, 4 Feb.; delivers an address; propositions considered . . . . . . 14-28 Feb. 1890
Prince Bismarck resigns the offices of premier and foreign minister, 18 March; succeeded by gen. George von Caprivi . . about 20 March, ,,
Death of count Moltke, see *Germany* 24 April, 1891
Much discussion on the primary education bill, which enacts, that in all schools some form of Christianity should be taught, to counteract socialism; read first time . . . 30 Jan. 1892
Ministerial crisis in relation to the education bill; count Caprivi resigns the premiership, but remains foreign minister and chancellor of the empire . . . . 22 March, ,,
Count Botho von Eulenburg becomes premier 24 March, ,,
The government withdraw the education bill, about 28 March, ,,
Certain privileges of the nobility abolished with compensation . . . . May, ,,
Blackpox epidemic in East Prussia; many deaths, 7 March, 1893
Important communal taxation bill, introduced by Dr. Miquel, passed . . . . . 3 July, ,,
Elections for the diet (lower house), little changed from that of 1888 . . . 31 Oct.–7 Nov. ,,
Opening of the diet, 16 Jan. 1894, see *Königsberg*, 1894.
Resignation of count Eulenburg, president of the council, 26 Oct.; succeeded by prince Clovis von Hohenlohe; Herr von Köller minister of the interior . . . . 29 Oct. 1894
Opening of the diet; budget shows a deficiency, 15 Jan. 1895
Law of association (amended) (a government) bill passed by the diet, 30 June; rejected by the lower house, 24 July, 1897; diet closed, 18 May, 1898
Expulsion of Danes and non-Prussians from Schleswig and elsewhere . . . . Oct. ,,
Diet opened by the emperor; financial surplus, announced . . . . 16 Jan. ,,
Chamber adjourns . . . . . 4 July, ,,
Herr Heinrich von Achenbach, chief president of the province of Brandenburg, 1879, dies, aged 69, 10 July, 1899
Great fire at Marienburg, near Dantzig . 26 July, ,,
Diet meets; government defeated on the Rhine Elbe canal bill, 16, 19 Aug.; crisis; the emperor holds a council, 23 Aug.; royal message, moderate and conciliatory, diet closed . 29 Aug. ,,
Landräthe and other officials placed on the retired list for opposing the canal bill . . 1 Sept. ,,
Baron von der Recke (interior) and Dr. Bosse (education) resign; baron von Rheinbaben and Herr Studt, conservatives, appointed . 4 Sept. ,,
Diet meets, speech from the throne read by prince Hohenlohe, reintroduction of the Rhine-Elbe canal bill, announced . . . . . 9 Jan. 1900
Diet meets, 24 April; joint sitting of the two houses, session closed . . . . 19 June, ,,
Imperial edict granting reforms in the higher schools, English to be compulsory . 2 Dec. ,,
Diet meets, speech from the throne read by count von Bulow; budget 1899–1900, surplus 88,000,000 marks . . . . 8, 9 Jan. 1901

Bicentenary of the Prussian monarchy celebrated in Berlin . . . . 17, 18 Jan. 1901
Crisis; agrarian victory, the canal bill given up; joint sitting of the two houses; diet closed; Dr. von Miguel (finance) and other ministers resign 3 May, „
Count William Bismarck, chief president of East Prussia, dies, aged 48 . . . . . 30 May, „
Dr. von Miguel, fiscal reformer, born 1829, died 7 Sept. „
Frau Piasecka sentenced to 2½ years' and 22 others to various terms of imprisonment for disturbances at the Wreschen school in Posen, owing to the children being punished for refusing to receive religious instruction in German, reported, 19 Nov. „
Anti-German agitation at Lemberg and Warsaw, early Dec. „
Interpellation introduced by prince Radziwill in the diet . . . . 10 Dec. „
Meeting of Polish women at Lemberg; resolution to boycott German goods, papers, and schools, carried . . . . 15 Dec. „
Religious instruction in German abandoned at Wreschen . . . . . . mid Dec. „
Diet meets; financial depression reported, 8 Jan. 1902
Visit of prince Henry of Prussia to the United States . . . . 23 Feb.–11 March, „
Death of prince George of Prussia, dramatic author, aged 76 . . . . 2 May, „
Germanisation of the Slav peoples urged by the emperor . . . . 5 June, „
Polish (German) settlement bill passed . June, „
Polish demonstration against ministerial Polish policy, Berlin . . . . . . 17 Aug. „
New State college for arts and music at Charlottenburg opened by the emperor . . . . 2 Nov. „
Diet opened, 13 Jan.; about 3,635,000*l.* deficit for 1903; to be covered by a loan . . . 14 Jan. 1903
Count von Bulow defends his Polish policy, 19 Jan. „

(See *Germany* 1871 *et seq.*)

MARGRAVES, ELECTORS, DUKES, AND KINGS.

MARGRAVES OR ELECTORS OF BRANDENBURG.

1134. Albert I., the Bear, first elector of Brandenburg.
1170. Otho I.
1184. Otho II.
1206. Albert II.
1221. John I. and Otho III.
1266. John II.
1282. Otho IV.
1309. Waldemar.
1319. Henry I. the Young.
1320. [Interregnum.]
1323. Louis I. of Bavaria.
1352. Louis II. the Roman.
1365. Otho V. the Sluggard.
1373. Wenceslas, of Luxemburg.
1378. Sigismund, of Luxemburg.
1388. Jossus, the Bearded.
1411. Sigismund, again emperor.
1415. Frederick I. of Nuremberg (of the house of HOHENZOLLERN).
1440. Frederick II., surnamed Ironside.
1470. Albert III., surnamed the German Achilles.
1476. John III., his son; as margrave; styled the Cicero of Germany.
1486. John III. as elector.
1499. Joachim I., son of John.
1535. Joachim II., poisoned by a Jew.
1571. John George.
1598. Joachim Frederick.
1608. John Sigismund.

DUKES OF PRUSSIA.

1618. John Sigismund.
1619. George William.
1640. Frederick William, his son, the "Great Elector."
1688. Frederick III., son of the preceding; crowned king, 18 Jan. 1701.

KINGS OF PRUSSIA.

1701. Frederick I.; king; died.
1713. Frederick William I., son of Frederick I.
1740. Frederick II. (or Frederick III.; styled the Great), son; made Prussia a military power.
1786. Frederick William II., nephew of the preceding.
1797. Frederick William III. (he had to contend against the might of Napoleon, and after extraordinary vicissitudes he aided England in his overthrow), died 7 June, 1840.
1840. Frederick William IV., son; born 15 Oct. 1795; died, 2 Jan. 1861
1861. William I., brother (born, 22 March, 1797); proclaimed emperor of Germany at Versailles, 18 Jan. 1871); married princess Augusta of Saxe-Weimar, 11 June, 1829; golden wedding kept, 11 June, 1879; died 9 March, 1888; she died 7 Jan. 1890.
1888. Frederick III. (William) son, "the noble"; born 18 Oct. 1831; (married Victoria, princess-royal of England, 25 Jan. 1858); died 15 June, 1888.
„ William II., son; born 27 Jan. 1859 (married princess Augusta Victoria of Schleswig-Holstein, 27 Feb. 1881); brother, Henry, born 14 Aug. 1862 (married princess Irene of Hesse, 24 May, 1888).

Heir: William; born 6 May, 1882.

PRUSSIC ACID (hydrocyanic acid), accidentally discovered by Diesbach, a German chemist, in 1709, and first obtained in a separate state by Scheele about 1782. It is colourless, smells like peach flowers, freezes at 5° Fahrenheit, is very volatile, and turns vegetable blues into red. Simple water distilled from the leaves of the *lauro-cerasus* first ascertained to be a most deadly poison by Dr. Madden of Dublin; see *Blue*.

PRUTH, a river in Moldavia, the boundary of Turkey. Peter the great crossed the Pruth, was surrounded by the Turks, and lost much by a convention, June, 1711. The Russians crossed it 2 July, 1853, and war ensued.

PRYTANIS, a magistrate of Corinth, annually elected from 745 B.C. till the office was abolished by Cypselus, a despot, 655 B.C.

PSALMS OF DAVID were collected by Solomon, 1000 B.C.; others added, 580 and 515 B.C. The Church of England Old Version in metre by Sternhold and Hopkins was published in 1562; the New Version by Tate and Brady in 1698.

The version of Francis Rous, provost of Eton, first published in 1641, was ordered to be used, by the parliament in 1646. It is the basis of the Scotch version, which appeared in 1650. The marquis of Lorne published a version in 1877. Many other versions published.
Mr. W. E. Gladstone's edition of "The Psalter," with concordance, &c., published, March, 1895.
"The Earliest known Coptic Psalter, the text in the dialect of Upper Egypt," edited by E. A. Wallis-Budge, published Feb. 1899.
The Anglo-Genevan edition, 1558, recovered 1902.

PSEUDONYM LIBRARY, a name given to a series of books by eminent writers in which the name of the publisher was substituted for that of the author. The publication began in 1891.

PSEUDOSCOPE (from *pseudos*, false), a name given by professor Wheatstone (in 1852) to the stereoscope, when employed to produce "conversions of relief," *i.e.*, the reverse of the stereoscope: a terrestrial globe appears like a hollow hemisphere.

PSYCHIC FORCE, see *Spiritualism*.

PSYCHOLOGY, the science of the soul and its phenomena, studied by Aristotle, Plato, Descartes, Leibnitz, Locke, Hume, James Mill, J. S. Mill, Herbert Spencer, sir Wm. Hamilton, Alex. Bain, and others. See *Telepathy*.

Psychological Society founded by serjt. Cox, 1875–79.
Professor Balfour Stewart, lord Rayleigh, and the bishops of Carlisle and Ripon were members, 1886.
Society for Psychical Research founded, 1882. At a meeting of the society, 29 Jan. 1897, prof. Wm. Crookes

(knt. 1897), presided, and gave an address.

International congress of Experimental Psychology, Paris, 1889; London, 1 Aug. 1892; Munich, 4 Aug. 1896; Paris, 20 Aug. 1900.

Prof. Wm. James' "Principles of Psychology," 1892.

Mr. F. Myers, hon. sec., poet and author of psychical works, died, aged 57, 17 Jan. 1901.

Sir Alex. Bain, an eminent psychologist, died, aged 85, 18 Sept. 1903.

Mr. Herbert Spencer, the illustrious psychologist, died, aged 83 . . . . 8 Dec. 1903

PSYCHROMETER (from *psychros*, cold), an apparatus for measuring the amount of elastic vapour in the atmosphere; invented by Gay Lussac (1778-1850), and modified by Regnault (about 1848). An electric psychrometer was described by Edmond Becquerel, 4 Feb. 1867.

PTOLEMAIC SYSTEM. Claudius Ptolemy of Pelusium, in Egypt (about A.D. 140), supposed that the earth was fixed in the centre of the universe, and that the sun, moon, and stars moved round once in twenty-four hours. The system (long the official doctrine of the church of Rome) was universally taught till that of Pythagoras (500 B.C.) was revived by Copernicus, A.D. 1530, and demonstrated by Kepler (1619) and Newton (1687).

PUBLICANS, farmers of the state revenues of Rome. Soon after the battle of Cannæ they were so wealthy as to be able to advance large sums to the government, payable at the end of the war. No magistrate was permitted to be a publican.

PUBLIC BATHS, &c., see *Baths*, *Education*.

PUBLIC DEPARTMENTS, Royal Commission to inquire generally into their state was appointed about 13 Sept. 1886. It consisted of sir M. W. Ridley (chairman), lords Brownlow, Lingen, Rothschild, Messrs. Sclater Booth, H. Fowler, Rylands, sir E. Guinness, and others; Mr. Walpole (secretary); first report issued, Oct. 1887; second, Sept. 1888. Important changes recommended. Public expenses act passed, 1 April, 1898.

PUBLIC ENTERTAINMENTS ACT, 38 Vict. c. 21, passed 14 June 1875, amends the Act 25 Geo. II. c. 36, 1752.

PUBLIC GOOD, see *Leagues*.

PUBLIC HEALTH ACTS. New act, consolidating all the previous sanitary and nuisance acts, passed, 11 Aug. 1875; another act passed in 1883. Amendment acts passed in 1890, and 1892. The Public Health (London) act, passed 5 Aug 1891, made very important changes. It came into operation 1 Jan. 1892; amended, 1893; it repealed 16 acts entirely, and partially 19 more, and consolidated their best provisions. The Public Health acts, relating to Scotland and Ireland, were amended in 1891. An act relating to supply of water passed 4 July, 1878. New Public Health act passed, 7 Aug. 1896. Public Health act (Scotland) passed, 1897. See *Health*, *Sanitation*.

British (made "Royal" 1898) institute of public health founded, 1886; annual congress met at Edinburgh, 27 July, 1893; London, July, 1894; Hull, 12 Aug. 1895; London, jubilee meeting, 16 June, 1897; Dublin, 18 Aug., 1898; Blackpool, the marquis of Lorne, president, 21 Sept. 1899; at Aberdeen, 2 Aug. 1900; Exeter, 21 Aug. 1902; Liverpool, 15-21 July, 1903.

In Dr. Legge's "Public Health in European Capitals," 1896, London is stated to be in the best condition.

RATE OF DEATHS PER 1,000.

England in 1660-79, 80; 1840-74, 22¼.

Average death-rate per 1,000 for 4 weeks, in London and 32 great English towns (published in the Registrar-General's weekly report)—1890, 15 Jan. 28·1; 15 Feb. 25·3; 15 March, 23·6; 12 April, 20·6; 10 May, 19·2; 14 June, 17·2; 12 July, 17·7; 16 Aug. 21·0; 13 Sept. 18·6; 11 Oct. 19·8; 15 Nov. 21·1; 13 Dec. (frost), 21·3; 20 Dec. 26·0; 27 Dec. 26·3. 1891, 3 Jan. 28·7; 17 Jan. 27·3; 24 Jan. 25·1; 31 Jan. (warmer), 22·3; 7 Feb. 19·8; 14 Feb. 19·9; 14 March, 22·1; 11 April, 22·9; 2 May (influenza), 26·8; 16 May, 30·1; 13 June, 23·8; 11 July, 16·8; 15 Aug. 18·8; 19 Sept. 17·7; 17 Oct. 18·2; 14 Nov. 20·6; 12 Dec. 19·8. 1892, 16 Jan. 33·0 (influenza); 23 Jan. 35·4; 13 Feb. 23·1; 12 March, 22·9; 16 April, 20·9; 14 May, 20·4; 11 June, 17·9; 16 July, 17·9; 20 Aug. 18·0; 17 Sept. 18·6; 15 Oct. 17·3; 19 Nov. 18·6; 17 Dec. 20·7. 1893, 14 Jan. 28·3; 11 Feb. 19·9; 18 March, 19·9; 15 April, 20·8; 13 May, 18·6; 10 June, 18·2; 15 July, 24·8; 12 Aug. 20·9; 16 Sept. 19·1; 14 Oct. 18·2; 11 Nov. 21·5; 16 Dec. 26·6. 1894, 13 Jan. 28·6; 17 Feb. 18·7; 17 March, 19·2; 14 April, 19·3; 12 May, 18·2; 14 July, 15·9; 11 Aug. 17·6; 15 Sept. 15·9; 13 Oct. 16·7; 17 Nov. 17·1; 15 Dec. 19·7. 1895, 12 Jan. 20·1 (frost); 16 Feb. 26·7 (9 March, London, 41·2); 16 March, 32·2; 14 April, 20·5; 11 May, 17·7; 15 June, 15·4; 13 July, 19·9 (London, 17 Aug. 17·3; 15 Sept. 15·4); 13 Oct. 21·0; 16 Nov. 19·1; 14 Dec. 17·8. 1896, 11 Jan. 18·5; 15 Feb. 19·3; 14 March, 20·0; 11 April, 20·0; 16 May, 18·4; 13 June, 16·7; 11 July, 19·9; 15 Aug. 19·9; 12 Sept. 15·8; 17 Oct. 16·3; 14 Nov. 20·8; 19 Dec. 18·2. 1897, 16 Jan. 19·2; 13 Feb. 19·6; 13 March, 18·6; 10 April, 18·6; 15 May, 16·5; 12 June, 15·6; 16 July. 17·6; 14 Aug. 29·5; 18 Sept. 18·5; 16 Oct. 16.9; 13 Nov. 19·0; 11 Dec. 20·8. 1898, 15 Jan. 20·6; 19 Feb. 20·4; 12 March, 21·1; 16 April, 19·5; 14 May, 16·6; 18 June, 14·7; 16 July, 14·7; 13 Aug. 20·5; 17 Sept. 24·0; 15 Oct. 19·0; 12 Nov. 17·2; 17 Dec. 16·6. 1899, 14 Jan. 18·3; 18 Feb. 19·5; 18 March, 23·3; 15 April, 19·5; 13 May, 17·7; 17 June, 16·5; 12 Aug. 24·3; 16 Sept. 21·1; 14 Oct. 18·7; 18 Nov. 17·3; 30 Dec. 30·6 (London, 35·2). 1900, 13 Jan. 29·1; 17 Feb. 25·8; 17 March, 20·3; 14 April, 22·4; 19 May, 18·2; 16 June, 18·0 (London, 13·3, 23 June); 14 July, 15·6; 18 Aug. 19·5; 15 Sept. 18·2; 13 Oct. 17·1; 17 Nov. 17·6; 15 Dec. 16·8. 1901, 19 Jan. 19·1; 16 Feb. 19·5; 16 March, 18·9; 13 April, 19·2; 18 May, 16·8; 15 June, 14·5 (London, 13·7); 13 July, 15·6; 17 Aug. 21·3; 14 Sept. 18·3; 12 Oct. 15·9; 16 Nov. 19·4; 14 Dec. 18·5. 1902, in London and 75 great towns, 18 Jan. 17·7; 15 Feb. 22·6; London only, 29·3, 22 Feb.; 15 March, 22·0; 19 April, 18·3; 17 May, 17·3; 14 June, 15·0; 12 July, 14·5; 16 Aug. 15·5; 13 Sept. 16·4; 18 Oct. 17·4; 15 Nov. 17·4; 13 Dec. 19·6. 1903, 17 Jan. 17·5; 14 Feb. 17·1; 14 March, 17·2; 18 April, 15·9; 16 May, 15·4; 13 June, 13·9; 18 July, 13·5; 15 Aug. 15·7; 12 Sept. 15·8.

PUBLIC HOUSES, see *Victuallers*, and *Sunday*.

PUBLIC LIBRARIES ACTS, passed 1855 and 1871; amended in 1877, 1887, 1889.; consolidated, 1892; amended, 1893; another passed 1901. Public Works Loans act passed 1890, 1901, and 1903.

PUBLIC LOAN COMMISSIONERS were constituted by the acts passed 13 Aug. 1875. Other acts passed 1879-83.

PUBLIC MEETINGS, for political purposes, were occasionally held in England in the latter part of the 17th century, but became very important in the reign of George III. The meetings in Devonshire in 1763 to protest against the Cider Tax, were very effective, and set an example speedily followed, with the warm approbation of Burke, Fox, and other statesmen. These meetings were prohibited by the Gagging acts, *which see*, passed in 1795; see *Sedition*. In the reign of George IV., the right of public meetings was fully assured, and they were very effectual in relation to the passing the Reform acts, the Repeal of the Corn Laws, and other important measures. See *Hyde Park*. The place on which the speakers stand is termed a "platform," corresponding to the Roman *rostrum*, and the French *tribune*. "The Platform," by Mr. H.

Jephson, was published in 1792. The term "platform" is also applied to a set of political or religious opinions held by a party; such as the "platform of Geneva." *Hooker*.

PUBLIC OFFICES SITE ACT (for the Admiralty and War) passed 24 July, 1882.

Public Buildings Expenses act passed, 1 April, 1898; estimated cost, 2,550,000*l*.

PUBLIC PROSECUTOR, see *Prosecutor*.

PUBLIC RECORDS, see *Records*.

PUBLIC SAFETY, COMMITTEE OF, was established at Paris during the French Revolution on 6 April, 1793, with absolute power, in consequence of the coalition against France. The severe government of this committee is termed the Reign of Terror, which ended with the execution of Robespierre and his associates, 28 July, 1794. A similar committee was established at Paris by the communists, March–May, 1871.

PUBLIC SCHOOLS ACT, 1868, amended by acts passed 1870 and 1872; see *Education*.

PUBLIC STORES. The laws relating to their protection were consolidated and amended by an act passed 29 June, 1875.

PUBLIC WORKS ACT, passed 21 July, 1863, to provide work for the unemployed persons in the manufacturing districts at the time of the cotton famine. It enabled corporate bodies to raise loans, and proved very successful. It was continued in 1864-75, 1886 and 1892-3. See under *Local Loans*. Public Works Loans act 1903, royal assent 14 Aug.

PUBLIC WORSHIP REGULATION ACT, 37 & 38 Vict. c. 85, principally for the repression of ritualism in the church of England, was introduced into the House of Lords by the archbishop of Canterbury, 21 April, and after very much discussion, received the royal assent, 7 Aug. 1874.

By it a new judge in the provincial courts of Canterbury and York was appointed: the first being lord Penzance (dies, 9 Dec. 1899); the act came into operation . . . . July, 1875

First cause, the parish of Folkestone *v.* rev. C. J. Ridsdale, the vicar, 4 Jan., 1876; tried at Lambeth palace; verdict for plaintiffs . . 3 Feb. 1876

Rev. Arthur Tooth of Hatcham, and rev. T. Pelham Dale of St. Vedast's, London; monition to discontinue practices . . . . 18 July, „

Rev. A. Tooth disregards monition; justifies himself and denies authority of court, 21 Dec. 1876; carries on ritualistic services up to 14 Jan.; pronounced contumacious by lord Penzance in court of Arches, 13 Jan.; imprisoned in Horsemonger-lane gaol from 22 Jan. to 17 Feb. The church was forcibly entered, and he celebrated holy communion in the censured form . . 14 May, 1877

Proceedings against him quashed by the Queen's Bench on appeal, because the trial did not take place in the diocese of Rochester . 19 Nov. „

Sentence upon Rev. T. P. Dale set aside through legal difficulty; he resumes service . 22 July, „ [Again convicted and admonished, 8 Feb. 1879.]

The Queen's Bench division assert the public worship regulation court is a new court, and not a modification of the court of Arches . 19 Nov. „

Rev. John Edwards of Prestbury suspended for six months, and Rev. A. H. Mackonochie warned, 23 March, 1878

Rev. A. H. Mackonochie sentenced by court of Arches to three years' suspension from benefice and office, for disobedience to monition of the court . . . . 1 June, „

Enforcement of the sentence prohibited by the Queen's Bench . . . . . . 8 Aug. „

Rev. J. Edwards' suspension also set aside . Aug. „

Sentence of court of Arches against Mr. Mackonochie affirmed by court of Appeal, 28 June; he is sentenced to 3 years' suspension from benefice (from 23 Nov. 1879), he protests . . . . 15 Nov. 1879

Mr. Sinclair, nominated to officiate, retires; Mr. Mackonochie officiates as usual . . 23 Nov. „

Martin *v.* Mackonochie, new trial; lord Penzance declines to decide, as the former sentence has not been carried out . . . . . . 5 June, 1880

Rev. T. Pelham Dale is imprisoned in Holloway gaol for contempt of court . . . 30 Oct. „

Rev. Sidney F. Green, rector of Miles Platting, Manchester, and Rev. Rd. Wm. Enraght, of Bordesley, Birmingham, convicted 20 Nov.; Mr. Enraght imprisoned in Warwick gaol 27 Nov. „

Mr. Dale applies to Queen's Bench for release on ground of illegal proceedings; his detention affirmed . . . . . . 6-13 Dec. „

Mr. Dale on appeal to house of lords released till 11 Jan. 1881; Mr. Enraght prefers to remain 18 Dec. „

Mr. Dale (and consequently Mr. Enraght) discharged through technical irregularity respecting the writ by decision of Appeal court, 15 Jan. 1881; he died in 1892

Rev. A. H. Mackonochie's appeal to the house of lords dismissed; sentence of 1878 to take effect 7 April, „

The judicial committee of privy council grant him a new trial, 3 Feb.; remit to Lord Penzance to decree suitable punishment . . . 22 Feb. 1882

Rev. S. F. Green imprisoned in Lancaster Castle March 1881; released . . . . 5 Nov. „

Sir Percival Heywood *v.* the bishop of Manchester, for refusing to institute Rev. Mr. Cowgill, curate of Rev. S. F. Green, as his successor, 10, 12 Dec. 1883; Baron C. Pollock decides for the bishop 21 Jan. 1884

Mr. Mackonochie sentenced to deprivation by court of Arches, 21 July, 1883. He resigns the benefice of St. Peter's, London Docks 31 Dec. 1883. Died, aged 62, by exposure to cold, having lost his way near Kinlochmore, Scotland about 15 Dec. 1887

Rev. James Bell Cox suspended for ritualistic practices after much litigation; committed to Walton gaol, by error for contempt of court, 5 May; release ordered by writ of *habeas corpus*, 20 May; this set aside on appeal, 22 Nov.; but affirmed by the house of lords . . . 5 Aug. 1890

A trial of the bishop of Lincoln, see under *Canterbury*.

The people's churchwarden of St. Mark's, Marylebone *v.* the rev. Morris Fuller, the vicar, for certain alterations and innovations in the church; verdict for plaintiffs with costs; notice of appeal, consistory court . . . . . . 7 Dec. 1897

Mr. John Kensit, an anti-Ritualist agitator, severely injured after speaking at a meeting in Birkenhead, 25 Sept.; died of *pneumonia* or *blood poisoning*, aged 49, 8 Oct.; John M'Keever, accused of murder, acquitted . . . . . 11 Dec. 1902

PUBLISHERS' CIRCULAR, first issued twice a month, weekly since Dec. 1890; organised chiefly by Mr. William Longman (died 1877), greatly assisted by Mr. Sampson Low, who first published it, 2 Oct. 1837.

In 1890 the London publishing firm of Messrs. Longman, which existed as Osman and Longman in 1726, purchased the business of Messrs. Rivington, which was established by Mr. Charles Rivington in 1710. "The Publishing House of Rivington," edited by Septimus Rivington, published, June, 1894.

Publisher's association inaugural meeting, Mr. C. J. Longman president, 21 April, 1896.

International congress of publishers in London, Mr. John Murray (president), 7–9 June, 1899; Leipzig, 10 June, 1901

Mr. George M. Smith, eminent publisher, died, aged 77, 6 April, 1901.

PUDDLING, making the walls of canals water-tight by means of clay, was largely adopted by Brindley in constructing the Bridgewater canals, 1761 *et seq.*; see also under *Iron Manufacture*.

PUEBLA, see *Mexico*, 1863.

PUERTO, see *Porto*.

PUGILISM, see *Boxing*.

PULLEY, vice, and other mechanical instruments, are said to have been invented by Archytas of Tarentum, about 400 B.C., or by Archimedes, 287-212. In a single movable pulley the power gained is doubled: in a continued combination the power is equal to the number of pulleys, less one, doubled.

PULLMAN CARS, see under *Railways*, 1874.

PULTOWA (Russia), where Charles XII. of Sweden was entirely defeated by Peter the Great of Russia, 8 July, 1709. He fled to Bender, in Turkey.

PULTUSK (Russia), where a battle was fought between the Saxons, under their king Augustus, and the Swedes, under Charles XII., in which the former were signally defeated, 1 May, 1703. Here also the French under Napoleon fought the Russian and Prussian armies: both sides claimed the victory, but it inclined in favour of the French, 26 Dec. 1806.

PUMPS. Ctesibius of Alexandria is said to have invented pumps (with other hydraulic instruments), about 224 B.C., although the invention is ascribed to Danaus, at Lindus, 1485 B.C. Pumps were in general use in England, A.D. 1425. An inscription on the pump in front of the late Royal Exchange, London, stated that the well was sunk in 1282. The air-pump was invented by Otto Guericke in 1654, and improved by Boyle in 1657; see *Air* and *Wells*.

PUNCH, the puppet show, borrowed from the Italian Polichinello, is descended from a character well known in the theatres of ancient Rome. *Fosbroke.* The satirical weekly publication, *Punch, or the London Charivari*, was established by Henry Mayhew, Mark Lemon, Douglas Jerrold, Gilbert a' Beckett, and others: amongst its early contributors were Wm. M. Thackeray; Prof. E. Forbes, and other eminent writers; first published 17 July, 1841. Mark Lemon, the first editor, died 23 May, 1870; 2nd, Shirley Brooks, died 23 Feb. 1874; 3rd, Tom Taylor, died July, 1880; 4th, Francis Cowley Burnand. Richard Doyle, who designed the wrapper, and was a frequent contributor, died 11 Dec. 1883; John Leech died 1864, and was succeeded by Mr. George Du Maurier, born in Paris, 6 March, 1834, died, 8 Oct. 1896. Mr. Percival Leigh, an early and long-continued contributor to *Punch*, died 24 Oct. 1889, aged 77. Charles Keene, artist, a contributor since 1850, died 4 Jan. 1891. Phil May, artist and clever caricaturist, died, aged 39, 5 Aug. 1903. John Tenniel, cartoonist, since 1851 (knt. 1893); resigns, Jan. 1901; succeeded by Linley Sambourne. Mr. W. H. Lucy (Toby, M.P.). Mr. Wm. Agnew, proprietor (bart. June, 1895). An interesting jubilee number of *Punch* was published 17 July, 1891. Mr. Wm. Hardwick Bradbury, born, 3 Dec. 1832, long printer of *Punch*, and of this volume, died, 13 Oct. 1892. "The history of *Punch*," by M. H. Spielmann, published autumn, 1895. Mr. Edwin James Milliken, contributor of the "'Arry papers," etc., died, aged 57, 26 Aug. 1897. *Punch* appears in an enlarged form, and with a story by Dr. Conan Doyle, 3 Jan. 1900. "*Punch's* Holiday Book," edited by Mr. E. T. Reed, July, 1901. The king receives Mr. Burnand (knt. 26 June, 1902); accepts a copy of the Coronation number, 21 June, 1902. See *Caricatures* and *Charivari*.

PUNCTUATION. The Hebrew accents for punctuation are very ancient. The period (.) is the most ancient; the colon (:) was introduced about 1485; the comma (,) was first seen about 1521, and the semicolon (;) about 1570. In sir Philip Sidney's "Arcadia" (1587), they all appear, as well as the note of interrogation (?), asterisk (*), and parentheses ( ).

PUNIC WARS, see *Carthage*, 264-241; 218-201; 149-146 B.C.

PUNISHMENTS, see *Beheading*, *Blinding*, *Boiling*, *Death*, *Drowning*, *Flogging*, and *Poisoning*.

PUNJAUB (N. W. Hindostan) was traversed by Alexander the Great, 327 B.C.; by Tamerlane, A.D. 1398; by Mahmoud of Ghizni, about 1000. It was an independent state under Runjeet Singh, 1791-1839. Our wars with the Sikhs began here, 14 Dec. 1845, and were closed on 29 March, 1849, when the Punjaub was annexed; see *India*. The Punjaub has since greatly flourished, and on 1 Jan. 1859, was made a distinct presidency (to include the Sutlej states and the Delhi territory); see *Durbar*. The Sirhind canal (502 miles) opened by the viceroy, marquis of Ripon, 24 Nov. 1882. Local self-government bill passed 10 Oct. 1883. Population in 1881, 18,843,186; in 1891, 20,803,000; in 1901, 22,455,769*l*. Capital, Lahore; population, 1901, 120,058.

[Dhuleep Singh (son of Runjeet Singh), born 1838, received a pension of 40,000*l*.; he resided in England till 1886 when he sailed for India; in consequence of an indiscreet proclamation to the Sikhs he was stopped at Aden about 3 May, 1886. After his release he wandered about Europe; in May 1889 he married a European in Paris; his manifesto to the Sikhs, inciting them to rebellion, indignantly rejected with strong censure, Nov. 1889. After severe illness, he expresses deep regret for his conduct, 27 July, and is pardoned by queen Victoria, 1 Aug. 1890; received by her at Grasse, 31 March, 1891; dies at Paris, 22 Oct. 1893.]

The new Jhelam irrigation canal (relief work), see *India*, 1896-7; 28,000 labourers employed, Jan. 1897; opened . . . . 29 Oct. 1901

Increase of plague, reported . . . . 11 Feb. 1898

Lord Curzon visits Lyallpur, a new town founded as the result of successful irrigation . 3 April, 1899

Punjaub land alienation bill becomes law, see *India* . . . . 19 Oct. 1900

Sir Mackworth Young installs the young maharajah of Patiala. . . . . 22 Oct. 1903

New north-west frontier province formed out of the 4 Trans-Indus districts, Feb. 1901; inauguration of col. Deane as chief commissioner at Peshawar. . . . . . . 9 Nov. "

Lieut.-governors: sir James Lyall, 1887; sir Dennis Fitzpatrick, March, 1892; Mr. (aft. sir) Wm. Mackworth Young, March, 1897; sir Charles Rivaz . . . . 6 March, 1902

PUPPETS (Italian, *puppi*; French, *marionnettes*), of which the eyes, arms, &c., were moved by strings, were used by the ancients, and are mentioned by Xenophon, Horace, and others. Skilful theatrical performances with puppets have been several times exhibited in London (at the Adelaide gallery, 1852). A performance with puppets as large as life, began at St. James's-hall, July, 1872. M. Ch. Magnin published a "*Histoire des Marionnettes*," 1852.

PURCELL CLUB, formed Aug. 1836; dissolved 1863.

PURCELL SOCIETY, founded 21 Feb. 1876, to publish and perform the works of Henry

Purcell. Bi-centenary of Purcell's death celebrated in Westminster Abbey, 21 Nov. 1895. Purcell operatic society founded, 1899.

PURCHASE OF LAND, see under *Land*.

PURCHASE SYSTEM in the army. The payment of a present or gratuity for a commission was prohibited by William III., 1693; but in 1702 purchase was legally re-organised. In 1711 the sale of commissions was forbidden without the royal permission; in 1719-20 regulations were issued; and a fixed scale of prices was adopted in consequence of a commission in 1765. Large over-regulation payments continued to be paid. Commissions of inquiry were held frequently since 1858; and in 1871 the system was abolished, with compensation, by royal warrant, 20 July, 1871, the bill for the purpose having been rejected by the house of lords. For amounts paid, see under *Army*.

PURGATIVES of the mild species (aperients), particularly cassia, manna, and senna, are ascribed to Actuarius, a Greek physician, 1245.

PURGATORY, the middle place between heaven and hell, where, it is believed by the Roman catholics, the soul passes through the fire of purification before it enters the kingdom of God. The doctrine was known about 250; was introduced into the Roman church in the 5th century, and made a religious dogma by Gregory I., 590-604. It was first set forth by a council at Florence, 1439; enforced by the council of Trent, Dec. 1563; see *Indulgences*.

PURIFICATION, after childbirth, was ordained by the Jewish law, 1490 B.C. (*Lev.* xii.); see *Churching*. The feast of the purification was instituted, 542, in honour of the Virgin Mary's going to the temple. (*Luke* ii.) Pope Sergius I. ordered the procession with wax tapers, whence Candlemas-day.

PURITANS, the name first given, it is said, about 1564, to persons who aimed at greater purity of doctrine, holiness of living, and stricter discipline than others. They withdrew from the established church, professing to follow the word of God alone, and maintaining that the church retained many human inventions and popish superstitions; see *Cathari*, *Nonconformists*, and *Presbyterianism*.

PURLEY, see *Diversions*.

PURPLE, a mixed tinge of scarlet and blue, discovered at Tyre. It is said that Hercules Tyrius having observed his dog's lips to be stained, after eating a shell-fish named *murex* or *purpura*, was thereby led to invent the dye. Purple was anciently used by the princes and great men for their garments. It was restricted to the emperor by Justinian I. 532, and *porphyrogenitus* attached to the names of some emperors signifies "born to the purple."

PURVEYANCE, an ancient prerogative of the sovereigns of England of purchasing provisions, &c., without the consent of the owners, led to much oppression. It was regulated by Magna Charta, 1215, and other statutes, and was only surrendered by Charles II. in 1660, for a compensation.

PUSEYISM, a name attached to the views of certain clergymen and lay members of the church of England, who proposed to restore the practice of the church of England to what they believed to be required by the language of her Liturgy and Rubrics, but which were considered by their opponents to be of a Romish tendency. The term was derived from the name of the professor of Hebrew at Oxford, Dr. Edwd. Pusey. The heads of houses of the university of Oxford passed resolutions censuring Dr. Pusey's attempts to renew practices which are now obsolete, 15 March, 1841; and his celebrated sermon was condemned by the same body, 30 May, 1843; he died 16 Sept. 1882; see *Tractarians*, and *Ritualism*.

PUTNEY, anciently Putilei and Putenheath, N.E. Surrey, on the Thames, opposite Fulham. A new granite bridge, founded by the prince of Wales (to replace the wooden one completed in 1729), 12 July, 1884. Opened by the prince, 29 May, 1886.

PYDNA (Macedon), where Perseus, the last king of Macedon, was defeated and made prisoner by the Romans, commanded by Æmilius Paulus, 22 June, 168 B.C.

PYRAMIDS OF EGYPT, about 75 in number, of various sizes, constructed for the preservation of mummies of the kings and their families.

The Stepped Pyramid of Sakkara is conjecturally assigned to Ouenephes of the first dynasty, see *Egypt*. Three great pyramids are situated near Gizeh on the W. bank of the Nile. The first or greatest, is said to have been erected as the tomb of Choofoo, fourth dynasty, the Cheops of Herodotus, dated by Brugsch, 3733–3666 B.C. Its height is said to have been originally 481 feet, and its base 774 square feet. The second pyramid is ascribed to Chafra, or Chephren, 3666–3633 B.C. The third pyramid is said to have been built by Menkaura or Mycerinus, 3633 B.C.

The pyramids have been visited and described by Belzoni, 1815; Vyse, 1836; C. Piazzi Smith, and others, see *Egypt Exploration Fund*.

Some of the eleven pyramids at Sakkara explored by M. Maspero, 1880 *et seq.*

At the *battles of the Pyramids*, Napoleon Bonaparte defeated the Mamelukes, and thereby conquered Lower Egypt, 13 and 21 July, 1798.

PYRENEES. After the battle of Vittoria (fought 21 June, 1813), Napoleon sent Soult to supersede Jourdan, with instructions to drive the allies across the Ebro; Soult retreated into France with a loss of more than 20,000 men, having been defeated by Wellington in a series of engagements from 25 July to 2 Aug. One at the Pyrenees on 28 July. A railway through the Pyrenees (from Bilbao to Miranda) was opened 21 Aug. 1862.—THE PEACE OF THE PYRENEES was concluded between France and Spain, by cardinal Mazarin, for the French king, and don Louis de Haro, on the part of Spain, in the island of Pheasants, on the Bidassoa. By this treaty Spain yielded Roussillon, Artois, and her right to Alsace; and France ceded her conquests in Catalonia, Italy, &c., and engaged not to assist Portugal, Nov. 1659.

PYROLETER, a mechanical and chemical apparatus for extinguishing fires, especially in ships, invented by Dr. Paton.

PYROMETER (fire-measurer), an apparatus employed to ascertain the temperature of furnaces, &c., where thermometers cannot be employed; Muschenbroek's pyrometer (a metallic bar) was described by him in 1731. Improvements were made by Ellicott and others. Wedgwood employed clay cylinders, 1782-6. In 1830 professor Daniell received the Rumford medal for an excellent pyrometer made in 1821. Mr. Ericsson's pyrometer appeared in the Great Exhibition of 1851. (*Eng. Cyc.*) Mr. (aft. sir) C. W. Siemens' electric pyrometer and those of Becquerel, and Le Châtelier are also in use.

PYROPHONE (Greek, *pur*, fire; *phone*, voice), a musical instrument, invented by M. Frédéric Kastner, of Paris. It consists of glass tubes of various lengths; the tones being produced by what are termed "singing flames." It is based upon the "chemical harmonicon." Keys are attached for playing, as in the piano. The invention was reported to the French Academy of Sciences, 17 March, 1873; exhibited at Vienna, same year; and at the Society of Arts, 17 Feb. 1875. M. Kastner died aged 31, 6 April, 1882.

PYROXYLIN, the chemical name of *Gun Cotton* (*which see*).

PYRRHONISM, see *Sceptics*.

PYTHAGOREAN PHILOSOPHY. Pythagoras, of Samos, head of the Italic sect, flourished in the 6th century B.C. He is said to have taught the doctrine of metempsychosis, or transmigration of the soul from one body to another, forbidden his disciples to eat flesh and beans, invented the multiplication table, improved geometry, and taught the present system of astronomy.

PYTHIAN GAMES, in honour of Apollo, near the temple of Delphi; asserted to have been instituted by himself, in commemoration of his victory over the serpent, Python. Also said to have been established by Agamemnon, or Diomedes, or Amphictyon, or lastly, by the council of the Amphictyons, 1263 B.C. They lasted till 394.

PYX, the casket in which Catholic priests keep the consecrated wafer. In the ancient chapel of the pyx, at Westminster abbey, are deposited the standard pieces of gold and silver, under the joint custody of the lords of the treasury and the comptroller-general. The "*trial of the pyx*" signifies the verification by a jury of goldsmiths of the coins deposited in the pyx or chest by the master of the mint; this took place on 17 July, 1861, at the exchequer office, Old Palace-yard, in the presence of twelve privy councillors, twelve goldsmiths, and others, and on 15 Feb. 1870. This trial is said to have been ordered in the reign of Henry II., 1154-89; King James was present at one in 1611. The first *annual* trial of the pyx, appointed by the Coinage act of 1870, took place 18 July, 1871; new regulations issued, Feb. 1901.

Q.

QUACKERY, or medical imposture, is very ancient. Quack medicines were taxed in 1783 *et seq.* An inquest was held on the body of a young lady, Miss Cashin, whose physician, St. John Long, was afterwards tried for manslaughter, 21 Aug. 1830; he was found guilty, and sentenced to pay a fine of 250*l.*, 30 Oct. following. He was tried for manslaughter in the case of Mrs. Catherine Lloyd, and acquitted, 19 Feb. 1831. Dr. Vriès, "the black doctor," a professed cancer-curer, at Paris, was condemned to fifteen months' imprisonment as an impostor in Jan. 1860. Alabone *v.* Morton, see *Trials*, 8 July, 1893.

QUADRAGESIMA SUNDAY, first Sunday in Lent and 40th day before Good Friday; see *Lent*, and *Quinquagesima*.

QUADRANT, a mathematical instrument in the form of a quarter of a circle. The solar quadrant was introduced about 290 B.C. The Arabian astronomers under the caliphs, in 995, had a quadrant of 21 feet 8 inches radius, and a sextant 59 feet 9 inches radius. Davis's quadrant for measuring angles was produced about 1600; Hadley's quadrant about 1731; see *Navigation*.

QUADRILATERAL or **QUADRANGLE**, terms applied to four strong fortresses in N. Italy, long held by the Austrians, but surrendered to the Italians, Oct. 1866;—Peschiera, on an island in the Mincio; Mantua on the Mincio; Verona and Legnago, both on the Adige; see *Italy*, *Peschiera*, &c.

The *Turkish Quadrilateral* was Shumla, Varna, Rustchuk, and Silistria, lost to the sultan by the treaty of Berlin, which established the autonomy of Bulgaria.

QUADRILLE, a dance (originally *quadrille de contre danse*, introduced into French ballets about 1745), in its present form became popular in France about 1804. It was introduced into this country about 1808 (*Miss Berry*), and promoted by the duke of Devonshire and others, in 1813. *Raikes.*

QUADRIVIUM, see *Arts*.

QUADRUPLE ALLIANCE. That between Great Britain, France, and the emperor (signed at London, 22 July, 1718), on the accession of the states of Holland, 8 Feb. 1719, obtained its name. It guaranteed the succession of the reigning families of Great Britain and France, settled the partition of the Spanish monarchy, and led to war.

QUADRUPLE TREATY, concluded in London 22 April, 1834, by the representatives of Great Britain, France, Spain, and Portugal, guaranteed the possession of her throne to Isabella II., the young queen of Spain.

QUADRUPLEX TELEGRAPHY, see under *Electricity*.

QUÆSTORS (seekers). Two *quæstores parricidii*, public prosecutors, in cases of murder and other capital crimes, acted in Rome under the kings; two *quæstores classici*, who had the management of the public treasure; appointed about 484 B.C. The number of quæstors was raised from time to time, as circumstances demanded. Plebeians were first elected in 409 B.C. There were eight quæstors in 265. Sylla raised the number to twenty; Julius Cæsar to forty.

QUAKERS or **SOCIETY OF FRIENDS**, originally called Seekers, from their seeking the truth. and afterwards Friends (3 *John*, 14). Justice Bennet, of Derby, gave the society the name of Quakers in 1650, because George Fox (the founder) admonished him and those present to quake at the word of the Lord. This sect was commenced in England about 1646, by George Fox (then aged 22), who was joined by George Keith, William Penn, and Robert Barclay, of Ury, and others. Fox rejected all religious ordinances, explained away the commands relative to baptism, &c.; discarded the ordinary names of days and months, and used *thee* and *thou* for *you*, as more consonant with truth. He published a book of instructions for teachers and professors, and died 13 Jan. 1691. Sir H. Nicolas explains the Quaker calendar in his Chronology of History. The first meeting-house in London was in White Hart-court, Gracechurch-street.

Their principles are contained in "Extracts of minutes" (from the beginning) published 1782: revised 1802, 1861, and 1883.

The Quakers early suffered grievous persecutions. At Boston, U.S., where the first Friends who arrived were females, they were cruelly scourged, and had their ears cut off; some put to death.

In 1659 they stated in parliament that 2000 Friends had endured sufferings and imprisonment in Newgate: and 164 Friends offered themselves at this time, by name, to government, to be imprisoned in lieu of an equal number in danger (from confinement) of death, 1659.

Fifty-five (out of 120 sentenced) were transported to America, by an order of council, 1664.

The masters of vessels refusing to carry them for some months, an embargo was laid on West India ships, when a mercenary wretch was at length found for the service. The Friends would not walk on board, nor would the sailors hoist them into the vessel, and soldiers from the Tower were employed. In 1665, the vessel sailed; but it was immediately captured by the Dutch, who liberated twenty-eight of the prisoners in Holland, the rest having died of the plague. Few reached America.

William Penn, with a company of Friends, colonised Philadelphia . . . 1682

First meeting of Quakers in Ireland in Dublin in 1658; and their first meeting-house there was opened in Eustace-street . . . 1692

The solemn affirmation of Quakers enacted to be taken in all cases in the courts below, wherein oaths are required from other subjects (see *Affirmation*) . . . 1696

John Archdale, a Quaker, elected M.P. for Chipping Wycombe; refused to take the oaths, and his election was declared void . . . 1699

Quakers emancipated their negro slaves . 1 Jan. 1788

The Quakers had in England 413 meeting-houses in 1800, and 372 in . . . 1872

A schism in the society was begun in America about 1827, by Elias Hicks publishing his opinions denying the divinity of Christ and his atonement and the authority of the Holy Scriptures. His numerous followers are styled Hicksite Friends.

Joseph Pease, a Quaker, was admitted to parliament on his affirmation . . . 15 Feb. 1833

At an annual assembly it was agreed to recommend that mixed marriages should be permitted, and that many of the peculiarities of the sect in speech and costume should be no longer insisted on. 2 Nov. 1858

An act passed rendering valid Quaker marriages when only one of the persons is a Quaker. May, 1860
The Quakers publish an address deprecating the continuance of the Franco-Prussian war . Jan. 1871
Said to be 14,441 Quakers in Great Britain, May, 1877; about 14,700, May, 1880; 15,381, May, 1885; 16,854, and 348 meeting-houses in 1898; in the world, 112,413 members, of whom 92,398 are in America, reported, 10 Jan. 1898; home and colonial membership, 21,629 . . . . Jan. 1903
Quaker summer school of theology opened at Scarborough . . . . 4–18 Aug. 1897
Their "appeal to the nation" against increase of army and navy and forward policy issued . Dec. „

QUALIFICATION FOR OFFICE ABOLITION ACT, passed May, 1866, rendered it unnecessary to make and subscribe certain declarations.

QUARANTINE, the custom observed at Venice as early as 1127, whereby all merchants and others coming from the Levant were obliged to remain in the house of St. Lazarus, or the Lazaretto, forty days before they were admitted into the city. Various southern cities have now lazarettos; that of Venice is built in the water. In the times of plague, England and all other nations oblige those that come from the infected places to perform quarantine with their ships, &c., a longer or shorter time, as may be judged most safe. Quarantine acts were passed in 1753 and in 1825. The system was abolished in England by an act passed 1896, and the old quarantine men-of-war in the Solent were broken up. Quarantine established throughout Europe, in consequence of the bubonic plague at Bombay (*which see*), 16 Jan. 1897. By order of council, 10 Nov. 1866, foreign cattle were made subject to quarantine.

QUARRIES. An act was passed for their regulation in 1894. See *Slate*.

QUARTER SESSIONS established 25 Edw. III. 1350-1. Days of sitting appointed, 2 Hen. V. 1413. In 1830 it was enacted that quarter sessions of the peace should be held in the first whole weeks after 11 Oct., 28 Dec., 31 March, and 25 June. Further regulated, 1842, 1848, and 1858. *Brewster Sessions* are regulated by the Licensing Act 1902.

QUARTERLY REVIEW, the organ of the Tory party. The publication was proposed to Mr. George Canning, and his support solicited by Mr. John Murray, the publisher, in a letter dated 25 Sept. 1807, in opposition to the opinions of the *Edinburgh Review*. Mr. Murray was assisted by Walter Scott, Robert Southey, John Gibson Lockhart (editor 1825-53), J. W. Croker, and other eminent persons. It first appeared Feb. 1809, with William Gifford, the celebrated translator of "Juvenal" as editor. He died 31 Dec. 1826. The rev. Whitwell Elwin, an able editor, 1853–1867, died, aged 84, 1 Jan. 1900. Dr. (aft. sir) William Smith, editor, from 1867 till his death, 7 Oct. 1893; succeeded by Mr. Rowland Prothero, Nov. 1893.

QUASI MODO, a name given to *Low Sunday* (the first Sunday after Easter) from the commencement of a hymn sung on that day.

QUATERNIONS, an important mathematical method or calculus, invented by Sir Wm. Rowan Hamilton, about 1843.

It is based upon the separation of multiplication from addition, and its fundamental idea is mental transference or motion by what he termed vectors. He attributed to addition motion from a point; to multiplication about a point. Four numbers are generally involved, hence the name quaternion. Hamilton's "Lectures on Quaternions," was published 1853: his "Elements," 1866. Other works by professors Kelland and Tait, published since.

QUATRE-BRAS (Belgium). Here on 16 June, 1815, two days before the battle of Waterloo, a battle was fought between the British and allied army under the duke of Brunswick, the prince of Orange, and sir Thomas Picton, and the French under marshal Ney. The British fought with remarkable intrepidity, notwithstanding their inferiority in number, and their fatigue through marching all the preceding night. The 42nd regiment (Royal Highlanders) suffered severely in pursuit of a French division by cuirassiers posted in ambush behind growing corn. The duke of Brunswick was killed.

QUEBEC a province of the dominion of Canada, formerly called Lower Canada, was settled by the French in the 16th and 17th centuries. Quebec the capital, was founded by them in 1608. Population of the province, 1881, 1,359,027; 1891, 1,489,062; 1901, 1,648,898. Town, 1881, 62,446; 1891, 63,090; 1901, 68,840.

Quebec reduced by the English, with all Canada, in 1629, but restored 1632
Besieged by the English, but without success . 1711
Conquered by them after a *battle* memorable for the death of general Wolfe in the moment of victory, and of the French general Montcalm 13 Sept. 1759
Besieged in vain by the American provincials, under general Montgomery, who was slain . 31 Dec. 1775
Bishopric established 1793
Public and private stores and several wharfs destroyed by fire; the loss estimated at upwards of 260,000*l*. . . . . Sept. 1815
Awful fire, 1650 houses, the dwellings of 12,000 persons, burnt to the ground . . . 28 May, 1845
Another great fire, 1365 houses burnt . 28 June, „
Fire at the theatre, 50 lives lost . . 12 Jan. 1846
Quebec made the seat of government . 17 April, 1856
Visited by the prince of Wales . 18-23 Aug. 1860
Great fire in French quarter; 2500 houses and 17 churches destroyed, and nearly 20,000 persons made homeless . . . . . . 14 Oct. 1866
Great fire; 500 houses burnt . . 24 May, 1870
Great fires at St. John's—commercial district; 9 churches and 7 hotels said to be destroyed. 18 June, 1876
Dissensions between the lieut.-governor Luc Letellier de St. Just and his ministers . . . . „
600 small wooden houses destroyed by fire . June, 1881
Parliament buildings burnt (incendiary) 19 April, 1883
Dynamite explosions destroying new parliament buildings . . . . . . 11 Oct. 1884
Destructive fire in the citadel; the powder magazine saved; about 30,000*l*. damage . 6–7 July, 1887
A. Real Angers appointed lieut.-governor . . „
Thunderstorm with great loss of life and property, 16 Aug. 1888
Fire in the suburb St. Sauveur; above 700 houses destroyed; great distress . . 15–16 May, 1889
Jesuits' Estate act passed, see *Canada* . Aug. „
Landslip below the citadel, 7 dwellings fell, 19 Sept.; 30 bodies recovered, 36 missing 21 Sept. „
The duke and duchess of Connaught received warmly 10 June, 1890
Visit of the Comte de Paris, banquet . 28 Oct. „
At St. Joseph de Levis, a railway train, crossing the bridge, is thrown into the river, about 10 lives lost . . . . 18 Dec. „
Destructive boiler explosion at Hare Point, about 30 persons killed . . . . . . 12 Feb. 1891
The Hon. Honoré Mercier, premier of Quebec, and Mr. Joseph Adolphe Chapleau, secretary of state, charged with misappropriating public money in relation to the Chaleurs Bay railway, &c.; the charge accepted by the Senate . 14 Sept. „
In consequence of the interim report of the Royal Commission of inquiry (three judges) appointed by lieut.-governor Réal Angers (issued Nov.), he dismisses the ministry . . . . 16 Dec. „
Mr. C. B. de Boucherville forms a ministry 21 Dec. „

Royal commission to inquire into the conduct of the ministry, 11 Jan. 1892; the report censures several persons and blames Mr. Mercier for negligence, 17 Feb.; investigations proceeding, April, 1892
New parliament opened (conservatives 55, opposition 17) . . . . . 27 April, ,,
Trial of Mr. Charles Langelier and Mr. Ernest Pacaud for conspiracy and fraud; judgment reserved . . . . . 21 May, ,,
Mr. Mercier and Mr. Pacaud committed for trial for conspiracy to defraud the province of money, 9 June; acquitted . . . . 4 Nov. ,,
Great fire at Hedley; 120 families homeless, 9 Sept. ,,
Sir J. A. Chapleau appointed lieut.-governor, Dec. ,,
Mr. C. de Boucherville resigns, succeeded by Mr. Taillon as premier . . . . 14 Dec. ,,
Mr. Mercier, in a manifesto, advocates Canadian independence; reported . . . 4 April, 1893
Death of sir Narcisse Fortunal Belleau, eminent official . . . . . . 14 Sept. 1894
Death of Mr. Honoré Mercier, ex-premier 30 Oct. ,,
Forest fires, many farmers ruined . about 23 Sept. ,,
Cabinet reconstructed, Mr. E. J. Flynn premier, 11 May, 1896
Ursuline convent at Roberval, Lake St. John, burnt down, 7 nuns perish . . . . 6 Jan. 1897
Legislature dissolved . . . . . 6 March, ,,
New ministry, Mr. F. G. Marchand, premier, 26 May, ,,
Victoria park opened by sir J. A. Chapleau (died, 13 June, 1898), Jubilee day . . . . 22 June, ,,
Disastrous floods; towns in the east under water, reported . . . . . . 15 July, ,,
Sir Louis Jette appointed lieut.-governor . 3 Jan. 1898
Card. Taschereau, archbishop of Quebec, born 17 Feb. 1820, died . . . . . . 12 April, ,,
Construction of a cantilever bridge over the St. Lawrence began . . . . . . Sept. 1900
Death of Mr. F. G. Marchand, premier, aged 68, 25 Sept. ,,
Duke and duchess of Cornwall and York visit the city . . . . 16, 17 Sept. 1901
Strike riot, factory raided . . . . 5 March, 1903

(See *Canada*, 1898 *et seq.*)

QUEEN (Saxon, *cwen;* German, *königin*). In 1554 an act was passed "declaring that the regall power of this realme is in the quenes majestie [Mary] as fully and absolutely as ever it was in any of her moste noble progenitours kinges of this realme." The Hungarians called a queen-regnant king; see *Hungary*. John Knox's "Monstrous Regiment of Women," published 1555, against Mary queen of Scots, greatly offended Elizabeth of England. See under *England*, kings and queens.

QUEEN ANNE'S BOUNTY, established by her in Nov. 1703, being the first-fruits with the tenths, to increase the incomes of the poorer clergy. There were 5597 clerical livings under 50*l*. per annum found by the commissioners under the act of Anne capable of augmentation. *Chalmers*. Act to consolidate the offices of first-fruits, tenths, and queen Anne's Bounty, passed 1 Vict. 1838. Benefactions in 1895, 53,467*l*.; in 1902, 35,126*l*. Total of benefactions and grants, 1703–1903, 7,782,057*l*. Joint commission, lords and commons, 1900–1, on reconstruction of the Bounty.

QUEEN ANNE'S FARTHINGS. The popular stories of the great value of this coin are fabulous, although some few of particular dates have been purchased by persons at high prices. The current farthing, with the broad brim, when in fine preservation, is worth 1*l*. The common patterns of 1713 and 1714 are worth 1*l*. The two patterns with Britannia under a canopy, and Peace on a car, R R R, are worth 2*l*. 2*s*. each. The pattern with Peace in a car is more valuable and rare, and worth 5*l*. *Pinkerton* (died 1826).

QUEEN CAROLINE'S TRIAL, &c.

Caroline Amelia Elizabeth, second daughter of Charles William Ferdinand, duke of Brunswick, born 17 May, 1768; married to George, prince of Wales . . . . 8 April, 1795
Their daughter, princess Charlotte, born 7 Jan. 1796
The "Delicate Investigation" (*which see*) 22 May, 1806
Charges against her again disproved . . . 1813
The princess embarks for the continent . Aug. 1814
Becomes queen, 20 Jan.; arrives in England, 6 June, 1820
A secret committee in the house of lords, appointed to examine papers on charges of incontinence, 8 June, ,,
Bill of pains and penalties introduced by lord Liverpool . . . . . . 5 July, ,,
The queen removes to Brandenburg-house, 3 Aug. ,,
Receives an address from the married ladies of the metropolis (and many others afterwards) 16 Aug. ,,
Her trial commences . . . . . 19 Aug. ,,
Last debate on the bill of pains and penalties, when the report was approved by 108 against 99; the numerical majority of nine being produced by the votes of the ministers themselves. Lord Liverpool moves that the bill be reconsidered *that day six months* . . . . . 10 Nov. ,,
Great public exultation; illuminations for three nights in London . . . . 10, 11, 12 Nov. ,,
The queen goes to St. Paul's in state . 29 Nov. ,,
She protests against her exclusion from the coronation, 19 July; taken ill at Drury-lane theatre, 30 July; dies at Hammersmith . . . 7 Aug. 1821
Her remains removed on their route to Brunswick; an alarming riot occurs; two persons were killed in an affray with the guards . . 14 Aug. ,,

QUEEN CHARLOTTE SHIP OF WAR, a first-rate ship of the line, of 110 guns, the flag-ship of lord Keith, then commanding in chief in the Mediterranean, was burnt by an accidental fire, off the harbour of Leghorn, and more than 700 British seamen out of a crew of 850 perished by fire or drowning, 17 March, 1800.

QUEEN'S ADVOCATE (see *King's*), prosecutes or defends on the part of the crown in all cases in the court of admiralty. Sir R. J. Phillimore, appointed in 1862, was succeeded by sir Travers Twiss, Aug. 1867, who resigned in March, 1872; no successor appointed.

QUEEN'S BENCH COURT AND PRISON, see *King's Bench*.

QUEEN'S COLLEGES, see *Cambridge* and *Oxford*. Queen's colleges, Ireland, from their unsectarian character termed the "Godless Colleges," were instituted in 1845, to afford education of the highest order to all religious denominations. They were placed at Belfast, Cork, and Galway; the last was opened on 30 Oct. 1849.—THE "QUEEN'S UNIVERSITY in Ireland," comprehending these colleges, was founded by patent, 15 Aug. 1850; the earl of Clarendon, lord lieutenant, the first chancellor. These were "condemned" by the Propaganda and the pope, and by a majority (a small one) of the Irish bishops in a synod held at Thurles, in Sept. 1850. A supplemental charter, granted in June, 1866, created much dissension when acted upon in October following, and was suffered to expire, 31 Jan. 1868; see *Colleges*.

A government commission of inquiry into the colleges was appointed about . . . . May, 1876
Dissolution of the Queen's University enacted, another to be created, by 42 & 43 Vict. c. 65, passed 15 Aug. 1879.
Queen's college, Harley-street, London, founded mainly by the rev. F. D. Maurice in 1848, its jubilee commemorated . . . . 2 May, 1898

QUEENSLAND, Moreton-bay, a British colony, comprising the whole of the north-eastern portion of Australia; was separated from New South Wales and made a distinct colony, in 1859, when Brisbane, the capital (pop. 1901, 119,428), founded by Oxley, 1823, was made a bishopric. Chinese immigrants are virtually excluded.

Sir George Fergusson Bowen, the first governor, 1859 (died 1899), succeeded by Mr. Blackall, 1868; the marquis of Normanby, 1871; Mr. Wm. Wellington Cairns, 1874; sir Arthur E. Kennedy, Jan. 1877; sir Anthony Musgrave, March, 1883 (died 9 Oct. 1888); sir Henry Arthur Blake Nov. (objected to by the colony); resigns about 27 Nov.; sir Henry Wylie Norman appointed Nov. 1888; well received 1 May.; opens the parliament with speech noticing the prosperity of the colony, 21 May, 1889

Report of royal commission, 25 April, 1885; on recruiting in South Pacific Isles for labourers for sugar plantations in North Queensland, discloses much deceit and cruelty, especially in the ship *Hopeful*, capt. Shaw, May; Neil McNeil, agent, and Williams, boatswain, were convicted of murder (not executed) 1884; 404 islanders sent home, announced . 6 June; others in July, 1885

North Queensland made a bishopric 1878; agitation of North Queensland for separation July, *et seq.* ,,

Loan of 1,554,000*l.* authorised . . 15 Nov. 1889

Mount Morgan, a grazing district of 640 acres, in central Queensland, bought by Donald Gordon for 5*s.* an acre, was sold by him to Messrs. Morgan for 1*l.* an acre: in 1882 they discovered gold, and formed a partnership with Messrs. Hall and others. The product of gold enormously increased, and in 1886, a new company was formed with a capital of 1,000,000*l.*, which is said to have paid very large dividends . . . Nov. ,,

Disastrous floods, about 800 miles of land submerged through heavy rains . . announced 5 Jan. 1890

The cabinet re-arranged; hon. B. D. Morehead still premier . . . . . announced 6 Jan. ,,

Destructive cyclone; Cardwell, a small township, nearly destroyed . . about 31 March, ,,

Resignation of Mr. Morehead's ministry, 7 Aug.; succeeded by sir S. W. Griffith's . . 8 Aug. ,,

Labour disputes and riots in central Queensland, about 21 March; suppressed . . 26 March, 1891

The Shearers' Union, very active . . . 1890–1

Strike of the shearers collapses reported 14 June, 1891

Very large crop of wheat and wool reported 8 Dec. ,,

Misunderstanding between sir Thomas M'Ilwraith and the Bank of England respecting a loan, Sept.–Dec., 1891; explanations given, March; amicable settlement . . . . . 3 May, 1892

North and Central Queensland petition for separation from the colony; the British government recommends delay . . . . May, ,,

Revival of the employment of Kanaka labourers, under restrictions; bill passed reported 6 May ,,

The separation question deferred by government, Aug.; the bill passed, 13 Oct.; rejected by the legislative council . . . 27 Oct. ,,

Destructive floods through heavy rains on the S. E. coast, a national calamity; Brisbane, Ipswich, and other towns greatly damaged; about 30 lives lost; relief funds opened in all the Australian colonies, London, &c., 5 Feb. *et seq.*; estimated loss about 3,000,000*l.*; relief funds, 69,000*l.*, 4 May, 1893

Resignation of sir Samuel Griffith; sir Thomas M'Ilwraith forms a ministry, about . 26 March, ,,

Stoppage of Queensland National bank and the bank of North Queensland, 15 May; of the Royal Bank of Queensland . . . . . 17 May, ,,

Meeting of parliament . . . . . 25 May, ,,

The Royal bank re-constructed . . 15 June, ,,

National bank declared solvent, 6 July; re-opened 2 Aug. ,,

Budget reported; deficit, 1,500,000*l.*; due to floods, &c., 25 July; the issue of 520,000*l.* of treasury bills authorized, 17 Oct.; issue suspended, 27 Oct. ,,

Resignation of sir Thomas M'Ilwraith, premier; succeeded by Mr. Hugh Muir Nelson . 27 Oct. ,,

Peace preservation bill for the suppression of outrages in the pastoral districts; passed . 19 Sep. 1894

A loan for 2,000,000*l.* authorized; passed 6 Dec. ,,

Lord Lamington appointed governor . . Sept. 1895

Fierce tornado and floods over N. Queensland, 20 deaths and destruction of shipping, etc. at Townsville . . . . . . 25, 26 Jan. 1896

Parliament dissolved . . . . . 22 Feb. ,,

Lord and lady Lamington arrive at Brisbane, 9 Apr. 1896

Federal enabling bill rejected by the legislative council, Oct.; Mr. H. Nelson, the premier, is requested by the premiers of the other colonies to reconsider the question, so that Queensland may be represented at the Federal convention; bill withdrawn . . . . . . 29 Nov. ,,

The national bank, loss of 1,183,000*l.*, with a deficit of 1,253,000*l.* declared; government bill guaranteeing current deposits for 12 months, passed, 12 Nov. ,,

Bill authorising a government loan passed, 11 Dec. ,,

Report of a committee of inquiry into the affairs of the National bank received; estimated losses up to 30 June 1896, 3,500,000*l.* . . 16 Nov. 1897

Destructive cyclone at Mackay . . . Feb. 1898

Mr. Byrnes, attor.-gen., becomes premier, 12 April, dies . . . . 27 Sept. ,,

Prosecutions begun against Mr. Hart (ex-chairman), Mr. Morehead, Mr. Webster (ex-directors), and 2 others at Sydney, 8 May; trial concluded, verdict *not guilty* . . . . 8 Nov. ,,

Mr. James Tyson, born 1822, a benefactor, formerly a squatter, died . . . . . early Dec. ,,

The legislative assembly dissolved . . 15 Feb. 1899

Hurricane off the coast; many deaths, reported, 10 March, ,,

Elections, government majority, 25 March; 13th parliament opened . . . . 16 May, ,,

Federal bill passed both houses, 20 June; *referendum*, 35,000 for and 29,000 against the bill, reported . . . . 1 Oct. ,,

Queensland offers troops for South Africa, 12 July; see *Colonies* . . . . ,,

National agricultural and industrial association's exhibition at Brisbane, opened by lord Lamington, 9 Aug. ,,

The ministry resigns, 25 Nov.; Mr. R. Philp forms a cabinet . . . . . . 7 Dec. ,,

Budget: good report, 47,800*l.* surplus . 30 Aug. 1900

Sir J. R. Dickson, premier, 1898, minister of defence in the 1st Federal cabinet, dies, aged 69, 10 Jan. 1901

Imperial troops welcomed at Brisbane, 17, 18 Jan. ,,

The duke and duchess of Cornwall warmly received at Brisbane . . . . 20 May, ,,

Lord Lamington leaves amid regrets . 20 June, ,,

Lord Hopetoun, gov.-gen. of Australia, welcomed, 19 Sept. ,,

Parliament dissolved . . . . . . 4 Feb. 1902

Major-gen. sir Herbert Chermside, governor, arrives at Brisbane . . . . . . 24 March, ,,

Parliament opened by the governor . . 9 July, ,,

Death of Brunton Stephens, poet, aged 67, early Aug. ,,

Appeal of 3,000 islanders against the Pacific island labour act, 1901, 23 June; refused . 30 Aug. ,,

Terrible cyclone at Townsville (see *Storms*) 9 March, 1903

Parliament opened . . . . . . 21 July, ,,

Death of Dr. Webber, bp. of Brisbane, aged 66, 3 Aug. ,,

Brisbane exhibition very successful, closed 15 Aug. ,,

New cabinet formed by Mr. Morgan . 17 Sept. ,,

Statement to the legislative assembly by Mr. Kidston *re* the financial position of the colony; anticipated revenue 185,000*l.* less than late treasurer's estimate, leaving a deficiency for year ending 30 June, 1904 of about 200,000*l.*; the government meant to effect economies by reform in administration, recognising the opposition of the country to fresh taxation, reported 13 Oct. ,,

Population in 1850, about 23,450; in 1871, 125,146; in 1875, about 163,182; in 1884, 301,577; in 1891, 393,718; 1901, 502,892.

Chief exports, wool, gold, copper, tallow, live stock, cotton, and sugar; value in 1871, 2,560,383*l.*; 1883, 5,276,608*l.*; in 1901, 9,249,366*l.*

Revenue 1887, 3,032,463*l.*; expenditure, 3,350,049*l.* 1888–9, revenue, 3,636,000*l.*; expenditure 3,510,000*l.* 1889–90, revenue, 3,260,308*l.*; expenditure, 3,745,217*l.*; imports, 5,066,700*l.*; exports, 8,554,512*l.*; revenue, 1894, 3,413,000*l.*; revenue, 1895, 3,642,000*l.*; revenue, 1901, 4,403,225*l.*; expenditure, 4,958,806*l.*; imports, 6,376,239*l.*; exports, 9,249,366*l.*

QUEENS OF ENGLAND, see under *England.*

QUEEN'S THEATRE, see *Opera House*.

QUEEN'S TITLE, see *Royal Style*.

QUEENSTOWN (Upper Canada). This town, on the river Niagara, was taken in the war with U.S.N.A. by the troops of the United States, 13 Oct. 1812; but was retaken by the British forces, who defeated the Americans with considerable loss in killed, wounded, and prisoners, on the same day. Queenstown suffered severely in this war.—The Cove of Cork was named QUEENSTOWN, 3 Aug. 1849, by the queen on her visit. The U. S. steamer *America* was burnt here, 29 Nov. 1893.

QUEEN'S UNIVERSITY (see *Queen's Colleges*), was directed to be dissolved by 42 & 43 Vict. c. 65 (1879), and was dissolved by proclamation, 31 Jan. 1882; see *University of Ireland*.

QUEEN'S YEAR, see *Jubilee*, 1887 and 1897.

QUEEN VICTORIA STEAM SHIP. Wrecked 15 Feb. 1853; see *Wrecks*.

QUENTIN, ST. (N. France). The duke of Savoy, with the army of Philip II. of Spain, assisted by the English, defeated the French under the constable De Montmorency, at St. Quentin, 10 Aug. 1557. In fulfilment of a vow made before the engagement, the king built the monastery, palace, &c., the Escurial, considered by the Spaniards the eighth wonder of the world; see *Escurial*. During the Franco-German war the army of the north, under Faidherbe, was defeated here by the Germans after seven hours' fighting, on 19 Jan. 1871; total loss about 15,000: the German loss about 3100.

QUERETARO (Mexico), was besieged and taken (through the treachery of Lopez) by the liberal general Escobedo, 15th May, 1867. The emperor Maximilian and his generals Miramon and Mejia, were taken prisoners, and, after trial were shot 19 June following.

QUERN or **HANDMILL**, is probably the implement spoken of in Isaiah xlvii. 2, about 712 B.C. So-called Roman querns have been found in Yorkshire.

QUESNOY (N. France), was taken by the Austrians, 11 Sept. 1793, but was recovered by the French, 16 Aug. 1794. It surrendered to prince Frederick of the Netherlands, 29 June, 1815, after the battle of Waterloo.—It was here that cannon were first used, and called bombards. *Hénault*.

QUETTAH, see *Beloochistan*.

QUIBERON BAY (W. France). A British force landed here, Sept. 1746, but was repulsed. In the bay admiral Hawke gained a complete victory over the French admiral Conflans, and thus defeated the projected invasion of Great Britain, 20 Nov. 1759. Quiberon was taken by some French regiments in the pay of England, 3 July, 1795; but on 21 July, through treachery, the French republicans, under Hoche, retook it by surprise, and many emigrants were executed. About 900 of the troops, and nearly 1500 royalist inhabitants who had joined the regiments in the pay of Great Britain, effected their embarkation on board the ships.

QUICKSILVER, in its liquid state, mercury. Its use in refining silver was discovered, 1540. There are mines of it in various parts, the chief of which are at Almaden, in Spain, and at Idria, in Illyria; the latter, discovered by accident in 1497, for several years yielded 1200 tons. A mine was discovered at Ceylon in 1797; and at New Almaden and other places in California. Quicksilver was congealed in winter at St. Petersburg, in 1759. It was congealed in England by a chemical process, without snow or ice, by Mr. Walker, in 1787. Corrosive sublimate, a deadly poison, is a combination of mercury and chlorine; see *Calomel*.

QUICUNQUE VULT, see *Athanasian Creed*.

QUIETISM, the doctrine of Miguel Molinos, a Spaniard (1627-96), whose work, the "Spiritual Guide," published in 1675, was the foundation of a sect in France. He held that religion consisted in an internal silent meditation on the merits of Christ and the mercies of God. Madame de la Mothe-Guyon, a quietist, was imprisoned in the Bastille for her visions and prophecies, but released through the interest of Fénélon, archbishop of Cambray, between whom and Bossuet, bishop of Meaux, arose a controversy, 1697. Quietism was finally condemned by pope Innocent XII. in 1699. See *Jansenists*, *Quakerism* and *Pietism*.

QUILLS are said to have been first used for pens in 553; authorities say not before 635.

QUINCE, the *Pyrus Cydonia*, brought to this country from Austria, before 1573. The Japan quince, or *Pyrus Japonica*, brought hither from Japan, 1796.

QUINDECEMVIRI, fifteen men, chosen to keep the Sybilline books. The number, originally two (duumviri), about 520 B.C., was increased to ten in 365 B.C., and afterwards (probably by Sylla) to fifteen, about 82 B.C. Julius Cæsar added one; but the precedent was not followed.

QUININE or **QUINIA**, an alkaloid (much used in medicine), discovered in 1820 by Pelletier and Caventou. It is a probable constituent of all genuine cinchona barks, especially of the yellow bark; see *Jesuits' Bark*. Artificial quinine was prepared (synthetically) by Mr. W. L. Scott, in Oct. 1865.—QUINOIDINE, see *Fluorescence*. John Eliot Howard, promoter of the cultivation of cinchona in India, and author of "Quinologia" (1862) died 22 Nov. 1883.

QUINQUAGESIMA SUNDAY. The observation is said to have been appointed by Gregory the Great (pope, 590-604). The first Sunday in Lent having been termed *Quadragesima*, and the three weeks preceding having been appropriated to the gradual introduction of the Lent fast, the three Sundays of these weeks were called by names significant of their position in the calendar: and reckoning by decades (tenths), the Sunday preceding Quadragesima received its present name, *Quinquagesima*, the second *Sexagesima*, and the third *Septuagesima*.

QUINTILIANS, heretics in the 2nd century, the disciples of Montanus, who took their name from Quintilia, a lady whom he had deceived by his pretended sanctity, and whom they regarded as a prophetess. They made the eucharist of bread and cheese, and allowed women to be priests and bishops. *Pardon*.

QUIRINUS, a Sabine god, whose name was given to Romulus after his death. L. Papirius Cursor, general in the Roman army, first erected a sun-dial in the temple of Quirinus, from which time the days began to be divided into hours, 293 B.C. *Aspin*. The sun-dial was sometimes called the Quirinus, from the original place in which it was set up. *Ashe.* The Sabines who became Roman citizens were termed QUIRITES.

QUITO (capital of the republic of Equator), founded in 1534, was the scene of the measurement of a degree of the meridian, by the French and Spanish mathematicians, 1736-42. Forty thousand persons perished by an earthquake which almost overwhelmed the city of Quito, 4 Feb. 1797. Since then violent shocks, but not so disastrous, occurred; till one, on 22 March, 1859, when about 5000 persons were killed; see *Earthquakes* and *Equator*.

QUIXOTE, see *Don Quixote*.

QUOITS, a game said to have originated with the Greeks, and to have been first played at the Olympic games, by the Idæi Dactyli, fifty years after the deluge of Deucalion, 1453 B.C. Perseus, the grandson of Acrisius, by Danaë, having inadvertently slain his grandfather, when throwing a quoit, exchanged the kingdom of Argos, to which he was heir, for that of Tirynthus, and founded the kingdom of Mycenæ, about 1313 B.C.

QUOTATIONS. Athenæus's "*Deipnosophistæ or Banquet of the Learned*" (compiled about 228), and Burton's "Anatomy of Melancholy" (1621), contain masses of extracts. Henry Ainsworth's "Communion of Saints" (died 1622), is a mosaic of Scripture quotations.

Macdonnel's "Dictionary of Quotations," 1796; Moore's 1831
Riley's "Dictionary of Latin Quotations," with a Selection of Greek, published by H. Bohn . . 1856
Collections of English Quotations are now numerous:
Friswell's "Familiar Words," 2nd ed. . . 1866
Bartlett's "Familiar Quotations" . . . 1869-91
Adams' "Cyclopædia of Poetical Quotations" . 1853
Bohn's "Dictionary of Poetical Quotations" . 1881-4
Several useful books since published.

QUO WARRANTO ACT, passed 1280. By it a writ may be directed to any person to inquire by what authority he holds any office or franchise. Charles II. directed a writ against the corporation of London in 1683, and the court of king's bench declared their charter forfeited. The decision was reversed in 1690. The proceedings have been regulated by various acts, 1710, 1792, 1837, 1843.

R.

RABBITS, see *New South Wales*, 1887.

The rabbit pest has spread devastation over the Australian colonies. Rabbit-proof wire-netting is at present the only means of checking its progress. The ravages of the *jack-rabbits* in California and adjoining states checked by hunters, 1895–6. Rabbits destroyed in Queensland by injection with chicken cholera, reported, 22 Oct. 1898.

RABELAIS CLUB, to promote the study of Rabelais and the illustration of his works; lord Houghton, sir W. Frederick Pollock and his sons, Walter Besant, and others; first meeting, Dec. 1879.

Rabelais Gallery, Pall Mall East, opened to the press, 13 Oct.; at the instance of the National Vigilance Association, four pictures were seized as indecent by the police, 3 Nov.; Mr. J. F. Sutton and Mr. H. Scarborough, the exhibitors, were prosecuted at Bow Street, 5 Nov.; committed for trial; 21 pictures ordered to be destroyed, 12 Nov.; Messrs. Sutton & Scarborough convicted, 18 Dec. 1890; fined 25*l*. each; the pictures ordered to be returned to France 18 April, 1891

Mr. W. F. Smith's translation of the works of Rabelais was issued by the club to subscribers, Feb. 1893

A hitherto unknown first edition of the fifth book of "Gargantua and Pantagruel," dated 1549, a duodecimo vol., discovered by Herr L. Rosenthal, reported . . . . Dec. 1900

RABIES, see *Hydrophobia*.

RACES, one of the ancient games of Greece. Horse-races were known in England in very early times. Fitz-Stephen, in the days of Henry II., mentions the delight taken by the citizens of London in the diversion. In James I.'s reign Croydon in the south, and Garterly in the north, were celebrated courses. Near York there were races, and the prize was a little golden bell, 1607. *Camden.* In the end of Charles I.'s reign, races were performed at Hyde Park. Charles II. patronised them, and instead of bells, gave a silver bowl, or cup, value 100 guineas. William III. added to the plates (as did queen Anne), and founded an academy for riding.

At Ascot, begun by the duke of Cumberland, uncle to George III.; mentioned . . . 1727

The first racing calendar is said to have been published by John Cheney . . . . . . ,,

Act for suppressing races by ponies and weak horses, 19 Geo. II. 1739

The most eminent races in England are those at Newmarket (*which see*), established by Charles II. 1667; and at Epsom, begun about 1711; by Mr. Parkhurst (annual since 1730, *Allen's Surrey*). [The earl of Derby began the Oaks, 1779; the Derby, 1780 (first won by Diomed)]. See *Derby Day*.

At Doncaster, by col. St. Leger (the *St. Leger* stakes were founded in 1776, and so named in 1777) . 1776

At Goodwood, begun by the duke of Richmond, in his park 1802

Lord Stamford, said to have engaged Jemmy Grimshaw, a light-weight jockey, at a salary of 1000*l*. a year. . . . . March, 1865

"Tattersall's," the "high-change of horse-flesh," was established by Richard Tattersall, near Hyde Park Corner (hence termed "the Corner") in 1766, for the sale of horses. The lease of the ground having expired, the new premises at Brompton were erected and opened for business on 10 April, ,,

The *Jockey Club*, which now chiefly regulates races and the betting connected with them, was founded in 1750. Its gradually accumulating rules were modified in 1828 and revised in 1857

Alterations recommended by a committee appointed in April; adopted by the club 16 July following . 1870

Rules revised, Nov. 1876; reforms made . . . 1880

Proceedings taken against the club by the Anti-Gambling league at Newmarket for keeping betting places . . . . 12 Feb. 1895

Summonses dismissed from want of proper evidence 16 Feb. ,,

Resolved that a shorthand-writer be present at the meetings . . . . 16 April, 1890

John Scott, a most eminent trainer, died, aged 77, Oct. 1871

Betting. Between 1858 and 1868, 75,000*l*. and 115,000*l*. have been won upon a single race. Betting is now much reprobated; see *Betting*.

Gate-meetings: Races held in fields by publicans and others; Metropolitan Race-course Act (42 & 43 Vict. c. 18), to check them, passed . 3 July, 1879

Tom Chaloner, celebrated jockey, dies March, 1886

Fred. Archer, very successful jockey, winner of 2,746 races, aged 29, committed suicide with a revolver when in a state of high fever (left by will 70,000*l*.) . . . . 8 Nov. ,,

Charles Wood, jockey, *v*. Cox, for libel in *Licensed Victuallers' Gazette*, charging Wood with pulling the head of Success in two races; nine days' trial in queen's bench division; verdict for plaintiff damages one farthing and no costs allowed . . . . 29 June, 1888

Sir George Chetwynd *v*. the earl of Durham, see *Trials* . . . . 29 June, 1889

Suspected poisoning of the duke of Westminster's *Orme*, to prevent his running . 28 April, 1892

The York race committee and the Gimcrack club's 131st annual dinner, the earl of Rosebery present, 7 Dec. 1897

George Barrett, very successful jockey, died, aged 34 . . . . 25 Feb. 1898

Mr. Edmund Tattersall, eminent horse auctioneer, died, aged 82 . . . . . 5 March, ,,

John Watts, many years the king's first jockey, died, aged 41 . . . . . . 29 July, 1902

RACE-HORSES.

Flying Childers, bred in 1715 by the duke of Devonshire, was allowed by sportsmen to have been the fleetest horse that ever ran at Newmarket, or that was ever bred in the world; he ran four miles in six minutes and forty-eight seconds, or at the rate of 35¼ miles an hour, carrying nine stone two pounds. He died in 1741, aged 26 years.

Eclipse was the fleetest horse that ran in England since the time of *Childers;* he was never beaten, and died in February, 1789, aged 25 years. His heart weighed 14 lb., which accounted for his wonderful spirit and courage. *Christie White's Hist. of the Turf.*

On the accession of queen Victoria, the royal stud was sold for 16,476*l*. on . . . . 25 Oct. 1837

The comte de la Grange's stud (in consequence of the war) was sold for 23,730*l*. *Gladiateur* fetched 5800*l*. 1870

Middle-park stud (property of Mr. Blenkiron, deceased) sold for 102,005 guineas; *Blair Athol*, for 12,000*l*. (to the English Stud Company); 4 days' sale . . . . 26 July, 1872

Lieut. Lubowitz, Hungarian, rode from Vienna to Paris, on his horse Caradoc, in 15 days, winning a wager, arriving . . . . . . 9 Nov. 1874

Death of Comte Frédéric Lagrange, eminent French studmaster . . . . 22 Nov. 1883

Lord Falmouth's stud sold for 36,420 guineas; (Harvester 8600 guineas; Busybody 8800 guineas) 28 April; and for 75,440 guineas . 30 June, 1884

Persimmon (owner, the prince of Wales), won the Derby, 3 June, 1896, and the Ascot gold cup, 17 June, 1897

RACK, an engine of torture, for extracting a confession from criminals, mentioned by Demosthenes, *de Coronâ*, B.C. 330, and in later times an instrument of the Inquisition. Lord Coke states from tradition that the duke of Exeter, in the reign of Henry VI., erected a rack of torture (thence called the duke of Exeter's daughter, now seen in the Tower), 1447. In the case of Felton, who murdered the duke of Buckingham, the judges of England protested against the proposal of the privy council to put the assassin to the rack, as contrary to the laws, 1628; the use of the rack was abolished 1640. See *Ravaillac* and *Torture*.

RACQUETS (Arabic *ra'hat*, "palm of the hand"). A game played in an open (now but seldom) or close court (60 ft. long, and 30 ft. wide and 40 ft. high, with high walls surrounding it, the floor being divided into two principal areas by the "short" line) with a bat resembling that used in tennis, and a small hard ball. 15 usually constitutes the game. Racquets first came into vogue during the early part of the 19th century, and Chas. Dickens refers to the game in "Pickwick" in connection with the Fleet prison, where insolvent debtors enlivened the monotony of their existence by playing this game against a single wall. In 1853, a racquet court was erected at Prince's Club, and since then courts have become common at the universities and public schools. On the sale of Prince's Club grounds in 1886, the Queen's Club, Kensington, became the headquarters of the game, and here the championship and the universities and public school matches take place. "Racquets" in the Badminton series by J. M. Heathcote, 1890.

Champion Players of England, Sir W. Hart Dyke, 1862; H. J. Gray, 1863; Wm. Gray, 1866; H. Fairs, 1876; Joseph Gray, 1878; P. Latham, 1887 to 1902 (retired); Jamsetjee (the Parsi professional), 1903.

RADCLIFFE LIBRARY, OXFORD, founded under the will of Dr. John Radcliffe, an eminent physician. He died 1 Nov. 1714, leaving 40,000*l.* to the university of Oxford for the founding a library, the first stone of which was laid 17 May, 1737, and the edifice was opened 13 April, 1749.—The RADCLIFFE OBSERVATORY, Oxford, founded by the exertions of Dr. Hornsby, Savilian professor of astronomy, about 1771, was completed in 1794. The publication of the observations was commenced in 1842, by Mr. Manuel J. Johnson, the director, appointed in 1839. Radcliffe Infirmary opened in 1770, see *Oxford*, 1893.

RADIATION, see *Heat*.

RADICALS or "RADICAL REFORMERS," persons who professed to aim at procuring a thorough reformation in the government and policy of England, became prominent in 1816, when Hampden clubs were formed, of which sir Francis Burdett, lord Cochrane, major Cartwright, and William Cobbett were prominent members. Samuel Bamford's "Life of a Radical," published in 1842, gives much information; he died 13 April, 1872. Many radicals were severely punished, 1817-20. Wm. Harris's "History of the Radical Party," published early in 1885.—The "Radicals" in the United States were the party headed by Thaddeus Stevens, bitterly opposed to the policy of president Johnson, as too favourable to the subdued Southern States.

The *Radical Programme*, advocated by the rt. hon. Joseph Chamberlain, widely circulated, first appeared July, 1885, in the *Fortnightly Review*; it included reform of the land laws, free education, increased local government, reform in taxation and finance, improvement of condition of agricultural labourers and of the poor, and religious equality and dis-establishment of national churches.

Mr. C. C. Greville (*Journal*, 25 Aug. 1837) describes "Tory Radicals." Some politicians were so termed in 1885

The National *Radical* Union at its fourth anniversary at Birmingham changed its name to National *Liberal* Union . . . . . 24 April, 1889

RADICLE, see *Compound*.

RADIOGRAPHS, a name given to the photographs obtained by Röntgen rays, see *Photography*, 1896.

RADIOMETER, &c., a little instrument constructed by Mr. (knt. 1897) Wm. Crookes, F.R.S., 1873-6. Two little disk arms, mounted on a pivot and placed in an exhausted glass-bulb, revolve when placed in bright light. The motion was attributed to heat-absorption, 1877; see *Light*.

Radiophone. By this apparatus professor Bell, at Philadelphia, showed how a ray of strong light, acting on a selenium cell, conveyed sound 500 feet, Sept. 1884.

RADIUM, a new metal found in pitchblende; its discovery by M. and Mdme. Curie, announced in 1903, see *Addenda*.

RADSTADT, Austria. Here Moreau and the French defeated the Austrians, 5 July, 1796.

RAFFAELLE WARE, see *Pottery*.

RAGGED SCHOOLS, free schools for outcast destitute ragged children, set up in large towns. The instruction is based on the scriptures, and most of the teachers are unpaid. John Pounds, a cobbler, of Portsmouth, who died in 1839, opened a school of this kind; and one was set up by Andrew Walker, in "Devil's Acre," Westminster, in 1839. *Knight.* They did not receive their name till 1844, when the "Ragged school union" was formed, principally by Mr. S. Starey and Mr. Wm. Locke (afterwards hon. secretary). The earl of Shaftesbury was chairman. In 1856 there were 150 Ragged school institutions. Sunday ragged schools reported in London in 1867, 226; in 1898, 231; day schools, in 1867, 204; in 1878, 58; week evening schools, in 1867, 207, in 1878, 147; 44 industrial schools in 1898. Ragged school buildings were exempted from rates, 1869. The day schools have now been superseded by those established by the London school board; but the sunday and night schools, mother's meetings, &c., are still maintained in very great efficiency (1903). The union reported 212 federated schools (1895). Dr. Guthrie, a founder of ragged schools in Edinburgh, &c., died 24 Feb. 1873. The earl of Shaftesbury an ardent supporter of the movement, died 1 Oct. 1885. Jubilee celebrated, 20 April, 1894. Annual meetings; the union was styled Shaftesbury society in May, 1898; total members 127,087, 1902. See *Shoeblack*.

RAGMAN ROLL (said to derive its name from Ragimunde, a papal legate in Scotland) contains the records of the homage and fealty to Edward I., sworn to by the nobility and clergy of Scotland at Berwick in 1296. The original was given up to Robert Bruce, king of Scotland, in 1328, when his son David was contracted in marriage to the princess Joanna of England.

RAGUSA, a city on the Adriatic, on the south confines of Dalmatia, was taken by the Venetians, 1171, but became an independent republic, 1358.

It suffered much by an earthquake, 1667; was taken by the French in 1806, and given up to Austria in 1814.

RAID OF RUTHVEN, see *Ruthven.*

RAILWAY COMMISSIONERS; see *Railways*, 1873 and 1880.

RAILWAYS. Short roads, in and about Newcastle, laid down by Mr. Beaumont, so early as 1602, are thus mentioned in 1676:—"The manner of the carriage is by laying rails of timber from the colliery to the river, exactly straight and parallel; and bulky carts are made with four rollers fitting those rails, whereby the carriage is so easy that one horse will draw down four or five chaldron of coals, and is an immense benefit to the coal merchants." *Roger North.* They were made of iron at Whitehaven, in 1738. See *Gauges, Tramroads.* For electric railways see *Electricity.*

An iron railway laid down near Sheffield by John Curr (destroyed by the colliers) 1776
The first considerable iron railway was laid down at Colebrook Dale 1786
The first iron railway sanctioned by parliament (except a few undertaken by canal companies as small branches to mines) was the Surrey iron railway (by horses), from the Thames at Wandsworth to Croydon 1801
Trevethick and Vivian obtained a patent for a high-pressure *locomotive* engine 1802
William Hedley of Wylam colliery made the first travelling engine (locomotive), or substitute for animal power in a colliery 1813
The first *locomotive* constructed by George Stephenson, travelled at the rate of 6 miles per hour . 1814
The Rocket travelled at the rate of 25 and 35 miles per hour 1829
(It obtained the prize of 500*l.* offered by the directors of the Liverpool and Manchester railway company for the best locomotive, Oct. 1829.)
The Firefly attained a speed of 20 miles per hour . 1834
The North Star moved with a velocity of 37 miles per hour 1839
At the present time locomotives have attained a speed of 70 miles per hour.
Stockton and Darlington railway, constructed by Edw. Pease and George Stephenson, first opened for passengers (see 1875-1881, *below*) . 27 Sept. 1825
The Liverpool and Manchester railway commenced in Oct. 1826, and opened (Wm. Huskisson, M.P., killed) . . . . . . 15 Sept. 1830
Act for transmission of mails by railways . . 1838
Duty on Railways:—½*d.* a mile for 4 passengers (2 & 3 Will. IV. c. 120), 1832; 5 per. cent. on gross receipts (5 & 6 Vict. c. 59) 1842
Railway clearing house established . . . . "
The examination of railway schemes, before their introduction into parliament, by the Board of Trade, was ordered 1844
7 & 8 Vict. c. 85, required companies to run *cheap trains* every day, and to permit erection of electric telegraphs, and authorised government, after 1 Jan. 1866, to buy existing railways with the permission of parliament . . . . . "
George Hudson, a draper, mayor of York in 1839, by his successful management as chairman of the Leeds and York railway and others, was styled the "railway king" . . . . "
Great Southern and Western Ry. (Ireland) opened. "
Midland Great Western Ry. (Ireland) opened . . 1845
Waterford, Limerick and Western Ry. opened . "
An act passed 10 Vict. for constituting commissioners of railways, who have since been incorporated with the Board of Trade . . 28 Aug. 1846
The Railway Mania and panic year, when 272 railway acts passed . . . . "
Act for compensating families of persons killed by accidents (see *Campbell's Act*) . . . . "
George Stephenson died . . . . 12 Aug. 1848
Buffer springs invented by Mr. John Brown of Sheffield in . . . . "
The absolute block system introduced . . . 1853
Act for the better regulation of railways . . . 1854
Railway Benevolent Institution, instituted May, 1858
Act to enable railway companies to settle differences with other companies by arbitration 1859
Belfast and Northern counties Ry.(Ireland) opened 1860
Railway Clauses Consolidation act passed . . . 1863
Joint committee of both houses of parliament appointed to report on railway schemes . 5 Feb. 1864
Murder of Mr. Briggs in a railway carriage (see *Trials* 1864) . . . . 9 July, "

(See *Atmospheric* and *Street Railways.*)

Period of "contractors' lines" 1859-6
London, Chatham, and Dover company suspend payment; directors censured for their policy . 1866
Railway Companies Securities act passed . Aug. "
A Welsh railway train (about to start) seized for debt . . . . 27 Nov. "
250 railway bills passed, 1865; only 98 1867
Strike of 350 men on London and Brighton line, 25-27 March, "
Strike of 500 on North Eastern line, 11 April; overcome by the company . . . 25 April, "
Railway commission report against the government buying the railways, &c. . . . . May, "
Railway acts amended by act passed . 20 Aug. "
A climbing locomotive, by means of central rails, ascended Mont Cenis in 1865. [The experiments were first tried on the High Peak railway, Sept. 1863 and Feb. 1864.] The railway completed and traversed by a locomotive and two carriages, containing Mr. Fell, the inventor of the plan, and others; an unexampled journey in regard to steepness of gradients and the elevation of the summit level, 6700 feet, 21 Aug. 1867. After successful trials in May, the railway was opened 15 June, 1868
Lord Cairns (on appeal) decides that holders of debentures are responsible as qualified proprietors, 28 Jan. "
Capt. Yolland, government inspector, reports that in his opinion electric communication between the passengers and the railway servants on trains stopping only at long intervals is necessary and practicable . . . . March, "
Railway Regulation acts passed . . . 1868, 1871
Conference of railway shareholders at Manchester, 14, 15 April, 1868
Southern Railways Amalgamation bill; opposed in the lords; withdrawn . . . . . June, "
Mont Cenis railway opened for traffic . 15 June, "
New act to amend the laws relating to railways, 30 & 31 Vict. c. 119; (it orders smoking compartments, and communication between passengers and railway servants in certain trains; and prohibits trains for prize-fights, &c.) passed, 31 July, "
Midland railway station, St. Pancras (*which see*), opened . . . . 1 Oct. "
New route to Liverpool (by a viaduct over the Mersey at Runcorn), opened . . . 1 April, 1869
Pacific railway: from the Atlantic to the Pacific; opened . . . . 12 May, "
"Abandonment of Railways act" passed 11 Aug. "
Railway Companies Powers act (1864) and Construction Facilities act (1864) amended by act passed . . . . 20 June, 1870
"*Railway Association*" established: (it consists of directors and representatives of shareholders, to watch legislation, &c.,) inaugural dinner, 21 July, "
Under the London, Chatham, and Dover railway act, the arbitrators, the marquis of Salisbury and lord Cairns, decide for the amalgamation of the general undertaking; extensions for award published . . . . Aug. 1871
Rigi Mountain railway (up to 4000 feet above sea level), opened . . . . . 23 May, "
Mansion-house station of the Metropolitan District railway inaugurated . . . . . 1 July, "
European and North American railway opened at Bangor, Maine . . . . . . 18 Oct. "
Proposed amalgamation of the Midland and Glasgow and South-Western . . . . . "
Amalgamation of the London and North-Western and the Lancashire and Yorkshire railways, voted by companies . . . . . . 20 Oct. "
Forged telegram announcing proposed amalgamation of the Midland and Manchester, Sheffield, and Lincolnshire railways (led to purchase of shares, and affected the market), about 23 Nov. "

George Hudson, the "railway king," died, aged 71, 14 Dec. 1871
Strike of porters of London and North-Western company; settled . . . . 26. 27 July, 1872
Death of Thos. Brassey, who made 6600 miles of railways, which cost 78,000,000*l.* (able, honest, kind) ,,
Parliamentary committee report in favour of railway amalgamation, published . . . Aug. ,,
First railway in Japan opened . . . 12 June, ,,
One-rail railway laid down at Paris by M. Larmenjat, reported successful for short distances Aug. ,,
Amalgamations already accomplished: London and North-Western, 61 branch lines; Great Northern, 37; Great Eastern, 27; London and Brighton, 22; London and South-Western, 22; Midland, 17 . ,,
Railway proposed by M. de Lesseps from Orenburg to Peshawur (2500 miles), to connect by means of Russian and East Indian railways Calais and Calcutta . . . . . . May, 1873
Bill for amalgamation of London and North-Western and Lancashire and Yorkshire companies rejected by the commons committee . . . 23 May, ,,
New Regulation of Railways Act passed (commissioners to be appointed to carry out the Act of 1854), 21 July; commissioners: sir Frederick Peel, Mr. Price, and Mr. Macnamara; met first time . . . . 11 Nov. ,,
First railway in Persia begun at Resht . 11 Sept. ,,
Railway accidents investigated by Capt. Tyler; 1871, 171; in 1872, 246; in the United Kingdom in 1872, 541 railway servants killed, 499 injured.
Circular from the Board of Trade, by Mr. Chichester Fortescue, to the railway companies respecting the increase of preventable accidents and unpunctuality . . . . . . 18 Nov. ,,
The justificatory replies of sir Edward Watkin for the London and Brighton Co., and of R. Moon for the L. and N. W. Co.; from other companies Dec. ,,
Ten railway servants convicted of robbing the luggage, severely sentenced . . . . 19 Nov. ,,
120 persons killed; 48 without their own fault; in six months 1873-4
The Board of Trade's reply (by Mr. Malcolm) to the railway companies, published about 24 Feb. 1874
The Pullman palace saloon cars (American, 1863) introduced on the Midland railway, 21 March; opened to the public . . . . . 1 June, ,,
Commission to inquire into causes of railway accidents agreed to by government, 27 April; nominated (duke of Buckingham and others) 11 June, ,,
Circular from sir C. Adderley, recommending punctuality and care, to avoid accidents . July, ,,
Railway Travellers' Protection Society organised; duke of Manchester, president . . 23 July, ,,
Board of Trade Arbitration Act passed . 30 July,
New standing orders respecting labourers' houses removed for making railways, passed 30 July, ,,
Statement of railway servants: that 632 were killed in 1872, and 773 killed in 1873; many injured; [asserted to be less than the truth] . . Sept. ,,
Midland railway company announces change of fares: first-class to 1½*d.* a mile; second-class abolished: no return tickets at lower fares; began . . . . 1 Jan. 1875
Other companies announce reductions in fares Jan. ,,
Persons employed on railways: England, 228,958; Scotland, 31,023; Ireland, 14,554; total, 274,535; (L. & N. W. company, about 40,000); announced Jan. ,,
House of lords on appeal decide that railway companies are responsible for negligence in conveying persons and goods, although they disclaim it on tickets . . . . 1 June, ,,
Great trial of continuous *railway brakes* on Midland railway, near Lowdham; Westinghouse automatic *air-pressure* brake considered the best June ,,
Extension of Metropolitan railway to Great Eastern opened, 10 July, ,,
Railway jubilee at Darlington; 50th anniversary of opening of the Stockton and Darlington railway; statue of Joseph Pease unveiled . . 27 Sept. ,,
Dr. Strousberg, "German railway king," tried for fraud, &c., at Moscow 1876
Great Northern Ry. (Ireland) opened . . . ,,
Metropolitan extension to Aldgate opened . 11 Nov. ,,
Elevated street railways erected in New York, U.S.A. . . . . 1877 *et seq.*
Folkestone and Dover tunnel injured by rains; fallings in . . . . . . 12, 15 Jan. 1877
Fusion of South-eastern and London, Chatham, & Dover companies, voted by former . . 18 Jan. ,,
Railway accident commission report: recommend that the companies' responsibilities be not diminished, &c. . . . . Feb. ,,
Proposed fusion of the Great Northern and Great Eastern, fails June; of the Manchester and Sheffield and Lincolnshire with the Great Northern and Midland, fails . . . . . . Nov. ,,
First railway in China, from Shanghai to Oussoon (11 miles), constructed by Europeans; at first opposed; trial trip, 16 March; publicly opened, 30 June, 1876; much opposed; stopped 31 Oct.; plant taken to Formosa; resumed . . . Dec. ,,
Many embarrassed subsidiary lines purchased by the French government (for about 11,000,000*l.*) . 1878
Great increase of third-class passengers, receipts, about 7,000,000*l.* 1869; about 14,000,000*l.* . . 1879
Sudden strike of goods-guards on Midland railway through alteration of mode of payment, 3 Jan., fails . . . . about 20 Jan. ,,
South-Eastern railway company *v.* Railway Commissioners (who had given orders for enlarging station at Hastings, &c.), Queen's Bench; verdict restricting powers of the commissioners (*see above*, 1873), two judges against one . . . . 13 Jan. 1880
Enlarged dividends on the principal lines for half-year . . . . 1 Jan. to 30 June, ,,
Expended on railways in the United Kingdom, about 720,000,000*l.* (since 1829); gross annual receipts about 62,000,000*l.*, net earnings about 30,000,000*l.* reported . . . . Aug. ,,
Packet of dynamite placed on rails between Bushey and Watford (L. & N. W. Railway), night, 12-13 Sept. ,,
Board of Trade circular respecting precautions against accidents, &c. (accidents of 10, 11 Aug. attributed to neglect) . . . . . 20 Sept. ,,
Railway rates select committee meet . 10 March, 1881
Siemens' & Halske's electrical railway at Berlin, 18¾ miles an hour, tried 12 May; opened to the public . . . . 16 May, ,,
Centenary of George Stephenson's birth celebrated at Newcastle, Chesterfield, the Crystal Palace, London, and throughout the counties of Durham and Northumberland . . . . . 9 June, ,,
Murder of Mr. Fk. Isaac Gold in a carriage on London and Brighton railway . . 27 June, ,,
[Percy Lefroy *alias* Mapleton arrested on suspicion, 8 July; committed for trial, 21 July; convicted, 8 Nov.; executed . . . . . 29 Nov.] ,,
Passenger duty received, 507,076*l.* for year 1872-3; 736,369*l.* for year 1875-6; 728,718*l.* for 1876-7; 741,919*l.* for 1877-8; 748,506*l.* for 1880-1; 798,364*l.* for 1881-2
International congress for the unification of the rolling stock on the railways at Berne opened 16 Oct. 1882
The committee on railway and canal rates for the conveyance of persons, merchandise, &c., defer their report, recommend re-appointment of the committee, and also the establishment of a tribunal to decide questions and enforce decisions; revision of rates, &c., early Aug. 1881; issue report with few recommendations . 27 July, ,,
A Pullman car burned near Hunslet, Dr. Arthur perishes . . . . 29 Oct. ,,
Railway passengers' protection association established . . . . ,,
Caledonian railway strike, traffic partly suspended; Glasgow, &c. . . . . 15, 16, 17 Jan. 1883
A compromise; strike ends . . . . 21 Jan. ,,
Proposed reduction of duty on third-class passengers April, ,,
Metropolitan railway carried 36,753,321 passengers in six months without accident . . . . ,,
Association of railway shareholders established; meeting held in London . . . . 8 Aug. ,,
Existing: railway and canal, railway companies, railway shareholders, associations . . . ,,
Another cheap trains act passed . . . 20 Aug. ,,
Northern Pacific railway (2,500 miles) opened 8 Sept. ,,

4,000*l.* awarded to rev. Joseph Lloyd Brereton, and 6,500*l.* to gen. Brereton for injuries caused by derangement of machinery, &c. 28 July, 1882; 25, 26 Feb. 1884
Parks railway bill rejected by committee 20 May, ,,
Railway regulation bill making it a permanent court of record, enlarging powers, &c., read first time, 22 May; dropped . . . . . 10 July, ,,
M. Lartigue's balance railway (single rail), reported successful in Normandy . . . June, ,,
Renewed agitation respecting brakes; the board of trade's recommendations neglected . . . ,,
Metropolitan Inner Circle completed; opened 1 Oct. ,,
312,047 railway servants in England . . Oct. ,,
Communication of the Canadian Pacific railway (Halifax, Nova Scotia, to Port Moody, British Columbia) 18 May; work completed . 7 Nov. 1885
Death of Dr. R. H. Gilbert, inventor of the elevated rail system used in New York, very poor Aug. ,,
Receipts of twelve leading companies, about 25,084,000*l.* . . . . . Jan–June, ,,
Wm. H. Vanderbilt, "Railway King," dies suddenly at New York, aged 64 . . . . . 8 Dec. ,,
Lawrie *v.* L. & S. W. Railway; companies may increase their fares on days of extra traffic such as Ascot races . . . . . 11 Dec. ,,
459 railway servants killed in 1886
International railway congress, Brussels, opens 8 Aug. 1885; at Berne, July, 1886; and June, 1887
Mr. Mundella introduces bill for constituting a new court of record for railway affairs with great powers; read first time 11, 12 March; second time 6 May, 1886; introduced (modified) into the lords by lord Stanley . . . . . 1 March, ,,
The South-Eastern railway company's present of 1,000*l.* to the Imperial Institute March; declared to be illegal . . . . . 6 May, ,,
Midland Railway; strike of 2,713 drivers, firemen, &c.; traffic continued 5 Aug.; strike gradually fails . . . . Aug.–Sept. ,,
International railway congress at Rome opens 17 Sept. ,,
Thirty-four principal railway lines of the United Kingdom; net divisible profit for ordinary shareholders first six months, 1886 4,390,517*l.*; 1887, 5,357,891*l.*
15th annual congress of Amalgamated society of Railway Servants at Newcastle-on-Tyne; prudent discussion; Midland strike censured 4–7 Oct. ,,
Trumpets employed for signalling near Glasgow, and introduced into the greater lines autumn, ,,
Leinwather, an Austrian, publishes his improvements in *portable* railways for military purposes Dec. ,,
A railway between Listowel and Ballybunion, county Kerry, on the Lartigue single-rail system opened . . . . 27 Feb. 1888
Railway and Canal Traffic Bill passed . . . ,,
State purchase of the railways negatived by the commons without a division . . 4 May, ,,
L. & N. W. company run trains between London and Edinburgh and Glasgow in 9 hours from 1 June; in eight hours 6 Aug; the Great Northern makes similar reductions . June and Aug. ,,
First railway constructed in Persia, from Teheran to Shah-Abdul-Azim, opened . . 25 June, ,,
Direct railway communication between Constantinople and Vienna completed . . . Aug. ,,
Central Asian railway from the Caspian to Samarcand opened . . . . May, ,,
Mr. justice Wills appointed president of the railway commission . . . . Dec. ,,
First regular railway in China, 86 miles, opened Nov. ,,
The new railway and canal commission begins 1 Jan. 1889
Railway up Mount Pilatus, Switzerland, inaugurated . . . . 4 June, ,,
Bill for the regulation of railways relating to the block system, brakes, &c., passed . . Aug. ,,
Great swing railway bridge, span 140 ft., over the Dee declared open by Mrs. Gladstone . 2 Aug. ,,
[It gives a direct route to the Manchester, Sheffield and Lincolnshire Railway into Wales, and also to the Great Northern and Midland systems.]
International railway Congress at Paris . 14 Sept. ,,
Death of sir Daniel Gooch, aged 73, able chairman of the Great Western . . . . 15 Oct. ,,
Increased dividends through improvement in trade July–Dec. 1889
International railway conference at Rome 15 Jan. 1890
City and South London Electric railway (see *Tunnels*) . . . . 4 Nov. and 18 Dec. ,,
Underground Central London Electric Railway bill (from Uxbridge-road to the Bank), passed by the commons . . . . ,,
Lynton and Lynmouth cliff railway, steep ascent, worked by water, opened . . . 7 April, ,,
Dispute between the South-Eastern and the London Chatham & Dover railway companies, on appeal decided by the house of lords in favour of the latter company . . . . . . 5 May, ,,
Board of Trade inquiry (by lord Balfour of Burleigh and Mr. Courtenay Boyle) as to the rates of charges for the carriage of goods, concluded Jan.–21 May
Tables of maximum rates issued . . . July, ,,
Proposed establishment of the New Grand Junction company to unite the Manchester, Sheffield and Lincolnshire railway, with the Metropolitan and other railways, so as to form a new line to the north, Oct. 1890; bill rejected 1891
First annual congress of railway employés of all grades opened at the Hope Town-hall, Bethnal-green-road . . . . 18 Nov. 1890
City and South London Electric railway formally opened by the prince of Wales, 4 Nov., to the public . . . . 18 Dec. ,,
Strike of the men employed in the Caledonian, North British, Glasgow and S.W. railways, for a ten hours' day, &c. 22 Dec. 1890–31 Jan. 1891
By the great exertions of Mr. Thompson, manager of the Caledonian railway, and Mr. Walker, manager of the North British railway, the passenger traffic was continued with much difficulty, but the goods traffic almost suspended. About 9,000 men were out at one time. Rioting at Motherwell, at the eviction of railway tenant strikers, was quelled by military and police, 5 Jan. *et. seq.* The strike ended by the submission of the men, North British, 29 Jan., Caledonian 31 Jan.
Select committee of the commons on the working hours of railway servants, sir M. H. Beach chairman, meets . . . . 10 March *et seq.* ,,
The Gliding railway, which is moved by hydraulic power over a thin layer of water was exhibited by M. A. Barré, at the Crystal Palace 26 March ,,
The nine Railway Rates and Charges bills passed . 5 Aug. ,,
Brienzer Rothhornbahn railway on the Alps, the highest in Europe, opened . . early Nov. ,,
Receipts of 12 great companies, 33,028,558*l.* . . July–Dec. ,,
Mr. Christopher Anderson's (of Leeds) invention for carrying off smoke and foul air in underground railways by tubes, tried and reported successful at Neasden, near Willesden . . 26 March, 1892
Death of sir James Joseph Allport, the eminent railway manager, especially of the Midland, aged 81 . . . . 25 April, ,,
Great demonstration of railway servants in Hyde-park, for shorter hours and increased wages . 15 May, ,,
The broad gauge totally superseded, on the Great Western . . . . 20–23 May, ,,
Sir James Brunlees, eminent railway engineer, dies, aged 76 . . . . 2 June, ,,
Lancashire, Derbyshire, and East Coast (East and West) railway begun (incorporated 1891) 7 June, ,,
Railway and canal traffic amendment act, passed, 27 June, ,,
Central London railway act passed . 28 June, ,,
Manchester, Sheffield & Lincolnshire railway (with extension to London) act; third reading in the lords suspended by dissolution . . 28 June ,,
[Act passed, 28 March; another act, 29 June, 1893; amended, 1894.]
International railway congress at St. Petersburg, 20–31 Aug. ,,
Mr. W. E. Gladstone cuts the first sod of the Wirral railway connecting Wales and Liverpool, 21 Oct. ,,
Railway Travellers' association instituted 17 Nov. ,,
The electric overhead system, connecting Walsall, Wednesbury, Darlaston, and Bloxwich opened, 31 Dec. ,,

New railway rates begin, 1 Jan. lead to controversy; sir James Whitehead, president of the Mansion-house railway traffic association; sir Henry Oakley, hon. sec. of the Railway Companies' association; compromises proposed, Jan. 1893

Great meeting at the Mansion-house opposing the new rates . . . . 30 Jan. ,,

Second-class carriages abolished on the East Coast "express" route between England and Scotland worked by the Great Northern, North Eastern, and North British companies, and also on the London & North-Western, and Caledonian lines, 1 May, ,,

The new "corridor train," G. W. R., goes from London to Penzance . . . . 1 June, ,,

Railway union conference at Berne 5 June, *et seq.* ,,

Railway Servants (Hours of Labour) act passed, 27 July, ,,

First international congress of railway servants at Zurich . . . . 14 Aug. ,,

Great loss by the Midland and other railways through the coal strike . . Aug.–Sept. ,,

Report of the select committee on railway rates issued . . . . . . mid. Dec. ,,

Great decrease in the dividends through the coal strike . . . July–Nov. 1893; Jan.–Feb. 1894

Lancashire, Derbyshire, and East Coast railway act passed . . . . 31 July, ,,

International congress of railway servants at Paris 3 Oct. ,,

The countess of Wharncliffe cuts the first sod of the Manchester, Sheffield, and Lincolnshire (extension) railway at Alpha-road, St. John's Wood 13 Nov. ,,

1st conference on "light railways," summoned by the board of trade, Mr. Brice, M.P., chairman, 6 Dec. ,,

Mr. justice Mathew decided that the London, Chatham, and Dover railway company had been making illegal charges for passage from London to Calais (Mr. C. N. Nicholson *v.* the company), 14 May, 1895

Charles Henry Parkes, born 1816, able and successful chairman of the Great Eastern railway company, Nov. 1874–93; died . . 9 May, ,,

International railway conference at Amsterdam, 150 delegates, 6 June; at the Imperial institute, London, 26 June; the delegates (1,100) received by the queen at Windsor . . . 6 July, ,,

Race to Aberdeen won by the West Coast route against the East (540 miles in 512 min.) 22 Aug. ,,

Wirral railway (see Oct. 1892) opened by Mr. Gladstone . . . . 28 March, 1896

Railway up Snowdon; on the descent of the first passenger train, at 12 a.m., the engine left the line at a sharp curve and plunged over the Cymglas precipice, 6 April, 1896; Mr. E. G. Roberts, of Llanberis, died of injuries, 7 April, 1896; "safety guard," the invention of sir Douglas Fox, laid down, railway re-opened to Clogwyn . 19 April, 1897

The Board of Trade report to the companies the necessity of protecting women travelling alone, *Times* . . . . 5 Aug. 1896

Baker-street and Waterloo railway act passed, 7 Aug. ,,

Light railways Act passed . . . . 14 Aug. ,,

The Board of Trade report the capital of the U. K. railway companies to have been more than 1,000 millions sterling in 1895 . . . . . 8 Oct. ,,

28 applications to construct light railways in Great Britain up to 31 Dec.; (121 up to July, 1898) ,,

Miss Camp murdered in a train near Waterloo, L. & S. W. R. . . . . 11 Feb. 1897

Board of Trade committee appointed to inquire respecting the means of communication between passengers and railway servants in charge of trains . . . . 4 May, ,,

Samuel Laing, late chairman of the L. and Brighton railway, died . . . . 6 Aug. ,,

Railway across Salisbury plain from Pewsey authorised . . . . Nov. ,,

S. Wales direct railway, first sod cut by the duchess of Beaufort . . . . 29 Nov. ,,

International conference at Frankfort-on-the-Main, accelerated service between London and Basle arranged . . . . Dec. ,,

Position of servants on the Great Eastern and London and North Western improved . Feb. 1898

Sir George Russell, M.P., born 1828, chairman of the S. Eastern railway, died (succeeded by Mr. Cosmo Bonsor, M.P.) . . . . . 7 March, 1898

New code of railway bye-laws submitted to the Board of Trade by the N. E. company . June, ,,

Working union between the S. E. and the L. C. & D. railways agreed to . . . . . . Aug. ,,

Electric (underground) railway between Waterloo station and the Mansion-house, opened by the duke of Cambridge . . . . . . 11 July, ,,

Mr. justice Mathews and a special jury awards 2,500*l.* damages against the Gt. Western railway to Mr. Pfeiffer (for injuries sustained Feb. 1898), 22 Feb. 1899

Gt. Central railway extension, Marylebone terminus, opened . . . . . . 9 March, ,,

Third-class train of increased breadth (to seat 12 instead of 10 passengers), Gt. Eastern railway, ran between Liverpool-street and Enfield, 10 April; widened carriages for suburban traffic adopted . . . . July, ,,

Royal commission appointed to inquire into accidents to railway servants meets, 16 June, 1899; recommends active state control and supervision, &c., report issued . . . . . 22 Jan. 1900

New daily fast service between Montreal and the Pacific; London brought within 10 days of Vancouver . . . . 18 June, ,,

Central London (electric tube) railway opened by the prince of Wales . . . . . 27 June, ,,

Sir Richard Moon, born 1814, chairman of the London and N.W. railway company 1847–91, a great organiser and of high financial probity, died . . . . 17 Nov. 1899

Col. sir Francis Marindin, born 1838, inspecting officer of railways to the Board of Trade 1877 *et seq.*, originated some important railway reforms, died . . . . 21 April, 1900

Experiments upon the atmospheric resistance to trains, special train used on the Baltimore and Ohio railway, U.S., 2 miles made in 81 sec., reported . . . . 9 June, ,,

Railways (prevention of accidents) act passed, 30 July, ,,

Internat. railway congress, at the exhibition, Paris . . . . Sept. ,,

Mr. Pearson murdered in a train (S.W. railway) near Wimbledon, by G. H. Hill, *alias* Parker, and Mrs. King also attacked by him, 17 Jan. 1901; he was convicted and sentenced to death, 1 March, 1901

Sir Edward Watkin, the "railway king," born 1819, died . . . . 14 April, ,,

Great reduction of dividends chiefly owing to continued increase of working expenses; tables of rates issued, *Times* . . . . . . 14 Aug. ,,

Mr. J. T. Marshall's new locomotive valve gear, which, with lower steam pressure, greatly augments the haulage power, reported . 13 Feb. 1902

Mr. W. L. Jackson, chairman of the Gt. Northern railway, made a peer . . . . 26 June, ,,

Internat. conferences at Brussels and St. Petersburg on the Trans-Siberian route . 9–21 Dec. ,,

Memorial at Euston to railway employés killed in the S. African war, unveiled by lord Roberts, 23 April, 1903

Electrification of the Mersey line completed, 1 May, ,,

Death of sir Joseph Wilkinson, general manager, G.W.R. . . . . 16 June, ,,

An express reaches Carlisle from Euston, 299 miles, without stopping, two minutes before time, 19 June, ,,

New Rhætian railway, Thusis to Pontresina, begun 1898, opened . . . . 27 June, ,,

Central Asian railway in progress, train reaches Turkestan . . . . 8 July, ,,

Line between Lulea and Narvik, within the Arctic circle, opened by the king of Sweden . 14 July, ,,

Railways (electrical power) act to come into force 1 Jan. 1904, royal assent . . . . 14 Aug. ,,

Mails for China, Japan, and Corea despatched by French mail service for first time by overland route *viâ* Trans-Siberian railway, reducing time of transit one-half . . . . . . 28 Sept. ,,

Electro-pneumatic signalling established at Bolton (Lancs. and Yorks. railway), reported, 30 Sept. ,,

Express service, *viâ* Dover and Ostend, between London, Berlin and St. Petersburg; the express leaves London 10 a.m., reaches Berlin 7.40 p.m., and St. Petersburg 2.25 p.m. the following day; quickest route between these capitals yet established; express night service, *viâ* Zurich, between London and Vienna, leaving London 9 p.m., reaching Vienna in 45 hours, commenced, 1 Oct.	1903
First train into Coomassie arrives . . 1 Oct.	,,
The *Novelty*, constructed by Messrs. Braithwaite & Wilson, one of the three engines that took part in the competitive locomotive trials in 1830 for the best engine to run on the Liverpool and Manchester railway (the others were the *Sans Pariel*, built by Hackworth, and the *Rocket*, which won the premium of 500*l.*, constructed by Stephenson; both these are in the South Kensington museum), discovered at Rainhill, announced early Oct.	,,
Congress of amalgamated society of railway servants at Peterborough opened . 5 Oct.	,,
Automobile service established on the Stroud valley line (G.W.R.) between Stonehouse and Chalford, mid Oct.	,,
First section of the Japanese railway from Seoul to Fusan, as far as Su-won, formally opened, 20 Oct.	,,
New electric railway (4⅔ miles) up Vesuvius, constructed by Messrs. Thos. Cook & Sons. reported early Nov.	,,
Miss Goss savagely assaulted and robbed in Harecastle tunnel . . . . 9 Dec.	,,

See *Strikes*, Feb.—Dec. 1897.

RAILWAYS OF GREAT BRITAIN AND IRELAND.

Year.	*Capital paid-up.*	*Miles opened.*	*Net Receipts.*
1851.	£240,897	6,890	
1854.	286,068.794	8,054	£11,009,519
1860.	348,130,127	10,433	14,579,254
1865.	455,478,143	13,289	18,602,582
1870.	529,908,673	15,537	23,362,618
1875.	630,223,494	16,658	28,016,272
1879.	717,003,469	17,696	29,731,430
1880.	728,316,848	17,933	31,890,501
1882.	767,899,570	18,457	33.206.688
1883.	784,921,312	18,681	33,693,708
1884.	801,464,367	18,864	33,305,446
1885.	815,858,055	19,169	32,767,817
1887.	845,971,654	19,578	33,880,110
1888.	864,695,763	19,812	30,851,320
1890.	897,472.026	20,073	36,760,146
1891.	919,425,121	20,191	36,731,624
1892.	944,357,320	20,325	36,374,075
1893.	971,323,353	20,646	34,936,773
1894.	985,387,355	20,908	37,102,518
1895.	1,001,110,221	21,174	38,046,065
1896.	1,029,475,335	21,277	39,926,698
1898.	1,134,468,462	21,659	40,291,958
1899.	1,152,317,501	21,700	41,576,378
1900.	1,176,001,890	21,855	40,058,338
1901.	1,195,564,478	22,078	39,069,076
1902.	1,216,861,421	22,152	41,628,502

Working expenses: 1854, 9,206,205*l.*; 1861, 13,843,337*l.*; 1870, 21,715,525*l.*; 1874, 32,612,712*l.*; 1877, 33.857,978*l.*; 1880, 33,601,124*l.*; 1883, 37,368,562*l.*; 1887, 37,063,266*l.*; 1888, 37,063,266*l.*; 1889, 40,094,116*l.*; 1890, 43,188,556*l.*; 1891, 45,144,778*l.*; 1892, 45,717,965*l.*; 1893, 45.695,119*l.*; 1894, 47,208,313*l.*; 1895, 47,876,637*l.*; 1896, 50,192,424*l.*; 1897, 53,083,804*l.*; 1898, 55,960.543*l.*; 1899, 60,090,687*l.*; 1900, 64,743,520*l.*; 1901, 67,489,739*l.*; 1902, 67,841,218*l.*

Number of passengers (not season-ticket holders): 1845, 33,791,253; 1854, 111,206,707; 1860, 163,483,572; 1865, 251,959,862; 1870, 331,701,801; 1877, 549,541,325; 1880, 603,885,025; 1883, 683,718,137; 1887, 733,678,531; 1890, 817,744,046; 1893, 873,177,052; 1894, 911,412,926; 1895, 929,770,909; 1896, 980,339,433; 1897, 1,030,420,201; 1898, 1,062,911,116; 1899, 1,106,691,991; 1900, 1,142,276,686; 1901, 1,172,395,900; 1902, 1,188,219,269.

Miles opened.

	1843.	1861.	1879.	1883.	1893.	1900.	1902.
England & Wales	1775	7820	12,547	13,215	14.440	15,187	15,358
Scotland	225	1626	2,864	2,964	3,215	3,485	3,580
Ireland .	31	1423	2,285	2,502	2,991	3,183	3,214

For 1847-9, it was calculated that out of 4,782,188 travellers by railway, *one* person was killed, from causes beyond his own control; for 1856-9, one in 8,708,411; 1866-8, one in 12,941,170. In 1878, one in 7,503,000. Passengers killed from causes beyond their control: in 1871, 12; 1862-72, 271; 1872, 24; 1876, 811.

United Kingdom.

1874, 1424 killed—211 passengers (not their fault, 86); 788 servants, 425 trespassers; 5041 injured.
1876, 1286 killed—138 (by own fault, 101) passengers; 6112 injured, 1883 passengers.
1877, 1175 killed—126 passengers; 4988 injured, 1283 passengers.
1878, 1112 killed; 6507 injured by various causes.
1879, 1032 killed; 160 passengers; 3513 injured, 1307 passengers.
1882, 1,121 killed; 127 passengers; 4,601 injured, 1,739 passengers; 1884, 1135 killed; 4100 injured; 1885, 957 killed, 3,467 injured; 1886, 938 killed, 3,539 injured.
1887, 919 killed, 3,590 injured; 1888, 905 killed, 3,826 injured.
1889. 1,076 killed; 4,836 injured.
1890. 1,076 killed; 4,721 injured.
1891. 1,168 killed, 5,060 injured.
Killed: 1892, 1,130; 1893, 1,011; 1894, 1,185; 1895, 1,090; 1896, 1093; 1897, 1,165; 1898, 1,179; 1899, 1,240; 1900, 1,250; 1901, 1,277; 1902, 1,171.
Railway servants killed: annual average (1872-5) 740; 1880, reduced to 483; 1896, 447; 1898, 522; 1899, 512; 1900, 559; 1901, 511; 1902, 447.
United States passengers and railway servants killed, 2,819; injured, 39,800 during year ended 30 June, 1902.

Compensation paid for injuries by companies.

	1873.	1883.	1902.
Passengers . .	£364,509	£247,032	£141,489
Goods . . .	231,707	197,941	483,807

PRINCIPAL RAILWAYS OF THE UNITED KINGDOM.

The railways are generally named after their termini.

Railways.	*Date of Opening.*	
Arbroath and Forfar	3 Jan.	1839
Atmospheric Railway (*which see*)		1840
Aviemore and Inverness (Highland)	1 Nov.	1898
Bangor and Carnarvon	July,	1852
Belfast and county of Down	April,	1850
Belfast and Northern counties opened		1860
Birmingham and Derby	12 Aug.	1839
Birmingham and Gloucester	17 Dec.	1840
Birmingham, Wolverhampton, and Stour Valley,	July,	1852
Brighton and Chichester	8 June,	1846
Brighton and Hastings	27 June,	,,
Bristol and Exeter	1 May,	1844
Bristol and Gloucester	July,	1845
Caledonian	Feb.	1848
Canterbury and Whitstable	May,	1830
Central London (Electric), *Tube* (2nd), Bank to Shepherd's Bush, opened	27 June,	1900
Charing Cross Railway, London, opened	11 Jan.	1864
Cheltenham and Gloucester	Oct.	1847
Chester and Birkenhead	22 Sept.	1840
Chester and Crewe		1848
City and South London, *Tube*, opened 4 Nov. and 18 Dec. 1890; new line to the Bank and Moorgate-street, opened, 26 Feb. 1900; extension from Stockwell to Clapham-common opened,	3 June,	1900
Cockermouth and Workington	28 April,	1847
Colchester and Ipswich	15 June,	1846
Cork and Bandon	8 Dec.	1851
Cornwall	1 May,	1859
Coventry and Leamington	2 Dec.	1844
Croydon and Epsom	17 May,	1847
Devon and Somerset	7 Nov.	1873
Dover and Deal, begun	29 June,	1878
Dublin and Belfast Junction	June,	1852
Dublin and Carlow	10 Aug.	1846
Dublin and Drogheda	26 May,	1844
Dublin and Kingstown	17 Dec.	1834
Dundee and Newtyle	Dec.	1831
Dundee and Perth	22 May,	1847
Durham and Sunderland	28 June,	1839
Eastern Counties (aft. Gt. Eastern)	18 June,	,,
Eastern Union (London and Colchester),	29 March,	1843

Railways.	*Date of Opening.*
East London	10 April, 1876
Edinburgh and Berwick	18 June, 1846
Edinburgh and Glasgow	8 Feb. 1842
Ely and Peterborough	Jan. 1847
Exeter and Plymouth (part)	29 May, 1846
Glasgow and Ayr	19 Sept. 1840
Glasgow and Greenock	24 March, 1841
Glasgow, Garnkirk, and Coatbridge	July, 1845
Gloucester and Chepstow	Sept. 1851
Gloucester and Swindon	May, 1845
Grand Junction (Birmingham to Newton)	July, 1837
Gravesend and Rochester	10 Feb. 1845
Great Central (name given to the Manchester, Sheffield and Lincolnshire) in 1897; extension to London opened	9 March, 1899
Great Eastern (name given to the eastern counties) in 1862, when incorporated.	
Great Southern and Western (Ireland) opened	1844
Great Northern (Ireland) opened	1876
Great Northern	1852
Great Western to Maidenhead, 4 June, 1838: to Bristol, 30 June, 1841; to Burryport, 15 March; to Goodwick	1 July, 1899
Hertford branch of Eastern Counties	31 Oct. 1843
Highland, 1865; to Fort George	1 July, 1899
Inner Circle, London	21 July, 1882-4
Ipswich and Bury St. Edmunds	24 Dec. 1846
Isle of Man	1 July, 1873
Kendal and Windermere	21 April, 1847
Lancaster and Carlisle	16 Dec. 1846
Lancaster and Preston	30 June, 1840
Leeds and Bradford	1 July, 1846
Leeds and Derby	July, 1840
Leeds and Huddersfield, *via* Spen valley,	1 Oct. 1900
Liverpool and Birmingham	4 July, 1837
Liverpool and Manchester	15 Sept. 1830
Liverpool and Preston	31 Oct. 1838
London and Birmingham	17 Sept. ,,
London and Blackwall	2 Aug. 1841
London and Brighton	21 Sept. ,,
London and Bristol	30 June, ,,
London and Cambridge	30 July, 1845
London, Chatham, and Dover, 29 Sept. 1860; united to South-Eastern	1 Jan. 1899
London and Colchester	29 March, 1843
London and Croydon	1 June, 1839
London and Dover	7 Feb. 1844
London and Greenwich	26 Dec. 1838
London and Richmond	27 July, 1846
London and Southampton	11 May, 1840
London and Southend	June, 1856
London and Warrington; branch of the Great Northern	Aug. 1850
Lowestoft branch; Norwich and Yarmouth	1847
Lynn and Ely	,,
Manchester and Birmingham	10 Aug. 1842
Manchester and Leeds	1 March, 1841
Manchester and Sheffield	22 Dec. 1845
Meon valley branch, shorter route to Portsmouth, *viâ* Aldershot, Farnham, and Alton	1 June, 1903
Metropolitan, London; act obtained, 1853; construction began, 1860; opened	10 Jan. 1863
Midland Counties	30 June, 1840
Midland and Great Western (Ireland) opened	1845
Newcastle and Berwick	July, 1847
Newcastle and Carlisle	18 June, 1839
Newcastle and North Shields	18 June, ,,
Newmarket and Cambridge	Oct. 1851
Northampton and Peterborough	2 June, 1845
North and South-Western Junction	Dec. 1852
North British	1862
North Eastern	July, 1854
Norwich and Yarmouth	1 May, 1844
Nottingham to Grantham	July, 1850
Nottingham and Lincoln	3 Aug. 1846
Nottingham branch; Rugby and Derby	30 May, 1839
Oxford branch of London and Bristol	12 June, 1844
Oxford, Worcester, and Wolverhampton	May, 1852
Penzance to Camborne	Jan. ,,
Rugby and Derby	July, 1840
Rugby and Leamington	Feb. 1851
St. Andrew's	July, 1852
St. Helen's; first act passed	1830
Salisbury branch of the London and Southampton.	1847
Settle and Carlisle	1 May, 1876
Southampton and Dorchester	1 June, ,,
South Devon	1850
South Eastern (London and Dover)	7 Feb. 1844
South Eastern; North Kent line	1849
Stockton and Darlington	27 Sept. 1825
Trent Valley	26 June, 1847
Ulster	Aug. 1839
Waterford, Limerick and Western opened	1845
Waterloo and City opened	1898
West and East India Docks and Birmingham Junction from the Blackwall railway to Camden Town,	Aug. 1850
West Highland, 11 Aug. 1894; extension to loch Ness	22 July, 1903
Worcester and Droitwich	Jan. 1852
York and Darlington (N. Eastern)	4 Jan. 1841
York and Newcastle ,,	17 June, 1847
York and Normanton ,,	30 June, 1840
York and Scarborough ,,	7 July, 1845
Yarmouth and Norwich	1 May, 1844
Yarmouth and Lowestoft	13 July, 1903

Alleged EXTENT OF RAILWAYS (in miles):—Germany, 34,069; Russia, 28,745; France, 26,382; Austria-Hungary, 22,670; Italy, 9,827; Spain, 8,301; Sweden, 6,702; Belgium, 3,871; Switzerland, 2,355; Roumania, 1,932; Turkey, 1,912; Denmark, 1,775; Holland, 1,715; Portugal, 1,470; Norway, 1,240; Greece, 605; Servia, 360; 1 Jan. 1900. United Kingdom, 22,078 in 1901; 22,152 in 1902; United States of America, 201,839, June, 1902.

Rolling Stock of railways in the United Kingdom, 1901: locomotive engines, 21,714; passenger carriages, 48,851; other vehicles attached, 19,065; waggons for live stock, goods, &c., 697,683; miscellaneous vehicles, 18,407.

Classes in which passengers were carried in 1901: 1st class, 34,622,141, an increase of 303,332 on 1900; 2nd class, 68,854,769, decrease of 229,860; 3rd class, 1,068,918,990, increase of 30,045,742; season or periodical ticket-holders, 1,879,136, increase of 129,332, with the following *receipts* respectively, 1st class, 3,520,963*l.*, increase on 1900 of 86,984*l.*; 2nd class, 3,101,463*l.*, increase 114,953*l.*; 3rd class, 28,900,249*l.*, increase 685,207*l.*; season and periodical ticket-holders, 3,573,378*l.*, increase 122,314*l.*

MEMORABLE RAILWAY ACCIDENTS.*

Very many (where only 2 persons killed) are not noted; in nearly all cases a large number were injured.

W. Huskisson, M.P., killed at the opening of the Liverpool and Manchester railway	15 Sept. 1830
Great Corby (Newcastle and Carlisle); train runs off line; 3 killed	3 Dec. ,,
Brentwood (Eastern Counties): carriages overturned; 3 killed	21 Aug. 1840
Cuckfield (London and Brighton): engine runs off line; 4 killed	2 Oct. 1841
Sonninghill cutting, near Reading: engine forced off line; 8 killed	24 Dec. ,,
Versailles: carriages take fire, passengers locked in; 52 or 53 lives lost, including admiral D'Urville,	8 May, 1842
Masborough (Midland Counties): collision; Mr. Boteler and others killed, many injured,	20 Oct. 1845
Stratford (Eastern Counties): collision through great carelessness; Mr. Hind killed, many mutilated,	18 July, 1846
Pevensey (Brighton and Hastings): collision; 40 injured	24 Aug. ,,
Clifton (Manchester and Bolton): express runs off line; 2 killed, many injured	15 Dec. ,,
Chester (Chester and Shrewsbury): train runs off bridge; 4 killed; greater number injured,	18 May, 1847
Wolverton (North Western): collision; 7 killed, many injured	5 June, ,,
Shrivenham (Great Western): collision; 7 killed, many injured	10 May, 1848
Carlisle (Caledonian): axletree of carriage breaks: 5 killed	10 Feb. 1849

* On Dec. 27, 1864, the queen wrote to the directors of the railway companies of London, requesting them "to be as careful of other passengers as of herself."

Frodsham Tunnel (Chester and Warrington Junction): collision; 6 killed . . . 30 April, 1851
Newmarket Hill (Lewes and Brighton): train runs off line; 4 killed . . . 6 June, „
Bicester (Oxfordshire): collision; 6 killed, 6 Sept. „
Burnley (Great Northern): collision; 4 killed, 12 July, 1852
Dixonfold (Great Northern): engine wheels broke; 7 killed . . . . . . 4 March, 1853
Near Straffan (Great Southern and Western, Ireland): collision; 13 killed . . . 5 Oct. „
Near Harling, Norfolk (Eastern Counties): collision; 6 killed . . . . 12 Jan. 1854
Croydon (Brighton and Dover): collision; 3 killed, 24 Aug. „
Burlington, between New York and Philadelphia: 21 killed . . . . . 29 Aug. „
Reading (Gt. Western): collision; 5 killed, 12 Sept. 1855
Near Paris: collision; 9 killed . . . 9 Oct. „
Between Thoret and Moret: collision; 16 killed 23 Oct. „
Campbell (N. Pennsylvania): collision; above 100 killed . . . . . 17 July, 1856
Dunkett (Waterford and Kilkenny): collision; 7 killed . . . . . 19 Nov. „
Kirby (Liverpool and Blackpool): collision; 200 injured; none killed . . . 27 June, 1857
Lewisham (North Kent): collision; 11 killed, 28 June, „
Between Pyle and Port Talbot: collision; 4 killed 14 Oct. „
Attleborough, Warwickshire (North Western): train thrown off the line through a cow crossing the rails: 3 killed . . . . 10 May, 1858
Near Mons, Belgium: coke waggon on the rails; 21 killed . . . . . . June, „
Chilham (South Eastern): either too great speed or broken axletree; 3 killed . . . 30 June, „
Near Round Oak Station (Oxford and Wolverhampton)—excursion train: collision; 14 killed, 23 Aug. „
Tottenham (Eastern Counties): engine wheel breaks; 6 killed . . . . 20 Feb. 1860
Helmshore (Lancashire and Yorkshire)—excursion train: collision; 11 killed . . . 4 Sept. „
Atherstone (North Western): collision of mail and cattle trains; 11 killed . . . 16 Nov. „
Near Wimbledon: Dr. Baly killed . . . 28 Jan. 1861
Railway tunnel falls in near Haddon Hall, Derbyshire; 5 men killed . . . . 2 July. „
Clayton Tunnel (London and Brighton): collision; 23 killed, 176 injured . . . 25 Aug. „
Kentish Town (Hampstead Junction): 16 killed, 320 injured . . . . . 2 Sept. „
Market Harborough: collision; 1 killed and 50 injured . . . . . 28 Aug. 1862
Near Winchburgh (Edinburgh and Glasgow): collision; 15 killed, 100 wounded . . 13 Oct. „
Near Streatham (London and Brighton): explosion of boiler through attempting too great speed; 4 killed; above 30 injured . . . . 30 May, 1863
Near Lynn (Lynn and Hunstanton): carriages upset through bullock on the line; 5 killed 3 Aug. „
Egham (South Western): collision; 5 killed, above 20 injured . . . . . . 7 June, 1864
Canada: train ran off a bridge at St. Hilaire in crossing; about 83 killed, 200 wounded, 29 June „
Blackheath Tunnel: fast train ran into a ballast train; 6 killed . . . . . 16 Dec. „
Near Rednal (on a branch of Great Western): train ran off insecure rails; 13 killed, about 40 injured, 7 June, 1865
Near Staplehurst (South Eastern): train ran off insecure rails, &c.; 10 killed and about 50 injured, 9 June, „
Near Colney Hatch (Gt. Northern): collision with coal trucks: above 50 persons injured . 30 Aug. „
Fall of a bridge at Sutton (S. coast line): 6 men killed, 28 April, 1866
Near Caterham junction (London and Brighton): 3 killed, 12 injured . . . . . 30 April, „
In Welwyn Tunnel (Great Northern): a steam tube burst; collision of three goods trains; and a great fire; 2 lives lost . . . 9, 10 June, „
Near Royston (Great Northern): train ran off line; 3 lives lost . . . . . . 2 July, „
Brynkir station (Carnarvonshire): points said to have been tampered with; train ran off line; 6 persons killed . . . . . . 6 Sept. 1866
20 miles from Carlisle (Lancaster and Carlisle): an axle of carriage of goods train broke; collision with another goods train; fire, and explosion of 5 tons of gunpowder; 2 killed . . 25 Feb. 1867
Between Bhosawul and Khundwah (Great Indian Peninsular): train precipitated into a chasm made in an embankment by a river torrent; many lives lost . . . . . 26 June, „
Walton Junction, Warrington (London and North Western): collision with coal train; error of pointsman; 8 lives lost . . . 29 June, „
At Brayhead, near Enniscorthy (Dublin, Wicklow, and Wexford): went off the line into a gorge; 2 killed, many injured . . . 9 Aug. „
Between New Mills and Peak Forest: 2 collisions; 5 lives lost . . . . . . 9 Sept. „
French Great Northern, about 14 miles from Paris: several killed, many wounded . . . 27 Oct. „
Lake Shore railway, New York: embankment fell; 41 persons burnt to death . . . 18 Dec. „
Carr's Rock, on river Delaware; Erie railway: carriages precipitated down an embankment; 26 persons killed, 52 very seriously injured, 14 April, 1868
Abergele, N. Wales (London and North-Western): collision between Irish mail train and luggage train; barrels of petroleum ignited; 33 persons burnt to death (see *Abergele*) . . . 20 Aug. „
Near Birdingbury station (Rugby and Leamington) carriages went over Draycot embankment; 2 persons killed . . . . . . 1 Oct. „
Near Bull's Pill, S. Wales (Great Western): mail train ran into a cattle train; 1 person and much cattle killed . . . . . . 6 Nov. „
Near Copenhagen tunnel, Holloway (Great Northern): coal train ran off the line; 2 killed, 18 Jan. 1869
Near Khandalla, Bombay (Great Indian Peninsular) train ran off the line; about 18 killed 26 Jan. „
Arch fell in at Bethnal Green (Great Eastern): coal train passing; 5 killed . . . 25 Feb. „
Newcross (London and Brighton): collision; 2 killed, many injured; loss to the company by compensation, about 70,000*l*. . . . 23 June, „
Near Barnet (Great Northern): collision; 1 man burnt to death . . . . . 16 Aug. „
Long Eaton Junction (Midland): collision; 7 killed 9 Oct. „
Near Welwyn (Great Northern): collision; 3 killed 24 Oct. „
Eureka, St. Louis, Missouri; collision; 19 killed. 12 May, 1870
Near Newark (Great Northern): collision; a waggon of a goods train, through the breaking of an old axle, went off the rails and met an excursion train; 19 deaths; 1.30 A.M. . 21 June, „
Near Carlisle: collision; 5 killed . . 10 July, „
Tamworth (London and North Western): Irish mail (late), sent into a siding; broke down a buttress and ran into the river Anker (error of a pointsman); 3 deaths . . 4.7 A.M. 14 Sept. „
Plessis near Tours: collision; between two trains; several killed . . . . 4 A.M. 20 Sept. „
Harrow (London and North-Western): collision with coal waggons; 7 killed . . 26 Nov. „
Brockley Whins (North Eastern): collision through mistake of Hedley, a pointsman; 5 killed 6 Dec. „
Barnsley (Manchester, Sheffield, and Lincolnshire railway): collision; goods trucks broke loose; 14 killed, many injured . . . . 12 Dec. „
Bell-bar, near Hatfield (Great Northern): tire of wheel broke; break and carriages overturned; 8 killed . . . . 26 Dec. „
Between Bandoz and St. Nizaire: explosion of gunpowder in casks; 60 killed . . 25 Feb. 1871
Revere (Boston and Portland, U.S.): collision; above 20 killed . . . . . 26 Aug. „
Near Champigny (Lyons Company): a spring broke; 11 killed . . . . 16 Sept. „
Ferry-hill (North British): collision; 2 killed, 16 Oct. „
Antibes railway between Nice and Cannes: train thrown into the river Brague; 12 said to be killed 24 Jan. 1872

Belleville (Grand Trunk of Canada): engine broke off the line; many burnt, scalded, &c.; about 30 killed . . . . 22 June, 1872
Connellsville (Baltimore and Pittsburg): collision; many hurt, 3 killed . . . . 22 June, ,,
Juvisy (Orleans railway): express ran into luggage train; boiler exploded; 5 burnt to death (including mother of the duchess of Malakoff) 26 June, ,,
Rose-hill junction (Newcastle and Carlisle): collision; 4 killed . . . . 5 July, ,,
Red-hill junction (Great Western and L. & N.W.), near Hertford; 2 killed . . . . 29 July, ,,
Clifton junction (Lancashire and Yorkshire): collision; 4 killed . . . . 3 Aug. ,,
Kirtlebridge, Dumfries (Caledonian): collision; express train late; error of pointsman; 12 killed, 2 Oct. ,,
Kelvedon, near Chelmsford (Great Eastern): locomotive driven off the line by a raised rail; 1 killed, many hurt . . . . . 17 Oct. ,,
Near Woodhouse junction (Manchester, Sheffield, and Lincolnshire): collision; two killed, 18 Oct. ,,
Corry, Pennsylvania, U.S.: train broke through a bridge; about 20 killed . . . . 24 Dec. ,,
Near Pesth: train ran off line; 21 killed, about 7 May, 1873
Near Shrewsbury (Great Western and London & N. W. Junction): axle of engine broke; carriages driven off the line; 4 killed . . 8 May, ,,
Near Higham, Derbyshire (Midland); engine-tire broke; train ran off the line; 2 killed . 21 June ,,
Wigan (London and North Western): carriages thrown off the line; sir John Anson and others (13 persons) killed . . . . . 23 Aug. ,,
Retford Junction (Great Northern, Manchester, and Sheffield): collision; 3 killed . . . 23 Aug. ,,
Near Hartlepool (North Eastern): train thrown off the line; 3 killed . . . . . 2 Sept. ,,
Peamarsh crossing, near Guildford (South Western): collision with a bullock; train thrown off the line; 3 killed . . . . 9 Sept. ,,
Barkston Junction, near Grantham (Great Northern): 2 killed . . . . 10 Jan. 1874
Near Manuel and Bo'ness Junction, between Edinburgh and Glasgow (North British): collision of London express with mineral train; 16 killed 27 Jan. ,,
Euxton Junction, between Preston and Wigan; collision through fog and too great speed; 2 killed 20 Feb. ,,
Merthyr-Tydvil (Great Western): coupling broke, causing collision; about 40 seriously injured; 1 death . . . . 18 May, ,,
Bargoed (Rhymney railway): collision; train ran away through brakes not acting; 2 killed; much damage . . . . 12 Aug. ,,
Thorpe, near Norwich (East Norfolk): collision; two trains met (mistake of Cooper and Robson, telegraph clerks, committed for trial for manslaughter); 26 deaths; about 50 injured; 8.30 p.m. 10 Sept. ,,
[Cost the company above 13,000*l.*, Cooper sentenced to 8 months' imprisonment, 7 April, 1875.]
Shipton, near Oxford (Great Western); tire of carriage-wheel broke; train driven over an embankment; 34 deaths ensued, about 70 injured 24 Dec. ,,
[Verdict of inquiry, accidental deaths; 16 March, 1875.]
Rothbury, near Morpeth (North Eastern): train ran off embankment; 4 killed . . . 3 July, 1875
Kildwick, near Skipton, Yorkshire (Midland): Scotch express ran into an excursion train; 7 deaths, 11.30 p.m. . . . . . . 28 Aug. ,,
Between Mutford and Somerleyton; train ran off the line; 3 killed . . . . 1 Jan. 1876
Near Odessa: train ran over embankment; about 68 killed . . . . 8 Jan. ,,
Abbot's Ripton (Great Northern), near Huntingdon; 2 collisions; first, Scotch express with coal train; and second, with Leeds express from London, whereby 14 deaths; including Mr. Thos. Mure, Scotch advocate, a son of Mr. Noble, the sculptor; a son of Mr. Dion Boucicault, dramatist; brother and 2 nieces of Dr. Burdon Sanderson; during a snow storm . . . . . . 21 Jan. ,,
[Coroner's inquest: verdict, virtually accidental deaths; directors censured for not having a separate line for mineral traffic, 3 Feb. 1876.]
Near Long Ashton (on Great Western), "Flying Dutchman" express: about 57 miles an hour; driver and stoker killed; defective condition of permanent way . . . . 27 July, 1876
Between Radstock and Wellow; about 4 miles from Bath (Somerset and Dorset), single line; collision between excursion trains; 14 killed; about 11 p.m. . . . . 7 Aug. ,,
[Inquest: verdict, manslaughter against James Sleep, station-master, 12 Sept. 1876.]
Wambrechie, near Lille (French great northern): collision with a conveyance on level crossing, 6 killed . . . . 5 Nov. ,,
Arlsey siding, near Hitchin (Great Northern): collision of Manchester express with goods train, 5 killed . . . . 23 Dec. ,,
[Verdict of inquest: neglect of Thos. Pepper, the driver (killed), in not observing the signal, 5 Jan. 1877.]
Near Ashtabula, U.S., Pacific express from New York: a bridge over a creek broke down during a snow-storm, above 100 perished by drowning, burning, &c. . . . . 29 Dec. ,,
Near Morpeth (North Eastern): Scotch express went off the line; 5 killed . early 25 March, 1877
Near Billing, Northamptonshire (London and North Western): collision, 2 deaths . . . 18 Oct. ,,
Buckstone Junction, near Grantham (Gt. Northern): express ran off the rails; 2 killed . 7 Dec. ,,
Holcombe, near Leeds (Midland): collision of trains; 2 killed . . . . 24 Dec. ,,
Chester: 2 carriages went off rails; 1 death; above 30 hurt . . . . 8 July, 1878
Newcross: collision between carriages of Brighton and S. Eastern Cos.: several injured, 7.45 p.m. (Bank Holiday) . . . . 5 Aug. ,,
Sittingbourne (London, Chatham, & Dover): cheap fast train, bringing home holyday-makers; run into luggage trucks; mistake of pointsman; midday . . . . 31 Aug. ,,
[Jacob Moden and Charles Clarke, committed for trial for manslaughter, 3 Sept. 1878.]
Curragheen, near Cork: engine uncoupled; ran off line; 3 killed and many injured . . 8 Sept. ,,
Near Pontypridd junction (Rhondda branch of Taff Vale line); collision through error of signals; 13 killed; about 40 hurt . . . . 19 Oct. ,,
Talybont (Brecon and Merthyr); engines uncontrolled; ran down steep descent; 4 killed; great destruction of property . . . . 2 Dec. ,,
Bloomfield, near Tipton, Staffordshire (London and North Western); collisions; about 30 severely injured . . . . 31 May, 1879
Near Manningtree (Great Eastern); train ran off line; 1 killed; several injured . . . 8 Dec. ,,
Tay bridge, Dundee; bridge and train blown into the river; about 74 lives lost . . . 28 Dec. ,,
Brickfield siding, Burscough junction (Lancashire and Yorkshire); collision; through error of signalman; 8 deaths . . . . . 15 Jan. 1880
Argenteuil, near Paris; collision; 7 killed 4 Feb. ,,
Lofthouse, near Wakefield (Great Northern); train runs off line; 2 deaths . . . . 20 March, ,,
A bridge fell near Hereford (Midland); 1 death 18 June, ,,
Marshall Meadows, 2 or 3 miles N. of Berwick (North British); "Flying Scotchman" engine ran off the line; carriages precipitated down embankment; guard, driver, and fireman killed; much damage to carriages; few passengers; (alleged cause, loose rails), about 11 a.m. 10 Aug. ,,
Near Wennington Junction, 12 miles N. of Lancaster (Midland); train went off the rails; 8 deaths . . . . 11 Aug. ,,
Near Manchester (Midland); train went off rails; 17 injured . . . . 2 Sept. ,,
Near Nine Elms station, Vauxhall (South Western); collision of train with a left engine; 5 killed; 20 injured . . . . 11 Sept. ,,
Kibworth: Leicestershire (Midland); Scotch express; driver by mistake reversed the engine; collision with advancing train; several severely injured . . . . 9 Oct. ,,
Leeds (Midland); collision; 2 deaths; many injured . . . . 21 Dec. ,,

Dalston Junction (North London); collision; through error in signalling; 2 deaths ensued; about 30 hurt . . . 26 Feb. 1881

Mexico; Morelos railway; through fall of bridge near Cuartla; train precipitated into river San Antonio; about 200 lives lost; night of 24 June, ,,

Blackburn (Lancashire and Yorkshire); collision; 5 deaths; about 40 injured . . . 8 Aug. ,,

Bow Station (Great Eastern); collision; 2 killed 3 Sept. ,,

Charenton (Lyons Railway); collision; about 20 killed . . . . . 5 Sept. ,,

Desford, near Leicester (Midland); collision; 5 killed, 22 Oct.; (Butler, pointsman, arrested for manslaughter) . . . . . 6 Nov. ,,

Tayport, Fife (North British); collision with goods train; 4 deaths . . . . . 25 Nov. ,,

Highbury Tunnel, near Canonbury (North London); collision of 3 trains; 5 deaths . . . 10 Dec. ,,

Slough (Great Western); express runs into a goods train; 12 killed . . . . . 24 Dec. ,,

Between Middlesbrough and Stockton; explosion of locomotive; 4 deaths . . . 26 Dec. ,,

Hudson river railway, near New York; collision and fire; 8 or 9 killed, including senator Wagner burned to death . . . 13 Jan. 1882

Hornsey (Great Northern); collision; fog; 2 deaths 25 Jan. ,,

Near Old Ford Station; collision of train with broken up coal trucks; 6 deaths . . . 28 Jan. ,,

Near Cork; collision; about 40 injured . 9 July, ,,

Between Tcherny and Bastigeur (Moscow Kursk, line); 8 carriages ran off the rails; about 178 killed . . . . . 13 July, ,,

Streatham Fen (Great Eastern): destruction of the express train, &c., by being thrown off the line 28 July, ,,

Hugstetten, between Freiburg and Colmar, Baden; excursion train ran off the line; about 70 killed . . . . . 3 Sept. ,,

Crewe (London and North Western); collision; many injured . . . . . 30 Sept. ,,

Bromley (London, Chatham and Dover): fall of a bridge; 7 killed . . . . . 24 Nov. ,,

Near Auchterless (Macduff and Turiff section of Great North of Scotland); train wrecked by fall of a bridge; about 5 killed . . . 27 Nov. ,,

Vriog, near Barmouth (Cambrian); cliff gave way, part of train falls over; 2 killed . 1 Jan. 1883

Near the Eglinton Street Station, Glasgow; collision; 4 killed . . . . 19 March, ,,

Near Lockerbie (Caledonian); collisions; 8 deaths, 11.30 p.m. . . . . . 14 May, ,,

Watford (London and North Western); express runs into empty carriages; 1 death . . 31 Oct. ,,

Near Toronto, Canada (Grand Trunk); collision; about 31 killed . . . . . 2 Jan. 1884

Stepney; collision; about 30 persons injured 22 March, ,,

Between Breamore and Downton (South Western); coupling broke, train falls over embankment; 5 killed and 41 injured . . . 3 June, ,,

Near Sevenoaks Station (South Eastern); collision; of goods trains; 2 killed . . . . 7 June, ,,

Bullhouse Bridge, near Penistone (Manchester, Sheffield, and Lincolnshire); express, 55 miles an hour; crank-axle of locomotive engine broke, train wrecked over an embankment; sharp curve; 24 deaths, afternoon . . . 16 July, ,,

Near Penistone; coal waggon, by breaking of an axle, thrown into the way of an excursion train; 4 deaths, many injured . . . 1 Jan. 1885

Earl's Court, Kensington (District), collision; one killed . . . . . 23 Aug. ,,

Whitland and Cardigan Railway, train went off the line through fast driving, 3 lives lost . 25 Aug. ,,

Finsbury Park station, collision of Great Northern and North London trains through fog; many injured; 1 death (March) . . . 11 Feb. 1886

Roccabrunna, between Monte Carlo and Mentone (Riviera) collision; about 8 killed; many injured 10 March, ,,

Portadown (Great Northern of Ireland), 4 killed 30 June, ,,

Collision near Niagara Falls; 18 killed . 14 Sept. ,,

Near Woodstock, Vermont, U.S. (Vermont Central) Boston and Montreal express; carriages fall over a bridge over the White River (frozen) and catch fire; about 45 lives lost . . . 4 Feb. 1887

Near Boston (Boston and Providence) U.S.; train broke through bridge; 32 killed . 14 March, ,,

Ibrox station (Glasgow and Paisley joint line), 4 surfacemen killed by an accident . 22 March, ,,

Collision at St. Thomas's, Ontario; ignition and explosion of petroleum, 14 killed and about 100 injured . . . . 16 July, ,,

East of Chatsworth, Illinois; excursion to Niagara; train overthrown by a burning bridge; 83 killed and many died afterwards . . . 11 Aug. ,,

Hexthorpe, near Doncaster; a Manchester and Sheffield train runs into a Midland excursion train during collection of tickets; 25 deaths 16 Sept.; Samuel Taylor (driver) and Robert Davis (fireman) committed for manslaughter 23 Sept.; acquitted; the directors and other officials censured 15 Nov. ,,

Hyde (Manchester, Sheffield and Lincolnshire); collision with a goods train; 4 women killed, midnight . . . . . 14–15 July, 1888

Hampton Wick (London and South Western), collision with a light engine, 4 persons killed, near midnight, officers censured for recklessness 6 Aug. ,,

Velars, between Blaisy and Lyons, train went off the rails, 9 persons killed early . 5 Sept. ,,

Lehigh Valley Railway, collision between excursion trains above Pennhaven; about 61 persons killed 10 Oct.; another collision on the same railway, 14 persons killed . . . . 16 Oct. ,,

Landslip between Salandra and Grassam Italy; destruction of an excursion train, about 22 persons killed . . . . . . 20 Oct. ,,

Near Borki Station in S. Russia, the engine of the imperial train (with the czar) ran off the line with four carriages (weak rails); 21 persons killed; the czar slightly injured . . . 29 Oct. ,,

By the falling in of Abergwynfi tunnel of the Rhondda and Swansea Bay railway, 7 persons were killed . . . . . 22 Jan. 1889

Near Grönendäl, Brussels; train crushed by collision with a bridge, about 12 lives lost 3 Feb ,,

Near St. George, Ontario, Canada, by collapse of a bridge, 11 persons killed . . . 27 Feb. ,,

Penistone station (Manchester, Sheffield and Lincolnshire), excursion train ran off the line, 1 life lost . . . . . . 30 March, ,,

Near Hamilton, Ontario (Grand Trunk), excursion train from Chicago to New York; carriages run off the line and burnt; 17 killed . 28 April, ,,

Killooney near Armagh (Gt. Northern of Ireland), collision between Sunday School excursion trains; about 80 deaths; 400 injured (officials charged with culpable negligence) . . . 12 June, ,,

Near Bucharest; collision of passenger and luggage trains, about 15 deaths . . . 8 July, ,,

Near Wildpark Station, between Stuttgart and Boblingen, train went down embankment; 7 killed . 1 Oct. ,,

Longsight, near Manchester (London & North-Western), collision of passenger and goods train, 6 deaths . . . . . . 4 Oct. ,,

Stirling, California, collision between Burlington and Union Pacific trains, about 30 deaths . 16 Oct. ,,

At Jarus Run, West Virginia, train upset by spreading rails; 10 killed . . . . 28 Dec. ,,

Near Cincinnati, U.S.A., collision of express train to New York; 6 persons killed . . 17 Jan. 1890

Near Salem, U.S.A., train runs off line; 6 killed . ,, 27 Jan. ,,

At Burnmouth, near Berwick (North British), collision; 3 deaths . . . . . . 25 Jan. ,,

Carlisle station (London & North Western), Scotch express ran into engine approaching (attributed to failure of vacuum or pneumatic brake through cold), 4 persons killed, 3 a.m. . . 4 March, ,,

Near Hamburg, U.S.A., Lake Shore railway, collision; 6 killed . . . . . 5 March, ,,

Quincey, near Boston, U.S.A., engine and cars left the rails; about 20 deaths . . . 20 Aug. ,,

At Schuylkill valley, near Reading U.S.A., collision of coal and goods trains; 23 deaths . 20 Sept. ,,

At Norton Fitzwarren, near Taunton (Great Western), collision of special express train from Plymouth and a shunted goods train; 10 passengers (from the Cape) killed; George Rice, signalman, through forgetfulness had declared the line clear, about 1.30 a.m. 11 Nov.; acquitted of manslaughter . . . . 22 Nov. 1890

Edinburgh, Georgia station (Suburban railway), collision of passenger and goods trains, through neglect of signalman; many persons injured . 11 Nov. ,,

Primrose-hill tunnel (London & North-Western), collision of passenger and goods trains; guard killed . . . . 13 Nov. ,,

At Topsin, near Salonica, train runs off the line; about 40 retired soldiers killed . . 14 Nov. ,,

Wreay, 5 miles S. of Carlisle (London and North-Western), express goods train; axle of a wagon broke, 20 wagons thrown over the embankment 25 feet high, 2 a.m. . . . . 3 April, 1891

Norwood Junction (London & Brighton), express train wrecked by the collapse of Portland bridge, through defect in the ironwork; about 10 a.m.; 6 persons injured . . . . 1 May, ,,

Moenchenstein, near Bâle, Switzerland, excursion train; by the collapse of a bridge several carriages thrown into the river Birse; about 70 persons perish . . . . 14 June ,,

Ravenna, Ohio, collision between heavy freight train and the Erie express for New York, above 25 persons perish . . . . . . 3 July, ,,

Charleston, W. Virginia, collapse of a trestle bridge, part of a train falls over 13 persons killed . . 4 July ,,

St. Mandé, near Paris, collision of a goods and an excursion train; about 44 killed . . 27 July, ,,

Near Port Byron, New York; collision; 11 persons killed . . . . 6 Aug. ,,

Pontypridd (Taff Vale) collision; 15 persons injured . . . . 15 Aug. ,,

At a junction between Münchenbuchsee and Zollikofen, near Berne; collision; about 14 deaths . 17 Aug. ,,

Trestle bridge over the Catawba river, N. Carolina, train plunged into the river; above 20 deaths 26 Aug. ,,

Near Burgos, Old Castile, collision of express and mixed trains; 25 deaths (including Mr. Maurice Long, British vice-consul at Malaga, and Mr. Wm. Cotton) . . . . 24 Sept. ,,

Kohlfurt (between Breslau and Berlin); collision; 5 deaths, midnight . . . . . 19 Oct. ,,

Near Nagpur, Bombay; train went off the line through wheel breaking; 11 British soldiers and 5 others killed . . . . 5 Nov. ,,

Near Domnino station on the Kosloff, &c., railway, Central Russia; train ran off the line on a bridge, 31 persons killed . . . 23 Nov. ,,

About 70 miles from Lahore, the N. W. railway of India; collision; about 30 persons killed . about 8 Dec. ,,

At Barnby (Great Eastern) collision of Lowestoft and Beccles trains; 3 persons killed . 24 Dec. ,,

Near Hastings, New York Central; collision of Buffalo and Niagara Falls, and St. Louis express trains; 10 persons killed . . . . 24 Dec. ,,

Near Medill, Missouri; train falls in the river through breaking down of the bridge; 7 persons killed . . . . 4 May, 1892

On the Cottonbelt, Arkansas, U.S.A., collision, 7 persons killed . . . . 20 May, ,,

Birmingham, collision between the L. & N. W. express train and a Midland train entering the station at the same time and partly on the same line; 2 deaths, many injured, 27 May, [T. E. Fear, the Midland driver, charged with manslaughter] . . . . 8 June, ,,

Near South Carrollton, Kentucky, collision, 4 deaths 5 June, ,,

Esholt junction near Leeds (Midland), collision; 4 deaths . . . . 9 June, ,,

Bishopsgate station (Great Eastern); collision of workmen's trains from Walthamstow and Enfield, containing 1,800 persons; 4 deaths, about 40 injured; between 6 and 7 a.m., 14 June; signalmen censured by the coroner . . . 17 June, ,,

Harrisburg, U.S.A., collision; 10 deaths . 25 June, ,,

Merreton, Grand Trunk railway, collision of two trains; carriages fall into the Welland canal; several persons drowned . . . . 18 July, 1892

Near Melton Mowbray (London and North-Western) train ran off the line; 3 persons killed 25 July, ,,

Near Clapham-junction (South-Western), collision, causing great fire; 1 death, many injured, 20 Aug. ,,

Leman-street, east (Great Eastern), collision; many injured . . . . 21 Aug. ,,

Near Cambridge station, Fitchburg railway, U.S.A., collision; about 14 deaths . 11 Sept. ,,

Clearfield and Cambria railway, Pennsylvania; collision; 8 persons killed . . . 9 Sept. ,,

At Shreve (Chicago railway); collision; 11 persons killed . . . . 21 Sept. ,,

Near Manayunk tunnel (Philadelphia and Reading railway); collision; 7 persons killed . 24 Oct. ,,

Manor-house cabin, near Thirsk (North-Eastern); collision of second part of Scotch express from Edinburgh with a goods train, through neglect of James Holmes, signalman; some of the wreckage takes fire; 10 persons killed; about 4 a.m. . . . . 2 Nov. ,,

James Holmes convicted of manslaughter and discharged; the company censured for the long term of duty of the signalmen . . . . Dec. ,,

Alton junction, on the Cleveland, Cincinnati, Columbus and St. Louis railway; collision of express with goods train; oil in tank-cars takes fire; 21 deaths, many fatally injured; reported 21 Jan. 1893

Camp, Tralee and Dingle light railway; the train ran off the steep gradient through failure of the brake; 3 deaths . . . . . . 22 May, ,,

Poulton-in-the-Fylde, near Blackpool, Preston and Wyre railway; engine went off the line at a curve; 3 deaths . . . . 1 July, ,,

Near Treforest station (Taff Vale railway); part of the train went over the embankment; 12 deaths 12 Aug. 1893

At Bushwick junction, Long Island, U.S.A.; collision; 16 deaths . . . . . 26 Aug. ,,

Near Chester, Massachusetts; collision; 15 deaths 31 Aug. ,,

Near Kankakee, on the Illinois Central railway; collision; 12 deaths . . . . . 18 Sept. ,,

At Jackson (Michigan Central railway); collision; 18 deaths . . . . 13 Oct. ,,

Battle Creek (Michigan); collision and fire; 26 deaths . . . . 19 Oct. ,,

At Limito, near Milan; collision; express and goods train; 13 deaths . . . . 28 Nov. ,,

Near Dunkirk, New York State; collision; 11 deaths . . . . 15 Dec. ,,

Near Leicester (Midland), an express goods train wrecked by a roll of web newspaper falling under the wheels; much damage to Market Harboro' station . . . . 14 Jan. 1894

Near Jersey City, New Jersey; collision; 15 deaths 15 Jan. ,,

Near Bilbao; heavy train fell over an embankment; 13 deaths . . . . . . 7 July, ,,

Near Winsford (London and North-Western railway); collision; 1 death . . . . 6 July, ,,

Newtonmore (Highland railway); collision; prof. Dobie, of Edinburgh University, killed 2 Aug. ,,

St. Pancras (Midland); through the failure of the brakes the Scotch express was wrecked in the station; 21 persons injured (morning). 12 Aug. ,,

At Apilly, between Noyon and Chauny; collision between Cologne express and a goods train; 5 deaths; 15 injured . . . . . . 9 Sept. ,,

Near Northallerton (North-Eastern railway); collision between Scotch express and coal train, 4 Oct.; driver died . . . . . 12 Oct. ,,

Near Canterbury (South-Eastern railway); collision between a goods train and a wagon carrying hop-pickers during a fog on a level crossing; 7 deaths 9 Oct. ,,

Chelford, near Crewe (London and North-Western); collision of the up-express with part of goods train which had been blown on to the line by the violent gale then raging; 14 deaths . 22 Dec. ,,
[Verdict of inquest: no criminal negligence, 11 Jan. 1895.]

Low Moor, near Bradford (Lancashire & Yorkshire railway); collision between two excursion trains; 16 persons injured . . . . 26 Dec. ,,

Near Mexico city; a train cast down a precipice; 140 lives lost . . . . . . 28 Feb. 1895

Near Thornhill station (London & North-Western railway); collision; 2 deaths . . 28 March, ,,

Near Leamington (London & North-Western); collision; 1 death and 18 injured . . 13 May, ,,

Craigshead station (Grand Trunk railway), E. Quebec; collision between two sections of a pilgrim train; 14 deaths . . . 9 July, ,,

At San Pablo, Argentine republic; collision; 15 deaths; reported . . . . 11 July, ,,

Near St. Brieuc, France, a pilgrim train ran off the line, 12 deaths . . . . . 26 July, ,,

Near Freiburg, collision between a military and goods train; 13 deaths . . . 20 Sept. ,,

Collision at Wellingborough (Midland), 1 death, 27 Sept. ,,

Collision, near Ottignies, Belgium; 17 deaths, many injured . . . . . . 6 Oct. ,,

At St. Neots (Gt. N. R.), train left the rails and collided with some coal wagons; Miss L. O'Hara killed, 10 Nov.; Mr. W. H. Corrie died of injuries, 18 Nov. ,,

Near Peterborough (Gt. N. R.), 2 carriages of the Leeds express left the rails; 2 deaths 7 March, 1896

Near Preston (L. & N. W.), express train left the rails; 1 death; much damage; after midnight, 12 July, ,,

Preston Junction (E. Lancashire), collision; 1 death . . . . 3 Aug. ,,

March station (Gt. E. R.), collision; 1 death, 21 injured . . . . 23 Sept. ,,

Louis & Nashville railway, 50 mi. from Birmingham, U. S. N. A. train went over a bridge; about 30 deaths . . . . . 27 Dec. ,,

Baroda line, near Golwood station, collision mail and passenger trains; 5 deaths, 24 injured 9 Jan. 1897

Accident, caused by a broken rail, near Dorchester, New Brunswick; 2 deaths . . . 26 Jan. ,,

By the fall of a platform on the Coldrenick viaduct, 134 ft. high, near Menheniot (Cornwall R.), 12 men killed . . . . 9 Feb. ,,

Excursion train left the line at Rothbury, Northumberland; 3 deaths . . . . 13 Feb. ,,

Excursion train left the rails, near Oswestry (Cambrian R.); 11 deaths . . . 11 June, ,,

Collision between a fast and excursion train, near Copenhagen (see *Denmark*) . . 11 July, ,,

A goods train ran over the points at Buxton (L. & N. W. R.); 1 death . . . . . 2 Aug. ,,

Express from Paris to Rouen left the rails at Petit Couronne, 1 death . . . . . 21 Aug. ,,

Near Mayfield (London, Brighton & S. Coast), passenger train left the rails; driver killed, many hurt . . . . 1 Sept. ,,

Collision at Tournay between 2 passenger trains, 12 deaths . . . . . . 24 Nov. ,,

See *France*, 24 Dec. 1897.

Collision near Dunbar (Scotch express and coal wagon), 1 death . . . . . . 3 Jan. 1898

Collision at Barassie between mail express and goods train (Glasgow & S. W. R.), 7 deaths, 4 Feb. ,,

Collision at St. John's-road station, Lewisham-road (S. E. R.), 3 deaths . . . 21 March, ,,

Collision at Bisley (L. & S. W. R.), between engine and standing train; many volunteers injured, 11 April, ,,

Collision between 2 excursion trains at Leyland, near Preston (L. and N. W. R.); 2 deaths, many injured, 9.30 P.M. . . . . . . 2 June, ,,

Wellingborough (Midland), 7 deaths; express ran into a van that had fallen on to the line 2 Sept. ,,

Collision between Montreal express and a car (Delaware and Hudson R.), near Cohoes, 18 deaths, 5 Sept. ,,

At Wrawby junction (Gt. Central R.) an express wrecked by the shunting of a goods train, 9 deaths . . . . 17 Oct. ,,

Collision (Grand Trunk R.) near Trenton, Canada, 12 deaths . . . . 15 Nov. ,,

Collision near Bound Brook (Lehigh valley R.), U.S.N.A., 12 deaths . . . . . 9 Jan. 1899

See *Storms*, Jan. 1899.

Collision between an express from Calais and a local trains at Forest, near Brussels, 21 deaths and 100 injured, some mortally . . 18 Feb. ,,

Collision, 2 passenger trains (Philadelphia and Reading R.), at Exeter, 34 killed . . 12 May, 1899

Near Waterloo, Iowa, U.S., a train left the rails, 8 deaths . . . . 27 May, ,,

At Flushing, the Berlin express dashed into the buffet, 3 deaths . . . . . 1 June, ,,

A shunting accident at Reading, 3 deaths, 24 June, ,,

Collision at Juvisy (Orleans R.) between 2 portions of a Paris express, 17 deaths and about 40 injured, 5 Aug. ,,

Express leaves the rails between Montreal and Ottawa, 7 deaths . . . . . . 9 Aug. ,,

In Chili, train leaves the rails and falls into the river Mapocho, 60 deaths . . . 24 Aug. ,,

Seven-sisters'-rd. station, Cape Colony, collision between 2 sections of a *refugee* train, 9 deaths, 13 Oct. ,,

Collision: Bordeaux express and goods train at Thouars, 4 deaths . . . . . 1 Nov. ,,

Collision in a fog: London express from Flushing with a mail train near Capelle (Holland), 5 killed and 15 mortally injured . . . . 15 Nov. ,,

Collision: Bordeaux express and fast train, Orleans line, near Montmoreau, 3 deaths . 18 Dec. ,,

Collision in a fog between the Newhaven boat train and the Brighton express at Wivelsfield, 6 deaths and 18 injured . . . . . . 23 Dec. ,,

Near Motherwell, branch of the Caledonian R., a train went over an embankment, 3 deaths and 12 injured . . . . 23 Dec. ,,

Collision: express and goods train at Bischweiler, Strasburg, 3 deaths . . . . . 4 Jan. 1900

Collision between 2 workmen's trains in Glasgow, near Charing-cross station, 7 deaths, 31 injured, 28 March, ,,

Electric railway accident near Budapest, 4 deaths, 4 June, ,,

Collision between stationary passenger train and Plymouth express at Slough (G. W. R.), 5 deaths and over 35 injured . . . . . 16 June, ,,

Accident near Frederickstad, S. Africa, 13 deaths, 39 injured . . . . 31 July, ,,

Collision on the Salario bridge near Rome, 15 deaths and many injured (the king and queen active in the work of rescue) . . . 12 Aug. ,,

Collision near Plevna, Bulgaria, 20 deaths, 20 Aug. ,,

Mail train leaves the line near Baripada, Orissa, 11 deaths, 25 injured, reported . 23 Aug. ,,

Collision at Hatfield, Philadelphia and Reading R., U.S.N.A., 15 deaths, 40 injured . . 2 Sept. ,,

Train disaster at Bolivar Point, on the Gulf and Inter-State R., U.S.N.A., 85 deaths . 8 Sept. ,,

Collision near Karlsthor, Germany, 4 deaths, over 70 injured . . . . 7 Oct. ,,

Collision between the Frankfurt express and local train near Offenbach, 8 deaths, 30 injured, 8 Nov. ,,

Collision between 2 passenger trains at Choisy-le-Roi, near Paris, 8 deaths, 25 injured . 11 Nov. ,,

Southern express falls over an embankment at Dax, near Bayonne; the duke of Canevaro and 16 others killed, 20 injured . . . . 15 Nov. ,,

Collision near Bethulie, Orange River colony, 4 deaths . . . . 2 Feb. 1901

Train falls down a declivity near Sydenham, New S. Wales, 10 deaths . . . . 15 Feb. ,,

Collision near Courtrai, Belgium, 3 deaths, 9 March, ,,

A train dashed down an incline at Saratoff, on the Volga, 5 deaths . . . . . 17 April, ,,

Train derailed near Lofa, Pekin railway, 19 Chinese killed, 23 injured . . . . 28 April, ,,

Collision near Pretoria, 9 deaths . . 7 June, ,,

Collision and explosion near Vestal, New York, 9 deaths . . . . 8 June, ,,

Collision at Chailland, France, 7 deaths . 15 June, ,,

A petroleum train dashed into an express at Palota, Hungary, 8 deaths and 9 injured 21 Sept. ,,

Locomotive-boiler explosion, many killed, at Lezama station, Bilbao, Spain . . . 4 Oct. ,,

Collision between passenger trains near Seneca, Wabash R., U.S.; one took fire; 20 killed and 30 injured . . . . 27 Nov. ,,

Collision between an express and passenger train near Paderborn, in Westphalia, 12 killed, 21 injured . . . . 20 Dec. ,,

Fire at Dingle station, Liverpool Overhead Electric railway, 6 deaths . . . . . 23 Dec. ,,

Collision in New York (Central Railroad), 15 deaths, 30 injured. . . . . . . 8 Jan. 1902

Train leaves the rails near Barberton, S. Africa; driver, stoker, 38 soldiers killed, 45 injured (6 mortally) . . . . 30 March, 1902
Another accident near Machavie, 13 soldiers killed and 13 injured . . . . . . 12 April, ,,
Accident (due to the breaking of an axle) to a workmen's train at Hackney downs station, 3 deaths, many injured, 10 seriously . 25 April, ,,
Pilgrim train from Brussels to Lourdes derailed near Compiègne, 8 killed, 25 injured . 6 May, ,,
Train blown over by a cyclone near Rampur-hat, E. India, 13 deaths, 15 injured . . 30 June, ,,
Collision on the Mountain and Lake electric railway, near Gloversville, Utica; 12 killed, 36 injured . . . . 4 July, ,,
Train derailed at Khatauli, Meerut, 16 deaths, 30 injured . . . . 31 July, ,,
Lille express derailed near Charleville, 3 deaths, 20 injured . . . . 10 Aug. ,,
Collision between a refugee train and an engine at Bloemfontein, several deaths . . 24 Aug. ,,
Negro excursion train fell down an embankment at Berry, Alabama, 26 deaths, many injured 1 Sept. ,,
Mail train wrecked by collapse of bridge, near Mangapatnan, Madras; 62 bodies found, many natives . . . . 11 Sept. ,,
Express leaves the rails near Douai, France, 20 killed, 41 injured . . . . . 27 Sept. ,,
Collision at Bloemfontein between goods trains, 6 natives killed, 10 injured . . . . 4 Oct. ,,
Train wrecked near Halifax. N.S., 7 deaths, 12 injured . . . . 6 Dec. ,,
Collision between an express and goods train (Grand Trunk R.) at Wanslead, Canada, 28 deaths, 28 injured, many fatally . . 26 Dec. ,,
Collision between a working train and a snow plough, at Chiwakum, Washington, U.S.A., 12 deaths . . . . 20 Jan. 1903
Collision near Tucson, Arizona, between 2 express trains; the débris caught fire, the driver and fireman burnt to death, 8 killed, 17 injured; collision at La Fox, Illinois, 3 killed, 12 injured, 28 Jan. ,,
Collision between an express and local train at Graceland, New Jersey, 21 killed and over 50 injured, reported . . . . . . 28 Jan. ,,
Collision at Newark, N. Jersey, U.S., school excursion train, 12 children killed, 30 injured, some fatally . . . . 19 Feb. ,,
Forepart of train derailed near Ballymoe, Ireland, 2 deaths . . . . 11 April, ,,
Collision between express and goods train, near Halifax, Canada, 4 deaths . . . 11 April, ,,
Collision between an express and goods train at Redhouse, N. York state; 6 deaths . 20 April, ,,
King's-cross (Met.) collision, between G.W. and Inner Circle trains; 5 persons seriously injured, 17 June, ,,
Train on the Bilbao-Zaragoza line ran into the Najerilla river, at San Asensio, Spain; over 100 killed, many injured . . . . 27 June, ,,
Train leaves the rails at Waterloo station, Liverpool; 7 deaths, 116 injured . . . . 15 July, ,,
At St. Enoch's, Glasgow, an excursion train from I. of Man, dashed into the station against the buffers, 2 carriages shattered; 15 deaths, over 30 injured (1 death subsequently) . 27 July, ,,
Collision at Preston between an excursion and empty passenger train, about 30 injured (1 death) . . . . 1 Aug. ,,
Collision between 2 sections of a circus train on the Grand Trunk railway, U.S., 19 deaths, reported, 7 Aug. ,,
Paris Underground Electric railway fire: the motor of a train failing, the train was joined to another (both having been emptied of passengers), and they were run past several stations towards the terminus; the station-master at Les Couronnes, seeing that the carriages were on fire, called to the driver to stop; he, however, dashed on, and soon after an explosion took place, the electric light wires became fused, and the current was cut off. Another train following was stopped about 300 yards off; a fearful panic ensued, 84 persons were killed by suffocation and in other ways, and a large number injured in their efforts to escape . . . . . 10 Aug. ,,
Train derailed near Rothenkirchen, Saxony; 3 killed, 20 seriously injured, reported . 17 Aug. 1903
Collision between a military and a goods train near Pasian, Italy; 18 deaths, many injured, reported 28 Aug. ,,
Fall of a mail train with crew of 16 men over a trestle bridge 75 ft. high, at Danville, Virginia, U.S., causes 9 deaths and serious injury to the other 7 men, reported . . . . 28 Sept. ,,
Collision on the Lancs. and Yorks. rly., 1 killed, 25 injured . . . . 22 Oct. ,,

RAINBOW. Its theory was developed by Kepler in 1611, and by René Descartes in 1629; see *Spectrum.*

RAIN-FALL. Mr. G. J. Symons printed a table of rain-fall in Britain for 140 years, 1726-1865, in the reports of the British Association in 1866; and another table in 1883 for the years 1866—1880. The wettest year was 1852, being 38 per cent. above the average; but 1872 was 58 per cent. He began to publish his "Annual Rainfall in the British Isles" in 1866–95. In 1867 he published, "*Rain: How, When, Where, Why, it is Measured.*" It contains an attempt at a rainfall table of the world. Mr. Symons died, aged 62, 10 March, 1900.

Rainfall observers in Britain for the tables, 168 in 1860; about 2000 in 1888; 3,506 stations in U.K. in 1902.
Deficient rainfall in 1887; average yearly fall at Bolton, Lancashire, for 56 years 47·07 in.; in 1887, 27·92 in. See *Drought.*
August 1891, the wettest in Britain for many years. Experiments for the artificial production of rain by means of explosives at El Paso in Texas . . 18, 19 Sept. 1891
Melbourne, "the rain-maker," contracts to water N.-W. Kansas in June–Aug. 1892 . . Oct. ,,
Rain-making experiments made in Madras presidency . . . . Nov. ,,
Extraordinary rainfall at Ilkley; estimated damage over 100,000*l* . . . . . . 12 July, 1900
Red rain with sand descends in Italy and Vienna, 10 March, 1901
Rain-making experiments successful in Italy and later at Brisbane . . . . . 2 Oct. ,,
Total fall in London, 21·48 in.; 126 rain days, 1 Jan.–31 Dec. ,,
Fall of red dust with rain in Cornwall, end of Jan. 1902
Fall of "blood rain," due to *(Carabus coccinella)* insects, in Hamburg . . . . . 24 May, ,,
1901, the driest (except 1888) since 1862, in the British Isles; 18 per cent. below the average rainfall in England, 15 per cent. Wales, 13 per cent. Scotland, and 10 per cent. Ireland. 1902: 20·84 in. fell in United Kingdom, 52 stations, 85 per cent. of average.
Heavy rain fell in London and the south of England daily 9–11 June; again without ceasing, when about 3½ in. fell, 13–15 June; more rainy days, 20 hrs., 19 June; total amount 6·43 in., with very low temperature; the wettest June since 1860 . . . . 8–19 June, 1903
Another heavy fall in London, Fleet-street offices flooded . . . . 25, 26 July, ,,
Total fall for June and July 11·62 ins. on 23 days, highest amount in 45 years, reported . 3 Aug. ,,
British Rainfall association, founded by the late Mr. Symons in 1860. Mr. Sowerby Wallis, his associate for 30 years, retires, and is succeeded by Dr. H. R. Mill . . . . . . 1 Sept. ,,
Rainfall 34·61 in. . . . from 1 Jan. to 27 Oct. ,,
[The wettest year recorded at Camden-square observatory since 1858 is that of 1903. During 46 years, in 6 complete years the annual rainfall exceeded 30 in., the wettest year in London previously to 1903 being that of 1878; of the British Isles, that of 1872.]

RAIN-GAUGE, an apparatus consisting primarily of a funnel-shaped receiver and a glass graduated measure of a much smaller size, measuring the amount of rain collected in tenths and hundredths of an inch. Those chiefly in use are Symons', the improved Glaisher's, Fleming's, and Jagga's.

RAISINS, dried grapes, produced chiefly in the S.W. provinces of Spain, in Asia Minor, the Greek Archipelago, Crete, S. Italy, and Provence. Imports, Great Britain, 1866, 493,600 cwt., value 813,000*l.*; 1887, 653,100 cwt., 1,022,400*l.*; 1902, 662,459 cwt. 1,201,378*l.*

RAJPUTANA, an administrative territory, N.W. India, embracing 20 native states and the British district of Ajmere-Merwara (27,11 sq. mi.; population, 460,722). Total area, 132,461 sq. mi.; population in 1881, 10,268,392; 1891, 12,089,330; 1901, 9,723,301. The Rajputs, the predominant race, are a proud aristocracy. At the time of the Mahometan invasions in the 11th century, the Rajputs ruled over half-a-dozen strong states. From the end of the 16th to the middle of the 18th century, these states acknowledged the supremacy of the Mogul emperor of Delhi; they were next subjected by the Mahrattas, but became independent when these were crushed by the British, 1817 *et seq.*, with whom they eventually became allies. The Rana of Jhalawar accused of misgovernment, etc., was deprived of full powers in 1887, reinvested, 1894.

RALEIGH'S CONSPIRACY, termed the *Main Plot* (*which see*).

"**RALLIED**" to republicanism, a name assumed by a party at the general election in France, Aug. 1893.

RAM, that portion of the bow of a battleship which projects below the water-line in the form of a beak, and designed by its momentum when striking a hostile vessel to crush in its side. All line-of-battleships are now constructed with rams. The ram was first used during the American civil war, when the federal frigate *Cumberland* was sunk by the confederate ram *Virginia*, 1862. During the Austro-Italian war the Austrian ironclad *Ferdinand Max* sunk the Italian ironclad *Re d'Italia* at the battle of Lissa, 1866. In the war between Chile and Peru, the Peruvian battleship *Huascar* sunk the Chilian corvette *Esmeralda*, 1879 Accidents by collision between battleships have occurred:—The *Vanguard* was rammed and sunk by the *Iron Duke*, 1875; the *Grosser Kurfürst* by the *König Wilhelm*, 1878 (280 of the crew of the former were drowned); the *Victoria* by the *Camperdown*; Adm. Tryon and 400 men perished, 1893.

RAMADÁN, otherwise Ramadhām, Ramazān, the ninth month of the Mahometan year, in which is kept a strict fast in memory of the first revelation to Mahomet; the fast is followed by the short festival Bairam (*which see*). The Mahometan year is lunar, consisting of 354 days 21 hours, and in about 33 years the Ramadān passes through all the seasons. Ramadān begins on 9 Nov. in 1904; on 30 Oct. in 1905 of our calendar.

RÂMÂYANA, the older of the two great Sanskrit epic poems, is said to have been written by the poet Valmiki, 5th cent. B.C. Its hero is Rama, an incarnation of Vishnu, as the son of the king of Oudh. The Râmâyana consists of 24,000 verses, divided in 7 books. A translation in English verse by R. T. H. Griffiths in 5 vols., published 1870-75.

RAMBOUILLET, a royal château, about 25 miles from Paris. Here Francis I. died 31 March, 1547; and here Charles X. abdicated, 2 Aug. 1830. After being owned by the count of Thoulouse and the duc de Penthièvre, it was bought by Louis XVI. 1778.

RAMILLIES (Belgium), the site of a brilliant victory gained by the English under the duke of Marlborough and the allies over the French commanded by the elector of Bavaria and the marshal de Villeroy, on Whitsunday, 23 May (O.S. 12), 1706. The French were soon seized with a panic, and a general rout ensued: about 4000 of the allied army were slain in the engagement. This accelerated the fall of Louvain, Brussels, &c.

RAMSGATE, Kent, a fishing village in the 17th century, became important through commerce after 1689. The erection of the pier began in 1750; the harbour was formed by George Smeaton, 1780-95, and the lighthouse erected soon after. Iron promenade pier, 1881; handsome Roman Catholic church, built by the Pugins, the elder of whom resided here; Jewish synagogue and college erected by sir Moses Montefiore, also a resident; the Granville hotel, a handsome structure. Ramsgate incorporated as a borough 1884. Frith's "Ramsgate Sands" painted 1854. Population, 1881, 22,683; 1891, 24,676; 1901, 27,693.

RANELAGH (near Chelsea), a public garden for concerts and dancing, occupying the grounds of Ranelagh House (built by Jones, earl of Ranelagh, about 1691), was opened with a breakfast, 5 April, 1742. The music for the orchestra was frequently composed by Dr. Arne. The gardens were closed, and the buildings taken down, in 1804.

RANGES ACT, 1891. See under *Commons*.

RANGOON, maritime capital of the Burmese empire, built by Alompra, 1753, was taken by sir A. Campbell on 11 May, 1824. In Dec. 1826, it was ceded to the Burmese on condition of the payment of a sum of money, the reception of a British resident at Ava, and freedom of commerce. Oppression of the British merchants led to the second Burmese war, 1852. Rangoon was taken by storm by general Godwin, 14 April, and annexed to the British dominions in December. An English bishopric founded, 1877. Destructive fire for two days about 18 April, 1884. Foundation stone of Cathedral laid by lord Dufferin, viceroy, 24 Feb. 1886. Prince Albert Victor of Wales hospitably received, 20 Dec. 1889. Population, 1891, 180,324; 1901, 232,326. Fighting between the Mahometans and Hindoos during a festival suppressed by government; many deaths, 23–25 June, 1893. Memorial of the officers who fell in the war, 1885–90, unveiled by the viceroy, the marquis of Lansdowne, 20 Nov. 1893. Mr. Macgregor, a merchant, bequeaths 75,000*l.* to the city, Jan. 1903. See *Burmah*.

RANK, RELATIVE, IN THE NAVY AND ARMY—

Navy	Army
*Admiral of the Fleet ranks with	*Field-marshal.
*Admirals	*Generals.
*Vice-Admirals	*Lieut.-generals.
*Rear-Admirals	*Major-generals.
*Commodores, 1st and 2nd class	*Brigadier-generals.
*Captains (of 3 years) with	*Colonels.
*Captains (under 3 years and staff captains) with	*Lieut.-colonels.
Commanders and staff commanders, with	†Lieut.-colonels.
Lieutenants and navig.-lieutenants of 8 years' standing, with	‡Majors.
Lieutenants and navig.-lieutenants under 8 years' standing, as with	‡Captains.
Sub-lieutenants with	‡Lieutenants.

* According to date of commission. † Senior to.
‡ According to date of commission or order.

RANSOME'S ARTIFICIAL STONE, the invention of Mr. Fred. Ransome, 1848, is made by dissolving common flint (silica) in heated caustic alkali, adding fine sand. The mixture is pressed into moulds and heated to redness.

RANTERS, a sect which arose in 1645, similar to the Seekers, now termed Quakers. The name is sometimes applied to the Primitive Methodists, separated from the *Wesleyans* in 1810.

RAPE was punished with death by the Jews, Romans, and Goths; by mutilation and loss of eyes in William I.'s reign. This was mitigated by the statute of Westminster 1, 3 Edw. I. 1274. Made felony by stat. Westminster 2, 12 Edw. III. 1338; and without benefit of clergy, 18 Eliz. 1575. Rape made punishable by transportation in 1841; by penal servitude for life, or a less period, 1861. The Criminal Law Amenpment Act, 1885, contains pr visions respecting rape.

RAPHIA, a port of Palestine. Here Antiochus III. of Syria was defeated by Ptolemy Philopater, king of Egypt, 217 B.C.

RAPHOE, a bishopric in N. Ireland. St. Columb-kille, a man of great virtue and learning, and of royal blood, founded a monastery in this place, and it was afterwards enlarged by other holy men: but it is the received opinion that St. Eunan erected the church into a cathedral, and was the first bishop of the see in the 8th century. Raphoe was united to the bishopric of Derry by act, 3 & 4 Will. IV. 1833; see *Bishops*.

RAPPAHANNOCK, see *Chancellorsville*, and *Trials*, 1865.

RASPBERRY, not named among the fruits early introduced into this country from the continent. The Virginian raspberry (*Rubus occidentalis*) before 1696, and the flowering raspberry (*Rubus odoratus*), about 1700, came from North America.

RASTADT, Baden. Here the preliminaries of a peace were signed, 6 March, 1714, by marshal Villars on the part of the French king, and by prince Eugène on the part of the emperor; the German frontier was restored to the terms of the peace of Ryswick.—The Congress of Rastadt, to treat of a general peace with the Germanic powers, was commenced 9 Dec. 1797; and negotiations were carried on throughout 1798. The atrocious massacre of the French plenipotentiaries at Rastadt by the Austrian regiment of Szeltzler took place 28 April, 1799.

RATCLIFFE HIGHWAY (now St. George's-street), East London. Mr. Marr, a shopkeeper here, with his wife, child, and boy, were brutally murdered, 7 Dec. 1811; and on 11 Dec., Mr. and Mrs. Williamson, their child, and servant, were also murdered. A man, named Williams, arrested on suspicion, committed suicide, 15 Dec.

RATES. See *Local Rates*.

RATHMINES (near Dublin). Colonel Jones, governor of Dublin castle, made a sally out, routed the marquis of Ormond at Rathmines, killed 4000 men, and took 2517 prisoners, with their cannon, baggage, and ammunition, 2 Aug. 1649.

RATING ACT. See *Local Rates*.

RATIONALISM, the doctrine of those who reject a divine revelation and admit no other means of acquiring knowledge but experience and reason. The leading writers are Reimarus of Hamburg (died 1768), Paulus of Heidelberg, Eichhorn, Reinhard, and Strauss. W. Lecky's (died 23 Oct. 1903) "History of Rationalism in Europe" appeared, July, 1865; and Dr. J. Hurst's, April, 1867. *Higher Criticism*, see *Addenda*.

RATISBON (in Bavaria) was made a free imperial city about 1200. Several diets have been held here. A peace was concluded here between France and the emperor of Germany, by which was terminated the war for the Mantuan succession, signed 13 Oct. 1630. In later times, it was at Ratisbon, in a diet held there, that the German princes seceded from the Germanic empire, and placed themselves under the protection of the emperor Napoleon of France, 1 Aug. 1806. Ratisbon was made an archbishopric in 1806; secularised in 1810; was ceded to Bavaria in 1815; became again an archbishopric in 1817. Population 1890, 37,567; 1900, 45,426.

RATTENING (from *rutten*, provincial for rat), the removing and hiding workmen's tools as a punishment for nonpayment to trades unions, or opposition to them. Much "rattening" was disclosed at the commission of inquiry at Sheffield in June, 1867; and at Manchester Sept. following; see *Sheffield*.

RAUCOUX (Belgium). Here marshal Saxe and the French army totally defeated the allies under prince Charles of Lorraine, 11 Oct. 1746.

RAVAILLAC'S MURDER of Henry IV. of France, 14 May, 1610. The assassin was fearfully tortured, and executed, 27 May.

RAVENNA (on the Adriatic), a city of the Papal states, founded by Greek colonists, fell under the Roman power about 234 B.C. It was favoured and embellished by the emperors, and Honorius made it the capital of the Empire of the West about A.D. 404. In 568 it became the capital of an exarchate. It was subdued by the Lombards in 752, and their king, Astolphus, in 754 surrendered it to Pepin, king of France, who gave it to the pope Stephen, and thus laid the foundation of the temporal power of the holy see. On the 11th of April, 1512, a battle was fought between the French, under Gaston de Foix (duke of Nemours and nephew of Louis XII.), and the Spanish and Papal armies. De Foix perished in the moment of his victory, and his death closed the good fortune of the French in Italy. Ravenna became part of the kingdom of Italy in 1860.

Many of the *Accoltellatori*, a secret society of assassins (said to have been formerly followers of Garibaldi), who long kept the city in terror, arrested, Sept.—Oct.; condemned to life imprisonment . . . . 12 Dec. 1874

RÉ, ISLE OF (W. coast of France, near Rochelle). Oyster beds planted here in 1862 have flourished. See *Rochelle*.

READERS, an order of ministrants in the church of England, received the assent of the archbishops and bishops in July, 1866. They are not ordained or addressed as reverend, but are licensed by the bishop of the diocese. Readers wear a special badge to denote their office. A monthly magazine devoted to the interests of licensed readers is in project, the first number to be issued 1 Jan. 1904.

READING (Berkshire). Here Alfred defeated the Danes, 871. The abbey was founded in 1121 by Henry I. The last abbot was hanged in 1539 for denying the king's supremacy. The palace prison was erected 1850. New town hall, free library, &c. opened 31 May, 1882. Royal County theatre burnt, 25 Aug. 1894. Mr. George Palmer, giver of Palmer park, &c., born 1818, died 19 Aug. 1897. University Extension (Oxford) college (4000*l.* presented by Mr. Walter Palmer), opened by the prince of Wales, 11 June, 1898. Lady Warwick hostel, to train women in the lighter side of agriculture, opened Oct. 1898; a donation of 50,000*l.* received Dec. 1900; exhibition, &c., 16 July, 1902. Population, 1881, 48,769; 1891, 60,054; 1901, 72,214.

Prince Christian unveils a statue of the king, 3 Dec. 1902

REAL ACTIONS LIMITATION ACT, passed 1874, comes into operation 1 Jan. 1879.

REALISTS, see *Nominalists.*

REAL PRESENCE, see *Transubstantiation.*

REAPING-MACHINES. One was invented in this country early in the present century, but failed from its intricacies. At the meeting of the British association at Dundee, Sept. 1867, the rev. Patrick Bell stated that he invented a reaping-machine in 1826, which was used in 1827; the principle being that on which the best American machines are now constructed. On 15 Jan. 1868, he was presented with a valuable testimonial, and 1000*l.* in money. McCormick's American machine was invented about 1831, and perfected in 1846; he received a gold medal from the jurors of the exhibition of 1851; and also at the Royal Agricultural society's competition at Bristol, 6 Aug. 1878. The sheaves are bound by these reaping machines. About 200 patented; few good. Hussey's machine, also American, exhibited in 1851, was highly commended.

John Ridley, the inventor of the reaping machine largely used n Australia, died 28 Nov. 1887.

REASON was decreed to be worshipped as a goddess by the French republicans, 10 Nov. 1793, and was personified by an actress.—Thomas Paine's "Age of Reason" was published in 1794-5; Immanuel Kant's "Critique of Pure Reason," ("Kritik der reinen Vernunft"), 1781.

REBECCA RIOTS, see *Wales*, 1843, 1878.

REBELLIONS or **INSURRECTIONS IN BRITISH HISTORY.** Details of many are given in separate articles. See *Conspiracies.*

Against William the conqueror, in favour of Edgar Atheling, aided by the Scots and Danes, 1069.

By Odo of Bayeux and others, against William II. in favour of his brother Robert, 1088; suppressed, 1090.

In favour of the empress Maude, 1139. Ended, 1153.

The rebellion of prince Richard against his father Henry II. 1189.

Of the barons, April, 1215. Compromised by the grant of *Magna Charta*, 15 June following.

Of the barons, 1261-67.

Of the lords spiritual and temporal against Edward II. on account of his favourites, the Gavestons, 1312. Again, on account of the Spencers, 1321.

Of Walter the Tyler, of Deptford, vulgarly called *Wat Tyler*, occasioned by the brutal rudeness of a poll-tax collector to his daughter. He killed the collector in his rage, and raised a party to oppose the tax itself, 1381; see *Tyler.*

In Ireland, when Roger, earl of March, the viceroy heir presumptive to the crown, was slain, 1398.

Of Henry, duke of Lancaster, who caused Richard II. be deposed, 1399.

Against king Henry IV. by a number of confederated lords, 1402-3.

Against Henry V. by earl of Cambridge and other lords, 1415

Of Jack Cade, against Henry VI. 1450; see *Cade's Insurrection.*

In favour of the house of York, 1452, which ended in the imprisonment of Henry VI. and seating Edward IV. of York on the throne, 1461.

Under Warwick and Clarence, 1470, which ended with the expulsion of Edward IV. and the restoration of Henry VI. the same year.

Under Edward IV. 1471, which ended with the death of Henry VI.

Of the earl of Richmond, against Richard III. 1485, which ended with the death of Richard.

Under Lambert Simnel, 1486, who pretended to be Richard III.'s nephew, Edward Plantagenet, earl of Warwick; his army was defeated, leaders slain, and he was discovered to be a baker's son; he was pardoned, and employed by the king as a menial.

Under Perkin Warbeck, 1492; defeated; executed 1499.

Under Thomas Flammock and Michael Joseph, in Cornwall, against taxes levied to pay the Scottish war expenses. They marched towards London, and lord Audley took the command at Wells. They were defeated at Blackheath, 22 June, and the three leaders were executed, 28 June, 1497.

The "Pilgrimage of Grace" against Henry VIII. 1536-7.

Of the English in the West, to restore the ancient liturgy, &c., 1549; suppressed same year.

In Norfolk, headed by Ket, the tanner, but soon suppressed, Aug. 1549.

In favour of lady Jane Grey, against queen Mary. Lady Jane was proclaimed queen of England on the death of Edward VI. 10 July, 1553; but she resigned the crown to Mary a few days afterwards: she was beheaded for high treason, in the Tower, 12 Feb. 1554, aged 17.

Of sir Thomas Wyatt, son of the poet, and others, against queen Mary's marriage with Philip of Spain, &c., fails; he is beheaded 11 April, 1554.

Of the Roman catholic earls of Northumberland and Westmoreland against queen Elizabeth, Nov. and Dec. 1567. The former fled to Scotland, but was given up by the regent Morton and executed.

Of the Irish under the earl of Tyrone, 1599, suppressed in 1601.

Under the earl of Essex, against queen Elizabeth, 1600; it ended in his death, 1601.

Of the Irish under Roger More, sir Phelim O'Neil, &c., against the English in Ireland, 1641-5.

The "Great Rebellion," 1641-60.

Rebellion of the Scots covenanters, 1666; soon put down.

Under the duke of Monmouth, 1685; executed 15 July.

Of the Scots in favour of the Old Pretender, 1715; quelled in 1716.

Of the Scots under the Young Pretender, 1745; suppressed in 1746; lords Lovat, Balmerino, and Kilmarnock beheaded.

Of the Americans on account of taxation, 1774. This rebellion led to the loss of our chief North American colonies, and the independence of the United States, 1782.

In Ireland, called the *Great Rebellion*, when great numbers took up arms, commenced 24 May, 1798; suppressed next year.

Again in Ireland, under Robert Emmett, a gifted enthusiast, 23 July, 1803, when lord Kilwarden was killed with several others by the insurgents.

Canadian insurrection (*which see*), Dec. 1837 to Nov. 1838.

Of Chartists at Newport (*which see*), 4 Nov. 1839.

Smith O'Brien's silly Irish rebellion; terminated in the defeat and dispersion of a multitude of his deluded followers by sub-inspector Trant and about sixty police constables, on Boulagh common, Ballingary, co. Tipperary, 29 July, 1848; see *Ireland.*

Sepoy mutiny in India (see *India*), 1857-8.

Of Fenians in Ireland; see *Fenians* and *Ireland*, 1865-7. See *Chili.*

RECEIPTS FOR MONEY were first taxed by a stamp duty in 1783. The act was amended in 1784, 1791 *et seq.*, and receipts were taxed by a duty varying according to the amount of the money received, in all transactions. Stamps required on bills of exchange, notes, and receipts in Ireland, by stat. 35 Geo. III. 1795; see *Bills of Exchange*. The uniform stamp of one penny on receipts, for all sums above 2*l.*, was enacted by 16 & 17 Vict. c. 59 (4 Aug. 1853); see *Stamps*. Penny postage-stamps used for receipts after 1 June, 1881.

RECIDIVISTS, the French term for habitual criminals. The proposal of the French government to transmit many of these to New Caledonia, with partial freedom, was opposed in France as dangerous to liberty, and very warmly protested against by our Australian colonies, especially Queensland and New South Wales, fearing their intrusion as dangerous to public security, 1883-4.

French legislation resumed; bill passed 12 May; came into operation . . . . . 1 Dec., 1885

RECIPROCITY ASSOCIATION, founded at Manchester Sept. 1869, in consequence of the restrictions on the importation of British manufactures into their territories imposed by foreign governments.

Reciprocity, a form of protection, was advocated by lord Bateman and others in 1878-9. His resolution was negatived by the lords, 29 April, 1879.

RECIPROCITY TREATY between Great Britain and the United States, regulating the relation between the latter and Canada, in regard to trade, fisheries, &c., negotiated by lord Elgin, and ratified 2 Aug. 1854. Its abrogation, proposed by the United States government in 1864, was effected 17 March, 1866. Its renewal was desired in the states in 1867. See *Canada and United States*, 1891.

RECITATIVE, a species of singing differing but little from ordinary speaking, and used for narratives in operas, is said to have been first employed at Rome by Emilio del Cavaliere, who disputed the claim of Rinuccini to the introduction of the opera, 1600; see *Opera*.

RECORD, Evangelical or Low Church, weekly newspaper, established 1828.

RECORDER, the principal judicial officer of great corporations. The first recorder of London was Jeffrey de Norton, alderman, 1298; right hon. Russell Gurney, Q.C., recorder, Dec. 1856—Jan. 1878. Sir Thomas Chambers, Feb. 1878, died 24 Dec. 1891, succeeded by sir Charles Hall, 8 Feb. 1892, died 9 March, 1900; sir Forest Fulton, 20 March, 1900. The salary, originally 10*l.* per annum, is now 3000*l.*

RECORDS, PUBLIC, IN ENGLAND, began to be regularly preserved in 1100, by order of Henry I. The repositories which possessed materials the most ancient and interesting to the historian were, the Chapter-house of Westminster Abbey, the Tower of London, the Rolls Chapel, and the Queen's Remembrancer's offices of the exchequer. The early records of Scotland, going from London, were lost by shipwreck in 1298. In Ireland, the council-chamber and most of the records were burned, 1711. Public records Act, 2 Vict. c. 94 (10 Aug. 1838).—A new RECORD OFFICE has been erected on the Rolls estate, between Chancery and Fetter lanes, to which the records have been gradually removed. New additional buildings occupied Oct. 1895 *et seq.* The Record Commissioners commenced their publications in 1802. Mr. F. Thomas's valuable "Handbooks to the Public Records," was published in 1853; Mr. Ewald's "Our Public Records," in 1873. Acts relating to the Public Records of Ireland, passed 1867 and 1875. The British Records society, which had published many documents, 1887 *et seq.*, was incorporated 1892. Annual meetings.

RECREATION, see *Playground*.

The Recreative Evening Schools Association for boys who have left school, founded, under royal patronage, 1886.

RECREATIVE RELIGIONISTS, a name given to an association of gentlemen for diffusing a knowledge of natural religion by the aid of science, formed in Dec. 1866. In Jan. 1867 lectures were given on Sunday evenings at St. Martin's-hall, London, by professor Huxley, Dr. W. B. Carpenter, and others, sacred music being performed at intervals during the evening. This was decided not to be an infraction of the Sunday act, 21 Geo. III. c. 49, in the trial, Baxter *v.* Baxter Langley, 19 Nov. 1868. See *Sunday Lecture Society*.

RECRUITING, see *Army*, 31 Oct. 1866. Recruits: 1878, 28,325; 1879, 25,662; 1880, 25,622; 1881, 26,258; 1882, 23,802; 1883, 33,096 (new regulations); 1884, 35,653; 1885, 39,971; 1886, 39,409; 1887, 31,225; 1888, 25,153; 1890, (for the regular army), 32,923; 1893, 35,195; 1894, 33,698; 1895, 29,583; 1896, 28,532; 1897, 35,015; 1898, 38,418; 1899, 42,700; 1900, 49,260, and 37,853 militia; 1901, 47,039, and 37,644 militia; 1902, 50,753, and 41,486, militia.

RECUSANTS, persons who refuse to attend church, 1 Eliz. c. 2, 1559; dissenters relieved from this act, 1689; it was repealed, 1844.

REDAN, a field fortification, consisting of two faces meeting in a salient angle directed towards the enemy; see *Russo-Turkish War*, 1855.

RED CRAG, deposits of fossil remains on the coast of Essex and Suffolk, so designated by Edward Charlesworth about 1835. They are much used in the manure manufacture.

RED CROSS on a white ground, the flag of the Geneva Convention (*which see*). Third international convention at Geneva, 1 Sept. 1884. The Russian Red Cross society, with others, was very active during the Servian war, July-Aug. 1876. The order of the Royal Red Cross for ladies who have acted as nurses in war, &c., and others, instituted by queen Victoria, 23 April, 1883. The princess of Wales and other ladies nominated, 25 May, 1883; conferred on Mrs. Grimwood for her services in the retreat of the troops from Manipur (*which see*), June, 1891; and on Miss Annie Myers and Miss Daisy Brazier for services in Pekin during the operations in China, Sept. 1902. The British Red Cross society active during the Greco-Turkish war, 1897; French aid received; the duke of Portland gives 10,000*l.*; the *Princess of Wales* hospital ship fitted up by the society; the princess of Wales gives 1,000*l.*, and hands over 9,000*l.*; the balance of the Egyptian campaign fund; and much help by Americans and others during the S. African war, Nov. 1899–1902. International conference held at St. Petersburg, 29 May, 1902.

REDE LECTURE, Cambridge; sir Robert Rede, chief justice of common pleas, in 1518 endowed some lectureships. In 1859 these were replaced by an annual lecture: which has been given by professors Owen, Phillips, Ansted, Tyndall, and other eminent persons.

REDEMPTORISTS, see *Liguorians*.

REDHILL, see *Reformatory Schools*.

REDISTRIBUTION OF SEATS ACT, see *Reform*, 1885.

REDOWA, a Bohemian dance in 3-4 time, introduced in 1846 or 1847, at Paris, and soon after in London.

RED RIVER SETTLEMENTS, a name given to part of the Hudson bay settlements.

RED SEA, the Mare Erythræum of the ancients, between Arabia and Africa, crossed by the Phœnicians and others in commerce, and by the Israelites in their escape from Egypt, 1491 B.C. In 1826 Ehrenberg discovered that the colour was due to marine plants, the *Trichodesmium Erythræum*; see *Suez*, *Soudan*, and *Somaliland*.—*Red Sea Littoral, Suakin*, &c., governor-general, col. Holled Smith, appointed 1888, resigned June, 1892; succeeded by col. Archibald Hunter, Oct. 1892; col. George Lloyd, Sept. 1894. Capt. N. E. Playfair, present governor (1903).

Much piracy and gun-running; 7 divers killed near Massowah . . . . 10 Sept. 1902

Active measures of suppression taken by the British and Italians; 3 dhows burnt and sunk; 2 Italians killed at Midi, reported 5 Nov.; agreement with Turkey settled. reported . 10 Nov. „

British chase a pirate off Hodeida, reported, 8 Dec. „

REFERENDUM, the name given to an article in the Swiss constitution of 29 May, 1874, by which certain laws passed by the Cantonal and Federal legislations might be referred to the people at large by *plébiscite*. The people have also the right of taking the *initiative* in proposing the enactment of new laws and the repeal of old ones. The *referendum* was much employed in Belgium in relation to the revision of the constitution, Feb., March, 1893.

REFLECTORS, see *Burning-glass* and *California*.

REFORM ASSOCIATION, instituted at Westminster to protect electors, 20 May, 1835.

National Reform Union: at the annual meeting at Manchester it was said to have 411 affiliated societies, 22 May, 1889.

REFORM BANQUETS, see *France*, 1847.

REFORM CLUB, established in 1886 by the right hon. Edw. Ellice, M.P., and others, to succeed the Westminster Club, 1834-6. The building in Pall-mall, designed by sir Charles Barry, was completed in 1841.

Jubilee ball; the prince of Wales and son, and above 2,000 persons of all parties present, 15 June, 1887.

A 2nd edition of the catalogue of the excellent library compiled by Mr. C. W. Vincent, the librarian, under the supervision of the library committee, with an historical introduction by Mr. W. Fraser Rae, was published in June, 1894. Mr. Louis Fagan's "The Reform Club; its Founders and Architect," 1886; he died early Jan. 1903.

REFORM IN PARLIAMENT. Mr. Pitt's motion for a reform in parliament was lost by a majority of 20, 7 May, 1782; of 144, 7 May, 1783; and of 74, 18 April, 1785; see *Radicals*. The measure of reform by earl Grey's administration was proposed in the house of commons by lord John Russell, 1 March, 1831.

BILL OF 1831.

First division; *second* reading: for it, 302; against it, 301; 22 March.

On motion for a committee, general Gascoyne moved an amendment, "that the number of representatives for England and Wales ought not to be diminished." Amendment carried on a division, 299 to 291; 19 April.

The bill abandoned, and parliament dissolved, 23 April.

A new parliament assembled, 14 June. Bill again introduced, 24 June.

Division on *second* reading: for it, 367; against it, 231—majority, 136; 7 July.

Division on *third* reading of the bill: for it, 345; against it, 236—majority, 109; 22 Sept.

In the LORDS:—first division, on *second* reading; lord Wharncliffe moved, "that the bill be read that day six months." For the amendment, 199; against it, 158—majority, FORTY-ONE; 8 Oct. [Parliament prorogued, 20 Oct. 1831.]

ACT OF 1832.*

Read in the COMMONS a *first* time without a division, 12 Dec. 1831. *Second* reading; division, viz.: for the bill 324; against it, 162—majority, 162; 17 Dec. 1831. *Third* reading; division, viz.: for the bill, 355; against it, 239—majority for it, 116; 23 March, 1832.

In the LORDS:—read a *first* time on motion of earl Grey, 27 March. *Second* reading: for the bill, 184; against it, 175—majority, NINE; 14 April. In the committee lord Lyndhurst moved, "that the question of enfranchisement should precede that of disfranchisement." The division was 151 and 116—majority against ministers, THIRTY-FIVE, 7 May.

Resignation of ministers, 9 May; great public excitement ensued, and they were induced to resume office on the king granting them full power to secure majorities by the creation of new peers.

In the LORDS, the bill was carried through the committee, 30 May; read a *third* time: 106 against 22—majority, EIGHTY-FOUR; 4 June. Received the royal assent, 7 June, 1832.

The royal assent given to the Scotch reform bill, 17 July; and to the Irish one, 7 Aug. 1832.

ABORTIVE REFORM BILLS.

Lord John Russell introduced a *new reform bill*, 13 Feb. 1854, which was withdrawn, 11 April, 1854, in consequence of the war with Russia.

On 28 Feb. 1859, Mr. Disraeli brought in a reform bill, which was rejected by the commons on 31 March, by a majority of 39. This led to a dissolution of parliament, and eventually to a change of ministry.

The new government (lords Palmerston and J. Russell) brought forward a new bill, 1 March, 1860; but withdrew it, 11 June. No reform bill was brought forward by the government, 1861-5; see *Commons*.

The discussion respecting parliamentary reform was revived in the autumns of 1864 and 1865.

Mr. Baines' reform bill was rejected by the commons, 8 May, 1865.

Mr. Gladstone introduced a *franchise bill*, 12 March, 1866; after much discussion, it was read a second time, 28 April. A re-distribution of seats bill was introduced, and incorporated with the franchise bill, 7 May; an amendment (on a clause, substituting "rateable" for "clear yearly value") was passed, in opposition to the government, 19 June; which led to the resignation of the government, 26 June; and the withdrawal of the bill (see *Adullam*), 19 July, 1866.

Numerous great reform meetings: London, Hyde-park (riotous), 23, 24 July; Agricultural-hall, 30 July; and Guildhall, 8 Aug.; Manchester, 24 Sept.; Leeds, 8 Oct.; Glasgow, 16 Oct.; Edinburgh, 17 Nov.; Conference at Manchester, 19 Nov. 1866.

* By this "Act to amend the Representation of the People in England and Wales" (2 & 3 Will. IV. c. 45), 56 boroughs in England were disfranchised (schedule A.), 30 were reduced to one member only (B.); 22 new boroughs were created to send two members (C.), and 20 to send one member (D.), and other important changes made.

Reform demonstration of trades-unions in London; procession of about 25,000; great order observed, 3 Dec., 1866.

Procession of about 18,000 men to Agricultural-hall, Islington: good order kept; 11 Feb. 1867.

Mr. Disraeli announced his plan of proceeding with reform by 13 resolutions, 11 Feb.; these withdrawn, 26 Feb. 1867.

"Ten Minutes' bill" introduced and withdrawn, 25 Feb. 1867.

[It comprised a 6*l.* franchise for boroughs, and 20*l.* for counties. Said by sir John Pakington to have been agreed to in the last ten minutes of a cabinet council.]

New bill (with household suffrage) introduced 18 March; read second time, 27 March, 1867.

The "Tea-room meeting" of liberals (Messrs. Owen Stanley, Dillwyn, Grant Duff, and others), who agree to support the bill in opposition to Mr. Gladstone's resolution, which is withdrawn, and the bill goes into committee, 8 April; Mr. Gladstone's amendment rejected by 22 (for 288, against 310), 12 April, 1867.

Peaceable reform meetings at Birmingham, 22 April; Hyde-park, 6 May; National Reform Union (first meeting), 15 May, 1867.

ACTS OF 1867-8.

The new Reform bill passed by the commons, 15-16 July; by the lords (with amendments, when lord Derby said, that it was "a great experiment," and "a leap in the dark") 6 Aug.; received the royal assent, 15 Aug. 1867.*

Scotch reform bill introduced by lord advocate, 17 Feb.; passed 13 July, 1868.

Irish bill introduced by the earl of Mayo, 19 March; passed 13 July, 1868.

The Reform league was dissolved 13 March, 1869; revived, Oct. 1876.

Bill for extending household suffrage to counties brought in annually by Mr. G. O. Trevelyan, see *Household Suffrage.*

ACTS OF 1884-5.

New bill for Representation of the People of the United Kingdom extending household and lodger suffrage to counties uniform with boroughs, adding about 2,000,000 voters introduced by Mr. Gladstone, the premier, 28 Feb., read first time 3 March; lord John Manners' amendment, declining to pass the bill without knowledge of re-distribution of seats, 24 March; negatived, (340-210), bill read second time, 7-8 April; third time, 27 June. Lords, first time, 27 June: rejected by earl Cairns's amendment (conservatives led by Marquis of Salisbury), (205-146), 8-9 July; earl of Wemyss's compromise rejected (182-132); earl Cadogan's amendment, (adjournment, instead of prorogation of parliament till the autumn), adopted 17 July. Commons, bill read first time, 24 Oct.; second time, (372-232) 7-8 Nov.; third time, 11 Nov. Lords bill read first time, 14 Nov.; second time, 18 Nov.; (compromise with the government); third time, 5 Dec.; passed 6 Dec. 1884.

Redistribution of Seats Act; commons, read first time, 1 Dec.; second time, 4 Dec. 1884; third time (116-33), 11-12 May, 1885. Lords, read first time, 12 May; second time, 15 May; third time, 12 June; Royal assent, 25 June, 1885.

REDISTRIBUTION OF SEATS ACT.—*Boroughs to cease as such* (having less than 15,000 inhabitants): England, 80; Scotland, 2; Ireland, 22. *To be included in their counties:* Berwick, Lichfield, Carrickfergus, and Drogheda. *Disfranchised for corruption:* Macclesfield, Sandwich. *To lose one member* (having less than 50,000 inhabitants): England, 34; Ireland, 3. *To have additional members* (with more than 50,000 inhabitants); England, 12; Scotland, 3; Ireland, 2. *New boroughs:* England, 43. 160 seats obtained by disfranchisement to be divided among counties and boroughs now under-represented. Certain boroughs and counties returning more than one member, formed into new subdivisions, returning one member. London only to have two members. Total number of members to be raised from 652 to 670; England to have 6 more, Scotland 12 more.

Mr. Stansfeld's resolution advocating the principle of "one man, one vote," negatived in the commons (291—189), 3 March, 1891.

* This act is divided into three parts:—

I. FRANCHISES. *Boroughs:* All householders rated for relief of the poor; lodgers, resident for twelve months, and paying 10*l.* a year. *Counties:* Persons of property of the clear annual value of 5*l.*; and occupiers of lands or tenements paying 12*l.* a year. At a contested election for any county or borough represented by three members, no person to vote for more than 2 candidates; in London, to vote for 3 only.

Disfranchised: Totnes; Reigate; Great Yarmouth; Lancaster.

II. DISTRIBUTION OF SEATS: Boroughs with less than 10,000 population, to return one member only (38 in Schedule A.). Manchester, Liverpool, Birmingham, and Leeds, to have 3 members instead of 2.

Chelsea (with Fulham, Hammersmith, and Kensington) made a borough: Merthyr Tydvil, and Salford, to return two members; Tower Hamlets divided into two boroughs—Hackney, and Tower Hamlets. (Other new boroughs in Schedule B.) University of London to return one member.

III. SUPPLEMENTARY PROVISIONS: Registration, &c. Boundary Commissioners (*which see*). Parliament not to be dissolved on any future demise of the crown. Members holding offices of profit from the crown not to vacate their seats on acceptance of another office.

REFORMATION, THE. Efforts for the reformation of the church may be traced to the reign of Charlemagne, when Paulinus, bishop of Aquileia, employed his voice and pen to accomplish it. The principal reformers were Wickliffe, Huss, Jerome of Prague, Savonarola, Erasmus, Luther, Zuinglius, Tyndal, Calvin, Melanchthon, Cranmer, Latimer, Knox, and Browne. Luther thus characterised himself and his fellow reformers: "Res non Verba—*Luther*." "Verba non Res—*Erasmus*." "Res et Verba—*Melanchthon*." "Nec Verba nec Res—*Carlstadt*;" see *Wickliffites, Protestants, Calvinists, Lutherans, Presbyterianism, Wittenberg,* &c. The eras of the reformation are as follows:—

In France (*Albigenses*), said to have been a surviving gnostic sect, not Christian reformers . about	1177
In England (*Wickliffe*)	1360
In Bohemia (*Huss*)	1405
In Italy (*Jerome Savonarola*)	1498
In France (*by Farel*) . before	1512
In Germany (*Luther*)	1517
In Switzerland (*Zuinglius*)	1519
In Denmark (*Andreas Bodenstein*)	1521
In Prussia	1527
In France (*Calvin*); see *Huguenots*	1529
Protestants first so called	..
In Sweden (*Petri*)	1530
In England (*Henry VIII.*)	1534
In Ireland (*Archbishop George Browne*)	1535
In England, completed (*Cranmer, Bucer, Fagius,* &c.), 1547; annulled by Mary, 1553; restored by Elizabeth	1558
In Scotland (*Knox*), established	1560
In the Netherlands, established	1562

REFORMATORY SCHOOLS, for juvenile delinquents.* The Reformatory School at Mettray, near Tours in France, was founded in 1839 by M. de Metz, formerly a councillor of Paris, warmly seconded by the vicomte de Courcelles, who gave the estate on which the establishment is placed. The one at Redhill, Surrey, is situated on land purchased in 1849 by the Philanthropic Society, and under the direction of the rev. Sydney Turner. The first stone of the building was laid 30 April, 1849, by the prince consort. The inmates of these establishments are instructed in farm labour, and divided into so-called families. In 1854 the Juvenile

* It was calculated (about 1856) that there were in London 30,000, and in England 100,000 youths under 17 leading a vagabond life, and that out of 15,000 of those who were committed for trial nearly half were in custody for the first time.

Offenders act was passed; amended act, 1901. In 1851 and 1853 great meetings were held on this subject; and in Aug. 1856, the first grand conference of the National Reformatory Union was held. See *Industrial Schools*.

North-West London Preventive and Reformatory Institution in the New-road, established: all kinds of trades taught 1852
Reformatory and Refuge Union founded . . 1856
Acts for establishing reformatory schools passed, 1857, 1858, 1866, 1868; amended . . 1872 & 1893
Fifty-one reformatory schools in England (and nine in Ireland), 1863; 53 reformatory schools (with 4674 boys; 1165 girls), 1872; Reformatory schools in England and Wales, 1889–90, 46; industrial schools, 1889, 134; 1890, 141; in Great Britain, 227 in 1893; 223 in 1901 (45 reformatory, 142 industrial, 14 truant, and 22 day industrial schools; 24,608 boys, 5297 girls in the reformatory and industrial schools).
An international exhibition of the works of these schools at the Agricultural-hall, Islington, near London, opened by the prince of Wales . . . 1865
Mr. T. Barwick Lloyd Baker, an eminent promoter of the reformatory system, died . Dec. 1886
Act passed abolishing imprisonment as a necessary preliminary to detention in reformatories . . 1899

"REFORMED CHURCH" (Calvinistic), established in Holland and in some parts of Germany. For the Reformed Presbyterian Church in Scotland, see *Cameronians*, note.

REFORMED EPISCOPAL CHURCH, founded in the United States of North America in 1873; in this country a secession from the Free Church of England in 1877.

Dr. Cummins, assistant bishop of Kentucky, after revising the prayer-book, consecrated C. E. Cheney as bishop, 14 Dec. 1873; others since consecrated and churches formed.

REFRACTION, see *Light*.

REFRESHMENT HOUSES for the sale of wine, &c., are licensed in pursuance of an act passed in 1860, amended in 1861: a new act passed in 1864, 1865. See *Licences*.

REFRIGERATORS, see *Provisions*.

REFUGE FOR THE DESTITUTE (criminal young females), Dalston, London, E.; instituted 1805, incorporated 1838.

REFUGEES' BENEVOLENT FUND, instituted in consequence of the Franco-German war, at a great meeting held at the Mansion-house, London, 21 Oct. 1870. It afforded temporary relief to many sufferers.

REFUGES, see *Poor*, 1864. Refuges for Destitute boys and girls, established in Great Queen-street in 1852. See *Chichester*.

REGALIA, see *Crown*.

REGATTA. A public boat race, introduced into this country from Venice in 1775: and in that year one took place on the Thames.

REGELATION. See *Ice*.

REGENCY BILLS. One was passed 1751. One was proposed to parliament in consequence of the mental illness of George III., and debated 10 Dec. 1788. It was relinquished on his majesty's recovery, 26 Feb. 1789. The return of the malady led to the prince of Wales (afterwards George IV.) being sworn in before the privy council as regent of the kingdom, 5 Feb. 1811. The Regency Bill providing for the administration of the government, should the crown descend to the princess Victoria while under eighteen years of age, passed 1 Will. IV., 23 Dec. 1830. A Regency Bill appointing prince Albert regent in the event of the demise of the queen, should her next lineal successor be under age; passed 4 Aug. 1840.

REGENTS, see *Protectorates*.

REGENT'S CANAL, begun at Paddington, where it joins a cut to the Grand Junction, passes under Maida-hill, continues its course by the Regent's-park to Islington, where another subterranean excavation, about three-quarters of a mile in length, was formed for its passage. It then proceeds by Hoxton, Hackney, Mile-end, to Limehouse, where it joins the Thames. The whole length of it is nine miles; it comprises twelve locks and thirty-seven bridges. Begun, 1812; opened 1 Aug. 1820. Great explosion of *gunpowder* (*which see*), 2 Oct. 1874. New bridge, near Gloucester gate, Regent's park, opened by the duke of Cambridge, 3 Aug. 1878. Regent's Canal and City Railway Co. act passed, 1882.

REGENT'S PARK, originally part of the grounds belonging to a palace of queen Elizabeth, near to the north end of Tottenham court-road, pulled down in 1791. Since 1600, the property was let to various persons, but the leases having expired it reverted to the crown; and in 1814 great improvements were commenced under the direction of Mr. Nash. The park consists of about 450 acres; within it are the gardens of the Zoological Society and the Royal Botanical Society. During a frost on 15 Jan. 1867, the rotten ice of one of the lakes gave way, and about 200 persons were immersed, of whom above 40 perished. Addition of 20 acres made to the public park, 1883.

Joseph Rumbold was murdered near York Gate, 24 May. Eight youths, George Gallesly, 17, William Elvis, 16, Francis Cole, 18, Peter Lee, 17, William Joseph Graefe, 17, William Henshaw, 16, Charles Henry Govier, 16, and Michael Duling, 15, all described as labourers, were charged with the wilful murder, 1 Aug.; Gallesly was convicted; the rest acquitted of murder, 2 Aug.; they pleaded guilty to minor charges, and were sentenced to various terms of penal servitude, 4 Aug. The evidence disclosed the existence of local bands of young roughs carrying on internecine warfare. Joseph Rumbold was not the intended victim; Gallesly reprieved, Aug. 1888.

REGENT STREET, London, W.; designed and executed by John Nash; authorised by act, 53 George III. 1813. The colonnades of the quadrant were removed in 1848.

REGGIO, see *Rhegium*.

REGICIDES, in English history, are the commissioners appointed to try king Charles I., 150 in number; of whom 70 acted, and 59 signed the death-warrant, Jan. 1649. Of these last, 29 were tried, and 10 executed: Harrison, 13 Oct.; Cook and Peters, 16 Oct.; Scott, Scroop, Clement, and Jones, 17 Oct.; Axtell and Hacker, 19 Oct. 1660. They asserted themselves to be martyrs. Others were imprisoned. See *Assassinations*.

Foreign Regicides.

James I. of Scotland, by nobles . . 20 Feb. 1437
James III. ,, ,, . . 11 June, 1488
Henry III. of France, by Clement, 1 Aug.; *d.* 2 Aug. 1589
Henry IV. ,, by Ravaillac . 14 May, 1610
Gustavus III. of Sweden, by Ankarström, 16 March; *d.* 29 March, 1792
Louis XVI. ,, by convention . 21 Jan. 1793
Paul of Russia, by nobles . . . . 24 March, 1801
Maximilian of Mexico . . . . . 19 June, 1867

REGIMENTAL EXCHANGE ACT, passed 28 May, 1875.

REGIMENTS OF INFANTRY were formed in France about 1588; see *Infantry*. The following are the approximate dates of the establishment of several British regiments:—

CAVALRY.

Oxford Blues are erroneously said to have been formed in the reign of Henry VIII.; they derive their name from their colonel, the earl of Oxford, in 1661

Three Indian regiments (19th, 20th, and 21st) added Aug. 1861

The Dragoon Guards, the Scots Greys, and the Royal Irish were formed about 1683-6

Several regiments of Light Dragoons were armed with lances and termed *Lancers* . . Sept. 1816

See *Germany*, June, 1894.

INFANTRY (see *Guards*).

1st Royal or Royal Scots regiment, 1633; the old title resumed . . . . Dec. 1871

Coldstream Guards, established by Monk, in . 1660

3rd Buffs, represent London train bands and have special privileges . . . . ,,

2nd Queen's Royal 1661

4th King's Own 1685

5th Northumberland Fusiliers . . . . . . ,,

26th Cameronian 1689

100th Canadian 1858

101st to 109th (Indian) added . . . . Aug. 1861

The Highland regiments are the old 42nd, 71st, 72nd, 78th, 79th, 92nd, and 93rd. See *Army Organization*.

NOTE.—By the reorganisation of the infantry in 1881 the numbers of the regiments by which they were formerly designated were (with some exceptions) merged into their territorial names.

The 3rd Buffs are now the Kent (East) regiment; the 2nd Queen's Royal, the Surrey (Royal West) regiment; 4th King's Own, the Lancaster (Royal) regiment; 5th Northumberland Fusiliers, the Northumberland Fusiliers; 26th Cameronians, the Cameronians (Scottish Rifles).

Highland Regiments.—The old 42nd (the Black Watch) is now the 1st battalion of the Royal Highlanders; the 71st, the 1st batt. Highland Light Infantry; the 72nd, the 1st batt. Seaforth Highlanders (the Ross-shire Buffs); the 78th, the 2nd batt. Seaforth Highlanders; the 79th, the Cameron Highlanders; the 92nd, the 2nd batt. Gordon Highlanders; the 93rd, the 2nd batt. Argyll and Sutherland Highlanders.

REGISTERS. The registering of deeds and conveyances disposing of real estates was appointed to be effected in Yorkshire and in Middlesex, 2 Anne, 1703, *et seq.* Greater security was thus given to purchasers and mortgagees; and the value of estates increased in those counties. Wills have been for a series of years kept and registered, in London, at Doctors' Commons; see *Wills*. The registering of shipping in the Thames was commenced, 1786; and throughout England, 1787; and several acts and amendments of acts have since followed for keeping and improving registers.

The duties and payments of the Lord Clerk Register of Scotland and his deputy were regulated by 42 & 43 Vict. c. 44 1879

REGISTERS, PAROCHIAL, were established by Cromwell, lord Essex, by which the dates of births, marriages, and burials, became ascertainable, Sept. 1538. This measure was opposed by the people, who feared some new taxation. A stamp-tax was laid on registers in 1784. Laws for their better regulation were enacted in 1813 *et seq.* The great Registration act (introduced by lord John Russell), 6 & 7 Will. IV. c. 86, passed 17 Aug. 1836, see *Bills of Mortality*, &c.

A new registration act for births and deaths, passed 7 Aug. 1874; another passed in 1901.

Births and Deaths Registration act for Ireland passed . . . . 2 Aug. 1880

Major George Graham, the first registrar-general (1838), was succeeded by sir Brydges Powell Henniker, appointed, Jan. 1880; retires, succeeded by Mr. Reginald Macleod . . . Feb. 1900

To the registrar-general's annual reports, supplements and decennial volumes are issued occasionally.

REGISTRATION OF VOTERS was enacted by the Reform act, passed 7 June, 1832, and by acts passed in 1868 and 1885; see *Revising Barristers.*

New Parliamentary and Municipal Registration act passed . . . . 22 July, 1878

New bill, second reading, 26 Apr.; withdrawn, Sept. 1893

Registration Acceleration act passed . 31 July, 1894

REGIUM DONUM (Royal gift), an allowance from the sovereign for the maintenance of the Presbyterian ministers in Ireland, commenced by Charles II. in 1672, and revived by William III. in 1690, was commuted by the Irish Presbyterian Church act passed June, 1871. The allowance to certain protestant dissenting ministers in Ireland was given up by them in 1857, in deference to the wishes of English dissenters.

REGULATION OF PUBLIC WORSHIP, see *Public Worship*.

REGULATION OF THE FORCES ACT passed 17 Aug. 1871. See *Army*.

REICHENBACH (Prussia). Here Duroc was killed during the conflicts between the French and the allies, 22 May, 1813; see *Bautzen*. Here was signed a subsidy treaty between Russia, Prussia, and England, whereby the last engaged to provide means for carrying on the war against Napoleon I. on certain conditions, 14, 15 June, 1813. Austria joined the alliance soon after.

REICHSRATH, the representative council of the empire of Austria, reconstituted by decree 5 March; met on 31 May, 1860. In May, 1861, the upper house consisted of 17 spiritual, 55 hereditary, and 39 peers. The lower house consisted of 136 elected deputies. No representatives came from Hungary, Transylvania, Venetia, the Banat, Slavonia, Croatia, and Istria. The Reichsrath was abolished by a rescript, 21 Sept. 1865, with the view of restoring autonomy to Hungary and other provinces. It again met 20 May, 1867. The Reichstag of Germany, the imperial parliament or diet, first met at Berlin, 21 Mar. 1871.

REIGATE (Surrey), sent two members to parliament in the reign of Edward I.; lost one by the Reform Act of 1832, and was wholly disfranchised for corruption by that of 1867. Population, 1881, 18,662; 1891, 22,646; 1901, 25,993.

REIGN OF TERROR. Maximilien Robespierre headed the populace in the Champ de Mars in Paris, demanding the dethronement of the king, 17 July, 1791. He was triumphant in 1793, and numbers of eminent men and citizens were sacrificed during his sanguinary administration. Billaud Varennes denounced the tyranny of Robespierre in the tribune, 27 July, 1794. The next day he suffered death, with many of his companions; see *France*. This has been termed the *Red* Terror. The reaction after the restoration of the Bourbons,

1815, disgraced by many atrocious acts of wanton cruelty, has been termed the *White* Terror. The Jesuits were then conspicuous in the destruction of their adversaries.

REIGNS OF SOVEREIGNS. The average duration, according to Newton, is 19 years each; according to Hales 22½ years; that of the sovereigns of England being 23½ years, and that of the popes, 7½ years. Pius IX. was the first pope who reigned above 25 years, 1846-78.

RELICS, the trade in these became general in the 7th century, fragments of bones, &c. being brought from Jerusalem. The sale of relics was prohibited by pope Innocent III. 1198, without effect.

RELIEF CHURCH, a secession from the church of Scotland, founded by Thomas Gillespie, who was deposed from his ministry for opposing the doctrine of passive obedience to the law of the church of Scotland respecting the settlement of ministers, 23 May, 1752. The church was constituted as the "presbytery of relief," 22 Oct. 1761. The Relief and Secession churches were united as the United Presbyterian Church, 13 May, 1847.

RELIEF OF DISTRESS (IRELAND) ACT, 43 & 44 Vict. c. 14, passed 2 Aug. 1880. See *Ireland, Dec.* 1890. Society for the relief of distress founded, 1860.

RELIGION (from *religo*, I bind again, in the sense of a vow or oath) comprehends a belief in the being and perfections of God, and obedience to his commandments. The Jewish religion is set forth in the Old, and the Christian religion in the New, Testament. Departure from these scriptures has been the origin of all corrupt forms of religion, as foretold in them. Buddhism differs from this. See *Mahometanism*, and other religions and sects under their names. The population of the globe with reference to religious worship, is given by Balbi (who assumed the total population to be 1,050,000,000), and Dieterici (who assumed it to be 1,288,000,000), as follows: A gallery of religions at the British museum, Bloomsbury, opened 19 Feb. 1894.

	Balbi (1836).	*Dieterici* (1859)
Jews	4,500,000	5,000,000
Christians	225,000,000	335,000,000
Roman Catholics	160,000,000	170,000,000
Mahometans	155,000,000	160,000,000
Idolators, &c. not professing the Jewish, Christian, or Mahometan worship	665,500,000	800,000,000

Estimate in 1869: 1,375,000,000.

Roman Catholics	195,460,200
Protestants	100,385,000
Eastern church	81,478,000
Buddhists	360,000,000
Other Asiatic religions	260,000,000
Pagans	200,000,000
Mahometans	165,000,000
Jews	7,000,000

In Europe (estimated) 1869 (*Almanach de Gotha*).

Roman Catholics	144,000,000
Protestants	68,500,000
Greek Church	68,000,000
Jews	4,400,000
Mahometans	6,642,000

RELIGION OF HUMANITY, see *Positive Philosophy* and *Secularism.*

RELIGIOUS TRACT SOCIETY, founded 1799; receipts (1887), including sales, &c., 203,446*l.* Centenary meeting in Exeter-hall, 5 May, 1899; centenary fund, total, 51,490*l.*, 20 April, 1900; receipts, 1902, 20,975*l.* Literature in 230 languages and dialects published. *Religious instruction* in board schools, see *Education*, 1870-94, and 7 Aug. 1902.

REMISSION OF PENALTIES ACT, see *Sunday.*

REMONSTRANCE, THE GRAND, drawn up by the house of commons, and presented to king Charles I., 1 Dec. 1641. It consisted of 206 articles, dwelt bitterly on all the king's illegal and oppressive acts, and was printed by order of the house.

REMONSTRANTS, see *Arminians.*

RENAISSANCE, a term applied to the revival of the study of classic literature and art in the 15th and 16th centuries, under the patronage of the Medici and others; see *Painters*, and *Sculptors*. Mr. John A. Symonds' "History of the Renaissance in Italy," with supplements, 7 vols., published 1875-86. He was born 1840 and died 19 April, 1893. "The Renaissance," vol. i. of the Cambridge Modern History, published Jan. 1903.

RENDSBURG (Holstein), was taken by the imperialists in 1627; by the Swedes in 1643; and by the Prussians and confederate troops in 1848. The first diet of Schleswig and Holstein met here 3 April, 1848. It was re-occupied by the Danes in 1852, and taken by the Prussians after a serious conflict, 21 July, 1864.

RENNES (capital of Brittany, N. W. France). Here was established by Henry II., in 1553, the parliament so celebrated for its independence, especially in its struggle with the court, 1788-89. On 20 May, 1788, it declared infamous every one who should take part in the *cour plenière* then proposed, but afterwards suppressed. Population in 1901, 74,006.

RENTS said to have been first made payable in money, instead of in kind, about 1135. Numerous statutes have been enacted in various reigns to define the relations and regulate the dealings between landlord and tenant. 8 & 9 Vict. c. 106 (1845) regulates leases. By the act 8 Anne, 1709, no goods are removable from tenements under an execution until the rent shall have been paid to the landlord by the sheriff, 1709. The rental of England, including land, houses, and mines, was 6,000,000*l.* about the year 1600, and twelve years' purchase the value of land. About 1690, the rental amounted to 14,000,000*l.*, and the land was worth eighteen years' purchase. *Davenant on the Revenues.* The rental of the United Kingdom was estimated during the nineteenth century at 127,000,000*l.*; Great anti-rent agitation in Ireland, 1879, *et seq.*; see *Land, Ireland*, and *Irish Land Act*, 1903.

REPEAL OF THE UNION, IRELAND. An Irish association was formed with this object under the auspices of Mr. O'Connell, in 1829. See *Home Rule* and *Ireland.*

A proclamation of the lord lieutenant prohibited the meetings of a society "leagued for the purpose of procuring a repeal of the union, under the name of the Irish Society for Legal and Legislative Relief, or the Anti-Union Society" . 18 Oct. 1830

The commons, by a majority of 484, reject Mr. O'Connell's motion for repeal . 27 April, 1834

A new association in 1841, 1842, and 1843 became more violent. Assemblies of the lower classes of the people were held in the last-named year, in various parts of Ireland, some of them amounting to 150,000 persons, and called "monster meetings."

A great meeting at Trim, 16 March; other meetings were held at Mullingar, Cork, and Longford, on 14, 21, and 28 May, respectively; at Drogheda, Kilkenny, Mallow, and Dundalk, on 5, 8, 11, and 29 June; at Donnybrook and Baltinglass, 3 and 20 July; at Tara, 15 Aug.; at Loughrea, Clifton, and Lismore, 10, 17, and 24 Sept.; and at Mullaghmast . . . . 1 Oct. 1843

A meeting to be held at Clontarf, on 8 Oct. was prevented by government; and Mr. O'Connell and his chief associates were brought to trial for political conspiracy, 15 Jan. 1844; and convicted 12 Feb.; but the sentence was reversed by the house of lords, 4 Sept.; see *Trials*.

The association for the repeal of the union continued for some time under the direction of Mr. John O'Connell, but was little regarded.

The total "repeal rent" is said to have amounted to 134,379*l*.

A fruitless attempt was made in Dublin to revive repeal agitation . . . . . . 4 Dec. 1860

REPLENISHER, see *Electricity* (*Frictional*).

REPORTING. The publication of the debates in parliament is forbidden as a breach of privilege, but was virtually conceded, after a severe struggle, in 1771.* Reporters' galleries were erected in the houses of parliament after the fire of 1834. To the unfettered liberty of reporting we doubtless owe much of our freedom and good government; see under *Law*. By the verdict for the defendant in the case of Wason *v. The Times* (for libel) reports of parliamentary debates were decided to be privileged, Nov. 1868. For the attempted exclusion of reporters, see *Parliament*, 1875. A commons committee on reporting recommend continuance of Hansard's debates with improvement, May, 1879.

The publication of Hansard's parliamentary debates began 1803 and closed in 1888. Latterly a subsidy was granted. The publication of the debates was taken up by Messrs. Macrae, Curtice & Co., Feb. 1889; and continued by the Hansard Publishing Union, limited, 1889; the Union ordered to be wound up, 13 May. See *Trials*, 1892-93.

Mr. Thomas Curson Hansard, formerly editor of the "debates," aged 78, dies . . . 12 Nov. 1891

Government contract with Reuter's Telegram company for printing and publishing reports of parliamentary debates, &c., 21 Dec. 1891; published 26 Feb. 1892

The contract accepted for 1893 by Messrs. Eyre & Spottiswoode.

A select committee of the commons on parliamentary reporting, sir J. T. Hibbert chairman, met 10 April, 1893

Tenders invited for three schemes of reporting, about 20 Dec. ,,

Tender accepted for 1895, by Waterlow, Sons & Co. Jan. 1895

* Very inaccurate reports of parliamentary debates were inserted in the *Gentleman's Magazine* and other periodicals in the middle of the last century. Miller, printer of the *London Evening Mail*, was arrested in the city of London, by order of the house of commons, for publishing the debates, but was discharged by the lord mayor, who for doing this was sent to the Tower, where he remained until the end of the session. No opposition was made to the publication of the debates in the next session, 1772.

REPRESENTATION OF THE PEOPLE ACT FOR ENGLAND, passed 15 Aug. 1867; for Ireland and Scotland, 13 July, 1868; a new act passed, 6 Dec. 1884. See *Reform*.

The *Representative*, a daily Tory paper, was started by Mr. John Murray, the bookseller, in opposition to the *Times*, in 1826. Although he was assisted by Mr. Benjamin Disraeli and other eminent persons, the project was unsuccessful; the first number appeared 25 Jan., the last . 29 July, 1826

"REPTILE BUREAUCRACY," term applied in Germany to certain journalists writing for government pay, 1871, *et seq*.

REPUBLICANS, see *Democrats*. The name adopted by the Northern party in the United States, N.A., opposed to the democrats in the South. It is stated that the first delegate-nominating convention in the United States that adopted the name Republican party, was held in Strong, Franklin county, Maine, 7 Aug. 1854. Sir Charles Dilke, M.P. professed himself a republican at public meetings and was much applauded, Nov. 1871; but at some places his appearance led to riotous proceedings. His motion for returns respecting the expenditure of the civil list by the queen was negatived in the house of commons (2—276), 19 March, 1872. A national republican conference of delegates was held at Sheffield, 1 Dec. 1872, when a national flag was adopted.

REPUBLICS, see *Athens*, *Rome*, *Genoa*, *Venice*, *France* (1792, 1848, 1870), *Spain* (1873), *Brazil* (1889), *Panama* (1903), and *America*.

REQUESTS, COURTS OF; see *Conscience*.

REQUIEM, a solemn mass, sung for the dead, so called from the introit "Requiem Æternam," &c. Palestrina's Requiem was printed at Rome, 1591; Vittoria's at Madrid, 1605; Mozart's last work was a requiem, 1791.

REREDOS, the screen or decorated portion of the wall behind the altar in a church.

A highly sculptured reredos, designed by sir G. G. Scott, was erected in Exeter cathedral, by subscription 1873

Prebendary Philpotts, the chancellor, and others who objected, brought their objections before the bishop's visitation court, on 7 Jan.; it was decided that the bishop had jurisdiction in the matter, and he ordered the reredos to be removed, 15 April, 1874. Dean Boyd appealed to the court of arches, and sir R. Phillimore reversed the previous decision . . . . 6 Aug. 1874

Prebendary Philpotts appealed to the judicial committee of the privy council, who decided that the reredos should remain . . . . 24 Feb. 1875

The magnificent reredos set up in St. Paul's Cathedral, London, was protested against as idolatrous by some of the London clergy, April, 1888. An action against the dean having been stopped by the bishop, the queen's bench division ordered the bishop to withdraw his veto upon the prosecution, 1 June, 1889. After further litigation, the house of lords sustained the bishop's veto . . . . 20 July, 1891

RESERVE FORCES. In the summer of 1859, acts were passed to provide for the establishment of a military reserve force of men who have been in her majesty's service (not to exceed 20,000), and a volunteer reserve force of seamen not to exceed 30,000. These acts were consolidated and amended in 1867, 1882 and 1896. The reserve forces called out by proclamation, on account of possible war with Russia,

2 April, 1878. About 35,000 good soldiers appeared, and were commended. They were disbanded 31 Aug. 1878. Again called out on account of war in Egypt, 25 July, 1882, and prospect of war with Russia, 27 March, 1885. Average of army reserve: 1888, 55,068; 1890, 56,082; 1893, 76,874; 1896, 78,057; 1898, 80,000. Important changes to be made to meet exigencies during war time, act passed, 1 July, 1898.

RESOLUTE, ship, see *Franklin Search*, 1854.

RESONATOR, a small apparatus, placed in the mouth to strengthen and increase the volume of the voice in singing, invented by signor Alberto Bach, who exhibited its effects at the Royal Academy of Music, 29 June, 1880.

RESPIRATORS, see *Charcoal* and *Fireman*.

RESTITUTION BILL, of Mr. Jesse Collings, proposes the surrender of lands illegally taken from commons, to be given to small cultivators, to become peasant proprietors, Jan. 1885.

RESTORATION, THE, of king Charles II. to the crown of England, after an interregnum of eleven years and four months, between 30 Jan. 1649, when Charles I. was beheaded, and 29 May, 1660, when Charles II. entered London amidst the acclamations of the people. The annual form of prayer, with thanksgiving, then appointed, was ordered to be disused by 22 Vict. c. 2, 25 March, 1849. See *France*, 1814, 1815.

RESTORATION CAMPAIGN, see *Zionists*.

RETREAT OF THE TEN THOUSAND GREEKS, who had joined the army of the younger Cyrus in his revolt against his brother, Artaxerxes Mnemon. The Greeks were victors, but Cyrus was defeated and slain at the battle of Cunaxa, 401 B.C. Artaxerxes having enticed the Greek leaders into his power and killed them, Xenophon was called to the command of his countrymen. Under continual alarms from sudden attacks, he led them across rapid rivers, through vast deserts, over the tops of mountains, till he reached the sea. The Greeks returned home after a march of 1155 parasangs or leagues (3465 miles), which was performed in 215 days, after the absence of fifteen months. This retreat has been immortalised by the account given by its conductor, in his "Anabasis Cyri" (Expedition of Cyrus).

REUNION, see *Evangelical Order*.

RÉUNION, isle of, see *Bourbon*.

REUSS-GREIZ AND REUSS-SCHLEIZ, two principalities in central Germany, with a united population of 166,502 in 1885; in 1890, 182,565; 1900, 208,000. The reigning family sprang from Ekbert, count of Osterode, in the 10th century. The princely dignity was conferred by the emperor Sigismond in 1426.

1859. Henry XXII., prince of Reuss-Greiz, 8 Nov.; born 28 March, 1846; married princess Ida of Schaumburg-Lippe in 1872; she died in 1891; son, Henry XXIV., *insane*, born 20 March, 1878.

REUTER'S INTERNATIONAL TELEGRAPHIC NEWS AGENCY, founded by baron Paul Julius de Reuter, born 1816, died 25 Feb. 1899. First line between Aix-la-Chapelle and Berlin, in 1849; chief office in London in 1851; cables laid between England and Germany and between France and United States, 1865 *et seq.* The agency was converted into a limited liability company in 1875.

REVELATION, see *Apocalypse*.

REVENUE AND EXPENDITURE OF ENGLAND. The revenue collected for the civil list, and for all the other charges of government, as well ordinary as extraordinary, was 1,200,000*l.* per annum, in 1660, the first after the restoration of Charles II. In 1690 it was raised to 6,000,000*l.*, every branch of the revenue being anticipated; this was the origin of the funds and the national debt, 2 William and Mary. *Salmon.* The revenue laws were amended in 1861. Previously to 1854 there had been an average *surplus* of 2,500,000*l.* since 1849. In consequence of the Russian war the *deficiency* in 1854 was 3,209,059*l.*; in 1855, 21,141,183*l.*; in 1856, 10,104,412*l.* In 1857 there was a *surplus* of 36,097*l.*; in 1858, of 1,127,657*l.*; in 1859, a *deficiency* of 2,019,584*l.*; in April, 1901, the deficit, owing to the S. African war, was 55,357,000*l.*; in April, 1902, it was about 23,924,000*l.*; see *Statistical Abstract.*

PUBLIC REVENUE.

William I. estimated	£400,000
William Rufus	350,000
Henry I.	300,000
Stephen	250,000
Henry II.	200,000
Richard I.	150,000
John	100,000
Henry III.	80,000
Edward I.	150,000
Edward II.	100,000
Edward III.	154,000
Richard II.	130,000
Henry IV.	100,000
Henry V.	76,643
Henry VI.	64,976
Edward IV.	* * *
Edward V.	100,000
Richard III.	130,000
Henry VII.	400,000
Henry VIII.	800,000
Edward VI.	400,000
Mary	450,000
Elizabeth	500,000
James I.	600,000
Charles I.	895,819
Commonwealth	1,517,247
Charles II.	1,400,000
James II.	2,001,855
William III.	3,895,205
Anne (at the Union)	5,691,803
George I.	6,762,643
George II.	8,522,540
George III., 1788	15,572,971
,, 1800, about	38,000,000
United Kingdom, 1820	65,599,570
George IV., 1825	62,871,300
William IV., 1830	55,431,317
,, 1835	50,494,732
Victoria, 1845, *net*	53,060,354
,, 1850	52,810,680
,, 1853	54,430,344

	Revenue.	Expenditure.
1855, *net*	£63,364,605	£65,692,962
1856	68,008,623	88,428,345
1857	66,056,055	75,588,667
1858	61,812,525	68,128,859

	Gross Revenue (Estimated).	Gross Expenditure, exclusive of Fortifications (Estimated).
1859, 31 March, *gross*	£65,477,284	£64,663,883
1860	72,089,669	69,502,289
1863	70,603,561	69,302,008
1864	70,208,964	67,056,286
1865	70,313,437	66,462,207
1866	67,812,292	65,914,357
1867	69,434,568	66,780,396
1868	69,600,219	71,236,242
1869	72,591,991	72,069,961
1870	75,454,252	68,864,752
1871	69,945,220	69,548,539
1872	74,708,314	71,490,020
1873	76,608,770	70,714,448
1874	77,335,657	76,466,510
1875	75,434,252	74,328,040
1876	77,131,693	76,621,773
1877	78,565,036	78,125,227
1878	79,763,298	82,403,495
1879	83,115,972	85,407,789
1880	81,265,055	84,105,754
1881	84,041,288	83,107,924
1882	85,822,282	85,472,556
1883	89,004,456	88,906,278
1884	87,205,184	86,999,564
1885	88,043,660	89,092,883
Vote of Credit, 27 April, 1885 . .		11,000,000
1886*	89,581,301	92,223,844
1887	90,772,758	89,996,752
1888	89,802,254	87,423,645
1889	88,472,812	87,683,830
1890	89,304,316	86,083,314
1891	89,489,112	87,732,855
1892	90,994,786	89,927,773
1893	90,395,377	90,375,365
1894	91,133,410	91,302,846
1895	94,683,762	93,918,421
1896	101,973,829	97,764,357
1897	103,949,885	101,476,669
1898	106,614,004	102,935,994
1899	108,336,193	108,150,236
1900	119,839,905	133,722,407
1901 (Edward VII.)	130,384.684	183,592,264
1902	152,601,637	195,522,214
1903	154,770,000	144,331,000

* Revised in relation to army, navy, and India.

The weekly instead of the quarterly publication of the public revenue and expenditure was begun by Mr. Robert Lowe, the chancellor of the exchequer, 16 Feb. 1870.

By an act passed 31 July, 1868, revenue officers are permitted to vote for the election of members of parliament.

Above 100 statutes relating to inland revenue fell into disuse 1 Jan. 1871.

The revenue friendly societies, and national debt act, 45 & 46 Vict., c. 72, passed 18 Aug. 1882. New revenue act passed, 1884.

REVEREND, an honorary appellation given to the clergy, since the middle of the 17th century.

In Tamworth parish register the minister is first styled "reverend," in 1657, occasionally afterwards; but regularly so after 1727. It first appears in the registry of All Hallows, Barking . 1732

The prefix on a family tombstone was refused to Mr. Keet, a Wesleyan preacher, by the bishop of Lincoln, but given by the archbishop of Canterbury 1874

On trial, Mr. Walter G. F. Phillimore, the chancellor of Lincoln, decided against Mr. Keet, who gave notice of appeal, 3 June. Sir R. Phillimore gave a similar decision in the court of arches, 31 July, 1875

On appeal to the privy council these decisions were reversed. It was decided that there is no law or usage restricting the epithet to ministers of the Church of England; it is merely laudatory. 21 Jan. 1876

REVIEWS. The *Journal des Scavans*, published on 5 Jan. 1665, by Denis de Salo, under the name of Hédouville, was the parent of critical journals. It was soon imitated throughout Europe, and was itself translated into various languages.* It is still published. George III. spoke of this publication to Dr. Johnson, in the private interview with which he was honoured by his majesty, in the library of the queen's house, in Feb. 1767. *Boswell.* The *Bibliothèque Anglaise* came out in 1716-27; the *Revue Britannique*, founded 1825, ceased Dec. 1901. For Military REVIEWS, see *Aldershot, Army*, and *Volunteers*. For Naval REVIEWS, see *Navy*.

Monthly Review . .	1749	Nineteenth Century .	1877
Critical . . .	1756	National Review .	1883
Anti-Jacobin . . .	1798	Law Quarterly .	1885
Edinburgh . . .	1802	English Historical Review. . . .	1886
Quarterly . . .	1809	Universal Review	1888–90
Eclectic . . .	1813	"New Review" .	1889
North American . .	1815	Paternoster Review .	1890
Retrospective . .	1820	Albemarle Review .	1891
Westminster . . .	1824	Progressive Review .	1896
Athenæum . . .	1828	Anglo-Saxon Review (quarterly), edited by lady Randolph Churchill, Vol. 1. June,	1899
Dublin . . .	1836	Empire Review .	1901
North British . .	1844	King and Country .	1902
British Quarterly . .	,,	New Liberal Review,	1903
National . . .	1855		
Saturday . . .	1855		
Fortnightly . . .	1865		
Contemporary . .	1866		
Academy . . .	1869		
Church Quarterly .	1875		

REVISERS, see under *Bible*.

REVISING BARRISTERS' COURTS, to examine the lists of voters for members of parliament, were instituted by the Reform Act of 1832.

REVISION, see under *Bible*. Advocates of the revision of the French constitution, chiefly Bonapartists or Jeromists, termed *Revisionists*, Feb. 1884.

REVIVALS on the subject of religion arose in the United States in 1857. In the autumn of 1859, they began in Scotland, the north of Ireland (particularly Belfast), and England. Many meetings were held for prayers and preaching throughout the week, as well as on Sundays. The "*twelve days' mission*," a series of revival services, took place in many London churches during advent, 1869.

Mr. Moody, preacher (born 1837, died 22 Dec. 1899), and Mr. Sankey, singer, American Revivalists, visited many towns in the United Kingdom, 1874-5. Their meetings in London began at the Agricultural-hall, 9 March, about 15,000 present; at the Queen's theatre, Haymarket, 12 April–31 May; farewell meeting, 12 July, 1875. Moody and Sankey again in London, 6 Oct. 1881; 3 Nov. 1883–23 June, 1884. See *Salvation Army*.

☛**REVOLUTIONARY CALENDAR,** see *French Revolution*, and *Calendar*.

REVOLUTIONARY TRIBUNAL, established at Paris, Aug. 1792.

Up to 27 July, 1794, when Robespierre was deposed, it had put to death 2774 persons, including queen Marie Antoinette, the princess Elizabeth, and a large number of nobility and gentry, male and female. The oldest victim was counsellor Dupin, aged 97; the youngest, Charles Dubost, aged 14. From 27 July to 15 Dec. 1794, only Robespierre and his accomplices (about 100) suffered by it.

REVOLUTIONS:—

The Assyrian empire destroyed, and that of the Medes and Persians founded by Cyrus the Great, B.C. 536

The Macedonian empire founded on the destruction of the Persian, by the defeat of Darius Codomanus, by Alexander the Great 331

The Roman empire established on the ruins of the republic by Julius Cæsar 47

The empire of the Western Franks begun under Charlemagne	A.D. 800
In Portugal	1640
In England	1649 and 1688
In Russia	1730 and 1762
In North America	1775
In Venice	1797
In Sweden	1772 and 1809
In Holland, 1795; counter-revolution	1813
In Poland	1704, 1795, and 1830
In the Netherlands	,,
In Brunswick	,,
In Brazil	1831
In Hungary	1848
In Rome	1798 and ,,
In France	1789, 1830, 1848, 1851, 1870, and 1871
In Italy	1859 and 1860
In United States	1860-5
In Danubian principalities	1866
In Papal States, suppressed	Oct. 1867
In Spain	Sept. 1868 and Dec. 1874
In Brazil	15 Nov. 1889
In Chili	Jan.—Sept. 1891
In Servia	11 June, 1903
In Colombia, new republic of Panama declared	3 Nov. ,,

Revolutions have been frequent in the South American republics.

[See the countries respectively.]

Among the results of the *Revolution* of 1688 in Great Britain, were the toleration act, the establishment of the presbyterian kirk of Scotland, the power of granting supplies limited to the house of commons, the purification of the administration of justice, and unlicensed printing.

REVOLVERS, see *Pistols*.

REVUE DES DEUX MONDES, the French literary and historical periodical published on the 1st and 15th of each month, first appeared in 1831. It includes among its contributors the most eminent writers in France.

REYNARD THE FOX, "REINEKE FUCHS," a satirical epic in low German, in which beasts are actors and speakers, was first printed as Reineke Vos, at Lubeck in 1498, and professes to be written by Hinreck van Alkmer. It has been frequently translated. Goethe's version in High (or literary) German hexameters appeared in 1794. Jacob Grimm has shown that the subject-matter of this "Thier-sage" or "beast-fable" is very ancient, many incidents being found in Pilpay and other oriental writers. The early French had a "Roman de Renart," and "Renart le Nouvel." A poem, entitled "der Reinaert," in Flemish, was known in the 11th century; Caxton's translation in English prose was printed 1481; a poetic English translation of Goethe's version, by T. J. Arnold, appeared in 1855.

REZONVILLE, BATTLE OF, 18 Aug. 1870, see *Metz*.

RHÆTIA (or RÆTIA), an ancient Alpine country, comprising the modern Grisons, Tyrol, and part of Lombardy, inhabited by a wild rapacious people, after a long struggle was conquered by Drusus and Tiberius, B.C. 15.

RHÉ, ISLE OF, see *Ré* and *Rochelle*.

RHEA, see *China Grass*.

RHEGIUM (now Reggio), S. Italy, a Greek colony, flourished in the 5th century, B.C. It was held by the Campanian legion, 281-271, afterwards severely punished for its rebellion. Reggio was taken by Garibaldi, Aug 1860.

RHEIMS (N. France). The principal church here, built before 406, rebuilt in the 12th century, is now very beautiful. The corpse of St. Remy, the archbishop, is preserved behind the high altar, in a magnificent shrine. The kings of France were crowned at Rheims; probably because Clovis, the founder of the French monarchy, when converted from paganism, was baptized in the cathedral in 496. Several ecclesiastical councils have been held here. The city was taken and retaken several times in the last months of the French war, 1814. University founded by cardinal Lorraine, 1547, suppressed about 1790. Strike of the workmen of Mr. Jonathan Holden, mill owner, a great benefactor to the town, May, 1890. Population, 1891, 104,186; 1901, 107,773.

RHEOMETER, see under *Electricity*.

RHETORIC. Rhetorical points and accents were invented by Aristophanes of Byzantium, 200 B.C. Rhetoric was first taught in Latin at Rome by Photius Gallus, about 87 B.C. He taught Cicero, who said "We are first to consider what is to be said; secondly, how; thirdly, in what words; and lastly, how it is to be ornamented." A regius professor of rhetoric was appointed in Edinburgh, 20 April, 1762, when Dr. Blair became first professor.

RHINE (Latin, *Rhenus*; German, *Rhein*; French, *Rhin*), a river, about 760 miles long, rising in Switzerland, receiving the Moselle, Main, Meuse, Neckar, and other rivers, terminating in many arms in Holland, and falling into the German ocean. On its banks are Constance, Basel, Strasbourg, Spires, Mannheim, Cologne, Düsseldorf, Utrecht, and Leyden. The possession of the banks of the Rhine has been the cause of many wars, and it has been crossed by the French above twenty times in a century. In the beginning of the revolutionary war, Custine invaded Germany by crossing it in 1792; and at the close of the war in 1815, France retained the left bank, but lost it at the close of the Franco-Prussian war, 1870-1 (*which see*). A navigation treaty with other powers was signed by France, 17 Oct. 1868. A central committee for the navigation exists, formed by members for Alsace, Lorraine, Baden, Bavaria, Hesse, Holland, and Prussia. Very great damage (about 4,000,000*l.*) and loss of life, caused by the rising of the river through excessive rain, end of November and December, 1882; relieved by government grants.

Becker's German song "They shall not have it, the free German Rhine;" and Alfred de Musset's reply, in French, "We have had it, your German Rhine," appeared in 1841. Max Schneckenburger, author of "The Watch on the Rhine," died 1851. All were popular during the war, 1870-71.

RHINOPLASTY, an operation performed by dissecting a flap of skin from the forehead and placing it over the nose.

RHODE ISLAND (N. America), settled by Roger Williams about 1636, was taken in the war of independence by the British, 8 Dec. 1776; but was evacuated by them, 25 Oct. 1779. Capitals, Providence and Newport. Population in 1880, 276,531; 1890, 345,506; 1900, 428,556; see *United States*.

RHODES, an island on the coast of Asia Minor, is said to have been peopled from Crete, as early as 916 B.C. The Rhodians were great navigators, and institutors of a maritime code afterwards adopted by the Romans. The city was built about 408 and flourished 300-200 B.C.; see *Colossus*. Rhodes, long an ally of the Romans, was taken by the emperor Vespasian, A.D. 71. It was held by the Knights Hospitallers from 1309 to 1522, when it was conquered by the Turks, who still retain it. The knights retired to Malta (*which see*). Rhodes suffered severely by an earthquake on 22 April, 1863.

RHODESIA, the name given (1895) to the territories subject to the S. Africa company (after the rt. hon. Cecil Rhodes, "the great empire builder," born at Bishop's Stortford, 5 July, 1853; died 26 March, 1902), about 2,000 mi. long, and 1,000 mi. broad; chief towns, Bulawayo and Salisbury. See *Zambesi* and *Mashonaland*, 1894.

Mr. Cecil Rhodes after the troubles in the Transvaal, visits London, 4 Feb. 1896; returns to Salisbury, and devotes himself to the development of Rhodesia; appointed administrator in conjunction with Earl Grey . . . Feb. 1896

Revolt of the Matabele, joined by many of the native police in the Insega and Filibusi districts and Matoppo hills; massacre of 8 whites, including inspectors Bentley and Jackson; several families murdered at outlying stations March, ,,

Skirmish between Mr. Selous with 5 troopers and the Matabele . . . . 25 March, ,,

The hon. Maurice Gifford's force repulses large body of natives . . . . . 27 March, ,,

Commissioners Graham, Handley, and 6 others attacked and killed, after a desperate fight with 300 natives at Inyati . . . . 27 March, ,,

Salisbury, Bulawayo, and other places fortified; relief parties sent out, 29 March; Mr. M. Gifford returns to Bulawayo after relieving Shangani and defeating the natives; Mr. Cecil Rhodes and col. Plumer arrive at Salisbury . . 30 March, ,,

Capt. Macfarlane repulses the natives at Queen's Reef in the hills, and returns to Bulawayo, 31 March, ,,

Enrolment of volunteers at Bulawayo 31 March, ,,

Olimo, instigator of the rebellion, styles himself king of the Matabele . . . . 1 April, ,,

The hon. Maurice Gifford repulses a large body of rebels in the Shiloh district, 5 engagements in 4 days, Mr. Gifford severely wounded; British loss, 3, Matabele loss, about 200; Gifford's party relieved by capt. Macfarlane . 4–8 April, ,,

Frequent murders; desultory attacks repulsed, April, ,,

Capt Brand's patrol attacked by 1,500 rebels on the Tuli road; 5 British and 150 Matabele killed, 10 April, ,,

Mr. Duncan, acting-administrator at Bulawayo, establishes 7 forts in the Mangwe Pass with 400 men . . . . 14 April–2 May, ,,

Insurrection attributed to losses by the rinderpest and locusts . . . . 17 April, ,,

Natives severely defeated by Mr. Duncan and capt. Napier on the Umgusa river, 22 April; repulsed again, after a desperate fight, by capt. Macfarlane and Mr. Duncan, 500 killed . . . 25 April, ,,

Earl Grey (administrator) arrives at Bulawayo, 28 April, ,,

Mr. Cecil Rhodes and the Salisbury column repulse an attack, near Gwelo . . . . . 1 May, ,,

General parade at Bulawayo, earl Grey compliments Mr. Duncan and officers . . 3 May, ,,

The enemy repulsed in several skirmishes, 9–15 May, ,,

Rebels outed at Thabas Induna, by col. Napier, 14 May, ,,

Col. sir Richard Martin, deputy-commissioner, arrives with reinforcements, at Bulawayo, 15 May, ,,

More murders in different parts . . May, ,,

Rebels defeated near Bulawayo and near the Umgusa river, with great loss . 24, 25, 26 May, ,,

Mr. Rhodes warmly received at Bulawayo 1 June, ,,

Sir Fredk. Carrington arrives at Bulawayo, 2 June, ,,

Rebels defeated, with heavy loss, by col. Spreckley and lieut.-col. Beal's column on the Gwelo road, 6 June; the Makalaka driven from the hills, by capt. Gibbs . . . . 9 June, ,,

Mr. Chamberlain reports to parliament, that Mr. Cecil Rhodes was managing director of S. Africa company without power over administrators, 11 June, ,,

Rebels in strong force on the Matoppos, more murders; Mazoe district in revolt 13–18 June, ,,

Martial law proclaimed at Salisbury, rising of the Mashonas . . . . 21 June, ,,

Escort from the Mazoe district attacked; Messrs. Blakiston and Routledge and 7 men killed, after a long fight, reported . . . . 22 June, 1896

Mr. Graham, native commissioner, and 3 others found murdered at Inyati; mission station at Ingwengwesi river destroyed; severe fighting with the Mashonas, on the Umfuli 22 June, ,,

Lieut. Bremner, the Meyers, and others murdered; the whole Ayrshire party killed on their way to Salisbury; M'Limo, the prophet, killed in the Matoppos; Fort Charter surrounded, 14 herd-boys killed, reported . . . 24 June, ,,

Resignation of the hon. Cecil J. Rhodes and Mr. Beit as directors (3 May), accepted by the company in London . . . . . . 26 June, ,,

The enemy surprised and defeated at Thabas-I-Mhamba, about 150 killed, 500 women and children, and much cattle, captured; British loss 8, and 2 mortally wounded . 5 July, ,,

Desultory fighting: kraals captured by major Hurrell . . . . 23–31 July, ,,

Rebel stronghold on Inyandi Mt. shelled 2 Aug. ,,

Capt. White relieves Hartley, after several fights; communication with Salisbury restored 4, 5 Aug. ,,

Matabele (5 impis) defeated by col. Plumer's force, at Secombo's stronghold in the Matoppos; heroic conduct of capt. Beresford's party, capt. Llewellyn, and the Cape "boys," under lieut. H. Howard; rebel loss, about 300; British, major F. Kershaw, lieut. H. F. Hervey, and 5 other officers killed . . . . . . 5 Aug. ,,

Col. Alderson captures Makoni's kraal; capt. Alfred E. Haynes and 3 troopers killed, rebel loss, 200; other kraals taken, and forts erected, 8 Aug. ,,

Terms of surrender proclaimed . . . 9 Aug. ,,

Select committee of the commons on the administration of the British S. Africa company and the "Jameson Raid": chairman, Mr. W. L. Jackson, sir Richard Webster, sir H. Campbell-Bannerman, Mr. Chamberlain, sir M. Hicks-Beach, sir Wm. Harcourt, Mr. Labouchere, and others, appointed, 11 Aug.; 1st meeting . 14 Aug. ,,

Capt. M'Callum murdered by Mashonas at Matelimi (25 June); 101 murders in Mashonaland up to . . . . 11 Aug. ,,

Marandella's kraal and others destroyed; W. B. Joliffe killed . . . . . . 19 Aug. ,,

Mr. Cecil Rhodes, Dr. Sauer, and Mr. J. Colenbrander unarmed, meet Secombo and other chiefs, who eventually surrender unconditionally, 21 Aug. ,,

Makoni, rebel chief, captured near Umtali by lieut. Richat, 4 Sept.; after several attempts to escape, tried by court martial, and shot, by order of major Watts, 7 Sept.; major Watts arrested, 9 Sept.; exonerated on inquiry, 30 Sept.

Major Ridley captures 2 chiefs and 60 natives, 12 Sept. ,,

Aweenya, rebel chief, convicted of atrocities, &c., shot . . . . 13 Sept. ,,

Major Tennant captures Simbanoatu, after much slaughter; 2 chiefs and 425 men surrender; major Jenner defeats Mtigeza (who surrenders) near Fort Charter, strongholds captured mid Sept. ,,

Gen. sir Frederick Carrington, Mr. Rhodes, and others hold an indaba with Babyan and other chiefs; terms accepted . . . . . 20 Sept. ,,

Judge Vintcent holds a meeting with the Mazoe chiefs, terms agreed to . . . . 21 Sept. ,,

Serious fighting on the Mazoe river 26–28 Sept. ,,

Mazoe, and other districts, cleared of rebels, 30 Sept. ,,

Explosion of a dynamite magazine at Bulawayo, B. W. Downes, W. Cooper, and 8 Kaffirs killed, 2 Oct. ,,

Desultory fighting, kraals captured, lieut. H. G. Morris and W. A. Smith, killed . . Oct. ,,

Earl Grey, Mr. Rhodes, and others hold a final meeting with chiefs in the Matoppos, peaceful settlement . . . . 13 Oct. ,,

Major Alderson takes Chena's kraal, after a hot fight; 180 natives surrender in the Somnabula forest to capt. Robinson and Mr. Driver, mid Oct. ,,

Gatze's kraal taken, major F. S. Evans, capt. Edw. Finucane, and trooper Earnshaw killed, 19, 22 Oct. ,,

Lieut.-col. Baden-Powell captures 8 kraals, 16, 28 Oct.; Dango's burnt, after a fight . . 30 Oct. 1896

Meeting of the British S. Africa company in London; the capital over a million, in hand (Feb. 1895), exhausted; issue of 500,000 *2l.* shares authorized . . . . . 6 Nov. ,,

Col. Paget disperses rebels on the Thaba Insimba hills, and returns to Gwelo . . 20 Nov. ,,

Much heroism shown during the war, by the settlers and troops; troops disbanded . 12 Dec. ,,

Mr. Cecil Rhodes warmly received at Port Elizabeth and Cape Town, 24, 30 Dec.; in London, 23 Jan. 1897.

Change of government announced to 85 Matabele chiefs by the hon. A. Lawley in the name of lord Grey, at Bulawayo; 12 districts to be under responsible paid chiefs and native commissioners, 5 Jan. 1897

Major Gosling captures Seka's kraal on his refusing to surrender his guns . . . . mid Jan. ,,

[The select committee of inquiry of the commons on the Transvaal Raid (14 Aug. 1896), re-appointed, 30 Jan. 1897; evidence of Mr. Cecil Rhodes, 16 Feb.–5 March, also of sir Graham Bower and Mr. Wm. P. Schreiner, 12, 26 March; Dr. Jameson, 26 March; col. Frank Rhodes, 29 March; sir John Willoughby, 2 April, he declined to answer certain questions, 6 April; Dr. Jameson recalled, explanations given by him and sir John Willoughby, 9 April; Dr. Harris, 30 April; the duke of Abercorn and the duke of Fife expressed their total ignorance of any raid, 12 May; Mr. Chas. Leonard, 14 May; Miss Flora Shaw, correspondent of the *Times*, 25 May (again 2 July); Mr. Chamberlain, 1 June; lord Selborne, 4 June. Report presented to parliament, 15 July. Conclusions: Discontent in Johannesburg previous to raid owing to grievances of the Uitlanders, Mr. Cecil Rhodes involved in grave breaches of duty, in his course of action. The imperial and colonial governments, the directors of the S. Africa company, with the exception of Mr. Beit and Mr. Maguire, exonerated from complicity in the raid. Mr. P. Stanhope's vote of censure on the report of the committee on Mr. Rhodes, and on the Chartered company, rejected in the commons, 304—77, 26 July, 1897.]

Many kraals captured, after much fighting, and native loss . . . . Feb. ,,

The Prospectors' association repudiate the reports of the pacification of the country, and appeal for imperial aid . . . . 23 April, ,,

Marandella's kraals captured, after a hard fight, 23–26 May, ,,

Mr. Cecil Rhodes returns to Bulawayo, 18 June; holds an indaba of Matabele chiefs, 23 June; lord Grey arrives . . . . . . 28 June, ,,

Medals granted to officers and men engaged in the war, from 24 March—31 Dec. 1896 . . 6 July, ,,

Severe fighting on the Unyami, 7, 10 July; 600 rebels and 40 guns captured, 111 rebels surrender, 13 July; desultory fighting near Fort Charter, district cleared, 3 British killed, 15 July; sir Richard Martin assumes command, 20 July; a kraal taken, 4 British killed; 600 prisoners liberated and located in Cherimba . . . 24 July, ,,

Dr. Jameson welcomed at Bulawayo, and Fort Salisbury . . . . 22, 24 July, ,,

Surrender of all the Mashona chiefs, reported, 29 Oct. ,,

Railway from Kimberley to Bulawayo projected by Mr. Cecil Rhodes, opened by sir A. Milner at Bulawayo . . . . 4 Nov. ,,

Col. Rivett Carnac appointed deputy-commissioner during the absence of sir R. Martin . 4 Jan. 1898

Mr. Chamberlain's scheme for the reconstitution of the S. Africa company, increasing government control, &c. issued; *Times* . . . 25 Feb. ,,

Escape of 51 native prisoners from the gaol at Salisbury . . . . 25 Feb. ,,

British S. Africa co.'s 2 yrs. report, ended 31 March, 1897, 360,000*l.* compensation to settlers for losses during the native rising; surplus over expenditure, 59,650*l.* for 1895–6; expenditure during the rebellion, 2,266,976*l.*, *Times*, 14 April, 1898; increase of capital, 1,500,000*l.*; Mr. Rhodes (arrived in London, 2 April), re-elected director, his scheme of administration approved, report adopted at a meeting, London . . 21 April, 1898

Meeting in London of the security holders of the Bechuanaland railway co., Mr. Cecil Rhodes in the chair; the railway from Vryburg to Bulawayo, 600 miles, cost 2,000,000*l.*; supplemental trust deed approved, 6 May; debate in the commons, defence of the Chartered company by Mr. Chamberlain . . . . 6 May, ,,

Growth of the gold industry and rapid development of the country, reported . . 25 Jan. 1899

Mr. Cecil Rhodes's negotiations in Berlin *re* the Trans-Atlantic telegraph, successful, 11–16 Mar.; he raises nearly 10,000,000*l.* in a few weeks, *Times* . . . . 3 May, ,,

Legislative council (S. Rhodesia) first meets at Salisbury . . . . 15 May, ,,

First train (E. Coast line) enters Salisbury, 1 May; first sod of the northern extension railway cut at Bulawayo . . . . 31 May, ,,

Expedition against Kazembe, a cruel chief; he flies into the Congo Free State . . 27 Oct. ,,

N.E. Rhodesia, including a large area north of the Zambesi (administrator, Mr. Codrington), constituted in . . . . ,,

Gen. sir Fred. Carrington arrives at Bulawayo, 27 June, 1900

Protectorate proclaimed over Marotseland under the title N.W. Rhodesia; major Coryndon appointed administrator . . . . Sept. ,,

Sir Marshal J. Clarke, resident commissioner, autumn, ,,

Death of Mr. Cecil Rhodes, aged 48, at Cape Town *which see*, 26 Mar. 1902; great demonstrations of grief and homage during the funeral ceremonies and along the route from Cape Town to the Matoppos, where he was buried (according to his own wish) in the hill which he called the "view of the world," thousands of natives and others being present . . . . . . 10 April, 1902

[By his will, dated 1 July, 1899, he practically bequeathed his immense fortune and possessions (about 6,000,000*l.*) to the public service, viz., his landed property near Bulawayo and at Inyanga, near Salisbury, to his trustees, lord Rosebery, lord Grey, lord Milner, Mr. A. Beit, Dr. Jameson, Mr. L. Michell, and Mr. B. F. Hawksley, to cultivate, for the instruction of the people of Rhodesia; 100,000*l.* to Oriel college, Oxford, nearly 52,000*l.* per annum for scholarships, viz., to be created at Oxford university, 60 colonial of 300*l.* each a year, 24 for S. Africa, 36 for Australasia and the North American and W. Indian colonies, and 2 for each of the 50 states or territories of the U.S.N.A.; also 15 of the value of 250*l.* per annum for German students, to be nominated by the German emperor. His residence, De Groote Schuur (*i.e.* the Great Granary, or Barn), near Cape Town, with contents, and all his land under Table Mountain, he left to the Federal government of S. Africa (when constituted), the house for the prime minister, and the other lands for public purposes, with an income of 1,000*l.* a year for maintenance; also 4,000*l.* per annum to be invested as a Matoppos and Bulawayo fund; and 2,000*l.* a year to be called the Inyanga fund, &c.; see *Times*, 5 April, 1902. Mr. G. R. Parkin, author of "The Great Dominion," principal of the Upper Canada college of Toronto, appointed by the trustees to prepare a scheme *re* the Colonial and American scholarships, reported 13 Aug. 1902.]

Virulent cattle disease (redwater) spreads, April–May, ,,

"The Ancient Ruins of Rhodesia," by R. N. Hall and W. G. Neal, result of their explorations between the Zambesi and the Limpopo, 1895–1900, published . . . . spring, ,,

Interesting discoveries in the ruins at Zimbabye, Aug. ,,

Outbreak of rabies, reported . . . . 4 Sept. ,,

Cape to Cairo railway, line from Buluwayo to Salisbury, *via* Gwelo, 300 miles, completed . 6 Oct. ,,

Mr. Milton, administrator, opens the legislative council . . . . 6 Nov. ,,

Irrigation scheme reported successful . 15 Nov. 1902
British S. Africa co.'s report—revenue, 435,255*l.*; expenditure, 710,563*l.*, 1901–2; revenue for 1903, 513,000*l.*; expenditure, 740,000*l.*, reported, 25 June, 1903
An order in council amending the provisions of the Southern Rhodesia Order in Council, 1898, published. Legislative council to consist of the administrator, the resident commissioner, with 7 nominated and 7 elected members . 17 Feb. ,,

RHODIUM, a rare metal, discovered in platinum ore, by Dr. Wollaston in 1804. It has been used for the points of metallic pens.

RHODOPE MOUNTAINS (Turkish, Despoto Dagh), a plateau in Roumelia.

In these about 150,000 Mahometans took refuge during the Russo-Turkish war, on the approach of the Russians in Dec. 1877, and Jan. 1878; and resisted the invaders. The Russians were accused of killing and outraging thousands of men, women, and children. A European commission of inquiry; met 21 July; closed, 26 Aug.; confirmed the statements, but issued no united report; some members seceded 1878
The insurgents asserted that they were not resisting the sultan himself, but maladministration. They are governed by an English chief, col. St. Clair, who receives the taxes, &c., and is styled "commander-in-chief of the national army of the Rhodope" . . . . Sept. ,,
About 40,000 destitute; reported . . 18 Jan. 1879
The insurrection gradually subsided.
Territory ceded to Bulgaria, reported . 16 July, 1895

RHUBARB. This plant was first cultivated for its stalks to be used as food by Mr. Myall, of Deptford, about 1820, and soon after came into general use.

RHUDDLAN, statute of, see *Wales*, 1283.

RIALTO, BRIDGE OF THE, at Venice (mentioned by Shakspeare in his "*Merchant of Venice*"), built about 1590, consists of a marble arch across the Grand Canal, 90 feet wide and 24 feet high.

RIBBONISM, a term given to the principles of a secret society in Ireland, organised about 1820, to retaliate on landlords any injuries done to their tenants. To the ribbonmen are attributed many of the agrarian murders, 1858-71-79. An act was passed to repress them, 16 June, 1871.

RICE, the *Oryza sativa* of botanists, in the husk termed paddy; largely grown in intertropical regions, occupying the same place as wheat in the warmer parts of Europe. It was conveyed to South Carolina near the end of the 17th century, and its cultivation greatly increased.

The duty on foreign rice, 15*s.*, on colonial rice, 1*s.* per cwt., was reduced by sir Robert Peel in 1842 to 6*s.* 3*d.* and 6$\frac{1}{10}$*d.* respectively. Further reductions were made in 1846, and in 1860 the duty was totally abolished.
Imported into Britain: 1846, 770,604 cwt.; 1856, 3,724,695 cwt.; 1866, 2,309,494 cwt.; 1877, 6,617,739 cwt.; 1881, 8,500,062 cwt.; 1883, 7,747,725 cwt.; 1885, 5,588,650 cwt.; 1887, 5,019,512 cwt.; 1889, 6,585,779 cwt.; 1890, 5,957,555 cwt.; 1893, 5,449,602 cwt.; 1896, 4,531,518 cwt.; 1900, 6,291,331 cwt.; 1901, 6,755,263 cwt.

RICHMOND (Surrey), anciently called Sheen, which in the Saxon tongue signifies *resplendent*. Here stood a palace in which Edward I. and II. resided, and Edward III. died, 1377. Here also died Anne, queen of Richard II., 1394. The palace was repaired by Henry V., who founded three religious houses near it. In 1497 it was destroyed by fire; but Henry VII. rebuilt it, and commanded that the village should be called Richmond, he having borne the title of earl of Richmond (Yorkshire) before he obtained the crown: and here he died in 1509. Queen Elizabeth was a prisoner in this palace for a short time during the reign of her sister. When she became queen it was one of her favourite places of residence; and here she died 24 March, 1603. It was afterwards the residence of Henry, prince of Wales. The beautiful park and gardens were enclosed by Charles I. 1,914 acres now open to the public. The observatory was built by sir W. Chambers in 1769. In Richmond, Thomson "sang the Seasons and their change;" and died 27 Aug. 1748.

The Star and Garter hotel burnt . 12 Jan. 1870
Mrs. Julia Martha Thomas was murdered at Richmond, her body cut up, put in bags and cast into river Thames, by Katherine Webster, aged 30, about 2 March; John Church, a publican, arrested on suspicion, discharged 17 April; Webster committed for trial, 16 May; convicted, 8 July; confessed; executed at Wandsworth . 29 July, 1879
Richmond incorporated 1890
Municipal buildings: foundation-stone laid by the mayor, sir J. Whittaker Ellis, M.P., 31 Oct. 1891; opened by the duke of York 10 June, 1893
Foot-bridge opened by the duke of York 19 May, 1894
New theatre opened by the mayor . 14 Sept. 1899
Petersham lodge and estate presented to the town by Mr. Max Waechter (knt. 9 Nov. 1902) to preserve the view from the hill; the house to be used as a holiday home for governesses . 14 Oct. 1902
Marble hill estate, Twickenham (cost 72,000*l.*) opened to the public . . . . 30 May, 1903
Body of Miss Hickman, the lady doctor, discovered in Richmond-park . . . . . 18 Oct. ,,
Population, 1881, 19,066; 1891, 22,684; 1901, 31,677.

RICHMOND (Virginia, U.S.) became the capital of the southern confederate states. The congress adjourned from Montgomery, Alabama, to Richmond, where it met 20 July, 1861. After a siege of 1452 days and many desperate battles, Richmond was evacuated by the confederates, 2, 3 April, 1865; see *United States*. By the fall of the flooring in the state capital building, about 60 persons were killed, 27 April, 1870. A statue of "Stonewall" Jackson (subscribed for by Englishmen), was unveiled here in presence of his wife and child, 26 Oct. 1875. A statue of gen. Robt. Lee at Richmond was unveiled 29 May, 1890. Population 1880, 63,600; 1890, 81,388; 1900, 85,050.

RIDING, see *Races*.

Leon, a Mexican, rode 100 miles, consecutively, in 4 hours 57 minutes, using 6 "Mustang horses," 15 July, 1876; 505 miles in 49 h. 51½ min. 8–10 Feb. 1877
Lord Dunmore rode from the Punjaub frontier, *viâ* the Pamirs, to Constantinople, Feb. 1892–15 Feb. 1893
Military ride. A number of German officers rode from Berlin to Vienna, and a number of Austrian officers from Vienna to Berlin (above 200 officers in all), 575 kilometres; 1st prize, 20,000 marks and a silver statuette given by the German emperor to count Stahremberg (Austrian), who rode the distance in 71 h. 20 m.; 2nd prize, 10,000 marks and a silver statuette, given by the emperor of Austria to baron von Reitzenstein (German), who rode 73 h. 6 m. Other prizes given, 1–7 Oct. 1892. An international military ride from Brussels to Ostend, 61 competitors, won by lieut. Madamet (French) . . 27 Aug. 1902

RIFLE CORPS, see *Volunteers*, and *Fire-arms*. *Rifle Brigade* formed, 1800. International rifle meeting, Washington, began 26 Sept. 1876. Another at Creedmoor, near New York, began 14 Sept.; the British victors, 1882; again victors at Ottawa, 13 Sept. 1902; the American team won at Bisley, 11 July, 1903. Mr. Astor gives 10,000*l.* to the nat. rifle assoc., reported, 25 Dec. 1901. For *Rifle Ranges*, see *Commons*.

RIGHTS, BILL OF. To the PETITION OF RIGHTS, preferred 17 March, 1627-8, Charles I. answered, "I will that right be done according to the laws and customs of the realm." Both houses addressed the king for a fuller answer to their petition of rights, whereupon he gave them an answer less evasive, "*Soit droit fait comme il est désiré*," 7 June, 1628. The petition thus became a statute 13 Car. I. c. 1. An important declaration was made by the lords and commons of England to the prince and princess of Orange on 13 Feb. 1689, in an act "declaring the rights and liberties of the subject, and settling the succession of the crown." The Bill of Rights, virtually the same as the declaration, was passed by parliament. It totally abolished the dispensing power of the crown, Oct. 1689. See *Claim of Right*.

RIG-VEDA. See *Vedas*.

RIMNIK (near Martinesti, Wallachia). Here the Austrians and Russians under prince Coburg and gen. Suwarrow, gained a great victory over the Turks, 22 Sept. 1789.

RINDERPEST, German for *cattle plague* (*which see*).

RING DES NIBELUNGEN, see *Nibelunge Nôt*.

RINGS anciently had a seal or signet engraved on them, to seal writings, and they are so used to this day. In *Genesis* xli. 42, it is said that Pharaoh gave Joseph his ring. Rings are now put upon women's fourth finger *at* marriage; but the Jews used them at the espousal or contract *before* marriage. Wedding-rings are to be of standard gold by statute, 1855.

RINK (from the Gaelic *rian*, or Saxon *hrinc*, a course), a term used in the Scotch game, "curling."

The Belgravia skating rink, London, S.W., was opened to the public . . . . . 2 Aug. 1875

Others since at Brighton and other places. Skates with rollers (said to have been introduced in a scene of Meyerbeer's "Prophète," at Paris, 16 April, 1849), are used. Mr. Plimpton, an American, patented roller-skates in 1865; his right was affirmed on a trial for infringement 28 Jan. 1876

See *Glaciarium*.

RIO DE JANEIRO (S. America), discovered by De Sousa, 1 Jan. 1531; see *Brazil*, 1889. In 1807 it was made capital of the empire of Brazil. Population of the city, 1885, 357,332; 1890, 876,884. See *Brazil*.

RIOTS. The riotous assembling of twelve or more persons, and their not dispersing upon proclamation, was first made high treason by a statute enacted 2 & 3 Edw. VI. 1548-9. The present *Riot Act* was passed 1 Geo. I. 1714.

Riots against Jews in London 1189

Some riotous citizens of London demolished the convent belonging to Westminster abbey; the ringleader was hanged, and the rest had their hands and feet cut off, 6 Hen. III. 1221

Goldsmiths' and Tailors' companies fought in the streets of London; several killed: the sheriffs quelled it; and thirteen hanged 1262

A riot at Norwich; the rioters burnt the cathedral and monastery; the king went thither, and saw the ringleaders executed 1271

Riot of Evil May-day (*which see*) 1517

Dr. Lamb killed by the mob . . . . June, 1628

A riot on pretence of pulling down houses of ill-fame; several of the ringleaders hanged 1668

Another, at Guildhall, at the election of sheriffs; several considerable persons, who seized the lord mayor, were concerned 1682

At Edinburgh and Dumfries, on account of the Union 1707

In London, on account of Dr. Henry Sacheverel, for preaching two sermons (one 5 Nov. 1709), voted by the house of commons to be scandalous and seditious; several dissenting meeting-houses were broken open and destroyed . . . . Feb. 1710

Riot of the Whig and Tory mobs, called Ormond and Newcastle mobs . . . . . 29 May, 1715

The *Mug-house* riot, in Salisbury-court, between the Whigs and Tories; the riot quelled by the guards; five rioters hanged . . . . . 24 July, 1716

Of the Spitalfields weavers, on account of employing workmen come over from Ireland; quelled by the military, but many lives lost 1736

Porteous riot at Edinburgh (see *Porteous*) 7 Sept. ,,

The nailers in Worcestershire march to Birmingham, and make terms with iron merchants there 1737

Of the Spitalfield weavers; the duke of Bedford narrowly escaped death; lives lost . . . May, 1765

A mob in St. George's-fields, to see Mr. Wilkes in the King's Bench prison; the military aid indiscreetly called for by the justices of the peace, and several innocent persons, particularly young Allen, fired upon, and killed . . . . 10 May, 1768

Gordon's "*No Popery*" riots . 10 May, 2-9 June, 1780

At Birmingham, on account of commemorating the French revolution, when several houses were destroyed . . . . . . 14 July, 1791

In various parts of Scotland, on account of the militia act, when several were killed . Aug. 1797

At Maidstone, at the trial of Arthur O'Connor and others, 22 May, 1798; the earl of Thanet, Mr. Ferguson, and others, were active in endeavouring to rescue O'Connor, for which they were tried and convicted . . . . . . 25 April, 1799

At Liverpool, occasioned by a quarrel between a party of dragoons and a press-gang . 27 June, 1809

O. P. riot (*which see*) at Covent-garden . . Sept. ,,

In Piccadilly, in consequence of the house of commons committing sir Francis Burdett to the Tower . . . . 6 April, 1810

Machinery destroyed by rioters at Nottingham from Nov. 1811 to Jan. 1812

In various parts of the north of England, by the Luddites, during . . . . 1811 and ,,

At Sheffield, during which 800 muskets belonging to the local militia were destroyed . 14 April, ,,

At the Theatre Royal, Dublin, on account of the celebrated *Dog of Montargis*, several nights, Dec. 1814

Alarming riots at Westminster, on account of Corn bill: lasted several days . . . March, 1815

At the depôt at Dartmoor, in quelling which seven American prisoners of war were killed, and thirty-five wounded . . . . April, ,,

Popular meetings at Spa-fields, when the shops of the gunsmiths were attacked for arms. Mr. Platt shot in that of Mr. Beckwith, on Snow-hill (Watson tried for high treason, but acquitted, June, 1817) . . . . 2 Dec. 1816

In St. James's park, on the prince-regent going to the house of lords; it was said that an air-gun was fired at him . . . . 28 Jan. 1817

At Manchester, at a popular meeting . 3 March, ,,

Affray at Manchester, called the "Field of Peterloo" (see *Manchester reform meeting*) . . 16 Aug. 1819

At the Theatre Royal, Dublin, of several nights' duration . . . . ,,

Riot at Paisley and Glasgow; many houses plundered . . . . 16 Sept. ,,

At Edinburgh, on the acquittal of queen Caroline, 19 Nov. 1820

In London, at the funeral of the queen 14 Aug. 1821

At Knightsbridge, between the military and the populace, on the funeral of Honey and Francis, (killed 14 Aug.) . . . . . . 26 Aug. ,,

At the theatre in Dublin; the riot called the "*Bottle conspiracy*," against the marquis Wellesley, lord-lieutenant . . . . . . 14 Dec. 1822
Riot at Ballybay; Lawless arrested . . 9 Oct. 1828
Riot at Limerick; the provision-warehouses plundered and mischief done . . . . 15 June, 1830
Fatal affrays at Castlepollard, 23 May; and Newtownbarry (*which see*) . . . . . 18 June, 1831
Alarming riots at Merthyr-Tydvil among the iron-workers; several fired upon by the military, killed and wounded . . . . . . 3 June, ,,
Riot at the Forest of Dean (see *Dean*) . 8 June, ,,
Nottingham castle burnt by rioters . . 10 Oct. ,,
Reform riots at Bristol (see *Bristol*) . . 29 Oct. ,,
Affray at Castleshock, county Kilkenny, when a number of police, attacked by the populace, were, with their commander, Mr. Gibins, killed, 14 Dec. ,,
Riot at Boughton, near Canterbury, produced by persons called *Thomites*, headed by a fanatic, Thom, or Courtenay, who. with others, was killed (see *Thomites*) . . . . . . 28-31 May, 1838
Great riots throughout the country, occasioned by the chartists (*which see*); Llanidloes, Montgomeryshire, 30 April, suppressed by military, 4 May; a proclamation . . . . . . 12 Dec. ,,
Riots in Birmingham; much mischief . July, 1839
Chartist riot at Newport (*which see*) . . 4 Nov. ,,
Meditated chartist outbreak at Sheffield, with most destructive objects, providentially discovered, and many persons arrested . . . 11 Jan. 1840
Rebecca riots against turnpikes in Wales 1843
Chartist demonstration (see *Chartists*) 10 April, 1848
Fatal affray at Dolly's Brae, near Castlewellan, in Ireland, between the Orangemen and the Roman catholics; several of the latter lost their lives, and some of their houses were ransacked and burnt . . . . 12 July, 1849
Serious riots at Yarmouth, through a dispute between the shipowners and the seamen 23 Feb. 1851
Riots occasioned by a procession of Orangemen at Liverpool, and several lives lost . . 14 July, ,,
Riot at Stockport, Cheshire; two catholic chapels destroyed and houses burnt . . 29 June, 1852
Fierce religious riots at Belfast, in Ireland, occur, 14 July, ,,
Fatal election riot at Six-mile-bridge, in the county of Clare, in Ireland; five persons shot dead by the military . . . . 22 July, ,,
Riots at Wigan, among the coal-miners, suppressed by the military without loss of life . 28 Oct. 1853
Bread riots at Liverpool . . . . . 19 Feb. 1855
Riots at Hyde-park, about Sunday bill, July, 1855: about dearness of bread . . . 14, 21, 28 Oct. ,,
Riots at Belfast through the open-air preaching of the rev. Hugh Hanna . . . 6, 13, 20 Sept. 1857
Religious riots at St. George's-in-the-East, London, on Sundays in . . . . Sept. and Nov. 1859
Break-out of the convicts at Chatham, suppressed by the military . . . . . 11 Feb. 1861
Violent riots at Belfast begin, through an Orange demonstration . . . . . . 17 Sept. 1862
Fierce rioting (caused by the Irish against the favourers of Garibaldi) at Hyde-park, London, 28 Sept. and 5 Oct.; and at Birkenhead, Cheshire, 8 and 15 Oct. ,,
Rioting at Stalybridge (on account of the mode of relief to the unemployed cotton-workers), principally Irish; put down by the military, 21 March, 1863
Fierce conflicts between Romanists and Protestants at Belfast; 9 persons killed, and about 150 injured 10-27 Aug. 1864
Reform riots in Hyde-park, London; much damage, and many hurt . . . . . 23, 24 July, 1866
Anti-popery riots at Birmingham, through the lecturing of Murphy: much damage done to houses, 17, 18 June, 1867
Col. Kelly and Deasy committed for trial as Fenians; rescued from the prisoners' van; Brett, a police sergeant, shot dead . . . . . 18 Sept. ,,
At Wigan; colliers on strike . . . end of April, 1868
Fierce riots against a colliery manager at Mold, Flintshire, put down by the military; 4 deaths, 2 June, 1869
Violent rioting at a colliery at Thorncliffe, near Sheffield; quelled by intervention of lord Wharncliffe and others . . . . . . 21 Jan. 1870
Rioting at Armathwaite, near Carlisle, between English and Irish navvies . . 15, 16 Oct. ,,
Violent riots at Belfast . . . . . 19, 20 Aug. 1872
Riots at Northampton, because Mr. C. Bradlaugh was not elected M.P.; suppressed by military 6 Oct. 1874
At Blackburn, Burnley, Accrington, Preston, and other places, through cotton strike and lock-out; several mills and houses destroyed; riots quelled by the military . . . . . 14, 15 May, 1878
At Camborne, Cornwall, against the Irish; a Romanist church destroyed . . 17-18 April, 1882
At Wrexham, of coal miners . . . . 19 April, ,,
Westminster colliery . . . . . . 19 April, ,,
In Skye, cottars against rent about 19 April-Sept. ,,
At Tredegar, Monmouthshire, Salvationists attacked by Irish roughs, retaliate with great violence; Irish quarter sacked, 8, 9 July; 1 Irishman died; 600 destitute Irish landed at Queenstown, 14 July; 6 rioters sentenced to 3 months' imprisonment . . . . 2 Aug. ,,
In Dublin, through resignation of police, suppressed by the military . . . . 1 Sept. ,,
At Kidderminster . . . . . . 4-8 April, 1884
Peaceable mass meeting of the unemployed in Trafalgar-square, joined by the social democrats with red flag led by Hyndman, Burns, and Champion, who, unchecked for about two hours (4 to 6 p.m.), from Pall-mall to Oxford-street and neighbourhood, smash windows, ransack shops, attack and rob private carriages: finally dispersed: police organisation inefficient (except by superintendent Cuthbert); estimated damage 11,000*l.*, 8 Feb.; other meetings; rioting checked 9, 10 Feb.; rioters sentenced to various terms of imprisonment . . . . . . March, 1886
Riots at Leicester occasioned by a strike; destruction of factories, &c.; partially checked by the police, 11, 12 Feb.; rioting continued 13–16 Feb. ,,
Riots Damages Act passed . . . . . . ,,
Destructive riot of coal-miners at Plas-Power colliery near Wrexham . . . . 30 Sept. ,,
Violent riots of Lanarkshire miners at Hamilton, Airdrie, &c.; 74 men arrested . 8–10 Feb. 1887
Riot at Lillie-bridge, West Brompton; structures destroyed and burnt by a crowd (about 5,000) disappointed at the non-performance of a race and their money not returned . . 19 Sept. ,,
Riotous assemblage of the unemployed in Trafalgar-square dispersed 17 Oct.; meeting at Hyde-park dispersed by the police after severe conflict, 18 Oct.; again dispersed 19 Oct.; meeting in Trafalgar-square, about 2,000 went to Westminster Abbey; disorderly, 23 Oct.; quiet meetings 24–27 Oct. and since; arrests for seditious language, &c., 4-8 Nov.; meetings in Trafalgar-square prohibited, 8 and 18 Nov.; processions of disorderly mob dispersed, and meetings in Trafalgar-square prevented by mounted and foot police aided by the 1st life guards; several severe conflicts with men using iron bars and knives; many seriously injured, chiefly police; Mr. Cuninghame Graham, M.P., a magistrate, and Mr. John Burns and many others arrested; moderate conduct of the police; sir C. Warren's arrangements thoroughly successful, Sunday, 13 Nov.; many sentenced to penal servitude . . . . . . 14 Nov. ,,
Funeral procession of Alfred Linnell, a law writer, accidentally killed in a crowd in Northumberland-avenue on Sunday, 20 Nov., from Soho to Bow cemetery: Messrs. Cuninghame Graham, M.P., Wm. Morris the poet, and others present; order was only maintained by a large body of police, 18 Dec. ,,
Much rioting connected with strikes 1890-92
Attacks of the coal mine strikers in Ebbw vale, Wales, defeated by the workers; military present 17 Aug. 1893
Riotous proceedings of the strikers in the coal districts checked by the military; 2 deaths; much property destroyed . . . . . 7–8 Sept ,,

See *Coal* and *Hull*, 1893.

Report of a committee on riots appointed, May, 1894; issued . . . . . . March, 1895

See *Strikes*, 1881; *Ireland*; *Crofters*, 1887-8; *Belfast*, *Southampton*, *Cardiff*, *Coal*, *Hull*, &c.

RIPON (Yorkshire), an ancient town. About 661 an abbey cell was built here by Eata. Ripon was made a bishopric by archbishop Wilfred, in 690, but did not endure so. It suffered much by the ravages of the Danes, the Normans (1069), and the Scots (1319 and 1323). The present see was erected 5 Oct. 1836, out of the archdeaconry of York in the West Riding. Income 4,200*l*. The cathedral was restored by sir G. G. Scott: the choir was re-opened 27 Jan. 1869. The thousandth anniversary of its incorporation was celebrated 25-27 Aug. 1886. Population, 1881, 7,390; 1891, 7,512; 1901, 8,225.

BISHOPS.

1836. Charles Thos. Longley, trans. to Durham, 1856.
1856. Robert Bickersteth, died 15 April, 1884.
1884. Wm. Boyd Carpenter, May.

RITCHIE'S ACT, see under *Local Government*.

RITUALISTS, a name given in 1866 to a party in the church of England, formerly termed Puseyites, who endeavoured to give a more imposing character to public worship, by the use of coloured vestments, lighted candles, incense, &c., professing to go back to the practices of the church in the time of Edward VI. An exhibition of these things was held during the church congress at York in Oct. 1866, but was not officially connected with it. The practices of the ritualists (said by Mr. Disraeli to be symbolical of doctrines they were bound to renounce), were censured in several episcopal charges in Dec. 1866; in two reports of the ritualistic commission, 19 Aug. 1867, and April, 1868, and by the judicial committee of the privy council on appeal, 23 Dec. 1868. See *Church of England* and *Trials*, 1867-9. At a general convocation of the American episcopal church at Philadelphia, 27, 28 Oct. 1868, after a warm discussion on ritualism, the discussion was adjourned. It was renewed at the convocation 10 Oct. 1874, and the ritualists were defeated by the evangelical party, a stringent canon on ceremonies being passed 27 Oct. The "Public Worship Regulation Act" was passed 7 Aug. 1874, for the repression of ritualism in England. Clerical declaration on ritual, see *Times*, 13 July, 1903. See *Public Worship* and *Church of England* 1903.

RIVERS COMMISSIONS, first appointed, 1865, Messrs. R. Rawlinson, J. T. Harrison, and Professor Way; second, 1868; sir Wm. Denison, Mr. J. Chalmers Morton, and Professor Frankland.

Published six blue books 1874
Association for preserving the rivers of Scotland, formed . . . . Jan. 1875
The Pollution of Rivers Act passed 15 Aug. 1876; amended, 1893; reported ineffectual by royal commission . . . . July, 1901

RIVOLI (near Verona, N. Italy). Near here the Austrians defeated the French, 17 Nov. 1796; and were defeated by Bonaparte 14, 15 Jan. 1797. Massena was made duke of Rivoli for his share in the actions.

ROAD CLUB, established in the autumn of 1874 in London, by gentlemen interested in the revival of coaching.

ROAD MURDER. On the night of 29-30 June, 1860, Francis Savile Kent, four years old, was murdered, and his body hid in a garden water-closet at Road. His step-sister Constance Kent (aged sixteen), and the nurse Elizabeth Gough (the first suspected), were discharged for want of evidence. The coroner was severely blamed for charging the jury improperly, but the court of queen's bench, in Jan. 1861, refused to issue a writ for a new inquiry. Constance Kent, on 25 April, 1865, before sir Thomas Henry at Bow-street, and at her trial at Salisbury, on 21 July following, confessed herself to be guilty of the murder. Her punishment was commuted to penal servitude for life. Let out on ticket-of-leave, 18 July, 1885. Road is near Frome, Somerset.

ROADS, see *Roman Roads*. The first general repair of the highways of this country was directed about 1285. Acts were passed for the purpose in 1524 and 1555, followed by others in Elizabeth's and succeeding reigns. Roads through the Highlands of Scotland were begun by general Wade in 1726. Loudon M'Adam's roads were introduced about 1818. Wooden pavements were tried with partial success in the streets of London: at Whitehall in 1839, and in other streets in 1840; asphalte pavement soon after. An act "for the better management of the highways" was passed in 1862 after much opposition; another, 16 Aug. 1878; also regulated the use of locomotives on roads. Steam road-rollers were tried in 1867; used in London 18 March, 1868: see *Macadamising*, *Tolls*, and *Wooden Pavements*. Committee on Highways appointed, 18 March, 1903, report issued, 29 Sept. 1903.

ROAD STEAMERS. Mr. R. W. Thomson, of Edinburgh, in 1868, by adding india-rubber to the tires of the wheels of locomotives is considered to have solved the question of steam traction on common roads. Road steamers have been successfully employed in Edinburgh and Leith for drawing heavy waggons up inclined planes, and are adaptable to any draught work. They were tried at Woolwich, 1 Oct. 1870, and reported successful by eminent authorities; and their application to ploughing by lord Dunmore was exhibited 1 Feb. 1871.

ROANOAKE, an island off N. Carolina, U.S., discovered by sir Walter Raleigh, 1584, and settled by him, 1585, without success. Other settlers also failed.

ROASTING ALIVE. An early instance is that of Bocchoris, king of Egypt, by order of Sabacon of Ethiopia, 737 B.C. *Lenglet*. Sir John Oldcastle, lord Cobham, was thus put to death in 1418, and Michael Servetus for heresy at Geneva, 27 Oct. 1553; see *Burning Alive*, and *Martyrs*.

ROBBERS were punished with death by Edmund I.'s laws, which directed that the eldest robber should be hanged. Remarkable robbers in England were Robin Hood, 1189 (see *Robin Hood*), and Claud Du Val, "executed at Tyburn," says an historian quaintly, "to the great grief of the women," Jan. 1670. In Ireland, the famous MacCabe was hanged at Naas, 19 Aug. 1691. Galloping Hogan, the rapparee, flourished at this period. Freney, the celebrated highwayman, surrendered himself, 10 May, 1749. The accomplished Barrington was transported, 22 Sept. 1790. See *Trials*.

ROBIN HOOD, captain of a band of robbers, in Sherwood forest, Nottinghamshire; traditionally reported to have been the earl of Huntingdon, disgraced and banished the court by Richard I. at his accession (1189). Robin Hood and Little John and their band are said to have continued their depredations till 1247, when Robin died. *Stow.* Lord Tennyson's drama, "The Foresters; Robin Hood and Maid Marian," first represented at New York on account of the American copyright law, end of March, 1892.

"ROBINSON CRUSOE," by Daniel De Foe; the first part appeared in 1719. See *Juan Fernandez*. Three old ladies, Mary Ann, Jane Amelia, and Sarah Frances De Foe, lineally descended from De Foe, pensioned by queen Victoria, May, 1877.

ROBURITE, a German explosive invented by Dr. Carl Roth, reported 1888.

ROCHDALE, Lancashire. A charter was obtained for a market by Edmund de Lacy, 1241, and the grammar school was founded 1564. Rochdale canal was opened 1804. The new town was commenced in 1865. Rochdale first sent a member to parliament in 1832. The woollen manufacture was carried on in the 16th century. The first cotton mill was erected in 1795. Theatre royal and opera house, built in 1867, destroyed by fire, 27 Jan. 1894. Population, 1881, 68,866; 1891, 71,458; 1901, 83,112.

ROCHEFORT (W. France), a seaport on the Charente. The port was made by Louis XIV. in 1666. In Aix-roads or Basque-roads, near Rochefort, capt. lord Cochrane attacked the French fleet and destroyed four ships, 11-12 April, 1809. Near Rochefort, the emperor Napoleon surrendered himself to capt. Maitland of the *Bellerophon*, 15 July, 1815.

ROCHELLE (W. France), a seaport on the Atlantic, belonging to the English for some time, but finally surrendered to the French leader, Du Gueselin, in 1372. As a stronghold of the Calvinist party, it was vainly besieged by the duke of Anjou in 1573; and was taken after a siege of thirteen months by cardinal Richelieu in 1628. The duke of Buckingham was sent with a fleet and army to relieve it; but the citizens declined to admit him. He attacked the isle of Rhé, near Rochelle, and failed, 22 July, 1627. He was repulsed 8 Nov. following. A conspiracy here in 1822 caused loss of life to sergeant Bories and others.

The new harbour opened by president Carnot 19 Aug. 1890

ROCHESTER, in Kent, the Roman *Durobrivæ*. The bishopric, founded by Augustin, 604, is the next in age to Canterbury. The first cathedral was erected by Ethelbert, king of Kent. St. Justus was bishop in 604. Alterations were made in the diocese in 1845. Rochester is valued in the king's books at 358*l.* 3*s.* 2½*d.* per annum. Present income 3,000*l.* The cathedral re-opened after repairs of the choir, 11 June, 1875; west front and towers restored, 25 July, 1894. The old castle and grounds were purchased for the public by the Corporation. 1883. The "ten churches fund" begun by the bishop, 1884. Population, 1881, 21,307; 1891, 26,309; 1901, 30,622.

Eastgate House, originally the residence of sir Peter Buck, clerk of queen Elizabeth's navy at Chatham. Date 1590 carved on woodwork. Referred to by Chas. Dickens in "Edwin Drood," opened as a public museum 31 March, 1903
Mr. Foord gives 10,000 gs. to St. Bartholomew's hospital, Rochester, and the cathedral . July, ,,

RECENT BISHOPS.

1793. Samuel Horseley, trans. to St. Asaph's, 1802.
1802. Thomas Dampier, translated to Ely, 1808.
1809. Walter King, died 22 Feb. 1827.
1827. Hugh Percy, translated to Carlisle, 27 Oct.
1827. George Murray, died 16 Feb. 1860.
1860. Joseph Cotton Wigram, died 6 April, 1867.
1867. Thos. Legh Claughton, translated to St. Albans.
1877. Anthony Wilson Thorold, consecrated, 25 July; translated to Winchester, 1890.
1890. Randall Thomas Davidson, Nov.; translated to Winchester, 1895; abp. of Canterbury, enthr. 12 Feb. 1903.
1895. Edward Stuart Talbot.

ROCKETS, destructive war implements, were invented by sir William Congreve about 1803. The carcase-rockets were first used at Boulogne, 8 Oct. 1806, when they set the town on fire, their powers being previously demonstrated in the presence of Mr. Pitt and several of the cabinet ministers, 1806. Improved rockets were made by Hales in 1846. Boxer's life-saving rope-carrying rocket, for communicating with stranded vessels, described in 1878. See *Wrecks*, March, 1892.

ROCKINGHAM ADMINISTRATIONS. The first succeeded the administration of Mr. Geo. Grenville; the second succeeded that of lord North.

FIRST ADMINISTRATION, 13 July, 1765 to 30 July, 1766.

Charles, marq. of Rockingham,* *first lord of the treasury.*
William Dowdeswell, *chancellor of the exchequer.*
Earl of Winchilsea and Nottingham, *lord president.*
Duke of Newcastle, *privy seal.*
Earl of Northington, *lord chancellor.*
Duke of Portland, *lord chamberlain.*
Duke of Rutland, *master of the horse.*
Lord Talbot, *lord steward.*
Henry Seymour Conway and the duke of Grafton, *secretaries of state.*
Lord Egmont, *admiralty.*
Marquis of Granby, *ordnance.*
Viscount Barrington, *secretary-at-war.*
Viscount Howe, *treasurer of the navy.*
Charles Townshend, *paymaster of the forces.*
Earl of Dartmouth, *first lord of trade.*
Lords Bessborough, Grantham, and Cavendish, &c.
See *Chatham administration.*

SECOND ADMINISTRATION, March to 1 July, 1782, when the marquis died.

Marquis of Rockingham, *first lord of the treasury.*
Lord John Cavendish, *chancellor of the exchequer.*
Lord Camden, *president of the council.*
Duke of Grafton, *privy seal.*
Lord Thurlow, *lord chancellor.*
William, earl of Shelburne and Charles James Fox, *secretaries of state.*
Augustus viscount Keppel, *first lord of the admiralty.*
Duke of Richmond, *master-general of the ordnance.*
Thomas Townshend, *secretary-at-war.*
Isaac Barré, Edmund Burke, John Dunning, &c.

ROCROY (N. France). Here, 19 May, 1643, the Spaniards were totally defeated by the French, commanded by the great Condé.

RODNEY'S VICTORIES. Admiral Rodney fought, near Cape St. Vincent, the Spanish admiral, Don Langara, whom he defeated and made prisoner, capturing six of his ships, one of which blew up, 16, 17 Jan. 1780. On 12 April, 1782, he encountered the French fleet in the West Indies, commanded by the count de Grasse, took five ships of the line, and sent the French admiral prisoner to England: Rodney was raised to the peerage, June, 1782.

ROGATION WEEK. Rogation Sunday, the Sunday before Ascension-day, received its title from the Monday, Tuesday, and Wednesday following it, called Rogation days, derived from the Latin *rogare*,

* Charles Watson Wentworth, marquis of Rockingham, was born 13 May, 1730; succeeded his father as marquis, 1750. He died without issue, 1 July, 1782; and his estates passed to his nephew, earl Fitzwilliam.

to beseech. Extraordinary prayers and supplications for these three days are said to have been appointed in the third century, as a preparation for the devout observance of our Saviour's ascension on the next day succeeding to them, denominated Holy Thursday or Ascension-day. The whole week in which these days happen is styled Rogation week; and in some parts it is still known by the other names of Crop week, Grass week, and Procession week. The perambulations of parishes have usually been made in this week.

ROHAN, an illustrious family, descended from the ancient sovereigns of Brittany. Henri de Rohan, son-in-law of the great Sully, after the death of Henry IV. (14 May, 1610), became head of the Protestant party, and sustained three wars against Louis XIII. He eventually entered the service of the duke of Saxe-Weimar, and died of wounds received in battle in 1638. Of this family was the cardinal de Rohan; see *Diamond Necklace*.

ROHILCUND, a tract of country, N.E. India, was conquered by the Rohillas, an Afghan tribe, who settled here about 1747. After aiding the sovereign of Oude to overcome the Mahrattas, they were treated with much treachery by him, and nearly exterminated. Rohilcund was ceded to the British in 1801. After the great mutiny, Rohilcund was tranquillised in July, 1858.

ROLLER SKATES, see *Rink*.

ROLLING-MILLS, in the metal manufactories, were in use here in the 17th century, and in 1784 Mr. Cort patented his improvements.

ROLLS, see *Master of the Rolls*, and *Records*.

ROLLS' CHAPEL (London), founded by Henry III., about 1233, for receiving Jewish rabbis converted to Christianity. On the banishment of the Jews in 1290 the buildings now called the Rolls, and the chapel, were annexed by patent to the office of the keeper or master of the rolls of chancery, from which circumstance they took their name. A number of public records from the time of Richard III., kept in presses in this chapel, have been removed to the Record Office (*which see*). The Rolls chapel was pulled down in July, 1892.

ROLT'S ACT, 25 & 26 Vict. c. 42 (1862), relates to the Chancery Court.

ROMAGNA, a province of the papal states, comprised in the legations of Bologna, Ferrara, Forli and Ravenna. It was conquered by the Lombards; but taken from them by Pepin, and given to the pope, 753. Cæsar Borgia held it as a duchy in 1501, but lost it in 1503. In 1859 the Romagna threw off the temporal authority of the pope, and declared itself subject to the king of Sardinia, who accepted it in March, 1860. It now forms part of the province of Emilia, in the new kingdom of Italy. Population, 1890, 1,218,392. See *Rome*.

ROMAINVILLE AND BELLEVILLE, heights near Paris, where Joseph Bonaparte, Mortier, and Marmont were defeated by the allies after a vigorous resistance, 30 March, 1814. The next day Paris capitulated.

ROMAN CATHOLICS, their religion was the established one in Britain since 597 till the Reformation; see *Church of England*. Since then many laws were made against them, which have been repealed; see *Rome*, *Religion*, *Leagues*, *Maynooth*. Among other disabilities, Roman Catholics were excluded from corporate offices, 1667; from parliament, 1691; forbidden to marry protestants, 1708; to possess arms, 1695, &c.

Roman Catholic Church in England and Wales, 1878; 1 archbishop, 12 bishops (Beverley, Birmingham, Clifton, Hexham, Liverpool, Newport, Northampton, Nottingham, Plymouth, Salford, Shrewsbury, Southwark); 1894, 14 bishops; 1903, 1 archbishop, 15 bishops, 2 auxiliary bishops (sees: Birmingham, Clifton, Hexham and Newcastle, Leeds, Liverpool, Middlesbrough, Newport, Northampton, Nottingham, Plymouth, Portsmouth, Salford, Shrewsbury, Southwark, Menevia, Wales. *Ireland*, 4 archbishops (metropolitan, Paul Cullen, archbishop of Armagh, 1850; of Dublin, 1852); 24 bishops; 1894, 23 bishops. Scotland, 1894, 2 archbishops, 4 bishops.

Roman Catholics in Great Britain and Ireland, 5,640,891; in Europe, 146,335,603; Asia, 9,234,000; Africa, 2,656,000; America, 51,033,790; Australia and Polynesia, 672,000; in the world, estimated nearly 210,000,000 (240,000,000 in 1903) . . 1891

British empire, 28 archiepiscopal, 102 episcopal sees, 166 archbishops and bishops in 1898; 28 archiepiscopal, 105 episcopal sees, 30 vicariates, 11 prefectures apostolic, 176 archbishops and bishops in 1903.

Great Britain, 5,414,956 Roman Catholics in 1897.

Ireland, 3,310,028 Roman Catholics . . . 1901

R.C. hierarchy consists of 55 cardinals, 11 patriarchs, 725 archbishops and bishops of the Latin rite, 49 of the Oriental rite, 367 titular bps. and archbps., and 10 prelates *nullius dioecsos*, Jan. ,,

United Kingdom, estimated Roman Catholic population, 5,250,000 . . . . . . Jan. 1902

Great Britain, priests, 3,500 . . . . Jan. ,,

Bishop Fisher, sir Thomas More, and others, executed for denying the king's supremacy . 1535

Catholics absolved from their allegiance to the king by Paul III. 1535; by Pius V. 1570

They rebel in . . . . 1549 and 1569

The Gunpowder Plot (*which see*) 1605

They suffer by Oates's fictitious popish plot . . 1678

They are excluded from the throne 1689

They suffer by the Gordon riots . . June, 1780

Various disabilities removed in . . 1780 and 1791

Mr. Pitt proposes measures for their relief, which he gives up 1801-4

Roman Catholic Association organised in Ireland, with the object of removing the political and civil disabilities of Roman catholics, "Catholic rents" subscribed . . . . . 1823 *et seq.*

Bills in their favour frequently brought in without effect from . . . . 1813 to 1828

An act of parliament passed for the suppression of the Catholic Association (it had voted its own dissolution, 12 Feb.) . . . . . 5 March, 1829

The duke of Wellington and sir Robert Peel carry the Catholic emancipation bill (10 Geo. IV. c. 7) in the commons, 30 March; in the lords, 10 April; received the royal assent . . . 13 April, ,,

The duke of Norfolk and lords Dormer and Clifford, the first Roman catholic peers, take their seats, 28 April, ,,

The first English R. C. member returned, the earl of Surrey, for Horsham . . . . 4 May, ,,

Mr. O'Connell elected for Clare, 1828, takes his seat (first Roman catholic M.P. since 1689) . Aug. ,,

Mr. Alexander Raphael, the first Roman catholic sheriff of London . . . . . 28 Sept. 1834

Sir Michael O'Loghlen, the first Roman catholic judge (as Master of the Rolls in Ireland), appointed, 30 Oct. 1836

St. George's cathedral, Southwark, erected by A. W. Pugin; founded 1840

Tablet newspaper established . . . . . ,,

Mr. O'Connell elected first Roman catholic lord mayor of Dublin 1841

"Catholic Poor School Committee" established . 1847

The "Papal Aggression" (*which see*); cardinal Nicholas Wiseman appointed archbishop of Westminster . . . . 30 Sept. 1850

Roman catholic university, Dublin, originated 5 May, 1851; established 1854

Universe newspaper established 1860

Agitation in favour of the pope 1860-2
Missionary college founded at Drumcondra, Ireland . . . . . . 20 July, 1862
Roman catholic chaplains permitted for gaols, by Prison Ministers act . . . . . July, 1863
Serjeant Wm. Shee made a justice of the Queen's Bench, the first Roman catholic judge since the Reformation [died 19 Feb. 1868] . . 15 Dec. ,,
Death of cardinal Wiseman, aged 63; 7th English cardinal since the Reformation . . 15 Feb. 1865
Henry Manning (formerly an archdeacon in the English church) consecrated archbishop of Westminster . . . . 8 June, ,,
Conference of Roman catholic bishops at Dublin; publish resolutions declining state help (in accordance with the papal injunctions, 1801 and 1805), and condemning mixed education and secret societies . . . . 17 Oct. 1867
In Great Britain 1639 Roman catholic priests; 1283 chapels and churches; 227 convents for women (principally educational); 21 colleges and large schools . . . . Dec. ,,
A proposal of the Derby government to endow a catholic university for Ireland, Oct. 1867, failed through the catholic bishops claiming the entire practical control . . . 31 March, 1868
Mr. Justice Thomas (aft. lord) O'Hagan, appointed lord chancellor of Ireland, is the first Roman catholic who has held that office since the revolution of 1688-9 . . . . . . Dec. ,,
Catholic truth society by Dr. (aft. cardinal) Vaughan, established about 1868; important conference at Hanley, end of Sept. 1896; annual meetings.
Catholic union of Great Britain, president the duke of Norfolk, constituted 1871
A Roman catholic made M.A. at Oxford, after the abolition of the test . . . . 22 June, ,,
The catholics opposing the dogma of papal infallibility term themselves "old catholics" (*which see*) ,,
The Ecclesiastical Titles act (see *Papal Aggression*) repealed . . . . 24 July, ,,
Pastoral issued by the R. C. bishops in Ireland claiming endowment for colleges, &c. under their sole control . . . . Oct. ,,
"Catholic Education Crisis Fund" established . ,,
Two R. C. bishops consecrated at Salford 28 Oct. 1872
"Catholic Union," Dublin, re-organised to obtain education under ecclesiastical control, abt. 4 Dec. 1873
A catholic union in Dublin formed . . . . . ,,
Roman Catholic university senate meet 21 May, 1874
Archbishop Manning made a cardinal . . . 1875
Catholic Congress at Venice met . . . 12 June, ,,
The marquis of Ripon becomes a Roman Catholic 7 Sept. ,,
Roman Catholic university college, Kensington; monsignor Capel, principal; opened . 15 Oct. ,,
Several English clergymen secede to Rome . Oct. ,,
New Catholic club opened in London by the duke of Norfolk, lords Denbigh and Petre, and others 27 Nov. ,,
Mr. Gladstone's pamphlet, "The Vatican Decrees" occasions declarations respecting papal infallibility, from abp. Manning, monsig. Capel, the Catholic Union and others for it; from lords Acton, Camoys, and sir George Bowyer, against it, Nov. ,,
R. C. hierarchy re-established in Scotland, by pope Leo XIII. . . . . 4 March, 1878
For the dissension between Church and State respecting the doctrine of papal infallibility, see *Prussia* and *Germany*.
Church in low state in Germany, 3 dioceses (of 12) occupied: 200 parishes without priests; 1500 priests expelled, reported . . . . April, 1879
The church of the Oratory opened at South Kensington . . . . 25 April, 1884
Lord Petre, a R. C. priest, takes his seat in the house of lords . . . . 3 Nov. ,,
Centenary of the establishment of the first R. C. diocese in the United States celebrated at Baltimore, 10 Nov. *et seq.*; cardinal Gibbons dedicates the new Catholic university at Washington 13 Nov. 1889
Rev. J. H. Newman, Anglican, professed Romanism, Oct. 1845; made cardinal, 12 May, 1879; died, aged 89 . . . . 11 Aug. 1890
New Spanish church, Manchester-square, London, W., opened . . . . . . 29 Sept. 1890
Mr. Gladstone's bill to enable a Roman Catholic to be lord chancellor of England or lord-lieutenant of Ireland, rejected by the commons (256—223) 4 Feb. 1891
Death of cardinal Manning, aged 83, 14 Jan.; solemn funeral service at the Brompton oratory; buried at the R. C. cemetery at Kensal green 21 Jan. 1892
Catholic congresses: Madrid, president, archbishop of Saragossa, 25 April *et seq.*; at Vienna, the high clergy and nobility present, 29 April, 1889; Malines, 8 Sept. 1891; Seville . . . 20 Oct. ,,
Dr. Herbert Vaughan, bishop of Salford, appointed archbishop of Westminster by the pope; confirmed, 3 April; enthroned, 8 May, 1892; created cardinal, 16 Jan. 1893; entertained with R. C. bishops at the Mansion-house, London, 11 April, 1893
The foundation stone of the cathedral at Westminster laid by cardinals Vaughan and Logue 29 June, 1895
Growth of organisation in the R. C. church, congresses, clubs, &c. 1870–1900
R. C. peers protest against the expressions used in the Declaration against Transubstantiation, subscribed by the king . . . . . 14 Feb. 1901
R. C. bishops protest against any special doctrines being denounced by the sovereign on his accession . . . . 9 July, ,,
Exodus from France (*which see*) of religious orders due to the new associations law of 1 July; many come to England . . . . July–3 Oct. ,,
Mass meeting of Catholics at Halifax (N.S.), protesting against the terms used in the accession and coronation oaths . . . . 22 Jan. 1902
Demonstration held by the Catholic league at Bermondsey in favour of financial equality between Catholic elementary schools and Board schools . . . . 10 Feb. ,,
St. Edward's tower, the Campanile of the new Westminster R. C. cathedral, illuminated by a beautiful crown and search-light . 9–12 Aug. ,,
Lord Grey's bill to abolish the Declaration made by the sovereign on his accession negatived by 109—62, on motion for second reading 25 June, 1903
Death of cardinal Vaughan, age 71, 19 June; laid in state in Westminster cathedral, buried at Mill-hill . . . . 26 June, ,,
Dr. Bourne, bishop of Southwark, elected archbishop of Westminster, 24 Aug.; confirmed by the pope 28 Aug.; receives the pallium at Rome, 12 Nov. ,,
New Westminster cathedral opened for public worship . . . . Dec. ,,

ROMAN LAW, see *Codes*; ROMAN LITERATURE, see *Latin*.

ROMAN ROADS IN ENGLAND. Our historians maintain, but are mistaken, that there were but four of these roads. *Camden.* "The Romans," says Isidore, "made roads almost all over the world, to have their marches in a straight line, and to employ the people;" and criminals were frequently condemned to work at such roads, as we learn from Suetonius, in his life of Caligula. They were commenced and completed at various periods, between the 2nd and 4th centuries, and the Roman soldiery were employed in making them, that inactivity might not give them an opportunity to raise disturbances. *Bede.*

1st, WATLING-STREET, so named from Vitellianus, who is supposed to have directed it, the Britons calling him in their language *Guetalin* (from Kent to Cardigan Bay).

2nd, IKNIELD, or IKENILD-STREET, from its beginning among the *Iceni* (from St. David's to Tynemouth).

3rd, FOSSE, or FOSSE WAY, probably from its having been defended by a fosse on both sides (from Cornwall to Lincoln).

4th, ERMIN-STREET, from *Irmunsul*, a German word, meaning Mercury, whom our German ancestors worshipped under that name (from St. David's to Southampton).

ROMAN WALLS. One was erected by Agricola (79 to 85) to defend Britain from the incursions of the Picts and Scots; the first wall extended from the Tyne to the Solway firth (80 miles); the second from the firth of Forth, near Edinburgh, to the firth of Clyde, near Dumbarton (36 miles). The former was renewed and strengthened by the emperor Adrian (121), and by Septimius Severus (208). It commenced at Bowness, near Carlisle, and ended at Wallsend near Newcastle. It had battlements and towers to contain soldiers. The more northern wall was renewed by Lollius Urbicus, in the reign of Antoninus Pius, about 140. Many remains of these walls still exist, particularly of the southern one; Dr. J. C. Bruce's "*Roman Wall,*" published 1853-1868.

ROMANCE, originally a composition in the Romance or Provençal idiom. The term in the middle ages was extended to narrative poetry in general. Heliodorus, a bishop of Tricca, in Thessaly, about 398, was the author of *Æthiopica* (relating to the loves of Theagenes and Charicleia), the first work in this species of writing. The first part of the "Roman de la Rose" was written by Guillaume de Lorres (1226-70); the second, a separate poem, by Jean de Meung (1285-1314), the Decameron of Boccaccio was published, 1358; Don Quixote, by Cervantes, 1605; Gil Blas, by Le Sage, 1715. Dunlop's "History of Fiction," published 1814. See *English Language; "Reynard the Fox."*

ROME. The foundation of the city, by Romulus, was laid on the 20th April,* according to Varro, in the year 3961 of the Julian period (753 years before the birth of Christ, and in the fourth year of the sixth Olympiad. Other dates given: Cato, 751; Polybius, 750; Fabius Pictor, 747; Cincius, 728 B.C.). The Romans conquered nearly the whole of the then known world. In the time of Julius Cæsar, the empire was bounded by the Euphrates, Taurus, and Armenia on the east; by Æthiopia on the south; by the Danube on the north; and by the Atlantic on the west. Numerous ecclesiastical councils have been held at Rome, from 197 to 1869-70. Population, 1872, about 240,000; 1877, 250,000; 1881, 300,467; 1890, 423,217; 1901, 463,000. Chiefly through the exertions of Mr. John Henry Parker of Oxford, the Roman exploration fund was established, for the preservation of ancient architectural remains. His "Archæology of Rome" (with many photographs) published, 1874-8. Professor J. H. Middleton's works on "Ancient Rome," published 1885, 1888, and 1892. The Italian government votes 1200*l.* a year for a similar purpose. The early history of Rome is legendary, and the dates *purely conjectural.* It has been greatly elucidated by the researches of B. G. Niebuhr, whose Roman history was published 1811 and 1827-30, and still further by Dr. Mommsen in his history of Rome, 1854. He died 1 Nov. 1903.

* In its original state, Rome was but a small castle on the summit of mount Palatine; and the founder, to give his followers the appearance of a nation or a barbarian horde, was obliged to erect a standard as a common asylum for criminals, debtors, or murderers, who fled from their native country to avoid the punishment which attended them. From such an assemblage a numerous body was soon collected, and before the death of the founder, the Romans had covered with their habitations the Palatine, Capitoline, Aventine, and Esquiline hills, with Mounts Cœlius and Quirinalis.

Foundation of the city by Romulus . . . B.C.	753
The Romans seize on the Sabine women at a public spectacle, and detain them for wives . . .	750
Rome taken by the Sabines; the Sabines incorporated with the Romans as one nation .	747
Romulus said to have been murdered by senators .	716
Numa Pompilius elected king, 715; institutes the priesthood, the augurs and vestals . . .	710
The Romans and the Albans contesting for superiority, agreed to choose three champions on each part to decide it. The three *Horatii*, Roman knights, overcame the three *Curiatii*, Albans, and united Alba to Rome . . . . . . about	667
War with the Fidenates; the city of Alba destroyed	665
Ostia, at the mouth of the Tiber, built . about	627
The capitol founded	615
The first census of the Roman state taken . . .	566
Political institutions of Servius Tullius . . .	550
Tarquinius II. and his family expelled for tyranny and licentiousness, royalty abolished: the Patricians establish an aristocratical commonwealth .	509
Junius Brutus and Tarquinius Collatinus first prætors or consuls; first alliance of the Romans with Carthage	"
The capitol dedicated to *Jupiter Capitolinus* . .	507
First dictator Titus Lartius	501
The Latins and the Tarquins declare war against the republic, 501; defeated at lake Regillus .	496
Secession of the Plebeians to the sacred mount; establishment of tribunes of the Plebeians . .	494
First agrarian law passed by Spurius Cassius; he is put to death by Patricians	486-5
Wars with the Æquians and Volscians; exploits and exile of Coriolanus; he besieges Rome, but retires at the intercession of his mother and wife about	491
Victory of Cincinnatus over the Æquians by stratagem, liberating the Roman army . . .	458
Destructive pestilences . . . 472, 466, 463 and	451
Wars with Veii and the Etruscans, indecisive, 475, 465; slaughter of the patriotic Fabii (*which see*)	477
The Aventine mount allotted solely to the plebeians	456
The appointment and fall of the Decemvirs (*which see*), 451—448. The Decemvirs were tried, Appius Claudius and Spurius Oppius died in prison, others were banished	448
The Canuleian law passed, permitting marriages between Patricians and Plebeians	445
Military tribunes first created	444
Office of censor instituted	443
The Veientes defeated, and their king Tolumnius slain	437
Great defeat of the Sabines	447
Spurius Mœlius, a benefactor during famine, judicially murdered by the Patricians . . .	436
War with the Etruscans	434
Æqui and Volsci defeated by Tubertus, dictator .	428
Two more quæstors appointed	421
Another dreadful famine at Rome	411
Three quæstors are chosen from the Plebeians for the first time	409
Veii taken by Camillus after ten years' siege . .	396
Banishment of Camillus	391
Great victory of the Gauls near the Allia, 16 July; they sack Rome, which is deserted, but are repulsed in an attack on the Capitol, which they blockade; they accept a heavy ransom, and retire	390
Proposed removal of the state, to Veii, rejected .	389
[Rome gradually rebuilt amid great distress and wars with neighbouring states.]	
M. Manlius, liberal to poor debtors, is executed as a traitor	384
Passing of the Licinian laws (*which see*); by them, one consul is to be a Plebeian (much resisted)	365
Marcus Curtius leaps into the gulf which had opened in the forum	362
The Gauls defeated in Italy	360
Treaty with Carthage to repress Greek piracy . .	348

War with the Etruscans, ended by a truce; war with the Latins; league renewed . . . . B.C. 365-342
First Samnite war, indecisive 343-340
Mutiny in the army in Campania, and rise of the commons in Rome; peace restored by concessions and the general abolition of the debts caused by the Gaulish invasion 341
The Publilian law passed, equalising the plebeians with the patricians in political rights . . . 339
The second Samnite war, a severe struggle, 326, *et seq.*; the Roman army, entrapped in the Caudine Forks (*which see*), 321; victories of L. Papirius Cursor; the Samnites and their allies compelled to submit 304
War with Etruria, 311; victories of Q. Fabius Maximus at the Vadimonian lake, &c.; the Etrurians and Umbrians submit 309
Appius Claudius Cæcus, censor, favours the lower classes; with the public money makes the road from Rome to Capua, termed the "Appian way," and erects the first aqueduct 312-308
Conquest of the Æquians, Marsians, &c. . . 304-302
Third Samnite war 300
Coalition of the Samnites, Etruscans, and Gauls (not continuous) against Rome; nine campaigns, with many conflicts and alternate invasions; great Roman victory at Sentinum (*which see*) . 295
The Samnites subdued after desperate struggles, 294-291; their general, C. Pontius, put to death at Rome 290
Conquest of the Sabines by M. Curius Dentatus . ,,
Great distress of the Plebeians, through war, pestilence and famine . . . . 300, *et seq.*
Secession of the people to the Janiculum; the Hortensian laws (*which see*) passed . . . 286
Census: 262,322 Roman citizens 293
Seven new temples erected, with statues by Greek artists 302-292
The Etruscans defeated at the Vadimonian lake . 283
The Tarentines form a coalition against Rome, and invite Pyrrhus, king of Epirus, to join them, 281; he defeats the Romans at Pandosia, 280; and at Asculum, 279; defeated by them at Beneventum 275
Subjugation of Tarentum, Samnium, Bruttium and their allies, 272-265; Rome supreme in Italy . 265
First Punic war (see *Carthage*) 264-241
First Roman fleet built 260
Temple of Janus closed 235
Corsica and Sardinia annexed . . . . 238 *et seq.*
Invasion of the Gauls; beaten by the consuls . . 225
Second Punic war, 218-201; Rome saved by the adhesion of 18 colonies, by the free-will offerings of gold, silver and money by the senate and people, and by the defeat of Hasdrubal at the Metaurus (see *Carthage*) 207
Syracuse taken by Marcellus 212
The Macedonian wars with Philip begin, 213 and 200; his defeat at Cynoscephalæ 197
Death of Scipio Africanus the elder 185
Third Macedonian war begins 171; Perseus beaten at Pydna; Macedon annexed 168
First public library erected at Rome 167
Philosophers and rhetoricians banished from Rome 161
Third Punic war begins 149
Corinth and Carthage destroyed by the Romans (see *Corinth* and *Carthage*) 146
Celtiberian and Numantine war in Spain . . 153-133
Attalus III. of Pergamos bequeaths his kingdom and riches to the Romans 133
The Servile war in Sicily 132
Two Plebeian consuls chosen . . . . . ,,
Agrarian disturbances: Gracchus slain . . . 121
The Jugurthine war 112-106
The Mithridatic war (*which see*) 108-63
The Ambrones defeated by Marius 102
The Social war 90-88
Rome besieged by four armies (viz.: those of Marius, Cinna, Carbo, and Sertorius) and taken . 87
Sylla defeats Marius: becomes dictator; sanguinary proscriptions, 82: abdicates 79
Bithynia bequeathed to the Romans by king Nicomedes 74
Revolt of Spartacus and the slaves 73-71
Syria conquered by Pompey 65
The Catiline conspiracy suppressed by Cicero . . 63
The first triumvirate: Cæsar, Pompey, and Crassus 60
Cæsar's campaigns in Gaul, 58; in Britain . . . 55

Crassus killed by the Parthians . . . . B.C. 53
Gaul conquered and made a province 51
War between Cæsar and Pompey 50
Pompey defeated at Pharsalia (*which see*) . . . 48
Cæsar defeats Pharnaces at Zela; and writes home "Veni, vidi, vici" 47
Cato kills himself at Utica; Cæsar dictator for ten years 46
Cæsar killed in the senate-house . . . 15 March, 44
Second triumvirate: Octavius, Antony, and Lepidus 43
Cicero killed, proscribed by Antony . . . . ,,
Battle of Philippi; Brutus and Cassius defeated . 42
Lepidus ejected from the triumvirate, 36; war between Octavius and Antony, 32; Antony defeated totally at Actium . . . . . 2 Sept. 31
Octavius emperor, as *Augustus Cæsar* 27
The empire now at peace with all the world; the temple of Janus shut; JESUS CHRIST born. (See *Jews*) 4
Varus defeated by Hermann and the Germans A.D. 9
Ovid banished to Tomi . . . . . . ,,
Death of Ovid and Livy 18
Tiberius retires to Caprea; tyranny of Sejanus . 26
A census being taken by Claudius, the emperor and censor, the inhabitants of Rome are stated to amount to 6,944,000.—[It is now considered that the population of Rome within the walls was under a million.] 48
Caractacus brought in chains to Rome 50
St. Paul arrives in bonds at Rome 62
Nero burns Rome to the ground and charges the crime upon the Christians 64
Seneca, Lucan, &c., put to death 65
Peter and Paul said to be put to death . . . 67
Jerusalem levelled to the ground by Titus 8 Sept. 70
Coliseum founded by Vespasian 75
The Dacian war begins (continues 15 years) . . 86
Pliny, junior, proconsul in Bithynia, sends Trajan his celebrated account of the Christians . . 102
Trajan's expedition into the East against the Parthians, &c.; subdues Dacia 106
Trajan's column erected at Rome 114
Adrian resides in Britain, and builds the wall . . 121
The capitol destroyed by lightning 188
Byzantium taken; its walls razed 196
The Goths are paid tribute 222
[The Goths, Vandals, Alani, Suevi, and other Northern nations attack the empire.]
Pompey's amphitheatre burnt 248
Invasion of the Goths 250
Pestilence throughout the empire 252
Great victory over the Goths obtained by Claudius II.; 300,000 slain 269
Dacia relinquished to the Goths 270
Palmyra conquered, and Longinus put to death . 273
The era of Martyrs, or of Diocletian 284
The Franks settle in Gaul. *Frèret* 287
Constantius dies at York 306
Four emperors reign at one time 308
Constantine the Great, it is said, in consequence of a vision, places the cross on his banners, and begins to favour the Christians 312
Constantine defeats Licinius, at Chrysopolis, and reigns alone . . . . . . 18 Sept. 323
He *tolerates* the Christian faith . . . . . ,,
Puts his son Crispus to death 324
Constantine convokes the first general council of Christians at Nice 325
The seat of empire removed from Rome to Byzantium, 321; dedicated by Constantine . . . 330
Constantine orders the heathen temples to be destroyed . . . . ,,
Revolt of 300,000 Sarmatian slaves suppressed . 334
Death of Constantine, soon after being baptized . 337
The army under Julian proclaims him emperor . 360
Julian, who had been educated for the priesthood, and had frequently officiated, abjures Christianity, and re-opens the heathen temples, becoming the pagan pontiff 361
Julian killed in battle in Persia; Christianity restored by Jovian 363
The empire divided into Eastern and Western by Valentinian and Valens, brothers: the former has the Western portion, or Rome 364
(See *Western and Eastern Empires*; and *Italy*.)
Rome placed under the exarchate of Ravenna . . 404
Taken by Alaric . . . . . . 24 Aug. 410
Taken and pillaged by Genseric . . . 15 July, 455

Odoacer takes Rome, and becomes king of Italy . 476
Rome recovered for Justinian by Belisarius . 536
Retaken by Totila the Goth, 546; recovered by Belisarius, 547: seized by Totila 549
Recovered by Narses, and annexed to the eastern empire; and the senate abolished . . 553
Rome at her lowest state . . . . . about 600
Rome independent under the popes . . about 728
Pepin of France compels Astolphus, king of the Lombards, to cede Ravenna and other places to the Holy Church 755
Confirmed and added to by Charlemagne . . . 774
Charlemagne crowned emperor of the West by the pope at Rome . . . . . . 25 Dec. 800
Rome taken by Arnulf and the Germans . . . 896
Otho I. crowned at Rome . . . . 2 Feb. 962
The emperor Henry IV. takes Rome . . March, 1084
Arnold of Brescia, endeavouring to reform church and state and to establish a senate, is put to death as a heretic 1155
The pope removes to Avignon 1309
Nicola di Rienzi, tribune of the people, establishes a republic, 20 May; is compelled to abdicate, 15 Dec. 1347
Returns; made senator, 1 Aug.; assassinated, 8 Oct. 1354
Papal court returns to Rome 1377
Rise of the families, Colonna, Orsini, &c. about ,,
Julius II. conquers the Romagna, Bologna, and Perugia 1503-13
The city greatly embellished by pope Leo X. 1513-21
It is captured by the constable de Bourbon, who is slain . . . . 6 May, 1527
Ferrara annexed 1597
St. Peter's dedicated . . . . . . 18 Nov. 1626
Expulsion of the Jesuits . . . . 16 Aug. 1773
Harassed by the French, German, and Spanish factions from the 16th to the 18th century.
The French invasion; the Legations incorporated with the Cisalpine republic 1796
The French proclaim the Roman republic, 20 March, 1798
Recovered for the pope by the Neapolitans, Nov. 1799
Retaken by the French, 1800; restored to Pius VII. July, 1801
Annexed by Napoleon to the kingdom of Italy, and declared second city of the empire . May, 1808
Restored to the pope, who returns . 23 Jan. 1814
He re-establishes the Inquisition and the Jesuits, 7 Aug. ,,
The papal government endeavour to annul all innovations, and thus provoke much opposition; the Carbonari increase in numbers 1815-17
Political assassinations in the Romagna . . . 1817
The "Young Italy" party established by Joseph Mazzini; temporary insurrections at Bologna suppressed by Austrian aid 1831
Election of Pius IX. . . . . . 16 June, 1846
He proclaims an amnesty; and authorises a national guard and municipal institutions . . . 1847
The Romans desire to join the king of Sardinia against the Austrians; the pope hesitates; the Antonelli ministry retires: and the Mamiani ministry is formed 1848
Count Rossi, minister of justice of the pontifical government, assassinated on the staircase of the Chamber of Deputies at Rome . . . 15 Nov. ,,
Insurrection at Rome, the populace demand a democratic ministry and the proclamation of Italian nationality; the pope (Pius IX.) hesitates, the Romans surround the palace, and a conflict ensues. The pope accepts a popular ministry (Cardinal Palma, the pope's secretary, shot in this conflict) . . . . 16 Nov. ,,
A free constitution published . . . 20 Nov. ,,
The pope escapes in disguise from Rome to Gaëta, 24 Nov. ,,
M. de Corcelles leaves Paris for Rome, a French armed expedition to Civita Vecchia having preceded him, to afford protection to the pope, 27 Nov. ,,
Protest of the pope against the acts of the provisional government . . . . 28 Nov. ,,
A constituent assembly meets at Rome . 5 Feb. 1849
The Roman National Assembly divests the pope of all temporal power, and adopts the republican form of government . . . . 8 Feb. ,,
Mazzini, Armellini, and Saffi appointed triumvirs Feb. ,,
The pope appeals to the Catholic powers, 18 Feb. 1849
Civita Vecchia occupied by the French force under Marshal Oudinot . . . . 26 April, ,,
A French force repulsed with loss . . 30 April, ,,
Engagement between the Romans and Neapolitans; the former capture 60 prisoners and 400 muskets, 5 May, ,,
The assembly refuses to receive the French as allies, 19 May, ,,
The French under marshal Oudinot commence an attack on Rome . . . . 3 June, ,,
After a brave resistance, the Romans capitulate to the French army . . . . . . 30 June, ,,
The Roman assembly dissolved . . . . 4 July, ,,
An officer from Oudinot's camp arrives at Gaëta, to present the pope with the keys of the two gates of Rome by which the French army had entered the city . . . . 4 July, ,,
The re-establishment of the pope's authority proclaimed at Rome . . . . . 15 July, ,,
Oudinot issues a general order stating that the pope (or his representative) now re-possesses the administration of affairs, but that public security in the pontifical dominions still remains under the special guarantee of the French army, 3 Aug. ,,
The pope arrives at Portici on a visit to the king of Naples . . . . 4 Sept. ,,
He arrives at Rome; cardinal Antonelli becomes foreign minister . . . . . . April, 1850
He issues the bull establishing a Roman catholic hierarchy in England (see *Papal Aggression*), 24 Sept. ,,
Important concordat with Austria . 18 Aug. 1855
The pope visits his dominions . . May-Sept. 1857
Insurrection in the Romagna, at Bologna, and Ferrara June, 1859
The pope appeals to Europe for help against Sardinia 12 July, ,,
The Legations form a defensive alliance with Tuscany, Parma, and Modena . . 20 Aug. ,,
The queen of Spain engages to send troops to Rome, if the French retire . . . 26 Aug. ,,
The assembly at Bologna vote annexation to Piedmont, 7 Sept.; the king engages to support their cause before the great powers, 15 Sept.; the pope annuls the acts of the assembly at Bologna; and announces the punishment due to those who attack the holy see, 26 Sept.; and dismisses the Sardinian chargé d'affaires at Rome . 1 Oct. ,,
The Romagna, Modena, and Parma formed into a province, to be called Æmilia . . 24 Dec. ,,
The Sardinian government annul the Tuscan and Lombard concordats . . 27 Jan., 20 March, 1860
Riots at Rome suppressed by the police with great cruelty . . . . 19 March, ,,
The pope excommunicates all concerned in the rebellion in his states . . . . 26 March, ,,
General Lamoricière takes command of the papal army, March; which is re-organised, and increased by volunteers from Ireland, &c. . May, ,,
Tuscan volunteers enter the papal states and are repulsed . . . . 19 May, ,,
Irish volunteers are severely treated for insubordination; many dismissed . . . . July, ,,
The papal army estimated at 20,000 . . . Aug. ,,
Insurrection in the Marches, 8 Sept.; Fossembrone subdued by the papal troops; the people appeal to the Sardinian government, whose troops, under Cialdini and Fanti, enter the Papal States, 11 Sept. ,,
Fanti takes Pesaro, 12 Sept.; and Perugia, including general Schmidt and 1600 prisoners, 14 Sept. ,,
Ancona besieged by sea and land . . 17 Sept. ,,
Severe allocution of the pope against France and Sardinia; he appeals to Europe for help, 28 Sept.
Cialdini defeats Lamoricière at Castel-Fidardo, 18 Sept.: and takes Ancona . . . 29 Sept. ,,
Additional French troops sent to Rome . . Oct. ,,
The Marches vote for annexation to Sardinia, Nov. ,,
Subscriptions raised for the pope in various countries; the formal collection forbidden in France and Belgium; permitted in England . . . Nov. ,,
Monastic establishments suppressed in the Legations; the monks pensioned; educational institutions founded . . . . Dec.

The French emperor advises the pope to give up his revolted provinces . . . 21 Dec. 1860

Publication of *Rome et les Evêques*, 6 Jan.; and of *La France, Rome et l'Italie*, 15 Feb.; great excitement, and strong advocacy of the pope's temporal government (attacked by prince Napoleon) in the French chambers . . . March, 1861

Cavour claims Rome as capital of Italy, 27 March, ,,

Petition to the emperor Napoleon to withdraw French troops from Rome . . . 10 May, ,,

The emperor of France declines a union with Austria and Spain for the maintenance of the pope's temporal power . . . June, ,,

Grand ceremony at the canonization of 27 Japanese martyrs (see *Canonization*) . . . 8 June, ,,

The pope declares a severe allocution against the Italians . . . 9 June, ,,

Garibaldi calls for volunteers, taking as his watchword, "Rome or death!" . . . 19 July, 1862

Railway between Rome and Naples completed; its opening opposed by the papal government, Nov. ,,

Earl Russell's offer to the pope of a residence at Malta, 25 Oct.; declined . . . 11 Nov. ,,

Antonelli's resignation of his office not accepted, 5 March, 1863

Convention between France and Italy: French troops to quit Rome within two years, 15 Sept. 1864

Encyclical letter of the pope, publishing a "syllabus," censuring 80 errors in religion, philosophy, and politics; (caused much dissatisfaction, and was forbidden to be read in churches in France and other countries) . . . 8 Dec. ,,

Jews persecuted at Rome . . . Dec. ,,

Fruitless negotiations between the pope and the king of Italy (by Vegezzi); mutual concessions proposed . . . 21 April to 23 June, 1865

Pope's severe allocution against secret societies (Freemasons, Fenians, &c.) . . . 25 Sept. ,,

Merode, the papal minister of war, dismissed, 20 Oct. ,,

A part of the French troops leave the papal dominions Nov. ,,

Rupture with Russia . . . Dec. 1865—Jan. 1866

A Franco-pontifical legion (1200 men) formed at Antibes, arrives; blessed by the pope, 24 Sept. ,,

Pope's severe allocution against Italy and Russia, 29 Oct. ,,

The pope invites all catholic bishops to meet at Rome to celebrate the 18th centenary of the martyrdom of Peter and Paul . . . 8 Dec. ,,

The pope's blessing given to French troops, 6 Dec., who all quit Rome . . . 2-12 Dec. ,,

Rome tranquil . . . 13 Dec. ,,

Law prohibiting protestant worship except at embassies in Rome enforced . . . 31 Dec. ,,

Negotiation with Italy fruitless; the Italian councillor Tonello quits Rome . . . April, 1867

599 bishops and thousands of priests present at the pope's allocution, 26 June; and canonization of 25 martyrs . . . 29 June, ,,

The pope receives an album and address from 100 cities of Italy . . . 8 July, ,,

Cholera in Rome; death of cardinal Altieri, while assisting the afflicted . . . 11 Aug ,,

The pope's allocution censures the sacrilegious audacity of the Sub-alpine kingdom, in confiscating ecclesiastical property . . . 20 Sept. ,,

Garibaldi arrested at Sinalunga, near the Roman frontier . . . 23 Sept. ,,

Irruption of Garibaldians in Viterbo—conflicts with various results; reported appeal of Antonelli for help from the great powers . . . Oct. ,,

Zouave barracks at Rome blown up, many killed, 22 Oct. ,,

Attempt at insurrection in Rome suppressed, 22 Oct.; state of siege proclaimed; Garibaldi within 20 miles of Rome, 24 Oct.; takes Monte Rotondo 26 Oct. ,,

French brigades enter Rome . . . 30 Oct. ,,

Italian troops cross the frontier, 30 Oct.; occupy several posts . . . 1 Nov. ,,

Garibaldians defeated by the papal and French troops at Mentana (*which see*) . . . 3 Nov. ,,

Italian troops retire from the papal states . . . Nov. ,,

The Roman committee of insurrection issue a narrative, and state that their watchword is "Try again and do better" . . . Dec. ,,

The papal army increased to about 15,000 . . . Dec. ,,

The pope's short allocution (thanking and blessing the French government) . . . 19 Dec. 1867

Nine cardinals made; Lucien Bonaparte one 13 March, 1868

Sudden death of cardinal Andrea . . . 15 May, ,,

The pope, in his allocution, censures the Austrian new civil marriage law . . . 22 June, ,,

Arrangement respecting the papal debt made with Italy . . . 30 July, ,,

Encyclical letter of the pope, summoning an œcumenical council at Rome on 8 Dec. 1869, and inviting ministers of the Greek and other churches 13 Sept. ,,

The patriarch of the Greek church declined to attend about 3 Oct. ,,

Monti and Tognetti (for complicity in the explosion of the Zouave barracks, 22 Oct. 1867), executed 24 Nov. ,,

The pope celebrates a jubilee . . . 11 April, 1869

In his allocution he deplores the opposition to the church in Austria and Spain . . . 25 June, ,,

He declares, in a letter to archbishop Manning, that no discussions on disputed points can take place at the council . . . 4 Sept. ,,

The council opened, see *Council XXI.* . . . 8 Dec. ,,

An exhibition of objects of Christian art opened by the pope . . . 7 Feb. 1870

British and American bishops protest against discussing the dogma of papal infallibility in the council, 11 April; the discussion begins 14 May, ,,

Count Arnim, on behalf of the North German confederation, protests against the dogma . . May, ,,

Papal infallibility adopted by the council and promulgated (533 for; 2 against; many retire); the council adjourns to 11 Nov. . . . 18 July, ,,

Rome completely evacuated by French troops in consequence of the war; 8 mortars and 15,000 shells said to be ceded to the pope, 8 Aug.; the troops sent from Civita Vecchia . . . 21 Aug. ,,

Conciliatory letter from Victor Emmanuel to the pope 8 Sept. ,,

Agitation in the papal provinces; the Italian troops invited to enter . . . about 10 Sept. ,,

The pope refuses terms offered him by the king of Italy (sovereignty of the Leonine city and retention of his income) . . . 11 Sept. ,,

Skirmish with papal Zouaves; several killed 14 Sept. ,,

The Italians occupy Civita Vecchia without resistance . . . about 15 Sept. ,,

Gen. Cadorna crosses the Tiber at Casale; sends flags of truce to gen. Kanzler, commander of the Zouaves, who refuses to surrender; baron Arnim in vain negotiates between them . . . 17 Sept. ,,

Letter from the pope to gen. Kanzler directing that a merely formal defence be made at Rome, and that bloodshed be avoided . . . 19 Sept. ,,

After a brief resistance from the foreign papal troops, stopped by order of the pope, the Italian troops under Cadorna make a breach and enter Rome amid enthusiastic acclamations of the people . . . 20 Sept. ,,

[Reported Italian loss, about 22 killed, 117 wounded; papal troops, 55 killed and wounded.]

Cardinal Antonelli issues a diplomatic protest against the Italian occupation of Rome 21 Sept. ,,

The papal troops surrender arms; about 8500 foreigners march out with honours of war; they insult the Italians; the native troops retained, 22 Sept. ,,

About 10,000 persons assemble in the Coliseum, choose 44 names for a provisional government (*giunta*) . . . 22 Sept. ,,

Protest of the pope . . . 26 Sept. ,,

Castle of St. Angelo occupied by Italian troops at the pope's request . . . 28 Sept. ,,

Circular letter from the pope to the cardinals complaining of the invasion and of his loss of liberty, and interference with his private post bag 29 Sept. ,,

A giunta of 14 (the duke Gaetani chief) selected from the 44 names chosen; approved by Cadorna 30 Sept. ,,

General Masi in command of Rome and the provinces; S.P.Q.R. appears on the proclamations 30 Sept. ,,

Plébiscite: out of 167,548 votes, 133,681 for union with the kingdom of Italy; 1507 against; the remainder did not vote . . . 2 Oct. 1870
Cardinal Antonelli issues a protest; published, 4 Oct. ,,
The pope said to have accepted 50,000 crowns (his monthly civil list) from the Italian government, 4 Oct. ,,
The result of the plébiscite sent to the king, 8 Oct., Rome and its provinces incorporated with the kingdom by royal decree . . . 9 Oct. ,,
General La Marmora enters Rome as viceroy; he proclaims that the pope shall be guaranteed in his sovereign powers as head of the church, 11 Oct. ,,
The Roman provinces united into one by decree 19 Oct. ,,
The pope issues an encyclical letter adjourning the meeting of the council . . . 20 Oct. ,,
Antonelli protests against the occupation of the Quirinal by the king . . . 10 Nov. ,,
Bill introduced into the Italian parliament respecting the transfer of the seat of government to Rome in about six months, and the preservation of the spiritual and temporal sovereignty of the pope . . . . about 12 Dec. ,,
Inundation of the Tiber; great suffering of the people, 27, 28 Dec.; the king gives 200,000 lire; visits Rome suddenly, the city illuminated 4 A.M. 31 Dec. ,,
Law guaranteeing to the pope full personal liberty and honours, a revenue of 3,225,000 livres, &c., 13 May; rejected by the pope in his allocution, 15 May, 1871
2624th anniversary of the city kept; the pope celebrates a jubilee on the 25th anniversary of his election . . . . . . 16 June, ,,
The Italian government remove to Rome, 2, 3 July, ,,
Allocution of the pope, appointing some Italian bishops; still rejecting guarantees . 27 Oct. ,,
Grand reception of the king . . . 21 Nov. ,,
He opens the parliament, saying, "The work to which we have consecrated our life is completed" 27 Nov. ,,
The pope receives an address from nobles and others 27 Nov. ,,
Commission appointed to dredge the bed of the Tiber to recover antiquities . . . Dec. ,,
Easter solemnities not performed by the pope 31 March, 1872
The pope delivers an allocution complaining of persecution of the church in Italy, Germany, and Spain . . . 23 Dec. ,,
American Protestant church dedicated to St. Paul; founded . . . 25 Jan. 1873
First Anglican church within the walls opened 25 Oct. 1874
Assassination of Raffaele Sonzogno, a republican printer and manager of "*Il Capitale*," 6 Feb.; trial of Pio Frezza, the murderer caught in the act with Luciani, Armati, and others, as incitors to the crime; convicted "with extenuating circumstances;" penal servitude for life . 13 Nov. 1875
Re-interment on the Janiculum hill of remains of Angelo Brunetti (termed Ciceruacchio) and other unarmed Italian patriots (shot by the Austrians 10 Aug. 1849) . . . . . . 12 Oct. 1879
International exhibition of fine art, opened 21 Jan. 1883
The German crown prince arrives a Rome, 17 Dec.; visits the pope . . . . 18 Dec. ,,
2,637th anniversary of the foundation of Rome 21 April, 1884
First Italian "Derby day" . . . 24 April, ,,
A sale of part of the Castellani collection, 21 days, about 48,000*l.* realized . . . April, ,,
Dispute; a cardinal stopped from visiting a cholera hospital without quarantine . . . Oct. ,,
Discoveries about the Temple of Vesta in the Forum by Prof. H. Jordan, announced April, 1885
Death of prince Torlonia, a great benefactor, aged 86, 7 Feb. 1886
Statue of Giordano Bruno, philosopher (burnt as a heretic at Venice, 17 Feb. 1600); unveiled, 9 June, 1889
Sig. Aurelio Saffi, one of the triumvirs of Feb. 1849, dies at Forli, aged 71 . . . . 10 April, 1890
Great explosion of the powder magazine at Fort Monteverde, 4 persons killed and about 150 wounded; the Vatican and several churches injured, and much property destroyed; the place visited by the king to relieve the sufferers 23 April, 1891
"Labour day," rioting suppressed with bloodshed; 4 persons killed, many wounded . . 1 May, ,,
Popular demonstration against foreign pilgrims for supposed insults to the memory of king Victor Emanuel; 3 pilgrims arrested . . 2-4 Oct. ,,
The Negroni Caffarelli palace burnt; great loss; 26 Aug. 1893
The 11th international medical congress opened; the king and queen present . . 29 March, 1894
National fine art exhibition opened by the king, 17 Sept. 1895
National fêtes, commemoration of the entry of the Italian troops into Rome, 1870; monument to Garibaldi on the Janiculum, unveiled by the king, 20 Sept.; the Humbert bridge opened, and the Cavour monument unveiled, 22 Sept.; other memorials unveiled . . . . 24 Sept. ,,
Anti-Anarchist conference (see *Anarchy*), 24 Nov. 1898
St. Bede's college, founded by cardinal Vaughan for English R.C. converts; papal constitution granted . . . . 29 Dec. ,,
Latin American council inaugurated, mgr. Casanova, president . . . . . 28 May, 1899
Earthquake shock in the city and environs, some damage . . . . 19 July, ,,
Excavations in and around the Forum and the basilica Æmilia, the Via Sacra, the Black stone, Fons and Sta. Maria (2,400*l.* from Mr. Lionel Phillips) discovered by sig. Boni, 1899 *et seq.*; visited by the king . . . . . 6 Nov. 1900
British school at Rome estab. Nov. 1899; excavations going on . . . . . . Jan. 1901
Statue of Goethe presented by the German emperor, 27 Jan. 1902
Prehistoric tomb (abt. 8th century B.C.) discovered in the Forum . . . . . . 2 April, ,,
Visit of the shah, grand review, the king and queen present . . . . . . 22 May, ,,
Death of cardinal Ledochowski, the Red pope, aged 79, 22 July; succeeded by cardinal Gotti, 29 July, ,,
The king opens an international historical congress, 2 April, 1903
Latin congress held in the Capitol . . 15 April, ,,
General strike, 7–10 April; printers' strike ends, 15 April, ,,
Centenary of the French Academy celebrated, the king and queen present . . . 18 April, ,,
Visit of king Edward VII., enthusiastic reception, the city handsomely decorated, 27 April; visits Pope Leo XIII. at the Vatican, 29 April; leaves Rome . . . . 30 April, ,,
Sig. Marconi visits Rome, received with enthusiasm, 1 May; receives the freedom of the city, 7 May, ,,
Students' anti-Austrian demonstration, university closed . . . . . . 1, 2 June, ,,
Death of pope Leo XIII., who bequeathed 90,000 lire to the poor of Rome . . . . 20 July, ,,
Pope Pius X. elected . . . . . 4 Aug. ,,
Fire in the Vatican (see *Pope*) . . . . 1 Nov. ,,

See *Popes*, Pius IX. *et seq.*, and *Italy*.

KINGS OF ROME.

(Dates conjectural.)

B.C.
735. Romulus; murdered by the senators.
[Titus Tatius, king of the Sabines, had removed to Rome in 747, and ruled jointly with Romulus six years.]
716. [Interregnum.]
715. Numa Pompilius, son-in-law of Tatius the Sabine, elected; died at the age of 82.
673. Tullus Hostilius; murdered by his successor, by whom his palace was set on fire; his family perished in the flames.
640. Ancus Martius, grandson of Numa.
616. Tarquinius Priscus; son of Demaratus, a Corinthian emigrant, chosen king.

578. Servius Tullius, a manumitted slave; married the king's daughter; and succeeded by the united suffrages of the army and the people.
534. Tarquinius Superbus, grandson of Tarquinius Priscus; assassinates his father-in-law, and usurps the throne.
510. [The rape of Lucretia, by Sextus, son of Tarquin, and consequent insurrection, leads to the abolition of royalty and the establishment of the consulate.]

REPUBLIC.

510-82. *First period.* From the expulsion of Tarquin to the dictatorship of Sylla.
2-27. *Second Period.* From Sylla to Augustus.
48. Caius Julius Cæsar; perpetual dictator; assassinated, 15 March, 44 B.C.
31. Octavianus Cæsar.

EMPERORS.

27. AUGUSTUS IMPERATOR, died 19 Aug. A.D. 14.
A.D.
14. Tiberius (Claudius Nero).
37. Caius Caligula: murdered by a tribune.
41. Claudius I. (Tiberius Drusus): poisoned by his wife Agrippina, to make way for
54. Claudius Nero; deposed; kills himself, 68.
68. Servius Sulpicius Galba; slain by the prætorians.
69. M. Salvius Otho; stabbed himself.
,, Aulus Vitellius; deposed by Vespasian, and put to death.
69. Titus Flavius Vespasian.
79. Titus (Vespasian), his son.
81. Titus Flavius Domitian, brother of Titus; last of the *twelve* Cæsars; assassinated.
96. Cocceius Nerva.
98. Trajan M. Ulpius (Crinitus).
117. Adrian or Hadrian (Publius Ælius).
138. Antonius Titus, surnamed Pius.
161. Marcus Aurelius (a philosopher) and Lucius Verus, his son-in-law; the latter died in 169.
180. Commodus (L. Aurelius Antoninus), son of Marcus Aurelius; poisoned by his favourite mistress, Martia.
193. Publius Helvius-Pertinax; put to death by the prætorian band.
[Four emperors now start up: Didianus Julianus, at Rome; Pescennius Niger, in Syria; Lucius Septimius Severus, in Pannonia; and Clodius Albinus, in Britain.]
,, Lucius Septimius Severus; died at York in Britain, in 211; succeeded by his sons,
211. M. Aurelius Caracalla and Septimius Geta. Geta murdered by Caracalla, 212; who is slain by his successor
217. M. Opilius Macrinus, prefect of the guards; beheaded in a mutiny.
218. Heliogabalus (M. Aurelius Antoninus), a youth; put to death for his enormities.
222. Alexander Severus; assassinated by some soldiers corrupted by Maximinus.
235. Caius Julius Verus Maximinus; assassinated in his tent before the walls of Aquileia.
237. M. Antonius Gordianus, and his son; the latter having been killed in a battle with the partisans of Maximinus, the father strangled himself in a fit of despair, at Carthage, in his 80th year.
238. Balbinus and Pupienus; put to death.
,, Gordian III., grandson of the elder Gordian, in his 16th year; assassinated by the guards, at the instigation of his successor.
244. Philip the Arabian; assassinated by his own soldiers; his son Philip was murdered at the same time, in his mother's arms.
249. Metius Decius; he perished with his two sons, and their army, in an engagement with the Goths
251. Gallus Hostilius, and his son Volusianus; both slain by the soldiery.
253. Æmilianus; put to death after a reign of only four months.
,, Valerianus, and his son Gallienus; the first was taken prisoner by Sapor, king of Persia, and flayed alive.
260. Gallienus reigned alone.
[About this time thirty pretenders to imperial power arise in different parts of the empire; of these Cyriades is the first, but he is slain.]
268. Claudius II. (Gallienus having been assassinated by the officers of the guard) succeeds; dies of the plague.
270. Quintillus, his brother, elected at Rome by the senate and troops; Aurelian by the army in Illyricum. Quintillus, despairing of success against his rival, who was marching against him, opened his veins and bled himself to death.
,, Aurelianus; assassinated by his soldiers on his march against Persia, in Jan. 275.
275. [Interregnum of about nine months.]
,, Tacitus, elected 25 Oct.; died at Tarsus in Cilicia, 13 April, 276.
276. Florianus, his brother; his title not recognised by the senate.
,, M. Aurelius Probus; assassinated by his troops at Sirmium.
282. M. Aurelius Carus; killed at Ctesiphon by lightning; succeeded by his sons.
283. Carinus and Numerianus; both assassinated, after transient reigns.
284. Diocletian; who associated as his colleague in the government,
286. Maximianus Hercules; the two emperors resign in favour of
305. Constantius I. Chlorus and Galerius Maximianus; the first died at York, in Britain, in 306, and the troops saluted as emperor his son,
306. Constantine, afterwards styled the Great; whilst at Rome the prætorian band proclaimed
306. Maxentius, son of Maximianus Hercules. Besides these were
,, Maximianus Hercules, who endeavoured to recover his abdicated power.
,, Flavius Valerius Severus, murdered by the last-named pretender; and
307. Flavius Valerianus Licinius, the brother-in-law of Constantine.
[Of these, Maximianus Hercules was strangled in Gaul, in 310; Galerius Maximianus died wretchedly in 311; Maxentius was drowned in the Tiber in 312; and Licinius was put to death by order of Constantine in 324.]
323. Constantine the Great now reigned alone; died on Whitsunday, 22 May, 337.
373. { Constantine II. Constans. Constantius II. } Sons of Constantine; divided the empire between them; the first was slain in 340, and the second murdered in 350, when the third became sole emperor.
360. Julian, the Apostate, so called for abjuring Christianity, having been educated for the priesthood; mortally wounded in a battle with the Persians, 363.
363. Jovian; reigned eight months; found dead in his bed, supposed to have died from the fumes of charcoal.
364. Valentinian and Valens.
375. Valens with Gratian and Valentinian II.
379. Theodosius I., &c.
392. Theodosius alone.
395. The Roman empire divided; see *Eastern Empire*, *Western Empire*, *Popes*, and *Italy*.

ROMILLY'S ACT, SIR SAMUEL, 52 Geo. III., c. 101 (1812) relates to charities.

The Romilly society, founded for the improvement of the criminal law, reform of prison regulations, abolition of cruel punishments, &c., inaugurated Essex hall, London, Lord Justice Vaughan Williams in the chair, 1 May, 1898; annual meetings.

RONCESVALLES (in the Pyrenees), where, it is said, Charlemagne's paladin, Roland or Orlando, was surprised, defeated and slain by the Gascons, 778. On 25 July, 1813, marshal Soult was defeated here by the British entering France.

RONDO, a short piece of music having one prominent subject to which returns are made; many composed by Beethoven, Chopin, and others.

RÖNTGEN RAYS, see *Surgery*, 1896. Prof. W. C. Röntgen while experimenting with a Crooke's vacuum tube, electrically excited, and enveloped in a black covering, observed that some rays proceeding from the tube passed through the black paper and affected a fluorescent screen at a distance of two yards, 8 Oct. 1895. See *Vacuum*.

The continued researches proved that many substances opaque to ordinary light were transparent to these rays, as flesh, wood, &c.; the shadows of such objects thrown on a screen can be photographed; the interior of a dead monkey was photographed with great distinctness, *Lancet*, March, 1896.

The movements of the bones in living animals were exhibited by these rays by means of a cinematograph, in 1897 *et seq.* These rays have the power of dis-electrifying electrified bodies.

The rays are much utilized in surgery; 416 cases at St. Thomas's hospital were reported in 1897; very successful in military surgery in 1898 *et seq.*

The Röntgen society founded, prof. Silvanus P. Thompson, president, June; first meeting in London, 5 Nov. 1897 (see *Radiographs*).

Experiments by dr. Heineke in Leipsig show röntgen rays exert a harmful effect on the internal organs of the body, reported, 9 Dec. 1903.

ROOF. The largest in the world was said to be that over a riding school at Moscow, erected in 1791, being 235 feet in span. The roof of the London station of the Midland railway, in Euston-road, London, N.W., is 240 feet wide, 690 feet long, 125 feet high. The extent of ground covered is about 165,000 square feet.

ROPE-MAKING MACHINE. One was patented by Richard March in 1784, and by Edmd. Cartwright, in 1792. Many improvements since.

RORKE'S DRIFT, boundary of British territory of Natal, in South Africa and Zululand. Behind extemporised trenches a handful of British soldiers, under lieuts. Chard and Bromhead, here successfully resisted a large Zulu army, and probably saved the colony, 22 Jan. 1879. See *Zululand*.

ROSAMOND'S BOWER. Rosamond was daughter of lord Clifford, and mistress of Henry II. about 1154. A conspiracy against her was formed by the queen, prince Henry, and the king's other sons. Henry kept her in a labyrinth at Woodstock, where his queen, Eleanor, it is said, discovered her apartments by the clue of a silk thread, and poisoned her. Buried at Godstow church, from whence Hugh, bishop of Lincoln, had her ashes removed, 1191.

ROSARY, see *Beads*.

In a brief of pope Pius IX., 30 Sept. 1852, it was asserted that 40 repetitions in a rosary of 40 beads of "Sweet Heart of Mary, be my salvation!" will obtain a large number of days of indulgence for souls in purgatory (23,300 days calculated).

ROSAS (N. E. Spain), BAY OF, where a brilliant naval action was fought by the boats of the *Tigre*, *Cumberland*, *Volontaire*, *Apollo*, *Topaze*, *Philomel*, *Scout*, and *Tuscan*, led by lieut. John Tailour (of the *Tigre*), which ended in the capture or destruction of eleven armed vessels in the bay, 1 Nov. 1809; for which purpose lord Collingwood had organised the expedition commanded by capt. Hallowell. Rosas was gallantly defended by lord Cochrane, 27 Nov.; but surrendered, 4 Dec. 1809.

ROSBACH (Rosebecque), Flanders. Here Charles VI. of France beat the Flemings, who had revolted against their count, 27 Nov. 1382.—At ROSBACH, in Prussia, a great battle was fought between the Prussians, commanded by Frederick the Great, and the combined army of French and Austrians, in which the latter were defeated with severe loss, 5 Nov. 1757.

"ROSCIUS, INFANT," Wm. Henry West Betty, born 13 Sept. 1791. After acting at Belfast, 16 Aug. 1803, and at other places, with much applause, he appeared at Covent-garden, 1 Dec. 1803, as Selim, in "Barbarossa," and is said to have gained in his first season, 17,210*l*.

After several years' retirement, he re-appeared. but soon after left the stage, not being successful. He retired on the fortune he had amassed, and died Aug. 1874

His portrait may be seen at the Garrick club.

Mr. Thos. Henry Betty, his son, died, aged 77 bequeathing large sums to form eventually the "Betty's Fund for poor actors and actresses, and to the Royal Theatrical fund, &c. 7 Feb. 1897

ROSE, see under *Flowers*. The rose, a symbol of silence, gave rise to the phrase *sub rosâ*, "under the rose;" said, by Italian writers, to have risen from the circumstance of the pope's presenting consecrated roses, which were placed over the confessionals at Rome, to denote secrecy, 1526. The pope sent a *golden rose* to the queen of Spain, which was given to her with much solemnity, 8 Feb. 1868. A "national rose society" opened its first annual show, St. James's hall, 4 July, 1877; shows now held at the Crystal palace.

The *League of the Rose*, under the patronage of the Comtesse de Paris, formed to promote the restoration of the monarchy in France, autumn 1888.

ROSEBERY ADMINISTRATION succeeded the fourth of Mr. W. E. Gladstone, who resigned 3 March, 1894; the ministry resigned in consequence of a minority on a vote of supply (132—125), virtually a vote of censure on the secretary of state for war (Mr. Campbell-Bannerman), who immediately resigned, 21 June. 1895.

First lord of the treasury and lord president of the council—Archibald Philip Primrose (earl of Rosebery).*
Lord high chancellor—Lord Herschell.
Lord privy seal—Edward Marjoribanks (baron Tweedmouth).
Chancellor of the exchequer and leader—Sir Wm. G. G. Vernon-Harcourt.
Secretaries—*home*, Herbert Henry Asquith.
foreign, earl of Kimberley.
colonial, George F. S. Robinson (marquis of Ripon).
war, Henry Campbell-Bannerman.
India, Henry H. Fowler.
Chancellor of the duchy of Lancaster, James Bryce; succeeded by lord Tweedmouth, 26 May.
First lord of the admiralty—John Poyntz (earl Spencer).
Chief secretary for Ireland—John Morley.
Secretary for Scotland—Sir George Trevelyan.
President of the board of trade—Anthony John Mundella; resigned about 12 May, 1894; James Bryce, about 26 May, 1894.
President of the local government board—George J. Shaw-Lefevre.
Vice-president of the committee of council on education—Arthur H. Dyke Acland.
Postmaster-general—Arnold Morley.

The above formed the cabinet.

President of the board of agriculture—Herbert Gardner.
First commissioner of works—Herbert J. Gladstone.
Financial secretary to the treasury—sir John T. Hibbert.

* Born 7 May, 1847; became 5th earl, 1868; president of the social science congress, 1874; lord rector of the university of Aberdeen, 1878; of Edinburgh, 1880; first commissioner of works, 1884; first chairman of the London county council, Feb. 1889—June, 1890; June, 1892; foreign secretary, Feb.—July, 1886; Aug. 1892—March, 1894; resigns the leadership of the liberal party, speech at Edinburgh, 6, 9 Oct. 1896. See *Liberals*.

Permanent secretary to the treasury—sir F. Mowatt.
Attorney-general—sir Charles Russell; sir John Rigby, May, 1894; sir Robert Threshie Reid, Oct. 1894.
Solicitor-general—sir John Rigby; Robert Threshie Reid, May, 1894; sir Frank Lockwood, Oct. 1894.
Secretaries—admiralty, sir Ughtred Kay Shuttleworth.
local government board, sir (Balthazar) W. Foster.
Under-secretaries—home, sir Godfrey Lushington; Kenelm E. Digby, Nov. 1894.
foreign, sir Edward Grey.
colonial, Sydney C. Buxton.
India, Donald James Mackay (lord Reay).
war, lord Sandhurst; lord Monkswell, Jan. 1895.
Ireland.—Lord-lieutenant.—Robert O. A. Milnes, baron Houghton (aft. earl of Crewe, 1895).
Lord chancellor—Samuel Walker.
Attorney-general—The Macdermot.
Solicitor-general—Charles Hare Hemphill.
Lord advocate for Scotland—J. B. Balfour.

ROSE'S ACT, 33 Geo. III. c. 54 (1793) brought benefit societies under the control of government.

ROSES, WARS OF THE, between the Lancastrians (who chose the red rose as their emblem) and the Yorkists (who chose the white rose), 1455-1485. It is stated that in the Wars of the Roses there perished 12 princes of the blood, 200 nobles, and 100,000 gentry and common people. The union of the roses was effected in the marriage of Henry VII. with the princess Elizabeth, daughter of Edward IV. 1486.

Richard II., who succeeded his grandfather Edward III. in 1377, was deposed and succeeded in 1399 by his cousin Henry IV. (son of John of Gaunt, duke of Lancaster, the fourth son of Edward III.), in prejudice to the right of Roger Mortimer (grandson of Lionel, duke of Clarence, Edward's *third* son), who was declared presumptive heir to the throne in 1385
Roger's grandson, Richard duke of York, first openly claimed the crown in 1449
Attempts at compromise failed, and the war began in 1455
The Lancastrians were defeated at St. Albans; the protector Somerset was slain; a truce was made, and Richard was declared successor to Henry VI. 23 May, 1455
The war was renewed, and the Yorkists defeated the Lancastrians at Bloreheath . . 23 Sept. 1459
The Yorkists eventually dispersed, and the duke was attainted.
He defeated his opponents at Northampton, took Henry prisoner, and was declared heir to the crown; but fell into an ambuscade near Wakefield, and was put to death . . . . 31 Dec. 1460
His son (Edward) continued the struggle; was installed as king . . . . 4 March, 1461
Defeated the Lancastrians at Towton . 29 March, ,,
Was deposed by Warwick, who restored Henry VI. Sept. 1470
Edward defeated the Lancastrians at Barnet, 14 April, and finally at Tewkesbury . . 4 May, 1471
The struggle ended with the defeat and death of Richard III. at Bosworth . . . 22 Aug. 1485

ROSETTA (in Egypt), taken by the French in 1798; and by the British and Turks, 19 April, 1801. The Turks repulsed the British here, 22 April, 1807. Near Rosetta was fought the battle of the Nile, 1 Aug. 1798; see *Nile*. Mehemet Ali rendered great service to his country by constructing a canal between Rosetta and Alexandria.

The *Rosetta Stone*, discovered by the French in 1799, was brought from Rosetta in a French vessel, from whence it was taken by Mr. Wm. R. Hamilton, who deposited it in the British Museum. In 1841, Mr. Letronne published the text and a translation of the Greek inscription. It is a piece of black basalt, about 3 ft. long and 2½ ft. wide, with an inscription in three languages, viz., hieroglyphics, modified hieroglyphics (demotic or enchorial), and Greek, setting forth the praises of Ptolemy Epiphanes (about 196 B.C.). It was studied by Dr. T. Young and especially by J. F. Champollion, whose works were published 1814-1845. Champollion's method was adopted by Rosellini, and extended by Lepsius, Bunsen, Birch, Brugsch, and others. Champollion discovered that the hieroglyphs represented sounds by an initial letter, and after studying the "Ritual of the dead," published a grammar and dictionary.

ROSICRUCIANS, a sect of mystical philosophers who appeared in Germany in the 14th century. It is asserted that their founder was a noble German monk named Christian Rosencreutz, born 1378, who travelled in Arabia, Egypt, Africa, and Spain; returned to Germany and founded the fraternity of the Rosy Cross, and died aged 102. The *Fama Fraternitatis* and the *Confessio Roseæ Crucis*, 1615, the latter attributed to Johann Valentin Andreas and others, are important works. They swore fidelity, promised secrecy, and wrote hieroglyphically, and affirmed that the ancient philosophers of Egypt, the Chaldeans, Magi of Persia, and Gymnosophists of the Indies, taught the same doctrine.

Mr. Arthur E. Waite's elaborate work "The Real History of the Rosicrucians" published in 1887.

ROSS, Cork (S. Ireland), a bishopric founded, it is supposed, by St. Fachnan, in the beginning of the 6th century. It was united to Cork in 1340, and Cloyne to both, by the Irish Church Temporalities act (1833); see *Bishops; New Ross*.

ROSTRUM (plural *rostra*), a beak, the name given to the prows of ships, which were affixed to the front of the platform (hence termed *rostra*), erected between the comitium and the forum in Rome, whence the tribunes addressed the people. The custom is said to have begun with the ships of Antium, taken during the Latin war, which ended 33 B.C.

ROTA CLUB, a society who met at Miles's Coffee-house in New Palace-yard, Westminster, during the administration of Oliver Cromwell; their plan was that all the great officers of state should be chosen by ballot: and that a certain number of members of parliament should be changed annually by rotation, from whence they took their title. Sir William Petty was one of the members in 1659. *Biog. Brit.*

ROTHAMSTED EXPERIMENTS, see *Agriculture*, 1843.

ROTHESAY, capital of the Isle of Bute. The ruined castle, founded about 1098, was repaired by the marquis of Bute, 1871-77. After 1398, the eldest son of the Scottish sovereign was styled duke of Rothesay. The Glenburn hydropathic establishment destroyed by fire, estimated loss, 45,000*l.*, 10 July, 1891. Population, 1881, 8,329; 1891, 9,034; 1901, 9,383.

ROTHESAY CASTLE, see *Wrecks*, 1831.

ROTHSCHILD FAMILY. Meyer Amschel, or Anselm, was born at No. 148, Judengasse (Jew-lane), Frankfort, in 1743. In 1772 he began business as a money-lender and dealer in old coins, in the same house, over which he placed the sign of the red shield (in German, Roth Schild). Having had dealings with the landgrave of Hesse, that prince entrusted him with his treasure (said to have been 250,000*l.*) in 1806, when the French held his country. With this sum as capital, Anselm traded and made a large fortune, and restored the 250,000*l.* to the landgrave in 1815. At his death his sons continued the business as partners. His son, Nathan, began at Manchester in 1798, removed to London in 1803; and died immensely rich, 28 July, 1836. The baron, James, head of the family, died at Paris, 15 Nov. 1868.

Sir Nathaniel de Rothschild, son of Lionel, created a peer; takes his seat, 9 July, 1885.

Hannah, daughter and heiress of the late baron Amschel de Rothschild, married to the earl of Rosebery, 1878, a great benefactress, dies, aged 39, 19 Nov. 1890.

Baron Ferdinand de Rothschild, born 1839, died, 17 Dec. 1898.

See *Jews* and *British Museum*, 1899.

Baron Wilhelm Carl von Rothschild, of Frankfort, benefactor, born, 16 May, 1828; died, 25 Jan. 1901.

ROTTERDAM, the second city in Holland. Its importance dates from the 13th century. The commerce of Antwerp was transferred to it in 1509. In 1572, Rotterdam was taken by the Spaniards by stratagem, and cruelly treated. It suffered much from the French revolutionary wars, and from inundations in 1775 and 1825. Desiderius Erasmus was born here in 1467. The museum and picture-gallery of Rotterdam were destroyed at the fire of the Schieland palace, 16 Feb. 1864. Strike of dock labourers about 27 Sept.-14 Oct. 1889. Population, 1887, 193,658; 1890, 209,136; 1900, 332,185. See *Danube*, 1890 *et seq.*

ROUEN (N. France), an archbishopric, 260, became the capital of Normandy in the 10th century. It was held by the English kings till 1204; and was retaken by Henry V., 19 Jan. 1419. Joan of Arc, the Maid of Orleans, was burnt here, 30 May, 1431. It was taken by Charles VII. of France in 1449; and by the duke of Guise from the Huguenots, Oct. 1562 and 1591. Rouen, after slight conflicts, 4, 5 Dec. 1870, surrendered to general Von Göben, 6 Dec. It was ordered to pay a contribution of 17,000,000 francs. Population, 1886, 107,163; 1891, 109,541; 1901, 115,914.

The theatre, destroyed by fire; many persons injured, and 13 killed . . . 25 April, 1876

Strike disturbances, many arrests . 22 Aug. 1899

International peace congress meets . 22 Sept. 1903

"ROUGH TERROR," a term given in 1874 to the prevalence of brutal assaults on women, children, and unprotected persons among the lower classes, especially in Lancashire and other manufacturing districts, for the repression of which the law appeared to be inadequate.

ROUMANIA, a kingdom, the name assumed by the Danubian principalities (*which see*) on 23 Dec. 1861, when their union was proclaimed at Bucharest and Jassy. Population in 1888, 5,376,000; 1902, 6,000,000 (estimated).

M. Catargi, the president of the council of ministers, assassinated as he was leaving the chamber of deputies . . . . 20 June, 1862

The united chambers of the two principalities meet at Bucharest . . . . . 5 Feb. ,,

Coup d'état of prince Couza against the aristocrats; a plébiscite for a new constitution, 2 May; which is adopted . . . . . 28 May, 1864

Law passed enabling peasants to hold land Aug. ,,

Revolt at Bucharest suppressed, 15 Aug.; amnesty, 11 Sept. 1865

Revolution at Bucharest; forced abdication of prince Couza; and provisional government established . . . . 22 Feb. 1866

The offered crown declined by the count of Flanders, Feb.; *prince Charles of Hohenzollern-Sigmaringen* elected hospodar by plébiscite, 20 April; enthusiastically received at Bucharest, 22 May; sworn to observe the constitution 12 July, 1866

Recognised hereditary hospodar by the sultan, and received at Constantinople . . 24 Oct. ,,

Roumania unsettled; "nationality" projects, Nov. 1867

The legislature proposes to repudiate the just claims of the German shareholders in the Roumanian railways; the prince assents reluctantly; Bismarck appeals to the Porte, which declines to interfere . . . . . . July-Aug. 1871

Peace between the prince and chambers . Nov. ,,

Austria, Germany, and Russia inform Turkey that they claim the right to conclude separate treaties with Roumania; the sultan objects . Oct. 1874

Convention with Russia, giving permission to cross Roumania, signed 16 April; Russians enter Moldavia . . . . 24 April, 1877

The Senate vote a declaration of independence and war with Turkey . . . . 21 May, ,,

The Roumanians actively engaged before Plevna.

See *Russo-Turkish War*, 1877.

Roumania declared independent by treaties of San Stefano (3 March) and of Berlin (losing the part of Bessarabia acquired in 1856, in exchange for the Dobrudscha) . . . . . 13 July, 1878

Independence recognised by England, France, and Germany . . . . . . 20 Feb. 1880

The prince and princess crowned king and queen, 23 May, 1881

Temporary rupture with Austria respecting the Danube, about . . . . . 1-27 Dec. ,,

Roumanian troops enter Silistria and seize territory, 3 Sept. 1885

Riotous meeting at Bucharest suppressed with loss of life, 25-27 March; M. Bratiano resigns (twelve years minister) . . . about 27 March, 1888

M. Rosetti forms a ministry . . . 3 April, ,,

Insurrection in the country towns and agricultural districts; increase reported; military called out; Bucharest threatened; revolt said to be encouraged by Russian emissaries 16 April; decrease, 24 April; the elections support the government, Oct.; assembly meets . 13 Nov. ,,

M. Catargi, minister, 12 April, resigns; succeeded by gen. Mano . . . . . 16 Nov. 1889

Proposed impeachment of M. Jean Bratiano, rejected by the chamber (86—67) . . 12 Feb. 1890

Resignation of gen. Mano's ministry . 27 Feb. 1891

Gen. Floresco forms a cabinet . 5 March, ,,

Prince Ferdinand, heir presumptive, said to be engaged to Mlle. Vacaresco, maid-of-honour; public disapproval . . . June, *et seq.* ,,

Sir H. D. Wolff, British minister . . . July, ,,

Mlle. Hélène Vacaresco leaves the queen at Venice 2 Sept. ,,

The king visits the German emperor at Potsdam 28 Oct. ,,

New ministry formed by M. Catargi . . 9 Dec. ,,

Vote of want of confidence in the ministry carried (78—74) . . . . 21 Dec. ,,

The senate and chamber dissolved . 23 Dec. ,,

Coalition of parties; M. Catargi's ministry reconstructed . . . . . about 30 Dec. ,,

Sir J. Walsham, British minister . about Jan. 1892

The government supported by a majority in the elections . . . . Feb. ,,

Prince Ferdinand betrothed to the princess Marie of Edinburgh, 2 June; received in London, 21 June; the king invited by queen Victoria, arrives with his brother, 27 June; at Windsor, 29 June; made K.G., 30 June; leaves England . 4 July, ,,

Dispute with Greece respecting the Zappa bequest, see *Greece* . . . . about 15 Oct. ,,

The king visits Vienna . . . 16-18 Nov. ,,

Treaty of commerce with Great Britain adopted, Dec. ,,

Marriage of prince Ferdinand and princess Marie of Edinburgh at Sigmaringen, near the Danube; present, the king of Roumania, the prince and princess of Hohenzollern, the dukes and duchesses of Edinburgh and Connaught, the emperor William, the grand-duke Alexis of Russia, and many other relatives, 10 Jan.; the prince and princess received at Bucharest . . . . 4 Feb. 1893
Opening of the parliament by king Charles 27 Nov. „
Resignation of many cavalry officers dissatisfied with recent changes in the service reported 16 Feb. 1894
The agitation subsides . . . . . 20 Feb. „
Gen. Lahovari, minister of war, resigns 6 March, „
About 50 persons drowned at Galatz, on the Danube, through the breaking-down of the landing stage . . . . . . 30 April, „
New Sulina canal, opened by king Charles 17 May, „
Parliament opened by the king; revenue surplus, reported 27 Nov. „
Political crisis: M. Demeter Sturdza forms a liberal ministry . . . . . 15 Oct. 1895
Elections: large government majority . 13 Dec. „
Visit of the emperor Francis Joseph to Bukharest, 28 Sept. *et seq.* 1896
Foundation stone of the new harbour laid by the king, at Constanza . . . . 28 Oct. „
Parliament opened by the king, with a cheerful speech . . . . . . 27 Nov. „
Riots in Bukharest against the deposition of the metropolitan Gennadius . . 28, 30 Nov. „
The ministry resigns, new cabinet formed by M. Aurelian, 2 Dec.; question of the deposition of Mgr. Gennadius settled by compromise, 14 Dec.; the metropolitan resigns . . . 17 Dec. „
Resignation of the cabinet . . . . 7 April, 1897
M. Demeter Sturdza forms a cabinet . 11 April, „
Prince Ion Ghika, eminent statesman, born, 1817; died . . . . 4 May, „
New university at Jassy opened by the king and queen . . . . 2 Nov. „
Anti-Semitic riots in Bukharest and Galatz; shops plundered, &c. . . . . . . 5 Dec. „
Parliament opened by the king . . 27 Nov. 1898
Agrarian rising suppressed by troops at Krajova, 5 Feb. 1899
Treaty respecting railways, &c., signed at Berlin, 1 March, „
Disorder in Bukharest, collision with the troops, 2 deaths . . . . 9 April, „
The cabinet resigns, 11 April; M. George Cantacuzene forms a ministry, 23 April; session opened by the king . . . . . 24 June, „
Parliament opened by the king, reform of taxation proposed. . . . . 27 Nov. „
Great exodus of Jews due to restrictive legislation and persecution . . . Jan.–July 19, 1900
Failure of the harvest; reported . . . . „
The ministry resigns . . . . . 17 July, „
Several political murders by Bulgarian revolutionists: Prof. Michaileano shot dead in Bukharest, 4 Aug. „
Strained relations between Bulgaria and Roumania, owing to the Macedonian agitation . . Aug. „
Satisfactory negotiations proceeding . Sept.–Oct. „
Many Bulgarians expelled from the country Oct. „
Conflict between peasants and troops at Pirkoff, 1 death . . . . 2 Nov. „
Nine prisoners convicted of the murder of Kiril Fitofski and prof. Michaileano and plotting against the life of King Charles; Dimitrof and Ilief the actual assassins.
Parliament opened by the king with a firm speech, 28 Nov. „
Decrease of revenue for 1900, reported . Jan. 1901
M. Carp's cabinet resigns; M. Sturdza forms a liberal cabinet . . . . . 26–27 Feb. „
New parliament opened by the king . 6 April, „
Great fire at Kalafat, three streets destroyed, 8 Oct. „
Parliament opened by the king . . 28 Nov „
Rioting in Bukharest, 130 arrests . . 25 Feb. 1902
The Sturdza ministry reconstituted, about 29 July,
American circular note, protesting against the treatment of Roumanian Jews as an international wrong, and as a breach of Article 44, Berlin treaty, 1878, 17 Sept.; British note of enquiry as to the action of the signatory powers, reported, 19 Sept. 1902
State anti-semitism, steady immigration of Jews, June; again . . . . . . Sept.-Oct. „
The king visits Bulgaria early . . . . Nov. „
Parliament opened by the king . . 27 Nov. „

PRINCES AND KING OF ROUMANIA.

1859. Alexander Couza; abdicated 1866.
1866. Charles I. (of Hohenzollern-Sigmaringen); born 20 April, 1839; elected 20 April, 1866; married Elizabeth, daughter of prince Hermann von Wied, 15 Nov. 1869; [scholar, poetess, popularly named Carmen Sylva, and "Mother of her people," visited Wales, at the Eisteddfod, Sept., received by queen Victoria, 2–4 Oct.; left England, 7 Oct. 1890], nominated KING 26 March, 1881, and crowned with the queen, 23 May, 1881.

Heir, Prince Ferdinand (of Hohenzollern), nephew; born 24 Aug. 1865; declared heir, 18 March, 1889; married to princess Marie of Edinburgh, 10 Jan. 1893. *Issue*, Carol, 16 Oct. 1893; Elizabeth, 12 Oct. 1894; Nicholas, 18 Aug. 1903.

ROUMELIA or ROMANIA (Turkey), part of Thrace (*which see*). The Roumelian railway opened 17 June, 1873. Population, 1880, 815,946; 1888, 960,901; 1899, 5,912,520.

By the treaty of Berlin, the province of Eastern Roumelia (termed South Bulgaria in 1886) was constituted, to be partly autonomous, with a Christian governor, nominated by the sultan 13 July, 1878
Sir H. D. Wolff appointed H.M.'s European commissioner for organisation of the province, 10 Aug. „
Russian prince Dondoukoff Khorsakoff rules here July-Nov. „
Scheme for government of the province approved by the sultan and the allied commissioners Nov. „
Russian evacuation begins . . . 5 May, 1879
Aleko Pasha (prince Alexander Vogorides, a Bulgarian) installed as governor at Philippopolis 30 May, „
Much political disorganisation reported Sept. „
Tranquillity restored . . . . . . Dec. „
Great prosperity reported . . . . . Sept. 1883
M. Chrestovitch (Gavril Pasha) appointed governor-general by the Porte, about . . 10 May, 1884
Bloodless revolution at Philippopolis; re-union with Bulgaria proclaimed 18 Sept.; prince Alexander at Philippopolis; all Bulgaria and Roumelia arming . . . . Sept.–Oct. 1885
About 75,000 Roumelians armed . . Nov. „
(see *Turkey* and *Bulgaria* for the war.)
Turkish delegates sent to Philippopolis . 2 Dec. „
Prince Alexander appointed governor for five years, (see *Bulgaria*) . . . . 5 April, 1886
State of siege at Philippopolis on account of brigandage and Russian agency . . 4 Nov. „
Diplomatic rupture with Greece respecting the nationality of a person who died at Bucharest, 13 Nov. 1887
A band of about 150 Montenegrins invading Bourgas repulsed with loss . . . 4 Jan. 1888
Amnesty granted to the insurgent peasantry, 15 Jan. 1889
First Bulgarian exhibition opened at Philippopolis by prince Ferdinand . . . 27 Aug. 1892
Fight between Turkish troops and Bulgarians in Radovishte, six Turks killed, reported . 3 Jan. 1903
Trial of 19 Bulgarian revolutionists at Salonika, three condemned to death, seven to life imprisonment, and others to lighter sentences, 28 March, „

ROUND. A species of musical canon in regular rhythm. Ancient rounds for six voices were composed in Italy, and introduced into England by the earl of Essex, about 1510. The first printed collection appeared in 1609. Warren's collection published 1763-94. Round, Catch, and Canon club founded in 1843.

ROUND-HEADS. In the civil war which began in 1642, the adherents of Charles I. were called Cavaliers, and the friends of the parliament Round-heads. The term, it is said, arose from those persons who had a round bowl or dish put upon their heads, and their hair cut to the edge of the bowl; see *Cavaliers*.

ROUND TABLE, see under *Garter* and *Liberals*, 1887.

ROUNDWAY DOWN (near Devizes, Wiltshire). Here the royalists defeated the parliamentarians with great slaughter, 13 July, 1643.

ROVEREDO (Austrian Tyrol) was held by the Venetians from 1416 till 1609, when it was acquired by Austria. It was taken by Bonaparte and the French, 4 Sept. 1796, after a brilliant victory.

ROWING, see *Boat Races*, *Doggett*, and *University*.

On 16 Oct. 1873, Mr. Reginald Herbert undertook to row on the Thames, from Maidenhead to Westminster bridge (47 miles 3 furlongs), in twelve hours, for 1000*l.* He did it in 10h. 2m. 19 sec.

ROWLAND HILL MEMORIAL FUND. See *Mansion House*. Mr. W. D. Keyworth was chosen to make a bust of sir Rowland Hill for Westminster abbey, March, 1881. A benevolent fund for the widows and orphans of postmen established 1882. A statue of him at the Royal Exchange uncovered by the prince of Wales, 17 June, 1882.

ROWTON HOUSES, buildings erected to afford respectable unmarried working-men cheap comfortable lodgings, with some of the advantages of the west-end clubs. The first in Bond-street, Vauxhall, was erected by lord Rowton, at a cost of 30,000*l.*, to accommodate 470 persons; opened by his niece, Miss Berta Corry, 15 Dec. 1892. Lord Rowton died, aged 65, 9 Nov. 1903.

The scheme proved very successful; a company was started in March, 1894, the first directors being lord Rowton, chairman; Mr. R. E. Farrant, the hon. C. Ashley and Mr. Walter Long. A new Rowton house was erected in Calthorpe-street, King's-cross-road. The building contains 677 cubicles, with good beds and large dining-room, &c., May, 1896; a third house still larger (804 cubicles), opened at Newington Butts, 23 Dec. 1897; a fourth (800 cubicles) opened, Hammersmith-road, 30 Nov. 1899; a fifth, in Fieldgate-st., Whitechapel (816 cubicles), opened, 11 Aug. 1902.

ROXBURGHE CLUB was instituted in 1812 by earl Spencer, for the republication of rare books, or unpublished MSS., in memory of John duke of Roxburghe. See under *Ballads*.

ROYAL AGRICULTURAL, ASTRONOMICAL, GEOGRAPHICAL, HORTICULTURAL, &c.; see under *Agriculture*, *Astronomy*, *Geography*, *Horticulture*, *Niger*, &c.

ROYAL ACADEMY. A society of artists met in St. Peter's-court, St. Martin's-lane, about 1739, which Hogarth established as the society of Incorporated Artists, who held their first exhibition at the Society of Arts, Adelphi, 21 April, 1760. From this sprang the Royal Academy, in consequence of a dispute between the directors and the fellows. On 10 Dec. 1768, the institution of the present Royal Academy was completed under the patronage of George III.; and sir Joshua Reynolds, knighted on the occasion, was appointed its first president. *Leigh.* The first exhibition of the academicians (at Pall-Mall) was on 26 April, 1769, when 136 works appeared. In 1771 the king granted them apartments in old Somerset-house, and afterwards, in 1780, in new Somerset-house, where they remained till 1838, when they removed to the National Gallery. Among the professors have been Johnson, Gibbon, Goldsmith, Macaulay, and Hallam. Turner, the painter, gave funds to the academy for the award of a medal triennially for landscape-painting, which was awarded to Mr. N. O. Lupton in 1857. A commission of inquiry into the affairs of the academy, appointed in 1862, recommended various changes in July, 1863, which were carried into effect. The hundredth anniversary of the foundation of the academy was celebrated 10 Dec. 1868. The Royal Academy held its first exhibition in Burlington-house, Piccadilly, 3 May, 1869. The annual exhibition of pictures by the old masters, with some British, began 3 Jan. 1870. The money received has been devoted to the establishment of a professorship of chemistry and a laboratory, &c. In 1874 the exhibition included many of Landseer's pictures.

Sir Francis Chantrey, sculptor, died 25 Nov. 1841. At the death of his wife Jan. 1875, in conformity with his will, about 3000*l.* a year accrued to the Academy for the purchase of works of art for the nation, and other purposes.

The court of appeal upholds Mr. justice North's decision that the works of sculpture purchased must be finished in marble or bronze, and not models, June, 1889.

The gallery containing the sculptures of John Gibson, bequeathed by him, was opened free, 27 Nov. 1876.

The number of the works of art exhibited in 1789 was about 620, in 1889, 2196, including sculptures.

Rembrandt exhibition, 95 oil paintings and collection of drawings, opened, 31 Dec. 1898.

10,000*l.* bequeathed by the late lord Leighton constituted a trust fund as "The Leighton Bequest," the interest to be devoted to the adornment of public places, &c.; announced, 11 Feb. 1899.

PRESIDENTS.

1768. Sir Joshua Reynolds.
1792. Benjamin West.
1805. James Wyatt (election not confirmed).
1806. Benjamin West.
1820. Sir Thomas Lawrence.
1830. Sir Martin A. Shee.
1850. Sir Charles Eastlake, died 24 Dec. 1865.
1866. Sir Edwin Landseer elected; declines, 24 Jan.
,, Sir Francis Grant, Feb. 1; died 5 Oct. 1878.
1878. Sir Frederick Leighton, 13 Nov.; created lord, Jan. 1896; died 25 Jan. 1896.
1896. Sir John Everett Millais; died 13 Aug. 1896.
,, Sir Edward John Poynter, 4 Nov. 1896 (bart., June, 1902).

ROYAL ACADEMY OF MUSIC was established in 1822, mainly by the exertions of lord Burghersh (afterwards earl of Westmorland, who died 16 Oct. 1859), and was incorporated by charter 23 June, 1830. The first concert took place 8 Dec. 1828. Its reconstruction was proposed in 1866, and since effected. Sir George Macfarren principal, 1876; died, 31 Oct. 1887; succeeded by dr. A. C. Mackenzie, Feb. 1888; knight, Jan. 1895. The duke of Edinburgh, president, July, 1893.

The academy unites with the Royal College of Music in regard to local examinations, announced 13 Nov. 1889

First meeting for the purpose at Marlborough-house . . . . 29 July, 1890

ROYAL ADELAIDE, see *Wrecks*, 1850.

ROYAL ARMY MEDICAL CORPS, name given by the queen to a corps formed out of the Army Medical Staff and the Medical Staff Corps, the officers of which will bear the same military titles as other officers of the army up to the rank of colonel, announced by lord Lansdowne at a banquet given by the lord mayor to members of the medical profession, 4 May, 1898.

ROYAL ASSENT. If the king assent to a public bill, the clerk of the parliament declares in Norman French, "*Le roy le veult*," the king wills it so to be. If the king refuses his assent, it is in the gentle language of "*Le roy s'avisera*," the king will consider it. *Hale*. By the statute 33 Hen. VIII., 1541, the king may give his assent by letters-patent. *Blackstone's Com.*

ROYAL BOUNTY, a fund from which sums are granted to female relatives of officers killed or mortally wounded during service.

ROYAL CHARTER, see *Wrecks*, 1859.

ROYAL COLLEGE, see MUSIC, 1878, and *Science and Art*, 1890. ROYAL ENGLISH OPERA HOUSE, see under *Theatres*.

ROYAL EXCHANGE (Cambium Regis), London. The foundation of the original edifice was laid by sir Thomas Gresham, 7 June, 1566, on the site of the ancient Tun prison. Queen Elizabeth opened it on 23 Jan. 1571, and her herald named it the *Royal* Exchange. *Hume*. It was totally destroyed by the great fire, Sept. 1666. Charles II. laid the foundation-stone of the next edifice, 23 Oct. 1667, which was completed by Mr. Hawkesmore, a pupil of sir Christopher Wren, in about three years; it was repaired and beautified in 1769. This also was burnt, 10 Jan. 1838. The new Royal Exchange, erected under the direction of Mr. Tite, was opened by the queen, 28 Oct. 1844.—Basement of Lloyd's offices damaged by fire, 27 Dec. 1894. Improvement and enlargement of the chimes inaugurated, 1 July, 1895. Decorations: paintings by sir F. (aft. lord) Leighton and others, 1895 *et seq.*; a fresco unveiled 30 Sept. 1903. Messrs. Smith's offices damaged by fire, 16 Jan. 1903. The ROYAL EXCHANGE, Dublin, commenced 1769, opened 1779.

ROYAL GEORGE, a man-of-war of 108 guns, lost off Spithead. While heeled over to repair a pipe, a sudden gust of wind washed the sea into her ports, and she went down. The rear-admiral Kempenfeldt, the crew, many marines, women, and Jews, in all about 600 persons, were drowned, 29 Aug. 1782. By the use of the diving-bell, the ship, embedded in the deep, was surveyed in May, 1817, *et seq.* Portions of the vessel and its cargo were brought up in 1839-42, under the superintendence of sir Charles Pasley, when gunpowder was ignited by the agency of electricity.

ROYAL GRANTS to members of the royal family:—

The queen on July 2 applied to parliament for a grant to prince Albert Victor of Wales for his maintenance, and for one to the princess Louise of Wales on her proposed marriage with the earl of Fife, a select committee was appointed consisting of 23 members (including Mr. Göschen, Mr. W. H. Smith, lord Hartington, Mr. J. Chamberlain, Mr. Gladstone, Mr. John Morley, Mr. Labouchere, Mr. Burt, dr. Cameron, Mr. Parnell, and Mr. Sexton), 8 July, the committee first met 10 July, 1889

After several meetings at which there was much discussion on various propositions, a report was submitted to the house of commons, who eventually resolved, after several amendments had been rejected, that 36,000*l.*, out of the consolidated fund should be paid annually (through trustees) to the prince of Wales for the support and maintenance of his family, the same to continue till six months after the queen's decease, 29 July, 1889. An act of parliament to this effect was passed . . . . . 12 Aug. 1889

ROYAL HUMANE SOCIETY (London), see *Humane Society*.

ROYAL INSTITUTION OF GREAT BRITAIN, the earliest of the kind in London, was founded 9 March, 1799, by count Rumford, sir Joseph Banks, earls Spencer and Morton, and several other noblemen and gentlemen. It received the immediate patronage of George III., and was incorporated 13 Jan. 1800, by royal charter, as "The Royal Institution of Great Britain, for the diffusing knowledge, and facilitating the general introduction of useful mechanical inventions and improvements, and for teaching, by courses of philosophical lectures and experiments, the application of science to the common purposes of life." It was enlarged and extended by an act of parliament in 1810; the original plan, as drawn up by count Rumford, in 1799, having been considerably modified. The members are elected by ballot, and pay ten guineas on admission, and five guineas annually, or a composition of sixty guineas. "The Royal Institution, its Founder, and its first Professors," by Dr. Bence Jones, hon. sec., published 1871.

The HOUSE (in Albemarle-street, Piccadilly) was purchased in June, 1799, and the present front was added by subscription in 1838. The Lecture theatre was erected in 1800–1, under the superintendence of Mr. T. Webster.

The Laboratory established in 1800; was rebuilt, with the modern improvements, 1872.

The LIBRARY was commenced in 1803, by the munificent subscriptions of the proprietors of the institution, It now comprises about 60,000 volumes. Classified catalogues (by W. Harris) were published in 1809 and 1821; new ones (by B. Vincent) in 1857 and 1882.

The MUSEUM contains original philosophical apparatus of Young, Cavendish, Davy, Faraday, and De la Rue.

The first LECTURE was delivered 4 March, 1800, by *Dr. Garnett*, he being the first professor of natural philosophy and chemistry.

In Aug. he was succeeded by *Dr. Thomas Young*, so celebrated for his researches in optics, resulting in the discovery of the interference of light, and the establishment of the theory of undulation. His "Lectures on Natural Philosophy and the Mechanical Arts," first published in 1807, are still considered a text-book of physical science. His works on antiquarian literature (hieroglyphic inscriptions, &c.) are highly esteemed.

In Feb. 1801, Mr. (afterwards sir *Humphry*) *Davy* was engaged as assistant lecturer and director of the laboratory, and on 31 May, 1802, he was appointed professor of chemistry. His lectures were eminently successful, and his discoveries in chemistry and electricity have immortalised his name, and conferred honour on the institution. By him the alkaline metals potassium and sodium, were discovered in 1807; the nature of chlorine was determined in 1810, and the safety-lamp invented in 1815.

William Thomas Brande succeeded sir Humphry Davy as professor of chemistry in 1813, and held that office till his resignation in 1852, since which time, till his death (Feb. 1866), he was hon. professor. From 1816 to 1850 he delivered, in the laboratory of this institution, his celebrated chemical lectures to students.

In 1813 *Michael Faraday* (born 22 Sept. 1791), on the recommendation of sir H. Davy, was engaged as assistant in the laboratory, and in 1825 as its director; in 1827 he became one of the permanent lecturers of the institution. In 1820 he commenced those researches in electricity and magnetism which form an era in the history of science. In 1823-4 he discovered the condensability of chlorine and other gases; in 1831 he obtained electricity from the magnet; in 1845 he exhibited the two-fold magnetism of matter, comprehending all known substances, the magnetism of gases, flame, &c.; in 1850 he published his researches on atmospheric magnetism: died, 25 Aug. 1867.

John Tyndall, F.R.S., professor of natural philosophy, July, 1853, hon. professor, 9 May, 1887; died 4 Dec. 1893; eminent for his researches on magnetism, heat, glaciers, &c.; bequeathed 1,000*l*. to the Royal Institution, received Jan. 1898.

Lord Rayleigh, F.R.S., professor of natural philosophy, 9 May, 1887; is eminent for his researches on sound, light, &c.

Edward Frankland, F.R.S. (after sir), professor of chemistry 1863-8, eminent for his discoveries in organic chemistry; he died, 9 Aug. 1899.

James Dewar, F.R.S. (born 20 Sept. 1842), professor of chemistry, 9 April, and director of the laboratory, 7 May, 1877; eminent for his discoveries and researches in the liquefaction and solidification of gases at high temperatures, air, oxygen, hydrogen, &c., 1878 *et seq.*

In 1804, sir J. St. Aubyn and other gentlemen proposed to form a SCHOOL OF MINES at this institution; but the plan, although warmly supported by the members, was withdrawn for want of encouragement by the government and by mining proprietors.

The WEEKLY EVENING MEETINGS, on the Fridays, from January to June, as now arranged, commenced in 1826. Discourses (of which abstracts have been printed, 1851 *et seq.*) are given at these meetings by the professors of the institution and other eminent scientific men.

ENDOWMENTS. In 1833, John Fuller, esq., of Rosehill, endowed two professorships, of chemistry and physiology; the former bestowed on Mr. Faraday for life; succeeded by Dr. Wm. Odling, 1868-73; by Dr. John Hall Gladstone, 1874, died 7 Oct. 1902; by James Dewar, 1877. The latter on Dr. Roget for three years, to be filled up afterwards by triennial election.—The Fullerian professors of physiology have been P. M. Roget, R. E. Grant, T. R. Jones, W. B. Carpenter, W. W. Gull, T. W. Jones, T. H. Huxley (*twice*), R. Owen, J. Marshall, Michael Foster, Wm. Rutherford, Alfred H. Garrod, and E. A. Schäfer (1878-81), J. G. McKendrick, 1881-4; A. Gamgee, 1884; G. J. Romanes, 1888, Victor Horsley, 1891; Charles Stewart, 1893; Augustus D. Waller, 1897; Edwin Ray Lankester, 6 Jan. 1898; Dr. Allan Macfadyen, Jan. 1901.—In 1838, Mrs. Acton gave 1000*l*. to be invested for paying every seven years 100 guineas for the best essay on the beneficence of the Almighty, as illustrative of a department of science; which have been awarded in 1844 to Mr. G. Fownes; in 1851 to Mr. T. Wharton Jones; in 1858 no award was made; in 1865 to Mr. George Warington; in 1872 to Rev. George Henslow and B. Thompson Lowne; in 1879, to Mr. G. S. Boulger; in 1886, to Prof. (aft. sir) G. G. Stokes, Pres. R.S.; Miss Agnes M. Clerke, 1893; sir Wm. and lady Huggins, 1900.

The "Fund for the Promotion of Experimental Research" was founded on 6 July, 1863, by sir Henry Holland, Professor Faraday, sir R. I. Murchison, Dr. Bence Jones, and others.

Many donations received, 1863 *et seq.*; since 1892 liberal donations have been received to support prof. Dewar's researches connected with low temperatures: Mr. Thomas G. Hodgkins, of Long Island, New York, 100,000 dollars; Goldsmiths' company, 1,000*l*., Nov. 1892; again 1,000*l*., Nov. 1899. The earl of Derby bequeaths 2,000*l*., 21 April, 1893 *et seq.*; Mr. Ludwig Mond, 1887–93, 1,540*l*.; others since.

In 1843 the establishment of a school of practical chemistry in the institution approved by profs. Faraday and Brande was proposed but failed.

On 2 July, 1894, the scheme was revived by Mr. Ludwig Mond, F.R.S. and M.R.I., who presented to the institution the house adjoining, with a proposal for its transformation into a laboratory, to be termed the DAVY-FARADAY RESEARCH LABORATORY. He supplied the funds necessary for the incidental expenses of the work, and also gave an endowment sufficient to maintain a staff of professors and assistants, and to supply everything necessary for the prosecution of scientific research, especially in pure chemistry and physical science. The laboratory is an adjunct to the Royal Institution, and is open, conditionally, to independent private research. The conveyance and deed of trust dated 8 June, 1896. The laboratory is subject to a committee appointed by the managers of the institution, the first directors being lord Rayleigh and prof. James Dewar. Dr. Alexander Scott appointed superintendent, 1896. The laboratory was opened by the prince of Wales, after an historical address by Dr. Ludwig Mond, followed by experiments in liquid air, by prof. Dewar, 22 Dec. *Times*, 23 Dec. 1896.

The *first officers* of the institution were sir Joseph Banks, *president*, till the charter was granted, afterwards the earl of Winchilsea; Mr. (afterwards sir Thomas) Bernard, *treasurer*; rev. Dr. Samuel Glasse, *secretary*.—Algernon duke of Northumberland, K.G., elected *president*, 1842; succeeded by sir Henry Holland, in 1865 (died 27 Oct. 1873); by Algernon George, duke of Northumberland, K.G., 1873 (died 2 Jan. 1899); by his son, Henry George, duke of Northumberland, 6 March, 1899. W. Pole, esq., *treasurer*, elected 1849; succeeded by Wm. Spottiswoode, esq., in 1865; by George Busk, esq., 1873; by Henry Pollock, esq., 1886; by sir James Crichton Browne, 1889. The rev. John Barlow, *secretary*, elected 1842; succeeded by Henry Bence Jones, M.D., 1860; by Wm. Spottiswoode, 1873; by Warren de la Rue, 1879; by sir Wm. Bowman, Bart., 1882; by sir Frederick Bramwell, Bart., 1885; by sir Wm. Crookes, 1900. *Librarians*: Wm. Harris, 1803-23; S. Weller Singer, 1826-35; Wm. Mason, 1835-48; Benjamin Vincent, 1849-89 (hon. librarian, 1889; died 3 May, 1899); Henry Young, 1889. 21 eminent foreign scientific men were elected honorary members, 4 May, 1891, in relation to the Faraday centenary, *which see*.

Centenary celebrations: 26 eminent foreign scientists elected honorary members, 1 May, 1899; banquet to the foreign delegates at the Merchant Taylors' hall, the prince of Wales, the dukes of Cambridge and Northumberland, the lord chancellor and others present, 5 June; the prince of Wales presides at a commemorative lecture by Lord Rayleigh on the "Discoveries of Thos. Young," 3 p.m., and presents diplomas to the foreign scientists, 4 p.m.; the lord mayor holds a reception in the evening, 6 June; at the second lecture (the duke of Northumberland in the chair), prof. Dewar produced liquid hydrogen, *which see*, in substantial quantities at about 21° absolute temperature, and by it solidified liquid oxygen and air, and exhibited a succession of beautiful experiments before lords Kelvin, Rayleigh, and a brilliant audience, Friday eve, 7 June, 1899.

Historical apparatus, &c., was exhibited in the upper library, 5–7 June, 1899.

Bust of sir Frederick Bramwell unveiled by the duke of Northumberland, 17 Jan. 1902.

Michael Faraday relics, bequeathed by Mr. Thos. Deacon, of Newcastle-on Tyne, received, Jan. 1902.

ROYAL LITERARY FUND, see *Literary Fund, Royal*.

ROYAL MARRIAGE ACT, &c., see *Marriage Act*; *Royal Military* and *Naval Asylums*; *Navy*, and *Prerogative*.

ROYAL NAVAL COLLEGE, see *Naval*.

ROYAL SOCIETY (London). In 1645 several learned men met in London to discuss philosophical questions and report experiments; the *Novum Organon* of Bacon, published in 1620, having given great impulse to such pursuits. Some of them (Drs. Wilkins, Wallis, &c.), about 1648-9, removed to Oxford, and with Dr. (afterwards bishop) Seth Ward, the hon. Robert Boyle, Dr. (afterwards sir) W. Petty, and several doctors of divinity and physic, frequently assembled in the apartments of Dr. Wilkins, in Wadham college, Oxford. They formed what has been called the Philosophical Society of Oxford, which only lasted till 1690. The members were, about 1658, called to various parts of the kingdom, on account of their respective professions; and the majority coming to London, constantly attended the lectures at Gresham college, and met occasionally till the death of Oliver Cromwell, 3 Sept. 1658; see *Societies*, and *Scientific Papers*. "Record of Royal Soc." issued 1897.

The society was organised in 1660, and constituted by Charles II. a body politic and corporate, by the appellation of "The President, Council, and Fellowship of the Royal Society of London, for improving Natural Knowledge," 22 April, 1662.

Henry Oldenburg, the first secretary, an eminent philosopher, a native of Bremen, a friend of Milton, Boyle, Wilkins, Wallis, and Petty, died Sept. 1677.

Evelyn records the first anniversary meeting, St. Andrew's-day, 30 Nov. 1663.

The *Philosophical Transactions* begin 6 March, 1664-5.

In 1668 Newton invented his reflecting telescope (now in the possession of the society), and on 28 April, 1686, presented to the society the MS. of his *Principia*, which the council ordered to be printed. This was done under the superintendence and at the expense of Halley the astronomer, at that time clerk to the society.

The society met for some years at Gresham College, and afterwards at Arundel House (1666), where it came into possession of a valuable library, presented by Mr. Howard, grandson of its collector, the earl of Arundel. After various changes the fellows returned to Gresham College, where they remained till their removal to Crane-court, in a house purchased by themselves, 8 Nov. 1710.

The Croonian lecture was founded in 1701; the Bakerian lecture by Henry Baker, 1774.

The first Copley medal was awarded to Stephen Gray in 1731; the royal medal to John Dalton, 1826; the Rumford medal (instituted in 1797) to count Rumford himself in 1800.

The society remove to apartments granted them in Somerset-house, 1780; to apartments in Burlington-house, Piccadilly, 1857.

Parliament votes annually 4000*l.* to the Royal Society for scientific purposes; raised to 5,000*l.* in 1895.

Regulations made by which only fifteen fellows are to be annually elected, who pay ten pounds on admission, and four pounds annually, or a composition of sixty pounds, March, 1847. In consequence, the number of fellows was reduced from 839 in 1847, to 626 in 1866; to 567 in 1875; to 552 in 1877; to 523 in 1888; 511 in 1893.

The entrance fee abolished, and the annual payment reduced to 3*l.*, announced, Nov. 1878.

The "Royal Society Scientific Fund" was founded in imitation of the "Literary Fund" in 1859; see *Scientific Fund*.

The Davy medal (*which see*) first awarded, Nov. 1877.

The Darwin medal (see *Development*) first awarded, 1890.

The Croonian lecture given by prof. Virchow, of Berlin, 16 March, 1893.

Sir Wm. Mackinnon bequeaths over 16,000*l.* to the society, announced Dec. 1897.

The "Hughes" medal for original discovery in physical science, particularly electricity and magnetism (from a bequest by prof. David Edw. Hughes), first awarded to Joseph John Thomson, Nov. 1902.

PRESIDENTS

1660. Sir Robert Moray.
1663. Lord Brouncker.
1677. Sir Joseph Williamson
1680. Sir Christopher Wren.
1682. Sir John Hoskyns.
1683. Sir Cyril Wyche.
1684. Samuel Pepys, author of Diary.
1686. John, earl of Carbery.
1689. Thomas, earl of Pembroke.
1690. Sir Robert Southwell.
1695. Chas. Montague (afts. earl of Halifax).
1698. John, lord Somers.
1703. Sir Isaac Newton (M.P. for Cambridge University, 1688–1705).
1727. Sir Hans Sloane.
1741. Martin Folkes.
1752. George, earl of Macclesfield.
1764. James, earl of Morton.
1768. James Burrow.
,, James West.
1772. James Burrow.
1772. Sir John Pringle.
1778. Sir Joseph Banks.
1820. Dr. W. H. Wollaston.
1820. Sir Humphry Davy.
1827. Davies Gilbert.
1830. Duke of Sussex.
1838. Marquis of Northampton.
1848. Earl of Rosse.
1854. Lord Wrottesley.
1858. Sir Benj. C. Brodie.
1861. Maj.-gen. sir Edward Sabine.
1871. Sir G. B. Airy.
1873. Dr., afterwards sir, Joseph Dalton Hooker.
1878. Wm. Spottiswoode, died 27 June, 1883.
1883. T. H. Huxley, 5 July.
1885. Sir George G. Stokes, 30 Nov. (M.P., 1887, Bart., 1889).
1890. Sir William Thomson, 1 Dec. (created Baron Kelvin, Feb. 1892.)
1895. Sir Joseph Lister, 30 Nov., baron Lister, Jan. 1897.
1900. Sir William Huggins, 1 Nov.

ROYAL SOCIETY OF EDINBURGH, incorporated 29 March, 1783, arose out of the Philosophical Society of Edinburgh, founded in 1739. It received a second charter in 1811.

ROYAL SOCIETY OF LITERATURE was founded under the auspices of king George IV. in 1823, and chartered 13 Sept. 1826.

ROYAL STYLE, &c., see *Style, Royal*, and *Titles*. Royal titles act passed by royal assent, 17 Aug. 1901.

ROYAL UNIVERSITY OF IRELAND, see *University*.

RUBICON, a small river flowing into the Adriatic sea, separated Cisalpine Gaul from Italy proper. Roman generals were forbidden to pass this river at the head of an army. Julius Cæsar did so, Jan. 49 B.C., and thereby began a revolt and deadly civil war.

RUBIDIUM, an alkaline metal, discovered by Bunsen by means of the spectrum analysis, and made known in 1861.

RUBRICS, directions in church offices, often printed in red. New ones for the English service agreed to by convocation, 4 July, 1879.

RUBY MINES OF BURMAH, Tavernier (middle of the 17th century) describes it as a place where rubies and other precious stones are largely obtained, in a country difficult of access. Similar accounts were given by Father Giuseppe d'Amato, about 1830. The largest stones were royal property. Mr. Bredemeyer had charge of these and other mines in 1868. Revenue about 1855, from 12,500*l.* to 15,000*l.* per annum. These mines are now British property (see under *Burmah*, 1885), and for the use of them a revenue is paid by the Shan tribes, 1887. An agreement respecting them made between the Indian Government and Messrs. Streeter & Co. of London, announced May, 1887; suspended July, 1887. Working licences issued to persons on the spot, 1887. Lease for seven years to the Streeter Syndicate signed at the India office, 22 Feb. 1889; formation of a company headed by Messrs. Rothschild, March *et seq.*, 1889. Visit of sir Lepel Griffin to the mines, satisfactory to the company, reported March, 1890. Lt.-governor, sir Hugh Shakespear Barnes, April 1903.

RUFFLES became fashionable about 1520; and went out about 1790.

RUGBY SCHOOL (Warwickshire), was founded in 1567 by Lawrence Sheriff, a London tradesman; its arrangements were affected by the Public Schools act 1868. Dr. Thomas Arnold, the historian, entered on the duties of head-master here in August, 1828, and under him the school greatly prospered. He died 12 June, 1842. His successors were Drs. Tait, Goulburn, Temple, Hayman, Jex Blake, Percival and H. A. James (since 1895). See *New Rugby*.

Dr. H. Hayman was opposed by the masters of the school, and after much dissension and discussion, was dismissed by the trustees, Dec. 1873, and Dr. Jex Blake elected in his room, Feb. 1874. Succeeded by Rev. J. Percival, Nov. 1886 (created bp. of Hereford, 1895); the rev. H. A. James elected, 21 March, 1895.

Vice-Chancellor Malins decided against Dr. Hayman in his attempt to set aside his dismissal, but expressed his own opinion on "the grievous hardship of Dr. Hayman's case," 21 March, 1874.

Mr. Disraeli, the premier, presented Dr. Hayman to the living of Aldingham, Lancashire, April, 1874.

Population of Rugby in 1881, 9,891; 1891, 11,262; 1901, 16,830.

Thomas Hughes, author of "Tom Brown's Schooldays," (at Rugby under Dr. Arnold), born 20 Oct. 1823, died 22 March, 1896.

The abp. of Canterbury unveils memorials to dean Goulburn and abp. Benson, 1 Oct. 1898.

RUGEN, an island in the Baltic, has frequently changed masters, having been held by the Danes, Swedes, and French. Transferred to Prussia 1815.

RUHMKORFF'S INDUCTION COIL, see *Induction*.

"RULE, BRITANNIA." The words are by James Thomson (altered by Mallet); the music, ascribed to Dr. Arne, is said by Schœlcher (in his life of Handel) to have been taken from an air in Handel's "Occasional Oratorio" composed 1746, but the song and music were really printed in Dr. Arne's masque of "Alfred," 1740. *Grove*.

RULE-OF-THE-ROAD, see *Seas*.

RULING MACHINES, used for ruling paper with faint lines, for merchants' account-books, &c. They were invented by an ingenious Dutchman, resident in London, in 1782, and were subsequently greatly improved by Woodmason, Payne, Brown, and others. They were improved in Scotland in 1803. An invention has lately rendered account-books perfect by the numbering of the pages with types, instead of the numbers being written by a pen, so that a page cannot be torn out from them without being discovered. The late Herr F. A. Nobert devised a ruling machine in 1845 for the production of microscopical test plates, diffraction gratings, and micrometers, specimens of which were exhibited in 1851. The test plates contain bands of lines in a graduated series of fineness from $\frac{1}{1000}$ to $\frac{1}{20000}$ of a Paris line.

RUM (French *rhum*), ardent spirit distilled from sugar lees and molasses, deriving its peculiar flavour from a volatile oil. Rum is principally made in the West Indies. The duty (since 1900) on rum imported into the United Kingdom is 11*s.* 4*d.* per gallon, 1*s.* additional per gallon if imported in bottle (since 1899).

Imported.	*Gallons.*	*Imported.*	*Gallons*
1848	6,858,981	1882	7,305,679
1851	4,745,244	1885	6,877,581
1857	6,515,683	1887	6,362,070
1863	7,194,738	1890	6,237,773
1871	7,526,890	1893	5,942,132
1877	7,920,150	1896	5,373,904
1879	6,946,657	1900	6,239,151
1880	6,107,661	1901	6,719,452
1881	4,816,887	1902	8,210,668

RUMFORD MEDAL, see *Royal Society*.

RUMP PARLIAMENT, see *Pride's Purge*.

RUNES. Alphabetic characters, probably of Phœnician origin, but popularly ascribed to the god Odin, cut or scratched on stone monuments, weapons, ornaments, implements, &c., which have been hypothetically dated from 1000 B.C. to 1000 A.D.; principally found in Scandinavia and England, and sometimes in Western Europe. Professor George Stephens, of Copenhagen, in his "Old Northern Runic Monuments in Scandinavia and England" (1866-84), has given the results of forty years' studies.

RUNNING, see *Athletic Sports*. Cross-country championships, the National won by A. Shrubb, S. London Harriers, 1902; Shrubb also ran 2 miles in 9 min. 11 sec., establishing a world's record, 30 May, 1903; T. Conneff, Travers Is., New York, ran 1 mile, in 4 min. 15¾ sec., 30 Aug. 1895.

RUNNY-MEDE (council-mead), near Egham, Surrey. Here king John granted Magna Charta, 15 June, 1215.

RUPEE. See *India*, 1892 *et seq.* The value of the coin varied during 1895; exchange on 11 Nov. 1896, stood about 1*s.* 3⅜*d.*; 1898-1903, at 1*s.* 4*d.*

RUPERT'S LAND (N. America), or *Red River Settlement*, now Manitoba, formerly the territories of the Hudson's bay company, was made a bishopric in 1849. By the Rupert's Land act, passed 1868, the Hudson's bay co. surrendered its rights over the entire region, which is now included in the dominion of Canada. See *Hudson's Bay*, *Canada*, and *Manitoba*.

RUPTURE SOCIETY, London, established 1804; see *Truss*.

RURAL CONFERENCES. A meeting in London of delegates from rural districts, organised in connection with the National Liberal Federation, claiming reform, 10 Dec. 1891. Mr. W. E. Gladstone addressed the conference, 11 Dec. 1891

A congress of labourers, &c., organized by the eastern counties conservative associations, was held at Ely. The Rt. Hon. Henry Chaplin present . . . . . . 29 Jan. 1892

Rural conference at Leicester . . . . 2 April, ,,

Rural Labourers' League: Mr. Jesse Collings, president; 3rd annual meeting, at Westminster; the duke of Devonshire and Mr. Joseph Chamberlain present, 17 Feb. 1892; again 6 June, 1893; 26 July, 1894 . . . . . . 27 Aug. 1895

RUSKIN MUSEUM, see *Sheffield*, 1881-90, and *Oxford*, 1899.

Ruskin Society of London, formed for the promotion of Mr. Ruskin's opinions in relation to art, inaugurated at the London Institution . 21 March, 1890

"The Life and Work of John Ruskin," by W. G. Collingwood, published . . . April, 1893

"John Ruskin" school, Walworth, opened by lord Reay . . . . . . 23 Feb. 1899

John Ruskin, born 1819, died at Coniston, 20 Jan. 1900

Ruskin Union, for the study, &c., of his works, founded at a meeting, Mr. Fred. Harrison in the chair, and council appointed, London, 8 Feb. 1900; first congress opened at Sheffield, lord Windsor president . . . . . 21 Sept. ,,

Ruskin exhibition at Coniston . . July–Sept. ,,

Memorial at Friars' Crag, Keswick, unveiled by Mrs. Arthur Severn . . . . . . 6 Oct. ,,

The Ruskin museum and institute opened, 31 Aug. 1901

"The Ruskin plot," 5 acres of land at Cothill, Berks, to be kept uncultivated, given by Mr. Henry Willett to the Ashmolean Nat. Hist. Soc., reported . . . . . . 21 Oct. ,,

Ruskin memorial fund; Mr. Geo. Cadbury gives 500*l.* . . . . . . March, 1902

Lord Avebury lays the first stone of the Ruskin memorial museum, &c., at Bournville, near Birmingham . . . . . . 21 Oct. ,,

RUSSELL ADMINISTRATIONS,* see *Palmerston Administration*, &c.

* Lord John Russell, third son of John, duke of Bedford, was born 19 Aug. 1792; M.P. for Tavistock

FIRST ADMINISTRATION (formed on the resignation of sir Robert Peel), July, 1846.

First lord of the treasury, lord John Russell.
Lord chancellor, lord Cottenham (succeeded by lord Truro).
Lord president of the council, marquis of Lansdowne.
Privy seal, earl of Minto.
Chancellor of the exchequer, Mr. (aft. sir Charles) Wood.
Foreign, home, and colonial secretaries, viscount Palmerston, sir George Grey, and earl Grey.
Boards of control and trade, sir John Hobhouse (aft. lord Broughton), and earl of Clarendon (succeeded by Mr. Labouchere).
Admiralty, the earl of Auckland (succeeded by sir Francis Thornhill Baring).
Duchy of Lancaster, lord Campbell (succeeded by the earl of Carlisle, late viscount Morpeth).
Secretary at war, Mr. Fox Maule.
Postmaster, marquis of Clanricarde.
Paymaster-general, T. B. Macaulay.
Lord John Russell and his colleagues resigned their offices, 21 Feb. 1851; but were induced (after the failure of lord Stanley's party to form an administration) to return to power, 3 March following.

SECOND ADMINISTRATION (or continuation of his first), March, 1851.

First lord of the treasury, lord John Russell.
President of the council, marquis of Lansdowne.
Lord privy seal, earl of Minto.
Chancellor of the exchequer, sir Charles Wood.
Home, foreign, and colonial secretaries, Sir George Grey, viscount Palmerston (succeeded by earl Granville, 22 Dec.), and earl Grey.
Lord chancellor, lord Truro.
First lord of the admiralty, sir Francis T. Baring.
Board of control, lord Broughton.
Board of trade, Mr. Labouchere.
Secretary at war, Mr. Fox Maule (aft. lord Panmure, and earl of Dalhousie).
Postmaster-general, marquis of Clanricarde.
Paymaster-general, earl Granville.
Lord Seymour, earl of Carlisle, &c.
This ministry resigned 21 Feb. 1852; see *Derby Administration*.

THIRD ADMINISTRATION. (On the decease of lord Palmerston, 18 Oct. 1865, earl Russell received Her Majesty's commands to reconstruct the administration.)

First lord of the treasury, John, earl Russell.
Lord chancellor, Robert, lord Cranworth.
Postmaster-general, John, lord Stanley of Alderley.
President of the poor-law board, Chas. Pelham Villiers.
Lord president of the council, George, earl Granville.
Lord privy seal, George, duke of Argyll.
Chancellor of the exchequer, Wm. E. Gladstone.
Secretaries—foreign affairs, George, earl of Clarendon; *colonies*, Edward Cardwell; *home*, sir George Grey; *war*, George, earl de Grey and Ripon, succeeded by Spencer, marquis of Hartington, Feb. 1866; *India*, sir Charles Wood, resigned (created viscount Halifax); succeeded by earl de Grey, Feb. 1866.
First lord of the admiralty, Edward, duke of Somerset.
President of the board of trade, Thos. Milner Gibson.
Chancellor of the duchy of Lancaster, George J. Göschen.
Secretary for Ireland, Chichester Fortescue.
This ministry resigned, 28 June, 1866, in consequence of a minority on 19 June (see under *Reform*, and *Derby Administrations*).

RUSSELL INSTITUTION (Great Coram-street, London), was founded in 1808 by sir Samuel Romilly, Francis Horner, Dr. Mason Good, Henry Hallam, sir James Scarlett (aft. lord Abinger), and others. The building comprises a library, news room, billiard room, &c.

1813; for London, 1841–61; was paymaster of the forces, 1830–34; secretary for home department, 1835–9; for the colonies, 1839–41; first minister, July 1846 to March 1852; secretary for foreign affairs, Dec. 1852 to Feb. 1853; president of the council, June 1854 to Feb. 1855; secretary for the colonies, March to Nov. 1855; secretary for foreign affairs, June 1859 to Oct. 1865, when he succeeded lord Palmerston as premier; created a peer, as earl Russell, 30 July, 1861. His motion for reform in parliament was negatived in 1822; adopted 1 March, 1831: he introduced the registration bill and a new marriage bill in 1836; introduced and withdrew a reform bill, 1860; died 28 May, 1878.

RUSSELL TRIAL. William, lord Russell's trial for complicity in the Rye-house plot was marked by a most touching scene. When he requested to have some one near him to take notes to help his memory, he was answered, that any of his attendants might assist him; upon which he said "My WIFE is here, and will do it for me." He was beheaded in Lincoln's-Inn-Fields, 21 July, 1683. Lady Russell survived him forty years, dying 29 Sept. 1723, in her eighty-seventh year. His attainder was reversed, 1 Will. III. 1689.

RUSSIA, the eastern part of ancient Sarmatia. The name is generally derived from the Roxolani, a Slavonic tribe. Ruric, a Varangian chief, appears to have been the first to establish a government, 862. His decendants ruled amid many vicissitudes till 1598. The progress of the Russian power under Peter the Great and Catherine II. is unequalled for rapidity in the history of the world. The established religion of Russia is the Greek church, with toleration of other sects, even Mahometans. By an imperial ukase, in 1802, six universities were established, viz., at St. Petersburg, Moscow, Wilna, Dorpat (in Livonia), Charcov, and Kasan; but literature made little progress till the present century, the native publications being very few, and the best books being translations. The Russian language, though not devoid of elegance, is, to a foreigner, of very difficult pronunciation; the number of letters and diphthongs is forty-two. The Anglo-Russian Literary Society, with library, &c., set up at the Imperial Institute, 1893. The population of the empire in 1867, 82,159,630; in 1872, about 85,685,945; in 1877 (estimated), 86,952,347; in 1885, 108,843,192; 1st general census of the empire, total, 129,211,113, 9 Feb. 1897. By the first Russian budget (1862), the estimated revenue was 34,500,000*l*.; expenditure, 37,850,000*l*; 1892, revenue, 118,025,000*l*.; expenditure, 112,549,000*l*.; 1897, revenue (estimate), 142,823,037*l*.; expenditure the same; 1902, total debt, 690,107,109*l*. Besides about 500 cathedrals, about 35,000 churches (Greek church, *which see*). Total armed strength of Russia, estimated at 3,460,000, 1903. Railways, 1893, 19,441 miles; 1902, 35,079 miles open.

	A.D.
Russia invaded by the Huns	376
Ruric the Norman or Varangian, arrives at Novgorod (or New City), and becomes grand duke [anniversary kept 20 Sept. 1862]	862
Oleg successfully invades the Greek empire	907
Baptism of Olga, widow of duke Igor, at Constantinople, about	955
Vladimir the Great marries Anne, sister of the emperor Basil II., and is baptized	988
The Golden Horde of Tartars conquer a large part of Russia about	1223
The grand duke Juric killed in battle	1237
Alexander Newski defeats the invading Danes	1241
The Tartars establish the empire of the khan of Kaptschak, and exercise great influence in Russia	1242
He is made grand duke of Russia by the Tartars	1252
Moscow made the capital	1300
Tartar war, 1380; Moscow burnt	1383
Tamerlane invades Russia, but retires	1395
Accession of Ivan III. the Great—able and despotic, founds the present monarchy	1462
Ivan introduces fire-arms and cannon into Russia	1475
Great invasion of the Tartars; consternation of Ivan	1479
His general Svenigorod annihilates their power	1481
War with Poland	1506–23
The English "Russian company" established	1553
Richard Chancellor sent to open the trade	1554
Discovery of Siberia	"

The royal body-guard (the Strelitz) established . 1568
Ivan solicits the hand of queen Elizabeth of England 1579
Murder of Feodor I., last of the race of Ruric, which had governed Russia for 700 years . . . 1598
The imposition of Demetrius (see *Impostors*).—Matins of Moscow . . . . . 29 May, 1606
Michael Fedorovitz, of the house of Romanoff, ascends the throne 1613
Finland ceded to Sweden 1617
Russian victories in Poland 1654
Subjugation of the Cossacks 1671
Reign of Ivan and Peter I. or the Great . . . 1682
Peter sole sovereign 1689
He visits Holland and England, and works in the dockyard at Deptford 1697
Recalled by a conspiracy of the Strelitz, which he cruelly revenges; 2000 tortured and slain; he beheads many with his own hand 1698
The Russians begin their new year from 1 Jan. (but retain the old style) 1700
War with Sweden; Peter totally defeated by Charles XII. at Narva . . . . . 30 Nov. ,,
Peter founds St. Petersburg as a new capital, 27 May, 1703
The Strelitz abolished 1704
Charles XII. totally defeated by Peter at Pultowa, and flees to Turkey . . . . 8 July, 1709
14,000 Swedish prisoners sent to Siberia . . . ,,
War with Turkey: Peter and his army cross the Pruth, and are surrounded by the Turks; they escape by the energy of the empress Catherine, who obtains a truce . . . . . June, 1711
Esthonia, Livonia, and a large part of Finland added to the empire 1715
Peter visits Germany, Holland, and France . . ,,
The Jesuits expelled 1718
Conspiracy and mysterious death of prince Alexis 7 July, ,,
Peter II. (last of the Romanoffs) deposed, and the crown given to Anne of Courland 1730
Elizabeth, daughter of Peter I., reigns, in prejudice of Ivan VI., an infant, who is imprisoned for life 1741
Peter III. dethroned and murdered, succeeded by Catherine his wife 1762
Ivan VI., the rightful heir, till now immured, put to death 1764
Treaty of Kutschouc Kainardji; independence of the Crimea and freedom of Black sea . July, 1774
Rebellion of the Cossacks, 1774: suppressed . . 1775
Successful invasions of the Crimea . . . 1769–84
Dismemberment of Poland; commenced by Catherine (see *Poland*), 1772; completed . . . 1795
Catherine gives her subjects a new code of laws; abolishes torture in punishing criminals; and dies 1796
Unsuccessful war with Persia . . . . . ,,
Russian treaty with Austria and England . . . 1798
Suwarrow, with an army joins the Austrians, and checks the French in Italy 1799
Mental derangement of Paul, 1800; murdered, 24 March, 1801
Alexander I. makes peace with England . May, ,,
He joins the coalition against France . 11 April, 1805
Allies defeated at Austerlitz . . . 2 Dec. ,,
Treaty of Tilsit with France . . . 7 July, 1807
Russians defeated by the Turks, near Silistria, 26 Sept. 1809
War with France . . . . . . June, 1812
The Russians defeated at Smolensko, 17 Aug.; and at the Borodino . . . . . 7 Sept. ,,
Moscow burnt by the Russians, 14 Sept.; retreat of the French begins . . . . 15 Oct. ,,
Alexander present at the battle of Leipsic, Oct. 1813; entered Paris . . . . . March, 1814
He visits England . . . . . . June, ,,
Forms the Holy Alliance 1815
The grand duke Constantine renounces the right of succession . . . . . . 26 Jan. 1822
Death of Alexander, 1 Dec.; Pestal's conspiracy against Nicholas I.; insurrection of troops at Moscow; suppressed . . . 26-29 Dec. 1825
Nicholas crowned at Moscow . . . 3 Sept. 1826
War against Persia . . . . . 28 Sept. ,,
Nicholas visits England; invested with the order of the Garter . . . . . . 9 July, 1827
Peace between Russia and Persia . . 22 Feb. 1828
War between Russia and the Ottoman Porte declared (see *Turkey* and *Battles*) . . . 26 April, ,,

Peace of Adrianople . . . . . . 14 Sept. 1829
The war for the independence of Poland against Russia (see *Poland*) . . . . 29 Nov. 1830
Failure of the expedition against Khiva . Jan. 1840
Treaty of London (see *Syria*) . . . 15 July, ,,
The emperor Nicholas arrives in London . 1 June, 1844
The grand duke Constantine arrives at Portsmouth in the *Ingermanland*, of 74 guns . 9 June, 1846
For the participation of Russia in the Hungarian [war of 1848-9, see *Hungary*.]
Russia demands the expulsion of the Hungarian and Polish refugees from Turkey (see *Turkey*) 5 Nov. 1849
They are sent to Konieh, in Asia Minor . Jan. 1850
Conspiracy against the emperor detected 6 Jan. ,,
Harbour of Sebastopol completed . . Feb. ,,
The emperor decrees seven men in each thousand of the population of Western Russia to be enrolled in the army, giving a total increase of 180,000 soldiers . . . . Aug. ,,
St. Petersburg and Moscow railway begun . 1851
The czar visits Vienna . . . . 8 May, 1852
Concentrates forces on frontiers of Turkey . Feb. 1853
Origin of the Russo-Turkish war (*which see*, and *Holy Places*) . . . . . . March, ,,
Conference between the emperors of Russia and Austria at Olmutz . . . . 24 Sept. ,,
And king of Prussia at Warsaw . . . 2 Oct. ,,
Interview of Mr. J. Sturge and other quakers with the czar to obtain peace . . . Feb. 1854
The northern provinces put in a state of siege, 5 March, ,,
The czar issues a manifesto to his subjects: he will combat only for the faith and Christianity, 23 April, ,,
Death of the czar Nicholas, and accession of Alexander II.; no change of policy . 2 March, 1855
Most extensive levy ordered by the czar (at Nicolaieff) . . . . 3 Nov. ,,
He visits his army at Sebastopol . . . 10 Nov. ,,
Death of prince Ivan Paskiewitsch, aged 74 1 Feb. 1856
Treaty of peace at Paris . . . 30 March, ,,
Alexander Gortschakoff foreign minister and chancellor . . . . 29 April, ,,
Amnesty granted to the Poles, 27 May; five political offenders, &c.; Alexander II. crowned at Moscow . . . . 7 Sept. ,,
Manifesto on account of the English and French interference in the affairs of Naples 2 Sept. ,,
St. Petersburg and Warsaw railway begun by government, 1851; ceded to Great Russian railway company (about 335 miles, the half completed) .
Grand duke Constantine visits France and England, April, 1857
The czar meets the emperor Napoleon at Stutgardt, 25 Sept.; and the emperor of Austria at Weimar, 1 Oct. ,,
Partial emancipation of the serfs on the imperial domains . . . . 2 July, 1858
A Russian naval station established at Villa Franca, on the Mediterranean, creates some political excitement . . . . Aug. ,,
New commercial treaty with Great Britain 12 Jan. 1859
Russia reproves the warlike movements of the German confederation during the Italian war, 27 May, ,,
The czar protests against the recognition of the sovereignty of peoples . . . 13 Feb. 1860
Fruitless meetings of the emperors of Russia and Austria and the regent of Prussia at Warsaw 20-25 Oct. ,,
Treaty with China for enlargement of commerce 1 Jan. 1861
Decree for the total emancipation of the serfs (23,000,000) throughout the empire in two years (19 Feb.) . . . . 3 March, ,,
Demonstrations and repression in Poland (*which see*) Feb.-April, ,,
Disturbances in South Russia, caused by an impostor asserting himself to be a descendant of Peter III.; many peasants shot or flogged, May and June, ,,
Inundations at Kiev, Moscow; 615 houses under water . . . . May, ,,
Death of prince Michael Gortschakoff, governor of Poland . . . . 14 May, ,,
Student riots at the university of St. Petersburg, which is closed, 6-9 Oct.: reopened . 24 Oct.

The nobles sign a petition for a political constitution Nov. 1861
Increased privileges granted to the Jews . 26 Jan. 1862
Death of Nesselrode, the chancellor of the empire, 20 March, ,,
Alarming increase of fires at St. Petersburg and Moscow ; the government suppresses various educational institutions . . . . June, ,,
Russia recognises the kingdom of Italy 10 July, ,,
1000th anniversary of the foundation of the Russian monarchy at Novgorod, celebrated 20 Sept. ,,
Re-organisation of the departments of justice decreed ; juries to be employed in trials, &c. 14 Oct. ,,
Trade tax bill introduced, admitting foreigners to merchants' guilds, &c. . . . . 26 Nov. ,,
Insurrection in Poland 22-24 Jan. 1863
[For events, see *Poland*.]
Termination of serfdom . . . . 3 March, ,,
Provincial institutions established throughout Russia . . . . 13 Jan. 1864
Great victory over the Oubykhs in the Caucasus, 31 March ; emigration of the Caucasian tribes into Turkey, April ; submission of the Aïbgas ; the war declared to be at an end. . . . 2 June, ,,
The cesarevitch betrothed to the princess Dagmar of Denmark . . . . . . 28 Sept. ,,
Serfdom abolished in the Trans-Caucasian provinces : new judicial system promulgated . . Dec. ,,
The Russian nobles request the emperor to establish two houses of representatives [declined] 24 Jan. 1865
New province, "Turkestan," in central Asia, created 14 Feb. ,,
The cesarevitch Nicholas dies at Nice . 24 April, ,,
Industrial exhibition at Moscow closes . 16 July, ,,
Censorship of the press relaxed ; law begins, 13 Sept. ,,
Rupture with the pope, on account of Russian severity to Polish clergy . . Jan. and Feb. 1866
Assembly of the nobility ; short, stormy session March, ,,
Inauguration of trial by jury in Russia . 8 Aug. ,,
Karakozow attempts to assassinate the czar, 16 April ; after long investigation into the origin of the plot, he is executed . . . . 15 Sept. ,,
War with Bokhara ; conflicts with varying results ; Russians advance in May, *et seq.* ; ended . Nov. ,,
Marriage of prince Alexander, heir to the crown, to princess Dagmar of Denmark . . . 9 Nov. ,,
Emancipation of many state serfs in Poland, 11 Nov. ,,
Three decrees for abolishing the remains of Polish nationality . . . . 1 Jan. 1867
Congress of Slavonian deputies at Moscow 5 May, ,,
Russian America sold to the United States for 7,000,000 dollars, by treaty, 13 March ; ratified 15 May, ,,
Amnesty in favour of the Poles . . . 29 May, ,,
The czar visits Paris (*which see*) . . . June, ,,
Escapes assassination by Berezowski, a Pole, 6 June, ,,
Decree for the use of the Russian language in the Baltic provinces . . . . . . 7 July, ,,
A Romanist college to replace the authority of the pope, established at St. Petersburg . 2 Aug. ,,
The separate interior government in Poland suppressed . . . . 29 Feb. 1868
Samarcand taken by Kaufmann . . . 26 May, ,,
Amnesty for political offences granted . 6 June, ,,
Polish language interdicted in public places in Poland . . . . July, ,,
The *Government Messenger*, official journal, published at St. Petersburg . . . . . 13 Jan. 1869
Socialist secret conspiracy among the students, headed by Sergius Netschajew, detected ; the informer assassinated . . . . . . Jan. 1870
Burlingame, Chinese envoy, arrives . . 2 Feb. ,,
Dies at St. Petersburg . . . . . 22 Feb. ,,
Russia neutral in the Franco-Prussian war July, ,,
Said to be arming, 20 Sept. ; contradicted 27 Sept. ,,
Fruitless visit of M. Thiers at St. Petersburg on behalf of the French government . . 27 Sept. ,,
Diplomatic circular of prince Gortschakoff, foreign minister, repudiating the clauses of the treaty of 30 March, 1856, respecting the Black Sea, 31 Oct. ; received by earl Granville, 9 Nov., who replies, maintaining the force of the treaty . 10 Nov. ,,
Vigorous protest of British and Austrian governments . . . . 16 Nov. ,,
Decree for forming military reserves, about 16 Nov. ,,
Conciliatory despatch from prince Gortschakoff to earl Granville, agreeing to a conference for revision of the treaty of 1856 . . 20 Nov. 1870
Prussian government expresses surprise at Gortschakoff's circular, and proposes a conference about 26 Nov. ,,
Firm courteous despatch from earl Granville, consenting to a conference which shall "assemble without any foregone conclusion" . 28 Nov. ,,
The other powers agree to a conference 7 Dec. ,,
Re-organisation of the army ordered . . Jan. 1871
The conference meets in London . . 17 Jan. ,,
The Black Sea clauses abrogated (see *Black Sea*), by treaty, signed . . . . . 13 March, ,,
Schamyl, the Circassian chief, dies about April, ,,
The grand duke Wladimir visits England . June, ,,
Military exercises, sham battles round St. Petersburg, 30,000 engaged ; emperor present, 15-23 Aug. ,,
Trial of persons implicated in a socialist conspiracy (at St. Petersburg) ; many condemned to imprisonment . . . . Sept. ,,
Electric telegraph between St. Petersburg and Nagasaki, Japan, completed . . . . . Nov. ,,
200th anniversary of the birth of Peter the Great, 30 May, 1672 (o.s.), solemnly observed by the court and nation . . . . 11 June, 1872
Peter the Great ironclad (incomplete) launched at St. Petersburg . . . . . . Aug. ,,
Great Russian Encyclopædia undertaken by prof. Beresina . . . . autumn ,,
Reconnoitring expedition to Khiva ; defeat of gen. Markosoff announced . . . . . Dec. ,,
Diplomatic visit of count Schouvaloff to London respecting this ; presented to the queen ; Russian concessions reported satisfactory . . 13 Jan. 1873
Expeditions against Khiva start . . . March, ,,
The emperor of Germany warmly received at St. Petersburg . . . . . . 27 April, ,,
The Shah of Persia visits St. Petersburg 22-31 May, ,,
Khiva surrenders, 10 June ; a rebellion suppressed, July, ,,
Jumuden Turcomans defeated at Tschandyr 25, 27 July, ,,
New treaty with Bokhara, published . . Dec. ,,
Marriage of the grand duchess Marie with the duke of Edinburgh . . . . 23 Jan. 1874
Visit of the emperor of Austria at St. Petersburg, 13 Feb. ; the czar in proposing his health, says, "In the friendship which binds us and also the emperor William and the queen Victoria, I see a most sure guarantee of peace" . . 15 Feb. ,,
The czar visits England . . . . 13-21 May, ,,
Count Schouvaloff succeeds Brunnow as ambassador in London . . . . . . autumn, ,,
New law for organization of the army . . Sept. ,,
Son born to the duke of Edinburgh and grand-duchess Marie . . . . 15 Oct. ,,
Visit of the empress and the cesarevitch to England 15 Oct.-24 Nov. ,,
Mitrophania, mother abbess, of Serpouchow, Moscow, prosecuted for fabricating commercial bills ; convicted, and sentenced to 14 years' exile, Nov. ,,
International telegraphic conference at St. Petersburg . . . . 1-19 July, 1875
Expedition (with scientific men) to Krasnovodsk, Central Asia, spoken of . . . . . Aug. ,,
War with Khokand (*which see*) . . 4 Sept.—Oct. ,,
Commercial panic through failure of Dr. Strousberg, a German railway speculator, at Moscow, Prague, and Berlin . . . . Nov. ,,
At a dinner of "Knights of St. George," the czar declares that the three emperors are united to maintain peace . . . . . . 8 Dec. ,,
Baltic provinces (formerly a provincial federation with a governor), incorporated with the empire under the ministry of the interior, on the death of the governor Bagration . . . 29 Jan. 1876
Khokand, formally annexed (as Ferghana) 29 Feb. ,,
Prosecution of a sect "White Doves" (Skoptzi) April, ,,
Warlike enthusiasm ; Russian volunteers in the Servian army . . . . . July-Sept. ,,
Depression through Servian defeats . . . Oct. ,,
Pacific declaration of the czar to lord Aug. Loftus 2 Nov. ,,

The czar, in an address at Moscow, says that if sufficient guarantees are not given by Turkey, he will act independently . . . 10 Nov. 1876
Dr. Strousberg and others tried for fraud, &c., Nov.; he is sentenced to banishment from Russia 14 Nov. „
Enthusiasm for Bulgarians; partial mobilisation of the army ordered . . . about 14 Nov. „
Internal loan of 10 million roubles . 19 Nov. „
Great enthusiasm for Bulgarians; war declared, and begun 24 April, 1877
See *Turkey*; and *Russo-Turkish War*, 1877.
The czar warmly received at Moscow, 4 May; and St. Petersburg . . . 7 May, „
Great trial of Nihilists for revolutionary propagandism, begun about . . . . 31 Oct. „
Russian loan of 15,000,000*l.* at 5 per cent. announced 12 Nov. „
The czar at St. Petersburg; celebrates centenary anniversary of birth of Alexander I. 23 Dec. „
Ill-feeling against Bulgarians . . . . Dec. „
Nihilist trial ended; about 160 sentenced to hard labour; about 90 acquitted, . about 9 Feb. 1878
Treaty of peace with Turkey signed at San Stefano; Europe dissatisfied . . . . . 3 March, „
Vera Zasulitch (or Sassulitch), a young woman, who acknowledged firing at gen. Trepoff, prefect of St. Petersburg (5 Feb.), for severity to prisoners, acquitted by jury . . . 12 April, „
Reported spread of Nihilism in Kieff, Moscow, &c. April, „
Public depression: feeling against Bulgarians; desire to get quit of the Eastern question May-June, „
Conference at Berlin (*which see*) meets 13 June; treaty signed . . . . . 13 July, „
Gen. Kaufmann's advance on the Oxus to occupy Balkh; reported . . . . Aug. „
Nihilists tried and condemned at Odessa; riots ensued . . . . . . 5 Aug. „
General disaffection to the government; general De Mesentzoff, chief of police, assassinated in the street in St. Petersburg . . 16 Aug. „
New 5 per cent. loan (300,000,000 roubles) issued on bonds . . . . 29, 30, 31 Aug. „
Ukase decreeing state offences to be punished by military law . . . . end of Aug. „
Gen. Drentelen made chief of police . . 6 Oct. „
Students at a college in St. Petersburg present an address to the cesarevitch complaining of grievances, 11 Dec.; they are attacked and punished by the police and cossacks, 12 Dec.; they issue an address soon after . . . . Dec. „
Prince Demetrius Krapotkine, governor, assassinated while returning from a ball at Kharkoff, 21 or 22 Feb. 1879
Attempted assassination of Drentelen, 25 March; and of the czar by Alexander Solovieff, a schoolmaster, with a revolver . . . . . 14 April, „
The poll tax abolished by ukase . . . April, „
Riots at Rostoff on the Don suppressed by military, 14 April, „
Ukase establishing martial law in the provinces of St. Petersburg, Moscow, Kieff, Odessa, and Warsaw, dated . . . . . 17 April, „
"Land and Liberty," a Nihilist newspaper, freely yet surreptitiously circulated . . . . April, „
Solovieff condemned, 7 June; executed . 9 June, „
Discontent at the small results of the war . July, „
Trials, convictions, and executions of Nihilists at Kieff and Odessa . . . . . May-Aug. „
Gen. Lazareff, commander of expedition against the Tekké Turkomans, dies at Tchat about 13 Aug. „
Gen. Lomakine succeeds in command; severe battle at Geok Tepe or Dengli Tepè; Russians said to be victorious, yet retreat with heavy loss 28 Aug. (O.S.), 9 Sept. „
Tergukasoff succeeds Lomakine in command, 25 Sept. „
Leon Mirsky condemned to death for attempted assassination of gen. Drentelen, chief of police 27, 28 Nov. „
Count Schouvaloff, ambassador at London, resigns, 27 Nov. (succeeded by prince Lobanof). . . „
Attempted assassination of the czar, by undermining railway train near Moscow; none hurt; baggage carriages destroyed . . . 1 Dec. „
The newspaper *Golos* suspended for 6 months, 4 Dec „
Proclamation of the executive revolutionary committee justifying the attempted assassination on 1 Dec. . . . . . . 4 Dec. 1879
Plot to blow up the Winter Palace, St. Petersburg, discovered . . . . . 12 Dec. „
"Will of the People" revolutionary paper freely circulated . . . . . Nov.-Dec. „
Explosion in a guard-room filled with dynamite and gun-cotton under the dining-room of the Winter Palace, St. Petersburg; the czar and family escape through being a little late for dinner; 11 soldiers killed; 47 wounded; between 6.0 and 7.0 P.M., 17 Feb. 1880
Hartmann, owner of a house near the explosion, arrested at Paris . . . about 20 Feb. „
Panic at St. Petersburg; ukase issued; appointing supreme executive commission, gen. Loris Melikoff, president, with extensive powers; virtual dictator . . . . . . 24 Feb. „
Extradition of Hartmann requested by Russia; declined . . . . March, „
Twenty-fifth anniversary of the czar's accession celebrated at St. Petersburg . . . 2 March, „
Hippolyte Molodzoff (Mladetsky, or Wladitsky, or Mlodecki), a converted Jew, fires at gen. Loris Melikoff, 4 March; hanged . . . 5 March, „
Hartmann expelled from France; goes to England; Prince Orloff, ambassador, quits France, about 6 March, „
Nihilist trials at St. Petersburg; sentences to death and imprisonment (Dr. Weimar and others); commuted . . . . May, „
Death of the empress after a long illness, 3 June, „
21 extreme Nihilists convicted at Kieff (capital sentences remitted) . . . . about 7 Aug. „
Ukase of 24 Feb. superseded; Melikoff, who had governed well, appointed minister of the interior, with charge of the police . . . 18 Aug. „
Count Loris Melikoff's scheme for administrative reform sanctioned by the czar; announced 3 Oct.; put into action . . . . . 25 Oct. *et seq.* „
"*Russia*," new national daily paper, published Oct. „
Great Nihilist trial at St. Petersburg for assassinations, explosion at Winter Palace, &c.; sentences, Kviatofski and 4 others condemned to death: 8 men and 3 women to imprisonment . 10 Nov. „
Kviatofski and Priessnakoff hanged . . 16 Nov. „
Gen. Skobeleff's expedition into Central Asia, 24 Dec. „
Severe conflicts with the Tekké Turkomans, 14 Jan. 1881
Geok Tepé besieged; taken . . . . 24 Jan. „
Assassination of the czar Alexander II. by explosion of a bomb; assassin himself killed; Risakoff seized . . . . . . 2 P.M. 13 March, „
A mine for explosion discovered in the middle of St. Petersburg . . . . about 15 March, „
Circular of the new czar Alexander III. to foreign powers; he will aim at moral and material development of Russia, and a pacific foreign policy 16 March. „
Manifesto from the Nihilist executive committee to the czar offering peace, if an amnesty with a legislative assembly to be elected by universal suffrage, free press, &c., be granted . . 22 March, „
Sophie Peroffskaja, and other Nihilists, arrested 23 March, „
The czar's magnificent funeral at St. Petersburg; the prince and princess of Wales present, 27 March, „
A representative council for St. Petersburg elected about 31 March, „
Trial of Risakoff, Sophie Peroffskaja, Jelaboff, Jessie or Hessie Heljmann, Kibaichick, and Michailoff (four men and two women), all condemned to death . . . . 8, 9 April, „
The Tekkés submit; maraudings cease; object of Skobeleff's expedition accomplished; announced 9 April, „
Risakoff and others hanged; Heljmann (*enceinte*) reprieved . . . . . . 15 April, „
Treaty of peace with China announced . April, „
Nihilist manifesto styling the assassins "martyrs," &c. . . . . 16 April, „
Changes in ministerial offices; tendency to reduce autocracy of the czar announced . about 4 May, „
Ukase supplementary to that of 19 Feb. 1861, for emancipating serfs, remitting payments to many peasant proprietors; announced . early May, „
Reactionary proclamations in favour of autocracy

(29 April), 11 May; resignation of count Loris Melikoff and other liberal ministers soon after, about 13 May, 1881
General Ignatieff, chief minister, issues manifesto, declaring for suppression of rebellion, and promising reforms; manifesto from Nihilists offering peace if reforms be granted . . 23 May, „
The czar, closely guarded, living in close seclusion; continued policy of repression . . June, „
The czar well received at Moscow, &c., 30 July; the czar meets the emperor of Germany at Dantzic 3 Sept.; stringent decree respecting public order 21 Sept. „
Treaty with Persia signed . . . . 22 Dec. „
Nihilist trials at St. Petersburg; 10 sentenced to death, 28 Feb.; commuted to penal servitude (except Suchanoff, to be shot) . . March, 1882
Gen. Strelnikoff, public prosecutor, assassinated at Odessa by two students, 30 March; executed 3 April, „
Retirement of the chancellor and foreign minister, Gortschakoff (his policy war-like); succeeded by his assistant De Giers . . about 9 April, „
Mine discovered under Moscow cathedral; 80 workmen arrested . . . . about 15 April, „
General Kaufmann died, aged 64 . . 16 May, „
Decree for the gradual abolition of the poll tax (imposed by Peter the Great) . beginning June, „
Ignatieff resigns; succeeded by count Tolstoy about 12 June, „
Death of general Scobeleff, the hero of Plevna, aged 39 . . . . 7 July, „
General Tchernaïeff appointed to command in Central Asia . . . . „
Successful exhibition of Russian arts and manufactures . . . . summer, „
Revival of the Russian navy determined on . . „
Tranquillity restored; great festivities through the visit of the duke and duchess of Edinburgh Jan.—Feb. 1883
Death of prince Gortschakoff, aged 85 11 March, „
Arrest of 200 persons at St. Petersburg about 20 March, „
Trial of Nihilists at St. Petersburg: some sentenced to death (remitted), others to imprisonment 19 April, „
The emperor and empress crowned with great ceremony at Moscow . . . . . 27 May, „
Patriotic and pacific manifesto, and amnesty, 27 May; and popular festival 2 June, „
Poll tax abolished for the poorest, reduced for others (1 Jan. 1884) on . . 8 June, „
The czar and the kings of Denmark and Greece breakfast with Mr. Gladstone on board the *Pembroke Castle*, Copenhagen . . . . 18 Sept. „
Reported discovery of a great conspiracy at St. Petersburg; many arrests . about 27 Sept. „
Government projects for re-modelling the communes . . . . published Oct. „
Grand funeral of Turgénieff at St. Petersburg, 9 Oct. „
Foundation of memorial church at the place where Alexander II. was assassinated at St. Petersburg laid by the czar . . . . 16 Oct. „
63 Nihilists sentenced to Siberia . . 19 Oct. „
Lieut. Sudeikin, chief of secret police, and his nephew, M. Sudovsky, assassinated at St. Petersburg; attributed to Nihilists aided by Jablonsky, a subordinate, whose life he had saved night of 28-29 Dec. „
37 students at Moscow arrested announced 9 Jan. 1884
Loyal address of the nobles to the czar, advocating union of nobles and peasantry . . . 25 Jan. „
Surrender of Merv to Russia, effected by general Komaroff . . . . . announced 14 Feb. „
Proposals for state loan not taken up, Nov. 1883; another loan at 6 per cent. offered in open market about 3 Dec. 1883; taken up . . April, „
Convention with Persia for cession of Sarakhs (threatening to Afghanistan) reported 6 May, „
The majority of the cesarevitch (aged 16) declared 18 May, „
Death of general Todleben, born 1818 . 1 July, „
Alleged dynamite conspiracy against the czar at Warsaw . . . . 8 Sept. „
Maria Wassilieona Kaliouchnaia, at Odessa, sentenced to 20 years' hard labour for attempt to shoot colonel Katensky . . . about 11 Sept. „
The czar meets the emperors of Germany and Austria at Skiernievice, near Warsaw 15, 16 Sept. 1884
The letters of "Stepniak" and others expose the cruel, dishonest, and unscrupulous conduct of government officials in prohibiting the diffusion of knowledge and literature; proposed united opposition of the nobility and peasantry Sept.-Oct. „
The circulation of many religious books prohibited „
14 Nihilists (including 6 officers and 3 women, one, Mary F. Figner) convicted by secret court martial; 8 sentenced to death at St. Petersburg, 11 Oct.; two men executed . . . . . 18 Oct. „
The Nihilist journal, *Narodnaia Volia*, reappears about 27 Oct. „
Sir Robert Morier, British ambassador at St. Petersburg . . . . „
Great discontent among workmen and peasantry Jan. 1885
Mission of M. Lessar, engineer-diplomatist to London respecting central Asian boundaries . Feb. „
Ship canal from St. Petersburg to Cronstadt completed, Feb.; opened . . . . 27 May, „
Russians advance to about 90 miles from Herat, and hold Zulfikar pass . . . . Feb. „
Three courses before them: to retire; to remain and negotiate; to make war . . . 1 March, „
(It was mainly through the urgent remonstrances of general Lumsden that a collision was avoided.)
Arrangement that no further advance on the "debated or debatable ground" be made by Russians or Afghans (since termed a "solemn covenant") . . . . 16 or 17 March, „
British government announce agreement to arbitration (by Denmark) . . . . 4 May *et seq.* „
The Russian general Komaroff, near the Kushk and Murghab rivers, commands the Afghans to retire; on their refusal, attacks them at Aktapa (or Aktepe or Pul-i-khusti), near Penjdeh; defeats them with much slaughter, and captures this important stragical position with artillery and stores; many Afghans perish in the retreat through exposure 30 March, 53 Russians killed and wounded; (sir Peter Lumsden reports the attack on the Afghans to have been unprovoked 14 April) . . . . „
The British government prepares for war with great energy; strongly supported by the colonies and Indian princes . . . . „
British government statement: new agreement with Russia; arbitration respecting fight on March 30 accepted 4 May; Denmark accepts work of arbitration . . . . May, „
Agreement on delimitation settled by earl Granville and earl of Kimberley, with MM. de Staal and Lessar; approval reported . 30 May, „
Cordial meeting of the czar and the emperor of Austria at Kremsier in Moravia . 25, 26 Aug. „
The Afghan boundary question settled 10 Sept. „
Discovery of plot against the czar; arrest of military officers and others . . . April, 1886
Tchesmé ironclad launched by the czar at Sebastopol (other vessels constructing) 18 May, „
Russia violates treaty of Berlin by declaring Batoum not to be a free port . . July, „
Honours and income of the younger members of the imperial family much diminished, announced July, „
Russian interference in Bulgaria (*which see*) Sept-Dec. „
Plot against the czar; students with dynamite and other explosives, detected 13 March; 200 arrested . . . . March, 1887
Three plotters executed 31 March; seven political offenders sentenced to death, the rest to various terms of imprisonment, 1 May; more arrests about 18 May; five executed . . 16 May, „
Prince Nicholas, the cesarevitch, made chief Ataman (Hetman) of all the Cossacks at Novo-Tcherkask . . . . 18 May, „
N. Katkoff, journalist and politician, editor of the *Moscow Gazette*, Russophile, died, aged about 69, 1 Aug. „
Statement in the *Cologne Gazette* of the existence of forged letters purporting to come from prince Bismarck (see *Germany*) . . . . . Nov. „
Baron Hirsch's present of 2,000,000*l.* for the establishment of primary Jewish schools in

Russia, accepted by the czar; the money to be paid into the bank of England, trustees, barons Rothschild and Henry de Worms, announced Nov.; said to be premature . . . Dec. 1887

Movement of troops on the Galician border causes excitement in Berlin and Vienna . Nov.–Dec. ,,

The *Invalide Russe*, a government organ, declares that Russia desires peace but is prepared for war, 15 Dec. ,,

The stringent restrictions on the studies of the universities lead to much insubordination among the students, and severe punishment; the universities of Moscow, St. Petersburg, Odessa, and many other academical institutions closed; nearly all the undergraduate class in a state of rebellion . . . . . Nov.–Dec. ,,

Lord Randolph Churchill visits Russia; received by the czar . . . . . . 26 Dec. ,,

Reported conspiracy; many arrests about 9 Jan. 1888

Reported surplus in the budget, yet a loan asked for; unsuccessful at Paris and Berlin . Jan. ,,

Moscow and other universities re-opened . Feb. ,,

For prince Ferdinand's position (see *Bulgaria*) Feb.–March, ,,

The highest courts of law decide against the claim of prince Hohenlohe to inherit the vast Wittgenstein estates in Lithuania, as a foreigner (in accordance with the ukase, 14 March, 1887), March, ,,

Attempted assassination of the czar by lieut. Timofeieff (mad ?) . . . . . . May, ,,

Visit of the emperor of Germany to the czar at Peterhof. . . . . . 19–23 July, ,,

Ninth centenary of the introduction of christianity celebrated at Kieff . . . . . 27 July, ,,

Central Asian (or Transcaspian) railway opened; promoted by general Anhenkoff . . . May, ,,

Near Borki station in S. Russia, the engine of the imperial train (with the czar) ran off the line with four carriages (weak rails); 21 persons killed, the czar slightly injured . . . . 29 Oct. ,,

Agreement for 20,000,000*l*. loan signed at St. Petersburg, 18 Nov.; chiefly taken up by the French Dec. ,,

The grand council disapproves of the administrative changes proposed by count Tolstoi substituting centralization for local self-government which, however, are approved by the czar (1888); the *Zemstvo*, established about 1864, being virtually abolished, Feb. 1889

Loan of 700,000,000 francs concluded with the Rothschilds and other bankers for the conversion of five per cent. loans into four per cent. . Feb. ,,

Captain Atchinoff, with a company of S. Cossacks (145 men with muskets and guns, also priests, women and children), evading French and Italian cruisers, landed at Tadjourah, in the bay of Obock, near the French settlement, on the Red Sea, on 18 Jan., professing to combine missionary and commercial enterprise in Abyssinia. He took possession of a fort at Sagallo, and hoisted the Russian flag. After useless negotiation, the French admiral Olry on 18 Feb. bombarded the fort, killing 6 Russians; the party then surrendered and were eventually conveyed to Russia. The French government virtually apologised for the precipitate conduct of the admiral . . Feb. ,,

Alleged discovery of a dynamite conspiracy, especially in the south, originating in Zurich (discredited) . . . . . . March, ,,

Death of count Tolstoy, minister of the interior, 7 May, ,,

Second four per cent. loan announced, completing the financial scheme . . . . . 13 May, ,,

The czarewitch, aged 21, appointed to military and political office . . . . . 18 May, ,,

Marriage of the archduke Paul and the princess Alexandra of Greece . . . . 16 June, ,,

M. Dournovo, minister of the interior, continues count Tolstoy's reactionary policy . July, Aug. ,,

Marriage of the grand duke Peta with princess Militza, of Montenegro . . . . 7 Aug. ,,

The czar visits Berlin . . . . 11–13 Oct. ,,

Great epidemic of influenza among all classes in St. Petersburg, spread . . . Nov., Dec. ,,

Capt. Solotouchine, chief of the Moscow secret police, assassinated by a female Nihilist, who commits suicide . . . . 11 Jan 1890

Ukase for a conversion loan of 90,000,000 roubles, taken up, especially in France . . Feb. 1890

Count Tolstoy's administrative changes carried into effect, together with increased Russification of the German provinces and Finland . Feb. ,,

The czar threatened (by letter, signed Maria Tshebrikova, a popular writer on education, &c.), for continuing to suppress liberty, 5 March; she is arrested, about 10 March; transported to the Caucasus . . . . . . April, ,,

Strong demonstrations of the students of Moscow, St Petersburg, Kieff, Charkoff, and other universities and schools, demanding changes; many arrests and police supervision, about Feb., March, ,,

The czar releases about 60 imprisoned soldiers. The man chosen to assassinate the czar by lot, commits suicide, leaving a letter incriminating associates; many arrests, reported . 31 March, ,,

Inquiry by special commission; some students expelled and others set at liberty, at St. Petersburg, &c.; order restored . . . 7 April, ,,

Great fires in the Ural district, iron works at Utaleisk and Newjansk, about 1,000 houses destroyed; about 40 persons perish, about 10 June, ,,

Revival of severe edict against the Jews (*which see*) reported July, ,,

The czar and the German emperor meet at Nava; military manœuvres . . . 17 Aug. *et seq.* ,,

A monster literary protest against the persecution of the Jews in preparation, headed by count Léon Tolstoy; publication forbidden by the government . . . . . . Nov. ,,

Decree for the revision of all foreign titles of nobility . . . . about 15 Dec. ,,

Gregory Petrovitch Danilesky, historian and novelist, dies . . . . . . 24 Dec. ,,

Trial of 47 Nihilists . . . . about 11 Jan. 1891

Coal-mine explosion near Jusoveja, about 40 men killed . . . . . . 17, 18 Jan. ,,

Arrest of Dedajeff, charged with the murder of col. Sudeikin in 1883 (*see above*), and other Nihilists, at Kostroma . . . . end of Feb. ,,

New law for the legitimatising of bastards promulgated . . . . April, ,,

Rescript from the czar, placing the great Siberian railway under the direction of the cesarevitch 19 May, ,,

Cloudburst at Ekaterinoslav, great destruction of life and property . . . . . 6 July, ,,

Count Tolstoy's administrative changes relative to the peasantry effected at St. Petersburg and other provinces . . . . . . July, ,,

A French naval squadron, under admiral Gervais, warmly received at Cronstadt, 23 July; the czar visits the fleet, 25 July; which leaves . 4 Aug. ,,

Failure of crops; exportation of grain (especially rye) forbidden (from 27 Aug.); relief works ordered and grants of money . about 11 Aug. ,,

The cesarevitch returns to Moscow after a tour 16 Aug. ,,

[He visited Vienna, 6 Nov.; at Athens, 12 Nov.; at Cairo, 23 Nov.; at Bombay, 23 Dec. 1890; received by the viceroy at Calcutta, 26–28 Jan. 1891; at Madras, 6 Feb.; Ceylon, 13 Feb.; Bankok, Siam, 26 March; travels in China, Japan, April, May; at Otsu, in Japan, he is wounded by a fanatical officer in a theatre, 11 May, 1891; traverses Siberia, June, July, 1891.]

Great distress through famine in certain districts of the Volga and other places, about 2 Sept. *et seq.* ,,

New 3 per cent. loan for 500,000,000 francs (for railways) negotiated in Paris, about 17 Sept.; opposed in Berlin, about 28 Sept.; taken up well Oct. ,,

Ivan Alexandrovitch Gontcharoff, popular novelist, aged 80, dies . . . . . . 27 Sept. ,,

In order to relieve famine, the czar forbids all state balls and festivities; great economy adopted by all classes . . . . Oct. ,,

Disputes with Great Britain respecting the Pamir ridge (*which see*) . . . . . Aug. ,,

The famine very severe in the central and eastern provinces . . . . Oct. ,,

Discovery of a political conspiracy at Moscow, 60 persons arrested, reported . . . 12 Nov. ,,

Decree issued prohibiting the exportation of wheat and all its products . . . . 22 Nov. 1891
Tour of M. de Giers in Italy, France, and Germany Sept.—Nov. ,,
The cesarevitch appointed president of a committee to deal with the effects of the famine by means of private charity, the ministry, the holy synod, and others, 5 Dec.; public relief works established . . . . Dec. ,,
The grand duke Constantine (brother of the czar, Alexander II.), learned, able and liberal, sometime viceroy of Poland, removed on suspicion of favouring the Poles, 1886; dies, aged 64 24 Jan. 1892
Count Tolstoy (the novelist), active reliever of the distressed people . . . early March ,,
Stoppage of the (baron) Günzburg bank of St. Petersburg and Paris, 15 March *et seq.*; liquidation arranged, reported . . 21 March *et seq.* ,,
Russian Jewish emigrants prohibited from entering Germany . . . . 25 March, ,,
Large supplies of American wheat, flour, and provisions transmitted for the relief of the famine by the citizens of Philadelphia, in the *Indiana*; from Minnesota, in the *Missouri*, arrive at Libau, Courland, March, April; transmitted to the distressed districts . . . . 4 April, ,,
Society of Friends famine fund: 35,989*l.* received up to . . . . 1 May, ,,
Meeting of the czar and German emperor at Kiel 7 June, ,,
About 125,370,500 roubles expended in relief of the sufferers by famine, Dec. 1891—May, 1892; reported . . . . 13 June, ,,
Removal of the restrictions on the exportation of grain, except rye, 21 June; of rye . . 23 Aug. ,,

See article *Cholera*.

See *Pamirs*, 1892.

Rurik, great ironclad cruiser, launched on the Neva, the czar present . . . . . . 3 Nov. ,,
Tour of the cesarevitch in Greece, &c.; he is received by the emperor at Vienna, 12 Nov.; arrives at the Caucasus, about . . . . . 17 Nov. ,,
"Darkest Russia," a periodical respecting persecution, published throughout the world . autumn, ,,
The grand duke Sergius and the grand duchess visit the queen at Windsor . 25 Nov.—8 Dec. ,,
Trial of 154 rioters against cholera regulations (at Saratoff, &c., 10 July); 23 sentenced to death, 56 to imprisonment; others acquitted 4 Nov.—3 Dec. ,,
Cholera rioters at Tashkend, in July; 20 at Astrakhan sentenced to death; others to imprisonment, 30 Dec. 1892; severe sentences mitigated Jan., Feb. 1893
Very severe winter . . . . Dec. 1892, Jan. ,,
A train on the Slatoust-Samara railway takes fire; about 49 persons perish . . . . 11 Jan. ,,
The cesarevitch warmly received at Berlin; leaves 28 Jan. ,,
Rescript of the czar for expediting the construction of the Siberian railway (*see above*, May, 1891), about . . . . 1 Feb. ,,
New internal loan, 100 millions of roubles, at 4½ per cent. for 81 years . . . 10 March, ,,
Cattle plague among the Don Cossacks; opposition to compulsory slaughter; reported . 12 April, ,,
Panic through alarm of fire in a church at Romanoff Borisogliebsk, Jaroslav; about 136 deaths 17 June, ,,
Tariff war; duties on German imports raised; German reprisals; mutual injury . . Aug. ,,
Loss of the *Roosalka*, ironclad, see *Wrecks*, 19 Sept. ,,
A Russian squadron (5 vessels) under admiral Avellan arrive at Toulon, warmly received, 13 Oct.; official banquet; grand ball at the arsenal, 14 Oct.; the admiral and officers received by pres. Carnot; banquet at the Elysée; Paris decorated, 17 Oct.; fêtes, &c., 18–24 Oct.; at Lyons, 25 Oct.; Marseilles, 26 Oct.; farewell banquet at Toulon, M. Carnot present, 27 Oct.; letter of thanks from the czar; the squadron leaves Toulon . . . . . . 29 Oct. ,,
The *Admiral Oushakoff* ironclad launched on the Neva, the czar present . . . . 8 Nov. ,,
Death of M. Tschaikowsky, musical composer; state funeral at St. Petersburg . . 9 Nov. ,,
Death of sir Robert Morier, British Ambassador, aged 66, at Montreux on the lake of Geneva 16 Nov. 1893
Religious persecution in Lithuania; reported 3 Jan. 1894
Commercial treaty with Germany for 10 years, signed, 10 Feb.; comes into force . 20 March, ,,
Sir Frank Cavendish Lascelles appointed British ambassador, about . . . . 9 March, ,,
Conspiracy of nihilists and anarchists suspected; many political arrests at St. Petersburg and other places . . . . April—May, ,,
Conversion of the 5 per cent. loans continued, May, ,,
Decree of the czar depriving his ministers and other officials of the power of appointing or dismissing their subordinates; and re-establishing an imperial committee of control, subject to himself; to commence on . . . . . 13 Nov. ,,
Sissoi the Great, battleship, launched at St. Petersburg in presence of the czar . . 1 June, ,,
Serious illness of the czar; he leaves for the Crimea, with the czarina and family . 30 Sept. ,,
Kwiatkowski, an officer, sentenced at Kieff to penal servitude for life for stealing official documents, and 26 others to varying terms of penal servitude; reported . . . . . . 29 Sept. ,,
The *Three Saints* ironclad launched at Nicolaieff 8 Oct. ,,
The princess Alix of Hesse is betrothed to the cesarevitch; received by the czar . 22 Oct. ,,
Death of the czar, Alexander III., at Livadia, aged 49; essentially a Russian conservative, orthodox, a promoter of peace . . . . . 1 Nov. ,,
Accession of Nicholas II. . . . . 1 Nov. ,,
Preliminary funeral of the czar at Moscow; the imperial family, the prince and princess of Wales and other eminent persons present, 11 Nov.; solemn service and interment at St. Petersburg; many royal personages present, including the king of Denmark, the prince of Wales, the duke of Saxe Coburg, the duke of York, and other distinguished persons . . . . 19 Nov. ,,
Launch of the *Poltava* at St. Petersburg, and the *Petropavlofsk*, twin ironclads . . 6, 9 Nov. ,,
The czar assures foreign powers, in a circular, of his adherence to his father's pacific policy, 9 Nov. ,,
Death of Anton Rubinstein, aged 65, pianist and composer, at Peterhof, 20 Nov.; state funeral at St. Petersburg . . . . . . 28 Nov. ,,
Marriage of the czar to princess Alix (Alexandra) of Hesse, at St. Petersburg . . 26 Nov. ,,
Imperial manifesto of clemency relating to political offences, debts to the crown, &c. . 26 Nov. ,,
New loan of 100,000,000 roubles at 3½ per cent. (issued at 94½ per cent., redeemable at par in 81 years), 6 Dec.; thoroughly taken up . 13 Dec. ,,
Death of M. de Giers, aged 74, minister of foreign affairs; peaceful policy; at St. Petersburg 26 Jan. 1895
The czar to the representatives of 120,000,000 of his subjects of all classes, who came to offer their congratulations and homage, declares his intention to maintain the principle of autocracy as firmly as did his father . . . . 29, 30 Jan. ,,
Delimitation of the Russo-Persian frontier, settled by commission . . . . . . Feb. ,,
Prince Lobanof, ambassador at Vienna, judicious and pacific, appointed foreign minister, 19 March, ,,
Colonel Gregorieff sentenced to 8 years' penal servitude, in Siberia, for selling plans to the Austrian government; 4 others exiled to Siberia, 24 March, ,,
Agreement with Great Britain respecting the Pamirs . . . . March, ,,
Relaxation of the press laws refused by the czar; reported . . . . . . 20 April, ,,
The town of Brest-Litofsk destroyed by fire, 30 deaths, 16 May; other fires, reported . June, ,,
Sebastopol, battleship, launched on the Neva by the czar . . . . 1 June, ,,
Russia guarantees a loan of 16,000,000*l.* for China, *which see* . . . . . . June, ,,
A Russian mission to Abyssinia returns with an embassy and presents to the czar from the Negus, 29 June; diplomatic relations proposed . July, ,,
The embassy leaves . . . . . . 7 Aug. ,,
Sir Nicholas Roderick O'Conor appointed British ambassador; announced . . . 13 Sept.

Much suffering and loss of life by storms in the south . . . . Nov. 1895

Increased development of the volunteer fleet for commerce, transport of troops and emigrants to the far East . . . . Nov. ,,

Capt. Roberofsky returns from a successful scientific expedition into Chinese Central Asia with rich collections . . . . . . Dec. ,,

Serge M. K. Stepniak (Kravchinsky), author of "Underground Russia," &c., killed on the railway at Chiswick . . . . . . 23 Dec. ,,

Naval budgets for seven years, confirmed . Jan. 1896

Sir Nicholas O'Conor (G.C.B.) arrives at St. Petersburg . . . . 2 April, ,,

Great increase of trade through influx of foreign capital . . . . April, ,,

The *Russia* and the *Gen. Adm. Apraxin*, warships, launched by the czar at St. Petersburg . 12 May, ,,

The czar enters Moscow with a grand procession, 21 May; coronation of the emperor and empress in the Cathedral of the Assumption, the royal family, foreign princes, including the duke and duchess of Connaught, Li Hung Chang, grand secretary, and other foreign representatives and dignitaries, the bishop of Peterborough, ministers of state, and others present . 26 May, ,,

Grand festivities and distribution of charities throughout the empire, imperial manifesto and general amnesty issued . . . . 26 May *et seq.* ,,

M. Witte appointed secretary of state . 27 May, ,,

At a special fête for the lower classes held on the Khodinsky plain, Moscow, an imperial dole of food, &c., was to be distributed among them; eager crowds began to assemble the previous night, and early next morning became uncontrollable, a great panic ensued through the broken ground and faulty arrangements, 1,429 persons were crushed to death and 644 injured, 30 May; immediate relief (40,000*l.*) for the sufferers was ordered by the czar; large public subscriptions . . . . June, ,,

Grand review of troops on the Khodinsky plain, 7 June, ,,

Pan-Russian exhibition opened at Nijni-Novgorod by M. Witte . . . . 9 June, ,,

The czar and czarina enter St. Petersburg in state, 4 July, ,,

The czar and czarina start on a foreign tour, 25 Aug.; at Vienna, 27 Aug; Kieff, 2 Sept.; Breslau (*which see*), 5 Sept.; Kiel, 8 Sept.; Copenhagen, 9–20 Sept.; received by the prince of Wales at Leith, and by the Queen at Balmoral (addresses of welcome presented on the way), 22 Sept.; at Portsmouth, 4 Oct.; convoyed by a British squadron, met mid-channel by the French fleet, received by pres. Faure at Cherbourg, 5 Oct.; Paris, much rejoicing, banquet at the Elysée, &c., 6 Oct.; visited Notre Dame, Panthéon, Invalides, &c., lays the corner stone of the Alexander III. bridge, and thereby of the exhibition of 1900, 7 Oct.; at the Louvre, Versailles, state banquet, 8 Oct.; Châlons, review of 70,000 troops, 9 Oct.; at Darmstadt, 10 Oct.; exchange visits of the czar and the German emperor at Wiesbaden, leaves 29 Oct.; at St. Petersburg, 31 Oct. ,,

Sudden death of prince Lobanoff, able and firm foreign minister, while travelling with the czar at Scheptowka . . . . 30 Aug. ,,

Rostislav, battleship, launched at Nikolaieff, 2 Sept. ,,

Several dragoon officers degraded for coercing soldiers to violence against the Jews in Podolia, whereby 5 Jews were killed, and buildings looted and burnt . . . . 2 Sept. ,,

Prince Khilkoff, minister of railways, &c. returns from his tour in the United States, &c. 30 Oct. ,,

Ceremonies and fêtes in memory of Catherine II., Nov. ,,

Imperial edict issued sanctioning the formation of the Eastern Chinese railway company, shareholders to be exclusively Russians and Chinese; line to be completed, 1,280 miles, in 6 yrs., 23 Dec.; subscription for shares largely over-subscribed . . . . 29 Dec. ,,

Count Muravieff appointed foreign minister, 11 Jan. 1897

Currency reform; resumption of specie payments, gold coins of 15 and 7½ roubles substituted for silver . . . . Jan. 1897

Explosion on the *Cissoi Veliki* warship in Crete, 21 deaths . . . . 15 March, ,,

Apollon Nickolaievitch Maikoff, eminent poet, died, aged 75 . . . . . . 20 March, ,,

Train wrecked, between Rockenhof and Elwa, 56 soldiers and 2 guards killed, abt. 100 injured, 14 May, ,,

Visit of the German emperor and empress to St. Petersburg . . . . . . 7–13 Aug. ,,

M. Nossiloff announces the discovery of a direct waterway between Siberia and Europe, and his exploration of the Yalmal peninsula . 17 Aug. ,,

Pres. Faure received by the czar at Cronstadt, arrives at Peterhof, 23 Aug.; warmly received at St. Petersburg, 24 Aug.; great review at Krasnoe Selo, 25 Aug.; leaves . . . . 26 Aug. ,,

Railway from Moscow to Archangel completed, 30 Sept. ,,

Fire panic in a church at Khmelovo (Kozloff), 74 deaths . . . . 24 Oct. ,,

New currency established on a gold basis 26 Nov. ,,

A general fund opened by the czar in aid of the Cretans . . . . 2 Dec. ,,

The sale of spirituous liquors made a state monopoly . . . . Jan. 1898

Explosion in a mine, Taganrog district, 53 deaths, and 30 horses killed . . . . . 18 Jan. ,,

Budget: deficit, 106,291,706 roubles . 16 Jan. ,,

Russia demands from China 99 yrs. lease over Port Arthur and Ta-lien-wan, 3 March; 25 yrs. lease of these ports, granted; railway concessions, 23 March; China to retain sovereign rights, agreement signed; Chinese garrisons withdrawn, Russian troops landed, 28 March; adm. Stark appointed commandant . . . . . July, ,,

Ta-lien-wan declared open to commerce, April, ,,

The disbursement of 90,000,000 roubles (7 yrs.) for warships ordered . . . . . . 10 March, ,,

Hsu-Ching-Cheng, Chinese ambassador, received by the czar . . . . 15 March, ,,

Death of admiral Popoff, aged 77, inventor of 3 *circular* ironclads (*which see*) . . 20 March, ,,

Naval officers (100) charged with bribery and corruption at Sebastopol, arrested, 5 commit suicide, 23 March, ,,

Perovnoff (privy councillor) and his daughter (20) sentenced to life exile in Siberia; 5 others to lighter sentences for high treason, at St. Petersburg . . . . 12 April, ,,

Agricultural distress and famine in the interior and S.E. . . . . . . Feb., April, ,,

Sir Chas. Stewart Scott (G.C.B. 1899) appointed British ambassador . . . . June, ,,

Russo-Japanese convention respecting Corea, signed . . . . 25 April, ,,

Pereswiet, 1st class battleship, launched at St. Petersburg, the czar present . . . . 19 May, ,,

Relaxation of the tariff of 1891 (favourable to England) . . . . June, ,,

Rear-adm. Stark appointed commandant at Port Arthur . . . . July, ,,

Death of gen. Tchernaieff . . . . . 17 Aug. ,,

Circular of count Muravieff on behalf of the czar proposing a conference of the Powers for the preservation of general peace by disarmament, 24 Aug.; sympathetic replies . . Sept.–Oct. ,,

[Second circular to European cabinets, 11 Jan. See *Peace Conference*, 1899.]

Famine through bad harvests . . . . Aug. ,,

The czar reviews the troops and the Black sea squadron at Sebastopol . . . . . 3 Sept. ,,

Oslyabya battleship launched on the Neva . 8 Nov. ,,

Labour strikes and riots frequent throughout the country . . . . Dec. ,,

Army pay increased . . . . Jan. 1899

Severe famine in the central and S.E. provinces; the czar gives 3,000,000, the czarina 50,000 roubles; great mortality in Kazan; over 15,000 deaths in Samara . . . . . . Jan.-May, ,,

Gen. Annenkoff, born 1835, constructed the Transcaspian military railway; died . . . mid Jan. ,,

Russification of Finland, *which see* . Feb. *et seq.* ,,

Students' agitation in the university at St. Petersburg against oppressive restrictions, &c.; the building cleared by the police and the students brutally charged by mounted police, 20 Feb.; general strike of students throughout the empire, March; M. Witte lays their grievances before the czar; committee of inquiry; gen. Vannofsky (ex-minister of war) and others appointed; many arrests in Moscow, 13 April; riots at Kieff, troops called out, 400 arrests, reported . 17 April, 1899

Gen. Vannofsky's report condemns M. Bogolepoff, minister of public instruction, and others, and exonerates the students, May; the czar censures both parties; the students ordered to return, reported . . . . 5 June, ,,

Anti-Jewish riots, 1 death, shops wrecked, at Nikolaieff, 400 arrests . . . . . 1–4 May, ,,

Adm. Possiet, eminent officer and statesman, died, 8 May, ,,

Severe measures against foreign as well as Russian Jews . . . . 9 May, ,,

Strike riots at Riga, 12 deaths . . . 15 May, ,,

Centenary of the birth of Pushkin (poet and nov.), memorials raised . . . . . 6, 7 June, ,,

The cesarevitch, grand duke George, born 9 May, 1871, dies suddenly at Abbas Tuman, in the Caucasus, 10 July; laid in state in St. Petersburg (see *Molokani*) . . . . 24–26 July, ,,

M. Delcassé, French foreign minister, received by count Muravieff, 4 Aug.; by the czar, 6 Aug.; leaves . . . . 9 Aug. ,,

Great fire at Grodno, in Lithuania, reported, 3 Aug. ,,

Measure passed imposing (1 to 3 yrs.) military service on rebellious students, reported . . Aug. ,,

Educational system for the aristocracy, largely at government expense, established . . Aug. ,,

The czar and czarina visit the German emperor at Potsdam . . . . 8 Nov. ,,

M. Witte's budget for 1900; growth of Russian industries, reported . . . . . . 11 Jan. 1900

Flattering rescript from the czar to count Muravieff (foreign minister) . . . . . 13 Jan. ,,

Trial of 43 officers and officials in the Russian navy for bribery and corruption, at Sebastopol, 17 Feb.; 16 persons acquitted, 26 found guilty 3 April, ,,

Ukase announcing the final redemption of the debt of the imperial exchequer to the state bank to the amount of 50,000,000 roubles . . 19 May, ,,

Count Muravieff, foreign minister, born 1845, dies suddenly . . . . 21 June, ,,

Mobilization of the E. Siberian army corps for China, ordered . . . . . . 25 June, ,,

Imperial ukase, largely abolishing banishment to Siberia, issued . . . . . . 3 July, ,,

Visit of the shah of Persia, 17 July; grand review at St. Petersburg . . . . . 19 July, ,,

Imperial ukase, reserves called out . 22 July, ,,

Import duties of the common tariff increased from 50 to 100 per cent. . . . . . 4 Aug. ,,

Anti-Jewish riots in Odessa and other districts, reported . . . . 5 Aug. ,,

Count Lamsdorff appointed foreign minister, Aug. ,,

Thibetan envoy received by the Czar . 13 Oct. ,,

Budget: net surplus for 1899, 84,000,000 roubles, passed . . . . 21 Oct. ,,

Illness of the czar in the Crimea . early Nov.–Dec. ,,

Count Tolstoi writes to the Czar appealing against religious persecutions . . . . 15 Dec. ,,

Budget for 1901: estimated surplus, 73,443,450 roubles, issued . . . . . . 14 Jan. 1901

The czar and czarina welcomed in St. Petersburg, 26 Jan. ,,

Gen. Gourko, distinguished commander, dies, aged 73 . . . . 29 Jan. ,,

Famine due to failure of crops, population of 24 millions affected; government relief organized, Feb. *et seq.* ,,

M. Witte increases the duties on imports from the U.S.A. . . . . Feb. ,,

Student disturbances in St. Petersburg and all the chief towns, many arrests . . Feb.–March, ,,

M. Bogoliepoff, minister of public instruction, mortally wounded by Peter Karpovich (sentenced to 20 years' imprisonment, 30 March), in St. Petersburg . . . . 27 Feb. ,,

Students' demonstration in St. Petersburg ends in serious rioting in Kazan square, 700 arrests, 17 March, ,,

Protest signed in Paris by 45 Russian authors against the cruel treatment of university students, 22 March, 1901

Severe snowstorms in the south, many deaths, Jan.–March, ,,

Riots in Kieff quelled by the troops . 24 March, ,,

The czar's rescript to gen. Vannovsky, new minister of public instruction, orders revision and reform in the present system, reported . . 7 April, ,,

Count Tolstoi excommunicated for his opinions, see *Times* . . . . . 19 March and 9 April, ,,

M. Lagovski sentenced to six years' imprisonment for attempting the life of the Procurator of the Holy Synod (22 March) . . . . . 9 April, ,,

Wholesale arrests, domiciliary visits in St. Petersburg . . . . 1–4 May, ,,

Centenary of the council of the empire celebrated, the cesarevitch appointed a member . 20 May, ,,

Epidemic of scurvy in the famine-stricken southern districts . . . . May, ,,

Count Tolstoi appeals to the czar and government on the situation in Russia, 15 March; see *Times*, 31 May, ,,

Strike riots in St. Petersburg and elsewhere, 20 May; again troops called out in St. Petersburg . . . . 14 June, ,,

The czar intervenes; many students pardoned, June, ,,

Thibetan mission received by the czar . 6 July, ,,

Moorish mission received by the czar . 5 Aug. ,,

Many bank and factory failures in S. Russia during the summer, reported . . . . 24 Sept. ,,

Forest fires, villages destroyed, reported, 12–19 Aug. ,,

State of siege in the province of Moscow continued, reported . . . . 23 Aug. ,,

The czar and czarina visit the king of Denmark, 2–10 Sept.; the czar meets the German emperor at Danzig, views the naval manœuvres, 11, 12 Sept.; visit France, *which see* . 18 Sept. ,,

Failure of crops, great distress in the east . Oct. ,,

Marqu. Ito from Japan decorated by the czar, 27 Nov. ,,

Student disorders, university at Kharkoff closed, 11–14 Dec. ,,

About 20 cities and towns placed under state of siege . . . . mid Dec. ,,

Death of M. de Bloch, state councillor, aged 66; his work on "War" helped to promote the Hague peace conference . . . . . 7 Jan. 1902

Budget for 1902, about 144,000,000 roubles deficit, issued . . . . 13 Jan. ,,

American note protests against Russian aggression in Manchuria . . . . . . 1 Feb. ,,

The archduke Franz Ferdinand received by the czar . . . . 7 Feb. ,,

Riots at Kieff and other university towns . 15 Feb. ,,

University of St. Petersburg closed owing to disorders, 20 Feb.–11 March; further disturbances, repressed by the troops and police, 16 March; riots and disorders in Moscow, 22 Feb. and 2 March; 567 students and others convicted of riot and *political disaffection* imprisoned (from 3 to 6 months, 95 banished to Siberia), announced, 25 March, ,,

New Russian 4 per cent. loan subscribed over 100 times in Germany, Holland, and Russia, 3 April, ,,

M. Sipiagnine, minister of the interior, a reactionist, assassinated at St. Petersburg by Palmascheff (executed 16 May), 15 April; state funeral, the czar present; M. de Plehve appointed minister of the interior . . . . 17 April, ,,

Increasing distress and poverty due to bad harvests and oppressive taxation, great economic and agricultural depression over the country, reported, April, ,,

The *Zemstvos*, local institutions, forbidden to collect rural statistics in S. Russia . . . spring, ,,

Rioting in Poltava and Kharkoff, many estates plundered (compensation granted by decree, 27 May) . . . . mid April, ,,

Great unrest in central and S. Russia; much incendiarism . . . . April, ,,

Gen. Vannovsky, minister of education, resigns, 19 April; succeeded by M. Sänger . 25 April, ,,

Martial law proclaimed in Poltava . . 5 May, ,,

Lieut.-gen. de Wahl, governor of Vilna, shot at and wounded by Hirsch Lekert . . 18 May, 1902

Revolutionary ourbreak at Saratoff suppressed by troops . . . . 18 May, ,,

Pres. Loubet visits the czar, 20 May; grand review of troops at St. Petersburg . . 21, 22 May, ,,

Lieut.-col. Grimm, charged with selling army secrets to a foreign power, sentenced to 12 years' imprisonment and life banishment to Siberia, 13 June, ,,

Prince Ferdinand of Bulgaria visits the czar, 10–14 June, ,,

Grave disturbances in Ekaterinoslaff, factories and farms sacked . . . . . end June, ,,

The king of Italy visits the czar . 13–17 July, ,,

Visit of count Matsugata, Japanese statesman, 25 July, ,,

Drought reported in the Trans-Caspian territory, 5 Aug. ,,

The czar and the German emperor meet at Reval, 6–8 Aug. ,,

Prince Obolenski, the governor, wounded by Katchoor, a peasant (death sentence commuted, Nov.) at Kharkoff; M. Bessonoff, chief of police, also wounded . . . . 11 Aug. ,,

The students imprisoned at Smolensk freed by the czar's orders . . . . . early Aug. ,,

Army manœuvres at Kursk . . . 13–16 Sept. ,,

The czar, at Kursk, exhorts the peasants to labour and thrift, &c., 14 Sept.; state banquet to the shah . . . . 17 Sept. ,,

Nine battleships built, 1900–1902; the *Knjaes Suwaroff* launched before the czar at St. Petersburg . . . . 25 Sept. ,,

Open discontent at existing systems, reported, 10 Oct. ,,

Turkish mission received by the czar . . 30 Oct. ,,

Labour troubles in the south, conflict with troops, 4 deaths, 102 arrests, 24, 30 Nov.; great distress, continued arrests . . . . . . Dec. ,,

Grand duke Alexander Mikhailovitch appointed director of the new department of commercial marine . . . . Nov. ,,

Severe weather in the south . . . . Dec. ,,

The czar pardons 62 exiles in Siberia, 26 Sept.; and 58 . . . . 19 Dec. ,,

Count Lamsdorff, foreign minister, visits Belgrade, Sofia, and Vienna, on the Macedonian question, 24–30 Dec. ,,

Special university commission of inquiry issue their report as to reforms, &c. . . about 5 Jan. 1903

Russian press jubilee suppressed . . . . Jan. ,,

Budget: 16,627,449 roubles surplus . . 13 Jan. ,,

Visit of the German crown prince . . 16–24 Jan. ,,

Lt.-col. Shavroff, chief of the Cronstadt police, sentenced to 2 years' imprisonment, and degraded for forgery . . . . 20 Feb. ,,

Manifesto from the czar, favouring religious freedom, reform of peasant taxation . 11 March, ,,

Labour disturbances at Slatonst, workmen's delegates imprisoned, crowd fired on, 34 killed, about 200 wounded, by order of M. Bogdanovitch, governor of Ufa; reported . . 28 March, ,,

Factory riot near Nishni-Novgorod, mob fired on, many killed and wounded . . . 8 April, ,,

Kishineff atrocities, S. Russia, houses and shops of the Jews sacked and pillaged, 45 Jews killed, 84 seriously wounded, 500 crippled and injured, 10,000 rendered destitute, "the soldiers looked on, passive if not sympathetic spectators, till at last ordered to act" . . . . 19, 20 April, ,,

[Gen. von Raahen the governor, the chief of the police, and other officials who had allowed the mob free play, dismissed, May–July, great agitation abroad; M. de Plehve, minister of interior, much censured, the *Bessarabetz* and other anti-Semitic journals also held responsible for the outrages.]

Loan of 72,000,000 roubles, 94½, at 4 per cent., for landowners raised . . . . 30 April, ,,

Political arrests and domiciliary visits in St. Petersburg, reported . . . . 8 May, ,,

Gen. Bogdanovitch, the governor, assassinated at Ufa . . . . 19 May, ,,

Mr. D. D. Braham, *Times* correspondent at St. Petersburg, arrested and ordered to leave Russia, 28 May, ,,

M. de Plehve issues a circular against the teaching of revolutionary doctrines among the peasants, 3 June, 1903

Anti-Semitic disturbances at Berestechko reported, 8 June, ,,

Expenditure more than doubled in ten years (1893–1903). M. Witte reports taxation to have reached its limit (Jan. 1903); estimated revenue for 1903, 33,000,000*l.*; Russian debt, 1902, 690,107,109*l.*, reported . . . . 15 June, ,,

Jewish meeting at Lodz attacked by the police, 10 killed, many seriously injured . . 15 June, ,,

Reform of district police in 46 provinces ordered, mid July, ,,

Agitation and unrest all over the empire, May *et seq.*; general strikes in the south, riots at Baku, Odessa, Kieff, and elsewhere, trains wrecked, oil wells set on fire and various other acts of outrage; murderous assaults on prince Urussoff in Tchernigoff, and on prince Gagarin, his wife, and prince Sherbatoff in Riazan, reported 27–31 July; conflicts with the troops resulting in great loss of life . . 5–7 Aug. ,,

Imperial viceroyalty appointed in the "Far East," by ukase issued . . . . . . 12 Aug. ,,

The czar and czarina return to St. Petersburg after the canonization of St. Seraphim at Saroff, *Times*, 13 Aug. ,,

Strike troubles at Odessa and Kieff subside, many imprisoned . . . . . . 11–16 Aug. ,,

Disturbances at Ekaterinoslav, mob fired on, many killed . . . . 20 Aug. ,,

Gloomy economic condition of the country manufactures generally stagnant, reported mid Aug. ,,

Army manœuvres between Riga and St. Petersburg . . . . 14–23 Aug. ,,

Battleship *Slava* launched at St. Petersburg, 29 Aug. ,,

Ministerial changes: M. Witte appointed president of the committee of ministers and members of the Imperial Council, M. Pleske, minister of finance . . . . 29 Aug. ,,

Serious strikes in Moscow . . . 22 Sept. ,,

Anti-Semitic riots at Gomel, terrible excesses and loss of life; houses wrecked 14–15 Sept.; Moghileff and suburbs placed under siege, reported, 26 Sept. ,,

The czar and czarina visit the emperor of Austria, 30 Sept. ,,

Three socialists sentenced to death, 2 exiled, and 7 imprisoned in connection with a strike demonstration at Rostoff, reported . . . 8 Oct. ,,

New law of expulsion of foreigners issued by imperial decree; special commission under the presidency of the czar appointed to consider affairs in the "Far East" . . . mid Oct. ,,

Russian substituted for Swedish at the opening of the Finnish senate . . . . . 22 Oct. ,,

Murderous attack on prince Galitzin, gov.-general of the Caucasus . . . . . . 27 Oct. ,,

Disturbances of a revolutionary character in S. Russia, revolutionary leaflets in great numbers distributed at Riesan, so many workmen arrested that accommodation for them could not be found in the prison; house of the inspector of the gymnasium partly destroyed by a bomb; many students arrested; 25 teachers and *zemstvo* officials arrested at Kursk; 74 male and female students arrested on the charge of socialism at Rostoff; proclamations by the revolutionists issued to the soldiers calling on them not to fire upon the people . . . . . . Oct.–mid Nov. ,,

M. Metlenko, chief of the police, fired at and slightly wounded in a public street in Bialystok (Grodno) . . . . 12 Nov. ,,

Sovereigns of Russia.

Dukes of Kiow or Kief.

850? Ruric.
879. Oleg.
913. Igor I.
945. Olga, widow; regent.
955. Swiatoslaw I.—victorious.
973. Jaropalk I.
980. Vladimir, Wladimir, the Great.
1015. Swiatopalk.
1018. Jaraslaw, or Jaroslaf I.
1054. Isiaslaw I.
1073. Swiatoslaw II.

1078. Wsewolod I.
1093. Swiatopalk II.
1113. Vladimir II.
1125. Mitislaw.
1132. Jaropalk II.
1138. { Wiatschelaw.
1139. { Wsewolod II.
1146. { Isiaslaw II. and Igor II.
1153. { Rostislaw.
1149. Jurie or George I.; the city of Moscow was built by this duke.

GRAND-DUKES AT WLADIMIR.

1157. { Andrew I. until 1175; first grand-duke.
1175. { Michael I.
1177. Wsewolod III.
1213. { Jurie or George II.
1217-18. { Constantine.
1238. Jaraslaw II.; succeeded by his son,
1245. Alexander-Nevski or Newski, the Saint.
1263. Jaraslaw III.
1270. Vasali or Basil I.
1275. Dmitri or Demetrius.
1281. Andrew II.
1294. Daniel-Alexandrovitz.
1303. Jurie or George III.; deposed.
1305. Michael III
1320. Vasali or Basil II.
1325. Jurie or George III: restored.
1327. Alexander II.
[The dates are doubtful, owing to the difficulty that occurs at every step in early Russian annals.]

GRAND-DUKES OF MOSCOW.

1328. Ivan or John I.
1340. Simeon, the proud.
1353. Ivan or John II.
1359. Demetrius II. prince of Susdal.
1362. Demetrius III. Donskoi.
1389. Vasali or Basil III. Temnoi.
1425. Vasali or Basil IV.

CZARS OF MUSCOVY.

1462. Ivan (Basilovitz) or John III.: took the title of czar, 1482.
1505. Vasali or Basil V. obtained the title of emperor from Maximilian I.
1533. Ivan IV. the terrible; a tyrant.
1584. Feodor or Theodor I.; and his son, Demetrius, murdered by his successor
1598. Boris-Godonof, who usurped the throne.
1605. Feodor II., murdered.
1606. Demetrius, the Impostor, a young Polish monk; pretended to be the murdered prince Demetrius; put to death.
" Vasali-Chouiski, or Zouinski.
1610. Ladislaus of Poland; retired 1613.
1613. Michael-Feodorovitz, of the house of Romanoff, descended from the czar Ivan-Basilovitz.
1645. Alexis, son; styled the father of his country.
1676. Feodor or Theodor II.
1682. { Ivan V. and
{ Peter I. brothers of the preceding.

EMPERORS AND EMPRESSES.

1689. Peter I. the Great, alone; took the title of emperor, 22 Oct. 1721; founded St. Petersburg.
1725. Catherine I. his widow; at first the wife of a Swedish dragoon, said to have been killed on the day of marriage.
1727. Peter II. son of Alexis-Petrovitz, and grandson of Peter the Great: deposed.
1730. Anne, duchess of Courland, daughter of the czar Ivan.
1740. Ivan VI. an infant, grand-nephew to Peter the Great; immured in a dungeon for 18 years, murdered in 1764.
1741. Elizabeth, daughter of Peter the Great, reigned during Ivan's captivity.
1762. Peter III. son of Anne and of Charles-Frederick, duke of Holstein-Gottorp: deposed, and died soon after, supposed to have been murdered.
1762. Catherine II. his consort: a great sovereign; extended the Russian territories on all sides; died 17 Nov. 1796.
1796. Paul, her son, murdered, 24 March, 1801.
1801. Alexander I. son (who, after many adverse battles, and a forced alliance with France, at length aided in the overthrow of Napoleon Bonaparte), died 1 Dec. 1825.
1825. Nicholas I. brother; died 2 March, 1855.
1855. Alexander II. son, born 29 April 1818; married 28 April, 1841, Mary princess of Hesse (she died 3 June, 1880); said to have married (morganatic) princess Dolgorouki, 19 (31) July; marriage announced, Oct. 1880; assassinated at St. Petersburg, 2 P.M., 13 March, 1881.
1881. Alexander III., born 10 March, 1845; married Mary (formerly Dagmar), princess of Denmark (born 26 Nov. 1847), 9 Nov. 1866; died 1 Nov. 1894.
1894. Nicholas II. (termed Educator), son, born 18 May, 1868; married Alexandra (formerly Alix), princess of Hesse (born, 6 June, 1872), 26 Nov. 1894. Grand duchess Olga Nicolaevna, born 15 Nov. 1895. Tatiana, born 10 June, 1897; Marie, born 26 June, 1899; Anastasia, born 18 June, 1901.

Heir presumptive: (George, brother, born 9 May, 1871, dies 10 July, 1899); Michael Alexandrovitch, brother, born 4 Dec. 1878.

RUSSIA COMPANY, see *Russia*, 1553-4. See *America*.

RUSSIAN congress of naturalists and physicians (10th), opened at Kieff, nearly 1,500 members, 3 Sept. 1898.

RUSSIAN LANGUAGE is a copious branch of the Slavonic family. There are many dialects, the predominant literary language being that of Moscow. The earliest literature consists of legendary poems and tales. The earliest preserved MS. is the codex of the Ostromir Gospels, written at Novgorod by the deacon Gregory, 1056–57. The first Russian book was printed at Moscow, 1504.

PRINCIPAL RUSSIAN AUTHORS.

	Born.	Died.
Simeon Polotski, *p.* and *d.*	1628	1680
Antiokh Kantemir, *p.*	1708	1744
Michael Lomonosov, *p.* and *hist.*	1711	1765
Denis von Visin, *d.*	1745	1792
Michael Kheraskov, *d.*	1733	1801
Gabriel Derzhavin, *p.*	1743	1816
Nicholas Karamzin, *hist.*	1766	1826
Alexander Pushkin, *p.*	1799	1837
Ivan Krilof (fables)	1768	1844
Michael Lermontoff, *p.*	1814	1841
Koltsov, *p.*	1809	1842
Nicholas Gogol, *ph.*	1809 or 1810	1852
Ivan Turgenief, *n.*	1818	1883
Count Leo Tolstoi, *p.*, *n.* and *l.*	1828	
James P. Polonsky, *p.*	1820	1898
Eduard Kunik, *hist.*	1814	1899

RUSSO-TURKISH WAR.* The Russian and French governments having each taken a side in the dispute between the Greek and Latin

* In 1844, when the czar was in England, he conversed with the duke of Wellington and lord Aberdeen (whom he had known many years) respecting the dissolution of the Turkish empire; and on his return he embodied his views in a memorandum drawn up by count Nesselrode, which was transmitted to London, but kept secret till March, 1854. In January and February of that year the czar had several conversations on the subject with the British envoy at St. Petersburg, sir G. H. Seymour, in one of which (Jan. 14) he compared Turkey to a "sick man" in a state of decrepitude, on the point of death, and made proposals to the British government as to the disposal of his property. He stated frankly that he would not permit the British to establish themselves at Constantinople; but said in another conversation, he would not object to their possessing Egypt. The purport of these conversations was conveyed in despatches to lord John Russell, who replied that the British government declined to make any provision for the contingency of the fall of Turkey. The czar made similar proposals to the French government with the same result.

churches as to the exclusive possession of the *Holy Places* (*which see*) in Palestine, the Porte advised the formation of a mixed commission, which decided in favour of the Greeks, and a firman was promulgated accordingly, 9 March, 1853: to this decision the French acceded, although dissatisfied.

The Russians make further claims, and prince Menschikoff (who arrived at Constantinople 28 Feb. 1853), by various notes (between 22 March and 18 May), demands that a convention should be signed by the sultan granting to the czar such a protectorate over the Greek Christians in Turkey, as the sultan considered inimical to his own authority . . . . . 22 March-18 May, 1853
Menschikoff's ultimatum rejected; he quits Constantinople . . . . . . 21 May, ,,
The sultan issues a hatti-scherif confirming all the rights and privileges of the Greek Christians, and appeals to his allies . . . . . 6 June, ,,
The English and French fleets anchor in Besika Bay, 13 June, ,,
The Russians, under gen. Luders, cross the Pruth and enter Moldavia . . . . . 2 July, ,,
Circular of count Nesselrode in justification, 2 July; lord Clarendon's reply . . . . . 16 July, ,,
The conference of representatives of England, France, Austria, and Prussia meet at Vienna, agree to a note, 31 July; accepted by the czar, 10 Aug.; the sultan requires modifications, 19 Aug.; which the czar rejects. . . 7 Sept. ,,
Two English and two French ships enter the Dardanelles . . . . 14 Sept. ,,
The sultan (with consent of a great national council) declares war against Russia . . . . 5 Oct. ,,
The Turkish fortress at Issaktocha fires on a Russian flotilla (the first act of war) . . . 23 Oct. ,,
The Turks cross the Danube at Widdin and occupy Kalafat . . . . . 28 Oct.-3 Nov. ,,
Russia declares war against Turkey . . . 1 Nov ,,
English and French fleets enter Bosphorus 2 Nov. ,,
Russians defeated at Oltenitza . . . 4 Nov. ,,
Turks (in Asia) defeated at Bayandur, Atskur, and Achaltzik . . . . 14, 18, 26 Nov. ,,
Turkish fleet destroyed at Sinope . . . 30 Nov. ,,
Collective note from the four powers requiring to know on what terms the Porte will negotiate for peace . . . . 5 Dec. ,,
Contests at Kalafat . . . 31 Dec. 1853–9 Jan. 1854
At the request of the Porte (5 Dec.), the allied fleets enter the Black Sea . . . . . 4 Jan. ,,
Russians defeated at Citate . . . . 6 Jan. ,,
Reply of the Porte to the note of Dec. 5, containing four points as bases of negotiation: viz., 1. The promptest possible evacuation of the principalities. 2. Revision of the treaties. 3. Maintenance of religious privileges to the communities of all confessions. 4. A definitive settlement of the convention respecting the Holy Places (dated 31 Dec.),—approved by the four powers 13 Jan. ,,
Vienna conferences close . . . . . 16 Jan. ,,
Kalafat invested by the Russians . . 28-31 Jan. ,,
Proposal in a letter from the emperor of the French to the czar (29 Jan.) declined . . . 9 Feb. ,,
Turkish flotilla at Rustchuk destroyed by the Russians under Schilders . . . . 15 Feb. ,,
Ultimatum of England and France sent to St. Petersburg . . . . 27 Feb. ,,
The czar "did not judge it suitable to give an answer" . . . . 19 March, ,,
Baltic fleet sails, under sir C. Napier . 11 March, ,,
Treaty between England, France, and Turkey, 12 March, ,,
Russians under Gortschakoff pass the Danube and occupy the Dobrudscha; severe conflicts; the Turks retire . . . . . 23, 24 March, ,,
France and England declare war against Russia, 27, 28 March, ,,
Rupture between Turkey and Greece 28 March, ,,
Gen. Canrobert and French troops arrive at Gallipoli, soon after followed by the English, 31 March, ,,
Russians defeated by the Turks at Karakai 30 May, ,,
English vessel *Furious*, with a flag of truce, fired on at Odessa . . . . 8 April, ,,
Four powers sign a protocol at Vienna guaranteeing the integrity of Turkey and civil and religious rights of her Christian subjects . . 10 April, 1854
Russians defeated at Kostelli by Mustapha Pacha, 10 April, ,,
Offensive and defensive alliance between England and France . . . . 10 April, ,,
Treaty between Austria and Prussia . . 20 April, ,,
Bombardment of Odessa by allied fleet 22 April, ,,
Russians, under gen. Schilders, assault Kalafat; repulsed; the blockade raised . 19-21 April, ,,
The *Tiger* steamer run aground near Odessa, captured by the Russians . . . . 12 May, ,,
Russians defeated at Turtukai . . . 13 May, ,,
Siege of Silistria begun . . . . . 17 May, ,,
Allied armies disembark at Varna . . 29 May, ,,
Mouths of the Danube blockaded by allied fleets, 1 June, ,,
Russians repulsed at Silistria; Paskiewitsch and many officers wounded . . . . 5 June, ,,
Turks defeated at Ozurgheti (in Asia) 16 June, ,,
Severe conflict before Silistria; the siege raised, 18-26 June, ,,
Batteries at the Sulina mouths destroyed by capt. Parker . . . . 26, 27 June, ,,
Captain Parker killed . . . . . 8 July, ,,
Russians defeated at Giurgevo . . . 7 July, ,,
10,000 French troops embark at Boulogne for the Baltic . . . . 15 July, ,,
Turks defeated at Bayazid in Armenia, 29, 30 July; and near Kars . . . . . . 5 Aug. ,,
Surrender of Bomarsund . . . . 16 Aug. ,,
In July and August the allied armies and fleets in the east suffered severely from cholera.]
The Russians defeated by Schamyl in Georgia, about 28 Aug. ,,
They evacuate the principalities . Aug.-20 Sept. ,,
By virtue of a treaty with Turkey (June 14) the Austrians, under count Coronini, enter Bucharest, 6 Sept. ,,
Allies sail from Varna, 3 Sept., and land at Old Fort, near Eupatoria* . . . . . . 14 Sept. ,,
Skirmish at the Bulganac. . . . . 19 Sept. ,,
Battle of the Alma (see *Alma*) . . . 20 Sept. ,,
Russians sink part of their fleet at Sebastopol. 23 Sept. ,,
Allies occupy Balaklava . . . . . 26 Sept. ,,
Death of marshal St. Arnaud . . . 29 Sept. ,,
General Canrobert, his successor . . 24 Nov. ,,
Siege of Sebastopol commenced—grand attack (without success) . . . . . 17 Oct. ,,
Battle of Balaklava—charge of the light cavalry, with severe loss . . . . . 25 Oct. ,,
Sortie from Sebastopol repulsed by generals Evans and Bosquet . . . . . . 26 Oct. ,,
Russian attack at Inkerman; defeated . 5 Nov. ,,
Miss Nightingale and nurses arrive at Scutari, 6 Nov. ,,
Great tempest in the Black Sea, loss of the *Prince* and store vessels . . . . . 14–16 Nov. ,,
Treaty of alliance between England, France, Austria, and Prussia—a commission to meet at Vienna; signed . . . . 2 Dec. ,,
Russian sortie . . . . 20 Dec. ,,
Omar Pacha arrives in the Crimea (followed by the Turkish army from Varna) . . 5 Jan. 1855
Sardinia joins England and France . 26 Jan. ,,
Great sufferings in the camp from cold and sickness, Jan. & Feb. ,,
Russians defeated by the Turks at Eupatoria, 17 Feb. ,,
Death of emperor Nicholas; accession of Alexander II. (no change of policy) . . 2 March, ,,
Sortie from the Malakhoff tower . . 22 March, ,,
Capture of Russian rifle-pits . . . 19 April, ,,
Arrival of Sardinian contingent . . . 8 May, ,,
Resignation of gen. Canrobert, succeeded by gen. Pelissier . . . . 16 May, ,,
Desperate night combats . . . . 22–24 May, ,,
Expedition into the sea of Azoff (under sir E. Lyons and sir G. Brown); destruction of Kertch and large amount of stores . . . 24 May–3 June, ,,
Taganrog bombarded . . . . . 3 June, ,,
Massacre of an English boat's crew with flag of truce at Hango . . . . 5 June, ,,

* 40,000 men, a large number of horses, and a powerful artillery, were landed in one day.

Russians evacuate Anapa . . 5 June, 1855
The White Works and Mamelon Vert taken, 6, 7 June, ,,
Unsuccessful attack on the Malakhoff tower and Redan . . 18 June, ,,
Death of lord Raglan; succeeded by general Simpson, 28 June, ,,
Russians invest Kars in Armenia, defended by gen. Williams . . . . . . 15 July, ,,
Bombardment of Sweaborg . . . 9 Aug. ,,
Defeat of the Russians at the Tchernaya 16 Aug. ,,
Ambuscade on the glacis of the Malakhoff taken; Russian sortie repulsed . . . 18 Aug. ,,
The French take the Malakhoff (*which see*) by assault; the English assault the Redan without success; the Russians retire from Sebastopol to the North Forts, and the allies enter the city; the Russians destroy or sink the remainder of their fleet, 8 Sept. &c. ,,
Tanan and Fanagorio captured . . 24 Sept. ,,
The Russians assaulting Kars are defeated with great loss . . . . . . 29 Sept. ,,
Russian cavalry defeated (50 killed, 105 prisoners) at Koughil, near Eupatoria, by the French, 29 Sept. ,,
Kinburn taken . . . . . . 17 Oct. ,,
Russians blow up Oczakoff . . . . 18 Oct. ,,
Large stores of corn destroyed near Gheisk, in the sea of Azoff . . . . . . 4 Nov. ,,
Defeat of the Russians, and passage of the Ingour by the Turks under Omar Pacha . . 6 Nov. ,,
The czar visits his army near Sebastopol 10 Nov. ,,
Sir Wm. Codrington takes the command in room of gen. Simpson . . . . . 14 Nov. ,,
Explosion of 100,000 lb. of powder in the French siege-train at Inkerman, with great loss of life, 15 Nov. ,,
Sweden joins the allies by a treaty . . 21 Nov. ,,
Capitulation of Kars to gen. Mouravieff, after a gallant defence by gen. Williams . . 26 Nov. ,,
Death of admiral Bruat . . . . 27 Nov. ,,
Russian attack on the French posts at Baidar repulsed . . . . 8 Dec. ,,
Proposals of peace from Austria, with the consent of the allies, sent to St. Petersburg . 12 Dec. ,,
Centre dock at Sebastopol blown up by the English, 2 Jan. 1856
Council of war at Paris . . . . . 11 Jan. ,,
Protocol signed accepting the Austrian propositions as a basis of negotiation for peace . 1 Feb. ,,
Destruction of Sebastopol docks . . . 1 Feb. ,,
Report of sir John M'Neill and col. Tulloch on state of the army before Sebastopol, published 5 Feb. ,,
Peace conferences open at Paris, an armistice till 31 March agreed on . . . 25 Feb. ,,
Suspension of hostilities . . . . 29 Feb. ,,
Treaty of peace concluded at Paris . 30 March, ,,
Proclamation of peace in the Crimea, 2 April; in London . . . . 29 April, ,,
The Crimea evacuated . . . . . 9 July,* ,,

RUSSO-TURKISH WAR, 1877. For the insurrections, Servian war, and the negotiations, see *Turkey*.

The czar addresses the army near Kischeneff, saying that "he has done everything in his power to avoid war, and patience is exhausted;" the Russian embassy quits Constantinople . . 23 April 1877
War declared; the czar's manifesto says that he is compelled, by the haughty obstinacy of the Porte, to proceed to more decisive acts; a justificatory circular to foreign powers sent out by prince Gortschakoff; the Russians enter the Turkish dominions in Roumania and Armenia . 24 April, ,,

* The English lost: killed in action and died of wounds, about 3500; died of cholera, 4244; of other diseases, nearly 16,000; total loss nearly 24,000 (including 270 officers); 2873 were disabled. The war added to the national debt 41,041,000*l*. The French lost about 63,500 men; the Russians about half a million. The army suffered greatly by sickness; see *Scutari*, *Times*, and *Nightingale*. The remains of the British soldiers and sailors were removed from Beicos to the Scutari Crimean Memorial cemetery with military honours, for which the queen returns thanks to the sultan, Feb. 1892.

The sultan's circular protests against the war, and refers to his reforms and the treaty of Paris 25 April, 1877
[Russian generals-in-chief in Bulgaria, grand duke Nicholas, in Armenia, grand duke Michael: Turkish generals, Abdul-Kerim in Europe; Mukhtar Pacha, in Asia Minor.
Russians defeated at Tchuruk Sou, near Batoum 26 April, ,,
The Russians, under the grand duke Michael and Loris Melikoff, advance into Armenia, defeat Turks and occupy Bayazid (deserted) 29, 30 April, ,,
The Turks stop the passage of the Danube, and blockade the Black Sea . . . . 3 May, ,,
The earl of Derby replies to the Russian circular; he refers to the treaty of 1856 as broken; does not consider that the war will benefit the Christians, and asserts that Russia has separated herself from European concert; the British government gives neither concurrence nor approval to the war 1 May, ,,
Kalafat occupied by Roumanians . . 3 May, ,,
Russians defeated in attacking Batoum . 4 May, ,,
The *Lufti-Djelil*, Turkish monitor, with 300 men, blown up near Ibraila, or Braila, on the Danube (said to be by Russian shells) . . 11 May, ,,
Much artillery firing down the river . May, ,,
Sukhum Khaleh, Russian fortress in the Caucasus, captured by Turks . . . . . 14 May, ,,
Ardahan, near Kars, Armenia, stormed by Melikoff 17 May, ,,
Insurrection in the Caucasus supported by the sultan . . . . . 18 May *et seq.* ,,
Explosion of Turkish monitor *Dar-Matoin*, by lieuts. T. Daubassoff and Sheshlakoff, with torpedoes . . . . 26 May, ,,
Neutrality of the Suez Canal assured: correspondence . . . . . . May–June, ,,
Kars invested by Russians . . . 3 June, ,,
The czar arrives at Plojesto (Ployesto) in Roumania 6 June, ,,
Turks defeated at Tahir, or Taghir, Armenia, 16 June, ,,
Turks victors at Zewin Dooz, Eshek-Khalian, Delibaba, and other places; Russians retreating 20 June, ,,
Turks successful in Montenegro; country reported subdued . . . . . 12-20 June, ,,
Russians cross Lower Danube by bridges at Galatz and Braila; 6 hours' conflict ensues; Turks retire, 22 June; Russians occupy Matchin, 23 June, and Hirsova . . . . . 25, 26 June, ,,
The grand duke Nicholas crosses the Danube at Simnitza by 208 pontoons, and enters Bulgaria; the Turks retire after severe conflicts; 289 Russians said to be killed . . . 27 June, ,,
The czar in his proclamation to Bulgarians encourages Christians and warns Mahometans 28 June, ,,
The Simnitza bridge destroyed by a storm or by Turks . . . . . about 30 June, ,,
The British fleet arrives at Besika bay . 3 July, ,,
Biela, Bulgaria, taken by Russians about 5 July, ,,
Plevna, Bulgaria, occupied by Russians 6 July, ,,
Tirnova, ancient capital of Bulgaria, captured by Russians under gen. Gourko . . 6, 7 July, ,,
Bayazid re-occupied by Turks . . . 12 July, ,,
Russians compelled to retire from Kars by Mukhtar Pasha . . . . . . 13 July, ,,
The invasion of Armenia considered a failure July, ,,
Gourko crosses the Balkans and enters Roumelia, 13 July; (this movement censured), several skirmishes . . . . . 14, 15, 20 July, ,,
Nicopolis (Nikopol) surrenders (after severe conflicts, 12-14 July); capture of 2 pashas, 6000 men, 2 monitors, and 40 guns . . 15, 16 July, ,,
The Turkish commander Abdul-Kerim replaced by Mehemet Ali (Jules Détroit, of French extraction); Russians retreating . . . July, ,,
Suleiman Pasha brought from Montenegro to the Schipka Passes . . . . about 21 July, ,,
Aziz Pasha (able and popular) killed in a rash conflict at Esirje, near Rasgrad . 26 or 28 July, ,,
Russians severely defeated; Plevna retaken by Osman Pasha, 19, 20 July; Russians again defeated . . . . . . 30, 31 July, ,,
Hostilities revive in Montenegro; the Turkish fortress Niksich besieged . . . July, ,,
The Roumanian army joins the Russians 9 Aug. ,,

Severe conflicts between Russians and Suleiman Pasha; the Turks eventually victors: Eski Saghra and Yeni Sagra, July; Kezanlik and Kalofer . . . . . 30 July *et seq.* 1877

Russians under Gourko expelled from Roumelia; retreat to Schipka passes . . about 11 Aug. ,,

Russians in the Schipka Passes relieved by Radetzky 21 Aug. ,,

Russians defeated at Kara Silar, near Osman Bazar, 14 Aug.; in the valley of the Lom, by Mehemet Ali . . . about 22–24 Aug. ,,

Russians defeated by Mukhtar Pasha at Kurukdara, or Kizil Tepe, between Kars and Alexandropol 24, 25 Aug. ,,

Desperate fruitless attempts of Suleiman Pasha to gain the Schipka Pass held by Gourko and Radetzky; great slaughter . . 20–27 Aug. ,,

Severe twelve hours' battle in valley of the Lom, near Szedina; Karahassankoi taken and re-taken six times; Russians (under the Czarewitch) retire in good order . . . . . . 30 Aug. ,,

Prince Charles with Roumanians crosses the Danube . . . . . about 31 Aug. ,,

Further successes of Mehemet Ali on the Lom at Katzelevo, Ablava, &c. . . . . 4–6 Sept. ,,

Lovatz or Luftcha (important) captured by Prince Imeritinsky and Russians after a sharp conflict 3 Sept. ,,

Niksich (left by Turks) captured by Montenegrines 7 Sept. ,,

Sanguinary conflicts at Plevna, greatly strengthened by Osman Pasha; artillery duel . 7–10 Sept. ,,

Fierce assault by Russians and Roumanians; they gain the strong Gravitza redoubt (with others, which are re-taken); the czar present; Russian loss about 20,000 . . . . 11, 12 Sept. ,,

Fort St. Nicholas in Schipka Pass taken by Suleiman Pasha and quickly lost; much bloodshed 17 Sept. ,,

Mehemet Ali repulsed in his attack on positions at Tchercovna, fifteen miles from Biela . 21 Sept. ,,

Siege of Plevna; Chefket Pasha enters with reinforcements after several skirmishes 22 Sept. ,,

Montenegrine successes continued . . Sept. ,,

Battles of the Yagni; severe conflicts; Russians repulsed near Ardahan, Asia about 27, 30 Sept. ,,

Russian losses, killed, wounded, and missing, 47,400 reported . . . . up to 20 Sept. ,,

Mehemet Ali retires to Kara Lom about 25 Sept. ,,

Gen. Todleben made chief of staff before Plevna 28 Sept. ,,

Mehemet Ali replaced by Suleiman Pasha; Raouf Pasha sent to Schipka . . . 2, 3 Oct. ,,

Battles near Kars; army of grandduke Michael attacks Turks under Mukhtar Pasha; severely defeated . . . . . . 2–4 Oct. ,,

Turkish monitor in the Danube exploded by torpedoes . . . . . . 8 Oct. ,,

Relief and supplies received by Turks at Plevna about 9 Oct. ,,

Battle of Aladja Dagh before Kars; Russians, under grand duke Michael, and generals Loris Melikoff, Lazareff, and Heimann, totally defeat Ahmed Mukhtar, taking 10,000 prisoners . 14, 15 Oct. ,,

Gravitza battery, near Plevna, captured by Roumanians, is quickly re-taken . . 19–20 Oct. ,,

Suleiman and his army said to be retreating from Kadikoi to Rasgrad . . . 22 Oct. ,,

Battle at Gornij Dubnik, near Plevna; Russians under Gourko said to be victorious; losses about equal (2,500) . . . . . . 24 Oct. ,,

Russians said to be defeated near Kara Ourgan, Armenia . . . . . 24 Oct. ,,

Battle of Sofia Road, near Plevna; Turkish position at Teliche captured . . . . 28 Oct. ,,

Mukhtar Pasha defeated by Heimann and Tergukasoff at Deve-Boyun, Armenia, after nine hours' conflict . . . . . . 4 Nov. ,,

Russians severely defeated at Azizi, before Erzeroum, by Mukhtar Pasha . . . . 9 Nov. ,,

Change in Turkish generals: Suleiman ordered to command the army of Roumelia, replaced by Azli Pasha; Mehemet Ali organises army to relieve Plevna . . . . early in Nov. ,,

Russian attack on Plevna repulsed . 12 Nov. ,,

Turks thrice repulsed near Plevna . 15 Nov. ,,

Kars taken by storm; the Russians climbed steep rocks; fierce conflict from 8 p.m. to 8 a.m.; 300 guns and 10,000 prisoners taken; about 5000 Turks killed and wounded; Russian loss about 2,500; the grand-duke Michael present 17-18 Nov. 1877

Russians said to be severely repulsed at Orchanié. 16 Nov. ,,

Plevna said to be thoroughly invested (30 miles round, with 120,000 men) . . . Nov. ,,

Osman Pasha, invited to surrender at Plevna, refuses . . . . . . about 16 Nov. ,,

Rahova on the Danube taken by Roumanians, 21 Nov. ,,

Entrepol (fortified) near Plevna taken by Russians, 24 Nov. ,,

Indecisive fighting in the valley of the Lom between the czarewitch and Mehemet Ali; Russians said to be defeated . . . . . . 30 Nov. ,,

Turks capture Elena with guns and prisoners, after sharp conflict . . . . . . 4 Dec. ,,

Skirmishing on the Lom . . . . 4-6 Dec. ,,

Osman Pasha endeavours to break out of Plevna, about 7 p.m. 9 Dec.; six hours' fierce conflict; surrounded; unconditional surrender; said to be 30,000 prisoners, 128 officers, 100 guns; great slaughter on both sides . . . 10 Dec. ,,

The Servians declare war against Turkey, 12 Dec.; cross the frontier and capture villages 15 Dec. *et seq.* ,,

Turkish circular note to the great powers, requesting mediation, 12 Dec.; merely acknowledged, action declined . . . . about 12 Dec. ,,

Montenegrines successful . . . . . Dec. ,,

Suleiman made general of the army of Roumelia; and Todleben of that of Rustchuk, about 19 Dec. ,,

Suleiman retires on the quadrilateral; visits Constantinople; armies concentrating near Adrianople . . . . . . about 20 Dec. ,,

Servians said to have taken Ak Palanka after 3 hours' fight . . . . . . 24 Dec. ,,

Erzeroum, Armenia, nearly invested; brave resistance by Mukhtar Pasha . . about 24 Dec. ,,

Many Turkish wounded prisoners perish from cold during removal . . . . . Dec. ,,

Turkish steamer with 875 men, said to be captured in Black Sea . . . . about 25 Dec. ,,

Alleged Russian losses, 80,435 men; Turkish much more, and 80,000 prisoners . . . Dec. ,,

Mukhtar Pasha recalled to Constantinople, about 29 Dec. ,,

The sultan requests mediation of England; the British government only convey to Russia the sultan's desire to make peace; Russia declines mediation . . . . 26—31 Dec. ,,

Servians advancing successfully . end of Dec. ,,

Gourko crosses the Balkans and advances on Sofia; Turks defeated in an engagement, about 31 Dec. ,,

Col. Baker gallantly protects the retreating Turkish army, defeating the Russians. . . 1 Jan. 1878

Sofia taken by Russians after an engagement, 3 Jan. ,,

Russians said to be defeated near Erzeroum, about 5 Jan. ,,

Servians defeated; Kurschumli reoccupied by Turks . . . . 6, 7 Jan. ,,

Gen. Radetzky crosses the Balkans; the Trojan pass taken about 9 Jan.; the Turkish army (about 32,000) and cannon taken by Skobeleff and Radetzky, after conflicts, 8, 9, 10 Jan. (see *Senova*); Gourko advances towards Adrianople . 11 Jan. ,,

Nisch taken by the Servians; Antivari by the Montenegrines . . . . about 10 Jan. ,,

Russians advance successfully; Turkish envoys proceed to treat for peace . about 16-18 Jan. ,,

Gourko advances toward Philippopolis; totally defeats Suleiman Pasha, who retreats to the sea, losing many prisoners and much cannon, 16, 17 Jan. ,,

Adrianople abandoned; occupied by Russians, 19, 20 Jan. ,,

Suleiman with remains of his army at Karala on the Ægean transporting his troops, about 21 Jan. ,,

Servians occupy nearly all Old Servia . 29 Jan. ,,

Russian attack on Batoum defeated . . 30 Jan. ,,

After much delay, an armistice signed at Adrianople 31 Jan. ,,

Russian losses announced 89,879 men . Feb. ,,

Continued advance of Russians towards Constantinople; great panic; flight of many Turks; many deaths and great sufferings . . Jan., Feb. 1878
Part of British fleet ordered to Constantinople to protect British life and property, 8 Feb.; enters Dardanelles without permission of the Porte, 13 Feb. „
Erzeroum evacuated by Turks . 17-21 Feb. „
Rustchuk occupied by Russians . . 20 Feb. „
Treaty of peace signed at San Stefano (see *Stefano*), 3 March; ratified at St. Petersburg . 17 March, „
The war lasted 322 days, 12 April, 1877, to 3 March, „
Long negotiation respecting a European congress, March-May, „
Grand duke Nicholas in Roumelia replaced by gen. Todleben, who assumes command . 30 April, „
Conference at Berlin, meets 13 June; treaty signed (see *Berlin*), 13 July; ratified . . 3 Aug. „
Grand review of about 80,000 Russians near Constantinople . . . . . . 17 Aug. „
40,000 Russians have sailed for home . 12 Sept. „
Definitive treaty of peace with Turkey signed at Constantinople . . . . 8 Feb. 1879
Estimated cost of the war to Russia, 120,000,000*l*.

RUSTCHUK, Turkish town on the Danube, one of the "quadrilateral" fortresses lost to Turkey with Bulgaria by treaty of Berlin, 13 July, 1878.

RUTHENIUM, a rare metal, discovered in an ore of platinum by M. Claus, in 1845.

RUTHERFURD'S ACT, LORD (13 & 14 Vict. c. 36), for simplifying law proceedings in Scotland, passed 1850.

RUTHVEN, RAID OF, a term applied to the seizure of the person of James VI. of Scotland by William Ruthven, earl of Gowrie, and other nobles, in 1582, to compel the king to dismiss his favourites, Arran and Lennox. Ostensibly for this, Gowrie was judicially put to death by his two opponents in 1584.

RUTLAND, STATUTE OF, 10 or 12 Edw. I. 1282 or 1284.

RYE-HOUSE PLOT, a plot (some think pretended) to secure the succession of the duke of Monmouth to the throne in preference to the duke of York (afterwards James II.), a Roman catholic. Some of the conspirators are said to have projected the assassination of the king, Charles II., and his brother. This design is said to have been frustrated by the king's house at Newmarket accidentally taking fire, which hastened the royal party away eight days before the plot was to take effect, 22 March, 1683; see *Newmarket*. The plot was discovered 12 June following. Lord William Russell on 21 July, and Algernon Sidney on 7 Dec. following, suffered death for being concerned in this conspiracy. Both were illegally convicted. The name was derived from the conspirators' place of meeting, the Rye-house at Broxbourne, Hertfordshire.

RYSWICK (Holland), where the celebrated peace was concluded between England, France, Spain, and Holland, signed, by their representatives, 20 Sept., and by the emperor of Germany, 30 Oct. 1697.

S.

SAALFIELD (Saxony, N. Germany). Here the Prussians, under prince Louis of Prussia, were defeated and their leader slain by the French under Lannes, 10 Oct. 1806.

SAARBRÜCK, the Roman *Augusti Muri* or *Saræ pons*, an open town on the left bank of the Saar, in Rhenish Prussia, founded in the tenth century, long subject to the bishops of Metz, afterwards ruled by counts (about 1237), and by the house of Nassau about 1380. It was captured by the French and retaken by the Germans 1676, reunited to France 1794-1814, and ceded to Prussia, 1815. On 2 Aug. 1870, it was bombarded by the French under Frossard (between 11 and 1 in the daytime), and the Prussians in small force were dislodged, and the town occupied by the French general Bataille. The mitrailleuses were said to be very effective. The emperor Napoleon, who was present with his son, said in a telegram to the empress, "Louis has gone through his baptism of fire. He has not been in the least startled. We stood in the foremost rank, and the rifle balls were dropping at our feet, and Louis picked up one that fell near him. His bearing was such as to draw tears from the soldiers' eyes." On the 6 Aug. the Prussian generals Gœben and Von Steinmetz, with the first army, recaptured Saarbrück, after a sanguinary conflict at the village of Spicheren. The heights taken by the French on the 2nd are in Germany, those taken by the Germans on the 6th are in France, and both battles were fought between Saarbrück and the town of Forbach, which was captured, and has given a name to the second conflict. The loss was great on both sides. The French general François was killed, and the 2nd corps under Frossard nearly destroyed. The French retreated to Metz. They were greatly superior in numbers at the beginning of the fight, but were badly commanded.

SABBATARIANS. Traces exist of Sabbatarii, or Sabbathaires, among the sects of the 16th century on the continent. Upon the publication of the "Book of Sports" in 1618, a violent controversy arose among English divines on two points: first, whether the Sabbath of the fourth commandment was in force among Christians; and secondly, whether, and on what ground, the first day of the week was entitled to be distinguished and observed as "the Sabbath." In 1628, Theophilus Brabourne, a clergyman, published the first work in favour of the Seventh-day or Saturday, as the true Christian Sabbath. He and several others suffered great persecution for this opinion; but after the restoration there were three or four congregations observing the last day of the week for public worship in London, and seven or eight in the country parts of England. In 1851 there were three Sabbatarian or Seventh-day Baptist congregations in England; but in America (especially in the New England states) they are more numerous.—Joseph Davis suffered imprisonment in 1670. He and his son bequeathed property to maintain the sect; and litigation respecting its disposal was settled by vice-chancellor Stuart in conformity with their intentions in June. 1870. Very few Sabbatarians then remained. The rev. Wm. Mead Jones, an eminent seventh-day Baptist in London, a profound scholar; died 22 Feb. 1895.

SABBATH: ordained by God. *Gen.* ii.; *Exod.* xx. 8; *Isaiah* lviii. 13. Jews observe the seventh day in commemoration of the creation of the world, and of their redemption from the bondage of the Egyptians; Christians observe the first day of the week in commemoration of the resurrection of Christ from the dead, and the redemption of man; see *Sunday*.

SABBATH SCHOOLS, see *Sunday Schools*.

SABBATICAL YEAR: a Jewish institution, 1491 B.C. *Exodus* xxiii. During every seventh year the very ground had rest, and was not tilled; and every forty-ninth year all debts were forgiven, slaves set at liberty, and estates, &c., that were before sold or mortgaged, returned to their original families, &c.

SABELLIANISM, from Sabellius (of Ptolemais in Egypt), who flourished in the 3rd century and who taught that there was but *one* person in the Godhead, the other persons of the Trinity being but different names of the same person This doctrine was condemned at a council at Rome, 260.

SABINES, an ancient people of central Italy, from whom the Romans, under Romulus, took away their daughters by force, having invited them to some public sports or shows on purpose. When the Sabines determined to revenge this affront, the women became mediators to their fathers in behalf of their husbands, the Romans, and a lasting peace was made between them, 750 B.C. The Sabines, who had supported the Samnites in their war with Rome, were thoroughly defeated by M. Curius Dentatus, and their lands annexed 290 B.C., and eventually the Sabines were combined with the Roman people. One of the ecclesiastical provinces is still called Terra Sabina; chief town, Magliano.

SACCHARINE, see *Benzole*.

SACCHAROMETER, an instrument for determining the amount of sugar in solutions. Soleil, an optician, of Paris, in 1847 made use of rotary polarised light for this purpose in a saccharometer, since improved by Duboscq.

SACHEVEREL RIOTS, see *Riots*, 1710.

SACKVILLE INCIDENT, see *United States*, Oct. 1888.

SACRAMENT (from *sacramentum*, an oath, obligation, also mystery). The Christian sacraments are baptism and the Lord's Supper. The council of Trent, in 1547, affirmed the doctrine of the schoolmen that there are *seven* sacraments: baptism, the Lord's Supper, confirmation, penance, holy orders, matrimony, and extreme unction. The name was given to the Lord's Supper by the Latin fathers. The wine was restricted to the clergy about the beginning of the 12th century. Communion in one kind only was authoritatively sanctioned by the council of Constance, 15 June, 1415. Henry VII. of Germany was poisoned by a priest by the consecrated wafer, 24 Aug. 1313. The sacramental wine was poisoned by the gravedigger of the church at Zürich, by which sacrilegious deed a number of persons lost their lives, 4 Sept. 1776. In 1614 members of both houses of parliament were ordered to take the sacrament, as a guard against the introduction of Roman Catholics. In 1673 the test act was passed; repealed in 1828; see *Transubstantiation*.

"Society of the Blessed Sacrament" (English churchmen), London, founded, 1860; "Confraternity of the Blessed Sacrament," founded 1862; the two united, 1867.

SACRAMENTARIANS, followers of Zwingli (1487-1531), who differed from the Romanists and Lutherans in regard to the sacrament.

SACRAMENTO, St., a Portuguese settlement in S. America, claimed by Spain in 1680, but relinquished in 1713; several times seized; ceded in 1777; acquired by Brazil in 1825, see *California*.

SACRED BAND, see *Thebes*.

SACRED BOOKS OF THE EAST. The publication of translations of the sacred books of the religion of the Brahmans, Buddhists, and Mohammedans, and of the followers of Khung-fu-tze and Lao-tze, edited by professor Max Müller, began in 1879. About 30 volumes have been published.

SACRED HARMONIC SOCIETY, see *Music*.

SACRED HEART OF JESUS; a form of devotion said to have been instituted in England in the seventeenth century, and much promoted by Marguerite Marie Alacoque, an enthusiastic French nun, who asserted that Christ had appeared to her, and taken out her heart, placed it in his own, glowing in flame, and then returned it. She died in 1690.

Her book "Dévotion au Cœur de Jésus," published in 1698, much advocated by father Joseph Gallifet about 1726; and introduced into France, by request 1765

A pilgrimage from England, specially blessed by the pope, and headed by the duke of Norfolk, went to the shrine of Marguerite, at Paray-le-Monial, and returned . . . . 1-6 Sept. 1873

The R.C. diocese of Salford dedicated to the Sacred Heart, 4 Sept. 1873: and a church at Montmartre, near Paris, founded for the same purpose, 16 June, 1875

The pope dedicated the universal church to "the Sacred Heart" . . . . 15 June, „

SACRED WARS.—I. Declared by the Amphictyons against Cirrha, near Delphi, for robbery and outrage to the visitors to the oracle, 595 B.C. Cirrha was razed to the ground, 586.—II. Between the Phocians and Delphians for the possession of the temple at Delphi, 448, 447.—III. The Phocians, on being fined for cultivating the sacred lands, seized the temple, 357. They were conquered by Philip of Macedon, and their cities depopulated, 346. See *Crusades*.

SACRIFICE was offered to God by Abel, 3875 B.C. Sacrifices to the gods were introduced into Greece by Phoroneus, king of Argos, 1773 B.C. Human sacrifices seem to have originated with the Chaldeans, from whom the custom passed into other Eastern nations. All sacrifices to the true God were to cease with the sacrifice of Christ, 33 A.D. *Heb.* x. 12-14. Pagan sacrifices were forbidden by the emperor Constantius II. 341.

SACRILEGE. In 1835, the punishment (formerly death) was made transportation for life. By 23 & 24 Vict. c. 96, s. 50 (1861), breaking into a place of worship and stealing therefrom was made punishable with penal servitude for life.

SACRIPORTUS (Latium, Italy). Here Sylla defeated the younger Marius and Papirius Carbo with great slaughter, B.C. 82, and became dictator, 81.

SADDLES. In the earlier ages the Romans used neither saddles nor stirrups. Saddles were in use in the 3rd century, and are mentioned as made of leather in 304, and were known in England about 600. Side-saddles for ladies were introduced by Anne, queen of Richard II. in 1388. *Stow*.

SADDUCEES, a Jewish sect, said to have been founded by Sadoc, a scholar of Antigonus, about 200 B.C., who, misinterpreting his master's doctrine, taught that there was neither heaven nor hell, angel nor spirit; that the soul was mortal, and that there was no resurrection of the body from the dead. The Sadducees rejected the oral law, maintained by the Pharisees. See *Matt.* xxii. 23; *Acts* xxiii. 8.

SADLER'S WELLS (N. London), so called after Mr. Sadler, who built an orchestra to entertain the invalids who used the waters medicinally, 1683. In time the orchestra was enclosed, and the building became a place for dramatic performances. The theatre was opened in 1765. Eighteen persons were trampled to death at this theatre, on a false alarm of fire, 18 Oct. 1807; see under *Theatres*. The theatre put up to auction and not sold, 31 Aug. 1875; and 30 July, 1878.

SADOWA, see *Königgrätz*.

SAFES. A National Safe Company, London, opened vaults for storage of valuables, 1876.

SAFETY LAMP. One was invented in 1815 by sir Humphry Davy, to prevent accidents which happen in coal and other mines. The safety-lamp is founded on the principle that flame, in passing through iron-wire meshes, loses so much of its heat as to be incapable of igniting inflammable gases. The father of all safety-lamps was Dr. Reid Clanny, of Sunderland, whose invention and improvements are authenticated in the *Transactions of the Society of Arts* for 1817. The "Geordy," constructed by George Stephenson, the engineer, in 1815, is said to be the safest. A miner's electric light, by MM. Dumas and Benoit, was exhibited in Paris on 8 Sept. 1862. On 14 Aug. 1867, safety-lamps were rigidly tested by several mining engineers, and serious doubts thrown upon their complete efficacy. Col. Shakespear's safety lamp (light extinguished by opening) exhibited at Royal Institution, &c., May, 1879. Messrs. Fleuss and Foster's new safety mining lamp approved, Jan. 1884.

Mr. J. Wilson-Swan's electric safety lamp, weighing 6½ lb. exhibited at Aberdeen meeting of British Association, Sept. 1885.

Mr. Charles D. Aria's safety lamp reported successful; the supply of mineral oil is isolated from the burner 1889.

The Thornbury miners' lamp tried at Aldwarke Main Collieries by Mr. C. E. Rhodes, and subjected to experiments by prof. Dewar and sir Frederick Abel, who declare that this lamp fulfils the conditions required by the royal commission in 1886. Paraffin and other mineral oils may be used in this lamp, reported Nov. 1889.

SAFFRON (*saffran*, French; *saffrano*, Italian), the flower of crocus, was first brought to England in the reign of Edward III. by a pilgrim, about 1339, probably from Arabia, as the word is from the Arabic *saphar*. *Miller*. It was cultivated in England in 1582.

SAGAS. Early Icelandic tales, dated from the 10th century, see *Eddas*.

SAGE (*Sauge*, French; *Salvia*, Latin), a wholesome herb *Mortimer*. The Mexican sage, *Salvia mexicana*, was brought from Mexico, 1724. The blue African sage, *Salvia africana*, and the golden African sage, *Salvia aurea*, were brought to England from the Cape of Good Hope in 1731.

SAGUNTUM, or ZACYNTHUS, now Murviedro, in Valentia, E. Spain, renowned for the dreadful siege it sustained, 219 B.C. The citizens, after performing incredible acts of valour for eight months, chose to be buried in the ruins of their city rather than surrender to Hannibal. They burnt themselves, with their houses, and the conqueror became master of a pile of ashes, 218 B.C.

SAHARA, a great sandy desert, North Africa, south of Barbary States. A project for making an inland sea here was entertained in 1883, and the construction of a railway was proposed in Algeria, Oct. 1890. A large natural reservoir of water at El Golea in the desert, was discovered early 1891. M. Foureau's 12 years' exploration, rich in scientific results, see *French West Africa*, 1898–1900. M. Blanchet's mission meets with many disasters; he dies, Oct. 1900. Twat, the region between Algeria and the Sudan, includes 3 districts, Gurara, Twat, and Tidikelt, occupied by the French; see *Algeria* and *Morocco*, 1900.

SAIGON, French colony in Cochin China, founded in 1860, after a defeat of the Chinese, 17 Feb. 1859.

SAILORS' HOME, in Well-street, London Docks, established by Mr. George Green, 1830; opened, 1835; enlarged, 1865. In one year it admitted 5444 boarders, who, besides home, had evening instruction, the use of a savings' bank, &c. The establishment is self-supporting, aided by subscriptions. Similar institutions have since been established. *Sailors' orphan girls' school and home*, Hampstead, established 1829. Sailors' and Firemen's Union, see *Shipping*. The Passmore Edwards Sailors' Palace, Limehouse, opened by the prince and princess of Wales; an "Ocean library" inaugurated (total 31,120*l.*, 15,000*l.* additional promised), 19 May, 1903.

SAINT. For names with this prefix, see the names themselves throughout the book. See *Acta Sanctorum*.

SAKYA MUNI, see *Buddhism*.

SALADO, a river, S. Spain; see *Tarifa*.

SALADS are stated to have been in use in the middle ages; lettuces are said to have been introduced into England from the Low Countries, 1520-47.

SALAMANCA (W. Spain), taken from the Saracens 861. The university was founded 1240, and the cathedral built 1513. Near here the British and allies, commanded by lord Wellington, totally defeated the French army under marshal Marmont, 22 July, 1812. The loss of the victors was most severe, amounting in killed, wounded, and missing, to nearly 6000 men. Marmont left in the victor's hands 7141 prisoners, 11 pieces of cannon, 6 stands of colours, and 2 eagles. This victory was followed by the capture of Madrid. Population, 1887, 22,199.

SALAMIS (near Athens). In a great sea-fight here, 20 Oct. 480 B.C., Themistocles, the Greek commander, with only 310 sail, defeated the fleet of Xerxes, king of Persia; which consisted of 2000 sail.—Near Salamis, in Cyprus, the Greeks defeated the Persian fleet, 449 B.C.; and Demetrius Poliorcetes defeated the fleet of Ptolemy and his allies, 306 B.C.

SALASSI, a turbulent Alpine tribe, were thoroughly subdued by Terentius Varro, 25 B.C., and a Roman colony established in their territories (now Aosta).

SALDANHA BAY, S. Atlantic Ocean; northward of the Cape of Good Hope. Here on 17 Aug. 1796, a Dutch squadron, under admiral Lucas, was captured by vice-admiral sir George Keith Elphinstone, without resistance; sir George was created lord Keith.

SALE OF FOOD AND DRUGS ACT, passed 11 Aug. 1875; repeals all adulteration acts, and makes new arrangements.

SALE OF GOODS ACT, codifying the law, passed 20 Feb. 1894.

SALENCKEMEN, on the Danube. Here a victory was gained by the imperialists, under prince Louis of Baden, over the Turks, commanded by the grand vizier Mustapha Kiuprigli, 19 Aug. 1691.

SALERNO (Salernum, S. Italy), an ancient Roman colony. Its university, with a celebrated school of medicine, reputed to be the oldest in Europe, was founded by Robert Guiscard the Norman, who seized Salerno in 1077. Salerno suffered much in the wars of the middle ages.

SALFORD, near Manchester. Population, 1881, 176,235; 1891, 198,136; 1901, 221,587.

An incendiary explosion at the barracks caused one death; Fenians suspected . . . 14 Jan. 1881.
New technical school opened by the duke of York, 25 March, 1896

SALIQUE or SALIC LAW, by which females are excluded from inheriting the crown of France, is said to have been instituted by Pharamond, 424, and ratified in a council of state by Clovis I., the real founder of the French monarchy, in 511. *Hénault*. This law, introduced into Spain by the Bourbons 1700, was formally abolished by decree 29 March, 1830; and on the death of Ferdinand VII. his daughter succeeded as Isabella II., 29 Sept. 1833; see *Spain*. By this law also Hanover was separated from England, when queen Victoria ascended the English throne, 1837.

SALISBURY (Wilts), founded in the beginning of the 13th century, on the removal of the cathedral hither from Old Sarum. National councils or parliaments were repeatedly held at Salisbury, particularly in 1296, by Edward I.; in 1328, by Edward III.; and in 1384. Henry Stafford, duke of Buckingham, was executed here by order of Richard III., in 1483.—On SALISBURY PLAIN is Stonehenge (*which see*). This plain was estimated at 500,000 acres. On it were so many cross roads, and so few houses to take directions from, that Thomas, earl of Pembroke, planted a tree at each milestone from Salisbury to Shaftesbury, for the traveller's guide. The autumn military manœuvres took place on Salisbury Plain, Aug., Sept. 1872; again 31 Aug., 1898; see under *Army*.—The first seat of the BISHOPRIC was at Sherborne, St. Aldhelm being prelate, 705. Herman removed the seat to Old Sarum, about 1072; and the see was removed to Salisbury by a papal bull, in 1217. It has yielded to the church of Rome one saint and two cardinals. The building of the cathedral commenced 28 April, 1220, and was completed in 1258. This edifice is reckoned one of our finest ecclesiastical erections. Its spire, the loftiest in the kingdom, was considered in danger in April,

1864, and subscriptions were begun for its immediate repair. The choir was re-opened, after restoration by sir G. G. Scott, 1 Nov. 1876; spire and turrets restored under sir Arthur Blomfield, March, 1898. The bishopric is valued in the king's books at 1367*l.* 11*s.* 8*d.* Present income 5000*l.* Population, 1881, 14,792; 1891, 15,980; 1901, 17,117.

RECENT BISHOPS.

1797. John Fisher, died 2 July, 1825.
1825. Thomas Burgess, died 19 Feb. 1837.
1837. Edmund Denison, died 6 March, 1854.
1854. Walter Kerr Hamilton, died 1869.
1869. George Moberly, elected 9 Sept., died 6 July, 1885.
1885. John Wordsworth. Aug.

SALISBURY ADMINISTRATIONS.—

Mr. Gladstone resigned in consequence of a defeat in the house of commons on the Budget Bill (264—252), 8-9 June, and was succeeded by lord Salisbury, whose ministry received the seals, 24 June, 1885.

Prime minister and foreign secretary—Robert Arthur Talbot Gascoigne-Cecil, marquis of Salisbury.*
First lord of the treasury—Sir Stafford Northcote (earl of Iddesleigh).
Lord chancellor—Sir Hardinge Giffard (lord Halsbury).
Lord president of the council—Gathorne Gathorne-Hardy, viscount Cranbrook.
Lord privy seal—Dudley Ryder, earl of Harrowby.
Secretaries: home—Sir Richard Assheton Cross.
the colonies—Col. Frederick Arthur Stanley.
India—Lord Randolph Henry Spencer-Churchill.
war—William Henry Smith; G. Gathorne Hardy, viscount Cranbrook, about 23 Jan. 1886.
Scotland—Charles Henry, duke of Richmond, about 14 Aug. 1885.
First lord of the admiralty—Lord George Hamilton
Chancellor of the exchequer—Sir Michael Hicks-Beach.
Lord lieutenant of Ireland—Henry H. M. Herbert, earl of Carnarvon; resigned Jan. 1886.
Lord Chancellor of Ireland—Edward Gibson (lord Ashbourne).
President of board of trade—Charles Henry Gordon-Lennox, duke of Richmond; Edw. Stanhope, about 17 Aug. 1885.
Postmaster-general—Lord John Manners.
Vice-president of the council—Edward Stanhope.

The above form the cabinet.

Chancellor of duchy of Lancaster—Henry Chaplin.
President of local government board—Arthur J. Balfour.
Chief secretary for Ireland—Sir William Hart-Dyke, resigned; W. H. Smith, about 23 Jan. 1886.

* He was born 3 Feb. 1830; married Georgina, daughter of baron Alderson, 1857, a lady of high intellect, she died 1899; lord Cranborne, on the death of his brother, 1865; succeeded his father as marquis in 1868; M.P. for Stamford, 1853-68; secretary for India, July, 1866, to March, 1867; and Feb. 1874 to April, 1878: for foreign affairs, April, 1878, to May, 1880; special ambassador to Constantinople, Nov. 1876; chancellor of the University of Oxford, 1860. Manifesto respecting the election issued, *Times*, 28 June, 1892; judicious speech on the eastern question, at the Guildhall, 9 Nov. 1896; another, on international politics, 9 Nov. 1898; resigns the premiership, which he had nobly and successfully held over 13½ years, made K.C.G. of the Roy. Victorian order, 11 July, 1902. He sat 15 years in the commons, 34 years in the lords, and held important posts in the cabinet about 20 years. He earned the gratitude and admiration of the nation as foreign secretary (four times held), and through the "great contest over home rule." Under his able leadership the unionist party was developed; "in Egypt, the Soudan, S. Africa and other African possessions he has secured our rights for all time, and during his last years in office has built up an excellent understanding between the empire and the United States, a fitting crown to a life devoted to the highest interests of the British people," *Times*, 14 July, 1902. He died at Hatfield, 22 Aug. 1903; buried there 31 Aug.

First commissioner of works—David Robert Plunket.
Attorney-general—Sir R. E. Webster.
Solicitor-general—John E. Gorst.
Resigned 27 Jan., in consequence of Mr. Jesse Collings' amendment on the address being carried (329-250) 26-27 Jan. 1886.

SECOND ADMINISTRATION (26 July, 1886)—

Prime minister and foreign secretary (Jan. 1887)—Robert Arthur Talbot Gascoigne-Cecil, marquis of Salisbury.
First lord of the treasury and leader of the commons—Wm. Henry Smith, 3 Jan. 1887; died 6 Oct. 1891. Arthur J. Balfour, 9 Nov. 1891.
Lord chancellor—Hardinge Stanley Giffard, lord Halsbury.
Lord president of the council—Gathorne Gathorne-Hardy, viscount Cranbrook.
Chancellor of the exchequer—Lord Randolph Henry Spencer-Churchill; resigned 22 Dec. 1886;* George Joachim Goschen, 3 Jan. 1887.
Secretaries: home—Henry Matthews (R.C.).
foreign—Stafford Henry Northcote, earl of Iddesleigh (died 12 Jan. 1887); marquis of Salisbury, Jan. 1887.
the colonies—Edward Stanhope; sir Henry Thurstan Holland (baron Knutsford), Feb. 1888 (Jan. 1887).
India—Sir Richard Cross (viscount Cross).
war—William Henry Smith; Edward Stanhope, 6 Jan. 1887; died 21 Dec. 1893.
First lord of the admiralty—Lord George Francis Hamilton.
Lord chancellor of Ireland—Edward Gibson, lord Ashbourne.
Chief secretary for Ireland—Sir Michael Edward Hicks-Beach; resigns, but remains in the cabinet (retires Jan. 1888); succeeded by Arthur J. Balfour, 5 March, 1887. Wm. L. Jackson, 9 Nov. 1891.
Chancellor of the duchy of Lancaster—Lord John Manners (duke of Rutland), 4 March, 1888.
President of the board of trade—Sir Frederick Stanley (lord Stanley of Preston); succeeded by sir M. E. Hicks-Beach, 15 Feb. 1888.
President of the board of agriculture, Henry Chaplin, 5 Sept. 1889.

The above form the Cabinet.

Lord privy seal—George Henry Cadogan (earl Cadogan).
Lord lieutenant of Ireland—Charles Stewart Vane Tempest Stewart, marquis of Londonderry: succeeded by Laurence Dundas, earl of Zetland, 30 May, 1889.
Secretary for Scotland—Arthur J. Balfour; succeeded by Schomberg Henry Kerr, marquis of Lothian, 8 March, 1887, died 17 Jan. 1900.
President of local government board—C. T. Ritchie.
Postmaster-general—Henry Cecil Raikes, died 24 Aug. 1891; sir James Fergusson, about 21 Sept. 1891.
First commissioner of works—David Robert Plunket.
Attorney-general—Sir Richard Everard Webster, Q.C.
Solicitor-general—Sir Edward Clarke, Q.C.
Resigned 12 Aug., in consequence of want of confidence voted by the commons, Mr. Asquith's amendment (350-310), 11 Aug. 1892. For chief measures, see *Education, Ireland, Local Government, Navy,* and *National Debt.*

THIRD ADMINISTRATION (25 June *et seq.* 1895)—

Prime minister and foreign secretary—the marquis of Salisbury.
First lord of the treasury and leader of the commons—Arthur James Balfour.
Lord high chancellor—Lord Halsbury; earl, 1 Jan. 1898.
Lord president of the council—Spencer C. Cavendish (duke of Devonshire).
Lord privy seal—Richard Assheton (viscount Cross).
Chancellor of the exchequer—sir Michael Hicks-Beach
Secretaries: home—sir Matthew White Ridley.
foreign—marquis of Salisbury.
colonial—Joseph Chamberlain.
war—marquis of Lansdowne.
India—lord George Hamilton.
Chancellor of the duchy of Lancaster—sir Henry James, lord James of Hereford.
First lord of the admiralty—George J. Goschen, retired 10 Nov. 1900.
Secretary for Scotland—Alexander H. Bruce (lord Balfour of Burleigh).
President of the board of trade—Charles T. Ritchie.

* The marquis of Hartington and the liberal unionists declined to form part of a coalition ministry, 30 Dec. 1886.

President of the local government board—Henry Chaplin.
Lord lieutenant of Ireland—George Henry, earl Cadogan.
Lord chancellor of Ireland—lord Ashbourne.
President of the board of agriculture—Walter Hume Long.
First commissioner of works—Aretas Akers-Douglas.

The above form the Cabinet.

Postmaster-general—Henry F. Howard (duke of Norfolk), *resigned* March, 1900; succeeded by lord Londonderry, April.
Vice-president of the committee of council on education—sir J. E. Gorst.
Financial secretary of the treasury—Robt. Wm. Hanbury.
Patronage secretary to the treasury—sir W. H. Walrond.
Attorney-general—sir Richard E. Webster; sir Robert Finlay, May, 1900.
Parliamentary secretary to the board of trade—earl of Dudley.
Solicitor-general—sir Robert B. Finlay, Aug.; Sir E. Carson, May, 1900.
Civil lord of the admiralty—J. Austen Chamberlain.
Secretaries: admiralty—W. E. Macartney.
local government board—T. W. Russell
Under secretaries: home—Jesse Collings.
foreign—George Curzon, *res.*, Aug.; succeeded by Wm. St. John Brodrick, Oct. 1898.
colonial—earl of Selborne.
India—earl of Onslow.
war—Wm. St. John Brodrick; succeeded by George Wyndham, Oct. 1898.
Chief secretary for Ireland—Gerald Wm. Balfour.
Attorney-general for Ireland—John Atkinson.
Solicitor-general for Ireland—William Kenny, Q.C; Dunbar Plunket Barton, Dec. 1897; Mr. George Wright, Jan. 1900.
Solicitor-general for Scotland—Andrew Graham Murray; Chas. Scott Dickson, May, 1896.
Lord advocate for Scotland—sir C. Pearson; Andrew Graham Murray, May, 1896.
Paymaster-general—earl of Hopetoun; duke of Marlborough, Jan. 1899.

For chief measures, see *Australasia, Education, London Government Act, Ireland, Money Lending, Companies.*

FOURTH ADMINISTRATION (reconstructed 12 Nov. *et seq.* 1900–11 July, 1902, see *Balfour Administration*).
Prime minister and lord privy seal—lord Salisbury (*resigned*, 11 July, 1902, cabinet remained unchanged).
First lord of the treasury and leader of the commons—Arthur James Balfour.
Lord high chancellor—lord Halsbury.
Lord president of the council—duke of Devonshire.
Chancellor of the exchequer—sir Michael Hicks-Beach.
Secretaries: home—Charles T. Ritchie.
foreign—lord Lansdowne.
colonial—Joseph Chamberlain.
war—hon. St. John Brodrick.
India—lord George Hamilton.
Scotland—lord Balfour of Burleigh.
First lord of the admiralty—lord Selborne.
Lord lieutenant of Ireland—George Henry, earl Cadogan.
Lord chancellor of Ireland—lord Ashbourne.
President of the board of trade—Gerald Wm. Balfour.
Chancellor of the duchy of Lancaster—lord James of Hereford.
President of the local government board—Walter Hume Long.
President board of agriculture—Robt. Wm. Hanbury.
First commissioner of works and public buildings—Aretas Akers-Douglas.
Postmaster-general—lord Londonderry.

The above formed the Cabinet.

Chief secretary for Ireland—George Wyndham (in the cabinet).
Attorney-general for Ireland—John Atkinson.
Solicitor-general for Ireland—James H. Mussen Campbell.
Vice-president of the committee of council on education—Sir John Gorst.
Junior lords of the treasury—Henry T. Anstruther, William Hayes Fisher, hon. Ailwyn Fellows.
Financial secretary to treasury—Austen Chamberlain.
Patronage secretary to treasury—sir Wm. Walrond.
Secretary to the admiralty—Hugh O. Arnold-Forster
Civil lord of the admiralty—capt. E. G. Pretyman.
Under secretaries: home—Jesse Collings.
foreign—lord Cranborne.
colonial—lord Onslow.
India—lord Hardwicke.
war—lord Raglan.
Secretary board of trade—lord Dudley.
Secretary local government board—John Grant Lawson.
Financial secretary war office—lord Stanley.
Attorney-general—sir Robert Finlay.
Solicitor-general—sir Edward Carson.
Lord advocate for Scotland—Andrew Graham Murray.
Solicitor-general for Scotland—Charles Scott Dickson.
Paymaster-general—duke of Marlborough.

SALISBURY'S ACT, see *Artisans.*

SALLEE, a port of Morocco, long a haunt for pirates, destroyed by the British in 1632, and about 300 captives released.

SALLENTINI, allies of the Samnites, the only Italian tribe not subject to Rome, were overcome in war in 267 and 266 B.C., and Brundisium, their port, taken.

SALMON FISHERIES. The laws relating to them were consolidated and amended in 1861, and the report of a commission of inquiry (including sir Wm. Jardine) was published, in Feb. 1862. An act restricting the capture of salmon at certain times, passed in 1863, was amended in 1869–1870, and 1873. During the "salmon fence," 14 Sept. to 1 Feb., it is unlawful to catch fish of the salmon kind. A salmon-fishery congress opened at South Kensington, 7 June, 1867. Salmon eggs sent to New Zealand, Jan. 1878.

SALMON OVA, packed in boxes with moss, charcoal, and ice, to retard development—a plan suggested and proved practicable by Mr. E. H. Moscrop in 1863—adopted successfully by Mr. J. A. Youl, who sent ova to Australia in the "Norfolk," . 1864
Salmon disease, in rivers, announced, 1879; commission of inquiry appointed, Mr. F. Buckland and others . . . . Jan. 1880
Mr. Henry Ffennell strongly recommends measures for its promotion, *Times*, 30 Dec. 1892.
Very great increase in the number of salmon caught, 1883
Royal commission appointed (the earl of Elgin, duke of Bedford, and others) to inquire into the deterioration of the fisheries in Great Britain, 20 March, 1900; report issued, a central authority, local fishery boards, &c. recommended . 6 Aug. 1902
Salmon introduced into the Thames, at Teddington, 1901, and Feb. . . . . ,,

SALONICA, see *Thessalonica.*

SALT (chloride of sodium, a compound of the gas chlorine and the metal sodium) is procured from the rocks in the earth, from salt-springs, and from sea-water. The famous salt-mines of Wielitzka, near Cracow in Poland, have been worked 600 years. The salt-works in Cheshire, called the WICHES (Nantwich, Northwich, and Middlewich), were of great importance in the time of the Saxon heptarchy. The salt-mines of Staffordshire were discovered about 1670. Salt duties were first exacted in 1702; they were renewed in 1732; reduced in 1823; and in that year were ordered to cease in 1825. During the French war the duty reached to 30*l.* per ton. For the salt-tax in France see *Gabelle.* The government salt monopoly in India was abolished in May, 1863, by sir C. Trevelyan. Since 1797 salt has been largely employed in the manufacture of chloride of lime or bleaching powder (by obtaining its chlorine), and soap (by obtaining its soda). On this are based the chemical works of Cheshire, Lancashire, and other places. See under *Alkalies.*

Much distress in the salt districts of Cheshire through the subsidence of land, 1887–8. The proprietors of the Cheshire salt mines combined to form a "trust" or syndicate in the autumn of 1888; central office, Northwich; the trade being nearly ruined by great competition, first meeting 27 Sept. 1888.

Great advance in the price of salt Oct. 1888.

A "salt museum" presented to the town of Northwich by Mr. Brunner, M.P., March, 1889.

Salt exported from the United Kingdom: 1876, 865,804 tons; 1880, 1,051,240 tons; 1885, 921,869 tons; 1890, 726,021 tons; 1896, 660,935 tons; 1900, 547,395 tons; 1901, 617,203 tons.

SALTAIRE, see *Alpaca*.

SALT LAKE, see *Mormonites*.

SALT-PETRE (from *sal petræ*, salt of the rock), or Nitre, is a compound of nitric acid and potash (nitrogen, oxygen, and potassium), and hence is called nitrate of potash. It is the explosive ingredient in gunpowder, many detonating powders, and lucifer matches. Boyle in the 17th century demonstrated that salt-petre was composed of aqua fortis (nitric acid) and potash; the discoveries of Lavoisier (1777) and Davy (1807) showed its real composition. Its manufacture in England began about 1625. During the French revolutionary war, the manufacture was greatly increased by the researches of Berthollet.

SALUTE AT SEA. It is a received maxim at sea, that he who returns the salute always fires fewer guns than he receives, which is done even between the ships of princes of equal dignity; but the Swedes and Danes return the compliment without regarding how many guns are fired to them. The English claim the right of being saluted first in all places, as sovereigns of the seas; the Venetians claimed this honour within their gulf, &c. The admiralty issued a code of rules for salutes, Dec. 1876. See *Flag*, and *Naval Salute*.

SALVADOR, SAN, one of the Bahamas, and the first point of land discovered in the West Indies or America by Columbus. It was previously called Guanahani, or Cat's Isle, and Columbus (in acknowledgment to God for his deliverance) named it San Salvador when he first saw it, 11 Oct. 1492. The capital, San Salvador, was destroyed by an earthquake, 16 April, 1854, and is now abandoned.

SALVADOR, SAN, one of the republics of Central America, with a constitution established 24 Jan. 1859. Capital, Libertade. General Barrios elected president 1 Feb. 1860, was compelled to flee in Oct. 1863; when Francis Dueñas became provisional president; his formal election took place April, 1865. The ex-president, Gerard Barrios, was surrendered by Nicaragua, tried and shot, Aug. 1865. A reattempted revolution failed; Zaldivar fled; general Gonzales president, 1 Feb. 1872; R. Zaldivar, May, 1876; Gen. Menendez, June, 1885; re-elected 1 March 1887 for four years. Population, 1886, 651,130; 1901, estimated 900,000. The capital, San Salvador, was nearly destroyed by an earthquake, 19 March, 1873, about 50 persons perished. The convulsion began 5 March and thus gave timely warning. A rebellion suppressed, 6–10 Sept. 1887.

General Rivas and an insurgent army defeated by government troops, announced . . . 31 Dec. 1889
Insurrection ended . . . . . Jan. 1890
Gen. Menendez dies suddenly, 22 June; revolution, sen. Carlos Ezeta becomes provisional president, . . . 25 June ,,
Guatemala and Honduras declare war against president Ezeta, several sanguinary battles; invading troops defeated, July; Guatemala invaded, July; gen. Rivas revolts against president Ezeta, and is, after a severe engagement, defeated by gen. A. Ezeta, captured, and publicly shot, 1 Aug. ,,
Gen. Ezeta re-elected president . about 13 Sept. 1890
Peace with Guatemala signed, announced 17 Nov. ,,
Gen. Ezeta confirmed as president for four years, 1 March, 1891
Rebellion in the island of Amapala suppressed, and the leader, gen. Bardales, killed . 6 May, ,,
Violent earthquake, great destruction of life and property . . . . 9 Sept. ,,
About 40 persons killed in the capital; Comasagua nearly destroyed; shocks still continue 13 Sept. ,,
Conspiracy suppressed; gen. Narcisso Avilez and others executed; reported . . 22 July, 1893
Insurrection, with bloodshed, Santa Ana held by the rebels; reported . . . . 13 May, 1894
Great railway accident through the removal of the rails on a steep gradient by the insurgents; about 200 deaths; reported . . . . 16 May, ,,
Gen. Antonio Ezeta, with government troops, defeated and killed; resignation and flight of president Ezeta; reported . . . 4 June, ,,
Gen. Rafael A. Guitierrez proclaimed president; reported . . . . . . 7 June, ,,
Pres. Gutièrrez deposed, in consequence of the proposed federation with Honduras and Nicaragua; gen. Tomas Regalado made president . 19 Nov. 1898
Señ. Escalon elected president; reported . 15 Jan. 1903
Dispute with Guatemala settled . 30 March, ,,

"SALVATION ARMY," a name assumed by a body of persons terming themselves the "Christian Mission" (formed by the combination of several revival societies in 1865, for the evangelization of the very lowest classes). Mr. William Booth was nominated "general" of the army. Deeds constituting Mr. Booth general superintendent of the affairs of the "Christian Mission" with plenary powers, and trustee of its property and income, and also with power to name his successor, were enrolled in Chancery, Aug. 1878.

A great "Hosanna" meeting to celebrate the formation of the 104th corps at Northampton, was held at the headquarters (with prayers, addresses, and singing), 272, Whitechapel-road, 30 June, 1879.
Gen. Booth set forth his principles in the *Contemporary Review* for August, 1882; he upholds the gospel; opposes sectarianism, and requires from his soldiers implicit obedience, aiming at the reformation of drunkards and other reprobates.*
The Eagle Tavern and Grecian Theatre, City Road, London, purchased; occupied, early 12 Aug.; devoted, 14 Sept. 1882; conditions of sale not kept, ordered to quit . . . . 6 July, 1883
Indian contingent (major Tucker and others), land at Bombay; fined; imprisoned on non-payment, 28 Sept. ,,
Their "invasion" opposed by the authorities in Switzerland, Jan. *et seq.*; severely opposed, June; Miss Booth imprisoned at Neufchâtel, Sept.; acquitted, 1 Oct.; expelled . . . 11 Oct. ,,
Great fighting between Salvation and Skeleton armies at Gravesend [and other places] 15 Oct. ,,
"553 army brigades in the United Kingdom; 182 abroad."—*Gen. Booth* . . . . April, 1884
West-end centre building founded . . . 14 June, ,,
Severe rioting at Worthing; the army attacked by the Skeleton army, 18-20 Aug.; a man wounded by a revolver fired by Mr. G. Head, 7 Sept.; rioting at Brighton . . . . 7 Sept. ,,
International congress in London 28 May–4 June, 1886
General Booth appeals to the army for a subscription of 5,000*l*. . . . . . . 20 Aug. ,,
Another appeal . . . . Dec. 1887
He reports "advance of the army" throughout the world with varying success, opposition and indifference; about 100,000*l*. received in . . . ,,
Celebration of the 23rd anniversary of the organization of the army at the Alexandra Palace, 9 July, 1888
Severe decree against the army in Berne, 2 Sept.; unconstitutional persecution, Aug.-Sept. 1884, continued 1888-9

* The army has officers of various grades; headquarters, 101, Queen Victoria Street, London; publishing offices, &c., Paternoster Square; official gazette, the *War Cry*, price ½d., in various languages, of which millions are sold The propagandism is very vigorous.

The offices in Queen Victoria Street, London, partly burnt . . . . . . 3 Dec. 1889
17th anniversary kept at the Alexandra Palace, 3 July, 1882; 25th at Crystal Palace . . . 1890
Death of Mrs. Catherine Booth, aged 61 . 4 Oct. ,,
Great funeral demonstration at Olympia, 13 Oct.; Abney Park . . . . . 14 Oct. ,,
Gen. Booth publishes his book "In Darkest England, and the Way Out," to renovate the very lowest classes ("the submerged tenth"); he proposes the formation of city, farm, and over the sea colonies (cost about 1,000,000*l.*) . Oct. ,,
Great meetings of the army at Exeter Hall, 43,171*l.* contributed . . . . 17, 18 Nov. ,,
Above 106,000*l.* subscribed or promised . Dec. ,,
Great progress of the army in India and the colonies reported . . . . . 13 Nov. ,,
Force of the army: 9,416 officers, 1,375 corps at home, and 1,499 in the colonies, capital, 750,000*l.*, reported . . . . . . Dec. ,,
General Booth visits Copenhagen, Hamburg, Berlin, and other places to inspect his army, Feb.; S. Africa, the East, and Australia, Aug. *et seq.* 1891; his welcome home, 12 days' festivities, 12 Feb. *et seq.* 1892
Mrs. David Bell, of Glasgow, bequeaths about 58,193*l.* and a hall in Dollar to gen. Booth in support of his work, announced . . 8 May, 1891
Gen. Booth urgently appeals for funds . May, 1892
A committee of inquiry respecting the expenditure of the funds (earl of Onslow, sir Henry James, Mr. Sydney Buxton, and others), 25 Oct. *et seq.*; a good report issued . . . . . 19 Dec. ,,
A lady leaves gen. Booth 20,000*l.* unconditionally; reported . . . . . 21 March, 1894
Jubilee meeting at the Crystal Palace, 80,000 British and foreign delegates present . 3 July, ,,
In Aug. 1894, there were 10,740 officers and 28,893 members; 41 countries occupied, 54 training institutions and 27 languages used.
Gen. Booth endeavours to establish peasant colonies, and village banks, 1895 *et seq.*
Dissension in the army, Mr. Ballington Booth, son of the "general," starts a separate army in the United States, N.A. . . . . March, 1896
Great exhibition (foreign and domestic) at the Royal Agricultural hall, Islington . 1–12 Aug. ,,
32nd annual festival at the Crystal Palace (60,000 present), commendatory letter from the queen, read by gen. Booth . . . . 20 July, 1897
Meeting at the Alexandra palace (50,328 officers, 14,500 bandsmen in the army) . 18 July, 1898
Meetings at the Mansion house in aid of the social work of the army . . . 1 April, ,,
Mansion house meeting, Mr. Cecil Rhodes testifies to the good done in S. Africa, and subscribes 200*l.* to the funds; lord Aberdeen praises the farm colony and the over-sea colony in W. Australia, 21 April, 1899
Salvation army international exhibition at the Agricultural hall (see *Essex*). . . 24 July, ,,
Army force: 4,164 corps; 15,500 officers; 81 rescue homes in Gt. Britain, 407 abroad, about 20,000 inmates . . . . in 1901
Gen. Booth speaks at an inaugural meeting of the new temperance crusade at Exeter hall . 3 Feb. 1902
Army force: 7,599 corps; 15,796 officers (302,000*l.* expended in 1902) . . . . 1 Jan. 1903

SALZBACH (Baden). Here the French general Turenne was killed, at the commencement of a battle, 27 July, 1675.

SALZBURG, an ancient city of Germany, was annexed to Austria, 1805; to Bavaria, 1809; to Austria again 1815. It was the birthplace of Mozart, 1756. The meetings of the emperors of Austria and France here, 18 Aug. 1867, and the emperors of Austria and Germany, 6 Sept. 1871, which caused some anxiety, were reported to be in favour of peace. Population, province, 1890, 173,510; 1900, 193,247; city, 1890, 27,741; 1900, 32,934.

SAMAJ, or **SOMAJ**, see *Deism*.

SAMANIDE DYNASTY, began with Ismail Samani, who overcame the army of the Safferides, and established himself in the government of Persia, 902; his descendants ruled till 999.

SAMARCAND (in Tartary) was conquered by the Mahometans, 707; by Genghis Khan, 1220, and by Timur, or Tamerlane, who ruled here in great splendour. Samarcand was occupied by the Russians under Kaufmann 26 May, 1868, after a conflict on the previous day. The garrison left, resisted a fierce siege till relieved by Kaufmann, 13-20 June, 1868.

SAMARITANS. Samaria was built by Omri, 925 B.C.; and became the capital of the kingdom of Israel. On the breaking up of that kingdom (721 B.C.), the conqueror Shalmaneser placed natives of other countries at Samaria. The descendants of these mixed races were abominable to the Jews, and much more so in consequence of the rival temple built on Mount Gerizim by Sanballat the Samaritan, 332 B.C., which was destroyed by John Hyrcanus, 130 B.C.; see *John* iv. & viii. 48, and *Luke* x. 33. The Samaritan Pentateuch (of uncertain origin) was published in his Polyglot by Morinus, 1632.

The Samaritan Free hospital, Marylebone; memorial stone laid by the prince of Wales, 24 July, 1889.

SAMNITES, a warlike people of S. central Italy, who strenuously resisted the Roman power, and were not subjugated till after three sanguinary wars, from 343 to 290 B.C. They afterwards joined Pyrrhus, Hannibal, and other enemies of Rome, without benefit to themselves. Their brave leader, Caius Pontius, who spared the Romans at Caudium, 320, having been taken prisoner, was basely put to death, 292. They did not acquire the right of citizenship till 88 B.C. See *Caudine Forks* and *Rome*.

SAMOAN ISLES (or Navigators), (nine inhabited), near the Fiji islands; christianized by rev. John Williams, 1830. King Malietoa succeeded, 8 Nov. 1880. The isles have a political constitution; their parliament voted annexation to New Zealand, March, 1885. R. L. Stevenson died at Vailima, 3 Dec. 1894. Population 1902, 33,700.

King Malietoa deposed for alleged robbery and insult by Germans, and replaced by Tamatese, the British and French consuls protest, announced 8 Sept. 1887
Insurrection against Tamatese, headed by Mataafa Oct. 1888
Victory of Mataafa, after a fierce battle 29 Nov. ,,
A party of Germans land, attacked by Mataafa's forces; 16 killed and the rest rescued 18 Dec. ,,
Difficulties regarding Samoa have arisen between the German, British, and United States governments . . . . . . Jan. 1889
The Germans declare war against Mataafa; 31 Jan. ,,
Prince Bismarck yields to U. States claims Feb. ,,
Cessation of hostilities reported 5 March, ,,
By a great storm three German and three American war vessels were driven ashore at Apia on the island of Upola and destroyed; about 50 Americans and 96 Germans drowned; H.M.S. *Calliope* escaped by steaming out 15, 16 March, ,,
[Capt. Kane of the *Calliope* was thanked by the admiralty for his skill and seamanship.]
Conference on Samoan affairs at Berlin; plenipotentiaries: England, sir Edward Malet; Germany, count H. Bismarck; United States, Mr. John Kasson; first met 29 April; closing conference, agreement signed subject to legislative ratification 14 June, ,,
The convention declares the Samoan Isles to be independent neutral territory; the three powers to have equal rights; Malietoa recognized as king; a supreme court created, with other provisions.

Mataafa supports Malietoa, who is warmly received on his return to Apia, 11 Aug.; he resigns kingship to Mataafa 1889
Mataafa elected king, and Malietoa vice-king, announced . . . . . . 14 Oct. ,,
Malietoa reinstated as king, with the assent of foreign powers . . . . . 10 Dec. ,,
Death of Tamasese, reported . . . 28 April, 1891
The powers promise the king needed help . Aug. 1892
Threatened war averted by intervention . Dec. ,,
A German white book, containing the diplomatic correspondence from spring, 1890, to 6 Dec. 1892 (supporting the statements of Mr. Robert L. Stevenson and describing the troubles attributed to the misconduct of baron Senfft von Pilsach, adviser to the king, and Herr von Cederkrantz, chief justice), issued at Berlin . . 16 Jan. 1893
Herr von Senfft Pilsach and Herr von Cederkrantz dismissed; reported . . . . . 11 May, ,,
Disputes between the king and Mataafa; reported 14 June; fighting began, 7 July; stopped by foreign warships . . . . . 19 July, ,,
Mataafa subdued and transported to Kakaofo island; reported . . . . . . 1 Sept. ,,
Mr. Henry Ide, an American citizen, appointed chief justice . . . . Sept. ,,
A rebellion against king Malietoa suppressed; reported . . . . 30 Jan. 1894
Civil war, caused by the repressive measures of the chief justice, Mr. Henry Ide; 35 men killed, many wounded . . . . 10 March *et seq.* ,,
A protectorate of the isles proposed by New Zealand, April; see *New Zealand*, Nov. 1894.
Cessation of war through foreign influence; reported 25 April, ,,
Insurrection in Atua; reported, 1 June *et seq.*; intervention of British and German warships; the rebel stronghold bombarded, 10 Aug.; fighting continued, 12, 13 Aug.; the rebels surrender, 15 Aug.; end of war . . . . . 6 Sept. ,,
Death of Mr. Robt. Louis Stevenson, at Apia, aged 44, 4 Dec.; much beloved by the Samoans, and buried by them on the top of Vaea mountain, 1,300 feet above sea-level . . . . 5 Dec. ,,
Depression of trade, reported . . . . April, 1898
Death of king Malietoa . . . . . 22 Aug. ,,
Combined demonstration of British and German warships against Mulinuu, reported 24 Nov. ,,
Dispute over the election of a king; chief justice Chambers decides in favour of Tanu, son of Malietoa, and against Mataafa (according to internat. compact, 14 June, 1889) . . 31 Dec. 1898
Mataafa, encouraged by the Germans, rebels; fighting ensues, houses looted and burnt in Apia; capt. Sturdee lands with British marines; Tanu, Mr. Chambers and others take refuge on H.M.S. *Porpoise* . . . . 1 Jan. 1899
Foreign consuls acknowledge Mataafa *de facto* king . . . . 4 Jan. ,,
Provisional government formed; dr. Raffel, president of the municipal court, proclaims himself acting-chief justice; British and U.S. consuls protest; capt. Sturdee, of H.M.S. *Porpoise*, threatens to open fire if any resistance is offered to chief justice Chambers, who resumes his court under escort . . . . 7 Jan. ,,
Negotiations between the British, American, and German governments . . . . . . Jan. ,,
German opposition to chief justice Chambers 9 Jan. ,,
Robt. Louis Stevenson's house looted by the rebels . . . . Feb. ,,
Dr. Raffel is recalled to Berlin; leaves Apia, Feb. ,,
Adm. Kantz U.S. *Philadelphia*, arrives, 6 March; negotiations held; a proclamation issued, denouncing Mataafa's government as illegal under the Berlin treaty, 12 March; a counter-proclamation issued by Herr Rose, German consul, 13 March; Apia surrounded by rebels, 14 March; British and American blue-jackets landed under capt. Sturdee; the Tivoli hotel attacked by the rebels, 3 British marines killed; the warships open fire, 15 March; rebels repulsed at the British consulate by blue-jackets under gen. Cutliffe, 17 March; Malietoa crowned king in presence of the foreign consuls (Germans excepted) . 23 March, ,,
Much friction and anarchy; 4 British marines, 1 private and 1 American guarding the consulates killed; German consul issues an aggressive proclamation: villages shelled by British and U.S. warships, brisk fighting . . . . 30 March, 1899
An Anglo-American force ambuscaded while reconnoitring at Vailele, British lieut. Freeman and 2 men, U.S. lieut. Philip Lansdale, ensign John Monaghan and 2 marines killed; 100 rebels killed and wounded . . . . 1 April, ,,
Rebel posts at Vailima and elsewhere captured by lieut. Gaunt's brigade, 12–17 April; much skirmishing; ultimatum; Mataafa and chiefs agree to keep outside boundary, 25 April; and surrender arms . . . . May, ,,
Internat. commission: Mr. Bartlett Tripp (U.S.), president; Mr. Eliot and baron Sternburg arrive at Apia . . . . 13 May, ,,
Mr. Chambers' decision concerning the kingship confirmed; Tanu voluntarily abdicates, 10–13 June, ,,
Further fighting, 3 chiefs arrested . . 4 July, ,,
Chief-justice Chambers resigns, and leaves Apia, 14 July, ,,
Rival parties sign an agreement abolishing the kingship; an administrator, with a council of 3, to be nominated by Great Britain, U.S. and Germany; a native assembly and high court of justice to be appointed, Mr. Osborne, U.S. consul, to act as chief justice, 17 July; the commissioners leave, 18 July; their report issued, 13 Oct.; government in the hands of Dr. Solf, the municipal president, and 3 consuls . . Aug. ,,
Samoa treaty: Anglo-German convention; Samoa ceded to Germany; the Tonga, Savage, and Solomon isles, &c., to Great Britain; Tutuila and adjacent isles to U.S.N.A.; Gold Coast and Togoland (Hinterland) frontiers settled, signed 14 Nov. 1899, ratified 16 Feb. 1900; German flag hoisted, Dr. Solf, governor . . . . 1 March, 1900
Convention signed by England, U.S. and Germany, referring compensation claims to the arbitration of the king of Sweden, 7 Nov. 1899; Great Britain and U.S.N.A. pronounced liable for losses to foreigners incurred during the fighting; award signed . . . . 14 Oct. 1902

SAMOS, an island on the W. coast of Asia Minor. Colonised by Ionians about 1043 B.C. The city was founded about 986. Polycrates, ruler of Samos (532-22 B.C.), was one of the most able, fortunate, and treacherous of the Greek tyrants, and possessed a powerful fleet. He patronised Pythagoras (born here) and Anacreon. Samos was taken by the Athenians, 440; and, with Greece, became subject to Rome, 146. It was taken by the Venetians, A.D. 1125, who here made velvet (*samet*), and became subject to the Turks, about 1459. Population, 1891, 44,953; 1900, 54,830.

It was made a principality under Turkish suzerainty by sultan Mahmoud in 1832.
New autonomous constitution granted, in 1850.
Prince Constantine Adossides, born 23 Feb., 1822; appointed 4 March, 1879. Alexander Karatheodory, born 20 July, 1833, appointed 1885; Georghi Pasha Berovitch appointed, Jan. 1895; succeeded by Stephanaky Musurus Bey, about 28 June, 1896; Costaki Valganis Effendi, March, 1899; Mihailaki Georgiadis, Aug. 1900; Alexander Mavrogeno, March, 1902.

SAN. For names with this prefix, see the names themselves throughout the book.

SANATORIUM, see *Tuberculosis*.

SAMPFORD COURTENAY (Devon). Here John, lord Russell, defeated the Cornish and Devonshire catholic rebels, the middle of Aug. 1549.

SANCTION, see *Pragmatic*.

SANCTUARIES, see *Asylums*. Privileged places for the safety of offenders are said to have been granted by king Lucius to churches and their precincts. St. John's of Beverley was thus privileged in the time of the Saxons. St. Burian's, in Cornwall, was privileged by Athelstan, 935; Westminster, by Edward the Confessor; St. Martin's-le-Grand, 1529. Being much abused, the privilege of sanctuary was limited by the pope in 1503 (at the request of Henry VII.), and much reduced in 1540. In London, persons were secure from arrest in certain localities: these were the Minories, Salisbury-court, Whitefriars, Fulwood's-rents, Mitre-court, Baldwin's-gardens, the Savoy, Clink, Deadman's-place, Montague-close, and the Mint. This security was abolished 1697, but lasted in some degree till the reign of George II. (1727).

SANDALS, see *Shoes*.

SAND-BLAST. Gen. B. C. Tilghman, of Philadelphia, has invented a method of cutting stone or hard metal by a jet of quartz sand impelled by compressed air or steam. A hole of 1½ inch diameter and 1½ inch deep was bored through a block of corundum, nearly as hard as diamond, in 25 minutes. The invention was submitted to the Franklin Institute, Philadelphia, 15 Feb. 1871. It may be employed in the arts, for etching, &c.; for this purpose a company was at work, 1874.

SANDEMANIANS, see *Glasites*.

SANDGATE, Kent, see *Landslips*.

SANDHURST, ROYAL MILITARY COLLEGE, founded, first at High Wycombe, in 1799; removed to Great Marlow in 1802, and to Sandhurst in 1812. It consists of the staff college and cadets' college. Competitive examination for entrance into the latter began in Feb. 1858. A wing of the college was destroyed by fire, 21 Jan. 1868; 5 fires from unknown causes occurred, 23 April, 7 May, 7, 25 June; 29 cadets rusticated, 3 July; 3 servants discharged, much indignation, see *Times*, 8, 12 July; all but two cadets exonerated by lord Roberts after special inquiry, 25 July, 1902.

SANDRINGHAM HOUSE, N.E. Norfolk, was purchased by the prince of Wales, 1861, rebuilt; occupied, 1871; much injured by fire, 1 Nov. 1891. Here the duke of Clarence and Avondale died, 14 Jan. 1892. *York cottage*, occupied by the duke and duchess of York, 6 July, 1893. An avenue (joining the Sandringham estate to the newly-acquired Anmer one) presented to the king by his tenants and labourers, 10 Nov. 1902. Fire in room over queen's bedroom, her majesty's happy escape, 11 Dec. 1903.

SANDWICH (*Portus Rutupensis*, Kent). It suffered by Danish invaders in 851, 993, and 1014, but was rebuilt by Canute, and became prosperous; it became chief of the cinque ports about 1066. It contributed 22 ships and 504 mariners to Edward III.'s French expedition. It was taken and plundered by the French under Brézé in Aug. 1457. Flemish silk and woollen manufactories were settled here by Elizabeth in 1561. Disfranchised 1885. Pop., 1881, 2,846; 1891, 2,796; 1901, 3,000.

SANDWICH ISLANDS or **HAWAII ARCHIPELAGO**, a group in the Pacific Ocean, discovered by captain Cook in 1778; but thought now to have been discovered by Juan Galtan, a Spaniard, about 1542. In *Owhyhee* or *Hawaii*, one of these islands, he fell a victim to the sudden resentment of the natives, 14 Feb. 1779. The king and queen visited London in 1824, and died there in July. These people have made great progress in civilisation and embraced Christianity before any missionaries were settled among them. Population in 1884, 80,578; 1890, 89,990; 1900, 63,592. Numbers of native population said to be stationary.

King Kaméhaméha I., a chieftain of the island Hawaii, subdued the other isles, and ruled from 1789 to 1819.

Idolatry gradually superseded by Christianity, 1819 *et seq.*

Kaméhaméha II., with his queen, visited England; both died of measles in London in 1824.

Kaméhàméha III. promulgation of constitution, 1840; independence of the state recognized by the great powers, 1843.

Kaméhaméha IV. married Miss Emma Rooker, 1856; she came to England and was received by the queen, 9 Sept. 1865.

Bishopric of Honolulu constituted, 1861; Dr. Thomas Staley, constituted, 18 Aug. 1862.

The king died; Kaméhaméha V. king . Nov. 1863

The duke of Edinburgh warmly received at Honolulu . . . . . 21 July, 1869

Bishop Staley resigns, Aug. 1870; bishop Alfred Willis consecrated . . . . . 2 Feb. 1872

Kaméhaméha V. died, unmarried . 11 Dec. ,,

Wm. C. Lunalilo crowned, 8 Jan. 1873; died, 3 Feb. 1874

Reciprocity treaty concluded between Hawaii and the United States 1875

David Kalakaua (born 16 Nov. 1836), elected king, in opposition to queen Emma 12 Feb.; visits the president at Washington 12 Dec. 1876; visits Europe; at Rome, 1 July; received by the queen at Windsor, 12 July, 1881; crowned . 12 Feb. 1883

Queen Kapiolani arrives at Liverpool to be present at the royal jubilee service 2 June; arrives in London . . . . . 8 June, 1887

Revolution against a corrupt ministry 25 June; the ministry deposed 30 June; the king powerless appeals to the foreign representatives, who recommend the formation of a new constitution; the king signs a new constitution 7 July; new ministry formed . . . . 10 July, ,,

Mr. Wilcox, a government military pupil, with 100 men, attempts the seizure of the palace at Honolulu, 30 July; fighting ensues, 6 rebels killed; Wilcox surrenders . . . . 31 July, 1889

Death of the king David Kalakaua at San Francisco, 20 Jan.; succeeded by his sister, Lydia Liliuokalani (who visited England in 1887), proclaimed . . . . . 29 Jan. 1891

Political troubles: the late king's ministers refuse to resign, Feb.; opposition to the queen; American intervention against civil war about 4 March, ,,

The ministry resigns; new one formed, 26 Feb.; princess Kaiulani declared heir apparent, 9 March, ,,

The queen nominates her privy council of 40 members, including her husband, Mr. John Owen Dominis, March; Mr. Dominis died . 27 Aug. ,,

Mr. Robert Wilcox heads a native party against the government, desiring a republic . Dec. ,,

Conspiracy of Wilcox and others suppressed, 20 May, 1892

The queen, proposing to change the constitution, is dethroned, and a provisional government set up (justice S. B. Dole and others), 17 Jan.; order maintained by troops from the U.S. warship *Boston*; the provisional government recognized by the British minister . . . 19 Jan. 1893

A mission sent to Washington desiring annexation, 14–16 Jan. 1893; the commissioners received at Washington. . . . . 4 Feb. *et seq.* ,,

Temporary protectorate established by Mr. John L. Stevens, the U. S. minister . . 1 Feb. ,,

Treaty for the annexation of the islands to the U.S.N.A.; proposed 16 Feb.; the treaty withdrawn from the senate by president Cleveland 9 March, ,,

Commissioners from the queen oppose the treaty, Feb.; appeal of the princess Kaiulani, published 21 Feb.; she arrives at New York . 1 March, ,,

Commissioner Blount sent to Honolulu from America, 20 March; he withdraws the protectorate and troops, 1 April; made U.S. minister May, ,,

Sympathizing letter from queen Victoria to the ex-queen Liliuokalani; reported . . April, ,,

The United States decline the annexation; the restoration of the queen opposed by the provisional government; reported . . Jan. 1894

U.S. admiral Walker authorized to establish an American naval station at Honolulu . 24 March, 1894
The senate of U.S.N.A. affirm the sole right of Hawaii to fix its own form of government, 31 May, „
Establishment of a republic proposed, 3 June; proclaimed; Mr. Sanford B. Dole elected president . . . . 4 July, „
Rising of the Hawaiians against the republican government; desultory fighting, Mr. C. L. Carter, late U.S. commissioner, killed; martial law proclaimed, 6, 7, Jan. 1895; rebellion over; many arrests, reported . . . 11 Jan. „
The ex-queen arrested for complicity, 19 Jan.; eloquent defence by the ex-queen before the military commission; sentenced after trial to 5 years' imprisonment and fine of 5,000 dollars; 3 of her adherents sentenced to death (remitted); many to long imprisonment . 24 Feb.–March, 1895
Walker and Rickard, British subjects, arrested; intervention of lord Kimberley, May, 1895; all political prisoners released . . . 1 Jan. 1896
The ex-queen and most of her supporters pardoned, reported, 13 Sept. 1895; the queen restored to civil rights, reported . . . . 29 Oct. „
Treaty for the annexation of Hawaii to the United States signed at Washington, 16 June, 1897; ratified by the Hawaii senate . . . 10 Sept. 1897
The ex-queen protests, announced . . 18 June, „
The island annexed by the United States; 7 July, 1898
Volcanic eruption of Mauna Loa, 4 July, 1899; violent eruption of Kilauea at Honolulu, 3 June, 1902

SANGIR ISLANDS, a group lying between the Philippines and Celebes, subject to the Dutch. Great Sangir has suffered much by volcanic eruptions. By one in 1856 about 2,000 persons perished, and by others, 7 June *et seq.* 1892, it was said that nearly all the population, about 12,000, was destroyed.

SANHEDRIM. An ancient Jewish council of the highest jurisdiction, of seventy, or, as some say, seventy-three members, usually considered to be that established by Moses, *Num.* xi. 16,—1490 B.C. It was yet in being at the time of Jesus Christ, *John* xviii. 31. A Jewish Sanhedrim was summoned by the emperor Napoleon I., 23 July, 1806. A meeting of Jewish deputies was held 18 Sept., and the Sanhedrim assembled, 9 March, 1807.

SANITARY INSTITUTE OF GREAT BRITAIN, founded 13 July, 1876; president, the duke of Northumberland; incorporated Aug. 1888. Congress at Leamington, 3 Oct. 1877; at Stafford, 2 Oct. 1878; at Croydon, 21 Oct. 1879; at Exeter, 1880; opened a School of Hygiene in London. Nov. 1879. Congress at Newcastle, 1882; at Glasgow, 27 Sept. 1883; at Dublin, 30 Sept. 1884; at Leicester, 22 Sept. 1885; York, 21 Sept. 1886; Bolton, 20 Sept. 1887; Worcester, 24 Sept. 1889; Brighton, 24 Aug. 1890; Portsmouth, 12 Sept. 1892; Liverpool, 24 Sept. 1894; Newcastle-on-Tyne, 2 Sept. 1896; Leeds, 14 Sept. 1897; Birmingham, 27 Sept. 1898; Southampton, 29 Aug. 1899; Manchester, 9 Sept. 1902. See under *Sanitation.*

SANITATION, the preservation of health. Strict cleanliness is enjoined in the law of Moses, 1490 B.C. Great attention has been paid to the public health in France since 1802. Tardieu published his "Dictionnaire de Hygiène," 1852-54. Sanitary commissions were appointed in 1838 and 1844. To Dr. Southwood Smith is mainly attributable the honour of commencing the agitation on the subject of public health in England about 1832; his "Philosophy of Health" having excited much attention. Since 1838 he has published numerous sanitary reports, having been much employed by the government. Professors of hygiene are now appointed. See *Health, Public Health*, and *Hygiene* (Congresses).

Investigations of the Poor Law Commissioners and consequent disclosures and the reports of the registrar-general lead to legislation, 1834 *et seq.*
Nuisances Removal act passed (repealed) . 1845-1860
Baths and Washhouses act 1846-1847
Public Health act (subsequent Supplemental acts). See *Health, Board of* 1848
Common Lodging Houses act 1851-1853
Labouring Classes Lodging Houses act . . . 1851
Smoke Nuisance Abatement act 1853
Diseases Prevention act 1855
Public Health act passed . . . . . . „
Metropolitan Interments acts . . . 1850-1855
International sanitary conferences at Paris, 1851; at Constantinople 1860
Labouring Classes Dwelling-house act passed, March, 1866
New Sanitary act (stringent) passed Aug. 1866; amended 1868, 1870
Public Health act passed . . . . 10 Aug. 1872
National health society founded 1873
International sanitary congress at Vienna, closed 1 Aug. 1874
Public Health act for Ireland passed . 7 Aug. „
Sanitary Laws Amendment act passed . 7 Aug. „
New Consolidated Public Health act passed . 1875
An international exhibition of objects relating to public health and safety was opened by the king of Belgium at Brussels, 26 June; a congress met 27 Sept. 1876

See *Hygiene* and *Sanitary Institute.*

Parkes "museum of hygiene," instituted 1876, at University college, London; incorporated and removed to Margaret-street, Cavendish-square, 1882; opened by the duke of Albany 26 May, 1883; incorporated with the Sanitary Institute of Great Britain . . . . Aug. 1888
Sanitary Assurance Association, formed by sir Joseph Fayrer, Drs. Andrew Clark, Corfield, Tyndall, and others; constituted . . . . 14 Dec. 1880
London Sanitary Protection Association, founded by sir Wm. W. Gull, professor Huxley, and others . 1881
International sanitary exhibition, royal Albert hall, 16 July—13 Aug. „
National health society's exhibition opened 2 June, 1883
International health exhibition, 1884; proposals adopted, Nov. 1883; opened by the duke of Cambridge, 8 May; closed, 30 Oct.; conferences held about 12 June; the juries inaugurated by the prince of Wales, 17 June; admitted, 4,153,390; medals awarded (242 gold, 5096 silver, and others), 27 Oct. 1884; estimated surplus, 19,000*l.* . Feb. 1885
International sanitary conferences at Washington, 1881; at Rome . . . . „
Stated result of fifty years' sanitation saving of about 500,000 lives; death rate reduced from above 22 to 19 per thousand . . . Nov. 1886
The College of State Medicine for the training of persons officially employed in matters relating to public health inaugurated; address by Mr. Brudenell Carter . . . . . 2 May, 1888
Congress of Hygiene met at Paris . . . 4 Aug. 1889
Sir Edwin Chadwick, a great promoter of sanitation, died, aged 90 . . . . 5 July, 1890
International sanitary conference at Venice, 5 Jan. *et seq.*; convention respecting quarantine, &c., signed by some of the delegates . . 30 Jan. 1892
Sanitary conference at Paris . . about 24 May, „
Church Sanitary Association, established 1893 (annual meetings) 1894
International sanitary conference at Dresden respecting cholera, &c., 11 March, 1893; closed 15 April, 1893; at Paris, 7 Feb. *et seq.* 1894; convention for the powers, 3 April, 1894, see *Plague*, 1897; Leeds, 14 Sept. 1897; Paris . 17 Oct. 1903
Sir Richard Thorne Thorne, K.C.B., a promoter of sanitary science and preventive medicine, died, aged 58 . . . . 18 Dec. 1899
Prof. W. H. Corfield died, aged 60 . 26 Aug. 1903

SANITAS (health), an antiseptic and disinfectant, invented by Mr. C. T. Kingzett, about 1875.

Having discovered that the salubrity of the air surrounding certain trees, such as the *Eucalyptus globulus* and pines, is due to their volatile oils producing peroxide of hydrogen and camphoric acid, he devised a method for procuring these re-agents by the decomposition of common turpentine, and in 1877 they were manufactured and sold as "Sanitas."

SAN JUAN ISLAND, see *Juan.*

SANOSIN, a new remedy for consumption, stopping coughing and fever and night sweats, and causing increase in weight. Papers on the new remedy read by Dr. Danelius and professor Sommerfield at Berlin Medical society, 13 May, 1903.

SAN SALVADOR, see *Salvador*.

SANSCULOTTES, a term of reproach applied to the leaders of the French republicans about 1790, on account of their negligence in dress, and afterwards assumed by them with pride. The complementary days of their new calendar were named by the Mountain party *Sansculottides*.

SANSKRIT, the language of the Brahmans of India, spoken at the time of Solomon, has been much studied of late years. Sir Wm. Jones, who published a translation of the poem Sakuntalá, in 1783, discovered that a complete literature had been preserved in India, comprising sacred books (the Vedas), history and philosophy, lyric and dramatic poetry. Texts and translations of many works have been published by the aid of the East India Company, the Oriental Translation Fund, and private liberality. The professorship of Sanskrit at Oxford was founded by colonel Boden. The first professor, H. H. Wilson, appointed in 1832, translated part of the Rig-veda Sanhitá, the sacred hymns of the Brahmins, and several poems, &c. Professor Monier Williams (elected 1860, knt. 1886, died 11 April, 1899) published an English and Sanskrit dictionary, 1851. Professor Max Müller published his history of Sanskrit Literature in 1859, and has edited the original text of the Vedas (he died 28 Oct. 1900). Philologists have discovered an intimate connection between the Sanskrit, Persian, Greek, Latin, Teutonic, Slavonian, Celtic, and Scandinavian languages. Prof. Buehler, eminent Oriental scholar, professor of Sanskrit at Vienna, drowned in the lake of Constance, 8 April, 1898; Dr. Peter Peterson, of Bombay, an eminent Sanscritist, dies Sept. 1899. Mr. Herbert Spencer's "Education" translated by Mr. H. Soobba Row into Sanskrit, 1899.

SAN STEFANO, see *Stefano*.

SANTA CRUZ (Teneriffe, Canary Isles). Here admiral Blake, by daring bravery, entirely destroyed sixteen Spanish ships, secured with great nautical skill, and protected by the castle and forts on the shore, 20 April, 1657. *Clarendon*. In an unsuccessful attack made upon Santa Cruz by Nelson, several officers and 141 men were killed, and the admiral lost his right arm, 24 July, 1797.* See *Virgin Isles*. Isles annexed by Great Britain, August, 1898.

SANTA FE DE BOGOTA, see *New Granada*.

SANTA HERMANDAD, see *Hermandad*.

SANTANDER. A thriving Spanish port in the Bay of Biscay; it has suffered by war, and was sacked by Soult, 1808. Population, 1887, city, 41,829; 1897, 50,640; province, 242,843; 1897, 263,673.

A vessel lying in the harbour caught fire, causing an explosion of dynamite, petroleum, &c., whereby other vessels were destroyed and part of the town burnt; the death of 500 persons, about 2,000 injured, reported; and much property destroyed, 3 Nov.; the place visited immediately by the minister of finance, sen. Gamazo; liberal subscriptions headed by the queen regent, sen. Gamazo and others, 7 Nov. 1893; see *Mansion House Funds*, 1893.

A second explosion in the vessel, 18 workmen, &c. killed; panic in the city, 21 March, 1894.

The ship blown up by order, 30 March, 1894.

SANTIAGO DE COMPOSTELLA (N.W. Spain), was sacked by the Moors in 995, and held by them till it was taken by Ferdinand III. in 1235. The order of Santiago, or St. James, was founded about 1170 to protect pilgrims to the shrine of St. James the Greater (Acts, xii. 2), said to be buried in the cathedral. The town was taken by the French in 1809, and held till 1814.—SANTIAGO, the capital of Chili, S. America, founded by Valdivia in 1541, has suffered much by earthquakes, especially in 1822 and 1829. Population, 1885, 189,332; 1899, 320,638. See *Spanish-American war*.

At a festival in honour of the Virgin Mary, 8 Dec. 1863, when the church of the Campania, brilliantly illuminated, was crowded, the combustible ornaments took fire, and above 2,000 persons, principally women, perished. On 20 Dec. the government ordered the church to be razed to the ground. See *Chili*, 1891.

SAPPERS AND MINERS, a name given in 1812 to the non-commissioned officers and privates of the corps of Royal Engineers. *Brande*.

SAPPHIC VERSE, invented by Sappho, the lyric poetess of Mitylene. She was equally celebrated for her poetry, beauty, and a hopeless passion for Phaon, a youth of her native country, on which last account it is said she threw herself into the sea from Mount Leucas, and was drowned, about 590 B.C. The Lesbians, after her death, paid her divine honours, and called her the tenth muse. Some consider the story fabulous.

SAPPHIRE, a precious stone of an azure colour, and transparent; in hardness it exceeds the ruby, and is next to the diamond. One was placed in the Jewish high priest's breast-plate, 1491. Thamas Kouli Khan is said to have possessed a sapphire valued at 300,000*l.*, 1733. Artificial sapphires were made in 1857 by M. Gaudin. Equal parts of alum and sulphate of potash were heated in a crucible. Mr. Pierpont Morgan presents two sapphires, one reported to be the largest and the other the most beautiful in the world, to the Nat. Hist. museum, New York, July, 1902.

SARABAND. A stately dance invented by Sarabanda, a dancer of Seville, in the 16th century.

SARACENS, a name of doubtful origin, popularly applied in the middle ages and since to the Arabs, Moors, and other Mahometans who conquered the East, Spain, Sicily, and parts of Africa, and resisted the Crusaders. See *Mahometanism*.

SARAGOSSA (N.E. Spain), anciently Cæsarea Augusta, founded 27 B.C., was taken by the Goths, 470; by the Arabs, 712; by Alfonso of Spain, 1118. Here Philip V. was defeated by the archduke Charles, 20 Aug. 1710. On 17 Dec. 1778, 400 of the inhabitants perished in a fire at the theatre. Saragossa, after successfully resisting the French in 1808, was taken by them after a most heroic defence by general Palafox, 20 Feb. 1809. The inhabitants, of both sexes, resisted until worn out by fighting, famine, and pestilence. Population, 1887, 92,407; 1897, 100,000.

SARAH SANDS, see *Wrecks*, 1857.

SARAKHS, see *Russia*, 1884.

SARATOGA (New York State, N. America). Here general Burgoyne, commander of a body of the

---

* Captain Fremantle, the friend of Nelson, and his companion in most of his brilliant achievements, was also wounded in the arm immediately before Nelson had received *his* wound in the same limb. The following note, addressed to the lady of Captain Fremantle (who was on board with her husband at the time he wrote), has been preserved, as being the first letter written by the hero with his left hand:—"MY DEAR MRS. FREMANTLE,—Tell me how Tom is, I hope he has saved his arm. *Mine is off;* but, thank God! I am as well as I hope he is. Ever yours, "HORATIO NELSON."

British army, after a severe engagement with the Americans at Germanstown, in which he was victorious, 3, 4 Oct., being surrounded, surrendered all his army (5791 men) to the American general Gates, 17 Oct. 1777. This was the greatest check the British suffered in the war.

SARAWAK, see *Borneo*.

SARDINIA, an island in the Mediterranean, successively possessed by the Phœnicians, Greeks, Carthaginians (about 500 B.C.), Romans (238), Vandals (A.D. 456), Saracens (720-40), Genoese (1022), Pisans (1165), Aragonese (1352), and Spaniards. From settlers belonging to these various nations the present inhabitants derive their origin. Victor Amadeus, duke of Savoy, acquired Sardinia in 1720, with the title of king; see *Savoy*. Population of the Sardinian dominions in 1858, 5,194,807; of Sardinia alone, 1887, 723,833; 9 Feb. 1901, 789,314. The king of Sardinia was recognised as king of Italy by his parliament in Feb. 1861; see *Italy*.

Conquered by the English naval forces, under sir John Leake and gen. Stanhope 1708
Ceded to the emperor Charles VI. 1714
Recovered by the Spaniards . . . 22 Aug. 1717
Ceded to the duke of Savoy with the title of *king*, as an equivalent for Sicily 1720
Victor-Amadeus abdicates in favour of his son . . 1730
Attempting to recover his throne, he is taken, and dies in prison 1732
The court kept at Turin, till Piedmont is overrun by the French 1792
Charles-Emmanuel resigns to his brother, duke of Aosta . . . . 4 June, 1802
Piedmont annexed to Italy . . . . 26 May, 1805
The king resides in Sardinia 1798-1814
Piedmont restored to its sovereign, with Genoa added . . . . Dec. „
King Charles-Albert promulgates a new code . . . 1837
Cavour establishes the newspaper "Il Risorgimento" ("the Revival") 1847
The king grants a constitution, and openly espouses the cause of Italian regeneration against Austria, 23 March, 1848
Defeats the Austrians at Goito; and takes Peschiera 30 May, „
Incorporation of Lombardy with Sardinia 28 June, and Venice . . . . 4 July, „
Sardinian army defeated by Radetzky . 26 July, „
Sardinians at Milan capitulate to Radetzky 5 Aug. „
Armistice signed . . . . 9 Aug. „
Hostilities resumed . . . . . . 12 March, 1849
Radetzky defeats a division of the Sardinians, and occupies Mortara . . . . . 21 March, „
Complete defeat of the Sardinians by the Austrians at Novara . . . . 23 March, „
Charles-Albert abdicates in favour of his son, Victor-Emmanuel . . . . . 23 March, „
The Austrians occupy Novara, &c. . . 25 March, „
Another armistice . . . . . . 26 March, „
Death of Charles-Albert, at Oporto . . 28 July, „
Treaty of Milan between Austria and Sardinia, signed . . . . 6 Aug. „
Adoption of the Siccardi law, which abolishes ecclesiastical jurisdictions . . . . 9 April, 1850
Arrest of the bishop of Turin . . . . 4 May, „
He is released from the citadel . . . 2 June, „
Cavour minister of foreign affairs 1851
Bill for suppression of convents and support of clergy by the state passed . . . 2 March, 1855
Convention with England and France signed; a contingent of 15,000 troops to be supplied against Russia . . . . 10 April, „
10,000 troops under general La Marmora arrive in the Crimea . . . . 8 May, „
Who distinguish themselves in the battle of the Tchernaya . . . . 16 Aug. 1855
The king visits London, &c. . . . 30 Nov. &c. „
Important note on Italy from count Cavour to England . . . . 16 April, 1856
Rupture with Austria; subsequent war (see *Austria*, 1857 *et seq.*)
Cavour declares in favour of free trade . June, 1857
Prince Napoleon Jerome marries princess Clotilde (see *Italy*) . . . . 30 Jan. 1859
Preliminaries of peace signed at Villa Franca, 11 July; count Cavour resigns, 13 July; Rattazzi administration formed . . . . . 19 July, „
The emperor Napoleon's letter to Victor-Emmanuel advocating the formation of an Italian confederation: the latter declares it to be impracticable, and maintains his engagements with the Italians, 20 Oct. „
Treaty of peace signed at Zurich . . . Nov. „
Garibaldi retires into private life . . . 17 Nov. „
Count Cavour returns to office . . . . 16 Jan. 1860
The Sardinian government refers the question of annexation of Tuscany, &c., to the vote of the people . . . . 29 Feb. „
Annexation of Savoy and Nice proposed by the French government; the Sardinian government refer it to the vote of the people . . . 25 Feb. „
Annexation to Sardinia voted almost unanimously by Æmilia, 14 March; by Tuscany, 16 March; accepted by Victor-Emmanuel . . 18-20 March, „
Treaty ceding Savoy and Nice to France, signed 24 March, „
Prussia protests against the Italian annexations 27 March, „
New Sardinian parliament opens . . . 2 April, „
Annexation to France almost unanimously voted for by Nice, 15 April; by Savoy . . 22 April, „
The government professes disapproval of Garibaldi's expedition to Sicily (*which see*) . . 18 May, „
The chambers ratify treaty of cession of Savoy and Nice . . . . 29 May, „
The Sardinian troops enter the papal territories (see *Italy* and *Rome*) . . . . . 11 Sept. „
Victor-Emmanuel enters the kingdom of Naples, 15 Oct. „
Naples and Sicily vote for annexation to Sardinia 21 Oct. „
Railway from Sassari to the sea opened . 9 April, 1872
Great storm; at Quarto, 200 houses, and at Quartuccie, 3 houses fell, about 15 people killed; at Pizzi, 10 houses destroyed . . . . . 7 Oct. 1889
A destructive hurricane, four bridges and many buildings destroyed, 12 persons killed, reported, 7 Dec. 1890
Destructive storm and floods, with loss of life, in the plain of Campedano, N. of Cagliari, 20 Oct. 1892
Tortoli ravaged by brigands . . . . 12 Nov. 1894
Report of a commission on the state of the island; recommendations: defences to be strengthened, garrisons and railways to be increased; work begun . . . . Sept. 1896
Visit of the king and queen, fêtes, &c., at Cagliari, 12 April, 1899; he lays the first stone of the new municipal buildings, 14 April; gives 4,000*l.* to the poor; unveils a monument to Victor Emmanuel at Sassari, 19 April; reviews British and Italian fleet in Aranci bay, visits adm. sir H. Rawson on H.M.S. *Majestic*, 22 April; Garibaldi's tomb at Caprera, and leave . . . . 23 April, 1899
300 persons arrested as accomplices and harbourers of criminals . . . . 14, 15 May, „
Brigandage in the Moro district suppressed, 10, 11 July, „
The forest of Anela on fire . . . . 24 Aug. 1903

[For the disputes, and war with Austria, and the events of 1859-61, see *Austria*, *France*, *Rome*, *Sicily*, and *Naples*.]

[For later history see *Italy*.]

KINGS OF SARDINIA. See *Savoy*.

1720. Victor-Amadeus I. king (as duke II.); resigned, in 1730, in favour of his son; died in 1732.
1730. Charles-Emmanuel I. (III. of Savoy), son.
1773. Victor-Amadeus II., son.
1796. Charles-Emmanuel II., son; resigned his crown in favour of his brother.
1802. Victor-Emmanuel I., brother; 4 June.
1805. [Sardinia merged in the kingdom of Italy, of which the emperor Napoleon was crowned king, 26 May, 1805.]
1814. Victor-Emmanuel restored; resigned in March, 1821; and died in 1824.
1821. Charles-Felix.
1831. Charles-Albert; abdicated in favour of his son, 23 March, 1849. Died at Oporto, 28 July, 1849.

1849. Victor-Emmanuel II., son; born 14 March, 1820; died, 9 Jan. 1878.
Humbert, king of Italy; born, 14 March, 1844; assassinated 29 July, 1900. See *Italy*, end.

SARDIS, see under *Seven Churches*.

SARMATIA, the ancient name for the country in Asia and Europe between the Caspian Sea and the Vistula, including Russia and Poland. The Sarmatæ or Sauromatæ troubled the early Roman empire by incursions. After subduing the Scythians they were subjugated by the Goths, in the 3rd and 4th centuries. They joined the Huns and other barbarians in invading Western Europe in the 5th century.

SARNO (S. Italy). Near this river, Teias, king of the Goths, was defeated and slain by Justinian's general Narses, March, 553.

SARUM, OLD (Wiltshire), an ancient British town, the origin of Salisbury (*which see*). Although completely decayed, it returned two members to parliament till 1832.

SASSANIDES, descendants of Artaxerxes or Ardishir, whose father, Babek, was the son of Sassan. He revolted against Artabanus, the king of Parthia; defeated him on the plain of Hormuz, 226; and re-established the Persian monarchy. This dynasty was expelled by the Mahometans, 652; see *Persia*.

SATAN, see *Devil Worship*.

SATELLITES, see *Planets, Jupiter, Mars, Saturn*.

SATIRE. About a century after the introduction of comedy, satire made its appearance at Rome in the writings of Lucilius, called the inventor of it, 116 B.C. *Livy*. The Satires of Horace (35 B.C.), Juvenal (about A.D. 100), and Persius (about A.D. 60), are the most celebrated in ancient times, and those of Churchill (1761) and Pope (1729), in modern times. Butler's "Hudibras," satirizing the presbyterians, first appeared in 1663. *Satire Menippée*, a celebrated satirical pamphlet, partly in verse and partly in prose, attacking the policy of the court of Spain and the league, written in the style of the biting satires of the cynic philosopher Menippus. The first part, "Catholicon d'Espagne," by Leroy, appeared in 1593; the second, "Abrégé des Etats de la Ligue," by Gillot, Pithou, Rapin, and Passerat, appeared in 1594. *Bouillet*.

SATRAPIES, divisions of the Persian empire, formed by Darius Hystaspes about 516 B.C.

SATTARA (W. India) was long a flourishing state, founded by Sevajee about 1646; subjugated by the Mahrattas about 1749; conquered by the British, 1818; ruled by a rajah under the protection of the company. The last rajah died without issue in 1848; when the country was annexed.

SATURDAY (the last, or seventh day of the week; the Jewish Sabbath; see *Sabbath*). It was so called from an idol worshipped on this day by the Saxons, and according to Verstegan, was named by them Saterne's day. *Pardon*. It is more probably from Saturn, *dies Saturni*. *Saturday Review*, an independent literary weekly journal, was first published, 3 Nov. 1855. See *Hospital* and *Lifeboat*.

SATURN, the planet, ascertained to be about 900 millions of miles distant from the sun, and its diameter to be about 77,230 miles. One of the 9 satellites was discovered by Huyghens (25 March, 1655); four by Cassini (1672-84); two by sir William Herschel (1789), one by Bond and Lassell (1848), and one by prof. Pickering in Arizona, U.S. (18 March, 1899). The ring was observed by Galileo, about 1610; its annular form determined by Huyghens, about 1655. The notion that the discovery of the two-fold character of the ring was by the Messrs. Ball, 1665, is exploded. Cassini discovered that the ring consisted in fact of two concentric rings, the inner brighter than the outer, in 1675. An inner ring was detected in 1850 by Dawes in England (29 Nov.), and by Bond in America. The ring, or series of concentric rings, is now considered to be composed of a multitude of small satellites. A bright spot observed by prof. Hall, Dec. 1876; spots seen by Mr. Denning 24 June, 9 July, 1903.

SATURNALIA, festivals in honour of Saturn, father of the gods, were instituted long before the foundation of Rome, in commemoration of the freedom and equality which prevailed on the earth in his golden reign. Some, however, suppose that the Saturnalia were first observed at Rome in the reign of Tullus Hostilius (673-640 B.C.), after a victory obtained over the Sabines: whilst others suppose that Janus first instituted them in gratitude to Saturn, from whom he had learned agriculture. Others assert that they were first celebrated after a victory obtained over the Latins by the dictator Posthumius, when he dedicated a temple to Saturn, 497 B.C. During these festivals no business was allowed, amusements were encouraged, and distinctions ceased. *Lenglet*.

SAVAGE CLUB, instituted by various literary men, in 1857, facetiously terming themselves "savages," on account of their freedom from conventionalism. On some occasions they gave a war-whoop. *Sala*. Mr. W. E. Gladstone was present at the 22nd anniversary, 14 June, 1879, and the king, then prince of Wales, was a visitor in 1882.

SAVAGE ISLAND was discovered by capt. Cook in 1774, and so named because of the fierce attack made by the natives on his party. The island has long been a field of missionary enterprise, the inhabitants, about 5,000, are now Christians, and it was ceded to Great Britain by the Samoa agreement, Nov. 1899.

SAVANDROOG or **SEVERNDROOG** (Mysore, S. India), a strong fortress, was captured by the British, 2 April, 1755, and 21 Dec. 1791.

SAVANNAH, a city and port of Georgia on the river Savannah, U.S.A., founded in 1733, and incorporated, 1789; it was taken by the British in the American war in 1778, and by gen. Sherman, the northern general, 21 Dec. 1864. Pop. 1880, 30,709; 1890, 43,189; 1900, 54,244.

SAVINGS' BANKS. The first of these was instituted at Berne, in Switzerland, in 1787, by the name of *caisse de domestiques*, being intended for servants only; another was set up in Basel, in 1792, open to all depositors. The rev. Joseph Smith, of Wendover, began a Benevolent Institution in 1799; and in 1803-4, a "charitable bank" was instituted at Tottenham by Miss Priscilla Wakefield. The rev. Henry Duncan established a parish bank at Ruthwell in 1810. One was opened in Edinburgh in 1814. The benefit clubs, among artisans, having accumulated stocks of money for their progressive purposes, a plan was adopted to identify these funds with the public debt of the country, and an extra rate of interest was held out as an inducement; hence were formed savings' banks to receive small sums, returnable with interest on demand.

Rt. hon. Geo. Rose developed the system, and brought it under parliamentary control, 1816.

In 1840 there were 550 banks; 766,354 depositors; amount, 22,060,904*l.*

Acts to consolidate and amend previous laws relating to savings' banks were passed in 1828 and 1847; extended to Scotland in 1835; again consolidated and amended in 1863, 1880, and 1887.

On 20 Nov. 1851, the number of savings' banks in Great Britain and Ireland was 574, besides above 20,000 friendly societies and charitable institutions. The depositors (in the banks) were 1,092,581, while the societies embraced a vast but unknown number of persons: the amount of deposits was 32,893,511*l.*

Amount of computed capital of savings' banks in the United Kingdom:—1853, 33,362,260*l.*; 1860, 41,258,368*l.*; 1870, 37,958,549*l.*—1871, England, 31,413,002*l.*; Wales, 1,066,543*l.*; Scotland, 4,119,735*l.*; Ireland, 2,220,383*l.*, total, 38,819,663*l.* In 1877, England, 34,750,747*l.*; Wales, 1,189,254*l.*; Scotland, 6,026,802*l.*; Ireland, 2,271,883*l.*; total, 44,238,686*l.* In 1883, England, 34,441,787*l.*; Wales, 1,103,201*l.*; Scotland, 7,359,586*l.*; Ireland, 2,082,549*l.*; total, 44,987,123*l.* In 1887, England, 35,595,889*l.*; Wales, 915,171*l.*; Scotland, 8,688,354*l.*; Ireland, 2,062,808*l.*; total, 47,262,222*l.* In 1890, England, 31,232,451*l.*; Wales, 852,455*l.*; Scotland, 9,533,971*l.*; Ireland, 2,011,675*l.*; total, 43,650,552*l.* Total in 1891, 42,858,434*l.*; 1894, 44,464,936*l.* 4*s.* 11*d.*; 1901, 52,680,000*l.*; 1902, 51,950,404*l.*

1877.	*Received by Trustees.*	*Paid.*
England	£6,590,428	£7,031,233
Wales	178,260	224,434
Scotland	2,090,480	1,927,283
Ireland	504,463	472,185
	9,363,631	9,655,135

1890.	*Received by Trustees.*	*Paid.*
England	£6,234,996	£8,607,201
Wales	124,055	165,502
Scotland	2,824,391	2,870,407
Ireland	380,965	483,290
1893.	*Received by Trustees.*	*Paid.*
England	£5,677,539	£6,819,089
Wales	91,639	203,111
Scotland	2,973,494	2,761,860
Ireland	355,457	500,552
1899.	*Received by Trustees.*	*Paid.*
England	£7,235,389	£7,345,193
Wales	89,207	95,745
Scotland	4,940,554	4,659,248
Ireland	472,495	469,765
	12,737,645	12,569,951

For *Post-office Savings' Banks*, established in 1861, see under *Post-office.*

Savings' Banks Investment acts, passed March, 1866, and Aug. 1869.

New Savings' Bank act, 43 & 44 Vict. c. 36, passed, 1880, came into effect, interest to depositors reduced to 2*l* 15*s.* per cent. 1 Nov. 1880.

449 old Savings' Banks in the United Kingdom, 1,506,714 accounts, deposits, 43,797,805*l.*, 1880; 380 banks in 1888.

Post-office and Trustee Savings bank deposits, 197,105,000*l.* in 1902.

The defalcations of the Cardiff savings' bank (*which see*), April, 1886, and irregularities in other banks, leads to demand for legislation; a new Savings Banks act was brought in and withdrawn in 1890; passed, 3 July, 1891; an inspection committee appointed, sir Albert Rollit, Mr. Lyulph Stanley, and others, April, 1893; first report issued, generally satisfactory, some laxity in regard to rules observed, April, 1893; Amendment act passed, 21 Dec. 1893.

CLASSIFICATION OF THE FIRST 20,000 DEPOSITORS.

Domestic servants	7245
Persons in trade, mechanics, &c.	7473
Labourers and porters	672
Miners	1454
Friendly and charitable societies	58
Persons not classed, viz., widows, teachers, sailors, &c.	3098

SAVONA

SAVONA (a manufacturing town, N. Italy, long held by the Genoese) was captured by the king of Sardinia in 1746; by the French in 1809, and annexed; restored to Sardinia at the peace. Pope Pius VII. was kept here by Napoleon I., 1809-12. Soap is said to have been invented here, and hence its French name *savon.*

SAVOY

SAVOY, the ancient *Sapaudia* or *Sabaudia*, formerly a province in N. Italy, east of Piedmont. It became a Roman province about 118 B.C. The Alemanni seized it in A.D. 395, and the Franks in 490. It shared the revolutions of Switzerland till about 1048, when Conrad, emperor of Germany, gave it to Humbert, with the title of count. Count Thomas acquired Piedmont in the 13th century. Amadeus, count of Savoy, having entered his dominions, solicited Sigismund to erect them into a duchy, which he did at Cambray, 19 Feb. 1416. Victor-Amadeus, duke of Savoy, obtained the kingdom of Sicily from Spain, by a treaty, in 1713, but afterwards exchanged it with the emperor for the island of Sardinia, with the title of king, 1720. The French subdued Savoy in 1792, and made it a department of France, under the name of Mont Blanc, in 1800. It was restored to the king of Sardinia in 1814; but with Nice annexed to France in 1860, in accordance with a vote by universal suffrage, 23 April, 1860. Savoy was visited by the emperor and empress of the French in August, 1860. The annexation was censured in England.

DUKES OF SAVOY.

1391. Count Amadeus VIII. is made duke in 1416; he was named pope, as Felix V. He abdicated as duke of Savoy, 1439: renounced the tiara, 1449; died in 1451.
1439. Louis.
1465. Amadeus IX.
1472. Philibert I.
1482. Charles I.
1489. Charles II.
1496. Philip II.
1497. Philibert II.
1504. Charles III.
1553. Emmanuel-Philibert.
1580. Charles-Emmanuel I.
1630. Victor-Amadeus I.
1637. Francis-Hyacinthe.
1638. Charles-Emmanuel II.
1675. Victor-Amadeus II. became king of Sicily, 1713; exchanged for Sardinia (*which see*) in 1720.

SAVOY PALACE

SAVOY PALACE (London), was built by Peter of Savoy, uncle of Eleanor, queen of Henry III., in 1245, on land granted to him. He gave it to the fraternity of Mountjoy (Monte Jovis), from whom it was purchased by queen Eleanor for her son Edmund. Here resided John, king of France, when a prisoner, 1357 *et seq.* The Savoy was burnt by Wat Tyler and his followers, 1381. It was restored as an hospital of St. John the Baptist by Henry VII. about 1505. The fruitless CONFERENCE of bishops and eminent puritans for the revision of the liturgy was held at the Savoy, April-July, 1661. The hospital was dissolved in 1702. The buildings (used as a military prison) were removed to make way for Waterloo-bridge and its approaches, 1817-19. The privilege of sanctuary which the ancient *Chapel* formerly possessed, and which was much abused, was abolished by parliament in 1697. The *Chapel* after several restorations, was destroyed by fire, 7 July, 1864, and was rebuilt at the queen's expense, and re-opened 26 Nov. 1865. The rev. Henry White, 30 years chaplain, died 7 Oct. 1890.

Savoy Theatre, erected for Mr. D'Oyly Carte by Mr. C. J. Phipps, opened 10 Oct. 1881; lit by Swan's incandescent electric light successfully (1194 lamps); 1000th performance of "Patience," by Sir A. Sullivan, libretto by W. S. Gilbert, 28 Dec. 1881. See *Operas.*

A list of the operas produced by sir A. Sullivan and Mr. W. S. Gilbert is given in the article *Operas. The Gondoliers*, 7 Dec. 1889–20 June, 1891; *The Nautch Girl*, 30 June, 1891–16 Jan. 1892; *The Vicar of Bray* (revived), 28 Jan.–18 June, 1892.

Haddon Hall, by sir A. Sullivan and Sidney Grundy 24 Sept.–15 April, 1892

Jane Annie, or *The Good Conduct Prize*, by Mr. Ernest Ford, and Mr. J. M. Barrie and Dr. Conan Doyle . . . . 13 May–1 July, 1893

Utopia (Limited): or, *The Flowers of Progress*, by W. S. Gilbert and sir Arthur Sullivan 7 Oct. 1893–9 June, 1894

Mirette, by Adrian Ross, music by Messager 3 July–11 Aug.; 6 Oct.–6 Dec. ,,

The Chieftain, book by F. C. Burnand, music by sir Arthur Sullivan . 12 Dec. 1894–16 March, 1895

Hanseland Gretel, fairy opera by Humperdinck (Carl Rosa Company). . 16 April–16 June, ,,

Eleanora Duse and company; *Magda* and other pieces . . . . . 27 June–13 July, ,,

The Mikado . . . . 6 Nov. 1895–4 March, 1896

The Grand Duke, or *The Statutory Duel*, by W. S. Gilbert and Arthur Sullivan 7 March–10 July, ,,

The Mikado . . 11 July, 1896–17 Feb. 1897

His Majesty, by F. C. Burnand and R. C. Lehmann, music by sir A. C. Mackenzie 19 Feb.–24 April, ,,

Yeomen of the Guard, by W. S. Gilbert and Arthur Sullivan; reproduced 5 May–20 Nov. ,,

The Grand Duchess of Gerolstein, music by Offenbach . . . . . 4 Dec. 1897–12 March, 1898

The Gondoliers; reproduced . 22 March–21 May, ,,

The Beauty Stone, musical drama, by A. W. Pinero, J. Comyns Carr, and Arthur Sullivan, 1st time, 28 May–16 July; *The Gondoliers*, 18 July–17 Sept.; *The Sorcerer*, 22 Sept.–31 Dec.; *The Lucky Star*, by Ivan Caryll, 7 Jan. 1899–31 May; *Pinafore*, reproduced, sir Arthur Sullivan conducting, 6 June–25 Nov.; *The Rose of Persia*, by Basil Hood and Arthur Sullivan, 29 Nov.–28 June, 1900; *Pirates of Penzance*, reproduced, 30 June–3 Nov.; *Patience*, 7 Nov.–20 April, 1901; *The Emerald Isle*, by Basil Hood, music partly by the late sir Arthur Sullivan, completed by E. German, 27 April–9 Nov.; *Ib and Little Christina*, by Basil Hood and Franco Leoni, 14–29 Nov.; *Iolanthe*, 7 Dec.–29 March, 1902; *Merrie England*, by Basil Hood, composed by Edward German, 2 April–30 July (Miss Kitty Loftus's season); *Naughty Nancy*, musical comedy, 8 Sept.–22 Nov.; *Merrie England*, reproduced, 24 Nov.–17 Jan. 1903; *A Princess of Kensington*, by Basil Hood and Edward German 21 Jan.–16 May, 1903

The Savoy Hotel on the Thames Embankment opened by a company, 6 Aug. 1889; the directors included the earl of Lathom, Mr. R. D'Oyly Carte, and sir Arthur Sullivan, who died suddenly, 22 Nov. 1900; Mr. D'Oyly Carte, died, aged 56, 3 April, 1901.

SAW. Invented by Dædalus. *Pliny.* Invented by Talus. *Apollodorus.* Talus, it is said, having found the jaw-bone of a snake, employed it to cut through a piece of wood, and then formed an instrument of iron like it. Saw-mills were erected in Madeira in 1420; at Breslau in 1427. Norway had the first saw-mill in 1530. The bishop of Ely, ambassador from Mary of England to the court of Rome, describes a saw-mill there, 1555. The attempts to introduce saw-mills in England were violently opposed, and one erected by a Dutchman in 1663 was forced to be abandoned. Saw-mills were erected near London about 1770. The excellent saw-machinery in Woolwich dockyard is based upon the invention of the elder Brunel, 1806-13. The circular saw was introduced into England about 1790. The *saw-gin* for separating cotton wool from the pod, invented by Eli Whitney, an American, in 1793, led to the immense growth of cotton in the southern states of the Union. Powis and James's band-saw was patented in 1858.

SAXE-ALTENBURG (formerly Hildburghausen), a duchy in central Germany. The dukes are descended from Ernest the Pious, duke of Saxony. Ernest, the first duke, died in 1715. The duke, Ernest, born 16 Sept. 1826; succeeded his father, George, 3 Aug. 1853; he entered into alliance with Prussia, 18 Aug. 1866. Heir, brother, Maurice, born 24 Oct. 1829. Population, 1900, 195,000.

SAXE-COBURG AND GOTHA (central Germany), capitals Gotha and Coburg. The reigning family is descended from John Ernest (son of Ernest the Pious, duke of Saxony), who died in 1729. Population 1900, 229,567.

DUKES.

1826. Ernest I. duke of Saxe-Saalfeld-Coburg; born, 2 Jan. 1784; married Louisa, heiress of Augustus, duke of Saxe-Gotha, and became by convention duke of Saxe-Coburg-Gotha, 12 Nov. 1826; died, 29 Jan. 1844.

[His brother, Leopold, married the princess Charlotte of England, 2 May, 1816; became king of the Belgians, 12 July, 1831; and Ferdinand, the son of his brother Ferdinand, married Maria da Gloria, queen of Portugal, 9 April, 1836.]

1844. Ernest II. son (brother of Albert, prince consort of Great Britain); born 21 June, 1818; married Alexandrina, duchess of Baden, 3 May, 1842; no issue; died 22 Aug. 1893; funeral at Coburg; present duke Alfred, the prince of Wales, the German emperor, and other princes, 28 Aug. He entered into alliance with Prussia, 18 Aug. 1866. Published Memoirs, 3 vols. 1887–9.

1893. Prince Alfred of England, duke of Edinburgh; born, 6 Aug. 1844 (in whose favour the prince of Wales resigned his rights, 19 April, 1863), formally received by the emperor at Potsdam; 28 Oct. 1893. *Heir:* Alfred, son, born, 15 Oct 1874; died, 6 Feb. 1899. *Presumptive heir:* Arthur, duke of Connaught; resigns in favour of his nephew, Charles Edward, the duke of Albany 30 June, 1899.

1900. Leopold Charles Edward, duke of Albany, born 19 July, 1884.
Regent: Hereditary prince of Hohenlohe-Langenburg, born, 1863.

See *England, issue.*

Grand reception of the duke and duchess at Gotha, 31 Jan. 1894.

Visit of queen Victoria, 17 April, 1894.

Duke of Connaught and family visit Gotha, 20 April, 1899.

Equestrian statue of duke Ernest II. unveiled at Coburg, 10 May, 1899.

Constitutional dispute of 6 years between Herr von Strenge, minister of state, and the diet, settled by duke Alfred in favour of the diet, 31 Jan. 1900

Sudden death of duke Alfred, an able and judicious ruler, much lamented, at Castle Rosenau, 30 July, 1900; funeral at Coburg (present duke Charles Edward, the Regent, the prince of Wales, the German emperor, and other princes), 4 Aug.

Tercentenary of the birth of duke Ernest the Pious, celebrated, the German emperor present, 25 Dec. 1901.

SAXE-MEININGEN (a duchy in central Germany). The dukes are descended from Ernest the Pious, duke of Saxony. The first duke, Bernard (1680), died in 1706. Bernard (duke, 24 Dec. 1803, died 3 Dec. 1882), abdicated in favour of his son George II., 20 Sept. 1866, who professed his adhesion to the Prussian policy; he was born, 2 April, 1826. Heir, his son, Bernard, born 1 April, 1851. By a fire at Meiningen, about 3000 persons became houseless, 6 Sept. 1874.

SAXE-WEIMAR-EISENACH (central Germany). The grand-dukes are descended from John Frederic, the Protestant elector of Saxony, who was deprived by the emperor in 1548; see

Saxony. The houses of Saxe-Coburg-Gotha, Saxe-Gotha, Hilburghausen, and Saxe-Meiningen also sprang from him. They are all termed the senior or *Ernestine* branch of the old family.—Saxe-Weimar became a grand duchy in 1815. The dukes have greatly favoured literature and art, and their capital Weimar has been called the Athens of Germany. Statue of Liszt unveiled at Weimar, 31 May, 1902.

GRAND-DUKES.

1815. Charles Augustus.
1828. Charles Frederic; died, 8 July, 1853.
1853. Charles Alexander; born, 24 June, 1818. He entered into alliance with Prussia, 18 Aug. 1866; died, 5 Jan. 1901.
Heir: Charles Augustus: born, 31 July, 1844; died, 20 Nov. 1894; son, William Ernest, born, 10 June, 1876.
1901. William Ernest, born, 10 June, 1876.

SAXONY, a kingdom in N. Germany. The Saxons were a fierce warlike race, the terror of the inhabitants of the later western empire, frequently attacked France, and conquered Britain (*which see*). After a long series of sanguinary conflicts they were completely subdued by Charlemagne, who instituted many fiefs and bishoprics in their country. Witikind, their great leader, who claimed descent from Woden, professed Christianity about 785. From him descended the first and the present ruling family of Wettin (the houses of Supplinburg, Guelf, and Ascania intervened from 1106 to 1421). Saxony became a duchy, 880; an electorate, 1180; and a kingdom, 1806. It was the seat of war, 1813; the king being on the side of Napoleon. In the conflict of 1866 the king took the side of Austria, and the army fought in the battle of Königgrätz, 3 July. The Prussians entered Saxony 18 June. Peace between Prussia and Saxony was signed 21 Oct. (subjecting the Saxon army to Prussia), and the king returned to Dresden, 3 Nov. Constitution of 4 Sept. 1831; modified, 1849, 1851, 1860, 1861, 1868, and 1874. Population, 1861, 2,225,240; 1871, 2,556,244; 1880, 2,972,805; 1885, 3,182,003; 1890, 3,500,513; 1900, 4,199,758.

Octocentenary of the house of Wettin was celebrated at Dresden with great magnificence 15–19 June, 1889; the many branches of the royal family and its connections were represented; the emperor William II., prince Alfred of Edinburgh for England, and princes representing Portugal and Belgium, and deputations from Austria and Russia were present. The festivities included church services, military equestrian performances, historical pageants and a procession of 12,000 costumed characters. The people presented about 150,000*l*. to the king, for the restoration of his palace.

Flight of the crown princess from Salzburg to Zurich, 12 Dec. 1902; her renunciation of all royal rights, titles, and dignities, 9 Jan.; confirmed by royal order, 14 Jan.; she was also suspended from all rights and honours as an Austrian archduchess, 28 Jan.; divorce of the crown prince and princess pronounced at Dresden, 11 Feb. 1903.

ELECTORS.

1423. Frederic I., first elector of the house of Misnia.
1428. Frederic II.
[His sons Ernest and Albert divide the states.]

1464. Ernest.	1464. Albert.
1486. Frederick III.	1500. George.
1525. John.	1539. Henry.
	1541. Maurice.

1532. John Frederic; deprived by the emperor Charles V.; succeeded by
1548. Maurice (of the Albertine line).
1553. Augustus.
1586. Christian I.
1591. Christian II.
1611. John George I.
1656. John George II.
1680. John George III.
1691. John George IV.
1694. Frederic Augustus I., king of Poland, 1697.
1733. Frederic Augustus II., king of Poland.
1763. Frederic Augustus III. becomes king, 1806.

KINGS.

1806. Frederic Augustus I.; increased his territories by alliance with France, 1806-9; suffered by peace of 1814.
1827. Anthony Clement.
1836. Frederic Augustus II., nephew (regent, 1830); died 9 Aug. 1854.
1854. John, brother (born 12 Dec. 1801); celebrated his golden wedding (50 years), 10 Nov. 1872; died, 29 Oct. 1873.
1873. Albert; born, 23 April, 1828; married, 18 June, 1853, Caroline of Wasa; he died, 19 June, 1902.
1902. George, brother; born 8 Aug. 1832; married Maria Anna, infanta of Portugal, 11 May, 1859 (she died, 5 Feb. 1884). *Heir*: Friedrich August, born 1865.

SCAFELL, a double-peaked mountain in Cumberland, the highest in England; the higher, called Scafell Pike, is 3,210 ft., the other 3,161 ft. Prof. A. M. Marshall, biologist, was killed by falling down the Pike, 31 Dec. 1893, and four tourists (Messrs. Jupp, Garrett, Broadrick, and Ridsdale) fell while attempting to climb the peak; three were killed outright. Mr. Ridsdale died while being carried down by a rescue party, who had made the ascent at night under circumstances of great difficulty, 21 Sept. 1903.

SCANDALUM MAGNATUM, a special statute relating to any wrong, by words or in writing, done to high personages of the land, such as peers, judges, ministers of the crown, officers in the state, and other great public functionaries, by the circulation of the scandalous statements, false news, or horrible messages, by which any debate or discord between them and the commons, or any scandal to their persons, might arise. *Chambers*. This law was first enacted 2 Rich. II. 1378.

SCANDINAVIA, the ancient name of Sweden, Norway, and great part of Denmark (*which see*), whence proceeded the Northmen or Normans, who conquered Normandy (about 900), and eventually England (1066). They were also called Sea-kings, or Vikings. They settled Iceland and Greenland, and, it is thought, visited the northern regions of America, about the 9th century. A "National Scandinavian Society" formed at Stockholm; see *Sweden*, Dec. 1864, *Stockholm*, 1897. Scandinavian Union, see *Norway* and *Sweden*, 1898.

SCARBOROUGH, Yorkshire (anciently Skardeburge), was ravaged by the Danes 1066. Incorporated by Henry II., 1181. The town was made a bonding port in 1841. A new drive and promenade, a great engineering work, costing 50,000*l*., opened by the duke of Clarence and the archbishop of York, 27 June, 1890; new town-hall opened and a statue of queen Victoria unveiled by princess Henry of Battenberg, 28 July, 1903. Population, 1881, 30,504; 1891, 33,776; 1901, 38,160.

SCARLET, or kermes dye, was known in the East in the earliest ages; cochineal dye, 1518. Kepler, a Fleming, established the first dye-house for scarlet in England, at Bow, 1643. The art of dyeing red was improved by Brewer, 1667. *Beckmann*.

SCARLET FEVER, was very prevalent in the metropolis from August, 1887, to Feb. 1888. Patients admitted into the hospitals, April, 1887—March, 1888, 7614. Arrangements for the crisis were made by the Metropolitan Asylums Board.

Increase of fever in the metropolis; scarlet fever 1,426, 8 Aug.; decreasing Dec. 1890; (scarlet fever cases in 1892, 13,093); (scarlet fever, 14,548 in 1893).

Total of fever patients, 19,937 (deaths, 1,999), scarlet fever cases, 11,598, during 1894. Decreasing in 1895. 4,133 scarlet fever cases week ending 24 Oct. 1896; 15,113 patients during 1897; 18,381 cases notified, 14,539 in hospitals in 1901; decrease in 1902-3.

SCEPTICS, the sect of philosophers founded by Pyrrho, about 334 B.C. He gave ten reasons for continual suspense of judgment; he doubted of everything, never made any conclusions, and when he had carefully examined the subject, and investigated all its parts, he concluded by still doubting of its evidence. He advocated apathy and unchangeable repose. These doctrines were held by Bayle (died 1706).

SCEPTRE, an emblem of royalty mentioned in the Bible (*Gen.* xlix. 10, *Psalm* xlv. 6, *Esther* iv. 11, &c.), and in Homer. The sceptre, originally a staff, was gradually ornamented till it assumed its present form.

SCHAFFHAUSEN (N. Switzerland), a fishing village in the 8th century, became an imperial city in the 13th; was subjected to Austria, 1330; independent, 1415; became a Swiss canton, 1501. Population, 1888; canton, 37,783; city, 12,315; 1901, 41,523; city, 15,430.

SCHAUMBURG-LIPPE (Germany) was formed into a county by Adolphus, of Sondersleben, 1033. In 1640, on the death of count Otho IV., his mother, Elizabeth, transferred the domains to Philip of Lippe, from whom descended the reigning prince (the title assumed in 1807). Adolphus, born 1 Aug. 1817, succeeded his father, 21 Nov. 1860; died 8 May, 1893. Succeeded by his son, George, born 10 Oct. 1846. Population of the principality, 1882, 35,753; 1885, 37,204; 1890, 39,163; 1900, 43,132.

SCHELDT TOLLS were imposed by the treaty of Munster (or Westphalia), 1648. The tolls were abolished for a compensation, 1867. The house of commons voted 175,650*l.* for the British portion, on 9 March, 1864. The Scheldt was declared free on 3 Aug. with much rejoicing at Antwerp and Brussels.

SCHIEHALLION, a mountain in Perthshire, where Dr. Neville Maskelyne, the astronomer-royal, made his observations with a plumb-line, 24 Oct. 1774, from which Hutton calculated that the density of the earth is five times greater than water.

SCHIPKA PASSES, on the Balkans, Turkey. Through these the Russian general Gourko entered Roumelia. After his retreat, they were fortified, and desperately, but on the whole unsuccessfully, assailed by the Turks under Suleiman Pasha, with great slaughter on both sides, 20-27 Aug. He took and lost fort St. Nicholas, 17 Sept. 1877. The Russians re-entered Roumelia, Jan. 1878.

SCHISM, see *Heresy* and *Popes*.

SCHISM ACT, 13 Anne, c. 7, introduced by lord Bolingbroke, 1713; repealed by 5 Geo. I. c. 4, in 1719. By it teachers were required to declare their conformity to the established church.

SCHLESWIG, see *Holstein*, *Denmark*, and *Gastein*.

SCHOOL BOARD, see *Education*.

SCHOOLMEN or **SCHOLASTIC PHILOSOPHY**, began in the schools founded by Charlemagne, 800-14; and prevailed in Europe from the 9th to the 15th centuries; see *Doctors*.

SCHOOLS. Charity schools were introduced into London to prevent the seduction of the infant poor into Roman catholic seminaries, 3 James II. 1687. *Rapin.* Charter schools were instituted in Ireland, 1733. *Scully.* In England there were, in 1847, 13,642 schools (exclusively of Sunday schools) for the education of the poor; and the number of children was 998,431. The parochial and endowed schools of Scotland were (exclusively of Sunday schools) 4836; and the number of children, 181,467. The schools in Wales were 841, and the number of children, 38,164; in Ireland, 13,327 schools, and 774,000 children. In 1851 there were 2310 schools in connection with the Education Committee actually inspected in England and Scotland. They included: 1713 church of England schools in England and Wales; 282 protestant dissenting schools in England and Wales; 98 Roman catholic schools in Great Britain; and 217 presbyterian schools in Scotland, whereof 91 were of the free church: the whole affording accommodation for 299,425 scholars; see *Education, Design, Ascham*, &c. For *Schoolboy Strikes*, see *Strikes*, Oct. 1889.

SCHOOL SHIPS, see *Chichester. Cornwall*, off Purfleet, established 1859; *Shaftesbury*, established, 1878, for vagrant lads.

SCHWARZBURG (the seat of two principalities, N. Germany). Gunther, count of Schwarzburg, whose family dates from the 12th century, was elected emperor of Germany in 1349. From the two sons of count Gunther, who died 1552, sprang the present rulers.

SCHWARZBURG-RUDOLSTADT
(a principality, 1697).

1807. Albert (28 June), born 30 April, 1798; died 26 Nov. 1869.
1869. George (born 23 Nov. 1838), 26 Nov.; died 19 Jan. 1890.
1890. Gonthier, brother (born, 21 Aug. 1852).

SCHWARZBURG-SONDERSHAUSEN
(a principality, 1710).

1835. Gunther (19 Aug.), born 24 Sept. 1801; abdicated.
1880. Charles, son (born 7 Aug. 1830), 17 July.

SCHWEIDNITZ, Prussia, often besieged and taken in the thirty years' and seven years' wars. Near it Frederick II. defeated the Austrians under marshal Daun, 16 May, 1762.

SCHWEIZ, a Swiss canton, which with Uri and Unterwalden renounced subjection to Austria, 7 Nov. 1307. The name Switzerland, for all the country, dates from about 1440.

SCIENCE, see *Education*, *Chemistry*, and other branches.

Science and Art Department began as the Normal School of Design, 1 Jan. 1837, with a grant of 1,500*l.* See under *Design.* The grant in 1885-6 was 391,573*l.*; 1888-9, 445,303*l.*; 1891-2, 530,000*l.*

100,000*l.* voted for the purchase of a site for new building, 25 Feb. 1890.

The Normal School of Science and Royal School of Mines, were directed to be called the Royal College of Science, London, Oct. 1890; the first dean, prof. Th. Huxley, died 29 June; was succeeded by prof. Judd, July, 1895.

Miss Marshall, of Warwick gardens, Kensington, bequeaths to the department 1,000*l.* for a scholarship and scientific books and instruments, 5 May, 1891.

The 36th report stated that in 1888 the department supported 1,952 schools, and 6,579 classes were examined in elementary science, with 112,808 pupils; the S. Kensington museum is in the charge of the department.

Estimates for 1894-5, 692,122*l.* See *Arts*, Sept. 1896.

Sir John Donnelly, K.C.B., inspector for science about 1858-9, energetic promoter of scientific education, died 5 April, 1902.

SCIENTIFIC APPARATUS. The International Loan Exhibition, at South Kensington, consisting of about 17,000 objects, many of great historical interest, from all countries except

America, was opened (by queen Victoria), 13 May, and closed 30 Dec. 1876. Conferences were held, 16 May—2 June, and many free lectures given by eminent persons. Reopened 30 June, 1877.

SCIENTIFIC ASSOCIATION, for promotion of research; proposed at the meeting of the American Association at Philadelphia, Sept. 1884. Mrs. Elizabeth Thompson promised liberal support.

SCIENTIFIC FRONTIER (in reference to Afghanistan), a term used by Lord Beaconsfield, 9 Nov. 1878.

SCIENTIFIC INDUSTRY, SOCIETY FOR PROMOTING, established at Manchester, in 1873. It proposed setting up a library and museum, the delivery of lectures, and the publication of reports. *Industries*, a weekly scientific periodical, first published, 2 July, 1886, combined with *Iron* (*which see*), 1893.

SCIENTIFIC PAPERS, published by eminent societies: of these a valuable catalogue has been prepared by the Royal Society of London, commencing with 1800, and continued to the present time; the 1st vol. appeared in 1867; 11 vols. issued, 1896.

An international conference to consider proposals for an international catalogue was held at Burlington house, London, 40 delegates present, 14 July, 1896; another at the Royal Society, lord Lister in the chair, 11–13 Oct. 1898; meetings held Aug. 1899; 3rd conference, London, 12, 13 June, 1900; an international council formed, 1st convention held Dec. 1900; the work started from 1 Jan. 1901; in 4 yearly instalments; vols. i. and ii. issued June-Sept. 1902; Dr. Ludwig Mond gives 8,000*l.* to the work, Mr. Carnegie, 1,000*l.*, 3 Nov. 1902; Vol. viii., Feb. 1903

SCIENTIFIC RELIEF FUND. In 1859, several fellows of the Royal Society (Messrs. Gassiot, Wheatstone, Miller, Tyndall, and others) commenced the collection of subscriptions with the view of establishing a permanent fund to be expended in aiding necessitous men of science and their families, in imitation of the "Literary Fund." In the spring of 1860, 3365*l.* had been subscribed; in Jan. 1865, 5320*l.*; in 1867, 6052*l.*; in 1877, 6428*l.*; and many cases had been relieved.

SCIENTIFIC SOCIETIES' HOUSE COMPANY, proposed March, 1873.

SCIENTIFIC SURVEYING EXPEDITION, see *Deep Sea*.

SCILLY ISLES (the Cassiterides or Tin-islands). They held commerce with the Phœnicians; and are mentioned by Strabo. They were conquered by Athelstan, 936; and given to the monks. They were granted by Elizabeth to the Godolphin family, by whom they were fortified; the works were strengthened in 1649 by the royalists, from whom they were taken by Blake, 1651. Mr. Augustus Smith, the owner, and termed the king of these isles, after a long paternal rule, died in Aug. 1872. Mr. Dorrien Smith was the proprietor in 1892. The appointment of a county council for 1 April, 1891, was ordered by the local government board, June, 1890. Population, 1891, 2,044; 1901, 2,096.

A British squadron under sir Cloudesley Shovel was wrecked here, when returning from an expedition against Toulon; he mistook rocks for land, and struck upon them. His ship, the *Association*, in which were persons of rank, and 800 brave men, went instantly to the bottom. The *Eagle*, captain Hancock and the *Romney* and *Firebrand*, were also lost; the rest of the fleet escaped, 22 Oct. 1707. Sir Cloudesley's body was conveyed to London, and buried in Westminster abbey, where a monument was erected to his memory.

Visit of the king, 8 April, 1902.

SCINDE, see *Sinde*.

SCIO MASSACRE, 11 April, 1822, see *Chios*.

SCLAVONIA, see *Slavonia*.

SCONE (near Perth). The Scotch coronation chair was brought from Scone to Westminster abbey by Edward I. in 1296. Here Charles II. was crowned, 1 Jan. 1651.

SCOPTZI, see *White Doves*.

SCORE, MUSICAL, was written by the monk Hucbald, who wrote "Enchiridion Musicae;" he died 930. Specimens written in the 13th century exist in the British Museum.

SCOTTISH - IRISH CONVENTION, see *United States*, May, 1889.

SCOTISTS. Those who adopted the doctrines of John Duns Scotus (who died 8 Nov. 1308) on divine grace, freewill, the origin of the moral law, the Conception of the Virgin Mary, &c., strongly opposed by the Thomists, disciples of St. Thomas Aquinas, who died 7 March, 1274.

SCOTLAND, see *Caledonia*. At the death of queen Elizabeth, 24 March, 1603, James VI. of Scotland, as the most immediate heir, was called to the throne of England, and proclaimed king of Great Britain, 24 Oct. 1604. Each country had a separate parliament till 1707, when the kingdoms were united; see *England*, *Population*, and *Edinburgh*. History of Scotland, by P. Hume Brown, vol. i. published April, 1899; vol. ii., April, 1902; another, by Mr. Andrew Lang, vol. ii., Nov. 1902.

Camelon, capital of the Picts, taken by Kenneth II. and every living creature put to the sword or destroyed, 843
The Norwegians occupy Caithness 9th century.
Scotland ravaged by Athelstan 933
The feudal system established by Malcolm II. . . 1004
Invaded by Canute 1031
Divided into baronies 1032
The Danes driven out of Scotland 1040
Duncan I. is murdered by his kinsman Macbeth, by whom the crown is seized . . . . . . "
Malcolm III., aided by Edward the Confessor, defeats the usurper at Dunsinane, 1054; Macbeth killed by Macduff . . . . 1056 or 1057
The Saxon-English language introduced into Scotland by fugitives from England escaping from the Normans 1080
Siege of Alnwick: Malcolm III. killed . . . 1093
Reign of David I., a legislator 1124-53
Scotland invaded by Hacho, king of Norway, with 160 ships and 20,000 men; the invaders are defeated by Alexander III., who now recovers the Western Isles 1263
Death of Margaret of Norway, heiress to the throne, 7 Oct. 1290
John Balliol and Robert Bruce contend for the throne, 1291; Edward I. of England, as umpire, decides in favour of John . . . . Nov. 1292
John Balliol, king of Scotland, appears to a summons, and defends his own cause in Westminster hall against the earl of Fife 1293
Edward, wishing to annex Scotland to England, dethrones John, ravages the country, destroys the muniments of Scottish history, and seizes the prophetic stone (see *Coronation*) . . . 1296
William Wallace defeats the English at Cambus Kenneth, and expels them, 1297; is defeated at Falkirk, 22 July, 1298; taken by the English, and executed at Smithfield . . . . 23 Aug. 1305
Robert Bruce, crowned, 1306; he defeats the English, 1307; and takes Inverness, 1313; defeats the English at Bannockburn . . . 24 June, 1314
Edward Balliol gains the throne for a little time by his victory at Dupplin, 11 Aug. 1332; and by the victory at Halidon-hill . . . 19 July, 1333
David II. taken prisoner at the battle of Durham (and detained in captivity 11 years) . . . 1346
Battle of Chevy Chase, between Hotspur Percy and earl Douglas (see *Otterburn*) . . . 10 Aug. 1388
Murder of duke of Rothesay, heir of Robert III., by starvation . . . . 3 April, 1401

The Scots defeated at Homildon-hill . 14 Sept. 1402
James I. captured by the English near Flamborough head on his passage to France . 30 March, 1406
St. Andrews university founded by bishop William Turnbull 1451
University of Aberdeen founded 1494
James IV. invades England, slain at Flodden Field, and his army cut to pieces . . . 9 Sept. 1513
James V. banishes the Douglases 1528
He establishes the court of session 1532
Order of St. Andrew, or the Thistle, is revived . 1540
Mary, the queen of Scots, born 7 Dec.; succeeds her father, James V., who dies . 14 Dec. ,,
The regent, cardinal Beaton, persecutes the reformers, 1539, 1546; he is assassinated at St. Andrews . . . . . . 29 May, 1546
The Scots defeated at Pinkie . . 10 Sept. 1547
Mary marries the dauphin of France . April, 1558
The parliament abolishes the jurisdiction of the pope in Scotland . . . 24 Aug. 1560
Francis II. dies, leaving Mary a widow . Dec. ,,
The Reformation in Scotland, by John Knox, and others, during the minority of Mary, between 1550 & ,,
Mary, after an absence of thirteen years, arrives at Leith from France . . . . 21 Aug. 1561
Upon an inquisition, which was officially taken, by order of queen Elizabeth, only 58 Scotsmen were found in London. *Stow*. 1562
Mary marries her cousin, Henry Stuart, lord Darnley . . . . . . 29 July 1565
David Rizzio, her confidential secretary, murdered by Darnley in her presence . 9 March, 1566
Lord Darnley blown up by gunpowder, in his house (Mary accused of conniving at his death), 10 Feb. 1567
James Hepburn, earl of Bothwell, carries off the queen, who marries him . . . 15 May, ,,
Mary made prisoner at Carberry hill by her nobles, 15 June, ,,
Resigns her crown to her infant son James VI.; the earl of Murray appointed regent . 22 July, ,,
Mary escapes from prison, and collects a large army, which is defeated by the regent Murray, at the battle of Langside, 13 May; enters England, 16 May, 1568
The regent Murray murdered . . . . 23 Jan. 1570
The earl of Lennox appointed regent . 12 July, ,,
The earl of Lennox murdered, 4 Sept.; the earl of Mar chosen regent . . . . Sept. 1571
Death of the reformer John Knox . 24 Nov. 1572
[His funeral in Edinburgh is attended by most of the nobility, and by the regent Morton, who exclaims, "There lies he who never feared the face of man!"]
The university of Edinburgh founded 1582
The raid of Ruthven (see *Ruthven*) . . . . ,,
Mary having taken refuge in England, 16 May, 1568, is after a long captivity, beheaded at Fotheringay castle (see *Fotheringay*) . . . 8 Feb. 1587
Gowrie's conspiracy fails . . . 5 Aug. 1600
Union of the crown of Scotland with that of England by the accession of James VI. . 24 March, 1603
James proclaimed "king of Great Britain, France, and Ireland" . . . . 24 Oct. 1604
Charles I. attempts in vain to introduce the English liturgy; tumult at Edinburgh . 23 July, 1637
Solemn league and covenant subscribed 1 March, 1638
A Scotch army enters England . . . 1640
Charles joins the Scotch army, 1646; betrayed into the hands of the English parliament . 30 Jan. 1647
Marquis of Montrose defeated at Philiphaugh, 13 Sept. 1645; defeated and taken prisoner, executed at Edinburgh . . . . . 21 May, 1650
Charles II. crowned at Scone, 1 Jan.; defeated at Worcester . . . . . 22 Aug. 1651
Scotland united to the English commonwealth by Oliver Cromwell . . . . . Sept. ,,
Charles II. revives episcopacy in Scotland . 1661
Argyll beheaded . . . . 27 May, ,,
Scottish hospital, London, incorporated . . 1665
The Covenanters defeated on the Pentland hills . 1666
Abp. Sharpe murdered near St. Andrews, by John Balfour of Burley and others . 3 May, 1679
The Covenanters defeat Claverhouse at Drumclog 1 June; are routed at Bothwell bridge 22 June, ,,
Richard Cameron's declaration for religious liberty 22 June, 1680
Resolution of a convention in favour of William III.; re-establishment of presbytery . . 14 March, 1689
The "claim of right" accepted by William and Mary . . . . 11 May, 1689
Insurrection of Claverhouse: killed at Killiecrankie, 27 July, ,,
Massacre of the Macdonalds at Glencoe 13 Feb. 1692
Parish schools established by the parliament. 1697
Legislative union of Scotland with England 1 May, 1707
Insurrection under the earl of Mar in favour of the son of James II. (see *Pretender*) 1715
The rebels defeated at Preston, 12 Nov.; and at Dumblane (or Sheriffmuir) . . 13 Nov. ,,
Captain Porteous killed by a mob in Edinburgh (see *Porteous*) . . . . 7 Sept. 1736
Prince Charles Edward proclaimed at Perth, 4 Sept.; at Edinburgh, 16 Sept.; with the Highlanders defeats sir John Cope at Prestonpans, 21 Sept.; takes Carlisle, 15 Nov.; arrives at Manchester, 28 Nov.; at Derby, 4 Dec.; retreats to Glasgow . . . . . . 25 Dec. 1745
Defeats general Hawley at Falkirk, 17 Jan.; is totally defeated at Culloden . . 16 April, 1746
The Highland dress prohibited by parliament, 12 Aug.
Lords Kilmarnock and Balmerino executed for high treason on Tower-hill . . . 18 Aug. ,,
Simon Fraser, lord Lovat, aged 80, executed 9 April 1747
Heritable jurisdictions abolished by parliament . ,,
Thomson, the poet, dies . . . 27 Aug. 1748
The Old Pretender, "Chevalier de St. George," dies at Rome . . . . . 30 Dec. 1765
Prince Charles Edward Louis Casimir, the Young Pretender, dies at Rome . . . . 31 Jan. 1788
Death of Robert Burns . . . . 21 July, 1796
Scott's "Lay of the Last Minstrel" published . 1806
Cardinal Henry duke of York (last of the Stuarts) dies . . . . . . 31 Aug. 1807
The Court of Session is formed into two divisions . ,,
Royal Caledonian asylum, London, founded . . 1813
Scott's "Waverley" published 1814
The establishment of a jury court under a lord chief commissioner 1815
Visit of George IV. to Scotland . . . Aug. 1822
Sir Walter Scott dies . . . . 21 Sept. 1832
Seven ministers of the presbytery of Strathbogie are deposed by the General Assembly of the Church of Scotland for obeying the civil in preference to the ecclesiastical law. (Their deposition was formally protested against by the minority of ministers and elders, headed by Dr. Cook) . . . 28 May, 1841
The General Assembly condemn patronage as a grievance to the cause of true religion that ought to be abolished . . . . . 23 May, 1842
Visit of the queen, prince Albert, and the court; she landed at Granton pier . . 1-13 Sept. ,,
Secession of the non-intrusion ministers of the church of Scotland (about 400) at the General Assembly (see *Free Church*) . . . 18 May, 1843
Death of Jeffrey . . . . . 26 Jan. 1850
National Association for vindication of Scottish rights formed . . . . . Nov. 1853
Forbes Mackenzie's act (16 & 17 Vict. c. 67), "for the better regulation of public-houses in Scotland"; it permits grocers to sell spirits, &c., but allows drinking on the premises only in duly licensed places, passed . . . . . ,,
Act for better government of the universities passed Aug. 1858
Salmon Fisheries act passed . . . July, 1864
The queen's visit to the borders, Kelso, Melrose, &c. 21-24 Aug. 1867
Scotch Reform bill introduced into the commons, 17 Feb., passed . . . . . 13 July, 1868
Procedure in court of session and justiciary and other courts amended . . . . July, ,,
Scotch Reform act passed . . . 13 July, ,,
Land Registers and Titles to Land act passed July, ,,
Commission appointed to inquire into the administration of justice . . . . . Oct. ,,
Municipal elections amendment act passed, 9 Aug. 1870
Act to unite counties for sheriffs' duties passed 9 Aug. ,,
Robert Chambers, author and publisher, died aged 69 17 March, 1871
Scott centenary celebrated in Edinburgh, &c. (Scott born 15 Aug. 1771) . . . . . 9 Aug. ,,
Scotch Education act passed . . . 10 Aug. 1872
Return of owners of land and heritages, 1872-3 (a kind of Domesday book), published by government . . . . April, 187

Patronage in the established church (see 1842) abolished by act passed . . . 7 Aug. 1874
Scottish Church Disestablishment Association: first annual meeting . . . 8 March, 1875
Visit of the queen to Edinburgh; the Scottish national monument, by J. Steell, to prince Albert, unveiled by her . . . 17 Aug. 1876
Romanist hierarchy revived by the pope; archbishopric of Glasgow, bishopric of Dunkeld, &c. 4 March; the Scotch protestant bishops protest against this . . . 13 April, 1878
Public Parks act passed . . . 18 March, ,,
Marriage Notice act passed . . . 8 Aug ,,
Education act amended, by act . . . 16 Aug. ,,
Visit of Mr. Gladstone to Mid-Lothian, Edinburgh, Glasgow, &c., many speeches . 24—29 Nov. 1879
About 40,000 Scottish volunteers reviewed in the Queen's Park, Edinburgh, by the queen 25 Aug. 1881
Agitation respecting rents in Aberdeen, Banff, &c. Sept.-Oct. ,,
Farmers' alliance founded at Aberdeen by delegates from above 4000 farmers . . . 1 Dec. ,,
Movement for home rule (*which see*) begun 4 April, 1882
Old Scottish regimental colours deposited in St. Giles's cathedral, Edinburgh, by the duke of Cambridge . . . 13 Nov. 1883
Death of Walter, duke of Buccleuch, aged 78; munificent patron of public works, agriculture, science, literature, and art . . 15 April, 1884
Agitation for the dis-establishment of the church (see *Church of Scotland*) . . . autumn, 1885
Secretary for Scotland act passed . . 14 Aug. ,,
Charles Henry, duke of Richmond, appointed secretary Aug. 1885; succeeded by G. O. Trevelyan about 6 Feb.; by Arthur J. Balfour 26 July 1886; by Schomberg H., marquis of Lothian, 8 March. 1887
Local government bill for Scotland introduced by J. P. B. Robertson, 8 April; passed . 26 Aug. 1889
Scotch universities bill, giving more freedom to teaching and increasing state grant to 42,000*l.* a year, passed . . . 30 Aug. ,,
New national portrait gallery for Scotland in Edinburgh, opened by the marquis of Lothian 15 July, ,,
The new universities commission and the special commission on the Western Highlands and islands, meet in Edinburgh . . . Jan. 1890
Great railway strike, see *Railways*, 22 Dec. 1890—31 Jan. 1891
Death of lord justice-general John Inglis, eminent lawyer, aged about 81, 20 Aug.; succeeded by rt. hon. James P. B. Robertson about . 17 Sept. ,,
Destructive plague of field-mice, or voles, in some agricultural districts, reported . April—June, 1892
[The committee on the subject reported, suggesting remedies, burning grass, &c., March, 1893.]
Education and Local Taxation Relief act passed 27 June, ,,
Sir George Trevelyan, secretary for Scotland, 18 Aug. ,,
Death of the duke of Sutherland, aged 64; promoter of railways, &c. . . . 22 Sept. ,,
Celebration of the jubilee of the free church, 18 May, 1893
Resolutions in favour of home rule (*which see*) rejected in the commons, 29 April, 1892; 23 June, ,,
Wedding of the duke and duchess of York; festive demonstrations at Edinburgh, Glasgow, &c. 6 July, ,,
Resolution for the appointment of a standing committee in the commons for Scotch affairs (70 Scotch members, 15 others), carried, 232–20, 27 April; 1st meeting, 31 May, 1894; committee again appointed . . . 23 May, 1895
Great miners' strike (see *Coal*) . 26 June–22 Oct. 1894
A Church Disestablishment bill read 1st time, 24 April (withdrawn).
Local Government bill; royal assent . 25 Aug. ,,
Severe snowstorms; railways blocked . 6 Feb. 1895
Death of lord Moncrieff (lord justice clerk; eminent lawyer); aged 83 . . . 27 April, ,,
Lord Balfour of Burleigh, secretary for Scotland, 25 June, ,,
Centenary of the death of Robert Burns celebrated at Dumfries, and throughout the country, 21 July, 1896
20,000*l.* voted by parliament for the relief of the Islands and Highlands of Scotland . 4 June, 1897
Public Health act (Scotland) passed . 6 Aug. ,,
Scottish universities commission discontinued, 31 Dec. ,,
Private legislation procedure (Scotland), passed, 9 Aug. 1899
Death of the duke of Argyll, aged 76, orator and statesman (for 50 years the personal friend of the queen) . . . 24 April, 1900
New elementary code introduced into public schools in . . . ,,
Union of the Free and United Presbyterian churches . . . 31 Oct. ,,
The general election proved that the liberal party, strong since 1832, had lost its hold on the people, Nov. ,,
Mr. Andrew Carnegie gives 2,000,000*l.* in trust to the universities for the benefit of poor students, May, 1901; committee appointed, the earl of Elgin, chairman, early June; charter of incorporation granted . . . 21 Aug. 1901
Education (Scotland) act, royal assent given, 9 Aug. ,,
Lands' valuation amendment act passed, 13 June, 1902
Immoral traffic bill passed . . . 4 July, ,,
Free church of Scotland *v.* the United Free church, respecting funds, &c., lord Low's decision against the Free church claimants (9 Aug. 1901) upheld by the second division of the Edinburgh court of session . . . 4 July, ,,
Centenary of the birth of Hugh Miller celebrated at Cromarty . . . 22 Aug. ,,
The king and queen visit Brodick, Arran, 26, 27 Aug. ,,
Committee appointed in reference to the board of manufactures and the administration of parliamentary grants for art . . early Sept. ,,
Mr. Balfour presented with the freedom of Haddington . . . 20 Sept. ,,
Royal commission (the earl of Mansfield chairman) on physical training . . . April–3 Oct. ,,
"Rapid increase in crime and disorder" since 1897, reported . . . Jan. 1903
Visit of the king and queen, warmly welcomed, 11–15 May ,,
Licensing act passed royal assent . . 14 Aug. ,,
Death of Dr. Alex. Bain, eminent psychologist, aged 85 . . . 15 Sept. ,,
Great speeches by Mr. Chamberlain on the new fiscal policy, at Glasgow 6 Oct.; Greenock 7 Oct. ,,
Mr. Wm. Quarrier, founder of the Scottish orphan homes, died . . . 16 Oct. ,,
Marriage of the duke of Roxburghe to Miss May Goelet, of New York . . . 10 Nov. ,,

KINGS OF SCOTLAND.

BEFORE CHRIST.

[The early accounts of the kings are in a great measure fabulous. The series of kings is carried as far back as Alexander the Great.]

330. Fergus I.: ruled 25 years; lost in the Irish Sea.

[Fergus, a brave prince, came from Ireland with an army of Scots, and was chosen king. Having defeated the Britons and slain their king Coilus, the kingdom of the Scots was entailed upon his posterity for ever. He went to Ireland, and, having settled his affairs there, was drowned on his return, launching from the shore, near the harbour, called *Carrick-Fergus* to this day, 3699 A.M. *Anderson.*]

AFTER CHRIST.

357. Eugenius I. son of Fincormachus; slain in battle by Maximus, the Roman general, and the Picts.

*** With this battle ended the kingdom of the Scots, after having existed from the coronation of Fergus I., a period of 706 years; the royal family fled to Denmark. *Boece; Buchanan.*

[Interregnum of 27 years.]

404. Fergus II. (I.) great-grandson of Eugenius, and 40th king; slain in battle with the Romans.
420. Eugenius II. or Evenus: reigned 31 years.
451. Dongardus or Domangard, brother: defeated and drowned.
457. Constantine I. brother: assassinated.
479. Congallus I. nephew; just and prudent.
501. Goranus, brother; murdered. *Boece.* Died while Donald of Athol was conspiring to take his life.
535. Eugenius III. nephew: "none excelled him in justice."
558. Congallus II. brother.
569. Kinnatellus, brother; resigned for
570. Aidanus or Aldan, son of Goranus.
605. Kenneth, son of Congallus II.
606. Eugenius IV. son of Aidanus.
621. Ferchard or Ferquhard I. son; confined for misdeeds to his palace, where he laid violent hands upon himself. *Scott.*

632. Donald IV. brother; drowned in Loch Tay.
646. Ferchard II. son of Ferchard I.; "most execrable."
664. Malduinus, son of Donald IV.; strangled by his wife for his supposed infidelity, for which crime she was immediately afterwards burnt.
684. Eugenius V. brother.
688. Eugenius VI. son of Ferchard II.
698. Amberkeletus, nephew; fell by an arrow from an unknown hand.
699. Eugenius VII. brother; some ruffians designing the king's murder, entered his chamber, and, he being absent, stabbed his queen, Spontana, to death. *Scott.*
715. Mordachus, son of Amberkeletus.
730. Etfinus, son of Eugenius VII.
761. Eugenius VIII. son of Mordachus; sensual and tyrannous; put to death by his nobles.
764. Fergus III. son of Etfinus; killed by his jealous queen, who afterwards stabbed herself to escape a death of torture.
767. Solvathius, son of Eugenius VIII.
787. Achaius: just and wise.
819. Congallus III.; a peaceful reign.
824. Dongal or Dougal, son of Solvathius; drowned.
831. Alpine, son of Achaius; beheaded by the Picts.
834. Kenneth II. son; surnamed Mac Alpine; defeated the Picts, slew their king, and united them and the Scots under one sceptre, and became the first sole monarch of all Scotland, 843.
854. Donald V. brother: dethroned; committed suicide.
858. Constantine II. son of Kenneth II.: taken in battle by the Danes and beheaded.
874. Eth or Ethus, surnamed Lightfoot; died of grief in prison; confined for sensuality and crime.
876. Gregory the Great; brave and just.
893. Donald VI. son of Constantine II.; excellent.
904. Constantine III. son of Ethus; became a monk, and resigned in favour of
944. Malcolm I. son of Donald VI.; murdered.
953. Indulfus or Gondulph; killed by the Danes in an ambuscade.
961. Duff or Duffus, son of Malcolm; murdered by Donald, the governor of Forres castle.
965. Cullen or Culenus, son of Indulfus; avenged the murder of his predecessor; assassinated
970. Kenneth III. brother of Duffus; murdered by Fenella, the lady of Fettercairn.
994. Constantine IV. son of Cullen: slain.
995. Kenneth IV. or Grimus, the Grim, son of Duffus; routed and slain in battle by Malcolm, the rightful heir to the crown, who succeeded.
1003. Malcolm II. son of Kenneth III.; assassinated on his way to Glamis; the assassins in their flight crossing a frozen lake were drowned.
1033. Duncan I. grandson; assassinated by his cousin.
1039. Macbeth, usurper; slain by Macduff, the thane of Fife.
⁂ Historians so differ up to this reign, in the number of the kings, the dates of succession, and the circumstances narrated, that no account can be taken as precisely accurate.
1057. Malcolm III. (Canmore), son of Duncan; killed while besieging Alnwick castle.
1093. Donald VII. (Donald Bane), brother; usurper; fled to the Hebrides.
1094. Duncan II. natural son of Malcolm; murdered.
,, Donald VII. again; deposed.
1098. Edgar, son of Malcolm (Henry I. of England married his sister Maud).
1107. Alexander I. the Fierce, brother.
1124. David I. brother; married Matilda, daughter of Waltheof, earl of Northumberland.
1153. Malcolm IV. grandson.
1165. William the Lion; brother.
1214. Alexander II. son; married Joan, daughter of John, king of England.
1249. Alexander III. married Margaret, daughter of Henry III. of England; dislocated his neck, when hunting near Kinghorn.
1285. Margaret, the "Maiden of Norway," grand-daughter of Alexander, "recognised by the states of Scotland, though a female, an infant, and a foreigner; died on her passage to Scotland.
A competition for the vacant throne; Edward I. of England decides in favour of
1292. John Balliol, who afterwards surrendered his crown, and died in exile.
[Interregnum.]
1306. Robert (Bruce) I. a great prince.
1329. David (Bruce) II. son; Edward Balliol disputed the throne with him.
1332. David II. again a prisoner in England, 1346-57 (Edward Balliol king, 1332-4.)
1371. Robert (Stuart) II. nephew; died 19 April.
1390. Robert (John Stuart) III. son; died 4 April.
1406. James I. second son; imprisoned 18 years in England; set at liberty in 1424; conspired against, and murdered at Perth, 21 Feb.
1437. James II. son; killed at the siege of Roxburgh castle by a cannon bursting, 3 Aug.
1460. James III. son; killed in a revolt of his subjects at Bannockburn-field, 11 June.
1488. James IV. son; married Margaret Tudor, daughter of Henry VII. of England; killed at the battle of Flodden, 9 Sept.
1513. James V. son; succeeded when little more than a year old; a sovereign possessing many virtues; died 14 Dec.
1542. Mary, daughter: born, 7 Dec. 1542; succeeded 14 Dec.; see *Annals*, above.
1567. James VI. son; succeeded to the throne of England, and the kingdoms were united, 1603.

See *England*.

SCOTT CENTENARY, celebrated in London and throughout Scotland, 9 Aug. 1871. Sir Walter Scott was born 15 Aug. 1771; died, 1832.

SCOTTISH CORPORATION, established 1665. It is maintained by voluntary contributions, and supports the Scottish hospital which greatly helps necessitous natives of Scotland in London. Annual income about 6,000*l*. The old hall, Crane-court, Fleet-street, built by Wren, burnt 14 Nov. 1877; new hall inaugurated 21 July, 1880.

SCOTTISH HISTORY society founded in Edinburgh in 1886. The earl of Rosebery, president, 23 Nov. 1897.

SCOURERS, see *Mohocks*.

SCOURING OF THE WHITE HORSE, see *Ashdown*.

SCREW, was known to the Greeks. The pumping-screw of Archimedes, or screw-cylinder for raising water, invented about 236 B.C., is still in use. It is stated that with the assistance of the screw, one man can press down or raise up as much as 150 men can do without it.—The SCREW-PROPELLER consists of two or more twisted blades, like the vanes of a windmill, set on an axis, running parallel with the keel of a vessel, and revolving beneath the water at the stern. It is driven by a steam-engine. The principle was shown by Hooke in 1681, and since by Du Quet, Bernouilli, and others. Patents for propellers were taken out by Joseph Bramah in 1784; by Wm. Lyttelton in 1794; and by Edward Shorter in 1799. But these led to no useful result. In 1836 patents were obtained by Francis Pettit Smith (knighted July, 1871; died, 12 Feb. 1874) and captain John Ericsson (died, aged 86, March, 1889); and to them the successful application of the screw-propeller must be attributed. The first vessels with the screw were the *Archimedes*, built on the Thames in 1838 by H. Wimshurst, and the *Rattler*, built in the United States (1844), and tried in England in 1845. Double screw-propellers are now employed. A new form of screw-propeller invented by col. W. H. Mallory, of U.S.A. army, was tried on the Thames and reported successful, Aug. 1878.

SCRIBLERUS CLUB, a literary club, founded by Swift in 1714, included amongst its members, Bolingbroke, Pope, Gay, and Arbuthnot.

SCRIPTURE KNOWLEDGE INSTITUTION, Bristol, was founded by George Müller, a Prussian (born 1805, died 10 March, 1898). He came to Bristol as a minister of the "Brethren" in

1832, and on 5 March, 1834, founded this institution, the objects of which are: 1. Assistance of schools giving instruction on scriptural principles; 2. Circulation of the scriptures; 3. Assistance to missions; 4. Circulation of tracts; 5. Provision for destitute orphans, see *Orphan-houses*. Without application, Mr. Müller. since he began, up to 26 May, 1895, had received by voluntary contribution, 1,373,348*l*. 6*s*. 2½*d*.

SCROFULA, see *King's-evil*.

SCRUTIN (French for ballot). In *scrutin de liste* the voter writes on his paper as many names as there are persons to be elected, for instance for the whole department. In *scrutin d'arrondissement*, the members are elected separately. The adoption of one of these modes was much discussed in France in 1875. The conservatives prefer the latter, the radicals the former. See *France*, Nov. 1875. The *scrutin de liste* was adopted in the elections of 1848, 1849, 1871, and 1875.

M. Bardoux's bill for adopting the *scrutin de liste* (warmly advocated by M. Gambetta), was passed by the chamber of deputies (243-235), 18 May, 1881; rejected by the senate (148-114), 9 June, 1881; again rejected, Jan. 1882.

M. Welbeck Rousseau's bill for the *scrutin de liste* passed by the deputies (412-99), 24 March, finally passed, 8 June, 1885.

The bill for the restoration of the *scrutin d'arrondissement* passed by the chamber 11 Feb. and senate 13 Feb. 1889.

The *scrutin de liste* was adopted by the Italian chamber, 14 Feb. 1882.

SCULLABOGUE, see *Massacres*, 1798.

SCULPTURE is said to have begun with the Egyptians. Bezaleel and Aholiab built the tabernacle in the wilderness, and made all the vessels and ornaments, 1491 B.C., and their skill is recorded as the gift of God. *Exod.* xxxi. 3. Dipœnus and Scyllis, statuaries at Crete, established a school at Sicyon. Pliny speaks of them as being the first who sculptured marble and polished it; all statues before their time being of wood, 568 B.C. Alexander gave Lysippus the sole right of making his statues, 326 B.C. He left no less than 600 pieces, some of which were so highly valued in the age of Augustus, that they sold for their weight in gold. Sculpture did not flourish among the Romans, and in the middle ages with some fine exceptions, was generally degraded. With the revival of painting, it revived also; and Donato di Bardi, born at Florence, A.D. 1383, was the earliest professor among the moderns. An institute of sculptors was established in 1861. See *Royal Academy* and *Statues*.

EMINENT SCULPTORS.

Pheidon flourished	B.C. 869
Myron	480
Phidias (the greatest)	442
Praxiteles	363
Lysippus	328
Chares	288
Michael Angelo Buonarotti	A.D. 1474–1564
Benvenuto Cellini	1500–1570
Giovanni L. Bernini	1598–1680
Caius Gabriel Cibber	1630–1700
Andreas Schlüter	1662–1714
Grinling Gibbons	1648–1721
Francis Bird	1667–1731
John Henry Danneker	1758–1741
Louis Roubiliac (statue of sir I. Newton)	*died* 1762
Peter Scheemakers	1691–1769
John M. Rysbrack	1693–1770
John Bacon	1740–1799
Thomas Banks	1735–1805
Joseph Nollekens	1737–1823
Antonio Canova	1757–1822
John Flaxman	1754–1826
Jean-Antoine Houdon	1741–1828
J. C. F. Rossi	1762–1839
Peter Turnerelli	1774–1839
William Pitti	1790–1840
Francis Chantrey	1781–1841
Albert Thorwaldsen	1770–1844
Sir Richard Westmacott	1775–1856
Christian Rauch	1777–1857
Thos. Campbell	1790–1858
M. Cortes Wyatt	1777–1862
John E. Jones	1806–1862
John Thomas	1813–1862
Wm. Behnes	1790–1864
C. Kiss	1802–1865
John Gibson	1791–1866
Edw. Hodges Baily	1788–1867
Richd. Westmacott	1799–1872
Hiram Powers	1805–1873
John Henry Foley	1818–1874
Alfred Geo. Stevens	1817–1875
Matthew Noble	1820–1876
Thos. Woolner	1826–1892
Sir Joseph Edgar Boehm	1834–1890
Mary Thornycroft (*née* Francis)	1814–1895
Hamo Thornycroft (her son)	1852
Alfred Gilbert	1852
John Mossman	1816–1890
William Theed	1804–1891
Sir John Steel	1807–1891
Prince Victor of Hohenlohe (formerly count Gleichen)	1833–1891
Charles Bell Birch	1832–1893
Giovanni Guiseppe Fontana	1821–1893
William Calder Marshall	1831–1894
John Bell	1811–1895
M. Chatrousse	1829–1896
Harry Bates	1850–1899
Paul de Vigne	1844–1901
Onslow Ford	1852–1901
Jules Dalou	1838–1902
Marc Antokolsky	1842–1902

SCUTAGE or **ESCUAGE**. The service of the shield (scutum) is either uncertain or certain. Escuage uncertain is where the tenant by his tenure is bound to follow his lord; and is called Castleward, where the tenant is bound to defend a castle. Escuage certain is where the tenant is set at a certain sum of money to be paid in lieu of such uncertain services. The first tax levied in England to pay an army, 5 Hen. II. 1159. *Cowel.*

SCUTARI, Asiatic Turkey, opposite Constantinople, of which it is a suburb. It was anciently called *Chrysopolis*, golden city, in consequence, it is said, of the Persians having established a treasury here when they attempted the conquest of Greece. Near here Constantine finally defeated Licinius, 323. The hospital was occupied by the sick and wounded of the Anglo-French army, in 1854-5, whose sufferings were much alleviated by the kind exertions of Miss Florence Nightingale and a band of nurses under her, aided by a large fund of money (15,000*l*.) subscribed by the public and placed in the care of the proprietors of the *Times* newspaper; see *Times*. Explosion of powder magazine by lightning, about 150 killed, 8 June, 1883. Population, 1901, about 82,400.

SCYTHIA, situate in the most northern parts of Europe and Asia. The boundaries were unknown to the ancients. The Scythians made several irruptions upon the more southern provinces of Asia, especially 624 B.C., when they remained in possession of Asia Minor for twenty-eight years, and at different periods extended their conquests in Europe, penetrating as far as Egypt; see *Tartary*.

SEA. Lieut. Maury first published his "Physical Geography of the Sea" in 1854, and other important works since; he died Feb. 1873; see *Deep Sea*.

SEA BIRDS' PRESERVATION ACT, passed 24 June, 1869.

SEA FIGHTS, see *Naval Battles.*

SEA FISHERIES, see *Fisheries,* and *Behring Straits.*

SEAL FISHERY ACT, passed 14 June, 1875; another act, 29 June, 1893, see *Behring Straits.* Seal fisheries (N. Pacific) act, relating to Russia, passed, 27 June, 1895.

SEALS or **SIGNETS.** Engraved gems were used as such by the Egyptians, Jews, Assyrians, and Greeks; see *Exod.* xxviii. 14. Ahab's seal was used by Jezebel, 899 B.C. (1 *Kings* xxi. 8.) The Romans in the time of the Tarquins (about 600 B.C.) had gemmed rings. They sealed rooms, granaries, bags of money, &c. The German emperor, Frederick I. (A.D. 1152) had seals of gold, silver, and tin. Impressions of the seals of Saxon kings are extant; and the English great seal is attributed to Edward the Confessor (1041-66). "A seal with armorial bearings before the 11th century, is certainly false." *Fosbroke.* The most ancient English seal with arms on it is said to be that of Richard I. or John. White and coloured waxes were used. Our present sealing-wax, containing shellac, did not come into general use in Germany and England until about 1556. Red wafers for seals came into use about 1624; but were not used for public seals till the 18th century. A seal acquired by the British Museum made of black hematite, thought to be Hittite, found at Yuzgat in Asia Minor, announced Nov. 1886. *Seal Society,* for publication of fac-similes of ancient seals, was established in 1883.—For SEALED LETTERS, see *Great Seal* and *Lettres de Cachet.*

SEAMEN. In consequence of the great loss of life by wrecks of merchant vessels, attributed to bad ships and overloading, a commission of inquiry was agreed to by parliament on the motion of Mr. S. Plimsoll (who published "Our Seamen: an Appeal"), 4 March, 1873. The duke of Edinburgh was on the commission; the duke of Somerset, chairman. Mr. Plimsoll has been censured for exaggeration.

The report issued in September tended to justify the public apprehensions, but suggested no remedy. The report presented to parliament, 2 July, 1874, condemned the present insurance system, and recommended increased responsibility of owners and others, and strengthening the powers of the Board of Trade for investigation.

The Merchant Shipping Survey bill was rejected (173—170) . . . . 24 June, 1874

After much excitement, an act was passed to give further powers to the Board of Trade to stop unseaworthy ships . . . . . 13 Aug. 1875

Another Merchant Shipping act (*which see*) passed, 15 Aug. 1876

Strong circular issued by the Board of Trade (Mr. Chamberlain); deaths of the employed in ships asserted to be 1 in 60; in coal mines 1 in 315; present system stated to be ineffectual . Jan. 1884

First annual congress of the National Seamen's and Firemen's union held at Cardiff, Mr. Plimsoll present (he died, aged 74, 3 June, 1898) . 8 Oct. 1889

See *Shipping.*

Seamen's hospital society, see *Dreadnought.*

SEAS, SOVEREIGNTY OF THE. The claim of England to rule the British seas is of very ancient date. Arthur is said to have assumed it, and Alfred afterwards supported this claim. It was maintained by Selden, and measures were taken by government in consequence, 8 Chas. I. 1633. The Dutch, after the death of Charles I., made some attempts to obtain it, but were roughly treated by Blake and other admirals. Russia and other powers of the north armed to avoid search, 1780; again, 1800; see *Armed Neutrality* and *Flag.* The international rule of the road at sea was settled in 1862; (new rules were issued in 1879 and 19 Aug. 1884), yet near Great Britain alone there have been 13,000 collisions in six years. Mr. Wm. Stirling Lacon proposed to reduce the rules from 749 words to 144, for simplicity and security. His form had been nine times before parliament, 1873. Revised rules issued by the admiralty in a "Fleet Circular," Nov. 1885.

The British Board of Trade appointed a committee, consisting of admirals N. Bowden Smith, sir Robert Molyneux, sir George S. Nares, and others, to consider measures for the establishment of a "new rule of the road at sea"; first meeting . . . . . . 1 Aug. 1890

The committee adopted the regulations recommended by the Washington conference in 1889 (see *Navigation Laws*), in spite of much opposition from the Chamber of Shipping of the United Kingdom, the General Shipowners' Society of London, the committee of Lloyd's, and other kindred bodies; reported Dec. 1894.

Committee appointed by the board of trade: sir Francis H. Jeune (chairman), and others, March, 1895; report issued, the new rules supported but simplification recommended, April, 1896; another committee appointed respecting collisions at sea, May, 1897; final report concluded 13 May; rules to be enforced . . . . 1 July, 1898

Blue-book issued . . . . . . 29 June, „

Load line committee, report issued . . Nov. „

International maritime congresses, Antwerp, 2 Sept. 1898; London, 1899; Paris, 1900; Hamburg, draft treaties as to collisions considered . Sept. 1902

SEA SERPENT, GREAT, the name given to an animal popularly believed to exist, especially in deep tropical seas, but much controverted by zoologists, sir Richard Owen and others.

Capt. M'Quhae described the appearance of such an animal in the South Atlantic ocean in 1848. Other descriptions have been since published, and many explanations have been suggested. "The Great Sea Serpent," by Mr. A. C. Oudemans, published in 1893, contains reports of 187 appearances, with 82 illustrations.

SEASONS. The four natural divisions of the year.

In the north temperate regions in 1884 the spring quarter began 20 March, 5 a.m., the summer, 21 June, 1 a.m., the autumn, 22 Sept. 3 p.m., the winter, 21 Dec. 10 a.m. See Lapland seasons under *Year.*

James Thomson's "Seasons" published: "Winter," 1726; "Summer," 1727; "Spring," 1728; "Autumn," 1730. Haydn's "Seasons" first performed, 1801.

SEATS BILL, see under *Reform.*

SEBASTIAN, ST. (N. Spain), was taken by the French, under the duke of Berwick, in 1719. It was besieged by the British and allied army under Wellington. After a most heavy bombardment, by which the whole town was laid nearly in ruins, it was stormed by general Graham (afterwards lord Lynedoch), and taken 31 Aug. 1813.—On 5 May, 1836, the fortified works, through the centre of which ran the high road to Hernani, were carried by the English auxiliary legion under general Evans, after very hard fighting. The British naval squadron, off St. Sebastian, under lord John Hay, lent very opportune aid to the victors in this contest.—A vigorous assault was made on the lines of general De Lacy Evans, at St. Sebastian, by the Carlists, 1 Oct. 1836. Both parties fought with bravery. The Carlists were repulsed, after suffering severely. The loss of the Anglo-Spanish force was 376 men and 37 officers, killed and wounded. General De Lacy Evans was slightly wounded. See under *Leagues*. The queen regent of Spain meets queen Victoria here, 27 March, 1889. Population, 1887, 29,047.

SEBASTOPOL or **Sevastopol**, a town and once a naval arsenal, at S.W. point of the Crimea, formerly the little village of Aktiar. The buildings were commenced in 1784, by Catherine II. after the conquest of the country. The town is built in the shape of an amphitheatre on the rise of a large hill flattened on its summit, according to a plan laid down before 1794, which has been since adhered to. The fortifications and harbour were constructed by an English engineer, colonel Upton, and his sons, since 1830. The population in 1834 was 15,000. This place underwent eleven months' siege, by the English and French in 1854 and 1855. Immediately after the battle of the Alma, 20 Sept. 1854, the allied army marched to Sebastopol, and took up its position on the plateau between it and Balaklava, and the grand attack and bombardment commenced 17 Oct 1854, without success.* After many sanguinary encounters by day and night, and repeated bombardments, a grand assault was made on 8 Sept. 1855, upon the Malakhoff tower and the Redans, the most important fortifications to the south of the town. The French succeeded in capturing and retaining the Malakhoff. The attacks of the English on the great Redan and of the French upon the little Redan were successful, but the assailants were compelled to retire after a desperate struggle with great loss of life. The French lost 1646 killed, of whom 5 were generals, 24 superior and 116 inferior officers, 4500 wounded, and 1400 missing. The English lost 385 killed (29 being commissioned and 42 non-commissioned officers), 1886 wounded, and 176 missing. In the night the Russians abandoned the southern and principal part of the town and fortifications, after destroying as much as possible, and crossed to the northern forts. They also sank or burnt the remainder of their fleet. The allies found a very great amount of stores when they entered the place, 9 Sept. The works were utterly destroyed in April, 1856, and the town was restored to the Russians in July; gen. Todleben, the able defender, died 1 July, 1884, and was buried here; his monument uncovered 28 June, 1890. See *Russo-Turkish War*. Population of Sebastopol, 1885, 33,803; 1897, 50,710. Made a naval port, Sept. 1895; new dock, opened, 18 May, 1898. Monument to adm. Nakhimoff unveiled by the czar, 30 Nov. 1898.

SECEDERS; SECESSION CHURCH, see *Burghers*.

SECONDARY EDUCATION, see *Education*, 1893-4.

SECONDARY of **London**, an ancient office, resembling that of under-sheriff in counties. The place was purchaseable till early in the present century, when it was bought up by the corporation.

* In consequence of the sufferings and disasters of the army in the winter of 1854-5, the Sebastopol Inquiry Committee was appointed, and the Aberdeen administration resigned, Feb. 1855. The committee sat from 1 March to 15 May, lord Aberdeen being the last person examined. Its report was presented 18 June. Mr. Roebuck, the chairman, moved on 17 July that the house should pass a vote of severe reprehension on every member of the Aberdeen administration. On 19 July his motion was lost by a majority of 107 against it. In 1855 the government sent sir John M'Neill and col. Tulloch to inquire into the state of the armies in the Crimea. Their report was presented to parliament in Feb. 1856. A commission was appointed to consider the statements in the report (which were very unfavourable to many officers), but the substance of the report was unshaken.

SECRET SOCIETIES, *Assassins, Fenians, Ribbonism, Vehmic Tribunal, Rosicrucians, Illuminati, Carbonari, Mary-Anne, Nihilists.*

SECRETARIES of **State**. The earliest authentic record of a secretary of state is in the reign of Henry III., when John Maunsell is described as "*Secretarius Noster*," 1253. *Rymer*. Towards the close of Henry VIII.'s reign, two secretaries were appointed; and upon the union with Scotland, Anne added a third as secretary for Scotch affairs; this appointment was afterwards laid aside; but in the reign of George III. the number was again increased to three, one for the American department. In 1782 this last was abolished by act of Parliament; and the secretaries were appointed for home, foreign, and colonial affairs. When there were but two secretaries, one held the *portefeuille* of the Northern department, comprising the Low Countries, Germany, Denmark, Sweden, Poland, Russia, &c.; the other, of the Southern department, including France, Switzerland, Italy, Spain, Portugal, and Turkey; the affairs of Ireland belonging to the elder secretary; both secretaries then equally directed the home affairs. *Beatson*. There are now six secretaries—home, foreign, colonial, war, (in 1858) India, and (in 1885) Scotland, all in the cabinet. Secretary of State for Scotland act passed 14 Aug. 1885, amended 1887, explained 1889. See *Administrations*, and separate articles.

The Institute of Secretaries was started at a meeting in London, 4 July, 1890, to collect information respecting the position, duties, and responsibilities of secretaries to be applied for their benefit. First dinner, 24 June, 1892. Annual meetings.

SECTS, RELIGIOUS, see under *Worship*, and their respective titles.

SECULAR GAMES (*Ludi Sæculares*), very ancient Roman games, celebrated on important occasions. Horace wrote his "Carmen Sæculare" for their celebration in the reign of the emperor Augustus (17). They took place again in the reign of Claudius (47), of Domitian (88), and for the last time, of Philip (248), believed to be 2000 years after the foundation of the city.

SECULARISM, a name given to the principles advocated by G. J. and Austin Holyoake, about 1846, and subsequently by Mr. Bradlaugh. He died 30 Jan. 1891.

Its central idea is free, not lawless thought, and it considers scepticism to be scrutiny. It advocates liberty of action without injury to others. It is not against Christianity, but independent of it. Its standard is utilitarian; it is the religion of the present life only; teaching men to seek morality in nature, and happiness in duty. Mr. Austin Holyoake and other secularists repudiated atheism

SECURITY from **Violence Act**, passed in 1863, appointed whipping as part of the punishment for attempts at garotting.

SEDAN, an ancient fortified city in the valley of the Meuse, N.E. of France, the seat of a principality long held by the dukes of Bouillon. On 6 July, 1641, a victory was gained at La Marfée, near Sedan, by the count of Soissons and the troops of Bouillon and other French princes, over the royal army supporting Richelieu; but the count was slain on 23 June, 1642. The duke was arrested in the midst of his army, and was made to cede Sedan to the crown. The protestant university was abolished after the revocation of the edict of Nantes, 22 Oct. 1685. Around this place a series of desperate conflicts on 29, 30, and 31 Aug. between the French army of the north, under marshal MacMahon (about 150,000 men) and the greater part of the three German armies under the king and crown-prince of Prussia and the crown-prince of Saxony (about 250,000 men) was brought to a close on 1 Sept. 1870.

The battle began with attacks on the French right and left about 5 a.m., and was very severe at 2 p.m. At 4 p.m. the Germans remained masters of the field, and the crown-prince of Prussia announced a complete victory, the chief part of the French army retreating into Sedan.

The emperor Napoleon was present during the battle, and, it is said, stood at Iges, near Sedan, exposed for four hours to the German grenades. The impossibility of further resistance was then evident. The Germans had contracted their circle close round Sedan; their formidable artillery held all the heights, from which they could at pleasure wholly destroy the town and the army, and only 2000 men were in a condition to respond to their commander's call, and to make a supreme effort to break through the enemy with the emperor and escape to Montmédy.

At first general de Wimpffen (called to the command when MacMahon was wounded) indignantly rejected the terms offered by the victor, and the emperor had a fruitless interview with count Bismarck to endeavour to mitigate them.

On 2 Sept. the emperor wrote in autograph to the king of Prussia, "Mon frère, n'ayant pu mourir à la tête de mes troupes, je dépose mon épée au pied de votre majesté. NAPOLEON." A capitulation of Sedan and the whole army therein was signed by generals Von Moltke and De Wimpffen at the château of Bellevue, near Frenois, at 11.30 a.m., and at 2 p.m. an interview took place between the king and the emperor, who was downcast but dignified.

The conflict was principally carried on by the artillery, in which (according to the emperor) the Germans had the advantage, not only in number (600 to 500), but also in weight, range, and precision. The carnage was awful, and the field the next day was a mass of shattered bones, torn flesh, and coloured rags.

About 25,000 French prisoners were taken in the battle, and 83,000 surrendered the next day, together with 70 mitrailleuses, 400 field-pieces, and 150 fortress guns. About 14,000 French wounded were found lying in the neighbourhood, and about 3000 escaped into Belgium and laid down their arms. The great army of the north had ceased to exist. Among the killed was lieut.-col. Pemberton, a correspondent of the *Times*, who had approached too near the conflict.

The French emperor and his suite arrived at Wilhelmshöhe, a castle near Cassel appointed for his residence (formerly inhabited by his uncle Jerome, when king of Westphalia), in the evening of 5 Sept.

On 1 Sept. the village of Bazeilles was stormed by the Bavarians and burnt, it was said, because the inhabitants fired on the ambulances; many women and children perished. The French denied the provocation. The place had been previously twice bombarded and stormed by the maddened combatants.

In a letter dated 12 May, 1872, the emperor Napoleon took upon himself the whole responsibility of the surrender of Sedan.

SEDAN CHAIRS (so called from Sedan), were first seen in England in 1581. One used in the reign of James I., by the duke of Buckingham, caused great indignation, and the people exclaimed that he was employing his fellow-creatures to do the service of beasts. Sedan chairs came into London in 1634, when sir Francis Duncomb obtained the sole privilege to use, let, and hire a number of such covered chairs for fourteen years. They came into very general use in 1649.

SEDANGS, a tribe dwelling on the borders of Annam. M. de Mayrena, an ex-officer of the French navy, having made himself their king, came to Paris. He was set aside, and the Sedangs were brought under French protection by the French resident-general in Indo-China; reported Oct. 1889.

SEDGMOOR (Somersetshire), where the duke of Monmouth (natural son of Charles II. by Lucy Walters), who had risen in rebellion on the accession of James II., was completely defeated by the royal army, 6 July, 1685. The duke was made a prisoner in the disguise of a peasant, at the bottom of a ditch, overcome with hunger and fatigue. He was tried and beheaded on 15 July following.

SEDITION. Sedition acts were passed in the reign of George III. The proclamation against seditious writings was published May, 1792. The celebrated Sedition bill passed Dec. 1795. Seditious societies were suppressed by act, June, 1797. The Seditious Meetings and Assemblies' bill passed 31 March, 1817. In Ireland, during the Roman Catholic and Repeal agitation, acts or proclamations against sedition and seditious meetings were published from time to time until 1848.

SEEDS. An act was passed to prevent the adulteration of seeds (a common practice), 11 Aug. 1869; amended in 1878.

SEEKERS, see *Quakers*.

SEGEDIN, or SZEGEDIN, Hungary. Here was concluded a treaty between Ladislaus IV. and Amurath II., 12 July, 1444. It was treacherously annulled at the instigation of cardinal Julian, who with Ladislaus perished in the fatal battle of Varna, 10 Nov. 1444. See *Varna*.

SEICENTO, see under *Italian*.

SEIDLICE (Poland), where a battle was fought 10 April, 1831, between the Poles and Russians. The Poles obtained the victory after a bloody conflict, taking 4000 prisoners and several pieces of cannon; but this success was soon followed by fatal reverses.

SEISMOMETER (from *seismos*, Greek for earthquake), an apparatus for measuring the violence of the shocks. One is described by Mr. Robert Mallet in his work on earthquakes, published in 1858. Many described by Prof. J. A. Ewing, 1880-8. Further advances described by prof. J. Milne, at the Royal Institution, 12 Feb. 1897. Dr. Ehlert's apparatus adopted as the standard system for international investigations, see *Switzerland*, Jan. 1899. Drs. Vicentini and Vacher improve their micro-seismograph for recording earthquake movements, vertical and horizontal, March, 1899.

A seismological society founded in Japan in . . 1880
First international seismological conference held at Strassburg, 11-13 April, 1901; second held there 24 July, 1903
An earthquake investigation committee formed in Japan, prof. Kikuchi and Dr. F. Omori, president and secretary, June, 1892; 32 vols. published, valuable information of seismic phenomena, &c., see *Nature* . . . . 18 April, 1901
Prof. Milne's horizontal pendulums used in 40 observatories, reported . . . . Aug. „

SELA, see *Petra*.

SELBORNE SOCIETY, for the preservation of birds, plants, and pleasant places, originated in the Selborne league (afterwards society) formed by Mr. and Mrs. G. A. Musgrave in Nov. 1885. It has included the plumage league since Jan. 1886 (see under *Birds*). The society met at Selborne to celebrate the centenary of the death of the rev. Gilbert White, author of the "Natural History of Selborne," 24 (for 26) June, 1893. Roundell Palmer, earl Selborne, born 27 Nov. 1812, died, 4 May, 1895, see *Parliament*, 20 May, 1895.

SELDEN SOCIETY, founded 29 Jan. 1887, for the study of English legal history, and publication of ancient MSS. and books, by lords justice Fry, Coleridge, and Lindley, and other eminent lawyers. John Selden, legal antiquary, born 16 Dec. 1584, died 30 Nov. 1654.

SELECT-MEN, the earliest officers of the townships formed by the first colonists of New England about 1635.

SELECTION, NATURAL, see *Species*.

SELENIUM, a grayish-white elementary substance (chemically resembling sulphur), discovered in the stone riolite by Berzelius, in 1817.

The variation in its resistance to the electric current when subjected to light was observed by Mr. Willoughby Smith in 1873, and utilised in the photophone (*which see*). Dr. C. Wm. Siemens constructed a "*selenium eye*."

SELEUCIA (Syria), made the capital of the Syrian monarchy by its builder, Seleucus Nicator, 312 B.C. On the fall of the Seleucidæ, it became a republic, 65 B.C. It was taken by Trajan, A.D. 116; several times given up and retaken; subjugated by the Saracens, and united with Ctesiphon, 636.

SELEUCIDES, ERA OF THE, dates from the reign of Seleucus Nicator. It was used in Syria for many years, and frequently by the Jews until the 15th century, and by some Arabians. Opinions vary as to its commencement. To reduce it to our era (supposing it to begin 1 Sept. 312 B.C.), subtract 311 years 4 months.

SELF-DENYING ORDINANCE, which ordained that no member of parliament should hold any civil or military office or command conferred by either or both of the houses, or by authority derived from them, after much discussion, was passed 3 April, 1645, by the influence of Cromwell, who thus removed the earl of Essex and other Presbyterians out of his way. A somewhat similar ordinance was adopted by the parliament at Melbourne in Australia, in 1858. The name was given to an arrangement made respecting British naval promotions and retirements in 1870.

SELLASIA (Laconia). Here the Spartans under Cleomenes were defeated by Antigonus Doson and the Achæans, 221 B.C.

SELSEY, see *Chichester*.

SEMAPHORE, see *Telegraphs*.

SEMATOLOGY (Greek *sēma*, a sign), the science of signs, a term proposed by B. H. Smart, who died 1872.

SEMINARA (Naples). Near here Gonsalvo de Cordova, the great captain, was defeated by the French, in 1495; but defeated them, 21 April, 1503.

SEMINARY-PRIESTS. A name given in the 16th and 17th centuries to English R. C. priests educated at Douay (*which see*) or other foreign colleges; when they became Jesuits they were prosecuted as traitors.

SEMINCAS, see *Simancas*.

SEMPACH (Switzerland). Here the Swiss gained a great victory over Leopold, duke of Austria, 9 July, 1386, under Arnold von Winckelried; the duke and Arnold were slain, and the liberty of Switzerland was established. The day is still commemorated. Especially on 5 July, 1886.

SEMPER EADEM ("Always the same"), one of the mottoes of queen Elizabeth, was adopted by queen Mary and queen Anne, 13 Dec. 1702.

SEMPERINGHAM, see *Gilbertines*.

SENATE (*Senatus*). In the ancient republics the government was divided between the *senatus* (from *senis*, old; in Greek, *gerousia*, from *gerōn*, old), an assembly of elders, and the popular assembly (*comitia*, Latin; *ecclesia*, Greek), the king being merely the executive. The Roman senate, said to have originally been composed of 100 members, was raised to 300 by Tarquinius Priscus; to about 600 by Sylla, about 81 B.C.; and to 900 by Julius Cæsar. It was reformed and reduced to 600 by Augustus; and gradually lost its power and dignity under the emperors. The mere form existed in the reign of Justinian. A second senate, formed at Constantinople by Constantine, retained its office till the 9th century. S.P.Q.R. on the Roman standard stood for "Senatus Populusque Romanus," "the Roman senate and people." A *senatus consultum* was a law enacted by the senate.

The French senate was created by the constitution of the year 8, promulgated 24 Dec. 1799, to watch over the administration of the laws. The number of senators was raised gradually from 60 to 137. The senate was replaced by the chamber of peers in 1814; re-established by Napoleon III. 14 Jan. 1852; and abolished, 5 Sept. 1870. Its re-establishment was proposed in 1873.

Establishment of a senate of 300 voted; 225 to be elected for 9 years by the departments; 75 (for life) by national assembly, 22 Feb. 1875.

The 75 elected, 9-21 Dec., 1875.

The congress of 13 Aug. 1884, ordered the gradual abolition of life senators as vacancies occurred; new senators were to be elected for 9 years by the departments; enacted, 5 Nov.; bill passed by the deputies and senate, 4-9 Dec. 1884. See *France*.

SENEFFE (Belgium). Near here was fought a severe but indecisive battle between the Dutch, under the prince of Orange (afterwards our William III.), and the French, led by the great Condé, 11 Aug. 1674.

SENEGAL, French colonies on the river of that name in Senegambia, W. Africa, settled about 1626; several times taken by the British, but recovered by the French, to whom they were finally restored in 1814.

The French opposed by two powerful chiefs, Samory and Ahmadou, sultan of Toucouleurs; Samory, defeated by the French, makes a treaty . . 1885

Very great loss of life and property by unexampled floods; towns and villages wholly submerged Aug., Sept. 1890

French war with the Sofas, 1890; the chief Ahmadou's army defeated in sharp battles; the French, under col. Archinard, enter Nioro, 1 Jan. 1891

Ahmadou again defeated by col. Archinard; many prisoners taken; Ahmadou fled; Nioro restored to the chiefs, reported . . . 18 Jan. ,,

The rebel tribes defeated, near Dienia; 600 rebels killed, 24 Feb. Dienia and Kinian taken by col. Archinard, reported . . . March, ,,

War with Samory renewed; he retires to his southern territories, after much carnage and desolation . . . . . . April–June, ,,

Intestine wars between the native chiefs, Ahmet-Saloum and Amar-Saloum, Ahmet-Saloum victor, reported Aug. ,,

Expedition of colonel Humbert against Samory in French Soudan, 1 Jan., whom he defeats, 9, 11 Jan., and takes two strongholds, 25 Jan.; fresh conflicts; capt. Menard killed, reported 6 April; colonel Humbert victorious, 14 March; 3 flying columns traverse the country; 14 fights, reported . . . . Dec. 1892–March, 1893

Col. Archinard appointed chief commander in the *French Soudan*, about 12 Nov. 1892; appointed governor; the tribes submit . . . April, ,,

Capt. Blachère defeats Ahmadou, and dies, 31 May, 1893
Col. Archinard divides the French Soudan into 3 great regions (the Moro, Segu, and Siguiri *cercles*), and returns to France, reported . . Dec. „
Succeeded by col. Bonnier (see *Timbuctoo*).
For disasters with the British, see *Sierra Leone*, 1894.
M. Grodet governor of the French Soudan, reported, 18 Feb. 1894
Guerilla warfare against Samory, reported . 8 Jan. 1895
Samory's army routed at Nzo, many captured, 9 Sept.; his fort at Guelemon seized, and he and his followers captured 29 Sept. 1898; he died at Libreville . . . . . . 2 June, 1900
Outbreak of yellow fever . autumn, 1900–Nov. 1901
Moors attack and burn a village . mid June, 1903

SENEGAMBIA, see *Gambia*.

SENESCHAL, a high officer of the French royal household. In the reign of Philip I. 1059, the office was esteemed the highest place of trust.

SENLAC, see *Hastings*.

SENONES (see *Gauls*), defeated by Camillus; 367 B.C. They defeated Metellus the consul at Arretium, 284, but were almost exterminated by Dolabella, 283. They invaded Greece in 279; were defeated by Antigonus Gonatas, 278; and sued for peace.

SENOVA, near Schipka, in the Balkans. Here Suleiman Pasha and the Turks were defeated by the Russian general Skobeleff, 9 Jan. 1878. This victory virtually closed the war, and opened the road to Adrianople. About 26,000 Turks and 283 officers were made prisoners, with 40 Krupp guns. About 8000 Turks and 2000 Russians were killed or wounded.

SENTINUM (central Italy). The site of a great victory of the Romans under Fabius Maximus, over the Samnites and Gauls, whose general, Gellius Egnatius, was slain, 295 B.C. P. Decius, the other consul, devoted himself to death during the conflict.

SEPARATISTS, a term applied to the Irish National Party, headed by Mr. Parnell, about 1883. In 1884 it vehemently attacked earl Spencer and the Irish executive.—The name is also assumed by a small Christian sect in Dublin, and some other places; originated by John Walker, a classical scholar, somewhat resembling the Glasites (Prov. xviii. 1); he died 25 Oct. 1833, aged 66. Mr. Lucas Chance, a philanthropic separatist, died at Birmingham, 24 Nov. 1897.

SEPHARDIM, the name given to the descendants of the highly civilised Jews of Spain and Portugal, who fled from the persecutions of the Inquisition, 1492-1505. The Jews interpret Sepharad, in *Obadiah* 20, as Spain.

SEPOYS (a corruption of *sipâhi*, Persian, a soldier), the term applied to the native troops in the British Service in India. The Turkish cavalry is named *Spahis*, a name also given to native cavalry in Algeria in the French service in 1834. Under able generals they greatly aided in establishing British rule in India. For their mutinies, see *Vellore*, 1806; *Madras*, 1809; and *India*, 1857.

SEPTEMBER, the seventh Roman month reckoned from March (from *septimus*, seventh). It became the ninth month when January and February were added to the year by Numa; 731 B.C. The Roman senate would have given this month the name of Tiberius, but the emperor opposed it; the emperor Domitian gave it his own name Germanicus; the senate under Antoninus Pius gave it that of Antoninus; Commodus gave it his surname, Herculeus; and the emperor Tacitus his own name, Tacitus.—"September 4 government," see *France*, Sept. 1870.

SEPTEMBRIZERS. In the French revolution a dreadful massacre took place in Paris, 2-5 Sept. 1792. The prisons were broken open, and the prisoners butchered, among them an ex-bishop, and nearly 100 non-juring priests. Some accounts state the number of persons slain at 1200, others at 4000. The agents in this slaughter were named Septembrizers.

SEPTENNALISTS, the party in France who supported the septennate or seven years' government of marshal MacMahon, enacted by the assembly, 19, 20 Nov. 1873. See *France*, 1874.

SEPTENNATE, in the German constitution, is the stipulation that every German fit for the duty is liable to serve for seven years in the Imperial army, 4 May, 1871.

SEPTENNIAL PARLIAMENTS. Edward I. held but one parliament every two years. In the 4th Edward III. it was enacted, "that a parliament should be holden every year once." This continued to be the statute-law till 16th Charles I. 1641, when an act was passed for holding parliaments once in three years at least; repealed in 1664. The Triennial act was re-enacted in 1694. Triennial parliaments thence continued till the 2 Geo. I. 1716, when, in consequence of the allegation that "a popish faction were designing to renew the rebellion in this kingdom, and the report of an invasion from abroad," it was enacted that "the then parliament should continue for seven years." This *Septennial act*, entitled "an act for enlarging the continuance of parliaments" (1715 in the statutes, 4to, given as 1 Geo. I. stat. 2, c. 38), was passed 7 May, 1716; see *Parliaments*. Several unsuccessful motions have been made for its repeal; one in May, 1837; again 24 Feb. 1880, and 8 April, 1892 (188-142).

SEPTIMANIA, a Roman province, S. France; see *Languedoc*.

SEPTUAGESIMA SUNDAY; see *Quadragesima Sunday* and *Week*. *Septuagesima* is the season between Epiphany and Lent.

SEPTUAGINT VERSION OF THE BIBLE, made from Hebrew into Greek, about 280-150 B.C. Seventy-two translators were shut up in thirty-six cells; each pair translated the whole; and on subsequent comparison the thirty-six copies did not vary by a word or letter. *Justin Martyr*. St. Jerome affirms that they translated only the Pentateuch; others say they translated the whole. Ptolemy Philadelphus gave the Jews about a million sterling for a copy of the Old Testament, and seventy translators half a million more for the translation. *Josephus*. Finished in seventy-two days. *Hewlett*. The above statements are merely *traditional;* see *Bible* and *Alexandrian Codex*.

SEQUESTRATION of Benefices Act passed 13 July, 1871.

SERAING, Belgium, on the Meuse, near Liège, formerly the site of a palace of the prince bishops of Liège; now containing great iron works, established in 1817, by John Cockerill, an Englishman. His father, who had works at Liège, died in 1813. Nearly the whole town has been built by Cockerill.

SERAJEVO, capital of Bosnia and Herzegovina, with about 50,000 inhabitants, was founded in 1465 by two nobles. It was taken by Mathias, king of Hungary, in 1480, and by prince Eugène, of Savoy, in 1698. In pursuance of the treaty of Berlin, 13 July, 1878, the Austrians entered Serajevo, after a sharp conflict with the Bosnians, and bombardment of the city, 19 Aug. 1878. By a fire 8, 9 Aug. 1879, above 20,000 persons were rendered homeless.

SERAPHINE, a free-reed musical instrument, a precursor of Debaine's harmonium, brought out by John Green in London, 1833.

SERAPIS, TEMPLE OF (near Naples), was exhumed in 1750. The remains of his temple at Memphis, termed Serapeum, were discovered by Mariette, 1850 *et seq.*

SERASKIER, the Turkish minister of war.

SERFS, see *Slavery* (note), and *Russia*, 1861, 1863.

SERINGAPATAM (S. India), the capital of Hyder Ali, sovereign of Mysore (*which see*). The battle of Seringapatam, called also the battle of Arikera, in which the British defeated Tippoo Sahib, was fought 15 May, 1791. The redoubts were stormed, and Tippoo was reduced by lord Cornwallis, 6 Feb. 1792. After this capture, preliminaries of peace were signed, and Tippoo agreed to cede one half of Mysore, and to pay 33,000,000 of rupees (about 3,300,000*l.* sterling) to England, and to give up to lord Cornwallis his two eldest sons as hostages.—In a new war the Madras army, under general Harris, arrived before Seringapatam, 5 April, 1799; it was joined by the Bombay army 14 April; and the place was stormed and carried by major-general Baird, 4 May, same year. In this engagement Tippoo was killed. Serious plague riot, troops called out, 134 taken prisoners, 18 Nov. 1898. See *Mysore*.

SERJEANTS-AT-LAW were pleaders from among whom the judges were ordinarily chosen, and who were called serjeants of the coif. The judges called them brothers; see *Coif*. Their exclusive rights of addressing court of common pleas suspended, 1834; restored, 1840; abolished, 1846. By the Supreme Court of Judicature act, judges on their appointment need not be made serjeants, 1873. Mr. F. L. Spinks, the last serjeant-at-law, died, aged 82, 27 Dec. 1899. See *Inns of Court*.

SERPENT, an ancient wind instrument, parent of the cornet family. A "contra serpent" was shown in the Exhibition, 1851, made by Jordan, of Liverpool. The "serpentcleid" was produced by Beacham in Jullien's orchestra about 1840. For H.M. cruiser *Serpent*, see *Navy*, 1887 and 1890, *Mansion House Fund*, and *Sea-Serpent*.

SERPENTINE, see *Hyde Park*.

SERVANTS. An act levying a duty on male servants was passed in 1777, which was augmented in 1781 *et seq.* A tax on female servants, imposed in 1785, was repealed in 1792. The tax on servants yielded in 1830 about 250,000*l.* per annum; in 1840 the revenue from it had fallen to 201,482*l.*; in 1850 it produced about the same sum. The licence duty for male servants is now 15*s.* each. It produced in the year 1876-7, 167,004*l.*; 1877-8, 154,641*l.*; 1878-9, 146,061*l.*; 1883-4, 139,631*l.*; 1887-8, 136,287*l.*; 1901-2, 158,320*l.* The law respecting servants was amended by the Master and Servants' act passed in 1867.

SERVIA, an independent kingdom, south of Hungary. The Servians or Serbs are of Slavonic origin. They embraced Christianity about 640. The emperor Manuel subjugated them in 1150; but they recovered their independence in 1180. Population in 1854, 985,000; 1873, 1,338,505; 1890, 2,162,759; 1901, 2,500,000. Belgrade is the capital (*which see*). Old Servia is still subject to Turkey.

Stephen Nemanya, a Servian chief, founds the Racian dynasty, under whom the country progressed . . . 1159 *et seq.*
Stephen Dushan subdues Bulgaria, &c., and aims at resisting the Turks 1336-56
The Servians, weakened by dissensions, defeated by the Turks 1371
The sultan Amurath I. defeated the combined Christian army of Servians, Hungarians, Albanians, &c., and was himself killed by a wounded Servian soldier in the plain of Cossova, or Kossova . . . . . 15 June, 1389
Servia, subdued by the sultan Mahomet II., is rigorously ruled, 1459 *et seq.*; ceded to Austria, 1718; regained by Turkey 1739
The Servians aid Austria by free companies . 1788-90
Again rebel, and capture Belgrade 1806
Kara George, chosen leader, 1801; aided by the Russians, establishes a government . . 1807-11
The Turks break a treaty, and Kara George flees . 1814
Their governor Milosch rebels . . . March, 1815
Kara George returning, is assassinated . . . 1817
Alexander Milosch I. Obrenovitch recognised as hereditary prince by the sultan . . 15 Aug. 1829
Milosch becoming despotic, made to abdicate, and a new constitution established . 13 June, 1839
His son and successor Milan soon dies, whose brother Michael also retires; Alexander, son of Kara George, chosen prince . . . . 14 Sept. 1842
Alexander becoming unpopular, made to abdicate by the national party; Alexander Milosch re-elected prince . . . . . 23 Dec. 1858
Plot against Milosch frustrated, 11 July; the Servian assembly meets . . . 13 July, 1860
Milosch dies; succeeded by his son Michael Obrenovitch (born 4 Sept. 1825) . . 26 Sept. „
Rising movement to render Servia independent of Turkey . . . . . . March, 1861
Disputes between the Servians and the Turkish garrison at Belgrade, which lead to bloodshed; the city bombarded, 15 June; submits 17 June; the Turkish pacha dismissed . . 19 June, 1862
A conference of the representatives of the great powers at Constantinople, Aug.; the Porte agrees to liberal concessions to the Servians, which their prince accepts . . . . 7 Oct. „
Servians demand withdrawal of Turkish garrisons from Belgrade and other fortresses . 5 Oct. 1866
Which are evacuated, March; prince Michael, at Constantinople, thanks the sultan . 30 March, 1867
Prince Michael assassinated in Belgrade 10 June, 1868
Milan IV. grand-nephew of prince Michael, chosen his successor, 22 June; 14 of the murderers were executed . . . . . . 28 July, „
Constitution affirming the hereditary rights of the Obrenovitch family 1869
Prince Karageorgevitch accused of complicity with murder; imprisoned at Pesth, Jan.; acquitted, May, 1871
The regents surrender the government to prince Milan at Belgrade . . . . 22 Aug. 1872
Excitement through insurrection in Herzegovina, new ministry hostile to Turkey, formed, about 31 Aug.; resign; announced, 4 Oct.; peace ministry formed . . . . 9 Oct. 1875
Ristitch, premier, opposed to Turkey . . July, 1876
See *Turkey*, for the war declared . . 1 July, „
Milan proclaimed king by Tchernayeff and the army at Deligrad; not approved . . . 16 Sept. „
Peace with Turkey ratified . . . 4 March, 1877
[Servian losses in the war, about 8000 killed, 20,000 wounded.]
Servians again declare war and enter Turkey (see *Russo-Turkish war*) . . . 14, 15 Dec. „
Sultan deposes prince Milan . . . 22 Dec. „
Servia declared independent, with new frontiers, by treaty of San Stefano, 3 March, and of Berlin . . . . . . 13 July, 1878

Execution of Markovitch and other rioters end of May, 1878

Proclamation of peace and national independence at Belgrade . . . . . . 22 Aug. ,,

The ministry re-modelled by Ristitch, about 15 Oct. ,,

Resignation of Ristitch (virtual dictator) announced 25 Oct. 1880

Milan proclaimed king by the Assembly about 6 March, 1882

[Married Natalie Keschko (born 1859), 17 Oct. 1875.]

Escaped assassination by mad. Markovitch 23 Oct. ,,

Resignation of the Pirochanitz ministry, 27 Sept.; succeeded by Nicolas Christitch . 3 Oct. 1883

New military organization leads to insurrection in S.E. Servia; soon suppressed . announced 5-10 Nov. ,,

Insurgents defeated . . . . about 10 Nov. ,,

18 members of the Radical committee arrested Nov. ,,

General tranquillity reported . . . 13 Nov. ,,

18 rebel leaders executed, about 19 Nov.; many others reprieved . . . . . Dec. ,,

Rebels enter Bulgaria; disputes with that country ensue; prospect of war . . . . June, 1884

M. Garachanine, premier . . . . 23 Oct. ,,

Dispute settled by arrangement . about 10 Nov. ,,

Political dissensions: Panslavist agitation by M. Ristitch . . . . . . Sept. 1885

Military movements consequent upon the *coup d'état* in Roumelia . . . . Oct. ,,

Declaration of war against Bulgaria (*which see*) 13 Nov. ,,

Invasion: success followed by disastrous retreat 14–24 Nov. ,,

Royal decree calling out the army . 11 Feb. 1886

Peace between Servia and Bulgaria signed at Bucharest 3 March; ratified by the sultan 13 March, ,,

M. Ristitch fails to form a new ministry about 3 April, ,,

M. Garachanine resigns; succeeded by M. Ristitch (pro-Russian) about 13 June, 1887; by colonel Gruics . . . . . . 1 Jan. 1888

Strong independent speech of the king . 13 Dec. 1887

New ministry under M. Nicolas Christitch 26–27 April, 1888

The king demands a divorce from the queen for disagreements; he favours Austria, she Russia; she refused the deed of terms offered; she gives up the crown prince and goes to Paris . 18 July, ,,

Queen Natalie protests against the divorce 20 Aug. & 30 Oct.; the divorce decreed by the metropolitan Theodosius, abp. of Belgrade (authority questionable) . . . . Oct. ,,

A royal commission recommends universal suffrage, all electors eligible to the Skuptschina, independence of the church, all religions free and protected, liberty of the press, &c. . 24 Oct. ,,

The king proclaims coming constitutional changes 26 Oct. ,,

Elections of the chambers annulled by the king as not free . . . . . . 28 Nov. ,,

New elections give majority to the radicals, headed by M. Ristitch, against the progressists under M. Christitch, the minister . . . . 16 Dec. ,,

The Skuptschina opened . . . . 30 Dec. ,,

The king informs a deputation desiring changes in the proposed constitution that the deputies must accept it unaltered; otherwise he will set it aside and rule absolutely . . . 1 Jan. 1889

The new constitution passed (494–73) 2 Jan.; the session closed . . . . . . 3 Jan. ,,

An amnesty proclaimed for political offences Jan. ,,

The Christitch ministry resigns but continues after others fail . . . . 8 Jan. *et seq.* ,,

The formation of a radical ministry stopped by the king on suspicion of conspiracy . 13 Feb. ,,

Abdication of the king; his son Alexander proclaimed; liberal regency—M. Ristitch, gen. Bolimarkovitch, and gen. Protitch; radical cabinet headed by M. Taushanovitch . . 6 March, ,,

The Servians celebrate with mourning the quincentenary of the battle of Cossova . 27 June, ,,

The king founds a monument in memory of the slain. The king was anointed by the metropolitan Michael in the church of Zitcha, near Kraljevo . . . . 2 July, ,,

Queen Natalie arrives at Belgrade, 29 Sept.; interview with her son . . . . 13 Oct. ,,

Elections: a great radical majority, 1 Oct.; new parliament meets . . . . 13 Oct. 1889

Ministerial crisis averted by arrangement between radicals and liberals. . . . . March, 1890

M. Patchitch, Russophil radical leader, president of the Skuptschina . . . . 20 March, ,,

Ministry re-constructed; gen. Gruitch premier, 28 March, ,,

The Servian vice-consul at Pristina, M. Marinkovite, assassinated, 1 July. The arrested assassins confess and are tried; the excessive demands of the Servian government refused by Turkey; the affair arranged . about 28 July, ,,

Elections: radicals 113, liberals 18, progressists 2 27 Sept. ,,

Queen Natalie agitates to annul her isolation from her son; her memorandum (22 Nov.) to the parliament dismissed . . . 8 Dec. *et seq.* ,,

Gen. Sava Gruitch's cabinet resigns, 29 Jan., but remains, 1 Feb.; again resigns . . 20 Feb. 1891

M. Ristitch writes to the queen, opposing her efforts to obtain political power; increasing agitation against her . . . . 9 Feb. *et seq.* ,,

M. Patchitch forms a radical ministry . 23 Feb. ,,

King Milan agrees to live out of Servia, till his son's majority, on receipt of a sum of money and a pension, about 14 April; he arrives at Vienna 19 April, ,,

Queen Natalie requested by the government to leave the country, refuses about 10 May: attempted expulsion stopped by students and people; 2 persons killed and several wounded by the troops, 18 May. The queen forcibly conveyed to Semlin in Hungary, early . 19 May, ,,

The king starts for St. Petersburg, 22 July; at Moscow, 29 July; St. Petersburg, 4 Aug.; at Vienna, 10 Aug.; received by the emperor at Ischl, 11, 12 Aug.; returns to Belgrade . 15 Sept. ,,

King Milan resigns definitely all his military and political rights, reported . . . 18 Nov. ,,

The ministry resigns, 8 March; re-constituted under M. Patchitch. . . . . . 2 April, 1892

Death of gen. Protitch, one of the regents; ministerial crisis . . . . . . 15 Aug. ,,

M. Avakumovitch forms a ministry . . 21 Aug. ,,

Truce concluded between the liberals and progressists headed by M. Garashanine . Oct. ,,

Election riots at Tchatchak and Semendria, with bloodshed; many arrests, reported . 13 Jan. 1893

Reconciliation of king Milan and queen Natalie at Biarritz; joy of the young king, announced, 19 Jan. ,,

Parliamentary elections; government majority, about 11 March, ,,

Severe earthquakes (*which see*) . . 8–10 April, ,,

Coup d'état: king Alexander, after a banquet, and appealing to the army, 13 April, proclaims his majority and dismisses the regents and their ministry, and appoints a radical ministry (Dr Dokitsch premier); the parliament dissolved; popular rejoicing . . . . . 14 April, ,,

King Alexander meets queen Natalie at Kladova, 19 May, ,,

The new parliament opened by the king; he takes the oath of the constitution, 16 June; the parliament closed, 21 Aug.; re-opened . 15 Nov. ,,

The impeachment of the Avakumovitch cabinet agreed to by the parliament . . 19 July, ,,

Resignation of Dr. Dokitsch, the premier . 8 Sept. ,,

Reconciliation of the king and the liberal party; public demonstration . . . . 15 Oct. ,,

M. Georgevitch, the Servian minister in Paris, stabbed by Leauthier in a restaurant there; not much injured, 13 Nov. 1893; Leauthier sentenced to life imprisonment . . . . 23 Feb. 1894

Ministerial crisis . . . . . . 25 Nov. 1893

New ministry; gen. Gruitch premier . 6 Dec. ,,

Death of Dr. Dokitsch, ex-premier . . 13 Dec. ,,

Trial of M. Avakumovitch and his former colleagues; began 21 Dec.; suspended . 26 Jan. 1894

Resignation of the Gruitch ministry on the arrival of king Milan invited by his son . 21 Jan. ,,

New coalition ministry, under M. Georgsimitch, formed; parliament prorogued . . 24 Jan. ,,

Amnesty to political offenders granted . 26 Jan. ,,

King Milan's divorce annulled by the episcopal synod, reported . . . . 18 March, ,,

Coalition ministry formed by M. Nicolaievitch, 3 April, 1894

Coup d'état: the king suspends the constitution of 1888 and re-establishes that of 29 June, 1869; despotic changes; the press restricted, &c.; M. Nicolas Christitch, president of the council of state . . . . 21 May, ,,

King Alexander warmly received at Berlin, 17 Oct.; at Vienna . . . . 21 Oct. ,,

M. Nicolaievitch resigns; new ministry formed by M. Nicola Christitch . . . . . 28 Oct. ,,

M. Ranko Taisitch and 3 others sentenced to 3 years' and M. Czebinatz to 2 years' imprisonment for treason, 12 Jan.; pardoned . . July, 1895

Elections; government majority . . 21 April, ,,

Return of queen Natalie to Belgrade; warmly received . . . . 10 May, ,,

A pension of 12,000*l.* per annum voted to king Milan . . . . 12 May, ,,

Resignation of the Christitch ministry . 3 July, ,,

Cabinet formed by M. Stojan Novakovitch, 7 July, ,,

Government conversion scheme adopted 19 July, ,,

M. Ristitch declared leader of the liberal party, 16 Sept. ,,

The king visits Vienna, mid Nov.; and Rome, received by the pope . . . . . 25 Nov. 1896

New cabinet formed by M. Simitch, foreign minister; M. Velimirovitch, prime minister, 30 Dec.; parliament dissolved . . . 31 Dec. ,,

Many Albanian raids, 204 notes in 3 yrs. addressed to the porte, on the subject . . . July, 1897

The ex-king Milan appointed commander-in-chief of the army . . . . 6 Jan. 1898

General elections: decisive government victory (moderates) 4 June; parliament opened by the king . . . . 1 July ,,

Note to the porte regarding the Albanian outrages in Kossovo, 31 Oct. 1898; claims disallowed by the porte . . . . 26 Jan. 1899

Albanian raids: Turkish troops engaged near Vrania, much bloodshed . . 14–16 June, ,,

Regulations for frontier service agreed to by a mixed commission . . . early Aug. ,,

The ex-king Milan shot at in Belgrade by Payitch, *alias* Knezevitch, a fanatic, 6 July (wholesale arrests followed); loyal demonstration in honour of the king and ex-king, 8 July; martial law proclaimed . . . . 9 July–2 Oct. ,,

State trial, 8–25 Sept.; Knezevitch and 27 others charged with high treason (M. Angjelitch commits suicide in his cell, 8 Sept.); 22 found guilty; Knezevitch and Ranko Tisitch (who escaped) sentenced to death, 10 others to 20 years' penal servitude, the rest to various terms of imprisonment (M. Pasitch, radical leader, afterwards pardoned); Knezevitch (reaffirming the absolute innocence of 10 of the condemned) shot in public, 25 Sept.; the trial regarded unjust, the prisoners' defence having been entirely ignored; see *Times* . . . . 26 Sept. ,,

M. Vesnitch, an able lawyer, prof. Paolovitch (without evidence), and 2 others accused of *lèse majesté*, sentenced from 2 to 8 years' penal servitude . . . . 27 Sept. ,,

M. Ristitch, eminent statesman, dies, aged 68, 4 Sept.; state funeral at Belgrade . 6 Sept. ,,

Parliament opened with a speech by the king, 4 Oct. ,,

Budget (surplus 1,500,000f.) adopted . 8 Feb. 1900

Betrothal of the king to Mdme. Draga Maschin (unpopular); ex-king Milan, commander-in-chief, resigns (afterwards banished) . 21, 22 July, ,,

New cabinet formed by M. Jovanovitch . 25 July, ,,

Political amnesty to radicals announced . 5 Aug. ,,

Gen. Sretchkovitch appointed commander-in-chief, Aug. ,,

The shah received by the king at Belgrade, 6 Oct. ,,

M. Genchitch, ex-minister, sentenced to 7 years' imprisonment for *lèse majesté* . . . 12 Dec. ,,

Parliament opened by the king . . . 12 Jan. 1901

Death of ex-king Milan at Vienna, aged 47, 11 Feb. ,,

Ministry resigns; M. Vuitch forms one, 2, 3 April, ,,

New liberal constitution promulgated; fuller civil liberties restored . . . . . 19 April, ,,

Frequent Albanian affrays on the frontier June, ,,

Elections, 4 Aug.: 110 ministerialists, 14 radicals, and 6 liberals in the new house . . 12 Aug. ,,

Supreme council of war (for 3 years) ordered, reported . . . . 4 Sept. ,,

New parliament opened by the king . 20 Oct. 1901

Alavantich, a Servian agitator, is mortally wounded in a revolutionary attempt at Shabatz, 5 March, 1902

George Schtrik sentenced to 15 years', and several others to varying terms of imprisonment, 25 May, ,,

The Vuitch ministry resigns, but is reconstructed, 20 May, ,,

Loan bill adopted, 28—7 . . . . . 6 Aug. ,,

Commercial agreements with Russia, reported, 26, 31 Aug. ,,

Vuitch ministry resigns, 14 Oct.; one formed by M. Velimirovitch, 20 Oct.; another by gen. Markovitch (assassinated 10 June, 1903). 20 Nov. ,,

Political riots in Belgrade, 18 killed . 6 April, 1903

Coup d'état chamber dissolved, laws annulled, liberal constitution of 1901 restored . 7 April, ,,

Elections, government victory, reported early June, ,,

Military *coup d'état* and revolution raised by the radicals at Belgrade; col. Maschin, the queen's brother-in-law, col. Misitch and a band of officers, forced their way into the palace (col. Naumovitch killed by the explosion of a bomb, which himself had thrown at one of the doors) and massacred king Alexander and queen Draga, gen. Petrovitch, 2 aides-de-camp, many of the guards and others who tried to defend them: gen. Markovitch, premier, gen. Pavlovitch (war minister), 2 other ministers, Nikodem (alleged heir to the throne), Nikola Lungevica, the queen's brothers, and 17 others, murdered, and about 10 wounded in the town at night between . . . 10–11 June, ,,

Provisional government formed, M. Avakumovitch premier, col. Maschin board of works . 11 June, ,,

The king and queen privately buried at dawn, 12 June ,,

Col. Zivanovitch and lieut. Ivanovitch, loyalists, commit suicide . . . . . . 12 June, ,,

Parliament meets, prince Peter Karageorgevitch elected king . . . . . . 15 June, ,,

The new king by proclamation asserts "that he will be faithful to the traditions of his ancestors, and that all that has passed will be buried in oblivion" . . . . 15 June, ,,

Thanksgiving service at Belgrade, the metropolitan thanked, and praised the army for its recent action . . . . 16 June, ,,

The liberal constitution of 1888 (amended) adopted, 17 June, ,,

Cloudburst over Zeruni, 54 houses destroyed, 38 deaths . . . . 21 June, ,,

Sir G. Bonham, British minister, recalled, 23 June, ,,

King Peter enthusiastically received, Russian and Austrian the only foreign ministers present, 24 June; he takes the oath of the constitution, and holds a review of troops, the provisional ministry retained . . . . 25 June, ,,

Political amnesty and perpetual indemnity for acts of treason up to the present time, issued, 28 June, ,,

Parliament prorogued . . . . . 30 June, ,,

King Edward VII.'s reply to the king's message concludes, "Whilst expressing my sincere desire that your reign may bring to the people entrusted to your charge the blessings of peace and prosperity, I hope that your majesty will succeed in restoring the good repute of your country upon which recent events have left so regrettable a stain" . . . . 30 June ,,

MM. Pasitch and Venitch, councillors, resign; reported . . . . 6 July ,,

Cabinet crisis, 12 Aug.; ministry reconstituted; a "military triumph" . . . . . 15 Aug. ,,

Great meeting in Belgrade in favour of the Macedonians, calls upon the government to intercede on their behalf . . . . . . 30 Aug. ,,

Rumours of unrest and conspiracies, col. Misitch removed from the war ministry . . 17 Sept. ,,

Continued unrest reported, the army divided between the "old conspirators" (assassins of the king and queen) still in power, and the "new conspirators," who are opposed to them, reported, 19 Sept. ,,

Elections: 80 radicals, 65 independent radicals, 14 liberals, 1 socialist . . . . 21 Sept. ,,

Servian nationality in European Turkey settled, iradé signed . . . . . . 26 Sept. ,,

New cabinet: gen. Gruitch, premier, col. Andrejvitch, war minister, reported . . . 4 Oct. ,,

The Skupshtina opened by the king: he requests it to work in earnest for the advancement of the country, both as regards economy and finances, 7 Oct. 1903

Six officers sentenced to 13 months' imprisonment for conspiring against officers connected with the murder of the late king and queen, reported 10 Oct. ,,

Gen. Mashin, who took a prominent part in the assassination of king Alexander and queen Draga, appointed to the command of the Belgrade-Danube division, reported . early Oct. ,,

HEREDITARY PRINCES.

1829. Milosch (Obrenovitch) I., recognised by Turkey, 15 Aug. 1833; abdicates 13 June, 1839.
1839. Michael II., son; dies 1840.
1840. Michael III., brother; abdicates 1842.
1842. Alexander (Karageorgevitch), son of Kara George; chosen, 14 Sept.; deposed 23 Dec. 1858; died 3 May, 1885; his son, Peter, b. 1846.
1858. Milosch (Obrenovitch), re-elected, 23 Dec.; dies, 1860.
1860. Michael III., son; succeeds, 26 Sept.; assassinated, 10 June, 1868.
1868. Milan (Obrenovitch) IV., grand-nephew, born, 22 Aug. 1854; married to Natalie Keschko, 17 Oct. 1875; again proclaimed, 2 July, 1868; he abdicated 6 March, 1889; died, 11 Feb. 1901.
1889. Alexander, son, born 14 Aug. 1876; married Mme. Draga, *née* Lungevica, 5 Aug. 1900; both assassinated 10 June, 1903.
1903. Peter I. (Karageorgevitch), born 1846; married princess Zorka of Montenegro, Aug. 1883; elected king, 15 June, 1903.

SERVILE WARS, insurrections of slaves against their masters. Two were quelled in Sicily after much slaughter, 135-132 and 102-99 B.C., see *Spartacus*.

SESSION COURTS in England were appointed to be held quarterly in 1413, and the times for holding them regulated in 1831; see *Quarter Sessions* and *Court of Session*. The *kirk session* in Scotland consists of the minister and elders of each parish. They superintend religious worship and discipline, dispense money collected for the poor, &c.

SESTUS, on the Thracian Chersonesus; see *Hellespont*. Near Sestus was the western end of Xerxes' bridge, across the Hellespont, 480 B.C. Sestus was retaken from the Persians by the Athenians, 478, and held by them till 404, giving them the command of the trade of the Euxine.

SETTLED ESTATES ACT, 40 & 41 Vict. c. 18, consolidates and amends the law relating to their leases, sales, &c. (passed 28 June, 1877). Other acts passed, 1882, 1884, and 1890.

In conformity with these acts, the earl of Radnor was authorised to sell pictures which were heirlooms for the National gallery, in 1890, *which see*. An appeal was disallowed by the court, 7 Aug. 1890.—The marquis of Ailesbury, on appeal, was authorised to sell the mortgaged family mansion, Savernake hall and estate, 12 Dec. 1891; affirmed by the house of lords . 9 Aug. 1892

SETTLEMENT, ACT OF, for securing the succession to the British throne, to the exclusion of Roman catholics, was passed in 1689. This name is also given to the statute by which the crown, after the death of William III. and queen Anne, without issue, was limited to Sophia, electress of Hanover, grand-daughter of James I., and her heirs being protestants, 1702. The Irish act of settlement, passed in 1662, was repealed in 1689; see *Hanover* and *Accession*.

SETTLEMENT, the subject of many statutes since 1535, by which the destitute poor were directed to be removed from place to place till their proper settlement was found; an act was passed in 1662, mainly to relieve the cities of London and Westminster. The law was somewhat changed by the poor law act of 1834.

SEVEN BISHOPS, see *Bishops*, 1688.

SEVEN BROTHERS, martyrs at Rome, under Antoninus; their feast is kept 10 July.

SEVEN CHAMPIONS OF CHRISTENDOM, THE, are: *England*, St. George; *Scotland*, St. Andrew; *Ireland*, St. Patrick; *Wales*, St. David; *France*, St. Denis; *Spain*, St. James; *Italy*, St. Anthony.

SEVEN CHURCHES OF ASIA, to the angels (ministers) of which the apostle John was commanded to write the epistles contained in the 2nd and 3rd chapters of his Revelation, viz., Ephesus, Smyrna, Pergamos, Thyatira, Sardis, Philadelphia, and Laodicea, 96.

1. *Ephesus* (*which see*). Paul founded the church here, 57. In 59, he was in great danger from a tumult created by Demetrius; to the elders of this church he delivered his warning address, 60 (Acts xix., xx.). Ephesus was in a ruinous state even in the time of Justinian (527), and still remains so.

2. *Smyrna*. An ancient Greek city, claiming to be the birthplace of Homer; was destroyed by the Lydians; about 627 B.C., rebuilt by Antigonus and Lysimachus. Its first bishop, Polycarp, was martyred here about 169. It has been frequently captured. It was sacked by Tamerlane in 1402; and finally taken by the Turks, 1424. It is now the chief city of Asia Minor, and the seat of the Levant trade. Earthquake, above 2000 perish, 12 May, 1875. Great fire; about 700 houses destroyed, 18 July, 1882. Massacre by the Kurds of over 200 Armenian workmen and foreign engineers, buildings and stores burnt, near Smyrna, 7 June, 1896. Disorders between refugee Mahomedan Cretans and local Christians, murders, &c., at Scala Mirva and in the coast towns, reported, 20 Feb. 1899. Population, 1896, 200,000.

3. *Pergamos*. Capital of the kingdom of the same name, founded by Philetærus, whom Lysimachus, one of Alexander's generals, had made governor, 283 B.C. He was succeeded by Eumenes I., 263; Attalus (who took the title of king), 241; Eumenes II. (who collected a great library), 197; Attalus II., 159; Attalus III., 138. He bequeathed his kingdom to the Romans, 133. It revolted, was subdued, and made the Roman province, Asia. Pergamos is still an important place, called Bergamo. Parchment is said to have been invented here. The explorations of the ancient citadel, instituted by the German government in 1878, resulted in the discovery of Greek marble statuary, which has been deposited in the museum at Berlin.

4. *Thyatira*. Now a mean town of 2000 houses, called Ak-hissar, "White Castle."

5. *Sardis*. Formerly the capital of Lydia, the kingdom of Crœsus (560 B.C.); taken by Cyrus, 548; burnt by the Greeks, 499; it flourished under the Roman empire; was taken by the Turks; and destroyed by Tamerlane about 1462; it is now a miserable village, named Sart.

6. *Philadelphia* was built by Attalus (III.) Philadelphus, king of Pergamos (159-138 B.C.); was taken by Bajazet I., A.D. 1390. It is now called Allah Shehr, "The city of God," and is a miserable town of 3000 houses.

7. *Laodicea*. In Phrygia, near Lydia; has suffered much from earthquakes. It is now a deserted place, called Eske-hissar, "The old castle."

SEVEN DAYS' WAR, see *Army*, 1871.

SEVEN SAGES, see *Greece*, 590 B.C.

SEVEN-SHILLING PIECES in gold were authorised to be issued 29 Nov. 1797.

SEVEN SLEEPERS. According to an early legend seven youths, in 251, commanded to worship a statue set up in Ephesus by the emperor Decius, refused, and fled to a cavern in the mountain, where they were enclosed, and slept, according to Durandus, for 300 years. Other writers give shorter periods, and various accounts of the incidents which accompanied the awakening. A festival in their honour is kept by the Roman church on 27 July.

SEVEN WEEKS' WAR, see *Prussia*, 1866.

SEVEN WONDERS OF THE WORLD, see *Wonders*.

SEVEN YEARS' WAR, the conflict maintained by Frederick II. of Prussia against Austria, Russia, and France, from 1756 to 1763; see *Battles*. He gained Silesia; see *Hubertsburg*.

SEVENTH-DAY BAPTISTS, see article *Sabbatarians*, *Adventists*, &c.

SEVERN, see under *Tunnels*.

SEVERNDROOG, see *Savandroog*.

SEVERUS'S WALL, see *Roman Walls*.

SEVILLE (S.W. Spain), the *Hispalis* of the Phœnicians, and the *Julia* of the Romans, was the capital until Philip II. finally established his court at Madrid, 1563. It opened its gates to the Saracens in 712, and was taken from them by the Christians in 1247, after an obstinate siege. The peace of Seville between England, France, and Spain, and also a defensive alliance to which Holland acceded, signed 9 Nov. 1729. In the peninsular war, Seville surrendered to the French, 1 Feb. 1810; and was taken by assault by the British and Spaniards, after the battle of Salamanca, 27 Aug. 1812. It was besieged but not taken by Espartero, July, 1843. Visit of prince of Wales, 20 April, 1876. The ancient cathedral was much renovated, 1889-90. Population, 1887, 143,182; 1897, 147,000.

Destructive cyclone, many injured . . 28 Oct. 1896
Death of the duchesse de Montpensier, daughter of Ferdinand VII. of Spain; benefactor . 1 Feb. 1897
Strike riots, state of siege proclaimed . 14 Oct. 1901
The remains of Columbus brought from Havana, and interred here . . . . . 17 Nov. 1902

SÈVRES, see *Pottery*.

SEWERS, see *Cloaca Maxima*. An act was passed in 1847 enforcing the conveyance of the sewage of houses in London into the public sewers. The commissioners of sewers in London were superseded by the metropolitan commissioners of sewers, nominated by the government. They abolished the large brick sewers, introducing pipe drains, and turned the contents of 30,000 cesspools into the river Thames. The necessity for purifying the defiled river led to the construction of a new system of drainage, under the superintendence of the Metropolitan Board of Works (*which see*). The main drainage (the plan of Mr. J. W. Bazalgette) consists of the northern high-level, middle-level, and low-level, and southern high-level and low-level. On 14 March, 1865, the works were said to be completed, except the low-level sewer on the north side, which was waiting for the completion of the Thames embankment, &c. On 4 April, 1865, the prince of Wales started the engines which commenced lifting the waters of the southern outfall, at Crossness Point, near Erith.* The main drainage works of the metropolis (82 miles), were finally completed Aug. 1875. The sewage is carried 14 miles down the river. Total cost, 4,500,000*l*. See *Carbolic Acid*.

Royal commission on the Metropolitan Sewage discharge (lord Bramwell, sir John Coode, prof. A. W. Williamson and others), appointed 22 June, 1882; reports on the great contamination of the Thames at the outfalls, and need of change; approves of the combination of chemical precipitation with filtration through earth, June and Dec. 1884.
Mr. Wm. Webster's method of decomposing London sewage by electricity set up at Crossness; reported successful on inspection . March, 1889
Mr. H. Wollheim's process, the "Amines" (or ammonia compounds), reported successful; exhibited at Wimbledon Sewage farm, Aug.; before the lord mayor and others . 18 Sept. „
City Commission of Sewers, after 230 years existence, absorbed by the corporation of London, by act passed, 1897, final meeting . . . 4 Jan. 1898
Messrs. Stone & Co.'s system of sewer ventilation and purification reported successful at Deptford, 1900–1901
Royal commission appointed, May, 1898; third report, scientific investigation needed, 3 March, 1903

SEWING-MACHINE. It is said that Thomas Saint patented one for boots and shoes in 1790. Similar inventions are ascribed to Duncan (1804); Adams and Dodge (American, 1818); Thimonnier (French, 1834); and Walter Hunt (1834). The first really practical sewing-machine was the invention of Elias Howe, an American mechanic, of Cambridge, in Massachusetts, about 1841, who died at Brooklyn, 2 Oct. 1867, aged 47. It is now known under an improved form as Thomas's shuttle machine, by whom it was introduced into England in 1846. Many improvements have been since made and new machines invented.

SEXAGESIMA SUNDAY, see *Quadragesima Sunday* and *Week*.

SEXTANT, an instrument used like a quadrant, containing sixty degrees, or the sixth part of a circle, invented by Tycho Brahe, at Augsburg, in 1550. The Arabian astronomers are said to have had a sextant of fifty-nine feet nine inches radius, about 995.

SEYCHELLES ISLES (Indian Ocean), settled by the French about 1768; captured by the British, 1794; ceded to them, 1815. A dependency of Mauritius until 9 Nov. 1903, when the isles were proclaimed a separate colony by letters patent. First governor, Mr. E. B. Sweet, 9 Nov. 1903. Population, 1894, 17,000; 1902, 19,772.

SFAXEES, see *Tunis*.

SHADOWING, a term applied in Ireland to the practice of the police, closely following persons

* *The utilisation of disinfected sewage* as manure is now much advocated. Great success is said to have been attained at Edinburgh, Carlisle, Croydon, and other places. Much hot controversy has arisen respecting this disposal of the London sewage. On 15 Nov. 1864, the Metropolitan board accepted a contract for its disposal from Messrs. Hope and Napier. Sewage Utilisation acts were passed in 1865 and 1867, and the Metropolitan Sewage and Essex Reclamation acts were passed in June, 1865. The sewage farm, near Barking, Essex, was reported to be flourishing in 1868: good grass and corn crops raised.

suspected of boycotting, or intimidating persons opposed to the National League, 1889-91.

SHAFTESBURY'S ACT, LORD, 18 & 19 Vict. c. 86 (1855), relates to religious worship.

SHAFTESBURY MEMORIALS, relating to the earl of Shaftesbury, celebrated for his life-long exertions to ameliorate the condition of the working classes, the poor and destitute, women and children. He died 1 Oct. 1885, aged 84. A large sum was subscribed for two statues and a national convalescent home, Oct. 1885. A statue uncovered in Westminster Abbey by the baroness Burdett-Coutts, 1 Oct. 1888. A memorial fountain and bust by Alfred Gilbert set up in Piccadilly circus, inaugurated by the duke of Westminster, 29 June, 1893. The *Shaftesbury* training-ship established 1878. See *Ragged Schools*, 1898.

Shaftesbury-avenue murder (see *Trials*) . July, 1894

SHAFTESBURY PARK ESTATE, near Wandsworth, London, S.W., a model village, and termed "a workman's city;" built here for clerks, artizans, and labourers, by a company, was opened by the earl of Shaftesbury, 3 Nov. 1873, and 18 July, 1874.

SHAKERS, an English sect, now chiefly found in America, arose in the time of Charles I., and derived its name from their voluntary convulsion. It existed for a short time only, but was revived by James Wardlaw in 1747, and still more by Ann Lee (or Standless), expelled quakers, about 1757. The sect emigrated to America, May, 1772, and settled near Albany, New York, 1774. They denounce marriage as sinful, regard celibacy as holy, oppose war, disown baptism and the Lord's supper, and use dancing as part of their worship. *Marsden.* One of their elders, Fred. W. Evans, lectured in London, Aug. 1871.

Above a hundred English persons, incorrectly termed shakers, settled in the New Forest, near Lymington, Hampshire, on property obtained for them by a Miss Wood in 1872; not paying the interest of a mortgage they were ejected in severe weather, and suffered much; end of Dec. 1874. They are called Girlingites, from Mrs. Girling, a leader among them, who died 18 Sept. 1886. The community then gradually dispersed.

Goods seized for debt, about 27 July; expelled, 22 Aug.; permitted to remain in the neighbourhood, Oct. 1878.

Miss Wood was confined as a lunatic, 27 Feb. 1875.

20 men and 40 women half-starved in the New Forest; will not work for hire, Jan. 1884.

SHAKSPEARE'S PLAYS. William Shakspeare was born at Stratford-upon-Avon, Warwickshire, (23) April, 1564, and died 23 April, 1616. [An act to incorporate the Trustees and Guardians of Shakspeare's birthplace was passed 26 March, 1891.] The first collected edition of his works is dated 1623 [a facsimile of this edition was published, 1862-5]; the second, 1632;* the third, 1664; the fourth, 1685; all in folio. Critical editions of the text, edited by Alexander Dyce, were published in 1857 and 1864-6; Boydell's edition, with numerous plates, was published in nine vols., folio, in 1802. Ayscough's Index to Shakspeare was published in 1790; Twiss's Index, in 1805, and Mrs. Cowden Clarke's Concordance, 1847, she died, aged 88, 12 Jan. 1898; "Key to Shakspeare," 1879; Shakspeare-Lexicon, by Alexander Schmidt, 1874-5; "A Life of Wm. Shakespeare," by Sidney Lee. illustrated, published, Nov. 1898; new edition, portion of Macmillan's "Eversley Series," to be in 10 crown 8vo vols., editor, prof. C. H. Herford, published, Feb. 1899.

Shakspeare's first plays were probably produced about 1590, and soon after represented, himself frequently taking a part at the "Theatre," or the "Curtain," near Shoreditch, E. London, and after 1594, at the new "Globe" theatre, Bankside, Southwark, of which Shakspeare himself was part proprietor. It was of a horse-shoe form, partly covered with thatch. After it was licensed, the thatch took fire, through the negligent discharge of a piece of ordnance, and the whole building was consumed, 29 June, 1613. The house was crowded to excess, to witness the play of *Henry VIII.*; but the audience escaped unhurt.

SHAKSPEARE'S JUBILEE, projected by David Garrick, was celebrated at Stratford-upon-Avon, 6-8 Sept. 1769. A similar festival was kept 23 April, 1836. The *tercentenary* of Shakspeare's birth was celebrated, with many festivities, at Stratford-upon-Avon, 23-29 April, 1864.

SHAKSPEARE'S HOUSE. In 1847, a number of persons of distinction interested themselves for the preservation of the house in which Shakspeare was born, then actually put up for sale: they held a meeting at the Thatched-house tavern, London, 26 Aug. in that year, and took measures for promoting a subscription set on foot by the Shakspearian Club at Stratford-upon-Avon; and a committee was appointed to carry out their object. In the end Shakspeare's house was sold at the Auction Mart in the city of London, where it was "knocked down" to the United Committee of London and Stratford for the large sum of 3000*l.* 16 Sept. 1847. In 1856, a learned oriental scholar, John Shakspeare (no relation of the poet), gave 2500*l.* to purchase the adjoining house, that it might be pulled down, in order to ensure the poet's house from the risk of fire.

His wife's (Anne Hathaway) cottage and furniture purchased for 3050*l.*, 5 May, 1893.

Mr. Matthias Mull, a remarkable emendator of Shakespeare's text, died early Oct. 1893.

SHAKSPEARE FUND, established in Oct. 1861, to purchase Shakspeare's garden, birth-place estate, and to erect and endow a public library and museum at Stratford-upon-Avon. The catalogue of the library and museum was published, Feb. 1868. Books bequeathed by Mrs. Cowden Clarke and gifts by the late Mr. Halliwell-Phillips and others in 1897.

SHAKSPEARE MEMORIAL ASSOCIATION established 1875; eleventh annual meeting at Stratford-upon-Avon 28 April, 1886. A monument surmounted by a statue of Shakspeare, including statues of Shakspearian characters, executed by lord Ronald Gower, presented by him to the association, set up at Stratford-upon-Avon, unveiled by lady Hodgson (the mayoress) 10 Oct. 1888.

Bronze statue of Shakspeare (presented by Mr. William Knighton) erected in the boulevard Haussmann, Paris, unveiled 14 Oct. 1888.

The hon. Ignatius Donnelly, an American, reports his discovery of a cryptogram of Francis Bacon in the text of one of the plays in the folio of 1623, and thereon asserts his belief that Bacon was the author of the Shakspeare plays, autumn 1887. His book entitled "The Great Cryptogram: Francis Bacon's cipher in the so-called Shakspeare Plays" was published in 1888. Mr. Donnelly died, 2 Jan. 1901; controversy renewed, see *Times*, 6 Jan. 1902.

The SHAKSPEARE LIBRARY, at Birmingham, was founded

* In 1849, Mr. J. P. Collier, editor of an edition of Shakspeare, purchased a copy of the second folio, on which was written in pencil a number of corrections, supposed to have been made soon after publication. At first he thought little of these marks; but in 1853 he was induced to publish "Notes and Emendations" derived from this volume. Much controversy ensued as to the authenticity of these corrections; and in 1859 it was generally agreed that they were of modern date, and so of little value. Mr. Collier died, aged 94, 17 Sept. 1883. New Variorum edition by H. Howard Furness, vol. ii., 1898.

in 1864, and formally opened, 23 April, 1868; burnt 11 Jan. 1879.

SHAKSPEARE FORGERIES, see *Ireland*.

SHAKSPEARE GALLERY, see *Boydell*.

SHAKSPEARE MEMORIAL THEATRE, Stratford (capable of holding 800); foundation laid by lord Leigh, 23 April, 1877; opened with ceremonies, 23 April, 1879. Shakspeare memorial week, Mr. F. R. Benson and company perform the entire play of *Hamlet* and other plays, 24 April *et seq*. 1899; held annually.

Mdme. Sarah Bernhardt and company play *Hamlet* here, 29 June, 1899.

A fine copy of the first folio edition of Shakspeare, 1623, sold for 1,700*l*., 11 July, 1899; facsimile printed, Oxford, 1902.

Revival of Shakspeare's plays, with splendid scenery, by Henry Irving, at the Lyceum (*which see* under *Theatres*, 1874 *et seq*.).

SHAKSPEARE SOCIETY, issued 20 volumes, 1841-53.

NEW SHAKSPEARE SOCIETY issues works, 1874 *et seq.*

SHAKSPEARIAN SHOW at the Royal Albert Hall, 30 May, 1884.

Halliwell-Phillipps, "Shakspearean Rarities" (portraits, personal relics, books, &c.), offered for sale, Jan. 1890.

Stratford-on-Avon visited by the prince of Wales, 18 May, 1895.

A bronze bust of Shakspeare, by the late Wm. Page, of New York, presented by his family, unveiled by sir W. Treloar at Stratford-on-Avon, 23 June, 1900; a first folio Shakspeare sold for 1,720*l*., 16 July, 1901.

Shakspeare commemorations: 338th anniversary of his birth celebrated, 23 April; 9 plays performed, 14-26 April, 1902; again, 23 April, 1903.

London Shakspeare commemoration league; committee, rev. Stopford Brooke, Mr. Wm. Poel, Mr. Walter Crane, and others, formed, early Aug. 1902.

SHAMROCK. It is said that the shamrock used by the Irish was adopted by Patrick M'Alpine, since called St. Patrick, as a simile of the Trinity, about 432. The shamrock to be worn by Irish troops on St. Patrick's day, to commemorate the bravery of the Irish in the South African war, by order of queen Victoria, 7 March, 1900. St. Patrick's day celebrated in London and elsewhere, 17 March, 1900. See also *Yacht*.

SHANGHAI, or **SHANGHAE** (China), captured by the British, 19 June, 1842; by the Taeping rebels, 7 Sept. 1853; retaken by the imperialists, 1855. The rebels were defeated near Shanghai by the English and French, allies of the emperor, 1 March, 1862. Population, 1890, about 380,000; see *China*.

Visit of the duke and duchess of Connaught; he unveils a statue of sir H. Parkes . 9 April, 1890
Great fire; about 1,000 houses destroyed, 3 April, 1894
Much trouble through the war (see *Corea*) . Oct. ,,

SHARPSBURG (Maryland), see *Antietam*.

SHAWLS, of oriental origin, were introduced into Paris after the return of Napoleon Bonaparte from Egypt, 1801. The manufacture was introduced by Barrow and Watson, in 1784, at Norwich. It began at Paisley and Edinburgh about 1805. *Ure*.

SHEEP were exported from England to Spain, and, the breed being thereby improved, produced the fine Spanish wool, which proved detrimental to our woollen manufacture, 1467. *Anderson*. Their exportation was prohibited on pain of fine and imprisonment, 1522. The number of sheep in the United Kingdom has been variously stated—by some at 43,000,000, by others at 49,000,000, and by more at 60,000,000, in 1840. In 1851 there were imported into England 201,859 sheep and lambs; in 1858, 184,482; in 1864, 496,243. See under *Cattle*. In Aug. and Sept. 1862, many sheep in Wiltshire died of smallpox; and on Sept. 11, government declared for enforcing the act for the prevention of contagion. The evil soon abated. In April, 1866, the disease reappeared and the regulations were re-issued.

Mortality amongst sheep through flukes, &c., April, 1880

In 1865, 914,170 sheep and lambs were imported; in 1868, 341,155; in 1871, 916,799; 1874, 758,915; 1875, 985,652; 1876, 1,041,329; 1877, 874,055; 1878, 892,125; 1879, 944,888; 1880, 941,121; 1881, 935,144; 1882, 1,124,391; 1883, 1,116,115; 1885, 750,886; 1887, 971,404; 1888, 956,210; 1889, 677,958; 1890, 358,458; 1891, 344,504; 1892, 79,048; 1893, 62,682; 1900, 382,833; 1901, 383,594.

For number in Great Britain, see under *Cattle*.

SHEEPSHANKS' DONATIONS. On 2 Feb. 1857, Mr. John Sheepshanks, by a deed of gift, presented to the nation his valuable collection of paintings and drawings, valued at 60,000*l*. In accordance with the donor's directions, the pictures were placed in the South Kensington museum. The collection is rich in the works of Mulready, Landseer, and Leslie. He died 5 Oct. 1863.—On 2 Dec. 1858, the trustees of his brother, the late rev. Richard Sheepshanks, presented 10,000*l*. stock to Trinity college, Cambridge, for the promotion of the study of astronomy, meteorology, and magnetism.

SHEERNESS (N. Kent), a royal dockyard, planned by Charles II. in 1663, was taken by the Dutch, under De Ruyter, 9 June, 1667. Improved since 1815; new fortifications still in progress. Population, 1881, 14,286; 1891, 13,281; 1901, 14,492.

The old dock church burned; 3 persons killed, 26 Nov. 1881.

SHEFFIELD, on the river *Sheaf*, West Riding, Yorkshire; renowned for cutlery, plated goods, &c. Sheffield thwytles are mentioned by Chaucer, in the time of Edward III. Sheffield in the time of the Conqueror was obtained by Roger de Buisli, and has since been held by the Lovetots, Nevils, Talbots, and Howards. See *Population*.

St. Peter's church built temp. Henry I.
Hospital and almshouses erected by the earl of Malmesbury 1616
Cutlers' company incorporated . . . 1624
The castle (built in the 13th century) was taken by the parliamentarians in 1644, and demolished . 1648
Cutlers' hall built 1726
Plate assay office established . . . 1773
Made a borough by the Reform act . . . 1832
Wesley college opened 1838
Sheffield and Manchester railway opened . 1845
Athenæum and Mechanics' institution opened . 1849
John A. Roebuck (grandson of Dr. Roebuck of Sheffield), M.P. for Sheffield . May, 1849-68
Embankment of the Bradfield water reservoir broke down, and flooded Sheffield and the country 12 or 14 miles round; about 250 lives were lost; many buildings and much property destroyed; estimated loss, 327,000*l*. . . . 11 March, 1864
The Atlas armour works constructed by sir John Brown in 1864, see *Iron*.
52,751*l*. collected for the sufferers by . 29 April, ,,
The Surrey music hall burnt . . 25 March, 1865
House of Fearnehough, a non-unionist saw-grinder, blown up (no deaths) . . . 8 Oct. 1866
Great excitement; meetings held; subscriptions made; a Sheffield manufacturers' protection society formed; and rewards offered, 12 Oct. &c. ,,

A commission (headed by Mr. Overend) to enquire into trade outrages met . . 3 June-8 July, 1867

[Several murders and outrages (including the above) confessed to by Crookes, Hallam, and others, instigated and paid by Wm. Broadhead, secretary to the saw-grinders' union; indemnity granted.]

A meeting of workmen expresses abhorrence, 8 July, „

Mr. Roebuck loses his election (through opposing rattening) . . . . Nov. 1868

Great loss of life and property by a gale 16 Dec. 1873

Mr. Roebuck re-elected M.P. . . . . Feb. 1874

Five board schools opened by the abp. of York, Mr. Roebuck, Mr. Forster, and others, 18 Aug. „

Prince and princess of Wales open Firth park, the gift of Mark Firth, the mayor; most euthusiastically received . . . . 16 Aug. 1875

Public museum and hall opened . . 6 Sept. „

Eighteenth Church Congress held here, 1–4 Oct. 1878

Great distress through stoppage of work, winter, 1878-9

Institution for the blind, endowed by Mr. Daniel Holy; opened . . . . 24 Sept. 1879

Firth College, built by Mr. Mark Firth, for 20,000*l.*; endowed by the town; inaugurated by prince Leopold . . . . 20 Oct. „

Death of Mr. Roebuck, M.P. for Sheffield, 30 Nov. „

Ruskin Museum of Art, &c., founded by Mr. John Ruskin, by gifts of historical sculpture, paintings, books, &c., 1881; lent to the corporation for 20 years; removed from Walkley to Meersbrook hall; re-opened . . . . April, 1890

New corn exchange, built by the duke of Norfolk, cost 55,000*l.*, opened . . . . . . 13 Dec. „

Ruskin Society formed . . . . . . Feb. 1882

Great conservative demonstration (marquis of Salisbury and others) . . . . . 22 July, 1884

Returns five M.P's. by act passed . 25 June, 1885

Technical school opened . . . . . 1 Feb. 1886

Explosion at Don steel works, Brightside, while casting a gun; 9 killed . . . . 6 Sept. 1887

Severe epidemic of small-pox March, 1887–April, 1888

New municipal buildings founded . . 9 Oct. 1891

Constituted a city 1893

Premises of Messrs. Hovey and other establishments burnt; 1 death . . . . 21 Dec. „

The earl of Rosebery at the 271st annual cutlers' feast . . . . 25 Oct. 1894

Visit of the duke and duchess of York 10–14 May, 1895

The town trustees vote 10,000*l.* towards the endowment of Firth college . . . July, „

Mr. G. Woofenden bequeaths 120,700*l.* to charities, June, „

Sheffield school system, groups of 15 pauper children isolated in cottages reported successful, 2 Dec. 1896

Death of sir John Brown, pioneer of armour-plate manufacture for defence of ships . . 27 Dec. „

Mrs. Jane E. Rodgers died, leaving 26,886*l.* and other charitable bequests to Sheffield . 11 Dec. „

Visit of the queen; received by the duke of Norfolk, the mayor; opened the new town hall; reviewed 50,000 children in the Norfolk park and visited the Cyclops works . . . . 21 May, 1897

Overhead electric tramway opened . . . 4 Sept. 1899

Lord Kitchener receives the freedom, &c., 30 Sept. 1902

Musical festival; the choir highly praised 1 Oct. „

Foundation stone of the new University college laid by the lord mayor of London . 30 June, 1903

Great conference of Nat. Union of Conservative and Constitutional associations, about 2000 delegates. Important speech on fiscal policy by Mr. A. J. Balfour at meeting in Artillery drill hall, 1 Oct. „

Lord Rosebery speaks on free trade at greal Liberal league demonstration in Albert hall . 13 Oct. „

SHELBURNE ADMINISTRATION, formed at the death of the marquis of Rockingham, July, 1782; terminated April, 1783; the "Coalition" administration followed.

The earl of Shelburne* (afterwards marquis of Lansdowne), *first lord of the treasury.*
William Pitt, *chancellor of the exchequer.*
Lord (afterwards earl) Camden, *president of the council.*
Duke of Grafton, *privy seal.*
Thomas, lord Grantham, and Thomas Townshend (afterwards lord Sydney), *secretaries.*
Viscount Keppel, *admiralty.*
Duke of Richmond, *ordnance.*
Lord Thurlow, *lord chancellor.*
Henry Dundas, Isaac Barré, sir George Yonge, &c.

* William Petty, earl of Shelburne, born 1737; secretary of state under lord Chatham, July, 1766; premier, 1782-3; created first marquis of Lansdowne, 1784; died, 7 May, 1805.

SHELLEY SOCIETY, founded by Dr. F. J. Furnivall, and Messrs. H. Sweet, W. M. Rossetti, Todhunter, and others, 1885. In July, 1892, it was proposed by lord Tennyson and others, to celebrate the centenary of the birth of Shelley, by establishing a library and museum at Horsham, Sussex, near which place he was born. A mural tablet commemorating his birth, 4 Aug. 1792, and his death, 8 July, 1822, was set up publicly in the parish church 4 Aug., 1892.

SHELLS, see *Bombs.*

SHERIFF, or *shire-reeve*, governor of a shire or county. London had its sheriffs prior to William I.'s reign; but some say that sheriffs were first nominated for every county in England by William in 1079. According to other historians, Henry Cornhill and Richard Reynere were the first sheriffs of London, 1 Rich. I., 1189. The nomination of sheriffs, according to the present mode, took place in 1461. *Stow.* Anciently sheriffs were hereditary in Scotland, and in some English counties, as Westmoreland. The sheriffs of Dublin (first called bailiffs) were appointed in 1308, and obtained the name of sheriff by an incorporation of Edward VI. 1548. Thirty-five sheriffs were fined, and eleven excused in one year, rather than serve the office for London, 1734; see *Bailiffs.* The high sheriffs of the counties of England and Wales, except Middlesex and Lancaster, are nominated on the morrow of St. Martin, Nov. 12. This somewhat vice-regal office, of Saxon origin, has gradually lost much of its importance.

The sheriffs' act passed 1887

SHERIFFMUIR, see *Dumblane.*

SHERIFF'S FUND, see *Prisons.*

SHETLAND ISLES, see *Orkneys.*

SHIBBOLETH, the word by which the followers of Jephthah tested their opponents the Ephraimites, on passing the Jordan, about 1143 B.C. *Judges* xii. The term is now applied to any party watchword or dogma.

SHIITES, the Mahometan sect predominating in Persia; see *Mahometanism.*

SHILLING. The value of the ancient Saxon coin of this name was fivepence, but it was reduced to fourpence about a century before the conquest. After the conquest the French *solidus* of twelve pence, in use among the Normans, was called *shilling.* The true English shilling was first coined, some say, in small numbers, by Henry VII., 1504. *Ruding.* A peculiar shilling, value nine pence, but to be current at twelve, was struck in Ireland, 1560; and a large but very base coinage in England for the service of Ireland, 1598. Milled shillings were coined 13 Chas. II. 1662; see *Coins.*

SHILOH, see *Pittsburg.*

SHIP-BUILDING, &c., according to the Greek legends, began with the Egyptians, and ancient drawings of their rude vessels are extant. The Greeks, Phœnicians, and Carthaginians were skilful shipbuilders, and Solomon's "navy of ships" (1 *Kings* ix. 26), was doubtless constructed by Tyrians, 992 B.C. The ships of Tarshish (probably in Spain), are mentioned in *Psalm* xlviii. 7, *Isaiah* ii. 16, &c. The Romans built their first fleet of boats, by copying a Carthaginian vessel wrecked on their coast, 260 B.C. The dangers of navigation are described in *Psalm* cvii. 23-30 and *Acts* xxvii. Strong vessels were constructed by the Norsemen for invasion and piracy in the 5th century A.D. *et seq.*, and by the Venetians and other Italians, for commerce and war in the Middle Ages. The first double-decked ship built in England was of 1000 tons burthen, by order of Henry VII., was called the *Great Harry*, and cost 14,000*l.* *Stow.* Port-holes and other improvements were invented by Descharges, a French builder at Brest, in the reign of Louis XII., about 1500. Ship-building was treated as a science by Hoste, 1696. Iron and steel are now greatly used in ship-building.

A prehistoric ship cut out of solid oak, 48 feet long, 4 feet 4 inches wide, and 2 feet deep, was found by the Brigg gas company while excavating near the river Ancholme in Lincolnshire, April, 1885. Mr. Justice Chitty decided 6 July, 1886, that the ship was the property of the owner of the land, Mr. Elwes.

The *France*, a great sailing ship, was built on the Clyde by Messrs. Henderson for a Bordeaux firm; five masts, 360 feet long, 48 feet wide, bowsprit 50 feet long; carrying power over 6,000 tons Sept. 1890

Ships, originally made of wood, and latterly of iron, are now frequently made of steel.

Internat. congress, 550 delegates (the earl of Glasgow, lord Brassey, and others) opened by the crown prince at Düsseldorf . . . 2 June, 1902

See *Navy*, *Steam*, *Carrack*, &c.

SHIPKA, see *Schipka*.

SHIP-MONEY was first levied about 1007, to form a navy to oppose the Danes. This impost, levied by Charles I. in 1634-6, was much opposed, and led to the revolution. He assessed London in seven ships, of 4000 tons, and 1560 men; Yorkshire in two ships, of 600 tons or 12,000*l.*; Bristol in one ship of 100 tons; Lancashire in one ship, of 400 tons. Among others, John Hampden refused to pay the tax; he was tried in the Exchequer in 1636. The judges declared the tax legal, 12 June, 1637. Ship-money was included in the grievances complained of in 1641. The five judges, who had given an opinion in its favour, were imprisoned. Hampden received a wound in a skirmish with prince Rupert, at Chalgrove, 18 June, and died 24 June, 1643.

SHIPPING, BRITISH. Shipping was first registered in the river Thames in 1786; and throughout the empire in 1787. In the middle of the 18th century, the shipping of England was but half-a-million of tons—less than London now. In 1830, the number of ships in the British empire was 22,785. The merchant shipping act of 1854 was amended in 1867; see *Merchant Shipping Act*, *Navy*, and *Navigation Acts*. *Trials*, 1893.

General Shipowners' Society; 57th annual meeting, London . . . . 18 July, 1893

Shipwrights' Company International Exhibition, opened at Fishmongers' Hall, London, by the duke of Edinburgh . . . . . 2 May, 1882

Chamber of Shipping of the United Kingdom was established in 1878, mainly by H. J. Atkinson, M.P., the first president. Meetings are held for discussing matters relative to shipping and to disseminate information. It holds annual meetings; 1878, Hull; 1879, Liverpool; 1880, London; 1881, Cardiff; 1882, London; 1883, Sunderland; 1884, London; 1885, Belfast; 1886, London; 1887, Newcastle-on-Tyne; London: 1888, 1889, 1890 (13 Feb.), 1891 (20 Feb.), 1892 (10 Feb.), 1893 (1 Feb.), 1894 (14 Feb.), 1895 (13 Feb.); 12 Feb. 1896; 17 Feb. 1897; 16 Feb. 1898; 8 Feb 1899; 20 Feb. 1903. The chamber has an office in London.

The London Shipping Exchange (sir D. Currie, chairman) opened by the lord mayor . 30 Jan. 1893

The National Seamen's and Firemen's Union established 1889

Federation of shipowners of the United Kingdom, established to resist strikes and maintain free labour, Sept.; joined by the London Association of shipowners, Nov. 1890; and by those of Liverpool . . . . . . Feb. 1891

Boycotting of free labour in the docks of London stopped by the Shipping Federation, Dec. 1890—Feb. ,,

Cardiff: strike of the shipping trades; conflicts between the Shipping Federation and the Seamen's Union; the latter defeated, Feb.; rioters punished; strike ends . . . 14 March, ,,

The crisis on the Thames ends; work resumed March, ,,

The Shipping Federation proposes a scheme for the insurance of the lives of its sailors and firemen against death by accident, about 14 April; the scheme adopted, May, 1891; carried into effect 1 Jan. 1892

Strike at Hull (*which see*) . . . April—May, 1893

Disputes in the trade begun by the Clyde engineers, 29 March *et seq.* 1895

Conference of Belfast and Clyde shipbuilders and their operative engineers, at Carlisle . 23 Oct. ,,

The master's terms temporarily accepted, except by the Belfast men, 25 Oct.; (closed at Belfast by concessions to the men, 17 Dec. 1895.)

Conference of employers at Glasgow, 1 Nov.; many engineers locked out on the Clyde, 5 Nov.; conference at Glasgow, under lord James of Hereford, 10 Dec.; the masters' proposals rejected by ballot, Dec.; close of the strike by the decisive action of the executive council of the Amalgamated engineers, 22 Jan.; agreement signed, 23 Jan. 1896

Advance of wages conceded on demand to workmen on the Tyne, Wear, and Tees . 1 April, ,,

Dispute revived on the Clyde, at Belfast, and on the Wear, Aug.—Sept.; ended on the Clyde, 8 Sept. ,,

The London Docks, &c. association determine to abide by the Mansion house agreement (see *Strikes*, 14 Sept. 1889) . . . 16 Sept. ,,

The Shipping federation issue a notice urgently maintaining free labour . . . Sept. ,,

North Atlantic Shipping Trust, see *Steam*, 19 April, 1902

Internat. congress held at Dusseldorf . 30 June, ,,

Shipping exhibition at Whitechapel opened, 6 Oct.; visited by the prince and princess of Wales, 13 Oct. 1903

NUMBER OF VESSELS REGISTERED IN THE BRITISH EMPIRE ON JAN. 1, 1840.

Country.	*Vessels.*	*Tonnage.*	*Seamen.*
England	15,830	1,983,522	114,593
Scotland	3,318	378,194	25,909
Ireland	1,889	169,289	11,288
Guernsey, Jersey, and Man	633	39,630	4,473
British Plantations	6,075	497,798	35,020
Total	27,745	3,068,433	191,283

The following are the numbers of the Registered Sailing and Steam Vessels (exclusive of River Steamers) of the United Kingdom, engaged in the home and foreign trade:—

	1849.		1861.		1877.		1887.		1901.	
	Vessels*	Tonnage.	Vessels†	Tonnage.	Vessels §	Tonnage.	Vessels‖	Tonnage.	Vessels ‡	Tonnage.
Sailing .	17,807	2,988,021	19,288	3,918,511	17,101	4,138,149	12,694	3,114,430	7,026	1,839,190
Steamers.	414	108,321	997	441,184	3,218	1,977,489	5,029	4,009,324	7,548	7,685,306
Total .	18,221	3,096,342	20,285	4,359,695	20,319	6,115,638	17,723	7,123,754	14,574	9,524,496

1890 : Sailing vessels, 14,181 ; Steamers, 7,410.
1891 ,, ,, 13,823 ,, 7,720.
1892 ,, ,, 13,578 ,, 7,950.
1893 ,, ,, 13,239 ,, 8,088.
1894 ,, ,, 12,943 ,, 8,263.
1895 ,, ,, 12,617 ,, 8,385.

1896 : Sailing vessels, 12,274 ; Steamers, 8,522.
1897 ,, ,, 11,911 ,, 8,590.
1898 ,, ,, 11,566 ,, 8,838.
1899 ,, ,, 11,167 ,, 9,029.
1900 ,, ,, 10,773 ,, 9,209.
1901 ,, ,, 10,572 ,, 9,484.

* Men employed—sailing vessels, 144,165 ; steamers, 8,446 ; total, 152,611.
† ,, ,, ,, ,, 144,949 ; ,, 27,008 ; ,, 171,957.
§ ,, ,, ,, ,, 123,563 ; ,, 72,999 ; ,, 196,562.
‖ ,, ,, ,, ,, 81,442 ; ,, 121,101 ; ,, 202,543.
‡ ,, ,, ,, ,, 46,492 ; ,, 201,481 ; ,, 247,973.

SHIP-RAILWAY, see *Railways*, Oct. 1889.

SHIPWRECKS, see *Wrecks*.

SHIRES, see *Counties* and under *Horse*.

SHIRTS are said to have been first generally worn in the west of Europe early in the 8th century. *Du Fresnoy*. Woollen shirts were commonly worn in England until about 1253, when linen, but of a coarse kind (fine coming at this period from abroad), was first manufactured in England by Flemish artisans. *Stow*.

SHODDY, a kind of soft woollen goods, manufactured from old woollen rags, or the refuse, to which new wool is added, is stated to have been first manufactured about 1813, at Batley, near Dewsbury, Yorkshire.

SHOEBLACK SOCIETY Brigades (Blue, Red, and Yellow) were established at various times, especially in 1850, by Mr. John MacGregor, "Rob Roy," in connexion with the Ragged School Union. In 1855, 108 boys had cleaned 544,800 pairs of boots and shoes, and thus earned 2270*l*.; of which 1235*l*. had been paid to the boys, 519*l*. to their bank, and 516*l*. to the society. The brigades earned 4548*l*. in 1859; 11,031*l*. in 1871; 10,936*l*. (in nine districts) in 1886. Ragged School Union reported 319 boys earning 6770*l*., 1895. There were eleven shoeblack societies in the metropolis in 1888.

SHOEBURYNESS (Essex). Some ground here, purchased in 1842 and 1855, by an act of parliament in 1862 was set apart as "ranges for the use and practice of artillery," and a school for gunnery was established; see *Cannon*, note. Experiments with Mr. Whitworth's projectiles on 12 Nov. 1862, showed their great improvement in form and material. Shells were sent through 5½ inch plate and the wood-work behind it. It was objected, that they might not do this with ships in motion. The National Volunteer Artillery Association began their annual meetings here in July, 1865.

During shell experiments with a new sensitive fuse, col. Francis Lyon (the inventor), col. Fox-Strangways, capt. Francis M. Goold-Adams, and four others were killed, 26 Feb. 1885.

SHOES, among the Jews were made of leather, linen, rush, or wood. Moons were worn as ornaments in their shoes by Jewish women. *Isaiah* iii. 18. Pythagoras would have his disciples wear shoes made of the bark of trees; probably that they might not wear what were made of the skins of animals, as they refrained from the use of everything that had life. The Romans wore an ivory crescent on their shoes, and Caligula enriched his with precious stones. In England, about 146,2 the people wore the beaks or points of their shoes so long that they encumbered themselves in walking, and were forced to tie them up to their knees; the fine gentlemen fastened theirs with chains of silver or silver gilt, and others with laces. This was prohibited, on the forfeiture of 20s. and on pain of being cursed by the clergy, 7 Edw. IV. 1467; see *Dress*. Shoes, as at present worn, were introduced about 1633. The buckle was not used till 1668. *Stow; Mortimer*. The buckle-makers petitioned against the use of *shoe-strings* in 1791. A strike of London shoemakers respecting wages, April, 1884.

SHOOTING STARS, see under *Meteors*.

SHOP HOURS' REGULATION ACT (Sir John Lubbock's), for the protection of young persons, passed, 1886, amended, 1892. His resolution against long hours adopted by the commons, 21 March, 1893. Amendment act passed, 21 Dec. 1893; another bill, withdrawn, April, 1895; stopped Aug. 1896. Shop assistants (seats) act passed, 9 Aug. 1899; shop clubs act, royal assent, 8 Aug. 1902; one passed (lords), 28 April, 1903.

SHOP-TAX enacted in 1785; caused so great a commotion, particularly in London, that it was deemed expedient to repeal it in 1789. The statute whereby *shoplifting* was made a felony, without benefit of clergy, was passed 10 & 11 Will. III. 1699. This statute has been some time repealed.

SHORE, JANE, the mistress of Edward IV. and afterwards of lord Hastings. She did public penance in 1483, and was afterwards confined in Ludgate; but upon the petition of Thomas Hymore, who agreed to marry her, king Richard III., in 1484, restored her to liberty: and sir Thomas More mentions having seen her. *Harleian MSS*.

SHORT-HAND, see *Stenography*.

"SHORT - LIVED" ADMINISTRATION—that of William Pulteney, earl of Bath, lord Carlisle, lord Winchilsea, and lord Granville, existed from 10 Feb. to 12 Feb. 1746.

SHOT. In early times various missiles were shot from cannon. Bolts are mentioned in 1413;

and in 1418 Henry V. ordered his clerk of the ordnance to get 7000 stone shot made at the quarries at Maidstone. Since then chain, grape, and canister shot have been invented, as well as shells, all of which are described in Scoffern's work on "Projectile Weapons of War, and Explosive Compounds," 1858; see *Bombs* and *Cannon*. For Palliser's chilled shot, see *Cannon*.

SHOWMEN'S SOCIETY held their first annual meeting and opposed the Movable Dwellings bill in 1892; second meeting, 25 Jan. 1893.

SHREWSBURY ADMINISTRATION. Charles, duke of Shrewsbury, was made lord treasurer, 29 July, 1714, two days before the death of queen Anne. His patent was revoked soon after the accession of George I., 29 Oct. following, when the earl of Halifax became first lord of the treasury; see *Halifax*. The office of lord treasurer has been executed by commissioners ever since.

SHREWSBURY (Shropshire), arose after the ruin of the Roman town Uriconium (see *Wroxeter*), and became one of the chief cities of the kingdom, having a mint till the reign of Henry III. Here Richard II. held a parliament in 1397.—On 21 July, 1403, was fought a sanguinary *battle* at Hateley field, near Shrewsbury, between the army of Henry IV. and that of the nobles, led by Percy (surnamed Hotspur), son of the earl of Northumberland, who had conspired to dethrone Henry. Henry was seen in the thickest of the fight, with his son, afterwards Henry V. The death of Hotspur by an unknown hand gave the victory to the king. *Hume*.—Shrewsbury grammar school was founded by Edward VI. in 1551, endowed by Elizabeth, and opened 1562. Its arrangements were modified by the public school act, 1868. A statue of Charles Darwin unveiled, 10 Aug. 1897. Population in 1881, 26,481; 1891, 26,962; 1901, 28,395.

250 voters deprived of franchise for receiving bribes at parliamentary election . . . . 24 Jan. 1903
500th anniversary of Shrewsbury battle celebrated, 19–22 July, „

SHROPSHIRE; by battles in this county the Britons were completely subjugated, and Caractacus, the king of the Silures, became, through the treachery of the queen of the Brigantes, a prisoner to the Romans, about 50.

SHROVE TUESDAY, the day before Ash-Wednesday, the first day of the Lent Fast; see *Carnival*.

SIAM, a kingdom in India, bordering on the Burmese empire. Siam was governed by two kings, one inferior, till Jan. 1887, when the second king being dead, the dignity was abolished. Siam was re-discovered by the Portuguese in 1511, and a trade established, in which the Dutch joined about 1604. A British ship arrived about 1613. In 1683, a Cephalonian Greek, Constantine Phaulcon, became foreign minister of Siam, and opened a communication with France; Louis XIV. sent an embassy in 1685 with a view of converting the king without effect. After several ineffectual attempts, sir John Bowring succeeded in obtaining a treaty of friendship and commerce between England and Siam, which was signed 30 April, 1855, and ratified 5 April, 1856. Two ambassadors from Siam arrived in Oct. 1857, and had an audience with the queen; they brought with them magnificent presents, which they delivered crawling, on 16 Nov. They visited Paris in June, 1861. By a treaty with France, the French protectorate over Cambodia was recognised; signed 15 July, ratified 24 Oct. 1867. The king Chulalonkorn, born 21 Sept. 1853, succeeded his father Mongkout, 1 Oct. 1868; the king was entertained at Calcutta, 7-12 Jan. 1872; a political constitution was decreed, 8 May, 1874. Queen Victoria receives the order of the White Elephant from the Siamese minister at Windsor, 2 July, 1880. Population of Siam (1891) about 9,000,000.

Various changes and political reforms were begun by the king, 16 Nov. 1873. On 9 Oct., 1874, he invited astronomers to Bangkok to view the eclipse of 5 April, 1875.

Death of the able ex-regent Somdetch Chau, 19 Jan. 1883.

Telegraphic communication with France opened, 14 July, 1883.

Gradual abolition of slavery nearly completed, Aug. 1886.

One of the king's sons (born 1878), declared the first crown prince, 1887.

Rebellion in N. Siam, headed by Phya Phraph Song Kuam, Sept. 1889; revived, May, 1890.

British boundary commission: complications, 1889–90; frontier question settled, reported Feb. 1893.

The king and queen visit the Straits Settlements, May, June, 1890.

The king turns the first sod for the Bangkok-Paknam railway (other railways promoted), announced 16 July, 1891; opened 11 April, 1893.

Prince Damrong, half-brother of the king, minister of education (on a mission), arrives at Paris, 27 Aug.; travels in Great Britain; received by the queen at Balmoral, 24 Sept.; arrives at Berlin, 6 Nov.; received by the czar at Livadia, 15 Nov.; by the sultan at Constantinople, 19 Nov.; at Athens by the king, 28 Nov.; at Rome by the king, 3 Dec.; by the khedive at Cairo, 24 Dec. 1891; at Bombay, 11 Jan.; at Rangoon, 12 March, 1892.

Dispute with France; conflict between a Franco-Annamite column and Laotian tribes on the Mekong river, subject to Siam; the French lose 3 men, 3 May, 1893; the Siamese retire from Cammon, reported 3 June; the French occupy Samit, an island, 13 June; reparation for the murder of M. Grosgurin demanded; Siam objects, about 18–20 June; more islands occupied by the French, about 3 July; admiral Humann, with French gunboats, goes up the Mekong; skirmish, with bloodshed on both sides, 13 July; French ultimatum sent, requiring payment of 3,000,000f. as an indemnity, and an enlargement of territory on the Mekong; the ultimatum partly accepted by the Siamese, 18, 19 July; M. Pavie, the French minister, recalled; capt. Adam de Villers takes Don-Dua and other forts; many Siamese killed, 19 July; Siam accepts the ultimatum unconditionally, 29 July; blockade of Siamese coast, 26 July; raised, 4 Aug.; the French envoy received by the king, reported 22 Aug.; difficulties overcome; a moderate draft-treaty signed, 3 Oct.; the French envoy leaves, 6 Oct. 1893.

Messages from queen Victoria and other foreign powers to the king of Siam on the silver jubilee of his reign, 6 Dec. 1893.

Phra Yot sentenced to 20 years' penal servitude for the murder of M. Grosgurin in 1893, 13 June, 1894.

Lamented death of the crown prince, aged 16; educated and trained after the English manner under Mr. Robert L. Morant, 4 Jan. 1895.

Royal decree, establishing a legislative council (ministers and nobles), 17 Jan. 1895.

Prince Damrong appointed chief minister, Jan. 1895.

Prince Chowfa Maha Vajiravudh, aged 16 (studying at Eton), proclaimed crown prince, 17 Jan.; invested with the honours at the Siamese legation, London, 8 March, 1895.

Dispute between England and France respecting the Mekong Mongsin territory, Aug. 1895.

Boundary treaty signed, the Mekong to be the boundary of the French possessions; Mongsin given over to France, 15 Jan.; evacuated 11 May, 1896.

Railway from Bangkok to Khorat constructed by Mr. M. Campbell; first half opened by the king at Bangkok, 27 March, 1897; second half to Lopburi, opened, July, 1901.

King Chulalonkorn arrives at Rome, received by king Humbert, 3 June; at Vienna, received by the emperor, 23 June; at Peterhof, 3 July; received by the czar, 7 July; at Copenhagen, received by the king, 23 July; received by the duke of York at Portsmouth, and by the duke of Cambridge in London at Buckingham palace, 30 July; with the queen at Osborne, 4 Aug.; Edinburgh, 10 Aug.; lord Armstrong's at Newcastle, 12 Aug.; received by the emperor at Potsdam, 26 Aug.; the Hague, 7 Sept.; Brussels, 9 Sept.; Paris, 11 Sept.; grand review (60,000) at St. Quentin, 14 Sept.; London, 17 Sept.; Oxford, 28 Sept.; Windsor, 29 Sept.; leaves London, 2 Oct.; Madrid, 16 Oct.; Lisbon, 21 Oct.; Cairo, reception by the khedive, 15 Nov.; arrives at Bangkok, amid festivities, 16 Dec. 1897.

"Five years in Siam," 1891–96, by H. Warington Smyth, published, May, 1898.

Great progress and reorganisation under British officials; Mr. Mitchell-Innes, financial adviser, leaves for Egypt; succeeded by Mr. Rivett-Carnac; Burmese village system introduced by prince Damrong, minister of finance, Prince Rabi, minister of justice, Jan. 1899.

Death of the king's son, prince Sommotwongse, June, 1899.

Perak boundary dispute settled by Mr. Greville, British minister, 19 Dec. 1899.

Mr. McCarthy, 12 years' exploration and map of Siam, completed, May, 1900.

Steady yearly increase of revenue; 65 gambling houses closed, 1899–1901.

British treaty of 1856 revised as to the land revenue; new agreement signed, early 1901.

Shan rebellion in the north, troops defeated, 23 July; Pray captured, buildings sacked, Siamese massacred, 25 July; Lakon abandoned by Europeans, early Aug.; the British consul from Nan persuades the Shans to leave Pray and give up other positions, 24 Aug. 1902.

Kelantan and Tringano virtually under British control, reported 3 Oct. 1902.

France restores Chentabun, but secures Meluprey, Bassak, &c.; treaty signed, 7 Oct. 1902.

Mr. Black appointed vice-minister of justice, reported, 28 Oct. 1902.

500 Shans surrender to the French across the Mekong, 15 Nov. 1902.

Rebels dispersed in the north, order restored, reported, 25 Nov. 1902.

Gold standard scheme accepted by foreign banks, early Dec. 1902.

Siamese Twins. Two persons born about 1811, enjoying all the faculties and powers usually possessed by separate and distinct individuals, although united together by a short cartilaginous band at the pit of the stomach. They were named Chang and Eng, and were first discovered on the banks of the Siam river by an American, Mr. Robert Hunter, by whom they were taken to New York, where they were exhibited. Captain Coffin brought them to England. After having been exhibited for several years in Britain, they went to America, where they settled on a farm, and married two sisters. In 1865 they were in North Carolina in declining health. Their exhibition in London began again 8 Feb. 1869. They died in America, within two hours of each other, 16, 17 Jan. 1874.

SIBERIA (N. Asia). In 1580 the conquest was begun by the Cossacks under Jermak Timofejew. In 1710 Peter the Great began to send prisoners thither. An insurrection broke out among the Poles in Siberia in June, 1866, and was soon suppressed. University founded, 1886. Population in 1885, 4,313,680. 9 Feb. 1897, 6,731,732.

Since 1863 efforts have been made to open up a sea route to central Siberia, especially by capt. Wiggins and his friends, 1874 *et seq.* In 1890 two vessels from London reached Karaoul on the Yenesei, stayed there 19 days, and returned in October.

The construction of a railway to Siberia, in ten years, was authorised, Feb. 1890; (see *Russia*, May, 1891).

A party of about 30 political exiles, including women and children, at Yakutsk, N.E. Siberia, were suspected of mutiny, very severely treated, and some persons were killed, 4 April. The exiles were tried by court-martial in May, and all were convicted, 18 June. Three men were hanged, 20 Aug. 1889. The story printed in the *Times*, 26 Dec. 1889, was at first contradicted and afterwards said to be exaggerated, March, 1890.

About 300 convicts, on their way to a penal settlement, rise against their warders, and are subdued after a conflict, with much bloodshed, reported 28 March, 1893.

Eastern section of the Trans-Siberian railway opened, Sept. 1893.

Capt. Wiggins' expedition through the Kara sea and up the Yenesei to deliver rails for the railway successful, reported 24 Jan.; he receives a handsome present from the czar at St. Petersburg, Feb. 1894.

Capt. Wiggins' steamship *Stjernen* wrecked in Yugor straits; all saved, 22 Sept.; arrives at Archangel, 15 Dec. 1894; arrives at St. Petersburg, 9 Jan. 1895; lectures to the London chamber of commerce, 18 March; an expedition under him to the Yenisei leaves the Tyne, 12 Aug. 1895; reported successful, 1896; British expedition in the *Glenmore* and *Scotia* arrives at Krasnoyarsk, autumn 1897.

Trans-Siberian railway, from Vladivostok to Nauraview Amurski (235 miles), opened for traffic, 20 Dec. 1894.

Important judicial reforms introduced, 14 July, 1897.

Successful expedition (11 steamers) of Mr. F. W. Popham in the *Naranja* (capt. Tinkler) and a flotilla through the Ob (or Obi) Gulf and up the Ob river, left London 20 July; returned 1 Oct. 1897.

The East Asiatic Ry. completed, 9 Nov. 1901.

New Siberian route from Port Arthur, S. Manchuria, to London in 18 days, opened 13 Jan. 1903.

SIBYLS, Sibyllæ, women believed to be inspired, who flourished in different parts of the world. Plato speaks of one, others of two, Pliny of three, Ælian of four, and Varro of ten. An Erythrean sibyl is said to have offered to Tarquin II. nine books containing the Roman destinies, demanding for them 300 pieces of gold. He denied her; whereupon the sibyl threw three of them into the fire, and asked the same price for the other six, which being still denied, she burnt three more, and again demanded the same sum for those that remained, when Tarquin conferring with the pontiffs was advised to buy them. Two magistrates were created to consult them on all occasions, 531 B.C.; see *Quindecemvirs*.

SICILIAN VESPERS, the term given to the massacre of the French (who had conquered Sicily, 1266), commenced at Palermo, 30 March, 1282.

On Easter Monday conspirators assembled at Palermo; and while the French were engaged in festivities, a Sicilian bride passed by with her train. One Drochet, a Frenchman, used her rudely, under pretence of searching for arms. A young Sicilian stabbed him with his own sword; and a tumult ensuing, 200 French were instantly murdered. The populace ran through the city, crying out, "Let the French die!" and, without distinction of rank, age, or sex, slaughtered all of that nation they could find, to the number of about 8000. Even the churches proved no sanctuary, and the massacre became general throughout the island.

SICILY (anciently *Trinacria*, three-cornered). The early inhabitants were the Sicani, or Siculi, a people of Spain, and Etruscans, who came from Italy. The Phœnicians and Greeks settled some colonies here (735–582); see *Syracuse*. In modern times its government has frequently been united with and separated from that of Naples (*which see*); the two now form part of the kingdom of Italy. Population of Sicily in 1856, 2,231,020; 1871, 2,565,323; 1887, 3,192,108; 1890, 3,285,472; 1901, 3,529,266.

Naxos built by the Greeks from Eubœa, about . B.C.	735
Syracuse founded by Archias from Corinth .	734

Leontini and other cities founded . . . 730 *et seq.*
Agrigentum founded by a Dorian colony, 579; ruled by Phalaris (see *Brazen Bull*), about 563
Gelon, tyrant of Gela, becomes supreme at Syracuse; the Carthaginians enter Sicily to found colonies, but are severely defeated by Gelon, at Himera 480
Gelon succeeded by his brother Hiero . . . 478
Syracuse becomes predominant in Sicily . . . 453
Great Athenian expedition under Nicias, 315; defeated by the aid of Gylippus, the Lacedemonian 413
An excellent code of laws established by Diocles . 412
Dionysius the elder, able and ambitious, becomes captain-general at Syracuse, 406; subdues the aristocracy, becomes tyrant, and gradually supreme in Sicily, 405; makes successful war with the Italian Greeks; declares war against Carthage 397
Syracuse closely besieged by the Carthaginians; their army is crippled by a pestilence; their fleet destroyed by Dionysius, a treaty made . 395
War renewed, 393; peace made 392
Dionysius plants colonies in Italy, 387; dies . . 367
His dissolute son, Dionysius II., succeeds him, 367; receives Plato and other philosophers; he is dethroned by Dion, his banished relative, who becomes ruler 356
Dion rules severely and becomes unpopular; is assassinated by Calippus 353
Dionysius II. (tyrant at Socri 10 years) recovers his authority at Syracuse, 346; rules till his expulsion by Timoleon with a small Corinthian army, and retires to Corinth 343
Timoleon restores the republic, deposes the other Sicilian tyrants, and becomes supreme, 343 *et seq.*; totally defeats the Carthaginians at the Crimissus, 339; rules Sicily till his death . . . 337
Agathocles overthrows the republic with bloodshed, and becomes "autocrat," and afterwards king, 317; defeated by the Carthaginians at the Himera, 310; he invades Africa, gains victories over the Carthaginians, but is compelled to return to Sicily by revolts, 307; dies 289
Political dissensions; Pyrrhus, king of Epirus, enters Sicily, and defeats the Carthaginians, 278; retires 276
Hiero II. made king of Syracuse, 270; makes war with the Romans, is defeated, and makes peace . 263
The first Punic war begins, see *Carthage* . . . 264
Hiero II. dies 216
Hieronymus, his grandson, succeeds, 216; renounces the alliance with Rome; and is assassinated . 214
The Roman consul, Marcellus, invades Sicily, and besieges Syracuse, which is vigorously defended by the aid of Archimedes, 214; it is taken, when Archimedes is slain 212
Sicily becomes a Roman province 210
The Servile wars; much slaughter . . 135, 134, 132
Tyrannical government of Verres (for which he was accused by Cicero) 73-71
Sicily held by Sextus Pompeius, son of the great Pompey, 42; defeated; expelled, 36; killed . 35

* * * * * * *

Invaded by the Vandals, A.D. 440; by the Goths, 493; taken for the Greek emperors by Belisarius, A.D. 536
Conquered by the Saracens and held . . . 832-78
Greatly recovered by the Greek emperor by the aid of Normans 1038
The Greeks and Arabs driven out by a Norman prince, Roger I., son of Tancred, 1058; who takes the title of count of Sicily 1061-1090
Roger II., son of the above-named, unites Sicily with Naples, and is crowned king of the Two Sicilies 1131
Charles of Anjou, brother of St. Louis, king of France, conquers Naples and Sicily, deposes the Norman princes, and makes himself king . 1266
The French massacred (see *Sicilian Vespers*) . . 1282
Sicily seized by a fleet sent by the kings of Aragon; Naples remains to the house of Anjou . . . ,,
Alphonso, king of Aragon, takes possession of Naples 1435
The kingdom of Naples and Sicily united to the Spanish monarchy under Ferdinand the Catholic 1501
Victor, duke of Savoy, by the treaty of Utrecht, made king of Sicily 1713
Which he gives up to the emperor Charles VI., and becomes king of Sardinia 1720
Charles, son of the king of Spain, becomes king of the Two Sicilies 1735
The throne of Spain becoming vacant, Charles, who is heir, vacates the throne of the Two Sicilies, in favour of his third son Ferdinand, agreeably to treaty 1759
Dreadful earthquake at Messina, in Sicily, which destroys 40,000 persons 1783
The French conquer Naples (*which see*); Ferdinand IV. retires to Sicily 1806
Political disturbances 1810
New constitution granted, under British auspices . 1812
The French expelled; kingdom of Two Sicilies re-established; Ferdinand returns to Naples; abolishes the constitution 1815
Revolution at Palermo suppressed 1820
The great towns in Sicily rise and demand the constitution; a provisional government proclaimed 12 Jan. 1848
The king nominates his brother, the count of Aquila, viceroy, 17 Jan.; promises a new constitution 29 Jan. ,,
The Sicilian parliament decrees the exclusion of the Bourbon family, 13 April; and invites the duke of Genoa to the throne . . . . 11 July, ,,
Messina bombarded and taken by the Neapolitans 7 Sept. ,,
Catania taken by assault, 6 April; Syracuse surrenders 23 April; and Palermo . . 15 May, 1849
Insurrections suppressed at Palermo, Messina, and Catania, 4 April *et seq.*; the rebels retire into the interior . . . 21 April *et seq.* 1860
Garibaldi and his followers (2200 men) embark at Genoa, 5 May; and land at Marsala, 11 May; he abandons his ships; and assumes the dictatorship in the name of the king of Sardinia . 14 May, ,,
He defeats the royal troops at Calatafimi, 15 May; storms Palermo, 27 May; which is bombarded by the royal fleet, 28 May; an armistice agreed to 31 May, ,,
A provisional government formed at Palermo, June: which is evacuated by the Neapolitans, 6 June, ,,
Garibaldi defeats the Neapolitans at Melazzo, 20, 21 July, ,,
Convention signed, by which the Neapolitans agree to evacuate Sicily (retaining the citadel of Messina) . . . . 30 July, ,,
New Sicilian constitution proclaimed . 3 Aug.
Garibaldi embarks for Calabria (see *Naples*), 19 Aug. ,,
Professor Saffi (late of Oxford), a short time dictator . . . . Sept. ,,
The Sicilians by universal suffrage vote for annexation to Sardinia (432,054 against 667) 21 Oct. ,,
Victor-Emmanuel visits Sicily . . . 1 Dec. ,,
Citadel of Messina blockaded, 28 Feb.; surrenders to general Cialdini . . . . 13 March, 1861
King Victor-Emmanuel warmly received at Messina, May, 1862
Imprudent speeches of Garibaldi at Marsala, 19 July; he enters Catania, and establishes a provisional government, 19 Aug.; embarks for Italy, 24 Aug. ,,
Sicily placed under blockade; removed in Sept.; tranquil . . . . Oct. ,,
Insurrection in Palermo, attributed to the priests and brigands, 16 Sept.; suppressed with bloodshed by Italian troops . . . . 21-26 Sept. 1866
Revival of brigandage and murder . . Aug. 1872
Martial law established in some places . Sept. 1874
Aliano, a brigand, tried at Potenza, for numerous murders, and other crimes . . . . . Nov.

Capraro, great brigand, killed during capture about 2 Oct. 1875
Mr. Forester Rose carried off by brigands, 3 Nov.; ransomed for about 4000*l*. . . . . Nov. 1876
Leone and other brigands surrounded and shot, 1 June, 1877
Five chief brigands surrender; abatement of brigandage announced . . . about 6 Nov. ,,
Successful visit of the king and queen; arrive at Palermo . . . . 4 Jan. 1880
Explosion in sulphur mine at Gessolungo, near Caltanissetta, about 30 killed . . 12 Nov. 1881
Violent cyclone in Catania, about 27 killed; 200,000*l*. damage . . . . 7 Oct. 1884
Grand banquet to sig. Crispi, Italian premier, at Palermo . . . . 14 Oct. 1889
Opening of the Italian National Exhibition at Palermo (*which see*) . . . . . 15 Nov. 1891
Increase of brigandage by secret societies; many arrests . . . . 26 Sept.—9 Oct. 1892
Despatch of troops to suppress brigandage; nearly a state of siege, reported . . . 23 Oct. 1893
Increase of socialism, 1893 (Fasci dei Lavoratori) . ,,
Violent rioting, with bloodshed (see *Palermo*), Dec.; rioting in Trapani against the *octroi* dues; reinforcements sent, 30 Dec. 1893; destructive rioting, with bloodshed, at different places; gen. Morra di Lavriano invested with full powers to establish order . . . . 2 Jan. 1894
State of siege in Sicily proclaimed at Palermo, 4 Jan. ,,
Frequent conflicts, with bloodshed . . 5 Jan. ,,
The rising attributed to misgovernment and oppression by the municipal authorities . Jan. ,,
Sig. de Felice Giuffrida (deputy) sentenced to 18 years, and 7 others to various terms of imprisonment, for connection with rioting (*see above*) 30 May, ,,
Order restored, reported . . . . . 25 Sept. ,,
Destructive earthquakes, with loss of life, at Messina, &c. . . . . 16 Nov. ,,
Severe shock in Catania; many persons buried by the fall of a church . . . 23 March, 1895
Disaster at a mine at Casteltermini, 35 deaths, 24 Sept. 1897
Riot at Siculiana, town hall sacked and burnt; 1 death . . . . 2 Jan. 1898
Jubilee celebration of the Sicilian revolution (1848); hearty welcome to the prince and princess of Naples, and sig. Crispi, at Palermo 10 Jan. ,,
A marble monument commemorative of the revolution, unveiled by the crown prince, at Palermo, 12 Jan. ,,
Demonstrations in honour of sig. Crispi . 4 Oct. 1899
The king and queen open the Sicilian agricultural exhibition at Palermo; British naval squadron well received . . . . . 27, 28, 29 May, 1902
Cyclone and floods in Modica and Catania; 400 deaths; the king sends 2000*l*. . 26–28 Sept. 1902
Fatal riot at Giarratana . . . . . 13 Oct. ,,
Visit of king Edward VII. . . 21, 22 April, 1903

SICK CHILDREN, Hospital for, Great Ormond-street, London; established 1851. The princess of Wales (now queen) laid the foundation of new buildings, 11 July, 1872. A branch has been set up at Highgate.

"SICK MAN," an epithet applied to Turkey, by the czar Nicholas, 14 Jan. 1854; see *Russo-Turkish War*, note.

SICYON, an ancient Grecian kingdom in the Peloponnesus, founded, it is said, about 2080 B.C. Its people took part in the wars in Greece, usually supporting Sparta. In 252 it became a republic and joined the Achæan league formed by Aratus. It was the country of the sculptors Polycletes (436) and Lysippus (328 B.C.).

SIDEROSTAT (from *sidus*, Latin for a star), an apparatus constructed by M. Leon Foucault, shortly before his death, 11 Feb. 1868, for observing the light of the stars in precisely the same way in which the light of the sun may be studied in the camera obscura. It consists of a mirror moved by clockwork, and a fixed objective glass for concentrating the rays into a focus.

SIDON or **Zidon** (Syria), a city of Phœnicia, to the north of Tyre. It was conquered by Cyrus about 537 B.C.; and surrendered to Alexander, 332 B.C.; see *Phœnicia*. The town was taken from the pacha of Egypt by the troops of the sultan and of his allies, assisted by some ships of the British squadron, under commodore Charles Napier, 27 Sept. 1840; see *Syria* and *Turkey*.

SIEGES. Azoth, which was besieged by Psammetichus the Powerful, held out for nineteen years. *Usher*. It held out for twenty-nine years. *Herodotus*. This was the longest siege recorded in the annals of antiquity. The siege of Troy was the most celebrated, and occupied ten years, 1184 B.C. Other an ient sieges: Tyre, 572 B.C., 332 B.C.; Syracuse, 414 B.C., 212 B C.; Saguntum, 219 B.C.; Jerusalem, 590 B.C.; A.D. 70. The following are the most memorable sieges since the 12th century; for details of many of them see separate articles.

Acre, 1192, 1799, 1832, 1840.
Algesiras, 1341.
Algiers, 1681 (*Bomb vessels first used by a French engineer named Renau*); 1816.
Alkmaer, 1573.
Almeida, 27 Aug. 1810.
Amiens, 1597.
Ancona, 1174, 1799, 1860.
Antwerp, 1576, 1583, 1585, 1746, 1832.
Arras, 1640.
Azoff, 1736.
Badajoz, 11 March, 1811; 6 April, 1812.
Bagdad, 1258.
Barcelona, 1697, 1714.
Belgrade, 1439, 1456, 1521, 1688, 1717, 1739, 1789.
Belle-Isle, 1761.
Bergen-op-Zoom, 1622, 1747, 1814.
Berwick, 1333, 1481.
Bethune, 1710.
Bilbao by Carlists, 1874.
Bois-le-Duc, 1603, 1794.
Bologna, 1512, 1796, 1799
Bommel: *the invention of the covered way*, 1794.
Bonn, 1672, 1689, 1703.
Bouchain, 1711.
Boulogne, 1544.
Breda, 1625.
Brescia, 1238, 1512, 1849.
Breslau, 1807.
Brisac, 1638, 1704.
Brussels, 1695, 1746.
Bomarsund, 1854.
Buda, 1541, 2 Sept. 1686.
Burgos, 1812, 1813.
Cadiz, 1812.
Calais, 1347 (*British historians affirm that cannon were used at Cressy, 1346, and here in 1347. First used here in* 1388. Rymer's Fœd.), 1558, 1596.
Calvi, 1794.
Candia: *the largest cannon then known in Europe, used here by the Turks*, 1667.
Carthagena, 1706-7, 1740, 1873-4.
Chalus, 1199.
Charleroi, 1693.
Charleston, U.S., 1864-5.
Chartres, 1568.
Cherbourg, 1758.
Chitral Fort, *which see*, 1895.
Ciudad Rodrigo, 1810, 1812.
Colchester, 1648.
Comorn, 1849.
Compiègne (*Joan of Arc*), 1430.
Condé, 1676, 1793, 1794.
Coni, 1691, 1744.
Constantinople, 1453.
Copenhagen, 1658, 1801, 1807.
Corfu, 1716.
Courtray, 1646.
Cracow, 1702.
Cremona, 1702.
Dantzic, 1734, 1793, 1807, 1813, 1814.
Delhi, 1857.
Douay, 1710.
Dresden, 1756, 1813.
Drogheda, 1649.
Dublin, 1500.

Dunkirk, 1646, 1793.
Famagosta, 1571.
Flushing, 15 Aug. 1809.
Fredrickshald: *Charles XII. killed*, 1718.
Gaëta, 1435, 1734, 1860-1.
Genoa, 1747, 1800.
Gerona, 1809.
Ghent, 1708.
Gibraltar, 1779, 1782-3.
Glätz, 1742, 1807.
Göttingen, 1760.
Graves, 1674.
Grenada, 1491, 1492.
Groningen, 1594.
Haerlem, 1572, 1573.
Harfleur, 1415.
Heidelberg, 1688
Herat, 1838.
Humaitá, 1868.
Ismail, 1790.
Kars, 1855.
Khartoum, 1884.
Kimberley, 15 Oct. 1899–15 Feb. 1900.
Kehl, 1733, 1796.
Ladysmith, 2 Nov. 1899–28 Feb. 1900.
Landau, 1702 *et seq.*, 1792.
Landrecy, 1712, 1794.
Laon, 988, 991.
Leipsic, 1757 *et seq.*, 1813.
Leith, 1560.
Lerida, 1647, 1707, 1810.
Leyden, 1574.
Liége, 1408, 1688, 1702.
Lille, 1708, 1792.
Limerick, 1651, 1691.
Londonderry, 1689.
Louisbourg, 1758.
Lucknow, 1857.
Luxemburg, 1795.
Lyons, 1793.
Maestricht, 1579, 1673; *Vauban first came into notice*; 1676, 1748.
Mafeking, 13 Oct. 1899–17 May, 1900.
Magdala, 1868.
Magdeburg, 1631, 1806.
Malaga, 1487.
Malta, 1565, 1798, 1800.
Mantua, 1797, 1799.
Marseilles, 1524.
Menin, 1706.
Mentz, 1689, 1793.
Messina, 1282, 1719, 1848, 1861.
Metz, 1552-3, 1870.
Mons, 1691, 1709, 1792.
Montargis, 1426.
Montauban, 1621.
Montevideo, Jan. 1807.
Mothe: *the French, taught by a Mr. Muller, first practised the art of throwing shells*, 1634.
Namur, 1692, 1746, 1794.
Naples, 1435, 1504, 1557, 1792, 1799, 1806.
Newark, 1644-5.
New Orleans, 1814.
Nice, 1706.
Novogorod, 1478.
Nieuport, 1600.
Olivenza, 1801, 1811.
Olmutz, 1758.
Orleans, 1428, 1563.
Ostend, 1601, 1798.
Oudenarde, 1706.
Padua, 1509.
Pampeluna, 1813.
Paris, 1420, 1594, 1870, 1871.
Parma, 1248.
Pavia, 1524, 1655.
Pekin legations, 20 June–14 Aug. 1900.
Perpignan, 1542, 1642.
Phalsbourg, 1814, 1815, 1870.
Philipsburg, 1644, 1676, 1688, *first experiment of firing artillery à ricochet*, 1734, 1799.
Plevna, 1877.
Pondicherry, 1748, 1793.
Prague, 1741-1744.
Quebec, 1759-60.
Quesnoy, 1793-1794.
Rheims, 1359.
Rhodes, 1521.
Richmond, U.S., 1864-5.
Riga, 1700, 1710.
Rochelle, 1573, 1628.
Rome, 1527, 1798, 1849.
Romorantin; *artillery first used in sieges* (VOLTAIRE), 1356.
Rouen, 1419, 1449, 1591.
Roxburgh, 1460.
St. Sebastian, 1813.
Saragossa, 1710, 1808, 1809; *the two last dreadful.*
Sebastopol, 1854-5.
Schweidnitz: *first experiment to reduce a fortress by springing globes of compression*, 1757-1762.
Scio (see *Greece*), 1822.
Seringapatam, 1799.
Seville, 1247-8.
Silistria, 1854.
Smolensko, 1632, 1812.
Soissons, 1870.
St. Quentin, 1557.
Stralsund: *the method of throwing red-hot balls first practised with certainty*, 1715.
Strasburg, 1870.
Tarragona, 1811.
Temeswar, 1716.
Thérouenne, 1513.
Thionville, 1792.
Thorn, 1703.
Tortosa, 1811.
Toulon, 1707, 1793.
Toulouse, 1217.
Tournay, 1340, 1513, 1583, 1667, 1709 (*this was the best defence ever drawn from counter-mines*), 1792.
Trèves, 1635, 1673, 1765.
Tunis, 1270, 1535.
Turin, 1640, 1706.
Valencia, 1705, 1707, 1712.
Valenciennes, 1677, 1793, 1794.
Vannes, 1342.
Venice, 1879.
Venloo, 1702.
Verdun, 1792.
Vicksburg, U.S., 1863.
Vienna, 1529, 1683.
Wakefield, 1460.
Warsaw, 1831.
Xativa, 1246.
Xeres, 1262.
York, 1644.
Yprès, 1648.
Zurich, 1544.
Zutphen, 1586.

SIENA (the ancient Sena Julia), Italy, in the middle ages a powerful republic rivalling Florence and Pisa; see *Tuscany*. It was incorporated with France, 1808-14. Population, 1881, 23,445.

The Sienese thoroughly defeated the Florentines at Montaperto in 1260; placed themselves under the duke of Milan, 1399; were ruled by Pandolfo Petrucci, 1487–1512; submitted to the emperor Charles V. 1524; rebelled, called in the French, 1555; were defeated and given up to Cosimo de Medici, 1557; who annexed Siena to Tuscany.

SIERRA LEONE (W. Africa), discovered by the Portuguese navigator, P. de Cintra, in 1462. An attempt to form a settlement here made by the British government by sending out from London about 400 freed negroes and 60 whites, Dec. 1786, failed; a second attempt by the Sierra Leone Company in 1791, was not much more successful, and in 1807 the settlement was given up to the crown. Capital, Freetown. Population in 1891, 30,033. The settlement was attacked by the French, Sept. 1794; by the natives, Feb. 1802. Sir Charles Macarthy, governor of the colony, was defeated and killed by the Ashantee chief, 21 Jan. 1824.—16 & 17 Vict. c. 16, relates to the government, &c., of this colony. It was made a bishopric in 1852; see *Ashantees* and *West Africa*. Population in 1891, 74,835; 1893, 136,000; 1901, 76,655.

Robarrie, the stronghold of the insurgent Yonnie tribe, captured by sir Francis De Winton, 21 Nov. 1887
The king was captured and the rebellion suppressed Nov.–Dec. ,,
The Gambia territory isolated and made an independent colony . . . . 22 Dec. 1888
Largoh, capital of the chief Mackiah captured by the British under governor Hay; 700 prisoners liberated; announced . . . . 14 Feb. 1889
In accordance with an agreement with the French government, 10 Aug. 1889, a commission was appointed for the delimitation of the British and French possessions in West Africa . . Oct. 1890
Agreement signed . . . . 21 Jan. 1895
Governors: sir James Shaw Hay, 1888; sir Francis Fleming, 1892; sir Frederick Cardew . Feb. 1894
British expedition sent to punish aggressions in May, 1891; fighting at Tambi; the British retreat; Tambi taken and destroyed . 7 April, ,,
A British expedition, under col. A. B. Ellis, against the Sofas, a marauding tribe, are mistaken for the Sofas by a French force, under lieut. Maritz, at Warina (or Waima), on the British border, and attacked; British loss: capt. Lendy; lieuts. Liston, Wroughton; serg.-major Carraher, and 2 privates; French loss: lieut. Maritz and 10 Sengalese; many wounded . . 23 Dec. 1893
[The collision attributed to the false statements of Korona, a chief, who was afterwards executed; the British awarded 9000*l.* by arbitration, 1902.]
Sub-inspector Taylor, at Tungea, with a detachment of frontier police and some natives, defeat a body of about 4000 Sofas; 50 killed, 150 taken prisoners . . . . . 29 Dec. ,,
The Sofas, after a destructive raid, severely defeated by col. A. B. Ellis at Bagwema . 2 Jan. 1894
Capture of Kerra-Yemma and rescue of 673 slaves, 29 Jan. ,,
Another conflict between the British and French

(native police) on the borders of Sierra Leone; several killed . . . . . 3 Feb. 1894
Col. A. B. Ellis, author of "The History of the Gold Coast," &c., dies at Teneriffe . 5 March, „
"Human Leopard" society (men clothed in leopard skins) vow to kill people to be eaten; efforts made for its suppression; 3 men hanged, July, 1895; 5 men hanged . . . . Sept. 1896
Great fire at Freetown . . . . 9–10 Jan. „
Delimitation of British and French territories, settled, May; British protectorate proclaimed . „
Serious rising due to the suppression of slavery, &c., and the hut tax in the Hinterland . . Feb. 1898
Conflicts between the natives and frontier police under major Tarbet at Karene, lieut. F. E. Yeld mortally wounded; Quiah burnt by capt. Moore, March, „
Serious fighting: Ekuta and Tabira occupied by the British . . . . . . 26 March, „
Death of col. Bosworth while on the march, April; capt. Macdonald dies of wounds, 6 April, and major Donovan . . . . . . 17 April, „
Desultory fighting round Port Lokko, the rev. W. J. Humphrey killed; Sorie Bunkey, the king, killed by Bai Bureh, rebel chief . . April, „
Rising spreading in the S.E., Benda in ruins; Mr. Hughes, native commissioner, and over 200 inhabitants, massacred by the Mendis; factories plundered in the Sherbro' district, April; 5 American missionaries massacred at Rotifunk; 2 others at Taiama . . . . May, „
British warships and reinforcements sent to Freetown, rebels repulsed at Kwellu by capt. Fairtlough, 3 chiefs arrested, May; col. Woodgate returns to Freetown, after successful operations against the rebels in Karene, 13 May; H.M.S. *Fox* returns to Freetown, after burning several villages . . . . 14 May, „
Rotifunk occupied by col. Woodgate's punitive expedition (about 100 men) after desperate fights with hordes of Mendis, who were finally driven off with great loss, 1 June; Bompeh, their stronghold, taken by lieut.-col. Cunningham and lieut. Russell; enemy's loss heavy . . . 13 June, „
Col. Marshall's punitive operations in the Karene and Kwellu districts successful; H.M.S. *Alecto* returns to Freetown with 41 natives rescued from Sherbro' district . . . . . 18 June, „
Sir David Patrick Chalmers appointed royal commissioner to inquire into the rising (computed loss of life about 1,000); arrives 18 July (leaves 22 Nov.) . . . . „
The expeditionary force returns to Freetown after destroying 4 towns in the Bompeh and Shengeh districts . . . . 12 July, „
Nigua, chief of Panguma, charged with complicity in the rebellion; brought to Freetown, 20 July, „
Rebels repulsed with loss at Songo Town, 21 July, „
The Mendis repeatedly defeated, the chiefs sue for peace, 10 Aug.; king of the Upper Mendis captured, Port Lokko chiefs fined and released, Sept. „
Further operations against Bai Bureh, Oct.; he is captured by capt. Goodwin, 14 Nov. (brought to Freetown with 4 other ringleaders, 25 Feb. 1899).
Lahai, rebel chief, and followers surrender to capt. Robertson at Karene, Dec. (Bai Forkey captured, Jan. 1899).
Hon. Colenso Bishop, mayor of Freetown, born in the colony, 1850; died . . . . 7 Dec. „
Frontier fighting (Meli river); Yebema occupied, enemy repulsed . . . . . . Dec. „
Judge Bonner tries 240 prisoners at Kwellu and elsewhere for murder during the rising (Aug.); 151 sentenced to death, about half commuted; he returns to England . . . . 12 Jan. 1899
General amnesty in Bandajuma district, with some exceptions; arrears of taxes remitted . Feb. „
The Sierra Leone railway (32 mi. to Songo town) opened by major Nathan, acting governor, 1 May, „
Col. Woodgate's (K.C.M.G. 1899) expedition to explore unknown country and overawe the Mendi and Kissi tribes, very successful; the Kissi chiefs submit after some days' continuous fighting, British loss slight . . Dec. 1898–1 March, „
Sir David Chalmers (died 5 Aug. 1899) issued his report condemning the hut tax, &c. . 26 July, „
Major Ronald Ross (K.C.B. 1902), head of the Liverpool malaria research expedition, arrives, 10 Aug.; discovers the *Anopheles* malarial mosquito (*which see*) in stagnant pools, &c.; grubs killed by kerosene oil; leaves . end Sept. 1899
Sir Chas. King-Harman, new governor, arrives, 11 Dec. 1900
The governor well received in tours through southern districts, 5–23 Feb.; Karene district, April, 1901; Panguma, Jan.; good report issued, 3 April, 1902
Anti-malaria work in Freetown very successful, reported . . . . April, „
The governor leaves Freetown on a tour . 14 Jan. 1903

SIGNALS are alluded to by Polybius. Elizabeth had instructions drawn up for the admiral and general of the expedition to Cadiz, to be announced to the fleet in a certain latitude; this is said to have been the first set of signals given to the commanders of the English fleet. A system for the navy was invented by the duke of York, afterwards James II. 1665. *Guthrie; see Fog-signals* and *Navigation Laws.*
Block system of signalling on railways, introduced 1853
The telephotos, an electrical system of signalling, invented by Mr. Claudius Victor Boughton, of New York state, was exhibited by him at a meeting in London; lord George Hamilton in the chair; incandescent lamps are employed . . 15 Dec. 1893
A new naval signalling apparatus invented by prince Louis of Battenberg and capt. Percy Scott, announced . . . . 14 Sept. 1894
Messrs. Thompson & Marsden's recording ship's indicator, an apparatus recording orders from the bridge to the engine-room, announced . Jan. 1895
International code of signals committee, final report issued; by the new code of 26 flags 375,076 signals can be made, April, 1897. See *Telegraphs*, June, 1897
New international maritime code introduced, 1 Jan. 1901

SIGNBOARDS were used by the Greeks and Romans. A "History of Signboards," by Jacob Larwood and John Hotten, was published in 1866.

SIGNETS, see *Seals*.

SIGN MANUAL, ROYAL, a stamp, imitating the royal signature, employed when the sovereign was so ill as to be unable to write: in the case of Henry VIII. 1547; James I. 1625; and George IV., 29 May, 1830. *Rosse.*

SIKHS, originally a Hindu religious sect (about 1500), a people of N. India, invaded the Mogul empire, 1703–8; see *Punjab* and *India*, 1849, 1897.

SIKKIM, a small Himalayan State, joining Tibet, allied to the Indian government since 1814. By a treaty in 1861 free trade and passage through the country were secured.
The erection of a fort by the Rajah under the influence of Tibetans in contravention of the treaty, led to a military demonstration; 1,000 troops sent ostensibly to repair the road to Tibet, Jan.; the rajah proving contumacious, the viceroy intervened ineffectually, March; about 2,000 men concentrated at Pedong, March; Lingtu fort quickly captured; flight of the Tibetans, 20 March; destruction of the fort ordered 21 March; slight skirmishes with the Tibetans, 24 killed, May; col. Graham defeats the attacking Tibetans, who are said to have lost 200 men . . . . . . 23 May, 1888
Troops ordered to return to Darjeeling 17 June, „
Return to Sikkim on appearance of Tibetan aggression . . . . July, „
The Tibetans defeated at Jelapla pass; about 400 killed and wounded, 25 Sept.; col. Graham's advance suspended and the expedition recalled, Sept. „
A Chinese amban, or resident, at Lhassa, arrives with a large following at Calcutta, 11 March. A treaty signed at Calcutta, 17 March, 1890; Sikkim is to be treated as a British feudatory state.

The rajah goes secretly to Tibet; arrested in Nepaul, April; lives in retirement 1892
Mr. Douglas Freshfield and prof. Garwood explore the glaciers of mount Kangchenjunga (28,156 feet high) . . . . Sept.-Oct. 1899

SILCHESTER, Hants. Here are the remains of the Roman town Calleva (built on the site of the British Caer Segeint or Segont); including walls of excellent masonry, a basilica and forum, private dwellings, &c. Many discoveries during excavations made by the rev. Mr. Joyce, under the patronage of the duke of Wellington, from 1864 till his death in 1878. Coins of Claudius I. and later emperors have been found.

A systematic investigation of these remains was begun, 23 June, 1890, under the superintendance of Mr. G. E. Fox and other fellows of the Society of Antiquaries, London.
Mr. Laurence Gomme, Mr. Hilton Price, gen. Pitt-Rivers, and Mr. St. John Hope co-operate in the work . . . . Sept. 1890
Many vases, tools and implements discovered; these remains constitute a veritable British and Roman Pompeii . . . . ,,
Exhibition of relics, models, &c. . . . . Jan. 1891
The work was recommenced . . . . April, 1892
The remains of a presumed Romano-British church, probable date 4th century, discovered in . June, ,,
Annual exhibition of relics at Burlington house, March, 1893, *et seq.*; the work still proceeding in 1092
Remains of Roman public baths and an altar discovered in 1903

SILESIA, formerly a province of Poland, was invaded by John of Bohemia, 1325, and ceded to him, 1355. It was taken by the king of Hungary, 1478, and added to the Austrian dominion, 1526. It was conquered and lost several times during the Seven years' war by Frederick of Prussia, but was retained by him at the peace in 1763. The emperor William was most enthusiastically received during his visit, Sept. 1875. Population, 1900, 680,529.

Strike of about 3,000 miners in the Strau district; order kept by the military . . 24 Sept. 1890
Another strike with rioting and bloodshed . May, 1894
By explosions of fire damp in the coal mines of Karwin, about 232 persons perished . 14 June, ,,
Another at Zaborze, 14 deaths, 15 Feb. 1895; another at Troppau, 49 deaths . 16 March, 1895
Fire in the Antonien colliery, 20 deaths . 10 June, ,,
Explosion in the Wrangel colliery, Waldenburg, 50 deaths . . . . 31 Dec. ,,
Explosion in the Hedwig-Wunsch colliery, Arnold Borsig, the owner, and 5 others killed, 1 April, 1897
Fire in a colliery at Zabrze, about 32 deaths, 16 Jan. 1898

SILICON or SILICIUM (from *silex*, flint), a non-metallic element, next to oxygen the most abundant substance in the earth, as it enters into the constitution of many earths, metallic oxides, and a great number of minerals. The mode of procuring pure silicon was discovered by Berzelius in 1823. *Gmelin*. See *Water-glass* and *Ransome's Stone*.

SILISTRIA, a strong military town in Bulgaria, European Turkey. It was taken by the Russians, 30 June, 1829, and held some years by them as a pledge for the payment of a large sum by the Porte; but was eventually returned. In 1854 it was again besieged by the Russians, 30,000 strong, under prince Paskiewitch, and many assaults were made. The Russian general was compelled to retire in consequence of a dangerous contusion. On 2 June, Mussa Pacha, the brave and skilful commander of the garrison, was killed. On 9 June, the Russians stormed two forts, which were retaken. A grand assault took place on 13 June, under prince Gortschakoff and general Schilders, which was vigorously repelled. On the 15th, the garrison assumed the offensive, crossed the river, defeated the Russians, and destroyed the siege works. The siege was thus raised, and the Russians commenced their retreat as Omar Pacha was drawing near. The garrison was ably assisted by two British officers, capt. Butler and lieut. Nasmyth, the former of whom, after being wounded, died of exhaustion. They were highly praised by Omar Pacha and lord Hardinge, and lieutenant Nasmyth was made a major. Population, 1888, 11,414; 1900, 12,133.

SILK. Wrought silk was brought from Persia to Greece, 325 B.C. Known at Rome in Tiberius's time, when a law passed in the senate prohibiting the use of plate of massive gold, and also forbidding men to debase themselves by wearing silk, fit only for women. Silk was at first of the same value with gold, weight for weight, and was thought to grow in the same manner as cotton on trees. Silkworms were brought from India to Europe in the 6th century. Charlemagne sent Offa, king of Mercia, a present of two silken vests, 780. The manufacture was encouraged by Roger, king of Sicily, at Palermo, 1146, when the Sicilians not only bred the silk-worms, but spun and wove the silk. The manufacture spread into Italy and Spain, and also into the south of France, a little before the reign of Francis I. about 1510; and Henry IV. propagated mulberry-trees and silk-worms throughout the kingdom, about 1600. In England, silk mantles were worn by some noblemen's ladies at a ball at Kenilworth castle, 1286. Silk was worn by the English clergy in 1534. Manufactured in England in 1604; and broad silk wove from raw silk in 1620. Brought to perfection by the French refugees in London at Spitalfields, 1688. A silk-throwing mill was made in England, and fixed up at Derby, by sir Thomas Lombe, merchant of London, modelled from the original mill then in the king of Sardinia's dominions, about 1714. He obtained a patent in 1718, and died 3 Jan. 1739. Six new species of silk-worm were rearing in France, 1861.*

The Silk association of Great Britain and Ireland begun, 1886-7; first exhibition St. James's-square, London, S.W. (opened by the duchess of Teck), 6-21 May, 1890; others since. See *Italy*, May, 1899.

SILKWORM DISEASE. In 1853 the annual produce of sericulture in South France was estimated at about 4,680,000*l*. Soon after a disease broke out in the worms, which reduced the value of the silk crop to about one-third that amount. In 1858 a commission was appointed to inquire into the nature of the disease, then termed *pébrine*; and M. Quatrefages, in 1869, proved that it is hereditary, contagious, and infectious. M. Filippi discovered in the blood of the diseased worms a multitude of cylindrical corpuscles, since named *pankistophyton*, which Pasteur, who took up the study in 1865, has demonstrated to be parasitical, and the cause of the disease. He has since devised a way by which, it is hoped, the organic germs may be got rid of, and the disease extirpated.

The manufacture of a fabric from wood pulp, invented by count Hilaire de Chardonnet about 1893, and carried on at Besançon, reported very successful; dress and other fabrics of this material sold in London, summer of 1896.

SILOTVOR, a new explosive invented by M. Rouckteshell, who asked 50,000*l*. for the patent, 1887.

SILURES, a British tribe, occupying the counties of Monmouth and Hereford, was subdued

* In 1858, M. Guérin-Méneville introduced into France a Chinese worm termed the *Cynthia Bombyx*, which feeds on the *Ailanthus glandulosa*, a hardy tree of the oak kind. The cynthia yields a silk-like substance termed *Ailantine*. It was brought to Turin by Fantoni in 1856.

by the Roman general Ostorius Scapula, 50; see *Shropshire*. From this tribe is derived the geological term "Silurian strata," among the lowest of the palæozoic or primary series, from their occurrence in the above-mentioned counties. *Murchison's "Siluria"* was published 1849.

SILVER exists in most parts of the world, and is found mixed with other ores in various mines in Great Britain. The silver mines of South America are far the richest. A mine was discovered in the district of La Paz in 1660, which was so rich that the silver of it was often cut out with a chisel. In 1749, one mass of silver weighing 370 lbs. was sent to Spain. From a mine in Norway, a piece of silver was dug, and sent to the Royal Museum at Copenhagen, weighing 560 lbs., and worth 1680*l.* In England silver plate and vessels were first used by Wilfrid, a Northumbrian bishop, a lofty and ambitious man, 709. *Tyrrell.* Silver knives, spoons, and cups were great luxuries in 1300; see *Mirrors.* The act of 1816 restricted the use of silver as legal tender to 40*s.* In 1855, 561,906 oz., in 1857, 532,866 oz., in 1865, 724,856 oz., in 1870, 784,562 oz.; in 1876, 483,422 oz.; in 1882, 372,544 oz.; in 1887, 320,345 oz.; in 1888, 321,425 oz.; in 1889, 306,149 oz.; in 1890, 291,724 oz.; 1893, 274,100 oz.; 1896, 283,826 oz.; 1899, 191,927 oz.; 1900, 187,842 oz.; 1901, 173,724 oz. were obtained from mines in Britain. Estimated annual production of silver throughout the world, 1477 tons; value, 37,360,000*l.* (1892). Pattinson's process for obtaining silver from lead ore was introduced in 1829. See *Bimetallism, Bullion, Coins, Goldsmiths, Mirrors, Plate, India,* 1876, *United States,* 1878, 1890-5; *Trials,* Nov. Dec. 1895.

Fall in price of silver through introduction of gold coinage in Germany, and increased produce from South American mines . . . . . spring, 1876
The report of a commission on the subject was issued in . . . . July, ,,
Another commission appointed, see under *Currency*, 7 Sept. 1886
Pure silver: United States, N. A., 1,000; England, 925, alloy 75; Europe, 900, 100 alloy; reported . 1890
Value of the rupee (2*s.*) in India, 1892: Jan., 1*s.* 5*d.*; Dec., 1*s.* 2$\frac{3}{4}$*d.*
General fall in silver caused by the Indian Currency act (see *India*) . . . . . . June, 1893
For silver coinage, &c., see *United States,* March, 1894, and . . . . May, 1895

Average price in London, 1845-9, 59*d.* and a fraction per oz.; 1850-72, 61*d.*; 1871, 60$\frac{7}{16}$*d.*; 1875, 56$\frac{7}{8}$*d.*; 1880, 52$\frac{1}{4}$*d.*; 1883, 50$\frac{9}{16}$*d.*; price 49$\frac{7}{8}$*d.* 7 May, 1885; 1886, 46$\frac{9}{16}$*d.*; 1887, 44$\frac{5}{8}$*d.*; 1888, 43$\frac{1}{16}$*d.*; 1889, Jan–March, 42$\frac{9}{16}$*d.*; 7 May, 42$\frac{1}{8}$*d.*; 22 July, 42$\frac{3}{16}$*d.*; 13 Sept., 42$\frac{9}{16}$*d.*; 1890: 9 Jan., 44$\frac{3}{8}$*d.*; 3 April, 43$\frac{7}{8}$*d.*; 3 July, 47$\frac{3}{4}$*d.*; 4 Sept., 54$\frac{5}{8}$*d.*; 1891: 1 Jan., 48$\frac{1}{8}$*d.*; 2 April, 44$\frac{3}{8}$*d.*; 11 July, 45$\frac{5}{8}$*d.*; 3 Sept., 45$\frac{3}{16}$*d.*; 1892: 7 Jan., 43$\frac{1}{2}$*d.*; 1 April, 39$\frac{7}{8}$*d.*; 1 July, 40$\frac{3}{16}$*d.*; 2 Sept., 38$\frac{1}{8}$*d.*; 6 Oct. 38$\frac{3}{8}$*d.*; 3 Nov. 38$\frac{11}{16}$*d.*; 3 Dec., 39*d.*; 1893: 5 Jan., 38$\frac{3}{16}$*d.*; 2 Feb., 38$\frac{1}{4}$*d.*; 9 March, 38$\frac{3}{16}$*d.*; 4 April, 37$\frac{3}{8}$*d.*; 3 May, 37$\frac{5}{8}$*d.*; 2 June, 37$\frac{1}{4}$*d.*; 1 July, 33$\frac{1}{2}$*d.*; 1 Aug. 32$\frac{11}{16}$*d.*; 1 Sept., 34*d.*; 2 Oct. 38$\frac{1}{8}$*d.*; 2 Nov., 32*d.*; 2 Dec., 41-16*d.*; 1894: 1 Jan., 31$\frac{1}{2}$*d.*; 1 Feb., 30 11-6*d.*; 1 March, 27$\frac{5}{8}$*d.*; 2 April, 28$\frac{1}{8}$*d.*; 1 May, 29$\frac{3}{16}$*d.*; 1 June, 28$\frac{5}{16}$*d.*; 2 July, 28$\frac{3}{4}$*d.*; 1 Aug., 28$\frac{3}{4}$*d.*; 1 Sept. 30$\frac{1}{4}$*d.*; 1 Oct., 29$\frac{3}{16}$*d.*; 1 Nov., 29$\frac{3}{16}$*d.*; 1 Dec. 28$\frac{1}{2}$*d.*; 1895: 1 Jan., 27$\frac{3}{8}$*d.*; 1 Feb. 27$\frac{1}{16}$*d.*; 1 March, 27$\frac{5}{8}$*d.*; 1 April, 30$\frac{3}{4}$*d.*; 2 May, 30$\frac{3}{16}$*d.*; 1 June, 30$\frac{11}{16}$*d.*; 1 July, 30$\frac{1}{2}$*d.*; 1 Aug. 30$\frac{1}{4}$*d.*; 2 Sept. 30$\frac{7}{16}$*d.*; 1 Oct. 30$\frac{11}{16}$*d.*; 1 Nov. 30$\frac{11}{16}$*d.*; 2 Dec. 30$\frac{5}{8}$*d.*; 1896: 1 Jan. 30$\frac{1}{2}$*d.*; 1 Feb. 30$\frac{3}{4}$*d.*; 2 March, 31$\frac{3}{16}$*d.*; 1 April, 31$\frac{1}{8}$*d.*; 2 May, 31$\frac{1}{16}$*d.*; 1 June, 31$\frac{3}{16}$*d.*; 1 July, 31$\frac{1}{2}$*d.*; 1 Aug. 31$\frac{3}{8}$*d.*; 1 Sept. 30$\frac{11}{16}$*d.*; 1 Oct. 30$\frac{5}{16}$*d.*; 2 Nov. 30*d.*; 1 Dec. 29$\frac{7}{8}$*d.* 1897: 1 Jan. 29$\frac{13}{16}$*d.*; 1 Feb. 29$\frac{11}{16}$*d.*; 1 Mar. 29$\frac{5}{8}$*d.*; 1 April, 28$\frac{1}{2}$*d.*; 1 May, 28$\frac{3}{16}$*d.*; 1 June, 27$\frac{5}{8}$*d.*; 1 July, 27$\frac{9}{16}$*d.*; 3 Aug. 26$\frac{1}{2}$*d.*; 1 Sept. 23$\frac{3}{4}$*d.*; 1 Oct. 26*d.*; 1 Nov. 27*d.*; 1 Dec. 27$\frac{1}{2}$*d.* 1898: 3 Jan. 26$\frac{9}{16}$*d.*; 1 Feb. 25$\frac{1}{16}$*d.*; 1 March, 25$\frac{9}{16}$*d.*; 1 April, 25$\frac{11}{16}$*d.*; 3 May, 25$\frac{7}{8}$*d.*; 1 June, 26$\frac{15}{16}$*d.*; 1 July, 27$\frac{1}{8}$*d.*; 2 Aug. 27$\frac{1}{8}$*d.*; 1 Sept. 27$\frac{11}{16}$*d.*; 3 Oct. 28$\frac{3}{16}$*d.*; 1 Nov. 28$\frac{5}{16}$*d.*; 2 Dec. 27$\frac{7}{16}$*d.*; 1899: 2 Jan. 27$\frac{5}{16}$*d.*; 1 Feb. 27$\frac{1}{2}$*d.*; 1 March, 27$\frac{1}{2}$*d.*; 4 April, 27$\frac{1}{2}$*d.*; 2 May, 28$\frac{1}{4}$*d.*; 1 June, 28*d.*; 1 July, 27$\frac{3}{4}$*d.*; 1 Aug. 27$\frac{3}{4}$*d.*; 1 Sept. 27$\frac{3}{16}$*d.*; 2 Oct. 26$\frac{13}{16}$*d.*; 1 Nov. 26$\frac{3}{4}$*d.*; 1 Dec. 27$\frac{1}{4}$*d.*; 1900: 2 Jan. 27$\frac{1}{8}$*d.*; 1 Feb. 27$\frac{3}{4}$*d.*; 1 March, 27$\frac{9}{16}$*d.*; 2 April, 27$\frac{1}{2}$*d.*; 1 May, 27$\frac{1}{2}$*d.*; 1 June, 27$\frac{9}{16}$*d.*; 2 July, 28$\frac{1}{4}$*d.*; 1 Aug. 28*d.*; 1 Sept. 28$\frac{7}{16}$*d.*; 1 Oct. 29$\frac{1}{4}$*d.*; 1 Nov. 29$\frac{7}{8}$*d.*; 1 Dec. 29$\frac{3}{4}$*d.*; 1901: 2 Jan. 29$\frac{9}{16}$*d.*; 4 Feb. 28$\frac{5}{16}$*d.*; 1 March, 28$\frac{3}{16}$*d.*; 1 April, 27$\frac{3}{16}$*d.*; 1 May, 27$\frac{3}{16}$*d.*; 1 June, 27$\frac{1}{2}$*d.*; 1 July, 27$\frac{1}{4}$*d.*; 1 Aug. 26$\frac{13}{16}$*d.*; 2 Sept. 27*d.*; 1 Oct. 26$\frac{7}{8}$*d.*; 1 Nov. 26$\frac{1}{8}$*d.*; 2 Dec. 25$\frac{1}{16}$*d.*; 1902: 1 Jan. 25$\frac{3}{4}$*d.*; 1 Feb. 25$\frac{1}{2}$*d.*; 1 March, 25$\frac{3}{8}$*d.*; 1 April, 24$\frac{3}{4}$*d.*; 1 May, 23$\frac{7}{16}$*d.*; 2 June, 23$\frac{15}{16}$*d.*; 1 July, 24$\frac{3}{16}$*d.*; 1 Aug. 24$\frac{7}{16}$*d.*; 1 Sept. 24$\frac{1}{8}$*d.*; 1 Oct. 23$\frac{5}{8}$*d.*; 1 Nov. 23$\frac{1}{4}$*d.*; 1 Dec. 22$\frac{3}{8}$*d.*; 1903: 1 Jan. 22$\frac{1}{4}$*d.*; 2 Feb. 22$\frac{1}{16}$*d.*; 2 March, 22$\frac{1}{8}$*d.*; 1 April, 22$\frac{13}{16}$*d.*; 1 May, 24$\frac{3}{4}$*d.*; 2 June, 24$\frac{9}{16}$*d.*; 1 July, 24$\frac{1}{4}$*d.*; 1 Aug. 25$\frac{1}{2}$*d.*; 1 Sept. 26$\frac{3}{4}$*d.*; 1 Oct. 27$\frac{3}{16}$*d.*; 2 Nov. 27$\frac{5}{8}$*d.*; 1 Dec. 26$\frac{7}{16}$*d.*

SILVER BOOK (Codex Argenteus), see under *Bible.*

SIMANCAS (Castile, Spain). Near it Ramirez II. of Leon, and Fernando of Castile, gained a great victory over Abderahman, the Moorish king of Cordova, 6 Aug. 939.

SIMLA CASE, see *India*, 1866.

SIMNEL CONSPIRACY, see *Rebellions*, 1486.

SIMONASAKI or SHIMONOSEKI, see *Japan*, 1864; *Corea*, April, 1895.

SIMONIANS, a sect named after the founder, Simon Magus, the first heretic, about 41. A sect of social reformers called ST. SIMONIANS, after their founder, Claude H. comte de St. Simon (born 1760), sprang up in France in 1819, and attracted considerable attention; the doctrines were advocated in England, particularly by Dr. Prati, who lectured upon them in London, 24 Jan. 1834. St. Simon died in 1825, and his follower, Père Enfantin, died 1 Sept. 1864.

SIMONY (trading in church offices) derives its name from Simon desiring to purchase the gift of the Holy Spirit (*Acts* viii. 18, 19). It is forbidden in England by the canon law, and by statute 31 Eliz. c. 6, "for the avoiding of simony and corruption in presentations, collations, and donations of and to benefices," &c., 1588-9; and by statute of 12 Anne 2, stat. 12 (1713). The rev. James John Merest was convicted of simony, 26-29 Nov. 1869, and deprived.

The bishop of Peterborough (Dr. Magee), moved for a committee on the laws relating to simony; appointed . . . . . . 21 April, 1874

SIMPLON, a mountain road, leading from Switzerland into Italy, constructed by Napoleon in 1801-7. It winds up passes, crosses cataracts, and passes by galleries through solid rock, and has eight principal bridges. The number of workmen employed at one time varied from 30,000 to 40,000. The new Simplon tunnel boring operations began 13 Nov. 1898; Herr Brandt, the chief engineer, died, Nov. 1899. The tunnel to be completed, 1 July, 1905.

SINAI, MOUNT. Here the ten commandments were promulgated, 1491 B.C. *Exod.* xx. After much investigation and discussion by many persons, Dr. Beke stated that he had discovered the true Sinai, Feb. 1874.

SINALUNGA or ASINALUNGA (near Siena, Italy). Here Garibaldi, when about to enter the papal territory, was seized and conveyed to Alessandria, 23 Sept. 1867; see *Italy.*

SINDE (N.W. India), was traversed by the Greeks under Alexander, about 326 B.C.; conquered by the Persian Mahometans in the 8th century A.D.; tributary to the Ghaznevide dynasty in the 11th century; conquered by Nadir Shah, 1739; reverted to the empire of Delhi after his death, 1747; after various changes of rulers, Sinde was conquered by the English under Sir Charles Napier, *see India* and *Meeanee*, and annexed, March, 1843. Population, 1901, 3,212,808.

SINGAPORE, see *Straits Settlements*.

SINGING, see *Music* and *Hymns*.

SINKAT, see under *Soudan*, 1884.

SINKING FUND. First projected by sir Robert Walpole to redeem the debt to the bank of England; act passed in 1716. The act establishing the sinking fund of Mr. Pitt, devised by Dr. Price, was passed in March, 1786. A then estimated surplus of 900,000*l.* in the revenue was augmented by new taxes to make up the sum of 1,000,000*l.* which was to be invariably applied to the reduction of the national debt. The fallacy of the scheme was shown by Dr. Hamilton in 1813. In July, 1828, the sinking fund was limited to one-fourth of the actual surplus of revenue.

A new sinking fund was established by act passed 2 Aug. 1875. The annual charge of the national debt of the year ending 31 March, 1877, to be 27,700,000*l.*; subsequent years to be 28,000,000*l.* This act was temporarily suspended in 1897; again during the S. African war in 1900 and 1901; restored 1902.

SINOPE, an important Greek colony on the Euxine, after resisting several attacks was conquered by Mithridates IV., king of Pontus, and made his capital. It was the birth-place of Diogenes, the cynic philosopher. On 30 Nov. 1853, a Turkish fleet of seven frigates, three corvettes, and two smaller vessels, was attacked by a Russian fleet of six sail of the line, two sailing vessels, and three steamers, under admiral Nachimoff, and totally destroyed, except one vessel, which conveyed the tidings to Constantinople. Four thousand lives were lost by fire or drowning, and Osman Pacha, the Turkish admiral, died at Sebastopol of his wounds. In consequence of this act (considered treacherous) the Anglo-French fleet entered the Black Sea, 3 Jan. 1854.

SION COLLEGE AND HOSPITAL, situated on the site of a nunnery, which, having fallen to decay, was purchased by William Elsynge, a citizen and mercer, and converted into a college and hospital, called from his name Elsynge Spital. In 1340 he changed it to an Austin priory, which was afterwards granted by Henry VIII. to sir John Williams, master of the jewel-office, who, with sir Roland Hayward, inhabited it till its destruction by fire. In 1623, Dr. Thomas White having bequeathed 3000*l.* towards purchasing and building a college and alms-house on the ancient site, his executors erected the present college. It is held by two charters of incorporation, 6 Chas. I. 1630 and 16 Chas. II. 1664. It contains a valuable library (easily accessible to the public), and an almshouse for ten men and ten women. New buildings erected on the Thames Embankment; memorial stone laid 21 April, 1885; opened by the prince of Wales, 15 Dec. 1886.

SIRENE, an instrument for determining the velocity of aërial vibrations corresponding to the different pitches of musical sounds, was invented by baron Cagniard de la Tour of Paris in 1819. The principle was shown in an apparatus exhibited by Robert Hooke before the Royal Society, 27 July, 1681.

SISTERHOODS in the English church were begun by Lydia Priscilla Sellon about 1846, in Devonshire; she died, Nov. 1876.

SISTERS OF CHARITY, an order for the service of the sick poor, was founded by Vincent de Paul, in 1634. Their establishment in London began in 1834.

SIX ACTS, a term given to certain acts, also named "Gagging Acts," 60 Geo. III. & 1 Geo. IV. cc. 1, 2, 4, 6, 8, 9, passed in 1819-1820 to suppress seditious meetings and publications.

SIX ARTICLES, see *Articles*.

SIX CLERKS, officers of the court of chancery, who were anciently *clerici* or *clergy*. They were to conform to the laws of celibacy, and forfeit their places if they married; but when the constitution of the court began to alter, a law was made to permit them to marry; statute 24 & 25 Hen. VIII. 1533. The six clerks continued for many years officers of the chancery court, and held their offices in Chancery-lane, London, where proceedings by bill and answer were transacted and filed, and certain patents issued. *Law Dict.* The six clerks were discontinued by 5 & 6 Vict. c. 103, 1841.

SIXTEEN (*seize*), a large French political club, in the reigns of Henry III. and IV., sixteen members of which took charge of the sixteen quarters of Paris. They at first supported the catholic league, and attempted to overthrow Henry III., in 1587, but vacillating in their policy, and committing many crimes, their power was annihilated by Mayenne in 1591, and several of them were executed.

SIXTY CLUB (constitutional), instituted by A. E. Southall, limited to 60 members; president, the earl of Hardwicke; inaugural dinner, 13 Jan. 1898.

SKALITZ (Bohemia), was stormed by the Prussian general Steinmetz, 28 June, 1866; whereby the junction of the divisions of the Prussians was greatly facilitated.

SKATING (with blunt skates) is said to have been practised in prehistoric times by northern nations. See *Rinks*.

Mentioned by the Danish historian Saxo Grammaticus . . . . . . about	1134
William Fitz Stephens speaks of it in London, about	1180
Figures of skates in Olaus Magnus's history, printed	1555
Edinburgh skating club, ...	1642
Blade-skates, probably introduced from Holland, about 1660, were seen in St. James's-park by Evelyn and Pepys . . . . . 1 Dec.	1662
Robert Jones's "Art of Skating," published . .	1772
London Skating club, 1830; Oxford club . .	1838
Severe frost, much skating . . . . Jan.	1880
International skating contest at Vienna . Jan.	1882
National Skating Association of Great Britain, established in	1890

SKIERNIEVICE, Poland; see *Russia*, 15, 16 Sept. 1884.

SKINS. The raw skins of cattle were usually suspended on stakes and made use of instead of kettles to boil meat, in the north of England and in Scotland, 1 Edw. III. 1327. *Leland.*

SKUPTSCHINA, the Servian legislative assembly.

SKYE, Isle of, N.W. Scotland. See *Crofters*.

SKY SIGNS, see *Advertisements*.

SLADE PROFESSORSHIP of Fine Art, Cambridge, established in pursuance of the will of Felix Slade, 24 June, 1869, sir Matthew Digby Wyatt, the first professor, 1869-73; Sidney Colvin, 1873-1885; Mr. J. H. Middleton, 1886; Dr. Waldstein, 1895; sir Wm. Martin Conway, 1901.

SLANDER of Women, act passed 5 Aug. 1891.

SLANG, see *Dictionaries*.

SLATE. Fifteen persons were killed by the fall of a mass of rock and rubble at the Delaboll slate quarries, Cornwall, 21 April, 1869.

Great strike at lord Penrhyn's slate quarries Bethesda, Wales, in Sept.-Oct.; end Nov. 1874; the management of the quarries entrusted to a committee of the men Nov. 1874 till 1885, when the committee was abolished; prosperous management of lord Penrhyn 1885–1895
The men publish their grievances, through a committee, Aug.; lord Penrhyn issues a stringent reply, 25 Sept.; the committee of 71 men dismissed, strike declared, 28 Sept.; fruitless intervention of the board of trade . . . . Dec. 1896
The quarries closed; pensions granted to loyal men (over 65 years) . . . . . . 31 Dec. ,,
Lord Penrhyn invites the men to return on his terms . . . . 18 Jan. 1897
Meeting without result . . . . 18 March, ,,
Dispute settled, 21 Aug.; work resumed . Sept. ,,
Fresh dispute, some rioting; troops called in, partial lock-out, about 24 Oct. 1900; military withdrawn, 23 Nov.; quarries closed, 9 Dec.; work resumed, 11 Jan. 1901; fresh riots, 31 Dec., and 1 Jan. 1902; mass meeting, arbitration proposed, 30 Aug., rejected by lord Penrhyn; over 2,000 men at work, 4 Sept.; conflicts between workers and strikers, 13 Sept.; dispute continued, Jan. 1903; work renewed by some, mid April; meeting favouring the men held in London, 28 April; strike subsequently ends . . 1903

SLAUGHTER HOUSES ACT for the metropolis, passed 7 Aug. 1874.

SLAVERY. The traffic in men came from Chaldæa into Egypt, Arabia, and all over the East. In Greece, in the time of Homer, all prisoners of war were treated as slaves. The Lacedæmonian youths, trained up in the practice of deceiving and butchering slaves, were from time to time let loose upon them to show their proficiency; and once, for amusement only, murdered, it is said, 3000 in one night, see *Helots*. Alexander, when he razed Thebes, sold the whole people for slaves, 335 B.C. There were 400,000 slaves in Attica, 317 B.C. In Rome slaves were often chained to the gate of a great man's house, to give admittance to the guests invited to the feast. By one of the laws of the XII. Tables, creditors could seize their insolvent debtors, and keep them in their houses, till by their services or labour they had discharged the sum they owed. Cæcilius Isidorus left to his heir 4116 slaves, 12 B.C. The first Janissaries were Christian slaves, 1329.

Slavery abolished in the French colonies by the agency of M. Schœlcher 1848
Serfdom was abolished by Frederick I. of Prussia in 1702; by Christian VII. of Denmark in 1766; by Joseph II. emperor of Germany, in his hereditary states in 1781; by Nicholas I. of Russia in the imperial domains in 1842; and by his successor, Alexander II. throughout his empire, 3 March, 1861.
Slavery ceased in the Dutch West Indies on 1 July, 1863
Slavery abolished in Porto Rico . 23 March, 1873
Immediate suppression of slavery in the colonies of St. Thomas, &c. by Portugal, announced, Feb. 1876
Gradual emancipation in Cuba; bill passed in Spanish senate, 24 Dec. 1879; by deputies, 21 Jan. promulgated, 18 Feb. 1880; total abolition by decree . . . . 6 Oct. 1886
Slavery to be abolished in Egypt . end of July, 1881
Abolition of slavery in Brazil (*which see*) . . 1867-88
Slavery gradually diminishing in Zanzibar, Oct. 1889; abolished by decree . . . 6 April, 1897
Anti-slavery Conference at Brussels: meeting of foreign plenipotentiaries and delegates from 17 states, 18 Nov. 1889. Conferences: 19 Nov.–Dec. 1889; 27 Jan.–28 May, 1890. Regulations for the suppression of the slave trade, and rules relating to the traffic in spirit agreed to. After much negotiation, the general act was ratified by all the powers for immediate effect . 2 April, 1892
The act accepted by the Egyptian government, 25 June, 1895

SLAVERY in England. Laws respecting the sale of slaves were made by Alfred. The English peasantry were commonly sold for slaves in Saxon and Norman times; children were sold in Bristol market like cattle for exportation. Many were sent to Ireland and to Scotland. Under the Normans the vassals (termed villeins, of and pertaining to the *vill*) were devisable as chattels during the feudal times.

Severe statutes were passed in the reign of Richard II., 1377 and 1385; the rebellion of Wat Tyler, 1381, arose partly out of the evils of serfdom.
A statute was enacted by Edward VI. that a runaway, or any one who lived idly for three days, should be brought before two justices of the peace, and marked V with a hot iron on the breast, and adjudged the slave of him who bought him for two years. He was to take the slave and give him bread, water, or small drink, and refuse meat, and cause him to work by beating, chaining, or otherwise; and, if within that space, he absented himself fourteen days, was to be marked on the forehead or cheek, by a hot iron, with an S, and be his master's slave for ever; second desertion was made felony. It was lawful to put a ring of iron round his neck, arm, or leg. A child might be put apprentice, and, on running away, become a slave to his master 1547
Queen Elizabeth ordered her bondsmen in the western counties to be made free at easy rates . 1574
Serfdom was finally extinguished in 1660, when tenures in capite, knights' service, &c., were abolished.
A slave named Somerset, brought to England, was, because of his ill state, turned adrift by his master. By the charity of Mr. Granville Sharp he was restored to health, when his master again claimed him. A suit was the consequence, which established, by decision of the Court of King's Bench, in favour of Somerset, that slavery could not exist in Great Britain 22 June, 1772
Act for the abolition of slavery throughout the British colonies, and for the promotion of industry among the manumitted slaves, and for compensation to the persons hitherto entitled to the services of such slaves by the grant from parliament of 20,000,000*l.* sterling, passed 28 Aug. 1833
Slavery terminated in the British possessions; 770,280 slaves became free . . . 1 Aug. 1834
Slavery was abolished in the East Indies 1 Aug. 1838
British and Foreign anti-slavery society established, 1839
In 1853 John Anderson, a runaway slave, killed Septimus Digges, a planter of Missouri, who attempted to arrest him, and escaped to Canada. The American government claimed him as a murderer. The Canadian judges deciding that the law required his surrender, Mr. Edwin James, Q.C. (15 Jan.), obtained a writ of habeas corpus for his appearance before the court of queen's bench. Anderson was discharged on technical grounds . . . . 16 Feb. 1861
Circular from the Admiralty concerning the surrendering fugitive slaves on board British ships to their owners, dated 31 July; much censured by the public, Sept., Oct.; withdrawn Nov. 1875

A revised circular issued near end of Dec., 1875; met with much adverse criticism . . Jan. 1876
Government commission appointed (the duke of Somerset, chief justice Cockburn, sir Henry S. Maine, and others), Feb.; report unfavourable to the circulars; published . . . 13 June, „
New admiralty instructions: fugitive slaves to be received and not given up; action left to captain's discretion; breach of international faith and comity to be avoided; issued . . 10 Aug. „
Jubilee meeting to celebrate the abolition of slavery in the British colonies at Guildhall, London, the prince of Wales in the chair . . 1 Aug. 1884
International congress on the "White Slave" trade opened at Frankfort . . . . 7 Oct. 1902

SLAVERY IN UNITED STATES. Before the war of independence all the states contained slaves. In 1783 the statement in the Massachusetts Bill of Rights, "All men are born free and equal," was declared in the supreme court at Boston to bar slave-holding in that state. Slaves in the United States in 1790, 697,897; in 1810, 1,191,364; in 1820, 2,009,031; in 1850, 3,204,313; in 1860, 4,002,996. In 1870, 4,889,193, free coloured persons.

Congress passes unanimously the celebrated ordinance "for the government of the territory to the N.W. of the Ohio," which contained an "*unalterable*" article, forbidding slavery or involuntary servitude in the said state, 13 July, 1787; after 1800, several of the states prayed, without effect, to be relieved from this prohibition.
Louisiana purchased, which was considered by many as fatal to the constitution 1803
The enormous increase in the growth of cotton in the southern states (see *Cotton*) led to a corresponding increase in the demand for slave labour. The *Missouri Compromise* (drawn up by Henry Clay, by which slavery was permitted in that state, but was prohibited in all that part of it to the north of 36° 30′ N. lat.), carried . Feb. 1820
Contest between the slave-holders and their opponents at the annexation of Texas; a similar division to that of Missouri obtained 25 Dec. 1845
Another compromise effected; California admitted as a free state: but the Fugitive Slave act passed (*which see*) 1850
The Missouri compromise was abrogated by the admission of Nebraska and Kansas as slave-holding states; civil war ensued (see *Kansas*) . 1854
Dred Scot's case (see *United States*) . . 1857
John Brown's attempt to create a slave rebellion in Virginia failed (see *United States*) . . Nov. 1859
Abraham Lincoln, the anti-slavery candidate, elected president of the United States 4 Nov. 1860
Secession of South Carolina (see *United States*), Dec. „
Slavery abolished in the district of Colombia 16 April, 1862
President Lincoln proclaims the abolition of slavery in the southern states, if they have not returned to the union on 1 Jan. 1863 22 Sept. „
The total abolition of slavery in the United States officially announced . . . . 18 Dec. „
Mr. William Lloyd Garrison, a fervent champion for emancipation, entertained at St. James's-hall, London (he started the *Liberator* in 1831, and had suffered much for his zeal) . . 29 June, 1867
A negro judge present in a court at New Orleans, 18 Sept. „
Negro equality with the whites completely recognised . . . . Feb. 1870
Slavery revived in the south, peonage trials, July, 1903

SLAVE TRADE. The slave trade from Congou and Angola was begun by the Portuguese in 1481. The commerce in man has brutalised a tract fifteen degrees on each side of the equator, and forty degrees wide, or of 4,000,000 of square miles; and men and women have been bred for sale to the Christian nations during the last 250 years, and war carried on to make prisoners for the Christian market. The Abbé Raynal computed (1777) that, at the time of his writing, 9,000,000 of slaves had been consumed by the Europeans. The slave-trade is now approaching extinction.

In 1768 the slaves taken from Africa amounted to 104,100. In 1786 the annual number was about 100,000.
In 1807 it was shown by documents, produced by government, that since 1792 upwards of 3,500,000 Africans had been torn from their country, and had either perished on the passage or been sold in the West Indies.

SLAVE TRADE OF ENGLAND: begun by sir John Hawkins His first expedition, with the object of procuring negroes on the coast of Africa, and conveying them for sale at the West Indies, took place in Oct. 1562; see *Guinea* and *Assiento*.
England employed 130 ships and carried off 42,000 slaves, 1786.
Thos. Clarkson, at a spot in Wadesmill, Hertford, devotes his life to the abolition of the slave-trade, June, 1785.
The "Society for the Suppression of the Slave Trade," founded by Clarkson, Wilberforce, and Dillwyn, 1787.
Slave-trade question debated in parliament, 1787.
The debate for its abolition; two days, April, 1791.
Mr. Wilberforce's motion lost by a majority of 88 to 83, 3 April, 1798.
The question introduced under the auspices of Lord Grenville and Mr. Fox, then ministers, 31 March, 1806.
The trade abolished by parliament, 25 March, 1807.
Thomas Clarkson, died, aged 85, Sept. 1846.
An obelisk as a memorial of Thos. Clarkson, erected by Mr. Arthur Giles Puller, at Wadesmill, inaugurated 9 Oct. 1879.
A statue unveiled at Wisbeach, Cambridge, 11 Nov. 1881.

FOREIGN COUNTRIES: the trade was abolished by Austria in 1782; by the French convention in 1794; by the United States in 1808.
The allies at Vienna declared against it, Feb. 1815.
Napoleon, in the hundred days, abolished the trade, 29 March, 1815.
Treaty for its repression with Spain, 1817; with the Netherlands, May, 1818; with Brazil, Nov. 1826; prohibition, 1831; not effected till 1852.
Its revival was proposed in the congress of the United States of America, 14 Dec. 1856, and negatived by 183 votes to 58.
In June, 1857, the French government gave permission to M. Regis to convey *free* negroes from Africa to Guadaloupe and Martinido, French colonies.
This having led to abuses and consequent troubles (see *Charles et Georges*), was eventually given up in Jan. 1859.
It is said that about 40,000 slaves were landed at Cuba in 1860.
A treaty between Great Britain and the United States for the abolition of the slave trade, was signed 7 April; ratified 20 May, 1862.
The Spanish government denounce the slave trade as piracy, Nov. 1865.
Sir Samuel Baker headed an expedition to put down slave-trading on the Nile (see *Egypt*), Jan. 1870; reported to be partially successful, 30 June, 1873. He published "Ismailia," a history of the expedition, 1874. He estimates that at least 50,000 are captured and sold as slaves, Nov. 1874.
A species of slave trade arose in the South Seas consequent upon natives being enticed on board certain British vessels and shipped to Queensland, Australia, and the Fiji isles; the subject was brought before parliament (see *Melanesia*), 1871-2.
The ship *Carl* (owner, Dr. James P. Murray; master, Joseph Armstrong) left Melbourne for South Sea isles; it anchored off Malokolo, Solomon's and Bougainville isles and kidnapped many natives as labourers for the Fiji isles; while about 20 miles from land, the prisoners rose and attempted to set fire to the ship; were fired on; about 50 killed and 20 wounded were cast into the sea. At Melbourne Murray gave evidence, and Armstrong was committed for trial, 16 Aug.; the master and mate sentenced to death, Nov. 1872.
Sir Bartle Frere went to Zanzibar on a mission to suppress the East African slave trade; see *Zanzibar*, 1872-3.
An act of parliament for consolidating with amendments the acts for carrying into effect treaties for the more effectual suppression of the slave trade (36 & 37 Vict. c. 88), was passed 5 Aug. 1873.

Several African kings and chiefs, at Cape Coast Castle, agreed to give up slave trade, at an interview with governor Strahan, 3 Nov. 1874.
The slave trade on the Gold Coast abolished, by proclamation of governor Strahan, 17 Dec. 1874.
Convention with Egypt forbidding the traffic, 4 Aug. 1877; col. Gordon's efforts in the Soudan reported successful, 1879.
Slave trade prohibited at West African conference, 7 Jan. 1885.
Slave trade in East Africa checked by British cruisers, 1886.
United action of England and Germany and other powers to check the maritime slave-trade and importation of arms on the east coast of Africa, which is to be blockaded for that purpose from Suakin to Zanzibar, Oct.–Nov.; proclamation of the commencement of the blockade, 2 Dec. 1888. See *Zanzibar*.
Mr. Sydney Buxton's resolution for urgent suppression of the slave trade passed in the house of commons, 26 March, 1889.
Slave trade reported nearly extinct in Egypt, and few slaves there, May, 1889.
Law for the repression of the slave trade published in Turkey, 30 Dec. 1889.
Dealing in slaves prohibited in Zanzibar, 1 Aug. 1890.
For conflicts, see *Congo*.

SLAVONIA or **SCLAVONIA**, a province of Austria, derives its name from the Slavs, a Sarmatian people who replaced the Avars in Pannonia early in the 9th century. In 864 Cyril and Methodius, Greek missionaries, preached here, and adapted the Greek alphabet to the Slavonian language; the letters of which have since been a little altered. The country, after having been held at times by the Greeks, Turks, and Hungarians, and the cause of sanguinary conflicts, was ceded finally to Hungary in 1699, at the peace of Carlowitz. Deputies from the Slavonian provinces of Austria were entertained at Moscow and St. Petersburg, May, 1867. The Croatian-Slavonian diet, at Agram, was dissolved, May, 1867. It protested against incorporation with Hungary. The Slavonian family of languages includes Russian, Polish, Servian, Bohemian, Bulgarian, Wendic, Slovak, and Polabic. For the war, see *Turkey*, 1875-6.

Estimated number of Slavs in Europe in 1875: 90,365,633; Russians and Ruthenians, 66,129,590; Serbo-Croats, 5,940,539; Bulgarians, 5,123,952; Slovenes, 1,260,000; Slovaks, 2,223,830; Czechs, 4,815,154; Poles, 9,492,162.
Lord Ilchester's bequest to promote the study of Slavonian literature at Oxford; lectures given, May, 1876.
Agitation against the Germans in Slavonic provinces of Austria, Aug.–Sept. 1883.
Political agrarian excitement and arrests among the peasantry, April, 1897.

SLEEP, see *Seven Sleepers*. M. Chauffat, awoke after a nineteen days' sleep at the Alexandra Palace, 28 Nov. 1888; many similar cases are reported. Johann Latus, at Myslowitz, in Silesia, is said to have slept four and a-half months, being kept alive by imbibing milk, reported 31 Jan.; he awoke about 9 Feb., 1892. The case was ascribed to catalepsy.

SLESWIG, see *Holstein*.

SLIDING-SCALE, see *Corn Laws*.

SLING. In *Judges* xx. 16, is mentioned the skill of the Benjamite slingers (about 1406 B.C.), and with a sling David slew Goliath 1063 B.C. (1 *Sam.* xvii.). The natives of the Balearic isles (Majorca, Minorca, and Iviça) were celebrated slingers, and served as mercenaries in the Carthaginian and Roman armies. Slings are said to have been used by the Huguenots at the siege of Sancerre, in 1672, to economise their powder.

SLOANE'S MUSEUM, see *British Museum*.

SLOYD or **SLOJD ASSOCIATION** OF **GREAT BRITAIN AND IRELAND**, its object to promote the training of the eye and hand; first meeting held in London, the earl of Meath in the chair, 5 Dec. 1888. The "Sloyd" or "Slojd" system is reported successful in Scandinavia; August Abrahamson, founder of the Sloyd seminary at Nääs, 1872, died, 6 May, 1898. Meeting in London; successful report, 10 Feb. 1894.

SLOUGH, near Eton, Bucks, Mrs. Ann Reville, a butcher's wife, was barbarously murdered early in evening, 11 April, 1881. Alfred Payne, a lad, was tried and acquitted, same month.

SLUYS (Holland), near which Edward III. gained a signal naval victory over the French. The English had the wind of the enemy, and the sun at their backs, and began this sanguinary action. Two hundred and thirty French ships were taken; thousands of Frenchmen were killed, with two of their admirals; the loss of the English was inconsiderable: 24 June, 1340.

SMALCALD (Hesse), **TREATY OF**, entered into between the elector of Brandenburg and the other princes of Germany in favour of Protestantism, 31 Dec. 1530; see *Protestants*. The emperor, apprehensive that the kings of France and England would join this league, signed the treaty of Passau, 31 July, 1532, allowing liberty of conscience.

SMALL HOLDINGS, See *Agricultural*.

SMALLPOX, *variola* (diminutive of *varus*, a pimple), a highly contagious disease, supposed to have been introduced into Europe from the East by the Saracens. Rhazes, an Arabian, described it accurately, about 900. From Europe it was carried to America, soon after its discovery, and raged there with great severity, destroying the Indians by thousands. In 1694, queen Mary of England died of smallpox, as did in 1711 and 1712 the emperor of Germany, the dauphin and dauphiness of France and their son, in 1730 the emperor of Russia, in 1741 the queen of Sweden, and in 1774 Louis XV. of France. It is stated that in the middle of the last century two millions perished by it in Russia. In London in 1723 one out of fourteen deaths was caused by smallpox, and in France in 1754 the rate was one in ten. For the attempts to alleviate this scourge, see *Inoculation*, introduced into England in 1722, and *Vaccination*, announced by Dr. Jenner in 1798. *Smallpox Hospital*, established 1746. Smallpox raged in parts of London, and thousands died, 1870-1; a temporary hospital was established at Hampstead (*which see*). Many parents have been fined for opposing the vaccination of their children, 1870-6. In Sept. and Oct. 1862, a great many sheep died of smallpox in the West of England, till successful preventive measures were resorted to. Many cases and deaths, adults and children, in London, 1876-8; and in 1901-2. The Vaccination act of 1898, which remains in force until 1 Jan. 1904, modified in many important particulars the law previously existing. It provides for domiciliary vaccination, the use of glycerinated calf lymph (supplied by the Local Government board), and exempts the conscientious objector from penalties, see *Vaccination*.

Smallpox prevalent in London, 88 deaths 1—7 May; 103 deaths 15—21 May; diminishing July, 1881.
Deaths, June, 1880—June, 1881, 1532 deaths, 637 not vaccinated; in N.E. London, May, deaths, about 36 a week, June, 1884; deaths decreasing reported, 24 July; reappears, but subsides, Dec. 1884.

Severe epidemic of smallpox at Sheffield and neighbourhood, March, 1887; still prevalent, Jan. 1888; disappearing, April, 1888.
Severe at Manchester and Leicester, about 16 Jan. 1893; at Gloucester, 1896.
Epidemics in London, August *et seq.*; 1,743 cases, 257 deaths in 1901; severe in winter; 1,604 cases in hospitals, 11 March, total cases 9,659, deaths 1,663, 1901-2. Outbreak at Cambridge, July, Aug. 1903; Newcastle-on-Tyne, Aug.; isolation hospitals cost over 500,000*l.*; subsides, June *et seq.* 1902; prevalent in United States, Feb. 1902.

See *Vaccination.*

SMALL TENEMENTS ACTS (59 Geo. III. c. 12, 1819); 1850 (13 & 14 Vict. c. 99), provided for owners paying rates of houses instead of the occupiers. This was annulled by the new Reform act, 30 & 31 Vict. c. 102, s. 7 (1867). Small Dwellings Acquisition act passed, 1899.

SMECTYMNUUS, the initials of certain nonconformist writers against episcopacy in the seventeenth century: Stephen Marshall, Edmund Calamy, Thomas Young, Matthew Newcomen, William Spurstow. They were answered by bishop Hall in his "Divine Right of Episcopacy," 1640.

SMITH'S CHARITY (FOR POOR KIN). Alderman Henry Smith, by will dated 26 April, 1647, left 1000*l.* for relief of captives held by Turkish pirates, and 1000*l.* for his poor kinsmen.

The former object having become obsolete, an act was passed in 1772 to divert all the property to the poor kinsmen. In 1868 these were 412 in number. The value of the property was 17,000*l.* a year in 1889. The master of the rolls decided in Dec. 1877, that the funds should be applied to general charitable purposes. On appeal, the decision was in favour of the "poor Smiths," 12 Feb. 1878.

SMITHFIELD, WEST, in the heart of London, was once a favourite walk of the London citizens, outside the city walls. Sir W. Wallace was executed here, 23 Aug. 1305. On 15 June, 1381, Wat Tyler was met by Richard II. at this place, and was stabbed by Walworth the mayor. Many tournaments were also held here. In the reign of Mary (1553-8), many persons perished by fire; and Bartholomew Leggatt, an Arian, was burnt here, 18 March, 1612.—Bartholomew fair was held here till 1853.—This place is mentioned as the site of a cattle market as far back as 1150. The space devoted to this purpose was enlarged from about three acres to four and a half, and in 1834 to six and a quarter. The ancient regulations were called the "statutes of Smithfield." In one day there were sometimes assembled 4000 beasts and 30,000 sheep. The annual amount of the sales was about 7,000,000*l.*

Sold here 226,132 beasts, 1,593,270 sheep and lambs, 26,356 calves, 33,531 pigs. (About 160 salesmen) 1846
The contracted space of the market, the slaughtering places adjoining, and many other nuisances, gave ground to much dissatisfaction, and after investigation, an act was passed appointing metropolitan market commissioners with powers to provide a new market, slaughtering places, &c.; and to close the market at Smithfield . 1 Aug. 1851
Smithfield was used as a cattle market for the last time on 11 June; and the new market in Copenhagen-fields was opened on 13 June (see *Metropolitan Market*) 1855
A dead-meat and poultry market ordered to be erected in Smithfield, and Newgate market to cease 1861
A tender for its erection, from designs by Horace Jones, accepted from Messrs. Browne and Robinson for 134,460*l.* . . . . Nov. 1866
The market inaugurated by the lord mayor Lawrence, 24 Nov.; opened to the public . 1 Dec. 1868
New poultry market, inaugurated by lord mayor Cotton . . . . 30 Nov. 1875
New central fruit and vegetable market determined on . . . . 14 July, 1879
A new poultry and provision market was opened in Farringdon road by lord mayor Isaacs, 11 Dec. 1889; the new fruit and vegetable market opened by lord mayor Evans . . . . 13 June, 1892
The *Smithfield Club*, to promote improvements in the breed of cattle, was established 17 Dec. 1798; first president, Francis, duke of Bedford; first secretary, Arthur Young. The members established an annual cattle show, held first in Dolphin-yard, Smithfield, Dec. 1799; next in Barbican, 1805; in Goswell-street, 1806; removed to Baker-street, 1839; and to the new Agricultural hall, Liverpool road, Islington, 1862.
The show, suspended in Dec. 1866, on account of the cattle plague, was partially resumed Dec. 1867; wholly, Dec. 1868.
Three of the highest prizes were awarded to queen Victoria; 110,000 visitors, 10-14 Dec. 1883. Large show opened, 339 cattle, 221 sheep, no pigs through swine fever, 10 Dec. 1894; the show is held annually in December.

SMITHSONIAN INSTITUTION, "for the increase and diffusion of knowledge among men," a handsome building at Washington, U.S., was founded in 1846, by means of a legacy of above 100,000*l.* bequeathed for the purpose to the United States government by James Smithson, illegitimate son of sir Hugh Smithson, who became duke of Northumberland in 1766. It includes the U.S. national museum, the zoological park, and the astrophysical observatory, and publishes and freely distributes scientific memoirs and reports. The library was burnt on 25 Jan. 1865. Professor Joseph Henry, the first secretary, died, 13 May, 1878; succeeded by Mr. Spencer F. Baird, died, 19 Aug. 1887; succeeded by Professor S. P. Langley. The Hodgkins medal (first gold medal given by the institution for scientific work) awarded to prof. James Dewar for his discoveries in the liquefaction of air, April, 1899.

SMOKE NUISANCE. An act was passed in 1853 to abate this nuisance, proceeding from chimney shafts and steamers above London bridge. In 1856 another act, obtained for its further application to steamers below London bridge, and to potteries and glass-houses previously exempted, came into operation, 1 Jan. 1858; enactments have been made for all the kingdom.

Meeting at Mansion-house for the abatement of smoke in London, 7 Jan. 1881.
An exhibition of appliances for this purpose in the Royal Albert Hall, opened 30 Nov. 1881; closed 14 Feb. 1882; opened at Manchester, 17 March, 1882.
National Smoke Abatement Institution founded, and Mr. R. E. W. Coles appointed smoke inspector, autumn, 1882.
Smoke abatement fund opened, 1883.
The Thompson smoke consuming furnace tried successfully on the Thames, 15 July, 1886.
Messrs. Ashworth and Kneen patent a furnace which saves about 35 per cent. of coal and consumes smoke, autumn, 1887.
A bill to abate the nuisance was rejected by the lords, 2 March, 1891.
The London county council authorised to deal with the smoke nuisance by the Public Health Act of 1891.
A smokeless fuel, invented by Herr Koopmann, was exhibited before the prince of Wales and others at Messrs. Brewis' premises, King's cross, London, N., 7 April, 1891. The fuel consists of coal-dust incorporated with pitch and other mineral substances in small proportions.
Smoke abatement, committee appointed—the duke of Westminster, sir Frederick Abel, lord Rayleigh, and other scientists—at Manchester, 8 Nov. 1889.
Other committees formed at Glasgow and other places; many reports with recommendations issued (*Times*) 3 Aug. 1896.

Coal smoke abatement society formed through the exertions of sir W. B. Richmond,; committee: the abp. of Canterbury, duke of Westminster and others, formed, 1898; some prosecutions, Nov. 1899 *et seq.*

SMOLENSKO (Russia). The French in most sanguinary engagements here were three times repulsed, but ultimately succeeded in entering Smolensko, and found the city, which had been bombarded, burning and partly in ruins, 16, 17 Aug. 1812. Barclay de Tolly, the Russian commander-in-chief, incurred the displeasure of the emperor Alexander because he retreated after the battle, and Kutusoff succeeded to the command.

SMUGGLING. The customs duties, instituted to enable the king to afford protection to trade against pirates, afterwards became a branch of public revenue, and gave rise to much smuggling. The Smugglers' act was passed in 1736, and its severity was mitigated in 1781 and 1784. A revision of these statutes took place 1826 and 1835. Lieut. the hon. H. N. Shore's "Smuggling Days and Smuggling Ways," published 1892.

SMYRNA, see *Seven Churches.*

SNEEZING. The custom of saying "God bless you" to the sneezer originated, according to Strada, among the ancients, who, through an opinion of the danger attending it, after sneezing made a short prayer to the gods, as "Jupiter, help me." The custom is mentioned by Homer, the Jewish rabbis, and others, and is found among savages. Polydore Vergil says it took its rise at the time of the plague, 558, when the infected fell down dead sneezing, though seemingly in good health.

SNIDER GUN, see under *Firearms.*

SNOWDON, see *Railways*, 1896; *Wales*, 1902.

SNUFF-TAKING took its rise in England from the captures made of vast quantities of snuff by sir George Rooke's expedition to Vigo in 1702, and the practice soon became general. In 1839 there were imported 1,622,493 lbs. of snuff, of which 196,305 lbs. were entered for home consumption; the duty was 88,263*l.*; see *Tobacco.* In 1853, 2,573,925 lbs. of snuff and cigars, in 1861, 2,110,430 lbs.; in 1871, 3,852,236 lbs.; 1877, 3,762,831 lbs.; 1883, 3,121,174 lbs.; 1887, 3,595,071 lbs.; 1902, 137 lbs. (snuff only) were imported.

SOANE MUSEUM, &c. No. 13, Lincoln's-inn-fields, was gradually formed by sir John Soane, the architect, who died in 1837, after making arrangements for its being open to the public by an act passed in 1833. It contains Egyptian and other antiquities, valuable paintings, rare books, &c. 150*l.* are distributed annually to distressed architects or their widows and children.

One of two sealed closets in the museum was opened 29 Nov. 1886; chiefly private legal documents discovered.

SOAP is a salt, a compound of a fatty acid with an alkali, soda or potash. The Hebrew *bôrith*, translated soap, is merely a general term for cleansing substances. *Job* ix. 30; *Jer.* ii. 22. Pliny declares soap to be an invention of the Gauls, though he prefers the German to the Gallic soap. Nausicaa and her attendants, Homer tells us, washed clothes by treading upon them with their feet in pits of water. *Odyssey*, book vi. The Romans used fuller's earth. *Savon*, the French word for soap, is ascribed to its having been manufactured at Savona, near Genoa. The manufacture of soap began in London in 1524, before which time it was supplied by Bristol at one penny per pound. The duty upon soap, imposed in 1711, after several reductions from 3*d.* per pound, was totally repealed in 1853. It then produced, according to the chancellor of the exchequer, Mr. Gladstone, about 1,126,000*l.* annually. Exported from the United Kingdom: 1876, 254,853 cwts.; 1880, 391,808 cwts.; 1885, 402,112 cwts.; 1890, 496,930 cwts.; 1896, 719,700 cwts.; 1900, 874,214 cwts.

SOBRAON (N.W. India). The British army, 35,000 strong, under sir Hugh (afterwards viscount) Gough, attacked the Sikh force on the Sutlej, 10 Feb. 1846. The enemy was dislodged after a dreadful contest, and all their batteries taken; and in attempting the passage of the river by a floating bridge in their rear, the weight of the masses that crowded upon it caused it to break down, and thousands of Sikhs were killed, wounded, or drowned. The British loss was 2338 men.

SOCIALISM, which proposes the re-organisation of society for the benefit of the community, and advocates the doctrine of the equal right of all to the material conditions of existence, was warmly advocated in London, 24 Jan. 1834, by Robert Owen. He had, beginning at New Lanark, in Scotland, about 1801, established a settlement at New Harmony in America in 1824. He died 17 Nov. 1858, aged 90. The French socialists, termed *Communists*, became a powerful political body in that country, were implicated in the revolution of 1848, and made an insurrection at Paris, 1871. See *France*, *Germany*, 1878 *et seq.*, *Positive Philosophy*, and *Working-men.* See *Individualism.* Socialism in England is represented by the Social Democratic federation, the Fabian society, and the Independent Labour party, and in a modified form, by the Christian Social union; in Germany by the Social Democrats; in France by the Workmen's party and the Republican socialists. Socialism is also active in Austria, Italy, Belgium, Denmark. The subject of municipal socialism is at the present time (1903) receiving considerable attention.

The rev. Charles Kingsley, Mr. Thomas Hughes, and others, endeavoured to set up *Christian Socialism*, about 1855-60

At a meeting of "Christian Socialists," including prince Johann Schwarzenburg, and prince Liechtenstein, and other eminent persons, at Vienna, it was resolved to erect a monument to baron Vogelsang, their founder . . . 13 March, 1893

Count Tolstoi's "The Kingdom of God is within you," translated by Mrs. Garnett, published Feb. 1894

[He renounces for himself all nationality, government, and law, &c., and proposes the adoption of Christ's sermon on the mount.—*Matt.* v., vi. vii.; he was excommunicated by the Greek church, March, 1901.]

P. J. Proudhon, an eminent socialist, to whom is ascribed the saying "*La propriété c'est le vol*"; died 20 Jan. 1865

Communist manifesto issued by Carl Marx, 1848; (he died 14 March, 1883).

Social democratic party organised by Ferdinand Lassalle 1863

International workmen's association formed . . 1864

"Gotha programme" (exalting labour) . . . 1875

A grand congress of socialists met at Ghent, Sept. 1877

Socialism said to be increasing in Germany . . ,,

Stringent bill to repress it passed in the parliament; socialists expelled from Germany by decree, Nov. many papers suppressed, Nov., Dec., 1878. Expulsions renewed . . . . autumn, 1880

See *Germany*, 1890.

Illegal meeting of socialists permitted in Dod-street, Limehouse, London . . 27 Sept. 1885

Social democratic federation holds meetings which tend to riots, see *Riots* . . 8 and 21 Feb. 1886
Meetings held in Trafalgar-sq., 29 Aug. and 21 Nov. ,,
About the end of 1886 they began "church parades" disturbing the service at several churches; ineffectually at St. Paul's cathedral . 27 Feb. 1887
The general council of the social democratic federation issues a manifesto exhorting to constant organized agitation for adequate relief works &c., to be provided by the government and local authorities; see *Hyde Park* and *Riots*, 13 Nov. ,,
Mr. William Morris, poet, author of the "Earthly Paradise," Mr. H. M. Hyndman, Mr. H. H. Champion, and Mr. John Burns became leaders of the "socialist league" formed in 1886.
A kind of state socialism instituted in Germany; see under *Working Men*, 1889.
The attempts of the federation to hold open-air meetings at Chelsea on Sunday evenings, prevented by the police, Oct., Dec. 1891, and Jan. 1892
Socialist congress at Marseilles . . 25 Sept. ,,
Great social democratic congress at Berlin, met, 14 Nov. *et seq.*, 1892; at Cologne, end of Oct. 1893; at Vienna . . . . . March, 1894
The Socialist union formed against the government at Paris by the combination of socialists and anarchists at a meeting opened by "gen." Cluseret (a communist) . . . 14 Jan. 1893
International socialist congress at Ghent, 2 April; at Zurich . . . . . . 6 Aug. ,,
Socialist congresses held at Frankfort, 22 Oct. 1894; at Breslau, Oct. 1895; Gotha, 11 Oct. 1896; Stuttgart, 3 Oct. 1898; Hanover, 8 Oct. 1899; Lübeck, 23 Sept. 1901; Munich, 15 Sept. 1902; Dresden, 13 Sept. 1903
Dissensions in Germany and France, between the moderates and ultras . . . . . Nov. 1894
Social democratic federation conference held at Birmingham (see *Germany*, 1895–6) . 4 Aug. 1895
Death of Frederick Engels, socialist leader Aug. ,,
International congress at Lille broken up by rioting; several arrests . . . 23 July, 1896
International congress in London (see *Hyde Park*), 26 July *et seq.* ,,
National socialist congress, 1st meeting at Erfurt, 23 Nov. ,,
Socialist and labour conferences held at Leeds, 31 March, 1899; at Glasgow . . . 13 April, 1900
Wilhelm Liebknecht, eminent socialist leader, editor of the *Vorwärts*, born 1826; died . 7 Aug. ,,
Internat. socialist congress, Mr. H. M. Hyndman and sig. Costa, presidents, Paris . Sept. ,,
Nat. socialist and labour conference at Leicester, 5 April, 1901
Internat. meeting in Brussels, the treatment of the Poles in Prussia (*which see*) condemned, 30 Dec. ,,
"Municipal socialism," 17 articles in the *Times*, mid Aug.–10 Nov. 1902

SOCIAL SCIENCE. The National Association for the Promotion of Social Science originated in a meeting at lord Brougham's in May, 1857. Its object was to promote improvements in the administration of law, in education, in public health, and in social economy. It held annual meetings, and published its proceedings.

Mr. Wm. Ellis and Mr. John Stuart Mill began to promote the study . . . . . about 1823
Birmingham, meeting opened . . 12 Oct. 1857
Liverpool . . . . . . 11 Oct. 1858
Bradford . . . . . . 10 Oct. 1859
Glasgow . . . . . . 24 Sept. 1860
Dublin . . . . . . 14 Aug. 1861
London . . . . . . 6 June, 1862
Edinburgh . . . . . . 7 Oct. 1863
York . . . . . . 22 Sept. 1864
Sheffield . . . . . . 4 Oct. 1865
Manchester . . . . . . 2 Oct. 1866
Belfast . . . . . . 18 Sept. 1867
Birmingham . . . . . . 30 Sept. 1868
Bristol . . . . . . 29 Sept. 1869
Newcastle-on-Tyne . . . . 21 Sept. 1870
Leeds . . . . . . 4 Oct. 1871
Plymouth . . . . . . 11 Sept. 1872
Norwich . . . . . . 1 Oct. 1873
Glasgow . . . . . . 30 Sept. 1874
Brighton . . . . . . 6 Oct. 1875
Liverpool . . . . . . 11 Oct. 1876
Aberdeen . . . . . . 19 Sept. 1877
Cheltenham . . . . . . 23 Oct. 1878
Manchester . . . . . . 1 Oct. 1879
Edinburgh . . . . . . 5 Oct. 1880
Dublin . . . . . . 3 Oct. 1881
Nottingham . . . . . . 20 Sept. 1882
Huddersfield . . . . . . 3 Oct. 1883
Birmingham (the last congress) . . . 17 Sept. 1884

SOCIAL WARS, see *Athens*, and *Marsi*.

SOCIETIES AND INSTITUTIONS, LITERARY AND SCIENTIFIC, in Great Britain. Further details of many of these will be found under their respective heads. All in the list below are in London, except otherwise stated. An act was passed, 11 Aug. 1854, "to afford facilities for the establishment of institutions for the promotion of literature and science," by grants of land, &c.; and for their regulation. The Royal and London Institutions were exempted from the operation of the act. See *Scientific Papers*.

The "Year-Book of Scientific and Learned Societies" first appeared in 1884
Royal Society . . . . . . Charter 1662
Christian Knowledge Society 1698
Spalding Gentlemen's Society 1712
Society of Antiquaries . . . (Charter 1751) 1717
Society of Dilettanti 1734
Society of Arts . . . . (Charter 1847) 1753
Medical Society of London 1773
Bath and West of England Society . . . 1777
Gaelic Society of London . . . . ,,
Manchester Literary and Philosophical Society . 1781
Royal Society of Edinburgh . (Charter 1783) 1782
Highland Society 1785
Royal Irish Academy . . . . Charter 1786
Linnæan Society . . . . (Charter 1802) 1788
Newcastle Literary and Philosophical Society . . 1793
Royal Institution (Act of parliament, 1810) Charter 1800
Glasgow Philosophical Society 1802
Royal Horticultural Society . . (Charter 1809) 1804
Royal Medical and Chirurgical Society (Charter 1834) 1805
London Institution . . . . . . ,,
Geological Society . . . (Charter 1826) 1807
Russell Institution 1808
Swedenborg Society 1810
Liverpool Literary and Philosophical Society . . 1812
Roxburghe Club . . . . . . ,,
Institution of Civil Engineers . (Charter 1828) 1818
Leeds Literary and Philosophical Society . . ,,
Egyptian Society 1819
Cambridge Philosophical Society . (Charter 1832) ,,
Hunterian Society . . . . . . ,,
Royal Astronomical Society . . (Charter 1831) 1820
Medico-Botanical Society 1821
Royal Scottish Society of Arts . . . . ,,
Hull Literary and Philosophical Society . . 1822
Yorkshire Philosophical Society . . . ,,
Sheffield Literary and Philosophical Society . ,,
Royal Society of Literature . . (Charter 1826) 1823
Royal Asiatic Society . . . (Charter 1824) ,,
Bannatyne Club, Edinburgh . . . . ,,
Mechanics' Institution, London . . . . ,,
Western Literary Institution 1825
Eastern Literary Institution . . . . ,,
Zoological Society . . . . (Charter 1829) 1826
Incorporated Law Society . . (Charter 1831) 1827
Society for Diffusion of Useful Knowledge . . ,,
Ashmolean Society, Oxford 1828
Royal Geographical Society 1830
Royal United Service Institution (Charter 1860) 1831
Royal Dublin Society . . . . . ,,
Harveian Society . . . . . . ,,
British Association . . . . . . ,,
Marylebone Literary Institution . . . 1832
British Medical Association . . . . ,,
Entomological Society 1833
Statistical Society 1834
Westminster Literary Institution . . . ,,
Surtees Society, Durham . . . . . ,,
Royal Institute of British Architects (Charter 1837) ,,

Leicester Literary and Philosophical Society	1835
Numismatic Society	1836
Ornithological Society	1837
Electrical Society	1837-8
English Historical Society	1838–56
Royal Agricultural Society (Charter 1840)	1838
Camden Society	,,
Microscopical Society (Royal, 1866)	1839
Ecclesiological Society	,,
Spalding Club, Aberdeen	,,
Royal Botanical Society of London	,,
Parker Society	1840-55
Percy Society	1840-52
Irish Archæological Society, Dublin	1840
London Library	,,
Shakespeare Society	,,
Chemical Society	1841
Pharmaceutical Society	,,
Wodrow Society, Edinburgh	1841-7
Philological Society	1842
Ælfric Society	1843-56
Chetham Society, Manchester	1843
Spottiswoode Society, Edinburgh	,,
British Archæological Association	,,
Royal Archæological Institute	,,
Sydenham Society	,,
Ethnological Society	,,
Law Amendment Society	,,
Handel Society	1844
Syro-Egyptian Society	,,
Ray Society	,,
Caxton Society	1844-54
Celtic Society, Dublin	1845-53
Pathological Society	1846
Sussex Archæological Society, Lewes	,,
Cambrian Archæological Association	,,
Cavendish Society	,,
Hakluyt Society	,,
Palæontographical Society	1847
Institute of Mechanical Engineers (Birmingham)	,,
Institute of Actuaries	1848
Arundel Society	,,
Philanthropic Society	1849
British (now Royal) Meteorological Society (Charter 1866)	1850
Epidemiological Society	,,
North of England Institute of Mining Engineers, Newcastle	1851
Photographic Society (Royal, 1894)	1852
Philobiblon Society	1853
Juridical Society	1855
Odontological Society	1856
Genealogical Society	1857
National Association for Social Science	,,
Horological Institute	1858
Society for the Encouragement of Fine Arts	,,
Institution of Naval Architects	1860
Clinical Society	1861
Anthropological Society	1863
Early English Text Society; began to publish	1864
Victoria Institute	24 May, 1865
London Mathematical Society	,,
Aëronautical Society	12 Jan. 1866
Dialectical Society	1866–88
Chaucer Society	,,
Holbein Society	1868
Royal Historical Society	,,
Colonial Institute (Royal Charter, 1882)	,,
Iron and Steel Institute	1869
Harleian Society	,,
Amateur Mechanical Society	,,
Christian Evidence Society	1871
Biblical Archæology Society	,,
Anthropological Institute (*which see*)	,,
Institution of Electrical Engineers (late Society of Telegraph Engineers)	,,
Marine Engineers' Institution	1872
Society for Organization of Academical Study	,,
London Anthropological Society (*extinct*)	1873-5
Palæographical Society, 1873; dissolved	1895
English Dialect Society (see *Wales*, 1890)	1873
(New) Shakspeare Society	,,
Physical Society	1874
Musical Association	,,
Public Analysts	,,
Psychological Society	1875–79
Education Society	1875
Royal Aquarium Society	,,
Anti-Vivisection Society	1876
Mineralogical Society	,,
Sanitary Institute of Great Britain	,,
Philosophical Society (Birmingham)	,,
Purcell Society	,,
Library Association	1877
Index Society	,,
Institute of Chemistry of Great Britain	,,
Zetetical Society	1878
Folk-Lore Society	,,
Astrological Society	1879
Carlyle Society	,,
Hellenic Society	,,
Society for promoting Hellenic Studies	,,
Rabelais Club	,,
Willoughby Society	,,
Institute of Bankers	,,
London Topographical Society	,,
Balloon Society	1880
Aristotelian Society	,,
Wordsworth Society	,,
Topographical Society of London	,,
Ascham Society	,,
Chemical Industry Society	1881
Browning Society	,,
Dante Society, London	,,
Society for Psychical Research	1882
Wycliffe Society	,,
Seal Society	1883
Marine Biological Association	1884
Society of Authors	,,
Pipe Roll Society	,,
Middlesex County Record Society	,,
Society of Medallists	1885
Bacon Society	,,
Selborne Society	,,
Shelley Society	,,
Goethe Society	1886
Selden Society	1887
Neurological Society	,,
Anatomical Society	,,
Gilbert Club	1889
Ruskin Society	1890
British Astronomical Society	,,
Japan Society	1892
British Records Society incorporated	,,
Anglo-Russian Society	1893
Navy Records Society	,,
Anglo-Norman Records Society	,,
Elizabethan Society	1894
Philosophical Society	1896
Romilly Society	1898
International Association of Academies	1900
Irish Literary Society (see *Irish language*)	,,
African Society	1901
Royal Economic Society, incorporated	2 Dec. 1902

SOCIETY ISLANDS, Pacific Ocean, discovered by De Quiros in 1606; re-discovered by capt. Wallis, 1767, who gave Otaheite or Tahiti the name of King George's Island. Capt. Cook, who visited them in 1769 and 1777, named them Society Islands in honour of the Royal Society; they now belong to France. An insurrection in Raiatea suppressed, 3 Jan. 1897. Destructive hurricane and huge wave; about 1000 natives killed and islands devastated, 13 Jan. 1903. See *Otaheite*.

SOCINIANS, persons who accept the opinions of Faustus Socinus (died 1562), and his nephew Lælius (died 1604), Sienese noblemen. They held —1. That the Eternal Father was the one only God, and that Jesus Christ was no otherwise God than by his superiority to all other creatures; 2. That Christ was not a mediator; 3. That hell will endure for a time, after which the soul and body will be destroyed; 4. That it is unlawful for princes to make war. *Hook*. The Socinians established a church at Rakow, in Poland, and made proselytes in Transylvania, 1563. They were expelled from Poland in 1658. The Rakovian catechism was published in 1574; see *Unitarians*.

SOCIOLOGY, a term applied by Comte to the study of mankind in their social relations; it recommends the prevention of national wars by arbitration, and the settlement of the war of classes by boards of conciliation. Schools or departments for the study of sociology are in operation in Edinburgh, Paris, and the United States.

Herbert Spencer published *The Study of Sociology*, 1872; *Principles of Sociology*, 1876–96, see *Political Economy*.

International Institute of Sociology, first congress held at Paris, sir John Lubbock, president, 1 Oct. 1894; Paris, 3 Oct. 1895; Paris 21 July, 1897; and 1903

"Social England," a Record of the Progress of the People, by various writers, edited by H. D. Traill, vol. i. *et seq.* 1894–5

SOCOTRA (*Dioscoridis insula*), an island in the Indian ocean, belonging to the imam of Muscat, 120 miles E. of cape Guardafui, Eastern Africa. In the summer of 1878, it was said to have been given up to the British; formally annexed, Nov. 1886. The island explored by Mr. Theodore Bent and Mr. E. N. Bennett, British resident, reforms needed, slavery existing, *Times*, 13 March, 1897. Results of a scientific expedition under Mr. W. R. Ogilvie-Grant and others, 7 Dec. 1898—22 Feb. 1899, reported in *Nature*, 1 June, 1899.

SODIUM, a remarkable metal, first obtained in 1807 by sir Humphry Davy, from soda (which was formerly confounded with potash, but proved to be a distinct substance by Duhamel in 1736). This metal, like potassium, was obtained by the agency of the electric battery. In consequence of Deville's improved processes, sodium manufactured by Bell Brothers, of Newcastle, at 10*s*. a pound (1868). It is an important agent in the modern production of aluminium. Common salt (chloride of sodium) is a compound of sodium and chlorine. Mr. H. Y. Castner's (of New York) new process for the enlarged production of sodium, and through sodium of aluminium and magnesium, announced in June, 1887. His works were set up at Oldbury, near Birmingham; he died Oct. 1899. See *Alkalies* and *Aluminium*.

SODOM AND GOMORRAH (Palestine), with their inhabitants, were destroyed by fire from heaven, 1898 B.C., *Gen.* xix.

SODOR, said to be derived from Sodor-eys, or south isles (the Æbrides or Hebrides), in distinction from Orkneys, the north isles. The southern or western isles were made an episcopal diocese by Magnus, king of Norway, 1098, and joined to the isle of Man about 1113. See *Man*.

SOFAS, a West African tribe, see *Sierra Leone* and *Senegal*.

SOFIA, a manufacturing town in Bulgaria; founded by Justinian on the ruins of the ancient Sardica; became the capital of the new principality. A palace and other buildings were erected, Aug. 1881. It contains 30 mosques and 10 churches. Destructive thunderstorm with loss of life, 31 May, 1890; see *Bulgaria*. Population, 1890, 42,000; 1900, 67,920.

SOFFARIDES DYNASTY reigned in Persia, 872-902.

SOFTAS, Mahometan students devoted to the Koran only. See *Turkey*, May, 1876.

SOHO BAZAAR AND THEATRE, see *Bazaars* and *Theatres*.

SOISSONS (France), capital of the Gallic Suessiones, was subdued by Julius Cæsar, 57 B.C. It was held by Syagrius, after his father Ægidius, till his defeat by Clovis, A.D. 486. Several councils have been held at Soissons (in 744, 1092, 1122). Its academy was established in 1674. During the Franco-Prussian war, Soissons, after three weeks' investment and four days' bombardment, surrendered to the Germans under the grand-duke of Mecklenburg, 16 Oct. 1870. 99 officers, 4633 men, 128 guns, &c., were said to be taken. The Germans thus obtained a second line of railway from Châlons to Paris.

SOLAR SYSTEM, nearly as now accepted, is said to have been taught by Pythagoras of Samos, about 529 B.C. He placed the sun in the centre, and all the planets moving in elliptical orbits round it—a doctrine superseded by the Ptolemaic system (*which see*). The system of Pythagoras, revived by Copernicus (1543), is called the Copernican system. Its truth was demonstrated by sir Isaac Newton in 1687. See *Planets*.

SOLDIERS' DAUGHTERS' HOME was established at Hampstead, near London, in Aug. 1857, by the surplus of the money collected by the central association in aid of the wives and families of soldiers in active service during the Crimean war, and opened by the prince consort, 18 June, 1858. It has been much indebted to the exertions of major Powys.

Soldiers' and Sailors' Families Association founded 1885

In Nov. 1890 *et seq.* it received subscriptions for the sufferers by the wreck of H.M.S. *Serpent*, see *Navy* Nov. 1890

The princess of Wales, president, appeals for funds, 31 Dec. 1900; warmly seconded by lord Roberts, 4 Jan. 1901; Mr. W. Astor, 5,000*l*., sir E. Cassel, 2,500*l*., the king of Portugal, 200*l*., Feb. 1901; the queen presides at a meeting in the queen's-hall; col. (knt. 1902) Gildea reports 1,310,019*l*. had been received since Oct. 1899; the queen gave 5,000*l*. from her war fund, over 1,250,000*l*. received; 1,204,050*l*. expended to about 200,000 families, reported, annual meeting . 26 June, 1903

SOLEBAY or **SOUTHWOLD BAY** (Suffolk), where a fierce naval battle was fought between the fleets of England and France on one side, and the Dutch on the other, the former commanded by the duke of York, afterwards James II., 28 May, 1672. The English lost four ships, and the Dutch three; but the enemy fled, and were pursued to their coasts. The earl of Sandwich was blown up, and thousands were killed and wounded.

SOL-FA SYSTEM, see *Music*.

SOLFERINO (in Lombardy), the site of the chief struggle on the great battle of 24 June, 1859, between the allied French and Sardinian army commanded by their respective sovereigns, and the Austrians under general Hess; the emperor being present. The Austrians, after their defeat at Magenta, gradually retreated across the Mincio, and took up a position in the celebrated quadrilateral, and were expected there to await the attack. But the advance of Garibaldi on one side, and of prince Napoleon and the Tuscans on the other, induced them to recross the Mincio and take the offensive, on 23 June. The conflict began early on the 24th, and lasted fifteen hours. At first the Austrians had the advantage; but the successful attack of the French on Cavriana and Solferino changed the fortune of the day, and the Austrians, after desperate encounters, were compelled to retreat. The French attribute the victory to the skill and bravery of their emperor and the generals MacMahon and Niel; the Austrians, to the destruction of their reserve by the rifled cannon of their adversaries. The Sardinians maintained a fearful contest of fifteen hours at San Martino, it is said against double their number. Loss of the Austrians, 630 officers, and 19,311 soldiers; of the allies, 8 generals, 936 officers, and 17,305 soldiers killed and wounded. This battle closed the war; preliminaries of peace being signed at Villa Franca, 12 July. On 24 June, 1870, on the site of the battle, three ossuaries, containing the bones of thousands of the slain, were consecrated in the presence of representatives of Austria, France, and Italy. The Ossuary tower inaugurated, and a colossal statue of king Victor-Emmanuel, unveiled by king Humbert, 15 Oct. 1893.

SOLICITOR, see *Attorney*. By the Supreme Judicature Act, attorneys in future are to be styled solicitors; an act for regulating their examination was passed, 23 July, 1877; amended in 1894; another bill passed, 6 June, 1899. See *Trials*, Jan. 1901.

SOLICITOR-GENERAL, the legal officer next in rank, and deputy to the attorney-general, whom he frequently succeeds.

1839. Sir Thomas Wilde (afterwards lord Truro), 5 Dec.
1841. Sir William Follett (second time), 6 Sept.
1844. Sir Frederick Thesiger (since lord Chelmsford), 17 April.
1845. Sir Fitzroy Kelly, 17 July.
1846. Sir John Jervis, 4 July.
,, Sir David Dundas, 18 July.
1848. Sir John Romilly, April 4, aft. lord Romilly.
1850. Sir Alex. J. E. Cockburn, 11 July.
1851. Sir W. Page Wood, 28 March, aft. lord Hatherley.
1852. Sir Fitzroy Kelly, Feb.
,, Sir Richard Bethell, Dec., aft. lord Westbury.
1856. Rt. Hon. James Stuart Wortley, Nov.
1857. Sir Henry Keating, May.
1858. Sir Hugh M. Cairns, 26 Feb., aft. earl Cairns.
1859. Sir Henry Keating, 18 June.
,, Sir William Atherton, Dec.
1861. Sir Roundell Palmer, 27 June, aft. lord Selborne.
1863. Sir Robert Porrett Collier, 2 Oct.
1866. Sir William Bovill, 13 July.
,, Sir John Burgess Karslake, 29 Nov.
1867. Sir Charles Jasper Selwyn, July.
1868. Sir Wm. Baliol Brett, Feb. (made judge, Sept.)
,, Sir Richard Baggallay, 14 Sept.
,, Sir John Duke Coleridge, 12 Dec., aft. ld. Coleridge.
1871. Sir George Jessel, Nov.
1873. Sir Henry James, 26 Sept.
,, Sir Wm. Vernon Harcourt, Nov.
1874. Sir Richard Baggallay, Feb.
,, Sir John Holker, 22 April.
1875. Sir Hardinge Stanley Giffard, 25 Nov., aft. lord Halsbury.
1880. Sir Farrer Herschell, 3 May, aft. lord Herschell.
1885. John E. Gorst, June.
1886. Sir Horace Davey, 15 Feb.
1886. Sir Edward Clarke, 26 July.
1892. Sir John Rigby, 18 Aug.
1894. Sir Robert Threshie Reid, 1 May.
,, Sir Frank Lockwood, 19 Oct.; died, Dec. 1897.
1895. Sir Robert Bannatyne Finlay, 23 Aug.
1900. Sir Edward Carson, 12 Nov.

SOLICITORS' ACT, passed 24 Dec. 1888.

SOLICITORS' REMUNERATION ACT, 44 & 45 Vict. c. 44; passed in 1881.

SOLIFIDIANS (from *solus*, only, and *fides*, faith) a name given to the Antinomians (*which see*).

SOLOMON ISLANDS, discovered by Mendaña in 1568: the southern isles in the W. Pacific belong to Gt. Britain, agreement signed with Germany, April, 1886; high commissioner, Mr. C. M. Woodford, 1897. The northern isles belong to Germany. Choiseul and Isabel, with surrounding isles, ceded to Gt. Britain, 8 Nov. 1899.

Baron Foullon, Austrian scientist, De Beaufort, a midshipman, and 2 sailors massacred by the natives at Guadalcanar . . . . . 10 Aug. 1896

SOLOMON'S TEMPLE, see *Temple*.

SOLWAY MOSS (Cumberland, bordering on Scotland). On 13 Nov. 1771, it swelled, owing to heavy rains. Upwards of 400 acres rose to such a height above the level of the ground, that at last it rolled forward like a torrent above a mile, sweeping along with it houses, trees, &c. It covered 600 acres at Netherby, and destroyed about 30 small villages. Near Solway Moss the Scots were defeated by the English, 25 Nov. 1542.

SOMAJ, see *Deism*.

SOMALI-LAND, termed the "Unknown Horn of Africa," a tract of land opposite Aden, which derives from it its chief supply of cattle and sheep. The inhabitants, about half a million, are Mahometans. Treaties with native chiefs were made by the British in 1840 and 1854. The country was practically annexed by Egypt between 1873–77, but was given up and eventually occupied by the British, who declared a protectorate in 1885 to the great satisfaction of the people. The British resident at Aden has the governing power. British expedition authorised to suppress raids of the tribes, July, 1895.

Successful expedition of Dr. Donaldson Smith (American), through new country, to lakes Rudolf and Stefanie, May, 1894; arrives at Aden, 4 Nov. 1895

Sig. Cecchi, Italian consul-gen., 7 officers, 6 Italians, and 18 Askaris (with a caravan) massacred by Wadans, 15 miles from Mukdishu, on the Benadir coast . . . . 26 Nov. 1896

Gezira, a village, bombarded by an Italian gunboat, 2 Dec. ,,

5 prisoners found guilty of the massacre, shot at Mukdishu . . . . Dec. ,,

Wadan villages destroyed . . . . 25 Feb. 1897

About 50 Somalis killed by an Italian force, 23 April, ,,

Results of the Bottego Italian expedition to lakes Rudolf and Stefanie, and the Valley of the Nile, published . . . . . 10 Sept. ,,

The Mullah raids British territory, proclaims himself Mahdi and occupies Burao, Aug.; his forces defeated by the British near Berbera, reported, 5 Aug. 1899

Dr. Donaldson Smith leaves Berbera 1 Aug. 1899, and explores new regions between the Omo and the Nile; lake Rudolf reached 10 Dec.; returns with valuable collections . . . June, 1900

Mullah's power increasing; murderous raids frequent . . . . mid June,

Mr. Jenner, inspector, attacked and murdered by Ogadens, and his escort cut up in Jubaland 16 Nov. ,,

Punitive expedition against Ogaden Somalis; col. Ternan occupies Afi Madu, 5 Feb. 1901; enemy routed . . . . 16 Feb. 1901

Sharp fighting, lieut.-col. Maitland and 17 others killed at Sannasa, 150 of the enemy killed, 16 Feb. ,,

British post formed at Mfudu . . . mid April, ,,

Successful British and Abyssinian expedition; the Mad Mullah is defeated and put to flight by col. Swayne and capt. MacNeill at Moyo, 30 May, and at Somali, 3, 4 June, and finally routed at Farddidih, 17 July; the Mullah again active, fresh operations successful, May–July, 1902; col. Cobbe defeats the enemy in the Nogal valley, 150 killed, large captures of camels and sheep, July, again 8 Aug.–3 Sept. 1902; again attacked in thick bush at Erego, capts. Phillips, Angus, and

99 men killed, enemy finally repulsed and 62 killed, 6 Oct. (lieut.-col. Cobbe made V.C. for great bravery in this action, 20 Jan. 1903); British reach Bohotle safely, reported 22 Oct.; fresh expedition decided on; col. Swayne in ill-health leaves, gen. Manning arrives at Burao, 14 Nov.; co-operation of the Italians, the Obbia-Mudug route agreed to . . . . . 16 Dec. 1902

Parliamentary paper, containing correspondence respecting the rising of the Mullah Muhammed Abdullah in Somali-land, and consequent military operations 1901-2, issued . . . 28 Jan. 1903

Yusuf Ali, sultan of Obbia, captured and removed to Aden . . . . end Jan. ,,

Galkayn and Damot occupied, 3, 4 March, enemy driven off Lasakante, 15 killed, 16 captured; Galadi occupied 30 March; successful operations in the south, heavy loss of the enemy 2, 5 April, ,,

The Abyssinians inflict a severe defeat on the Dervishes at Burhilli, N.E. of Bori, 300 killed 15 April, ,,

British reverse: Col. Cobbe's reconnoitring column left Galadi 10 April; a patrol was attacked near Gumburru, capt. Chichester killed, enemy repulsed, 16 April; capt. Olivey was attacked on all sides by overwhelming numbers near Gumburru the British force fought with heroic courage until the last, only 40 (34 of whom were wounded) escaped; the colonel, 8 officers, 48 Sikhs and about 171 British were killed; the Mullah's loss about 2,000, 17 April; col. Cobbe relieved by gen. Manning . . . . . 18, 19 April, ,,

Force under gen. Gough attacked at Daratoleh, capts. Bruce and Godfrey and 13 men killed; enemy's loss about 150 . . . . 22, 23 April, ,,

The Abyssinians under gen. Gabriz surprise and rout the Mullah's force at Zeyd, 1,000 killed, 31 May, ,,

The chief of the Ker Ali tribe deserts the Mullah and joins gen. Gabriz at Hahi, reported, 27 June, ,,

The Ogaden Somalis defeated by the Abyssinians, reported 24 June; Mullah's forces retreat to the N.E. . . . . . . end of June, ,,

Maj.-gen. sir C. Egerton takes command, 15 July, ,,

Col. Swaine returns to Berbera, reported, 2 Sept. ,,

Illig looted and the Mullah 6 miles from Obbia, reported . . . . 10 Oct. ,,

Illig shelled by Italian cruiser *Lombardia*, 15 Oct. ,,

Forward movement under gen. Manning in preparation, date and direction kept secret, reported, 6 Nov. ,,

SOMBRERO (West Indies). On this desert isle, Robert Jeffery, a British man-of-war's man, was put ashore by his commander, the hon. captain W. Lake, for having tapped a barrel of beer when the ship was on short allowance. After sustaining life for eight days on a few limpets and rain-water, he was saved by an American vessel, 13 Dec. 1807; and returned to England. Sir Francis Burdett advocated his cause in parliament, and he received 600*l*. as a compensation from captain Lake, who was tried by a court-martial, and dismissed the service, 10 Feb. 1810.

SOMERSET-HOUSE (London), formerly a palace, founded on the site of several churches and other buildings levelled in 1549, by the protector Somerset, whose residence fell to the crown after his execution, 22 Jan. 1552. Here resided at times queen Elizabeth, Anne of Denmark, and Catherine, queen of Charles II. Old Somerset-house, a mixture of Grecian and Gothic, was demolished in 1775, and the present edifice, from a design by sir William Chambers, was erected for public offices. The Royal Academy of Arts first assembled in the apartments given to the members by the king, 17 Jan. 1771. The Royal Society met here, 1780-1857; and apartments here were also held by the Society of Antiquaries and the Geological Society; all three now at Burlington House. Large suites of government buildings were erected in 1774. The Navy-office, Pipe-office, Victualling and other offices, were removed herein 1788, and various government departments since. The east wing forming the King's College (see *King's College*) was completed in 1833. By an act passed in 1854, the offices of the duchy of Cornwall were transferred to Pimlico.

CHIEF OFFICES AT SOMERSET HOUSE.

Probate and Divorce Division of high court of justice and Registry Offices.	Stamp Offices, &c.
Appeals Registry Office.	Excise and Tax-Offices.
Register of Births, Deaths, and Marriages.	Legacies and Succession Duty Offices.
Exchequer and Audit Department.	Inland Revenue Offices.
Property and Income Tax Offices.	Bank Returns Office.
	Laboratory Department.
	Solicitors' Offices.
	Companies' Register Offices, &c., &c.

SOMERSET THE BLACK, see *Slavery in England*.

SOMERS-TOWN, a populous district in St. Pancras parish, N. London: named after earl Somers, whose family acquired the property about 1695. The building began about 1786; and many French refugees settled in it. Much of the district has been occupied by the railway companies.

SOMMERVILLE COLLEGE, see *Women*.

SOMNATH GATES, the gates of an ancient Hindoo temple at Guzerat, which was destroyed by Mahmoud of Ghuznee in 1025. The priests wished to preserve the idol; but Mahmoud broke it to pieces and found it filled with diamonds, &c. He carried the gates to Ghuznee. When that city was taken by general Nott, 6 Sept. 1842, lord Ellenborough ordered the gates to be restored after an exile of 800 years, and issued a proclamation much censured at the time. The gates are made of sandal wood, and are described and figured in the Archæologia of the Society of Antiquaries, vol. xxx.

SOMOFORM, an anæsthetic composed of chloride, bromide, and iodide of ethyl, possesses the property of producing complete insensibility in 30 to 60 seconds. First used 1902. No recorded case of accident from its use.

SOMORROSTRO, see *Spain*, 1874.

SONATA (Italian, sound-piece), the highest form of instrumental music, consisting of three or four movements, intending to express diverse kinds of human feelings.

It was developed from the *suite*, varied dance music (Tartini, 1624, and others). The form fixed by Corelli (1653-1713), was adopted and modified by Scarlatti, the Bachs, Handel, Mozart, Haydn, and culminated in the master-pieces of Beethoven (1770-1827). Fine sonatas have been composed by Dussek, M. Clementi, Weber, Schubert, Mendelssohn, Schumann, Wm. Sterndale Bennett, Chopin, Liszt, and Rubinstein.

SONDERBUND, see *Switzerland*, 1846.

SONNET, a poem in fourteen lines, with rhymes adjusted by rules, was invented, it is said, by Guido d'Arezzo, about 1024. The most celebrated sonnets are those by Petrarch (about 1327), Shakspeare (1609), Milton (about 1650), and Wordsworth (1820).

SONNITES, the orthodox Mahometans who now possess the Turkish empire; see *Mahometanism*.

SONS OF THE CLERGY, see *Clergy*.

SONTAY, see *Tonquin*, Dec. 1883.

SONTHALS, a tribe of Northern India, brought to Bengal about 1830, where they prospered, till, partly from the instigation of a fanatic, and partly from the exactions of money-lenders, they broke out into rebellion in July, 1855, and committed fearful outrages. They were quite subdued early in 1856, and many were removed to the newly-conquered province of Pegu.

SOOLOO, see *Sulu*.

SOPHIA, ST. (in Constantinople). The first church was dedicated to St. Sophia (holy wisdom) by Constantius II., 360; this having been destroyed, the second, the present edifice, was founded by Justinian, 531, and dedicated 537. Since the Mahometan conquest in 1453, it has been used as an imperial mosque. Its length is 269 feet, and its breadth 243 feet. Six of its pillars are of green jasper, from the temple of Diana, at Ephesus; and of porphyry, from the temple of the Sun, at Rome. Four minarets were added by Selim II., who reigned in 1566. The interior of the dome is beautifully ornamented with mosaic work.

SOPHIA, see *Sofia*.

SOPHISTS, teachers of youth in Athens, who were censured by Socrates, and consequently were instrumental in causing his judicial murder, 399 B.C. The controversy against them was carried on by Plato and his disciples.

SORBONNE, a society of ecclesiastics at Paris, founded by Robert de Sorbonne in 1252. The members lived in common, and devoted themselves to study and gratuitous teaching. They soon attained a European reputation as a faculty of theology, their judgment being frequently appealed to, from the 14th to the 17th centuries. The influence of the Sorbonne was declining when the society was broken up in 1789. The buildings are now devoted to education. The new Sorbonne buildings were opened on 5 Aug. 1889; this is the virtual reconstruction of the university of Paris. Gymnastic education introduced, 1892.

SORCERERS AND MAGICIANS. A law was enacted against their seductions, 33 Hen. VIII. 1541; and another statute equally severe was passed, 5 Eliz. 1563. The pretension to sorcery was made capital, 1 James I. 1603; see *Witchcraft*.

SORGHUM, see under *Sugar*.

SOUDAN or **SOUJAH**, the title of the lieutenant-generals of the caliphs, which they bore in their provinces and armies. The officers afterwards made themselves sovereigns. Saladin, general of the forces of Noureddin, king of Damascus, was the first that took upon him this title in Egypt, 1165, after having killed the caliph Caym.

SOUDAN or **NIGRITIA**, a region of Central Africa, partly subjected to the Khedive of Egypt since 1874, capital Khartoum. It was well governed, by col. Gordon, till 1879. See *Egypt*. For FRENCH SOUDAN, see *Senegal*.

Insurrection headed by Sheik Mahomed Ahmed of Dongola, declaring himself to be a prophet (Mahdi or Muhdi, foretold by Moslem prophets), July, 1881

Defeated; retires up the Blue Nile; crosses White Nile with increased army . . . winter, ,,

Defeats the Egyptians . . . . Nov. 1881

Surrounds and massacres 6000 Egyptians under Yussuf Pasha, 14 June; occupies Shala, July; defeated at Bara, 19 Aug.; at Duem, 28 Aug.; repulsed at Obeid, 8, 14 Sept.; defeats the Egyptians, 15 Sept.-24 Oct.; rebels defeated at Bara, 4 Nov.; Col. Stewart at Khartoum, 16 Dec. 1882

The Mahdi captures Bara and Obeid, 5 Jan.; he is repulsed . . . . 23-26 Feb. 1883

Col. Hicks pasha with an army starts for the Kordofan; arrives at Berber, 1 March; totally defeats the Mahdi with great loss; the enemy pursued 29 April, ,,

The Mahdi defeated at Khartoum about 14 May, ,,

The Sennaar chiefs submit; announced 25 June, ,,

Hicks marches up the Nile, 9 Sept.; arrives at Duem . . . . 20 Sept. ,,

Surprise and defeat of Egyptian detachment at Tokar, near Suakin; about 150 killed, including the brave and able British consul . . 6 Nov. ,,

Battle of El-Obeid, or Kashgal; col. Hicks decoyed into a defile; about 11,000 men attacked by overwhelming multitudes, they form squares and resist till nearly all are killed, including col. Hicks, col. Farquhar, and other European officers, only two said to have escaped; reported desertion of some of Hicks' troops; the Mahdi gains cannon and much ammunition 3-5 Nov. ,,

Egyptian force concentrated at Khartoum under col. Coetlogon . . . . . Nov. ,,

General rising throughout the country; the British government sends gunboats to defend Suakin and Red Sea ports, about 23 Nov.; attack on Suakin forts, 26 Nov.—1 Dec.; about 720 Egyptians surrounded and 682 killed (asserted) 2 Dec. ,,

V. Baker pasha sent to Suakin with plenary powers about 18 Dec. ,,

Khartoum garrison strengthened about 26 Dec. ,,

Osman Digna, a ruined slave-dealer, commander for the Mahdi . . . . . . Dec. ,,

General (Chinese) Gordon sent to the Soudan (to report) 18 Jan., starts 19 Jan.; appointed governor-general of the Soudan by the Khedive 25 Jan. 1884

Sinkat closely besieged . . . Nov. 1883—Jan. ,,

Tokar besieged by rebels; surrenders, 21 Feb.; Baker pasha with 3500 men defeated near Tokar, loses about 2250 men (demoralised), with the remnant retreats to Trinkitat, 4 Feb.; received by H.M.S. *Ranger*, 5, 6 Feb.; reinforcements ordered to be sent to adm. Hewett at Suakin, 6 Feb.; Baker pasha recalled; remains; Suakin in state of siege; adm. Hewett in full command, 7-9 Feb.; desperate sortie of the garrison, headed by Tewfik bey, from Sinkat, all killed; women and children prisoners, town taken . 8 Feb. ,,

Reinforcements sent to Suakin . 11, 12 Feb.

General Gordon arrives at Berber, 11 Feb.; enthusiastically received as a deliverer at Khartoum; proclaims the Mahdi sultan of Kordofan; remission of half the taxes, and non-interference with the slave trade, releases prisoners, remits debts . . . . 18 Feb. ,,

Restoration of the former sultanate of Darfour proposed; Kassala besieged by Osman Digna Feb. ,,

The Black troops at Suakin mutiny and disperse; announced . . . . . . 25 Feb. ,,

Battle of El-Teb, near where Baker pasha was defeated, 4 Feb. After fruitless attempt at negotiation, gen. Gerald Graham, with about 4000 men (consisting of 10th and 19th Hussars, Gordon Highlanders, the Black Watch, Lancashire and Yorkshire battalions, and Marines), at 11 a.m., advanced on the rebels, about 12,000, who, after a most desperate, heroic resistance, were totally defeated with the loss of about 2000 men, at 2.30 p.m.; the British loss was major M. M. Slade, lieuts. F. H. Probyn, F. A. Freeman, and Frank Royds, and quartermaster James Wilkins and 24 men killed, and 142 wounded, 29 Feb. 1884

Tokar surrendered, and the rebel garrison fled 1 March, ,,

Osman Digna at Tamanieb . . . 3 March, 1884
Several Arab sheikhs come into Suakin, 6, 7 March, ,,
Osman Digna disregards gen. Graham's proclamation, about 8 March. Osman Digna disdainfully rejects British proposals, and proclaims death to infidels . . . . . about 10 March, ,,
Battle of Tamanieb. The British advance to capture Osman Digna's camp at Tamasi, near El-Teb, 7.20 a.m.; the British were massed in oblong squares, one square broken into by a violent onslaught of hidden Arabs, who creep under and capture the Gatling and other guns, desperate hand-to-hand conflict; the British driven back; no panic; col. Wood with 700 cavalry charges the Arabs in flank, and drives them back, the infantry rally and recover the guns, the other square perfectly successful; the camp taken, 12.30 p.m. The British loss, killed, capts. H. G. V. Ford, Walker, and Aitken; lieuts. Montresor, Almack, and Houston Stewart, and 86 men, 111 wounded, and 19 missing; 2000 of the enemy killed out of above 10,000. The Black Watch and Naval Brigade suffered much 13 March, ,,
Osman Digna's camp with stores captured on 4 Feb.; burnt . . . . . 14 March, ,,
Gordon defeats rebels and brings off garrison of Halfyeh . . . . . about 15 March, ,,
Through cowardice and treachery Gordon's troops (1500) defeated by about 60 rebels with great slaughter . . . . 16 March, ,,
Reward of 5000 dollars offered for capture of Osman Digna, alive or dead, 15 March; countermanded from home . . . . . 17 March, ,,
Troops march to Handoub wells . 18 March, ,,
Friendly sheikhs coming in . . . 20 March, ,,
Hassan and Said pashas, Turko-Egyptian generals, tried and shot . . . . . . 23 March, ,,
The Mahdi rejects Gordon's offers; announced 23 March, ,,
General Graham advances on Tamanieb; slight skirmish; the Arabs flee; Osman Digna's villages burnt . . . . 27 March, ,,
Three regiments at Suakin embark for home, &c. 29 March, ,,
March to Berber reported safe . 29 March, ,,
Gordon contending with the rebels, with varying success; Kassala closely besieged, announced 30 March, ,,
Khartoum said to be closely invested; the rebels frequently defeated . . . . . April, ,,
General Gordon, col. Stewart, and Mr. Power, the *Times* correspondent, the only British there 8 April, ,,
The Mahdi said to have been twice defeated by the Jagalla tribes; reported . . . . 9 April, ,,
Egyptian troops arrive at Suakin . . 10 April, ,,
Adm. Hewett's mission well received by Ras Aloola about 13 April, ,,
The Marines depart . . . . about 15 April, ,,
Shendy closely besieged; 51 fugitives from it killed by Arabs; announced . . . . . 19 April, ,,
Berber said to be closely invested . 20 April, ,,
Reported evacuation of Berber; troops withdrawn to Korosko; announced . . . . 26 April, ,,
The whole country in insurrection; Egyptian troops joining the Mahdi . . . . April, ,,
The government declining to send help, Gordon writes to sir Evelyn Baring, "I shall hold on here as long as I can, and if I can suppress the rebellion, I will do so. If I cannot, I shall retire to the equator."
Col. Stewart and Mr. Power decide to remain with him . . . . May, ,,
Subscriptions proposed to support Gordon . May, ,,
Adm. Hewett well received by the king of Abyssinia at Adowa; treaty signed . about 26 May, ,,
Fruitless attacks on Suakin checked by Marines, 27, 28, 31 May, 2, 4, 10 June, ,,
Gordon said to have been opposed by government in all his propositions . . . April, May, ,,
Highly successful sally from Khartoum; major Chermside made governor of Suakin; refugees from Korosko arrive at Assouan; reported rise of another Mahdi . . . . . . 28 May, ,,
The Mudir of Dongola said to have defeated the rebels . . . . May, 1884
Advance of Egyptian troops . . . . . May, ,,
Fall of Berber announced . . . . . 10 June, ,,
Assouan fortified . . . . . . June, ,,
Rebels defeated at Debbeh with great loss, 29-30 June, ,,
Advance of the Mahdi said to be checked by another Mahdi; announced . . . . . . 2 July, ,,
Assouan occupied by the British . 12 July, ,,
Additional troops sent to Alexandria from Malta, July, ,,
Gordon dominant and successful at Khartoum; reported . . . . 22 July, ,,
Continued desertion of Egyptian troops, announced July; Gordon reports Khartoum and Sennaar holding out . . . . 2 Aug. ,,
Mudir of Dongola said to have greatly helped Gordon . . . . July, Aug. ,,
Gen. Gordon repulses severe attack, 10 Aug.; defeats rebels . . . . 12 Aug. ,,
Osman Digna, near Suakin, frequently defeated, Aug. ,,
Preparation for the expedition to relieve Khartoum, gen. Earle commander; British troops arrive at Wady Halfa . . . . . . 23 Aug. *et seq.* ,,
The expedition to ascend the Nile in about 800 flat-bottomed boats, navigated by Canadian Indians (*voyageurs*); Sarras . . . . . Sept.-Oct. ,,
Defeat of the Mahdi's troops by the Mudir of Dongola at Ambikol . . . . . . 8 Sept. ,,
Gen. Earle to be at Wady Halfa; col. Stewart and lord Airlie at Dongola; col. Maurice at Assiout Sept. ,,
Another defeat of Mahdi's troops reported 15 Sept. ,,
Telegrams from Gordon requiring assistance Sept. ,,
Friendly tribes defeat rebels, and relieve Suakin, about 17 Sept. ,,
Victories of Gordon on 24 July and 30 Aug., and raising of the siege of Khartoum reported, 20 Sept. ,,
British army in Egypt, 13,559 . about 22 Sept. ,,
Lord John Hay arrives with the fleet at Alexandria, 24 Sept. ,,
Several camel corps start from Woolwich for the Soudan . . . . . . about 25 Sept. ,,
Mr. Power's journal of the siege of Khartoum, from April to 31 July published in the *Times*, 29 Sept.
Lord Wolseley arrives at Wady Halfa . 5 Oct. ,,
Shendy taken . . . . 6 Oct. ,,
Col. J. D. Stewart, with Mr. Power and M. Herbin, and about 40 men in a steamer, wrecked near Wady Garna, fifth cataract; land; massacred by Arabs offering guidance; announced about 6 Oct. ,,
Gordon defeats rebels and returns to Khartoum; announced . . . . 1 Nov. ,,
Lord Wolseley arrives at Dongola . . 3 Nov. ,,
Attacks on Suakin repulsed . . 3, 4 Nov. ,,
Gordon reports all well at Khartoum . 4 Nov. ,,
Rebels often repulsed . . . . . Nov. ,,
Above 200 whalers on the Nile conveying troops, &c. 15 Nov. ,,
Two steamers disabled by rebels near Khartoum; announced . . . . 18 Nov. ,,
Lord Wolseley's proclamation to the soldiers and sailors issued . . . . 1 Dec. ,,
Two hours' attack of the rebels on Suakin without effect, 3 Dec.; rebels defeated with loss 8 Dec. ,,
Lord Wolseley arrives at Korti . . 15 Dec. ,,
Successful sally of the garrison of Kassala, 26 Dec. ,,
Forward movement of the army . . 28 Dec. ,,
Rapid marches of gen. sir Herbert Stewart . Dec. ,,
Successful march in the desert . . . Jan. 1885
Gen. Earle proceeding up the Nile, and gen. Stewart crossing the desert with troops, towards Metammeh . . . . Jan. ,,
Near Abu Klea wells, about 120 miles from Khartoum, gen. Stewart, with 1500 men, defeats about 10,000 Arabs, who retire after a fierce conflict within the square, leaving about 800 dead. The British lose 9 officers (col. Fred. A. Burnaby, majors Atherton, Carmichael, and Gough, capts.

Law and Darley, lieuts. Pigott, Delisle, and Wolfe), and 65 men killed, with 85 wounded 17 Jan. 1885

Gen. Stewart, marching towards Metammeh, is severely wounded by hidden sharpshooters; 12 killed, including correspondents of the *Morning Post* and *Standard*, Thos. St. Leger Herbert, and John A. Cameron; sir Charles Wilson takes command . . . . 18 Jan. ,,

At Gubat, near Metammeh, fierce Arab onset on the British square is repulsed with very heavy loss . . . . 19 Jan. ,,

Message from gen. Gordon received, dated 29 Dec.: "Khartoum is all right; could hold out for a year" . . . . about 19 Jan. ,,

Communications opened with Khartoum . 24 Jan. ,,

Gen. Earle with army marches to Handoub for Berber . . . . 24 Jan. ,,

Successful skirmishes of gen. Earle . . Jan. ,,

Gen. Stewart succeeded by sir Redvers Buller Jan. ,,

Surrender of Khartoum; Gordon and his faithful followers killed . . . . . early 26 Jan. ,,

Sir Charles Wilson sails up the Nile . 28 Jan. ,,

Reconnaissances of gen. Fremantle; heavy Arab loss, about 30 Jan.; Handoub captured and burnt by a party which is intercepted by Arabs, and lose 12 men . . . . 2 Feb. ,,

The Italian flag hoisted beside Egyptian at Massowah (*which see*) . . . . 6 Feb. ,,

Sir Charles Wilson and party, within 800 yards of Khartoum, fired upon; retreats; his steamer is wrecked by treachery of Arab pilots; lands on an island; is rescued from peril by the daring courage of lord Charles Beresford in face of batteries; arrives at Korti . . . . 9 Feb. ,,

Victory at Kirbekan: the Arabs on a ridge, surrounded by gen. Earle's column (the Black Watch and Staffordshire regiments), many killed; gen. Earle and lieut.-cols. Eyre and Coveney, and nine others killed; attack well planned and gallantly executed; gen. Brackenbury takes the command . . . . 10 Feb. ,,

Gen. Buller retreats from Gubat to Abu-Klea wells, 13-15 Feb. ,,

Death of sir H. Stewart at Gakdul . . 16 Feb. ,,

Railway between Suakin and Berber ordered to be constructed . . . . Feb. ,,

Near Abu-Klea, Arabs demoralised by skilful feat of major Wardrop, who takes the heights after much skirmishing; Arabs flee . . . . . 17 Feb. ,,

Sir Evelyn Wood arrives at Gakdul . . 17 Feb. ,,

Gen. Gerald Graham, with Coldstream and Grenadier Guards and others, start for the Soudan; farewell given by the queen and prince of Wales, 19-21 Feb. ,,

Osman Digna massing his forces near Suakin, about 21 Feb. ,,

Rebels' attack on Kassala garrison defeated with great loss; announced . . . . . 22 Feb. ,,

Gen. Buller reaches Gakdul . . . 26 Feb. ,,

Gen. Buller's column marches to Korti 1 March, ,,

Gen. Graham's staff and 15th Sikh regiment arrive at Suakin . . . . 4 March, ,,

Successful sally from Kassala announced 4 March, ,,

The queen's address of thanks read to the army at Korti by lord Wolseley . . . . . 7 March, ,,

The 17th Bengal Infantry and the Royal Engineers balloon corps arrive at Suakin . 7 March, ,,

Arab raids on Suakin camp; sentries killed 11 March, ,,

The bulk of lord Wolseley's army at Korti, 12 March, ,,

Gen. Graham arrives at Suakin with 5th Lancers, 12, 13 March, ,,

The last of the desert troops arrive at Korti, 16 March, ,,

Gen. Graham calls on Osman Digna to surrender, to avoid bloodshed . . . . about 16 March, ,,

Battle of Hasheen: Graham, with part of his army, starts at daybreak; several of Osman Digna's positions on the hills taken after conflicts: about 21 British killed . . 20 March, ,,

Gen. McNeil's brigade unexpectedly attacked by about 4500 Arabs, about 6 miles from Suakin; they are repulsed with heavy loss (about 1500), after a severe fight; British loss about 100 killed, including lieuts. Swinton, Seymour, and Newman, capt. Romilly and others 22 March, ,,

Manifesto of the Mahdi claiming the caliphate published . . . . March, 1885

Fever at Korti; evacuated by the army, about 28 March, ,,

Arab attacks repulsed by the guards 24 March, ,,

Attacks on British convoy repulsed 24-26 March, ,,

The last Egyptian troops leave Suakin 26 March, ,,

Zebehr Pasha arrested at request of lord Wolseley, 14 March; sent to Gibraltar . . 29 March, ,,

[Released under conditions, 3 Aug. 1887.]

New South Wales contingent arrives at Suakin 29, 30 March, ,,

Graham advances; finds Tamai deserted; burns it and returns to Suakin . . . 2, 3 April, ,,

The railway to Berber constructing under military protection . . . . April, ,,

Handoub (deserted) occupied by the British 8 April, ,,

Successful raid of capt. Briggs, capturing prisoners, cattle, &c. . . . . 15 April, ,,

Numerous night attacks . . . . . April, ,,

Rebellion against the Mahdi; his troops said to be defeated near Kordofan . . . . April, ,,

Lord Wolseley arrives at Suakin . . 2 May, ,,

Takool burnt and cattle captured by gen. Graham; organised force of Arabs dispersed midnight, 5-6 May, ,,

Proposed armed defence of line from Assouan to Wady Halfa announced . . 11 May, ,,

General Graham with British troops, and the Indian (part) and New South Wales contingents, quit Suakin . . . . . 17 May *et seq.* ,,

Major-gen. sir G. Greaves assumes command at Suakin, 18 May; leaves . . 15 June, ,,

Handoub evacuated by the British, 22 May; occupied by the Arabs, many of whom join Osman Digna . . . . June, ,,

Dongola evacuated . . . . 15 June, ,,

Sir F. Stephenson commander-in-chief . 6 July, ,,

Lord Wolseley arrives in London . . 13 July, ,,

Repulse of attack on Kassala, about 3,000 of the rebels killed; the garrison capture much cattle in a sortie . . . . . . 15, 16 June, ,,

Death of the Mahdi by small-pox, reported June 20, 21, or 22; said to be succeeded by his kinsman Khalifa Abdullah . . . . June, ,,

Olivier Pain sent by the Irish in Paris to join the Mahdi at El Obeid, July, 1884; reported death, time uncertain; Selikovitch, an interpreter dismissed by the British, asserts without any evidence that Pain was executed by order of col. Kitchener in April, 1885; no British investigation; much excitement in Paris caused by M. Rochefort, ... Aug.–Sept. ,,

Sennaar surprised and taken . . 16 Aug. ,,

Rebels defeated and stores captured near Suakin, 19 Aug. ,,

Major Chermside sent to relieve Kassala . Aug. ,,

Khalifa Abdullah El Taashi reported successor of the Mahdi . . . . autumn, ,,

Successful skirmish of the hussars and Egyptians with Arabs near Giniss; fighting on the Nile; announced . . . . 3 Dec. ,,

Advance of rebels northward; two battalions sent from Britain . . . . about 10 Dec. ,,

Attack of 3,000 Arabs on Mograkeh, near Kosheh; repulsed . . . . 12 Dec. ,,

6,000 Arabs defeated at Giniss, near Kosheh, 3½ hours' fight; one officer (lieut. Soltau) killed; 19 Egyptians killed and wounded; about 600 Arabs killed . . . . 30 Dec. ,,

Attack on Suakin repulsed . . . . 11 Feb. 1886

Osman Digna and the rebels active, about 2 March, ,,

Rebels defeated by friendly Arabs and the British, 13 March, ,,

Sir C. Warren appointed governor at Suakin, about 16 Jan.; [made commissioner of police, London]; gen. Dixon left in command . . . March, ,,

Country south of Wady Halfa abandoned by the Egyptians, announced . . . . . April, ,,

General Watson nominated governor of the Red Sea territories about 14 April; arrives 8 May, ,,

British evacuation of Suakin completed 16 May, ,,

Fighting near Sheik Barghut; victory of friendly Arabs who take prisoners and recover captives, about 28 May, ,,

Major Kitchener succeeds general Watson, Aug.; arrives . . . . 7 Sept. ,,

By judicious advice of gen. Watson and col. Kitchener, the Arabs combine to overthrow Osman Digna; after serious losses he quits his stronghold at Tamai, which, with all its military stores is captured, with much slaughter of his followers . . . . 7 Oct. 1886

Emin Bey (Austrian physician), an associate of gen. Gordon, holds Wadelai as governor of Equatorial Africa since 1878, with black troops; news brought by Dr. Junker . . . . . Nov. ,,

Retreat of the rebels on British advance 3 Dec. ,,

Expedition of Mr. Henry Morton Stanley on behalf of the Emin Pasha committee (*which see*), with a small armament with able volunteer officers, starts from London . . . 21 Jan. *1887

Messengers from the new Mahdi with arrogant message, received and dismissed by the khedive, 19 April, ,,

Col. Chermside, with the Egyptians, defeats the Dervishes at Sarras, near Wady Halfa, after stubborn resistance; about 190 killed, 29 April, ,,

Great defeat of the Dervishes announced about 29 Aug. ,,

Successful skirmish of col. Wodehouse with the Dervishes . . . . 24 Oct. ,,

Arab attack on Wady Halfa repulsed, 25 Oct.; reinforcements sent . . . . . 27 Oct. ,,

Expedition of the hon. Montague Kerr to Emin Pasha's station at Wadelai, starts . . Nov. ,,
[He is struck down by fever; returns to Europe; dies in France, 23 April, 1888.]

Osman Digna defeated with great loss by the friendly tribes . . . . . . 29 Dec. ,,

Unsuccessful attacks on Suakin Dec. 1887.–3 Jan. 1888

His camp at Handoub captured and his followers dispersed; they return and retake the camp; the friendly tribes forced to retreat, col. Kitchener and major McMurdo wounded . . . 17 Jan. ,,

Colonel Kitchener leaves for Cairo; succeeded by col. Shakspear . . . . . . 19 Jan. ,,

A band of Dervishes dispersed after fierce conflict near Suakin, col. Tapp killed . . . 4 March, ,,

Return of col. Kitchener to Suakin . 15 March, ,,

Affairs quiet; Osman Digna's followers dispersing, April, ,,

Col. Kitchener leaves for England . 26 May, ,,

Defeat of the Dervishes near Wady Halfa 20 July, ,,

The Dervishes severely defeated in an attack on Fort Khormoussa . . . midnight, 27 Aug. ,,

Attempted raid of Osman Digna checked 12 Sept. ,,

Lt. col. Holled Smith succeeds col. Kitchener as governor-general and commandant at Suakin, 13 Sept. ,,

Continued investment of Suakin by Arabs (Dervishes) with guns, &c.; severe night attacks; reinforcements ordered . . 22 Sept., Oct. ,,

German expedition for the relief of Emin Pasha organized; supported by prince Hohenlohe Langenburg and other nobles . . . Sept. ,,

A sharp attack on Suakin vigorously repulsed, 30 Oct. ,,

General Grenfell with reinforcements arrives at Suakin . . . . 5 Nov. ,,

* They embarked with a number of natives at Zanzibar for the west coast, 25 Feb., and sailed up the river Congo. After undergoing great dangers and much suffering through famine, disease and native opposition, Mr. Stanley fell in with Emin Pasha on lake Nyanza, 29 April, 1888; and eventually, with him and the remains of his party, arrived at the German station Bogamoya, 5 Dec. 1889. Mr. Stanley and his officers arrived at Cairo, 14 Jan. 1890; at Rome, 11 April; at Brussels, 19 April; in London, 26 April; dined with the queen, 6 May; with his companions, lieut. Stairs, surgeon Thomas H. Parke, capt. Nelson, Mr. A. M. Jephson, and Mr. Bonny, received the gold medals of the Royal Geographical Society, from the prince of Wales, 5 May. Besides other honours Mr. Stanley was presented with the freedom of the city of London, 13 May; of Edinburgh, 11 June; and of Glasgow, Dundee, Aberdeen, Newcastle-on-Tyne, and Manchester, in June. His book, entitled "In darkest Africa; or, the Quest, Rescue and Retreat of Emin, governor of Equatoria," was published, 28 June. He married Miss Dorothy Tennant at Westminster Abbey, 12 July, 1890; elected M.P. for Lambeth, July, 1895.

Defeat of the nominal Mahdi by the sultan of Wadai's people; gen. Grenfell reconnoitres; the enemy very strong; the Mahdi afterwards captures Wadai, and the sultan flees Nov. 1888

More British troops sent to Suakin . . Dce. ,,

The enemy's redoubts stormed by the black brigade under gen. Grenfell; great slaughter, slight British loss; total flight of the enemy with loss of about 400; 7.30 a.m. . 20 Dec. ,,

General Grenfell and part of his army leave Suakin, 4 Jan. 1889

Handoub abandoned and burnt . . 11 Feb. ,,

Suakin declared open to commerce . . 20 Feb. ,,

Dr. Carl Peters, with 100 soldiers, &c., starts to relieve Emin Pasha . . . . 26 Feb. ,,

The Dervishes repulsed with loss after their attack on Haliab, 19 April; again repulsed, 29, 30 April; again repulsed, and an outpost captured . . . . 2 June, ,,

Colonel Wodehouse, with three Egyptian black battalions, &c., defeats about 3,500 Dervishes at Arguin near Wady Halfa; they lose about 500 killed, Egyptian loss about 70 killed and wounded . . . . 2 July, ,,

The Dervishes repulsed with the loss of about 100 men, 4 July; they break up their camp, 7 July; which is occupied by the British 8 July ,,

Reinforcements from Malta; which is proclaimed to the natives by gen. Grenfell, 10 July . . ,,

Reinforcements sent from Malta to strengthen the garrison at Assouan . . . . . July, ,,

Dervish deserters come in; prisoners sent to Cairo; their loss estimated to be since 1 July 2,500 killed and wounded . . . . . about 14 July, ,,

Gen. sir F. W. Grenfell arrives at Col. Wodehouse's camp at Bellana; the enemy hold a strong position at Khor; their fighting force estimated at 2,500 . . . . 15 July, ,,

The R. Irish Rifles arrive at Assouan . 16 July, ,,

Gen. Grenfell summons Wad-el-N'jumi to surrender, all lives to be spared; the messenger beaten . . . . 17 July, ,,

Wad-el-N'jumi calls on the Egyptians to surrender, and threatens them with the fate of gen. Gordon, reported . . . . 19 July, ,,

A large number of additional troops sent from Cairo 20 July, ,,

British field force at Assouan commanded by major-gen. hon. R. H. de Montmorency, 23 July, ,,

Party of 300 Dervishes repulsed with loss; reported . . . . 21 July, ,,

Frequent skirmishes; many killed and prisoners 25–31 July, ,,

Dervishes defeated with loss of 70 men by lieut. D'Aguilar at Anabi . . . . . 31 July, ,,

Battle of Toski; after seven hours' hard fighting about 3,000 Dervishes are defeated by gen. sir Francis Grenfell. Wad-el-N'jumi with his principal emirs, and about half his army are killed, the other half are either wounded or fugitives; the repeated desperate charges of the Dervishes are chiefly repulsed by the 20th Hussars and the Egyptian cavalry, who pursue them till they are utterly routed and their arms and standards captured. (The commanders under gen. Grenfell were col. Kitchener, mounted troops; col. Wodehouse, infantry; Rundle, artillery, Irwin and Beech, English and Egyptian cavalry; Settle, sen. staff officer); the British loss 17 killed (1 English 16 Egyptians); wounded, 131; above 1,000 Dervishes prisoners and wounded; parts of the Shropshire and Lancashire regiments and the Royal Irish Rifles were engaged 3 Aug; gen. Grenfell arrives at Cairo . . . . 17 Aug. ,,

The Egyptian troops occupy Matuka; the British ordered to return to Cairo . . . 7 Aug. ,,

Emin Pasha, after a long illness, occasioned by a fall from a window at Bogamoya, 5 Dec., closely attended by Dr. Parke, arrives at Zanzibar, 2 March; accepts the offers of major Wissmann, enters the German service, and proceeds with a military expedition to Victoria Nyanza 31 March *et seq.* 1890
[For his connection with capt. Casati, see *Italy*, 14 July, 1890.]

Military movements of the Mahdi, reported, 8 May, ,,

Famine and great distress in E. Soudan through drought, partly relieved by government and others . . . . Jan.—Aug. 1890
The Khalifa Abdullahi reported supreme in the south . . . . July, ,,
Osman Digna's forces broken up by desertion, reported . . . . Oct. ,,
Emin Pasha, in good health at Tabora, Aug.; his letter received at Brunswick, about 25 Nov.; he establishes German stations on the shores of lake Victoria Nyanza, reported 7 Dec.; recalled to the coast by major von Wissmann, the imperial commissary, reported . . . . . 19 Dec. ,,
A raid of the Dervishes on Suakin; they are pursued and defeated, 27 Jan.; after a sharp engagement, the governor-general takes possession of Handoub, 28 Jan.; several Dervish leaders captured, peace restored . . . about 4 Feb. 1891
Col. Holled Smith, governor-general of the Red Sea littoral, conducts an expedition of 2,000 Soudanese and Egyptian troops, aided by friendly Arabs; El Teb occupied and fortified . . 17 Feb. ,,
Col. H. Smith, with brigade of Egyptian troops, advances at daybreak from El Teb against Tokar, strongly held by Osman Digna with 2,000 Dervishes; after a desperate fight of one and a half hours, Tokar is occupied; all the principal emirs and about 700 Dervishes killed; Osman Digna fled south with 30 horsemen. Our loss—capt. Hugh Lusada Barrow, of South Lancashire regiment, and 15 Egyptian soldiers killed; the Egyptians fought bravely and steadily; guns, ammunition and other stores captured. After the action, the troops advance 4 miles to Osman Digna's deserted camp at Afafil, a large village, where about 100 Arabs surrender . . . . 19 Feb. ,,
The Red Sea littoral reported clear of rebels; the sheikhs solicit and obtain pardon, general rejoicing, reported . . . . 23 Feb. ,,
Gen. Grenfell, col. Holled Smith, with the troops, &c., return to Suakin, 7 March; an amnesty proclaimed; joyfully received by the sheikhs 8 March, ,,
Capt. Hackett Pain appointed governor of the Tokar sub-district . . . . about 8 March, ,,
The country reported quiet and prosperous, 5 May, ,,
Defeat of the Dervishes by the Shilluks about the end of Nov., reported . . . . . . 17 Dec. ,,
Father Ohrwalder and two R. C. sisters, long prisoners in the Mahdi's camp, Omdurman, Khartoum, escape, 29 Nov., and arrive at Cairo, 21 Dec. ,,
Rupture between Khalifa Abdullah and two other chiefs, reported . . . . 21 Jan. 1892
Incursion of about 100 Dervishes near Wady Halfa, led by Osman Azrak . . . about 12 May, ,,
Archibald Hunter pasha, appointed governor-general of the Red Sea littoral in place of col. Holled Smith who resigned, reported . 17 Oct. ,,
Osman Digna encamped near Suakin with about 300 followers, Oct. 1892; retires to Amet, 2 Nov.; a raid on Tokar repulsed, reported . 24 Nov. ,,
A force of 400 dervishes defeated at the Temerin fort . . . . 23 Nov. ,,
Two dervish attacks at Gemai and Sarras near Wady Halfa, repulsed 31 Dec. 1892 and 1 Jan. 1893
Sharp engagement at Ambigol Wells, heavy loss on both sides; capt. Pyne (adjutant) killed . 2 Jan. ,,
Gen. Kitchener visits Wady Halfa about 16 Jan. ,,
Osman Digna, with a band moving about Suakin, Jan., Feb., defeated after a raid . . 8 April ,,
Central Soudan: insurrection of Rabah, he takes Baghirmi; fight with the troops of the sultan of Wady at Fizzan, reported . . . . 10 Sept. ,,
Osman Azrak with 300 Dervishes repulsed with loss after a severe engagement at Murhat Wells; Saleh Bey the Egyptian leader and 12 other friendly Arabs killed . . . . 10–12 Nov. ,,
Severe defeat of the dervishes by the Italians, at Fort Agordat. See *Massowah* . . . 20 Dec. ,,
Col. Archibald Hunter appointed governor of the frontier province and col. George Lloyd governor of Suakin and Red Sea littoral . . . Sept. 1894
Dervish raid near Wady Halfa . . . 10 Dec. 1895
British advance up the Nile to check the Dervishes and to reconquer territory up to Dongola; Akasheh occupied without resistance, 20 March, 1896
Sir H. H. Kitchener, commander-in-chief, arrives at Wady Halfa . . . . . . 29 March, ,,
Osman Digna repulsed with loss at Erkowit, 8, 11 April; again by col. Fenwick and major Sidney near Tokar . . . . 15 April, 1896
Dervishes severely repulsed by major Burn-Murdoch, near Akasheh . . . . . 1 May, ,,
Murat wells occupied by the British after a march of 120 miles in 65 hours, 117° in the shade, 4 May, ,,
Indian troops (4,341), under col. C. Egerton, arrive, June, ,,
Akasheh fortified, railways constructed, Apr.–June, ,,
The Dervishes surprised and defeated by gen. sir H. H. Kitchener at Ferkeh (*which see*) 7 June, ,,
Suarda, a strong position, occupied, Dervish camp, 40 boats, &c., captured by col. Burn-Murdoch, road clear to Dongola . . . . . 8 June, ,,
Cholera at Kosheh; major M. Fenwick and surgeon-captain S. Trask died, 25 July; 244 deaths among the troops between Assuan and Suarda up to 2 Aug.; decreasing . . . . . mid. Aug. ,,
Advance of the army; Absarat occupied, 25 Aug.; 7 steamers successfully pass the cataracts and arrive at Kosheh, 23, 25 Aug.; destructive storms, railway destroyed by a flood, 25 Aug.; cyclone in the camp . . . . . . 27 Aug. ,,
Railway collision near Moghrat, 1 death, 22 injured . . . . 4 Sept. ,,
Garrisons established along the route to Absarat, 9 Sept.; Fereig occupied, 14 Sept.; Kubudeh, 18 Sept.; Kerman occupied unresisted; a strong Dervish fort at Hafir bombarded by 3 Egyptian gunboats under commander Colville, and heavy fire of Maxims from the opposite banks; a Dervish gunboat sunk and the fort evacuated, 19 Sept. ,,
Dongola found undefended; grain and stores seized by the British, 20 Sept.; the gunboat *Abu Klea*, under lieut. Beatty, bombards and dismantles the fort and works . . . . . . 21 Sept. ,,
Dongola occupied with little resistance, the Dervishes retreat into the desert; several important emirs surrender; all the guns and stores captured; about 200 Dervishes killed, 900 prisoners taken . . . . 22, 23 Sept. ,,
Dervish force completely disorganised . 25 Sept. ,,
Relatives of the Mahdi come in and are pardoned, 28 Sept. ,,
Col. Hunter left in command of the frontier; the province of Dongola settled and clear of Dervishes . . . . Oct. ,,
Sir H. H. Kitchener and staff arrives at Cairo, 13 Oct. ,,
Rebel sheikhs tender submission to the government . . . . Oct. ,,
Dervish raids near Tokar; friendly Arabs organised to guard the roads, &c.; repulsed after a sharp fight . . . . Nov. ,,
Sir H. H. Kitchener arrives at Dongola abt. 18 Dec. ,,
Dervish raid on Beni Amer (Italian territory), 30 Askaris killed . . . . Jan. 1897
Osman Digna appointed governor of Berber, "Emir of Emirs," by the Khalifa, summons 25,000 Dervishes to rise . . . . 15 Jan. ,,
The Arabs defeat the Dervishes, and recapture women and cattle . . . . . . March, ,,
Dervishes defeated by Egyptians, north of Dongola, 1 June; advance of sir Herbert Kitchener and the army to Merawi . . . . 13 July, ,,
Dervishes defeat the Jaalin, 2,000 killed; Metammeh occupied, and massacres by the Dervishes, 1 July, ,,
Abu-Hamed held by 1,000 Dervishes, captured, after severe fighting, by major-gen. Hunter's column, major H. M. Sidney, lieut. Fitzclarence, and others killed; emir Mahomed Zein, Dervish commander, and 50 others captured . 7 Aug. ,,
Berber evacuated by the Dervishes; occupied by the Anglo-Egyptian troops, under gen. Hunter, 7–13 Sept. ,,
Six garrisons along the river, and screen-posts across the desert, established . . . . Sept. ,,
Many wells sunk along the route, Berber–Suakin road . . . . Sept.–Dec. ,,
All the E. Soudan tribes renounce Mahdism 2 Oct. ,,
Railway from Abu-Hamed to Wady-Halfa completed; Dervish raids opposite Berber repelled, Nov. ,,
Dervish grain boats (6) captured at Metammeh, 8 Dec. ,,
Fashoda occupied by the French . . . Dec. ,,

Es-Sofiyeh Mugatta captured from the Dervishes by col. Parsons' Kassala troops . . 13 Jan. 1898
Gen. sir H. H. Kitchener returns to Wady-Halfa from a successful tour of inspection, 530 mi. in 39 hrs. . . . . 8 Feb. ,,
Mahmud, the Dervish general, joins Osman Digna at Shendy . . . . . about 27 Feb. ,,
Strong position of Anglo-Egyptian troops, from Berber to the Atbara; march across the desert from Abu Dis to Berber . 25 Feb.–10 March, ,,
Dervishes driven from Shebaliya island by major Sitwell, 38 killed, 14 March; repulsed again at Adarama, 42 killed, 18 March; Dervish cavalry repulsed with loss by Anglo-Egyptian cavalry, near Ras el Hudi . . . . . 21 March, ,,
Shendy attacked, and forts destroyed by major Hickman and capt. Keppel, 160 Baggara killed, 645 slaves freed, cattle, &c. captured; Mahmud checkmated by gen. Kitchener . 26 March, ,,
Successful cavalry reconnaissances at Ras el Hudi, 30 March; and up the W. bank of the Atbara to Mahmud's camp; enemy's cavalry driven in, 8 Dervishes captured, 3 April; sharp fight outside the Dervish camp, 200 Dervishes and 6 British killed . . . . 5 April, ,,
Battle of the Atbara, brilliant victory: rout of the Dervish army (16,000), Mahmud captured, flight of Osman Digna; British loss, capt. Urquhart and major Napier (died, 24 May), capts. Findlay and Baillie (died, 18 May), lieut. P. A. Gore, and 21 men killed: 18 Egyptian officers, and 51 men killed; Dervishes, 3,000 (many emirs) killed; 2,000 surrendered, 10 guns, and over 100 flags, &c. taken: Dervish camp ushed . . . . 8 April, ,,
Triumphant entry of gen. sir H. Kitchener and the army into Berber, enthusiastic reception by the natives, 13 April; further operations suspended till . . . . end of July, ,,
A band of Dervishes defeated with loss on the Atbara, about 19 May.
Dervish forces retreat from Shabluka to El Boga, about 40 mi. from Khartoum; Anglo-Egyptian advance post formed at Shendy . . 3 June ,,
The Khalifa's army concentrated at Omdurman, July, ,,
Advance of the Anglo-Egyptian force under Sir H. Kitchener and the flotilla of gunboats up the Nile, 31 Aug.–1 Sept. ,,
The battle of Omdurman (5.30 a.m.–11.50 a.m.), 2 Sept.; total defeat of the Dervishes (50,000), after desperate resistance, and flight of the Khalifa Abdullahi; Col. Hector Macdonald and others displayed fine leadership and heroism. Grand charge of the 21st Lancers, under col. Martin, against enormous odds, lieut. R. Grenfell and 23 men killed; capt. Guy Caldecott, the hon. Hubert Howard, *Times* correspondent, and 23 others killed; 334 wounded, some mortally. Dervish loss, 10,800, and about 400 killed in the town, between 3,000 and 4,000 prisoners, about 150 European prisoners released. The sirdar (Sir H. Kitchener) joyfully received at Khartum, 3 Sept. ,,
The British and Egyptian flags hoisted on the palace at Khartum . . . . . . 4 Sept. ,,
European congratulations . . . . Sept. ,,
Hostilities over, more surrenders, 8 Sept.; Sir H. Kitchener finds major Marchand and a French force at Fashoda, *which see*, who refuse to retire without orders from their government, 19 Sept.; sir H. Kitchener establishes garrisons at Fashoda and Sobat, and returns to Omdurman, 24 Sept. ,,
Col. Parsons defeats the Dervishes (500 killed) and captures Gedarif, their last stronghold, after a desperate fight, 22 Sept.; Ahmed Fedil, Dervish leader, defeated again, 28 Sept. his army broken up and followers surrender . 23 Oct. *et seq.*
Major-gen. Sir H. Kitchener, K.C.B., created a peer of U.K. (lord Kitchener of Khartum), Sept.; arrives in London, 27 Oct.; received by the queen at Balmoral, 31 Oct.; many honours . Nov. ,,
The khalifa attacked by "friendlies" on the frontier of Kordofan; several emirs are brought to Omdurman . . . . 9 Nov. ,,
The khalifa defeated near Sherkela, about 18 Nov. ,,
Sudan honours and promotions announced, 1 Nov. ,,
Col. Parsons welcomed by the natives at Suakin, 10 Dec. ,,

Lord Kitchener arrives at Khartum . . 30 Dec. 1898
Col. Lewis defeats Ahmed Fedil near Roseires, on the Nile; 500 Dervishes killed and 1,500 taken prisoners . . . . 26 Dec. ,,
Lord Cromer addresses the sheikhs at Omdurman, promises religious freedom, local government, &c. 5 Jan. 1899
Dervishes (2,000) surrender to lieut. Strickland, 8 Jan. ,,
Anglo-Egyptian convention signed at Cairo, 19 Jan. ,,
Lord Kitchener appointed gov.-general of the Sudan . . . . 21 Jan. ,,
The duke and duchess of Connaught arrive at Omdurman, 18 Feb.; the duke reviews 9,000 troops, holds a levee, and visits Khartum . . 20 Feb. ,,
The khalifa defeats and raids local tribes, reported, 22 Feb. ,,
The *Sudan Gazette*, in English and Arabic, first No. published at Omdurman . . . 7 March, ,,
Ibrahim Ali, with escort of 150 men, routed by Ali Dinar, the usurper of the sultan of Dar Fur, 120 killed, reported . . . . . . 3 May, ,,
Over 360 deserters from the khalifa surrender at the White Nile . . . . . . 3 May, ,,
Total expenditure for military operations in the Sudan charged on the public revenues of the United Kingdom, 1883–97, 7,890,112*l.*, announced, 19 May, ,,
Thanks of parliament to the army, queen's message, and vote of 30,000*l.* to lord Kitchener, carried, 5–8 June, ,,
Majors Maxse and Capper explore the Sobat river and its tributary the Pibor; favourable report issued . . . . June, ,,
The Atbara bridge opened by lord Kitchener, 26 Aug. ,,
Mahdist revolt on the Blue Nile; sharp fighting; 2 sons of the Mahdi killed at Shukaba, 27 Aug. ,,
"A Prisoner of the Khalifa: 12 Years' Captivity at Omdurman," by Chas. Neufeld, published, Oct. ,,
Sir Francis Reginald Wingate's Anglo-Egyptian force defeats Ahmed Fedil (about 2,400 men) at Abu Adil (White Nile); 400 Dervishes killed, many prisoners captured, reported, 23 Nov.; the khalifa Abdullahi overtaken, defeated, and killed, "disdaining surrender," at Om Debrikat; Ahmed Fedil, 4 chief emirs, and many others died with him; 1,000 Dervishes killed and wounded, and 9,400 prisoners, including women and children; Egyptian loss slight . 24 Nov. ,,
Egyptian government grants 10,000*l.* to cut the *sudd* of the White Nile, early . . . Dec. ,,
Sir Francis (aft. Reginald) Wingate appointed sirdar and gov.-general . . . . . 23 Dec. ,,
Budget: total deficit estimated for 1900, 427,000*l.*, reported . . . . 16 Dec. ,,
Lord Kitchener leaves Khartum for S. Africa, 18 Dec. ,,
The first through train from Cairo reached Khartum, 10 Jan. 1900
Osman Digna captured by capt. Burges near Tokar, 19 Jan.; taken to Suez . . . . . 25 Jan. ,,
Court of inquiry (4 Egyptian and 3 British officers) into alleged insubordination of Egyptian officers; 10 degraded; the khedive confirms the sentence, 14 March,
Lord Cromer addresses the sheikhs and notables at Khartum and reports progress; law courts established, the land tax reduced, &c.; reviews the Egyptian troops and receives chiefs of the Dinkas . . . . 24, 26 Dec. ,,
Col. H. W. Jackson appointed lieut.-gov. of the Soudan . . . . Jan. 1901
Sultan Ibrahim of Wadai assassinated; civil war over, reported . . . . 9 June, ,,
The Bahr-el-Ghazal occupied by an Anglo-Egyptian force, end . . . . June, ,,
Sir R. Wingate arrives at Cairo after a successful tour through the provinces . 31 Jan.–3 July, ,,
Major Austin's survey expedition from Omdurman to Mombasa underwent much suffering, 45 Soudanese died . . . . Dec. 1900–26 Aug. ,,
Frontier questions relating to Erythrea settled 26 Nov. ,,
The khedive welcomed at Berber and Khartum; witnesses a sham fight at Omdurman, 2, 3 Dec.; holds a review at Khartum and opens the new mosque; leaves . . . . . 5–7 Dec. ,,

Agreement with Abyssinia *re* boundary signed, about . . . . 31 May, 1902
Lord Cromer visits stations as far as Gondokoro, abt. 500 miles south of Khartum; finds order, progress and content, but railways and other reforms needed . . . . Jan. 1903

SOULAGES COLLECTION. About 1827, M. Soulages of Toulouse collected 790 specimens of Italian art and workmanship, &c. These were bought for 11,000*l.* by 73 English gentlemen, with the view of first exhibiting them to the public, and afterwards selling them to the government (who gradually purchased them between 1858 and 1865). They formed part of the "Art Treasures" exhibited at Manchester in 1857.

SOUND, see *Acoustics.*

SOUND DUTIES. Till the year 1857 no merchant ship was allowed to pass the Sound (a narrow channel separating Zealand from Sweden) without clearing at Elsinore and paying toll. These duties had their origin in an agreement between the king of Denmark and the Hanse towns (1348), by which the former undertook to maintain lighthouses, &c., along the Cattegat, and the latter to pay duty for the same. The first treaty with England in relation to this was in 1450; other countries followed. In 1855 the United States determined to pay the dues no more; and in the same year the Danish government proposed that these dues should be capitalised; which was eventually agreed to, the sum being 30,476,325 rix-dollars. In Aug. 1857, the British government paid 10,126,855 rix-dollars (1,125,206*l.*) to the Danes as their proportion.—The passage of the Sound was effected, in defiance of strong fortresses, by sir Hyde Parker and lord Nelson, 31 March, 1801; see *Baltic Expedition.*

SOUNDINGS AT SEA. Captain Ross, of H.M.S. *Œdipus*, in 1840, took extraordinary soundings at sea. In the latitude 33° S. and longitude 9° W. about 300 miles from the Cape of Good Hope, 2266 fathoms were sounded; the weight employed amounted to 450 lbs. On 13 July, 1857, lieut. Joseph Dayman, in the North Atlantic Ocean, lat. 51° 9′ N., long. 40° 2′ W., in sounding, found a bottom at 2424 fathoms. The deepest sounding known (3875 faths.) was taken by the *Challenger*, capt. Nares, 24 March, 1873, in the North Atlantic, north of St. Thomas's. See *Deep Sea Soundings.*

SOUTH AFRICAN ASSOCIATION, established July, 1881, to promote the commercial and social interests of the South African colonies. A league formed to uphold British supremacy, with recognition of colonial self-government, April, 1896; first annual conference at Port Elizabeth, 11 Feb. 1897; 140 meetings held in Great Britain in 1897. The association accepts the co-operation of the South African league, Queen's Town, S. Africa (requested 1 June), 26 June, 1896. Mr. Cecil Rhodes, president, May, 1899; died 22 March, 1902.

SOUTH AFRICAN ASSOCIATION for the Advancement of Science, sir David Gill, K.C.B., first president, started autumn, 1902; opened at Cape Town (762 ordinary members, 36 associates) 27 April, 1903

SOUTH AFRICA COMPANY (BRITISH). See *Zambesi* and *Rhodesia*, 11 Aug. 1896.

SOUTH AFRICAN HOSPITAL Commission of Inquiry (Royal), see Mr. Burdett-Coutts' letters, *Times*, 27–29 June, 1900; lord justice Romer, sir David Richmond, Dr. Church (knt. 1901), and others appointed, 23 July; first meeting held at Cape Town, 21 Aug.; report, stating difficulties and urging reforms, issued . . . . . 22 Jan. 1901

SOUTH AFRICA CONFEDERATION: to comprise the three British colonies—Cape Town, Natal, and West Griqualand (1873)—and the two Dutch republics, Orange River free state, and the South Africa or Transvaal republic (1852). The formation was proposed by the earl of Carnarvon, colonial secretary, in a despatch to sir Henry Barkly, governor of Cape Town, 4 May, 1875, and advocated by the historian, J. A. Froude, on a visit. It was much opposed at the Cape. See *Cape.* A conference of delegates in London was opened, 5 Aug. 1876.

The South Africa Act "for the union under one government of such of the South Africa colonies and states as may agree thereto," was passed 10 Aug. 1877.
South African customs union convention (preferential treatment for British imports) passed July, came into force, 15 Aug. 1903.

SOUTH AFRICAN EXHIBITION, INTERNATIONAL, see *Griqualand*, 1892.

SOUTH AFRICA REPUBLIC, name assumed by the Boers in the Transvaal (*which see*) in 1880-1, adopted by treaty Feb. 1884.

SOUTH AFRICAN WAR (Boer Republics).

For the origin of this war, see *Transvaal*, 1876 *et seq.*
Boer ultimatum, demanding arbitration, withdrawal of troops from the frontier, compliance within 48 hours demanded, 9 Oct. 1899; rejected by Gt. Britain . . . . . . 11 Oct. 1899.
Gen. sir George White arrives at Ladysmith, 11 Oct. ,,
Natal train commandeered by Orange Free Staters, 11 Oct. ,,
General advance of Boers, 11 Oct.; they invade Natal at Laing's Nek and Van Reenen's pass, 12 Oct. ,,
Armoured train under capt. Nesbit captured by Boers at Kraaipan . . . . . 12 Oct. ,,
British reconnaissance from Ladysmith . 13 Oct. ,,
Newcastle occupied by the Boers . . 15 Oct. ,,
MAFEKING INVESTED: Boers repulsed; sorties under col. Baden-Powell, 2 British killed . 15, 16 Oct.
SIEGE OF KIMBERLEY: garrison, 500 Lancashires and about 3,000 colonials, under col. Kekewich, aided by Mr. Cecil Rhodes; successful sorties, 15 Oct. *et seq.* ,,
Patrols from Ladysmith have sharp encounter with Boers at Acton Homes . . . . . 18 Oct. ,,
Boers occupy Vryburg and Klipdam (under cover of the white flag) . . . . 19, 20 Oct. ,,
Desultory skirmishing on the Limpopo, Rhodes Drift, and elsewhere . . . . . . Oct. ,,
BATTLE OF GLENCOE OR DUNDEE: Boers under comm. Lucas Meyer storm the British camp; TALANA HILL captured by the King's Royal Rifles and the Irish Fusiliers, Boers routed and 6 guns taken; gen. sir Wm. Penn Symons mortally wounded (died 23 Oct.), cols. Sherston and Gunning, 6 officers killed; total casualties, 432; Boer casualties estimated, 500 . . 20 Oct. ,,
A party of 18th Hussars under col. Möller, in pursuit of the Boers after the battle, was surrounded and the *survivors* captured and taken to Pretoria, 22 Oct.]
Gen. Joubert's combined force attacks Dundee without success . . . . 21 Oct. ,,
BATTLE OF ELANDSLAAGTE: French and Ian Hamilton rout the Boers under Ben Viljoen, their guns, camp, and position taken; col. Scott-Chisholme and 4 officers killed; total casualties, 223; Boer loss, gen. Koch mortally wounded, 208 killed and wounded, 188 prisoners taken, 21 Oct ,,
Mafeking bombarded; Boers repulsed, 23 Oct. *et seq.* ,,
RIETFONTEIN: White routs the O.F.S. Boers, col. Wilford and 11 men killed; total British casualties, 111 . . . . 24 Oct. ,,

Sortie from Kimberley; comm. Botha and others killed; British loss, 3 . . . . 24 Oct. 1899

Yule joins White at Ladysmith after a hard march, 22–26 Oct. ,,

Plumer engages the Boers near Tuli . 26 Oct. ,,

Successful sortie from Mafeking . . 27 Oct. ,,

LOMBARD'S KOP OR FARQUHAR'S FARM: position captured and Boers put to flight; major Myers (eminent art collector) killed . . 30 Oct. ,,

NICHOLSON'S NEK disaster: attempt to turn the Boers' position failed through a stampede of the battery mules, with the guns, &c.; after desperate fighting, col. Carleton and 870 surrendered, 30 Oct. ,,

[British casualties in these 2 actions, 1,227. Gen. White nobly took *all the blame* for last affair.]

Brilliant sorties from Mafeking; capt. Pechell, lieut. Marsham and 10 others killed; Boer loss heavy . . . . . . 27–31 Oct. ,,

Gen. sir Redvers Buller lands at Cape Town, 31 Oct. ,,

Cape Colony invaded by Boers . . 1 Nov. ,,

LADYSMITH ISOLATED and bombarded: capt. Lambton's naval guns used effectively on Boer camp; lieut. F. G. Egerton, of H.M.S. *Powerful*, mortally wounded; treacherous use of the white flag by the Boers . . . . . . 2 Nov. ,,

British garrison evacuates Colenso, retires on Estcourt; Boers repulsed by the Dublin Fusiliers, 2 Nov. ,,

British evacuate Naauwport and Stormberg 3, 4 Nov. ,,

Successful cavalry action by Brocklehurst outside Ladysmith, near Dewdrop . . . 6 Nov. ,,

Brilliant sortie from Mafeking . . . 7 Nov. ,,

General attack on Ladysmith repulsed; Boer casualties over 800 . . . . 9 Nov. ,,

Reconnoitring force engaged near Belmont; lieut.-col. Keith Falconer killed . . . 10 Nov. ,,

Free Staters occupy Aliwal North . . 14 Nov. ,,

Boers capture an armoured train near Chieveley; Mr. Winston Churchill, war correspondent *Morning Post* (he escaped from Pretoria, 12 Dec.), and over 100 British captured or missing . 15 Nov. ,,

Kuruman besieged; Boers repulsed . 13–19 Nov. ,,

Estcourt in Natal isolated . . 19 Nov. ,,

BELMONT: lord Methuen, advancing to relieve Kimberley, attacks the Boers under gen. Cronje and drives them with heavy loss from their positions (grand charge of the Guards); British casualties, 270 (53 killed) . . . . 23 Nov. ,,

Major Leuchars' Natal troops repulse the Boers at Tugela Drift . . . . 23 Nov. ,,

Hildyard repulses the Boers at Ulundi and near Estcourt . . . . . 18, 23 Nov. ,,

Col. Kitchener encounters a strong Boer force and drives them back on Colenso . 23 Nov. ,,

Successful sortie from Kimberley on Carter's Ridge, 23 or 25 Nov. ,,

ENSLIN OR GRASPAN: Methuen defeats the Boers with heavy loss; commander Ethelston, R.N., killed; total British casualties, 185 . 25 Nov. ,,

Gen. sir Redvers Buller arrives in Natal . 25 Nov. ,,

Naval brigade, under capt. E. P. Jones, follows Buller . . . . . 26 Nov. *et seq.* ,,

Gatacre occupies Bushman's Hoek and Putter's Kraal . . . . . . 27 Nov. ,,

MODDER RIVER: Methuen attacks 11,000 Boers under Cronje and forces them to quit their positions after 10 or 16 hours' fierce fighting; cols. Northcott and Stopford, 2 officers and 66 men, killed; total casualties, 461; Boer loss unknown, 70 captured . . . . . 28 Nov. ,,

Gallant sortie from Kimberley, Boer redoubts *rushed*, major Scott-Turner and 22 British killed, 28 Nov. ,,

Col. Plumer's column invades the Transvaal, 3–8 Dec. ,,

Methuen repulses an attack on his line at Enslin, 8 Dec. ,,

Successful sorties from Ladysmith under sir A. Hunter; Gun hill surprised, 2 guns destroyed and 1 taken, 8 Dec.; Surprise hill captured and gun destroyed by col. Metcalfe's 2nd Rifle Brigade, bayonet charge, 28 Boers and 12 British killed, 10 Dec. ,,

STORMBERG REVERSE: Gatacre (misled by guides) attacks an impregnable position by night, after a hard march, and is driven back; complete disaster averted by the artillery; 31 killed, about 500 captured; total casualties, 702 . . . 10 Dec. 1899

MAGERSFONTEIN: Methuen's attack on the Boer lines repulsed with loss; grand courage shown by the Black Watch, Gordons, Yorks, and artillery under a terrific fire; major-gen. Wauchope, lord Winchester, lieut.-cols. Downman, Coode, 19 officers and 167 men killed; total casualties, 395; Boer loss estimated over 700 . 10, 11 Dec. ,,

Col. Porter repels the Boer advance on Naauwpoor, near Vaal Kop . . . . . 13 Dec. ,,

Capt. Bradshaw killed in an action near the Orange river; Boers fled to Goemansberg . 14 Dec. ,,

COLENSO, Natal: Buller's advance from Chieveley on the Boer lines repulsed; attempt to cross the Tugela fails, 12 guns lost, lieut. F. Roberts, V.C. (lord Roberts' only surviving son), mortally wounded in trying to save the guns; 6 officers and 134 men killed; total casualties, 1,100 . 15 Dec. ,,

[Sir Wm. MacCormac (died 4 Dec. 1901), in attendance on the wounded, reports fine work of the ambulance corps.]

Lord Roberts appointed commander-in chief in S. Africa (lord Kitchener as chief of staff); leaves Southampton . . . . . . 23 Dec. ,,

Col. Dalgety occupies Dordrecht . . 24 Dec. ,,

The queen sends Xmas greeting to all the troops, 25 Dec. ,,

Attack on Game Tree fort; sortie from Mafeking repulsed, capts. Sandford and Vernon, lieut. Paton and 21 killed . . . . . 26 Dec. ,,

Skirmish near Dordrecht: small force under lieuts. Milford and Turner cut off, Dec. 30; rescued, and Boers defeated with heavy loss by capt. Goldsworthy and Cape police . . . . 31 Dec. ,,

Col. Pilcher, with colonials and regulars, captures Boer camp at Sunnyside, many killed and 48 taken prisoners . . . . . . 1 Jan. 1900

Mafeking bombarded, the hospital and women's laager shelled with loss . . 1 Jan. *et seq.* ,,

British garrison surrenders at Kuruman after sharp resistance . . . . . 2 Jan. ,,

Boer attack repulsed near Molteno, Gatacre dislodges them from a strong position . 3 Jan. ,,

French captures Boer outposts near Colesberg and again repulses them . . . . 1, 4 Jan. ,,

LADYSMITH: Boer attack repulsed; "a soldier's battle," Cæsar's Camp and Wagon hill attacked, British intrenchments 3 times taken and again retaken, enemy finally driven off after 17 hours' fighting by bayonet charge of the Devons under col. Park, and great gallantry displayed by the Imperial Light Horse (Boer casualties estimated 1,700, over 200 killed); British loss, lord Ava (lord Dufferin's son) mortally wounded, lieut.-col. Dick-Cunyngham, 13 officers and 164 men killed; total casualties, 453 . . . . 6 Jan. ,,

Suffolk regiment attacks a hill at Colesberg at dawn, but are overcome by treachery; lieut.-col. Watson, 7 officers and 33 men killed, over 100 captured . . . . . . 6 Jan. ,,

Successful British reconnaissance from Sterkstrom towards Stormberg . . . . . 8 Jan. ,,

Lords Roberts and Kitchener arrive at Cape Town, 10 Jan. ,,

Buller again advances towards Ladysmith; Dundonald surprises the Boers and occupies Zwart Kop . . . . 10 Jan. ,,

Cavalry reconnaissances into the Free State, 7–11 Jan. ,,

Dundonald seizes Potgeiter's Drift on the Tugela, 11 Jan. ,,

Buller again retires on his lines . . 13 Jan. ,,

New Zealanders and Yorks repulse Boer attack on French's post near Rensburg . . 15 Jan. ,,

New S. Wales Lancers surprised, 13 captured, near Rensburg . . . . . 16 Jan. ,,

Boer position shelled at Modder River . 16 Jan. ,,

British under Lyttelton and Warren cross the Tugela . . . . . . 16–18 Jan. ,,

Dundonald engages the Boers near Acton Homes, 20 killed and 23 captured . . 18 Jan. ,,

Clery's force captures ridge after ridge near Venter's spruit . . . . 20 Jan. ,,

Warren attacks Boers on Tabamyama, capt. Hensley mortally wounded, major Childe and 16 others killed and missing . . . . 20, 21 Jan. 1900
SPION KOP captured by Buller's forces, 23, 24 Jan.; found untenable, being exposed to a *raking shell fire*, and evacuated, major-gen. sir Edw. Woodgate mortally wounded (died 24 March), col. Buchanan Riddell killed; total casualties, 595; Boer loss about 53 killed . . 24, 25 Jan. ,,
[British loss, Spion Kop, &c., 30 officers, 276 men killed; total casualties, 1,437, 17–24 Jan.; Spion Kop despatches issued, see *Times*, 18 April, 1902.]
Buller's force retires across the Tugela, 26, 27 Jan. ,,
Loyal message to the queen from Mafeking on the 100th day of siege . . . . . . 27 Jan. ,,
British success, hills rushed and taken round Rensburg . . . . 2 Feb. ,,
Hector Macdonald (knt. 1901), with Highland brigade, marches from Modder River and occupies Koodoesberg (died 25 March, 1903) . 2–4 Feb. ,,
Potgieter's Drift: Buller again crosses the Tugela; VAAL KRANTZ captured, 5 Feb.; but evacuated after severe fighting, and the army again withdrawn . . . . 6, 7 Feb. ,,
Boer attack on Gatacre's outposts at Penhoek repulsed, Brabant's patrol captured; Edw. Dampier, wounded prisoner, shot by the Boers, 7 Feb. ,,
Boers repulsed with heavy loss at Koodoesberg, 8 Feb. ,,
Lord Roberts arrives at Modder River; Macdonald's force recalled from Koodoesberg, 9 Feb. ,,
British pickets driven in at Bastard's Nek and Hobkirk's farm . . . . . 10 Feb. ,,
Boers attack Rensburg; lieut.-col. Coningham mortally wounded, about 28 killed . . 12 Feb. ,,
Operations for the relief of Kimberley at Magersfontein successful; col. Hannay marches to Ramdam from Orange River . . . . 12 Feb. ,,
French leaves Modder River, 11 Feb., and by rapid marches seizes Dekiel's Drift, Riet River, capt. Majendie mortally wounded, 12 Feb.; crosses the Modder at Klip's and Rondeval Drifts, 5 laagers captured, Boers fled . . . . . . 13 Feb. ,,
Clements, hard pressed, retires from Rensburg on Arundel, grand charge of the Inniskillings; 20 of the Victoria cavalry entrapped, died fighting to the last man; Rensburg occupied by the enemy, 14 Feb. ,,
Buller moves from Chieveley and captures Hussar hill . . . . 14 Feb. ,,
Jacobsdal captured by the City Imp. Volunteers and others; lord Roberts enters . . . 15 Feb. ,,
RELIEF OF KIMBERLEY (total casualties during the siege since 15 Oct. 1899, 163; from other causes, 1,694): French with cavalry division marches rapidly from Klip Drift, joins col. Kekewich, drives the Boers out of Alexandersfontein and the district, and enters Kimberley, 15 Feb. ,,
Cronje evacuates Magersfontein and Spytfontein and retreats towards Paardeberg . . 15 Feb. ,,
French routs the Boers S. of Kimberley 16 Feb. ,,
Brabant's colonials capture a laager near Dordrecht, 16 Feb. ,,
Kelly-Kenny pursues Cronje's army (10,000) *viâ* Modder towards Bloemfontein, constant rear-guard action; 2 laagers captured by Knox at Koodoosrand Drift . . . . . 16, 17 Feb. ,,
PAARDEBERG: Kelly-Kenny's and Colvile's divisions under lord Kitchener attack Cronje at Woolvekraal Drift, desperate fighting, *cordon* round the Boers completed by the Welsh regiment seizing the drift; major Day mortally wounded, British casualties over 1,100; armistice 24 hours granted to Cronje . . 18 Feb. ,,
Brabant with colonials enters Dordrecht . 18 Feb. ,,
Buller advances steadily; Dundonald captures Cingolo hill, 17 Feb.; Monte Christo won by Lyttelton and Hildyard's brigades; Colenso reoccupied . . . . 18 Feb. ,,
Hlangwane hill taken . . . . . . 19 Feb. ,,
Lord Roberts reaches Paardeberg, revokes armistice, issues a proclamation promising protection to the Free Staters if they cease hostilities, 19 Feb.; enemy repulsed with loss, about 50 captured; Cronje asks for 24 hours' armistice and is told to surrender; he refuses, and his camp is heavily bombarded . . . 20 Feb. 1900
Buller's 5th division crosses the Tugela, Boers driven back . . . . 21 Feb. ,,
Cronje refuses lord Roberts's offer of safe-conduct for the women and children and medical aid, 21 Feb. ,,
Buller advances again, Grobler's Kloof boldly taken by the Dublin Fusiliers . . . . 22 Feb. ,,
Buller attacks Railway hill unsuccessfully, 3 officers killed; total casualties, 97 . . 23 Feb. ,,
[The queen sends a message of sympathy to her "brave Irish soldiers and her admiration for their splendid qualities," 24 Feb.]
Boer reinforcements for Cronje defeated; 88 prisoners taken . . . . . . 23, 24 Feb. ,,
Capt. R. de Montmorency, V.C., and lieut.-col. Hoskier and others killed in a reconnaissance on Stormberg . . . . 24 Feb. ,,
Brabant occupies Jamestown; Boers routed, 25 Feb. ,,
Col. Sandbach finds a new passage of the Tugela; Buller's army crosses . . . 25, 26 Feb. ,,
PIETER'S HILL: Railway and Terrace hills; *Tugela Heights*: the Boer main positions between the Tugela and Ladysmith carried by Hildyard and Warren, 60 Boers captured; British loss: lieut.-col. McCarthy O'Leary, maj. Lewis, capt. Sykes, and many others killed . . . 27 Feb. ,,
Clements drives the Boers back from Arundel and reoccupies Rensburg . . . . 25–27 Feb. ,,
CRONJE SURRENDERS UNCONDITIONALLY AT PAARDEBERG, 27 Feb. (the anniversary of *Majuba*); the British had drawn in closer each night, and a heavy bombardment had been kept up; at 3 a.m. the Canadians, backed by the Gordons and Shropshires, rushed the enemy's trenches, thus "clinching matters," for at 6 a.m. they surrendered; total Boer prisoners 4,000 (including 1,150 Free Staters) and 46 officers, all afterwards sent to St. Helena.
[British loss at Paardeburg, 18 officers, 245 men killed; total casualties, 1,440, 15–27 Feb.]
Buller, *en route* to Ladysmith, drives back Louis Botha's forces, severe fighting; British loss: 22 officers, 241 men killed; total casualties, 1,782, 19–27 Feb. ,,
RELIEF OF LADYSMITH (besieged since 2 Nov. 1899; total casualties, 805): Lord Dundonald, with Natal Carbineers and Imperial Horse, entered first, Buller arriving later; reported complete defeat of the Boers and district clear to the south . . . . 28 Feb. ,,
[Queen's message to sir Redvers Buller: "Thank God for news you have telegraphed to me."]
Colesberg occupied by gen. Clements . 28 Feb. ,,
Colonial Dutch rising round Prieska, Kenhardt occupied . . . . 28 Feb. ,,
Buller advances to Nelthorpe . . . 1 March, ,,
French shells and checks Boer advance near Osfontein, O.F.S. . . . . . 2, 3 March, ,,
Brabant captures Labuschagne Nek, defeats and pursues the Boers . . . . 4, 5 March, ,,
Stormberg occupied by Gatacre . . . 5 March, ,,
Troops arrive in Carnarvon to stop Dutch rising, 6 March, ,,
Lord Roberts routs Delarey at Poplar Grove, 7 March, ,,
DRIEFONTEIN: Boers defeated by lord Roberts, 102 killed and about 20 captured; British loss: col. Umphelby mortally wounded, 4 officers and 58 men killed, 4 mortally wounded . 10 March, ,,
Lord Roberts protests against the Boers' gross abuse of the white flag witnessed by himself at Driefontein . . . . 11 March, ,,
Peace overtures made by the Boer president, 5 March; rejected by lord Salisbury . 11 March, ,,
Brabant occupies Aliwal North after sharp fighting . . . . 11 March, ,,
French seizes the hills and railway commanding Bloemfontein; maj. Hunter-Weston, with 10 men, gets through the Boer lines, cuts the telegraph, and blows up the railway N. of the town; pres. Steyn escapes . . . . 12 March, ,,
LORD ROBERTS ENTERS BLOEMFONTEIN: Boers retreat to Kroonstad . . . . . 13 March, ,,

Barkly East re-occupied by the Cape Police; rebel movement collapsing . . . 13 March, 1900
Methuen seizes Bishop, N.W. of Free State, 14 March, ,,
Proclamation issued at Bloemfontein; surrender of arms ordered . . . . 15 March, ,,
Methuen, advancing towards Mafeking, seizes the ferry at Warrenton . . . 16 March, ,,
Plumer, after advancing to Lobatsi, is forced to retire to Crocodile Pools . . . 16 March, ,,
Boers repulsed at Fourteen Streams by Drummond and Peakman's column . . 16–18 March, ,,
Imperial military railways inaugurated at Bloemfontein . . . . . . 18 March, ,,
Lord Kitchener enters Prieska without resistance; 200 rebels surrender, 33 prisoners taken, 19 March, ,,
Rouxville and Zastron occupied by the British, 19, 21 March, ,,
Clements occupies Philippolis; Free Staters surrender . . . . . . 23 March, ,,
Lieut. the hon. Edw. Lygon killed and 3 officers wounded and captured, 13 mi. N. of Bloemfontein . . . . . . 23 March, ,,
Mr. Fraser, member of the late Free State Government, appointed administrator of the Free State, announced . . . . . . 24 March, ,,
Gen. "Piet" Joubert dies at Pretoria, aged 66, 27 March, ,,
[Succeeded by comm. Louis Botha, 30 March.]
Sir A. Milner, from Cape Town, received by Lord Roberts at Bloemfontein . . 27 March, ,,
Methuen, at Warrenton, opposed by a large force of Boers, artillery duel, 21–27 March; he is recalled to Kimberley . . . 28 March, ,,
Sir George White leaves Cape Town for England, 28 March, ,,
Karee Siding, near Brandfort: Boers defeated and their position seized by Tucker; British loss, 20 men and 1 officer killed . . 29 March, ,,
Col. G. H. Gough dies at Norval's Pont, 29 March, ,,
Broadwood, hard pressed by comm. Olivier and about 10,000 Boers at Thabanchu, retires to Bloemfontein waterworks . . 30 March, ,,
Sanna's Post or *Koorn Spruit*; De Wet attacks Broadwood; 2 batteries of R.H.A. and a large convoy were entrapped at Waterval Drift and, with 6 guns, lost; total casualties, 350; Boer loss unknown . . . 30, 31 March, ,,
Plumer repulsed at Ramathlabama, near Mafeking, 31 March, ,,
Reddersburg, S. of Bloemfontein: a detachment of Irish Rifles and mounted infantry surrounded and captured when all their ammunition was gone; total casualties, 440 . . 3, 4 April, ,,
Clements arrives at Bloemfontein after a successful march . . . . . . 5 April, ,,
Methuen surrounds the Boers near Boshof and takes 51 prisoners; col. De Villebois-Mareuil and 7 Boers killed . . . . 5 April, ,,
Col. Dalgety and Cape Mounted Rifles isolated near **Wepener**; heavily engaged . 7, 9 April, ,,
Boers repulsed with great loss near Kenhardt, 13 April, ,,
Chermside leaves Reddersburg to relieve Wepener, 15 April, ,,
Rundle engages the Boers and seizes their position near Dewetsdorp . . . . 21 April, ,,
Pole-Carew seizes Leeuw Kop; Boers fled, 22, 23 April, ,,
Ian Hamilton re-occupies Bloemfontein waterworks . . . . . . 23 April, ,,
Maxwell's brigade seizes hills commanding the Modder at Kranz Kraal . . 23 April, ,,
Sir Charles Warren appointed military gov. of Griqualand West, leaves Durban . 23 April, ,,
Pole-Carew reaches Roode Kop, driving the Boers back with loss . . . . 24 April, ,,
Wepener relieved by Brabant and Hart, co-operating with Rundle; Louis Botha retreats North . . . . . . 25 April, ,,
Ian Hamilton outflanks the enemy and drives them off *the Waterworks* and their position at Israel's Poort . . . . . . 24, 25 April, ,,
Ian Hamilton and Smith-Dorrien defeat strong Boer force at Houtnek, 1 May (a day's halt ordered, his men having fought 7 out of 10 days) 1900
Lord Roberts begs Mafeking to hold out until 18 May, announced . . . . . 2 May, ,,
Brandfort captured by Pole-Carew . . 3 May, ,,
Sir A. Hunter crosses the Vaal river at Windsorton, 3 May, ,,
Cavalry routs the Boers at Welkorn; their right dislodged by Macdonald's Black Watch . 4 May, ,,
Barton routs the Boers at Ruidam . . 5 May, ,,
Lord Roberts advances: Hutton turns the enemy's right and crosses the Vet river, great gallantry of colonials; a maxim and 25 men captured, 5 May, ,,
Winburg surrenders to Hamilton . . 6 May, ,,
Hunter defeats the Boers at Fourteen Streams, 7 May, ,,
Boer white flag treachery: capt. Elworthy killed, 2 officers and 21 men entrapped, near Kroonstad, 10 May, ,,
Lord Roberts crosses the Zand river; Boers in full retreat . . . . . . 10 May, ,,
Lord Roberts enters **Kroonstad** without resistance; pres. Steyn flies to *Heilbron*, which he proclaims his new capital . . . 12 May, ,,
Mafeking: Boers repulsed, comm. Eloff and 108 Boers captured . . . . 12 May, ,,
Col. Mahon, with Mafeking relief column, defeats the Boers at Koodoosrand . . 13 May, ,,
Grenfell captures Newberry's mills, with stores, 13 May, ,,
Buller drives the Boers from the Biggarsberg, after a hard march over a *waterless* country, 9–14 May, ,,
Boer white flag treachery near Kroonstad; officer wounded, 2 men killed . . 14 May, ,,
Buller occupies Dundee and Glencoe; Boer rout complete . . . . . . 15 May, ,,
Hunter enters the Transvaal and occupies Christiania . . . . . . 16 May, ,,
Mahon marches rapidly from Barkly West and joins Plumer; they drive the Boers from their western positions, and by an action at Malopo river the advance to Mafeking is secured, 14–16 May, ,,
Methuen occupies Hoopstad; gens. Duprez and Daniels, with 40 Boers, surrender . 17 May, ,,
Ian Hamilton occupies Lindley, slight resistance; 25 Boers captured by Hutton's M.I. . 17 May, ,,
Relief of Mafeking, gallantly defended by maj.-gen. R. Baden-Powell and all under him since 13 Oct. 1899; siege raised; Mahon, with a flying column, enters the town 4 a.m. . 17, 18 May, ,,
Bethune's mounted infantry ambushed near Vryheid; 66 casualties . . . 20 May, ,,
Ian Hamilton occupies Heilbron after several actions with retreating enemy . 22 May, ,,
Lord Roberts advances; French crosses the Rhenoster . . . . . . 22, 23 May, ,,
Hunter occupies Vryburg after forced march, 24 May, ,,
French crosses the Vaal at Parys and pushes on towards Johannesburg; Rundle occupies Senekal, 24 May, ,,
Ficksburg occupied, 24 May; Boer attack repulsed, 26 May, ,,
Annexation of the *Orange Free State*, under the name of **Orange River Colony**, proclaimed at Bloemfontein . . . . . . 28 May, ,,
Lord Roberts occupies Vereeniging . 27 May, ,,
Col. Adye defeats the Boers at Kheis . 27 May, ,,
Utrecht surrenders to Hildyard . . 27 May, ,,
Buller, sweeping eastwards, drives back the enemy; reaches Newcastle . . . . 28 May, ,,
Brabant's patrols (2) entrapped; 3 men killed, the rest taken prisoners, near Hammonia . 28 May, ,,
Senekal: Rundle severely defeats the Boers; 38 British killed . . . . . 29 May, ,,
Sir H. Colvile's force reaches Heilbron from Ventersburg, after hard fighting . . 29 May, ,,
British advance to **Johannesburg**: lord Roberts arrives at Germiston; Boers defeated and their positions carried by the Gordon Highlanders and City Imp. Volunteers, under French and Ian Hamilton, near Roodepoort . . . 29 May, ,,
Comm. Botha, 100 men and Creuzot gun captured at Doornkop . . . . . 29 May, ,,

Warren defeats the enemy at Fabers; col. Spence and about 17 killed . . . 29, 30 May, 1900

Pres. Kruger flies from Pretoria to Waterval-boven . . . . 30 May, „

Lord Roberts grants 24 hours' armistice to comm. Krause (see *Trials*, 18 Jan. 1902) at Johannesburg . . . . 30 May, „

Johannesburg entered; British flag hoisted, 31 May, „

Col. Spragge, with Imp. Yeomanry (Irish), after a brave defence, captured by De Wet at Lindley; British casualties, 78 . . . . 27–31 May, „

Methuen's relief force defeats the Boers at Lindley, 1, 2 June, „

Capt. Corballis with convoy surrenders to De Wet, 4 June, „

Lord Roberts marches north, 3 June; routs the Boers at Six Miles Spruit and bivouacs outside Pretoria . . . . . . 4 June, „

Pretoria entered; British flag hoisted . 5 June, „

Buller advances in Natal; Talbot Coke seizes Van Wyk hill . . . . 6 June, „

British reverse: 4th Derbyshires and Imp. Yeomanry surrounded at Roodeval by De Wet; lieut.-col. Baird-Douglas and 35 killed, 5 officers and 111 wounded, the rest captured . 6, 7 June, „

Botha's Pass captured by Hildyard; Buller's army through the Drakensberg . . . . 8, 9 June, „

Methuen routs De Wet at the Rhenoster and seizes railway . . . . . . 11 June, „

Gans Vlei and Almond's Nek forced by Buller's forces; heavy Boer losses; Langs Nek and Majuba evacuated . . . . 10, 11, 12 June, „

Gen. Villiers (French) mortally wounded and comm. Olivier killed at Rooikrantz, announced, 11 June, „

French, Ian Hamilton, and Pole-Carew attack Botha at Eerste Fabrieken; hard fight on **Diamond Hill**, E. of Pretoria, Boers routed; the earl of Airlie, maj. Fortescue, lieut. the hon. Chas. Cavendish, and others killed; great gallantry of the C.I.V.'s (lieut. Alt and 2 men killed) and troops . . . . 11, 12 June, „

Kelly-Kenny defeats the Boers at Honing Spruit, 12 June, „

Buller enters the Transvaal, occupies Volksrust, 12 June, „

Wakkerstroom surrenders to Lyttelton . 13 June, „

Boer attack on Ficksburg again repulsed, 14 June, „

Knox defeats the Boers at Sand river; maj. Seymour (American engineer) and 2 men killed; lieut. Harrison mortally wounded . . 14 June, „

Hunter occupies Klerksdorp; comm. Andreas Cronje surrenders . . . . 9–15 June, „

Baden-Powell occupies Rustenburg; comm. Steyn and 2 officers captured . . . . 15 June, „

Buller relieves Natal volunteers from service, with high praise . . . . . . 15 June, „

Lord Roberts's offer of 5 days' armistice, 12 June, declined by gen. Louis Botha . . . 15 June, „

Methuen defeats De Wet at Heilbron . 19 June, „

Hutton's M.I. capture 2 guns near Pretoria, 19 June, „

Railway restored from Pretoria to Cape Town, 20 June, „

De Villiers' commando surrenders to Warren in Cape Colony . . . . 20 June, „

Honing Spruit attacked by Boers; maj. Hobbs and 5 others killed . . . . . 22, 23 June, „

Ian Hamilton occupies Heidelberg after slight resistance . . . . 23 June, „

Clements drives the enemy N. of the Zand, 24 June, „

British successes; much skirmishing, 22–26 June, „

British convoy reaches Lindley after a heavy rearguard action; 10 killed, many wounded, 26 June, „

Senekal, Roodeval Spruit, and Hammonia attacked; Boers repulsed . . 26, 27, 29 June, „

Clery occupies Greylingstad with slight opposition, 2 July, „

Andries Wessels, head of the *Afrikander Bond*, captured by Methuen, near Paardekraal, about 2 July, „

Paget defeats the Boers near Leeuwkop, and pursues them towards Bethlehem; flight of ex-pres. Steyn . . . . . . 3, 4 July, „

Roberts and Buller join at Vlakfontein; railway to Natal clear . . . . 4 July, 1900

Boers' final attack on Ficksburg repulsed . . 4 July, „

Bethlehem captured by Clements and Paget; British casualties about 100 . . . 7 July, „

Boer attack on Rustenburg repulsed; 3 British officers and 4 men killed . . . . 7 July, „

Guerilla warfare adopted by the Boers, early July, „

Free State government officials surrender at Heilbron . . . . 8–10 July, „

Uitvals Nek: surrender Scots Greys and Lincolns; 3 officers and 16 men killed; total casualties, 255; Boer loss also heavy . . . . 11 July, „

Mahon captures Boer positions near Rietfontein, 11 July, „

Boers lose severely at Derdepoort and Krugersdorp . . . . 11 July, „

Lord Roberts repulses the enemy in 2 actions near Eerste Fabricken . . . . 11, 12 July, „

Much skirmishing; Dundonald captures a laager, 13–15 July, „

Boers repulsed near Pretoria . . . . 16 July, „

Boers break through British cordon between Bethlehem and Ficksburg, 17 July; overtaken and dispersed by col. Little . . . . 19 July, „

Maj. English, with Dublin Fusiliers, repels a strong attack near Heidelberg . . 21 July, „

Methuen routs the Boers at Oliphant's Nek, relieves Rustenburg and joins Baden-Powell, 21 July, „

Bruce Hamilton seizes a strong post at Spitzray, 21 July, „

Ian Hamilton forces the Boers from Rusfontein, 22 July, „

Cols. Airey and Lushington rout the Boers at Magato Pass; British loss, capt. Robinson and 5 men killed . . . . 22 July, „

Hunter seizes a kopje S. of Bethlehem and forces Retief's Nek at dusk . . . . . 23 July, „

Lord Roberts's general advance east begins, 23 July, „

Boers driven back; Vredefort reached . 24 July, „

Boers twice repulsed at Vlaklaagte . 26 July, „

Gen. Prinsloo and over 3,000 Boers surrender (De Wet escaped) to Hunter at Naauwpoort, in Brandwater Basin . . . . 29, 30 July, „

Two sappers and 3 natives murdered by Boers near Frederickstad . . . . . . 30 July, „

Collapse of Boer resistance in the Caledon valley and Basuto border . . . . . . Aug. „

Ian Hamilton drives the Boers off the Magaliesberg . . . . 2 Aug. „

Maj. Gough routs the Boers near Standerton, 4 Aug. „

Harrismith surrenders to Macdonald - 4 Aug. „

De Wet crosses the Vaal, Kitchener in pursuit, 6 Aug. *et seq.* „

Guerilla warfare: desultory fighting . Aug. *et seq.* „

Bergendal Farm: here Botha's force checked for 24 hours the combined efforts of Buller, French, and Pole-Carew, but was finally routed on the arrival of lord Roberts . . . . 7 Aug. „

Boer Plot in Pretoria to seize lord Roberts and murder British officers, discovered; 15 arrests, 9, 10 Aug. „

Field-cornet and 182 men surrender to Clery, 12 Aug. „

Col. Helyar murdered by the Boers, 31 July; his body found by Col. Hickman . . . 13 Aug. „

Elands River garrison of 300 Australians under col. Hore besieged by Delarey since 28 July (17 killed), relieved by Kitchener . . 16 Aug. „

Ian Hamilton captures 2 Krupp guns at Oliphant's Nek . . . . 17 Aug. „

Baden-Powell attacks comm. Grobler's rearguard E. of Pienaar's river, lieut.-col. Spreckley and 4 men killed; Boer loss heavy . . 21 Aug. „

Buller reaches Van Wyk's Vlei after sharp fighting, 21 Aug. „

Baden-Powell rescues 100 British and captures 25 Boers near Warmbaths . . . 22 Aug. „

Buller strongly opposed at Geluk's farm; Liverpool regiment cut off, 10 killed and 32 missing, 23 Aug. „

BOER PLOT to kidnap lord Roberts and the British garrison at Johannesburg; Hans Cordua found guilty, 21 Aug., and executed . . 25 Aug. 1900

Lord Roberts joins Buller at *Belfast* . 25 Aug. ,,

Boers defeated at Winburg by Ridley and Bruce Hamilton; gen. Olivier and his 3 sons captured by Queenstown volunteers . . . . 26 Aug. ,,

BERGENDAL, N. Transvaal, captured by Buller from Louis Botha; fine charge of Inniskillings and 2nd Rifles; Boer general and 19 men taken, about 20 killed: British officer and 13 men killed . . . . 27 Aug. ,,

DALMANUTHA, sharp fighting . . 26, 27 Aug. ,,

Maj. Brooke routs a Boer force at Kraai . 27 Aug. ,,

MACHADODORP captured by Buller; Botha retreats to the hills . . . . 28 Aug. ,,

Lord Roberts takes Waterval Boven . 29 Aug. ,,

French releases British prisoners at Nooitgedacht, 30 Aug. ,,

TRANSVAAL REPUBLIC ANNEXED to Gt. Britain by lord Roberts; proclamation issued, 1 Sept. *et seq.* ,,

Ladybrand garrison hard pressed; relieved by Bruce Hamilton . . . . . . 4, 5 Sept. ,,

LYDENBURG taken by Buller and Ian Hamilton, 6, 7 Sept. ,,

Comm. Theron killed in a skirmish near Krugersdorp, about . . . . 6 Sept. ,,

Buller storms and captures the Mauchberg, 8, 9 Sept. ,,

Methuen scatters the Boers at Molopo and captures 30 . . . . 9 Sept. ,,

KRUGER and other officials fly to Lorenzo Marques, 11 Sept. ,,

Transvaal placed under martial law . 11 Sept. ,,

Douglas defeats the Boers at Wonderfontein, 11 Sept. ,,

Hart captures many Boers and reoccupies Potchefstroom . . . . 11 Sept. ,,

BARBERTON occupied by French, over 100 Boers captured; 74 British released . . 13 Sept. ,,

Macdonald routs the enemy near Tapel Kop, Vet river . . . . 13 Sept. ,,

Roberts calls on burghers to surrender; proclamation issued . . . . . . 13 Sept. ,,

Boer peace delegates at the Hague issue an appeal to the powers for intervention . . 15 Sept. ,,

Bultfontein garrison, under lieut. Slater, relieved after a gallant defence . . . . 16 Sept. ,,

Over 400 foreigners under suspect deported . Sept. ,,

Lord Roberts occupies Nelspruit; further successes, 17 Sept. *et seq.* ,,

Lord Roberts returns to Pretoria from the front, 21 Sept. ,,

Gen. Pienaar and 3,000 Boers surrender to the Portuguese, and are sent to Delagoa bay, 23 Sept. ,,

KOMATI POORT; Portuguese frontier, occupied by the Guards with slight opposition . 24, 25 Sept. ,,

Rundle captures stores, &c. . . . 26 Sept. ,,

Buller seizes Pilgrim's hill after a night march; Boers fled . . . . . . 27, 28 Sept. ,,

Gen. Maxwell appointed administrator of the Transvaal . . . . 1 Oct. ,,

Baden-Powell assumes command of the Transvaal and Orange river police . . . 2 Oct. ,,

Skirmishes; capt. Wiltshire killed near Lindley, 4 Oct. ,,

Reconnoitring party ambushed near Vlakfontein; capts. Stewart and Paget and others killed, 8 Oct. ,,

Col. de Lisle drives De Wet out of Orange River Colony, N. of the Vaal . . . . 5–9 Oct. ,,

Boers defeated at Dwarsvlei and Frankfort, 9, 11 Oct. ,,

Lord Roberts issues army order thanking sir Redvers Buller for great services in Natal, 11 Oct. ,,

Mahon's column heavily attacked at Dalmanutha, 3 officers and 8 men killed . . 13 Oct. ,,

Theunis Botha surrenders at Valksrust . 13 Oct. ,,

Settle enters Bloemhof and captures 50 Boers, 14 Oct. ,,

Desultory fighting; casualties on both sides, Oct. ,,

KRUGER leaves Lorenzo Marques for Europe in the *Gelderland*, Dutch cruiser . . 20 Oct. ,,

Paget captures 65 Boers and 25,000 cattle near Pienaars river . . . . . 21–23 Oct. 1900

Success near Zeerust, 20 Boers killed and 39 captured . . . . 24 Oct. ,,

Buller leaves Cape Town for England . 24 Oct. ,,

Plucky defence of the little garrison under lieut. Tonkin at Philippolis until relieved by Kelly-Kenny . . . . 18–24 Oct. ,,

Boers driven out of Jacobsdal, comm. Bosman killed . . . . 25 Oct. ,,

Barton captures 2 guns and scatters De Wet's force with loss . . . . 24, 25 Oct. ,,

SOUTH AFRICAN BOER REPUBLIC formally annexed and styled *Transvaal Colony* . . 25 Oct. ,,

Knox inflicts heavy loss on De Wet at Rensburg, 27 Oct. ,,

Prince Christian Victor of Schleswig-Holstein, an able soldier, aged 33, dies of *enteric*, at Pretoria; much liked and lamented . . . . 29 Oct. ,,

Further British successes . . 30 Oct.–3 Nov. ,,

Many natives shot in cold blood by the Boers, Oct.–Nov. ,,

De Wet and Steyn severely defeated by cols. Le Gallais and De Lisle near BOTHAVILLE, 8 guns and 100 Boers captured; col. Le Gallais, major Legge and 10 men killed . . . . 5 Nov. ,,

Smith-Dorrien drives the enemy near Belfast east of Komati river; gen. Fourie and comm. Prinsloo killed . . . . 6, 7 Nov. ,,

Boers defeated near Edenburg . . 16 Nov. ,,

Suspected anarchist plot against lord Roberts, several arrests at Johannesburg . . 16 Nov. ,,

Clements defeats Delarey at Baberspan . 18 Nov. ,,

De Wet captures Dewetsdorp after hard fighting, 17–23 Nov. ,,

Paget defeats Viljoen and seizes Rhenoster Kop; lieut.-col. Lloyd and 13 killed . . 27 Nov. ,,

LORD KITCHENER takes supreme command, 29 Nov. ,,

Knox sharply engages De Wet east of Slick Spruit, 2, 3 Dec. ,,

Lord Roberts's farewell army order testifies to the courage, endurance, and humanity of the troops, 3 Dec. ,,

Delarey attacks a convoy near Rustenburg; 15 British killed and stock destroyed . . 3 Dec. ,,

De Wet's attempt on Cape Colony defeated by Knox; Krupp gun captured near Bethulie, 5–8 Dec. ,,

Mr. Kruger's appeal for European intervention fails . . . . Dec. ,,

Vryheid fiercely attacked; Botha retreats with heavy loss . . . . 11 Dec. ,,

Lord Roberts leaves Cape Town for England, 11 Dec. ,,

Delarey and Beyers attack Clements before daybreak at Nooitgedacht; British outpost seized; Clements retires on Commando Nek; lieut.-col. Legge, 4 officers and 9 men killed, about 500 captured; Boer loss heavy . . . 13 Dec. ,,

British successes in many places; gen. Lemmer and many Boers killed . . . . 4–13 Dec. ,,

Brabant's Horse trapped near Zastron, 8 killed, 13 Dec. ,,

Knox drives De Wet in a running fight north of Helvetia . . . . 11, 12 Dec. ,,

De Wet and Steyn, after being twice repulsed and 2 guns seized, escaped through *Springhaan's Pass*, 14 Dec. ,,

Boers defeated at Scheeper's Nek and elsewhere, 13–18 Dec. ,,

Herzog and Kritzinger invade Cape Colony, 16–19 Dec. ,,

French and Clements rout the Boers at Thorndale and drive them from the Magaliesberg; about 130 killed . . . . 19, 20 Dec. ,,

Martial law in northern districts of Cape Colony, 20 Dec. ,,

Lord Kitchener's offer of protection to the burghers on surrender well received at Pretoria, 20, 21 Dec. ,,

De Wet fails to get back into Cape Colony; raiders driven back . . . . . . 26, 28 Dec. ,,

Helvetia: Boers capture gun and garrison, 11 British killed . . . . 29 Dec. ,,

Colonial defence force called out in Cape Colony, 1 Jan. 1901

Botha defeats British bodyguard near Lindley; lieut.-col. Laing, 2 officers and 15 men killed, 3 Jan. ,,

Bruce-Hamilton relieves Bultfontein after 2 months' siege . . . . 4 Jan. 1901

Disaster to the Imperial Light Horse after a gallant charge, 18 killed and 6 mortally wounded, 6 Jan. ,,

Burgher peace committee at Pretoria issue earnest appeals to the Boers to surrender . early Jan. ,,

Boer night attacks on Belfast, Dalmanutha, Machadodorp, repulsed after fierce fighting and much loss along the Delagoa railway, British officer and 20 men killed . . . . 7, 8 Jan. ,,

Farms burnt in South Africa up to . . . Jan. ,,

Guerilla warfare continues: *incessant raids, small victories and defeats;* slow but steady weakening of the enemy's forces; *Times* . . Jan. *et seq.* ,,

Ermelo occupied, and Smith-Dorrien defeats Louis Botha at Bothwell, near lake Chrissie; gen. Spruit and many Boers killed; 23 British killed, 28 Jan. ,,

Col. Grey routs Delarey near Ventersburg, 17, 18 Jan. ,,

French (knt. May, 1901) drives Beyers from posts covering the Wilge river valley; and Knox hotly engages De Wet on the Tabaksberg . 28, 29 Jan. ,,

King Edward wires to lord Kitchener: "One of the queen's last inquiries was after yourself and the gallant army under your command," 30 Jan. ,,

Modderfontein: British post rushed, 2 officers and others killed . . . . 31 Jan. ,,

Mr. Piet De Wet, president of the Boer peace committee at Bloemfontein, urges his brother, gen. De Wet, to surrender, 11 Jan.; announced, 5 Feb. ,,

Morgendaal and De Kock (at Belfast, 12 Feb.), peace envoys, shot by the Boers; natives flogged and murdered . . . . . Jan.–Feb. ,,

De Wet again enters Cape Colony, 10 Feb.; Plumer repulses him at Philipstown, 12, 13 Feb.; captures a maxim, 20 men and stock, at Wolvekuil, 14, 15 Feb. ,,

Botha's attempt on Natal fails; French inflicts heavy loss on the enemy; Luneburg and other places occupied (major Howard, a Canadian, killed, 17 Feb.) . . . . 11–22 Feb. ,,

De Wet, hotly pursued, is driven out of Cape Colony; recrosses Orange river between Sand Drift and Colesberg, having lost guns, stock, 200 prisoners and many killed . 23–28 Feb. ,,

Peace conference between lord Kitchener and gen. Botha at Middelburg . . . . 27, 28 Feb. ,,

Delarey repulsed at Lichtenburg, maj. Fletcher and 15 others killed . . . . 3 March, ,,

Mr. Boyd and 4 others shot by Delarey's orders at Wolmaranstad . . . . 9 March, ,,

Boers capture a train near Wilge river, Transvaal, and murder 10 *unarmed natives* . . 11 March, ,,

Lord Kitchener's offers of peace and *amnesty*, 7 March, rejected by Botha . . 15, 16 March, ,,

Philip Botha killed at Doomberg . mid March, ,,

VENTERSDORP: Babington routs Delarey; 3 guns and 6 maxims captured . . 22, 23 March, ,,

Dartnell and Alderson work successfully in east Transvaal; 200 Boers surrender . end March, ,,

French's operations very successful; 11 guns, many men and stock, &c., captured in S.E. district, reported . . . . . . 5 April, ,,

Zekoe river fight in Cape Colony; British (about 100) surrounded, 4 killed, 13 wounded, 25 escaped, 6 April, ,,

Pietersburg captured by Plumer; Bosman Kop and 16 men, &c., seized by Byng . . . 8 April, ,,

Maj. Twyford's small escort ambushed near Badfontein; he was shot and the rest overpowered, mid April, ,,

Klerksdorp; Rawlinson captures a laager and 2 guns . . . . 14 April, ,,

Sir Bindon Blood takes command in E. Transvaal; train wrecking stopped . . . . April, ,,

Lieut. Reid and 20 Australians seize a laager and 41 Boers at Klipdam . . . . 24 April, ,,

The Tantesberg and Bothasberg cleared; 1,081 Boers taken or surrendered . . . . April, ,,

Babington defeats the Boers at Hartebeestfontein and Lopfontein . . . . 27, 28 April, ,,

Boers defeated with loss, S. of Maraisburg and at Zwagershoek . . . . 13 and 16 May, ,,

Zeerust relieved by Methuen after several months' siege . . . . 22 May, 1901

British successes in Cape Colony and O.R.C., comm. Swarts and others captured . . 22 May, ,,

Boers routed near Brandfort and Kenhardt, 23 May, ,,

VLAKFONTEIN: Dixon (K.C.B. 26 June, 1902) defeats Delarey, 41 Boers left *dead on the field;* 6 British officers and 51 men killed, 5 mortally wounded (*Boers shot several of the wounded*) . . 29 May, ,,

Laager at Pienaar's river rushed by Kitchener's Scouts, 27 Boers killed, 86 wounded; 5 British killed and 21 wounded . . . . . 31 May, ,,

JAMESTOWN, Cape Colony, taken by Kritzinger, 2 June; one of his forces is routed near Roodenek, 6 June, ,,

Elliot defeats De Wet at Graspan, near Reitz, convoy and 45 Boers captured (lieut. Mair and 2 others shot in cold blood by the Boers), 6 June, ,,

Comm. Van Rensburg and force surrender at Pietersburg . . . . about 10 June, ,,

Disaster to Victorians (350), 18 killed, 42 wounded, 2 guns lost at Wilmansrust, Transvaal, 12 June, ,,

Boers defeated with heavy loss near Zeerust, mid June; at Orange Pan . . . . 19 June, ,,

Cape Mounted Rifles severely defeated at Waterkloof . . . . 20 June, ,,

Boer attacks along the Delagoa railway repulsed, 26 June, ,,

Train wrecked by Boers near Naboomspruit, lieut. Best, 11 soldiers and 7 others killed . 4 July, ,,

Kruger telegraphs to Botha, in reply to inquiries, to *continue fighting* . . . . . 5 July, ,,

Broadwood captures 29 officials of the late Orange Free State; ex-pres. Steyn escaped, but his papers were seized, at Reitz . . . 12 July, ,,

French very successful; drives Scheepers' commando out of the Camdeboos . . 8–15 July, ,,

Boers defeated near Jamestown . . 14 July, ,,

Lord Kitchener commutes 34 death sentences to penal servitude . . . . . . mid July, ,,

Gen. Spruyt killed near Vlakfontein . 20 July, ,,

Yeomanry (20) and some native scouts surrender at Doornriver, O.R.C; a soldier and natives shot in cold blood by the Boers . . . . . 27 July, ,,

W. Kitchener captures gun and 32 men from Viljoen near Middelburg . . . . 30 July, ,,

Many laagers captured in July; comm. H. Steyn killed at Ficksburg . . . . . 31 July, ,,

Lord Kitchener reports shooting of unarmed natives by Boers . . . . . . 1 Aug. ,,

Van Rhyns Dorp captured by Boers after 7 hours' fighting . . . . 6 Aug. ,,

Jas. Madhaila, native constable (unarmed), shot by Boers at Steytleville . . . . 7 Aug. ,,

Comm. de Villiers and 2 field cornets surrender at Warmbaths . . . . 8 Aug. ,,

Gorringe routs Kritzinger's commandos near Steynsburg, 2 leaders mortally wounded and about 20 killed . . . . 13 Aug. ,,

Proclamation, calling on the Boers to surrender before 15 Sept. under pain of banishment and confiscation of property, issued . . 15 Aug. ,,

Laager rushed near Middlesburg by S.A. constabulary, over 23 Boers killed . 17 Aug. ,,

Lord Kitchener reports inefficiency of certain reinforcements, published . . . 21 Aug. ,,

French's operations in Cape Colony result in expulsion of Kritzinger and disorganisation of other commandos . . . . . . Aug. ,,

Laager surprised at Doornberg, O.R.C., Boer loss about 60 . . . . . . about 21 Aug. ,,

Boer attack on a convoy repulsed near Rooikopje, 9 British killed, 23 wounded . . 24 Aug. ,,

Methuen, cols. Hickie and Williams clear district between Taungs and Mafeking, Krugersdorp and Magaliesberg regions, reported . 29, 30 Aug. ,,

TRAIN WRECKED and fired by Boers near Waterval, lieut.-col. Vandeleur, 13 men and 3 others killed, 25 wounded . . . . 31 Aug. ,,

Concentration camps: 35,000 Boers and 74,589 women and children . . . . Aug. ,,

Trains wrecked and looted by Boers in Cape Colony. . . . . early Sept. ,,

LOTTER'S COMMANDO near Petersburg, Cape Colony, captured by col. Scobell, 19 Boers killed; Lotter and Breedt and 102 prisoners taken . 5 Sept. 1901

Methuen operates successfully in Great Maries valley, gen. Lemmer and 19 Boers killed, 44 prisoners and stock seized . 1–5 Sept. ,,

Scheepers' commando routed at Laingsburg by col. Crabbe, Van de Merwe killed, Du Plessis and 37 Boers captured . . . 10 Sept. ,,

Concentration camp at Middelburg visited by lieut. Malan, gen. Viljoen's aide-de-camp, and reported satisfactory . . . 11 Sept. ,,

Patrol of Guards surrounded, lieut. Rebow and others shot dead at close range . 16 Sept. ,,

[Boer leaders encouraged by pro-Boer speakers and press, reported, Sept.]

BLOOD RIVER POORT, near UTRECHT: maj. Gough's force trapped by Botha, capt. Mildmay, lieuts. Blewitt, Lambton and 31 killed, 25 wounded, 17 Sept. ,,

Lancers (17th) surprised at Elands River Poort by Smuts' commando, lieuts. R. Brinsley Sheridan, Morritt and 24 killed, 33 wounded, 3 mortally; enemy, in khaki, also suffered heavily . 17 Sept. ,,

Boers attack an escort at Vlakfontein, lieut. Barry and 5 men killed, 2 guns captured (recovered, 2 Oct.) . . . . . . 19 Sept. ,,

British successes: Williams captures 55 of Koch's force and transport, W. of Edenburg; Benson captures, S.E. of Carolina, P. J. Botha, 53 men and transport . . . . . 20 Sept. ,,

Lovat's Scouts rushed by Kritzinger, who fails to cross the Orange river, lieut.-col. and capt. Murray and 16 killed; 20 Boers captured, 20 Sept. ,,

Thorneycroft's men retake gun (captured 19 Sept.), 1 Boer killed, 20 captured . . 22 Sept. ,,

Basutos attacked by Boers, severe fighting, 24 Sept. ,,

Capt. R. Miers murdered by Boers bearing a white flag at Riversdraai . . . . . 25 Sept. ,,

FORTS ITALA and PROSPECT, on the Zulu border, bravely defended by maj. Chapman and capt. Rowley; Botha's army defeated and Natal saved from invasion; 19 hours' heavy fighting, estimated Boer loss, 128 killed, 270 wounded; British loss, lieut. Kane and 11 others killed, many wounded . . . . . 25, 26 Sept. ,,

Brigg's force surrounds Reitz and captures 21 Boers, stock, &c. . . . . . 29 Sept. ,,

MOEDWILL: Delarey and Kemp's attack on Kekewich defeated, heavy loss on both sides; 1 British officer and 46 killed, 26 officers and 124 (some mortally) wounded . . . 29, 30 Sept. ,,

Guerilla warfare, many engagements . early Oct. ,,

Martial law extended in Cape Colony . 8 Oct. ,,

Comm. Lotter convicted of murder, &c., executed, 11 Oct. ,,

French captures comm. Scheepers at Kopjeskraal, 11 Oct. ,,

Sir H. Rawlinson captures Meyer's transport, Boer loss 20 . . . . . . 14 Oct. ,,

Many death sentences commuted: J. S. Kruger and lieut. Breda executed . . . 17 Oct. ,,

Many minor British successes; Dawkins captures 3 laagers and 76 Boers, W. of Nylstroom, without loss . . . . . . 17–20 Oct. ,,

Botha narrowly escapes capture, his papers seized by Rimington, E. of Ermelo . 21–24 Oct. ,,

Badfontein blockhouse line attacked by Viljoen; Kemp repulsed by Von Donop's column, near Marico river, 40 Boers left dead, comm. Ouisterhuysen mortally wounded; 2 British officers and 26 men killed, 55 wounded . . 24 Oct. ,,

Byng's column, after a long night march from Coalmine Drift, captures Spanneberg's laager; Damant disperses the enemy near Villiersdorp, 25 Oct. ,,

Convoy to Clanwilliam captured by Maritz, 29 Oct. ,,

BRAKENLAAGTE: here Botha's force, about 1,000, attacked col. Benson's column, charging close under cover of violent rain and hail; Benson, lieut.-col. E. Guinness, maj. F. D. Murray, capts. Thorold, Eyre and 56 others killed; 16 officers and 149 wounded; about 44 Boers killed, many wounded (Boers charged with cruel and brutal treatment of the wounded), 30, 31 Oct.; the fight lasted till the arrival of col. Barter's relief column, when the Boers retired . . . . early 1 Nov. 1901

Kekewich captures Van Albert's laager at Beestekraal . . . . . . 1 Nov. ,,

Dutoit's laager at Doornhoek captured . 11 Nov. ,,

Imp. Yeomanry from Brakspruit surrounded, 6 killed, 16 wounded; Boers driven off by relief column . . . . . . 13 Nov. ,,

De Wet attacks Byng near Heilbron . 14 Nov. ,,

Bluebook issued on the concentration camps reports the ignorance and prejudice of the Boers on sanitation, &c. . . . . 15 Nov. ,,

Plot discovered in Johannesburg to betray the town to Delarey, 20 arrests . . . 19 Nov. ,,

Comm. Buys captured (after attacking railway pioneers' patrol near Villiersdorp, maj. Fisher mortally wounded) by Rimington's column, 20 Nov. ,,

Gens. Celliers and Andries Cronje form a volunteer burgher corps on the British side . . Nov. ,,

Minor successes: Boer raids repelled, 13–20 Nov. ,,

Knox's column capture comm. Joubert . 26 Nov. ,,

Blockhouse system reported successful; concentration of Boer forces prevented . Sept.–Dec. ,,

Hon. col. A. Wools-Sampson (K.C.B. 26 June, 1902) captures a laager in Ermelo district . 3, 4 Dec. ,,

Dawkins captures part of Beyer's laager near Nylstrom . . . . 4 Dec. ,,

National Scouts corps established . . 7 Dec. ,,

Extension of blockhouse lines . . . 11 Dec. ,,

Bruce Hamilton's columns, after a rapid march, capture nearly *the whole Bethel commando*, 10 Dec.; also Piet Viljoen's at Witkranz, 16 killed, 70 taken prisoners, gun recaptured . 12 Dec. ,,

Comm. Badenhorst and 14 captured at Sterkfontein . . . . . . 14, 15 Dec. ,,

Comm. Kritzinger (wounded) and others captured near Hanover road . . . . 16 Dec. ,,

Comm. Haasbroek and 2 others killed in a fight near the Doornberg . . . . 16 Dec. ,,

Methuen surprises Potgieter near the Makwasi hills, captures his family and papers, 19 men, &c., 18 Dec. ,,

Dartnell repulses De Wet with loss near Landberg, 18 Dec. ,,

Allenby captures Staats Artillerie under Pretorius, 19 Dec. ,,

TAFELKOP, O.R.C.: col. Damant's force surprised, repels a fierce attack of Wessels, over 27 Boers killed; 2 British officers and about 30 killed, 23 wounded [Boers charged with cruelty] . 20 Dec. ,,

Kitchener's 2nd report of natives murdered by Boers, issued . . . . . . 23 Dec. ,,

TWEEFONTEIN disaster: col. Firman's camp on a hill slope rushed from the other side by De Wet with about 1,200 men (about 2 a.m.), maj. Williams, 5 officers and 51 men killed, 88 wounded; Boer loss about 30 killed and 50 wounded . 25 Dec. ,,

Mounted infantry corps organised in S. Africa, 28 Dec. ,,

Bruce Hamilton, operating E. of Ermelo, captures 105 Boers, also gen. Erasmus and 40 S. of Amsterdam . . . . . 29 Dec.–2 Jan. 1902

Scots Greys ambushed near Bronkhorst Spruit, 7 killed, enemy finally driven off; reported, 4 Jan. ,,

ONVERWACHT: Plumer drives the Boers from their positions, gen. Opperman killed; maj. Vallentin and 7 killed, 37 (2 mortally) wounded . 3, 4 Jan. ,,

Col. Wing surprises a laager N.W. of Ermelo, Wolmarans, Malan and 42 Boers captured . 10 Jan. ,,

Liebenberg, Boer leader, executed for the murder of lieut. Neumeyer, Aliwal North . 11 Jan. ,,

Comm. Scheepers, convicted of murder, &c., executed at Graaf Reinet . . . . 18 Jan. ,,

Maj. Whitehead and 4 men killed near Griquatown, Boer loss severe; reported . . . . 18 Jan. ,,

Gen. Ben Viljoen captured near Lydenburg, 25 Jan. ,,

Plumer, Pulteney and Colville capture 55 Boers between Spitzkop and Castrols Nek . 25 Jan. ,,

Abraham's Kraal, Riet river, Boers repulsed with loss; lieut.-col. du Moulin and 8 men killed, 28 Jan. ,,

Laager captured by Price, comm. Vanzyl killed at Klaarfontein; Marais, rebel leader, captured near Laingsburg . . . . . 30, 31 Jan. 1902

Dutch government's proposals for negotiations with the Boers, 25 Jan.; declined by the British government, 29 Jan.; correspondence issued, 4 Feb. ,,

Successful British operations in the Liebenberg Vlei district, O.R.C.: Byng defeats comm. Wessels, 3 guns taken, 72 Boers captured, 3 Feb.; maj. Leader captures comm. Alberts and 130 men from Delarey, near Krugersdorp, 4 Feb.; British lines close round the Boers; De Wet and a few others break through the Lindley-Kroonstad blockhouse lines . . . . . 5, 6 Feb. ,,

Col. von Donop surprises Potgieter's laagers, S.W. Transvaal, 36 Boers taken . . . 8 Feb. ,,

Sharp fighting near Fraserburg: Boers finally repulsed, 24 killed; major Crofton and 12 British killed . . . . 8 Feb. ,,

KLIP RIVER, S. of Johannesburg: Mounted Infantry heavily engaged, lose 11 killed, 45 wounded, 12 Feb. ,,

Parliamentary paper, list of natives (unarmed) murdered by the Boers, issued . . 12 Feb. ,,

Protest repudiating continental slanders on the British army signed by Germans in Natal; similar meetings at Cape Town, Johannesburg and elsewhere . . . . 12, 14, 16 Feb. ,,

Col. Edw. Locke Elliot (K.C.B. 26 June) engages De Wet at Trommel, 10 Boers captured, 16, 17 Feb. ,,

Judge Kock captured in Cape Colony . 17 Feb. ,,

KLIPDAM: disaster to Scots Greys, 2 killed, maj. Fielden and capt. Ussher mortally wounded, 46 captured, afterwards released . . 18 Feb. ,,

Col. Park surprises Trichardt's commando, 164 captured at Nooitgedacht, no British casualties, 20 Feb. ,,

Christian Botha, Natal rebel, sentenced to 10 years' imprisonment . . . . . 21 Feb. ,,

Committee of ladies, Mrs. Fawcett, E. C. Scarlett, M.D., Jane Waterston, M.D. and others, appointed to visit the refugee camps, arrived in S. Africa, July; report favourably as to food, hospitals, &c., over 100,000 men, women and children provided for; the high mortality at one time, due to an epidemic of measles and the gross ignorance of the Boers themselves, 12 Dec. 1901; blue-book issued; death-rate normal . . 21 Feb. ,,

Mackenzie captures Hans Grobelaar's force near Lake Chrissie . . . . . . 22 Feb. ,,

KLERKSDORP: Von Donop's convoy, under col. Anderson, captured by Delarey near Wolmaransstad, 5 officers, 48 men killed . . 23 Feb. ,,

SUCCESSFUL MOVEMENT against De Wet in the Harrismith district began about 16 Feb.; the enemy's efforts to break through the British lines by night at Langverwacht, near Bothasberg (De Wet escaped, 24 Feb.), defeated by the gallantry of the New Zealanders, who lost 27 killed, 41 wounded (out of 84); total Boer casualties, 819, 25 Feb.; on the last day of the operations, comm. Truther, being hemmed in between the Wilge river and Natal frontier, was granted an hour's armistice, and 600 surrendered . . 27 Feb. ,,

Court-martials held at Pietersburg, 16 Jan. and 5 Feb. (resulting from evidence collected by the court of inquiry, held first 16 Oct. 1901); 4 Australian officers of the Bushveldt Carbineers (an irregular *colonial* corps recruited in N. Transvaal) tried and "found guilty as principals or accessories in 12 Boer murders" during Aug. 1901; lieuts. P. J. Handcock and H. H. Morant executed, 26, 27 Feb. [lieut. G. R. Witton sentenced to life imprisonment, lieut. H. Picton found guilty of manslaughter and cashiered, *Times*, 5 April, 1902]; meeting at Kroonstad condemning "slander and lies" against the British army, resolutions carried by gen. Piet de Wet, Mr. C. Born and others . . . . . . 25 Feb. ,,

KLIP DRIFT OR TWEEBOSCH: lord Methuen's force, moving in 2 parties, was charged and routed by Delarey, Kemp, Cellier and 4 other leaders with about 1,500 men; gallant stand made by Northumbrians and Lancastrians, lieuts. Nesham and Venning and their men were all shot down beside their guns; 4 British officers and 64 men killed, 10 officers and 111 men wounded; lord Methuen wounded, captured by the Boers (but afterwards released and taken to Klerksdorp, 13 March), 7 March, 1902

Successful "drive" in the West against De Wet, 190 Boers captured . . . . 9–15 March, ,,

Bruce Hamilton captures gen. Cherry Emmett, 15 March, ,,

Mr. Schalk Burger and other members of the "Boer government," with flag of truce, arrive at Pretoria, to treat, and then leave for Kroonstad to consult with the other leaders . . 23 March, ,,

Combined movement against Delarey; W. Kitchener recaptures Methuen's 5 guns, 8 Boers killed, 165 prisoners . . . . . 23–25 March, ,,

Death of Mr. Cecil Rhodes . . . 26 March, ,,

Railway disaster near Barberton, 42 soldiers and 3 others killed, 38 injured . . 30 March, ,,

BRAKSPRUIT OR BOSCHBULT, *Hart's River*: Delarey, Kemp and 4 other leaders repulsed on all sides by cols. Keir and Cookson, great gallantry of the troops; the Canadians (21) under lieut. Bruce Carruthers held their position bravely, the lieut. and 5 men killed and 12 wounded; total British loss, 27 killed, 149 wounded . . 31 March, ,,

BOSCHMAN'S KOP, near *Leeuwkop*: severe action fought here by the Queen's Bays under lieut.-col. Fanshawe; on the arrival of col. Lawley with reinforcements the Boers retreated with loss; 13 British killed, 5 officers and 59 wounded, 1 April, ,,

Comm. Erasmus killed near Boshof . . 3 April, ,,

Caspar Kruger, eldest son of the ex-president, and other burghers take the oath of allegiance; announced . . . . 5 April, ,,

Comm. Kritzinger acquitted of the charge of murdering native scouts . . . . 6 April, ,,

Colenbrander captures Beyers' laager and over 100 Boers near Pietersburg . . . 8 April, ,,

Mr. Steyn, gens. Delarey and De Wet join the peace delegates at Klerksdorp. . . . 9 April, ,,

Railway accident near Machavie, 13 New Zealanders killed, 13 injured . . . 12 April, ,,

ROOIWAL: here Kekewich's column severely repulsed Kemp and Vermaas; comm. Potgieter and 43 Boers killed, and 39 and 2 guns captured, 11 April, ,,

Death of commandant Theron . . 14 April, ,,

Bloemfontein–Sanna's Post railway extension opened . . . . 16 April, ,,

Schweizer Reneke captured . . . 16 April, ,,

Maj.-gen. Bruce Hamilton's (K.C.B. 26 June) eastern move successful . . 17–20 April, ,,

Boer peace delegates at Pretoria, 12 April; consult the commandos . . . . 18–24 April, ,,

Vryheid and Utrecht districts added to Natal; announced . . . . . 30 April, ,,

Col. Barker captures Manie Botha . . . 1 May, ,,

John Potgieter's force raids and burns Sikobobo's kraals, 3 natives burnt alive; the Zulus forthwith attacked him at Holkrantz; 56 Boers and 52 Zulus killed . . . . . . 6 May, ,,

Ookiep, Cape Colony, invested by rebels, 1 May; relieved by col. Cooper . . . 7 May, ,,

Operations in O.R. colony successful, 321 prisoners brought in . . . . . . 7 May, ,,

Armoured train derailed near Pretoria; lieut. Campbell and 11 men killed . . 5 or 7 May, ,,

Ian Hamilton's drive on the Bechuanaland blockhouse line very successful, Van Zyl's convoy captured and many prisoners . . 7–13 May, ,,

Peace conference, 15, 16 May; Louis Botha, De Wet, Delarey, Smuts and Hertzog leave Vereeniging to confer with lords Milner and Kitchener in Pretoria . . . . 18 May, ,,

Boers attack Aberdeen in Cape Colony, Van Heerden killed . . . . 18 May, ,,

Visaye, with 50 men, surrenders at Balmoral, 20 May, ,,

Lord Lovat captures Fouché's laager at Stapleford, 21 May, ,,

Jack Hindon, train-wrecker, and his force surrender at Balmoral . . . . 16 and 25 May, ,,

Comm. Malan, mortally wounded, captured at Ripon Road, Cape Colony . . . 27 May, ,,

British government's final answer received at Pretoria; Boer delegates return to Vereeniging, 28, 29 May

British terms: unconditional surrender, imperial grant of 3,000,000*l.* and loans for Boer repatriation, &c.; no death penalty on rebels; Dutch language to be used in law courts when necessary; accepted and signed by the Boers before lords Milner and Kitchener at Pretoria . . . . . 31 May, 1902

The king sends a message of thanks to lord Kitchener . . . . 1 June, „

Lord Kitchener congratulated the Boers on the good fight they had made; welcomed them as citizens of the British empire . . . 2 June, „

Great goodwill and fellowship on both sides; loyal speeches by Boer leaders, reported, during surrenders . . . . June, „

Thanks of the king and parliament to the army and navy, colonials, Indian force, volunteers, &c.; grant of 50,000*l.* to lord Kitchener (visct. 26 June), *who had dealt with 90 mobile Boer columns over an area larger than the European states;* carried, 380–44 . . . . 4 June, „

Lord Kitchener sailed for England, leaving lieut.-gen. Lyttelton (K.C.B. 26 June), in command, 23 June, „

List of coronation (S. African honours), *Times*, 26 June, „

[Splendid service done during the campaign by the crews of the *Terrible* and *Powerful*.]

Total Boer force during the war about 75,000; about 3,700 killed or mortally wounded; about 32,000 prisoners of war, 700 of whom died, announced . . . . 8 July, „

Boer archives delivered up to the British at Pilgrim's Rest, reported . . . . 8 July, „

Total Boer surrenders: 21,256 (Transvaal, 11,166; O.R.C., 6,455; Cape Colony, 3,635).

Cost of the war: 222,974,000*l.* up to end of financial year . . . . „

Dr. (knt. 26 June, 1902) Conan Doyle's "Great Boer War" published, Oct. 1901, and his "Cause and Conduct of the War" published, Jan. 1902; widely circulated.

The Times "History of the War," edited by L. S. Amery, vol. ii., 23 May; "Three Years of War," by Chris. De Wet and many others, published in „

Sudden death of gen. Lucas Meyer, aged 56, at Brussels . . . . 8 Aug. „

Parliamentary paper, with telegrams and correspondence between gens. sir G. White and sir R. Buller, *re* the siege and relief of Ladysmith, issued, 19 Aug.; *Times* . . . 8 July, 20 Aug. „

Total British force in S. Africa, 9,940, 1 Aug. 1899; total sent there up to 31 May, 1902, 396,021; from home, 337,219; India, 18,534; Colonies, 30,238; raised in S. Africa, 52,414; grand total, 448,435; killed in action, 5,744; wounded, 22,829; died of wounds or disease in S. Africa, 16,168. Returned to England, *sound*, 68,531; *invalided*, about 75,430; to India, 10,134; to Colonies, regulars, 3,967; colonials, 12,294; total, 170,356; report issued . . . . 4 Sept. „

Royal commission (lord Alverstone, Mr. Justice Bigham, and sir John Ardagh) to inquire into the sentences passed by martial law during the war, left for S. Africa, 9 Aug.; 794 cases tried, 26 Aug.–8 Oct.; 119 prisoners released, many sentences lightened; report signed, 28 Oct.; issued . . . . 2 Dec. „

The Boers generals visit Europe and issue an appeal for the "General Boer Relief Fund" (Mr. H. Phipps, of U.S.N.A., gives 20,586*l.* 14*s.* 5*d.*, 20 Sept.); *Times* . . . . . . 25 Sept. „

Boer meeting held at Pretoria to hear the report of the generals on their tour; total amount collected in Europe, 105,000*l.* . . . 7 Jan. 1903

Royal commission of inquiry into the conduct of the war up to the occupation of Pretoria; adm. sir John Hopkins, sir Henry Norman, sir George Goldie, lord Elgin, chairman, and others; holds many meetings, 7 Oct. *et seq.* 1902; sittings resumed, 7 Feb.; report issued (see *Addenda*), 25 Aug. „

SOUTH AMERICA, see *America*.

SOUTHAMPTON, a seaport (S. England), a county of itself, near the Roman Clausentum and the Saxon Hamtune. It frequently suffered by Danish incursions: Canute, when king, occasionally resided here. The charter was granted by Henry I. and confirmed by Richard I. and John; and the free grammar school was founded by Edward VI. On 17 July, 1861, a monument to Dr. Isaac Watts, a native, was uncovered; and on 15 Oct. 1862, the Hartley institution was opened by lord Palmerston. The prince of Wales laid the foundation of the parish church of St. Mary, built as a memorial of Samuel Wilberforce, bishop of Winchester, 12 Aug. 1878; consecrated 19 June, 1879. The British Association met here 1846 and 1882. Population 1881, 60,051; 1891, 65,325; 1901, 104,911. See *Docks*, Aug. 1895.

New deep-water dock inaugurated as the Empress dock, by the queen . . . . . 26 July, 1890

Great strike of dock labourers, seamen and firemen begun; trade paralysed; violent rioting; conflict with the military, 8, 9 Sept.; gun-boats sent for; order restored, 10 Sept. The strike, not recognized by London union, fails, 11 Sept.; work resumed, 17 Sept. The Union Steamship company import 46 foreign seamen from Hamburg as a check to strikes . . . . . 21 Sept. „

Arrival of the *New York* from New York, first steamer of the American line (6 days 21½ hours) 4 March, 1893

American and Italian warships in Southampton water, officers entertained by the mayor, 5 June *et seq.*, 1895; the graving dock opened by the prince of Wales in 1895, and the deep-water quays opened by Mr. W. B. Beach, M.P., 12 Oct. 1898

Princess Henry of Battenberg opens the Victoria wing of the South Hants hospital . . 7 Feb. 1900

Sir Redvers Buller receives the freedom on his return from S. Africa . . . . 10 Nov. „

Mr. A. Barlow gives 13,650*l.* to local hospitals and other charities . . . . . end Aug. 1901

Lord Kitchener receives the freedom on his return from S. Africa . . . . . 12 July, 1902

Dr. Lyttleton, bishop suffragan of Southampton, died 19 Feb.; succeeded by Dr. J. MacArthur, bishop of Bombay . . . . . . 9 Sept. 1903

SOUTH AUSTRALIA was visited by capt. Sturt in 1830, and explored shortly after by capt. Parker and Mr. Kent, the former of whom was killed by the natives. The boundaries of the province were fixed by 4 & 5 Will. IV. c. 95 (1834); and it was occupied 26 Dec. 1836, by capt. Hindmarsh, the first governor. It was colonised according to Mr. E. Gibbon Wakefield's scheme, which was carried out by the South Australian Colonisation Association. The colony for several years underwent severe trials through the great influx of emigrants, land-jobbing, building speculations, &c., which produced almost universal bankruptcy in 1839. In five years after, by the energy and liberality of Sir George Grey, the colonists had overcome their difficulties, and the prosperity of the colony appeared fully established. In 1842 the highly productive Burra Burra copper mines were discovered, and large fortunes were suddenly realised; but in 1851 the discovery of gold in New South Wales and Victoria almost paralysed this province by drawing off a large part of the labouring population. Very little gold was found in South Australia; but a reaction took place in favour of the copper mines and agriculture, &c. Before the discovery of gold, little trade existed between Adelaide (the capital of South Australia) and Melbourne; but in 1852 gold was transmitted from the latter to the former to the amount of 2,215,167*l.* principally for breadstuffs, farm produce, &c. The bishopric of Adelaide was founded in 1847. Discovery of alluvial gold at Tatulpa, Waukaringa, Oct.; favourable report Dec. 1886. Sir Dominic Daly, appointed governor in Nov. 1861, died 19 Feb. 1868; succeeded by sir James Fergusson, Dec. 1868; by Anthony Musgrave, Jan 1873; by Wm.

Wellington Cairns, Jan. 1877; Sir W. F. D. Jervois, June, 1877; sir W. Robinson, Nov. 1882; the earl of Kintore, Dec. 1888; Sir Thos. Fowell Buxton, April, 1895; sir G. R. Le Hunte, 1903. Population in 1855, 85,821; in 1865, 156,605; in 1871, 185,626; in 1877, 225,677; in 1882, 293,509; in 1891, 315,048; 1901, 362,604.

See *Adelaide*. 1887, revenue, 2,014,102*l.*; expenditure, 2,145,133*l.* Imports, 1887, 5,096,293*l.*; exports, 5,330,780*l.*; 1890, imports, 8,262,673*l.*; exports, 8,827,378*l.*; 1893, revenue, 2,671,495*l.*; expenditure, 2,583,481*l.*; imports, 7,934,200*l.*; exports, 8,463,936*l.*; 1894, revenue, 2,424,385*l.*; 1897, revenue, 2,561,520*l*; 1900–1, revenue, 2,818,712*l.*; 1901–02, deficit, 239,000*l.*

Resignation of the ministry; new one formed by the hon. J. A. Cockburn . . . 24, 25 June, 1889

He resigns; succeeded by hon. T. Playford, reported . . . . 18 Aug. 1890

The earl of Kintore and party cross the continent from Port Darwin to Adelaide (see *Australia*) 9 April–23 May, 1891

Resignation of Mr. Playford, 17 June; Mr. Holder forms a ministry . . . . 20 June, 1892

Resignation of Mr. Holder, 12 Oct.; cabinet formed by sir John Downer . . . . 14 Oct. ,,

Income tax raised from 3*d.* to 5½*d.*, &c. . 22 Nov. ,,

A loan for 1,016,000*l.* for railways and waterworks authorized . . . . . . 9 Dec. ,,

The ministry reconstructed, 11 May, 1893; resignation of sir John Downer, 14 June; Mr. Kingston forms a ministry . . . . 15 June, 1893

Income-tax doubled to make up the deficiency of 57,000*l.* in the revenue for one year, 14 Dec.; passed, 20 Dec. . . . . . . ,,

A loan of 850,000*l.* at 3½ per cent., passed 20 Dec. ,,

Women's suffrage, increased taxation, and other bills passed . . . . . . 18 Dec. 1894

Destructive storm at Adelaide and other places, 9 Dec. 1895

Federal enabling bill passed by the assembly, 17 Dec. ,,

Exploring expedition, supported by Mr. Calvert, leaves Adelaide . . . . . 22 May, 1896

Failure of crops through drought in the north; relief fund started at Adelaide . . . Oct. ,,

Federal enabling bill passed by both houses, 3 March, 1899

The *referendum* results in 65,990 votes for, and 17,053 against, the federation or commonwealth bill . . . . 29 April, ,,

Lord Tennyson opens parliament . . 22 June, ,,

Ministry defeated by majority of one, and resigns, 28, 29 Nov.; Mr. V. L. Solomon's cabinet, 30 Nov., defeated, 6 Dec.; Mr. Holder forms a ministry, 8 Dec. ,,

Century (arts) exhibition opened by the governor at Adelaide . . . . . 15 March, 1900

Mr. Holder's 9th budget statement; good report; country prosperous . . . . 23 Aug. ,,

Mr. See, premier, issues a manifesto stating the policy of the state government . 26 April, 1901

Mr. Jenkins forms a ministry . . . 14 May, ,,

Constitution bill passed, 17 Dec.; Mr. Jenkins' ministry reconstituted, 31 March, 1902; parliament opened . . . . . . 3 July, 1902

Drought ends; good rains reported . . . 10 Sept. ,,

SOUTHCOTT, JOANNA, a fanatic, born in 1750, came from Exeter to London, where her followers at one period amounted to many thousands. In 1792 she announced herself as the woman spoken of in *Revelation*, chap. xii.; and a disease favoured the delusion that she would be the mother of the promised Shiloh. She died 27 Dec. 1814. In 1851 there existed in England four congregations, professing to expect her return. Her successor, Mrs. Peacock, died March, 1875.

SOUTH-EASTERN RAILWAY, from London to Folkestone, opened, 28 June, 1843; to Dover, 7 Feb. 1844.

SOUTHEND, Essex, at the mouth of the Thames, a watering-place, principally built by Sir S. Morton Peto (1809—89), has a pier above a mile in length with electric tramway and concert-room; theatre burnt, 6 Jan. 1895. Population, 1851, 2,462; 1871, 4,561; 1891, 12,333; 1901, 28,793. See *Trials*, Nov. 1894. *Corporation act*, passed 6 July, 1895.

Statue of the queen presented by alderman Tolhurst, unveiled by lady Rayleigh . 24 May, 1898

Lord Avebury opens a new technical school, 24 Sept. 1901

Westcliff hotel burnt down . . . . 27 June, 1902

Technical school (cost 20,000*l.*) opened by lady Warwick . . . . 13 Sept. ,,

SOUTHERN CONFEDERATE STATES, see *Confederates*.

SOUTHERN CONTINENT. The Southern Ocean was first traversed by Magellan in 1520; and explored by Wallis and Carteret in 1766; and by Cook in 1773 and 1774. Of the southern continent little more is known than that it is ice-bound, and contains active volcanoes. It was discovered in the first instance by capt. John Biscoe, on 27 Feb. 1831, in lat. 65° 57′ S., long. 47° 20′ E., extending east and west 200 miles,—this he named Enderby Land, after the gentleman who had equipped him for the voyage. Capt. Biscoe also discovered Graham's Land on 15 Feb. 1832, situated in lat. 67° 1′ S., long. 71° 48′ W. The Messrs. Enderby equipped three other expeditions in search of the southern continent, the last (in connection with some other gentlemen) in 1838, when capt. Balleny had command, who, on 9 Feb. 1839, discovered the Balleny Islands, in lat. 67° S., long. 165° E., and in March, 1839, Sabrina Land, in lat. 65° 10′ S., long. 118° 30′ E. In 1840, a French expedition, under the command of admiral D'Urville, and an American expedition, under the command of commodore Wilkes, greatly added to our knowledge in respect to the existence of a southern continent, and this was again increased by the expedition which sailed from England in 1839, under the command of capt. sir James Clark Ross, who discovered Victoria Land in 1841, and subsequently penetrated as far south as 78° 11′. Antarctic expedition proposed by the Argentine republic and the Genoese, Sept. 1881; the objects collected to be divided. Italian expedition under lieut. Booe, 1881-2. See *Antarctic Pole*.

New South Polar expedition proposed by the Antarctic Exploration committee at Melbourne, supported by the governor and others . Aug. 1890

Th sum required for the expedition is 15,000*l.* Sir Thomas Elder subscribed 5,000*l.*, other persons 5,000*l.*; appeal for the other 5,000*l.*

Committee appointed by the Roy. Geographical Soc. to promote Antarctic research . . Nov. 1893

Meeting at the Royal Society to discuss Antarctic exploration; addresses by Drs. John Murray, Nansen, and others, 24 Feb.; the government declines to support further exploration; the Roy. Geog. Soc. decides to send out an expedition, and to raise a fund of 50,000*l.*, 9 June, 1898; the society gives 5,000*l.* and Mr. Harmsworth, 5,000*l.*, Nov. 1898; Mr. L. W. Longstaff, 25,000*l.* March; 45,000*l.* from government, June; total, 90,000*l.* autumn, 1899; an expedition was organized by a joint committee of the Roy. Soc. and the Roy. Geo. Soc; the *Discovery* (Antarctic ship) launched at Dundee, 21 March, 1901; visited by the king and queen, 5 Aug.; leaves Spithead with capt. Robt. F. Scott, commander, Mr. George Murray, F.R.S., head of the scientific staff, and 46 others, 6 Aug. 1901; leaves Port Chalmers, New Zealand, for Victoria Land . . 24 Dec. 1901

The German government grants 60,000*l.* towards an Antarctic expedition under prof. von Drygalski, March, 1899; the *Gauss* launched at Kiel, 2 April; leaves the Elbe, 15 Aug. 1901; and Kerguelen, 31 Jan. 1902

The Swedish expedition, under Dr. Otto Nordenskjöld, in the *Antarctic*, left Gothenburg, 16 Oct. 1901; passes the S. Shetlands to Graham's Land, winters on the ice, and surveys district of the

unknown sea between Falkland isles and South Georgia, U.S.A. . . . April–4 July, 1902
Morning, relief ship to the *Discovery*, under capt. Wm. Colbeck, with crew 29 (total fund 23,000*l*., 100*l*. from the king and 50*l*. from the prince of Wales, raised mainly through the exertions of sir Clements Markham, president of the Roy. Geographical Soc.), leaves London 9 July, 1902; leaves Lyttelton, N.Z., 6 Dec.; Scottish Antarctic expedition in the *Scotia*, commanded by lieut. W. S. Bruce, reaches Kingstown . . . 3 Nov. „

SOUTH KENSINGTON MUSEUM, near Brompton old church (containing the pictures presented by Mr. Vernon, Mr. Sheepshanks, Mrs. Ellison, and those bequeathed by Turner, the great painter, as well as specimens of sculpture and art, educational collections, products of the animal, vegetable, and mineral kingdoms, &c.), was opened on 22 June, 1857. A special exhibition of works of art, of immense value, lent for the occasion, was opened here in the summer of 1862, and closed in November. In July, 1873, a testimonial to Mr. (aft. sir) Henry Cole, C.B., was proposed for his exertions in organizing this museum, and in promoting its objects. Directors, sir P. Cunliffe-Owen, 1873—93, died 23 March, 1894; major-gen. Festing and prof. J. H. Middleton, 1893 (prof. Middleton died from an overdose of morphia, 10 June, 1896); Mr. C. Purdon Clarke, June, 1896. See *Design* and *Arts*, Sept. 1895. *Needles*.

Mr. John Forster, biographer of Dickens, bequeathed his library of books, MSS., paintings, and drawings to this museum. He died 1 Feb. . 1876
Scientific Apparatus Loan Exhibition (*which see*) opened 13 May, closed . . . . . 30 Dec. „
Mr. John Jones bequeaths a collection of works of art, &c.; estimated value, 500,000*l*. . . Jan. 1882
Report of committee on the museum . . May, 1897
Queen Victoria lays the memorial stone of the Victoria and Albert museum . . . . 17 May, 1899

SOUTHPORT, Lancashire, a watering place, founded in 1792 on a sandy waste, has rapidly progressed, now possessing an esplanade 3 miles long, and many fine buildings. It was made a municipal borough in 1867, and received the British Association 19 Sept. 1883. Population, 1851, 4,765; 1871, 18,085; 1891, 43,026; 1901, 48,083.

SOUTH-SEA BUBBLE commenced with the establishment of the South-sea company in 1710, which was at first unwisely and afterwards dishonestly managed. It exploded in 1720, ruining thousands of families; and the directors' estates, to the value of 2,014,000*l*., were seized in 1721 and sold. Mr. Knight, the cashier, absconded with 100,000*l*.; but he compounded the fraud for 10,000*l*., and returned to England in 1743. Almost all the wealthy persons in the kingdom had become speculators; the artifices of the directors having raised the shares, originally 100*l*., to the price of 1000*l*. A parliamentary inquiry took place in Nov. 1720, and Aislabie, chancellor of the exchequer, and several members of parliament were expelled the house in 1721; see *Law's Bubble*.

SOUTHWARK (S. London) was governed by its own bailiffs till 1327. The city, however, found great inconvenience from the number of malefactors who escaped thither, in order to be out of the reach and cognizance of the city magistrates; and a grant was made of Southwark to the city of London by the crown, for a small annuity. In Edward VI.'s reign it was formed into a city ward, and was named Bridge Ward Without, 1550.—*Southwark bridge* was designed by John Rennie, and built by a company, 1815-19, at an expense of 800,000*l*. It consists of three great cast-iron arches, resting on massive stone piers and abutments; the distance between the abutments is 708 feet; the centre arch is 240 feet span, the two others 210 feet each; and the total weight of iron 5308 tons. The bridge was freed from toll on 8 Nov. 1864, the company receiving a compensation from the city. An act for the payment of dividends to shareholders was passed in 1872.—*Southwark park* was opened, 19 June, 1869. By the Seats act (1885), Southwark sends three members to parliament.

City and South London Electric Railway (see *Tunnels*) opened . . . 4 Nov. and 18 Dec. 1890
The priory church of St. Marie Overie, dating from the 13th century, was leased from the crown to the united parishes of St. Margaret and St. Mary Magdalene, and became the parish church as St. Saviour's in 1540. Since then many changes have been made; Mr. G. Gwilt repaired the tower, the lady chapel, and the choir, 1818 *et seq*. The roof of the nave was removed in 1831, and in 1839 replaced by lath and plaster. The prince of Wales laid the memorial stone of a new nave, 24 July, 1890; the church re-opened after restoration at a total cost of 95,000*l*., the prince of Wales, the archbishop of Canterbury and others present, 16 Feb. 1897; memorial windows to the prince consort and others unveiled, new clock and bells started by the duke of Connaught, 22 June, 1898.
The prince and princess of Wales visit the Evelina hospital; he lays the foundation stone of the new buildings of the R. S. London Ophthalmic Hospital . . . . 24 July, 1897
Petition of Southwark for incorporation with the city, April, 1896; bill rejected by the commons, 22 March, „
St. Olave's and St. John's institute, Tooley-st., opened by the duke of Cambridge . 28 Nov. 1898
King visits Southwark in royal progress through South London . . . . . 25 Oct. 1902
The prince and princess of Wales inaugurated new buildings of St. Saviour and St. Olave's Grammar school for girls in New Kent-road . 14 March, 1903

SOUTHWELL, Nottinghamshire, an ancient Saxon town, where a church was founded by Paulinus, archbishop of York, 627; made collegiate before the conquest, refounded by Henry VIII., and made a bishopric by Henry VIII., 1541; dissolved by Edward VI. Collegiate church restored by Elizabeth, 1586. Near here Charles I. surrendered himself to the Scotch army in 1646. The Bishoprics act, authorising the establishment of a see at Southwell, was passed, 16 Aug. 1878. Constituted (to consist of the counties of Derby and Nottingham), 2 Feb. 1884. The restored minster re-opened as cathedral, 2 Feb. 1888.

FIRST BISHOP, George Ridding, consecrated 1 May, 1884.

SOUTHWOLD, see *Solebay*.

SOVEREIGN, an ancient and modern British gold coin. In 1489 22½ pieces, in value 20*s*., "to be called the sovereign," were ordered to be coined out of a pound of gold. *Ruding*. In 1542 sovereigns were coined in value 20*s*., which afterwards, in 1550 and 1552 (4 & 6 Ed. VI.), passed for 24*s*. and 30*s*. "Sovereigns" of the new coinage were directed to pass for 20*s*. 1 July, and half-sovereigns for 10*s*. 10 Oct. 1817; see *Coin* and *Gold*. By the Coinage act, 1870, the weight of the sovereign is fixed at 123·27447 grains troy; specific gravity, 17·57; (916·67, gold being 1000); half-sovereigns, 61·63723 grains. The *dragon* sovereigns were re-issued in 1871.

SPA-FIELDS (N. London). Here about 30,000 persons assembled to vote an address from the distressed manufacturers to the prince regent, 15 Nov. 1816. A second meeting, 2 Dec. following, terminated in an alarming riot; the shops of several gunsmiths were attacked for arms by the rioters; and in the shop of Mr. Beckwith, on Snow-hill, Mr. Platt was wounded, and much injury was done before the tumult was suppressed. For this riot, Cashman, a seaman, was hanged, 12 March, 1817. Watson, the ringleader, escaped to America.

Spa-fields Chapel, a dome building, originally a place of entertainment named the Pantheon, erected, 1770, was after several changes purchased by the countess of Huntingdon and used as a place of worship for her "connection" (see *Whitefieldites*).
This chapel was pulled down in 1887

SPAHIS, see *Sepoys*.

SPAIN (the ancient Iberia and Hispania), the S.W. peninsula of Europe. The Phœnicians and Carthaginians successively planted colonies on the coasts, which were all conquered by the Romans, 206 B.C. Population of Spain in 1857, 15,464,078; of the colonies, 6,333,887; 1883, total 25,022,880; in 1887, 17,564,588; 1897, 18,089,500. Revenue: 1822, about 6,000,000*l.*; 1850, 12,722,200*l.*; 1871, about 26,000,000*l.*; 1883-4, 32,095,075*l.*; 1891, 32,222,055*l.*; expenditure, 32,456,530*l.*; 1894, 30,765,074*l.*; 1901, revenue (budget), 35,486,166*l.*; expenditure, 36,184,930*l.*

The Carthaginians, enriched by the mines of Spain (480 B.C. *et seq.*), form settlements . . . B.C. 360
New Carthage (Carthagena) founded by Hasdrubal 242
Hamilcar extends their dominions in Spain . 238-233
At his death, Hannibal, his son, takes the command, 221; prepares for war, 220; takes Saguntum, 219; crosses the Alps, and enters Italy . 218
The Romans carry the war into Spain; two Scipios defeated and slain by Hasdrubal . . . 212
Pub. Cornelius Scipio Africanus takes New Carthage, 210 or 209; drives the Carthaginians out of Spain 207
Celtiberian and Numantine war . . . 153-133
Viriathus, general of the Celtiberians and Lusitanians, subdued all West Spain, 145; makes peace with the consul Fabius Servilianus, 142; assassinated by order of the Romans . . . 140
Insurrection of Sertorius, 78; subdued by Pompey, and assassinated 72
Julius Cæsar quells an insurrection in Spain . . 67
Pompey governs Spain 60-50
Revolt through the rapacity of Crassus . . 48-47
Era of Spain: conquest by Augustus begun, 1 Jan. 38
The Vandals, Alani and Suevi, wrest Spain from the Romans . . . . . . A.D. 409
Adolphus founds the kingdom of the Visigoths . . 414
The Vandals pass over to Africa 429
Theodoric I. vanquishes the Suevi 452
Assassinated by his brother Euric, who becomes master of all Spain 466
Recared I. expels the Franks 587
He abjures Arianism, and rules ably . . till 601
Wamba's wise administration; he prepared a fleet for defence against the Saracens . . 672-677
The Arabs invited into Spain against king Roderic. 709
His defeat and death at Xeres 711
Establishment of the Saracens at Cordova . . ,,
Victorious progress of Musa and Tarik . . 712-13
Emirs rule at Cordova; Pelayo, of Gothic blood, rules in Asturias and Leon 718
The Saracens defeated at Tours by Charles Martel, 732 or 733
Abderahman the first king at Cordova . . . 755
Invasion of Charlemagne 777-78
Sancho Iñigo. count of Navarre, &c. . . . 873
Sancho of Navarre becomes king of Castile . 1026
The kingdom of Aragon commenced under Ramirez I. 1035
Leon and Asturias united to Castile . . . 1037
Portugal taken from the Saracens by Henry of Besançon (see *Portugal*) 1095
The Saracens, beset on all sides by the Christians, call in the aid of the Moors from Africa, who seize the dominions they came to protect, and subdue the Saracens . . . . . 1091 *et seq.*
Exploits of the Cid Rodrigo; dies . . about 1099
Dynasty of the Almoravides at Cordova . 1094-1144
The Moors defeated in several battles by Alfonso of Leon . . . . ,,
Dynasty of the Almohades at Cordova . . 1144-1225
Cordova, Toledo, Seville, &c., taken by Ferdinand of Castile and Leon 1233-48
The kingdom of Granada begun by the Moors, last refuge from the power of the Christians . . . 1238
The crown of Navarre passes to the royal family of France 1274
200,000 Moors arrive to assist the king of Granada . 1327
They are defeated at Tarifa by Alfonso XI. of Castile with great slaughter 1340
Reign of Pedro the Cruel 1350
His alliance with Edward the Black Prince . . 1363
Defeated at Montiel and treacherously slain . . 1369
Ferdinand II. of Aragon marries Isabella of Castile, 18 Oct. 1469; and nearly the whole Christian dominions of Spain are united in one monarchy . 1479
Establishment of the Inquisition 1480-4
Persecution of the Jews 1492-8
Granada taken after a two years' siege; and the power of the Moors is finally extirpated by Ferdinand 1492
Jews expelled . . . . ,,
Columbus is sent from Spain to explore the western ocean . . . . . . 17 April, ,,
Mahometans persecuted and expelled . . 1499-1502
Death of Columbus . . . . . 20 May, 1506
Ferdinand conquers great part of Navarre . . 1512
Accession of the house of Austria to the throne of Spain; Charles I. of Spain 1516
Able administration of Ximenes; ungratefully used, 1516; his death 1517
Charles elected emperor of Germany . . . 1519
Insurrection in Castile 1520-21
Philip of Spain marries Mary of England 25 July, 1554
Charles abdicates and retires from the world . 1556
War with France; victory at St. Quentin 10 Aug. 1557
Philip II. commences his bloody persecution of the protestants 1561
The Escurial begun building 1563
Revolt of the Moriscoes, 1567; suppressed . . . 1570
Naval victory of Lepanto over the Turks 7 Oct. 1571
Portugal united to Spain by conquest . . . 1580
The Spanish Armada destroyed; see *Armada*. . 1588
Philip III. banishes the Moors (900,000) . 1598-1610
Ministry of the duke of Lerma 1598-1618
Ministry of Olivarez 1621-43
Philip IV. loses Portugal 1640
Death of Charles II., last of the house of Austria; accession of Philip V. of the house of Bourbon . 1700
War of the Succession 1702-13
Gibraltar taken by the English 1704
Siege of Barcelona 1713
Able government of cardinal Alberoni; he re-established the authority of the king, reformed many abuses; and raised Spain to the rank of a first power, 1715-20; ordered to quit Spain . . . 1720
Charles, son of Philip V., conquers Naples . . 1735
Charles III. king of the Two Sicilies, succeeds to the crown of Spain 1759
War with England, 1762-3; and 1796
Battle of Cape St. Vincent . . . 14 Feb. 1797
Spanish treasure-ships, valued at 3,000,000 dollars, seized by the English . . . . Oct. 1804
Battle of Trafalgar (see *Trafalgar*) . 21 Oct. 1805
Sway of Godoy, prince of the peace 1806
The French enter Spain; a Spanish army sent to the Baltic 1807
Conspiracy of the prince of Asturias against his father . . . . . . 25 July, ,,
Treaty of Fontainebleau . . . 27 Oct. ,,
The French take Madrid . . . . March, 1808
The prince of the peace dismissed . 18 March, ,,
Abdication of Charles IV. in favour of Ferdinand, 19 March; and at Bayonne, in favour of his "friend and ally" Napoleon, when Ferdinand relinquished the crown . . . . 1 May, ,,
Revolution: the French massacred at Madrid, 2 May, ,,
The province of Asturias rises *en masse* . 3 May, ,,
Napoleon assembles the notables at Bayonne 25 May, ,,
Joseph Bonaparte enters Madrid as king of Spain, 12 July; retires . . . . . 29 July, ,,
Battle of Vimiera; French defeated . . 21 Aug. ,,
Supreme junta installed . . . . . Sept. ,,
Madrid taken by the French, and Joseph restored 2 Dec. ,,
Napoleon enters Madrid . . . . . 4 Dec. ,,
The royal family of Spain imprisoned in the palace of Chambery in Savoy . . . . 5 Dec. ,,
The French defeated at Corunna, 16 Jan.; take Ferrol, 27 Jan.; Saragossa, 21 Feb.; Oporto,

29 Feb. ; Cordova and Seville, Nov. ; Gerona, 12 Dec. 1809
Ney takes Ciudad Rodrigo . . . . 10 July, 1810
The Spanish cortes meet . . . . 24 Sept. ,,
Wellington defeats Massena at Fuentes de Onoro, 5 May, 1811
Soult defeated at Albuera . . . . 16 May, ,,
Constitution of the cortes (democratic) . 8 May, 1812
Wellington takes Ciudad Rodrigo, 19 Jan. ; storms Badajoz, 6 April ; defeats Marmont at Salamanca, 22 July, ,,
He occupies Madrid, and totally defeats the French at Vittoria, 21 June ; defeats Soult in the Pyrenees, 28 July ; takes St. Sebastian, 31 Aug. ; and enters France . . . . . . 8 Oct. 1813
Ferdinand VII. restored (constitution set aside), 14 May, 1814
Slave trade abolished for a compensation . . . 1817
Insurrection at Valencia repressed 1819
Spanish revolution begun by Riego . . Jan. 1820
Ferdinand swears to the constitution of the cortes, 8 March, ,,
The cortes remove the king to Seville, and thence to Cadiz . . . . . . March, 1823
The French enter Spain, 7 April ; and invest Cadiz, 25 June, ,,
Battle of the Trocadero . . . . 31 Aug. ,,
Despotism resumed ; the cortes dissolved ; executions of liberals . . . . . . Oct. ,,
Riego put to death . . . . . 7 Nov. ,,
The French evacuate Cadiz . . . . 21 Sept. 1828
Cadiz made a free port . . . . 24 Feb. 1829
Salique law abolished, 29 March ; Carlist and Christina parties formed 1830
Queen of Spain appointed regent during the king's indisposition ; change in the ministry, 25 Oct. 1832
Don Carlos declares himself legitimate successor to the king . . . . . . 29 April, 1833
Death of Ferdinand VII. ; his queen assumes the title of governing queen until Isabella II., her infant daughter, attains her majority 29 Sept. ,,
Constitution termed "Estatuto Real" granted by advice of Martinez de la Rosa . . . . . ,,
The royalist volunteers disarmed with some bloodshed at Madrid . . . . . . 27 Oct. ,,
Queen Christina marries Ferdinand Muñoz (afterwards duke of Rianzarés) . . . 28 Dec. ,,
The quadruple treaty establishes the right of Isabella to the throne . . . . 22 April, 1834
Don Carlos suddenly appears in Spain . 10 July, ,,
The peers vote his exclusion . . . 30 Aug. ,,
Mendizabal, prime minister ; Mina and Espartero commanded the royalists ; the rebel leader, Zumalacarregui, killed near Bilbao . June, 1835
Sir De Lacy Evans and others raise a British legion for the queen of Spain . . . . . ,,
They defeat the Carlists at St. Sebastian 1 Oct. 1836
Espartero gains the battle of Bilbao . 25 Dec. ,,
General Evans takes Irun . . . 17 May, 1837
Constituent cortes proclaimed . . . . . ,,
Dissolution of the monasteries . . . . . ,,
The Carlists under Maroto desert Don Carlos and conclude a treaty of peace with Espartero, at Vergara . . . . . . 31 Aug. 1839
Don Carlos seeks refuge in France . 13 Sept. ,,
Surrender of Morello . . . . 28 May, 1840
Cabrera, the Carlist general, unable to maintain the war, enters France . . . . 7 July, ,,
The British auxiliaries evacuate St. Sebastian and Passages . . . . . . 25 Aug. ,,
Revolutionary movement at Madrid : the authorities triumphant . . . . . 1 Sept. ,,
Dismissal of the ministry, and dissolution of the cortes . . . . . . 9 Sept. ,,
Espartero, minister, makes his triumphal entry into Madrid . . . . . . 3 Oct. ,,
The queen regent appoints a new ministry, who are nominated by Espartero, 5 Oct. ; she abdicates and leaves the kingdom ; visits France and Sicily ; returns to France . . . . 12 Oct. ,,
Espartero, duke of Victory, expels the papal nuncio 29 Dec. ,,
The Spanish cortes declare Espartero regent during the queen's minority . . . 12 April, 1841
Queen Christina's protest . . . . 19 July, ,,
Insurrection in favour of Christina commenced at Pampeluna by general O'Donnell and Concha, 2 Oct. ,,
Don Diego Leon attacks the palace at Madrid ; his followers repulsed, and numbers slain by the queen's guards, 7 Oct. ; he is shot at Madrid, 15 Oct. 1841
Zurbano captures Bilbao . . . . 21 Oct. ,,
Rodil, constitutional general, enters Vittoria, 21 Oct. ,,
Montes de Oca shot . . . . . 21 Oct. ,,
General O'Donnell takes refuge in the French territory . . . . 21 Oct. ,,
Espartero decrees the suspension of queen Christina's pension . . . . . 26 Oct. ,,
Fueros of the Basque provinces abolished 29 Oct. ,,
Borio and Gobernado, implicated in the Christina plot, put to death at Madrid . . . 9 Nov. ,,
Espartero enters Madrid . . . . 23 Nov. ,,
General pardon of all persons not yet tried, concerned in the events of October . . 13 Dec. ,,
The effective strength of the army fixed at 130,000 men . . . . 28 June, 1842
An insurrection at Barcelona ; the national guard joins the populace, 13 Nov. ; battle in the streets between the national guard and the troops : the latter lose 500 in killed and wounded, and retreat to the citadel . . . . . . 15 Nov. ,,
Barcelona blockaded, 26 Nov. ; Espartero arrives before it, 29 Nov. ; its bombardment and surrender . . . . 3, 4 Dec. ,,
The disturbances at Malaga . . . . 25 May, 1843
The revolutionary junta is re-established at Barcelona . . . . 11 June, ,,
[Corunna, Seville, Burgos, Santiago, and numerous other towns, shortly afterwards "pronounce" against the regent Espartero.]
Arrival of general Narvaez at Madrid, which surrenders . . . . 15 July, ,,
Espartero bombards Seville . . . 21 July, ,,
The siege is raised . . . . . 27 July, ,,
[The revolution is completely successful, and Espartero flees to Cadiz, and embarks on board her Majesty's ship *Malabar*.]
The new government deprives Espartero of his titles and rank, 16 Aug. ; he arrives in London, 23 Aug. ,,
Reaction suppressed at Madrid . . . . Aug. ,,
Isabella II. 13 years old, is declared by the cortes to be of age ; Narvaez (friend of the queen-mother), lieutenant-general . . . . . 8 Nov. ,,
The queen-mother returns to Spain . 23 March, 1844
Zurbano's insurrection, 12 Nov. 1844 ; he is shot, 21 Jan. 1845
Don Carlos relinquishes his right to the crown in favour of his son . . . . . 18 May, ,,
Reactionary constitution . . . . . . ,,
England removed from "favoured nation" clause (treaty of Utrecht, 1713) . . . . . ,,
Narvaez and his ministry resign, 12 Feb. ; return to power, 17 March ; again resign . 28 March, 1846
Escape of Don Carlos from France . . 14 Sept. ,,
Marriage of the queen to her cousin, Don Francisco d'Assiz, duke of Cadiz, and marriage also of the infanta Louisa (she died 1 Feb. 1897) to the duc de Montpensier . . . . . . 10 Oct. ,,
[The Spanish marriages disturb the friendly relations of the French and English governments.]
Amnesty granted to political offenders . 18 Oct. ,,
Two shots fired at the queen by an assassin, La Riva, 4 May, 1847
He suffers "death by the cord" . . . 23 June, ,,
Espartero restored . . . . . . 3 Sept. ,,
Sir Henry Lytton Bulwer, British envoy, ordered to quit Spain in 48 hours . . . . 17 May, 1848
Narvaez dismissed and recalled 1849
Diplomatic relations with England restored, 18 Apr. 1850
The queen of Spain delivered of a male child, which lives but ten minutes . . . . 12 July, ,,
The American expeditions under Lopez against Cuba (see *Cuba* and the *United States*) . 1850, 1851
Resignation of Narvaez . . . . . 10 Jan. ,,
The infante don Henrique permitted to return to Spain . . . . 2 Feb. ,,
Madrid-Aranjuez railway opened . . . 9 Feb. ,,
Law respecting the public debt (which has since excluded Spain from the European money-markets) . . . . 1 Aug. ,,
Death of Godoy, prince of the peace . . 4 Oct. ,,
The queen pardons the prisoners taken in the attempt upon Cuba . . . . . 11 Dec. ,,
Her majesty gives birth to a princess . 20 Dec. ,,

Attempt made on the life of the queen; she is slightly wounded by the dagger of Merino, a Franciscan . . . . . 2 Feb. 1852
Gen. Castaños, duke of Baylen, renowned in the French war, dies, aged 95 . . . . 23 Sept. ,,
Narvaez exiled to Vienna . . . . . Jan. 1853
Ministerial changes—Lersundi forms a cabinet, 11 April; resigns: Sartorius' cabinet . Sept. ,,
Birth and death of a princess . . . 5 Jan. 1854
General O'Donnell, Concha, and others banished, 17 Jan. ,,
Disturbances at Saragossa, &c. . . . Feb. ,,
Don Francisco (father of the king consort), marries an "unfortunate" woman . . . March, ,,
Military insurrection, under O'Donnell, near Madrid, 28 June, ,,
The movement headed by Espartero; Barcelona and Madrid pronounce against the government; barricades in Madrid . . . 1-17 July, ,,
Triumph of the insurrection: resignation of the ministry; the queen sends for Espartero, 19 July, ,,
Peace restored: the degraded generals reinstated, &c.; Espartero forms an administration, 31 July, ,,
The queen mother impeached; she quits Spain 28 Aug. ,,
Ministerial crisis; Espartero resigns, but resumes office . . . . . 21-30 Nov. ,,
New constitution of the cortes . . . 13 Jan. 1855
The cortes vote that all power proceeds from the people; they permit liberty of belief, but not of worship . . . . Feb. ,,
Don Carlos dies . . . . . . 10 March, ,,
Insurrection of Valencia . . . . 6 April, 1856
Resignation of Espartero; new cabinet formed, headed by marshal O'Donnell; insurrection in Madrid, 14 July; O'Donnell and the government troops subdue the insurgents; the national guard suppressed . . . . 15-16 July, ,,
Insurrection at Barcelona and Saragossa quelled by O'Donnell, as dictator . . . 15-23 July, ,,
O'Donnell compelled to resign; Narvaez becomes minister . . . . . 12 Oct. ,,
Amnesty granted to political offenders . 19 Oct. ,,
Espartero resigns as senator . . . . 1 Feb. 1857
Insurrection in Andalusia; quickly suppressed; cruel military executions; 98 insurgents shot (24 at Seville) . . . June and July, ,,
Ministerial changes; Armero minister . 26 Oct. ,,
Birth of the prince royal . . . 28 Nov. ,,
Isturitz, minister, 14 Jan.; O'Donnell, minister, 1 July, ,,
Cessation of state of siege at Barcelona, &c. 20 Sept. 1858
Joint French and Spanish expedition against Cochin China announced . . . . 1 Dec. ,,
War with Morocco (*which see*) . . Nov.-Dec. 1859
An association for reforming the tariff, &c., formed ,,
O'Donnell commands the army in Africa; indecisive conflicts reported; battle at Castillejos; a Spanish "Balaklava" charge . . . 1 Jan. 1860
The Moors defeated near Tetuan, which surrenders 4 Feb. ,,
An ineffectual truce . . . 16-23 Feb. ,,
The Moors defeated at Guad-el-ras . 23 March, ,,
Treaty of peace signed; 400,000,000 reals to be paid by Moors, and Tetuan to be held till paid 26 Mar. ,,
General Ortega, governor of the Balearic Isles, lands near Tortosa, in Valencia, with 3000 men, and proclaims the comte de Montemolin king, as Charles VI.; his troops resist, and he is compelled to flee, with the comte and others, 3 April; Ortega shot 19 April, ,,
The comte de Montemolin and his brother Ferdinand arrested at Tortosa, 21 April; renounce their claim to the throne . . . . 23 April, ,,
An amnesty proclaimed . . . . 2 May, ,,
Their brother Juan asserts his right, 5 June; and they, when at Cologne, annul their renunciation, 28 June, ,,
The emperor Napoleon's proposal to admit Spain as a first-class power is opposed by England, and given up . . . . Aug. ,,
The comte de Montemolin and his wife die at Trieste 14 Jan. 1861
The annexation of St. Domingo to Spain ratified; slavery not to be re-established . . 19 May, ,,
Insurrection at Loja suppressed . . . July, ,,
The queen said to be governed by the nun Patrocinio Dec. 1861
Intervention in Mexico (see *Mexico*) . 8 Dec. ,,
Much church property in course of sale . April, 1862
José Alhama and Manuel Matamoras, protestant propagandists, sentenced to 10 years' imprisonment . . . . 14 Oct.
Don Juan de Bourbon renounces his right to the throne . . . . . . 8 Jan. 1863
Resignation of the premier, marshal O'Donnell, 26 Feb.; marquis de Miraflores minister, 4 March, ,,
Insurrection in St. Domingo; war ensues (see *Domingo*) . . . . . . 1 Sept. ,,
Empress of France visits the queen . . Oct. ,,
Rupture with Peru (*which see*) . . . April, 1864
General Prim exiled for conspiracy . . 13 Aug.
Arrazola ministry, Jan.; Mon forms a ministry, 1 March; resigns, 13 Sept.; Narvaez forms a cabinet . . . . Sept. ,,
Queen Christina returns to Spain . . 26 Sept. ,,
English government recognises the insurrection at St. Domingo; Narvaez advises abandonment of the contest; the queen refuses; the ministry resign; but resume office . . . 14-18 Dec. ,,
Peace with Peru, which has to pay a heavy indemnity 27 Jan. 1865
The queen orders the sale of crown lands, giving up three-fourths to the nation . . . 20 Feb. ,,
Student riots at Madrid; several persons killed, 10 April, ,,
[Bravo Murillo accused of cruelty on this occasion.]
Decree relinquishing St. Domingo . . 5 May, ,,
Suppression of a conspiracy at Valencia to reunite Spain and Portugal . . . . 10 June, ,,
Resignation of Narvaez, 19 June; O'Donnell forms a liberal cabinet . . . . 22 June, ,,
Kingdom of Italy recognised by Spain 26 June, ,,
Father Claret dismissed from court . 20 July,
Dispute with Chili; M. Tavira's settlement (20 May) disavowed by the government . 25 July, ,,
Emperor Napoleon visits the queen at St. Sebastian, 9 Sept.: she visits him at Biarritz, 11 Sept. ,,
Disturbances at Saragossa suppressed . 3 Oct. ,,
Admiral Pareja, at Valparaiso, insults the Chilian government, 18 Sept.; which declares war, 25 Sept.; Pareja declares a blockade . . Oct. ,,
The Chilian captain Williams captures the Spanish vessel *Covadonga* (Pareja commits suicide) 26 Nov. ,,
Intervention fruitless . . . . . . Dec. ,,
Claret returns to court . . . . 25 Dec. ,,
New cortes elected; the great Progresista party still abstains from action in public affairs; queen opens cortes . . . . . . 27 Dec. ,,
Military insurrection at Aranjuez, headed by gen. Prim, 3 Jan.; martial law in Madrid, 4 Jan.; Concha and Zabala march against rebels, 4 Jan.; &c.; riots at Barcelona, 9, 10 Jan.; state of siege in New Castile, Catalonia, and Aragon 6-12 Jan. 1866
Prim enters Portugal and lays down arms; the insurrection ends . . . . . . 20 Jan. ,,
Queen Victoria, British sloop, seized by a guarda-costa . . . . 15 Jan. ,,
Admiral Mendez bombards Valparaiso, destroying much property, 31 March; he is repulsed at Callao with loss . . . . . . 2 May, ,,
The queen declares the campaign in the Pacific ended, 15 June, ,,
Great military revolt in favour of Prim at Madrid; about 1200 men, headed by non-commissioned officers, with cannon, quelled summarily by marshals O'Donnell and Narvaez, with much bloodshed; 200 prisoners shot, 22 June; 21 sergeants shot; (Sen. Castelar escaped to France) 26 June, ,,
Military revolts at Barcelona and at various other places . . . . 23 June, ,,
Resignation of O'Donnell as minister, succeeded by Narvaez and Bravo, who adopt severe measures against the liberals . . . . . July, ,,
The queen said to be subject to the influence of the "bleeding nun," Patrocinio, and the priests, July, ,,
Freedom of the press abolished, and writers transported to the colonies; a "reign of terror," Aug.-Sept.
British screw steamer *Tornado*, com. E. Collier, seized by Spaniards (charged with aiding Chili), and carried to Cadiz . . . . 21-22 Aug. ,,

33 persons condemned to death, many of whom had fled . . . . 23 Sept. 1866
Re-establishment of tranquillity declared at Madrid 3 Oct. ,,
Public instruction placed under the clergy Oct. ,,
Reform of the municipal institutions decreed on account of revolutionary proceedings . . Oct. ,,
Crew of *Tornado* detained as prisoners, 31 Oct. the case referred to law . . . . Nov. ,,
King and queen visit Lisbon . . . . 11 Dec. ,,
Taxes for 1867 received in advance . . Dec. ,,
The queen dismissed the cortes (and imprisoned many eminent deputies for petitioning against it) 30 Dec. ,,
O'Donnell and his colleagues residing in Paris, Jan. 1867
Decision in *Tornado* case—the ship a prize and the crew prisoners of war, 18 Dec. 1866; lord Stanley protests against the proceedings . 8 Feb. ,,
Decree for making secret publication of journals and pamphlets penal . . . . 16 Feb. ,,
The *Tornado* prisoners released . . Feb. ,,
State of siege raised . . . . 7 March, ,,
Queen Victoria sloop declared by Spain to have been wrongfully seized and reparation to be made, 21 April, ,,
Amnesty to revolters of June 1866 . 25 April, ,,
Son of duchess of Montpensier born . 1 May, ,,
Attempted insurrection in different parts (attributed to Prim) failed through want of organisation, about 15 Aug. ,,
Insurrectionary movements reported in Catalonia and Aragon . . . . July, Aug. ,,
State of siege proclaimed . . . . 17 Aug. ,,
Insurrection suppressed; amnesty . . Sept. ,,
Death of marshal O'Donnell, duke of Tetuan 5 Nov. ,,
Martial law annulled . . . . . . 16 Nov. ,,
Parliament opened by the queen in person 27 Dec. ,,
An armament bill adopted by the chamber of deputies . . . . 22 Jan. 1868
Proposed settlement with national creditors at 20 per cent. of the debt . . . . Jan. ,,
General amnesty proclaimed . . . . 25 Jan. ,,
Death of marshal Narvaez, duke of Valencia, aged 67) 23 April, ,,
New ministry formed by Gonzalez Bravo Murillo, 24 April, ,,
Marriage of princess Isabella, the queen's eldest daughter, to the count of Girgenti, brother of ex-king of Naples 13 May, ,,
Law enacted abolishing normal schools and subjecting education to the priests . . . 2 June, ,,
Ministerial changes . . . . . . 16 June, ,,
Duke and duchess of Montpensier arrested and exiled . . . . 6 July, ,,
Marshal Serrano, general Dolce, and others exiled, about 10 July, ,,
Insurrection begins in the fleet, 18 Sept.; joined by the garrison and city of Cadiz, 19 Sept.; accepted by nearly all Spain . . . . . 19-30 Sept. ,,
Prim arrives at Cadiz, 17 Sept.; announces a provisional government . . . . 19 Sept. ,,
The ministers resign, 19, 20 Sept.; José Concha becomes president of the council, 22 Sept.; Bravo Murillo and his colleagues flee to Bayonne 23 Sept. ,,
[*Royalist leaders:* José Concha, marquis de Havaña, Manuel Concha, marquis de Duero, at Madrid; the marquis de Pezuela at Barcelona; Eusebio de Calonge in the north; Pavia y Lacy, marquis de Novaliches in Andalusia.]
Novaliches, the royalist general, defeated at Alcolea by Serrano, 27 Sept.; surrenders . 28 Sept. ,,
The queen flies to Bayonne and thence to Pau, and protests . . . . . . 29, 30 Sept. ,,
The deposition of the queen declared at Madrid, 29 Sept. ,,
A national guard organised . . . . 30 Sept. ,,
Don Juan, son of Don Carlos, renounces his hereditary rights in favour of his son, Carlos, 3 Oct. ,,
Serrano enters Madrid, 3 Oct.: Serrano, Prim, and Olozaga constitute a provisional government, 5 Oct. ,,
Prim enthusiastically received at Madrid 7 Oct. ,,
The education law of 2 June annulled; the Jesuits and other religious orders suppressed; the laws expelling the Jews abrogated; freedom of religious worship decreed . about 12, 13 Oct. ,,
All the local juntas dissolved by manifesto of the provisional government . . . . 20 Oct. ,,
The provisional government recognised by the United States, 13 Oct.; by England, France, and Prussia, 25 Oct.; by Austria, Sweden, and Belgium about 31 Oct. 1868
Manifesto of the government declaring for universal suffrage, and free press and education 26 Oct. ,,
Prim created a marshal . . about 6 Nov. ,,
The queen arrives at Paris . . . . 6 Nov. ,,
The joint electoral committee at Madrid declare in favour of a limited monarchy . 14 Nov. ,,
Decree for formation of a citizen force of the Volunteers of Freedom . . . . . . 18 Nov. ,,
Loan of 20,000,000*l.* proposed by Figueras, minister of finance; 4,000,000*l.* said to be undertaken by Rothschilds; about 2,000,000 subscribed in Spain . . . . . . about 25 Nov. ,,
Insurrection against the provisional government breaks out at Cadiz, 5 Dec.; murderous conflicts, 6 Dec.; the city invested; surrenders; entry of general Caballero de Roda, general of the army of Andalusia . . . . 12 Dec. ,,
Peaceful elections for constituent cortes, 19, 20 Dec. ,,
Manifesto of the duc de Montpensier, justifying his recent entry into Spain . . dated 19 Dec. ,,
Violent insurrection at Malaga suppressed with much slaughter . . . . . . 31 Dec. ,,
Election of members for the cortes . 17 Jan. 1869
The Spanish envoy at Rome not received 23 Jan. ,,
Gutierez de Castro, civil governor of Burgos, murdered in the presence of priests while taking an inventory of the artistic treasures of the cathedral 24 Jan. ,,
Insurrection in Cuba increasing . . Feb. ,,
Meeting of the cortes, 11 Feb.; Rivero elected president . . . . 13 Feb. ,,
The provisional government resign; Serrano reappointed head of the government with same ministry . . . . 25, 26 Feb. ,,
Riots at Xeres on account of conscription, 16 March, ,,
Spanish Protestant religious service at Madrid 28 March, ,,
Insurrection in Cuba fomented by Americans, April, ,,
61st anniversary of the Madrid revolution and massacre of the French (1808) . . . 2 May, ,,
The cortes vote for a monarchy (214 to 71), 21 May, ,,
The new constitution promulgated . 6 June, ,,
Marshal Serrano elected regent by the cortes, 15 June; sworn . . . . . . 18 June, ,,
New ministry under Prim . . about 18 June, ,,
Carlist risings in La Mancha and at Ciudad Real, suppressed . . . . . July-Aug. ,,
United States' overtures respecting Cuba indignantly rejected . . . . about 18 Sept. ,,
Candidature of the duke of Genoa discussed, Sept. Oct. ,,
Republican risings at Tarragona, Barcelona, and other places, suppressed with bloodshed, Sept.; republicans defeated near Reus, 4 Oct.; Saragossa cannonaded, 8 Oct.; Valencia surrendered, 16 Oct.; tranquillity generally restored . 20 Oct. ,,
Warm discussions respecting the election of a king; Topete, minister of marine, resigns . 2 Nov. ,,
General Dulce dies . . . . . . 23 Nov. ,,
Powerful republican speech of Castelar in the cortes about 18 Dec. ,,
Resignation of Prim and the ministry on the Italian government opposing the nomination of the duke of Genoa as king of Spain . . . . 4 Jan. 1870
Prim resumes office with Topete and Rivero, 10 Jan. ,,
Majority in the assembly for Prim against the combined unionists and liberals . . 3 April, ,,
Conscription riots at Barcelona; soon suppressed 7, 8 April, ,,
The duc de Montpensier, after great provocation, kills don Enrique de Bourbon, brother of the ex-king, in a duel, 12 March; tried, condemned, and fined . . . . 12 April, ,,
The offered crown declined by Espartero . May, ,,
Bill for gradual abolition of slavery in the colonies presented to the cortes . . . 28 May, ,,
Two Englishmen of Gibraltar seized by brigands; ransomed for 5200*l.*; brigands afterwards attacked by the Spanish civil guard; several of them killed, and part of the ransom recovered . . June, ,,
Rojo Arias carries a resolution requiring an absolute majority in the cortes for any proposed sovereign (179 out of 356); this excludes all present candidates . . . . June, ,,

Isabella II. abdicates in favour of her son Alfonso, 25 June, 1870

Prince Leopold of Hohenzollern-Sigmaringen nominated king, accepted by the regent and ministry, 6 July; this justified by the government in a circular, 7 July; on the strong opposition of France he resigns . . . . 12 July, ,,

Neutrality in the war announced . . 27 July, ,,

Renewed agitation for a republic about 9 Aug. ,,

Amnesty for all political offences since 29 Sept. 1868, published . . . . 10 Aug. ,,

Irruption of Carlists into Navarre, 27 Aug.; defeated, 28 Aug. ,,

The Basque provinces put into a state of siege, 28 Aug. ,,

The French republic warmly recognised Sept. ,,

Ministerial crisis . . . . . . 15 Sept. ,,

Claret, the ex-queen's confessor, dies . 4 Oct. ,,

Amadeus, duke of Aosta (born 30 May, 1845), accepts the candidature for the crown . . 20 Oct. ,,

Elected by the cortes by 191 votes: (63 for a republic; 27 for the duc de Montpensier) . 16 Nov. ,,

Proclaimed king . . . . 17 Nov. ,,

The ex-queen, on behalf of her son Alfonso, protests against the election . . . . . 21 Nov. ,,

The duke accepts the crown from a deputation of the cortes at Florence, and says "that his honesty should rise above the struggle of parties, and that he had no other object than the peace and prosperity of the nation" . . . . . 4 Dec. ,,

Stormy session in the cortes respecting arrangements for the new king, 19 Dec.; Rivero, the president, resigns . . . . . 25 Dec. ,,

Prim fired at and wounded in his carriage by six men, who escaped; great indignation at Madrid, 27 Dec.; Topete rejoins the ministry; vote of confidence in it . . . . . . 28 Dec. ,,

Prim dies in the evening (aged 56); the king received by Topete at Cartagena . . . . 30 Dec. ,,

Funeral of Prim . . . . 31 Dec. ,,

The king enters Madrid, visits the body of Prim, and takes the oath . . . . . . 2 Jan. 1871

New ministry under Serrano . . . 5 Jan. ,,

Warm reception of the queen at Madrid 19 March, ,,

New cortes opened; the king's speech much applauded . . . . 3 April, ,,

Del Castillo and other Alfonsists recognise the king . . . . April, ,,

Olozaga elected president of the cortes 4 April, ,,

The *Tornado* difficulty settled (Aug.–Nov. 1866), compensation to be paid by the Spanish government . . . . May, ,,

Ministerial crisis through financial affairs; settled by the king . . . . June, ,,

Marshal Serrano fails in forming a cabinet, 23 July; a ministry formed by Zorrilla . . 24 July, ,,

The king visits the provinces; warmly received, 1 Sept. *et seq.*; welcomed by Espartero at Logroño, 30 Sept. ,,

Cortes opened, 1 Oct.; Sagasta elected president in opposition to Rivero (123-113), 3 Oct.; the Zorrilla ministry resigns, 4 Oct.; Malcampo forms a ministry . . . . 5 Oct. ,,

Republican meeting at Madrid; strong resolutions passed . . . . 15 Oct. ,,

Defeat of the ministry in the cortes; dissolution, 24, 25 Nov. ,,

Angulo, the finance minister, proposes to tax the foreign national creditors 18 per cent. 27 Nov. ,,

Suicide of the count of Girgenti . . . 27 Nov. ,,

Ministry formed under Sagasta . . . 21 Dec. ,,

Espartero, duke of Victory, made prince of Vergara, Jan. 1872

Resignation of Sagasta and the ministry for a trifling defeat; refused by the king, dissolution of the cortes; much excitement; troops under arms . . . . 25, 26 Jan. ,,

Ministry reconstituted by Sagasta and Topete, 20 Feb. ,,

Union of the opposition against the ministry, who determine to support the throne, about 8 March, ,,

Elections; majority of about 100 for ministers; Madrid elects for the opposition 4-6 April, ,,

Insurrection of Carlists incited by priests in Navarre, Leon, &c.; manifesto of don Carlos, duke of Madrid; Diaz de Rada, his general about 20 April, ,,

The new cortes opened; the king says, "I will never impose myself on the Spanish people, but neither will I allow myself to be accused of deserting the post which I occupy by their will" . 24 April, 1872

Navarre, &c., in state of siege . . 25 April, ,,

Marshal Serrano enters Navarre with an army; don Carlos, calling himself Carlos VII., crosses the frontiers near Véra, and takes the command, Rada retiring, 2 May; totally defeated at Oroquieta (*which see*) . . . . . . 4 May, ,,

The Carlists surrender by hundreds, or disperse, 8, 9, 20, 21 May, ,,

Reported small defeats at Onate, &c. . 13, 20 May, ,,

Resignation of the Sagasta ministry . . 22 May, ,,

Band of Carlists defeated near Gerona, about 22 May, ,,

New ministry (supported by Serrano), adm. Topete president . . . . 25 May, ,,

Serrano offers amnesty to Carlists who surrender, 25 May; it is accepted, 27 May; he is censured, but exonerated by the cortes, 8 June; he assumes the presidency of the ministry . . 4 June, ,,

Carlism increases; the ministry propose martial law; the king opposes it; the ministry resign, 12 June, ,,

Ruiz Zorrilla (who had just retired from political life) becomes president of a new ministry, 14 June, ,,

Letter of the duc de Montpensier advocating the rights of prince Alfonso, 17 April; published, June, ,,

Dissolution of the cortes . . . . 29 June, ,,

Don Carlos calls on Catalonia, Arragon, and Valencia, to rise, promising to restore their ancient liberties . . . . 16 July, ,,

Attempted assassination of the king and queen by about 15 men; one assassin killed, two taken; a little after midnight of . . . 18-19 July, ,,

The king's popular visit to the provinces, travelling nearly 2000 miles . . 26 July-24 Aug. ,,

Elections for the cortes; highly favourable to the Zorrilla ministry . . . . 25 Aug. *et seq.* ,,

The cortes opened by the king with a fine speech, 15 Sept. ,,

Republican rising at Ferrol; red flag displayed; 1500 men under Montojo and Bozas, 11 Oct.; town captured by the captain-general of Galicia, 13 Oct. ,,

The insurgents disperse or surrender; about 500 prisoners . . . . 17 Oct. ,,

Impeachment of the Sagasta ministry for financial corruption proposed in the cortes; much agitation, end of Oct. ,,

The country disturbed by Carlists and republicans, Nov., Dec. ,,

Gen. Hidalgo appointed to a military command; the artillery officers resigned: punished . Nov. ,,

Outbreak in Madrid suppressed . . . 11 Dec. ,,

Changes in the ministry announced . 20 Dec. ,,

Bill for abolition of slavery in Porto Rico, for compensation, brought into congress . . 24 Dec. ,,

Carlist bands defeated and several generals killed, Jan. 1873

King Amadeus' message to the cortes, announcing his abdication; he states that he sees Spain in a continual struggle, the era of peace more distant; he sought for remedies within the law, and did not find them; his efforts were sterile. The two chambers combine as the sovereign cortes of Spain, and vote for a republic (126-32) . 11 Feb. ,,

Reported success of the Carlists; agitation for the duc de Montpensier among the Orleanists in France . . . . 12 Feb. ,,

New ministry under Figueras . . . 12 Feb. ,,

King Amadeus arrives at Lisbon . . 13 Feb. ,,

Irruption of Carlists; they hold part of Catalonia; demonstrations in favour of a federal republic, 22, 23 Feb. ,,

Ministry reconstituted; Figueras chief, 24, 25 Feb. ,,

Powerful circular to European powers from Castelar, foreign minister . . . . . . 27 Feb. ,,

Appointment of a permanent committee of the cortes . . . . 22 March, ,,

Great dissensions between the radicals and republicans; fighting with Carlists in the provinces, early in March, ,,

Slavery in Porto Rico abolished . . 23 March, ,,

Proclamation of the government calling for volunteers against the Carlists . . . 25 March, ,,

Mutinous spirit in the army . . . April, ,,

The Carlists beaten in several encounters; don Alfonso de Bourbon re-enters France . 23 April, 1873

The old "monarchical volunteers" take possession of the bull-ring at Madrid; are disarmed and dispersed by the government troops; the "permanent committee" dissolved by the government, which assumes supreme power . . 26 April, ,,

Serrano and Sagasta have left Spain . 29 April, ,,

More defeats of the Carlists; Madrid tranquil, 29, 30 April-4 May, ,,

Elections for the cortes commence; monarchists abstain from voting . . . . . . 10 May, ,,

Mr. Bradlaugh, the English republican, entertained at Madrid . . . . 24 May, ,,

More Carlist defeats reported; their alleged cruelties denied by the Carlist committee . May, June, ,,

The Intransigentes or Irreconcilables (extreme republicans) very powerful . . . June, ,,

The new cortes opened; a speech by Figueras, 1 June, ,,

The federal republic voted by the cortes (210-2) and proclaimed, 8 June; Pi y Margall, president of a new ministry, rejected; Figueras and his ministry resume office . . . . . . 9 June, ,,

Carlists besieging Irun . . . . . 7 June, ,,

Ministerial crisis renewed, 10 June; Pi y Margall becomes minister; Figueras quits Spain, 11 June, ,,

Carlists defeat Castañon near Murieta . 26 June, ,,

Cadiz, Seville, Malaga, and Valencia very insubordinate . . . . 29 June, ,,

The Intransigentes withdraw from the cortes, 1 July, ,,

Defeat and death of Calvinety by Carlists; insurrection at Alcoy, promoted by Internationalists; the mayor and others killed, announced, 11 July ,,

Don Carlos (as Carlos VII.) enters Spain, "to save the country" . . . . . . 13 July, ,,

Desperate fighting at Igualada, Catalonia 17, 18 July, ,,

Four prevailing parties:—1. The government, highly democratic; 2. The Intransigentes, or irreconcilables: extremely democratic; 3. The International, or communists; 4. The legitimists, Carlists.

Murcia and Valencia proclaim themselves federal cantons . . . . 18 July, ,,

Pi y Margall compelled to resign; Salmeron forms a ministry opposed to the Intransigentes, 18 July, ,,

Igualada taken by the Carlists under Don Alfonso, 19 July, ,,

The government determine to put down insurrection . . . . . . 24 July, ,,

Don Carlos enters Biscay . . . . 31 July, ,,

Carlists hold chief of N. Spain . . . Aug. ,,

Insurgents repulsed in their attack on Almeria; beaten in fights at Seville, 28-30 July; gen. Pavia warmly received . . . . . . 31 July, ,,

Cadiz surrenders to him . . . . . 4 Aug. ,,

Troops attack Valencia, 26 July; it surrenders, 8 Aug. ,,

New constitution printed, 27 July; discussed, Aug. ,,

[118 Articles: includes separation of church and state; free religious worship; nobility abolished; 15 states in and near peninsula; 2 in the Antilles; cortes (senate and congress) to have legislative power; one deputy to 50,000 souls; cortes to be renewed in 2 years; members to be paid; executive: president and ministry; president elected for 4 years.]

Bombardment of Malaga stopped by the British and German admirals . . . . . 1 Aug. ,,

Alleged Carlist victories at Elgueta, &c. 5-10 Aug. ,,

Reported total defeat of the insurgents at Chinchilla, while marching on Madrid . . 10 Aug. ,,

Cartagena, held by Intransigentes, besieged, 22 Aug. ,,

The *Deerhound*, English yacht, conveying stores to Carlists, seized by the Spaniards, 11½ miles off Biarritz; crew imprisoned, and captain sent to Ferrol . . . . 13 Aug. ,,

Capt. Werner, of German ship, *Friedrich Karl*, captures *Almanza* and *Vittoria*, Spanish ironclads, held by rebels, gives them up to adm. Yelverton, who prepares for action against Intransigentes, claiming them, and sends them to Gibraltar unmolested . . . . 1 Sept. ,,

Carlists defeat republicans at Arrichulegui, near Renteria, many killed . . . . 21 Aug. ,,

They take Estella after a conflict at Dicastillo, 25 Aug. ,,

Castelar elected president of the cortes . 26 Aug. 1873

The ministry propose abolition of capital punishment in the army, defeated in the cortes; resign 5 Sept. ,,

Castelar heads a ministry; proposes calling out 150,000 men, to end the war . . 7, 8 Sept. ,,

Carlists successful; yet do not advance . 5-8 Sept. ,,

Salmeron elected president of the cortes 9 Sept. ,,

Castelar made virtually dictator . . 15 Sept. ,,

Ferdinand Muñoz, duke of Rianzarès, husband of queen Christina, dies at Havre . . 12 Sept. ,,

The *Deerhound* and crew given up; announced about 18 Sept. ,,

Reported victories of Loma over Carlists 18 Sept. ,,

Speech of Castelar, the cortes to be closed 2 Jan. 1874 . . . . 18 Sept. ,,

Carlist attack on Tolosa repulsed by Loma, 19 Sept. ,,

The cortes prorogued . . . . 21 Sept. ,,

The Carlist Merendon killed and his band dispersed, about 26 Sept. ,,

The *Vittoria* and *Almanza* given up to the Spanish government . . . . . 26 Sept. ,,

Carlists in Navarre defeated by Moriones, 27 Sept. ,,

The Intransigentes' ironclads, *Mendez Nuñez* and *Numancia*, bombarding Alicante, repulsed, 28 Sept. ,,

Combination of parties to support Castelar, about 6 Oct. ,,

Battle at Maneru, near Puenta de la Reyna, in Navarre, between republicans, under Moriones, and Carlists, under Ollo; both claim a victory; advantage with Carlists . . . . 6 Oct. ,,

Carlists said to be repulsed at La Junquera, in Catalonia . . . . . about 8 Oct. ,,

Battle of Escombrera bay; the Intransigentes' ships attempt to break blockade of Cartagena; repulsed by admiral Lobo . . . . . 11 Oct. ,,

Many Carlists escape into France . about Oct. ,,

Lobo declines to fight, and retires, pursued by the Intransigentes, 13 Oct.; justifies himself at Madrid . . . . 22 Oct. ,,

Collision of the Intransigentes' vessels *Numancia* and *Fernando del Catolico*, the latter sunk and 66 drowned . . . . . . 18 Oct. ,,

Unsuccessful sortie at Cartagena . . 21 Oct. ,,

Tristany, with 2,500 Carlists, defeated by Salamanca 25 Oct. ,,

Death of Rios Rosas, statesman . . 3 Nov. ,,

The *Murillo* (see *Wrecks*, 1873) captured; condemned to be sold by the British court of admiralty . . . . Nov. ,,

Indecisive conflicts at Monte Jurre and Monjardin, victories claimed by Carlists . 7, 8, 9 Nov. ,,

Cartagena bombarded . . . 26 Nov. *et seq.* ,,

Reported victory of Moriones near Tolosa, 7 Dec. ,,

Lopez Dominguez becomes commander before Cartagena . . . . . . 13 Dec. ,,

Tetuan, insurgent vessel, at Cartagena, blew up (? purposely) . . . . . . 30 Dec. ,,

Pronunciamento:—Meeting of the cortes; speech of Castelar; vote of confidence in him lost by 20; he resigns; Salmeron attempts to form a ministry, 2, 3 Jan.; Pavia, captain-general of Madrid, forcibly dissolves the cortes . . . . 3 Jan. 1874

Marshal Serrano made president of a new ministry, including Topete; the national guard of Madrid disarming . . . . 4 Jan. ,,

Insurrection at Saragossa, suppressed with bloodshed . . . . 4 Jan. ,,

The new government issue a moderate manifesto, 9, 10 Jan. ,,

Cartagena captured by Lopez Dominguez, 12 Jan. ,,

Insurrection at Barcelona quelled . 12, 13 Jan. ,,

Numancia ironclad, with Intransigentes leaders and convicts, escapes; they land at Mers el Kebir, near Oran, on the African coast; are interned by the French . . . . . . 12 Jan. ,,

Blockade of the coast of Spain announced 31 Jan. ,,

The Carlists besiege Bilbao. Moriones defeated at Somorrostro . . . . . 25 Feb. ,,

Marshal Serrano resigns presidency of the ministry, and becomes chief of the executive, succeeded by Zabala; Serrano proceeds to Bilbao, 28 Feb. *et seq.* ,,

Serrano assumes command . . about 8 March, ,,

The blockade of the coast (31 Jan.) raised, 2 March, ,,

Asserted victory of the Carlists at San Felice, Burgos . . . . 15 March, ,,

Three days' conflict at Somorrostro, near Bilbao; the Carlists defeated, but retain their positions (about 2000 killed and wounded on both sides) 25, 26, 27 March, 1874
Armistice for three days . . . 28 March, „
General Manuel da Concha joins Serrano at Santander . . . . about 8 April, „
Great national effort to relieve Bilbao; union of parties; hostilities resumed . . 20 April, „
After several days' conflict, Carlists retreat; marshal Concha enters Bilbao, which is much injured by long bombardment . . . . . 2 May, „
A battle at Prats de Llusanés, indecisive 6 May, „
New ministry formed under Zabala . . 13 May, „
Carlists repulsed in severe attack at Ramales, about 20 May, „
Carlists defeated at Gondesa . about 6 June, „
Republicans repulsed before Estella . 25-27 June, „
Concha killed (succeeded by Zabala) . 27 June, „
Carlists accused of butchering prisoners, June and July, „
Alleged Carlist victories at Peña Mura (or Plata), near Abarzuza . . . . 25-27 June, „
Schmidt, a German correspondent, shot as a spy by Carlists . . . . about 28 June, „
German intervention for killing of captain Schmidt by Carlists . . . . . . July, „
Carlists hold Navarre, Guipuscoa, Biscay, and Alara . . . . July, „
The Carlists capture Cuenca (about 80 miles from Madrid) . . . . 13 July, „
Don Carlos's manifesto promising constitutional government . . . . . . 16 July, „
Massacre of 86 republican prisoners by Carlists under Saballo at Valfogona . . . 17 July, „
All Spain placed under martial law; levy of 125,000 men . . . . . . about 18 July, „
Government circular to foreign courts respecting Carlist atrocities . . . . . . 29 July, „
The government appeals to the French government respecting French assistance to Carlists; justificatory reply . . . . 3 Aug. „
The British Mediterranean squadron under admiral Drummond sails from Malta for Barcelona, 4 Aug. „
Don Carlos appeals to the chief powers not to intervene; justifies Dorregaray's severities, and the execution of Schmidt . . . . . 6 Aug. „
Moriones' alleged defeat of Mendiri and Carlists at Oteiza . . . . 12 Aug. „
Duty of 5*d*. a ton on imported iron granted to Bilbao for repairs . . . . . 13 Aug. „
Serrano's government recognised by Great Britain, Germany, France, and other powers (not by Russia) . . . . . . about 14 Aug. „
Letter of sympathy and encouragement from the comte de Chambord to don Carlos . Aug. „
183 prisoners of war at Olot said to be shot by Carlists . . . . Aug. „
Puycerda vigorously besieged by Carlists, Aug.-Sept. „
Zabala resigns; ministry formed under Sagasta, 4 Sept. „
Carlists fire on German gunboats *Nautilus* and *Albatross* near San Sebastian; the Germans fire shells into the town . . . about 5 Sept. „
Lopez Dominguez said to have defeated Carlists five times, and relieved Puycerda . about 6 Sept. „
Carlists fire on German and Austrian ambassadors on the road to Madrid . . . 6 Sept. „
Carlists defeated by Lopez Pinto near Mora, about 9 Sept.; by Moriones at Barasoam near Tafalla, about 25 Sept. „
The ruthless Carlist general Dorregaray retires to Bayonne; said to have been superseded by Mendiri . . . . Oct. „
Pavia superseded by Jovellar in Valencia, early in Oct. „
Note sent to French government complaining of neglect respecting the Carlists on the frontiers, early in Oct. „
Carlists said to have been defeated at Fortuna, in Murcia, 11 Oct.; and at Villa Fortuna, 30 Oct. „
Carlists begin to bombard Irun, 4 Nov.; repulsed, 10 Nov. „
Serrano commander of the army in the north, Nov. „
Prince Alfonso issues a manifesto in reply to address, declaring himself to be "a true Spaniard, catholic, and liberal" . . . . . 1 Dec. „
The army at Murviedro pronounces in favour of Alfonso; he is proclaimed king by gen. Martinez Campos, 29 Dec.; recognised by the other armies and the navy, 30 Dec.; proclaimed by gen. Primo da Rivera at Madrid; Antonio Canovas del Castillo head of a royal ministry . . 31 Dec. 1874
The president marshal Serrano withdraws to France, 1 Jan. 1875
Proclamation of Carlos against Alfonso 6 Jan. „
Alfonso XII. recognised throughout Spain; well received at Barcelona, 9 Jan.; enters Madrid, 14 Jan. „
Orders of knighthood re-established; payments to clergy to be renewed . . . . . Jan. „
Increased barbarities of the Carlists reported, Jan. „
Alfonso reviews 30,000 troops near Tafalla, 22 Jan.; issues proclamation to northern provinces, promising amnesty, and respect to local rights, 22 Jan. „
Serrano returns to Madrid . . . . . Feb. „
Carlists surprise and defeat royalists at Lucar, 3 Feb. „
Carlists retreat from Pampeluna; entered by the king, 6 Feb.; he exchanges decorations with Espartero at Logroño . . . . . 9 Feb. „
Resignation of generals Moriones, Loma, and Blanco; Concha sent for from Cuba . Feb. „
Serrano received by the king . . . . 8 March, „
Cabrera, an old Carlist general (see 1840) publishes an address, declaring for Alfonso XII., 11 March, „
Several professors seized and exiled for liberal opinions . . . . . . March, April, „
Eight prisoners shot by Carlist general Mendiri, in reprisal . . . . 7 April, „
Papal nuncio received by the king . . 3 May, „
Aguirre, Carlist general, joins the royalists, about 9 May, „
Jovellar, commander of royal army, about 7 June, „
Martinez Campos said to have taken fortress of Miraveti . . . . 24 June, „
Vigorous action of the government troops; Carlists expelled from Castile; stringent measures ordered against those who favour them . July, „
Carlists defeated by Quesada and others, 31 July, „
Strong citadel at Urgel surrendered by Carlists to Campos, after a gallant defence; the bishop and the brave general Lizarraga captured, 26 Aug. „
New conscription ordered, 12 Aug; reported successful . . . . Sept. „
Resignation of "conciliation ministry," 11 Sept.; liberal cabinet headed by gen. Jovellar, 12 Sept. „
The papal nuncio issues a circular against toleration, about 13 Sept. „
Dorregaray said to be nominated to the chief command; declaration from don Carlos stating that his mission is "to quell the revolution, and that it will die" . . . . Sept. „
Bombardment of San Sebastian, 28 Sept.-2 Oct.; resumed, 11 Oct.
The government declare the civil war at an end, and purpose summoning the cortes to assist the king in re-organising the country, early in Oct. „
Reported defection of Mendiri from the Carlists, and trial of Dorregaray and Caballi for misconduct; and Carlist successes . . . Oct. „
Reported interference of United States respecting Cuba . . . . Oct., Nov. „
Alleged victories of Quesada, near Pennacerada, 4, 5, Nov. „
Correspondence of ministry with the pope respecting ecclesiastical affairs . . . . Nov. „
Letter from don Carlos to the king proposing a truce, and offering help if war occurs with the United States (not answered) . . 9 Nov. „
Formation of a new constitutional party under Sagasta . . . . Nov. „
New proclamation of don Carlos to encourage his supporters . . . . . . 23 Nov. „
Serrano and Sagasta greet the king on his birthday, 28 Nov. „
Ministry reconstructed under Canovas del Castillo, 27 Nov. „
Cortes elected, 364 nominal ministerialists out of 406, Jan. 1876
Cortes opened by the king . . . . 15 Feb. „
Carlists defeated at Estella, Vera, and Tolosa, by Quesada and Moriones . . . . . Feb. „
The king assumes command; Estella surrenders to Primo da Rivera: severe loss . . 18 Feb. „

Reported letter from the pope recommending Carlos to retire from the contest . . . 22 Feb. 1876

Many Carlists submit or flee into France, 24-26 Feb. ,,

Don Carlos with general Lizarraga and five battalions surrender to the governor of Bayonne, at St. Jean Pied de Port, 27 Feb.; he lands with some officers at Folkestone, and proceeds to London . . . . 4 March, ,,

Triumphal entry of Alfonso XII. into Madrid, 20 March, ,,

Draft of new constitution submitted to the cortes, 28 March, ,,

The pope opposes moderate religious toleration in Art. 11 of the constitution . . . April, ,,

The Jews (expelled in 1492) petition for re-admission April, ,,

The prince of Wales at Madrid by invitation, 25-30 April, ,,

Outbreaks in the Basque provinces reported; martial law . . . . . about 27 May, ,,

Long debate in the cortes; confidence in ministry voted (211-26); the constitution passed; cortes adjourns . . . . about 21 July, ,,

Queen Isabella received by the king at Santander; declares that "her share in public affairs is at an end" . . . . 31 July, ,,

Repression of public worship of protestants by authority . . . . Sept. ,,

Ex-queen Isabella quietly received at Madrid, 13 Oct. ,,

Alleged federalist conspiracy of Ruiz Zorrilla and Salmeron; about 150 arrests . . . 23 Oct. ,,

State of siege in Old Castile raised . . 1 Feb. 1877

Treaty favoured nation clause in regard to England abrogated . . . . ,,

Royal progress in the provinces; the king well received . . . . March, ,,

General amnesty to Carlists and others surrendering . . . . April, ,,

Meeting of the new cortes; cheerful royal speech, 25 April, ,,

The cortes suddenly closed . . . . 11 July, ,,

New tariff passed; customs duties raised in respect to Great Britain, France, and United States, 17 July, ,,

The ex-queen, after visiting her son, disapproves of his proposed marriage, and associates with don Carlos in Paris, who is privately forbidden to remain, and goes to England; she is forbidden to return to Spain; her pension stopped, end of Dec. ,,

The king married to his cousin Mercedes, daughter of the duc de Montpensier . . . 23 Jan. 1878

End of the insurrection in Cuba announced, 21 Feb. ,,

Death of queen Mercedes, deeply lamented, 26 June, ,,

Budget receipts, 30,025,208*l.*, expendit. 30,127,114*l.* announced . . . . Aug. ,,

Death of the queen dowager Christina . 21 Aug. ,,

The king fired at (not injured) by Juan Oliva Moncasi, a member of the International Society, aged 23 . . . . 25 Oct. ,,

Moncasi executed . . . . 4 Jan. 1879

Espartero, duque de Victoria, dies . . 8 Jan. ,,

Castillo ministry (1874) resigns; marshal Campos forms a ministry . . . . 3 March, ,,

The cortes dissolved, 16 March; to meet, 1 June, ,,

Heavy rains, 14 Oct.; consequent disastrous inundations in the provinces of Malaga, Almeria, Granada, Seville, and especially in Murcia and Alicante; about 1000 persons perish; about 10,000 houseless . . . . . 15-17 Oct. ,,

Fresh storms and inundations; 21 persons drowned at Vera, in Almeria . . . . 29, 30 Oct. ,,

The king married to the archduchess Maria Christina of Austria . . . . . 29 Nov. ,,

Vines attacked by phylloxera in Malaga, &c. Nov. ,,

Resignation of the Campos ministry; Canovas del Castillo forms a cabinet . . . . 9 Dec. ,,

Attempted assassination of the king and queen by Francisco Otero y Gonzalez by shooting, 30 Dec. ,,

Promulgation of law for gradually abolishing slavery in Cuba . . . . . 18 Feb. 1880

Manifesto from 279 senators and deputies claiming liberty of religion, the press, &c., and education, universal suffrage, &c. . . . 6 April, ,,

Otero executed . . . . . . 14 April, ,,

Resignation of ministry; Sagasta forms a ministry (liberal), 8 Feb.; the chambers adjourned, 9 Feb. 1881

Calderon centenary, Madrid, begins . 23 May, ,,

Conference of advanced radicals at Biarritz to organize the party . . . . . 13 June, 1881

Permission said to be given to about 60,000 Russian Jews to come to Spain . . . . June, ,,

Don Carlos expelled from France for expressing sympathy with legitimists (goes to London) 17 July, ,,

Elections; majority for the ministry . . Aug. ,,

The cortes opened by the king . . 20 Sept. ,,

Consolidation of the National debt (60,000,000*l.*) proposed, Sept.; law published . 10 Dec. ,,

The king invested with the order of the Garter, 7 Oct. ,,

The kings of Spain and Portugal open a new railway between Madrid and Lisbon . . 8 Oct. ,,

Great agitation against the free trade policy of the minister Camacho, in Catalonia, &c. (see *Barcelona*) . . . . ,,

Treaty with France passed by the cortes (237-65), 22 April, 1882

Continued disputes with England respecting tariff, Aug. *et seq.* ,,

"Dynastic Left," a new party formed by marshal Serrano and others, constituted (dividing the liberals) . . . . 27 Oct. ,,

Gen. Maceo and five Cuban insurgent leaders surrendered at Gibraltar to the Spaniards (they had escaped from Cadiz, 20 Aug.); they petition queen Victoria to ask for their release; application made for inquiry; gen. Baynes, colonial secretary at Gibraltar, and Mr. Blair, the chief inspector of police, dismissed for exceeding their authority, announced . . . . . 4 Dec. ,,

The "Dynastic Left" in cortes pronounce in favour of advanced liberalism . . . 15 Dec. ,,

Majority for government in elections for councils general . . . . 17 Dec. ,,

Resignation of the ministry . . . . 6 Jan. 1883

New cabinet formed by Sagasta . . 8 Jan. ,,

Socialist and anarchist disturbances in Seville, &c., Feb. ,,

A secret society, entitled the "Black Hand (Mano Negra)," reported; arrests, 28 Feb.; total suppression reported . . . . 4 March, ,,

Release of two Cuban refugees; Maceo retained, March, ,,

The king and queen of Portugal at Madrid, 22 May, ,,

Temporary republican military insurrection at Badajoz, said to be planned by Ruiz Zorrilla; on the approach of troops, mutineers enter Portugal, and are disarmed . . . 4, 5, 6 Aug. ,,

Brief military outbreaks near Logroño and at Barcelona, 8 Aug.; Seo-de-Urgel . . . 9 Aug. ,,

Spain reported tranquil . . . 13 Aug. ,,

The king's military tour, Valencia, Barcelona, Saragossa, &c., well received . . 17 Aug. *et seq.* ,,

He visits Vienna, 10 Sept.; Berlin, Homburg, and Brussels . . . . . . 27 Sept. ,,

The king honourably received by president Grévy, but hissed and reviled by the Paris mob (on account of his having been made a colonel of Uhlans by the emperor William); behaved with dignity and courage . . 29, 30 Sept. 1 Oct. ,,

Resignation of Sagasta and his ministry; succeeded by Posada Herrera and others . 11-13 Oct. ,,

The crown prince of Germany arrives at Madrid, 23 Nov. ,,

Amnesty granted to insurgent soldiers announced, 27 Nov. ,,

Treaty for new commercial tariff signed . 1 Dec. ,,

The king opens the cortes, with speech promising important reforms . . . . 15 Dec. ,,

Treaty with England condemned by the council of state; free traders indignant . . . Jan. 1884

Government defeated in the cortes (221-126) 17 Jan. ,,

Ministry resigned; Canovas del Castillo (conservative) forms a ministry . . . 18 Jan. ,,

Dissolution of the cortes . . . . 31 March, ,,

Suspected military insurrection; about 25 persons arrested, about 17 March; 7 of 15 condemned; Black Hand conspirators garrotted at Xeres, 14 June; Commander Fernandez and lieut. Telles shot as rebels . . . . . . 28 June, ,,

Fall of the Alcudia railway bridge near Badajoz, great loss of life (said to be 90); believed to be due to criminal work of republicans . 26 April, ,,

New cortes (three-fourths conservative) meets, 20 May; business begun . . . . 10 June, ,,

Sir Robert Morier, British envoy, 1881; succeeded by sir Francis Clare Ford 1884
Last section of the Great Asturian railway opened by the king . . . . 15 Aug. ,,
Indiscreet speech of sen. Pidal y Mon, minister of instruction, causes revival of agitation in favour of the pope; resented by Italy; apology made . . . . Aug. Sept. ,,
Speech of professor Moraytor against clericals; university students at Madrid forbidden to attend his lectures by Sen. Pidal, resist; conflict with the police; many wounded, 20 Nov.; professors and students expelled from the university; many liberal newspapers suspended; other universities agitated . . . . Nov. ,,
Passive resistance of the students . 1 Dec. *et seq.* ,,
Much sufferings by *Earthquakes*, which see, 25-31 Dec. ,,
National subscription proclaimed by the king, 3 Jan. 1885
The king visits the afflicted districts, 11-23 Jan.; liberal subscriptions in London . 11 Jan. ,,
Protocol restoring Great Britain to position of most "favoured nation" in regard to commerce (lost since 1845); wine duties modified; signed at Madrid, 21 Dec. 1884; gazetted . 6 Feb. ,,
Commercial treaty with England ratified by the deputies, 11 March; by the senate, 28 March; by the king . . . . 1 April, ,,
Failure of the negotiations for the treaty announced, 18 May, ,,
Break out of cholera in Valencia (see *Cholera*), May, ,,
The ministers resign on account of the king's intention to visit Valencia; he gives in; they resume office . . . . . . 20, 21 June, ,,
Riots at Madrid through the Germans occupying Yap, a Caroline isle; the German legation attacked, 4, 5 Sept.; quiet restored 6 Sept; Spanish note of apology sent to Berlin about 26 Sept.; mediation of the pope accepted (see *Caroline Islands*) . . . . about 26 Sept. ,,
British legation insulted by claim of taxes, about 29, 30 Sept. ,,
Attempted military insurrection at Cartagena, 1 Nov.; suppressed . . about 4, 5 Nov. ,,
Death of king Alfonso XII., 25 Nov.; resignation of Canovas del Castillo; ministry formed by senor Sagasta . . . . . 26, 27 Nov. ,,
Death of marshal Serrano . . . . 26 Nov. ,,
Amnesty granted to press and political offenders, 10 Dec. ,,
Manifesto of the Spanish bishops to their dioceses, declaring the distinction to be observed between religion and politics, and the submission of the church to any lawful form of government, monarchical or republican . . . 6 Jan. 1886
50 soldiers at Cartagena mutiny; most escape to a ship, 10, 11 Jan.; general Fajardo wounded; dies 27 Jan.; ringleader of mutiny shot, 3 March, ,,
Suspected intrigue of Zorrilla and his followers, Jan. ,,
The duke of Seville sentenced to eight years' imprisonment, &c., for insulting, &c., the queen regent . . . . . . about 27 Feb. ,,
Assassination of the bishop of Madrid (see *Madrid*), 19 April, ,,
The commercial treaty with England (till 1892) again accepted by the cortes, May; ratified, 24 July; royal assent, 29 July; comes into operation . . . . 15 Aug. ,,
Destructive cyclone at Madrid (*which see*), 12 May, ,,
Don Carlos protests against recognition of Alphonso XIII. . . . . 20 May, ,,
Revolt of 300 of Madrid garrison under brigadier Villacampa; unsupported, quickly suppressed; three officers killed, 19 Sept.; capital punishment of insurgents commuted . . . Oct. ,,
Republican manifesto of the duke of Seville issued at Tarbes . . . . . about 30 Sept. ,,
Changes in M. Sagasta's cabinet . . 10 Oct. ,,
Solemn commemoration of the death of king Alphonso XII. . . . . . 25, 26 Nov. ,,
Attempted assassination by a Frenchman of marshal Bazaine . . . . . 18 April, 1887
The regent queen Christina visits the N. provinces; well received . . . . . . Aug. ,,
The Philippine exhibition at Madrid; the queen distributes the prizes . . . . . 17 Oct. ,,
Opening of the cortes; the infant king enthroned; speech of the queen regent; the country prosperous and quiet . . . . . 1 Dec. 1887
Sir Francis Clare Ford, British envoy, &c., nominated ambassador; received by the queen regent . . . . 21 Jan. 1888
Rioting at the Rio Tinto mines suppressed with bloodshed . . . . 4, 5 Feb. ,,
Trial by jury introduced by the senate . 27 Feb. ,,
Ruiz Zorrilla's revolutionary manifesto issued, demanding a *plébiscite* for the form of national government . . . . . . 4 March, ,,
Resignation of the ministry . . . 13 June, ,,
Senor Sagasta forms a new ministry . 14 June, ,,
Republican outbreak at Saragossa against conservatives; senor Canovas del Castillo attacked, 20 Oct.; outbreak at Seville, 7 Nov.; outbreak at Madrid . . . . 11 Nov. ,,
Resignation of the ministry, 9 Dec.; reconstituted by senor Sagasta. . . . . . 10 Dec. ,,
Amnesty to political offenders and mutinous soldiers decreed . . . . . . 23 Jan. 1889
The queen regent meets queen Victoria at San Sebastian . . . . . . 27 March, ,,
Long debate in the chamber, victory of ministers (227-65) . . . . 22 May, ,,
Trial by jury first put in force (at Madrid), 29 May, ,,
Parliamentary deadlock, the session closed by the queen regent . . . . . 2 June, ,,
Powerful speech by senor Sagasta to his supporters, 12 June; the cortes reopened . . 14 June, ,,
Victory of senor Sagasta over senor Canovas del Castillo and the combined conservatives and dissentient liberals, reported . . 14 July, ,,
Dispute with Morocco (*which see*) settled 29 Sept. ,,
The cortes opened . . . . . . 29 Oct. ,,
Death of sen. Julian Gayarré, a popular tenor singer . . . . 2 Jan. 1890
Resignation of the ministry, 3 Jan.; Senor Sagasta forms a slightly modified cabinet . 20 Jan. ,,
Illness of the king, 4 Jan.; serious, 9 Jan.; convalescent . . . . 16 Jan. ,,
Death of the duc de Montpensier, 4 Feb.; buried in the Escurial . . . . . . 7 Feb. ,,
The duke of Seville, who had escaped from prison (*see above*, 1886), pardoned by the queen regent, 27 Feb. ,,
Strike of about 40,000 workmen in Barcelona and other parts of Catalonia, chiefly for reduction of time of labour . . . . . . 30 March, ,,
Barcelona placed under martial law; the anarchists and socialists opposed by the people, 1 May *et seq.*; tranquillity restored . . 5 May *et seq.* ,,
Resignation of the Sagasta ministry . . 3 July, ,,
Sen. Antonio Canovas del Castillo (Castelár) forms a coalition ministry . . . 5 July *et seq.* ,,
Strikes of workmen in Catalonia . 15 July *et seq.* ,,
Infanta Marie Teresa, first class belted cruiser, launched at Bilbao by the queen regent 30 Aug. ,,
Choleraic disease in Valencia and other places, about 2,840 deaths . . . . May—Sept. ,,
The cortes dissolved . . . . . . 30 Dec. ,,
Death of sen. Alonzo Martinez, eminent statesman, 14 Jan. 1891
Patrocinio, the "bleeding nun," who had been banished and returned 1875, lived in retirement, and died, aged 91 . . . . . . 28 Jan. ,,
Conservative majority at the general election—of the deputies 1 Feb., of the senate . . 15 Feb. ,,
The cortes opened by the queen regent 2 March ,,
Republican disturbances at Corunna, supported by the corporation; its powers suspended, 8 Sept.; affair settled . . . . 16 Sept. ,,
Violent storms, causing great floods, especially in the province of Toledo; all the towns and villages on the banks of the Amarguillo, especially Consuegra, 30 miles S.E. of Toledo, inundated; deaths estimated at 2,000, 11, 12 Sept. *et seq.* The queen regent sends immediate relief, and orders a national subscription . 13 Sept. *et seq.* ,,
Destructive storm at Valencia; inundations at Almeria with loss of life; grape harvest destroyed, 15 Sept. ,,
Consuegra nearly destroyed, above 1,781 deaths; the minister of public works visits the place; large subscriptions for relief, 16 Sept.; railway and telegraphic communications greatly sus-

pended; the staple crops in many places almost annihilated . . . . 11 Sept. *et seq.* 1891
Spanish inundation fund started in London, about 14 Sept. ,,
Above 100,000 persons homeless through floods of the Amarguillo, Tagus, Guadalquivir, and other rivers; palaces and country houses open to receive sufferers, reported . . . 18 Sept. ,,
See *Railway accidents*, 24 Sept. 1891
Reported government financial difficulties; the queen attends a meeting of the cabinet, about 14 Nov. ,,
Resignation of the ministry, 21 Nov.; reconstituted by sen. Canovas del Castillo . 22 Nov. ,,
Decree for new loan of 250,000,000 pesetas, at 4 per cent., 18 Dec.; opened . . . . 28 Dec. ,,
Anarchist attack on Xeres suppressed with bloodshed, 9 Jan.; 4 rioters sentenced to death, others to imprisonment, 4 Feb.; executed . 10 Feb. 1892
Sir Henry Drummond Wolff succeeds sir Francis Clare Ford as British ambassador, about 15 Jan. ,,
Rupture with France through the new commercial tariff . . . . 1 Feb. ,,
Anarchist disturbances at Barcelona; evidence of plots at other places; the military employed, about 10 Feb.; 7 anarchists arrested at Reus, Catalonia. . . . . . 30 March, ,,
Alleged discovery of a plot to blow up the chamber of deputies, the palace, and other places; Jean Marie Delboche, a Frenchman, and Manuel Ferriera, a Portuguese, arrested with documents, 4 April; 13 anarchists arrested at their club, 5 April. Philip Munoz, an anarchist chief arrested, 10 April; released . . 24 April, ,,
Explosions or attempts at Barcelona and other places, arrests made . . . 16 April *et seq.* ,,
A commercial *modus vivendi* with France signed by the queen . . . . . 28 May, ,,
Celebration of the fourth centenary of the sailing of Columbus from Palos, near Huelva, 3 Aug. 1492; ships from all nations present, 3 Aug.; grand banquet at Huelva, 4 Aug.; national holiday . . . . . 12 Oct. ,,
National celebration of the discovery of America, especially at Huelva; the queen regent, the king, and foreign dignitaries present 12 Oct. *et seq.*; historical exhibition at Madrid, opened, 30 Oct. ,,
Visit of the king and queen of Portugal at Madrid, 10–17 Nov. ,,
Resignation of the minister of the interior and all the civil authorities at Madrid, 30 Nov.; reappointments made . . . . . 2 Dec. ,,
Trial of anarchists: 18 sentenced to imprisonment, 29 acquitted . . . . . 5 Dec. ,,
Resignation of sen. Canovas del Castillo, 7 Dec.; succeeded by sen. Sagasta as prime minister, 10 Dec. ,,
The chambers dissolved . . . . . 6 Jan. 1893
José Zorilla, poet and dramatist, died, aged 75, 24 Jan.; public funeral . . . 25 Jan. ,,
Elections; majority for government . 5 March, ,,
The cortes opened by the queen regent, 5 April, ,,
The government defeats the republicans in the chamber (after sitting nearly 60 hours) 12 May, ,,
Explosion at the house of sen. Canovas del Castillo; 1 man killed . . . . 20 June, ,,
Retirement of sen. Canovas del Castillo (Castelár) from political life . . about 28 July, ,,
Much suffering by intense heat and drought; Madrid, 112 deg. F. . . . . Aug. ,,
Destructive floods, with great loss of life, in the province of Toledo; villages destroyed and roads impassable . . . . about 15 Sept. ,,
Much damage in New Castile and other parts, reported . . . . . 16 Sept. ,,
Anarchist movements in Catalonia; dynamite explosions in Barcelona; Pallas, a leader, who threw a bomb amongst a group of officers, Sept.; executed . . . . 6 Oct. ,,
Fighting with the Moors at Melilla . . 2 Oct. ,,
See *Morocco*.
Depression of the finances; national subscriptions to support the war with the Moors, about 7 Nov. ,,
Disastrous explosion at Santander (*which see*), 3 Nov. ,,
Destructive bomb explosion (by anarchists) at Barcelona (*which see*) . . . 7 Nov. ,,
Close of dispute with Morocco (*which see*) . 23 Feb. 1894
Resignation of the cabinet, 8 March; re-constituted under sen. Sagasta, 12 March; meeting of the cortes; legislation against anarchism, 4 April, ,,
The marriage of don Carlos, duke of Madrid, to princess Maria Bertha of Rohan, celebrated at Prague . . . . . 28 April, ,,
Anarchists' trial and execution . April, May, ,,
See *Barcelona*.
Cortes closed by decree . . . 11 July, ,,
Señor Cabrera consecrated first bishop of the reformed church . . . . 23 Sept. ,,
See *Spanish Reformed Church*.
Resignation of sen. Sagasta and cabinet, 30 Oct.; reconstituted by him, 4 Nov. . . . . ,,
Opening of the cortes; improvement of the finances, reported . . . . 12 Nov. ,,
Introduction of the budget for 1895–96, deficit, 1 Feb. 1895
Heavy snowfall, Madrid blocked . . 4 Feb. ,,
Reina Regente cruiser, sunk during a storm between Cape Tarifa and Trafalgar; over 400 lives lost, about 10 March, ,,
The *Resumen*, Madrid newspaper, accuses military officers of want of zeal in the royal cause.
The offices of the *Resumen* and others attacked by officers and the staff ill-treated; rioting suppressed by the capt.-gen. of Madrid, 16–17 March, ,,
Debate in the cortes, which favours the officers; resignation of the Sagasta cabinet, 16–17 March, ,,
Sen. Canovas del Castillo (conservative) forms a cabinet . . . . . 23 March, ,,
Marshal Martinez Campos appointed commander in Cuba; arrives there . . . 16 April, ,,
Attempted assassination of gen. Primo de Rivera, capt.-gen. of Madrid by capt. Primitivo Clavijo, 3 June, ,,
Capt. Clavijo shot . . . . . 5 June, ,,
A vote of censure passed in the chamber on the government . . . . . . 3 June, ,,
Railway communication with France, etc., stopped by a landslip . . . . . 6 June, ,,
A loan of about 24,000,000*l.* authorized by the senate . . . . . 12 June, ,,
Ruiz Zorrilla, the republican leader, died 13 June, ,,
Count Casa Valencia appointed ambassador at London . . . . . 2 July, ,,
Spanish fleet warmly received at Cherbourg, 16 July; at Plymouth, 20–29 July; telegram of welcome from queen Victoria . . 22 July, ,,
Destructive floods in Andalusia . . Sept. ,,
Death of capt. gen. Concha, marquis de Habaña, eminent statesman, aged 87 . . . 5 Nov. ,,
Cortes dissolved . . . . . 26 Feb. 1896
Much resentment against the United States (*which see*) for the resolutions of the senate, relating to Cuba . . . . . 28 Feb. *et seq.* ,,
Duke of Tetuan appointed foreign minister, 4 March, ,,
Sen. Canovas del Castillo defends his policy, and declines American intervention . . 7 March, ,,
Rioting at Valencia, and other towns . 8 March, ,,
The chambers opened by the queen-regent, reforms in Cuba promised; increased expenditure and taxation, required . . . . . 11 May, ,,
Budget presented, large deficit for 1895–6, 20 June; ordinary budget adopted . . . 11 Aug. ,,
Reported conspiracy for the independence of Philippines, 25 arrests at Madrid . . 21 Aug. ,,
Anti-Anarchist bill adopted by the senate Aug. ,,
Railway subventions bill granting concessions to the companies till 1980 in return for a large loan, passed . . . . . . 1, 3 Sept. ,,
New loan ordered, 10 Nov.; largely taken up, 16 Nov. *et seq.* ,,
Cuban reform bill drawn up by sen. Canovas, signed by the queen-regent (see *Cuba*) . 4 Feb. 1897
Royal decree authorizing a war loan for Cuba and the Philippines . . . . . 8 May, ,,
The United States senate recognize the Cubans as belligerents, great excitement in the cortes, 21 May, ,,
Budget statement: new loan proposed 22 May, ,,
Deadlock: the Canovas ministry resigns, 2 June; but agree to remain in office . . 6 June, ,,
Sen. Canovas del Castillo assassinated at Santa Agueda, by Michele A. Golli, to avenge the Bar-

celona anarchists), 8 Aug.; state funeral at Madrid, 13 Aug.; Golli executed . 20 Aug. 1897

Gen. Azcarraga appointed premier (same policy), 9 Aug.; the cabinet resigns . . . 29 Sept. ,,

Sen. Sagasta forms a ministry . . . 4 Oct. ,,

Disastrous floods in Saragossa, 15 deaths, early Nov. ,,

Rejoicing at Madrid at the end of the rebellion in the Philippines . . . . 16 Dec. ,,

Scarcity of food in the provinces, high price of wheat, bread riots in Salamanca . 24 Feb. 1898

Special performance at the Royal theatre in aid of the national navy fund, the queen-regent present; large subscriptions; great patriotism and enthusiasm . . . . 31 March, ,,

United States proposals respecting Cuba: Spain to proclaim an armistice till Oct., to relieve the starvation and distress, and the United States to assist, 31 March; Spain agrees to an armistice if asked for by the Cubans . . . . 1 April, ,,

Mediation of the pope, 6 April; an armistice granted on the recommendation of the 6 powers, 9 April, ,,

Elections, large government majority; demonstrations for Spain and the army, in Madrid, many arrests . . . . 10 April, ,,

See *United States*, 11–13 April, 1898.

National patriotic fund for increase of the navy headed by the queen-regent, 14 April; over 22,000,000 pesetas . . . . . 22 June, ,,

The council rejects United States intervention, 14 April; note issued to the powers protesting against the resolution of U.S. congress 18 April, ,,

The *Times* correspondent requested to leave Havana . . . . 19 April, ,,

The cortes opened with a firm speech by the queen-regent, the king present; U.S. ultimatum sent, 20 April; diplomatic relations broken off; gen. Woodford leaves Madrid . . . 21 April, ,,

Spanish reserve (30,000) called out . . 22 April, ,,

Cortes united in support of the government, 25 April: Budget: surplus estimated, 506,095 pesetas . . . . 26 April, ,,

Martial law proclaimed in Madrid, city quiet, 2 May; riots at Valencia, Talavera, and elsewhere owing to the rise of bread, state of siege proclaimed, 3 May; corn duties reduced . 5 May, ,,

Riots at Murcia, the law courts pillaged and burnt, prisoners in the gaol set free, 5 May; state of siege in Catalonia, Badajos, Alicante, Lináres, and other places, with loss of life 8–10 May, ,,

War expenditure bill passed by the chamber and senate, after a hot debate . 10, 12 May, ,,

Resignation of the ministry, señ. Sagasta commissioned to reconstruct the cabinet 16 May, ,,

The senate meets, señ. Sagasta, the premier, denounces the conduct of the United States and declares that Spain will carry on the war *à outrance* till an honourable peace be obtained, 20 May, ,,

Bill passed to prevent the exportation of silver, 31 May, ,,

Bank panic, arrangements for a loan of 1,000,000,000 pesetas at 4 per cent. . . . . . 1 June, ,,

Serious mining agitation in Catalonia, over 17,000 men out of work . . . . . June, ,,

The cortes closed after an exciting debate on the political situation and the war . . 24 June, ,,

The government opens an issue of 5 per cent. treasury bonds . . . . 11 July, ,,

Decree suspending the constitutional guarantees (martial law) proclaimed . . . . 15 July, ,,

The cortes meets, 5 Sept.; peace protocol adopted, 13 Sept.; the cortes prorogued, 14 Sept. ,,

Destructive hurricane in Seville and Granada, many deaths . . . . 18 Sept. ,,

The National union formed by the middle classes, calling for financial and administrative reform, Nov. ,,

Carlist agitation in Catalonia and Bilbao, Nov.; clubs closed, some arrests . . . 19 Dec. ,,

Amnesty for press offences issued . . 6 Jan. 1899

Col. San Martin, who surrendered Puertorico to the Americans, sentenced to life imprisonment, 6 Jan. ,,

Colonial ministry abolished . . . . 7 Jan. ,,

Stormy debates in the cortes on the government policy and conduct f the late war, 20–25 Feb.; the ministry resigns . . . . . 28 Feb. ,,

New cabinet, señ. Silvela, premier and foreign minister; the cortes suspended . 5, 6 March, 1899

Army discontent; meetings held; some disorder in Madrid . . . . 6 March, ,,

The Saragossa commissioners' (chamber of commerce) proposals for political and financial reforms, &c., well received by señ. Silvela, 10 March, ,,

Peace treaty with U.S. ratified, cortes dissolved, 17 March, ,,

Election riots at Bilbao and elsewhere . 16 April, ,,

Carlist plot reported; 5 arrests, arms, &c., seized, at Barcelona . . . . . . 21 April, ,,

General elections; government majority about 40, 23 April, ,,

Financial decree against existing abuses . 14 May, ,,

Don Emilio Castelar, eminent orator, leader of the republican party, born 1832, died 25 May; public funeral in Madrid . . . . . . 29 May, ,,

The cortes opened by the queen-regent; the Carolinas, Pelews, Marianne, and Ladrones ceded to Germany for 837,500*l*., announced . 2 June, ,,

See *Storms*, 9 June, 1899.

Budget, 1899-1900: suspension of the sinking fund, reduction of interest on bonds, increased taxation proposed; 5 per cent. loan of 300,000,000 pesetas to be issued . . . . 17 June, ,,

Anti-budget riots; troops called out at Zaragoza, Valencia, and other towns; martial law proclaimed, 26, 27 June; 1 death; debate in the chamber, 28 June; further rioting, see *Barcelona* and *Badalona*, 4 deaths, reported . 1 July, ,,

The queen-regent gives up another 2,000,000 pesetas of her civil list . . . . . 13 July, ,,

Bill for reorganising internal debts passed by the chamber . . . . 28 July, ,,

Decree calling out 60,000 men for the army, signed, Aug. ,,

Catholic congress at Burgos; many divisions; recent prescriptions of the Vatican resisted, 4 Sept. ,,

Regionalism, a desire for more self-government, active in Catalonia and other provinces, reported, Sept. ,,

Martial law decreed throughout Vizcaya, due to increase of *Separatism* . . . 13 Sept. ,,

Card. Cascajares and the bps. issue a statement demanding Catholic ascendancy in education and civil affairs . . . . 18 Sept. ,,

Clearance of goods through the customs stopped to non-payers of the new industrial tax at Barcelona . . . . Sept. ,,

Adm. Montojo, who surrendered to the Americans at Cavite, dismissed from the service by court-martial . . . . 22 Sept. ,,

Strike riots at the naval arsenal at Ferrol; town in a state of siege . . . . . 23 Sept. ,,

Ministerial crisis regarding military expenditure; gen. Polavieja resigns; succeeded by gen. Azcarraga . . . . 30 Sept. ,,

Anti-taxation riots at Barcelona, 13 Oct.; state of siege proclaimed; press censorship . 17 Oct. ,,

Negotiations with trade guilds, Nov.; state of siege raised, but the "suspension of guarantees" still in force . . . . . . 22 Dec. ,,

Mass meetings of the "National Union" organised by the Spanish chambers of commerce; wholesale reforms demanded . . . . 14 Jan. 1900

Conversion of debt bill signed by the queen-regent, 26 March, ,,

Cabinet reconstructed; señ. Silvela, premier and minister of marine; marquis of Aguilar Campo, foreign minister . . . . 18 April, ,,

Martial law proclaimed in Barcelona and Valencia, 11 May, ,,

New consolidation loan subscribed for 25½ times over, announced . . . . . . 6 June, ,,

Royal decree suspending constitutional guarantees in Madrid province; city quiet . 21 June, ,,

Sir H. Mortimer Durand appointed ambassador at Madrid . . . . 7 Aug. ,,

Death of marshal Martinez de Campos, aged 66, 23 Sept. ,,

Gen. Weyler appointed capt.-gen. of Madrid; señ. Silvela, premier, resigns, 21 Oct.; gen. Azcarraga forms a cabinet . . . . 22 Oct. ,,

Carlist rising near Barcelona; fatal rioting at Badalona, 28 Oct.; the movement repudiated by don Carlos; many arrests in Madrid . 2 Nov. 1900
The Cagayan and Sibutu islands ceded to the U.S. for 100,000 dols.; convention signed at Washington . . . . 7 Nov. ,,
Budget, 7,930,230 pesetas surplus for 1900, 22 Nov. ,,
Mercedes, princess of the Asturias, married to prince Carlos of Bourbon, son of the count de Caserta, at Madrid . . . . . 14 Feb. 1901
Anti-Jesuit rioting (due to a law case) in Madrid, spreads to other towns; monasteries, &c., attacked, 7–13 Feb.; the case is decided against the Jesuits . . . . . . 19 Feb. ,,
Cabinet resigns, 26 Feb.; señ. Sagasta forms one; gen. Weyler (war), duke of Almodovar (foreign), señ. Moret (interior) . . 6 March, ,,
Rioting against the octroi duties in Madrid; strike riots in Barcelona and elsewhere, 10–18 March, ,,
Anti-clerical demonstrations in Barcelona, Valencia, and other places . . . 31 March–April, ,,
Cortes dissolved . . . . . 24 April, ,,
Elections: 238 ministerialists, 163 of the opposition, returned . . . . . 19 May, ,,
Fatal strike riots in La Coruña . . . 31 May, ,,
Elections of senators . . . . . 2 June, ,,
The cortes opened; proposed reform of monetary circulation . . . . . 11 June, ,,
Anti-clerical riots at Zaragoza . . 17, 18 July, ,,
Convents and churches closed and guarded, 19 July, ,,
Cortes suspended . . . . . . 22 July, ,,
Decree ordering the registration of religious associations, issued . . . . . 19 Sept. ,,
Students' riots frequent in Madrid and Barcelona, 19–22 Nov. ,,
Budget: revenue, 974,000,000 pesetas; expenditure, 971,000,000 pesetas; passed . . 31 Dec. ,,
General strike in Barcelona and neighbouring towns; conflicts with troops; over 40 deaths; bill suspending the constitutional guarantees passed by the senate; martial law proclaimed in Zaragoza and Tarragona . . 17–20 Feb. 1902
Bill for the reconstruction of the Bank of Spain fails; the ministry resigns . . 13 March, ,,
Arbitration treaties signed between Spain and Spanish America . . . . March, ,,
Señ. Sagasta reconstructs the cabinet . 18 March, ,,
Bank of Spain bill passed by the chamber, 197—32, 28 April, ,,
The queen-regent, after over 16 years' noble constitutional rule, bids farewell to her ministers, 12 May (her letter published 18 May) . . . ,,
Protest of don Carlos against the king's accession, published . . . . . . 13 May, ,,
Alfonso XIII. enthroned as a constitutional ruler in Madrid . . . . . . 17 May, ,,
Anarchist plot discovered; 6 arrested . 17 May, ,,
The king reviews the troops; opens an exhibition of national portraits, 19, 20 May; present with the duke of Connaught and other foreign princes at a state bull-fight . . . . 21 May, ,,
Señ. Canalejas (agriculture) and other ministers later resign . . . . . 27 May, ,,
Cortes suspended by royal decree . 30 May, ,,
Labour troubles; rioting at Badajoz; martial law, 1 June, ,,
Total religious communities in Spain, 2,586 for women, with 40,188 members; 529 for men, with 10,745 members; announced . 20 June, ,,
New 5 p.c. loan of 338,400,000 pesetas, issued, 5 June; well taken up, 16 times over . 23 June, ,,
Decree for the regulation of non-official instruction signed by the king . . . 1 July, ,,
New bank law passed, May; convention signed by contracting parties for the loan . 16 July, ,,
Mine explosion at Camargo; 14 deaths, 5 houses destroyed; reported . . . . 7 Aug. ,,
The king visits Santander and San Sebastian, &c., 8–14 Aug. ,,
Cabinet crisis: señ. Sagasta forms a ministry 11–14 Nov. ,,
Arrests of Carlists at Barcelona . . 17 Nov. ,,
Señ. Sagasta resigns on a hostile division in the chamber . . . . . . 2 Dec. ,,
Señ. Silvela, conservative, forms a cabinet; señ. Abarzuza (foreign), señ. Villaverde (finance), señ. Maura (interior), gen. Linares (war) . 6 Dec. 1902
Cortes suspended by decree . . . 9 Dec. ,,
Señ. Sagasta, liberal leader, died, aged 75, 5 Jan.; public funeral . . . . . 7 Jan. 1903
The duke of Sotomayor shot at by a delusionist in Madrid . . . . . . 10 Jan. ,,
Budget (1904): 31,656,729 pesetas (estimated) surplus, announced . . . . . 28 Jan. ,,
Strikes in Barcelona begin 30 Dec., and Reus, Feb. ,,
Duke of Tetuan, ex-minister (foreign), dies, 9 Feb. ,,
Fatal rioting at Bilbao between a religious procession and an anti-clerical crowd; 1 killed, 47 injured . . . . 11 Oct. ,,
Great strike of 40,000 miners and others at Bilbao; dynamite and other outrages, several killed, many injured; state of siege proclaimed, mid Oct. ,,
Banquet in honour of the adm. and officers of H.M. battleship *Prince George* given by Spanish authorities at Ferrol . . . . . 21 Oct. ,,

See *Spanish-American war*.

Sovereigns of Spain.

Gothic Sovereigns.

411. Ataulfo; murdered by his soldiers
415. Sigerico; reigned a few days only.
,, Valia, or Wallia.
420. Theodoric I.; killed in a battle, which he gained, against Attila.
451. Thorismund, or Torrismund; assassinated.
452. Theodoric II.; assassinated.
466. Euric, the first monarch of all Spain.
483. Alaric II.; killed in battle.
506. Gesalric; his bastard son.
511. Amalric, or Amalaric; legitimate son of Alaric.
531. Theudis, or Theodat; assassinated by a madman.
548. Theudisela, or Theodisele; murdered.
549. Agila; taken prisoner, and put to death.
554. Atanagildo.
567. Liuva, or Levua I.
568. Leuvigildo; associated on the throne with Liuva, in 568; and sole king in 572.
586. Recaredo I.
601. Liuva II.; assassinated.
603. Vitericus; also murdered.
610. Gundemar.
612. Sisibut, or Sisebuth, or Sisebert.
621. Recaredo II.
,, Suintila; dethroned.
631. Sisenando.
636. Chintella.
640. Tulga, or Tulca.
642. Cindasuinto; died in 652.
649. Recesuinto; associated; in 653 became sole king.
672. Vamba, or Wamba; dethroned, and died in a monastery.
680. Ervigius, or Ervigio.
687. Egica, or Egiza.
698. Vitiza, or Witiza, associated; in 701 sole king.
711. Rodrigo, or Roderic; slain in battle.

[Six independent Suevic kings reigned 409-469; and Two Vandalic kings: Gunderic, 409-425; his successor Genseric with his whole nation passed over to Africa.]

Mahometan Spain.

Cordova.

Emirs. The *first*, Abdelasis; the *last*, Yussuf-el-Tehri: A.D. 714-755.

Kings. The *first*, Abderahman I.; the *last*, Abu Ali; 755-1238.

Granada.

Kings. The *first*, Mohammed I.; the *last*, Abdalla; 1238-1492.

Christian Spain.

Kings of Asturias and Leon.

718. Pelagius, or Pelayo; overthrew the Moors, and checked their conquests.
737. Favila; killed in hunting.
739. Alfonso the Catholic.
757. Froila; murdered his brother Samaran, in revenge for which he was murdered by his brother, and successor,

768. Aurelius or Aurelio.
774. Mauregato, the Usurper.
788. Veremundo (Bermuda) I.
791. Alfonso II., the Chaste.
842. Ramiro I.: he put 70,000 Saracens to the sword in one battle. *Rabbe.*
850. Ordoño II.
866. Alfonso III., surnamed the Great; relinquished his crown to his son,
910. Garcias.
914. Ordoño II.
923. Froila II.
925. Alfonso IV., the Monk; abdicated.
930. Ramiro II., killed in battle.
950. Ordoño III.
955. Ordoño IV.
956. Sancho I., the Fat; poisoned with an apple.
967. Ramiro III.
983. Veremundo II. (Bermuda), the Gouty.
999. Alfonso V.; killed in a siege.
1027. Veremundo III. (Bermuda); killed.

KINGS OF NAVARRE.

873. Sancho Iñigo. *Count.*
885. Garcia I., king.
905. Sancho Garcias; a renowned warrior.
924. Garcias II., surnamed the Trembler
970. Sancho II., surnamed the Great (king of Castile through his wife).
1035. Garcias III.
1054. Sancho III.
1076. Sancho IV., Ramirez, king of Aragon.
1094. Peter of Aragon.
1104. Alfonso I., of Aragon.
1134. Garcias IV., Ramirez.
1150. Sancho V., surnamed the Wise.
1194. Sancho VI., surnamed the Infirm
1234. Theobald I., count of Champagne
1253. Theobald II.
1270. Henry Crassus.
1274. Joanna; married to Philip the Fair of France, 1285.
1305. Louis Hutin, of France.
1316. John; lived but a few days.
,, Philip V., the Long, of France.
1322. Charles I., the IV. of France.
1328. Joanna II., and Philip, count d'Evreux.
1343. Joanna alone.
1349. Charles II., or the Bad.
1387. Charles III., or the Noble.
1425. Blanche and her husband John II., afterwards king of Aragon.
1479. Eleanor.
,, Francis Phœbus de Foix.
1483. Catherine and John d'Albret.
1512. Navarre conquered by Ferdinand the Catholic, and united with Castile.

KINGS OF LEON AND CASTILE.

1035. Ferdinand the Great.
1065. Sancho II., the Strong, son of Ferdinand; Alfonso in Leon and Asturias, and Garcias in Galicia.
1072. Alfonso VI., the Valiant, king of Leon.
1109. Uraca and Alfonso VII.
1126. Alfonso VII., Raymond.
1157. Sancho III., surnamed the Beloved.
1158. Alfonso VIII., the Noble.
[Leon is separated from Castile under Ferdinand II., 1157-88.]
1188. Alfonso IX., of Leon.
1214. Henry I.
1217. Ferdinand III., the Saint and the Holy. By him Leon and Castile were permanently united.
1252. Alfonso X., the Wise (the Alphonsine Tables were drawn up under his direction).
1284. Sancho IV., the Great and the Brave.
1295. Ferdinand IV.
1312. Alfonso XI.
1350. Peter the Cruel: deposed; reinstated by Edward the Black Prince of England; slain by his natural brother and successor,
1369. Henry II., the Gracious; poisoned by a monk.
1379. John I.: he united Biscay to Castile.
1390. Henry III., the Sickly.
1406. John II., son of Henry.
1454. Henry IV., the Impotent.
1474. Isabella, sister (had married Ferdinand of Aragon, 18 Oct. 1469).
1504. Joanna (daughter of Ferdinand and Isabella) and Philip I. of Austria. On her mother's death Joanna succeeded, jointly with her husband Philip; but Philip dying in 1506, and Joanna becoming imbecile, her father Ferdinand continued the reign; and thus perpetuated the union of Castile with Aragon.

KINGS OF ARAGON.

1035. Ramiro I.
1065. Sancho Ramirez (IV. of Navarre).
1094. Peter of Navarre.
1104. Alfonso I., the Warrior, king of Navarre.
1134. Ramiro II., the Monk.
1137. Petronilla, and Raymond, count of Barcelona.
1163. Alfonso II.
1196. Peter II.
1213. James I.; succeeded by his son,
1276. Peter III.; conquered *Sicily* (*which see*) in 1282.
1285. Alfonso III., the Beneficent.
1291. James II., surnamed the Just.
1327. Alfonso IV.
1336. Peter IV., the Ceremonious.
1387. John I.
1395. Martin.
1410. [Interregnum.]
1412. Ferdinand the Just, king of Sicily.
1416. Alfonso V., the Wise.
1458. John II., king of Navarre, brother of Alfons ; died 1479.
1479. Ferdinand II., the Catholic, the next heir; by marriage with Isabella of Castile (*styled the Catholic kings*), the kingdoms were united.

SPAIN.

1512. Ferdinand V. (of Castile), the Catholic; having conquered Granada and Navarre, became king of all Spain.
1516. Charles I., grandson, son of Joanna of Castile and Philip of Austria (emperor of Germany, as Charles V., in 1519); resigned both crowns, and retired to a monastery.
1556. Philip II., son, king of Naples and Sicily; a merciless bigot; married Mary of Portugal, 1543, Mary of England, 1554, and Isabella of France, 1559.
1598. Philip III., son, drove the Moors from Granada and the adjacent provinces.
1621. Philip IV., son: wars with the Dutch and French; lost Portugal in 1640.
1565. Charles II., son; last of the Austrian line; nominated, by will, as his successor,
1700. Philip V., duke of Anjou, grandson of Louis XIV. of France: hence arose the "war of the Succession," terminated by the treaty of Utrecht in 1713; resigned.
1724. Louis I., son; reigned only a few months.
,, Philip V. again.
1746 Ferdinand VI., the Wise, son; liberal and beneficent.
1759. Charles III., brother, king of the Two Sicilies, which he gave to his third son, Ferdinand.
1788. Charles IV., son; the influence of Godoy, prince of the peace, reached to almost royal authority in this reign; Charles abdicated in favour of his son in 1808, and died in 1819.
1808. Ferdinand VII., whom Napoleon of France also forced to resign.
,, Joseph Bonaparte, brother of Napoleon; forced to abdicate.
1813. Ferdinand VII. restored; married Maria Christina of Naples, 11 Dec. 1829; died 29 Sept. 1833; succeeded by
1833. Isabella II., daughter (born, 10 Oct. 1830); declared of age, 8 Nov. 1843; married her cousin, don Francis d'Assisi, 10 Oct. 1846 (born 13 May, 1822; died 17 April, 1902); deposed 30 Sept. 1868; separated from her husband, March, 1870; and abdicated, 25 June, 1870, in favour of her son, Alfonso, prince of Asturias (born, 28 Nov. 1857). Visits queen Victoria at Windsor, 20 May; leaves England 29 May, 1890.
1870. Amadeo I. (duke of Aosta, son of Victor-Emanuel II. king of Italy); born, 30 May, 1845; married Maria Victoria of Pozzo della Cisterna, 30 May, 1867; accepted the crown offered him by the cortes, 4 Dec. 1870; abdicated 11 Feb. 1873; died 18 Jan. 1890.

REPUBLIC founded, 11 Feb. 1873. Very unsettled, 1873-4.

KINGS.

1874. Alfonso XII., son of Isabella II. (born 28 Nov. 1857); proclaimed 30 Dec. 1874; married 1st, his cousin Mercedes, daughter of the duc de Montpensier (born 24 June, 1860), 23 Jan. 1878; she died 26 June, 1878; 2nd, archduchess Maria Christina of Austria (born 21 July, 1858), 29 Nov. 1879. He died 25 Nov. 1885.

1885. Maria *Mercedes* Isabella (princess of Asturias), born 11 Sept. 1880; replaced by her brother; married prince Carlos of Bourbon (born 1870), 14 Feb. 1901; son, Alfonso, born 30 Nov. 1901.

1886. Alphonso (Leon, &c.) XIII., born 17 May; formally enthroned 17 May, 1902.

CARLIST LEGITIMIST PRETENDERS.

(See above 1833 *et seq.*)

Carlos V., brother of Ferdinand VII., born 29 March, 1788; died, 10 March, 1855.

Carlos VI., his son (conde de Montemolin), died 14 Jan. 1861.

Carlos VII. (son of don Juan, brother of Carlos VI., who renounced his right, 8 Jan. 1863); born, 30 March, 1848; see above 1873-6.

SPALATO (Dalmatia), the ancient Spalatum and Salona. At his palace here, Diocletian spent his last nine years, and died July, 313. R. Adam published the "Antiquities of Diocletian's Palace," 1764.

SPANISH AMERICA, ARMADA, &c., see *America*, *Armada*, and *Eras*.

SPANISH-AMERICAN WAR, see *Spain* and *United States*, April, 1898.

The *Buenaventura* and the *Pedro*, Spanish ships, captured by the *New York*, U.S. flagship, and the *Nashville*, cruiser . . . . . . 22 April, 1898

CUBA, blockade of Havana and other ports, also San Juan in Puertorico, by rear-adm. Sampson, with the N. Atlantic squadron . 22 April, *et seq.* ,,

6 Spanish vessels captured . . 23, 24 April, ,,

Spanish circular to the powers accusing the United States of aggression . . . . . 25 April, ,,

Lieut. A. S. Rowan lands on the S.E. coast of Cuba to arrange co-operation with the insurgents about . . . . . . 26 April, ,,

Matanzas bombarded, batteries destroyed by adm. Sampson; the *Guido*, Spanish steamer, captured, 27 April, ,,

The *Argonauta*, mail steamer, with 10 Spanish officers and soldiers, captured by the *Nashville*, off Cuba . . . . 29 April, ,,

Rear-adm. Sampson bombards San Juan, Puertorico, forts, &c., destroyed . . . 12 May, ,,

American attempts to land at Cabañas, Cardenas and Cienfuegos repulsed; forts destroyed by the U.S. gunboats . . . . . . 12 May, ,,

Santiago forts bombarded by 3 U.S. warships, 18 May; Spanish squadron under adm. Cervera arrives, 19 May; U.S. ships withdraw; frequent skirmishes; conflicting reports: bombardment of forts by U.S. ships checked by Spanish warships, 31 May; the U.S. *Florida* lands 400 Cubans, with stores and ammunition, on the N. coast of Santiago . . . . . . about 31 May, ,,

The U.S. collier, *Merrimac*, sunk at night in the harbour channel of Santiago, to block the Spanish squadron in the harbour, through the heroism of lieut. R. P. Hobson and 7 men; they were afterwards taken up by a Spanish ship, and made prisoners, 3 June (prisoners exchanged, 7 July); an American force lands, and joins insurgents in an attack on forts . . 6 June, ,,

Bombardment of Puertorico by the U.S. squadron, 10 Spaniards killed, reported, 6 June; Guantanamo bay taken by rear-adm. Sampson, 7 June; American force, under lieut.-col. Huntingdon, occupies Guantanamo, earthworks, &c. destroyed; the U.S. flag hoisted, 10 June; adm. Sampson with 8 ships bombards Santiago; sharp fighting, the Spaniards repulsed, 11 June; Caimanera shelled by U.S. squadron . . . . . 15 June, ,,

Santiago bombarded, forts dismantled; Americans repulsed on attempting to land at Punta Cabrera, W. of Santiago, by col. Aldea's column, 16 June; again driven back with loss by Spanish infantry at Cabañas . . . . 17 June, 1898

Major-gen. Shafter arrives with 47 U.S. ships and troops, S.E. of Santiago, 21 June; 6,000 troops successfully landed at Baiquiri, under the direction of adm. Sampson, gen. Shafter, and gen. Lawton; the country for 6 miles occupied by the Americans, with little or no resistance, 9 A.M., 22 June—1 A.M. . . . . . . 23 June, ,,

Advance of American troops under gen. Lawton, 24 June; a severe engagement fought near Santiago between about 1,000 Americans, under gen. Wheeler, col. Wood, and gen. Young, and 2,000 Spaniards, under gen. Linares and gen. Rubin; Spaniards driven back from Sevilla, to the city; capt. Capron, serg. H. Fish, Mr. Edw. Marshall, newspaper correspondent, and about 34 others killed; Spanish loss 265 . 24 June, ,,

Sharp engagement between 2,000 Cubans, under Castillo, and the Spaniards at Guasima . 24 June, ,,

Calixto Garcia, with 5,000 Cubans, joins the Americans at Juragua . . . . 26 June, ,,

Extension of the blockade by U.S. ships 28 June, ,,

Gen. Shafter begins the attack on Santiago, 8 A.M. 1 July; El Caney and El Paso captured by the Americans; gen. Linares severely wounded, gives up the command to gen. Toral; San Juan captured by the Americans, the Spaniards retreat to Santiago . . . . . . 2 July, ,,

Adm. Cervera's squadron (ordered to sea by the Madrid government) leaves Santiago harbour, and is destroyed by adm. Sampson's squadron (one ship only surrendered); Spanish loss about 600; adm. Cervera wounded, and 692 Spaniards taken prisoners . . 3 July, ,,

Santiago summoned to surrender, 4 July; armistice, till 9 July; gen. Toral's offer of honourable surrender declined; American reinforcements land to co-operate with Garcia, 10 July; bombardment resumed, and the line of investment extended, 9 A.M. till about noon; gen. Shafter sends a flag of truce, again demanding the unconditional surrender of the city; negotiations; gen. Miles arrives off Santiago; truce extended till 16 July . . . . . . 11 July, ,,

Alfonso XII., warship, attempting to escape from Havana, destroyed near Mariel . . 5 July, ,,

The abp. of Santiago appeals to Madrid, advising the surrender of the city; the government determines on stubborn resistance . 5 July, ,,

Yellow fever (mild type) appears among the American troops; several deaths; Siboney, a suburb, ordered to be burnt for sanitary reasons, by gen. Miles; 18,000 refugees starving; reported . . . . 13 July, ,,

Surrender of Santiago and province, successfully concluded, 16 July; Santiago evacuated by the Spanish troops, 20,000 surrender, the U.S. flag hoisted noon . . . . 17 July, ,,

Pres. McKinley issues instructions for the government, &c. of the province of Santiago . 19 July, ,,

Guantanamo and Caimamera surrender, 18, 19 July, ,,

Naval engagement off Manzanillo, 3 Spanish merchantmen and 5 gunboats destroyed, about 100 Spaniards killed . . . . . 18 July, ,,

Surrender of Spanish troops at San Luis and Dos Palmas . . . . 22 July, ,,

Expedition to Nipe successful, the Spanish cruiser, *Jorge Juan*, destroyed, reported . . 22 July, ,,

Jibara surrendered to the insurgents; Tunas and Zaza besieged by the Americans; reported, 24 July, ,,

Condition of Santiago improving . . 25 July, ,,

Gen. Miles lands at Guanica, Puertorico 25 July, ,,

Castillo appointed military governor . 26 July, ,,

PHILIPPINES.—The *Saranga*, U.S. sailer, captured by a Spanish gunboat off Manila, about 27 April,

Battle of Manila: the Spanish squadron, 11 ships, under adm. Montojo, attacked and destroyed by the American fleet, 9 ships, under commodore Dewey; don Luis Cadarso, capt. of the *Reina Christina*, the chaplain, and about 400 Spaniards killed; Spanish ships inefficient, none surrendered, great bravery shown by the Spaniards under unequal conditions; no American loss;

Cavite bombarded, and fortifications destroyed; blockade of Manila . . . 1 May *et seq.* 1898
Memorial from the British residents at Manila to rear-adm. Dewey, pointing out their critical position, the population starving . . 10 May, ,,
Spanish gunboat, *Leyte*, captured off Iloilo, reported, 30 May; Spanish position at Manila desperate, the city surrounded by insurgents, Aguinaldo, their leader, brought back from Hong Kong, and supplied with arms, &c., by the Americans; he captures the province of Cavite; night and day fighting, Spanish outposts driven in; their 3,000 prisoners well treated by the rebels; great scarcity of food, and suffering amongst the Spanish soldiers, 31 May–4 June; Gen. Augustin, the capt.-gen., appeals to Madrid for help, holds a council of war; proposes surrender, and resigns to the general, second in command, 5 June; the whole archipelago in revolt, except the Visayas isles; concerted attack by insurgents on all sides; Aguinaldo issues a proclamation, independence of the Philippines, &c., declared at Cavite; 4,000 Spaniards and 1,000 natives prisoners . . . . . 12 June, ,,
Three days' fierce fighting at Bulacan, north of Manila, 500 Spaniards surrendered; rebel attack at Marabon, which was captured, reported, 17 June, ,,
The Ladrone islands seized by U.S. *Charleston*, the governor, officers and men surrender, 20 June; U.S. sovereignty over the isles proclaimed, 22 June; the *Charleston* arrives at Manila, 30 June, ,,
Gen. Peña, with 1,000 soldiers, surrenders, reported . . . . 28 June, ,,
The *Bohul*, Spanish sailing ship, captured in Kayabas bay; the province of Bulacan occupied and the governor captured by the insurgents, reported . . . . 1 July, ,,
Gen. Monet, with 1,000 men, at Bulacan, made prisoners by the insurgents, reported 10 July, ,,
Spanish squadron under adm. Camara prohibited from coaling at Port Said by the Egyptian government; called on to leave the harbour, 30 June; ordered to quit Suez, 6 July; leaves, 11 July, ,,
Aguinaldo proclaims the Philippine republic, provisional government established . 3–8 July, ,,
Gen. Augustin's sortie from Manila repulsed with loss, reported . . . . . . 5 July, ,,
The island taken, no resistance offered . 7 July, ,,
The gov. gen. issues a proclamation promising autonomy, &c., reported . . . 9 July, ,,
Heavy fighting round Malate . . 15–17 July, ,,
Provisional native government, Aguinaldo president, formed at Bacolor, reported . 21 July, ,,
Insurgents twice repulsed with loss (500) at Manila, reported . . . . 23 July ,,
Spain sues for peace . . . . 26 July, ,,
Gen. Shafter's army leaving Santiago . Aug. ,,
Desultory fighting; famine and disease reported Aug. ,,
Gen. Augustin retires . . . . . . 5 Aug. ,,
Protocol; terms: Spain to evacuate Cuba, and to cede to United States Puertorico, her islands in the Antilles and one of the Ladrones; United States to hold Manila temporarily; Cuban rule to be established later; signed by Mr. Day and M. Cambon . . . . 12 Aug. ,,
Manila surrenders . . . . 13 Aug. ,,
Gen. Blanco resigns . . . . . . 15 Aug. ,,
Conference at Paris . . . . . . 7 Oct. ,,
Desultory fighting; anarchy in the Southern isles, reported . . . . 20 Oct. ,,
Spanish evacuation of Puertorico completed, 24 Oct. ,,
Spain abandons Cuba, the Philippines, and other islands for an indemnity of 20,000,000 dols., 28 Nov.; treaty signed 10 Dec., ratified 6 Feb. 1899.
American loss in the war 336 men killed, 125 mortally wounded, 5,277 died of disease, 1 May, 1898–18 Feb. 1899.
Spanish loss, 80,000; the majority dying from disease, reported . . . . . . 25 Jan. 1899
General Chaffee appointed military, and judge Taft civil governor of the Philippines; local government established in 765 towns, reorganisation of judicial administration, and a native police force established in 1901
Inquiries by a court-martial into the charges brought by maj. Gardener against the military administration of the islands, with allegations of cruelty to the natives and the burning of their houses by American officers . . 25 April, 1902
[Gen. Smith was admonished, and subsequently retired from the U.S. army.]
Cost of operations in the Philippines to June 1902, 170,326,586 dols.
Philippines civil government bill passes house of representatives . . . . . . 27 June, ,,
Amnesty to all political prisoners, including Aguinaldo, proclaimed . . . . 4 July, ,,
Import duties on goods to U.S. from Philippines reduced from 75 to 25 per cent. by bill passed by house of representatives . . . 10 Dec. ,,
Further fighting at Cus and Surigao, March; insurgents routed with loss near Mariguina, reported, 27 March, ,,
Gen. Miles's report confirming some American cruelties during the war, published . 27 April, ,,
A stronghold captured, 100 natives killed, reported 10 April; 10 forts captured, heavy loss of enemy, reported . . . . 7 May, ,,
Continuance of agricultural and commercial depression, reported . . . . . . 8 Aug. ,,

SPANISH EXHIBITION of Arts and Industries, Earl's Court, West Brompton, London, W., chairman, the duke of Wellington, a grandee of Spain.

The exhibition, although unfinished, was informally opened with a fine display of pictures, 1 June, 1889
In July, 1889, it included representations of the Alhambra, Madrid market-place, cosmorama of a journey through Spain, a Spanish band and strolling players, &c., closed . . 31 Oct. ,,

SPANISH GRANDEES, the higher nobility, at one time almost equal to the kings of Castile and Aragon, and often setting their authority at defiance, were restrained on the union of the crowns by the marriage of Ferdinand and Isabella in 1474, who compelled several to relinquish the royal fortresses and domains which they held. Charles V. reduced the grandees to sixteen families (Medina-Sidonia, Albuquerque, &c.), dividing them into three classes.

SPANISH LANGUAGE (Lengua Castellana), is a dialect of Latin largely intermingled with Arabic, which was the legal language till the 14th century. Spanish did not become general till the 16th century. See *Drama*.

EMINENT SPANISH AUTHORS.

	Born	*Died*
Garcilasso de la Vega	1503	1536
Boscan	1496	1543
Jorge de Montemayor	1520	1562
Las Casas	1474	1566
Ercilla	1533	1595
Cervantes (author of Don Quixote)	1547	1616
Mariana	1536	1623
Herrera	1565	1625
Gongora	1561	1627
Alarcon y Mendoza		1634
Lope de Vega	1568	1635
Quevedo	1570	1647
Gabriel Tellez	1585	1648
Calderon	1601	1682
Solis	1610	1686
Feyjos	1701	1765
Yriarte	1750	1798
Leandro F. Moratin	1760	1828
José de Larra	1809	1837
Manuel Breton de los Herreros	1796	1873
José Zorilla	1818	1893
Antonio Canovas del Castillo	1830	1897
Ramon de Campoamor	1818	1901

SPANISH REFORMED CHURCH, constituted at Gibraltar, 25 April, 1868. By permission of general Prim its missionaries entered Spain soon after the revolution, in Sept. following.

15 congregations with about 2,500 members; at Madrid, Seville, and other places.
The consecration of a church at Madrid by lord Plunket, archbishop of Dublin, proposed but strenuously opposed by the authorities; he licenses the building and departs, Dec. 1892; permission granted under conditions, 3 Jan. 1893; the church opened . . . . 18 March, 1893
The church and senor Cabrera, the first bishop of the reformed church, consecrated by the archbishop of Dublin and the bishops of Clogher and Down . . . . 23 Sept. 1894

SPANISH SUCCESSION AND MARRIAGES, see *Spain*, 1700, and 10 Oct. 1846.

SPARTA, the capital of Laconia (Greek, Laconica), or Lacedæmon, the most considerable republic of the Peloponnesus, and the rival of Athens. Though without walls, it resisted the attacks of its enemies by the valour of its citizens for eight centuries. Lelex is supposed to have been the first king. From Lacedæmon the fourth king, and his wife Sparta, who are also spoken of as the founders of the city, it obtained names. The Lacedæmonians were a nation of soldiers, and cultivated neither the arts, sciences, commerce, nor agriculture. The early history is traditional and the dates conjectural.

Sparta founded. *Pausanias*. . . . B.C. 1490
Tyndarus marries Leda: Helen born 1388
Helen stolen by Theseus, king of Athens, but recovered by her brothers 1228
The princes of Greece demand Helen in marriage; she makes choice of Menelaus of Mycenæ . . 1216
Paris, son of Priam, king of Troy, carries off Helen 1204
The Trojan war 1194
After a war of ten years, and a disastrous voyage of nearly eight, Menelaus and Helen return to Sparta 1176
The kingdom seized by the Heraclidæ 1104
Establishment of two kings, Eurysthenes and Procles, by their father Aristodemus . . . 1100
Rule of Lycurgus, who establishes the senate, and enacts a code of laws. *Eusebius*. (Mythical) 884-850
Charilaus declares war against Polymnestor, king of Arcadia 848
Alcamenes, known by his apophthegms, makes war upon the Messenians 813
Nicander succeeds his father, Charilaus; war with the Argives 800
Theopompus introduces the Ephori . . about 757
War declared against the Messenians, and Amphia taken 743
The progeny of the Partheniæ, the sons of Virgins . 733
Battle of Ithome; Messenians beaten 730
Ithome taken; the Messenians become vassals to Sparta, and the war of nineteen years ends . . 724
Conspiracy of the Partheniæ with the Helots to take Sparta 707
The Partheniæ colonise Tarentum 706
The Messenians revolt, and league with Elis, Argos, and Arcadia, against the Lacedæmonians. [This war lasted fourteen years.] 685
Carnian festivals instituted 675
The Messenians settle in Sicily 669
War with the Argives, and celebrated battle between 300 select heroes of each nation . . 547
War with Athens 505
The Spartans resist the king of Persia . . . 491
The states of Greece unite against the Persians . . 482
Leonidas, at the head of 300 Spartans, withstands the Persian arms at the defile of Thermopylæ (see *Thermopylæ*) 480
Persians defeated by Pausanias, king of Sparta, at Platæa 479
He is put to death for treason; the Grecian armies choose an Athenian general 472
An earthquake at Sparta destroys 30,000 persons; rebellion of the Helots 466
Sparta joins Macedon against Athens . . . 454
Beginning of the Peloponnesus war 431
Platæa taken by the Spartans . . . . B.C. 428
The Spartans, under Agis, enter Attica, and lay waste the country 426
Agis (king 427) gains a great victory over the Argives and the Mantinæans 418
The Lacedæmonian fleet, under Mindarus, defeated at Cyzicum, and Mindarus slain . . . 410
The Spartans, defeated by land and at sea, sue for peace, which is denied by the Athenians . . 409
Reign of Pausanias 408
The Athenians defeated at Ægospotami by Lysander 405
Athens taken by him; end of Peloponnesian war . 404
Agesilaus (king 398) enters Lydia 396
The Athenians, Thebans, Argives, and Corinthians enter into a league against the Spartans, which begins the Corinthian war 395
Agesilaus defeats the allies at Coronea . . . 394
The Lacedæmonian fleet, under Lysander, defeated by Conon, the Athenian commander, near Cnidos; Lysander killed in an engagement . . . ,,
Peace of Antalcidas 387
The Thebans drive the Spartans from Cadmea . 378
The Spartans lose the dominion of the seas; their fleet totally destroyed by Timotheus . . . 376
The Spartans defeated at Leuctra 371
Epaminondas, heading 50,000 Thebans, appears before Sparta 369
Battle of Mantinea; the Thebans victors 27 June, 362
Philip of Macedon overcomes Sparta 344
Pyrrhus defeated before Sparta 294
Agis IV. endeavours to revive laws of Lycurgus . 244
Leonidas II. vacates the throne, and flies . . 243
Recalled: becomes sole sovereign; Agis killed . 241
Reign of Cleomenes III., the son of Leonidas . . 236
He re-establishes most of the laws of Lycurgus . 225
Antigonus defeats Cleomenes, and enters Sparta . 222
Cleomenes retires to Egypt . . . . . . ,,
The Spartans murder the Ephori 221
Machanidas ascends the throne, and abolishes the Ephori 210
He is defeated and slain by Philopœmen, prætor of the Achæan league 207
Cruel government of Nabis . . . . . . ,,
The Romans besiege Sparta; Nabis sues for peace 197
The Ætolians seize Sparta: Nabis assassinated . 192
The laws of Lycurgus abolished 188
Sparta, under the protection or rather subjugation of Rome, retains its authority for a short time . 147
Taken by Alaric . . . . A.D. 396
Taken by Mahomet II. 1460
Burnt by Sigismund Malatesta 1463
Rebuilt as Misitra; it is now called Sparta, and is part of the kingdom of Greece.
Ancient buildings discovered here during excavations by Dr. Waldstein . . . . March, 1892

SPARTACUS'S INSURRECTION (or Servile War). Spartacus was a noble Thracian, who served in an auxiliary corps of the Roman army. Having deserted and been apprehended, he was reduced to slavery and made a gladiator. With some companions he made his escape, collected a body of slaves and gladiators, 73 B.C.; ravaged southern Italy; and defeated the Roman forces under the consuls sent against him. Knowing the impossibility of successfully resisting the republic, he endeavoured to conduct his forces into Sicily, but was defeated and slain by Crassus, 71 B.C.

"SPASMODIC SCHOOL" of poetry, a name sarcastically given to Philip James Bailey ("Festus," 1839), Alex. Smith, Sydney Dobell (died in Aug. 1874), and others (precursors of Morris, Algernon Swinburne, and Rossetti, sarcastically termed the "fleshly school"), ridiculed by professor Aytoun in his "Firmilian," published 1854.

SPEAKERS OF THE HOUSE OF COMMONS. Peter de Montford, afterwards killed at the battle of Evesham, was the first speaker, 45 Hen. III., 1260; sir Thos. Hungerford is said to have been the first named "Speaker," 1372; but sir Peter de la Mare is supposed to have been the first regular speaker, 50 Edw. III., 1376. The king refused his assent to the choice of sir Edward Seymour, as speaker, 6 March, 1678; and serjeant William Gregory was chosen in his room. Sir John Trevor was expelled the chair and the house for taking a gratuity after the act for the benefit of orphans had passed, 12 March, 1694-5; a deputy speaker was appointed Aug. 1853.

RECENT SPEAKERS.

1789. Henry Addington (aft. viscount Sidmouth), 5 June.
1801. Sir John Mitford (aft. baron Redesdale), 15 Feb.
1802. Charles Abbot (aft. lord Colchester), 10 Feb.
1817. Charles Manners Sutton (afterwards viscount Canterbury), 2 June.
1835. James Abercromby (afterwards baron Dunfermline), 19 Feb.
1839. Charles Shaw Lefevre (afterwards viscount Eversley), 27 May.
1857. John Evelyn Denison, 30 April (afterwards viscount Ossington).
1872. Sir Henry Wm. Bouverie Brand (afterwards viscount Hampden), 9 Feb.-25 Feb. 1884.
1884. Arthur Wellesley Peel, 26 Feb.; resigned, 9 April; created viscount Peel, 1895.
1895. William Court Gully, 10 April; re-elected, 12 Aug.

The Speaker, a weekly liberal (Gladstonian) newspaper, edited by Mr. T. Wemyss Reid, first appeared 4 Jan. 1890.

SPEAKER'S COMMENTARY, a name given to an edition of the Bible with a revised text and a commentary by several bishops and other theologians, edited by F. C. Cook. The undertaking originated, it is said, chiefly with Mr. John Evelyn Denison, speaker of the house of commons, with the view of opposing the interpretations of Dr. Colenso, and was announced in Nov. 1863. The publication, begun in 1871, was completed in 1881. The Apocrypha published in 1888.

SPEAKING-TRUMPET, used by ships at sea. One is said to have been used by Alexander, 335 B.C. One was constructed from Kircher's description by Saland, 1652; philosophically explained and brought into notice by Morland, 1670.

SPECIAL COMMISSION ACT, passed 13 Aug. 1888. A commission constituted to try certain charges and allegations against certain members of parliament. See *Parnellites* and *Ireland*, 1888.

SPECIAL CONSTABLES are sworn in for the preservation of the public peace when disturbances are feared. The laws relative to their appointment were amended in 1831 and 1835. Louis Napoleon, afterwards emperor, aided as a special constable in London, 10 April, 1848; see *Chartists* and *London*, Dec. 1867. Instructions for their organisation were issued, 13 Jan. 1868. On 28 Jan. 52,974 in the metropolis, and 113,674 in the United Kingdom, had been sworn in. Their services were not required, and they were honourably dismissed by an order issued 31 March, 1868.

Special constables were sworn in in relation to the disturbances in Trafalgar-square (see *Riots*) 17 Nov. *et seq.*; 1,500 held Trafalgar-square, Sunday, 20 Nov. 1887; served till 18 Jan. 1888, and thanked.

SPECIES. Much controversy among naturalists arose in consequence of the publication, in 1859, of Mr. Charles Darwin's "Origin of Species," in which he suggests that all the various species of animals were not created at one time, but have been gradually developed by what he terms "natural selection," and the struggle for life in which the strong overcome the weak.

"This preservation of favourable individual differences and variations, and the destruction of those which are injurious, I have called *natural selection*, or the survival of the fittest."—*Darwin*.

The idea was put forth by Lamarck in his "*Philosophie Zoologique*," 1809. Similar views appear in the "Vestiges of Creation," 1844. Mr. Darwin says that he infers "from analogy that probably all the organic beings which have ever lived on the earth have descended from some one primordial form, into which life was first breathed by the Creator." See *Development* and *Evolution*.

Charles Darwin was born 12 Feb. 1809; and died 19 April, 1882.

Statue of Darwin by J. E. Boehm, paid for by universal subscription, received at the British Museum of Natural History by the prince of Wales, and uncovered by professor Huxley, 9 June, 1885.

His Life and Letters, edited by his son Francis Darwin, published Nov. 1887.

Professor G. J. Romanes' elaborate work, "Darwin and after Darwin," was published in 1892.

SPECIFIC GRAVITIES. See under *Weights*.

SPECTACLES, unknown to the ancients, are generally supposed to have been invented by Alexander de Spina, a monk of Florence, in Italy, about 1285. According to Dr. Plott, they were invented by Roger Bacon, about 1280. Manni attributes them to Salvino, who died 1317. On his tomb at Florence is the inscription, "Qui giace Salvino degli Armati, inventore degli occhiali: Dio gli perdoni le peccata" ("Here lies Salvino degli Armati, inventor of spectacles: May God pardon his sins").

SPECTATOR. The first number of this periodical appeared on 1 March, 1711; the last was No. 635, 20 Dec. 1714. The papers by Addison have one of the letters C L I O at the end. The most of the other papers are by sir Richard Steele, a few by Hughes, Budgell, Eusden, Miss Shephard, and others.—The *Spectator* newspaper (philosophical, whig), begun 5 July, 1828. Mr. Richard Holt Hutton, an able scholar, was editor from 1861 for 40 years, he died 9 Sept. 1897.

SPECTRUM, the term given to the image of the sun or any other luminous body formed on a wall or screen, by a beam of light received through a small hole or slit, and refracted by a prism. The colours thus produced are red, orange, yellow, green, blue, indigo, and violet. The phenomena were first explained by Newton, whose "Optics" was published in 1704. Several of these colours are considered to be compounds of three primary ones: by Mayer (1775), red, yellow, and blue;—by Dr. Thos. Young (1801), red, green, and violet;—by Prof. Clerk Maxwell (1860), red, green, and blue. As the colour of a flame varies according to the substance producing it or introduced into it, so the spectrum varies. This led to the invention of a method of chemical analysis by professors Bunsen and Kirchhoff (1860), by which they discovered two new metals, and drew conclusions as to the nature of the atmosphere of the sun and stars, and of the light of the nebulæ, by comparing the spectrum with that produced by flames into which iron, sodium, and other substances have been introduced. For the invisible rays of the spectrum, see *Calorescence*, *Fluorescence*, *Bolometer*, and *Röntgen Rays*.

Fraunhofer's Lines. In 1802 Dr. Wollaston observed several dark lines in the solar spectrum; in 1815 Joseph Fraunhofer not only observed them, but constructed a map of them, giving 590 lines or dark bands. By the researches of Brewster and others the number observed is now above 2000.

Mr. Fox Talbot observed the orange line of strontium in the spectrum in 1826; and sir David Brewster observed other lines, 1833-42-3. In 1862-3 Mr. William Huggins analysed the light of the fixed stars and of the nebulæ; and in 1865 Dr. Bence Jones, by means of spectrum analyses, detected the presence of minute quantities of metals in the living body, introduced only a few minutes previously.

A spectroscopic society in Italy published a journal early in 1872.

H. Schellen's "Spectralanalyse" published 1870; new edition 1883.

Sir H. Roscoe's "Spectrum Analysis" published 1867-85.

Lecoq de Boisbaudran's "Spectres Lumineux" . 1874

Oxygen detected in the solar spectrum by Mr. Draper 1877

The experiments of professor Dewar and others have shown that the spectra of various gases are affected by temperature and pressure, 1888-9.

"The Michelson-Echelon spectroscope, by prof. Michelson and Mr. A. Hilger. See *Nature*, 27 April, 1899.

Spectrum of radium investigated, 1903.

SPECULATIVE SOCIETY, Edinburgh (which had included among its members David Hume), celebrated its hundredth anniversary on 14 Oct. 1863; see *Philosophy*.

"SPELLING-BEES," meetings to test the proficiency in correct spelling; introduced into London from the United States of America; the first at Holloway, London, N., in the autumn of 1875. Geographical, musical, and other bees followed, and all soon ceased.

SPELLING REFORM. A resolution in favour of it was adopted by the London School Board, in 1877; a conference and public meeting were held at the Society of Arts, 29 May, 1877.

A Spelling Reform Association formed: Dr Temple, bishop of Exeter (archbp. of Canterbury), Robert Lowe, E. B. Tylor, and Max Müller were among the members, 1879; another association formed in the United States; professor F. A. March, president 1887

Mr. T. B. Sprague's article on a Marriage and Mortality Table, in the Journal of the Institute of Actuaries, is printed according to phonetic spelling July, 1879

SPHERES. The celestial and terrestrial spheres and sun-dials are said to have been invented by Anaximander, 552 B.C.; and the armillary sphere by Eratosthenes, about 225 B.C. The planetarium was constructed by Archimedes before 212 B.C. Pythagoras maintained that the motions of the twelve spheres must produce delightful sounds, inaudible to mortals, which he called the music of the spheres.

SPHYGMOGRAPH (from the Greek, *sphygmos*, a pulsation), an instrument for investigating disease, by showing the state of the pulse, invented by M. E. J. Marey, of Paris, and described by him in 1863.

SPICES. Imported into Great Britain: cinnamon and other spices, exclusive of pepper; 1846, 1,910,584 lbs.; 1856, 4,154,167 lbs.; 1867, 12,831,953 lbs.; 1877, 17,186,572 lbs.; 1879, 19,340,817 lbs.; 1883, 24,344,895 lbs.; 1887, 23,783,960 lbs.; 1890, 23,508,493 lbs.; 1902, 27,000,290 lbs.

SPICHEREN, see *Saarbruck*.

SPINET, a clavichord or keyed instrument, used in the 17th century, a modification of the virginals, *which see*. Bull, Gibbons, Purcell, and especially Domenico Scarlatti composed for this instrument.

SPINNING was ascribed by the ancients to Minerva, the goddess of wisdom. Arcas, king of Arcadia, taught his subjects the art about 1500 B.C. Tradition reports that Lucretia with her maids was found spinning, when her husband Collatinus paid a visit to her from the camp, that the wife of Tarquin was an excellent spinner, and that a garment made by her, worn by Servius Tullius, was preserved in the temple of Fortune. Till 1767, the spinning of cotton was performed by the hand spinning-wheel, when Hargreaves, an ingenious mechanic, near Blackburn, made a spinning jenny, with eight spindles, and also erected the first carding machine, with cylinders. Arkwright's machine for spinning by water was an extension of the principle of Hargreaves; but he also applied a large and small roller to expand the thread, for which he took out a patent in 1769. At first he worked his machinery by horses; but in 1771 he built a mill on the stream of the Derwent, at Cromford. In 1774-9, Crompton invented the mule (*which see*).

SPINTHARISCOPE, a contrivance for showing the scintillations of radium nitrate, exhibited at Royal Society soirée, May 15, 1903.

SPIRES (in Bavaria). The emperors held many diets at Spires since 1309, and it was the seat of the imperial chamber till 1689, when the city was burned by the French, and not rebuilt till after the peace of Ryswick, in 1697. The diet to condemn the reformers was held at Spires, called there by the emperor Charles V. 1529; see *Protestants*.

SPIRIT-LEVEL. The invention is ascribed to J. Melchisedec Thevenot, who died 1692.

SPIRIT-MOTOR, Mr. Yarrow explained to the Institute of Naval Architects his method of employing vaporised spirit instead of steam in the propulsion of steam launches, thus dispensing with the use of a boiler, &c., March, 1888. Petroleum is used as fuel in some locomotives on the Great Eastern railway, and petrol as the generating power for driving motor-cars.

SPIRITS, see *Distillation*. In all nations spirituous liquors have been considered as a proper subject of heavy taxation for the support of the state; the duty imposed on spirits in 1746 led to much smuggling, *which see*; see *Alcohol, Brandy, Rum, Methylated Spirits, Whisky*, &c.

In 1840 England made about ten millions of gallons of spirits, Scotland about seven millions of gallons, and Ireland about nine millions of gallons.

In 1851 the number of gallons on which duty was paid for home consumption was 23,976,596. The total amount paid was 6,017,218*l*., of which 3,758,186*l*. were paid by England, 1,252,297*l*. by Scotland, and 1,006,735*l*. by Ireland.

The total duty on home consumption paid in 1853 was 6,760,422*l*.

In 1858, 9,195,154*l*. were paid as duty on 27,370,934 gallons.

In 1855, *methylated* spirits of wine, for use in the arts and sciences, were made duty free.

In 1859, 27,657,721 gallons of spirits were distilled in the United Kingdom. The uniform duty of 8*s*. per gallon was paid on 24,254,403 gallons for home consumption, producing 9,701,764*l*. In the year 1865-6 the tax produced about 13,955,000*l*., being the largest sum then ever raised by indirect taxation. In 1871-2, 16,798,344*l*. (customs and excise); in 1875-6, 21,295,663*l*; in 1877-8, 20,675,928*l*.; in 1883-4, 18,435,957*l*.; in 1887-8, 17,312,550*l*.; in 1888-9, 17,175,797*l*.; in 1889-90, 18,531,277*l*.; in 1890-1, 19,263,541*l*.

In 1861 an act was passed repealing wholly or in part 26 previous acts, and embodying all regulations for the guidance of manufacturers and dealers in spirits.

In 1870, about 89,000,000*l.* spent in spirits; 58,000,000*l.* by working classes.

Proof spirits distilled in the United Kingdom in 1873, 36,479,648 gallons (England, 9,531,058; Scotland, 16,421,701; Ireland, 10,526,889) in 1874, 35,352,232 gallons; duty paid, 10*s.* a gallon.

Exported from the United Kingdom: 1876, 1,308,456 gallons; 1880, 2,060,193; 1885, 2,760,041; 1889, 3,431,320; 1890, 3,658,658; 1893, 3,407,282; 1896 4,678,862; 1900, 5,721,434.

Additional duty of 6*d.* per gallon on spirits imposed, 17 April, 1890; addition of 6*d.*, June, 1894.

SPIRITS ACT (43 & 44 Vict. c. 24), passed 26 Aug., 1880, consolidated and amended the law relating to the manufacture and sale of spirits.

SPIRITUAL COMBATANTS (Dukhobortsy). A Russian communistic religious sect formed by a quaker missionary near the end of the last century, now settled in the Caucasus, about 20,000 members. Its leading tenet, the refusal of all military service, so important in a country like Russia, has led to its repression and severe punishment. The sect also opposes legal tribunals, oaths, &c. Peter Veriguin, their energetic leader, was exiled to Siberia, 1894–5; count Leo Tolstoi gave a description of the sect and its sufferings, *Times*, 23 Oct. 1895. Continued prosecution of the sect, Oct. 1896. 1,129 exiles land at Larnaka, Cyprus, under British protection, 30 Aug. 1898; the climate being unsuitable about 7,000 leave for Manitoba, Canada, 1898–9; count Tolstoi gives 5,000 dols. for their relief, Dec. 1899; deeming it wrong to keep animals in servitude, they turn their horses, cows, &c., adrift, Aug. 1902; their petition for land to live in under no authority than that of God, refused by the British Columbian Government, 23 Oct. 1902; they leave their homes to Christianize the world, about 28 Oct.; great suffering and distress; their march stopped at Minnedosa by mounted police; all sent back by special trains to their homes, 9–12 Nov. 1902.

SPIRITUALISM or SPIRIT-RAPPING. Spiritual manifestations (so called) began, it is said, in America about 1848, and attracted attention in this country about 1851, in the shape of rapping table-turning, &c. Many inquisitive or credulous persons visited Mr. Daniel Dunglas Hume or Home and Mr. Forster, noted "spiritual mediums." Mr. Home, secretary of the Spiritual Athenæum, Sloane-street, Chelsea, published, in 1863, "Incidents of my Life," in which he states that the only benefit he derived from the "gift" was the convincing many unbelievers of the certainty of a life to come; the *Trials*, April, May, 1868. The "Spiritual Magazine" began Jan. 1860; the "Spiritualist," 9 Nov. 1869. The London Dialectical society published a report on spiritualism in Nov. 1871. Mr. (afterwards sir) Wm. Crookes, in 1871, investigated the phenomena, and ascribed them to "psychic force" ("Quarterly Journal of Science," July and Oct. 1871). Miss Kate Fox, said to be the earliest American medium (about 1852) was married to Mr. H. D. Jencken, in London, Dec. 1872. London Spiritualistic Alliance founded, 1884, incorporated 1896; publishes *Light*, started in 1881. The first president of the Alliance and editor of *Light* was Mr. W. Stainton-Moses; president and editor (1903), Mr. E. Dawson Rogers. In connection with the Alliance is an extensive library of works on physic science.

The impostures of the Davenport bros. exposed in 1865.

In 1874 Messrs. Maskelyne and Cooke, and Dr. Lynn, exhibited tricks by which they said they demonstrated the imposture of spiritualism.

Spiritualism discussed by a section of the British Association at Glasgow (supported by Messrs. Wm. Crookes, A. Russel Wallace, and other eminent men), without result, 12 Sept. 1876.

20 spiritualist journals publishing, 1876.

Dr. Henry Slade, a medium, and Geoffrey Simmons, his assistant, charged at Bow-street by prof. E. Ray Lankester and others, with "unlawfully using certain subtle and crafty means and devices to deceive"; dealt with under Vagrant Act; 2, 10, 20 Oct.; Simmons discharged, Slade sentenced to 3 months' imprisonment with hard labour, 31 Oct. 1876; sentence quashed for a technical error, 29 Jan. 1877.

Wm. Lawrence sentenced to 3 months' imprisonment for receiving money as a "medium," 16 Jan. 1877.

International congress of spiritualists, Mr. E. Dawson Rogers president, at St. James's hall, 21 June *et seq.* 1898.

See *Trials*, 1881.

SPITALFIELDS (East London), so named from the priory of St. Mary Spittle, founded by Walter Brune and his wife Rosia, 1197; dissolved 1534. Here the French protestant refugees, after the revocation of the Edict of Nantes, settled and established the silk manufacture in 1685. In consequence of commercial changes the weavers endured much distress about 1829. Great poverty in 1898.

SPITHEAD, a roadstead near the Spit, a sandbank between Portsmouth and the Isle of Wight. See *Naval Reviews*, under *Navy of England*. Here in 1797 the sailors of the channel fleet mutinied for higher pay.

SPITZBERGEN, an archipelago in the Arctic ocean, discovered in 1553 by sir Hugh Willoughby, who called it Greenland, supposing it to be a part of the western continent. In 1595 it was visited by Barents and Cornelius, two Dutchmen, who pretended to be the original discoverers, and called it Spitzbergen, or sharp mountains, from the many sharp pointed and rocky mountains with which it abounds; see *Phipps*.

A scientific expedition to Spitzbergen organized by Herr Stänglin of Stuttgart, left Bremen about 29 July; returned . . . . 26 Aug. 1891

An expedition under sir Martin Conway, Mr. Trevor-Battye and others arrives at Advent Bay, 20 June; crosses from west to east, reaching Agardh bay, 17 July, 1896; Hornsund Tind ascended, 17 Aug.; arrives at Hammerfest, 18 Aug. 1896; another expedition . . . . June, 1897

"The First Crossing of Spitzbergen," by sir W. M. Conway and others published, 1897.

Russo-Swedish scientific expedition arrives at Horn Sound, reported . . . . . . 2 Aug. 1899

SPITZCAP, see *Majuba*.

SPITZER COLLECTION, formed by Frederick Spitzer, a Jew, consisted chiefly of articles of *vertu* connected with the Middle Ages and Renaissance with some antiques but no paintings. It included metal work, *faïence*, and majolica ware, arms and jewelry. He built an hotel at Paris to receive them, and died in 1890, aged about 75. The collection, valued at about 500,000*l.*, was sold for about 400,000*l.*, 17 April—17 June, 1893.

SPONGE, the name applied to a class of animals, *porifera*, intermediate between the *protozoa* and *cœlenterata*. Sponges are in general composed of an internal supporting framework of horny fibres interlaced with calcareous or siliceous spires (spicula) covered with a soft gelatinous substance, called sarcode. Their food consists chiefly of microscopic organisms contained in the water which constantly circulates through the minute pores of the sponge, and finds its outlet by the larger apical openings. Sponges exist in a variety of forms; one is the beautiful Venus's flower-basket. Several species of sponges are used for economic purposes; two species are chiefly brought from the Levant, and one of a coarser kind from the W. Indies and Florida. They are also artificially cultivated in the Adriatic by planting cuttings in waters favourable to their growth. A considerable trade is carried on in sponges, about 600 boats and some 5,000 men being employed in the Levant, and a similar number in the W. Indian trade, to the annual value respectively of 100,000*l.* and 70,000*l.* In addition to its domestic and economic uses, sponges are employed in surgery, and burnt sponge was formerly used as a specific for scrofulous diseases and goitre; iodine and bromine (which gave it its therapeutic value) are now administered in other ways.

SPONTANEOUS COMBUSTION of the human body, declared by most chemists to be impossible, although some cases have been recorded. The case of the countess of Görlitz, 1847, disproved by confession of her murderer, March, 1850.

SPONTANEOUS GENERATION. The origin of the germs of infusorial animalcules developed during putrefaction, &c., has been warmly debated by naturalists. Spallanzani (about 1766), and especially M. Pasteur and others, assert that these germs are really endowed with organic life existing in the atmosphere. Needham (about 1747), and especially M. Pouchet and his friends in our day, assert that these germs are spontaneously formed out of organic molecules.—Pouchet's "*Hétérogénie*" appeared in 1859. Bastian's "Beginnings of Life," 1872. The researches of professor Tyndall, supporting Pasteur, and opposing Bastian, were published 1876-8. The late professor Huxley, in his presidential address to the British Association at Liverpool, 1870, affirmed that the doctrine of *biogenesis* (that life proceeds only from life) "was victorious all along the line" (see his article in *Nineteenth Century*, Jan. 1878).

"Spontaneous generation" (also termed *generatio æquivoca, epigenesis,* and *abiogenesis*) has been still further disproved by the laborious microscopic investigations of Dr. W. H. Dallinger, 1875-8. He found germs to stand a much greater heat than perfect organisms.

SPORTING NEWSPAPERS: Bell's Life in London, began 1820; Sporting Life, 16 March, 1859; Sporting Gazette, 1862; Sporting Times, 1865; Sportsman, Aug. 1865; The Field, 1853; Illustrated Sporting and Dramatic News, 1874; Referee, 1877.

SPORTS. The *first* "Book of Sports," under the title of "The King's Majestie's Declaration to his Subjects concerning Lawful Sports to be used" on Sundays after evening prayers, was published by king James I., 24 May, 1618. The *second* "Book of Sports," with a ratification by his majesty Charles I., is dated 18 Oct. 1633. On the publication of the first "Book of Sports," there arose a long and violent controversy among English divines on certain points; see *Sabbatarians*, *Sunday*, &c.—The book was ordered to be burnt by the hangman, and the sports were suppressed by the parliament. The sportsman's annual exhibition, at the Agricultural Hall, London, began in 1882. The "*Sporting League*" established to maintain British sports in opposition to the Anti-Gambling league, first meeting in London, earl of Coventry in the chair, 19 Dec., 1894. "The Encyclopædia of Sport," edited by the earl of Suffolk and others, Part I. published Feb. 1897. "The Sportman's Library" (Arnold), edited by sir Herbert Maxwell, 1899 *et seq.* See *Badminton Library*.

SPOTTSYLVANIA (Virginia), see *United States*, May, 1864.

SPRINGFIELD (Missouri), near which was fought the desperate battle of Wilson's Creek, in which the federals had the advantage over the confederates, but lost their brave general, Nathaniel Lyon, 10 Aug. 1861.

SPURS. Anciently the difference between the knight and esquire was that the knight wore gilt spurs (*eques auratus*), and the esquire silver ones. Two sorts of spurs seem to have been in use at the time of the Conquest, one called a pryck, having only a single point, the other a number of points of considerable size. Spurs nearly of the present kind came into use about 1400; see *Plating*.

SPURS, BATTLE OF. Henry VIII. of England, the emperor Maximilian, and the Swiss, in 1513, entered into an offensive alliance against France. Henry VIII. landed at Calais in the month of July, and soon formed an army of 30,000 men. He was joined by the emperor with a good corps of horse and some foot, the emperor as a *mercenary* to the king of England, who allowed him a hundred ducats a day for his table! They invested Teroüenne with an army of 50,000 men; and the duc de Longueville, marching to its relief, was signally defeated on the 16th of August, at Guinegate. This battle was popularly called the battle of *Spurs*, because the French used their *spurs* more than their *swords*. The name was really obtained from the village of Spours near which it was fought. *Lodge*. The English king laid siege to Tournay, which submitted in a few days. *Hénault*. See *Courtrai*, for another "battle of spurs."

S. S., see *Collar*.

STABAT MATER, a Latin hymn, by Jacopone, 14th century, sung during Passion week in Catholic churches. Rossini's music to this hymn (1842) is often performed.

STADE DUES. At a castle near the town of Stade, in Hanover, certain dues on goods were charged by the Hanoverian government. The British government settled these dues in 1844. They were resisted by the Americans in 1855, and were abolished in June, 1861. Great Britain paid 160,000*l.* as her share of the compensation (3,000,000*l.*).

STADION, see *Athens* and *Olympic Games*.

STADTHOLDER, see *Holland*.

STAFFA, a small uninhabited island in the Hebrides, 6 miles distant from Iona, celebrated for its caves and the columnar basalt cliffs. Here is the famous *Fingal's Cave*, the sides of which are formed of basaltic columns, while from the roof, 66 feet in height, hang clusters of short columns, whitened with calcareous stalactite. The cave is 227 ft. in length and 42 ft. wide at the entrance.

STAFF COLLEGE (Sandhurst), for providing an education to qualify military officers for the duties of the staff. The foundation stone was laid by the duke of Cambridge on 14 Dec. 1859.

STAFFORD, Staffordshire, a municipal and parliamentary borough, returning, since 1885, one

M.P. A castle was erected here by Ethelfleda, countess of Mercia, 913; taken by the parliamentarian forces in 1643, it was demolished; a new castle, not completed, built by sir G. Jerningham, 1810-15. A charter was granted by king John, 1207, and the grammar-school was rebuilt and endowed by Edward VI., 1550. The two old churches of St. Mary and St. Chad are of interest. Isaac Walton was baptised in the former. Principal industries are boot and shoe manufacture and brewing. Population, 1881, 19,977; 1891, 20,270; 1901, 20,894. Fire at the workhouse infirmary, 7 deaths, 16 May, 1901.

STAGE COACHES, so called from the stages or inns at which the coaches stopped to refresh and change horses. *Bailey*. The stage-coach duty act passed in 1785. These coaches were made subject to salutary provisions for the safety of passengers, in 1810; to mileage duties, 1815. The acts were consolidated in 1832, and amended in 1833 and 1842. See *Mail Coaches*, &c.

STAGYRITE, properly Stagirite, see *Aristotelian*.

STAMFORD BRIDGE (York). In 1066 Tostig, brother of Harold II., rebelled against his brother, and joined the invading army of Harold Hardrada, king of Norway. They defeated the northern earls and took York, but were defeated at Stamford-bridge by Harold, 25 Sept., and were both slain. The loss by this victory no doubt led to his defeat at Hastings, 14 Oct. following. The claim of Mr. William Grey for the *earldom of Stamford*, was granted by the house of Lords, 3 May, 1892.

STAMP-DUTIES. By 22 & 23 Charles II. (1670-1) duties were imposed on certain legal documents. In 1694 a duty was imposed upon paper, vellum, and parchment. The stamp-duty on newspapers was commenced in 1711, and every year added to the list of articles upon which stamp-duty was made payable.

Stamp act, which ordered a stamp to be affixed to all legal documents, in the colonies, and thereby to assist the revenue of Great Britain was passed, 22 March, 1765. It excited great opposition in N. America, with rioting, and consequently was repealed, 21 Feb. 1766. The resistance of the colonists to taxation, without representation in parliament, led to the American war, 1775–83.

Stamp duties in Ireland commenced 1774

Stamps on notes and bills of exchange in . . 1782

The stamp-duties produced in England, in 1800, a revenue of 3,126,535*l*.

Many alterations made in 1853 and 1857. In June, 1855, the stamp-duty on newspapers as such was totally abolished; the stamp on them being henceforth for postal purposes.

In July and Aug. 1854, 19,115,000 newspaper stamps were issued; in the same months, 1855, only 6,870,000.

Drafts on bankers to be stamped 1858

Additional stamp duties were enacted in 1860 (on leases, bills of exchange, dock warrants, extracts from registers of births, &c.); in 1861 (on leases, licences to house-agents, &c.).

tamp-duties reduced in 1864, 1865.

All fees payable in the superior courts of law, after 31 Dec. 1865, are to be collected by stamps, by an act passed in June, 1865. Also in Public Record office 1868

144,623,014 inland revenue penny stamps sold, besides other stamps 1869

By the Stamp acts, 10 Aug. 1870, newspaper stamps were abolished after . . . . . 1 Oct. 1870

New stamp duties imposed; came into effect 1 Jan., 1871

1*d*. receipt and postage stamps used for each other after . . . . 1 June, 1881

Stamp-duties imposed on foreign or colonial share certificates, bonds, &c. by Customs Act, 1888.

A new consolidating act relating to stamps passed, 21 July, 1891

Certain exemptions made by the Finance Act, 31 July, 1894

The changes are noticed in the Finance Act passed annually.

AMOUNT OF STAMP DUTIES RECEIVED IN THE UNITED KINGDOM.

Year	Amount	Year	Amount
1840	£6,726,817	1888	£13,056,950
1845	7,710,683	1889	12,270,000
1850	6,558,332	1890	13,060,000
1855	6,805,605	1891	13,413,831
1860 (to 31 Mar.)	8,040,091	1892	13,730,184
1865	9,542,645	1893	13,788,383
1870	9,288,553	1894	12,783,633
1876	11,023,374	1895	14,440,000
1880	11,306,914	1896	7,350,000
1881	11,933,114	1897	7,350,000
1882	12,348,175	1898	7,650,000
1883*	11,691,025	1899	7,630,000
1884	11,681,431	1900	8,500,000
1885	11,886,185	1901	7,825,000
1886	11,600,614	1902	7,800,000
1887	11,780,333	1903	8,200,000

STANDARD for gold and silver in England fixed by law, 1300. Standard gold is 22 parts out of 24 of pure gold, the other two parts or carats being silver or copper. The standard of silver is 11 oz. 2 dwts. of fine silver alloyed with 18 dwts. of copper, or 37 parts out of 40 pure silver, and three parts copper. In 1300 these 12 oz. of silver were coined into 20 shillings; in 1412 they were coined into 30 shillings; and in 1527 into 45 shillings. In 1545 Henry VIII. coined 6 oz. of silver and 6 oz. of alloy into 48 shillings; and the next year he coined 4 oz. of silver and 8 oz. of alloy into the same sum. Elizabeth, in 1560, restored the old standard in 60 shillings; and in 1601 in 62 shillings. The average proportions of silver to gold at the royal mint are 15½ to 1. The standard of plate and silver manufactures was affirmed, 6 Geo. I. 1719 *et seq.*; see *Gold*, *Goldsmiths*, *Silver*, *Coinage*, and *Currency*.

STANDARD, BATTLE OF THE, see *Northallerton*.

STANDARD MEASURES. In the reign of Edgar a law was made to prevent frauds arising from the diversity of measures, and for the establishment of a legal standard measure to be used in every part of his dominions. The standard vessels made by order of the king were deposited in the city of Winchester, and hence originated the well-known term of "Winchester measure" of the time of Henry VII. (1487). The bushel so made is still preserved in the museum of that city. Henry I. also, to prevent frauds in the measurement of cloth, ordered a standard yard of the length of his own arm to be made and deposited at Winchester, with the standard measures of king Edgar. The Guildhall contains the standard measures of succeeding sovereigns. *Camden*.—The standard weights and measures were settled by parliament in 1824. The pound troy was to be 5760 grains, and the pound avoirdupois 7000 grains. The "Standard yard of 1760," in the custody of the clerk of the house of commons, was declared to be the Imperial Standard yard and the unit of measures of extension. This standard having been destroyed by the fire in 1834, a new commission was appointed to reconstruct it, and researches for this purpose, in conformity with the act, which directed the comparison of the standard with a

* Fee and patent stamps now omitted.

pendulum vibrating seconds of time in the latitude of London, were begun by Francis Baily (died in 1844), continued by the rev. R. Sheepshanks till his death in 1855, and completed by G. B. Airy, astronomer royal. In 1855 was passed "an act for legalising and preserving the lost standards of weights and measures." The parliamentary copies of the standard pound and yard are deposited at the Royal Observatory, Greenwich. The standard weights and measures act was passed Aug. 1866. The Standard Commission published reports, 1866 *et seq.*

The old standard yard and other measures and weights, supposed to have been burnt at the fire of the parliament houses in 1834, were discovered by Mr. Bull's agents in the Journal Office, where they had been deposited and left unnoticed, July, 1891. The rude standards of the reign of Henry VII. and Elizabeth are still in existence.

"STANDARD," 1*d.* conservative newspaper; begun, morning, 1827; evening, 29 June, 1857. It is the semi-official organ of the conservative party, and its church news, foreign intelligence, and articles on commerce are leading features of the paper.

STANDARDS, see *Banners*, *Flags*, &c. The practice in the army of using a cross on standards and shields is due to the asserted miraculous appearance of a cross to Constantine, previously to his battle with Maxentius; Eusebius says that he received this statement from the emperor himself, 312. The standard was named LABARUM. For the celebrated French standard, see *Auriflamme*.—STANDARD OF MAHOMET; on this ensign no infidel dared look. Christians have been massacred by the Turkish populace for looking on it.—The British IMPERIAL STANDARD was first hoisted on the Tower of London, and on Bedford Tower, Dublin, and displayed by the Foot Guards, on the union of the kingdoms, 1 Jan. 1801.

STANFORD COURT, Worcestershire, the ancient mansion of sir Francis Winnington, burnt 5-7 Dec. 1882; valuable portraits, books, MSS. &c., destroyed.

STANHOPE ADMINISTRATION was formed by James (afterwards earl) Stanhope and the earl of Sunderland, 15 April, 1717. Stanhope was premier and chancellor of the exchequer; lord (afterwards earl) Cowper, lord chancellor; earl of Sunderland and Joseph Addison, secretaries of state, &c. In March, 1718, Addison resigned, and the earl of Sunderland became premier.

STANHOPE DEMONSTRATOR, see *Logic*.

STANLEY, AND AFRICAN EXHIBITION. Patrons, queen Victoria and the king of the Belgians; Mr. Joseph Thomson, the traveller, chief superintendent, opened at Victoria Gallery, Regent street, 24 March; closed 8 Nov. 1890.

The exhibition included pictures and portraits, African weapons, historical maps, and many interesting objects collected by Livingstone, Grant, Speke, Johnstone, and other travellers.

STANLEY FUND. Mr. Stanley's wish that the surplus of the receipts from the exhibition should form a fund for placing a steamer on the lake Victoria Nyanza (17 May), agreed to at a meeting at the Mansion house, 5 June; 50*l.* given by the queen, 16 July; 2,300*l.* received Oct. 1890.

STANNARY COURTS of Devon and Cornwall for the administration of justice among the tin miners, whose privileges were confirmed by 33 Edw. I. 1305. They were regulated by parliament in 1641, and at many times since. A "Stanneries act" was passed in 1869; another act in 1887. The Stannaries court (abolition) act, passed, 14 Aug. 1896, came into force, 1 Jan. 1897.

STAPLE (literally that which is fixed). The chief English staple commodities which were traded in by privileged merchants, and on which customs were levied, were wool, skins, leather, tin, lead and sometimes cloth, butter, and cheese; certain towns were appointed for the collection of the duties; statutes relating to the staple were passed by Edward III., Richard II., and Henry VI. Edward III.'s "ordinacio stapularum" (ordinance of the staple) was enacted in 1353.

STARCH is a sediment produced at the bottom of vessels wherein wheat has been steeped in water: it is soft and friable, easily broken into powder, and is used to stiffen and clear linen, with blue; its powder is employed to powder the hair. The art of starching linen was brought into England by Mrs. Dinghein, a Flemish woman, 1 Mary, 1553. *Stow.* Patents for obtaining starch from other substances have been taken out: from potatoes by Samuel Newton and others in 1707; from the horse-chestnut by Wm. Murray in 1796; from rice by Thomas Wickham in 1823; from various matters by Orlando Jones in 1839-40.

STAR-CHAMBER, COURT OF. So called haply from its roof being garnished with stars. *Coke.* This court of justice was called Star-Chamber, not from the *stars* on its roof (which were obliterated even before the reign of queen Elizabeth), but from the *Starra*, or Jewish covenants, deposited there by order of Richard I. No *star* was allowed to be valid except found in those repositories, and here they remained till the banishment of the Jews by Edward I. The court was instituted or revived, 3 Hen. VII. 1486, for trials by a committee of the privy council, which was in violation of Magna Charta; as it dealt with civil and criminal causes unfettered by the rules of law. In Charles I.'s reign it exercised its power upon several bold innovators, who gloried in their sufferings, and contributed to render government odious and contemptible. It was abolished in 1640. There were in this court from 26 to 42 judges, the lord chancellor having the casting voice. The judicial committee of the privy council is the Star-chamber revived under another name.

STAR OF INDIA, a new order of knighthood for India, instituted by letters patent 23 Feb., gazetted 25 June, 1861, enlarged in 1866 and 1903. It comprised the sovereign, the grand master, 25 knights (Europeans and natives), and extra or honorary knights, such as the prince consort, the prince of Wales, &c. Queen Victoria invested several knights on 1 Nov. 1861. The prince of Wales held a grand chapter at Calcutta, 1 Jan. 1876.

STARS, THE FIXED. They were classed into constellations (*which see*), it is supposed, about 1200 B.C. Hicetas, of Syracuse, taught that the sun and the stars were motionless, and that the earth moved round them, about 344 B.C. (this is mentioned by Cicero, and perhaps gave the first hint of this system to Copernicus). Job, Hesiod, and Homer mention several of the constellations. The Royal Library at Paris contains a Chinese chart of the heavens, made about 600 B.C., in which 1460 stars are correctly inserted. The aberration of the stars was discovered y Dr. Bradley, 1727; see *Astronomy*, and *Solar System*. Maps of the stars were published by the Society for the Diffusion of Useful Knowledge in 1839, and a set of Celestial Maps, issued under the superintendence of the Royal Prussian Academy, was completed in 1859. See *Photometer*.

Tycho Brahe discovered a new star in Cassiopeia in 1572.

Temporary stars were observed in 1876 and 1885.

A list of about 200 stars, which vary in their brightness and sometimes disappear, has been published by Mr. G. F. Chambers in his "Handbook on Astronomy," 1889–90. A variable star, named *a* Ceti, or Mira Ceti, observed by David Fabricius in Aug. 1596, disappeared in Oct. following. It was observed again in 1603 and 1638, and since.

Bessel discovered the annual parallax of star 61 Cygni (hence he calculated its distance from the earth to be about 60 billions of miles) 12 Feb. 1841

Struve made it 40 billions [supported by Brünnow and R. S. Ball] 1853

The calculations of T. Henderson (at the Cape) 1832 supported by D. Gill and others showed that probably *a* Centauri, is the star nearest to the earth 1883-4

A new star in Auriga in the Milky Way was discovered at Edinburgh, by Dr. Anderson, 1 Feb. 1892. It had been photographed by prof. Pickering, 1, 10, 20 Dec. 1891. It has been named Nova Aurigæ. Its brilliancy diminished, May; revived . . . . Aug. 1892

Dr. (after sir) Wm. Huggins reported his spectroscopic observations on the star to the Royal Institution . . . . 3 May, „

A new star in Centaurus discovered by Mrs. Fleming . . . . 12 Dec. 1895

Four variable stars discovered by Mr. R. T. Innes at the Cape Observatory, reported, 26 Aug. 1897. A new one in Andromeda discovered by Mr. T. Anderson, reported 26 Jan. 1899. Another in Sagittarius, by Mrs. Fleming, from the Draper memorial photos, 1897 or early 1898 (5 by her since 1885), May, 1899.

A new variable of *Algol* type discovered by photography by M. Ceraski in *Cygnus*, May–June, 1899. Two new variables, one in *Hercules* and the other in *Cygnus*, 24 and 28 Aug. 1899, discovered by Dr. T. D. Anderson, Edinburgh.

A new star, *Nova Persei*, of the first magnitude, discovered by Mr. Anderson, Edinburgh, in Perseus, and by M. Borissiak, at Kieff, 21 Feb. 1901. Much studied and photographed. Gradual decrease of magnitude; in June, 1902, and since its spectrum showed the characteristics of planetary nebulæ; on Dec. 1 its magnitude had diminished to 9·5.

Double stars discovered at the Cape of Good Hope from time to time, total reported, 259 up to Dec. 1901

STARVATION: Deaths attributed to it in the metropolitan districts, 1873, 107; 1875, 46; 1879, 80; 1888, 29. In London, 1889, 27; 1891, 30; 1892, 31; 1893, 51; 1894, 39; 1895, 71; 1896, 43; 1897, 41; 1899, 68, 1900, 53. In England and Wales: 1887, 250; 1888, 237. See *Abstinence*.

STATE CHILDREN'S ASSOCIATION, a movement to obtain individual treatment for children under the state guardianship, to bring up children in families in place of existing aggregated schools; to disassociate children with the workhouse system and to secure further power for the state over neglected children.

STATE MEDICINE, see under *Sanitation*, 2 May, 1888.

STATE PAPER OFFICE was founded in 1578, now merged into the Public Record Office. In 1856 the British government began the publication of Calendars of State Papers, invaluable to future historians; brought down to William and Mary, 1898.

STATES-GENERAL OF FRANCE. An ancient assembly of France, first met, it is said, in 1302 to consider the exactions of the pope. Previous to the Revolution, it had not met since 1614. The states consisted of three orders, the clergy, nobility, and commons. They were convened by Louis XVI., and assembled at Versailles, 5 May, 1789 (308 ecclesiastics, 285 nobles, and 621 deputies or *tiers état*, third estate). A contest arose whether the three orders should make three distinct houses, or but one assembly. The commons insisted upon the latter, and assuming the title of the National Assembly, declared that they were competent to proceed to business, without the concurrence of the two other orders, if they refused to join them. The nobility and clergy found it expedient to concede the point, and they all met in one hall; see *National Assembly*. Centenary, see *France*, 5 May, 1889.

STATESMAN'S YEAR-BOOK, statistical and historical annual of the states of the world, first published in 1864, edited by Frederick Martin. Present editor, J. Scott Keltie, assisted by T. P. A. Renwick, 1900–2.

STATES OF THE CHURCH, see *Pope*, and *Rome*.

STATIONERS. Books and papers were formerly sold only at stalls; hence the dealers were called stationers. The company of stationers of London is of great antiquity, and existed long before printing was invented, yet it was not incorporated until 3 Philip & Mary, 1557. Their old dwelling was in Paternoster-row; 500th anniversary celebrated 10 June, 1903.

STATISTICS, the science of the state, political knowledge, is said to have been founded by sir Wm. Petty (1623—1687), in his "Political Arithmetic," published 1691. The term is said to have been invented by professor Achenwall of Göttingen in 1749. The first statistical society in England was formed at Manchester in 1833; the Royal Statistical Society of London, which publishes a quarterly journal, was established 15 March, 1834, for the purpose of procuring, arranging, and publishing "facts calculated to illustrate the condition and prospects of society." Jubilee kept, 22, 23, 24 June, 1885; incorporated, 1887. The gold medal presented to Mr. Robert Giffen (K.C.B. 1895), the able government statistician, 20 Nov. 1894; resigns office 30 Sept. 1897; succeeded by Mr. A. E. Bateman. Similar societies have been established on the continent. International Statistical Institute constituted in 1885, met at Rome, 12-16 April, 1887. International Statistical Congresses are now held occasionally. The first at Brussels, chiefly through the agency of M. Quetelet, in 1853; 2nd at Paris, 1855; 3rd at Vienna, 1857; 4th at London, under the presidency of the prince consort, 16-21 July, 1860; 5th at Berlin; 6th at Florence; 7th at the Hague; 8th at St. Petersburg, was opened 22 Aug. 1872; 9th at Pesth, 31 Aug. 1876 and since; ..e at Vienna 28 Sept. 1891. The eminent statistician, Dr. Wm. Farr, died 14 April, 1883. *Statistical Abstracts* have been published annually by the government for many years, gives much information respecting the revenue, expenditure, commerce, etc., of the empire for 15 years. Mr. M. G. Mulhall's "Dictionary of Statistics" published 1891.

STATUES, see *Sculpture*, &c. Two statues of Rameses II. and one of his queen (about 1322 B.C.), 10 feet high, discovered at Aboukir by Daninos Pasha, Oct. 1891. Phidias, whose statue of Jupiter passed for one of the wonders of the world, was the greatest statuary among the ancients, 440 B.C. He had previously made a statue of Minerva at the request of Pericles, which was placed in the Parthenon. It was made of ivory and gold, and measured 39 feet in height. Lysippus invented the art of taking likenesses in plaster moulds, from which he afterwards cast models in wax, 326 B.C. Michael Angelo was the greatest artist among the moderns. The first equestrian statue erected in Great Britain was that of Charles I. in 1678.* By 17 & 18 Vict. c. 10 (10 July, 1854), public statues were placed under the control and protection of the Board of Works. The following are the chief public statues in London:—

Achilles, Hyde-park, in honour of the duke of Wellington, by the ladies of Great Britain 18 June, 1822
Albert, prince consort, Royal Exchange, 1850; Horticultural Society gardens, 1863; Holborn circus, 1873
Anne, queen, St. Paul's Churchyard, 1712; replaced, 1886
Barry, sir Charles, Westminster 1865
Bedford, duke of, Russell-square 1809
Bentinck, lord George, Cavendish-square . after 1848
Bright, John, the palace, Westminster . 11 Feb. 1896
Boadicea (by the late), Thos. Thornycroft, Westminster . . . . Jan. 1902
Burns,† Thames embankment . . 26 July, 1884
Byron, lord, Hamilton-place, Hyde-park, 24 May, 1880
Canning, Geo., New Palace-yard, Westminster . . 1832
Carlyle, Thos., embankment, Chelsea . Oct. 1882
Cartwright, major, Burton-crescent 1831
Charles I., Charing-cross 1678
Charles II., Soho-square . . . . * * *
Churchill, lord Randolph (bust), house of commons 18 April, 1898
Clyde, lord, Waterloo-place 1868
Cobden, Richard, Camden-town . . . June, 1868
Cromwell (bust, by Bernini), given to the commons by Mr. Charles Wertheimer . . . March, 1898
Cromwell (by Hamo Thornycroft), Westminster, 14 Nov. 1899
Cumberland, duke of, Cavendish-square . . . 1770
Derby, Edward, earl of, Parliament-square . . 1874
Disraeli, Benj., lord Beaconsfield, Parliament-square . . . . 19 April, 1883
Elizabeth, queen, St. Dunstan's, Fleet-street . . 1586
Faraday, Michael, Royal Institution 1867
Forster, W. E., Victoria embankment . 1 Aug. 1890
Fox, Charles James, Bloomsbury-square 1816
Franklin, sir John, Waterloo-place 1866
George I., Grosvenor-square 1726
George III., Somerset-house 1788
George III., Cockspur-street 1836
Gladstone, William Ewart, Houses of Parliament (Central Hall) . . . . . . 19 May, 1900
Gordon, gen. C. G., Trafalgar-square . 25 Sept. 1888
Granville, earl, the palace, Westminster, 11 June, 1896
Havelock, sir Henry, Trafalgar-square . . . 1861
Herbert, lord, Pall Mall . . . 3 June, 1867
Hill, Rowland, Royal Exchange 1882
Howard, John; first erected in St. Paul's . . . 1796
James II., Whitehall [removed 1897 (?)] . . . 1687
Jenner, Edward, Trafalgar-square, 1858; removed to Kensington-gardens 1864
Kent, duke of, Park-cres., Portland-place, between 1820 and 1827
Lawrence, lord, Waterloo-place (a new statue since) April, 1885
Macgregor, sir James, Chelsea hospital 1868
Mill, John Stuart, Thames embankment, 26 Jan. 1872
Myddelton, sir Hugh, Islington-green 1862
Napier, gen. sir Chas. J., Trafalgar-square . . 1856
Napier of Magdala, lord, Waterloo-place, uncovered 8 July, 1891
Nelson, lord, Trafalgar-square, by E. H. Baily [the lions at the base, designed by sir E. Landseer, were uncovered 31 Jan. 1867] 1843
Outram, sir James, Thames embankment 17 Aug. 1871
Palmerston, viscount, Parliament-street . 29 Jan. 1876
Peabody, George, Royal Exchange 1869
Peel, sir Robert, Cheapside, 1855; near Westminster abbey, 1868; Parliament-square 1877
Pitt, William, Hanover-square 1831
Queen Victoria, Royal Exchange, 1845; Temple-bar site, 1880; Kensington-gardens, 28 June, 1893; Royal Exchange, 19 June, 1896; Victoria embankment . . . . 21 July, 1896
Raikes, Robert, Thames embankment . 3 July, 1880
Richard Cœur de Lion, near Westminster abbey . 1860
Shakespeare, &c., Leicester-square 1874
Stephenson, Robert, Euston-road, near L. & N. W. station 1871
Strathnairn, lord, equestrian statue by Mr. E. Onslow Ford in Knightsbridge, unveiled by the duke of Grafton . . . . . . 19 June, 1895
Tyndale, Wm., Thames embankment 1884
Wales, Prince of, Temple-bar site, 1880; princess R. College of Music, by prince Victor of Hohenlohe-Langenburg . . . . . . Oct. 1893
Wellington, duke of, Royal Exchange 1844
Wellington, duke of, arch, Hyde-park-corner, 1846; equestrian statue, height 27 feet, weight 40 tons, chiefly gun metal (cannon taken by the duke) designed by Matthew Cotes Wyatt, set up 1 Oct. 1846; taken down, 24 Jan., 1883; set up at Aldershot camp 1848
Wellington, duke of, new equestrian statue with figures of four Waterloo soldiers at the base, by sir J. E. Boehm, facing Hyde Park Corner, set up 13 Nov.; unveiled by the prince of Wales 21 Dec. 1888
William III., St. James's-square 1717
William IV., King William-street 1845
York, duke of, Waterloo-place 1834

* This statue is of brass, cast by Le Sueur, in 1633, at the expense of the Howard-Arundel family. During the civil war, the parliament sold it to John River, a brazier, in Holborn, with strict orders to break it to pieces; but he concealed it underground till the Restoration, when it was erected, in 1678, on a pedestal executed by Grinling Gibbons. The first equestrian statue of bronze, founded at one cast, was that of Louis XIV. of France, 1699; it was elevated about 1724.

† By sir John Steell, the gift of Mr. John Gordon Crawford.

STATUTES, see *Acts of Parliament*, *Clarendon*, *Merton*, &c. Statute Law Revision acts were passed in 1863-1894. The subject was referred to a joint committee of both houses, 14 March, 1892. Statute Law Revision and Civil Procedure act, 44 & 45 Vict. c. 59, passed 27 Aug. 1881. "Statutes: Revised Edition: (1325-1878)," in 18 volumes, published 1870-85. The number of volumes since greatly reduced. Select commons' committee on the subject, met 17 July, 1891.

STATUTORY DECLARATIONS. By 5 & 6 Will. IV. c. 62 (1835), persons objecting to oaths are permitted to make declarations before magistrates, judges, &c.; commencing: "I ——, do solemnly and sincerely declare that"—an indulgence sometimes abused.

Mr. Alexander Chaffers having made a declaration against the character of Lady Twiss, wife of sir Travers Twiss, was prosecuted for libel. She withdrew during the examination, and the prosecution ceased: but Chaffers was severely censured by the magistrate, and by the attorney-general in parliament . . . . March, 1872

STEAM CARRIAGE (for ordinary roads), invented by the earl of Caithness, was said to be successful in 1860. It travels over rough roads at the rate of 8 miles an hour, at a cost of less than 1*d*. per mile. His lordship made a journey of 140 miles in two days; see *Road Steamers*.

STEAM ENGINE* AND NAVIGATION.

Hero of Alexandria, in his "Pneumatics," describes various methods of employing steam as a power; and to him is ascribed the Æolopile, which, although a toy, possesses the properties of the steam-engine: he flourished about 284-241 B.C. Roger Bacon appears to have foreseen the application of steam-power; see *Railways, Locomotives, Road Steamers,* &c.

Solomon de Caus, a French protestant, publishes a work which Arago on insufficient grounds considers to have contained the germs of the steam-engine . 1615

The marquis of Worcester describes his steam-engine in his "Century of Inventions" 1663

Papin's *digester* invented 1681-2

Captain Savery's engine constructed for raising water 1698

Papin's engine exhibited to the Royal Society about 1699

[He is said to have made a steamboat which was destroyed by boatmen of the Weser.]

Thomas Newcomen, of Dartmouth, is stated to have constructed "the first self-acting steam-engine;" (used for nearly a century without alteration or amendment) 1712

[He died in London while endeavouring to obtain a patent, 1729.]

First idea of *steam navigation* set forth in a patent obtained by Jonathan Hulls 1736

Watt's invention of performing condensation in a separate vessel from the cylinder 1765

His first patent, 1769; his engines erected in manufactories, and his patent renewed by parliament . 1775

Thomas Paine proposes steam navigation in America 1778

Engines made to give a rotary motion . . . . ,,

Watt's expansion engine . . . . . . ,,

Double-action engines proposed by Dr. Falck on Newcomen's principle 1779

Watt's double engine and his first patent for it . 1781

Hornblower's double-cylinder engine . . . . ,,

Claude comte de Jouffroy constructed an engine which propelled a boat (pyroscaphé) on the Saône. 1783

Wm. Patrick Miller patented paddle-wheels . . 1787

[He and Mr. Symington are said to have constructed a small steamboat which travelled at about 4 miles an hour soon after.

W. Symington made a passage on the Forth and Clyde canal 1790

First steam-engine erected in Dublin by Henry Jackson 1791

First experiment with steam navigation on the Thames 1801

Trevethick's high-pressure engine . . . . ,,

Woolf's double-cylinder expansion engine constructed 1804

Manufactories warmed by steam 1806

Fulton's steamboat *Clermont* on the Seine, 9 Aug. 1803; at New York, 1806; started a steamboat on the river Hudson, America 1807

Steam power to convey coals on a railway employed by Blenkinsop 1811

Comet, built by Henry Bell, sailed on the Clyde [John Robertson, who made the engine, died 20 Nov. 1868, aged 86] . . . . 18 Jan. 1812

The *Comet* sailed from Glasgow to Greenock three times a week; fares. 3*s.* and 4*s.*; speed, 7½ miles an hour.]

Steam applied to printing in the *Times* office (see *Printing machines*) 1814

There were five steam-vessels in Scotland (*Parl. Returns*) . . . . ,,

First steam-vessel on the Thames, brought by Mr. Dodd from Glasgow 1815

First steamer built in England (*Parl. Returns*) . ,,

Rising Sun, a steamer built by lord Cochrane, crossed the Atlantic 1818

The *Savannah*, aided by steam, of 350 tons, came from New York to Liverpool in 26 days 15 July, 1819

First steamer in Ireland 1820

Steamboats established between Dover and Calais and London and Leith 1821

Steam-gun, invented by Perkins 1824

Steam-jet applied by George Stephenson, 1814; by Timothy Hackworth, about 1825

Captain Johnson obtained 10,000*l.* for making the first steam voyage to India, in the *Enterprise*, which sailed from Falmouth . . . 16 Aug. ,,

The locomotive steam-carriages on railways at Liverpool . . . . Oct. 1829

The railway opened (see *Liverpool*) 1830

The *Royal William*, steamship, built at Quebec by Mr. James Grondie in 1830-1, said to have crossed the Atlantic in 21 days 1833

Capt. Ericsson's screw steamer, "*Francis Bogden*," speed 10 miles an hour, constructed: see *Screw-Propeller* 1837

The *Sirius* sailed from Queenstown 4 April; arrived at New York . . . . 21 April, 1838

The *Great Western* sails from Bristol to New York, being her first voyage . . . . 8-23 April, ,,

War-steamers built in England . . . . . ,,

War-steamers built at Birkenhead, named the *Nemesis* and *Phlegethon*, carrying each two thirty-two pounders, sent by government to China . . 1840

Hall's method of economising fuel introduced about ,,

The first Cunard steamer, the *Britannia*, sailed . . . . 4 July, ,,

[Sir Sam. Cunard died 28 April, 1865, aged 78.]

The Peninsular Company was formed in 1837; became the Peninsular and Oriental Steam Navigation Company in . . . . ,,

[They possessed 53 steamers and a fleet of tugs, Dec. 1866.]

The *Great Britain* sailed from the Mersey 26 July, 1845

[She arrived at New York 10 Aug. During her second voyage, she ran aground in Dundrum bay, Ireland, 22 Sept. 1846. Her passengers were landed; and she was extricated with little injury, after long-continued and strenuous efforts, by I. Brunel, jun. and Bremner, 27 Aug. 1847.]

The Collins steamers began 1850

Inman Company: began by Wm. Inman, first vessel *City of Glasgow*, 1850; the company became the Liverpool, New York, and Philadelphia company, 1857; *City of Richmond*, sailed from Liverpool 6 p.m. 15 July, arrived at New York 12.30 p.m. 24 July, 1875. (Apparent time 7 days, 19 hours, 45 minutes; average 365 miles a day, 15 knots an hour.)

The *Pacific* crosses the Atlantic in 9 days, 19 hours, 25 minutes, arriving at Holyhead . . 20 May, 1851

The British India Steam Navigation Company initiated by Mr. (afterwards sir) Wm. Mackinnon, afterwards extended to Australia, 1855. [Had a fleet of 110 vessels, 1893.]

Manchester Steam-Users Association established about 1855

Steam packets leave Galway for America . . . 1858

The merits of an attacking vessel termed a *steam-ram*, advocated by sir G. Sartorius, discussed 1859-60

Giffard's valuable steam-injector invented about 1859

An iron-plated frigate, *La Gloire*, completed in France (see *Navy, French*) 1860

The *Warrior*, an iron-plated vessel, launched 29 Dec. ,,

The *Far East*, a vessel with two screws, launched at Millwall . . . . 31 Oct. 1863

A *cigar ship*, a steam yacht, designed by Mr. Winan, built by Hepworth, launched on the Thames 19 Feb. 1866

Trial trip of the *Nautilus*, with a hydraulic propeller worked by steam, Ruthven's patent; no paddle or screw required . . . . . . 24 March, ,,

Successful trial trip of the *Water-witch*, a government hydraulic propeller iron-clad gun-vessel (Ruthven's patent), on the Thames . 19 Oct. ,,

* "The best known mechanical arrangement for converting heat into work." *A. Rigg*, 1878. "*Gas, Oil and Air Engines*," by Bryan Donkin, un., 1895.

* Since then many great steamers have been wrecked or burnt: viz., *Governor Fenner*, 19 Feb., 1841; *President*, March, 1841; *Ocean Monarch*, Aug. 1848; *St. George*, 24 Dec. 1852; *George Canning*, 1 Jan. 1855; *Pacific*, 1856; *Austria*, 13 Sept., 1858; *Indian*, 21 Nov., 1859; *Hungarian*, Feb., 1860; *Anglo-Saxon*, 27 April, 1863; *City of Boston*, Feb., 1870; *Germania*, 21 Dec., 1872; *Atlantic*, April, 1873; *Ville de Havre*, 22 Nov., 1873; *Cashmere*, 5 July, 1877; *Eten*, 15 July, 1877, &c.

Mr. Ruthven patented his system in 1849, and exhibited his machinery at the International Exhibition in 1851. His object is to increase speed and save fuel. In the *Water-witch* a steam-engine gives the power of absorbing and expelling the water, and no screw or paddle is required. The water-wheel is 14½ feet in diameter.

Trial trip of H.M. gun-boat *Thistle*; explosion of boiler, 8 killed . . . 3 Nov. 1869

Channel Steamers: "Twin-ship" *Castalia*, steamer (two hulls, separated by 26 feet), 290 feet long; invented by capt. W. T. Dicey, for the English Channel steam company, to prevent sea-sickness when crossing the Channel; (really a single ship, with the middle part of her bottom raised out of the water throughout her whole length); launched, 2 June; tried in calm weather; reported successful but slow, 2 Aug. 1875; successful, June, 1876; sold Nov. 1876.

Bessemer, saloon steamer, designed by Mr. Bessemer and E. J. Reed; built by the Earles company; launched at Hull, 24 Sept. 1874; first voyage from Hull to Gravesend, 5 March, 1875; sailed to Calais, 10 April, 1875. [Success doubtful, 1876.] Modified by Mr. E. J. Reed; trial near Hull, reported successful, 26 March, 1877.

Express, twin steamer; built by A. Leslie, of Newcastle; sailed from the Tyne to Coquet Island, 22½ miles, in 1h. 22m., reported satisfactory, 13 March, 1878.

Folkestone, twin steamer, launched at Hull, 23 March, 1878.

Pizarro, steamer (the first built of Siemens-Martin steel; 340 feet long by 40 feet broad, 3400 tons), launched at Napier's yard, Govan, near Glasgow, 5 Aug. 1879.

Livadia, a turbot-shaped steam yacht (broad and flat), built by Elder & Co. of Glasgow for the czar of Russia, launched on the Clyde, 7 July, 1880.

Faraday, steam-ship (for laying electric cables, 360 feet long, 52 feet wide, 36 feet deep, 5000 tons register; to carry 6000 tons dead weight); next in size to *Great Eastern*; built for Messrs. Siemens by Messrs. Mitchell, at Newcastle; launched (much employed, 1881 *et seq.*), 17 Feb. 1874; she laid cables from Nova Scotia to New York . . . . Dec. 1889

Orient, steamer, built by Elders of Glasgow, for Australian traffic; length, 460 feet; breadth, 46 feet; depth, 37¾ feet; sailed from Greenock to West India Dock, London . . 10-12 Sept. 1879

Servia, Cunard royal mail steamer, 530 feet long, 52 feet broad, 44 feet depth; gross tonnage, 8500 tons; 5 decks and promenade; next in size to *Great Eastern*; launched in the Clyde, 1 March, 1881; sailed from America to Liverpool (by long route) in 7 days, 8 hours, 15 min., quickest passage hitherto made . . 26 Jan. 1882

City of Rome, mail steamer, length 586 feet, breadth 52 feet, left the Clyde . . . . 28 Sept. 1881

Alaska, Guion mail steamer crossed the Atlantic, 6 days, 22 hours . . . . 31 May-6 June, 1882

The Guion steamer *Arizona*, left Queenstown at 2.10 p.m. Sept. 11, and reached Sandy Hook at 6.20 p.m. on the 18th, which, including the difference in time, 4 hours, 22 min., makes the passage 7 days, 8 hours, 12 min. On the return passage she made the voyage in 7 days, 7 hours, 48 min.

The Guion steamer *Alaska* arrived at Sandy Hook on Sunday, in 7 days, 17 min. . . 31 July, ,,

Black Star Line of steamers between Grimsby and America . . . . ,,

Victoria, steamer (jubilee of the P. and O. company), built by Messrs. Caird & Co.; length 465 feet, breadth 52 feet, depth 37 feet; sailed from Greenock to Southampton . . . . 16 July, 1887

Mr. Thomas Lishman's steam generator said to economize fuel without producing smoke, employed at Elswick Works, Newcastle, and other places . . . . ,,

Arcadia (P. and O. steamer), arrived at Albert Docks . . . . . . 18 May, 1888

Etruria, Cunard line, sailed from Roches Point, Cork, to New York in 6 days, 1 hour, 47 minutes 2 June, ,,

Parisian, boat of the Allan line, said to have crossed the Atlantic from land to land in 4 days, 17 hours and 10 minutes . . . . . Aug. ,,

City of New York, length 560 feet, breadth 63¼ feet, first voyage across Atlantic . . . 1 Aug. ,,

Said to have crossed from New York to Queenstown in 5 days, 23 hours, and 14 minutes . 17–23 Sept. 1890

Campania, twin-screw Cunard liner, with a gross tonnage of 12,500, 620 feet long by 65 feet 3 inches broad and 43 feet deep, launched on the Clyde, 8 Sept., 1892. She left New York 2 Sept.; arrived at Queenstown, 8 Sept. 1893 (5 days, 14 hours, 55 min.); *Lucania*, a similar vessel, launched 2 Feb. 1893

The *Umbria*, Cunard liner, captain M'Kay, with 380 passengers, left Liverpool for New York, 17 Dec., endured bad weather and seas till 23 Dec., when the propeller-shaft broke and disabled her near Newfoundland; the attempt of the *Bohemia*, Hamburg liner, to take her in tow, failed; at length the injury was repaired by the exertions of chief engineer Tomlinson and his staff, the *Umbria* proceeded on her voyage, and arrived at New York, amid great rejoicing, noon 31 Dec. 1892

The *New York*, the first steamer of the American line from New York, arrives at Southampton 6 days, 21½ hrs. . . . . . . 4 March, 1893

The *Gothic*, White Star line, exhibited in Royal Albert Docks, London . . . . 16 Dec. ,,

Sir Thomas Sutherland at a meeting of the Institute of Marine Engineers stated that the *Lucania*, Cunard line, has attained an average speed of 25 statute miles per hour or 600 miles per day, and that the mails are conveyed from Charing Cross to Bombay in 13 days . . . 24 Oct. 1894

The great cargo steamer *Georgic* (10,000 gross tonnage) launched at Belfast . . . 22 June, 1895

The *India*, large P. and O. steamer, launched at Greenock . . . . . . 15 April, 1896

The *Ernest Bazin*, new roller-ship, named after the inventor, launched at St. Denis . 19 Aug. ,,

The *Arabia*, large P. and O. steamer, launched at Greenock, 10 Nov. 1897; the *Isis*, launched, 9 April; the *Osiris*, launched 6 June . . . 1898

The *Oceanic*, White Star liner, will carry, grand total, 2,104 persons, launched . . 14 Jan. 1899

The *Omrah*, Orient liner, 507 ft. long, 56 ft. 9 in. broad, starts on first voyage . 3 Feb. ,,

Kinfauns Castle, twin screw Castle liner, 532 ft. long, 59 ft. 3 in. broad, launched at Gowan, 12 May, ,,

Amalgamation of the Union and the Castle lines of steamers, announced . . . 16 Dec. ,,

Lord Inverclyde, head of the Cunard Co., died, aged 79 . . . . 12 Feb. 1901

Imperial direct service from Avonmouth, Bristol, to Jamaica, started . . . . 16 Feb. ,,

The *Celtic*, White Star liner, 700 ft. long, 75 ft. wide, 49 ft. deep, will carry 2,859 passengers and crew of 335, launched at Belfast . . 4 April, ,,

Deutschland, Hamburg-American liner, sails from New York to Plymouth in 5 days, 11 hrs. and 5 min. . . . . 17 July, ,,

Combination formed of the leading British and American North Transatlantic lines (no change of flag, &c., involved), Mr. Pierpont Morgan syndicate manager, reported, 19 April, 1902; agreement with the Hamburg-American and the North-German Lloyd, issued, *Times*, 27 May, 1902

Kaiser Wilhelm II., N. German Lloyd co., 20,000 tons register, launched at Stettin, the emperor present . . . . 12 Aug. ,,

Messrs. Yarrow's new type of shallow draught steamer tried on the Thames . . 19 Aug. ,,

Cedric, White Star liner, 700 ft. long, 75 ft. beam, launched at Belfast . . . 21 Aug. ,,

Improved service to S. American ports (British and German combination), started . . 19 Sept. ,,

New monthly line from Canada to S. Africa to be started by *Ontario*, Allan s.s. from Montreal, 18 Oct. ,,

Satisfactory agreements between the British government and the N. Atlantic Shipping Combination and also with the Cunard line, formally incorporated at Trenton, New Jersey, U.S.A., and styled the Internat. Mercantile Marine co. (capital about 24,000,000*l.*), *Times* . 1–3 Oct. ,,

Death of Mr. John Penn, M.P., aged 55, head of the marine engineering firm of Penn & Sons, 21 Nov. 1903

See *Navy*, and *Shipping*.

LARGE STEAM VESSELS OF ENGLAND.

	Long.	Broad.
reat Western	236 ft.	35 ft.
uke of Wellington	240 ft.	60 ft.
itish Queen	275 ft.	61 ft.
reat Britain	322 ft.	51 ft.
imalaya	370 ft.	43 ft.
rsia	390 ft.	45 ft.
rvia	530 ft.	52 ft.
ceanic	705 ft. 6 in.	68 ft. 4 in.
altic	726 ft.	76 ft.
REAT EASTERN, for a short time (1857-8) called *Leviathan* . .	692 ft.	83 ft.

Horse Power: — Paddles, 1000; screw, 1600: *Weight* of ship, 12,000 tons; ordinary light draught, 12,000 tons; said to have cost 732,000*l.*

he was designed by Mr. I. K. Brunel [who died 15 Sept. 1859], and built by Messrs. Scott Russell and Co., at Millwall; launching lasted from 3 Nov. 1857, to 31 Jan. 1858.

he capital subscribed having been all expended, a new company was formed to fit her for sea.

n 7 Sept. 1859, she left her moorings at Deptford for Portland-roads. On the voyage an explosion took place (off Hastings), through some neglect in regard to the casing of one of the funnels, when ten firemen were killed and many persons seriously injured. After repairs she sailed to Holyhead, arriving there 10 Oct.; she endured the storm of 25-26 Oct. well; and proceeded to Southampton for the winter, 4 Nov.

She was fitted up to convey 5000 persons from London to Australia, a distance of 22,500 miles, with accommodation for 800 1st class passengers, 2000 2nd class, and 1200 3rd class. Her able captain (Harrison) was drowned in the Solent 22 Jan. 1860, deeply regretted. She sailed for New York 17 June, under command of captain Vine Hall, and arrived there 28 June. After being exhibited she left New York 16 Aug. and returned to England 26 Aug.

Owing to a lawsuit in April, the ship came into the hands of sheriff's officers; but was released and sailed for New York on 1 May, 1861. On 12 Sept. she suffered much loss through a violent gale.

In 1862 she performed several voyages to and from New York; but in Aug. ran on a rock near Long Island and injured her bottom.

She was repaired and arrived at Liverpool 17 Jan. 1863, and sailed to New York (16-27 May).

She was bought by Glass, Elliot, and Co. in March or April, 1864, and was chartered to convey the Atlantic telegraph cable; sailed from Sheerness 15 July; and returned 19 Aug. 1865; see under *Electric Telegraph.*

She sailed for New York, prepared for 2000 passengers, 26 March, and returned with 191. She was seized by the seamen, claiming their wages, May, 1867; and the case was carried into Chancery in July.

At the meeting of the shareholders 10 Feb. 1868, no dividend was declared.

She conveyed the French Atlantic telegraph cable, successfully laid . . . . . . Oct. 1869

Arrived at Bombay with Bombay and Suez cable, 27 Feb.; returned to Sheerness . . June, 1870

Sailed with the fourth Atlantic telegraph cable 8 June; which was completely laid 3 July, 1873

Sailed with the fifth Atlantic telegraph cable: laid . . . . . . Aug., Sept. 1874

Put up for sale at 30,000*l.*; not bought 19 Oct. 1881

[John Scott Russell died, aged 74] . 8 June, 1882

Proposed to be employed as a coal hulk in Gibraltar Bay . . . . . . April, 1884

Sold by auction to Mr. Frederick de Mattos for 26,200*l.* for the London traders (limited) 28 Oct. 1885

The ship reported in good condition . 20 April, 1886

Sold to Mr. Worsley for 26,000*l.* . . . „

In the Mersey . . . 12 May–12 Oct. „

Largely visited; drink licence refused . April, 1887

Sold to Mr. Craik for 21,000*l.* . . 20 Oct. „

In the Clyde, sold to Messrs. Henry Bath, metal brokers, for 16,500*l.* . . . . Dec. 1887

Messrs. Henry Bath and Sons cause the vessel to be moved to the Mersey, where she is beached 25 Aug. 1888

Total receipts of the sale at Liverpool 58,000*l.* 24 Nov. „

STEAM GUN; suggested by Wm. Murdoch, 1803. One patented by Messrs. Perkins, in 1824, was ineffectual.

In Oct. 1870, Mr. H. Bessemer proposed the application of steam power to artillery.

STEAM HAMMER, invented by Mr. James Nasmyth in 1838, and patented by him 18 June, 1842. Its main feature is the absolutely direct manner by which the elastic power of steam is employed to lift up and let fall the mass of iron constituting the hammer, which is attached direct to the end of a piston-rod passing through the bottom of an inverted steam cylinder placed immediately over the anvil.

In 1842, Mr. Nasmyth applied his steam-hammer to driving piles, which has importantly assisted in the execution of great public works. Owing to its vast range of power, forged iron-work can now by its means be executed on a scale, and for a variety of purposes, with an ease and perfection not previously possible. Parts of gigantic marine steam-engines, anchors, and Armstrong guns, as well as the most minute details of machinery, as in Enfield rifles, are executed by the steam-hammer.

A steam-hammer, said to be the then largest in the world, completed at Woolwich: the falling portion weighs 40 tons, and when used with top steam (51 tons) has the force of 91 tons, April, 1874. One at Schneider's works, Creuzot, France; weight between 75 and 80 tons, Dec. 1877.

Mr. Nasmyth, aged 81, died 7 May, 1890. His Autobiography, edited by Dr. S. Smiles, was published in 1883.

STEAM-MAN. A figure constructed to drag a phaeton received this name in New York in March, 1868.

STEAM NAVIGATION, see under *Steam.*

STEAM-PLOUGHS were patented by G. Callaway and R. A. Purkes, 1849; H. Cowing, 1850; and others. John Fowler's of 1854 is much approved.

STEAM-RAM (to be used in naval warfare), was invented by Mr. James Nasmyth in 1836, and communicated to the Admiralty in 1845. Steam-rams built by Mr. James Laird of Birkenhead for the Confederates in N. America, were stopped and eventually bought by the British government, 1864.

STEAM-WHISTLES and **STEAM-TRUMPETS**, used in factories to summon or dismiss workmen, prohibited by an act passed Aug. 1872.

STEARINE (from *stear*, suet), that part of oils and fats which is solid at common temperature. The nature of these substances was first made known by Chevreul, in 1823, who showed that they were compounds of peculiar acids, with a base termed *glycerine*; of these compounds the chief are stearine, margarine, and elaine; see *Candles.*

STEEL, metal, a compound of iron and carbon, exists in nature, and has been fabricated from the earliest times. It was certainly used by the Egyptians, Assyrians, and Greeks. It now largely replaces cast iron in ship building, &c.

Reaumur discovered the direct process of making steel by immersing malleable iron in a bath of cast iron 1722

A manufactory for cast steel is said to have been set up by Benjamin Huntsman at Handsworth, near Sheffield 1740

The manufacture of shear steel began in Sheffield, about 1800

German steel was made at Newcastle previously by Mr. Crawley.

The inventions of Mushat (1800), Lucas (1804), and Heath (1839), were important steps in this manufacture; see *Engraving*.

Reipe patented his "puddled steel" . . . 1850

Mr. (aft. sir) H. Bessemer made steel by passing cold air through liquid iron, 1856. By this method 20 tons of crude iron have been converted into cast steel in 23 minutes.*

Tungsten steel was made in Germany, 1859; and M. Fremy made steel by bringing red-hot iron in contact with carbonate of ammonia . . . 1861

M. Alfred Krupp exhibited an ingot of steel weighing 4500 lbs. in 1851, and one weighing 20 tons in 1862 [about 15,000 men are employed at his works at Essen, 1887; 46,000 in 1902.]

The subject much investigated by M. Caron, 1861-5; much attention was excited by cutlery made from a metallic sand, brought from Taranaki or New Plymouth, in New Zealand 1860

A steel bridge, in connection with the exhibition, constructed at Paris by M. Joret 1866

Mr. John Heaton published his process . . . 1867-8

Dr. Siemens, by means of his "regenerative gas furnaces," produced excellent steel, cheaply, in large masses . . . . 1876, *et seq.*

Cutlers' Company, London, opened an exhibition, 1 May, 1879

Messrs. Bolckow, Vaughan & Co. of Middlesbrough, by Thomas and Gilchrist's process, convert Cleveland iron ore into Bessemer steel, by lining the furnace with radial bricks of magnesian limestone and adding cold basic material, phosphorus being thereby removed . . ,,

The process reported successful . . . Oct. 1880

Mr. J. S. Jeans published his important work, "Steel: its History, Manufacture, Properties, and Uses" . . . . Feb. ,,

The Garfield, a steel sailing ship, 2,220 tons, 292 ft. length, 24 ft. 9 in. depth, 41 ft. breadth, launched at Belfast . . . . 7 Jan. 1882

Umbria, Cunard liner, above 8,000 tons, 520 ft. long, 57 ft. 3 in. broad, 41 ft. deep, launched on the Clyde . . . . Sept. 1884

Mr. B. H. Thwaite, of Liverpool, and Mr. A. Stewart, of Bradford, introduce an improved "rapid" process for the manufacture of steel, announced Oct. 1887

New process of steel manufacture from Cleveland ironstone at Port Clarence on the Tees, reported, 4 Jan. ,,

See under *Steam*.

STEEL PENS. "Iron pens" are mentioned by Chamberlayne in 1685. Steel pens, made long before, began to come into use about 1820, when the first gross of three-slit pens was sold wholesale for *7l. 4s.* In 1830 the price was *8s.*, and in 1832, *6s.* A better pen is now sold for *6d.* a gross. Birmingham in 1858 produced about 1000 million pens per annum. Women and children are principally employed in the manufacture. Perry, Mitchell, and Gillott are eminent makers. Joseph Gillott, originally a mechanic, made a large fortune by steel-pen making. He died 5 Jan. 1872, aged 72.

STEEL-YARD. An ancient instrument, the same that is translated *balance* in the Pentateuch. The *Statera Romana*, or Roman steel-yard, is mentioned in 315 B.C.—The STEEL-YARD or STILL-YARD COMPANY, London merchants, who had the steel-yard in Thames-street assigned to them by Henry III., about 1232, were Flemings and Germans, and the only exporters, for many years after, of the staple commodities of England. *Anderson.* The company lost its privileges, finally, in 1578; and the merchants were expelled from England in 1597.

STEENKIRK, see *Enghien*.

* For this invention he had received by royalties 1,507,748*l.* up to 1879; also many foreign honours; knighted June, 1879; born 19 Jan. 1813, died 15 March, 1898.

STEFANO, SAN, a small village on the sea of Marmora, S.W. of Constantinople; here the grand duke Nicholas established his head quarters, 24 Feb.; and here was signed a treaty of peace with Turkey, 3 March, 1878, much modified by the treaty of Berlin, signed 13 July, following. The Russians quitted San Stefano, 22 Sept. 1878.

It established independence of Montenegro, Servia, and Roumania; constituted Bulgaria a tributary principality; required a heavy indemnity from Turkey for Russia, who was to gain a port on the Black Sea and Kars; to exchange the Dobrudscha for Bessarabia; to obtain rights for Christians; to open the Bosphorus and Dardanelles in peace and war; &c.

STELLA, see *Wrecks*, 30 March, 1899.

STELLA-LAND, see *Trans-vaal* and *Bechuana-land*.

STENOCHROMY, see *Printing in Colours*.

STENOGRAPHY (from *stenos*, narrow), the art of short-hand, said to have been practised by the ancients. Its improvement is attributed to the poet Ennius, to Tyro, Cicero's freedman, and still more to Seneca. The *Ars Scribendi Characteris*, written about 1412, is the oldest system extant. Dr. Timothy Bright's "Characterie, or the Arte of Shorte, Swifte, and Secrete Writing," published in 1588, is the first English work on short-hand. Peter Bales, the famous penman, published on stenography in 1590; and John Willis published his "*Stenographie*" in 1602. Since then many systems and modifications have been produced. See *Phonography*.

Edmund Willis's system, 1618; Thomas Shelton's system, 1620 (used by Samuel Pepys); Wm. Cartwright's, 1642–69 (known as Rich's); Wm. Mason's, 1672, improved by Thos. Gurney (1720) (known as Gurney's, officially used in parliament since 1813); John Byrom's, published after his death, 1767; Wm. Mavor's, 1780; Sam Taylor's, on which are based ("Odell's and Harding's") 1786; Rev. Richard Roe's, 1820, first Script system; James H. Lewis's, 1812–15; Isaac Pitman's (phonographic), 1837, see *Phonography*; A. M. Bell's, 1849; Prof. Everett's, 1877; T. Cooper ("Parliamentary shorthand," Gurney's), 1858; E. Pocknell's ("Legible shorthand"), 1880; J. M. Sloan's, 1882; Thomas Anderson's, 1884; "A text-book of the Gurney system," edited by W. B. Gurney and Sons, 18th edition, 1884; J. Barker's, 1885; A. Jane's ("Shorthand without complication") . . . . . . 1885-9[illegible]

Various systems are in use, in France, Germany, America, and the East; Pitman's adapted to the Japanese language, and employed for reporting proceedings of the diet, in 1879

Shorthand Society founded . . . . . . 188[illegible]

Sig. A. Michela's stenographic machine for the graphic representation of phonetic sounds (about 200 words per minute); like a harmonium with a key-board, exhibited at the Turin exhibition of 1884, successfully adopted by the Italian Senate.

International Shorthand Congress at the Geological Museum, London, S.W. (482 systems noticed) 26 Sept.–1 Oct. 1887; Paris, 1889; Munich, 1890; Berlin . . . . 30 Sept. 18[illegible]

Shorthand placed on the government education code, no fixed system . . . . . . 189[illegible]

Mr. J. F. Hardy's shorthand writing machine (silent), reported successful . . . . 4 Jan. 1897

STEPHEN'S CHAPEL, ST. (Westminster), built by king Stephen, about 1135. It was rebuilt by Edward III. in 1347, and by him made a collegiate church, to which a dean and twelve secular priests were appointed. Soon after its surrender to Edward VI., about 1548, it was applied to the use of Parliament; see *Parliament*. It was destroyed by fire, 16 Oct. 1834. The Society of Antiquaries published memorials of it about 1810; and Mr. Mackenzie's work appeared in 1844. The restoration of the beautiful crypt was complete in Jan. 1870.

STEPNEY, a parish, E. London, the Stebenhide of Domesday book. Edward I. summoned a parliament here, 1299. Stepney suffered severely by the plague, 1625 and 1665. Stepney-green was restored and opened as a park by the Metropolitan Board of Works, Aug. 1872. Stepney church, built 1470, restored 1899, much damaged by fire, 12 Oct. 1901; re-opened 21 June, 1902. One of the divisions of the Tower Hamlets; returns one M.P. Constituted a municipal borough by London Government act 1899. (10 aldermen, 60 councillors). Population, 1881, 58,543; 1891, 57,599; 1901, 298,600.

STEREOCHEMISTRY, the chemistry of atoms, carbon, &c., in space, connected with the researches of M. Pasteur and his colleagues, Van't Hoff and Le Bel; was so named about 1890 by Victor Meyer. Van't Hoff's "Chemistry in Space," translated by J. E. Marsh. "Handbuch der Stereochemie," by Dr. C. A. Bischoff and Dr. Paul Walden, published 1893. Prof. J. Wislicenus, one of its earliest exponents, died in 1902.

STEREOCHROMY, a mode of painting in which water-glass (an alkaline solution of flint, silex) serves as the connecting medium between the colour and the substratum. Its invention is ascribed to Von Fuchs, who died at Munich on 5 March, 1856. Fine specimens of this art by Kaulbach and Echter exist in the Museum at Berlin, and also at Munich.

STEREOMETER, by which is compassed the art of taking the contents of vessels of liquids by gauging, invented about 1350. *Anderson.* M. Say's stereometer, for determining the specific gravity of liquids, porous bodies and powders as well as solids, was described in 1797.

STEREOSCOPE (from *stereos*, solid, and *skopein*, to see), an optical instrument for representing in apparent relief natural objects, &c., by uniting into one image two plane representations of these objects as seen by each eye separately. The first stereoscope by reflection was constructed and exhibited by professor Charles Wheatstone in 1838, who had announced its principle in 1833. Since 1854 stereoscopes have been greatly improved. By Mr. John Anderton's lantern stereoscope, remarkable effects were exhibited on a screen in the Royal Society's lecture room, 7 June, 1893.

STEREOTYPE, a cast from a page of movable printing-types, so named by the Parisian printer, Didot, 1798. It is said that stereotyping was known in 1711. It was practised by Wm. Ged of Edinburgh, about 1730. Some of Ged's plates are at the Royal Institution, London. A Mr. James attempted to introduce Ged's process in London, but failed, about 1735.* *Nichols.* Stereotype printing was in use in Holland, in the last century; and a quarto Bible and a Dutch folio Bible were printed there. *Phillips.* It was revived in London by Wilson in 1804. Since 1850 the durability of stereotypes has been greatly increased by electrotyping them with copper or silver. Stereotyping used for printing the *Times*, 1856, *et seq.*

In the library of the Royal Institution is an edition of Sallust, with this imprint: "Edinburgi, Gulielmus Ged, auri faber Edinensis, non typis mobilibus, ut vulgo fieri solet, sed tabellis seu laminis fusis, excudebat. 1744." (Printed at Edinburgh by William Ged of Edinburgh, goldsmith, not with moveable types, as is commonly done, but with cast tablets or plates.)

* It was hotly opposed by the journeymen printers.

STERLING (money). Ducange says (1733), "Esterlingus, sterlingus, are English words relating to money, and hence familiar to other nations, and applied to the weight, quality, and kind of money." "Denarius Angliæ, qui vocatur sterlingus," stat. Edw. I. (The penny of England, which is called sterling.) Camden derives the word from *easterling* or *esterling*, observing that the money brought from Germany, in the reign of Richard I., was the most esteemed on account of its purity, being called in old deeds "*nummi easterling.*" Others derive the word from the Easterlings, the first moneyers in England.

STETHOSCOPE. In 1816 Laënnec, of Paris, by rolling a quire of paper into a kind of cylinder, and applying one end to the patient's chest and the other to his own ear, perceived the action of the heart in a much more distinct manner than by the immediate application of the ear. This led to his inventing the stethoscope, or "breast-explorer," the principle of which, now termed "auscultation," was known by Hippocrates (357 B.C.), and by Robert Hooke, 1681. See *Water*, 1895.

STETTIN (Pomerania), an ancient city, formerly held by the Sidini and Venedes, was taken by Boleslas of Poland in 1121. After being conquered by the Swedes, Russians, and French, it was awarded to Prussia in 1814. Population, 1890, 116,239; 1900, 210,680.

Visited by emperor William during military manœuvres	12 Sept. 1887
A new harbour opened by the emperor,	23 Sept. 1898
Deutschland, Hamburg-American liner, launched; the emperor present	10 Jan. 1900

STEWARD OF ENGLAND, LORD HIGH. The first grand officer of the crown. This office was established prior to the reign of Edward the Confessor, and was formerly annexed to the lordship of Hinckley, Leicestershire, belonging to the family of Montfort, earls of Leicester, who were, in right thereof, lord high stewards of England; but Simon de Montfort, the last earl of this family, having raised a rebellion against his sovereign, Henry III., was attainted, and his estate forfeited to the king, who abolished the office, 1265. It is now revived only *pro hâc vice*, at a coronation, or the trial of a peer. The first afterwards appointed was Thomas, second son of Henry IV. The first for the trial of a peer was Edward, earl of Devon, on the arraignment of the earl of Huntingdon, in 1400. The last was lord Denman at the trial of the earl of Cardigan, 16 Feb. 1841. The duke of Hamilton was lord high steward at the coronations of William IV. 1831, and Victoria, 1838.

STEWARD OF THE HOUSEHOLD, LORD (an ancient office), has the sole direction of the king's house below-stairs; he has no formal grant of his office, but receives his charge from the sovereign in person, who, delivering to him a white wand, the symbol of his office, says, "*Seneschal, tenez le bâton de notre maison.*" This officer has been called lord steward since 1540; previously to the 31st of Henry VIII. he was styled grand master of the household. His function as a judge was abolished in 1849.

STEWART, see *Stuart*.

STICKLESTADT (Norway). Here Olaf II., aided by the Swedes, was defeated in his endeavours to recover his kingdom from Canute, king of Denmark, and slain, 29 July, 1030. He was afterwards sainted, on account of his zeal for Christianity.

STIPENDIARY MAGISTRATES, see *Magistrates.*

STIRLING (S. Scotland). For the battle of Stirling (1297), see *Cambuskenneth*. The strong castle was taken by Edward I. of England, 1304. Here James II. stabbed the earl of Douglas, 13 Feb. 1452, and here James VI. was crowned, 24 July, 1567. Stirling surrendered to Monk, 14 Aug. 1651. The statue of king Robert Bruce unveiled, 24 Nov. 1877.

A gigantic bronze statue of sir William Wallace unveiled at the National Wallace Monument 25 June, 1887.
Population, 1881, 16,013; 1891, 16,895; 1901, 18,403.

STIRRUPS were unknown to the ancients. Gracchus fitted the highways with stones to enable the horsemen to mount. Warriors had projections on their spears for the same purpose. Stirrups were used in the 5th century, but were not common even in the 12th.

STOCKACH, a town in Baden, near which the Austrians, under the archduke Charles, defeated the French, 25 March, 1799; and Moreau defeated Kray, 3 May, 1800.

STOCKHOLM, capital of Sweden (built on *holmen*, or islands), was fortified by Berger Jarl about 1254. Here the Swedish nobility were massacred by Christian II. in 1520; see *Sweden*. Population, 1887, 227,964; 1890, 246,154; 1900, 300,624.

Peace of Stockholm, between the king of Great Britain and the queen of Sweden, by which the former acquired the duchies of Bremen and Verden as elector of Brunswick . . . . 20 Nov. 1719
Treaty of Stockholm, between Sweden and Russia, in favour of the duke of Holstein-Gottorp, 24 March, 1724
Another between England and Sweden . 3 March, 1813
And one between England, France, and Sweden, 21 Nov. 1855
Great fire, 25 houses destroyed . . . 21 Sept. 1892
Scandinavian exhibition of arts and industries opened, end of . . . . Aug. 1897

STOCKINGS of silk are said to have been first worn by Henry II. of France, 1547. In 1560 queen Elizabeth was presented with a pair of knit black silk stockings, by her silk-woman, Mrs. Montague, and she never wore cloth ones any more. *Howell.* He adds, "Henry VIII. wore ordinary cloth hose, except there came from Spain, by great chance, a pair of silk stockings; for Spain very early abounded with silk." Edward VI. was presented with a pair of Spanish silk stockings by his merchant, sir Thomas Gresham; and the present was then much taken notice of. *Idem.* Others relate that William Rider, a London apprentice, seeing at the house of an Italian merchant a pair of knit worsted stockings from Mantua, made a pair like them, the first made in England, which he presented to the earl of Pembroke, 1564. *Stow.* The art of weaving stockings in a *frame* was invented in England by the rev. Mr. Lee, of Cambridge, in 1589, twenty-five years after he had learnt to knit them with wires or needles. Cotton stockings were first made in 1730; see *Cotton*. *Digitated stockings* (like gloves), introduced 1882.

STOCKPORT (in Cheshire) has become eminent on account of the cotton trade. Heaton Norris, in Lancashire, is united to it by a bridge over the river. Here the Manchester blanketeers were dispersed, 11 March, 1817; and here was a serious religious riot, when two Roman catholic chapels were destroyed, and the houses of man[y] Roman catholics gutted, and their furniture an[d] other contents smashed or burnt, 29 June, 185[2]. Great mill fire, 9 deaths, 5 Nov. 1902.

STOCKS, in which drunkards were placed. The last in London was removed from St. Clemen[t] Danes, Strand, 4 Aug. 1826.

STOCKS. The public funding system originated in Venice, about 1173, and was introduced int[o] Florence in 1340. The term *stocks* is applied t[o] money invested in public securities such as our National Debt (*which see*). The Stock Exchange, in Capel Court, London, was established in 1801.

The Forged Transfer of Stock Act was passed 5 Aug. 1891
"*Bulls*" are persons who buy stock and thus cause the market to rise; "*Bears*" those who sell and cause it to fall.
Act to prevent *stock-jobbing* passed March, 1734; repealed 1860
Stockbrokers' rents to the city of London abolished 1884; came into effect . . . . . Sept. 1886
The foundation of the Stock Exchange, in Capel-court, the residence of the lord mayor, sir Wm. Capel, in 1504, was laid on 18 May, 1801. It was stated on the first stone that the public debt was then 552,730,924*l*. Members, 1864, about 1100; above 2000 in 1878; 4,673 members and 3,147 clerks in 1901
The memorable Stock Exchange hoax, for which admiral lord Cochrane (afterwards lord Dundonald), Johnstone, and others, were convicted, 22 Feb. 1814. Lord Cochrane was in consequence expelled the house of commons. His innocence was afterwards proved, and he was restored to his rank by king William IV., and to the honours belonging to it by queen Victoria.
Stock-exchange coffee-house destroyed by fire, 11 Feb. 1816
Royal Commission (lord Penzance, justice Blackburn, Mr. Spencer Walpole, and others) to examine into the constitution and management of the London stock exchange, agreed to, 20 March, 1877; report issued; the majority recommend incorporation and other changes; signed 31 July, 1878
The number of stock-holders in 1840 amounted to 337,481.
Three per cent. annuities created 1726
Three per cent. consols created 1731
Three per cent. reduced 1746
Three per cent. annuities, payable at the South Sea-house 1751
Three-and-a-half per cent. annuities created . . 1758
Long annuities 1761
Four per cent. consols 1762
Five per cent. annuities . . . . 1797 and 1802
Five per cents. reduced to four 1822
Old four per cents. reduced to three-and-a-half in 1824
Further reductions made in 1825, 1830, 1834, 1841, and 1844; the maximum being now three per cent.
Further reductions proposed by Mr. Goschen (2¾ to 2½ in 15 years under specified conditions) 9 March; new threes all converted or paid off . 6 April, 1888
Messrs. Thomas and Co., bankrupts, for a large amount, suspected frauds . . . 31 Jan. 1884
Three per cents. convertible into 2¾, and 2½ per cent. by Act of 2 Sept., 1884.
The local loans stock exchangeable for the three per cents. consols created by the National Debt and Local Loans Act passed . . . 12 July, 1887
National War Loan (S. Africa) 30,000,000*l*. at 2¾ per cent. issued in consols . . . . March, 1900
New issue of 60,000,000*l*. at 2¾ per cent. in consols, amply and promptly taken up, 20 April, 1901; see *Budget.*
New loan in 32,000,000*l*. consols at 93½ issued, and 16,000,000*l*. placed, 16 April, closed . 18 April, 1902
Lord Goschen stated that the country had borrowed practically 159,000,000 since 1899, leaving about 122,000,000*l*. additional permanent debt, 6 June, 1902

By a return of the average price of the public funds by the Commissioners for the reduction of the national debt, it appears that *Consols* (*i. e.*, consoli dated annuities, paying 3 per cent. per annum) averaged in the year—

Year	£	s.	d.	Year	£	s.	d.
1749	£100	0	0	1815	£58	13	9
1780	63	13	6	1820	68	12	0
1785	68	6	6	1825	90	0	8
1790	71	2	6	1830	89	15	7
1795	74	8	6	1840	89	17	6
1798	39	10	0	1845	93	2	6
1800	66	3	3	1848	86	15	0
1805	58	14	0	1850	96	10	0
1810	67	16	3	1852 (Dec. 101*l*. 10s.)	99	12	6

The price of £100 stock varied in

1853,	from	£101	to	£$90\frac{5}{8}$
1854,	,,	96	,,	$85\frac{3}{4}$
1855,	,,	$93\frac{3}{4}$	,,	$86\frac{1}{2}$
1856,	,,	$96\frac{1}{8}$	,,	$87\frac{5}{8}$
1857,	,,	$95\frac{1}{8}$	,,	$86\frac{1}{8}$
1858,	,,	$98\frac{5}{8}$	,,	94
1859,	,,	$97\frac{5}{8}$	,,	89
1861,	,,	$94\frac{1}{4}$	,,	$89\frac{1}{2}$
1862,	,,	$94\frac{3}{4}$	,,	$90\frac{3}{8}$
1863,	,,	94	,,	90
1864,	,,	$91\frac{7}{8}$	,,	$87\frac{1}{8}$
1865,	,,	$87\frac{7}{8}$	,,	$86\frac{1}{4}$
1866,	average	88	June	$86\frac{1}{4}$
1867,	,,	93	,,	$94\frac{1}{2}$
1868,	,,	$93\frac{7}{8}$	,,	$94\frac{5}{8}$
1869,	,,	$92\frac{7}{8}$	,,	$92\frac{3}{8}$
1870,	,,	$92\frac{1}{8}$	,,	$92\frac{3}{4}$
1871,	,,	$92\frac{5}{8}$	,,	92
1872,	,,	$92\frac{1}{2}$	,,	$92\frac{3}{8}$
1873,	,,	$92\frac{1}{2}$	,,	$92\frac{1}{4}$
1874,	,,	$92\frac{1}{4}$	,,	$92\frac{5}{8}$
1875,	,,	$93\frac{1}{4}$	,,	93
1876,	,,	95	,,	$94\frac{1}{2}$
1877,	,,	$95\frac{3}{8}$	,,	$94\frac{1}{2}$
1878,	,,	$95\frac{3}{16}$	,,	$95\frac{7}{8}$
1879,	,,	$97\frac{1}{2}$	,,	$97\frac{1}{4}$
1880,	,,	$98\frac{3}{8}$	,,	$98\frac{7}{8}$
1881,	,,	100	,,	$100\frac{3}{4}$
1882,	average	$100\frac{1}{2}$	June	$100\frac{1}{4}$
1883,	,,	$101\frac{3}{16}$	,,	$100\frac{1}{2}$

1884, highest $102\frac{5}{8}$; lowest, 31 Dec. $98\frac{15}{16}$.
1885, average . . $99\frac{1}{8}$
1886, ,, $100\frac{3}{8}$; 13 May, (highest price recorded) $103\frac{1}{2}$.
1887, average . . . $101\frac{3}{8}$

New Consols ($2\frac{3}{4}$)

1888, 9 June . . $99\frac{1}{8}$
Average $97\frac{11}{16}$.
1889, 2 Jan. $99\frac{3}{4}$; 28 June $98\frac{3}{8}$. Average 98.

1890, 2 Jan.	$97\frac{1}{4}$
,, 10 April	98
,, 5 June	$97\frac{3}{4}$
,, 3 July	$96\frac{5}{8}$
,, 4 Sept.	$95\frac{7}{8}$
,, 2 Oct.	$94\frac{7}{8}$
,, 15 Nov. (Baring difficulty)	$93\frac{7}{8}$
,, 4 Dec.	96
Average $96\frac{3}{8}$.	
1891, 2 Jan.	$95\frac{7}{8}$
,, 5 March	96
,, 4 June	$94\frac{7}{8}$
,, 2 July	96
,, 1 Oct.	$94\frac{1}{2}$
,, 3 Dec.	95
Average $95\frac{3}{8}$.	
1892, 7 Jan.	$95\frac{5}{8}$
,, 1 April	$96\frac{1}{2}$
,, 5 May	$97\frac{3}{8}$
,, 2 June	$96\frac{7}{8}$
,, 1 July	97
,, 3 Nov.	$96\frac{7}{8}$
,, 1 Dec.	$96\frac{7}{8}$
Average $96\frac{11}{16}$.	
1893, 5 Jan.	$98\frac{1}{4}$
,, 4 April	$98\frac{5}{8}$
,, 1 Sept.	$97\frac{7}{8}$
,, 2 Oct.	$98\frac{5}{8}$
,, 2 Nov.	$97\frac{3}{4}$
,, 2 Dec.	98
Average $98\frac{3}{8}$	
1894, 2 Jan.	$98\frac{1}{2}$
,, 1 Feb.	99
,, 2 May	$100\frac{3}{8}$
,, 1 June	$101\frac{3}{8}$
,, 1 Aug.	$101\frac{7}{8}$
,, 1 Sept.	$102\frac{3}{8}$
,, 1 Oct.	$101\frac{1}{4}$
,, 2 Nov.	102
,, 1 Dec.	$103\frac{3}{8}$
1895, 22 Jan.	105
,, 1 Feb.	$103\frac{1}{4}$
,, 1 March	$104\frac{1}{4}$
,, 1 April	$104\frac{3}{4}$
,, 2 May	$105\frac{3}{8}$
,, 4 June	$106\frac{9}{16}$
,, 1 July	$107\frac{1}{16}$
,, 1 Aug.	$107\frac{1}{2}$
,, 2 Sept.	$107\frac{1}{2}$
,, 1 Oct.	$107\frac{11}{16}$
,, 2 Nov.	107
,, 2 Dec.	$106\frac{9}{16}$
1896, 2 Jan.	$106\frac{3}{8}$
,, 1 Feb.	$107\frac{15}{16}$
,, 21 Feb.	110
,, 2 March	$108\frac{15}{16}$
,, 1 April	$109\frac{11}{16}$
,, 2 May	$111\frac{3}{8}$
,, 1 June	113
,, 1 July	$113\frac{11}{16}$
,, 1 Aug.	$113\frac{3}{8}$
,, 1 Sept.	$111\frac{13}{16}$
,, 1 Oct	$110\frac{1}{16}$
,, 3 Nov.	$108\frac{3}{8}$
,, 1 Dec.	$111\frac{7}{16}$
1897, 2 Jan.	$111\frac{15}{16}$
,, 1 Feb.	$112\frac{11}{16}$
,, 1 March	$111\frac{13}{16}$
,, 1 April	$111\frac{13}{16}$
,, 3 May	$112\frac{9}{16}$
,, 1 June	$112\frac{3}{4}$
,, 1 July	$112\frac{7}{8}$
,, 3 Aug.	$113\frac{1}{2}$
,, 1 Sept.	$111\frac{7}{16}$
,, 1 Oct.	$111\frac{15}{16}$
,, 2 Nov.	112
,, 1 Dec.	$112\frac{7}{8}$
1898, 3 Jan.	113
,, 1 Feb.	$112\frac{7}{16}$
,, 1 March	$112\frac{3}{4}$
,, 1 April	$111\frac{13}{16}$
,, 1 June	$111\frac{5}{16}$
,, 1 July	112
,, 2 Aug.	111
,, 1 Sept.	110
,, 1 Oct.	$109\frac{7}{8}$
,, 1 Nov.	$108\frac{3}{4}$
,, 1 Dec.	$110\frac{3}{8}$
1899, 3 Jan.	$110\frac{7}{8}$
,, 1 Feb.	111
,, 1 March	$110\frac{1}{4}$
,, 4 April	$110\frac{3}{4}$
,, 2 May	$110\frac{5}{16}$
,, 1 June	$109\frac{5}{8}$
,, 3 July	$107\frac{13}{16}$
,, 1 Aug.	$106\frac{5}{8}$
,, 1 Sept.	105
,, 2 Oct.	$102\frac{3}{4}$
,, 1 Dec.	$102\frac{3}{8}$
1900, 2 Jan.	$99\frac{5}{8}$
,, 1 Feb.	$100\frac{1}{2}$
,, 1 March	$100\frac{5}{16}$
,, 2 April	$101\frac{3}{16}$
,, 2 May	$100\frac{9}{16}$
,, 1 June	$102\frac{5}{8}$
1900, 2 July	$100\frac{1}{2}$
,, 1 Aug.	$97\frac{5}{16}$
,, 1 Sept.	$98\frac{11}{16}$
,, 1 Oct.	$98\frac{5}{16}$
,, 2 Nov.	$98\frac{3}{4}$
,, 1 Dec.	98
1901, 2 Jan.	$97\frac{5}{16}$
,, 4 Feb.	$96\frac{11}{16}$
,, 1 March	$97\frac{1}{16}$
,, 1 April	$95\frac{9}{16}$
,, 2 May	$94\frac{1}{2}$
,, 1 June	$94\frac{1}{16}$
,, 1 July	$93\frac{7}{16}$
,, 1 Aug.	$93\frac{1}{4}$
,, 2 Sept.	$94\frac{1}{16}$
,, 1 Oct.	$93\frac{7}{16}$
,, 2 Nov.	$91\frac{11}{16}$
,, 2 Dec.	$91\frac{1}{4}$
1902, 2 Jan.	$93\frac{15}{16}$
,, 1 Feb.	$94\frac{3}{8}$
1902, 1 March	$94\frac{11}{16}$
,, 1 April	$94\frac{3}{16}$
,, 2 May	$94\frac{13}{16}$
,, 2 June	$96\frac{9}{16}$
,, 1 July	$96\frac{5}{16}$
,, 1 Aug.	$95\frac{5}{8}$
,, 1 Sept.	94
,, 1 Oct.	$93\frac{3}{16}$
,, 3 Nov.	$93\frac{3}{8}$
,, 1 Dec.	$92\frac{7}{8}$
1903, 2 Jan.	$93\frac{1}{4}$
,, 2 Feb.	$93\frac{3}{8}$
,, 2 March	$92\frac{1}{4}$
,, 1 April	$90\frac{1}{4}$
,, 2 May	$91\frac{7}{8}$
,, 2 June	$91\frac{7}{8}$
,, 1 July	$92\frac{5}{8}$
,, 4 Aug.	$91\frac{1}{8}$
,, 1 Sept.	$90\frac{3}{4}$
,, 1 Oct.	$88\frac{3}{8}$

"During the greatest crisis ever developed in the history of the world the funds remain day after day without a fractional movement." *Times*, 11 Oct. 1870.

Purchase of stock for 10*l*. legalised, 1880.

Mr. (aft. sir) H. C. Burdett's "Official Intelligence of British, American, and Foreign Securities," published under the sanction of the Stock Exchange Committee, 1882 *et seq.*; he was secretary at the Stock Exchange, 1880–97. "The Story of the Stock Exchange, its History and Position," by Chas. Duguid, pub. 1901.

Consols lowest point ($87\frac{3}{8}$) since 1866, 29 Sept. 1903.

STOICS, disciples of Zeno, the philosopher (about 290 B.C.); obtained the name because they listened to his instructions in a porch (Greek, *stoa*) at Athens. Zeno taught, that man's supreme happiness consisted in living agreeably to nature and reason, and that God was the soul of the world. *Stanley.*

STOKE, EAST (near Newark, Nottinghamshire). Near here, on 16 June, 1487, the adherents of Lambert Simnel, who personated Edward, earl of Warwick, and claimed the crown, were defeated by Henry VII. John de la Pole, the earl of Lincoln, and most of the leaders, were slain. Simnel was afterwards employed in the king's household.

STONE. Stone buildings erected in England by Benedict Biscop about 670. A stone bridge built at Bow, in the 11th or 12th centuries, is accounted the first; but a bridge exists at Crowland, which is said to have been built in 860; see *Bridges*. The first stone building in Ireland was probably a round tower; see *Building*. Stone china-ware was made by Wedgwood in 1762. *Artificial stone* for statues was manufactured by a Neapolitan, and introduced into England, 1776. Stone paper was made in 1776; see *Ransome's Artificial Stone*, and *Lithotomy*. For stone implements, see *Flints*, and *Piano-forte*. An orchestra composed of wind instruments made of terra-cotta appeared in London in 1874.

STONEHENGE (on Salisbury Plain, Wiltshire) is said to have been erected on the counsel of Merlin, by Aurelius Ambrosius, in memory of 460 Britons, who were murdered by Hengist the Saxon about 450. *Geoffrey of Monmouth.* Erected as a sepulchral monument of Ambrosius, 500. *Polydore Vergil.* An ancient temple of the Britons, in which the Druids officiated. *Dr. Stukeley.* The Britons are said to have held annual meetings at Abury and Stonehenge, when laws were made and justice administered. The cursus near Stonehenge was discovered by Dr. Stukeley, 6 Aug. 1723. The origin and object of these remains are still very obscure. See W. M. Flinders Petrie's "Stonehenge: Plans, Description, and Theories." 1880.

The thorough preservation of Stonehenge strongly advocated Aug. 1886. Fall of one of the uprights and capstone, 31 Dec. 1900, afterwards restored, Stonehenge enclosed within a fence, 1901.

STONEWALL BRIGADE, see *United States*, 1862, note.

STONYHURST COLLEGE, N.E. Lancashire. This institution for the education of Roman Catholics was begun by the arrival in 1794 of 18 Jesuit fathers, with their pupils, of the seminary of St. Omer (*which see*), by invitation of Mr. Thos. Weld of Lulworth, himself formerly a pupil. At first they were placed in an old mansion here. The undertaking prospered, and during this century the present spacious buildings were erected, including a chapel, library, museum, and observatory. In 1892 there were 300 pupils and 30 masters. In 1840 the college was affiliated to the University of London.

The chief of the observatory, Father Stephen Joseph Perry, F.R.S., at Kerguelen, an isle in the S. Indian Ocean, observed the transit of Venus, 8 Dec. 1874. He died at Salut island, near Demerara, where he had gone to observe the eclipse of the sun . . . . . 22 Dec. 1889

STORM-WARNINGS, see under *Meteorology*.

STORMS, see *Meteorology*, *Cyclones*, and *Waterspouts*. The following are recorded:—

In London a storm raged which destroyed 1500 houses, 944.

In several parts of England, the sky being very dark, the wind coming from the S.W.; many churches were destroyed; and in London 500 houses fell, 5 Oct. 1091.

On the coast of Calais, when Hugh de Beauvais and several thousand foreigners, on their voyage to assist king John against the barons, perished, 1215. *Holinshed.*

It thundered 15 days successively, with tempests of rain and wind, 1233.

Storm with violent lightnings; one flash passed through a chamber where Edward I. and his queen were conversing, did them no damage, but killed two of their attendants, 1285. *Hoveden.*

Violent storm of hail near Chartres, in France, which fell on the army of Edward III. then on its march. The hail was so large that the army and horses suffered very much, and Edward was obliged to conclude a peace, 1339. *Matt. Paris.*

When Richard II.'s queen came from Bohemia, on her setting foot on shore an awful storm arose, and her ship and a number of others were dashed to pieces in the harbour, Jan. 1382. *Holinshed.*

Richard's second queen also brought a storm with her to the English coasts, in which the king's baggage was lost, and many ships cast away, 1396. *Holinshed.*

Hurricane, throughout Europe, which did very considerable damage, on 3 Sept. 1658, the day that Cromwell died. *Mortimer.*

Storm on east coast of England: 200 colliers and coasters lost, with most of their crews, 1696.

The "*Great* Storm," one of the most terrible that ever raged in England. The devastation on land was immense; and in the harbours and on the coasts the loss in shipping and in lives was still greater, 26-27 Nov. 1703. The loss sustained in London alone was calculated at 2,000,000*l*. sterling. The number of persons drowned in the floods of the Severn and Thames, and lost on the coast of Holland, and in ships blown from their anchors and never heard of afterwards, is thought to have been 8000. Twelve men-of-war, with more than 1800 men on board, were lost within sight of their own shore. Trees were torn up by the roots, 17,000 of them in Kent alone. The Eddystone light-house was destroyed, and in it the ingenious contriver of it, Winstanley, and the persons who were with him. The Bishop of Bath and Wells and his lady were killed in bed in their palace in Somersetshire. Multitudes of cattle were also lost: in one level 15,000 sheep were drowned.

Snow-storm in Sweden, when 7000 Swedes, it is said, perished upon the mountains, in their march to attack Drontheim, 1719.

One in India, when many hundreds of vessels were cast away, a fleet of Indiamen greatly damaged, and some ships lost, and 30,000 persons perished, 11 Oct. 1737.

Dreadful hurricane at the Havannah: many public edifices and 4048 houses were destroyed, and 1000 inhabitants perished, 25 Oct. 1768.

Awful storm in the north of England, in which many vessels were destroyed, and four Dublin packets foundered, 29 Oct. 1775.

One at Surat, in the East Indies; destroyed 7000 of the inhabitants, 22 April, 1782.

One hundred and thirty-one villages and farms laid waste in France, 1785.

One general throughout Great Britain: several hundred sail of shipping destroyed or damaged, 6 Oct. 1794.

One which did vast damage in London, and throughout almost the whole of England, 8 Nov. 1800.

A tremendous storm throughout Great Britain and Ireland, by which immense damage was done, and many ships wrecked, 16-17 Dec. 1814.

An awful gale, by which a great number of vessels were lost, and much damage was done to the shipping in general on the English coast, 31 Aug. 1816.

Dreadful hurricane, ravaged the Leeward Islands, from the 20th to the 22nd Sept. 1819. At the island of St. Thomas alone, 104 vessels were lost.

Great storm along the coast from Durham to Cornwall; many vessels lost, Nov. 1821.

In Ireland, particularly in the vicinity of Dublin, many houses were thrown down, and vast numbers unroofed, 12 Dec. 1822.

Awful storm on the coast of England: many vessels lost, and 13 driven ashore and wrecked in Plymouth alone, 12-13 Jan. 1828.

At Gibraltar, where more than 100 vessels were destroyed, 18 Feb. 1828.

Dreadful storm at the Cape of Good Hope, where immense property was lost, 16 July, 1831.

A hurricane visited London and its neighbourhood, which did great damage to the buildings, but without the destruction of human life, though many serious accidents occurred, 28 Oct. 1838.

Awful hurricane on west coast of England, and in Ireland. The storm raged through Cheshire, Staffordshire, and Warwickshire; 20 persons were killed in Liverpool, by the falling of buildings, and 100 were drowned in the neighbourhood; the coasts and harbours were covered with wrecks, the value of two of the vessels lost being nearly half-a million sterling. In Limerick, Galway, Athlone, and other places, more than 200 houses were blown down, and as many more were burnt, the winds spreading the fires. Dublin suffered dreadfully; London and its neighbourhood scarcely sustained any damage, 6-7 Jan. 1839.

[The winter of 1852-3 (Dec. and Jan.) was one of storms, many of which were very destructive.]

Great storm in the Black Sea, 13-16 Nov. 1854, causing much loss of life, shipping, and stores sent for the allied armies in the Crimea.

Great storm on N. coast of Europe, &c., 31 Dec. 1854.

Great storm on N.E. coast of Scotland; 42 fishermen lost, 23 Nov. 1857.

Dreadful storm on the night 25-26 Oct.; the Royal Charter totally lost, and many other vessels; another storm, 31 Oct. and 1 Nov. 1859.

Great storm in the channel, causing much loss of life and property, 1 Jan. 1860.

Dreadful gales, doing much mischief, 26, 27, 28 Feb.: 28 May; and 2 June, 1860.

Great storm; part of the Crystal Palace blown down Chichester cathedral steeple fell, 20-21 Feb. 1861.

Great storm on British coasts, 143 wrecks, 28 May, 1861.

Storm on the north-east; 50 wrecks, 13-14 Nov. 1861.

At Market Laverton, &c.; much damage to crops by hail, 2 Sept. 1862.

Storm on British coasts; many wrecks, 19, 20 Oct. 1862.

There were severe gales, doing much damage, and loss of life, 19 Jan. &c. 1863; and 14 Jan. &c. 1865 (see under *Wrecks*).

Dreadful hurricane in the Indian Ocean, &c. (see *Calcutta*), 5 Oct. 1864.

Hurricane at Lisbon, causes much damage, worst for many years, 13 Dec. 1864.

Severe gales; many vessels and lives lost (see *Wrecks*), 6-11 Jan. 1866; 2-4 Dec. 1867; 22 Jan. and 31 Jan. and 1 Feb. 1868; 11-12 Sept. 1869.

Severe storm; much damage; barometer very low, 24 Jan. 1872.

After several days' intense heat, violent storms, and deluges of rain in midland and southern counties; several persons killed, 24-26 June, 1872.
Very stormy in July and August, 1872.
Violent gale; much destruction (wind. greatest velocity 57 miles an hour), 8 Dec. 1872.
Awful storms in Scotland, and N. England; loss of life, and much damage, 22, 23 July; in Lancashire and Yorkshire, 16 Dec. 1873.
Awful storm, N. E. London; several persons killed; churches and buildings fired; railways flooded, 11 July, 1874.
Violent gales, with destruction of life and property, 21 Oct.; Nov. 29; 7, 8, 10, 11 Dec. 1874.
Much destruction by typhoon at Macao, Hong Kong, &c., 22 Sept. 1874.
Severe snowstorms in Scotland, several lives lost, 1, 3 Jan. 1875.
Destructive storms at Buda-Pesth, about 200 killed, 26 June, 1875.
On coast of Texas: Galveston, and other places much injured; villages washed away by the sea; great loss of life, 15–18 Sept. 1875.
Severe snowstorm, south England: destruction of life and property; telegraph wires broken, 12 March, 1875.
Severe storms; great loss of shipping, 11-13 Nov.; 2, 3, and 22-24 Dec. 1876, and 2 Jan. 1877.
Most violent gale; great destruction of property on land and shipping throughout England, with loss of life, 14, 15 Oct. 1877.
Again; much damage on S.E. coast, &c., 24, 25 Nov. 1877.
Storm and heavy rain in London; inundations, 10, 11 April, 1878.
Many thunderstorms, destroying life and property in England, Aug. 1878.
At Kew and neighbourhood, 2, 3 Aug.; in Cheshire and Wales, 16, 17 Aug. 1879.
Violent gale; Tay bridge (*which see*) blown down, 28 Dec. 1879.
Destructive tornadoes, &c., western states North America; great loss of life and property, about 18 April, 1880.
Many thunderstorms in England, July, 1880.
Severe storms in England, with much destruction by inundations, 27, 28 Oct. 1880.
Severe snowstorm, or blizzard; railways and other traffic largely stopped; great loss of life at sea, 17-21 Jan. 1881.
Violent hurricane in England: great destruction of life and property: houses thrown down or unroofed; large trees torn up by the roots; telegraph wires and poles blown down; about 130 wrecks (105 British), &c., 14-19 Oct. 1881.
Many wrecks on south and west coasts of England with much loss of life, 19-20 Oct. 1881.
Great destruction of life and property by gales, 26, 27 Nov. 1881.
Lighthouse, Calf Rock, in Bantry Bay destroyed, 27 Nov. 1881.
Six men left on the rock got off, 9 Dec. 1881.
By a typhoon in Haifong, &c., China, about 300,000 persons perished, 8 Oct. 1881.
Destructive gales in England, &c.; many wrecks and loss of life by sea and land, 17-21 Dec. 1881.
Severe gale; much destruction in England and Scotland, 6 Jan.; another, 29 April, 1882.
Tornado in Iowa, &c., Grinnell and other towns nearly destroyed; great loss of life, about 16 June, *et seq.*, 1882.
Violent gales with damage, 22, 23 Aug.; 24 Oct. 1882; 26, 27, 28 Jan., 10 Feb., 6 March, 1883.
Tornadoes in southern states, U.S.A., about 150 killed, April, 1883.
Violent gale in British channel, &c.; many wrecks, 1-2 Sept. 1883.
Destructive gale on the Scotch and Irish coasts, 26 Sept. 1883.
Another with great loss of life and damage in London and other parts of Britain, morning, 12 Dec. 1883.
Violent S.W. gales; destruction of life and property; 23-24 Jan. 1884; very severe; many disasters, 26, 27 Jan. 1884.
Tornadoes in southern states, U.S.A.; about 600 killed, about 18 Feb. 1884.
Storm in Catania, Sicily (see *Sicily*), 7 Oct. 1884.
Destructive snowstorms in Piedmont (see *Italy*), 16 Jan. *et seq.* 1885.
Heavy storms on the Labrador coast, about 80 craft wrecked and about 300 lives lost 12–15 Oct. 1885
Storm off Colon, Panama, 15 vessels wrecked, 50 lives lost 2 Dec. 1885.
Heavy snowstorm, N.E. England, &c.; locomotion stopped 1, 2, 3 March, 1886.
Destructive hurricane at Madrid, 32 lives lost, 320 wounded 12 May, 1886.
Destructive tornadoes in S. Ohio, Indiana, Illinois, &c., U.S.A. 12–15 May, 1886.
Violent storm N.E. France, much damage at Rheims, Nancy, &c. 10 Aug. 1886.
Hurricane at St. Vincent; great loss of life and property 16 Aug. 1886.
Violent gale in Texas, &c., causing inundation, above 250 persons drowned, 12 Oct. 1886.
Severe gale; very destructive on sea and land (see *Wrecks*) 15–16 Oct. 1886.
Destructive gale and storm, especially in S. & W. England; many wrecks and loss of life 8, 9 Dec. 1886 (see under *Lifeboat*).
Destructive snowstorm, specially E. and S. England; many wrecks; telegraphic and railway communications stopped; trees blown down, &c., 26–27 Dec. 1886.
Destructive hurricane at Bordeaux and S. France with loss of life 16 Aug. 1887.
Violent thunderstorm in London with destruction of property, several persons killed, about 5.30 p.m.; lasted about 4 hours 17 Aug.; many storms throughout the country, 17 Aug. *et seq.* 1887.
W. gale; destruction of life and property in France, the Channel, and S. England 30 Oct., another gale on the W. coast, destruction at Holyhead, Liverpool and in the Bristol channel 31 Oct.–1 Nov.; another gale on the S.E. coast, 3 Nov. 1887.
Snowstorm (blizzard) in N.W. of United States; about 235 persons perish and much cattle 11–13 Jan.; another in New York 26 Jan. 1888.
Cyclone in Illinois, U.S.A.; great destruction of life and property 19 Feb. 1888.
Violent gale; several wrecks and loss of life, 9–11 March, 1888.
A destructive blizzard from the N.W. desolated the eastern coast of United States; communication between New York, Philadelphia and Boston suspended; many wrecks; great loss of life (about 400) and property; food at famine prices 11–13 March, 1888.
Town of Ninnescah in Kansas destroyed by a gale 27 March, 1888.
Great storm and a tidal wave, much destruction, near Wellington, New Zealand 28 March, 1888.
Destructive hurricane in Dacca, N.E. India; about 69 persons killed 7 April, 1888.
Great storm in Ontario and Quebec, many persons killed by lightning and fright, estimated loss in Quebec, 1,500,000 dollars 16 Aug. 1888.
Destructive cyclone in the West Indies (Cuba, &c.), 4 Sept. 1888.
Destructive gale; Scotland, N. England and Ireland; many shipwrecks; Forth bridge damaged, 15–16 Nov. 1888.
Severe storm on the N. American E. coast; more than 50 vessels wrecked and about 45 lives lost 25 Nov. 1888.
Tornado in eastern states U.S., especially in Pennsylvania; great destruction and loss of life in about 200 miles, especially at Pittsburg (14 killed) and at Reading (24 killed), through collapse of a silk-mill; suspension-bridge, Niagara, wrecked 9 Jan. 1889.
Destructive gales over Britain; wrecks and loss of life 2, 3, 8 Feb. 1889.
Violent hurricane in the Pacific (see *Samoan Isles*) 15, 16 March, 1889.
Destructive storm on the east coast of the United States 10 May, 1889.
Great storm in South Germany, especially in Austria, Bohemia, &c., great loss of life and property, 17 May; in Switzerland 3–4 June, 1889.
Destructive storm, Flintshire, Cheshire and Lancashire; heavy rain and large hail causing floods, crops much injured, buildings struck and fired 2 June, 1889.
Great storms over the United Kingdom; wrecks with loss of life, 21 Aug. and 5-7 Oct. 1889.
Easterly gales on the Atlantic coast; wrecks with loss of life off Long Island, New Jersey, &c., 11-12 Sept. 1889.
29 vessels wrecked in Delaware Bay, about 31 lives lost, 13 Sept. 1889.

Great storm in Sardinia (*which see*), 7 Oct. 1889.
Destructive storm on the coast of Carolina, 26, 27 Oct. 1889.
Destructive storms in the Western States, U.S.A., 12 Jan.; in Canada, 14 Jan. 1890.
Destructive gale with loss of life in the Atlantic and on British coast, especially S. and S.W., high tides and floods, 17–27 Jan. 1890.
Destructive storm on the continent from Paris to Vienna, 23, 24 Jan. 1890.
[68 British wrecks and 67 lives lost in Jan. 1890.]
Tornadoes in the Ohio valley, from Cincinnati to Cairo; very great destruction at Louisville, where about 93 persons perish; many places in Illinois, Missouri and Indiana, suffer greatly; total loss of life about 175, 27 March, 1890.
Cyclone in Texas, much destruction, 15 persons killed, 4 May, 1890.
Tornado in Lee county, Illinois, 15 deaths, 20 June, 1890.
Great cyclone at Muscat, causing floods, about 700 persons said to have perished, reported 9 July, 1890.
Terrible cyclone in Minnesota (*which see*), July, 1890.
Destructive cyclone at Slonim, Russia, 19 lives lost, 20 July, 1890.
Cyclone in south Lawrence, Merrimac valley, Massachusetts, 100 buildings destroyed, 9 deaths, 26 July, 1890.
Destructive storms in Austria, France, Switzerland and in the United States, August, 1890.
Violent gale over Great Britain and Ireland, great destruction of life and property, especially at sea; 114 lives saved by lifeboats; viscount Cantelupe drowned and his yacht wrecked in Belfast Lough, 7 Nov. 1890.
Violent N.W. gale in the channel, several wrecks on the S. coast, 23 Nov. 1890.
Violent gales throughout Europe (see *Inundations*), 23–25 Nov. 1890.
Gale in the Gulf of St. Lawrence, 40 vessels said to be wrecked, reported 3 Dec.; much destruction of shipping and buildings, Newfoundland, reported 8 Dec. 1890.
Violent storms in the N. Atlantic, above 60 vessels lost, reported, 24 Dec. 1890.
Violent blizzard in Nebraska, South Dakota, &c., U.S.A., many perished, 7 Feb. *et seq.* 1891.
Destructive cyclone over the Fiji and Navigation Isles, great loss of life and shipping, 12, 13 Feb. 1891.
Another blizzard in Minnesota, Iowa, Illinois and Wisconsin, 8, 9 March, 1891.
Great snow storm, or blizzard, throughout England, especially in the south and west; railway traffic, post and telegraph greatly impeded, in some places totally stopped; many wrecks and loss of life in the channel; hurricanes near Dover and Plymouth; wrecks of fishing boats at Hastings and other places. The *Victoria* (capt. Shirley) had a long dangerous passage from Dover to Calais. Great Western and South-Western railways disorganized; 14 ships lost; about 60 lives lost, 9–13 March, 1891.
Destructive cyclone in S. Dakota, 2 June, 1891.
By a cyclone, the village of Ponikwa in Galicia destroyed and about 30 persons killed, 10 June, 1891.
Destructive storm in Iowa, Minnesota, and other states, about 24 June, 1891.
Destructive storm and cloud-burst in the Rhine provinces, 26 June; and over a large part of Germany, chiefly in the Crefeld district and in Brunswick, 1 July; Salzburg, 9 July, 1891.
Destructive storm at Bâton Rouge, Louisiana, with loss of life, 6 July, 1891.
Violent hurricane and rain in lower Austria, Moravia, and Upper Hungary; the season's vintage destroyed, 5 Aug. 1891.
Cloud-burst at Kollmann, between Botzen and Brixen (Tyrol), the lowlands flooded, about 60 deaths, 18 Aug. 1891.
Destructive storms and floods in Great Britain, especially on the N.W. coast, 24–26 Aug. 1891.
Destructive storm off Nova Scotia, about 20 vessels wrecked, with loss of life, about 9 Sept. 1891.
Great storm throughout S. Spain (*which see*), 11–13 Sept. 1891.
Violent storms with loss of life in midland and northern English counties, and parts of Scotland, 20, 21 Sept. 1891.
Violent cyclone over the British Isles; much destruction of houses, shipping, trees, &c.; moderate loss of life, 13–15 Oct. 1891.
Severe storm on the S. and W. coasts of England, and in Spain and S. France, 22–24 Oct. 1891.
Destructive cyclone in the bay of Bengal, &c., with loss of life (see *Andaman Islands* and *Wrecks*), 2 Nov. 1891.
Destructive gale in England, especially on the S. and W. coasts; many wrecks, with loss of life, off Sandgate, Dover, Folkestone, St. Leonards, Brighton, &c.; telegraphic communication greatly suspended 10 (night), 11 Nov. 1891.
Great damage by the gale at Boulogne, Paris, Havre, Roubaix, Rouen, Bilbao, Madrid, and other places, 11 Nov. *et seq.* 1891.
Violent gale at Liverpool and on the Irish coasts, with loss of life, 11 Nov. 1891.
Violent gales in the channel, causing wrecks and loss of life, 7–11 Dec. 1891.
Violent gales, causing wrecks and loss of life in the English Channel and France, 8, 9 Dec., over N.W. Europe and the British Isles, 10–13 Dec. 1891.
Violent blizzard in Omaha and other N.W. states, U.S.A., 26 Dec. 1891.
Destructive cyclone in Georgia, 6 Jan. 1892.
Disastrous blizzard in Wisconsin, Minnesota, and North Dakota, 9, 10 March, 1892.
Destructive tornado in the N.W. states, U.S.A., above 30 persons killed, 31 March, 1892.
Disastrous hurricane in Mauritius (*which see*), 29 April, 1892.
Destructive storms in Minnesota, &c., and in Canada, with great loss of life, 15, 16, June, 1892.
Cyclone on the Cape Verd islands, houses, shipping, plantations, and cattle destroyed, 12 Sept. 1892.
Great storm in the Black Sea, 8 ships said to have been wrecked, including the *Lord Byron*, about 7 Nov. 1892.
Destructive storm in the Black Sea, loss of 30 steamers reported, including the *City of Manchester*, Dec. 1892.
Destructive gale with loss of life through the United Kingdom, the Channels, and the North Sea, 10 Feb. 1893.
Violent cyclone in the United States, N. A., with great destruction of property and loss of life, especially in Mississippi and Georgia, 4 March; another in the Mississippi valley, reported 24 March, 1893.
Hurricane over New Caledonia and the New Hebrides; great damage to property and loss of 18 lives, reported 20 March, 1893.
Destructive cyclone in Iowa, Illinois, Indiana, Nebraska, Kansas, and Missouri, &c., many deaths, 11 April; also in Illinois, Texas, and Oklahoma, 25–28 April, 1893.
Destructive cyclones in N.W. Iowa, about 100 persons killed and much property destroyed, 6 July; on the coast of New Jersey, many wrecks with loss of life, 23, 24 Aug.; in Georgia, N. and S. Carolina and Virginia, 28, 29 Aug. 1893, see *Georgia*.
Destructive storm at New Orleans (*which see*), and along the S.E. coast, about 1200 lives lost, 2 Oct. 1893.
Violent gales over the British Isles and the continent, much property and shipping destroyed, 293 deaths reported, 16–19 Nov. 1893; wrecks (*which see*), *Hampshire*, steamship, 18 Nov.; *Princess*, of Sunderland, sunk off Flamboro', all lost, 18 Nov.; many French fishing smacks off Calais, more than 300 lives lost, 18 Nov. 1893.
Destructive gale in London and S. and W. coasts, 12 Dec. 1893.
Captain Parry, collier, wrecked off Holyhead, 12 lives lost, 12 Dec. 1893.
Violent blizzard in the west of United States, 12 Feb. 1894.
S.W. gale over the British isles, much damage on land, 6 persons killed, many wrecks, 11, 12 Feb. 1894.
Great storm over Europe and the United States, N.A., 12, 13 Feb. 1894.
Destructive storms in S. and S.W. United States, N. A., reported 20 March, 1894.
Severe gale on the coast of New Jersey, and heavy fall of snow, 10, 11 April, 1894.
Violent hailstorm at Vienna and other parts of Hungary, with loss of life, vineyards, &c., destroyed, 7 June, 1894.
Destructive cyclone at Herencia in Spain, great loss, 12 Aug. 1894.

Disastrous cyclone over Iowa, Minnesota, and Wisconsin, towns destroyed and much loss of life, 21 Sept. 1894.
Violent gale off Newfoundland, many wrecks and loss of life, reported 11 Oct. 1894.
Severe gale on the N. E. coast and in the channel, several vessels driven ashore with loss of life; also in the Bristol Channel, 20–25 Oct. 1894.
Destructive storms with much rain and floods in S.E. and W. of England, and on the continent; telegraphic communication stopped, 11–13 Nov. 1894.
Violent gale over the United Kingdom and Holland, Belgium, &c., great loss of life, much shipping and other property destroyed, especially in Liverpool, Hull, Leeds, Manchester, Belfast, Aberdeen, and other places, 21, 22 Dec. 1894.
Another gale with loss of life, 28–30 Dec. 1894.
Disastrous gale N. and S.E. coast, wrecks and loss of life, 12 Jan. 1895.
Violent gale over S. France, N. Spain, and on the Portuguese coast, 15, 16 Jan. 1895.
Destructive S.W. gale over the United Kingdom, very severe in London and midlands, with loss of life, 24 March, 1895.
Destructive cyclonic storms in Kansas, Iowa, Dakota, Sioux centre, with great loss of life, 1 May, 1895.
Violent northerly gale in the channel, 15, 16 May, 1895.
Destructive tornadoes in Kansas and Missouri, U.S., with loss of life, 6 July, 1895.
Severe thunderstorms in London and S.W. counties, with loss of life and much destruction of property, 17–22 Aug.; again, a series of thunderstorms, especially over London and S. England, 6–7 Sept. 1895.
Destructive gale on the W. coast of England, with loss of life, 1–2 Oct. 1895.
Gale and floods in different parts of British isles, with loss of life, 10, 11 Nov. 1895.
N.E. gale in the channel, with loss of life, 23–25 Nov. 1895.
Destructive storms in S. Russia and Black Sea, great loss of life, reported, 25 Nov. 1895.
N.W. gale throughout the United Kingdom, 13 Dec. 1895.
S.E. gale over the United Kingdom, great loss of life, 23–25 Dec. 1895.
Violent storms in the Black sea: 3 Russian, 4 foreign steamers, 18 sailing ships wrecked, over 100 lives lost, reported 19 Feb. 1896.
Destructive cyclones, great loss of life at Sherman, Texas, 15 May; and at St. Louis (*which see*), 27 May; another at Seneca, Missouri, 30 deaths, 30 May, 1896.
Tornado in Paris (*which see*), 10 Sept. 1896.
Destructive gales over the S.W. of the United Kingdom, with loss of life, 25 Sept.; again (see *Wrecks and Inundations*), 6, 7 Oct. 1896.
Disastrous storm in the Eastern states, U. S. N. A., with much loss of life; bridge at Columbia destroyed; the town of Cedar Keys destroyed, 29 Sept. 1896.
Destructive cyclone at Seville, 28 Oct. 1896.
Destructive storm at Athens (*which see*), 26 Nov. 1896.
Destructive gales on the E. and S. Channel coasts, 4, 5 Dec.; Bordeaux, Dieppe, and in the Mediterranean, 6, 7 Dec. 1896.
Port Darwin in Victoria wrecked by a hurricane, many deaths, reported, 7 Jan. 1897.
Destructive S.W. gales, with great loss of life, 2, 3, 4 March, 1897.
Destructive gale in Irish sea and W. coast of Gt. Britain (see *Wrecks*, *Foudroyant*, and *Manchester*), 15, 16 June, 1897.
Very destructive hailstorm and cyclone in central Essex: farmers ruined; 70 sq. miles devastated, 24 June, 1897 (see *Mansion house fund*, 1897).
Cyclone near Brindisi, much damage, 45 deaths, 21 Sept. 1897.
Destructive gale over British isles, Norway, and Denmark, many wrecks, with loss of life; damage done at London, Woolwich, Margate, Sheerness, Whitstable, and other places, 28, 29, 30 Nov.; again (see *Lifeboat*), 3 Dec.; relief funds started, Dec. 1897.
Severe gales in the channel, and elsewhere, 29 Dec. 1897; another on the West and N.E. coasts, 1, 2 Feb. 1898.
Destructive snowstorm in S.W. counties, 21–22 Feb. 1898.
Severe gales with snow, over United Kingdom, with loss of life, etc., 24–26 March, 1898.
Destructive tornadoes with loss of life, in Iowa, Illinois, Minnesota, etc., about 18 May, 1898.
Destructive tornado at St. Catherine's and Merriton Niagara, 5 deaths, 26 Sept. 1898.
Severe gale round Gt. Britain, many deaths, 15 Oct. 1898.
Again, with loss of life, 2, 3 Nov.; blizzard and floods in the Midlands and Channel, some deaths, 23–25 Nov. 1898.
Violent gale off New England, 6 vessels wrecked, 180 deaths, 27 Nov. 1898.
Destructive S.W. gale over the United Kingdom, 26, 27, 31 Dec. 1898.
Gale in the Channel and Irish sea, with loss of life, 2, 3 Jan. 1899.
Violent gales over the United Kingdom and continent, some deaths, 12–16 Jan. 1899.
Again, with floods in Wales and Thames valley, 20–24 Jan. 1899.
Destructive S.W. gale and tidal wave in Wales, 11–13 Feb. 1899.
Blizzard in New York and United States, 40 deaths, 9–13 Feb. 1899.
Destructive storm in Buenos Ayres, reported, 7 March, 1899.
Hurricane in Queensland, 411 persons drowned, 11 March, 1899.
S.W. gale over the United Kingdom, with loss of life, 7 April, 1899.
Cyclone at Kirkville, Newtown and Missouri, about 100 deaths, 27, 28 April, 1899.
Destructive hailstorms at Madrid, San Pedro and Toledo, with loss of life, 9 June, 1899.
Tornado on the Upper Mississippi, Wisconsin and Minnesota, New Richmond almost destroyed, about 200 killed and many injured, 12, 13 June, 1899.
Destructive storm off Florida, many deaths, 3 Aug. 1899.
Fearful hurricane in the West Indies (*which see*), 100 deaths, at Montserrat, 1,500 injured, 8,000 homeless, total deaths about 2,000, 7–12 Aug. 1899.
Destructive storms in S. America, see *Chili*, 8–15 Aug. 1899.
Hurricane in the Azores, wrecks and loss of life, 3 Sept. 1899.
Gale off Nova Scotia, many deaths, 8 Sept. 1899, and off Newfoundland, 400 fishing vessels reported lost, 15, 16 Sept. 1899.
Gale in the Channel, wrecks and loss of life, 29, 30 Sept. and 2 Oct. 1899.
Typhoon in Central and E. Japan, train blown off a bridge, 50 deaths, 7 Oct. 1899.
Destructive storm and floods in Salerno, about 40 deaths, 8 Oct.; again in S. Italy, much damage and 3 deaths, 20 Oct. 1899.
Destructive storm in Jamaica, several deaths, 27–30 Oct. 1899.
Gales and floods in the N., over 61 deaths, 13–17 Feb. 1900.
Cyclone in Huelva, Spain, with damage, reported, 29 April, 1900.
Destructive cyclone at Mafeking, some deaths, 29 Aug. 1900.
Destructive hurricane and tidal wave at Galveston, Texas, over 4,500 deaths, 8, 9 Sept. 1900.
Storms and floods in Granada, Spain, with loss of life, &c., reported, 2 Oct. 1900.
Hurricane off Newfoundland and Prince Edward island, French fishing fleet lost, great loss of life, 12 Sept. 1900.
Heavy rainstorm and destructive floods in the Newcastle district, 5 deaths, 26, 27 Oct. 1900.
Gale with loss of life on the E., S. and W. coasts, 6, 7 Nov. 1900.
Destructive typhoon off Guam, Philippines, hundreds killed, 11–13 Nov. 1900.
Typhoon at Hong-Kong, over 70 deaths, early Nov. 1900.
Destructive cyclone at Columbia, Tennessee, many deaths, 20 Nov. 1900.
Gale over United Kingdom, with loss of life (20*l.* from the queen, Jan. 1901), 22 Shetland fishermen drowned, 20, 21 Dec. 1900.
Destructive gale over the United Kingdom, see *Wrecks*, 27, 29 Dec. 1900.
Storm off the W. coast of Japan, 400 fishermen missing, 10 Jan. 1901.
Destructive hurricane over Herro, Norway, 35 deaths, 22 Jan. 1901.
Severe westerly gale over the British isles, 27, 28 Jan. 1901.

Destructive gale over S. and W. of U.S.A., many deaths, 9, 10 March, 1901.

Destructive hurricane at Levuka, Fiji isles, 13 March, 1901.

Destructive storms and floods in the United States, some deaths at Pittsburg, mid April, 1901.

Disastrous gale on the Great lakes, U.S.A., 24, 25 May, 1901.

Destructive gale at St. Vincent, West Indies, reported, 26 Aug. 1901.

Hurricane along the coasts of Louisiana and Texas, much damage and several deaths, reported, 9 Sept. 1901.

Destructive gales and floods general over Gt. Britain, many wrecks and great loss of life, 12–14 Nov.; again, over the United Kingdom, 12, 13 Dec. 1901.

Destructive storms and floods, with some loss of life, in the United States, reported, 16 Dec. 1901

N.E. gale in the Channel and North sea, with serious loss of life, 31 Jan.–3 Feb. 1902.

Destructive windstorm, with loss of life, in Pennsylvania, 29 March, 1902.

Terrific gale, herring fleet and 250 lives lost, off Yezo, Japan, 30 April, 1902.

Fearful hurricane in Sinde, India, 40 miles of railway washed away, many deaths, much stock destroyed, mid May, 1902.

Destructive tornado at Goliad, Texas, 98 deaths, 103 injured, 18 May, 1902.

Severe snowstorms in Cape Colony, sheep and cattle perish, reported, 16 June, 1902.

Destructive cyclone over Karachi, mid June, 1902.

Destructive storm at Kieff, 23 deaths, 20 July, 1902.

Destructive storm and high wind over Cologne district, 1 death, 26 July, 1902.

Destructive cyclone in Majorca, several deaths, reported, 27 Aug. 1902.

Great gale, estimated loss of 51 lives in Algoa bay and Port Elizabeth, 1 Sept. 1902.

Severe thunderstorms and destructive floods, 2 deaths, S. England, 10 Sept. 1902.

Cyclone and floods in Catania and Modica, E. Sicily, 400 deaths, 26–28 Sept. 1902.

Severe typhoon at Yokohama, about 200 deaths, shipping damaged, 29 Sept. 1902.

Destructive hurricane at Diamante, Argentina, about 15 deaths, reported, 24 Oct. 1902.

Destructive hurricane over San Urbano, Argentina, 5 deaths, 15 injured, reported, 24 Nov. 1902.

Destructive gales in Newcastle and N.E. coast and Copenhagen, 25 Dec. 1902.

Severe westerly gales over Ireland and W. coast of Scotland; numerous casualties to shipping, 27, 28 Dec. 1902.

Heavy snowstorms in N. Wales, the greater part of Ireland, and parts of Scotland, 29 Dec. 1902.

Hurricane in the Society Islands, Hao and Marakan depopulated, 800 to 1,000 lives lost, 13–15 Jan. 1903.

Violent gale with much rain, in some parts heavy snowstorms, over the whole of Great Britain, 24 Feb. 1903.

Tornado in the southern states of U.S.; loss of 64 lives and great destruction of property at Gainesville, Georgia, 10 June, 1903.

Hurricane in Jamaica, great destruction to crops, 10 Aug. 1903.

Violent S.W. gale over British islands and N.W. France, with heavy rains, causing great damage to property, trees, crops, &c., several lives lost, 10 Sept. 1903.

Hurricane over Venetian provinces, much injury to crops and destruction of property at Vincenza, 13 Sept. 1903.

Hurricane in Florida and southern states U.S., later New York and district, great damage done; worst storm experienced for many years along New Jersey coast; 40 houses and hotels unroofed at Atlantic city, reported, 16 Sept. 1903.

Violent storm N.W. coast of Portugal, casualties to shipping, 11 lives lost, 72 men shipwrecked, end Sept. 1903.

Great storms and floods in the United States, 10 Oct. 1903.

Magnetic storm in Great Britain, on the continent, and in the United States, telegraphic communication interrupted, 31 Oct. 1903.

Gale in the Channel, several vessels wrecked, and much damage done at various inland places, 27 Nov. 1903.

STORTHING, the Norwegian parliament, said to have been first held at Bergen by Haco V. in 1223.

STOVES. The ancients used stoves which concealed the fire, as the German stoves yet do. They lighted the fire also in a large tube in the middle of the room, the roof being open. Apartments were warmed by portable braziers. Stoves on this old principle, improved, continue in use in many houses and public establishments in England, and generally on the continent. Dr. Franklin and count Rumford (who invented a stove) pointed out the waste of fuel in our open fires; and Dr. Neil Arnott patented his "improvements in the production and agency of heat," 14 Nov. 1821. Dr. C. William Siemens described his smokeless stove in "*Nature*" for 11 Nov. 1880. See *Chimneys*, and *Cottager's Stove*.

Mr. T. Pridgin Teale publishes his inventions, in which he revives the principles of count Rumford with additions, 1885–6.

STOWMARKET EXPLOSION, see *Gun-Cotton*, 1871.

STRAIGHT-OUT DEMOCRATS, a party which advocated limiting the powers of a government to police purposes arose in the United States of America in 1872, and nominated Charles O'Connor for the presidency. A state convention was convoked to meet at Harrisburg, 16 Oct. 1872.

STRAITS SETTLEMENTS, including Malacca, Penang or Prince of Wales island, and Singapore, secured to Great Britain in 1824, were made a separate dependency in 1853, and placed under the governor-general of India. They were separated from India, and constituted an independent settlement by an act passed 10 Aug. 1866, which took effect April, 1867. Governor, sir Harry St. George Ord, 1867; sir Andrew Clarke, 1873; sir William F. D. Jervois, Oct. 1875; sir W. C. F. Robinson, 1877; sir Frederick A. Weld, 1880; sir Cecil Clementi-Smith, Aug. 1887; lieut.-col. sir Charles Bullen Hugh Mitchell, June, 1893; died, 7 Dec. 1899; sir Fred. Cardew, 1900; sir Frank A. Swettenham, 1901. Population, 1891, 512,342; 1901, 572,249.

Singapore, the capital, founded by sir T. Stamford Raffles in 1819, who compiled the constitution, laws, &c.

Traders complained to Sir H. Ord, governor, who said they must submit to their risks 1872

Sir Andrew Clarke made a treaty establishing Abdullah as sultan in place of Ismail, and a British resident as his adviser, with plenary powers at Perak . . . . Jan. 1874

Mr. J. W. Birch, the resident, issues a proclamation, 1 Nov.; is suddenly attacked and killed, 2 Nov. 1875

The Malays rise, and besiege the residency, which is relieved by Capt. Innes, 6 Nov. He is killed in attacking a stockade . . . . . 15 Nov. „

The Malays thoroughly defeated by troops from Hong Kong and Calcutta, under Gen. Colborne, 7 and 22 Dec. „

Kinti taken; Ismail retreats . . . . 17 Dec. „

British power supreme at Perak . . . 27 Dec. „

Major Hawkins killed in an ambuscade; the village burnt . . . . 4 Jan. 1876

Ismail surrenders, about 21 March; Birch's assassin hanged . . . . 20 May, „

Great prosperity of the settlement reported, Aug. 1884

Secret societies successfully suppressed by the governor, reported . . . . . . June, 1890

Five prosperous protected states on the Malay peninsula are subject to the governor 1891

The neighbouring state of Pahang was much disturbed by turbulent miners and others in Dec. 1891 *et seq.* Order only restored by the help of the British . . . . Dec. 1891—July, 1892

Substitution of the British rule for that of the sultan proposed . . . . . July, 1892
Arrival of sir Charles Mitchell at Singapore, 31 Jan. 1894
Rising in Pahang, reported 18 June; suppressed by col. Walker . . . . . . 29 July, ,,
Members of the legislative council and others protest against changes in military contribution made by the home government, 4 Jan. 1895; lord Ripon's terms of 28 June accepted . 16 Oct. 1895
The council allot 17½ per cent. of the revenue to military tribute . . . . . . May, 1896
The British steamer *Pegu* raided by 10 Achinese passengers, capt. Ross and 13 others killed, July, 1897
The duke and duchess of Cornwall visit Singapore (the sultan of Perak made G.C.M.G.), 21–23 April, 1901
Increasing prosperity, reported . . Sept. ,,

STRALSUND (Pomerania), a strongly fortified Hanse-town, built about 1230. It resisted a fierce siege by Wallenstein in 1628; was taken by Frederick William, of Brandenburg, in 1678; restored to the Swedes, 1679; re-captured by the Prussians and their allies, Dec. 1715. It surrendered to the French under Brune, 20 Aug. 1807; was awarded to Prussia, 1815.

STRAND (London). Houses were first built upon the Strand about 1353, at which period it was the court end of the town, or formed the communication between the two cities of London and Westminster, being then open to the Thames and to the fields. Somerset and other palaces were erected 1547-1605.—*Stow*. The Strand bridge was commenced 11 Oct. 1811; see *Waterloo bridge*. The Strand improvements were commenced in 1829.

Strand returns one M.P. by act passed in 1885.
Strand improvements bill proposed by the "London county council," much opposed Dec. 1889 and Jan. 1890; the bill brought in, but withdrawn 15 Aug. 1890; passed, 7 Aug. 1896. Widening of the Strand, 1900–3. New roads, Aldwych and Kingsway, from Strand to Holborn, in progress, 1903.

STRANGERS in house of commons; see *Parliament*, May, 1875.

STRASBURG, the Roman *Argentoratum*, the capital of Alsace. Here Julian defeated the Alemanni, 357, who captured it, 455. It was annexed to Germany, 870. Louis XIV. seized it 28 Sept. 1681, and retained it by the treaty of Ryswick, 1697. The citadel and fortifications, which he constructed, have been so much augmented that Strasburg may be considered one of the strongest places in Europe. It was confirmed to France by the peace of Ryswick in 1697, but captured by the Germans, 28 Sept. 1870, and retained at the peace, May, 1871. The cathedral, an epitome of Gothic art, was founded by Clovis, and reconstructed by Pepin and Charlemagne. After destruction by lightning, 1007, it was principally rebuilt by Erwin de Steinbach and his son in the 14th century. The lofty tower was completed in 1439. The celebrated astronomical clock, after a long stoppage, was repaired by M. Schwilgué, and inaugurated 1 Jan. 1843. Population, 1890, 123,499; 1900, 150,268.

An attempt at insurrection in the city was made by prince Louis Napoleon (afterwards president of the French republic, and emperor), aided by two officers and some privates . . . 30 Oct. 1836
It was instantly suppressed by their arrest, and the prince was shipped off to America by the French government.
Strasburg invested by the Germans, principally from Baden, during the Franco-Prussian war 10 Aug. 1870
Gen. von Werder assumed the command of the besiegers, and the bombardment began 14 Aug., and a vigorous sally was repulsed . 16 Aug. ,,
Gen. Uhrich, the commander, declared that he would not surrender except upon a heap of ashes; but after a heroic resistance, and when a breach had been made and an assault was impending, notice was given, and the place surrendered at 2 A.M.; at 8 A.M. 17,150 men and 400 officers laid down their arms . . 27 Sept. 1870
The German loss was said to be 906 men, of whom 43 were officers . . . . . 28 Sept. ,,
The Germans entered Strasburg on the anniversary of its surrender to the French in 1681 by a surprise . . . . 30 Sept. ,,
Uhrich received the grand cross of the legion of honour . . . . Oct. ,,
The invaluable library was destroyed and the cathedral much injured. About 400 houses were destroyed, and 8000 persons rendered homeless.
Visit of the emperor of Germany well received; but "France is still there" . . . 19 Sept. 1879
William II. very well received, 20 Aug. 1889; again . . . . early Sept. 1899

STRATFORD-UPON-AVON (Warwickshire), see *Shakspeare*.

STRATHCLUYD, a kingdom formed by the Britons, who retired northward after the Saxon conquest, about 560. It extended from the Clyde to Cumberland. The Britons in it submitted to Edward the Elder, in 924.

STRATHCLYDE CASE, see *Wrecks*, 1876

STRATHFIELD-SAYE, in Hampshire, in which is situate the estate bought of lord Rivers by the nation for 263,000*l*., and presented to the duke of Wellington, 1817. An act to provide a suitable residence for his grace and his heirs was passed 11 July, 1815.

STRATHMORE ESTATES. Miss Bowes, of Durham, the then richest heiress in Europe, whose fortune was 1,040,000*l*., with vast additions on her mother's death and immense estates on the demise of her uncle, married the earl of Strathmore, 25 Feb. 1766. Having, after the earl's death, married Mr. Stoney, she was forcibly carried off by him and other armed men, 10 Nov. 1786. She was brought up to the King's Bench by *habeas corpus* and released, and he committed to prison, 23 Nov. The lady recovered her estates, which she had assigned to her husband under the influence of terror, in May, 1788.

STRATTON-HILL, BATTLE OF, in Cornwall, 16 May, 1643, between the royal army under sir Ralph Hopton, and the forces of the parliament under the earl of Stamford. The victory was gained over the parliamentarians, who lost numbers in killed and wounded.

STRAWBERRY, see *Fruits*.

STRAWBERRY-HILL, Surrey, the Gothic villa of Horace Walpole, constructed 1750, at Twickenham, near London. In April and May, 1842, his collection of pictures and articles of taste and virtu were sold by auction for 29,615*l*. 8*s*. 9*d*. The villa was enlarged by Mr. Chichester Fortescue, created lord Carlingford, and the countess of Waldegrave, daughter of John Braham, the singer. She died 5 July, 1879. The place bought by baron H. de Stern, July, 1883.

STREET MUSIC. An act was passed in 1864 for the better regulation of street music in the metropolitan police districts.

STREET RAILWAYS, see *Tramways*.

STRELITZ, the imperial guard of Russia, established by Ivan IV. about 1568. Becoming frequently seditious, it was suppressed by Peter the

Great; great numbers were put to death, many by the czar's own hand, 1698-1704.

STRIKES, see under *Agriculture*, *Preston*, *London*, *Newcastle*, *Trials*, Aug. 1867; *Railways*, *Shipping and Coal*, *Cotton*, *Bristol*, *Slate*, and other seaports and towns.

Strikes in 1888, 504 (249 reported successful, 332 settled by conciliation). In 1889, 1,145; in 1890, 1,028; in 1891, 893; in 1896, 926; in 1900, 648; in 1901, 642; in 1892: Jan. 63; Feb. 48; March, 39; April, 65; May, 93; June, 59; July, 35; Aug. 35; Sept. 54; Oct. 42; Nov. 44; Dec. 24; strikes termed *Trade Disputes* in the *Board of Trade Journal*; in 1893: Jan. 38; Feb. 37; March, 59; April, 73; May, 87; June, 71; July, 55; Aug. 54; Sept. 54; Oct. 42; Nov. 34; Dec. 16; in 1894: Jan. 50; Feb. 57; March, 100; April, 13; May, 118; June, 85; July, 66; Aug. 86; Sept. 69; Oct. 55; Nov. 56; Dec. 43; in 1895: Jan. 57; Feb. 55; March, 49; April, 83; May, 84; June, 65; July, 49; Aug. 52; Sept. 66; Oct. 77; Nov. 38; Dec. 37; in 1897: Jan. 48; Feb. 66; March, 113; April, 85; May, 126; June, 53; July, 65; Aug. 66; Sept. 51; Oct. 49; Nov. 41; Dec. 28; in 1898: Jan. 28 Feb. 25; March, 27; April, 44; May, 56; June, 49; July, 62; Aug. 44; Sept. 52; Oct. 53; Nov. 44; Dec 29; in 1899: Jan. 26; Feb. 36; March, 53; April, 63 (none of great magnitude); May, 94; June, 59; July, 51; Aug. 33; Sept. 54; Oct. 38; Nov. 32; Dec. 28; in 1900: Jan. 37; Feb. 33; March, 40; April, 52; May, 44; June, 45; July, 41; Aug. 32; Sept. 29; Oct. 30; Nov. 48; Dec. 20; in 1901: Jan. 29; Feb. 25; March, 52; April, 66; May, 64; June, 39; July, 28; Aug. 32; Sept. 33; Oct. 26; Nov. 25; Dec. 14; in 1902: Jan. 33; Feb. 18; March, 21; April, 32; May, 23; June, 11; July, 25; Aug. 15; Sept. 18; Oct. 23; Nov. 24; Dec. 15; in 1903: Jan.

[United States: 1,115 in 1899; 1,164 in 1900].

The tailors of London struck for increase of wages; they yield . . . . . . April, 1834

The strike of the calico printers of Glasgow . . ,,

Staffordshire potters' strike; obtained an advance after much loss . . Nov. 1834-March, 1835

The strike of the amalgamated engineers took place 1852

Strike of the London cabmen . . . 27-30 July, 1853

Builders' strike . . . . . Aug.-Oct. 1859

A strike among the silk-workers at Coventry came to an end . . . . . . 30 Aug. 1860

An unsuccessful attempt to get up a strike in the building trade began . . . 23 March, 1861

A strike of the puddlers in the iron trade occurred in the spring of (see *Iron*, and *Railways*) . . 1865

Strike of London west-end tailors (about 2000), lasted . . . . . . 22 April-Oct. 1867

Great strike of colliers near St. Helens, April, 1867; about 40,000 men on strike . . . April, 1868

Colliery strike at Thorncliffe, near Sheffield; dreadful riots and devastation . . . 21 Jan. 1870

Strike of 10,000 miners at Le Creuzot, Burgundy, the property of M. Schneider; soon over Jan. 1871

Engineers' strike at Newcastle (see *Newcastle*) May-Oct. ,,

Strike of builders employed by Messrs. Brass and Jackson & Shaw, for a 9 hours' day, at 9d. an hour, 1 June; after negotiation led to a lock-out by the masters, beginning . . . 19 June, 1872

The lock-out of the masons ceased, the carpenters going on, 9 July; arrangements were made. and strike ceased . . . . about 27 Aug. ,,

Strike of London journeymen bakers, 23 Sept.-9 Oct. ,,

Strike of firewood cutters . . . . . Sept. ,,

Lock-out of miners in Wales for their excessive demands . . . . Oct. ,,

Strike of London gas-stokers (see *Gas*) . 2 Dec. ,,

Strike of about 60,000 colliers in S. Wales, refusing to submit to 10 per cent. reduction in wages, 1 Jan. Strike ended . . . about 25 March, 1873

Powerful speech of earl Fitzwilliam to his colliers of Low Stubbin after a strike . . 5 June, ,,

Strike of about 50,000 miners, South Wales, 2 Jan.; led to a lock-out, 1 Feb.; given up; gradual return of men to work end of . . . . May, 1875

Strike of Warwickshire miners . . May-Aug. ,,

Strikes at Oldham and Dundee . . July-August ,,

Strike of earl Fitzwilliam's colliers on account of the compulsory use of safety lamps; he closes his mines and rejects their submission . Dec. ,,

Erith, strike of workmen of Eastons and Anderson, engineers, in opposition to piece-work, 18 Dec.; supported by amalgamated engineers, Dec., 1875; on trial for conspiracy, the men plead guilty; no sentence passed . . . . . 14 July, 1876

Strike of 1600 miners against 15 per cent. reduction of wages, Bolton . . . . 24 Aug. ,,

"Operative Spinners' Association" of N. and N.E. Lancashire propose to set aside the "standard list of prices" after 1 Nov. The masters thereupon announced a lock-out of about 80,000 men (after 23 Nov.), 26 Oct. The association submits 18 Nov. ,,

Strike of Doulton's bricklayers respecting employment of others on terra-cotta work (settled) Oct. ,,

Great strike and lock-out of about 10,000 shipwrights, &c., on the Clyde, May; closed, Oct.; the arbitrator, lord Moncrieff, decided against the men . . . . Nov. 1877

Northumberland miners (about 12,000), began, 29 May; over about . . . . 12 June, ,,

Great railway strike, see *United States* . July, ,,

Bolton cotton workers' strike, about 1 Sept.; closed by agreement . . . . ,,

Railway strike on Great Southern and Western line, Ireland . . . . . about 14-22 Sept. ,,

181 strikes, result mostly against workmen . . ,,

Lock-out of about 8000 miners in Northumberland, about 15 Dec. 1877; closed . . . . Feb. 1878

Strike of masons of London (employed on the law courts, &c.), demanding increased pay and less working hours, 31 July; some firms yield, about 20 Sept.; Germans and others engaged, Oct.—Dec. 1877. Strike ends (cost about 60,000*l.*) 14 March, ,,

Strike and lock-out of cotton spinners in N. and N.E. Lancashire (about 120,000 men); masters required reduction of 10 per cent. on wages; began about 18 April; ended by the men submitting to arrangements . . about 17 June, ,,

Partial strike and lock-out of labourers in Kent and Sussex . . . . . . Oct.-Dec. ,,

Cotton strike at Oldham, at reduction of wages 5 per cent., 25 Nov.; submission . . 28 Dec. ,,

277 strikes in the year . . . . . . ,,

Midland railway; sudden strike of goods guards 3-20 Jan. 1879

London engineers, 18 firms, against reduction of wages, began about 7 Feb.; closed . 4 Oct. ,,

Durham coal miners, against reduction of wages, began 5 April; stoppage of Cleveland and other iron works; about 70,000 men unemployed, April; settled by arbitration . . . about 16 May, ,,

Bristol builders' 2 months' strike ends . 30 July, ,,

Strike of cotton-workers at Blackburn, 15 May *et seq.* ,,

Strike of Lancashire miners; about 40,000 out, 12 Jan.; rioting with loss of life near Bolton, 25-28 Jan.; strike reported over . . . 21 Feb. 1881

Strike in the potteries, 70 firms and 30,000 men, begun . . . . about 25 Nov. ,,

The men agree to arbitration . . . . 6 Dec. ,,

Ironworkers' strike at Hopton and Darlington, 2 Feb -9 June, 1882

Strike of Staffordshire colliers, about 8000, 12 May, ends . . . . . . about 3 Sept. 1883

Great strike of South Staffordshire ironworkers at reduction of wages . . . . about 5 July, ,,

Many submit, about 17 July; strike closed, 24 July, ,,

Cotton weavers on strike, opposition to the reduction of wages, in the N.W. districts, about 18,500, 18 Dec. 1883; men yield under conditions, about 8 Feb. 1884

Strike in the cotton trade; mass meeting at Burnley reject the masters' terms . . 16 July, ,,

Determined to maintain the strike against reduction of wages . . . . 24 July, ,,

End of Barnsley coal miners' long strike . 23 Dec. ,,

Strike of about 2000 miners in west Cumberland, 16 March, 1885

Strike of about half the colliers in S. and W. Yorkshire . . . . . . 1 April-May, ,,

Chorley, Lancashire, about 3000 cotton weavers 16 July, ,,

Cotton weavers on strike at Oldham (25,000 out) against 10 per cent. reduction, 20 July *et seq.*; compromise 5 per cent. accepted for three months about 16 Oct. ,,

Strike of 4,700 men at Elswick Iron Works, Newcastle; ascribed to two managers, 2 Sept.; closed 17 Sept. 1885

Close of engineers' strike (2½ years) at Sunderland; cost above 200,000*l.* . . . Nov. ,,

Strike of shipwrights in the Tyne and Wear about Jan.–24 Feb. 1886

Increase of strikes in France, Belgium, Germany, and United States . . . . March, ,,

Shropshire ironworks strike (twenty weeks) ends; masters yield . . . . 14 July, ,,

Northumberland miners' strike about 30 Jan.; terms arranged at a conference, and work resumed, twelve weeks . . . 23–28 May, 1887

Strike (wrought nail trade) in South Staffordshire of about 15,000 operatives . . . 12 Sept. ,,

Strike of engineers at Bolton respecting wages, overtime, &c., 14 May; intimidation and boycotting of men at work; strike closes by conciliation . . . . 27 Oct. ,,

Shoemakers' strike at Northampton; about 20,000 out 3 Dec.; closed by arbitration, about 24 Dec. ,,

Strike of engineers at Blackburn, 21 weeks, closed by compromise . . . . . 12 March, 1888

Strike of match-girls at Bryant and May's factory (see *Lucifers*) . . . . . . 5 July, ,,

Colliery strikes begin 22 Oct.; about 30,000 miners on strike in S.W. Yorkshire and the Midland counties 24 Oct.; the colliers' demands, 10 per cent. increase generally, acceded to, the owners gradually yield . . . . 27–31 Oct. ,,

Strike of coal miners in Westphalia (*which see*) May, ,,

Strikes in Silesia, Bohemia, and Belgium, May, June, ,,

Temporary strikes of seamen and firemen in the steamers in the ports of Glasgow (ended 27 June), Leith, Aberdeen (ended), and Dundee for an advance of wages, end of May; gradually collapsing, end of June *et seq.*; Liverpool, May–July, ,,

Strike of the *dock labourers* of the port of London, demanding not less than 4 hours' engagement, pay to be raised from 5*d.* to 6*d.* per hour, and redress of other grievances, 15 Aug.; they are joined by stevedores, lightermen, and nearly every class of riverside workers; about 25,000 men out, 22 Aug.; negotiations of the London and India docks committee (for the directors, Mr. C. M. Norwood, Mr. H. Morgan, sec.); with the dock labourers' strikes committee (leaders, Messrs. John Burns, Benjamin Tillett, sec., Henry Champion, and Tom Mann), demands refused, 27 Aug.; 80,000 said to be out, 30 Aug.; dock directors reject the compromise proposed by shipowners and others, 31 Aug. Close of the strike; greatly due to the intervention of the lord mayor Whitehead, cardinal Manning, the bishop of London, sir John Lubbock, Mr. Sydney, and others: terms of agreement, pay for ordinary work raised from 4*d.* to 6*d.* per hour, 8*d.* per hour overtime, contract work to be changed to piece work, with other concessions, to begin on 4 Nov., 14 Sept.; work at the docks resumed . . . . 16 Sept. 1889

[During the strike there were many processions of labourers and sympathisers through the streets. Great meetings were held in Hyde park on Sundays 25 Aug., 1, 8, 15 Sept. There was much picketing; the extreme distress in the east end was relieved by liberal public subscriptions, and the Australian colonies gave about 31,000*l.*; received in December from Melbourne, 3,792*l.*; from Sydney 720*l.*, Dec. 1889.]

Great strike of Jewish tailors and other operatives in East London, 3 Sept., about 10,000 out; they demand an increase of pay, and reduction of time and labour to 12 hours daily; settled by compromise . . . . 2 Oct. ,,

Ridiculous strike of schoolboys for shorter hours and fewer lessons, in Hawick, Dundee, Aberdeen, Glasgow, Greenock, Edinburgh, Cardiff, Liverpool, Leeds, Northampton, parts of London and Brighton, and other places . . . Oct. ,,

Strike at Messrs. Silvers' india-rubber works at Silvertown . . . . . . Nov.–Dec. ,,

Many strikes and much agitation in London, and throughout the country . . Sept.–Dec. ,,

Strike of about 1,000 of the stokers and others employed by the South Metropolitan gas company, against "the bonus" system successfully resisted by Mr. G. Livesey, the secretary, 12 Dec. 1889; the strike ends . . . . 5 Feb. 1890

Strike of about 11,000 bootmakers, E. London, 29 March–29 April, ,,

Strike of Kentish bargemen and lock-out of brickmakers, early March; closed . about 28 April, ,,

Strike of Thames shipjoiners . 1 March–3 May, ,,

Strike at Cardiff of the servants of the Taff Vale, Rhymney and Barry railways, dockers and others, respecting time-working; the merchants and other employers, support the railway companies, 7 Aug.; traffic suspended, 8 Aug.; great meeting, sir E. Read, M.P., president; no result, 9 Aug.; about 50,000 men out, 10 Aug.; compromise effected, the strike ends . 15 Aug. ,,

Strikes in Australia (see *Melbourne* and *Sydney*), Aug. *et seq.* ,,

Strike at Manningham Mills, see *Bradford*, 1891.

Great strike of colliers in Durham, on account of the eviction of miners at Silksworth, lord Londonderry's colliery, 20 Feb. *et seq.*; strike ends, 20 March, 1891

Five weeks' great strike of cotton-spinners at Huddersfield, closed . . . . 20 March, ,,

Close of the strike of the Scotch furnace men (21 works) . . . . . . 5 March, ,,

Strike in the building trades in London, leading firms; mass meeting in Hyde park, 3 May; referred to arbitration, 20 Oct.; award given (no increase of pay), about 19 Nov.; work resumed, 23 Nov. ,,

Strikes in Belgium, France, Austria, Westphalia, Great Britain . . . . . April, May, ,,

Many strikes in London and the provinces, May *et seq.* ,,

End of 11 weeks' strike at Messrs. Wostinholm, cutlers, Sheffield . . . . 27 June, ,,

Strike of tailors at Southport, Liverpool, July; the delegates of the Master Tailors' Association of the United Kingdom at Liverpool, order a general lock-out throughout the United Kingdom unless the strikers return to work before the 29th, 22 July; settlement . about 29 July, ,,

End of the strike at Brooks' cotton mill, Clitheroe (25 weeks) . . . . . . 12 Aug. ,,

Strike of Durham coal-miners, see under *Coal*, 11 March, 1892

End of three months' strike of seamen and firemen at Sunderland . . . . . 13 June, ,,

Strike of the workmen of the salt union in Cheshire closed, and threatened strike and lock-out of the tailors averted by compromises . . Sept. ,,

Carmaux strike (see *France*) . . Aug.–Sept. ,,

Bedminster district of Bristol, end of about 18 months' strike . . . . . . 30 Jan. 1893

Disputes between employers and men of the boot and shoe trade (about 200,000 persons interested), arranged at a national conference at Leicester, sir Henry James, M.P., appointed umpire, 10 Aug. 1892; he meets the conference, 19 Aug. *et seq.*; his award, advocating compromises, to last till 1 Sept. 1896, issued 25 Aug. 1892; national conference at Leicester . . . 17 April *et seq.* ,,

Strikes against the employment of free labour in the docks, London, Hull, Bristol . April, May, ,,

For strikes of coal miners, see *Coal*, 1890 *et seq.*

Strike of 1,000 men in the shoe trade at Northampton . . . . 1 Jan. 1894

Pullman car railway strike . . . . . July, ,,

See *United States.*

Strike of ironworkers on N.E. coast (1,500 moulders) . . . . . June–July, ,,

See *Newcastle.*

Lock-out in the boot and shoe trade, Leicester and Northampton . . . . . . 6 March, 1895

Strike ensues; 200,000 men out . 8 March, ,,

Defensive measures of employers in London, 14 Mar. ,,

London lock-out . . . . . 16 March, ,,

Mr. Labouchere's proposal for arbitration approved by Mr. Asquith; rejected by both parties, March, ,,

Strike in the building trade at Leicester, 30 March, ,,

The employers' federation and the operatives' union accept the government proposal to send 8 delegates to sir Courtenay Boyle at the board of trade; preliminary conference . 4 April, 1895
Agreement arrived at . . . . 19 April, „
Sir Wm. Markby appointed arbitrator in the carpenters' and joiners' strike at Leicester, 1 June, „
See *Shipbuilding*, 1895–6.
Strike in the London and Dublin building trades for advance of ½*d*. per hour in wages and new code in working rules, 1 May; concessions to the men, 20 May; closed by settlement, 1 July; closed mainly by the mediation of archbishop Walsh in Dublin, 21 Aug. See *Leeds* and *Belfast*, 1896
Strike of tailors averted by concessions to the men, Sept. „
Strike in the flax-spinning trade Belfast . Jan. 1897
See *Hamburg*, 1896–7.
Strike of men on the N.E. railway and general labour disputes, Newcastle district affected, 20 Feb.; arbitration accepted, 5 April; award of lord James of Hereford, concessions to the men, 9 Aug.; address presented to lord James by the men . . . . 3 Dec. „
Strike of the Amalgamated Society of Engineers and allied trade unions for an eight hours' day, &c., throughout the country . . 3 July *et seq.* „
Federation of engineering and shipbuilding employers issue a manifesto . . . . 4 Aug. „
10th distribution of strike pay, 30,000*l*., 57,000 out, 18 Sept.; 70,000 out . . . . 8 Oct. „
Boilermakers' dispute, about 1,000 men in London strike work, 15 Oct.; work resumed . 16 Nov. „
Letter of mediation from sir Courtenay Boyle (died 1901) (Board of Trade) proposing a joint conference . . . . . . 20 Oct. „
Preliminary conference between col. Dyer, Messrs. A. Henderson and Biggart for the employers. Messrs. Barnes and Sellicks (men), London 17 Nov. „
Conferences, 24, 25, 26 Nov.; the employers' ultimatum rejected by ballot of the men, 11 Dec.; 80,000 men out . . . . . . Dec. „
Conf. of delegates at Westminster, 15, 17, 19 Dec. „
The federated employers meet at York and refuse to shorten the hours of labour . . 30 Dec. „
The demand for a 48-hours' week withdrawn by the men, 15 Jan.; work generally resumed . 24 Jan. 1898
Strike and lock-out closed, 28 Jan.; 10 per cent. of the men re-engaged . . . . . 1 Feb. „
S. Wales coal dispute, increase of wages demanded, 50,000 men idle, 1 April *et seq.*; defence statement of the employers issued, 27 April; conferences: provisional committee appointed to negotiate, 26 May; 10 per cent. advance refused, 31 May; great distress in Cardiff; some disturbance at Tirphil, 21 June; sir Edw. Fry appointed to act as conciliator, 2 July; declined by the masters, 13 July; negotiations fruitless, 22 July; masters' terms accepted . 31 Aug. „
Dispute in Lancashire cotton trade closed, 2½ per cent. advance in wages adopted . 9 May, 1899
Taff Vale railway dispute, increase of wages and modification in hours of labour demanded, &c.; a strike begins, 20 Aug. 1900; dispute provisionally settled through the medium of sir W. T. Lewis . . . . 29 Aug. 1900
Gt. Eastern railway dispute, Aug. (concessions granted, Jan. 1901) (see *Trials*, July, 1901, and Dec. 1902); concessions accepted by the men, mid Sept. „
Trawlers' dispute, see *Grimsby* . . July–Dec. 1901
Eviction of miners at Denaby, after strike lasting 28 weeks at the Denaby and Cadeby collieries, S. Yorks . . . . . . 6 Jan. 1903
Dispute between Grimsby shore fishermen's society and the federated vessel owners closed . 12 Jan. „
Denaby miners return to work . . mid March, „
Strike of scholars in secondary schools (see *Italy*), mid March, „
Labour disturbances at Slatoust, Russia; workmen's delegates imprisoned; 34 workmen killed and 200 injured in conflict with the troops, reported . . . . . . 28 March, „
Great railway and dock strikes in Amsterdam (see *Holland*) . . . . . . 6–13 April, „
Strikes general in the south of Russia, riots at Odessa, Kieff, Baku, and other places, oil wells set on fire, trains wrecked, and other outrages, reported . . . . . 27–31 July, 1903
Strikes at Odessa and Kieff subside, many workmen imprisoned . . . . . . 11–16 Aug. „
Employés of the 40 associated tin works in S. Wales cease work, the establishments closed down, throwing out of employment 16,000 hands, and affecting 40,000 other workpeople 29 Aug. „
Strike at Niagara in connection with the construction works being carried on by three Canadian power companies, the contractors having issued an order reducing the wages of the men 25c. per diem, reported . . . . . . 3 Nov. „
Strike at Bilbao, Spain; much rioting, early Nov. „
Mass meeting at Bethesda; 161 vote in favour of continuing strike, 192 for returning to work at the Penrhyn quarry; strike practically over after lasting for 3 years, costing the district in wages alone 364,000*l*. reported . . . . 7 Nov. „
[Before the strike, which began Oct. 1900, the quantity of slates imported into England was practically *nil*. For the quarter ended 31 March, 1901, 15,702 tons were imported, for the quarter ended 30 Sept. 31,581 tons.]
Serious coal strike in Colorado, most important coalfield in the West; coal famine at Denver threatened, began . . . . . 9 Nov. „
See *United States*, 1903, and *France*, Oct. 1902.

STROME CASE, see *Trials*, 1883.

STRONTIUM. The native carbonate of strontia was discovered at Strontian, in Argyleshire, in 1787. Sir Humphry Davy first obtained from it the metal strontium in 1808.

STRYCHNIA, a poisonous vegetable alkaloid, discovered in 1818 by Pelletier and Caventou in the seeds of the strychnos ignatia and nux vomica, and also in the upas poison. Half a grain blown into the throat of a rabbit occasions death in four minutes; its operation is accompanied by lock-jaw. Much attention was given to strychnia in 1856, during the trial of William Palmer, who was executed for the murder of Cook, 14 June, 1856.

STUART (properly STEWART), HOUSE OF, see under *Scotland, England*; and *Pretenders*.

A collection of portraits and relics of the house of Stuart was exhibited in the New Gallery, Regent-street, autumn, 1888. The surplus receipts amounting to about 1,800*l*. were judiciously distributed.

STUCCO WORK was known to the ancients, and was much prized by them, particularly by the Romans, who excelled in it.—*Lenglet*. It was revived by D'Udine, about 1550; and in Italy, France, and England in the 18th century.

STUD Company, to improve the breed of British horses, held its first annual meeting, 20 Sept. 1873.

STUHM (W. Prussia). Here Gustavus Adolphus of Sweden defeated the Poles, 1628.

STUNDISTS, a puritan sect in south Russia, said to be descendants of Russian soldiers converted from the Greek church by German missionaries; some were cruelly persecuted by the bigoted peasantry of Vossnessensk in Kherson in 1879; thirteen of the ringleaders were tried for the crime, 8 Nov. 1879. Strong repressive measures against the sect, with persecution, were taken by the government, autumn, 1891 *et seq.*

STURGES BOURNE'S ACT, 58 Geo. III. c. 69 (1818), relates to parish vestries.

STUTTGART (Würtemburg), first mentioned in 1229, was made his residence by count Eberhard, 1320; enlarged by Ulric, 1436; and made capital of the state, 1482. It has been greatly adorned during the last and present centuries. International rifle meeting here, 1 Aug. 1875. Theatre Royal, built, 1811, reconstructed, 1846 and 1883, burnt, 19 Jan. 1902. Population, 1885, 125,901; 1890, 139,659; 1900, 176,705.

STYLE, see *New Style*.

STYLE ROYAL, see *England*, *King*, *Majesty*, and *Titles*. The *styles* of the English sovereigns are given in the later editions of Nicolas's "Chronology of History." The Royal Style and Titles Act, giving power to add to the queen's titles "empress of India," after much opposition in the commons, received royal assent 27 April; proclamation issued 28 April; announced in India, by the viceroy, 19 Aug. 1876; proclamation announcing the insertion of the words "and of the British dominions beyond the seas" in the king's style of titles, 4 Nov. 1901.

STYLITES, see *Monachism*.

STYRIA (Austria), part of the ancient Noricum and Pannonia, was held successively by the Romans, Ostrogoths, and Avars. It was conquered by Charlemagne, and divided among his followers, styled counts, among whom the count of Styria, about 876, was the most powerful. The count became margrave about 1030; and Ottocar VI., in 1180, was made duke. At his death, 1192, Styria was annexed to the duchy of Austria. In 1246 it was acquired by Bela IV. of Hungary; in 1253, by Ottocar II. of Bohemia; after whose defeat and death, at Marchfeld, in 1278, it reverted to Rudolph of Austria, and was annexed to his possessions. Population, 1890, 1,282,708; 1900, 1,356,058.

SUAKIN, a seaport town of the Red Sea on an island off its W. coast. See *Soudan*, 1883, *et seq.* Under the rule of colonel Kitchener and lieut. Gordon, R.E., Suakin has become a nearly impregnable fortress and commerce has revived, 1888. Col. George Lloyd appointed governor of Suakin and of the Red Sea littoral, Sept. 1894. Lieut.-col. Parsons appointed gov.-gen. arrives at Suakin, 17 Oct. 1896.

SUBMARINE BOAT, see under *Boats*.

SUBMARINE LAMP, one invented by Siebe and Gorman, has been in use since 1850, especially at Cherbourg. Heinke and Davis's lamp was exhibited, 1871.

SUBMARINE TELEGRAPH, see *Telegraph* (under *Electricity*), 1840 *et seq.*

SUBSCRIPTION ACT, see *Clerical Subscription Act*.

SUBSIDIES to the kings of England were formerly granted in kind, particularly in wools, 30,000 sacks were voted to Edward III. on account of the war with France, 1340.—*Anderson*. Subsidies were raised upon the people of England by James I. 1624; but they were included in a bill for the redress of grievances, 1639. Four subsidies (the last) were granted to Charles II. in 1663.*

SUBWAY, see *Tunnels*.

SUCCESSION ACTS, see *Settlement*.

* England granted subsidies to foreign powers in several wars, particularly in the war against the revolutionists in France, and against Bonaparte.

SUCCESSION, WAR OF (1702–1713), distinguished by the achievements of the duke of Marlborough and the earl of Peterborough, and their unprofitable results, arose on the question whether an Austrian prince or a French prince should succeed to the throne of Spain. The British court opposed Louis, and Marlborough was victorious; but the allies withdrew one after another, and the French prince succeeded; see *Spain* and *Utrecht*.

SUCCESSION DUTY ACT (16 & 17 Vict. c. 51), after much discussion, was passed 4 Aug. 1853. By this act the legacy duty was extended to real estate, and was made payable on succession to both landed and personal property; see *Legacies*. Additional duties imposed by customs, &c., acts of 1888 and 1889. The probate and succession duty replaced by the estate duty, 1894 (*which see*).

SUDAN, see *Soudan*.

SUDBURY, in Suffolk, chartered by queen Mary, 1554, was disfranchised for bribery in 1844.

SUEVI, a warlike Gothic tribe, which, with the Alani and the Visigoths, entered Spain about 408, were overcome by the latter, and absorbed into their kingdom about 584.

SUEZ CANAL. The caliph Omar about 640 opposed cutting the isthmus. A plan for a canal between the head of the Red Sea and the bay of Pelusium was brought forward by M. Ferdinand de Lesseps in 1854. He undertook to cut a canal through 90 miles of sand, to run out moles into the Mediterranean; to deepen the shallow waters; to create ports to receive the ships from India and Australia, and to adapt the canal to irrigation. The consent of the Egyptian, Turkish, Russian, French, and Austrian governments was gradually obtained, but not that of the British. M. Ferdinand de Lesseps visited the queen and prince Albert, 6 May, 1856. A company was formed, 1856, and the work commenced in 1859 by Mr. Daniel Lange (knighted 1870). The cost was estimated at 8,000,000*l*. Engineer, M. L. Monteit.

M. Delacour, a French engineer, after viewing the works which were "employing 25,000 men in the desert," expressed his conviction that they would be completed in four or five years . . 7 Nov. 1862
The waters of the Mediterranean admitted into a narrow channel communicating with Lake Timsah . . . . . . Dec. ,,
The new town Timsah named Ismaila . 4 March, 1863
The works visited by the Sultan and by Mr. Hawkshaw . . . . ,,
The company compelled by the Egyptian government to give up employment of compulsory labour; litigation ensued . . . . Aug. ,,
M. de Lesseps reported that a vessel containing 30 persons had been tugged along the canal the whole distance between the two seas . Feb. 1865
Delegates from the British chambers of commerce visited the works, and reported that the success of the scheme was only an affair of time and money . . . . . . 17 April, ,,
The flood gates of the smaller Suez canal were opened, the fresh water of the Nile admitted; a coal vessel passed from the Mediterranean to the Red Sea . . . . 15 Aug. ,,
The *Primo*, 80 tons burden, passed through the canal from the Mediterranean into the Red Sea, 17 Feb. 1867
A loan raised in France . . . . . . ,,
French and English vessels enter the canal . Nov. 1868
Mr. John Fowler, the engineer, reported the canal as suitable for steamers and mail traffic, but not for vessels requiring tugs . . . . 5 Feb. 1869
Water of the Mediterranean admitted to the salt lakes . . . . . . 18 March, ,,
The works visited by the prince and princess of Wales . . . . . . 23 March, ,,

The canal successfully opened in the presence of the emperor of Austria, the empress of the French, the viceroy of Egypt, and others . . 16 Nov. 1869
M. de Lesseps entertained in London . 4 July, 1870
Traffic in 1870-1 doubled 1872-3
Charges upon vessels passing through the canal increased 50 per cent.; the British appeal for a national conference . . . . . . April, 1873
International conference on Suez dues met at Constantinople; 21 sittings; report dated 18 Dec.
Proposals of the sultan accepted by European powers . . . . Dec. ,,
M. de Lesseps protests; the lords of the admiralty informed (by D. A. Lange) that the canal will be closed unless the old dues are paid, 22 April; he gives way about . . . 26 April, 1874
Col. Stokes, after a survey, reported to the earl of Derby that the canal generally was in a satisfactory state . . . . 20 April, ,,
British government authorise Messrs. Rothschild to buy for 4,080,000*l.* the Khedive's shares (176,602 shares of 20*l.*, out of 400,000) in the canal; (5 per cent. to be paid till 1 July, 1894, after which dividends will be received) . . . . Nov. 1875
M. de Lesseps in a circular says he regards "as a fortunate circumstance the powerful union between English and French capitalists for the purely industrial and necessarily peaceful working of the universal maritime canal" . 29 Nov. ,,
The subject discussed in the commons, 14 Feb.; money (4,080,000*l.*) voted, 21 Feb.: act passed 15 Aug. 1876
Neutrality of the canal claimed by Great Britain May, June, 1877
Freedom of the canal secured by settlement of Egypt 1882-3
Receipts about 5,000,000 francs, 1870; 60,523,815 francs 1882
Second canal determined on by British shipowners; Mr. (aft. sir) James Laing very efficient; syndicate appointed . . . . . . 10 May, 1883
Arrangements made by the government for the construction of the canal and advancement of capital, to be virtually under control of De Lesseps' company, announced, 11 July: great dissatisfaction and opposition in England, 12 July; the proposed convention withdrawn by the government, 23 July, ,,
Sir Stafford Northcote's resolution against De Lesseps' monopoly negatived (284-185) . 31 July, ,,
De Lesseps visits London; agrees with the steam shipowners to enlarge the present canal, or create a new one, giving additional power and influence in the direction of the company, and to reduce dues, &c. . . . . . . 30 Nov. ,,
The agreement approved by the British government, 25 Feb.; the shareholders at Paris protest against it, but ratify it (2608-556) . . . 29 May, ,,
International commission sits at Paris; English and French schemes discussed, April—May, 1885; parts of these schemes incorporated in treaty, May, 1885; last sitting . . . 13 June, 1886
The widening of the present canal decided on, after investigation by commission, Dec. 1884; plans adopted by the commission 9 Feb. 1885; arrangements with the Egyptian government completed 27 Dec. ,,
Convention signed at Paris for England and France neutralising the canal and placing it under a joint commission . . . . 24 Oct. 1887
Adhesion of the other powers announced July; ratified by the sultan 25 Oct.; by the powers 29 Oct. and 22 Dec. 1888
M. Charles de Lesseps, manager and secretary, arrested for bribery in relation to the Panama canal (*which see*) . . . . . . 16 Dec. 1892
A provisional board appointed; M. Guichard, senator, appointed chairman . . 20 Dec. ,,
M. Ferdinand de Lesseps nominated hon. chairman, 13 Feb. 1894; pensions granted to him and his family, June; he died . . . . 7 Dec. 1894
Strike of the company's dredgermen . Aug.-Sept. ,,
M. Lemasson, chief engineer of the company, fatally stabbed at Suez, 29 Sept.; strike ended by compromise . . . . . . 18 Oct. ,,
Prince d'Arenberg elected president of the company, at Paris, 3 Aug. 1896, 1897, and 1898.
A statue of Ferdinand de Lesseps at Port Said unveiled by the Khedive . . . 17 Nov. 1899

Traffic passed through canal:

Year.	No. of Ships.	Gross Tonnage.	Gross Receipts.
1870	486	435,911	£255,488
1871	765	761,467	464,091
1872	1,082	1,439,169	758,659
1873	1,173	2,085,073	971,882
1874	1,264	2,423,672	1,029,492
1875	1,494	2,940,709	1,204,387
1876	1,457	3,072,107	1,229,157
1877	1,663	3,418,950	1,337,617
1878	1,593	3,291,535	1,272,435
1879	1,477	3,236,942	1,214,443
Total 10 years.	12,454	23,105,535	£9,737,651
1880	2,026	4,344,519	£1,672,836
1881	2,727	5,794,401	2,187,047
1882	3,198	7,122,125	2,536,343
1883	3,307	8,051,307	2,645,506
1884	3,284	8,319,967	2,480,000
1885	3,624	8,985,411	2,601,998
1886	3,100	8,183,313	2,241,095
1888	3,444	9,437,957	2,680,000
1890	3,389	9,749,129	2,679,340
1894	3,352	8,039,175	2,951,072
1896	3,409	8,560,283	3,255,061
1899	3,607	9,895,630	3,652,751
1900	3,441	9,738,152	3,624,944
1901	3,699	10,823,840	4,015,456
1902	3,708	11,248,413	4,148,800

SUFFRAGAN BISHOPS. Power to appoint them was given by parliament in 1534 to Henry VIII. as head of the church. Suffragan bishops bill passed, 1 July, 1898. See ***Bishops*** and ***Supremacy***.

SUGAR* (*Saccharum officinarum*) is supposed to have been known to the ancient Jews. Found in the East Indies by Nearchus, admiral of Alexander, 325 B.C.—*Strabo*. An oriental nation in alliance with Pompey used the juice of the cane as a common beverage.—*Lucan*. It was prescribed as a medicine by Galen, 2nd century. Brought into Europe from Asia, A.D. 625;—in large quantities, 1150. Attempted to be cultivated in Italy; not succeeding, the Portuguese and Spaniards carried it to America about 1510.

The sugar-cane transported from Syria to Cyprus about 1148; from Madeira about 1420; and to the West Indies . . . . about 1506
It is not known at what date sugar was introduced into England, but it seems to have been prior to the reign of Henry VIII. Mr. Whittaker, in the History of Whalley, p. 109, quotes an instance in 1497
A manuscript letter from sir Edward Wotton to lord Cobham, dated Calais, advertises him that sir Edward had taken up for his lordship twenty-five sugar-loaves at six shillings a loaf, "whiche is eighte pence a pounde" . . . 6 March, 1546
Sugar first taxed (by James II.) 1685
Duties on free and slave-grown sugars equalized, Aug. 1846
Duties reduced and regulated . . . . Sept. 1848

* Sugar, long considered a neutral substance, without congeners, has of late years become the head of a numerous family, viz.: Cane-sugar (*sucrose*, from the sugar-cane; boiled with dilute acids it becomes *glucose*) Fruit-sugar (from many recent fruits); Grape-sugar (*glucose*, from dried fruits and altered starch); sugar of milk; *melitose* (from eucalyptus, by Berthelot in 1856); *sorbin* (from the berries of the mountain ash, by Pelouze); *inosite* (from muscular tissue, Scherer); *dulcose* (by Laurent); *mannite* (from manna, obtained from the fraxinus ornus, a kind of ash); *quercite* (from acorns); to these have been added *mycose*, by M. Mitscherlich, and *melezetose* and *rehalose*, by M. Berthelot.

Duty increased (war) 1855
Reduced, 1857, 1864; modified, 1867; greatly reduced, 1 Aug. 1870; further reduced, May, 1873; abolished from . . . . . . 1 May, 1874
Sugar industries committee recommend a protective duty on the import of sugar from certain countries . . . . Aug. 1880
Sugar-refining was made known to Europeans by a Venetian, 1503, and was first practised in England in 1659, though some say we had the art a few years earlier. The invaluable vacuum-pan was invented by Howard, 1812. Dr. Scoffern's processes were patented in 1848-50, but not adopted in Britain.
Sugar manufactured from *sorghum* in United States Dec. 1882; success reported . . March, 1888
Manufacturers and colonies protest strongly against French and German bounties on beet sugar . 1882-9
International Conference on Sugar Bounties, representatives from Germany, France, Austria and others, not United States; first meeting in London, baron H. de Worms chosen president. 24 Nov.; a protocol with a convention signed condemning bounties and recommending legislation for their abolition . . . . . 19 Dec. 1887
The mission of baron de Worms to various courts reported successful . . . . . . Feb. 1888
Another protocol with convention signed, 12 May, ,,
Finally signed for Great Britain, Germany, Austria-Hungary, Italy, Russia, Spain, Belgium, and the Netherlands, declined at present by France, Denmark, and Sweden . . . . . 30 Aug. ,,
International commission to examine the laws to enforce the convention meet . . . 1 May, 1889
Bill for the adoption of the convention brought into the commons May; deferred by the government 17 June, ,,
A secret process of refining sugar by electricity said to have been invented by prof. Henry C. Friend of New York, announced 1885. He succeeded in organizing the New York Electric Sugar Refining company to carry out the invention; the scheme collapsed and occasioned much loss in America and England by credulous persons, the whole affair being an imposture 1888
It caused a temporary panic in Liverpool Jan.; Mrs. Friend, then a widow, and her daughter were arrested in Michigan . . . . Feb. 1889
William E. Howard, one of the company, was sentenced to imprisonment for "grand larceny," 21 June, ,,
Sugar commission (royal), see *West Indies*, 1896–7.
Great fluctuations in the price of sugar since 1884.
International conference on sugar bounties at Brussels, 7 June *et seq.*, adjourned 1898
Sugar cane experiments in Barbadoes and other islands, reported successful . . . . Jan. 1901
Sugar bounties international conference held at Brussels, 16 Dec.; bounties to be abolished Sept. 1903, and *maximum* of the surtax limited; convention signed . . . . 5 March, 1902
World's consumption of sugar, 9,369,685 tons, 1901–2.

For *Saccharine*, see *Benzole*.

RAW SUGAR IMPORTED INTO UNITED KINGDOM.—1853, 7,284,290 cwts.; 1860, 8,817,277 cwts.; 1865, 10,250,524 cwts.; 1871, 12,126,508 cwts.; 1875, 16,264,711 cwts.; 1877, 16,620,944 cwts.; in 1879, 17,734,223 cwts.; in 1883, 20,366,627 cwts.; in 1887, 18,010,366 cwts.; in 1890, 15,717,476 cwts.; 1893, 16,032,113 cwt.; 1902, 13,221,492 cwts.

REFINED SUGAR exported from the United Kingdom: 1876, 1,192,277 cwts.; 1880, 965,446 cwts.; 1885, 994,353 cwts.; 1890, 709,416 cwts.; 1896, 993,698 cwts.; 1900, 606,353 cwts.

See *Beet-root*.

SUICIDE (from *sui*, self; *cædere*, to kill), the slayer of himself. The first instances recorded in Jewish history are those of Samson, about 1120, and Saul, 1055 B.C. The Greek and Roman philosophers deemed it a crime, and burned the offending hand apart from the rest of the body. In the reign of Tarquin I., the Roman soldiers, thinking themselves disgraced by being ordered to make common sewers, destroyed themselves, 606 B.C. Cato committed suicide, 46 B.C.* In the Roman catholic church, in the 6th century it was ordained that no commemoration should be made in the Eucharist for such as committed self-murder. This ecclesiastical law continued till the Reformation, when it was admitted into the statute law of England by the authority of parliament, with the confiscation of land and goods. Till 1823 the body of the suicide was directed to be buried in a cross-road, and a stake to be driven through it. A new act, suppressing the barbarous customs, was passed in 1882. It is now usually buried in consecrated ground without a religious ceremony. Thomas Cooper, the eminent Chartist, author of "The Purgatory of Suicides," an epic poem, published in 1845, died, aged 87, 15 July, 1892. Dr. Henry Morselli published "Suicides: an Essay," 1881. There were 7,572 suicides in France in 1887.

MEMORABLE RECENT CASES OF SUICIDE.

Gen. Pichegru . . . . 7 April, 1804
Miss Champante . . . . 15 Aug. ,,
Sellis, valet of the duke of Cumberland . 31 May, 1810
Abraham Goldsmid, an eminent merchant . . . ,,
Williams, supposed murderer of the Marr family and others . . . . 15 Dec. 1811
Lord French . . . . 9 Dec. 1814
Marshal Berthier . . . . . . 1 June, 1815
Samuel Whitbread, esq. . . . . . 6 July, ,,
Sir Richard Croft . . . . . . 13 Feb. ,,
Sir Samuel Romilly . . . . . . 2 Nov. 1818
Christophe, king of Hayti . . . . 8 Oct. 1820
Adm. sir George Campbell . . . . 23 June, 1821
Marquis of Londonderry . . . . . 12 Aug. 1822
Hon. colonel Stanhope . . . . . 26 Jan. 1825
Mr. Montgomery in Newgate (see *Prussic Acid*), 4 July, 1828
Miss Charlotte Both . . . . . . 3 Jan. 1830
Lord Greaves . . . . 7 Feb. ,,
Colonel Brereton . . . . 13 Jan. 1832
Major Thompson . . . . 13 June, ,,
Mr. Simpson, the traveller . . . . 24 July, 1840
Lord James Beresford . . . . . 27 April, 1841
Gen. sir Rufane Shaw Donkin . . . . 1 May, ,,
The earl of Munster . . . . . . 20 March, 1842
Lord Congleton . . . . 8 June, ,,
Laman Blanchard . . . . 15 Feb. 1845
Colonel J. Gurwood, editor of "Wellington's Despatches" . . . . 25 Dec. ,,
Rear-admiral Collard . . . . . . 18 March, 1846
Haydon, the eminent painter . . . . 22 June, ,,
Count Bresson . . . . 2 Nov. 1847
Colonel King, in India . . . . . 12 July, 1850
Walter Watts, lessee of Olympic theatre, 13 July, ,,
Rev. Dr. Rice . . . . 20 Jan. 1853
Lieut.-col. Layard . . . . . . 27 Dec. ,,
Rev. T. Robinson (threw himself off Shakspere's Cliff, Dover) . . . . 16 Aug. 1854
Dr. Franks, late editor of the *Allgemeine Zeitung*, after killing his son . . . . . . 3 Nov. 1855
John Sadleir, M.P. (in 1852, a lord of the treasury), by prussic acid; on Hampstead Heath. (He was found to have been guilty of enormous frauds upon the Tipperary bank, &c.) . . . . 16 Feb. 1856
A. Smart, a watchmaker, threw himself from the whispering-gallery in St. Paul's . . 14 March, ,,
Charles Russell, esq., late chairman of Great Western Railway . . . . . . 15 May, ,,
Hugh Miller, geologist, author of *The Old Red Sandstone* (insane, through overwork) . . 23 Dec. ,,
Major-gen. Stalker, C.B., of Indian army (14 March), and commodore Ethersey, of the Indian navy. (Both through physical and mental depression

* Three instances of self-destruction by fire: the philosopher Empedocles threw himself into the crater of Mount Etna; a Frenchman threw himself, in 1820, into the crater of Vesuvius; and an Englishman, who jumped into the furnace of a forge about the year 1811. Plutarch relates that an unaccountable passion for suicide seized the Milesian virgins, from which they could not be prevented by the tears and prayers of their friends; but a decree being issued that the body of every young maid who did self-murder should be drawn naked through the streets, a stop was soon put to the extraordinary frenzy.

while on the expedition against Persia: see *Bushire*) . . . . . 17 March, 1857
Major Warburton, M.P. for Harwich, brother of Eliot, lost in the *Amazon* . . . 23 Oct. ,,
Henry M. Witt, a promising young chemist, at the Government School of Mines . . 19 June, 1858
Dr. Sadleir, Senior Fellow of Trinity College, Dublin, July, ,,
Rev. G. Martin, chancellor of the diocese of Exeter, 27 Aug. 1860
Lord Forth, son of earl of Perth . . . 8 Oct. 1861
Wm. G. Prescott, banker . . . . 29 April, 1865
Admiral Robert Fitz-Roy (see *New Zealand*, and *Meteorology*) . . . . . 30 April, ,,
Col. Hobbs (connected with the suppression of Jamaica outbreak) on his way to England, 9 May, 1867
G. W. Green, merchant, jumped off Clifton Suspension bridge . . . . . 11 May, ,,
Dr. A. W. Warder, murderer of his wife, at Brighton, 12 July, ,,
Thos. Lee, threw himself from the north tower of the Crystal palace . . . . . 18 Feb. 1868
Theodore, emperor of Abyssinia . . 13 April, ,,
Mr. Stephenson, bettor on races; the "leviathan bookmaker" . . . . . . 9 Feb. 1869
G. H. Townsend, historical scholar . . 25 Feb. ,,
Lord Cloncurry . . . . . . 3 April, ,,
Sir Robert H. J. Harvey, Norwich banker, 15 July; died . . . . 19 July, 1870
M. Prévost-Paradol, the accomplished French minister at Washington, formerly a correspondent for the *Times* . . . . . 19 July, ,,
Mr. Robert K. Bowley, 15 years manager of the Crystal palace company . . . 25 Aug. ,,
Dr. Augustus Matthiessen, eminent chemist, professor at St. Bartholomew's hospital . 6 Oct. ,,
Lord Walsingham . . . . . . 31 Jan. 1871
Sir James Shaw Willes, justice of common pleas (overwrought mind) . . . . 2 Oct. 1872
Earl Delawarr (insane) . . . . 22 April, 1873
Rev. Arthur Holmes, dean of Clare College, Cambridge, a great scholar; (overwrought mind) 17 April, 1875
George Lord Lyttelton, eminent scholar; temporary insanity; 18 April; died . . 19 April, 1876
Abdul Aziz, sultan of Turkey, deposed 29 May; said to have committed suicide (see *Turkey*, 1881), 4 June, ,,
Dr. Sam. Butcher, bishop of Meath; insane, 29 July, ,,
Harriet Mary, dowager countess Howe; insane through grief . . . . . 29 Jan. 1877
Raphael Brandon, architect . . . 8 Oct. ,,
J. W. Stevens, insane; threw himself from whispering gallery, St. Paul's . . . . 10 Jan. ,,
E. M. Ward, *genre* painter; insane . . 15 Jan. 1879
Isaac Fletcher, M.P., F.R.S. . . . 3 April, ,,
Rev. W. Gunson, able tutor of Christ's College, Cambridge (insane) . . . . 30 Sept. 1881
Carl Engel (musical archæologist) . 18 Nov. 1882
Dr. William Whitfield Edwards, surgeon at Hounslow . . . . 27 Dec. ,,
Count Wimpffen, Austrian ambassador at Paris, 30 Dec. ,,
Morris Simeon Oppenheim, barrister . . 3 Jan. 1883
Joseph Dimsdale, Gutter-lane, E.C. . . 13 Jan. ,,
Sir John Savage, formerly mayor of Belfast, 15 June, ,,
Rev. Alexr. Taylor, preacher of Gray's Inn 11 April, 1884
H. T. Edwards, dean of Bangor . . 24 May, ,,
The eighth earl of Shaftesbury (insane) in a cab in Regent-street . . . . 13 April, 1886
Fred Archer, celebrated jockey (insane) 8 Nov. ,,
Louis II., king of Bavaria . . . 13 June, ,,
Nagayori Asana, Japanese prince, law student (melancholia), at south Kensington . 24 Dec. ,,
John K. Cross, formerly M.P. and under-secretary for India (1883–5) . . . 20 March, 1887
Dr. Ridley of Tullamore gaol (see under *Ireland*,) 20 July, 1888
Richard Pigott (see *Ireland*) . . . 1 March, 1889
M. Denfert-Rochereau, manager of the Comptoir d'Escompte (see *France*) . . . 5 March, ,,
Sir Wm. Tindal Robertson, M.P. . . . 6 Oct. ,,
Sir Thos. Sidgreaves . . . . . 23 Dec. ,,
Professor Lant Carpenter (insane) . . 23 Dec. 1890
The duke of Bedford (insane) . . 14 Jan. 1891
Charles Verrall Willett, M.D. (insane) . 6 March, ,,
Lord James E. Sholto Douglas (insane) 5 May, ,,
Sen. José M. Balmaceda, president of Chili 19 Sept. 1891
Georges E. J. M. Boulanger (see *France*) 30 Sept. ,,
Dr. Philip H. Carpenter, at Eton College 21 Oct. ,,
Arthur Goring Thomas, musical composer (insane), 20 March, 1892
Mr. J. H. Ferris, deputy-coroner of Cornwall, through grief . . . . . . 26 March, ,,
M. Henri Dupeyrier, African explorer . April, ,,
M. Anatole de la Forge, French author . 6 June, ,,
Dr. Alexander Woodburn Heron . . 25 Oct. ,,
Mr. Hilton Cassenet Barker . . . 22 Feb. 1893
Dr. Lombard J. N. Tanner . . . 28 April, ,,
Mr. Scotton, eminent cricketer . . 9 July, ,,
Mr. Leo Percy, electrician, after killing Miss Montague and Mr. Samuel Garcia in Regent's-square, W.C. (jealousy) . . . . . 21 Sept. ,,
Mr. John L. G. Mowat, fellow and librarian of Pembroke College, Oxford . . . 7 Aug. 1894
Mr. Patrick Henderson (British consul at Cadiz), at the foreign office . . . . 10 Oct. ,,
Mr. Arthur Dacre, actor, after killing his wife (formerly Miss Amy Roselle), by agreement, at Sydney, N.S.W. . . . . . . 17 Nov. ,,
Dr. Daniel Robert Wynter, coroner (Warwickshire), 24 Feb. ,,
Mr. I. B. Barnato, aged 45, insane, mid June, see *Cape* . . . . ,,
Mr. P. Scott Fishe, actor . . . . . Aug. 1898
Edith and Ida Bowyer (Yeoland), actresses, aged 28 and 25 (unsound mind) . . 16 July, 1901
Hugh Jervis Smith, lt. 3rd batt. Somerset lt. inf., aged 22 . . . . . . 5 Feb. 1903
Maj.-gen. sir Hector MacDonald, "Fighting Mac," 33 years in army, distinguished service in India, Egypt, and S. Africa; Paris . . 25 March, ,,
Arthur Shrewsbury, noted cricketer . 19 May, ,,
Miss Hickman, a lady doctor, disappeared mysteriously from the Free Hospital, Gray's-inn-road, 15 Aug., her body found in Richmond park, 18 Oct.; verdict of suicide by morphia poisoning during temporary insanity . . 12 Nov. ,,
Mr. Andrew Pattullo, a member of the Ontario legislature . . . . 29 Dec. ,,

INQUESTS ON SUICIDES IN ENGLAND AND WALES.

	Males.	Females.	Total.
1858	909	366	1275
1860	961	396	1357
1861	961	363	1324
1862	938	346	1284
1863	1048	337	1385
1864	978	359	1337
1865	1028	369	1397
1866	973	387	1360
1867	985	371	1356
1868	1138	408	1546
1869	1165	397	1562
1870	1135	382	1517
1871	1073	391	1464
1872	1057	398	1455
1873	1099	382	1481
1874	1106	383	1549
1875	1170	407	1577
1876	1270	443	1713
1877	1253	383	1636
1878	1279	430	1709
1879	1461	480	1941
1880	1450	480	1930
1881	1440	478	1918
1882	1388	502	1890
1883	1437	507	1944
1884	1537	482	2019
1885	1504	484	1988
1886	1663	559	2222
1887	1672	555	2227
1888	1720	577	2297
1889	1603	535	2138
1890	1610	544	2154
1891	1851	608	2459
1892	1884	661	2545
1893	1880	643	2523
1894	2027	684	2711
1895	2059	712	2771
1896	1971	668	2639
1898	2163	714	2877
1899	2077	703	2780
1900	2138	725	2863

SUITORS' FUND (in the court of chancery) in 1862 amounted to 1,290,000*l*. As this money has no specific owner, a proposal was made by government to apply it to the building of new law-courts, payment of all legal claims being guaranteed, which was directed by the "Courts of Laws Fees" act, passed 20 Aug. 1867.

SULPHUR has been known from the earliest times. Basil Valentine mentions its production from green vitriol. Sulphuric acid (vitriol), produced by him from burning sulphur, was introduced into England about 1720. Sulphur has been the object of research of many eminent chemists during the present century, and many discoveries have been made, such as its allotropic condition, &c. It is the inflammable constituent in gunpowder, and a deleterious ingredient in coal gas. The sulphur mines of Sicily have been wrought since the 16th century, but the exportation was inconsiderable till about 1820; in 1838 the trade increased so much that Great Britain alone imported 38,654 tons. In that year the Neapolitan government was induced to grant a monopoly of the trade to a French company; but a firm remonstrance from the British government led to a discontinuance of this impolitic restriction in 1841, which, however, gave a great and lasting impetus to the British sulphur manufacture.

SULPHURYL FLUORIDE, a new colourless, odourless gas, which can be liquefied and solidified at low temperatures; prepared by Moissan and Lebeau, by the action of fluorine on sulphur dioxide; reported, 17 Aug. 1901.

SULTAN, or ruler, a Turkish title, from the Arabic, given to Mahometan rulers and especially to the grand signior or emperor of Turkey.

For the wreck of H.M.S. *Sultan*, see *Navy of England* 1889

SULU, Sooloo or Soluk Archipelago, a group of above 60 islands in the Malay Archipelago. The Spanish under colonel Arolas, the governor, defeated the rebels at Maiburg, and burnt the town, announced 1 May, 1887.

SUMATRA, an island in the Indian ocean, called Java Minor by Marco Polo, and visited by Nicolo di Conti prior to 1449. Mainly on account of the pepper trade, the Dutch formed a settlement at Padang about 1649, and the British at Bencoolen about 1685. The Dutch possessions with Java were acquired by the British in 1811; but were restored in 1816. In 1824 the Dutch acquired all the British settlements in Sumatra, in exchange for Malacca and some possessions in India. Restrictions on their progress in Sumatra were removed by treaty Feb. 1872. Severe fighting between the Dutch and the Achinese natives with varying results, mostly in favour of the Dutch, April 1873 to 1879. Dutch successful in war, peace announced, Aug. 1879. New war; great victory of the Dutch, 13 Sept. 1882. Sumatra suffered much by the volcanic eruptions and earthquakes of 26-27 Aug. 1883. See *Java* and *Holland*, 1896 *et seq.*

SUMMARY JURISDICTION ACT, 42 & 43 Vict. c. 49, 11 Aug. 1879. It amends the law respecting the jurisdiction of magistrates, in regard to fines, imprisonments, &c. It came into operation 1 Jan. 1880. Amended 1881, 1884 and 1895; again, powers extended, 1899. Summary convictions in 1893 in England and Wales, 649,371.

SUMPTUARY LAWS restrain excess in dress, furniture, eating, &c. The laws of Lycurgus were severe against luxury, probably 9th century B.C. Those of Zaleucus ordained that no sober woman should go attended by more than one maid in the street, or wear gold or embroidered apparel, 450 B.C.—*Diog. Laert.* The *Lex Orchia* among the Romans (181 B.C.) limited the guests at feasts, and the number and quality of the dishes at an entertainment; and it also enforced that during supper, which was the chief meal among the Romans, the doors of every house should be left open. The English sumptuary laws, chiefly of the reigns of Edward III. and Henry VIII., were repealed in 1856; see *Dress*.

SUN.* Pythagoras taught that the sun was one of the twelve spheres, about 529 B.C. The relative distances of the sun and moon were first calculated geometrically by Aristarchus, who also maintained the stability of the sun, about 280 B.C. Numerous theories were ventured during fifteen centuries, and astronomy lay neglected till about A.D. 1200, when it was brought into Europe by the Moors of Barbary and Spain. The Copernican system was made known in 1530; see *Copernican System* and *Solar System*. Galileo and Newton maintained that the sun was an igneous globe. The transit of Mercury was observed by Gassendi, 1631. For recent discoveries, see *Eclipses*, *Spectrum*, and *Venus*.

By the observations of Dr. Halley on the spot which darkened the sun's disc in July and August, 1676, he established the certainty of its motion round its own axis.

Parallax of the sun, Dr. Halley 1702

Solar spots were observed by Fabricius and Harriot in 1610. A macula three times the size of the earth passed the sun's centre, 21 April, 1766, and frequently since.

Dr. Wilson observed the motion of a spot . . 1769

Herschel measured two spots, whose length together exceeded 50,000 miles . . . . 19 April, 1779

Many sun spots observed . early 1892 and 1894

Schwabe discovered that a cycle of changes (from maximum to minimum and minimum to maximum) in the number of spots occurs in 11 years, confirmed by Wolf and others . . . 1826-51

Mr. Warren de la Rue took two photographs at the time of total obscuration . . . . 18 July, 1860

Mr. James Nasmyth discovers the lenticular-shaped objects on the sun (termed by him "willow-leaves," by Stone "rice-grains") . . 28 Aug. ,,

Red flames, or protuberances, during an eclipse of the sun, observed by capt. Stannyan, 1706; by Halley, 1715; by F. Baily (hence termed "Baily's beads,") 1842.

Determined by M. Janssen to be due to the accumulated hydrogen of the photosphere, at the solar eclipse (see *Eclipses*) . . . . 18 Aug. 1868

Mouchot constructed a solar boiler for distillation, &c. . . . . Oct. 1860

Mr. Ericsson proposed condensation of the sun's rays and their employment as a motive power, Oct. 1868

The observations of the eclipse of 22 Dec. 1870 and 12 Dec. 1871 led to the opinion that an unknown substance (represented in the spectrum by line 1474) existed in the sun.

"*Solar physics*" especially studied by Messrs. Warren de la Rue, Balfour Stewart, &c. . . 1865-6

Apparatus for cooking by the *condensed solar rays* in the Paris exhibition 1878

* The estimated diameter is 840,000 miles, and the distance from the earth, till lately given as 95,000,000 miles, has been recently corrected to 94,000,000, by the result of the experiments and calculations of MM. Fizeau and Foucault (1864). "The error corrected corresponds to the apparent breadth of a human hair at 125 feet, or of a sovereign 8 miles off."—*Herschel*. Distance computed by sir G. B. Airy from results of the observation of transit of Venus (9 Dec. 1874), 93,321,000 miles, Oct. 1877; 92,600,000, June, 18-8. From the transit of 1882 by professor Harkness (an American), 92,385,000 miles, October, 1888. The sun is now described as consisting of a solid or liquid nucleus, surrounded by a luminous envelope (photosphere), over which is a dense atmosphere, containing the vapours of various metals and other elements; see *Spectrum*.

M. Mouchot at Algiers, by a mirror, collected solar rays, and boiled water, drove an engine, &c., March, 1880; see under *Heat*.

Intensely red sunsets and after-glow, and very red sun-rises, seen in England and other parts of the globe, Nov. and Dec. 1883; attributed by Dr. Meldrum, Dr. Norman Lockyer and others, to the volcanic dust projected by the eruptions of Krakatoa (see *Java*, Aug. 1883), Dec. 1883; other causes, such as cosmic dust, were suggested. Similar sunsets in the autumn . 1884 and 1885

Interesting photographs of the sun's corona exhibited by Dr. Huggins at the Royal Institution, 20 Feb. ,,

Photographic researches of sir W. and lady Huggins on the presence of calcium vapour in the sun's rays, reported to the Royal society . 17 June, 1897

A sun spot, diameter 30,000 miles, observed by Mr. G. F. Chambers at Eastbourne . . 9 Aug. ,,

A fine sun spot, connected with aurora and magnetic disturbance, appeared, March; another, with a train of small spots, appeared, 2 Sept. *et seq.*; another outburst . . . 22 Oct. 1898

12 groups of spots, including 392 individual spots, observed in 1901

Large sun spots, one 180,000 mi., visible, Oct.-Nov. 1903

SUNCION, Treaty of, between general Urquiza, director of the Argentine confederation, and C. A. Lopez, president of the republic of Paraguay, recognising the independence of Paraguay, 14 July, 1852.

SUNDA ISLES, include Java and Sumatra (*which see*).

SUNDAY was the day on which, anciently, divine adoration was paid to the Sun. Among Christians it is commonly called *Dies Dominica*, or Lord's day, on account of our Saviour's appearance on that day, after his resurrection. The first civil law that was issued for the observance of this day, combined it with that of the seventh-day Sabbath and other festivals (*Eusebius*, *Life of Constantine*), and it was followed by several imperial edicts, in favour of this day, which are extant in the body of Roman law, the earliest being that of Constantine the Great, dated 7 March, 321. See *Sabbath*, *Sabbatarians*, *Sports*, *Book of*, &c.—For Sunday Letter, see *Dominical Letter*.

The council of Orleans prohibited country labour . 538

The Sabbath-day was ordained to be kept holy in England, from Saturday at three in the afternoon to Monday at break-of-day, 4th Canon, Edgar . 960

Act of parliament, levying one shilling on every person absent from church on Sundays, 3 James I. 1606

James I. authorised certain sports after divine service on Sundays (see *Sports*) 1618

Act restraining amusements, 1 Charles I. . . . 1625

Act restraining the performance of servile works, and the sale of goods except milk at certain hours and meat in public-houses, and works of necessity and charity, on forfeiture of five shillings, 29 Charles II. 1676

The Sunday act (of bishop Porteus), 21 Geo. III. c. 49, passed 1781

Lord Robert Grosvenor (aft. lord Ebury), introduced a bill to suppress Sunday trading. (It met with much opposition and was withdrawn), April-July, 1855

The Jews released from the compulsory observance of Sunday . . . . . began 28 May, 1871

Sunday act (1676) amended . . . . 17 Aug. ,,

Opening of public museums and galleries on Sunday often proposed in parliament; negatived (271-68), 19 May, 1874; (229-87) 8 June, 1877

"Sunday Society" established 6 Aug. 1875, "to maintain and enhance the value and importance of the English Sunday." Annual meeting; Dr. A. P. Stanley, the dean of Westminster, professors Tyndall and Huxley, &c., present 12 May, ,, See *Museum*.

The Brighton Aquarium Company fined for opening on Sunday, 27 April; much agitation; petitions to government for and against, May; an act was passed to enable the Home Secretary to remit the penalties, 13 Aug., 1875; the company again fined . . . . . . 28 April, 1877

Grosvenor gallery and other collections opened on Sundays, summer 1878

Act for closing public-houses in Ireland on Sundays, passed . . . . . . 16 Aug. ,,

Free libraries opened on Sundays at Manchester and other places . . . . . Sept. ,,

Proposed opening of museums and galleries in London, negatived in the lords (67-59), 5 May, 1879; (34-41), 22 Feb. 1880; (91-67) 8 May, 1883; assented to (76-62), 19 March, 1886; agreed to by resolution—178-93—commons . 10 March, 1896

Opening of Guildhall library on Sundays, negatived by the common council . . . . 16 Oct. 1879

Welsh Sunday Closing act passed 1881

Alexandra Palace religious services on Sundays for a time . . . . . . Sept.-Oct. ,,

Jubilee memorial to the queen signed by 1,132,608 women of England, requesting the prohibition of the sale of intoxicating liquors on Sundays, given in . . . . 30 Dec. 1887

Protest of the bishops in convocation against increasing desecration of the Lord's day by the upper classes . . . . . 2 March, 1888

Closing of public houses in England on Sunday frequently negatived; Sunday closing bill read second time in the commons . . 27 March, 1889

Sunday Rest League formed at Paris . . . . ,,

National federation of Sunday societies; second congress held in London . . . 1 July, 1895

SUNDAY LECTURE SOCIETY was founded 25 Nov. 1869. It began its proceedings by a lecture delivered by Dr. W. B. Carpenter at St. George's hall, Regent-street, 16 Jan. 1870. Its success was reported at the first annual meeting, 7 July, 1870. "Sunday concert society," formed for the promotion of Sunday concerts (carried on by Mr. Robert Newman, 1894 *et seq.* at the Queen's hall), Sir E. Clarke chairman, duke of Newcastle vice-pres., 9 Dec. 1898; the duke of Portland president, Jan. 1899. See *Recreative Religionists*.

SUNDAY NEWSPAPERS, see *Newspapers*.

SUNDAY SCHOOLS. Cardinal Sr. Charles Borromeo introduced Sunday instruction of children at Milan, about 1580; in the next century his example was followed in England by the rev. Joseph Alleine; by rev. David Blair, at Brechin, about 1760; by the rev. Theophilus Lindsey, at Catterick, Yorkshire, about 1763; and more especially organised by Robert Raikes, an eminent printer of Gloucester, conjointly with rev. Thos. Stock, 1780. Ludweek Hacker set up a Sabbath school at Ephrata, Pennsylvania, between 1740 and 1747.

Sunday-school buildings exempted from rates . 1869

Church of England Sunday-school Institute . . 1843

Sunday-school union was founded in 1802; it supported 4204 schools, 1878; 6162 schools in . . 1892

Monument in memory of twelve originators of Sunday-schools, Essex-street, Strand (names inscribed, 1st, cardinal Borromeo, Milan, 1580; last, rev. Thomas Stock and Robert Raikes, Gloucester, 1780); inaugurated by Henry Richard, M.P., the Italian ambassador, and others 26 June, 1880

National centenary celebration of the establishment of Sunday-schools, in London, &c., promoted by the royal family, archbishop of Canterbury, the lord mayor, and others . 27 June—3 July, ,,

Grand reception of scholars at Lambeth palace-gardens by the archbishop; prince and princess of Wales, &c., present . . . . . . 3 July, ,,

World's Sunday-school convention, 1st held in London, 1889; 2nd at St. Louis, Missouri, 1893; 3rd, 2500 delegates present, London, 12-15 July, 1898

Centenary of the Sunday-school Union, 2-8 July, 1903

See *Education* and *Sabbath Schools*.

SUNDERLAND, seaport, N.E. Durham, anciently South Wearmo', made a borough by Reform bill, 1832. Returns two members (1885). The magnificent bridge over the Wear, designed by Wilson, 236 feet in span, was built 1793-6.

Population, 1881, 116,542; 1891, 130,921; 1901, 146,828.

On 16 June, 1883, 186 children were crushed to death against a doorway whilst rushing down from a gallery in Victoria-hall to obtain toys given away by Fay, a conjuror, at the close of his performances.

Great distress of the unemployed . Sept. *et seq.* 1884
See *Strikes*, 1892.

Great fire, began at Mr. G. H. Robinson's, draper, Fawcett-st., business premises in High-st. and John-st. also destroyed . . 18, 19 July, 1898

SUNDERLAND ADMINISTRATION, formed in 1718, arose out of a modification of the Stanhope ministry. After various changes, it was broken up in 1721.

Charles, earl of Sunderland, *first lord of the treasury*.
Earl Cowper, *lord chancellor*.
Earl Stanhope and Mr. Craggs, *secretaries*.
Mr. Aislabie, *chancellor of the exchequer*, &c.

SUNDERLAND LIBRARY, see under *Libraries*.

SUN DIALS, see *Dials*.

SUNNITES, or SONNITES (*which see*).

SUNSHINE RECORDER, a sphere of glass so disposed as to char a marked piece of paper, by concentrating the sun's rays. The instrument (invented by Mr. J. F. Campbell in 1857), in its present form was devised by sir G. G. Stokes (died 1 Feb. 1903) and made by Mr. R. J. Lecky (1880). A more delicate form of instrument for recording photometrically the duration and intensity of sunshine has been invented by Mr. J. B. Jordan, 1884; much improved, April, 1888.

SUPERANNUATION ACTS for the Civil Service were passed in April, 1859, Aug. 1866, June, 1892.

SUPPER, see *Lord's Supper*.

SUPREMACY over the church was claimed by pope Gelasius I. as bishop of Rome, 494. On 15 Jan. 1535, Henry VIII. by virtue of the act 26 Hen. VIII. c. 1, formally assumed the style of "on earth supreme head of the church of England," which was retained by Edward VI., Mary I. (for a time), but was refused by Elizabeth, and has never been revived by succeeding sovereigns. The bishop of Rochester (Fisher) and the ex-lord chancellor (sir Thomas More) and many others were beheaded for denying the king's supremacy in 1535; and in 1578, John Nelson, a priest, and Thomas Sherwood, a young layman, were executed at Tyburn for the same offence. The "act of Supremacy," repealed by 1 & 2 Phil. and Mary, c. 8 (1554), was re-enacted 1 Eliz. c. 1 (1559).

SUPREME COURT OF JUDICATURE was constituted by the Judicature act 36 & 37 Vict. c. 66, passed 5 Aug. 1873, to come into operation 1 Nov. 1874. In 1874 this was deferred to 1 Nov. 1875. The "Council of Judges" appointed by this act met to consider questions relating to the reform of the law, 18 Jan. 1892. See under *Judges*.

The existing courts were to be united into one Supreme Court, divided into the High Court of Justice and the Court of Appeal. The High Court to consist of the lord chancellor, the two lord chief justices, the vice-chancellors, and the other judges: (hereafter the court to consist of 21 judges.)

Five divisions: 1. Chancery, 2. Queen's Bench, 3. Common Pleas, 4. Exchequer, and 5. Probate, Divorce, and Admiralty; subject to alteration.

The Court of Appeal to consist of five ex-officio judges (viz., lord chancellor, two lord chief justices, lord chief baron, master of the rolls), and such others as may be appointed (§§ 20, 21, 22).

Appeals to the house of lords or the judicial committee of the privy council to be discontinued.

Law and equity to be concurrently administered; law terms abolished; and sittings in vacation provided for. See under *Terms*.

The act passed 11 Aug., 1875, suspended §§ 20, 21, and 55, converted the proposed court of appeal into an intermediate court till 1 Nov., 1876. (See below.)

The Supreme Court of Judicature (comprising the High Court of Justice, Chancery division, Queen's Bench, Common Pleas, and Exchequer subdivisions, Probate, Divorce, and Admiralty division (*all which see*) began . . . . . . 2 Nov. 1875

After one term, it was said in the *Times*, "Its operation has tended to economise judicial power and to prevent delay of justice" . . 29 Nov. ,,

By the Appellate Jurisdiction act (1876) the house of lords retains its powers as a court of ultimate appeal; the court to consist of the lord chancellor, two lords of appeal (to be created peers for life, with 6000*l.* salary), and any peers who are or have been lawyers. Act to come into operation . . . . . . 1 Nov. 1876

The court may sit during prorogation of parliament. The statute relating to the judicial committee of the privy council and to the intermediate court of appeal is amended . . . . . ,,

By this act also the Queen's Bench, Common Pleas, and Exchequer divisions of the Supreme Court are converted into 15 courts of first instance or primary courts.

Additional judge for chancery division appointed.

Style of ordinary judges:—of the court of appeal to be "lord justices of the appeal;" other judges, "justices of the high court;" by act passed 24 April, 1877

An amendment act (42 & 43 Vict. c. 78), relating to offices, fees, &c., passed . . . . 15 Aug. 1879

At a meeting of the judges it was resolved to recommend the abolition of the exchequer and common pleas, and their consolidation into one, termed the "queen's bench division," under the lord chief justice of England, 30 Nov.; order in council 16 Dec. 1880

Carried into effect; old divisions at an end; judicature act carried out for the first time 7 March, 1881

Further changes made by the act 44 & 45 Vict. sec. 68, passed 27 Aug. 1881, by it the master of the rolls was made a judge of appeal only, and the chief justice of England was endowed with the powers of the chief justice of common pleas and the chief baron of the exchequer.

New code of rules of procedure issued about 9 July; came into force 24 Oct. 1883. See *Circuits*. Amendment act passed (combining other acts), 14 Aug. 1884; other acts passed 14 Aug. 1890, 11 May, and 5 Aug. 1891 and 1894

New rules issued, published . . . . 3 July, ,,

Commercial causes (398) tried in a court, queen's bench division . . . . March, 1895

Decrease in business of the courts, attributed to acceleration in the proceedings; reported June, ,,

Judicial statistics: published annually since 1893, in two parts [civil and criminal].

Supreme court (appeals) bill passed, 6 June, 1899; another passed in 1902

SUPREME COURT OF JUDICATURE FOR IRELAND constituted by act passed 14 Aug. 1877. Amended by an act passed 23 May, 1887, by which the titles of chief baron of the exchequer and chief justice of the common pleas are to be abolished at the next vacancies; again, 6 Aug. 1897.

COURT OF APPEAL: *ex-officio members*, lord chancellor, lord chief justice of Ireland, master of the rolls, lord chief justice of common pleas, and lord chief baron of exchequer. *Ordinary members*, two lords justices of appeal.

HIGH COURT OF JUSTICE: *Chancery division*, lord chancellor, master of the rolls, vice chancellor and two land judges.

Queen's Bench division: lord chief justice and three judges.

Common Pleas division: lord chief justice, and two judges.
Exchequer division: lord chief baron, and two judges.
Probate and Matrimonial division: one judge.

See under *Chancery* and the other divisions.

SURAT (E. Indies). Before the English East India company obtained possession of Bombay, the presidency of their affairs on the coast of Malabar was at Surat; and they had a factory here established under captain Best in 1611. The Great Mogul had here an officer who was styled his admiral. An attack of the Mahratta chief Sivajee, on the British factory, was defeated by sir George Oxenden, 1664. The English were again attacked in 1670 and 1702, and often subsequently. The East India company, in 1759, fitted out an armament, which dispossessed the admiral of the castle; and, soon after, the possession of this castle was confirmed to them by the court of Delhi. Surat was vested in the British in 1800 and 1803. A fourth part of Surat was destroyed by fire 6, 7 April, 1889.

SURGEONS. Barbers and surgeons were united in one company in 1540; but it was enacted that "no person using any shaving or barbery in London shall occupy any surgery, letting of blood, or other matter, excepting only the drawing of teeth." In 1745 the surgeons and barbers of London were made distinct corporations. The college of surgeons obtained charters in 1745, 1800, and 1843 (when it was styled the "Royal College of Surgeons of England"), 1852 and 1859. Since that period, various legislative and other important regulations have been adopted to promote their utility and respectability; and no person is legally entitled to practise as a surgeon in the cities of London and Westminster, or within seven miles of the former, who has not been examined at this college. The college in Lincoln's-inn-fields was remodelled in 1836, and the interior completed in 1837. The premises were enlarged in 1852-3. The museum began with the Hunterian collection, 1800; and the library was founded in 1801. Death of the president, Mr. J. W. Hulke, 19 Feb. 1895; succeeded by sir Wm. MacCormac; centenary of the college celebrated, 26 July, 1900 (he died, aged 65, 4 Dec. 1901); H. G. Howse, knt., June, 1902. Mrs. Mary Emily Dowson, the first lady surgeon duly qualified to act, was invested with the letters testimonial of the Irish college of surgeons, June, 1886. See *Anatomy*, *Physic*, and *Medical Council*.

Royal college of surgeons, Edinburgh, received its charter from James V. 1505; another received in 1778, and a fuller one, 1851; Dublin, incorporated, 1786.

SURGERY. It was not until the age of Hippocrates that diseases were made a separate study from philosophy, &c., about 410 B.C. Hippocrates mentions the *ambe*, the ancient instrument with which they reduced dislocated bones. Celsus flourished about A.D. 17; Galen, 170; Aëtius, 500; Paulus Ægineta, in 640. The Arabians revived surgery about 900; and in the 16th century a new era in the science began; between these periods surgery was confined to ignorant priests and barbers. Anatomy was cultivated under Vesalius, the father of modern surgery, in 1538. Surgeons and doctors were exempted from bearing arms or serving on juries, 1513, at which period there were only 13 in London; see *Physic* and *Photography*, 1896. For antiseptic treatment see *Germ Theory*. Great improvements in surgery in the 19th century reported by sir Joseph (aft. lord) Lister in his address to the British association at Liverpool, 16 Sept. 1896.

SURGICAL AID SOCIETY, founded 1862; supplies the poor with instruments, waterbeds, &c.

SURINAM (Dutch Guiana), discovered by Columbus, 1498. The factories established by the English in 1640 were occupied by the Portuguese, 1643; by the Dutch, 1654; taken by the British, 1799, 1804; and restored to the Dutch, 1802, 1814.

Plantation riot, Mavor the manager killed, troops fire on the rioters, 13 killed and 40 wounded, reported . . . . 31 July, 1902

SURNAMES were introduced into England by the Normans, and were adopted by the nobility about 1100. The old Normans used *Fitz*, which signifies son, as Fitz-herbert. The Irish used O, for grandson, O'Neal, O'Donnell. The Scottish Highlanders used Mac, as Macdonald, son of Donald. The Welsh used Ap, as Ap Rhys, the son of Rhys; Ap Richard. The prefix Ap eventually was combined with the name of the father, hence Prys, Pritchard, &c. The northern nations added the word son to the father's name, as Williamson. Many of the most common surnames, such as Johnson, Wilson, Dyson, Nicholson, &c., were taken by Brabanters and other Flemings, who were naturalised in the reign of Henry VI., 1435. M. A. Lower's "Dictionary of English Surnames" was published in 1860.

SURPLICES were first worn by the Jewish priests, and are said to have been first used in churches in the fourth century, and encouraged by pope Adrian, 786. "Every minister saying public prayers shall wear a comely surplice with sleeves," *Canon* 58. The garb prescribed by stat. 2 Edw. VI. 1547; again 1 Eliz. 1558; and 13 & 14 Chas. II. 1662.

SURREY CHAPEL, Blackfriars-road, was built for Calvinistic dissenters in 1783; the rev. Rowland Hill, their minister, who died in 1833, was buried in a vault here. The congregation under the rev. Newman Hall (died 18 Feb. 1902) removed to Christ church, in Westminster-road, July, 1876. See *Lincoln Tower*.

SURREY HOUSE MUSEUM, Forest Hill, containing the collections of Mr. F. Horniman, cost about 100,000*l*., presented by him to the public, was opened by sir Morell Mackenzie, 24 Dec. 1890.

SURREY ZOOLOGICAL GARDENS (near London) were established in 1831, by Mr. Edward Cross, who brought hither the menagerie formerly at Exeter change. Various picture models have been exhibited here since 1837, viz., Vesuvius, Iceland, &c., accompanied by fireworks. In 1856, a company which had taken the gardens, erected a large yet elegant building for concerts; the architect being Mr. Horace Jones. On 19 Oct. 1856, when the hall contained about 9000 persons, attending to hear the rev. C. H. Spurgeon, seven were killed and thirty seriously injured, by a false alarm of fire. It was burnt 11 June, 1861; see *Fires*. In 1862 the hall was temporarily taken for the reception of the patients of St. Thomas's hospital.

SURTEES SOCIETY for publishing MSS. relating to the northern counties, established 1834; 84 volumes have been published, 1889.

SURVEY ACT, passed 12 May, 1870. See *Ordnance Survey*.

SURVEYORS, INSTITUTION OF, London, founded in 1868, to promote the "knowledge which constitutes the profession of a surveyor."

Incorporated by royal charter as "The Surveyors' Institution" in 1881. The number of members, 1,200 in 1886; about 3,000 in 1897.

SUSA, or **Shushan**, capital of Susiana, a province of Persia, was taken by Alexander the Great, 331 B.C.

SUSPENDING POWER, see *Dispensing Power*.

SUSPENSION BRIDGES are ancient in China. The Hungerford (or Charing-cross) suspension bridge, opened May 1, 1845, was removed to Clifton and opened there, 8 Dec. 1864. Parliament empowered the commissioners of woods to erect (among other improvements there) a suspension bridge at Battersea, Sept. 1846; and many bridges of similar construction have been erected in various parts of the kingdom. Lambeth and Westminster suspension bridge was opened 10 Nov. 1862; see *Menai Strait*, *Hungerford*, *Clifton*, &c.

SUSPENSORY BILL, the name given to "a bill to prevent for a limited time [to 1 Aug. 1869] new appointments in the church of Ireland; and to restrain, for the same period, in certain respects, the proceedings of the Ecclesiastical Commissioners for Ireland." This bill was introduced into the commons by Mr. Gladstone, 14 May, and passed through committee, 5 June; rejected by the lords (192 to 97), 30 June, 3 A.M., 1868. A similar bill, with limitations relating to Wales and Monmouthshire, introduced by Mr. Asquith, read first time (301 to 245), 23 Feb. 1893; withdrawn, Sept. 1893; see *Church of England*, May, 1893.

SUSSEX, see *Britain*.

SUTLEJ, a river in N.W. India, the ancient Hyphasis or Hypana, on the banks of which were fought the desperate battles of Aliwal, 28 Jan., and Sobraon, 10 Feb. 1846 (*which see*).

SUTTEE, the burning of widows. This custom began in India from one of the wives of "Bramah, the Son of God," sacrificing herself at his death, that she might attend him in heaven. Seventeen widows have burnt themselves on the funeral pile of a rajah; and in Bengal alone, 700 have thus perished in a year. The English government, after long discouraging suttees, by the agency of lord William Bentinck, formally abolished them, 7 Dec. 1829; but they have since occasionally taken place. The wife of the son of the rajah of Beygoon thus perished, June, 1864, and several wives of sir Jung Bahadoor, minister of Nepaul, 1 March, 1877. Suttees still occur; one, voluntary, at Poona, Nov. 1890.

About 20,000,000 women in enforced widowhood; much profligacy, 1885. Legislative interference with the Hindoo marriage laws declared by lord Dufferin, viceroy, to be ineffectual and unnecessary; moral influence progressing (see Brahmo Somaj, under *Deism*) announced . . . Oct. 1886

SUWANOW, or **(SUWOROFF)**, a group of small uninhabited isles in the Pacific, about 450 miles NNW. of the Samoan isles, annexed by Great Britain, 1889.

SWABIA, a province in S. Germany; was conquered by Clovis, and incorporated into the kingdom of the Franks, 496. After various changes of rulers, it was made a duchy by the emperor Conrad I., in 912, for Erchanger; according to some, in 916, for Burckhardt. The duchy became hereditary in the house of Hohenstaufen in 1080. Duke Frederick III. became emperor of Rome, commonly styled of Germany, as Frederick I. (usually styled Barbarossa, red beard), in 1152. Conradin, his descendant, was defeated at the battle of Tagliacozzo (*which see*), in 1268, and beheaded shortly after. The breaking up of the duchy gave rise to many of the small German states; part of Swabia is included in Würtemberg and Switzerland. Swabia was made a circle of the empire in 1387 and 1500. A league, composed of Swabian cities and states, about 1254, was the germ of the great Swabian league, formed for the preservation of the peace of Germany, under the auspices of the emperor Frederick, in 1488.

SWAN RIVER SETTLEMENT, see *Western Australia*.

SWANSEA, Glamorganshire, an ancient Welsh town; seat of the copper trade since 1719. New dock opened by the prince of Wales, 18 Oct. 1881. Population, 1881, 76,430; 1891, 90,423; 1901, 94,514.

The British association met here Aug. 1848, and Aug., Sept. 1880
Lewis L. Dillwyn, 37 years M.P. for Swansea, died suddenly . . . . 19 June, 1892
Boating disaster in the bay, 14 persons drowned, 7 Aug. 1893
Lord Rosebery receives the freedom . . 21 Dec. 1901
The Mumbles lifeboat capsized in the bay, 6 lives lost . . . . 1 Feb. 1903
British medical association met here, 28–31 July, „

SWAT, or **Svat**, a river, N.W. India. The Akhond, Abdul Ghafur, originally an austere Mahometan fanatic, about 1822, gradually obtained temporal power over the tribes in the hills near Afghanistan, dying in high reputation, about 1878.

SWAZILAND, South Africa, a tract of about 8,000 square miles, nearly surrounded by the Transvaal territory; population, about 60,000 natives and 600 whites, 1889.

Great disorders through the weakness of the king, Umbandeni; influenced successively by opposing white factions, English and Boers; the king dies, 6 Oct. 1889
To settle the government of the country, sir Francis de Winton was appointed British commissioner, sailed 8 Oct.; at Pretoria, about 12 Nov.; Boer commissioners were appointed . about 21 Oct. „
Boon, eldest son of Umbandeni, elected king; Mr. Shepstone appointed to take charge of European affairs . . . . . . about 23 Oct. „
Sir Francis de Winton and the Transvaal commissioners meet 100 head-men of the Swazis; results: the independence of the nation to be preserved; the accession of the king recognized; the queen-mother to be regent during his minority; Mr. Shepstone to be adviser; the commissioners to govern the whites during their stay, to be succeeded by 3 delegates; a legal tribunal to be appointed to enquire respecting concessions of land to the whites . . . . 11 Dec. „
The queen-regent (by Mr. Shepstone) proclaims submission to the commissioners, about 16 Dec.; the commissioners appoint 3 delegates (British, Boer, and Swazi) to help the queen, pending the decision of the British and Transvaal governments, and leave . . . . . . Dec. „
At a conference with president Krüger at Blignauts Pont, it was agreed to defer the settlement for four months . . . . . . 12 March, 1890
Independence of the Swazis re-affirmed by a convention; a joint administration over the white settlers to be established with other conditions; signed by president Krüger; reported 4 Aug.; ratified by the volksraad. . . . 8 Aug. „
Conference of commissioners, sir H. B. Loch and president Krüger at Colesberg, 18–20 April, 1893; sir H. B. Loch arrives at Pretoria, . 3 June, 1893
Convention of 1890 prolonged . . . . 8 Aug. „

Convention transferring Swaziland to the Transvaal government, signed at Pretoria . . 13 Nov. 1893
Renewed political complications, the queen-regent refuses to sign the convention, reported 13 April, 1894
New convention agreed to, dual control extended for 6 months . . . . 29 June, ,,
A deputation of 6 indunas (chiefs) from the queen, desiring a British protectorate for their country, accompanied by Mr. J. Stuart and Mr. Hulett, arrive at Plymouth, 27 Oct. 1894; interview with the marquis of Ripon, 31 Oct.; entertained by the baroness Burdett-Coutts, 7 Nov., and others; by the queen at Windsor, 15 Nov.; leave Southampton . . . . 17 Nov. ,,
Conference between sir Henry Loch and president Krüger in the Transvaal, 7 Dec.; a new convention signed . . . . 10 Dec. ,,
Sir Henry Loch delivers the queen's message to the envoys . . . . 15 Dec. ,,
British residents and others oppose annexation to the Transvaal. . . . . 27 Nov. ,,
The Transvaal volksraad adopt the new *convention* without the consent of Swaziland . . 13 Feb. 1895
Mr. T. Krogh appointed administrator, 19 Feb.; the government taken over . . . . 21 Feb. ,,
Resignation of col. Martin, British commissioner, 10 March, ,,
King Bunu installed as chief captain . 16 March, ,,
Financial agreement between the king and the Transyaal government . . . . . . Dec. ,,
The Transvaal volunteer force, with an advance guard, crosses the border on the king disobeying an ultimatum summoning him to appear at Bremersdorp to answer for the murder of the head induna, 21 June, 1898; fails to obey the summons, 5 July; an indaba held at Bremersdorp, commissioner Krogh president, gen. Joubert and the British consul present, the queen to stand in Bunu's place as chief of the Swazi nation, 14 July, 1898
Protocol of the convention, "a wise and satisfactory settlement," signed . . . . . 5 Oct. ,,
King Bunu fined 500*l*. for allowing acts of rapine, he dies later . . . . Nov. 1899
The queen-regent appoints Isitoso, her son, king; reported . . . . April, 1900

SWEABORG, a strong fortress in Finland, the Gibraltar of the north, 3½ miles south of Helsingfors; it is situated on seven rocky islands; the fortifications were commenced by the Swedes in 1748, and completed after Finland was united to Russia in 1809. On 6 Aug. 1855, the English and French fleet anchored off Sweaborg, and bombarded it by mortar and gun-boats from the 9th to the 11th, causing the destruction of nearly all the principal buildings, including the dockyard and arsenal. Few casualties and no loss of life ensued in the allied squadron, but this success was not followed up.

SWEARING ON THE GOSPELS, first used about 528, and introduced in judicial proceedings about 600.—*Rapin*. PROFANE SWEARING made punishable by fine; a labourer or servant forfeiting 1*s*., others 2*s*. for the first offence; for the second offence, 4*s*.; the third offence, 6*s*.; 6 Will. III. 1695; see *Oaths*.

SWEATING SICKNESS, see *Plague*.

SWEATING SYSTEM, a term applied, especially in the east end of London, to the practice carried on by large tradesmen of entrusting orders to middlemen termed "sweaters," who employ men, women, and children (principally foreigners) to make up clothes, boots, and furniture in their own houses at excessively low wages with many evil consequences. Lord Dunraven's motion for a select committee of inquiry was carried in the lords, 28 Feb.; archbishop of Canterbury, earl of Derby, and others appointed 9 March, 1888. Painfully distressing evidence was obtained. The origin of the evil is attributed to the great competition in producing extreme cheapness. The new and foreign workmen are termed "greeners." It is stated that about 5*s*. are sometimes paid for a week of days of 14 hours, May. The sufferings of the Cradley Heath chainmakers, nailmakers, and others were disclosed to the committee . . . . . March, 1889
Anti-sweating league formed in London. . 1 Oct. ,,
The fifth and final report recommends that where legislation cannot intervene capitalists should enquire into the way in which their work is carried on, with the view of improvement 5 May, 1890
Blue Book published . . . . . 19 May ,,

SWEDEN (N. Europe). The ancient inhabitants were the Fins, now the modern inhabitants of Finland, who retired to their present territory on the appearance of the Scandinavians or Goths, who have ever since been masters of Sweden; see *Scandinavia*, and *Norway*, 1891. The internal state of this kingdom is little known previous to the 11th century. By the union of Calmar in 1397, Sweden became a province of Denmark, and was not wholly rescued from this subjection till 1521, when Gustavus Vasa recovered the kingdom from the Danish yoke. He became king in 1523, and his descendants ruled till 1809. The government of Sweden is a limited monarchy. The diet consists of four orders, the nobles, the clergy, the peasants, and the burghers, and meet every three years. The king is, as in Britain, the head of the executive. There are two universities, Upsal and Lund; and Sweden can boast, among its great men, Linnæus, Celsius, Scheele, Bergman, Berzelius, Thorwaldsen, and Andersen. Population (31 Dec. 1887) of Sweden, 4,734.901; of Norway (1875), 1,806,900. Sweden, 1890, 4,784,675. Norway, 1891, 1,988.997. Norway, 1900, 2,239,880; Sweden, 1901, 5.175,228. Sweden, 1890-91, 4,911,894*l*. Norway, 1891-2, estimated revenue, 2,733,333*l*.; expenditure, 2,738,889*l*.

The mythical hero Odin said to arrive in the north, and died . . . . B.C. 40
His son Skiold reigns
The Skioldungs reign till Olaf the infant is baptized, and introduces Christianity among his people, about A.D. 1000
Waldemar I. of Denmark subdues Rugen, and destroys the pagan temples 1168
Stockholm founded 1260
Magnus Ladulæs establishes a regular form of government 1279
The crown of Sweden, which had been hereditary, is made elective; and Steenchel Magnus, surnamed Smæk, or the foolish, king of Norway, is elected 1319
Waldemar lays Gothland waste 1361
Albert of Mecklenburg reigns 1363
Treaty or union of Calmar (*which see*), by which Sweden is united to Denmark and Norway, under Margaret 1397
University of Upsal founded 1476
Christian II. of Denmark, "the Nero of the North," massacres the Swedish nobility 1520
The Swedes delivered from the Danish yoke by the valour of Gustavus Vasa 1521
Gustavus Vasa raised to the throne 1523
He introduces Lutheranism and religious liberty . 1527
Makes the crown hereditary 1544
Gustavus Adolphus heads the protestant cause in Germany 1628
He takes Magdeburg and Munich, 1630; slain at Lutzen . . . . 16 Nov. 1632
Rugen ceded to Sweden by Denmark 1648
Abdication of Christina . . . . 16 June, 1654
Charles X. overruns Poland 1655
Arts and sciences begin to flourish 1660
University of Lund founded 1666
Charles XII., "the Madman of the North," begins his reign; he makes himself absolute; abolishes the senate, 1699; and defeats the Russians at Narva . . . . 30 Nov. 1700
Battle of Pultowa, where Charles is defeated by the czar of Russia (see *Pultowa*) . . . 8 July, 1709
He escapes to Bender, where, after three years' protection, he is made a prisoner by the Turks . . 1713

He is restored; and after ruinous wars, and fighting numerous battles, is killed at the siege of Frederickshald . . . . 11 Dec. 1718
Queen Ulrica abolishes despotism 1719
Bremen and Verden ceded to Hanover . . . Nov. ,,
Royal Academy founded by Linnæus 1741
Conspiracy of counts of Brahe and Horne, who are beheaded 1756
The Hats and Caps (French and Russian parties), 1738-57: put down by Gustavus III. 1770
Despotism re-established 1772
Order of the Sword instituted . . . . . . ,,
Assassination of Gustavus III. by count Ankerström, at a ball, 16 March; he expired 29 March, 1792
The regicide was scourged with whips of iron thongs three successive days; his right hand was cut off, then his head, and his body impaled, 18 May, ,,
Gustavus IV. dethroned and the government assumed by his uncle, the duke of Sudermania (Charles XIII.) . . . . . 13 March, 1809
Representative constitution established . 7 June, ,,
Sweden cedes Finland to Russia . . 17 Sept. ,,
Marshal Bernadotte, the prince of Ponte Corvo (one of Bonaparte's generals), chosen the crown prince of Sweden . . . . . . 21 Aug. 1810
Gustavus IV. arrived in London . . . 12 Nov. ,,
Swedish Pomerania seized by Napoleon . 9 Jan. 1812
Alliance with England . . . . . 12 July, ,,
Sweden joins the grand alliance against Napoleon, 13 March, 1813
Norway is ceded to Sweden by the treaty of Kiel, 14 Jan.; carried into effect . . . Nov. 1814
Bernadotte king, as Charles John XIV. . 5 Feb. 1818
Canals and roads constructed 1822
Treaty of navigation between Great Britain and Sweden . . . . 19 May, 1826
Death of Charles John; his son Oscar I. king, 8 Mar. 1844
Alliance with England and France . 21 Nov. 1855
Banishment decreed against catholic converts from Lutheranism . . . . Oct. 1857
Demonstration in favour of Italy . . . 17 Dec. 1859
Increased religious toleration . . . . May, 1860
The king visits England and France . . Aug. 1861
He is warmly received in Denmark . 17 July, 1862
Treaty of commerce with Italy, signed . 14 June, ,,
Demonstration in favour of Poland . . April, 1863
Inauguration of free trade . . . . . 1 Jan. 1864
Sweden protests against the occupation of Sleswig by the allies . . . . 22 Jan. ,,
Excitement throughout the country; March: preparation for war; (no result) . . . April, ,,
Foundation of a "National Scandinavian Society" at Stockholm to obtain by legal means a confederation of the three kingdoms for military and foreign affairs, reserving independent interior administration . . . . Dec.
New constitution passed by the chambers, 4-8 Dec. ,,
Commercial treaty with France approved . Feb. 1866
Severe famine in North Sweden . . Oct.-Dec. 1867
Resignation of ministers, 9 April; new ministry under M. Wachtmeister . . . . 4 June, 1868
Princess Louisa was married to Frederic, crown-prince of Sweden . . . . 28 July, 1869
Neutrality in the Franco-Prussian war was proclaimed . . . . 4 Aug. 1870
The queen dies . . . . . . 13 March, 1871
Prince Oscar visits England; lays foundation of a Scandinavian church at Rotherhithe 27 July, ,,
Re-organization of the army proposed, Aug.; negatived . . . . Oct. ,,
Death of king Charles XV. . . . . 18 Sept. 1872
The diet opened by king Oscar II. . 20 Jan. 1873
The king and queen crowned . . . 12 May, ,,
Ministry under baron de Geer . . . 11 May, 1875
The king and queen visit Copenhagen and Berlin; warmly received . . . . . 26-28 May, ,,
Ministry under Dr. Forssell . . . 19 April, 1880
The king with the queen at Bournemouth for his health . . . . May, 1881
Ministry of count Posse defeated on the army bill, resigns . . . . 25 May, 1883
M. Thyselius appointed premier . . 13 June, ,,
The crown prince made viceroy of Norway 19 March, 1884
M. O. R. Themptander appointed premier 16 May, ,,
The king visits Britain, July, Aug. 1884; at Constantinople . . . . 9 April, 1885
New ministry formed under baron Bildt, 6 Feb. 1888
Prince Oscar married to Miss Munck at Bournemouth, England; his mother present 15 March, ,,
The king visits England . . . . early June, ,,
Norway agitates for autonomy in foreign affairs; opposed by Sweden . . . . Feb. 1892
Extraordinary session of the diet to consider the national defences . . . . 22 Oct. *et seq.* ,,
Bills for the reorganization of the army adopted by the legislature . . . . . . 27 Nov. ,,
The parliament opened by the king with a cheerful speech . . . . 18 Jan. 1893
A national assembly of radicals (130) elected by non-electors, meets at Stockholm . 13 March, ,,
Sir Spenser St. John appointed British minister, May, ,,
Telephonic communication opened between Stockholm and Christiania . . . . . 2 Sept.
The 300th anniversary of the Swedish reformation celebrated at Upsala, the king present, 5-7 Sept. ,,
General election, 145 grain free traders and 83 protectionists . . . . 30 Sept. ,,
Revision of the constitution of the two chambers, 1 March, 1894
Celebration of the birth of Gustavus Adolphus (9 Dec. 1594) throughout Sweden . . . 9 Dec. ,,
The king receives the committee of Union, and deprecates change . . . . . . 5 Dec. 1895
The king in opening parliament, maintains the union with Norway, announces a large surplus of revenue, provision for national defence proposed, 18 Jan. 1896
The hon. F. Pakenham appointed British minister, Jan. ,,
Karl Herman Sätherberg, poet and physician, born 1812, died . . . . 9 Jan. 1897
Parliament opened by the king . . . 19 Jan. ,,
Celebration of the 25th anniversary of the accession of Oscar II., at Stockholm 18 Sept. *et seq.* ,,
Parliament opened by the king . . . 18 Jan. 1898
Report of the Swedish committee on the Union, to Parliament . . . . 7 March, ,,
Swedish Arctic (scientific) expedition, under Dr. A. G. Nathorst, to explore the region between Spitzbergen and Franz Josef Land, starts spring, ,,
Parliament opened with a speech from the throne, 18 Jan. 1899
Parliament opened by the king; budget introduced, 18 Jan. 1900
Large sums voted for the army and navy, 19 April, ,,
The king heartily received at Cambridge; made D.C.L., 14 May; visits Woolwich arsenal, 25 May; visits Paris; leaves . . . 16 June, ,,
Johan P. Nordlund sentenced to death for murdering 7 persons and wounding 5 others on board a steamer near Quicksund (7 May) . . . 30 June, ,,
M. Boström, premier, resigns, succeeded by adm. von Otter . . . . mid Sept. ,,
Illness of the king, the crown prince regent, 17 Oct.; the king resumes his office . . 21 Jan. 1901
Army reorganisation and military service law, ratified . . . . 25 June, ,,
Prof. baron von Nordenskjöld, great Arctic explorer, dies, aged 69 . . . . . 12 Aug. ,,
Dr. Otto Nordenskjöld's S. Polar expedition leaves, 16 Oct. ,,
Universal suffrage demonstrations in Stockholm and other towns . . . . . . 20 April, 1902
Ministry resigns, 28 June; M. Boström forms one, 5 July, ,,
Sir Wm. Curzon Barrington appointed British minister . . . . 14 Oct. ,,
Parliament opened, extension of the franchise proposed . . . . 17 Jan. 1903
The council meets; in consequence of the continued ill-health of the king, the crown prince assumes the regency . . . . . 27 Jan. ,,
Expedition for the relief of Dr. Nordenskjold's south polar expedition, under command of capt. Glyden, of the Swedish navy, leaves Stockholm on board the "Frithjof" . . . . 17 Aug. ,,

KINGS OF SWEDEN (*previously Kings of Upsal*).

1001. Olaf Schotkonung, or Olif Schœtkonung the Infant, is styled king, 1015.
1026. Edmund Colbrenner.
1051. Edmund Slemme.
1056. Stenkill.

1066. Halstan.
1090. Ingo I. the Good.
1112. Philip
1118. Ingo II.
1129. Swerker or Suercher I.
1155. St. Eric IX.
1161. Charles VII. ; made prisoner by his successor.
1167. Canute, son of Eric I.
1199. Swerker or Suercher II. ; killed in battle.
1210. Eric X.
1216. John I.
1222. Eric XI. the Stammerer.
1250. Birger Jarl, regent.
,, Waldemar I.
1275. Magnus I. Ladulæs.
1290. Birger II.
1319. Magnus II. Smæk ; dethroned
1350. Eric XII.
1359. Magnus restored ; deposed 1363.
1363. Albert of Mecklenburg : his tyranny causes a revolt of his subjects, who invite Margaret of Denmark to the throne.
1389. Margaret, queen of *Sweden and Norway* now also of *Denmark*, and Eric XIII.
1397. [Union of Calmar, by which the three kingdoms are united under one sovereign.]
1412. Eric XIII. governs alone ; deposed.
1440. Christopher III.
1448. Charles VIII. Canuteson, king of Sweden only.
1471. [Interregnum.] Sten Sture, *Protector*.
1483. John II. (I. of Denmark).
1502. [Interregnum.]
1503. Swante Sture, *Protector*.
1512. Sten Sture, *Protector*.
1520. Christiern, or Christian II., of Denmark, styled the "Nero of the North ;" deposed for his cruelties.
1523. Gustavus I. Vasa ; by whose valour the Swedes are delivered from the Danish yoke.
1560. Eric XIV., son ; dethroned and slain by
1569. John III., brother.
1592. Sigismund III., king of Poland, son ; disputes for the succession continued the whole cf this reign.
1604. Charles IX. brother of John III.
1611. Gustavus II. Adolphus, the Great, son ; fell at the battle of Lutzen, 16 Nov. 1632.
1632. [Interregnum.]
1633. Christina, daughter of Gustavus. Resigned the crown to her cousin, 16 June, 1654 ; died at Rome in 1689.
1654. Charles X. Gustavus, son of John Casimir, count palatine of the Rhine.
1660. Charles XI. son ; the arts and sciences flourished in this reign.
1697. Charles XII., son ; styled the "Alexander" and the "Madman of the North ;" killed at Fredericks-hall, 11 Dec. 1718.
1718. Ulrica Eleanora, sister, and her consort, Frederick I. landgrave of Hesse Cassel. Ulrica relinquishes the crown, and in
1741. Frederick reigned alone.
1751. Adolphus Frederick of *Holstein Gottorp*, descended from the family of Vasa.
1771. Gustavus III. Adolphus, son ; assassinated by count Ankarström at a masked ball, 16 March ; died 29 March, 1792.
1792. Gustavus IV. Adolphus, son ; dethroned, and the government assumed by his uncle, the duke of Sudermania.
1809. Charles XIII. duke of Sudermania.
[Treaty of Kiel (1814), by which Norway falls under the sovereignty of Sweden.]
1818. Charles (John) XIV. *Bernadotte*, the French prince of Ponte Corvo : died 8 March, 1844.
1844. Oscar I., son ; born 4 July, 1799 ; died 8 July, 1859.
1859. Charles XV., son ; born 3 May, 1826 ; died 18 Sept. 1872 ; a poet ; brave and impulsive ; much beloved.
1872. Oscar II., brother ; born 21 Jan. 1829 ; married princess Sophia of Nassau, 6 June, 1857.

Heir : Gustavus, son, born 16 June, 1858 ; married to Victoria of Baden, 20 Sept. 1881.

PRINCIPAL SWEDISH AUTHORS.

Olaus Petri, 1497–1552, and his brother Laurentius, 1499–1573, translated the Bible into Swedish in 1541.

	Born.	*Died.*
Linnæus, *nat.*	1707	1778
Karl Fredrik Dahlgren, *p.* and *hum.*	1791	1844
Geijer, *p.* and *hist.*	1783	1847
Tegner, *p.*	1782	1846
Almqvist, *m.*	1793	1866
Johan Ludvig Runeberg, *p.*	1804	1877
Frederika Bremer, *n.*	1801	1865
Wetterbergh, "Uncle Adam"	1804	1889
Magnus Jakob Crusenstolpe, *n.* and *h.*	1795	1865
August Strindberg, *n.*	1849	
Fryxell, *hist.*	1795	1881
Johan Jakob Berzelius, *ph.*	1779	1848
Baron Nordenskiöld, *nat.* and explorer	1832	

SWEDENBORGIANS is the name given to those who adopt the theological teachings of Emanuel Swedenborg, but the organisation these have formed they call the New Church, or New Jerusalem Church.

Swedenborg was born in Stockholm, 29 January, 1688, died in London 29th March, 1772 ; interred in a vault of the Swedish church in Prince's-square, near the Tower of London.

Assessor in the Swedish Royal College of Mines, 1717–1747, with a seat in the Upper House of the Legislature.

Ennobled by queen Ulrica Eleanora, 1719.

Wrote many scientific and philosophical works, his *Principia, Economy of the Animal Kingdom, &c.*, being published at the expense of the duke of Brunswick.

In 1743 he began his work as a theologian, writing *Arcana Cœlestia, Heaven and Hell, True Christian Religion, Divine Love and Wisdom, Divine Providence, Apocalypse Revealed, &c., &c.*

In London meetings of his followers began in 1783 ; they organised for public worship 1787.

Swedenborg Society for publishing his works founded 1810.

Missionary and Tract Society of the New Church, 1821.

National Missionary Institution, 1857.

New Church Orphanage, 1881.

In 1903 there were 71 churches in Great Britain connected with the General Conference, and 9 independent congregations. In America there were 81 connected with the General Convention, and many important circles in affiliation. In Canada there were 5 places of worship, and others in Australia, New Zealand, and South Africa. Also in France, Germany, Austria, Hungary, Sweden, Denmark, &c.

Their belief is that the whole Godhead is centred in Jesus Christ, who is Father, Son, and Holy Spirit ; Creator, Redeemer, and Saviour ; one in essence and person ; in whom is a Trinity of Love, Wisdom, and Power, answering to the trinity in man of soul, body, and their operation ; that Salvation is effected by faith in Him and obedience to Him, the Lord operating with the man, and the man co-operating with the Lord, and that Charity and Faith are together in good works ; that the Sacred Scripture is the Word of God or the Divine Truth itself, the literal sense being the basis and continent of a spiritual sense in all and every part, and that the word is in all the heavens and the wisdom of the angels is thence derived ; that man is a spiritual being fitted for life in the spiritual world, clothed temporarily with a material body for life in this world, which at "death" he lays aside for ever ; that the last Judgment was effected in the spiritual world during Swedenborg's lifetime ; and that the Lord's Second Coming has taken place in the revelation to man by the Lord, through the instrumentality of Swedenborg, of a new system of truth derived from the inner or spiritual sense of Scripture, based upon the literal sense when properly understood, and having special application to the spiritual life and needs of man, here and hereafter. Publishing house, 1, Bloomsbury-street, W.C.

SWEET-BAY, *Laurus nobilis*, was brought to these realms from Italy before 1548. *Laurus indica*, or Royal Bay, was brought from Madeira in 1665. The Sweet-Fern bush, *Comptonia asplenifolia*, came from America, 1714. *Laurus aggregata*, or the Glaucous Laurel, came from China in 1806.

SWIMMING. Leander is said to have swum across the Hellespont, between Sestos and Abydos, about one mile; and Lord Byron and lieut. Ekenhead did the same, 3 May, 1810. On 24 Aug. 1872, Mr. Johnson, styled the "hero of London-bridge," and swimming champion of the world, attempted to swim from Dover to Calais, but was prevented by cold. He was said to have swum seven miles in about sixty-five minutes. "Swimming," by Archibald Sinclair and William Henry (Badminton Library), 1894, contains remarkable records.

Public swimming bath on the Thames opened, 6 July, 1875

Capt. Matt. Webb swam from Blackwall to Gravesend, 20 miles, in 4 hours 53 minutes, 3 July; and from Dover to Calais (22½ miles) in 23¾ hours, 24-25, Aug. 1875; drowned while attempting to cross the rapids of Niagara . . . . 24 July, 1882

Agnes Beckwith, aged 14, swam from London bridge to Greenwich, 5 miles, in 1 h. 8 min. 1 Sept. 1875

Emily Parker, aged 15, swam from London bridge to Blackwall, 7 miles, in 1 h. 35 min. . 4 Sept. ,,

Mr. Cavill swam from Dover to Calais in 12 hours, 20, 21 Aug. 1877

Miss Beckwith said to have swum 30 continuous hours . . . . 7, 8 May, 1880

Taylor wins the amateur swimming championship of Great Britain at Birmingham . 19 Aug. 1882

Davis Dalton, an American, aged 38, swam on his back across the Channel, accompanied by a lifeboat from Boulogne to Folkestone 17–18 Aug. 1890

Willie Beckwith, an eminent swimmer, aged 36, dies . . . . 13 Dec. 1892

World's swimming championship won by J. A. Jarvis, 500 mètres in 8 min. 33 3-5 sec. at Paris, 16 Aug. 1903

William Finney, a professional diver, aged 28, died, at Walsall hospital, from injuries received in diving from a platform 30 feet high into a tank containing 4 feet of water. He was engaged for some years at the Westminster Aquarium, where he dived in a burning sack into a shallow tank; he performed three years in Berlin (his brother James was champion swimmer of the world at nearly all distances from 1883 to 1889), end of Aug. ,,

Mr. Montague Holbein makes his fourth attempt to swim across the Channel, Dover to Calais; when within about 7 miles of the French coast, he abandons the attempt, after being 17½ hours in the water (his best performance was on 27 Aug. 1902, from Cape Grisnez to Dover, when he got within 2 miles of Dover, after remaining in the sea 22½ hours) . . . . . . 1, 2 Sept. ,,

Boyton's Apparatus, see under *Life Boat*.

SWING. Between 1830 and 1833 many haystacks and barns were fired in the rural districts of England, and attributed to an imaginary person named "Swing." Many persons were caught and punished. The probable cause was disputes between the farmers and their dissatisfied labourers.

SWISS GUARDS, Royal, in France, formed in 1616; massacred while defending the Tuileries, 10 Aug. 1792; re-organised Sept. 1815; defeated during the insurrection, 28 July, 1830; dismissed by Charles X. Aug. 1830.

SWITHIN'S DAY, ST., 15 July. St. Swithin lived in the 9th century; and, having been the preceptor to king Ethelwulf, was made bishop of Winchester in 852, and died 2 July, 862. The tradition states that it rained forty days in consequence of the proposed removal of his remains from the churchyard to the cathedral.

SWITZERLAND was in ancient times inhabited by the Helvetii (*which see*). The country was colonised by the Romans after Cæsar's victory over the Helvetii in their invasion of Gaul, 58 B.C., and the people were gradually combined with the Romans and partook of the fortunes of their empire. The canton Schweitz has given name to the whole confederacy.—The present national council is elected every third year, at the rate of one member for 2000 persons. The president of the confederation of the 22 cantons is elected annually. The revised federal constitution was voted 19 April, 1874. See *Referendum*.—Population, Dec. 1860, 2,507,170; 1870, 2,669,147; 1880, 2,846,102; June 1888, 2,917,754; Dec. 1900, 3,313,817. Revenue, 1890, 2,704,850*l.*; expenditure, 2,667,535*l.*; 1900, revenue, 4,041,348*l*; expenditure, 4,110,313*l*.

"The Swiss Confederation," by sir F. O. Adams and C. D. Cunningham; published by Macmillan & Co. 1889

SWISS CONFEDERATION OF 1815.

Uri, 1307	first confederation.	Schaffhausen
Schweitz		Appenzell
Unterwalden		St. Gall
Zurich		Glaris
Berne		Zug
Lucerne		Freiburg
Solothurn		Tessins
Basle		Pays de Vaud
Grisons		Valais
Aargau		Neufchatel
Thurgau		Geneva

Helvetia ravaged by the Huns 909

Becomes subject to Germany 1032

Friburg built by Berthold IV. 1179

Berne built 1191

Tyranny of Gesler, heroism of William Tell, and revolt (demonstrated to be mythical), dated 1306

Confederation against Austria; declaration of Swiss independence . . . . 4 Nov. 1307

The men of Uri, Unterwalden, and Schwytz made a solemn defensive league and covenant for ever against the Austrians; this is regarded as the foundation of the Swiss Confederation, 1 Aug. 1291; said to have been confirmed by the leaders, Werner Stauffacher (of Schwytz), Walter Fürst (Uri), and Arnold von Melchthal (Unterwalden), determined to free their country from a foreign yoke . . . . 17 Nov. ,,

A malignant fever carries off, in the canton of Basle, 1100 persons 1314

Form of government made perpetual . . . 1315

Leopold of Austria defeated at Morgarten, 15 Nov. ,,

Lucerne joins the confederacy 1332

The canton of Zurich joins and becomes head of the league 1350

Berne, Glaris, and Zug join 1351

8 cantons form a perpetual league 1353

Leopold II. of Austria defeated and slain at Sempach, 9 July, 1386

The Austrians defeated at Näfels, 9 April, 1388; make peace 1389

The Grisons league (see *Caddee*) 1400

Second league of the Grisons 1424

The third league of the Grisons 1436

Battle of St. Jacobs on the Birs, near Basle (1600 Swiss resist 30,000 French, and are all killed, the enemy losing 10,000) . . . . . 26 Aug. 1444

The Swiss defeat Charles the Bold at Granson, 5 March; and at Morat . . . . 22 June, 1476

And aid the duke of Lorraine at Nancy, where Charles is slain . . . . . . 5 Jan. 1477

Swiss soldiers first enter into the pay of France, under Louis XI. 1480

Fribourg and Soleure join; confederation formed . 1481

Maximilian I. emperor, acknowledges Swiss independence 1499

Schaffhausen and Basle join the union . . . 1501

Confederation of 13 cantons 1513

The Swiss invade Milan and defeat the French at Novara . . . . 6 June, ,,

Defeated by them at Marignano . . 13, 14 Sept. 1515

The Swiss confederacy acknowledged by France and other powers 1516

The Reformation begins at Basle; the bishop compelled to retire 1519

The Reformation adopted by some cantons; battle of Cappel, Zwingli killed and reformers defeated, 12 Oct. 1531

The Grison leagues join the Swiss confederacy as allies 1544

Appenzel joins the other Cantons 1597
Charles Emanuel of Savoy attempts Geneva by surprise, scales the walls, and penetrates the town, but in the end is defeated 1602
[This circumstance gave rise to an annual festival commemorative of their escape from tyranny.]
Independence of Switzerland recognised by the treaty of Westphalia (see *Westphalia*) . . . 1648
Peace of Aargau, end of religious war . Aug. 1712
[From this period until the French revolution the cantons enjoyed tranquillity, disturbed only by the changes arising out of their various constitutions.]
Alliance with France . . . . . . 25 May, 1777
Strife in Geneva, between the aristocratic and democratic parties; France interferes. . . . 1781
1000 fugitive Genevese seek an asylum in Ireland (see *Geneva*) 1782
Swiss guards ordered to quit France 1792
Helvetic confederation dissolved; its subjugation by France 1798
Helvetian republic formed . . . . . . ,,
Switzerland the seat of war 1799-1802
The number of cantons increased to 19; the federal government restored; and a landamman appointed by France . . . . . . 12 May, ,,
Uri, Schweitz, and Underwald separate from the republic . . . . . . 13 July, ,,
Switzerland joins France with 6000 men 24 Aug. 1811
The allies entered Switzerland in the spring of . 1814
The number of cantons increased to 22, and the independence and neutrality of Switzerland secured by the treaty of Vienna 1815
Revision of the constitution of the cantons . . . 1839
Law to make education independent of the clergy . 1830
leads to dissensions between the catholics and protestants 1840-4
Dispute about the convents of Aargau, 1844; to put education into the hands of the Jesuits, &c.; opposition of the protestant cantons . . . 1846
Lucerne, Uri, Schweitz, Unterwalden, Freiburg, Zug, and Valais (Roman catholic cantons), form a separate league (Sonderbund) to support education by the Jesuits, &c. . . . . . ,,
Insurrection at Geneva against Jesuit teaching; a temporary provisional government established, 7 Oct. ,,
The diet declares the Sonderbund illegal, and dissolves it, 20 July; the seven cantons protest, 22 July; the diet orders the expulsion of the Jesuits, 3 Sept.; communal assemblies held to resist it, 26 Sept.; 3, 10 Oct.; appeal to arms 21 Oct. 1847
The diet prepares to repress the Sonderbund, 4 Nov.; Friburg surrenders, 14 Nov.; civil war; the Sonderbund defeated by gen. H. Dufour, near Lucerne, 23 Nov.; end of the Sonderbund; it submits to the expulsion of the Jesuits, and the secularisation of monastic property. . 29 Nov. ,,
New federal constitution . . . . 12 Sept. 1848
Dispute about Neufchâtel (*which see*) 1857
Declaration of neutrality in the coming Italian war, 14 March, 1859
Mutiny and punishment of the Swiss mercenary troops at Naples; the confederation forbid foreign enlistment . . . . . July and Aug. ,,
Swiss government protests against the annexation of Savoy to France . . . . 15 March, 1860
150 Swiss attempt to enter Savoy; stopped by Genevese government . . . . 30 March, ,,
M. Thorel, a Swiss, obtains a prize at the national shooting match at Wimbledon . . . July, ,,
The government forbid the Swiss to enlist in foreign service without permission . . . 30 July, ,,
Proposed European congress to preserve Swiss neutrality, put off . . . . . July, ,,
Glarus destroyed by fire . . . . . 3 May, 1861
French troops occupy Vallée des Dappes, 28 Oct.; the Swiss announce the violation of their territory, 5 Nov. ,,
Treaty of France settles the question of the Vallée des Dappes by mutual cession of territory; no military works to be constructed on territory ceded; signed . . . . . 8 Dec. 1862
Serious election riots at Geneva, with bloodshed, 22 Aug.; federal troops arrive . . 23 Aug. 1864
Federal troops quit Geneva . . . 11 Jan. 1865
International Social Science Congress meets at Berne . . . . 28 Aug. ,,
Revision of the constitution; deliberations begin 23 Oct. 1865
Nearly all the revised articles of the federal constitution rejected by the vote of the Swiss burgesses 14 Jan. 1866
J. J. Stehlen elected president . . . 1 July, 1867
Workmen's international congress at Lausanne, 2-7 Sept. ,,
Meeting of the federal assembly . 6-25 July, 1868
Queen Victoria visits Lucerne . . Aug. Sept. ,,
International peace and liberty congress, at Geneva, 9-12 Sept. 1867; at Berne, 22-26 Sept. . . . ,,
Neutrality in the Franco-Prussian war proclaimed, July, ,,
New constitution adopted by Zurich . 18 April, 1869
The French army under Clinchant (84,000), crosses the frontiers and is disarmed . . . 1 Feb. 1871
The French soldiers interned at Zurich, and oppose German demonstrations . . 9-12 Mar. ,,
Extraordinary session of the federal assembly to revise the constitution . . . . 6 Nov. ,,
Plebiscite respecting a new constitution, re-organizing the army, and promoting uniform education, &c., rejected by majority of 4967 out of 509,921 . . . . . . 12 May, 1872
M. Favre engaged to construct a tunnel through St. Gothard in 8 years, for 2,000,000*l*. . 8 Aug. ,,
The papal nuncio, Mermillod, expelled . 16 Jan. 1873
Revised federal constitution voted (321,870 for, 177,800 against) . . . . . 19 April, 1874
Swiss national catholic church constituted June, ,,
19 Catholic priests deprived for refusal to take constitutional oath . . . . 5 Sept. ,,
International postal congress at Berne, 15 Sept.; protocol signed (see *Postal Convention*) 9 Oct. ,,
Civil marriage law and registration adopted by universal suffrage (212,854—204,700) . 23 May, 1875
President of the national council for three years, J. Philippin, elected . . . . 6 June, 1877
Continued deficit in revenue, announced, 16 March, 1878
Death of James Fazy, eminent statesman, 6 Nov. ,,
National voting for St. Gothard, railway and tunnel (161,000 majority) . . . . . 19 Jan. 1879
Suicide of Herr Anderwert, the president elect, 27 Dec. 1880
Opening of St. Gothard railway from Milan to Lucerne . . . . . . 20, 21 May, 1882
Invasion of the salvation army (*which see*), autumn, 1883, much resisted at Berne, Geneva, &c., Jan. *et seq.* 1884
The watch-tool making village, Vallorbes, almost destroyed by fire . . . . 7 April, ,,
National exhibition at Zurich . 1 May—27 Dec. ,,
M. Schenck elected president . . . . Dec. ,,
Village of Mulligan, Aargau, destroyed by fire, 23 April, 1885
Fifth centenary of the battle of Sempach (9 July, 1386), celebrated . . . . . . 5 July, 1886
Grand funeral of Mr. Hertenstein, the president at Berne, who died after a surgical operation, 30 Nov.; vice-president Bernard Hammer elected president . . . . 13 Dec. 1888
The German government protests against the expulsion of its police officer, Wohlgemuth, from Switzerland, May; the great powers protest against the asylum given to political criminals; the Swiss propose new legal measures, June; the Swiss government repels the charge, but prepares legal measures for redress, June, 1889
The Swiss government in a reply note to Berlin, stands firm . . . . . . 14 July, ,,
Loan for 25,000,000 francs, to supply new arms for the federal troops, subscribed for by Berne alone . . . . . reported 23 July, ,,
M. Ruchonnet elected President for 1890 about 10 Dec. ,,
Destructive storms in the poorest districts, much distress . . . . . . 18–23 Aug. 1890
Insurrection at Ticino (*which see*) . 12–14 Sept. ,,
Railway accident near Bâle; by the collapse of a bridge several carriages of an excursion train were thrown into the river Birse. Above 70 persons perish . . . . . 14 June, 1891
600th anniversary of the foundation of the Swiss confederation celebrated in the province of Schwytz . . . . 1–2 Aug. ,,
Meiringen, canton of Berne, totally burnt; 2 deaths, about 2,000 persons homeless . . 25 Oct. ,,

President, A. A. Lachenal . . . . 1 June, 1891
Bill for giving effect to the popular vote of July, affirming the right of the people to take the initiative in constitutional reforms, considered by the national council . . . 7 Dec. „
Dr. E. Welti, president of the confederation, resigns in consequence of a plébiscite on 6 Dec., refusing to purchase the Swiss railways reported 8 Dec. „
M. Walter Hauser, president . . . 1 Jan. 1892
The commercial treaties with Germany and Austria-Hungary adopted by the states council 28 Jan. „
Great fire at Grindelwald, near Interlachen; the Bear hotel, the English church, the telegraph office and other buildings destroyed; estimated damage, 2,000,000 francs . . . 18 Aug. „
Rejection of the Franco-Swiss convention by France; duties on French goods increased, 1 Jan. 1893
Carl Schenk president of the Swiss confederation, 1 Jan. „
Extreme socialists defeated in national elections, 29 Oct. „
Col. Emile Frey elected president of the Swiss confederation for 1894 . . . . 14 Dec. „
A state loan of 20,000,000 f. authorized 21 Dec. „
Decree for a referendum respecting representation of Switzerland abroad . . . . 30 Oct. 1894
M. Zemp elected president of the confederation for 1895 . . . . 13 Dec. „
A Franco-Swiss liberal commercial agreement signed . . . . 25 June, 1895
Carl Schenk, 6 times president of the confederation, death by an accident . . . 18 July, „
M. Lachenal, of Geneva, radical, elected president for 1896 . . . . 12 Dec. „
National exhibition opened at Geneva . 1 May, 1896
Railway traffic suspended through floods, reported 11 Aug. „
Prof. Grunert and 2 guides killed on the glacier while descending the Lyskamm, near Zermatt, 10 Sept.; and Mr. Gilbert Betjemann killed on the Grindelwald glacier . . . 10 Sept. „
M. Adolphe Deucher, radical, elected president for 1897 . . . . . 17 Dec. „
M. Ruffy, radical, elected president for 1898, 15 Dec. 1897
Archæological discoveries at Windisch, 30 Nov. 1897; an ancient Roman hospital, &c., near Zurich discovered . . . . June, 1898
Travelling from Basle to London (595 miles) accomplished in 14 hrs. 35 mins. . . July, „
Dr. John Hopkinson, electrician, with his son and two daughters, perished by a fall while ascending the Petite Dent de Veisivi, 27 Aug. (see *Cambridge*, Feb. 1900). Mr. Norman Neruda, experienced climber, killed by a fall on the Schmidkamin, Dolomites, 11 Sept.; Mr. Aston-Binns and a guide killed on the Aiguille de Charmoz . . . . 16 Sept. „
Expulsion of anarchists . . . . Sept. „
Unification of civil and penal codes accepted by a *referendum* . . . . Nov. „
M. Müller, radical, elected president for 1899, 15 Dec. „
See *Landslips* . . . . . „
Switzerland admitted by America as a favoured nation . . . . . 31 Dec. „
M. Welti (6 times president) died, aged 73, 24 Feb. 1899
M. Guyer-Zeller, banker, "railway king," died, 3 April, „
Prof. Socin, eminent orientalist, born 1844, died, June, „
Mr. Jones and 3 guides killed by a fall while ascending the Dent Blanche; Mr. Hill, one of the party, reached Zermatt after having passed 48 hours on the mountain, reported . . 30 Aug. „
M. W. Hauser, elected president . . 15 Dec. „
Mr. J. G. Cockin, an experienced climber, killed by a fall on the Weisshorn; a guide killed and others injured on the Matterhorn 27 July, 1900
Two Americans killed on the Engadine . 2 Aug. „
The "double initiative," viz., the election by proportional representation of members of the national council and the election of the federal council by the people, rejected by the nation, 4 Nov. „
M. Breuner, radical, elected president for 1901, 12 Dec. „
M. Zemp (catholic conservative) elected president for 1902 . . . . . . 12 Dec. 1901
New palace of the Swiss parliament begun, 1894; opened . . . . . . 1 April, 1902
Museum of war and peace founded by the late M. de Bloch at Lucerne, opened . 7 June, „
Rupture with Italy (*which see*), 10 April; relations resumed . . . . . 30 July, „
The king of Italy received by the president at Göschenen . . . . 26 Aug. „
Dr. Largin, chief judge of the Berne court, killed on the Nadelhorn, about 15 Aug.; many fatal Alpine accidents, reported . . Aug. „
Elections: strong radical-democratic majority, 26 Oct. „
Dr. Adolph Deucher elected president . 11 Dec. „
Bomb explosion at entrance to Geneva cathedral, Machetto, an Italian, arrested . . 24 Dec. „
Swiss government give one year's notice to terminate the commercial treaty, dated 19 April, 1892, between Switzerland and Italy, but is prepared to negotiate a new treaty, reported, mid Sept. 1903
Subvention for construction of the projected Jura tunnel for a line between Soleure and Münster agreed to by grand council of Berne; also agreement between federal council and the Simplon tunnel company . . . . early Oct. „

Swiss Literature is included either in German or French literature. *Chambers*. To the German division belong Huldreich Zwingli, *theo.*, 1484–1531; Heinrich Bullinger, *theo.* and *hist.*, 1504–1575; Tschudi Bodmer, *p.*, 1698–1783; Salomon Gessner, *p.*, 1730–1788; Johann Zimmermann, *ph.*, 1728–1795; Albrecht von Haller, *p.* and *phy.*, 1708–1777; Johann Kaspar Lavater, *p.*, 1741–1801; Johann Heinrich Pestalozzi, *educational theorist*, 1745–1827; Johannes von Muller, *hist.*, 1752–1809; Gottfried Keller, *p.* and *n.*, 1819–1890; Albert Bitzius "Gotthelf," *n.*, 1797–1854; Conrad Ferd Meyer, *p.*, 1825–1898; to the French: François de Bonivard, *hist.*, 1496–1570; Jean Jacques Rousseau, *m.*, 1712–1778; Chas. de Bonnet, *nat.* and *ph.*, 1720–1793; Benj. Constant de Rebecque, *e.* and *n.*, 1767–1830; Jean Sismondi, *hist.*, 1773–1842; Jacques Necker, *e.*, 1732–1794; and his daughter, mdme. de Staël, *e.* and *n.*, 1766–1817; Pierre Dumont, *e.*, 1759–1829; Rudolf Töpffer, *n* 1799–1846; Alex. R. Vinet, *theo.* and *c.*, 1797–1847; Victor Cherbuliez, *n.* and *e.*, born, 1829.

SWORDS. The Roman swords were from 20 to 30 inches long. The broadsword and scimitar are of modern adoption. Damascus steel swords were most prized; the next the sword of Ferrara steel. The Scotch Highlanders, from the artificer Andrea di Ferrara, called their swords *Andrew Ferraras*. The large sword shown at Dumbarton castle as Wallace's was transferred to the Wallace monument (*which see*), 17 Nov. 1888. The broadsword was forbidden to be worn in Edinburgh in 1724. International sword-play competitions in Gray's-inn-garden, London, 17 June, 1901. New cavalry sword for British army adopted, 1903.

SYBARIS, a Greek colony in S. Italy, founded about 720 B.C.; destroyed by the Crotonians about 510 B.C. The people were greatly addicted to luxury; hence the term Sybarite.

Archæological investigations disclosed evidences of the existence of a great city and civilization anterior to the Greek invasion 1888

SYCAMORE, or SYCOMORE TREE, In Mrs. Jameson's "Memoirs of Female Sovereigns" we are told that Mary queen of Scots brought over from France a little sycamore tree, which she planted in the garden at Holyrood, and that from this have sprung all the beautiful groves of sycamore now to be seen in Scotland.

SYDNEY, capital of New South Wales; founded by governor Phillip, on a cove on Port Jackson, 20 Jan. 1788, as a British settlement for the colony of convicts originally intended for Botany bay. It was named after lord Sydney, secretary for the colonies. Population 1891, 386,400; 1901, 488,968. See *Australia*, *New South Wales*, *Convicts*.

A legislative council first held . . . 13 July, 1829
Sydney erected into a bishopric (afterwards an archbishopric) 1836
Lit with gas, the first place so lit in Australia, May, 1841
Bishop of Australia made bishop of Sydney and metropolitan 1847
University founded 1852
Roman Catholic cathedral burnt, and valuable property destroyed . . . 29 June, 1865
Visited by the duke of Edinburgh . . . Feb. 1868
At Port Jackson he narrowly escaped assassination; O'Farrell, a Fenian, who shot him in the back on 12 March, was convicted on 31 March, and executed . . . 21 April, „
The duke sailed for England 4 April, and arrived 26 June, „
New cathedral consecrated . . . 30 Nov. „
Foundation of capt. Cook's monument laid by the duke of Edinburgh . . . . 28 March, 1869
A conference of delegates from the Australian colonies met here for customs, postal and railway purposes, without effect . . . . Jan. 1873
Exhibitions opened here, April, 1873, and 11 April, 1874
Captain Cook's statue uncovered . . . 2 Feb. 1878
International exhibition opened by the governor, lord A. Loftus . . . . . 17 Sept. 1879
Direct railway to Melbourne completed . June, 1883
Canon Barry consecrated bishop of Sydney and metropolitan 1 Jan. 1884; resigns, . . Dec. 1888
Meetings of loyalists opposing the home rule delegates (Mr. Dillon, sir Thomas Esmonde, and Mr. Deasy, M.P.'s) . . . . . . May, 1889
Death at Sydney of Mr. J. B. Watson (aged 64) termed the Australian "quartz reef king," said to have left to his family about 30,000,000*l.* the results of gold digging at Bendigo, Victoria, and other places and of railway and other speculations . . . . . . about 12 July, „
Rev. canon William Saumarez Smith, D.D., announced as the new bishop and metropolitan of Australia, 9 Aug. 1889, elected 21 March arrived 30 Sept. 1890
Strike of men connected with shipping, about 5,000; reported 20 Aug.; rioting in Newcastle checked by military . . . . . 27 Aug. „
Conference of Australian employers, 9 Sept.; labour conference . . . . 11–24 Sept. „
Great fire in Pitt-street and other streets; estimated damage 750,000*l.* . . . . 1 Oct. „
Departure of lord Carrington; grand demonstration in his honour . . . . . 1 Nov. „
The strike practically closed . . . . 5 Nov. „
Reception of the earl of Jersey . . . 15 Jan. 1891
Meeting of the National Australasian Federation Convention, see *Australasia* . . 2 March, „
Sir Alfred Roberts, eminent surgeon, promoter of the prince Alfred hospital, the Australian museum, &c., born 1823, died . . 24 Jan. 1899
Outbreak of bubonic plague, spring *et seq.*; total cases, 303; total deaths, 103, 1 Sept.; town free, 8 Sept. 1900
The new Australian commonwealth inaugurated; lord Hopetoun sworn in as gov.-gen.; great rejoicings and celebrations . . . 1 Jan. *et seq.* 1901
Messrs. Hordern's premises burnt down, 4 deaths; over 500,000*l.* damage . . . . 10 July, „
Loyal demonstration; resolutions carried expressing confidence in the British government, &c., 10 Feb. 1902
Her majesty's theatre burnt, properties, &c., valued, 14,000*l.* lost . . . . 23 March, „
Death of dean Cowper, aged 92, reported, 16 June, „
University jubilee celebrated . . . 1 Oct. „
The prefix *lord* conferred on the mayor . 23 Nov. „
Bronze statue of Burns on pedestal of granite, executed by Mr. F. W. Pomeroy, to be erected on site given by government, and set up in . . 1904

SYLLABUS OF ERRORS in modern times. 80 paragraphs divided into 10 chapters, issued by pope Pius IX., with an encyclical letter, 8 Dec. 1864. It condemned heresy, modern philosophy, and liberalism in politics; was forbidden to be read in French churches, and was generally opposed, but was adopted by the council at Rome 1870.

SYMPHONIES. Short pieces of instrumental music between songs in operas; early in the 17th century. These were gradually developed by the great masters, such as Lulli, into independent pieces; of these the symphonies of Corelli, Handel, Mozart, Haydn, and Beethoven are eminent examples.

SYMPHONION, an improved form of the musical box capable of performing many more tunes, invented by Mr. Ellis Parr, 1887.

SYMPIESOMETER, a species of barometer invented by Adie of Edinburgh in 1819.

SYNAGOGUE (literally an assembly), a congregation of the Jews, and the place where such assembly is held for religious purposes. When these meetings were first held is uncertain; some refer them to the times after the Babylonish captivity. In Jerusalem were 480 synagogues. In 1851 there were in London 10 synagogues, in England and Wales, 53. A magnificent synagogue was consecrated at Berlin, 5 Sept. 1866; see *Jews*.

SYNDICATE, originally a body of syndics, officers of a government or any ruling body; the term is now frequently used as synonymous with a company or body of trustees, 1888. See *Trusts*.

SYNOD. The first general synods were called by emperors, and afterwards by Christian princes; but the pope ultimately usurped this power, one of his legates usually presiding; see *Councils*. The first national synod held in England was at Hertford, 673; the last was held by cardinal Pole in 1555. Made unlawful to hold synods but by royal authority, 25 Henry VIII. 1533; see *Dort* and *Thurles*.

SYNONYM, a word having the same or nearly the same meaning as another, as valour, courage. Books of Greek and Latin synonyms were early compiled. G. Crabbe's dictionary appeared, 1816; Dr. P. M. Roget's excellent "Thesaurus of English Words and Phrases," 1852.

SYPHILIS, a disease said to have been introduced into Europe at the siege of Naples, 1495; but was probably known to the ancients.

SYRACUSE, S.E. Sicily, founded by Archias, 734 B.C. The city gradually included five towns, Ortygia (an island, containing the citadel, or acropolis), Achradina, Tyche, Neapolis, and Epipolae. The ancient history is given in the article *Sicily*.

Syracuse taken by the Saracens and ransomed 669; burnt by them 878
Retaken by count Roger, the Norman . . . 1088
Destroyed by earthquakes in 1542, Jan. 1693; and nearly destroyed . . . . 6 Aug. 1757
In the insurrection, Syracuse surrendered to the Neapolitan troops . . . . . 8 April, 1849
Remains of an ancient city discovered by Dr. Orsi at Pantalica, reported . . . . Dec. 1895
Further discoveries reported . . . 14 Feb. 1897

SYREN, see *Sirene*.

SYRIA, a country of W. Asia. The capital was originally Damascus; but after the battle of Ipsus, Seleucus founded Antioch.

Alliance of David king of Israel and Hiram king of Syria . . . . B.C. 1049
Syria conquered by David 1040
Liberated by Rezin 980
Benhadad, king of Syria, makes war on the Jews 898
Benhadad II. reigns . . . . . . about 830
Syria subjugated by Tiglath-pileser, king of Assyria 740

Syria conquered by Cyrus 537
And by Alexander 333
Seleucus *Nicator* enters Babylon 312
Æra of the Seleucidæ (*which see*) . . . . ,,
Great battle of Ipsus; death of Antigonus, defeated by Ptolemy, Seleucus, and Lysimachus . . . 301
The city of Antioch founded 299
Antiochus, son of Seleucus, falling in love with his father's queen, Stratonice, he pines away nearly to death; but the secret being discovered, she is divorced by the father, and married by the son . 297
Battle of Cyropedium; Lysimachus slain by Seleucus 281
Seleucus foully assassinated by Ceraunus; Antiochus I. king 280
Antiochus I. (*Soter*, or Saviour) defeats the Gauls . 275
Antiochus II. surnamed by the Milesians *Theos* (God) king 261
Poisoned by Laodice 246
Seleucus II. (king, 246) makes a treaty of alliance with Smyrna and Magnesia 243
Seleucus III. *Ceraunus* (or Thunder), king . . 226
Antiochus III. the Great (king, 223), conquers Palestine, but is totally defeated at Raphia . . 217
Again conquers Palestine, 198; but gives it to Ptolemy 193
Enters Greece, 192; defeated by the Romans at Thermopylæ, 191; and at Magnesia . . . 190
Makes peace with the Romans, giving up to them Asia Minor 188
Seleucus Philopator, king 187
Antiochus IV. king, who assumes the title of *Theos-Epiphanes*, or the illustrious God . . . 175
He sends Apollonius into Judea; Jerusalem is taken; the temple pillaged; 40,000 inhabitants destroyed, and 40,000 more sold as slaves . . 168
Antiochus V. Eupator (king, 164), murdered by Demetrius Soter, who seizes the throne . . . 162
Demetrius is defeated and slain by his successor Alexander Bala, 150; who is also defeated and slain by Demetrius Nicator 146
Antiochus VI. Sidetes (son of Demetrius Soter) rules during the captivity of his brother Demetrius Nicator (after slaying the usurper Trypho) . 137
Antiochus grants peace to the Jews, and placates the Romans, 133; invades Parthia, 129; and is defeated and slain 128
Demetrius Nicator restored . . . . . . ,,
Cleopatra, the queen, murders her son Seleucus with her own hand 124
Her son Antiochus VII. Grypus (king, 125), whom she attempts to poison; but he compels his mother to swallow the deadly draught herself . 123
Reign of Antiochus VIII. Cyzicenus at Damascus, and of Grypus at Antioch 111
Seleucus, king 95
Antiochus IX. Eusebes, king 94
Dethroned by Philip 85
Tigranes, king of Armenia, acquires Syria . . . 83
Antiochus X. Asiaticus, solicits the aid of the Romans 75
Defeat of Tigranes by Lucullus, 69; he submits to Pompey, who enters Syria, and dethrones Antiochus Asiaticus 65
Syria made a Roman province 63

* * * * * *

Syria invaded by the Parthians . . . . A.D. 162
By the Persians 256
Violent earthquakes 341
Invaded by the Saracens, 497, 502, 529; by the Persians 607
Conquered by the Saracens 638
Conquest of Syria by the Fatimite caliphs . A.D. 970
Revolt of the emirs of Damascus 1067
The emirs of Aleppo revolt 1068
The crusades commence (see *Crusades*) . . . 1095
Desolated by the Crusades (*which see*) . . 1096-1272
Noureddin conquers Syria 1166
Saladin dethrones the Fatimite dynasty . . . 1171
The Tartars overrun all Syria 1259
The sultans of Egypt expel the Crusaders . . . 1291
Syria overrun by Tamerlane 1400
Syria and Egypt conquered by the Turks . . 1516-17
Syria continued in possession of the Turks till the invasion by the French, 1799; Bonaparte overruns the country, Gaza and Jaffa taken . March 1799
Siege of Acre begun by the French, 16 March; raised . . . . 20 May, ,,
Bonaparte returns to France from Egypt 23 Aug. 1799
Egypt and Syria evacuated by the French army, 10 Sept. 1801
Mehemet Ali attacks and captures Acre, and overruns the whole of Syria 1831
Ibrahim Pacha, his son, defeats the army of the grand signior at Konieh . . . . 21 Dec. 1832
Numerous battles and conflicts follow with various success; the European powers intervene, and peace is made . . . . 6 May, 1833
The war renewed, May; Ibrahim defeats the Turks at Nezib . . . . 24 June, 1839
The Turkish fleet deserts to Mehemet Ali, and arrives at Alexandria . . . . . 14 July, ,,
The five powers unite to support the Porte July, ,,
Death of lady Hester Stanhope . . . 23 June, 1840
Treaty of London (not signed by offended France), 15 July, ,,
Capture of Sidon (see *Sidon*) . . . . 27 Sept. ,,
Fall of Beyrout (see *Beyrout*) . . . . 10 Oct. ,,
Fall of Acre (see *Acre*) . . . . . 3 Nov. ,,
Long negotiations; the sultan grants hereditary rights to Mehemet, who gives up Syria . Jan. 1841
The Druses said to have destroyed 151 Christian villages and killed 1000 persons (see *Druses*), 29 May–1 July, 1860
The Mahometans massacre Christians at Damascus: about 3300 slain; many saved by Abd-el-Kader, 9 July, &c. ,,
The English and French government intervene; a convention signed at Paris; 12,000 men to be sent by France . . . . 3 Aug. ,,
Vigour of Fuad Pacha; he punishes the Mahometans implicated in the massacres at Damascus very severely; 167 of all ranks, including the governor, executed . . . . 20 Aug. *et seq.* ,,
4000 French soldiers, under general Hautpoul, land at Beyrout . . . . 22 Aug ,,
Lord Dufferin, the British commissioner in Syria, arrives at Damascus . . . . . 6 Sept. ,,
The French and Turks advance against Lebanon; 14 emirs surrendered . . . . . Oct ,,
Pacification of the country effected . Nov. ,,
The French occupation ceases . . . 5 June, 1861
Prince of Wales visits Syria . . . . April, 1862
Insurrection of Joseph Karam, Maronite, in Lebanon; suppressed . . . . . March, 1866
Another suppressed Karam flies to Algeria, 31 Jan. 1867
Midhat Pasha appointed governor-general to inaugurate reforms, Nov. 1878; experiences great difficulty, Oct.; resigns, but continues, Oct. 1879-June, 1880
Hamed Pasha, governor of Smyrna, and Midhat Pasha change places . . . . Aug. ,,
Midhat Pasha, charged with complicity in the murder of the sultan Abdul Aziz, surrenders (see *Turkey*, 1881) . . . . about 17 May, 1881
Dr. Robert Payne-Smith, dean of Canterbury, author of a great Syriac dictionary, died, aged 76, 31 March, 1895
Disturbances between the Druses and the Mutualis in the Lebanon; agitation at Damascus against the Christians . . . . 16 Oct. ,,
Conflicts and pillaging, Nov.; the Druses routed by Circassians and Arabs, aided by the Turks; villages burned, women and children killed, 1 Dec.; again defeated, 19, 21 Dec. 1895. (The Turks suffered much by the incapacity of their generals, and deficient commissariat, *Times*, 17 Feb. 1896.)
Turkish troops totally defeated by the Druses and Arabs, near Damascus . . . . June, 1896
Indecisive fighting; mutiny of troops, Aug.; cessation of hostilities . . . . . Sept. ,,
Abdullah pasha appointed commander-in-chief, Oct. ,,
The German emperor visits Syria . 25 Oct.–Nov. 1898

SYSTON, see under *Libraries*.

SZEGEDIN (Hungary), on the Theiss at its junction with the Maros, the seat of revolutionary government, 1849. Rebuilt under superintendence of Ludwig Tisza. Grand festival, the emperor present, 16 Oct. 1883. See *Inundations*, 1879 and 1887. Population, 1900, 100,552.

T.

TABERNACLE, the Holy Place of the Israelites, till the erection of Solomon's temple, was constructed by Divine direction, 1491 B.C. The tabernacle set up at Shiloh by Joshua, 1444 B.C. was replaced by the temple erected by Solomon, 1004 B.C. The chapel erected for George Whitefield in Moorfields in 1741, being of a temporary nature, received the name of Tabernacle, which was afterwards given to their chapels by the Calvinistic Methodists. Whitefield's Tabernacle in Tottenham-court-road was erected in 1756, and enlarged in 1760. His lease expired in 1828; the chapel was opened by the Independents in 1830, and taken down in 1890. A large metropolitan tabernacle, erected for the ministrations of Rev. C. H. Spurgeon, in Newington Butts, was opened on 31 March, 1861; burnt down, 20 April, 1898; rebuilt, 1899.

TABINET, see *Poplin*.

TABLES, see *Decemvirs*.

TABLET, Roman Catholic weekly paper, established 1840.

TABLE TURNING. This delusion, which came from America, and was popular in 1853, was attributed by Faraday and others to involuntary mechanical action. See *Spirit-Rapping*.

TABOR, in Bohemia, was founded by Ziska in 1420, and became a chief seat of the Hussites; see *Hussites*.

TADMOR, see *Palmyra*.

TAEPINGS, see *China*, 1851, note.

TAFFETY, an early species of silken manufacture, more prized formerly than now, woven very smooth and glossy. It was worn by our elder queens, and was first made in England by John Tyce, of Shoreditch, London, 41 Eliz. 1598. —*Stow's Chron*.

TAGLIACOZZO, in the Abruzzi mountains, S. Italy, where, on 23 Aug. 1268, Charles of Anjou, the usurping king of Naples, defeated and made prisoner the rightful monarch, young Conradin (the last of the Hohenstaufens, and grandson of the emperor Frederick II.), who had been invited into Italy by the Ghibelline or Imperial party; their opponents, the Guelfs, or papal party, supporting Charles. Conradin was beheaded, 29 Oct. following.

TAGLIAMENTO, a river in Lombardy, N. Italy, near which the Austrians, under the archduke Charles, were defeated by Bonaparte, 16 March, 1797.

TAHERITES, a dynasty of Persia, 813-872.

TAHITI. The French abbreviated name for Otaheite; see *Otaheite*.

TAILLEBOURG (W. France). Near here Henry III. of England was defeated and nearly captured by Louis IX. of France, 20 July, 1242.

TAKU FORTS, China, taken by the allies, 21 Aug. 1860; again, 17 June, 1900.

TALAVERA DE LA REYNA (central Spain), was taken from the Mahometans by Ordoño, king of Leon, 913. Here a battle was fought 27, 28 July, 1809, between the united British and Spanish armies under sir Arthur Wellesley, and the French army commanded by marshals Victor and Sebastiani. After a conflict on the 27th, both armies remained on the field during the night, and the French at break of day renewed the attack, and were again repulsed by the British with great slaughter. At noon Victor charged the whole British line, was repulsed at all points, and retreated with a heavy loss. As Soult, Ney, and Mortier were in the rear, the British retired after the victory.

TALBOTYPE, see *Photography*.

"TALISMAN" affair, see *Peru*, 1874-6.

TALKING-MACHINE, see *Automatons*.

TALLY OFFICE in the Exchequer took its name from the French word *tailler*, to cut. A tally is a piece of wood written upon both sides, containing an acquittance for money received; which, being cloven asunder by an officer of the exchequer, one part, called the stock, was delivered to the person who paid, or lent, money to the government; and the other part, called the counter-stock, or counter-foil, remained in the office, to be kept till called for, and joined with the stock. This manner of striking tallies is very ancient.—*Beatson*. The practice was ordered to be discontinued in 1782. See *Exchequer*. On 16 Oct. 1834, the houses of parliament were burnt down by too many of these tallies being used in heating the stoves in the house of lords.

TALMUD (from *lamad*, to teach), the compendium of ancient Jewish oral or unwritten law, as distinguished from the Pentateuch, or written law; its origin is coeval with the return from the Babylonish captivity, 536 B.C. Its compilation in Hebrew was begun by the Scribes, and by their successors the work was carried on till 220 B.C. It is composed in prose and poetry, and contains two elements, legal and legendary. The morality resembles that of the New Testament, and the philosophy is rather Platonic than Aristotelian.

The Mischna, comprising the work of the rabbis, termed Thanaïm, was compiled by Jehuda Hanassi, in the middle of the second century, A.D., and forms the Jerusalem Talmud, written at Tiberias, in Palestine, about 230. The Babylonian Talmud contains also the Gemera or Ghemara, the work of the rabbis termed Amoraïm, criticisms and comments on the Mischna. The part named *Halacha*, is dogmatic, legal, and doctrinal; the *Agaba*, is illustrative, narrative, and legendary.

After being almost universally condemned, and the MSS. often burnt, the defence of the Talmud was undertaken by the German reformer Reuchlin, in the 16th century, and between 1520 and 1523, the "Talmud Babylonicum," in 12 vols. fol., and the "Talmud Hierosolytanum," in one vol. fol., were printed at Venice. A discourse on the Talmud was given at the Royal Institution, 15 May, 1868, by Mr. Emanuel Deutsch, whose article in the "Quarterly Review," Oct. 1867, had attracted much attention.

Vol. I. of the first English translation of the Jerusalem Talmud by Dr. Moise Schwab, appeared in 1885; he had published part of a French translation.

TAMANIEB, or **TAMASI**, battle of, 13 March, 1884; see *Soudan*.

TAMATAVE, see *Madagascar*, 1883.

TAMMANY FRAUDS, see *New York*, 1871, and Nov. 1897.

TANAGRA (Bœotia). Here the Spartans defeated the Athenians 457 B.C., but were defeated by them in 456 and in 426, when Agis II. headed the Spartans and Nicias the Athenians.

TANCRED'S CHARITIES. Valuable exhibitions for students at Cambridge are maintained by Christopher Tancred's endowment, 1721; established by chancery, 1757.

TANDY ARREST. James Napper Tandy proposed a plan of reform in 1791. In the French expedition against Ireland he acted as a general, Aug. 1798. After its failure he fled to Hamburg, and was there delivered up to the English, 24 Nov.; for which Bonaparte declared war upon Hamburg, 15 Oct. 1799. Tandy was liberated after the peace of Amiens in 1802.

TANGIER (Morocco, N. W. Africa), besieged by prince Ferdinand of Portugal, who was beaten and taken prisoner, 1437. It was conquered by Alfonso V. of Portugal in 1471, and given as a dower to princess Catherine, on her marriage with Charles II. of England, 1662; who, in 1683, caused the works to be blown up, and the place abandoned. Tangiers afterwards became a piratical station. See *Morocco*.

Great storm, about 40 vessels destroyed 9 March, 1895

TANISTRY (in Ireland), the equal division of lands, after the decease of the owner, amongst his sons, legitimate or illegitimate. If one of the sons died, his son did not inherit, but a new division was made by the tanist or chief. Abolished 1604. *Davies*.

TANJORE (W. India). About 1678, Vencajee, a Mahratta chief, brother of the great Sevajee, made himself rajah. In 1749 a British expedition endeavoured to restore a deposed rajah without success; the reigning prince bought them off by the cession of territories. Much intervention ensued. In 1799 the company obtained possession of the country, engaging to support the rajah with nominal authority. The last is said to have died in 1855.

TANNENBERG (E. Prussia). Here Ladislaus V. Jagellon of Poland defeated the Teutonic knights with great slaughter, the grand master being among the slain, 15 July, 1410. The order never recovered from this calamity.

TANNHÄUSER, the name of one of Wagner's operas, founded on the German legend of the hero of that name.

TANNING leather with the bark of trees was early practised. Great improvements have been made in tanning by chemical processes.

TANTALUM, a rare metal, discovered in an American mineral by Hatchett, in 1801, and named by him columbium; and in a Swedish mineral by Ekeberg, who gave it its present name. Wollaston pointed out the identity of the two metals in 1809; and Berzelius prepared pure metallic tantalum in 1824. In 1846 Rose discovered that tantalum was really a mixture of three metals, which he named tantalum, niobium, and pelopium.—*Gmelin*.

TANZIMAT, see *Turkey*, 1839-44.

TAOISM, one of the three religions of China. The name is derived from the Tâo, or "Way," a treatise written by Li Urh, a contemporary of Confucius in the sixth century B.C. The "Way" is the quiet, passionless discharge of all our duties, "Heaven" not being a ruler, but a pattern. Tâoism was modified by the introduction of Buddhism.

TAPESTRY. An art of weaving borrowed from the Saracens, and hence its original workers in France were called *Sarazinois*. The invention of tapestry hangings belongs [the date is not mentioned] to the Netherlands.—*Guicciardini*. Manufactured in France under Henry IV. by artists invited from Flanders, 1606. The art was brought into England by William Sheldon; and the first manufactory of it was established at Mortlake by sir Francis Crane, 17 James I. 1619.—*Salmon*. Under Louis XIV. the art of tapestry was much improved in France; see *Gobelin Tapestry*. Very early instances of making tapestry are mentioned by the ancient poets, and also in Scripture; so that the Saracens' manufacture is a revival of the art. For the tapestry said to have been wrought by Matilda, queen of England, see *Bayeux Tapestry*.

Tapestry manufactory established at Windsor by Mr. H. Henry, supported by the royal family, and others; exhibition opened in the town-hall, 6 December, 1878; works said to be closed, June, 1892.

Manufacture revived by Messrs. Trollope of London, 1882-3

TAPIR, the American water-hog, a pachydermatous animal. The first born in England at Zoological Gardens, London, 12 Feb. 1882.

TAR. The chemist Becher first proposed to make tar from pit-coal; the earl of Dundonald's patent was granted 1781. The mineral tar was discovered at Coalbrookdale, Shropshire, 1779; and in Scotland, Oct. 1792. Tar-water was first recommended for its medicinal virtues by Dr. Berkeley, bishop of Cloyne, about 1744. From benzole, discovered in coal-tar, many brilliant dyes are now produced; see *Benzole*.

TARA, a hill in Meath, Ireland, where the early kings of Ireland were inaugurated. Near here, on 26 May, 1798, the royalist troops, 400 strong, defeated the insurgent Irish (4000 men), 500 killed. On 15 Aug. 1843, Daniel O'Connell held a monster meeting here (250,000 persons said to have been assembled).

TARBES (S. France, near the Pyrenees), capital of Bigorre, the property of the English kings in the middle ages. The French, under Soult, were forced from their position at Tarbes, with considerable loss, by the British army commanded by Wellington, 20 March, 1814. See *Toulouse*.

TARENTUM (now *Taranto*, S. Italy), was founded by the Greek Phalantus, B.C. 708. The people of Tarentum assisted by Pyrrhus, king of Epirus, supported a war which had been undertaken B.C. 281 by the Romans, to avenge the insults the Tarentines had offered to their ships when near their harbours; it was terminated after ten years; 300,000 prisoners were taken, and Tarentum became subject to Rome. Except the citadel, Tarentum was captured by Hannibal, 212, but recovered by Fabius, 209 B.C. Tarentum has shared in the revolutions of Southern Italy, and only ruins remain.

TARGUMS or **EXPLANATIONS**, names given to certain ancient Chaldee paraphrases of the Old Testament. The most remarkable are those of Onkelos, Jonathan-ben-Uzziel, and Joseph the Blind. The Targum of Onkelos is referred by some writers to the first century A.D.

TARIFA (S. Spain), the ancient Joza and Julia Traducta, where Muza landed when invading Spain, 712. It was taken from the Moors by Sancho IV. of Castile, 1291 or 1292; and was relieved, when besieged by them, after a great victory over the kings of Morocco and Granada, by Alfonso XI. of Castile and Alfonso IV. of Portugal, 28 or 30 Oct. 1340. The conflict is called the battle of Salado, having been fought on the banks of that river. Tarifa was taken by the French in 1823.

TARIFF (said to have been derived from Tarifa, where duties were formerly collected), a book of duties charged on goods exported or imported. Our tariff in 1840 comprised 1042 articles; the number was reduced (by sir Robert Peel) in 1845 and 1847. It comprised 439 articles in 1857; this number was greatly reduced in 1860. For Mr. McKinley's tariff bill, see *United States*, Oct. 1890.

What is called "the war of tariffs," very injurious to free trade, began in . . . . Oct. 1890

International office for the publications of all customs tariffs, in the five principal European languages at Brussels, begins the work of translation, &c. . . . . 1 April, 1891

TARIFF REFORM LEAGUE, inaugurated 21 July, 1903, for the employment of the tariff with a view to its use to consolidate and develop the resources of the Empire, and to defend the industries of the United Kingdom. The league, which is independent of political parties, carries on its propaganda by means of meetings, lectures, and literature on the subject; it also supports members of parliament and parliamentary candidates who are in favour of tariff reform. Branches of the league are being formed in every constituency in England and Wales, with the exception of the counties of Worcestershire, Warwick, Shropshire, and Staffordshire, which form the area worked by the Imperial tariff committee at Birmingham. President of the league, the duke of Sutherland.

TARPEIAN ROCK (Rome), owed its name to the tradition that Tarpeia, daughter of Tarpeius, the keeper of the Roman citadel, was here crushed to death by the shields cast on her by the Sabines, whom she treacherously admitted, having bargained for the gift of what they wore on their left arms, meaning their bracelets; about 750 B.C.

TARRAGONA (N.E. Spain), occupied as a naval station by the British before their capture of Gibraltar in 1704. It was stormed and sacked by the French under Suchet, 29 Jan. 1811, and the inhabitants put to the sword. Population, 1887, 27,225.

TARTAN or **HIGHLAND PLAID**, the dress of the Scottish Highlanders, said to have been derived from the ancient Gauls, or Celtæ, the *Galli non braccati*.

TARTARIC ACID is said to have been the first discovery of the eminent chemist, Scheele, who procured it in a separate state by boiling tar with lime, and in decomposing the tartrate of lime thus formed by means of sulphuric acid, about 1770. In 1859 baron Liebig formed tartaric acid from other sources.

TARTARY, a name given in the middle ages to a part of Central Asia and Eastern Europe, see *Turkestan* and *Crimea*. The Tatars, or Tartars, or Mongols, or Moguls, were known in antiquity as Scythians. During the decline of the Roman empire, these tribes began to seek more fertile regions; and the first who reached the frontier of Italy were the Huns, the ancestors of the modern Mongols. The first acknowledged sovereign of this vast country was the famous Genghis Khan. His empire, by the conquest of China, Persia, and all central Asia (1206-27), became one of the most formidable ever established; but it was split into parts in a few reigns. Timur, or Tamerlane, again conquered Persia, broke the power of the Turks in Asia Minor (1370-1400), and founded the Mogul dynasty in India, which began with Baber in 1525, and formed the most splendid court in Asia till the close of the 18th century; see *Golden Horde*. The Calmucks, a branch of the Tartars, expelled from China, settled on the banks of the Volga in 1672, but returned in 1771, and thousands perished on the journey.

TASIMETER, see *Micro-tasimeter*.

TASMANIA, the name now given to the British settlement in Van Diemen's Land (*which see*).

TATE GALLERY, see *National Gallery*, July, 1897; new rooms added, Nov. 1899.

TATTERSALL'S, see *Races*.

TAUNTON (Somerset) was taken by Perkin Warbeck, Sept. 1497; and here he was surrendered to Henry VII. 5 Oct. following. The duke of Monmouth was proclaimed king at Taunton, 20 June, 1685; and it was the scene of the "bloody assize" held by Jeffreys upon the rebels in August. The castle restored and a fine museum opened by lord Cork, 21 May, 1902. Population, 1881, 16,614; 1891, 18,026; 1901, 21,078.

TAVERNS may be traced to the 13th century. "In the raigne of king Edward the Third, *only three taverns* were allowed in London: one in Chepe, one in Walbrok, and the other in Lombard-street."—*Spelman*. The *Boar's Head*, in East-cheap, existed in the reign of Henry IV., and was the rendezvous of prince Henry and his dissolute companions. Shakspeare mentions it as the residence of Mrs. Quickly, and the scene of Falstaff's merriment.—*Shakspeare*, "Henry IV." The *White Hart*, Bishopsgate, established in 1480, was rebuilt in 1829. Taverns were licensed in 1752.

Taverns were restricted by 7 Edward VI. 1552-3, to 40 in London, 8 in York, 4 in Norwich, 3 in Westminster, 6 in Bristol, 3 in Lincoln, 4 in Hull, 3 in Shrewsbury, 4 in Exeter, 3 in Salisbury, 4 in Gloucester, 4 in Chester, 3 in Hereford, 3 in Worcester, 3 in Southampton, 4 in Canterbury, 3 in Ipswich, 3 in Winchester, 3 in Oxford, 4 in Cambridge, 3 in Colchester, 4 in Newcastle-upon-Tyne.

TAXES were levied by Solon, the Athenian legislator, about 594 B.C. The first class of citizens paid an Attic talent of silver, about 55*l*. of our money. Darius, the son of Hystaspes, levied a land-tax by assessment, which was deemed so odious that his subjects styled him, by way of derision, Darius the Trader, 480 B.C.—*D'Eon*. Taxes in specie were first introduced into England by William I., 1067, and he raised them arbitrarily; yet subsidies in kind, as in wool, leather, and other products of the country, continued till the accession of Richard II., 1377.—*Camden*; see *Revenue* and *Income Tax*. "TAXES ON KNOWLEDGE" (see *Advertisement Duty*, *Newspaper Stamp*, and *Paper Duty*). For his exertions in repealing these, a testimonial was presented to Mr. T. Milner Gibson in 1861. The *assessed* taxes now include *land tax*, *house duty*, and *property* and *income tax*. The Taxes Management act, 43 & 44 Vict. c. 19, passed 6 Aug. 1880 (see below). Mr. Stephen Dowell's "History of Taxation and Taxes in England," published in 1884-8. The elder Wm. Pitt, in his great speech on the Stamp act imposed on the colonies without their consent, 1765—66, said that taxation and representation should go hand in hand. See *Stamp Duties*.

The Statistical Abstract published annually by the government gives much information respecting taxation, revenue, and expenditure for 15 years. Receipts from general taxation, 1887-8, 75,660,000*l*.

Assessed Taxes.		*Land Tax*	
1800	£3,468,131	1800	£1,307,941
1805	4,508,752	1805	1,596,481
1810	6,233,161	1810	1,418,337
1815	6,524,766	1815	1,084,251
1820	6,311,346	1820	1,192,257
1825	5,176,722	1825	1,288,393
1830	5,013,405	1830	1,189,214
1835	3,733,997	1835	1,203,579
1840	3,866,467	1840	1,298,622

Assessed Taxes.—Gross Amount.

1851 (to Jan. 5)	£4,365,033
1855 (year ending March 31)	3,160,641
1860 ,, ,,	3,232,000
1865 ,, ,,	3,292,000
1866 ,, ,,	3,350,000
1867 ,, ,,	3,468,000
1868 ,, ,,	3,509,000
1869 ,, ,,	3,494,000
1870 ,, ,,	4,500,000
1871 { Land tax and house duty *only*,	2,725,000
1872 see *Licences*. }	2,330,000
1873	2,337,000
1874	2,324,000
1875	2,440,000
1876	2,496,000
1877	2,532,000
1878	2,670,000
1879	2,720,000
1880	2,670,000
1883	2,843,154
1884	2,899,223
1886	2,890,000
1888	2,970,000
1890–1	2,600,000
1892–3	2,450,000
1893–4	2,460,000

See *House Duty* and *Land Tax*.

TAY BRIDGE at Dundee, above two miles across the Tay; act passed 1870, work begun June, 1871; Mr. De Bergue, first contractor, died, succeeded by Messrs. Hopkins, Gilke & Co., of Middlesbrough. Engineer, sir Thomas Bouch. It was much injured by a gale, 4 Feb. 1877; completed, 30 Aug.; tried, 25 Sept. 1877; opened, 31 May, 1878. Length, 10,612 feet; it consisted of 85 spans, some above 90 feet above water level; cost said to be 350,000*l*. Above 20 lives lost during its construction.

The bridge was partly destroyed by a gale, while a N. British mail-train was passing over it; a gap of about 3,000 feet was made; between 75 and 90 persons perished; about 7.15 P.M. Sunday, 28 Dec. 1879
46 bodies were recovered . . up to 27 April, 1880
Liberal collections were made for sufferers by the loss of relatives.
After the Board of Trade inquiry, Mr. H. C. Rothery, in the report, stated "that the bridge had been badly designed, badly constructed, and badly maintained" . . . . . . 3 July, ,,
Sir Thomas Bouch died . . . . 30 Oct. ,,
Mr. Barlow's (died, aged 90, 12 Nov. 1902) plans for a new bridge approved . . . . . May, 1881
Plans for new bridge approved . . . . Jan. 1882
Fourteen piers erected . . . . . Dec. 1885
Opened for public traffic . . . . 20 June, 1887

TCHERNAYA, a river in the Crimea. On 16 Aug. 1855, the lines of the allied army at this place were attacked by 50,000 Russians under prince Gortschakoff, who was repulsed with the loss of 3329 slain, 1658 wounded, and 600 prisoners. The brunt of the attack was borne by two French regiments under general D'Herbillon. The loss of the allies was about 1200; 200 of these were from the Sardinian contingent, which behaved with great gallantry, under the command of general La Marmora. The Russian general Read, and the Sardinian general Montevecchio, were killed. The object of the attack was the relief of Sebastopol, then closely besieged by the English and French.

TEA was brought to Europe by the Dutch, 1610. It is mentioned as having been used in England on very rare occasions prior to 1657, and sold for 6*l*. and even 10*l*. the pound. Price of inferior kinds, 1801, 4*s*. 2½*d*. the pound; in 1871, 1*s*. 10*d*.; in 1903,
For *Théine*, see *Cafeine*.

Samuel Pepys records his first "cup of tea," 25 Sept. 1660
A duty of 8*d*. was charged upon every gallon of tea made for sale (12 Ch. II. c. 13) . . . . ,,
The East India Company first import it . . . 1669
Brought into England in 1666, by lord Ossory and lord Arlington, from Holland: and being admired by persons of rank, it was imported from thence, and generally sold for 60 shillings per pound, till our East India Company took up the trade.—*Anderson*.
Green tea began to be used 1715
Price of black tea per lb. 13*s*. to 20*s*.; of green, 12*s*. to 30*s*. 1728
The duty imposed on tea in America, 1767: this tax occasioned the destruction of 17 chests at New York, and 340 at Boston, Dec. 1773, and ultimately led to the American war (see *Boston*).
The tea-plant brought to England . . . about 1768
Tea-dealers obliged to have sign-boards fixed up, announcing their sale of tea . . . . Aug. 1779
Commutation act for reducing the duty on tea from 50 to 12½ per cent.; taxing windows in lieu, June, 1784
"Millions of pounds' weight of sloe, liquorice, and ash-tree leaves, are every year mixed with Chinese teas in England."—*Report of the House of Commons*, 1818
"The consumption of the whole civilised world, exclusively of England, is about 22,000,000 of pounds, while the annual consumption in Great Britain is 30,000,000."—*Evidence in House of Commons* 1830
The first tea-sale in London on the abolition of the exclusive privilege of the East India Company took place in Mincing-lane . . . 19 Aug. 1834
New duties were charged, 1796; the duty was 96 and 100 per cent., made 2*s*. 1*d*. per pound . . . 1836
The duty derived from the import of tea in 1850 amounted to 5,471,461*l*.; and the amount was 5,902,433*l*. . . . . . . in 1852
Various changes made in 1854, 1855 . . . and 1856
Duty of 1*s*. 5*d*. per pound begun . . . April, 1857
Duty upon tea gradually reduced from 2*s*. 2½*d*. to 1*s*. per pound; reduced to 6*d*. per pound, 1 June, 1865
Licences to sell tea abolished 1869
Tea duty 6*d*., continued 1871
Produced, 3,709,450*l*. year 1875-6; 4,002,210*l*. 1877-8; 4,268,734*l*. 1883-4; 4,613,311*l*. . . 1887-8
The duty reduced to 4*d*. per pound . 17 April, 1890
Tea duty raised to 6*d*. . . . . . 9 April, 1900
Area under tea cultivation in India at end of 1902, 525,252 acres; nine-tenths of total in Assam and Bengal; government report issued . . Sept. 1903

TEA IMPORTED INTO ENGLAND.

1726	lb 700,000	1875	lb 197,505,316
1766	7,000,000	1876	185,536,371
1792	13,185,000	1877	187,515,284
1800	23,723,000	1878	204,872,899
1805	24,133,000	1879	184,076,472
1810	25,414,000	1880	206,971,570
1815	26,368,000	1881	209,801,522
1820	25,662,474	1882	210,663,133
1825	24,803,668	1883	222,262,431
1830	30,544,404	1884	213,877,759
1835	44,360,550	1885	212,143,820
1840	38,068,555	1886	230,669,292
1845	44,193,433	1887	221,841,490
1850 *govt. retns.*	50,512,384	1889	222,147,661
1856	86,200,414	1890	223,494,511
1858	75,432,535	1892	239,445,467
1861	96,577,383	1893	249,546,451
1864	124,359,243	1894	244,310,500
1866	139,610,044	1895	255,360,128
1868	154,845,863	1896	265,394,127
1870	141,020,767	1898	271,593,683
1871	169,898,303	1900	298,900,200
1872	184,927,128	1901	229,000,000
1873	163,765,269	1902	236,000,000

The importation of tea grown in India has very greatly increased.

A consignment of tea from the Gallebodde Estate, Ceylon, was sold in London at the rate of 87*s.* per pound, 13 Jan.; re-sold for 110*s.* per pound, to the United Kingdom Tea Company, Jan.; some tea, Ceylon, sold for 10*l.* 12*s.* 6*d.* per pound, 10 March; 17*l.* per pound, 5 May; 25*l.* 10*s.* per pound . . . . 7 May, 1891

TEACHERS, NATIONAL UNION OF ELEMENTARY, established about 1869. The *Teachers' Association* held their 3rd annual conference at University College, London, 9 Jan. 1878. The Teachers' Guild held its first public meeting, Mr. Mundella in the chair, 23 Jan. 1884. Conferences held annually; the duke and duchess of York receive 9,000*l.* for the benevolent fund at Brighton, 9 April, 1896. 1901, 35,000 members.

TEACHING, see *Apostles* and *University*.

"TEARLESS VICTORY," was won by Archidamus III, king of Sparta, over the Arcadians and Argives, without losing a man, 367 B.C.

TEA-ROOM MEETING of members of the house of commons, 8 April, 1867. See *Reform*, 1867

TEB, Battle of, 29 Feb. 1884. See *Soudan*.

TECHNICAL EDUCATION, defined as "science and art applied to industry." Polytechnic schools in Darmstadt established 1830; in Hanover 1835; the trade association of the grand duchy of Hesse, 1836; Berlin working mens' union, 1843; Wurtemburg workmen's school, 1848; society for promoting the interests of the working classes at Amsterdam, 1854. The first real practical technical school in England was formed in the Chester Diocesan Training College, by the rev. Arthur Rigg, principal, 1839-69.

Conference of masters of city companies at the Mansion-house to promote technical education 5 Nov. 1869

National university for industrial and technical training, proposed . . . . . . Oct. 1870

City and Guilds of London Institute for the advancement of technical education formally constituted, 11 Nov. 1878; foundation laid by prince Leopold . . . . 10 May, 1881

Central Institution of City and Guilds Institute, South Kensington; foundation laid by the prince of Wales . . . . 18 July, ,,

A royal commission (Mr. B. Samuelson, prof. H. E. Roscoe (since knighted) and others) to inquire as to technical instruction in foreign countries, Aug. ,,

Technical college, Finsbury, opened . . 19 Feb. 1883

Technical schools (Scotland) act passed . . . 1887

Royal commission on technical instruction appointed (Mr. Bernhard Samuelson, prof. H. E. Roscoe, and four others), to inquire abroad and at home, 5 Aug. 1881; reports (reassuring as to English work), about 17 Feb. 1882, and 16 May, 1884

Technical instruction bill introduced in Parliament; dropped . . . . . . 10 July, 1888

Great meeting at the Mansion House to promote technical education in the metropolis, 27 March, 1889

The technical instruction act, authorising local authorities to supply aid for the purpose, passed 30 Aug. 1889; another act passed . 26 March, 1891

Technical and Industrial Institutions act passed . 1892

National association for the promotion of technical education formed, lord Hartington (since duke of Devonshire), president, 1 July, 1887; annual meetings. 1893

Association of technical institutions constituted at the Society of Arts . . . . 26 Jan. 1894

Mr. T. H. Adams, of Newport, bequeathes about 50,000*l.* for technical education in agriculture, announced . . . . 27 Jan. ,,

International congress on technical education at the Society of Arts . . . . . 15 June, 1897

New mining and technical college at Wigan opened by the countess of Crawford . . . . 12 Jan. 1903

See *Polytechnic Institution* and *Whitworth*.

TE DEUM, a song of praise used by the Romish and English churches, beginning "*Te Deum Laudamus*—We praise thee, O God," supposed to be the composition of Augustin and Ambrose, about 390. The original music is very ancient.

TEETOTALER, a term applied to an abstainer from all fermented liquors, originated with Richard Turner, an artisan of Preston, who, contending for the principle at a temperance meeting about Sept. 1833, asserted "that nothing but *te-te-total* will do." The word was immediately adopted. He died 27 Oct. 1846. These facts are taken from the "Staunch Teetotaler," edited by Joseph Livesey, of Preston (an originator of the movement in 1832, he died, aged 90, 2 Sept. 1884), Jan. 1867. See *Encratites*, *Good Templars*, *Temperance*, and *United Kingdom*.

TEFLIS, see *Tiflis*.

TEGYRA, Bœotia. Here Pelopidas defeated the Spartans, 375 B.C.

TEHERAN became capital of Persia about 1795. Estimated population, 210,000.

TELEGRAPHONE, a development of the telephone and phonograph invented by Mr. Poulsen, a Dane, by which the voice may be directed to any number of points simultaneously, *Nature*, 17 May, 1900; another by Mr. Kumberg, reported, 27 Oct. 1900.

TELEGRAPHS (from the Greek, *tele*, afar, and *grapho*, I write). Æschylus, in his Agamemnon (B.C. 500), describes the communication of intelligence by burning torches as signals. Polybius, the Greek historian (who died about 122 B.C.), calls the different instruments used by the ancients for communicating information, *pyrsiæ*, because the signals were always made by fire. In 1663, a plan was suggested by the marquis of Worcester, and a telegraph was suggested by Dr. Hooke, 1684. M. Amontons is also said to have been the inventor of telegraphs about this period. James II., while duke of York, originated a set of navy signals, which were systematised by Kempenfeldt in 1780; and a dictionary was compiled by sir Home Popham. M. Chappe then invented the telegraph first used by the French in 1792, and two were erected over the Admiralty-office, London, 1796. The semaphore was erected there 1816. The naval signals by telegraph enabled 400 previously concerted sentences to be transmitted from ship to ship, by varying the combinations of two revolving crosses. Baron Reuter's telegraph agency founded at Aix la Chapelle, 1851. Acts relating to telegraphs were passed in 1863 and 1866. The telegraph act, passed 31 July, 1868, enabled the postmaster-general to purchase existing electric telegraphs (not less than 1*s.* for a telegram, 20 words). Mr. Scudamore was appointed director, Jan. 1872. The principle of a 6*d.* telegram adopted by the commons, 29 March, 1883, and enacted to come into operation 1 Oct. 1883, deferred; bill introduced by Mr. Shaw-Lefevre 30 March; act passed 14 Aug.; came into operation 1 Oct. 1885. Another telegraph act passed 28 June, 1892, and 1899. See *Telephone*. Great destruction of telegraph posts and wires by gale and snowstorm; London streets blocked by fallen wires 26-27 Dec. 1886. The Society of Telegraph Engineers founded 1871; held first general meeting, 28 Feb. 1872, Chas. Wm. Siemens, president;

incorporated 1883. Present title "Institution of Electrical Engineers" (1903). See *Electric Telegraph* and *Wireless Telegraphy*, under *Electricity* and *Telegraphs*, under *Post Office*, 1869 *et seq.* The *Telegraphic Journal* began 15 Nov. 1873

International Telegraph Conferences (commercial), have been held at Brussels, 1858; Paris, March, 1865; Vienna, 1868; Rome, 1871–2; St. Petersburg, 1 June, 1875; London, 18 June, 1879; Paris, 16 Oct. 1882; Berlin, 10 Aug.–17 Sept. 1885; Paris (114 delegates, representing 38 states and 23 great companies) . 15 May–21 June, 1890

Telautography: successful experiments made with prof. Elisha Gray's machine; messages transmitted in *facsimile* writing between the General Post-office, London and St. Margaret's Bay (83 miles), 22 July, 1894; further improvements in 1898 and 1900

Prof. Rowland's multiplex system of printing to telegraphy, successful . . . . April, 1900

TELEKOUPHONON, or speaking telegraph, consisted of piping of gutta percha, caoutchouc, glass, or earthenware, with a terminal mouthpiece of ivory, bone, wood, or metal. It was used for dockyards and large establishments. It was described by Mr. Francis Whishaw at the meeting of the British Association at Swansea, August, 1848.

TEL-EL-KEBIR, Egypt, the site of the entrenched camp of the rebel general, Arabi Pasha, his force being about 17,500 regular infantry, 2500 cavalry, 6000 Bedouins and other irregulars, and 70 guns; captured by the British 13 Sept. 1882.

Sir Garnet Wolseley broke up his camp at Ismailia on the night of 12 Sept. and began his advance at 1.30 a.m., his force being about 11,000 infantry, 2000 cavalry, and 40 guns: the troops marched rapidly in the dark, each regiment endeavouring to be first. At daybreak they arrived at the camp. The surprised Egyptians filled the trenches and fought well under cover; but when the British scaled the parapets, they at first resisted bravely, but afterwards fled, being hotly pursued by the British cavalry, leaving all their guns, ammunition, &c., in the hands of the victors. Thousands were killed or made prisoners. Arabi Pasha fled towards Cairo. Among our killed were majors Colville, Underwood, and Somervell, and lieut. McNeill. The British general's masterly plans of the campaign were thus successfully carried out by his efficient staff and gallant army, which included many young soldiers; the Irish and Highland regiments and the Guards being specially distinguished. Arabi Pasha's army was completely broken up, and the British entered Cairo the next day, 14 Sept. British killed about 52, and 380 wounded; Egyptian killed and wounded about 1500. The Highlanders bore the brunt of the action.

TELEMETER, &c., an instrument for determining the distance between a gun and the object fired at. Lieut. von Ehrenberg and major Montaudon, in Baden, constructed a telemeter the size of a watch, by which the distance is determined and shown on a dial by the action of sound, 1878-85. *Teletopometer*, another apparatus for ascertaining the distance from point to point, invented by Dr. Luigi Cerebotani, was announced in Sept. 1885; two telescopes are employed.

TELEPATHY, "the supersensory transference of thoughts and feelings from one mind to another"; the principal subject of "Phantasms of the Living," edited by Messrs. Edmund Gurney, Frederic Myers, and Frank Podmore, and issued by the society for psychical research about 30 Oct. 1886. See *Psychology*, 1897.

TELEPHONE (from Greek, *tēle*, afar, *phōnē*, voice, sound), a name now given to apparatus for transmitting articulate and musical sounds, by means of wire, vibrating rods, threads, or magneto-electricity. See *Electrophone* [in article *Electricity*], *Phonograph*, *Microphone*, *Phonopore*.

Robert Hooke conveyed sounds to a distance by distended wire 1667

Wheatstone conveyed the sounds of a musical-box from a cellar to upper rooms by means of a deal rod (termed "Enchanted Lyre") 1821

Page produced galvanic musical tones by magnetising and demagnetising an iron bar 1837

The principle advanced by De la Rive 1843

Professor Pepper lectured on Wheatstone's telephone before the queen at the Polytechnic, 10 May 1855

Philip Reis exhibited a partially articulate electric telephone at Frankfort . . . . 25 April 1861

Cromwell Varley produced a musical one, 1870; played on at the Queen's theatre, Long-acre, 12 Feb. 1877

Elisha Gray improved Reis's telephone, and is said to have anticipated prof. Bell's discovery . 1873

Professor A. Graham Bell's articulating telephone produced: (he employs a thin disk of iron vibrating in front of a permanent magnet, surrounded by a coil of insulated copper wire; the sound or voice causes the vibration of the disk, thereby generating a current of electricity which, sent round a similar coil on a distant magnet, sets vibrating another disk, and thus the sound is reproduced; sound is converted into electricity and electricity reconverted into sound;) experiments at Boston and Salem, United States (18 miles apart); speech, music, singing, laughing, &c., distinctly heard . . . . 12 Feb. 1877

This telephone exhibited by Mr. W. H. Preece before the British Association, Plymouth, 23 Aug. 1877; before the queen at Osborne, Isle of Wight, 14, 15 Jan. 1878

Debates in the house of commons, reported by it for *Daily News* (unsuccessful) . . . 22 Jan. „

Telephone company established . . . summer „

Edison's carbon "loud speaking" telephone; conversation heard between London and Norwich; 115 miles of wire . . . . . 11 Nov. „

Mr. Frederick Allen Gower improves Bell's telephone; shown at Royal Institution, London, 20, 21 March, 1879

Telephone Exchange (Edison's system), Lombard-street; ten offices connected; private conversation between two persons in either a loud or low tone carried on; successfully tried . 6 Sept. „

New building in Lime-street 1894

The Bell and Edison companies become the United Telephone Company; announced . 26 July, 1880

The telephone tried by lord Elphinstone in his coalmines near Carberry, Scotland . Sept. „

Telephone communication established between Liverpool and Manchester; exchange of messages between the mayors . . . . 9 Nov. „

20,000 Gower-Bell telephones said to have been ordered by the post-office . . . Dec. „

The attorney-general applies for injunction against the Telephone company and the Edison telephone company; case deferred; the companies directed to keep accounts, 20 Jan. 1880; decision that the Telephone company is an infraction of the electric telegraph monopoly bought by the act of 1868, 20 Dec. 1880; legal arrangements with the company . . . . 11 April, 1881

The postmaster-general now grants licences . . „

Professor Dolbear of Tuft's college, Massachusetts, announced a new system, with improved telephone receiver (an articulating air condenser), different to Bell's and Edison's . . . . Aug. „

Opera at Royal Comedy theatre, Panton-street, London, heard at Bristol hotel, Burlington-gardens . . . . 21 Dec. „

National Telephone company 2nd annual meeting, report gross revenue 30 June, 1881, 15,050*l.*; 30 June, 1882, 26,996*l.*; dividend 6 per cent. announced . . . . Aug. 1882

Telephonic communications between Brighton and London established . . . . . 21 Dec. „

The system largely developed in Europe and America . . . . „

United Telephone company *v.* Harrison, Cox, Walker & Co., for infringements of patents (Gordon, Bell and Edison); verdict for plaintiffs on appeal . . . . 6 Feb. 1883
Distinct communication between New York and Chicago 1000 miles (by steel wire coated with copper) reported . . . . .. 24 March, ,,
Sermons at churches and chapels transmitted at Bradford . . . . Aug. ,,
The post-office makes large concessions to the companies . . . . Sept. 1884
Successful experiments between Uxbridge and Liverpool (200 miles) . . . . 9 July, 1885
Simple mechanical telephone of Messrs. A. A. Knudson and T. G. Ellsworth of New York announced . . . . Aug. ,,
Telephonic communication between Brussels and Paris opened by means of Dr. Cornelius Herz's micro-telephone . . . . . . 2 Feb. 1887
A telephone palace at Stockholm . . Feb. ,,
Communication by telephone between Paris and Marseilles opened . . . . . 6 Aug. 1888
Proposed amalgamation of the United Telephone company with other companies opposed by the postmaster-general in regard to their licences from government . . . . . . June, 1889
The Pulsion telephone, in which sounds are communicated by an ordinary wire, without electricity, invented by Mr. Lemuel Mellett, successfully used on railways in America, 1888; tried with good results on the Midland railway near London . . . . Dec. ,,
Mr. Edison, said to have invented a process of combining photography with the telephone, Feb. 1890
Telephonic communications open between London, Birmingham, and Liverpool, 11 July; Manchester 30 Sept. ,,
The telephone almost universally adopted . 1890–2
Telephone communication between London and Paris, proposed by the French, and assented to by the English Government; the necessary works were completed by the construction of the first sub-marine telephonic cables, and their submerging by the *Monarch*, 14 March; officially tested by the engineers, 17 March; the first communications were from the prince of Wales and president Carnot exchanging congratulations; others followed between Mr. Raikes, the postmaster-general, and M. Roche, French minister of commerce, and other officials, 18 March; opened to the public (day and night) . . . 1 April, 1891
Telephonic communication from London to Marseilles and Brussels, completed 19 April, 1891; between Dublin and Belfast, opened . 5 April, 1892
Treasury minute to promote the development of the telephone system in the United Kingdom by promoting the co-operation of the post-office and the telephone companies, &c. . 23 May, ,,
The government authorised to raise 1,000,000*l.* to purchase the trunk lines of the telephone companies, by the telegraph act passed . . June, ,,
Telephone from New York to Chicago (950 miles) opened . . . . Oct. ,,
A "Manual of Telephony," by W. H. Preece and A. J. Stubbs, published . . . . Dec. 1893
Telephone from Berlin to Vienna (410 miles) opened, 29 Nov. 1894
Telephone between the post-office, London, Edinburgh, and other principal towns of the kingdom inaugurated . . . . . . 12 June, 1895
The Apostoloff automatic telephone, system described in the *Times* . . . . 17 Aug. 1896
All the trunk telephone lines in the United Kingdom transferred to the post-office . 6 Feb. 1897
Second telephone cable—24 miles long—between Abbot's-cliff, near Dover, and Sangatte, near Calais, laid . . . . 8 May, ,,
Telephone communication with and through Ireland begun . . . . 9 Sept. ,,
Report of telephone committee issued . 12 Aug. 1898
Communication between farms by instruments on wire fences used in Australia, announced, Sept. ,,
The history of the telephone service, from 1877–1892, *Times* . . . . . . 20, 23 Jan. 1899
Telegraphs (telephonic communication) act passed, 4 Aug. ,,
Successful experiments with the Brussels–London telephone (cable between Ostend and St. Margaret's bay, near Dover), reported . 3 Oct. 1900
Telephone convention between Gt. Britain and France signed . . . . . . 29 July, 1902

TELEPHOTOGRAPHY, a process for transmitting to a distance images of objects by the agency of electricity and selenium, was invented by Mr. Shelford Bidwell, early in 1881.

TELERADIPHONE, an arrangement of apparatus in which M. Mercadier has adapted prof. Graham Bell's photophone to telegraphy, announced Jan. 1882.

TELESCOPES. Their principle was described by Roger Bacon about 1250, and Leonard Digges (who died about 1573) is said to have arranged glasses so that he could see very distant objects.

Telescopes constructed by John Lipperhey and Zacharias Jansen, spectacle-makers of Middleburg, and James Metius of Alkmaer . . about 1608
Galileo (from a description of the above) constructed telescopes (May, 1609), gradually increasing in power, till he discovered Jupiter's satellites, &c. Jan. 1610
The telescope explained by Kepler 1611
Huyghens greatly improved the telescope; discovered the ring and satellites of Saturn, &c. 1655-6
Telescopes improved by Gregory . . about 1663
Reflecting telescope invented by Newton . . 1668
Achromatic telescopes made by Chester More Hall, about 1723; re-invented by John Dollond . 1758
Sir Wm. Herschel (originally an organist at Bath) greatly improves telescopes, and discovers the planet Uranus (*which see*), 21 March, 1781, and a volcanic mountain in the moon, in 1783; he completes his forty-feet focal length telescope in 1789, and he discovers two other volcanic mountains; he lays before the Royal Society a catalogue of 5000 nebulæ and clusters of stars . 1802
A telescope made in London for the observatory of Madrid, which cost 11,000*l.*, in . . . . . . ,,
Telescopes improved by Guinand and Fraunhofer. 1805-14
The great telescope taken down, and one of twenty-feet focal length erected by sir John Herschel (who afterwards took it to the Cape of Good Hope, and made with it his observations) . 1822
The earl of Rosse erected at Parsonstown, in Ireland, a telescope (at a cost exceeding 20,000*l.*) 6 feet in diameter, and 54 feet in length; it is moved with ease 1828-45
Mr. Lassell constructed a telescope by which he discovered the satellite of Neptune, 1846; and the eight satellites of Saturn 1848
One of gigantic size, 85 feet in length (very imperfect), completed at Wandsworth by the rev. John Craig 1852
Magnificent equatorial telescopes set up at the national observatories at Greenwich and Paris . 1860
M. Foucault exhibits at Paris a reflecting telescope, the mirror 31½ inches in diameter; the focal length 17⅞ feet 1862
Mr. R. S. Newall's telescope (with object glass 25 inches diameter; tube nearly 30 feet), set up at Gateshead by Cookes of York 1870
One at United States Observatory, Washington; object-glass, 26 inches diameter, 33 feet length 1881
Mr. A. Ainslie Common's reflecting telescope; speculum 37½ inches diameter; length, 20 feet; said to be the most powerful in existence; Ealing, Middlesex; completed, Sept. 1879; a paper on a new form of his reflecting telescope read by Dr. Common at the Roy. Astron. Society, 11 Jan. 1895
The largest refracting telescope yet made; by Howard Grubb at Dublin (for Vienna), approved by the commissioners . . . . 16 March, 1881
A very large refracting telescope by Messrs. Clark of America was set up in the observatory at Mount Hamilton, California, named after Mr. Lick (who left money for its foundation) . . 1888

A giant telescope, largest in the world, due to M. François Deloncle, erected at the Paris exhibition (see *Nature*) . . . . . 11 Oct. 1900
The Victoria telescope, the gift of Dr. Frank McClean, F.R.S., of Kent, mounted at the Cape, June, 1898; unveiled . . . . Sept. 1901
Great telescope erected in the Yerkes observatory in . . . . „

TELL, WILLIAM. The popular stories respecting him were demonstrated to be mythical by Professor Kopp of Lucerne, 1872.

TELLERS, see under *Exchequer*.

TELLURIUM, a rare metal, in its natural state containing small quantities of iron and gold, was discovered by Müller of Reichenstein, in 1782, and named by Klaproth.

TELODYNAMIC TRANSMITTER, invented by M. Hirn, is an arrangement of water-wheels, endless wires, and pulleys, for conveying and using the power of water-falls at a distance, and has been much used since 1850. The apparatus was shown at Paris in 1862.

TELPHERAGE, an application of electrical motion, invented by professor Fleeming Jenkin, aided by professors Ayrton and Perry, for conveying heavy goods, 2*d*. a ton per mile, 4 miles an hour, shown at Millwall, 1884.

A Telpherage company was formed. A Telpher line at the estate of lord Hampden at Glynde near Lewes, opened . . . . 17 Nov. 1885

TEMESWAR (Hungary), capital of the Banat, often besieged by the Turks. On 10 Aug. 1849, Haynau totally defeated the Hungarians besieging this town, and virtually ended the war.

TEMNOGRAPH, an instrument designed to plot to any accurate scale a section of the ground over which it travels. It works by frictional motion governed by two pendulous weights. Invented by A. M. Rymer-Jones in 1879.

TEMPERANCE SOCIETIES originated with Mr. Calhoun, who, while he was secretary of war in America, in order to counteract the habitual use of ardent spirits among the people, prohibited them altogether in the United States' army, 1818. See *Teetotaler* and *Permissive Bill*.

The first public temperance society in America was projected in 1825, and formed . . . 13 Feb. 1826
Many temperance societies immediately afterwards formed in America, England, and Scotland.
British and foreign temperance society formed, 29 June, 1831
The "Rechabites" (see Jer. xxxv.) began . about 1838
In Ireland, the rev. Dr. Edgar, of Belfast, published upon temperance in 1829-31; and Father Theobald Mathew, a Roman catholic clergyman, affirmed that he had made more than a million of converts to temperance 1841
Father Mathew arrived in America in July, 1849; was not so successful there; he died, aged 66, 8 Dec. 1856; centenary of his birth celebrated, 10 Oct. *et seq.* 1890; his statue at Dublin unveiled, 8 Feb. 1893
Anti-alcohol congress at the Hague . . 16 Aug. „
In England, the National temperance society, formed 1843
London temperance league 1851
The United Kingdom alliance for the legislative suppression of the sale of intoxicating liquors, 1 June, 1853; annual meetings up to 1896 *et seq.*
The National Temperance league, formed . . . 1856
Mr. J. B. Gough lectures in London, &c. . . „
United Kingdom Band of Hope Union formed 1855, by Mr. Stephen Shirley (died 24 Feb. 1897); 11,400 societies with 1,414,900 members, 1888; 26,881 societies, and 3,308,988 members . . 189
The National union for suppression of intemperance by means of "few houses, shorter hours, and better provisions," established end of . . . 1871
Church of England temperance society inaugurated by the archbishop of Canterbury and others at Lambeth . . . . 18 Feb. 1873
A Temperance hospital, where no alcoholic drinks are to be given for disease, was opened . 6 Oct. „
British Women's temperance association inaugurated at Newcastle-on-Tyne . . . . April, 1876
Mr. J. B. Gough lectures in London, Sept. 1878; Oct. 1879
London Temperance hospital, Hampstead-road, London, building (21,000*l*. out of 30,000*l*. subscribed) . . . . Sept. „
International exhibition of objects connected with temperance opened at the Agricultural hall, Islington 22 Aug. 1881
The Green and Blue Ribbon Armies of persons advocating temperance were prominent in 1882
A *Yellow Army* of moderate drinkers proposed (gen. Hicks) . . . . about Sept. „
National Temperance Jubilee at the Crystal palace; above 50,000 present [other fetes since] . 5 Sept. „
International temperance conferences: Brussels, 1880; London 1882; Antwerp 1885; London, June, 1895; Vienna . . . . 9 April, 1901
Mr. J. B. Gough dies in Philadelphia, aged 69, about 17 Feb. 1886
British and colonial congress in London, bishop of London president . . . . 14-16 July, „
"National Prohibition Party," Mr. Alex. Gustafson, in the *Christian Commonwealth*, strongly urges the total abolition of alcohol . April, 1887
The African anti-alcoholic international conference meets at Brussels . . . . . 20 April, 1899
A world's temperance congress, the abp. of Canterbury president, in London . . . . 11 June, 1900
See *Licenses*, 1899-1902.
Temperance demonstrations in the parks, London, 15 June, 1901
The abp. of Canterbury inaugurates a week's temperance mission at Leicester . 14 Oct. „
Salvation army temperance campaign started by a meeting at Exeter hall . . . . . 3 Feb. 1902
Band of Hope jubilee building, foundation-stone laid by the lord mayor in Old Bailey . 18 Feb. „
New association against drinking between meals, earl Roberts and lord Alverstone president and vice-president, reported . . . . 6 Feb. 1903
Mr. W. S. Caine, M.P., prominent spokesman of advanced temperance views in the house of commons, died, aged 59 . . . . 17 Mar. „

TEMPERED GLASS, see *Glass*.

TEMPLARS. The military order of "soldiers of the Temple," to protect pilgrims, was founded about 1118 by Baldwin II., king of Jerusalem, confirmed by pope Honorius II., 1128. The Templars were numerous in several countries, and came to England before 1185. Their wealth having excited the cupidity of the French kings, the order was suppressed by the council of Vienne, and part of its revenues was bestowed upon other orders about 1312. Numbers of the order were tried, condemned, and burned alive or hanged in 1308-10, and it suffered much persecution throughout Europe; 68 knights were burnt at Paris, 1310. Pope Clement V. abolished the order, April, 1312. The grand master Molay was burnt alive at Paris, 18 March, 1314. Their property in England was given to the Hospitallers, and the head of the order in England died in the Tower. See *Good Templars*.

TEMPLE (London), the dwelling of the Knights Templars, consecrated by Heraclius, patriarch of Jerusalem, 1185, at the suppression of the order, was purchased by the professors of the common law, and converted into inns, 1311, afterwards called the Inner and Middle Temple. Essex house, also a part of the house of the Templars, was called the Outer Temple, because it was situated without Temple-bar.

The *Temple hall* was built in 1572
St. Mary's, or the Temple church, situated in the Inner Temple, is a Gothic stone building, erected by the Templars in 1240, and is remarkable for its circular vestibule, and for the tombs of the crusaders, who were buried here. The church was recased with stone by Mr. Smirke in 1828; resignation of Dr. Charles John Vaughan, dean of Llandaff, Master of the Temple in 1869; succeeded by the rev. Canon Alfred Ainger, formerly reader (26 years) . . . . . June, 1894
The Middle Temple new library was opened by the prince of Wales, 31 Oct. 1861; he becomes treasurer of the Middle Temple . . . . Nov. 1886
New Inner Temple hall opened by princess Louise, 14 May, 1870
TEMPLE BAR, erected outside the gates; ordered to be rebuilt 27 June, 1669; erected by sir C. Wren; completed March 1672-3; cost 1397*l.* 10*s.*; room above contained books of Child and Co. for 200 years; reported dangerous March, 1868; began to sink 30 July; shored up 1868
Its removal voted by the common council, 27 Sept. 1876; the removal began 2 Jan., 1878; last stones removed . . . . . . 13 June, 1879
The stones, &c., given to sir H. B. Meux to be erected at Theobald's park, near Cheshunt, June, 1887; the bar set up . . . . . Nov. 1888
The memorial to mark the site (including statues of the queen and prince of Wales); cost about 11,550*l.*; inaugurated by prince Leopold, 8 Nov. 1880
"*Temple" at Paris*, formerly an asylum for debtors, and a prison during the republic, was made the site of a market in 1809, and rebuilt in 1864.
The "*City Temple*," a dissenters' chapel (minister, Dr. Parker, died 28 Nov. 1902), Holborn Viaduct, was opened . . . . . . 19 May, 1874

TEMPLES. The Egyptians were the first who erected temples to the gods.—*Herodotus*. The first erected in Greece is ascribed to Deucalion. —*Apollonius*.

The temple of Jerusalem built by Solomon, 1012 B.C. consecrated 1004; pillaged by Shishak, 971; repaired by Joash, 856; profaned by Ahaz, 740; restored by Hezekiah, 726; pillaged and fired by Nebuchadnezzar, 588, 587; rebuilt, 536; pillaged by Antiochus, 170; rebuilt by Herod, 18; destroyed by Titus, A.D. 70.
The temple of Apollo, at Delphi, first a cottage with boughs, built of stone by Trophonius, about 1200 B.C.; burnt by the Pisistratidæ, 548; a new temple raised by the family of the Alcmæonidæ, about 513.
Temple of Diana at Ephesus, built seven times; planned by Ctesiphon, 544 B.C.; fired by Eratostratus or Herostratus, to perpetuate his name, 356 B.C.; to re-build it employed 220 years; destroyed by the Goths, A.D. 260.
The temple of Piety was built by Acilius, on the spot where once a woman had fed with her milk her aged father, whom the senate had imprisoned, and excluded from all aliments.—*Val. Max.*
Temple of Theseus, built 480 B.C., is at this day the most perfect ancient edifice in the world.
Most of the heathen temples were destroyed throughout the Roman empire by Constantine the Great and Theodosius, 331-392. See *separate articles*.

TENANT, see *Rent*. Bills to amend the position of Irish tenants in relation to their landlords were brought into parliament by Mr. Sharman Crawford, 1835, sir Joseph Napier, 1852, Mr. Cardwell, 1860, Mr. Chichester Fortescue, 1866, Lord Naas, 1867. The Irish land bill settling the question passed 8 July, 1870. See *Ulster*.

The TENANTS' DEFENCE ASSOCIATION was formed in consequence of a declaration by Mr. Parnell and his party, at a meeting in the house of commons, that a new league was necessary to defend the Irish tenant farmers against their landlords, 14 July, 1889. The tenants were invited to contribute to the fund, and preliminary meetings were held. The association was inaugurated at Thurles, Tipperary, by Mr. Sexton, Mr. Redmond, and other M.P.'s., 600 delegates being present, 28 Oct. 1889. 40,000*l.* had been subscribed up to 30 Jan. 1890. In April, 1891, the scheme was reported unsuccessful.

TENASSERIM (N.E. India), ceded by Burmah to the British, 24 Feb. 1826.

TENERIFFE (Canaries, N.W. coast of Africa). The peak of Teneriffe, 12,198 feet above the level of the sea, was ascended in 1856 by professor C. Piazzi Smyth for astronomical observations. An earthquake in this island destroyed several towns and many thousands of people in 1704. See *Santa Cruz*. The governor, col. Pedro Bastanica, was hanged for murder of his mother-in-law, 28 Oct. 1890.

TEN MINUTES' BILL, see *Reform*.

TENNESSEE, a southern state of North America, was settled about 1760, and admitted into the union 1 June, 1796. An ordinance of secession from the union was passed—it is asserted illegally —on 6 May, 1861. On 23 Feb. 1862, the federal general Nelson entered Nashville, and in March, Andrew Johnson (afterwards the president of the United States) was made military governor over a large part of Tennessee. In Sept. 1863, Rosencrans expelled the confederate government. The representatives of Tennessee were re-admitted to the congress, July, 1866. Population, 1880, 1,542,359; 1890, 1,767,518; 1900, 2,020,616. Capital, Nashville.

Riots at Knoxville, through the employment of convicts in the mines; about 500 liberated by the mob, 30 Oct. *et seq.*; recaptured, 4 Nov. 1891.
See *United States*, 1892.

TENNIS. This game, brought from France, in the middle ages, became fashionable in England in the reign of Charles II. 1660-85; see *Jeu de Paume*. "Lawn Tennis" became fashionable in 1877, replacing croquet. Julian Marshall's "Annals of Tennis" published June, 1878. "Ping Pong," table tennis, very popular, 1901 *et seq*.

A National Lawn Tennis Association started Jan. 1888
Winners of the amateur championship, sir Edward Grey, 1889, 1891, 1895, 1896, 1898; Mr. F. B. Curtis, 1890; Mr. H. E. Crawley, 1892, 1893, 1894; Mr. J. B. Gribble, 1897; Mr. E. H. Miles, 1899-1903.

TEN TABLES, see *Decemvirs*.

TENTERDEN'S ACT, LORD, 2 & 3 Will. IV. c. 71, for shortening the time of prescription in certain cases (such as rights of way, and use of light), passed 1 Aug. 1832.

TEN THOUSAND, see *Retreat*.

TENTHS, see *Tithes*.

TENURES, the mode in which land is held. Military tenures in England were abolished in 1660. Lyttelton's book on Tenures is dated 1481.

TERBIUM, a metal sometimes found with yttrium (*which see*).

TERCEIRA, see *Azores*.

TERMS OF LAW AND VACATIONS. They were instituted in England from the Norman usage, the long vacation being suited to the time of the vintage in France, 14 Will. I. 1079.—*Glanville de Leg. Anglic.* They were gradually formed.—*Spelman.* The terms were fixed by statute 11 Geo. IV. and 1 Will. IV. 22 July, 1830: *Hilary Term* to begin 11 Jan. and end 31 Jan.; *Easter*, 15 April, to end 8 May; *Trinity*, 22 May, to end 12 June; *Michaelmas*, 2 Nov. to end 25 Nov. This act was amended 1 Will. IV. 15 Nov. 1830. New law terms (now sittings) were appointed under the Supreme Court of Judicature act, passed 5 Aug. 1873.

Michaelmas sittings: 2 Nov. to 21 Dec.
Hilary: 11 Jan. to Wednesday in Passion week.
Easter: Thursday in Easter week to Friday before Whit-Sunday.
Trinity: Tuesday after Whit-Sunday to 8 Aug.
The new *legal vacations* ordered to be as follows:—
Christmas: 24 Dec. to 6 Jan. *Easter*: Good Friday to Easter-Tuesday. *Whitsun*: Saturday before Whit-Sunday to Whit-Tuesday. *Long vacation*: 10 Aug. to 24 Oct.

TERNOVA, see *Tirnova*.

TERRITORIAL WATERS JURISDICTION ACT, passed, 16 Aug. 1878. It regulates the law relating to the trial of offences committed on the sea within a certain distance of the coasts of her majesty's dominions.

TERROR, see *Reign of*.

TERRY ALTS, insurgents of co. Clare, who committed numerous outrages after the union, 1801. They resembled the "Thrashers" of Connaught, the "Carders," the followers of "capt. Rock," 1822, and the Fenians (*which see*). *Brewer*.

TEST ACT, directing all officers, civil and military, under government, to receive the sacrament according to the forms of the church of England, and to take the oaths against transubstantiation, &c.; enacted 29 March, 1673. The Test and Corporation acts were repealed, 9 May, 1828. See *University Tests*.

TESTAMENT, see *Bibles* and *Wills*.

TESTER, *testone*, a silver coin struck in France by Louis XII. 1513; and also in Scotland in the time of Francis II. and of Mary, queen of Scots, 1559. It was so called from the head of the king, stamped upon it. In England the tester was of 12*d*. value in the reign of Henry VIII., afterwards of 6*d*. (still called a tester).

TESTRI (N. France). Pepin d'Heristal, invited by malcontents, here defeated and captured Thierry III., king of Austrasia, and established himself as duke, 687.

TETTENHALL (Staffordshire). It was probably at this place, then named Teotenheal, that the Danes were defeated by the Saxon king, Edward the Elder, 6 Aug. 910.

TETUAN (Morocco) was entered by the Spaniards 6 Feb. 1860, after gaining a decisive victory on 4 Feb. The general O'Donnell was made a grandee of the first class.

TEUTOBERG FOREST (the Teutobergiensis saltus, *Tacitus*), probably situate between Detmold and Paderborn, where Hermann, or Arminius, and the Germans defeated the Romans under Varus, with very great slaughter, A.D. 9. Varus and many of his officers preferred suicide to captivity. This defeat was regarded at Rome as a national calamity, and Augustus, in agony, cried, "Varus, give me my legions!"

TEUTONES, a people of Germany, who with the Cimbri made incursions upon Gaul, and cut to pieces two Roman armies, 113 and 105 B.C. They were at last defeated by the consul Marius at Aix, and a great number made prisoners, 102 B.C. (see *Cimbri*), with whom authors commonly join the Teutones. The appellation came to be applied to the German nation in general (hence *Deutsche*).

TEUTONIC ORDER, military knights established in the Holy Land about 1191, through the humanity of the Germans (Teutones) to the sick and wounded of the Christian army in the Holy Land, under Guy of Lusignan before Acre. The order was confirmed by a bull of pope Cœlestine III. On their return to Germany, the knights were invited to subdue and christianise the country now called Prussia and its neighbourhood, which they gradually accomplished. Their territories were invaded, and their army was defeated, with great slaughter, near Tannenberg, in East Prussia, by Jagellon, duke of Lithuania, 15 July, 1410, when the grand master and many of the knights were slain. A large part of their possessions was incorporated into Poland in 1466, and into Brandenburg about 1521. In 1525, the grand master was made a prince of the empire, and the order much weakened. Its remaining possessions were seized by Napoleon I. in 1809. Marienburg castle (about 1274) and chapel restored and dedicated by the emperor, 5 June, 1902. See *Prussia*, &c.

TEWKESBURY (Gloucestershire), where Edward IV. gained a decisive victory over the Lancastrians, 4 May, 1471. Queen Margaret, the consort of Henry VI., was taken prisoner, and her son killed. The queen was conveyed to the Tower of London, where king Henry expired soon after this fatal engagement; being, as is generally supposed, murdered by the duke of Gloucester, afterwards Richard III. The queen was ransomed in 1475 by the French king, Louis XI., for 50,000 crowns. Population, 1881, 5,100; 1891, 5,269; 1901, 5,500.

The *abbey*, founded by Robert Fitz-Hamon, cousin of William I., completed and consecrated 1123; grandly altered, 14th century; a monastery destroyed by Henry VIII.; the abbey spared; restored by G. G. Scott, 1877-9.

TEXAS (N. America) was settled by the French, 1687, who were expelled soon after. It revolted from Mexico in 1835; was helped by the Americans in 1836. Its independence was acknowledged in 1840. Its proposed annexation led to war between Mexico and the United States. It was admitted into the Union by the latter in 1845; seceded from it in 1861; submitted in 1865; re-admitted to state rights, March, 1870. The coast was desolated by a great storm, 15-18 Sept. 1875. Population 1880, 1,591,749; 1890, 2,235,523; 1900, 3,048,710; capital, Austin. See *Storms*.

Great fire at Galveston, above 700 residences burnt, loss about 800,000*l*.	13 Nov.	1885
About 1,000 Mexicans entered Rio Grande and caused disturbances, soon quelled	Sept.	1888
Diplomatic correspondence respecting the conduct of Mr. Lyall, British consul at Galveston, in relation to an Englishman convicted of burglary; he defends himself	Dec.	1890
Hurricane and great wave, 38 deaths, at Port Arthur and Sabine Pass	12 Sept.	1897
Overflow of the Brazos river; great damage; estimated deaths, 100 to 300	30 June–5 July,	1899
Great cloud-burst and floods, about 40 deaths and vast loss of property, reported	7 April,	1900
Hurricane and tidal wave, Galveston wrecked, nearly 8,000 perished; enormous loss, 9 Sept.; much looting, troops called in, about 25 persons shot, reported	12 Sept.	„
Tornado at Goliad, 98 deaths, 103 injured; estimated damage, 200,000 dol.	18 May,	1902

Oilfields discovered in Eastern Texas in 1900; rapid development, reported . . . June, 1902
Rapid rise of the seaport La Porte, San Jacinto bay, reported . . . . . . Dec. ,,

TEXEL (at the mouth of the Zuyder Zee, Holland). Its vicinity has been the scene of memorable naval engagements. An engagement between the English under Blake, Dean, and Monk, and the Dutch under Van Tromp and De Ruyter, in which the latter were worsted and admiral Van Tromp was killed, 31 July, 1653. Again, in the mouth of the Texel a sharp indecisive action took place between the allied English and French fleets under prince Rupert and comte d'Estrées, and the Dutch fleet under De Ruyter, 11 Aug. 1673. The Dutch fleet was vanquished by admiral Duncan on 11 Oct. 1797; see *Camperdown*. The Dutch fleet of 12 ships of war and thirteen Indiamen surrendered to admiral Mitchell, who, entering the Texel, possessed himself of them without firing a shot, 30 Aug. 1799.

TEXTILE. International conference, met at Manchester, 179,000 operatives represented, 24 July, 1894.

THALLIUM, a metal, occurring in the sulphuric acid manufacture, discovered by Mr. Wm. Crookes, by means of the spectrum analysis, March, 1861.

THAMES (London), the Roman Tamesis or Tamesa, Saxon Temese, Temesa, rises in four springs, at Ullen farm, near Coates, Gloucestershire. The head of the river in Wiltshire is about 170 miles from London bridge, and its whole course from source to mouth about 220 miles. See *London*, *London-bridge*, and *Frosts*.

The river rose so high at Westminster that the lawyers were brought out of the hall in boats . . 1235
It rose to a great height, 1736, 1747, 1762 . . 1791
The conservation of the Thames was given to the mayors of London 1489
The Thames was made navigable to Oxford . . 1624
It ebbed and flowed twice in three hours, 1658; again, three times in four hours, 22 March, 1682; again, twice in three hours . . . . 24 Nov. 1777
An act of parliament gave the conservation of the Thames to the corporation of London; twelve conservators were to be appointed—three by the government 1857
In consequence of the great contamination of the Thames by the influx of the sewage of London, and the bad odours emanating from it in the summer of 1858, an act was passed empowering the Metropolitan Board of Works (*which see*) to undertake its purification by constructing new drainage 1858
The Thames Angling Preservation Society (established about 1838) is revived in . . . 1863
Mr. Leach, engineer of the conservators, reported that "the river is dreadfully mismanaged from its source to its mouth" . . . . . 23 July, ,,
The Thames navigation acts, appointing five more conservators, &c., and prohibiting pollution by sewage, &c., passed . . . . . Aug. 1866
The powers of the act extended up to Staines . 1867
New bye-laws to protect the fish in the Upper Thames passed by the conservators . 14 June, 1869
Highest tide known for many years; river overflowed from Gravesend to its tidal limit; great damage and distress in Blackfriars and Lambeth; Woolwich arsenal flooded and suffered; river said to have risen above 29 feet . . 15 Nov. 1875
The lord mayor and others (with carriages and horses) cross by ferry from Rotherhithe to Wapping . . . . 1 Nov. ,,
Thames Steam Ferry; first pile of a landing-place at Wapping struck by Lord Mayor Stone, 11 Oct., 1875; first steam ferry boat, *Jessie May*, launched . . . . 26 Feb. 1876
In consequence of the wreck of the saloon steamer *Princess Alice*, by collision with the *Bywell Castle*, 3 Sept., a committee appointed by the Board of Trade to inquire into matters connected with safety of navigation, &c., in the river . Sept. 1878
Thames traffic committee of the Board of Trade appointed 1879
Floods on the south side, through heavy rains and high tides, 2, 3, Jan. 1877; during severe frost, 18, 19 Jan. 1881
Very high tide, 19 Feb.; another, very destructive, Charing-cross pier carried away . . 28 Oct. 1882
Appointment of committee to inquire into the acts for preserving the Thames for recreation agreed to . . . . 11 March, 1884
Thames Preservation act passed . . 14 Aug. 1885
Greenwich great steam ferry formally opened 13 Feb. 1888; one between North and South Woolwich (free) formally opened by lord Rosebery 23 March, 1889
Thames Conservancy act, repealing previous acts, passed 1894
Destructive overflow of the Thames (see *Inundations*) . . . . Nov. ,,
The upper Thames frozen over at Windsor, &c.; navigation impeded at Sheerness and London, Feb. 1895
Appeal respecting prevention of floods by a deputation to the Board of Trade . . 19 March, 1896
New works undertaken at Teddington, Staines, &c. ,,
Lower Thames navigation commission appointed, Nov. 1894; report presented . . . April, ,,
The Thames Conservancy open a new channel at Teddington and other improvements at Maidenhead . . . . 22 Nov. 1897
Salmon (600) placed in the river at Teddington in 1901; other consignments in 1902
THAMES TUNNEL. One proposed, 1799; shaft sunk, 1804. The present one proposed by I. K. Brunel to form a communication between Rotherhithe and Wapping, 1823. The bill received the royal assent . . . 24 June, 1824
The shaft was begun, and the first brick laid by Mr. Smith, 2 March; the excavation commenced, 1 April; the first horizontal excavation in Dec. 1825
At a distance of 544 feet from the shaft, the first irruption took place . . . . 18 May, 1827
The second irruption, by which six workmen perished . . . . 12 Jan. 1828
The tunnel was opened throughout for foot-passengers, 25 March, 1843. [The length of the tunnel is 1300 feet; its width is 35 feet; height, 20 feet; clear width of each archway, including foot-path, about 14 feet; thickness of earth between the crown of the tunnel and the bed of the river, about 15 feet.]
The Thames Tunnel company was dissolved in . 1866
The tunnel, transferred to the East London railway company, was closed . . . . . 21 July, ,,
The *Tower subway*, an iron tube tunnel beneath the Thames, constructed by Messrs. Barlow, was begun 16 Feb. 1869, and privately opened, April, 1870. It was said to have cost only 16,000*l*.
A *tubular Thames tunnel*, chiefly for workmen, between North and South Woolwich, begun 23 Aug. 1876
Blackwall Tunnel (see *Tunnel*) 1891
New Greenwich and Millwall tunnel opened to the public . . . . 4 Aug. 1902
New bridge at Kew opened by the king . 20 May, 1903
Widening of London bridge, commenced 1901, completed 1904
New bridge to replace Southwark bridge, announced 1903

THAMES EMBANKMENT: recommended by sir Christopher Wren, 1666, and by Wm. Paterson, founder of the bank of England, about 1694. It was the corporation embanked a mile in 1767. It was further recommended by Gwynne, 1767; by sir Frederick Eden, 1798; by sir Frederick Trench, 1824; by James Walker; by the duke of Newcastle, 1844; and by John Martin the painter, 1856. In 1860, the Metropolitan Board of Works recommended that the north bank of the Thames should be embanked, whereby the bed of the river would be improved; a low-level sewer could be easily constructed beneath a broad roadway; docks to be constructed within the embankment wall; the expense to be defrayed by the city duties on coal, and by means provided by government. The principle of this recommendation was approved by parliament, and a committee was appointed, which sat for the first time, 30 April, 1861

An act for "embanking the *North* side of the Thames from Westminster bridge to Blackfriars bridge, and for making new streets in and near thereto," passed 7 Aug.; the work begun in Nov. 1862

First stone of the northern (Victoria) embankment (designed by Mr. [aft. sir] Joseph W. Bazalgette) laid by Mr. Thwaites near Whitehall stairs, 20 July, 1864; the footway opened to the public, 30 July, 1868; the roadway opened by the prince of Wales . . . . . . 13 July, 1870

The proposal to build public offices upon the reclaimed land negatived by the house of commons, July, ,,

"*Cleopatra's Needle*" (see *Obelisk*), set up on the embankment . . . . . 12 Sept. 1878

Mr. J. W. Bazalgette (aft. sir) presented a report, with a plan for embanking the *South* side of the Thames, 6 Nov. 1862; act for carrying it out passed . . . . . . 28 July, 1863

Southern (Albert) Embankment. First stone laid by Mr. (aft. sir Wm.) Tite, 28 July, 1866; partially opened . . . . . . 24 Nov. 1869

Thames Mystery. See *London*, 1873.

Chelsea (Victoria) Embankment. Authorised by parliament, 13 July, 1868; commenced 5 Aug., 1871, opened by the duke of Edinburgh 9 May, 1874

Kingston, Kew, Hampton Court, and other bridges freed from the toll by acts passed 1869 and 1874, 1870–1878

Avenue theatre opened . . . . . 11 March, 1882

The Thames at Windsor and other places frozen, end of Dec. 1890

Steamboat service stopped, about 26 Dec. 1890; resumed . . . . . . about 30 Jan. 1891

The Thames, from Westminster to London Bridge, nearly closed by ice . . . . . . 6 Jan. ,,

Thames Embankment tramways act passed, 27 June, 1892

Memorial to sir Joseph Bazalgette unveiled, 6 Nov. 1901

THANE, a Saxon title of nobility, abolished in England at the conquest, upon the introduction of the feudal system, and in Scotland by king Malcolm III., when the title of earl was adopted, 1057.

THANET (Kent) was the first permanent settlement of the Saxons, about 449. The Danes held a part of it, 853-865, and ravaged it 980, 988 *et seq.*

THANKSGIVINGS, special national, were offered up at St. Paul's cathedral for the defeat of Spanish Armada, queen Elizabeth present, 8 Sept. and 24th Nov. 1588; for Marlborough's victories, 12 Nov. 1702, and 7 Sept. 1704; for George III.'s recovery from illness, 23 April, 1789; for Duncan's and other naval victories, 19 Dec. 1797; for the recovery of the prince of Wales, 27 Feb. 1872; for the 60th year of the queen's reign, 22 June, 1897; for the conclusion of peace in S. Africa, 8 June, 1902; and for the recovery of the king 26 Oct. 1902.

THAPSUS (N. Africa). Near here Julius Cæsar totally defeated the army of the party which supported the policy of Pompey, Feb. 46 B.C. The suicide of Cato followed soon after.

THEATINES, a religious order, the first who assumed the title of regular clerks, founded by Caraffa, bishop of Theate, or Chieti, in Naples (afterwards pope Paul IV.), 1524, to repress heresy. They first established themselves in France, according to Hénault, in Paris, 1644. The Theatines vainly endeavoured to revive among the clergy the poverty of the apostles.

THEATRE (Greek *theatron*, "a place for seeing"). Greek theatres for the exhibition of the drama and musical performances were gradually developed from the ring in which songs and choruses were performed in honour of Dionysus or Bacchus. Greek theatres are well described and illustrated in Mr. Robert W. Lowe's article *Theatre* in Chambers's Encyclopedia, 1892. The theatre of Dionysus at Athens could contain 30,000 spectators, and that at Megalopolis (*which see*), 44,000. The revival of the drama in the 16th century led to the construction of modern theatres on Greek models such as that at Rome by Bramante, 1580; the *Teatro Olimpico* at Vicenza by Palladio, 1584. "Modern Opera Houses and Theatres," by Edwin O. Sachs, Vol. II., published Jan. 1898. See *Amphitheatres*, *Comédie Française*, and *Operas*.

THEATRES IN ENGLAND. The first royal licence for a theatre in England was in 1574, to master Burbage and four others, servants of the earl of Leicester, to act plays at the Globe, Bankside. It is stated the first play-house in London was erected at Shoreditch, and called the "Theatre" in 1576, and that the Curtain near it, was erected in 1577. The Blackfriars was built in 1596. The other London theatres in Elizabeth's reign were Whitefriars, Rose, Hope, Swan, Red Bull, Cockpit or Phœnix, and several others. Shakespeare and his fellow actors erected the Globe theatre on Bankside, about 1594. The prices of admission are said to have been—gallery, *2d.*; lords' rooms, *1s.*; see *Drama*, *Drury Lane*, and other theatres. The theatres were closed by parliament, 1642-60.

The first play-bill was dated 8 April, 1663, and issued from Drury-lane; it runs thus: "By his Majestie his company of Comedians at the New Theatre in Drury-lane, will be acted a comedy called the *Humovrous Lievtenant.*" After detailing the characters, it concludes thus: "The play will begin at three o'clock exactly" . . 8 April, 1663

Lincoln's-inn theatre (the Duke's theatre) opened by sir Wm. Davenant's patent, 25 April, 1662; rebuilt 1695

Acts for licensing plays and play-houses (placing them under the lord chamberlain) 10 Geo. II. c. 28 1737

Act for regulating theatres (6 & 7 Vict. c. 68), 22 Aug. 1843

See *Independent Theatre*, 1891–2.

See *Trials*, 1843.

Marionettes or Puppets produced at the Adelaide gallery 1852

Several of the theatres first opened on Sunday evenings for religious worship, and filled . Jan. 1860

Lord Chamberlain warned managers against indecent dances and scanty dresses 28 Jan. 1869 and 21 Dec. 1874

Introduction of the *queue*, as at French theatres, by Mr. D'Oyly Carte, at the Savoy . 29 Dec. 1882

The employment of children under ten years of age forbidden in theatres by the Home Secretary about 5 Dec. 1886

Theatres in Great Britain, 166; in London, 33, summer of 1868

In London, Jan. 1876, 45; Jan. 1885, 43; Dec. 1891, 55; Dec. 1894, 60.

Actors' Association (protective) initiated at Manchester, constituted at the Lyceum, London, 16 March, 1891

Parliamentary committee on theatres and music-halls appointed, March; recommend in their report that the lord chamberlain's control be continued . . . . 2 June, 1892

Mr. Henry Irving, in a lecture at the Royal Institution, claims for acting the position of a fine art, 1 Feb. 1895

Mr. Wm. Archer's "Theatrical World," 1893–4–5, published 1894–6

DRURY LANE.

Killigrew's patent . . . . . . 25 April, 1662
Opened . . . . 8 April, 1663
Nell Gwynn performed 1666
Theatre burnt down with 60 houses . . Jan. 1672
Rebuilt by sir C. Wren, and opened 26 March, 1674
Cibber, Wilkes, Booth 1712
Garrick's *début* here 1742
Garrick and Lacy's tenure (revival of Shakspeare) . 1747
Theatrical fund founded by Mr. Garrick, 1766; incorporated 1775
Interior rebuilt by Adams; opened . 23 Sept. ,,
Garrick's farewell . . . . . 10 June, 1776
Sheridan's management . . . . . ,,
Mrs. Siddons' *début* as a *star* . 10 Oct. 1782
Mr. Kemble's *début* as *Hamlet* . . 30 Sept. 1783
The theatre rebuilt on a large scale, and re-opened, 12 March, 1794
Charles Kemble's first appearance (as *Malcolm* in *Macbeth*) . . . . . 21 April, ,,
Dowton's first appearance (as *Sheva* in the *Jew*), 11 Oct. 1796
Hatfield fired at George III. . . . . 11 May, 1800
The theatre burnt . . . . . 24 Feb. 1809
Rebuilt by Wyatt, and re-opened with a prologue by lord Byron . . . . . 10 Oct. 1812
Edmund Kean's appearance (as *Shylock*) 26 Jan. 1814
Mr. Elliston, lessee . . . . . 3 Oct. 1819
Madame Vestris's first appearance . 19 Feb. 1820
Real water introduced in the *Cataract of the Ganges*, 27 Oct. 1823
Mr. Price, lessee . . . . . . July, 1826
Ellen Tree's appearance (as *Violante*) . 23 Sept. ,,
Charles Kean's appearance (as *Norval*) 1 Oct. 1827
Mrs. Nisbet's first appearance (as the *Widow Cheerly*) 9 Oct. 1829
Mr. Alexander Lee's and captain Polhill's management 1830
Mr. Alfred Bunn, lessee 1831
Mr. Forrest's first appearance (as *Spartacus*), 17 Oct. 1836
Mr. Hammond's management 1839
German operas commenced here . . 15 March, 1841
Mr. Macready's management . . . . ,,
Mr. Bunn again lessee 1843
Miss Clara Webster burnt on the stage, 14 Dec.; and died . . . . . . 16 Dec. 1844
Mr. Anderson's management 1849
Mr. Macready's farewell . . . 26 Feb. 1851
Mr. Bunn, lessee and manager 1852
Mr. E. T. Smith 1853-9
English opera (Mr. Harrison and Miss Pyne) . . 1858
Italian opera, part of 1859-78
Opened by Mr. E. T. Smith . . . 15 Oct. 1860
Suddenly closed . . . . . 20 April, 1861
Mr. G. V. Brooke appears (as *Othello*) . 27 Oct. ,,
[Drowned in the *London*: see *Wrecks*, 11 Jan. 1866.]
Mr. Falconer . . . . . . Dec. 1862-1865
Messrs. Falconer and Chatterton, managers, Jan. 1866
Re-opened with Halliday's *King of Scots*, 26 Sept ,,
Re-opened with *Antony and Cleopatra* . 20 Sept. 1873
Balfe's posthumous *Talisman* produced 11 June, 1874
Balfe's statue uncovered . . . . 25 Sept. ,,
Salvini as *Othello* 1 April; as *Hamlet* . 31 May, 1875
Wagner's *Lohengrin* . . . . . 12 June, ,,
Boucicault's new drama the *Shaughraun* produced 4 Sept. ,,
Manager and lessee, F. B. Chatterton . . 1876-78
Re-opened with *Richard III.* . . . 23 Sept. 1876
Mr. Wills's *Charles II.* . . . . 24 Sept. 1877
Theatre suddenly closed; strike of actors, &c. 4 Feb. 1879
Saxe-Meiningen Court Company (Germans), *Julius Cæsar* . . . . . 30 May *et seq.* 1881
Mad. Ristori as *Lady Macbeth* . . . July, 1882
Mr. (afterwards sir) Augustus Harris, lessee and manager . . . . . Sept. 1879-92
Carl Rosa's opera company . . . part of 1883-5
Re-opens the house (*Le Nozze de Figaro*) 31 May, 1886
Re-opens with the *The Spanish Armada* by Messrs. H. Hamilton and A. Harris . . 22 Sept. 1888
The *Royal Oak* performed . 23 Sept.—30 Nov. 1889
Jack and the Beanstalk . . . 26 Dec. *et seq.* ,,
Carl Rosa company, Mr. Henry Bruce, director, Gounod's *Romeo and Juliet*, &c. 5 April—10 May, 1890
Mr. Cowen's new opera *Thorgrim* 22 April *et seq.* ,,
House closed . . . . 7 June, ,,
Re-opened; *A Million of Money* . 6 Sept. *et seq.* 1890
Beauty and the Beast . 26 Dec. 1890—4 April, 1891
Never too Late to Mend . . 11 April—23 May, ,,
Boucicault's *Formosa* . . . 26 May *et seq.* ,,
Drink . . . . . . 23 June—4 Aug. ,,
House closed.
A Sailor's Knot, new drama by Henry Pettitt, 5 Sept.—5 Dec. ,,
Special English opera performances on Saturdays, 26 Sept.—17 Oct. ,,
Humpty-Dumpty . . 26 Dec. 1891—9 April, 1892
Overflow from Covent Garden, foreign operas, occasionally . . . 13 June—29 July, ,,
The Prodigal Daughter, by H. Pettitt and sir A. Harris . . . . 17 Sept.–10 Dec. ,,
Little Bo-Peep, Little Red Riding-Hood, and *Hop O' My Thumb* . . . 26 Dec. 1892–25 March, 1893
Operas: *The Bohemian Girl, Carmen*, and others, 3–29 April, ,,
Comédie Française: Plays by Racine, Molière (Windsor Castle, 27 June) . 12 June–12 July, ,,
Operas: Wagner's *Die Walküre*, &c. 15–24 July, ,,
The duke of Bedford renews the lease for 7 years, July, ,,
A Life of Pleasure, by Henry Pettitt and sir Augustus Harris . . . 21 Sept.–9 Dec. ,,
[See *Princess's*, below.]
The Bohemian Girl brought out, 27 Nov. 1843; performed in memory of Balfe . . . 27 Nov. ,,
Genoveva, opera by Robt. Schumann, performed by students (Royal College of Music) . 6 Dec. ,,
Robinson Crusoe (pantomime), by Harry Nicholls and sir Augustus Harris, 26 Dec. 1893–10 March, 1894
English opera: *Maritana*, &c. 24 March *et seq.* ,,
Gentleman Jack (American drama), 21 April–12 May, ,,
German opera: 8 performances (Tuesdays and Saturdays) . . . . 19 June–21 July, ,,
The Derby Winner . . . . 15 Sept.–15 Dec. ,,
Dick Whittington (pantomime), 26 Dec. 1894–16 March, 1895
English opera: *Bohemian Girl*, &c., 13 April–1 June, ,,
Eight performances by Eleonora Duse and company . . . . 3 June, ,,
Coburg court company; comic operas, &c., 17 June–13 July, ,,
Cheer, Boys, Cheer . . . . 19 Sept.–14 Dec. ,,
Cinderella (pantomime) . 26 Dec.–21 March, 1896
English opera season: *Faust*, etc. 4 April–9 May, ,,
Cheap summer season: Chas. Dickens' *Jo*, 13 May; closed . . . . 29 May, ,,
Sir Augustus Harris, born 1852, died . 22 June, ,,
Autumn season: Mr. John Coleman, manager, *The Duchess of Coolgardie*, by Messrs. Euston Leigh and Cyril Clare, 19 Sept.–26 Nov.; *The Kiss of Delilah*, by George Grant and James Lisle, 27, 28 Nov. ,,
Aladdin (pantomime): manager, Mr. Oscar Barrett, 26 Dec.–end of March, 1897
Mr. Arthur Collins becomes managing director, on behalf of a company (limited) . . 29 March, ,,
The White Heather, by Cecil Raleigh and Henry Hamilton, 1st time . . 16 Sept. *et seq.* ,,
The Babes in the Wood (pantomime), 27 Dec.–26 March, 1898
Performance (selections) for the benefit of Miss Nellie Farren, over 6,000*l.* realised . 17 March, ,,
The White Heather (revived) . 12 May–25 June, ,,
The Great Ruby, by Cecil Raleigh and Henry Hamilton . . . . . 15 Sept.–10 Dec. 1898
The Forty Thieves, pantomime, 26 Dec.–18 March, 1899
Hearts are Trumps, spectacular drama, by Cecil Raleigh, first time . . 16 Sept.–9 Dec. ,,
Jack and the Beanstalk, pantomime, 26 Dec.–21 March, 1900
Marsac of Gascony, by Edward Vroom, 21 April–11 May, ,,
Grand dramatic and musical matinée for Homes of Rest for Soldiers . . . . 15 May, ,,
Canadian matinée: Ottawa fire fund . 19 June, ,,
The Price of Peace, by Cecil Raleigh, first time, 22 Sept.–12 Dec. ,,
The Sleeping Beauty and the Beast, pantomime, 26 Dec.–30 March, 1901
The Great Millionaire, by Cecil Raleigh, first time, 19 Sept.–7 Dec. ,,

Blue Beard, pantomime . 26 Dec.–19 March, 1902
Ben-Hur, by gen. Lew Wallace, dramatised by Wm. Young . . . . . . 3 April–18 July, „
The Best of Friends, by Cecil Raleigh, first time, 18 Sept.–6 Dec. „
Mother Goose, pantomime . . . 26 Dec. „

COVENT GARDEN.

The theatre opened by Rich . . . . 7 Dec. 1732
Beef-steak Society, founded by Rich and Lambert . 1735
Theatrical fund instituted 1760; incorporated . 1764
Mr. Harris's tenure 1767
Lewis's first appearance (as *Belcour*) . 15 Sept. 1773
Miss Reay killed by Mr. Hackman, coming from the house . . . . . . 7 April, 1779
Jack Johnstone's first appearance in Irish characters 3 Oct. 1783
Munden's appearance . . . . . 2 Dec. 1790
Fawcett's first appearance (as *Caleb*) . 21 Sept. 1791
G. F. Cooke's appearance (as *Richard III.*), 31 Oct. 1800
Braham's appearance . . . . 9 Dec. 1801
Mr. Kemble's management 1802
Appearance of Master Betty, the *Infant Roscius*, 1 Dec. 1804
Lewis's last appearance (as the *Copper Captain*), 28 May, 1808
Theatre burnt down . . . . . 20 Sept. „
Rebuilt by R. Smirke, R.A., and re-opened with *Macbeth* . . . . . . 18 Sept. 1809
The O. P. Riot (*which see*) . 18 Sept. to 10 Dec. „
Horses first introduced; in *Bluebeard* . 18 Feb. 1811
The farewell benefit of Mrs. Siddons (immense house) 29 June, 1812
Mrs. Siddons performed once afterwards, in June, 1819, for Mr. and Mrs. C. Kemble's benefit.
Miss Stephens' first appearance (as *Mandane*), 7 Sept. 1813
Miss Foote's appearance here (as *Amanthis*), 26 May, 1814
Miss O'Neill's appearance (as *Juliet*) . 6 Oct. „
Miss Kelly fired at by George Barnet, in the house, 7 Feb. 1816
Mr. Macready's first appearance (as *Orestes*), 16 Sept. „
Mr. J. P. Kemble's farewell (as *Coriolanus*), 23 June, 1817
Henry Harris's management 1818
Charles Kemble's management 1823
Miss Fanny Kemble's appearance (as *Juliet*), 5 Oct. 1829
Mr. Fawcett's farewell . . . . 21 May, 1830
Charles Young's farewell . . . . 30 May, 1832
Mr. Macready's management 1837
Madame Vestris's management 1839
Miss Adelaide Kemble's appearance (as *Norma*), 2 Nov. 1841
Charles Kemble again . . . . 10 Sept. 1842
Mr. Laurent's management . . . . 26 Dec. 1844
Opened by F. Gye for Italian opera . 6 April, 1847
Destroyed by fire (during a *bal masqué*, conducted by Anderson the Wizard) . . . 5 March, 1856
New theatre (by Barry) opened by Mr. F. Gye (*Les Huguenots*) . . . . . . 15 May, 1858
English opera (Miss Pyne and Mr. Harrison), Oct. 1859
All principal actors perform parts of plays for the benefit of the Dramatic College . 29 March, 1860
Balfe's *Bianca* brought out . . . . 6 Dec. „
Italian opera (Mr. Gye) . . . . . April, 1861
Last appearance of Grisi . . . . 3 Aug. „
English opera (Pyne and Harrison) . . 31 Oct. „
Italian opera (Mr. Gye) . . . . . April, 1862
English opera (Pyne and Harrison) . . 25 Aug. „
Italian opera (Mr. Gye) . . . . 7 April, 1863
Gounod's *Faust* . . . . . . July, „
English opera (Pyne and Harrison . . 12 Oct. „
Italian opera (Mr. Gye) . . . . . April, 1864
English opera, &c. (Opera Company, Limited), 17 Oct. „
Italian opera (Mr. Gye) . . . 28 April, 1865
Becomes the property of a company, Mr. Gye, manager . . . . Aug. „
Reopened (Mr. Gye) April, 1866; 2 April, 1867; 31 March, 1868
Opened by Mr. Mapleson's company . 24 Oct. „
Opera season (Gye and Mapleson) . 29 May, 1869
Mr. Dion Boucicault lessee and manager 29 Aug. 1872
Italian opera 1873-8
Mr. F. Gye, many years lessee, died through accident with gun . . . . . 5 Dec. 1878
A. & S. Gatti, managers . . . . . Dec. 1878
Mr. Lionel Gye, lessee 1878-81
"Royal English opera" under Mr. T. H. Friend; short season . . . . . . 7 Jan. 1884
Sig. Salvini's company, *Othello*, &c. . 28 Feb. „
Grand International cirque . 26 Dec. *et seq.* „
William Holland, lessee and manager 1884-5
Mr. Mapleson, with Italian opera June and July, 1885
Grand demonstration to Madame Adelina Patti 25 July, „
Revival of Italian opera, signor Bevignani, conductor . . . . . . 25 May, 1886
Italian opera, opened under Mr. Mapleson (Verdi's *Traviata* performed) . . . 12 March, 1887
Donizetti's *La Favorita* performed . 24 May, „
Donizetti's *Lucrezia Borgia* performed 14 May; successful season; closed . . 21 July, 1888
Italian opera season, Mr. A. Harris, director, 20 May–27 July, 1889
Promenade concerts, Mr. F. Thomas Sept.—Nov. „
Cinderella and grand circus . 26 Dec. *et seq.* „
Italian opera, Gounod's *Faust*, &c. 19 May—28 July, 1890
Promenade concerts (Mr. F. Thomas), 9 Aug.—4 Oct. „
Italian opera (Sig. Lago) . . 18 Oct.—29 Nov. „
Million of Money . . 15 Dec. 1890—17 Jan. 1891
Carnival balls . . . 3, 17 Feb.; 4, 8 March, „
Lent oratorios, *Elijah*, &c. . 14 Feb.—7 March, „
Italian opera (Mr., afterwards sir, A. Harris), *Orfeo* &c. . . . . . 6 April—27 July, „
Promenade concerts . . . 12 Sept.—10 Oct. „
Opera season: *Roméo et Juliette*, &c. 20 Oct.—20 Nov. „
Carnival balls, 30 Dec. 1891; 13 Jan., 10 Feb., 1 March, 23 March, 20 April, 1892.
Italian Opera . . . . 16 May, 1892
Cavalleria Rusticana, by Mascagni, and other pieces, 16 May, „
German opera, &c. . . . 8 June—28 July, „
Opera season: *Orfeo* and *Cavalleria Rusticana*, &c., 10 Oct.–Dec. „
The Prodigal Daughter . 12 Dec. 1892–14 Jan. 1893
Carnival season: fancy dress balls, 25 Jan., 8 Feb., 22 Feb., 8 March, 21 March, 12 April . „
Opera season: dress recitals . 28 Jan.–4 Feb. „
Operas: *Lohengrin*, &c. . . 15 May–29 July, „
[State performance of Gounod's *Roméo et Juliette*, 4 July, 1893; *The Veiled Prophet*, by Mr. Villiers Stanford; libretto by Mr. Barclay Squire, 26 July, 1893.]
Promenade concerts; Farley Sinkins, manager; Mr. Cowen, conductor . . . 9 Oct. „
William Holland's *Noah's Ark*, 26 Dec. 1893–March, 1894
Carnival season: fancy dress balls, 31 Jan., 14 Feb., 28 Feb., 14 March, 4 April, 18 April . . „
Royal opera season: *Manon Lescaut*, by Puccini (1st time) . . . . . . 14 May, „
Verdi's *Falstaff* . . . . . . 19 May, „
House closed . . . . . . 30 July, „
Fancy dress balls, 30 Nov., 11 Dec., 14 Dec., 31 Dec. (juvenile fancy fête, 26 Dec. 1894), 18 Jan. 1, 15, 26 Feb., 15, 29 March, 24 April 1895
Royal opera season: Verdi's *Otello*, 13 May, &c.; F. H. Cowen's *Harold*; libretto by sir Edward Malet; 1st performance, 8 June; closed 29 July, „
English opera season: *Tannhäuser*, *Valkyrie*, etc., 12 Oct.–9 Nov. „
Fancy dress balls . . . Dec.; Jan.–April, 1896
Royal opera season: *Roméo et Juliette*, etc., 11 May–28 July, „
Fancy dress balls . . . 18 Nov.–9 April, 1897
Grand concert: in aid of the prince of Wales's hospital fund . . . . . . 8 May, „
Royal opera season: *Faust*, etc. . 10 May–July, „
State performance: *Tannhäuser*, etc. 23 June, „
Carl Rosa opera season (see *Opera, English*): Puccini's new opera *La Bohème*, 2 Oct.; *Tannhäuser*, 4 Oct., etc.; closed . . . . 30 Oct. „
Fancy dress balls . . . 17 Nov.–5 April, 1898
Royal opera season: *Lohengrin*, etc. . 9 May. „
Wagnerian cycle: *Das Rheingold*, &c., 6 June–26 July, „
Fancy dress balls . . 4 Nov. 1898–10 March, 1899
Royal opera: special Wagner performances: *Lohengrin*, 8 May *et seq.*, and other operas; *Romeo et Juliette* . . . . 23 July, „
Promenade concerts . . . . 2 Sept.–Oct. „
Fancy dress balls . . 27 Oct. 1899–23 March 1900

Opera season: *Faust*, 14 May; other operas; Wagner cycle, 6 June *et seq.*; Puccini's *La Tosca*, first time here, 12 July; other operas . 30 July, 1901
Fancy dress balls . . 26 Oct. 1900–29 March, ,,
Royal opera: *Romeo et Juliette*, 13 May; *Much Ado About Nothing*, by Dr. Villiers Stanford, first time, 30 May; closed . . 29 July, ,,
Fancy dress balls . . 11 Oct. 1901–14 March, 1902
Popular concerts, Sousa's band, begin . 23 Nov. ,,
Opera season: Wagnerian cycle: *Lohengrin*, &c. (and other operas) . . . 8 May, ,,
Der Wald, by Miss E. M. Smyth, first time, 18 July; closed with *Rigoletto* . . 28 July, ,,
Domino ball . . . . 8 Aug. ,,
Moody-Manners' opera season: *Carmen*, &c., 25 Aug.–27 Sept. ,,
Fancy dress balls (Fridays) . . 10 Oct. *et seq.* ,,

HIS MAJESTY'S THEATRE, OR ITALIAN OPERA-HOUSE.

Opera-house opened. *Pennant*. (See *Opera-house*). 1705
Madame Rachel's appearance . . 10 May, 1841
Mr. Lumley's management . . . 1842
Jenny Lind's first appearance . . 4 May, 1847
Association formed for conducting financial affairs of the house 1852
Jullien's concerts . . . . Oct. 1857
Festive performances on the marriage of the princess royal . . . . Jan. 1858
Macfarren's *Robin Hood* brought out . . 11 Oct. 1860
[Not opened in 1861.]
Italian opera (Mr. Mapleson) . . . 1862-67
Burnt down; great loss . . . 6 Dec. 1867
Rebuilt—its affairs in Chancery . . . 1872
Sold for 31,000*l.* . . . 20 May, 1874
[Lease to earl Dudley, till 1891.]
Opened for Italian opera by Mr. Mapleson 1877 *et seq.*
Carl Rosa's company, Wagner's operas, &c., part of 1879-80
Carl Rosa, Wagner's *Lohengrin* . 14 Jan. *et seq.* 1882
Sig. Rossi as *Lear* . . . 10 June, ,,
Opened by M. Carillon (Cargill); Gounod's *Faust*; performance stopped by strike of unpaid company, carpenters, &c., riot . . 6 March, 1886
Mr. Mayer, lessee; appearance of madame Sarah Bernhardt in *Fedora*, &c. . 26 April, *et seq.* ,,
French opera . . . . 22 Nov. ,,
Promenade concerts inaugurated by colonel Mapleson 20 Aug.; by Mr. Van Biene . . 12 Nov. 1887
Italian opera season begins (under Mr. Mapleson) 1 June, 1889
The establishment of a company "Her Majesty's Theatre (limited)," with a capital of 40,000*l.* to restore the theatre to its original position, proposed by lord Hay, Mr. Henry J. Leslie, and others . . . . June, ,,
Promenade concerts . . . 17 Aug.—Oct. ,,
Opera company (lessees), *Cinderella* 26 Dec. *et seq.* ,,
The house suddenly closed; the company bankrupt . . . . 29 Jan. 1890
French plays. Gymnase company, including S. Bernhardt, 2–16 June. Mr. M. L. Mayer, manager . . . . . ,,
House closed, 12 July, 1890; pulled down, 1892–3; new theatre on the same site designed by Mr. C. J. Phipps (died 25 May, 1897).
House opened, proprietor and manager, Mr. H. Beerbohm Tree, *The Seats of the Mighty*, by Gilbert Parker, 28 April–5 June; short runs: *Trilby*, 7 June; *The Red Lamp*, 12 June; *The Silver Key*, adapted from the French by Sydney Grundy, 10 July–11 Aug: *Hamlet*, 12 and 13 Aug. 1897
The Hedmondt opera season: *Rip Van Winkle*, opera by Wm. Akerman and F. Leoni, 1st time, 4 Sept.; Humperdinck's *Hansel and Gretel*, 22 Sept.; new one-act opera, *The Prentice Pillar*, by Guy Eden and Reginald Somerville . 24 Sept. ,,
The Silver Key, by Sydney Grundy . 1–20 Nov. ,,
A Man's Shadow, revival . . 27 Nov.–15 Jan. 1898
Julius Cæsar (scenery and costumes under the supervision of Mr. Alma Tadema, R.A.) 22 Jan.–18 June ,,
Ragged Robin, Mr. Louis Parker's version of *La Chemineau*, produced . . 23 June. ,,
The Termagant, by L. N. Parker and Murray Carson (short run) . . . 1 Sept. ,,
The Musketeers, adapted by Sydney Grundy from Dumas' novel . . . 3 Nov.–7 April, 1899
(Revived, 17 June–7 July).
Carnac Sahib, by Henry Arthur Jones, first time, 12 April–12 May; *Capt. Swift*, by Haddon Chambers (revival) . . 13 May–June, 1899
King John, Mr. Tree's company; Constance, Miss Julia Neilson . . 20 Sept. 1899–6 Jan. 1900
Midsummer Night's Dream . . 10 Jan.–26 May, ,,
Rip Van Winkle, new version . 30 May–21 July, ,,
Julius Cæsar (revival) . . 6 Sept.–27 Oct. ,,
Herod, by Stephen Phillips (first time), 31 Oct. 1900–21 Jan. 1901
Twelfth Night . . . . 5 Feb.–31 May, ,,
Mme. Sarah Bernhardt season; M. Coquelin French plays *L'Aiglon* . . . 3 June, ,,
Twelfth Night: Mr. Tree's company . 7–19 Oct. ,,
The Last of the Dandies, by Clyde Fitch, first time, 24 Oct. 1901–25 Jan. 1902
Ulysses, by Stephen Phillips; music by Coleridge Taylor, first time . . 1 Feb.–31 May, ,,
Twelfth Night, 2–9 June; *Trilby* . 21 June–5 July, ,,
Merry Wives of Windsor (Mrs. Kendal and Ellen Terry) . . . 10 June–8 Aug. ,,
House styled "His Majesty's Theatre" . 23 Aug. ,,
The Eternal City, by Hall Caine . 2 Oct.–16 Jan. 1903
Merry Wives of Windsor . . . 17 Jan. ,,
Resurrection (Tolstoy), by H. Bataille and H. Morton . . . . 17 Feb. ,,
See *Addenda*.

HAYMARKET.

Built 1702
Opened by French comedians . . . 29 Dec. 1720
Fielding's Mogul company . . . 1734-5
A French company prohibited from acting by the audience 1738
Mr. Foote's patent 1747
The Bottle-conjuror's dupery (see *Bottle Conjuror*), 16 Jan. 1748
The theatre rebuilt 1767
Mr. Colman's tenure . . . 1 Jan. 1777
Miss Farren's appearance here (afterwards countess of Derby) . . . . ,,
Royal visit—great crowd—16 persons killed and many wounded . . . 3 Feb. 1794
Mr. Elliston's *début* here . . 24 June, 1796
First appearance of Mr. Mathews (as *Lingo*) 16 May, 1803
Mr. Morris's management . . . 1805
Appearance of Mr. Liston (as *Sheepface*) . 8 June, ,,
The tailors' riot . . . 15 Aug. ,,
Appearance of Mr. Young (as *Hamlet*) . 22 June, 1807
Of Miss F. Kelly (as *Floretta*) . 12 June, 1810
Present theatre rebuilt by Nash; opened 4 July, 1821
Miss Paton's (Mrs. Wood) appearance (as *Susannah*), 3 Aug. 1822
Mr. Webster's management . . 12 June, 1837
Mr. Charles Kean's appearance here . . 1839
Mr. Webster's management (16 years) terminated with his farewell appearance . 14 March, 1853
First appearance of *Our American Cousin* (said to be by Tom Taylor, and to have been acted 800 times in America), Mr. Sothern, *Lord Dundreary* (played 496 nights) . . . . 11 Nov. 1861
Mr. Buckstone's management . . 1853-76
Mr. John S. Clarke . . . 1878
Re-opened; pit removed, and other changes; temporary riot . . . 31 Jan. 1880
Mr. S. B. (knt. June, 1897) & Mrs. Bancroft . 1879-85
Grand closing performance . . 20 July, 1885
Opened by Messrs. Russell and Bashford 26 Sept. ,,
Interior re-constructed and re-opened by Mr. Beerbohm Tree, lessee . . Sept. 1887–9
A Man's Shadow (from the French), by Mr. R. Buchanan . 12 Sept. 1889—29 March, 1890
A Village Priest, by Mr. S. Grundy, 3 April—12 July; 6 Oct– 6 Nov. ,,
Beau Austin, by W. E. Henley and R. L. Stevenson . . . 3 Nov. *et seq.* ,,
Called Back, by Hugh Conway and Comyns Carr, 10 Nov., and other pieces on different days, Nov., Dec. 1890—Jan. 1891
The Dancing Girl . . 15 Jan.—27 June, ,,
House closed, 27 June; re-opened with *The Dancing Girl* . . 5 Oct. 1891—15 Jan. 1892
Mr. Beerbohm Tree, lessee and manager . Jan. ,,
Hamlet, with *Peril* occasionally in the afternoon, 21 Jan.—27 May, ,,
Peril, with *Hamlet* occasionally in the afternoon, 28 May—5 July, ,,

Hamlet, season terminates . . . . 6 July, 1892

Mrs. Langtry, manager: *The Queen of Manoa*, by Messrs. Haddon Chambers and Outram Tristram, 15 Sept.–17 Oct. ,,

Agatha Tylden, Merchant and Shipowner, by Edwd. Rose . . . . . . 18 Oct.–10 Dec. ,,

Hypatia (adapted from Kingsley), 2 Jan.–25 March; 1–15 April, 1893

A Woman of No Importance, by Mr. Oscar Wilde, 19 April–16 Aug. ,,

Ibsen's play, *An Enemy of the People* (afternoon), 14, 21 June; 20, 21, 22 July, ,,

The Tempter, by Henry A. Jones . 20 Sept.–1 Dec. ,,

Captain Swift, by Haddon Chambers, 2 Dec.–17 Jan. 1894

The Charlatan, by Robert Buchanan, 18 Jan.–17 March, ,,

Once Upon a Time (adapted from the German), by Mr. Louis N. Parker . . 28 March–21 April, ,,

A Bunch of Violets, by Sydney Grundy (adapted from the French) . . 25 April–19 July, ,,

An Enemy of the People, by Henrik Ibsen, 20 July, House closed.

[*The Ballad-monger*, by Walter Besant and Walter Pollock, and *The Red Lamp*, by W. Outram Tristram, at Balmoral, 24 Sept.; after a rapid journey of 591 miles, *A Bunch of Violets* at Dublin, 25 Sept.]

A Bunch of Violets (London) . . 8 Oct.–3 Nov. ,,

John a' Dreams, by Mr. C. Haddon Chambers, 8 Nov.–27 Dec. ,,

Hamlet . . . . 28–29 Dec. ,,

Mr. Beerbohm Tree and company go to New York, Jan. 1895

An Ideal Husband, by Mr. Oscar Wilde (under the management of Messrs. Morell and Waller), 3 Jan.–6 April, ,,

Mr. Tree's company: *John a' Dreams* 2–22 May, ,,

Fedora, by Sardou; translation by Herman Merivale . . . . 25 May–20 July, ,,

Trilby, by George Du Maurier 30 Oct.–28 March, and 4 April–15 July, 1896

Special matinées, etc.: *King Henry IV.*, 8 May–10 July, ,,

Retirement of Mr. Tree from the management, 15 July, ,,

Under the Red Robe, produced by Mr. Fred Harrison and Mr. Cyril Maude . 17 Oct.–2 June, 1897

A Marriage of Convenience (Alex. Dumas), adapted, by Sydney Grundy, 5 June–24 July; resumed, 4 Sept.–4 Nov. ,,

The Little Minister, by J. M. Barrie 6 Nov.–22 July, 1898 (Revived, 3 Sept.–26 Oct. 1898).

The Manœuvres of Jane, comedy, by Henry A. Jones, first time, 29 Oct.; preceded by the *Golden Wedding* (one-act), by Mr. Eden Philpotts and Mr. Charles Groves . 30 Nov. 1898–21 July, 1899

The Degenerates, by Sydney Grundy; Mrs. Langtry's company . . . . . . 31 Aug. ,,

The Black Tulip (by Alex. Dumas *père*), adapted by Sydney Grundy . 28 Oct. 1899–6 Jan. 1900

She Stoops to Conquer (Goldsmith), 9 Jan.–24 March ,,

The Rivals (Goldsmith) . . 27 March–16 June, ,,

School for Scandal . . . 19 June–21 July, ,,

Sweet Nell of Old Drury, by Paul Kester, 30 Aug.–13 Oct. ,,

The School for Scandal . . 16 Oct.–24 Nov. ,,

The Second in Command, by Robt. Marshall, first time, 27 Nov. 1900–20 July, 1901; again, 14 Oct. 1901–1 Jan. 1902

Frocks and Frills, adapted from the French of Scribe and Legouvé, by Sydney Grundy, 2 Jan.–25 April, ,,

Caste, by T. W. Robertson . . 26 April–5 July, ,,

(*The Little Minister*, special (charity) matinée), 6 May, ,,

"*There's many a Slip*," adapted from the French of Scribe and Legouvé, by Robt. Marshall, 25 Aug.–29 Nov. ,,

The Unforeseen, new play, by Robt. Marshall, 2 Dec. ,,

The Clandestine Marriage, by Geo. Colman and David Garrick, revived . . . . March, 1903

LYCEUM, FORMERLY ENGLISH OPERA-HOUSE.

Built by Dr. Arnold 1794-5

Winsor experiments with gas-lighting . . . 1803-4

Opened as the Lyceum in 1809

Appearance of Mr. Wrench (as *Belcour*) . 7 Oct. ,,

Re-opened with an address by Miss Kelly 15 June, 1816

House destroyed by fire . . . . . 16 Feb. 1830

Rebuilt, and re-opened . . . . 14 July, 1834

Equestrian performances . . . . 16 Jan. 1844

Mrs. Keeley's management . . . . 8 April, ,,

Madame Vestris and Mr. C. Mathews' management, Oct. 1847-56

Retirement of Mr. C. Mathews . . . . March, 1855

Appearance of Madame Ristori . . . . June, 1856

Taken by Mr. Gye for Italian opera for forty nights, 14 April, 1857

Opened for English opera by Miss Louisa Pyne and Mr. Harrison . . . . . . 21 Sept. ,,

Balfe's opera, *Rose of Castile*, produced . . Oct. ,,

Mr. B. Webster and Mr. Falconer, July, 1858; closed, April, 1859

Opened by Madame Celeste Nov. 1859, and Oct. 1860

The "Savage Club" perform before the queen and prince . . . . . . 7 March, ,,

Italian opera . . . . . . 8 June, 1861

Mr. Falconer, manager (English comedy) 19 Aug. ,,

Peep o' Day brought out . . . . 9 Nov. ,,

Mr. Fechter . . . . . . 10 Jan. *et seq.* 1863

Japanese troupe . . . . Spring, 1868

Lord Lytton's *Rightful Heir* brought out 3 Oct. ,,

Mr. H. Irving as *Hamlet* (long run) . . 31 Oct. 1874

,, *Macbeth* . . . . 25 Sept. 1875

,, *Othello* . . . . 14 Feb. 1876

Tennyson's *Queen Mary* performed 19 April, ,,

Mr. H. L. Bateman, lessee and manager . . 1873-6

Mrs. Bateman, ditto . . 1876-8

Mr. H. Irving, lessee and manager (knt. 1895), Sept. *et seq.* 1878

Re-opens with *Hamlet* . . . . . 30 Dec. ,,

Mr. Chippendale's benefit (68 years on the stage), 24 Feb. 1879

Much Ado about Nothing; grand scenery . 11 Oct. 1882

Miss M. Anderson and American actors . 1 Sept. 1883

Faust, adapted by W. G. Wills, 19 Dec. 1885; 250th performance . . . . . . 22 Nov. 1886

Miss Mary Anderson, autumn season 10 Sept. 1887

Revival of *Macbeth* with new rendering by Mr. Irving and Miss E. Terry . . . 29 Dec. 1888

His company performs the *Bells* before the queen at Sandringham . . . . . 26 April, 1889

Mr. Mayer with Italian opera and French plays: Verdi's *Otello*, 5 July–27 July; Madame Sarah Bernhardt in *Léna* . . . . . . 9 July, ,,

The Dead Heart revived . . . . . 9 May, 1890

The Bells, *Louis XI.*, *Olivia* . . . . May, ,,

Mr. Augustin Daly's company, from New York, 10 June—16 Aug. ,,

Ravenswood, by Herman Merivale . 20 Sept. *et seq.* ,,

Much Ado About Nothing, *Charles I.*, *Corsican Brothers*, and other pieces 5 Jan.—25 March, 1891

Mr. Augustin Daly's company . 9 Sept.—13 Nov. ,,

King Henry VIII., with *Richelieu* occasionally in the afternoon or evening . 5 Jan.—30 July, 1892

The Bells . . . . . . 24 Sept. *et seq.* ,,

King Henry VIII. . . . . 1 Oct.–5 Nov. ,,

King Lear . . . . . 10 Nov. 1892–1 Feb. 1893

Becket, by lord Tennyson . . 6 Feb.–25 March, ,,

[At Windsor Castle, 18 March.]

Becket (other plays occasionally), afternoons and evenings . . . . . . April–22 July, ,,

[The company went to America.]

Cinderella, pantomime; Mr. Oscar Barrett, 26 Dec. 1893–17 March, 1894

Return of the Lyceum company.

Faust . . . . . . 14 April–7 July, ,,

Becket . . . . . . 9 July–20 July, ,,

Merchant of Venice, 21 July. House closed . ,,

Under direction of Henry E. Abbey and Maurice Grau: *The Queen of Brilliants*, comic opera; adapted by Brandon Thomas; music by Edwd. Jakobowski . . . . 8 Sept.–18 Oct. ,,

Santa Claus; Mr. Oscar Barrett, 26 Dec.; afterwards daily, till . . . . . March, 1895

Return of Mr. Irving and Miss Ellen Terry.

King Arthur, by J. Comyns Carr; choral and incidental music by Arthur Sullivan, 12 Jan.–6 April, ,,

Closed; re-opens . . . 15 April–3 May, ,,

A Story of Waterloo, by Conan Doyle; *Don Quixote*, by the late W. G. Wills; *Bygones*, by A. W. Pinero . . . . . 4 May–1 June, ,,

Nance Oldfield, *The Bells*, &c. . . . . 3 June, ,,

Testimonial to sir Henry Irving from 4,000 professionals . . . . 19 July, ,,

The company sail to America . . . 31 Aug. 1895
Romeo and Juliet (under the management of Mr. Forbes Robertson and Mr. Frederick Harrison), 21 Sept.–21 Dec. „
The PURCELL COMMEMORATION: his opera, *Dido and Æneas*, performed by pupils of the Royal college of Music . . . . . 20 Nov. „
Reception of and presentations to Mrs. Robert Keeley, on her 90th birthday; her reply to an address, etc. . . . . 22 Nov. „
Pantomime matinées: Mr. Oscar Barrett's *Robinson Crusoe*, twice daily . . 26 Dec.–22 Feb. 1896
Michael and his Lost Angel, by Henry Arthur Jones, 15–22 Jan. „
For the Crown (from the French), adapted by John Davidson, 27 Feb.–30 May; *Magda*, by Hermann Sudermann, translated by Louis N. Parker, 3–19 June; *School for Scandal*, 20 June–24 July; end of tenancy of Mr. Forbes Robertson and Mr. Frederick Harrison . . . . 25 July, „
Cymbeline (Lyceum company), 22 Sept.–11 Dec.; *The Bells*, 25 Nov., 5, 12, 14, 15 Dec.; *Richard III.*, 19 Dec. (closed); *Cymbeline*, 26 Dec., 29 Jan. 1897; *Olivia*, 30 Jan.; *Richard III.*, 27 Feb.–6 April; *Madame Sans Gêne*, by M.M. Sardou and Moreau, adapted by J. Comyns Carr, 10 April–23 July; *The Bells*, *Merchant of Venice*, Saturdays in June–22 July, 1897
Mr. Forbes Robertson's season: *Hamlet*, 11 Sept.–18 Dec. „
Peter the Great (new play), by Laurence Irving, 1 Jan.–14 Feb. 1898
Don Giovanni (Mozart), performed by the students of the Royal college of music; matinée 27 Jan. „
Madame Sans Gêne . . . . . 15 Feb. „
Merchant of Venice, and other plays, 17 Feb.–26 April, „
The Medicine Man, new melodramatic comedy, by H. D. Traill and R. S. Hichens, first performance, 4–27 May; *Waterloo* and *The Bells*, and other plays, 28 May–1 July; M. Coquelin and French company, *Cyrano de Bergerac*, by Rostand, 4 July, „
Macbeth, *Hamlet*, and *Pelleas and Melisande*, by M. Maeterlinck (Mr. Forbes Robertson and Mrs. Patrick Campbell) . . . 17 Sept.–10 Dec. „
Royal Carl Rosa company: *Tannhäuser*, &c., 2 Jan. *et seq.* 1899
The Only Way, adapted by Freeman Wills, from Dickens's novel, "A Tale of Two Cities," 16 Feb.–25 March, „
Robespierre, written by M. Victorien Sardou for Sir Henry Irving, Mr. Laurence Irving's translation, first time . . . . 15 April–29 July, „
Lydia Thompson, farewell matinée . . 2 May, „
M. Jules Claretie, director of the Théâtre Français, gives an address on Shakespeare and Molière, 13 July, „
Mr. Wilson Barrett's season: *The Silver King*, by Henry A. Jones and Henry Herman, 2 Sept.–5 Oct. „
Man and his Makers, by Wilson Barrett and Louis N. Parker, 7–17 Oct.; *Sign of the Cross*, by Wilson Barrett, 19 Oct.–18 Nov.; matinées, &c., *The Silver King*, *Othello*, *Hamlet*, 20 Nov.–16 Dec. „
The Snow Man, a fairy play, adapted from the French by Arthur Sturgess, music by Walter Slaughter . . . 21 Dec. 1899–31 Jan. 1900
Mr. F. K. Benson's Shakespeare season: *Henry the Fifth* . . . . . 15 Feb. „
Midsummer Night's Dream, 22 Feb.; *Hamlet* in its entirety, 9 March; *The Rivals*, 13 March; *Richard the Second*, &c. . . . 15 March–5 May, „
Signora Eleonora Duse's season: *Magda* and other pieces, 10 May–15 June; matinée of *Magda*, 18 June, „
Olivia, revival, by W. G. Wills (Henry Irving and Ellen Terry) . . . . . . 16 June, „
Waterloo and *The Bells*, 30 June and 4–7 July; and other plays . . . . . 28 July, „
Mr. Wm. Mollison's season: *For Auld Lang Syne*, by Seymour Hicks and F. G. Latham, first time, 6 Oct.–31 Oct. „
The Three Musketeers (Henry Hamilton's version), 3 Nov.–15 Dec. „
Henry the Fifth . . . 22 Dec. 1900–16 March, 1901
Coriolanus (Henry Irving and Ellen Terry), 15 April, „
Waterloo and *The Bells*, 22 May; *Robespierre*, 27 May; *King Charles I.*, 24 June; and other plays, 20 July, 1901
Sherlock Holmes, by Conan Doyle, 9 Sept. 1901–12 April, 1902
Faust (Henry Irving), 26 April–11 July; matinées, *King Charles I.*, 28 June, 5 July; *Louis XI.*, 14–16 July; *Waterloo* and *The Bells* . 17, 18 July, „
Merchant of Venice, 7, 14, 21 June; 12, 19, 26 July; closed . . . . „

ADELPHI THEATRE

Formerly called the *Sans Pareil*, opened under the management of Mr. and Miss Scott . . 27 Nov. 1806
Under Rodwell and Jones, who gave it the present name, 1820-21; Terry and Yates . . 1825
Messrs. Mathews and Yates' management join (*Mathews at Home*) 1828
New front 1840
Madame Celeste's management . . 30 Sept. 1844
Rebuilt and opened, with improved arrangements, 27 Dec. 1858
Colleen Bawn represented . . . 10 Sept. 1860
[Immense run; above 360 nights.]
Miss Bateman appears as *Leah*, 1 Oct. 1863, to 11 June, 1864
Messrs. F. B. Chatterton and B. Webster, lessees 1844-73
Messrs. Gatti, lessees and managers . . 1879 *et seq.*
London Day by Day, by G. R. Sims and Mr. Pettitt, 14 Sept. *et seq.* 1889
Green Bushes revived . . . 19 April *et seq.* 1890
The Bride of Love, by R. Buchanan . May *et seq.* „
The English Rose, by G. R. Sims and R. Buchanan, 2 Aug. 1890—2 May, 1891
The Streets of London, by D. Boucicault 7 May *et seq.* „
The Trumpet Call, by G. R. Sims and R. Buchanan, 1 Aug. 1891–21 April, 1892
The White Rose, by G. R. Sims and R. Buchanan, 23 April—10 June, „
Lights of Home, by same authors 30 July–17 Dec. „
The Lost Paradise, by Henry C. de Mille, from Ludwig Fulda . . 22 Dec. 1892–11 March, 1893
The Black Domino, by G. R. Sims and R. Buchanan, 1 April–27 May, „
A Woman's Revenge, by Henry Pettitt, 1 July–16 Nov.; 26 Dec. 1893–3 March, 1894
The Cotton King, by Sutton Vane, 10 March–8 May, „
The Two Orphans . . . . 12 May–18 June, „
Shall We Forgive Her? by Frank Harvey, 20 June–18 Aug. „
The Fatal Card, by C. Haddon Chambers and B. C. Stephenson . . . . 6 Sept.–16 March, 1895
The Girl I Left Behind Me, by Franklin Fyles and David Belasco . . . 13 April–10 Aug. „
The Swordsman's Daughter . . 31 Aug.–30 Nov. „
One of the Best, by Seymour Hicks and George Edwardes 21 Dec.–6 June, 1896; closed . „
Boys Together, by Haddon Chambers and Comyns Carr . . . . 26 Aug.–Dec. 1896
Black Ey'd Susan, by Douglas Jerrold, 23 Dec.–8 May, 1897 (Mr. Agostino Gatti, manager, died 14 Jan. 1897).
Secret Service, by Wm. Gillette, New York company . . 15 May–mid June, again 22 July, 1897
French plays, Mdme. Sarah Bernhardt, *Lorenzaccio*, etc.. . . . . . . 18 June–July, „
In the Days of the Duke, by Haddon Chambers and Comyns Carr . . . . 9 Sept.–20 Nov. „
Secret Service (revival), 24 Nov.–mid Jan. 1898.
Mr. Wm. Terris (Lewin), aged 49, leading actor, fatally stabbed by Richard Archer Prince (32), actor, at the private stage door, Maiden-lane, in revenge for non-employment, about 7 p.m. 16 Dec.; buried at Brompton, thousands present, 21 Dec. (theatre closed till 27 Dec.). See *Trials*, 13 Jan. 1898
Charlotte Corday . . . . . . 21 Jan. „
Lady of Lyons . . . . 12 Feb.–17 March, „
The Heart of Maryland, by David Belasco (New York company) . . . 9 April–25 June, „
The Gipsy Earl, by G. R. Sims . 31 Aug.–10 Dec. „
Dick Whittington . . . 26 Dec. 1898–18 Feb. 1899
The Man with the Iron Mask (Mr. Norman Forbes' season) . . . . . 11 Mar.–20 May, „

French plays: Sarah Bernhardt, *La Tosca*, 8, 9 June; *La Dame aux Camellias*, 10 June; *Hamlet*, 12–24 June; M. Coquelin as *Cyrano de Bergerac*, *Tartufe*, &c. . . . . 26 June–15 July, 1899
With Flying Colours, by Seymour Hicks and Fred Latham, first time . . . . 19 Aug.–6 Nov. ,,
Children of the Ghetto, by I. Zangwill (short run), 11 Dec. ,,
Drink, revived (Mr. Chas. Warner), 26 Dec. 1899–13 Jan. 1900
Two Little Vagabonds, by G. R. Sims and A. Shirley, revived . . . . . 15 Jan.–3 Feb. ,,
The Better Life, adapted from the rev. Chas. Sheldon's book *In His Steps*, by Arthur Shirley and Sutton Vane . . . . . 5–17 Feb. ,,
Bonnie Dundee, by Laurence Irving, 10 March–April, ,,
Quo Vadis, adapted from Sienkiewicz's novel, by S. Stange . . . . . . 1 May–1 June, ,,
[The theatre re-opened under the name of the CENTURY, but resumed its old name, 2 Feb. 1902.]
The Whirl of the Town, by Hugh Morton, music by Gustav Kerker . . . . . . 11 Sept. 1901
The Belle of New York, 27 Nov. *et seq.*
Arizona, by Augustus Thomas (American company) 2 Feb.–26 April, 1902
Sapho, adapted from Daudet's novel, by Mr. Clyde Fitch (Miss Olga Nethersole's season), 1 May–12 July, ,,
Magda, *Camille*, &c. (Miss Nance O'Neil's season), 1–20 Sept. ,,
Capt. Kettle, adapted from Cutcliffe Hyne's story by M. Watson and Murray Carson, produced, 23 Oct. ,,
The Christian King, by Wilson Barrett; *Silver King*, *Manxman* . . 18 Dec. 1902–31 Jan. 1903
A Queen of Society, by Cecil Raleigh . . 5 Feb. ,,
The Worst Woman in London, by W. Melville, 7 March, ,,

ST. JAMES'S, LATE PRINCE'S.

This theatre was built by and opened under the management of Mr. Braham . . . . 14 Dec. 1835
German operas performed here under the management of Mr. Bunn 1840
Mr. Mitchell's tenure; performance of French plays, 22 Jan. 1844
German plays 1852
Mrs. Seymour's tenure . . . . 22 Oct. 1854-5
French plays 1857
Neapolitan buffo-opera . . . . . . Nov. ,,
Italian plays 1858
French operas . . . . Jan. 1859
French plays . . . . May, ,,
English comedy, under Mr. F. Chatterton, manager, Oct. ,,
French plays . . . . 28 May, 1860
English plays . . . . 12 Aug. ,,
Mr. Wigan, manager 1860-2
French plays . . . . May, 1868, April, 1869
French plays 1871-3
The Ironmaster . . . . 17 April, 1884
Messrs. Hare & Kendal, lessees and managers . . 1885
Mr. Rutland Barrington 1888
Mrs. Langtry . . . . March, 1890
As You Like It . . . . April, ,,
Esther Sandraz, by Sydney Grundy . 3 May *et seq.* ,,
House closed, 7 June; re-opened (Mr. Bourchier, manager), *Your Wife* . . . . 26 June, ,,
Mr. Mayer, French plays . . . . 27 Oct. *et seq.* ,,
Mr. G. Alexander (from the Avenue) lessee and manager . . . . 15 May, ,,
Sunlight and Shadow, 100th time . . . 31 Jan. 1891
The Idler . . . . . . 26 Feb.—17 July, ,,
Molière, new piece . . . . . . 17 July, ,,
The Idler (*Molière* sometimes) . 30 Sept.—4 Nov. ,,
Lord Anerley, by Mark Quinton and Henry Hamilton . . . . 7 Nov.—23 Dec. ,,
Forgiveness, by J. C. Carr . 30 Dec. 1891—10 Feb. 1892
Lady Windermere's Fan, by Oscar Wilde, 20 Feb.—29 July, ,,
Lady Windermere's Fan . . . 31 Oct.–30 Nov. ,,
Liberty Hall, by R. C. Carton, 3 Dec. 1892–20 May, 1893
The Second Mrs. Tanqueray, 27 May–28 July; 11 Nov.–20 Dec.; begins 26 Dec.–21 April . . 1894
The Masqueraders, by Henry Arthur Jones; 28 April–28 July; 10 Nov.–22 Dec. . . . . .
Guy Domville, by Henry James . 5 Jan.–5 Feb. 1895
The Importance of being Earnest, by Oscar Wilde, 14 Feb.–10 April; 15 April–8 May, ,,
The Triumph of the Philistines, by Henry Arthur Jones . . . . . . 11 May–19 June, 1895
The Second Mrs. Tanqueray . 20 June–3 July, ,,
The Idler, by C. Haddon Chambers . 4–10 July, ,,
Bogey, by H. V. Esmond . . . . . 10 Sept. ,,
Liberty Hall, by R. C. Carton . 7 Nov.–22 Nov. ,,
The Mysogynist, by G. W. Godrey; *The Divided Way*, by H. V. Esmond . 23 Nov.–14 Dec. ,,
The Prisoner of Zenda (Anthony Hope), 7 Jan.–18 July . . . . . . 20 Oct.–28 Nov. 1896
As You Like It . . . . . 2 Dec.–20 March, 1897
The Princess and the Butterfly, by A. W. Pinero, 29 March–30 June, ,,
The Prisoner of Zenda . . . . 1–31 (?) July, ,,
The Tree of Knowledge, by R. C. Carton, 25 Oct.–5 Feb. 1898
Much Ado About Nothing . . 17 Feb.–2 April, ,,
The Conquerors, by Paul M. Potter, 14 April–28 May, ,,
The Ambassadors, comedy, by John Oliver Hobbes, 2 June–22 July, ,,
The Elder Miss Blossom, by Ernest Hendrie and Metcalfe Wood (Mr. and Mrs. Kendal's season), 22 Sept.–23 Dec. ,,
The Ambassador (revived) . . 9 Jan.–21 April, 1899
A Repentance (one-act drama), by John Oliver Hobbes; overture and incidental music by sir Hubert Parry; first performance . . . 28 Feb. ,,
In Days of Old, by Edward Rose; first time, 26 April–23 June, ,,
Rupert of Hentzau, by Anthony Hope (Mr. George Alexander's company) . 1 Feb.–27 March, 1900
The Man of Forty, by Walter Frith, 28 March–6 June, ,,
A Debt of Honour, by Sydney Grundy, 1 Sept.–17 Nov. ,,
The Wisdom of the Wise, by John Oliver Hobbes, first time . . . . . 22 Nov. 1900–11 Jan. 1901
The Awakening, by C. Haddon Chambers, 6 Feb.–1 April, ,,
The Wilderness, by H. V. Esmond; produced, 11 April–11 July, ,,
The Elder Miss Blossom (Mr. and Mrs. Kendal's season), 16 Sept.–26 Oct.; *The Likeness of the Night*, by Mrs. W. K. Clifford, first time, 28 Oct.–21 Dec.; *The Wilderness* and *Liberty Hall* (revived) . . . . . 26 Dec. 1901–4 Jan. 1902
The Importance of being Earnest, by Oscar Wilde, 7 Jan.–28 Feb. ,,
Paolo and Francesco, by Stephen Phillips; music by Percy Pitt; first time . 6 March–5 July, ,,
If I were King, by Justin Huntly McCarthy; first time . . . . . 30 Aug. 1902–21 Feb. 1903
Old Heidelberg, English version of Meyer-Foster's comedy, by R. Bleichmann . . . . 19 Mar. ,,

ROYAL PRINCESS'S THEATRE, OXFORD STREET.

First opened for concerts . . . . . Sept. 1840
Sold for 16,400*l*. . . . . 9 Sept. 1841
Opened for plays by Mr. J. Maddox . 26 Dec. 1842
Mr. Bartley's farewell here . . . 18 Dec. 1852
Mr. Charles Kean's management, 1850: closed, 29 Aug. 1859
Mr. A. Harris's management; opened 29 Sept. ,,
Zouave Crimean company . . . 23 July, 1860
Mr. Harris, lessee 1860-1
Mr. Fechter appears (as *Hamlet*) . . 20 March, 1861
Mr. Lindus, manager . . . . . 20 Oct. 1862
Mr. G. Vining, lessee and manager . . May, 1863-66
Mr. F. B. Chatterton, lessee 1872-78
Carl Rosa's Opera company 1875
Mr. Walter Gooch, lessee and manager . . 1878-81
Closed for rebuilding, 19 May; rebuilt; opened (1st appearance of Edwin Booth) . . . 6 Nov. 1880
G. R. Sims' *Lights o' London* . . . . Sept. 1881
Mr. Wilson Barrett, lessee and manager . . Aug. 1883
Claudian, by Herman and Wills . . . 6 Dec. ,,
Miss G. Hawthorne, lessee . . . . Jan. 1888-9
Mr. Wilson Barrett closes his season, going to America for a year . . . . 18 May, 1889
Sole lessee, Miss Grace Hawthorne; manager, Mr. W. W. Kelly . . . . ,,
Gold Craze . . . . . . 30 Nov.—14 Dec. ,,
Theodora, by Sardou . . . . . . 5 May, 1890
Mrs. Langtry, sole lessee and manageress . Nov. ,,
Antony and Cleopatra . . 18 Nov. 1890—Feb. 1891
Lady Barter, by Mr. Coghlan . 28 Feb.—20 March, ,,

Linda Grey . . . . 8 April, 1891
House closed . . . . . . 17 April, ,,
Manager, Mr. Sidney Herberte-Basing; *Fate and Fortune* . . . . . 27 July—28 Aug. ,,
Revival of *Arrah-na-Pogue* . 29 Aug.—7 Nov. ,,
After Dark, by D. Boucicault . 9 Nov.—19 Dec. ,,
Alone in London . 21 Dec. 1891—16 Jan. 1892
The Swiss Express . . . 18 Jan.—3 Feb. ,,
The Great Metropolis . . 11 Feb.—9 April, ,,
The Life we Live . . . 16 April *et seq.* ,,
Strathlogan, new piece . . 9 June *et seq.* ,,
House to let, advertised . . . 22 June, ,,
Royal Divorce, altered by Miss Grace Hawthorne 25 July *et seq.* ,,

Mr. W. W. Kelly, manager . 15 July–26 Oct. ,,
Mr. Rollo Balmain, lessee and manager; *Uncle Tom's Cabin* (an American combination), by Charles Hermann . 29 Oct.–19 Nov. (closed), ,,
Hoodman Blind . . . . 26 Nov.—3 Dec. ,,
Eagle Joe, by Mr. Henry Herman 26 Dec. 1892–7 Jan. 1893

Advertised to be let or sold . . . 10 Jan. ,,
Reopened, Mr. John Hollingshead, director; *Miami*, new melodramatic opera, by Haydn Parry, 16–28 Oct. ,,
A Life of Pleasure (for Drury Lane) . . 11 Dec. ,,
The World, by Paul Meritt, Henry Pettitt, and sir Augustus Harris . . 24 Feb.–14 April, 1894
Jean Mayeux, mimo-drama, by Blanchard de la Bretesche (French company) . 12–19 May, ,,
The Texan, by Tyrone Power . 20 May–29 June, ,,
Mrs. Harriet Gooch, proprietress; *Odette*, adapted from Sardou . . . 29 Sept.–13 Oct. ,,
Robbery under Arms, a composite entertainment, 22 Oct.–Nov. ,,
The Derby Winner . 22 Dec. 1894–16 Feb. 1895
Hansel und Gretel, a fairy opera by Humperdinck (Carl Rosa company) . 2 March–15 April, ,,
Reopened, at reduced prices . . 3 Aug. *et seq.* ,,
Shirley and Landeck's *Saved from the Sea*, 3 Aug.–7 Sept. ,,

[Plays with short runs.]

A Dark Secret, 14 Nov.–24 Jan. 1896; *The Colleen Bawn*, 25 Jan. *et seq.*; *The Star of India*, by G. R. Sims and Arthur Shirley, 6 April–16 May; *The Span of Life*, by Sutton Vane, 19 May–27 June; *The Grip of Iron*, 29 June–11 July; *Drink*, 13–30 July; *In Sight of St. Paul's*, by Sutton Vane, 3 Aug.–19 Sept.; *Two Little Vagabonds* (adapted from the French), by G. R. Sims and A. Shirley, 23 Sept.–29 May, 1897; *The County Fair*, by Chas. Barnard, 5 June *et seq.*; *In Sight of St. Paul's*, 26 June–17 July; *Tommy Atkins*, 31 July–2 Oct.; *Two Little Vagabonds*, revival, 4 Oct.–18 Dec.; *How London Lives*, by Martyn Field and Arthur Shirley (from the French), 27 Dec.; closed 16 April, 1898; *The Crystal Globe*, by Sutton Vane, 26 Dec. 1898; *White Heather* (revived), 30 Jan. 1899. Short seasons, 1899 *et seq.*

OLYMPIC, NOW NEW OLYMPIC.

Erected by the late Mr. Astley, and opened with horsemanship . . . . . 18 Sept. 1806
Here the celebrated Elliston (1813), and afterwards Madame Vestris, had managements; the latter until 1839
Mr. George Wild's tenure 1840
Miss Davenport's tenure . . . . 11 Nov. 1844
Mr. Watts's management 1848
The theatre destroyed by fire . . 29 March, 1849
Rebuilt and opened—Mr. Watts resumes his management . . . . . . 26 Dec. ,,
Mr. William Farren's management . . . 1850
Lessee and manager, Mr. A. Wigan . 17 Oct. 1853-7
Messrs. Robson and Emden's management, Aug. 1857-62
Mr. Horace Wigan, manager 1864-68
Lessee, Mr. B. Webster 1868
Lessee and manager, Miss Ada Cavendish . . 1873
Mr. Wills's *Buckingham* produced . . Dec. 1875
Mr. Henry Neville 1873-78
Mrs. A. Conover, lessee 1885
Mr. J. Pitt-Hardacre 1889
Opened by Mr. Wilson Barrett; *The People's Idol*, and other pieces, by Mr. Barrett and Mr. V. Wednell . . . . . . 4 Dec. *et seq.* 1890

Lights o' London . . . . . . 9 Feb. 1891
Hamlet . . . . 13–18 April, ,,
The Acrobat, or *Belphegor* . . . 21 April, ,,
House closed, 9 May; re-opened by Mr. Charles Wilmot; manager, Mr. W. W. Kelly . . ,,
Theodora, by Sardou . . . 1 Aug.—8 Sept. ,,
A Royal Divorce, by W. G. Wills 10 Sept.—19 Dec. ,,
Oliver Twist . . . . . . 21 Dec. *et seq.* ,,
East Lynne . . . . . 2 Feb.—5 March, 1892
The Black Flag . . . . . 7 March *et seq.* ,,
Called Back . . . . 22 March—2 April, ,,
Theodora revived . . . . . 4 April *et seq.* ,,
Lessee and manager, Mr. Edmund Tearle; *Julius Cæsar*, *Richard III.*, *Virginius*, *Othello*, 16 April—28 May, ,,
Royal opera season, by signor Lago, 17 Oct.–3 Nov. ,,
Closed.
Mr. Wm. Hogarth, acting manager: *Dick Whittington* (pantomime) . . 26 Dec. 1892–March, 1893
Made a music-hall . . . . 7 Aug. *et seq.* ,,
Opened by sir Augustus Harris, *Cheer boys, Cheer!* 19 Dec. *et seq* 1895
True Blue (and other plays with short runs), by Leonard Outram and lieut.-Stuart Gordon, R.N. 19 March, 1896
The Free Pardon, by Messrs. F. E. Philips and Leonard Merrick . . . . . 28 Jan. 1897
The Mariners of England, by Messrs. Robert Buchanan and "Charles Marlowe" . 9 March, ,,
Mr. Ben Greet's Shakspearean season: *Hamlet*, etc. . . . . 10 May–12 June, ,,

SAVOY THEATRE, see under *Savoy*. Opened 10 Oct. 1881

STRAND THEATRE.

First opened—Mr. Rayner and Mrs. Waylett . . 1831
Mr. William Farren's management . . . 1849
Lessee, Mr. F. Allcroft; manager, Mr. T. Payne . 1855
Lessee, Miss Swanborough 1858-61
Mr. Swanborough, sen. . . . . . Dec. 1862
Mrs. Swanborough, 1865-88; she died (aged 84) 6 Jan. 1889
Rebuilt; re-opened . . . . . . 18 Nov. 1882
Mr. J. S. Clarke, lessee . . . . . . Jan. 1888
Re-opens; Mr. C. Wyndham and Mr. Wm. Duck, managers . . . . 6 Feb. 1889
Mr. Arthur Rousbey's opera company perform *Figaro* . . . . 14 March, ,,
Lessee, J. S. Clarke . . . . . . Sept. ,,
Mr. Willie Edouin . . . . . . 13 March, 1890
Our Flat, 645th and last performance . . 3 Jan. 1891
Private Inquiry, by F. C. Burnand 7 Jan.—13 Feb. ,,
Turned Up . . . . . . 14 Feb.—18 April, ,,
Our Daughters . . . . . 22 April—9 May, ,,
A Night's Frolic . . . . . 1 June *et seq.* 1891
Katti . . . . 27 June, ,,
The Late Lamented . . . 1 Aug. 1891—8 Jan. 1892
The New Wing, by H. A. Kennedy 9 Jan.—9 April, ,,
Niobe (All Smiles), a mythological comedy, by H. and E. Paulton (550 performances) . 11 April, 1892—21 July 1893
Our Flat (revived) . . . . 2 July–11 Oct. 1894
Babes (burlesque); Willie Edouin, lessee, 30 Jan.–4 Feb. 1895
Fanny, by George R. Sims and Cecil Raleigh, 15 April–1 June, ,,

[Plays with short runs.]

In a Locket, 16 Sept.–30 Oct. 1895; *The Lord Mayor*, by H. and E. A. Paulton, 1–5 Nov.; *Niobe*, by H. and E. A. Paulton, 14 Nov.–7 Feb, 1896; *On 'Change*, 15 Feb. *et seq.*; *Josiah's Dream*, by Chas. Rogers, 21 May–10 June; *Playing the Game*, musical farce, by W. Younge, A. Flaxman, F. Eplett, 12–16 June; *Teddy's Wives*, by Fergus Hume, 24 Sept., *et seq.*; *The Prodigal Father*, Mr. J. S. Clarke, manager, 1 Feb. 1897; *The Queen's Proctor*, adapted from the French, by Herman Merivale, 17 April–8 June; *John Gabriel Borkman*, by Ibsen, 5 matinées by the New Century theatre association, 3–7 May; *All Alive, Oh!* farce, 16 June *et seq.*; *The Purser*, by John T. Day, 13 Sept.–16 Oct.; *The Fanatic*, by John T. Day, 21 Oct.; *A Brace of Partridges*, farce, by Robt. Ganthony, 10 Feb.–mid March, 1898; *The "J. P.,"* farce, 9 April–2 July; *What happened to Jones*, 12 July, 1898–22 April, 1899; *Why Smith Left Home*, by Geo. W. Broadhurst . 1 May, 1899

A Chinese Honeymoon, by Geo. Dance and Howard Talbot, 608th performance . . 31 March, 1903

ROYAL ENGLISH OPERA HOUSE.

Erected for Mr. D'Oyly Carte by Mr. T. E. Colcutt in Cambridge Circus, Shaftesbury Avenue, a magnificent fireproof building to accommodate 2,000 persons, opened with *Ivanhoe*, music by sir Arthur Sullivan, libretto by Mr. Julian Sturgis, 31 Jan.—31 July, 1891

House closed . . . . 31 July, ,,

The Basoche, composer M. André Messager; librettist, M. Albert Carré; *Ivanhoe* (on some intervening days), 3–28 Nov. 1891; 5 Dec. 1891—16 Jan. 1892

House closed.

Madame Sarah Bernhardt; Sardou's *Cleopatra*, &c. 28 May—23 July, ,,

Named the PALACE THEATRE OF VARIETIES by a company, to whom it was sold; managing director, sir Augustus Harris, Oct.; opened, 10 Dec. ,,

ASTLEY'S AMPHITHEATRE.

Built by Philip Astley, and opened . . . 1773

Destroyed by fire, with numerous adjacent houses, 17 Sept. 1794

Rebuilt 1795

Burnt again, with forty houses . . 1 Sept. 1803

Ducrow's management 1825

Again destroyed by fire . . . 8 June, 1841

Rebuilt and re-opened by Mr. Batty . 17 April, 1843

Lessee and manager, Mr. W. Cooke . . 1855-60

Mr. W. Cooke's farewell benefit . . 30 Jan. 1860

A man killed by a lion . . . . Jan. 1861

Opened by Mr. Batty . . . . 6 Dec. ,,

Opened by Mr. Boucicault, as the THEATRE ROYAL, WESTMINSTER . . . . 26 Dec. 1862

Horsemanship and opera (under Mr. E. T. Smith), June, 1865

Sold by auction 1868

SURREY THEATRE (FORMERLY CIRCUS).

[Originally devoted to equestrian exercises, under Mr. Hughes] . . . . 4 Nov. 1782

Opened for performances . . . 4 Nov. 1783

Destroyed by fire . . . . 12 Aug. 1805

Mr. Elliston's management 1809

Mr. Elliston again . . . . 4 June, 1827

Mr. Davidge's tenure 1833

Mr. Shepherd and Mr. Anderson, managers, 12 Sept. 1863-5

Destroyed by fire, 31 Jan.: rebuilt and opened, 26 Dec. 1865

Used for melodramas pantomimes, &c. at low prices, 1889 *et seq.*

VICTORIA (FORMERLY COBURG).

[The erection was commenced under the patronage of the late princess Charlotte and the prince Leopold of Saxe-Coburg] 1816

The house was opened 1818

Messrs. Egerton and Abbott had the management in 1833

Mr. Osbaldiston's tenure 1840

Alarm of fire, sixteen persons killed . 27 Dec. 1858

Now *Victoria Hall*, used for popular lectures, concerts, &c. 1889

SADLER'S WELLS.

Opened as an orchestra 1683

Present house opened 1765

Eighteen persons trampled to death on a false alarm of fire . . . . 15 Oct. 1807

Management of Mrs. Warner and Mr. Phelps, 20 May, 1844-59

Management of Mr. Josephs . . 25 March, 1861

Re-opened by Mr. Phelps . . . 7 Sept. ,,

Lessee, Miss C. Lucette . . . 27 Sept. 1862

Miss Marriott, manager . 5 Sept. 1863—20 May, 1864

Miss C. Lucette, for opera 1865

Miss Marriott, legitimate drama (with intervals) 1865-8

Miss Hazlewood, Miss Marriott, and others . 1868-73

Opened by Mrs. Bateman as New Sadler's Wells 9 Oct. 1879

Mrs. Bateman dies (Miss I. Bateman succeeds), 13 Jan. 1881

Opened by Miss Roze de Vane . . 12 April, 1884

Closed and re-opened occasionally . . 1887 *et seq.*

Renovated and reopened by Mr. F. Macnaghten, 10 Nov. 1902

OTHER THEATRES.

Queen's Theatre, Tottenham-court-road . . . 1828

Garrick Theatre, Goodman's-fields 1830

City Theatre, Norton-Folgate 1837

Miss Kelly's Theatre (since named *Soho* and *New Royalty*) 1840

Marylebone, opened 1842

Standard Theatre, built 1854; burnt, 21 Oct. 1866; rebuilt 1868

Pavilion Theatre burnt . . . . 23 Feb. 1856

Alhambra, Leicester-square, opened, 1858; burnt, 7 Dec. 1882; and re-opened . . . 3 Dec. 1883

New Royalty (Soho) . . . . . 31 Aug. 1863

Holborn Theatre (afterwards called the *Mirror*, and the *Duke's*), opened, 16 Oct. 1866; burnt, 4 July, 1880

Royal Amphitheatre (for horses, &c.), Holborn, opened . . . . . . 25 May, 1867

New East London, opened . . . 12 Oct. ,,

"New Queen's Theatre," formerly St. Martin's hall, opened by Alfred Wigan . . . 24 Oct. ,,

St. George's Opera-house, Langham-place, opened by Mr. German Reed . . . . 18 Dec. ,,

The Globe, Strand, opened . . . 28 Nov. 1868

The Gaiety, Strand, opened . . . 21 Dec. ,,

Charing Cross, opened . . . . 19 June, 1869

Vaudeville, opened . . . . 16 April, 1870

Opéra Comique, 299, Strand, opened (for Mdlle. Déjazet) . . . . . . 29 Oct. ,,

Court Theatre, Chelsea, opened . . 25 Jan. 1871

Royal Alexandra Theatre, Park-street, Camden-town, opened, 31 May, 1873; burnt . 10 Sept. 1881

Criterion, Regent's-circus, Piccadilly, opened by Spiers and Pond, 21 March, 1874; closed, Feb. 1883; re-opened, 4 Oct. 1884; Mr. (aft. sir) Charles Wyndham's last appearance here, after 23 years' management; *David Garrick*, one of his greatest triumphs, produced here in 1886; special performance of *Rosemary*, by Louis N. Parker and Murray Carson, 21 July, 1899 (1,474*l.* proceeds for the prince of Wales's Hospital fund).

National Opera-house (*which see*), founded 7 Sept. and 16 Dec. 1875

Charing Cross re-opened as the "Folly" . 16 Oct. 1876

"Imperial theatre," at Westminster Aquarium . 1878

Holborn theatre reopened as the "Royal Connaught theatre" . . . . . . 1 Nov. 1879

Savoy Theatre opened (*which see*) . . 10 Oct. 1881

Toole's Theatre, formerly the Folly, opened in . 1882

Avenue Theatre, Thames Embankment, opened, 11 March, ,,

Prince's Theatre, Coventry-street (Mr. Bruce), opened . . . . . . 18 Jan. 1883

New Alhambra Theatre opened . . . 3 Dec. ,,

Empire Theatre, formerly Pandora, opened 14 April, afterwards music hall 1884

Mr. Terry's new theatre, Strand, opened 17 Oct. 1887

Grand Theatre, Islington, opened 4 Aug. 1883; burnt 29 Dec. 1887; rebuilt 1888

New Court Theatre opened . . . 24 Sept. ,,

Shaftesbury Theatre, London, opened . 20 Oct. ,,

Lyric Theatre, London . . . . 17 Dec. ,,

Garrick Theatre, Charing-cross-road, opened by Mr. Hare . . . . . 24 April, 1889

Trafalgar Theatre, St. Martin's-lane, opened 10 Sept. 1892; named Duke of York's, 1895.

Daly's Theatre, Leicester-square (American company), opened (*The Taming of the Shrew*), 27 June, 1893 [death of Mr. Augustin Daly, 7 June, 1899].

Borough Theatre at Stratford; proprietor, Mr. Albert Fredericks; opened by Mr. Beerbohm Tree and the Haymarket company with *King Henry IV.* . . . . . . 31 Aug. 1896

Grand Theatre, Fulham, opened by George Edwardes' *Geisha* Company on Monday, 23 Aug. 1897

Alexandra Theatre and Opera-house, Stoke Newington-road, N., opened . . . 27 Dec. ,,

Coronet Theatre, at Notting-hill-gate, opened, 28 Nov. 1898

Princess of Wales's Theatre, Kennington, opened, 28 Nov. ,,

The Century, formerly the Novelty, opened, Oct. 1899

Royal Duchess Theatre, Balham, opened by Mr. Chas. Wyndham (knt. June, 1902) . 16 Sept. ,,

Wyndham's Theatre, Charing-cross-road, Mr. Chas. Wyndham (knt. June, 1902), sole proprietor, opened with a performance of *David Garrick*; proceeds of first night (4,000*l*.) given to Transvaal War relief fund . . 16 Nov. 1899–7 Feb. 1900
Camden Theatre, High-st., Camden-town, erected by Mr. E. G. Saunders, to seat 3,000 persons, cost 50,000*l*., opened by Miss Ellen Terry, 21 Dec. ,,
Apollo Theatre, Shaftesbury-avenue, opened, 21 Feb. 1901
Elephant and Castle (reconstructed), opened, 4 Aug. 1902
New Theatre, St. Martin's-lane, proprietor, sir Chas. Wyndham, opened with a revival of *Rosemary*; receipts of the first night given to the British Soldiers' wives and families assoc., 12 March, 1903

DUBLIN THEATRES.

Werburg-street, commenced 1635
Orange-street, now Smock-alley 1662
Aungier-street (*Victor*) 1728
Ditto, management of Mr. Hitchcock . . . 1733
Crow-street Music-hall 1731
Rainsford-street Theatre 1732
Smock-alley Theatre, rebuilt 1735
Fishamble-street Music-hall 1741
Capel-street Theatre 1745
Crow-street, Theatre Royal 1758
Peter-street, Theatre Royal 1789
Hawkin's-street, Theatre Royal 1821
Destroyed by fire . . . . . . 9 Feb. 1880
Queen's Theatre, Brunswick-street 1844

EDINBURGH THEATRES.

Theatre of Music 1672
Allan Ramsay's 1736
The Caledonian Theatre 1822
Adelphi Theatre burnt down . . . 24 May, 1853
Royal Theatre burnt down (several lives lost), 13 Jan. 1865, again 6 Feb. 1875

FIRST OR LAST APPEARANCES.

Quin's first appearance 1716
Macklin at Lincoln's-inn-fields 1725
Garrick's at Goodman's-fields, as *Richard III.*, 19 Oct. 1741
Miss Farren (afterwards countess of Derby) first appears at Liverpool 1773
Garrick's last appearance . . . . . 10 June, 1776
Mrs. Robinson, *Perdita*: her last appearance, 24 Dec. 1779
Braham's first appearance at the Royalty, 20 April, 1787
Madame Storace; her first appearance in London, 24 Nov. 1789
Incledon's first appearance 1790
Miss Mellon, her first appearance as *Lydia Languish*, 31 Jan. 1795
Master Betty (*Infant Roscius*) *début* in London, enthusiastically received . . . . . 1 Dec. 1804
Liston's first appearance in London . 1 June, 1805
Miss F. M. Kelly's first appearance 1807
Romeo Coates appears as *Lothario* . . 10 April, 1811
Mrs. Jordan's last appearance, as *Lady Teazle*, 1 June, 1814
Miss O'Neill, as *Juliet* . . . . . 6 Oct. ,,
Mr. Macready's first appearance at Bath, as *Romeo*, 29 Dec. ,,
Booth's first appearance . . . . . 12 Feb. 1817
W. Farren's first appearance 1818
Munden's last appearance . . . . . May, 1824
Fanny Kemble's first appearance . . . 5 Oct. 1829
Edmund Kean's last appearance, as *Othello*, 25 March, 1833
Liston's last appearance . . . . . 31 May, 1838
Adelaide Kemble's first appearance . . . 2 Nov. 1841
Jenny Lind's first appearance . . . . 4 May, 1847
Mrs. Glover's farewell . . . . . 12 July, 1850
Mr. Bartley's farewell . . . . . 18 Dec. 1852
Mr. W. Farren's farewell 1855
Clara Novello's farewell . . . . . 21 Nov. 1860
Adelina Patti's first appearance at Covent Garden, 14 May, 1861
Miss Bateman appears as *Leah* . . . . 1 Oct. 1863
Her farewell at H.M.'s theatre . . . . 22 Dec. 1865
Madlle. Nilsson's first appearance at H.M.'s theatre as *Violetta* . . . . . . 8 June, 1867
Miss Kate Terry's last appearance (*Juliet* at the New Adelphi) . . . . . . 31 Aug. 1867
Madlle. Kellogg's *début* at Drury-lane . . 2 Nov. ,,
Mr. Bandmann's *début* . . . . . 17 Feb. 1868
Mr. Paul Bedford's farewell at New Queen's theatre, 16 May, ,,
Madlle. Marimon's *début*, as *Amina* . . 6 May, 1871
Mario's farewell in *La Favorita* at Italian opera, 19 July, ,,
Miss Isabella Bateman's *début* . . . 12 Sept. ,,
Mr. and Mrs. Alfred Wigan's last appearance (at Drury Lane) . . . . . . 6 July, 1872
Mr. H. Irving first appears as *Hamlet*, 31 Oct. 1874, 200th performance . . . . . 29 June 1875
Our Boys by H. J. Byron, 1st time 16 Jan. 1875 (at the Vaudeville); 1350th, 1 April; and last 18 April, 1879
Mr. Byron's *The Girls*, 1st performance 19 April, ,,
Mr. Sims Reeves' farewell at the R. Albert Hall, 11 May, 1891; appeared again at intervals, and died, aged 82 . . . . 25 Oct. 1900

MEMORANDA.

Richard Burbage 1567–1619
Edward Alleyn 1566–1626
Thomas Betterton 1635–1710
Mrs. Elizabeth Barry 1658–1713
Mrs. Pritchard 1711–1768
Mrs. Jordan 1762–1816
David Garrick 1717–79
Charles Macklin died 1797
Mr. Palmer died on the stage at Liverpool, 2 Aug. 1798
Bannister retired from the stage 1815
John P. Kemble died 1823
Talma died in Paris 1826
Weber came to London . . . . . Feb. ,,
The Brunswick theatre fell, owing to the weight of a newly-erected roof, and numbers of persons were wounded and some killed . . 29 Feb. 1828
Sarah Siddons died, 1831; her statue at Paddington Green unveiled by sir H. Irving on . 14 June, 1897
Edmund Kean died 1833
Charles Mathews died . . . . . 28 June, 1835
Madame Malibran died at Manchester . 23 Sept. 1836
Paganini died . . . . 27 May, 1840
Power lost in the *President* steamer, about 13 March, 1841
Elton lost in the *Pegasus* . . . . 18 July, 1843
Madlle. Mars died at Paris . . . 23 March, 1847
Madame Catalini died at Paris . . . 13 June, 1849
W. C. Macready retired . . . . 26 April, 1851
Alexander Lee died . . . . . . 9 Oct. ,,
Mrs. Warner died . . . . . . 5 Sept. 1854
Charles Kemble died . . . . . 12 Nov. ,,
John Braham died . . . . . . 17 Feb. 1856
Madame Vestris died . . . . . 8 Aug. ,,
Madlle. Rachel died . . . . . . 4 Jan. 1858
Mrs. Nisbet (lady Boothby) died . . . 16 Jan. ,,
Louis Lablache (buffo singer) died . . 23 Jan. ,,
John Pritt Harley died . . . . . 22 Aug. ,,
Flexmore, celebrated clown, died . . . 20 Aug. 1860
Mrs. Yates died . . . . . . 30 Oct. ,,
Alfred Bunn died . . . . . . 20 Dec. ,,
William Farren died . . . . . 25 Sept. 1861
Mr. Vandenhoff died . . . . . . 4 Oct. ,,
M. Tree (Mrs. Bradshaw) died . . . . Feb. 1862
Subscription testimonial (value 2001.) presented to C. J. Kean: Mr. Gladstone in the chair, 22 March, ,,
Sheridan Knowles died . . . . . . 30 Nov. ,,
Mrs. Wood (Miss Paton) died . . . . 21 July, 1864
Mr. F. Robson died . . . . . . 11 Aug. ,,
Madame Pasta died, aged 66 . . . 1 April, 1865
Charles J. Kean died . . . . . 23 Jan. 1868
Robert Keeley died, aged 74 . . . 3 Feb. 1869
Madame Grisi died . . . . . . 25 Nov. ,,
Wm. Brough, burlesque-writer, died, aged 44, 13 Mar. 1870
Paul Bedford died . . . . . . 11 Jan. 1871
T. W. Robertson, dramatist, died . . . 3 Feb. ,,
Lady Wrixon Becher (Miss O'Neill, *Juliet*), died 29 Oct. 1872
William C. Macready died . . . . 27 April, 1873
Wm. Hy. West Betty (the *Infant Roscius*) died, aged 82 . . . . Aug. 1874
Charles James Mathews died . . . 24 June, 1878
Alfred Wigan died . . . . . . 29 Nov. ,,
Frederick Gye, died (accidentally shot), nearly 30 years lessee and manager of Royal Italian Opera, Covent Garden . . . . . . 5 Dec. ,,

Wm. H. Schofield Payne, "King of Pantomime" (aged 70), died . . . . . . 18 Dec. 1878
Mrs. Wybert Rousby died . . . . 19 April, 1879
J. B. Buckstone died . . . 31 Oct. ,,
Mrs. Charles Kean (Miss Ellen Tree), died 20 Aug. 1880
Countess of Essex, formerly Miss Stephens, died. 22 Feb. 1882
Benjamin Nottingham Webster died . . 8 July, ,,
Miss Francis M. Kelly, aged 92, died . . 6 Dec. ,,
Grand dinner to Mr. H. Irving . . . 4 July, 1883
Miss Mary Anderson's *début* . . . . 1 Sept. ,,
Sig. Giuseppe Mario, aged 75, died . . 11 Dec. ,,
H. J. Byron, author, died . . . . 11 April, 1884
Mr. Frederick Balsir Chatterton, lessee of Drury Lane, &c. died . . . . . 18 Feb. 1886
Jenny Lind (Madame Lind Goldschmidt) died, aged 67 . . . . 2 Nov. 1887
Mrs. Swanborough died . . . . 6 Jan. 1889
Mrs. Dallas, known as Miss Glyn, died, aged 66 18 May, ,,
James Albery, dramatist, died . about 16 Aug. ,,
H. B. Farnie, dramatist, died . . 22 Sept. ,,
Frederic Emes Clay, operatic composer, died, about 24 Nov. ,,
Westland Marston, dramatist, died . . 6 Jan. 1890
John Barnett, operatic composer, died, aged 87, 17 April, ,,
Dion Boucicault, dramatist, died . . 18 Sept. ,,
Wm. Gorman Wills, dramatist, died, announced, 15 Dec. 1891
Maddison Morton, dramatist, author of "Box and Cox," &c., died . . . . . 19 Dec. ,,
Samuel Brandram, M.A., able reciter; died, aged 68 . . . . 7 Nov. 1892
Mrs. Frances Ann (Kemble) Butler, daughter of Charles Kemble, died aged 83 . . 15 Jan. 1893
Eleanor Bufton (aft. Mrs. Arthur Swanborough), died . . . . . . about 11 April, ,,
Mr. Edwin Booth, American actor, died . 7 June, ,,
Mr. David James (Belasco), comedian, aged 54, died, 2 Oct. ,,
Miss Ada Swanborough, of the Strand Theatre, died . . . . 12 Dec. ,,
Mr. Henry Pettitt, dramatist, died . . 24 Dec. ,,
Mr. James Anderson, tragedian; born 1819, died 3 March, 1895
Priscilla Horton, actress, 1832 *et seq.*; married Mr. German Reed; died . . . . 18 March, ,,
Mr. Corney Grain died . . . . 19 March, ,,
Ada Cavendish died . . . . . 5 Oct. ,,
Amy Roselle (Mrs. Arthur Dacre), born 1854; died (see *Suicide*, 1895) . . . 17 Nov. ,,
Lady Gregory (Mrs. Stirling, died, aged 79, 30 Dec. ,,
Mr. Henry Howe, died aged 84 . . . 9 March, 1896
Mr. Temple E. Crozier (aged 24) accidentally killed while acting at the Novelty theatre by Wilfrid Moritz Franks, also acting . . . 10 Aug. ,,
Mr. William Chas. Jas. Terriss (Lewin), aged 49, assassinated at the Adelphi (*which see*) . 16 Dec. 1897
The collections of Edmund Kean and his son Charles, realized 1,653*l.* 11*s.* . . 24 June, 1898
Lady Martin (Helen Faucit), born, 11 Oct. 1820; died . . . . 31 Oct. ,,
Mrs. Keeley (Mary Ann Goward), born, 22 Nov. 1805; died . . . . . . 12 March, 1899
Mrs. Sara Lane, over 50 years manager of the Britannia theatre, for which she wrote many plays, died, aged 76 . . . . Aug. ,,
Mr. Franklin McLeay, a clever Canadian actor, died, aged 33 . . . . early July, 1900
Mr. George Conquest, a *pantomimist* and manager of the Surrey theatre, died . . 14 May, 1901
Edith and Ida Yeoland, aged 26 and 21, died (see *Suicide* 1901) . . . . 16 July, ,,
Mrs. Hermann Vezin (Mrs. Chas. Young) died, 10 April, 1902

THEATRICAL FUNDS. The Theatrical fund of Covent Garden was established in 1760, incorporated 1774; that of Drury Lane by Garrick 1766; incorporated 1775. They grant pensions to members and their families. The Royal General Theatrical fund was established in 1839, incorporated 1853.

The *Theatrical Mission and Institute* for the benefit of theatrical employés, started in 1876. The princess Christian inaugurated for them "Macready" house, Covent Garden 30 Nov. 1887.

THEATROGRAPH, see *Kinetoscope*, March, 1896.

THEATROPHONE, a form of the telephone specially adapted for hearing theatrical performances at a distance. The apparatus of the "compagnie du theatrophone" of Paris was exhibited at the Savoy hotel, and by its means the performance of the "Nautch Girl" at the Savoy theatre was said to be well heard, 11 Dec. 1891.

THEBAN LEGION, according to tradition, was composed of Christians, and submitted to martyrdom rather than attack their brethren during the persecution of the emperor Maximin, or sacrifice to the gods, about A.D. 286. Their leader Maurice was canonised.

THEBES or **LUXOR**, in Upper Egypt, called also Diospolis, as being sacred to Jupiter. *Homer.* Its foundation is mythically attributed to Osiris. It is said to have been the magnificent capital of Egypt about 1600 B.C., having a circuit of about 14 geographical miles. It was then the chief seat of the worship of Ammon, or Ammun, the Zeus Ammon of the Greeks, and the Jupiter Ammon of the Romans, and hence was called No Ammon by the Hebrews. Thebes was ruined by Cambyses, king of Persia, 525 B.C., and by the foundation of Alexandria, 332 B.C.; it rebelled and was taken by Ptolemy Lathyrus, 86 B.C., and few traces of it were seen in the age of Juvenal; see *Memnoneium.* After centuries of neglect, its wonderful ruins have been greatly visited since the explorations of Belzoni, 1817.—The tombs of Amenophis II. abt. 1500 B.C., XVIII. dynasty, and 7 other royal mummies, discovered by M. Loret in perfect preservation, March, 1898. THEBES, N. Greece (the capital is mythically said to have been founded by Cadmus.) The legendary history of Œdipus and his family, celebrated by the Greek tragic poets, belongs to Thebes. It became a republic about 1120 B.C., and flourished under Epaminondas 378-362 B.C. The "sacred band" formed by him, 377 B.C., was revived in 1877. Thebes' seven gates are mentioned by Homer. See *Bœotia* and *Greece.* Thebes suffered much by earthquake shocks, end of May, 1893, and was nearly destroyed by earthquakes, 20 April *et seq.* 1894; active relief measures were organized.

THEFT was punished by heavy fines among the Jews; by death at Athens, by the laws of Draco; see *Draco.* The Anglo-Saxons nominally punished theft with death, if above 12*d.* value; but the criminal could redeem his life by a ransom. In the 9th of Henry I. this power of redemption was taken away, 1108. The punishment of theft was very severe in England, till mitigated by Peel's acts 9 & 10 Geo. IV. 1829. The laws respecting theft were consolidated in 1862. Larceny act passed 14 Aug. 1896; another passed, 2 Aug. 1901.

THEINE, see *Cafeine.*

THEISTS (*Theos*, God), a name given to deists about 1660.—*Dean Martin.* See *Deism*, *Unitarians*, and *Voysey.*

THELLUSSON'S WILL, a most singular document. Mr. Peter Isaac Thellusson, a Genevese and an affluent merchant of London, left 100,000*l.* to his widow and children; and the remainder of his property, more than 600,000*l.*, he left to trustees, to accumulate during the lives of his three sons, and the lives of their sons; then the estates, directed to be purchased with the produce of the accumulated fund, were to be conveyed to the eldest lineal male descendant of his three sons, with the benefit of survivorship. Should no heir then exist, the whole was to be applied, by the agency of the sinking fund, to the discharge of the national debt. It is said that Mr. Thellusson held much property in trust, and that he desired a sufficient interval of time to elapse for the appearance of just claimants. He died 21 July, 1797. His will incurred much public censure, and was contested by the heirs-at-law, but finally established by a decision of the house of lords, 25 June, 1805. The last surviving grandson died in Feb. 1856. A dispute then arose whether the eldest male descendant or the male descendant of the eldest son should inherit the property. The question was decided on appeal by the house of lords (9 June, 1859), in favour of the latter, lord Rendlesham and Charles S. Thellusson confirming the decision of the Master of the Rolls in 1858. In consequence of the legal expenses the property is said not to exceed greatly its value in the testator's lifetime. On 28 July, 1800, the Thellusson act was passed, restraining testators from devising their property for purposes of accumulation for longer than 21 years after death; any other direction to be void.

THEOCRACY, government by God, existed among the Israelites till Saul was made king, about 1095 B.C. (*Sam.* viii. 7.)

THEODOLITE, an instrument for measuring horizontal angles, used in surveying, consists of a telescope and a divided circle. It was probably first constructed in the 17th century. Jesse Ramsden, in 1787, completed the great theodolite employed in the trigonometrical survey of England and Wales by general Roy.

THEODOSIAN CODE, see *Codes*.

"THEOLOGIA GERMANICA," or "Teutsche Theologey" (printed 1528; Latin and French editions, 1558), a German mystical work, written about the 14th century. In it the "good man," disgusted with the corruptions in church and state, is led to seek for God in the temple of the heart. Luther is said to have placed the work next to the Bible and St. Augustin.

THEOLOGY (from the Greek *Theos*, God), the science which treats of the nature and attributes of God, of his relations to man, and of the manner in which they may be discovered. It is generally divided into two heads. 1. *Inspired*, including the Holy Scriptures, their interpretation, &c. 2. *Natural;* which lord Bacon calls the first part of philosophy. — Butler's "Analogy of Religion" (1736) and Paley's "Natural Theology" (1802) are eminent books on the latter subject.—Abelard (died 1142) wrote "Theologia Christiania." The "Summa Totius Theologiæ" by Thomas Aquinas (born about 1224), a standard Roman catholic work, was printed with commentaries, &c., in 1596. Modern theology much influenced by the results of the higher criticism.

Death of prof. A. B. Davidson, eminent British Hebraist . . . . 2 Feb. 1902

THEOPHILANTHROPISTS (lovers of God and man), a sect formed in France in 1796; and headed by one of the five directors, Lepaux, in 1797; was dissolved in 1802.

THEOSOPHY (*theos*, God; *sophia*, wisdom), divine wisdom, a name that has been given since the time of Ammonius Saccas, in the third century, to various schools of philosophy and their mystical tenets respecting the spiritual nature of man and his relation to the universe. Followers of Giordano Bruno and Paracelsus, in the 16th century, are termed theosophists.

The *Theosophical Society* was founded in America by Madame Blavatsky, aided by colonel Olcott, about 1875–6. Aims at universal brotherhood, the study of Eastern philosophy, and to investigate unexplained laws of nature and powers latent in man. It has a station in London, and 350 branches in India (headquarters, Madras, 1879), America, and the colonies. Mrs. Anna Kingsford, M.D., president in 1883, died 22 Feb. 1888. Annual conventions.

Mrs. Besant's lecture on Theosophy and Occultism at St. James's hall, London, 9 Oct. 1891, related especially to "Esoteric Buddhism" as described by Mr. Sinnett.

Prof. Max Müller's "Theosophy or Psychological Religion" (a sequel to Psychical and Anthropological religion, all combined in Christianity), published April, 1893.

THERMIDOR REVOLUTION. On the 9th Thermidor of the 2nd year (27 July, 1794), the Convention deposed Robespierre, and on the next day he and twenty-two of his partisans were executed.

THERMO-ELECTRICITY and **THERMOPILE**, see under *Electricity*, and *Heat*.

THERMOMETER. Freezing point: *Fah.* 32°; *R.* 0°; *C.* 0°. Boiling point: *Fah.* 212°, *R.* 80°, *C.* 100°.

Invented by Galileo, before 1597. *Libri.*
Invented by Drebbel of Alcmaer, 1609. *Boerhaave.*
Invented by Paulo Sarpi, 1609. *Fulgentio.*
Invented by Sanctorio in 1610. *Borelli.*

Fahrenheit's thermometer invented about 1726; Réaumur's and Celsius's (the latter now termed centigrade) soon after. [Fahrenheit's scale is usually employed in England, and Réaumur's and the centigrade on the continent.

The mode of construction by substituting quicksilver for spirits was invented some years subsequently. Halley proposed it in 1697.

Mr. L. M. Casella issued a minimum thermometer in Sept. 1861. It registers degrees of cold by means of mercury. Mr. Casella made many improvements in thermometers, &c., and died, 23 April, 1897.

Negretti and Zambra's registering minimum thermometers, adapted for deep-sea purposes, made known early in 1874.

Letter from Mr. James J. Hicks, of London, stating that since 1861, he makes about 250,000 or more thermometers of all kinds, annually, hundreds of which are tested at the Kew Observatory, and are superior to those of foreign manufacture, *Times*, 23 March, 1897.

THERMOPHONE, in which sonorous vibrations are produced by the expansion of heated bodies connected with an electro-magnet. The apparatus was constructed by Theodor Wiesendanger and described by him in October, 1878.

THERMOPYLÆ (Doris, N. Greece). Leonidas, at the head of 300 Spartans and 700 Thespians, at the defile of Thermopylæ, withstood the whole force of the Persians during three days, 7, 8, 9 Aug. 480 B.C., when Ephialtes, a Trachinian, perfidiously leading the enemy by a secret path up the mountains, brought them to the rear of the Greeks, who, thus placed between two assailants, perished gloriously on heaps of their slaughtered foes. One Greek only returned home, and he was received with reproaches for having fled.* Here Antiochus the Great, king of Syria, was defeated by the Romans, 191 B.C.

* The distich, in the Greek Anthology, by Simonides, their contemporary, is thus translated by Bowles:—

"Go, tell the Spartans, thou that passest by,
That here, obedient to their laws, we lie."

THERMUM, THERMUS, or THERMA (Greece), a strong city, the Acropolis of Ætolia, N. Greece, was captured and ravaged by Philip V. of Macedon, 218 and 206 B.C., on account of its favouring the Romans.

THESAURUS (treasury), a title given in the 17th and 18th centuries to large collections of small works on history and archæology. The most celebrated are—

"Thesaurus Antiquitatum Græcorum," by J. Gronovius. 13 vol. fol. 1697-1702
"Thesaurus Antiquitatum Romanorum," by J. G. Grævius. 12 vol. fol. 1694
"Thesaurus Antiquitatum et Historicum Italiæ, Siciliæ," &c., by G. Grævius and P. Burmannus. 45 vol. fol. 1725
"Thesaurus Antiquitatum Sacrarum," by B. Ugolinus. 34 vol. fol. 1744-09

THESPIÆ, a city of Bœotia, N. Greece. 700 of its citizens perished with Leonidas at Thermopylæ, Aug. 480 B.C. It suffered through the jealousy of the Thebans, who destroyed its walls in 372 B.C.

THESSALONICA (now Salonica), a city in Macedonia, N. Greece, originally Therme, but rebuilt by Cassander, and said to have been named after his wife, Thessalonica, daughter of Philip, after 315 B.C. Here Paul preached, 53; and to the church here he addressed two epistles in 54. In consequence of seditions, a frightful massacre of the inhabitants took place in 390, by order of the emperor Theodosius. Thessalonica partook of the changes of the Eastern empire. Thessalonica was taken by the Saracens, with great slaughter, 30 July, 904; by the Normans of Sicily, 15 Aug. 1185; and after various changes was taken from the Venetians by the Turks under Amurath, 1430. Population, 1885, 159,000; 1901, *about*, 105,000.

A young Bulgarian Christian girl, said to be an unwilling convert to Mahometanism, was rescued from the Turks and taken to the American consul's, 5 May; riots ensued on 6 May; the German and French consuls, Abbott and Moulin, were murdered; the Western powers intervened; reparation was ordered by the Sultan; several murderers were executed 16 May; other persons were imprisoned; and 40,000*l.* said to be paid to the families of the victims, Aug. 1876.

Destructive fire; 10,000 persons homeless; the mosque and church, &c., destroyed; estimated loss, 800,000*l.*, 4 Sept., see *Mansion House Fund*, 1890.

Dynamite plot and outrage, Ottoman bank, and other buildings destroyed by bombs, many people killed and injured, 28 April, 1903.

THESSALY (N. Greece), the seat of many of the adventures described by the poets. The first king of whom we have any certain knowledge was Hellen, son of Deucalion, from whom his subjects were called Hellenists, a name afterwards extended to all Greeks. From Thessaly came the Achæans, the Ætolians, the Dorians, the Hellenes, &c. The two most remarkable events in the early history of this country are the deluge of Deucalion, 1548 B.C., and the expedition of the Argonauts, 1263 B.C.; *see them severally*. Thessaly long aimed at neutrality in Grecian affairs, but became involved through its rulers, the tyrants of Pheræ;—Lycophron, about 404 B.C.; his son Jason, 374, assassinated 370; Alexander, the most eminent, defied Athens and Thebes; assassinated 359. Philip of Macedon, after a defeat (353 B.C.), gained a victory over the tyrants, 352; and subjugated the country wholly, 343. The Romans gave a nominal freedom to Thessaly after their victory at Cynoscephalæ, 197. It is now included in the kingdom of Greece by the treaty of 24 May, signed 2 July, and occupied Aug. — Sept. 1881. Railway from Volo to Larissa the capital, opened by the king, 4 May, 1884. See *Inundations*, 1883; *Greco-Turkish War* and *Greece*, 1897-8.

THETFORD (Norfolk), said to have been the Roman Sitomagus, and an important Saxon town, was a bishopric from 1075 to 1091, when the see was removed to Norwich. It was made a suffragan bishopric by Henry VIII.; the power given him 1534. Dr. A. T. Lloyd (bp. of Newcastle, 1903); Dr. J. P. A. Bowers, 29 June, 1903. Pop. 1891, 4,247; 1901, 4,600.

THIBET or TIBET (central Asia), is said to have been a kingdom 313 B.C., conquered by Genghis Khan 1206, and gradually subdued by and annexed to China, 1255-1720. Buddhism, introduced about 639, became the dominant religion about 905; and the Lamas have absolute power in religious and temporal affairs. Thibet was visited by Marco Polo, 1278; by Jesuits about 1661-2; Bogle and Hamilton, 1774; and Thomas Manning, 1810. An astronomical survey was carried on surreptitiously by two pundits of semi-Thibet origin, under the superintendence of capt. Montgomerie, 1865-7. War with Nepaul, May; peace, June, 1884. Hon. Colman Macaulay's expedition to Lachen valley, to promote commerce; well received, announced 30 Nov. 1884.

A mission to Tibet, including Mr. Macaulay with scientific assistance, organised in India; scheme suspended July, 1886. See *Sikkim*.

The progress of the Russian exploring expedition under colonel Pevtsoff reported, summer 1890.

Much geographical knowledge has been obtained, and maps constructed. The Chinese oppose the expedition.

M. Gabriel Bonvalot, prince Henry of Orleans, and father Dedeken, gave an illustrated account of their recent exploration of Thibet, &c., to the French Geographical society, at Paris, 31 Jan. 1891.

"Across Thibet," by M. Bonvalot, published, 1891.

Capt Bower, Dr. Thorold and party cross Thibet, June, 1891, and arrive at Simla, April, 1892.

See *Nepaul*, 1896.

Mahometan rebellion, much slaughter, Oct. 1895; desperate fighting, Mahometan forts destroyed, rebellion crushed, Feb. 1896.

"Through Unknown Tibet, 1896," by capt. M. S. Wellby, published 1898; he died of his wounds in S. Africa, 5 Aug. 1900.

Capt. Deasy successfully explores W. Thibet; see *Asia*, 1896-99.

Mr. Douglas Freshfield explores the Kanchenjunga glaciers, autumn, 1899.

Capt. Kozloff explores unknown lands; the source of the Hoang-ho, the Yang-tse, and the Mekong; May, 1900-Oct. 1901.

Dr. Sven Hedin's successful explorations, 1899-1902; see *Asia*.

Mission under col. Younghusband despatched by the Indian government to meet the Tibetan and Chinese officials to discuss questions of trade, reaches Kanba Jong, July, 1903.

Advance of the British mission to be made, the Chumbi valley, "the key of Tibet," to be occupied, and an advance made to Gyangtse, 150 miles from Lhassa, reported mid Nov. 1903.

THIEVES' ISLAND, see *Ladrones*.

THIEVES' SYNOD, at Ephesus, 349 or 449, where the doctrines of Eutyches respecting Christ's incarnation were approved, received the name because his opponents were silenced or excluded.

THIMBLES are said to have been found at Herculaneum, and long ago used by the Chinese. Their invention in Europe is traditionally ascribed to Nicolas van Benschoten, of Amsterdam, in the 17th century. The art of making them was brought to England by John Lofting, a mechanic, from Holland, who set up a workshop at Islington, near London, and practised the manufacture in various metals with profit and success, about 1695.

A *Thimble League* patronised by queen Victoria 1886; the object being to provide employment for distressed needlewomen; there was a sale of the work at lady Winchilsea's house, 23, Ennismore-gardens, 24–25 Oct. 1888.

THIONVILLE, the ancient *Theodonis villa*, a fortified city on the Moselle, N. E. France. It was the occasional residence of Charlemagne and his successors, and on the extinction of his race it was successively held by private lords, the counts of Luxemburg, the dukes of Burgundy, the house of Austria, and the kings of Spain. It was taken by the duke of Guise, 23 June, 1558, after an obstinate defence, and returned to Philip II. by the peace of Cateau-Cambrésis. It successfully resisted the marquis de Feuquières in 1637, but was taken after four months' siege by the duc d'Enghien, 10 Aug. 1643, and remained with France. It successfully resisted the Austrians in 1792, and the Prussians in 1814. It was invested by the Germans in Aug. 1870, and after bombardment, being in flames, surrendered 24 Nov. following.

THIRTEEN CLUB, about 130 members, formed in London, Oct. 1889, to counteract vulgar prejudices respecting unlucky numbers, days, &c.

THIRTY-NINE ARTICLES, see *Articles*.

THIRTY TYRANTS, a term applied to the governors of Athens, in 404 B.C., who were expelled by Thrasybulus, 403; and also to the numerous aspirants to the imperial throne of Rome during the reigns of Gallienus and Aurelian, A.D. 259-274.

THIRTY YEARS' WAR, in Germany, between the catholics and protestants. It began in Bohemia in 1618, and ended with the peace of Westphalia in 1648. It is renowned for the victories of Wallenstein and Gustavus Adolphus of Sweden, and for its history by Schiller, published 1790-93. See *Battles*, 1618-48.

THISTLE,* ORDER OF THE, SCOTLAND, founded by James V. 1540. It consisted originally of himself, as sovereign, and twelve knights, in imitation of Christ and his twelve apostles. In 1542, James died, and the order was discontinued, about the time of the Reformation. The order was renewed by James VII. of Scotland and II. of England, by making eight knights, 29 May, 1687; increased to twelve by queen Anne in 1703; to sixteen by George IV. in 1827. The original knights of 1687 were

George, duke of Gordon.
John, marquis of Athol.
James, earl of Arran, afterwards duke of Hamilton; killed in a duel, 1712.
Alexander, earl of Moray.
James, earl of Perth; attainted.
Kenneth, earl of Seaforth; attainted.
George, earl of Dumbarton.
John, earl of Melfort; attainted.

* Some Scottish historians make the origin of this order very ancient. The abbot Justinian says it was instituted by Achaius I. of Scotland, 809, when that monarch made an alliance with Charlemagne, and then took for his device the thistle. It is stated that the king Hungus, the Pict, had a dream, in which St. Andrew made a midnight visit, and promised him a sure victory over his foes, the Northumbrians; and that the next day St. Andrew's Cross (×) appeared in the air, and the Northumbrians were defeated. On this story, it is said, Achaius framed the order more than 700 years before James V.

THISTLEWOOD'S CONSPIRACY, see *Cato-street Conspiracy*.

THOMAS'S HOSPITAL, ST. (Southwark), was founded as an almshouse by Richard, prior of Bermondsey, in 1213, and surrendered to Henry VIII. in 1538. In 1551 the mayor and citizens of London, having purchased of Edward VI. the manor of Southwark, including this hospital, repaired and enlarged it, and admitted into it 260 poor, sick, and helpless objects; upon which the king, in 1553, incorporated it, together with Bethlehem, St. Bartholomew's, &c. It was rebuilt in 1693. In 1862, the site was sold to the South-eastern railway company, and the patients were removed to the Surrey music hall. The foundation stone of the new hospital, erected at Stangate, near the Surrey side of Westminster-bridge, was laid by queen Victoria, 13 May, 1868; and the new hospital was opened by her majesty, 21 June, 1871.

The appointment of a paid resident treasurer, instead of an honorary one, and other changes recommended by committees, were negatived by the general committee, Nov. 1877.

Establishment of wards for paying-patients . Nov. 1878

Meeting at the Mansion-house to raise 100,000*l.* to increase the accommodation, the duke of Connaught present, 13 Feb. 1895; the queen gave 100*l.*, 15 Feb.; 1000*l.* from Messrs. Barclay & Perkins; 1000*l.* from lord Iveagh, &c., April, 26,249*l.* 13*s.* 7*d.* received up to Dec. 1895; 35,000*l.* bequeathed by sir Robert Rawlinson, announced, 4 July, 1898; over 500,000*l.* bequeathed by Mr. C. Gassiot . . . . May, 1902

THOMAS, ST., see *Virgin Isles*.

THOMISTS, see *Scotists*.

THOMITES or **TOMITES**, a body of enthusiasts who assembled at Boughton, near Canterbury. An insane Cornish publican named John Nicholls, called Thom, or Tom, assumed the name of sir W. Courtenay, knight of Malta and king of Jerusalem, came into Kent, was an unsuccessful candidate for parliament, and incited the rabble against the Poor Law act. On 31 May, 1838, a farmer of the neighbourhood, whose servant had joined the crowd which attended Thom, sent a constable to fetch him back; but on his arrival on the ground he was shot dead by Thom. The military were then called out, and lieut. Bennett proceeded to take the murderer into custody; but Thom advanced, and, firing a pistol, killed the lieutenant on the spot. One of the soldiers fired at Thom, and laid him dead by the side of lieut. Bennett. The people then attacked the military, who were compelled to fire, and eight more persons were killed before the mob dispersed.

THORACIC DUCT, discovered first in a horse, by Eustachius, about 1563; in the human body, by Ol. Rudbec, a Swedish anatomist. Thomas Bartholine, of Copenhagen, and Dr. Joliffe, of England, also discovered it about 1654. See *Lacteals*.

THORINUM, a very rare metal (a heavy gray powder), discovered by Berzelius in 1828.

THORN (on the Vistula, Poland) was founded by the Teutonic Knights in 1231. Here they acknowledged themselves to be vassals of Poland in 1466. Thorn was taken by Charles XII. of Sweden in 1703. Many protestants were slain here (after a religious riot) at the instigation of the Jesuits, 7 Dec. 1724. Thorn was acquired by the Prussians in 1793; taken by the French in 1806; restored to Prussia at the peace in 1815. Population, 1890, 27,007.

THOROUGH. The name given by Thos. Wentworth, earl of Strafford, to his unsuccessful scheme for making Charles I. an absolute monarch. He was attainted and beheaded, 12 May, 1641.

THORPE, see *Railway Accidents*, 1874.

THOUGHT READING. In 1881 Mr. W. Irving Bishop professed to be able to read a person's thoughts by touching some part of the skin. On June 11 in the presence of Mr. G. J. Romanes, professor E. Ray Lankester, Mr. F. Galton, and others; he was successful with some persons, and failed with others (*Nature*, No. 608).

In 1883 he was challenged by Mr. Labouchere, M.P., to operate under certain conditions, at St. James's Hall on 12 June, but virtually declined the tests. Other experiments by Mr. Bishop, 3, 4 June, 1884; success doubted.

Mr. Bishop sentenced to pay 10,000*l.* damages to Mr. Maskelyne for libel in *Truth* (23 July, 1884), 15 Jan.; appeal disallowed, 28 Jan.; damages reduced to 500*l.*, 2 July, 1885. He died of catalepsy at New York, 13 May, 1889.

Experiments by Mr. Stuart Cumberland reported successful on the prince of Wales and others, 19 July, 1884; by sefi. Odrap, London, 15 Oct. 1902.

THRACE (now *Roumelia*, in Turkey) derived its name from Thrax, the son of Mars.—*Aspin.* The Thracians were a warlike people, and therefore Mars was said to have been born and to have had his residence among them.—*Euripides.* See *Odrysæ.*

Byzantium, the capital, founded by the Megarians, about B.C.	675
Invasion of Darius I. 513; Thrace subdued by Megabazus	508
Xerxes marches against Greece through Thrace, and retreats	480
Other Greek colonies established	450-400
Wars between Macedon and the Odrysæ (*which see*)	429-343
Philip II. acquires Amphipolis, 358; and gradually all the Greek colonies	357-341
Death of Alexander; Thrace allotted to Lysimachus, 323; who builds Lysimachia	309
Lysimachus defeated and slain by Seleucus at Corupedion	281
Thrace overrun by the Gauls	279
Lysimachia and the chief towns seized by the fleet of Ptolemy Euergetes	247
Recovered by Philip V. of Macedon	205-200
Lost by him to the Romans	196
Seized by Antiochus III. of Syria, who is defeated at Magnesia, 190; and surrenders Thrace	188
Perseus defeated in his attempt to regain Thrace,	171-168
The Thracian kings rule nominally under the Romans	148 *et seq.*
Rebellion of Vologæsus quelled	14
Rhœmetalces II. last king A.D.	38
Thrace made a Roman province, about	47
Invaded by the Goths	255
Settled by Sarmatians	334-376
Ravaged by Alaric, 395; by Attila	447
Conquered by the Turks, who made Adrianople their capital	1341-53
Constantinople captured by Mahomet II., 29 May,	1453

THRASHING-MACHINES. The flail was the only instrument formerly in use for thrashing corn. The Romans used a machine called the *tribulum*, a sledge loaded with stones or iron, drawn over the corn-sheaves by horses. The first machine attempted in modern times was invented by Michael Menzies, at Edinburgh, about 1732; Andrew Meikle invented a machine in 1776. Many improvements have been since made, and steam is employed. An act for the prevention of accidents by these machines was passed in 1879.

THRASYMENE or **TRASIMENE** (more correctly Trasimenus), a lake (N. Italy). A most bloody engagement took place near the Trasimene lake between the Carthaginians under Hannibal and the Romans under Flaminius, 217 B.C. No less than 15,000 Romans were left dead on the field of battle, and 10,000 taken prisoners; or, according to Livy, 6000; or Polybius, 15,000. The loss of Hannibal was about 1500 men. About 10,000 Romans made their escape, all covered with wounds. Flaminius was killed during the fight.—*Livy; Polybius.* On the same day, an earthquake occurred, which desolated several cities in Italy.

THREATENING LETTERS. Sending letters, whether anonymously written, or with a fictitious name, demanding money, or threatening to kill a person, or fire his house, was made punishable as a felony, without benefit of clergy, by the Black Act, in 1722. Persons extorting money by threatening to accuse others of such offences as are subjected to death, or other infamous punishments, were to be adjudged imprisonment, whipping, or transportation, by 30 Geo. II., 1756, and other acts; another, 24 & 25 Vict. cc. 96, 97 (1861).

THREE DENOMINATIONS, see *Denominations.*

THREE CHOIRS (Gloucester, Worcester, and Hereford). Festivals held in 1724, if not earlier, at Gloucester, for the performance of cathedral music on a grand scale for charitable purposes, still continued.

THREE F.'s, *see* F.

THREE ACRES AND A COW, see *Land*, 1885.

THRIFT, see under *National.*

THROAT AND EAR DISEASES, a hospital for them opened near Gray's-inn-road, March, 1874; foundation of a new building laid by madame Adelina Patti, marchesa de Caux, 16 Sept. 1875.

THUGS, organised secret fanatical murderers in India, who considered their victims to be sacrifices to their goddess Kali or Bhowain. The English commenced suppressing them about 1810, but did not succeed till about 1830, when a plan for the purpose was adopted by lord Wm. Bentinck.

THUMB-SCREW, an instrument used in the first stages of torture by the Spanish inquisition. In Great Britain, rev. Wm. Carstares, a presbyterian minister, was the last who suffered by it, before the Scotch privy council, to make him divulge secrets entrusted to him, which he firmly resisted. After the revolution in 1688, the thumb-screw was presented to him by the council. King William expressed a desire to see it, and tried it on, bidding the doctor to turn the screw; but, at the third turn, he cried out "Hold—*hold!* doctor: another turn would make *me* confess anything."

THUNDERER, see *Navy of England*, 1872, 1876, 1879.

THUNDERING LEGION. During a contest with the invading Marcomanni, the prayers of some Christians in a Roman legion are said to have been followed by a storm of thunder, lightning, and rain, which tended greatly to discomfit the enemy; and hence the legion received the name, 174.

THURII or THURIUM, a Greek city, S. Italy, founded after the fall of Sybaris, about 443 B.C. It suffered from the incursions of the Lucanians, by whom the Thurians were severely defeated, 390 B.C. It became eventually a dependent ally of Rome; was ravaged by the troops of Hannibal, 204; was established as a colony by the Romans, 194; and was captured by Spartacus in the Servile war, who levied upon it heavy contributions, 72.

THURINGIA, an early Gothic kingdom in central Germany, was overrun by Attila and the Huns, 451; the last king, Hermanfried, was defeated and slain by Thierry, king of the Franks, who annexed it to his dominions, 530. It formed two duchies, 630-717, and 849-919; a margraviate, 960-1090; landgraviate and county, 1130-1247; and was, after various changes and many conflicts, absorbed into Saxony in the 15th century. In 1815 it was surrendered to Prussia.

THURLES (S. Ireland). Here was held a synod of the Roman catholic archbishops, bishops, inferior clergy, and religious orders, under the direction of archbishop Cullen, the Roman catholic primate, 22 Aug. 1850. It condemned the Queen's Colleges, and recommended the foundation of a Roman catholic university, 10 Sept. following. The acts were forwarded to Rome for approval of the pope, Pius IX., and published, 1 Jan. 1852.

THUROT'S INVASION. Thurot, an Irish commodore in the French service, became a terror to all the merchant-ships of this kingdom. He had the command of a small armament, and landed 1000 men at Carrickfergus in Ireland, and plundered the town. He reached the Isle of Man, and was overtaken by captain Elliot, with three frigates, who engaged his little squadron, which was taken, and the commodore killed, 28 Feb. 1760. Thurot's true name was O'Farrell. His grandfather had followed the fortunes of James II.; but his mother being of a family of some dignity in France, he assumed her name.—*Burns*.

THURSDAY, the fifth day of the week, named from Thor, the most valiant son of Odin, a deified hero worshipped by the northern nations, particularly by the Scandinavians and Celts. His authority was said to extend over the winds, seasons, thunder and lightning, &c. Thursday is in Latin *dies Jovis*, or Jupiter's day.

THYATIRA (Asia Minor), the place assigned for the battle at which the rebel Procopius was defeated by the army of the emperor Valens, 366. See *Seven Churches*.

THYMBRA (Asia Minor). Here Cyrus the Great defeated the confederate army aiding Crœsus, and obtained supremacy in Asia, B.C. 548.

TIARA, head ornament of the ancient Persians. The name is given to the triple crown of the pope (anciently called regnum), indicative of his civil rank, as the keys are of his ecclesiastical jurisdiction. The right to wear a crown is said to have been granted to the bishops of Rome by Constantine the Great, and by Clovis, founder of the French monarchy. Their ancient tiara was a high round cap. Pope Damasus II. first caused himself to be crowned with a tiara, 1048. "Boniface VIII. encompassed the tiara with a crown; Benedict XII. added a second; and John XXIII. a third." —*Rees*.

TIBER (central Italy), the river on whose banks Rome was built. In the flourishing times of the city the navigation of the river was enormous. Livy states that the Tiber was frozen over, 398 B.C. A commission was appointed to dredge the bed of the river near Rome, Dec. 1871. Garibaldi's scheme for improving the river, making a new port, &c., laid before the Italian parliament, 25 May, 1875; works begun, March, 1877.

TIBERIAS, a city in Palestine, built by Herod Antipas, and named after the emperor Tiberius, 39. Near it Guy de Lusignan, king of Jerusalem, and the crusaders, were defeated by Saladin, 3, 4 July, 1187; and Jerusalem fell into his hands.

TIBET, see *Thibet*.

TIBUR (now Tivoli), a Latin town more ancient than Rome, and frequently at war with it. The Tiburtines were defeated 335 B.C., and the subjection of all Latium followed; for which Furius Camillus obtained a triumph and an equestrian statue in the forum.

TICHBORNE CASE, see *Trials*, 1871-4. Dr. Kenealy, the claimant's counsel, elected M.P. for Stoke, moves for a royal commission to inquire into the trial; rejected, 433 to 3 (Dr. Kenealy, Mr. Whalley, and the O'Gorman); 26 April, 1875. See *Englishman*.

TICINO or TESSIN, a Swiss canton south of the Alps, conquered by the Swiss early in the 16th century; made a separate canton in 1815. It suffered by internal disputes 1839 and 1841. Population, 1888, 126,751.

Insurrection in Bellinzona and Lugano, the conservative ultramontane government overthrown by the liberals, and a provisional government formed. M. Rossi, director of the interior, found killed. Revision of the constitution demanded, 11 Sept. Intervention of federal troops. The insurrection suppressed; the provisional government superseded by a federal commission, 12-14 Sept. 1890

Change in the constitution voted by the people, 5 Oct.; the conservative government reinstated, 14 Oct. ,,

Angelo Castioni, accused of the murder of councillor Rossi, arrested in London, 3 Oct.; extradition demanded by Switzerland, not granted by the queen's bench division . . . . 11 Nov. ,,

Reconciliation of the parties effected . 26 Nov. ,,

Revised ultramontane constitution accepted by popular vote . . . . 8 March, 1891

Trial of the revolters of 1890, 30 June; acquitted, 14 July, ,,

TICINUS, a river, N. Italy. Here Hannibal defeated the Romans, 218 B.C.

TICKETS OF LEAVE, see *Transportation*, and *Crime*.

TICONDEROGA (N. America). The French fortress here was unsuccessfully besieged by Abercromby in July, 1758; taken 26 July, 1759. The Americans took it 10 May, 1775, but retired July, 1777. The British retired from it shortly after.

TIDES. Homer is the earliest profane author who speaks of the tides. Posidonius of Apamea accounted for the tides from the motion of the moon, about 79 B.C.; and Cæsar speaks of them in his fourth book of the Gallic war. The theory of the tides was first satisfactorily explained by Kepler, 1598; but the honour of a complete explanation of them was reserved for sir Isaac Newton, about 1683; see *Thames*. Sir Wm. Thomson, at the Royal Institution, 9 April, 1875, described a valuable tide-calculating machine.

TIEN-TSIN, see *China*, June, 1858-Jan. 1861, 1870, and 1900.

TIERRA DEL FUEGO, see under *Missions*.

TIERRA DEL FUEGO (*The Land of Fire*)—A group of five large islands, and many smaller ones, the extreme S.W. of South America, misnamed by Magellan from the fires seen on the coast 1520. Recent discoveries have shown that the country is not so inhospitable and the natives not so degraded as was formerly supposed.

Expedition under M. Otto Nordenskjöld arrives in San Sebastian bay, 5 Dec. 1895.

TIERS-ETAT, see *States-General*.

TIFLIS (Asiatic Russia), built about 469 by Vakhtang; became the capital of Georgia. It was taken by Genghis Khan in the 12th century; by Mustapha Pacha, 1576; by the Persians, 1796; and by the Russians, 1801, who have made it the capital of their Trans-caucasian possessions. Population in 1885, 89,551; 1900, 160,000.

By the fall of a temporary bridge over the river Kura, during a religious ceremony, a number of persons were drowned or crushed to death, 18 Jan. 1892

Collision of two petroleum trains on the Trans-caucasian railway; 6 men burnt to death, 21 Jan. „

TIGRANO-CERTA, capital of Armenia, built by Tigranes the Great, and taken by Lucullus and the Romans, after a great victory, B.C. 69.

TIGRIS, a river forming the eastern boundary of Mesopotamia, celebrated for the cities founded on its banks: Nineveh, Seleucia, Ctesiphon, and Bagdad. It was explored by an English steamer in 1838. Colonel Chesney, in 1850, published an account of his survey in 1836-7.

TILBURY (Essex). The camp formed here in 1588 to resist the Spanish invasion was visited by queen Elizabeth. See *Docks*, 1886.

TILES are said to have been first made in England about 1246. They were taxed in 1784. The number of tiles taxed in England in 1820 was 81,924,626; and in 1830, 97,318,264. The tax was repealed in 1833.

TILSIT (on the Niemen), on which river, on a raft, the emperors of France and Russia met, 25 June, 1807. By a treaty concluded between France and Russia, signed 7 July, Napoleon restored to the Prussian monarch one-half of his territories, and Russia recognised the Confederation of the Rhine, and the elevation of Napoleon's three brothers, Joseph, Louis, and Jerome, to the thrones of Naples, Holland, and Westphalia.

TILTS, see *Tournaments*.

TIMBER. The annual demand of timber for the royal navy, in war, was 60,000 loads, or 40,000 full-grown trees, a ton each, of which 35 will stand on an acre; in peace, 32,000 tons, or 48,000 loads. A 74 gun ship consumed 3000 loads, or 2000 tons of trees, the produce of 57 acres in a century. —*Allnutt*. Iron is now largely used in preference to timber. In 1843 we imported 1,317,645 loads of timber (cut and uncut); in 1857, 2,495,964 loads; in 1866, 3,638,344 loads; in 1871, 4,497,136 loads; in 1875, 5,092,394 loads; in 1877, 6,788,789 loads; in 1883, 6,609,942 loads; in 1887, 5,653,791 loads. In 1866, we imported 53,458 tons of mahogany; in 1871, 29,256 tons; in 1875, 80,705 tons; in 1877, 53,600 tons; in 1883, 50,158 tons; in 1887, 37,650 tons. The duties on timber were modified in 1851. Annual estimated excess of imports over exports, Britain, 20,523,758*l*., reported, 1901.

TIMBER BENDING. Apparatus was invented for this purpose by Mr. T. Blanchard, of Boston, U.S., for which a medal was awarded at the Paris Exhibition of 1855. A company was formed for its application in this country in 1856.

TIMBUCTOO (N.W. Africa), S. edge of the Sahara, a city built by Mansa Suleiman, a Mahometan, about 1214, and frequently subjugated by the sovereigns of Morocco. Since 1727 it has been partially independent; recently it has been governed by a council.

Timbuctoo visited by major Laing, who was murdered, on his return journey, in 1826

René Caillié wrote an account of the town, 1828; Dr. Barth, 1853; Lenz 1880

Col. Flatter's surveying expedition massacred by the tribes 1881

A French flotilla at Kabara, on the Upper Niger, attacked by Tuaregs; navy-ensign Aube and others killed . . . . . . Jan. 1894

Col. Bonnier, commander in the French Soudan, with two gunboats, proceeds to and enters Timbuctoo without resistance . . 10 Jan. „

Col. Bonnier's flying column annihilated by the Tuaregs, near Timbuctoo; himself, 10 Europeans, and 70 natives killed, about 13 Jan.; another column, under commandant Joffre, capture a village, 100 natives killed, 23 Jan.; enters Timbuctoo . . . . 12 Feb. „

Several bands of Tuaregs surprised and defeated by the French between Lake Fati and Goundam; about 400 Tuaregs surrender; peace made March, „

Two French officers and 29 natives killed in a rising of the Hogar Tuaregs near Racho . . July, 1897

The Tuaregs routed by the French and 300 prisoners released . . . . Sept. „

The Tuaregs defeated and their leader killed at Emmela . . . . Nov. 1898

TIME. See *Hour*, *Day*, *Month*, *Year*, *Geodesy*, *Dials*, *Clocks*, and *Watches*.

TIMES NEWSPAPER. On 1 Jan. 1785, Mr. John Walter published the first number of the *Daily Universal Register*, price 2½*d*., printed on the logographic system (invented by Henry Johnson, a compositor), in which types containing syllables and words were employed instead of single letters.

On 1 Jan. 1788, the paper was named the *Times*.

In 1803, when Mr. John Walter gave up the paper to his son John, the circulation was about 1000; that of the *Morning Post* being 4500.

Mr. John Walter (I.), born, 1739; died, 16 Nov. 1812.

Dr. Stoddart (satirised as Dr. Slop by Moore the poet) became editor in 1812, but five years after retired and set up in opposition the *New Times*, an unprofitable speculation. Thomas Barnes became next editor. He died 7 May, 1841, and was succeeded by his assistant John Thaddeus Delane (son of W. F. A. Delane, financial manager) who retired in 1877, and died 22 Nov. 1879.

On 28 Nov. 1814, the *Times* was first printed by steam power (the invention of F. König), 1200 per hour, afterwards increased to 2000 and 4000.

It is asserted that the *Times* was termed the "*Thunderer*" in consequence of an article by Edward Sterling in which are the words, "We thundered forth articles on reform, &c." when Barnes was editor.

On 19 Jan. 1829, the first double number appeared.

In July, 1834, an attack of Mr. O'Connell in the house of commons on the correctness of the reports of the debates in the *Times* was signally defeated.

Shortly after began the convenient summary of the debates, written in the first instance by Mr. Horace Twiss.

In 1841 the *Times* was instrumental in detecting and exposing a scheme organised by Allan George Bogle and others, to defraud by forgery all the influential bankers of Europe. This brought on the proprietors an action for libel (in the case Bogle *v.* Lawson). The jury found the charge to be true, giving a verdict of *one farthing* damages, but the judges refused costs. Subscriptions were set on foot at the Mansion-house and in all parts of Europe to reimburse the proprietors for the immense outlay in defending the action. This they firmly declined; and the money was expended in establishing *Times Scholarships* at Oxford and Cambridge, and at Christ's Hospital, and other schools; a marble tablet also, commemorating the event, was set up in the Royal Exchange and at the *Times* office. These were the greatest honours ever conceded to a newspaper.

In Oct. 1845, the *Times* express was for the first time conveyed to India overland, by the agency of lieut. Waghorn.

Of the number of the *Times* containing the life of the duke of Wellington for 19 Nov. 1852, 70,000 were sold—the ordinary number being then 36,000; the circulation is stated to vary from 50,000 to 60,000 (1868).

The *Times* (a slip) announcing permission to relax restriction of issue of bank-notes, published 24 Oct. 1847.

Mr. John Walter (II.) died 28 July, 1847.

In 1854, the proprietors sent Mr. W. H. Russell as their special correspondent to the seat of war in the Crimea; in 1857 to India.

Times Fund.—On the 12th of Oct. 1854, sir Robert Peel originated by a letter in the *Times* a subscription for the sick and wounded in the Crimean war, and in less than a fortnight 15,000*l.* were sent to the *Times* office to be thus appropriated. Mr. Macdonald was sent out by the proprietors as special commissioner to administer the fund, from which large quantities of food and clothing were supplied to the sufferers, with inestimable advantage; see *Scutari* and *Nightingale.*

In Dec. 1858, the *Times* drew attention to the state of the houseless poor of London; and in a few days 8000*l.* were subscribed for their relief.

In 1851, 13,000,000 copies were sold; in 1857, 16,100,000; in 1859, 16,900,000; in 1860, 16,670,000.

The *Times* of 21 June, 1861, contained 4076 advertisements (about 1810 it contained 150 advertisements).

Stereotypes from papier-mâché moulds introduced, 1856; much improved 1860.

The "Walter press" invented by John Cameron Macdonald (aft. manager) and Joseph Calverley, prints about 15,000 an hour, perfected, 1862-71.

A list of the contents, inserted over the first leader, appeared first, 3 Feb. 1869.

3½ pages tables of metropolitan charities appeared 11 Feb. 1869.

John Walter (IV.) drowned 24 Dec. 1870.

Special train for conveying the *Times*, North-Western Railway, began to run, 4.55 a.m., 16 Feb. 1875.

Annual summaries, 1851-75, reprinted, price 1*s.* (type set-up by composing-machines).

12,000 perfect sheets per hour printed by "Walter press," Jan. 1876.

Weekly issue, price 2*d.*, began, 5 Jan. 1877.

The Rapieff electric lamp adopted in the machine-room, Nov. 1878.

Summary of the *Times* published daily, ½*d.* about 26 July, 1883; stopped, Oct. 1884.

Death of Thomas Chenery, six years editor, long correspondent, 11 Feb.; succeeded by G. E. Buckle, Feb. 1884.

Death of Chas. Ross, aged 84, 63 years a parliamentary reporter and 30 years a chief, 6 Dec. 1884.

Edwin Murray (watch dealer) *v. Times*, libel case, farthing damages, 26-27 Oct. 1886.

Articles "Parnellism and Crime," published 7, 10, 14 March; article on Mr. Dillon, 2 May, declared by the commons not to be a breach of privilege, 4-6 May, 1887.

Centenary of the publication of the *Times;* special leader 2 Jan. 1888.

O'Donnell *v.* Walter and another (see under *Parnellites*); verdict for the defendant, 2-5 July, 1888.

No. 31,725 (5 April, 1886) published as a book at Leipsic with German notes by Dr. F. Landmann, Oct. 1888; the number for 14 Nov. 1888, published as a book at Paris, with French notes by M. M. A. & G. Elwall. Dec. 1889.

For the trial by the special commission see under *Parnellites.*

Rev. lord Sidney G. Osborne (S.G.O.), long a philanthropic writer to the *Times*, dies 9 May, 1889.

Death of Mr. J. C. Macdonald, aged 67, successively reporter, writer, and manager (see above, 1854 *et seq.*), 10 Dec. 1889.

Walter *v.* Steinkoppf, see *Trials*, 2 June, 1892.

Death of Mr. J. S. Oswald from cholera while assisting patients at Jeddah (formerly correspondent at Suakin), 4 July, 1893.

Capt. H. J. Borrow, war correspondent, killed (see *Mashonaland*), about 5 Dec. 1893.

Mr. John Walter (III.) born 1818, able and successful during 50 years; died (succeeded by his son and associate Arthur) 3 Nov. 1894.

Sir George Dasent, sub-editor 1845-70, died 11 June, 1896.

The "*Times Atlas*" (formerly "*Universal Atlas*"), published April *et seq.* 1895; new edition, 21 May, 1900.

The *Times* consisted of 24 pages 21, 26 June, 1861; 14 June, 1884; 5 times in 1886; 3 times in 1887; 6 times in 1888; 11, 18, 25 May, 1, 22, 29 June, 1889; 3, 10, 17 May, 7, 14 June, 1890; 30 May, 6, 13, 20, 27 June, 1891; 7, 14, 21, 28 May, 4, 11, 18, 25 June, 2 July, 1892; 5, 19, 26 May, 29, 16, 23, 30 June, 1894; 11, 18, 25 May, 15, 22 June, 6, 13 July, 1895; 2, 9, 16, 23 May, 6, 13, 20 June, 1896; 10 April, 22, 29 May, 12, 21, 23 June; 10, 17 July 1897; 25 June, 1898; 6, 13 May, 1899; and once early July, 1901; 26 April, 3 May, 30 Sept. 1902.

Mr. Palmer's "Index to the *Times*" was begun 1867, and has been continued backward to 1817, and forward to 1898. (Mr. Palmer died 26 Aug. 1899.)

Walter v. *Central News*, for supplying telegrams, fabricated, altered, or expanded, 1894-5, a breach of contract: verdict for plaintiff; charge of fraud withdrawn, nominal damages with costs, 14 April, 1896.

Facsimile of the *Times*, 9 Nov. 1796, produced by photozincograph, issued, 9 Nov. 1896.

First number of Miss Nancy Bailey's annual index to the *Times* appeared Feb. 1899 (issued in monthly instalments).

Mr. Fred. Hawkins, born 1849, sub-editor 1876-1894, and dramatic critic, died 30 June, 1900.

Walter *v.* Lane, see *Trials*, Aug.-Nov. 1899; Aug. 1900.

The *Times* of 31 Dec. 1900, and of 1 Jan. 1901 *et seq.*, contained extracts from the paper for every year of the 19th century.

Mr. W. J. Stillman, an eminent American correspondent, died aged 73, 6 July, 1901.

The *Times* "Life of Queen Victoria" published 9 Nov. 1901.

Weekly literary supplements, first one 17 Jan. 1902.

The *Times* "History of the War in S. Africa," edited by L. S. Amery, Vol. II., May, 1902.

M. de Blowitz, *Times* correspondent in Paris, 31 Dec. 1871-Dec. 1902, died, aged 78, 18 Jan. 1903.

Mr. D. D. Braham, *Times* correspondent at St. Petersburg, ordered to leave Russia, 28 May, 1903.

Mr. L. Ashe, army tutor, wins 1000*l.* prize in the *Times* competition, announced 1 Dec. 1903.

Encyclopædia Britannica, with *Times* supplement, issued on the instalment system at half-price until 19 Dec. 1903.

TIN. The Phœnicians traded with England for more than 1100 years before the Christian era. Under the Saxons, our tin mines appear to have been neglected; but under the Normans, they produced considerable revenues to the earls of Cornwall, particularly to Richard, brother of Henry III. A charter and various immunities were granted by Edmund, earl Richard's brother, who framed the Stannary Laws (*which see*), laying a duty on the tin. Edward III. confirmed the tinners in their privileges, and erected Cornwall into a dukedom, with which he invested his son, Edward the Black

Prince, 1337. Since that time the heirs-apparent to the crown of England, if eldest sons, have enjoyed it successively. Tin mines were discovered in Germany, which lessened the value of those in England, till then the only tin mines in Europe, 1240.—*Anderson*. Discovered in Barbary, 1640; in India, 1740; in New Spain, 1782; near Cape Town, Feb. 1903. In 1857, 9783 tons; in 1860, 10,462 tons; in 1864, 10,108 tons; in 1865, 10,039 tons; in 1870, 10,200 tons; in 1874, 9942 tons; in 1876, 8500 tons; in 1879, 9532 tons; 1882, 9158 tons; in 1884, 9,574 tons; in 1887, 9,282 tons; in 1888, 9,241 tons; in 1889, 8,912 tons; in 1890, 9,602 tons; 1893, 8,837 tons; 1896, 4,838 tons; 1899, 4,013 tons; 1900, 4,268 tons of metallic tin were procured from British mines. Of tin plates we exported in value, in 1847, 484,184*l.*; in 1854, 1,075,531*l.*; in 1860, 1,500,812*l.*; in 1864, 1,263,246*l.*; in 1866, 1,896,192*l.*; in 1871, 2,900,625*l.*; in 1873, 3,953,042*l.*; in 1877, 3,033,126*l.*; in 1879, 3,507,977*l.*; in 1883, 4,705,403*l.*; in 1887, 4,792,854*l.*; in 1888, 5,546,228*l.*; in 1889, 6,030,005*l.*; in 1890, 6,361,477*l.*; in 1893, 4,991,300*l.*; 1900, 3,976,796*l.*

The great tin-plate manufacture in S. Wales suffered greatly by the operation of the McKinley tariff, 1 July *et seq.* 1891.

TINCHEBRAY (N.W. France), where a battle was fought between Henry I. of England and his brother Robert duke of Normandy. England and Normandy were reunited under Henry, at the decease of William Rufus, who had already possessed himself of Normandy by a mortgage from his brother Robert, at his setting out for Palestine. Robert, on his return, recovered Normandy by an accommodation with Henry; but having afterwards quarrelled, Robert was defeated in the battle of Tinchebray, 28 Sept. 1106, and Normandy was annexed to the crown of England.—*Hénault*.

TINTOMETER, an apparatus invented by Mr. J. W. Lovibond, to determine the purity, &c. of a given substance by means of tinted glasses, reported, Nov. 1895.

TIPPERARY, S. Ireland, made a county by king John, 1210.

The shopkeepers of the town of Tipperary, tenants of Mr. Smith Barry, accepted the plan of campaign, paid no rent, and were evicted. *New Tipperary*, built to receive them, was inaugurated by Mr. W. O'Brien, M.P., and others 12 April, 1890

Some of the tenants make terms and return to their homes . . . . . Dec., 1890, Jan. 1891

Failure of New Tipperary, the property put up for sale, June; buildings pulled down . . Aug. 1892

Mr. Smith Barry warmly received by his tenants, 16 Sept. „

TIPPERMUIR (near Perth). Here the marquis of Montrose defeated the covenanters under lord Elcho, 1 Sept. 1644.

TIRNOVA on the Jantra, a tributary of the Danube, capital of the ancient kingdom of Bulgaria, and the seat of a patriarch. It was occupied without resistance by general Gourko, 6, 7 July, 1877, and made the Russian head-quarters.

TIRYNS, an ancient city of Greece, S.E. of Argos, with massive cyclopœan remains. Excavations of Dr. Schliemann in 1884 led to the discovery of what he termed "the Prehistoric Palace of the kings of Tiryns." His book on Tiryns was published in 1886. As Byzantine remains are also found some of his conclusions are disputed by eminent antiquaries.

TITANIUM, a rare metal, discovered by Gregor in menaccanite, a Cornish mineral, in 1791, and in 1794 by Klaproth.

TITHES, or TENTHS, were commanded to be given to the tribe of Levi, 1490 B.C. (*Lev.* xxvii. 30). Abraham returning from his victory over the kings (*Gen.* xiv.), gave tithes of the spoil to Melchisedek, king of Salem, priest of the most high God (1913 B.C.) For the first 800 years of the Christian church they were given purely as alms, and were voluntary.—*Wickliffe.* "I will not put the title of the clergy to tithes upon any divine right, though such a right certainly commenced, and I believe as certainly ceased, with the Jewish theocracy."—*Blackstone.* They were established in France by Charlemagne, about 800, and abolished 1789. Tenths were confirmed in the Lateran councils, 1215.—*Rainailda.* The payment of tithes appears to have been claimed by Augustin, the first archbishop of Canterbury, and to have been allowed by Ethelbert, king of Kent, under the term "God's fee," about 600.

The first mention of them in any English written law is a constitutional decree made in a synod strongly enjoining tithes, 786.

Offa, king of Mercia, gave unto the church the tithes of all his kingdom, to expiate the death of Ethelbert, king of the East Angles, whom he had caused to be basely murdered, 794.

Tithes were first granted to the English clergy in a general assembly held by Ethelwold, 844. *Henry.*

In England, in 1545, tithes were fixed at the rate of *2s. 9d.* in the pound on rent; since then, many acts have been passed respecting them.

The Tithe Commutation act, passed 13 Aug. 1836. It was amended in 1837, 1840, 1846, 1860, and 1878.

A *rector* is entitled to all the tithes; a *vicar* to a small part only, frequently to none.

Several acts relating to tithes in Ireland have been passed in 1832-47, altering and improving the tithe system.

Tithe redemption trust appointed, 1846.

Agitation against "extraordinary tithes," 11 Aug. *et seq.* 1881.

An Anti-Extraordinary Association existed in 1882.

Extraordinary Tithe Redemption act passed 1886.

Riotous opposition to tithes in Wales, Aug.; anti-tithe league formed Sept. 1886; riots (see *Wales*) 1887.

Tithe bill brought in; dropped Aug. 1887.

Much agitation against tithes in Wales, 1889. A tithes recovery bill withdrawn, 16 Aug. 1889.

Royal commission on Tithe Redemption nominated: lord Basing and others, 30 Jan; met 6 March *et seq.* 1891.

An act for the recovery of tithe rent charge in England and Wales passed, 26 March, 1891. The liability for the payment of tithes is transferred from the tenant to the landowner.

Tithe rent-charge (rates) act, over 10,000 clergy benefited, passed, 1 Aug. 1899.

Tithe rent-charge (Ireland) act passed, 8 Aug. 1900.

TITHING. The number or company of ten men with their families knit together in a society, all of them being bound to the king for the peaceable and good behaviour of each of their society; of these companies there was one chief person, who, from his office, was called (toothingman) tithingman; but now he is nothing but a constable, formerly called the headborough. *Cowel.*

TITLES ROYAL. Henry IV. had the title of "Grace" and "My liege," 1399. Henry VI., "Excellent Grace," 1422. Edward IV., "Most High and Mighty Prince," 1461. Henry VII., "Highness," 1485; Henry VIII. the same title, and sometimes "Grace," 1509 *et seq.* Francis I. of France addressed Henry as "Your Majesty" at their interview in 1520; see *Field of the Cloth of Gold.* Henry VIII. and James I. were styled "Dread Sovereign" ("Bible" dedication, 1611). James I.

coupled to "Majesty" the present "Sacred," or "Most Excellent Majesty." "Majesty" was the style of the emperors of Germany; the first king to whom it was given was Louis XI. of France, about 1463. Royal titles act passed, by royal assent, 17 Aug. 1901; see *Style*.

TITLES TO LAND CONSOLIDATION ACT (Scotland), passed 31 July, 1868, and amended in 1869.

TIVOLI, see *Tibur*.

TOBACCO,* *Nicotiana tabacum*, received its name from Tabacco, a province of Yucatan, New Spain; some say from the island of Tobago, one of the Caribbees; others from Tobasco, in the Gulf of Florida. It is said to have been first observed at St. Domingo, in Cuba, 1492; and to have been used freely by the Spaniards in Yucatan in 1520. Tobacco was either first brought to England in 1565, by sir John Hawkins; or by sir Walter Raleigh and sir Francis Drake, in 1586. It was manufactured only for exportation for some years. *Stow's Chron.* The Pied Bull inn, at Islington, is said to have been the first house in England where tobacco was smoked. In 1584 a proclamation was issued against it. James I. published "A Counterblaste against Tobacco," and the star-chamber ordered the duties to be 6*s.* 10*d.* per pound, 1614. Its cultivation was prohibited in England by Charles II., 1684. Act laying a duty on the importation was passed 1684. The cultivation was allowed in Ireland, 1779. The tax was increased and put under the excise, 1789. *Anderson; Ashe.* Various statutes have passed relative to tobacco. Act to revive the act prohibiting the culture of tobacco in Ireland passed 2 Will. IV., Aug. 1831. Act directing that tobacco grown in Ireland be purchased in order to its being destroyed, 24 March, 1832. The quantity consumed in England in 1791 was nine millions and a half of pounds, and in 1829 about fifteen millions of pounds. We imported in 1850, 35,166,358 lbs., and 1,557,558 lbs. manufactured (cigars and snuff); in 1855, 36,820,846 lbs., and 2,651,544 lbs. manufactured; in 1860, 48,936,471 lbs., and 2,110,430 lbs. manufactured; in 1864, 61,042,667 lbs., and 6,578,707 lbs., manufactured; in 1866, 54,374,800 lbs., and 3,171,906 lbs. manufactured; in 1871, 73,042,305 lbs., and 3,852,236 manufactured; in 1876, 76,814,974 lbs., and 3,818,682 lbs. manufactured; in 1879, 38,861,220 lbs., and 3,591,558 lbs. manufactured; in 1883, 56,475,199 lbs., and 3,121,174 lbs. manufactured; in 1887, 72,178,994 lbs. and 3,595,071 manufactured; in 1890, 65,729,970 lbs.; and 3,678,846 lbs. manufactured; 1896, 83,558,757 lbs. and 5,037,198 lbs. manufactured; 1898, 79,631,955 lbs. and 4,621,230 lbs. manufactured; 1900, 98,348,500 lbs. and 6,362,140 lbs. manufactured. The tobacco duties were modified in 1863; raised April, 1878. 2*d.* a lb. extra duty on cigars added, April, 1879. Net customs duties paid for tobacco and snuff in the year 1875-6, 7,744,977*l.*; 1877-8, 8,006,836*l.*; 1883-4, 8,991,205*l.*; 1886-7, 9,367,186*l.*; 1887-8, 8,713,944*l.*; 1888-9, 8,858,781*l.*; 1889-90, 9,061,984*l.*; 1890-91, 9,533,888*l.*; 1895-6, 7,350,000*l.*; 1901-2, 10,585,819*l.*

Permission to grow tobacco in England with conditions granted by the Board of Trade, April, 1886.

Tobacco successfully cultivated by Messrs. James Carter and Co., near Bromley, Essex, Sept. 1886; and by others in 1887.

Duty per lb. on unmanufactured tobacco reduced from 3*s.* 6*d.* to 3*s.* 2*d.*; cigars 5*s.*; snuff 3*s.* 9*d.* or 4*s.* 6*d.* 1887; 1898-9, tobacco reduced 6*d.* per pound.

TOBAGO (West Indies), discovered by Columbus in 1498; settled by the Dutch 1642. Taken by the English, 1672; retaken, 1674. In 1748, it was declared a neutral island; but in 1763 it was ceded to the English. Tobago was taken by the French under De Grasse in 1781, and confirmed to them in 1783. Again taken by the English, 14 April, 1793, but restored at the peace of Amiens, 6 Oct. 1802. The island was once more taken by the British under general Grinfield, 1 July, 1803, and was confirmed to them by the peace of Paris, in 1814. Population in 1887, 19,937. Tobago is one of the Windward isles, *which see*. Tobago was united with Trinidad by parliament in 1887. Population of Tobago, 1891, 18,353.

TOBITSCHAU (Moravia). In a sharp action here, on 15 July, 1866, the Austrians were defeated by the army of the crown prince of Prussia with the loss of 500 killed and wounded and 500 prisoners, and seventeen guns.

TOBOGGANNING, the name of a sport very popular in Canada and the northern United States. The toboggan in popular use for "coasting" is formed of a single plank curved backward in front and held in position by leather cords, and is guided by the foot of the steerman, which drags behind with the toe turned downward. International contest at Davos; the Symonds shield won by Mr. J. A. Bott of Moritz, Jan. 1903.

TOGOLAND, a large German West African territory between the Gold Coast and Dahomey, extending inland. Anglo-German delimitation expedition began work, autumn, 1901; finished, Aug. 1902.

TOISON D'OR or GOLDEN FLEECE (*which see*).

TOKAR, in the Soudan. Here Osman Digna's forces were defeated by col. Holled Smith, 19 Feb. 1891; see under *Soudan*.

TOKAY, a town in Upper Hungary, celebrated for its wines, made here by dressers, brought from Italy by Bela IV., king, 1235-70. The wine is principally used by sovereigns, and 50 bottles were presented to queen Victoria at her jubilee, 1887.

The town, with its six churches and public buildings, was destroyed by fire, 26 Aug. 1890. About 4,000 persons rendered homeless.

TOKENS, BANK, silver pieces issued by the Bank of England, of the value of 5*s.*, 1 Jan. 1798. The Spanish dollar had a small profile of George III. stamped on the neck of the Spanish king. They were raised to the value of 5*s.* 6*d.* 14 Nov. 1811. Bank tokens were also current in Ireland, where those issued by the bank passed for 6*s.* and lesser sums until 1817. They were called in on the revision of the coinage. Tradesmen were permitted to issue tokens as small coins from 1648 till 16 Aug. 1672, when their circulation was prohibited by royal proclamation. These tokens are figured and described in a work by Wm. Boyne, 1858.

TOKIO, the name given to Jedo, the capital of Japan, about 1869. Great fire; 5,000 houses destroyed, and 45 persons perish, 10 April, 1892. Another great fire, 600 houses destroyed; reported 14 Nov. 1892. See *Jedo*. Population, 1887, 1,552,457.

---

* *British Anti-Tobacco Crusade*, originated by the late Thos. Reynolds in 1853. 60,000 of its publications had been circulated gratuitously in 1876.

TOLBIAC (now ZULPICH), near the Rhine, where Clovis totally defeated the Allemanni, 496.

TOLEDO, the ancient Toletum (Central Spain), made capital of the Visigothic kingdom by Athanagild, 554; taken by the Saracens, 712. Toledo was taken after the war begun 1081, by Alfonso I. of Castile, 25 May, 1085. In 1088 the archbishop was made primate of Spain. The university was founded in 1499. Toledo sword-blades have been famed since the 15th century. Population, 1887, 20,837.

The alcazar, ancient Moorish palace, used by the emperor Charles V., destroyed by fire, 9–10 Jan. 1887.

TOLENTINO (Italy, formerly in the Papal states), where a treaty was made between the pope and the French, 19 Feb. 1797. Here Joachim Murat, having resumed arms against the allies, was defeated by the Austrians, 3 May, 1815, taken prisoner, and shot.

TOLERATION ACT, passed in 1689, to relieve Protestant dissenters from the church of England. Their liberties were, however, greatly endangered in the latter days of queen Anne, who died on the day that the Schism bill was to become a law, 1 Aug. 1714.

The toleration granted was somewhat limited. It exempted persons who took the new oath of allegiance and supremacy, and made also a declaration against popery, from the penalties incurred by absenting themselves from church and holding unlawful conventicles; and it allowed the quakers to substitute an affirmation for an oath, but did not relax the provisions of the Test act (*which see*). The party spirit of the times checked the king in his liberal measures.

TOLLS were first paid by vessels passing the Stade on the Elbe, 1109. They were first demanded by the Danes of vessels passing the Sound, 1341; see *Stade* and *Sound*. *Tollbars* in England originated in 1267, on the grant of a penny for every waggon that passed through a certain manor; and the first regular toll was collected a few years after for mending the road in London between St. Giles's and Temple-bar. Gathered for repairing the highways of Holborn-inn-lane and Martin's-lane (now Aldersgate-street), 1346. Toll-gate or *turnpikes* were set up in 1663. In 1827, 27 turnpikes near London were removed by parliament; 81 turnpikes and toll-bars ceased on the north of London on 1 July, 1864; and 61 on the south side, ceased on 31 Oct. 1865; and many others on the Essex and Middlesex roads ceased on 31 Oct. 1866; the remainder on the north of London ceased 1 July, 1872. The tolls on the Commercial roads, London, E., were abolished 5 Aug. 1871. The tolls on Waterloo and other metropolitan bridges abolished, 1878-9. The high road from Brighton to London free from toll, 31 Oct. 1881. Many private gates and bars in London since removed, several in Nov. 1893. See *Wales*, 1843 and 1889.

TOLOSA. On the plain named las Navas de Tolosa, near the Sierra Morena, S. Spain, Alfonso, king of Castile, aided by the kings of Arragon and Navarre, gained a great victory over the Moors, 16 July, 1212. This conflict is sometimes termed the battle of Muradal.

TONGA ISLES, the name now given to the Friendly isles (*which see*).

TONIC SOL FA SYSTEM. See *Music*.

TONK, Rajpootana, India. The nawab and his minister, for a massacre of Hindoo chiefs, 1 Aug. 1867, were deposed by the British. In 1872 he demanded investigation, and his case came before parliament without any issue.

TONNAGE. The Tonnage Act of 1694 established the Bank of England (*which see*). See *Tunnage*.

TONOMETER, a delicate apparatus (consisting of 52 forks) for tuning musical instruments, by marking the number of vibrations, was invented by H. Scheibler of Crefeld, and described in his "Tonmesser," 1834. It received little notice till Dr. Rudolph Kœnig removed some of the difficulties opposed to its successful use, and exhibited it at the International Exhibition of 1862.

TONQUIN, S.E. Asia, the delta of the river Songkoi, formerly a province of Annam, subject to France. Here a French missionary bishop, Melchior, was murdered with great barbarity 27 July, 1858: the abbé Neron was also murdered, 3 Nov. 1860; see *Annam* and *Indo-China*.

Successful attack and death of lieut. Garnier . . 1873
Naomdink captured by the French announced, 11 April, 1883
Lin-Yang-Fu declares war against French aggressors, 8 May; a new expedition voted for 15 May, „
Commander R. T. Rivière (French), and 32 others besieged by the Black Flags* at Hanoi; captured and killed in a sortie . . . . 20 May, „
[He was buried at the Madeleine, Paris, 30 Jan. 1885.]
Gen. Bouet arrives 7 June; fortifies Hanoi 16 June, „
China firmly opposed to French aggression; Tu Duc, emperor of Annam, opposed to the French, „
Successful French sortie from Nam Din; much slaughter . . . . 19 July, „
Proclamation of capt. Morel Beaulieu offering protection to the people, deserted by Annam, announced . . . . 20 July, „
The Black Flags severely defeated . . 7 Aug. „
French advance, under gen. Bouet, checked at Cachao . . . . 15 Aug. „
Bombardment and capture of the Hue forts, great slaughter of natives . . . . . 18-20 Aug. „
Armistice granted, submission of the Annamite government; treaty signed, recognising French protectorate, ceding province of Bin-Huam, &c. 25 Aug. „
The Black Flags defeated at Phokhai by gen. Bouet with great loss, the French suffer severely, 1-2 Sept. „
Negotiations of Jules Ferry and Mandarin Tseng respecting the protectorate of Tonquin . Sept. „
Disbandment of the Annamite troops, yellow flags opposed to the French . . . about 15 Sept. „
Gen. Bouet replaced by adm. Courbet as commander of the French forces . . announced 20 Sept. „
Admiral Courbet begins actual occupation of Tonquin . . . . about 3 Nov. „
Ninh-Binh and Kuang-Yen occupied by the French without resistance . . . . announced 4 Nov. „
The Black Flags repulsed in a violent attack on the French gun-boat *Carabine* and on Haidzuong, 17 Nov. „
The Yellow book on Tonquin, published . 5 Dec. „
The French take forts on the Red river opposite Sontay . . . . about 16 Dec. „
Sontay captured, the Black Flags retire, alleged French loss, about 77 killed, 231 wounded 16, 17 Dec. „
Sontay fortified and left . . . . . Dec. „
The unarmed native Tonquinese suffer on all sides by the war . . . . Aug.-Dec. „
Namdinh attacked by pirates, houses burnt, people killed . . . . 1, 2 Jan. 1884
Arrival of Chinese troops to defend Hainan against the French . . . . . . about 20 Jan. „

* The Black Flags originated with Li-Hung-Chang, an able leader of the Canton rebels, who about 1863 with his followers took refuge in Tonquin, where he was at first tolerated by the emperor of Annam, but afterwards, being strengthened by many adherents, established an independent despotic government. He strenuously opposed the French.

Gen. Millot (successor in command to adm. Courbet) captures Bacninh, after hard fighting Chinese flee, 25 French killed . . . . 12 March, 1884
Gen. Brière de L'Isle captures citadel of Thai-Nguyen . . . . 22 March, ,,
Rainy season . . . . . March—Oct. ,,
Honghoa fired by the Chinese and quitted, about 9 April, ,,
Treaty signed by capt. Fournier and Li-Hung-Chang at Tientsin; French protectorate of Tonquin and Annam recognised . . . 11 May, ,,
The Chinese garrison of Langson resist capt. Dugenne and a French column (700), (unauthorised), advancing to occupy it; 10 killed; a violation of the treaty of 11 May . . . . 23 June, ,,
The French appeal to Pekin for indemnity; the Chinese deny the ratification of the treaty about 1 July; but order the evacuation of Langson and other places, announced . . . . 18 July, ,,
Gen. Millot resigns, succeeded by gen. Brière de l'Isle . . . . 30 Aug. ,,
Fighting resumed . . . . Oct. ,,
Chinese regulars, attacks repulsed with great loss; French suffer little (at Kep); gen. Négrier in command . . . . 6–8 Oct. ,,
Victory of col. Donnier, great Chinese loss; 20 French killed . . . . . 10, 11 Oct. ,,
Chinese hold strong camps with reinforcements; their attacks repulsed at Tuguen Quan-hung with great loss . . . . 13 Oct. ,,
Fighting: the Black Flags defeated about 20 Nov. ,,
Chinese pirates said to be severely defeated, announced . . . . Dec. ,,
Gen. Négrier defeats 12,000 Chinese E. of Chu, announced . . . . . . 6 Jan. 1885
Dong Song camp captured by the French after severe conflict . . . . . . 5 Feb. ,,
Several forts captured . . . . . 10–25 Jan. ,,
Severe conflict with about 10,000 Chinese, who are compelled to retreat 12 Feb.; the French flag placed on the captured citadel of Langson 13 Feb. ,,
Mutiny on the *Bayard* on account of deficient rations, &c.; 12 sailors shot; announced end of Jan. ,,
30 French killed and many wounded 9–12 Feb. ,,
Chinese 18 days' siege of Thuyen-Quan raised after 18 desperate assaults . . . . 2 March, ,,
The Chinese defeated by col. Duchesne, 4–7 March, ,,
French attack Dong-dang, successful 22 March, ,,
Heavy Chinese attack on French positions; gen. Négrier wounded, compelled to retreat; Langson evacuated . . . . 28 March, ,,
Preliminaries of peace signed at Pekin; Tonquin to be abandoned by the Chinese, &c. . 5 April, ,,
Luh Vinh Phuoc, chief of the Black Flags, rewarded for his services by the Chinese government . . . . April, ,,
The Chinese troops retiring . . . . May, ,,
Reported massacre of christians . . . Aug. ,,
The Black Flag bands very troublesome, Oct.; defeated by Négrier . . . . . Dec. ,,
Reported massacre of 700 christians; and destruction of 30 villages . . . . . . Aug. 1886
Renewed warfare; French successes . . Nov. ,,
M. Paul Bert, French resident, appointed 21 Jan.; dies 11 Nov. 1886; succeeded by M. Bibourd, Jan. 1887
Much fighting; insurgents defeated by the French Jan. ,,
Col. Bosc captured Muong losing 9 men 19 April, 1888
Establishment of the civil native guard for suppression of piracy, and other organizations reported . . . . Sept. ,,
Renewed fighting by pirates; defeated by gen. Borgnis des Bordes with French loss 17 Jan. 1889
Surrender of Doivan, chief of the Bac Ninh pirates; country reported quieter . . . . 16 March, ,,
French success against the pirates March, April, 1890
Pirates defeated in several engagements, followed by executions, 21 April—28 July; again 15 Dec. 1891
Sharp fighting with the pirates, who are dispersed with heavy loss, reported, 2 July; 3 French officers and 10 men killed in a sharp conflict, 9 July, 1892
Duc, a noted pirate chief, with some of his followers, surrenders . . . . 5 Nov. ,,
Renewed Chinese attacks; results vary . April, 1893
The delta entirely flooded; heavy rains and hurricane . . . . June–Aug. 1893
The hill country in revolt; reported . 12 Nov. ,,
De Tham, a pirate chief, killed, and his bands defeated . . . . 19, 25 May, 1894
Railway opened . . . . . . 25 Dec. ,,
Fight between the French Duclonin column and pirates at Panai, 40 French killed . . Oct. 1895
The *Raphael* steamer sunk in collision with a Chinese junk near Nam-Dinh, 30 deaths, reported, 13 Oct. 1897
M. Breugnot's force captures Lasa Sor, a noted pirate . . . . Aug. 1899
Rebellion in Laos, French posts attacked, reported, 24 Sept. 1902

TONSURE, the clerical crown, adopted, it is said, in imitation of St. Peter, or of Christ's crown of thorns, was disapproved of in the fourth century as pertaining only to penitents, and not made essential till the end of the fifth or beginning of the sixth century.

TONTINES, loans given for life annuities with benefit of survivorship, invented by Laurence Tonti, a Neapolitan. They were first set on foot at Paris to reconcile the people to cardinal Mazarin's government, by amusing them with the hope of becoming suddenly rich, 1653. *Voltaire*. Tonti died in the Bastile after seven years' imprisonment. A Mr. Jennings was an original subscriber for a 100*l*. share in a tontine company; and being the last survivor of the shareholders, his share produced him 3000*l*. per annum. He died aged 103 years, 19 June, 1798, worth 2,115,244*l*.; see *Alexandra Park*.

By the termination of a tontine begun by M. Lafarges in 1791 to diminish the national debt the French government received 1,218,000 francs Dec. 1888

TOOLS. Many of the tools in common use are described and represented in Rosellini's magnificent work, "Monumenti dell' Egitto e della Nubia," 1832-44. The tools used by Bezaleel and Aholiab in the construction of the tabernacle, described in Exodus xxxi. and xxxv. B.C. (1491), were doubtless Egyptian or Phœnician. In building Solomon's temple (1014-04) B.C., "there was neither hammer nor axe nor any tool of iron heard," the stone and other materials being previously prepared (1 Kings vi. 7). The invention of many tools is mythically ascribed to Dædalus, the Athenian artificer in the 14th century B.C. The multimplement invented by lord Wemyss combines many tools in a small compass, April, 1902.

TÖPLITZ (Bohemia). Here were signed, in 1813, two treaties—one between Austria, Russia, and Prussia, 9 Sept.; and one between Great Britain and Austria, 3 Oct.

TOPOGRAPHICAL SOCIETY OF LONDON was founded 1879; inaugurated at the Mansion-house, 28 Oct. 1880; reconstituted, the earl of Rosebery president, annual meetings, 9 March, 1899, *et seq*.

TORBANEHILL MINERAL. Mr. Gillespie, of Torbanehill, granted a lease of all the coal in the estate to Messrs. Russell. In the course of working, the lessees extracted a combustible mineral of considerable value as a source of coal-gas, and realised a large profit in the sale of it as gas-coal. The lessor then denied that the mineral was coal, and disputed the right of the lessees to work it. At the trial in 1853 there was a great array of scientific men and practical gas engineers, and the evidence was most conflicting. One side maintained the mineral to be coal, the other that it was a bituminous schist. The judge set aside the scientific evidence, and the jury pronounced it to be coal. The authorities in Prussia have since pronounced it *not* to be coal. *Percy.*

TORDESILLAS (near Valladolid). Here was signed, 7 June, 1494, a treaty modifying the boundary line which pope Alexander VI. had assigned, in May, 1493, in his division of the new world between Spain and Portugal.

TORGAU (Saxony, N. Germany), the site of a battle between Frederick II. of Prussia and the Austrians, in which the former obtained a signal victory; the Austrian general, count Daun, being wounded, 3 Nov. 1760. He had, in 1757, obtained a great victory over the Prussian king. Torgau was taken by the allies in 1814; and given to Prussia, 1815.

TORIES, a term given to a political party about 1678; see *Whig*. Dr. Johnson defines a Tory as one who adheres to the ancient constitution of the state, and the apostolical hierarchy of the Church of England. The Tories long maintained the doctrines of "divine hereditary indefeasible right, lineal succession, passive obedience, prerogative," &c. *Bolingbroke*; see *Conservatives*. For the chief Tory administrations, see *Pitt*, *Perceval*, *Liverpool*, *Wellington*, *Peel*, *Derby*, *Disraeli*, *&c.* For TORY DEMOCRACY see *Fourth Party*.

TORNADOS. See *Storms*.

TORONTO, the capital of Canada West, now Ontario, founded in 1794 as York; it received its present name in 1834. It was made a bishopric in 1839. Population 1886, 118,403; 1891, 181,220; 1901, 208,040.

Opera-house burnt, 8 Feb. 1883.
Industrial exhibition opened by marquis of Lorne, 12 Sept. 1883; another opened by lord Lansdowne, 6 Sept. 1887.
The university, with its hall, library, and museum, destroyed by fire, 14 Feb.; a committee was formed in London, including the marquis of Salisbury, the archbishop of Canterbury, representatives of the universities, the lord mayor, and other eminent persons, to restore the library, March; an appeal was liberally responded to, the queen being among the contributors; donations were received from other countries . . . . . reported 15 May, 1890
The duke and duchess of Connaught warmly received at Toronto . . . . . . 29 May, ,,
Meeting of the British association . . 18 Aug. 1897
Visit of the duke and duchess of Cornwall and York . . . . 10 Oct. 1901

TORPEDO SHELLS, a name given to explosives placed under ships, an invention ascribed to David Bushnell, an American, in 1777. His attempt to destroy H.M.S. *Cerberus* failed. The action of Fulton's torpedoes was successful in Britain 1805; but their use was declined by the government. Torpedo shells ignited by electricity were successfully employed in the war in the United States, 1861-5. On 4 Oct. 1865, Messrs. M'Kay & Beardslee tried them at Chatham before the duke of Somerset and others. An old vessel, the Terpsichore, was speedily sunk. Torpedoes, made by professor (aft. sir Frederick) Abel, of Woolwich, were tried in May, 1866. A torpedo invented by Mr. Wightman and an Austrian, tried and reported successful at Sheerness; an old hulk was sunk, 8 Oct. 1870. Torpedoes to be ignited from a distance by an electric battery are now made at Woolwich. A Turkish monitor in the Danube was blown up by a torpedo (see *Russo-Turkish war, II.*), 26 May, 1877. Whitehead's fish torpedoes, projected by compressed air from a boat; very destructive if skilfully directed; described Nov. 1884.

The first fast torpedo-boat built by Messrs. Donaldson & Thornycroft, at Chiswick, for Norway, in 1873; Mr. Donaldson, an able engineer, dies, aged 57 . . . . 4 Oct. 1899
The new torpedo boat *Peacemaker* invented by prof. J. H. L. Tuck announced . . . . Aug. 1886
Nordenfelt's submarine torpedo boat tried in Southampton Water (see under *Boats*) . 19, 20 Dec. 1887
Several severe accidents with torpedo boats July, 1888
Mr. A. Légé's torpedo, based upon the principle of a flying kite, announced . . 16 March, 1889
See under *Cannon* 1889.
The powerful Brennan Torpedo, with the Watkin position finder, successfully tried at Cliff End Fort, on the western side of the Solent . 5 July, 1890
The controllable torpedo of Mr. Scott Sims and Mr. Edison tried at Portsmouth and reported successful . . . . . . 3, 15 Feb. 1892
Lieut. Padillo and several others killed by a torpedo explosion at Cadiz . . . . 3 July, 1901

TORQUAY, a seaport in Devonshire. The pier harbour was made in 1803-7, and enlarged in 1870. Torre abbey was founded in 1196. The prince of Orange landed at Torbay, 5 Nov. 1688. Population, 1881, 24,767; 1891, 25,534; 1901, 33,611.

In Kent's Hole, a cavern near Torquay, the rev. Mr. McEnery discovered a quantity of bones of extinct and recent animals, 1825-9. The investigations were continued by Mr. Godwin-Austen, 1840; by the Torquay Natural History Society, and by a committee of the British Association, 1865, by whom the results were published. Mr. William Pengelly, of Torquay, was actively engaged in the researches.
The princess Louise laid the memorial stone of the new pier and harbour works, 6 May, 1890.
Charter granted to Torquay, Aug. 1892.
Mr. Wm. Pengelly, founder of the Torquay Natural History society and of the Devonshire association for the advancement of science, literature, and art in 1862, died, aged 82, 16 March, 1894.

TORRES STRAIT, dividing Australia from Papua or New Guinea, was discovered by Torres, a Spaniard, in June, 1606. Anthropological expedition from Cambridge, conducted by Dr. A. Haddon, arrived at Murray island, and was heartily welcomed by the natives, mid May–Dec. 1898.

TORRES VEDRAS (a city of Portugal). Near here Wellington, retreating from the French, took up a strong position, called the *Lines of Torres Vedras*, 10 Oct. 1810.

TORTOLA, see *Virgin Isles*.

TORTURE was only permitted by the Romans in the examination of slaves. It was applied to heretics by the Roman catholic clergy, and was used in England so late as 1640 (when Archer, who took part in an attack on Laud's palace, was racked), and in Scotland until 1690. The trial by torture was abolished in Portugal, 1776; in France, by Louis XVI., in 1789; and in Sweden by Gustavus III., 1786. General Picton was convicted of allowing Louisa Calderon to be tortured in Trinidad, in accordance with the old law of the island, at his trials, 21 Feb. 1806, and 11 June, 1808.

TOSKI, battle of, see *Soudan*, 3 Aug. 1889.

TOTAL ABSTINENCE, see *Teetotaller*.

TOTNES (Devon): thought to be the Roman *Ad* Durium Amnem. It was held by Judhael de Totneis, who built the castle about 1085. It was disfranchised for gross corruption and bribery, by the Reform act, 15 Aug. 1867.

TOUGHENED GLASS, see *Glass.*

TOUL, the Roman *Tulli Leucorum*, a fortified town on the Moselle, N.E. France, one of the most ancient in the empire. The city and diocese acquired great privileges from Charles the Simple, 925, when it was united with the German empire. It was reunited with France, 1552. The fortifications, begun in 1238, were rebuilt and enlarged in 1700, according to the plans of Vauban. After a vigorous resistance to the Germans, commencing 14 Aug. 1870, Toul surrendered with its garrison of 3000 men, 23 Sept., when the town was burning in twenty-three places. The Germans thus acquired an uninterrupted railway communication to Paris.

TOULON, the ancient *Telo Martius* (S. France), an important military port. It was taken by the constable of Bourbon, 1524, and by the emperor Charles V. in 1536. In 1707 it was bombarded by the allies, both by land and sea, by which almost the whole town was reduced to a heap of ruins, and several ships burned; but the allies were at last obliged to raise the siege. It surrendered 27 Aug. 1793, to the British admiral, lord Hood, who took possession both of the town and shipping, in the name of Louis XVII., under a stipulation to assist in restoring the French constitution of 1789. A conflict took place between the English and French forces, when the latter were repulsed, 15 Nov. 1793. Toulon was retaken by Bonaparte, 19 Dec., when great cruelties were exercised towards such of the inhabitants as were supposed to be favourable to the British.—A naval battle off this port was fought 11 Feb. 1744, between the English under Mathews and Lestock, against the fleets of France and Spain: in this engagement the brave captain Cornewall fell. The victory was lost by a misunderstanding between the English admirals. Mathews was afterwards dismissed for misconduct. Population in 1901, 101,172. See *Cholera*, 1884.

Visit of Queen Victoria . . . . 13 April, 1892
Destructive fire in the arsenal . . . . 9 July, 1894
The Lagouban naval magazine exploded; over 50 deaths . . . . 5 March, 1899
Pres. Loubet entertains the duke of Genoa and officers of the Italian squadron . . 10 April, 1901
Bones of more than 1,000 persons (supposed victims of 1793) discovered in layers, reported . 3 Sept. 1902

TOULOUSE, the ancient TOLOSA (S. France), founded about 615 B.C.; was the capital of the Visigothic kings in A.D. 419; and was taken by Clovis in 508. The dukes of Aquitaine reigned here, 631-761. A university was established here, 1229, and a parliament, 1302. The inquisition was established here to extirpate heretics, 1229. The troubadours, or rhetoricians of Toulouse, had their origin about 850, and consisted of a fraternity of poets, whose art was extended throughout Europe, and gave rise to the Italian and French poetry; see *Troubadours*. The allied British and Spanish army entered this city on 12 April, immediately after the BATTLE OF TOULOUSE, fought between the British Peninsular army under lord Wellington, and the French led by marshal Soult, 10 April, 1814. The French were forced to retreat, after twelve hours' fighting. Neither of the commanders knew that Napoleon had abdicated the throne of France. Population, 1886, 147,617; 1891, 148,220; 1901, 147,696.

TOULOUSE. The county was created out of the kingdom of Aquitaine by Charlemagne, in 778. It enjoyed great prosperity till the dreadful war of the Albigenses (*which see*), when the count Raymond VI. was expelled, and Simon de Montfort became count. At his death, in 1218, Raymond VII. obtained his inheritance. His daughter Jane and her husband, Alphonse (brother of Louis IX. of France), dying without issue, the county of Toulouse was united to the French monarchy in 1271. A large part of Toulouse destroyed by an inundation of the Garonne; St. Cyprien like a sepulchre; 23 June, 1875.

TOURAINE, the garden of France, was conquered by the Visigoths about 480. It was ceded to Geoffroy count of Anjou, 1044, and thus became the property of the Plantagenet kings of England. It was seized by Philip Augustus in 1203, and was made a duchy by John, 1360. It was finally united to the crown on the death of the duke of Anjou, 1584.

TOURNAMENTS, or JOUSTS, were martial sports of the ancient cavaliers. Tournament is derived from the French word *tourner*, "to turn round." Tournaments were frequent about 890; and were regulated by the emperor Henry I., about 919. Tournaments were introduced into England early in the 12th century; prohibited by Henry II., but revived by Richard I., his son. Solemn tournaments were held by Edward III., 25 Sept. 1329, in London; and 19 Jan. 1344, at Windsor; and by Richard II. in Smithfield, London, 10 Oct. 1319; and also by Henry VIII., in May 1513. The Lateran council published an article against their continuance in 1136. Henry II. of France, in a tilt with the comte de Montgomery, had his eye struck out, an accident which caused the king's death in a few days, 29 June, 1559. Tournaments were then abolished in France.—A magnificent feast and tournament, under the auspices of Archibald, earl of Eglintoun, took place at Eglintoun castle, 29 Aug. 1839, and the following week: many of the visitors (among whom was the late emperor of the French) assumed the characters of ancient knights, lady Seymour, aft. duchess of Somerset, being the "Queen of Beauty." She died 14 Dec. 1884. Among the festivities at the marriage of prince Humbert, at Turin, was a tournament, 24 April, 1868. Tournaments held at the Agricultural hall, London, N. (for benefit of soldiers' widows, &c.), 21 June *et seq.* 1880; 11 June, 1887; 14 June, 1888; 20 June, 1889; 18 June, 1890; 26 May, 1891; 17 May, 1892; 25 May, 1893; 31 May, 1894: 23 May, 1895; 28 May, 1896. Opened by the prince of Wales, 27 May, native Indian (22) officers and other colonials present, prizes given by the duchess of Connaught, 10 June, 1897; 19 May, 1898; (amount received 28,992*l.* 3*s.* 7½*d.*); 25 May, 1899; 18 May, 1900; 30 May, 1901, opened by the king and queen; 22 May, 1902. In Oct. 1883, these tournaments were organized as "Royal Military Tournaments" for development of skill in arms in the army. Tournaments on Woolwich common, directed by col. Curzon, 21-23 Aug. 1889. Manchester, 9 Oct. 1901.

Historical tournament at Rome in relation to the silver wedding of the king and queen and the house of Savoy . . . . . . 25 April, 1893
Grand military tournament at the Crystal palace, March, 1894
Volunteer tournament at the Crystal palace, 8 Aug. 1896; again 3 July, 1897; and 20 July, 1898.

TOURNAY (S. Belgium) was very flourishing till it was ravaged by the barbarians in the 5th century. It has sustained many sieges. Taken by the allies in 1709, and ceded to the house of Austria by the treaty of Utrecht; but the Dutch were allowed to place a garrison in it, as one of the barrier towns. It was taken by the French under general La Bourdonnaye, 8 Nov. 1792. Several battles were fought near Tournay in May, 1793, and May, 1794. Population, 1890, 35,403; 1900, 37,069.

TOURNIQUET (from *tourner*, to turn), an instrument for stopping the flow of blood into a limb, by tightening the bandage employed in amputations, is said to have been invented by Morelli at the siege of Besançon, 1674. J. L. Petit, in France, invented the screw tourniquet in 1718.

TOURS, an ancient city, central France, near which Charles Martel gained a great victory over the Saracens, and saved Europe, 10 Oct. 732, and from which he acquired the name of *Martel*, signifying *hammer*. This conflict is also called the battle of Poitiers. When Paris was invested by the Germans, M. Crémieux and several of the members of the French government of defence went to Tours, together with the representatives of foreign powers, 18 Sept. 1870. On 9 Oct. these were joined by Gambetta, minister of the interior, afterwards of war (who escaped from Paris by a balloon, 7 Oct.). In consequence of the defeat of the army of the Loire near Orleans, the government removed to Bordeaux, 11 Dec.

TOWERS. That of Babel, the first of which we read, built in the plains of Shinar (*Gen.* xi.) 2247 B.C.; see *Babel*. The Tower of the Winds at Athens, built 550 B.C. The Tower of Pharos (see *Pharos*), 280 B.C. The *round towers* in Ireland were the only structures of stone found at the arrival of the English, 1169, except some buildings in the maritime towns founded by the Danes. These towers are tall hollow pillars, nearly cylindrical, but narrowing towards the top, pierced with lateral holes to admit the light, and covered with conical roofs. Fifty-six of them still remain, from 50 to 130 feet high; see *Pisa*.

TOWER OF LONDON. The tradition that Julius Cæsar founded a citadel here (about 54 B.C.) is very doubtful. A royal palace, consisting of no more than what is now called the White Tower, which appears to have been first marked out by William the Conqueror, 1076, was commenced in 1078, and completed by his son, William Rufus, who, in 1098, surrounded it with walls and a broad deep ditch. Several succeeding princes made additions to it, and king Edward III. built the church. In 1638, the old White Tower was rebuilt; and under king Charles II. it was thoroughly repaired, 1680-5, and a great number of additional buildings made to it. Here are the Armoury, Jewel-office, and various other divisions and buildings of peculiar interest. Here took place many executions of illustrious persons, and many murders (king Henry VI., 1471; king Edward V. and his brother, 1485; sir Thomas Overbury, 1613). The armoury and 280,000 stand of arms, &c., were destroyed by fire, 30 Oct. 1841. The "New Buildings" in the Tower were completed in 1850. See *Blood*; for *Tower-Subways*, see *Thames*. The more recent constables of the Tower have been the duke of Wellington, lord Combermere, and sir John Burgoyne. Sir George Pollock, constable Oct. 1871, died 6 Oct. 1872; sir Wm. Gomm, 31 Oct. 1872, died 15 March, 1875; sir Charles Yorke, April, 1875, died 20 Nov. 1880; sir W. Fenwick Williams, April, 1881; gen. sir R. J. Dacres, Aug. 1881, died 6 Dec. 1886; lord Napier of Magdala, Dec. 1886, died 14 Jan. 1890; gen. sir Daniel Lysons, 3 March, 1890, died 29 Jan. 1898, aged 81; gen. sir Frederick C. Stephenson, 2 March, 1898.

The menagerie, long here, was removed to the Zoological Gardens, 1831; the state papers were removed to the Record Office, 1857.

Opened free to the public (Mondays and Saturdays) from 3 April, 1875.

Lanthorne Tower rebuilt and other restorations, 1884-5.

The White Tower and other parts greatly damaged by an explosion of dynamite; about 16 visitors seriously hurt, about 2 p.m. 24 Jan. John Gilbert Cunningham and Harry Burton apprehended, 24 Jan.; committed for trial, 27 March, 1885. See *Trials*.

Tower Bridge act passed, 14 Aug. 1885; foundation of the bridge laid by the prince of Wales, 21 June, 1886.

The work practically completed, 27 March, 1894.

The bridge is a compound suspension and bascule bridge of three spans, of which the centre opening is fitted with a bascule or drawbridge; Mr. J. Wolfe Barry, engineer, K.C.B., 1897; the bridge opened by the prince and princess of Wales; a procession of vessels passed under the bridge, 30 June, 1894.

Opened to the public, 9 July, 1894, *et seq.*

Cost of bridge and approaches, reported to be nearly 1,000,000*l.*

TOWN HOLDINGS in Great Britain and Ireland. A committee appointed in 1886-9 (Mr. Lewis Fry, sir H. James, sir Wm. Marriott, and others), to enquire into terms of occupation, facilities for purchase by tenants, rating, improvements, &c. The report issued 13 July, 1889, was stated to be a compromise.

Report of the committee, dealing with questions relating to local taxation, the liability of ground rents, &c., published . . . 20 May, 1892

TOWNLEY MARBLES, in the British Museum, were purchased in 1805 and 1814.

TOWTON (Yorkshire), where a sanguinary battle was fought, 29 March, 1461, between the houses of York (Edward IV.) and Lancaster (Henry VI.), to the latter of whom it was fatal, and on whose side more than 37,000 fell. Edward issued orders to give no quarter, and the most merciless slaughter ensued. Henry and his queen, Margaret, fled to Scotland; and Edward IV. was settled on the throne.

TOXOPHILITES (from *toxon*, a bow, and *philos*, a lover), a society established by sir Aston Lever in 1781. The Toxophilites formed a division of the Artillery Company about 1784-1803. In 1834 they took grounds in the inner circle of Regent's-park, and built the archery lodge. They possess a very curious piece of plate, given by Catherine, queen of Charles II., to be shot for by the Finsbury archers, of whom the Toxophilites are the representatives.

TOYNBEE HALL, see under *University Teaching*.

TRACT SOCIETIES. The Society for Promoting Christian Knowledge was founded in 1698; the Religious Tract Society, London, in 1799; and other similar societies since.

TRACTARIANISM, a term applied to certain opinions on church matters propounded in the "Tracts for the Times," of which ninety numbers were published, 1833-41. The principal writers were the revs. Dr. E. Pusey, J. H. Newman, J. Keble, J. Froude, and I. Williams—all of the university of Oxford; see *Puseyism*. The tracts (specially No. 90, ascribed to rev. J. H. Newman) were condemned by the authorities at Oxford, 15 March, 1841.

TRACTION-ENGINES were used on common roads in London in 1860, but afterwards restricted. In Aug. 1862, one of Bray's traction-engines conveyed through the city a mass of iron which would have required 29 horses; see *Road-steamers* and *Railways*.

TRADE OF GREAT BRITAIN, see *Exports* and *Imports*. In 1861 the value of the two amounted to 377,017,522*l.*; in 1871 to 614,590,180*l.*; in 1875 to 655,551,900*l.*; in 1877, to 646,765,702*l.*; in 1879, 611,775,239*l.*; in 1881, 694,105,264*l.*; in 1883, 732,328,649*l.*; 1884, 685,986,152*l.*; 1885, 642,442,263*l.*; 1886, 618,822,935*l.*; 1887, 643,490,449*l.*; 1888, 686,213,284*l.*; 1890, 748,944,115*l.*; 1901, 869,854,466*l.* See *Commerce.*

Trade with the United States doubled in value in ten years. 1877, 77,805,000*l.*; 1878, 89,070,000*l.*

Royal commission for enquiry into causes of depression of trade, 31 Aug. 1885. Earls of Iddesleigh and Dunraven, Mr. G. Sclater Booth, prof. Bonamy Price, and twenty others. First meeting 7 Oct. 1885; final report issued Feb. 1887. The majority refer to over-production, rise in value of gold, and in regard to agriculture, fall of prices, as probable causes; improved condition of the working classes noted, Jan. 1887.

See blue book on British trade and industry, issued 16 Sept. 1903.

TRADE AND PLANTATIONS, BOARD OF. Cromwell seems to have given the first notions of a board of trade: in 1655 he appointed his son Richard, with many lords of his council, judges, and gentlemen, and about twenty merchants of London, York, Newcastle, Yarmouth, Dover, &c., to meet and consider by what means the trade and navigation of the republic might be best promoted. *Thomas's Notes of the Rolls.* Charles II., on his restoration, established a council of trade for keeping a control over the whole commerce of the nation, 1660; he afterwards instituted a board of trade and plantations which was remodelled by William III. This board was abolished in 1782; and a new council for the affairs of trade on its present plan was appointed, 2 Sept. 1786.

The parliamentary recommendation in 1880 to appoint a "minister of trade and commerce" was dropped by Mr. Gladstone in March, 1881.

Board of trade journal of tariffs, &c. published, 15 Sept. 1886 *et seq.* For the presidents, see successive *Administrations:* Sir M. E. Hicks-Beach, 15 Feb. 1888; Mr. A. J. Mundella, Aug. 1892. (Secretary, Mr. Thomas Burt, originally a coal-hewer, Dec. 1892.) Mr. Charles T. Ritchie, 25 June, 1895. (Secretary, sir Courtenay Boyle, 1893; died, 19 May, 1901.)

Lord Farrer, nearly 40 years secretary, died, aged 80, 11 Oct. 1899.

TRADE CONGRESSES, see *Working-men.*

TRADE MARKS REGISTRATION ACT, passed 13 Aug. 1875. The registration office, Quality-court, Chancery-lane (Mr. H. Reader Lack, registrar), was opened 1 Jan. 1876; a similar act passed in the United States, 1881. 3,118 trade-marks registered in 1879; 3,522 in 1893; 3,358 in 1897. See *Merchandise Marks Act.*

TRADES MUSEUMS. The formation of one was undertaken in 1853, jointly by the commissioners of the Great Exhibition of 1851, and the Society of Arts. The animal department was opened 17 May, 1855, when a paper on the mutual relations of trade and manufactures was read by professor E. Solly. The contents of this museum were removed to the South Kensington Museum, which was opened 24 June, 1857. The French "Conservatoire des Arts et Métiers" was established 1795.

TRADE, NATIONAL CHAMBER OF, inaugural meeting at Manchester, Mr. R. Thornton-Varley elected president (from 8,000 to 10,000 members), 24 Nov. 1897.

TRADES UNIONS defined as "continuous associations of wage-earners, for the purpose of maintaining or improving the conditions of their employment," were gradually formed after the repeal of the "combination laws" in 1825, to withstand the undue influence of capital and competition. As trades unions formed for maintaining the rate of wages, &c., are not recognised by law, a commission (including lord Elcho, Thomas Hughes, and others, with sir Wm. Erle as chairman) was appointed to enquire into their constitution, 14 Feb. 1867, and an act to facilitate their proceedings was passed 5 April following. Their reports were issued during the year, disclosing the existence of murderous practices, with great intimidation; see *Sheffield* and *Manchester*. An act to protect union funds from embezzlement was passed in 1869. A trade union act passed 29 June, 1871, amended by act passed 30 June, 1876. To counteract the influence of trades unions, the National Federation of Employers was formed Dec. 1873; see *Employers* and *Working-men.* Trades unions were legalised in France in 1884. Trades unions in the United States, N.A., previously local, were legalised in 1845, and were gradually consolidated and became very powerful. See *United States.* "History of Trade Unionism," published 1894, and "Industrial Democracy," by Sidney and Beatrice Webb, published 1897.

207 trades unions in England in 1885; 1,330 in 1896; 1,236, 1901.

Trades Union Congress opened at Liverpool, 18 Jan. 1875, 1876; at Leicester, 17 Sept. 1877; at Bristol, 9 Sept. 1878; at Edinburgh, 15 Sept. 1879; Dublin, 13 Sept. 1880; London, 12 Sept. 1881; Manchester, 18 Sept. 1882; Nottingham [134 unions, 552,091 members], 10 Sept. 1883; Aberdeen, 8 Sept. 1884; Southport, 7 Sept. 1885; Hull, 6 Sept. 1886; Swansea, 5 Sept. 1887; Bradford, 3 Sept. 1888; Dundee, 2 Sept. 1889; Liverpool, 1 Sept. 1890; Newcastle-on-Tyne, 7 Sept. 1891; Glasgow, 5 Sept. 1892; Belfast, 4 Sept. 1893; Norwich, 3 Sept. 1894; Cardiff, 2 Sept. 1895; Edinburgh, 7 Sept. 1896; Birmingham, 6 Sept. 1897; Bristol, 29 Aug. 1898; Plymouth, 4 Sept. 1899; Huddersfield, 3 Sept. 1900; Swansea, 2 Sept. 1901; London, 1 Sept. 1902; Leicester, 7 Sept. 1903.

A special congress (280 delegates) in favour of national trade federation, at Manchester, 24–26 Jan. 1899.

Internat. congress at Stuttgart, mid June, 1902.

Amalgamated society of railway servants hold special meetings at Holborn Town hall and discuss the verdict and judgment given in favour of the Taff Vale rly. co. (see *Trials* 22, July, 1901). Resolution not to appeal, but to support trade unions if they decide to appeal and to bear proportion of cost. Gen.-secretary estimates total cost of dispute to the society at 50,000*l.*; rules revised, and resolution carried in favour of direct labour representation in parliament, 6-8 Jan. 1903.

Conference at the offices of Taff Vale rly. co., Cardiff, between the manager and solicitor of the company and a deputation of the Amalgamated Society of Railway Servants on the question of damages in the action against the society. Agreed that the society should pay 23,000*l.* for damages and cost, 11 Feb. 1903.

Trade Union Congress at Leicester passes a resolution in favour of the legislative limitation of hours of labour to 8 hours per diem, and of making this a test question at all elections, 10 Sept. 1903.

TRAFALGAR (Cape S. Spain), off which a great naval victory was gained by the British, under Nelson, over the combined fleets of France and Spain, commanded by admiral Villeneuve and two

Spaish admirals, 21 Oct. 1805. The enemy's force was eighteen French and fifteen Spanish vessels, all of the line: that of the British, twenty-seven ships. After a protracted fight, Villeneuve and the other admirals were taken, and nineteen of their ships captured, sunk, or destroyed. Nelson was killed, and admiral Collingwood succeeded to the command. Nelson's ship was the *Victory;* and his last signal was, "England expects every man will do his duty;" see *Nelson*. The day specially celebrated in London, 21 Oct. 1896 *et seq.* TRAFALGAR-SQUARE, London, begun 1829; completed 1845. Act passed in 1844, declaring that the square is Crown property, the charge of it placed in the hands of the Commissioners of Woods and Forests and under police regulations. In 1851, the charge was transferred to the Commissioners of Works. The right of preventing public meetings in the square by the executive affirmed by the commons (316—224), 2 March, 1888. Grand Hotel opened by Lord Mayor, 29 May, 1880. See *Riots*.

Public meetings in the square on Saturday afternoons, Sundays, and bank holidays, subject to regulations, 31 Oct. 1892, were resumed, 5 Nov. Generally the unemployed met. Louise Michel there . . . . 11 Dec. 1892

Meeting of 1,000 anarchists to protest against the employment of military and police in strike riots, 17 Sept. 1893; meeting on behalf of the midland coal-strikers . . . . 1 Oct. 1893

Anarchist meeting in memory of the executions in Chicago . . . . 12 Nov. ,,
See *United States*, 1887.

A meeting of anarchists proposed for 3 Dec. prohibited . . . . ,,

A meeting of the Bermondsey vestry and several M.P.s against the house of lords' action on the Parish Councils bill on Sunday . 18 Feb. 1894

Demonstration in favour of Crete and Greece, 14 March, 1897

Demonstration against the S. African war fails completely; the speakers refused a hearing by the crowd . . . . . . 24 Sept. 1899

Demonstration of shop assistants, clerks, and warehousemen; resolution carried against the "living-in" system, long hours, and low pay . 28 Sept. 1902

Mass meeting to consider the distress; resolution passed in favour of a permanent national system to provide work for every deserving citizen, 21 Dec. ,,

Demonstration of the unemployed . . 14 Feb. 1903

TRAFFIC in the metropolis is now regulated by the Metropolitan Streets act, passed 20 Aug. 1867.

LONDON TRAFFIC COMMISSION, appointed 1903 to inquire into the subject of metropolitan locomotion. Evidence is being taken of the London County Council, and of witnesses from the municipal borough councils and other authorities in the vicinity of London who are interested in the question of metropolitan traffic, including the great railway companies and tube railway companies. The commission propose to personally examine the means of transit existing in the chief cities of Europe and in the United States. A sub-commission of six members visited (Sept.-Oct.) New York, Boston, Philadelphia, and Chicago to investigate the methods adopted in these cities with special reference to the merits of subways and tube railways. The report of the commission will probably be presented to parliament towards the end of 1904.

TRAGEDY, see *Drama*.

TRAINING SCHOOLS, begun by the National Society, 1811. One was founded at Battersea in 1840, by sir J. Kay Shuttleworth, and Mr. E. C. Tufnell; the latter, who was then in the Poor Law Commission, devoting a year's salary towards the expenses. Mr. Mann stated, in 1855, that there were about forty of these schools in different parts of the country.

Maria Grey training college, established 1878; extension fund started, 1891.

Finsbury training college established about 1883.

TRAINING SHIPS, see *Marine Society*, *Chichester*, and *Shaftesbury Memorials*.

TRAJAN'S COLUMN (in Rome), erected 114, by the Roman senate and people, to commemorate his victories, and executed by Apollodorus. It was built in the square called the *Forum Trajanum;* it is of the Tuscan order, and from its base, exclusive of the statue and pedestal, is 127½ feet high.

TRAM-ROADS. The name is probably derived from being made of *trams* or bars of wood; the statement that it was derived from Mr. Benjamin Outram (the father of sir James Outram, the Indian general), who improved the colliery railroads about 1800, is very doubtful. The iron tram-road from Croydon to Wandsworth was completed on 24 July, 1801. The Preston Outram-way was opened 1 June, 1803. Street railways or tramways for omnibuses drawn by horses, previously established by Mr. Train in New York, were opened by him at Birkenhead, Cheshire, 30 Aug. 1860, and at Bayswater, London, 23 March, 1861. (See *Ireland*, 1868.) A street railway bill was rejected by the house of commons in April, 1861. Several of these railways existed for a time in various parts of the metropolis in 1861, but were all taken up in 1862. An act to facilitate the construction of tramways passed 9 Aug. 1870. Tramways from Brixton to Kennington, and from Whitechapel to Bow, were opened 9 May, 1870; and others since. Their introduction into the city was much recommended but opposed, March-May, 1873. Dividend of the North Metropolitan tramways company, 8 per cent. Aug. 1876. The use of steam locomotives proposed: approved in Paris, July, 1876.

Elevated street railways erected in New York, 1877-8.

233 miles of tramways constructed in England and Wales, 1870-80.

Steam cable tramway on Highgate Hill, N. London (the first in Europe), opened 29 May, 1884; stopped Dec. 1892; cars again running (1898).

Steam employed by the North London Tramways company, 1 April, 1885. See under *Air*.

886 miles of tramways in the United Kingdom in 1887; 904 miles in 1888; 1889, 949 miles; 811,943*l.* net receipts in 1890; 1893, 768,649*l.* net receipts, 960 miles; 1895, 982 miles: 855,200*l.* net receipts; 1896, 1009 miles: 1,046,505*l.* net receipts; 1901, 1305 miles: net receipts, 1,435,883*l.*; 1902, 1484 miles: net receipts, 1,861,418*l.*

An international tramway congress opened at Brussels, 5 Sept. 1888.

Mr. Lineff's mode of traction on tramways by magneto-electricity was tried at Chiswick, 25 June, 1890. His patent has been purchased by a syndicate.

Overhead electric tramway opened at Leeds, 29 Oct. 1891.

The Connelly tramcar motor in which the vapour of mineral oil is employed, adopted by tramcars on part of the London and Greenwich system, March, 1893.

London Street Tramways, valued at 64,540*l.*, proposed purchase by the London County Council, March, 1893.

Propulsion of tramcar by compressed coal-gas successfully tried at Croydon, 19 June, 1894.

London Tramways act passed 31 July, 1894.

All night service from Stratford to Aldgate (Metrop. Tram. co.) begins, Jan. 2; further extensions, Feb. *et seq.* 1899.

Internat. tramways and light railways exhibition opened at the Agricultural hall, 22 June, 1900; another congress opened by Mr. Gerald Balfour, 30 June, 1902.

First section of South London electric system opened by the prince of Wales, 15 May, 1903.

TRANQUEBAR (East Indies), the Danish settlement here, founded in 1618, was purchased by the English in 1845.

TRANSCASPIAN RAILWAY, see under *Railways*, 1888.

TRANSFIGURATION. The change of Christ's appearance on Mount Tabor, in the presence of Peter, James, and John, A.D. 32 (*Matt.* xvii.). The feast of the Transfiguration, kept on 6 Aug., was instituted in the East before 700, and seems to have been observed in the West as early as 450. Pope Calixtus III. in 1456 issued a bull making it a "feast of obligation" to be generally observed in honour of the defeat of the Turks at Belgrade in that year.

TRANSFORMATION PRINTS. A method of printing one picture over another, the former being easily effaced, patented by Mr. Andrew Reid of Newcastle-on-Tyne, and others, 1885.

TRANSFUSION OF BLOOD, see *Blood*.

TRANSIT, see *Mercury* and *Venus*.

TRANSLATION TO HEAVEN. The translation of Enoch to heaven at the age of 365 years, 3017 B.C. The prophet Elijah was translated to heaven in a chariot of fire, 896 B.C.—The possibility of translation to the abode of eternal life has been maintained by some extravagant enthusiasts. The Irish house of commons expelled Mr. Asgill from his seat, for his book asserting the possibility of translation to the other world without death, 1703.

TRANSPADANE REPUBLIC, comprising Lombardy and part of the Venetian territories, was established by Bonaparte after his victory at Lodi, 10 May, 1796. With the Cispadane republic, it merged into the Cisalpine republic, Oct. 1797.

TRANSPORTATION, see *Banishment*. Judges were given the power of sentencing offenders to transportation "into any of his majesty's dominions in North America," by 18 Charles II. c. 3 (1666), and by 4 Geo. I. c. 11 (1718). Transportation ceased in 1775, but was revived in 1786. The reception of convicts was successfully refused by the Cape of Good Hope (in 1849) and by the Australian colonies (1864). Transportation, even to West Australia, where labour is wanted, ceased after a few years, through the fierce opposition of the eastern colonies. In consequence of the difficulty then experienced in transporting felons, 16 & 17 Vict. c. 99 was passed to provide other punishment, namely, penal servitude, empowering the queen to grant pardon to offenders under certain conditions, and licences to others to be at large: such licences being liable to be revoked if necessary; and many have been. These licences are termed "tickets of leave." The system is said to have originated in Australia under the superintendence of captain Maconochie. It was much assailed in Oct. and Nov. 1862, on account of violent crimes being traced to *ticket-of-leavers;* and was modified by the Penal Servitude Act, 1864; and the Prevention of Crimes Acts, 1871 and 1879. It is now considered successful. See *Crime*.

John Eyre, esq., a man of fortune, was sentenced to transportation for stealing a few quires of paper. —*Phillips* . . . . 1 Nov. 1771

The Rev. Dr. Halloran, tutor to the earl of Chesterfield, was transported for forging a frank (10*d.* postage) . . . . 9 Sept. 1818

The first transportation of felons to Botany Bay was in May, 1787; where governor Phillip arrived with about 800 on 20 Jan. 1788; convicts were afterwards sent to Van Diemen's Land, Norfolk Island, &c.

Transportation superseded by penal servitude . . 1853

Returning from transportation was punishable with death until 5 Will. IV. c. 67, Aug. 1834, when an act was passed making the offence punishable by transportation for life.

A shipment of convicts to West Australia (which had already received 10,000) in 1867.

TRANSUBSTANTIATION, the doctrine of the "real presence." That the bread and wine in the Eucharist are changed into the very flesh and blood of Christ by the consecration, was broached in the days of Gregory III. (731), and accepted by Amalarius and Radbertus (about 830), but rejected by Rabanus Maurus, Johannes Scotus Erigena, Berengarius, Wicliffe, and others. In the Lateran council, held at Rome by Innocent III., the word "Transubstantiation" was used to express this doctrine, which was decreed to be incontrovertible; and all who opposed it were condemned as heretics. This was confirmed by the council of Trent, 18 Jan. 1562. John Huss, Jerome of Prague, and other martyrs of the reformation, suffered for denying this dogma, which is renounced by the church of England (28th article), and by all protestant dissenters. The declaration against transubstantiation, invocation of the saints, and the sacrifice of the mass, on taking any civil office, was abolished by an act passed 25 July, 1867; see *Sacrament*.

Luther maintained the doctrine of *con-substantiation*, viz., that after consecration the body and blood of Christ are substantially present in the bread and wine. He was opposed by Bucer, Carlstadt, Zwingle, and others (termed sacramentarians), who asserted that the Lord's supper is only a commemorative rite.

TRANSVAAL REPUBLIC, named South African Republic in 1883, founded by Dutch Boers (farmers) in 1848, after several years' severe conflict with the natives. Its independence was declared 17 Jan. 1852, S. J. P. Krüger elected president 7 May, 1853; and its constitution proclaimed 13 Feb. 1858; capital Pretoria. President for four years, T. F. Burgers, 27 May, 1872. Population about 38,000 Boers, 5000 English settlers, 770,000 blacks (1881); 1894 (estimated), 800,000, of whom about 90,000 are whites; 1895 (estimated), 15,000 Boers, 60,000 Uitlanders, "outsiders" (mixed), 250,000 Kaffirs. Estimated revenue, 4,886,499*l.* 1897–8. The republic was annexed to Gt. Britain, 1 Sept., and styled TRANSVAAL COLONY, 25 Oct. 1900. See *below* and *South African War*. Estimated revenue, 4,000,000*l.*; expenditure, 3,702,765*l.* 1902–3; imports, 13,067,671*l.* 1902.

War with the Kaffirs begun; Cetewayo, king; Secocœni (Sickakuni), an eminent chief . . July, 1876

Republican government blamed; its troops defeated; Sir Theophilus Shepstone sent to mediate Sept. ,,

Dutch boers assisted by the Amazwasies, a warlike tribe, who check Kaffirs . . . . Sept. ,,

Severe dispatch of the earl of Carnarvon, censuring burgers for aggression on Kaffirs . . Oct. ,,

Secocœni threatening Leydenburg . . . Nov. ,,

Schlickman, the Dutch general, killed in an attack, 17 Nov. ,,

Sir T. Shepstone well received; a desire expressed for federation, Feb.; opposition to it March, 1877

Anarchy in the Transvaal; annexation of the Transvaal (for protection) to the British dominions proclaimed by sir T. Shepstone, 12 April; he is sworn in as administrator . . . 30 May, ,,

Conflict with Secocœni (disapproved); some volunteers killed . . . . . . 17 June, 1878

Sir Wm. Owen Lanyon made governor of the Transvaal . . . March, 1879

Great opposition to the British rule; appeased after much discussion . . . . 12 April, „

Sir G. Wolseley appointed governor of Natal, &c., May „

War with Secocœni continues . . . Aug. *et seq.* „

His stronghold captured by col. Baker Russell (under sir Garnet Wolseley), with British and native troops . . . . . . 28 Nov. „

Secocœni surrenders . . . . . 2 Dec. „

The Transvaal declared a crown colony . . Dec. „

The Boers meet and claim independence; Bok, Kruger, and Pretorius arrested for signing a document issued by the Boer committee, Dec. 1879, and Jan. 1880

The Boers seize Heidelberg, 16 Dec.; establish the South Africa republic, Paul Kruger president 17 Dec. „

A party of Boers stop at Bronker's Spruit about 250 British troops of the 94th regiment, who resist; some killed or wounded; others disarmed and dismissed . . . . . . 20 Dec. „

Potchefstrom seized by Boers, who retire when the place is shelled; col. Bellairs besieged in it, 27 Dec. *et seq.* „

Capt. J. M. Elliot said to be treacherously killed while fording the Vaal . . . . 29 Dec. „

The South Africa Republic proclaimed by a triumvirate; Kruger, Joubert, and Pretorius 30 Dec. „

Troops sent from Britain, &c., Dec., 1880, and Jan. 1881

Sir George P. Colley (appointed governor of Natal 1880) takes command in the war . . . Jan. „

Gen. Colley's attack on Laing's Nek, a pass, repulsed with heavy loss; col. Bonar Millet Deane, majors Ruscombe Poole and Wm. Hunt Hingeston killed . . . . 28 Jan. „

Severe conflict on the Ingogo river; the British 12 hours under fire; repulsed with heavy loss, 8 Feb. „

Sir Evelyn Wood arrives with reinforcements and joins gen. Colley . . . . . . 17 Feb. „

The Orange Free State proclaim neutrality and mediation . . . . . about 22 Feb. „

Gen. Colley marches in the night to Majuba hill (*which see*); defeated and killed after a desperate conflict . . . . . . 26-27 Feb. „

Gen. sir F. Roberts sent to Africa . . . 28 Feb. „

Armistice proposed by the Boers; accepted for 6-14 March; armistice extended, 14 March; Boers agree to British terms, 21, 22 March; peace proclaimed; the Boers disperse; gen. Roberts recalled 24 March, „

Potchefstrom surrenders with honours of war, 21 March; given up as occupied by mistake April, „

Vote of censure on the Government policy in the commons negatived (314-205) . . 25, 26 July, „

Commissioners to carry out treaty of peace appointed 5 April, agree to convention ceding virtually all the territory to "The TRANSVAAL STATE" on 8 August, subject to suzerainty of the Queen, and a British resident; with debt of about 420,867*l*. &c.; independence of the Swazies guaranteed; signed by Royal commissioners and Martin W. Pretorius and Peter J. Joubert (Stephen J. P. Kruger not present), 3 Aug.; effected . . . . 8 Aug. „

Meeting of the volksraad, 21 Sept.; treaty confirmed, 25 Oct. „

Mr. G. Hudson appointed first British resident, Nov. „

Departure of the British troops . about 28 Dec. „

Fighting with the natives . . . . . Feb. 1882

Secocœni killed by a rival chief . . . . Aug. „

War with the insubordinate chief Mapoch . Oct. „

Renewed troubles with the natives . . Sept.-Oct. „

Fighting with the natives, who are repulsed, under their chief Mapoch . . . 16-17 Nov. „

Again defeated . . . . Jan. 1883

Combination of chiefs against the Boers announced, March, „

Negotiations for peace begun by Mapoch announced, 5 April, „

Paul Kruger, president . 9 May, 1883, and 8 May, 1883

Peace concluded . . . . July, „

Transvaal deputies, Paul Kruger and others, received by lord Derby . . . . . 7 Nov. „

Definite proposals submitted to the government, 22 Dec.; amended boundary lines accepted, 2 Feb.; convention signed, the republic to be styled the "South Africa Republic" under British suzerainty . . . . . 27 Feb. 1884

The convention adopted by the Transvaal assembly, 8 Aug. „

The filibustering settlers of Goshen and Stellaland break the convention; seize and annex Montsioa's lands in Bechuanaland; sanctioned by a proclamation; withdrawn on remonstrance, Sept., Oct. „

Sir H. Robinson's ultimatum from Cape Town requiring protection of the frontiers . about 14 Oct. „

Short war with the natives, refusing to pay taxes; Mamusa taken; battle . . . . . 2 Dec. 1885

Johannesburg founded through the development of gold mining; inhabitants chiefly English . 1887

Defensive treaty with the Orange Free State, about 13 March, 1889

A great commercial development of commerce since the discovery of goldfields, rapid growth of Johannesburg . . . . reported Sept. „

Famine in Johannesburg, relieved by government, about 23 Oct. „

Visit of president Kruger to Johannesburg, resisted by a violent crowd . . . . . 4 March, 1890

He signs the agreement for Swaziland, about 4 Aug. „

Gen. Joubert entertained in London . . . Dec. „

Heavy rains and destructive floods; Johannesburg suffers greatly, ... middle Jan. 1891

About 100 Boers prevented by the police from crossing the Limpopo . . . about 2 July, „

Destructive storm and inundation, about 10, 11 Feb. 1893

Paul Kruger re-elected president, 7,881; gen. Joubert, 7,009; M. Kotze, 76; reported 12 April, „

Malaboch's stronghold in Zoutpansberg stormed by the Transvaal forces; reported . 20 June, 1894

Sir Henry B. Loch, the high commissioner, visits Pretoria to obtain redress of the grievances of British and foreign residents . . . 26 June, „

British subjects exempted from military service by the Transvaal government; friendly agreement . . . . 28 June, „

Destructive revolt of the Kaffirs (Zoutpansberg district), reported . . . . . . 13 Aug. „

Malaboch and 200 followers imprisoned at Pretoria, 18 Aug. „

The Kaffirs defeated after severe fighting and sue for peace . . . . 29 Aug. „

The chiefs surrender; reported . . . 13 Sept. „

The Swaziland convention passed by the Volksraad; see *Swaziland* . . . . . . 13 Feb. 1895

Rebellion in Zoutpansberg suppressed after severe fighting . . . . 11 June, „

The Delagoa railway opened at Pretoria, sir Hercules Robinson and other British governors present; much festivity . . . . . . 8 July, „

Protest of the British government at the closing of the Vaal river drifts as contrary to the convention of London, 4 Nov.; agreed to . 8 Nov. „

Increased opposition to the despotic government of pres. Kruger; Mr. Esselen, state attorney, Mr. Christian Joubert, and other officials resign; the Uitlanders (settlers) demand a voice in public affairs, &c., reported . . . . . 16 Dec. „

The National union, chairman, Mr. Chas. Leonard, issues a liberal manifesto . . . 26 Dec. „

Dr. Jameson having received an appeal for help from the Uitlanders in Johannesburg, crosses the frontier with a force from Pitsani Pitlogo, 29 Dec.; col. Grey and others start from Mafeking, with about 460 men (volunteers) of the British S. Africa company's troops . . . . 30 Dec. „

Sir Hercules Robinson telegraphs to Dr. Jameson to retire . . . . 30 Dec. „

Mr. Chamberlain and sir H. Robinson intervene to stop hostilities, and offer co-operation to pres. Kruger . . . . 31 Dec. „

Dr. Jameson's party, outnumbered and without resources, defeated by the Boers near Krugersdorp . . . . 1 Jan. 1896

They surrender conditionally, after another fight at Vlakfontein, 2 Jan.; British loss, 21 killed, 46 wounded; 9 officers and 550 men prisoners at Pretoria . . . . 3 Jan. ,,

Johannesburg surrenders unconditionally, on the advice of the British government . . 2 Jan. ,,

The German emperor congratulates pres. Kruger, 2 Jan.; who replies gratefully . . 5 Jan. ,,

Correspondence between Mr. Chamberlain and pres. Kruger respecting the prisoners, 3, 4, 5 Jan. ,,

Sir H. Robinson, sir Graham Bower, capt. Dawkins, and others arrive in Pretoria . . 5 Jan. ,,

Some of the Reform committee at Johannesburg arrested . . . . 6 Jan. ,,

Dr. Jameson and other prisoners handed over to sir H. Robinson* . . . . . . 7 Jan. ,,

The British South Africa company in London request a judicial inquiry relating to Dr. Jameson's entry into the Transvaal (29 Dec.) . . . . 9 Jan. ,,

General amnesty (with exceptions) at Johannesburg . . . . 9 Jan. ,,

Between 50 and 60 members of the Reform committee of the Uitlanders, col. Rhodes, sir Drummond Dunbar, Mr. Lionel Phillips, and others, arrested, and sent to Pretoria . . . 10 Jan. ,,

The parliament votes thanks to the Orange Free State and to sir H. Robinson, and adjourns, 13 Jan. ,,

Sir Hercules Robinson leaves Pretoria 14 Jan. ,,

Preliminary trial of the Reform leaders begins at Pretoria, 3 Feb.; confiscation of property adjudged . . . . 25 Feb. ,,

Pres. Krüger invited to London . . . . 4 Feb. ,,

Explosion of shunted trucks of dynamite, at Vrededorp, a suburb of Johannesburg; the whole district in ruins, thousands homeless, about 80 deaths; vigorous measures of relief adopted, 19 Feb. ,,

1,000*l.* contributed by the Cape government to the relief fund; total, 104,000*l.* . . . . 22 Feb. ,,

Friendly but firm despatch from Mr. Chamberlain to the president, insisting on redress of Uitlander's grievances, and requesting an answer to the invitation, 1 April; pres. Krüger defers his visit for the present . . . . . . 24 April, ,,

Trial of the Reform leaders: they plead guilty of high treason, sentence of death passed on Mr. Lionel Phillips, Mr. Hays Hammond, George P. Farrar, and col. Frank Rhodes (commuted to imprisonment and banishment, 29 April), 24–28 April, ,,

[59 principal men of the Rand, sentenced to 2 yrs. imprisonment, 3 yrs. banishment, and heavy fines, 28 April, 1896.]

The volksraad opened by pres. Krüger, who refers to the drought, locusts, and rinderpest . 4 May, ,,

Resignation of sir Jacobus de Wet, British agent in Pretoria . . . . 11 May, 1896

Dr. Jameson and major Robt. White write to the *Times* emphatically denying the receipt of any message from Mr. Cecil Rhodes directing them to move to Johannesburg . . . . 12 May, ,,

Mr. Grey, one of the reform committee, became insane and commits suicide in prison, 16 May; 9 released and shorter sentences on the others, 20 May; insanitary condition of the gaol; illness among the prisoners, 45 released under conditions, 30 May, ,,

The executive decide to release the reform leaders on payment of 25,000*l.* each, or in default 15 years' banishment; fines paid; col. Rhodes, not accepting conditions, banished . 11 June, ,,

Bill for the education of Uitlanders' children passed by the volksraad . . . . . 4 Aug. ,,

Mr. Wm. Conyngham Greene appointed British agent at Pretoria, Aug.; arrives . . 1 Dec. ,,

Aliens (dangerous) expulsion bill comes into force, 30 Sept.; aliens immigration restriction law passed, 26 Nov. (comes into operation, 1 Jan. 1897)

Pacific speech of pres. Krüger at a banquet in Pretoria . . . . 27 Nov. ,,

Pres. Krüger opens the new railway from Krugersdorp to Potchefstroom . . . . 22 Jan. 1897

Volksraad opened, 1 Feb.; 826 Uitlanders admitted to the franchise . . . . . 11 Feb. ,,

Collision between the volksraad and the high court of justice; deadlock, Feb.; the new high court law passed, 25 Feb.; the judges (high court) adjourn, 5 March; compromise, negotiations, 19 March; court resumed *pro tem.* 14 July, Aug.; [compromise ended, 5 Feb. 1898].

Firm conciliatory despatches of Mr. Chamberlain, 6 March; and again . . . . 16 Oct. ,,

Indemnity claimed for the Jameson raid, 677,938*l.* 3*s.* 3*d.*, "moral or intellectual damage, 1,000,000*l.*," total, 1,677,938*l.* 3*s.* 3*d.* . 19 March, ,,

Dr. Jameson examined by the S. Africa committee (see *Rhodesia*) . . 26 March *et seq.* ,,

Defensive alliance with the Orange Free State, June, ,,

Construction of forts round Pretoria April *et seq.* ,,

Alien immigration bill repealed . . 7 May, ,,

Epidemic in the north attributed to the pollution from the rinderpest; great mortality . June, ,,

Suicide of Mr. I. B. Barnato (temporary insanity), see *Cape of Good Hope* . . . . June, ,,

Messrs. Sampson and Davies, Uitlander reformers, who refused pardon, not accepting conditions, released on Jubilee day . . . . 22 June, ,,

Pres. Krüger, in the volksraad, denies the suzerainty of Great Britain, but maintains the convention of 1884 and desires peace . 24 Aug. ,,

Diamond mine near Pretoria discovered . Sept. ,,

Presidential election, candidates: Mr. Krüger, gen. Joubert, and Mr. Burger, 4 days' poll, closed, 22 Jan.; Mr. Krüger re-elected, majority, 9,005, announced . . . . 10 Feb. 1898

Chief Justice Kotze (see *above*, Feb.) dismissed from office (unconstitutional); succeeded by state-attorney Gregorowski . . . 16 Feb. ,,

Mr. Kotze supported by the lawyers, 12 March (over 5,000*l.* subscribed for him, April); his manifesto issued, 16 March; *Times*, 7 April; entertained in London . . . . 20 June, ,,

The volksraad opened by the president . 2 May, ,,

The government's reply to Mr. Chamberlain's despatch of 16 Oct. 1897, to the effect that it cannot recognise British suzerainty since the convention of 1884, but that it will abide by the stipulations of that convention, and re-affirms its right to arbitration, published . 24 May, ,,

Aliens expulsion amendment bill passed . 13 June, ,,

Mr. Kotze, ex-chief justice, allowed to practise as advocate . . . . Nov. ,,

Punitive expedition under gen. Joubert against Mpefu, Kaffir chief, in the Zoutpansberg district, much fighting, 21 Oct.; Magato's mountain captured . . . . . . 16 Nov. ,,

---

* Dr. Jameson and his party (350 officers and men) sail from Durban, 21 Jan. 1896; arrive in London, 25 Feb.; charged, after examination, before sir John Bridge at Bow st., 25 Feb. *et seq.*; Leander Starr (Dr.) Jameson and 5 others were committed, and bailed, 15 June; trial at bar, before lord chief justice Russell, Mr. baron Pollock, and Mr. justice Hawkins: counsel for the crown, attorney-gen. sir R. Webster, sol.-gen. sir R. B. Finlay, and others: for Dr. Jameson and defendants, sir Edward Clarke, and others; South Africa Republic represented by Mr. Cohen, and others; verdict, guilty of offences under the Foreign enlistment act: appeal for new trial declined by defendants; sentences: imprisonment without hard labour: Dr. Jameson, 15 months [ill; released, 2 Dec. 1896]; sir John Willoughby, 10 months; major Robt. White, 7 months; col. Henry White, col. Grey, and major Coventry, 5 months: 20–28 July, 1896. Major Coventry, ill, released, 22 Aug. 1896; the 5 officers permitted to retire from the army, 8 officers unconvicted, reprimanded, and return to duty, reported, 15 Sept. 1896. [A trooper awarded 500*l.* damages from the B. S. A. company as compensation for losses, July, 1898.]

Mpefu captured by the Chartered company's force and sent to Bulawayo, reported . . 30 Dec. 1898

Mr. Edgar, British subject, shot dead by Jones, a policeman, 19 Dec. 1898; Jones is acquitted, 25 Feb. 1899

Stormy British meeting at Johannesburg to protest against the arrest of Messrs. Webb and Dodd, of the S. African league, 14 Jan.; the British vice-consul refuses to appear at the trial, which is adjourned, 19 Jan.; prisoners discharged, 14 April, „

A petition to the queen, signed by 23,000 Uitlanders, stating their grievances (the franchise, dynamite monopoly, &c.), 24 March, forwarded by sir A. Milner, 3 April (over 40,000 signatures, July).

Negotiations: Mr. Chamberlain declares the dynamite monopoly to be a breach of the convention, April, „

Much intimidation of Uitlanders . April *et seq.* „

Mrs. Applebee, wife of a Wesleyan minister (who had denounced the illegal liquor traffic), murdered, 28 April; 2 other murders near Johannesburg, May, July (crimes unpunished).

Volksraad opened by pres. Kruger, 1 May; hot debate; some slight concession in respect to the franchise proposed. . . . . 23 May, „

The British government, through Mr. Conyngham Greene, British agent at Pretoria, expresses sympathy with the Uitlanders, and hopes for a speedy change in their position, announced, 27 May, „

Bloemfontein conference: sir A. Milner's franchise proposals rejected by pres. Kruger; negotiations fail; see *Orange Free State*, 30 May–5 June, „

Mass meeting at Johannesburg, the Uitlanders assert sir A. Milner's proposals to be the irreducible *minimum* they could accept . 9 June, „

Gen. Joubert opens the Pietersburg railway, 31 May, „

Pres. Kruger's franchise proposals adopted by the raad, 14 June, see *below*.

Blue-book relating to the wrongs of the Uitlanders, issued . . . . 14 June, „

Boer meetings throughout the country endorse pres. Kruger's franchise proposals . . June, „

Exodus of miners begins . . 19 June *et seq.* „

Firm speech of Mr. Chamberlain at Birmingham, 26 June, „

See *Cape Town* . . . . 28 June, „

Despatches on the suzerainty of Great Britain, published at Pretoria . . . . . 3 July, „

Great meeting at Johannesburg endorsing sir A. Milner's policy . . . . . . 4 July, „

Ministers from the Cape and Orange Free state confer with pres. Kruger on sir A. Milner's franchise proposals at Pretoria, 5, 6 July; secret session of the raad, pres. Kruger, Mr. Fischer (O.F.S.), present . . . . . 6 July, „

Green-book published, protesting against the annexation of Zambaansland by Great Britain, July, „

Trial of 4 *alleged* Johannesburg conspirators against the government (May), a "bogus affair"; charge withdrawn and prisoners discharged, 25 July, „

Draft franchise law, 7 years' prospective and retrospective franchise to Uitlanders, passed by the raad, 11 July; ratified . . 26 July, „

The British government adhere to sir A. Milner's *minimum* franchise scheme . . 13 July, „

Blue-book, with despatches, sir A. Milner declares the new franchise law inadequate, issued, 27 July, „

Overflow meeting in Johannesburg against the new franchise law, reforms demanded, guaranteed by the imperial government . . 26 July, „

Mr. Chamberlain proposes a joint inquiry into the new law, 31 July; Mr. Conyngham Greene asks the Transvaal government to appoint delegates, 2 Aug.; rejected; pres. Kruger proposes a five years' retrospective franchise, 10 members from the goldfields, renunciation of British suzerainty, and international arbitration . . 19 Aug. „

Mr. Chamberlain proposes an inquiry by the British agent, and insists on the terms of the conventions 1881 and 1884 . . . . 28 Aug. 1899

Mr. Chamberlain's firm, warning speech at Birmingham, 26 Aug., hailed with satisfaction by the Uitlanders . . . . . . 28 Aug. „

Crisis, business suspended at Johannesburg . Aug. „

Military preparations amongst the Boers; ammunition for the Transvaal stopped at Delagoa bay; released . . . . 31 Aug. „

The Transvaal withdraws its proposal of a 5 years' and returns to the 7 years' franchise . 2 Sept. „

Attempted arrest of Messrs. Pakeman and Moneypeny, press editors . . . . . 2 Sept. „

Boer troops gathered on the frontiers . . Sept. „

Panic and exodus of Uitlanders from Johannesburg, 3 Sept. *et seq.*

Urgent British despatch, demands 5 years' franchise, a quarter representation for the goldfields, and equality of Dutch and English in the volksraad, 8 Sept.; Boer reply, negative and inconclusive . . . . 17 Sept. „

Two firm despatches from Mr. Chamberlain maintaining the terms of previous despatches, and announcing that the imperial government would now formulate its own proposals . . 22 Sept. „

Boer troops (about 30,000) mobilised, posted along the frontier . . . . . . 2 Oct. *et seq.* „

Exodus of Uitlanders; mail train from Natal stopped by Government order, passengers sent back at Volksrust, 30 Sept.; another stopped and 800,000*l.* worth of Uitland gold confiscated, 2 Oct. „

The raads prorogued . . . . . 2 Oct. „

Boer Ultimatum presented by Mr. Reitz (secretary of state) to Mr. C. Greene, at Pretoria, demanding arbitration; withdrawal of British troops on the border, &c., 9 Oct.; due compliance to be intimated by 5 p.m., 11 Oct.; British reply states that these demands are such as are impossible to be discussed . . 11 Oct. „

Martial law proclaimed at Pretoria . . 11 Oct. „

Mr. C. Greene recalled; leaves Pretoria . 12 Oct. „

War proclaimed in Johannesburg, Boer manifesto issued to the Afrikanders . . . 12 Oct. „

See *South African War*.

Mr. A. F. Hay appointed U.S. consul at Pretoria, Dec. „

Special war tax in accordance with the volkraad resolution (28 Sept. 1899), levied, reported, 3 Feb. 1900

Cartridge factory at Modderfontein blown up, 70 deaths, reported . . . . 15 Feb. „

The Robinson bank at Johannesburg seized by Boer officials, reported, 8 Feb.; cash and securities restored and bank re-opened, reported, 25 Feb. „

Pres. Kruger arrives in Pretoria from the front and holds a hurried meeting of the executive, 9 March, „

The government's appeal to the powers for intervention, declined . . . . . 12 March, „

Death of gen. Piet Joubert, an able general and politician, aged 66 . . . . 27 March, „

The Rand mines closed and all British expelled from the republic . . . . . 29 March, „

The Boer peace mission received at the Hague, 19 April–2 May; at Washington, 18 May; neutral policy to be maintained, announced, 21 May; at Paris . . . . 7 July, „

Commandant Prinsloo sentenced to 9 months' imprisonment for treason . . . 24 April, „

Begbie's foundry, under the management of the Creuzot firm, wrecked by explosion at Johannesburg, 30 deaths and 54 injured, many arrests, 24 April; Mr. Begbie, jun., and 3 others acquitted, charges withdrawn by the state prosecutor . . . . . 24 May, „

Volksraad opened by pres. Kruger, 7 May; his speech approved, session closed . . 9 May, „

Rev. Adrian Hofmeyr imprisoned 7 months without

trial for speeches in favour of the progressives; released at Pretoria . . . . 14 May, 1900

For other events see *S. African War.*

TRANSVAAL annexed to Great Britain; proclamation issued by lord Roberts, 1 Sept.; formal annexation took place . . . . 25 Oct. ,,

Transvaal concessions commission (the hon. A. Lyttelton, Mr. A. M. Ashmore, and Mr. R. K. Loveday) met in S. Africa, end of Aug.; public sittings at Pretoria during . . . Oct. ,,

Sir A. Milner, high commissioner for S. Africa, appointed governor of the Transvaal, Jan. 1901; arrives at Pretoria . . . . 4 March, 1901

Civil jurisdiction re-established in Pretoria and 4 chief towns; military tribunals abolished in Pretoria and Johannesburg . . . 10 April, ,,

Mine accident at Johannesburg, 26 natives killed, 13 April, ,,

The Meyer and Charlton mine re-started, lord Kitchener and others present . 4, 6 May, ,,

Municipal government started in Johannesburg, 8 May, ,,

Frequent breaches of the oath of neutrality; stricter regulations enforced . . June, ,,

Blue-book, with report of Transvaal concessions commission issued, 11 June; and sir David Barbour's report on the finances of the Transvaal and Orange River colony, considered just and generous, total expenditure of the home government, estimated, 64,332,000*l.*, *Times*, 12 June, ,,

Mrs. Kruger dies at Pretoria, aged 67 . 20 July, ,,

Major O'Meara appointed administrator in Johannesburg, Sept. 1900; made government commissioner and chairman of the new town council, March; good report . . 20 July, ,,

Blue-book issued relating to cruel treatment of natives by the late republic, *Times*, 1 Aug. 1901; laws modified.

Seven Rand mines in operation . . . 23 Aug. ,,

Mr. Broeksma, ex-public prosecutor (tried and sentenced to death for treachery and treason, 13–29 Sept.), shot at Johannesburg . 30 Sept. ,,

S. African Compensation Commission, Mr. Milvain, chairman (sir John Ardagh and others for the imperial government); long negotiations: total foreign claims, 1,631; amount claimed, 1,116,450*l.*; amount awarded, 106,050*l.*; Holland claimed, 706,355*l.*; amount awarded, 37,500*l.*; sittings closed in London . . . . . . 9 Nov. ,,

Werneck, a *surrendered* burgher, convicted of high treason, &c., shot at Johannesburg . 22 Nov. ,,

The British return to the owners 23,000 oz. of gold commandeered by the late Boer government and found in the Pretoria mint . . . 26 Nov. ,,

A commission appointed to inquire into the working of the Gold Law; sir Richard Solomon, chairman . . . . 27 Nov. ,,

Proclamations issued prohibiting betting houses and abolishing various laws of the late republic relating to the High Court, the franchise, &c., about 30 Nov. ,,

Regulations controlling native labour; *flogging*, forced labour, &c., strictly forbidden, published, 11 Dec. ,,

Growth of revenue, financial prospects good, 11 Dec. ,,

Johannesburg stock exchange re-opened, 17 Dec. ,,

Education and industries gradually re-established, Jan.–Dec. ,,

Blue-book issued relating to treatment of natives (lord Milner's despatch and policy, 6 Dec. approved, 27 Jan.) . . . . . 30 Jan. 1902

Mining industry progressing, influx of natives, 7 Feb.–March, ,,

Military governorship of Pretoria relinquished by sir J. Maxwell . . . . . 19 March, ,,

First general meeting of the chamber of mines since the war; estimated loss due to the war, over 6,000,000*l.* . . . . . . 3 April, ,,

Transvaal high court in the new palace of justice at Pretoria, opened . . . . 10 May, ,,

New mining tax, 10 per cent. on net produce, issued . . . . 9 June, 1902

Lord Kitchener (made visct. and gen., June) and troops enthusiastically received at the end of the war; banquet at Johannesburg, speeches by lords Milner and Kitchener . . 17 June, ,,

Lord Milner installed governor of the Transvaal and commander-in-chief at Pretoria . 21 June, ,,

German banquet at Johannesburg, lord Milner (made a peer, 26 June) present . 25 June, ,,

Teachers' conference, Mr. Sargant, director of education, president, at Johannesburg, 2 July; received by lord Milner . . . 8 July, ,,

Sir Percy Girouard appointed railway commissioner, line to be styled Central S. African railway . . . . early July, ,,

Advocates Smuts, Jacobs, and De Wet (of the staff of the late government) admitted into the supreme court, reported . . . . 4 Aug. ,,

Gens. Botha, De Wet, and Delarey announced their intention to start a Boer fund abroad, 4 Aug. (see end of *S. African War*).

Transvaal political association to support lord Milner meets . . . . . 14 Aug. ,,

Outbreak of redwater; precautionary measures issued . . . . 29 Aug. ,,

Sir Arthur Lawley appointed lieut.-gov.; arrives, 31 Aug. ,,

Customs tariff revised . . . . 8 Oct. ,,

Lord Milner tours successfully through the west and north . . . . Sept.–Oct. ,,

J. P. Fitz-Patrick, author of "The Transvaal from Within," and George Farrar (sentenced to death, 28 April, 1896), knighted . . . Oct. ,,

Grant of 8,000,000*l.* for the Transvaal and Orange River colony voted in the commons . 5 Nov. ,,

70,000 persons repatriated . . June–Nov. ,,

Martial law withdrawn . . . . 19 Nov. ,,

Land department established . . . 21 Nov. ,,

Coal struck, 30 ft. thick, at Grootvlei . mid Dec. ,,

Mr. Chamberlain's successful tour to promote reconciliation and unity; grand reception and banquet at Pretoria, 5, 6 Jan.; Boer address received, their demands refused; the Vereeniging treaty to be kept, 8 Jan.; at Johannesburg: Transvaal war contribution, 30,000,000*l.*, to be raised in 3 years, agreed to by the mine leaders; an imperial loan of 35,000,000*l.* for the new colonies guaranteed, 13 Jan.; visits many villages; at Mafeking . . . . . 28 Jan. 1903

Report (majority and minority) of the commission appointed 1901 to inquire into the working of the gold law, issued . . . . end Jan. ,,

Ordinance issued empowering municipality of Johannesburg to raise loans . . end Jan. ,,

Sir William Harcourt writes letter to *Times* on native labour in the Transvaal . . 5 Feb. ,,

Report on labour immigration commission issued; legislative council approves Asiatic labour, 30 Dec. ,,

TRANSYLVANIA, an Austrian province, was part of the ancient Dacia (*which see*). In 1526, John Zapoly rendered himself independent of the emperor Ferdinand I. by the aid of the Turks. His successors ruled with much difficulty till Jan. 1699, when the emperor Leopold I., by the treaty of Carlowitz, finally incorporated Transylvania into the Austrian dominions. The Transylvanian deputies did not take their seat in the Austrian parliament till 20 Oct. 1863. A decree for the convocation of the Transylvanian diet was issued 12 Sept. 1865. The inhabitants are about 1,100,000 ignorant Roumans, 1,500,000 Saxon colonists, and 550,000 Magyars, the last being the ruling class. The union of Transylvania with Hungary in 1848, which has caused much discontent, was ratified by the Transylvanian diet, 25 Dec. 1866.

Serious agrarian riots at Föeldvar suppressed with bloodshed, 27 June, 1888.

PRINCES OF TRANSYLVANIA.

1526. John Zapoly.
1540. John Sigismund.
1571. Stephen Zapoly I. Bathori.
1576. Christopher Bathori.
1581. Sigismund Bathori.
1602. Emperor Rodolph.
1605. Stephen II. Bottskai.
1607. Sigismund Ragotzski.
1608. Gabriel I. Bathori.
1613. Gabriel II. (Bethlem Gabor).
1631. George I. Ragotzski.
1648. George II. Ragotzski.
1660. John Kemin.
1662. Michael I. Abaffi.
1690-99. Michael II. Abaffi.

TRAPPISTS. The first abbey of La Trappe in Normandy was founded, in 1140, by Rotrou, comte de Perche. The present order of Trappists owes its origin to the learned Jean le Bouthillier de la Rancé (editor of *Anacreon* when aged 14), who renounced the world, and sold all his property, giving the proceeds to the abbey of La Trappe, to which he retired in 1662, to live there in great austerity. After several efforts he succeeded in reforming the monks, and in establishing a new rule, which commands silence, prayer, reading, and manual labour, and which forbids study, wine, fish, &c. Rancé was born in 1620, and died in 1700. The Trappists' new building was consecrated in Aug. 1833.

A number of these monks, driven from France in the revolution of 1790, were received by Mr. Weld, of Lulworth, Dorsetshire, who gave them some land to cultivate and a habitation, where they remained till 1815. This order was charged with rebellion and conspiracy in France, and sixty-four English and Irish Trappists were shipped by the French government at Paimbœuf, 19 Nov., and were landed from the *Hebé*, French frigate, at Cork, 30 Nov. 1831. They established themselves at Mount Melleray, county of Waterford.

TRASIMENE, see *Thrasymene*.

TRAUTENAU (Bohemia). On 27 June, 1866, the first corps of the army of the crown-prince of Prussia seized Trautenau, but was defeated and repulsed by the Austrians under Gablenz; on the 28th, the Prussians defeated the Austrians with great loss.

TRAVELLERS' CLUB (Pall-mall), established in 1815. A member must have "travelled out of the British islands to a distance of at least 500 miles from London, in a direct line."

TRAVELLING IN ENGLAND. In 1707 it took in summer one day, in winter nearly two days, to travel from London to Oxford (55 miles). In 1817 the journey was accomplished in six or seven hours. By the Great Western Railway express (63 miles) it is done in $1\frac{1}{2}$ hour. In 1828, a gentleman travelled from Newcastle to London (273 miles) inside the best coach in 35 hours, at an expense of 6*l*. 15*s*. 3*d*. or 6*d*. per mile (including dinner, &c.). In 1857, the charge of the Great Northern railway ($275\frac{1}{4}$ miles) first-class express (6 hours) was 50*s*. 9*d*.; in 1903, 38*s*. 3*d*.

TRAWLING. Deep-sea fishing with a boat (sometimes driven by steam) having a very large net attached to it, and thereby catching the fish which mostly live at the bottom of the sea; principally practised on the N.E. coast of Britain.

Commissions reported in 1864 and since, that trawling was not injurious to the supply of fish as suggested; but another commission, with scientific advice, reported in Feb. 1885, that there was some ground for the fishermen's complaints.

TREAD-MILL, an invention of the Chinese, to raise water for the irrigation of the fields. The complicated tread-mill introduced into the prisons of Great Britain is the invention of Mr. (afterwards sir William) Cubitt, of Ipswich. It was erected at Brixton gaol, 1817, and soon afterwards in other large prisons.

TREASON, see *High Treason*. PETTY TREASON (a term abolished in 1828, defined by the statute of 25 Edw. III. 1352) was a wife's murder of her husband; a servant's murder of his master; and an ecclesiastical person's murder of his prelate or other superior. *Misprision* of treason, knowledge and concealment of the crime, punishable with forfeiture of goods and imprisonment for life.

TREASON-FELONY. By the Crown and Government Security Act, 11 Vict. c. 12 (1848), certain treasons heretofore punishable with death were mitigated to felonies, and subjected to transportation or imprisonment. The Fenians in Ireland were tried under this act; see *Trials*, 1865.

TREASURER OF ENGLAND, LORD HIGH, the third great officer of the crown, a lord by virtue of his office, having the custody of the king's treasure, governing the upper court of exchequer, and formerly sitting judicially among the barons. The first lord high treasurer in England was Odo, earl of Kent, in the reign of William I. This great trust is now confided to a commission, and is vested in five persons, called "lords commissioners for executing the office of lord high treasurer," and of these the chancellor of the exchequer is usually one; the first lord being usually the premier; see *Administrations*, for a succession of these officers. Sir Stafford Northcote (aft. Earl of Iddesleigh) was first lord of the treasury and not premier, 24 June, 1885, as was Mr. W. H. Smith, 26 July, 1886; see *Salisbury Administrations*. A third lord of the treasury (Mr. Stansfeld) was appointed, Dec. 1868, succeeded by Mr. W. H. Gladstone, Dec. 1869.

The first of this rank in IRELAND was John de St. John, Henry III. 1217; the last, William, duke of Devonshire, 1766; vice-treasurers were appointed till 1789; then commissioners till 1816, when the revenues of Great Britain and Ireland were united.

The *first* lord high treasurer of SCOTLAND was sir Walter Ogilvie, appointed by James I. in 1420; the *last*, in 1641, John, earl of Traquair, afterwards commissioners were appointed.

TREASURER OF THE CHAMBER, formerly an officer of great consideration, and always a member of the privy council. He discharged the bills of all the king's tradesmen, and had his office in Cleveland-row, in the vicinity of the royal palace. His duties were transferred and the office suppressed at the same time with the offices of master of the great wardrobe and cofferer of the household in 1782. *Beatson*.

TREATIES. A formal and written treaty made in England with any foreign nation was entered into at Kingston between Henry III. and the dauphin of France (then in England and leagued with the barons), 11 Sept. 1217. The first commercial treaty was with Guy, earl of Flanders, 2 Edw. 1274; the second with Portugal and Spain, 1308. *Anderson*. The chief treaties of the nations of Europe will be found described in their respective places: the following forms an index; see *Coalitions, Commerce, Leagues*, &c. Hertslet's "Commercial Treaties," 16 vols. 1820-85.

Abo, peace . . 7 Aug. 1743
Adrianople, peace . 14 Sept. 1829
Aix-la-Chapelle . 2 May, 1668
Aix-la-Chapelle, peace . 1748
Akermann, peace . 4 Sept. 1826
Allahabad (Bahar, &c., ceded to E. I. Company) . . 1765
Alt Radstadt, peace 24 Sept. 1706
America, peace . . 3 Sept. 1783
Amiens, peace 25 Mar. 1802
Ancon (Chili and Peru) 20 Oct. 1883
Anglo-Abyssinian, frontiers, &c. 15 May, 1902
Anglo-Chinese, commercial 5 Sept. 1902
Anglo-French, etc. agreements, *which see* 1890 . . 1903
Anglo-Japanese agreement 30 Jan. 1902
Anglo-Spanish convention, 29 July, 1886
Anglo-Turkish convention, 4 June, 1878
Antananarivo (Madagascar), 1 Oct 1895
Antwerp, truce . . 4 April, 1609
Armed Neutrality, convention, 16 Dec. 1800
Arras . . . 22 Sept. 1435
Arras 1482
Augsburg, league of . . . 1686
Austria with England, convention; the latter agrees to accept 2,500,000*l*. as a composition for claims on Austria, amounting to 30,000,000*l*. sterling 1824
Baden, peace . . . Sept. 1714
Bagnalo (Venice, Naples, &c.) . 1484
Balta Liman . 1838 and 1849
Barcelona (France and Spain) . 1493
Barrier treaty . 15 Nov. 1715
Barwalde (France and Sweden) . 1631
Basel, peace (France and Spain) 22 July, 1795
Bassein (Great Britain and Mahrattas) 1802
Bayonne . . . 5 May, 1808
Belgrade, peace . 18 Sept. 1739
Berlin, peace . 28 June, 1742
Berlin, decree . 29 Nov. 1806
Berlin convention 5 Nov. 1808
Berlin, peace (Prussia & Saxony) 21 Oct. 1866
Berlin treaty (Russia, Turkey, &c.) 13 July, 1878
Berlin (Russia and Germany, commercial) . . March, 1894
Beyara . . . 31 Aug. 1839
Breda, peace . 25 July, 1667
Bretigny, peace . 8 May, 1360
Bucharest, 28 May, 1812; (Servia and Bulgaria) . . 3 March, 1886
Cambray, league 10 Dec. 1508
Cambray, peace . 5 Aug. 1529
Campo Formio 17 Oct. 1797
Canton . . 29 Aug. 1842
Capua, convention . 20 May, 1815
Carlowitz, peace . 26 Jan. 1699
Carlsbad, congress of 1 Aug. 1819
Cateau-Cambrésis, peace . 1559
Chaumont . . 1 Mar. 1814
Chefoo, convention 17 Sept. 1876
China and Japan, peace (see Corea) . . 17 April, 1895
Chunar, India . . . 1781
Cintra, convention . 22 Aug. 1808
Closterseven, convention 8 Sept. 1757
Coalition, first, against France 26 June, 1792
Coalition, second 22 June, 1799
Coalition, third . 8 Sept. 1805
Coalition, fourth . 6 Oct. 1806
Coalition, fifth 9 April, 1809
Coalition, sixth . 1 March, 1813
Commerce (Great Britain and Turkey) 16 Nov. 1839
Commerce (Great Britain and the Two Sicilies) 25 June, 1845

Concordat, with France, 15 July, 1801
Conflans . . . 1465
Constantinople, peace, 16 April, 1712
Constantinople . 8 July, 1833
Constantinople . 8 May, 1854
Constantinople (Russia and Turkey, definitive) . . 8 Feb. 1879
Constantinople (settling boundaries of Greece) 24 May and 2 July, 1881
Constantinople (peace between Turkey and Greece) 4, 19 Dec. 1897
Copenhagen, peace 27 May, 1660
Copenhagen (composition for Sound dues) . 14 March, 1857
Crecy 1544
Dover 1670
Dresden, peace 25 Dec. 1745
Egypt, viceroy and admiral Codrington, convention 6 Aug. 1828
Eliot convention . April, 1835
England, convention with Austria, Russia, Prussia, and Turkey, for settlement of the East 15 July, 1840
England and United States, convention . . 13 Nov. 1826
Evora Monte 26 May, 1834
Family Compact . 15 Aug. 1761
Fommanah (Ashantee war) 13 Feb. 1874
Fontainebleau, peace 2 Sept. 1679
Fontainebleau 8 Nov. 1785
Fontainebleau, concordat 25 Jan. 1813
France and England, convention respecting the slave trade 29 May, 1845
France and Italy, convention respecting the occupation of Rome . . 15 Sept. 1864
France and Siam, convention 7 Oct. 1902
Frankfort (peace between Germany and France) 10 May, 1871
French commercial treaty, 23 Jan. 1860
Friedwald . . 5 Oct. 1551
Fuessen, peace . 23 April, 1745
Gandamak (with Afghanistan), 26 May, 1879
Gastein convention 14 Aug. 1865
Ghent, pacification 8 Nov. 1576
Ghent, peace (America) 24 Dec. 1814
Golden Bull . . . 1356
Grand alliance . 12 May, 1689
Hague . . . 21 May, 1659
Hague . . . 7 May, 1669
Halle . . . 1610
Hamburg, peace . 2 May, 1762
Hanover . 3 Sept. 1725
Hanover and England 22 July, 1834
Holy alliance . 26 Sept. 1815
Hubertsburg, peace 15 Feb. 1763
Hué (France and Annam) 25 Aug. 1883
"Interim" . . . 15 May, 1548
Italo-Abyssinian . Oct. 1889
Japan and Great Britain 26 Aug. 1858
Jay's treaty . 19 Nov. 1794
Kaynardji, or Koutschouc-Kaynardji . . 21 July, 1774
Kiao-chau (Germany and China) 6 March, 1898
Kiel . . 14 Jan. 1814
Laybach, congress 6 May, 1821
League, holy . . . 1576
Leipsic, alliance . April, 1631
Leoben, peace . . 1797
Lisbon, peace . 13 Feb. 1668
London (settlement of Greece) 6 July, 1829
London (separating Belgium from Holland) . 15 Nov. 1831
London (convention respecting Belgium) . 19 April, 1839
London (Turkey and Egypt) July, 1840

London (succession to crown of Denmark) . . . 1852
London (neutrality of Luxemburg settled) . 11 May, 1867
London, Alaska award 20 Oct. 1903
Lübeck, peace . 22 May, 1629
Luneville, peace . 9 Feb. 1801
Madrid, concord . . 1526
Methuen treaty . . . 1703
Milan decree . . 17 Dec. 1807
Milan (Austria and Sardinia) 6 Aug. 1849
Munster, peace . 24 Oct. 1648
Nankin, peace 29 Aug. 1842
Nantes, edict . . 13 April, 1598
Naumberg . . . 1554
Nice . . . 1518
Nimeguen, peace . 10 Aug. 1678
Noyon 16 Aug. 1516
Nuremberg . . 2 Aug. 1532
Nystadt . . 30 Aug. 1721
Oliva, peace . 3 May, 1660
Paris, peace (*Paris*) . 10 Feb. 1763
Paris . . . 20 June, 1784
Paris . . . 15 May, 1796
Paris, peace (Sweden) 6 Jan. 1810
Paris . . . . 11 April, 1814
Paris . . . . 10 June, 1817
Paris . . . . April, 1856
Paris (settlement of Neufchâtel affair) . . 26 May, 1857
Partition, first . 11 Oct. 1698
Partition, second . . 1700
Passarowitz, peace . 13 Mar. 1718
Passau . . 12 Aug. 1552
Pekin, peace, 24 Aug. 1860; 5 April, 1885
Persia, peace . . 3 March, 1857
Petersburg, St., peace 5 May, 1762
Petersburg, St. . 5 Aug. 1772
Petersburg, St. . 8 April, 1805
Peterswald, convention 8 July, 1813
Pilnitz, convention . 20 July, 1791
Poland, partition . 25 Nov. 1795
Pragmatic sanction . . 1438
Pragmatic sanction 17 April, 1713
Prague, peace . 30 May, 1635
Prague (peace between Austria and Prussia) . 23 Aug. 1866
Presburg, peace . 26 Dec. 1805
Pretoria (see *Transvaal*) 3 Aug. 1881
Pretoria, peace . 31 May, 1902
Public good, league for the . 1464
Pyrenees, peace . 7 Nov. 1659
Quadruple alliance . 2 Aug. 1718
Radstadt, peace 6 March, 1714
Radstadt, congress . 9 Dec. 1797
Ratisbon, peace . 13 Oct. 1630
Ratisbon . . 1 Aug. 1806
Reichenbach, treaties . June, 1813
Religion, peace of . . 1555
Rhine, confederation . 1 Aug. 1806
Ryswick, peace 20 Sept. 1697
Samoa, conventions . 16 Feb. 1900
St. Cloud, convention 3 July, 1815
St. Germains, peace . . 1570
St. Germain-en-Laye. peace 29 June, 1679
St. Ildefonzo, alliance 19 Aug. 1796
San Stefano (peace between Russia and Turkey), see *Berlin* 3 March, 1878
Shimonoseki (peace between China and Japan) . 17 April, 1895
Siöröd, peace 1613
Sistowa, peace . . 4 Aug. 1791
Smalcald, league . 31 Dec. 1529
Spain, pacification . 22 April, 1834
Spain, convention, satisfying British claims . 26 June, 1828
Spain (peace with America), 10 Dec. 1898; ratified . 6 Feb. 1899
Stettin, peace . 13 Dec. 1570
Stockholm, peace . 20 Nov. 1719
Stockholm . . 24 March, 1724
Stockholm . . 3 March, 1813
Stockholm, treaty of (Sweden and allies) . . 21 Nov. 1856

Suncion . . . 15 July, 1852
Temeswar, truce . 7 Sept. 1664
Teschen, peace . . 12 May, 1779
Teusin, peace . . 18 May, 1595
Tien-Tsin, China, peace 26 June, 1858; . . . 11 May, 1884
Tilsit, peace . . . 7 July, 1807
Tolentino . . . 19 Feb. 1793
Töplitz . . . 9 Sept. 1813
Triple alliance . . 28 Jan. 1668
Triple alliance . . 4 Jan. 1717
Triple alliance (Austria, Germany, and Italy), 13 March, 1887; 28 June, 1891
Troppeau, congress . 20 Oct. 1820
Troyes . . . 21 May, 1420
Turin (cession of Savoy and Nice . . . 24 March, 1860
Turkmauchay, peace 22 Feb. 1828
Ulm, peace . . 3 July, 1620
Unkiarskelessi . . 8 July, 1833
Utrecht, union . . 22 Jan. 1579
Utrecht, peace . . 11 April, 1713
Valençay . . . . 8 Dec. 1813
Verona, congress . . 25 Aug. 1822
Versailles, peace . . 20 Jan. 1783
Vienna . . . . 30 April, 1725
Vienna, alliance . . 16 March, 1731
Vienna, peace . . 18 Nov. 1738
Vienna, peace . . 14 Oct. 1809
Vienna, convention . 28 Sept. 1814
Vienna, 25 March; 31 May; 9 June, 1815
Vienna (Austria and Prussia), commercial . . 19 Feb. 1853
Vienna . . . 30 Oct. 1864
Vienna (Austria & Great Britain, commercial) . . 16 Dec. 1865
Vienna (peace between Austria and Italy) . . 3 Oct. 1866
Villa Franca (*prelim.*) 12 July, 1859
Vossem, peace . . 16 Jan. 1673
Warsaw, alliance . 31 March, 1683
Warsaw. . . . . 24 Feb. 1768
Washington, reciprocity treaty between Great Britain and the United States, respecting Newfoundland fishery, commerce, &c. . . . . 2 July, 1854
Washington (settling Alabama claims, &c.) . 8 May, 1871
Washington (fishery dispute), 15 Feb. 1888
Westminster, peace . 19 Feb. 1674
Westminster (with Holland) . 1716
Westphalia, peace . 24 Oct. 1648
Wilna, treaty of 1561
Wurms, edict of 1521
Wurtzburg league 1610
Zurich, convention . 20 May, 1815
Zurich (Austria, France, and Sardinia) . . 10 Nov. 1859

TREBIA, now *Trebbia*, a river in North Italy, near which Hannibal defeated the Roman consul Sempronius, 218 B.C.: and Suvarrow, after a struggle, defeated the French marshal Macdonald and compelled him to retreat, 17-19 June, 1799.

TREBIZOND, a port of Asia Minor in the Black Sea, was colonised by the Greeks, and became subject to the kings of Pontus. It enjoyed self-government under the Roman empire, and when the Latins took Constantinople in 1204, it became the seat of an empire which endured till 1461, when it was conquered by the Turks under Mahomet I. Population in 1885, 45,000.

EMPERORS.

1204. Alexis I. Comnenus.
1222. Andronicus I.
1235. John I.
1238. Manuel I., great captain.
1263. Andronicus II.
1266. George.
1280. John II.
1285. Theodora.
,, John II.
1297. Alexis II.
1330. Andronicus III.
1332. Manuel II.
,, Basil.
1340. Irene.
1341. Anna.
1343. John III.
1344. Michael.
1349. Alexis III.
1390. Manuel III.
1417. Alexis IV.
1446. John IV. (Calo-Joannes).
1458-61. David.

TRECENTO, see *Italian*.

TREES in London. Many were planted by John Evelyn in the Mall, St. James's, &c. He recommended this in his "Fumifugium," published 1661. The planting of rows of trees in suburban roads began in 1875.

TREES OF LIBERTY were planted in Paris and other parts of France during the revolutionary eras, 1790 and 1848. These trees were cut down in Paris in Jan. 1850, when riots ensued, put down by the military.

The celebrated tree *Février*, planted in 1789 near the National Library, Paris, was felled early in 1884.

English arboricultural society founded at Hexham in 1880, about 420 members in 1897. Annual meetings.

TRENT (the ancient Tridentum), in the Tyrol, belongs to Austria. The council held here is reckoned in the Roman catholic church as the 18th general council. Its decisions have been implicitly received as the standard of faith, morals, and discipline in that church. It first sat 13 Dec. 1545, and continued (with interruptions) under pope Paul III., Julius III., and Pius IV. to 4 Dec. 1563; its last sitting (the 25th). A jubilee in relation to this council was celebrated in June, 1863. Trent was several times taken during the French war. Population, 1890, 21,653.

At the council was decreed, with anathemas: the canon of scripture (including the apocrypha), and the church its sole interpreter; the traditions to be equal with scripture; the seven sacraments (baptism, confirmation, the Lord's supper, penance, extreme unction, orders, and matrimony); transubstantiation; purgatory; indulgences; celibacy of the clergy; auricular confession, &c.

TRENT STEAMER, see *United States*, Nov.-Dec. 1861.

TREVECCA, see *Cheshunt*.

TRÈVES, or **TRIER**, the Roman Treviri, in Rhenish Prussia, was a prosperous city of the Gauls, 12 B.C. The emperor Gallienus held his court here A.D. 255. The church of St. Simeon dates from the 4th century. Trèves was made an electorate in the 14th century, and became subject to the archbishop in 1585. Councils held here, 385-1423. The archbishopric is said to have been founded before the 7th century and to be the oldest in Germany. After various changes, Trèves was acquired by Prussia, June 1815. In 1844 much excitement was occasioned by miracles said to have been wrought by a "Holy Coat" in the cathedral. The coat was exhibited to thousands, Aug., Sept. 1891. Population, 1890, 36,162; 1900, 43,324.

"*TRIA JUNCTA IN UNO*" (three joined in one), the motto of the knights of the military order of the Bath, signifying "faith, hope, and charity;" see *Bath*.

TRIAL AT BAR, signifies by the whole court or a plurality of judges. This plan was adopted at Bristol after the riots in 1832; also at O'Connell's trial, 1844; and arranged for the trial of the claimant of the Tichborne estates for perjury, in April, 1873. See *Juries*.

TRIALS. Regulations for conducting trials were made by Lothaire and Edric, kings of Kent, about 673 to 680. Alfred the Great is said to have begun trial by jury; but there is good evidence of such trials before his time. Arrangements were made for more speedy trials by "the Winter Assizes Act," 1876. See *Appeal*.

REMARKABLE TRIALS.

King Charles I.: 20 Jan.; condemned . 27 Jan. 1649
Oates's Popish Plot: Edward Coleman, convicted, 27 Nov.; Wm. Ireland and other priests 17 Dec. 1678
—— Robt. Green and others, 10 Feb.; Thos. Whitbread and other Jesuits, 13 June; Richard Langhorne, counsellor, 14 June; convicted . . 1679
Sir George Wakeman, the queen's physician; acquitted . . . . 13 July, ,,
Viscount Stafford: convicted . 30 Nov.-7 Dec. 1681

Rye House Plot: convicted; William lord Russell, 13 July; Algernon Sidney . . . 21 Nov. 1683
The Seven Bishops; acquitted . . . 29 June, 1688
Captain Porteous, for murder, see *Porteous*, 22 June, 1736
Jenny Diver, for felony, executed . 18 March, 1740
William Duell, executed for murder at Tyburn, but who came to life when about undergoing dissection at Surgeons' Hall . . 24 Nov. ,,
Lords Kilmarnock and Balmerino for high treason 28 July, 1746
Mary Hamilton, for marrying with her own sex, 14 wives . . . 7 Oct. ,,
Lord Lovatt, 80 years of age, for high treason; beheaded . . . 9 March, 1747
Freney, the celebrated Irish robber, who surrendered himself . . 9 July, 1749
Amy Hutchinson, burnt at Ely, for the murder of her husband . . . 5 Nov. 1750
Miss Blandy, the murder of her father (hanged) 3 March, 1752
Ann Williams, for the murder of her husband, burnt alive . . . 11 April, 1753
Eugene Aram, for murder at York; executed 13 Aug. 1759
Earl Ferrers, for the murder of his steward; executed . . . 16 April, 1760
Mr. MacNaughten, at Strabane, for the murder of Miss Knox . . . 8 Dec. 1761
Ann Bedingfield, for the murder of her husband; burnt alive . . . 6 April, 1763
Mr. Wilkes, alderman of London, for an obscene poem ("Essay on Woman") . . 21 Feb. 1764
Murderers of captain Glas, his wife, daughter, mate, and passengers, on board the ship *Earl of Sandwich*, at sea . . 3 March, 1766
Elizabeth Brownrigg, for the murder of one of her female apprentices; hanged . . 12 Sept. 1767
Lord Baltimore, the libertine, and his female accomplices, for rape . . 28 March, 1768
Great cause between the families of Hamilton and Douglas . . . 27 Feb. 1769
Great Valencia cause in the house of peers, in Ireland 18 March, 1772
Cause of Somerset the slave (see *Slavery*) 22 June ,,
Elizabeth Herring, for the murder of her husband; hanged, and afterwards burnt at Tyburn 13 Sept. 1773
Messrs. Perreau brothers, bankers, forgery; hanged 17 Jan. 1776
Duchess of Kingston, for marrying two husbands; guilty (see *Kingston*) . . . 15 April, ,,
Dr. Dodd, for forging a bond of 4200*l.* in the name of the earl of Chesterfield, 22 Feb. (see *Forgery*) executed . . . 27 June, 1777
Admiral Keppel, by court-martial; honourably acquitted . . . 11 Feb. 1779
Mr. Hackman, for the murder of Miss Reay, when coming out of the theatre-royal, Covent-garden 16 April, ,,
Lord George Gordon, on a charge of high treason; acquitted . . . 5 Feb. 1781
Capt. John Donellan, for murder of sir Theodosius Boughton; executed . . 2 April, ,,
Mr. Woodfall, the celebrated printer, for a libel on lord Loughborough, afterwards lord chancellor 10 Nov. 1786
Lord George Gordon, for a libel on the queen of France; guilty . . . 28 Jan. 1788
Mr. Warren Hastings: a trial which lasted seven years and three months (see *Hastings, Trial of*), commenced . . . 13 Feb. ,,
The printer of *the Times* newspaper, for libels on the prince of Wales, and dukes of York and Clarence; fined 200*l.* and imprisoned one year, 3 Feb. 1790
Renwick Williams, called the "Monster," for stabbing women in London . . 8 July, 1790
Barrington, the pickpocket, most extraordinary adept; transported . . 22 Sept. ,,
Thomas Paine, political writer and deist, for libels in the *Rights of Man*; guilty . . 18 Dec. 1792
Louis XVI. of France (see *France*) . . 1792-3
Archibald Hamilton Rowan, for libel; imprisoned and fined . . . . 29 Jan. 1794
Mr. Purefoy, for the murder of colonel Roper in a duel: acquitted . . . 14 Aug. 1794
Mr. Robert Watt and Downie, at Edinburgh, for treason . . . . 3 Sept. ,,
Messrs. Hardy, Horne Tooke, Thelwall, and Joyce, for high treason; acquitted . 29 Oct. ,,
Earl of Abingdon, for his libel on Mr. Serman; guilty . . . . 6 Dec. ,,
Major Semple, *alias* Lisle, for felony . 18 Feb. 1795
Redhead Yorke, at York, libel . . 27 Nov. ,,
Lord Westmeath *v.* Bradshaw, for *crim. con.*; damages, 10,000*l.* . . . 4 March, 1796
Lord Valentia *v.* Mr. Gawler, for adultery, damages, 2000*l.* . . . . 16 June, ,,
Daniel Isaac Eaton, for libels on kingly government; guilty . . . 8 July, ,,
Sir Godfrey Webster *v.* lord Holland, for adultery; damages, 6000*l.* . . . 27 Feb. 1797
Parker, the mutineer at the Nore, called admiral Parker (see *Mutinies*) . 27 June, ,,
Boddington *v.* Boddington, for *crim. con.*; damages, 10,000*l.* . . . 5 Sept. ,,
William Orr at Carrickfergus, for high treason; executed . . . 12 Oct. ,,
Mrs. Phepoe, *alias* Benson, murderess . 9 Dec. ,,
The murderers of col. St. George and Mr. Uniacke, at Cork . . . 15 April, 1798
Arthur O'Conner and O'Coigley, at Maidstone, for treason; latter hanged . . 21 May, ,,
Sir Edward Crosbie and others for high treason; hanged . . . 1 June,
Beauchamp Bagenal Harvey, at Wexford, for high treason . . . 21 June, ,,
Two Messrs. Sheares, at Dublin, for high treason; executed . . . 12 July, ,,
Theobald Wouffe Tone, by court-martial (he committed suicide, died on the 19th) . 10 Nov. ,,
Sir Harry Brown Hayes, for carrying off Miss Pike of Cork . . . 13 April, 1800
Hatfield, for shooting at George III. (see *Hatfield*) 26 June, ,,
Mr. Tighe of Westmeath *v.* Jones, for *crim. con.*; damages, 10,000*l.* . . . 2 Dec. ,,
Mutineers at Bantry Bay, hanged (see *Bantry Bay*) 8 Jan. 1802
Governor Wall, for cruelty and murder, twenty years before (tried under 33 Hen. VIII. c. 23) (see *Goree*) 20 Jan. ,,
Crawley, for the murder of two females in Peter's-row, Dublin . . . 6 March, ,,
Colonel Despard and his associates, for high treason; hanged on the top of Horsemonger-lane gaol (see *Despard*) . . . . 7 Feb. 1803
M. Peltier, for libel on Bonaparte, first consul of France, in *l'Ambigue*: guilty . 21 Feb. ,,
Robert Aslett, cashier at the bank of England, for embezzlement and frauds; the loss to the bank, 320,000*l.*; found *not guilty*, on account of the invalidity of the bills . . . 18 July, ,,
Robert Emmett, at Dublin, for high treason; executed next day . . . 19 Sept. ,,
Keenan, one of the murderers of lord Kilwarden; hanged . . . . 2 Oct. ,,
Mr. Smith for the murder of the supposed Hammersmith Ghost . . . 13 Jan. 1804
Lockhart and Laudon Gordon for carrying off Mrs. Lee . . . . 6 March, ,,
Rev. C. Massy *v.* marquis of Headfort, for *crim. con.*; damages, 10,000*l.* . . . 27 July, ,,
William Cooper, the Hackney Monster, for offences against females . . . 17 April, 1805
General Picton, for applying the torture to Louisa Calderon, to extort confession, at Trinidad, tried (under 42 Geo. III. c. 85) in the court of King's Bench; guilty [new trial, same verdict, 11 June, 1808] . . . . 24 Feb. 1806
Mr. Patch, for the murder of his partner, Mr. Bligh . . . . 6 April, ,,
Lord Melville, impeached by the house of commons; acquitted . . . 12 June, ,,
Hamilton Rowan, in Dublin; pleaded the king's pardon . . . . 1 July, ,,

The Warrington gang, for unnatural offences; executed . . . . 23 Aug. 1806
Palm, the bookseller, by a French military commission at Brennau . . . . . 26 Aug. ,,
Judge Johnson, for a libel on the earl of Hardwicke; guilty . . . . . 23 Nov. ,,
Lord Cloncurry *v.* Sir John B. Piers, for *crim. con.*; damages, 20,000*l.* . . . . . . 19 Feb. 1807
Holloway and Haggerty, the murderers of Mr. Steele; thirty persons were crushed to death at their execution, at the Old Bailey . 20 Feb. ,,
Sir Home Popham, by court-martial; reprimanded . . . . 7 March, ,,
Knight *v.* Dr. Wolcot, *alias* Peter Pindar, for *crim. con.* . . . . 27 June, ,,
Lieut. Berry, of H.M.S. *Hazard*; for an unnatural offence . . . . 2 Oct. ,,
Lord Elgin *v.* Ferguson, for *crim. con.*; damages, 10,000*l.* . . . . 22 Dec. ,,
Simmons, the murderer of the Boreham family, at Hoddesdon . . . . . 4 March, 1808
Sir Arthur Paget, for *crim. con.* with Lady Borrington . . . . . . 14 July, ,,
Major Campbell, for killing Captain Boyd in a duel; hanged . . . . 4 Aug. ,,
Peter Finnerty and others, for a libel on the duke of York . . . . 9 Nov. ,,
The duke of York, by inquiry in the house of commons, on charges preferred against him by colonel Wardle from 26 Jan. to 20 March . . 1809
Wellesley *v.* Lord Paget, for *crim. con.*; damages, 20,000*l.* . . . . 12 May, ,,
The king *v.* Valentine Jones, for breach of duty as commissary-general . . . . 26 May, ,,
Wright *v.* colonel Wardle, for Mrs. Mary Ann Clarke's furniture . . . . 1 June, ,,
The earl of Leicester *v. Morning Herald*, for a libel; damages 1000*l.* . . . . . 29 June, ,,
William Cobbett, for a libel on the German legion; convicted . . . . 9 July, ,,
Hon. captain Lake, for putting Robert Jeffery, a British seaman, on shore at Sombrero; dismissed the service (see *Sombrero*) . . 10 Feb. 1810
Mr. Perry for libels in the *Morning Chronicle*; acquitted . . . . 24 Feb. ,,
The Vere-street gang, for unnatural offences; guilty . . . . 20 Sept. ,,
Peter Finnerty, for a libel on lord Castlereagh; 31 Jan. 1811
The king *v.* Messrs. John and Leigh Hunt, for libels; guilty . . . . . 22 Feb. ,,
Ensign Hepburn, and White the drummer; both were executed . . . . . . 7 March, ,,
Walter Cox, in Dublin, for libels; he stood in the pillory . . . . . . 12 March, ,,
The king *v.* W. Cobbett, for libels; convicted 15 June, ,,
Lord Louth, in Dublin; sentenced to imprisonment and fine, for oppressive conduct as a magistrate . . . . 19 June, ,,
The Berkeley cause, before the house of peers, concluded . . . . 28 June, ,,
Dr. Sheridan, physician, on a charge of sedition; acquitted . . . . 21 Nov. ,,
Gale Jones, for seditious and blasphemous libels; convicted . . . . 26 Nov. ,,
William Cundell and John Smith, for high treason (see *High Treason*) . . . . . 6 Feb. 1812
Daniel Isaac Eaton, on a charge of blasphemy; convicted . . . . 6 March, ,,
Bellingham, for the murder of Mr. Perceval, prime minister . . . . 15 May, ,,
The king *v.* Mr. Lovell, of the *Statesman*, for libel; guilty . . . . . . 19 Nov. ,,
Messrs. John and Leigh Hunt, for libels in the *Examiner*; convicted . . . . . 9 Dec. ,,
Marquis of Sligo, for concealing a sea-deserter 16 Dec. ,,
The murderers of Mr. Horsfall; at York; executed . . . . 7 Jan. 1813
Mr. Hugh Fitzpatrick, for publishing Scully's *History of the Penal Laws* . . . . 6 Feb. ,,
The divorce cause against the duke of Hamilton for adultery . . . . . . 11 April, ,,
Mr. John Magee, in Dublin, for libels in the *Evening Post*; guilty . . . . . . 26 July, ,,
Nicholson, the murderer of Mr. and Mrs. Bonar; hanged . . . . 21 Aug. 1813
Tuite, murder of Mr. Goulding; executed 7 Oct. ,,
The celebrated Mary Ann Clark, for a libel on the right hon. Wm. Vesey Fitzgerald, afterwards lord Fitzgerald . . . . 7 Feb. 1814
Lord Cochrane, Cochrane Johnstone, Berenger, Butt, and others, for frauds in the public funds, 22 Feb.; convicted (see *Stocks*) . 8, 9 June, ,,
Admiral Bradley, at Winchester, for frauds in ship letters . . . . 18 Aug. ,,
Colonel Quentin, of the 10th Hussars, by court-martial . . . . 1 Nov. ,,
Sir John Henry Mildmay, bart., for *crim. con.* with the countess of Rosebery; damages, 15,000*l.* . . . . 5 Dec. ,,
George Barnett, for shooting at Miss Kelly, of Covent Garden theatre . . . 8 April, 1816
Captain Hutchinson, sir Robert Wilson, and Mr. Bruce, in Paris, for aiding the escape of count Lavalette (see *Lavalette*) . . . . 24 April, ,,
"Captain Grant," the famous Irish robber at Maryborough . . . . 16 Aug. ,,
Vaughan, a police officer, Mackay, and Browne, for conspiracy to induce men to commit felonies to obtain the reward; convicted . . 21 Aug. ,,
Colonel Stanhope, by court-martial, at Cambray, in France . . . . . . 23 Sept. ,,
Cashman, a seaman, for the Spafields riots and outrages on Snowhill; convicted and hanged (see *Spafields*) . . . . . . 20 Jan. 1817
Count Maubreuil, at Paris, for robbing the queen of Westphalia . . . . . . 2 May, ,,
Mr. R. J. Butt, for a libel on lord chief-justice Ellenborough . . . . . . 23 May, ,,
Mr. Wooler, for libels on the government and ministers . . . . 6 June, ,,
Thistlewood, Dr. Watson, Hooper, and others, for treason . . . . 9 June, ,,
The murderers of the Lynch family at Wildgoose-lodge, Ireland . . . . . . 19 July, ,,
Mr. Roger O'Connor, on a charge of robbing the mail; acquitted . . . . . . 5 Aug. ,,
Brandreth, Turner, and others, at Derby, for high treason . . . . 15 Oct. ,,
Hone, the bookseller, for parodies; three trials before Lord Ellenborough: extemporaneous and successful defence . . . 18, 19, 20 Dec. ,,
Mr. Dick, for abduction and rape of Miss Crockatt 21 March, 1818
Appeal of murder case; Ashford, the brother of Mary Ashford, against Abraham Thornton, accused of her murder (see *Appeal*) and acquitted 16 April, ,,
Rev. Dr. O'Halloran, for forging a frank (see *Transportation*) . . . . . . 9 Sept. ,,
Robert Johnston, at Edinburgh; his dreadful execution . . . . 30 Dec. ,,
Sir Manasseh Lopez, for bribery at Grampound (see *Bribery*) . . . . . 18 March, 1819
Mosely, Woolfe, and other merchants, for conspiracy and fraud . . . . . . 20 April, ,,
Carlile, for the publication of Paine's *Age of Reason*, &c. . . . . . . 15 Oct. ,,
John Scanlan, at Limerick, for murder of Ellen Hanly . . . . 14 March, 1820
Sir Francis Burdett, at Leicester, for a seditious libel . . . . 23 March, ,,
Henry Hunt, and others, for their conduct at the Manchester meeting; convicted (see *Manchester Reform Meeting*) . . . . . 27 March, ,,
Sir Charles Wolseley and rev. Mr. Harrison, for sedition; guilty . . . . . 10 April, ,,
Thistlewood, Ings, Brunt, Davidson, and Tidd, for conspiracy to murder the king's ministers; commenced (see *Cato-street*) . . . 17 April, ,,
Louvel, in France, for the murder of the duke de Berri . . . . 7 June, ,,
Lord Glerawley *v.* John Burn, for *crim. con.* 18 June, ,,
Major Cartwright and others at Warwick, for sedition . . . . 3 Aug. ,,
"Little Waddington," for a seditious libel; acquitted . . . . 19 Sept. ,,
Lieutenant-colonel French, 6th dragoon guards, by court-martial . . . . . 19 Sept. ,,
Caroline, queen of England, before the house of

lords, for adultery, commenced 16 Aug.; it terminated (see *Queen Caroline's Trial*) . 10 Nov. 1820
The female murderers of Miss Thompson, in Dublin: hanged . . . . . . 1 May, 1821
David Haggart, an extraordinary robber, and a man of singularly eventful life, at Edinburgh, for the murder of a turnkey . . . . 9 June, ,,
Samuel D. Hayward, the favourite man of fashion, for burglary . . . . . 8 Oct. ,,
The murderers of Mrs. Torrance, in Ireland, convicted and hanged . . . 17 Dec. ,,
Cussen, Leahy, and others, for the abduction of Miss Gould . . . . 29 July, 1822
Barthelemi, in Paris, for the abduction of Elizabeth Florence . . . . 23 Sept. ,,
Cuthbert *v.* Browne, singular action for deceit 28 Jan. 1823
The famous "Bottle Conspirators," in Ireland, by *ex-officio* . . . . 23 Feb. ,,
The extraordinary "earl of Portsmouth's case" commenced . . . 18 March, ,,
Probert, Hunt, and Thurtell, murderers of Mr. Weare; Probert turned king's evidence; afterwards hanged for horse-stealing (see *Executions*) 5 Jan. 1824
Mr. Henry Fauntleroy, banker of London, for forgery; hanged . . . . . 30 Oct. ,,
Foote *v.* Hayne, for breach of promise of marriage; damages, 3000*l.* . . . . 22 Dec. ,,
Mr. Henry Savary, a banker's son at Bristol, for forgery . . . . . 4 April, 1825
O'Keefe and Bourke, murderers of the Franks family . . . . . . 18 Aug. ,,
The case of Mr. Wellesley Pole and the Misses Long; commenced . . . 9 Nov. ,,
Captain Bligh *v.* the hon. Wm. Wellesley Pole, for adultery . . . . . 25 Nov. ,,
Fisher *v.* Stockdale, for libel in *Harriette Wilson* 20 March, 1826
Edward Gibbon Wakefield, and others, for abduction of Miss Turner . . . 24 March, 1827
Rev. Robert Taylor for blasphemy; found guilty 24 Oct. ,,
Richard Gillan, or the murder of Maria Bagster, at Taunton . . . . . . 8 April, 1828
Mr. Montgomery, for forgery; he committed suicide in prison on the morning appointed for his execution . . . . . . 4 July, ,,
Brinklett, for the death of lord Mount Sandford by a kick . . . . . 16 July, ,,
William Corder, for murder of Maria Marten; executed . . . . . . 6 Aug. ,,
Joseph Hunton, a quaker merchant, for forgery; hanged . . . . . . 28 Oct. ,,
Burke, at Edinburgh, for the Burking murders; Hare, his accomplice, became approver (see *Burking*) . . . . . 24 Dec. ,,
The king *v.* Buxton, and others, for fraudulent marriage . . . . . 21 March, 1829
Jonathan Martin, for setting fire to York minster 31 March, ,,
Stewart and his wife, noted murderers, at Glasgow; hanged . . . . . 14 July, ,,
Reinbauer, the Bavarian priest, for murders of women . . . . . . 4 Aug. ,,
Captain Dickenson, by court-martial, at Portsmouth; acquitted . . . . 26 Aug. ,,
Mr. Alexander, editor of the *Morning Journal*, for libels on the duke of Wellington; convicted 10 Feb. 1830
Clune, &c., at Ennis, for cutting out the tongues of the Doyles . . . . 4 March, ,,
Mr. Comyn, for burning his house in the county of Clare; hanged . . . . 6 March, ,,
Mr. Lambrecht, for murder of Mr. Clayton in a duel . . . . . . 2 April, ,,
Captain Moir, for murder of William Malcolm; hanged . . . . . . 30 July, ,,
Captains Smith and Markham, for killing Mr. O'Grady in a duel . . . . 24 Aug. ,,
Captain Helsham, for murder of lieut. Crowther in a duel . . . . . . 8 Oct. ,,
Mr. St. John Long, for manslaughter of Miss Cashin (see *Quacks*) . . . 30 Oct. ,,
Polignac, Peyronnet, and others, ministers of France (see *France*) . . . 21 Dec. ,,
Richard Carlile, for a seditious libel, inciting to a riot; guilty . . . . . 10 Jan. 1831
Mr. D. O'Connell, for breach of proclamation; pleaded guilty . . . . . 12 Feb. 1831
St. John Long, for manslaughter of Mrs. Lloyd (see *Quacks*) . . . . . . 19 Feb. ,,
Major Dundas, for the seduction of Miss Adams; damages, 3000*l.* . . . . 26 May, ,,
Rev Robert Taylor (who obtained the revolting distinction of "the *Devil's Chaplain*"), for reviling the REDEEMER: convicted . . . 6 July, ,,
Mr. Cobbett, for a seditious libel; the jury could not agree . . . . . . 7 July, ,,
Mr. and Mrs. Deacle *v.* Mr. Bingham Baring, M.P. 14 July, ,,
John Any Bird Bell, 14 years of age, for the murder of Richard Taylor, aged 13; hanged at Maidstone 1 Aug. ,,
The great cause, earl of Kingston *v.* lord Lorton; commenced . . . . . 9 Nov. ,,
Bishop and Williams, for murder of the Italian boy (see *Burking*) . . . . 3 Dec. ,,
Earl of Mar, in Scotland, for shooting at Mr. Oldham . . . . . . 17 Dec. ,,
Elizabeth Cooke, for murder of Mrs. Walsh, by "Burking" . . . . . 6 Jan. 1832
Colonel Brereton, by court-martial, at Bristol (see *Bristol*) . . . . . 9 Jan. ,,
The murderers of Mr. Blood, of Applevale, county of Clare . . . . . 28 Feb. ,,
William Duggan, at Cork, for murder of his wife and others . . . . 26 March, ,,
Mr. Hodgson (son of the celebrated Miss Aston) *v.* Greene . . . . . 26 July, ,,
Mayor of Bristol, for neglect of duty in the Bristol riots . . . . 26 Oct. ,,
Rev. Mr. Irving, by the Scots church, for heresy 13 March, 1833
Lord Teynham, and Dolan, a tailor, for swindling; guilty . . . . . . 10 May, ,,
Attorney-general *v.* Shore (lady Hewley's charity, which is taken from the Unitarians) . 23 Dec. ,,
Captain Wathen, 15th hussars, by court-martial, at Cork; honourably acquitted; his colonel, lord Brudenell, cashiered . . . . . Jan. 1834
Proprietors of the *True Sun*, for libels; guilty, 6 Feb. ,,
Mary Ann Burdock, the celebrated murderess, at Bristol . . . . . . 10 April, 1835
Sir John de Beauvoir, for perjury; acquitted, 29 May, ,,
Fieschi, at Paris, for attempting the life of the king, Louis Philippe, by exploding an infernal machine (see *Fieschi*) . . . 30 Jan. 1836
Hon. G. C. Norton *v.* lord Melbourne, in court of Common Pleas, for *crim. con.* with the hon. Mrs. Norton; verdict for defendant . . . 22 June, ,,
Lord de Roos *v.* Cumming, for defamation, charging lord de Roos with cheating at cards; verdict in favour of Mr. Cumming . . . . 10 Feb. 1837
James Greenacre and Sarah Gale, for the murder of Hannah Browne; Greenacre convicted and hanged; Gale transported . . . 10 April, ,,
Bolam, for murder of Mr. Millie; verdict, manslaughter . . . . 30 July, ,,
Rev. Mr. Stephens, at Chester, for inflammatory language . . . . . . 15 Aug. ,,
John Frost, an ex-magistrate, and others, for high treason; guilty: sentence commuted to transportation (see *Newport*) . . . . . 31 Dec. ,,
Benjamin Courvoisier, for murder of lord William Russell; hanged . . . . . 18-20 June, 1840
Gould, for murder of Mr. Templeman; transported 22 June, ,,
Edward Oxford, attempted the life of the queen; adjudged insane, and confined in Bethlehem (see *Oxford*) . . . . 9, 10 July, ,,
Madame Lefarge, in France, for the murder of her husband; guilty . . . . . . 2 Sept. ,,
Prince Louis Napoleon, for his descent upon France (see *France*) . . . . . . 6 Oct. ,,
Captain J. W. Reynolds, 11th hussars, by court-martial; guilty: the sentence excited great popular displeasure against his colonel, lord Cardigan 20 Oct. ,,
Lord Cardigan before the house of peers, capitally charged for wounding captain Harvey Tucket in a duel; acquitted . . . . . 16 Feb. 1841
The Wallaces, brothers, merchants, for having wilfully caused the destruction of the ship *Dryad* at sea, to defraud the underwriters; transported 4 March, ,,

Josiah Mister, for attempting the life of Mr. Mackreth; guilty . . . . . 23 March, 1841

Bartholomew Murray, at Chester, for the murder of Mrs. Cook . . . . 5 April, ,,

Earl Waldegrave and captain Duff, for an aggravated assault on a police constable; guilty: judgment, six months' imprisonment, and fines of 200*l.* and 20*l.* . . . . 3 May, ,,

Madame Lefarge again, for robbery of diamonds 7 Aug. ,,

The great case, Allen Bogle *v.* Mr. Lawson, publisher of the *Times* newspaper, for an alleged libel, in stating the plaintiff to be connected with numerous bank forgers throughout Europe in their schemes to defraud Messrs. Glyn and Company, bankers of London, by means of fictitious letters of credit: damages, one farthing. This exposure, so honourable to the *Times*, led to the *Times Testimonial* . . . . 16 Aug. ,,

Mr. MacLeod, at Utica, America, for taking part in the destruction of the *Caroline*, commenced: acquitted after a trial that lasted eight days, 4 Oct. ,,

Robert Blakesley, for murder of Mr. Burdon, of Eastcheap; hanged . . . . . . 28 Oct. ,,

Mr. Beaumont Smith, for forgery of Exchequer bills to an immense amount; he pleaded guilty, and was sentenced to transportation for life 4 Dec. ,,

Sophia Darbon *v.* Rosser; breach of promise of marriage; damages, 1600*l.* . . . . 8 Dec. ,,

Mr. John Levick and Antonio Mattei, principal and second in the duel in which lieut. Adams was killed at Malta: both acquitted . . . 10 March, 1842

Vivier, courier of the *Morning Herald*, at Boulogne, for conveying the Indian mail through France, for that journal, contrary to the French regulations . . . . 13 April, ,,

Daniel Good, for murder of Jane Jones; the Roehampton murder; found guilty, and sentenced to be hanged . . . . 13 May, ,,

John Francis, for attempting to assassinate the queen (see *Francis*) . . . . . 17 June, ,,

Thomas Cooper, for the murder of Daly, the policeman; hanged . . . . 4 July, ,,

Nicholas Suisse, valet of the late marquis of Hertford, at the prosecution of that nobleman's executors, charged with enormous frauds; acquitted 6 July, ,,

M'Gill and others, for abduction of Miss Crellin; guilty . . . . 8 Aug. ,,

Nicholas Suisse again, upon like charges, and again acquitted . . . . 24 Aug. ,,

Bean, for pointing a pistol at the queen: 18 months' imprisonment . . . . . . 25 Aug. ,,

The rioters in the provinces, under a special commission, at Stafford . . . . . 1 Oct. ,,

The Cheshire rioters, under a special commission, before lord Abinger . . . . 6 Oct. ,,

The Lancashire rioters, also under a special commission . . . . 10 Oct. ,,

Alice Lowe, at the prosecution of lord Frankfort; acquitted . . . . 31 Oct. ,,

Mr. Howard, attorney, *v.* sir William Gosset, serjeant-at-arms . . . . . . 5 Dec. ,,

Mr. Egan, in Dublin, for the robbery of a bank parcel; acquitted . . . . . 17 Jan. 1843

Rev. W. Bailey, LL.D., for forgery; guilty: transportation for life . . . . . 1 Feb. ,,

MacNaughten, for the murder of Mr. Drummond, secretary to sir Robert Peel: acquitted on the ground of insanity . . . . . 4 March, ,,

The Rebeccaites, at Cardiff, under a special commission . . . . 27 Oct. ,,

Samuel Sidney Smith, for forgery; sentenced to transportation for life . . . . 29 Nov. ,,

Edward Dwyer, for the murder of his child at Southwark; guilty . . . . . . 1 Dec. ,,

Mr. Holt, of the *Age*; libel on the duke of Brunswick; guilty . . . . . . 29 Jan. 1844

Lieut. Grant, second to lieut. Munro, in his duel with col. Fawcett; acquitted . . . 14 Feb. ,,

Fraser *v.* Bagley, for *crim. con.*; verdict for the defendant . . . . 19 Feb. ,,

Lord William Paget *v.* earl of Cardigan, for *crim. con.*; verdict for defendant . . . 26 Feb. ,,

Mary Furley, for the murder of her child in an agony of despair . . . . . 16 April, ,,

The will-forgers, William Henry Barber (since declared innocent), Joshua Fletcher, Georgiana Dorey, William Saunders, and Susannah his wife: all found guilty, 15 April: sentenced 22 April, 1844

[In 1848 Mr. Barber returned to England with a free pardon, and an acknowledgment of his innocence by his prosecutors: he was re-admitted to practise as an attorney; and on the 3rd of August, 1859, in conformity with the recommendation of a select committee of the house of commons, the sum of 5000*l.* was voted him "as a national acknowledgment of the wrong he had suffered from an erroneous prosecution."]

Crouch, for the murder of his wife; found guilty, 8 May; hanged . . . . 27 May, ,,

Messrs. O'Connell, sen., O'Connell, jun., Steele, Ray, Barrett, Grey, Duffy, and rev. Thomas Tierney, at Dublin, for political conspiracy: the trial commenced 15 Jan., and lasted twenty-four days: all the traversers were found guilty, 12 Feb. Proceedings on motions for a new trial, &c., extended the case into Easter term; and sentence was pronounced upon all but the clergyman, on whom judgment was remitted . . . 30 May, ,,

Augustus Dalmas, for the murder of Sarah Macfarlane; guilty . . . . 14 June, ,,

Wm. Burton Newenham, for the abduction of Miss Wortham; guilty . . . . . 17 June, ,,

Bellamy, for the murder of his wife by prussic acid; acquitted . . . . . . 21 Aug. ,,

John Tawell, for murder of Sarah Hart; hanged 13, 14 March, 1845

Thomas Henry Hocker, for murder of James Delarue . . . . 11 April, ,,

Joseph Connor, for murder of Mary Brothers, 16 May, ,,

The Spanish pirates, for murder of ten Englishmen at sea . . . . 26 July, ,,

Rev. Dr. Wetherall, for *crim. con.* with Mrs. Cooke, his own daughter . . . . . 16 Aug. ,,

Captain Johnson, of the ship *Tory*, for the murder of several of his crew . . . . . 5 Feb. 1846

Miss M. A. Smith *v.* earl Ferrers; breach of promise of marriage . . . . . . 18 Feb. ,,

Lieut. Hawkey, for the murder of Mr. Seton, in a duel; acquitted . . . . . . 16 July, ,,

Richard Dunn, for perjury and attempted fraud on Miss A. Burdett Coutts . . . 27 Feb. 1847

Mitchell, the Irish confederate; transported for 14 years (see *Ireland*) . . . . 26 May, 1848

Wm. Smith O'Brien, Meagher, and other confederates, sentenced to death; the sentence afterwards commuted to transportation (pardoned in 1856) . . . . 9 Oct. ,,

Bloomfield Rush, for murder of Messrs. Jermy, at Norwich; hanged . . . . . 29 March, 1849

Gorham *v.* the bishop of Exeter; ecclesiastical case; judgment given in the court of Arches against the plaintiff . . . . . 2 Aug. ,,

[The bishop had refused to institute the rev. Mr. Gorham into the living of Brampton-Speke, in Devonshire, alleging want of orthodoxy in the plaintiff, who denied that spiritual regeneration was conferred by baptism; the court held that the charge against the plaintiff of holding false doctrine was proved, and that the bishop was justified in his refusal. Mr. Gorham appealed to the Judicial Committee of the Privy Council, which pronounced its opinion (8 March, 1850) that "the doctrine held by Mr. Gorham was not contrary or repugnant to the declared doctrine of the church of England, and that Mr. Gorham ought not, by reason of the doctrine held by him, to have been refused admission to the vicarage of Brampton-Speke." This decision led to subsequent proceedings in the three courts of law, successively, for a rule to show cause why a prohibition should not issue, directed to the judge of the Arches court, and to the archbishop of Canterbury, against giving effect to the judgment of her majesty in council. The rule was refused in each court, and in the end Mr. Gorham was instituted into the vicarage in question, 7 Aug. 1850.]

Manning and his wife, for murder of O'Connor; guilty: death . . . . 27 Oct. ,,

Walter Watts, lessee of the Olympic theatre, for forgery, &c. . . . . 10 May, 1850

Robert Pate, a retired lieutenant, for an assault on the queen . . . . 11 July, ,,

The Sloanes, man and wife, for starving their servant, Jane Wilbred . . . . 5 Feb. 1851

The Board of Customs *v.* the London Dock Company, on a charge of defrauding the revenue of duties; a trial of 11 days ended in a virtual acquittal . . . . 18 Feb. 1851
Sarah Chesham, for murder of husband, by poison; she had murdered several of her children and others by the same means; hanged . 6 March, ,,
Thomas Drory, for the murder of Jael Denny: hanged . . . . 7 March, ,,
Doyle *v.* Wright, concerning the personal custody of Miss Augusta Talbot, a Roman catholic ward of chancery, before the lord chancellor: protracted case . . . . . . 22 March, ,,
The murderers of the rev. George Edward Hollest, of Frimley, Surrey; guilty . . 31 March, ,,
Achilli *v.* Newman, for libel; tried before lord chief justice Campbell in the Queen's Bench: verdict for the plaintiff, Nov. 1851 . 31 Jan. 1852
Miller *v.* ald. Salomons, M.P., for voting as a member without having taken the required oath; verdict against the defendant . . . 19 April, ,,
The case "Bishop of London *v.* the rev. Mr. Gladstone:" judgment of the Arches court against the defendant . . . . . . 10 June, ,,
Lord Frankfort, for scandalous and defamatory libels; guilty . . . . . . 3 Dec. ,,
Richard Bourke Kirwan, for the murder of his wife; guilty . . . . 10 Dec. ,,
Eliot Bower, for murder of Mr. Saville Morton, at Paris; acquitted . . . . . . 28 Dec. ,,
Henry Horler, for murder of his wife; hanged at the Old Bailey . . . . . . 15 Jan. 1853
James Barbour, for murder of Robinson: hanged at York . . . . 15 Jan. ,,
George Sparkes and James Hitchcock, for the murder of William Blackmore at Exeter; guilty 19 March, ,,
Five Frenchmen (principal and seconds) for the murder of a sixth Frenchman in a duel at Egham; verdict, manslaughter . . . . 21 March, ,,
Moore and Walsh, for the murder of John Blackburn, at Stafford; hanged . . . 21 March, ,,
Saunders, for murder of Mr. Toler; hanged at Chelmsford . . . . 30 March, ,,
The Stackpole family, four in number; two of them females, and wives to the others, for the murder of their relative, also a Stackpole; hanged at Ennis . . . . 28 April, ,,
Case of Holy Cross Hospital, Winchester, decided against rev. earl of Guildford . . 1 Aug. ,,
Smyth *v.* Smyth, ended in the plaintiff being committed on a charge of forging the will on which he grounded his claim . . . 8, 9, 10 Aug. ,,
The Braintree case respecting liability to church-rates, decided by the house of lords, against the rate . . . . 12 Aug. ,,
Case of Lumley *v.* Gye, respecting Mdlle. Wagner; decided . . . . 22 Feb. 1854
Mr. Jeremiah Smith, mayor of Rye, convicted of perjury . . . . 2 March, ,,
Duchess of Manchester's will case . . April, ,,
Mr. Carden, for abduction of Miss E. Arbuthnot, and assault upon John Smithwick; convicted 28, 29 July, ,,
Mary Anne Brough, for murdering her six children; not guilty (insanity) . . . . . 9 Aug. ,,
Case of Pierce Somerset Butler *v.* viscount Mountgarret; verdict for plaintiff, who thus came into a peerage, defendant being proved illegitimate Aug. ,,
Courts-martial on lieuts. Perry and Greer; sentences reversed by lord Hardinge 29 July-Aug. ,,
Courts-martial on sir E. Belcher, captain McClure, &c., for abandoning their ships in the Arctic regions; acquitted . . . . . . Oct. ,,
Emanuel Barthélémy, for murder of Charles Collard and Mr. Moore (executed) . . 4 Jan. 1855
Handcock *v.* Delacour, otherwise De Burgh (cruelty to Mrs. Handcock, and charges against lord Clanricarde); compromised . . . . . ,,
Earl of Sefton *v.* Hopwood (will set aside) 3-10 April, ,,
Luigi Baranelli, for murder of Joseph Latham (or Lambert); (executed 30 April) . 12 April, ,,
Charles King, a great thief-trainer; transported 13 April, ,,
Wm. Austin (governor), for cruelties in Birmingham gaol; acquitted . . . . 3 Aug. ,,
Sir John Dean Paul, William Strahan, and Robert M. Bates, bankers, for disposing of their customers' securities (to the amount of 113,625*l.*): convicted . . . . 27 Oct. 1855
Joseph Wooler, on charge of poisoning his wife; acquitted . . . . 7 Nov. ,,
Westerton *v.* Liddell (on decorations, &c., in church in Knightsbridge; decision against them) 5 Dec. ,,
[Decided again by privy council, partly for both parties; each to pay his own costs, 21 March, 1857.]
Celestina Sommers, for murder of her child; convicted (but reprieved) . . . 6 March, 1856
Wm. Palmer, for murder of J. P. Cook by poison 14-27 May, ,,
[He was executed at Stafford on 14 June, in the presence of 50,000 persons. If he had been acquitted, he would have been tried for the murder of his wife and brother.]
Wm. Dove, for murder of his wife (executed 9 Aug.) 19 July, ,,
Ditcher *v.* archdeacon Denison, respecting the doctrine of the eucharist; defendant deprived, and appeal disallowed [verdict set aside by privy council] . . . . 22 Oct. ,,
W. S. Hardwicke and H. Attwell; convicted of forgery . . . . 31 Oct. ,,
Wm. Robson, for frauds of Crystal Palace Company (to the amount of about 28,000*l.*); transported for twenty years . . . 1 Nov. ,,
Earl of Lucan *v.* *Daily News*, for libel; verdict for defendant . . . . 3 Dec. ,,
Pearce, Burgess, and Tester (see *Gold Robbery*) 14 Jan. 1857
Leopold Redpath, for forgeries (to the amount of 150,000*l.*) upon Great Northern railway company: transported for life . . . 16 Jan. ,,
Jem Saward, a barrister (called the Penman), Wm. Anderson, and others, convicted of extensive forgery of bankers' cheques . . 5 March, ,,
Miss Madeline Smith, on charge of poisoning Emile L'Angelier, at Glasgow; not proven 30 June-9 July, ,,
Thos. Fuller Bacon, for poisoning his mother, convicted . . . . 25 July, ,,
[He was acquitted on a charge of murdering two children, 13, 14 May, same year. His wife confessed the murder, but appeared to be insane.]
James Spollen, on charge of murder of Mr. Little, near Dublin; acquitted . . . 7-11 Aug. ,,
W. Attwell and others, convicted of stealing the countess of Ellesmere's jewels (value 15,000*l.*) from the top of a cab . . . . . 15 Dec. ,,
Strevens *v.* Campion, for slander, in charging the plaintiff with complicity in the murder of his aunt, Mrs. Kelly; damages 6*d.* . . 31 Dec. ,,
The directors of the British Bank, Humphry Brown, Edw. Esdaile, H. D. Macleod, alderman R. H. Kennedy, W. D. Owen, James Stapleton, and Hugh Innes Cameron, for fraud (see under *Banks*); convicted . . . . . . 13-27 Feb. 1858
Rev. S. Smith and his wife, for murderous assault on John Leech; convicted . . . 6-7 April, ,,
Edw. Auchmuty Glover, M.P., for false declaration of qualification of M.P. . . . . 9 April, ,,
Simon Bernard, as accessory to the conspiracy against the life of the emperor Napoleon; acquitted 12-17 April, ,,
The earldom of Shrewsbury case; earl Talbot's claim allowed . . . . 1 June. ,,
James Seal, for the murder of Sarah Guppy; convicted (and executed) . . . . 23 July, ,,
The Berkeley peerage case, see *Berkeley* ,, ,,
Patience Swynfen *v.* F. H. Swynfen; a will case; the will affirmed . . . . . 27 July, ,,
[The plaintiff was Patience Swynfen, widow of Henry John Swynfen, son of the testator, Samuel Swynfen. Her husband died 15 June, 1854, and his father on 16 July following, having made a will 19 days before his death, devising the Swynfen estate (worth about 60,000*l.*) to his son's wife, but leaving a large amount of personal estate undisposed of. The defendant, F. H. Swynfen, son of the testator's eldest half-brother, claimed the estate as heir-at-law on the ground of the testator's insanity. The issue was brought to trial in March, 1856; but proceedings were stayed by Mrs. Swyn-

fen's counsel, sir F. Thesiger, entering into an agreement with the opposite counsel, sir Alexander Cockburn, without her consent, and in defiance of her instructions. After various proceedings, the court of chancery ordered a new trial. She gained her cause, mainly through the energy of her counsel, Mr. Chas. R. Kennedy, to whom she had promised to pay 20,000*l.* for his extraordinary services. Mrs. Swynfen, however, married a Mr. Broun, and repudiated Mr. Kennedy's claim. The latter, in an action against her, obtained a verdict in his favour on 29 March, 1862, which was, on appeal, finally reversed in Feb. 1864. Mrs. Swynfen was non-suited in an action brought against her counsel (afterwards lord Chelmsford and lord chancellor), in July, 1859, and June, 1860.]

Lemon Oliver, a stockbroker, convicted of extensive frauds . . . . 10 Nov. 1858

Marchmont *v.* Marchmont; a disgraceful divorce case, begun . . . . . . 30 Nov. ,,

W. H. Guernsey, for stealing Ionian despatches from the Colonial Office; acquitted . 15 Dec. ,,

Evans *v.* Evans and Rose, divorce case . Dec. ,,

Lieut.-col. Dickson *v.* earl of Wilton, for libel; verdict for the plaintiff . . . . . 14 Feb. 1859

Black *v.* Elliott, 850 sheep poisoned by a sheep-wash sold by defendant; damages 1400*l.* 23 Feb. ,,

Wagner, Bateman, and others, a gang of bank forgers; convicted . . . . . . 13 May, ,,

Earl of Shrewsbury *v.* Hope Scott, and others; the earl gains the Shrewsbury estates . 3 June, ,,

Thellusson will case decided (see *Thellusson*) 9 June, ,,

T. R. Marshall, E. A. Mortimer, and H. S. Eicke, convicted of illegal sale of army commissions, 29 June, ,,

Thomas Smethurst, a surgeon, for the murder by poison of Isabella Bankes, whom he had married during his wife's lifetime; convicted 15-19 Aug. ,,

[He was reprieved on the ground of insufficient evidence; but was tried and found guilty of bigamy, 16 Nov. 1859. On 11 Nov. 1862, he proved Miss Bankes's will, and obtained her property.]

Oakley *v.* the Moulvie Ooddeen, "ambassador of the king of Oude." Verdict for the defendant, who seems to have fallen among bill-sharpers, 17 Dec. ,,

David Hughes, an attorney, convicted of gross frauds upon his clients . . . . . Jan. 1860

George Pullinger, cashier of the Union Bank of London, sentenced to 20 years' imprisonment for fraud (see *Banks*, foot-note) . . . 15 May, ,,

Eugenia Plummer, aged 11 years, convicted of perjury against rev. Mr. Hatch . . . . 14 May, ,,

Mr. W. H. Leatham, M.P., convicted of bribery at Wakefield . . . . 19 July, ,,

Thomas Hopley, a schoolmaster, convicted of manslaughter of Reginald Cancellor, by flogging, 23 July, ,,

Nottidge *v.* Prince (see *Agapemone*) . 25 July, ,,

Rev. J. Bonwell, of Stepney, degraded for immorality, 29 Aug. ,,

James Mullens, convicted for the murder of Mrs. Elmsley; by endeavouring to inculpate one Ems, he led to his own conviction . . . 25 Oct. ,,

Miss Shedden *v.* Patrick. (The plaintiff ably pleaded her own cause when the case was opened; her object, to prove the legitimacy of her father, was not attained) . . . . . 9 Nov. *et seq.*

Hooper *v.* Ward; disgraceful profligacy of a magistrate; verdict for plaintiff . . . 19, 20 Dec. ,,

Constance Kent inquiry; trial refused (see *Road Murder*) . . . . Jan. 1861

Thelwall *v.* hon. Major Yelverton. The plaintiff sued for expenses incurred by defendant's wife; the major denied the validity of his marriage with Miss Longworth, having since married the widow of professor Edward Forbes, the eminent naturalist. The court in Dublin supported the first marriage . . . . 21 Feb. to 4 March, ,,

[Miss Longworth endeavoured to establish her marriage. On appeal, the Scotch court annulled the marriage, July, 1862, and this judgment was affirmed by the house of lords, 28 July, 1864, and again finally, 30 July, 1867. An attempt to set aside the judgment of the house of lords rejected by the court of session, 29 Oct. 1868.]

Brook *v.* Brook; see *Marriage with Wife's Sister.*

The house of lords on appeal decided against the validity of such marriages, even when celebrated in a foreign country . . . . 18 March, 1861

Reade *v.* Lacy; the dramatising a novel restrained, 17 April, ,,

Beamish *v.* Beamish; the lords on appeal decide that a clergyman cannot perform the ceremony of marriage for himself . . . . . 22 April, ,,

Emperor of Austria *v.* Day; verdict for plaintiff. The defendant had printed 100 million florin notes on the bank of Hungary, for Louis Kossuth. The notes were ordered to be destroyed within one month, 6 May; judgment affirmed 12 June, ,,

Cardross case. John MacMillan, a free-church minister, was expelled for drunkenness and misconduct, May, 1858. The Glasgow synod and the general assembly of the free church affirmed the sentence. He appealed to the court of session, which set aside the decree (which involved temporalities), asserting that the assembly had only spiritual authority . . . July, ,,

W. B. Turnbull *v.* Bird, secretary of protestant alliance; libel; verdict for defendant 8-10 July, ,,

J. C. Charlesworth, M.P., convicted of bribery at the Wakefield election . . . . . 20 July, ,,

Baron de Vidil; convicted of wounding his son; the latter refused to give evidence against his father, 23 Aug. ,,

Vincent Collucci: convicted of obtaining money on false pretences, from Miss F. Johnstone 23 Oct. ,,

John Curran, a Dublin cabman; convicted of a violent assault on Miss Jolly, who heroically defended herself . . . . . . 25-30 Oct. ,,

Patrick McCaffery; shot col. Crofton and capt. Hanham, at Preston; convicted . . 13 Dec. ,,

Inquiry into sanity of Wm. Fred. Wyndham (on behalf of his relatives), with a view of annulling an injudicious marriage; trial lasted 34 days: 140 witnesses examined; verdict sane mind (see *Lunacy*) . . . 16 Dec. 1861, and 30 Jan. 1862

[Each party adjudged to pay its own costs, March, 1862.]

Capt. Robertson, by court-martial; convicted of submitting to ungentlemanly conduct from his brother-officers:—30 days' inquiry: ended, 24 March, ,,

[The court was much blamed by the public and the sentence was annulled.]

Mrs. A. C. Vyse for poisoning her two children; acquitted as insane . . . . 9 July, ,,

Roupell *v.* Waite; during the trial, W. Roupell, M.P., a witness, confessed himself guilty of forging a will, and other frauds . 18, 19 Aug. ,,

Jessie McLachlan; convicted for the murder of Jessie Macpherson, at Glasgow; she confessed to being accessory after the murder, which she imputed to Mr. Fleming, a gentleman 80 or 90 years old . . . . 17-20 Sept. ,,

[She was respited 27 Oct. 1862.]

Wm. Roupell, M.P., for forgery; convicted on his own confession (released Sept. 1876) . 24 Sept. ,,

Catherine Wilson, convicted of poisoning Mrs. Soames in 1856 . . . . . . 25-27 Sept. ,,

27 indictments and 24 convictions for savage personal outrages in the streets of the metropolis during the month . . . . . . Nov. ,,

Wm. Digby Seymour, M.P. *v.* Butterworth; libel; verdict for plaintiff, damages 40*s.* . . 3 Dec. ,,

Hall *v.* Semple; verdict for plaintiff, who had been consigned to a lunatic asylum through his wife's getting the defendant to sign a certificate of lunacy with culpable negligence; damages 150*l.* 10 Dec. ,,

George Buncher, Wm. Burnett, Richd. Brewer, and James Griffiths, for forging bank-notes, printed on paper stolen from the paper-mill at Laverstoke; convicted . . . . 7-12 Jan. 1863

Clare *v.* The Queen; petition of right for infringement of a patent; verdict for defendant 2-6 Feb. ,,

Rev. John Campbell *v.* Spottiswoode (as printer of a libel in *Saturday Review*): verdict for plaintiff, 27 Feb. ,,

Queen on appeal of earl of Cardigan *v.* col. Calthorpe for libel, charging the earl with deserting his men at Balaclava, 25 Oct. 1855; verdict for defendant (who, however, admitted his error), 9, 10 June, ,,

Attorney-general *v.* Sillim and others, for having

built the *Alexandra* for the Confederates, against the Enlistment act; verdict for defendants, 25 June, 1863
[Decision finally affirmed on appeal to the house of lords, 6 April, 1864.]
Col. Lothian Dickson *v.* viscount Combermere, earl of Wilton, and gen. Peel, for conspiracy to expel him from the army; verdict for defendants, 27 June *et seq.* ,,
Morrison (Zadkiel) *v.* sir Edward Belcher; libel; verdict, 20s. damages . . . . . 29 June, ,,
Richard Roupell *v.* Haws: arising out of Roupell forgeries; no verdict . . . 16-24 July, ,,
Woolley *v.* Pole, for Sun Fire Office; verdict for plaintiff, awarding him his claim for 29,000*l.* for his insurance of Campden-house; burnt 23 March, 1862 . . . . 29 Aug. ,,
George Victor Townley, for murder of Miss Goodman, through jealousy; convicted . . . 12 Dec. ,,
He escaped execution through a certificate of insanity, too hastily signed: and committed suicide in prison, 12 Feb. 1865.]
Lieut.-col. Crawley, by court-martial at Aldershot, for alleged oppression and cruelty to sergeant-major John Lilley, in consequence of a court-martial at Mhow, in India; honourably acquitted, 17 Nov.-23 Dec. ,,
Franz Müller, for murder of Mr. Briggs in a railway carriage, 9 July; convicted . . . 27-29 Oct. 1864
Gedney *v.* Smith, a supposititious child detected and deprived of much property . . . 10 Nov. ,,
E. K. Kohl, for murder of Theodore Fuhrkop; convicted . . . . 11, 12 Jan. 1865
Queen *v.* Wm. Rumble, for infringement of Foreign Enlistment act, in equipping the *Rappahannock* for the Confederate government; acquitted, 4 Feb. ,,
Woodgate *v.* Ridout (for *Morning Post*), for libel respecting the great will case of the earl of Egmont *v.* Darell; verdict for plaintiff, 1000*l.*, 10 Feb. ,,
Bishop Colenso's appeal to privy council against decision of bishop of Capetown, deposing him, which is annulled . . . . . . 21 March, ,,
Roberts, Jeffery, Casely, and others, for jewel robberies in London; convicted . . . 13 April, ,,
J. W. Terry and Thos. Burch, for misdemeanor in connection with the Unity Bank; acquitted, April, ,,
Edw. Wm. Pritchard, M.D., for murder of his wife and her mother, by poisoning; guilty . 3-7 July, ,,
Charlotte Winsor, a child-murderer, convicted on the evidence of an accomplice . . . July, ,,
[On account of legal irregularities in her trial, her execution was long deferred, and her sentence was commuted to life-imprisonment, 23 May, 1866.]
Constance Kent tried (see *Road Murder*) 21 July, ,,
Trials of Fenians for treason-felony; Thos. Clarke Luby, convicted and sentenced to 20 years' penal servitude, 28 Nov.-1 Dec.; O'Leary and others convicted; O'Donovan Rossa (previously convicted) sentenced to imprisonment for life, 13 Dec.; others convicted at Cork . . . Dec. ,,
Stephen Forwood (or Ernest Southey), for murder of his wife and children: guilty . 20-21 Dec. ,,
Other Fenians convicted at Dublin (see *Fenians*), Jan. 1866
Breadalbane peerage: succession decided in favour of Campbell of Glenfalloch . . . 26 Jan. ,,
Ryves and Ryves *v.* the attorney-general; an endeavour to prove the marriage of king George III. with Hannah Wilmot, and that of his brother Henry, duke of Cumberland, with Olive Wilmot; the jury decided that the claim was not made out, and that Olive Serres, the alleged mother of Mrs. Ryves, was not the legitimate daughter of the duke of Cumberland, and that the 82 documents brought in evidence were forged (Mrs. Ryves died 7 Dec. 1871) . . . . 13 June, ,,
Banda and Kirwee prize case (Indian mutiny); court of admiralty decide that 700,000*l.* are to be divided between the soldiers commanded by generals Whitelocke, Rose, Roberts, and others, 30 June, ,,
Bishop Colenso *v.* Gladstone and others, trustees of colonial bishopric fund (for withholding his stipend); verdict for plaintiff, with costs 6 Nov. ,,
Hunter *v.* Sharpe (*Pall Mall Gazette*), for libel (charging him with quackery); one farthing damages gained by plaintiff . . . 1 Dec. 1866
James F. Wilkinson, manager of joint stock discount company, convicted of fraud . . 9 *et seq.* Jan. 1867
[Liberated with free pardon, after investigation, July, 1868.]
Bryant *v.* Foot; decision against prescriptive right of a rector to claim a marriage-fee . . 23 Jan. ,,
C. W. Lee Webb, Lionel Holdsworth, and others, convicted of fraud (scuttling a ship, and claiming insurance) . . . . 4 Feb. ,,
C. Anderson, a Swede; convicted of murdering a mulatto, from superstition . . . 12 April, ,,
Breadalbane peerage; Wm. J. Campbell declared heir, on appeal to house of lords . . 16 July, ,,
Smith *v.* Tebbitt and others; a will case, disposing of upwards of 400,000*l.*; verdict for defendants, annulling the will of Ann Thwaites, who is declared of unsound mind, after a long trial, in April and May; judgment given . . . 6 Aug. ,,
Oakes *v.* Turquand, and others; appeal case, house of lords; decision affirming liability of shareholders of the company of Overend, Gurney, and Co. (limited) . . . . . . 15 Aug. ,,
Geo. Druitt, M. Lawrence, and John Anderson, leaders of the operative tailors' association, convicted of a misdemeanor (organising the system of "picketing," or watching men on strike; and intimidating non-unionists; which began 24 April, 1867) . . . . . . 21 Aug. ,,
13 tailors convicted of "picketing" . . 22 Aug. ,,
Fenian trials at Manchester, Allen, &c. (see *Fenians*) . . . . . . 30 Oct.-12 Nov. ,,
Frederick Baker convicted of brutal murder of a child . . . . 6 Dec. ,,
Mr. Rigby Wason *v.* Walter (for publication of an alleged libel in the *Times*; viz., a correct report of a debate in the house of lords, &c.); verdict for defendant, settling that such a report is privileged . . . . 18-20 Dec. ,,
[Verdict affirmed again, 25 Nov. 1868. Mr. Wason died July, 1875.]
Martin *v.* Mackonochie (for ritualistic practices); before dean of arches, 4 Dec. 1867, and 14 days; recommenced; closed . . . . 18 Jan. 1868
Flamank *v.* Simpson; similar case; begun 5 Feb.; verdict condemning elevation of sacrament, use of incense, and mixture of water with the wine in the communion service . . . 28 March, ,,
Crossley *v.* Elsworthy for fraudulent misrepresentation; verdict for plaintiff, damages 35,000*l.* 18 Feb. ,,
Trial of Fenians for Clerkenwell outrage (see *Fenians*), begun 20 April; all acquitted except Michael Barrett . . . . . 20-27 April, ,,
Richard Burke (*alias* Geo. Berry, &c.), Theobald Casey, and Henry Shaw (*alias* Mullady), Fenians, for treason felony, at Old Bailey; Burke and Shaw convicted, Casey acquitted . 28-30 April, ,,
Mornington *v.* Wellesley, and Wellesley *v.* Mornington, a 29 years' suit in chancery, decided (costs above 30,000*l.*); 22,000*l.* awarded to the countess of Mornington . . . . . . 7 May, ,,
Lyon *v.* Home (the spiritual medium). The plaintiff, a widow, sought to recover 60,000*l.* stock, given to Home at the alleged command of her deceased husband's spirit, between Oct. 1866 and Feb. 1867; suit instituted 15 June, 1867; trial, 21 April to 1 May, 1868; verdict given for plaintiff, by the vice-chancellor, sir G. M. Giffard, 22 May, ,,
[The judge, in concluding, said, regarding spiritualism, that "the system, as presented by the evidence, is mischievous nonsense; well calculated on the one hand to delude the vain, the weak, the foolish, and the superstitious; and on the other to assist the projects of the needy and the adventurer."]
Esmonde will case, Dublin; Lady Esmonde bequeathed property to support protestantism in Ireland, by endowing a college, &c.: will disputed by her family: no verdict by jury . 3-13 June, ,,
[New trial; will affirmed, Aug. 1869.]
Thomas Edgeley, convicted of fraud against Leeds Banking Company . . . . 11-13 June, ,,
Risk Allah *v.* Whitehurst (for *Daily Telegraph*): libel case; damages for plaintiff, 960*l.*, 19 June, ,,
Attorney-general *v.* Dakin: appeal case; decision

that privilege of exemption from execution of legal process does not extend to Hampton Court palace . . . . . . 20 June, 1868
Madame Sarah Rachel Leverson convicted of conspiracy . . . . . . 25 Sept. ,,
[Writ of error: new trial refused, 11 May, 1869.]
Chornford *v.* Lingo: female suffrage declared illegal 7-9 Nov. ,,
Baxter *v.* Langley: Sunday evening lectures declared not illegal . . . . 19 Nov. ,,
Martin *v.* Mackonochie: see *Church of England*, 23 Dec. ,,
Phillips *v.* Eyre: verdict for defendant; see *Jamaica* . . . . 20 Jan. 1869
Saurin *v.* Star and another (convent case; a sister sued her mother superior, for ill-usage and expulsion); verdict for plaintiff, damages 500*l.* 3-26 Feb. ,,
[Case compromised, April, 1870.]
James Thos. Gambier, admiralty clerk, and Wm. Rumble, engineer, convicted of fraud and seeking bribes from contractors . . . 9 April, ,,
Cooper *v.* Gordon: verdict for plaintiff; the vice-chancellor decides that the majority of a congregation of dissenters may dismiss their minister for any cause . . . . 28 May, ,,
Major Frederick Beswick, constable of Birkenhead, convicted of forgery . . . . 10 June, ,,
Farrer (president of the Amalgamated Carpenters' Society) *v.* Close (the secretary), for misappropriation of money. In 1867 the justices dismissed the charge because the society had illegal rules. At the trial at the Queen's bench the court was equally divided, and no verdict given . 3 July, ,,
Fanny F. M. Oliver convicted of murder of her husband . . . . . . 20 July, ,,
Lyons *v.* Rev. N. Thomas and others, for abduction of Esther Lyons, a Jewish girl, a proselyte; damages 50*l.* . . . . . . 31 July, ,,
Frederick Hinson convicted of murder of his paramour, Maria Death, and Wm. Douglas Boyd 24 Nov. ,,
Rev. James John Merest, convicted of simony; deprived . . . . . . 26-29 Nov. ,,
Martin *v.* Mackonochie: before judicial committee of privy council, defendant censured for evading verdict, and condemned in costs . . 4 Dec. ,,
Mrs. Kelly *v.* Rev. J. Kelly; judicial separation for ill usage (not violence) decreed . . 7 Dec. ,,
Messrs. Gurney and others, for conspiring to defraud; acquitted . . . . 13-23 Dec. ,,
Smith *v.* Earl Brownlow: after long litigation decision against the enclosure of the common at Berkhampstead by lord of the manor 14 Jan. 1870
James Clifford, a retired artilleryman, convicted of "sweating" sovereigns by the voltaic battery, 1 Feb. ,,
Jacob Spinass, a Swiss, convicted of murder of Cecilia Aldridge, an unfortunate . 3 March, ,,
Dr. Kinglake convicted of bribery on behalf of his brother at Bridgewater . . . . 26 March, ,,
Wicklow peerage case: claim for an infant declared to be unfounded by house of lords (remarkable evidence) . . . . . . 31 March, ,,
Demetrius Pappa, a bank manager, sentenced to 5 years' penal servitude for embezzlement, 6 May, ,,
Sir Charles Mordaunt *v.* lady Mordaunt, and others, for divorce: preliminary trial of her sanity (declared insane on 30 April, 1869), 16-25 Feb. 1870; appeal, 27 April, 1870; judgment affirmed 2 June, ,,
Bishop Goss (R.C.) *v.* Hill and Whittaker: will case; Mr. Moreton's will, bequeathing the chief of his property to the bishop, set aside 16 June, ,,
Phillips *v.* Eyre, for imprisonment during Jamaica rebellion; verdict for defendant . . 23 June, ,,
Chelsea Murders: Walter Miller convicted of murder of Rev. Elias Huelin and Anne Boss, his housekeeper (8 or 9 May, 1870) . . 13, 14 July, ,,
Michael Davitt and John Wilson, treason felony; see *Fenians* . . . . . . 18 July, ,,
John Jones or Owen, convicted of murder of Emanuel Marshall and family (7 persons, early 22 May, 1870), at *Denham*, near Uxbridge . 22 July, ,,
Shepherd *v.* Bennett (Arches); decision that defendant had retracted heresy; appeal to privy council, 23 July, ,,
Margaret Waters convicted of murder of John Cowen, infant; her sister and accomplice, Sarah Ellis, was convicted of fraud, 22 Sept. (baby farming case; see *Infanticide*) . 21-23 Sept. 1870
Rev. C. Voysey *v.* Noble: appeal to privy council judicial committee against condemnation for heresy . . . . . . 10 Nov. ,,
Ebdy *v.* McGowan: verdict against an architect for refusing to give up the plans of a building he was about to erect . . . . . 16 Nov. ,,
Catch *v.* Shaen: for libel on master of Lambeth workhouse; verdict for plaintiff, 600*l.* damages; execution stayed . . . . 15 Dec. ,,
Diamond Robbery: London and Ryder's man made insensible and robbed of diamonds, 12 Jan.; Martha Torpey acquitted, 1 March; James Torpey pleaded guilty (sentenced to 8 years' penal servitude) . . . . . . 1 May, 1871
E. Boulton, L. C. Hurt, F. W. Park, and others (frequently dressed as women) tried for a conspiracy; acquitted . . . . 9-15 May, ,,

Tichborne *v.* Lushington: the plaintiff declared himself to be sir Roger Charles Tichborne, supposed to have been lost at sea; and claimed the baronetcy and estates, worth about 24,000*l.* a year.

Roger Charles Tichborne, son of sir James, born . 1829
Educated in France till . . . . . about 1843
Entered the army 1849
Proposed marriage to his cousin Kate Doughty; declined . . . . Jan. 1852
Sailed from Havre for Valparaiso (March), and arrived there . . . . . 19 June, 1853
Sailed from Rio Janeiro in the *Bella*, which foundered at sea . . . . . 20 April, 1854
[A Chancery suit was instituted, and his death legally proved.]
His mother advertised for her son . 19 May, 1865
The claimant (found by Gibbes and Cubitt in Australia) asserted that he and eight of the crew were saved from the wreck of the *Bella;* that he went to Australia, and lived there, roughly, 13 years under the name of Castro; married as Castro, Jan.; as Tichborne . . . . . 3 July, 1866
He set up his claim; and was accepted by the dowager lady Tichborne as her son at Paris . Jan. 1867
[No others of the family accepted him; but sir Clifford Constable and some brother-officers did.]*
His claim was resisted on behalf of sir Henry (a minor), son of sir Alfred Tichborne; and after chancery proceedings (begun March, 1867) a trial began in the court of common pleas before chief justice Bovill . . . . . . 11 May, 1871
The claimant was examined 22 days; the trial adjourned on 40th day, 7 July; resumed, 7 Nov.; case for claimant closed . . . 21 Dec. ,,
Trial resumed, 15 Jan.; the attorney-general, sir J. D. Coleridge, spoke 26 days; on 4 March the jury expressed themselves satisfied that the claimant was not sir Roger; on the 103rd day he was declared nonsuited . . . . 6 March, 1872
The law proceedings are said to have cost the estate nearly 92,000*l.*
He was lodged in Newgate to be tried for perjury, 7 March; indicted as Thos. Castro, otherwise Arthur Orton, for perjury and forgery 9 April, ,,
The court of queen's bench decide that he may be admitted to bail, 23 April; released . 26 April, ,,
The trial of the claimant for perjury and forgery begun before chief justice Cockburn, and justices Mellor and Lush at bar 23 April; case for the prosecution closed, 10 July: resumed (for defence) 21 July, ,,
Lady Doughty, mother of sir Henry Tichborne, dies 13 Dec. ,,
[Up to 27 June (47th day of the trial), out of 150 witnesses above 100 had sworn that the claimant was not Tichborne; and about 40 that he was Arthur Orton.]
The claimant forbidden to attend public meetings, 19 Sept. 1873
Case for the defence closed on 124th day, 27 Oct. adjourned from 31 Oct. to 17 Nov., then to 27 Nov.; rebutting evidence heard, 27, 28 Nov. ,,

* Mr. Guildford Onslow, who spent about 15,000*l.* in supporting the claimant, died 20 Aug. 1882.

Dr. Kenealy's summing-up,* 2 Dec.-14 Jan. 1874; Mr. Hawkins's reply . . . 15 Jan.-28 Jan. 1874
[Mr. Whalley, M.P., fined for contempt of court, 250*l*., 23 Jan.]
The chief-justice's summing-up, 29 Jan.-28 Feb. ,,
Verdict: that the claimant did falsely swear,—that he was Roger Charles Tichborne, that he seduced Catherine N. E. Doughty in 1851, and that he was not Arthur Orton; † sentence, 14 years' imprisonment with hard labour . . 28 Feb. ,,
[*Longest trial known in England.*]
New trial refused by the judges . . 29 April, ,,
On appeal, sentence affirmed by the house of lords, 10, 11 March, 1881; released on ticket of leave, 20 Oct. 1884; his confession printed in the *People*, May, 1895; born 1835; died . 1 April, 1898

Eltham Murder: E. W. Pook for murder of Jane Maria Clousen; acquitted . . 12-15 July, 1871
Hannah Newington, or Flora Davey; convicted of manslaughter of Frederick Moon; she was his mistress, and excited by insult . . 15 July, ,,
Capt. H. Hamilton Beamish and others tried for stranding the *Agincourt* (see *Navy*), 26 July; reprimanded by the court . . . . 8 Aug. ,,
Robert Kelly: for murder of Talbot (a police-constable and informer against Fenians) on night of 12 July; acquitted (extraordinary verdict) 30 Oct.-10 Nov. ,,
Peek *v.* Gurney and others (Overend and Co.) plaintiff's claim for loss incurred through misrepresentations in the company's prospectus; disallowed by master of rolls on account of his neglecting to verify the prospectus and his too late claim; costs refused to defendants . . . 6 Nov. ,,
Mr. Pigott condemned to imprisonment for illegal comments on a trial, in the *Irishman* . 13 Nov. ,,
Rev. John Selby Watson, eminent scholar, killed his wife in a fit of passion, 8 Oct.; convicted and imprisoned for life . . . . 10-12 Jan. 1872
Christiana Edmunds; convicted of poisoning at Brighton; she purchased chocolate creams, and returned poisoned ones to the confectioner, and thus caused death to one child and nearly killed other persons; reprieved as insane 15, 16 Jan. ,,
The Queen *v.* the Lords of the Treasury: for not repaying expenses for prosecutions to the county of Lancaster; mandamus refused . . 29 Jan. ,,
Park-lane Murder: Margaret Dixblancs, a Belgian emigrant, murdered her mistress, madame Riel, on Sunday, 7 April; escaped; taken at Paris; confessed to killing her mistress in a quarrel; convicted, but recommended to mercy, 11-14 June; sentence commuted to penal servitude for life . . . . 21 June, ,,
Ellen Kettel: charged with poisoning her husband's first wife in order to marry him; acquitted, 24, 25 Oct. ,,
Chelsea Tragedy: Hermann Nagel and Paul May, young Prussians, came to London to avoid conscription; their money being spent, they agreed to commit suicide; after wounding May, Nagel shot himself dead, 21 Aug.; May recovered, and was indicted for murder, tried, and acquitted, 21 Nov. ,,
[He was convicted and punished for forgery at Berlin, Feb. 1873.]
Baker *v.* Loader: widow, to whom 107,000*l.* had been bequeathed; in ten years is reduced to poverty by imposition; she sues the widow of her friend Loader and solicitors; verdict of vice-chancellor Malins, ordering deeds to Loader to be cancelled; the solicitor to pay his own costs, 20 Nov. ,,
Mr. Hepworth Dixon *v.* Smith (*Pall-Mall Gazette*), for libel; damages, one farthing . 26-29 Nov. ,,
Mr. Guildford Onslow and Mr. G. H. Whalley, M.P.'s, fined for contempt of court in speeches respecting the Tichborne case, 20 Jan.; Mr. Skipworth, barrister, for same offence, condemned to three months' imprisonment and fined; the claimant made to give securities for 1000*l.*, for a similar offence . . . . 29 Jan. 1873
Parke *v.* Harvey Lewis, sir Joseph McKenna, and others: for misuse of a company's funds while directors; 10 days' trial; verdict for plaintiff, 30 Jan. 1873
Omagh Murder: (of Mr. Glass, 29 June, 1871); sub-inspector Montgomery tried; 12 days; strong evidence; jury not agreed . . . 19 March, ,,
Broughton *v.* Knight: will of Mr. Knight set aside on account of unsound mind . 31 March, ,,
Andrews *v.* Salt: decision by lord-chancellor that a child shall be educated as a protestant by grandmother, not by Roman catholic uncle; confirmed on appeal . . . . . . 6 May, ,,
Rev. O'Keeffe *v.* Cardinal Cullen (for libel, and virtually suspending him from his office); consideration of demurrer; judges (at Dublin) divided in opinions; three decide that the papal ordinance on which the cardinal relied was prohibited by the statutes of Elizabeth; demurrer set aside, 7 May; the trial begun 12 May; verdict for plaintiff; the jury gave one farthing damages, 27 May, ,,
[Mr. O'Keeffe submitted to the cardinal, May, 1876.]
Sub-inspector Montgomery, at his third trial for the brutal murder of Mr. Glass, at Newton-Stewart, Ireland, on 8 June, 1871; convicted and confessed, 28 July [executed, Aug. 26] . ,,
Great jewellery frauds; Michael and Rebecca Goldsmid convicted . . . . 8 July, ,,
Farrell *v.* Gordons; much property left to R. C. church; will affirmed . . . . 9 July, ,,
Todd *v.* Lyne (father Ignatius); son of the plaintiff rescued from convent (where he had taken vows) by chancery . . . . . 25 July, ,,
Bank Forgery: Austin Biron Bidwell, George Macdonnell, George Bidwell, and Edwin Noyes, Americans, forged bills for discounting at the Bank of England, West-Branch, and obtained 102,217*l.*; detected through not dating one bill; convicted; penal servitude for life [their plot to escape by bribing the warders failed] 18-26 Aug. ,,
Rev. John Berrington (after 30 years' swindling) sentenced to 15 years' penal servitude 22 Aug. ,,
Cheltenham Chronicle fined 150*l.* for commenting on trial of the Tichborne claimant . . 23 Sept. ,,
Marshal Bazaine; see *France* . . 6 Oct. ,,
Gilbert *v.* Enoch (for *Pall Mall Gazette*) for libel in critique on "*The Wicked World,*" a play; verdict for defendant (both regarded harmless) 27 Nov. ,,
Capt. Charles S. Maunsell sentenced to a month's imprisonment with hard labour for assaulting the duke of Cambridge on 6 Jan. . 4 Feb. 1874
Miss Fairland gave her fortune to St. Mary's Dominican convent, Belfast; her trustees oppose the transfer; the master of the rolls affirms the gift, 24 Feb. ,,
Dr. Hayman *v.* the governing body of Rugby school; judgment for the defendants . 21 March, ,,
Jean Luie (Lindgren) and "capt." Brown convicted of perjury in the Tichborne case (7 years' and 5 years' penal servitude) . . . 9, 10 April, ,,
Mordaunt case (see 1870), divorce court; 3 judges hold that insanity is no bar to suit for divorce; 2 judges hold that it is . . . . . 15 May, ,,
Callan, M.P., *v.* O'Reilly Dease; for libel (termed "wilful and malicious" by ch.-just. Whiteside), Dublin; damages one farthing . . 2 July, ,,
E. Welby Pugin, convicted of libel against J. R. Herbert, R.A., 23 Sept.; not sentenced 24 Sept. ,,
Epping forest case; decision against the enclosures of the lords of the manors as illegal (see *Commons*) 10 Nov. ,,
Frederick *v.* Attorney-General: col. Charles Edward Frederick declared heir to baronetcy; the validity of the marriage of his grandparents affirmed in divorce court . . . . 18 Dec. ,,
Rubery *v.* baron Albert Grant and M. B. Sampson (long city editor of the *Times*) for libel; the article in *Times*, 18, 20 Nov. and 20 Dec. 1872, charged Rubery with connection with a fraud in a certain diamond mine in Colorado; 10 days' trial; Grant cleared; Sampson fined 500*l.* . . 18 Jan. 1875
[By these articles the public were protected from a bad scheme.]
Alleged False Prospectus Case: (Canadian Oil-Works Corporation), Charlton *v.* sir John Hay, Mr. Eastwick, and others grossly deceived; 17 days' trial; jury divided; discharged; no verdict 24 Feb. ,,
[Oil-wells in Ontario, Canada, property of Prince's company got up to buy them, by Longbottom;

* See *Englishman*.
† Charles Orton declared the claimant to be his brother Arthur, at the *Globe* office, 10 March, 1874.

scheme not accepted in the city; taken up at west-end; sir John Hay, Mr. M'Cullagh Torrens, Mr. Eastwick, and others induced to become directors; wells bought; company collapsed.]

Philpotts *v.* Boyd: see *Reredos*: settled by judicial committee of privy council . . . . 24 Feb. 1875

Mordaunt *v.* Mordaunt and viscount Cole (see above, May, 1874); divorce granted 11 March, „

Terry *v.* Brighton Aquarium Company, for opening on Sundays; verdict; penalty 200*l.* (see *Sunday*) 27 April, „

Jackson *v.* Grand Junction Canal Company (see *Gunpowder Explosion*, 2 Oct. 1874); company adjudged responsible for damages . 14 May, „

Keith Johnston *v.* Proprietors of *Athenæum*, for libel in criticism of an atlas; Edinburgh; damages, 1275*l.*: 24 March, new trial; damages reduced to 100*l.* . . . . 16 June, „

John Neave, Arthur Keen (or Murrell) and Annie Bolwell, convicted of coining and uttering false coin at railway stations . . . . 12, 13 July, „

Jenkins *v.* Rev. Flavel Cook (for excluding him from the communion for heresy (denying personality of Satan and eternal punishment); verdict for defendant in Court of Arches . 16 July, „

Col. Valentine Baker sentenced to fine of 500*l.*, and 12 months' imprisonment for indecently assaulting Miss Dickenson in a railway carriage 2 Aug. „

Mrs. Gladstone *v.* capt. Gladstone (long case concluded); divorce granted . . . . . 6 Aug. „

Wm. Thompson Hunt convicted of manslaughter for administering strychnia to Mrs. Hudson (who died) and others, as a remedy for intoxication; 5 years' penal servitude . . . . . 25 Sept. „

Wm. Talley, a solicitor, for dissuading a person bound over to prosecute from fulfilling his engagement; sentence 1 year's imprisonment 25 Sept. „

Sugden and others *v.* St. Leonards, will case (lord St. Leonards' will missing; many codicils left); verdict for plaintiffs, affirming the lost will on his daughter's, Miss Sugden's, recollection of its provisions . . . . 17-26 Nov. „

[Verdict affirmed on appeal, 14 March, 1876.]

Whitechapel Murder (*which see*).

Henry Wainwright for murder of Harriet Lane, and his brother Thomas as accessory before and after the fact; before chief justice Cockburn (nine days); Henry sentenced to death; Thomas, as accessory after fact, to 7 years' penal servitude 22 Nov.-1 Dec. „

Smith *v.* Union Bank of London (see *Drafts*); verdict for defendants . . . . . 29 Nov. „

Rev. H. Keet *v.* Rev. G. E. Smith (see *Reverend*); appeal to privy council; verdict for the plaintiff 21 Jan. 1876

Persons representing the parish of Folkestone *v.* Rev. C. J. Ridsdale, vicar (for ritualistic practices); verdict for plaintiffs; the vicar to be admonished and pay costs . . . . 3 Feb. „

Jenkins *v.* Rev. F. S. Cook, appeal from the dean of Arches to the privy council judicial committee; verdict for plaintiff (Rev. F. Cook resigned) 16 Feb. „

Eupion Gas Company (1874); Queen *v.* Aspinall and others, directors, for fraud; long trial; verdict, Aspinall and another convicted of improperly obtaining settlement of quotation on Stock Exchange; acquitted of charge of fraud . 17 Feb. „

[The lord chief justice declared the company to be "a fiction and a sham from beginning to end;" sentence, Joseph Aspinall and Charles Knocker, 12 months' imprisonment, John Saunders Muir and William Whyte, 2 months' imprisonment, 1 July, 1876.]

W. K. Vance and Ellen Snee, conspiracy to murder (ostensibly herself); singular case; sentenced to imprisonment . . . . . . 1 June, „

Robert Buchanan, the poet, *v.* P. A. Taylor, M.P., proprietor of *Examiner*, libels in papers 27 Nov. and 1 Dec. (letter said to be by Mr. A. Swinburne, the poet); damages, 150*l.* . . . . 1 July, „

Twycross (representing many others) *v.* baron Albert Grant and others, to recover money paid for shares in Lisbon tramway company, promoted by defendant and others; long trial; able speech of Grant; verdict, 700*l.* damages . 13 July, „

[Judgment affirmed on appeal, 2 June, 1877.]

Buckhurst peerage, claimed by earl Delawarr and by his brother, Mortimer Sackville West; house of lords decide in favour of the earl 18 July, 1876

Blackburn Murder; Wm. Fish convicted of murder and violation of Emily Mary Holland, aged 7 (28 March); pleaded temporary insanity . 28 July, „

Richard Banner Oakley, manager of Co-operative Credit Bank, convicted of obtaining money by false pretences; much credulity in victims; 5 years' penal servitude . . . . . 9-12 Aug. „

Will Frauds: Charles Howard (count von Howard, &c.), sentenced to 5 years' penal servitude for obtaining 380*l.* from John Harvey, for a pretended will (other cases) . . . . . . 26 Oct. „

Frederick Henry Vane *v.* sir Henry Ralph Vane (his nephew); verdict for defendant, maintaining his father's legitimacy; chancery division 25 Nov. „

Lewis *v.* Higgins, for alleged slander in speech as counsel; verdict for defendant, affirming privilege of counsel . . . . . . 4 Dec. „

Coe (stage manager, Haymarket, dismissed as accused of receiving payments from actors engaged) *v.* Sothern and Buckstone; verdict for plaintiff; damages, 1035*l.* . . . . 13 Dec. „

Lord Longford *v.* Wellington Purdon; will giving property to the plaintiff's young son set aside; the testator, Cooke, having been under the undue influence of Rev. Wm. Lyster (plaintiff not blamed); 25 days' trial . . . . Feb. 1877

Lynall Thomas *v.* the Queen (petition of right); for patent of cannon, &c.; verdict for plaintiff, with damages . . . . . . 10 March, „

Great Turf Frauds: forgery of cheques for 10,000*l.*, &c.; about 13,000*l.* obtained; five sentenced to penal servitude; Henry Benson, 15 years; Wm. and Fred. Kerr and Chas. Bate, 10 years; Edwin Murray, accessory, 18 months 12—23 April, „

Cresswell and others *v.* Walrond; will of Bethell Walrond set aside by arrangement (he had bequeathed his property to strangers and dogs, had been cruel to his children, decorated his bed with skulls and hearse plumes, &c.) 13 June, „

Queen *v.* Charles Bradlaugh and Annie Besant, for publication of "Fruits of Philosophy," by Dr. Knowlton, which they defended, on grounds of humanity, in long speeches; verdict, the book calculated to deprave, but not intended, 18—21 June; sentence (through the defendants not submitting to the court), 6 months' imprisonment, 200*l.* fine for both, 28 June; appeal, on ground of legal informality, disallowed by queen's bench 16 Nov. „

Nathaniel Druscovitch, John Meiklejohn, and Wm. Palmer, police inspectors, and Edward Froggatt, solicitor, charged with conspiracy to defeat the ends of justice in respect to turf frauds (see *above* 12—23 April); examination began, 12 July; Froggatt committed, 6 Sept.; chief inspector Clarke arrested, 8 Sept.; 28 days' examination; committed, 22 Sept.; trial began, 24 Oct.; all convicted except Clarke; sentence, 2 years' imprisonment with hard labour . . 20 Nov. „

Wm. Swindlehurst, secretary, and Dr. John Baxter Langley, director of Artisans' Dwelling Company, and Edward Saffery, convicted of defrauding shareholders of about 24,312*l.*; officers sentenced to 18 months', Saffery 12 months' imprisonment . . . . . . 23-26 Oct. „

Thos. Hyslop (aged 19) and John Denham (aged 18) convicted of highway robbery at Blackheath 23 Oct. „

Penge Case: Louis A. E. Staunton, Patrick L. Staunton his brother, and Eliz. Ann, his wife, and her sister, Alice Rhodes, mistress of Louis; tried for murder by starvation of Harriet, wife of Louis (a woman of weak intellect, married for her property, and soon deserted), 19 Sept.; all convicted, 26 Sept.; respited, 13 Oct.; Alice Rhodes pardoned; the others sentenced to penal servitude for life; announced . . 30 Oct. „

Coote (solicitor) *v.* Kenealy; for payments; verdict for plaintiff . . . . . 14 Nov. „

Forged Leases: Frederick Dimsdale, solicitor, Chas. Burrell Moore, clerk, and others; forged leases, and borrowed money on them (above 300,000*l.*); many lenders did not appear; pleaded guilty; sentence, Dimsdale, penal servitude for life; Moore, 7 years; others less . 16, 17 Jan. 1878

Madame Rachel (Levison, or Leverson), convicted of misdemeanour; obtained money and jewels from Mrs. Pearce, for "beautifying;" 5 years' penal servitude . . . 10, 11 April, 1878

Eugene Marie Chantrelle, Frenchman, convicted of murder of wife, at Edinburgh; much cruelty disclosed . . . 10 May, ,,

Will case, Dublin; Christopher Neville Bagot, made a fortune in Australia; made will, disinheriting his son as illegitimate; died, 23 May, 1877; trial, 23 days; painful disclosures; the will set aside (*see below*, 1879) . . 20 May, ,,

Harrington *v.* Victoria Graving Dock Company; he claimed remainder of commission for obtaining an order from Great Eastern railway company; nonsuited; such commissions declared illegal by queen's bench . . . 4 June, ,,

Jas. T. Northcott, Geo. Thompson, Thos. G. Wood (of the Albion Life Insurance company); sentenced to 5 years' penal servitude for conspiracy, and obtaining money on false pretences; subordinates sentenced to less imprisonment 8 June, ,,

Charles Marvin, copying-clerk of foreign office, examined for copy of an Anglo-Russian agreement published in *Globe*, 14 June, 27 June; discharged 16 July, ,,

Taylor *v.* Gwyn; claim for Jermy estates (see Jermy murders by Rush, *Trials*, 1849); claim denied; trial set aside by statute of limitations 5 Aug. ,,

In re Agar Ellis; the husband's promise before marriage that his children should be brought up Romanists, permitted to be withdrawn by chancery . . . . . . 6 Aug. ,,

The Board of Works *v.* rev. F. G. Lee, of All Saints, Lambeth; queen's bench division decide that the incumbent of a church is not its owner, and therefore not responsible for keeping it in repair. 11 Nov. ,,

Annie Louisa lady Gooch (with Ann Walker); she tried to pass a child as her own and her husband's, committed for trial 30 Nov., indictment ignored, 11 Dec. ,,

Paul and others *v.* Summerhayes; appeal; sentence against plaintiffs affirmed (foxhunters may not trespass), queen's bench . . . . 16 Nov. ,,

Queen *v.* Bandmann (for assault on Mrs. Rousby), not guilty . . . . . 19-20 Nov. ,,

Henry Sturt Marshall, asst. sec. of curates' augmentation fund, convicted of embezzling about 7,000*l.*; confessed . . . . . 24 Oct. ,,

Whistler *v.* Ruskin, for libellous criticism in "*Fors Clavigera*," one farthing damages . 25, 26 Nov. ,,

Hill and others *v.* managers of Metropolitan Asylums District 11 (days), verdict, that Hampstead smallpox hospital was a nuisance (verdict affirmed on appeal, 28 Jan. 1879) . . . . 29 Nov. ,,

Mr. Wybrow Robertson (manager of Westminster Aquarium) *v.* Labouchere, for libel in *Truth*, 27 Nov., verdict for defendant . . 20 Dec. ,,

Muir and others; court of session, decides that trustees who have invested in the "City of Glasgow bank," are responsible [affirmed on appeal to house of lords, 7 April, 1879] . . . 20 Dec. ,,

Stephen Gambrill for murder of Mr. Arthur Gillow (on 5 Dec. when defending agricultural machinery), at Wednesborough, near Sandwich, Kent, convicted . . . . . 14-15 Jan. 1879

Long firm forgeries, Kettle and others convicted, sentenced to various terms of imprisonment, 16-17 Jan. ,,

City of Glasgow Bank directors and managers (see under *Banks*, note) convicted . 20 Jan.-1 Feb. ,,

Charles Peace (or John Ward), committed many burglaries in skilful manner, convicted of attempting life of policeman, 19 Nov.; convicted of murder of Arthur Dyson, at Bannercross near Sheffield, 29 Nov. 1876 . . . . 4 Feb.

[He jumped from a moving railway train near Sheffield, and was nearly killed, 22 Jan.; confessed to murders, &c.; exonerated William Habron, convicted as an accomplice in a murder (therefore released, 18 March); executed at Leeds, 25 Feb.] ,,

Dr. Julius *v.* Bishop of Oxford (for not prosecuting rev. T. T. Carter of Clewer for ritualistic practices), queen's bench, (verdict for plaintiff, set aside on appeal, 30 May, Mr. Carter resigned 24 March, 1880 . . . . 8 March, ,,

Kentish Town murder, Thomas Perryman convicted of murder of his mother . . 2 April, 1879

Queen *v.* Booker & Wyman (for libel in *Truth*, against Mr. Lambri), verdict against Wyman; long trial . . . . . . 30 April, ,,

Duke of Norfolk *v.* Arbuthnot, claiming ownership of Fitz-alan chapel in Arundel church, verdict for plaintiff, common pleas . . . . 17 May, ,,

[Decision affirmed on appeal, 7 June, 1880.]

Bagot will case, appeal, new trial ordered 5 June, ,,

Shepherd *v.* Francis (for libel in a review in the "Athenæum"), damages, 150*l.* . . 16 June, ,,

The Queen *v.* sir Charles Reed; the queen's bench decide that the metropolitan school board have power to borrow money . . . 27 June, ,,

Sturla *v.* Freccia: Antonio Mangini, born 1735, consul here about 1771, died 1803; his daughter married Aquila Brown, 1792; after 8 years contest established her disputed legitimacy, 1811: died intestate in London, aged 93, 1871, her property, after a trial, awarded to the Freccia family, 1876. the claim of Madame Sturla set aside by vice-chancellor . . . 24 June, ,,

Richmond murder, Katherine Webster, convicted of murder of Mrs. Julia Martha Thomas (see *Richmond*) . . . . . . 8 July, ,,

Edmund Galley convicted of murder, by error, and transported; declared innocent by the house of commons . . . . . 25 July, ,,

Euston-square mystery, Hannah Dobbs, for murder of Matilda Hacker, acquitted . . 23 July, ,,

The mutilated remains of Matilda Hacker, eccentric, about 50 years old, were found in a coal-cellar, No. 4, Euston-square. Hannah Dobbs was maid-servant there. She published her autobiography, in which she attacked her former master, Sewerin Bastendorff, who, after bringing an action for libel, was convicted of perjury . . Dec. ,,

(He was awarded by consent 500*l.* damages for the libel, 27 Jan. 1881.)

Rev. Christopher Newman Hall *v.* Mrs. Hall, and Mr. Richardson, long trial, divorce granted, 8 Aug. ,,

Jonathan Gaydon (or Geyden), for murder of Miss Mary White at Chingford, 21 June, 1857, confessed, retracted, convicted (reprieved) . . 24 Oct. ,,

Adolphus Rosenberg, for libel against Mrs. Langtry and Mrs. West, in *Town Talk*, convicted, 18 months' imprisonment . . . 25, 27 Oct. ,,

Tranmere baby-farming case (near Birkenhead), John and Catherine Barns, convicted of manslaughter; (they received illegitimate infants with premiums of 30*l.*, &c.) . . . . . 28, 29 Oct. ,,

Dr. Arthur H. Nowell *v.* George Williams (for placing him in a lunatic asylum), verdict for the defendant, medical men censured by the jury, 13 Nov. ,,

Phillips, surgeon, *v.* S. W. railway company, for injury, awarded 7000*l.* by justice Field; new trial, awarded 16,000*l.* by lord ch. justice Coleridge, common pleas, new trial refused 6 Dec. ,,

Smee *v.* Smee and corporation of Brighton, will set aside, Brighton loses a free library bequeathed, 5 Dec. ,,

Hilliard *v.* Rose & Todd, will affirmed, singular case, 12 Dec. ,,

Edward Froggatt (see above, 20 Nov. 1877), sentenced to 7 years' penal servitude for fraudulent conversion of trust property (8000*l.*) . 17 Dec. ,,

James Lewis Paine and Fanny Matthews, for murder of Miss Annie Maclean, aged 34, daughter of col. Maclean, C.B., a deformed lady of property, by starving, administering spirits, and ill-usage, committed 15 Dec.; Fanny Matthews acquitted 16 Feb., Paine sentenced to penal servitude for life . . . . 24 Feb. 1880

Railway commissioners, powers limited (see *Railways*, 1880) . . . . . 13 Jan. ,,

Martin *v.* Mackonochie, new action for deprivation, first movement, see *Public Worship* . 17 Jan. ,,

Alexander Schosser attempted to kill priests in the Italian chapel, Hatton-garden, 10 Jan., tried, sentenced to imprisonment for life . 10, 11 Feb. ,,

Wm. Henry Walter, forger by chemicals, &c., sentenced to 20 years' penal servitude . 23 March, ,,

Dr. Caleb Charles Whitefoord sentenced to 2 months' imprisonment and fine of 50*l.* for forging letter to stop execution of Charles Shurety, 24 March, ,,

West of England bank directors (Jerome Murch

and others), for publishing false balance-sheets, acquitted . . . . 28 April—5 May, 1880
Lambri *v.* Labouchere, for libel in *Truth*, verdict for defendant . . . . . . 15 May, „
Tichborne case, writ of error before court of appeal, granted 13 Jan., sentence affirmed . 24, 25 June, „
Northern Counties Insurance Company, James E. Crabtree, manager, Geo. Edw. Nesbitt, accountant, and four directors, sentenced to imprisonment for making and circulating false accounts, 22 July, „
Pleasance Louisa Ingle, nurse at Guy's hospital, convicted of manslaughter (she putting Louisa Morgan, a patient, into a cold bath and leaving her), 3 months' imprisonment . . 9 Aug. „
Henry Perry, for robbing Clarence Lewis in a Kensington railway carriage, and attempting to throw him out of the carriage, &c.; whipping and 20 years' penal servitude . . . . 15 Sept. „
Thomas Wheeler for murder of Edward Anstee at Marshall's Wick farm, near St. Albans, 22 Aug. convicted . . . . 6, 8 Nov. „
Sergeant Wm. Marshman (by court-martial), for alleged fraudulent marking at the volunteer rifle meetings at Wimbledon, 1878, 1879, 1880, acquitted . . . . 13 Aug.—16 Sept. „
George Pavey convicted of murder of Ada Shepherd, aged ten (*Acton murder*), and Wm. Herbert, convicted of murder of Jane Messenger in Finsbury park . . . . 24 Nov. „
Mr. P. Callan, M.P., convicted of libel against Mr. A. M. Sullivan, M.P. (fine 50*l.*) . . 30 Nov. „
Debenham & Freebody *v.* Mellon, appeal, house of lords decide that a husband is not responsible for wife's debts if he allow her sufficient means, 27 Nov. „
Attorney-general *v.* Edison Telephone company, 29 Nov. *et seq.*, verdict against company, establishing monopoly bought by Government 20 Dec. „
Trial of Charles Stewart Parnell, Thomas Sexton, Timothy Daniel Sullivan, John Dillon, Joseph Gillis Biggar, all M.P.'s, Thomas Brennan, Patrick Egan and Michael O'Sullivan, secretary, treasurer, and assist. secretary of the land league, Michael Boyton, Patrick Joseph Gordon, Matthew Harris, John W. Mally, John W. Walsh, and P. J. Sheridan, indicted for conspiracy to prevent tenants paying rent, &c. Queen's Bench, Dublin; lord chief justice May retires, as having been alleged to have given an opinion on the case previously; trial began 28 Dec. 1880, jury disagreeing were discharged . . . . 25 Jan. 1881
Jones and others (trustees) *v.* rev. John Turner Stannard, nonconformist minister, and others, to dismiss him for doctrine contrary to trust deed; verdict for plaintiffs, chancery division 1 Feb. „
Mary Annie Wilmot, nurse, attempt to poison Mrs. Booth (whose son and daughter had died under doubtful circumstances), at Sheffield, strong case, acquitted . . . . . 16 Feb. „
Hampstead small-pox hospital case (*see* above, 1878-9), on appeal, to the house of lords, preceding judgments reversed . . . . 7 March, „
Dysart peerage legitimacy case, Wm. John Manners claims by an English marriage of lord Huntingtower, Albert Edwin Tollemache by a Scotch marriage, which is declared not proved, house of lords (painful details) . . . . 7 March, „
Clarke *v.* Bradlaugh, suit for penalty of 500*l.* for sitting and voting as M.P. without taking the oath, on July 2, 1880; verdict for plaintiff; appeal, sentence confirmed* . . 30, 31 March, „
Edward Levi Lawson *v.* Labouchere, M.P. for libels in *Truth*, seven days' trial, jury disagree, no verdict . . . . 28 March, „
Spiritualist case, Susan Wills Fletcher (wife of a spiritualist doctor in America, who was concerned in the case), convicted of obtaining by false pretences about 10,000*l.* (in jewellery, &c.), of Mrs. Hart-Davies, long trial, twelve months' imprisonment with hard labour . . . . 12 April, „

* Verdict affirmed (see *Barratry*), 22 July; Bradlaugh appeals, 12—14 Nov.; new trial granted, 2, 3 Dec. 1881; appeal allowed by lords justices, 22—24 Feb.; sentence confirmed, 30 March 1882; sentence reversed by the ords, 9 April, 1883.

Johann Most, convicted of libel against Alexander II. of Russia, and incitement to murder in the *Freiheit* for 19 March, 25 May; sentence affirmed on appeal, 18 June; 16 months' imprisonment with hard labour . . 29 June, 1881
Saunders *v.* Richardson, 5 judges decide that parents must either pay board-school fees for child beforehand or apply for pecuniary help; coming without fee considered non-attendance 27 June, „
Bend Or libel, Barrow *v. Morning Post* for accusation of doctoring the horse, verdict for plaintiff, damages 1750*l.* . . . . 27, 28 June, „
Big Ben libel, Stainbank (for Mears) *v.* sir E. C. Beckett, 27 June, verdict for plaintiff, 200*l.* damages . . . . 5 July, „
Percy Lefroy *alias* Mapleton committed for trial for murder of Mr. Fk. I. Gold on the London and Brighton railway (27 June), 21 July; convicted, 8 Nov.; confessed; executed . . . . 29 Nov. „
Notting Hill Fire, William Nash and Maria Wright, for murder of Elizabeth Jane Clark and others by fire, 30 May; he sentenced to death (reprieved), she acquitted . . . . . . 3, 4 Aug. „
Ledru Rolin Reynolds, adventurer, with many aliases, convicted of remarkable frauds connected with the silver mine company, two years' penal servitude . . . . 15 Sept „
Mabel Wilberforce, an adventuress, convicted of gross perjury in action against Mr. Philip; nine months' hard labour . . . . 24 Oct. „
Kate Dover, for murder of Chas. Skinner, artist, at Sheffield, convicted of manslaughter . 7 Feb. 1882
Dr. G. H. Lamson, for murder of Percy M. John (see *Wimbledon*); convicted, 8—14 March; executed . . . . 28 April „
Roderick Maclean, for shooting at the queen, acquitted as insane . . . . . 19 April, „
Esther Pay, for murder of Georgiana Moore (see *Pimlico*), acquitted . . . 27—29 April, „
Albert Young, for threatening to shoot at the queen, 10 years' penal servitude . 26 May, „
Mr. Thomas Scrutton *v.* Miss Helen Taylor, a libel concerning St. Paul's industrial school; damages 1000*l.* . . . . 30 June, „
Sir Henry Tyler, M.P., *v.* Wm. Jas. Ramsey, Geo. Wm. Foote, and Edwd. Wm. Whittle, also Chas. Bradlaugh, for blasphemous libel in the *Freethinker* (lord mayor, 11 July), committed for trial, 21 July, „
Next of Kin Fraud, J. E. Rogers, A. McKenzie, J. H. Shakspear, and W. Evans sentenced to imprisonment . . . . . . 21 July, „
Thomas Walsh, for treason felony (see *Fenians*), 7 years' penal servitude . . . 7—9 Aug. „
John Saunders, desperate ruffian, convicted of burglary and attempt to murder at Stamford-hill; penal servitude for life . . . 19 Oct. „
Charles Soutar, for stealing the body of the earl of Crawford; Edinburgh; 5 years' penal servitude, 23, 24 Oct. „
Wm. Meager Bartlet, a manager of mines, convicted of murder of illegitimate child, Exeter, 27 Oct. „
Charles Brookshaw, for threatening to kill the prince of Wales, 10 years' penal servitude, 21 Nov. „
St. Luke's Mystery, Franz Felix Stum, convicted of forgery of signature of Urban Napoleon Stanger, baker, who had disappeared; 10 years' penal servitude . . . . 11 Dec. „
Plumstead Murder, Louisa Jane Taylor, convicted of poisoning Mary Ann Tregillis, aged 81, 15 Dec. „
Richard Claude Belt (sculptor) *v.* Charles Lawes (sculptor), for libel in *Vanity Fair*, 20 Aug. 1881, *et seq.*; (charges of fraudulent imposture, &c.) before Baron Huddleston, Exchequer division, 21 June *et seq.*, 14 Nov. *et seq.*; verdict on 43rd day for plaintiff, damages 5000*l.* . 28 Dec. „
Goodacre *v.* Watson, to restrain deposition of pestilential refuse on building ground, as a nuisance at Fulham; injunction granted with costs, 22 Feb. 1883
Bethell *v.* Sir Percy Shelley, for infringement of the Theatre act, verdict for defendant, 1*s.* damages 23 Feb.
G. W. Foote, editor, W. J. Ramsey, printer, and

H. A. Kemp, publisher, sentenced to imprisonment for blasphemous libels in the *Freethinker*, 5 Mar. 1883
Clarke *v.* Bradlaugh, verdict for defendant on appeal to lords (see *above*, March, 1881) 9 April, ,,
C. Bradlaugh, for blasphemy in the *Freethinker*, 10 April, acquitted . . . . . 14 April, ,,
Bradlaugh *v.* Newdegate, for supporting an action by a common informer, verdict for plaintiff with costs . . . . 23 April, ,,
Phœnix park murders (see under *Ireland*) . April, May, ,,
Belt *v.* Lawes: appeal for new trial, 24 May—9 June, ,,
Dynamite Plot (see *Birmingham, England,* and *London*, 1883), Thomas Gallagher, Henry Wilson, John Curtin, and Alfred Whitehead, for treason-felony, sentenced to penal servitude for life; William Ansburgh and Bernard Gallagher, acquitted . . . . . . 11—14 June, ,,
STROME FERRY CASE. Ten men were sentenced to four months' imprisonment for violently stopping the transmission of fish by Highland railway on Sunday, 3 June . . . . . . 23 July, ,,
Dynamite conspiracy, Timothy Featherstone, and three other Fenians, convicted at Liverpool, 7—9 Aug. ,,
Wm. Gouldstone convicted of murder of his five children at Walthamstow (on 8 Aug.), 14 Sept.; respited as insane . . . . . . 3 Oct. ,,
Bournemouth case. Mrs. Miller, the *Joy* breach of promise; conflicting evidence; damages for plaintiff, 2350*l.* . . . . . . 15 Nov. ,,
French *Date Coffee Co.*, Bellairs *v.* Haymen and others, promoters; misleading prospectus, verdict for plaintiff . . . . . . 22 Nov. ,,
London and River Plate Bank robbery, George Warden pleads guilty to robbery of securities (about 116,000*l.*), 26 Nov., and John Davis Watters convicted of receiving the same; both sentenced to 12 years' penal servitude . . . . 27 Nov. ,,
Dobbs *v.* Grand Junction water works co.; on appeal the house of lords decides that houses are to be rated for water on the rated, not the gross value . . . . 30 Nov. ,,
Patrick O'Donnell, convicted of murder of James Carey, the informer (see *Ireland*), 30 Nov., 1 Dec. ,,
Priestman *v.* Thomas; *Whalley will case;* incredible incidents; verdict for plaintiff; a forged will; fraudulent compromise proposed by defendant; 15 days' trial . . . . 4 Dec. ,,
Central News v. *Judy*, for libel respecting telegrams, verdict for defendant . . . . . 13 Dec. ,,
Belt *v.* Lawes, again; the judges decide for a new trial unless Mr. Belt accepts 500*l.* instead of 5,000*l.*; Belt accepts, defendant objects, 21 Dec. ,,
Wm. Wolff and Edwd. Bondurand, for plot to blow up German embassy, arrested in Westminster, 22 Nov. 1883; jury disagree, 14—19 Jan.; prisoners discharged . . . . . 28 Jan. 1884
Bradlaugh *v.* Gosset; verdict for defendant (see *Parliament*) . . . . 9 Feb. ,,
Attorney-general *v.* Birkbeck, for contravention of the Bank act of 1844; verdict for the crown, 9 Feb. ,,
Liverpool poisoning case, Catherine Flanagan and Margaret Higgins, convicted of the murder of Thomas Higgins; other charges, 16 Feb.; executed . . . . 3 March, ,,
Belt *v.* Lawes, appeal before Master of the Rolls and others, 3 March, sentence of the other court affirmed with costs . . . . 17 March, ,,
London Financial Association *v.* Kelk and others; case dismissed (see *Alexandra park*) 8 March, ,,
Earl *v.* countess of Euston, divorce sought on ground that she had a husband living when she married; as it was proved that this man had a wife living when he married her, and that thus she was free, divorce was refused . 4 April, ,,
Parks-place Club declared by the Queen's Bench to be a gaming-house; Mr. Jenks, the proprietor and others fined . . . . . 24 June, ,,
Mrs. Weldon *v.* Dr. Semple, for signing certificate of lunacy; ten days; verdict for plaintiff, 1000*l.* damages . . . . 28 July, ,,
Daley and Egan, Aug. 1884 (see *Dynamite*) . May, ,,
Thomas Henry Orrock, convicted of murder of policeman Cole (on 1 Dec. 1882); remarkable evidence . . . . . . 19, 20 Sept. 1884
Tichborne Claimant (see *above*, 1871—4) released on ticket-of-leave . . . . . . 20 Oct. ,,
Mignonette Case (see *Wrecks*) . . . . 6 Nov. ,,
Miss Finney *v.* viscount Garmoyle; breach of promise of marriage; a verdict by consent for 10,000*l.* 20 Nov. ,,
Defence society for innocent prisoners; Morley Jervis sentenced to 2 years' penal servitude, Vernon Garland 15 months' and Charles Kemp 9 months', for fraud . . . . . . 21 Nov. ,,
Adams *v.* Hon. B. Coleridge, for libel in a letter to Miss M. Coleridge; verdict of jury for plaintiff, 3,000*l.*; verdict by judge Manisty for defendant, the letter being privileged . . 21, 22 Nov. ,,
Whalley Will Case (see Dec. 1883), Charles Thomas and Thomas William Nash, convicted of forgery, 15 years' penal servitude, Edward Gunnell acquitted . . . . . . 24 Nov.—2 Dec. ,,
Mrs. Weldon *v.* Dr. Forbes Winslow, for treating her as a lunatic, 500*l.* awarded to plaintiff, 4th trial, 25—29 Nov. ,,
Eliz. Gibbons, for murder of husband; she asserted his suicide, 18-19 Dec.; life imprisonment, 31 Dec. ,,
Mr. Edmund Yates sentenced to 4 months' imprisonment, for libel against the earl of Lonsdale (in *The World*), July, 1883-April, 1884; appeal disallowed . . . . 16 Jan. 1885
Mr. Irving Bishop fined, 10,000*l.* for libel (reduced to 500*l.* on appeal) (see *Thought Reading*) 15 Jan. ,,
John Lee, footman, convicted of murder of Miss Emma A. W. Keyse, his mistress (at Babbicombe, near Torquay, 15 Nov.), 2-4 Feb.; when about to be hanged at Exeter, the drop failed three times, and Lee was removed and reprieved . 23 Feb. ,,
The earl of Durham's petition for annulling his marriage, on account of his wife's alleged insanity at the time of their union dismissed with costs by sir James Hannen, after 8 days' trial, 10 March, ,,
Mrs. Georgina Weldon sentenced to 6 months' imprisonment for libel on M. Jules Prudence Rivière . . . . 30 March, ,,
James Lee, convicted of murder of Inspector Simmons at Romford (25 Jan.) . . 28 April ,,
John Gilbert Cunningham and Harry Burton convicted of treason-felony (see under *Tower*), and for complicity with criminal explosions (25 Feb. *et seq.*); sentenced to penal servitude for life, 11-18 May, ,,
Weldon *v.* Gounod for libel; 10,000*l.* awarded 7 May, ,,
Eugene Loraine, engraver, an accomplished swindler, and chief of a seminary of crime, convicted of attempted fraud by forgery, 22 May, ,,
Benj. Warburton's will; Warburton *v.* Childs, Hobson & Moss; testator declared insane and intestate; legacies lost by Royal Society and others; seven days' trial . . . . 23 June, ,,
Mrs. Lotinga *v.* Commercial Union Insurance Co. Policy of her husband Isaac for 2,000*l.* established; conflicting evidence respecting his death and temperance (14 days' trial) . . 2 July, ,,
James Malcolm (otherwise capt. Macdonald) for bigamy (gross case), Emma Dash, at Brighton, 4 April; doubtful identity; jury disagree 25 Sept.; second trial, 16 Oct.; convicted, seven years' penal servitude . . . . . . 24 Oct. ,,
W. T. Stead, editor of *Pall Mall Gazette*, (2) Sampson Jacques (assistant) (3), Bramwell Booth, of Salvation Army, (4) Rebecca Jarrett, and (5) Louise Mourey, connection with abduction of Eliza Armstrong, under 16, and indecent assault: (1) three months' imprisonment, (2) one month, (3) acquitted, (4) six months', (5), six months' with hard labour . . . . 23 Oct.–10 Nov. ,,
Mrs. Weldon *v.* sir Henry De Bathe for slander, 19 Nov.; 1,000*l.* damages awarded . 23 Nov. ,,
Anthony Benjamin Rudge, James Baker, and John Martin convicted for burglary at Netherby Hall, Cumberland 28 Oct., and murder of police constable Byrnes at Plumpton, 29 Oct. (captured by railway servants) . . . . 18–20 Jan. 1886
John Magee, photographer, sentenced to seven years' penal servitude for threatening the prince of Wales . . . . 15 Jan. ,,
Richard Belt, sculptor, sentenced to twelve

months' imprisonment with hard labour for fraudulent sale of jewellery to sir Wm. Abdy; his brother Walter acquitted . . 15 March, 1886
John Burns, Henry Hyde Champion, Henry Mayers Hyndman, and John Edward Williams, for seditious words; acquitted but censured, 6–10 April, „
Mrs. Adelaide Bartlett tried for the murder of her husband by chloroform; (Rev. George Dyson charged as an accessory before the fact discharged, 12 April); Mrs. Bartlett acquitted 12–17 April, „
Dr. Lyell, for heirs-at-law, *v.* Kennedy, agent for Anne Duncan, intestate; long litigation respecting property; verdict for plaintiff, 22 June, „
Crawford *v.* Crawford; divorce of Mrs. Crawford, decreed, 12 Feb.; confirmed; serious charges against sir Charles Dilke, denied by him but accepted by jury . . . . . 23 July, „
Diamond robbery with violence to Mr. Julius Tabak, the owner, 25 March; conviction and sentences: Adolphe Weiner, instigator, seven years' penal servitude; James Palmer, perpetrator ten years'; accomplices, Leon Weiner, Daniel Jacoby, and Samuel Scandland, each five years, ... 1–4 Nov. „
[Principal witness, Toussaint or Denuncis, who was sentenced to 15 years' penal servitude in June for his joint action with Palmer, who escaped when Toussaint was taken.]
Mary Lena Sebright (formerly Scott) *v.* Arthur Sebright; a merely formal marriage contract entered into by the terrorised plaintiff annulled, 16 Nov. „
Adams *v.* lord Coleridge and his son, the hon. B. Coleridge, for libel in letters sent to an arbitrator (lord Monkswell), wrongly delivered; verdict for defendants with costs . . 17–25 Nov. „
Lord and lady Colin Campbell divorce, double suit (previous judicial separation; numerous charges on both sides not proved); suits for divorce dismissed . . 27 Nov.–20 Dec. „
Miss Allcard *v.* Miss Skinner (superior of the "Sisters of the Poor", an Anglican convent, Rev. Henry Nihill, director), to recover property given as under undue influence; verdict for defendant, 31 Jan.; appeal rejected . 9 July, 1887
Thomas William Carroll convicted for atrocious murder of Lydia Green, at 8, Baches-street, Hoxton, 5 Feb. . . . 30 March–2 April, „
Mr. Dillon and other M.P.'s for conspiracy; jury disagree (see *Ireland*) . . . 14–24 Feb. „
Col. Sandoval sentenced to one month's imprisonment and fined 500*l.* for fitting out vessel against Venezuela . . . . 21 March, „
Mr. James Davis, proprietor of the *Bat*, convicted for libel against Mr. Robert Peck; three months' imprisonment, and fine of 500*l.* 30 March, „
Mr. Edward St. John Brenon *v.* Messrs. Ridgway, publishers of the "Black Pamphlet" (relating to Irish republican brotherhood &c.); 500*l.* awarded as damages . . . . . 3 May, „
Professor Caird *v.* Syme (a bookseller); after differing decisions of the courts, the house of lords, on appeal, decides against the publication of university lectures without the consent of the lecturers . . . . 13 June, „
Beyfus *v.* Jonas and others, charge of fraudulent conspiracy; thirteen days' trial; verdict for plaintiff, 40*s.* damages . . . . 5 July, „
Samuel Taylor, driver, and Robert Davis, fireman, tried for manslaughter (see *Railway Accidents*, Doncaster) . . . . 14 Oct. „
Police constable Endacott acquitted of perjury (see under *Police*) . . . 31 Oct.–1 Nov. „
Joyce (the marquis's agent) *v.* the marquis of Clanricarde, for libel in a letter; verdict for plaintiff; damages 2,500*l.* . . . 6, 7 Dec. „
Long firm fraud; thirteen men convicted; sentenced to various terms of imprisonment . 21 Dec. „
Cuninghame Graham, M.P., and John Burns tried for assaulting police, &c., on 13 Nov. 1887 (see *Riots*); convicted of taking part in an unlawful assembly; six weeks' imprisonment without hard labour . . . 16–18 Jan. 1888
Dynamite conspiracy (see under *Dynamite*), Thomas Callan and Michael Harkins sentenced to fifteen years' penal servitude . . . . 3 Feb. „
Slater *v.* Slater; a chancery forgery case; the court defrauded of about 4,000*l.*, the property of Miss Rose Maud Maxwell, by the forgeries of William Bowden, a solicitor's clerk: the money ordered to be paid to her by the court of chancery; Bowden in Nebraska; John Francis Lidiard, a solicitor, his friend, ordered to repay the money to the court . . . 4 Feb. 1888
Marquis of Abergavenny *v.* bishop of Llandaff, after much litigation, verdict for the bishop who had refused to induct the Rev. Robert W. Gosse into a living, being ignorant of the Welsh language . . . . 22 Feb. „
Major Borrowes fined 400*l.* and costs for assaulting his brother-in-law, lord Howard de Walden, 10 March, „
Major Templer honourably acquitted of charge of divulging secret information concerning military ballooning, &c. . . . . . 9 April, „
Mr. Samuel Peters *v.* Mr. C. Bradlaugh, M.P., for libel respecting cheques given him by lord Salisbury and others for the relief of the unemployed; 300*l.* awarded to the plaintiff . . 18 April, „
Warne & Co. *v.* Seebohm (see *Copyright*), 10 May, „
Hutt and another *v.* The governors of Haileybury college (see under *Haileybury*) . . 19 June, „
Wood *v.* Cox (see under *Races*) . . 29 June, „
O'Donnell *v.* Walter and another (for libel in the *Times*); verdict for the defendants (see under *Parnellites*). . . . . . 2–5 July, „
Trials respecting electric light patents (see under *Electricity*) 1886–8
George and Kelynge Greenway, bankers, of Warwick and Leamington, sentenced to imprisonment, &c., for frauds. . . 31 July, 1888
Trial of Regent's park murderer (see *Regent's Park*), July, „
R. P. B. Frost and his presumed wife, Annie Frost (clever and fascinating), who as Mrs. Gordon Bailie and other names, had carried on a long series of frauds at home and abroad by means of fictitious cheques, convicted of cheating tradesmen of goods and money; he sentenced to eighteen months' imprisonment with hard labour, she to five years' penal servitude . . . 24 Oct. „
Anthony Isidor Glika sentenced to ten years' penal servitude for defrauding his employers, Messrs. Vagliano Bros., and the Bank of England, of 71,500*l.*, 27 June,–7 July; in a subsequent trial the Queen's Bench Division adjudged the bank to bear the loss . . . . . 2 Nov. „
[Sentence confirmed by court of appeal, 21 May, 1889; reversed by the House of Lords, 5 March 1891.]
Mrs. Weldon *v.* M. Rivière and others; verdict for defendants . . . . 15 Nov. „
Charles Richardson and Edgell, who had confessed to burglary at Edlingham vicarage, near Alnwick, on 7 Feb. 1879; sentenced to five years' penal servitude . . . . . 24 Nov. „
[Michael Brannagham and Peter Murphy, who had been wrongfully convicted for this crime, and attempt to murder, had been sentenced to penal servitude for life, April, 1879; each received 800*l.* as compensation, Dec. 1888; the police were acquitted of perjury, and doubts were thrown on the confession of Richardson and Edgell, Feb. 1889.]
Lyster, Burdett, and Clarke convicted of burglary and attempt to murder Mr. George Atkin at Muswell Hill; sentenced to penal servitude for life . . . . 7 March, 1889
Mrs. Sophia Irwin *v.* *Pall Mall Gazette* for libel; damages awarded, 1,000*l.* . . . 4 April, „
Sir George Chetwynd *v.* the earl of Durham, for libels relating to racing transactions, the damages claimed, 20,000*l.* After some litigation and much discussion, the case was referred to the arbitration of the stewards of the jockey club, Mr. Jas. Lowther, M.P., the earl of March, and prince Soltikoff; they awarded sir George Chetwynd ½*d.* damages, each person to pay his own costs . . . . . . 29 June, „
[Sir George Chetwynd, who was exonerated from the graver, but censured for the lighter charges, quitted the club, 5 July, 1889.]
W. O'Brien, M.P. *v.* the marquis of Salisbury for libel in a speech at Watford, 10 March; charging him with inciting to crime in a speech at

Ballyneale, near Clonmel, 30 Sept. 1888; damages claimed, 10,000*l.*; trial at Manchester; verdict for defendant . . . . 20 July, 1889
[New trial refused by the queen's bench, 21 Dec. 1889; appeal disallowed, 8 May, 1890.]

Mrs. Florence Elizabeth Maybrick charged with poisoning her husband, James Maybrick, at Aigburth, by arsenic, tried at Liverpool by Mr. justice Stephen; convicted 21 July–7 Aug.; sentence of death commuted to penal servitude for life . . . . 22 Aug. „

Gweedore trials, see *Ireland* . . . . Oct. „

John Watson Laurie (at Edinburgh) convicted of the murder of Edwin Robert Rose, his fellow traveller, in the Island of Arran (on 15 July), 8, 9 Nov. 1889; respited as of unsound mind, 28 Nov.; penal servitude for life . about 1 Dec. „

Rev. Percy G. Benson, vicar of Hoo, Kent, suspended from duty for one year for excluding Mrs. Swayne from the communion, for schism, 25 Oct.; directed by the bishop of Rochester to receive her; yields . . . . . . 29 Nov. „

Mr. Herbert J. Gladstone *v.* Colonel George B. Malleson, for libel in *Allahabad Morning Post*, damages awarded 1,000*l.* . . . . 16 Jan. 1890

Mr. Ernest Parke, sentenced to one year's imprisonment for libel against the earl of Euston in the *North London Press* . . . . . 16 Jan. „

Parnell *v.* Walter (see under *Parnellites*) . 3 Feb. „

Trial of the bp. of Lincoln, see *Canterbury* 4 Feb. „

Crewe murder; Richard and George Davies, youths, aged 19 and 16, convicted of the murder of their father, Richard Davies, a clothier, on 25 Jan. while riding home in a pony chaise, 20, 21 March; Richard executed, George reprieved (penal servitude for life) . . . . 8 April, „

Miss Florence Jennie Day *v.* Mr. Morris Roberts, for breach of promise of marriage, Birmingham; damages awarded, 2,500*l.* . . . 26 March, „

Miss Emily Mary Hairs *v.* sir George Elliot, M.P. (aged 75), for breach of promise of marriage; damages claimed 5,000*l.*; jury disagree, 18 April, „

Lord Dunlo (son of the earl of Clancarty) *v.* lady Dunlo and Mr. T. E. Wertheimer, six days' trial; divorce refused . . . . . . 30 July, „

Miss Gladys Knowles *v.* Mr. Leslie Duncan, proprietor and editor of the *Matrimonial News*, for breach of promise of marriage; damages awarded, 10,000*l.* . . . . 11, 12 Aug. „

Reginald John Birchall convicted of the murder of Mr. F. J. Benwell, see *Canada*, 29 Sept.; executed . . . . 14 Nov. „

Capt. O'Shea *v.* Mrs. C. O'Shea, and Mr. C. S. Parnell, M.P.; divorce granted . . 15–17 Nov. „

Catherine Theresa Riordan sentenced to six years' penal servitude for attempting to kill Dr. James Frank Bright, master of University College, Oxford (6 Nov.) . . . . . . 15 Nov. „

Mr. R. Buchanan *v.* Mrs. Langtry, respecting a non-accepted play; damages awarded, 150*l.* 21 Nov. „

Mary Eleanor Wheeler (otherwise Pearcey) convicted of the murder of Mrs. Phœbe Hogg and infant . . . . 1–3 Dec. „
[Mrs. Wheeler had been connected with her victim's husband, Frank S. Hogg, before their marriage; she invited Mrs. Hogg to her rooms at No. 2, Priory-street, Kentish-town, and there murdered her; she then in a perambulator conveyed the body of the mother to near Crossfield-road, Hampstead, and that of the child to a field near Finchley-road, 24 Oct. 1890; her motive appears to have been jealousy, executed 23 Dec. 1890.]

Bellamy *v.* Wells, proprietor of the Pelican Club, Gerrard-street, Soho, to restrain a nuisance by noise caused by boxing matches, concerts, &c.; justice Romer, in the chancery division, forbids the assembling of crowds and calling cabs between midnight and 7 A.M. . . . . 6 Dec. „

Thomas Macdonald, convicted on his own confession of the murder of Miss Elizabeth Ann Holt, at Belmont, near Bolton . . . . 12 Dec. „

Mr. Harry H. Marks (editor of the *Financial News*) *v.* Mr. George Washington Butterfield, for libel respecting gold mines; verdict, not guilty; libel proved, but publication justified 8–17 Dec. „

Walter Alfred Hargan, tried for murder, convicted of manslaughter, for killing two roughs in Kingsland, London, N.E., in alleged self-defence; sentenced by Mr. justice Charles to 20 years' penal servitude, 8 Sept.; commuted to 12 months' 17 Dec. 1890

Charles Lyddon, acquitted of the murder of his half brother, William Recks-Lyddon, of Faversham, who had been much ill-used 18–21 March, 1891

Clitheroe case (see under *Wives*) . . . . . „

Baccarat case; sir William Gordon-Cumming *v.* Mr. and Mrs. Lycett Green and others, for slander, charging him with cheating in the game of baccarat, in the house of Mr. Arthur Wilson, Tranby Croft, near Doncaster, Sept. 1890; counsel for plaintiff, sir Edward Clarke; sol. gen. for the defendants, sir Charles Russell, and others; queen's bench division, lord Coleridge; evidence was given by the prince of Wales; verdict for the defendants . . . . . . 1–9 June, „

Coombs *v.* Barber and others, in relation to the Great Eastern Steamship company; queen's bench division; the case stopped; Mr. Barber exculpated from criminal charges . 26 June, „

The Cathcart case; after 17 days' investigation, Mrs. Cathcart is declared to be of sound mind by Mr. Bulwer, a master in lunacy, and a special jury, and ordered to be released from custody 23 July, „

Berkeley Peerage case, *which see*; decision 31 July, „

Mr. Francis Du Bedat, president of the Dublin Stock Exchange, pleads guilty to charges of fraud relating to bankruptcy and breaches of trust; sentence, one year's imprisonment with hard labour, and seven years' penal servitude 20 Oct. „

The rev. James C. Clutterbuck, D.C.L., an inspector of workhouse schools, convicted of obtaining money on false pretences, on his own confession; sentenced to 4 years' penal servitude; Wells [he died 18 Nov. 1892] . . . 21 Nov. „

The petition of Mabel Edith, countess Russell, to the divorce court, for judicial separation from earl Russell, on account of cruelty, dismissed with costs . . . . 1–4 Dec. „

Pinnock *v.* Chapman & Hall, for libel in "West African Stories," by major A. B. Ellis; 200*l.* damages awarded . . . . . 7–9 Dec. „

Miss Ethel Florence Elliot (afterwards Mrs. Osborne) *v.* major and Mrs. Hargreaves, for slander in charging her with stealing jewels while their guest at Torquay, 9–18 Feb.; verdict by consent for the defendants . . . . 15–22 Dec. „
[It was proved that Miss Elliot sold the jewels to Messrs. Spinks, in Gracechurch street, for 550*l.*, 19 Feb.; that she cashed the cheque at the bank of Messrs. Glyn, Mills & Co., receiving gold, 23 Feb.; that through Messrs. Benjamin, of Conduit street, W., she changed gold for bank notes, at the National and Provincial bank, in St. James's square, early in March; and that she endorsed one of these notes for 50*l.*, and paid it to Messrs. Maple, which note was passed into the Bank of England. Information was given to the judge, Mr. Justice Denman, and the trial was suspended, 19 Dec. It was admitted by all the parties concerned that capt. Osborne, the plaintiff's husband, had acted throughout as an honourable and chivalrous gentleman. Mrs. Osborne, at her trial for larceny and perjury, was sentenced to 9 months' imprisonment, with some hard labour, 9 March; released in the summer, 1892. The jewels were sold by auction for major Hargreaves for 1,076*l.*, 29 March, 1892.]

Mr. Alexander Jacob, a jeweller of Simla, charged at Calcutta by the Nizam of Hyderabad of criminally misappropriating 23 lakhs of rupees (above 100,000*l.*) deposited by his highness as earnest money for the purchase of the gem known as the "imperial diamond," after a long trial, was acquitted . . . . 22 Dec. „

Nettlefold (limited), Birmingham screw-makers, *v.* Reynolds, an American agent, for alleged infringement of patent; 14 days' trial; verdict for defendant with costs . . . . . 22 Jan. 1892

Mr. George W. Hastings, M.P., misappropriating to himself, a trustee, about 20,000*l.*, the property of the children of major John Brown, pleaded guilty; sentenced to 5 years' penal servitude, 11 March, 1892

Maitland Francis Morland, a law tutor at Cambridge, not connected with the university, charged with sending threatening letters to extort money, pleaded guilty; sentenced to 10 years' penal servitude . . . . 11 March, „

Miss Mary E. T. Knox *v.* canon Hayman, D.D., and co-directors of the Canadian Pacific Colonization corporation; verdict for plaintiff; to be repaid 258*l.*, the amount claimed . . 25 March, „

Concha, pauper, *v.* Concha and wife; a series of intricate suits respecting property, which commenced in 1858, closed by the house of lords varying the decision of the court of appeal, 28 March, „

Frederick Charles, Victor Cailes, John Westley, William Ditchfield, Joseph Thomas Deakin, and Jean Battolla, anarchists, tried for unlawfully possessing explosive substances (with evil intentions) at Walsall, 1 Nov. 1891—7 Jan.; Charles, Battolla, and Cailes, at Stafford, sentenced to 10 years' penal servitude, Deakin to 5 years' penal servitude, Westley and Ditchfield acquitted, 30 March—4 April, „

Hansard Publishing Union, sir Henry and Mr. Joseph M. Isaacs, Mr. Charles Dollman, Mr. Horatio Bottomley, directors, charged with defrauding the company and applicants for shares; 11 days' examination; committed for trial, 6 April, „
[Trial, 24 days; against sir Henry Isaacs and Mr. Joseph Isaacs no case, 20 April; Mr. Dollman and Mr. Bottomley acquitted; Mr. Justice Hawkins and the jury urgently affirm the necessity of amendment of the law relating to the directors of public companies, 30 Jan.—28 Feb.; 17–26 April, 1893.]

Mr. Lane Fox *v.* Kensington Electric Lighting company for infringement of patent; verdict for defendants with costs . . . 30 March, „

Mrs. Montagu sentenced at Dublin to one year's imprisonment for cruel manslaughter of her daughter, aged 3 years . . . . 4 April, „

David John Nicoll, journalist, sentenced to 18 months' imprisonment, with hard labour, for inciting persons to murder Mr. H. Matthews, the home secretary, and others, by writing in the *Commonweal*, condemning the punishment of the Walsall anarchists (Jan.) . . 6 May, „

Walter (the *Times*) *v.* Steinkopff (the *St. James's Gazette*), to restrain the copying of articles; verdict for plaintiff with some of the costs, 13, 17 May; 2 June, „

Buckley *v.* Edwards, see under *Judges* . 21 May, „

Mr. Henry de Vere Vane's claim to the ancient barony of Barnard in Durham, vacant by the death of the duke of Cleveland, granted by the house of lords . . . . 30 May, „

Mrs. Carlill *v.* the Carbolic Smoke Ball company, claiming 100*l.*, which the company had engaged to give to any person who had tried the smoke ball as a preventive of influenza without success (by advertisement, 13 Nov. 1891); verdict for plaintiff . . . . 4 July, „

Mr. Bottems, contractor, *v.* corporation of York; the court of appeal decides (against the plaintiff) that the terms of a ruinous contract must be fulfilled . . . . . 16 July, „

"International Society of Literature, Science and Art" started Dec. 1890; 4 days' trial for frauds; sir Gilbert E. Campbell, bart., sentenced to 18 months' imprisonment, with hard labour, for conspiracy; Wm. James Morgan and Joseph S. Tomkins (organizers), 8 and 5 years, for fraud; Wm. H. Steadman, 15 months; David Tolmie, 6 months; Charles M. Clarke, 4 months, 27 Sept. „

Margaret J. Smith sentenced to 10 years' penal servitude for forging a deed, in which she claimed part of the property of the late Mr. Park; her accomplices: Wm. Micklethwaite, 7 years; John Paul, 5 years; Thomas Allistone, 12 months; Sarah Ingram, 6 months . . . 27 Sept. „

Thomas Neill, *alias* Cream, M.D. Am., convicted of the murder of Matilda Clover (an unfortunate) by strychnine, 21 Oct.; executed . . 15 Nov. „
[He was accused of the murder of 3 other women.]

Mrs. Claudine Olivia Leader (wife of lieut. H. P. Leader) *v.* Mrs. Eleanor C. Smyth (wife of major-general J. G. Smyth), for slander, in accusing her of stealing a diamond brooch; Mr. Justice Day, queen's bench; Mr. Lockwood for plaintiff; sir Edward Clarke for defendant; verdict for plaintiff, 500*l.* damages . . . . 1–4 Nov. 1892
[For comments adverse to the plaintiff in the *Morning*, 31 Oct., 1 Nov., Mr. Bennett, editor, was fined 100*l.*, and Mr. Boyle, publisher, 50*l.*, 2 Nov.]

Manslaughter of Dr. Wm. P. Kirwan, 12 Oct., at Whitecross-st., S.E.; Edward Waller and Charles Balch sentenced to penal servitude for 20 years; John James Noble to 14 years . 18–19 Nov. „

Mr. Charlewood, registrar to the bishop of Manchester *v.* the rev. J. P. Foster, for libel; verdict for plaintiff, 200*l.* damages . . . 26 Nov. „

Will of Miss Ellen Roe, sometimes a lunatic, sustained against medical opinions . . 9 Dec. „

Mr. Harry Parminter (a promoter of the unsuccessful Edison phonographic toy and automaton company) *v.* London stereoscopic company, for alleged slander; verdict for defendants, with costs . . . . . . 13 Jan. 1893

Rev. Wilding *v.* canon Hayman and Mr. Fortescue Harrison (similar case to that of Miss M. E. T. Knox, 25 March, 1892); verdict for plaintiff, 450*l.*, 23 Jan. „

Messrs. Samuel Hope Morley and Arnold Morley (executors of their brother Henry Morley an epileptic, who, when insane, committed suicide) *v.* Mr. William H. Loughnan, and his brothers, Alfred and Henry Loughnan, members of the "close order" of the Plymouth brethren, and Mr. Charles Sleeman, not called, to recover about 140,000*l.*, alleged to have been obtained at various times by undue influence; 7 days' trial; painful evidence; verdict for the plaintiffs . . . . 27 Jan. „

For the Yelverton and Moseley case, see *Bahama Isles*, 2 Feb. 1893.

Missing Word Competition, see *Lotteries*, 9 Feb. 1893.

Coxon (family) *v.* Mrs. Schofield; the voluntary settlement in 1879 on a boy, falsely asserted by Mrs. Schofield to be the son of herself and her late husband, F. C. Coxon (killed while hunting, March, 1877), set aside, and the money received by her ordered to be repaid to the Coxon family; Chancery division . . . . . 16 Feb. „

Charles Wells, engineer (a large winner at Monte Carlo), for fraudulently obtaining money (about 30,445*l.*) for bogus patents; sentenced to 8 years' penal servitude . . . . 9–15 March, „

Lord Howard de Walden's suit for divorce from his wife rejected, and judicial separation granted to her and custody of the child . 8–11 March, „

Worth (the celebrated Paris costumier firm, established 1858) *v.* Mrs. Bradley, for inserting in her advertisement "Worth et Cie;" compromise, 17 March, „

Edward S. W. de Cobain sentenced to 1 year's imprisonment for gross misdemeanour at Belfast, 21 March, „

Liberator building society, see under *Building societies*: trials, 17 March *et seq.*; James W. Hobbs and Horace Granville Wright sentenced to 12 years' penal servitude for forgery, and to 5 years (concurrently) for fraud (J. Hobbs released on medical grounds, Jan. 1898); George Newman to 5 years for fraud . . 27 March, „

The dowager duchess of Sutherland ordered to pay a fine of 250*l.* and costs, and to be imprisoned for 6 weeks, for contempt of the probate division in burning a letter brought to her for inspection (on 12 April), 18 April; arrested . . 21 April, „

Hansard publishing union (*see above*, April, 1892) trial closed . . . . . . 26 April, „

Charles T. Gatty *v.* Henry R. Farquharson, M.P. for W. Dorset, for libel; queen's bench; damages awarded 5000*l.*, 20 June; appeal . 21 June, „

The dowager duchess of Sutherland *v.* the duke of Sutherland, respecting leases; her case dismissed . . . . 21 June, „

Aimé H. Meunier convicted of the murder of Charlotte Pearcey, aged 71, at Longeye, near Bromsgrove, on 13 Jan. . . . . 28 June, „

Mr. Hormuzd Rassam (see *Abyssinia*, 1864, *British Museum*, 1884, *Nineveh*, 1854) *v.* Mr. E. A. Budge, for libel and slander in 1891; verdict for plaintiff, damages 50*l*. . . . . 28 June—3 July, 1893

Dr. Edwin W. Alabone (American) *v.* Mr. Henry E. Morton, at first associates, afterwards rivals in professing to cure consumption by bogus remedies; verdict for plaintiff; Mr. Justice Wright hopes that further legal notice will be taken of the case in regard to both parties, 8 July, ,,

Mr. J. H. Wilson, M.P., general secretary of the Seamen's and Firemen's union *v.* Spottiswoode and another, for libel in the *Shipping Gazette;* verdict for defendants . . . . 26 July, ,,

Messrs. Allan & Co., steamship owners, *v.* Mr. J. H. Wilson, M.P., for libel in a handbill and pamphlet; damages awarded to the plaintiffs, 200*l*. . . . . 9 Aug. ,,

Daniel Phelan and his wife Constance sentenced to 6 and 9 months' penal servitude for brutal cruelty to their 2 children, aged 3 years and 21 months, Chester . . . . . . 19, 20 Oct. ,,

Miss J. Mighell *v.* the sultan of Johore (see *Johore*), Nov. ,,

James Barber Edwards (a trustee), 76, pleaded guilty of defalcation of 70,000*l*.; sentence, 8 years' penal servitude . . . . . . 21 Nov. ,,

Paul Joly, aged 25, and Celestan Joly, aged 17 (French), sentenced to 20 years' and 5 years' penal servitude respectively, for extorting 650*l*. from Mr. Pardoe, of Brighton, by threats of false accusation . . . . . . 29 Nov. ,,

Alfred John Monson tried at Edinburgh for the murder (or attempt) of lieut. W. C. Hambrough, at Ardlamont, Argyllshire, in Aug.; a mysterious case connected with insurance; verdict, *not proven* . . . . . . 12–22 Dec. ,,

Zierenberg and wife *v.* Labouchere, for libel in *Truth* respecting St. James' home for female inebriates, charging the plaintiffs with cruel tyranny; 20 days' trial; verdict for defendant, 13 Dec. ,,

The Nobel's Explosives company *v.* Dr. Anderson (see *Cordite*) . . . . 30 Jan.—14 Feb. 1894

Martin and wife *v.* trustees of British museum (*which see*) . . . . . . 27 Feb. ,,

Trial respecting the collision of the *Ibis* and the *Fortuna;* 6 days; verdict, not caused by wilful action of Henry Rumbell or incitement of Mr. Henry Smethurst . . . . . 19 March, ,,

Anarchists possessing explosives; Farnara sentenced to 20 years' and Francis Polti to 10 years' penal servitude . . . . 4 May, ,,

New Zealand loan and mercantile agency company (*which see*) in chancery . . . April—May, ,,

Hopegood *v.* French (will case); 7 days' trial; settled by arrangement . . . . . 5 June, ,,

The case of the duke of Sutherland and the dowager duchess in the probate division settled by arrangement . . . . . . 7 June, ,,

Mr. Henry J. B. Montgomery (author of *The British Navy*, published in 1885–6) *v.* prof. Laughton and others, for libel; Mr. Montgomery's book is described in prof. Laughton's article in the *Army and Navy Gazette* as "a mass of impudent and scurrilous falsehoods;" verdict for the defendants, with costs . . . . 12 June, ,,

Ella Gillespie, nurse, sentenced to 5 years' penal servitude for cruelty to children in the Hackney workhouse school at Brentford . . . 20 June, ,,

Miss Trebelli-Bettini *v.* the Royal Academy of Music; Madame Trebelli's will, bequeathing property to the academy, affirmed, with recommendations; 10 days' trial . . . . 28 June, ,,

Paul Koczula and George Schmerfeld, accessory (respited), sentenced to death for murder of Sophia F. M. Rasch, keeper of a restaurant in Shaftesbury-avenue, 28 July; Koczula executed, 14 Aug. ,,

Trial of 30 anarchists begins . . . . 6 Aug. ,,

James Canham Read (very depraved), for murder of Florence Dennis, one of his victims, at Prittlewell, Southend, 24 June; Chelmsford, 12–15 Nov.; executed . . . . 4 Dec. ,,

Haufstengl *v. Daily Graphic*, see *Copyright*, 1894.

Mr. Geo. Edwd. Brock, Mr. Geo. Dibley, Mr. Morrell Theobald, major John Thos. Wright and Mr. Frank M. Coldwells (died 29 July), "the Balfour group" directors of Liberator building society and the Lands allotment company, &c., prosecuted for conspiracy and fraud, 11 Feb. 1895; committed and bailed . . . 4 April, 1895

Patrick A. Chance *v.* Wm. O'Brien, M.P., for debt; verdict for plaintiff, 407*l*. 0*s*. 11*d*. . . . 14 Feb. ,,

Henry Fredk. Nash, secretary of Bayswater and Kensington building society, pleads guilty of misappropriating 196*l*. 17*s*. 9*d*.; sentenced to 5 years' penal servitude . . . . 26 March, ,,

The marquis of Queensberry charged with publishing a libel against Mr. Oscar Wilde, author; acquitted, the case being withdrawn . 3–5 April, ,,

Mr. Oscar Wilde and Alfred Taylor tried for misdemeanours, 19 April; partial acquittal; jury disagree; new trial ordered, 1 May; Mr. Wilde bailed, 7 May; Alfred Taylor convicted, 21 May, and Oscar Wilde, 25 May; both sentenced to 2 years' imprisonment with hard labour . 25 May, ,,

Dunham *v.* Russell; claim for 40,183*l*., the property of Mrs. Mabel L. Theobald, an intestate widow of Mr. James Theobald, M.P.; an intricate case; verdict for the defendant, Miss Kate Russell, sister of Mrs. Theobald . . 9 April, ,,

Countess Russell *v.* earl Russell; verdict for defendant; judicial separation decreed, April, 1894; her appeal dismissed and separation annulled . . . . 7 Aug. ,,

Jabez Spencer Balfour, ex-M.P., prosecuted for conspiracy and fraud (see *Building Societies*) at Bow-street, 6 May; committed for trial, appeal set aside . . . . . . 1 July, ,,

House of lords: appeal of Mr. Osgood Hanbury Mackenzie for divorce from his wife, Minnie Amy, for desertion (4 years); appeal dismissed, the desertion being justified by her husband's great cruelty . . . . 16 May, ,,

Georgina Priestly Salisbury, infant (born April, 1894), claiming property of alleged father, George Henry Salisbury (died 7 Jan. 1894) *v.* Rawson (chancery division), 23 May *et seq.;* on 14th day a statement was read from Dr. Capon asserting that the claimant was the daughter of Miss Florence Wright; Mr. Jelf, the plaintiff's counsel, gave up her case, and Mr. Justice Hawkins adjourned the trial, 17 June; verdict for defendant (18th day), 7 Aug.; case dismissed, 30 Nov.; appeal rejected . . . . 9 Dec. ,,

Mr. W. T. Stead fined 100*l*. for contempt of court for an article in *Review of Reviews* against Jabez Balfour; appeal set aside . . . . 1 July, ,,

Michael Cleary and others tried for murder (see *Witchcraft*) . . . . 5 July, ,,

John Lynchehaun, a bailiff, for attempt to murder his mistress, Mrs. Agnes M'Donnell, in Achill island, Ireland, by thrusting her into a burning building, &c., sentenced to penal servitude for life . . . . 17 July, ,,

Messrs. Wright & Co. *v.* Mr. Daniel Hennessy, sec. of Nat. association of plasterers, for interference with their business and libel; verdict for plaintiffs, 800*l*. damages . . . . . 26 July, ,,

Frances Rose, lady Gunning, sentenced to 1 year's hard labour for forgery . . . . . 10 Sept. ,,

Robt. A. Coombes (13), murderer of his mother, acquitted as insane . . . . . 17 Sept. ,,

Jabez Spencer Balfour and four others (see *above*), 4 April, 1895, tried for fraud in relation to the Liberator building society, and the Lands allotment co. and other companies, &c., before Mr. justice Bruce; counsel for the crown, sir Richard Webster, the attorney-gen., and 5 others, 25 Oct.; all convicted, except Dibley, on whom the jury disagreed, 20 Nov.; 2nd trial of Balfour, 21 Nov.; convicted, 27 Nov.; sentences, imprisonment: Balfour, 14 years' penal servitude [public examination as to his affairs, 27 Jan. 1898]; Brock, 9 months; Theobald, 4 months; the others discharged . . . . 28 Nov. ,,

Henry Wright, lodger, convicted, 4 Dec., of the murder of Mrs. Reynolds, her two sons, Wm. and Charles Reynolds, and grandson, Wm. Peck (11 Aug.); executed . . . . . . 24 Dec. ,,

Henry Bailey, sentenced to 3 years and 6 months' penal servitude, for stealing 31 ingots of silver, value 4,900*l*., the property of the Midland railway co., in Ossulston-street, N.W., 19 Nov.; Alexander Edw. Sarti, sentenced to 3 years' penal servitude for robbing Messrs. Elkington & Co., silversmiths, his employers, and for complicity in the silver robbery, 20 Dec.; George Barratt sentenced to 5 years' penal servitude, and Henry Gray to 18 months' hard labour for receiving the stolen ingots . . . . 22 Dec. 1895

John Skates and others convicted of fraud (see *Marriage*) . . . . 5 March, 1896

John Havelock Wilson, M.P. *v.* Collison and Rogers, for libel; verdict for plaintiff, one farthing damages 14 March; his request for parliamentary inquiry, refused by the commons, 17 March (see *above*, July, Aug. 1893).

Mrs. Arthur Kitson *v.* Dr. William S. Playfair and wife, for libel and slander; verdict for plaintiff, damages awarded by jury, 12,000*l.*; 7 days' trial, 21–27 March (execution stayed by consent; sum to be paid unconditionally) . . . 30 March, ,,

Tower Hamlets (St. George's division) election petition; Mr. Marks retains his seat, 40 days' trial, before baron Pollock and justice Bruce, 13 Feb.—1 April, ,,

Albert Millsom, 32, and Henry Fowler, 31, charged with the murder of Mr. Henry Smith, at Muswell-hill, on 13 Feb.; captured at Bath, after a desperate fight, 12 April; convicted, 21 May; executed . . . . 9 June, ,,

Walter *v.* *Central News*, see *Times* . 14 April, ,,

William Seaman, convicted of the murder of John Goodman Levy, 75, and Sarah Ann Gale, servant, at Mile-end . . . . 18 May, ,,

Amelia E. Dyer, convicted of infanticide (*which see*), 22 May; executed . . . . . 10 June ,,

Mrs. Langtry *v.* the Union bank of London (see *Jewels*) . . . . 5 May, ,,

Trollope and others *v.* the London Building Trades Federation and others, for posting a placard with a black border, containing a list of names of men charged with working; "Trollope's black list"; verdict, that the list is vindictive and malicious, and a perpetual injunction granted; damages, 500*l.* . . . . . . 24 April—4 May, ,,

Dr. Jameson and others, see *Transvaal*, Dec. 1895, July, 1896, *footnote*; and *Rhodesia*, Aug. 1896, Jan. 1897.

Elijah Galley, sentenced to 20 years' penal servitude, for killing Mr. and Mrs. Riley, in a fit of passion, in North-street, Pentonville, on 4 July, 11 Sept. ,,

See *Companies' Acts*, 16 Nov. 1896.

Mary Selina Elizabeth, lady Scott, John Cockerton, Fred. Kast (died, 11 Dec.), and Wm. Aylott, tried for libel (17 Sept.) against earl Russell, lady Scott's son-in-law, 23 Nov.; convicted, 7 Jan. 1897; sentence, 8 months' imprisonment without hard labour, 8 Jan. 1897.

Stiven *v.* Welsford, medical slander, 7 days' trial, verdict for the plaintiff, 75*l.* damages . 17 Dec. ,,

Messrs. Bailey & Co. *v.* the Officials of the Glass-bevellers' Union for malicious interference with their trade by picketing with violence, verdict for plaintiffs, 674*l.* 13*s.* damages . . 13 Jan. 1897

Hugh Campbell Browning *v.* Mostyn and others, 6 days' trial, verdict for the plaintiff, sustaining the will of Chas. Stuart Coningham, an important judgment . . . . . . 27 Jan. ,,

Maxim *v.* Anderson, see *Cordite* . . 4 March, ,,

The will of Mr. E. Hunter bequeathing between 80,000*l.* and 90,000*l.* &c., for ecclesiastical purposes, set aside as indefinite, 6 March [decision reversed by the court of appeal, 21 May; their finding reversed by the house of lords, and that of the court below restored, 18 May, 1899] . . ,,

Hawke *v.* Dunn, see *Betting Houses* . 13 March, ,,

Catherine Kempshall, 32, sentenced to death, 19 March, for the murder of Edgar S. Holland, merchant, Liverpool (29 Oct. 1896), respited, as insane . . . . 31 March, ,,

Mr. Samson Fox *v.* Mr. Jerome K. Jerome and others for alleged libels in *To-Day*, 31 March; 16 days' trial; verdict for plaintiff, farthing damages . . . . 7 May, ,,

The will of Mr. T. P. Hounsell, of Chertsey, who died in 1894, set aside by the probate court, on account of his gross delusions, described in papers found after his death . . . 1 April, ,,

Joseph Yates, solicitor, convicted of fraud, perjury, &c., penal servitude for life . . . . 21 May, ,,

Capt. Hill Kennedy sentenced to 5 years' penal servitude for perjury in a libel action . 2 June, ,,

Earl and countess Russell, judgment of court of appeal (see above, 1895) affirmed by the house of lords . . . . July, 1897

Charlton *v.* Phillips, disputed will, verdict for the plaintiff (5 days trial), testator not insane, 25 Nov. ,,

Labouchere *v.* H. Hess, proprietor of the *African Critic*, for an injunction to restrain the publication of his letters to the late G. A. Sala, granted, with costs as regards Mr. Hess, but refused with costs in regard to Mrs. Sala . . . 27 Nov. ,,

Allen *v.* Flood and Taylor, see *Times* . 16 Dec. ,,

Flood and Taylor *v.* Allen, shipwrights, for malicious injuries (dismissal from employment), verdict for plaintiffs in 1895; verdict upheld in court of appeal, 1895; verdict reversed by the house of lords, 6 judges against 3 (much discussed) . . . . 14 Dec. ,,

Lewis *v.* Clay, 11,113*l.* 15*s.* claimed by the plaintiff on two promissory notes, endorsed by defendant on assurances by lord Wm. Nevill that he was only witnessing a document, which he did not see; verdict for the defendant . . 18 Dec. ,,

Richard Archer Prince, 32, actor, convicted of the wilful murder of Wm. Charles Lewin, see *Adelphi*, Dec. 1897; detained as a criminal lunatic . . . . 13 Jan. 1898

Queen's bench: Jay (a money lender) *v.* sir Tatton Sykes, to recover 15,872*l.* odd, advanced on 5 promissory notes, signed by sir Tatton and lady Sykes; lady Sykes admitted her signature: verdict for the defendant, signatures to the other notes being forgeries; 5 days' trial . 18 Jan. ,,

Vladimir Bourtzeff, journalist, sentenced to 18 months, and Klement Wierzbicki, printer, to 2 months' imprisonment for publishing incitements to kill the czar . . . . 11 Feb. ,,

Lord William Nevill (37), sentenced to 5 years' penal servitude for fraud respecting securities (against Mr. Jas. Spender Clay) . . . . . 15 Feb. ,,

Mr. Russell Spokes for the Grosvenor Hotel company *v.* the directors, manager, and Mr. R. C. Drew, for conspiracy; verdict for plaintiff, with arrangements (9 days' trial) . . . 19 Feb. ,,

Mrs. Camilla Nicholls convicted of the manslaughter of her servant, Jane Popejoy, by ill-treatment and starvation (5 days' trial); sentenced to 7 years' penal servitude . 2 May, ,,

Thomas Edw. Brinsmead, and 5 other directors and promoters of the company of Thomas Edw. Brinsmead & Sons (Ltd.), convicted of conspiracy to defraud, and sentenced to various terms of imprisonment . . . . . 7 May, ,,

Walter Horsford convicted of the murder of Annie Holmes, by strychnine . . . . . 6 June, ,,

John Trodd, bootmaker, charged with attempting to murder count Arco-Valley, of the German embassy, and police-constable Whitefield by shooting them at Carlton House terrace, 15 June; prisoner certified to be a lunatic . 22 June, ,,

Wm. Maunsell Collins, 48, surgeon, charged with the wilful murder of Emily Edith Uzielli, 27 June; convicted of manslaughter, sentenced to 7 years' penal servitude . . . . 2 July, ,,

The hypnotic will case—Kingsbury *v.* Howard. The will of Mrs. Howard (who died Dec. 1897), devising to Dr. Kingsbury, her medical attendant and friend (who had in her case applied hypnotism up to 1894), her residuary estate (a vast sum), was declared to be valid by the probate court . . . . . . 13–19 July, ,,

Fred. Tomlinson, 34, sentenced to life imprisonment for attempts to wreck trains . 18 Nov. ,,

John Lloyd Whitmarsh, surgeon, convicted of the murder of Alice Bayley, sentenced to death, 26 Oct.; commuted to 12 years' penal servitude, 25 Nov. ,,

Albert Davies sentenced to 3 years' penal servitude for fraud and forgery respecting col. Shipway's pedigree, &c. . . . . . . 23 Nov. ,,

Mrs. Athalie Mills, Christian science "healer," and Kate Lyon charged with the manslaughter of the late Harold Frederic, author, by neglecting to provide him with proper medical treatment; both found *not guilty* and discharged for want of evidence . . . . 5 Dec. ,,

Robert John (lieut.) Wark, tried for the murder of Jane Yates, sentenced to death, with a strong recommendation to mercy, 8 Dec. 1898; reprieved, 10 Dec.; petition to the Home Office, 54,000 signatures, 5 Jan. 1899; sentence commuted to 3 years' penal servitude . . 9 Jan. 1899

See *Blackmailing*, 1899.

Miss Bertha Petersen charged with the murder of John Whibley (whom she shot at Biddenden), 5 Feb.; proved insane . . . . . 12 July, „

George R. Birt charged with falsifying the half-yearly balance-sheets of the Millwall docks co., sentenced to 9 months' hard labour . 13 May, „

Mrs. Keighley, palmist, *v.* printers and publisher of the *Society* newspaper, for libel; 1,000*l.* damages for plaintiff . . . . 14 June, „

Joseph Slater and Robt. James sentenced to 20 years' penal servitude for manslaughter of a policeman at Harwell, Berks (3 April), 16 June, „

Mostyn *v.* Atherton: an action by sir Pyers Mostyn and G. Chator and Co., for an injunction to restrain the defendant from diverting or abstracting water from St. Winifred's well and the Holywell stream, Flintshire, and from interfering with the flow of water in the stream through the plaintiff's land; injunction granted, with costs, 29 June, „

George and Sigmund Wolff, convicted of keeping a common lottery, and of fraud in connection with bogus "missing word" competitions, sentenced respectively to 10 and 4 months' imprisonment, 30 June, „

Mary Ann Ansell, convicted of murdering her sister (inmate of an asylum), by sending her by post poisoned cake, found guilty, after 2 hours' consultation, and sentenced to death . 30 June, „

Arthur Kirby and Morris Clifford charged with conspiracy to defraud in connection with the Coolgardie mint and Iron King gold mines (limited), sentenced to 6 months' hard labour each . . . . 4 July, „

See *Glasgow*, Oct. 1899.

Walter *v.* Lane. Mr. Justice North grants an injunction restraining Mr. John Lane from further publication of "Appreciations and addresses of lord Rosebery," containing reports of speeches taken from the *Times*, 10 Aug. 1899; his decision reversed in the court of appeal, 9 Nov. [the last judgment reversed and Mr. Justice North's decision restored by the house of lords, 6 Aug. 1900].

Beall, Singleton, Lambert, and Wain tried (15 days) for conspiring to defraud in connection with the London and Scottish banking and discount corporation; Lambert acquitted; Beall sentenced to 4 years' imprisonment; Singleton to 18 and Wain to 12 months' imprisonment . . 18 Nov. „

Dumbell's bank trial, see *Man, isle of*, Nov. 1900.

Sir Robt. Peel's application for leave to sell certain heirlooms, pictures, &c., for provision for lady Peel and her child, granted, in court of appeal; lord Peel, on whose appeal against a former order the action took place, ordered to pay the costs . . . . 4 Dec. „

Louise Masset, 36, a governess, convicted of the murder of her illegitimate son, aged 3½ years, at Dalston railway station, and sentenced to death, 18 Dec. „

Wm. Chard Williams, 41, and Ada Chard Williams, 24, charged with the murder of Selina Ellen Jones, 21 months old (entrusted to the care of the female prisoner, Aug. 1899); the woman found guilty and sentenced to death, the man acquitted, 17 Feb. 1900

Mr. E. Vizetelly, journalist, *v.* Mudie's library (limited), for a libel in "Emin Pasha, his Life and Work"; plaintiff awarded 100*l.* damages, 6 March (appeal dismissed with costs, 27 April) . „

Howard Gray charged with contempt of court in regard to a scurrilous article on Mr. Justice Darling in the Birmingham *Daily Argus*, fined 100*l.* and 25*l.* costs . . . . 28 March, „

Reg. *v.* Stoddart: Mrs. Ada Stoddart fined 50*l.*, with costs, under the Betting Act, 1853, for keeping or using a house or office for betting or receiving money in lieu of payment of money dependent on the result of a race . 21 Nov. „

Reg. *v.* Cockerton, see *Education* . . 20 Dec. 1900

Benjamin Green Lake, 62, solicitor of high standing, sentenced to 12 years' imprisonment for converting to his own use trust funds . 22 Jan. 1901

Thos. Sismey, 37, solicitor, pleaded guilty to conspiring to defraud a Mrs. Clarke of 14,000*l.*, and J. Arnold, 39, solicitor, pleaded guilty to appropriating trust funds; Arnold sentenced to 10 years' imprisonment and Sismey to 15 months' hard labour; James Greenfield, 56, solicitor, sentenced to a year's imprisonment for converting 960*l.*, a client's money, to his own use (pleaded guilty) . . . . . 25 Jan. „

Barnet Abrahams, 41, sentenced to 20 years' imprisonment for the manslaughter of a constable, 5 Feb. „

Mr. Justice Byrne's decision *re* the ownership of 7 tapestries in the late Mme. de Falbe's drawing-room at Luton Hoo reversed in court of appeal, her executors' appeal granted, as the tapestries were affixed as chattels and not for the improvement of the freehold . . . . . 7 Feb. „

[This decision upheld by the lords, appeal dismissed with costs, 6 Feb. 1902.]

Chas. B. Smith pleads guilty to converting trust funds to his own use, sentenced to 6 months' imprisonment . . . . . 8 Feb. „

Maidstone election petition: election of Mr. J. Barker, liberal, declared void for bribery, by Messrs. Justices Kennedy and Channell, 13 Feb. „

Robt. Porteous, solicitor, sentenced to 3 years' imprisonment for conspiracy to defraud, in connection with a bogus firm of stockbrokers, 15 Feb. „

Yarmouth murder: Herbert John Bennett, convicted of the murder of his wife on the beach, Yarmouth (22 Sept. 1900), 6 days' trial before the lord chief justice; sentenced to death, 2 March, „

Mr. Arthur Chamberlain, brother of Mr. Joseph Chamberlain, colonial secretary, *v.* the *Star* newspaper co. for libels in reference to firms and companies with which the plaintiff was connected: verdict for plaintiff, with 200*l.* damages, 20–26 March, „

Mr. Neville Chamberlain, son of Mr. Joseph Chamberlain, *v.* the same defendants, for libel in the *Morning Leader*; apology, and 1,500*l.* accepted for damages and costs . . . . 26 March, „

Countess Russell *v.* earl Russell, suit undefended, divorce granted, 28 March [made absolute, 28 Oct.] . . . . „

Charles McCarthy *v.* the *Evening News*, for libel, verdict for plaintiff, 1,000*l.* damages . 24 April, „

Mr. Joseph Stoddart, proprietor of *Sporting Luck*, sentenced to 6 months' imprisonment and 50gs. costs for infringing the Betting Acts, 30 April (his appeal dismissed with costs 6 Nov.) . „

The *Daily Mail* (newspaper) ordered to pay 2,500*l.* damages to Miss Hettie Chattell, for libel, 15 July (damages 1,000*l.* on appeal, or a new trial ordered, 12 Dec.) . . . . „

Earl Russell tried by the house of lords for bigamy, and sentenced to 3 months' imprisonment, 18 July, „

Taff Vale Railway *v.* the Amalgamated Railway Servants' Society: the house of lords decide that a trade union can be sued in its registered name as a corporate body, restoring a judgment of Mr. Justice Farwell given in Sept. 1900 (reversed in Nov. by court of appeal) . . . 22 July, „

The proprietor of *Sporting Luck*, a journal, fined 50*l.* and sentenced to 3 months' imprisonment for publishing an advertisement of a "Derby" sweepstake to be drawn in Holland . 25 July, „

The house of lords upholds the decision of the court of appeal, allowing lord Cowley's late wife, who had obtained a divorce from him, to style herself countess Cowley . . . . . 30 July, „

Quinn *v.* Leathem (case of appeal), *re* the boycotting case at Lisburn, near Belfast; verdict for Leathem, the *plaintiff*, in the first trial, with 200*l.* damages, and 50*l.* additional damages against 4 others concerned in the publication of "black lists"; the decision confirmed by the Irish appeal court, and again by the house of lords, 5 Aug. „

George Stephens, *alias* Thompson, and Chas. McNelly, *alias* McMay, sentenced to 5 years' imprisonment for conspiring to obtain money, &c., from Mrs. Annie Renwick, widow, 18 Sept. 1901
Chas. Tibbets and Chas. Windust found guilty at Bristol assizes of conspiring to prevent the due course of justice by publishing certain articles in the *Weekly Dispatch*, 13 July; the convictions confirmed by lord Alverstone and others, 9 Nov. ,,
Rev. Joseph Nesbitt *v.* Mr. Mercer, of Rodmersham house, and another, for libel; damages 1,100*l.*, end Nov. ,,
Marais case: see *Cape Colony*, 18 Dec. 1901.
Frank and Laura Jackson, *alias* Horos, tried for offences under the Criminal Law Amendment act, 18 Dec.; the man sentenced to 15 years', the woman to 7 years' penal servitude . 20 Dec. ,,
Samuel Stanton, ex-manager of a branch of Messrs. Foster's bank, pleaded guilty to embezzling bank money, and was sentenced to 3 years' imprisonment . . . . 30 Dec. ,,
Dr. Fred. E. Krause, 33, barrister-at-law (special commandant of Johannesburg when it surrendered to lord Roberts), arrested 2 Sept.; sentenced to 2 years' imprisonment for attempting to solicit Cornelius Broeksma to murder Mr. J. D. Forster in the Transvaal . . . . 18 Jan. 1902
King *v.* the abp. of Canterbury and C. A. Cripps, esq., K.C. (vicar-general); see *Church of England*, 10 Feb.
Chas. Bank Nelson, ex-director of Dumbell's bank, Isle of Man, *which see*, appeals against a conviction and sentence of 5 years' imprisonment for applying to his own use the money of the bank, granted by the lords, and *that part* of the conviction set aside . . . . 12 Feb. ,,
Mr. J. D. Forster, barrister, of the Transvaal, *v.* A. B. Markham, M.P., for libel in a letter in the *Times*, 25 Feb. 1901; damages 2,000*l.* . 12 Feb. ,,
Goudie, clerk (pleaded guilty), Burge, Kelly, and Stiles charged with forgery, fraud, conspiracy, and false pretences, whereby the bank of Liverpool was robbed of over 160,000*l.*, 17 Feb.; Goudie and Burge sentenced to 10 years', Kelly and Stiles (who pleaded guilty to conspiracy to defraud) to 2 years' imprisonment . 22 Feb. ,,
Bottomley *v.* Hess, for libel; verdict for plaintiff, 1,000*l.* damages . . . . 8 March, ,,
Arthur S. Francis, solicitor, pleaded guilty to appropriating, as *trustee*, 6,500*l.* of the countess of Orkney's funds; sentenced to 5 years' imprisonment . . . . 13 March, ,,
Cowen *v.* Labouchere and another, libel action, 1 May; jury unable to agree, discharged, 13 May, ,,
Countess Cowley awarded 100*l.* damages and costs in a libel action *v.* the editor and publishers of the paper *Candid Friend* . . . . . 13 May, ,,
Bank of England forgery case; see *Forgery*, 16 May, ,,
Rosalie Mansell *v.* the proprietors of the *Sun* newspaper for an alleged libel; damages 600*l.*, king's bench . . . . 27 May, ,,
Father Bernard Vaughan, a Jesuit, *v.* the proprietors of the *Rock* newspaper, for libel published in a letter; damages 300*l.* . . . . 3 June, ,,
Mr. Le Mesurier *v.* Mr. Van Cuylenberg, proprietor of a Ceylon newspaper, for libel; damages 1,500*l.*, 11 June, ,,
London and Globe Finance Corporation *v.* Basil Montgomery & Co. and others, king's bench (9 days' trial), verdict for all defendants, on the jury answering in the negative two questions: "Did the defendants agree not to sell the Lake View shares deposited with them below 17*l.* a share?" "Was there an agreement that the profits of the sale of such shares should be divided with the plaintiffs?" etc. . . . 12–16 June, ,,
[The attorney-gen. refused to instruct the public prosecutor to take the case up, see *Times*, 29 Dec. 1902].
Henry Beels, 27, a rough, see *Hooligan*, sentenced to 7 years' imprisonment for the manslaughter of Mr. Herbert Murray Spicer (2 June) in Upper Woburn-place . . . . 3 July, ,,
Henry White, 22, sentenced to 10 years' imprisonment for blackmailing Mr. Austin Neame, 16 Sept. ,,
Gerald and Herbert Kennaway sentenced to 7 years' imprisonment for various elaborately-schemed forgeries . . . . . 16 Sept. 1902
Mrs. Watt *v.* lady Violet Beauchamp, for libel; verdict for plaintiff, with 5,000*l.* damages . 30 Oct. ,,
Mr. T. C. McQuire, actor and theatrical manager, awarded 100*l.* damages, with costs, from the *Western Morning News* co. (limited) *re* a disparaging criticism (25 June, 1901) on *The Major*, a musical piece . . . . . . 3 Nov. ,,
Mr. J. C. Kenworthy, author and lecturer, *v.* the *Sun* newspaper, for alleged libel, 140*l.* damages for plaintiff. . . . . . . 13 Nov. ,,
Cowen *v.* Labouchere, libel action, 11 days' trial; verdict for defendant . . . . . 17 Nov. ,,
Central criminal court: John Goodfellow, analytical chemist, pleaded guilty to forgery, sentenced to 3 years' imprisonment; Wm. Armstrong, late manager of the Richmond branch (London, City and Midland bank), pleaded guilty to embezzlement, sentenced to 4 years' imprisonment, 18 Nov. ,,
Walter Butters, cashier, Bayswater branch (Union of London and Smith's bank), pleaded guilty to embezzlement, sentenced to 4 years' imprisonment . . . . 19 Nov. ,,
Mrs. Annie Elizabeth Penruddocke, 38, of Compton-park, Wilts, tried for alleged cruelty and neglect of her daughter Constance, aged 6, found guilty on two counts of the charge, and fined 50*l.*, central criminal court (Dr. C. Penruddocke entrusted with the care of the child, 27 Feb. 1903), 21 Nov. ,,
John M'Keever charged with the murder of the late Mr. John Kensit, see *Public Worship*, acquitted, Liverpool . . . . . 11 Dec. ,,
Robt. Milward, 64, solicitor, sentenced to 6 years' imprisonment for frauds, Birmingham . 11 Dec. ,,
Mary Spillane, 28, sentenced to death for murder of her illegitimate infant, 11 Dec.; reprieved, 18 Dec. ,,
The Bootle Murder: Ethel Rollinson, 20, and Eva Eastwood, 17, sentenced to death for the murder by suffocation of Miss Eliza Marsden, 71 (commuted to life imprisonment 22 Dec.) . 13 Dec. ,,
Ada Kirk, 25, laundress, convicted of the murder of infant daughter (but found insane) . 16 Dec. ,,
Emma "Kitty" Byron, 24, sentenced to death, but *recommended to mercy*, for the murder of Arthur Reginald Baker, stock-jobber (in Post-office court, Lombard-street, 10 Nov.), 17 Dec. (commuted to life-imprisonment, 22 Dec.) . ,,
Taff Vale railway co. *v.* Amalgamated soc. of railway servants, concerning the strike, Aug. 1900, *which see*; verdict for plaintiffs (with damages 23,000*l.*, settled 23 Feb. 1903) . . 19 Dec. ,,
Philip Bernstein, Solomon and William Barmash sentenced respectively to 20, 15 and 10 years' imprisonment for forging bank of England notes (Solomon Barmash committed suicide in the cell the same day) . . . . 7 Jan. 1903
"Col." Lynch (see *High Treason*) . 23 Jan. ,,
PEASENHALL MURDER: Wm. Gardiner, 35, carpenter, charged with the murder of Rose Harsent, on 1 June, 1902; the jury, unable to agree after 5 hours' deliberation, were discharged, 10 Nov.; and again at the second trial, after over 2 hours', 24 Jan. 1903; a *nolle prosequi* was decided on and Gardiner was released at Ipswich . 29 Jan. ,,
Annie Walters, 54, Amelia Sach, 29, sentenced to death for baby-farming murders, 16 Jan.; executed . . . . 23 Feb. ,,
Edgar Edwards, 44, convicted of the murder of Mr. and Mrs. Darby and infant child, in Camberwell, sentenced to death, 13 Feb. (executed 3 March) ,,
Court of Session, Edinburgh: the Spanish minister of marine and others *v.* the Clydebank engineering and shipping co., for failure to deliver 4 torpedo-boat destroyers, which the defendants had contracted to build for the Spanish government; plaintiffs awarded 67,500*l.*, with interest, 18 Feb. ,,
Mr. S. H. Wallace sues Tenessee, lady Cook, for remuneration for services, and damages for an alleged libel and slander; granted 550*l.* 3 March, ,,
[Application for new trial allowed by court of appeal, 15 June, 1903.]

Divorce suit, Gordon *v.* Gordon and Gordon, president of the court refuses to vary previous order directing the child Cecily Margot to be given into the custody of her father, 10 March; writ of attachment and order for contempt of court against lady Granville Gordon, who had given an undertaking not to remove the child from her residence in Hereford-square without leave of the court, but had taken her over to Dunkirk in a tug from Tilbury, 8 March . . . . . . 12 March, 1903

Bethesda Libel Case: Lord Penrhyn awarded 500*l.* damages in action for libel against Mr. W. J. Parry, formerly secretary of the Quarrymen's union . . . . 13 March, ,,

Southwark Poisoning Case: Severino Klosowski (George Chapman) convicted of the murder, by antimonial poisoning, of Maud Marsh (19), at the "Crown" public-house, Borough High-street; two other indictments for antimonial poisoning of Isabella Spink in 1897, and Elizabeth Taylor in 1901; (executed 7 April) . . . 19 March, ,,

Court of Appeal upholds decision that the bicycle toll for crossing the Cressage bridge over the river Severn is 1*d.*, a bicycle not being a "two-wheeled carriage"; the trustees demanded 6*d.*, 23 March, ,,

The landlord of the "Royal Crescent" hotel, Filey, Yorks, fined 20*s.* for permitting a party of ladies and gentlemen to use a room in the hotel for a progressive whist drive, in which prizes were competed for . . . . 27 March, ,,

Mr. Richard Ganthony recovers 200*l.* damages from proprietors of *Daily Express*, owing to paragraph ascribing the success of his play "A Message from Mars" to its alleged re-writing by Mr. G. Hawtrey . . . . 3 April, ,,

Cavendish *v.* Strutt and others, to annul a voluntary settlement on the ground of improper influence through the medium of a "planchette," end Feb.; judgment for plaintiff . . . . 13 May ,,

Otto Monson, Gustav Rau, and Willem Smith, found guilty of the murder of the captain and 6 of the crew of the barque *Veronica* while on a voyage from Ship island, Mississippi to Montevideo . . . . 14 May, ,,

Henry George, private detective, sentenced to 5 years' penal servitude for perjury in divorce suit of Worsley *v.* Worsley . . . . 25 May, ,,

Stewart *v.* Webber and others, the defendants (excluding Webber) found guilty of fraudulent representations to induce the public to buy shares of the Anglo-Dutch exploration company, 26 May, ,,

Head *v. Morning Post*, for alleged libel in connection with his candidature for a directorship of the Royal Steam Packet company; verdict for defendants . . . . 27 May, ,,

Mr. Hugh Watt non-suited in action against Mr. Horatio Bottomley to recover 7,160*l.* interest on 65,000*l.*; both parties to pay own costs, 28 May, ,,

Moat Farm Murder, Samuel Herbert Dougal, ex-soldier, convicted of the murder of Miss Camille Cecile Holland, with whom he had resided, at Moat farm, Clavering, near Chelmsford. Miss Holland mysteriously disappeared 19 May, 1899; the discovery of the murder was occasioned by the prosecution of Dougal on the charge of forging a cheque in the name of his victim; sentenced to death 23 June; executed 14 July, ,,

Rev. Chas. Garnett, a nonconformist minister, nonsuited in his action against the *Christian World* for alleged libel, imputing that various degrees he held from the university of Harriman, Tennessee, U.S., were "bogus and worthless," . 16 June, ,,

Alfred Samuel Nelson, 26, a cabinetmaker, found guilty of the murder of Edith Alice Fitt, at Lakenham; recommended to mercy on ground of his mental condition . . . . mid June, ,,

Crown v. *British Museum*, to establish the right of the crown to certain gold articles as treasure-trove, discovered in 1896 on the shores of lake Foyle, Ireland, and bought by the trustees of the British Museum; judgment in favour of the crown . . . . 20 June, ,,

Committee of privileges reject petition for the Poulett peerage presented by William Turnour Thos. Poulett, declaring him to be illegitimate, mid July, ,,

Springfield *v. Evening Standard*, for alleged infringement of copyright in a paragraph published in the *Daily Mail;* suit dismissed . 27 July, 1903

Judicial committee of the privy council on appeal of Messrs. H. Graves & Co. printsellers, Pall Mall, decided with the Canadian court that the Fine Art Copyright act of 1862 is limited to the United Kingdom . . . . . 28 July, ,,

Resolution of the Royal Aquarium company directing that on its liquidation 7,800*l.* should be distributed among its officers and servants, set aside . . . . 29 July, ,,

Demetrius S. Constantinidi having sought a divorce from his wife, Julia, *née* Ralli (from whom in 1889 he was judicially separated on the ground of her desertion), is awarded by the jury damages assessed at 25,000*l.* (Mrs. Constantinidi in 1902 obtained a divorce in S. Dakota, U.S., and married the co-respondent, Dr. H. W. Lance), 29 July, ,,

Injunction granted to Miss Olga Nethersole to prevent Mr. and Mrs. Bell infringing her play *Sappho*, adapted from Daudet's novel by Mr. B. Espinasse . . . . 30 July, ,,

The purchase of certain gold mining shares by the British America corporation from the London and Globe Finance corporation, declared not to be binding on the former corporation, 31 July, ,,

Arthur Wilkes, 21, soldier, sentenced to death for the murder of John James, at Altcar, on 16 May, 31 July, ,,

Court of Appeal allows appeal of the Glamorgan coal company against decision in favour of the North Wales Miners' federation, who were sued for inducing the workmen in plaintiff's collieries to break their contract of service. . 11 Aug. ,,

Judgment on appeal in favour of Messrs. Barclay, bankers, against the corporation of Sheffield to recover 11,487*l.* 17*s.* 5*d.* on loss by a forged transfer which the corporation had to make good, and sought to recover from Messrs. Barclay, 11 Aug. ,,

Chancellor of the Consistory court refuses to grant a faculty to the vicar and churchwardens of St. Sepulchre's church, Holborn viaduct, to enlarge their schools on the ground that, although desirable, it would be a contravention of the Disused Burial Grounds act . . . 17 Aug. ,,

Jacob Blitz, 35, committed for trial for the alleged attempted murder of John Lang, the prisoner having stabbed Lang with a knife, the point of which penetrated his heart; the wounded man was taken to the London hospital, his chest opened, and the wound in his heart sewn up, effecting a complete recovery . . 18 Aug. ,,

G. E. T. Edalji sentenced to 7 years' penal servitude for maiming cattle . . . 23 Oct. ,,

Richard Palmer, 24, labourer, found guilty of the murder of Esther Swinford, a barmaid, whom he shot with a revolver . . . . . 28 Oct. ,,

The editor of *Lloyd's Weekly News* fined 50*l.* for contempt of court in publishing comments on case of G. L. James, charged with murder, 3 Nov. ,,

Saghitiel Sagouni, an Armenian, murdered at Nunhead, 26 Oct.; two more Armenians shot at Peckham, the assasin, Dakran, commits suicide, 4 Nov.; inquest, verdict of murder and suicide, 9 Nov. ,,

Whitaker Wright Case: Mr. Wright, formerly the managing director of the London and Globe, British America, and Standard Exploration corporations, was prosecuted by the official receiver in companies liquidation (order granted 10 March) on the alleged charge of manipulating the balance sheets of these corporations so as to show large profits and cash balances which had no real existence, the total loss to the shareholders and creditors being estimated at 5,000,000*l.* Mr. Wright, who had left England for America, was arrested at New York on landing 15 March; extradition proceedings taken; Mr. Wright voluntarily returns to England; charged at the Guildhall, committed for trial 17 Sept.; bail allowed, 25,000*l.* himself, two sureties 25,000*l.*; rule *nisi* made absolute in King's Bench division for removing the indictment from the Central Criminal court to the crown side of the King's Bench division . . . . 17 Nov. ,,

Dr. W. M. Bayliss, assist. prof. of physiology at University college, London, obtained 2,000*l.* damages from hon. S. Coleridge for libel and slander, imputing cruelty to a dog on which Dr. Bayliss was performing an operation . 18 Nov. 1903

Aldershot murder: W. Brown and J. Dunbar, soldiers, and T. Cowdrey, labourer, were tried at Winchester for the murder of Esther Atkins, an unfortunate, on 6 Oct. Brown and Cowdrey were sentenced to death; Dunbar was acquitted, 27 Nov. „

W. Haywood, at Hertford assizes, charged with the murder of his wife on 11 July, sentenced to death . . . . 28 Nov. „

G. F. Robinson, 27, a mining engineer, charged with firing a revolver at Mr. K. Grahame, secretary of the Bank of England, 24 Nov.; jury return verdict of insanity, Robinson ordered to be detained in a lunatic asylum . . . 17 Dec. „

Miss Bertha Cave's application to be admitted to Gray's inn, which had been refused, considered by a special tribunal of judges, the lord chancellor presiding; her appeal was rejected on the ground that there was no precedent for ladies being called to the English bar . . . . 2 Dec. „

See *Executions and Addenda*.

TRIBUNES OF THE PEOPLE (*Tribuni Plebis*), magistrates of Rome, first chosen from among the commons to represent them, 494 B.C., when the people, after a quarrel with the senators, had retired to Mons Sacer. The first two tribunes were C. Licinius and L. Albinus; but their number was soon after raised to five, and 37 years after to ten, which number remained fixed. The office was annual, and as the first had been created on the 4th of the ides of December, that day was chosen for the election. In A.D. 1347, Nicolo di Rienzi assumed absolute power in Rome as tribune of the people, and reformed many abuses; but committing extravagances, he lost his popularity and was compelled to abdicate. He returned to Rome and was assassinated, 8 Sept. 1354.

TRICHINIASIS, a fatal disease, occasioned by eating raw or underdone pork containing a minute worm named *Trichina spiralis*. Professor Owen discovered these worms in cysts, in human muscle, in 1832. The trichinæ are thoroughly destroyed by proper cooking. The disease excited much attention in 1865, and Dr. Thudichum lectured on it at the Society of Arts on 18 April, 1866.

TRICOLOR FLAG (red, white, and blue, white representing the ancient monarchy; red and blue, Paris) invented by La Fayette, adopted by France, 1789.

TRICOTEUSES (knitters), a name given to a number of French republican females, who zealously attended political meetings and executions in 1792, knitting at intervals.

TRIDENTINE, see *Trent*, and *Catechism*.

TRIENNIAL PARLIAMENTS. On 15 Feb. 1641, an act was passed providing for the meeting of a parliament at least once in three years. This law was broken by the Long Parliament, and was repealed in 1664. Another triennial bill, passed in 1694, was repealed by the Septennial act, 1716; see *Parliaments*, and *Septennial Parliaments*.

TRIESTE, an Austrian port on the Adriatic, declared a free port by the emperor Charles VI., 1719, confirmed by Maria Theresa in 1750. It was held by the French in 1797 and 1805. Since the establishment of the overland mail to India, it has risen to great commercial importance. After various changes of rulers it was restored to Austria in 1814; see *Lloyd's*, note. The emperor and empress were warmly received here mid Sept. 1882. Population of city and territory in 1890, 157,466; 1900, 176,672.

Cordial reception of the duke of Edinburgh and the Mediterranean fleet . . . . 15 Sept. 1887

The city suffered much by an earthquake 14, 15, 17 April, 1895

Strike riot, mob fired on by the troops, about 12 killed, many wounded, 14, 15 Feb.; martial law proclaimed . . . . 16 Feb. 1902

TRIGONOMETRICAL SURVEY, see *Ordnance*.

TRIMMER, a term applied to George Savile, marquis of Halifax, and others who held similar political opinions, midway between those of the extreme Whigs and Tories, about the latter part of the 17th century. He assumed the title as an honour, asserting that it could be rightly given to the British constitution and church. Macaulay says that Halifax was a trimmer on principle, and not a renegade. He died in 1695. See *Opportunists*.

TRINACRIA, a name of Sicily. The title "King of Trinacria," was temporarily assumed by Frederick II. (1302), and Frederick III. (1373).

TRINCOMALEE (Ceylon), was taken from the Dutch, by the English, in 1782; it was retaken by the French the same year; but was restored to the Dutch by the peace of 1783. It surrendered to the British, under colonel Stewart, 26 Aug. 1795, and was confirmed to England by the peace of Amiens, in 1802; see *Ceylon*. Of a series of actions off Trincomalee between sir Edward Hughes and the French admiral Suffren, one was fought 18 Feb. 1782, the enemy having eleven ships to nine; on 12 April following, they had eighteen ships to eleven, and on 6 July, same year, they had fifteen ships to twelve. In all these conflicts the French were defeated.

TRINIDAD, an island in the West Indies, discovered by Columbus in 1498, was taken from the Spaniards by sir Walter Raleigh in 1595; by the French from the English in 1676. Taken by the British, with four ships of the line, and a military force under command of sir Ralph Abercromby, to whom the island capitulated, 18 Feb. 1797; they captured two, and burnt three Spanish ships of war in the harbour. This possession was confirmed to England by the peace of Amiens in 1802. The insurrection of the negroes occurred 4 Jan. 1832. Population in 1861, 84,438; in 1881, 153,128; in 1891, 196,172; 1901, 253,250. The capital Port of Spain nearly destroyed by fire, 5 March, 1895. Governor: hon. Arthur H. Gordon, 1866; James R. Longden, 1870; sir H. T. Irving, 1874; sir Sandford Freeling, 1880; sir Wm. Robinson, Aug. 1885; sir Frederick Napier Broome, July, 1891, died, 26 Nov. 1896; sir Hubert Jerningham, Jan. 1897; sir Alfred Moloney, Oct. 1900. Trinidad united with Tobago by parliament in 1887.

Port of Spain nearly destroyed by fire 28 Jan. *et seq.* 1884

The Indian coolies at San Fernando forbidden to go in festival procession to cast their taboots (small shrines) on the last day of Mohurrum, disobey, and are fired upon by the police and soldiers; 12 killed, and many wounded 30 Oct. „

This course was justified, after due investigation, by sir Henry Norman, governor of Jamaica; blue book published . . . . . 14 April, 1885

Reciprocity treaty (reduced duties) with United States signed at Washington . . 14 Feb. 1900

Good report, island prosperous . . . . Jan. 1903

Great riot at Port of Spain, arising out of an organised struggle for right of public entry during proceedings of legislative council: popular feeling having been aroused by the denial of this right during debate by the legislative council on the second reading of a new waterworks ordinance, March 16. Mob stoned council chamber, including law courts and other government offices, and set it on fire. Dispersed by police; 18 people killed, 40 wounded . . . . 23 March, 1903
Commissioners appointed to inquire into the rioting arrived in England . . . 3 June, „
Parliamentary paper and blue book report of commission of inquiry published . . 22 July, „
TRINIDAD—A small desolate island in the S. Atlantic, 700 miles east of Rio de Janeiro, which has successively belonged to Portugal and Brazil. To obtain a place for telegraph cables a party from H.M.S. *Barracouta* landed on the isle and formally annexed it to the British empire, Jan. 1895, the gunner being nominated governor, as reported by lieut. Ryan. The affair caused much indignation at Rio . . . . . . July, 1895
The island given up to Brazil according to the award of Portugal . . . . . . Aug. 1896

TRINITY AND TRINITARIANS. Theophilus, bishop of Antioch, who flourished in the 2nd century, was the first who used the term Trinity, to express the three sacred persons in the Godhead. His "Defence of Christianity" was edited by Gesner, at Zurich, in 1546. *Watkins.* An order of the Trinity, termed Mathurins, was founded about 1198 by John de Matha and Felix de Valois. See *Crutched Friars.* The Trinity fraternity, originally of fifteen persons, was instituted at Rome by St. Philip Neri, in 1548. The act to exempt from penalties persons denying the doctrine of the Trinity (such as Unitarians and Swedenborgians) passed in 1813. *Trinitarian Bible Society* founded, 1831.

TRINITY COLLEGES, see *Cambridge, Oxford, Dublin, Glenalmond,* &c. Trinity College, Dublin, called the University: grant of the Augustine monastery of All Saints within the suburbs for erecting this college, conferred by queen Elizabeth, 1591. First stone laid by Thomas Smith, mayor of Dublin, 1 Jan. 1593. New charter, 1637. Made a barrack for soldiers, 1689. *Burns.* The principal or west front erected, 1759. Library erected, 1732. This college grants degrees upon examination without residence. The Roman Catholics desire exemption from mixed education and special privileges. Great changes were proposed by the Irish University bill, which was brought into parliament Feb. 1873, but withdrawn. Religious tests were abolished in the same year.

A proposal to establish a Roman catholic college within the university was negatived by the senate (74-7) . . . . 18 May, 1874
The church choral society incorporated as Trinity College, London 1875
Report of Irish University commission, 11 March, 1903
Degree of Litt.D. conferred on lord Roberts, 31 May, „
Women admitted to degrees . . . . June, „

TRINITY HOUSE, LONDON, founded by sir Thomas Spert, 1512, as an "association for piloting ships," was incorporated in 1514, and re-incorporated in 1604, 1660, and 1685. The present Trinity House was erected in 1795. By their charter the brethren of the Trinity House have the power of examining, licensing, and regulating pilots, and of erecting beacons and lighthouses, and of placing buoys in the channels and rivers. Spert, the first master, died 8 Sept. 1541.—TRINITY HOUSES, originally guilds or fraternities, founded at Deptford, Hull, and Newcastle, were incorporated by Henry VIII., 1536-41.

The Trinity almshouses, Mile-end-road, London, E., erected by sir Christopher Wren, for decayed mariners, containing statuary, tablets, stained glass and other relics, transferred from the Trinity house, Deptford, about a century ago. The proposed sale of the land, demolition of the buildings with a suitable provision for the pensioners, was successfully opposed . . Nov. 1895

RECENT MASTERS.

William Pitt 1790
Earl Spencer 1806
Duke of Portland 1807
Earl Camden 1809
Earl of Liverpool 1815
Marquis Camden 1828
Duke of Clarence 1829
Marquis Camden 1831
Duke of Wellington 1836
The Prince Consort 1852
Viscount Palmerston . . . . . 16 June, 1862
Duke of Edinburgh . . . . . 15 March, 1866
Duke of York (prince of Wales, re-elected 26 May, 1902), 21 May, 1894

Scientific adviser—lord Rayleigh, Jan. 1896. The office was successively held by profs. Faraday and Tyndall. See *Lighthouse.*

TRINITY SUNDAY, the Sunday following Whitsunday. The festival of the Holy Trinity was instituted by pope Gregory IV. in 828, on his ascending the papal chair, and is observed by the Latin and protestant churches on the Sunday next following Pentecost or Whitsuntide, of which, originally, it was merely an octave. The observance of the festival was first enjoined in the council of Arles, 1260. It was appointed to be held on the present day by pope John XXI. in 1334.

TRINOBANTES, a British tribe which occupied Middlesex and Essex, and joined in opposing the invasion of Julius Cæsar, 54 B.C., but soon submitted. They joined Boadicea and were defeated by Suetonius Paulinus near London, A.D. 61.

TRIPARTITE TREATY, name given to treaty of Paris, 1856.

TRIPLE ALLIANCE was ratified between the States-General and England against France, for the protection of the Spanish Netherlands; Sweden afterwards joining the league, it was known as the Triple Alliance, 23 Jan. 1668.—Another Triple Alliance was that between England, Holland, and France against Spain, Jan. 1717.—Another between Great Britain, Russia, and Austria, 28 Sept. 1795. Another between Germany, Austria, and Italy, said to have been proposed June, 1882, and adopted 1883, and signed 13 March, 1887: to expire 1892; renewed for six years, 28 June, 1891. The alliance was strengthened by commercial treaties, ratified Dec. 1891; again renewed, 28 June, 1902.

TRIPOLI (three cities). I., in Syria, comprised three quarters built by the Tyrians, Sidonians, and Arabians; was taken by the Crusaders 1109, and made a county for Raymond of Toulouse. It was conquered by the Egyptians in 1832; restored to the Porte 1835; surrendered to the British 1841. II., a Turkish province, N. Africa, comprised the cities Sabrata, Œa (the present Tripoli, the capital), and Leptis (the ancient Tripolitana), after having been held by Greeks, Romans, Vandals, and Saracens, was conquered and annexed by the Turks 1551. Hamet Bey, pacha in 1741, made himself independent, and the government remained in his family till 1835, when Tripoli was restored to nominal subjugation to the sultan. Population (1884) about 1,000,000. Panic through fear of insurrection about 20 July, 1882. In conflicts with the troops, about 160 natives were killed, reported 19 Dec. 1891. Severe drought in the country, Dec. 1892 *et seq.* Gov.-gen., Ahmed Rassim, 1881; succeeded by Ismail Bey, Jan. 1895; Namyk Bey, June, 1896; Hashem Bey, March, 1899; Hafiz Mehemet, July, 1900.

TRIPOLITZA (Greece), was stormed by the Greeks, who committed dreadful cruelties, 5 Oct. 1821; retaken by the Egyptians, 30 June, 1825; given up to the Greeks, 1828.

TRIREMES, galleys with three banks of oars, are said to have been invented by the Corinthians, 784 or 700 B.C.

TRISTAN D'ACUNHA, a small island in the S. Atlantic, inhabited by about 100 persons. Before the opening of the Suez Canal, the island prospered, through the visits of ships, now very rare; the duke of Edinburgh was there in 1867, and showed great kindness to the people. Patriarchal government under Mr. Peter Green, who received a portrait from queen Victoria in 1897; 64 inhabitants in Nov. 1897.

TRIUMPHS were granted by the Roman senate to generals of armies after they had won great victories. They were received into the city with great magnificence and public acclamations. There were the great, called *the* Triumph; and the less, the Ovation; see *Ovation*.

TRIUMVIRATES, ROMAN. In 60 B.C., Julius Cæsar, Pompey, and Crassus formed a coalition to rule the state. This lasted ten years, and the civil war ensued. The second triumvirate, 43 B.C., was formed by Octavius Cæsar, Mark Antony, and Lepidus, through whom the Romans totally lost their liberty. Lepidus was expelled in 36; Antony was subdued in 31, and Octavius made himself absolute; see *Rome*. In Feb. 1849, a triumvirate was appointed at Rome, consisting of Joseph Mazzini, Armellini, and Saffi, which resigned on 1 July, 1849, when the city was taken by the French.

TRIVIUM, see *Arts*.

TROCADERO, Paris, a mount on the right bank of the Seine, so named in memory of a fort near Cadiz, captured by the French while suppressing the insurrection in 1823. On this ground was erected the palace of the "Trocadéro," in connection with the international exhibition of 1878; see *Paris*.

TROGLODYTES, or "cave dwellers," the name given by the ancient Greeks to various savage races inhabiting natural caverns or holes in the earth which they had excavated. This term was more especially applied to the cave dwellers on the coast of the Red Sea, and along the banks of the Upper Nile in Nubia and Abyssinia, this district being called *Troglodytike*. The Troglodytes are mentioned by Herodotus, Aristotle, and Diodorus. Mr. Chamberlain, in his speech on "fiscal reform" at Tynemouth, 21 Oct. 1903, applied the term to the Cobden club and free trade party.

TROPICAL DISEASES. Medical schools for the study of these diseases founded, see *Liverpool*, April, 1899, and *Sierra Leone*, Aug. 1899. One established at the Dreadnought hospital, London (1,000*l.* from lord George Hamilton, 3,500*l.* from the colonial office, 200*l.* from the king of the Belgians), spring, 1899; others since.

TROPPAU, CONGRESS OF, in Austrian Silesia. The emperors Francis of Austria and Alexander of Russia met at Troppau, 20 Oct. 1820. The congress between them and the king of Prussia, against Naples, took place 10 Nov.; and the conference was transferred to Laybach, as nearer to Italy, 17 Dec. 1820; see *Laybach*.

TROUBADOURS AND TROUVÈRES (from *troubar*, *trouver*, to find or invent), the poets of the middle ages (from the 11th to the 15th century). The former flourished in the south of France and north of Spain, and used the Langue d'oil (that is, *oc* for *oui*, yes); the latter flourished in the north of France, and used the Langue d'oïl (that is, *oïl* for *oui*). The Troubadours produced romances, but excelled chiefly in lyric poetry; the Trouvères excelled in romances, several of which are extant; as, the *Brut d'Angleterre*, and the *Rou*, by Wace; the "Romance of the Rose," by Guillaume de Lorris and Jean de Meung. The Troubadours were usually accompanied by *Jongleurs*, who sang their masters' verses, with the accompaniment of the guitar. Histories of these French poets, and specimens of their works, have been published in France. These poets, although frequently very licentious, tended to promote civilisation during those warlike times.

TROY (or Troja), the common name of ILIUM, capital of the Troas, Asia Minor; see *Homer*. Its history mythical, and dates conjectural.

Teucer succeeds his father . . . . . B.C. 1502
Dardanus succeeds; builds Dardania 1480
Reign of Erichthonius 1449
Reign of Tros; from whom the people are called Trojans, and the city Troas 1374
Ilus, his son, reigns; the city called Ilium . . . 1314
Reign of Laomedon 1260
Arrival of Hercules in Phrygia. Hesione delivered from the sea monster. *Blair; Usher* . . . 1225
War of Hercules and Laomedon 1224
Reign of Priam or Podarces . . . . . . ,,
Rape of Helen, by Alexander Paris, son of Priam, 20 years before the sacking of Troy. *Homer's Iliad*, book xxiv. 1204
Commencement of the invasion of the Greeks to recover Helen 1193
Troy taken and burnt in the night of the 11th of June, *i.e.*, 23rd of the month Thargelion. *Parian Marbles.* 408 years before the first Olympiad. *Apollodorus, Hales,* and *Clinton*, 1183; others . 1184
Mr. W. E. Gladstone dates the war . . 1316-1307
Æneas arrives in Italy. *Lenglet.* 1183
[Some time after the destruction of Troy, a new city was built with the same name, about thirty stadia distant from the old site. It was favoured by Alexander the Great in his Asiatic expedition, but never rose to much importance, and in the age of Strabo was nearly in ruins. *Priestley.*]
Dr. H. Schliemann, during his excavations at Hissarlik in the Troad, discovered the remains of a very ancient city with temples, which he named "Novum Ilium" . . . . . A.D. 1872-3
He published *Troy and its Remains* (trans. by Dr. P. Smith) 1875
His Trojan antiquities arranged at South Kensington Museum, for exhibition . . . Dec. 1877
Dr. Schliemann resumes excavations at Hissarlik; discovers Trojan houses and many antiquities, a dagger, earrings, bracelets, idols, shells, &c., 30 Sept.-1 Dec. 1878
Again with professor Virchow and M. Burnouf, 1 March; makes fresh discoveries described in letter 5 June, 1879; desists investigation; published his book *Ilios*, 1880, and *Troja* . . . 1883
Excavations renewed by the Germans at Hissarlik; the city wall, buildings, &c. discovered . Sept. 1894
See *Mycenæ*, 26 Dec. 1890.

TROY WEIGHT. The Romans introduced their ounce, our avoirdupois ounce, into Britain. The present ounce was brought from Grand Cairo into Europe, about the time of the Crusades, 1095, and was first adopted at Troyes, a city of France, whence the name. It is used to weigh gold, silver, and precious stones. The Troy weight, Scots, was established by James VI. (our James I.) in 1618; see *Standard*.

TROYES (Central France), where a treaty was concluded between England, France, and Burgundy, whereby it was stipulated that Henry V. should marry Catherine, daughter of Charles VI., be appointed regent of France, and, after the death of Charles, should inherit the crown, 21 May, 1420. Troyes was taken by the allied armies, 7 Feb.; retaken by Napoleon, 23 Feb.; and again taken by the allies, 4 March, 1814.

TRUCE OF GOD (*Frera* or *Treuga Dei*), a term given to a cessation of the private feuds and conflicts so general during the middle ages all over Europe, said to have been strongly advocated by the bishop of Aquitaine, in 1032. The clergy strenuously exerted their influence for the purpose. A synod at Roussillon, 1027, decreed that none should attack his enemy between Saturday evening (at nones) and Monday morning (at the hour of prime). Similar regulations were adopted in England, 1042 (sometimes Friday and Wednesday being chosen for the time). The truce of God was confirmed by many councils of the church, especially the Lateran Council, in 1179.

TRUCK SYSTEM of paying workmen's wages in goods (sold at "*tommy shops*") instead of money, was prohibited by parliament in 1831. By the Truck act a commission to inquire into its alleged prevalence was appointed; act passed 10 Aug. 1870; amended 1887 and 1896.

TRUMPET. Some of the Greek historians ascribe the invention of the trumpet to the Tyrrhenians, and others to the Egyptians. It was in use in the time of Homer. First torches, then shells of fish sounded like trumpets, were the signals in primitive wars. *Potter*. The Jewish feast of trumpets was appointed 1490 B.C. (*Lev.* xxiii. 24). Offa, king of Mercia, is said to have had trumpets sounded before him when travelling, about A.D. 790. The *speaking trumpet* is said to have been used by Alexander the Great in 335 B.C.; improved by Kircher in A.D. 1652; by Salland, 1654; and philosophically explained by Morland, 1671.

Trumpet blasts employed for railway signalling in Scotland 1887
Thomas Harper, celebrated trumpeter, died (aged 81) . . . . 27 Aug. 1898

TRUMPET-FLOWER, *Bignonia radicans*, was brought hither from North America, about 1640. The Trumpet Honeysuckle, *Lonicera sempervirens*, came from North America in 1656. The *Bignonia capensis* was brought to England from the Cape in 1823. The Large-flowered Trumpet-flower, or *Bignonia grandiflora*, was brought from China in 1800.

TRURO, W. Cornwall. The town was founded by Richard de Lucy, chief justice of England in the 12th century, and chartered by Reginald, earl of Cornwall, illegitimate son of Henry I. An act to provide for the foundation of a bishopric of Truro passed 11 Aug. 1876, and money sufficient for its endowment having been subscribed, the see was constituted by order in council, 9 Dec. same year. Act amended in 1887. Truro was made a city, Aug. 1877; absorbed into the county, 1885. Population, 1881, 10,619; 1891, 11,131; 1901, 11,562.

Foundation of new cathedral (St. Mary's) laid by the prince of Wales, 20 May, 1880; it includes part of the old parish church; the eastern part erected, consecrated and opened for public worship in the presence of the prince of Wales and the archbishop of Canterbury, 3 Nov. 1887; architect, Mr. Pearson, died 11 Dec. 1897; the first cathedral erected since St. Paul's, London. Canon Richard F. Wise, a munificent contributor to the cathedral, died, aged 80, April, 1896. An anonymous gift of 10,000*l*. for the cathedral, received, March, 1901
Mr. J. H. Dennis gives 15,000*l*. for the tower, May, ,,
Dedication of the nave, prince and princess of Wales present . . . . . . 15 July, 1903

See *Mansion House Fund*.

BISHOPS.

1877. Edward White Benson, consecrated, 25 April; trans. to Canterbury, Dec. 1882.
1883. George Howard Wilkinson, consecrated 25 April; resigned 1891.
1891. John Gott, D.D., June.

TRUSS. A transverse spring-truss for ruptures was patented by Robert Brand in 1771, and by many other persons since. The National Truss Society to assist indigent persons, was established in 1786; and many similar societies since.

TRUSTEES, see *Fraudulent*.

Trustees' act passed, 1888, and Trust Funds' act . 1889
The Trustees' Appointment act (1850 to 1890), 25 July, 1890
The Trustees' and Executors' Association initiated, Aug. 1891
The Trustee (Consolidation) act passed 22 Sept. 1893; amended 1894
Trusts (Scotland) act, 1867; amended, 1887 and 1897

TRUSTS and COMBINES. Terms applied in the United States to the union of manufacturers and traders as corporate bodies for the purpose of creating and maintaining strict monopolies and thereby controlling the output and the prices of goods of all kinds and the wages of workmen, a system injurious to all classes of society.

In the autumn of 1888, legislation for the repression of the evil was urgently demanded. There is a petroleum trust, a cotton trust, a steel rail trust &c. (see *Corner*). The proprietors of the salt mines in Cheshire combined to form a "trust" in the autumn of 1888. Similar trusts have been projected and opposed. Central Publichouse trust association, formed 1901 (lord Grey, president; Mr. Chamberlain and the bp. of Chester, vice-presidents), to promote temperance, &c.; 37 companies reported . . Feb. 1903

TRUTH, "a society journal," established by Mr. H. Labouchere in 1877. See *Trials*, 1893.

TSAR, see *Czar*.

TSUNG-LI-YAMÊN OR YAMEN, the Chinese imperial parliament.

TUBE RAILWAYS. See *Railways* and *Tunnels*.

TUAM (W. Ireland). St. Jarlath, the son of Loga, who lived about 501, is looked upon as the first founder of the cathedral of Tuam, though the abbey is said to have been founded in 487. The church was anciently called *Tuaim-da-Gualand* In 1151, Edan O'Hoisin was the first archbishop, at least the first who received the pall, for some of his predecessors are sometimes called bishops of Connaught, and sometimes archbishops, by Irish historians. The see of Mayo was annexed to Tuam in 1559. Tuam is valued in the king's books, by an extent returned *anno* 28 Eliz., at 50*l*. sterling per annum. *Beatson.* It ceased to be archiepiscopal, conformably with the statute 3 & 4 Will. IV., 1833; and is now a bishopric only, to which Killala and Achonry, a joint see, has been added; see *Archbishops.* New protestant cathedral of St. Mary, consecrated by the bishop, the Hon. Dr. Charles B. Bernard, 9 Oct. 1878.

TUBERCULOSIS, a disease caused by the development of tubercles, small masses of diseased matter in the lungs (phthisis or consumption), in the face and other parts (lupus).

Dr. Robert Koch, of Berlin, discovered and isolated a minute organism, named *bacillus tuberculosis*, to whose action he attributed the disease, 15 Aug. 1881. In the autumn of 1890, he reported his invention of a lymph (*see below*, 15 Jan. 1891), by the injection of which into the system, as in vaccination, he hoped to cure the diseases. In Berlin he made many experiments on tuberculosed guinea-pigs and human beings, with some success in respect to lupus, but not to phthisis. Dr. Koch was much honoured by the emperor, and was aided by the state. Dr. Koch's full account of his method was published in the *British Medical Journal*, London, 15 Nov., and other papers. Medical men flocked to Berlin from all parts of the world, to obtain the lymph. Exaggerated cases of successful application were published, and it soon appeared that time was required to test the efficacy of the remedy. Much discussion ensued. Dr. Koch, on 15 Jan. 1891, published the statement that his lymph, named *tuberculine*, was a glycerine extract from the pure cultivation of the tubercle bacilli.

Royal commission on tuberculosis (Dr. Koch's method, &c.), actively inquiring at home and abroad (lord Basing (died), profs. Brown, Burdon Sanderson, Dr. Payne, sir George Buchanan), Dec. 1890 *et seq.*; re-constituted, sir G. Buchanan chairman, Nov. 1894; died 5 May, 1895; special researches respecting animals, and much evidence reported, 1895; the continent visited, 1897; report issued . . . . . April, 1898

Professor Badenheuer, of Cologne, asserted that out of 100 surgical cases no perfect cure had been effected by the lymph . . end of Jan. 1891

Prof. Virchow, Berlin, in regard to 21 cases of injection of the lymph, reported unfavourable results . . . . Jan. ,,

Drs. Bertin, Picq, and Bernheim proposed the cure of tuberculosis by the transfusion of goat's blood, Jan., Feb. ,,

Dr. Lannelongue at Paris, proposed a new remedy, which he explained and illustrated to the members of the second congress for the study of tuberculosis . . . . . 27 July, ,,

Dr. Koch appointed director of the Institute for Infectious Diseases at Berlin . . . July, ,,

He acknowledges the failure of his remedy, and proposes an improvement by the addition of alcohol . . . . 22 Oct. ,,

National association for the Prevention of Tuberculosis founded, meeting at Marlborough house, the prince of Wales in the chair, lord Salisbury and many scientists present; Messrs. Wernher, Beit & Co. give 20,000*l.* for a new sanatorium, 20 Dec. 1898. Annual meetings (lord Derby, chairman), branch societies formed at Belfast and Dublin . . . . . April-May, 1899

Internat. congress at Berlin (180 delegates) opened by the duke of Ratibor, the empress present, 24-27 May, 1899; report issued, *Times* 13 July, ,,

Internat. congress, over 1,000 delegates, opened at Naples, the king and queen present . 25 April, 1900

The light cure of lupus (discovered by Dr. Finsen, of Copenhagen, about 1896) started at the London hospital through the generosity of queen Alexandra, and proved successful (Mr. Alfred Harmsworth gives 10,000*l.*) . . . . May, 1901

Internat. congress in London, opened by the duke of Cambridge with a message from the king; lords Lansdowne, Cadogan, Derby, Lister, Strathcona, and sir William Broadbent among the speakers; profs. Koch, Brouardel, 148 foreign delegates, and others, 22 July; prof. Koch speaks hopefully of the scientific treatment of the disease, believes it to be not hereditary, that human and bovine tuberculosis are not interchangeable, 23 July; prof. Brouardel states *alcoholism to be the most potent factor in propagating the disease*, and commends England's efforts since 1836 in improving artisan's dwellings, &c., 24 July; closed . 26 July, 190

Royal (scientific) commission appointed (profs. Woodhead, Martin, McFadyean and Boyce), sir Michael Foster, K.C.B., chairman, to inquire whether tuberculosis is the same disease in animals and man, whether it is communicable from animals to man, and if so, how the transmission occurs . . . . 3 Sept. ,

Sir Ernest Cassel presents the king with 200,000*l.* for charitable or utilitarian purposes, which the king devotes to provide additional sanatoria for tuberculous patients, announced . 6 Jan. 1902

Internat. congress at Berlin . . 23–26 Oct. ,,

Meeting held at Vienna to found an Austrian anti-tuberculosis union . . . . . 4 Jan. 1903

Foundation-stone of the king Edward VII. Sanatorium, near Midhurst, Sussex, for the open-air treatment of tuberculosis, laid by the king, 3 Nov. ,,

Church costing 20,000*l.* for the Midhurst Sanatorium to be built by Mr. J. Brickwood, announced, end Nov. ,,

TÜBINGEN SCHOOL of historico-philosophical theology was founded by professor F. C. Baur about 1835.

TUBMAN, see *Postman.*

TUBULAR BRIDGES. The Britannia Tubular Suspension Bridge, then the most wonderful enterprise in engineering in the world, was constructed, 1846-50 (Mr. R. Stephenson and Mr. Fairbairn, engineers), about a mile southward of the Menai Strait Suspension Bridge.*

On the Britannia rock, near the centre of the Menai Strait, the surface of which is about ten feet above low water level, is built a tower two hundred feet above high water (commenced building, May, 1846), and on which rest two lines of tubes or hollow girders strong enough to bear their weight and laden trains in addition, the ends resting on the abutments on each shore; each tube being more than a quarter of a mile in length. The height of the tube within is thirty feet at the Britannia tower, diminishing to twenty-three feet at the abutments. The lifting of these tubes to their places was a most gigantic operation, successfully performed, 27 June, 1849

The first locomotive passed through . March, 1850

The Conway tubular bridge, a miniature copy of the Britannia (principal engineers, Mr. Robt. Stephenson and Mr. Fairbairn) erected . . 1846-8

At Chepstow, a railway tubular bridge . . . 1852

A bridge or viaduct on the tubular principle (called the Albert viaduct) over the river Tamar at Plymouth, opened by the prince consort . 2 May, 1859

See *Victoria Railway Bridge* and *Tay Bridge.*

TUDELA (N. Spain). Near here marshal Lannes totally defeated the Spaniards, 23 Nov. 1808; see *Ebro.*

* The Britannia tubular bridge was intended to supply the place of one of the finest bridges in the kingdom; and the railway, of which the tubular bridge forms a part, is in like manner a substitute for one of the finest mail-coach roads ever constructed. The road from London to Holyhead has been long regarded as the highway from the British metropolis to Dublin; and the late Mr. Telford was applied to by the government to perfect this route by the London and Holyhead mail-coach road, which he did by erecting a beautiful suspension bridge over the river Conway and over the Menai Strait; commenced in July, 1818, and finished in July, 1825.

TUDOR SOVEREIGNS; see *England*, 1485-1603.

TUDOR EXHIBITION, New Gallery, Regent street; patron, the queen; committee, the prince of Wales, and other eminent persons. The collection included portraits and miniatures by Holbein and others, armour and weapons, personal relics, plate, bibles, prayerbooks, Shakespeare's and other books. Opened 1 Jan. 1890, and continued several months. A similar exhibition was opened at the British Museum about 22 Jan. 1890

Another opened by the duke of Devonshire at Manchester . . . . . . 29 April, 1897

TUESDAY, in Latin *Dies Martis*, the day of Mars, the third day of the week, so called from *Tuisto*, *Tiw*, or *Tuesco*, a Saxon deity, worshipped on this day. Tuisto is mentioned by Tacitus; see *Week Days*.

TUGENDBUND ("league of Virtue"), formed in Prussia soon after the peace of Tilsit, June, 1807, ostensibly for relieving the sufferers by the late wars, and for the revival of morality and patriotism. Its head-quarters were at Königsberg. It excited the jealousy of Napoleon, who demanded its suppression in 1809. It was dissolved at the peace in 1815.

TUILERIES (Paris), the imperial palace of France, commenced by Catherine de Medicis, after the plans of Philibert de l'Orme, 1564; continued by Henry IV.; and finished by Louis XIV. This palace was stormed by the mob, 10 Aug. 1792; and ransacked in the revolutions of July, 1830, and Feb. 1848. Louis Napoleon made it his residence in 1851, and greatly renovated it. The restoration of the Tuileries (much injured by fire by the communists, May 1871) was determined on, Oct. 1872; not proceeded with. The ruins were sold for 32,200*l*. to M. Picard, 4 Dec. 1882.

TULCHAN BISHOPS; a mere nominal episcopacy set up in Scotland by the regent Morton, who, with other nobles, absorbed the larger portion of the revenue, 1572-3. *Tulchan* was a stuffed calf's skin set before a cow to facilitate milking.

TULIPS, indigenous in the east of Europe, came to England from Vienna about 1578. It is recorded in the register of Alkmaer in Holland, that in 1639, 120 tulips, with the offsets, sold for 90,000 florins: and that one, called the *Viceroy*, sold for 4203 guilders! The States stopped this ruinous traffic. The *tulip tree*, *Liriodendron tulipifera*, was brought to England from America, about 1663.

TUMUT, New South Wales, a small town on the Tumut river, a tributary of the Murrumbidgee, 264 miles S.W. of Sydney. It is the centre of a rich agricultural district, and mines are worked. Tumut was placed first on the list of places by the committee appointed to consider the choice of a site for the federal capital of Australia. Committee's selection rejected by the senate, Oct. 1903.

TUNBRIDGE WELLS (Kent). The springs were discovered, it is stated, by Dudley, lord North, who, when very ill, was restored to health by the use of the waters, 1606. The wells were visited by the queens of Charles I. and II., and by queen Anne, and soon became fashionable. Population, 1881, 24,119; 1891, 27,895; 1901, 35,000.

The town was incorporated by royal charter early in 1889

Mr. John Stone-Wigg, the first mayor, a great benefactor, died, end of . . . . . Dec. 1897

TUNGSTEN (also called wolfram and scheelium), a hard whitish brittle metal. From tungstate of lead, Scheele in 1781 obtained tungstic acid, whence the brothers De Luyart in 1786 obtained the metal. In 1859 it was employed in making a new kind of steel.

TUNIS (N. Africa) stands nearly on the site of Carthage. Tunis was besieged by Louis IX., of France, who died near it 25 Aug. 1270. It remained under African kings till taken by Barbarossa, for Solyman the Magnificent, 1531. Barbarossa was expelled by the emperor Charles V., when 10,000 Christian slaves were set at liberty, June, 1535. The country was recovered by the Turks under Selim II. 1575. The bey of Tunis was first appointed in 1574; Tunis was reduced by admiral Blake, on the bey refusing to deliver up the British captives, 1655. The Hussein dynasty was founded 1705. In July, 1856, the bey agreed to make constitutional reforms. He died 22 Sept. 1859; and his brother and successor Mohamed-es-Sadok took the oath of fidelity to the constitution. He died, and was succeeded by his brother Sidi Ali, 28 Oct. 1882; died, 11 June, 1902; succeeded by his son Mohamed. Tunis is now under French protection. Estimated total population, 1,800,000, 1902.

Insurrection, 18 April; ships of war sent to protect Europeans . . . . May, 1864

Tunis decreed to be an integral part of the Turkish empire . . . . 25 Oct. 1871

Commercial treaty with Great Britain, 1875 *et seq.*

A dispute with France settled by submission of the bey . . . . Jan. 1879

The bey, embarrassed by debt (5,000,000*l*.), places his finances in hands of an international commission 1880

Disputes between France and Italy respecting railway concessions . . . . Aug. ,,

Dispute between a British subject here and a French company respecting purchase of the Enfida estate, decision left to the legal tribunals . . Feb. 1881

Dispute with France; predatory incursions of the Kroumirs, nomadic shepherd tribes, on Algerian territory, March: the bey appeals to Turkey, 11 April; and the Great Powers, 27 April: military expedition sent from France; lands in Tabarka, bombards fortress, and occupies Bizerta, 30 April, ,,

The Kroumirs said to be enclosed by the French; the bey's army retreats . . . early May, ,,

Alleged battle with the Kroumirs . about 2 May, ,,

The French approach Tunis, alleging the object to be to restrain warlike tribes and protect their frontier . . . . 11 May, ,,

Treaty with France signed; it assures to France the right to occupy the positions which the French military authorities might deem necessary for the maintenance of order and the security of the frontier and the coast, and to send a resident minister to the capital. The French government guarantees to the bey the security of his person, his states, and his dynasty, and the maintenance of existing treaties with the European powers; while the bey undertakes not to conclude any international convention without a previous understanding with the French government, and to prevent the introduction of arms into Algeria through Tunis. The financial system of the regency to be regulated by France in concert with the bey, 12 May, ,,

Reported conflict between the French under gen. Bréart and the Arabs; the French enter Mater, 18 May, ,,

The Sultan of Turkey protests against the treaty, May, ,,

M. Séguin, a news correspondent, murdered at Beja by a fanatic (who is executed) . . 28 May, ,,

M. Brangard, inspector of telegraphs, and assistants, murdered by Arabs, near Oran . about 5 June, ,,

M. Roustan, the consul, appointed French resident minister (said to be virtual ruler, replacing bey), French army returning home . . June, ,,

Mustapha Ben Ismail, the bey's chief minister, received by president Grévy, at Paris . 21 June, ,,

Insurrection at Sfax, revolt of great chief Ali Ben Khalifa, announced . . . . . 30 June, 1881
Europeans attacked, nearly all flee to ships, alleged massacres . . . . 31 July, ,,
Sfax bombarded by the French, 5 July, *et seq.*; captured after severe conflict . . 16 July, ,,
Arabs revolting; anarchy reported . 20 July, ,,
Enfida case; decision against the English, Mr. Levy . . . . Aug. ,,
Collapse of bey's authority . . about 15 Aug. ,,
Asserted conflict at Hammamet, the French repulsed about 31 Aug.; the French retreating about 8 Sept. ,,
Arrival of 2,000 French troops at Goletta 9 Sept. ,,
General Sabattier with troops at Zaghouan surrounded by Arabs . . . . about 13 Sept ,,
28,000 men sent to Tunis announced . 26 Sept. ,,
Alleged defeat of the bey's troops under Ali Bey; 4 hours' conflict . . . about 25 Sept. ,,
Ali Bey's army surrounded . about 4 Oct. *et seq.* ,,
Union of the French and Ali Bey's army, about 8 Oct. ,,
Tunis occupied by the French . . 10 Oct. ,,
Gen. Sabattier defeats the Arabs; six hours' conflict; 800 killed, French loss slight . . 13 Oct. ,,
Continued fighting . . . . about 22 Oct. ,,
The French under Gen. Etienne enter Kairwan, without resistance . . . . . 26 Oct. ,,
The French treaty with the bey (11 May) confirmed by the chambers . . . . . 9 Nov. ,,
Alleged defeat of Arabs, near Gerid, by Gen. Logerot . . . . . . about 16 Nov. ,,
Gen. Saussier reports his capture of a large rebel convoy . . . . . . about 17 Nov. ,,
The insurrection virtually suppressed; army of occupation to be 20,000 . announced 29 Nov. ,,
M. Levy (see Aug. 1881) expelled . about 14 Dec. ,,
M. Roustan in Paris; M. H. Rochefort acquitted of bitter libel against M. Roustan . . 15 Dec. ,,
M. Roustan returns . . . . about 29 Dec. ,,
Transferred to Washington . . about 23 Feb. 1882
Victory of insurgents . . . about 1 April, ,,
Enfida case amicably settled . . . May, ,,
Treaty with France (taking over debt about 5,000,000*l.*) draft . . . . . . July, ,,
Renewed Arab incursions . . . about 3 Oct. ,,
French courts of law established; foreign consular jurisdictions abolished (capitulations) 1 Jan. 1884
Tunis made a seaport by the construction of a canal 1885–93
Meeting of the French association . . 1–4 April, 1896
The rev. Mr. Leach, eminent missionary, and family murdered at Sfax . . . . . . 6 May, ,,
The marquis de Mores murdered by Tuaregs in the Tunisian Sahara . . . . about 8 June, ,,
Treaty between France and Italy signed . 30 Sept. ,,
Railway between Tunis and Susa completed, 6 Nov. ,,
Visit of the princess of Wales . . 14 May, 1899
Sir Harry Johnston's report on Tunis describes the "Mosque of the Olive Tree," an Arab university, about 400 students and 100 professors . June, ,,
Hafiz Mehmet Pasha, Bey of Tunis . . July, 1900
M. Pichon, new resident-gen., arrives . Dec. 1901
French residents, 1891 about 10,000; about 25,000, and over 75,000 Italians . . . . Feb. 1903

TUNNAGE AND POUNDAGE were ancient duties levied on every tun of wine and pound of other goods, imported or exported, and were the origin of our "customs." They commenced in England about 1346, and were granted to the kings for life, beginning with Edward IV. Charles I. gave great offence by levying them on his own authority, 1628. They were granted to Charles II. for his lifetime, 24 June, 1660. By the act 27 Geo. III. c. 13, these and other duties were repealed, 1787, and a new arrangement of excise and customs was introduced.

TUNNELS, for drainage, are ancient. The earliest tunnel for internal navigation was executed by M. Riguet, in the reign of Louis XIV., at Bezières in France. The first in England was by Mr. Brindley, on the duke of Bridgewater's canal, near Manchester, about 1766. Project of the Gravesend tunnel, 1800—the report upon it, 1801. The Thames Tunnel was projected by Mr. Brunel in 1823, and opened for foot passengers, 25 March, 1843; see *Thames Tunnel*. Innumerable tunnels have been made for railways. The railway tunnel at Liverpool was completed in the middle of 1829, lit up with gas, and exhibited once a week. On the London and Birmingham railway there are eight tunnels (the Primrose-hill, Watford, Kilsby, &c.), their total length being 7336 yards. *Smiles.* It was computed by Mr. Fowler, that there were 80 miles of tunnels in the United Kingdom in 1865, which cost about 6,500,000*l.*, at the average of 45*l.* a yard; see *Alps* [Mont Cenis, etc.] and *Thames.*

Tunnel between Dover and Calais, suggested by M. Mathieu . . . . about 1802
Tunnel for a railway beneath the channel from Dover to Calais, proposed by Messrs. J. F. Bateman and J. Revy . . . . . 30 Aug. 1869
M. Thomé de Gamond, after many years' study, exhibited his plans in Paris, 1867; his scheme revived in France, July, 1871 and Nov. 1873; a convention in its favour was signed for France by M. Michel Chevalier, Jan., 1875; engineers, sir John Hawkshaw and M. Lavally; monopoly for 30 years granted; chairman for English company, lord Richard Grosvenor; plan of boring through 20 miles chalk by Mr. D. Brunton.
M. Thomé de Gamond died . . . . . Feb., 1876
Boring at Sangatte, near Calais, begun 25 Feb.: 200 feet deep . . . . 3 June, ,,
Memorandum of basis of proposed treaty between England and France issued . . . Aug. ,,
Other plans have been proposed by G. Remington, P. J. Bishop, A. Austin, &c.
The French government's concession for preliminary works granted in 1875, renewed for 3 years from 2 Aug. 1880
Experimental boring going on, April, 1881; 800 mètres from the coast . . . . May, 1883
Meeting of Channel Tunnel Company 2 Feb.; of submarine Continental railway company 3 Feb. 1882
Channel Tunnel near Dover; about 1 mile excavated; visited by Mr. Gladstone and others 11 March, ,,
The Channel Tunnel disapproved of by sir G. Wolseley, and other officers, British and foreign March, *et seq.* ,,
The works stopped by government about 1 May; by order of Mr. Justice Kay . . . . 6 July, ,,
Two channel tunnel bills discharged in the commons 16 Aug. ,,
Report of a commission on the channel tunnel (sir A. Alison, chairman) unfavourable on political grounds issued . . . . 11 Oct. ,,
The question referred to a committee of lords and commons 4, 6 April, which meets 24 April; decide against the tunnel (6-4) . . . about 10 July, 1883
The company resolutely determine to wait 17 Aug. ,,
Bill rejected by the commons (222-84) 14 May, 1884; (281-99) . . . . 12 May, 1885
Boring of the Channel tunnel still continued, 2 Feb. 1887
The Channel tunnel bill again rejected by the commons (153–107) . . . . . 3 Aug. ,,
Sir E. Watkin's bill for experimental works opposed by the government and rejected in the commons (307–165), 27 June, 1888; again rejected (234–153) 5 June, 1890; bill withdrawn . 20 July, 1893
Mersey tunnel, between Liverpool and Birkenhead, one mile long, projected 1866, execution frequently suspended, boring renewed by the energy of major Samuel Isaac, 1880, boring completed under his superintendence, 17 Jan. 1884 (he died, 22 Nov. 1886); tunnel opened, 13 Feb. 1885; first passenger train run through, 22 Dec. 1885; formally opened by the prince of Wales, 20 Jan. 1886

The Severn tunnel near Bristol, constructed by W. C. Richardson, for the Gt. Western company's railway begun, March, 1873; official train passed through, 5 Sept. 1885; opened for traffic, 1 Sept., for passengers . . . . 1 Dec. 1886

"Joseph II. mining adit," Schemnitz, begun 1782, after many delays, finished, 16,538 metres long, 5 Sept. 1878

Arlberg tunnel, Austria, 10,270 metres long; begun June, 1880; completed, and train passed through, 13 Nov. 1883

Two tunnels for the City and South London Electric Railway, from the Monument to Stockwell, completed, March; the railway opened by the prince of Wales, 4 Nov.; to the public 18 Dec. 1890

The construction of a tunnel under the Irish Channel recommended by sir Roper Lethbridge at the Society of Arts . . . 11 Feb. 1891

Tunnel between Blackwall and Charlton reaches, on the Thames, constructed by the London county council (Messrs. S. Pearson & Son's tender, 871,000*l*.), designed by Mr. A. R. Binnie, knt., June, 1897, length, 6,200 ft., 19 ft. wide, 80 ft. depth from high water level, with road and footpaths, begun the end of 1891; opened by the prince and princess of Wales, 22 May, 1897; opened for traffic 10 p.m. . . . 24 June, 1897

Central London (tube) railway, Shepherd's Bush to the Bank, opened for traffic by the prince of Wales . . . . 27 June, 1900

Tunnel between Millwall and Greenwich constructed at a cost of about 120,000*l*. by the London County Council as a footway tunnel for passenger traffic between Greenwich and the Isle of Dogs, opened . . . . . . 4 Aug. 1902

Tunnel gardens, Poplar, opened by the mayor, 30 Aug. „

Simplon Tunnel (21,576 yds.) in course of construction by the Jura-Simplon company, at the estimated cost of 2,800,000*l*., to which the Swiss government, the Swiss cantons and the Italian government contribute, was commenced at Iselle, 15 Aug. 1898; its completion expected in 1904.

TURAN, see *Turkestan*.

TÜRCKHEIM, see *Türkheim*.

TURIN, the ancient Augusta Taurinorum in Piedmont, capital of the Sardinian States, and of the kingdom of Italy, till 1864, when it was superseded by Florence. Its importance dates from the permanent union of Savoy and Piedmont in 1416. The French besieged this city; but prince Eugène defeated their army, and compelled them to raise the siege, 7 Sept. 1706. In 1798, the French republican army took possession of Turin, seized all the strong places and arsenals of Piedmont, and obliged the king and his family to remove to the island of Sardinia. In 1799, the French were driven out by the Austrians and Russians; but the city and all Piedmont surrendered to the French, June 1800. In May 1814, it was restored to the king of Sardinia; see *Italy*, 1864. Here prince Humbert was married to his cousin Margherita amidst great rejoicing, 22 April, 1868. The monument to Cavour was inaugurated, 8 Nov. 1873. An exhibition opened by the king, 25 April, 1880; another opened by the king, 1 May, 1898. Monuments to prince Amadeus of Savoy (ex-king of Spain) and to king Humbert, inaugurated, 7, 8 May. Internat. art exhibition opened by the king, 10 May; closed, 12 Nov. 1902. See *Treaties*, and *Italy*, 1884. Population, 1890, 320,808; 1900, 335,539.

TURKESTAN, called by the Persians Turan, formerly Independent Tartary (*which see*), the original country of the Turks, in Central Asia, was reached by Alexander, 331 B.C., and has since undergone many changes, forming successively part of the empires of Genghis Khan and Tamerlane (see *Tartary*). For Eastern or Chinese Turkestan, see *Kashgaria*; for Western, see *Bokhara* and *Khiva*. The Russians gradually encroached on this country; on 14 Feb. 1865, a new province, Turkestan, was created by decree, and gen. Kauffmann made governor, 26 July, 1867; died 16 May, 1882. The rule of the czar accepted by the chief tribes at Merv (*which see*), announced 8 Feb. 1884. Gen. Dukhofski appointed gov.-gen. of Turkestan and the Transcaspian territory, April, 1898. Explorations and discoveries by Dr. Sven Hedin in 1895, and by Dr. Stein, June–Dec. 1900. Severe earthquake shocks at Andijan, in Ferghana, 10,000 deaths, 15,000 houses destroyed, 16 Dec. 1902.

TURKEY. The Turks were originally a tribe of Tartars; but, by incorporation with the peoples they have conquered, have become a mixed race. About 760, they obtained possession of a part of Armenia, called from them Turcomania. They gradually extended their power; but in the 13th century, being harassed by other Tartar tribes, they returned to Asia Minor. The Turkish empire till 1878 comprehended the almost independent principalities of Moldavia and Wallachia, Servia, and Montenegro, the hereditary vice-royalty of Egypt, and Tunis. The Turkish quadrilateral fortresses were Shumla, Varna, Silistria, and Rustchuck. The population of the empire was estimated in 1887 at 32,978,100; (immediate Possessions, 21,633,000, tributaries and protectorates, 11,345,100); in Europe, 8,987,000; Asia, 16,174,100; Africa, 7,817,000; 1901, in Europe, about 6,000,000; total, including Asia, &c., about 39,732,900. By the treaty of Berlin (13 July, 1878) Turkey is said to have

	Square Miles.	Inhabitants.	Mohammedans.
Ceded to Roumania . . .	5,935	246,000	142,000
„ Servia . . .	4,326	264,000	75,000
„ Montenegro . .	1,549	40,000	9,000
„ Austria . . .	15	2,000	—
„ Greece (?) . . .	5,300	750,000	40,000
To be occupied and administered by Austria . .	28,125	1,061,000	513,000
Formed into the Principality of Bulgaria . . .	24,404	1,773,000	681,500
Included in Eastern Roumelia	13,646	746,000	265,000

If we exclude the provinces "indefinitely" to be occupied by Austria, Bulgaria, and Eastern Roumelia, there remain to Turkey in Europe only 74,790 square miles, with 4,779,000 inhabitants, of whom 2,521,500 are Mohammedans. In Armenia Russia takes 10,000 square miles, with about 350,000 inhabitants. Cyprus, entrusted to the keeping of England, has an area of 3,584 square miles, and 186,173 inhabitants in 1881. Thessaly ceded to Greece by convention, 24 May; treaty signed, 2 July, 1881. See *Greco-Turkish War*, May, 1897.

Alp Arslan and the Turks conquer Armenia and Georgia 1065-8

Asia Minor conquered, 1074-84; Jerusalem taken . 1076

Soliman Shah drowned in the Euphrates, while on the march; his son Ertoghul, granted territories near Angora, dies 1283

Osman, or Othman, his son, emir of the sultan of Iconium, whose followers were named Osmanlis, founded the Ottoman empire at Prusa, Bithynia, by policy and conquest, in 1299

Organisation of Janissaries by Orcan about . . 1330

Nicæa conquered, 1330; and the Morea . . . 1346

The Turks enter Thrace, and take Adrianople . 1361

Amurath I. remodels the Janissaries 1362

Bajazet I. overruns provinces of the Eastern empire 1389 *et seq.*

He defeats Sigismund of Hungary at Nicopolis, 28 Sept. 1396
He besieges Constantinople; but is interrupted by the approach of Tamerlane (or Timour), by whom he is defeated and made prisoner, at Ancyra, 28 July, 1402
Macedonia annexed 1430
Ladislas of Hungary defeated and slain at Varna by Amurath . . . . . . 10 Nov. 1444
Amurath defeats John Huniades at Kossova Oct. 1448
The Turks, invading Hungary, repelled by Huniades 1450
Constantinople taken by the Turks under Mahomet II., which ends the Eastern Roman empire, 29 May, 1453
Belgrade relieved by Huniades' victory over the Turks . . . . July, 1456
Greece subjected to the Turks (see *Greece*) 1458-60
The Turks take Otranto, diffusing terror throughout Europe 1480
Selim I. raised to the throne by the Janissaries; murders his father, brothers, &c. 1512
He takes the islands of the Archipelago . . . 1514
He overruns Syria 1515
Gains Egypt by defeat of Mamelukes . . Aug. 1516
Solyman takes Belgrade, Aug. 1521; and Rhodes, Dec. 1522
Defeats Hungarians at Mohatz . . . 29 Aug. 1526
Repulsed before Vienna. . . . . . Oct. 1529
Peace with Austria 1533
Cyprus taken from the Venetians . . . Aug. 1571
Great battle of Lepanto (*which see*) . . 7 Oct. ,,
Treaty of commerce with England 1579
Turks driven out of Persia by Shah Abbas . . 1585
Great fire in Constantinople 1606
War with the Cossacks, who take Azof . . . 1637
The Turks defeat the Persians and take the city of Bagdad 1638
Candia (Crete) taken from Venice, after a 25 years' siege 1669
Vienna besieged by Mahomet IV. but relieved by John of Poland . . . . . . 12 Sept. 1683
Peace of Carlovitz . . . . . . 26 Jan. 1699
Mustapha II. deposed by Janissaries 1703
The Morea retaken by the Turks 1715
The Turks defeated at Peterwardein 1716
They lose Belgrade; and their power declines . 1717
Peace of Erivan (with Persia) 1732
Belgrade taken from Austria; and Russia relinquishes Azof 1739
The Turks defeated at Kars 1745
Insurrection of Wahabees 1749
Great sea-fight in the channel of Scio; the Russian fleet defeats the Turkish 1770
The Crimea ceded to Russia . . . . Jan. 1784
Disastrous war with Russia and Austria, the Turks lose more than 200,000 men 1787-91
Cession of Oczacow 1791
War with the French, who invade Egypt . . . 1798
Insurrection of Mamelukes at Cairo 1803
War against Russia and England . . . 7 Jan. 1807
Passage and repassage of the Dardanelles effected by the British fleet, but with great loss; see *Dardanelles* . . . . 19 Feb. ,,
Murder of Hali Aga . . . . . . 25 May, ,,
The Janissaries massacre the newly disciplined troops 1808
The Russians defeated at Silistria 1809
Treaty of Bucharest (*which see*) . . 28 May, 1812
A caravan consisting of 2000 souls, returning from Mecca, destroyed by a pestilential wind in the deserts of Arabia; 20 saved . . . 9 Aug. ,,
Subjugation of the Wahabees (*which see*) . 1818-19
Ali Pacha of Janina, in Greece, declares himself independent 1820
Insurrection in Moldavia and Wallachia, 6 March, 1821
Persecution of Christians, 6 March; the Greek patriarch put to death at Constantinople, 23 April, ,,
[For the events in connection with the independence of Greece, see *Greece*.]
Horrible massacre at Scio (see *Chios*). 23 April, 1822
Sea-fight near Mitylene; Turks defeated . 6 Oct. 1824
New Mahometan army organised . . 29 May, 1826
Insurrection of the Janissaries at Constantinople; they are suppressed and massacred, 14-16 June, 1826
6000 houses burnt at Constantinople . 30 Aug. ,,
Battle of Navarino; the Turkish fleet destroyed by the fleets of England, France, and Russia (see *Navarino*) . . . . 20 Oct. 1827
Banishment of 132 French, 120 English, and 85 Russian settlers from the empire . 5 Jan. 1828
War with Russia . . . . . . 26 April, ,,
The czar Nicholas takes the field . . 20 May, ,,
Capitulation of Brahilow . . . . 19 June, ,,
Surrender of Anapa . . . . . 23 June, ,,
Eminences of Shumla taken by Russians, 20 July, ,,
The czar arrives before Varna . . . 5 Aug. ,,
Battle of Akhalzic . . . . . . 24 Aug. ,,
Fortress of Bajazet taken . . . . 9 Sept. ,,
The sultan proceeds to the camp with the sacred standard . . . . 26 Sept. ,,
Dardanelles blockaded . . . . . . 1 Oct. ,,
Surrender of Varna . . . . . . 11 Oct. ,,
Russians retreat from Shumla . . . . 16 Oct. ,,
Surrender of the castle of the Morea to the French, 30 Oct. ,,
Siege of Silistria raised by Russians . 10 Nov. ,,
Victory of the Russians at Kuleftscha, near Shumla 11 June, 1829
Battle near Erzeroum . . . . . 2 July, ,,
Adrianople is entered by the Russians, 20 Aug.; armistice agreed on . . . . . 29 Aug. ,,
Treaty of peace at Adrianople . . . 14 Sept. ,,
Fire at Constantinople; extinguished by the men of H.M.S. *Blonde* . . . . . 22 Jan. 1830
The porte acknowledges the independence of Greece, 25 April, ,,
Treaty with America . . . . . 7 May, ,,
Great fire at Pera; British embassy destroyed, 2 Aug. 1831
New military "order of glory" (Nischan) founded, 19 Aug. ,,
St. Jean d'Acre taken by Ibrahim Pacha, son of Mehemet Ali . . . . . . 2 July, 1832
He defeats the army of the sultan at Konieh, 21 Dec. ,,
Ibrahim Pacha marches within eighty leagues of Constantinople, and the sultan asks the aid of Russia . . . . Jan. 1833
The Russians enter Constantinople . 3 April, ,,
Treaty with Russia, offensive and defensive, 8 July, ,,
Office of grand vizier abolished . . 30 March, 1838
Treaty of commerce with England, concluded by lord Ponsonby, ratified . . . . 16 Aug. ,,
[For the events of 1839 and 1840 in relation to Syria; see *Syria*.]
Hatti-sherif promulgated decreeing many reforms, termed the Tanzimat (regulations), 3 Nov. 1839; again, at Rhodes 6 Jan. 1840; again 1844.
Christians admitted to office in Turkey . June, 1849
The Turkish government refuses to surrender the Hungarian and Polish refugees on the joint demand of Russia and Austria . . 16 Sept. ,,
[The porte (countenanced by England) firmly resists this demand.]
Russia suspends intercourse with the Porte, 12 Nov. ,,
The British fleet, under sir W. Parker, anchors in Besika bay . . . . 13 Nov. ,,
Diplomatic relations between Russia and the porte resumed, 31 Dec.; the latter sending the refugees to Konieh . . . . Jan. 1850
Turkish Croatia in a state of rebellion . . Jan. 1851
Treaty with France respecting the holy places (*which see*) . . . . . . 13 Feb. 1852
Imperial order of Medjidie founded . . Aug. ,,
Prince Menschikoff repairs to Constantinople as Russian negotiator, 28 Feb.; his peremptory demands rejected . . . . . 19 April, 1853
Reschid Pacha becomes foreign minister; the ultimatum being rejected, Menschikoff quits Constantinople . . . . . . 21 May, ,,
Hatti-sheriff issued, confirming the rights of the Greek Christians . . . . . . 6 June, ,,
Russian manifesto against Turkey . . 26 June, ,,
Russian army crosses the Pruth . . . 2 July, ,,
Grand national council—war to be declared if the principalities are not evacuated . . 26 Sept. ,,
War declared against Russia . . . . 5 Oct. ,,
[See *Russo-Turkish War*.]

Commencement of national debt (see *Loans*, 1854) . 1853

Insurrection in Epirus and Albania, favoured by the Greek government at Athens—Hellenic empire proclaimed . . . . 27 Jan. ,,

Volunteers from Athens join it . . 14 March, ,,

Rupture between Greece and Turkey 28 March, ,,

[Several conflicts ensue with varied success.]

Osman Pacha storms Peta, the central point of the insurrection . . . 25 April, ,,

English and French governments, after many remonstrances, send troops, which arrive at the Piræus; the king of Greece submits, and promises strict neutrality: the Greek volunteers are recalled . . . 25 and 26 May, ,,

Abdi Pacha and Fuad Effendi take the intrenched camp at Kolampaka, and the insurrection shortly after ceases . . . . 18 June, ,,

Reschid Pacha, having retired (3 June), resumes his office . . . . 1 July, ,,

Convention between Turkey and Austria . 14 June, ,,

The Russians retire from the principalities, which are thereupon occupied by the Austrians, Sept. ,,

Turkish loans . . . . . . Aug. 1855

[See *Loans* 1854-5.]

Firman authorising free exercise of religion 18 Feb. 1856

Peace with Russia by treaty of Paris . 30 March, ,,

Great Britain, France, and Austria guarantee integrity of Turkish empire . . 15 April, ,,

Austrians quit the principalities . . March, 1857

Misunderstanding among the allied powers respecting Moldavian elections, which are annulled, July, ,,

Death of Reschid Pacha . . . 7 Jan. 1858

Massacre of Christians at Jedda (*which see*), 15 June, ,,

Lord Stratford de Redcliffe, many years English ambassador at Constantinople, returned to England, Jan.; he is succeeded by sir H. Lytton Bulwer; accredited . . . 12 July, ,,

Indecisive conflicts in Montenegro between the natives and the Turks . . . July, ,,

Turkish financial reforms begun . . Aug. ,,

The first Turkish railway opened (from Aidan to Smyrna) . . . . 19 Sept. ,,

Base coinage called in; a fictitious Turkish coinage begun at Birmingham suppressed . . Oct. ,,

The allied powers determine the Montenegrine boundaries . . . . 8 Nov. ,,

Prince Alexander Cousa elected hospodar of both Moldavia and Wallachia . 5 and 7 Feb. 1859

[The porte at first objects, but afterwards accedes to the double election.]

Electric telegraph completed between Aden and Suez . . . . . . May, ,,

Great fire at Constantinople; 1000 houses destroyed, 10-14 Sept. ,,

Conspiracy against the sultan, 17 Sept.; his brother implicated; several condemned to die; reprieved, Sept. and Oct. ,,

Great agitation for financial reform . Oct. ,,

Alleged ill treatment of Christians in Turkey; proposed intervention of the great powers, 5 May; the Turkish government promises investigation and redress, 30 May; all the powers satisfied except Russia . . . June, 1860

War between the Druses and Maronites in Lebanon; massacres (see *Druses*) . . . June, ,,

Massacre of Christians at Damascus (see *Damascus* and *Syria*) . . . 9-11 July, ,,

Convention on behalf of the great powers at Paris; armed intervention of the French agreed to, 2 Aug. ,,

Inundations at Galatz; loss about 175,000*l.* 24 Feb. 1861

Christians revolt in the Herzegovina, aided by the Montenegrins . . . March, ,,

Great need of financial reform: the British ambassador, sir H. Lytton Bulwer, proposes a scheme . . . . . April, ,,

Discussion respecting the French occupation of Syria; it ceases . . . 5 June, ,,

Death of the sultan, Abdul-Medjid; accession of Abdul-Aziz, his brother . . 25 June, ,,

Economical reforms begun; Fuad Pacha made president of the council . . July, ,,

The late sultan's jewels sold in London . Aug. ,,

Imperial order of knighthood (Osmaneh) to include civil as well as military persons, founded, Sept. ,,

Imperial guard reorganised . . . . Oct. 1861

Fuad Pacha made grand vizier . 22 Nov. ,,

He puts forth a budget; treaties of commerce with Sweden, Spain, &c. . . . March, 1862

A Turkish loan (8,000,000*l.*) taken up in London, May, ,,

Secularisation of the property of the mosques, (value about 3,000,000*l.*) said to be determined on, Oct. ,,

Insurgents in the Herzegovina submit; peace made with Montenegro . . . 23 Sept. ,,

Dispute with Servia (*which see*) settled . 7 Oct. ,,

Ministerial crisis through the sultan's attempt at reaction; Fuad Pacha and others resign, but resume office . . . . . 7 Jan. 1863

A new bank established . . . 28 Jan. ,,

Fuad Pacha becomes seraskier . . 12 Feb. ,,

The sultan visits Egypt . . . 7-17 April, ,,

Fuad Pacha made grand vizier . 1 June, ,,

Exhibition of the produce of the empire opened in March; closed . . . 26 July, ,,

Great immigration of the Caucasian tribes April, 1864

Financial reforms; conversion and verification of the Turkish debt . . . . Aug. 1865

Cholera rages at Constantinople, nearly 50,000 deaths, Aug.: cholera subsides, Sept.; great fire there, about 2500 buildings (mosques, dwellings, &c.) destroyed . . . 6 Sept. ,,

Fuad Pacha proposes confiscation of the property of the mosques: opposition of the Sheikh-ul-Islam 21 Sept. ,,

Lord Lyons, ambassador at Constantinople . Oct. ,,

Revolt of the Maronites under Joseph Karam, 30 Dec. ,,

The grand vizier, Fuad Pacha, superseded by Mehemet Ruchdi . . . . 5 June, 1866

Revolution in Bucharest (see *Danubian principalities*).

Insurrection in Candia (*which see*) . . Aug. ,,

International conference respecting cholera at Constantinople . . 13 Feb.-26 Sept. ,,

European Turkey very unsettled . . Jan. 1867

Maronite revolt, under Joseph Karam, suppressed; his flight, Jan.; Turks leave . 28 March, ,,

Ministerial changes: Ali Pacha becomes grand vizier; Fuad Pacha, foreign minister 11 Feb. ,,

The recommendation of the European powers to the sultan to give up Candia finally declined, 31 Mar. ,,

Omar Pacha, commander-in-chief of the Turkish army . . . . . . April, ,,

Destruction of the dockyards in the Golden Horn by fire . . . . . 2 April, ,,

The sultan, with his son and nephew, visits Paris, 1-12 July; arrives at Buckingham Palace, London, 12 July; entertained by the queen at Windsor, 13 July; by the lord mayor, 18 July; at a ball at New India House, 19 July; gives 2500*l.* to the poor of London, 22 July; sails from Dover, 23 July; at Vienna, 27 July-1 Aug.; returns to Constantinople . . . 7 Aug. ,,

The sultan declines the proposition of Russia for the suspension of hostilities in Crete, and an international commission . . . 4 Sept. ,,

Ministerial crisis; Fuad Pacha resigns, but resumes his office . . . . Jan. 1868

Meeting of the new council of state (including Jews and Christians), with legislative, but not executive, functions . . . 18 May, ,,

Arrival of prince Napoleon Jerome at Constantinople . . . . . 26 June, ,,

Arrests on account of a supposed plot against the sultan . . . . . 30 Sept. ,,

Dispute with Greece for intervention in the Cretan insurrection; see *Greece* . . . . Dec. ,,

Fuad Pacha dies . . . . . Feb. 1869

The prince and princess of Wales's visit April, ,,

Memorial of the porte to the European powers desiring the abolition of the consular jurisdictions termed "capitulations" . . . June, ,,

The khedive or viceroy of Egypt censured for assuming sovereign powers encroaching on those of the sultan . . . . . Aug. ,,

System of compulsory education promulgated, Oct. ,,

Arrival of the empress of the French at Constantinople . . . . . 15 Oct. ,,

Inauguration of the Suez canal . 17 Nov. ,,

The khedive submits to the sultan . . Dec. ,,

Modification of the "capitulations" . April, 1870
Great fire at Pera; British embassy and about 7900 houses destroyed; great loss of life . 5 June, ,,
Another fire at Constantinople: about 1500 houses burnt . 11 July, ,,
Change in the cabinet; Mustapha Fazyl, finance minister . . . . 14 Aug. ,,
Reported treaty between Turkey and Greece to resist European aggression in the East . 21 Oct. ,,
Russia repudiates the treaty of Paris, 1856, 31 Oct. ,,
A note delivered to the porte (see *Russia*), 15 Nov. ,,
The sultan agrees to a conference on the Black Sea question alone . . about 3 Dec. ,,
Mustapha Fazyl, replaced by Mehemet Ruchdi, about 15 Jan. 1871
The Black Sea question settled by the conference at London (see *Russia*) . . 13 March, ,,
Omar Pacha, general, dies . . . . 18 April, ,,
Insurrection in Yemen, subdued . . . May, ,,
Great fires at Constantinople . . 7 June, ,,
Aali Pacha, grand vizier, an able statesman, dies 6 Sept. ,,
Mahmoud Pacha, grand vizier . . . . Sept. ,,
Tunis made an integral part of the empire, by decree . . . . 23 Oct. ,,
Political reforms inaugurated by the new ministry Nov. ,,
Important speech of the sultan to his council respecting the finances . . . . 16 May, 1872
Mahmoud Pacha, grand vizier, having made enemies through dismissing foreign employés, &c., is dismissed and replaced by Midhat Pacha, about 30 July, ,,
Midhat Pacha, who favoured Austria, dismissed; replaced by Mehemet Ruchdi . . . 19 Oct. ,,
Essad Pacha, grand vizier, 15 Feb.; Mehemet Ruchdi again . . . . . . April, 1873
The Roumelian railway connecting Constantinople, Adrianople, &c., opened . . . 17 June, ,,
The sultan's jewels, &c. (valued at 8,000,000*l.*) exhibited at Vienna . . . . . Aug. ,,
The shah of Persia arrives at Constantinople 19 Aug. ,,
Inability to raise a loan: the sultan gives up a large sum; great financial reforms proposed . Oct. ,,
Turkish aggressions on South Arabia checked by Great Britain . . . . Nov. ,,
Great improvements in the army; formation of reserves . . . . ,,
Hussein Avni, pacha made grand vizier . Feb. 1874
Improved financial arrangements reported April. ,,
The sultan ill; he recognises his nephew Murad as successor . . . . about 5 Oct. ,,
Austria, Germany, and Russia inform Turkey that they consider they have the right to conclude separate treaties with Roumania . . 20 Oct. ,,
Mésoudivé or *Mesoudiyé*, Turkish ironclad, launched at Blackwall . . . . . . 28 Oct. ,,
Turkish debt 3,000,000*l.* in 1854; 180,000,000*l.* ,,
Budget: estimated receipts, 21,711,764*l.*; expenditure, 26,299,178*l.* . . . . . June, 1875
Insurrection in Herzegovina (*which see*); great excitement in Bosnia, Servia, and Montenegro, July-Aug. ,,
Mahmoud Pacha made grand vizier, with a strong ministry, about . . . . . 25 Aug. ,,
Decree (in consequence of the deficit of 5,000,000*l.* in the budget) that for 5 years half the interest on the debt be paid in cash and half in 5 per cent. bonds . . . . 6 Oct. ,,
Circular note remitting taxes and promising economical and commercial reform, 7 Oct.; another stating object of the government to stop onerous loans, develop the resources of the empire, &c., 20 Oct. ,,
Remonstrances of British and Russian ambassadors with the government respecting expenditure and treatment of Christian subjects . Sept.-Nov. ,,
Raschid Pasha new foreign minister . . Nov. ,,
Midhat Pasha, reformer, resigns . . 4 Dec. ,,
Firman issued; ordering great reforms, equality of rights to Christians, &c. . . . Dec. ,,
Note of Andrassy, Austrian minister, respecting reforms, 30 Dec.; adopted by Germany and Russia, Jan.; by Great Britain, 18 Jan.; transmitted to the porte, about 7 Feb., agreed to . 10 Feb. 1876

Payment of April dividends deferred to July April 11, 1876
Insurrection in Bulgaria, promoted by foreign agitators, 1, 2 May; quickly suppressed by troops sent 7 May; about 65 villages burnt by the Bashi-bazouks and other Turkish troops; several towns destroyed; about 15,000 persons killed; atrocious cruelties to women and children; a few Turks killed by Bulgarians in self-defence (report by Mr. Schuyler, *see below*) . . . . May, ,,
Riots at Constantinople; the softas, fanatical students, and others, demand reforms; their cry, "Turkey for the Turks;" ministerial changes; Mahmoud Pacha, the grand vizier, replaced by Mehemet Ruchdi; Europeans much alarmed, 10 May *et seq.* ,,
British fleet arrives in Besika Bay . . 26 May, ,,
Meeting at Berlin of ministers of Austria, Germany, and Russia; they agree to a note to Turkey, requiring an armistice of two months, and other measures, 11, 12 May; the note accepted by France and Italy, not by Great Britain, 19 May; not presented through the revolution . 30 May, ,,
The grand vizier Mehemet Ruchdi, Hussein Avni, and Midhat Pacha, request the sultan to give up some of his treasure to save the nation from ruin; he refuses and is deposed, 29 May; his nephew proclaimed as Murad V.; joyfully accepted by the people, and recognised by the western powers . . . . 30 May *et seq.* ,,
Manifesto recognising the danger of the empire through misgovernment, and promising amendment . . . . 2 June, ,,
Abdul-Aziz recognises Murad; said to have committed suicide by cutting arteries in the arm; said to be insane; (decided, by trial, to have been murdered; *see below*, June, 1881) . 4 June, ,,
Assassination of Hussein Avni, the war minister, Raschid Pacha, the foreign minister, and others, by Hassan, a disgraced Circassian officer, 15 June, who is hanged . . . . . 17 June, ,,
Declaration of war by Servia, 1 July; by Montenegro . . . . 2 July, ,,
Tchernayeff and Servians enter Turkey; battle at Saitschar or Zaicar; Turks said to have the advantage . . . . 3 July, ,,
Severe conflict of Turks with Servians at Yavor, near Novi Bazar, 6 July; with Montenegrins at Nevesinje . . . . 27 July, ,,
League in aid of Turkish Christians formed in London . . . . 27 July, ,,
Mukhtar Pacha defeated by prince Nikita at Urba or Urbitza in Herzegovina . . . 28 July, ,,
Issue of paper money announced . . 28 July, ,,
Several days' conflict; the Turks enter Servia, and capture Gurgosavatz; Servians retreat 7 Aug. ,,
Turkish barbarities in Bulgaria reported by *Daily News'* correspondent, substantiated by report of Mr. Schuyler, the American commissioner from Constantinople, dated . . . . . 10 Aug. ,,
Asserted victory of prince Nikita at Medun, near Kutchi, about . . . . . . 14 Aug. ,,
Advance of the Turks under Abdul-Kerim Pacha upon Alexinatz; severe fighting . . 9 Aug. ,, 19-30 Aug. ,,
Servia invites the mediation of the guaranteeing powers . . . . . about 24 Aug. ,,
Murad V. deposed on account of bad health; his brother Abdul-Hamid II. proclaimed 31 Aug. ,,
The great powers propose an immediate armistice, the restoration of the *status quo ante bellum*, payment of an indemnity by Servia, &c.; memorandum presented . . . . . . 3, 4 Sept. ,,
Servians said to be severely beaten before Alexinatz 1, 2 Sept.; continued indecisive fighting . . ,,
Armistice till 25 Sept. agreed to about 17 Sept. ,,
Prince Milan proclaimed king by the army at Deligrad; disapproved . . . . . 16 Sept. ,,
Report of Mr. Baring, the British commissioner in Bulgaria, published . . . . . 19 Sept. ,,
[It establishes the facts "that a ferocious Mussulman soldiery, in revenge for a feeble and abortive insurrection, were let loose on the inhabitants of a large province; that the population were barbarously massacred, men, women, and children included; and that during the storm of savage fury crimes of all descriptions and outrages un-

mentionable were perpetrated on the inhabitants."—*Times.*]

Firm incisive despatch from Lord Derby to Sir H. Elliot, referring to Mr. Baring's report, proposing longer armistice, &c. . . . . . . 21 Sept. 1876

The porte receives the propositions of the six great powers . . . . 26 Sept. „

Lord Derby informs the deputation from the city of London that, in regard to the Eastern question, the government is labouring for local self-government for the Turkish provinces in Europe, equal treatment of Mahometans and Christians, better administration for both, security for life and property, and effectual guarantees against repetition of outrages . . . . 27 Sept. „

Servia rejects the renewal of the armistice; Tchernayeff and army dominant; fighting renewed, 26, 27 Sept. „

Servian attacks on the Turks near Alexinatz severely repulsed . . . . 28, 29 Sept. „

In reply to the great powers the porte declines an armistice, opposes administrative autonomy to the provinces as impracticable, proposes a senate, and guarantees incisive reforms . . 2 Oct. „

Mukhtar Pacha said to defeat Montenegrines, 7 Oct. „

Montenegrine victory at Danilograd . 13 Oct. „

Turkey's proposal of an armistice for 6 months, 10 Oct.; declined by Russia, who proposes 4 to 6 weeks, longer being injurious to commerce, &c. . . . . 14 Oct. „

Continued fighting, generally unfavourable to Servians . . . . 15-19 Oct. „

Alexinatz bombarded . . . . . 16-19 Oct. „

Medun surrenders to Montenegrines . 20 Oct. „

Krevet taken by Turks . . . . . 21 Oct. „

Result of fighting very favourable to Turks, 19-24 Oct. „

Alleged conspiracy at Constantinople against the reform ministry; many arrests . about 23 Oct. „

Important Turkish successes in the valley of the Morava . . . . 19-24 Oct. „

Servians and Russians defeated; armies under Tchernayeff and Horvaritch divided, 19-24 Oct.; Djunis taken by Turks; Deligrad untenable; severe Russian loss . . . . . 29 Oct. „

Neutral despatch of lord Derby . dated 30 Oct. „

Alexinatz captured by Turks; Russian ultimatum given, demanding 6 weeks' armistice within 48 hours . . . . dated 31 Oct. „

Armistice for two months signed . . 1 Nov. „

Deligrad captured by Turks, now virtually masters of Servia . . . . 1 Nov. „

Pacific declaration of the czar to lord Aug. Loftus, 2 Nov. „

Deligrad evacuated by Turks; farewell address of Tchernayeff to officers, exhorting to constancy, 4 Nov. „

Czar's speech at Moscow; he will act independently if guarantees are not obtained . . 10 Nov. „

Marquis of Salisbury appointed special ambassador for conference at Constantinople; he arrives at Paris, 18 Nov.; Berlin, 20 Nov.; Vienna, 24 Nov.; Rome, 29 Nov.; Constantinople . . 5 Dec. „

Alleged abortive conspiracy to restore Murad, about 8 Dec. „

Preliminary meetings of conference of representatives of six great powers begin (Great Britain, Russia, Austria, Germany, France, and Italy), 12 Dec. „

Ruchdi Pacha, grand vizier, replaced by Midhat Pacha, a reformer . . . . . . 19 Dec. „

Armistice extended to Feb. 1877 . . . Dec. „

New political constitution proclaimed: (chief provisions: indivisibility of the empire; the sultan supreme; individual liberty; freedom of all creeds, of the press, and of education; equal legal taxation; a senate and two chambers; general elections by ballot every fourth year; irremovable judges, &c.) . . . . 23 Dec. „

Opening of the conference . . . . 23 Dec. „

Financial decree of 6 Oct. 1875, abrogated, 27 Dec. „

Armistice extended to 1 March . . . 28 Dec. „

The great national council of Turkey rejects the propositions of the conference, 18 Jan.; it closes, 20 Jan.; chief ambassadors leave soon after 22 Jan. „

Negotiations for peace opened with Servia and Montenegro . . . . . . about 26 Jan. „

Midhat Pacha, the grand vizier, dismissed and banished; succeeded by Edhem Pacha (educated at Paris); reforms to go on . . . . 5 Feb. 1876

Gortschakoff's circular to great powers, inquiring what they intend to do, signed 19 Jan.; published . . . . about 7 Feb. „

Protocols of the conference published in *Times*, &c. early in Feb. „

In Turkey "there is no aristocracy, no governing class; no organised democracy; no representative government" (marquis of Salisbury), 20 Feb. „

Peace with Servia signed . . . 1 March, „

First Turkish parliament opened: 30 senators, 90 deputies; speech from the sultan read, 19 March, „

Gen. Ignatieff visits Berlin, Paris, London, Vienna, &c. . . . . March, „

Protocol signed for six powers: principles—to wait for Turkish reforms and watch; conditional disarmament in Russia and Turkey (voidable under certain conditions) . . . . 31 March, „

Protocol rejected by Turkey, 12 April; justificatory circular sent to the powers; Mr. Layard sent as temporary ambassador to Turkey . . April, „

Insurrection of Mirdites or Miridites, April; armistice with Montenegro not renewed . 13 April, „

Arrival of Mr. Layard as ambassador, at Constantinople; he affirms the neutrality of Great Britain, about 24 April, „

War declared by Russia (see *Russo-Turkish war*, 1877) . . . . 24 April, „

Riotous manifestation by the softas, soon subsides, 24 May, „

A *jihad* or holy war against Russia propounded by the sheikh-ul-islam . . . about 28 May, „

Suleiman Pacha successful in Montenegro; relieves Nicksics, besieged . . . . May *et seq.* „

Miridite leaders captured . . . . June, „

The parliament closed without a speech . 28 June, „

Safvet Pacha, foreign minister, replaced by Aarifi Pacha . . . . about 18 July, „

Other ministerial changes . . . . July, „

Protests against alleged Russian atrocities, July —Aug. „

Bosnian revolt reported to be ended . . Aug. „

Proclamation for increase of army by 150,000—Christians and others to serve . . 26 Nov. „

Reported intrigues at Constantinople by peace and war parties . . . . Nov. „

The sultan issues a rather vague proclamation of amnesty to Bulgaria . . . about 27 Nov. 1877

Surrender of Plevna, 10 Dec.; circular note to the great powers requesting mediation . 12 Dec. „

Parliament opened; the sultan's speech censures the war, and praises his generals and soldiers, 13 Dec. „

The ministry censured, resigns; still holds office; Suleiman dismissed; crisis at Constantinople, 5, 6, 7 Jan. 1878

Hamed Pacha, grand vizier . . . . 11 Jan. „

New ministry under Ahmed Nefik; grand viziership abolished . . . . 4, 5 Feb. „

British fleet enter the Dardanelles without permission of the sultan . . . . . 13 Feb. „

The parliament dissolved by the sultan . 14 Feb. „

Insurrection in Crete, Thessaly, Epirus, &c. (see *Greece*) . . . . Feb., March, „

Treaty of peace with Russia signed at San Stefano (see *Stefano*), 3 March; ratified at St. Petersburg, 17 March, „

Osman Pacha honourably received by the sultan, 24 March, „

Grand-duke Nicholas and the sultan exchange visits at Constantinople . . . . . 26 March, „

Ahmed Nefik replaced by Sadyk as prime minister, about 18 April, „

Insurrection near Rhodope, in Roumelia, against Russians going on; see *Rhodope* . . . April, „

Insurrection (said doubtfully to be in favour of the ex-sultan Murad) in Constantinople, suppressed; Ali Suavi, a softa and fanatical reformer, with others, killed . . . . 20 May, „

Public offices, &c., at Constantinople destroyed by fire; attributed to incendiaries . . 22 May, „

Office of grand vizier revived for Mehemet Ruchdi, May; soon replaced by Safvet . . 29 May, „

Secret agreement between the marquis of Salisbury and count Schouvaloff, Russian ambassador, 30 May,

Secret British convention with Turkey (defensive alliance): if by the treaty of Berlin, Russia acquires Kars, Ardahan, or Batoum, Great Britain is to join the sultan in arms in defending his dominions, he engaging to reform his government; Cyprus to be held by Great Britain till Russia returns its acquisitions . . . . 4 June, 1878
Cyprus ceded to Great Britain . . . 3 July, „
Berlin conference meets, 13 June; treaty signed (see *Berlin*) . . . . 13 July, „
A conspiracy against the sultan suppressed, about 10 July, „
A ministerial crisis ends; the vizier Safvet Pacha's policy approved by the sultan, who gives him a present; ratification of the treaty of Berlin announced . . . . 4 Aug. „
Trial of Suleiman Pacha for misconduct during the war begun . . . . Aug. „
The Turks said to be grossly ill-treated in Bulgaria, and other surrendered places . . . . Aug. „
Safvet Pacha's circular to foreign powers refusing to recognise Greek proposal for annexation of Candia, Thessaly, &c. . . . . . 8 Aug. „
Murder of Mehemet Ali Pacha at Ipek, near Scutari, by Albanian rioters . . . . . . 6 Sept. „
Alleged conspiracies on behalf of the ex-sultan Murad; instigated by the ulemas, about 10 Sept. „
Albanian leader with 40,000 men said to be ruling from Janina to Montenegro . . 12 Sept. „
German circular to the powers on Turkish delays in carrying out the Berlin treaty . middle Sept. „
The sultan accepts the reforms proposed by the British government; announced . . 24 Oct. „
Insurrectionary movements in Macedonia Oct. „
Midhat Pacha appointed governor-general of Syria, to inaugurate reforms . . about 11 Nov. „
Suleiman Pacha sentenced to degradation and imprisonment, 2 Dec.; absolved by the sultan 4 Dec. „
New ministry; Kheredine Pacha (grand vizier); Caratheodori, and others . . . . 4 Dec. „
Macedonian insurrection ended . . . . 3 Jan. 1879
Definitive treaty of peace with Russia, signed, 8 Feb. „
British fleet leaves the sea of Marmora March, „
Definitive treaty with Austria, published 26 May, „
Mahmoud Nedem, old statesman, returns to Constantinople on invitation . . . 30 June, „
Kheredine, Caratheodori, and others compelled to resign through opposition of the assembly of ulemas (their policy said to be against the Khoran); succeeded by Aarifi Pacha 28, 29 July, „
The Russians evacuate Turkey . July, Aug. „
New ministry under Said Pacha . 18, 19 Oct. „
Pressure for reforms put upon the government by the British; admiral Hornby and the fleet enter Turkish waters; quit . . early in Nov. „
Baker Pacha appointed inspector-general of gendarmerie in Asia Minor . announced 18 Nov. „
Great financial depression . . Nov., Dec. „
Official relations with Great Britain temporarily suspended on account of the imprisonment of Dr. Köller, a German missionary, and Ahmed Tewfik, who assisted him in translations . 31 Dec. „
Successful intervention of sir A. H. Layard, 1-10 Jan. 1880
Note of Savas Pacha to the powers acknowledging corruptions in judicial affairs and promising efficient reforms (in *Times*) . . . 30 Jan. „
Col. and Mrs. Synge (distributors of relief to Mussulmans) captured by Greek brigands, near Salonica, about 19 Feb.; released for 10,000*l.* about 24 March, „
Mr. Goschen sent as temporary ambassador; arrives at Constantinople . . . 28 May, „
New ministry under Kadri Pacha about 8 June, „
Identic note from European powers, 11 June; given in . . . . 12 June, „
Osman Pacha, war minister, dismissed about 10 July, „
Naval demonstration by the European powers at Dulcigno, suggested by earl Granville . July, „
Collective note of the Berlin conference presented, 15 July, „
Madame Skobeleff, mother of the Russian general, robbed and murdered near Philippopolis by Ouzalis, a Russian . . . . 18 July, „
Midhat Pacha, governor of Syria, and Hamed Pacha of Smyrna exchange offices . . Aug. 1880
Collective note from the powers urging cession of Dulcigno, &c., to Montenegro, and proposing to aid the prince in taking possession . 3 Aug. „
The ministry modified under Said Pacha, premier, 12 Sept. „
A final note from the powers respecting cession of Dulcigno to Montenegro, delivered . 15 Sept. „
Admiral Beauchamp Seymour, commander of combined fleet at Ragusa, sent to make a demonstration near Dulcigno . . . . . 20 Sept. „
The sultan refuses to surrender Dulcigno; the French decline to partake in attack on the town, about 27 Sept. „
Note from the sultan limiting his concessions and resisting coercion; presented . . 3 Oct. „
Immediate cession of Dulcigno ordered by the sultan, about 23 Oct.; effected . . 26 Nov. „
The combined fleet disperses . . . 4 Dec. „
Note from the sultan to the powers respecting the Greeks arming . . . . . 14 Dec. „
Circular from the powers recommending arbitration, 24 Dec. 1880; declined by Turkey and Greece . . . . early in Jan. 1881
Circular from Turkey proposing conference at Constantinople, &c. . . . . about 15 Jan. „
Notes from the powers presented . . 21 Feb. „
Conference at Constantinople; agreement between Turkey and the powers; proposals referred to Athens . . . . . . 30 March, „
Mr. Henry Suter, engaged in mines, seized by brigands at Cassandra, in Salonica, about 8 April, „
Rebellion in Albania (*which see*) suppressed May, „
Midhat Pacha's palace surrounded by soldiers; he escapes and appeals to the powers . 17 May, „
The sultan protests against French invasion of Tunis (*which see*) . . . . May, „
Midhat surrenders, claiming a fair trial, about 17 May, „
Turkey protests against the Tunis treaty of 12 May, May, „
Mr. Suter's release for 15,000*l.* ransom announced, 23 May, „
Convention between Turkey and Greece arranged at Constantinople settling frontiers: Thessaly ceded by Turkey . . . . . . 24 May, „
Mr. Goschen leaves Constantinople; his mission successful; succeeded by lord Dufferin, 26 May; who arrives at Constantinople . 15 June, „
Trial of Midhat Pacha and others for murder of the late sultan Abdul-Aziz; convicted; Mustapha Fahri Bey and Hadj Mehmed actual assassins; others, Mahmoud and Nouzi Pachas, the sultan's brothers-in-law, Midhat Pacha, and others accomplices . . . . . 27, 28 June, „
Sentence; death to all, except two subordinates to imprisonment . . . . . . 29 June, „
Turco-Greek convention ceding Thessaly to Greece, signed at Constantinople . . . 2 July, „
The trial of Midhat and others said to be a mockery; punishment commuted to exile on intercession of the British Government; announced 31 July, „
The captors of Mr. Suter taken in Greece, about 15 Aug. „
Turkish mission at Cairo . . . . 7-18 Oct. „
Continued negotiations at Constantinople respecting national debt . . . Oct. *et seq.* „
The German vessel *Vulcan* laden with dynamite (said to belong to Russia) cargo unshipped near Constantinople . . . . about 8 Oct. „
Decree signed for a satisfactory settlement of the national debt . . . . . . 28 Dec. „
Capt. Selby, R.N., wounded by Albanians at Artaki, announced 16 Feb.; died . . . . 20 Feb. 1882
Mehemet Ruchdi Pasha dies . . 26 March, „
Russian-war indemnity convention ratified, 6 May, „
The minister Said Pasha dismissed, succeeded by Abdurrahman Pasha, about 2 May; who resigns, 7 July, „
Said Pasha reinstated . . . about 8 July, „
Sultan protests against bombardment of forts at Alexandria (see *Egypt*) . . about 11 July, „
Protractive negotiations respecting a military convention; agreed to . . . . . 29 Aug. „
Alleged conspiracy of Fuad Pasha and others to dethrone the sultan . . . about 28 Nov. „

Said Pasha dismissed; Circassian guard dismissed, 29 Nov. 1882

Frontier disputes with Montenegro . . Nov. ,,

Said Pasha restored with honours, made grand Vizier 3 Dec. Fuad Pasha restored to favour, 7 Dec. ,,

Excitement of the sultan through dread of assassination . . . . about 13 Dec. ,,

Fight among the sultan's body guard (Albanians and Negroes), about 30 killed or wounded 17 Jan. 1883

Turkish note to the powers against British Egyptian circular . . . . . about 23 Jan. ,,

Difficulties with the Greek church respecting political reforms; resignation of the Œcumenical patriarch Yoachim II.; not accepted; conciliation proposed . . . . 29 Dec.–3 Jan. 1884

Resignation maintained . . . . 9 Jan. ,,

Amicable settlement of dispute, announced April, ,,

The Imperial prince and princess of Austria hospitably entertained by the sultan . . April, ,,

Death of Midhat Pasha, great statesman and reformer in exile, aged 62 . . . . May, ,,

Circular to the six great powers announcing the stoppage of the post offices in Constantinople, 20 July, resisted; the Turkish arrangements fail, and are withdrawn . . . . . Aug. ,,

Sir Edward Thornton appointed to succeed lord Dufferin . . . . Sept. ,,

Greek patriarch elected . . . . . 13 Oct. ,,

Mutiny of troops at Monastir, for want of pay and clothing; settled by concession . about 21 Nov. ,,

Petitions to the sultan from Macedonia respecting Turkish atrocities signed . . . . 12 Oct. ,,

Hassan Fehmy Pasha sent to London to confer on the Egyptian question; his proposals not received, end of . . . . Jan. 1885

Turkey protests against Italian occupation of Massowah on the Red Sea . . about 23 Feb. ,,

New tariff with England signed . . 9 July, ,,

Sir H. D. Wolff arrives at Constantinople on a mission respecting Egypt, 22 Aug.; well received by the sultan . . . . . . 29 Aug. ,,

Revolution in Roumelia (*which see*), 18 Sept.; firm Turkish note to the powers about 22 Sept. ,,

Said Pasha, grand vizier, and other ministers dismissed; succeeded by Kiamil Pasha, 24 Sept. ,,

Conference of ambassadors, 4 Oct.; the ambassadors present a collective note condemning the revolution in Roumelia as breaking the treaty of Berlin, 14 Oct. ,,

Decree for Turkish commission to go with sir H. D. Wolff to Cairo, about 12 Oct.; convention signed . . . . 24 Oct. ,,

Turkey asks assistance of the powers to settle the Roumelian affair . . . . . . 19 Oct. ,,

Conference of ambassadors at Constantinople, 5 Nov.; collective declaration for maintenance of *status quo ante*, about 7 Nov.; division of opinion as to enforcement . . . 11 Nov. ,,

Rustem Pasha succeeds Musurus Pasha (1856–85) as ambassador in London . . . Nov. ,,

The Sultan ratifies the treaty between Bulgaria and Servia . . . . . . 13 March, 1886

Sir Edward Thornton, British ambassador, received by the Sultan . . . . . . 11 March, ,,

Hobart Pasha, Turkish admiral, dies, aged 64, 19 June ,,

Sir William White appointed British ambassador, Oct.; received . . . . . . 2 Nov. ,,

Four English gentlemen captured near Smyrna by brigands who demand 3,000*l.* ransom, 24 Sept.; released by payment of a ransom of 750*l.* 26 Sept. 1887

Reported deficit of 1,000,000*l.* in the budget; increase of brigandage . . . . Nov. ,,

After the celebration of the feast of Mevlud, the Sultan delivers an optimist speech to the officials on the state of the empire . 27 Nov. ,,

Direct railway communication between London and Constantinople via Dover and Calais in 94 hours; first train from Vienna . 12–14 Aug. 1888

The government contracts a loan for 1,350,000*l.* from the "German" bank; consequent rupture with the Ottoman bank, its usual financial agent, Oct. ,,

80,000 men of the reserve called out . . Aug. 1889

The Ottoman bank, sir Edgar Vincent, director, lends the sultan 150,000*l.*, reported 28 Oct. ,,

Trial of Moussa Bey, see *Armenia* 23 Nov. *et seq.* 1889

The German emperor and empress warmly received by the sultan at Constantinople, 2 Nov.; a review, &c. . . . . 3–6 Nov. ,,

Five new war vessels launched at Constantinople, 30 Jan. 1890

New 5 per cent. conversion loan at 93, successfully effected by the grand vizier, aided by sir Edgar Vincent; agreement signed . . . 30 April, ,,

The Russian government demands payment of the arrears of the Russo-Turkish war indemnity, about 15 May, ,,

Troubles in Old Servia by bands of Arnauts; severe fight, with much slaughter . . . June, ,,

Turkey defers payment of indemnity till Nov., Russia demands immediate payment; note sent, about 18 June, ,,

British cotton and woollen yarn-spinning factory opened at Constantinople . . . 22 June, ,,

For Armenian troubles see *Armenia*, 1889–90.

The government frigate *Ertogrul* founders on the S. coast of Japan, during a gale; out of 653, 584 persons perish, including vice-admiral Osman Pasha . . . . 18 Sept. ,,

Sir Edgar Vincent thanked by the leading merchants of Constantinople for his services to them . . . . 12 Jan. 1891

Arnaut revolt in Old Servia; the government buildings in Drenitza burnt, reported, about 4 Feb. ,,

Death of Musurus pasha, diplomatist, aged 84; 33 years ambassador in London . . 12 Feb. ,,

The Arnauts again attack the Christians in Old Servia, who bravely resist, but are defeated with loss . . . . . . about 14 May, ,,

Railway train at Tcherkesskeni, near Constantinople, attacked by brigands; two persons killed; five carried off for ransom, 1 June; active measures taken by the porte, June; captives liberated, 4–8 June, ,,

M. Eugène de Raymond, sub-manager of a vineyard company captured by brigands at Ormoudja, 7 Aug.; ransomed by the sultan . . 12 Aug. ,,

Dismissal of Kiamil pasha, president of ministry or grand vizier (appointed 1890) by the sultan, 3 Sept. 1891; succeeded by Djevad pasha.

Sir William A. White, the able British ambassador, dies at Berlin, while on a visit, 28 Dec. 1891; succeeded by the right hon. sir Francis Clare Ford . . . . about 8 Jan. 1892

Payment of the war indemnity resumed, reported, 27 Jan. ,,

Sir Francis Clare Ford arrives at Constantinople, 26 Feb.; received by the sultan . 8 March, ,,

The Russian government remonstrates against the reception of M. Stamboloff, the Bulgarian premier, 18 Aug. *et seq.*; the porte replies courteously that this is not a violation of the treaty of Berlin . . . . 18 Oct. ,,

Russia again demands payment of war indemnity about 7 Nov. ,,

The retreat of the robbers of the railway train in June, 1891, discovered; about 2,000*l.* recovered by the police, reported . . . 14 April, 1893

Sir Philip Currie appointed British ambassador 20 Dec. ,,

Arrival of the khedive in Constantinople, 25 June, and of the king of Servia . . . 27 June, 1894

Earthquake at Constantinople, &c. (*which see*) 10, 11 July, ,,

Six war vessels launched in the Golden Horn, autumn, ,,

Further instalment of the war indemnity paid to Russia . . . . 8 Nov. ,,

Diplomatic relations with the powers suspended in relation to Armenia (*which see*) . . 9 Dec. ,,

Financial deficit; economical reforms proposed, April, 1895

The grand vizier, Djevad pasha, opposed to Armenian reforms; dismissed; succeeded by Said pasha; Turkhan pasha, president of the Armenian commission, appointed foreign minister, 8 June, ,,

The great powers demand the disarmament of the Beduin and indemnity for the attacks at Jedda (*which see*) . . . . 10 June, ,,

Reply of the porte accepting in principle the proposed reforms, but objecting to supervision of the powers . . . . . 17 June, 1895
A commission appointed for reforms in Armenia; Turkhan pasha to be inspector of certain provinces . . . . . . 29 June, „
Scheme submitted to the sultan; reported 15 July, „
Shakir pasha appointed to supervise the carrying out of reforms in Armenia . . . . 20 July, „
Approved by the powers . . . . 31 July, „
Visit of the khedive to the sultan 18 July–16 Sept. „
The porte rejects the control of the powers in the administration of Armenia, reported, 19 Aug.; and appeals to France and Russia against England, without effect, about 29 Aug.; the porte communicates some concessions . . 7 Sept. „
An Armenian demonstration at Constantinople resisted by the mob and police with much cruelty; 172 killed, 30 Sept., 1 Oct.; churches filled with Armenian destitute refugees; a fierce fight at Scutari; massacre of Armenians at Pera; the ambassadors of 6 powers remonstrate with the porte; Kiamil pasha appointed grand vizier in place of Said pasha; Rifat pasha, minister of interior, resigns, 3 Oct.; Said pasha, a Kurd, re-appointed foreign minister; 95 corpses delivered up to the patriarchate, 6 Oct.; conflicts and massacre of 800 Armenians at Trebizond, by Turkish soldiery, 8 Oct.; refugees quit the churches, under protection of the dragomans, 10–12 Oct.; over 700 killed, injured and missing during the riots; British fleet at Lemnos, reported . . . . 10 Oct. „
Armenians attacked by Mahometans at Ak Hissar, 45 killed . . . . 9 Oct. „
Armenian reform scheme accepted and decreed by the porte . . . . . . 17, 20 Oct. „
Decree authorizing the conversion of the 5 per cent. customs loan into 4 per cent. . . . 18 Oct. „
Financial crisis: run on the Ottoman bank, 2, 3 Nov. „
The ambassadors urgently demand that immediate measures be taken to suppress anarchy and bloodshed . . . . . . 5 Nov. „
The "Young Turkey" party in Paris demand general reforms . . . . Nov. „
Kiamil pasha, grand vizier, superseded, 6 Nov.; appointed gov.-gen. of Aleppo; Halil Rifat pasha appointed grand vizier; a palace anti-reform cabinet appointed . . . . . 7 Nov. „
Evil influence of the "palace party": needful intervention of the diplomatic body; arrests of Armenians in Constantinople . 9 Nov. *et seq.* „
Arrival of gold, end of financial crisis . 14 Nov. „
Gradual formation of the Constitutional party, desiring reform, rational government, &c.; their views published . . . . . . 15 Nov. „
Extra powers and forces granted by the powers to their ambassadors, for the defence of Christians, 18 Nov. „
Insurrection in Arabia (*which see*) . . . Nov. „
Death of Rustem pasha, ambassador in London, a Christian and patriot, 20 Nov.; succeeded by Costaki pasha . . . . . . Dec. „
Foreign naval demonstration in the Levant, 26 Nov. „
The sultan, after delay, accedes to the entrance of extra foreign despatch boats, 10 Dec.; martial law decreed . . . . . . 14 Dec. „
Newspaper started by the "Young Turkey" reform party in Paris . . . . . . Dec. „
Many Armenians in Constantinople released, 21 Dec.; 182 arrests for disaffection to the sultan, Jan. 1896
Contract for a loan of 3,000,000*l.* sanctioned by the Porte . . . . 18 Feb. „
Scheme for administrative reform in European provinces, published . . . . . 28 April, „
Despatches of vice-consul Fitzmaurice describing the atrocities and misery at Orfa, and other places, in Armenia, received at Constantinople, April, „
Successful intervention of sir Philip Currie and the ambassadors regarding the forced conversions of Armenians at Biredjik, and elsewhere, 7–15 May, „

Circulation of British journals prohibited, Jan.—May, 1896
Increased persecution of Armenians in Constantinople; many Turkish students sentenced to 10 years' penal servitude for aiding the Armenians at Zeitun . . . . 16 May, „
Sir Philip and lady Currie leave Constantinople for London . . . . 18 May, „
Conference of ambassadors respecting Crete, 20 June; the Porte accedes to all their recommendations, conditionally, 3 July; again 25 Aug. „
The Armenian revolutionary committee, with the view of inciting the ambassadors to more active measures on behalf of the Armenians, take possession of the Ottoman bank at Constantinople. Dynamite and bombs were secretly introduced into the building by a band of about 25 armed men; and at 1.30 p.m. revolvers were fired and bombs thrown, many gendarmes and 5 of the conspirators were killed; the staff of the bank took refuge in the upper rooms, from which sir Edgar Vincent, the governor, and several directors, escaped by a balcony. The conspirators, after threatening to destroy the building if their demands were not granted, sent a message to the palace, where sir Edgar Vincent and others were consulting, offering to surrender, if permitted to leave the country; their terms were agreed to; and 15 of them were taken on board sir Edgar Vincent's yacht at night, 26 Aug. (thence they were conveyed to Marseilles by the *Gironde*, 4 Sept.).
A great massacre of Armenians (estimated between 5,000 and 6,000) by Mahometans ensued, 26–30 Aug. „
Remonstrance of the ambassadors to the sultan respecting the conduct of the troops in promoting the massacres; energetic action of the hon. Michael Herbert and the consuls; British and foreign marines landed to protect the embassies, &c. . . . . 29 Aug. „
Judicial committee of inquiry appointed, 400 persons arrested . . . . . . 30 Aug. „
The embassies abstain from celebrating the sultan's accession; collective note to the Porte, respecting the massacres, 31 Aug.; the Porte replies, practically denying the truth of their statements . . . . 12 Sept. „
Extraordinary tribunal appointed for the trial of the rioters, 3 Sept.; many Armenians transported; some Mahometan murderers acquitted, Sept. *et seq.* „
Return of sir Philip Currie; British embassy intercedes . . . . 5–8 Sept. „
Bomb factory discovered at Scutari, 2 leaders and 14 of the Armenian revolutionaries arrested, Sept. „
Disorder and panics at Constantinople, trade paralysed, foreign merchants ruined; collective note from the embassies to the porte; 3000*l.* sent to sir Philip Currie from England for Armenian relief . . . . 15 Sept. „
Repression of the "Young Turkey" party, arrests and deportation in Constantinople . 16 Sept. „
3000 Armenian refugees leave under consular assistance up to 19 Sept.; exodus of all races continues . . . . . . 26 Sept. *et seq.* „
Extraordinary tribunal condemns Mahometan murderers to 15 years' imprisonment; Armenians suspected of having taken part in the Armenian *coup* at the bank sentenced to death . 29 Sept. „
Armenian circular letter of complaint received by the embassies . . . . 1 Oct. „
Continued arrests and injustice to Armenians; the porte demands the right to search foreign vessels for Armenians, 6 Oct.; rejected by the embassies, 9 Oct. „
The ambassadors complain to the porte of the non-execution of its promises to Crete . 10 Oct. „
Note from the Italian embassy to the porte demanding an indemnity for the massacre of an Italian at Constantinople and Father Salvatore in a convent near Marash in 1895, early Oct. „
The Austrian embassy demands the punishment of those in command of the soldiers who recently murdered M. Zlatko and an indemnity of 6000*l.* 12 Oct.; paid . . . . . . 22 Oct. „
Death of Mr. W. H. Wrench, British consul, able and upright, deeply lamented, 13 Oct.; public funeral . . . . 14 Oct. „

Decree ordering the return of Armenian emigrants under pain of confiscation of property, &c., 10 Oct. 1896

Poll tax, &c., on Mahometans decreed . 21 Oct. ,,

Great destitution in Constantinople . Oct., Nov. ,,

French intervention; release of innocent Armenians in Constantinople and provinces ordered; the vali of Diarbekr dismissed; execution of reforms in Armenia, &c., promised, 7 Nov.; delayed . . . . 19 Nov. ,,

Total, 55,000*l.* from the Armenian relief fund remitted to sir Peter Currie . . . Nov. ,,

Special tribunal dissolved by decree . 17 Nov. ,,

Many members of the "Young Turkey" party and others exiled . . . . . . Dec. ,,

All London newspapers of 30 Nov. refused entry, Dec. ,,

Manifesto issued by the "Ottoman liberal committee" denounces the sultan, and demands the restoration of the constitution of 1876 . 6 Dec. ,,

Anglo-Russian agreement concerning the execution of reforms in Turkey, announced . 6 Dec. ,,

Recall of Saadeddin pasha from Crete (within 48 hours) granted on demand of the ambassadors, 15 Dec. ,,

Amnesty to Armenians and Mahometans; death sentences to 100 Armenians commuted to imprisonment . . . . 21 Dec. ,,

Sir Edgar Vincent's financial report to the sultan on the revenue and expenditure (with recommendations); shows a yearly deficit since 1890 of 1,000,000*l*T. . . . . . . 26 Dec. ,,

Ato Jossef, the emperor Menelik's envoy, received by the sultan and decorated . . 1 Jan. 1897

Col. Mazhar Bey acquitted at Marash of the murder of Father Salvatore; new trial ordered by the sultan at Aleppo, Jan.; sentenced to life imprisonment . . . . 3 March, ,,

Anarchy reported in N.E. provinces of Asia Minor, 12 Jan. ,,

Irade issued accepting the demands of the Armenian patriarch with certain modifications, 20 Jan. ,,

Arrests of Armenians in Constantinople recommenced . . . . 6 Feb. ,,

Collective note from the six powers presented to the porte (see *Crete*), and the porte calls on the powers to abide by the treaty of Paris, 1856, 2 March, ,,

The porte agrees to the establishment of Cretan autonomy; 2nd note from the powers calling on Turkey to withdraw her troops from the interior, 5 March, ,,

Disturbed condition of Asia Minor, bloodshed at Everek and Tokat . . . . March, ,,

Mobilization of the fleet in the Bosphorus, 22 Mar. ,,

The powers declare that the aggressor on the Greek frontier in case of conflict shall be held responsible and shall derive no advantage . 5 April, ,,

War declared against Greece (the aggressor) (see *Greco-Turkish War*) . . . . . 17 April, ,,

Bomb outrages in Constantinople, one death, 18 Aug.; 8 men sentenced to death . 2 Sept. ,,

Peace preliminaries signed at Constantinople, 18 Sept. ,,

Prince Mavrocordato appointed Greek minister, announced . . . . 6 Oct. ,,

Sir R. Hamilton Lang appointed director-general of the Ottoman bank at Constantinople . Oct. ,,

Peace conferences at Constantinople, 8 articles agreed to, 23 Oct.; the Turkish protocol accepted . . . . 2 Dec. ,,

Rupture between Austria and Turkey concerning the severe ill-usage of Herr Brazzifolli, agent for the Austrian-Lloyd at Mersina, Asia Minor, Oct.; reparation promised by the porte but delayed; ultimatum 15–18 Nov. ,,

Full submission of Turkey . . . . 18 Nov. ,,

Indemnities claimed by the powers for injuries to their subjects during the troubles in Anatolia and Constantinople . . . . 29 Nov. ,,

Treaty of peace signed at Constantinople, 4 Dec. (text in *Times*, 11 Dec. 1897); ratified by the sultan . . . . 16 Dec. ,,

Memorial presented by the Armenian patriarch to the sultan . . . . . . 23 Dec. ,,

Sir Vincent Caillard's special report on the Ottoman public debt (1892–93 to 1896–97, *Times*, 20 Dec. 1897); he is decorated by the sultan . 24 April, 1898

An Abyssinian mission received with honours by the sultan . . . . . . 28 Jan. 1898

The sultan demands the application of autonomy to Crete as existing in Lebanon and Samos, with a Christian governor (Ottoman subject), 27 Mar. ,,

Collective note from the powers notifying the evacuation of Thessaly from 6 May, the Greek war indemnity to be completed after the evacuation; presented to the porte . . . 6 May, ,,

Russian note demanding payment of the arrears of the Russo-Turkish war indemnity, presented May; 300,000*l*T. paid, the rest guaranteed by the Ottoman bank . . . . . 30 June, ,,

Note to the porte from the British embassy complaining of grievances of British merchants, &c. 18 May; some compensation paid . . July, ,,

Sir Philip Currie leaves Constantinople (succeeded by sir Nicholas O'Conor) . . . . 26 May, ,,

Turco-Greek frontier settled, the foreign delegates return to Volo . . . . . 31 May, ,,

Russian note to the porte demands the repatriation of 40,000 Armenians in the Caucasus 13 June, ,,

The Porte refuses compensation for losses suffered by British, French and Italian subjects during the massacres in Constantinople . 18 July, ,,

Visit of the German emperor and empress, 18–22 Oct. ,,

Visit of the grand duke Nicholas of Russia, monument to Russian soldiers who fell in 1878 unvailed at Galataria . . . . 17, 18 Dec. ,,

Ghani Bey, Albanian col. and the sultan's aide-de-camp, shot at Pera by Hafyz pasha . 22 Dec. ,,

Alleged plot to assassinate the sultan, 4 arrests, 26 Jan.; 50 Softas arrested for seditious language . . . . mid Feb. 1899

Kurdish outrages, the superior of the Pirnaschen monastery and 2 monks assassinated, Serouk and 5 villages burnt, many killed, reported, 12 June, ,,

Over 100 fires in Constantinople since 1 June; commission of inquiry appointed . . 11 July, ,,

Russian note demanding cessation of frontier raids, often assisted by Hamidian cavalry . 29 July, ,,

Visit of the prince and princess of Montenegro, honoured by the sultan . . . . 2–6 Sept. ,,

Frequent arrests among the young Turks, Sept; 40 week ending . . . . . . 7 Oct. ,,

Sir Nicholas O'Conor's proposals regarding the quay arrangement agreed to by the porte, 26 Oct. ,,

32 Mussalmans implicated in the Tokat massacres (1897) pardoned . . . . . . Oct. ,,

Mahomedan officials banished to Yemen for sedition, and many young Turks arrested, reported, 27 Nov. ,,

Baghdad railway concession granted to a German syndicate . . . . . . end Nov. ,,

Flight of Mahmud pasha, the sultan's brother-in-law . . . . 14 Dec. ,,

Italian ultimatum to the porte, demanding the restoration of a kidnapped Italian girl, promptly acceded to . . . . . . 30, 31 Jan. 1900

Rebellion against the spy system at the military school of medicine at Stambul, 16 April; 14 students exiled without trial . . 23 April, ,,

Russian demands for railway concessions in Asia Minor; accepted by the porte . . 31 March, ,,

Death of Osman pasha, the defender of Plevna; state funeral at Constantinople . 4, 5 April, ,,

The powers protest against the proposed 3 per cent. increase of the customs duties (14 May), 27 May, 7 and 18 April, ,,

The *Seham*, torpedo boat, sunk by explosion at Beirut, 27 deaths . . . . . 21 April, ,,

Many young Mahomedans, denounced by spies, exiled . . . . 30 April, ,,

Manifesto by the Young Turks, urging the powers to put an end to the sultan's *régime*, presented to the embassies . . . . . 23 June, ,,

About 100 Armenians arrested . . . 7 July, ,,

The sultan's jubilee, adm. sir John Fisher received with honours, the British fleet illuminated, in Constantinople . . . 31 Aug., 1 Sept. ,,

11 Armenian relief agents pardoned, due to British intervention . . . . . . Sept. ,,

Major Maunsell, British vice-consul at Van, attacked and robbed by Turks . . . . mid Aug. ,,

Kurds defeated by Turks at Elk, reported, 6 Sept. 1900
The shah received by the sultan at Constantinople, 30 Sept. ,,
Armenian persecution continues, arrests daily, Oct.; many released through Russian intervention . . . . 22 Oct. ,,
Russian note demands punishment of Kurds who attacked the Russian vice-consul at Erzerum, 3 Oct. ,,
Greek notes respecting the frequent murders of Greeks in Macedonia, indemnity demanded, 22, 31 Dec. ,,
Destitution in the army, desertions, increased brigandage, reported . . . . 26 April, 1901
The porte seizes foreign mail-bags, 5 May; regular service resumed after negotiations . 23 May, ,,
Money scarce, financial trouble . June, July, ,,
America claims 95,000 dols. for losses in Armenia, April; again, 23 June; paid, reported, 10 July, ,,
Settlement of monetary claims demanded by French bankers in the quays company, early Aug. ,,
M. Constans leaves Constantinople . . 26 Aug. ,,
Diplomatic rupture . . . . 3 Sept. ,,
Flight of adm. Faik pasha, disgusted with the government . . . . . early Sept. ,,
French ultimatum presented . . . 4 Nov. ,,
Adm. Caillard's fleet seizes the custom-houses at Mytilene . . . . 7 Nov. ,,
French demands conceded by the porte, ratified by the sultan; diplomatic relations resumed, 7, 11 Nov. ,,
Death of Halil Rifat pasha, grand vizier, aged 94, 9 Nov. ,,
French fleet leaves Mytilene for Syra . . 12 Nov. ,,
Austro-Hungarian affairs settled . . 10 Nov. ,,
British claim for 16,000*l*., respecting the Sariyeri mines, paid . . . . . 12 Nov. ,,
Said pasha, grand vizier in 1895, reappointed, 17 Nov. ,,
Foreign notes presented *re* mining regulations, 16, 17 Dec. ,,
Mutinies of unpaid Albanian troops, reported, Dec. ,,
Mubarakh, sheikh of Koweyt in the Persian Gulf, shakes off the Turkish yoke . . Dec. ,,
Congress of Ottoman liberals held in Paris, 4–10 Feb. 1902
Miss Stone, an American missionary, and mme. Tsilka kidnapped by brigands in Macedonia, Sept. 1901; ransomed by subscription and released, 23 Feb. ,,
Collective note (British, French, Russian, and Italian) protesting against hindrances to commerce, &c., in Crete . . . 6 March, ,,
The sultan under the sway of spies and evil favourites, reported . . . end March, ,,
Marshal Fuad pasha (loyal and honourable) charged with conspiracy, March; sentenced to life-imprisonment by iradé issued (fate unknown), 5 June, ,,
M. Rouvier's project for the unification of the Ottoman debt with British, French, and German syndicates, adopted, 2 July; iradé issued, 2 Aug. ,,
The Porte demands the suppression of Cretan money with prince George's effigy . . 12 July, ,,
Budget statement: advance of about 3 millions needed . . . . 15 July, ,,
Commission appointed to consider reforms, &c., for Macedonia; report issued with recommendations, 24 July, ,,
Alleged plot against the sultan's life, reported, 23 July, ,,
Afium Karahissar, a commercial town in Anatolia, nearly destroyed by fire, reported . 30 Aug. ,,
Muzaffer pasha (Tchaikowsky) appointed governor of the Lebanon; made field marshal and vizier, 27, 30 Sept. ,,
Visit of the grand duke Nicholas . . 2 Oct. ,,
Visit of the Khedive . . . 20 Sept.-11 Oct. ,,
Circular note to the powers asserting the bad frontier supervision by Bulgaria, 12 Oct.; satisfactory replies received . . . 13 Oct. ,,
Frequent violations of the Aden frontier, sir Nicholas O'Conor's demand for the withdrawal of Turkish troops agreed to . . 30 Oct. ,,
Death of Costaki pasha, a christian, ambassador in London, aged 70, 10 Nov.; succeeded by Musurus bey (pasha Jan. 1903), a christian . . 12 Dec. ,,
The powers urge effective reforms in Macedonia, Nov., 10, 13 Dec.; sir Nicholas O'Conor again calls attention to the reports of cruelty by the Turks . . . . 30 Dec. 1902
Italian indemnity, 12,000*l*. for losses, in 1896; paid, 29 Dec. ,,
Said pasha, grand vizier, resigns; succeeded by Ferid pasha, president of the Macedonian reforms commission . . . . . 12, 13 Jan. 1903
British embassy protests against the passage of Russian torpedo boats through the Dardanelles; afterwards dropped . . . . Jan. ,,
Mgr. Ormanian, Armenian patriarch, wounded in the Kum Kapu cathedral, 19 Jan.; 2 men sentenced to death (one escaped), 2 others to life imprisonment . . . . . . 7 Feb. ,,
Turco-German convention for Konia-Baghdad railway concluded . . . . . 10 Feb. ,,
Austro-Russian reform scheme for Macedonia; recommending an inspector-gen., with wider powers, an effective *gendarmerie* organised by European officers, political amnesty, &c.; accepted by the powers, mid Feb.; presented to the porte, and agreed to by the sultan, 21, 23 Feb.; ordered to be applied also to 6 Rumelian vilayets, 25 Feb. ,,
Sultan orders the application of the Austro-Russian reforms to all six Rumelian vilayets, reported, early March, ,,
Violent revolt of Albanians against the reform scheme; sultan promises Russian ambassador that he will deal firmly with the revolutionaries, 27 March, ,,
Attack by an Albanian soldier, Ibrahim, on M. Stcherbina (who died by his injuries, 10 April), the Russian consul at Mitrovitza, 31 March; sultan tenders his regret to the Russian ambassador . . . . 1 April, ,,
Russian and Austrian ambassadors urge the immediate military occupation of all the Albanian centres, to which the sultan promises compliance . . . . 3 April, ,,
[For development of the revolutionary movement and its cruel suppression in the Macedonian vilayets, see *Macedonia*.]
Earthquake in the vilayet of Van (see *Earthquakes*).
Turkish note addressed to the Bulgarian government by the porte respecting the dynamite outrages by Bulgarians at Salonica, 28 April, early May, ,,
Serious outbreak at Monastir . . . 6 May ,,
Bulgarian government opens direct negotiations with the porte on the Macedonian question, mid May, ,,
Imperial iradé promulgated approving of scheme of Ottoman bank for the unification of the debt, 2 June, ,,
Turkish forces occupy strategic positions in Kossovo, Monastir, and Adrianople districts; Bulgaria calls the attention of the great powers to this occupation . . . . end June, ,,
First section of Baghdad railway begun at Konia, 27 July, ,,
Circular issued by the porte on the subject of Macedonia to its representatives abroad, end July, ,,
Russian consul at Monastir, M. Roskowsky, shot dead by a gendarme; full satisfaction demanded by the Russian ambassador . . . 8 Aug. ,,
Strained relations between Bulgaria and Turkey, Sept. ,,
The sultan expresses regret to the Russian ambassador for excesses committed by the Turkish troops, and states that orders had been given to prevent their recurrence; iradé issued purporting to embody the reforms for Macedonia already communicated verbally to the Bulgarian government; instructions given to Hilmi pasha to carry out reforms without delay and ordering punitive measures against the Bulgarians to be discontinued . . . . 18 Sept. ,,
New Turkish cruiser *Abdul Hamid* launched at Elswick . . . . 25 Sept. ,,
Identical note sent by Austrian and Russian governments to Turkey and Bulgaria stating their intention to institute "a more efficacious mode of control" in connection with Macedonia, 5 Oct. ,,

Refusal of the sultan to receive the identical note; iradé issued stating the resolution of his ministers with respect to reforms in Macedonia and relief for refugees . . . . 17 Oct. 1903

Austro-Russian instructions for the execution of the reforms in Macedonia presented to the sultan. The chief items are: the appointment of Austrian and Russian civil agents to direct the inspector-general; the reorganisation of the gendarmerie by a foreign general in the service of the porte assisted by officers of the Great Powers; the changing of the territorial division of the administrative districts to facilitate a more regular grouping of the various nationalities; mixed commission to be appointed in the chief towns composed of an equal number of Christian and Mohammedan delegates; the reorganisation of administrative and judicial institutions, and the dismissal of the second-class reserves or Ilavehs and Bashi-Bazouks; these reforms to be carried without delay by the Turkish government (additions made subsequently by Austria and Russia reserving their right to increase their consular establishment in Macedonia, and to demand an amnesty for the insurgents) . 22 Oct. „

British, French, German, and Italian embassies receive instructions from their governments to support the scheme; reply of the porte (practically a rejection of the scheme) communicated to the embassies . . . . . . 3 Nov. „

Pressure put by Austrian and Russian ambassadors on the Porte to accept the scheme . 10 Nov. „

The Porte assents to all points of the amended scheme, but stipulates that anything in its application calculated to humiliate Turkey shall be avoided . . . . 25 Nov. „

See *Candia*, *Egypt*, *Greece*, *Montenegro*, *Servia*, *Macedonia*, and *Addenda*.

TURKISH SULTANS.

1299–1301. Othman, Osman, or Ottoman, founded the empire, retained the title emir, but ruled despotically.
1326. Orchan, son, took the title "sultan."
1360. Amurath (or Murad), I.; stabbed by a soldier, of which wound he died.
1389. Bajazet I., Ilderim, son: defeated by Tamerlane, and died imprisoned.
1403. Solyman, son: dethroned by his brother.
1410. Musa-Chelebi: strangled.
1413. Mahomet I., son of Bajazet.
1421. Amurath II., son.
1451. Mahomet II., son: took Constantinople, 1453.
1481. Bajazet II., son.
1512. Selim I., son.
1520. Solyman I. or II., the Magnificent, son.
1566. Selim II., son.
1574. Amurath III., son: killed his five brothers; their mother, in grief, stabbed herself.
1595. Mahomet III., son: strangled all his brothers, and drowned his father's wives.
1603. Ahmed (or Achmet) I., son.
1617. Mustapha I., brother: deposed by the Janissaries and imprisoned.
1618. Osman II., nephew; strangled by Janissaries.
1622. Mustapha I. again: again deposed, sent to the Seven Towers, and strangled.
1623. Amurath IV., brother of Osman II.
1640. Ibrahim, brother: strangled by the Janissaries.
1648. Mahomet IV., son: deposed by
1687. Solyman II. or III., brother.
1691. Ahmed (or Achmet) II., son of Ibrahim, nephew.
1695. Mustapha II., eldest son of Mahomet IV.: deposed.
1703. Ahmed (or Achmet) III., brother: deposed, and died in prison in 1736.
1730. Mahmud I. (or Mahomet V.), son of Mustapha II.
1754. Osman III., brother.
1757. Mustapha III., brother.
1774. Abdul-Ahmed or Hamid I. (or Achmet IV.) brother.
1789. Selim III., son of Mustapha III.; deposed by the Janissaries.
1807. Mustapha IV., son of Abdul-Ahmed; deposed, and, with the late sultan Selim, murdered.
1808. Mahmud II., or Mahomet VI., brother.
1839. Abdul-Medjid (son), 2 July (born 23 April, 1823); died 25 June, 1861.
1861. Abdul-Aziz, brother, born 9 Feb. 1830, deposed 29 May; alleged suicide 4 June, 1876 (see 1881).
1876. Amurath V. (Murad) son of Abdul-Medjid, born 21 Sept. 1840; proclaimed 30 May; deposed for bad health, 31 Aug.
„ Abdul-Hamid II., brother, 31 Aug. born 21 Sept., 1842.
Son: Mehemed Selim, born 11 Jan. 1870.

TURKEY TRADE, commenced in the year 1550. The Turkey or Levant Company of London was instituted by charter of Elizabeth, in 1579.

TURKEYS AND GUINEA FOWLS, first brought to England about 1523, and to France in 1570. Turkeys are natives of America, and were consequently unknown to the ancients.

TÜRKHEIM (E. France). Here the elector of Brandenburg and the Imperialists were defeated by the French under Turenne, 5 Jan. 1675.

TURKISH BATHS, see *Baths*.

TURKISH COMPASSIONATE FUND, instituted by the *Daily Telegraph*, and supported by lady Burdett-Coutts, the abp. of Canterbury, and others, to relieve sufferers by the war, Aug. 1877.

TURKOMANS, see *White Sheep*, and *Turkestan*.

TURNER'S ACT, 13 & 14 Vict. c. 35 (1850), relates to the court of chancery.

TURNER'S LEGACIES. Joseph M. W. Turner, a great landscape painter, was born in April, 1775, and died 19 Dec. 1851. He bequeathed to the nation all the pictures and drawings collected by him and deposited at his residence, 47, Queen Anne-street, London, on condition that a suitable gallery should be erected for them within ten years; and directed his funded property to be expended in founding an asylum at Twickenham for decayed artists. The will was disputed by his relatives, but a compromise was made. The oil-paintings (100 in number) and the drawings (1400) were obtained by the nation, and the engravings and some other property were transferred to the next of kin. The drawings were cleaned and mounted under the careful superintendence of Mr. Ruskin, and the pictures were sent to Marlborough-house for exhibition. In 1861, many of the pictures were removed from the South Kensington Museum to the National Gallery, others in 1869. The sketches, plates, &c., of *Turner's Liber Studiorum*, were sold for about 20,000*l.* 28 March, 1873.

TURNING, see *Lathe*. In our dockyards, blocks and other materials for our ships of war are now produced by an almost instantaneous process, from rough pieces of oak, by the machinery of Mr. (afterwards sir Mark Isambard) Brunel (died 1849); see *Blocks*.

TURNPIKES, see *Tolls*.

TURPENTINE TREE, *Pistacia Terebinthus*, came from Barbary, before 1656. Spirits of turpentine were first applied, with success, to the rot in sheep; one-third of the spirit diluted with two-thirds water, 1772.

TURRET SHIPS, see *Navy of England*.

TUSCAN ORDER OF ARCHITECTURE, a debased Doric, used in Tuscany for buildings in which strength is chiefly required. *Wotton.*

TUSCANY, formerly a grand duchy in Central Italy, the northern part of the ancient Etruria (*which see*). It formed part of the Lombard kingdom, after the conquest of which by Charlemagne, 774, it was made a marquisate for Boniface about 828. His descendant, the great countess Matilda, bequeathed the southern part of her domains to the pope (1115). In the northern part (then called Tuscia), the cities, Florence, Pisa, Sienna, Lucca, &c., gradually became flourishing republics. Florence became the chief under the government of the Medici family; see *Florence*. The duchy in that family began in 1531; and the grand-duchy in 1569. After the extinction of the Medicis in 1737, Tuscany was given by the treaty of Vienna (1738) to Francis, duke of Lorraine (married to Maria Theresa of Austria in 1736), who had ceded his hereditary estates to France. Population in 1882, 2,226,265; 1890, 2,274,191; 1901, 2,548,154.

The French enter Florence . . . 28 March, 1799
The grand-duke is dispossessed, and his dominions given to Louis duke of Parma (of the royal house of Spain), with the title of king of Etruria . 1801
Tuscany incorporated with the French empire . 1807
The grand-duchy given to Eliza, sister of Napoleon 1808
Ferdinand III. restored 1814
Lucca united to Tuscany 1847
Leopold II. grants a free constitution . 15 Feb. 1848
Insurrection at Florence; republic proclaimed; the grand-duke flies . . . . . 11 Feb. 1849
He is restored by the Austrians . . . July, 1850
Rigorous imprisonment of the Madiai, husband and wife, converts to protestantism, for reading the Bible . . . . . . May, 1852
The earls of Shaftesbury and Roden and others in vain intercede for them at Florence . Oct. ,,
They are released after the intervention of the British government . . . . . March, 1853
[An annuity was provided for them by subscription.]
The Tuscan army demand alliance with the Sardinians; the grand-duke refuses, and departs to Bologna; the king of Sardinia is proclaimed dictator, and a provisional government formed 27 April, 1859
The king assumes the command of the army, but declines the dictatorship . . . 30 April, ,,
The Sardinian commissary Buoncompagni invested with the powers of government . 11 May, ,,
Prince Napoleon arrives at Leghorn, addresses the Tuscans, and erects his standard . 23 May, ,,
The grand-duke Leopold II. abdicates in favour of his son Ferdinand . . . 21 July, ,,
Tuscan constituent assembly meets . 11 Aug. ,,
It declares against the house of Lorraine, and votes for annexation to Sardinia . . Sept. ,,
Prince Eugene of Savoy-Carignan elected governor-general of central Italy; he declines: but recommends Buoncompagni, Nov.; who is accepted by the Tuscans . . . . 8 Dec. ,,
Annexation to Sardinia voted by universal suffrage, 11, 12 March; decreed . . . 22 March, 1860
Prince Eugene appointed governor . 26 March, ,,
Florence made the capital of Italy, by decree published . . . . 11 Dec. 1864

(See *Italy*, and *Florence*.)

SOVEREIGNS OF TUSCANY.

DUKES.

1531. Alexander I.
1537. Cosmo I.

GRAND-DUKES.

1569. Cosmo I., *Medici*.
1574. Francis I.
1587. Ferdinand I.
1608. Cosmo II.
1621. Ferdinand II.
1670. Cosmo III. (visited England, and wrote an account of his travels).
1723. John Gaston (last of the Medici).
1737. Francis II. (duke of *Lorraine*), became emperor of Germany in 1745.
1765. Leopold I. (emperor in 1790).
1790. Ferdinand III. (second son of Leopold I.); expelled by the French in 1800.

KINGS OF ETRURIA.

1801. Louis I., duke of Parma.
1803. Louis II.

GRAND-DUCHESS.

1808-14. Eliza Bonaparte (married to Bacciochi, made prince of Lucca).

GRAND-DUKES.

1814. Ferdinand III. restored.
1824. Leopold II., 18 June (born 3 Oct. 1797; abdicated 21 July, 1859), died 29 Jan. 1870.
1859. Ferdinand IV., 21 July (born 10 June, 1835); protested against the annexation of his grand duchy, 26 March, 1860.
Son, Leopold Ferdinand, born 2 Dec. 1863.

TUSCULUM (now Frascati), a city of Latium (S. Italy). The Tusculans supported Tarquinius Superbus against the Romans, by whom they were totally defeated, 498 B.C. The Tusculans, on account of their friendship with Rome, suffered much from the other Latins, who took their city, 374, but were severely chastised for it. Here Cicero during his retirement wrote his "Tusculanæ Disputationes," about 46 B.C.

TWELFTH-DAY, the feast of the Epiphany, or manifestation of Christ to the Gentiles, 6 Jan.; see *Epiphany*.

TWENTIETH CENTURY MILLION GUINEAS FUND, see under *Wesleyan Methodists*.

"TWENTIETH CENTURY LEAGUE," founded to promote the welfare of the youthful working classes by healthy recreation, &c.; meeting held at the Mansion house, 22 Feb. 1901; first annual meeting, 50,000 out of 1,500,000 *catered for*, reported, 28 Jan. 1903.

TWELVE TABLES, see *Decemviri*.

TWINS, joined together, have been born frequently, but seldom lived long. Helen-Judith, joined Hungarian twins, were born in 1715, and died in 1723. Millie-Christine, negro twins, born in North Carolina in 1851, were wholly distinct in the upper part of the body, but one in the lower part of the spinal column and pelvis; the four legs obeying nerves from a common centre. They sang and danced well, and were named the "Two-headed Nightingale." The will, understanding, and conscience were distinct. Exhibited in London 17 Feb. 1885. See *Siamese Twins*.

TWIN-SHIP, see under *Steam*.

"TWOPENNY TRASH," a term given to W. Cobbett's *Weekly Political Register*, after 2 Nov. 1816, when he reduced the price from 12½*d*. to 2*d*., the sale greatly increased.

TYBURN (W. London), at the west end of Oxford-road (now street), the chief place in London for the execution of malefactors till 1783. Pennant (who died 1798) remembered Oxford-street as "a deep, hollow road, and full of sloughs, with here and there a ragged house, the lurking-place of cut-throats."

In conformity with an act passed in 1697, a so-called "Tyburn ticket" was given to the prosecutor of a criminal executed at Tyburn. The ticket gave exemption from serving on juries and parochial offices. The act was repealed in 1818.

"TYBURNIA" (a N.W. suburb of London), was built between 1839 and 1850, on the green fields and nursery grounds in Paddington belonging to the see of London.

TYLER'S INSURRECTION, in opposition to the poll-tax imposed on all persons above 15, 5 Nov. 1380. One of the collectors, acting with indecent rudeness to Wat Tyler's daughter, was struck dead by the father, June, 1381. His neighbours took arms, and in a short time almost the whole of the population of the southern and eastern counties rose, extorting freedom from their lords, and plundering. On 12 June, 1381, they gathered upon Blackheath to the number of 100,000 men, and on 14 June murdered Simon of Sudbury, archbishop of Canterbury, and sir Robert Hales, the royal treasurer. The king, Richard II., invited Tyler to a parley, which took place on the 15th at Smithfield, where the latter addressed the king in a menacing manner, now and again lifting up his sword. On this the mayor, Walworth, stunned Tyler with a blow of his mace, and one of the king's knights named Cavendish, dispatched him. Richard temporised with the multitude by promising a charter, and thus led them out of the city, when sir R. Knollys and a band of knights attacked and dispersed them with much slaughter. The insurrection in Norfolk and Suffolk was subdued by the bishop of Norwich, and 1500 of the rebels were executed.

TYNDALE MEMORIAL. A statue of William Tyndale, protestant martyr, translator of the new testament, published 1525, was set up on the Thames Embankment in 1883. Sculptor, Mr. J. E. Boehm.

TYNEMOUTH, Northumberland. Here are remains of a monastery built by king Edwin, 625; destroyed by the Danes; rebuilt by king Egfrid, 671-85; often ravaged by Danes, 795-993; re-founded and made a castle, by Rob. de Mowbray, 1090; plundered by Scots, 1316 and 1389; fortified for Charles I., 1642; taken by Scots, 1644; finally ruined, 1665; and made a depot, 1783. The chapel has been restored. Tynemouth was made a borough, returning one member to parliament, 1832. An aquarium, winter-garden, &c., was opened, 27 Aug. 1878. Population, 1881, 44,118; 1891, 46,267; 1901, 51,514.

Mr. Chamberlain addresses a great meeting on "fiscal reform" . . . . . . 21 Oct. 1903

TYPE-COMPOSING MACHINES, see under *Printing*.

TYPE-FOUNDING, see under *Printing*, 1452, 1720.

TYPE-WRITERS. M. Foucault sent to the Paris exhibition of 1855, a writing-machine for the blind; and several were invented by Wheatstone. After successive improvements, Messrs. Remington, in America, in 1873, contracted to construct 25,000. The standard speed is between 60 and 70 words per minute, the record 208.

The action of the type-writer somewhat resembles that of a pianoforte. Pressure upon a key marked with a letter causes a hammer with a type-cut letter, to press upon paper; provision is made for inking the type, shifting, &c.

The Hall type-writer exhibited in London, 1883.

Mr. E. Peacock's new compact and expeditious type writer exhibited in April, 1885.

T. G. and H. Daw's type-writer for reporters commended May, 1885.

Hammond type-writer 1886.

The "Simplex" type-writer (cost about 10s. 6*d*.) introduced into London by a company April, 1887.

A speed contest with the Remington type-writer at St. James's Hall; several prizes awarded by the proprietors, Messrs. Wyckoff & Co., Jan. 1889.

The Bar-lock type-writer exhibited by Messrs. Richardson & Co., in London, 14 Dec. *et seq.*, 1889.

The pneumatic type-writer introduced, Nov. 1894.

Other well-known machines in general use are the Yost, Smith-Premier, Oliver, Blickenderfer, &c.

TYRANT. In early Greek history, the term was applied to any man who governed with irresponsible power. Solon objected to the term, and chose the name Archōn (ruler), 594 B.C. The earliest tyrants were those at Sicyon, beginning with Cleisthenes, in the 7th century B.C. Tyranny declined in Greece about 490 B.C., and revived after the close of the Peloponnesian war, 404 B.C.; see *Thirty Tyrants*.

TYRE (Phœnicia), a great city, said to have been first built by Agenor. Another city was built 1257 (about 2267, *Hales*) B.C. It was besieged by the Assyrians, who retired from before it, after a siege of upwards of five years, 713 B.C. Taken by Nebuchadnezzar, 572 B.C., and the city demolished, when the Tyrians removed to an opposite island, and built a new and magnificent city. It was taken by Alexander with much difficulty, after a siege of seven months, July, 332 B.C. He joined the island to the continent by a mole. *Strabo*. Tyre was captured by the Crusaders, 7 July, 1124; by the French, 3 April, 1799; and by the allied fleet, during the war against Mehemet Ali, 1841.

TYRE, ERA OF, began on 19 Oct. 125 B.C., with the month of Hyperberetæus. The months were the same as those used in the Grecian era, and the year is similar to the Julian year. To reduce this era to ours, subtract 124; and if the given year be less than 125, deduct it from 125, and the remainder will be the year before Christ.

TYROL, the eastern part of ancient Rhætia, now a province of the Austrian empire, was ceded to the house of Hapsburg in 1363 by Margaret, the heiress of the last count. It became an appanage of the younger (or Tyrol) branch of the imperial house, which came to the throne in the person of Maximilian II., in 1618. The French conquered the Tyrol in 1805, and united it to Bavaria; but in 1809 an insurrection broke out, headed by Andreas Hofer, an innkeeper, who drove the Bavarians out of the Tyrol, thoroughly defeated some French detachments, but laid down his arms at the treaty of Vienna. He was subsequently accused of corresponding with the Austrians, captured and sent to Mantua, and there shot by order of the French government, 20 Feb. 1810. The Austrian emperor ennobled his family in 1819, and erected his statue in Innsbruck in 1834; another statue on the Iselberg was unveiled in the presence of the emperor Francis Joseph, 28 Sept. 1893. The Tyrolese riflemen were very effective in the Italian war in 1859. The Arlberg tunnel railway from Innsbruck to Bregenz inauguurated by the emperor 20 Sept. 1884. Population in 1890, 812,696; 1900, 850,062.

TYRONE (near Ulster, N. Ireland), formerly the territories of the O'Neills, and the seat of the insurrection in 1641.

TYRRHENI, included the ancient Etruscans, and other tribes, said to have come from Lydia, Asia Minor.

U.

UBIQUITARIANS or **UBIQUARIANS**, a small German sect, originated by John Brentius about 1560, who asserted that the body of Christ was present everywhere (*ubique*).

UGANDA. A kingdom in Equatorial Africa, near the head of the Nile; capital, Mengo.

Missionaries sent out by the Church Missionary society . . . . July, 1877
French R. C. missionaries arrive 1879
The king Mtesa, friendly to Grant, Stanley, and other travellers and missionaries, dies . 10 Oct. 1884
His son M'wanga, jealous and suspicious, kills bishop Hannington, for advancing by a new route . . . . . . about 29 Oct. 1885
Persecutions well endured; native Christians killed, June *et seq.* 1886
Revolution with bloodshed, Sept. 1888; M'wanga deposed and replaced by his brother Kawewa (Oct.), whose attempts to revive his father's policy are frustrated by the Arab slave-dealers; much persecution ensues; the Europeans flee and their settlements are destroyed Nov. 1888. King Kawewa resists the Arabs, and is expelled, they set up his brother Kalema; civil war . Nov. 1888
M'wanga defeated in an attempt to recover his crown; Kalema burns his own relatives, reported, 2 Sept. 1889
M'wanga severely defeats the Arabs, 4 Oct.; takes Rubaga, 5 Oct., and re-establishes his power; Kalema a fugitive . . . . . 11 Oct. ,,
M'wanga professes himself a Christian, and appoints Catholic officials, reported . 5 March, 1890
He places Uganda under the influence of the British East African company, by treaty with Mr. Jackson, reported . . . . 30 April, ,,
M'wanga driven from the capital by Kalema; retires with the missionaries to Sesse island, reported . . . . . . 9 May, ,,
Final defeat of Arabs by M'wanga, who regains all his kingdom, reported . . . . 15 June, ,,
Uganda placed within the sphere of British influence by the Anglo-German treaty . 1 July, ,,
Capt. (now brig.-gen. sir) F. D. Lugard and capt. W. H. Williams lent by the British war-office to assist the company; they arrive . . 31 Dec. ,,
They strenuously endeavour to maintain peace between the French Catholics and British Protestant missionaries and their converts; they hold Kampala, a fortified station near Mengo; capt. Lugard constructs and garrisons several forts in the country; about 1450 Soudanese placed there (about 450 being soldiers), who afterwards, under Selim bey, join capt. Lugard Jan. *et seq.* 1891
Revival of religious feuds and outrages; a Protestant murdered in the street, 20 Jan.; capt. Lugard demands redress, the king refuses it, and threatens him and his party; fruitless negotiations; other murders of Protestants; the Catholics arm and attack Kampala, and are repulsed with severe loss by capt. Williams, who is compelled to use Maxim guns, 24 Jan.; the Catholic houses wrecked; bishop Hirth and the priests taken to Kampala, 24 Jan.; the king, with 300 of the Catholic party, flees to the isle of Burenguge, where he is joined by the bishop; the isle is taken by capt. Williams, with bloodshed; the king and bishop flee to Sesse . . . . 30 Jan. 1892
[Reported in capt. Lugard's letter of 11 Feb., received 15 July.]
Letters received from bishop Hirth by the French government, accusing the British of outrages, and claiming compensation; on appeal, the British government promises investigation, June, July, ,,
The king rejoins the Protestants; order restored at Mengo, about 30 March; the company predominant, reported . . . . . . 27 July, 1892
The Imperial East Africa company accepts the offered support of the government in postponing the evacuation of Uganda from 31 Dec. 1892, to 31 March, 1893 . . . . 3 Oct. ,,
Capt. Lugard arrives in London (capt. Williams left in command) . . . . . 4 Oct. ,,
King M'wanga and the native Christians in Uganda petition against British evacuation (16 June) received . . . . Oct. ,,
The retention of Uganda strongly advocated at various public meetings . . 5 Nov. *et seq.* ,,
Capt. Lugard's reply to French charges against him, *Times* . . . . . . 13 Dec. ,,
Bishop Hannington's remains found and interred in the new church, bishop Tucker present; 31 Dec. ,,
British commission, headed by Sir Gerald Portal, starts for Uganda *viâ* Mombasa, 1 Jan. 1893; he arrives at Mengo, 17 March, and is received by the king, 20 March; engages the Soudanese troops and leaves capt. Macdonald in command at Kampala . . . . . . early April, 1893
The Imperial East Africa company evacuates Uganda . . . . . . 31 March, ,,
Major Eric Smith and capt. W. H. Williams arrive at Kikuyu; the company's officers and stores taken over by government . . . 15 May, ,,
Dispute between Mahomedans and Christian natives respecting escaped slaves . April, ,,
Insurrection of Mahomedans, joined by Selim Bey; the Catholics and Protestants united under capt. Macdonald defeat and expel the insurgents from Uganda, the Soudanese remaining faithful, 17 June *et seq.* ,,
Selim Bey taken prisoner 20 June, and dies in exile . . . . Aug. ,,
Capt. Macdonald reports peace in Uganda, 25 Aug. ,,
Sir Gerald Portal arrives at Zanzibar, 22 Oct. 1893; leaves for England with Mr. R. Rodd 4 Nov.; arrives in London . . . . 27 Nov. ,,
Col. Colvile (adminstratr.) arrives in Uganda 4 Nov. ,,
Kabarega, king of Unyoro, an aggressive slave raider, severely defeated about . . 13 Dec. ,,
Wadelai taken by Major Owen 4 Feb.; he leaves for Mombasa 24 March; in London . . 5 June, 1894
Death of Sir Gerald Portal, 25 Jan.; his report published . . . . April, ,,
Lord Rosebery announces a future British protectorate . . . . 12 April, ,,
50,000*l.* voted for expenses . . . . . 1 June, ,,
The protectorate formally announced in the *London Gazette* 19 June; proclaimed at Mengo with good effect . . . . 29 Aug. ,,
"Sir Gerald Portal's mission to Uganda" published June, ,,
Kabarega's assault on Fort Hoima repulsed by capt. Thurston and garrison . . . end Sept. ,,
Col. sir Henry Colvile arrives in London; reports peace about 26 March; his book published, Oct. 1895
Mr. (knt. 1897) E. L. Berkeley (from Zanzibar) appointed commissioner of Uganda, &c. about 11 May; arrives at Kampala . . . . 24 Aug. ,,
Kabarega's forces annihilated, reported . 13 Aug. ,,
Slaughter of a government caravan party (1200) in the Eldoma ravine by the Masai; Mr. Andrew Dick killed by them on the Uganda road, 26 Nov. ,,
Uganda railway act passed, 14 Aug. 1896; progressing; station at Mombasa . . . . Sept. 1897
Unyoro made a British protectorate; the road to Victoria Nyanza completed . . . . March, ,,
Revolt in the Buddu district, 20 July; king M'wanga defeated by major Ternan at Kiango, 24 July; again at Marongo, 28 July; Mr. Grant's force attacked, rebels driven off, 23 Aug.; M'wanga surrenders to the Germans . about 26 Aug. ,,

Chowa, infant son of M'wanga, made king with a regency at Mengo . . . . . Nov. 1897
Soudanese troops (Nubians) refuse to go with an expedition, under major Macdonald, to explore and delimit the boundary near the Italian sphere fixed by treaty (1891); mutiny ensues . 23 Sept. „
Fort Lubwas, in Usoga, betrayed by the Soudanese garrison to the mutineers, 17 Oct.; major A. B. Thruston, Mr. N. Wilson, and Mr. W. Scott massacred by them, 19 Oct.; the fort besieged by major Macdonald's forces, 18 Oct.; heavy fighting, lieut. Fielding and 15 others killed, enemy's loss severe . . . . . 19 Oct. „
Severe 10 hours' fight, heavy loss on both sides, 10 Nov. „
Sir Arthur Hardinge reviews loyal Soudanese troops at Ravine . . . . . 17 Nov. „
Several engagements, lieut. Macdonald and the rev. Geo. L. Pilkington, eminent missionary (33), killed . . . . 11 Dec. „
M'wanga escapes from the Germans and attacks Koki, missions, &c. burnt, Jan.; his force routed by major Macdonald in Ankoli . . . 19 Jan. 1898
The mutineers escape from fort Lubwas, 15 Jan., and cross the Nile, Feb.; overtaken by major Macdonald and capt. Harrison, their stockades at Kabagambi, lake Kioga, captured after severe fighting, capt. Maloney mortally wounded, British loss 15, rebels' loss about 55, survivors dispersed, 23 Feb. „
The country still very unsettled; much raiding in Buddu and Koki . . . . . . March, „
New railway (100 miles) opened from Kilindini to Voi . . . . mid May, „
Revolt in Unyoro; the ex-king M'wanga ravaging the west of Uganda, churches burnt, &c., March, „
Mr. Berkeley, British commissioner, enters Kampala fort with great ceremony, country settling down . . . . 11 April, „
Major Macdonald reports 280 killed (30 Europeans and regulars), 1,300 rebels (estimated) in 7 months' fighting . . . . 30 May, „
Soudanese rebels totally defeated at Mruli by lieut.-col. Martyr, 40 killed, 34 taken prisoners, 4 Aug. „
Col. Macdonald's E. African expedition, to explore unknown country N. of Uganda, starts, 3 May, 1898 (divided into 3 columns); capt. Kirkpatrick and 7 men treacherously murdered at Nakwai by natives, who are afterwards routed by col. Macdonald, Nov. 1898; major Austin's and lieut. Hanbury-Tracy's columns, after adventurous marches with good results, join col. Macdonald, and all return to Mombasa . . . . 5 March, 1899
Lieut. Hannyngton's party attacked at Kisiliza, 13 British and 100 rebels killed, 10 Oct. 1898; further fighting, 7 British killed, early Nov.; Bilal (major Thurston's murderer) killed in action, mutineers dispersed by Cole's force . 6 Dec. 1898
Major Martyr's expedition down the Nile; Wadelai and other posts occupied as far as Rejaf, Sept. 1898; Fort Berkely, the last built by the expedition, early 1899; further progress stopped by *sudd* (river swamps) . . . . . March, 1899
Col. Evatt's force defeats and captures Kabarega and M'Wanga in Unyoro . . . . 9 April, „
The Macupa railway bridge, between Mombasa and the mainland, opened . . . . . 8 July, „
Mr. Berkely resigns; sir H. H. Johnston appointed special commissioner . . . . . July, „
Uganda railway act passed . . . . 25 June, 1900
Caravans attacked and telegraphs cut by natives in the Nandi district . . . . . . Aug. „
Col. Evatt's punitive expedition reaches Nandi, 24 Sept. „
Dr. J. Sherlock and 10 natives killed in action, 13 Oct.; the tribes submit . . . . . Oct. „
Sir H. Johnston tours through the Toru and Nkole districts and the western districts; ascends mount Ruwenzori (probably the highest in Africa) to 14,800 ft. alt., May *et seq.*, reported . Dec. „
Operations against the raiding Suk and Turkana tribes well conducted . . . . . June, 1901
Sir H. Johnston's interesting and satisfactory report issued, *Times* . . . . . 29 July, „
Maj. Delmé-Radcliffe's operations against raiding Lango tribes, some Soudanese mutineers, May; successfully completed . . . . . 24 Aug. „
Mr. Kühlewindt explores unknown country north of Satuka; journeys from Mombasa to Khartoum in 10 months, reported . . . . 23 Oct. 1901
Lieut.-col. Sadler appointed commissioner and consul-general . . . . Dec. „
Uganda railway, 584 miles, completed, to lake Victoria Nyanza; estim. cost, 5,550,000*l.*, 20 Dec. „
"The Uganda Protectorate," 2 vols., by sir Harry Johnston, published in 1902
Eastern Province annexed to the E. Africa Protectorate . . . . 1 April „
The Katikiro (prime minister) of Uganda received by the king, London . . . . . 8 Aug. „
Epidemic of sleeping sickness rapidly extending; great mortality; isolation and other schemes in operation, reported . . . . 20 Dec. *et seq.* „
Uganda railway practically finished, early March, 1903
M'wanga, ex-king of Uganda, died . . 8 May, „
Great commercial development of the country as result of the new railway, present working stated to represent a saving to Uganda and E. Africa protectorates of 31,000*l.* per annum in transport expenses.

(See *Addenda.*)

UHLANS, the German lancers, very effective in the war in 1870.

UKRAINE (Polish for a frontier), a vast fertile plain in Russia, ceded to the Cossacks by Poland in 1672, and obtained by Russia in 1682. The country was divided, Poland having the west side of the Dnieper, and Russia the east. The whole country was assigned to Russia by the treaty of partition in 1795.

ULM, in Würtemberg, S. Germany, where a PEACE was signed, 3 July, 1620, by which Frederick V. lost Bohemia (having been driven from it previously). Ulm was taken by the French in 1796. After a battle between the French and Austrians, in which the latter, under general Mack, were defeated with dreadful loss by marshal Ney, Ulm surrendered with 28,000 men, the flower of the Austrian army, 17-20 Oct. 1805. The cathedral was built 1377-1494; the spire, 530 feet high, said to be the loftiest in the world, was completed Aug. 1894, with great rejoicings. Population, 1890, 36,201; 1900, 42,985.

ULPHILAS'S BIBLE, see under *Bible*.

ULSTER, the N. division of Ireland. After the death of Strongbow, 1176, John de Courcy was made earl of Ulster; Hugh de Lacy was earl, 1243; and Walter de Burgh, 1264; whose descendant, Elizabeth, married Lionel, son of Edward III., 1352. He thus became earl of Ulster. In 1611, the British colonisation of the forfeited lands (termed the *Ulster settlements* or *plantations*) began, much land being granted to the corporation of London; see *Irish Society*. The consequent rebellion of the Irish chieftains, Roger More, Phelim O'Neale, McGuire, earl of Inniskillen, and others, broke out on 23 Oct. 1641 (see *Ireland*).—*Ulster King of Arms* appointed for Ireland, 1553.—By the ancient "Ulster tenant-right," the outgoing tenant of a farm received from his successor a sum of money for the privilege of occupancy. A modified form of this right was adopted in the Irish land act, passed 8 July, 1870.

The ULSTER CONVENTION, proposed 8 April, met at Belfast 17 June, 1892, in a large pavilion erected for the purpose. 12,000 delegates of various classes and opinions, from all parts of the province, with many other persons, were present, the duke of Abercorn being in the chair. The proceedings, which were of a grave, earnest character, began with a prayer and the singing of part of psalm xlvi. Five resolutions for firmly maintaining the Union of Great Britain and Ireland in opposition to the scheme for home rule were passed unanimously.

Ulster Convention League formed (2,000*l.* subscribed) . . . . 2 Aug. 1892

Great meetings at Belfast and Armagh, 17 Jan.; Dungannon, 20 Jan.; Omagh, 21 Jan.; Derry, 23 Jan.; Ballymena, 24 Jan.; Newry, 25 Jan.; Monaghan, 1 Feb. 1893 (annual meetings).

Meeting at Belfast to get up petitions from all parts of Ulster against the home rule bill 24 Feb.; mass meeting at Belfast (15,000) . . 28 Feb. 1893

Manifesto of the Ulster Defence Union, signed by the Duke of Abercorn, Marquis of Londonderry, and others, issued 16 March; 169,870 signatures up to . . . . June, „

Mr. A. J. Balfour, instead of the marquis of Salisbury, arrives at Belfast 3 April; after a march past of about 80,000 persons, gives an address; all classes and creeds represented, 4 April; leaves . . . . 5 April, „

Visit of the marquis of Salisbury; great demonstrations and speeches at Belfast and other places, 23 May; address in Ulster hall, 24 May; at Londonderry . . . . 26, 27 May, „

Joyful demonstrations at the rejection of the home rule bill by the lords . . . . . 9 Sept. „

ULTRAMONTANISTS (from *ultra montes*, beyond the mountains), a term originally applied in France to those who upheld the extreme authority of the pope in opposition to the freedom of the Gallican church, which had been secured by various bulls, and especially by the concordat of 15 July, 1801. Ultramontanists now are those who maintain the *official* infallibility of the bishop of Rome.

ULUNDI, Zululand, South Africa. On 4 July, 1879, the Zulus, commanded by their king, Cetywayo, who had refused the conditions of peace, were totally defeated near here by lord Chelmsford, after a severe conflict. Capt. Wyatt-Edgell, 17 Lancers, and 9 men were killed, and about 53 wounded. The British were attacked in the open country by the Zulus, who enveloped our hollow square and charged on all sides up to within 60 yards, when they broke and fled under the heavy fire. They were pursued and routed by cavalry. About 23,000 Zulus engaged, 1,500 killed. The British showed much firmness and the Zulus displayed great courage. The royal kraal at Ulundi and other military kraals were burnt.

UMBRELLA, described in early dictionaries as "a portable pent-house to carry in a person's hand to screen him from violent rain or heat." Umbrellas appear in the carvings at Persepolis. Niebuhr saw a great Arabian prince returning from a mosque, he and each of his family having a large umbrella carried by his side. Old chinaware shows the Chinese shaded by umbrellas. It is said that the first person who generally used an umbrella in the streets of London was the benevolent Jonas Hanway, who died in 1786.

John Macdonald, a footman, who wrote his own life, informs us that he had "a fine silk umbrella, which he brought from Spain; but he could not with any comfort to himself use it, the people calling out, 'Frenchman! why don't you get a coach?'" The hackney-coachmen and chairmen were clamorous against their rival. The footman says he "persisted for three months, till they took no further notice of this novelty. Foreigners began to use theirs; and then the English." 1778.

Mr. Samuel Fox, inventor of the hollow-steel paragon frame, strong, light, and elastic, having made a great fortune, especially at Lille in France, died 25 Feb. 1887.

In 1885 Mr. Gladstone's political programme was termed his *umbrella*, by lord Rosebery.

UMBRIA, an ancient division of Italy, west of Etruria, finally subjugated by the Romans at Sentinum (*which see*), 295 B.C. For the steamer *Umbria*, see *Steam Engine*, 1892-3.

UNCLAIMED MONEY, &c., a pamphlet with this title, by Mr. Edward Preston, was published in 1883, describes six classes and recommends legislation to facilitate publication for the benefit of claimants.

1.—Dividends on government, East India and Colonial stocks (government stocks 4 Jan. 1887, 537,815*l.*).
2.—Dividends of companies, surplus assets in bankruptcy, &c.
3.—Army and navy prize-money.
4.—Funds in chancery (28 Feb. 1886, 77,677,581*l.*).
5.—Intestates' estates in the United Kingdom, India, and the colonies.
6.—Deposits in banks (including plate, jewellery, &c.).

Mr. Sidney H. Preston published similar returns in the *Times*, 22 Aug. 1890, 8 Oct. 1892, and 22 Aug. 1896.

"UNCLE TOM'S CABIN," a story by Mrs. H. Beecher-Stowe (born, 1812, died, 1 July, 1896), published in portions in a newspaper in 1850; complete in March, 1852; setting forth the evils of negro slavery. The sale was enormous, and the translations numerous, and it greatly contributed to emancipation. The Rev. Josiah Henson, the original "Uncle Tom," was received by the queen at Buckingham palace, 2 March, 1877, and was much benefited by his visit to Britain; he died May, 1883, aged 93.

UNCTION, EXTREME, see *Anointing*.

UNDULATORY THEORY OF LIGHT, supposes a progressive wave-like motion between the eye and the luminous body seen. It is said to have been suggested by Francisco Grimaldi about 1665, and was propounded by Robert Hooke and Huyghens, about 1672; opposed by Newton; but confirmed by Thomas Young by experiments in 1801, and is now generally adopted. "Die Wellenlehre auf Experimente gegründet," by Ernst and Wilhelm Weber, published in 1825; see *Emission*, and *Light*.

UNEMPLOYED, see under *Riots*, 1886-7, and *Mansion House Funds*, 1886.

A plan for providing work proposed by the bishops of London, Rochester and Bedford, cardinal Manning, Mr. Spurgeon and Mr. Reaney Nov. 1886. A conference of poor-law guardians at Exeter Hall declare that there is no exceptional distress in the country 8 Dec. 1886.

Disorderly demonstrations of so-called unemployed in London early Oct. 1887; conference at Memorial Hall, lord Herschel in the chair 5 Dec. 1887.

Deputation (not unanimous) to lord Salisbury recommending public works, inquiry, and registration, state-aided emigration and repression of alien pauper immigrants 1 Feb. 1888.

Lord mayor de Keyser, aided by the earl of Meath and rev. Harry Jones, puts forth a scheme for employment of the London poor in making open spaces, gardens and recreation grounds with due stipulations (20,000*l.* wanted) *Times* 22 Dec. 1887.

The Gardens and Pleasure Grounds Fund started (see under *Mansion House*) about 24 Dec. 1887.

The scheme in action reported partially successful Aug. 1888.

Meeting of the unemployed at Tower hill, led by Mr. Power (after an attempt at the Royal Exchange), 4 Oct. 1890.

Attempt in St. Paul's Churchyard, Power arrested, 11 Oct. 1890.

Meetings at Tower hill renewed, 8 April *et seq.* 1892, and at Trafalgar-square, 5 Nov. 1892.

See *Clearing-house* (for the unemployed), 1892.

Letter from the rev. Samuel A. Barnett, Mr. Sydney Buxton, M.P., and 15 others, suggesting a system of relief, *Times*, 29 Dec. 1892.

Circular issued to local authorities, by the local government board, recommending the setting up relief works, 2 Oct 1893.

Manifesto issued by the central unemployed organisation committee, stating that there are nearly two million unemployed in the United Kingdom, demanding legislation for the exclusion of foreigners, prevention of sweating, amendment of the poor laws, grants for public works, &c., 29 Oct. 1893.
Conference respecting the unemployed, at the Mansion house: the lord mayor, bishop of London, M.P.'s, Cardinal Vaughan, the chief rabbi present; a committee for relief appointed, 31 Oct. 1893.
Meeting of between 2000 and 3000 men on Tower hill, 12 Dec. 1893.
Disorderly procession and meeting at Trafalgar square; Mr. J. Williams the leader, 3 Feb. 1894.
The works at the Abbey mills, West Ham, of 1893, resumed through liberal subscriptions, Feb.; reported successful, Dec. 1894; work resumed, March, 1895.
Select committee of the commons appointed on the unemployed; sir H. Campbell-Bannerman, chairman, 13 Feb.; interim report, 11 March; 3rd report, with recommendations, issued July, 1895; final report issued, Feb. 1896; committee reappointed, Mr. T. W. Russell, chairman, 17 April, 1896.
Metropolitan visiting and relief association largely supported; the queen gave 250*l.* Feb. 1895.
Number of paupers registered in London 2nd week of Feb. 144,116; 37,623 excess of 1894.
Demonstration of about 5,000 unemployed in Hyde-park, 23 Jan.; another in Trafalgar-square, 14 Feb., 1903.
Conferences at the Guildhall, sir A. Rollit, sir John Gorst, and delegates from all parts present; restriction of alien immigration, labour bureaus, &c., recommended, 27, 28 Feb. 1903. See *Addenda*.

UNIFICATION, see *London*, March, 1893, *et seq.* Mr. John Leighton's ingenious plan published, 1895.

UNIFORMITARIANS, see *Continuity*.

UNIFORMITY ACTS. That of 2 & 3 Edward VI., 15 Jan. 1549, ordained that the order of divine worship, drawn up by Cranmer and others, "with the aid of the Holy Ghost," should be the only one used after 20 May. The penalties for refusing to use it were fine and imprisonment. This act was confirmed in 1552; repealed by Mary, 1554; and re-enacted by Elizabeth in 1559. The act of Uniformity, 14 Charles II. c. 4, was passed in 1662. It enjoined uniformity in matters of religion, and obliged all clergy to subscribe to the thirty-nine articles, and use the same form of worship, and same book of common prayer. Its enforcement on 24 Aug. 1662, termed Black Bartholomew's day, caused, it is said, upwards of 2000 ministers to quit the church of England. This day was commemorated by dissenters in 1862. The Act of Uniformity Amendment act, whereby shortened services were authorised, and other changes made, was passed 18 July, 1872. The *Uniformity of Process* act, which made many law changes, was passed 23 May, 1832.

UNIFORMS. Military uniforms were first used in France, "in a regular manner" by Louis XIV. about 1668. In England the uniform was soon afterwards adopted in the military service, but with little analogy to the modern dress. See under *Navy*.

UNIGENITUS, see *Bull*.

UNINFLAMMABLE SALTS. At the British Association, 15 Sept. 1859, MM. Versmann and Oppenheim announced their discovery that fabrics steeped in solutions of tungstate of soda, or sulphate or phosphate of ammonia, burn without flame.

UNION CHAPEL, see under *Islington*.

UNION OF CALMAR, 1397; of Utrecht, 1579.

UNION OF ENGLAND AND SCOTLAND by the accession of James VI. of Scotland as James I. of England, 24 March, 1603. The legislative union of the two kingdoms (as Great Britain) was attempted, but failed in 1604 and 1670; in the reign of Anne, commissioners were appointed, the articles discussed, and, notwithstanding a great opposition made by the Tories, every article in the union was approved by a great majority, first in the house of commons, and afterwards by the peers, 22 July, 1706; was ratified by the Scottish parliament, 16 Jan. 1707, and became law, 1 May, same year.

UNION OF GREAT BRITAIN AND IRELAND effected, 2 July, 1800.

Proposed in the Irish parliament . . 22 Jan. 1799
Rejected by the commons of Ireland, the votes being 105 for, to 106 against the union, 24 Jan. ,,
Passed . . . . 7 June, 1800
The English house of commons on the same question divided, 140, 141, and 149 for the union; against it, 15, 25, and 28 respectively . . . . ,,
Lord Castlereagh detailed his plan of the union, in the Irish house of lords, founded on the resolutions of the British parliament thereon 5 Feb. ,,
Votes of the commons agreeing to it, 161 against 115, 17 Feb.; and again, 152 against 108 21 Feb. ,,
The houses of lords and commons wait on the lord-lieutenant with the articles of union, 27 March. ,,
The act passed in the Irish parliament, 13 June, and in the British parliament . . . 2 July, ,,
The imperial united standard first displayed at the tower of London, and upon Bedford Tower, Dublin Castle, on the act of legislative union becoming an operative law . . . . 1 Jan. 1801
For attempts to *dissolve* this union, see *Repeal, Ireland* 1886
National Union Club, Albemarle Street, London, established . . . . . . 18 Jan. 1887

UNION JACK. The original flag of England was the banner of St. George, *i.e.*, white with a red cross, which, 12 April, 1606 (three years after James I. ascended the throne) was incorporated with the banner of Scotland, *i.e.*, blue with a white diagonal cross. This combination obtained the name of "Union Jack," in allusion to the union with Scotland, and the word Jack is considered a corruption of the word Jacobus, Jacques, or James. This arrangement continued until the union with Ireland, 1 Jan. 1801, when the banner of St. Patrick, *i.e.*, white with a diagonal red cross, was amalgamated with it, and forms the present Union flag. Mansion house meeting in aid of a "Union Jack" club in memory of the soldiers and sailors who died in the S. African war, 25 Feb. 1903.

UNION CHARGEABILITY ACT, providing for the better distribution of the charge for relieving the poor in unions, was passed in June, 1865. One object of the act is the improvement of the dwellings of agricultural labourers.

UNION RELIEF ACT, passed in 1862, continued in 1863, to enable boards of guardians of certain unions to obtain temporary aid to meet the extraordinary expenditure for relief occasioned by the distress in the cotton manufacturing districts.

UNION REPEAL ASSOCIATION, IRELAND, see *Repeal of the Union*.

UNIONIST LIBERALS, opposed to Mr. Gladstone, see *Liberals*, 1886, *et seq.*; *Ireland* and *Ulster*, 1892; *Salisbury Administration*, 1895, *et seq.*

Irish Unionist Alliance formed in Dublin . April, 1891
Liberal Unionist Association, 3rd annual meeting of the council at Westminster . . 16 Feb. 1892

UNIONISTS. A Spanish political party, long headed by marshal Serrano. In 1869 they advocated the election of the duc de Montpensier as king. See *Progresistas* and *Spain*.

UNIONS, see *Poor* and *Trades*.

UNION GÉNÉRALE, see *France*, Dec. 1882.

UNIT, a gold coin, value 20*s.*, issued by James I. in 1604.

UNITARIANS, termed Socinians from Lælius Socinus, who founded a sect in Italy about 1546. They profess to believe in and worship one only self-existent God, in opposition to those who worship the Trinity in unity. They consider Christ to have been a mere man; and do not admit the need of an atonement or of the complete inspiration of the Scriptures. Michael Servetus printed a tract in disparagement of the doctrine of the Trinity. In 1553, proceeding to Naples through Geneva, Calvin induced the magistrates to arrest him on a charge of blasphemy and heresy. Servetus, refusing to retract his opinions, was condemned to the flames, which sentence was carried into execution, 27 May, 1553. Servetus is numbered among those anatomists who made the nearest approach to the doctrine of the circulation of the blood, before Harvey established that doctrine. Matthew Hamont was burnt at Norwich for asserting Christ not to be the Son of God, 1 June, 1579. The Unitarians were numerous in Transylvania in the 17th century; they came to England about 1700, and many of the original English presbyterian churches became Unitarian about 1730. They were not included in the Toleration act till 1813. There were 229 congregations in England in 1851. Their tenets resemble those of the Arians and Socinians (*which see*). The Unitarian marriage bill was passed, June, 1827. In Dec. 1833, by a decision of the vice-chancellors the Unitarians (as such) lost the possession of lady Hewley's charity; the decision was affirmed on appeal in 1842. *British and Foreign Unitarian Association* founded, to promote Unitarianism, 1825; meeting in London, 64th anniversary kept in London, 12 June, 1889. There were 320 Unitarian churches in the United Kingdom in Feb. 1884; 364 in Jan. 1903. The rev. Dr. Martineau, LL.D., an eminent preacher and writer, died, aged 94, 11 Jan. 1900. The internat. Unitarian council met in London, 27 May; received by the lord mayor, 1 June, 1901; in Amsterdam, Sept. 1903.

UNITED BRETHREN, see *Moravians*.

UNITED EMPIRE TRADE LEAGUE, formed for the advancement of British industry throughout the world, by abandoning free trade doctrines, and substituting a differential tariff for colonial produce. This scheme, which was originated by Mr. Hofmeyr, was opposed by sir Thomas Farrer and others in London, March, 1891. First annual report by col. Howard Vincent; 5,120 members April, 1892.

UNITED IRISHMEN, a political society founded in 1791, was at first loyal, but afterwards met secretly, to establish a republic, became active in 1795. Theobald Wolf Tone, the founder, was captured by sir John Warren in the *Hoche*, one of six frigates destined to support the rebellion, in Oct. 1798. He anticipated his punishment by suicide in prison Nov. 1798.

United Ireland newspaper first published July 1881. See under *Ireland*.

UNITED KINGDOM. England and Wales were united in 1283; Scotland to both in 1707; and the British realm was named the United Kingdom on the union of Ireland, 1 Jan. 1801; see *Union* and article *Population*—The UNITED KINGDOM ALLIANCE, for the total suppression of liquor traffic, was founded, 1 June, 1853. See *Permissive Bill*. The subscribed manifesto of this alliance occupied a page of the *Times*, 11 Dec. 1871. Annual reports. United Kingdom Beneficent Association, founded 1863, grants annuities to poor persons of a better class.

UNITED PRESBYTERIAN CHURCH, in Scotland, was formed 13 May, 1847, see *Burghers* and *Relief Church*. The United Presbyterians formed a union with the Free Church of Scotland (*which see*), 31 Oct. 1900, the two bodies now being designated the United Free Church of Scotland.

UNITED PROVINCES (Holland, Zealand, Utrecht, Friesland, Groningen, Overyssell, and Guelderland), the deputies of which met at Utrecht, 23 Jan. 1579, and signed a treaty for their mutual defence: see *Holland*.

UNITED SERVICE INSTITUTION, ROYAL, Whitehall, London, initiated as a naval and military library and museum in June, 1831, named the United Service Institution in 1839, received the royal charter in 1860. The institution has been warmly supported by the duke of Cambridge and by capt. Boughey Burgess, the able secretary. Its museum contains many remarkable military and naval relics. The lectures given are reported in its journal, which first appeared in 1857. The institution met in the Whitehall Chapel Royal (*which see*) 7 March, 1891. The memorial stone of the new buildings was laid by the prince of Wales, 6 June, 1893; opened by him, 20 Feb. 1895.

The *United Service Gazette* first published 9 Feb. 1833.

UNITED STATES OF AMERICA were so styled by the congress of the revolted British provinces, 9 Sept. 1776. Their flag was declared to be thirteen stripes, alternately red and white and thirteen stars in a blue field, corresponding with the then number of states of the union, 20 June, 1777. There are now 45 states. The government of the United States is a pure democracy. Each of the states has a separate and independent legislature for the administration of its local affairs, but all are ruled in matters of imperial policy by two houses of legislature, the senate, elected for six years, and the house of representatives (356 members in 1891) elected for two years, to which delegates are sent from the different members of the confederacy. The president of the United States is elected every fourth year by the free voice of the people. He and his ministers have no seat in the legislative assemblies. His veto may be nullified by the vote of two-thirds of the house. The election of Abraham Lincoln as president on 4 Nov. 1860, was followed by the secession of eleven slaveholding states, and led to the great civil war, 1861-5; see *Confederates*, *English Language*, *Cuba*, 189°.

The thirteen states of the union at the declaration of independence in 1776; the italics indicate the then slaveholding states; those with a * prefixed *seceded* from the federal government in 1860 and 1861, and were subdued in 1865.

New Hampshire.	*Delaware.*
Massachusetts.	*Maryland.*
Rhode Island.	**Virginia.*
Connecticut.	**North Carolina.*
New York.	**South Carolina.*
New Jersey.	**Georgia.*
Pennsylvania.	See *separate articles.*

The following have been added:—

Vermont (from New York) 1791
Tennessee (from North Carolina) 1796
Kentucky (from Virginia) 1792
Columbia district (under the immediate government of congress) contains Washington, the seat of government 1790–1
Ohio (created) 1802
**Louisiana* (bought from France in 1803) . . . 1812
Indiana (created) 1816
**Mississippi* (from Georgia) 1817
Illinois (created) 1818
**Alabama* (from Georgia) 1819
Maine (from Massachusetts) 1820
Missouri (from Louisiana) 1821
**Arkansas* 1836
Michigan 1837
**Florida* (ceded by Spain, 1820); made a state . 1845
**Texas* . . . . ,,
Iowa 1846
Wisconsin 1848
California 1850
New Mexico (state) 1902
Minnesota (territory, 1849); state 1858
Oregon (territory, 1850); state 1859
Kansas (territory, 1854); state 1861
Utah (territory), 1850; state 1896
Washington (territory 1853); state 1889
Nevada (territory, 1861); state 1864
Colorado (territory 1861); state 1876
Dakota (territory 1861); north and south state . 1889
Arizona (state) 1902
Idaho (territory 1863); state 1890
West Virginia (from Virginia); state 1863
Montana (territory 1864); state 1889
Nebraska (territory 1854); state 1867
Wyoming (territory 1868); state 1890
Alaska (territory) 1868
Oklahoma (state) 1902
Hawaii 1898
Puerto Rico . . . . ,,
Philippine islands . . . . ,,
Guam . . . . ,,
Samoan islands 1899

Electoral College in 1872, 366 members; 40 for New England, 95 for the southern States, 12 for the Pacific States, 84 for the middle States, and 135 for the western States.

POPULATION. See *Slavery in America*.

	Slaves.	*Total.*		*Slaves.*	*Total.*		*Slaves.*	*Total.*
1776		2,614,300	1840		17,069,453	1870	no slaves	38,558,371
1800	896,849	5,309,756	1850	3,204,313	23,191,876	1880	,, ,,	50,497,057
1810	1,191,364	7,239,903	1860	3,952,801	31,445,980	1890	,, ,,	62,622,250
1830	2,009,050	12,858,670				1900	,, ,,	76,891,220

The Census of 1880 thus classifies the population: Males, 25,518,820; females, 24,636,963. Native born, 43,475,840; foreign born, 6,679,043. Whites, 43,402,970; coloured, 6,580,793. The remaining 339,098 are composed of Indians not in tribal relations and under Government care, Chinese, and other Asiatics. The Chinese are estimated at 105,613.

The *senate* is composed of 2 members for each state, elected for 6 years. The *representatives* in congress were formerly elected for 2 years in the ratio of 1 in 93,423 persons (five slaves were counted as three persons); but this system ended with the abolition of slavery. In 1872 the number of representatives was raised from 233 to 283, to commence 3 March, 1873; increased to 386 by bill passed, 8 Jan. 1901.

Revenue.—

			Dollars.
Total receipts, year ending	30 June,	1855,	65,003,930
ditto	ditto	1859,	53,405,071
ditto	ditto	1863,	888,082,128
ditto	ditto	1866,	1,273,960,215
ditto	ditto	1875,	284,020,771
ditto	ditto	1877,	269,000,586
ditto	ditto	1880,	333,526,610
ditto	ditto	1884,	348,519,869
ditto	ditto	1888,	379,266,072
ditto	ditto	1889,	388,591,675
ditto	ditto	1891,	392,612,447
ditto	ditto	1894,	390,000,000
ditto	ditto	1895,	390,373,203
ditto	ditto	1896,	409,475,409
ditto	ditto	1897,	347,721,705
ditto	ditto	1900,	567,240,852
ditto	ditto	1901,	587,685,337
ditto	ditto	1902,	684,326,280

Expenditure—

		Dollars.
Year ending 30 June,	1855	56,365,393
ditto	1859	66,346,226
ditto	1863	714,709,996
ditto	1866	1,141,072,666
ditto	1875	274,623,392
ditto	1877	238,660,008
ditto	1880	267,642,957
ditto	1884	244,126,244
ditto	1888	267,924,801
ditto	1889	300,064,795
ditto	1891	355,372,684
ditto	1894	433,000,000
ditto	1895	433,178,426
ditto	1896	434,678,654
ditto	1897	365,774,160
ditto	1899	700,093,564
ditto	1900	544,258,348

Expenditure—

		Dollars.
Year ending 30 June,	1901	566,452,044
ditto	1902	593,038,904

Public Debt—

June, 1867, 2,515,615,936 dollars.
June, 1871, 2,292,030,835 dollars.
June, 1875, 2,237,813,048 dollars.
June, 1876, 2,176,947,758 dollars.
June, 1880, 2,120,415,370 dollars.
June, 1884, 1,830,528,923 dollars.
Dec. 1888, 1,690,975,251 dollars.
June, 1891, 1,610,620,103 dollars.
Nov. 1894, 1,690,777,469 dollars.
Nov. 1895, 985,713,148 dollars.
Nov. 1896, 1,044,926,743 dollars.
Nov. 1897, 1,817,672,666 dollars.
Oct. 1901, 1,106,170,671 dollars.
Nov. 1902, 958,507,722 dollars.

YEAR ENDING 30 JUNE.	VALUE OF IMPORTS.	EXPORTS.
1872	£114,502,161	£112,361,676
1875	106,600,905	109,013,805
1877	90,261,510	117,933,898
1880	133,590,660	164,789,270
1884	133,539,538	144,992,970
1888	$723,957,114	$683,862,104
1891	844,916,196	884,480,810
1894	654,994,622	892,140,572
1896	842,000,000	1,023,300,000
1900	849,941,184	1,394,483,082
1901	823,172,165	1,487,764,991
1902	903,320,948	1 381,719,401

ARMY.—That which achieved independence was disbanded at the end of the war. In 1789, a war department was established, and in 1790 the army consisted of 1216 men for the Indian frontier. In 1808, the militia was newly equipped. When war with Great Britain was declared on 18 June, 1812, 35,000 men were voted; and this army was disbanded at the peace in 1815. Armies were voted for the wars in 1833 and 1835, afterwards disbanded.

In 1855, Army, 11,658. Militia, 1,873,558. *Fleet*, 72 vessels (2290 guns).

In 1860, the United States Militia were 3,070,987. *Fleet*, 92 vessels (of all kinds); in Oct. 1862, 256 vessels of war.

Federal Army, 29 July, 1861, estimated at 660,971. In Dec. 1862, nearly 1,000,000 men. In April, 1865, about 1,500,000, at the end of the war, when the reduction began at once. Number of soldiers in 1867, 54,890; in July, 1871, 32,135; 1875, 27,525 men; in 1883, 25,478 men; in 1888, 26,270 men; in 1891, 26,073 men; 1901, 84,513 men; 1902, 63,686 men.

Fleet, in July, 1867, 261 vessels of all kinds, 2218 guns; Jan. 1871, 179 vessels, 1440 guns; 1875, 155 vessels, 1203 guns; 1884, 92 vessels; 1888, 66 vessels; 1901, 307 vessels.

In 1890 and 1891, the congress authorised the construction of three battleships, two protected cruisers, and one torpedo cruiser, and one torpedo boat. The *Texas* battleship was launched, 28 June, 1892.

Railways, miles: 1839, 23; 1861, 31,286; 1873, 73,533; in 1884, 121,532; in 1888, 150,710; in 1902, 200,000.

Act of the British parliament, imposing new heavy duties on imports . . . . . 11 March, 1764
Obnoxious stamp-act passed . . . 22 March, 1765
First American congress held at New York, June; the stamp-act resisted . . . . . 1 Nov. ,,
Stamp-act repealed . . . . . 18 March, 1766
British act, levying duties on tea, paper, painted glass, &c. . . . . . . 14 June, 1767
Gen. Gage sent to Boston . . . . . Oct. 1768
840 chests of tea destroyed by the populace at Boston, and 17 chests at New York . . 18 Dec. 1773
Boston port bill (port rights annulled) 25 March, 1774
Deputies from the states meet at Philadelphia, 5 Sept.; Declaration of Rights issued 4 Nov. ,,
First action between the British and Americans, at Lexington; British retreat . . . 19 April, 1775
Act of perpetual union between the states 20 May, ,,
George Washington appointed commander-in-chief, May; battle of Bunker hill, the Americans retire after a severe conflict, 17 June; petitions from the colonists for reconciliation, styled the "Olive Branch," rejected by the British government, contrary to the counsel of the earl of Chatham and other eminent statesmen . Nov. ,,
America declared "free, sovereign, and independent" . . . . . 4 July, 1776
General Howe takes Long Island, 27 Aug.; new York, 15 Sept.; victor at White Plains, 20 Oct.; takes Rhode Island . . . . . 8 Dec. ,,
The Hessians surrender to Washington 25 Dec. ,,
La Fayette and other French officers join the Americans 1777
Washington defeated at Brandywine . 11 Sept. ,,
Lord Cornwallis takes Philadelphia . Sept. ,,
Burgoyne victor at Germantown, 3, 4, Oct.; surrounded; capitulates at Saratoga . . 17 Oct. ,,
A federal government adopted by congress 15 Nov. ,,
The states recognised by France . . 16 Dec. ,,
Alliance with France . . . . 6 Feb. 1778
The king's troops quit Philadelphia . June, ,,
Americans defeated at Brier's Creek . 3 March, 1779
Charleston surrenders to the British . 13 May, 1780
Cornwallis defeats Gates at Camden 16 Aug. ,,
Major André hanged as a spy . . . . 2 Oct. ,,
André (born 1751) was an adjutant-general in the British army, and was taken in disguise on his return from a secret expedition to the traitorous American general Arnold, 23 Sept. 1780. He was sentenced to execution as a spy by a court of general Washington's officers at Tappan, New York, and suffered death, 2 Oct. following. His remains were removed to England in a sarcophagus, 10 Aug. 1821, and interred in Westminster abbey. Impartial judges justify the severity of this punishment.]
American Academy of Arts and Sciences at Boston founded . . . . ,,
The federal government accepted by all the states, 1 March; congress assembles . . 2 March, 1781
Cornwallis defeats Green at Guildford, 15 March; Arnold defeats the Americans at Eutaw 8 Sept. ,,
Surrender of lord Cornwallis and his whole army of 7000 men to generals Washington and Rochambeau, at Yorktown . . . . . 19 Oct. ,,
Arrival of sir Guy Carleton to treat for peace, 5 May; provisional articles signed at Paris by commissioners . . . . 30 Nov. 1782
Definitive treaty of peace signed at Paris, 3 Sept. 1783; ratified by congress . . . 4 Jan. 1784
Samuel Seabury consecrated bishop of the episcopal church in America at Aberdeen . . 14 Nov. ,,
John Adams, first American ambassador's first interview with the king of England . . 1 June, 1785
The cotton plant introduced into Georgia . . 1786
New constitution signed by a convention of states, 17 Sept. 1787
The same ratified . . . . . 23 May, 1788
The quakers of Philadelphia emancipate their slaves, 1 Jan. ,,
New government organised, 4 March; *George Washington, 1st president*, 6 April; present departments of state established . . 27 July, 1789
An act protecting native industry passed . . ,,
Death of Benjamin Franklin . . . . 17 April, 1790
Bank instituted; capital, 10,000,000 dollars, 7 June, 1791
City of Washington chosen the capital of the states, 8 July, 1792
Eli Whitney's invention of the cotton-gin gives an immense impetus to the growth of American cotton 1793
Re-election of general Washington as president, 4 March, 1793; resigns . . . 17 Sept. 1796
John Adams, 2nd president . . . 4 March, 1797
Washington dies; universal sorrow . 14 Dec. 1799
The seat of government removed to Washington . 1800
Thomas Jefferson, 3rd president . . . 4 March, 1801
Louisiana purchased from the French . 30 April, 1803
Discussion between England and America respecting the rights of neutrals 1807
American ports closed to the British, July; trade suspended . . . . 9 Dec. ,,
Importation of slaves abolished . . . . 1 Jan. 1808
James Madison, 4th president . . . 4 March, 1809
War with Great Britain (New England States opposed to it, threatened to secede) . 18 June, 1812
Action between the American ship *Constitution*, and the British frigate *Guerrière*, an unequal contest, 19 Aug. ,,
Fort Détroit taken . . . . . 21 Aug. ,,
The British sloop *Frolic* taken by the American sloop *Wasp*, 18 Oct.; the privateer *Defiance* also captured by the *Wasp* . . . . . . ,,
The ship *United States* of 54 guns, great calibre (commodore Decatur), captures the British frigate *Macedonia* . . . . . . 25 Oct. ,,
Battles of Frenchtown (*which see*) . . 22-24 Jan. 1813
The *Hornet* captures the British sloop of war *Peacock*, 25 Feb. ,,
Fort Erie and Fort George abandoned by the British, 27 May, ,,
The American frigate *Chesapeake* captured by the *Shannon* frigate, captain Broke . . 1 June, ,,
At Burlington Heights, Americans defeated, 6 June, ,,
H.M. sloop *Pelican* takes the sloop *Argus* 14 Aug. ,,
Buffalo town burnt by the British . . Dec. ,,
American frigate *Essex* taken by the *Phœbe* and *Cherub* . . . . 29 March, 1814
The British defeat the Americans in a severe conflict, 2 July, ,,
[Several engagements with various success followed.]
The British, under Ross, defeat the Americans at Bladensburg; the city of Washington taken and public edifices burnt . . . . . 24 Aug. ,,
The British sloop of war *Avon* sunk by the American sloop *Wasp* . . . . . . 8 Sept. ,,
The British squadron on Lake Champlain captured, 11 Sept. ,,
Attack on Baltimore by the British; general Ross killed . . . . 12 Sept. ,,
Treaty of peace with Great Britain, signed at Ghent, 24 Dec. ,,
The British repulsed at New Orleans . 8 Jan. 1815
The British ship *Endymion* captures the *President*, 15 Jan. ,,
The Ghent treaty ratified . . . . . 17 Feb. ,,
James Monroe, 5th president . . . 4 March, 1817
Treaty with Canada respecting fisheries . . . 1818
Centre foundation of the capitol of Washington laid, 24 Aug. ,,
The "Missouri Compromise" of Henry Clay, regarding slavery, passed . . . . Feb. 1820
Spain cedes Florida to the American States 24 Oct. ,,
The States acknowledge the independence of South America . . . . 8 March, 1822
Treaty with Columbia . . . . . 3 Oct. 1824

John Quincey Adams, 6th president . 4 March, 1825
Death of the two ex-presidents, Adams and Jefferson, on the 50th anniversary of the independence of the American States . 4 July, 1826
Convention with Great Britain concerning indemnities for war 1812-14 . 13 Nov. ,,
American Tariff Bill imposing heavy duties on British goods, termed the "tariff of abominations" 13 May, 1828
General Jackson, 7th president . 4 March, 1829
Treaty between the United States and the Ottoman Porte . 7 May, 1830
Ports re-opened to British commerce . 5 Oct. ,,
First railway made . ,,
New tariff laws . 14 July, 1832
Commercial panic . ,,
Great fire at New York, 674 houses and many public edifices burnt; loss estimated at 20,000,000 dollars . 16 Dec. 1835
National debt paid off . 1836
Martin Van Buren, 8th president . 4 March, 1837
In the Canadian insurrection, many Americans assist the insurgents . Oct. to Dec. ,,
The American steamboat *Caroline* is attacked and burnt by the British, near Schlosser, to the east of the Niagara, on the territory of the United States . 29 Dec. ,,
Proclamation of the president against American citizens aiding the Canadians . 5 Jan. 1838
The *Great Western* steam-ship first sails from Bristol to New York . 8-15 April, ,,
American banks suspend cash payments . Oct. 1839
Alexander MacLeod, charged with aiding in the destruction of the *Caroline;* true bill found against him for murder and arson . 6 Feb. 1841
The United States bank again suspends payment, 7 Feb. ,,
Gen. W. H. Harrison, 9th president . 4 March, ,,
Died . 4 April, ,,
Mr. Fox, British minister, demands the release of Mr. MacLeod . 12 March, ,,
John Tyler, 10th president . April, ,,
The case of MacLeod removed to supreme court at New York . 6 May, ,,
A party of British volunteers from Canada carry off col. Grogan . 9 Sept. ,,
Resignation of all the United States ministers, with the exception of Mr. Webster . 11 Sept. ,,
President's proclamation against lawless attempts of American citizens to invade British possessions, and to suppress secret lodges, clubs, and associations . 25 Sept. ,,
Grogan restored to the Americans . 4 Oct. ,,
Trial of MacLeod at Utica, 4 Oct.; acquitted, 12 Oct. ,,
Colossal statue of Washington placed in the capitol at Washington . 1 Dec. ,,
Affair of the *Creole;* dispute with England Dec. ,,
[This American vessel was on her voyage to New Orleans with a cargo of slaves: they mutinied, murdered the owner, wounded the captain, and compelled the crew to take the ship to Nassau, New Providence, where the governor, considering them passengers, allowed them, against the protest of the American consul, to go at liberty.]
Announcement of lord Ashburton's mission to the United States . 1 Jan. 1842
Arrest of Hogan, implicated in the *Caroline* affair, 2 Feb. ,,
Lord Ashburton arrives at New York . 1 April, ,,
Washington treaty, defining the boundaries between the United States and the British American possessions, and for suppressing the slave trade, and giving up fugitive criminals; signed at Washington, by lord Ashburton and Mr. Webster, 9 Aug. ,,
The tariff bill is passed . 30 Aug. ,,
Lord Ashburton leaves the United States . 5 Sept. ,,
Death of Dr. Channing . 2 Oct. ,,
James Knox Polk, 11th president . 4 March, 1845
War declared against the United States by Mexico, on account of the proposed annexation of Texas, 4 June, ,,
[Several actions are fought between the belligerents, adverse to Mexico.]
Resolution of the senate and house of representatives for terminating the joint occupancy of Oregon . 20 April, 1846
Annexation of New Mexico to the United States, after a protracted war . 23 Aug. 1846
Mexicans defeated by Taylor at Palo Alto, 8, 9 May, ,,
Treaty fixing the north-west boundary of the U.S. at the 49th parallel of latitude, and giving the British possession of Vancouver's island, the free navigation of the Columbia river, &c., signed 12 June, ,,
Treaty with Columbia guaranteeing neutrality of the isthmus of Panama . ,,
The Mexicans defeated by general Taylor, at Bueno Vista . 22, 23 Feb. 1847
Vera Cruz taken by storm, 29 March; the Mexicans everywhere worsted. Great battle of Sierra Gorda; the Mexicans signally defeated by general Scott, 18 April, ,,
Treaty between Mexico and the United States, ratified . 19 May, 1848
Gen. Zachary Taylor, 12th president . 4 March, 1849
Riot at the theatre, New York, occasioned by the dispute between Mr. Forrest and Mr. Macready, 10 May, ,,
Proclamation of the president against the marauding expedition to Cuba . 11 Aug. ,,
[Lopez, a Spanish adventurer, landed 600 men at Cuba; after a short but obstinate struggle they took the town of Cardenas; and soon after had a land engagement with some Spanish soldiers, in which many of them were killed or taken prisoners; the others embarked with Lopez in the *Creole* steamer, and thus escaped from a Spanish war steamer, the *Pizarro*, May, 1850.]
The French ambassador dismissed from Washington. 14 Sept. ,,
Treaty with England for a transit way across Panama (see *Bulwer*). 10 April; ratified . 4 July, 1850
President Zachary Taylor dies; death of M. Calhoun . 31 March, ,,
Millard Fillmore, 13th president. . March, ,,
California admitted a state . 15 Aug. ,,
Fugitive slave bill passed . Aug. ,,
President Fillmore issues a second proclamation against the promoters of a second expedition to Cuba, and the ship *Cleopatra*, freighted with military stores destined for that island, is seized, 25 April, 1851
Census of the United States taken, the population ascertained to amount to 23,347,884, in the whole union . 16 June, ,,
Henry Clay, American statesman, dies . 29 June, ,,
Failure of the second expedition against Cuba by Lopez and his followers; they are all defeated and taken: 51 are shot by the Cuban authorities, Lopez is garotted, and the rest are sent prisoners to Spain, where, after some negotiation, they are mercifully set at liberty (see *Cuba*) Aug.-Sept. ,,
J. F. Cooper, American novelist, dies . 14 Sept. ,,
The president issues a proclamation against the sympathisers with the revolutionary movement in Mexico . 22 Oct. ,,
Part of the capitol of Washington, and the whole of the library of the United States congress, destroyed by fire . 24 Dec. ,,
M. Kossuth, the Hungarian chief, arrives at Washington, on the invitation of the United States legislature . 30 Dec. ,,
Publication of "Uncle Tom's Cabin," by Mrs. Stowe . 20 March, 1852
The dispute with England relating to the Fisheries occurs about this time; Mr. Webster's note upon the subject . 14 July, ,,
Lone Star Society (see *Lone Star*) . Aug. ,,
The United States Ship *Crescent City* boarded at Havannah, and not allowed to land her mails or passengers . 3 Oct. ,,
Death of the eminent statesman Daniel Webster in his 70th year . 24 Oct. ,,
Expedition to Japan . ,,
Address to the women of America on slavery adopted by the duchess of Sutherland and other ladies (signed afterwards by 576,000 Englishwomen) . 26 Nov. ,,
Gen. Franklin Pierce, 14th president . 4 March, 1853
Affair of Koszta at Smyrna (see *Koszta*) 21 June, ,,
Crystal palace opens at New York . 14 July, ,,
Duel between M. Soulé (American minister at Madrid) and M. Turgot . 18 Dec. ,,

Great fire at New York—*Great Republic* clipper destroyed . . . . 26 Dec. 1853
Astor Library, New York, opened . . 9 Jan. 1854
William Walker proclaims the republic of Sonora divided into two states—Sonora and Lower California . . . . 18 Jan. ,,
American steamer *Black Warrior* seized at Cuba. 28 Feb. ,,
The Spanish government remitted the fine, but considered the seizure legal . . . . . April, ,,
Commercial treaty concluded between Japan and United States by commodore Perry (sent there for the purpose) . . . . . . 23 March, ,,
Reciprocity treaty between Great Britain and United States (respecting Newfoundland fishery, international trade, &c.) concluded . 7 June, ,,
Captain Hollins in American sloop *Cyane*, bombards San Juan de Nicaragua . . . . 13 July, ,,
Negotiation for the annexation of the Sandwich Islands . . . . Oct. ,,
Dreadful election riots in Kansas, March and April, 1855
Indian war: they are defeated . 25, 29 April, ,,
Dispute with British government on enlistment (see *Foreign Legion*) . . . . . . July ,,
Gen. Harney gains a victory over the Sioux Indians, 3 Sept. ,,
Senator Charles Sumner savagely assaulted by ~~senator~~ Preston Brooks in the senate-house for speaking against slavery . . . . 2 May, 1856
Mr. Crampton, British envoy, dismissed, 28 May, ,,
John C. Fremont nominated the "Republican" candidate for the presidency . . . 17 June, ,,
Battle in Kansas; the slavers (under Capt. Reid) defeat Brown and the abolitionists . 30 Aug. ,,
James Buchanan, elected 15th president . 4 Nov. ,,
The *Resolute* presented to queen Victoria (see *Franklin*) . . . . 12 Dec. ,,
Lord Napier appointed British envoy to United States (16 Jan.); warmly received 18 March, 1857
Central American question settled . . March, ,,
Judgment given in the "Dred Scott" case in the supreme court. (He was claimed as a slave in a free state: 2 judges declared for his freedom, 5 against it, which causes great dissatisfaction throughout the free states) . . . . March, ,,
Disorganised state of Utah; troops march to support new governor . . . May and June, ,,
Riots in Washington against Irish electors; and in New York on account of changes in the police arrangements . . . . June, ,,
Insurrection in Kansas quelled . . . July, ,,
Commercial panic in New York . . . . Aug. ,,
Outrage at Staten Island; quarantine house burnt, 7 Sept. ,,
The import duties of the protective tariffs reduced from 23 to 15 per cent. . . . . . . ,,
Dispute respecting right of search, settled May, 1858
Tranquillity restored in Utah . . . June, ,,
Great rejoicing at the completion of the Atlantic telegraph (see *Electric Telegraph*) . . . Aug. ,,
A massacre of emigrants at Mountain Meadows, Utah (Mormons suspected) . . . 18 Sept. ,,
Lieut. Moffat seizes the American slave ship *Echo* and takes her to Charleston . . . Sept. ,,
Death of W. H. Prescott, the historian . 28 Jan. 1859
Daniel Sickles, a government official, killed Philip Barton Key, for adultery with his wife; acquitted of murder . . . . 26 Feb. ,,
The American commodore Tatnall assists the English at the Chinese engagement on the river Peiho, saying, "Blood is thicker than water," 25 June, ,,
Gen. Ward, the United States envoy, goes to Pekin, but does not see the emperor . . . July, ,,
Gen. Harney sends troops to San Juan Island, near Vancouver's Island, "to protect the American settlers;" moderation of the British, who have a naval force at hand; governor Douglas also sends troops . . . . 27 July, ,,
Insurrection at Harper's Ferry . . . 16 Oct. ,,
[John Brown, called captain Brown and old Brown, was a prominent leader in the violent conflicts in Kansas, during the agitation respecting the question of its becoming a slave state. He was a monomaniac on the slavery question, and contended that all means for annihilating slavery were justifiable. He gathered together a band of desperate characters, who so much annoyed Missouri and other slave states, that a reward was offered for his head. He had arranged for the successful issue of the insurrection above mentioned, so far as to devise a provisional government and a new constitution. On 16 Oct. he and his band, aided by a mob, seized the arsenal at Harper's Ferry, a town on the borders of Virginia and Maryland, stopped the railway trains, and cut the telegraph wires; a conflict with the military ensued, when many of the insurgents were killed. Temporary panic in southern states.]
Gen. Harney superseded by Gen. Scott at San Juan, who makes conciliatory overtures; accepted by governor Douglas . . . . . . Nov. 1859
Death of Washington Irving . . . 28 Nov. ,,
John Brown captured and tried; executed 2 Dec. ,,
Great agitation in the congress, Nov. 1859; no speaker elected till . . . . . 1 Feb. 1860
President Buchanan protests against a proposed inquiry into his acts . . . . . 28 March, ,,
Companions of John Brown executed . March, ,,
The national republican convention meet at Chicago; Abraham Lincoln chosen as candidate for the presidency . . . . . 16 May, ,,
Japanese embassy received by the president at Washington . . . . 17 May, ,,
Fresh disputes at San Juan, through gen. Harney, who is recalled . . . . . . May, ,,
William Goodrich (Peter Parley) dies . May, ,,
The national democratic convention meet at Baltimore; a large number of delegates secede; the remainder nominate Stephen Douglas as president: the seceders nominate John Breckinridge, 18 June, ,,
The *Great Eastern* arrives at New York 23 June, ,,
The prince of Wales arrives at Detroit, in the United States, 20 Sept.; visits Washington, 3 Oct.; Philadelphia, 9 Oct.: New York, 11 Oct.; Boston, 17 Oct; embarks at Portland . 20 Oct. ,,
Abraham Lincoln, the republican candidate, *elected 16th president* (see *Southern Confederacy*), 6 Nov. ,,
[303 electors are appointed to vote for a president; 152 to be a majority. The numbers were, for A. Lincoln, 180; John C. Breckinridge, 72; John Bell, 39; Stephen A. Douglas, 12.]
Intense excitement at Charleston, South Carolina, and in other southern states . . . Nov. ,,
South Carolina secedes from the union . 20 Dec. ,,
Major Anderson, of United States army, occupies Fort Sumter in Carolina . . . 26 Dec. ,,
Delegates from South Carolina not received by the president . . . . 30 Dec. ,,
Vacillating policy of president Buchanan; the secretaries Cass, Cobb, Floyd, and Thompson resign, Dec. 1860–Jan. 1861
New York and other northern states protest against the secession; a general fast proclaimed; observed on . . . . 4 Jan. ,,
Vicksburg, Mississippi, fortified . . . 12 Jan. ,,
Kansas admitted a state . . . . 21 Jan. ,,
Secession (by convention) of Mississippi, 8 Jan.; Alabama, Florida, 11 Jan.; Georgia, 19 Jan.; Louisiana, 26 Jan.; Texas (by legislature), 1 Feb. ,,
Jefferson Davis, elected by the six seceding states, 8 Feb.; is inaugurated president of the "southern confederacy," at Montgomery, Alabama, 18 Feb. ,,
New (Morrill) tariff bill passed (nearly prohibits commerce with England) . . . 2 March, ,,
President Davis prepares for war (100,000 men to be raised) . . . . March, ,,
Abm. Lincoln, inaugurated president at Washington, says, "the central idea of secession is the essence of anarchy" . . . . 4 March, ,,
Southern commissioners not received by the president at Washington . . . 12 March, ,,
Gen. Winfield Scott, in a letter to president Lincoln, sets before him four courses: either, I., to surrender to slavery half the territory acquired or to be acquired; II., to blockade all revolted ports; III., to say to seceding states, "Wayward sisters, go in peace!" or IV., to conquer the south, which would require 300,000 men and afterwards a resident army [the letter became public Oct. 1862] March, ,,
(Statement denied in 1874.)

Great excitement at the operation of the new Morrill tariff, which begins . . . 1 April, 1861

The war begins: Major Anderson refuses to surrender Fort Sumter, Charleston, when summoned, 11 April; it is taken by the secessionists, after a bloodless conflict . . . . . 13 April, „

President Lincoln summons the congress to meet on 4 July; issues a proclamation, calling on the states to furnish a contingent of 75,000 men, &c. 15 April, „

Massachusetts, New York, Pennsylvania, and other states zealously respond, with vigorous preparations for war; Kentucky, North Carolina, Virginia, Tennessee, and Missouri decidedly refuse, asserting the proposed coercion to be wicked, illegal, and unconstitutional . . April, „

The mob in Baltimore, Maryland, attack some Massachusetts regiments on their way to Washington; several persons killed in the conflict, 19 April, „

President Davis issues letters of marque, 17 April; president Lincoln proclaims the blockade of the ports of seceding states . . . 19 April, „

U.S. Arsenal at Harper's Ferry, Virginia, fired by command, and 15,000 stand of arms destroyed, 18 April; 9 ships of war and naval stores in the navy yard, Norfolk, Va., burnt to prevent them falling into the hands of the southern confederates, who occupy the place . . 21 April, „

Virginia (except West Virginia) secedes by ordinance (the 8th state) . . . 25 April, „

Lincoln calls for 42,034 volunteers for three years, 3 May, and informs foreign powers of his intention to maintain the union by war . 4 May, „

The confederates under Beauregard and Johnston, in Virginia, threaten Washington, defended by the federals under generals Winfield Scott and George McClellan . . . . . . May, „

The British queen commands her subjects to be neutral in the ensuing war . . 13 May, „

The federals enter Virginia; Beauregard calls on the Virginians to rise and expel them 1 June, „

Formal *secession* of Arkansas, 6 May; North Carolina, 20 May; Tennessee (9th, 10th, and 11th), 8 June, „

Several British vessels seized while endeavouring to break the blockade; the southern privateer *Savannah* captured . . . . . June, „

Neutrality announced by the French emperor 10 June, „

Fast-day in confederate states . . 13 June, „

Missouri.—Gen. Lyon raises a federal army, and defeats the state troops, 17 June; the federals successful at Carthage, 5 July; Fremont takes command in West Missouri, 26 July; federals victorious at Athens, 5 Aug.; at Wilson's Creek (gen. Lyon killed), 10 Aug.; Fremont proclaims martial law, and freedom to slaves or rebels, 31 Aug.; Lexington surrenders to confederates, 20 Sept.; Fremont blamed, retires; succeeded by Hunter . . . . 2 Nov. „

Virginia.—Federals defeated at Big Bethell, 10 June; occupy Harper's Ferry, evacuated by the confederates, 16 June; col. Pegrim and 600 confederates surrender at Beverley . 13 July, „

[Very many skirmishes, with various results.]

McClellan defeats confederates at Rich Mountain, 11 July; Paterson permits the junction of the confederates under Johnston and Beauregard near Manassas, 15 July; who are repulsed at Blackburn's Ford, near Centreville . 18 July, „

Battle of Bull Run (*which see*) or Manassas, Virginia; the federals, seized with panic, flee in utter disorder . . . . . 21 July, „

Meeting of U.S. Congress, 4 July; a loan of 250 million dollars authorised . . . 17 July, „

Meeting of confederate congress at Richmond, Virginia . . . . . . 20 July, „

Passport system introduced into the northern states, and the liberty of the press greatly restricted . . . . Aug. „

The charges in the Morrill tariff greatly raised; the confederates prohibit exportation of cotton except by southern ports . . . Aug. „

Battle of Springfield or Wilson's Creek; confederates defeated . . . . . . 10 Aug. „

McClellan assumes command of the army of the Potomac . . . . 20 Aug. 1861

Federal gen. Butler takes Fort Hatteras, N. Carolina (700 prisoners and 1000 stand of arms), 29 Aug. „

Fast-day in federal states . . . . 26 Sept. „

Garibaldi declines command in the federal army, Sept. „

Battle of Ball's Bluff; federals defeated and gen. Baker killed, near Leesburg, Virginia; hundreds drowned . . . . 21 Oct. „

The federals and confederates enter Kentucky; the governor protests; many skirmishes, Sept.-Dec. „

Resignation of lieut.-gen. Scott, 31 Oct.; George McClellan made commander-in-chief of the federal army . . . . . . 1 Nov. „

The federal general Sherman takes Port Royal forts, S. Carolina . . . . . . 7, 8 Nov. „

Capt. Wilkes, of federal war steamer *San Jacinto*, boards the Royal British mail packet *Trent*, and carries off Messrs. Mason and Slidell, confederate commissioners, and their secretaries, 8 Nov., and conveys them to Boston . 19 Nov. „

Great rejoicings in the northern states at the capture of Mason and Slidell . . . Nov. „

McClellan reviews 70,000 men . . . 20 Nov. „

Capt. Pegram, of confederate steamer *Nashville*, burns the federal ship *Harvey Birch*, 19 Nov., and brings the crew on to Southampton . 21 Nov. „

A secession ordinance passed by a party in Missouri, 2 Nov.; the same in Kentucky . 30 Nov. „

Dissensions increase between the republicans (abolitionists) and the democrats in New York, &c. Nov. „

Jefferson Davis elected president of confederate states for six years . . . . 30 Nov. „

President Lincoln states that the federal armies comprise 660,971 men . . . . 2 Dec. „

Meeting of congress, which votes thanks to capt. Wilkes, 2 Dec.; the foreign envoys at Washington protest against his act . . . . 3 Dec. „

The federals commence sinking hulks filled with stones to block up Charleston harbour (S. Carolina) [much indignation in England] 21 Dec. „

Banks at New York, &c., suspend cash payments, 30 Dec. „

A firm despatch from the British government arrives, 18 Dec. 1861; Mason, &c., surrendered, sail for Europe . . . . . . 1 Jan. 1862

Phelps' fruitless expedition to Ship Island, Mississippi Sound . . . 3 Dec. 1861-Jan. „

Confederate general Zollicoffer defeated by Thomas and slain at Mill Springs or Somerset, Kentucky, 19 Jan. „

Tennessee.—The federals (Grant) take Fort Henry, 6 Feb.; Fort Donnelson, with 15,000 prisoners, 16 Feb.; and Nashville . . . 23 Feb. „

Confederates defeated at Pea Ridge, Arkansas, 6, 7, 8 March, „

Confederate iron-plated ship *Merrimac* destroys federal vessels *Cumberland* and *Congress* in Hampton roads, 8 March; is repulsed by federal iron-clad floating battery *Monitor* . 9 March, „

McClellan and his army (100,000) cross the Potomac and find the confederate camp at Bull Run evacuated . . . . . . 10 March, „

McClellan resigns general command, and assumes that of the army of the Potomac only; Fremont that of the Mountain department; and Halleck that of the Mississippi . . . 11 March, „

Burnside's expedition sails, 11 Jan.; takes Roanoke, N. Carolina, 7, 8 Feb.; Newbern . 14 March, „

Capt. Wilson (British) boldly rescues his vessel, *Emily St. Pierre*, a merchantman, from the federals 21 March, „

[She was sailing from Calcutta to New Brunswick, and while attempting to inquire whether a blockade existed, was captured off Charleston bar by a federal ship of war. Her captain, and his cook and steward, were permitted to remain on board on her voyage to Philadelphia. On 21 March, Wilson with his two associates succeeded, by stratagem and courage, in recovering the command of the vessel, overcoming two U.S. officers and 13 sailors, and brought her into Liverpool. The owners of the ship gave him 2000 guineas, and the Liverpool merchants presented him with a magnificent testimonial of their admiration of his gallantry. The British government refused to restore the vessel when claimed by the Americans.]

Confederates defeated at Winchester 23 March, 1862

General Burnside occupies Beaufort and Fort Macon 1 April, ,,

Slavery abolished in district of Columbia, 4 April, ,,

McClellan advances into Virginia, with the view of taking Richmond; he besieges Yorktown, held by 30,000 confederates . . . 5 April, ,,

Correspondents of English newspapers excluded from federal army . . . . . . 5 April, ,,

Great battles of Shiloh or Pittsburg Landing, near Corinth, Tennessee; confederates victorious, but lose their able gen. Albert Johnston; they retire 6, 7 April, ,,

Treaty between Great Britain and the United States for the suppression of the slave trade, 7 April, ,,

Federals take Fort Pulaska on the Savannah, 11 April; and New Orleans 25-28 April, ,,

Yorktown evacuated by confederates . 3 May, ,,

The Seward-Lyons treaty between Great Britain and the United States, for suppression of the slave trade, signed 7 April; ratified 20 May, ,,

Confederates repulsed at Williamsburg, 5 May; their naval depôt at Norfolk, Virginia, surrenders, 10 May; they burn the *Merrimac* . 11 May, ,,

Commodore Farragut with a flotilla ascends the Mississippi . . . . . . May, ,,

Little Rock, Arkansas, taken by federals . May, ,,

Stonewall Jackson defeats Banks at Winchester, 18 May, ,,

McClellan takes Hanover court-house . 27 May, ,,

Skirmishes in Virginia; success varying . May, ,,

Severe battles of Fair Oaks, before Richmond (indecisive) . . . . 31 May, 1 June, ,,

Beauregard and the confederates retreat from Corinth, Tennessee, 30 May; pursued by Halleck and the federals . . . . . . June, ,,

Memphis, on the Mississippi, taken . 6 June, ,,

Federals defeated near Charleston . 16 June, ,,

Federal forces under Fremont, Banks, and McDowell, placed under Pope; Fremont resigns, 27 June, ,,

Federals suffer through several severe engagements in Virginia . . . . 25-30 June, ,,

General Butler excites great indignation by his military rigour at New Orleans May and June, ,,

Seven days' conflict on the Chickahominy before Richmond; the confederate gen. Lee compels McClellan to abandon the siege and retreat 17 miles, taking up a position at Harrison's Landing, on James's river . . 25 June-1 July, ,,

The tariff still further raised . . . . July, ,,

Many conflicts in Kentucky, Missouri, and Tennessee, through confederate guerilla parties. June and July, ,,

Lincoln visits and encourages the army of McClellan, and calls for 300,000 volunteers . . July, ,,

Lincoln's assent to a bill confiscating the property and emancipating the slaves of all rebels in arms after 60 days 17 July, ,,

Halleck supersedes McClellan as commander-in-chief 26 July, ,,

Slow volunteering; many emigrations to Canada and Europe; habeas corpus suspended; the president ordains a draft if the volunteers are not ready by 15 Aug. . . . . . . July, ,,

Public debt of United States estimated at 1,222,000,000 dollars . . . . . 1 July, ,,

Pope takes command in Virginia . . 14 July, ,,

Lincoln's proclamation of confiscation of property of rebels 26 July, ,,

Fierce attack of Breckenridge (confederates) on Bâton Rouge; the federals soon after retire, 5 Aug. ,,

Pope's troops ravage Virginia; Banks, his subordinate, defeated at Cedar Mountain by gen. Thos. "Stonewall" Jackson . . . . 9 Aug. ,,

[According to some accounts he obtained the name by promising Beauregard, at the battle of Bull Run, that his brigade should stand like a "stone wall;" others say that Beauregard gave the name himself.]

McClellan retreats from Harrison's Landing (said to have lost 70,000 men, killed, wounded, prisoners, and deserters) . . . . 16 Aug. ,,

The federals surprised, and Pope loses his baggage, 25 Aug. 1862

Jackson turns the flank of Pope's army, and attacks him at Groveton, 29 Aug.; and when reinforced by Lee, defeats him and McDowell at Bull Run, 30 Aug.; Pope retreats to Centreville 1 Sept. ,,

The remains of Pope's army flee behind the lines of Washington, 2 Sept.; he is removed to the north-west to act against the Indian insurrection 3 Sept. ,,

McDowell superseded; charged with treachery, he claims a trial . . . . . . Sept. ,,

McClellan appointed commander-in-chief, saves Washington, and marches against the confederates under Lee, who have crossed the Potomac and entered Maryland . . . 5, 6 Sept. ,,

Severe conflicts at South Mountain Gap (or Middletown), 14-16 Sept.; confederates, after a great fight near Antietam Creek and Sharpsburg road, retreat . . . . . . 17 Sept. ,,

Harper's Ferry surrendered to Jackson, 15 Sept.; he crosses Potomac and joins Lee's army, 17 Sept. ,,

Federal cause declining in the west; they lose Lexington, Aug.; and Munsfordville . 17 Sept. ,,

Thanksgiving-day in southern states 18 Sept. ,,

Rosencrans defeats the confederates at Iuka1, 9 Sept. ,,

Confederates re-enter Virginia laden with stores 22 Sept. ,,

Lincoln proclaims freedom to the slaves in the confederate states, on 1 Jan. 1863, if the states have not returned to the union . . 22 Sept. ,,

Secret convention of 16 governors of states at Altoona, Pennsylvania, approve Lincoln's policy 24 Sept. ,,

Draught of 40,000 men ordered in New York state by 12 Oct. . . . . Sept. ,,

Lincoln suspends habeas corpus writ, and authorises severe measures against disloyal persons, 25-27 Sept. ,,

Desperate but indecisive conflicts near Corinth, Tennessee, 3-5 Oct.; and at Perrysville, Kentucky 8, 9 Oct. ,,

Confederate gen. Stuart crosses Upper Potomac, and enters Pennsylvania; enters Chambersburg and other places, carrying off horses, ammunition, &c.; rides round the federal army, and returns to his camp . . . . . . 10, 13 Oct. ,,

Gold at 29 premium at New York . . Oct. ,,

Great democratic meeting at New York, condemning the president's policy . . . . . 12 Oct. ,,

At New Orleans Butler compels all persons who refuse to take the oath of allegiance to send in their names and register their property to the provost marshal . . . . 12 Oct. ,,

McClellan's head-quarters at Harper's Ferry, 17 Oct. ,,

Raid of confederate gen. Morgan in Kentucky; he carries off 80 federal waggons of ammunition, &c. 18 Oct. ,,

Ten confederate prisoners at Palmyra shot by order of gen. McNeil in consequence of the disappearance of Abraham Allsman 18 Oct. ,,

Rosencrans supersedes Buell in the west 30 Oct. ,,

Elections for next congress; great majority for the democratic (opposition) candidates in New York and several other states . . . 4 Nov. ,,

McClellan, while advancing towards Richmond, is superseded by gen. Burnside, 5 Nov., who advances towards Richmond . . 7 Nov. ,,

M. Drouyn de Lhuys, on behalf of the French government, proposes joint mediation in the American conflict to Great Britain and Russia, 30 Oct.; declined by Gortschakoff, 8 Nov.; by earl Russell . . . . . . 13 Nov. ,,

The confederate steamer *Alabama*, capt. Semmes, captures many U.S. vessels, and excites much alarm at New York . . . Oct.-Dec. ,,

President Davis threatens reprisals if general McNeil is not surrendered (see 18 Oct.) 17 Nov. ,,

Burnside summons Fredericksburg to surrender; confederate gen. Lee with about 80,000 men near 22 Nov. ,,

100,000 federal soldiers on the sick list . Nov. ,,

Great honour shown to McClellan; he is proposed as the next president . . . . Nov. ,,

The federal government orders release of disaffected persons in prisons . . . . 25 Nov. ,,

Annual session of U.S. congress; the president recommends compensated emancipation of all slaves in the loyal states before the year 1900, 1 Dec. 1862

Battle of Fredericksburg (*which see*); Burnside crosses the Rappahannock, 10 Dec.; bombards Fredericksburg, 11 Dec.; a series of desperate attacks on the confederates; Burnside totally defeated, 13 Dec.; recrosses the river 15 Dec. „

Engagements in Tennessee with varying results, Dec. „

Discovery of frauds in the U.S. army financial accounts; public dissatisfaction with the government; secretaries Chase and Seward resign, but resume office . . . . . . Dec. „

Homestead and Pre-emption act (relating to settlement of free land) passed . . . . . . „

Battles near Murfreesboro', or Stone River, between Rosencrans and the federals and Braxton Bragg and the confederates: begin 29 Dec.; severe but indecisive, 31 Dec.; battle continued, 1 Jan.; Bragg defeated, retreats . . . 2 Jan. 1863

["There have been about 2000 battles and skirmishes since the commencement of the war."—*American Almanack.*]

President Lincoln proclaims the freedom of slaves in the rebel states, except in parts held by the U. S. army . . . . 2 Jan. „

Burnside superseded by Joseph Hooker in command of army of the Potomac . . 26 Jan. „

The French government's offer of mediation, 9 Jan. declined . . . . . . 6 Feb. „

The *George Griswold*, a vessel containing provisions and other relief for the distressed cotton workers in Lancashire, arrives . . . . 9 Feb. „

A conscription bill (for men between 18 and 45) passed . . . . 25 Feb. „

The congress authorises the suspension of the habeas corpus act, 3 March; and establishes a National Academy of Sciences at Washington 4 March. „

Confederate loan for 3,000,000*l.* well taken up in Europe . . . . March, „

Charleston, South Carolina, attacked by monitors and gunboats; the Keokuk, a monitor, sunk 7 April, „

Battle of Chancellorsville (*which see*); the federals under Hooker cross the Rappahannock, 28 April; defeated (gen. Stonewall Jackson is mortally wounded), 2-4 May; Hooker recrosses the Rappahannock . . . . . . 5 May „

Stonewall Jackson dies . . . . . 10 May, „

Grant's successful campaign in Tennessee; he defeats the confederates under Joseph Johnston at Jackson, 14 May; and under Pemberton at Champion Hills, 16 May; and invests Vicksburg, Mississippi, which is strongly fortified, 18 May, a dreadful assault on it repelled . . 22 May, „

Great peace meeting at Norfolk . . 5 June, „

Confederate invasion under Lee; invade Maryland and Pennsylvania, and take various towns 14 June *et seq.* „

The federal gen. Hooker superseded by George H. Meade . . . . 27 June, „

Meade advances against Lee; great battle of Gettysburg, indecisive; but the confederates evacuate Pennsylvania and Maryland 1-3 July, „

Vicksburg bombarded, 3 July; surrendered by Pemberton to Grant and Porter . 4 July, „

Port Hudson, a confederate fortress on the Mississippi, surrenders . . . . 8 July, „

Fierce riots at New York against the conscription; many negroes murdered, and much property destroyed . . . . . . 13-16 July, „

The Sioux defeated, 7 Aug.; gen. Pope reports that the Indian war is ended . . . . Aug. „

New York rioters tried and convicted, 12 Aug.: conscription going on peaceably . . 21 Aug. „

Siege of Charleston; defended by Beauregard; attacks with varied success, July: Fort Sumter bombarded and destroyed (and so-called Greek fire employed); attacks on the ruins repulsed 21, 22 Aug. „

Knoxville occupied by Burnside . . 10 Sept. „

A Russian squadron warmly received at New York Sept. and Oct. „

Battles of Chickamauga, Tennessee; Rosencrans defeated by Bragg . . . . 19, 20 Sept. „

Mason, the confederate commissioner in England, protests against the mode of his reception, and quits . . . . 22 Sept. 1863

Confederates defeated at Blue-Springs, Tennessee 10 Oct. „

Lincoln calls for 300,000 volunteers . 17 Oct. „

Rosencrans' command of the federal army in Tennessee superseded by Grant, and Thomas, and Sherman . . . . 19 Oct. „

The steam rams *El Tousson* and *El Monassir*, built by Mr. Laird at Birkenhead, and suspected to be for the confederates, are placed under charge of a government vessel in the Mersey . 31 Oct. „

British consuls dismissed from southern states Oct. „

Meade captures a part of Lee's army on the N. side of the Rappahannock . . . . 7 Nov. „

The chief justices Lowrie, Woodward, and Thompson declare that the Conscription act is unconstitutional . . . . . . 12 Nov. „

Longstreet defeats Burnside, and compels him to retire into Knoxville . . . 14-17 Nov. „

Sherman and Thomas defeat Bragg at Chattanooga 23, 24 Nov. „

Longstreet's attack on Knoxville, defended by Burnside, fails, and he retreats into Virginia 29 Nov. and 1 Dec. „

The confederate general Bragg superseded by Hardee . . . . 2 Dec. „

Lincoln's message to congress warlike; he proffers amnesty to all except heads of governments, &c., 4 Dec.: Davis's message, firm, but acknowledging reverses . . . . . . 7 Dec. „

Gen. Joseph Johnston takes command of the confederate army in Georgia . . . 27 Dec. „

President Lincoln orders a draft of 500,000 men in 3 years . . . . 1 Feb. 1864

Federal expedition into Florida; defeated at Olustee . . . . 20 Feb. „

Failure of attack of Kilpatrick and Dahlgren on Richmond . . . . . 27 Feb.-4 March, „

Ulysses Grant made commander-in-chief, succeeding Halleck . . . . 12 March, „

Confederate raids into the Western states March, „

Sherman's expedition against Mobile, 2 March, defeated by Kirby-Smith . . . 5 April, „

James E. Stuart, the celebrated confederate cavalry officer, killed . . . . . 11 May, „

Campaign in Virginia; the army of the Potomac crosses the Rapidan; advance of Lee (now supported by Longstreet), 2 May; severe battle in the "Wilderness" (near Chancellorsville), indecisive, 5, 6 May; battle of Spottsylvania; the federals remain on the field; much carnage 10-12 May, „

Sherman (in Georgia) beats the confederates at Resacca, 14 May, and at Dallas . 28 May, „

Fugitive slave act repealed by the house of representatives . . . . 13 June, „

After a succession of attacks on both sides, Grant compels Lee to retire gradually, and by a flank movement marches to the other side of Richmond, and faces Petersburg, 15 June; where, having taken the first intrenchments after desperate assaults, he is repulsed with considerable loss 18 June, „

The confederate steamer *Alabama* (capt. Semmes) attacked and sunk by the U.S. corvette *Kearsage* (capt. Winslow) near Cherbourg, France, 19 June, „

Mr. Chase, secretary to the U.S. treasury, resigns; succeeded by Mr. Fessenden . . . July, „

Part of Lee's army invades Maryland, 1 July; defeats Wallace near Monocracy river, 9 July; threatens Baltimore and Washington, and retreats 12, 13 July, „

Sherman's 3 battles at Atlanta (Georgia), 20, 22 July; victory remains with the federals . 28 July, „

Confederates again invade Maryland and Pennsylvania, and destroy Chambersburg . 30 July, „

Grant orders the explosion of a mine at Petersburg, whereby 250 confederates are killed: but the assault following is repulsed with great slaughter 30 July, „

The *Tallahassee* confederate steamer (built in London) destroys many U.S. merchantmen July, Aug. „

Severe conflicts in the Shenandoah valley: the federals victors . . . . . . Aug. „

The confederate flotilla near Mobile destroyed by Farragut, 5 Aug.; Fort Gaines taken 8 Aug. „

McClellan nominated for the presidency by the "Democratic" Chicago convention 1 Sept. 1864
Sherman occupies Atlanta; the confederate general Hood retires . . . . 1 Sept. ,,
Sherman orders the depopulation of Atlanta, 7 Sept. ,,
McClellan declares for maintaining the union; the democratic party divided . . . 13 Sept. ,,
Sheridan (federal) defeats Early at Winchester, in the Shenandoah valley, but with very great loss 19 Sept. ,,
Longstreet replaces Early in the command of the confederates . . . . Oct. ,,
Longstreet defeats the federals at Cedar Creek; Sheridan arrives, rallies his troops, and defeats the confederates . . . 19 Oct. ,,
St. Alban's Raid.—Between 20 and 30 armed men enter St. Alban's, Vermont; rob the bank and carry off horses and stores; fire on and kill several persons, and flee to Canada, 19 Oct.; where 13 of them are arrested . . 21 Oct. ,,
Lincoln re-elected president; McClellan resigns his command in U.S. army . . . . 8 Nov. ,,
Sherman destroys Atlanta and begins his march through Georgia to Savannah . 13 Nov. ,,
Hood's attack on Thomas (federal), at Franklin, repulsed with severe loss . . . . 30 Nov. ,,
Lincoln's message to congress considered "bold" 6 Dec. ,,
The St. Alban's raiders discharged by Judge Coursol; general Dix issues an intemperate order for reprisals (disannulled by the president) 14 Dec. ,,
Hood defeated by Thomas (federal) near Nashville 14-16 Dec. ,,
Sherman storms fort M'Allister, 13 Dec.; enters Savannah . . . . 21 Dec. ,,
Wilmington bombarded; the attack of general Butler and admiral Porter repulsed 24, 25 Dec. ,,
The St. Alban's raiders recaptured and committed for trial . . . . 27 Dec. *et seq.* ,,
The federal congress abolishes slavery in the United States . . . . 1 Feb 1865
Fruitless meeting of president Lincoln and secretary Seward with the confederate secretary Stephens and 2 commissioners to treat for peace at Fort Monroe . . . . 2, 3 Feb. ,,
The Canadian government surrenders Burley, a raider, to the federals . . . . . Feb. ,,
Lee takes the general command of the confederate armies; he recommends enlistment of negroes 18 Feb. ,,
Wilmington captured by Schofield; Charleston evacuated by the confederates; retreat of Beauregard . . . . 22 Feb. ,,
The confederate congress decree the arming of the slaves . . . . 22 Feb. ,,
Abraham Lincoln and Andrew Johnson inaugurated as president and vice-president . . 4 March, ,,
A new stringent tariff comes into operation, 1 April, ,,
Three days' sanguinary conflict at Five Forks, began 31 March; Sheridan turns Lee's front, and totally defeats him, 1 April; Lee retreats, 2 April, ,,
Richmond and Petersburg evacuated by the confederates and occupied by Grant . 2, 3 April, ,,
Sheridan overtakes and defeats Lee at Sailor's Creek, 6 April; Lee surrenders with the army of Northern Virginia to Grant, at Appomatox court-house . . . . 9 April, ,,
Mobile evacuated by the confederates 12 April, ,,
The Union flag replaced at Fort Sumter, Charleston, 14 April, ,,
President Lincoln shot at Ford's Theatre, Washington, about 11 o'clock, p.m., 14 April, by Wilkes Booth, who escapes; Mr. Seward, the foreign secretary, and his son, wounded in his own house by an assassin about the same time; Lincoln dies at 7.30 a.m., 15 April; *Andrew Johnson, vice-president, sworn in as 17th president,* 15 April, ,,
The convention between Sherman and Johnston (favourable to confederates), 17 April, disavowed by the government, 21 April; Johnston surrenders on same terms as Lee 26 April, ,,
Wilkes Booth shot, and his accomplice Harrold captured, in a farmhouse . . . 26 April, 1865
The confederate general Dick Taylor (near Mobile) surrenders . . . . 4 May, ,,
President Jefferson Davis captured at Irwinsville, Georgia; imprisoned . . . . 10 May, ,,
The confederate general Kirby Smith, in Texas, surrenders; end of the war . . . 26 May, ,,
President Johnson proclaims the opening of the southern ports, 22 May; and an amnesty with certain exemptions . . . . . . 29 May, ,,
Solemn fast observed for death of president Lincoln, 1 June, ,,
The armies on both sides rapidly disbanding; fierce riots at New York between whites and negroes, June, ,,

[Registered loss of the Federals 359,496; of which officers 9,584.]

Galveston, Texas, the last seaport held by the south, surrendered by Kirby-Smith . 5 June, ,,
The British and French governments rescind their recognition of the confederates as belligerents, 2, 6 June, ,,
President Johnson, uniting with the democrats, and acting leniently towards the south; reorganisation of the state governments . . . June, ,,
Close of the long trial of the assassination conspirators, 29 June; execution of Payne, Atzerott, Harrold or Herold, and Mrs. Suratt 7 July, ,,
The president declines recognition of the emperor of Mexico . . . . 18 July, ,,
All southern prisoners of war to be released on parole on taking oath of allegiance . 29 July, ,,
Federal debt declared 2,757,253,275 dollars, 31 July, ,,
The confederate privateer *Shenandoah* (captain Waddell) captures and destroys many federal vessels (about 30) . . . . . . Aug. ,,
Pacific policy of president Johnson; he declares himself opposed to centralisation and in favour of state rights; and is bitterly opposed by the radicals . . . . Sept. ,,
Correspondence between earl Russell and Mr. Adams (U.S. minister, London) respecting the *Alabama*, confederate privateer; proposal of a commission to whom claims for reparation shall be referred . . . . 7 April-18 Sept. ,,
Alex. Stephens and other southern officials pardoned . . . . 11 Oct. ,,
Great meeting of Fenians at Philadelphia; the Irish republic proclaimed - 16-24 Oct. ,,
Much public discussion respecting equal negro suffrage . . . . July-Oct. ,,
The national debt stated to be 600,000,000*l*. Oct. ,,
General Robert Lee becomes president of Washington College, Virginia . . . . 2 Oct. ,,
Several southern states pass ordinances annulling secession, abolishing slavery, and renouncing confederate debt . . . . Sept. Oct. Nov. ,,
National thanksgiving for the peace . . 2 Nov. ,,
Captain Waddell arrives at Liverpool, 6 Nov.; surrenders the *Shenandoah* to the British government, stating that he had not heard of the end of the war till 2 Aug.; he and his crew paroled, 8 Nov.; the vessel given up to the American consul . . . . 9 Nov. ,,
Capt. Wirz, after long military trial, executed for cruelty to the federal prisoners at Andersonsville, 10 Nov. ,,
A negro convention at Charleston, appeals for justice and generosity . . . . . 25 Nov. ,,
Ex-president Buchanan publishes his justification, Nov. ,,
Habeas corpus act restored in N. states . 1 Dec. ,,
Close of correspondence between the British and U.S. governments respecting depredations of *Alabama, Shenandoah, &c.* The earl of Clarendon maintains that "no armed vessel departed during the war from a British port, to cruise against the commerce of the United States" . . 2 Dec. ,,
Congress and government protest against the French intervention in Mexico, Nov.; 6, 16 Dec. ,,
Opening of 39th congress; president Johnson's message conciliatory and firm (he requires from the southern states—repeal of their act of secession, abolition of slavery, and repudiation of confederate debt) . . . . . . 4 Dec. ,,

The radical party, opposed to the president, and to clemency to the south, predominate in the congress, and move violent resolutions against restoration of southern states to the union . Dec. 1865
Estimated federal debt, 600,000,000*l.*; revenue, 80,000,000*l.* . . . . Dec. ,,
85 members for the southern states excluded from congress; the conservative party support the president in his endeavours to reconstruct the union; the radicals violently oppose his policy, requiring the south to undergo previously a severe probation; the president has restored state government to all the southern states except Texas and Florida . . . 29 Dec. ,,
The radicals demand for the negroes, personal, civil, and political rights, equal to those of the whites; the president proposes gradual enfranchisement, in separate states . . . Feb. 1866
The president vetoes the Freedmen's Bureau bill, 21 Feb.; and the bill for the civil rights of the blacks . . . . 27 March, ,,
The president fiercely opposed by the radicals; the conservatives and democrats unite to support him . . . . March, ,,
He proclaims the rebellion at an end . 3 April, ,,
The Civil Rights bill passed in spite of the veto, 9 April, ,,
The veto on the admission of Colorado as a state, 15 May; set aside . . . . . . May, ,,
Fenian raids in Canada . . . 31 May-7 June, ,,
The radical reconstruction clause termed the "constitutional amendment" (granting negro suffrage to be enforced by the different states; the whites and the blacks to be equal in the sight of the law, &c.), passed by the senate . 13 June, ,,
Death of general Winfield Scott, aged 80, 29 May; and of Lewis Cass, aged 83 . . . 17 June, ,,
Continued dissension between the president and the congress . . . . July, ,,
The representatives of Tennessee re-admitted to the congress (10 states still excluded) . July, ,,
The Atlantic telegraph completed (see *Electric Telegraph*) . . . . 27 July, ,,
The congress adjourns . . . . . . 28 July, ,,
Great meeting at Philadelphia of the National Union Convention, consisting of delegates (the moderate men of all the parties, in every state, north and south, now termed the conservative party), whose object is to establish the national union, restore the south to its rights, and vindicate the president's policy . . . 14 Aug. ,,
Tour of the president; he visits Philadelphia, New York, Chicago, &c.; he is very enthusiastically received; and speaks warmly, and often injudiciously . . . . . 28 Aug.-18 Sept. ,,
Elections for congress go in favour of the republicans . . . . Oct. ,,
[They demand that three-fifths of the blacks in the south shall be entitled to vote; that where negro suffrage is not established, only whites shall count; and that all persons who have taken any part in the rebellion shall be disqualified to vote.]
Death of Martin Van Buren, ex-president Oct. ,,
Trial of Jefferson Davis deferred till spring Oct. ,,
Elections in all the states except Delaware and Maryland in favour of the radicals (about 2,200,000 to 1,800,000); two coloured deputies elected in Massachusetts . . . . . Oct.-Nov. ,,
Government policy declared to be "dead" Nov. ,,
Meeting of congress; president's message; he declares that he adheres to his policy . 3 Dec. ,,
Bills to provide territorial governments in southern states; and restriction of president's appointing powers proposed . . . . . . 3 Dec. ,,
The president charged with being "silent and motionless;" congress absorbs all the power Dec. ,,
A bill admitting negroes to the suffrage in district of Columbia passed . . . . . 13 Dec. ,,
Veto of president set aside . . . . . Jan. 1867
Supreme court decides that congress has not power to appoint military tribunals . . . Jan. ,,
Impeachment of president by a judicial committee agreed to . . . . 7 Jan. ,,
Division among the radicals; Stevens successfully opposed by Ashley . . . . . 29 Jan. ,,
Debt of the United States reported 2,543,000,000 dollars . . . . 1 Feb. ,,
Nebraska admitted as the 37th state, over president's veto . . . . 9 Feb. 1867
Bill for establishing military government in the southern states, divided into five districts, discussed . . . . 13-15 Feb. ,,
Modified and passed, 20 Feb.; vetoed by the president . . . . 28 Feb. ,,
Mr. Peabody gives 1,000,000 dollars to promote education in the south . . . . Feb. ,,
40th congress opened . . . . . 4 March, ,,
Supplementary reconstruction bill for the south passed . . . . 20 March, ,,
Tenure of Office act passed . . . . March, ,,
Russian America purchased for 7,000,000 dollars; treaty ratified by the senate . . . 9 April, ,,
"Protection" rife: taxation on British manufactures 80 per cent.; much smuggling; public debt not diminishing; many strikes amongst operatives . . . . April, ,,
Jefferson Davis released on bail, 13 May; proceeded to New York, and thence to Canada, 20 May, ,,
Supplementary reconstruction bill adopted over the president's veto . . . . 15 July, ,,
Long trial of John H. Suratt, for complicity in assassination of president Lincoln; jury not agreed on verdict (discharged, 6 Nov. 1868), 10 Aug. ,,
Insubordination of gen. Sheridan, favoured by Edw. Stanton, secretary of war, who refuses to resign at the requisition of the president, 5 Aug.; suspended; succeeded by gen. Grant 12 Aug. ,,
General amnesty proclaimed by the president, 9 Sept. ,,
Removal of gen. Sheridan from the government of Louisiana, and of Sickles from N. Carolina, for insubordination to the president . Aug.-Sept. ,,
National cemetery at Antietam (*which see*) dedicated in presence of the president . 17 Sept. ,,
Sir Fred. Bruce, British ambassador, died at Boston, 9 Sept. ,,
Russian America ceded . . . . . 8 Oct. ,,
Jefferson Davis's trial adjourned . . 26 Nov. ,,
Elections in the south give supremacy to the negroes; in the north, great majorities for the democrats . . . . Oct.-Nov. ,,
President's message, maintaining his principles on reconstruction . . . . 3 Dec. ,,
Revenue of the states fallen off; public debt about 520,000,000*l.* . . . . Dec. ,,
Proposed impeachment of the president negatived in congress (108 to 57) . . . . . 8 Dec. ,,
Treaty for purchase of Danish West Indies (St. Thomas and St. John), for 7,500,000 dollars, signed . . . . Dec. ,,
Great general storm of snow and sleet; many perish; many wrecks . . . . 11-15 Dec. ,,
President Johnson censured; and gen. Sheridan thanked by house of representatives (*see* Aug. 1867) . . . . 4 Jan. 1868
General Grant replaced by Stanton (by the senate), 14, 15 Jan. ,,
The house of representatives declare that there is no valid government in the south; and transfer the jurisdiction from president Johnson to Grant, as general of the army . . . . 21 Jan. ,,
Great commercial depression; Mr. Wells, the revenue commissioner, recommends "peace, retrenchment, and reform" . . . . . . Jan. ,,
The inland cotton tax repealed . about 1 Feb. ,,
Edward Thornton, new British ambassador, and Charles Dickens received by the president, 7 Feb. ,,
Angry correspondence between the president and gen. Grant . . . . . 28 Jan.-14 Feb. ,,
President Johnson orders dismissal of Stanton, and appoints gen. Thomas secretary of war, 21 Feb.: declared illegal by the senate . . 22 Feb. ,,
The impeachment of the president voted by house of representatives (126 to 47), 24 Feb.; reported at the bar of the senate by Thaddeus Stevens and Bingham . . . . 25 Feb. ,,
Nine articles of impeachment (for issuing order for removal of E. M. Stanton from war-office, and following proceedings) adopted by representatives (127 to 47) . . . . . . 2 March, ,,
Bill of impeachment of Johnson sent up to the senate by the house of representatives, 4 March,

Judicious speech of lord Stanley in the British house of commons on the *Alabama* claims, 6 March, 1868
Trial of president Johnson comes before the senate, 23 March, „
Impeachment opened by gen. Butler 30 March, „
Mr. Dickens sails from New York, after most affectionate parting . . . . . . 22 April, „
National republican convention at Chicago; announce their "platform"; approving the congress reconstruction policy; severely condemning president Johnson; denouncing repudiation of the debt; declaring for protection of naturalised citizens, &c., 20 May; and proposing general Ulysses Grant as the next president, and Mr. Colfax as vice-president . . . . 21 May, „
The senate reject the 11th article of the impeachment . . . . 16 May, „
Reject 2nd and 3rd articles; and adjourn *sine die*; intense excitement among republicans, 26 May, „
Mr. Stanton resigns, 27 May; succeeded by gen. Schofield . . . . 30 May, „
Death of the ex-president James Buchanan, 1 June, „
Chinese embassy received by the president, 5 June, „
Bill for re-admitting North and South Carolina, Georgia, Louisiana, Florida, and Alabama, to representation in congress, passed by the senate, 11 June, „
Mr. Reverdy Johnson nominated ambassador to Great Britain . . . . . . 12 June, „
Arkansas re-admitted over the president's veto, 20 June, „
The democratic convention nominate Horatio Seymour for president, and Francis P. Blair for vice-president . . . . 4–7 July, „
General amnesty (with exceptions) issued 4 July, „
Wyoming territory organised . . . . 22 July, „
Act for protection of naturalised citizens abroad passed . . . . 27 July, „
Thaddeus Stevens dies . . . . 12 Aug. „
Total debt declared, 2,641,002,572 dollars . 1 Nov. „
General Ulysses Grant, elected 18th president 3 Nov. „
General Sheridan's victory over insurgent Indians; a village burnt . . . . . . 27 Nov. „
Any repudiation of debt renounced by the house of representatives (154 to 6) . . . . 14 Dec. „
General pardon issued . . . . . 25 Dec. „
Cornell university (*which see*) founded . . . . „
Convention respecting *Alabama* claims signed by lord Clarendon and Mr. Reverdy Johnson, 14 Jan. 1869
Prosecution of Jefferson Davis dropped; a *nolle prosequi* entered . . . . 6 Feb. „
Indian war reported over . . . . . . Feb. „
Alabama treaty rejected by committee of senate, 18 Feb. „
Suffrage bill, abolishing all distinctions of race, colour, and property, passed . . . 21 Feb. „
General Schenk's bill, declaring that all national obligations shall be paid in coin, passed 3 March, „
Adjournment of 40th congress; meeting of 41st congress; gen. Grant assumes office . 4 March, „
Schenk's bill for cash payments passed by senate, 15 March, „
Convention respecting *Alabama* claim rejected by the senate . . . . 13 April, „
John Lothrop Motley appointed minister at London, April, „
Naturalisation treaty with Great Britain ratified by senate . . . . 15 April, „
Great peace jubilee held at Boston; colossal concert (10,371 voices, 1094 instruments, with anvils, bells, &c.) began . . . . . 15 June, „
Wm. Pitt Fessenden, financier, died 8 Sept. „
Steam-boat, *Stonewall*, burnt on the Mississippi; about 200 persons perish . . . . 27 Oct. „
Free-trade agitation prevalent . . . Oct.–Dec. „
Adm. Charles Stewart, "old iron-side," aged 92, died 6 Nov. „
Correspondence respecting *Alabama* claims, &c., between lord Clarendon and Mr. Hamilton Fish (June—Oct. 1869), published . . . Dec. „
Renewal of the reciprocity treaty with Canada rejected by congress . . . . . 13 Dec. „
U.S. corvette *Oneida* sunk by collision with British P. & O. steamer *Bombay*; 112 lives lost, 24 Jan. 1870
[Capt. Eyre, of the *Bombay*, severely censured for not waiting to give succour.]

Darien canal scheme approved by congress, Jan.; treaty signed . . . . 26 Jan. 1870
Virginia (15 Jan.) and Mississippi re-admitted to congress . . . . 3 Feb. „
Prince Arthur presented to president Grant, 24 Jan.; attended Mr. Peabody's funeral . 8 Feb. „
Bill for purchase of St. Thomas's isle rejected by senate . . . . 23 March, „
Texas (15 Mar.) and Georgia re-admitted to congress, 20 April, „
By amendments of the constitution, negroes admitted to equal rights with whites . . April, „
The tariff bill opposed by freetraders . . May, „
Non-recognition of Cuba affirmed . . . June, „
Lincoln state (out of New Mexico) constituted, June, „
Strong opposition to Chinese immigration; citizenship refused by the senate . . . . 4 July, „
Admiral J. A. Dahlgren died . . 12 or 13 July, „
Session of congress closed . . . . 15 July, „
J. L. Motley, minister to Great Britain, recalled, July, „
New tariff bill passed (new rates take effect, 1 Jan. 1871) . . . . „
Admiral David Farragut died, aged 70 14 Aug. „
Strict neutrality in the Franco-Prussian war proclaimed . . . . Aug. „
Senator Oliver P. Morton accepts the embassy to Great Britain . . . . 23 Sept. „
Great loss of life and property through floods in Virginia and Maryland, end of . Sept.-2 Oct. „
Total public debt, the principal and interest, 2,346,913,652 dollars . . . . 1 Oct. „
Great reduction of the heavy internal taxation begins . . . . 1 Oct. „
Movement against the Mormons on account of their polygamy . . . . 1 Oct. „
Meeting of the southern convention at Cincinnati for political and commercial affairs . 4 Oct. „
General Robert Lee dies, aged 62 . . . 12 Oct. „
President Grant issues a proclamation against Fenianism, and attacks on Cuba . . 13 Oct. „
Mr. Morton declines the embassy to Britain for party reasons . . . . about 25 Oct. „
The republican majority in the congress greatly reduced by the "fall" election (the first in which all races are duly represented) . . . Nov. „
Gen. Cox, secretary of interior, dismissed; quarrel between him and the president . . Nov. „
Total debt, 2,334,308,494 dollars . . 1 Dec. „
Annual message of the president: he regrets failure of proposal for annexing St. Domingo; and of the non-settlement of the *Alabama* claims; and complains of Canadian aggression . 5 Dec. „
Population: 33,581,680 whites; 4,879,323 coloured; Indians, 25,733; Chinese, 63,196; Japanese, 55; total, 38,549,987 . . . . Dec. „
Mr. Motley terms his recall "an outrage" 7 Dec. „
Gen. Robert Schenck appointed minister in London; accepts . . . . 21 Dec. „
New tariff in operation . . . . . 1 Jan. 1871
George Ticknor, historian, dies . . . 26 Jan. „
Statue of Abraham Lincoln in the capitol at Washington, unveiled . . . . . . 25 Jan. „
42nd congress meets (senate, 47 republicans; 15 democrats) . . . . 4 March, „
Proclamation against the Ku Klux in N. Carolina, 5 March, „
Commission to settle disputes with Great Britain respecting the *Alabama*, &c., fishery question, and the San Juan affair: for the British, the earl de Grey (since marquis of Ripon), sir Stafford Northcote, and others; for the Americans, secretary Fish, gen. Schenck, and others; announced 10 Feb.; meet at Washington, 27 Feb.; sign treaty, agreeing to arbitration at Geneva, &c. (see *Alabama* and *San Juan*), 8 May; ratified . 26 May, „
General Schenck warmly received at Liverpool, 3 June, „
An American fleet, accompanied by English and French and German ships, arrives at Corea to conclude a treaty for protection of mariners; on attempting to explore the island the Europeans are assailed from masked batteries, the Corean forts are then attacked and destroyed; and negotiations renewed . . . . June, „

Formation of the "new departure" democrat party advocating perfect freedom of all males irrespective of race and colour, full political restoration of the southern states, and free trade; about July, 1871

Chicago destroyed by fire; great exertions to relieve the sufferers; see *Chicago*; about 2000 lives lost by fires in N.W. forests . . . 8-11 Oct. ,,

Col. Hodge, paymaster of the regular army, confesses great defalcations since 10 Sept. 1864; condemned to long imprisonment . . . Nov. ,,

European and North American railway opened at Bangor, Maine, by lord Lisgar and gen. Grant, 18 Oct. ,,

Dispute between the U.S. foreign minister, Hamilton Fish, and the Russian envoy Katakazy (for undue interference); Katakazy dismissed Nov. ,,

Grand duke Alexis of Russia warmly received at New York . . . . 18 Nov. ,,

Congress opened; president in his message refers to peace abroad and prosperity at home . 4 Dec. ,,

Formal meeting of the *Alabama* arbitration commission at Geneva (adjourned to 15 June) . 18 Dec. ,,

Gen. Halleck died . . . . Jan. 1872

General amnesty bill passed . . . 16 Jan. ,,

American case under the treaty of Washington; claims indirect damages by *Alabama* and other vessels; much excitement in England . Jan. ,,

Despatch from the British minister sent 2 Feb.; reply received (not divulged to parliament), 14 March; further correspondence (see *Alabama*), March, April, ,,

Formation of Yellowstone National Park (*which see*) authorised by congress . . . March, ,,

Horace Greeley, editor of the *New York Tribune*, nominated president by many republicans, 4 May, ,,

New tariff, reduced duties to begin from 1 Aug.; passed . . . . 4 June, ,,

General Grant nominated for re-election as president by the republicans at Pennsylvania . 6 June, ,,

Continued negotiations respecting the *Alabama* affair, May; nothing settled; congress adjourns to December . . . . 10 June, ,,

Dispute with Spain respecting unjust imprisonment of Dr. Howard, an American citizen, in Cuba since 13 Dec. 1870; settled; Dr. Howard released . . . . June, ,,

Formation of "straight-out" democrat party, about June, ,,

Great international musical peace jubilee at Boston, 17 June–4 July, ,,

Coalition between the democrats and the liberal republicans at Baltimore to support Greeley, 10 July, ,,

Trial of Edward S. Stokes for murder of James Fisk of the Erie Ring (see *New York*, 1872), 15 July, ,,

United States squadron at Southampton, England, visited by the prince of Wales . . 13 Aug. ,,

Judge Barnard convicted of corruption, and removed from office and disqualified . . . 19 Aug. ,,

The "straight-out democrats" nominate Charles O'Connor for president . . . . Sept. ,,

Announcement of the award of the Geneva arbitration on the *Alabama*, &c. (about 3,229,166*l.*) Sept. ,,

Wm. Henry Seward, statesman, died . 10 Oct. ,,

The emperor of Germany, arbitrator in the San Juan difficulty, awards the island to the United States . . . . 23 Oct. ,,

Total debt of the States, 2,276,828,101 dollars, 1 Nov. ,,

Gen. Grant re-elected president (by 300 electoral votes; 68 for Greeley) . . . . 5 Nov. ,,

Death of Horace Greeley, aged 61 . 29 Nov. ,,

Sergeant William Bates walked from Gretna Green to London, carrying the American flag; warmly received everywhere (the feat originated in a wager); arrived 29 Nov.; rode through London to Guildhall . . . . 30 Nov. ,,

Gen. Grant in his message says that the results of the arbitration leave Great Britain and the United States without a shadow upon their friendly relations . . . . 2 Dec. ,,

Modoc Indians, near Oregon, defeat troops sent to expel them . . . . . . 17 Jan. 1873

Visit of professor Tyndall; he lectures in Boston, Philadelphia, Washington, New York, &c., Sept. 1872–Feb.

Vice-president Colfax accused of perjury . Feb. 1873

Civil war in Louisiana, fighting at New Orleans, Feb. ,,

The congress opened, great Credit Mobilier scandal, members accused of bribery . . . March, ,,

Death of chief justice Chase . . . 7 May, ,,

General Canby and others massacred (see *Modocs*), 11 April; capt. Jack and others captured; end of the war . . . . 1 June, ,,

Hiram Powers, sculptor of "the Greek Slave," died at Florence . . . . 27 June, ,,

Steamer *Wawasset* takes fire on the Potomac; about 70 perish . . . . 8 Aug. ,,

Cash payments (in silver) resumed . . 28 Oct. ,,

Great excitement through the execution of Americans taken in the *Virginius* (see *Cuba*) Nov. ,,

Public debt (less money in treasury) 2,141,833,476 dollars (about 4*s.* gold per dollar) . 1 Nov. ,,

President Grant's message: (calm) . . 2 Dec. ,,

Great deficiency in the revenue (about 17,000,000*l.*) announced . . . . Dec. ,,

Alex. H. Stephens, the great confederate leader, returns to political life and the legislature Dec. ,,

Women's *whisky-war* in S. Ohio: endeavour to suppress the liquor traffic by prayers, singing, &c., opposite the shops, Feb.: in New York 27 Feb. 1874

Ex-president Fillmore died . . . 8 March, ,,

Charles Sumner, senator, died . . 11 March, ,,

Women's whisky-war resisted; subsides March, April, ,,

President Grant's veto of the currency bill for creating inconvertible paper money, advocated by the Butler party . . . . . 22 April, ,,

Total debt, 2,285,786,818·89 dollars . 1 Aug. ,,

Fierce white and black riots at Austin, Mississippi, quelled by the military (after loss of 15 lives) 12 Aug. ,,

Great excitement respecting the Beecher-Tilton scandal; the rev. H. Beecher, a great preacher, accused of adultery with Mrs. Tilton, July; acquitted by a committee of his church . 27 Aug. ,,

Pennsylvania Republican Convention choose governor John F. Hartranft for next president Aug. ,,

Insurrection of negroes at Trenton, Tennessee; suppressed; leaders hanged . . . Aug. ,,

Centenary of the meeting of delegates at Philadelphia celebrated . . . . . Sept. ,,

Insurrection of whites at New Orleans against R. D. Kellogg, the governor of Louisiana, whom they depose, 15 Sept.; they submit to the president; and Kellogg is restored . 18 Sept. ,,

Great fire at Fall River cotton mills, Mass., about 60 lives lost . . . . . . 19 Sept. ,,

Reported massacre of whites by Indians in N.W. provinces . . . . Oct. ,,

The Republic, new government paper, started, Oct. ,,

Lincoln monument, Springfield, Illinois, inaugurated . . . . 15 Oct. ,,

Triennial convention of the episcopal church; canon passed against ritualism . . . 27 Oct. ,,

Majority for democratic party in elections for congress reported . . . . . 4 Nov. ,,

President Grant's message, moderate . 7 Dec. ,,

The senate passes a bill for the resumption of cash payment, 1 Jan., 1879 . . . . . Dec. ,,

Disturbances in New Orleans: government troops eject conservative members from the legislative assembly as unduly elected . . . . 4 Jan. 1875

New York, Boston, and other cities protest; the president's excuse in his message . . Jan. ,,

Senate rejects new reciprocity treaty with Canada 4 Feb. ,,

Colorado and New Mexico to be made states Feb. ,,

Civil rights (of negroes) bill passed . . Feb. ,,

The 44th congress comes into office, 4 March; (to meet on 6 Dec.) . . . . ,,

Centenary of battle of Lexington celebrated 19 April, ,,

Centenary of battle of Bunker's hill celebrated June, ,,

Trial of Tilton *v.* Beecher ends: jury disagreeing, discharged . . . . 2 July, ,,

Andrew Johnson, ex-president, dies . 31 July, ,,

Democratic conventions of New York declare in favour of hard money and resumption of cash payments . . . . 16 Sept. ,,

John McCloskey, R. C. archbishop of New York, made the first North American cardinal, received in his church at Rome . . . . 30 Sept. 1875
President Grant, in addressing the Tennessee army in Iowa, protests against Roman catholic aggression . . . . . . 30 Sept. ,,
Democratic inflationists defeated at elections for governor in Ohio and Iowa . about 12 Oct. ,,
Virginia city destroyed by fire (see *Nevada*) 26 Oct. ,,
State official elections give large majority for republicans . . . . . about 2 Nov. ,,
President Grant's message; alludes to attacks on and defends unsectarian education; notices unsatisfactory state of Cuba, and hints at ultimate intervention . . . . . . 7 Dec. ,,
Centennial year begun with great demonstrations at Philadelphia, &c. . . . . 1 Jan. 1876
General Babcock, secretary to president, acquitted of complicity in "Whisky frauds;" (resigned) 24 Feb. ,,
Mr. Belknap, secretary at war, accused of selling official places; resigns; impeached by congress 2 March, ,,
General Schenck, minister in London, charged with complicity in "Emma Mine frauds;" resigns and proceeds to America; R. H. Dana appointed in his room (opposed); John Walsh appointed next; John Walsh comes . . . . March *et seq.* ,,
Salary of next president proposed to be reduced from 50,000 to 25,000 dollars . . March, ,,
Increased opposition to Chinese immigration, March, ,,
Dana's appointment as minister to Britain rejected by the senate . . . . about 5 April, ,,
Lincoln monument, Washington; (erected by coloured people;) unveiled . . . 14 April, ,,
Other scandals in government offices reported, April, ,,
The president vetoes the bill for reduction of president's salary . . . . . 19 April, ,,
Issue of silver coin for small notes . . . May, ,,
Dispute with Great Britain respecting the extradition of Winslow, an American forger March-May, ,,
Mr. Pierrepoint, attorney-general, nominated minister for London . . . . . 5 May, ,,
International exhibition opened (see *Philadelphia*) 10 May, ,,
Political conferences at Philadelphia urge reforms May, ,,
Governor Rutherford B. Hayes, of Ohio, nominated president, and Wm. A. Wheeler vice-president, by the republican convention, Cincinnati 16 June, ,,
The arrangements for surrendering fugitive criminals in the treaty of 1842 nullified by the release of Winslow and Brent (see *Extradition*) . June, ,,
General Custer and his army attack the Sioux Indians, fall into an ambuscade, and are nearly all killed . . . . 25 June, ,,
Mr. Tilden nominated president by the democratic convention, St. Louis . . . . 29 June, ,,
Centenary of the foundation of the republic 4 July, ,,
Massacre of negro militiamen by whites at Hamburg, S. Carolina, 9 July; 53 whites indicted for murder . . . . Aug. ,,
Mr. Belknap's case in the senate: 35 vote him guilty of official corruption; 25 not; acquittal 1 Aug. ,,
Death of gen. Braxton Bragg . . . . Sept. ,,
The president's proclamation against unlawful combinations (of whites) in S. Carolina . 17 Oct. ,,
He declines to receive a centennial address from Irish home-rulers . . . . . Oct. ,,
Election of electors for the president . 7 Nov. ,,
International Exhibition at Philadelphia closed 10 Nov. ,,
President Grant's message; he declares the electoral system to have failed . . . 5 Dec. ,,
Election for president by delegates; Mr. Tilden, 184; Mr. Hayes, 185; (some votes challenged) 6 Dec. ,,
End of dispute with the British Government announced (see *Extradition*) . . . . Dec. ,,
Electoral tribunal (to settle the election for president) chosen in congress . . . 30 Jan. 1877
President in his message urges a speedy return to cash payments . . . . . . 3 Feb. ,,
Mr. R. B. Hayes' election confirmed; Mr. Wm. A. Wheeler, vice-president, 2 March; sworn, 4 March; inaugurated; in his message he professes impartial devotion to the public good, 5 March; and forms an impartial ministry . . . March, 1877
Gen. Grant visits Britain. . . 28 May *et seq.* ,,
"Molly Maguire," murderous terrorist rioters in Pennsylvanian coal-fields; subdued; several executed . . . . June, ,,
Strike of railway servants on Baltimore and Ohio railway through reduced pay; violent riots in West Virginia; reign of terror; successful resistance to the military; many killed and wounded at Pittsburg; held by rioters: sheriff killed; cannon used . . . . . 16-22 July, ,,
Strike extending to New York railways (not in New England) . . . . 24 July, ,,
Mob (many foreign communists) beaten by military at Chicago (15 killed, about 100 wounded), 26 July, ,,
Gen. Sheridan sent to Pittsburg, 22 July; damage about 8,000,000*l.*; tranquillity restored about 4 Aug. ,,
Death of Brigham Young . . . . . 29 Aug. ,,
General movement for the rights of labour during the year . . . . ,,
President Hayes warmly received in the south, Sept. ,,
Formation of a Cuban league on behalf of insurgents, announced . . . . . . Sept. ,,
Opposition to the president in Ohio, and other states; in elections . . . . . Oct. ,,
The new congress opened (democratic majority in the house of representatives; gaining in the senate); Sam. J. Randall, democrat, re-elected speaker . . . . 15 Oct. ,,
Many suspicious failures of commercial companies and others . . . . . . Sept., Oct. ,,
Reduction of the federal army from 25,000 to 20,000 voted by congress, refused by senate Oct. Nov. ,,
Anti-resumption bill passed by house of representatives . . . . 23 Nov. ,,
President Hayes' message; recommends resumption of cash payments on 1 Jan. 1879; pacification of the south; good treatment of the negroes, 3 Dec. ,,
The government defeated in the senate by Conkling and party; opposing civil service reform, cash payments, &c. . . . . . . 12 Dec. ,,
Bland's "silver bill," making silver the standard instead of gold; (injurious to fundholders, &c.,) passed by senate, veto of the president, (specie payments in silver to be resumed 1 Jan. 1879;) dollar 412½ grains said to be 8 per cent. less value than gold . . . . 16 Feb. 1878
Committee appointed to investigate charges of corruption against boards returning delegates to elect the president . . . . . June, ,,
Gen. Butler secedes from the republicans, and joins a new "National party" connected with Kearney, a violent agitator from California; (they are popularly termed "Greenbackers," as contending for soft money, and opposing return to cash payments) . . . . Aug. *et seq.* ,,
Desire expressed for a new reciprocity treaty with Canada . . . . Aug. ,,
American association meet at St. Louis . 21 Aug. ,,
Many deaths by yellow fever in southern states Aug., Sept., Oct. ,,
Autumn elections (mostly on 5 Nov.) . . . . ,,
46th congress elected; 149 democrats, 130 republicans, 10 greenbackers . . . . Nov. ,,
President's address to congress expresses gratitude "for countless blessings" . . . 2 Dec. ,,
Gold at par (1st time since 1862) . . 18 Dec. ,,
Resumption of cash payments; no great demand 2 Jan. 1879
Death of Caleb Cushing, U.S. minister at Madrid; aged about 79 . . . . . . 11 Jan. ,,
Meeting of 46th congress . . . . 4 March, ,,
Great emigration of negroes from the southern to the western states . . . March, April, ,,
30,000,000*l.* 5 per cents. converted into 4 per cents. at par . . . . April, ,,
Mr. John Walsh, minister in London, resigns, July; leaves England [succeeded by James Russell Lowell the poet] . . . . . 19 Aug. ,,
"Knights of Labour," a secret society for protection and advancement of workmen, active in the middle states . . . . ,,
Largest grain crops for many years . autumn, ,,

Public debt, 2,027,202,452 dollars . . . 1 Oct. 1879
Elections specially favour republicans . . Oct. „
Much distress of freed negroes in Kansas, &c. 1 Jan. 1880
The republican convention at Chicago choose gen. Garfield and Mr. Arthur as president and vice-president, 9 June; the democratic convention at Cincinnati choose gen. Winfield Scott Hancock and Wm. H. English . . . . 24 June, „
Gen. Garfield sets forth his proposed policy in a letter; says, "We legislate for the people of the United States, not for the whole world;" proposes a check for Chinese immigration, &c. . 12 July, „
97,000 office holders said to be liable to change Aug. „
Public debt reduced to 1,915,594,813 dollars 1 Oct. „
Gen. Garfield elected president; Mr. Chester A. Arthur vice-president (213-156) . . . 2 Nov. „
Treaty with China . . . . 17 Nov. „
Dispute between the president and senator Conkling respecting appointment of collector of customs at New York; Conkling resigns . May, 1881
Assassination of president Garfield by Charles Jules Guiteau, a lawyer of Chicago, at railway station, Washington; two pistol shots; ball enters the body . . . . 2 July, „
Destructive forest fires in Michigan; about 500 persons perish; 10,000 homeless . . 5 Sept. „
General Garfield, after much suffering, died 19 Sept. „
Queen Victoria's message to Mrs. Garfield: "Words cannot express the deep sympathy I feel with you at this terrible moment. May God support and comfort you as He alone can" . 20 Sept. „
After lying in state at Washington the general is buried at Cleveland, in Ohio . . 23 Sept. „
Court mourning in Great Britain . 21–28 Sept. „
334,000 dollars collected for Mrs. Garfield up to 30 Sept. „
Centenary of the capture of Yorktown celebrated (English flag saluted) . . 16 Sept. *et seq.* „
Mr. Blaine's letter to the European powers asserting the treaty respecting neutrality at Panama in 1846 to be sufficient, and protesting against their interference . . . . . . 25 Oct. „
The hon. Sackville West, the new British minister, warmly received at Washington . . 4 Nov. „
Guiteau's trial begins . . . . . 14 Nov. „
Meeting of Congress . . . . . . 5 Dec. „
Mr. Frelinghuysen succeeds Mr. Blaine as foreign minister. . . . . 12 Dec. „
Guiteau in the prison van shot at by Wm. Jones; his head grazed, 19 Nov. 1881; verdict, guilty 25 Jan. 1882
Chinese immigration suspended for 20 years; bill passed by senate about 10 March; vetoed by representatives, March; by the president about 4 April, „
Bill abolishing polygamy passed . 23 March, „
Great floods in the west (see *Mississippi*) March, „
United States constitution translated into Chinese by Tsai Sih Yung, completed . . . . . „
Representatives pass immigration bill excluding Chinese for ten years . . . . . 17 April, „
Great strike of iron-workers (about 150,000) in Pennsylvania begun 1 June; going on 13 July, „
Meeting of masters at Pittsburg to organise resistance . . . . 7 June, „
Guiteau executed . . . . . . 30 June, „
The Chinese exclusion act comes into operation 4 Aug. „
Act imposing a tax of 2s. per head (opposed by government) comes into operation . . Aug. „
One of only two copies of a life of general Garfield presented to queen Victoria; the other to Mrs. Garfield . . . . „
End of the iron-workers' strike . about 12 Sept. „
Robert E. Lee steamer burned on the Mississippi; about 20 deaths . . . . . 29 Sept. „
Elections greatly in favour of the Democrats 7 Nov. „
Death of Thurlow Weed, politician and journalist, aged about 85 . . . . . . 22 Nov. „
Meeting of Congress; president's address; comments on financial prosperity; recommends reduction of taxation and tariff . . 4 Dec. „
Civil service reform bill adopted by the senate 27 Dec. „
Immigration, 1881, about 719,000; 735,000 in . „
Presidential succession bill passed . 9 Jan. 1883
National debt, net, 1,607,543,676 dollars 1 Jan. „
The marquis of Lorne visits Washington . 26 Jan. 1883
Reduction in internal revenue and revision of the tariff by the senate and congress . 3 March, „
Last sitting of the congress . . . . 4 March, „
Great East River bridge, connecting New York and Brooklyn, opened . . . . . 24 May, „
Great strike of telegraph clerks in various states July, ends about 15 Aug. „
Visit of chief justice Coleridge; very warmly received . . . . . . Sept.—Oct. „
Gen. Sheridan succeeds gen. Sherman in command of the United States army . . . 31 Oct. „
Autumn elections; favour republicans . Nov. „
The new congress meets . . . . . 3 Dec. „
Death of Wendell Phillips, energetic abolitionist, aged 72 . . . . 4 Feb. 1884
Excitement concerning the wreck of the *Daniel Steinmann* (see *Wrecks*); investigation 8 April, „
Financial embarrassment of gen. Grant through endeavouring to support his son [relieved by government, 1885] . . . . . May, „
Mr. James G. Blaine and gen. Logan nominated republican candidates for the presidency and vice-presidency at Chicago, 6 June; great dissatisfaction thereat . . . . . . June, „
Meetings at New York, and other cities, about 21 June, „
Colossal statue of Liberty, by Bartholdi, the gift of the French to the United States, delivered at Paris by M. Jules Ferry, 4 July [received at New York, 19 June, 1885] . . . . . . „
Mr. Grover Cleveland, governor of New York, and Mr. Thomas A. Hendricks, nominated democrat candidates for the presidency and vice-presidency at Chicago . . . . . 11, 12 July, „
Gen. Butler offers himself as people's candidate 19 Aug. „
Great strike of miners in Hocking valley, Ohio, on account of foreigners; rioting . 1 Sept. *et seq.* „
Governor Cleveland, president, and Mr. Hendricks, vice-president, elected (defeat of the republicans) 4 Nov. „
Roman Catholic plenary council at Baltimore (about 70 archbishops and bishops) opened 9 Nov. „
Cattle-men s convention at St. Louis (see under *Cattle*) . . . . . . 18–22 Nov. „
About 56,000,000 acres appropriated by the Homestead act of 1862, up to 1880; announced Jan. 1885
Public indignation at the criminal explosions in London; stringent dynamite bill introduced in the senate by government . . . . 26 Jan. „
Public debt, 1,409,128,325 dollars, announced 2 Feb. „
The Chinese expelled from California; indemnity to be claimed by their government; announced Feb. „
Memorial obelisk of George Washington, 555 feet high, at Washington, inaugurated . 21 Feb. „
President Cleveland installed amid great acclamations . . . . 4 March, „
A new ministry; secretary of state, Thomas F. Bayard . . . . 4 March, „
Mr. Edward J. Phelps appointed U.S. minister in London, March; arrives at Southampton 16 May, „
Currency crisis; the banks oppose the Bland Act, and the compulsory coinage of silver . July, „
Death of gen. Grant, 23 July; he lies in state at New York, 5, 6, 7 Aug.; funeral procession 6 miles long includes the family, president Cleveland, government officials, gen. Hancock, and others of U.S. army; gen. Johnson (confederate), soldiers, marines, &c.; about 400 carriages; starts at 9 A.M.; arrival at the temporary tomb in Riverside Park on the Hudson 5 P.M. . 8 Aug. „
Murderous attacks on the Chinese workmen at Rock Springs in Wyoming territory 29 Aug.; quelled by government . . . about 3 Sept. „
Violent action against Chinese capitalists and workmen in Washington territory; proclamation for its suppression by the president . . 9 Nov. „
Death of gen. G. B. McClellan, com.-in-chief Nov. 1861, aged 59 . . . . 28 Oct. „
Death of T. A. Hendricks, vice-president U.S., aged 66 . . . . 25 Nov. „
Gen. Sherman elected vice-president . . 7 Dec. „
Wm. H. Vanderbilt, aged 64, "railway king," dies suddenly at New York; said to be worth about 50 million pounds . . . . 8 Dec. „

Meeting of congress . . . . 8 Dec. 1885
Much money subscribed for promoting Irish Home Rule 1885–6
Great ovation of Jefferson Davis through the Southern States . . . . April, 1886
German socialist agitation, eight hours' movement; riots at Chicago; dynamite employed; mob dispersed by police after fighting, 4 May; riots at Milwaukee 5 May; 10 killed, 115 wounded; 25 arrests, about 6 May; Herr Most (anarchist) arrested at New York, 12 May; convicted of inciting to riot, May; sentenced to fine and imprisonment . . . . 2 June, ,,
Gradual cessation of strikes in different states about 24 May, ,,
Chinese Indemnity Bill passed . . June, ,,
Large subscriptions to the Parnellite fund for elections, &c. . . . . . June *et seq.* ,,
The president promotes civil service reform; political action of officials checked . July, ,,
Election tour of Mr. James G. Blaine in Pennsylvania, &c.; strongly advocating Protection 16 Oct. ,,
Bartholdi Statue of Liberty, 150 feet high, set up at the harbour of New York, 305 feet above the sea level, on Bedloe Island, publicly dedicated by the president . . . . 28 Oct. ,,
Alien's Landlord's Bill (almost limiting holding of land and mines in "territories" to citizens) passed . . . . 2 Aug. ,,
Ex-president Arthur dies . . . . . 18 Nov. ,,
Great increase of speculation in railway stocks and trade . . . . . . Nov.–Dec. ,,
Mr. Henry George (see under *Land*) propagates his doctrines of Land Nationalisation; much opposed 1886–7
Edmunds' Canadian Fisheries Bill passed senate (46–1) . . . . 24 Jan. 1887
Fisheries Retaliation Bill passed . . . 3 March, ,,
American Exhibition (*which see*) opened in London 9 May, ,,
Seven socialists sentenced to death for murders during riots at Chicago, May, 20 Aug. 1886; ordered for execution . . . . 14 Sept. ,,
Centenary of the adoption of the Federal constitution celebrated at Philadelphia; five miles' procession illustrating the progress of trade and industry; fall of a great stand, many spectators injured, 15 Sept.; review of the army by the president, &c. . . . . . . 17 Sept. ,,
After great efforts for remission of sentence four of the Chicago anarchists executed (two sentenced to life imprisonment, one committed suicide) 11 Nov. ,,
Mr. Barnum's menagerie at Bridgport, Connecticut, burnt (see *Menagerie*) . . . . . 10 Nov. ,,
Mr. J. Chamberlain warmly received at New York; grand dinner at the chamber of commerce, 15 Nov. ,,
President Cleveland's message strongly urges fiscal reform, large reduction of protective duties and other taxation; surplus income 1886–7 above 11,000,000*l.* (annually increasing) 6 Dec.; approved by the Democrats, opposed by the Republicans, Dec. ,,
Naturalization of British emigrants increasing; strongly advocated by the *British American* newspaper to neutralize Irish influence (see *George, St.*) . . . . autumn ,,
The Knights of Labour order strikes of colliers and railway men; total on strike about 50,000, end of Dec.; end of railway strike reported 28 Dec. ,,
Snowstorm in the N.W. states; about 235 persons perish and many cattle . . . 11–13 Jan. 1888
Reform club at New York to support tariff reform; first banquet . . . . . . 21 Jan. ,,
Treaty respecting fisheries signed at Washington (see *Fisheries*) . . . . . . 15 Feb. ,,
Destructive blizzard (see *Storms*) . 11–13 March, ,,
Deadlock in the House of Representatives on the Direct Tax Bill; ended . . . 13 April, ,,
Mr. James G. Blaine announces positively his retirement from his candidature for the presidency 17 May, ,,
Mr. Cleveland nominated by acclamation for re-election as president by the Democratic convention at St. Louis, 6 June; gen. Benjamin Harrison (born 20 Aug. 1833) nominated candidate by the Republican convention at Chicago . 25 June, ,,
Lock-out of about 100,000 ironworkers near New York . . . . 30 June, ,,
President Cleveland at New York declares vigorously for reduced import duties and fiscal reform 5 July, 1888
American Tariff Bill passed lower House 21 July, ,,
Death of gen. Philip Henry Sheridan, commander-in-chief of the army, aged 57, 5 Aug.; succeeded by gen. John M. Schofield . . . 14 Aug. ,,
Treaty with China to prohibit Chinese immigration for 20 years 14 March; bill passed . 20 Aug. ,,
The senate refuses to ratify the fisheries treaty 21 Aug. ,,
The president in a message censures this, but declares for a policy of retaliation against Canada 23 Aug. ,,
Retaliation Bill passed by the House . 8 Sept. ,,
Agitation against "Trusts and Combines" (*which see*) . . . . autumn, ,,
Chinese Exclusion Bill approved by president Cleveland . . . . Oct. ,,
Chinese Exclusion Act vigorously carried out at San Francisco and at other places middle Oct. ,,
Lord Sackville, British minister at Washington, dismissed by president Cleveland for conversations with a reporter, and for writing a private "reply to an alleged" naturalised Englishman in California respecting the presidential election 30 Oct.; lord Sackville admitted indiscretion but repudiated other charges . . . . 26 Oct. ,,
Gen. Benjamin Harrison elected president, Mr. Levi P. Morton, vice-president; great defeat of the Democrats (233–168) . . . . 5 Nov. ,,
Resolution introduced into the House proposing negotiations for the annexation of Canada, 13 Dec. ,,
The American Commonwealth, by professor James Bryce, M.P., an elaborate work published . ,,
Destructive tornado in the Eastern states (see *Storms*) . . . . 9 Jan. 1889
Bill introduced in the House for stringent repression of immigration, especially labourers and criminals . . . . 19 Jan. ,,
New Tariff Bill passed by the senate . 22 Jan. ,,
The Anglo-American Extradition Treaty rejected by the senate (38–15) . . . . . 1 Feb. ,,
The senate and house pass the Nicaragua Canal Bill . . . . 7 Feb. ,,
Explosion at Park Central Hotel in Hartford, U.S.; about 40 persons killed . . . . . 18 Feb. ,,
Gen. Harrison assumes office; his cabinet formed; Mr. Blaine, secretary of state . . 4 March, ,,
Demonstrations and subscriptions in honour of Mr. Parnell at Philadelphia and other places (see *Ireland*) . . . . March, ,,
Storm at Samoa; three American war-vessels with loss of 4 officers and 46 men (see *Samoa*), 16 March, ,,
Oklahoma (*which see*) reserved lands (virgin soil) near Kansas, Arkansas, and Texas, proclaimed open to settlers; thousands of farmers and others with their goods, cattle, &c., migrate thither; riotous proceedings with bloodshed precede and attend the entering . . . . . 22 April, ,,
Sir Julian Pauncefote becomes British minister at Washington, Feb.; arrives . . . 23 April, ,,
Guthrie and two other towns founded 23 April, ,,
Order maintained by the military and lynch law 24 April *et seq.* ,,
Many unsuccessful settlers return, reported April, ,,
Celebration at New York of the centenary of gen. Washington's inauguration as first president 29 April–1 May, ,,
Naval procession; 300 vessels sail round the harbour 29 April; military procession (65,000 men) 30 April, civic and industrial procession 1 May, ,,
A convention met at Columbia, Tennessee, and organized an American-Scottish-Irish Association to perpetuate race memories and history 8 May, ,,
Cyclone from Maryland to Connecticut, much damage . . . . 10 May, ,,
Mr. Robert T. Lincoln, son of Abraham, appointed minister to Great Britain, March; arrives in London . . . . 22 May, ,,
Dr. Patrick Henry Cronin, Irish dynamite nationalist (expelled from the Clan-na-Gael, and denounced as a spy by Alex. Sullivan and the leaders, termed the "Triangle," and condemned to death by them for accusing them of embezzling funds allotted for dynamiting in England, Feb.) 4 May; found murdered at Lake View, Chicago 22 May; several men arrested . 29 May *et seq.* ,,

The coroner's jury declare the murder to be the result of a conspiracy of which Alexander Sullivan, P. O'Sullivan, Daniel Coughlin and Frank Woodruff (connected with the Clan-na-Gael) were the principals. Alex. Sullivan and others arrested 12 June; Alexander Sullivan released on high bail . . . . . 15 June, 1889

Martin Burke arrested at Winnipeg, Canada, indicted about 20 June. The grand jury at Chicago after 16 days' investigation, presents an indictment against Martin Burke, John F. Beggs, Daniel Coughlin, Patrick O'Sullivan, Frank Woodruff, Patrick Cooney, and John Kunz, with others unknown, of conspiracy and of the murder of Patrick Henry Cronin . . . . 29 June, „

[The conspiracy is said to have originated in camp 20 of the Clan-na-Gael.]

About 6,000 persons perish by the overflow of the dam of a lake in Conemaugh valley (see *Pennsylvania*) . . . . 31 May, „

Destructive floods in the eastern states; 8 persons drowned at Harper's Ferry, Virginia, and 13 at Corning, New York; estimated loss at Washington, 1,000,000 dollars; floods subsiding end of May, and 1, 2 June, „

Message of sympathy from queen Victoria to the president . . . . 8 June, „

Visit of American civil, mechanical, mining, and electrical engineers; well received in London, &c.; early June, „

Death of Simon Cameron, aged 90, war secretary during the civil war . . . . . 26 June, „

Great public meeting at Chicago impeaching the Clan-na-Gael as "an association of assassins," "existing under the protection of the United States, usurping the highest acts of government, in that it decrees death, exacts fealty, and levies war" . . . . 2 July, „

A meeting of Irish-Americans at Chicago propose the formation of an "Irish-American Republican Association," to be settled in Lower California 5 July, „

Inundation in Mohawk Valley, New York; 14 persons drowned at Johnstown . . . 9 July, „

Martin Burke (otherwise Frank Williams) at Winnepeg ordered for extradition 10 July; given up . . . . 3 Aug. „

The British sealer, *Black Diamond*, seized by the U.S. revenue cutter *Rush* (captain Shepard), in Behring sea (see *Behring Straits*) . 30 July, „

Reception at Liverpool of 50 representatives of American industries (on a tour of trade observation in Europe) . . . . . . 1 Aug. „

The national monument at New Plymouth, Massachusetts, commemorating the landing of the "Pilgrim Fathers" (*which see*) dedicated 1 Aug. „

The Sioux and the Chippewa Indians sell a large part of their reservations, which are to be opened for settlement . . . . . . Aug. „

David Terry, formerly a judge, shot dead at Lathorp, California, by Marshal Nagle, for striking judge Field in revenge . . . . 14 Aug. „

[Nagle was exonerated, 17 Sept.]

Destructive storm on the east coast (see *Storms*), 11, 13 Sept. „

Pan-Anglican Congress (*which see*), meeting of delegates at Washington . . . . 30 Sept. „

Maritime conference (*which see*) at Washington, 16 Oct. „

Fine evolutionary fleet (4 vessels) sails from New York for the Mediterranean under rear-admiral Walker. . . . . 10 Nov. „

President Harrison's message, moderate and pacific, 3 Dec. „

Death of Mr. Jefferson Davis, aged 81, late president of the Confederate States, 6 Dec.; solemnly buried at New Orleans . . . . 11 Dec. „

[Re-interred at Richmond, Virginia, 31 May, 1893.]

The new Anglo-American extradition treaty ratified by the senate . . . . . . 18 Feb. 1890

Mr. Blaine and sir J. Pauncefote agree to refer the Behring sea affair to arbitration, reported, 25 Feb. „

Inundations in the west through excessive rains, destructive snowstorms on the east coast, end of Feb. „

A national convention of the delegates of the coloured citizens of the U.S., at Washington, issues an address . . . . 7 Feb. 1890

Cronin trials. The case called on 26 Aug. 1889; 1,115 talesmen were examined before a jury of 12 could be obtained (a plot to corrupt the jury having been discovered, 4 persons pleaded guilty, one convicted, Feb. 1890) . . . . 23 Oct. 1889

The trial began at Chicago before judge M'Connell: Mr. Longenecker, state attorney, counsel for the prosecution, Mr. Forrest for the defence, 24 Oct.; the jury acquitted John F. Beggs; found Daniel Coughlin, Patrick O'Sullivan, and Martin Burke guilty of murder, and sentenced them to imprisonment for life; John Kunz, as accessory, to 3 years' imprisonment . . . 16 Dec. „

[Frank Woodruff discharged, April, 1890.]

A new trial granted to John Kunz, the other sentences confirmed . . . . . 14 Jan. 1890

"World's Fair" ordered to be in 1893 . March, „

Bills introduced for greatly raising the minimum of the coinage of silver, fixed by the Bland act of 1878; bills dropped through disagreement, reported . . . . 19 April, „

The World's Fair bill passed; signed by the president . . . . 25 April, „

Congress votes 150,000 dollars for relief of sufferers by the Mississippi floods; sent to the president, 25 April, „

Naval Supply bill passed by the senate; three battleships to be built . . . . 27 May, „

The president proclaims the Behring sea closed to unlicensed seal-fishing . . . . 25 March, „

The president approves of the new silver bill passed to enlarge the currency . . . . 14 July, „

John C. Fremont, scientist, explorer, statesman, &c., dies, aged 77 . . . . . . 13 July, „

The British sealing schooners, *George R. White* and *Ariel*, seized in Behring seas reported . 31 July, „

Silver purchase circular issued by the secretary of the treasury, offering to sell silver bullion in lots, not under 10,000 ozs., to mints, on and after 13 Aug. . . . . 1 Aug. „

Strikes of workmen, railway men, &c., in New York, Chicago, &c. . . . . . . Aug. „

Labour day, orderly demonstration in New York, Chicago, and other cities . . . 1 Sept. „

Mr. McKinley's tariff bill, highly protectionist, to encourage home manufactures, after long discussion and opposition from the democrats, passed by the congress, 30 Sept.; approved by the president, 1 Oct.; comes into operation . 6 Oct. „

[The bill greatly affected Great Britain, Canada, France, Austria, and other states; the act includes a policy of retaliation and reciprocity.]

The count of Paris arrives at New York, 3 Oct.; at Philadelphia, 6 Oct.; at Washington, 7 Oct.; Richmond, 9 Oct.; New York, 17 Oct.; leaves for Canada . . . . 21 Oct. „

Elections for the 52nd congress; great majority for the democrats . . . . 4 Nov. *et seq.* „

For Indian rising, see *Indians* . Nov. *et seq.* „

The president's message to congress, defending the McKinley tariff, &c. . . . . 1 Dec. „

Convention at Ocala, Florida, to organize a new political party to be named the National Union party, to include the Farmers' Alliance, the Knights of Labour and similar bodies, early Dec. „

A free silver coinage bill hastily passed by the senate . . . . 15 Jan. 1891

Great distress in the west attributed to the McKinley act . . . . Jan. „

Death of George Bancroft, historian and diplomatist, aged 90 . . . . . . 17 Jan. „

Destructive snowstorm on the Atlantic coast, starting from Alabama (see *New York*) 24, 25 Jan. „

Death of admiral David Dixon Porter, eminent commander in the Civil war, aged 76 . . 13 Feb. „

Gen. Wm. Tecumseh Sherman, commander-in-chief (1869-84) dies, aged nearly 71, 14 Feb.; funeral ceremony at New York; present, president Harrison and state officials, chief army officers with about 10,000 troops, 19 Feb.; burial at St. Louis, Missouri . . . . 21 Feb. „

Mr. Charles Foster appointed secretary of the treasury . . . . 21 Feb. „

The senate's free coinage bill defeated by the house, 22 Feb.; end of the great speculation in Wall-street, New York, termed the "silver pool," or syndicate . . . . . . 24 Feb. 1891
Gen. Joseph Johnston, confederate, aged 87, dies, 21 March, „
President Harrison's tour to the Pacific coast; visiting the S. and W. states . April, May, „
The Farmers' Alliance form a "third party" to oppose the republicans and democrats, end of May, „
Mr. John Bardsley, city treasurer of Philadelphia, sentenced to 15 years' solitary confinement, and heavy fine, for defalcations . 2 July, „
Threatened revolt of the Indians (*which see*), 12 July, „
James Russell Lowell, statesman and popular writer, dies, aged 72 . . . . 12 Aug. „
Dispute with Chili (*which see*) . . . Oct. „
Fight between supporters of the Farmers' Alliance and their opponents, 5 deaths at Bucksport, Arkansas . . . . . . 28 Oct. „
Destructive storm over the city of Washington, and a waterspout, much damage done at Baltimore, and along the coast . . . . 23 Nov. „
Meeting of the 52nd congress; republican majority lost; president Harrison's message 9 Dec. „
A new "reciprocity" party formed, headed by Mr. Blaine, about 80,000 members . . 9 Jan. 1892
The arbitration treaty respecting the Behring seas signed at Washington, (see *Behring Straits*) 29 Feb. „
Death of Walter Whitman, national poet, author of "Leaves of Grass," aged 72 . . 26 March, „
Destructive tornado in the N.W. states; about 30 persons killed . . . . . 3 April, „
The difficulty with the Italian government closed (see *New Orleans*) . . . . . 14 April, „
Above 450,000,000 of silver dollars in the treasury vaults, reported . . . . . 25 April, „
The corner stone of general Grant's monument in Riverside-park, New York, laid by president Harrison . . . . . . 27 April, „
The invitation to an international conference on the silver question, accepted by Great Britain and other powers (see *Monetary Conferences*) May, June, „
The National Bi-metallic League formed in Washington . . . . May, „
Resignation of Mr. Blaine as secretary, 4 June; succeeded by Mr. John W. Foster . 29 June, „
President Harrison nominated for re-election by the republican convention at Minneapolis, Mr. Whitelaw Reid as vice-president . . 10 June, „
Mr. Grover Cleveland (president 1885) nominated for election as president at Chicago, Mr. Adlai E. Stevenson as vice-president . 23 June, „
The *Texas*, battleship, launched at Norfolk, Virginia . . . . . . 28 June, „
The "Prohibition" (temperance) Convention at Cincinnati nominates gen. John Bidwell for president . . . . . . 1 July, „
Senator W. M. Stewart's Free Silver bill passed the senate, 1 July; rejected by the house . 13 July, „
The "People's Party" convention at Omaha, nominates gen. James B. Weaver for president, and gen. J. G. Field for vice-president . 5 July, „
Great heat throughout the greater part of the United States, about 23 July; many deaths; 99°-102°, 28 July; the hottest day for 21 years, 29 July; traffic impeded by death of horses, 29 July; 107°, 223 deaths at New York, 29 July; 90 deaths, 30 July; 296 deaths, 31 July; cooler, 31 July, „
The congress adjourns till Dec. 1892 . 6 Aug. „
The *Marblehead*, warship, launched at Boston 11 Aug. „
Great strike on several railways in New York State, 13 Aug.; severe conflicts between strikers and non-strikers; about 150 cars burnt, 14, 15 Aug.; the Buffalo railway guarded by troops; traffic suspended; troops massed; more strikes, with conflicts like civil war, 17 Aug. *et seq.*; traffic resumed under military protection, 18, 19 Aug.; end of strike reported . . . . 24 Aug. „
Rising of miners in Tracy City, Tennessee, against the employment of convicts in state labour, 13 Aug.; convicts attacked and expelled and their stockades demolished; fighting between the convict guard and the strikers; the strikers victors at Coal Creek; much slaughter; progress of troops on the line temporarily stopped; the miners surrender to gen. Carnes after severe fighting; order restored at Coal Creek 18, 19 Aug. 1892
Western Reserve, steamer, wrecked on Lake Superior; 26 lives lost . . . . . 30 Aug. „
Hattie, U.S. fishing schooner, seized by the Canadian cruiser *Curlew*, while unlawfully fishing in the Bay of Fundy . . . reported 6 Sept. „
Death of John Greenleaf Whittier, eminent poet, and opponent of slavery, aged 84 . . 7 Sept. „
Cholera panic on Long Island, New York; the landing on Fire Island of passengers from foreign vessels violently resisted by an armed mob, causing much distress; the landing only effected by governor Flower and the military, 11–13 Sept. „
Grand celebration of the discovery of America by Columbus (12 Oct. 1492) at New York, Philadelphia, and throughout the union, 12 Oct. *et seq.* „
Solemn dedication of the buildings of the World's Columbian exposition at Chicago (*which see*), 21 Oct. „
Death of Mrs. Caroline Scott Harrison, wife of the president; an accomplished lady; aged 58, 25 Oct. „
General drought throughout the country, Aug.–Oct. „
Grover Cleveland re-elected president, 277; Harrison, 145; Weaver, 22; total, 444; Mr. Adlai E. Stevenson vice-president . . . . 8 Nov. „
Coinage in year 1891–2: gold, value 35,506,978 dollars; silver dollars, 8,329,467; total coinage, 51,792,976 dollars; mint report . about 18 Nov. „
Mr. Jay Gould, successful speculator in railways and telegraphy, realizes between 72,000,000 dollars; termed "little wizard of Wall-street;" dies at New York, aged 56 . . . 2 Dec. „
Congress opened by president Harrison, 5 Dec.; his message very cheerful . . . . 6 Dec. „
Death of gen. Benjamin Franklin Butler, aged 75; energetic republican . . . . Jan. 1893
Death of ex-president gen. Rutherford B. Hayes, aged 70 . . . . 17 Jan. „
James Gillespie Blaine, statesman and orator; born 31 Jan. 1830, died 27 Jan.; state funeral, 30 Jan. „
The commissioners from Honolulu received (see *Sandwich Isles*) . . . . . . 11 Feb. „
Treaty for the annexation of the Sandwich isles proposed . . . . „
Gen. Pierre G. T. de Beauregard, confederate (*see above*, 1861), dies, aged 75, reported . 22 Feb. „
The president hoists the U.S. flag on the mail steamer *New York* . . . . . 22 Feb. „
Judge Walter Q. Gresham as secretary of state; Mr. John G. Carlisle, secretary of the treasury; Daniel S. Lamont, war; Hilary A. Herbert, navy; Mr. Hoke Smith, interior; Mr. Richard Olney, attorney-general; appointed . . . . Feb. „
Indiana, great battleship, launched at Philadelphia, 28 Feb. „
Inauguration of Grover Cleveland as president; in his address, he declares for a stable currency, condemns protection and state paternalism and favouritism; proposes reform of the civil service and the tariff, and justice and humanity to the Indians . . . . 4 March, „
Sir Julian Pauncefote, British minister at Washington; Mr. Robert T. Lincoln, U.S.A. minister in London; nominated "ambassadors" . March, „
Mr. Thomas F. Bayard appointed first "ambassador" for London; (died 28 Sept. 1898), 30 March, „
Grand international naval review at New York; 2 columns of war-ships, extending about 3 miles; present: president Cleveland and his cabinet, American superior officials, diplomatic body, &c., the duke of Veragua, and many eminent persons; many presentations to president Cleveland; all operations successful; in the evening, illuminations and fireworks and parade of troops and seamen in the city . . . . . 27 April, „
New immigration law comes into effect, 3 May; the Chinese exclusion act much opposed . 5 May, „
Launch of the *Massachusetts*, great battleship, at Philadelphia . . . . . . 10 June, „
Fall of price of silver through the Indian currency act, end of June; silver mining and works suspended in Colorado and other places . 29 June, „

Extra session of congress opens . . 7 Aug. 1893
President Cleveland, in his message, referred to the silver troubles . . . . 8 Aug. ,,
Award of the arbitrators at Paris issued (see *Behring Straits*) . . . . 15 Aug. ,,
Two compulsory silver purchase repeal bills: Mr. Voorhees' before the senate, 28 Aug.; Mr. Wilson's passed by the house, 28 Aug.; prolonged discussion in the senate . . . . Oct. ,,
Cherokee Strip, near Arkansas (*which see*), given up for settlement . . . 16 Sept. ,,
The world's fair closed (see *Chicago*) 30 Oct. ,,
The silver purchase repeal bill passed by the senate (victory of pres. Cleveland) 43–32, 30 Oct.; signed by him . . . 1 Nov. ,,
The Chinese exclusion bill passed by the senate, 2 Nov. ,,
Death of Francis Parkman, historian of French America, aged 70 . . . . . 9 Nov. ,,
President Cleveland's message to congress firm, liberal and pacific . . . 4 Dec. ,,
Out of work in New York, 80,000; Chicago, 120,000; Philadelphia, 60,000, reported . 21 Dec. ,,
The tariff bill, with internal revenue bill and income-tax clause, passed (204–140) by the house, 1 Feb. 1894
The *Kearsage* (battle-ship) wrecked in the Caribbean sea, on Roncadore reef; all saved . . 2 Feb. ,,
Mr. Bland's silver seigniorage coinage bill, authorizing a large coinage of silver, passed by the house, 1 March; by the senate, 15 March; vetoed by pres. Cleveland . . . . 29 March, ,,
Decline of the democratic party through ministerial mismanagement respecting the finances and currency (not due to president Cleveland), Feb., March, ,,
The Behring sea treaty bill passed . . 7 April, ,,
Great strike of colliers (about 126,600) in Pennsylvania, Ohio, Maryland, and other coal districts, reported, April; rioting, with bloodshed, in Illinois and other places, May; troops called out, 27 May *et seq.*; subsidence of the coal strike through compromise, reported . 10 June, ,,
Coxey's commonweal, and other "industrial armies," formed by Mr. Coxey, of Ohio, throughout the states, proceeding to Washington to demand legislation for work and better payment; conflict with the railway authorities at Omaha, Council Bluffs, Nebraska, 20 April; 1st section arrives, 21 April; trains seized and successfully held against the authorities in Montana and Indiana; some re-captured by troops in Dakota, &c., April; total of Coxeyite bands, 7,250; the main body of Coxeyites (about 400) arrive at Washington . . . . . . 29 April, ,,
Messrs. Coxey, Browne and Jones committed for illegal acts, 2 May; imprisoned and fined, about 21 May; the movement collapsing, reported, 11 May, ,,
Settlement of the claims against Chili (*which see*, 1894)
Arrival of rear-admiral Erben and capt. A. T. Mahan (naval historian) in the U.S. war-ship *Chicago* in the Thames, 9 May; banquet given to them in St. James's hall, 24 May; reception and dance on the *Chicago* off Gravesend . 11 June, ,,
Capt. Mahan made LL.D. at Cambridge, 18 June; D.C.L. at Oxford . . . . 20 June, ,,
Railway strikes: "Pullman car," reported, 28 June; above 60,000 men out; service partially blocked throughout the states, 29 June; the government orders the military to raise the blockade of the railways and quell rioting; Mr. Edward Phelan, strike leader, arrested at Cincinnati, 3 July; conflicts ensue, reported . 6 July, ,,
[See *Chicago*.]
Martial law proclaimed in Illinois and other states, 9–10 July, ,,
Strike subsides . . . . . 13 July, ,,
Collapse of the railway union . . . 15 July, ,,
Senator Gorman's new tariff bill passed by the senate . . . . . . 3 July, ,,
Disagreement between the senate and house respecting tariff bill, 19 July; long conference of delegates fruitless, 8 Aug.; compromise; the senate's tariff bill, favouring free trade, passed by the house (181–105), 13 Aug.; comes into force, 27 Aug. ,,
Bill for the exclusion and deportation of anarchists passed . . . . . . 16 Aug. 1894
New treaty between United States and China ratified, reported . . . . . 28 Aug. ,,
Session closed . . . . . . Sept. ,,
Nine weeks' drought leads to great forest fires in Minnesota, Wisconsin and Michigan; 13 towns and many villages destroyed, 31 Aug.–3 Sept.; 400 deaths, reported . . . . 4 Sept. ,,
Oliver Wendell Holmes, M.D., physiologist, poet, novelist and essayist; "Autocrat of the Breakfast-table;" born 29 Aug. 1809; died . . 7 Oct. ,,
Gen. Schofield advocates increase of the army to support the authority of the federal government, Oct. ,,
Autumn elections: 248 republicans; 95 democrats; 13 populists, in the house . . 7 Nov. *et seq.* ,,
Congress opens with the president's message, 3 Dec. ,,
Message from the president to the congress respecting the withdrawal of gold . . 28 Jan. 1895
Gold received from Philadelphia, Cincinnati, &c., Jan. ,,
The national board of trade vote confidence in president Cleveland's financial proposals, 30 Jan. ,,
Pres. Cleveland's bond bill for the relief of the treasury rejected by the house . . 7 Feb. ,,
The president's 2nd message to congress, stating that he has made arrangements to issue a 3 per cent. gold bond at par in place of the 4 per cent., 8 Feb. ,,
The 3 per cent. gold bill rejected by the house, 14 Feb. ,,
The bond syndicate deposits in the treasury over 30,000,000 dollars in gold (1,000,000 from Canada), 15 Feb. ,,
Death of Fredk. Douglass at Washington, aged 78; half-negro; abolitionist orator . . 21 Feb. ,,
The supreme court at Washington decides that the imposition of an income-tax (2 per cent.) on rents, estates, &c., to meet the deficit is unconstitutional . . . . 8 April, ,,
General opposition to the tax increasing; collection begun . . . . 12 April, ,,
Dr. James Dwight Dana, born 12 Feb. 1813; eminent naturalist, geologist and writer; Silliman professor at Yale university; attached to the U.S. exploring voyage under capt. Wilkes to the South seas in 1838; illustrated reports of his observations, &c., published 1846 *et seq.*; died, 15 April, ,,
Increased agitation for and against free coinage of silver . . . . April, ,,
A silver convention of 17 states W. of the Mississippi to increase the use of silver, held at Salt Lake city; formation of a bimetallic union proposed . . . . . . 15–18 May, ,,
The supreme court decides the entire income-tax to be unconstitutional . . . 20 May, ,,
A "sound money" convention at Memphis, Tennessee, opposing unlimited silver coinage, opened; pres. Cleveland's policy commended, 23 May, ,,
Mr. W. Q. Gresham, secretary of state; born 17 March, 1832; died 28 May, 1895; state funeral, 29, 30 May; succeeded by Mr. Richard Olney; Mr. Judson Harmon, att.-gen. . . . 7 June, ,,
Agitation in favour of bimetallism . . . May, ,,
Proclamation of strict neutrality in regard to Cuba, 13 June, ,,
Much agitation throughout the states on the silver question . . . . June, ,,
The bond syndicate complete the transfer of gold to the treasury; gold balance, 107,553,774 dollars; cash balance, 192,620,422 dollars, reported, 28 June, ,,
Death of Howell Edmunde Jackson, eminent judge, aged 63, reported . . . . 9 Aug. ,,
The Irish-American convention to promote complete Irish independence, John F. Finerty, president, held at Chicago . . . 24 Sept. ,,
Chicago Fenians adopt the name of "Irish national alliance of the world" . . . . 26 Sept. ,,
Wm. Wetmore Story, sculptor and author, died in Italy, aged 75 . . . . . . 7 Oct. ,,

Pres. Cleveland declares in favour of a vigorous democratic state platform . . . . 31 Oct. 1895

Congress meets, 2 Dec.; the president's message, relating to finance (new measures), Argentine, China, Hawaii, Japanese treaty, Mosquito strip, Nicaragua, Russia, Armenia, Behring Sea dispute, Venezuela, &c. . . . . 3 Dec. ,,

For dispute with Great Britain see *Venezuela*, 1895.

The president's views on the Monroe doctrine much censured; heavy falls in the New York stock market . . . . 20 Dec. ,,

Message of peace and goodwill to the American people from the prince of Wales and the duke of York in response to an appeal of the New York *World*, 24 Dec.; cordially received in most parts, 26 Dec. ,,

New tariff bill increasing the revenue passed by the house of representatives . . . . 26 Dec. ,,

The president's policy severely censured by the New York chamber of commerce . . 2 Jan. 1896

Resolution of the senate and the house deprecating the civil war in Cuba, asserting the rights of the insurgents to good civil government and to be regarded as belligerents . . . . . 29 Jan. ,,

State loan (100,000,000 dollars) fully taken up, announced . . . . 6 Feb. ,,

The free silver bill of the senate rejected by the house (216—91) . . . . 14 Feb. ,,

Arbitration conference held at Philadelphia, an approving letter from pres. Cleveland read, 22 Feb. ,,

Concurrent resolution in the senate recognising the Cuban insurgents as belligerents and requesting the Spanish government to recognise the independence of Cuba, 28 Feb.; adopted by the house, 2 March; resented in Spain . March, ,,

The Washington arbitration conference appoint a permanent committee, and urge action in favour of arbitration between the U.S. and other countries . . . . 23 April, ,,

Presidential campaign: candidates — Mr. Wm. McKinley, republican, Mr. Reed, and others, May, ,,

The senate passes Mr. Butler's bill prohibiting the further issue of interest-bearing bonds against a gold standard and favouring the silver party, 2 June, ,,

Mrs. Harriet Beecher-Stowe, born 1812, died 1 July, ,,

A silver vase from the president presented to capt. A. Nicholl, at Manchester, for saving 8 men from the schooner *Elisha Gibbs*, of New Bedford, Massachusetts, 6 March, 1896 . . . . . 12 Aug. ,,

"Coin's Financial School" (a mixture of fiction and truth), published in 1894 by a company supporting a silver standard, and opposed by "Sound Money" in 1895, much controversy . Aug. ,,

Law congress at Saratoga Springs, N.Y.; address of lord Russell, chief justice of England, on international arbitration and mediation, warmly received . . . . 20 Aug. ,,

Mr. William McKinley elected president, over 7,123,234 votes; majority, 1,000,000, . 3 Nov. ,,

General revival of trade; great rise in the price of wheat . . . . 9 Nov. ,,

Increased agitation on behalf of Cuba . Nov. ,,

Thanksgiving on the result of the elections, 26 Nov. ,,

Pres. Cleveland's dignified message to the last session of the 54th congress; refers to Armenia, Turkey, Cuba, Venezuela, financial reforms, and foreign relations . . . . 7 Dec. ,,

Senate committee on foreign relations report their recognition of the independence of the republic of Cuba, and that the United States will use its friendly offices to close the war between Spain and Cuba . . . . 18 Dec. ,,

Many bank failures in the west . Dec. 1896–Jan. 1897

Gen. Walker, eminent economist, dies . . Jan. ,,

Arbitration treaty (5 years) between Great Britain and United States signed by Mr. Olney and sir Julian Pauncefote (peer, 1899) at Washington, 11 Jan.; text in *Times* . . . . 19 Feb. ,,

Modified and referred to the senate, 31 Jan.; virtually nullified by amendments, 23 March; senate refuses to ratify the treaty as amended, 5 May, ,,

Capt. Hart, owner of the *Laurada*, steamer, convicted of filibustering, appeals for new trial, released on bail, 23 Feb.; sentenced to 2 years' imprisonment and a fine (pardoned, June 1898) . 8 March, ,,

Bill passed for an international monetary conference . . . . 3 March, 1897

Mr. McKinley's cabinet: Mr. John Sherman, secretary of state; Mr. Lyman J. Gage, treasury; Mr. Russell A. Alger, war; Mr. John D. Long, navy; Mr. Cornelius R. Bliss, interior; Mr. Joseph M'Kenna, attorney-general; Mr. James Gary, postmaster-general . . . . . 3 March, ,,

Inauguration of William McKinley as president; in his address he recommends a revision of the coinage, higher tariff, currency laws, protection, arbitration, etc. 4 March; message to congress, financial review, 15 March; new tariff, *Times*, 15 March, ,,

The Dingley tariff bill passed by the house, 31 March; passed by the senate, 7 July, and becomes law . . . . 24 July, ,,

National monument to gen. Grant at Riverside, New York, inaugurated by pres. McKinley, 27 Apr. ,,

Col. John Hay, diplomatist and author, received by the queen at Windsor as U.S. ambassador, 3 May, ,,

Resolution recognising Cuban belligerency passed by congress (41—14) . . . . . 20 May, ,,

International commercial congress at Philadelphia opened by president McKinley . . 2 June, ,,

Treaty for the annexation of Hawaii (Sandwich islands) to the United States signed at Washington, 16 June (annexed 7 July, 1898) . . . . ,,

Congratulations to the queen on her diamond jubilee, 28 May; presented . . . June, ,,

Coalminers strike for increase of wages in 5 states, July, ,,

Gen. Neal Dow, philanthropist, born, 1804, died, 2 Oct. ,,

International fur seal conference; see *Behring Straits*, 23 Oct. 1897.

Sir Wilfrid Laurier's unofficial visit to Washington, 11 Nov. *et seq.* ,,

Pres. McKinley's message to congress; currency reform; Hawaii; Cuban question . 6 Dec. ,,

Mr. Teller's resolution for free silver, adopted in the senate, 47—32, 29 Jan.; rejected in the house, 182—132, 31 Jan. 1898. (The republican party unsettled.)

Destructive blizzard in New York and New England, with loss of life, railways blocked, etc., 31 Jan. 1898

Sen. Dupuy de Lôme, Spanish minister at Washington, resigns on the publication of a private letter, reflecting against pres. McKinley; leaves 15 Feb.; regret expressed by Spain . 16 Feb. ,,

Explosion on the cruiser *Maine* (*which see*), 15 Feb. ,,

Bill for 2 new regiments of artillery passed, 7 March, ,,

Appropriation bill for 50,000,000 dollars for national defence, passed by the house, 8 March, and the senate, becomes law . . . . . 9 March, ,,

Sen. de Bernabe well received as Spanish minister, 12 March, ,,

Two warships bought from Brazil, March; the *Kearsarge* and *Kentucky* battleships, launched at Newport . . . . 24 March, ,,

The hon. Blanch K. Bruce, born a slave in Virginia, 1 March, 1841; self-educated; elected senator, 1875–81; register of the treasury; died, 17 March, ,,

Message to Spain, regarding Cuba (*which see*), 31 March, ,,

An appeal for peace to the president from the powers . . . . 7 April, ,,

An armistice in Cuba granted by Spain 9 April, ,,

The president's message to congress, requiring the end of the war, and the establishment of a stable government in Cuba . . . . . 11 April, ,,

The Spanish ministry in a semi-official note declares the message incompatible with the rights of Spain . . . . 12 April, ,,

Great revival of prosperity in the west after 4 yrs. depression, 1897–8.

The foreign committee's resolutions: the Cubans right to be free and independent, Spain to withdraw her forces; that the U.S. president be empowered to give effect to these resolutions, agreed to by both houses, after a stormy scene, 13 April, ,,

Debates in the senate, 14–16 April; conferences between the senate and house, the resolutions of 13 April, passed, senate, 40–35; house, 310—6, 18, 19 April; signed by the president, and an

ultimatum sent to Spain; the Spanish minister, sen. Polo de Bernabe, received his passports, and left Washington, 20 April; diplomatic relations at once broken off; gen. Woodford left Madrid, 21 April, 1898
President McKinley calls out 125,000 volunteers for 2 years, service . . . . . . 23 April, „
The president's message to congress declares that war exists between Spain and United States, since 21 April. . . . . . . 25 April, „
Mr. Sherman, the secretary of state, resigns, succeeded by Mr. Day . . . . 25, 26 April, „
Commodore George Dewey thanked by congress, and promoted, for the victory at Manila (see *Spanish-American war*, 1 May); a sword to be presented to him, and medals to his officers and men . . . . 2, 9 May, „
International commission to settle differences between Canada and United States agreed on, 31 May; see *Behring Straits*, and *Canada*, June, „
War revenue bill (increased tonnage dues), passed by congress . . . . 9 June, „
Count Cassini received as Russian ambassador, 23 June, „
Thanks of congress voted to lieut. Hobson and his crew, 29 June; and message of thanks to adm. Sampson on the destruction of the Spanish fleet at Santiago, 4 July; congress adjourns, 8 July, „
Mr. John Hay nominated secretary of state, 16 Aug. „
Controversy respecting the conduct of the war; gen. Miles publishes his statement, criticising the war office . . . . 8 Sept. „
Mr. Hay, U.S. ambassador, leaves London, 14 Sept. „
The *Illinois* battleship launched . . . . 4 Oct. „
Elections: republican majority . . . 8 Nov. „
Society founded at Boston against imperialism and annexation of foreign territory; Mr. Andrew Carnegie contributes 1,000 dollars . 19 Nov. „
Spanish-American treaty signed at Paris, see *Spanish-American War* . . . . 10 Dec. „
Congress meets: the president's message, proposed increase of the army and navy, and occupation of Cuba, 5 Dec. 1898; meets 4 Jan. 1899; debate on expansion policy . . . . . 9, 10 Jan. 1899
Mr. Joseph H. Choate appointed ambassador to Great Britain . . . . 11 Jan. „
Mr. N. Dingley, supporter of a protective tariff policy, died, aged 66 . . . . . 13 Jan. „
The *Albany*, U.S. cruiser, launched at Elswick, Newcastle-on-Tyne . . . . . 14 Jan. „
The Nicaragua canal bill (U.S. control and neutrality guaranteed) passed by the senate 21 Jan. „
Army reorganization (increase) bill passed by the house, 31 Jan.; amended temporary increase till 1901, passed senate . . . . . 28 Feb. „
Peace treaty with Spain ratified (57–27), 6 Feb.; bill passed by the house for payment of 20,000,000 dollars to Spain for the Philippines (219–34), 21 Feb. „
Destructive storm and heavy snow-fall, 30 to 38 deg. of frost; great distress throughout the States . . . . 9–14 Feb. „
War commission appointed (Sept.) to investigate alleged abuses; report issued, acquitting Mr. Alger, sec. for war, and all officials, of blame, 12 Feb. „
Lord Charles Beresford, in New York, advocates the co-operation of the powers for keeping the "open door," *which see*, in China . . 23 Feb. „
Congress closed . . . . 4 March, „
Diplomatic relations with Spain resumed, 3 June, „
Algerism, a term expressing the inefficiency of the war office, see *Times* . . . . 14 July, „
Reciprocity treaties with Great Britain and France signed . . . . . 16 June and July, „
Mr. Alger, sec. of war, resigns; succeeded by Mr. Elihu Root . . . . 1 Aug. „
Mr. Cornelius Vanderbilt, benefactor and financier, director of 34 railway companies, dies suddenly, aged 56 . . . . 12 Sept. „
Demonstrations in honour of adm. Dewey, "the hero of Manila," in New York, 29, 30 Sept.; Mr. McKinley presents him with a sword of honour at the capitol, Washington . . . . 3 Oct. „
Mr. Garret Hobart, vice-pres. U.S.N.A., highly esteemed died . . . . . . 21 Nov. „
Great Britain's S. African policy warmly approved, Oct., Nov. 1899
The president's message to congress: prosperity reported; the existing gold standard, a canal uniting the Atlantic with the Pacific, and a cable to Manila, advocated . . . . 5 Dec. „
The currency bill passed by the house . 18 Dec. „
Maintenance of the "open door" policy in China; negotiations with the powers successfully concluded by Mr. Hay, reported . . . 2 Jan. 1900
Death of Mr. R. B. Osborne, aged 85, an eminent civil engineer, and author of "Lyons' Tables," &c. . . . . about 8 Jan. „
Convention revising the Clayton-Bulwer treaty of 1850 respecting a canal across the Central American isthmus, signed by lord Pauncefote and Mr. Hay at Washington . . . . . 5 Feb. „
Gold standard bill, favouring bimetallism, passed by the senate . . . . . . 15 Feb. „
Mr. E. J. Phelps, ex-minister to Great Britain, 1885–9, born 1822, died . . . 9 March, „
Financial bill signed by pres. McKinley, reported, 14 March, „
Boer delegates received by pres. McKinley; their mission fails; neutrality maintained . 22 May, „
Congress adjourns *sine die* . . . . 7 June, „
Presidential campaign: Mr. McKinley nominated republican candidate at Philadelphia; col. Theodore Roosevelt, vice-president, 21 June; Mr. W. J. Bryan, democratic candidate, nominated, 5 July, „
Coal strikes (70,000 men) in Pennsylvania, mid Sept.; martial law proclaimed at Shenandoah, about 22 Sept.; 10 per cent. advance in wages from Oct. till April, and abolition of the sliding scale, accepted by the men . . . 23 Oct. „
Mr. McKinley re-elected president, large majority, 6 Nov. „
The Cagayan and Sibutu islands ceded by Spain for 100,000 dols. . . . . 7 Nov. „
Pres. McKinley at Philadelphia; speaks in favour of the gold standard, "open door" in China, reciprocal trade, U.S. sovereignty in the Philippines, &c. . . . . 24 Nov. „
The president's message to congress: U.S. pacific policy as to China, protection of foreign rights by treaty; recommends the reduction of internal revenue taxes, maintenance of the army at 100,000 men, and the Hay-Pauncefote treaty, 3 Dec. „
Deep sympathy with England on the death of queen Victoria; the exchanges closed in New York and other cities on the funeral day; memorial services held . . . . . 2 Feb. 1901
The president's policy maintaining the *status quo* in Cuba and the Philippines, carried in both houses . . . . 1 March, „
Inauguration of Mr. McKinley as president: in his address he recommends broader trade with other countries, fulfilment of obligations imposed by the war with Spain, moderate Chinese policy, &c. 4 March, „
The senate's three amendments to the Hay-Pauncefote treaty of 5 Feb. 1900, 20 Dec. 1900, rejected by Great Britain . . . . . . 11 March, „
Death of ex-president Harrison, aged 68, 13 March, „
Mr. Andrew Carnegie gives 5,200,000 dollars for libraries in New York, and 1,000,000 dollars for one in St. Louis, see *Pittsburg* (his total gifts 22,563,252 dollars) . . . . . 12 March, „
Prof. H. A. Rowland, eminent scientist, born 27 Nov. 1848, died . . . . . mid April, „
Cuban commission received by the president, demands refused . . . . . . 25 April, „
The president's tour begins, 29 April; stopped at San Francisco by the illness of Mrs. McKinley, 15 May, „
Strike riots at Albany, troops called out, two deaths . . . . 16 May, „
Great coal strike begins 12 May, and others, 20 May *et seq.* „
The supreme court's decision on the "insular cases" regarding the levying of duties on imports from the Spanish acquired territories; legalises expansion in any direction approved by congress, 27 May, „

Heat wave; many deaths, 106° F., 28 June; drought ends . . . . about 29 July, 1901

Steel strike in Pittsburg, 1 July; ends in defeat of the men . . . . 14 Sept. ,,

Pres. McKinley shot in the exhibition at Buffalo, by Czolgosz, who was at once seized, 5 Sept. [executed by electricity, 29 Oct.]; Mr. McKinley dies at 2.15 p.m.; *Theodore Roosevelt, vice-president, sworn in as president* . . . 14 Sept. ,,

World-wide sympathy expressed on the president's death; the lying-in-state in Buffalo and at the capitol, Washington, attended by thousands, 15–17 Sept.; funeral at Canton, Ohio, over 70,000 present; general suspension of business in London, and memorial services held, 19 Sept. ,,

Mr. Choate, American ambassador, presents the thanks of the nation to the king and queen of England for their sympathy . . 27 Sept. ,,

Johann Most, an anarchist, sentenced to a year's imprisonment for an article in his journal inciting to the murder of rulers . . . . . 14 Oct. ,,

Naval estimates for 1902, 99,000,000 dollars, Oct. ,,

The new Hay-Pauncefote isthmian canal (connecting the Gulf of Mexico with the Pacific ocean) treaty, superseding the Clayton-Bulwer treaty, signed by Mr. Hay and lord Pauncefote at Washington . . . . . . 18 Nov. ,,

National reciprocity convention opened at Washington . . . . 19 Nov. ,,

Mr. Hay, secretary of state, expounds the Monroe doctrine, the creation of an isthmian canal under American ownership and control, but for the use of all nations, and a fair field and no favour in commerce, as American foreign policy . 19 Nov. ,,

Congress opened, the president's message; the exclusion and deportation of anarchists strongly urged; favours reciprocity, but yet maintains protection in commerce; upholds the Monroe doctrine; commends the isthmian canal (Hay-Pauncefote) treaty; emphasises the need of a strong navy; re-enactment of the Chinese exclusion law, &c. . . . . . . 2, 3 Dec. ,,

Governor Shaw of Iowa appointed minister of finance . . . . Dec. ,,

Gifts to education in the States amount to over 15,000,000*l.* in . . . . ,,

Danish W. Indies, proposed purchase by treaty, signed 24 Jan.; ratified, 17 Feb. (rejected by Denmark, 22 Oct.). 1902

Epidemic of smallpox . . . . Feb. ,,

Hay-Pauncefote canal treaty finally ratified, 21 Feb. ,,

Russian government, in reply to Mr. Hay's note, 1 Feb., states that Manchuria will always be open to U.S. trade, &c. . . . . . 23 Feb. ,,

Philippines tariff bill passed by the senate, 25 Feb. ,,

Pres. Roosevelt informs the Boer delegates that the United States cannot interfere in the war in South Africa . . . . 5 March, ,,

Prince Henry of Prussia visits New York, Washington, St. Louis, Chicago, Niagara; made LL.D. of Harvard university, Philadelphia, 23 Feb.–11 March, ,,

Gen. Wade Hampton, who distinguished himself in the civil war, died, aged 84 . . . 11 April, ,,

The president's visit to South Carolina and Columbia very successful, reported . 11 April, ,,

Munificent gifts to universities from Mr. J. D. Rockefeller and others . . March–April ,,

The rev. Dr. Talmage, eminent Presbyterian preacher, died, aged 72 . . . . 13 April, ,,

Democratic victory in the house of representatives; the Cuban reciprocity bill, with amendment removing the differential duty on sugar, passed (majority 195) . . . . . . 18 April, ,,

Major Gardener, civil governor of Tayabas, reports cruelty and outrages of American troops, 16 Dec. 1901; investigation ordered, 19 Feb. and 2 April; see *Philippines* . . . . April, ,,

Mr. W. H. Moody appointed naval secretary in succession to Mr. Long, resigned . . 29 April, ,,

Chinese exclusion bill ratified. . . . 30 April, ,,

Adm. Sampson, eminent naval commander, died, aged 62 . . . . 6 May, ,,

Mr. E. L. Godkin, eminent publicist and editor, died, aged about 68 . . . . . 21 May, ,,

Lord Pauncefote (British minister, 1889; *ambassador*, 1893 *et seq*) died, much regretted, aged 74, 24 May; state funeral at Washington, 28 May (his body conveyed to England on the *Brooklyn*, U.S. man-of-war; interred at Stoke, 15 July); hon. (aft. sir) Michael Herbert appointed British ambassador . . . . 4 June, 1902

The president's message to congress urging reciprocity to Cuba (on the sugar question), *failed*, 13 June, ,,

Increase of shipping, 2,087 vessels constructed in 1900, reported . . . . . . June, ,,

Mr. Spooner's Panama canal bill passed by congress, 26 June; signed . . . . 28 June, ,,

Congress adjourns . . . . 1 July, ,,

Philippines civil government bill passed, 26 June; signed . . . . 2 July, ,,

Pres. Roosevelt tours in New England; he strongly advocates the repression of "trusts," 23 Aug. [declares the Monroe doctrine to be the belief of Americans that "the nations on that continent must be left to work out their own destinies, and that America was not to be regarded as the colonizing ground of any European power," 26 Aug.] . . . . ,,

Naval manœuvres; blue squadron captures white squadron off Magnolia . . . . 24 Aug. ,,

Narrow escape of the president; two men killed in his coach by collision with an electric car near Pittsfield . . . . 3 Sept. ,,

Forest fires in Oregon and Washington; about 38 deaths, many missing, reported . . 15 Sept. ,,

Death of Mr. Horace Gray, eminent judge, aged 74, reported . . . . 27 Sept. ,,

Coal famine due to the strike; colliery near Mt. Carmel, New York, attacked by strikers, troops called out, reported . . . . . 30 Sept. ,,

Pres. Roosevelt's warm appeal at a conference in Washington with the mine owners and strike leaders to come to a settlement, fails, 3–10 Oct. ,,

Visit of the crown prince of Siam . . . 11 Oct. ,,

Conferences between pres. Roosevelt and Mr. Pierpont Morgan and Mr. Mitchell, the miners' leader . . . . 13–15 Oct. ,,

Coal strike (158 days) ends; arbitration commission appointed, 16 Oct.; miners' convention accepts pres. Roosevelt's proposals, 20, 21 Oct. ,,

Californian pious fund case, see *Mexico*. . . Oct. ,,

Elections; republican majority over 20 . 4 Nov. ,,

Mr. Mosely's British industrial commission received by pres. Roosevelt . . . . . 26 Nov. ,,

Congress meets; the president's message similar to that of Dec. 1901 . . . . . 2 Dec. ,,

Death of Mr. Thos. B. Reed, eminent statesman, aged 63 . . . . 7 Dec. ,,

Coal famine; great distress . . . . . Dec. ,,

Commercial treaty with Cuba, signed . 12 Dec. ,,

Death of Mr. Thos. Nast, the caricaturist, aged 62, Dec. ,,

Pres. Roosevelt declines to act as arbitrator in the Venezuelan dispute; arbitration by the Hague tribunal agreed to by the powers . . 25 Dec. ,,

Battleships: *Maine, Illinois, Alabama* and *Wisconsin* launched during the year . . . . ,,

Bill passed repealing the duties on anthracite coal, and reducing other coal duties, for a year, 14 Jan. 1903

Panama canal treaty, between U.S. and Colombia, signed . . . . 22 Jan. ,,

Forty lives lost, many injured, by three railway collisions and a boiler explosion, about 25 Jan. ,,

Coal miners' convention accepts 12½ per cent. average increase in wages in Illinois and elsewhere, reported . . . . 8 Feb. ,,

Alaska boundary treaty signed, 24 Jan.; ratified, 11 Feb. ,,

Venezuela dispute settled; foreign protocols signed, Washington . . . . . . 13–17 Feb. ,,

Mr. Root, secretary for war, and senators Lodge and Turner selected as U.S. members of the Alaska boundary arbitration tribunal; Mr. Cortelyou officially appointed to the new post of secretary of commerce, reported . mid Feb. ,,

The supreme court's decision in the *lottery cases* virtually settles the power of congress to exercise control over inter-state commerce . 23 Feb. ,,

Philippine currency bill passed . . . 25 Feb. ,,

Sir M. Herbert, British ambassador, made K.C.M.G., 26 Feb. 1903

The president defends his negro policy in a letter to Mr. Clark Howell, editor of the *Atlanta Constitution*, reported . . . . . 2 March, ,,

Navy bill, 81,000,000 dollars credit, agreed to, 3 March, ,,

Extra session of the senate, president's message, urging the ratification of the Cuban and Panama canal treaties . . . . . . 5 March, ,,

Coal strike commission appointed by president Roosevelt awards anthracite miners increase of 10 per cent. from 1 Nov. 1902; decrees working day of nine hours, and fixes a sliding-scale; award to remain in force until March, 1906, reported . . . . 25 March, ,,

Labour troubles, epidemic of strikes: strikes among employees of the American bridge co. extending; great cotton mills at Lowell (Mass.), closed, reported . . . . 1 April, ,,

President Roosevelt begins his great journey through the States, 1 April; speaks at Chicago on the Monroe doctrine (*which see*), makes an appeal for a strong navy on the ground that it is necessary to support the doctrine by force; recited course of recent events in Venezuela acknowledging fully the loyal conduct of the Powers to the U.S., 2 April; speaks on trusts at Milwaukee, 3 April; at Minneapolis on the tariff, practically abandoning the idea of its revision . . . . 4 April, ,,

Anthracite miners' unions refuse to work nine hours daily as ordered by the commission, reported . . . . 6 April, ,,

Ex-president Cleveland declares against president Roosevelt's attitude on the negro question, early April, ,,

Lock-out at most of the collieries of the Philadelphia and Reading coal company, affecting 30,000 men, reported . . . . mid April, ,,

Strike of some 30,000 labourers employed on the Rapid transit railway, New York, leave work; strikes among the millwrights, ironworkers, and teamsters, reported . . . . . 1 May, ,,

Attempt to blow up the Cunard liner *Umbria* with dynamite at New York . . . about 13 May, ,,

Sir Michael Herbert, the British ambassador, entertained by Society of Pilgrims, speech by Mr. Roob, secretary of war, "England is our true friend, war between England and the United States would not only be a crime, but would argue an incapacity of the governing powers worse than crime" . . . . . . 25 May, ,,

Celebration of the centenary birth of Emerson, 25 May, ,,

250th anniversary of the foundation of the civic government of New York . . . . 26 May, ,,

Permanent treaty with Cuba signed (see *Cuba*), end May, ,,

90,000 textile workers strike in Philadelphia for shorter hours and increased wages . end May, ,,

Tornado at Gainsville, Georgia, 64 persons killed; great floods in the west, causing enormous damage and serious loss of life, especially at Topeka, reported . . . . 30 May, ,,

Cloud-burst in Oregon, the greater part of the town of Heppner destroyed, about 300 lives lost; forest fires in New England and in other eastern states; much damage done . . early June, ,,

90 per cent. of building operations in New York at a standstill owing to strikes, 110,000 mechanics and labourers unemployed; building capital unemployed estimated at 200,000,000 dols., reported . . . . 8 June, ,,

Sir Thos. Lipton's *Shamrock III.* and *Shamrock I.* arrive at New York . . . . . 14 June, ,,

Explosion at Hanna, Wyoming, at Union Pacific coal company's mine, 75 killed . . 30 June, ,,

Trial of landlords, constables, and others charged with cruelties in connection with the "peonage" system of virtual slavery in Georgia and Alabama . . . . 30 June, ,,

Russian government refuses to receive from president Roosevelt the Jewish petition of the executive council of the B'nai B'rith requesting better treatment for Russian Jews; also refuses to recognise American passports to American Jews, end June, 1903

Lynching riots at Evansville and elsewhere (see *Lynching*) . . . . . . early July, ,,

Negotiations for opening the ports demanded by United States and Japan reported successful; prince Ching refuses on behalf of Chinese government to open towns in Manchuria for foreign trade; American treaty negotiations opened by Chang-Chi-tung, who asks for modifications of articles relating to mining rights and protection of patents . . . . . . mid July, ,,

Builders' lock-out at Pittsburg, 25,000 men affected, end July, ,,

Meeting under auspices of the Clan-na-Gael; Mr. Redmond denounced for accepting the Irish Land bill . . . . 30 July, ,,

President Roosevelt on lynching, letter to Mr. Durbin, governor of Indiana (see *Lynching*), early Aug. ,,

Collision between two sections of a circus train on the Grand Trunk railway, 19 killed, 30 injured, 7 Aug. ,,

Judge Taff to become secretary of war on the retirement of Mr. Roob in Jan. 1904, reported end Aug. ,,

Attempt by Weilbrenner, a lunatic, to shoot president Roosevelt at his home at Sagamore hill, Oyster bay . . . . . . 1 Sept. ,,

Sir Thos. Lipton ill with appendicitis at Chicago, early Sept. ,,

President Roosevelt at the State fair at Syracuse, reviews a great labour parade; delivers address, urging as watchwords for all, "honesty, decency, fair dealing, and common sense" . . 7 Sept. ,,

Hurricane in New York, Florida, and the southern states . . . . 16 Sept. ,,

The period during which the congress of Columbia might decide affirmatively respecting the Panama canal treaty having expired, 22 Sept.; the treaty becomes dead . . . . . . 23 Sept. ,,

The United States government denounce the action of the Dominican government in sending a project to congress for establishing the neutrality of the Dominican waters, and making certain ports free, and refuses to permit the establishment of coaling ports in San Domingo, or cession of any of its territory to any European power, or any territory to be classed as "neutral" . end Sept. ,,

Death of sir Michael Herbert, 30 Sept.; memorial service at Washington, president Roosevelt and members of his cabinet present . . 6 Oct. ,,

Greatest rainfall recorded by the New York weather bureau since its foundation in 1867; streets flooded, traffic disarranged, 50 houses swept away at Paterson, many bridges on the Delaware river carried away, great damage on the coast from Virginia to Rhode Island by hurricanes and high tides, beginning . 8 Oct. ,,

Delegation of hon. artillery company of London arrive at Boston; city elaborately decorated, British flag seen for the first time on Bunker's hill monument, 2 Oct.; received by president Roosevelt at the White House . . 10 Oct. ,,

Special reception in honour of the Mosely educational commission at the White House . 20 Oct. ,,

Tammany victory in the New York municipal elections, Mr. Geo. B. McClellan elected mayor, 3 Nov. ,,

Mr. A. H. Green, "the father of Greater New York," fatally shot by a negro . . 13 Nov. ,,

M. Varilla received by president Roosevelt as minister of the new republic of Panama (*which see*) . . . . 13 Nov. ,,

Labour riots and outrages in Chicago, Colorado, and Denver, reported . . . . mid Nov. ,,

Sir M. Durand, new British ambassador, received by president Roosevelt . . . . 2 Dec. ,,

Great excitement and speculation in the cotton market . . . . . early Dec. *et seq.* ,,

Report of Mr. Shaw, secretary of the Treasury, shows a surplus of over 54,297,667 dols. for the fiscal year 1903: revenue, 694,621,117 dols., increase, 10,294,837 dols.; expenditure, 640,323,450 dols., increase, 47,284,545 dols.; surplus, 54,297,667 dols.: estimates for 1904: revenue, 674,767,664 dols.; expenditure, 660,767,664 dols.; surplus, 14,000,000 dols.: estimates for 1905, revenue, 704,472,060 dols.; expenditure (not including sinking fund), 727,474,206 dols.; deficit, 23,002,146 dols., submitted to congress . . 7 Dec. 1903

See *Addenda.*

PRESIDENTS OF THE UNITED STATES OF AMERICA.

1789 & 1793. General George Washington, elected first president. 6 April.
1797. John Adams. 4 March.
1801 & 1805. Thomas Jefferson. 4 March.
1809 & 1813. James Madison. 4 March.
1817 & 1821. James Monroe. 4 March.
1825. John Quincy Adams. 4 March.
1829 & 1833. General Andrew Jackson. 4 March.
1837. Martin Van Buren. 4 March.
1841. General William Henry Harrison. 4 March. Died 4 April, succeeded by
,, John Tyler (formerly vice-president).
1845. James Knox Polk. 4 March.
1849. General Zachary Taylor. 4 March. Died 9 July, 1850, succeeded by the vice-president,
1850. Millard Fillmore.
1853. General Franklin Pierce. 4 March.
1857. James Buchanan. 4 March.
1861 & 1865. Abraham Lincoln. 4 March. Shot 14 April; died 15 April, 1865; succeeded by vice-president,
1865. Andrew Johnson. 15 April.
1869 & 1873. Ulysses S. Grant. 4 March.
1877. Rutherford Birchard Hayes. 4 March.
1881. Gen. James Abram Garfield. 4 March. Shot 2 July; died 19 Sept. 1881.
,, Gen. Chester A. Arthur. 19 Sept.
1885. Grover Cleveland. *Dem.* 4 March.
1889. Gen. Benjamin Harrison. 4 March (grandson of the president of 1841); died 13 March, 1901.
1893. Grover Cleveland. *Dem.* again.
1896. William McKinley. *Republican*; re-elected 6 Nov. 1900; shot 5 Sept.; died 14 Sept. 1901.
1901. Theodore Roosevelt, *Republican.* 14 Sept.

UNIVERSALISTS, who believe in the final salvation of all men. This doctrine, declared in the Talmud, and ascribed to Origen, about 230, was advocated by other early fathers, but opposed by St. Augustin, about 420; and condemned by the 5th general council at Constantinople, May, June, 553. It was received by the Unitarians in the 17th century, and avowed by numerous clergymen of the church of England. James Relly, who published his "Union" in 1760, founded the sect of Universalists in Britain; and John Murray, in America, about 1770. The sect flourishes in America.

UNIVERSAL REVIEW, edited by Mr. Harry Quilter, devoted to fine art, literature, &c., first published 15 May, 1888. Publication ceased Dec. 1890.

UNIVERSAL SUFFRAGE (*Plebiscitum*), one of the six points of the charter (see *Chartists*), was adopted by the French in their constitution of 1791; and used in the election of their president in 1851, and of their emperor in 1852; and by the Italian States in voting for annexation to Sardinia in 1860, 1861, 1866, and 1870.

UNIVERSAL TIME, see under *Day.*

UNIVERSITIES. The most ancient in Europe are said to be those of Bologna, Oxford, Cambridge, Paris, and Salamanca. In old Aberdeen was a monastery, in which youths were instructed in theology, the canon law, and the school philosophy, at least 200 years before the university and King's College were founded; see *Degrees.* Mr. Hastings Rashdall's "Mediæval Universities," an important work, published in 1895. The following dates are generally given, many traditional:

Aberdeen founded	1494
Abo, Finland	1640
Adelaide, Australia	1876
Andrews, St., Scotland	1411
Angers, chiefly law	1364
Anjou, 1349; enlarged	,,
Athens	1836
Barcelona, revived	1841
Basle, Switzerland	1460
Berlin	1810
Berne	1834
Besançon, Burgundy	1676
Birmingham	1900
Bologna, Italy	1116
Bonn	1784, 1818
Bordeaux	1472
Bourges	1465
Breslau	1702
Bruges, French Flanders	1665
Brussels	1834
Caen, Normandy, 1436; revived	1803
Cambridge, 12th century.	
Cambridge, New England, projected	1630
Christiania	1811
Cologne, n Germany, refounded	1385
Compostella, Spain	1517
Coimbra, Portugal	1279
Copenhagen	1476
Cordova, Spain	968
Corfu	1823
Cracow, Poland, 700, revived	1364
Dijon, France	1722
Dillingen, Swabia	1565
Dole, Burgundy	1422
Dorpat	1632
Douay, French Flanders	1568
Dresden, Saxony	1694
Dublin (see *Trinity College*)	1591
Dublin College (catholic)	1851
Durham	1831
Edinburgh, founded by James VI.	1582
Erfurt, Thuringia; enlarged	1390
Erlangen	1743
Evora, Portugal	1533
Florence, Italy, enlarged	1439
Frankfort-on-the-Oder	1506
Franeker	1585
Fribourg, Germany	1460
Geneva	1368
Ghent	1816
Glasgow	1450
Göttingen	1735
Granada, Spain	1537
Gripswald	1547
Groningen, Friesland	1614
Halle, Saxony	1694
Harvard, U.S.	1638
Heidelberg	1386
Helmstadt	1575
Ingolstadt, Bavaria	1593
Irish new	1879
Jena, or Sala, Thuringia	1547
Kiel, Holstein	1665
King's College, London (*which see*)	1829
Königsberg, Prussia	1544
Leipsic, Saxony	1409
Leyden, Holland	1575
Liège	1816
Lima, in Peru	1614
Lisbon, 1290; removed to Coimbra	1391
London University (*which see*)	1826
Louvaine, Flanders, 926; enlarged	1426
Lyons, France	30, 1300
Madrid	1836
Mantua	1625
Marburg	1527
Mechlin, Flanders	1440
Melbourne, Victoria	1855
Mentz	1477
Milan	1565
Montpellier	1289
Moscow, 1754; again	1829
Munich	1826
Munster	1492
Nancy	1769
Nantes	1460
Naples	1224
Orange	1365
Orleans, France	1305
Oxford (see *Oxford*)	1879
Paderborn	1592
Padua, Italy	1228
Palenza, 1209; removed to Salamanca	1249
Palermo	1447
Paris, 792; renovated	1200
Parma	1482
Pau	1722
Pavia, 1360; enlarged	1599
Perpignan	1349
Perugia, Italy	1307
Petersburg, St., 1747; again	1819
Pisa, 1343; enlarged	1552
Poitiers	1431
Prague	1348
Queen's University (Ireland)	1850
Rheims, 1145; enlarged	1548
Rome	1245
Rostock, Mecklenburg	1419
Salamanca	1239
Salerno	1233
Salzburg	1623
Saragossa, Aragon	1474
Seville	1504
Sienna	1380
Siguenza, Spain	1517
Sorbonne, France	1253
Strasbourg	1538
Stutgardt	1775
Sydney, N. S. W.	1852
Toledo, Spain	1499
Toulouse	1229
Treves, Germany	1473
Tübingen, Würtemberg	1477
Turin	1405

Upsal, Sweden	1476	Venice	1592	Würtzburg	1403
Utrecht, Holland	1634	Victoria, N. England	1880	Wilna	1803
Valence, Dauphiné	1454	Vienna	1365	Yale, United States	1701
Valencia	1209	Wales	1893	Zurich	1832
Valladolid	1346	Wittenburg	1502		

UNIVERSITIES OF OXFORD AND CAMBRIDGE. Royal commission appointed to inquire into their income and property, in 1872; reported in Oct. 1874, that the united income for 1871, was 754,405*l.* 5*s.* 1½*d.*; see *Cambridge and Oxford*. The Universities Act passed, 10 Aug. 1877, appoints commissioners with power to make statutes and other provisions.

UNIVERSITY BOAT-RACE. The contest between the universities of Oxford and Cambridge, at first near Oxford, afterwards on the river Thames, began 10 June, 1829, and has been annual since 1856. In 1864, after 20 contests, the opposing parties were equal; but on 8 April, 1865, 24 March, 1866, 13 April, 1867, 4 April, 1868, and 17 March, 1869, Oxford won; the last time being the 9th in succession. Cambridge won, 6 April, 1870, 1 April, 1871, 23 March, 1872, 29 March, 1873, and 28 March, 1874. Oxford won, March 20, 1875; Cambridge won, 8 April, 1876. Dead heat; neither won, 24 March, 1877; Oxford won, 13 April, 1878; Cambridge won, 5 April, 1879; Oxford won on Monday, 22 March, 1880; Friday, 8 April, 1881; Saturday, 1 April, 1882; and Thursday, 15 March, 1883; Cambridge, Monday, 7 April, 1884; Oxford, Saturday, 28 March, 1885; Cambridge, Saturday, 3 April, 1886; 26 March, 1887; 24 March, 1888. (E. T. Campbell killed at Cambridge, 24 Feb. 1888); 30 March, 1889; Oxford, 26 March, 1890, 21 March, 1891, 9 April, 1892; 22 March, 1893; 17 March, 1894; 30 March, 1895; 28 March, 1896; 3 April, 1897; 26 March, 1898; Cambridge, 25 March, 1899; 31 March, 1900; Oxford, 30 March, 1901; Cambridge, 22 March, 1902; Cambridge, 1 April, 1903. In the international boat-race between the universities of Oxford and Harvard, Massachusetts, U.S., Oxford won, 27 Aug. 1869.

The Oxford crew rowed from Dover to Calais in 4¼ hours . . . . 25 July, 1885

UNIVERSITY COLLEGES (London), see *London University*, and *Oxford*.

UNIVERSITY EDUCATION (Ireland) Act, 42 & 43 Vict. c. 85, passed 15 Aug. 1879. It provides for the dissolution of the "*Queen's University*," and the foundation of the "*Royal University of Ireland*," the charter of which was signed by the queen, 19 April, 1880.

UNIVERSITY ELECTIONS, see *Dodson's Act*.

UNIVERSITY TEACHING, Society for its extension formed in London about 1875, and supported by Cambridge, Oxford, and London universities; great meeting for its support at the Mansion-house, 19 Feb. 1879. Courses of lectures given in various parts of London, Oct. 1879.

Proposed establishment of a settlement in east London, by university men of Oxford and Cambridge, to improve social intellectual condition, May, 1884; at *Toynbee Hall*, Whitechapel, volunteer lectures on science, art, &c. given; also instruction in music, athletic sports &c.; and a social club formed. The hall was organized by the rev. S. A. Barnett and others as a memorial of Arnold Toynbee, an earnest supporter of the movement, who died in 1883, aged about 31.

Oxford House, at Bethnal Green; a kind of club for social and intellectual improvement, and for the extension of university teaching, opened by the archbishop of Canterbury . . . . 18 Feb. 1888

The new buildings, founded 30 Nov. 1891, were opened by the duke of Connaught . 23 June, 1892

Congress held at the university of London 22 June, 1894

See *Passmore Edwards' Settlement*.

UNIVERSITY TESTS (Religious). A bill for their abolition was rejected by the lords, 19 July, 1869, and 14 July, 1870; passed, and received royal assent, 16 June, 1871. A similar act for Trinity College, Dublin, was passed in May, 1873. In April, 1878, on trial it was affirmed, that an endowment with a religious test at Hertford college, Oxford, was valid.

UNKNOWN TONGUES, see *Irvingites*, note.

UNLEARNED PARLIAMENT, see *Parliament*, 1404.

UNSEAWORTHY SHIPS COMMISSION, see *Seamen* and *Merchant Shipping Act*.

UPSAL (Sweden). The Swedish rulers were kings of Upsal till 1001. The university was founded in 1476, by Sten Sture, the "protector," and opened 21 Sept. 1477. Celebration of foundation of university, Sept. 1877.

URANIUM, a brittle grey metal discovered by Klaproth in 1789, in the mineral pitch-blende. It has lately been employed in the manufacture of glass for certain philosophical purposes.

The discovery of a new lode in the Union mine, Grampound Road, Cornwall, Sept. 1889, and improvements in treating the ore, have greatly cheapened the metal . . . . . Feb. 1890

Its radio-activity discovered by M. Henri Becquerel in 1896, studied by lord Kelvin, Mdme. and M. Curie and others . . . . . 1897 *et seq.*

URANUS, a planet discovered by sir William Herschel, 13 March, 1781, first called Georgium Sidus, after George III.; next Herschel; and, finally, Uranus. It is about twice as distant from the sun as the planet Saturn. The anniversary of its first revolution (in 84 years 7 days) since its discovery, was celebrated on 20 March, 1865. Its perturbations led to the discovery of Neptune, in 1846. Uranus has 4 satellites; 2 discovered by Herschel in 1787, and 2 by Lassell, 1 of which almost simultaneously by Struve, in 1847. Herschel was mistaken in supposing that he had discovered other satellites, 2 in 1790 and 2 in 1794; they were probably faint stars.

URBANISTS, see *Clementines*, and *Clare*.

URBINO, the ancient Urbinum Hortense, central Italy, capital of a duchy created for Malatesta, 1474. It was treacherously seized by Cæsar Borgia, 1502; captured by Julius II., 1503; and given to Borgia, 1504; given to Lorenzo de' Medici by Leo X. 1516; after many vicissitudes recovered by the duke Francesco, 1522; on the duke's resignation annexed to the papal states, 1631; annexed to Italy, 1860.

URGENCY, see *Parliament*, 1881.

URICONIUM, see *Wroxeter*.

URIM AND THUMMIM, LIGHT AND PERFECTION (*Exodus* xxviii. 30), words connected with the breastplate worn by the high priest when he entered into the holy place, with the view of obtaining an answer from God (1490 B.C.).

URSULINE NUNS (so called from St. Ursula), founded originally by St. Angela of Brescia), about 1537. Several communities existed in England; and some still exist in Ireland.

URUGUAY, BANDA ORIENTAL, a republic in South America, formerly part of the vice-royalty of Buenos Ayres; declared its independence, 25 Aug. 1825; recognised 4 Oct. 1828; constitution proclaimed 18 July, 1830. Capital, Montevideo. Population in 1886 (estimated) 632,250; 1893, 728,447; 1901, 964,577.

The president of the executive, G. A. Pereyra, elected in 1856; succeeded by B. P. Berro . . 1860
Civil war broke out in consequence of the invasion of the ex-president, general Venancio Florès, 26 June, 1863
The vice-president Aguirre became president, 1 March, 1864
He refused to modify his ministry according to the desire of general Florès, who marched towards the capital . . . . June, „
Florès became provisional president . . Feb. 1865
F. A. Vidal elected president . . 1 March, 1866
Two opposing parties in the state, Blancos and Colorados . . . . „
During an insurrection of the Blanco party (headed by Berro), at Montevideo, general Florès was assassinated; the troops remained faithful; insurrection soon suppressed, and Berro shot, 19 Feb. 1868
Gen. Lorenzo Battle elected president . 1 March, „
Blanco insurrection repressed, July, 1871; ended, Jan. 1872
Revolution at Montevideo; Ellazio's government overthrown; Pedro Varela provisional president, about . . . . 15 Jan. 1875
Col. L. Latorre president . . . 11 March, 1876
Dr. F. A. Vidal, president, died, 17 March 1880; gen. Maximo Santas, president . 1 March, 1882
Insurrection by general Arredondo, 29 March; reported defeat of government troops, 30 March, 1886
Flight of general Arredondo to Brazil, March–April, „
Insurgents completely defeated . . . 2 April, „
Resignation of general Santas, 18 Nov.; general Maximo Tajes as president . . . 18 Nov. „
Dr. Herrera y Obes, president . . . 1 March, 1890
State financial difficulties; run on the banks for gold; paper currency authorised, not accepted, 8–19 July, „
Conversion of the state debt and reduction of interest proposed by the government, accepted by the creditors in London . . . 31 Aug. 1891
Attempted revolution at Montevideo by the Blanco party suppressed with bloodshed; martial law set up . . . . 11 Oct. „
Don Juan Idiarte Borda (a Colorado, and despotic) elected president . . . . . 21 March, 1894
The new chambers opened with a message from the president, improved financial and commercial arrangements, announced . . . 15 Feb. 1897
Revolt of the Blancos: state of siege in Montevideo, proclaimed . . . . 3 March, „
Severe fighting at Paysandu, much slaughter, retreat of government troops . . 17 March, „
Desultory fighting: insurgents routed in 2 engagements, by gen. Muniz, March–April; and again, by gen. Villar, near San Fructuoso . . 16 May, „
War loan authorized, 6 per cent. 4,000,000 pesos, 18 May, „
Government troops repulsed, at Rivera, in May, and at Canudos . . . . . . July, „
Pres. Borda assassinated in Montevideo, by Avelino Arredondo [released on public appeal, Aug. 1899], 25 Aug. „
Sen. Juan Cuestas becomes president (till March, 1898) . . . . 10 Sept. „
Compromise concluded with the insurgents; peace signed, 15 Sept.; ratified by the chambers, 18 Sept. 1897
Drs. Herrera and Aguirre and gen. Tajes exiled to Argentina, on a charge of conspiracy, 30 Nov.; rescinded . . . . 31 Dec. „
Coup d'État: sen. Cuestas assumes a dictatorship, 8 Jan. 1898
New council of state: important administrative changes, 12 Feb.; favourable report . 18 Feb. „
Revolutionary conspiracy suppressed, col. Lamas, the leader, killed by a fall from his horse; reported . . . . 31 May, „
Revolt of 2 regiments, in favour of ex-pres. Julio Herrera; the arsenal seized, and fighting in Monte Video, about 50 killed; a state of siege declared; British marines landed to defend the consulate, 4 July, „
The ringleaders, military and civilian, submit on condition of an amnesty being granted, and are deported to Buenos Ayres, order restored 5–6 July „
Revolt quelled, country tranquil . early Feb. 1899
Señ. Juan Cuestas elected president . 1 March, „
Amnesty granted to political offenders, 8 March, „
Treaty of commerce, &c. (1885) renewed with Great Britain . . . . 15 July, „
Chambers meet, president's message, good report, 15 Feb. 1900
Arbitration treaty with Argentina, announced, mid March, 1901
First stone of the new port works laid at Montevideo . . . . 18 July, „
Parliament opened by the president, good report, 18 Feb. 1902
Alleged plot against pres. Cuestas, some arrests, 2 senators banished, mid July; but withdrawn, 19 July, „
Chambers meet, sound financial and administrative progress since 1897, reported 15 Feb. 1903
Señ. Batele elected president . . 1 March, „
New cabinet formed, seňs. Romieu and Martinez, foreign and finance ministers, reported, 5 March, „
Nationalist rebellion in six departments of the interior, railway at Montevideo destroyed, 8000 men prepare to attack the city, reported, mid March, „
End of Nationalist rising; rebels accept terms offered by the president, amnesty granted, reported . . . . 25 March, „
Budget, revenue and expenditure balanced at 3,483,300*l*. . . . . . . mid June, „
Customs revenue for 1902, 2,130,000*l*.; increase over 1901, 85,000*l*. . . . . mid July, „
Decision of government to construct harbour at Paysandu, and piers at Salto and other places, and further development works, reported, Oct. „

USEFUL KNOWLEDGE SOCIETY; see *Diffusion*.

USES, STATUTE OF, 27 Hen. VIII. c. 10 (1535-6); see *Charitable Uses*.

USHANT, an island near Brest, N.W. France, near which two naval battles were fought between the British and French fleets.

(1.) On 27 July, 1778, after an indecisive action of three hours, the French, under cover of the night, withdrew into the harbour of Brest. Admiral Keppel commanded the English fleet; the count d'Orvilliers the French. The failure of a complete victory was attributed to admiral sir Hugh Palliser's non-compliance with the admiral's signals. Palliser preferred articles of accusation against his commander, who was tried and acquitted, and the charge against him declared to be "malicious and ill-founded."

(2.) Lord Howe with 25 ships signally defeated the French fleet (26 ships, under Villaret-Joyeuse), taking six ships of the line, and sinking one (the *Vengeur**),

* Various French histories, on the authority of the French demagogue Barrère, state that the English had 36 ships of the line, and the French only 26, and that the crew of the *Vengeur* sang the *Marseillaise* while the ship sank, displaying the tricolor flag. All this was denied in 1802, and disproved by rear-admiral Griffith in

1 June, 1794. While the two fleets were engaged in this action, a large fleet of merchantmen, on the safety of which the French nation depended for its means of prosecuting the war, got safely into Brest harbour, which gave occasion to the enemy to claim the laurels of the day, notwithstanding their loss in ships, and in killed and wounded, which was very great. The day was long termed in England the "glorious first of June." The victory commemorated, 1 June, 1894.

USURY from a stranger was permitted to the Jews, but forbidden from their brethren, 1491 B.C. (*Exod.* xxii. 25., *Deut.* xxiii. 13.) This law was enforced by Nehemiah, 445 B.C. (*Neh.* v.) Usury was prohibited by the English parliament, 1341. Until the 15th century, no Christians were allowed to receive interest of money, and Jews were the only usurers, and therefore often banished and persecuted; see *Jews*. By the 37th of Henry VIII. the rate of interest was fixed at 10 per cent., 1545. This statute was repealed by Edward VI., but re-enacted 13 Eliz. 1570. For later legislation, see *Interest*.

UTAH, a western territory of North America, was organised 9 Sept. 1850; the capital, Salt Lake City, became the chief seat of the *Mormonites* (*which see*). Population in 1880, 143,963; 1890, 207,905; 1900, 276,749. Salt Lake city, 1890, 44,843; 1900, 53,531.

Gold discovered near the Colorado river, about 22 Dec. 1892
Utah admitted as a state, 13 July, 1894; proclaimed, ... 4 Jan. 1896
Fresh polygamy prohibited . . . . 4 Jan. „
Emigration of Mormons to N.W. Canada, reported, May, 1899
Colliery explosion at Schofield, over 200 deaths, 1 May, 1900

UTICA (N. Africa), an ancient Tyrian colony, an ally of Carthage, named in the treaty with the Romans 348 B.C. Here Cato the younger, after the defeat of the partisans of Pompey at Thapsus, committed suicide, 46 B.C. Utica flourished greatly after the fall of Carthage, and was made a Roman city by Augustus on account of its favouring Julius Cæsar. It suffered by the invasion of the Vandals, 439; and of the Saracens, about 700. See *New York*, 1895.

UTILITARIANISM, termed the "greatest happiness principle," the philosophy which proposes the attainment of the greatest happiness of the greatest number; a doctrine ascribed to Priestley by Bentham. The doctrine is found in the writings of Locke, Hartley, Hume, and Paley; but was chiefly propounded by Jeremy Bentham in his "Introduction to the Principles of Morals and Legislation," 1780-89, by John Stuart Mill, who died 9 May, 1873, and by sir Edwin Chadwick, who died 5 July, 1890. Mill founded a small "utilitarian society," in 1822. He took the name from an expression in Galt's "Annals of the Parish." "The English Utilitarians," 3 vols., by Leslie Stephen, see *Athenæum*, 8 & 15 Dec. 1900.

Nov. 1838. The *Vengeur* surrendered to the British, who exerted themselves to save the crew. The French statement was accepted by Alison, and at first by Carlyle, but afterwards contradicted by both.

UTOPIA, the name given by sir Thomas More to an imaginary isle, representing the "best state of a public weale," described in a book written in Latin, published 1548. The work is considered to be an ironical satire on the state of Europe at the time, Utopia signifying "Nowhere." An English translation was published in 1551; the rev. J. H. Lupton's edition was published by the Clarendon Press, Nov. 1895. For the loss of the *Utopia*, emigrant steamer, see *Wrecks*, 17 March, 1891.

UTRAQUISTS, see *Calixtins*.

UTRECHT (the Roman *Trajectum ad Rhenum*) became the seat of an independent bishopric about 695. The last prelate, Henry of Bavaria, weary of his turbulent subjects, sold his temporal government to the emperor Charles V. in 1528. The union of the Seven United Provinces began here (see *United Provinces*); signed 23 Jan. 1579; 300th anniversary celebrated 23 Jan. 1879. The *treaty of Utrecht*, which terminated the wars of queen Anne, was signed by the ministers of Great Britain and France, and all the other allies, except the ministers of the empire, 11 April, 1713. This treaty secured the Protestant succession in England, the separation of the French and Spanish crowns, the destruction of the works of Dunkirk, the enlargement of the British colonies and plantations in America, and a full satisfaction for the claims of the allies. Utrecht surrendered to the Prussians, 9 May, 1787; was acquired by the French, 18 Jan. 1795, and restored at the peace, 1814. Population, 1887, 81,398; 1890, 86,116; 1897, 96,349; 1900, 104,194.

UXBRIDGE (W. Middlesex). On 30 Jan. 1645, commissioners met here to discuss terms of peace between Charles I. and the parliament; they separated without effect, 22 Feb. The latter required absolute control of the army and navy, the abolition of the episcopacy, liturgy, &c. Uxbridge murder, see *Trials*, Dec. 1884.

V.

VACATIONS, see *Terms*.

VACCINATION (from *Variola Vaccina*, the cow-pox), discovered by Dr. Edward Jenner. He was born in 1749, and educated for the medical profession, partially under John Hunter. Having heard that milkmaids who had had the cow-pox never took the small-pox, he, about 1780, conceived the idea of vaccination. He made the first experiment by transferring to a healthy child on 14 May, 1796, the *pus* from the pustule of a milkmaid who had caught the cow-pox from the cows. He announced his success in a memoir published 1798, and vaccination, begun 21 Jan. 1799, soon became general, after much opposition. For this Dr. Jenner received 10,000*l*. from parliament, 2 June, 1802, and 20,000*l*. in 1807. The first national institution for vaccination, the Royal Jennerian Institution, was founded 19 Jan. 1803. The emperor Napoleon valued Dr. Jenner so highly, that he liberated Dr. Wickham, when a prisoner of war, at Jenner's request, and subsequently whole families of English, making it a point to refuse him nothing that he asked. Vaccination, although much opposed, was practised throughout all Europe previously to 1816. Dr. Jenner died suddenly, 26 Jan. 1823.

Royal Jennerian and London Vaccine Institution, founded 1802
The Vaccination act, 3 & 4 Vict. passed . 23 July, 1840
An important blue-book, entitled "Papers on the History and Practice of Vaccination," edited by Mr. John Simon, was published by the board of health in 1857
A statue, subscribed for by all nations, was erected to Jenner's memory in Trafalgar-square 30 April, 1858
It was removed to Kensington in 1862
Vaccination was made compulsory in England in 1853, and in Ireland and Scotland 1863
A statue was erected by the French at Boulogne, and inaugurated . . . . . 11 Sept. 1865
These laws were consolidated and amended by 30 & 31 Vict. c. 84, 12 Aug. 1867 (see *Small-pox* and *Inoculation*), and amended in 1871
Much opposition to vaccination; an anti-vaccination society formed, 1870-71; a parliamentary commission appointed . . . . 13 Feb. „
A government bill respecting punishment for compulsory vaccination dropped . . . . Aug. 1880
Vaccination direct from the cow or calf advocated and practised in Brussels, &c. . . . 1879 *et seq.*
Successful vaccination of 68,900 sheep by M. Pasteur of Paris . . . . . up to 1 Oct. 1881
The Grocers company of London offer prize of 1000*l*. for a plan for propagating vaccine contagium apart from the animal body . 30 May, 1883
Great anti-vaccination demonstration at Leicester (many persons had been fined) . . 23 March, 1885
London society for abolition of compulsory vaccination, held 7th annual meeting . . 11 May, 1887
Estimated: 750,000 infants vaccinated annually; 50 die of disease in consequence; stated Oct. „
Royal commission of inquiry appointed 29 May, 1889
Interim report issued . . . . . 1892 and 1893
Amendment bill read 1st time, commons, 11 May; withdrawn, Sept. 1893.
Increase of small-pox, especially in parts of London, attributed to anti-vaccination . June–Aug. 1894
Report presented to the queen, 13 Aug.; the delay said to have been injurious, see *Small-pox*, 1896, and *Jennerian Institution*; final report issued Nov. 1897
Vaccination act passed (experimental for 5 years); glycerinated lymph authorised; conscientious objections recognised with conditions . 12 Aug. 1898
(203,413 conscientious objectors down to Dec. 1898; 32,341 in 1899.)
Nat. anti-vaccination league meets at Eastbourne, 5 Dec. 1900
Imperial vaccination league formed, 30 June, 1902, first meeting, London, duke of Northumberland, president, 12 Dec. 1902; report issued with recommendations . . . . . . 9 Jan. 1903
Deputation from the Imperial vaccination league on president of the Local government board to urge the amendment of the Vaccination Act, to ensure more efficient primary vaccination, to require revaccination at school age, and to make better provision for the supply of pure lymph, . 14 Jan. „
Very important report by Dr. G. S. Buchanan on an epidemic of small-pox in union of Orsett, 1901-2, containing much evidence that small-pox hospitals may become grave sources of danger to the inhabitants in their vicinity; issued by the Local government board . . . . March, „

VACUUM, is produced by reducing the pressure of the atmosphere, whereby its power of absorbing moisture is greatly increased. The Aristotelian philosophers asserted that "nature abhors a vacuum." It has been proved that an absolute vacuum cannot be obtained by the air pump, a small residuum of gaseous matter remains after extreme exhaustion. To study the effects of the projection of an electric discharge upon this matter, prof. W. Crookes (knt. June, 1897) invented his celebrated *vacuum tubes*, which he exhibited with interesting experiments at the Royal Institution, 4 April, 1879. At the same place, on 21 Jan. 1881, Dr. Warren De La Rue exhibited splendid results which he had obtained with the assistance of Dr. Hugo Müller, by means of an electric discharge from a battery of 14,400 chloride of silver cells into vacuum tubes. See *Röntgen Rays*. 32 forms of vacuum tubes are described in *Nature*, 28 Jan. 1897. The power of absorbing moisture possessed by a vacuum has been utilised by M. Emil Passburg, of Breslau, in his drying apparatus which has been successfully employed for drying grains by Messrs. Guinness, of Dublin, since the spring of 1888.

VADIMONIS LACUS, the Vadimonian lake, Umbria, central Italy, near which the Etruscans were totally defeated in two severe engagements by the Roman consuls: 1, by Fabius Maximus, 309 B.C.; 2, by Cornelius Dolabella, 283.

VAGRANTS. By law, after being whipped, a vagrant was to take an oath to return to the place where he was born, or had last dwelt for three years, 1530. A vagrant a second time convicted was to lose the upper part of the gristle of his right ear, 1535; a third time convicted, death. A vagabond to be branded with a V, and be a slave for two years, 1547. If he absconded and was caught, he was to be branded with S, and be a slave for life. Vagrants were punished by whipping, gaoling, boring the ears, and death for a second offence, 1572. The milder statutes were those of 17 Geo. II.; 32, 35, and 59 Geo. III. The present

Vagrant Act (5 Geo. IV. c. 83) was passed in 1824; amendment act passed, 12 Aug., 1898. There were about 33,000 tramps in England and Wales in 1865. For vagrants in London, see under *Poor*.

VALDENSES, see *Waldenses*.

VALENÇAY, a château near Châteauroux, central France, where Napoleon I. imprisoned Ferdinand of Spain from 1808 to 1813. His kingdom was restored to Ferdinand by a treaty signed 8 Dec. 1813.

VALENCIA (E. Spain), the *Valentia Edetanorum* of the Romans, became the capital of a Moorish kingdom, 1000; annexed to Aragon 1238. Its university, founded, it is said, in the 13th century, was revived in the 15th. Valencia was taken by the earl of Peterborough in 1705, but submitted to the Bourbons after the unfortunate battle of Almanza, in 1707. It resisted the attempts made on it by marshal Moncey, but was taken from the Spaniards with a garrison of more than 16,000 men, and immense stores, by the French under Suchet, 9 Jan. 1812. Population of the city, 1887, 170,763; 1897, 204,768.

VALENCIENNES (N. France). This city (the Roman Valentianæ), after many changes, was taken by Louis XIV. in 1677, and annexed 1678. It was besieged from 23 May to 28 July, 1793, when the French garrison surrendered to the allies under the duke of York. It was retaken, together with Condé, by the French, 27-30 Aug. 1794; on capitulation, the garrison and 1100 emigrants were made prisoners, with immense stores.

VALENTIA, a Roman province, including the country between the walls of Severus and Adrian, was reconquered from the Picts and Scots by Theodosius, and named after Valentinian I. the reigning emperor, 368.

VALENTINE'S DAY (14 Feb.). Valentine is said to have been a bishop, who suffered martyrdom under Claudius II. at Rome; others say under Aurelian, in 271. 618,000 letters passed through the post-office on 14 Feb. 1856. 530,300 was the estimated number of valentines delivered in 1864; in 1870, 1,545,755. The origin of the ancient custom of "choosing a valentine" has been much controverted; see *Post*.

VALENTINIANS, followers of Valentine, a priest, who, on being disappointed of a bishopric, forsook the Christian faith, declaring there were thirty gods and goddesses, fifteen of each sex, which he called Æones, or Ages. He taught in the 2nd century, and published a gospel and psalms: his followers added other errors.

VALLADOLID (Spain), the Roman Pintia and the Moorish Belad Walíd: was recovered for the Christians by Ordoño II., the first king of Leon, 914-23. It became capital of Castile in the 15th century. It was taken by the French Jan. 1808; and captured by the English, 4 June, 1813. Here died Christopher Columbus, 20 May, 1506. Population, 1887, 62,012; 1897, 68,746.

VALLOMBROSA (Central Italy). A Benedictine abbey was founded here by John Gualbert, about 1038. The monks were termed Vallambrosians.

VALMY (N.E. France). Here the French, commanded by Kellermann, defeated the Prussians, commanded by the duke of Brunswick, 20 Sept. 1792. The victory was of immense moral advantage to the republicans; and Kellermann was made duke of Valmy in 1808.

VALOIS, a county (N. France) given by Philip III. to his younger son Charles, whose son Philip became king as Philip IV. in 1328; see *France*.

VALOR ECCLESIASTICUS, a report of the annual value of church property, made by order in 1534, was published by the Record Commission in 1810-34.

VALPARAISO, principal port of Chili, South America, was bombarded by the Spanish admiral Mendez Nuñez, on 31 March, 1866, when much property was destroyed. It suffered by earthquakes in 1822, 1829, and 1851. Population, 1895, 122,447; 1900, 143,022. See *Chili*, 1891.

VALTELLINE (N. Italy), a district near the Rhætian Alps, seized by the Grison league, 1512, and ceded to it, 1530. At the instigation of Spain, the catholics rose and massacred the protestants, 19-21 July, 1620. After much contention between the French and Austrians, the neutrality of the Valtelline was assured in 1639. It was annexed to the Cisalpine republic in 1797; to Italy, 1807; to Austria, 1814; to Italy, 1860.

VALUATION OF PROPERTY ACT, to provide for the uniform assessment of rateable property in the metropolis, was passed 9 Aug. 1869.

VALVASOR (or "VAVASOR"). Camden holds that the "Vavasor" was next below a baron. Du Cange maintains that there were two sorts of vavasors: the greater, who held of the king, such as barons and counts; and the lesser, called "valvasini," who held of the former, such as vassals holding land under a nobleman himself a vassal. Valvasors are mentioned in the Domesday book, 1086.

VANADIUM (from Vanadis, the Scandinavian Venus), metal discovered by Sefström, in 1830, combined with iron ore. A similar metal, discovered in lead ore by Del Rio in 1801, and named *Erythronium*, was proved by Wöhler to be Vanadium. Vanadium was discovered in the copper-bearing beds in Cheshire, in 1865, by Mr. (aft. Sir) H. E. Roscoe, by whom its peculiarities were further studied, and published in 1867-8. It is useful in photography and dyeing.

VANCOUVER'S ISLAND, North Pacific ocean, near the main land. Settlements were made here by the English in 1781, which were seized by the Spaniards in 1789, but restored. By a treaty between the British government and that of the United States in 1846, this island was secured to the former. It has become of much greater importance since the discovery of gold in the neighbouring main land in 1858, and the consequent establishment of the colony of British Columbia (*which see*). Victoria, the capital, was founded in 1857. The island was united with British Columbia by act passed in Aug. 1866; and on 24 May, 1868, Victoria was declared the capital. Lord Dufferin, governor-general of Canada, was warmly received here, 15 Aug. 1876. See *Juan, San*. Chinese immigrants are virtually excluded by a poll-tax, 1878.

Vancouver nearly destroyed by fire, about 15 June; again . . . . 6 July, 1886
Wellington colliery explosion; 76 lives lost, Jan. 1888
Visit of the duke and duchess of Cornwall, 30 Sept. 1901

VANCOUVER'S VOYAGE. Captain Vancouver served as a midshipman under captain Cook, and was appointed to command during a voyage of discovery, to ascertain the existence of any navigable communication between the North Pacific and North Atlantic oceans. He sailed 7 Jan. 1791, and returned 24 Sept. 1795. He compiled an account of this voyage of survey of the north-west coast of America, and died in 1798.

VANDALS, a Germanic race, attacked the Roman empire in the 3rd century, and began to ravage Germany and Gaul, 406-14; their kingdom in Spain was founded in 411; under Genseric they invaded and conquered the Roman territories in Africa, 429, and took Carthage, Oct. 439. They were subdued by Belisarius in 534. They were driven out by the Saracen Moors. The dukes of Mecklenburg style themselves princes of the Vandals.

VANDAL KINGS IN AFRICA.

429. Genseric (see *Mecklenburg*).
477. Hunneric, his son.
484. Gundamund.
496. Thrasimund.
523. Hilderic.
531. Gelimer.

VAN DIEMEN'S LAND (called Tasmania since 1853), was discovered by Abel Jansen Tasman, 24 Nov. 1642, and named after the governor of the Dutch East Indies. Capital, Hobart Town, now Hobart.

Population, 1857, 81,492; 1865, 95,201 (only four remained of the aborigines); 1870, 99,328; 1880, 114,762; 1891, 146,667; 1901, 172,475. Revenue, 1887–8, 594,976*l.*; expenditure, 668,759*l.*; imports, 1887, 1,449,371*l.*; exports, 1,596,817*l.* 1890: Revenue, 753,305*l.*; expenditure, 718,604*l.* Imports, 1,897,512*l.*; exports, 1,486,992*l.* 1893: revenue, 706,972*l.*; expenditure, 836,417*l.*; imports, 1,057,683*l.*; exports, 1,352,184*l.* 1896: revenue, 807,696*l.*, 1898, surplus, 109,000*l.* 1901: revenue, 954,000*l.*

Visited by Furneaux, 1773; Cook 1777
Proved to be an island by Flinders, who explored Bass's Straits 1798–9
Taken possession of by lieut. Bower 1803
Arrival of col. Collins, the first governor, with convicts; Hobart Town founded 1804
Bishopric of Tasmania established 1842
Transportation abolished 1853
Representative government granted 1855
Col. Thos. Gore Brown, governor 1862
Visited by the duke of Edinburgh . . 7-18 Jan. 1868
Charles Ducane, governor . . . Aug. ,,
Fred. Aloysius Weld, governor 1874
Gen. sir John Henry Lefroy, governor . . 21 Aug. 1880
Sir George C. Strahan, governor . . . Dec. 1881
Discovery of gold at Mount Lyell . . . July, 1886
Sir Robert G. Hamilton, governor . . . Nov. ,,
Silver-field discovered in the Zeehan country about 1885 or 1886; about 200 mining companies established; the town Zeehan established; about 6,000 people settled in the district . . . 1889–90
Loan of 6,000,000*l.* authorized 1891
The Tasmanian exhibition, Launceston; the fine arts section opened by sir Robert Hamilton, 25 Nov. 1891 exhibition closed . 22 March, 1892
Resignation of Mr. Fysh, 12 Aug.; Mr. Henry Dobson forms a new ministry; retrenchments proposed to meet deficit . . . 16 Aug. ,,
Great discovery in Maria island of carboniferous limestone, from which Portland cement is made, reported . . . . . 13 Feb. 1893
Viscount Gormanston appointed governor, March, ,,
An income-tax bill rejected . . . 6 Oct. ,,
Probate duties passed by 1 vote . . . 10 Oct. ,,
Budget, 363,243*l.* deficit . . . 2 March, 1894
The ministry, under Mr. Dobson, defeated on the land-tax proposals by 1 vote, 10 April; resigns, 11 April, ,,
Sir Edward Braddon forms a ministry . 12 April, ,,
A conference of Australian premiers (sir E. C. Braddon, president) meets at Hobart (see *Australasia*) . . . . . 29 Jan. 1895
Weather observatory erected on Mount Wellington, reported . . . . . 22 May, 1895
Federal enabling bill passed . . . . 9 Jan. 1896
Bush fire in co. Montagu, Pengana nearly destroyed, many homeless . . . . 13 Dec. ,,
Diamond jubilee celebrations throughout the country . . . . 20 June *et seq.* 1897
Serious bush fires, many lives lost . . . Feb. 1898
Referendum on the commonwealth (bill 10,000 for and 712 against the bill) . . . 27 July, 1899
General election: strong government majority, reported . . . . 10 March, 1900
The duke and duchess of Cornwall visit Hobart (see *Australasia*) . . . . 3–6 July, ,,
Budget: 131,000*l.* surplus, announced . 8 Aug. ,,
Sir J. S. Dodds, administrator . . . autumn, ,,
Sir Arthur E. Havelock appointed governor, May; arrives . . . . . 8 Nov. ,,
Budget: deficit for 1901, 97,000*l.* . . 25 July, 1902
Expenditure reduced by 30,000*l.*; revenue and expenditure equalised at about, 865,000*l.* for 1903, reported . . . . . 13 Dec. ,,

VANGUARD, see *Wrecks*, 1875.

VARANGIANS, OR VARAGIANS, a name given to northern pirates, who invaded Flanders, about 813; France, about 840; Italy, 852. Their leader, Ruric, invited by the Novgorodians to help them, founded the Russian monarchy, 862.

VARENNES, a town in N.E. France, is celebrated for the arrest of Louis XVI., his queen, sister, and two children. They fled from the Tuileries on 21 June, 1791; were taken here the next day, and conducted back to Paris, mainly through Drouet, the postmaster, who, at an intermediate town, recognised the king.

VARNA, a fortified seaport in Bulgaria, formerly European Turkey. A great battle was fought near this place, 10 Nov. 1444, between the Turks under Amurath II. and the Hungarians under their king Ladislaus and John Hunniades. The latter were defeated with great slaughter: the king was killed, and Hunniades made prisoner, who had opposed the Christians breaking the truce for ten years, recently made at Szegedin. The emperor Nicholas of Russia arrived before Varna, the headquarters of his army, then besieging the place, 5 Aug. 1828. The Turkish garrison made a vigorous attack on the besiegers, 7 Aug.; and another on the 21st, but were repulsed. Varna surrendered, after a sanguinary conflict, to the Russian arms, 11 Oct. 1828. It was restored at the peace in 1829; its fortifications were dismantled, but have since been restored. The allied armies disembarked at Varna, 29 May, 1854, and sailed for the Crimea, 3 Sept. They suffered severely from cholera. In conformity with the treaty of Berlin, Varna was evacuated by the Turks, and occupied by Russians, autumn, 1878. Population, 1888, 25,256; 1900, 33,443.

VASSALAGE, see *Feudal Laws*, and *Slavery*.

VASSAR COLLEGE (on the east bank of the Hudson, United States), for the higher education of women, was founded by Matthew Vassar in 1861.

VASSY (N.E. France). The massacre of the protestants at this place by the duke of Guise on 1 March, 1562, led to desolating civil wars.

VATICAN (Rome), the ancient Mons Vaticanus, a hill of Rome. The commencement of the palace is ascribed to Constantine, Liberius, and Symmachus, and also to pope Eugenius III., 1146. It became the residence of the pope at his return from Avignon, 1377. The palace is said to contain 7000 rooms, rich in works of art, ancient and modern. The library, founded by pope Nicholas V., 1448, is exceedingly rich in printed books and MSS.—Pistolesi's description of the Vatican, with numerous plates, was published 1829-38.—The phrase "Thunders of the Vatican" was first used by Voltaire, 1748.—The ancient Vatican Codex of the Old and New Testament in Greek was published at Rome in 1857. For "Vatican Decrees," see *Councils*. See *Observatories*.

Theft of bonds, &c., value over 14,000*l.*, from the pope's private safe . . . . . 2 Oct. 1900
Fire in room over the library . . . . 1 Nov. 1903

VAUD, a Swiss canton, after having been successfully held by the Franks, the kings of Burgundy, emperors of Germany, dukes of Zähringen, and dukes of Savoy, was conquered by the Bernese, Jan. 1536, and annexed, 1554. Vaud, made independent in 1798, joined the confederation in 1815. A new constitution was obtained in 1830, after agitation.

VAUDOIS, see *Waldenses*.

VAUXHALL BRIDGE, constructed of iron under the direction of Mr. Walker, at an expense of 150,000*l.* (to be defrayed by a toll). The first stone was laid 9 May, 1811, by prince Charles, eldest son of the duke of Brunswick; and the bridge was opened on 4 June, 1816; freed from toll, 24 May, 1879. Design for a new bridge to be built of granite backed with concrete approved by London County Council, Feb. 1898; parliamentary estimate of cost, 380,000*l.* Owing to difficulties, revealed by boring, due to softer clay, the council adopted, 25 Nov. 1902, the design of a steel elliptical-arch bridge with ornamental facings.

VAUXHALL GARDENS (London), were so denominated from the manor of Vauxhall, Falkeshall, Fox-hall, or Faukeshall, said to have been the property of Fulke de Breauté about 1282. The premises were the property of Jane Vaux in 1615, and the mansion-house was then called Stockden's. From her it passed through various hands, till it became the property of Mr. Tyers in 1732. The New Spring Gardens at Vauxhall are mentioned by John Evelyn in his diary 2 July, 1661, Pepys 29 May, 1662, Wycherley 1672, and in the *Spectator* 1711, as a place of great resort. The gardens were opened for a "ridotto al fresco" 7 June, 1732, by Jonathan Tyers. The greatest season was in 1823, when 133,279 persons visited the gardens, and the receipts were 29,590*l.* The number on the then *supposed last* night, 5 Sept. 1839, was 1089 persons. Vauxhall was sold by auction, 9 Sept. 1841, for 20,200*l.*, and again 20 Aug. 1859. The last performances at Vauxhall took place on 25 July, 1859. The ground has been sold for building purposes. Six persons killed and many injured by fall of stack of wood at Buckley's saw-mills, 25 Feb. 1880.

Vauxhall park (formerly the lawn, &c., including the residence of Mr. H. Fawcett, M.P., purchased for 45,000*l.*) opened by the prince of Wales . . . . 7 July, 1890
The statue of professor Fawcett, by Mr. Tinworth, the gift of sir Henry Doulton, was unveiled by the archbishop of Canterbury . . 7 June, 1893

VAVASOR, see *Valvasor*.

VEDAS, the sacred books of the Hindoos, in Sanskrit, were probably written about the sixth or seventh century B.C. Veda means knowledge. These books comprise hymns, prayers, and liturgical formulæ. The edition by professor Max Müller, printed under the patronage of the East India Company, appeared in 1849-74. Four volumes of a translation by H. H. Wilson appeared in 1850-67.

Vol. V. & VI., edited by professor Cowell & W. F. Webster, completing the work, appeared in 1889.
In 1887 the Maharajah of Vizianagram proposed to bear the expense of a new edition of the text, edited by professor Max Müller. Two vols. of this edition, printed at Oxford, appeared in 1890. He died, 28 Oct. 1900.

VEGETABLES for the table were brought from Flanders about 1520; see *Gardening*.

VEGETARIAN SOCIETY, founded 1847, whose members restrict themselves to a vegetable diet, held their fifteenth anniversary in London, 4 Sept. 1862. A federation of societies throughout the world known as the Vegetarian Federal Union is active in the propaganda of the doctrines of vegetarianism.

Meetings held at Manchester, 14 Oct. 1874, and other places since.
"Fraternia," a settlement of vegetarians, existed in California in 1880. International Congress in London, 11 Sept. 1890; again, Mr. A. F. Hills president, 13 Sept. *et seq.* 1897. See *China*, Aug. 1895.
London vegetarian association, annual meetings; 14 societies reported in London, 28 Jan. 1898.
A national congress and exhibition at the Memorial hall, London, 12–17 Sept. 1898; again, mid Sept. 1899.
Oriolet (vegetarian) hospital at Loughton, founded by Mr. A. F. Hills, the president, in 1895, reported successful, 16 Sept. 1899.
Internat. congress held in London, 26 June, 1901.

VEHMIC TRIBUNALS: *Vehmgerichte*, *Fehmgerichte*, or *Femgerichte*, secret tribunals established in Westphalia to maintain religion and the public peace, had their origin in the time of Charlemagne, and rose to importance in 1182, when Westphalia became subject to the archbishop of Cologne. Persons of the most exalted rank were subjected to their decisions, being frequently seized, tried, and executed. The emperors endeavoured to suppress them, but did not succeed till the 16th century. Their last court, it is said, was held in 1568. Sir W. Scott has described them in "Anne of Geierstein." A remnant of these tribunals was abolished by Jerome Bonaparte, king of Westphalia, in 1811.

VEII, an independent Etruscan city near Rome. There were frequent wars between Veii and Rome, for above three centuries; see *Fabii*. Veii was taken by the dictator Camillus, it is said, after a siege of ten years, 396 B.C. When Rome was destroyed by the Gauls in 390, the Romans, who had fled to Veii, desired to remain there, and make it their capital, but were dissuaded from it by the entreaties of Camillus, and Veii was abandoned. It was restored by the Emperor Augustus, but had fallen into decay, at the time of Hadrian.

VELLORE (S.E. India) became the residence of the family of the dethroned sultan of Mysore, and was strongly garrisoned by English troops, 1799. The revolt of the sepoys, in which the family of the late Tippoo took an active part, took place 10 July, 1806. The insurgents were subdued by colonel Gillespie, and mostly put to the sword; about 800 sepoys were killed.

VELOCIPEDES. A machine of this kind was invented by Blanchard the aëronaut, and described in the *Journal de Paris*, 27 July, 1779; and one was invented by Nicéphore Niepce in 1818. The "dandy-horse" or "Draisena, a machine called a velocipede," was patented for the Baron von Draise in Paris and London in 1818, and described in "Ackermann's Repository," Feb. 1819. These machines came again into use in 1861; and since 1867 have been very common under various forms, termed bicycles and tricycles. M. Michaux, of Paris, introduced the bicycle proper in 1866, and it was imported into England about 1869. The chief inventor in England, James Starley, an ingenious mechanic of Albourne, Sussex, was buried at Coventry, June, 1881. The popular "Otto" bicycle, first patented in 1881, much improved since. Velocipede races took place at the Crystal Palace, 26 May, 1869, and frequently since. Mr. John Mayall and two friends travelled to Brighton on velocipedes, 17 Feb. 1869.

Mr. Stanton went from London to Bath, 106 miles, on a bicycle, in 8 h. 28 min. . . . 17 Aug. 1874
Similar feats since performed. Ordinary speed with bicycles 8 (now 10) miles an hour; with tricycles 10 miles may be attained.—*Field*. Oct. ,,
A gentleman said to have travelled 1000 miles in Ireland and Wales; expenses 25*l*. . . . . ,,
Bicycle clubs formed in London, &c. 1875
Above 1500 velocipedes at a meeting at Hampton Court . . . . 26 May, 1877
Middlesex magistrates decide that a bicycle is a carriage, and fine a rider for damage . 31 July, 1878
John Rankin went from Kilmarnock to London and back to Glasgow, with stoppages (112 miles one day) . . . . 23 July–10 Aug. ,,
The Bicycle Union, the National Cyclists' Union, and the Cyclists' Touring club founded . . ,,
Six days' contest, Agricultural Hall, London, Mr. George Waller won prize-belt (100*l*.) and 105*l*., rode 1172 miles, 28 April—3 May. Mr. Waller again won, rode 1404 miles (6 days of 18 hours), 1–6 Sept. 1879
Ivan Zmertych, Hungarian, travelled on his velocipede from Ostend to Pesth (about 1200 miles), 10–30 June, 1880
Mr. Alfred Nixon, hon. sec. London tricycle club, on 'Premier' tricycle from John o' Groat's to Land's End in 13 days, 23 hours, 55 minutes, 16–30 Aug. 1882; Mr. E. Oxborrow did the reverse in a week, 1–8 June, 1885; Mr. H. R. Goodwin, on a bicycle, did the double journey, 1–16 June, 1885
F. J. Lees, of Sheffield, covers 20 miles within an hour with a bicycle . . . . . 18 Aug. 1883
Switzerland crossed by bicycles and tricycles Aug.–Sept. ,,
17th annual exhibition of bicycles, &c., at the Floral Hall, Covent Garden . . . 4 Feb. 1884
Mr. Alfred Nixon went from London to Edinburgh on a tricycle in three days . . 28–31 Aug. ,,
Crypto-dynamic gearing invented by Mr. W. T. Shaw 1885
Annual congress of cyclists held at Colchester, 2 June, 1886
The cycling championship of Europe gained by Mr. E. Hall of Gainsborough at Berlin, 16 Aug. ,,
Mr. Thomas Stevens, on a bicycle, travelled 11,700 miles through America, across Europe to Asia, April, 1884–Jan. 1887
Messrs. Wilkins' bicycle for travelling rough roads and up hills exhibited at Hanwell, Middlesex, 8 Sept. ,,
The Rev. Hugh Callan, of St. Andrews, Glasgow, travelled to Jerusalem, through Europe and Asia Minor, and back on a bicycle . . autumn, 1888
The use of bicycles, &c., regulated by local government act of 1888, Part I., sect. 84.
The 13th annual show of the Stanley Cycle Club (at the Crystal Palace), 1,500 cycles exhibited, Jan. 1890; Islington, 20 Nov. 1896; 26th, Islington . . . . 21 Nov. 1902
1036 cyclists observed on the Brighton Road, Good Friday, April, 1892
Under the heading, "tyranny of the road," a great many letters complaining of the danger caused by the excessive speed of cyclists, appeared in the *Times* . . . . . . April–July, ,,
Speed and length of rides much increased . 1889–92
The first national cycle show at the Crystal Palace opened, 20 Jan. 1893; others since.
International cyclist congress at Antwerp . 13 Aug. 1894
The property of the Dunlop company sold at Dublin to the new Pneumatic Tyre company for 3,000,000 . . . . . . 8 May, 1890
Cycles largely manufactured in America, 1894–96, and specially at Birmingham and Coventry in England 1895–97
"Cyclist Year Book" states the capital of limited companies to be nearly 6,000,000*l*. up to end of 1895.
"Bicycles and Tricycles," by Archibald Sharp, published 1897
Miss Jane Yatman (24) completed 700 miles of cycling in Long island; total time taken, 81 hours and 5 minutes . . . . . 20 Sept. 1899
Mr. J. Kemp Starley, inventor of the safety bicycle, died, aged 46 . . . . . 29 Oct. 1901
J. Michael accomplished 46 miles in an hour at the Parc des Princes, Paris . . . . . 7 Sept. 1902
Winners of world's championships, 1902: at Rome, 1000 metres (amateur), Picard (France), 2 min. 16⅗ sec.; (professional), Ellegaard (Denmark), 3 min. 54⅘ sec. At Berlin, 100 kilometres (amateur), Goerneman (Germany), 1 hr. 24 min. 23 sec.; (professional), Robl (Germany), 1 hr. 42 min. 49 sec. These last two performances are world's records.

VELVET. The manufacture, long confined to Genoa, Lucca, and other places in Italy, was carried to France, and thence to England, about 1685. Velvet is mentioned by Joinville in 1272; and our king Richard II., in his will, directed his body to be clothed "in velveto," 1399. Jerome Lanyer in London patented his "velvet paper" in 1634.

VENAISSIN COMTAT, or COMTAT (S. France), after various changes, was ceded to pope Gregory X. 1274; and retained by his successors till 1791, when, with Avignon, it was re-united to France.

VENDÉE, see *La Vendée*.

VENDÉMIAIRE, 12, 13, 14 (3, 4, 5 Oct.), 1795, Barras and Napoleon Bonaparte suppress a royalist revolt against the convention.

VENDÔME COLUMN (132 feet 2 inches high), erected in the Place Vendôme, Paris, by Napoleon I. in 1806, to commemorate his successful campaign in Germany in 1805. On its side were bas-reliefs by Launay. It was pulled down by the communists "in the name of international fraternity," 16 May, 1871; restored by the national assembly, 31 Aug. 1874; statue of Napoleon I. on the top, replaced 28 Dec. 1875.

VENETI, maritime Gauls inhabiting Armorica, N.W. France. They rose against the Romans 57 B.C., and were quelled by Julius Cæsar, who defeated their fleet, 56, and cruelly exterminated an active commercial race.

VENETIA, see *Venice*.

VENEZUELA, the seat of a South American republic. When the Spaniards landed here in 1499, they observed some huts built upon piles, in an Indian village named Cora, in order to raise them above the stagnated water that covered the plain; and this induced them to give it the name of Venezuela, or Little Venice. This state in July, 1814, declared in congressional assembly the sovereignty of its people, which was recognised in 1818. It formed part of the republic of Columbia till it separated from the federal union, Nov. 1829. The population in 1881, 2,075,245; in 1891, 2,323,527; capital, Caracas.

Its independence was recognized by Spain . . 1845
General D. T. Monagas was elected president . . 1855
A new constitution promulgated . . . Dec. 1858

Revolution; José Castro became president, March, 1858; compelled to resign in Aug. 1859; and Dr. Pedro Gual assumed the government . Aug. 1859
General José Paez elected president . . 8 Sept. 1861
He resigned; and Juan E. Falcon succeeded, 17 June, 1863
General Febres Cordero protested, and set up a rival government at Porto-Cabello . . Oct. „
Marshal J. C. Falcon proclaimed president, 18 March, 1865
A revolution in Caracas; president Falcon fled, 22–26 June, „
The president Monagas dies, 18 Nov., and Pulgar becomes provisional president . . Dec. „
Caracas captured by general Guzman Blanco, after three days' conflict . . . . 27 April, 1870
He is made president, virtually dictator 13 July, „
A rebel general, Salazar, tried and shot about 17 May, 1872
Blanco re-elected president . . . 20 Feb. 1873
Severity towards the church for opposition to civil marriages; bishop of Merida expelled . July, 1874
Renunciation of papal authority announced Sept. 1876
Gen. F. L. Alcantara president, elected . 27 Feb. 1877
Gen. A. Guzman Blanco, president, elected 12 May, 1879
Gen. Joaquin Crespo, president, elected . 20 Feb. 1884
Gen. A. Guzman Blanco elected president (died, 28 July, 1899) . . . . 14 Sept. 1886
Dispute respecting territories containing gold mines; diplomatic relations broken off with Great Britain . . . . Feb. 1888
Dr. J. Pablo Rojas Paul, president, elected 29 June, „
The dictatorship of Don G. Blanco (envoy at Paris) set aside by the congress, about 10 June, 1889
Senor Palazio elected president, 20 Feb. 1890; insurrection against him as a dictator, headed by gen. Crespo, with about 8,000 men, March; guerilla warfare in the provinces, reports uncertain, April, 1892; the government troops massed at Valencia and Puerto Cabello 22 April, 1892
Junction of gen. Crespo's forces with those of gen. Mora . . . . . . 27 April, „
The government general, Juan Quevedo, killed by the people at Los Teques . . . 18 April, „
Valencia besieged by the insurgents; sorties defeated . . . . . . about 6 May, „
Outbreaks in Caracas against the president, about 12 May; his troops join the insurgents in Bolivia, after several conflicts . . . May, „
Gen. Crespo's army increased by desertions from the president's army, near Caracas, reported, 12 June, „
Several conflicts; president Palacio resigns, and leaves the country; sen. Villegas provisional president, reported . . . . 10 June, „
Gen. Crespo defeats the government troops and advances towards Caracas, reported . 11–14 Aug. „
Civil war continues; generals Urdaneta and Luciano Mendoza declare themselves dictators, Aug.; ex-president Villejas imprisoned, Aug.; congress dissolved . . . about 26 Aug. „
Sen. Pulido said to have formed a cabinet at Caracas, reported . . . . . 6 Sept. „
Gen. Luciano Mendoza at Caracas with 6,000 men, reported . . . . . . 6 Sept. „
Gen. Mendoza, dictator, proclaims blockade of Ciudad-Bolivar and Puerto Cabello; gen. Mendoza defeats gen. Martin Vegas near Petare, reported . . . . . . 10 Sept. „
Gen. Mendoza's attempted confiscations resisted by the foreign consuls at La Guayra; he resigns the dictatorship and proclaims sen. Pulido president, reported . . . . 11 Sept. „
Negotiations between gen. Pulido and gen. Crespo, reported . . . . . . 24 Sept. „
Troops of gen. Urdaneta board British brig *Chislehurst*, carry off 3 passengers, and imprison several merchants reported . . . 26 Sept. „
Government army defeated at Los Teques, about 5 Oct.; gen. Crespo enters Caracas, is proclaimed provisional president, and appoints a cabinet, 7 Oct. *et seq.*; recognized by the United States N.A. . . . . . . 25 Oct. „

[Reports uncertain.]

Disastrous floods, with great loss of life, S.E. of Caracas . . . . about 19 Oct. 1892
Gen. Crespo disbands his army . about 5 Dec. „
Gen. Crespo resigns; succeeded by gen. Guzman Alvarez, reported . . . . . 6 Oct. 1893
Gen. Crespo assumed office . . . 14 March, 1894
Government troops defeated by rebels near Bolivar, reported . . . . . . 11 Aug. „
Rupture with France, Germany, and other powers respecting claims of their subjects for losses sustained during the war of 1892 . . 9 March, 1895
Boundary dispute with British Guiana, continued, autumn, „
Lord Salisbury's ultimatum demanding reparation for insults to British officials at Uruan, in British Guiana. Dec. [1,500*l.* indemnity paid, Jan. 1897.]
A United States commission of inquiry on the boundary question: chief justice Alvey, justice Brewer, Mr. Andrew D. White, and others, appointed, 1 Jan. 1896; the British government supplies information . . . . . . Feb. 1896
Attempted assassination of pres. Crespo at Caracas, during a bull-fight; the assassin killed . 2 Feb. „
Resignation of Mr. Boulton, the British consul, at Caracas, announced . . . . 19 Feb. „
Conciliatory message to congress by pres. Crespo, reported . . . . 26 Feb. „
Blue book containing diplomatic correspondence on the Venezuelan case since 1822, presented to the commission at Washington, 10 March; commission sat at New York, 14 April *et seq.*
The *Mariscal Ayacuche* warship, burnt, off Margarita, 8 deaths . . . . 22 March, „
The British and American governments agree to a form of arbitration, announced . 18 June, „
Mr. Harrison, crown surveyor of British Guiana, arrested by Venezuelans, 15 June; a colonial force despatched to protect the surveyors, on the Cuyuni river, at Acarabisco . . 24 June, „
Negotiations resumed, between sir Julian Pauncefote and Mr. Olney . . . . 23 Oct. „
Lord Herschell and Mr. justice (aft. sir R.) Henn Collins, British members of the tribunal to decide the boundary question; treaty signed, by sir Julian Pauncefote and sen. Andrade at Washington, 2 Feb. 1897; ratified by congress, 5 April, 1897.
Diplomatic relations with Gt. Britain suspended in 1887; restored, announced . 2 March, 1897
Dr. Juan Pietri appointed British minister, 12 March, „
The Anglo-American Venezuelan boundary treaty, ratified at Washington . . . 14 June, „
New ministry, sen. Luis Castillo, treasurer, reported . . . . 28 June, „
Gen. Andrade elected president . . 16 Sept. „
Revolutionary plot suppressed, 500 arrests at Caracas, 185 arrests elsewhere . 27, 29 Oct. „
Financial crisis: trade paralyzed, etc., 31 Oct.; end of the crisis . . . . . . 11 Dec. „
New ministry, under ex-pres. Crespo formed, 28 Dec. „
The Venezuelan Amazon territory, with privileges, granted to an English syndicate, reported, 9 Feb. 1898
Ex-president Crespo killed in a skirmish with rebels, under gen. Hernandez, abt. 18 April; Hernandez captured, end of the rising, 12 June, „
Lands ceded by the government for 15 yrs. to an Italian colonization society . . . . June, „
Revolt in the province of Los Andes, reported, 9 June, 1899
Government troops defeated near Barquisimeto, 23 Aug.; gen. Castro captures Valencia and Maracay, 15, 16 Sept.; defeats pres. Andrade's force near Valencia, and invests Caracas, reported . . . . 28 Sept. „
BRITISH GUIANA BOUNDARY dispute, see *above*: arbitration tribunal meets at Paris, 25 Jan. 1899; lord Russell of Killowen succeeds lord Herschell (died March), April; case opened, prof. Martens (Russia) president, 15 June *et seq.*; British case ably stated by sir Richard Webster (bart. Nov. 1899), 13 July–19 Sept.; 32 days occupied by the Venezuelan and 23 by the British case, closed, 27 Sept.; goldfields, &c., settled within British territory; Barima Point and mouth of the Orinoco given to Venezuela . . . . . 3 Oct. „

Ultimatum from gen. Castro delivered at Caracas, 18 Oct.; pres. Andrade flies to La Guayra, peace proposals accepted, 20 Oct.; gen. Castro, provisional president, and a new ministry formed, reported . . . . 24 Oct. 1899
Puerto Cabello taken by gen. Castro after severe fighting, reported . . . . . 12 Nov. ,,
Insurgents occupy Maracaybo, reported . 3 Dec. ,,
Mr. James Lyall, British consul, assassinated at Bolivar . . . . 28 Feb. 1900
Rebels defeated near Bolivar city . 22 March, ,,
Peace proclaimed; political prisoners released, 24 July, ,,
The Venezuela and British Guiana boundary commission, demarcation begins . . Nov. ,,
Government's troops defeated near Giuria, mid Jan. 1901
Rebels defeated near Carupano, reported, 30 Jan. ,,
Tachira district invaded from Colombia, rebels defeated at San Cristobal . 29, 30 July, ,,
Further fighting, the Venezuelans invade Colombia and are severely routed at La Hacha . 14 Sept. ,,
Gen. Castro elected president . . 28 Oct. ,,
[Ratified by congress for 6 years, Feb. 1902.]
Continued fighting, conflicting reports, Dec.–Jan. 1902
Señ. Pulido, ex-minister, and others arrested in Caracas . . . . 27 Jan. ,,
Convention (customs) settled with France . Feb. ,,
Colombian invaders severely repulsed near Lafrias, reported . . . . 1 March, ,,
Revolutionary rising, government troops defeated near Carupano, and near El Pilar, 3, 4 April; again near San Antonio, gen. Castillo mortally wounded, 22 April; rebels repulsed at La Guaira, 7 June; vice-pres. Ayala and 1,744 men surrender to the rebels at Coro, 20 June; rebels capture Barquisimeto, about 4 July; and Barcelona after hard fighting and great slaughter, 3–9 Aug.; Carupano reoccupied by troops, 22 Aug.; rebels defeated at Taguay, 28 Aug.; 550 of the troops desert to the enemy near Ocumare, 600 others defeated and Los Teques captured, 29 Aug.; troops defeated near Tinaquillo, 11–15 Sept. ,,
Two bridges blown up on the English railway at La Guaira by the insurgents . . . 18 Sept. ,,
Severe fighting near La Victoria, 11–17 Oct.; pres. Castro occupies La Victoria; further fighting, 26 Oct. ,,
Rebels attack Carupano, and retreat after hard fighting . . . . . . 26, 27 Oct. ,,
Four British merchant ships seized . . Nov. ,,
British and German cruisers arrive . early Dec. ,,
British notes urging claims for outrages on persons and property (Jan. 1901–Oct. 1902), presented, July, Aug. and 2 Dec. ,,
British and German ultimatums presented, the ministers leave Caracas . . . . 7, 8 Dec. ,,
5 Venezuelan gunboats seized . . . 9 Dec. ,,
Pres. Castro proposes arbitration . . 12 Dec. ,,
Topaze, British s.s., seized at Puerto Cabello, 10 Dec.; released, the fort and custom-house bombarded . . . . 13 Dec. ,,
Pres. Castro forbids reprisals on foreigners, 14 Dec. ,,
Claims urged by other powers . 15–19 Dec. ,,
Blockade of ports proclaimed . . 20 Dec. ,,
Armistice with insurgents ends . . 24 Dec. ,,
Severe fighting at Barquisimeto . . 27 Dec. ,,
Arbitration by the Hague tribunal agreed by the powers, 25 Dec.; and by pres. Castro, early Jan. 1903
Insurgents defeated at Guatire and at Cumana, 4, 6 Jan. ,,
Mr. Bowen, U.S. minister, leaves to act for Venezuela at Washington . . . 11 Jan. ,,
Insurgents attack Coro, but eventually retire with heavy loss . . . . . . 19 Jan. ,,
Fort San Carlos shelled by German cruisers, the village burnt, many killed (great indignation in U.S.A. and elsewhere) . . 17, 21–23 Jan. ,,
Insurgents defeated near Camatagua, 250 captured, reported . . . . 3 Feb. ,,
Guatire captured by the troops . . 9 Feb. ,,
Settlement of British and German first-class claims agreed to, other questions to be referred to the Hague; protocols signed at Washington, 13 Feb. ,,
Blockade of ports raised . . . 14, 15 Feb. ,,
Insurgents capture Carupano, reported . 28 Feb. ,,
Other foreign protocols signed . Feb.–March, 1903
Venezuelan warships returned by the British, 3 March, ,,
British minister protests against the closing of ports on the Orinoco; government troops recapture Ciudad Bolivar from insurgents after three days' fighting . . . mid June, ,,
Formal presentation of the claims of the Powers against Venezuela: United States, 10,900,000 dols.; Great Britain, 2,500,000 dols.; Germany, 1,417,000 dols.; France, 16,040,000 dols.; Italy, 8,300,000 dols.; Belgium, 3,093,800 dols.; Holland, 1,048,451 dols.; Spain, 600,000 dols.; Sweden, 200,000 dols.; Mexico, 500,000 dols., reported mid Sept. ,,
Sittings of Venezuelan arbitration court at the Hague . . . . Oct. ,,
(See *Columbia*; *Trials*, 21 March, 1887.)

"VENGEUR STORY," see *Ushant*, note.

VENI, VIDI, VICI,—"I came, I saw, I conquered;" see *Zela*.

VENICE (N. Italy). The province of Venetia, held by the Veneti, of uncertain origin, was invaded by the Gauls about 350 B.C. The Veneti made an alliance with the Romans, 215 B.C., who founded Aquileia, 181, and gradually acquired the whole country. Under the empire, Venetia included Padua, Verona, and other important places. Population of the city of Venice in 1857, 118,173; in 1881, 129,445; in 1890, 158,019; 1901, 151,841; of the province Venetia, 1890, 2,985,036; 1901, 400,030. New line of steamers for the east started from Venice by the Peninsular and Oriental Company, July, 1872.

Venice, founded by families from Aquileia and Padua fleeing from Attila . . . about A.D. 452
First doge (or duke) chosen, Anafesto Paululio . . 697
Bishopric founded 733
The doge Orso slain; an annual magistrate (maestro di militi, master of the militia) appointed . . 737
Diodato, son of Orso, made doge 742
Two doges reign: Maurizio Galbaio, and his son Giovanni 777
The Rialto made the seat of government 811
Venice becomes independent of the eastern empire, and acquires the maritime cities of Dalmatia and Istria 997
Its navy and commerce increase . . . 1000–1100
The Venetians aid at the capture of Tyre and acquire the third part, 1124; and ravage the Greek archipelago 1125
Bank of Venice established 1157
Ceremony of wedding the Adriatic instituted, about 1177
Zara captured by the Venetians . . 24 Nov. 1202
The Venetians aid the crusaders with men, horses, and ships . . . . ,,
Crete purchased 1204
Venice helps in the Latin conquest of Constantinople, and obtains power in the East . . 1204-5
The four bronze horses by Lysippus, brought from Constantinople, placed at St. Mark's by the doge Pietro Ziani, who died 1229
The Venetians defeat the Genoese near Negropont, 1262
War with Genoa 1293
The Venetian fleet severely defeated by the Genoese in the Adriatic, 8 Sept. 1298; peace between them 1299
Louis of Hungary defeated at Zara . . 1 July, 1346
Severe contest with Genoa 1350-81
The doge Marino Faliero, to avenge an insult, conspires against the republic; beheaded 17 April 1355
The Venetians lose Istria and Dalmatia . . . 1358
War with the Genoese, who defeat the Venetians at Pola, and advance against Venice, which is vigorously defended 1377
The Genoese fleet is captured at Chiozza . . . 1380
And peace concluded 1381
Venice flourishes under Antonio Vernieri . 1382-1400
War with Padua; conquest of Padua and Verona . 1404
War against Milan; conquest of Brescia 1425 of Bergamo 1428
The city suffers from the plague 1447

War against Milan, 1430; conquest of Ravenna . . 1454
War with the Turks; Venice loses many of its eastern possessions 1461-77
The Venetians take Athens, 1466; and Cyprus . . 1475
Venice excommunicated, 1483; joins league against Naples, 1493; helps to overcome Charles VIII. of France 1495
Injured by the discovery of America (1492), and the passage to the Indies 1497
The Venetians nearly ruined by the league of Cambray formed against them 1508
They assist in defeating the Turks at Lepanto, 7 Oct. 1571
The Turks retake Cyprus . . . . ,,
Destructive fire at Venice 1577
The Rialto bridge and the Piazza di San Marco erected . . . . . . about 1592
Paul V.'s interdict on Venice (1606) contemptuously disregarded 1607
Naval victories over the Turks; at Scio, 1651; and in the Dardanelles 1655
The Turks take Candia, after 24 years' siege . . 1669
Venice recovers part of the Morea, 1683-99; loses it, 1715-39
Venice occupied by Bonaparte, who, by the treaty of Campo Formio, gives part of its territory to Austria, and annexes the rest to the Cisalpine republic 1797
The whole of Venice annexed to the kingdom of Italy by the treaty of Presburg . 26 Dec. 1805
All Venice transferred to the empire of Austria . . 1814
Venice declared a free port . . . 24 Jan. 1830
Insurrection begins 22 March, 1848; the city, defended by Daniel Manin, surrenders to the Austrians after a long siege . . . 22 Aug. 1849
During the Italian war in 1859, the country was much disorganised, and many persons emigrated in 1860-1.]
Venetian deputies will not attend the Austrian parliament at Vienna . . . . May, 1861
Venetia surrendered to France for Italy (by the treaty of Vienna, signed 3 Oct.), and transferred to Italy . . . . . . 17 Oct. 1866
Plebiscitum: 651,758 votes for annexation to Italy; 69 against . . . . . 22 Oct. ,,
Result reported by Venetian deputies, and the iron crown given to the king at Turin . . 4 Nov. ,,
He enters Venice . . . . . . 7 Nov. ,,
Masterpiece of Titian ("Death of Peter Martyr") destroyed at the burning of a chapel . 15 Aug. 1867
The remains of Daniel Manin (brought from Paris) buried in St. Mark's . . . . 23 March, 1868
His statue unveiled . . . . . 22 March, 1875
The emperor of Austria and king of Italy at Venice 5-7 April, ,,
The bronze equestrian statue of Victor Emmanuel II. by Ferrari unveiled in the presence of the king and queen of Italy; great festivities . . 1 May, 1887
Art exhibition opened by the king . . 2 May, ,,
The restoration of the palace of the Doges was completed, and the building exposed to view in Nov. 1889
Launch of the ironclad *Sicilia*, the royal family present . . . . 6 July, 1891
Representations of Venice at the Olympia, London (*which see*) . . . . 26 Dec. 1891; 7 Jan. 1893
Visit of the emperor of Germany; received by king Humbert, 8 April, 1894; again in . . April, 1896
International art exhibition, opened by the king and queen, 30 April, 1895; another opened by the prince of Naples . . . . . 28 April, 1897
Sanitary convention signed, see *Plague*. 19 March, ,,
The king and queen of Italy arrive to visit the exhibition . . . . . 22-25 Oct. 1899
Internat. art exhibition opened by the duke of the Abruzzi . . . . 27 April, 1901
Fall of the campanile (bell tower) of St. Mark, 323 ft. high, 42 ft. wide at base . 14 July, 1902
20,000*l*. voted by the municipality for its reconstruction; also 40,000*l*. for repairing monuments of the city; crack in two arches of the Procuratie Vecchie on the Piazza of St. Mark occasions alarm . . . . Jan. 1903
[Venice has had 122 doges; Anafesto, 697, to Luigi Manin, 1797.]

VENLOO (Holland), surrendered to the allies, under Marlborough, 23 Sept. 1702; and to the French, under Pichegru, 26 Oct. 1794.

VENNER'S INSURRECTION, see *Anabaptists*, 1661.

VENTILATORS were invented by the rev. Dr. Hales, and described to the Royal Society of London, May, 1741; and the ventilator for the use of ships was announced by Mr. Triewald, in November, same year. The marquis of Chabannes' plan for warming and ventilating theatres and houses for audiences was applied to those of London about 1819. The systems of Dr. Reid (about 1834) and others followed, with much controversy. Dr. Arnott's work on this subject was published in 1838. A commission on warming and ventilation issued a report in 1859.

New air machine in the house of commons started 5 June, 1874
Mr. Tobin's plan, a horizontal tube from without communicating with vertical tube inside; successful at Leeds; described (in *Times*), 12 April, 1875
Mr. D. G. Hoey's system was exhibited at Messrs. Barclay's bank, Lombard-street, London, and reported successful . . . . . Jan. 1891

VENTRILOQUISM (speaking from the stomach), was known to the Greeks, who termed ventriloquists "belly-prophets." The name is a misnomer, as the sounds are produced by regulating the breathing and organs of voice, without motion of the lips. Among eminent ventriloquists were baron Mengen and M. Saint Gille, about 1772 (whose experiments were examined by a commission of the French Academy); Thomas King (about 1716); Charles Mathews (1824); and M. Alexandre (1822); others since.

VENUS, the Roman goddess of love and beauty (the Greek Aphrodité). *Statues:* Venus de Medicis, found near Tivoli and removed to France, 1680; the Venus found at Milo or Melos, 1820, placed in the Louvre, Paris, 1834. The transit of the planet over the sun was predicted by Kepler to take place 6 Dec. 1631, but was not observed; he died 15 Nov. 1630. The first transit observed, was by the rev. Jeremiah Horrox, or Horrocks, and his friend, Wm. Crabtree, on 24 Nov. 1639, as predicted by Horrox in 1633. The astronomer-royal Maskelyne observed her transit at St. Helena, 6 June, 1761. Capt. Cook made his first voyage in the *Endeavour*, to Otaheite, to observe a transit of Venus, 3 June, 1769; see *Cook's Voyages*. The diurnal rotation of Venus was discovered by Cassini in 1667. This is contested by Schiaperelli and others, who assert her rotation to be as long as her revolution in her orbit. See *Sun*, note.

Halley suggested the observation of the transit as a means of estimating the distance of the earth from the sun, and devised a method for this purpose 1716
Another method was invented by Delisle about . 1743
Both plans were used in . . . . Dec. 1874
Expeditions for the accurate observation of the phenomena, on 8 Dec. astronomical day; ordinary day, 9 Dec. 1874, were sent to different parts of the globe by all the great powers, and favourable results have been reported . . . 1875-6
The transit, on 6 Dec. 1882, was observed at Bath, Penzance, Cork, Cape Town, Washington, Melbourne, and many other places. The next transits will take place 8 June, 2004, and 6 June, 2012.
Venus was both a morning and evening star, rising 43 min. before the sun, and setting 43 min. after it . . . . 14 Feb. 1894
Dr. W. R. Brooks obtained some good photographs by the light of Venus when a morning star, Sept. 1900

VERA CRUZ (Mexico), built about 1600; was taken by the Americans in 1847, and by the allies on 17 Dec. 1861, during the intervention; retaken by the liberals, under Juarez, 27 June, 1867.

VERCELLI, the ancient Vercellæ, Piedmont, near which Marius defeated the Cimbri, 101 B.C. It was the seat of a republic in the 13th and 14th centuries. It was taken by the Spaniards, 1630; French, 1704; and allies, 1706; and afterwards partook of the fortunes of Piedmont.

VERDEN (Hanover). Here Charlemagne massacred about 4500 Saxons, who had rebelled and relapsed into idolatry, 782.

VERDUN (the ancient Verodunum), a first-class fortress on the Meuse, N.E. France, made a magazine for his legions by Julius Cæsar. It was acquired by the Franks in the sixth century, and formed part of the dominions of Lothaire by the treaty of Verdun, 843, when the empire was divided between the sons of Louis I. It was taken and annexed to the empire by Otho I. about 939. It surrendered to France in 1552; and was formally ceded in 1648. It was taken and held by the Prussians 43 days, Sept.—Oct. 1792. Gen. Beaurepaire, the commandant, committed suicide before the surrender, and 14 ladies were executed on 28 May, 1794, for going to the king of Prussia to solicit his clemency for the town. Verdun surrendered to the Germans 8 Nov. 1870, after a brave defence; two vigorous sallies being made 28 Oct. Above 4000 men were captured, with a large number of arms and ammunition. It was the last place held by the Germans; and was given up 15, 16 Sept. 1873, and the troops retired.

VERGARA, N. SPAIN. Here the Carlist general, Maroto, made a treaty, termed "The pacification of Vergara," with Espartero, 31 Aug. 1839. The monument to celebrate it was destroyed by the Carlists in Aug. 1873.

VERMANDOIS (N. France), a county given by Charlemagne to his second son Pepin, whose family held it till the 11th century; in 1156 it came, by marriage, to the counts of Flanders; and in 1185 it was seized by Philip II., and incorporated with the monarchy in 1215.

VERMONT, a northern state in North America, was settled by the French, 1724-31; and ceded to Great Britain in 1763. It was freed from the authority of New York, and admitted as a state of the union in 1791. Population 1880, 332,286; 1890, 332,422; 1900, 343,641; capital, Montpelier.

VERNEUIL (N.W. France), the site of a battle fought 17 Aug. 1424, between the Burgundians and English under the regent duke of Bedford, and the French, assisted by the Scots, commanded by the count de Narbonne, the earls of Douglas and Buchan, &c. The French at first were successful; but some Lombard auxiliaries, who had taken the English camp, commenced pillaging. Two thousand English archers came then fresh to the attack; and the French and Scots were totally defeated, and their leaders killed.

VERNON GALLERY. The inadequate manner in which modern British art was represented in the National Gallery was somewhat remedied in 1847 by the munificent present to the nation, by Mr. Robert Vernon, of a collection of 157 pictures, all but two being by first-rate British artists. They were first exhibited at Mr. Vernon's house in Pall-mall, next in the vaults beneath the National Gallery, afterwards at Marlborough house, and are now at the South Kensington Museum. In 1857, Mr. John Sheepshanks followed Mr. Vernon's example; see *Sheepshanks' Donations*.

VERONA (N. Italy) was founded by the Gauls or Etruscans; see *Campus Raudius*. The amphitheatre was built by Titus, A.D. 82. Verona has been the site of many conflicts. It was taken by Constantine 312; and on 27 Sept. 489 Theodoric defeated Odoacer, king of Italy. Verona was taken by Charlemagne 774. About 1260 Mastino della Scala was elected podestà, and his descendants (the Scaligeri) ruled, till subdued by the Visconti, dukes of Milan, 1387. Verona was conquered by the Venetians 1405, and held by them with some intermissions till its capture by the French general Massena, 3 June, 1796. Near to it Charles Albert of Sardinia defeated the Austrians 6 May, 1848. Verona is one of the four strong Austrian fortresses termed the Quadrangle, or Quadrilateral (*which see*), and here the emperor Francis Joseph, on 12 July, 1859, in an order of the day, announced to his army that he must yield to circumstances unfavourable to his policy, and thanked his people and army for their support. It was surrendered to the Italian government, 16 Oct. 1866; and the king was received by 70,000 persons in the amphitheatre, 18 Nov. 1866. Above 50,000 coins of Gallienus and other emperors, chiefly bronze, discovered near Verona, Jan. 1877. Population, 1881, 60,768; 1901, 74,261.

VERSAILLES (near Paris) was a small village, in a forest thirty miles in circuit; where Louis XIII. built a hunting-seat about 1632. Louis XIV. between 1661 and 1687 enlarged it into a magnificent palace, which became the usual residence of the kings of France. By the treaty between Great Britain and the revolted colonies of British North America, signed at Paris, the latter power was admitted to be a sovereign and independent state, 3 Sept. 1783. On the same day a treaty was signed at Versailles between Great Britain, France, and Spain, by which Pondicherry and Carical, with other possessions in Bengal, were restored to France, and Trincomalee restored to the Dutch. Here was held the military festival of the royal guards 1 Oct. 1789, which was followed (on the 5th and 6th) by the attack of the mob, who massacred the guards and brought the king back to Paris. Versailles became the residence of Louis-Philippe in 1830. The historical gallery was opened in 1837. Versailles, with the troops there, surrendered to the Germans 19 Sept. 1870, and the crown prince of Prussia entered the next day; and on 26 Sept. he awarded the iron cross to above 30 soldiers at the foot of the statue of Louis XIV. The palace was converted into a hospital. The royal head-quarters were removed here from Ferrières 5 Oct. After the peace, Versailles became the seat of the French government (see *France*). March, 1871. Removed to Paris 27 Nov. 1879. The congress for the revision of the constitution met here 4—13 Aug. 1884. See *France*, 1889. Visited by the members of the British parliamentary party, 28 Nov. 1903, on the occasion of their visit to Paris.

VERSE, see *Poetry*, *Hexameter*, *Elegy*, *Iambic*, &c. Surrey's translation of part of *Virgil's Æneid* into *blank verse* is the first English composition of the kind, omitting tragedy, extant in the English language (published in 1547). The verse previously used in our grave compositions was the stanza of eight lines, the *ottava rima* (as adopted with the addition of one line by Spenser in his *Faëry Queene*), who probably borrowed it from Ariosto and Tasso. Boccaccio introduced it into Italy in his *Teseide*, having copied it from the old French *chansons*. Trissino is said to have been the first introducer of blank verse among the moderns, about 1508. *Vossius*.

VERULAM, see *Alban's, St.*

VERVINS (N. France). Here was concluded the peace between Philip II. of Spain and Henry IV. of France, with mutual concessions, 2 May, 1598.

VESERONCE (S.E. France), near Vienne. Here Gondemar, king of the Burgundians, defeated and killed Clodomir, king of Orleans, and revenged the murder of his brother Sigismond and his family, 524. This conflict is called also the battle of Voiron.

VESPERS, see *Sicilian Vespers*. In the house of the French ambassador at Blackfriars, in London, a Jesuit was preaching to upwards of three hundred persons in an upper room, the floor of which gave way with the weight, when the whole congregation was precipitated to the street, and the preacher and more than a hundred of his auditory, chiefly persons of rank, were killed. This catastrophe, termed the *Fatal Vespers*, occurred 26 Oct. 1623. *Stow.*

VESTA. The planet Vesta (the ninth) was discovered by Dr. Olbers, of Bremen, on 29 March, 1807. She appears like a star of the sixth magnitude.

VESTALS, virgin priestesses, took care of the perpetual fire consecrated to Vesta. The mother of Romulus was a vestal. Numa is said to have appointed four, 710 B.C., and Tarquin added two. Minutia was buried alive for breaking her virgin vow, 337 B.C.; Sextilia, 273 B.C.; and Cornelia Maximiliana, A.D. 92. It is said that only eighteen vestals had been condemned since the time of Numa. The order was abolished by Theodosius, 389.

"**VESTIGES OF THE NATURAL HISTORY OF CREATION**," a work which upholds the doctrine of progressive development as a hypothetic history of organic creation, ascribed to Robert Chambers, and other persons, first appeared in 1844, and occasioned much controversy. See *Origin of Species.*

VESUVIUS, MOUNT, S. Italy. Near it, the Latin confederacy were totally defeated by the Romans, whose general, P. Decius Mus, had devoted himself to death, 340 B.C. By an eruption of Mount Vesuvius, the cities of Pompeii and Herculaneum (*which see*) were overwhelmed 24 Aug. 79 A.D., and more than 200,000 persons perished, among them Pliny the naturalist. Numerous other disastrous eruptions have occurred. Torre del Greco, with 4000 persons, was destroyed, 17 Dec. 1631. There was a dreadful eruption, took place suddenly, 24 Nov. 1759, and another 8 Aug. 1767. The violent burst in 1767 was the 34th from the time of Titus. One in June, 1794, was most destructive: the lava flowed over 5000 acres of rich vineyards and cultivated land, and Torre del Greco was a second time burned; the top of the mountain fell in, and the crater is now nearly two miles in circumference. A great eruption in Oct. 1822, and others in May, 1855, May and June, 1858, caused great destruction. A series of violent eruptions causing much damage occurred in Dec. 1861, and in Feb. 1865. Torre del Greco was again destroyed in Dec. 1861. Another eruption began 12 Nov. 1867, and continued increasing in grandeur and danger, March, 1868. The phenomena were observed by professors Tyndall and Miller, sir John Lubbock, and other scientific men, in April, 1868. A great eruption began 8 Oct. 1868, and continued, causing much destruction, 19, 20 Nov. A severe eruption began 23 April and ended about 3 May, 1872; above 60 lives were lost. The mountain was disturbed in 1876; and another eruption began about 20 Sept. 1878; lava was spouted to the height of 300 feet; an eruption began 11 June, 1879; an intermittent eruption 2 May, 1885. A new crater formed 7 June; continued flowing of lava, 11 June; ceases 16 June, renewed; a Brazilian tourist fell into the crater, July, 1891. Increasing eruptions, 9 June *et seq.*; active, 13 Sept. 1892. Professor John Phillips' "Vesuvius" was published 1869.

Vesuvius was ascended by the princess of Wales and her family . . . . 25 March, 1893

A fissure on the N.W. side of the great cone, increased activity, reported (*Nature*, 8 Aug.) 3 July, 1895

Active eruption, lava streams, 8 Nov. 1897; again, Aug.; violent eruption, 7 new craters, 15–17 Sept.; again, 31 Dec. 1898–Jan. 1899; and again 4–7 May; new eruptive cone formed, Sept. 1900–April, 1901

VETERINARY COLLEGES. The Royal College of Veterinary Surgeons, at Red Lion-square, London, which alone grants diplomas, was chartered in 1844. The Veterinary Surgeons act, 44 & 45 Vict. sec. 62; passed 27 Aug. 1881, deals only with this college; amendment act passed, 30 July, 1900. The Royal Veterinary College at Camden Town, London, N.W., was founded in 1791. Centenary festival, the duke of Cambridge in the chair, the prince of Wales present, 19 Oct. 1891. There are veterinary colleges in Edinburgh and Glasgow; new one opened at Ballsbridge, Dublin, 1 Oct. 1902.

Internat. congress of veterinary surgeons at Baden-Baden, 6–12 Aug. 1899.

VETO. See *Permissive Bill.*

VEXATIOUS ACTIONS Act passed, 14 Aug. 1896. Act for Scotland passed, Aug. 1898.

VICE, an instrument of which Archytas of Tarentum, disciple of Pythagoras, is said to have been the inventor, along with the pulley and other implements, 420 B.C. *Society for the Suppression of Vice*, established 1802. Internat. federation congress for the abolition of state regulation of vice, meets in London, 12–15 July, 1898.

VICE-ADMIRALTY COURTS ACT, 1863, was extended and amended in 1867.

VICE-CHANCELLOR OF ENGLAND, an equity judge, appointed by parliament, first took his seat 5 May, 1813. A new court was erected for him about 1816 contiguous to Lincoln's-inn-hall. Two additional vice-chancellors were appointed under act 5 Vict. c. 5, 5 Oct. 1841. The office of vice-chancellor *of England* ceased in August, 1850, and a *third* vice-chancellor was appointed in 1851, when two more equity judges, styled *lords justices*, were appointed.

VICE-CHANCELLORS OF ENGLAND.

1813. Sir Thomas Plumer, 13 April.
1818. Sir John Leach, 13 Jan.
1827. Sir Anthony Hart, 4 May.
1827-50. Sir Lancelot Shadwell, 1 Nov. THE LAST.

VICE-CHANCELLORS.

1852. Sir John Stuart, sat last, 27 March, 1871.
1853. Sir Wm. Page Wood, made a justice of appeal, 1868; lord chancellor, Dec. 1868.
1868. Sir Geo. Markham Giffard, died 1870.
1869. Sir Wm. M. James, Jan.; made a lord justice of appeal, June, 1870.
1871. Sir John Wickens, April; died, 23 Oct. 1873.
1866. Sir Richard Malins, resigned 1881; died 15 Jan. 1882.

1870. Sir James Bacon, the last of the vice-chancellors, resigned 10 Nov. 1886; died, aged 97, 1 June, 1895.
1873. Sir Charles Hall, Nov.; died 12 Dec. 1883.
} now included in the chancery division.

VICENZA (the ancient Vicentia, N. Italy) was the seat of a republic in the 12th century. It greatly suffered by the ravages of Alaric, 401, and Attila, 452. Having joined the Lombard league, it was sacked by Frederic II. 1236. After many changes it was subjected to Venice, and with it fell under the French domination, 1796; and was given to Austria in 1814. Having revolted, it was retaken by Radetzky, 11 June, 1848. It was annexed to the kingdom of Italy, Oct. 1866.

VICE-PRESIDENT OF THE BOARD OF TRADE. This office was abolished in 1867, and a secretary with a seat in parliament substituted.

VICKSBURG, see *United States*, 1863.

VICTORIA, formerly PORT PHILLIP (Australia), situated between New South Wales and South Australia. In 1798, Bass, in his whale-boat expedition, visited Western Port, one of its harbours; and in 1802 Flinders sailed into Port Phillip Bay. Governor, col. sir George Clarke, Aug. 1895.

Population of the colony in 1836, 224; in 1841, 11,738; in 1846, 32,879; in 1851, 77,345; 31 Dec. 1852, about 200,000; in March 1857 there were 258,116 males and 145,403 females; in all 403,519. In 1859, in all 517,366; in 1861, 540,322; Dec. 1865, 626,630; in 1871, 729,654; 1877, 849,021; in 1881, 858,582; 1891, 1,140,411; 1901, 1,200,914. 1886–7, revenue, 6,733,867*l.*; expenditure, 6,665,863*l.*; 1889–90, revenue, 8,519,159*l.*; expenditure, 9,811,251*l.*; imports, 22,954,015*l.*; exports, 13,266,222*l.* 1892–93, revenue, 6,959,229*l.*; expenditure, 7,989,757*l.*; imports, 13,283,814*l.*; exports, 13,308,551*l.*; revenue, 1899, 7,450,676*l.*; expenditure, 7,318,945*l.* (war, 63,000*l.*); 1900-1901, 8,087,264*l.*; expenditure, 7,709,033*l.*

Colonel Collins lands with a party of convicts with the intention of founding a settlement at Port Phillip, but afterwards removed to Van Diemen's Land 1804
Messrs. Hume and Hovell, two stock-owners from New South Wales, explore part of the country, but do not discover its great advantages . . 1824
Mr. Edward Henty (of a Sussex family), comes from Tasmania with cattle, sheep, shepherds, &c., and settles in Portland Bay; his brothers, Stephen George and John, follow soon . . 1832
Mr. John Batman enters between the heads of Port Phillip, and purchases a large tract of land from the aborigines for a few gewgaws and blankets: he shortly after, with fifteen associates from Hobarton, took possession of 600,000 acres in the present Geelong country . . . May, 1835
The Launceston associates and Mr. John Pascoe Falkner ascend the Yarra-Yarra (or everflowing) river, and encamp on the site of Melbourne ,,
The colonists (450 in number) possess 140,000 sheep, 2500 cattle, and 150 horses; sir R. Bourke, governor of New South Wales, visits the colony, determines the sites of towns, and causes the land to be surveyed and resold, setting aside many contending claims; he appoints captain Lonsdale chief-magistrate (see *Melbourne*) . . 1837
The colony named Victoria 1839
Mr. C. J. Latrobe appointed lieutenant-governor under sir G. Gipps . . . . . . ,,
Its prosperity brings great numbers to it, and induces much speculation and consequent embarrassment and insolvency 1841-2
The province declared independent of New South Wales; a reward of 200*l.* offered for the discovery of gold in Victoria, which was soon after found near Melbourne, and was profitably worked Aug. 1851
7000 persons were at Ballarat, Oct.; 10,000 round Mount Alexander . . . . . . Nov. ,,
From 30 Sept. to 31 Dec. 1851, 30,311 ounces of gold were obtained from Ballarat; and from 29 Oct. to 31 Dec. 94,524 ounces from Mount Alexander—total 124,835 ounces
The production was still very great 1859
Immense immigration to Melbourne (see *Melbourne*) 1852
Sir Charles Hotham, governor . . . . June, 1854
A representative constitution granted . . . 1855
Sir Henry Barkly appointed governor . . . 1856
The parliament was opened . . . . 26 Nov. 1857
Four administrations had been formed in . . 1857-1860
Exhibition of the products of the colony opened by the governor . . . . 1 Oct. 1861
Sir Charles Darling appointed governor, May: arrives . . . . 10 Sept. 1863
Great opposition to reception of convicts in any part of Australia; a ship containing them sent back . . . . Oct. 1864
Important land act passed . . . 22 March, 1865
The assembly passes the new government tariff, Jan., which is rejected by the legislative council; the governor raises money for the public service irregularly . . . . July, ,,
The crisis still continues; appeal to the queen proposed . . . . Oct. ,,
Parliament prorogued . . . . Dec. ,,
Sir Charles Darling recalled . . . . 26 Feb. 1866
Ministerial difficulties: Mr. M'Culloch becomes premier . . . . April, ,,
The assembly votes 20,000*l.* to lady Darling; sir Charles departs . . . . May, ,,
New governor, sir John H. T. Manners Sutton, (viscount Canterbury in 1869) arrived 13 Aug. ,,
Intercolonial Exhibition opened . . . 25 Oct. ,,
Vote of 20,000*l.* to lady Darling rejected by legislative council . . . . . . 20 Aug. 1867
Ministerial crisis; dispute continues between the assembly and the council . . . . Oct. ,,
Duke of Edinburgh arrives; great rejoicings 23 Nov. ,,
An address presented to him by Mr. Edward Henty, the first settler, and others . . . ,,
Parliament dissolved . . . . . . 30 Dec. ,,
New parliament; ministry resigned because the governor objected to insertion of the Darling grant in the appropriation bill . . 12 March, 1868
First woollen and paper manufactories established May, ,,
The M'Culloch ministry arrange the Darling affair July, ,,
The M'Pherson ministry announced . . . Oct. 1869
Mr. M'Culloch forms a ministry including Mr. M'Pherson, April; is knighted . . . May, 1870
Mr. M'Culloch resigns . . . . . 14 June, ,,
The federation of the Australian colonies, proposed by Mr. Gavan Duffy in 1857, revived by him and discussed in the legislative assembly . June, ,,
Industrial Museum at Melbourne, opened 8 Sept. ,,
Mr. Chas. Gavan Duffy minister (knt. 1873), July, 1871
He resigns on a vote against him . . . 29 May, 1872
Mr. Francis forms a ministry . . . . June, ,,
Payment (300*l.* a year) to M.P.s begins . . . ,,
Sir George Ferguson Bowen succeeds viscount Canterbury . . . . Feb. 1873
Ministerial crisis: Mr. Kerford premier; Mr. Service's budget; expenditure, 4,500,000*l.*; deficit, about 340,000*l.*; he proposes a moderate free-trade policy; reduction of taxation and a loan; rejected by the parliament; Mr. Kerford resigns, as sir Wm. Stowell, the acting governor, would not dissolve . . . . Aug. 1875
Mr. Graham Berry, premier; would continue protection and tax the richer colonists heavily (a financial *coup d'état*); defeated; resigns Oct. ,,
Sir James M'Culloch forms a coalition ministry, Oct.; proposing tax on income, land, and realised property . . . . Nov. ,,
Passes his income-tax bill with a majority of 3 announced June, 1876
Dispute of government with Messrs. Stevensons, respecting their alleged undervaluing goods for payment of duties; their letters opened March–June, ,,
Elections; triumph of protectionists; sir James M'Culloch resigns; Mr. Berry again premier, May; a land-tax enacted . . . . . Oct. 1877
Legislative council rejects Mr. Berry's appropriations, defence, and exhibition bills, end of Oct. ,,

County court and other judges dismissed by the council; sir G. Bowen, the governor, supports the ministry . . . . . . Jan. 1878
The lower house overrules the council; orders public creditors to be paid on its sole vote, about 13 Feb. ,,
Berry ministry and the lower house predominant March–Aug. ,,
The marquis of Normanby appointed governor, Feb. 1879
Mr. Berry's fruitless visit to England . . . ,, ,,
He introduces a reform bill, Sept.; which is withdrawn . . . . Dec. ,,
Parliament dissolved about 9 Feb.; elections give majority against Mr. Berry, 28 Feb.; his cabinet resign, 2 March; new ministry under Mr. James Service . . . . . . 3 March, 1880
Mr. Service's reform bill rejected, 24 June; dissolution of the assembly, 29 June; the ministry resigns . . . . 14 July, ,,
Mr. Berry forms a cabinet . . . . 28 July, ,,
Ned Kelly and some of his gang of bush-rangers after committing many murders and robberies (since autumn of 1878) captured and sent to Melbourne . . . . . 27, 28 June, ,,
International exhibition at Melbourne, open 1 Oct. ,,
Kelly hanged . . . . 11 Nov. ,,
Vote of confidence in Mr. Berry in parliament lost; sir Brien O'Loghlen forms a ministry . July, 1881
The marquis of Normanby resigns, March; sir Henry Brougham Loch succeeds . . April, 1884
Mr. Service, premier, promotes a confederation bill about 30 June, ,,
Chinese immigrants are now virtually excluded . 1885
Prosperity budgets; surplus 392,000*l.*, 22 July, 1885; 837,415*l.* . . . . . . 24 July, 1888
New ministry under hon. Duncan Gillies, formed 18 Feb. 1886
Naval defence act passed with royal assent, 21, 25 Nov. 1887
Prevalence of strikes among workmen and opposition to Chinese immigration . . autumn, 1888
Parliament opened by Mr. W. C. F. Robinson, acting governor.
(Continued three years prosperity reported), 4 June, 1889
The earl of Hopetoun appointed governor about 22 July, ,,
The government submits to the protectionists; the import duties increased, and new ones imposed . . . . . about 13 Sept. ,,
The irrigation works of Messrs. Chaffey Bros., an American firm on the Murray river, reported successful; sir Henry Parkes protests, claiming both sides of the river for New South Wales, about 13 Sept. ,,
Large subscriptions for the dock labourers of London subscribed, 22,000*l.* up to . . Oct. ,,
The new tariff bill passed by the council, under protest . . . . . . about 31 Oct. ,,
The protectionist budget passed . . 5 Nov. ,,
Departure of sir Henry B. Loch, much honoured (diamond tiara presented to lady Loch by the ladies of Victoria) . . . . . 15 Nov. ,,
Arrival of the earl and countess of Hopetoun, 28 Nov. ,,
Irrigation conference at Melbourne (25 trusts established, 280,000*l.* advanced by the state), 25 March *et seq.* 1890
Mr. D. Gillies' prosperous budget . . 1 Aug. ,,
His ministry defeated by a majority of 20, 30 Oct.; Mr. James Munro forms a ministry . 4 Nov. ,,
Failure of the British Bank of Australia at Melbourne (established April, 1888), reported liabilities, 640,440*l.* . . . . . 14 Sept. 1891
The loan bill for 6,000,000*l.* passed . . 30 Oct. ,,
Brief monetary crisis at Melbourne . . early Dec. ,,
Resignation of Mr. James Munro; new ministry; hon. William Shiels, premier . . 3 Feb. 1892
Distress through want of work; relief works ordered . . . . 4 Feb. ,,
Parliament dissolved, 7 April; new parliament supports the ministry; the labour party defeated, 20 April *et seq.*: parliament opened, 11 May, ,,
Failure of the Mercantile bank of Australia (Melbourne); about 1,000,000*l.* due to English creditors; 2 liquidators appointed at a meeting, 6 Oct. ,,
Deadlock; difference between the two houses respecting new stamp duties, about 19 Oct.; terminated . . . . . . 29 Nov. 1892
Death of sir James MacBain, president of the legislative council, aged 64 . . . 4 Nov. ,,
Death of chief justice George Higinbotham, statesman, &c., aged 65, reported 2 Jan.; succeeded by Mr. Madden . . . . . 6 Jan. 1893
The Shiels ministry defeated (45–42), 18 Jan.; resigns 19 Jan.; Mr. J. B. Patterson forms a ministry, 20 Jan.; policy of retrenchment, 1 Feb. ,,
Tour of the earl of Hopetoun in Australia, &c., 24 Jan. ,,
Messrs. Charles Staples and Sydney Allright, directors of the Anglo-Australian bank, and others, sentenced to imprisonment (Staples, 5 years; Allright fined 100*l.*; Robert Dilley, 2 years) . . . . . 8–24 March, ,,
Directors, manager, and auditors of the Mercantile bank of Australia charged with conspiracy to defraud, 8 March; all acquitted, except sir Matthew Davies and Mr. F. Millidge, 3 May, who are committed for trial, 11 May; prosecution stopped, *nolle prosequi* . . . . 17 May, ,,
Suspension of London Chartered bank of Australia, 25 April, ,,
Banking crisis in Melbourne; 5 bank holidays proclaimed, 30 April; disregarded by some banks, May, ,,
The City of Melbourne bank stopped payment, 16 May, ,,
[See *Australia*, May, 1893.]
Sir M. Davies escapes; Mr. Millidge detained, 31 May; sir M. Davies arrested at Colombo, 16 June; both committed for trial . . 26 June, ,,
Estimated financial deficit in 1892–3 about 1,068,000*l.*; balance of debt, 960,000*l.* . 30 June, ,,
The bank of Victoria and the City of Melbourne bank re-open . . . . . . 19 June, ,,
Meeting of parliament; retrenchment proposed by the governor . . . . . . 28 June, ,,
Other banks re-open . . . . 29 June and July, ,,
Sir M. Davies at Melbourne, July; proceedings stopped . . . . 3 Aug. ,,
The annual budget shows a deficit of 960,188*l.*, 19 July; the issue of 1,250,000 treasury bonds authorized . . . . . . 17 Oct. ,,
The trial of sir Matthew Davies, Mr. F. Millidge, and Mr. Muntz, on charges of fraud, begun, 19 Feb. 1894; acquitted . . . . 7 March, 1894
Annual budget: revenue, 6,719,000*l.*; expenditure, 7,384,000*l.* . . . . 31 July, ,,
The parliament prorogued . . . . 29 Aug. ,,
General election; opposition majority; defeat of free-traders . . . . . . 20 Sept. ,,
Resignation of sir James Patterson; ministry formed by Mr. George Turner . . 27 Sept. ,,
Parliament re-opened; the earl of Hopetoun proposes financial reform and revision of the tariff, &c. . . . . 30 Oct. ,,
Mr. (aft. sir) G. Turner's budget; 528,000*l.* deficit on the year, to be met by direct taxation on land and incomes, &c. . . . . 7 Nov. ,,
The government defeated on a motion for reduction of salaries of members and others . 8 Jan. 1895
The proposed land and income tax bill rejected, 10 Jan. ,,
Salary of future governors reduced to 7,000*l.*, 24 Jan. ,,
Lord Brassey appointed governor . . . Jan. ,,
The income-tax bill passed, 18 Jan.; by the council, 23 Jan. ,,
Parliament prorogued . . . . 19 March, ,,
Departure of the earl and countess of Hopetoun from Melbourne; much regretted . 26 March, ,,
Expenditure to be reduced to avoid extra taxation announced . . . . April, ,,
Revenue for 1894, 6,719,151*l.*, reported . 30 June, ,,
Immediate liquidation of the Melbourne bank ordered . . . . 6 Aug. ,,
Tariff reform bill passed (new duties and some reductions). . . . . 15 Oct. ,,
Arrival of lord and lady Brassey . . . 25 Oct. ,,
Death of sir James Patterson, statesman . 25 Oct. ,,
One man one vote and woman's suffrage bill, passed by the legislative assembly . . . 28 Nov. ,,
Women's suffrage bill rejected by the legislative council . . . . 12 Dec. ,,

Federal enabling bill passed by both houses, 28 Feb. 1896
Parliament opened by lord Brassey with a cheerful speech . . . . 23 June, ,,
Deficit for 1895-96, 76,829*l.*; reported . 16 Sept. ,,
Constitution amendment bill (female suffrage and one man one vote) read 2nd time, after an all night sitting, 9 Oct.; bill passed by the assembly, 29 Oct.; suspended by the council . Dec. ,,
Sir Ferdinand von Mueller, K.C.M.G., F.R.S., born June, 1825, eminent botanist, explorer, 1847 *et seq.*, died . . . . . . 9 Oct. ,,
Strike of marine engineers; traffic suspended, Dec.–Jan. 1897
Sudden death of sir Wm. John Clarke, benefactor, aged 65, at Melbourne . . . . 15 May, ,,
Diamond jubilee celebrations . . 20 June *et seq.* ,,
Parliament opened by lord Brassey, congratulatory addresses to the queen . . . . 23 June, ,,
Long drought relieved by rain, announced 5 July, ,,
Australian commonwealth bill passed by the assembly . . . . 20 Aug. ,,
Parliament dissolved, 28 Sept.; opened . 26 Oct. ,,
Several towns in the Wimmera district wrecked by a cyclone . . . . . . 19 Nov. ,,
A conference of premiers meets at Melbourne, 13 Jan. 1898
Acute distress on account of bush fires, relief fund opened . . . . 16 Jan. ,,
Great heat, renewed bush fires, many homeless, reported . . . . 4 Feb. ,,
General rains, end of the drought . . 25 May, ,,
100,520 votes for, 22,099 against the Commonwealth bill; reported . . . . . 17 June, ,,
Sir James Service, ex-premier, died, aged 76, 12 April, 1899
Sir Frederick McCoy, K.C.M.G., eminent geologist, scientist (founded the Melbourne museum), born, 1823, died . . . . 16 May, ,,
Sir John Madden appointed governor . June, ,,
Royal commission appointed to inquire into technical education . . . . . June, ,,
Parliament opened by the governor; federal enabling bill passed by the assembly, 29 June; by the council . . . . 5 July, ,,
The *referendum* on the Commonwealth bill results in 151,000 for and 9,000 against federation, about 27 July, ,,
Sir G. Turner's budget, surplus 351,427*l.*, income-tax to be reduced one-eighth all round . 9 Aug. ,,
The ministry defeated after an all-night sitting; lord Brassey declines to dissolve parliament; sir G. Turner, premier, resigns . . . . 1 Dec. ,,
Bush fires in the west; great destruction of sheep, reported . . . . 29 Jan. 1900
Parliament prorogued . . . . . 20 Feb. ,,
Victoria subscribes 67,000*l.* to the S.A. war funds, reported . . . . . . 12 March, ,,
Parliament opened by the governor . 27 June, ,,
Budget statement: surplus for 1899, 131,731*l.*, 15 Aug. ,,
Parliament prorogued, 17 Oct.; sir G. Turner's vote of want of confidence carried (51—42), 14 Nov.; he forms a cabinet . . . . . 17 Nov. ,,
Old-age Pension bill (10*s.* weekly to the indigent, over 65) passed by both houses . . 20 Dec. ,,
Federal cabinet meets first in Melbourne, 11 April, 1901
The duke and duchess of Cornwall arrive in Melbourne, see *Australasia* . . 6 May *et seq.* ,,
Sir John Madden opens parliament . 18 June, ,,
Col. sir George Clarke appointed governor, Aug.; arrives . . . . 11 Dec. ,,
Death of lieut.-gen. sir Andrew Clarke, eminent for his services to the colony . . 29 March, 1902
State meeting 250 delegates, urging economy in parliamentary and other expenditure, 18 April, ,,
Parliament opened by sir George Clarke, 27 May, ,,
Mr. Irvine forms a cabinet . . . 9 June, ,,
Railway strike averted by the premier . 15 Aug. ,,
Ministry defeated on the Retrenchment bill (44—33); parliament dissolved . . 9 Sept ,,
Good rainfall reported . . . 10–26 Sept. ,,
The premier issues a manifesto appealing for support in retrenchment and reform . 15 Sept. ,,
Elections: government majority 36, announced, 1 Oct. ,,
Parliament opened by Sir George Clarke . 15 Oct. ,,
Mr. Shiels reports 836,000*l.* deficit for 1902.
Reform bill passed by the assembly; budget deficit 356,278*l.*; increase of income-tax, probate duties, &c., proposed . . . . . 18 Dec. 1902
Ministry reconstructed; Mr. Irvine, premier, att.-gen., and sol.-gen. . . . . . . 7 Feb. 1903
Official statistics show population of Victoria on 31 Dec. 1902, to be 1,205,513, a decrease in 12 months of 3,192, chiefly due to the emigration of young men of the farming class; efforts being made by the minister of lands to stop the exodus by opening up crown lands for selection, 29 April, ,,
Parliament opened by sir George Clarke, who referred to the improved financial position of the colony, the copious rainfall, the railway strike, and various legislative measures, including industrial legislation, and the establishment of a court of industrial appeal; irrigation work on a large scale to be pushed forward . . 7 Sept. ,,

VICTORIA, on Vancouver's island, founded 1857; declared capital of British Columbia, *which see.* Mining convention held here, Feb. 1903.

VICTORIA, see *Hong Kong*, *Vancouver's Island*, *Docks*, *Thames* 1870, *Wrecks* 1852, *British Columbia*, *Navy of England*, 22 June, 1893, and *Mansion-house Fund*, 1893, 1901–03.

VICTORIA, a British colony in Ambas bay, on the West African coast, originally a Baptist missionary settlement, annexed 19 July, 1884.

Ceremoniously transferred to Germany by consul Hewett and annexed to Cameroons . 28 March, 1887

VICTORIA AND ALBERT MUSEUM, see *South Kensington Museum.*

VICTORIA COUNTY HISTORY, edited by Mr. Doubleday, vol. i., of Norfolk, issued, Aug. 1901.

VICTORIA CROSS, an order of merit, instituted to reward the gallantry of persons of all ranks in the army and navy, 29 Jan. 1856. It is a Maltese cross made of Russian cannon from Sebastopol. The queen conferred the honour on 62 persons (of both services) on Friday, 26 June, 1857; and on many of the Indian army, 2 Aug. 1858, and on many since in relation to recent wars. *Victoria and Albert Royal Order* of Knighthood for ladies, India, instituted 10 Feb. 1862, enlarged 1864, 1865, and 1880. *Royal Victorian Order* of Knighthood, England, instituted by queen Victoria, to confer honour on persons, British and foreign, who have rendered service to herself, 23 April, 1896.

VICTORIA EMBANKMENT, &c., see under *Thames.*

VICTORIA INSTITUTE, or **PHILOSOPHICAL SOCIETY OF GREAT BRITAIN**, established 22 June, 1865; its primary object being the attempt to reconcile apparent discrepancies between Christianity and science. Annual meetings.

VICTORIA NYANZA, a lake in E. Central Africa, 300 miles long, 90 miles broad, discovered by capt. John H. Speke in 1858, and explored by him and capt. J. A. Grant in 1862; circumnavigated by Mr. H. M. Stanley in 1875. Col. J. H. Speke was accidentally killed by his own gun, 15 Sept. 1864. Col. J. A. Grant died 11 Feb. 1892. The steamer *William Mackinnon* launched on the lake, 15 Nov. 1900. The Uganda railway completed here, 19 Dec. 1901.

ALBERT NYANZA, 140 miles long and 40 miles broad, situated 80 miles N.W. of Victoria Nyanza. It was discovered by capts. Speke and Grant, 1862, and visited by Mr. (afterwards sir) Samuel White Baker in 1864 (see *Nile* and *Africa*).

ALBERT EDWARD NYANZA was discovered by Mr. H. M. Stanley in 1887, and named in 1889. These lakes are considered to be reservoirs from which the Nile flows.

VICTORIA PARK (E. London), was originated by an act passed in 1841, which enabled her majesty's commissioners of woods and forests to purchase certain lands for a royal park, with the sum of 72,000*l.* raised by the same act, by the sale of York-house to the duke of Sutherland. The act described the land to be so purchased, containing 290 acres, situate in the parishes of St. John, Hackney; St. Matthew, Bethnal-green; and St. Mary, Stratford-le-bow. The park was completed and opened to the public in 1845. Lady (then Miss) Burdett-Coutts presented a handsome drinking fountain, and was present at its inauguration, 28 June, 1862. The park was visited by queen Victoria, 2 April, 1873; and in memory of her reception, she presented a clock and peal of bells to St. Mark's church; recognition service, 21 May, 1874. See *Parks*.

VICTORIA RAILWAY BRIDGE (tubular), over the St. Lawrence, Montreal, erected by Mr. James Hodges, under the superintendence of Mr. Robert Stephenson and Mr. A. M. Ross, engineers, was begun 24 May, 1854, and formally opened by the prince of Wales, 25 Aug. 1860. It forms part of the Grand Trunk railway, which connects Canada and the seaboard states of North America. The length is about sixty yards less than two English miles, and about 7½ times longer than Waterloo bridge, and ten times longer than new Chelsea bridge; the height sixty feet between the summer level of the river and the under surface of the central tube. It is supported by 24 piers. The cost was 1,700,000*l.* On 5 Jan. 1855, while constructing, the bridge was much injured by floating ice, but the stonework remained firm.

VICTORIA REGIA, the magnificent water-lily brought to this country from Guiana by sir Robert Schomburgk, in 1838, and named after the queen. Fine specimens are at the Botanic Gardens at Kew, Regent's Park, &c. It was grown in the open air in 1855, by Messrs. Weeks, of Chelsea.

Mr. J. B. Sowerby, sec. of the Roy. Botanic soc., Regent's Park, was photographed seated on a leaf floating on the water, Sept. 1895.

VICTORIA STEAMER; sunk; see *Wrecks*, 24 May, 1881.

VICTORIAN EXHIBITION, illustrating the reign of queen Victoria from 1837 to 1887, was opened in the New Gallery, Regent street, 2 Dec. 1891, and closed 2 April, 1892. The queen was patron, and the prince of Wales was active in the management. It succeeded the Tudor, Stuart, and Guelph exhibitions, *which see*.

The Victorian exhibition illustrated events in the life of the royal family, and the progress of the nation in politics, philanthropy, literature, science, art, and manufactures, by means of portraits, pictures, statues, relics, books, models, costumes, &c.

VICTORIAN ERA Exhibition at Earl's-court, fine art, &c., opened by the duke of Cambridge, 24 May, 1897. Another opened, see *Crystal Palace*, 6 May, 1897.

VICTORIA UNIVERSITY constituted for men and women with identical privileges; combines Owens college, Manchester, and others; the charter was granted in April; the first council met, 14 July, 1880.

Jubilee fund closed 31 May, 1902; nearly 103,000*l.*; total capital, 1,070,363*l.*

VICTORY, MAN-OF-WAR, of 100 guns, the finest first-rate ship in the navy of England, was lost in a violent tempest near the race of Alderney, and its admiral, sir John Balchen, and 100 gentlemen's sons, and the whole crew, consisting of 1000 men, perished, 8 October, 1744.—The *Victory*, the flag-ship of Nelson, at the battle of Trafalgar, 21 Oct. 1805, has been kept in a condition of fine preservation at Portsmouth. The historic old vessel was much damaged by the *Neptune*, an old iron-clad, colliding with her, 23 Oct. 1903 (see *Navy*).

VICTUALLERS, an ancient trade in England. The Vintners company of London was founded 1437; their hall rebuilt in 1823.

None shall sell less than one full quart of the best beer or ale for 1*d.* and two quarts of the smaller sort for 1*d.* 1603
The power of *licensing* public-houses was granted to sir Giles Mompesson and sir Francis Mitchel . 1621
The number in England then was about 13,000 . ,,
In Great Britain about 76,000 public-houses . . 1790
England, 59,335; Scotland, 15,081; Ireland, 14,080; total, 88,496 in 1850
In England and Wales, 23,028 in 1889
Public-houses allowed to be opened on Sundays from 1 o'clock till 3, and from 5 till 11 P.M. . . 1828
The prescribed time enlarged 1855
127,352 licences were issued for the sale of beer, cider, and perry in the United Kingdom, producing a revenue of 304,688*l.*; and 93,936 licences for the sale of spirits: revenue 560,557*l.* . . 1858
Licensed Victuallers' School established . . . 1803
Licensed Victuallers' Asylum established 22 Feb. 1827
Between 100,000,000*l.* and 150,000,000*l.* said to be invested in the liquor trade. The licensed victuallers actively opposed Mr. Bruce's licensing bill, which was withdrawn . . summer of 1871
Licensed Victuallers in the United Kingdom 99,465 1872
New licensing act, regulating hours of opening and shutting, &c., passed and came into execution 10 Aug. ,,
[It caused much irritation, and was said to have conduced to the fall of the Gladstone ministry, 1874.]
Public-houses in Ireland closed on Sundays, by act passed . . . . 16 Aug. 1878
Payment for licenses raised . . . . June, 1880
Sale of intoxicating liquors to children act . . 1901
Important licensing act, 1902 (royal assent, 8 Aug.), containing provisions respecting the sale of liquor to habitual drunkards, and the control of retail off-licences by the licensing justices, came into operation . . . . 1 Jan. 1903
Public-house trust movement active, 1901–3; 34 public-house trust companies registered in Great Britain and Ireland in 1902.

VICTUALLING OFFICE (London), for managing the victualling of the royal navy, was instituted Dec. 1663. The number of commissioners was five, afterwards seven, and then reduced to six. The various departments on Tower-hill, St. Katharine's, and Rotherhithe, were removed to Deptford in Aug. 1785, and the office to Somerset-house, 1783. In 1832 the office of commissioners was abolished, and the victualling-office made one of five departments under the lords of the admiralty.

VIENNA (the Roman *Vindobona*), was capital of the margraviate of Austria, 984; virtual capital of the German empire, 1273; since 1806, capital of the Austrian dominions only. Population in 1857, 476,222; 1872, 901,000; 1880, 1,103,857; 1890, 1,364.548; 1900, 1,656,662; see *Austria*.

Vienna made an imperial city 1136
Walled and enlarged, with the ransom paid for Richard I. of England, 40,000*l.* 1194

Besieged by the Turks under Solyman the Magnificent, with an army of 300,000 men; but he was forced to raise the siege with the loss of 70,000 of his best troops 1529
Besieged by the Turks . . . . . July, 1683
The siege raised by John Sobieski, king of Poland, who defeats the Turkish army of 100,000, 12 Sept. ,,
Vienna taken by the French under prince Murat, 14 Nov. 1805, evacuated . . . . 12 Jan. 1806
Captured by Napoleon I. . . . . 13 May, 1809
Restored on the conclusion of peace . 14 Oct. ,,
Congress of sovereigns at Vienna . . Nov. 1814
Imperial Academy of Sciences founded . . . 1846
The revolt in Hungary induces an insurrection in Vienna . . . . . . 13 March, 1848
Conferences respecting the Russo-Turkish war held at Vienna* 1853-5
The fortifications demolished, and the city enlarged and beautified 1857-8
The imperial parliament (Reichsrath) assembles here . . . . 31 May, 1860
The Prussians encamp near Vienna; state of siege proclaimed . . . . . . July, 1866
Visited by the sultan . . . . 27 July, 1867
New palace of the fine arts founded by the emperor about 18 Sept. 1868
The great international exhibition opened by the emperor; the prince of Wales and many dignitaries present . . . . . 1 May, 1873
[The enormous building with annexes was designed by Mr. Scott Russell, most ably supported by the Austrian engineers; the grand central rotunda 312 feet in diameter, with lofty dome, is an exaggerated Pantheon, suspended on iron girders in place of masonry, and dwarfs St. Peter's at Rome.]
Great financial failures; affect all Europe. 9 May, ,,
Visit of the czar, 1-7 June; of the shah of Persia 30 July, ,,
Prizes to exhibitors presented by the archduke Albert . . . . 18 Aug. ,,
Visit of Victor Emmanuel, king of Italy, 17-22 Sept.; of the emperor of Germany 17–23 Oct. ,,
Waterworks inaugurated by the emperor 24 Oct. ,,
The exhibition closed . . . . . 2 Nov. ,,
New bed of the Danube inaugurated . 30 May, 1876
Johann Zich throws a stone at Russian ambassador 19 Jan. 1882
International art exhibition opened . 1 April, ,,
The Ring theatre destroyed by fire, caused by the fall of a large spirit lamp, 447 persons perished out of about 2000, 8 Dec. 1881; [accusations of culpable negligence]; imprisonment decreed . . . . 16 May, ,,
Riot of shoemakers and others suppressed by military . . . . 7–8 Nov. ,,
International exhibition of graphic art, &c. 15 Sept.–1 Nov. 1883
Electric exhibition . . . . 16 Aug.–3 Nov. ,,
Anarchist conspiracy to burn Vienna on the nights of 3, 4 Oct.; detected; premises in the suburbs fired, 27 Sept.; 17 men arrested and houses searched, bombs, &c., discovered, and police disguises; announced . . . . 10 Oct. 1883
Great international hygienic congress opened by crown prince Rudolph . . . 26 Sept. ,,
Bi-centenary of the siege raised by John Sobieski, king of Poland, celebrated . . 12 Sept. ,,
The imperial parliament meets in its new grand house early in . . . . . Dec. ,,
Much disaffection; see *Austria* . . . . Jan. 1884
Awful storm; destruction of life and property 10 Dec. ,,
Joseph Pircher, a gilder, secretly climbs up the steeple of St. Stephen's cathedral and places a banner on the cross (432 German feet high) and descends safely . . . . 17, 18 Aug. 1886
The emperor retires, 17 May; returns . Aug. ,,
A second insurrection: Count Latour, the war minister, is murdered . . . . 6 Oct. ,,
The emperor again takes flight . . 7 Oct. ,,
Vienna is bombarded by Windischgrätz and Jellachich, 28 Oct.; its capitulation . 30 Oct ,,
International art exhibition opened . 3 March, 1888
Grand monument of the empress queen Maria Theresa inaugurated in the presence of the emperor and empress . . . . 13 May, ,,
National industrial exhibition opened in honour of the 40th year of the emperor's reign, 14th May; closed . . . . 31 Oct. ,,
Grand funeral of Beethoven on the removal of his remains from Währing cemetery to the central cemetery at Simmerung . . . 22 June, ,,
Goldsmiths' exhibition opened . . . 22 April, 1889
Strike of tram-car men, anti-semitic rioting suppressed by the military; close of strike, 22–24 April, ,,
The grand Natural History museum opened by the emperor . . . . 10 Aug. ,,
Strike of about 15,000 masons for increased pay, 31 March, 1890
General agitation, with intimidation, of workmen, April, ,,
Riots suppressed by military . 8 April *et seq.* ,,
The great enlargement of the city by the incorporation of the suburbs ordered, Dec. 1890; completed . . . . Dec. 1891
Frank Schneider and Rosalie his wife, sentenced to death for the cruel murder of several servant maids, whom they decoyed into a wood near Vienna, June *et seq.*, 16–29 Jan.; he is executed (she is imprisoned for life) . . 17 March, 1892
International musical and dramatic exhibition, president, arch-duke Charles Louis, opened by the emperor . . . . 7 May, ,,
Visit of prince Bismarck, 19–23 June; marriage of his son Herbert . . . . . 21 June, ,,
Many strikes, early May; labour riots, 22 Aug. 1893
International fine art exhibition, opened, 6 March, 1894
International exhibition, relating to military and sporting affairs, &c., opened by the emperor 20 April, ,,
About 50,000 men on strike . . . . May, ,,
Destructive hailstorm, 4 deaths, much property and trees destroyed, birds killed . 7 June, ,,
Monumental triumphal arch commemorating the deliverance of Vienna by John Sobieski in 1683; unveiled by the emperor Francis Joseph in St. Stephen's cathedral . . . 13 Sept. ,,
Municipal election; Dr. Lüger, anti-semitic leader, elected burgomaster. anti-semitic demonstrations against the liberals; the council dissolved; an imperial commission appointed; re-election deferred; government censures of demonstrations, 29, 30 May, 1895; Dr. Lüger re-elected, 29 Oct.; his election not sanctioned by the emperor . . . . 5 Nov. 1895
Dr. Lüger re-elected; the town council dissolved; Dr. Friebeis appointed imperial commissary; rioting suppressed . . . . 13 Nov. ,,
Disorderly scene in the reichsrath . . 16 Nov. ,,
Municipal election: anti-semite victory, 5 March, 1896
Dr. Lüger re-elected burgomaster, 18 April; resigned . . . . 27 April, ,,
Socialist demonstrations in the Prater, suppressed by the military . . . . . . 1 May, ,,

* A conference of the four great powers, England, France, Austria, and Prussia, was held 24 July, when a note was agreed on and transmitted for acceptance to St. Petersburg and Constantinople, 31 July. This note was accepted by the czar, 10 Aug., but the sultan required modifications, which were rejected by Russia, 7 Sept. The sultan's note (31 Dec.) contained four points:—1. The promptest possible evacuation of the principalities. 2. Revision of the treaties. 3. Maintenance of religious privileges to the communities of all confessions. 4. A definite settlement of the convention respecting the holy places. It was approved by the four powers, and the conferences closed on 16 Jan. 1854.—A new conference of plenipotentiaries, from Great Britain (lord John Russell), France (M. Drouyn de l'Huys), Austria (count Buol), Turkey (Arif Effendi), and Russia (count Gortschakoff), took place, March, 1854. Two points, the protectorate of the principalities and the free navigation of the Danube, were agreed to; but the proposals of the powers as to the reduction of the Russian power in the Black Sea were rejected by the czar, and the conference closed, 5 June, 1854. The English and French envoys' assent to the Austrian propositions was not approved of by their governments, and they both resigned their official positions.

Herr Strobach elected burgomaster; Dr. Lüger, deputy . . . . . . 6 May, 1896
Visit of the czar . . . . . 27 Aug. *et seq.* „
Agrarian conference, 10,000 present . 13 Sept. „
Exhibition commemorative of the centenary of the birth of Franz Schubert, opened by the emperor, 20 Jan. 1897
Municipal elections: defeat of the anti-semites, 22 March, „
Dr. Lüger re-elected burgomaster . . 8 April, „
Exhibition of M. Verestchagin's pictures (Napoleon series) . . . . Nov. „
Fire at the Stock exchange . . . 20 April, 1898
Jubilee of the emperor's reign, he opens the exhibition . . . . . 8 May, „
Anti-semitic demonstration, over 5,000 present, 2 Oct. „
Bubonic plague in the Pathological institute, some deaths; Dr. Müller died, age 32 . 23 Oct. „
Visit of the czar . . . . 29 Sept. 1903
Death of Dr. Falb, eminent meteorologist, 30 Sept. „

TREATIES OF VIENNA.

1. The treaty between the emperor of Germany and the king of Spain, by which they confirmed to each other such parts of the Spanish dominions as they were respectively possessed of; and by a private treaty the emperor engaged to employ a force to procure the restoration of Gibraltar to Spain, and to use means for placing the Pretender on the throne of Great Britain. Spain guaranteed the Pragmatic Sanction, 30 April, 1725.
2. Treaty of alliance between the emperor of Germany, Charles VI., George II., king of Great Britain, and the states of Holland, by which the Pragmatic Sanction was guaranteed, and the disputes as to the Spanish succession terminated. (Spain acceded to the treaty on the 22nd of July.) Signed 16 March, 1731.
3. Treaty of peace between the emperor Charles VI. of Germany and the king of France, Louis XV., by which the latter power agreed to guarantee the Pragmatic Sanction, and Lorraine was ceded to France. Signed 18 Nov. 1738; see *Pragmatic Sanction*.
4. Treaty between Napoleon I. of France and Francis (II. of Germany) I. of Austria, by which Austria ceded to France the Tyrol, Dalmatia, and other territories, which were shortly afterwards declared to be united to France under the title of the Illyrian Provinces, and engaged to adhere to the prohibitory system adopted towards England by France and Russia. 14 Oct. 1809.
5. Treaty between Great Britain, Austria, Russia, and Prussia, confirming the principles on which they had acted by the treaty of Chaumont, 1 Mar. 1814. Signed 25 March, 1815.
6. Treaty between the king of the Netherlands on the one part, and Great Britain, Russia, Austria, and Prussia on the other, agreeing to the enlargement of the Dutch territories, and vesting the sovereignty in the house of Orange. 31 May, 1815.
7. Treaty by which Denmark ceded Swedish Pomerania and Rugen to Prussia, in exchange for Lauenburg, 4 June, 1815.
8. Commercial treaty for twelve years between Austria and Prussia. Signed at Vienna, 19 Feb. 1853.
9. Treaty for the maintenance of Turkey, by the representatives of Great Britain, France, Austria, and Russia. Signed 9 April, 1854.
10. Treaty between Austria and Prussia and Denmark, by which Denmark ceded the duchies. 30 Oct. 1864.
11. Treaty of peace between Austria and Italy; Venetia given up to Italy. 3 Oct. 1866.

VIENNE, the ancient Vienna Allobrogum (S.E. France). Here the emperor Valentinian II. was put to death by Arbogastes, 15 May, 392, and a short reaction in favour of paganism followed. Vienne was capital of the kingdom of Burgundy in 432 and 879, and sometimes gave its name to the kingdom. A general council was held here in 1311. Vienne was annexed to the French monarchy, 1448.

VIGILANCE ASSOCIATION, see under *National*.

VIGILANCE MURDER ASSOCIATION, see *Ireland*, 1883.

VIGO (N.W. Spain) was attacked and burned by the English, under Drake and Norris in 1589. Sir George Rooke, with the combined English and Dutch fleets, attacked the French fleet and the Spanish galleons in the port of Vigo, when several men-of-war and galleons were taken, and many destroyed, and abundance of plate and other valuable effects fell into the hands of the conquerors, 12 Oct. 1702. Vigo was taken by lord Cobham in 1719, but relinquished after raising contributions. It was again taken by the British, 27 March, 1809.

VIKINGS. Scandinavian chiefs, Swedes, Danes, and Norsemen, who in the 4th century migrated—eastward, to the countries beyond the Baltic; westward and southward, chiefly to the British isles.

M. Paul B. Du Chaillu (died 30 April, 1903), in his "Viking Age," describes the Vikings as the ancestors of "the English-speaking nations," Oct. 1889

VIKING CLUB, founded in 1892 as the Orkney, Shetland, and Northern Society, to promote an interest in the North, and its literature and antiquities. To promote these objects, meetings are held for the discussion of papers on Northern history, literature, art, music, archæology, folk-lore, and anthropology; the formation of a library of books, MSS., maps, &c., relating to Northern history and antiquities, and the translation of Sagas and other works on Northern subjects, and the exhibition of Northern antiquities. Proceedings (Saga-book) are published; vol. iii., part ii., Jan. 1903.

VILLA FRANCA. Near here, and Llerena, Spain, the British cavalry, under sir Stapleton Cotton, defeated the French cavalry under marshal Soult, 11 April, 1812.—VILLA FRANCA, a small port on the Mediterranean, near Genoa, was bought for a steam-packet station by a Russian company, about Aug. 1858, which caused some political excitement.—At VILLA FRANCA, in Lombardy, the emperors of France and Austria met, on 11 July, 1859 (after the battle of Solferino), and on 12 July signed the preliminaries of peace, the basis of the treaty of Zurich (*which see*).

VILLA VICIOSA. 1. in Portugal. Here the Portuguese, under the French general Schomberg, defeated the Spaniards, 1665. 2. in Castile, Spain. Here the struggle for the Spanish crown was decided in favour of Philip V. by Vendôme's victory over Staremberg and the Austrians, 10 Dec. 1710.

VILLAIN, or VILLEIN, see *Slavery in England*.

VILLE DU HAVRE, French Atlantic mail steamer, 5,100 tons, sailed from New York for Havre, 15 Nov. 1873; was run into by a Glasgow clipper, *Lochearn*, about 2 a.m., 22 Nov., and sank in twelve minutes; 226 out of 313 persons perished.

The crew of the *Lochearn* rescued 87, who were conveyed to Cardiff by the American vessel *Tremountain*, capt. Urquhart, arriving there 1 Dec. 1873
The *Lochearn*, beginning to sink, 28 Nov., was abandoned by her crew, who were rescued by the *British Queen*, and brought to Plymouth 7 Dec. „
On judicial examination, the *Lochearn* was exonerated in England, but censured in France Jan. 1874

VILLETA (Paraguay, South America). Here Lopez and the Paraguayans were totally defeated by the Brazilians and their allies, 11 Dec. 1868. Lopez and 200 men fled; 3000 prisoners were made; and the war was considered to be ended.

VIMIERA (in Portugal), where the British and Spanish forces, under sir Arthur Wellesley, defeated the French, under marshal Junot, duke of Abrantes, 21 Aug. 1808. The attack, made with great bravery, was gallantly repulsed; it was repeated by Kellermann at the head of the French reserve, which was also repulsed. The French, charged with the bayonet, withdrew on all points in confusion, leaving many prisoners.

VINCENNES a strong castle near Paris; a residence of the French kings from the 12th to the 14th centuries. Henry V. of England died at the Bois de Vincennes, 31 Aug. 1422. At the fosse of the castle, Louis duc d'Enghien was shot by order of Napoleon, after a hasty trial, early on the morning of 22 March, 1804.

VINCENT, CAPE ST. (S. W. Portugal). See *Cape St. Vincent* and *Rodney's Victories*.

VINCENT, ST. (West Indies), long a neutral island; but at the peace of 1763, the French agreed that the right to it should be vested in the English. The latter soon after engaged in a war against the Caribs, on the windward side of the island, who were obliged to consent to a peace, by which they ceded a large tract of land to the British crown. In 1779 the Caribs greatly contributed to the reduction of this island by the French, who, however, restored it in 1783. In 1795 the French landed some troops, and again instigated the Caribs to an insurrection, which was not subdued for several months. Mt. Soufrière (abt. 3,623 ft. high) erupted 24 April, 1718; and again, 1 May, 1812, a violent eruption took place, 3 craters opened, 1,295 dead bodies found, total deaths, 1,565, 100 hopelessly injured, 3,000 homeless, 16 sq. miles covered with lava. ash fell on Barbadoes, 90 miles off; 7 May, 1902, disturbances took place in the adjoining islands, and earthquake shocks were frequent at Kingstown and Georgetown, whilst the village of Wallibon partly sank, and that of Richmond rose, 17 May (*Nature*, 27 May, 1902); eruptions continued, violent, 18, 24 May; earthquake shocks and another eruption, 10 July (see *Martinique*, 8 May, 1902); slighter ones, 21 July *et seq.*; violent, 3, 5, 21 Sept., 16 Oct.; Messrs. Quinton, Powell, and Foster ascended the mountain, while in a state of activity, 28 Oct. 1902. Population in 1861, 31,755; in 1881. 40,548; in 1891, 41,054; in 1901, 47,548; see *Windward Isles*.

Great destruction of life and property by a hurricane, 16 Aug. 1886; again, 300 deaths, 10-12 Sept. 1898. See *West Indies*.

VINCENT DE PAUL, ST., CHARITABLE SOCIETY founded in 1833, in France, by twelve young men. It extends its extremely beneficial operations into Britain. Its power excited the jealousy of the French government, which suppressed its central committee of Paris, in Oct. 1861. St. Vincent de Paul was born, 1576; established the congregation of Lazarists, or Vincentines, 1625; Sisters of Charity, 1634; a foundling hospital, 1648. He died 1660.

VINCY, N. France. Here Charles Martel defeated the Neustrians, 21 May, 717, and acquired their country.

VINE. The vine was planted by Noah, 2347 B.C. *Gen.* ix. 20. A colony of vine-dressers from Phocea, in Ionia, settled at Marseilles, and instructed the South Gauls in tillage, vine-dressing, and commerce, about 600 B.C. Some think that vines are aborigines of Languedoc, Provence, and Sicily, and that they grew spontaneously on the Mediterranean shores of Italy, France, and Spain. The vine was carried into Champagne, and part of Germany, by the emperor Probus, about A.D. 279. The vine and sugar-cane were planted in Madeira in 1420. In the gardens of Hampton-court palace is an old and celebrated vine, said to surpass any known vine in Europe; see *Grapes* and *Wine*. The Tokay vines were planted in 1350.

Vine Disease. In the spring of 1845, Mr. E. Tucker, of Margate, observed a fungus (since named *Oïdium Tuckeri*) on grapes in the hot-houses of Mr. Slater, of Margate. It is a whitish mildew, and totally destroys the fruit.

The spores of this *oïdium* were found in the vineries at Versailles in 1847. The disease soon reached the trellised vines, and in 1850 many lost all their produce.

In 1852, it spread over France, Italy, Spain, Syria, and in Zante and Cephalonia attacked the currants, reducing the crop to one-twelfth of the usual amount.

Through its ravages, the wine manufacture in Madeira ceased for several years.

Many attempts have been made to arrest the progress of this disease, but without much effect. Sulphur dust is the most efficacious remedy.

The disease had much abated in France, Portugal, and Madeira, in 1863. In 1862 Californian vines were introduced into the two latter.

New malady (microscopic insect, *phylloxera vastatrix*) in S. France, observed 1865

Remedy, sulphuret of carbon, recommended by M. Dumas . . . . Aug. 1873

Not successful; great destruction; 12,000*l.* offered for a remedy . . . . July, 1876

Phylloxera prevalent in Malaga and France; reported July, Aug. 1878; Portugal, Italy, Spain; Sept.-Nov. 1879; appears in Victoria, Australia, Nov. 1880

Phylloxera congress at Bordeaux . . 10-15 Oct. 1881

The phylloxera is said to be exterminated in Switzerland by fire . . . . Nov. 1882

Phylloxera ravaging vines on the Douro; consequent emigrations to Brazil . . . . 7 Feb. 1884

Disappearance of the phylloxera in W. France through the experimental researches of M. Pasteur: prosperous vintages reported . . 1883-91

VINEGAR. The ancients had several kinds, which they used for drink. The Roman soldiers were accustomed to take it in their marches. The Bible represents Boaz, a rich citizen of Bethlehem, as providing vinegar for his reapers (1312 B.C.), a custom still prevalent in Spain and Italy.

VINEGAR-HILL (near Enniscorthy, in Wexford, S.E. Ireland). Here the Irish rebels, headed by father John, a priest, encamped and committed many outrages on the surrounding country. They were gradually surrounded by the British troops, commanded by Lake, 21 June, 1798, and after a fierce struggle, with much slaughter, totally dispersed.

VINTNERS, see *Victuallers*.

VIOL AND VIOLIN. The lyre of the Greeks became our harp, and the viol of the middle ages became the violin. The violin is mentioned as early as 1200, in the legendary life of St. Christopher. It was introduced into England, some say, by Charles II. Straduarius (or Stradivarius) of Cremona, was a renowned violin-maker (1700 to 1722). The eminent violinist Paganini visited England, 1831; died at Nice, 27 May, 1840. Mr. J. T. Carrodus, an eminent English violinist, died, aged 59, 12 July, 1895. "Old Violins," by the rev. H. R. Haweis (died 29 Jan. 1901), published 1899.

VIRGINALS; an early keyed instrument of the kind termed clavichords; used in the 16th and

17th centuries; played on by queen Elizabeth and Mary queen of Scots. According to Johnson, it owed its name to young women being the usual performers. Tallis, Morley, Purcell, Gibbons, and Bull composed for this instrument.

VIRGINIA, see *Rome*, 449 B.C.

VIRGINIA, the first British settlement in North America, was discovered by John Cabot in 1497, and was taken possession of for Raleigh, and named after the virgin-queen Elizabeth, 13 July, 1584. Vain attempts were made to settle it in 1585. Two expeditions were formed by patent in 1606, and others in 1610. In 1626 it reverted to the crown; and a more permanent colony was established soon afterwards. George Washington was delegate for Virginia in the congress of 1774. Eastern Virginia seceded from the Union, 25 April, 1861, but Western Virginia declared for the Union, 13 Feb. and elected a governor, 20 Feb. 1861; became a state 1863. Virginia was a chief seat of the war. The state was readmitted to the congress, Jan.-Feb. 1870; see *United States* and *Richmond*. Population in 1880, 1,512,565; 1890, 1,655,980; 1900, 1,854,184; capital, Richmond. Western Virginia, population, 1880, 618,457; 1890, 762,794; 1900, 518,103; capital, Wheeling. By the overflowing of a lake near Staunton, houses were swept away and many lives lost, reported 1 Oct. 1896. Cloudburst and bursting of a dam in the west, about 100 deaths, about 22 June, 1901.

VIRGINIA CITY, see *Nevada*.

VIRGIN ISLANDS (West Indies), an eastern group discovered by Columbus (1494): Virgin Gorda, Tortola, Anegada, &c., and the Danish Isles, St. Thomas, Santa Cruz, and St. John. Population of the British possessions in 1891 was 4,639; 1901, 4,908. See *Leeward Isles*.

Tortola settled by Dutch buccaneers about 1648; expelled by the English (who have held it since) . 1666

St. Thomas settled by Danes 1672, and St. John a few years after; held by the British 1801-2; 1807-15; proposed sale to the United States for 1,500,500*l*. to be made a "territory." Danish proclamation, 25 Oct. 1867; purchase declined by U.S. senate . . . . 23 March, May, 1870

By a dreadful hurricane off St. Thomas, the Royal Mail steamers *Rhone* and *Wye* were entirely wrecked; the *Conway* and *Derwent*, and above 50 other vessels, driven ashore; about 1000 persons said to have perished . . . . . . 29 Oct. 1867

Much suffering was occasioned in Tortola; houses blown down or unroofed, &c. (a report reached London that the isle was submerged).

Earthquake at St. Thomas's and other isles; much damage; few lives lost . . . . Nov. „

Santa Cruz. A negro insurrection, in which M. Fontaine, a planter, was killed; Fredrikstadt and 36 out of 50 sugar plantations were burnt, and about 3000 whites rendered homeless. During the suppression by col. Garde, the governor, about 200 negroes were killed . . . . . 1-5 Oct. 1878

VIRGINIUS, American blockade-runner, see *Cuba*, 1873.

VIRGIN MARY. The Assumption of the Virgin is a festival in the Greek and Latin churches, in honour of the miraculous ascent of Mary into heaven, according to their belief, 15 Aug. A.D. 45. The Presentation of the Virgin is a feast celebrated 21 Nov., said to have been instituted among the Greeks in the 11th century; its institution in the West is ascribed to pope Gregory XI. 1372; see *Annunciation* and *Conception, Immaculate*.

VIRTUE, LEAGUE OF, see *Tugendbund*.

VISCONTI, the name of a noble Italian family, which ruled in Milan from about 1277 to 1447; the heiress of the family was married to Francesco Sforza, who became duke 1450.

VISCOUNT (*Vice Comes*), anciently the name of the deputy of an earl. The first viscount in England created by patent was John, lord Beaumont, whom Henry VI. created viscount Beaumont, giving him precedence above all barons, 10 Feb. 1440. *Ashmole*. This title is of older date in Ireland and France. John Barry, lord Barry, was made viscount Buttevant, in Ireland, 9 Rich. II. 1385. *Beatson*.

VISIBLE SPEECH, a term applied by Mr. Alex. Melville Bell to his "Universal Self-Interpreting Physiological Alphabet," comprising thirty symbols representing the conformations of the mouth when uttering sounds. He stated that about fifty different types would be required to print all known languages with these symbols. He expounded his system to the Society of Arts, London, 14 March, 1866; and published a book in 1867.

VISIGOTHS, separated from the Ostrogoths about 330; see *Goths*. The emperor Valens, about 369, admitted them into the Roman territories upon the condition of their serving when wanted in the Roman armies; and Theodosius the Great permitted them to form distinct corps commanded by their own officers. In 400, under Alaric, they invaded Italy, and in 410 took Rome. They founded their kingdom of Toulouse, 414; conquered the Alani, and extended their rule into Spain, 414; expelled the Romans in 468; and finally were themselves conquered by the Saracens under Muza, in 711, when their last king, Roderic, was defeated and slain; see *Spain* for a list of the Visigothic kings. Their rule in France ended with their defeat by Clovis at Vouglé, in 507.

VISITATIONS, see *Heralds*.

VITAL FORCE, defined by Humboldt "as an unknown cause preventing the elements from obeying their primitive affinities." This theory is now opposed by many physiologists, and animal motion is attributed to muscular and nervous irritability, illustrated by the researches of Galvani, Humboldt, sir Charles Bell, Marshall Hall, and others. The subject has been much discussed by the late professor Huxley and other eminent physiologists.

VITI ISLES, see *Fiji*.

VITTORIA (N. Spain), the site of a victory obtained by Wellington over the French army commanded by Joseph Bonaparte, king of Spain, and marshal Jourdan, 21 June, 1813. The hostile armies were nearly equal, from 70,000 to 75,000 each. After a long and fearful battle, the French were driven, towards evening, through the town of Vittoria, and in their retreat were thrown into irretrievable confusion. The British loss was 22 officers and 479 men killed; 167 officers and 2640 men wounded. Marshal Jourdan lost 151 pieces of cannon, 451 waggons of ammunition, all his baggage, provisions, cattle, and treasure, with his bâton as a marshal of France. Continuing the pursuit on the 25th, Wellington took Jourdan's only remaining gun. Population, 1887, 27,660; 1897, 30,514.

VIVARIUM, see *Aquavivarium*.

VIVISECTION, physiological experiments upon living animals, as practised by William Harvey, John Hunter, and other eminent physiologists, it is said, with good results. The societies for the prevention of cruelty to animals in Dresden and Paris in 1859 requested the opinion of a committee of eminent scientific men on the merits of the knowledge thus acquired. Their judgment was not unanimous. The London society took up the question in 1860; and printed a pamphlet by Mr. G. Macilwain against vivisection. In Aug. 1862 an international conference to discuss the question was held at the Crystal Palace, Sydenham. The subject was discussed in 1866, and a prize awarded by the London society. Sir Charles Bell's opinion of vivisection was, that it either obscured the subject it was meant to illustrate, or misled men into practical errors of the most serious character.

Discussion revived in consequence of the prosecution of Dr. Schiff in Florence, who justified vivisection when chloroform or any other anæsthetic is used 1873-6
Rival societies: 1. Society for the abolition of vivisection, 1875; Mr. G. R. Jesse, the founder (died June, 1898), leaves 10,000*l.* to the society; 2. International Association for total suppression of vivisection 1876
Commission (viscount Cardwell, professor Huxley, and others) to inquire into the practice, appointed 23 June, 1875; report signed, 8 Jan.; published, March, 1876; a bill to regulate vivisection (cruelty to animals act) brought into parliament; strongly opposed by the medical profession in general, June, July; passed, 15 Aug. 1876. Vivisectors are to have a licence or certificate.
Resolution in favour of vivisection passed by the International Medical Congress, London 9 Aug. 1881
The prosecution of prof. Ferrier (who had experimented on the brains of monkeys under anæsthetics) and others failed . . . . . Nov. „
Dr. Koch, of Berlin, demonstrates that tubercular disease can be propagated by organisms termed *bacilli* 1882
Mr. R. T. Reid's bill to prohibit vivisection, talked out . . . . 4 April, 1883
Report for 1883: Great Britain, 44 licences; 535 experiments; Ireland, 8 licences: 34 experiments; anæsthetics employed when required.
441 experiments in Great Britain in 1884
Report for 1886 and 1887: Great Britain 64 licences. In 1888 55 licences and 1,069 experiments.
Instructed by Dr. Ferrier's vivisection experiments, Dr. Hughes Bennett localized in a man's brain a tumour, which was removed by Mr. Godlee 25 Nov. „
The publication of the "Nine Circles, or the Hell of the Innocents," by the Anti-Vivisection society, occasioned much controversy at the church congress at Folkestone and sharp correspondence between prof. V. Horsely and Miss Frances M. Cobbe and others . . . . Oct. 1892
Prof. Virchow in the Croonian lecture warmly advocates vivisection . . . . . 16 March, 1893
Controversy revived in the *Times* . . March, 1902

See *Trials*, 18 Nov. 1903.

VIZIANAGRAM, a town in Madras presidency, formerly a kingdom, among the last bulwarks against the Mahomedan invasion, and a refuge for Hindoo learning. The sovereigns date from the 14th century. See *Vedas*.

VIZIER, GRAND, an officer of the Ottoman Porte, said to have been first appointed by Amurath I., about 1386. The office was abolished in 1838; but since been frequently revived and suppressed; see *Turkey*.

VLADIMIR (central Russia), a city founded in the 12th century, and the capital of a grand duchy from 1157 to about 1328.

VOCALION, a new musical instrument in which tones are produced from strings made to vibrate by currents of air, the joint invention of Mr. James Baillie Hamilton and Mr. John Farmer assisted by Mr. Hermann Smith, described and illustrated by Mr. Hamilton at the Royal Institution, 21 May, 1875, and tried successfully at Harrow, 23 March, 1882, and soon after at Westminster Abbey; and at other places.

VOICE FIGURES, in a variety of beautiful forms, such as trees, flowers, ferns, stars, &c., are produced by directing the voice against an elastic membrane upon which powder, paste, or some similar substance has been placed. The Eidophone, an apparatus used for this purpose, was invented by Mrs. Watts-Hughes, and many interesting specimens of voice figures were exhibited by her at the Royal Society about 1885.

VOIRON, see *Veseronce*.

VOLAPÜK (from 'world' and 'speak'), universal commercial language invented by M. Schleyer, who taught it in Paris in Feb. 1886. The Philological Society of London advocated its use in diplomacy and science, in 1887. The roots chiefly borrowed from Romanic, Germanic, and especially English languages shortened. There is a Volapük Academy at Munich, and about 500,000 people are using or learning it.

Mr. C. E. Sprague's handbook of Volapük published . . . . Jan. 1888
Volapük reported successful and spreading in Europe and America . . . . . . „
Mr. P. Hoinix publishes his "Anglo Franca" in opposition to Volapük . . . March, 1889

VOLCANOES. In different parts of the earth there are above 200 volcanoes which have been active in modern times; see *Etna*, *Vesuvius*, *New Zealand*, *Owhyhee*, and *Iceland*. In Mexico, a plain was filled up into a mountain more than a thousand feet in height by the burning lava from a volcano, in 1759. A volcano in the isle of Ferro broke out 13 Sept. 1777, which threw out an immense quantity of red water, that discoloured the sea for several leagues. A new volcano appeared in one of the Azore islands, 1 May, 1808. Lectures on vulcanology delivered by Dr. H. J. Johnston-Lavis, in Naples, in 1894. "The Ancient Volcanoes of Great Britain," by Archbd. Geikie, published April, 1897. "Volcanoes," by T. G. Bonney, F.R.S., 1899. Much volcanic activity in 1902; see *Martinique* and *Vincent St.*

VOLHYNIA, a Polish province, annexed to Russia 1793.

VOLSCI, an ancient Latin people, frequently at war with the Romans. From their capital, Corioli, Caius Martius (who defeated them about 490 B.C.) derived his name Coriolanus. The story of his banishment by his ungrateful countrymen; of his revenge on them by bringing the Volsci to the gates of Rome, yet afterwards sparing the city at the entreaties of his mother, Volumnia (487 B.C.), is considered by many as a poetical legend. The Volsci and their allies were totally defeated at Sutrium by the consul Valerius Corvus (346), and incorporated with the Roman people about 338.

VOLSINII, the inhabitants of an Etrurian city, who, after a sharp contest, were completely overcome by the Roman consul Titus Coruncanius 280 B.C.

VOLTAIC PILE or **BATTERY**, was constructed by Galvani; see *Galvanism* in article *Electricity*. The principle was discovered by Alessandro Volta, of Como (born 1745), for thirty years professor of natural philosophy at Pavia, and announced by him to the Royal Society of London in 1793. The battery was first set up in 1800. Volta was made an Italian count and senator by Napoleon Bonaparte, and was otherwise greatly honoured. While young he invented the electrophorus, electric pistol, and hydrogen lamp. He died in 1826, aged 81. The form of the Voltaic battery has been greatly improved by the researches of modern philosophers. The nitric acid battery of sir W. R. Grove was constructed in 1839; Alfred Smee's battery in 1840; the carbon battery of professor Robert Bunsen (died 16 Aug. 1899) in 1842. The first is very much used in this country; that of Bunsen on the continent; see *Copper-Zinc Couple* and *Italy*, 1899.

VOLTURNO, a river in S. Italy, near Capua, near to which Garibaldi and his followers held a strong position. This was furiously assailed by the royal troops on 1 Oct. 1860, who were finally repulsed after a desperate struggle, the fiercest in which Garibaldi had yet been engaged. He was aided greatly by a band of Piedmontese from Naples. On 2 Oct. general Bixio completed the victory by capturing 2500 fresh Neapolitan troops and dispersing others.

VOLUNTARY CONTRIBUTIONS. Public contributions for the support of the British government against the policy and designs of France amounted to two millions and a half sterling in 1798. About 200,000*l.* were transmitted to England from India in 1799. Sir Robert Peel, of Bury, among other contributions of equal amount, subscribed 10,000*l.* *Annual Register*; see *Patriotic Fund*. In 1862 nearly a million pounds were subscribed in the British empire for the relief of the Lancashire cotton spinners; see *Cotton* and *Mansion House*, where voluntary contributions for beneficent purposes are continually received.

VOLUNTARY SCHOOLS, see *Education*.

VOLUNTEERS were enrolled in England for the American war, 1778, and especially in consequence of the threatened invasion of revolutionary France, 1793-4. Besides our large army, and 85,000 men voted for the sea, we subsidised 40,000 Germans, raised our militia to 100,000 men, and armed the citizens as volunteers; the yeomanry formed cavalry regiments. Between 1798 and 1804, when this force was of greatest amount, it numbered 410,000, of which 70,000 were Irish;* Yeomanry in 1884, 11,400. On 26 Oct. 1803, king George III. reviewed in Hyde Park 12,401 London volunteers, and on 28 Oct. 14,676 more. The English volunteers were, according to official accounts, 341,600 on 1 Jan. 1804; see *Naval Volunteers*. In May, 1859, in consequence of the prevalence of the fear of a French invasion, the formation of volunteer corps of riflemen commenced under the auspices of the government, and by the end of the year many thousands were enrolled in all parts of the kingdom. The volunteers were said to be "a force potentially the strongest defence of England," 19 April, 1870. Dr. J. C. Bucknill, regarded as the originator of the movement, knighted, May, 1894; see *Artillery Association* and *Naval Artillery Volunteer Force*.

YEOMANRY were enrolled by lord Chatham in 1761.
The present 49 regiments of cavalry (about 300 each) cost 80,000*l.* 1870
The number of yeomanry - 1876, 12,093; 1880, 11,598; 1885, 11,590; 1890, 10,697; 1894, 10,014; 1897, 10,184.
By War-office regulations the whole yeomanry force was re-organized and appointed a definite place in the mobilization scheme (commencing 1 April), 4 Jan. 1893
Volunteer (military service) act passed . 6 July, 1895
[The first Middlesex volunteers were formed in 1803 as the duke of Cumberland's sharpshooters. They retained their organisation as a rifle club, when other volunteers were disbanded. In 1835 they were permitted by the duchess of Kent to take the name of the Royal Victoria Rifle Club.]
Circular letter from col. Jonathan Peel, proposing organization of *National Volunteer Association* for promoting the practice of rifle-shooting, 12 May, 1859. It was established in London, under the patronage of the queen and prince consort, Mr. Sidney (afterwards lord) Herbert, secretary at war, president, and the earl of Derby, earl Spencer, lord Elcho, and other noblemen vice-presidents. (Annual subscription one guinea, or a composition for life of ten guineas) . . . 16 Nov. 1859
2500 volunteer officers presented to the queen; a dinner followed, with the duke of Cambridge in the chair; and a ball . . . . 7 March, 1860
The queen reviews about 18,450 volunteers in Hyde-park . . . . . 23 June, ,,
[Mr. Tower, of Wealdhall, Essex, aged 80, was present as a private; he had been present as an officer in a volunteer review in 1803.]
First meeting of the National Association for rifle-shooting held at Wimbledon. The queen fired the first shot, a "centre"; captain Edw. Ross (North York) obtained the queen's prize of 250*l.* and the gold medal and badge of the association, 2-7 July, ,,
[M. Thorel, a Swiss, obtained a prize.]
Successful sham-fight at Bromley, Kent . 14 July, ,,
Above 20,000 volunteers reviewed by the queen at Edinburgh . . . . . . 7 Aug. ,,
Above 10,000 Lancashire volunteers reviewed by the earl of Derby at Knowsley . . 1 Sept. ,,
Lord Herbert stated that the association had a capital of 3000*l.* and an annual income of 1500*l.*, 16 Feb. 1861
Volunteers in Britain estimated at about 160,000, May, ,,
Second meeting at Wimbledon; Mr. Jopling (S. Middlesex) gains the queen's prize and the association medal . . . . . 4-10 July, ,,
Review of 11,504 volunteers at Wimbledon, 13 July; of 9000 at Warwick . . . . . 24 July, ,,
Registered number of volunteers, 162,681 1 April, 1862
20,000 volunteers reviewed by lord Clyde at Brighton . . . . . . 21 April, ,,
Third meeting at Wimbledon; Mr. Pixley (S. Victoria) gains the queen's prize, &c. 1-14 July, ,,
A commission recommends that an annual grant of either 20*s.*, 30*s.*, or 34*s.*, be given to each volunteer according to circumstances . . Oct. ,,
Fourth meeting at Wimbledon, 7 July, &c.; queen's prize, &c., won by sergeant Roberts (12th Shropshire) . . . . . . 14 July, 1863
An act to amend and consolidate the acts relating to the volunteer force of Great Britain was passed, 21 July, ,,
[Annual grant of 30*s.* to each volunteer authorised.]
22,000 volunteers reviewed by the prince of Wales in Hyde-park (great improvement noticed), 28 May, 1864

* The first regiment of Irish volunteers was formed at Dublin, under command of the duke of Leinster, 12 Oct. 1779. They armed generally to the amount of 20,000 men, and received the unanimous thanks of the houses of lords and commons in Ireland, for their patriotism and spirit, for coming forward and defending their country. At the period when the force appeared Irish affairs bore a serious aspect; manufactures had decreased, and foreign trade had been hurt by a prohibition of the export of salted provisions and butter. No notice of the complaints of the people had been taken in the English parliament, when, owing to the alarm of an invasion, ministers allowed the nation to arm, and an immense force was soon raised. The Irish took this occasion to demand a free trade, and government saw there was no trifling with a country with arms in its hands. The Irish parliament unanimously addressed the king for a free trade, and it was granted, 1779.

Fifth meeting at Wimbledon, 11 July, &c.; the queen's prize, &c., won by private John Wyatt (London rifle brigade) . . . . 23 July, 1864

Volunteers estimated at 165,000 in 1864.

Sixth meeting at Wimbledon, began 11 July; the queen's prize was won by private Sharman (4th West York), 18 July; the meeting ended with a review by the duke of Cambridge . . 22 July, 1865

Seventh meeting at Wimbledon, began 9 July; queen's prize won by Angus Cameron (6th Inverness), 17 July; the value of about 7000*l.* distributed in prizes; and review by duke of Cambridge . . . . 21 July, 1866

The volunteers reviewed by the prince of Wales at Brighton, 2 April; at York, 11 Aug.; by duke of Cambridge at Hyde-park . . . . 23 June, ,,

Estimate of volunteers: 135,000 infantry, 27,000 artillery, and 4000 engineers.—*Times* . 9 Oct. ,,

About 1100 volunteers visit Brussels, headed by col. Loyd Lindsay: warmly received; first prize gained by Curtis, of the 11th Sussex rifles, 11-22 Oct. ,,

Parliamentary vote for volunteers, 361,009*l.* 6 June, 1867

Metropolitan and Berkshire volunteers reviewed in Windsor Great Park . . . . . 10 June, ,,

Eighth meeting at Wimbledon, began 8 July; Belgian Garde civique and volunteers (above 2000) received by prince of Wales, 13 July; resignation of lord Elcho, chairman of the council; succeeded by earl Spencer, 18 July; grand review by prince of Wales, the sultan, &c.; the queen's prize given to sergeant Lane (Bristol) by the princess of Teck, 20 July, ,,

Grand review in New Sefton park, Liverpool, 5 Oct. ,,

About 28,000 volunteers reviewed by the queen at Windsor . . . . . . 20 June, 1868

Review of regulars and volunteers at Edinburgh, 4 July, ,,

Ninth meeting at Wimbledon, 13 July; the queen's prize gained by lieut. Carslake (5th Somerset), 25 July, ,,

Lord Elcho re-elected chairman of the council (earl Spencer resigned) . . . . . . Feb. 1869

Memorial to government respecting the capitation grant; signed by noblemen and gentlemen, 19 Feb. ,,

Volunteers reported to number 170,000 . . . . ,,

Review of volunteers of southern and western counties at Portsmouth . . . 26 April, ,,

Tenth meeting at Wimbledon 3 July; queen's prize gained by corporal Angus Cameron (6th Inverness), 2nd time, 13 July; grand review 24 July, ,,

Volunteers act, 1863, amended . . . 9 Aug. ,,

"*Army Service Corps*" to be composed of volunteers; established by royal warrant 12 Nov. ,,

Eleventh meeting at Wimbledon, 11 July; queen's prize won by corporal Humphries (6th Surrey), 19 July, 1870

Letter from the lord mayor recommending the enlargement of the volunteer system, and its greater efficiency . . . . . 22 Sept. ,,

Establishment of an extensive rifle range, drill ground, armoury, &c., for the London volunteers resolved on . . . . . . 3 Oct ,,

Distribution of breech-loaders commenced Nov. ,,

The volunteers recognised as part of the national army 1871

Lord Elcho (chairman) resigned; succeeded by the earl of Ducie . . . . . June, ,,

Twelfth meeting at Wimbledon, 8 July; queen's prize won by ensign A. P. Humphry, undergraduate (Cambridge university), aged 19 18 July, ,,

Vote for volunteer force, 1872-3, 473,200*l.* 24 June, 1872

Thirteenth meeting at Wimbledon, 8 July; queen's prize won by colour-sergeant Michie (London Scottish) . . . . 16 July, ,,

The Elcho shield, the International trophy, and the Irish International trophy (all won by the English) placed in the custody of the lord mayor, 27 July, ,,

Some volunteers visit Ghent . . 14-21 Sept. ,,

Fourteenth meeting at Wimbledon, 7 July; queen's prize won by sergeant Robert Menzies (1st Edinburgh) . . . . 15 July, 1873

Volunteers visit Havre; shoot for prizes; 50 obtain prizes, end of May; given 29 June, 1874

Fifteenth meeting at Wimbledon, 6 July; queen's prize won by private W. C. Atkinson (1st Durham) 14 July, 1874

An "efficient volunteer" defined by order in council (substitute for schemes of 27 July, 1863, and 15 Oct. 1872) . . . . . . Aug. ,,

Resignation of earl of Ducie as chairman . April, 1875

Sixteenth meeting at Wimbledon, 12 July; queen's prize won by capt. George Pearse (15th Devon) 20 July, ,,

175,387 enrolled volunteers 1874; 181,080, . . ,,

30,000 volunteers reviewed by the prince of Wales in Hyde Park ("complete success."—*Times*) 1 July, 1876

Seventeenth meeting at Wimbledon, 10-22 July; queen's prize won by sergeant Pullman, 2nd (South) Middlesex . . . . 18 July, ,,

185,501 enrolled volunteers . . . . . . ,,

Eighteenth meeting at Wimbledon, 9-21 July; queen's prize won by private George Jamieson (a Scot), of 15th Lancashire corps (Liverpool) 17 July, 1877

Nineteenth meeting at Wimbledon, 8-20 July; queen's prize won by private Peter Ray (a Scot), 11th Stirling . . . . . . 16 July, 1878

203,213 enrolled volunteers . . . . Nov. ,,

Twentieth meeting at Wimbledon, 14-26 July; queen's prize won by corporal George Taylor, 47th Lancashire . . . . . 22 July, 1879

International trophy won by England . 19 July, ,,

Standard of efficiency: 69 per cent. 1863; 85 per cent. 1868; 96 per cent. 1880

Earl Stanhope elected chairman in room of earl Wharncliffe . . . . May, ,,

Twenty-first meeting at Wimbledon, 12-24 July; Queen's prize won by Alexander Ferguson, private 1st Argyll . . . . 21 July, ,,

East York volunteer artillery corps resign on account of dismissal of col. Humphrey (through continued personal disagreements), 16 June; resignations said to be illegal . . 29 June, ,,

Sergeant Wm. Marshman, tried by court-martial for alleged fraudulent marking at the rifle meetings, 1878, 1879, 1880, acquitted . 13 Aug.-16 Sept. ,,

Earl Stanhope, chairman, succeeded by earl Brownlow . . . . 4 May, 1881

Above 52,000 volunteers reviewed by the queen at Windsor, 9 July. ["A magnificent success; the crowning achievement of the volunteer movement."—*Times*, 11 July] . . . . . ,,

About 40,000 Scotch volunteers reviewed by the queen, in Queen's-park, Edinburgh . 25 Aug. ,,

Twenty-second meeting at Wimbledon, 11-23 July; queen's prize won by private Thomas Beck, 3rd Devon . . . . 19 July, ,,

Twenty-third meeting at Wimbledon, 10-22 July; queen's prize won by sergeant Lawrence, 1st Dumbarton . . . . . . 18 July, 1882

Enrolled volunteers, 207,336 . . . 1 Nov. ,,

Twenty-fourth meeting at Wimbledon, 9-21 July; queen's prize won by sergeant Mackay, 1st Sutherland . . . . . . 17 July, 1883

International rifle match between British and Americans: won by British . . 21 July, ,,

Twenty-fifth meeting at Wimbledon, 14-26 July; queen's prize won by private Gallant, 8th Middlesex . . . . 22 July, 1884

Volunteers exercised in camping out; sham conflicts in Berkshire and other counties . . Aug. ,,

Volunteers Forces' Benevolent Association, inaugurated . . . . 6 July, 1885

Twenty-sixth meeting at Wimbledon, 13-25 July; queen's prize won by sergeant Bulmer, 2nd Lincoln . . . . 21 July, ,,

Twenty-seventh meeting at Wimbledon, 12-24 July; queen's prize won by private Jackson, of 1st V. B. Lincoln (one of three ties) 21 July, 1886

Enrolled volunteers, 224,012, Nov. 1885; 226,752 Nov. ,,

28,000 volunteers reviewed by the queen at Buckingham palace; march past in $1\frac{1}{4}$ hours . 2 July, 1887

Twenty-eighth meeting at Wimbledon, 11-23 July; queen's prize won by lieut. R. O. Warren, 1st Middlesex, (Victoria) rifles, Middlesex 19 July, ,,

Lord Wantage elected chairman, 1887; active in search of a site in place of Wimbledon. . 1888

Order issued for the formation of 95,000 volunteers into 19 brigades for immediate mobilization for home defence . . . . . . 3 July, 1888

Twenty-ninth meeting at Wimbledon, 9–21 July; queen's prize won by private Fulton, 13th Middlesex (queen's Westminsters) rifles, 17 July ,,

Brookwood, to be called Bisleycommon, chosen for 1890 . . . . 28 Feb. 1889

Estimated grant for 220,000 men, 742,700*l.* April, ,,

Thirtieth meeting at Wimbledon . . 8–20 July, ,,

Queen's prize won by sergeant Reid (1st Lanark engineers) . . . . . . 16 July, ,,

Patriotic volunteer fund started by lord mayor Whitehead in the spring; he appeals for subscriptions for the full equipment of a citizen army, equal to that of the regulars. The prince of Wales 105*l.*, 1 June; the queen 200*l.* 2 July; many others; about 42,000*l.* subscribed . . 20 Nov. ,,

Enrolled volunteers, 224,021 . . . . 1 Nov. ,,

Capt. St. John Mildmay, secretary since 1860, resigns, 6 Sept.; succeeded by Mr. A. P. Humphry, Nov. ,,

The council determines to appeal to the public for funds, and to obtain a charter of incorporation, 11 Feb.; this was granted and signed by the queen . . . . 25 Nov. ,,

Parliament votes 100,000*l.* for volunteer equipment, 17 April, 1890

Thirty-first meeting (the first at Bisley common), 12–26 July; the camp opened, the prince and princess of Wales and the duke of Cambridge present; the princess fired the first shot, a "bull's eye" . . . . 12 July, ,,

Queen's prize won by sergeant Bates (1st Warwick), 22 July, ,,

Meeting very successful . . . . ,,

[The Rifle Association includes 76 county associations in Great Britain, 4 in Ireland, and 64 in India and the colonies.]

Enrolled volunteers, 221,048 . . . . 31 Oct. ,,

Review of about 25,000 volunteers at Wimbledon by the German emperor . . . . 11 July, 1891

Thirty-second meeting (the second at Bisley common) . . . . 13–24 July, ,,

Queen's prize won by private D. Dear (Queen's Edinburgh). . . . . . . 21 July, ,,

Thirty-third meeting (the third at Bisley common), 11–23 July; queen's prize won by major Pollock (3rd Renfrew) . . . . . . 23 July, 1892

About 13,000 volunteers engaged in the army manœuvres . . . . Aug. ,,

"The Volunteer Officers' Decoration" (an oak wreath in silver tied with gold, having in the centre the royal cipher and crown in gold) for commissioned officers who have served 20 years, instituted by the queen, 25 July; conferred on certain officers, Nov., Dec. 1892; decorations granted to non-commissioned officers, 12 Sept. 1893; to the rank and file after 20 to 34 years' service . . . . Sept. 1894

Thirty-fourth meeting Bisley 10–22 July; queen's prize won by serjeant Davies (1st. V. B. Welsh); 22 July, 1893

Thirty-fifth meeting, Bisley 10–21 July; queen's prize won by private Rennie (3rd Lanark) 21 July, 1894

Enrolled volunteers; 231,328 (1894) reported; April, 1895

Total volunteer vote for 1895; 824,200*l.* April, ,,

Thirty-sixth meeting, Bisley, 8–20 July; queen's prize won by private Hayhurst, queen's hundred Canada, formerly private of the 1st. V. B. Lancashire . . . . 20 July, ,,

Enrolled volunteers, officers and men, 235,977, 31 Oct. ,,

Special army order granting new and increased allowances to officers and men . 16 May, 1896

Thirty-seventh meeting, Bisley, 13–25 July; queen's prize won by lieut. J. L. Thomson (Queen's Edinburgh) . . . . 25 July, ,,

Volunteer act of 1863, amended 1897

Capitation grant of 250,000*l.* agreed to . 29 Jan. ,,

Thirty-eighth meeting, Bisley, 12–24 July; queen's prize won by private Ward (1st Devon), 24 July, ,,

Enrolled volunteers, officers and men, 231,798 in ,,

Thirty-ninth meeting, Bisley, 11–23 July; queen's prize won by lieut. D. Yates (3rd Lanark) 23 July, 1898

Review of 25,965 metropolitan volunteers by the prince of Wales on the Horse Guards' parade, 8 July, 1899

Fortieth meeting, Bisley, 10–22 July; queen's prize won by private Priaulx (Guernsey) . 22 July, 1899

Enrolled volunteers, officers and men, 249,968, 31 Oct. ,,

Regulations issued for a contingent for South Africa . . . . 19 Dec. ,,

Enrolment of the city imperial volunteers for South Africa, 25,000*l.* voted by the city, 20 Dec.; 1st draft formed at the Guildhall, 1 Jan. 1900; embark, 13 Jan.; 2nd and 3rd drafts sailed, 20 and 27 Jan. 1900; see *London*, 12–27 Jan. 1900; imperial yeomanry, about 1,000, leave for South Africa . . . . 27, 28 Jan. 1900

Volunteer fund: prince of Wales 100 guineas; total, 117,643*l.* . . . . ,,

Reinforcements, 3 officers and 147 men, for South Africa, leave . . . . . 12 July, ,,

Forty-first meeting, Bisley, 7–21 July; queen's prize won by private Ward (1st Devon) . . 21 July, ,,

Volunteers' act passed . . . . . 6 Aug. ,,

Return of the C.I.V.'s: total sent 59 officers, 1,667 men (lieut. Alt and 13 men killed, 48 died of wounds or disease), see *London*, 29 Oct. 1900 (total volunteers who served in the war, about 700 officers and 25,000 others, besides some 7,000 who enlisted in the army—*Times*, 20 June, 1902).

Forty-second meeting, Bisley, 8–20 July; king's prize won by lance-corporal H. Ommundsen (Queen's Edinburgh) . . . . . . 20 July, 1901

Mr. Astor gives 10,000*l.* to the national rifle association, Dec. 1901; the duke of Cambridge reelected president; Mr. Astor, vice-president, 5 Feb. 1902

Revised volunteer regulations issued . 22 April ,,

Forty-third meeting, Bisley, 14–26 July; king's prize won by lieut. E. D. Johnson (London rifles), 26 July, ,,

Forty-fourth meeting, Bisley, 10–25 July; king's prize won by col.-serg. T. Davies (3rd Glamorgan), 25 July, 1903

Enrolled volunteers, total of all ranks for year 1902, 268,550 against 288,476 in 1901.

EASTER MONDAY REVIEWS AND SHAM FIGHTS.

(Operations from Good Friday to Easter Monday.)

Brighton . . . 21 April, 1862, and 5 April, 1863

Guildford . . . . 28 March, 1864

Brighton . . . 17 April, 1865; and 2 April, 1866

Dover . . . . 22 April, 1867

Portsmouth (the most successful hitherto, 29,490 volunteers present) . . . . . 13 April, 1868

Dover (bad weather) . . . . . . 29 March, 1869

Brighton, 18 April, 1870; (considered a failure) 10 April, 1871

——— Mock battle between sir Arthur Horsford (12,180 men, 22 guns) and gen. Lysons (11,082 men, 20 guns) . . . . 1 April, 1872

Small reviews at Wimbledon and other places, 14 April, 1873; 6 April, 1874; 29 March, 1875; at Tring, &c., 17 April, 1876; at Dunstable, &c., 2 April, 1877; at Staines, &c., 22 April, 1878; at Dover, Reigate, Wimbledon, &c., 14 April, 1879; Brighton, battle, successful; 29 March, 1880; 18 April, 1881; Portsmouth, 20,000 ("Genuine success," *Times*), 10 April, 1882; Brighton (evolutions very successful), 26 March, 1883; Dover, Portsmouth, &c., (12-)14 April, 1884; Brighton and Dover, 6 April, 1885; at Dover, Portsmouth, Colchester &c., 26 April, 1886; successful military operations at Dover, Eastbourne, and Aldershot, 11 April, 1887; campaign operations and battles, invasions, &c. at Portsmouth, Dover, Eastbourne &c., 30, 31 March; battles: invaders successful at Portsmouth . 2 April, 1888

Meetings for brigade drill, &c., Eastbourne, Portsmouth, Dover, Brighton, and other places, 22 April, 1889; Folkestone, Eastbourne, Portsmouth, &c., 7 April, 1890. Portsmouth, Dover, Brighton, &c., 30 March, 1891. At Dover, battle of St. Margaret's; invaders under col. J. C. Russel, defenders under col. J. B. Sterling. At Chatham, battle of the Bells; invaders under lieut. gen. Goodenough, defenders under major-gen. Dawson Scott . . . . . 18 April, 1892

Sham fights at Eastbourne, Canterbury, Chatham and Brighton, &c. . . . . . 3 April, 1893

Manœuvres at Dover, Canterbury, Chatham, Guildford, and Winchester . . . . 26 March, 1894
Great improvement in order and efficiency since 1888; reported 1895
Manœuvres at Windsor, Canterbury, and Marden Park, Surrey . . . . . 12–15 April, „
Field days at Winchester, Canterbury, Folkestone, Brighton, etc. . . . . . . 6 April, 1896
Manœuvres, sham-fights, etc., at Winchester, Shorncliffe, Dover, Folkestone, Brighton, etc. 17, 19 April, 1897
Manœuvres, abt. 16,000 men left London, 7 April; sham fights, etc., near Canterbury, Aldershot, Chatham, Dover, Colchester, 9–11 April; many injured in a railway collision at Bisley . 11 April, 1898
Manœuvres at Aldershot, Canterbury, Winchester, Chatham, Gravesend, etc., tactical operations, etc. . . . . 1– April, 1899
Manœuvres at Winchester . . . . 12–16 April, 1900
Manœuvres betweeen London and Colchester, and other places . . . . . . 5–8 April, 1901
Manœuvres at Bisley, Wimbledon, and elsewhere, 28–31 March, 1902
Elcho Challenge Shield, shot for by teams, and kept by the winning nation:
Won by England: 1862, 1863, 1865, 1867, 1868, 1870, 1871, 1872, 1876, 1881 (July 22), 1882 (July 20), 1885 (July 23), 1887 (July 21), 1891 (July 23), 1893 July 15), 1895 (July 13); 1896 (July 18) 1897 (July 17); 1898 (July 16); 1899 (July 15); 1901 (July 12); 1902 (July 18).
Scotland: 1864, 1866, 1869, 1874, 1879 (July 24), 1892 (23 July), 1894 (July 14).
Ireland: 1873, 1875, 1877, 1878, 1880 (July 22), 1883 (19 July), 1884 (24 July), 1886 (22 July), 1888 (19 July), 1889 (18 July), 1890 (24 July), 1900 (13 July), 1903 (17 July).
Volunteer Medical Staff Corps established, 23 March, 1885

VOSSEM, Peace of, between the elector of Brandenburg and Louis XIV. of France; the latter engaged not to assist the Dutch against the elector; signed 6 June, 1673.

VOTING PAPERS. See *Dodson's Act*. The proposal to use them was negatived in the debates on reform in 1867; adopted by the ballot act in 1873. A bill against plural voting was read first time in the commons, 30 April, 1895. See *Ballot*.

VOUGLÉ or **Vouillé**, S.W. France (near Poitiers), where Alaric II., king of the Visigoths, was defeated and slain by Clovis, king of France, 507, who subdued the whole country from the Loire to the Pyrenees. A peace followed between the Franks and Visigoths, who had been settled above one hundred years in that part of Gaul called Septimania. Clovis soon afterwards made Paris his capital.

VOYAGES. It is mythically stated that by order of Pharaoh-Necho, of Egypt, some Phœnician pilots sailed from Egypt down the Arabian Gulf, round what is now called the Cape of Good Hope, entered the Mediterranean by the Straits of Gibraltar, coasted along the north of Africa, and at length arrived in Egypt, after a navigation of about three years, 604 B.C. *Herodotus*. The first voyage round the world was made by a ship, part of a Spanish squadron which had been under the command of Magellan (who was killed at the Philippine Islands in a skirmish) in 1519-20; see *Circumnavigators*, *North-West Passage*, and *Periplus*.

VOYSEY ESTABLISHMENT FUND. The Rev. Charles Voysey having been deprived for heresy (see *Church of England*, 1871), began a series of services at St. George's hall, Langham-place, 1 Oct. 1871. The fund for their maintenance was supported by Bp. Hinds of Norwich (retired), Sir John Bowring, and other eminent liberals. Services now (1903) held in Swallow-street, Piccadilly, the congregation worshipping as the "Theistic Church."

VULCAN, see *Planets*. The Greek god Hephaistos answered to the Roman Vulcan.

VULCANITE (vulcanised india-rubber), also termed *Ebonite*.

VULGATE (from *vulgatus*, published), a term applied to the Latin version of the Scriptures which is authorised by the council of Trent (1546), and which is attributed to St. Jerome, about 384. The older version, called the Italic, is said to have been made in the beginning of the 2nd century. A critical edition was printed by order of pope Sixtus V. in 1590, which, being considered inaccurate, was superseded by the edition of pope Clement VIII. in 1592. The earliest printed vulgate is without date, by Gutenburg and Fust, probably about 1455, the first dated (Fust and Schœffer) is 1462.

W.

WACHT DES DEUTSCHEN VATERLAND ("Watch of the German Fatherland"). German national hymn, by Reichardt, first performed 2 Aug. 1825. Very popular during the war 1870-71.

WADHAM COLLEGE (Oxford). Founded by Nicholas Wadham, and Dorothy, his wife, in 1613. In this college, in the chambers of Dr. Wilkins (over the gateway), the founders of the Royal Society frequently met prior to 1658.

WAGER OF BATTLE, see *Appeal*.

WAGES IN ENGLAND. The wages of sundry workmen were first fixed by act of parliament 25 Edw. III. 1350. Haymakers had but one penny a day. Master carpenters, masons, tilers, and other coverers of houses, had not more than 3*d*. per day (about 9*d*. of our money); and their servants 1½*d*. *Viner's Statutes*.*

By the 23 Henry VI. the wages of a bailiff of husbandry was 23*s*. 4*d*. per annum, and clothing of the price of 5*s*. with meat and drink; chief hind, carter, or shepherd, 20*s*., clothing, 4*s*.; common servant of husbandry, 15*s*., clothing, 40*d*.; woman-servant, 10*s*., clothing, 4*s*. 1444

By the 11 Henry VII., a like rate of wages with a little advance: as, for instance, a free mason, master carpenter, rough mason, bricklayer, master tiler, plumber, glazier, carver or joiner, was allowed from Easter to Michaelmas to take 6*d*. a day without meat and drink; or, with meat and drink, 4*d*.; from Michaelmas to Easter, to abate 1*d*. A master having under him six men was allowed 1*d*. a day extra 1495

Agricultural labourers per week: Warwickshire, 3*s*. 6*d*. and 4*s*.; Devonshire, 5*s*.; Suffolk, 5*s*. and 6*s*.; wool-weavers, about 3*s*. and 4*s*. (Macaulay) about 1685

In 1866 the annual amount of wages paid in the United Kingdom was estimated by Mr. Gladstone at 250,000,000*l*.; by Mr. Bass at 350,000,000*l*.; and by professor Leone Levi at 418,300,000*l*., earned by 10,697,000 workers, ages 20 to 60.

In 1872-8 many trades struck for increase of wages and frequently were successful; in 1877-9, unsuccessful.

In 1878 professor Levi estimated that 503,000,000*l*. were earned (by men, 390,000,000*l*.; by women, 113,000,000*l*.); after deducting for holidays, &c., 422,700,000*l*.

He says, that "In no other country are wages more liberal, but in no other country are they more wastefully used." See *Strikes*.

Payment of wages in public-houses prohibited by act passed in 1883

Classified census of wages paid in the United Kingdom in 1885, published by the Board of Trade at various times; part iv. in 1892; decrease in the weekly wages bill for 1901, 1,584,000*l*. against 6,000,000*l*. increase in 1900, reported . 27 Aug. 1902

	Labourers wages per week. s.	d.	Corn per quarter. s.	d.
1824	7	7	62	0
1837	8	0	55	10
1860	9	6	53	3
1869	11	0	48	7
1872	11	9	57	1

WAGES OF HARVEST-MEN IN ENGLAND AT DIFFERENT PERIODS.

Year.		s.	d.	Year.		s.	d.	Year.		s.	d.
In 1350	per diem	0	1	In 1716	per diem	0	9	In 1800	per diem	2	0
1460	,,	0	2	1740	,,	0	10	1811	,,	2	1½
1568	,,	0	4	1760	,,	1	0	1850	,,	3	0
1632	,,	0	6	1788	,,	1	4	1857	,,	5	0
1688	,,	0	8	1794	,,	1	6	Since then increased.			

WAGGONS were rare in the 18th century. They, with carts, &c., not excepting those used in agriculture, were taxed in 1783. The carriers' waggons are now nearly superseded by the railways.

WAGHORN'S NEW OVERLAND ROUTE TO INDIA. Lieut. Waghorn devoted a large portion of his life to connect India with England. On 31 Oct. 1845, he arrived in London, by a new route, with the Bombay mail of the 1st of that month. His despatches reached Suez on the 19th, and Alexandria on the 20th, whence he proceeded by steamboat to a place twelve miles nearer London than Trieste. He hurried through Austria, Baden, Bavaria, Prussia, and Belgium, and reached London at half-past four on the morning of the first-mentioned day. The authorities of the different countries through which he passed eagerly facilitated his movements. The ordinary express, *viâ* Marseilles, reached London 2 Nov. following. Mr. Waghorn subsequently addressed a letter to the *Times* newspaper, in which he stated that in a couple of years he would bring the Bombay mail to London in 21 days. He died 8 Jan. 1850. On 3 Feb. 1884, at a meeting at the Mansion-house, London, it was determined to erect a national monument to his memory.

The Overland Mail, which had left Bombay on 1 Dec. 1845, arrived early on the 30th in London, by way of Marseilles and Paris. The speedy arrival was owing to the great exertions made by the French government to show that the route through France was shorter and better.

WAGNERISM, see under *Music*.

WAGRAM, a village near Vienna, where Napoleon I. totally defeated the archduke Charles, 5, 6 July, 1809. The slaughter on both sides was dreadful; 12,000 Austrians were taken by the French, and the defeated army retired to Moravia. An armistice was signed on the 12th; and on 24 Oct., by a treaty of peace, Austria ceded all her sea-coast to France; the kingdoms of Saxony and Bavaria were enlarged at her expense; part of Poland in Galicia was ceded to Russia; and Joseph Bonaparte was recognised as king of Spain.

WAHABEES OR WAHABITES, a warlike Mahometan reforming sect, considering themselves the only true followers of the prophet, established themselves in Arabia about 1750, under the rule of Abd-el-Wahab, who died 1787. His grandson, Saoud, in 1801, defeated an expedition headed by the caliph of Bagdad. In 1803 this sect seized

* Mr. J. E. Thorold Rogers, "Six Centuries of Work and Wages," published in 1884.

Mecca and Medina, and continued their conquests, although their chief was assassinated in the midst of his victories. His son, Abdallah, long resisted Mahommed Ali, pacha of Egypt, but in 1818 was defeated and taken prisoner by Ibrahim Pacha, who sent him to Constantinople, where he was put to death. The sect, now flourishing, is well described by Mr. W. Gifford Palgrave, in his "Journey and Residence in Arabia in 1862-3," published in 1865. It is influential in India, and is suspected of a tendency to insurrection.

WAHLSTATT, see *Katzbach*.

WAIFS and STRAYS (children). Church of England Central Society for providing Homes for Waifs and Strays, founded 1882. The society was very active in 1892, being supported by the bishops and clergy; 71,551*l.* received 1896, 73,679*l.* in 1901.

Miss Rye, a pioneer in promoting the emigration of neglected children to Canada, since 1860, presents to the society her training homes at Peckham and Niagara and 600*l.* . . . . . Aug. 1897

WAITS, the night minstrels who perform shortly before Christmas. The name was given to the musicians attached to the king's court. We find that a company of waits was established at Exeter in 1400 to "pipe the watch." The waits in London and Westminster were long officially recognised by the corporation.

WAKEFIELD (W. Yorkshire), an ancient town. Near it a battle was fought between the adherents of Margaret, the queen of Henry VI., and the duke of York, in which the latter was slain, and 3000 Yorkists fell upon the field, 31 Dec. 1460. The earl of Warwick supported the cause of the duke's son, the earl of March, afterwards Edward IV., and the civil war was continued. An art and industrial exhibition was opened at Wakefield, 30 Aug. 1865. The Bishoprics act, authorising the establishment of a see at Wakefield, was passed 16 Aug. 1878. The required funds subscribed Jan. 1888. Population, 1881, 30,854; 1891, 33,146; 1901, 41,413.

Bishopric founded by queen Victoria, 17 May, 1888; Rev. W. W. How (suffragan bishop of Bedford) first bishop, Feb. 1888; died . . . 11 Aug. 1897
George Rodney Eden, suffragan of Dover, succ. Aug. "
New municipal buildings opened by the marquis of Ripon . . . . 22 Feb. 1898
Anonymous gift of 3,000*l.* for enlarging the cathedral, 11,000*l.* promised, Jan. 1899; foundation-stone laid by the abp. of Canterbury, 18 June, 1901

WAKES, the ancient parish festivals on the saint's day to commemorate the dedication of the church; regulated in 1536, but gradually became obsolete.

WALBROOK CHURCH (London), a masterpiece of Sir Christopher Wren, completed in 1679. There was a church here in 1135, and a new church was erected in 1429.

WALCHEREN (an island at the mouth of the Scheldt, Holland). The unfortunate expedition of the British to this isle in 1809 consisted of 35 ships of the line, and 200 smaller vessels, principally transports, and 40,000 land forces, the latter under the command of the earl of Chatham, and the fleet under sir Richard Strachan. For a long time the destination of the expedition remained secret; but before 28 July, 1809, when it set sail, the French journals had announced that Walcheren was the point of attack. Flushing was invested in August; a dreadful bombardment followed, and the place was taken 15 Aug.; but no suggestion on the part of the naval commander, nor urging on the part of the officers, could induce the earl to vigorous action, until the period of probable success was gone, and necessity obliged him to return with as many of the troops as disease and an unhealthy climate had spared. The place was evacuated, 23 Dec. 1809. The house of commons instituted an inquiry, and lord Chatham resigned his post of master-general of the ordnance, to prevent greater disgrace; but the policy of ministers in planning the expedition was, nevertheless, approved. The following epigram, of which various readings exist, appeared at the time:—

> "Lord Chatham [or *the warrior earl*] with [his] sabre drawn,
> Stood waiting for sir Richard Strachan;
> Sir Richard, longing [or *eager*] to be at 'em,
> Stood waiting for the earl of Chatham."

A lychgate erected by queen Victoria at Dovercourt parish church, in memory of British soldiers who died there of disease contracted during the expedition 1809–11, was opened by gen. Gatacre, 22 Sept. 1899.

WALDECK AND PYRMONT, united German principalities, established in 1682. The late reigning family claim descent from the Saxon hero, Witikind, who flourished about 772. Prince George Victor, born 14 Jan. 1831, succeeded his father, George, 15 May, 1845; died May, 1893; succeeded by Frederic, son, born 20 Jan. 1865. On 22 Oct. 1867, the states approved a treaty of annexation, and the administration was transferred to Prussia, 1 Jan. 1868. Population, 1900, 57,918.

WALDENSES (also called Valdenses, Vallenses, and Vaudois), a sect inhabiting the Cottian Alps, derives it name, according to some authors, from Peter de Waldo, of Lyons (1170). They had a translation of the Bible The Waldenses settled in the valleys of Piedmont about 1375, but were frequently dreadfully persecuted, especially in the 17th century, when Charles I. of England interceded for them (1627-9) and Oliver Cromwell by threats (1655-6) obtained them some degree of toleration. All the Waldensian Barbes or pastors, save two, died in the great plague of 1630. Gilles and Gros went to Geneva and Lausanne for Swiss Calvinist ministers to fill the vacancies. The new ministers were no sooner inducted than they deposed the surviving Barbes and abolished all the distinctive teaching and usages of the community, substituting the Genevese model. They were permitted to have a church at Turin, Dec. 1853. They became French subjects when Savoy was annexed by Napoleon III. in 1860. In March, 1868, it was stated that there were in Italy 28 ordained Waldensian ministers, and 30 other teachers.

Mr. Thos Morton, a British merchant, who died 11 Sept. 1897, besides other bequests to religious bodies, left a large sum to the "Waldensian Church in Italy."

WALES, Cambria, Cymru, the land of the Cymry, called by the Romans *Britannia Secunda*. Welsh and Wales are corruptions of Teutonic epithets applied to foreigners, especially Gauls. After the Roman emperor Honorius gave up Britain, Vortigern was elected king of South Britain. He invited over the Saxons to defend his country against the Picts and Scots; but the Saxons perfidiously sent for reinforcements, consisting of Saxons, Danes, and Anglers, by which they made themselves masters of South Britain. Many of the Britons retired to Wales, and defended themselves against the Saxons, in their inaccessible mountains, about 447. In this state Wales remained unconquered till Henry II. subdued South Wales in 1157; and in 1282 Edward I. entirely reduced the whole country, an end being put to its independence by the death of Llewelyn, the last prince.* In 1284 the queen gave birth to a son at Caernarvon, whom Edward styled prince of Wales, now title of the heir to the crown of Great Britain. Wales was united and incorporated with England by act of parliament, 1536; see *Britain*, *Bards* and *Population*: 1891, 1,518,914; 1901, 1,698,148.

Ostorius Scapula, proprætor of Britain, defeats the Cymry . . . . A.D. 50
The supreme authority in *Britannia Secunda* intrusted to Suetonius Paulinus, who caused desolating wars 58-61
Conquests by Julius Frontinus 70
The Silures totally defeated . . . . ,,
The Roman, Julius Agricola, commands in Britain. 78
Bran ab Llyr, the Blessed, dies about . . . 80
The Druidical class gradually dissolved by the influence of Christianity in 300-400
The Britons defeat the Saxons 447-448
Vortigern king 448
The renowned Arthur elected king . . about 500
Defeats Saxons . . . . . . about 527
Cadwallawn, king of Gwynedd, defeated and slain by the Saxons at Denisburn . . . about 634
Dyvnwal Moelmud, said to have come from Armorica, and to have established his authority west of the Tamar and Severn as king of the Cymry about 640
Reign of Roderic the Great 844
He unites the petty states into one principality; his death 877
Division of Wales—into north, south, and central (or Powys-land) . . . . ,,
The Welsh princes submit to Alfred 885
The Danes land in Anglesey 900
Laws enacted by Howel Da, prince of all Wales, about 920
Athelstan subdues the Welsh 933
Civil wars at his death . . . . . about 948
Great battle between the sons of Howel Da and the sons of Idwal Voel; the latter victorious . 954
Edgar invades Wales . . . . . . about 973
Devastations committed by Edwin, the son of Eineon 980
Danes invade Wales; lay Anglesey waste, &c. 980-1000
The country reduced by Aedan, prince of North Wales 1000
Aedan, the usurper, slain in battle by Llewelyn . 1015
Part of Wales laid waste by the forces of Harold . 1063
William I. claims feudal authority over Wales . 1070
Rhys ab Owain kills king Bleddyn, 1073; defeated and slain 1077
Ravaging invasion of Hugh, earl of Chester . 1079-80
Invasion of the Irish and Scots 1080
William I. invades Wales 1081
Battle of Llechryd 1087
[In this conflict the sons of Bleddyn ab Cynvyn were slain by Rhys ab Tewdwr, the reigning prince.]
Rhys ab Tewdwr slain; S. Wales conquered by the English 1090
Invasion of the English under William II. . 1095-7
The settlement in Wales of a colony of Flemings . 1106
Violent seizure of Nest, wife of Gerald de Windsor, by Owain, son of Cadwgan ab Bleddyn . . . 1108
Cardigan conquered by Strongbow 1109
Cadwgan assassinated 1112
Gruffydd ab Rhys lays claim to the sovereignty . 1113
Another body of Flemings settle in Pembrokeshire ,,
[The posterity of these settlers are still distinguished from the ancient British population by their language, manners, and customs.]
Civil war in South Wales and Powysland leads to the subjugation of the country by the English; Henry I. erects castles in Wales . . . 1114 *et seq.*

* The statute of Wales, enacted at Rhuddlan, 19 March, 1284 (or March, 1283), alleges that—"Divine Providence has now removed all obstacles, and transferred wholly and entirely to the king's dominion the land of Wales and its inhabitants, heretofore subject unto him in feudal right." The ancient laws were to be preserved in civil causes; but the law of inheritance was to be changed, and the English criminal law to be put in force. *Annals of England.*

Owain killed in battle with Gerald de Windsor . 1116
Revolt of Owen Gwynedd on the death of Hen. I.; part of South Wales laid waste 1135
The English defeated in several battles . . . 1136
Strongbow, earl of Pembroke, invested with the powers of a count palatine in Pembroke . . 1138
Henry II. invades Wales, receives a stout resistance from Owen Gwynedd, but subdues S. Wales . . 1157
Confederacy of the princes of Wales for the recovery of their independence 1164
Prince Madoc said to have emigrated to America (Southey's epic "Madoc" is based on the tradition.) 1169
Anglesey devastated 1173
The crusades preached in Wales by Baldwin, archbishop of Canterbury 1188
The earl of Chester's inroad into North Wales . . 1210
King John invades Wales, laying waste a great part of the principalities; exacts tribute and allegiance 1211
The pope incites the Welsh to resist John . . 1212
Revolt of the Flemings 1220
Llewelyn, prince of North Wales, commits great ravages; overcomes Henry III. 1228
The earl of Pembroke and other nobles join Llewelyn against Henry III., 1233; a truce . . . 1234
Prince David ravages the marches, &c. . . . 1244
Invasion of Henry III. 1245
Anglesey cruelly devastated by the English Sept. ,,
Llewelyn ap Griffith, the last prince . . . 1246
Welsh princes combine against the English . . 1256
Great invasion of the English; threatened extermination of the Welsh, compelled to retreat with loss 1257
Welsh offers of peace refused 1257-62
Llewelyn's incursions into English territory . 1263
Reported conference between him and Simon de Montfort against the Plantagenets . . . 1265
Llewelyn does homage to Henry III. for a treaty Sept. 1267
Edward I. summons Llewelyn to Westminster; on his refusal to come, deposes him, 1276; and invades Wales . . . . . . June, 1277
Llewelyn submits and obtains good terms 10 Nov. ,,
He marries Eleanor de Montfort . . 13 Oct. ,,
The sons of Gruffydd treacherously drowned in the river Dee, by the earl Warrenne and Roger Mortimer; great insurrection 1281
Hawarden castle taken by surprise by Llewelyn and his brother David, 21 March; they destroy Flint and Rhuddlan castles. Fruitless negotiations Nov. 1282
Battle between Llewelyn and the English near Aber Edw: Llewelyn slain, after the battle, by Adam Frankton . . . . 11 Dec. ,,
Prince David surrenders, and is executed . . 1283
Wales finally subdued by Edward I. . . . . ,,
The first English prince of Wales, son of Edward, born at Caernarvon castle (see *Princes of Wales*, next page) . . . . 25 April, 1284
Statute of Wales (see footnote, preceeding column) enacted . . . . 19 March, ,,
Many insurrections suppressed and the leaders executed 1287-1320
Great rebellion of Owain Glyndwr, or Owen Glendower (descendant of the last prince, Llewelyn), commences 1400
Radnor and other places taken by Owain Glyndwr 1401
Allies with the Scots and the Percies: besieges Caernarvon 1402
And seizes Harlech castle 1404
Makes a treaty with France . . . . 10 May, ,,
Harlech castle retaken by the English forces . . 1407
Loses his allies by their defeat at Bramham moor 19 Feb. 1408
Ravages the English territories 1409
Refuses to ask for terms or submit; dies . 21 Sept. 1415
His son submits . . . . 24 Feb. 1416
Margaret of Anjou, queen of Henry VI., takes refuge in Harlech castle 1459
Town of Denbigh burnt 1460
The earl of Richmond, afterwards Henry VII., lands in Pembroke, and is aided by the Welsh . Aug. 1485
Palatine jurisdictions in Wales abolished by Henry VIII. 1535
Monmouth made an English county; counties of Brecknock, Denbigh, and Radnor formed . . ,,

Act for "laws and justice to be administered in Wales in same form as in England," 27 Henry VIII. 1535
Wales incorporated into England by parliament . 1536
Divided into twelve counties 1543
Dr. Ferrar, bishop of St. David's, burnt at the stake for heresy . . . . . . 30 March, 1555
Lewis Owain, a baron of the exchequer, attacked and murdered while on his assize tour . . . ,,
The bible and prayer-book ordered to be translated into Welsh, and divine service to be performed in that language 1562
Welsh bible printed 1588
First congregation of dissenters assembled in Wales; Vavasour Powel apprehended while preaching . 1620
Beaumaris castle garrisoned for king Charles I. . 1642
Powys castle taken by sir Thos. Myddelton . Oct. 1644
Dr. Laud, formerly bishop of St. David's, beheaded on Tower hill . . . . . . 10 Jan. 1645
Surrender of Hawarden castle to the parliament general Mytton . . . . ,,
Charles I. takes refuge in Denbigh . . . . ,,
Rhuddlan castle surrenders . . . . . . ,,
Harlech castle surrenders to Cromwell's army under Mytton 1647
Battle of St. Fagan's; the Welsh defeated by col. Horton, Cromwell's lieutenant . 8 May, 1648
Beaumaris castle surrenders to Cromwell . . ,,
Pembroke castle taken; Colonel Poyer shot, 25 Apr.* 1649
The lords marchers court suppressed . . . 1688
"Charitable society of Ancient Britons" and Welsh charity schools, established (now at Ashford) 1715
Cymmrodorion Society (for charitable purposes), established 1751-81
The French land in Pembrokeshire, and are made prisoners . . . . Feb. 1797
"Rebecca and her daughters," a name taken from Gen. xxiv. 60, by bands of rioters in female dress, who destroyed the toll-gates and houses in parts of S. Wales, Feb. *et seq.*; an old woman, a toll-keeper, was murdered, 10 Sept.; many persons were tried and punished . . . . . Oct. 1843
Cambrian Archæological Association founded . 1846
Subscriptions begun for a university in Wales Dec. 1863
A national unsectarian University college at Aberystwyth opened . . . . . 9 Oct. 1872
Great strike of colliers in S. Wales, 1 Jan.; ends about . . . . 27 March, 1873
Cymmrodorion society, to promote literature and art, re-established 1877
Great distress in South Wales through decay of coal trade by strikes and commercial depression 1877-8
"Rebecca" riots; people of Rhayader on the Wye capture fish out of season illegally; and resist the water bailiffs . . . . . Dec. 1878-Jan. 1879
Welsh Sunday closing act 1881
A Cambrian academy of arts settled to be established at Llandudno . . . . . Jan. 1882
A university college of South Wales and Monmouthshire established at Cardiff; professors appointed 6 Sept.; opened . . . . . . 4 Oct. 1883
North Wales university college, Bangor, opened, 18 Aug. 1884
The college at Aberystwith burnt; prof. Macpherson and three others perish; damage about 50,000*l.* . . . . . . night, 8, 9 July, 1885
Proposed disestablishment of the church negatived in the commons (241-229) . . . 9 March, 1886

* At the commencement of the civil war, Pembroke castle was the only Welsh fortress in the possession of the parliament, and it was entrusted to the command of col. Laugharne. In 1648, he, and colonels Powel and Poyer, embraced the cause of the king, and made Pembroke their head-quarters; after the defeat at St. Fagan's, they retired to the castle, followed by an army led by Cromwell. They capitulated, after having endured great sufferings from want of water. Laugharne, Powel, and Poyer were tried by a court-martial, and condemned to death; but Cromwell having been induced to spare the lives of two of them, it was ordered that they should draw lots for the favour, and three papers were folded up, on two of which were written the words, "Life given by God;" the third was left blank. The latter was drawn by colonel Poyer, who was shot in London accordingly on the above-mentioned day, after long imprisonment. *Pennant.*

Anti-tithe league formed; intimidation of payers, Aug.-Sept. 1886
Tithe riots at Mochdre, Clwyd; many injured; suppressed by military and police . 16 June, 1887
Three weeks' fire on Ruabon and Berwyn mountains; extinguished after much destruction of life and game . . . . 25 July, ,,
Inauguration of the national council of Wales at Aberystwith; disestablishment and disendowment of the church, home rule &c., advocated, Stuart Rendel, M.P. president, 7 Oct. 1887; annual meeting at Newtown . . . 8 Oct. ,,
Formation of a Welsh land league advocated in America; this league issues a manifesto 24 Dec. ,,
A Welsh clergy defence association formed about Nov. ,,
Marquis of Abergavenny *v.* bishop of Llandaff; after much litigation, verdict for the bishop who had refused to induct the rev. Robert W. Gosse into a living, being ignorant of the Welsh language . . . . 22 Feb. 1888
Death of Henry Richard "M.P. for Wales," ardent nonconformist and peace advocate . 20 Aug. ,,
1,000 miles of road freed from toll in S. Wales by local government act . . . . 2 April, 1889
Mr. Dillwyn's motion for disestablishment of the church in Wales, rejected by the commons (284-231) . . . . 14 May, ,,
The Welsh Intermediate Education act passed, 12 Aug. ,,
Visit of the queen; arrives at Llanderfel, Merionethshire (resides at Palé, seat of Mr. Henry Robertson), 23 Aug.; went to Bala, 23 Aug.; to Wrexham, 24 Aug.; leaves Llangollen 27 Aug. ,,
Welsh Dialect society, prince Louis Lucien Bonaparte, president, established, reported . April, 1890
Great strike of railway servants at Cardiff (see *Strikes*) . . . . 7-15 Aug. ,,
Tithes collected by the help of the military . Aug. ,,
The duke of Clarence visits South Wales, 15-18 Sept. ,,
Dr. Edward Thomas, of Manchester, bequeaths 39,500*l.* to University College of North Wales, announced . . . . Oct. ,,
Mr. David Evans, the first Welsh lord mayor of London in the century . . . . 9 Nov. ,,
Proposed disestablishment of the church in Wales negatived by the commons (235—203), 20 Feb. 1891; again negatived (267—220) . 23 Feb. 1892
The Welsh national council met at Rhyl, 10 Nov. ,,
The Suspensory bill (*which see*) read first time, 23 Feb.; opposed at Anglesey, Swansea, &c., 14 March *et seq.*, at a great meeting at St. James's hall, London, 24 April; bill withdrawn, 18 Sept. 1893
University of Wales charter signed by the Queen, 23 Nov. ,,
The queen's prize at Bisley common first won by a Welshman, serjeant Davies . . 22 July, ,,
Diocesan conferences protest against the Welsh disestablishment bill . . . . June, 1894
A conference at Grosvenor house in defence of the Welsh church, the duke of Westminster chairman, 5,000*l.* subscribed . . . . . 18 June, ,,
Welsh land commission appointed, lord Carrington chairman, March, met 23 May, 1893 . Nov. ,,
Welsh church disestablishment bill, introduced 26 April, withdrawn; 18 July, Mr. Asquith introduces another bill, commons, read 2nd time (304-260) 1 April; committee stage, 6 May *et seq.*; stopped by the dissolution . . . 8 July, 1895
Lord Aberdare, "father of Welsh education," elected chancellor of the Welsh university 25 Jan. died . . . . 25 Feb. ,,
Daniel Owen, popular novelist in Welsh, died Oct. ,,
Death of the rev. Richard Parry, aged 95, eminent bard . . . . 8 Feb. 1897
Land tenure (Wales and Monmouthshire bill), to establish a land court, rejected by commons, 278—154 . . . . 19 May, ,,
Sir G. Osborne-Morgan, liberal politician, born 8 May, 1826; died . . . . . 25 Aug. ,,
S. Wales coal strike, see *Strikes* . 1 April 31 Aug. 1898
See *Liberals* 1899
The duke and duchess of York visit N. Wales, 24-28 April, ,,
The duchess of York and the duke of Connaught open a new pier at Tenby, see *Yachts* . 9 May, ,,
Death of principal Viriamu Jones, of Cardiff, a promoter of higher education . . spring, 1901

The king, chancellor of the Welsh university, resigns, but assumes the title of "Protector," 22 Nov.; Mr. W. Jones's resolution for disestablishment of the Welsh church, rejected, 218–177, 4 Feb. 1902

Local government (Wales and Monmouthshire) bill, 2nd reading rejected by commons, 201–163, 16 April, ,,

Prince and princess of Wales visit N. Wales, the prince installed chancellor of the university, lays the first stone of a new wing to the infirmary at Bangor, and opens the new Alexandra hospital at Rhyl . . . 8, 9, 12 May, ,,

University of Wales (graduates) act, royal assent, 22 July, ,,

Coal crisis in S. Wales, end of sliding scale agreement . . . . 31 Dec. ,,

Resolution in house of commons to grant self government to Wales negatived, 146–74, 25 March, 1903

End of the Penrhyn quarries dispute, reported 7 Nov. ,,

SOVEREIGNS OF WALES.

630. Cadwallawn, king of Gwynedd.
634. Cadwaladr, his son.
661. Idwal, son.
728. Rhodri, or Roderic; heroic defender.
755. Cynan and Howel, sons; incessant war.
818. Mervyn; son-in-law, and Essyllt (wife).
844. Roderic the Great, son.
(Early dates uncertain.)

PRINCES OF GWYNEDD OR NORTH WALES AND FREQUENTLY OF ALL WALES.

877. Anarawd, son of Roderic.
915. Idwal Voel.
943. Howel Da the Good, prince of all Wales.
948. Iefan and Iago; sons of Idwal.
972. Howel ap Iefan, the Bad.
984. Cadwallon, brother.
985. Meredith ap Owen ap Howel Da.
992. Idwal ap Meyric ap Idwal Voel: able, brave.
998. Aedan, a usurper.
1015. Llewelyn ap Sitsyllt, good sovereign.
1023. Iago ap Idwal ap Meyric.
1039. Griffith ap Llewelyn ap Sitsyllt; killed.
1067. Bleddyn.
1073. Trahaern ap Caradoc.
1079. Griffith ap Cynan; able; warlike; generous.
1137. Owain Gwynedd; energetic, successful warrior.
1169. Howel, son.
,, David ap Owain Gwynedd, brother; married sister of Henry II.
1194. Llewelyn, the Great.
1240. David ap Llewelyn.
1246. Llewelyn ap Griffith, last prince of the blood; slain after battle, 11 Dec., 1282.

ENGLISH PRINCES OF WALES.*

1284. Edward Plantagenet (afterwards king Edward II.), son of Edward I., born in Caernarvon Castle on the 25th April, 1284. It is asserted that immediately after his birth he was presented by his father to the Welsh chieftains as their future sovereign, the king holding up the royal infant in his arms, and saying, in the Welsh language, "*Eich Dyn*," literally in English, "This is your man," but signifying, "This is your countryman and king." See, however, "*Ich Dien.*"
1301. Edward of Carnarvon made prince of Wales and earl of Chester.
1343. Edward the Black Prince.
1376. Richard, his son (afterwards Richard II.).
1399. Henry (afterwards Henry V.), son of Henry IV.
1454. Edward, son of Henry VI.; slain at Tewkesbury, 4 May, 1471.
1471. Edward (aft. Edward V.), son of Edward IV.
1483. Edward, son of Richard III.; died in 1484.
1489. Arthur, son of Henry VII.; died in 1502.
1503. Henry, his brother (afterwards Henry VIII.).
Edward, his son (afterwards Edward VI.) was duke of Cornwall, and not prince of Wales.

* WALES, PRINCESS OF. This title was held, some authors say, during the early period of her life, by the princess Mary of England, eldest daughter of Henry VIII., and afterwards queen Mary I. She was created, they state, by her father princess of Wales, in order to conciliate the Welsh people and keep alive the name, and was the only princess of Wales in her own right; a rank she enjoyed until the birth of a son to Henry, who was afterwards Edward VI., born in 1537. This is denied by Banks.

1610. Henry Frederic, son of James I.; died 6 Nov. 1612.
1616. Charles, his brother (afterwards Charles I.).
Charles, his son (afterwards Charles II.), never created prince of Wales.
1714. George Augustus (afterwards George II.).
1729. Frederic Lewis, his son; died 20 March, 1751.
1751. George, his son (afterwards George III.).
1762. George, his son (afterwards George IV.): born 12 Aug.
1841. Albert Edward, son of queen Victoria (afterwards Edward VII.): born 9 Nov.; baptized, king of Prussia a sponsor, 15 Jan. 1842.

Travelled on the continent, and studied at Oxford and Edinburgh, in 1859.

Visited Canada, with the dignity of a viceroy, and the United States, 1860.

Entered the university of Cambridge in Jan.; attended the camp at the Curragh, Kildare, July to Sept.; opened New Middle Temple Library, 31 Oct. 1861.

Ordered to be prayed for as Albert Edward, 8 Jan.; visited the continent, Syria, and Egypt, March-June; Germany and Italy, Aug-Dec. 1862.

Admitted to the house of peers, 5 Feb.; a privy councillor, 8 Dec. 1863.

Married to princess Alexandra of Denmark, 10 March, 1863.

Visited Denmark and Sweden, Sept.-Oct. 1864; Russia, Nov.-Dec. 1866.

Visited International Exhibition, Paris, May, 1867.

Visited Ireland; arrived at Dublin, 15 April, 1868.

Installed knight of St. Patrick, 18 April, 1868.

Opened Leeds Fine Arts Exhibition, 19 May, 1868

With the Princess at Glasgow, laid foundation of new university, 8 Oct. 1868.

Sailed for the continent, 17 Nov.; called at Paris; arrived at Copenhagen, 29 Nov.; visited Berlin, Vienna, and arrived at Cairo, 3 Feb. 1869.

Examined the Suez canal, Feb.; arrived at Constantinople, 1 April; at Sebastopol, 13-17 April; at Athens, 19-24 April; landed at Dover, 13 May, 1869.

Inaugurated Victoria Embankment (Thames), 13 July, 1870.

Opened Workmen's International Exhibition, Islington, 16 July, 1870.

Attacked with typhoid fever, about 19 Nov.; greatest danger, 6-13 Dec.; amendment began 14 Dec., 1871.

Went to St. Paul's with the queen for thanksgiving, 27 Feb.; sailed for the continent, 11 March; visited the Pope, 27 March; opened new grammar school at Yarmouth, 6 June; the Bethnal Green Museum, 24 June, 1872.

At the opening of the great exhibition at Vienna, 1 May, 1873.

At the duke of Edinburgh's wedding at St. Petersburg, 23 Jan.; visit to France: entertained by the duc de Rochefoucauld Bisaccia, duc d'Aumale, and others, about 17 Oct.; at Birmingham, 3 Nov. 1874.

Installed grand master of the freemasons of England, 28 April, 1875.

112,000*l.* voted for his visit to India [more than sufficient] July, 1875.

Sailed from Dover, 11 Oct.; warmly received at Athens, 18 Oct.; at Cairo, invested Mohammed Tewfik, the son of the Khedive, with the Star of India, 25 Oct. 1875.

Arrived at Bombay, 8 Nov.; Poonah, 13 Nov.; Goa, 27 Nov.; Colombo, Ceylon, 1 Dec.; Madras, 13 Dec.; Calcutta, 23 Dec. 1875.

At Benares, 5 Jan.; Lucknow, 6 Jan.; Delhi, 11 Jan.; Lahore, 18 Jan.; Jummoo, Cashmere, 20 Jan.; Agra, 25 Jan.; Gwalior, 31 Jan.; in Nepaul, 12 Feb.; at Allahabad, 7 March; sailed from Bombay, 13 March; arrived in Malta, 6 April; Gibraltar, 15 April; Seville, 21 April; Madrid, 25 April; Lisbon, 1 May; London, with about 500 animals for the Zoological gardens, 11 May; banquet at Mansion house, 19 May; reviewed 30,000 volunteers in Hyde Park, 1 July, 1876.

President of the British commissioners at the Paris exhibition, 1878.

Presided at National Water Supply conference, 21 May; laid foundation of St. Mary's, Wilberforce memorial church, Southampton, 12 Aug. 1878.

Laid foundation of new hospital, Norwich, 27 June; opened new dock at Great Grimsby 22 July, 1879.

Laid foundation of new cathedral at Truro, 20 April; opened new dock at Holyhead, 17 June, 1880.
Laid foundation of central Institution of City and Guilds of London Institute, South Kensington, 18 July, 1881.
Opens the Royal College of Music, 7 May, 1883.
Opens the International Fishery Exhibition, 12 May; closes it 31 Oct. 1883.
Inaugurated the juries at the Health Exhibition, 17 June, 1884.
Visits Newcastle and opens Armstrong park, museum, &c., 20, 21 Aug. 1884.
Visit to Dublin (enthusiastically received), 8 April; Cork, 15 April; Killarney, 16 April; Limerick (warmly received), 20 April; from Dublin to Belfast (warm reception), 23 April; Londonderry, 25 April; sailed from Larne, 27 April, 1885.
Opens art gallery, &c., at Birmingham, 27, 28 Nov. 1885.
Formally opens the Mersey tunnel, 20 Jan. 1886.
Kept his silver wedding, 10 March, 1888.
Opens the international exhibition at Glasgow, 8 May, 1888.
Founds a technical school at Blackburn, 9 May, 1888.
Visits Austria and Hungary, Sept.; Roumania, &c. 4 Oct.; returns to London, 22 Oct. 1888.
"Speeches and Addresses," 1863–1888; published 12 Jan. 1889.
Uncovers several Jubilee statues of the queen, &c. (*see Jubilee*), 1887–9.
Visits the universal exhibition at Paris, June, 1889.
Acts for the queen at the royal agricultural show (*see Windsor*), 24–29 June, 1889.
Receives and attends the Shah of Persia, 1 July *et seq.*
Annual payment of 36,000*l.* to the prince as a provision to his family, voted by the commons 29 July, 1889. Act passed (see *Royal Grants*), 12 Aug. 1889.
The prince and princess at the marriage of the duke of Sparta, 27 Oct. 1889.
Visits the Khedive at Cairo, 1 Nov. *et seq.* 1889.
Lays foundation stone of the new municipal buildings, &c., Westminster, 18 March, 1890.
Visit to Berlin with prince George, 21–28 March, 1890; unveils statue of the duke of Albany at Cannes, 6 April, 1890.
Visits Southwark (*which see*), 24 July, 1890.
Opens new town hall at Portsmouth, 9 Aug. 1890.
Opens the City and S. London Electric Railway, 4 Nov. 1890.
Many similar acts noticed under their respective headings, 1891 *et seq.*
The princess of Wales with the duke of York and her daughters, travel in Italy, Greece, etc. March *et seq.* 1893.
Welsh present to the duke and duchess of York, a centre piece weighing 3,000 oz. made of Welsh gold and silver; 16 Dec. 1893.
The visit of the prince and princess of Wales and the duke of York to Russia (*which see*) Nov. 1894.
Opens the Blackwall tunnel (see *Tunnel*), 22 May, 1897.
Created great master and principal knight, grand cross of the order of the Bath, 21 June, 1897 (see *Hospitals*, 1897).
"H.R.H. The Prince of Wales," by Grant Richards, published, Jan. 1898.
By a fall fractures his knee-cap, 18 July; recovery reported, 6 Aug. 1898.
Shot at by Sipido, aged 15, at the Nord station, Brussels, while travelling with the princess, 4 April, 1900; widespread sympathy; Sipido and 3 accomplices tried at Brussels, 1 July; 3 acquitted, Sipido held *irresponsible*, to be kept in government charge till he becomes 21, 5 July, 1900.
(See *England*, 22 Jan. *et seq.* 1901.)

1901. George Frederick, son of Edward VII., born 3 June, 1865; created duke of York, earl of Inverness, and baron Killarney, 24 May, 1892; capt. R.N. 2 Jan.; married princess Victoria Mary (May) of Teck (see *England*), 6 July, 1893; appointed capt. of the *Crescent* cruiser, 12 May, 1898; made rear-adm., and takes the title of duke of Cornwall, Jan. 1901.
With the duchess sailed for the colonies, 16 March; at Gibraltar, 20–22 March; at Malta, opens arts and crafts exhibition, 25–27 March; at Ceylon, 12–16 April (see *Australia* and other colonies); travelled, 50,718 miles; warmly received in London, 2 Nov. 1901.
The title of prince of Wales and earl of Chester, &c., conferred by the king, 9 Nov. 1901.
Visited St. Bartholomew's and received as president of the hospital, 3 Dec. 1901.
Entertained with the princess at the Guildhall, 5 Dec. 1901.
Visited the German emperor, 25–29 Jan. 1902.
Admitted as a Fellow of the Royal Society, 6 Feb. 1902.
Reviewed 12,000 lads of the Boys' Brigade, 14 June, 1902.
Entertained over 2,400 children from London charities, 26, 27 June, 1902.
Acts for the king at the grand reviews of colonial and Indian troops, 1, 2 July; receives the Indian princes and other distinguished guests, 4 July, 1902.
Charity children's entertainments at Marlborough house in June and 9 Aug. 1902.
Receives and attends the shah of Persia, 18 Aug. *et seq.* 1902.
Issue: Edward Albert Christian, *born*, 23 June, 1894; Albert Frederick, *b.* 14 Dec. 1895; Victoria Alexandra, *b.* 25 April, 1897; Henry William, *b.* 31 March, 1900; George Edward Alexander Edmund, *b.* 20 Dec. 1902.

WALES, UNIVERSITY OF, comprehending colleges at Aberystwith, Cardiff, and Bangor, charter signed by the queen, 23 Nov. 1893; equality of the sexes in regard to professors, &c.; annual government grant, 3,000*l.*, 200,000*l.* subscribed; first court held in London, earl of Rosebery, chairman, 6 April 1894

Meeting of the court at Shrewsbury, lord Aberdare elected chancellor, 25 Jan. 1895; he died, 25 Feb. 1895, succeeded by Albert Edward prince of Wales, 2 July, 1895; installed, 26 June, 1896; succeeded by George Frederick prince of Wales, 1902; installed 8 May.

WALHALLA or **VALHALLA** (the Hall of Glory), a temple near Ratisbon, erected by Louis, king of Bavaria, to receive the statues and memorials of the great men of Germany, commenced 18 Oct. 1830, and inaugurated 18 Oct. 1842. The name is derived from the fabled meeting-place of Scandinavian heroes after death.

WALKERITES, see *Separatists.*

WALKING, see *Pedestrianism.*

WALKING-STICKS, a term satirically applied to candidates for the house of commons nominated by political associations, and subject to them in their parliamentary votes, 1878.

WALLACE COLLECTION, THE, of paintings and other works of art in Hertford house, Manchester-square, London, W., formed by the marquis of Hertford, who resided chiefly in Paris from 1842, till his death, 25 Aug. 1870; spending his large fortune in the acquisition of about 700 pictures and other art treasures.

His heir, Mr. (aft. sir) Richard Wallace, lent a portion of these treasures to the Bethnal Green museum (*which see*). He died 20 July, 1890. His widow, lady Julie Amelia Charlotte Wallace (daughter of M. Bernhard Castlenau), died, 16 Feb. 1897, having bequeathed the whole of the priceless collection to the British nation on certain conditions. Will, dated 20 May, 1894, published, *Times* . . . . 30 March, 1897
A committee appointed, lord Lansdowne chairman, recommends the purchase of Hertford house, and the retention of the collection in it; Mr. (aft. sir) John Murray Scott (trustee by the will),

the earl of Rosebery, sir E. Malet, and others, appointed trustees; and Mr. Claude Phillips keeper, announced, 31 July; report issued, 2 Aug. 1897

Hertford house, after reconstruction as the repository of the collection, opened by the prince of Wales . . . . 22 June, 1900

WALLACE MONUMENT, at Abbey Craig, near Stirling, was inaugurated 27 Aug. 1869, and soon after given into the charge of the magistrates of Stirling. It cost about 13,000*l*. Wallace's sword was transferred from Stirling castle, by order of the secretary of state for war, to the custodians of the Wallace monument, 17 Nov. 1888. The telescope there was presented by the Scotch inhabitants of Ipswich, 24 June, 1865.

WALLACHIA, see *Danubian Principalities*. On 23 Dec. 1861, the union of Wallachia and Moldavia, under the name of Roumania, was proclaimed at Jassy and Bucharest.

WALLER'S PLOT. Edmund Waller, the poet, and others, conspired to disarm the London militia and let in the royalists, May, 1643. The plan was detected and punished, June-July, 1643. Waller betrayed his confederates, and was suffered to emigrate.

WALLIS'S VOYAGE. Captain Wallis sailed from England on his voyage round the world, 26 July, 1766; and returned to England, 19 May, 1768.

WALLOON. This name was given to those inhabitants of the low countries who retained the ancient German language, and to those who adopted the Walloon language (based on the Gaulish), which though surviving as a patois, has been supplanted in France by the modern French. The language of the Walloon protestant refugees in 1556 was French.

A church was given to Walloon refugees by queen Elizabeth at Sandwich, and they still have one at Canterbury. "The History of the Walloon and Huguenot church at Canterbury," by Francis W. Cross, published, Sept. 1898.

The frontier line of Flemish and German towns may be traced from the north through Gravelines to Luxemburg; that of the Walloon towns from Calais to Metz.

WALLS, see *Roman Walls, China*.

WALNUT-TREE has long existed in England.* The black walnut-tree (*Juglans nigra*) was brought to this country from North America before 1629.

WALPOLE'S ADMINISTRATIONS. Mr. Walpole (afterwards sir Robert, and earl of Orford) was born in 1676; became secretary-at-war in 1708; was expelled the house of commons on a charge of misappropriating the public money, 1711; committed to the Tower, 17 Jan. 1712; became first lord of the treasury and chancellor of the exchequer in Oct. 1715. He resigned, on a disunion of the cabinet, in 1717, bringing in the sinking fund bill on the day of his resignation. On the earl of Sunderland retiring in 1721, he resumed his office, and held it till Feb. 1742. He died 18 March, 1745.

SECOND WALPOLE ADMINISTRATION (APRIL, 1721).

Sir Robert Walpole, *first lord of the treasury.*

Thomas, lord Parker, created earl of Macclesfield, *lord chancellor.*

Henry, lord Carleton (succeeded by William, duke of Devonshire), *lord president.*

Evelyn, duke of Kingston (succeeded by lord Trevor), *privy seal.*

James, earl of Berkeley, *first lord of the admiralty.*

Charles (viscount Townshend), and John, lord Carteret (the latter succeeded by the duke of Newcastle), *secretaries of state.*

Duke of Marlborough (succeeded by the earl of Cadogan), *ordnance.*

George Treby (succeeded by Henry Pelham), *secretary-at-war.*

Viscount Torrington, &c.

WALRUS. One placed in the Zoological Gardens in 1853 lived a few days only; another was placed there in the autumn of 1867, and died 25 Dec.

WALTZ, the popular German national dance, was introduced into England by baron Neuman and others in 1813. *Raikes.*

WANDEWASH (S. India). Here the French, under Lally, were severely defeated by colonel Eyre Coote, 22 Jan. 1760.

WANDSWORTH, Surrey. Here was organised a "presbytery," 20 Nov. 1572. In Garratt-lane, near this place, a mock election of a mayor of Garratt was formerly held, after every general election of parliament, to which Foote's dramatic piece, *The Mayor of Garratt* (1763), gave no small celebrity. The iron bridge here was opened 26 Sept. 1873. Constituted a municipal borough by London Government act, 1899 (10 aldermen, 60 councillors). Population, 1881, 103,172; 1891, 155,524; 1901, 232,034.

Wandsworth returns one M.P. by act passed 25 June, 1885.

WAR, called by Erasmus "the malady of princes." Osymandyas of Egypt, the first warlike king, passed into Asia, and conquered Bactria, 2100 B.C. *Usher.* He is supposed by some to be the Osiris of the priests. It is computed that, up to the present time, no less than 6,860,000,000 of men have perished on the field of battle; see *Battles*; *Secretaries*; *Neutral Powers*. An international conference on "usages of war" began at Brussels, 27 July, 1874, and closed without important results. See *Brussels Conference*. In 1880, about 4,000,000 men in arms, annual cost, 500,000,000*l*.

* Near Welwyn, in Hertfordshire, there was the largest walnut-tree on record; it was felled in 1627, and from it were cut nineteen loads of planks; and as much was sold to a gunsmith in London as cost 10*l*. carriage; besides which there were thirty loads of roots and branches. When standing it covered 76 poles of ground; a space equal to 2299 square yards, statute measure.

FOREIGN WARS OF ENGLAND SINCE THE CONQUEST.

War with		Peace.	War with		Peace.	War with		Peace.
Scotland	1068	1092	France	1422	1471	Spain	1588	1604
France	1116	1118	Scotland	1480	1486	Spain	1624	1629
Scotland	1138	1139	France	1492	1492	France	1627	1629
France	1161	1186	France	1512	1514	Holland	1651	1654
France	1194	1195	France	1522	1527	Spain	1655	1660
France	1201	1216	Scotland	1522	1542	France	1666	1668
France	1224	1234	Scotland	1542	1546	Denmark	1666	1668
France	1294	1299	Scotland	1547	1550	Holland	1666	1668
Scotland	1296	1323	France	1549	1550	Algiers	1669	1671
Scotland	1327	1328	France	1557	1559	Holland	1672	167
France	1339	1360	Scotland	1557	1560	France	1689	169
France	1368	1420	France	1562	1564	Peace of Ryswick, 20 Sept.		169

War of the *Succession*, commenced 4 May, 1702. Peace of Utrecht, 13 March, 1713.
War with Spain, 16 Dec. 1718. Peace concluded, 1721.
War; *Spanish War*, 23 Oct. 1739. Peace of Aix-la-Chapelle, 30 April, 1748.
War with France, 31 March, 1744. Closed also on 30 April, 1748.
War; the *Seven Years' War*, 9 June, 1756. Peace of Paris, 10 Feb. 1763.
War with Spain, 4 Jan. 1762. General peace, 10 Feb. 1763.
War with the United States of North America, 14 July, 1774. Peace of Paris, 30 Nov. 1782.
War with France, 6 Feb. 1778. Peace of Paris, 20 Jan. 1783.
War with Spain, 17 April, 1780. Closed same time, 20 Jan. 1783.
War with Holland, 21 Dec. 1780. Peace signed, 2 Sept. 1783.
War of the *Revolution*, 1 Feb. 1793. Peace of Amiens, 27 March, 1802.
War *against Bonaparte*, 29 April, 1803. Finally closed, 18 June, 1815.
War with America, 18 June, 1812. Peace of Ghent, 24 Dec. 1814.
War with Russia, 27 March, 1854. Peace of Paris, 31 March, 1856.
War with the Boer republics (Transvaal and Orange Free state), 11 Oct. 1899. Peace signed at Pretoria, 31 May, 1902.
For the wars with India, China, Persia, Abyssinia, Ashantee, Afghanistan, Zululand, Burmah, Mashonaland, Soudan, Somaliland, see those countries.

WAR AFFAIRS. On account of the war with Russia, the duke of Newcastle, previously colonial secretary, was appointed a secretary for war affairs, and a cabinet minister, 9 June, 1854; see *Secretaries*. War Office act, passed 20 June, 1870, appoints a financial secretary (who may sit in parliament) and other officers. An act for the protection of war department stores was passed in 1867. By the warrant abolishing purchase in the army, in 1871, Mr. Cardwell became virtually uncontrolled minister of war. For WAR OFFICE CHARGE, see under *Army* and *Admiralty*.

New war offices erected by virtue of the Public Offices site act, passed . . . . 24 July, 1882
War Exhibition of trophies, &c., from Egypt, opened at Knightsbridge . . 14 Feb. 1883
Important changes in the war office announced; increased responsibilities of heads of departments, &c. . . . . Feb. 1888
Mr. Campbell-Bannerman, war secretary, reported to the commons important changes to be made in the war office, based on the recommendations of the Hartington commission of 1888: establishment of distinct departments with administrative, consultative and executive functions, the whole to form a deliberative council responsible to the minister; this led to the resignation of the duke of Cambridge, commander-in-chief; 21 June, 1895
War secretary, the marquis of Lansdowne, . 25 June, ,,
The order in council of 1870 assigned the administration of the army to the commander-in-chief, the surveyor-general of the ordnance, and the finan. secretary of the war office; in 1888 the surveyor-general was removed. By an order in council, 21 Nov. 1895, the administration was consigned to 6 officers—the commander-in-chief, adjutant-gen., quartermaster-gen., inspector-gen. of fortifications, inspector-gen. of ordnance, and the financial secretary, all responsible to the secretary of state.
War secretary, Mr. St. John Brodrick . 12 Nov. 1900
Committee on war office reform appointed, Mr. Clinton Dawkins (K.C.B., June, 1902), chairman, sir Chas. Welby, and others, Dec. 1900; col. Ward, permanent under-sec., April; report issued, *Times*, 11 June; by an order in council, 4 Nov. 1901, the adjutant-gen., the director-gen. of mobilization, &c., and the military sec., were placed under the control of the commander-in-chief, the others to be under his supervision, but *are to advise the secretary of state direct.*
War seretary, Mr. Arnold Forster . . . 5 Oct. 1903

WAR, GAME OF (German, *Kriegspiel*), based on the game of chess, was described in a pamphlet in 1780, and rules for it laid down by Domänenrathe von Reisswitz about 1820, and published by his son in 1824-8. Capt. (earl Cromer, 1901) Evelyn Baring published a translation of works on the subject in 1872. A society (including von Moltke) was formed at Magdeburg to study it. Prince Arthur (now duke of Connaught) lectured on this game at Dover, 13 March, 1872. A home district war society has since been established.

WARBECK'S INSURRECTION. Perkin Warbeck, the son of a Florentine Jew, to whom Edward IV. had stood godfather, was persuaded by Margaret, duchess of Burgundy, sister to Richard III., to personate her nephew Richard, Edward V.'s brother, which he did first in Ireland, where he landed, 1492. The imposture was discovered by Henry VII. 1493. Some writers consider that Warbeck was not an impostor.

Warbeck attempted to land in Kent, with 600 men, 169 were taken prisoners, and executed, July, 1495.
Recommended by the king of France to James IV. of Scotland, who gave him his kinswoman, lord Huntley's daughter, in marriage, when he assumed the title of Richard IV. James IV. invaded England in his favour, 1496.
Left Scotland, and went to Bodmin, in Cornwall, where 3000 joined him, Sept. 1497.
On the approach of Henry took sanctuary at Beaulieu; surrendered; taken to London, Oct. 1497.
Said to have been set in the stocks at Westminster and Cheapside, and sent to the Tower, June, 1499.
Accused of plotting with the earl of Warwick to escape out of the Tower, by murdering the lieutenant, Aug.; the plot failed, and he was hanged at Tyburn, 23 Nov.; the earl beheaded, 28 Nov. 1499.

WARBURG (N. Germany). Here the French were defeated by the duke of Brunswick and the allies, 31 July, 1760.

WARDIAN CASES. In 1829, Mr. N. B. Ward, from observing a small fern and grass growing in a closed glass bottle, in which he had placed a chrysalis covered with moist earth, was led to construct his well-known *closely glazed* cases, which afford to plants light, heat, and moisture, and exclude deleterious gases, smoke, &c. They are particularly adapted for ferns. In 1833 they were first employed for the transmission of plants to Sydney, &c., with great success, and professor Faraday lectured on the subject in 1838.

WARDMOTES, meetings of the citizens of London in their wards, where they elect annually their common councilmen. The practice is said to have begun in 1386. They had previously assembled in Guildhall; see *Plough Monday*.

WARRANTS, GENERAL, do not specify the name of the accused. They were declared to be illegal by lord chief justice Pratt, 6 Dec. 1763, in relation to the seizure and committal of Mr. Wilkes for a libel on the king; see *North Briton*.

WARRIOR, see under *Navy of England*, 1860.

WARSAW, the metropolis of Poland. The diet was transferred to this city from Cracow in 1566, and it became the seat of government in 1689. Population in 1890, 443,426; 9 Feb. 1897, 638,208.

The Poles defeated in three days' battle by the Swedes . . . . . 28-30 July, 1656
Alliance of Warsaw, between Austria and Poland, against Turkey, in pursuance of which, John Sobieski assisted in raising the siege of Vienna (September following), signed . . 31 March, 1683
Warsaw surrenders to Charles XII. 1703

Treaty of Warsaw between Russia and Poland, 24 Feb. 1768
The Russian garrison here expelled with the loss of 2000 killed and 500 wounded, and 36 pieces of cannon . . . . 17 April, 1794
The Poles defeated by the Russians at Maciejovice, 4 Oct. ,,
The king of Prussia besieges Warsaw, July; compelled to raise the siege, Sept.; it is taken by the Russians with great slaughter, especially of the armed citizens . . . . . . 9 Nov. ,,
Warsaw constituted a duchy, and annexed to the house of Saxony . . . . Aug. 1807
The duchy overrun by the Russians; Warsaw made the residence of a Russian viceroy . . 1813
The last Polish revolution commences at Warsaw, 29 Nov. 1830
Battle of Grochow, near Warsaw, in which the Russians were defeated, and forced to retreat with the loss of 7000 men . . . . . 25 Feb. 1831
Battle of Warsaw, when, after two days' hard fighting, the city capitulated, and was taken possession of by the Russians; and great part of the Polish army retired towards Plock and Modlin, 6-8 Sept. ,,
The czar meets the emperor of Austria and the regent of Prussia; no result . . 20-25 Oct. 1860
Panic in a church; great loss of life . 25 Dec. 1881
Alexander III. visits Warsaw; great precautions, 8 Sept. 1884
Suspected conspiracy, arrest of 30 students and a novelist named Smolnicky . about 30 Dec. 1891
Railway collision at the terminus (Pushto-Warsaw line), 11 deaths . . . . . . 30 Nov. 1897
Statue of Adam Mitskevitch, poet and patriot, unveiled . . . . 24 Dec. 1898
(See *Poland*, 1861-5.)

WARTBURG, a castle in Saxony (N. Germany), where Luther was conveyed for safety after the diet of Worms, April, 1521, and where he translated the Bible into German.

WARWICK CASTLE (Warwickshire), the seat of the Beauchamps, Nevilles, Plantagenets, Dudleys, Riches, and Grevilles, successively, and frequently besieged; suffered much by fire, 3 Dec. 1871; some of the more ancient part was destroyed. The town, incorporated in 1553, was nearly destroyed by fire in 1694. The show of the Agricultural society here was opened by the prince of Wales and the duke of York, 20 June, 1892. Visit of the prince of Wales to the castle, 17 May, 1895. "Warwick Castle," by the countess of Warwick, published Oct. 1903. Population, 1881, 11,800; 1891, 11,903; 1901, 11,889.

WASH-HOUSES, see *Baths*.

WASHING MACHINES. Several have been invented by Americans. At an hotel in New York hundreds of garments are washed in a few minutes by steam, and dried by a centrifugal machine (1862). The ingenious machines of Messrs. Hornsby, of Norwich, appeared in the great exhibition of London, 1862; many improvements since.

WASHINGTON. A northern state of the American Union, first settled in 1845, organized as a Territory in 1853, as a State 1889; population in 1880, 75,116; 1890, 349,390; 1900, 958,800. Capital, Olympia.

The flourishing town of Seattle was nearly destroyed by fire about 6 June, 1889; estimated loss about $15,000,000; few lives lost.
Ellensburg, a small town also nearly destroyed by fire, 4 July, 1889; estimated loss, $2,000,000; also Spokane Falls, loss about $10,000,000, about 4 Aug. 1889
Coal mine explosion near Roslyn, 43 deaths, 10 May, 1892
Fire in the Franklin mine near Seattle, 37 lives lost . . . . 24 Aug. 1894
Forest fires, loss of life, &c., reported . 15 Sept. 1902

WASHINGTON (in Columbia district, partly in Virginia and partly in Maryland, on the bank of the Potomac, N.E. Virginia), the capital of the United States, founded in 1791, and made the seat of government in 1800. The capital was founded in 1793. Population, 1880, 147,293; 1890, 230,392; 1900, 278,718.

The house of representatives opened . . 30 May, 1808
Washington was taken by the British forces under general Ross, after his victory at Bladensburg; its superb structures and national library burnt, 24 Aug. 1814
General Ross killed by some American riflemen, in a desperate engagement at Baltimore 12 Sept. ,,
Naval observatory founded 1842
Smithsonian institute (*which see*) founded . . . 1846
Part of the capitol and the whole of the library of the United States congress destroyed by fire, 24 Dec. 1851
The prince of Wales entertained by the president here . . . . Oct. 1860
Washington fortified in . . . . April, 1861
President Lincoln shot by Booth in Ford's theatre, 14 April; died . . . . . 15 April, 1865
Memorial obelisk to George Washington, 555 feet high, inaugurated . . . . . 21 Feb. 1885
National theatre burnt down . . . 27 Feb ,,
Fire at the house of the hon. Benjamin Tracy, secretary of the navy; he escapes, but his wife, daughter, and a servant perish . . 3 Feb. 1890
Collapse of government offices, formerly Ford's theatre, through excavations, 23 persons killed and many injured . . . . . 9 June, 1893
(Col. Frederick Ainsworth and others censured for negligence).
Fire at the capitol through an explosion of gas, 6 Nov. 1898
Peace celebrations (Spanish-American war), 23 May, 1899
Mr. A. Carnegie gives 2,000,000*l.* for a scientific research institute . . . . . 29 Jan. 1902
The German emperor offers a statue of Frederick the Great . . . . 14 May, ,,
Marshal Recambeau's statue unveiled . . 24 May ,,
Pres. Roosevelt lays first stone of the new army college . . . . 21 Feb. 1903
See *United States*.

IMPORTANT TREATIES OF WASHINGTON.

Fixing N.W. boundary of British America and United States, &c. . . . . . . 12 June, 1846
"Reciprocity" treaty regulating trade with Canada, 7 June, 1854
Referring the *Alabama* claims and the San Juan boundary question to arbitration; settling disputes respecting fisheries (see *Alabama* and *Juan*), and laying down three rules; asserting that it is the duty of a neutral state, which desires to remain at peace with belligerents, and to enjoy the rights of neutrality, to abstain from taking any part in the war by affording military aid to one or both of the belligerents; and to take care that no acts which would constitute such co-operation in the war be committed by any one within its territory . . . . 8 May, 1871

WASIUM (named from the royal house of Wasa or Vasa), a supposed new metal, discovered by F. Bahr, of Stockholm, in 1862. In Nov. 1863 Nicklès declared it to be a compound of didymium, yttrium, and terbium.

WASTE LANDS. The inclosure of waste lands and commons, in order to promote agriculture, first began in England about the year 1547, and gave rise to Ket's rebellion, 1549. Inclosures were again promoted by the authority of parliament, 1785. The waste lands in England were estimated in 1794 to amount to 14 millions of acres, of which there were taken into cultivation, 2,837,476 acres before June, 1801. In 1841, there were about 6,700,000 acres of waste land, of which more than half was thought to be capable of improvement; see *Agriculture*.

WATCH OF LONDON, at night, appointed 1253, proclaimed the hour with a bell before the introduction of public clocks. *Hardie.* The old watch was discontinued, and a new police (on duty day and night) commenced, 29 Sept. 1829; see *Police.*

WATCHES are said to have been first invented at Nuremberg, 1477, although it is affirmed that Robert, king of Scotland, had a watch about 1310.

Watches first used in astronomical observations by Purbach 1500
Authors assert that the emperor Charles V. was the first who had anything that might be called a watch, though some call it a small table-clock . 1530
Watches first brought to England from Germany in 1577
A watch which belonged to queen Elizabeth is preserved in the library of the Royal Institution, London.
Spring pocket-watches (watches properly so-called) have had their invention ascribed to Dr. Hooke by the English, and to M. Huyghens by the Dutch. Dr. Derham, in his *Artificial Clockmaker*, says that Dr. Hooke was the inventor; and he appears certainly to have produced what is called the pendulum watch about 1658; manifest, among other evidences, from an inscription on one of the double-balance watches presented to Charles II., "Rob. Hooke, inven. 1658; T. Tompion, fecit, 1675."
Repeating watches invented by Barlowe . . . 1676
Harrison's first time-piece produced (see *Harrison*), 1735
Watches and clocks were taxed in 1797
The tax was repealed in 1798. See *Clocks.*
Arrangements made at Kew observatory for testing high-class watches, and granting graduated certificates; fees, 1*l.* 1*s.*, 10*s.* 6*d.*, &c.; announced April, 1884
Great revival of the old manufacture by the Lancashire watch company, at Prescot, near Liverpool . . . . Jan. 1893

WATER. Thales of Miletus, founder of the Ionic sect, considered water to be the original principle of everything, about 594 B.C. *Stanley.*

Cavendish and Watt demonstrated that water is composed of 8 parts of oxygen and 1 part of hydrogen 1781–4
Water was decomposed into oxygen and hydrogen gases by Lavoisier, 1783; by the voltaic battery by Nicholson and Carlisle, 1800; by the heat of the oxy-hydrogen flame by W. R. Grove . 1846
In freezing, water contracts till it is reduced to 42° or 40° Fahr.; it then begins to expand till it becomes ice at 32°.
Water was first conveyed to London by leaden pipes, 21 Henry III. 1237. *Stow.* It took nearly fifty years to complete it; the whole being finished, and Cheapside conduit erected, only in . . . 1285
The New River water (*which see*) brought to London from Chadwell and Amwell in Hertfordshire, at an immense expense, by sir Hugh Myddelton, in 1609–13
The city was supplied with its water by conveyances of wooden pipes in the streets and small leaden ones to the houses, and the New River Company was incorporated, 1620. So late as queen Anne's time there were water-carriers at Aldgate-pump.
The water-works at Chelsea completed, and the company incorporated 1722
London-bridge ancient water-works destroyed by fire . . . . 29 Oct. 1779
An act to supply the metropolis with water, 15 & 16 Vict. c. 84, was passed, 1 July, 1852. This act was amended by an act passed 21 Aug. 1871. The companies were bound to provide a constant supply when required; the owner or occupier of the house to provide the prescribed fittings.
[The supply is now considered to be much improved in quality and quantity.]
Since 1829 filtration gradually adopted; made compulsory in 1856.
A company was formed to carry out Dr. Normandy's patent for converting salt water into fresh, in Jan 1857
Messrs. Pamphlett & Ferguson's process for producing fresh from salt water was exhibited at Messrs. George Wailes & Co., Euston Road, London, and considered successful . . 15 Oct. 1889
Commissioners for metropolitan water supply appointed, 27 April, 1867; report signed 9 June, 1869
London supplied by nine companies: the New River (the best), East London, Chelsea, Grand Junction, Southwark and Vauxhall, Kent, West Middlesex, Lambeth, and South Essex; who deliver about 108,000,000 gallons daily, 1867; about 116,250,000 gallons 1877
New schemes for supplying London with water, 1867:—
1. Mr. Bateman; from the sources of the Severn.
2. Messrs. Hemans and Hassard; from the Cumberland lakes.
3. Mr. Telford Macneill; Thames water filtered through Bagshot sand.
4. Mr. Bailey Denton; storage reservoirs near the sources of the Thames.
5. Mr. Remington; from the Derbyshire and Staffordshire hills.
The water from the first two sources analysed and highly approved by professors Frankland and Odling . . . . April, 1868
Water from the chalk districts softened by Homersham's process strongly recommended, Jan, 1871 Aug. 1878
Metropolitan Board of works undertook to supply water from the chalk districts and also from the Thames above Teddington, for 12,000,000*l.* ,,
Conference on the national water supply at Society of arts (suggested by the prince of Wales, president) . . . . . . 21, 22 May ,,
Letter from the prince of Wales to the earl of Beaconsfield suggesting the appointment of a commission on water supply, dated 24 March, 1879
National Water Supply Exhibition, Alexandra Palace; opened . . . . . . 14 Aug. ,,
Government proposal to buy companies' works for 34,398,700*l.* (New River company, 9,146,000*l.*), dropped . . . . April, 1880
Negotiations with the water companies by Mr. Smith, begun Oct. 1879; proposals not accepted, ,,
London water supply commission (Sir William Harcourt, chairman) appointed 3 June; reported, recommending water supply to be placed under control of some responsible public body, signed 3 Aug. ,,
Annual revenue, according to Mr. E. J. Smith's calculations, above 1,500,000*l.* 1881
Atkins' process for softening hard water an improvement upon Clarks' process, announced July, 1882
Metropolitan water bill, checking the systems of the companies, rejected in the commons (197–152) 11 March, 1884
Water companies (regulation of powers) act, passed 1887
The purchase of the companies' works recommended by the London County Council, 1890, and by a committee of the London corporation; report published . . . . . . 17 Oct. 1890
At a conference of representatives of the district boards of London, it was resolved to support sir Algernon Borthwick's bill, which proposes to confer upon an elected Water Trust the exclusive powers of supplying water within the metropolitan area, with an equalization of charges, &c., 27 Feb. 1891
Hybrid committee in the commons on the London Water Commission appointed: sir M. White Ridley, sir H. E. Roscoe, sir A. Borthwick, and six others . . . . . 20 March, ,,
Report disapproving of the two bills before parliament, and requiring further information 14 July, ,,
London Water act passed . . . . . 27 June, 1892
Royal commission on the metropolitan water supply appointed: lord Balfour of Burleigh, sir G. Barclay Bruce, prof. James Dewar, sir A. Geikie, Dr. Wm. Ogle, and others (frequent meetings up to July), reported . . 14 March, ,,
Twenty-ninth and last sitting, 15 Feb.; report with statistics and recommendations presented about 15 Sept. 1893; existing sources of supply from the Thames, Lea, etc. sufficient for 40 years; 8 bills for the acquisition of the undertakings of the Metropolitan water companies by the London county council deposited at private bill office, 21 Dec. 1894

Scarcity of water in London through severe frost, board of trade inquiry . . . Feb.–March, 1895
Progress of the water (transfer) bills stopped by the dissolution . . . 8 July, „
Water famine in east London . . . June–Aug. „
Increased supply through new works, reported Feb. 1896
Lord James's metropolitan water bill instituting a representative body (30 members) for inner and outer London read 1st time, 16 March; withdrawn . . . . Aug. „
Water famine in E. London much relieved by rain, 3 Sept. *et seq.* (another famine, Aug. 1898) . . „
Chelsea water bill rejected in the commons, 258—123; 7 other water bills withdrawn . 11 March, 1897
New Royal commission: visc. Llandaff, Mr. J. W. Mellor, sir J. Dorington, sir J. Bruce, and others, April; 1st sitting . . . . 22 Nov. „
Proposed formation of a "sinking fund" by the London water companies, trustee, the chamberlain of the city of London . . . May, „
The Metropolitan water act passed; brought into action . . . . Oct. „
Constant service in E. London begins . 7 Dec. 1898
Metropolitan water companies bill passed, 6 June, 1899
Roy. commission's report issued, 19 Jan. 1899; central water board to acquire the undertakings of the companies recommended in report, issued, 22 Jan. 1900
County council's London water (purchase) bill rejected . . . . . . 26 March, 1901
Conference on water supply and river pollution in London . . . . . 16 Oct. 1901
London water bill (*see above*, Jan. 1900) passed, 16 Dec. 1902
Local government board's inquiry as to lead poisoning through, reports issued 1887, 1895, and 16 Feb. 1903

See *Artesian Wells, Aqueducts, Birmingham, Liverpool,* and *Metropolitan Water Supply.*

WATER-BED, CLOCKS, see *Beds, Clocks.*

WATER-COLOUR PAINTING was gradually raised from the hard dry style of the last century to its present brilliancy, by the efforts of Nicholson, Copley Fielding, Sandby, Varley, the great Turner, Pyne, Cattermole, Prout, George A. Fripp, born 1813, died 17 Oct. 1896, and George Price Boyce, born 24 Sept. 1826, died 9 Feb. 1897; George Henry Andrews, born 1816, died 31 Dec. 1898; Birket Foster, born 1825, died 27 March, 1899. David Law, died 28 Dec. 1901, &c., within the past century. The Water-colour Society's exhibition, which began in 1805, was made Royal in 1881, the diplomas were to be signed by the queen after Nov. 1882. The Institute of Painters in Water-colours, established about 1831 (made Royal in 1883), open new galleries in Piccadilly, and propose to give free instruction, 27 April, 1883.

Dr. John Percy's unique historical collection of water-colour drawings was sold for 8,230*l.*, reported . . . . 26 April, 1890

WATERFORD (S. Ireland), built about 879, was totally destroyed by fire in 981. Rebuilt and considerably enlarged by Strongbow in 1171, and still further in the reign of Henry VII., who granted considerable privileges to the citizens. Richard II. landed and was crowned here in 1399; in 1690, James II. embarked from hence for France, after the battle of the Boyne; and William III. resided here twice, and confirmed its privileges. Memorable storm here, 18 April, 1792. The cathedral of Waterford, dedicated to the blessed Trinity, was first built by the Ostmen, and by Malchus, the first bishop of Waterford, after his return from England from his consecration, 1096. This see was united with that of Lismore in 1363. It was valued in the king's books, by an extent returned 29 Henry VIII., at 72*l.* 8*s.* 1*d.* Irish per annum. By stat. 3 & 4 Will. IV., c. 37 (the Irish Church Temporalities act), the see of Waterford and Lismore was united with the see of Cashel and Emly, 14 Aug. 1833. The interior of the cathedral, organ, &c., were destroyed by fire, 25 Oct. 1815. Population, 1891, 21,693; 1901, 26,743.

Waterford returns three M.P.s by act passed 25 June, 1885
Mr. John Redmond, M.P., presented with the freedom . . . . 12 Sept. „

WATER GAS, see *Gas-lights.*

WATER-GLASS, a name given to a liquid mixture of sand (silex) and one of the alkalies (potash or soda). Glauber (*De Lithiase*) mentions a similar mixture in 1644. Dr. Von Fuchs, the modern inventor, gave an account of his process in 1825; and Mr. Frederick Ransome, of Ipswich, ignorant of Von Fuchs's discovery, patented a mode of preparing water-glass in 1845, which he afterwards greatly improved upon. In 1857, M. Kuhlmann, of Lille, published a pamphlet setting forth the advantageous employment of water-glass in hardening porous stone and in stereochromy (*which see*). It has been applied to the exterior of many buildings in France and England. The memoirs of Von Fuchs and Kuhlmann translated and printed in England, 1859, by direction of the prince consort.

WATERING STREETS. Mr. Cooper's plan for using solutions of chloride of lime or of sodium (which dry slowly and attract moisture and ammonia and other gases, and combine them with the material of the road) was partially used in the parish of St. Mary-le-bone in 1868, and also in Liverpool, Boston, and other towns. The plan was ordered to be tried in Westminster in July, 1870.

WATERLOO, in Belgium, the site of the great battle, on Sunday, 18 June, 1815, between the French army, of 71,947 men and 246 guns, under Napoleon, and the allies, commanded by the duke of Wellington; the latter, with 67,661 men and 156 guns, resisted the various attacks of the enemy from about ten in the morning until five in the afternoon. About that time, 16,000 Prussians reached the field of battle; and by seven, the force under Blucher amounted to above 50,000 men, with 104 guns. Wellington then moved forward his whole army. A total rout ensued, and the carnage was immense. Of the British (23,991), 93 officers and 1916 men were killed and missing, and 363 officers and 4560 men wounded—total, 6932; and the total loss of the allied army amounted to 4206 killed, 14,539 wounded, and 4231 missing, making 22,976 *hors de combat*. Napoleon, quitting the wreck of his army, returned to Paris; and, finding it impossible to raise another, abdicated. *P. Nicolas.*

Napoleon attributed his defeat to the failures of marshal Grouchy, Wellington said unjustly.
Proposed monument over the British officers and men who died of their wounds, 7 Jan. 1888.
By the side of the chapel of Waterloo, which was uninjured by shot or shell on 18 June, 1815, Marlborough cut off a large division of the French forces, 17 Aug. 1705. The conquerors on the same field are the only British commanders whose career brought them to dukedoms.
Waterloo monument over the officers and men who fell in the campaign of 1815, in a cemetery at Brussels, erected by queen Victoria, unveiled by the duke of Cambridge . . . . . 26 Aug. 1890
Gen. George Whichcote, born 21 Dec. 1794, who fought in the Spanish campaigns and at Waterloo, died . . . . 26 Aug. 1891
German emperor congratulates the German legion "on having saved the British army from destruction at Waterloo" . . . . . . 19 Dec. 1903

WATERLOO BRIDGE, LONDON. A bridge over this part of the Thames was repeatedly suggested during the last century, but no actual preparations to carry it into effect were made till 1806, when Mr. G. Dodd procured an act of parliament, and gave the present site, plan, and dimensions of the bridge; but, in consequence of some disagreement with the committee, he was superseded by Mr. John Rennie, who completed this noble structure. It was commenced 11 Oct. 1811, and opened 18 June, 1817, on the anniversary of the battle of Waterloo, when the prince regent, the duke of Wellington, and other distinguished personages, were present. Its length within the abutments is 1242 feet; its width within the balustrades is 42 feet; and the span of each arch, of which there are nine, is 120 feet. Bought for 475,000*l.* by metropolitan board of works; opened toll free, 5 Oct. 1878; lit by electric light from 10 Oct. 1879.

On Oct. 9, 1857, two youths, named Kilsby, found on one of the abutments of the bridge a carpet bag, containing human bones and flesh, which had been cut up, salted, and boiled, and some foreign clothes. No clue could be found respecting these remains, which were interred in Woking cemetery.

WATERLOO CUP, see *Dogs*, 1871 and 1903.

WATERLOW PARK, S. Hampstead or Highgate, was presented to the metropolis with 6,000*l.* to the London county council, by sir Sydney H. Waterlow, 12 Nov. 1889. The park was opened to the public by sir John Lubbock (lord Avebury, 1900) chairman of the council, 17 Oct. 1891. A statue of sir Sydney Waterlow unveiled by princess Louise, duchess of Argyll, 28 July, 1900.

WATER-MILLS, used for grinding corn, are said to have been invented by Belisarius, the general of Justinian, while besieged in Rome by the Goths, 555. The ancients parched their corn, and pounded it in mortars. Afterwards mills were invented, which were turned by men and beasts with great labour; yet Pliny mentions wheels turned by water. See *Telo-dynamic transmitter*.

WATERSPOUT. Two waterspouts fell on the Glatz mountains in Germany, and caused dreadful devastation to Hautenbach and many other villages; many persons perished, 13 July, 1827. A waterspout at Glanflesk, near Killarney, in Ireland, passed over a farm of Mr. John Macarthy, destroying farm-houses and other buildings; seventeen persons perished, 4 Aug. 1831. The estimated length of one seen near Calcutta, 27 Sept. 1855, was 1000 feet. It lasted ten minutes, and was absorbed upwards. One seen on 24 Sept. 1856, burst into heavy rain. The town of Miskolcz, Hungary, destroyed by a waterspout; great loss of life and property, 30 Aug. 1878. 61 persons said to have been killed by a waterspout in Algeria, Oct. 1881. A waterspout at Arequipa, Peru, caused immense damage, several persons drowned, 14 Feb.; one at Pachuca, Mexico, 30 deaths, 27 Sept. 1884; another near Lagos, very destructive, 6 or 7 June, 1885. Destructive waterspout at Swansea 4 Sept. 1886; another on Batcombe hills, Dorsetshire, greatly damaged the villages of Chatnole, Cerne, and Mintern, 7 June, 1889. By the bursting of a waterspout at Voiron, near Grenoble, France, much damage was done with loss of life, 5 June, 1897; Steelville, Missouri, nearly destroyed by one, 13 deaths, 8 July, 1898. At Saffi, Morocco, about 100 deaths, great damage, 29 Dec. 1901. See *Wurtemburg*, June, 1895.

WATER TOFANA, see *Poisoning*.

WATKIN TOWER, Wembley Park, near Harrow, N.W. of London. In 1889, the Metropolitan tower company was formed, sir Edward W. Watkin, chairman, for the erection of a tower resembling the Eiffel tower, see *Paris*, 1889.

Premiums were offered for designs, and 500 guineas were awarded to Messrs. A. D. Stewart, J. M. MacLaren, and W. Dunn, joint authors. The designs were exhibited at Drapers' Hall, 29 April *et seq.*, 1890. Part of the Wembley Park estate was leased by a new company for 999 years, from 21 Oct. 1892, at a rental of 2,000*l.* a year. The structure, solely of steel, to be erected by Messrs. Heenan and Froude of Manchester (Dec. 1892), under the direction of Sir Benjamin Baker. Work proceeding, base 90,000 sq. ft., Oct. 1893.

Wembley Park opened, 12 May, 1894.

Erection of the tower stopped, Aug. 1894; the first platform opened, 155 feet from the ground, 18 May, 1896.

WATLING-STREET, see *Roman Roads*.

WATTIGNIES (N. France). Here Jourdan and the French republicans defeated the Austrians under the prince of Coburg, and raised the siege of Maubeuge, 14-16 Oct. 1793.

WAT TYLER'S INSURRECTION, see *Tyler*.

WAVE PRINCIPLE (in accordance with which the curves of the hull of a ship should be adapted to the curves of a wave of the sea) formed the subject of experiments begun by Mr. John Scott Russell in 1832, with the view of increasing the speed of ships. Colonel Beaufoy is said to have spent 30,000*l.* in researches upon this matter. It was also taken up by the British Association, who have published reports of the investigations. The principle has been adopted by naval architects; see *Undulatory Theory* and *Yacht*.

WAVERLEY NOVELS. The publication of the series began with "Waverley; or, 'Tis Sixty Years since," in 1814, and closed with "Tales of my Landlord," fourth series, in 1831. The authorship was acknowledged by sir Walter Scott, at a dinner, 23 Feb. 1827. The original MSS. of several of Scott's poems and novels were sold by auction by Christie and Manson for 1255 guineas, 6 July, 1867.

WAWZ or WAWER (Poland). The Poles under Skrzynecki attacked the Russians at Wawz, and after two days' hard fighting, all the Russian positions were carried by storm, and they retreated with the loss of 12,000 men and 2000 prisoners, 31 March, 1831. The loss of the Poles was small, but their triumph was soon followed by defeat and ruin.

WAX came into use for candles in the 12th century; and wax candles were esteemed a luxury in 1300, being but little used. In China, candles of vegetable wax have been in use for centuries; see *Candleberry*. The wax tree, *Ligustrum lucidum*, was brought from China before 1794.—SEALING-WAX was not brought into use in England until about 1556. Its use has been much superseded by the introduction of adhesive envelopes, about 1844.

WAXWORK.—Exhibition of models in wax were popular in the 17th and 18th centuries. The collection of wax figures exhibited by Mrs. Salmon at Aldgate, early in the last century, were removed to Fleet-street and shown there till 1812, when they were sold, it is said, for 50*l.* Madame Tussaud, a skilful modeller, exhibited her remarkable collection of models and casts of eminent persons with costumes and other interesting relics in the boulevard du Temple, Paris, 1785. In 1802 she exhibited her collection at the Lyceum, Strand, London, and afterwards at other places. The interest of the exhibition has been energetically sustained for many years at Baker-street, London, W., and latterly at

Marylebone-road, by madame Tussaud and her family; she died 15 April, 1850, aged 90. Early in 1889 the collection was purchased by a company, Mr. John Tussaud being engaged as manager. The exhibition well sustained, 1898.

Mr. Louis Tussaud opened a new exhibition of wax-works at 207, Regent-street, 24 Dec. 1890; it was destroyed by fire, 20 June, 1891, estimated loss, 10,000*l*.

See *Trials*, Jan. 1894.

WE. Sovereigns generally use *we* for *I*, which style began with king John, 1199. *Coke*. The German emperors and French kings used the plural about 1200.

WEALD of Kent and Sussex, the site of very large, ancient forests; St. Leonard's still remaining; near which, in the Wealden formation, Dr. G. A. Mantell discovered the remains of huge extinct animals, 1825 *et seq.* Mr. R. Furley published an exhaustive "History of the Weald of Kent," 1871-4.

WEATHER, see *Meteorology*.

WEAVING appears to have been practised in China more than a thousand years before it was known in Europe or Asia. The Egyptians ascribed the art to Isis; the Greeks to Minerva; and the Peruvians to the wife of Manco Capac. Our Saviour's vest, or coat, had not any seam, being woven from the top throughout, in one whole piece. The print of a frame for weaving such a vest may be seen in *Calmet's Dictionary*, under the word *Vestments*. Two weavers from Brabant settled at York, where they manufactured woollens, which, says king Edward, "may prove of great benefit to us and our subjects" (1331). Flemish dyers, cloth drapers, linen-makers, silk-throwsters, &c., settled at Canterbury, Norwich, Colchester, Southampton, and other places, on account of the duke of Alva's persecution, 1567; see *Loom* and *Electric Loom*.

WEDDINGS. Silver weddings are celebrated after a union of 25 years; golden weddings after a union of 50 years; and diamond weddings after a union of 60 years, some apply it to 75 years. John, king of Saxony, celebrated his golden wedding, 10 Nov. 1872.

WEDDING-RINGS were used by the ancients, and put upon the wedding finger, from a supposed connection with a vein there with the heart. According to Pliny they were made of iron; in the time of Tertullian of gold. Wedding-rings are to be of standard gold, by statute, 1855; see *Adriatic*.

WEDGE-LIKE CHARACTERS, see *Cuneiform*.

WEDGWOOD WARE, pottery and porcelain produced by Mr. Josiah Wedgwood, of Staffordshire, in 1762. His potteries, termed Etruria, were founded in 1771. Previously to 1763, much earthenware was imported from France and Holland.

WEDNESDAY, the fourth day of the week, so called from the Saxon idol Woden or Odin, worshipped on this day. Woden was the reputed author of magic and the inventor of all the arts, and was thought to answer to the Mercury of the Greeks and Romans.

WEEDON INQUIRY (Northamptonshire). Commissioners were appointed to inquire into the accounts of Mr. Elliot, superintendent of the great military clothing establishment at this place, in July, 1858, and commenced sitting in September. Many of the statements were afterwards disputed, and caused much dissatisfaction.

WEEK, the space of seven days, supposed to be first used among the Jews, who observed the sabbath every seventh day. They had three sorts of weeks—the common one of seven days; the second of years, seven years; the third of seven times seven years, at the end of which was the jubilee. All the present English names are derived from the Saxon:—

Latin.		*French.*
Dies Solis,	Day of the Sun,	Dimanche.
Dies Lunæ,	Day of the Moon,	Lundi.
Dies Martis,	Day of Mars,	Mardi.
Dies Mercurii,	Day of Mercury,	Mercredi.
Dies Jovis,	Day of Jupiter,	Jeudi.
Dies Veneris,	Day of Venus,	Vendredi.
Dies Saturni,	Day of Saturn,	Samedi.

English.	*Saxon.*	*German.*
Sunday,	Sun's day,	Sonntag.
Monday,	Moon's day,	Montag.
Tuesday,	Tiw's day,	Dienstag.
Wednesday,	Woden's day,	Mittwoche.
Thursday,	Thor's day,	Donnerstag.
Friday,	Friga's day,	Freitag.
Saturday,	Saterne's day,	Samstag, or Sonnabend.

WEEKLY DISPATCH, liberal weekly Sunday paper, established 1801.

WEIGHTS AND MEASURES. These and the stamping of gold and silver money, are attributed to Pheidon, tyrant of Argos, 895 B.C.; see *Arundelian Marbles*. Weights were originally taken from grains of wheat, the lowest being still called a grain. *Chalmers*. See *Crith*.

Much information is given by Mr. H. W. Chisholm in his work "On the Science of Weighing and Measuring," 1877.

The Jews ascribed weights and measures to Cain; the Egyptians to Theuth, or Thoth; the Greeks, to Hermes (the Roman Mercury).

The basis of ancient measures was the natural proportions of the human body; the digit, or breadth of the middle part of the first joint of the fore finger, being the lowest unit of the scale.

The Egyptian cubit (six palms), under the Pharaohs, was about 18.24 English inches; the cubit of Ptolemy about 21.87 inches; he determined the length of a stadium, and of a degree.

The sacred cubit of the Jews (Newton), 24·7 inches.

Assyrian weights are described by Mr. Layard in his "Nineveh."

The standard measure was originally kept at Winchester by the law of king Edgar 972

Standards of weights and measures were provided for the whole kingdom of England by the sheriffs of London, 9 Rich. I. 1197

A public weighing-machine was set up in London, and all commodities ordered to be weighed by the city-officer, called the weigh-master, who was to do justice between buyer and seller, stat. 3 Edw. II. (*Stow*) 1309

Edward III. ordered that there should be "one weight, measure, and yard," throughout the kingdom 1353

First statute, directing the use of avoirdupois weight, of 24 Hen. VIII. 1532

Weights and measures ordered to be examined by the justices at quarter-sessions, 35 Geo. III. . . 1795

Again regulated 1800

Statute for establishing a uniformity of weights and measures, 1824, took effect throughout the United Kingdom . . . . 1 Jan. 1826

New acts relating thereto passed in 1834, 1835, 1855, and in 1859

16 & 17 Vict. c. 29, regulates the weights to be used in the sale of bullion, and adopts the use of the Troy ounce 1853

A commission (consisting of Mr. G. B. Airy, gen. E. Sabine, lord Rosse, Mr. T. Graham, and others), appointed to examine the standards . 9 May, 1867

d report of the Standards commission states that errors exist in official standards, dated 24 July, 1868

A new Weights and Measures act passed to enforce uniformity in all markets in the United Kingdom, and abolish local measures, 8 Aug. 1878; this act was combined with another passed 26 July, 1889; another act passed . . . 29 June, 1893
Weights and Measures (metric system) act passed, 1897
Specific gravities (unit, pure water): iridium, 22·38; platinum, 21·45; osmium, 21·4; gold, 19·32; lead, 11·35; silver, 10·51; copper, 8·94; iron, 7·87; tin, 7·29; zinc, 7·19; iodine, 4·95; carbon, 3·52; aluminium, 2·56; sulphur, 2; sodium, 0·97; lithium, 0·59; oxygen, 0·001431; nitrogen, 0·001257; hydrogen, 0·0000896, *Dr. O. J. Broch* . 1878
The 15th annual report of the international committee of weights and measures was published at Paris 1892
Internat. congress (third sitting) meets in Paris, 18 Oct. 1901

(See *Standard* and *Metrical System.*)

WEI-HAI-WEI, see *England*, April, 1898. Population, 1902, about 123,750.

WEIMAR, capital of the grand-duchy of Saxe Weimar (*which see*).

WEINSBERG, see *Guelphs*.

WEISMANNISM, see *Heredity*.

WEISSENBURG, see *Wissembourg*.

WELLINGTON, a town in New Zealand, North Island, settled in 1840, made a bishopric in 1858, became a seat of government, 24 Dec. 1864. Population in 1891, 33,224; 1901, 49·344.

WELLINGTON ADMINISTRATION, succeeded that of viscount Goderich, Jan. 1828. The duke resigned 16 Nov. 1830.

Duke of Wellington, *first lord of the treasury.*
Lord Lyndhurst, *lord chancellor.*
Henry Goulburn, *chancellor of the exchequer.*
Earl Bathurst, *president of the council.*
Lord Ellenborough, *privy seal.*
Mr. (afterwards sir) Robert Peel, earl Dudley, and Mr. Wm. Huskisson, *home, foreign*, and *colonial secretaries.*
Viscount Melville, *board of control.*
Mr. Charles Grant, *board of trade.*
Lord Palmerston, *secretary-at-war.*
J. C. Herries, *master of the mint.*
Earl of Aberdeen, *duchy of Lancaster.*
Mr. Huskisson, earl Dudley, viscount Palmerston, and Mr. Grant quitted the ministry, and various changes followed in May and June same year.
The earl of Aberdeen and sir George Murray became, respectively, *foreign* and *colonial secretaries.*
Sir Henry Hardinge, *secretary-at-war.*
Mr. Vesey Fitzgerald (afterwards lord Fitzgerald), *India board.*
Lord Lowther, *first commissioner of land revenues*, &c., May and June, 1828.
Mr. Arbuthnot, Mr. Vesey Fitzgerald, &c.

WELLINGTON COLLEGE (Sandhurst), was erected by subscription in memory of the great duke of Wellington, for the support and education of orphan sons of commissioned officers. The first stone was laid by queen Victoria on 2 June, 1856; and the building was opened by her majesty on 29 Jan. 1859. Out of the 159,000*l.* subscribed, 55,000*l.* were expended on the building, and the rest invested for the maintenance of the institution.

A controversy respecting its management; certain charges explained or rebutted . . Aug.-Oct. 1878
Proposal for royal commission of inquiry negatived in the commons . . . . . 1 April, 1879
Commission appointed; lord Penzance, bishop of Exeter, Mr. R. Lowe (afterwards lord Sherbrooke), col. Chesney, &c., June, 1879; report recommending greater economy and improvement of income . . . . Aug. 1880
Much illness among the boys, 3 deaths; investigation of the premises made during 1891; the scholars were temporarily transferred to Malvern, early in 1892; good report . . . 18 June, 1898
Queen Victoria visits the college and reviews the boys . . . . 19 May, 1900

WELLINGTONIA GIGANTEA (sequoia), the largest tree in the world, a native of California, was discovered by W. Whitehead, June, 1850; a specimen first gathered by Mr. W. Lobb in 1853, and described by Dr. John Lindley. When full grown it is about 450 feet high, and 116 feet in circumference. The prince consort (5 June, 1861) and the queen (24 July, 1861) planted Wellingtonias at the new gardens of the Royal Horticultural Society. The trees did not live; the gardens were given up in 1887.

WELLINGTON'S VICTORIES, &c. For details see separate articles.

Arthur Wellesley was born, according to some authorities, in March or April (baptized 30 April); incorrectly said by others . . 1 May, 1769
Appointed to command in the Mahratta war in India, takes Poonah and Ahmednuggur, 12 Aug.; gains his first victory at Assaye, 23 Sept.; defeats Scindiah at Argaum, Nov.; and at Gawalghur 13 Dec. 1803
Becomes secretary for Ireland 1807
Takes the command in Portugal, defeats Junot at Vimiera . . . . . . 21 Aug. 1808
Passes the Douro and defeats Soult . 12 May, 1809
Defeats Victor at Talavera, 28 July; created viscount Wellington . . . . 4 Sept. ,,
Repulses Massena at Busaco, 27 Sept.; and occupies the lines at Torres Vedras . . 10 Oct. 1810
Defeats Massena at Fuentes de Onoro, 5 May; takes Almeida . . . . . 10 May, 1811
Storms Ciudad Rodrigo, 19 Jan.; and Badajos, 6 April; defeats Marmont at Salamanca, 22 July; enters Madrid . . . 12 Aug. 1812
Defeats Joseph Bonaparte and Jourdan at Vittoria, 21 June; (St. Sebastian stormed by gen. Graham (aft. lord Lynedoch), 31 Aug.); enters France, 8 Oct. 1813
Defeats Soult at Orthez, 27 Feb.; and at Toulouse 10 April, 1814
Created duke of Wellington, with an annuity of 13,000*l.* and a grant of 300,000*l.* . . May, ,,
First appeared in the house of lords; his patents of creation as baron, earl, marquis, and duke being read at the same time . . 28 June, ,,
Commands the army in the Netherlands; repulses an attack of Ney at Quatre Bras, 16 June; defeats Napoleon at Waterloo, 18 June; invests Paris 3 July, 1815
Commands the army of occupation in France July, 1815, till Nov. 1818
His assassination attempted by Cantillon, who escapes . . . . . . 10 Feb. ,,
Appointed master-general of the ordnance . . 1819
The Wellington shield and supporting columns designed by Stothard, commemorating all the above-mentioned victories, presented to the duke by the merchants and bankers of London. (It was manufactured by Green and Ward, and cost 11,000*l.*) . . . . . . 16 Feb. 1822
The duke appointed commander-in-chief, 22 Jan.; resigns . . . . . . 30 April, 1827
Becomes first minister . . . . 8 Jan. 1828
Aids in carrying the Catholic Emancipation bill April, 1829
Asserts that no reform in parliament is needed, 2 Nov.; resigns . . . . 16 Nov. 1830
Transacts all the business of the country, after the resignation of lord Melbourne, till the arrival of sir R. Peel from Italy, Nov.; and becomes foreign secretary under sir R. Peel, Dec. 1834; resigns April, 1835
Again commander-in-chief . . . . 15 Aug. 1842
Dies at Walmer castle* . . . . 14 Sept. 1852

* His favourite old horse, Copenhagen, (born 1808, at Waterloo), died 1836.

Removed to Chelsea hospital, where he lay in state 10 Nov. 1852
Removed to the Horse Guards . . 17 Nov. ,,
Public funeral at St. Paul's cathedral . 18 Nov. ,,
A multitude of all ranks, estimated at a million and a half of persons, were congregated in the line of route, a distance of three miles, to witness and share in the imposing spectacle.
The military consisted of the household regiments of horse and foot guards, the 2nd battalion of the rifles, a battalion of the Royal Marines, the 33rd regiment, the 17th Lancers, and the 18th Light Dragoons, the regiment of Scots Greys; a body of Chelsea pensioners, and men of different arms of the Indian army.
The body was placed upon a sumptuous funeral car, drawn by twelve horses richly caparisoned, and the coffin was thus seen by the whole of the crowd.
The procession moved about seven o'clock, and it was three o'clock before the body was lowered into the vault beside the remains of Nelson, under the dome of St. Paul's cathedral.
Memorial by Marochetti erected by the then duke, his son, the late duke of Wellington, and tenants at Strathfieldsaye, July, 1866.
See *Statues.*

WELLINGTON MONUMENT, in St. Paul's.
A number of models exhibited in Westminster hall; none chosen, 1857.
The execution of the monument entrusted to Mr. Alfred Stevens, sculptor, and Mr. Penrose, architect. The stone sarcophagus was completed in 1858.
In Aug. 1870, above 17,000*l.* had been expended, and it was stated that 15,000*l.* more were required. Parliament had granted 20,000*l.* Fresh arrangements were made with Mr. Stevens. He died 1 May, 1875. Monument reported complete, 1 Feb.; uncovered, 20 April, 1878.
The removal of the monument to a different part of the cathedral, and the addition of the equestrian statue modelled by Mr. Stevens, proposed in April, 1892; work completed Jan. 1894.

WELLS were dug by Abraham, 1892 B.C., and Isaac, 1804 (*Gen.* xxi. 30, and xxvi. 19). Danaus is said to have introduced well-digging into Greece from Egypt. Norton's "tube-well," patented Oct. 1867, is said to be the invention of Hiram J. Messenger, Stephen Brewer, and Byron Mudge, Americans of the state of New York. The apparatus consists of an iron tube perforated with holes at the lower end, and shod with a steel point, which readily enters the hardest soil when forcibly driven. It was used with great advantage during the civil war 1861-4; by the British in their campaign in Abyssinia in 1867-8; and by the Russians in Khiva, 1873.

Messrs. Meux, brewers, New Oxford-street, London, boring, found water beneath the greensand, about 1000 feet deep, April, 1877.

WELLS (Somerset). The cathedral church was built by Ina, king of the West Saxons, 704, and by him dedicated to St. Andrew. Other West Saxon kings endowed it, and it was erected into a bishopric in 909, during the reign of Edward the Elder. The present church was begun by Robert, 18th bishop of this see, and consecrated in 1148, and completed by his successors and finally consecrated by Jocelin. The first bishop was Æthelm or Adelmus (afterwards bishop of Canterbury). The see was united with Bath (*which see*) in 1088. Population, 1881, 4,634; 1891, 4,822; 1901, 4,849.

WELSH CHARITY SCHOOLS; established in Gray's-inn-road, London, 1715; removed to Ashford, near Staines, Middlesex, 1852. *Welsh National Council*, see *Wales*, Oct. 1887 *et seq.*

WELSH CHURCH, see *Wales*, 1893, *et seq.* *Welsh Land Commission* appointed, lord Carrington, chairman, March; met 23 May, 1893; sittings concluded Nov. 1894; report, with recommendations, including the establishment of a land court, issued, Oct. 1896. *Welsh University*, see *Wales, University of.*

WEMBLEY PARK, see *Watkin Tower.*

WENDS, a branch of the Slavonic family which spread over Germany in the 6th century, and settled especially in the north-eastern parts.

WESLEYAN METHODISTS, a sect founded by John Wesley (born 1703, died 1791) and his brother Charles, who in 1727 with a few other students formed themselves into a small society for the purpose of mutual edification by religious exercises. From their strictness of life they were called *Methodists*, in 1729. John Wesley went to Georgia in America, in 1735, with a view of converting the Indians. On his return to England, in 1738, a great change took place in his mind (24 May), he commenced itinerant preaching, and gathered many followers. On finding many churches shut against him, he built spacious meeting-houses in London, Bristol, and other places. The Wesleyan Methodist society, as such, began in 1739. For some time he was united with George Whitefield; but differing with him respecting the doctrine of election, they separated in 1741; see *Whitefield.* Wesley was almost continually engaged in travelling through the United Kingdom. His two leading doctrines were the instantaneousness of conversion, and Christian perfection, or deliverance from all sin. His society was well organised, and he preserved his influence over it to the last. "His genius for government was not inferior to that of Richelieu." *Macaulay.* The deed of declaration, establishing the conference, is dated 28 Feb. 1784. In 1851 there were 428 circuits in Great Britain, with between 13,000 and 14,000 local or lay preachers, and about 920 itinerant preachers, and 6,579 chapels; 8,993 chapels in 1902.

The *Conference*, the highest Wesleyan court, till lately, composed of 100 ministers, who meet annually. It was instituted by John Wesley in . 1784
At the centenary of the existence of Methodism 216,000*l.* were collected, to be expended on the objects of the society 1839
An œcumenical conference to be held in the autumn of 1881, settled . . . . . 31 July, 1880
138th annual conference opened . . 19 July, 1881

Out of the original connexion have seceded:—
Chapels in 1851
New Connexion (1796) 301; (1902) . . . 42,929
Primitive Methodists (1810) 2,871; (1902) . 195,651
Bible Christians, or Bryanites (from Wm. O'Bryan) (1815) 403; (1902) 28,877
Wesleyan Methodist Association (1834) . . . 329
Wesleyan Methodist Reformers (1849) 2000
The last arose out of the publication of "Fly Sheets," advocating reform in the body (1844-8). The suspected authors and their friends were expelled. By these disruptions the main body is thought to have lost 100,000 members.—This sect in America numbered about a million in 1844, when a division took place on the slavery question.
The *United Methodist Free Churches*, an amalgamation of the Protestant Methodist (1828), Wesleyan Methodist Association (1834) and the Wesleyan Reform Association (1849), effected in . . 1857
Wesleyan Methodist church members in Great Britain in 1868, 342,380; in 1872, 346,580; in 1876, 372,538; 1878, 380,867 (1412 ministers); 1885, 413,163; March, 1889, 421,784; 1892, 424,959; 1894, 433,350; 1902, 525,360.
Letter from Dr. Pusey requesting aid in opposing Coleridge's bill for admitting dissenters to the universities, read at the conference, but not received . . . . . 13 Aug. 1868

The establishment of a high school for Wesleyans at Cambridge (to prepare for the university) proposed . . . . May 1872

The chapel in the City-road, London, founded by John Wesley, 1 April, 1777, was nearly destroyed by fire . . . . 7 Dec. 1879

Œcumenical Methodist conference (at City-road chapel, London), of 400 delegates, ministers, and laymen from all parts of the world (representing nearly 4,000,000) . . . . 6 Sept. *et seq.* 1881

Centenary of the death of the celebrated John Wesley; his statue by Mr. Adams Acton, in front of the City-road chapel, unveiled by the Rev. D. Moulton . . . . . 2 March, 1891

Conference at Newcastle-on-Tyne . . 21 July 1885
" " Camborne, Cornwall . . 24 July 1888
" " Sheffield (146th) . . 23 July 1889
" " Bristol . . . . . July, 1890
" " Nottingham (148th) . 21 July, 1891
" " Bradford (149th) . . . 1 Aug. 1892
" " Birmingham . . . 23 July, 1894
" " Plymouth . . . . 23 July, 1895
" " Liverpool . . . . 21 July, 1896
" " Leeds . . . . . 20 July, 1897
" " Hull . . . . . 20 July, 1898
" " London . . . . . 24 July, 1899
" " Burslem . . . . 30 July, 1900
" " Newcastle-on-Tyne . . 23 July, 1901
" " Manchester (159th) . . 22 July, 1902
" " Camborne . . . . 21 July, 1903

Œcumenical conference at Washington, U.S., 7 Oct. 1891

The chapel in the City-road, London (restored since 2 March, 1891), re-opened by lord Strathcona; a bust of the late Dr. W. F. Moulton unveiled by sir Henry Fowler, 7 July, 1899; memorial window to bp. Simpson unveiled by Mr. Choate, U.S. ambassador . . . . 14 Nov. 1902

Dedication and endowment of John Wesley's house in the City-road . . . . . . 2 March, 1898

The rev. James Hocart, father of the French Wesleyan conference, died, aged 87, end Feb. 1899; the rev. Hugh Price Hughes, popular preacher, died, aged 55 . . . . . . 17 Nov. 1902

The Twentieth Century Million Guineas fund started Nov. 1898; 944,000*l.* received up to 2 Feb. 1903; Roy. Aquarium, Westminster, acquired, celebration meeting held . . . . 2 Feb. 1903

Bicentenary of Wesley's birth celebrated in Wesley's chapel, City-road, London, and at Epworth, 17 June, "

WESSEX, see *Britain.*

WEST AFRICAN SETTLEMENTS—Sierra Leone, Gambia, &c. Governor, sir Arthur E. Kennedy, 1867; sir Garnet Wolseley, Aug. 1873; Cornelius H. Kortright, 1875; Dr. Samuel Rowe, 1876; capt. Arthur E. Havelock, 1881; sir Samuel Rowe, 1884, died 1888. See *Ashantees.*

Turbulent chiefs subdued . . . . . June, 1883

International conference at Berlin, on West African affairs.* Freedom of trade on the Congo; Rights of States occupying open territory; proposed by Germany, accepted by France, England, Portugal, Spain, Holland, Belgium, the United States, and Turkey . . . . . 8 Oct. 1884

Conference opened, prince Bismarck president, 15 Nov. "

The conference declares free trade in the Congo valley and affirms British protectorate over the Niger, and recognises the International African Association . . . . Dec. "

Prohibits slave trade . . . . . . 7 Jan. 1885

Approves rules for future annexations on the coast 1 Feb. "

Result of the conference embodied in a general act signed . . . . 26 Feb. "

International limitations on the lower Congo, settled 15 Feb. "

Delimitation treaty between Great Britain and Germany signed at Berlin . . . . 15 Nov. 1893

WESTERN AUSTRALIA, formerly SWAN RIVER SETTLEMENT, which was projected by colonel Peel in 1828. Regulations issued from the colonial office, and Captain (aft. sir James) Stirling, appointed lieut.-gov., Jan. 17, 1829, arrived at the appointed site in August following. The three towns of Perth, Freemantle, and Guildford were founded same year. In March, 1830, fifty ships, with 2000 emigrants, with property amounting to 1,000,000*l.*, had arrived before hardly any dwellings had been erected or land surveyed. The more energetic settlers left for home, or the neighbouring colonies, and the colony languished for twenty years for want of suitable inhabitants—the first settlers, from their previous habits and rank in life, proving unfit for the rough work of colonisation. In 1848, the colonists requested that convicts might be sent out to them, and in 1849 a band arrived, who were kindly received and well treated. The best results ensued. By 1853, 2000 had arrived, and the inhabitants of Perth had requested that 1000 should be sent out annually. The reception of convicts is to cease in after-years, in consequence of the energetic opposition of the other Australian colonies (1865).—The settlement of King George's Sound was founded in 1826 by the government of New South Wales. It was used as a military station for four years. In 1830, the home government ordered the settlement to be transferred to Swan River. Since the establishment of steam communication, the little town of Albany here, employed as a coaling station, has become a thriving sea-port. It possesses an excellent harbour, used by whalers. A journal called the *Freemantle Gazette* was published here in March, 1831. Bishopric of Perth founded 1857. Population of Western Australia in 1859, 14,837; Dec. 1883, 31,233; April, 1891, 49,782; 1901, 187,660; 1887, revenue, 377,903*l.*; expenditure, 456,897*l.*; imports, 832,213*l.*; exports, 604,656*l.*; 1890, revenue, 414,314*l.*; expenditure, 401,737*l.*; imports, 874,447*l.*; exports, 671,813*l.*; 1893, revenue, 570,651*l.*; expenditure, 640,801*l.*; imports, 1,494,438*l.*; exports, 918,147*l.*; 1895-6, revenue, 2,440,390*l.*; 1896-7, revenue, 2,842,751*l.*; expenditure, 2,839,453*l.*; 1901-02, surplus, 123,194*l.* Governor John Stephen Hampton, appointed 1861; sir Benjamin C. C. Pine, May, 1868; Frederick A. Weld, 1869; Wm. C. F. Robinson, 1874; major-gen. sir Harry St. George Ord, 1877; sir W. F. Robinson, 1880; sir Frederick Napier Broome, 1882; sir William C. F. Robinson, Aug. 1889; col. sir Gerard Smith, Sept. 1895; sir Arthur Lawley, Jan. 1901; adm. sir F. Bedford, Jan. 1903.

New gold field at Perth discovered, May; gold discovered in N.W. Australia . . . . (?) May, 1886

The legislative council petition for responsible self-government instead of being a crown colony, autumn, 1887; a bill granting this was passed by the house of lords, 16 July, withdrawn in the commons, Aug. 1889; re-introduced and received the royal assent, 25 July; proclaimed at Perth, with great rejoicings . . . . . 22 Oct. 1890

The hon. John Forrest forms the first ministry, 28 Dec.; the first parliament meets . . 20 Jan. 1891

Bill granting virtual manhood suffrage passed 6 Oct. 1893

Prosperous budget: revenue, 961,670*l.*; expenditure, 934,508*l.* . . . . . . 28 Sept. 1894

The Gold Fields National league formed at Perth, Nov. 1895

Railway opened from Perth to Coolgardie, by the governor . . . . 23 March, 1896

Constitutional Reform bill read 2nd time in the legislative assembly . . . . 31 July, "

The Mueller botanical society established at Perth, June, 1897

Death of Mr. Wm. E. Powell Giles at Coolgardie, successful explorer . . . . . 23 Nov. "

Foundation-stone of the Gold Fields cathedral laid by sir Gerard Smith at Coolgardie . . 30 Nov. "

New railway line from Coolgardie to Menzies, opened . . . . 22 March, 1898

* Mr. H. Stanley, at Berlin.

Early closing act passed by the assembly, 28 Oct. 1898
Exhibition at Coolgardie opened by the governor, 21 March, 1899
Federation proposals rejected by the legislative council . . . . early Dec. ,,
Federal Enabling bill passed by the council, 7 June, 1900
Commonwealth bill adopted on the *referendum* by 44,704—19,691, the federation of Australia thereby completed . . . . . . 1 Aug. ,,
Sir J. Forrest's budget statement, 1899; surplus, 79,900*l*. . . . . 9 Oct. ,,
Mr. Throssel succeeds sir J. Forrest as premier, Feb. 1901; Mr. G. Leake forms a cabinet, 27 May, 1901
The ministry, defeated, resigns, 10, 12 Nov.; Mr. Morgan forms one, 18 Nov., resigns, and Mr. George Leake premier, 20 Dec.; dies 24 June, 1902; succeeded by Mr. James . 30 June, ,,
Good rains, revenue increasing, reported, 11 Sept. ,,
The Coolgardie water supply inaugurated by sir J. Forrest . . . . 24 Jan. 1903

WESTERN CHURCH (called also the LATIN or ROMAN) broke off communion with the Greek or Eastern Church, 653; see *Greek Church*. Its history is mainly comprised in that of the popes and of the European kingdoms; see *Popes*. This church was disturbed by the Arian heresy about 345 and 500; by Pelagianism, about 409; by the introduction of image-worship about 600; by the injunction of the celibacy of the clergy and the rise of the monastic orders about 649; by the contests between the emperors and the popes respecting ecclesiastical investitures between 1073 and 1173; by the rise and progress of the Reformation in the 15th and 16th centuries; by the contests between the Jesuits and Jansenists in the 17th and 18th centuries; and by the progress of modern philosophy and rationalism, and by ultramontanism, in the 19th; see *Roman Catholics*.

WESTERN EMPIRE. The Roman empire was divided into Eastern and Western by Diocletian in 296; but was reunited under Constans in 340. It was again divided into Eastern and Western by Valentinian and Valens, the former having the Western portion or Rome, 364; see *Eastern Empire, Italy*, and *Rome*.

EMPERORS.

364. Valentinian, son of Gratian, takes the Western, and his brother Valens the Eastern empire.
367. Gratian, a youth, son of Valentinian, made a colleague in the government by his father.
375. Valentinian II., another son, also very young, is, on the death of his father, associated with Gratian, who is assassinated by his general, Andragathius in 383. Valentinian murdered by one of his officers, Arbogastes, in 392.
392. Eugenius, a usurper, assumes the imperial dignity; he and Arbogastes are defeated by
394. Theodosius the Great, who becomes sole emperor. [Andragathius threw himself into the sea, and Arbogastes died by his own hand.]
395. Honorius, son of Theodosius, reigns, on his father's death, in the West, and his brother Arcadius in the East. Honorius dies in 423.
423. Usurpation of John, the Notary, defeated and slain near Ravenna.
425. Valentinian III., son of the empress Placidia, daughter of Theodosius the Great: murdered at the instance of his successor
455. Maximus: he marries Eudoxia, widow of Valentinian, who, to avenge the death of her first husband and the guilt of her second, invites the African Vandals into Italy, and Rome is sacked. Maximus stoned to death.
455. Marcus Mæcilius Avitus; forced to resign, and dies in his flight towards the Alps.
457. Julius Valerius Majorianus; murdered at the instance of his minister, Ricimer, who raises
461. Libius Severus to the throne, but holds the supreme power; Severus poisoned by Ricimer.
465. [Interregnum. Ricimer retains the authority, without assuming the title of emperor.]
467. Anthemius, chosen by the joint suffrages of the senate and army; murdered by Ricimer, who dies soon after.
472. Flavius-Anicius Olybrius: slain by the Goths soon after his accession.
473. Glycerius: forced to abdicate by his successor,
474. Julius Nepos: deposed by his general, Orestes, and retires to Salonæ.
475. Romulus (called Augustulus, or Little Augustus), son of Orestes. Orestes is slain, and the emperor deposed by
476. Odoacer, king of the Heruli: takes Rome, assumes the style of king of Italy, and completes the fall of the Western empire.

See *Italy, Rome*, and *Germany*.

WEST HAM, S.W. Essex (called London over the border), parish containing Plaistow, Stratford, &c., the population in 1841, 12,738; owing to the large increase of factories and other works rose to 99,142 in 1871, and 200,752 in 1881; 1891, 365,130; 1901, 367,308.

West Ham returns two M.P.'s by the act of 1885; and was incorporated by royal charter, July, 1886. West Ham is outside of the jurisdiction of the metropolitan board of works. The dreadful sanitary condition of 1855 gradually improved by the action of a new local board, now succeeded by a municipal corporation. Rateable value 79,000*l*. in 1856; nearly 700,000*l*. in 1886.
The Essex museum of Nat. History opened, and the Municipal Technical institute, recently burnt down, reopened by Mr. Passmore Edwards, 18 Oct. 1900
The 8th free picture exhibition opened by Mr. Seymour Lucas, R.A. . . . . 26 April, 1902

WESTERN ISLES OF SCOTLAND. Royal commission to inquire into extreme destitution appointed 20 March, 1883 (lord Napier and Ettrick, Mr. Donald Cameron, M.P., and others). See *Mansion House*.

WESTERN PACIFIC ISLANDS; under a high commissioner, the governor of Fiji (*which see*).

WESTERN TERRITORIES, North British America, contain four districts, Assiniboia, Saskatchewan, Alberta, and Athabasca, formed by the Dominion government in 1882. They were part of the Hudson Bay territories till 1870, when they were annexed to Canada. The Yukon, Mackenzie, Franklin, and Ungana annexed 1895. Population in 1891, about 67,554; 1901, 220,000. Capital, Regina. Lieut.-gov., Joseph Royal (1891; died, 23 Aug. 1902); C. H. M'Intosh (1894); M. C. Cameron, May (1898), died Sept.; Amadée E. Forget, 1898.

The north-west territories constituted a province, Oct. 1897
The legislature opened at Regina . . . 28 Oct. ,,
Visit of the duke and duchess of Cornwall, 27 Sept. 1901

WEST INDIES, islands discovered by Columbus, St. Salvador being the first land he made in the New World, and first seen by him in the night between the 11th and 12th Oct. 1492. The largest are Cuba, Hayti (or St. Domingo), Jamaica, Porto Rico, Trinidad, and Guadaloupe; see *the Islands respectively; Denmark*, 24 Jan. 1902.

A royal commission to inquire into their condition appointed in 1882, reported on their great need of important judicial and fiscal reforms April, 1884: Depressed condition through increased use of beet sugar; inadmissible remedies proposed by deputation to lord Derby, 28 Aug. 1884.
A royal commission of inquiry appointed, sir Henry Wylie Norman, sir Edw. Grey, sir David Barbour, and others, Dec. 1896; began taking evidence in British Guiana, end of Jan. 1897; depressing report as to sugar, 1 Oct. 1897; the islands suffer through sugar

bounties in foreign countries; grants in aid annually voted by parliament.
Terrible hurricane, tremendous rain and tidal wave, great loss of life and destruction of property, thousands homeless, over 300 deaths at St. Vincent, 87 deaths at Barbadoes, Guadaloupe, and St. Lucia . . . . 10–12 Sept. 1898
Relief fund opened at the Mansion house, and at Kingston, Jamaica, 17 Sept.; 250*l.* from the queen and 105*l.* from the prince of Wales, 27 Sept. ,,
Government grants for the restoration of damaged property, 40,000*l.* to Barbadoes, 25,000*l.* to St. Vincent, and a loan of 50,000*l.* to each island, announced . . . . . 10 March, 1899
Treaty for reciprocal trade between United States and West Indies signed at Washington, 16 June, ,,
Dreadful hurricane, Monserrat devastated; great loss of life and destruction of property throughout the islands, 7–14 Aug.; relief works opened, see *Mansion house* . . . . . . Aug. ,,
West Indian agricultural (2nd) conference opened at Barbadoes . . . . . 6 Jan. 1900
Grand Bourg in the French island of Marie Galante nearly destroyed by fire . . 18, 19 Aug. 1901
Fearful volcanic eruptions, see *Martinique* and *Vincent, St.* . . . . . May, 1902
Imperial government grants 250,000*l.* to the West Indies . . . . . . July, ,,
Hurricane, causing great damage . . 10 Aug. 1903
Government grant of 50,000*l.* for relief of planters, end Aug. ,,

WEST INDIAN SETTLEMENTS, see *Jamaica.*

WESTMINSTER, so called on account of its western situation with regard to St. Paul's cathedral, or from there being formerly a monastery named East Minster, on the hill now called Great Tower-hill. This city joins London at Temple-bar. Formerly Westminster was called Thorney, or Thorney Island: and in ancient times Canute had a palace here, burnt in 1263. Westminster and London were one mile asunder in 1603, when the houses were thatched, and there were mud walls in the Strand. It is said that the great number of Scotsmen who came over after the accession of James I. occasioned the building of Westminster, and united it with London. *Howel's Londinopolis.* See *Parliament*, 1834-52, 1884. By the Seats act of 1885, Westminster returns one M.P. Population, Westminster (borough), 1881, 46,549; 1891, 37,295, Strand, 1881, 32,587; 1891, 25,107. St. George's, Hanover-sq., 1881, 149,748; 1891, 134,122; 1901, 182,977. Westminster reconstituted a city under the London Government act, 1899 (10 aldermen, 60 councillors); the duke of Norfolk first mayor, his portrait unveiled in the council chamber, 12 Feb. 1903. See under *Roman Catholics.*

Earl Grosvenor created marquis of Westminster, 1831; the marquis created duke 1874
Westminster industrial exhibition, opened 24 May, closed . . . . 9 Aug. 1879
Baroness Burdett-Coutts lays foundation of New Town Hall, near Victoria Street, 29 March, 1882; opened . . . . 19 July, 1883
The prince of Wales lays the foundation stone of St. Martin's municipal buildings, &c., 18 March, 1890; which are opened by Mr. A. J. Balfour, 16 July, 1891; bust of Mr. W. H. Smith unveiled by Mr. A. J. Balfour . . . . 13 June, 1893
Foundation stone of the R. C. Cathedral laid by cardinal Vaughan . . . . . 29 June, 1895
Collapse of Abbey mansions, Orchard-st., 7 men killed . . . . 21 April, 1898
Bill for the improvement of Westminster and extension of the embankment, rejected by the commons, 336—84 . . . . 26 April, ,,
New municipal building, formerly St. Martin's town-hall, enlarged, &c., opened by the duke of Cambridge . . . . . . 29 May, 1902

WESTMINSTER ABBEY. Christopher Wren, in his survey of the present edifice, found nothing to countenance the belief that it was erected on the ruins of a pagan temple. The erection of the first abbey in the 7th century is ascribed to St. Sebert, king of Essex.

The church becoming ruinous, splendidly rebuilt by Edward the Confessor (1055-65) and filled with monks from Exeter (Pope Nicholas II. constituted it the place for the inauguration of the kings of England); dedicated . . . . 28 Dec. 1065
Rebuilt in a magnificent style by Henry III. 1220-69
In the reigns of Edward II., Edward III., and Richard II. the great cloisters, abbot's house, and principal monastic buildings, erected . 1300-1400
The western parts of the nave and aisles rebuilt between . . . . . . 1340 and 1483
The west front and the great window built by Richard III. and Henry VII.; the latter commenced the chapel which bears his name; the first stone laid . . . . . 24 Jan. 1502-3
The abbey dissolved and made a bishopric . . . 1540
Made a collegiate church by Elizabeth . . . 1560
Made a barrack for soldiers (*Mercurius Rusticus*), July, 1643
The great west window and the western towers rebuilt in the reigns of George I. and II. . . 1714-60
The choir injured by fire . . . . . 9 July, 1803
Mr. Wyatt commenced restoring the dilapidated parts at an expense of 42,000*l.* in 1809
A fire, without any serious injury . 27 April, 1829
The evening services for the working classes, when a sermon was preached by the dean, Dr. Trench, commenced on . . . . . 3 Jan. 1858
The 800th anniversary of the foundation celebrated, 28 Dec. 1865
7000*l.* voted by parliament to restore the chapter-house (G. Gilbert Scott employed), 1 May, 1866; re-opened . . . . 29 April, 1872
Lectures in the Abbey on foreign missions: professor Max Müller, a layman, 3 Dec. 1873; principal Caird, of Scotch church, 30 Nov. 1874; rev. Robert Moffat, father-in-law of Livingstone 30 Nov. 1875
Sir Charles Lyell, sir Wm. Sterndale Bennett, and bishop Connop Thirlwall, buried in the Abbey, 1875; G. E. Street, 29 Dec. 1881; C. R. Darwin, 26 April, 1882; Robert Browning, 30 Dec. 1889; lord Tennyson, 12 Oct. 1892; W. E. Gladstone, 28 May 1898
Repairs connected with the principal entrance after designs by Gilbert Scott, completed at a cost of about 20,000*l.* . . . . Nov. 1881
New Abbey gardens opened . . . . 12 April, 1882
New organ set up . . . . . . May, 1884
Thanksgiving jubilee services for the queen (see *Jubilee*) . . . . . . 21, 22 June, 1887
Proposed transfer of the charge of restoring and maintaining the abbey to the ecclesiastical commissioners who are to advance 10,000*l.* March; legalised by act passed . . . 28 June, 1888
Royal commission appointed to inquire in regard to the facilities for the interment of illustrious persons: the dean Bradley, sir F. Leighton, Mr. Alfred Waterhouse, and others, 29 April; report indecisive . . . . June, 1891
Restoration of the exterior of the north transept, as designed by sir Gilbert Scott, completed June, 1890
Special service on the death of sir John Macdonald, premier of Canada . . . . . 12 June, 1891
Memorial window and a bust to James Russell Lowell in the chapter house unveiled by Mr. Leslie Stephen . . . . . . 28 Nov. 1893
Mr. H. Yates Thompson offers 38,000*l.* for the erection of a monumental chapel, under certain conditions . . . . Feb. 1894
Houses in Old Palace Yard ordered to be demolished . . . . June,
New "Celestial organ" with electric action (connected with the other in the choir), built by Messrs. W. Hill and Son, presented by Mr. A. D. Clarke, inaugurated by prof. J F. Bridge (knt. June, 1897) . . . . 16 July, ,,
"Annals of Westminster Abbey," by Mrs. A. Murray Smith, daughter of Dean Bradley, published, Nov. ("The Roll of the Abbey," by her, July, 1902) . ,,
A bust of sir Walter Scott unveiled by the duke of Buccleuch . . . . 21 May, 1897

Medallion of John Ruskin unveiled by Mrs. Arthur Severn . . . . . 8 Feb. 1902
A fine "annexe" of the Abbey, designed by Mr. A. Y. Nutt, built and used for the coronation (June), 9 Aug.; the statues of the seven Edwards removed to Windsor castle . . . . Aug. ,,
CORONATION of king Edward VII. and queen Alexandra . . . . . . 9 Aug. ,,
The abbey and coronation fittings viewed by 96,907 persons (receipts over 4,949*l.*) . . 12-19 Aug. ,,
Memorial window to the late duke of Westminster, s. transept dedicated . . . . . 26 Sept. ,,

WESTMINSTER AQUARIUM, see *Aquarium*.

WESTMINSTER BISHOPRICS AND DEANERY. At the dissolution of monasteries, Westminster abbey was valued at 3977*l.* per annum; king Henry VIII. in 1539 erected it into a deanery; and in 1540 into a bishopric, and appointed Thomas Thirlby prelate. He was translated to Norwich in 1550, and with him ended the bishopric of Westminster; Middlesex, his diocese, being restored to London. The dean presided until the accession of Mary, who restored the abbot. Elizabeth displaced the abbot, and erected the abbey into a collegiate church of a dean and twelve prebendaries, as it still continues. On the revival of the order of the Bath, in 1725, the dean of Westminster was appointed dean of that order, which honour has been continued. Dr. Nicholas Wiseman was created *archbishop of Westminster* by the pope Pius IX. 30 Sept. 1850; see *Papal Aggression.* Dr. Wiseman died 8 Feb. 1865; Henry Manning was consecrated his successor 8 June, following; he died 14 Jan. 1892, and was succeeded by Dr. Herbert Vaughan about 30 March; enthroned 8 May; invested with the *pallium*, the first since 1556, 16 Aug. 1892; died 19 June, 1903, succeeded by Dr. Bourne, Aug. 24, enthroned 24 Dec. 1903. See *Roman Catholics.*

RECENT DEANS.

1793. Samuel Horsley; bishop of St. Asaph, 1802.
1802. William Vincent; died 21 Dec. 1815.
1815. John Ireland; died 21 Sept. 1842.
1842. Thomas Turton; bishop of Ely, 1845.
1845. Samuel Wilberforce; bishop of Oxford, 1846.
1846. William Buckland; died 14 Aug. 1856.
1856. Richard C. Trench; abp. of Dublin, 1 Jan. 1864.
1864. Arthur Penrhyn Stanley; died 18 July, 1881.
1881. George Granville Bradley, 14 Sept.; resigned, 1902; died, 13 March, 1903.
1902. Joseph Armitage Robinson, 28 Oct.

WESTMINSTER BRIDGES. The handsome old bridge was begun (after a design of M. Labelye), 13 Sept. 1738, the first stone laid 29 Jan. 1738-9; opened for passengers 18 Nov. 1750; cost 426,650*l.* It was built of Portland stone, and crossed the river where the breadth is 1223 feet.

Owing to the sinking of several of its piers, most of the balustrades on both sides were removed, to relieve the structure of its weight.
By 16 & 17 Vict. c. 46 the estates of its commissioners were transferred to her majesty's commissioners of works, who were empowered to remove the then existing bridge, and build a NEW BRIDGE (near the old one) . . . . . 4 Aug. 1853
The contract required the completion of the works by . . . . 1 June, 1857
The works were suspended for a time, in consequence of the failure of Messrs. Mare the contractors. The government eventually undertook the building, which they entrusted to Mr. Thomas Page, the engineer. One half of the new bridge was opened for use early in 1860; the whole on 24 May, 1862

WESTMINSTER CONFESSION OF FAITH AND CATECHISMS were drawn up by the "Assembly of Divines" (partly consisting of laymen), who sat by authority of parliament in Henry VII.'s chapel, Westminster, from 1643 to 1647. These have ever since been the doctrinal standards of Scotch Presbyterians.

WESTMINSTER HALL (London), first built by William Rufus in 1097, for a banqueting-hall; and here in 1099, on his return from Normandy, "he kept his feast of Whitsuntide very royally." The hall became ruinous before the reign of Richard II., who repaired it in 1397, raised the walls, altered the windows, and added a new roof, as well as a stately porch and other buildings. In 1236 Henry III. on New-year's day caused 6000 poor persons to be entertained in this hall, and in the other rooms of his palace, as a celebration of queen Eleanor's coronation; and here Richard II. held his Christmas festival in 1397, when the number of the guests each day the feast lasted was 10,000. *Stow.* The courts of law were established here by king John. *Idem.* Westminster hall was stated to be the largest room in Europe unsupported by pillars (except a hall of justice at Padua); it is 270 feet in length, 74 feet broad. The hall underwent a general repair in 1802. Concurrently with the erection of the palace of Westminster, many improvements and alterations have lately been made in this magnificent hall. The Volunteer Rifle corps were drilled in the hall in the winter of 1859, and since. The courts of law removed to the new buildings in the Strand Jan. 1883. Restorations proposed by Mr. J. L. Pearson, R.A., July, 1884. The roof and windows greatly damaged by an explosion of dynamite (?) about 2 p.m. 24 Jan. 1885.

WESTMINSTER HOSPITAL, founded, 1719; chartered, 1836.

WESTMINSTER PALACE, see under *Palace of Westminster* and *Parliament.*

WESTMINSTER REVIEW, liberal in religion and politics, first appeared, 1824, as the organ of the philosophic radicals, termed the Westminster school, friends of Jeremy Bentham. See *Utilitarianism.*

WESTMINSTER SCHOOL OR ST. PETER'S COLLEGE, was founded by queen Elizabeth in 1560, for the education of forty boys, denominated the Queen's scholars, who are prepared for the university. It is situated within the abbey enclosure. Besides the scholars on the foundation, many of the nobility and gentry send their sons to Westminster for instruction. The annual performance by the scholars of a Latin play is in conformity with the statute of queen Elizabeth. A proposal in 1860 to remove the school was disapproved of in 1861.

Westminster Schools, United, comprise Emanuel and St. Margaret's hospitals, and rev. James Palmer's and Emery Hill's school charities, which were abolished by the endowed school commissioners 27 June, 1873. New schools are to be erected.
Bicentenary celebration of the death of Dr. Richard Busby, 6 April. 1695 (headmaster 1638–95); exhibition of portraits, &c., 18 Nov. 1895.

WESTMINSTER, STATUTES OF, are 3 and 13 Edward I., 1275-90; see *Acts of Parliament.*

WESTMORELAND. This county and Cumberland were granted as a fief to Malcolm of Scotland by Edward the Elder in 945; but resumed by Henry III. in 1237. Neville, earl of Westmoreland, revolted against Elizabeth in 1569, and was attainted in 1570. Woodland and meadows acquired by the National Trust declared open by the princess Louise, 15 Oct. 1902.

WESTPHALIA (Germany). This duchy belonged in former times to the dukes of Saxony, and afterwards became subject to the archbishop of

Cologne. On the secularisation in 1802, it was made over to Hesse Darmstadt; and in 1814 was ceded for an equivalent to Prussia. The *kingdom* of Westphalia, one of the temporary kingdoms of Bonaparte, composed of conquests from Prussia, Hesse-Cassel, Hanover, and the smaller states to the west of the Elbe, was created by decree 18 Aug. 1806, and Jerome Bonaparte appointed king, 1 Dec. 1807. Hanover was annexed to it, 1 March, 1810. The kingdom was abolished in 1813, and the countries were restored to their former rulers.

Through strike of the coal miners for increased pay and shorter hours of labour, Herr Krupp, of Essen, had to stop his iron and steel works at several places for want of coal about 4 May. A conflict took place near Gladbeck between the troops and miners, and three miners were killed, 7 May; the owners stand firm; about 39,000 men on strike, 8 May; nearly 100,000 strikers out, 13 May; the government intervenes to effect a compromise, about 13 May; the emperor receives three delegates from miners, 14 May, and advises both parties to come to a compromise, about 15, 16 May; strike spreading to Silesia &c., 15 May; strikers in Westphalia about 110,000, in Silesia 10,000, 16 May—20 May; 40 members of the striking committee arrested 26 May; strike ends by a compromise, 31 May, 1889. Fresh demands of the miners (increase of 50 per cent. of wages, shorter hours, &c.), rejected by the masters, 23 Jan. 1890.

Explosion at the Hibernia pit, near Gilsenkirchen, about 44 deaths, reported . . . . 25 Jan. 1891

Great strike of coal miners near Essen, about 15,000 men out, 19 April; close of strike, reported, 3 May, „

Colliery explosion at Hamme, 115 deaths, 17 Feb. 1898

Rhenish-Westphalian exhibition at Düsseldorf opened by the crown prince . . 1 May, 1902

WESTPHALIA or **Münster, Peace of**; the treaties signed at Osnaburg 6 Aug., and at Münster 24 Oct. 1648, between France, the emperor, and Sweden; Spain continuing the war against France. By this peace (ending the thirty years' war) the principle of a balance of power in Europe was first recognised; Alsace given to France, and part of Pomerania and some other districts to Sweden; the Lower Palatinate restored to the elector palatine; the religious and political rights of the German states established; and the independence of the Swiss Confederation recognised by Germany.

WEST SAXONS, see *Wessex*, in *Britain*.

WEYMOUTH, Dorsetshire, was given by Henry I. to St. Swithin's, Winchester. Taken from Charles I., by the parliamentarians, 1644; visited and brought into note by George III., 1789. First Dorset industrial exhibition was opened here, 25 July, 1878. Statue of queen Victoria unveiled by princess Henry of Battenburg, 20 Oct. 1902. Princess Christian Sanitorium (cost 15,000*l.*), opened, 19 Nov. 1902. Population 1901, 22,000.

WHALE-FISHERY, it is said, was first carried on by the Norwegians in the ninth century. *Lenglet*. Whales were killed at Newfoundland and Iceland, for their oil only, 1578; the use of their fins and bones was not yet known, consequently (a writer adds) no stays were worn by the ladies. The English whale-fishing commenced at Spitzbergen in 1598; but the Dutch had been previously fishing there. The fishery was much promoted by an act of parliament passed in 1749. From 1800 to 2000 whales have been killed annually on the coast of Greenland, &c. The quantity of whale-oil imported in 1814 was 33,567 tuns; in 1826, when gas-light became general, 25,000 tuns; in 1840, about 22,000 tuns; in 1850, 21,360 tuns; in 1861, 19,176 tuns; in 1864, 14,701 tuns; in 1867, 15,945 tuns; in 1871, 24,679 tuns; in 1872 18,719 tuns; in 1878, 20,656 tuns; in 1883, 17,156 tuns; in 1887, 17,698 tuns; in 1890, 20,307 tuns. *A living whale* from Labrador, 9 feet 6 inches long, placed in the Westminster aquarium, 26 Sept., died 29 Sept. 1877. White whale (Beluga), arrived 28 May; died in latter part of June. 159 bottlenosed whales captured at Barns, Tankerness, near Kirkwall, 20 Nov. 1889; 166 captured at Hillswick, Shetland, 6 Sept. 1902.

WHARNCLIFFE MEETINGS of public companies (held to give enlarged powers under certain prescribed conditions) are so called because the standing orders of the house of lords, under which they are held, were introduced by lord Wharncliffe, about 1846.

WHEAT. The Chinese ascribe to their emperor, Ching-Noung, who succeeded Fohi, the art of husbandry, and method of making bread from wheat, about 2000 years before the Christian era. Wheat was introduced into Britain in the 6th century, by Coll ap Coll Frewi. *Roberts.* The first wheat imported into England of which we have a note was in 1347. Various statutes have regulated the sales of wheat, and restrained its importation, in order to encourage its being raised at home. In 1862 attention was drawn to the probable utility of considering the pedigree of wheat. In 1871 it was estimated that 3,571,894 acres in the United Kingdom were devoted to wheat; in 1876, 3,124,342. See *Bread* and *Corn Laws*. Greatest producers (in order), United States, Russia, France, Great Britain, &c. The wheat crop for Great Britain is said to have yielded 71,939,647 bushels in 1888; 37,176,257 in 1895. See *Corner*, 1898, and *Agriculture*, 1843. "The Wheat Problem," by sir Wm. Crookes, published, 1899. Steady shrinkage of area assigned to wheat, reported, Sept. 1901.

IMPORTED INTO THE UNITED KINGDOM.

	Wheat.	*Flour.*
1854,	2,656,455 *qrs.*	6,329,038 *cwts.*
1861,	29,955,532 „	6,152,938 „
1864,	23,196,714 *cwts.*	4,512,391 „
1866,	23,156,329 „	4,972,280 „
1868,	32,639,768 „	3,093,022 „
1871,	39,389,803 „	3,977,933 „
1874,	41,527,638 „	6,236,044 „
1877,	54,269,800 „	7,377,303 „
1879,	59,591,795 „	10,728,252 „
1880,	55,261,924 „	10,558,312 „
1881,	57,147,933 „	11,357,381 „
1883,	64,138,631 „	16,329,312 „
1884,	47,306,156 „	15,095,301 „
1885,	61,498,864 „	15,832,843 „
1886,	47,435,806 „	14,689,560 „
1887,	55,802,518 „	18,063,234 „
1888,	57,261,363 „	16,910,442 „
1889,	58,551,887 „	14,672,082 „
1890,	60,474,180 „	15,773,336 „
1891,	66,312,962 „	16,723,003 „
1892,	64,901,799 „	22,106,009 „
1893,	65,461,988 „	20,408,168 „
1894,	70,126,232 „	19,134,605 „
1895,	81,749,955 „	18,368,410 „
1896,	70,025,980 „	21,320,200 „
1897,	62,740,180 „	18,680,669 „
1898,	65,227,930 „	21,017,109 „
1899,	66,636,078 „	22,945,708 „
1900,	68,669,490 „	21,548,131 „
1901,	69,747,830 „	22,575,230 „
1902,	81,002,227 „	19,386,341 „

VALUE OF WHEAT IMPORTED INTO THE UNITED KINGDOM.

Year	Value	Year	Value
1854	£11,593,737	1876	£23,178,011
1855	9,679,578	1877	33,885,437
1856	12,716,349	1878	27,433,444
1857	9,563,099	1879	31,468,171
1858	9,050,467	1880	30,621,711
1859	8,713,532	1881	31,531,535
1860	16,554,083	1882	34,259,126
1861	19,051,464	1883	31,454,481
1862	23,203,800	1884	19,901,794
1863	12,015,006	1885	24,085,913
1864	10,674,654	1886	17,909,630
1865	9,775,616	1887	21,337,918
1866	12,983,090	1888	21,995,974
1867	24,985,096	1889	22,510,502
1868	22,069,353	1890	23,583,844
1869	19,515,758	1891	29,448,204
1870	16,264,027	1892	24,857,902
1871	23,318,883	1893	21,070,028
1872	26,169,185	1894	18,760,505
1873	28,538,746	1899	22,281,219
1874	25,236,932	1900	23,345,929
1875	27,510,469	1901	23,081,372

Average Annual Price per Quarter in England and Wales.

Year	s.	d.	Year	s.	d.	Year	s.	d.	Year	s.	d.
1801	119	6	1865	41	10	1878	46	5	1891	31	0
1805	89	9	1866	49	11	1879	43	10	1892	30	3
1810	106	5	1867	64	5	1880	44	4	1893	26	4
1815	65	7	1868	63	9	1881	45	4	1894	22	10
1820	67	10	1869	48	2	1882	45	1	1895	23	1
1825	68	6	1870	46	10	1883	41	7	1896	26	2
1830	66	4	1871	56	8	1884	35	8	1897	30	2
1835	39	4	1872	57	0	1885	32	10	1898	34	0
1840	66	4	1873	58	8	1886	31	0	1899	25	8
1845	50	10	1874	55	8	1887	32	6	1900	26	11
1850	40	3	1875	45	2	1888	31	10	1901	26	9
1855	74	8	1876	46	2	1889	29	9	1502	28	1
1860	53	3	1877	56	9	1890	31	11			

1894, 17s. 6d.; 22s. 10d.; 26s., at different places.
1896, 33s. 4d., 28 Nov.
1897, 34s. 4d., 25 Dec.
1898, 35s. 8d. 19 wks., 42s. 4d., 7 May, 40s. 8d., 25 June.

WHEEL, BREAKING ON THE. A barbarous mode of death, of great antiquity, ordered by Francis I. for robbers, about 1535; see *Ravaillac.*

"The Great Wheel," made of steel (300 ft. high, axle 7 ft. in diameter, supported on 8 columns 150 ft. high). 40 cars are swung round the wheel, each capable of holding about 40 persons, with adjuncts; the wheel was designed and constructed by Mr. Bassett. The wheel was named by lady Dowell, and started, carrying several hundreds of people at the Empire of India exhibition, Earl's Court, the revolution being successfully accomplished in about 40 minutes, 6 July, 1895. Through a stoppage of the machinery, between 60 and 70 persons were detained 16 hrs. in the upper cars, 21–22 May, 1896.

WHIGS. In the reign of Charles II. the name *Whig* was a term of reproach given by the court party to their antagonists for holding the principles of the "whigs," or fanatical covenanters in Scotland; and in return the name *Tory* was given to the court party, comparing them to the Tories, or popish robbers in Ireland. *Baker.* The distinction arose out of the discovery of the Meal-tub plot (*which see*) in 1678. Upon bringing up the meal plot before parliament, two parties were formed: the ones who doubted the plot styled those who believed in it *Whigs;* these styled their adversaries *Tories.* In time these names, given as marks of opprobrium, became honoured distinctions. *Hume.* The Whigs brought about the revolution of 1688-9, and established the protestant succession. They were chiefly instrumental in obtaining the abolition of the slave trade and slavery, the repeal of the Test and Corporation act, Catholic emancipation, parliamentary and municipal reform, the repeal of the corn laws, and similar measures. The Whig Club was established by Charles James Fox; one of its original members was the great Francis, duke of Bedford, who died in 1802. See *Liberals.* For the principal Whig ministries, see *Halifax, Walpole, Rockingham, Grenville, Grey, Melbourne, Russell, Palmerston,* and *Gladstone.*

WHIP, the popular title of the patronage secretary of the treasury, whose duty it is to collect members to make a house on important occasions, &c. Sir Wm. Hayter, the liberal "whip," 1850-8, received a testimonial for his energetic services, early in 1861. The right hon. Wm. P. Adam, an able whip, died governor of Madras, 24 May, 1881. It is the duty of both conservative and liberal whips to promote the interest of their party in every conceivable way.

The management of the house of commons by bribery is said to have begun with Clifford of the "Cabal" ministry, and continued by Whigs and Tories. Mr. Roberts (under Henry Pelham), is said to have paid members sums of 1,000*l.*, 500*l.*, &c., to each at the close of a session for their support. *Wraxall.*

WHISKY, the spirit distilled from malt and other corn in Scotland and Ireland, of which about eight millions of gallons have been distilled annually in the former, and upwards of nine millions of gallons in the latter. The duty upon this article once produced annually about three millions. The distillation of whisky is referred to the 16th century; but some authors state it to have been earlier; see *Distillation.* In 1855 the duties on spirits distilled in Scotland and Ireland were equalised with those distilled in England; additional duty of 6*d.* per gallon imposed, 1894. *Women's Whisky War,* see *United States,* 1874.

WHIST, a game at cards, became general at the end of the 17th century.

Edmund Hoyle, who published his "Short Treatise" about 1742, died in 1769, aged 97; lord Peterborough introduced short whist early in the past century; the laws were revised in 1864
"Whist," a poem 1791
James Clay, M.P., an eminent player, died 26 Sept. 1871
Mr. Henry Jones, "Cavendish," his "Laws and Principles of Whist," published 1862, died, aged 68 . . . . . 10 Feb. 1899
A committee formed to revise the laws of whist; first meeting . . . . . 12 May, ,,

WHITBY, N.R. Yorkshire. The monastery here, under St. Hilda, founded by king Oswy, 657, destroyed by the Danes 876, was restored by William de Percy about 1100. The Cholmleys established alum works here in 1615. Whitby was made a borough in 1832, and absorbed into the county in 1885. Population, 1881, 14,086; 1891, 13,274; 1901, 11,748.

WHITEBAIT DINNER, when the cabinet ministers met at the end of each session, is said to have begun at the end of the 18th century, through sir Robert Preston and Mr. George Rose inviting Mr. Pitt and his colleagues to dine at Dagenham, and afterwards at Greenwich. Another account dates its origin in 1721. The annual whitebait dinner, stopped by the Gladstone ministry, was revived by the Disraeli ministry, 1 Aug. 1874, and continued by the Gladstone, 1 Sept. 1880. No dinner since 1883; was revived by the Rosebery ministry, 15 Aug. 1894. The whitebait (*clupea alba*) is a subject of controversy. Albert Günther, of the British Museum, in his Catalogue of Fishes, says the whitebait is "a purely nominal species," and that all the examples which he has examined were young herrings (1868).

At the inquiry in June, 1878, James Henry Cannon, fisherman, claimed the discovery of the fish for his grandfather, Richard, who named it 1780. It was mentioned in a letter in the life of lord Malmesbury, 2 July, 1763.

WHITEBOYS, a body of ruffians in Ireland, so called on account of their wearing linen frocks over their coats. They committed dreadful outrages in 1761, but were suppressed by a military force, and their ringleaders executed in 1762. They rose and were again suppressed in 1786-7. The insurrection act was passed on their account in 1822.

WHITE CAPS, a self-constituted organisation in the United States, which professes to take cognizance of offences against morality and social order, punishing the offenders by severe whippings. Called "White caps" from the members wearing white hoods to conceal their faces when visiting the houses of alleged delinquents.

WHITECHAPEL, a parish in East London, was part of Stepney till 1329. The church, built in 1673, was replaced by one consecrated 2 Feb. 1877, which was burnt 26 Aug. 1880. Population, 1881, 71,363; 1891, 74,462.

Annual Loan Art exhibitions, 4 April, 1882, *et seq.*
Free library and museum, gift of Mr. Passmore Edwards, opened by the earl of Rosebery, 25 Oct. 1892. He also gave 4,250*l.* to establish a free library in Shoreditch, which was opened by the duke of Devonshire, 10 May, 1893.
London hospital medical college, new buildings opened by lady Knutsford . . 18 July, 1899
Lord Rosebery opens a new art gallery, the gift of Mr. Passmore Edwards and others . 12 March, 1901
Whitechapel and Bow railway opened . 31 May, 1902

WHITECHAPEL MURDERS, &c. Henry Wainwright, a brushmaker, murdered Harriet Lane, his mistress, on his premises, 215, Whitechapel-road, and buried the body, Sept. 1874.

While conveying the mutilated remains to be concealed in his cellars in Southwark, Wainwright and Alice Day were apprehended, through the courage and activity of Alfred Philip Stokes, 11 Sept. Day was discharged; Henry and his brother Thomas were committed for trial 13 Oct. 1875
Nine days' trial before chief justice Cockburn; Henry convicted of murder; Thomas as accessory after the fact (seven years' penal servitude), 22 Nov.-1 Dec.; Henry executed . . 21 Dec. "
1232*l.* subscribed for Henry's family.
30*l.* awarded to Stokes.
Much excitement was caused by the murder and brutal mutilation of unfortunate women at different times—Smith, 3 April; Martha Turner, 7 Aug.; Nichols, 31 Aug.; Chapman, 7, 8 Sept. Coroners return open verdict. The evidence showed the murderer possessed surgical knowledge, his object being to get possession of certain organs. Two more women murdered in a similar manner near Commercial Road and Aldgate; E. Watts or Stride and C. Conway or Eddowes between 1 and 2 A.M. 30 Sept. The lord mayor offers 500*l.* reward in relation to the murder near Aldgate; Mary Jane Kelly's body found dreadfully mutilated in 26. Dorset Street, Spitalfields . 9 Nov. 1888
Rose Milett or Davis (?) strangled at Poplar, 28 Dec. "
Alice McKenzie found with throat cut, &c., in Castle Alley, Whitechapel . . 17 July, 1889
The mutilated trunk of a woman discovered under a railway arch in Ruchin-street . . 10 Sept. "
Frances Coles found murdered in an archway, Orman-street, Whitechapel-road . 13 Feb. 1891
James Thomas Sadler arrested, 16 Feb.; discharged . . . . . 3 March, "
Marie Damyon, Thomas Street . . 17 Nov. 1894
Olga M. Wysocka (27) and Clement Kuczmierowich (22), shot dead by Frederick Karacrewski (39); Ada Varinski injured at 115, Brick-lane 5 Feb. 1898

WHITE CROSS ARMY, the shorter title of the Church of England Purity Society, established by Miss Ellice Hopkins, supported by the bishops of Durham and Lichfield and other prelates, highly successful at Oxford, Edinburgh, Liverpool, and other places, 1884.

WHITE DOVES, a South Russian religious sect, said to be wealthy and superstitious, strongly advocating celibacy: under a chief named Koudrine. Members were tried for moral offences about April, 1876.

WHITEFIELDITES. George Whitefield, the founder of the "*Calvinistic Methodists*," born 1714, was the son of an innkeeper at Gloucester, where he received his first education. He was admitted a servitor at Oxford in 1732, became a companion of the Wesleys there, and aided them in establishing Methodism. He parted from them in 1741, on account of their rejection of the doctrine of election. He was the most eloquent preacher of his day. His first sermon was preached in 1736, and he commenced field preaching in 1739. He is said to have delivered 18,000 sermons during his career of 34 years. He visited America in 1737, 1739, and 1744. His followers are termed "the countess of Huntingdon's connexion," from his having become her chaplain in 1748, and from her energetic support of the sect, by establishing a college at Trevecca, 1767. See *Spafields*. There were 109 chapels of this connexion in 1851; 36 chapels in 1896, but many of his followers have joined the Independents. He died 30 Sept. 1770, and the countess died 17 June, 1791; see *Tabernacle*.

WHITE FLAG, see *Flag*.

WHITE FRIARS, see *Carmelites* and *Sanctuaries*.

WHITEHALL (London), built by Hubert de Burgh, earl of Kent, before the middle of the 13th century. It afterwards devolved, by bequest, to the Black Friars of Holborn, who sold it to the archbishop of York, whence it received the name of York-place, and continued to be the town residence of the archbishops till taken by Henry VIII. from cardinal Wolsey, in 1530. At this period it became the residence of the court. Queen Elizabeth, who died at Richmond in 1603, was brought from thence to Whitehall, by water, in a grand procession. It was on this occasion, Camden informs us, that the following quaint panegyric on her majesty was written:

"The queen was brought by water to Whitehall,
At every stroke the oars did *tears* let fall.
More clung about the barge: fish under water
Wept out their *eyes of pearl*, and swam blind after.
I think the bargemen might, with easier thighs,
Have rowed her thither in her people's eyes;
For howsoe'er thus much my thoughts have scann'd,
She had come by *water*, had she come by *land*."

Whitehall was partly burnt 9-10 April, 1691; totally destroyed by fire, 4 Jan. 1697-8, except the banqueting-house, which had been added to the palace of Whitehall by James I., according to a design of Inigo Jones, in 1619. In the front of Whitehall Charles I. was beheaded 30 Jan. 1649. George I. converted the hall into a chapel 1723-4. The exterior of this edifice underwent repair between 1829 and 1833. The chapel was ordered to be permanently closed, 28 Oct. 1890; lent during queen Victoria's reign, to the Royal United Service Institution, from 1 Jan. 1891; first meeting held, 7 March, 1891.

WHITE HATS, a party in the Low Countries formed about 1377, against Louis, count of Flanders. The struggle lasted till 1384, when it was settled by Philip, duke of Burgundy.

WHITE HOODS, see *Catechumens*.

WHITE HORSE, see *Ashdown*.

WHITE HOUSE (Washington), built of freestone, the residence of the president, gives name to the United States government, as St. James's palace does to that of Great Britain.

WHITE LEAD, see *Lead*.

WHITE LEAGUE, formed in Louisiana and other southern states of North America, to resist the aggressions of the emancipated negroes and their friends, termed "carpet-baggers." See *New Orleans*, 1874.

WHITE PASHA, see *Soudan*, July, 1888.

WHITE PLAINS (N. America), where a battle was fought 28 Oct. 1776, between the revolted Americans and the British forces under sir William Howe. It terminated in the defeat of the Americans, who suffered considerable loss in killed, wounded, and prisoners.

WHITE ROSE, ORDER OF THE, includes men and women of many shades of opinion, who regard the revolution of 1688 as a national crime, and Jacobitism as true loyalty. The order has no religious test, its sole object being to maintain the doctrine of the divine right of kings, and revive public interest in the sufferings of the house of Stuart.

WHITE SHEEP, a name given to the Turcomans who conquered Persia about 1468, and persecuted the Shiites, but were expelled by Ismail, who founded the Sophi dynasty in 1501.

WHITE TOWER, the keep or citadel in the Tower of London, a large, square, irregular building, erected in 1070 by abbot Gundulph, afterwards bishop of Rochester. It measures 116 feet by 96, and is 92 feet in height: the walls, which are 11 feet thick, having a winding staircase continued along two of the sides, like that in Dover Castle. It contains an extensive armoury. Within this tower is the ancient chapel of St. John, originally used by the English monarchs. The turret at the N.E. angle, the highest of the four by which the White Tower is surmounted, was used for astronomical purposes by Flamsteed previously to the erection of the royal observatory at Greenwich.

WHITSUNTIDE, a festival appointed to commemorate the descent of the Holy Ghost upon the apostles: the newly-baptized persons, or catechumens, are said to have worn white garments on Whitsunday. This feast is movable, being always exactly seven weeks after Easter. Rogation week (*which see*) is the week before Whitsunday. Whitsunday 1892, 5 June; 1893, 21 May; 1894, 13 May; 1895, 2 June; 1896, 24 May; 1897, 6 June; 1898, 29 May; 1899, 21 May; 1900, 3 June; 1902, 18 May; 1903, 31 May; 1904, 22 May; 1905, 11 June.

Whitsunday, a Scotch quarter-day, is always on 15 May, as settled by an act of 1693, but local usage varies.

WHITTINGTON'S CHARITIES. Sir Richard Whittington, a citizen and mercer of London, served the office of lord mayor three times, the last in 1419. Many false stories are connected with his name, and his munificent charities are little known. He founded his college, dedicated to the Holy Ghost an (the Virgin Mary, in 1424; and his almshouses in 1429; the latter, originally built in London, now stand on Highgate-hill (built 1808) near the supposed site of the supposed famous stone which commemorated the legend of his return to London, after leaving it in despair.

WHITWORTH FOUNDATIONS. Mr. (aftd. sir) Joseph Whitworth, the eminent engineer (born 21 Dec. 1803; died 22 Jan. 1887), in a letter to the first lord of the treasury, dated 18 March, 1868, offered to found 30 scholarships of the annual value of 100*l.* each, to be applied for the further instruction of young men, natives of the United Kingdom, selected by open competition for their intelligence and proficiency in the theory and practice of mechanics and its cognate sciences, with a view to the promotion of engineering and mechanical industry in this country; and he expressed hopes that means might be found for bringing science and industry into closer relation with each other than at present obtains here. This offer was accepted by the lords of the committee of the privy council, 28 March, 1868. In 1875, sir Joseph assigned an estate to support these scholarships. For the results of sir Joseph Whitworth's will, see *Manchester*, 1888-90.

WHO? WHO? ADMINISTRATION, *Derby's*, earl of, Feb. 1852 (*which see*).

"WHOLE DUTY OF MAN;" (the authorship doubtfully attributed to abps. Sancroft, Frewen, and Sterne; to bishops Fell and Chapel; to Dorothy, lady Packington, and others;) first published, 1659. *Lowndes.* It is attributed by some to John Ischam.

WICKLIFFITES, the followers of John Wickliffe (born 1324), a professor of divinity in the university of Oxford and rector of Lutterworth in Leicestershire. He was a forerunner of the reformation of the English Church from popery, being among the first who opposed the authority of the pope, transubstantiation, the celibacy of the clergy, &c. Wickliffe, protected by John of Gaunt, Edward's son and Richard's uncle, was virulently persecuted by the church, and only saved from martyrdom by a paralytic attack, which caused his death, 31 Dec. 1384, in his 60th year. The Council of Constance, in 1414, decreed his bones to be disinterred and burnt, which was done by the bishop of Lincoln, and his dust was cast into the river Swift, 1415. Wickliffe's English version of the Bible was commenced in 1380; a noble edition of it was printed at Oxford in 1850. *Wycliff Society*, founded in 1882 to publish his works. Quincentenary of his death celebrated in London, &c., 21 May, 1884. See *Lollards*. A band of protestants organised by the late Mr. Kensit under the name of Wickliffites has been active in carrying on an anti-ritualistic propaganda.

WIDOWS. The Jewish law required a man's brother to marry his widow if without children (1490 B.C.). For the burning of widows in India, see *Suttee*. Among the numerous associations in London for the relief of widows are, one for the widows of musicians, instituted in 1738; for widows of naval men, founded in 1739; for widows of medical men, 1788: a law society, for widows of professional gentlemen, 1817; and a society for artists' widows, 1827.—WIDOWERS were taxed in England as follows: a duke, 12*l.* 10*s.*; lower peers, smaller sums; a common person, 1*s.*; 7 Will. III. 1695.

WIEN, see *Vienna*.

WIFE, see *Wives*.

WIG, see *Peruke*.

WIGAN (Lancashire). The king's troops, commanded by the earl of Derby, were defeated and driven out of the town in 1643 by the parliamentary forces under sir John Smeaton. The earl was again defeated by colonel Ashton, who razed the fortifications of Wigan to the ground, same year; and once more by a greatly superior force commanded by colonel Lilburne, 1651. In this last engagement, sir Thomas Tildesley, an ardent royalist, was slain; a pillar was erected to his memory in 1679. The colliers in the neighbourhood struck, and acting riotously 17, 18 April, 1868, were quelled by the military. Arrangements were soon after made with the employers. The prince and princess of Wales at their visit, 4 June, 1873, opened a new hospital, &c., and received a hearty welcome. See *Railway Accidents*, 2 Aug. 1873. Population, 1881, 48,194; 1891, 55,013; 1901, 60,774.

WIGHT, Isle of, the Roman *Vecta* or *Victis*, was conquered by Vespasian in the reign of Claudius. It was conquered by the Saxons under Cerdic about 530; by the Danes, 787, and in 1001, when they held it for several years. It was invaded by the French, July, 1377, and has several times suffered from invasion by them. In 1442, Henry VI. alienated the Isle to Henry de Beauchamp, first premier earl of England and then duke of Warwick, and afterwards crowned him king of the Isle of Wight, with his own hands; but dying without heirs male, his regal title died with him, and the lordship of the isle returned to the crown. Charles I., after his flight from Hampton-court, was a prisoner in Carisbrook castle, in 1647. In the time of Charles II. timber was very plentiful. In this isle was queen Victoria's marine residence, Osborne-house, which she bequeathed to king Edward VII.; he gave it to the nation to be used as a convalescent home for officers in the navy and army, 9 Aug. 1902. Population, 1901, 82,387.

Prince Henry of Battenberg appointed governor Jan. 1889; died, 20 Jan. 1896; the princess appointed governor . . . . 1 May, 1896

As a national memorial to lord Tennyson, a resident on the island, the erection of "the Tennyson Beacon" on Freshwater Down, designed by Mr. Pearson, R.A.; subscriptions of 750*l.* (200*l.* from United States) have been received, 1895. The beacon unveiled . . . . . . 6 Aug. 1897

Royal infirmary at Ryde, new children's wing, opened by the queen, and bust of the queen unveiled by princess Beatrice . . . 28 July, 1899

"Battenberg" block of the Royal Consumptive hospital at Ventnor opened by princess Beatrice, 9 Aug. ,,

Capt. Bray and several others killed by a gun accident at Freshwater . . . . 25 June, 1901

The king visits the island, end March; Ventnor hospital, Carisbrooke . . . . 1, 2 April, 1902

Princess Henry opens the new Western (Jubilee, 1897) esplanade at Ryde, 25 July; and a recreation-ground, the gift of Mr. Tankerville Chamberlayne, at Newport . . . . . 28 Aug. ,,

Royal naval college at Osborne opened by the king . . . . 4 Aug. 1903

WILD BIRDS' PROTECTION ACTS, passed 10 Aug. 1872, 24 July, 1876, and 7 Sept. 1880; amendment, 1894, passed, 14 Aug. 1896; amendment act passed, 12 June, 1902. International conference at Paris, 25 June, 1895.

WILDERNESS BATTLES, see *United States*, May, 1864.

WILHELMSHAFEN, at Hippens, bay of Jahde, Oldenburg, the first German military port, was inaugurated by William, king of Prussia, 17 June, 1869. Since 1871 it has become the Chatham of Germany. By explosion of a gun on the *Mars*, 8 men killed and 20 injured, 27 April, 1881. Visit of the emperor, 3 March, 1903.

WILKES'S NUMBER, 45, see *North Briton*, and also *Warrants, General*.

WILLIAMS' LIBRARY, see *Libraries*.

WILLIS'S ROOMS, see *Almack's*.

WILLOW-LEAVES, see *Sun*.

WILLS and Testaments are of very high antiquity, see *Genesis* xlviii. The private will of Sennacherib, king of Assyria, 680 B.C., found at Nineveh, is translated in *Records of the Past*, Vol. I. Solon introduced them at Athens, 578 B.C. There are regulations respecting wills in the Koran. Trebatius Testa the civilian, introduced codicils to wills at Rome, 31 B.C. The power of bequeathing lands by the last will and testament of the owner was confirmed to English subjects 1 Henry I. 1100; but with great restrictions and limitations respecting the feudal system, which were taken off by the statute of 32 Hen. VIII. 1541. *Blackstone's Commentaries*. The first will of a sovereign on record is stated (but in error) to be that of Richard II. 1399; Edward the Confessor made a will, 1066. Various laws have regulated the wills and testaments of British subjects. All previous statutes were repealed by the "Wills Act," 7 Will. IV. & 1 Vict. c. 26, 1837, and the laws with relation to wills amended.* The present Probate Court (*which see*) was established in 1857. An office for the reception of the wills of living persons was opened in Jan. 1861. See *Thellusson's Will*, *Legacies*, *Estate*, *Succession Duties*, *Trials*, 1 April, 1897. In 1869 twenty probates of wills or letters of administration were stamped for personal property, each exceeding a quarter of a million; one had a stamp of 21,000*l.* The Wills Office, removed from Doctors' Commons to Somerset House, was opened 24 Oct. 1874.

The will of Peter the Great, described in the "*Mémoires de la Chevalière d'Eon*," as a "plan for compassing European supremacy," left for his successors, and deposited in the archives of the palace of Peterhoff near St. Petersburg. It advocated "approach as near as possible to Constantinople, and towards the Indies: wars with Turkey and Persia; possession of the shores of the Black Sea, and the Baltic;" &c. The existence of the will (denied by the czars) was first announced by M. Lesur in his "*Progrès de la Puissance Russe*," published at Paris in 1812. In 1863, Dr. Berkholz of Riga asserted that the will was a forgery, probably dictated by Napoleon I. Mr. W. J. Thoms, the antiquary, and others, contend for the genuineness of the will, June, 1878.

EXTRACTS FROM THE LAST WILL OF NAPOLEON I., EMPEROR OF FRANCE.†

[He died 5 May, 1821, eleven days after he had signed these documents. The original in French occupies about twenty-six pages in Peignot's "Testamens Remarquables," 1829.]

"This day, 24 April, 1821, at Longwood, in the island of St. Helena. This is my testament, or act of my last will: . . . . .

"I leave to the comte de Montholon 2,000,000 francs as a proof of my satisfaction for the attentions he has paid to me for these six years, and to indemnify him for the losses which my residence in St. Helena has occasioned him. I leave to the comte Bertrand 500,000 francs. I leave to Marchand, my first valet-de-chambre, 400,000 francs; the services he has performed for me are those of a friend. I desire that he may marry a widow, sister, or daughter of an officer or soldier of my old guard. To St. Denis, 100,000 francs. To Novarre, 100,000 francs. To Pijeron, 100,000 francs. To Archambaud, 50,000 francs. To Cuvier, 50,000 francs. To Chandelle, *idem*.

* By this act the testator must be above 21, not a lunatic or idiot, not deaf and dumb, not drunk at the time of signing, not an outlawed or unpardoned felon. All kinds of property may be devised. The will must be written legibly and intelligibly, and signed by the testator, or by his direction, in the presence of two or more witnesses, who also must sign, and not be legatees.

† These documents, dated from 15-24 April, deposited since 1821 in England, have been given up to the authorities at Paris, at the request of the French Government.

"To the Abbé Vignali, 100,000 francs. I desire that he may build his house near Ponte Novo de Rossino. To the comte Las Casas, 100,000 francs. To comte Lavalette, 100,000 francs. To the surgeon-in-chief, Larrey, 100,000 francs. He is the most virtuous man I have known. To general Brayer, 100,000 francs.

"To general Lefevre Desnouettes, 100,000 francs. To general Drouet, 100,000 francs. To general Cambronne, 100,000 francs. To the children of general Muton Duvernais, 100,000 francs. To the children of the brave Labédoyère, 100,000 francs. To the children of general Girard, killed at Ligny, 100,000 francs. To the children of general Chartrand, 100,000 francs. To the children of the virtuous general Travost, 100,000 francs. To general Lallemand, the elder, 100,000 francs. To general Clausel, 100,000 francs. To Costa Bastilica, also 100,000 francs. To the baron de Menevalle, 100,000 francs. To Arnault, author of *Marius*, 100,000 francs.

"To colonel Marbot, 100,000 francs: I request him to continue to write for the defence and glory of the French armies, and to confound the calumniators and the apostates. To the baron Bignon, 100,000 francs: I request him to write the history of French Diplomacy from 1792 to 1815. To Poggi de Talaro, 100,000 francs. To the surgeon Emmery, 100,000.

"These sums shall be taken from the six millions which I deposited on leaving Paris in 1815, and from the interest at the rate of 5 *per cent.* since July, 1815; the account of which shall be adjusted with the bankers by the counts Montholon and Bertrand and by Marchand.

"These legacies, in case of death, shall be paid to the widows and children, and in their default, shall revert to the capital. I institute the counts Montholon, Bertrand, and Marchand my testamentary executors. This present testament, written entirely by my own hand, is signed and sealed with my arms.

"NAPOLEON.

"24 April, 1821, Longwood."

The following are part of the eight *Codicils* to the preceding will of the emperor:—

"On the liquidation of my civil list of Italy—such as money, jewels, plate, linen, coffers, caskets of which the viceroy is the depository, and which belong to me, I dispose of two millions, which I leave to my most faithful servants. I hope that without their showing any cause, my son Eugene Napoleon will discharge them faithfully. He cannot forget the forty millions which I have given him in Italy, or by the right (*parage*) of his mother's inheritance.

"From the funds remitted in gold to the empress Maria Louisa, my very dear and well-beloved spouse, at Orleans, in 1814, there remain due to me two millions, which I dispose of by the present codicil, in order to recompense my most faithful servants, whom I beside recommend to the protection of my dear Maria Louisa. I leave 200,000 francs to count Montholon, 100,000 francs of which he shall pay into the chest of the treasurer (Las Casas) for the same purpose as the above, to be employed according to my dispositions in legacies of conscience.

"10,000 francs to the sub-officer Cantillon (died July, 1869), who has undergone a prosecution, being accused of a desire to assassinate lord Wellington, of which he has been declared innocent. Cantillon had as much right to assassinate that oligarch, as the latter had to send me to perish on the rock of St. Helena," &c. &c. &c.

LETTER TO M. LAFITTE.

"MONSIEUR LAFITTE,—I remitted to you in 1815, at the moment of my departure from Paris, a sum of nearly six millions, for which you gave me a double receipt. I have cancelled one of these receipts, and I have charged comte de Montholon to present to you the other receipt, in order that you may, after my death, deliver to him the said sum with interest at the rate of five *per cent.*, from the 1st of July, 1815, deducting the payments with which you have been charged in virtue of my order. I have also remitted to you a box containing my medallion. I beg you will deliver it to comte Montholon.

"This letter having no other object, I pray God, Monsieur Lafitte, that He may have you in His holy and worthy keeping.

"NAPOLEON.

"Longwood, in the island of St. Helena, 25 April, 1821."

The following WILL OF NAPOLEON III. was published in the *Times*, 30 April, 1873:—

"April 24, 1865.

"This is my will. I commend my son and my wife to the high constituted authorities of the state (aux grands corps de l'Etat), to the people, and the army. The empress Eugénie possesses all the qualities requisite for conducting the regency well, and my son displays a disposition and judgment which will render him worthy of his high destinies. Let him never forget the motto of the head of our family, 'Everything for the French people.' Let him fix in his mind the writings of the prisoner of St. Helena; let him study the emperor's deeds and correspondence; finally, let him remember, when circumstances so permit, that the cause of the peoples is the cause of France. Power is a heavy burden, because one cannot always do all the good one could wish, and because your contemporaries seldom render you justice, so that, in order to fulfil one's mission, one must have faith in, and consciousness of, one's duty. It is necessary to consider that from heaven on high those whom you have loved regard and protect you; it is the soul of my illustrious uncle that has always inspired and sustained me. The like will apply to my son, for he will always be worthy of his name. I leave to the empress Eugénie all my private property. It is my desire that on the majority of my son she shall inhabit the Elysée and Biarritz. I trust that my memory will be dear to her, and that after my death she will forget the griefs I may have caused her. With regard to my son, let him keep as a talisman the seal I used to wear attached to my watch, and which comes from my mother; let him carefully preserve everything that comes to me from the emperor, my uncle, and let him be convinced that my heart and my soul remain with him. I make no mention of my faithful servants. I am convinced that the empress and my son will never abandon them. I shall die in the Catholic, Apostolic, and Roman religion, which my son will always honour by his piety. Done, written, and signed with my hand at the palace of the Tuileries, the 24th of April, 1865. (Signed) "NAPOLEON."

The WILL OF PRINCE LOUIS NAPOLEON was written with his own hand, and signed 26 Feb. 1879, the night before he sailed for South Africa (where he was killed while on a reconnoitring party, 1 June, 1879). He states that he dies in the Catholic religion; expresses his love for his country, his mother the empress, and his friends; and his gratitude to the queen and royal family of England, and to the English people for their cordial hospitality. He constitutes his mother sole legatee; bequeaths legacies and memorials to prince J. N. Murat, M. F. Pietri, baron Corvisart, M. Rouher, and others; and assigns to Victor, the eldest son of prince Napoleon Jerome, the task of continuing the work of Napoleon I. and Napoleon III. Executors, MM. Rouher and Pietri.

WILLUGHBY SOCIETY, devoted to the study of birds; founded in 1879; was named after Francis Willughby (1635-72), who wrote *Ornithologia*, published 1676.

WILMINGTON (N. Carolina, U.S.) was held by the confederates; resisted severe attacks of the federals in Dec. 1864. Fort Fisher was taken by assault on 15 Jan., and Wilmington was evacuated by the confederates, 22 Feb. 1865.

WILMINGTON ADMINISTRATION, succeeded that of sir Robert Walpole, Feb. 1742.

Earl of Wilmington, *first lord of the treasury*.
Lord Hardwicke, *lord chancellor*.
Earl of Harrington, *president of the council*.
Earl Gower, *lord privy seal*.
Mr. Sandys, *chancellor of the exchequer*.
Lord Carteret and the duke of Newcastle, *secretaries of state*.
Earl of Winchilsea, *first lord of the admiralty*.
Duke of Argyll, *commander of the forces* and *master-general of the ordnance*.
Mr. Henry Pelham, *paymaster of the forces*.
With several of the household lords.

[On lord Wilmington's death, 26 July, 1743, Mr. Pelham became prime minister; and in Nov. 1744, he formed the "Broad-bottom" administration; see *Pelham*.]

WILMOT'S ACT (SIR E.), 3 & 4 Vict. c. 77 (1840) relates to schools.

WIMBLEDON, ancient village 8 miles S.W. of London. See *Volunteers*, 1860-89. Population, 1881, 15,950; 1891, 25,758; 1901, 41,604.

Percy Malcolm John, student at Blenheim house, died suddenly at his school at Wimbledon, 3 Dec. 1881; his brother-in-law Dr. George Henry Lamson suspected of poisoning him, with aconitine, 2 Dec.; was convicted of the murder, 14 March, confessed his guilt 27 April, and was executed 28 April, 1882

WINCHESTER (Hampshire), a most ancient city, whose erection may reasonably be ascribed to the Celtic Britons, with the fabulous date 392 B.C. It was made the capital of the West Saxon kingdom under Cerdic, about 520; and of England by Egbert, 827; it became the residence of Alfred, 879-991. In the reign of William I. London began to rival it; and the destruction of religious houses by Henry VIII. almost ruined it. Several kings resided at Winchester, and many parliaments were held there. Memorials of its ancient superiority exist in the national denomination of measures of quantity, as Winchester ell, Winchester bushel, &c., the use of which has but recently been replaced by imperial measures. The cathedral church was first founded and endowed by Cynegils, or Kenegilsus, the first Christian king of the West Saxons. Becoming ruinous, the present fabric was begun by bishop Walkelyn, the 34th bishop, 1073; repairs to the roof began March, 1896; completed (cost, 12,670*l.* 10*s.* 11*d.*) Dec. 1898. The church was first dedicated to St. Amphibalus, then to St. Peter, and afterwards to St. Swithin, once bishop here. Dedicated to the Holy Trinity by Henry VIII. St. Birinus was the first bishop of the West Saxons, his seat Dorchester, 636; Wina, in 660, was the first bishop of Winchester. The see is valued in the king's books at 2793*l.* 4*s.* 2*d.* annually. Present income, 6,500*l.* Population, 1881, 17,780; 1891, 19,073; 1901, 20,919.

Taken by the Danes, 871-3; ravaged by Sweyn . 1013
William Rufus buried here 1100
Hospital of Holy Cross, founded by bishop Henry de Blois 1132
"Almshouse of Noble Poverty," engrafted on the Holy Cross by cardinal Beaufort, revived in 1883.
Winchester school, founded by bishop William of Wykeham 1382-7; the 500th anniversary of the laying of the first stone of New College, 26 March, 1387, celebrated 26 March, 1887.
Winchester several times taken and re-taken, 1641-3; taken by Cromwell and the castle dismantled . 1645
Charles II. began a palace here by Wren 1683
Charitable Society of Natives founded . . . 1699
Winchester Cross restored 1866
New Guildhall opened by lord Selborne 11 May, 1873
700th anniversary of the incorporation of the city, celebrated . . . . . . 3, 4 July, 1884
800th anniversary of the consecration of the cathedral celebrated, 8 April, 1893; subscriptions for restoration of the roof of the cathedral; from the queen, 150*l.* . . . . . . April, 1896
The queen, in passing, receives an address from the mayor . . . . 20 July, 1897
Large meeting at the Guildhall in connection with the millenary of king Alfred to take place in 1901, early June; other meetings held . . . 1898
The prince of Wales lays the first stone of the new barracks . . . . 8 June, 1899
THE KING ALFRED millenary celebration; delegates from the colonies, United States and all parts of the kingdom; lectures by Mr. Fred. Harrison and sir John Evans, and a Tennyson reading by sir Henry Irving; reception at the Guildhall; the king's statue, by Mr. Hamo Thornycroft, unveiled by lord Rosebery . . . 18, 19, 20 Sept. 1901
Indian princes received by the mayor and lord Northbrook . . . . . . 12 June, 1902
Lord Roberts presented with the freedom, 9 Oct. 1902

RECENT BISHOPS. (Prelates of the Order of the Garter.)

1781. Brownlow North, died 12 July, 1820.
1820. George Pretyman Tomline, died 1827.
1827. Charles Richard Sumner, resigned 1869; died, 15 Aug. 1874.
1869. Samuel Wilberforce, elected Nov.; killed, through the fall of his horse, 19 July, 1873.
1873. Edward Harold Browne, translated from Ely, Aug. 1873; resigned, 1890; died, 17 Dec. 1891.
1891. Anthony Wilson Thorold, translated from Rochester, Jan.; died, 25 July, 1895.
1895. Randall Thomas Davidson, translated from Rochester, Aug; translated to Canterbury, Jan. 1903.
1903. Herbert E. Ryle, translated from Exeter, Feb. 1903.

WINCHESTER SCHOOL, the oldest of our great schools, "Seinte Marie College of Wynchestre," the charter of which is dated Oct. 1382, was founded in 1387 by William (Long) of Wykeham, bishop of Winchester, who had established a school here in 1373. The ancient statutes were revised in 1855; and still further altered by the Public Schools act of 1868. In Nov.-Dec. 1872 there was much published correspondence respecting the *tunding*—the excessive punishment of the boys by *boy prefects*. In May, 1892, it was arranged that the quincentenary of the school should be celebrated 25 July, 1893.

Erection of memorial buildings determined on 4 May, 1893; buildings opened by the warden, the rev. Godfrey Bolles Lee, 16 June, 1897.
The quincentenary of the foundation of the school (or college) was celebrated . . . 25 July, 1893
[Besides special services in the buildings, there was a solemn service in the cathedral, processions, meetings, and festivities. Among the visitors were the prince of Wales and the duke of Connaught (part of the day), the archbishops of Canterbury and York, bishops of Winchester, London, Salisbury, and other prelates, a great number of Wykehamists, old and young, dating from 1821, and many eminent persons.]
"Winchester College," 1393–1893; prose, verse, and illustrations; edited by A. K. Cook, published . . . . Dec. 1893

WINDING-UP ACTS (to facilitate the winding up the affairs of joint-stock companies which are unable to meet their engagements) were passed in 1848, 1849, 1857, and 1862. Cases are tried by one of the judges of the chancery division.

WINDMILLS are of great antiquity, and stated to be of Roman or Saracen invention. They are said to have been originally introduced into Europe by the knights of St. John, who took the hint from what they had seen in the crusades. *Baker*. Windmills were first known in Spain, France, and Germany, in 1299. *Anderson*. Wind saw-mills were invented by a Dutchman, in 1633, when one was erected near the Strand, in London.

WINDOWS. There were glass windows in Pompeii, A.D. 79, as is evident from its ruins. It is certain that windows of some kind were glazed so early as the 3rd century, if not before, though the fashion was not introduced until it was done by Benedict Biscop, about 674. Windows of glass were used in private houses, but the glass was imported 1177. *Anderson*. In England, in 1851, about 6000 houses had fifty windows and upwards in each; about 275,000 had ten windows and upwards; and 725,000 had seven windows, or less than seven.

Window-tax first enacted in order to defray the expense of and deficiency in the re-coinage of silver 1695

The tax increased, 5 Feb. 1746-7; again in 1778; and again on the commutation-tax for tea 1 Oct. 1784
The tax again increased in . 1797, 1802, and 1808
Reduced 1823
The revenue derived from windows was in 1840 about a million and a quarter sterling; and in 1850 (to April 5), 1,832,684*l*.
The tax repealed by act 14 & 15 Vict. c. 36 (which act imposed a duty upon inhabited houses in lieu thereof) . . . . 24 July, 1851
International Window Cleaning Company, advertising . . . . May, 1892

WINDSOR (Berkshire). The *Castle*, a residence of the British sovereigns, begun by William the Conqueror, and enlarged by Henry I. about 1110. Edward III., who was born here, 13 Nov. 1312, caused the old building, with the exception of three towers at the west end, to be taken down, and re-erected the whole castle, under the direction of William of Wykeham, 1356, and built St. George's chapel. He assessed every county in England to send him workmen. James I. of Scotland was imprisoned here, 1406-23. Several additions were made by Henry VIII. Elizabeth made the grand north terrace; and Charles II. repaired and beautified it, 1676-80. Population, New Windsor, 1881, 12,273; 1891, 12,327; 1901, 13,958.

The chapel repaired and opened . . . . Oct. 1790
The castle repaired and enlarged, 1824-8; George IV. took possession . . . . . 8 Dec. 1828
Royal stables built 1839
A serious fire in the prince of Wales's tower, owing to some defect in the heating apparatus, 19 March, 1853
Our sovereigns have here entertained many royal personages, as the emperor and empress of the French, in . . . . April, 1855
Here died the prince consort . . . 14 Dec. 1861
The Albert memorial chapel, on the site of Wolsey chapel, was opened . . . . . 30 Nov. 1875
Windsor Forest, situated to the south and west of the town of Windsor, was formerly 120 miles in circumference; in 1607, it was 77½ miles round, but it has since been reduced in its bounds to about 56 miles. It was surveyed in 1789, and found to contain 59,600 acres.
Virginia Water and the plantations about it were taken out of the forest.
The marshes were drained and the trees planted for William, duke of Cumberland, about 1746; and much was done by George IV., who often resided at the lodge.
On the south side is Windsor Great Park; it contains about 3800 acres.
The Little Park, on the north and east sides of the castle, contains about 500 acres. The gardens are elegant, and have been considerably improved by the addition of the house and gardens of the duke of St. Albans, purchased by the crown.
Cumberland Lodge partially destroyed by fire; pictures burnt . . . . . . 14 Nov. 1869
Albert Institute, Windsor, opened by the prince of Wales . . . . 10 Jan. 1880
About 52,000 volunteers reviewed by the queen, 9 July, 1881
Jubilee fêtes and illuminations; the queen uncovers a statue of herself near the castle; torchlight procession of the Eton boys . . 22 June, 1887
The queen being here her 70th birthday is kept with great enthusiasm . . . . . . 24 May, 1889
Royal Agricultural Society to meet here; the queen president . . . . ,,
The Royal Agricultural Society held its jubilee show, the greatest one of the kind in the century in Windsor Great Park . . 24–29 June, ,,
The prince of Wales acted on behalf of the queen, who was president for the year; her majesty visited the show . . . . 27, 28 June, ,,
The weather was very fine during the week, and the show was reported to be a great success
Mr. Jacob Wilson, the hon. director of the show, knighted . . . . 30 June, ,,
[A fund was started at the Mansion House, London, in aid of the expenses 24 June; 5,516*l*. had been received up to 1 Aug., 1889.]
The royal pavilion with its decorations was presented to the queen by Mr. Charlton Humphreys and Messrs. Shoolbred and accepted about 29 June, 1889
The bronze equestrian statue of the prince consort (see under *Jubilee*) in the great park uncovered by the queen . . . . . . 12 May, 1890
Sir A. Sullivan's opera, "The Gondoliers," performed before the queen and court, by Mr. R. D'Oyly Carte's Savoy company, 6 March, 1891; Lord Tennyson's "Becket," Lyceum company 18 March, 1893
Other performances, 1892 *et seq.*
Visit of the German emperor and empress . 4 July, ,,
Silver wedding of the prince and princess Christian, 5 July; marriage of their daughter, princess Louise, to prince Aribert of Anhalt, 6 July; state banquet in St. George's hall . 7 July, ,,
Military funeral of the duke of Clarence and Avondale . . . . 20 Jan. 1892
The marquis of Lorne appointed constable of Windsor castle . . . . 22 Jan. ,,
The Comédie Française company perform 27 June, 1893
"La Locandiera" performed by Signora Eleonora Duse's company; the queen presents her with a diamond brooch . . . . . . 18 May, 1894
Gounod's "Faust" performed by the Royal Opera company . . . . 19 Jan. ,,
Destructive overflow of the Thames through heavy rains; Eton school closed; stoppage of traffic; much distress; relieved by the queen and others mid Nov. ,,
Sudden death at the castle of sir John Thompson. See *Canada*. 12 Dec. ,,
"The Governor's Guide to Windsor Castle," by the marquis of Lorne, issued . . April, 1895
The queen's 80th birthday celebrated with great enthusiasm; a serenade by Eton and other choirs, under sir Walter Parratt, in the quadrangle; Mr. J. T. Soundy, the mayor, knighted; *feu de joie*, military parade; the queen plants a commemoration oak; thanksgiving service in St. George's chapel, 24 May, 1899; she reviews the Honourable artillery company in the park, 1 July, 1899; visits the Victoria barracks, inspects the Grenadier guards and kindly addresses the wives and families of soldiers on service in S. Africa, 29 Nov. 1899
Colonial and Indian troops visit the castle, &c., 2, 19 July, 1902
Princess Christian opens the Alexandra gardens, 15 July, ,,
Lease (19 years) of Windsor racecourse sold for 22,000*l*. . . . . 30 Sept. 1903

WINDSOR KNIGHTS, see *Poor Knights*.

WINDWARD ISLES (West Indies)—Barbadoes, St. Vincent, Grenada, Trinidad, Tobago, and St. Lucia (*which see*). Governor, Rawson W. Rawson, 1868; J. Pope Hennessy, Feb. 1875; capt. Strahan, Nov. 1876; sir Henry Bulwer, April, 1880; William Robinson, 1881; Walter J. Sendall, May, 1885; hon. sir Walter Hely Hutchinson, Sept. 1889; sir Charles Bruce, Aug. 1893; sir C. A. Moloney, Jan. 1897; sir Robt. B. Llewelyn, Oct. 1900. Population, 1901, *about* 160,881.

WINE. "Noah planted a vineyard, and drank of the wine," 2347 B.C. (*Gen.* ix. 20); see *Vine*. Christ changed water into wine at the marriage of Cana in Galilee, A.D. 30. *John* ii. 3–10; see *Vine*.

Wine sold in England by apothecaries as a cordial in 1300, and so continued for some time after, although there is mention of "wine for the king" so early as John.
The price regulated by statute, 5 Richard II. . . 1381
The price was twelve shillings the pipe in . . 1400
A hundred and fifty butts and pipes condemned, for being adulterated, to be staved and emptied into the channels of the streets, by Rainwell, mayor of London. *Stow's Chron.* 1427
An act for licensing sellers of wine in England passed . . . . 2 April, 1661

By the Methuen treaty, Portuguese wines, port, &c., were highly favoured, and French wines discouraged by heavy duties 1703
Wine duties to be 2*s.* 9*d.* per gallon on Cape wine, and 5*s.* 6*d.* on all other wines 1831
In year ending 31 March, 1856, the customs duties on wines produced 1,856,120*l.*; in 1858, 1,733,729*l.*; 1867, 1,391,192*l.*; 1876, 1,755,710*l.*; 1884, 1,268,842*l.*; 1888, 1,085,046*l.*; 1890, 1,302,160*l.*; 1891, 1,318,006*l.*
By the French treaty of commerce, 1860, the duty on wines was reduced from 5*s.* 9*d.* to 2*s.* 6*d.* and 1*s.* according to the alcoholic strength . Jan. 1860
Licences granted to refreshment houses by an act passed in . . . . "
The Oporto Wine Company (a monopoly), established in 1756, and abolished 1865
Commission on the wine duties appointed by the commons . . . . April, 1879
The ancient duties on wine paid to the corporation on its entering the port of London, 4*s.* 9½*d.* per tun of 252 gallons amounted to 8,488*l.* net, in 1885
The abolition of these dues was discussed in 1889; the city dues on coal were abolished by parliament 8 July, 1889
Additional import duties on wine imposed by customs 1888
The *ad valorem* duty of 2*s.* 6*d.* and 1*s.* per gallon on sparkling wines, altered to 2*s.* all round 14 April, 1892

WINE IMPORTED INTO UNITED KINGDOM.

	Gallons.		Gallons.
1800	3,307,460	1879	15,162,857
1815	4,306,528	1880	17,385,496
1830	6,879,558	1882	15,715,813
1839	9,909,056	1883	15,559,795
1845	8,469,776	1884	15,106,271
1850	9,304,312	1885	14,629,739
1854	10,875,855	1886	14,552,864
1857	10,336,485	1887	15,383,641
1859	8,195,513	1888	14,745,161
1861	11,052,436	1889	15,900,749
1864	15,451,593	1890	16,194,107
1868	16,953.429	1892	17,319,477
1869	17,184,330	1893	14,675,201
1870	17,774,782	1896	16,695,560
1871	18,224,900	1898	18,139,652
1875	18,429,305	1900	16,803,829
1876	19,950,723	1901	16,546,206

WINNIPEG, capital of the province of Manitoba, Canada, has recently risen to great importance. The population, which was 215 in 1870, had risen to 20,238 in 1891; 1902, 55,000. A period of depression from 1882 to 1884 has been followed by great prosperity, especially since the suppression of Riel's rebellion in 1885; large numbers of immigrants reported in 1903. See *Canada*.

WINTER. Recent mild winters, 1862, 1868, 1873, 1876, 1881. See *Frosts*.

WINTER ASSIZES ACT, 39-40 Vict. c. 57, (11 Aug. 1876), gives power, by order in council, to unite counties for the purpose of winter assizes, for more speedy trials of prisoners.

WIRE. The invention of drawing wire is ascribed to Rodolph of Nuremberg, about 1410. Mills for this purpose were first set up at Nuremberg in 1563. The first wire-mill in England was erected at Mortlake in 1663. *Mortimer*.

WIRELESS TELEGRAPHY, see *Electricity*, page 413.

WIRTEMBERG, see *Würtemberg*.

WISCONSIN, a N.W. state of N. America, was organised as a territory in 1836; and received into the union, 29 May, 1848. Population in 1880, 1,315,497; 1890, 1,686,880; 1900, 2,069,042. Capital, Madison. Destructive forest fires, see *United States*, 31 Aug.-Sept. 1894; and storms, 1899.

WISSEMBOURG, or WEISSENBURG, N.E. France, in the department of the Lower Rhine, situate on the right bank of the river Lauter, the boundary of France and the Palatinate. It was formerly an imperial city of Alsace, and was seized by Louis XIV. in 1673, and annexed to France by the treaty of Ryswick, 1697. The "lines" of Wissembourg, erected by Villars 1705, were taken by the Austrians and retaken by the French, 1793, after Hoche's victory at Geisberg. On 4 Aug. 1870, the crown-prince of Prussia crossed the Lauter and gained a brilliant but bloody victory over the French (a part of MacMahon's division), storming the lines and the Geisberg. General Abel Douay was mortally wounded, and about 800 prisoners were made. The killed and wounded on both sides appear to have been nearly equal. The German army, composed of Prussians, Bavarians, and Würtembergers, were, it is said, about 40,000, against about 10,000 French, who fought with desperate bravery.

WITCHCRAFT. The Jewish law (*Exodus* xxii. 18), 1491 B.C., decreed, "Thou shalt not suffer a witch to live." Saul, after banishing or condemning witchcraft, consulted the witch of Endor, 1056 B.C. (1 *Sam.* xxviii.) Reginald Scots' "Discoverie of Witchcraft" (against its existence) published 1584. Reprinted, 1886. Bishop Hutchinson's historical "Essay on Witchcraft" was published in 1718. Pope Innocent VIII. issued a bull against witchcraft in 1484. Thousands of innocent persons were burnt, and others killed by the tests applied.

Many Templars burnt at Paris for witchcraft, &c., 1309.
Joan of Arc burnt at Rouen as a witch, 30 May, 1431.
About five hundred witches burnt in Geneva, in three months, 1515.
Many burnt in the diocese of Como in a year, about 1524.
A great number in France, about 1520, when one sorcerer confessed to having 1200 associates.
Nine hundred burnt in Lorraine, 1580-1595.
One hundred and fifty-seven burnt at Wurtzburg, old and young, learned and ignorant, between 1627 and 1629.
Grandier, the parish priest at Loudon, burnt on a charge of having bewitched a whole convent of nuns, 1634.
In Bretagne, twenty poor women put to death as witches, 1654.
Disturbances commenced on charges of witchcraft in America, at Massachusetts, 1648-9; and persecutions raged dreadfully in Pennsylvania in 1683.
At Salem, in New England, nineteen persons hanged (by the Puritans) for witchcraft, eight more condemned; fifty confessed themselves to be witches and were pardoned, 1692.
Maria Renata burnt at Wurtzburg in 1749.
At Kalisk, in Poland, nine old women charged with having bewitched and rendered unfruitful the lands belonging to that palatinate, were burnt 17 Jan. 1775.
Five women condemned to death by the Brahmins, at Patna, for sorcery, and executed, 15 Dec. 1802.

WITCHCRAFT IN ENGLAND.

A statute enacted declaring all witchcraft and sorcery to be felony without benefit of clergy. 33 Hen. VIII. 1541. Again, 5 Eliz. 1562, and 1 James I. 1603.
The 73rd canon of the church prohibits the clergy from casting out devils, 1603.
Barrington estimates the judicial murders for witchcraft in England in 200 years at 30,000.
Matthew Hopkins, the "*witch-finder*," causes the judicial murder of about 100 persons in Essex, Norfolk, and Suffolk, 1645-7.
Sir Matthew Hale burnt two persons for witchcraft in 1664.
Seventeen or eighteen persons burnt at St. Osyths, in Essex, about 1676.
Two pretended witches were executed at Northampton in 1705, and five others seven years afterwards.
In 1716, Mrs. Hicks, and her daughter, aged nine, were hanged at Huntingdon.
Northamptonshire and Huntingdon preserved the superstition about witchcraft later than other counties.

In Scotland, thousands of persons were burnt in the period of about a hundred years. Among the victims were persons of the highest rank, while all orders in the state concurred. James I. even caused a whole assize to be prosecuted for an acquittal. The king published his *Dæmonologie* in Edinburgh, 1597. The last sufferer in Scotland was at Dornoch in 1722.

The laws against witchcraft had lain dormant for many years, when an ignorant person attempting to revive them (by finding a bill against a poor old woman in Surrey for the practice of witchcraft), they were *repealed*, 10 Geo. II. 1736.

Credulity in witchcraft still abounds in the country districts of England. On 4 Sept. 1863, a poor old paralysed Frenchman died in consequence of having been ducked as a wizard at Castle Hedingham, Essex, and similar cases have since occurred.

Ann Turner, old; killed as a witch by a half-insane man at Long Compton, Warwickshire, 17 Sept. 1875.

Bridget Cleary, aged 27, burnt to death as a witch at Baltyvadhen, co. Tipperary, 15 March, 1895.

The husband sentenced to 20 years', and 5 others to different terms of imprisonment, 5 July, 1895.

WITENA-MOT or **WITENA-GEMOT**, the assembling of the wise men, the great council of the Anglo-Saxons. A witena-mot was called in Winchester by Egbert, 800, and in London, 833, to consult on the proper means to repel the Danes; see *Parliament*.

WITEPSK (in Russia), where a battle was fought between the French under marshal Victor, duke of Belluno, and the Russians commanded by general Wittgenstein. The French were defeated after a desperate engagement, with the loss of about 3000 men on both sides, 14 Nov. 1812.

WITNESSES. Two or more witnesses were required by the law of Moses, 1451 B.C. (*Deut.* xvii. 6), and by the early Christian Church in cases of discipline (2 *Cor.* xiii. 1), A.D. 60. The evidence of two witnesses required to attaint for high treason, 25 Edw. III. 1352. In civil actions between party and party, if a man be subpœnaed as a witness on a trial, he must appear in court on pain of 100*l.* to be forfeited to the king, and 10*l.*, together with the damages equivalent to the loss sustained by the want of his evidence to the party aggrieved. Lord Ellenborough ruled that no witness is obliged to answer questions which may tend to degrade himself, 10 Dec. 1802. New act relating to the examination of witnesses passed 13 Geo. III. 1773. Act to enable courts of law to order the examination of witnesses upon interrogations and otherwise, 1 Will. IV. 30 March, 1831. The Witnesses Protection act (see under *Parliament*, April, 1892), passed 28 June, 1892.

WITTENBERG, the capital of Upper Saxony, Prussian since 1815, the cradle of the reformation, suffered much during the thirty years', seven years', and Napoleonic wars. Here are the houses, tombs, and statues of Luther and Melanchthon.

On the wooden door of the castle church (consecrated 1499) Martin Luther, an Augustinian monk, then a professor at the university, affixed his theses against the sale of indulgences, and thus inaugurated the protestant reformation 31 Oct. 1517

The church, restored by the emperor William I. and his successors, was solemnly re-opened by the emperor William II. in the presence of the protestant princes of Germany and representatives of those of Europe, including the duke of York and other dignitaries, during the Luther celebration . . . . 31 Oct. 1892

WITU, or *Vitu*. See *Zanzibar*, 1890.

WIVES, see *Marriage*. By the Divorce and Matrimonial Causes Act, passed in 1857, the condition of married women has been much benefited. When ill-used they can obtain a divorce or judicial separation; and while in the latter state any property they may acquire is secured to them personally, as if unmarried. By another act passed in 1857, they are enabled to dispose of reversionary interests in personal property or estates. An act to amend the law relating to the property of married women was passed 9 Aug. 1870. By it the separate earnings of a wife were secured to her own use, as well as personal and freehold property bequeathed to her. She may maintain an action at law, and acquires other rights. The husband is declared not liable for debts contracted by his wife prior to marriage, and she may be sued for them. This act was amended in 1874. Husband and wife may be jointly sued for her debts before marriage. By the Matrimonial Causes Act, 1878, a magistrate can grant judicial separation, with maintenance, to a wife suffering from her husband's ill-usage.

House of lords decide that the husband is not responsible for his wife's debts if he allow sufficient for dress, &c. *Debenham* v. *Mellon* . 27 Nov. 1880

Married Women's Property Act, 45 & 46 Vict. c. 75, passed 18 Aug. 1882, making their powers almost equal to those of single women, and increasing their responsibilities in regard to debt, &c., came into effect, 1 Jan. 1883; amended 5 Dec. 1893

Provision made for deserted wives made by Act passed in 1886

Clitheroe case.—Miss Emily Hall (born 1860) was married to Mr. E. Haughton Jackson at Blackburn, 5 Nov. 1887. They never lived together; she returned to her friends, and he soon after went to New Zealand. He returned to England, 17 July, 1888. After some correspondence and one interview (16 Jan. 1889) she steadily refused to live with him. Some litigation ensued, and a decree against her was obtained, 30 July, 1889. On 8 March, 1891, Mr. Jackson and others seized her when coming from church at Clitheroe, and carried her off to his house at Blackburn, where she was closely confined in charge of a nurse. By means of a writ of *habeas corpus*, she was brought before the court of appeal, who decided that a husband has no legal power to detain his wife against her will, 19 March. Mrs. Jackson then returned to her friends

Summary Jurisdiction (Married Women) Act passed 6 July, 1895

WIVES' POISON or **WATER TOFANA** see *Poisoning*.

WIZARD: WIZARD OF THE NORTH, a name given to sir Walter Scott, on account of his romances; also to Mr. Anderson, the conjurer, who died 3 Feb. 1874, see *Covent Garden* and *Witchcraft*.

Robert - Houdin's *Confidences d'un Prestidigitateur* published in 1859.

Herr Hermann, an eminent rich beneficent conjurer or prestidigitateur, died at Carlsbad aged 71, June, 1887. See *Automaton Figures*.

The feats of Maskelyne and Cooke in recent years are well known.

WOERTH SUR SAUER, a town in the department of the Lower Rhine, N.E. France. After storming Wissembourg (*which see*) on 4 Aug. 1870, the crown-prince of Prussia, with the 3rd army (about 150,000) marched rapidly forward and surprised part of the French army under Marshal MacMahon, including the corps of Canrobert and part of that of Failly (about 47,000), and defeated it in a long, desperate, and sanguinary engagement near this place 6 Aug. The battle lasted from 9 a.m. till 4 p.m. The chief struggles occurred in the country round Reichshoffen and in the village of Froeschweiller; the French are said to have charged the German line eleven times, each time breaking it, but always finding a fresh mass behind. The ridge on which Woerth stands was not captured until the French were taken in flank by the Bavarians and Würtembergers. Nearly all MacMahon's staff were killed, and the marshal himself, unhorsed, fell fainting into a ditch, from which he was rescued by a soldier. He then, on foot, directed the retreat towards Saverne, to cover the passes of the Vosges. The victory is attributed to the very great numerical superiority of the Germans as well as to their excellent strategy. The French loss has been estimated at 5000 killed and wounded, and 5000 prisoners, 2 eagles, 6 mitrailleuses, 35 cannon, and much baggage. The Germans are stated to have had above 8000 men put *hors de combat*. It was admitted that MacMahon had acted as an able and brave commander.

WOLVERHAMPTON (Staffordshire), an old town formerly named Hamton; owes its present name to the foundation of a college here by Wulfrana, sister of king Edgar, and widow of Aldhelm, duke of Northampton, 996. The queen was present at the inauguration of the prince consort's statue here, 30 Nov. 1866, and the church congress was opened here 1 Oct. 1867. Wolverhampton is eminent for its manufactures in metal. Statue of hon. C. P. Villiers (its M.P., 1835-98) was uncovered, 6 June, 1879; he voted personally, when aged 90, for confidence in the Salisbury ministry, 11 Aug. 1892; died 16 Jan. 1898. Population, 1881, 75,766; 1891, 82,680; 1901, 94,179.

Wolverhampton returns three M.P.'s by act passed 25 June, 1885.

Mr. Edwin Butler bequeaths 10,000*l*. for a public reading-room, music for the parks, &c., Sept. 1893.

Celebration of the 900th anniversary of lady Wulfrana (sister of Ethelred II.), charter to the town, &c., 24 June *et seq*. 1894.

Wrottesley hall, with valuable library, burnt down, 16 Dec. 1897.

The duke and duchess of York open a new infirmary, and lay the stone for the new free library, 23 July, 1900 (opened, Mr. A. Carnegie presents 1,000*l*., 11 Feb. 1902).

Fine art and industrial exhibition opened by the duke and duchess of Connaught, 1 May, 1902; deficit of 34,000*l*. reported, 5 Dec. 1902.

Sir Joseph Dimsdale, lord mayor of London, presented with the freedom, 29 July, 1902.

Boiler explosion at Messrs. Tupper's ironworks, Bilston; 4 deaths, 12 injured, 20 Jan. 1903.

WOLVES were once very numerous in England. Their heads were demanded as a tribute, particularly 300 yearly from Wales, by king Edgar, 961, by which step they were falsely said to be totally destroyed. *Carte*. Edward I. issued his mandate for the destruction of wolves in several counties of England, 1289. Ireland was infested by wolves for many centuries after their extirpation in England; for there are accounts of some being found there so late as 1710, when the last presentment for killing wolves was made in the county of Cork. Wolves still infest France, in which kingdom 8384 wolves and cubs were killed in 1828-9. They were troublesome in the Vosges, Oct. 1875; premiums introduced by the state for their destruction, 1,316 killed in 1883; 171 in 1896; 197 in 1898; 207 in 1899; 115 in 1900.

WOMEN. The employment of women is regulated by the ***Factory and Workshop Regulation Acts*** (*which see*).

(See *Degrees*, *Female Medical School*, *Jubilee*, *Marriage*, *Wives*, and *Clubs*.)

Mary Wollstonecraft's Vindication of the Rights of Women, published 1791

Women disfranchised by the insertion of the word (male) before *person* in the Reform bill of . . 1832

Great advances in the legal rights, position, and employment of women 1837-89

Women's hospitals founded: Soho 1842

J. S. Mill's Subjection of Women, published . 1869

Female medical society and obstetrical college founded . . . . about 1864

Female suffrage for members of parliament was proposed by J. S. Mill, and negatived by 196 against 73 . . . . 20 May, 1867

Lily Maxwell, a shopkeeper at Manchester, voted for Jacob Bright . . . . . . 26 Nov. ,,

First annual meeting of the Manchester national society for women's suffrage . . . 30 Oct. 1868

Female suffrage decided to be illegal, by the court of common pleas . . . . 7, 9 Nov. ,,

Women's Club and Institute, Newman-street, London, W. opened . . . . . Jan. 1869

Women's Disabilities removal bill rejected by the commons (220 to 94) 12 May, 1870; (222-143) 1 May, 1872; (223-155) 30 April, 1873; withdrawn, 1874; (187-152) 7 April, 1875; (239-152) 26 April, 1876; hustled out, 6 June, 1877; (219-140) 19 June, 1878; (217-103) 7 March, 1879; (130-114) 6 July, 1883

Miss Garrett and Miss Davies elected members of the metropolitan school-board . . 29 Nov 1873

Medical school for women opened (see *Physic*, 1876) Oct. 1874

Working women's college (see under *Working-men*), 12 Oct. ,,

Women's Protective and Provident League founded by Mrs. Paterson and others, Great Queen Street, (out of this has arisen several independent trade unions, book-binders, upholsterers, &c.) . . ,,

Women's Whisky War, see *United States*, 1874.

Miss Merington elected guardian of the poor for Kensington (the first case in London) . April, 1876

Women's Education Union, president, the princess Louise, founded at the Society of Arts, in 1871, to promote the better education of women; said to be languishing in . . . . . Oct. 1877

University of London: senate vote for granting degrees to women, 28 Feb.: convocation vote against it, 8 May and July, 1877; vote for a supplemental charter granting it (242-132), 15 Jan.; charter granted . . . . . 28 March, 1878

Great meeting for female suffrage; St. James's Hall, 6 May, 1880

Elective suffrage granted to women in the Isle of Man . . . . ,,

Women excluded from government employment in the United States, by order . about 27 Dec. 1881

Women to be admitted to examinations for honours at Oxford; by statute . . . . 29 April, 1884

Female householders' suffrage (widows and spinsters), proposed by Mr. Woodall in the commons, 10 June; negatived (271-135) 12-13 June; in consequence Miss H. Müller refuses to pay queen's taxes, and her goods are distrained . . 2 July, ,,

Women's suffrage bill; lords read 1st time, 3 July; negatived 10 July, 1884; again 28 July, 1885; read second time commons 18-19 Feb.; blocked March; negatived by the lords 16 March, 1886; again 13 Sept. 1887; 13 April, 1888; and 18 March, 1889; again . . . . . . 1891 and 1892

Female suffrage granted in Madras presidency announced 28 Sept. 1885

Enactments for the protection of women and girls formed part of the Criminal Law Amendment Act passed . . . . 14 Aug. ,,

Women's National Suffrage Society annual meetings, July, 1886, *et seq.*

Many women's liberal associations (Unionist and Gladstonian) formed 1886-98

Miss A. F Ramsay and Miss B. M. Hervey obtain high university honours (see *Cambridge*), 18 June, 1887; and Miss G. P. Fawcett . . 7 June, 1890

International "council of women," advocating women's rights, met at Washington, U.S. 25 March, 1888; a similar one at Paris 25 June, 1889

Suffrage granted to female ratepayers, under the local government act, passed . . 13 Aug. 1888

Women's hospital with female practitioners begun in Marylebone 1871; the new building in Euston Road founded by the princess of Wales 7 May, 1888
Mrs. Scharlieb made M.D. . . . . 16 May, ,,
Two ladies elected for the London County Council; this declared illegal, a bill to legalise it rejected by the lords, 20 May, 1889, and 9 June, 1890; by the commons . . . . . 26 May, 1891
Women's trade union association, proposed by the bishop of Bedford and others at a meeting held in the Assembly-hall in the Mile-End-road 8 Oct. 1889
Another meeting at Piccadilly . . . 10 Feb. 1890
Women in New Zealand authorized to serve in parliament and vote at elections; bill passed, 4 Sept.; rejected by the legislative council, 10 Sept. 1891
Slander of Women Act passed . . . 5 Aug. ,,
Discrimination of sex in elections abolished by act passed in New York . . . . . 15 April, 1892
Bill for the extension of the parliamentary franchise to women, rejected by the commons (175—152), 27 April, 1892; by the lords, 11 Sept. 1893; withdrawn, commons, May, 1895; read 3rd time, lords, 1896; read 2nd time, commons, 3 Feb. 1897; bill withdrawn, commons, 14 July, 1898.
Conferences at Bristol and other places, respecting women's suffrage, &c. . . . . . Nov. ,,
Association of women pioneer lecturers; public meeting in London . . . . . 8 March, 1893
Miss Maria M. Ogilvie made D.Sc. of London university . . . . June, ,,
Act passed in New Zealand conferring elective franchise on women . . . . . 29 Sept. ,,
Women sanitary inspectors, under the factory and workshop act, Jan. 1892; reported very efficient in Kensington . . . . . . Jan. 1894
The national women's council organized by lady Aberdeen at Ottawa reported successful, 13 April, 1894; meetings in London, 12 Dec. 1895, and 19 July, 1897.
A great meeting held in the Queen's hall, Langham-place, W., in favour of the parliamentary franchise to women . . . . 9 June, ,,
Women's suffrage appeal started, June, 1893; received 249,000 signatures . . . . July, ,,
Women's christian education league, active . 1893–4
By the act passed 1894, women declared eligible for parish councils, &c.
Death of the dowager lady Stanley of Alderley, aged 87, an active promoter of female education; 7 years president of the women's liberal unionist association . . . . 16 Feb. 1895
Election manifesto issued by the women's franchise league . . . . 2 July, ,,
The proposal to admit women to the B.A. degree rejected at Oxford (215–140), 3, 10 March, 1896; rejected at Cambridge, 12 March, 1896; degrees by diploma recommended to the Cambridge senate, by the syndicate, 2 March, 1897; much controversy; rejected, 21 May, 1897.
Poor law Guardians (Ireland) Women act passed, 31 March, 1896
Women's international congress at Berlin, 21 Sept. ,,
The National union (since termed council) of women workers, conference at Manchester, 27 Oct., 1896. Annual meetings.
Women's suffrage bill passed in Victoria 29 Oct. ,,
Women admitted to the bar by benchers of the Ontario law society, under act of Provincial legislature . . . . 18 Nov. ,,
Mathilde Blind, poet, novelist, and critic, born 21 March, 1847, died . . . . . 26 Nov. ,,
"Woman under the English law, from the Saxons to the present time," by Arthur R. Cleveland, published 1897
Miss Frances E. Willard, great worker in the temperance movement; born 28 Sept. 1839, died, 18 Feb. 1898
Miss Gulvin and Miss Hutchings, from the Horticultural college, Swanley, Kent, employed as gardeners at Kew; 28 professional appointments held by women . . . . Feb. ,,
Women's local government society, annual meetings in London, lady Frederick Cavendish presiding, 18 March, 1898 (lady Aberdeen presided 21 March, 1901).
Women's liberal federation annual meeting at St. James's hall . . . . 22 June, ,,
Women's international congress (about 28 countries represented) opened at Westminster; lady Aberdeen, president; public meetings at the Queen's hall, many questions discussed; 1,250,000 members . . . . . 26 June–4 July, 1899
Mrs. Ellen Johnson, governor of the Massachusetts Women's reformatory prison, died suddenly at the congress, aged 69 . . . . 28 June, ,,
About 150 delegates received by the queen at Windsor . . . . 7 July, ,,
Women's international Christian temperance league, founded in America, 1874; 40 countries represented in . . . . ,,
Miss F. M. Skene, born 23 May, 1821, philanthropist and writer, died . . . . . 5 Oct. ,,
Miss Anna Swanwick, writer and transcriber of Æschylus and Goethe, leader in social and educational reforms, died, aged 86 . . . 2 Nov. ,,
Women's institute, founded by Mr. Wynford Philipps (1898), over 45 societies associated and 300 members; weekly conferences, &c.; great progress, reported . . . . . 15 March, 1900
An exhibition, "women of all nations," at Earl's court, opened by the lady mayoress, 5 May, 1900; closed . . . . 13 Oct. ,,
Miss Mary Kingsley, traveller, writer and lecturer, "West African Studies," &c., died, aged 37, of fever, while nursing Boer prisoners, at Simonstown, S. Africa . . . . . . 3 June, ,,
Women admitted as members to the committees of the British association, by resolution passed, 12 Sept. ,,
Law, in France, enabling women to practise as barristers, published 4 Dec.; Mme. Petit sworn in at Paris . . . . 5 Dec. ,,
Mansion house meeting in support of lady Warwick's agricultural scheme for women; see *Reading* . . . . 12 July, 1901
Mrs. Elizabeth Hanbury, philanthropist, active in the anti-slavery movement, died, aged 108, 31 Oct. ,,
Full suffrage for the federal parliament granted to the women of Australia . . . . . May, 1902
The maharajah Sindhia of Gwalior speaks warmly in favour of female education in India, London, 17 June, ,,
Women's suffrage granted by parliament of New South Wales . . . . Aug. ,,
Miss Cornelia Sorabji, B.C.L., Oxford, appeals for female legal assistance for purdah women in India; *Times* . . . . . . 26 Sept. ,,
Great progress of women in the medical and other professions . . . . . . 1870 *et seq.* ,,
Mrs. Elizabeth Stanton, of New York, who, with others, inaugurated the first woman's rights convention and the woman suffrage movement (1848), died, aged 86 . . . . . . 26 Oct. ,,
Death of Miss Helen Blackburn, sec. and subsequently hon. sec. to the central committee for women's suffrage in London, also edited the *Englishwoman's Review* . . . early Jan. 1903
Death of Louisa lady Ashburton, philanthropist, aged 76, 2 Feb.; and of "Edna Lyall," Miss Ada Bayly, novelist and able exponent of women's social and political rights . . . . . 7 Feb. ,,
The king and queen receive from the committee of the Queen's Nurses' Endowment Fund, 71,914*l*., collected as a women's memorial to the late queen Victoria . . . . . . mid May, ,,
Senate of Dublin University decides by large majority to open its degrees to women . mid June, ,,
Hon. degree of Mus.D. conferred on the princess of Wales by University of London . . 24 June, ,,
Mdlle. Marguerite Dilhan called to the bar at Toulouse 13 July, 1903, briefed as counsel for the defence of prisoner in a murder case of that town; first instance on record in France of a feminine barrister pleading in a criminal court, 26 Nov. ,,
Special tribunal of judges, house of lords, the lord chancellor presiding, considered the case of Miss Bertha Cave, who had been refused admission to Gray's Inn; the tribunal decided against the applicant on the ground that there was no precedent for women being called to the English bar, and that the tribunal was unwilling to create such precedent . . . . 2 Dec. ,,

WONDERS OF THE WORLD. 1. The pyramids of Egypt. 2. The mausoleum or tomb built for Mausolus, king of Caria, by Artemisia, his queen. 3. The temple of Diana, at Ephesus. 4. The walls and hanging gardens of the city of Babylon. 5. The vast brazen image of the sun at Rhodes, called the Colossus. 6. The ivory and gold statue of Jupiter Olympus. 7. The pharos or watch-tower, built by Ptolemy Philadelphus, king of Egypt; see *separate articles*.

WOOD (see *Silk*, 1895, and *Paper*) rendered non-inflammable by a chemical process, adopted in the United States, successfully tried on a building at Millbank, London, the surface being only charred, the prince of Wales and others present, 11 May, 1897.

WOOD-CUTS, see *Engraving on Wood.*

WOODHALL SPA, Lincolnshire, celebrated for mineral waters, especially containing iodine. On 22 May, 1888, Mr. E. Stanhope, M.P., sir Richard Webster, M.P. (lord Alverstone 1900), and others, inspected the pump-room, baths, hotel, and other buildings erected to promote the use of the waters by all classes of invalids. A hospital was opened 29 May, 1890.

WOODITE, a combination of india-rubber, cork, and other substances for the coating of life-boats and other vessels to defend them against collision and attacks of guns, &c. invented by Mrs. A. M. Wood, recommended by sir E. J. Reed, July, 1886.

WOODS. FORESTS, &c., see *Forests*. The board of woods, forests, and land revenues was constituted in 1810. The oversight of works and public buildings was added to its duties in 1832, but transferred to a separate board of commissioners in 1851. See *Works*. In 1874 the annual revenue of the crown woods and forests was 487,695*l.*; 1882-3, 308,000*l.*; 1886, 492,624*l.*; 1901, 666,109*l.*; 1902, 618,356*l.* Report of a commission issued, Nov. 1897.

WOOD'S HALF-PENCE, for circulation in Ireland and America, were coined by virtue of a patent, passed 1722. Against them, Dr. Jonathan Swift, by his letters signed M. B. Drapier published about 1723, raised such a spirit of opposition that the patent was withdrawn. Wood received a compensation, but was virtually banished the kingdom. The half-pence were assayed in England by sir Isaac Newton, and proved to be genuine, in 1724.

WOOD PAVEMENT was laid down at Whitehall in 1839; and in Oxford-street, the Strand, and other streets. The principal part was soon taken up. In Nov. 1872, the improved wood pavement company put forth a prospectus; and in May, 1876, wood was laid down in many places. It is said to be the best pavement in London, and its use has diminished the noise of the traffic.

Oxford-street was paved by Henson's street paving company, with a compound of wood, asphalt, felt, and Portland cement in 1876; with wood, 1878. Bond-street and many other streets paved with wood, 1879–81. Wood is now (1903) generally adopted as the paving for the principal thoroughfares of the metropolis.

WOODSTOCK (Oxfordshire). In Woodstock, now Blenheim-park, originally stood a royal palace, in which king Ethelred held a parliament, and Alfred the Great translated *Boethius de Consolatione Philosophiæ*, 888. Henry I. beautified the palace; and here resided Rosamond, mistress of Henry II. 1154. In it were born Edmund, second son of Edward I., 1301, and Edward, eldest son of Edward III., 1330; and here the princess Elizabeth was confined by her sister Mary, 1554. A splendid mansion, built at the expense of the nation, for the duke of Marlborough, was erected here to commemorate his victory at Blenheim in 1704. At that time every trace of the ancient edifice was removed, and two elms were planted on its site; see *Blenheim*. Scott's romance, "Woodstock," was published, June, 1826. Marshall's "History of Woodstock," 1873.

WOOL. From the earliest times to the reign of queen Elizabeth the wool of Great Britain was not only superior to that of Spain, but accounted the finest in the universe; and even in the times of the Romans a manufacture of woollen cloths was established at Winchester for the use of the emperors. *Anderson*. In later times wool was manufactured in England, and is mentioned 1185, but not in any quantity until 1331, when the weaving of it was introduced by John Kempe and other artizans from Flanders. This was the real origin of our now unrivalled manufacture, 6 Edw. III. 1331. *Rymer's Fœdera.*

Duties on exported wool were levied by Edw. I. . 1275
The exportation prohibited 1337
Staples of wool established in Ireland, at Dublin, Waterford, Cork, and Drogheda, 18 Edw. III. . . 1343
Sheep were first permitted to be sent to Spain, which has since injured our manufacture. *Stow*. 1467
First legislative prohibition of the export of wool from Ireland 1521
The exportation of English wool, and the importation of Irish wool into England, prohibited . 1696
The export forbidden by act passed 1718
Bill to prevent the running of wool from Ireland to France 1738
The duty on wool imported from Ireland taken off 1739
Woolcombers' act, 35 Geo. III. 1794
The non-exportation law was repealed, 5 Geo. IV. . 1824

In 1851 we imported 83,311,975 lb. of wool and alpaca, &c.; in 1856, 116,211,392 lb.; in 1859, 133,284,634 lb.; in 1861, 147,172,841 lb.; in 1864, 206,473,645 lb.; in 1866, 239,358,689 lb.; in 1871, 323,036,299 lb.; in 1875, 365,065,578 lb.; in 1879, 417,110,099 lb.; in 1881, 450,141,735 lb.; in 1883, 495,946,779 lb.; in 1888, 639,267,975 lb.; in 1889, 700,903,057 lb.; in 1890, 633,028,131 lb.; in 1893, 677,947,464 lb.; in 1898, 689,446,139 lb.; in 1901, 692,374,231 lb.

We imported from Australasia, in 1842, 12,979,856 lb.; in 1856, 56,052,139 lb.; in 1861, 68,506,222 lb.; in 1866, 113,773,694 lb.; in 1871, 182,710,567 lb.; in 1875, 238,631,824 lb.; in 1877, 281,247,190 lb.; in 1879, 287,831,804 lb.; in 1881, 329,665,855 lb.; in 1883, 351,685,606 lb.; in 1887, 383,506,395 lb.; in 1889, 431,303,391 lb.; in 1890, 418,771,604 lb.; in 1893, 472,367,225 lb.; in 1900, 386,367,117 lb.; in 1901, 334,355,000 lb.

WOOL-COMBERS in several parts of England have a procession on 3 Feb., in commemoration of bishop Blaise, who is reported to have discovered their art. He is said to have visited England, and to have landed at St. Blazy, in Cornwall. He was bishop of Sebaste, in Armenia, and is said to have suffered martyrdom in the Diocletian persecution, 289. Sir Isaac Holden, a great inventor of machinery and proprietor, died, aged 90, 13 Aug 1897.

WOOLLEN CLOTH. Woollen cloths were made an article of commerce in the time of Julius Cæsar, and are familiarly alluded to by him see *Weaving*.

The Jews were forbidden to wear garments of woollen and linen together . . . . . B.C. 1451

70 families of cloth-workers (from the Netherlands) settled in England by Edward III. *Rymer.* A.D. 1331
Worsted manufacture in Norfolk 1340
A kind of blankets were first made in England. (*Camden*) . . . . about 1340
Woollens made at Kendal 1390
No cloth but of Wales or Ireland to be imported into England 1463
Medleys, or mixed broad-cloth, first made . . . 1614
Manufacture of fine cloth began at Sedan, in France, under the patronage of Cardinal Mazarin . . 1646
Broadcloth first dressed and dyed in England, by Brewer, from the Low Countries 1667
British and Irish woollens prohibited in France . 1677
All persons obliged to be buried in woollens, and the persons directing the burial otherwise to forfeit 5*l*., 29 Charles II. 1678
The manufacture of cloth greatly improved in England by Flemish settlers 1688
Injudiciously restrained in Ireland, 11 Will. III. . 1698
The exportation from Ireland wholly prohibited, except to certain ports of England . . . 1701
English manufacture encouraged by 10 Anne, 1712, and 2 Geo. I. 1715
Greater in Yorkshire in 1785 than in all England at the revolution. *Chalmers.*
Value of woollen manufactures of all kinds exported in 1847, 6,896,038*l*.; in 1854, 9,120,759*l*.; in 1861, 11,118,692*l*.; in 1864, 18,569,089*l*.; in 1871, 27,182,385*l*.; in 1875, 21,659,325*l*.; in 1877, 17,343,203*l*.; in 1879, 15,861,166*l*.; in 1881, 18,128,756*l*.; in 1883, 18,315,575*l*.; in 1887, 20,594,962*l*.; in 1889, 21,324,892*l*.; in 1890, 20,418,482*l*.; in 1891, 18,446,640*l*.; in 1892, 17,906,608*l*.; in 1893, 16,404,035*l*.; in 1900, 15,682,154*l*.; in 1901, 17,725,014*l*.
International Woollen Exhibition at the Crystal Palace, Sydenham, opened by the duke of Connaught . . . . 2 June, 1881
Association for the encouragement of British woollen manufactures founded by the countess of Bective and about 200 other ladies . . . „
Dr. Jager's "Sanitary Woollen System of Clothing" was published in 1887

WOOLSACK, the seat of the lord high chancellor of England in the house of lords, so called from its being a large square bag of wool, without back or arms, covered with red cloth. Wool was the staple commodity of England in the reign of Edward III., when the woolsack first came into use.

WOOLWICH (Kent), the most ancient military and naval arsenal in England. Its royal dockyard, where men-of-war were built in the reign of Henry VIII., was closed, 1 Oct. 1869. Here *Harry Grâce de Dieu* was built, 1512; and here she was burnt in 1552. The royal arsenal was formed about 1720, on the site of a rabbit-warren; it contains vast magazines of great guns, mortars, bombs, powder, and other warlike stores; a foundry, with many furnaces, for casting ordnance; and a great laboratory, where fireworks, cartridges, grenades, &c., are made for the public service. The Royal Military Academy was erected in the royal arsenal, but the institution was not completely formed until 19 Geo. II. 1745. Woolwich returns one M.P., by act of 1885. Constituted a municipal borough by London Government act, 1899 (6 aldermen, 36 councillors). Population, 1881, 80,845; 1891, 107,324; 1901, 131,000.

The arsenal, storehouses, &c., burnt (loss of 200,000*l*.) 20 May, 1802
Another great fire . . . . . 30 June, 1805
Fatal explosion of gunpowder . . . 20 Jan. 1813
The hemp-store burnt down . . . . 8 July, 1813
Another explosion by gunpowder . . 16 June, 1814
The Royal Military Academy nearly destroyed by fire; loss about 100,000*l*. . . . 1 Feb. 1873
Visited by the shah of Persia . . . 21 June, „
Subway beneath the Thames between North and South Woolwich, begun . . . . 23 Aug. 1876
Explosion in the rocket factory; the town bombarded, with little damage; the armoury burnt, only two men killed in the factory, 10 a.m. 24 Sept. 1883
Construction of great free steam ferry authorized by the commons . . . . . 1 May, 1885
Free steam-ferry (between North and South Woolwich) inaugurated in great state by lord Rosebery 23 March, 1889

(*Woolwich Infant*, see *Cannon*, 1872.)

Extensive fire in the arsenal, saw mills, cork shop, &c. 6 Dec.; and at Messrs. Arnold and Co., timber merchants . . . . . 20 Dec. 1896
Explosion in a rocket factory averted . 12 May, 1898
Queen Victoria visits wounded soldiers at the Herbert hospital . . . . 22 March, 1900
Grand theatre, erected by Mr. Clarence Sounes, opened by sir Henry Irving . . . 18 Oct. „
Lord Avebury opens a free library . . 8 Nov. 1901
Visit of the king and queen; a new nursing department at the Herbert hospital opened . 16 Feb. 1903
Explosion in the arsenal, 14 killed, 17 injured, 18 June, „
Royal Artillery theatre burnt down. . 18 Nov. „

WORCESTER, successively an important British, Roman, and Saxon town, was burnt by the Danes (1041) for resisting the tribute called Danegelt. William I. built a castle, 1090. The city was frequently taken and retaken during the civil wars of the middle ages, and by Cromwell in 1651.—The BISHOPRIC was founded by Ethelred, king of the Mercians, 680, and taken from the see of Lichfield, of which it composed a part. The married priests of the cathedral were displaced, and monks settled in their stead, 964. The church was rebuilt by St. Wulstan, 25th bishop, 1030; the remains of his hospital are described by the rev. T. H. Marsh, in its "Annals," published in 1890. The see has yielded to the church of Rome four saints, and to the English nation five lord chancellors and three lord treasurers. It is valued in the king's books at 1049*l*. 16*s*. 3¼*d*. per annum. Present income, 5000*l*. Population, 1881, 38,270; 1891, 42,905; 1901, 47,000.

The renovated cathedral opened . . 8 April, 1874
Much excitement through the refusal of the dean and chapter to permit the cathedral to be used as a concert room for the three choirs festival Oct.-Nov. „
The festival held as strictly religious services 22, 23 Sept. 1875
The foundation stone of the jubilee Victoria institute laid by the duke of York, 3 April, 1894; opened by the mayoress, lady Mary Lygon, 1 Oct. 1896
Severn End-house, the ancient seat of the Lechmere family, near Worcester, destroyed by fire, 24 Oct. „
Theatre (enlarged) reopened by lord Coventry, 19 Jan. 1903

RECENT BISHOPS.

1781. Richard Hurd, died 28 May, 1808.
1808. Folliott H. Cornwall, died 5 Sept. 1831.
1831. Robert James Carr, died 24 April, 1841.
1841. Henry Pepys, died 13 Nov. 1860.
1861. Henry Philpott, resigned Aug. 1890, died 10 Jan., 1892.
1890. John James Stewart Perowne, Oct.; resigned Nov. 1901.
901. Charles Gore, appointed 11 Jan.; consecrated 23 Feb. 1902.

WORCESTER, BATTLE OF, 3 Sept. 1651, when the Scots army which came to England to reinstate Charles II. was defeated by Cromwell, who called it his *crowning mercy*. Charles with difficulty escaped to France. More than 2000 of the royalists were slain, and of 8000 prisoners most were sold as slaves to the American colonists; see *Boscobel.*

WORDSWORTH SOCIETY, formed "as a bond of union among those who are in sympathy with the general teaching and spirit of Wordsworth" and "to promote and extend the study of the poet's works," &c., was inaugurated at Grasmere, Westmoreland, 30 Sept. 1880. First President, Dr. Charles Wordsworth, bishop of St. Andrews. The society dissolved 7 July, 1886.

WORKHOUSES, see under *Poor.*

WORKING MEN. Since the great Exhibition of 1851, much has been done to benefit the labouring classes by organisation. See *Artisan.*

Working Men's Clubs considered to have begun with the Working Men's Mutual Improvement and Recreation Society, established in Lancaster by the instrumentality of the rev. H. Solly in . . 1860

The Westminster Working Men's Club, in Duck-lane, originated with Miss Adeline Cooper; opened in Dec. ,,

The Working Men's Club and Institute Union for the promotion of clubs, institutes and similar societies for the instruction and recreation of the working classes, was mainly established by the strenuous exertions of the rev. Henry Solly (died 27 Feb. 1903, aided by lord Lyttelton, sir Harcourt Johnstone, sir Hugh Owen, lord Frederick Cavendish, and others; the Union was constituted at a meeting, lord Brougham in the chair, 14 June, 1862. It has been eminently successful. The new Central hall in Clerkenwell-road opened by lord Brassey, 15 Sept. 1893.

The Working Men's Club and Lodging-house, Old Pye-street, Westminster, was opened 20 April, 1866

Working Men's Colleges, &c. The first, established in Sheffield, by Mr. Bayley in 1842, and reconstituted by some of the students in 1848. The second, in Great Ormond-street, London, by the rev. professor Frederick D. Maurice, as principal, in Oct. 1854 (died 1 April, 1872), succeeded by Thos. Hughes, "Tom Brown" 1873–83, and sir John Lubbock, 1883 (lord Avebury 1900), resigns; succeeded by prof. A. V. Dicey, 16 Feb. 1899; average number of students risen from 130 to over 1,000 per annum, reported, July, 1899. A third in Cambridge, 1855, Wolverhampton, 1857, Manchester, 1858, and elsewhere, but have not all survived; all wholly for the working classes, and undertaking to impart such knowledge as each man feels he is most in want of. The colleges engage to find a teacher wherever 10 or 12 members agree to form a class, and also to have lectures given. There were eleven classes at the one in Bloomsbury, London, in 1856; Mr. Ruskin gave lessons in drawing. Some of these colleges have been found to be self-supporting.

A Working Women's College, begun at Queen's-square, Bloomsbury, 1864; afterwards changed to the "New College for men and women," inaugural meeting . . . . 12 Oct. 1874

Working Women's College, Fitzroy-street, inaugurated . . . . 16 Oct. ,,

Act to establish councils of conciliation, to adjust differences between masters and workmen, passed 20 Aug. 1867

The Arbitration (Masters and Workmen) Act passed 6 Aug. 1872

Working Men's Institute, for South London, opened with a lecture by professor Huxley 4 Jan. 1868

The Samuel Morley Memorial College for working men and women at Victoria hall in connection with the Borough-road Polytechnic, was opened in 1889. See *Polytechnic.*

Workmen's International Exhibition proposed by the duke of Argyll, lord Elcho, and others, March, 1868; meeting for arrangements, 10 Jan. 1870, held in the Agricultural Hall, Islington (16 classes and a fine arts department); opened by the prince of Wales, 16 July; closed by Mr. Gladstone . . . . 31 Oct. 1870

National trades societies congress meet at Manchester, 1868; at Birmingham . . . Aug. 1869

Demonstration of working men in Hyde park against certain clauses relating to masters and servants in the Criminal Law Amendment Act, 2 June, 1873

International Working Men's Association (termed the *International*) owes its origin to some German socialists in London, 1847, and was much promoted by the foreign visitors to the great exhibition in 1862. It was definitely organised, 28 Sept. 1864, George Odger first president. Its professed object is the complete emancipation of labour from the tyranny of capitalists. It has held congresses at Geneva, Sept. 1866; Lausanne, Sept. 1867; Brussels, 6–13 Sept. 1868; Basel, 6–11 Sept. 1869; Barcelona, June, 1870; at the Hague, when great dissensions arose between the "authoritarians," who consider a government needful, and the "anarchists," who deny it. One party including the council seceded from the trade portion, and adjourned to New York, 3–10 Sept. 1872

Four of its members were elected into the French national assembly . . . . . . Feb. 1871

The association took part in the communist insurrection at Paris . . . . . . Dec. ,,

It made a demonstration at New York 18 Mar. 1872
It is said to have about 2,500,000 members in all countries, and to be allied with several secret societies, such as Fenians, the Mary Anne, &c.

A proposal from Spain that European governments should combine for its suppression, 9 Feb., was declined by Great Britain, 8 March. It was proscribed in France by the national assembly, 14 March, ,,

The British section met at McQueen's club-house, Parliament-street . . . . . 21 July, ,,

One party took the name of International Association, and held annual congresses: Geneva, Sept. 1873; Brussels, 7 Sept. 1874; Berne, 1876; Verviers, 7 Sept. 1877. A congress of socialists met at Ghent (partly united the two divisions), Sept. 1878

International congress, Paris, assembled, 2–12 Sept ,,

Report of an alliance between conservative peers and the working men for the improvement of the condition of the latter, about 15 Oct.; explained by Mr. Scott Russell (*Times,* 14 Nov. 1871), who issued a programme . . . . . Jan. 1872

Workmen's Peace Association held its first annual meeting in London . . . . . 20 Sept. 1871

A "Workman's city," Shaftesbury Park, Clapham, was inaugurated by the earl of Shaftesbury, 3 Nov. 1873

Annual trade congress at Sheffield . 12–17 Jan. 1874

Alex. Macdonald and Thos. Burt, working-men, elected M.P.'s for Stafford and Morpeth . Feb. ,,

Royal commission on labour laws appointed (chief justice Cockburn, lord Winmarleigh, Messrs. Roebuck, T. Hughes, Alex. Macdonald and others) . . . . March, ,,

Dwellings of working classes protected from railway bills by new standing orders . 30 July, ,,

Employers and Workmen Act passed . 13 Aug. 1875

Annual trade congress at Glasgow . 11–16 Oct. ,,

Church of England Working Men's Society founded at St. Alban's, Holborn . . . . 5 Aug. 1876

Working-Lads' Institutes, London; meeting at the Mansion House to found them, 27 Oct.; first institute opened at Whitechapel . . 14 Nov. ,,

Workmen's Social Education League, founded June, 1879; professor J. R. Seeley, president, announced . . . . 10 June, 1879

Employers' Liability Act (to compensate workmen for injuries) passed . . . . . 7 Sept. 1880

International conference of workmen at Paris closes . . . . 29 Oct. 1883

International trades union congress at Paris; main objects, shorter hours, safety and comfort; British, most moderate 29 Oct. *et seq.* 1883; again 23 Aug. 1886; London (79 English and 44 foreign delegates) . . . . 6 Nov. 1888

Workmen, &c., of the United Kingdom, about 9,000,000; average wages each 19*l.* per annum (1835); about 13,000,000, average wages each nearly 42*l.* per annum (1885). *R. Giffen* . 19 Jan. 1886

Working Men's Jubilee Festival held at the Crystal Palace . . . . . . 25 June 1878

Accounts of a new *International* formed to replace the old one, which had gradually disappeared, were published in the autumn of 1888. It was stated to have branches in the United States, and in various cities in Europe.

The German parliament, influenced by prince Bismarck, passed bills to compel the working classes, with the assistance of their employers and the state, to provide for sickness (1883), for accidents (1884), for old age and infirmity 24 May, 1889

International congress of workers, respecting accidents, etc., at Paris . . . . . 14 July, „
[Second congress at Berne, 21 Sept. 1891.]

The grand council of the National Federation of all Trades and Industries, recommends that a demonstration be made to promote improvement in the condition of working men on 1 May, to be termed "Labour day," 15 April. A moderate demonstration was made at the Victoria-embankment and Hyde-park; a very large and orderly meeting was held at Hyde-park, Sunday (speakers, Messrs. M. Davitt, John Burns, Cunninghame Graham, Mrs. Aveling, and others), 4 May, 1890

The great May-day demonstration of the working classes throughout Europe in favour of an eight-hours' labour day and other improvements in their condition, passed off with general tranquillity, adequate precautions having been taken at Paris, Vienna, Berlin, and other towns, 1 May, „

International congress of miners at Jolimont, Belgium (see *Mineralogy*) . . . 20 May *et seq.* „

Formation of the "Factory, Operative, and General Labour union" projected by Messrs. John Burns and Tom Mann . . . . . . Aug. „

First congress of Dock, Wharf, and Riverside Labourers' union . . . 30 Sept.—4 Oct. „

"Labour day" generally peaceably observed throughout Europe, except in France and Rome (*which see*), 1 May; meetings in Hyde-park (*which see*) . . . . . 1-3 May, 1891

International Labour Congress at Brussels, 16-22 Aug. 1891; London, 27 July–1 Aug. 1896; Zurich, 23 Aug. 1897

"Labour day" on the continent peaceably kept through precautionary measures (see *Hyde-park*), Sunday, 1 May, 1892; partially kept, 1 May, 1893, 1894, 1895, 1899; in United States, 4 Sept. 1893

National workmen's exhibition, Islington, opened by the prince of Wales, 1 July; prizes distributed by the lord mayor, 26 July, awards declared by Mr. Gladstone . . . . . . 5 Aug. „

Eleventh labour conference in Paris . . 7 Oct. „

Labourers' congress at Leeds . . . May, 1894

Rev. Henry Solly, founder, 1862, of the Working Men's Club and Institute Union, which now has 900 affiliated clubs and 300,000 members, died, aged 89 . . . . March 1903

See *Co-operative Societies, Employers, and Trades-Unions. Berlin conference,* 1890.

WORKMEN'S COMPENSATION for Accidents bill, royal assent, 6 Aug. 1897; the act, faulty and inconsistent, leads to much litigation; extension (agriculture) bill act passed, 30 July, 1900. See *Employers.*

WORKS AND PUBLIC BUILDINGS. Board of commissioners appointed in 1851. Commissioners of Works act of 1852 amended, 1894. Public works and buildings estimates, 1894-95, 1,737,720*l.* See *Woods.*

WORKSHOPS, see *Ateliers* and *Factories.*

WORKSHOP REGULATION ACT, supplement to Factory Acts, passed 21 Aug. 1867; amended, 1871.

WORLD, see *Creation,* and *Globe.* WORLD weekly society newspaper began 8 July, 1874; Mr. Edmund Yates, the editor (joined by Mr. Henry Labouchere, M.P., in 1875), died suddenly, 20 May, 1894; see *Trials,* 1884-5. *The World's Columbian Exposition,* see *Chicago,* 1890 *et seq.*

WORLD'S WOMEN'S CHRISTIAN TEMPERANCE UNION, a movement founded by the late Miss Frances Willard, to unify and consolidate women's work in temperance and social reform in the various countries of the world. The union also seeks to suppress the trade in opium. Its badge is a knot of white ribbon. Convention held at Geneva, June, 1903.

WORMS, a city on the Rhine, in Hesse-Darmstadt. The Roman city, Borbetomagus, was plundered by the Alemanni, 354, and by Attila, 451; rebuilt by Clovis I. about 475. Here Charlemagne resided in 806. Here was held the imperial diet before which Martin Luther was summoned, 4 April, 1521, and by which he was proscribed. Luther was met by 2000 persons on foot and on horseback, at the distance of a league from Worms. When Spalatin sent to warn him of his danger, he answered, "If there were as many devils in Worms as there are tiles upon the roofs of its houses, I would go on." He appeared before the emperor, the archduke Ferdinand, six electors, twenty-four dukes, seven margraves, thirty bishops and prelates, and many princes, counts, lords, and ambassadors, 17 April, acknowledged his writings and opinions, and left Worms, in fact, a conqueror. Yet, to save his life, he had to remain in seclusion under the protection of the elector of Saxony for about a year. The *edict* putting him under the ban of the empire was issued 26 May, 1521. Worms was burnt, by order of Louis XIV., 1689, the cathedral excepted; and was taken by the French, under Custine, 4 Oct. 1792. A memorial statue of Luther at Worms was uncovered, 25 June, 1868, in the presence of the king of Prussia and other sovereigns. Population, 1890, 25,504; 1900, 40,705.

WORSEMENT, see *Betterment,* 1895.

WORSHIP. The first worship mentioned is that of Abel, 3872 B.C. (*Gen.* iv.) "Men began to call on the name of the Lord," 3769 B.C. (*Gen.* iv.) The Jewish order of worship was set up by Moses, 1490 B.C. Solomon consecrated the temple, 1004 B.C. Athotes, son of Menes, king of Upper Egypt, is supposed to be the *Cops* of the Egyptians, and the *Toth,* or *Hermes,* of the Greeks, the *Mercury* of the Latins, and the *Teutatte* of the Celts or Gauls, 2112 B.C. *Usher.*

WORSHIP IN ENGLAND. The Druids were the priests here, at the invasion of the Romans (55 B.C.), who eventually introduced Christianity, which was almost extirpated by the victorious Saxons (455), who were pagans. The Roman catholic form of Christianity was introduced by Augustine, 590, and continued till the Reformation (*which see*). See *Hymns, Liturgies, Prayers, Public Worship, Ritualists.*

PLACES OF WORSHIP IN ENGLAND AND WALES IN 1851.

	Places of Worship.	*Sittings.*
Church of England	14,077	5,317,915
Wesleyan Methodists	6,579	2,194,298
Independents	3,244	1,067,760
Baptists	2,789	752,343
Roman Catholics	570	186,111
Society of Friends	371	91,559
Unitarians	229	68,554
Scottish Presbyterians	160	86,692
Latter-day Saints (*Mormonites*)	222	30,783
Brethren (Plymouth)	132 (?)	18,529
Jews	53	8,438
New Church (Swedenborgians)	50	12,107
Moravians	32	9,305
Catholic and Apostolic Church (Irvingites)	32	7,437
Greek Church	3	291
Countess of Huntingdon's Connexion	109	35,210
Welsh Calvinistic Methodists	828	198,242
Various small bodies, some without names	546	105,557

June, 1884, total sittings in the metropolis (population 4,019,361), 1,388,792 ; Church of England, 677,645.

See *Wesleyan Methodists*, note.

116 sects having 20,330 places of worship, Oct. 1871.

Certified Places of Worship, registered, 4 Nov. 1884, 23,341 ; 1 Nov. 1891, 27,253 ; 23,388 (6,000 cancelled), announced, 1 Nov. 1897.

WORSTED, spun wool, obtained its name from having been first spun at a town called Worsted, in Norfolk, in which the inventor lived, and where manufactures of worsted are still extensively carried on, 14 Edw. III. 1340. *Anderson.* "A worsted-stocking knave" is a term of reproach or contempt used by Shakspeare. Great increase of manufacture in W.R. Yorkshire, 1895 *et seq.*

WORTH, see *Woerth.*

WORTHIES, NINE, a term long ago given to the following eminent men:—

	Died.
Jews.	
Joshua	B.C. 1426
David	1015
Judas Maccabæus	161
Heathens.	
Hector of Troy	1184
Alexander the Great	323
Julius Cæsar	44
Christians.	
King Arthur of Britain	A.D. 532
Charlemagne of France	800
Godfrey of Bouillon	1100

In some lists, Gideon and Samson are given, instead of Hector and Arthur. In Shakspeare's *Love's Labour's Lost*, act v. sc. 2, Hercules and Pompey appear as worthies.

WOTHLYTYPE, see under *Photography.*

WOUNDED IN BATTLE, see *Geneva Convention*, and *Aid to Sick and Wounded.*

WOUNDING. Malicious wounding of another was adjudged death by the English statutes. The Coventry Act was passed in 1671 ; see *Coventry Act.* By lord Ellenborough's Act, persons who stab or cut with intent to murder, maim, or disfigure another were declared guilty of felony without benefit of clergy. Those guilty of maliciously shooting at another in any dwelling-house or other place, are also punishable under the same statute in the same degree, 43 Geo. III. 1802. This offence is met by some later statutes, particularly the act for consolidating and amending the acts relating to offences against the person, 9 Geo. IV., June, 1828. This last act is extended to Ireland by 10 Geo. IV., 1829. An act for the prevention of maliciously shooting, stabbing, &c., in Scotland, 6 Geo. IV., 1825 ; amended by 10 Geo. IV., 4 June, 1829, for the prevention and punishment of assaults on women and children.

WRECKS. The loss of merchant and other ships by wreck upon lee-shores, coasts, and disasters in the open sea, was estimated at Lloyd's, in 1800, to be about an average of 365 ships a year. In 1830, it appeared by *Lloyd's Lists* that 677 British vessels were totally lost, under various circumstances, in that year. The laws respecting wrecks were consolidated in 1846 and 1854. See *Seamen* (commission of inquiry).

Abstracts of the returns made to the Board of Trade of shipping casualties on or near the coast, &c., of the United Kingdom, and also of the casualties to British vessels elsewhere, and also to foreign vessels, published annually since 1855.

Wrecks on British coasts : July, 1887—July 1888, 4,004 ; 1888–9, 4,272 ; 1889–90, 4,344 ; 1890–1, 4,198 ; 1891–2, 4,710 ; 1893–4, 4,951 ; 1894–5, 4,917 (740 lives lost) ; 1895–6, 4,620 (458 lives lost) ; 1898–9, 5,040 (520 lives lost).

Between 1861 and the 30th June, 1890, 4,742 British, colonial, and foreign vessels were wrecked on our coast, 21,426 lives lost.

British vessels wrecked in 1848, were, sailing vessels, 501 ; steamers, 13 ; tonnage, 96,920.

In 1851, there were wrecked 611 vessels, of which number 11 were steamers : the tonnage of the whole being 111,976.

The year 1852-3, particularly the winter months (Dec. and Jan.), was very remarkable for the number of dreadful shipwrecks and fires at sea : but a few of them are recorded. Wrecks in 25 years (1854-79), 49,322 ; lives lost, 18,319.

Many vessels were lost in the great storms, 25, 26 Oct. 1859 ; 28 May, 1861 ; 19, 20 Oct. 1861 ; and 13, 14 Nov. 1862 : by a cyclone, India, 5 Oct 1864 ; in the West Indies, Oct. 1867.

See under *Life Boat.*

BRITISH VESSELS (EXCLUSIVE OF THE ROYAL NAVY) TOTALLY LOST AT SEA :

	Vessels.	*Lives lost.*		*Vessels.*	*Lives lost.*
1875	657	1,694	1889	447	1,045
1876	661	1,976	1890	528	1,544
1877	677	1,732	1891	587	1,926
1878	637	1,302	1892	416	1,329
1879	621	1,652	1893	523	1,487
1880	835	2,075	1894	539	2,735
1881	973	3,165	1895	478	1,443
1882	733	1,927	1897	475	876
1883	793	2,698	1898	413	972
1884	616	1,644	1899	397	1,308
1885	557	1,431	1900	341	1,044
1886	644	1,340	1901	546	1,280
1887	500	1,888	1902	556	2,048
1888	543	1,917			

REMARKABLE CASES OF BRITISH VESSELS WRECKED OR BURNT.

Mary Rose, 60 guns, going from Portsmouth to Spithead, upset in a squall ; all on board perished, 20 July, 1545

Coronation, 90 guns, foundered off the Ramhead ; crew saved : *Harwich*, 70 guns, wrecked on Mount Edgcumbe ; crew perished . 1 Sept. 1691

Royal Sovereign, 100 guns ; burnt in the Medway, 29 Jan. 1696

Stirling Castle, 70 guns ; *Mary*, 70 guns ; *Northumberland*, 70 guns, lost on the Goodwin ; *Vanguard*, 70 guns, sunk at Chatham ; *York*, 70 guns, lost near Harwich ; all lost but four men ; *Resolution*, 60 guns, coast of Sussex ; *Newcastle*, 60 guns, at Spithead, 193 drowned ; *Reserve*, 60 guns, at Yarmouth, 173 perished ; in the night of 26 Nov. 1703

Association, 70 guns, and other vessels, lost with admiral sir C. Shovel, off the Scilly isles (*which see*) 22 Oct. 1707
Solebay, 32 guns, lost near Boston neck; crew perished . . . . 25 Dec. 1709
Edgar, 70 guns, blew up at Spithead; all on board perished . . . . 15 Oct. 1711
Wager, part of commodore Anson's South Sea expedition; wrecked on desolate island, lat. 47° S. 14 May, 1741
Victory, 100 guns, near the isle of Alderney; all perished . . . . 5 Oct. 1744
Colchester, 50 guns, lost on Kentish Knock; 50 men perished . . . . 21 Sept. ,,
Namur, 74 guns, foundered near Fort St. David, East Indies; all perished except 26 persons; *Pembroke*, 60 guns, near Porto Novo; 330 of her crew perished . . . . 13 April, 1749
Prince George, 80 guns, burnt in lat. 48 N., on way to Gibraltar; about 400 perished . 13 April, 1758
Lichfield, 50 guns, lost on the coast of Barbary; 130 of the crew perished . . . . . 29 Nov. ,,
Tilbury, 60 guns, lost off Louisbourg; most of the crew perished . . . . . . 25 Sept. 1759
Ramilies, 90 guns, lost on the Bolt-head; only 26 persons saved; *Conqueror*, lost on St. Nicholas's Island, Plymouth . . . . . . 15 Feb. 1760
Duc d'Aquitaine, 64 guns, and *Sunderland*, 60 guns, lost off Pondicherry; all perished . 1 Jan. 1761
Raisonnable, 64 guns, lost at the attack of Martinique . . . . 3 Feb. 1762
Repulse, 32 guns, foundered off Bermuda; crew perished 1775
Thunderer, 74 guns; *Stirling Castle*, 64; *Defiance*, 64; *Phœnix*, 44; *La Blanche*, 32; *Laurel*, 28; *Shark*, 28; *Andromeda*, 28; *Deal Castle*, 24; *Penelope*, 24; *Scarborough*, 20; *Barbadoes*, 14; *Cameleon*, 14; *Endeavour*, 14; and *Victor*, 10 guns: all lost in the same storm, in the West Indies, in Oct. 1780
Gen. Barker, Indiaman, off Scheveling . 17 Feb. 1781
Grosvenor, Indiaman, coast of Caffraria . 4 Aug. 1782
Swan, sloop of war, off Waterford; 130 drowned, 4 Aug. ,,
Royal George; above 600 perished . 29 Aug. ,,
Centaur, 74 guns, foundered on her passage from Jamaica; capt. Inglefield and 11 of the crew saved 21 Sept. ,,
Ville de Paris, of 104 guns, one of admiral Rodney's prizes; the *Glorieux*, of 74 guns, lost in the West Indies . . . . 5 Oct. ,,
Superb, 74 guns, wrecked in Tellicherry roads, East Indies . . . . 5 Nov. 1783
Cato, 50 guns, admiral sir Hyde Parker, on the Malabar coast; crew perished . . . . . ,,
Count Belgioioso, Indiaman, off Dublin Bay; 147 souls perished . . . . . . 13 March, ,,
Menai, ferry-boat, in the Menai Strait 60 drowned, 5 Dec. 1785
Halsewell, E. Indiaman; 386 persons perished, 6 Jan. 1786
Hartwell, Indiaman, with immense wealth on board 24 May, 1787
Charlemont, packet, from Holyhead to Dublin; 104 drowned . . . . 22 Dec. 1790
Pandora, frigate, on a reef; 100 perished . 28 Aug. 1791
Union, packet of Dover, lost off the port of Calais; a similar occurrence had not happened for 105 years before . . . . 28 Jan. 1792
Winterton, E. Indiaman: many perished 20 Aug. ,,
Impétueux, 74 guns, burnt at Portsmouth 24 Aug. ,,
Scorpion, 74 guns, burnt at Leghorn . 20 Nov. 1793
Ardent, 64 guns, burnt off Corsica . . April, 1794
Boyne, by fire, at Spithead (see *Boyne*) . 4 May, 1795
Courageux, 74 guns, capt. B. Hallowell, near Gibraltar; crew, except 124, perished . 18 Dec. 1796
La Tribune, 36 guns, off Halifax; 300 souls perished 16 Nov. 1797
Proserpine, frigate; in the Elbe; 15 lost . 1 Feb. 1798
Resistance, blown up in the straits of Banca, 24 July, ,,
Royal Charlotte, East Indiaman, blown up at Culpee, 1 Aug. 1798
H.M.S. *Lutine*, 32 guns, was wrecked off Vlieland, coast of Holland; only one saved, who died before reaching England * . . . . 9-10 Oct. 1799
Impregnable, 98 guns, wrecked between Langstone and Chichester . . . . . . 19 Oct. ,,
Nassau, 64 guns, on the Haak Bank; 100 perished, 25 Oct. ,,
Sceptre, 64 guns, wrecked in Table Bay, cape of Good Hope; 291 of the crew perished . . . 5 Nov. ,,
Ethalion, frigate, 38 guns, on the Penmarks, 24 Dec. ,,
Queen, transport, on Trefusis Point; 369 souls perished . . . . 14 Jan. 1800
Mastiff, gunbrig, on the Cockle Sands . 19 Jan. ,,
Repulse, 64 guns, off Ushant . . . 10 March, ,,
Queen Charlotte (which see), burnt; 673 perish 17 March, ,,
Queen, W. Indiaman, by fire, off Brazil . 9 July, ,,
Brazen, sloop of war, off Newhaven; all lost except one man . . . . ,,
Invincible, 74 guns, near Yarmouth; capt. John Rennie, and the crew, except 126 souls, perished, 16 March, 1801
Margate, Margate-hoy, near Reculver; 23 persons perished . . . . 10 Feb. 1802
Bangalore, E. Indiaman, Indian Sea . 12 April, ,,
Active, West Indiaman, in Margate Roads 10 Jan. 1803
Hindostan, East Indiaman, went to pieces on the Culvers . . . . 11 Jan. ,,
La Déterminée, 24 guns, in Jersey Roads; many drowned . . . . 26 March, ,,
Resistance, 36 guns, off Cape St. Vincent . 31 May, ,,
Lady Hobart, packet, on an island of ice 28 June, ,,
Seine, frigate, 44 guns, off Schelling . 31 July, ,,
Antelope, capt. Wilson, off Pelew Islands 9 Aug. ,,
Victory, Liverpool ship, at Liverpool; 27 drowned, 30 Sept. ,,
Circe, frigate, 32 guns, off Yarmouth . 16 Nov. ,,
Nautilus, E. Indiaman, on Ladrones . 18 Nov. ,,
Fanny, in Chinese Sea: 46 souls perish 29 Nov. ,,
Suffisante, sloop, 16 guns, off Cork . 25 Dec. ,,
Apollo, frigate, on coast of Portugal . 1 April, 1804
Cumberland, packet, on Antigua coast . 4 Sept. ,,
Romney, 50 guns, on Haak Bank, Texel 18 Nov. ,,
Venerable, 74 guns, at Torbay; lost 8 men 24 Nov. ,,
Severn, on a rock, near Grouville . . 21 Dec. ,,
Doris, frigate, on the Diamond Rock, Quiberon Bay, 12 Jan. 1805
Abergavenny, East Indiaman, on the Bill of Portland; more than 300 persons perished 6 Feb. ,,
Naias, transport, on Newfoundland coast 23 Oct. ,,
Æneas, transport, off Newfoundland; 340 perished, 23 Oct. ,,
Aurora, transport, on the Goodwin Sands; 300 perished . . . . 21 Dec. ,,
King George, packet, from Park-gate to Dublin, lost on the Hoyle bank; 125 persons, passengers and crew drowned . . . . . . 21 Sept. 1806
Athénien, 64 guns, near Tunis; 347 souls perished, 27 Oct. ,,
Glasgow, packet, off Farm Island; several drowned, 17 Nov. ,,
Felix, 12 guns, near Santander; 79 souls lost 22 Jan. 1807
Blenheim, 74 guns, admiral sir T. Troubridge, and *Java*, 23 guns, foundered near island of Rodriguez, East Indies . . . . 1 Feb. ,,

* *La Lutine* was a French ship captured by admiral Duncan. She contained much bullion and money, belonging to merchants; a great loss to the underwriters at Lloyd's. The Dutch government claimed the wreck, and granted one third of the salvage in 1801 to the bullion fishers. After much discussion, and occasional recoveries, the king of the Netherlands ceded to Great Britain (for Lloyd's) half the remainder of the wreck. A Dutch salvage company began operations in Aug. 1857. At the end of 1859, Lloyd's had received 22,162*l.* 6*s.* 7*d.* About 99,893*l.* recovered; about 1,175,000*l.* remaining. A chair and table at Lloyd's were made of the rudder, recovered in 1859. *Martin's History of Lloyd's.*

Ajax, 74 guns, by fire, off the island of Tenedos; 250 perished . . . . 14 Feb. 1807
Blanche, frigate, on the French coast; 45 men perished . . . . 4 March, „
Ganges, East Indiaman, off the Cape of Good Hope, 29 May, „
Prince of Wales, Park-gate packet, and *Rochdale*, transport, on Dunleary point, near Dublin; nearly 300 souls perished . . . . . . 19 Nov. „
Boreas, man-of-war, upon the Hannois rock in the Channel . . . . 28 Nov. „
Anson, 44 guns, wrecked in Mount's Bay; 60 lives lost . . . . 29 Dec. „
Agatha, near Memel; lord Royston and others drowned . . . . 7 April, 1808
Astrea, frigate, on Anagada coast . . 23 May, „
Frith, passage-boat, in the Frith of Dornoch; 40 persons drowned . . . . . 13 Aug. 1809
Foxhound, 18 guns, foundered on passage from Halifax; crew perished . . . . 31 Aug. „
Sirius, 36 guns, and *Magicienne*, 36 guns, wrecked when advancing to attack the French, off Isle of France . . . . 23 Aug. 1810
Satellite, sloop of war, 16 guns, upset, and all on board perished . . . . . 14 Dec. „
Minotaur, of 74 guns, wrecked on the Haak Bank; 360 persons perished . . . 22 Dec. „
Pandora, sloop of war, off Jutland; 30 persons perished . . . . 13 Feb. 1811
Saldanha, frigate, on the Irish coast; 300 persons perished . . . . . . 4 Dec. „
St. George, of 98, and *Defence*, of 74 guns, and the *Hero*, stranded on the coast of Jutland, adm. Reynolds and all the crews (about 2000 persons) perished, except 18 seamen . . . . 24 Dec. „
Manilla, frigate, on the Haak Sand; 12 persons perished . . . . 28 Jan. 1812
Atalante, H.M. frigate, off Nova Scotia . 10 Nov. 1813
British Queen, packet, from Ostend to Margate, wrecked on the Goodwin Sands, and all on board perished . . . . 17 Dec. 1814
Duchess of Wellington, at Calcutta, by fire 21 Jan. 1816
Seahorse, transport, near Tramore Bay; 365 persons, chiefly soldiers of the 59th regiment, and most of the crew, drowned . . . . . . 30 Jan. „
Lord Melville and *Boadicea*, transports, with upwards of 200 of the 82nd regiment, with wives and children, lost near Kinsale; almost all perished, 31 Jan. „
Harpooner, transport, near Newfoundland; 200 persons drowned . . . . . . 10 Nov. „
William and Mary, packet, struck on the Willeys rocks, near the Holmes lighthouse, Bristol Channel; nearly 60 persons perished . . . 23 Oct. 1817
Queen Charlotte, East Indiaman, at Madras; all on board perished . . . . . . 24 Oct. 1818
Ariel, in the Persian Gulf; 79 souls perished, 18 March, 1820
Blendon Hall, on Inaccessible Island, many perished, 23 July, 1821
Earl of Moira, on the Burbo Bank, near Liverpool 40 drowned . . . . 8 Aug. „
Juliana, East Indiaman, on the Kentish Knock; 40 drowned . . . . 26 Dec. „
Thames, Indiaman, off Beachey Head; several drowned . . . . 3 Feb. 1822
Drake, 10 guns, near Halifax; several drowned, 20 June, „
Ellesmere, steamer; 11 persons lost . 14 Dec. „
Alert, Dublin and Liverpool packet; 70 souls perished . . . . 26 March, 1823
Robert, from Dublin to Liverpool; 60 souls perished, 16 May „
Kent (*which see*), East Indiaman; burnt . March, 1825
Fanny, in Jersey Roads; lord Harley and many drowned . . . . 1 Jan. 1828
Venus, packet, from Waterford to Dublin, near Gorey; 9 persons drowned . . . 19 March, „
Newry, from Newry to Quebec, with 360 passengers; cast away near Bardsy, about 40 persons were drowned . . . . 16 April, 1830
Lady Sherbrooke, from Londonderry to Quebec; lost near Cape Ray; 273 souls perished; 32 only were saved . . . . 19 Aug. 1831
Experiment, from Hull to Quebec; wrecked near Calais . . . . 15 April, 1832
Hibernia, burnt in W. long. 22°, S. lat. 4°; 150 persons (out of 232) perished . . . 15 Feb. 1833
Earl of Wemyss, near Wells, Norfolk: the cabin filled, and 11 ladies and children were drowned; all on deck escaped . . . . 13 July, „
Amphitrite, ship, with female convicts to New South Wales; lost on Boulogne Sands; out of 131 persons, 3 only were saved . . . . 30 Aug. „
United Kingdom, W. Indiaman, with rich cargo; run down by the *Queen of Scotland* steamer off Northfleet, near Gravesend . . . . . 15 Oct. „
Waterwitch, steamer, on the coast of Wexford; 4 drowned . . . . 18 Dec. „
Lady Munro, from Calcutta to Sydney; of 90 persons on board, not more than 20 were saved, 9 Jan. 1834
Cameleon, cutter, run down off Dover by the *Castor* frigate; 13 persons drowned . . . 27 Aug. „
Earl of Eldon, East Indiaman; burnt . 27 Sept. „
Killarney, steamer, off Cork; 29 persons perished, 26 Jan. 1838
Forfarshire, steamer, from Hull to Dundee; 38 persons drowned. Owing to the courage of Grace Darling and her father, 15 persons were saved (see *Forfarshire*) . . . . 6 Sept. „
Protector, E. Indiaman, at Bengal; of 178 persons on board, 170 perished . . . . . 21 Nov. „
Diligence, naval cutter, capt. sir J. Reid, bart., and 56 souls perish in the Irish channel . 7 Jan. 1839
William Huskisson, steamer, between Dublin and Liverpool; 93 passengers saved by capt. Clegg, of the *Huddersfield* . . . . . 11 Jan. 1840
Lord William Bentinck, off Bombay; 58 recruits, 20 officers, and 7 passengers perished; the *Lord Castlereagh* also wrecked, most of her crew and passengers lost . . . . . . 17 June, „
H.M.S. *Fairy*, captain Hewitt; sailed from Harwich on a surveying cruise, and was lost next day in a violent gale, off the coast of Norfolk . 13 Nov. „
City of Bristol, steam packet, 35 perished 18 Nov. „
Thames, steamer, captain Gray, from Dublin to Liverpool, wrecked off St. Ives; the captain and 55 persons perished . . . . 4 Jan. 1841
Governor Fenner, from Liverpool for America; run down off Holyhead by the *Nottingham* steamer out of Dublin; 122 persons perished . . 19 Feb. „
Amelia, from London to Liverpool; lost on the Herne Sand . . . . 26 Feb. „
President, steamer, from New York to Liverpool, with many passengers on board; sailed on 11 March, encountered a terrific storm two days afterwards, and has never since been heard of, 13 March, „

[In this vessel were, Mr. Tyrone Power, the comedian; a son of the duke of Richmond, &c.]

William Browne, by striking on the ice; 16 passengers who had been received into the long boat were thrown overboard by the crew to lighten her 19 April, „
Isabella, from London to Quebec; struck by an iceberg . . . . 9 May, „
Solway, steamer, on her passage between Belfast and Port Carlisle: crew saved . . 25 Aug. „
Amanda, off Metis; 29 passengers and 12 of the crew lost . . . . . . 26 Sept. „
James Cooke, of Limerick, coming from Sligo to Glasgow . . . . 21 Nov. „
Abercrombie, *Robinson* and *Waterloo* transports, in Table Bay, Cape of Good Hope: of 330 persons on board the latter vessel, 189, principally convicts, perished . . . . . . 28 Aug. 1842
Spitfire, war-steamer, off Jamaica . . 10 Sept. „
Reliance, East Indiaman, from China to London, off Merlemont, near Boulogne: of 116 persons on board, seven only were saved . . 13 Nov. „
Hamilton, on the Gunfleet sands, near Harwich; 11 of the crew perished . . . . . 15 Nov. „
Conqueror, East Indiaman, homeward bound, near Boulogne; crew and passengers lost . 13 Jan. 1843

Jessie Logan, East Indiaman, on the Cornish coast; many lives lost . . . . 16 Jan. 1843
Solway, royal mail-steamer, near Corunna; 28 lives lost, and the mail . . . 7 April, ,,
Catherine, trader, blown up off the Isle of Pines; most of the crew were massacred by the natives, or afterwards drowned . . . 12 April, ,,
Amelia Thompson, near Madras, part of crew saved 23 May, ,,
Albert, troop-ship, from Halifax, with the 64th regiment on board, which was miraculously saved 13 July, ,,
Pegasus, steam-packet, from Leith; off the Fern Islands; of 59 persons (including Mr. Elton, the actor), 7 only were saved . . . 19 July, ,,
Phœnix, in a terrific snow-storm, off the coast of Newfoundland; many lives were lost 26 Nov. ,,
Elberfeldt, iron steam-ship, from Brielle 22 Feb. 1844
Manchester, steamer, from Hull to Hamburg, off the Vogel Sands, near Cuxhaven about 30 lives lost, 16 June, ,,
John Lloyd, by collision, in the Irish sea; several lives lost . . . . . 25 Sept. 1845
Margaret, Hull and Hamburg steamer; many lives lost . . . . . . 22 Oct. ,,
Tweed, steamer; off Yucatan . . . 12 Feb. 1846
Great Britain, iron steam-ship, grounded in Dundrum bay (see *Great Britain*) . . 22 Sept. ,,
[Recovered by Brunel, &c., 27 Aug. 1847.]
Tweed, W. India mail-packet; 72 souls perished, 19 Feb. 1847
Exmouth, emigrant-ship, from Londonderry to Quebec; of 240 persons on board, nearly all were drowned . . . . . . 28 April, ,,
Carrick, brig; a gale in the St. Lawrence; 170 emigrants perished . . . . 19 May, ,,
Avenger, H.M. steam-frigate; off N. coast of Africa; officers and crew (nearly 200) lost 20 Dec. ,,
Ocean Monarch (*which see*) . . . . 24 Aug. 1848
Forth, steamer; off Campeachy . . . 13 Jan. 1849
Caleb Grimshaw, emigrant-ship, fire; 400 persons miraculously escaped . . . . 12 Nov. ,,
Royal Adelaide, steamer, wrecked on the Tongue Sands, off Margate, above 400 lives lost, 30 March, 1850
Orion, steam-ship, off Portpatrick (see *Orion*), 18 June, ,,
Rosalind, from Quebec; a number of the crew drowned . . . . . 9 Sept. ,,
Edmund, emigrant-ship, with nearly 200 passengers from Limerick to New York (of whom more than one-half perished), wrecked off the Western coast of Ireland . . . . . . 12 Nov. ,,
Amazon, W. India mail-steamer (see *Amazon*), 4 Jan. 1852
Birkenhead, troop-ship, iron paddle-wheeled, and of 556 horse-power, sailed from Queenstown, 7 Jan. 1852, for the Cape, having on board detachments of the 12th Lancers, 2nd, 6th, 12th, 43rd, 45th, and 60th Rifles, 73rd, 74th, and 91st regiments. It struck upon a pointed pinnacle rock off Simon's bay, South Africa, and of 638 persons only 184 were saved by the boats; 454 of the crew and soldiers perished . . . . . 26 Feb. ,,
Victoria, steam-packet, wrecked near Wings beacon off Gottenburg; many lives lost . 8, 9 Nov. ,,
Lily, stranded and blown up by gunpowder, on the Calf-of-Man; by which more than 30 persons lost their lives . . . . . 24 Dec. ,,
St. George, steam-ship, bound from Liverpool to New York, with 121 emigrant passengers (chiefly Irish), and a crew consisting of twenty-nine seamen (the captain inclusive), was destroyed by fire at sea. The crew and seventy of the passengers were saved by the American ship *Orlando*, and conveyed to Havre, in France; 51 supposed to have perished . . . . . . 24 Dec. ,,
Queen Victoria, steam-ship, bound from Liverpool, was wrecked off the Bailey lighthouse, near Dublin; mistook her course in a snow-storm: 67 lost out of 120 . . . . . 15 Feb. 1853
Independence, on the coast of Lower California, and which afterwards took fire: 140 persons were drowned or burnt to death, a few escaping, who underwent the most dreadful additional sufferings on a barren shore . . . . . 16 Feb. ,,
Duke of Sutherland, steamer, from London to Aberdeen; struck on the pier at Aberdeen, and the captain (Edward Howling) and 16 (of the crew and passengers) perished . . . 1 April, 1853
Rebecca, on west coast of Van Diemen's Land, capt. Shephard and many lives lost . . 29 April, ,,
William and Mary, an American emigrant ship, near the Bahamas. She struck on a sunken rock; about 170 persons perished . . . 3 May, ,,
Aurora, of Hull; sailed from New York, 26 April, and foundered; about 25 lives lost . 20 May, ,,
Bourneuf, Australian emigrant vessel; struck on a reef near Torres Straits; the captain (Bibby) and six lives lost . . . . 3 Aug. ,,
Annie Jane, of Liverpool, an emigrant vessel, driven on shore on the Barra Islands, on west coast of Scotland; about 348 lives lost 29 Sept. ,,
Harwood, brig, by collision with the *Trident* steamer, near the Mouse light near the Nore; foundered; six of the crew perished . 5 Oct. ,,
Dalhousie, foundered off Beachey Head: the captain (Butterworth), the passengers, and all the crew (excepting one), about 60 persons in all, perished; the cargo was valued at above 100,000*l.* 19 Oct. ,,
Marshall, screw-steamer, in the North Sea, ran into the barque *Woodhouse*; about 48 persons supposed to have perished . . . 28 Nov. ,,
Tayleur, emigrant ship, driven on the rocks off Lambay Island, north of Howth; about 380 lives lost . . . . 20 Jan. 1854
Favourite, in the Channel, on her way from Bremen to Baltimore, came into violent contact with the American barque *Hesper*, off the Start, and immediately went down; 201 persons were drowned 29 April, ,,
Lady Nugent, troop-ship, sailed from Madras, 10 May, 1854; foundered in a hurricane; 350 rank and file of the Madras light infantry, officers, and crew, in all 400 souls, perished . . . May, ,,
Forerunner, African mail-steamer, struck on a sunken rock off St. Lorenzo, Madeira, and went down directly afterwards, with the total loss of ship and mails, and 14 lives . . . 25 Oct. ,,
Nile, iron screw-steamer, struck on the Godevry rock, St. Ives' Bay, and all perished . 30 Nov. ,,
City of Glasgow, a Glasgow steamer, with 480 persons on board, disappeared in . . . . . ,,
In the storm which raged in the Black Sea, 13-16 Nov. 1854, eleven transports were wrecked and six disabled. The new steamship *Prince* was lost with 144 lives, and a cargo worth 500,000*l.* indispensable to the army in the Crimea. The loss of life in the other vessels is estimated at 340 ,,
George Canning, Hamburg and New York packet, near the mouth of the Elbe: 96 lives lost, and *Stately*, English schooner, near Neuwiek, in a great storm . . . . 1 Jan. 1855
Mercury, screw-steamer, by collision with a French ship: passengers saved . . . 11 Jan. ,,
Janet Boyd, bark, in a storm off Margate Sands; 28 lives lost . . . . . . 20 Jan. ,,
Will o' the Wisp, screw-steamer, on the Burn Rock, off Lambay; 18 lives lost . . . 9 Feb. ,,
Morna, steamer on rocks near the Isle of Man; 21 lives lost . . . . . 25 Feb. ,,
John, emigrant vessel, on the Muncles rocks off Falmouth; 200 lives lost . . . . 1 May, ,,
Pacific, Collins steamer, left Liverpool for New York, with 186 persons on board; never since heard of (supposed to have struck on an iceberg) 23 Jan. 1856
Josephine Willis, packet-ship, lost by collision with the screw-steamer *Mangerton*, in the Channel: about 70 lives lost . . . . . 3 Feb. ,,
John Rutledge, from Liverpool to New York, ran on an iceberg and was wrecked; many lives lost 20 Feb. ,,
Many vessels and their crews totally lost 1-8 Jan. 1857
Violet, royal mail-steamer, lost on the Goodwin; many persons perished . . . . 5 Jan. ,,
Tyne, royal-steamer, stranded on her way to Southampton from the Brazils . . . . 13 Jan. ,,
St. Andrew, screw-steamer, totally wrecked near Latakia; loss about 145,000*l.* . . 29 Jan. ,,
Charlemagne, iron clipper, wrecked by the coast of Canton; passengers saved; loss, about 110,000*l.* 20 March.

H.M.S. *Raleigh*, 50 guns, wrecked on south-east coast of Macao . . . . . 14 April, 1857

Catherine Adamson, Australian vessel, wrecked 25 miles from Sydney, 20 lives lost about 3 June, ,,

Erin, P. & O. Co.'s steamer, wrecked on coast of Ceylon . . . . June, ,,

H.M.S. *Transit*, wrecked on a reef in the Straits of Banca . . . . 10 July, ,,

Dunbar, clipper wrecked on the rocks near Sydney: 121 persons, and cargo valued at 22,000*l.*, lost; one person only saved, who was on the rocks 30 hours . . . . 20 Aug. ,,

Sarah Sands, an iron screw-steamer, sailed from Portsmouth to Calcutta, in Aug. 1857; 300 soldiers on board. On 11 Nov. the cargo (government stores) took fire. By the exertions of major Brett and captain Castle, the master of the vessel, who directed the soldiers and the crew, the flames were subdued, although a barrel of gunpowder exploded during the conflagration. A new danger then arose—the prevalence of a strong gale: water was shipped heavily where the port quarter had been blown out. Nevertheless, after a fearful struggle, the vessel arrived at the Mauritius, 21 Nov., without losing a single life 11-21 Nov. ,,

Windsor, emigrant-ship, struck on a reef near the Cape de Verde Islands . . . . . . 1 Dec. ,,

Ava, Indian mail-steamer, with ladies and others from Lucknow on board, wrecked near Ceylon 16 Feb. 1858

Eastern City, burnt about the equator on her way to Melbourne; by great exertions all on board were saved . . . . 23, 24 Aug. ,,

Austria, steam-emigrant ship, burnt in the middle of the Atlantic. Of 538 persons on board, only 67 were saved. The disaster due to carelessness 13 Sept. ,,

St. Paul, captain Pennard, from Hong Kong to Sydney, with 327 Chinese emigrants, wrecked on the island of Rossel, 30 Sept. 1858. The captain and eight of the crew left the island in search of assistance, and were picked up by the *Prince of Denmark* schooner. The French steamer *Styx* was despatched to the island, and brought away one Chinese, 25 Jan. 1859. All the rest had been massacred and devoured by the natives . . ,,

Czar, steamer, wrecked off the Lizard; 14 lives lost 23 Jan. 1859

Eastern Monarch, burnt at Spithead; out of 500, eight lives lost. The vessel contained invalid soldiers from India, who, with the crew, behaved admirably . . . . 2 June, ,,

Alma, steamer, grounded on a reef near Aden, Red Sea, about 35 miles from Mocha; all persons saved; after 3½ days' exposure to the sun, without water, they were rescued by H.M.S. *Cyclops*: sir John Bowring, who was on board, lost valuable papers . . . . 12 June, ,,

Admella, steamer, running between Melbourne and Adelaide, struck on a reef; of about 72 persons, only 23 were saved; many perished through exposure to cold . . . . 6 Aug. ,,

Royal Charter, screw-steamer, captain Taylor, totally wrecked off Moelfra, on the Anglesea coast: 446 lives lost. The vessel contained gold amounting in value to between 700,000*l.* and 800,000*l.*; much of this has been recovered night of 25-26 Oct. ,,

Indian, mail-steamer, wrecked off the coast of Newfoundland; out of 116, 27 lives lost 21 Nov. ,,

Blervie Castle, sailed from London docks for Adelaide; lost in the Channel and all on board, 57 persons; last seen on . . . . . 25 Dec. ,,

Northerner, steamer, wrecked on a rock near Cape Mendorino, between San Francisco and Oregon; 38 lives lost . . . . 6 Jan. 1860

Endymion, sailing-vessel, burnt in the Mersey; loss above 20,000*l.* . . . . 31 Jan. ,,

Dreadful gales and many wrecks on the coast, 15-19 Feb. ,,

Ondine, steamer; lost through collision with the *Heroine*, of Bideford, abreast of Beachy Head; the captain and about 50 persons perished 19 Feb. ,,

Luna, American emigrant vessel, wrecked on rocks off Barfleur; about 100 lives lost . . 19 Feb. ,,

Hungarian, new mail-steamer, wrecked off coast of Nova Scotia; all on board (205) lost on the night of . . . . 19-20 Feb. ,,

Nimrod, steamer, wrecked on rocks near St. David's Head; 40 lives lost . . . . . . 28 Feb. 1860

Malabar, iron ship, on her way to China, with lord Elgin and baron Gros: wrecked off Point de Galle, Ceylon. The ambassadors displayed much heroism; no lives lost. Of much specie sunk, a good deal was recovered . . . . 22 May, ,,

Lady Elgin, an American steamer, sunk through collision with schooner *Augusta* on lake Michigan; of 385 persons on board, 287 were lost, including Mr. Herbert Ingram, M.P., founder of the "Illustrated London News," and his son; morning of 8 Sept. ,,

Arctic, Hull steamer, wrecked off Jutland; many persons saved by Mr. Earle, who lost his own life while endeavouring to save others . . . 5 Oct. ,,

Connaught, steamer, burnt; crew saved through the gallantry of the crew of an American brig. 7 Oct. ,,

Juanita, wrecked through collision with an American vessel, *Joseph Fish*, 13 lives lost . 15 March, 1861

Canadian, steamer, struck on a field of ice in the straits of Belle-isle, and foundered in half an hour; 35 lives lost . . . . 4 June, ,,

H.M.S. *Conqueror*, stranded on Rum Cay, near Bahamas, and lost [the captain and master were censured for neglect of duty] . . . . 29 Dec. ,,

Harmony, lost with all hands off Plymouth 27 Feb. 1862

Ocean Monarch, 2195 tons, sailed from New York, 5 March, laden with provisions; foundered in a gale . . . . 9 March, ,,

Upwards of 60 merchantmen lost during gales in March, ,,

Mars, Waterford steamer, struck on a rock near Milford haven; about 50 lives lost. . April, ,,

Bencoolen, East Indiaman, 1400 tons; struck on sands near Bude haven, Cornwall; about 26 lives lost . . . . 19 Oct. ,,

Lotus, merchantman, off Chale Bay, in the great storm; crew all lost except two . . . 19 Oct. ,,

Many vessels lost during storm . . . . 19 Oct. ,,

Colombo, East India mail steamer, in thick weather, wrecked on Minicoy Island; 440 miles from Point de Galle, Ceylon; no lives lost (the crew and passengers taken off by the *Ottawa* from Bombay, 30 Nov.) . . . . 19 Nov. ,,

Lifeguard, steamer, left Newcastle, with about 41 passengers; never since heard of; supposed to have foundered off Flamborough head 20 Dec. ,,

Orpheus, H.M.S. steamer, new vessel, 1700 tons; commander Burnett; wrecked on Manakau bar, W. coast New Zealand; 70 persons saved; about 190 perished . . . . 7 Feb. 1863

Anglo-Saxon, mail steamer, captain Burgess, in dense fog, wrecked on reef off Cape Race, Newfoundland; about 237, out of 446, lives lost, 27 April, ,,

All Serene, Australian ship; gale in the Pacific; above 30 lives lost (the survivors suffered much till they reached the Fiji isles in a punt) 21 Feb. 1864

Many shipwrecks in consequence of the cyclone at Calcutta . . . . 5 Oct. ,,

H.M.S. *Racehorse*, off Chefoo Cape, Chinese coast; 99 lives lost . . . . 4 Nov. ,,

The *Stanley*, *Friendship*, &c., in the gale off Tynemouth; and the *Dalhousie*, screw steamer, mouth of the Tay; same gale; 34 lives lost . 24 Nov. ,,

H.M.S. *Bombay*, burnt off Flores Island, near Monte Fideo; 91 lives lost . . . . 14 Dec. ,,

Lelia, cutter, off Great Orme's Head, during a gale; several lives lost; 7 persons drowned by upsetting of the lifeboat . . . . 14 Jan. 1865

Eagle Speed, emigrant vessel, foundered near Calcutta; 265 coolies drowned; great cruelty and neglect imputed . . . . 24 Aug. ,,

Duncan Dunbar, wrecked on a reef at Las Rocas, S. America; no lives lost . . . . 7 Oct. ,,

Samphire, mail-steamer; collision with an American barque; several lives lost . . . 13 Dec. ,,

Ibis, steamer, machinery damaged, off Ballycroneen bay; 15 lives lost; sailed from Cork . . 18 Dec. ,,

London, steamer, on her way to Melbourne; foundered in Bay of Biscay; about 220 persons perished (including captain Martin, Dr. Woolley, principal of the university of Sydney, G. V. Brooke, the tragedian); about the same time the *Amalia* steamer went down with a cargo worth 200,000*l.*; no lives lost . . . . . 11 Jan. 1866

Many wrecks and much loss of life during gales, especially off Torbay . . . . 6-11 Jan. 1866
Spirit of the Ocean, steamer; wrecked on a rock near Dartmouth; all lost except 4 23 March, „
General Grant, on voyage from Melbourne to London, wrecked off Auckland isles; only 13 out of about 100 saved. . . . . . . May, „
Amazon, H.M. screw sloop, and screw steamer *Osprey*, sunk by collision near Plymouth; several passengers and sailors drowned 10 July, „
Bruiser, steamer, sunk by collision with the *Haswell*, off Aldborough; about 15 lives lost 19 Aug. „
Bhima, Indian steamer; foundered through collision with *Nana*, steamer, between Bombay and Suez; 19 lives lost . . . . . 11 Sept. „
H.M.S. *Berenice*, burnt in Persian Gulf; none perished . . . . . 13 Oct. „
Ceres, near Carnsoe, Ireland; about 36 lives lost [captain Pascoe censured for neglecting to sound] 10 Nov. „
Many wrecks in the Channel . . . . 5, 6 Jan. 1867
James Crosfield, iron ship; wrecked off Langness, Isle of Man; all on board lost . . . . 5 Jan. „
Singapore, Peninsular and Oriental steamer, struck on a sunken rock, and went down; no lives lost, 20 Aug. „
Rhone and *Wye*, Royal Mail steamers, totally lost, and about 50 other vessels driven ashore; great loss of life by a hurricane, off St. Thomas (see *Virgin Islands*) . . . . . 29 Oct. „
Hibernia, screw steamer; the shaft of screw propeller broke, 600 miles off coast of Ireland; many lives lost . . . . . 24 or 25 Oct. or Nov. 1868
Many wrecks on the Cornish coast during a gale, 19-20 March, 1869
Italian, merchant steamer, struck on a rock near Finisterre; about 26 lives lost about 21 March. „
Carnatic, Peninsular and Oriental steamer, wrecked off Shadwan in the gulf of Suez; about 25 lives lost, 13 Sept. „
Oneida, American vessel, run down by collision with P. & O. steamer *Bombay* off Yokohama; about 115 lives lost (captain of *Bombay* suspended for 6 months) . . . . . . 24 Jan. 1870
City of Boston, sailed from New York, long missing; a board stating that she was sinking found in Cornwall . . . . . 11 Feb. „
Normandy, S.W. company's steamer, by collision with the steamer *Mary*, off the Isle of Wight, sunk; the captain, C. B. Harvey, and 33 others perish, 17 March, „
H.M.S. *Slaney*, wrecked by a typhoon near Hong Kong; about 42 lives lost . . . . 9 May, „
H.M.S. *Captain*, iron-clad, sank in a squall off Finisterre (see *Captain* & *Navy of England*) 7 Sept. „
Cambria, iron screw-steamer, lost in a storm off Inishtrahul island, N.W. Ireland; about 170 lives lost . . . . 19 Oct. „
Queen of the Thames, magnificent vessel, sailed from London to Sydney by the Cape in 58 days; returning, was lost by striking on sands off Cape Agulhas, Africa; 4 lives and valuable cargo lost; the captain was censured . . . . 18 March, 1871
Cornwall, wrecked by collision with the *Himalaya* steamer off Hartlepool . . . . 19 March, „
Megæra, government iron screw-steamer, sailed with about 400 on board for Australia, Feb. 1871; sprang a leak, 8 June; when it was discovered that her bottom was nearly worn away by corrosion; she was beached on St. Paul's Isle, in the Indian ocean, 16 June; huts were erected, and the crew settled, and stores landed; lieut. Jones was taken on board a Dutch vessel, 16 July; the *Oberon* brought provisions, 26 Aug.; the crew was carried off during a storm, the stores being left behind, by the *Malacca* . . . . 3 Sept. „

[The vessel was reported unfit for service in 1867; capt. Thrupp was tried and acquitted of blame, 17 Nov.; sir Spencer Robinson and various admiralty officials were censured by a government commission, 6 March, 1872.]

Rangoon, Peninsular and Oriental steamer, valued at 78,000*l*., wrecked on Kadir rock, off Point de Galle; cargo lost; no lives lost . . . 1 Nov. „
Norfolk Hero, fishing lugger, lost off Norfolk coast, 2 Dec. „
Delaware, large steamer; wrecked off Scilly rocks; only 2 out of 47 saved . . . . . 20 Dec. 1871
Severe gales many wrecks, and lives lost
Kinsale, steamer, off Waterford; *Albion*, schooner, off Looe; *Dee*, schooner, &c. . . 22-23 Nov. 1872
Royal Adelaide, emigrant vessel; went ashore on Chesil beach, between Weymouth and Portland; 5 lost . . . . 25 Nov. „
Germania, mail packet; wrecked off La Rochelle; about 24 perished . . . . . 21 Dec. „
Northfleet, vessel laden with railway iron for Van Diemen's Land, and railway navvies, run into by a foreign steamer (probably the *Murillo*,* a Spanish vessel) off Dungeness, about 10.30 p.m.; about 300 lost. . . . . . . 22 Jan. 1873
Chacabuco, iron ship; sunk in the Channel, 15 miles from Orme's head, by collision with the *Torch* steamer; 24 lost . . . . . 1 March, „
Boyne, barque; wrecked off Mohilo bay, Cornwall; about 20 lost . . . . . . 1 March, „
Atlantic, steamer, of White Star company, struck on Meagher rock, west of Sambro; said to have fallen short of coals steaming for Halifax; 442 (including capt. Williams) saved; about 560 lost, 1 April, 1873; many on the rigging perished through cold and want. The case was investigated, and the captain was suspended for two years . . . . 18 April, „
Eden, ship, with 150 tons of gunpowder, sailing for Valparaiso; set on fire by her mad captain, and blew up: (the crew in a boat were rescued by the *Juanita*) . . . . 7, 8 Nov. „
Nagpore, from Calcutta, took fire and ran into Kingstown harbour, doing much damage till it went to pieces; the captain of the *Echo* and some sailors were drowned. . . . . . . 9 Nov. „
Lochearn lost, through collision with the *Ville du Havre* (*which see*), 22 Nov.; quitted by her crew 28 Nov. „
Ella, London and Hamburg steamer; crew, 32; left Thames 14 Dec., supposed to have foundered in a gale . . . . 16 Dec. „
Queen Elizabeth, Glasgow steamer from India; went ashore near Tarifa; about 20 perished; middle of March, 1874
Tacna, steamer, from Valparaiso; foundered; about 19 lost (see *Chili*) . . . . . March, „
Liberia, British and African Steamship Co.; wrecked by collision with *Barton* steamer, off Scilly isles; probably all lost on board both vessels about 13 April, „
British Admiral, emigrant ship; wrecked on King's island, Bass's strait; about 80 out of 89 lost 23 May, „
Milbanke, iron steamer; laden with zinc from Carthagena; sunk through collision with *Hankow* steamer off Dungeness; 14 perish; 1.30 a.m. 28 July, „
Calcutta, ship, from Shields to Aden; took fire; nearly all lost . . . . . about 11 Sept. „
Malvern, barque, from Sunderland; foundered off Singapore; all hands lost. . . . 23 Sept. „
Kingsbridge, iron ship, sunk off the Lizards, by collision with the *Candahar*, iron ship; the master, his wife and daughter, and 8 of the crew perish 14 Oct. „
Maju, iron ship, of London; new clipper; wrecked off the Hebrides in a gale; crew, about 24, lost 20 Oct. „
Chusan, from Glasgow for Shanghai; sunk in a gale off Ardrossan; about 7 lost . . . 20 Oct. „
Cutter of H.M.S. *Aurora* swamped in the Clyde; 15 lost . . . . 19 Nov. „
La Plata, steamer (capt. Dudden), 1600 tons; sailed from Gravesend with telegraph cable for Brazil, 26 Nov.; foundered in a gale in the Bay of Biscay; 17 escape out of 85 . . . . . . 29 Nov. „
Cospatrick, emigrant vessel (capt. Emslie), on her way to Auckland, New Zealand; took fire, midnight, 17-18 Nov.; only 5 or 6 (out of 476) escaped; picked up, 27 Nov.; arrived at St. Helena 6 Dec. „
Japan, Pacific Mail steamer, from Yokohama; took fire off Hong Kong; many lost about 17 Dec. „

* This vessel was captured near Dover, 22 Sept. and condemned by the court of admiralty to be sold; (the officers severely censured ;) 4 Nov. 1873.

Delfine, steamer; struck on sunken rock, west coast of Africa; nearly all lost 1874
Scorpio, steamer, from Cardiff to Charente; not heard of, 30 Dec. . . . . . 4 Dec. ,,
Cortes (s), of London, foundered in Bay of Biscay; laden with coal for Aden; capt. E. King; about 25 lost . . . . 16 Dec. ,,
Hong Kong, steamer; wrecked on sunken rock near Aden; about 12 lost . . . . . 22 Feb. 1875
Stuart Hahnemann, sailed from Bombay, 4 April; capsized; about 40 drowned; (some rescued by *Blandina*, Austrian barque, 27 April) . 14 April, ,,
Cadiz, London steamer; wrecked on Wizard Rock, Brest; about 62 lost . . . . 8 May, ,,
Vicksburg, steamer, left Quebec, 27 May; struck on ice, 30 May; sank, 1 June; between 40 and 50 lost . . . . 1 June, ,,
Strathmore, emigrant vessel, wrecked in a fog near the Crozet isles, South Indian ocean, on way to New Zealand; 45 out of 89 lost . . . 1 July, ,,
Boyne, mail steamer, from Brazil; ran on a rock during a fog, 15 miles off Ushant; 2 lives lost 13 Aug. ,,
Mistletoe, Mr. Heywood's pleasure yacht; sunk by collision with H M.'s steamer *Alberta* (the queen on board), in the Solent, near Isle of Wight; Miss Annie Peel and two others drowned 18 Aug. ,,

[Coroner's inquest on Nathaniel Turner; verdict, accidental death, with a note alleging error of navigating officers, 10 Sept.; another inquest, closed without verdict, 7 Dec. 1875; captain Welch, of the *Alberta*, was reprimanded; 3000*l*. paid to Mr. Heywood, and others compensated; announced, April, 1876.] See under *Navy of England*.

H.M.S. *Vanguard*, double-screw iron-clad, 3774 tons; cost about 350,000*l*. (captain Dawkins) struck by ram of the *Iron Duke* during a fog off the coast of Wicklow; crew (about 400) saved; 50 m. past noon . . . . . 1 Sept. ,,
Pacific, steamer, from Victoria, British Columbia, to California; foundered off Cape Flattery; abov 150 lost . . . . . . about 4 Nov. ,,
Goliath, old man-of-war, fitted up as a training-ship for poor boys; burnt through a lamp falling on the dirty floor of the lamp-room; about a dozen lives lost out of about 500; the boys were highly commended for their courage and discipline under the command of captain Bourchier . 22 Dec. ,,
Many wrecks autumn and winter, 1875.
Warspite, old training-ship of the Marine Society's boys, on the Thames between Woolwich and Charlton, burnt; no loss of life; good discipline shown . . . . 3 Jan. 1876
Strathclyde, Glasgow steamer, sunk by collision with Hamburg ship *Franconia*, in Dover bay, in daylight; about 17 lost; (verdict of manslaughter against Kuhn, captain of *Franconia**) . 17 Feb. ,,
Edith, steamer, sunk by collision with the *Duchess of Sutherland* (both owned by the London and North-Western Railway Company) off St. John's Point, Ireland; 2 lives lost . . . 8 Sept. ,,
Shannon, mail steamer; struck on a shoal, 80 miles S.S.W. of Port Royal, Jamaica; no lives lost, 8 Sept. ,,
Western Empire, in Gulf of Mexico; a leak sprung, 13 Sept.; vessel left (10 lost) . . 18 Sept. ,,
Great Queensland, with impure patent gunpowder, and ordinary gunpowder; 569 persons on board; sailed for Melbourne, 5 Aug.: supposed to have exploded (pieces of wreck found), near Finisterre after 12 Aug. ,,

[Verdict of wreck commission against owners, 21 July, 1877.]

St. Lawrence, troopship, capt. Hyde; ran aground in St. Helena's bay, Africa; no loss of life 8 Nov. ,,
Ambassador, steamer; sunk by collision with an American ship, *George Manson*, returning from Calcutta; lat. 58° 6′ N., lon. 73° 27′ E.; 23 lost (crew, 43) . . . . 25 Dec. ,,
Cairo, iron ship; bound for Australia; carried much gunpowder; (said to have been wrecked off Tristan or Gough island); disappeared about middle of . . . . Jan. 1877

* Verdict quashed on appeal; 7 judges (against 6), decide against British jurisdiction, 13 Nov. 1876.

Cashmere, steamer (British India Steam Navigation company); wrecked off Guardafui; 7 drowned 12 July, 1877
Eten, steam ship (English Pacific Steam Navigation company); wrecked about 70 miles N. of Valparaiso; about 100 (of 160) lost; many rescued by H.M.S. *Amethyst* . . . . . 15 July, ,,
Avalanche, emigrant iron vessel; from London to New Zealand; above 100 on board; struck by *Forest* (of Windsor, Nova Scotia), 21 crew; both sank; about 12 lives saved; in channel, 15 miles S. by W. of Portland, 9.15 p.m. . . 11 Sept. ,,
Many losses by severe gale . . . 14, 15 Oct. ,,
Knapton Hall, steamer; sank through collision with *Lochfyne*, to whose assistance she was coming; 9 perish . . . . 15 Oct. ,,
Atacama, steamer; wrecked 22 miles S. of Caldera, near Copiapo; about 104 lost . end of Nov. ,,
European, Clyde steamer, from Algoa Bay; wrecked off Ushant; diamonds, &c., lost; no lives, 5 Dec. ,,
Mizpah, steamer; sunk by collision with unknown vessel, 15 miles S.W. of Beachy Head; above 6 lost; early . . . . 6 Dec. ,,
C. M. Palmer, steamer, of Newcastle; lost by collision with *Ludworth* steamer, near Harwich; about 14 lives lost; fog, 10 a.m. . . . . 17 Feb. 1878
Eurydice, H.M.S., frigate; training ship; returning from Bermudas; founders off Dunnose headland, near Ventnor, Isle of Wight; through a squall; capt. A. S. Hare, lieut. Tabor, and about 300 men perish . . . . 24 March, ,,

[Raised with much skill and labour, and taken into Portsmouth, Aug.]

Childwall Hall, Hull steamer; wrecked near Cape St. Vincent, Portugal; about 14 lost 11 April, ,,
Princess Alice (*which see*), run into by the screw steamer, *Bywell Castle*, in the Thames, near Woolwich, and sunk; between 600 and 700 lost; about 7.40 p.m. . . . . . . 3 Sept. ,,
Fanny, coastguard cruiser; run down by National steamer *Helvetia*, off Tuskar, Irish channel; 17 lost . . . . 31 Oct. ,,
Much damage and loss of life by gales . 8-10 Nov. ,,
Mesopotamia, steamer, run ashore at Peniche, coast of Portugal; 8 perished . . . 18 Dec. ,,
Ava, British India Navigation Steam company steamer, sank by collision with sailing ship *Brunhilda*, in the Bay of Bengal; capt. Dickenson and about 70 perish . . . . 24 April, 1879
City of London, Aberdeen steamer; run down and sunk by the *Vesta*(s), in the Thames, near Barking Reach; no lives lost . . . . 13 Aug. ,,
Borussia, a Dominion steamer, left Liverpool 20 Nov.; sprang a leak in the Atlantic after leaving Corunna, 1 Dec.; went down; about 160 lost; 10 out of 184 saved by boats . . . 2 Dec. ,,
Valentine foundered in a gale near Falmouth; about 16 lost . . . . . . 8 Feb. 1880
Many wrecks in the North Atlantic during terrific gale (see *Atalanta*) . . . . 12-16 Feb. ,,
Strathnairn, of Dundee: collision with *Edith Hough*, steamer, off Ushant; all lost 13 Feb. ,,
Hindoo, steamer, from New York; loaded with grain, which shifted; abandoned; three officers lost and much cattle . . . . 22 Feb. ,,
Vingorla, steamer; sprang a leak 70 miles N. of Bombay; captain and 65 persons perish: announced . . . . 1 March, ,,
Barita, British steamer, sunk in a fog by collision with an Australian mail steamer near Galatz; 16 perish . . . . 9 April, ,,
American, steamer (Union Steamship company), capt. Maclean Wait, foundered off Cape Palmas; all passengers and crew escaped in boats: (picked up by vessels, and carried to Madeira, St. Paul de Loanda, the Canaries, &c.) . . 23 April, ,,
Hydaspes, sailing ship; sank by collision with *Centurion*, screw steamer, off Dungeness, in a fog; both blamed; no lives lost . . . 17 July, ,,
James Harris, steamer, loaded with iron; sunk by collision with the *Andalusia*, steamer, off the Ferne isles . . . . . . 14 April, 1881
H.M.S. *Doterel* destroyed by explosion in the Straits of Magellan (see *Navy*) . . 26 April, ,,
Tararua, Union company's steamer, wrecked off Waipara Point, New Zealand, 130 lives lost, 28 April, ,,

Victoria, steamer, on the Thames, Canada; overloaded; upset; several hundreds drowned; between 600 and 700 on board . . 24 May, 1881

Ten fishing boats sunk off the Shetland isles in a storm; about 58 lives lost . . . 20 July, ,,

Teuton, Union Company's mail screw steamer, struck on a rock near Cape Agulhas, Cape of Good Hope; and foundered a few hours after; of above 200 persons, not many saved; capt. E. Manning and most of the officers lost . . 30 Aug. ,,

[Inquiry: attributed to the captain's imprudent navigation . . . 19 Sept.] ,,

Govino, British steamer; about 13 perished, 7 Oct. ,,

130 wrecks (105 British) with great loss of life and property by the gales . . 10-15 Oct. ,,

Corsica, steamer; stranded near mouth of the Tagus; 21 deaths . . . 11 Oct. ,,

[The captain exonerated, 8 Nov.]

Cyprian, iron steamer, lost in Carnarvon bay; capt. Strachan and another drowned . . 14 Oct. ,,

——, Glasgow steamer, wrecked in the Irish sea; many lost . . . . about 20-22 Oct. ,,

Clan Macduff, steamer, capt. Webster; foundered off the Irish coast (over-loaded) 32 lives lost [captain censured] . . . 21 Oct. ,,

Albion, steamer, wrecked on the Atlantic coast of Columbia; 32 lost . . . . 5 Nov. ,,

Crown, British steamer, stranded near Jutland; 7 drowned . . . . . 15 Nov. ,,

Solway, channel steamer, capt. W. Fry; during a storm off the Skerries; greatly burned through ignition of naphtha oil flooding the decks through bursting of casks, about 14 burned, and 5 drowned (the steamer got back to Kingston harbour); officers exonerated from blame 16 Nov. ,,

Culzean, iron steamer; capt. Pirnie, while being towed to be repaired during a gale, stranded on rocks in the sound of Java; crew of 17 lost 22 Nov. ,,

Many wrecks with loss of life and property during a gale . . . . . 26-27 Nov. ,,

Kildare, barque, stranded off Aberdeen coast in gale . . . . . . Dec. ,,

Helenslea, barque, collision with *Catalonia*, Cunard steamer; 9 of the crew lost . . 25 Dec. ,,

Lanarkshire, screw steamer, stranded off Codling Bank, Wicklow; some of the crew lost 15 Jan. 1882

Bahama, steamer, foundered between Porto Rico and New York; 20 lives lost . . . 4 Feb. ,,

Kosmos, steamer, sank off Kilia; captain and 20 of crew drowned . . . . . Feb. ,,

Livadia, steamer, from Shields, sunk off Yarmouth; 23 lives lost . . . . . 28 Feb. ,,

Douro, royal mail steamer; collision with Spanish steamer, *Yurrac Bat*, both sunk; about 23 English and 36 Spanish lost, about 11 p.m. (captain of *Douro* blamed) . . . 1 April, ,,

Novara, ship; on voyage from Newcastle to San Francisco, burned; 19 missing . 13 April, ,,

Alexandrina, Liverpool ship, wrecked off Swanage; crew all lost . . . early in May, ,,

Pera, iron steamer; foundered 30 miles S.W. Cape Race; about 10 men lost . . . 10 June, ,,

Escambia, British screw steamer, wrecked at Escambia, near San Francisco; crew (about 20) lost, announced . . . 20 June, ,,

Alice, steam-tug, wrecked on Bondecao rocks, Northumberland; 16 lives lost . . 29 June, ,,

Fleurs Castle, steamer, run aground, near Cape Guardafui, N.E. Africa; several perished, 9 July, ,,

Ethiopia, African mail steamer, run on a reef, 28 July, ,,

Armenian, Liverpool steamer, lost in the Baltic; crew about 23 perish, announced . . 23 Aug. ,,

Ponoma, Glasgow iron ship, foundered off Yarmouth; about 20 perish, announced 9 Sept. ,,

Constantia and *City of Antwerp*, steamers, sunk by collision off the Eddystone; about 14 lives lost 16 Oct. ,,

Winton, lost off Ushant: 24 perish . . 16 Nov. ,,

Wearmouth, steamer, lost off Magdalen Island 21 Nov. ,,

Cambronne, steamer, sunk by collision with *Marion*, near Lundy . . . . . 26 Nov. ,,

St. George, steamer; lost off Portreath, Cornish coast; 11 perish . . . . 29 Nov. ,,

Cedar Grove, steamer, lost off Cape Canto, Nova Scotia; 17 persons missing . about 30 Nov. ,,

Many wrecks, with loss of life . . . Dec. 1882

Langrigg Hall, barque, wrecked off Wexford; 24 deaths . . . . . 15 Dec. ,,

35 wrecks during a storm off Newfoundland about 19 Dec. ,,

British Empire, ship, burnt off Aleppo; several persons perish . . . . . 5 Jan. 1883

City of Brussels (s), sunk by collision with the *Kirby Hall* (s), in the Mersey: 10 drowned . 7 Jan. ,,

Kenmure Castle, steamer, wrecked in Bay of Biscay; 30 drowned . . . . about 1 Feb. ,,

King Arthur, Hull steamer, sunk near the mouth of the Bosphorus; 14 lost . . . 22 Feb. ,,

Wrecks through gales in North sea, 382 lives lost, 6 March, ,,

Navarre, Scotch steamer; sunk near Christiansand; about 45 lost . . . . . 7 March, ,,

Dunstaffnage, Liverpool ship, wrecked off Aberdeen; 23 perished . . . . 17 March, ,,

Wykeham, steamer, of Whitby, foundered near Lisbon; 22 drowned; sailed from Cardiff, March, ,,

British Commerce, sunk by collision with *County of Aberdeen*, off Selsey Bill; 25 perish . 24 April, ,,

Grappler burnt near Bute Inlet (Vancouver Island), about 70 perish . . . . about 3 May, ,,

H.M.S. *Lively* stranded on rocks off Stornoway, 7 June, ,,

[Commander Parr dismissed, 28 June.]

Waitara, sunk by collision with *Hurunui* (New Zealand Steamship Co.,) off Beachy Head; 25 perish . . . . . . 22 June, ,,

Daphne, coasting steamer, heeled over, during launch in the Clyde; about 124 drowned 3 July, ,,

79 wrecks on British coasts reported through violent gale . . . . . 1-2 Sept. ,,

Holyhead, L. & N. W. railway's cattle steamer and German barque, *Alhambra*, sailing vessel, sunk by collision between Dublin and Holyhead; 15 deaths; midnight . . . . 31 Oct. ,,

Iris, sunk off Cape Villano; about 35 perish; announced . . . . . 8 Nov. ,,

Auk, Liverpool steamer, at South Henden; 22 lives lost . . . . . . 11 Dec. ,,

Simla, wrecked by collision with the *City of Lucknow*, both of Glasgow, Australian sailers, near the Needles, English channel; about 20 perish; 3 p.m. 25 Jan. 1884

Very many wrecks . . . . 23-27 Jan. ,,

Nakomis, barque, struck on Black Rock, Antrim; 16 perish . . . . . . 26 Jan. ,,

Juno, iron ship, stranded in the Mersey by a gale; the crew (30) perish . . . 26, 27 Jan. ,,

State of Florida, Glasgow steamer, and *Ponema*, barque, sunk by collision in mid-ocean off the Canadian coast; about 123 perish . 18 April, ,,

Laxham (capt. Lothian), English steamer, and *Gijon*, Spanish steamer, sunk by collision in a fog off Cape Finisterre; about 130 perish; many picked up by *Santo Domingo* (s) . night, 21 July, ,,

Dione, steamer, sunk by collision with *Camden*, steamer, near Gravesend; about 17 drowned; soon after midnight . . . . 2-3 Aug. ,,

[capt. of the *Dione* punished for reckless navigation, Aug.]

Wasp, H.M. gun-boat (see under *Navy*).

"*Little Beck*," stranded near the mouth of the Maas; 14 drowned . . . . 26 Oct. ,,

Indus, P. & O. company's steamer, wrecked on coast of Ceylon . . . . . 8 Nov. ,,

Durango, screw steamer, run down by *Luke Bruce*, iron barque, in the English channel; 20 lives lost 27 Nov. ,,

Pochard, steamer, foundered off Holyhead; crew lost . . . . 7 Dec. ,,

Mignonette, yacht; sailed from Southampton to Australia, 19 May; foundered in a storm about 1600 miles from the Cape; 3 men and a boy escaped in a boat, without provisions, 5 July; proposed killing of one by lot rejected by Brooks, boy (Richard Parker) killed by captain, and eaten, 20th day, *et seq.*; men picked up by German barque, *Montezuma*, 24th day, and carried to Falmouth; capt. Thos. Dudley and Edwin Stephens, mate, tried for murder at Exeter; facts affirmed, 6 Nov.; affirmed by lord chief justice and other judges in Queen's bench, 4 Dec.; sentence of death passed, 9 Dec.;

reprieved, 6 months' imprisonment without labour . . . . 13 Dec. 1884
Admiral Moorsom, L. and N. W. R.'s steamer, sunk near Holyhead by collision with *Santa Clara* (American); capt. Weeks, and about 4 perish 15 Jan. 1885
Cheerful, Liverpool steamer, collision with H.M.S. *Hecla* in the Bristol channel, 13 lives lost in a fog, 4 a.m. . . . . 21 July, ,,
Yarra Yarra, Liverpool barque, 27 lives lost, announced . . . . 11 Sept. ,,
Dolphin, steamer (Gen. Nav. St. Co.), sunk by collision with the *Brenda*, eight perish, 18 Sept. ,,
Merchantman, lost on Sand Heads; about 70 lives lost . . . . Sept. ,,
Albula, British ship, wrecked during typhoon off Loochoo islands, 10 perish . . . . 14 Oct. ,,
Algoma, Canadian steamer, foundered in lake Superior; 45 lives lost . . . . 7 Nov. ,,
Corinth, Union line steamer, sunk by collision with H.M.S. *Firebrand* . . . . March, 1886
Oregon, Cunard steamer, foundered (without loss of life), by collision with an unknown schooner near Long Island in America; schooner sunk with all on board . . . . . . 14 March, ,,
Ly-ee-Moon, an iron steamer, Australasian steam navigation company, wrecked off Green Cape, between Melbourne and Sydney; 76 persons drowned . . . . . . 30 March, ,,
Ferntower, British steamer, foundered near Saigon; about 50 lives lost . . . . . 26 Aug. ,,
Malleny, Liverpool iron steamer, foundered on the Tuskar reef, Bristol channel; all hands lost in the gale (about 20) . . . . . 15 Oct. ,,
Many vessels lost, many injured, and great loss of life during a severe gale . . 14–16 Oct. ,,
Teviotdale, steamer of Glasgow, lost on the Carmarthen coast; 18 lives lost . . . 15 Oct. ,,
Keilawarra and *Helen Nicholl* collision (42 lives lost) off the coast of Queensland; announced 9 Dec. ,,
Sultan, British ironclad, and *Ville de Victoria*, French steamer, collision in Lisbon harbour; the latter vessel sunk; 35 lives lost . 23 Dec. ,,
Kapunda, emigrant ship for Australia, said to have foundered by collision with *Ada Melmore* off Brazil; about 298 perish, 3 a.m. 20 Jan.; officers of the *Ada Melmore* censured . . . 29 March, 1887
Victoria, London & Brighton company's steamer, during fog struck on rock at Point D'Ailly; no fog horn sounded, about 16 lives lost out of 90 passengers through panic and recklessness; the rest saved by skill and courage of the captain and officers . . . . . . 13 April, ,,
Tasmania, P. & O. steamer wrecked on Monachi rocks, Corsica; 23 lives lost, including captain Perrin . . . . 17 April, ,,
Volta, Eastern Telegraph company's steamer, wrecked off Myconos, Greece; 12 lives lost, 18 April, ,,
Benton, steamer, of Singapore, foundered, with collision; about 150 lives lost, announced 28 April, ,,
Destruction of a Pearl fishing fleet, N.E. coast of Australia, with a loss of 550 lives, in a hurricane on 22 April: reported . . . . 28 April, ,,
John Knox, British steamer, wrecked at St. John's; 27 lost . . . . 4 May, ,,
City of Montreal (cotton ship), Inman steamer, burnt 400 miles off Newfoundland on her way from New York to Liverpool . . . 10 Aug. ,,
Monarch, pleasure yacht, founders near Ilfracombe; 11 lives lost . . . . . . 26 Aug. ,,
Falls of Bruar, of Glasgow, sunk off Yarmouth; 24 lives lost . . . . . . 2 Sept. ,,
Lydia, British schooner, lost in a hurricane in the North Atlantic; 15 lives lost . . Sept. ,,
Lanoma, iron barque, wrecked near Weymouth; 12 lives lost . . . . . . 8 March, 1888
City of Corinth sunk by collision with *Tasmania* near Dungeness . . . . . 9 March, ,,
Smyrna, sailing vessel, loses 12 men by collision with the *Moto*, steamer, off Dorset coast, 28 April, ,,
Trevelyan, emigrant ship, sunk off Cape Agulhas, all on board lost . . . . 3 June, ,,
Star of Greece wrecked in Aldinga Bay, near Adelaide; 17 lives lost . . . 13 July, 1888
Earl of Wemyss and *Ardencaple*, Glasgow barques, collision, 16 lives lost . . . . 8 Sept. ,,
Collision between Glasgow steamer *Neptune* and Russian steamer *Archangel* at Christiania; 18 lives lost . . . . 19 Oct. ,,
Nor, Norwegian barque, and *Saxmundham*, steamer from the Tyne; collision; 12 lives lost, 4 Nov. ,,
Steamer *Hartlepool* wrecked on a rock at Naalevig; 17 lives lost . . . . . . 6 Dec. ,,
British steamer *Priam*, wrecked near Cape Finisterre; about five lives lost . . . 12 Jan. 1889
Nereid, steamer, of Newcastle, collision with the Scotch ship *Killochan* off Dungeness; 23 lives lost . . . . 3 Feb. ,,
Collision of ship *Largo Bay* with steamer *Glencoe* which founders off Beachy Head; all hands lost, 4 Feb. ,,
Wreck of the Grimsby fishing fleet; 73 lives lost, 9 Feb. ,,
Cotopaxi, Pacific steamer, struck on unknown reef, Smyth's channel, straits of Magellan, and foundered; no lives lost . . . . 15 April, ,,
Altmore, British steamer, struck on rocks off Fiji islands; about 12 persons drowned 22 April, ,,
The *German Emperor*, screw steamer, ran into the *Beresford*, anchored off Dover, in a fog, and sank; nine missing . . . . . . 21 May, ,,
Gettysburg, barque, of Aberdeen, wrecked on a coral reef off Morant Cayes, 33 miles from Jamaica, with a crew of 16 hands, 30 March–1 April; by very great exertions, the captain and part of the crew succeeded in getting on the desolate isle, where they stayed, living on shell-fish, &c. On 22 April two men on a raft started for Jamaica and landed seven miles from Morant Bay, 24 April. On their reaching Kingston, H.M.S. *Forward* was sent off, and brought the captain and the rest of the crew to Kingston, 27 April, whence they were conveyed to England, having lost seven of their number, where they arrived . . . . 18 May, ,,
Isaac Houston, British schooner, foundered in a storm off Milwaukee; 16 lives lost; reported 14 June, ,,
The *Rapel* steamer wrecked on Huamblin island, S. American coast; 11 men drowned, reported, 2 Aug. ,,
Earnmore, Newcastle steamer, foundered in a cyclone off the Bahamas; the crew entered two boats, the captain, with 18 men, not heard of since—the first mate and 6 men nearly starving, were picked up and landed at Nassau, New Providence, 30 Sept. . . . . . 5 Sept. ,,
H.M.S. *Lilly* wrecked off Labrador coast (see *Navy*), 16 Sept. ,,
The *Florence*, screw steamer, foundered off Calf of Man, 10 lives lost. . . . . about 17 Sept. ,,
Minnie Swift, a Nova Scotian sailing ship, sunk by collision with the *Géographique*, off St. Pierre, France, 15 persons drowned . . . 20 Oct. ,,
Santiago, British screw steamer, on her way from New York to Hull, burnt; all hands saved by *A. J. Fuller* . . . . 29 Nov. ,,
Cleddy, steamer, sank after collision with *Isle of Cyprus*, steamer, off St. Catherine's, about 13 lives lost . . . . 20 Dec. ,,
Ovington, steamer, sunk by collision with *Queen Victoria*, near Greenock, six lives lost . 29 Dec. ,,
Loch Moidart, British iron ship, run ashore at Callandzoog, near Dieppe; 30 lives lost, reported, 27 Jan. 1890

[See *Storms* in Jan. 1890.]

Highgate, steamer, and *Sovereign*, ship, both sunk by collision off Lundy Island, 12 lives lost 19 Feb. ,,
Quetta, Queensland liner, struck on unknown rock, off cape York, Torres strait, and sank; about 133 lives lost out of 282; captain exonerated, 28 Feb. ,,
Virent, steamer, wrecked off Ferrol, 15 lives lost, about 22 March, ,,
Ethel Gwendoline, steamer, foundered off Rattray-head, Aberdeenshire; 7 men drowned 21 March, ,,

City of Paris, Inman Atlantic steamer, with above 680 passengers and 370 crew, left New York, 19 March, and was due at Queenstown, 26 March; on 25 March, about 5.45 P.M., the starboard engine broke down; the inflow of water stopped the other engine, and eventually the vessel was without machinery or sailing apparatus, a helpless log; a lifeboat was launched on 27 March, help arrived on 28 March, and without losing a single life, the vessel was towed into Queenstown 29 March, 1890

Dacca, British India company's steamer, foundered on a reef of rocks 400 miles from Suez; passengers, mostly emigrants to Queensland, got on to the reef, the officers and crew remained on board, were saved by the *Rosario* steamer; the *Palamcotta* took those on the reef to Suez 16 May *et seq.* ,,

[The disaster attributed to the unskilful navigation of the chief officer, 30 June.]

Gulf of Aden, steamer, foundered on the way from Liverpool to Valparaiso; 73 lives lost . 12 May, ,,

Ethel, barque, bound for Brisbane, sunk in the channel near Portland, by collision with the *Umbilo*, screw steamer; 4 lives lost . 25 June, ,,

The fishing fleets on the north and west coasts of Scotland suffered much by disasters; about 60 persons perished, reported . . 28 June, ,,

Egypt, Atlantic liner, of Liverpool, left New York 10 July; burnt at sea, 17, 18 July; all hands (95) saved by the *Gustav Oscar*; carried to Dover by the *Manhattan* . . . . . 24 July, ,,

Halcyon, British steamer, sunk by collision with *Rheubina*, off coast of Spain; 13 lives lost, reported . . . . 11 Aug. ,,

The *Portuense*, Liverpool steamer, founders during a cyclone, 250 miles from Barbadoes, the captain and most of the crew drowned . . 28 Aug. ,,

The *Melmerby*, Liverpool barque, wrecked off Roys Island; 15 men in the longboat drowned . 5 Oct. ,,

H.M.S. *Serpent*, cruiser, wrecked off the coast of Corunna; about 173 lives lost (see *Navy*), 11 Nov. ,,

Calypso, Bristol screw steamer, sunk by collision with the *Pinzon*, Spanish steamer, off Folkestone, 24 Nov. ,,

Uppingham, Cardiff steamer, bound for China, struck on a rock below Hartland Quay, Cornwall; about 7 men drowned . . . 23 Nov. ,,

Westbourne, Hull steamer, wrecked off Theodosia, Black Sea; 18 lives lost . . . . 24 Nov. ,,

Talookdar, British steel ship, sunk by collision with the *Libussa*, German ship, between the Cape de Verde and Cape Rocque; 22 lives lost 13 Dec. ,,

Shanghai, China Navigation Co.'s steamship (capt. Martin); near Ching Kiang, burnt; nearly 300 lives said to be lost . . . . . 25 Dec. ,,

Bear, steamer, sunk by collision off St. Abb's Head, Firth of Forth; 13 men drowned . 11 Jan. 1891

Chiswick, London steamer, struck on a reef off Scilly; 11 out of 19 men drowned . . 5 Feb. ,,

The *Queen*, British barque, sunk by collision with the *Ipswich*, between Antwerp and Cardiff; the captain and 6 men drowned . 5 A.M. 21 Feb. ,,

Bay of Panama, steel ship, from Calcutta, for Dundee (about 27 lives lost); *Marana*, iron steamer (about 22 lives lost), and about 13 other vessels (about 40 persons drowned), all wrecked off the Falmouth coast, during the great snowstorm, 9, 10 March, ,,

The *Utopia*, British steamer, capt. M'Keague, conveying 830 Italian emigrants, with 50 crew, from Naples to New York, sunk during a gale by collision with H.M.S. ironclad *Anson*, at anchor in the Bay of Gibraltar; about 538 passengers and 26 of the crew drowned. Heroic exertions were promptly made by the crews of all the ships in the harbour, to save life; of these, two brave men of the *Immortalité*, James Croton and George Hales, were drowned, 7 P.M. 17 March; above 1,150*l*. (Italian government, 200*l*.) subscribed for the relief of the survivors . . . March, ,,

The marine court censures capt. M'Keague for grave error of judgment, . . 25 March, ,,

[The *Utopia* was raised under the direction of Mr. Armit, 8 July, 1891.]

Strathairly, British steamer, wrecked off the coast of North Carolina; 19 lives lost, reported, 26 March, 1891

Chapman, missionary schooner, wrecked off the coast of Tahiti; 16 persons drowned, reported, 30 March, ,,

Glamorgan, steamer, sunk by collision with *P. Caland*, Dutch American steamer, in mid-channel, between Dover and Folkestone, 15 April, ,,

St. Catharis, steamer, wrecked off the Caroline Islands, reported; 90 persons drowned . April, ,,

Lestris and *Mersey*, two steamers, sunk by collision in the Mersey; several lives lost . 23 May, ,,

Dunholme, steamer, of W. Hartlepool, sunk by collision with the Glasgow steamer *Kinloch*, near Dover; 17 lives lost . . 2.30 A.M. 7 July, ,,

Gambier, screw-steamer, sunk by collision with the *Easby* in Port Phillip Bay, Melbourne; about 21 lives lost . . . . . 28 Aug. ,,

Dunmurry, British steamer, sunk during a hurricane, 250 miles from Halifax, Nova Scotia; 8 lives lost . . . . . . about 1 Sept. ,,

*Wolviston*e, steamer, left Bristol for New York, 11 Sept.; disabled by a gale, crew takes to lifeboats, 22 Sept.; 9 men rescued, the captain and 11 men missing . . . . . . 15 Oct. ,,

30 vessels wrecked off the coast of Labrador, and about 50 lives lost during a gale, reported, 23 Oct. ,,

Charlwood, barque, sunk by collision with the *Boston*, near the Eddystone lighthouse; 15 lives lost . . . . . . 4 A.M. 26 Oct. ,,

Moselle, royal mail steamer, struck on a reef, 10 miles from Colon; totally wrecked, only the captain drowned . . . . . . 28 Oct. ,,

Parsee, schooner, coming from Funck island, wrecked on a reef; 7 lives lost, reported 6 Nov. ,,

Enterprise, Indian marine steamer, founders off Port Blair, Andaman islands, during a cyclone: about 70 lives lost, 6 saved . . . . 2 Nov. ,,

Benvenue, full-rigged ship, bound for Sydney, wrecked off Sandgate; 27 persons suspended in the rigging for 16 hours, were saved with great difficulty by the Sandgate lifeboat, and taken to Folkestone; capt. James Moddrel and 4 men drowned . . . . 11 Nov. ,,

Many wrecks during gales . . . 10 Nov. *et seq.* ,,

Enterkin, steel sailing ship sunk off Ramsgate, near Galloper sands, during a gale; about 27 lives lost . . . . 11 Dec. ,,

Abyssinia, Guion screw-steamer, burnt, 5 days out from New York; the passengers and crew rescued by the *Spree* . . . . . 18 Dec. ,,

Childwall, barque, sunk by collision with *Noordland*, steamer, off Flushing; 15 men drowned, 2 Jan. 1892

Namchow, a British steamer, foundered off Cupchi Point, China; about 509 lives lost, about 14 Jan. ,,

Forest Queen, steamer, sunk by collision with the *Loughborough*, steamer, near Flamborough Head; about 14 lives lost . . . . . 24 Feb. ,,

County of Salop, steamer, stranded in Widemouth Bay, Cornwall; the 30 persons on board saved by the Bude Rocket Brigade . . 10 March, ,,

Walmer Castle, Deal lugger, foundered near the Isle of Wight during a gale; 7 men drowned, 15 March, ,,

Earl of Aberdeen, barque, wrecked on the Pembrokeshire coast; 16 lives lost . . 15 May, ,,

Petrolea, British petroleum steamer, blown up in Blaye harbour, near Bordeaux: 18 deaths, 14 June, ,,

City of Chicago, Inman Atlantic liner, run ashore near Old Head of Kinsale, during a fog; passengers, &c., landed, 1 July; totally wrecked, 7 July; Mr. Arthur Redford the master's certificate suspended for 9 months . . 21 July, ,,

Peter Stuart, British ship, struck on a rock near Yarmouth, Nova Scotia; 14 deaths . 4 July, ,,

Ajax, steamer, sunk by collision with *Rundeberg*, steamer; 35 deaths . . . . . 9 Aug. ,,

Thracia, barque, capsized near Port Erin, Isle of Man; 17 lives lost . . . . . 14 Aug. ,,

Anglia, Anchor Line steamer, capsized near the mouth of the Hooghly; 12 lives lost . 24 Aug. ,,

Stranger, British schooner, capsized in the Gulf of Mexico; 16 deaths . . . . . 10 Sept. ,,

Cashier, British schooner, sunk by collision with an unknown ship, on the Grand Bank of Newfoundland; 19 lives lost, reported . 20 Sept. 1892

The *Premier*, Canadian steamer, crushed by collision with the steam-collier *Williamette* off Whidby Island in the Pacific; five deaths, 8 Oct. ,,

The *Bokhara*, Peninsular and Oriental steamer, on her way from Shanghai to Hong Kong, during a typhoon, wrecked off Sand Island, in the Pescadores group; the fires were put out and the engines stopped; Capt. Sams and about 125 persons drowned; 23 persons saved . 10 Oct. ,,

Roumania, British Anchor line steamer, wrecked during a gale, off Gronho, on the coast of Portugal, on her way from Liverpool to Bombay; about 106 persons drowned, 9 saved . 28 Oct. ,,

The *Chishima*, Japanese cruiser, sunk in collision with the *Ravenna*, P. & O. steamer, in the Gogo Shima straits, 75 deaths, Nov. 1892; much litigation, 1892–5; appeal of the company to the judicial committee (privy council) allowed, and suit dismissed with costs . 20 July, 1895

Greystroke, Hartlepool steamship, wrecked outside Cuxhaven; the crew, about 24, lost, about 28 Nov. 1892

Dilsberg, Glasgow steamer, wrecked on the Long Sands, Kent; about 7 deaths . . . 9 Dec. ,,

Trinacria, Glasgow steamer, wrecked off Cape Vilaño, Spain; about 31 persons drowned 7 Feb. 1893

Pomeranian, Glasgow steamer, left Greenock for New York on 27 Jan., damaged during a gale; 12 deaths, 4 Feb.; returned to Greenock 11 Feb. ,,

Coanza, British steamer, wrecked on Baiyah Rock, near Sinou, W. Africa; many lives lost, reported 22 Feb. ,,

Countess Evelyne, Cardiff screw steamer, sunk by collision with the *City of Hamburg* near Trevose Head; about 24 lives lost . . . . 3 May, ,,

H.M.S. *Victoria* disaster, see *Navy of England*, 22 June, ,,

Many wrecks through gales . . . 16–19 Nov. ,,

Hampshire steamer, of London, owners Messrs. MacBeth and Grey of Glasgow (Capt. Weir and 22 men), sunk off St. Ives, Cornwall; all lost except Mr. James Swanson, chief officer 18 Nov. ,,

Jason, from Calcutta to Boston, U.S., off Eastham, Massachusetts; 27 deaths . reported 6 Dec. ,,

Colleen, Belfast barque, wrecked off Ballycotton, Ireland; capt. Bartlett and 10 men drowned 7–8 Jan. 1894

Allonby, steamer, in the bay of Biscay; 11 lives lost 14 Jan. ,,

Clytha, sunk by collision with the *Cadoxton* in the Barry Roads; 7 deaths . . . . 17 Feb. ,,

Port Yarrock, a Glasgow barque, left Cardiff for Mexico, 27 Oct. 1893, insufficiently manned and badly provisioned; the crew suffered greatly during the voyage; on her return, she was driven ashore in Brandon bay, co. Kerry, and the crew of 21 perished, 29 Jan. 1894; the court of inquiry severely blamed Robert John Rowat, the managing owner, for neglect of duty, and fined him 75*l*. . . . . . . 27 March, ,,

The *Valkyrie*, cutter, formerly belonging to lord Dunraven, foundered off the coast of Africa; all hands lost . . . . . reported 16 May ,,

Cambuswallace, barque, from Glasgow, wrecked off Stradbroke island; 5 deaths . reported 4 Sept. ,,

Brandon, British barque, driven on the Caïcos reef off U.S.A.; the capt. and 13 sailors drowned 26 Sept. ,,

Tormes, steamer, from Malaga to Liverpool, wrecked off Crow rock, near Pembroke; 21 lives lost 30 Oct. ,,

Wairarapa, Union steamer, from Sydney to Auckland, wrecked on Gt. Barrier island off New Zealand; the captain and 125 lives lost 29 Oct. ,,

Culmore of Londonderry, from Hamburg to Barry, wrecked off Spurn Head; 22 deaths . 14 Nov. ,,

Earl of Zetland, iron ship from London to Melbourne, went ashore off Dungeness . . . . 4 Dec. ,,

Abydos, steamer, of Glasgow, foundered off Isle of Man; 19 lives lost . . . . about 22 Dec. ,,

Many wrecks in the gale . . . 21–22 Dec. ,,

Ossco, iron barque, wrecked at Holyhead; 26 lives lost . . . . 30 Dec. ,,

Reported loss of the British steamer *Prescott*, from Sunderland to Marseilles; capt. Hind and 22 others drowned . . . . . . 29 Dec. 1894

Escurial, steamer, of Glasgow, wrecked off Cornwall; 11 lives lost . . . . 25 Jan. 1895

Colima, Pacific company's steamer from San Francisco to Panama, wrecked off S.W. coast of Mexico; 108 deaths . . . . 27 May ,,

Dundrennan, of Liverpool, sunk off Struis point; 25 deaths . . . . reported 11 April, ,,

Maritana, steamer, of Sunderland, sunk by collision off Brest with the *Esmeralda* of Glasgow; 11 deaths 13 May, ,,

Cleveland, steamer, from Newcastle, sunk in collision with the *Duffield* off Dover, crew saved 27 July, ,,

Catterthun, steamer from Sydney to Hong Kong, wrecked on the Seal rocks off Cape Hawk; 65 deaths . . . . 8 Aug. ,,

Seaford, Channel steamer, on her way from Dieppe to Newhaven, sunk by collision with the *Lyon*, cargo steamer, in a fog; all saved . 20 Aug. ,,

Iona, Scotch steamer, by a fire off Gunfleet, Thames; 6 women and a child perished; fire extinguished by the crew . . . 1.20 a.m. 16 Sept. ,,

Livonia, British steamer, sunk by collision with the *Napier*, British steamer, off Oeland; 11 deaths, reported . . . . . . 10 Oct. ,,

Leo, British steamer, wrecked off Stalman, Denmark; 15 deaths, reported . . . 16 Nov. ,,

Joseph, schooner, sank off the Lizard; the captain and 2 of the crew drowned . . about 24 Nov. ,,

Principia, steamship (capt. Stannard), from Dundee to New York, after a fire, wrecked off the Faroe isles; 28 lives lost, only one of the crew saved . . . . 21 Nov. ,,

Alicia, steamer, of West Hartlepool, sunk in collision with the *Netley Abbey*, off Cromer; 4 deaths, reported . . . . . 23 Dec. ,,

Moresby, Liverpool schooner, wrecked in Dungarvan bay, Waterford; 19 lives lost . . 24 Dec. ,,

Fortuna, schooner, sunk in collision with the *Barnstaple* steamer, off Highland Light, Cape Cod, U.S., 9 deaths . . . . 13 Jan. 1896

Matadi, British steamer, destroyed by an explosion of gunpowder, at Boma, Congo State; 25 deaths 7 March, ,,

The Queen of Mistley, sunk in collision with the steamer *Sayn*, of Rotterdam, off Newhaven; the captain and 3 others drowned . 12 March, ,,

Firth of Solway, barque, sunk in collision with the *Marsden* steamer, in Dublin bay; 15 deaths, 19 April, ,,

Bertha, steamer, sunk in collision with the *Claverley*, steamer, off Southwold; 6 deaths . 14 June, ,,

Drummond Castle (which see), wrecked off Ushant, France, 247 deaths . . . . 16 June, ,,

Royalist, schooner, foundered in a gale, at Holyhead; 1 man saved . . . . . . 8 Oct. ,,

Moss Brow, British steamer, wrecked off Finland; the captain and 14 men perish . . 21 Oct. ,,

P. H. Dawson, British schooner, wrecked off Point Barfleur; the captain, his wife, and crew drowned, 8 Nov. ,,

Memphis, steamer, from Montreal, ran ashore on Mizen Head; 9 deaths . . . . 17 Nov. ,,

Warren Hastings, troopship, wrecked off the Isle of Réunion; 2 deaths . . . . 14 Jan. 1897

John o' Gaunt, Liverpool barque, burnt; captain killed by an explosion, at Tocopilla . 23 Jan. ,,

City of Agra, British steamer, wrecked off Corunna; capt. Frame and 55 out of 75 persons saved; reported . . . . 6 Feb. ,,

Cyanus, Glasgow steamer, from Bilbao, wrecked near Ushant; 20 deaths; reported . 12 Feb. ,,

Zuleika, British ship; capt. Bremmer and 11 men drowned off Palliser, New Zealand; announced, 21 April, ,,

Collynie, steamer, sunk in collision with the *Girnigoe*, near Aberdeen; 11 deaths . . 3 May, ,,

Pearl, schooner, sunk in the channel by the *Aral*, steamer; 4 deaths . . . . . . 5 June, ,,

Susannah Kelly, steamer, sunk in a gale in Belfast Lough; the captain and 9 men drowned 16 June, ,,

Aden, P. and O. steamer, wrecked off Socotra, Indian ocean; the captain, 13 officers, the crew (20 Europeans, and 33 natives), and 25 passengers drowned (45 saved by the *Mayo* steamer), 9 June, ,,

Tasmania, steamer, from Wellington to Sydney, wrecked off North island, New Zealand; 10 deaths . . . . 29 July, 1897

Cordillera, British barque, wrecked after leaving Valparaiso; capt. Everitt and 16 men drowned, 7 Nov. ,,

The *Labarrouere*, Cardiff steamer, sunk in collision with unknown sailing vessel, off Lundy island; capt. Young and 4 others drowned . 25 Nov. ,,

Cleveland, steamer, from San Francisco, wrecked in Barclay sound; 9 deaths; reported 16 Dec. ,,

Clarissa Radcliffe, Cardiff steamer, wrecked off Cape St. Vincent; 16 deaths . . . . . 1 Jan. 1898

Channel Queen, steamer, from Plymouth, wrecked on the Black Rock, off Guernsey; 12 passengers and some of the crew drowned . . 1 Feb. ,,

Legislator, steamer, from Liverpool for Colon, burnt; 4 deaths . . . . . 13 Feb. ,,

Asia, British ship, from Manila, wrecked off Nantucket; 15 deaths; reported . . . 23 Feb. ,,

Midas, sailing ship, capt. Messenger and 22 men lost off Japan . . . . . . Feb. ,,

Helen W. Almy, barque, from San Francisco to Copper river, capsized, 41 deaths, about 23 Mar. ,,

Leechmere, steamer, lost in a gale, capt. Lawson and crew, about 18, perished . . 24–26 March, ,,

Marlborough, British ship, wrecked in the N. Atlantic, 15 deaths . . . . . 3 April, ,,

Maitland, steamer, wrecked, 18 deaths and 28 missing, and the *Merksworth*, steamer, 9 deaths, off Sydney . . . . 8, 9 May, ,,

Benholm, steamer (Liverpool), sunk in collision with the *Klondyke*, steamer (Antwerp), off the Skerries, 10 deaths . . . . . 14 May, ,,

Mecca, steamer, sunk by collision with the *Lindula*, in the Bay of Bengal, capt. Parkman and about 52 others drowned . . . . . 24 May, ,,

Gypsy Princess, Nova Scotia schooner, sunk in collision with the German steamer *Ems*; 6 deaths; reported . . . . 15 June, ,,

A number of fishing-boats wrecked in the Baltic, about 120 deaths . . . . . 19 Sept. ,,

The *Rheubina*, British steamer, sunk in collision with the *Cartagena*, Spanish steamer, 15 deaths, 22 Sept. ,,

Atlanta, sailing vessel, wrecked off Newport, Oregon, 28 deaths . . . . . 18 Nov. ,,

Mohegan, Atlantic Transport co. steamer, wrecked on the Manacles, off Cornwall (error of navigation), capt. R. Griffith and 106 drowned, 14 Oct. ,,

Blengfell, petroleum ship, from New York to London, burnt by an explosion off the N. Foreland, capt. J. Johnston and 8 others killed, 17 Oct. ,,

Many wrecks in the North Sea, with loss of life, 17–20 Oct. ,,

FitzJames, steamer, wrecked off Beachy Head, the capt. and 8 men drowned . . . . 24 Nov. ,,

Clan Drummond, Clan Line steamer, wrecked in the Bay of Biscay, capt. Crockett and 36 others drowned . . . . 28 Nov. ,,

Village Belle, schooner, wrecked off Havana, the capt. and 7 men drowned, reported . 2 Dec. ,,

Londonian, liner of Hull, wrecked off the Fastnet, 17 deaths. . . . . 29 Nov. ,,

Ilios, steamer, sunk by collison with the *Pierremont* steamer off Soutar, South Shields, 20 deaths, 16 Dec. ,,

Collision between the *Du Guesclin*, French steamer, and the *Ross-shire*, steamer, 12 deaths 4 Jan. 1899

Wooller, steamer, wrecked off Ushant, 19 deaths, 2 Jan. ,,

Andelana, British ship, capsized off Tacoma, the capt. and 18 men lost . . . . 14 Jan. ,,

Arno, steam collier, wrecked near Selsey Bill, 13 deaths . . . . 11 Feb. ,,

Many wrecks during gales . . . . . Feb. ,,

Missing steamers in the Atlantic through storms: 8 British, 1 American, 1 German, 255 deaths, reported . . . . 16 March, ,,

Stella, excursion steamer, from Southampton to Guernsey (S.W. Ry.), wrecked while going at full speed in a fog, at 4 p.m., on the Black rock, near the Casquets, 8 miles off Alderney (140 passengers, crew 40), capt. Reeks and 104 others drowned; no panic, great heroism shown (she sank in 8 minutes), 30 March; the queen's message and French sympathy expressed, 4 April; fund closed, grand total, 15,605*l.* 5*s.* 9*d.*, Sept. 1899

General Whitney, steamer, sunk off Florida, 27 deaths, reported . . . . . 23 April, ,,

Loch Sloy, barque, wrecked on Kangaroo island, S. Australia; 30 deaths . . . . 24 April, ,,

Resolute, steamer, sunk in collision with the *Scindia* steamer, off Calcutta in the Hooghli, the captain and 53 of the crew drowned . 14 Aug. ,,

Scotsman, Dominion liner, wrecked off Belle isle, Newfoundland; 15 deaths . . . 21 Sept. ,,

Niagara, Canadian steamer, wrecked near Long Point, Lake Erie, 16 deaths . . . 5 Dec. ,,

Ariosto, steamer, wrecked off N. Carolina, U.S.; 21 deaths . . . . 24 Dec. ,,

Planet Mercury, steamer, of Liverpool, wrecked off Yarmouth, N.S.; crew of 40 and several others and about 160 cattle lost . . end of Feb. 1900

Chibine, pilgrim ship to Mecca, wrecked in the Red sea with loss of life . . . 8 March, ,,

Cuvier, Glasgow steamer, sunk in collision with an unknown steamer, 27 deaths . 9 March, ,,

Glenelg, Melbourne steamer, wrecked off Gippsland, 30 deaths . . . . . 25 March, ,,

Embleton, sailer, sunk in a fog by the *Campania* Cunard liner, in St. George's channel, 11 deaths, 21 July, ,,

Dromedary, steamer, run into in a fog by the *Alligator* steamer, in Belfast lough, 12 deaths and 50 injured . . . . . . 21 July, ,,

Gordon Castle, Glasgow steamer, and the Hamburg steamer *Stormarn*, sunk by collision during a fog in Cardigan bay; capt. Casey and 19 others of the *Gordon Castle* lost . . . . 16 Sept. ,,

Charkieh, Khedivial Co.'s steamer, wrecked near the isle of Andros, about 50 deaths, reported, 21 Sept. ,,

City of Vienna, Dublin steamer, sunk in collision with unknown steamer (believed to have also sunk) off Land's End, 20 deaths . 7 Nov. ,,

Monticello, steamer, sunk off Nova Scotia, 36 deaths, 10 Nov. ,,

St. Olaf, steamer, wrecked off the mouth of the St. Lawrence, 26 deaths . . . . . 21 Nov. ,,

Rossgull, steamer, wrecked off Jersey; capt. Blamfield and 9 of the crew drowned . . 4 Dec. ,,

Mobile, steamer, with 26 hands, lost in the Atlantic Dec. ,,

Primrose Hill, a sailing ship, wrecked near Holyhead, 33 deaths . . . . . . 28 Dec. ,,

Kaisari, steamer, of London, wrecked off Réunion, 25 deaths . . . . 23 Nov. ,,

Holland, steamer, wrecked in the Nieuwe Waterweg, Rotterdam, 15 deaths . . . 28 Jan. 1901

Lucerne, steamer, lost off Newfoundland, 24 deaths, reported . . . . 13 Feb. ,,

Homer, steamer, sunk in collision with the *Hopper*, Russian barque, off Spurn Head, 16 deaths, 15 Feb. ,,

Rydalmere, sailer, lost off Cape de Gata, 25 deaths, 19 March, ,,

Tay, steamer, sunk in collision with German steamer *Chemnitz* off Flushing, 16 deaths, 21 March, ,,

Taher, steamer, wrecked at Port Louis, Mauritius, 20 deaths . . . . 22 March, ,,

Falkland, barque, wrecked off the Scilly isles, 6 deaths . . . . 22 June, ,,

Kincora, steamer, sunk in collision with the *Oceanic*, Atlantic liner, in St. George's channel, 7 deaths . . . . 8 Aug. ,,

Islander, steamer, Canadian Pacific liner, sunk off Douglas island, Alaska, 65 deaths, no panic, 15 Aug. ,,

Noranmore, steamer, sunk in a gale in the Black sea, 39 deaths . . . . . . 25 Aug. ,,

Perseverance, barque, with 14 men, lost in the Arctic regions . . . . . after 22 Oct. ,,

Cobra, disaster, over 60 lost, and *Active*, wrecked at Granton, 19 lost (see *Navy*). 18 Sept. and 12 Nov. ,,

Many shipping disasters and great loss of life round the coast . . . . 12–14 Nov. ,,

Alfonso, steamer, run into in a fog by a Spanish collier, s. of Finisterre; both sank, 18 British and 1 of the Spanish steamer drowned . 4 Jan. 1902

Huronian, Allan steamer, lost at sea, left the Clyde . . . . 11 Feb. 1902
Tiber, steamer, lost off Halifax, U.S., 21 deaths, reported . . . . 4 March, ,,
Athena, steamer, wrecked off Campana island, Patagonia, capt. Jones and 16 men lost, 22 March, ,,
Cambrian Princess, sunk in a fog in collision with the *Alma*, Channel steamer, 11 deaths, end March, ,,
Camorta, steamer, lost in a cyclone, in the Bay of Bengal; crew 89 and 650 native passengers, 6 May, ,,
Highfields, barque, sunk in collision with the German steamer *Kaiser*, at Cardiff, 23 deaths, 17 Aug. ,,
Elliott, barque, crew 16, missing since 19 Dec., reported 27 Aug. ,,
Great gale in Algoa bay, S. Africa; loss of shipping and about 51 lives . . . . 1 Sept. ,,
Bewick, steamer, sunk in a gale in the North sea, 11 deaths . . . . 12 Sept. ,,
Ventnor, steamer, struck off Cape Egmont, New Zealand, and sunk, 12 deaths . 26, 27 Oct. ,,
Defender, fishing-boat, wrecked at Lowestoft, 6 deaths . . . . 4 Nov. ,,
Elingamite, steamer, from Sydney for Auckland, wrecked on Three Kings island, over 38 lost; great heroism shown, 149 saved . 9 Nov. ,,
Sylvanus J. Macy, steamer, sunk in a gale on lake Erie, 15 deaths . . . . . . 28 Nov. ,,
Marlay, steam collier, sunk in Dublin Bay, 14 deaths . . . . 16 Dec. ,,
Grecian, steam trawler, lost in the North Sea, 9 deaths . . . . . . about 31 Dec. ,,
Manchester Merchant, steamer, with 7,000 bales of cotton on fire, scuttled in Dingle Bay, Kerry, 14, 15 Jan. 1903
Collision between the cruiser *Pioneer* and the torpedo-boat destroyer *Orwell*, off Corfu, 15 deaths . . . . 30 Jan. ,,
Mumbles lifeboat capsized in Swansea Bay, 6 lives lost . . . . 1 Feb. ,,
Olive, steamer, sunk in a gale near Edenton, N. Carolina, 18 deaths . . . . 10 Feb. ,,
Kelvinside, steamer, sunk at the mouth of the Para, Brazil, the captain and 8 men drowned, 18 Feb. ,,
Ottercaps, steamer, wrecked in a gale at Feuntenot, near Audierne, about 30 deaths . 26 Feb. ,,
Huddersfield, steamer, Antwerp to Grimsby, with foreign emigrants, sunk in the Schelde, 22 passengers drowned . . . . . . 26 May, ,,
Asequipa, of the Steam Navigation co., foundered at Valparaiso, 17 out of 80 persons reported saved . . . . 2 June, ,,
Rosa, with cargo of benzine, burnt at Vlaardingen, death of captain, 3 of crew injured . 21 Aug. ,,
Sutlej, cruiser, collides with and sinks barque *Charles Chalmers*, in North Sea, 4 drowned, 18 Sept. ,,
David Watson, with 200 passengers, on the St. John river (N.B.), totally burnt, 3 deaths, 20 Sept. ,,
Lady Head, Hudson's Bay co. ship, wrecked on the Gasket Shoal, in Hudson's Bay . . 25 Sept. ,,
Hardwick Hall, Ellerman steamer, Delagoa Bay to Calcutta, struck on Farquhar Island . 18 Oct. ,,
Loch Maree, Dundee steamer, founders near Cape Serrat, 9 of officers and crew missing . 31 Oct. ,,
Ovalau, steamer, burnt, near Lord Howe Island, 18 Nov. ,,
Spennymoor, steamer, foundered in open sea, 7 Dec. ,,

REMARKABLE CASES OF FOREIGN VESSELS WRECKED OR BURNT.

Arctic, U.S. mail steamer, by collision in a fog with the *Vesta*, French steamer, off Newfoundland; above 300 lives lost . . . . 27 Sept. 1854
Northern Belle, a large American vessel, was wrecked near Broadstairs. The American government sent 21 silver medals and 270*l.* to be distributed among the heroic boatmen of the place, who saved the crew . . 5-6 Jan. 1857
Pomona, an American ship, captain Merrihew (419 persons on board, from Liverpool to New York), was wrecked on Blackwater Bank, through the master mistaking the Blackwater for the Tuskar light, only 24 persons saved, night of 27-28 April, 1859
Lima, American barque with emigrants, wrecked off Barfleur; above 100 lives lost, 17 Feb. 1860. On the same rock, on 25 Nov. 1120, was wrecked the *Blanche Nef*, containing the children of Henry I. and a large number of attendants; in all 363 persons perished.
Schiller, Hamburg mail steamer, wrecked in a fog, on rocks off the Scilly isles; about 331 drowned, 7 May, 1875
Deutschland, fine Atlantic steamer, from Bremen to New York, during a gale, went on sandbank, the Kentish Knock, at mouth of the Thames; about 70 lost (many emigrants), 6 Dec. 1875. The *Liverpool*, tug steamer, saved a great many lives; on investigation, it was shown that there had been no delay in helping, and no robbery, 31 Dec. The captain censured for error in navigation, and want of judgment.
Grosser Kurfürst, the German ironclad, sunk by collision with *König Wilhelm*; about 300 lost, 31 May, 1878
Pomerania, Hamburg-American mail steamer, sunk off Folkestone, by *Moel Eilian*, iron bark, of Carnarvon; 162 saved by boats; about 48 missing; a little after midnight . . . 25 Nov. ,,
French steamer *Byzantin* sunk (losing above 200 lives) by collision with English steamer *Rinaldo*, in Dardanelles, during a fearful gale . 18 Dec. ,,
Arrogante, French ironclad battery, sank off Hyères isles; 47 drowned . . . 19 March, 1879
Vera Cruz, U.S. steamer, foundered through hurricane in N. Atlantic, 30 miles from shore; 11 out of 82 saved . . . . 4 Sept. 1880
Oncle Joseph, French steamer, sunk by collision with *Ortigia*, Italian steamer, off Spezzia; about 50 out of 300 saved . . . . . 24 Nov. ,,
Asia, N.W. transit service steamer, foundered near Lonely Island, in the Georgian bay, 20 miles from Point au Barrie; about 98 lost . 14 Sept. 1882
Cimbria, Hamburg steamer, sunk by collision with English steamer, *Sultan*, off coast of Holland; about 454 perish . . . . . 19 Jan. 1883
City of Columbus, U.S. passenger ship, ran on reef, coast of Massachusetts; 29 lives saved; about 97 perish: alleged negligence . . 18 Jan. 1884
Daniel Steinmann, White Cross steamer, struck on rock off Sambro' Isle, Nova Scotia; about 120 perish . . . . . . about 3 April, ,,
Senorine, French brig, wrecked off Great Bank, Newfoundland; about 62 perish . 6 May, ,,
W. A. Scholten, Dutch steamer, sunk by collision with *Rosa Mary* of Hartlepool, at anchor off Dover; about 130 persons perish, many saved by the crew of the *Ebro* of Sunderland, 19 Nov. 1887
Alfred D. Snow, American vessel, wrecked off Waterford; 28 perish . . . . 4 Jan. 1888
Collision between *Thingvalla* and *Geiser*, German steamers, off Sable Island, N. Atlantic; 105 lives in the *Geiser*, lost . . . . . 14 Aug. ,,
Collision between steamers *La France* (French) and *Sud America* (Italian) off the Canary Islands; about 87 lives lost . . . . 13 Sept. ,,
John Hanna, steamer, laden with cotton, burnt on the Mississippi; about 20 persons perish, 24 Dec. ,,
German and American war vessels wrecked off Samoa (see *Storms*) . . . 16 March, 1889
The *Comtesse de Flandre* cut in half by collision with the *Princess Henriette*, both Belgian mail boats; the captain and 14 others killed, prince Napoleon Bonaparte escapes; about 1.45 p.m. 20 March, ,,
Danmark, Danish emigrant vessel, sank in the Atlantic about 800 miles from Newfoundland; captain Murrell of the *Missouri*, Atlantic transport line, and his crew, with great energy rescued all on board (735). [He landed part on the Azores and part in Philadelphia.]* . . . 6 April, ,,

* At the Mansion House, on 24 May, 1889, captain Murrell, in the presence of distinguished company, received from the lord mayor a silver salver with an inscription, and a purse of money (about 500*l.*) from the citizens of London; the officers and crew also received testimonials.

Prins Frederik, Dutch mail steamer, outward bound for Java with troops and specie, sunk by collision with the *Marpessa*, British steamer, in a dense fog in the Channel. Great order maintained on the *Prins Frederik*; only 7 Dutch soldiers perished, out of the 170 persons on board, 25 June; the *Marpessa*, much injured, got to Falmouth . . . . . 27 June, 1890

Ertogrul, Turkish government cruiser, and the *Musasha Maru*, Japanese mail steamer (crews lost), founder in Japanese waters during a heavy gale (see *Turkey* and *Japan*) 18 Sept. ,,

Collision of the Spanish steamer *Vizcaya* with the *Cornelius Hargraves*, schooner, off New Jersey; both vessels sunk; the captain and about 60 persons of the *Vizcaya* drowned 30 Oct. ,,

The *Taormina*, Italian mail steamer, sunk by collision with the Greek steamer *Thessalia*, off Cape Sunium; about 60 lives lost, 2 A.M. . 12 Sept. 1891

Eider, German iron-screw steamer, six-masted (North German Lloyd's), from New York to Bremen, struck on rocks near the Isle of Wight during a fog, 31 Jan; capt. Heineke, crew 166, and 227 passengers, together with the mails, bars of silver, and other parts of the cargo saved by the great exertions of the lifeboats, 1–3 Feb.; the *Eider* lifted off the rocks about 7 March, and floated to Southampton* 29 March, 1892

Roosalka, Russian ironclad, foundered off the Finnish coast, possibly through an explosion; deaths reported 12 officers, 166 men, capt. Yenish, commander, total deaths about 200, 19 Sept. 1893

The *Vladimir* (Russian), sunk by collision with the *Columbia* (Italian), midnight off Tarhankut; about 100 deaths . . . . . 8 July, 1894

Elbe, N. German Lloyd steamer, from Bremen to New York, sunk in collision with the *Crathie* of Aberdeen off Lowestoft about 6 A.M.; 334 lives lost, including capt. von Gössel, the watch; 20 saved by Mr. Wm. Wright of the smack *Wildflower*, 30 Jan., 1895. The *Crathie* arrested at Rotterdam. Coroner's inquest at Lowestoft, the mate and look-out man of the *Crathie* censured for negligence; the captain exonerated, 1 May; the mate's certificate cancelled by the board of trade, 17 June, 1895. The court at Rotterdam declare the *Crathie* to be solely in fault, and adjudge 565,500*fl.* damages, with interest, 15 April, 1896

Reina Regente, Spanish cruiser, sunk off Cape Trafalgar; 400 lives lost (see *Spain*) . 10 March, 1895

Gravina, Spanish coasting steamer, wrecked off the Philippine isles in a cyclone; 168 drowned, 3 saved, reported . . . . . 22 May, ,,

Don Pedro, French steamer from Havre to La Plata with emigrants, wrecked off N. W. coast of Spain, 87 deaths . . . . 27 May, ,,

Maria P., Italian emigrant steamer to Brazil, sunk in collision with the *Ortigia* at the mouth of the Gulf of Spezzia; 148 deaths . 21 July, ,,

Sanchez Barcaiztegui, Spanish cruiser, sunk in collision with the *Mortera* steamer; about 20 deaths, including adm. Parejo, dr. Martin, and 4 officers . . . . . 19 Sept. ,,

Pacific, coal barque, of Dunkirk, sunk by collision with the *Emma*, German steamer; the captain, pilot, and 10 men drowned . . 14 Oct. ,,

Solferino, Italian emigrant steamer, wrecked off Ceuta; 20 deaths, reported . . 17 Nov. ,,

On Wo, steamer, sunk by collision with the steamer *Newchwang*, at Woosung, China; capt. Stessar and 5 English officers drowned; total deaths 200, 30 April, 1896

Alexandra, Swedish steamer, sunk by collision with the *Goole*, steamer, from Rotterdam, in the Humber; 10 lives lost . . . 8 Oct. ,,

Salier, North German Lloyd steamer, wrecked off Cape Corrubedo, N. Spain; capt. Wempe and 280 lives lost . . . . 7 Dec. ,,

Rajah, German ship of Bremen, foundered off Lundy island; 17 deaths . . . 8 Dec. ,,

* The German emperor presented 200*l.* to the Lifeboat Institution, and gold watches to some of the masters of lifeboats, April 1892.

Marie Fanny, French steamer, wrecked off the Casquets; 15 deaths . . . . 14 Dec. 1896

Siracusa, of Hamburg, wrecked off Newquay; all (24) lost . . . . . 3 March, 1897

Utrecht, steamer, from Rotterdam to Java, wrecked off Ushant; about 100 deaths . 4 or 5 March, ,,

Ville de St. Nazaire, French liner, lost off Cape Hatteras; about 65 deaths . . 8 March, ,,

Henri, French steamer, lost; 30 deaths, reported, 26 April, ,,

Vaillant, French fishing vessel, foundered off the Grand Banks, Newfoundland; 65 deaths, 14 April, ,,

Roedvar, Norwegian barque, and the *Firdene*, Dutch steamer, sunk in collision in the North sea; 19 deaths . . . . . 11 May, ,,

Ville de Malaga, French steamer, wrecked off the Casquets; 6 deaths . . . . 14 Aug. ,,

The *Ika*, Austrian pleasure steamer, sunk in collision with the *Tyria*, British steamer, off Fiume; 30 or 40 deaths . . . 20 Sept. ,,

The *Jokai*, Austrian steamer, sunk by collision with the *Baron Ardrossan*, in the Channel; 4 deaths . . . . . 25 Nov. ,,

Flachat (s), French liner, from Marseilles to Colon, wrecked off Point Anaga, Teneriffe; about 77 deaths . . . . . 16 Feb. 1898

Lydie, French steamer, lost in the Channel, 30 deaths . . . . . 24 March, ,,

La Bourgogne, French liner, bound from New York to Havre (160 miles N. of her true course and going at great speed), sunk in collision, during a dense fog, with the *Cromartyshire*, British barque, some 60 miles off Sable island, Nova Scotia; capt. Deloncle, and 545 passengers and crew drowned; 165 saved—including 1 woman, 104 of the crew, and 61 passengers* . 4 July, ,,

Portland, steamer, wrecked off Cape Cod, U.S. 157 deaths; 56 other vessels and barges lost along the New England coast; total deaths about 180 . . . . . 27 Nov. ,,

Algerois, French steamer, foundered near Bona 11 deaths . . . . . 5 Dec. ,,

Voorwaarts, Italian steamer, wrecked off Trevose Head, Cornwall, about 13 drowned . 2 Jan. 1899

Esperanza, Norwegian barque, wrecked off Cornwall, crew about 12 lost . . . 2 Jan. ,,

Idraet, Norwegian steamer, foundered in the North sea, 12 deaths . . . . 10 March, ,,

Hoche, French fishing boat, wrecked off Mizen Head, 24 deaths . . . . 11 April, ,,

Pierre le Grand, lost in a gale in the Mediterranean, about 60 drowned . . . mid Dec. ,,

Panillac, Atlantic steamer, from New York to Havre, lost, 37 deaths . . . mid Feb. 1900

Faidherbe, steamer, sunk in collision with the *Mitidja*, 24 deaths, reported . . 24 Oct. ,,

Gneisenau, German training-ship, wrecked off Malaga, 38 deaths . . . 16 Dec. ,,

Sente, Japanese dredger (built at Renfrew), wrecked off Queenstown, 12 deaths . . 26 Dec. ,,

City of Rio de Janeiro, Pacific mail steamer, U.S., wrecked off San Francisco, 122 deaths, 79 saved, panic among Chinese . . . . 22 Feb. 1901

Aslan, Turkish transport, wrecked in the Red Sea, over 180 deaths . . . . 1 April, ,,

City of Paducah, Mississippi steamer, sank off Grand Tower, 23 deaths . . . 13 May, ,,

City of Golconda, steamer, capsized in a squall on the Ohio, about 40 deaths . . 19 Aug. ,,

Ville d'Ys, a pleasure-boat, lost off Treguier, Brittany, 14 deaths, including 5 near relatives of M. Anatole le Braz, the Breton poet . 21 Aug. ,,

Polarstjernen, Danish steamer, lost on a sandbank in the North sea, 22 deaths, reported, 1 Jan. 1902

Walla Walla, San Francisco steamer, sunk by collision with *Max*, a French barque, 9 deaths, 33 missing . . . . . . 2 Jan. ,,

* Relief fund started; 500*f.* from pres. Faure, 10,000*f.* from Havre, 10 July; official inquiry at Halifax, Nova Scotia, 12 July; capt. Henderson, of the *Cromartyshire*, exonerated from blame, 28 July, 1898. The *Bourgogne* held alone to blame for the collision, 12 Jan. 1899; again on appeal, 11 May, 1899.

Chanaral, sailer, of Dunkirk, sunk off Ushant, 21 deaths . . . . 31 Jan. 1902
Luga, steamer, capsized on the Luga, Russia, about 30 deaths . . . . . 15 July, „
Primus, pleasure steamer, sunk in collision with *Hausa*, on the Lower Elbe, 112 deaths, 21 July, „
Prins Alexander sunk in collision with the *Ban Hire Guan*, off Malacca, 40 deaths, reported, 30 July, „
Enero, Spanish steamer, sunk in collision with the *St. Regulus*, steamer, off Dungeness, 22 deaths . . . . 31 Oct. „
Knud, Danish steamer, sunk in collision with the *Swaledale* steamer, off the Tyne, 8 deaths, 20 Nov. „
Neptuno, Spanish steamer, sunk in the Bay of Biscay, abont 29 deaths, reported . 3 Dec. „
Parthenon, lost on the Asiatic coast near the Bosphorus, 28 deaths, reported . 22 Dec. „
Prince Arthur, Norwegian barque, sunk off Cape Flattery, U.S.A., 18 deaths . . . . 2 Jan. 1903
Santa Pologna, barque, foundered off Spanish coast, all hands lost . . . . . . 13 Jan. „
Van Stabel, French barque, lost off the Outer Hebrides, 27 deaths . . . . . Jan. „
Luna, of Hamburg, lost on the Brissons, off Longships, 17 deaths . . . . 1 March, „
Norwegian barque *Tabitha*, totally lost by fire, 1 March, „
Collision off Hastings, between steamship *Poveña* and *Miraflores*, both of Bilbao, 3 killed 14 March, „
Liban, steamer, of Fraissinet co., with 150 passengers, sunk by collision with steamer *Insulaire*, of same co., near Mareeilles . . . June 7 „
Total loss of the King line steamer *Mexicano* on voyage from Philadelphia to Vera Cruz, reported mid Sept. „
French barque *François Coppée*, from Newcastle, N.S.W., for San Francisco, wrecked near Tonali Bay, Solomon Is., captain and 19 of crew missing, reported . . . . 24 Nov. „
Norwegian barque *Capella* of Arendal, bound for Table Bay with timber cargo, wrecked off Bovbjerg, Jutland, crew of 15 drowned 22 Nov. „

WRECK COMMISSION, a court established to inquire into the causes of shipwrecks; first sat, 30 Oct. 1876, Mr. H. C. Rothery, president.

WREXHAM, S. E. Denbighshire, the Saxon Wrightesham, given to earl Warren by Edward I.; made a borough by the reform act, 1832. An exhibition of art treasures of North Wales, and the border counties, was opened here by the duke of Westminster, 22 July, 1876. Musical festival here 1883, *et seq*. Population, 1881, 10,978; 1891, 12,552; 1901, 14,966.

WRITING. Pictures are considered to be the first essay towards writing. The Egyptian papyri are very ancient, see *Dead, Book of the*. The most ancient remains of writing are upon hard substances, such as stones and metals, used by the ancients for edicts, and matters of public notoriety. Cadmus, the founder of Cadmea, 1493 B.C., is mythically said to have brought the Phœnician letters into Greece. *Vossius*. The commandments were written on two tables of stone, 1491 B.C. *Usher*. The Greeks and Romans used wax table-books, and continued the use of them long after papyrus was known; see *Papyrus*, *Parchment*, *Paper*. Thos. Astle's "History of Writing" was first published in 1784; Natalis de Wailly's "Elémens de Paléographie," 1838; E. M. Thompson's "Handbook of Greek and Latin Palæography"; see *Hieroglyphics*, *Cuneiform inscriptions*, *Bible*, *Diplomatics*, *Palæography* and *Type-Writers*.*

WROXETER (in Shropshire), the Roman city *Uriconium*. Roman inscriptions, ruins, seals, and coins were found here in 1752. New discoveries having been made, a committee for further investigation met at Shrewsbury on 11 Nov. 1858. Excavations were commenced in Feb. 1859, which were continued till May. Large portions of the old town were discovered; also specimens of glass and pottery, personal ornaments and toys, household utensils and implements of trade, cinerary urns, and bones of man and of the smaller animals. A committee was formed in London in Aug. 1859, with the view of continuing these investigations, which were resumed in 1861, through the liberality of the late Beriah Botfield, M.P. The investigations, stopped through want of funds, were resumed for a short time in 1867. Mr. Thomas Wright published "Uriconium" in 1872.

WURSCHEN, see *Bautzen*.

WUNTHO, see *Burmah*, 1891.

WÜRTEMBERG, originally part of Swabia, was made a county for Ulric I., about 1265, and a duchy for Eberhard in 1494. The dukes were protestants until 1722, when the reigning prince became a Roman catholic. Würtemberg has been repeatedly traversed by armies, particularly since the great French revolution of 1793. Moreau made his celebrated retreat, 23 Oct. 1796. The political constitution is dated 25 Sept. 1819. Würtemberg opposed Prussia in the war, June, 1866, but made peace, 13 Aug. following; in Oct. 1867, joined the Zollverein (*which see*), but sent a contingent to Prussia in the war, 1870. Population of Würtemberg in 1871, 1,818,539; 1880, 1,971,118; 1885, 1,995,185; 1890, 2,035,443; 1900, 2,300,000.

Elections for 70 members of the diet; 47 by manhood suffrage . . . . 1 Feb. 1895
The diet demands revision of the constitution and other reforms . . . . . . March, „
Much destruction by a cloud-burst in the Black Forest district, 50 lives lost, 5 June; visit of the king to organize relief . . . . 8 June, „

DUKES.

1494. Eberhard I.
1496 Eberhard II.
1498. Ulric; deprived of his states by the emperor Charles V.; recovers them in 1534.
1550. Christopher the Pacific.
1568. Louis the Pious.
1593. Frederic I.
1608. John Frederic; joined the protestants in the Thirty years' war.
1628. Eberhard III.
1674. William Louis.
1677. Eberhard Louis; served under William III. in Ireland; and with the English armies on the continent.
1733. Charles Alexander.
1737. Charles Eugene.
1793. Louis Eugene (joins in the war against France).
1795. Frederic I., makes peace with France, 1796.
1797. Frederic II. marries Charlotte, princess royal of England, 18 May; made *elector* of Germany, 1803; acquired additional territories, and the title of king in 1805.

KINGS.

1806. Frederic I. supplies a contingent to Napoleon's Russian army; yet joined the allies at Leipsic in 1813. Died in 1816.
1816. William I., 30 Oct.; son; born 27 Sept. 1781. He abolished serfdom in 1818; instituted representative government in 1819; entered into a concordat with Rome in 1857; was the oldest living sovereign, 1862; died 25 June, 1864.

* "I would check the petty vanity of those who slight good penmanship, as below the notice of a scholar, by reminding them that Mr. Fox was distinguished by the clearness and firmness, Mr. Professor Porson by the correctness and elegance, and sir William Jones by the ease and beauty of the characters they respectively employed.' *Dr. Parr*.

1864. Charles I., son; born 6 March, 1823; married princess Olga of Russia, 13 July, 1846. No issue; died 6 Oct. 1891.

1891. William II., cousin; born, 25 Feb. 1848; married, 1. Marie, princess of Waldeck and Pyrmont, 15 Feb. 1877; 2. Charlotte, princess of Schaumburg Lippe, 8 April, 1886; attempt on his life by Martin Müller, lunatic anarchist, 20 Oct. 1889.

Heir presumptive (William, born 20 July, 1828, died 6 Nov. 1896; Nicolous, born 1 March, 1833, died 23 Feb. 1903), next in succession, duke Philip and his son Albrecht.

WÜRZBURG (in Bavaria), was formerly a bishopric, and its sovereign one of the greatest ecclesiastic princes of the empire. It was given as a principality to the elector of Bavaria in 1803; and by the treaty of Presburg, in 1805, was ceded to the archduke Ferdinand of Tuscany, whose electoral title was transferred from Salzburg to this place. In 1814 this duchy was again transferred to Bavaria, in exchange for the Tyrol, and the archduke Ferdinand was reinstated in his Tuscan dominions. Ministers from the second-rate German states met at Würzburg to promote union amongst them, 21-27 Nov. 1859. Near here the archduke Charles defeated the French under Jourdan, 3 Sept. 1796; and the Prussians defeated the Bavarians, 28 July, 1866.

WYATT'S INSURRECTION, see *Rebellions*, 1554.

WYCLIFFITES, see *Wickliffites*.

WYOMING, a western territory of the United States of America, constituted in 1868, admitted a state 1890. Capital, Cheyenne. Lynch Law has not long been superseded. Women have been enfranchised. It includes Yellowstone park (*which see*). The desolation of Wyoming, in Pennsylvania, by an incursion of Indians allied with the British, 3 July, 1778, forms the subject of Campbell's poem, "Gertrude of Wyoming" published 1809. Wyoming abounds in iron, coal, natural soda, mineral oil, &c. Explosion in a coal mine at Red Canyon, about 68 deaths, 21 March, 1895; another at Hanna, 175 killed, 30 June, 1903. The U.S. settlers attack the Bannock Indians on their hunting grounds; several killed; troops sent, 24 July, 1895. Population 1880, 20,789; 1890, 60,705; 1900, 92,531.

X.

XANTHIAN MARBLES, see *British Museum*.

XANTHICA, a military festival observed by the Macedonians in the month called Xanthicus (our April), instituted about 392 B.C.

XANTHUS, Lycia, Asia Minor, was taken by Harpagus for Cyrus, about 546 B.C., when the inhabitants buried themselves in the ruins. It was besieged by the Romans under Brutus 42 B.C. After a great struggle the inhabitants set fire to their city, destroyed their wives and children, and perished. The conqueror wished to spare them, and offered rewards to his soldiers if they brought any of the Xanthians into his presence, but only 150 were saved. *Plutarch.*

XENOPHON, see *Retreat of the Greeks*.

XERES DE LA FRONTERA (S.W. Spain), the *Asta Regia* of the Romans, and the seat of the wine-trade in Spain, of which the principal wine is that so well known in England as Sherry, an English corruption of Xeres. The British importations of this wine in 1850 reached to 3,826,785 gallons; and in the year ending 5 Jan. 1852, to 3,904,978 gallons. Xeres is a handsome and large town, of great antiquity. At the battle of Xeres, 26 July, 711, Roderic, the last Gothic sovereign of Spain, was defeated and slain by the Saracens, commanded by Tarik and Muza.

XERXES' CAMPAIGN. Xerxes crossed the Hellespont by a bridge of boats, and entered Greece in the spring of 480 B.C., with an army which, together with the numerous retinue of servants, eunuchs, and women that attended it, amounted (according to some historians) to 5,283,220 souls. Herodotus states the armament to have consisted of 3000 sail, conveying 1,700,000 foot, besides cavalry and the marines and attendants of the camp. This multitude was stopped at Thermopylæ (*which see*) by the valour of 300 Spartans under Leonidas, 7-9 Aug. 480 B.C. The fleet of Xerxes was defeated at Artemisium and Salamis, 20 Oct. 480 B.C.; and he hastened back to Persia, leaving behind Mardonius, the best of his generals, who, with an army of 300,000 men, was defeated and slain at Platæa, 22 Sept. 479 B.C. Xerxes was assassinated by Artabanus, 465 B.C.

XESIBELAND, a district in S. Africa, situated between Griqualand East and Pondoland; annexed in 1886 to Cape Colony.

XIMENA (S. Spain), the site of a battle between the Spanish army under the command of general Ballasteros, and the French corps commanded by general Regnier, 10 Sept. 1811. The Spaniards defeated their adversaries; the loss was great on both sides.

XYLOIDINE, an explosive resembling guncotton. It is produced by treating starch or some material of a fibrous, woody nature with strong nitric acid.

XYLONITE, a celluloid preparation used as a substitute for ivory, bone, coral, &c., for making combs, pianoforte keys, napkin rings, card cases, and numerous other articles, for which lightness and durability, combined with cheapness, are required.

XYLOTECHNOGRAPHICA, a process for staining wood various colours, invented and patented by Mr. A. F. Brophy; announced early in 1875.

Y.

YACHT (from the Dutch *jaght*); a light vessel for pleasure or races.

Queen Elizabeth had a yacht built at Cowes, Isle of Wight, 1588, and in 1660 one was presented by the Dutch to Charles II., who soon after had others constructed, and yacht races began.

The principal royal yachts: the *Royal George*, launched at Deptford by the Duke of York in 1817 (still used at Portsmouth as a depôt ship 1899); *Victoria and Albert*, first royal steam yacht, designed by sir W. Symonds, launched in 1843; second of the same name launched at Pembroke, 16 Jan. 1855; third, designed by sir Wm. White (larger and with all the latest improvements) launched by the duchess of York (the duke of Connaught, Mr. Goschen, and others present) at Pembroke, 9 May, 1899.

First royal cup presented to the Royal Yacht Squadron by king William IV. 1834

YACHT RACES.—The *America*, an American yacht schooner, built on the wave principle, 171 tons; at Cowes regatta, in a match round the Isle of Wight, open to all comers, came in first by 8 miles, gaining the Royal Yacht Squadron's International queen's cup worth 100*l*. . 22 Aug. 1851

Three American yachts, the *Henrietta*, *Vesta*, and *Fleetwing*, sailed from New York, 11 Dec. 1866, at 1 P.M. The *Henrietta* arrived at Cowes at 5.40 on 25 Dec., the quickest voyage ever made in a sailing vessel. Her rivals were only a few hours after her.

In a contest off the Isle of Wight, between the American vessel *Sappho* and the English cutters *Aline*, *Cambria*, *Oimara*, and *Condor*, the *Oimara* won . . . . 25 Aug. 1868

In a triangular race between *Sappho* and *Cambria*, *Sappho* won, 10 May; no race, 14 May; won 17 May, 1870

In a yacht race off Staten island, New York, for the squadron or queen's cup, the *Magic* won, *Cambria* being the 8th in 16 . . . . Aug. ,,

In a series of matches off Staten island between Mr. Ashbury's *Livonia*, and the vessels of the New York Club, she was beaten by the *Columbia*, 16, 18 Oct.; by the *Dauntless*, 21 Oct. The two vessels were disabled by a gale in attempting the race . . . . 25 Oct. 1871

In consequence of the collision of Mr. Heywood's yacht, *Mistletoe*, with her majesty's steam yacht, *Alberta*, 18 Aug. 1875 (see under *Wrecks*), a letter was written on behalf of the queen to the marquis of Exeter, commodore of the Royal Victoria Yacht Club, desiring yachts not to be brought too near to her majesty's, whether from loyalty or curiosity . . . . . . Sept. 1875

Yacht Racing Association formed as a court of appeal . . . . 17 Nov. ,,

Death of George Inman, of Lymington, head of the firm which built the *Alarm*, and many other swift sailing yachts . . . . 20 Oct. 1883

Match between the British *Genesta* and the American *Puritan*; the *Puritan* won by 1½ minutes . . . . 16 Sept. 1885

Genesta beat the *Dauntless* in a race, 26–28 Sept. 1885; the *Mayflower* beat the *Galatea*, 11 Sept. 1886.

Ocean yacht race from New York to Roche's Point, Queenstown, Ireland, between *Coronet* and *Dauntless* (American), 12 March; *Coronet* arrives at Roche's Point, 0·50 a.m. 28 March; *Dauntless* arrives 6·45 p.m. . . . . . 28 March, 1887

Jubilee yacht race; twelve yachts start from Southend, 14 June; the *Genesta* (sir Richard Sutton) arrives at Dover at 5 a.m.; the *Sleuthhound* 11·45 p.m. 27 June; first prize 1,000gs.

Race between the Scotch yacht *Thistle* and American yacht *Volunteer* for America cup over the New York yacht club course; *Volunteer* wins first race 27 Sept.; second race 30 Sept. ,,

The German emperor's yacht *Meteor* gained much distinction; but Mr. West's *Queen Mab* was most successful in regard to prizes in the season of . 1892

The prince of Wales's yacht *Britannia* wins prizes on the Thames, 25, 26 May, and wins the Victoria gold challenge cup at Ryde . . 11 Sept. 1893

International race for the America cup, Sandy Hook, New Jersey; won by the *Vigilant* (American) against lord Dunraven's *Valkyrie*, after a desperate struggle . . . . . 13 Oct. ,,

Second international exhibition of historical, modern, and scientific pictures and models of yachts, &c., at the Royal Aquarium, Westminster, Feb. 1894

The prince of Wales's yacht *Britannia* 1st in an international match at Cannes, 13 March (again victor, 23 Feb. 1895); victorious over the American *Vigilant* in the Clyde; lord Dunraven's *Valkyrie* sunk by collision . . . 5 July, ,,

"Yachting," in the Badminton series, published . ,,

Col. Lewis Conway-Gordon, R.E., an eminent yachtsman, drowned in the collision of ss. *Penzance* with his yacht *Scotia* . . . 25 June, 1895

Victory of the *Vigilant* over the *Britannia* on the Solent . . . . 4 Aug. ,,

The queen's cup won by adm. Montague's *Carina*, against the *Britannia*, *Meteor*, and others, 7 Aug. ,,

The *Britannia* wins the Meteor shield at the royal regatta, Cowes . . . . . . 9 Aug. ,,

The America cup won by the *Defender* (American) against lord Dunraven's *Valkyrie* at New York, 7 Sept. 1895; disputes respecting the race, Sept.–Nov.; lord Dunraven's charges declared unproved by a committee appointed by the New York Yacht Club, 18 Nov.; report issued, 21 Jan. 1896

The *Britannia* beaten by the German emperor's *Meteor* at Gravesend, 4 June; again at Cowes, 11 June; Ryde, 12, 13 Aug. . . . . . ,,

Royal Munster Y. C. match won by *Satanita* at Queenstown . . . . . . 19 June, ,,

Britannia wins at Southampton, 13 June; at Ramsay Bay, 25 June; Clyde . . . 27 June, ,,

Royal Mersey Y. C. at Liverpool, match won by *Ailsa* . . . . 23 June, ,,

The queen's cup won by capt. Orr-Ewing's *Mohawk* on her time allowance . . . . . 4 Aug. ,,

The German emperor's Meteor shield won by *Ailsa* at Cowes . . . . 7 Aug. ,

The Albert cup won by the *Meteor*, Southsea, 17 Aug. ,

Collision of the *Meteor* with the *Isolde* in the Solent, the owner, baron von Zedtwitz, killed . 18 Aug. 1898

The German emperor's Jubilee cup, race from Dover to Heligoland, won by Mr. W. Cook's *Freda*, 25 June, 1897; by the *Merry Thought* 24 June, ,,

Britannia beats the *Meteor* in the race for the queen's cup, Cowes . . . . . 3 Aug. 1897

Isolde wins the big yachts race, Cowes; *Latona* wins the German emperor's cup . . . 5 Aug. ,,

Britannia wins the emperor's Meteor shield, 6 Aug. ,,

The Jubilee cup won by *Latona* at Southampton, 9 Aug. ,,

The duke d'Abruzzi's *Bona* wins several races for big yachts, Aug. 1897; wins the queen's cup, 2 July; again . . . . . . 20 July, 1898

Annual yachting exhibition (6th) at the Westminster aquarium . . . . 1 Feb. ,,

Lord Dunraven wins the Vasco da Gama cup at the international regatta at Lisbon . May, ,,

Queen's cup won by the German emperor's *Meteor*, at Cowes . . . . 1 Aug. 1899

America cup won by the *Columbia* (American) against the *Shamrock* (sir Thos. Lipton's) 16, 17, 20 Oct. ,,

Queen's cup won by sir M. Fitzgerald's *Satanita*, defeating the German emperor's *Meteor*, 7 Aug. 1900

America cup won by *Columbia* (American) against sir Thos. Lipton's new yacht *Shamrock II.*, 4 Oct. 1901

German emperor's new yacht *Meteor* launched at Jersey city, New York . . . 25 Feb. 1902
Lasca wins the German emperor's cup (Heligoland to Dover) . . . . 16 July, „
King's cup won by Mr. W. P. Burton's *Lucida*, 5 Aug. „
Coronation cup won by *Bona* . . . 26 Aug. „
Launch of sir Thos. Lipton's yacht *Shamrock III.* at Leven shipyard, Dumbarton . . 17 Mar. 1903
America cup won by *Reliance* (American) against sir Thos. Lipton's new yacht *Shamrock III.*, 3 Sept. „

Yacht clubs:—The Cork harbour water club, now the Royal Cork yacht club, 1720; Royal Yacht Squadron, Cowes, 1812; Royal Albert, 1864; Alfred, 1864; Barrow, 1871; Channel Islands, 1863; Cinque Ports, 1872; Clyde, 1856; Cork, 1720; Cornwall, 1871; Dartmouth, 1866; Dorset, 1875; R. Eastern, 1835; R. Forth, 1868; R. Harwich, 1843; R. Highland, 1881; R. Irish, 1846; R. London (Arundel, 1838), 1849; R. Mersey, 1844; R. Northern, 1824; R. Portsmouth, 1880; R. St. George, 1838; R. Southampton, 1875; R. Southern, 1843; R. Thames, 1823; R. Torbay, 1875; R. Ulster, 1867; R. Victoria, 1844; R. Welsh, 1847; R. Western of England, 1827; R. Yorkshire, 1847; Solent, 1879, made Royal, 1902; Temple, made Royal, 1897, and a few others.

YANKEE, from "Yengees," a corruption of "English," the name originally given by the Massachusetts Indians to the colonists: applied solely to the New Englanders by the British soldiers in the American war (1775-81); afterwards by foreigners to all natives of the United States; and by the confederates of the south to the federals of the north during the war 1861-64.

YARD. The word is derived from the Saxon *geard*, or *gyrd*, a rod or shoot, or from *gyrdan* to enclose, being anciently the circumference of the body, until Henry I. decreed that it should be the length of his arm; see *Standard Measures*.

YARKAND, the chief town and commercial capital of Eastern Turkestan, situated on the river Yarkand, an affluent of the river Tanim, which enters Lob Nor, in the midst of a fertile oasis, 100 miles S.E. of Kashgar. The town is surrounded by a strong mud wall, inside which are numerous rich and well-watered gardens. The inhabitants are chiefly Persians, who are enterprising merchants. Near to Yarkand are mountains abounding in minerals. Yarkand was visited by Marco Polo, but comparatively little was known of it until Mr. R. Shaw, who resided there for a time, published in 1871 an account of the town and its people. Population about 60,000.

YARMOUTH, GREAT (Norfolk), was a royal demesne in the reign of William I., as appears from Domesday Book, 1086. It obtained a charter from John, and one from Henry III. In 1348, a plague here carried off 7000 persons; and did much havoc again in 1579 and 1664. The parish church of St. Nicholas, founded by bp. Herbert de Losinga, 1101, is one of the largest churches in Great Britain; restored 1847-84. A feature of Yarmouth are its narrow lanes or "rows," 145 in number, which intersect the main streets; a monument, 144 feet high, was erected here to Nelson in 1818. There are numerous public buildings and institutions, some of which are of considerable architectural merit. Yarmouth is the chief seat of the English herring fishery, and the curing of this fish, known as "Yarmouth bloaters," constitutes an important industry; a considerable trade is also carried on in connection with mackerel fishing. Associated with the town is Chas. Dickens' charming creation "Peggotty." Returns one M.P. by act of 1885. Population, 1881, 46,767; 1891, 49,318; 1901, 51,316.

Theatre built 1778
Nelson's pillar, a fluted column 140 feet in height, erected 1817
Suspension chain bridge over the Bure, built by Mr. R. Cory, at an expense of about 4000*l.*; owing to the weight of a vast number of persons who assembled on it to witness an exhibition on the water, it suddenly gave way, and seventy-nine lives (mostly children) were lost . . . 2 May, 1845
Yarmouth disfranchised for bribery and corruption by the Reform Act . . . . . . Aug. 1867
The prince of Wales opened a new grammar school, 6 June, 1873
Aquarium and winter garden opened . 5 Sept. 1876
New municipal buildings opened by the prince of Wales . . . . 31 May, 1882
Created a county borough 1888
The prince of Wales received by the mayor, 25 May; reviews the Norfolk artillery, &c., 26 May, 1899
Duke of York opens seamen's institute, 26 April, 1900
Mary Jane Bennett murdered here on the beach, 22 Sept. 1900; see *Trials* . . . . 25 Feb. 1901
Lady Claud Hamilton opens the new Britannia pier, length 810 feet, cost 70,000*l.* . 21 June, 1902

YARMOUTH, a small seaport in the Isle of Wight, 10 miles W. of Newport. Prior to the Reform bill of 1832 it returned two members to parliament. The name also of a seaport in *Nova Scotia*, and the chief shipbuilding centre of the province; situated 205 miles S.W. of Halifax. Population, 1901, about 7000.

YASHGAR, a country, Central Asia; Yakoob, its able despotic chief, was contending with China and Russia, 1875.

YEAR. The Egyptians, it is said, were the first who fixed the length of the year.

The Roman year introduced by Romulus, 738 B.C.; corrected by Numa, 713 B.C.; and again by Julius Cæsar, 45 B.C. (see *Calendar*).

The *solar* or astronomical year was found to comprise 365 days, 5 hours, 48 minutes, 51 seconds, and 6 decimals, 265 B.C.

The *lunar* year (twelve lunar months, or 354 days, 8 hours, 48 minutes) was in use amongst the Chaldæans, Persians, and Jews. Once in every three years was added another lunar month, so as to make the solar and the lunar year nearly agree. But though the months were lunar, the year was solar; that is, the first month was of thirty days, and the second of twenty-nine, and so alternately: and the month added triennially was called Ve-Adar or the second Adar. The Jews afterwards followed the Roman manner of computation.

The *sidereal* year, or return to the same star, is 365 days, 6 hours, 9 minutes, 11 seconds.

The Jews dated the beginning of the sacred year in March, and civil year in September; the Athenians began the year in June; the Macedonians on 24 Sept.; the Christians of Egypt and Ethiopia on 29 or 30 Aug.; and the Persians and Armenians on 11 Aug. Nearly all Christian nations now commence the year on 1 January.

In France, the Merovingian kings began the year with March; the Carlovingians sometimes began the year with Christmas, 25 Dec.; and sometimes with Easter, which, being a movable feast, led to much confusion.

Charles IX. of France, in 1564, published an arrêt, the last article of which ordered the year for the time to come to be constantly and universally begun, and written on and from 1 January.

The beginning of the year has been reckoned from the day celebrating the birth of Christ, 25 Dec.; his circumcision, 1 Jan.; his conception, 25 March; and his resurrection, Easter.

The English began their year on the 25th of December, until the time of William the Conqueror. This prince having been crowned on 1 Jan. gave occasion to the

English to begin their year at that time, to make it agree with the then most remarkable period of their history. *Stow.* Until the act for altering the style, in 1752 (see *Style*), when the year was ordered to begin on Jan. 1, it did not legally and generally commence in England until 25th March. In Scotland, at that period, the year began on the 1st of January. This difference caused great practical inconveniences; and January, February, and part of March sometimes bore two dates, as we often find in old records, 1745-1746, or 1745-6, or 174⅚. Such a reckoning often led to chronological mistakes; for instance, we popularly say the "revolution of 1688," as that event was completed in February, 1688, according to the then mode of computation: but if the year were held to begin, as it does now, on the first of January, it would be the revolution of 1689.

The year in the northern regions of Siberia and Lapland is described in the following calendar, given by a traveller:—"23 *June*, snow melts. 1 *July*, snow gone. 9 *July*, fields quite green. 17 *July*, plants at full growth. 25 *July*, plants in flower. 2 *Aug.*, fruits ripe. 10 *Aug.*, plants shed their seed. 18 *Aug.*, snow." The snow continues upon the ground from 18th Aug. of one year to 23rd June of the year following, being 309 days out of 365; so that while the three seasons of spring, summer, and autumn are together only fifty-six days, or eight weeks, the winter is of forty-four weeks' duration in these countries.

See *New Style, Platonic Year, Sabbatical Year, Mahometanism, French Revolutionary Calendar.*

Year of our Lord; see *Anno Domini.*

Year of the Reign. From the time of William the Conqueror, 1066, the year of the sovereign's reign has been given to all public instruments. The king's patents, charters, proclamations, and all acts of parliament have since then been generally so dated. The same manner of dating is used in most of the European states for all similar documents and records; see List of Kings under *England.*

Year and a Day. A space of time in law, and in many cases establishes and fixes a right; as in an estray, on proclamation being made, if the owner does not claim it within the time, it is forfeited. The term arose in the Norman law, which enacted that a beast found on another's land, if unclaimed for a year and a day, belonged to the lord of the soil. It is otherwise a legal space of time.

YEAR-BOOKS contain reports in Norman-French of cases argued and decided in the courts of common law. The printed volumes extend from the beginning of the reign of Edward II. to nearly the end of the reign of Henry VIII., a period of about 220 years; but in this series there are many omissions. These books are the first in the long line of legal reports in which England is so rich, and may be considered as, to a great extent, the foundation of our unwritten law, "*Lex non scripta.*" In 1863 *et seq.* various year-books of Edward I. (1292-1304) edited by Mr. A. J. Horwood, for the series of the Chronicles and Memorials, were published at the expense of the British government. Year-books 16 Edward III., published, 1897; the 17th year, 1342-3, published 1902. "Year-Book of Science," published 1892 *et seq.* "The Englishwoman's Year-book," published 1881 *et seq.*

YEAST, a substance causing fermentation, was discovered by Cagniard de la Tour and Schwann, independently, in 1836, to be a vegetable cell or fungus.

YELLOW FEVER, an American pestilence, made its appearance at Philadelphia, where it committed great ravages, 1699. It appeared in several islands of the West Indies in 1732, 1739, and 1745. It raged with unparalleled violence at Philadelphia in Oct. 1762; and most awfully at New York in the beginning of Aug. 1791. This fever again spread great devastation at Philadelphia in July 1793; carrying off several thousand persons. *Hardie.* It again appeared in Oct. 1797; and spread its ravages over the northern coast of America, Sept. 1798. It reappeared at Philadelphia in the summer of 1802; and broke out in Spain, in Sept 1803. The yellow fever was very violent at Gibraltar in 1804 and 1814; in the Mauritius, July 1815; at Antigua, in Sept. 1816; and it raged with dreadful consequences at Cadiz, and the isle of St. Leon, in Sept. 1819. A malignant fever raged at Gibraltar in Sept. 1828, and did not terminate until the following year. Yellow fever raging in the southern of the United States, Sept. Oct. 1878; at Memphis, autumn, 1879; in Florida (specially in Jacksonville) and other southern states, autumn 1888. Mr. R. A. Proctor, the astronomer, died of it at New York on his way from Florida to England, 12 Sept. 1888; the epidemic abating Oct. 1888; 4,583 cases, and 396 deaths in Jacksonville to Nov. 17, 1888; slight outbreak, with some deaths, July–Sept. 1899; and at Senegal, autumn, 1900; Messrs. Reed, Carroll, and Agromonte investigate into the cause of the fever in Cuba during 1900, and finally prove the disease to be conveyed by a species of mosquito (*Culex fasciatus*), reported Feb. 1901. Dr. W. Myers, one of the commission, died of the fever, 22 Jan. 1901; maj. Reed died mid Dec. 1902.

YELLOWSTONE NATIONAL PARK, about 3300 square miles, in territory of Wyoming.

It includes Yellowstone lake, about 330 square miles, with numerous geysers, volcanic and other grand natural phenomena, rugged mountains, forests, meadows, rivers, and much beautiful scenery. Its formation was authorised by congress in March, 1872.

YELVERTON CASE, see *Trials*, 1861.

YEMEN, a province of Asiatic Turkey, on the Red Sea, the Arabia Felix of the Romans; see *Arabia.*

YENIKALE, see *Azoff.*

YEOMANRY, see under *Volunteers.*

YEOMEN OF THE GUARD, a peculiar body of foot guards to the king's person, instituted at the coronation of Henry VII. 30 Oct. 1485, which originally consisted of fifty men under a captain. They were called beef-eaters, a corruption of *buffetiers*, being attendants on the king's buffet or sideboard; see *Battle-Axe.* They were of a larger stature than other guards, being required to be over six feet in height, and were armed with arquebuses and other arms. The band was increased by Henry's successors to one hundred men, and seventy supernumeraries; and when one of the hundred died, it was ordered that his place should be supplied out of the seventy. They were clad after the manner of king Henry VIII. *Ashmole's Instit.* This is said to have been the first permanent military band instituted in England. John earl of Oxford, was the first captain in 1486. *Beatson's Pol. Index.*

YEOVIL, a municipal borough in Somerset, situated on the river Yeo, 22 miles S.E. of Bridgewater and 40 miles S. of Bristol. The parish church, St. John's, called the "Lantern of the West," is a fine cruciform structure of the perpendicular style, dating from the 15th century, restored 1864. The town was formerly noted for its woollen industry; at the present time (1903) it carries on an extensive trade in gloves manufactured here. In 1449 a great fire destroyed 117 houses. Population, 1891, 9,648; 1901, 9,861.

YERMUK (Syria). Near here the emperor Heraclius was totally defeated by the Saracens, after a fierce engagement, Nov. 636. Damascus was taken, and his army expelled from Syria.

YEW-TREE (*Taxus*). The origin of planting yew-trees in churchyards was (these latter being fenced) to secure the trees from cattle, and in this manner preserve them for the encouragement of archery. A general plantation of them for the use of archers was ordered by Richard III. 1483. *Stow's Chron.* Near Fountains Abbey, Yorkshire, were seven yew-trees, called the Seven Sisters, supposed to have been planted before 1088; the circumference of the largest thirty-four feet seven inches round the trunk. In 1851 a yew-tree was said to be growing in the churchyard of Gresford, North Wales, whose circumference was nine yards nine inches, being the largest and oldest yew-tree in the British dominions; but tradition states that there are some yews in England older than the introduction of Christianity. The old yew-tree mentioned in the survey taken of Richmond palace in 1649, is said to be still existing.

YEZIDIS, an eastern tribe, living near the Euphrates, visited by Mr. Layard in 1841: see *Devil Worship*.

YEZDEGIRD, or PERSIAN ERA, was formerly universally adopted in Persia, and is still used by the Parsees in India, and by the Arabs, in certain computations. This era began on the 26th June, 632, when Yezdegird was elected king of Persia. The year consisted of 365 days only, and therefore its commencement, like that of the old Egyptian and Armenian year, anticipated the Julian year by one day in every four years. This difference amounted to nearly 112 days in the year 1075, when it was reformed by Jelaledin, who ordered that in future the Persian year should receive an additional day whenever it should appear necessary to postpone the commencement of the following year, that it might occur on the day of the sun's passing the same degree of the ecliptic.

YNGLINGS (youths, or off-shoots), descendants of the Scandinavian hero Odin, ruled Sweden till 830, when the last of the pontiff kings, Olaf Trætelia, being expelled, led to the foundation of the Norwegian monarchy.

YOKE is spoken of as a type of servitude. The ceremony of making prisoners pass under it was practised by the Samnites towards the Romans, 321 B.C.; see *Caudine Forks*. This disgrace was afterwards inflicted by the Romans upon their vanquished enemies. *Dufresnoy*.

YOKOHAMA, see *Japan*.

YORK (N. England), a town of the Brigantes, named Evrauc, settled by the Romans during the second campaign of Agricola, about 79, and named *Eboracum* or *Eburacum*, and became the metropolis of the north. See *Population*.

The emperor Severus died here . . 4 Feb. 211
Here Constantius Chlorus died, and his son Constantine the Great was proclaimed emperor, 25 July, 306
Abbey of St. Mary's, founded by Seward the Dane 1050
York burnt by the Danes, allies of Edgar Atheling, and all the Normans slain 1069
The city and many churches destroyed by fire, 3 June, 1137
Massacre and suicide of many Jews 1190
York received its charter from Richard II., and the mayor was made a lord 1389
The Guildhall erected 1446
Richard III. crowned again here . 8 Sept. 1483
At a parliament held here Charles I. professed his intention to govern legally . . 13 June, 1642
York taken for the parliament, after the battle of Marston-moor . . . . 16 July, 1644
Injured during the civil war by Fairfax . April, „
The corporation built a mansion-house for the lord mayor 1728
The castle was built by Richard III., 1484, and was rebuilt as a gaol 1741
The York petition to parliament, to reduce the expenditure and redress grievances . . Dec. 1779
Yorkshire Philosophical Society established . . 1822
First meeting of the British Association held here 27 Sept. 1831
British Association (2nd time) 1844
Population, 45,385 1861
Fall of the iron bridge over the Ouse; five persons killed . . . . . 27 Sept. „
Social Science Association met here . 22 Sept. 1864
Fine Arts and Industrial Exhibition opened, 24 July, 1866
Visit of prince and princess of Wales . 9-11 Aug. „
Meeting of the Church Congress . 9 Oct. „
The provincial mayors gave a festival to the lord mayor of London, &c., at York . 25 Sept. 1873
Permanent Fine Art Exhibition opened by the archbishop . . . . . 7 May, 1879
British Association jubilee meeting 31 Aug.-8 Sept. 1881
Royal Agricultural Society's annual meeting, 16 July, 1883
Yorkshire Institute, memorial stone laid by the prince of Wales 18 July, 1883; opened by the marquis of Lorne . . . . 10 June, 1885
Yorkshire college of science opened 26 Oct. 1874; new building opened by the prince of Wales, 15 July, „
New Courts of Justice, memorial stone laid by the duke of Clarence, 16 July, 1890; opened by the lord mayor, John Close . . . . 19 Oct. 1892
Visit of the duke and duchess of York; he receives the freedom of the city . . . . 5 Oct. 1893
Mr. W. F. Rawdon bequeaths valuable pictures to the city, and about 9000*l.* to various institutions, Jan. 1895
Death of the rev. James Raine, D.C.L., chancellor and canon of York, antiquary . . 20 May, 1896
The Yorkshire Agricultural society's show visited by the duke and duchess of York . 24 July, „
Sir Joseph Terry, born 1828, benefactor and thrice lord mayor, died . . . . 12 Jan. 1898
The prince of Wales reviews about 4000 militia, 5 July, „
Strike in S. Yorkshire, June, 1902, *et seq.*, followed by evictions at Denaby . . . 6 Jan. 1903

DUKES.

1385. Edmund Plantagenet (fifth son of king Edward III.); created duke, 6 Aug.; died 1402.
1406. Edward (his son), was degraded by Henry IV. in 1399, but restored in 1414; killed at Agincourt, 1415; succeeded by his nephew,
1415. Richard (son of Richard, earl of Cambridge, who was beheaded for treason in 1415); became regent of France in 1435; quelled the rebellion in Ireland in 1449; claimed the throne, and was appointed protector in 1454: his office was annulled, and he began the civil war in 1455, and was slain after his defeat at Wakefield in 1460.
1460. Edward (his son) afterwards king Edward IV.
1474. Richard (his second son), said to have been murdered in the Tower, 1483.
1494. Henry Tudor, afterwards Henry VIII.
1605. Charles Stuart, afterwards Charles I.

DUKES OF YORK AND ALBANY.

1643. James Stuart (his second son), afterwards James II.
1716. Ernest (brother of George I.); died 1728.
1760. Edward (brother of George III.); died 1767.

1784. Frederic (son of George III.), born 16 Aug. 1763
Marries princess Frederica of Prussia, 29 Sept. 1791
Commands the British forces at Antwerp, 8 April, 1793
Present at the siege of Valenciennes 23 May, „
Defeated at Dunkirk . . . . 7 Sept. „
At Bois-le-Duc, 14 Sept.: and at Boxtel, 17 Sept. 1794
Appointed commander-in-chief . . . 1798
Defeated near Alkmaar, 19 Sept. and 6 Oct. 1799
Accused by colonel Wardle of abuse of his patronage; he resigns . . 27 Jan. 1809
Becomes again commander-in-chief . . 1811
Strongly opposes the catholic claims . . 1825
Dies . . . . 5 Jan. 1827
See *Albany*.

Prince George of Wales created duke of York, 24 May, 1892
See under *Wales* (princes of).

YORK, ARCHBISHOPRIC OF. The most ancient metropolitan see in England, being, it is said, so made by king Lucius about 180, when Christianity was first partly established in England. The bishop Eborius was present at the council of Arles, 314. The see was overturned by the Saxons, and was revived by pope Gregory on their conversion, and Paulinus is said to have been consecrated archbishop, 21 July, 625. York and Durham were long the only two sees in the north of England, until Henry I. erected a bishopric at Carlisle, and Henry VIII. another at Chester. York was the metropolitan see of the Scottish bishops; but during the time of archbishop Nevil, 1464, they withdrew their obedience, and had archbishops of their own. Much dispute arose between the two English metropolitans about precedency, as by pope Gregory's institutions it was thought he meant, that whichever of them was first confirmed, should be superior: appeal was made to the court of Rome by both parties, and it was determined in favour of Canterbury. The archbishop of York was allowed to style himself primate of England, while the archbishop of Canterbury styles himself primate of *all* England. The province of York now contains the dioceses of York, Carlisle, Chester, Durham, Sodor and Man, Manchester, Liverpool, Newcastle, Wakefield and Ripon (*which see*). York has yielded to the church of Rome eight saints and three cardinals, and to England twelve lord chancellors, two lord treasurers, and two lord presidents of the north. It is rated in the king's books, 39 Henry VIII. 1546, at 1609*l.* 19*s.* 2*d.* per annum. *Beatson.* Present income 10,000*l.*

ARCHBISHOPS.

1501. Thomas Savage, died, 3 Sept. 1507.
1508. Christopher Bainbrigg, poisoned at Rome, 14 July, 1514.
1514. Thomas Wolsey, died, 29 Nov. 1530.
1531. Edward Lee, died, 13 Sept. 1544.
1545. Robert Holgate, deprived, 23 March, 1554.
1555. Nicholas Heath, deprived.
1561. Thomas Young, died, 26 June, 1568.
1570. Edmund Grindal, translated to Canterbury, 10 Jan. 1576.
1577. Edwin Sands or Sandys, died, 10 July, 1588.
1589. John Piers, died, 28 Sept. 1594.
1595. Matthew Hutton, died, 16 Jan. 1606.
1606. Tobias Matthew, died, 29 March, 1628.
1628. George Mountaigne, died, 24 Oct. 1628.
„ Samuel Harsnet, died, 25 May, 1621.
1632. Richard Neyle, died, 31 Oct. 1640.
1641. John Williams, died, 25 March, 1650.
[*See vacant ten years.*]
1660. Accepted Frewen, died, 28 March, 1664.
1664. Richard Sterne, died, 18 June, 1683.
1683. John Dolben, died, 11 April, 1686.
[*See vacant two years.*]
1688. Thomas Lamplugh, died, 5 May, 1691.
1691. John Sharp, died, 2 Feb. 1714.
1714. Sir William Dawes, died, 30 April, 1724.
1724. Launcelot Blackburn, died, 23 March, 1743.
1743. Thomas Herring, translated to Canterbury, Oct. 1747.
1747. Matthew Hutton, translated to Canterbury, March, 1757.
1757. John Gilbert, died, 1761.
1761. Robert Hay Drummond, died, 10 Dec. 1776.
1777. William Markham, died, 3 Nov. 1807.
1808. Edward Venables Vernon, died, 5 Nov. 1847.
1847. Thomas Musgrave, died, 4 May, 1860.
1860. Charles T. Longley, translated to Canterbury (from Durham), 1862.
1862. William Thomson, translated from Gloucester; died 25 Dec. 1890.
1891. Wm. Connor Magee, translated from Peterborough, elected Feb., died 4 May, 1891.
„ William Dalrymple Maclagan, translated from Lichfield, May.

YORK MINSTER (dedicated to St. Peter). The first Christian church erected here, which appears to have been preceded by a Roman temple, was built by Edwin, king of Northumbria, of wood, about 625, and of stone about 635. It was damaged by fire in 741, and was rebuilt by archbishop Albert, about 780. It was again destroyed by fire in the year 1069, and rebuilt by archbishop Thomas, of Bayeux. It was once more burnt down in 1137, with St. Mary's abbey, and 39 parish churches in York. Archbishop Roger built the choir, 1154-81; Walter Gray added the south transept in 1227; John de Romayne, the treasurer of the cathedral, built the north transept in 1260. His son, archbishop Romanus, laid the foundation of the nave in 1291. In 1330, William de Melton built the two western towers, which were finished by John de Birmingham in 1342. Archbishop Thoresby, in 1361, began to rebuild the choir, in accordance with the magnificence of the nave, and he also rebuilt the lantern tower. The minster was set on fire by Jonathan Martin, a lunatic, and the roof of the choir and its internal fittings destroyed, 2 Feb. 1829; the damage, estimated at 60,000*l.*, was repaired in 1832 under sir Robert Smirke. An accidental fire broke out, and in one hour reduced the belfry to a shell, destroyed the roof of the nave, and much damaged the edifice, 20 May, 1840. This was restored by Sidney Smirke, at a cost of 23,000*l.*, 1841.

YORK AND LANCASTER, WARS OF, see *Roses*.

YORK (Upper Canada), founded in 1794; since 1834 named Toronto. In the war between the United States and Great Britain, the United States' forces made several attacks upon the province of Upper Canada, and succeeded in taking York, the seat of the government, 27 April, 1813; but it was soon afterwards evacuated by the Americans.

YORKSHIRE Exhibition of Arts and Manufactures, opened at Leeds, by the duke of Edinburgh, 13 May, 1875. The Yorkshire Registries Act passed 7 Aug. 1884.

YORK TOWN (Virginia, United States). Lord Cornwallis had taken possession of York town in Aug. 1781; but after sustaining a disastrous siege, he was obliged to surrender his army, consisting of about 7000 men, to the allied armies of France and America, under the command of general Washington and count Rochambeau, 19 Oct. 1781. This mischance was attributed to sir Henry Clinton, who had not given the garrison the necessary succour they expected; and it mainly led to the close of the war. The centenary was celebrated 16 Oct. 1881 *et seq.* On 19 Oct. the

British flag was saluted generally. The town was strongly fortified by the confederates in the American civil war, but surrendered to M'Clellan, May, 1862.

YOUNG ENGLAND, a name given to a number of young tory gentlemen earnestly opposed to the repeal of the corn laws and other liberal measures, and very desirous of reviving the old relations between the upper and lower classes mixing in rural sports, &c., yet preserving the due distinctions (1842-6). Lord John Manners (duke of Rutland, 1888), and the hon. G. Smythe, were eminent leaders, and their ideas were favoured by Mr. Disraeli (lord Beaconsfield) in his novel "Coningsby," published 1844.

YOUNG IRELAND, see *Ireland, Young*.

YOUNG ITALY, see *Italy*, 1831.

YOUNG MEN'S CHRISTIAN ASSOCIATION, for improvement of young men by means of classes, meetings, &c., founded 1844; jubilee celebrated, with the 13th triennial international conference in London; about 1,700 delegates present; sir George Williams, president; meetings at Guildhall, &c., 1 June, *et seq.* 1894; 15th at Christiania, dean Christian Hall, pres., 20 Aug. 1902. Exeter-hall, Strand, was bought for the association about July, 1880. It met there, 29 March, 1881. The Young Men's Christian Institute bought the Polytechnic Institute, about Dec. 1881. In 1902 there were 7505 centres of the Association in various parts of the world, numbering 620,721 members; in the United Kingdom 1512 centres, 120,550 members; in London 65 centres with 13,000 members. The YOUNG WOMEN'S CHRISTIAN ASSOCIATION, founded 1857, has branches all over the world with a membership (1902) of some 500,000; in London about 14,000 members. In connection with the Association are various institutes and homes, including holiday homes at seaside resorts where board and lodging is provided for the members at a small cost. There is also a teachers' department, a nurses' union, a home for barmaids and other organisations for meeting the various requirements of its members. Head offices 25 and 26 George-street, Hanover-square. The World's Young Women's Christian Association for extending the movement in all parts of the world, held its second triennial international conference at Geneva, July, 1902.

YOUNG PEOPLE'S SOCIETY OF CHRISTIAN ENDEAVOUR, founded 1881, by the rev. F. E. Clark, D.D., in connection with the Congregational church in Portland, Maine, U.S., of which he was the minister. Its objects are "to promote an earnest christian life among its members, to increase their mutual acquaintances, and to make them useful in the service of God." The society has rapidly increased, in 1885 it numbered 11,000 members, now (1903) the total number of members is 3,750,000, associated with 66,000 societies, including about 8000 societies in the United Kingdom.

YOUNG TURKEY, see *Turkey*, 1895. All students abroad ordered to return to Turkey, April, 1896.

YOUTHFUL OFFENDERS' ACT, making a parent liable for the misdeeds of his child, passed 1901.

YTTRIUM, a rare metal. The earth yttria was discovered by professor Gadolin in a mineral at Ytterby, in Sweden, 1794. The metal was first obtained by Wöhler in 1828. It is of a dark grey colour, and brittle.

YUCATAN, Mexico, discovered by Hernandez Cordova, 1517; conquered by Bernal Diaz, 1522; declared for independence, 1813. Its ancient cities are described in works by the American traveller Stephens, 1838 and 1842.

YUKON GOLDFIELDS, see *Canada*, 1897.

YVRES (now IVRY, N. W. France), where a battle was fought, 14 March, 1590, between Henry IV. of France, aided by his chief nobility, and the generals of the catholic league, over whom the king obtained a complete victory.

Z.

ZAGRAB (Hungary). Here Andrew III. defeated the invader Charles Martel, to whom the pope had assigned his crown, 1292.

ZÄHRINGEN (Baden), the seat of dukes, ancestors of the grand dukes of Baden, descended from Herman I., margrave, 1074; see *Baden*.

ZAMA (near Carthage, N. Africa), the scene of the battle between the two greatest commanders in the world at the time, Hannibal and Scipio Africanus. The victory was won by Scipio, and was decisive of the fate of Carthage, 202. It led to an ignominious peace, which closed the second Punic war, 201 B.C. The Romans lost about 2000 killed and wounded, while the Carthaginians lost in killed and prisoners more than 40,000; some historians make the loss greater; 202 B.C.

ZAMBAANSLAND, territory between Swaziland and the sea, annexed by Gt. Britain, 1899.

ZAMBESI, river of E. Africa, explored by Livingstone 1851-6, 1858-64; the beautiful Victoria Falls, 900 mi. from the sea, discovered and named by him in 1855, are $1\frac{1}{4}$ mi. wide and nearly 400 ft. high. His book published Nov. 1865.

BRITISH ZAMBESIA.—A charter was granted to the British South Africa company 15 Oct., signed 29 Oct., 1889, to settle the immense area lying between Lower and Central Zambesi on the north, and the Transvaal border on the south. The company included Mr. Cecil J. Rhodes, the African explorer, the duke of Abercorn the duke of Fife (resigned about 1896), earl Gifford, and other eminent persons. The Portuguese exploring expedition under lieut. Cordon; he receives the allegiance of several tribes; the limits of the districts sanctioned by royal decree, and the province named Zumbo . . 7 Nov. 1889

The marquis of Salisbury protests against the assumption of Zumbo by the Portuguese, referring to the agreement of Great Britain with Lobengula, ruler of Mashona and Makalakaland, of 11 Feb. 1888, and also to British agreements with other tribes (referred to by consul Johnston, 26 Aug., and by consul Buchanan, 30 Sept. 1889), and to the results of British explorations, 21 Nov. ,,

Senhor de Barros Gomes, Portuguese foreign minister, in his reply sustains the claims of Portugal, based on discoveries and consequent effective occupation of the territories in question for centuries, relics of which still remain . 29 Nov. ,,

Major Serpa Pinto, with about 4,000 men with cannon, forms a camp in the Makololo country, quarrels with the natives, conquers them, and calls on the British settlers to submit to Portugal, reported by bishop C. A. Smythies 5 Dec. ,,

Lord Salisbury telegraphs to the Portuguese government in relation to major Serpa Pinto's action, that they should not permit any such attacks on British settlements, or on any other settlement under British protection or influence, 17 Dec. ,,

Sen. Barros Gomes, in his reply, justifies the actions of major Serpa Pinto, by referring to the disturbed state of the country . . 20 Dec. ,,

Lord Salisbury, in a despatch, declines to recognise the claims of Portugal as antiquated, and unsupported by action in modern times 26 Dec. ,,

A peremptory note sent by lord Salisbury, requiring immediate withdrawal of major Serpa Pinto, delivered . . . . . 6 Jan. 1890

Sen. Barros Gomes' reply being deemed unsatisfactory, lord Salisbury declares that his government will order that no acts of force be committed against any British settlements or others specified by him, and requests that the matters in dispute be referred to a conference of the powers, in accordance with the treaty of Berlin 8 Jan. ,,

Lord Salisbury, by telegram, requires to know that explicit instructions have been sent from Mozambique for the immediate withdrawal of Portuguese forces from the territories in question; sen. Barros Gomes informs the British minister, Mr. Petre, that such instructions had been sent 9 Jan. Lord Salisbury, having learned from consul Churchill at Mozambique, that major Serpa Pinto's forces still occupied his positions, and treated Nyassaland as a conquered country, directs Mr. Petre to require acceptance of the British demands before 10 P.M. 11 Jan.; if not accepted he is to order H.M.S. *Enchantress*, at Vigo, to enter the Tagus, and to prepare for the withdrawal of the British legation from Lisbon, 10 Jan. ,,

The council of state decide to yield under protest, reserving all Portuguese rights . . 12 Jan. ,,

[All the correspondence, from 16 Nov. 1889 to 13 Jan. 1890, was published in the *London Gazette*, 17 Jan. 1890.]

The surveying expedition under Mr. Selous, on behalf of the British South Africa company, starts . . . . Feb. ,,

The Portuguese evacuate the disputed territory in the Shiré district, reported . . 8 March, ,,

Telegraph lines rapidly constructed, reported, 11 June, ,,

Expedition of the South Africa company into Mashonaland under lieut.-col. E. G. Pennefather, with other military men, July; favourable progress, Aug.; arrives at its goal at mount Hampden, well received by the natives, reported, 12 Sept.; the force disbands to occupy the land granted them . . . . . about 24 Oct. ,,

Part of the Manica country ceded to the company by the chief Umtasa, by treaty . 14 Sept. ,,

H.M.S. gunboats, the *Herald* and *Musquito*, enter the Zambesi, accompanied by other vessels with stores . . . . 8 Oct. ,,

H.M.S. *Redbreast*, man-of-war, leaves Zanzibar, 3 Sept., amid many difficulties and some Portuguese opposition, with other vessels, proceeds up the Zambesi, reaches Zumbo, and returns to Zanzibar . . . . 17 Oct. ,,

Mr. Colquhoun, the administrator of the company, assumes the government at Fort Salisbury, 10 Oct. ,,

The Anglo-Portuguese agreement of 20 Aug. withdrawn, and a *modus vivendi* agreed on 14 Nov. ,,

Col. Paiva d'Andrade and the baron de Rezendi, with Gouveia, a half-breed native chief, and about 300 followers, seize Umtasa's kraal at Massi Kesse, and replace the British by the Portuguese flag, 8 Nov.; major Forbes, with the company's police, re-takes the kraal, restores the British flag, and temporarily imprisons the Portuguese officers; Gouveia, with his men, flee . 15 Nov. ,,

The South Africa company ordered by the British government to withdraw from Manica, about 19 Dec. ,,

Gungunhama, nominal king of Manica, said to have replaced the Portuguese flag by the English, reported . . . . 31 Dec. ,,

Gold discovered in Mashonaland; many claims for working and tracts assigned . Dec. *et seq.* ,,

Col. Paiva d'Andrade arrives in Lisbon, and complains of the conduct of major Forbes and others (in Nov.), and denies the truth of the company's statements respecting it . . . . 19 Jan. 1891
Mr. H. H. Johnston appointed British resident of the district N. of the company's territories, to be called "British Central Africa" . . March, ,,
The *Countess of Carnarvon*, steamer, conveying Messrs. Jameson, Doyle, Stevens, and Moodie to Cape Town, to meet Mr. C. Rhodes, captured by a Portuguese customs' steamer on the river Limpopo, which was declared open by the chief, Gungunhama, free to British commerce, about 8 March; Gungunhama repudiates vassalage to Portugal . . . . 14 March, ,,
Mr. Jameson and others at Delagoa Bay set free, 17 March; go to Cape Town . . March, ,,
The British steamer, *Norseman*, containing sir John Willoughby and party, with the imperial British mail for Mashonaland, stopped by the Portuguese at Port Beira, in the Pungwé river, although the prescribed duty of 3 per cent. on the stores had been offered, according to the *modus vivendi*; the British flag replaced by the Portuguese. Two steam launches seized, and the crews imprisoned, reported by sir John at Delagoa bay, 20 April; on the remonstrance of lord Salisbury the Portuguese government declares the Pungwé river open to British subjects; three of H.M.'s ships sent to the Pungwé, announced . 23 April, ,,
Massi Kessi evacuated by the British by government orders, reported . . . . 30 April, ,,
Gungunhama, king of Gazaland, sends an embassy to queen Victoria, soliciting perpetual alliance, April, May, ,,
Two envoys honourably received, May, June; by the Queen at Windsor . . . . . 10 July, ,,
Portuguese attack on the company's police post, W. of Massi Kesse, repulsed . . 11 May, ,,
Mr. Cecil Rhodes, commissioner, arrives at Fort Salisbury . . . . . . 16 Oct. ,,
First annual meeting of the British South Africa company, the duke of Abercorn in the chair; report and balance-sheet accepted . 22 Dec. ,,
The British parliament votes 20,000*l*. for a survey for the construction of a railway from Mombasa to the Victoria Nyanza . . . 10 March, 1892
Agreement between Great Britain and Portugal respecting the navigation of the Zambesi, about 19 March, ,,
Second annual meeting of the company in London; prosperity reported by Mr. Cecil Rhodes (telegraph between fort Salisbury and Cape Town completed; railway constructing to the coast; territories enlarged (N. and S.) . . 29 Nov. ,,
War with Lobengula (see *Mashonaland*) . . 1893
Extraordinary meeting of the company in London, confirming the agreements between the company and the United Concessions company and other companies (1890, *et seq.*), 20 Nov. 1893; 3rd annual meeting held in London; report adopted, 19 Dec. ,,
Governing ordinances gazetted . . 16 March, 1894
Mr. Cecil Rhodes, Dr. Jameson, and others, arrive in England . . . . . . 16 Nov. ,,
Agreement between the British government and the company relating to administration north of the Zambesi, signed . . . . 24 Nov. ,,
Satisfactory report of the company for 1894; speeches by Mr. Cecil Rhodes (died 26 March, 1902), Dr. Jameson, and others . 18 Jan. 1895
Creation of 500,000 1*l*. shares (issue price 70*s*.) to redeem debentures, at a meeting in London, 12 July, ,,
The directors of the company disapprove of Dr. Jameson's entering the Transvaal (*which see*) and order him to retire . . . . . 2 Jan. 1896
Frontier arrangements with Portugal prolonged till 1898, reported . . . . . 7 Feb. ,,
Report issued by the directors of the company for 1895; revenue, 118,883*l*.; expenditure, 142,423*l*. See *Rhodesia*, 1896 *et seq.*, *Times* 27 Feb. ,,
Portuguese gunboat captured and crew massacred by natives at Chinde . . . . July, 1897
Satisfactory report of the company for 1899; a supplemental charter and deed of settlement approved . . . . 14 Dec. 1899
The Middle Zambesi navigated first by steam, and its source discovered by maj. Gibbons, reported, 20 Aug. 1900
Col. Arnold's exploring expedition successful; the chief Macombi submits to the Portuguese, 8 Dec. ,,
Barotseland under British protection since 1890; definite agreement signed, king Lewanika granting administrative powers to the chartered company, and receiving an annual subsidy, in 1897; he arrives in England 24 May; is received by the king in London . . . . . 30 May, 1902
Livingstone, the first steamship launched on the Upper Zambesi, above the Victoria Falls, 19 Aug. ,,
Portuguese expedition routs Macombi, chief of Barue, reported . . . . . 27 Aug. ,,

ZAMORA (Spain). Here Alphonso the Great defeated the Moors, in 901.

ZANTE. One of the Ionian Islands (*which see*).

ZANZALEENS. This sect rose in Syria, under Zanzalee, 535; he taught that water baptism was of no efficacy, and that it was necessary to be baptized by fire, with the application of a red-hot iron. The sect was at one time very numerous.

ZANZIBAR or **ZANGUEBAR**, an island, east Africa, metropolis of the possessions of the Imaum of Muscat, and chief market for ivory, gum, coral, and cloves, and also for slaves. At the death of the Seyyid (or lord), miscalled "imaum" and "sultan," of Muscat, 1856, his dominions were divided between his sons; see *Muscat*. Majid obtained Zanzibar, after a contest with his brother, Barghash Seyyid, who, however, succeeded at his death, 7 Oct. 1870. An expedition for the purpose of suppressing the slave trade was sent to Zanzibar, under the command of sir Bartle Frere, 20 Nov. 1872, arrived about 12 Jan. 1873. After some delay and negotiation by Dr. Kirke, a treaty was signed, abolishing the trade, 5 June, 1873. The contract for the mail to Zanzibar was censured as too expensive in July, 1873, and altered. The Seyyid Barghash visited England in 1875, arrived 9 June; received by the queen, 21 June; received freedom of London, 12 July; sailed for France, 15 July. He decreed confiscation of slaves brought to Zanzibar, 18 April, 1876. The sultan's offer to concede large territories on the mainland to sir Wm. Mackinnon (founder of the British East Africa Company, 1888), not accepted by the British government, 1878. The sultan made knight of St. Michael and St. George, 14 Sept 1883. Zanzibar and Pemba, population 250,000, about 1904.

Treaty with Germany comes into force, 19 Aug. 1886. The sultan's rights recognised by Anglo-German treaty . . . 29 Oct. & 1 Nov. 1886
Rupture with Portugal respecting non-cession of territories (see *Mozambique*) . Feb.–March, 1887
Seyyid Barghash died; succeeded by his brother Seyyid Khalifah . . . . 26 March, 1888
Dispute with Italy respecting cession of territories by the late sultan . . . . . 6 June, ,,
Territories ceded to the British East Africa company; treaty signed . . . . 9 Oct. ,,
Lieut. Cooper captures a dhow but is killed: much regretted . . . . . 17 Oct. ,,
The universities' mission warned to retire from the mainland of Africa by government on account of operations against slave traders by England and Germany . . . . Oct. ,,
The coast blockaded by Germany and England, 2 Dec.; the Germans make war on the chiefs who burn Bagamoyo and retire . . 7 Dec. ,,
The Arab slave dealers attack some German stations and carry off the freed slaves; eight missionaries killed . . . . 11–13 Jan. 1889
Mr. Brooks and 26 others, missionaries, murdered near Saadani . . . . . 21 Jan. ,,

Meeting of the sultan's bodyguard stopped by the intervention of Mr. Portal and gen. Mathews, 19, 20 July, 1889
The sultan signs a concession of territory to the British East Africa company (headquarters Mombasa) . . . . 1 Sept. ,,
The blockade on the coast abandoned after 1 Oct. ,,
Ordered that all native children born in Zanzibar after 1 Jan. 1890, to be free subjects of the sultan Oct. ,,
The marquis of Salisbury receives the two envoys from Zanzibar, 25 Oct.; they are taken by Mr. Berkeley and capt. Gissing to Windsor and other places, 26 Oct.; received by the queen at Balmoral . . . . 29 Oct. ,,
Mr. Gerald Portal, much respected by the sultan and Europeans, leaves Africa . . 14 Nov. ,,
Mr. Stanley and party arrive at Zanzibar . 6 Dec. ,,
The sultan receives grand cross of St. Michael and St. George, and grand cross Red Eagle. 16 Dec. ,,
The sultan surrenders all control over the British East Africa company's territory for an annual payment, reported . . . . . 26 Dec. ,,
Twelve H.M.'s ships at Zanzibar . . 8 Jan. 1890
Expedition from Aden to Harrar under gen. Hogg, to chastise the Eesa tribe for a murderous raid on Bulhar, Somaliland, a place under British protection (17 Aug. 1889) on 11 Jan., reported successful, with some loss . . . 16 Feb. ,,
Adm. Fremantle, with 11 men-of-war, at Mombasa . . . . 31 Jan. ,,
Death of the sultan, Seyyid Khalifah, by apoplexy, succeeded by his brother, Seyyid Ali, 13 Feb.; duly recognised . . . . . . 17 Feb. ,,
The protectorate of Zanzibar, Witu, &c., assumed by Great Britain with the consent of the sultan, in conformity with the Anglo-German convention, announced . . . . . . 18 June, ,,
Adm. Fremantle with fleet at Zanzibar; the sultan received by the admiral on the *Boadicea* 25 July ,,
Decree of the sultan against slavery; the sale, purchase, or exchange of slaves strictly prohibited; slaves of persons dying without lawful heirs, declared free; slaves not to be disposable by will, &c. . . . . 1 Aug. ,,
6 houses of slave-brokers permanently closed, 2 Aug. ,,
Herr Küntzel and a party of Germans in Witu, or Vitu, disarmed by the sultan . . 14 Sept. ,,
Küntzel's violent conduct leads to the massacre by the natives of all the party except Menschel, 15 Sept. ,,
Redress demanded by the British and Germans; the sultan of Witu refuses to surrender the criminals . . . . 23 Oct. ,,
An expedition under captain Curzen-Howe and commander M'Quhae; certain evacuated villages on the coast burnt; adm. Fremantle at Kipini; the admiral, with nearly 1,000 men, advances on Witu . . . . . . 25, 26 Oct. ,,
Witu captured and destroyed, the enemy disperse; there were 13 British wounded; the success of the expedition was mainly attributed to capt. Curzon-Howe, the chief of the staff; between 80 and 90 natives were killed . . . . 27 Oct. ,,
Col. C. B. Euan-Smith, consul-general, made K.C.B., announced . . . . . . 10 Nov. ,,
The grand cross of the Star of India conferred on the sultan of Zanzibar, invested . 14 Nov. ,,
Death of the deposed sultan of Witu, reported, 14 Jan. 1891
Sir C. B. Euan-Smith makes terms with the Witu chiefs; a younger brother of the late sultan elected successor, announced, 26 Jan.; peace and amnesty proclaimed . . . . about 29 Jan. ,,
Sir C. B. Euan-Smith leaves for Europe (succeeded by Mr. Gerald Portal, (K.C.M.G., 1892) consul-general . . . . 6 March, ,,
The sultan opens the Cooper Royal Naval Institute, 8 July, ,,
Tipoo Tib at Zanzibar, received by the sultan, 20 July, ,,
Great increase of commerce under British protectorate . . . . . March—Sept. ,,
New government formed, gen. Mathews, president, 20 Oct. ,,
Import duties, except on alcohol and dangerous objects, abolished . . . . 20 Dec. ,,
Zanzibar declared a free port . . . 1 Feb. 1892
The international bureau, for the suppression of the slave trade, first meeting at Zanzibar; sir Gerald Portal, president . . . . 9 Nov. 1892
Sir Gerald Portal sent to Uganda (*which see*).
Mr. Rennell Rodd, deputy . . . about 12 Dec. ,,
Death of the sultan; succeeded by Said Hamed bin Thwain, grand-nephew, proclaimed by Mr. Rodd; the king's son set aside . . . . 5 March, 1893
Rescue of 60 children from an Arab dhow, with French colours, by *Philomel*, an English cruiser, reported . . . . . 10 April, 2 May, ,,
The Benadir ports and territories conceded to Italy for 3 years . . . . 12 July, ,,
Capt. Filouardi starts an Italian trading company, headquarters at Magadoxo, reported . 22 Nov. ,,
Death of sir Gerald Portal, consul-general, 25 Jan.; succeeded by Mr. Arthur Henry Hardinge, Feb. 1894
British E. Africa company's territory transferred to the British government under the jurisdiction of Mr. (aft. sir) A. Hardinge, K.C.M.G. 1897, 1 July, 1895
Four slavers captured by H.M.S. *Barossa*, and the persons implicated imprisoned . . . May, 1896
Death of the sultan, aged about 40; Said Khalid, his cousin, at once takes possession of the palace, and proclaims himself sultan . . . 25 Aug. ,,
British ultimatum, sent by rear-adm. Rawson, 7 a.m., bombardment began, 9 a.m.; firing ceased, 9.40 a.m.; sultan's corvette, *Glasgow*, sunk; usurper Khalid surrenders to the German consul; enemy's loss heavy; the late sultan's brother, Said Hamud bin Mahomed, proclaimed sultan, and saluted by the warships; looting, &c. in the town suppressed by the British . . 27 Aug. ,,
The sultan in full accord with the British; the military, financial, and executive departments placed under their control . . . Sept. ,,
The usurper, Said Khalid, taken on board the German sloop, *Seeadler* . . . . . 2 Oct. ,,
Slavery abolished, with compensation, by the sultan's decree . . . . . 6 April, 1897
British judicial system introduced, by orders in council . . . . 9 July, ,,
Heavy rainfall and gale; bridges and native houses, &c., destroyed . . . . . . 23 April, 1899
New 5 per cent. duty on imports, with a few exceptions . . . . 15 Sept. ,,
Gen. sir Lloyd Wm. Mathews, prime minister and treasurer, dies, aged 51, deeply regretted by all, 11 Oct. 1901; succeeded by Mr. Rogers . Nov. 1901
Death of the sultan Hamud, aged 51 . 18 July, 1902
Seyyid Ali, aged 18, proclaimed sultan; Mr. Rogers, regent . . . . 20 July, ,,
Visit of Mr. and Mrs. Chamberlain . 21 Dec. ,,

ZARA, capital of Dalmatia, a Roman colony under Augustus. It revolted from Venice and was recaptured, 18 Nov. 1202; unsuccessfully besieged by the Turks 1572, 1577; given up to Austria, 1791.

ZE, ZOW, ZIERES, for *ye, you*, and *yours*. The letter *z* was retained in Scotland, and was commonly written for the letter *y* so late as the reign of queen Mary, up to which period many books in the Scottish language were printed in Edinburgh with these words, 1543.

ZEALAND, one of the 13 provinces which formed the League of Utrecht, 1579; see *Holland*, and *New Zealand*.

ZELA, N.E. Asia Minor, where Julius Cæsar defeated Pharnaces, king of Pontus, son of Mithridates. Cæsar, in announcing his victory, sent his famous despatch to the senate of Rome, in these words: "*Veni, vidi, vici*,"—"I came, I saw, I conquered" (perhaps the shortest despatch on record). This battle ended the war; Pharnaces escaped into Bosporus, where he was slain by his lieutenant, Asander; Pontus was made a Roman province, and Bosporus given to Mithridates of Pergamus, 47 B.C.

ZELL (Hanover), see *Denmark*, 1772.

ZEMSTVOS, local representative councils in Russia established by Alexander II., 1855–81.

ZEND-AVESTA, ancient sacred books of the Parsees; of which 3 out of 21 are extant. The age of these books is much disputed. Professor Max Müller says that the MSS. had been preserved by the Parsee priests at Bombay, where a colony of fire-worshippers had fled in the 10th century. Anquetil Duperron's French translation, from a modern Persian version, was published in 1771; edition by Eugene Burnouf, 1829–43. A French translation was published by prof. James Darmesteter, professor of Zend, in Paris; he died 19 Oct. 1894, aged 45. Zend, a language akin to Sanskrit and the Afghan tongue, has been studied by Bopp and other philologists.

ZENO or **ZENON**, see *Stoics*.

ZENOBIA, Queen of the East, see *Palmyra*.

ZENTA, in Hungary, the scene of a battle where the Germans, under prince Eugene, defeated the Turks, 11 Sept. 1697. This victory led to the peace of Carlowitz, ratified January, 1699.

ZETETICAL SOCIETY, established in 1878, to afford opportunities for the unrestricted discussion of a variety of questions.

ZETUNIUM. After defeating Samuel king of Bulgaria here, 29 July, 1014, the emperor Basil II. blinded his 15,000 prisoners, except one in a hundred, to whom he left one eye. The king died of grief.

ZHOB VALLEY, see *Beloochistan*.

ZIDON, see *Sidon*.

ZIEGLER EXPEDITION, see *N.E. and N.W. Passages*.

ZINC. The ore of zinc, calamine or spelter, known to the Greeks, who used it in the manufacture of brass. It is said to have been known in China also, and is noticed by European writers as early as 1231; though the method of extracting it from the ore was unknown for nearly five hundred years after. The metal zinc is mentioned by Paracelsus (died 1541). A mine of zinc was discovered on lord Ribblesdale's estate, Craven, Yorkshire, in 1809. Zincography was introduced in London shortly after lithography became known in England, in 1817; see *Lithography*. Zinc is much used in voltaic batteries; and its application in manufactures has greatly increased of late years; see *Photozincography*.

ZINC OBTAINED IN THE UNITED KINGDOM.

	tons.	*value.*
1875.	6,713	162,790*l.*
1880.	7,162	123,544*l.*
1882.	16,130	286,710*l.*
1885.	9,778	146,100*l.*
1888.	10,002	191,455*l.*
1890.	8,582	203,358*l.*
1893.	9,284	167,770*l.*
1896.	7,110	123,240*l.*
1899.	8,698	220,132*l.*
1900.	9,066	188,573*l.*

ZIONIST CONGRESS, to acquire Palestine by purchase from Turkey with a view to establishing the Jews in the Holy Land, 200 European delegates present, Dr. Herzl and Herr Nordau, presidents, opened at Basel, 29 Aug. 1897; again 28 Aug. 1898; London, 13 Aug. 1900; Basel, 26 Dec. 1901; Basel, 23 Aug. 1903.

The Chovevi Zion association of England, 8th annual conference, 200 delegates present; at Clerkenwell Town hall . . . . 6 March, 1898

English Zionist federation, sir Francis Montefiore, chairman, inaugurated . . . . 22 Jan. 1899

Zionist congress at Basel pass resolution, 295–177, to send a committee to Uganda to investigate its suitability for Jewish colonization, 25 Aug.; National fund to end of Aug. 1903, 18,668*l.*, fund to be raised to 200,000*l.* to acquire land in Palestine and Syria, 27 Aug. 1903; Jewish Colonization act, royal assent . . . . 14 Aug. 1903

Public mass meeting, great assembly hall, Mile-end road, under auspices of English Zionist federation . . . . 5 Sept. ,,

ZIONISTS, the name given to the adherents of the rev. Dr. Dowie, previously a presbyterian minister in Australia, who, in 1894, founded the "Christian Catholic Church" at Chicago, where is the huge building, called the Zion tabernacle, from which his followers derive their name. Dr. Dowie, who claims to be the second Elijah foretold by the prophet Malachi (Mal. iii. 1), professes to reform the church on the model of the primitive apostolic times, and claims to possess the apostolic gift of healing. The Zionists give tithes of all their possessions, and abstain from eating pork; and in sickness depend solely for their cure on faith and prayer; connected with the Zionist settlement are lace and candy manufactures, which carry on an extensive business. In Oct. 1903, Dr. Dowie and a large number of his followers, calling themselves "the Zionist Restoration league," visited New York with the view to its conversion; Dr. Dowie's meetings in Madison-square were the scene of much confusion and derision, and the expenses and losses connected with the propaganda led to financial difficulties with his creditors. Mrs. Dowie, with her son, visited London, and conducted a service at Caxton hall, 8 Nov. 1903.

ZIRCONIUM, the metallic base of the earth Zirconia, discovered by Klaproth in 1789; from this Berzelius obtained the metal in 1824. Zirconia is found in the sand of the rivers of Ceylon. The metal exists in the form of a black powder.

ZIZYPHUS VULGARIS. A shrub brought from the south of Europe about 1640. The *Zizyphus Paliurus* shrub (Christ's Thorn) was brought from Africa before 1596; see *Flowers*.

ZODIAC. Its obliquity was discovered, its twelve signs named, and their situations assigned them by Anaximander, about 560 B.C. The Greeks and Arabians borrowed the zodiac from the Hindus. *Sir W. Jones.* The zodiacal light was observed by Tycho Brahe, Descartes, and others, and named by Cassini, 1683.

ZOLLVEREIN (*Customs' Union*), the name given to the German commercial union, projected by Prussia 1818, and gradually joined by nearly all the German states except Austria. On 19 Feb. 1853, an important treaty of commerce and navigation, between Austria and Prussia, to last from Jan. 1854 to Dec. 1865, was signed, to which the other states of the Zollverein gave in their adhesion on 5 April, 1853. In Nov. 1861, Prussia threatened to withdraw unless certain changes were made. By the treaty of 8 July, 1867, between the North German confederation, and the southern states (Bavaria, Würtemberg, Baden, and Hesse), various changes were made, and by other treaties signed in Oct. these states agreed to send delegates to a customs parliament to be held at Berlin. A session of this parliament was opened by the king of Prussia, 27 April, and closed 23 May,

1868. Federal chancellor, the count von Bismarck. Imports, 1882, valued at 158,235,000*l.*; exports, 1882, 162,235,000*l.*

ZOOLOGY (from *zoōn*, Greek for animal) is the division of biology which treats of animals; Aristotle (322-284 B.C.) the founder of the science. Systems of classification have been made by John Ray (1628-1705), Charles Linné (1707-78), G. Buffon (1707-88), and George Cuvier (1769-1832).

Linnæus divided the animal kingdom into six classes.—*Mammalia*, which includes all animals that suckle their young; *Aves*, birds; *Amphibia*, or amphibious animals; *Pisces*, fishes; *Insecta*, insects; *Vermes*, worms; 1741.

Cuvier (died in Paris, 13 May, 1832), in his great work, *Règne Animal*, published in 1816, distributed the animals into four great divisions, the *Vertebrata* (backboned); the *Mollusca* (soft-bodied); the *Articulata* (jointed); and the *Radiata* (the organs disposed round a centre).

In 1859, professor Owen made known a system of arranging the class *Mammalia* according to the nature of their brains.

The ZOOLOGICAL SOCIETY OF LONDON (originally the Zoological Club) was founded in 1826; the society was mainly founded by sir Stamford Raffles, sir H. Davy, and its gardens in the Regent's Park were opened in April, 1827; the society was chartered 27 March, 1829. 2072 animals in the gardens, 31 Dec. 1871; about 500 animals from India given by the prince of Wales, May, 1876; 15 animals from the late queen Victoria's menagerie, received 4 April, 1901. 2,585 animals, 31 Dec. 1887. 1 Jan. 1892, 2,985 members; total receipts, 24,054*l.*: 3,158 members; 28,713*l.* receipts, 31 Dec. 1897; 2,922 animals, 1901; 3,413 members; 29,077*l.* receipts, 31 Dec. 1902.

Dr. James Murie was appointed by the society to be their first "anatomical prosector," 3 May, 1865.

New reptile house opened, 6 Aug. 1883.

On the demolition of Exeter 'Change, in 1829, the menagerie of Mr. Cross was temporarily lodged in the King's Mews, whence it was removed to the Surrey Zoological Gardens, 1832.

The Zoological Gardens of Dublin were opened, 1832.

Zoological Station for study, open to the public, established at Naples by professor Anton Dohrn, opened 1 Oct. 1873.

Wombwell's (latterly Edmonds') great collection of trained animals sold, 29, 30 July, 1884. Bought by Mr. R. T. Barnum, Jan. 1888.

Mr. Charles Jamrach, who succeeded his father, an eminent importer of wild animals, which he supplied to the Zoological Society, and menageries, &c., died, 6 Sept. 1891.

International zoological congresses, Paris, 1889; Moscow, 1892; Leyden, 16–21 Sept. 1895; Cambridge, 22 Aug. 1898; Berlin, 12 Aug. 1901.

Mr. W. E. de Winton succeeds Mr. C. Bartlett, for many years superintendent of the Zoological gardens, Jan. 1903.

Reorganisation of the gardens, rebuilding of houses for giraffes, hippopotami, bears' dens, and other improvements and alterations, reported at annual meeting, 22 April 1903.

Dr. Chalmers Mitchell, on retirement of Dr. P. L. Sclater, elected secretary of the Zoological society, 29 Jan. 1903.

See *Aquarium, Hippopotamus, Giraffe*, and *Acclimatization, Olympia*, &c.

ZOOPRAXISCOPE, optical apparatus invented by Mr. Eadweard J. Muybridge to exhibit photographs of moving animals, about 1881.

The apparatus was successfully employed at the Royal Institution (in the presence of the prince of Wales) 13 March, 1882, and again in March and May, 1889; also at the Royal Society and other places in the same year. His great work on the subject was published in 1887-9, and his "Animals in Motion," in 1899.

ZORNDORFF, Prussia, where a battle was fought between the Prussian and Russian armies; the former, commanded by the king of Prussia, obtained a victory over the forces of the czarina, whose loss amounted to 21,529 men, while that of the Prussians was about 11,000: 25, 26 Aug. 1758.

ZOUAVES AND FOOT CHASSEURS. When the French established a regency at Algiers, in 1830, they hoped to find the employment of native troops advantageous, and selected the *Zooaouas*, a congregation of daring Arab tribes. In time, numbers of red republicans, and other enthusiastic Frenchmen, joined the regiments, adopting the costume, &c.: eventually the Africans disappeared from the ranks, and no more were added. Among their colonels were Lamoricière and Cavaignac. The French Zouaves formed an important part of the army in the Crimean war, 1854-5.*

ZUG, the smallest canton of Switzerland, joined the confederation, 1352, and the Sonderbund, 1846. Population, 1888, 23,029.

Many persons killed by fall of about 27 houses into the lake of Geneva . . . . 5–7 July, 1887

ZUIDER ZEE, or **SOUTH SEA**, a large gulf in the Netherlands, about 60 miles long, 210 miles in circumference, and some 40 miles at its greatest breadth, Texel, Vlieland and other islands separate it from the North sea, with which it communicates by various channels. The greater part of it was formerly covered with forests and towns, and was inundated in the twelfth and thirteenth centuries. In 1875, the Dutch chamber voted 9,500,000*l.* to reclaim the submerged land by drainage, and to erect a dyke, 26 feet high above the water, and 25 miles long; thus adding 759 square miles to the country; the new canal was inaugurated by the late king, 1 Nov. 1876. The Dutch Texel fleet here surrendered to admiral Mitchell, 30 Aug. 1799. A royal commission, appointed Sept. 1892, endorsed the proposals for reclaiming land from the sea, &c., set forth in the report of the Zuider Zee association, and in May, 1901, a bill was introduced by the government, but a change of ministry caused its subsequent withdrawal. The scheme comprises the union of the coasts of North Holland and Friesland by a great sea-wall or dyke, reclaiming an area of 478,720 acres of cultivable land, at an estimated cost of 29,625,296*l.*, its worth will extend over a period of 36 years.

ZUINGLIANS, or Zwinglians, the followers of the reformer, Ulric Zuingli, who at Zurich declaimed against the church of Rome, and effected the same separation for Switzerland from the papal dominion which Luther did for Saxony. He procured two assemblies to be called; by the first he was authorised to proceed, by the second, the ceremonies of the Romish church were abolished 1519. Zuingli died in arms, being slain in a skirmish against his popish opponents, 11 Oct. 1531. The Zuinglians were also called Sacramentarians.

ZULLICHAU (Prussia). Here the Russians, under Soltikow, severely defeated the Prussians under Wedel, 23 July, 1759.

ZULPICH, see *Tolbiac*.

ZULU CELIBATE MILITARY SYSTEM, founded by Godongwana, confirmed by Chaka and Dingaan; completed by Cetywayo.

* The Zouave organization and drill were introduced into the federal army in the great civil war in America, by Ephraim E. Ellesworth, early in 1861. He was assassinated on 24 May same year, at Alexandria, just after taking down a secession flag.

ZULULAND, South-east Africa; capital, Eshowe; near the British colony, Natal, to which it has been annexed. In the last century, the Zulus were a peaceful pastoral people.. Population about 205,000.

Godongwana, a chief, (termed Dingiswayo, "the Wanderer," from his early life,) began a military organisation by forming a celibate army; killed in battle and succeeded by his vigorous and merciless ally, Chaka, styled king, by whom Zulu supremacy was mainly established over the Fingoes and other tribes . . . . about 1812

Chaka assassinated; succeeded by his brother Dingaan, crafty, treacherous, and cruel; at first friendly with the British at Natal (*which see*); made treaty with capt. Allen Gardiner . 6 May, 1835

Massacres Retief, 70 Boers, and their servants (who had recovered his stolen cattle), 2 Feb., and about 600 afterwards; defeats the British and Dutch in several encounters; but is severely beaten by Andries Pretorius . . . . Dec. 1838

Dingaan again defeated; killed by one of his chiefs; succeeded by his brother Umpanda, peaceful and crafty; who keeps peace with the English and Dutch . . . . 1840, *et seq.*

Cetywayo (pronounced Ketchwāyo) his eldest son, kills his brothers; succeeds at his father's death; organizes still further his army, named by Frere "the celibate man-slaying war-machine" . Oct. 1872

Recognized on behalf of the British by Mr. Shepstone; crowned . . . . . . 1 Sept. 1873

Opposes missionaries; organizes armed resistance to the British; when remonstrated with for outrages, defies them 1876

Sir Bartle Frere, governor of the Cape, requests help from England; 90th regiment and a battery sent . . . . Jan. 1878

Cetywayo refuses to give up leaders of a raid on British territory (in July); and tenders a fine; sir Bartle Frere demands, as an ultimatum, their surrender within 30 days . . . . . Dec. ,,

The time (extended) having elapsed, 11 Jan., the British, under lord Chelmsford, cross the Tugela and enter Zululand . . . . . . 12 Jan. 1879

Col. Pearson defeats the Zulus and advances to Echowe (which he fortifies) . . . 21 Jan. ,,

British camp at Isandula or Isandlwana, about 10 miles from Rorke's Drift (on the Tugela), surprised and attacked by about 15,000 Zulus; 5 companies of the 24th regiment, and many natives killed, with cols. Durnford and Pulleine, and other officers; total loss about 837; 2000 Zulus said to have been killed; (lieuts. Melville and Coghill perished while preserving the colours) 22 Jan. ,,

Rorke's Drift severely attacked; successfully defended by lieuts. Chard and Bromhead 22 Jan. ,,

Zulus attack Inkanyana; defeated by col. Evelyn Wood . . . . 24 Jan. ,,

Reinforcements requested; troops rapidly sent off from England . . . . . 19 Feb. *et seq.* ,,

Prince Louis Napoleon requesting to join the British, permitted to go as a guest; sails 27 Feb. ,,

Arrival of the *Tamar* with 800 men, &c., at Pietermaritzburg . . . . 11 March, ,,

British convoy near Itombi river cut to pieces by Zulus; waggons and stores captured; capt. David Moriarty killed . . . . . 12 March, ,,

Cetywayo's brother Oham, with 600 men, joins the British; announced . . . . 18 March, ,,

Col. Evelyn Wood attacks the Zulus on the Zlobani mountains; suffers much loss, 28 March; gains victory at Kambula . . . . . 29 March, ,,

British advance to relieve Echowe . 29 March, ,,

Zulus defeated at Ginghilovo . . 2 April, ,,

Col. Pearson marches out of Echowe . 2, 3 April, ,,

Sir Garnet Wolseley appointed commander-in-chief, governor of Natal, &c., sails for the Cape May, ,,

British total loss; 1186 killed; 86 died of disease; announced . . . . 27 May, ,,

Cetywayo said to have suppressed an insurrection, and retired to his kraal (or village) at Ulundi, May, ,,

Reconnoitring party, under capt. J. Brenton Carey, on Imbabani, near the Mozani river, surprised; prince Louis Napoleon (acting as commander) killed . . . . . . 1 June, 1879

Ultimatum sent to Cetywayo, requiring restitution of cannon, and total submission; time expired, 12 June, ,,

Sir G. Wolseley arrives at the Cape . 23 June, ,,

Stafford House South African aid committee formed, June, ,,

Zulu raid on cattle; which are recovered 25 June, ,,

Sir Garnet Wolseley sworn in as high commissioner at Pietermaritzburg . . . . 28 or 29 June, ,,

Cetywayo totally defeated at Ulundi (*which see*), 4 July, ,,

Sir G. Wolseley receives chiefs 12 July, *et seq.* ,,

Lord Chelmsford resigns . . . . . 15 July, ,,

Sentence upon capt. Carey, respecting death of prince Napoleon, quashed . . . 22 Aug. ,,

Pursuit of Cetywayo: captured by major Richard Marter . . . . 28 Aug. ,,

Meeting of Sir G. Wolseley with Zulu chiefs; settlement by treaty; Zululand to be divided into 13 independent districts; John Dunn to be a chief; lands reserved for the British; British residents in each district (to be eyes and ears); celibate military system abolished; no arms to be imported; ancient laws and liberties retained; [John Dunn, 20 years in Zululand; conformed to Zulu ways] . . . . . . 1 Sept. ,,

Sir G. Wolseley's despatch, announcing end of the war, dated . . . . 3 Sept. ,,

Cetywayo arrives at Cape Town . . 15 Sept. ,,

His petition to the Queen for restitution declined, about 11 July, 1881

John Dunn energetically subdues a revolting chief about 30 July, ,,

Cost of Zulu war, 4,922,141*l*.

Sir Evelyn Wood visits Zululand and makes important changes . . . . . . Sept. ,,

Reported fighting among the chiefs . . Nov. ,,

The country reported quiet by John Dunn . Dec. ,,

Cetywayo lands at Plymouth and proceeds to London . . . . 3 Aug. 1882

Visited Mr. Gladstone 9 Aug.; received by the Queen, 14 Aug.; by the prince of Wales 16 Aug. ,,

His restoration to part of his kingdom with restrictions, proposed by the British government Aug.; sails from Southampton . . . . . 1 Sept. ,,

Changes made in the territories previous to Cetywayo's return, announced . . . . 29 Dec. ,,

Cetywayo's restoration accepted; proclaimed at Ulundi . . . . 29 Jan. 1883

Struggle between Cetywayo and chiefs, announced 25 April, ,,

Cetywayo defeated by Oham and others with heavy loss, announced . . . . . . 16 May, ,,

Mr. Fynn, British resident, resigns, announced June, ,,

Cetywayo is attacked at Ulundi, by Usibepu, 20 July; and said to be killed . . . . 21 July, ,,

Usibepu said to be all-powerful, Cetywayo a living fugitive, announced . . . . . 8 Aug. ,,

Great battle; Usibepu defeated by Cetywayo's supporters, announced . . . . 16 Aug. ,,

Cetywayo demands a British enquiry into his treatment, announced . . . . . 20 Aug. ,,

Cetywayo surrenders to Mr. Osborn, and is taken to Durban, about 15 Oct.; at Ekowe . 5 Nov. ,,

Defeats of Usibepu by other chiefs . . Nov. ,,

Flight, and recapture of Cetywayo . 27, 28 Jan. 1884

Zibedu defeats Usutus . . about 31 Jan. ,,

Cetywayo dies of heart disease . . 8 Feb. ,,

Much warfare . . . . March-May, ,,

Dinizulu, son of Cetywayo, crowned king by the Boers, in presence of 10,000 people; grants an amnesty, and promises fidelity to the British, 21 May, ,,

Usibepu, severely defeated by the Boers and Usutus, flies, announced . . . 14 June, ,,

A Boer republic established; Joubert, president, Aug. ,,

British flag hoisted at St. Lucia's bay . . Dec. ,,

Quietness in Zululand reported . . . . Jan. 1886

Proposed annexation of Zululand to Natal declined, Oct.; British protectorate over the Zulu territories planned by government . . . Nov. ,,

Agreement with the Boer republic announced, 4 Nov. ,,

Annexation of Zululand as a British possession; the governor to rule by proclamation, May; proclaimed at Durban . . . . 21 June, 1887
Troubles with Dinizulu announced 5 Nov.; his uncle Undabuko and others submit to sir Arthur Havelock, announced 7 Nov.; military preparations; Dinizulu submits, 13 Nov.; Usibepu reinstated in his lands . . . 15 Nov. ,,
The chiefs attacked by the police and military for stealing cattle . . . . . 2 June, 1888
Zulu rebels under Ishingana defeated after a severe conflict . . . . 2 July, ,,
Rebellion of Dinizulu announced . . . 11 July, ,,
Somkeli, the rebel chief, surrenders; announced 1 Aug. ,,
Dinizulu and about 1,000 rebels with cattle enters into the Transvaal territory, 10 Aug.; revolt ended; reported . . . . . 29 Aug. ,,
Dinizulu surrenders conditionally to the Transvaal government . . . . Sept. ,,
Surrender of Undabuko, 19 Sept; his trial began 27 Sept. ,,
Ishingana, rebel chief, surrenders . 12 Nov. ,,
Trial of Undabuko and Somkeli for treason, began 15 Nov. ,,
Dinizulu surrenders to the British . . Nov. ,,
Somhlolo sentenced to five years' hard labour for high treason . . . . . . 22 Nov. ,,
Several chiefs convicted of high treason and sentenced to imprisonment for five years, 1 Dec. ,,
Dinizulu sentenced to ten years', Undabuko to 15 years', and Ishingana to 12 years' imprisonment, 27 April, 1889
Douglas M'Kenzie, appointed bishop of Zululand in 1880, dies, announced . . . 15 Jan. 1890
Dinizutu, Undabuko, and others, transported to St. Helena . . . . 7 Feb. ,,
General tranquillity of the country, reported, 2 April, ,,
Annexation of the Trans-Pongolo territories, 30 May, 1895
Death of John Dunn, announced . . . 6 Aug. ,,
Report of the resident commissioner for 1896; rinderpest, crops destroyed by drought and locusts; European population, estimated, 1,101; native, about 180,000, announced . . . 20 Sept. 1897
Rev. Wilmot Vyvyan appointed bishop of Zululand on translation of Dr. Carter to diocese of Pretoria . . . . Jan. 1903
Col. Mills's report on fight between Boers and Zulus at Holkrantz (see *S. African war*, 6 May, 1902) exonerates the Zulus, published . end Jan. ,,
Engineer's report on the scheme for a harbour in Zululand condemns St. Lucia Bay, and recommends Umlatoosi lagoon . . . . early Feb. ,,
Zulu railway extension opened at Hlabisa, 17 Sept. ,,

See *South African War*.

ZURICH was admitted a member and made head of the Swiss confederacy, 1351, and was the first town in Switzerland that separated from the church of Rome; see *Zuinglians*. A grave-digger at Zurich poisoned the sacramental wine, by which 8 persons lost their lives and many others were grievously injured, 4 Sept. 1776. The French, under Massena, after repelling an attack of the Austrians, retired from Zurich, 5 June, 1799. The Imperialists were defeated by Massena, the former losing 20,000 men in killed and wounded, 25, 26 Sept. 1799; see *Switzerland*. A new democratic constitution was adopted, 18 April, 1869. Population, 1888; canton, 337,183; city, 90,088; 1901, 152,942.

On 24 June, 1859, the Austrians were defeated by the allied French and Sardinian army at Solferino.
Preliminaries of peace were signed at Villa Franca by the emperors of Austria and France on 12 July following.
A conference between the representatives of the powers concerned having been appointed, the first meeting took place at Zurich, on 8 Aug.
After many delays a treaty was signed 10 Nov. Lombardy was ceded to Sardinia; the formation of an Italian Confederation, under the presidency of the pope, was determined on, and the rights of the ex-sovereigns of Tuscany, Modena, and Parma were reserved.
The formation of the kingdom of Italy in 1861 annulled the treaty of Zurich.
Swiss National exhibition, 1 May—27 Dec. 1883.
The theatre destroyed by fire, no fatality; attributed to an incendiary, 1 Jan. 1890.
Rioting between Swiss and Italians suppressed by police and military . . . 25–29 July, 1896
National Swiss museum inaugurated by M. Ruffy, president of the Confederation . 25 June, 1898

ZUTPHEN, in Holland. At a battle here 22 Sept. 1586, between the Spaniards and the Dutch, the amiable sir Philip Sidney, author of "Arcadia," was mortally wounded. He died 7 Oct. He was serving with the English auxiliaries, commanded by the earl of Leicester.

ZUYDER ZEE, see *Zuider Zee*.

ZUYPER SLUYS (Holland). Here sir Ralph Abercromby defeated an attack of the French under Brune; the latter suffered great loss, 9 Sept. 1799.

ZWITTAU, Moravia. Here the Prussians defeated the Austrians and captured provisions, 10 July, 1866.

INDEX.

The references are to *articles* in the body of the work; the italics refer to articles in this Index. The year given is A.D. when B.C. is not mentioned; *b.*, born; *d.*, died; *m.*, murdered; *k.*, killed.

B.

D.

E.

G.

H.

I.

J.

K.

L.

N.

O.

P.

Q.

S.

U.

V.

W.

W.

Z.

ADDENDA.

PAGE

5\. **ABYSSINIA.**—The emperor Menelik prohibits the slave trade, reported, mid Oct. 1903
Lt.-col. sir J. Harrington appointed British minister . . . . Dec. ,,
Treaty signed with the United States, opening friendly commercial relations, reported . . . . 31 Dec. ,,

6\. **ACADEMIES.**—International Association of Academies, founded 1901, met at the Royal Society, London . . . . June, 1903

7\. **ACADEMY.**—Last line, *for* rev. T. Shore *read* T. Shore.

8\. **ACHEEN.**—Conflicts between Dutch and natives, reported, 21 July; submission of the Achenese leaders, reported . 27 Sept. 1903

10\. **ACTS OF PARLIAMENT.**—47 general acts passed in 1903.

11\. **ADEN.**—Punitive operations for native outrages, a village near Jimil destroyed, 7 Oct.; successful fighting with natives of the Kutebi tribe, many killed, 28 Oct. *et seq.*; country reported quiet . . 19 Nov. 1903

ADMIRAL.—*Adm. of the fleet*, hon. sir Henry Keppel died, aged 94 . 17 Jan. 1904

21\. **AFGHANISTAN.**—36 sepoys charged with inciting to rebellion put to death at Cabul, reported . . . . . . 25 Oct. 1903

23\. **AFRICA.**—Maj. Powell-Cotton's exploration in E. Equatorial Africa, completed; unknown country mapped, 6 new tribes, one called "Magician," discovered, reported . . . . 6 Oct. ,,

N.W. Africa.—Capt. Lenfant, French explorer, reaches Shari in a launch; waterway proved from Lake Chad to the Binné, reported . . . . . . 30 Dec. ,,

German S.W. Africa.—Hottentot rising, reported, Oct.; severe fighting at Sandfontein . . . . . . 20, 21 Nov. ,,
Sharp fighting at Hartebeeste river, 12 Dec. ,,
Disturbances north of the Herero territory in districts worked by the Otavi mining co.; unrest among the Ovambo tribes, some 60,000 strong; lieut. von Zülow with 120 men force a passage and join the besieged garrison at Okahandja, reported . 23 Jan. 1904
Rebels capture and burn small stations north of Windhoek, Otjimbigue; Omaruru captured by another body of Hereros, murdering the inhabitants, reported . 26 Jan. ,,

37\. **ALEXANDRA PARK.** — Kite-flying contest won by Mr. S. F. Cody, inventor of naval signalling kites . . . . 3 Oct. 1903

39\. **ALGIERS.**—French convoy attacked by brigands at El Mungar, 37 killed, 47 wounded, capt. Vauchez mortally . 5 Sept. ,,

49\. **ANDES.**—Mr. Reginald Rankin ascended Aconcagua alone, 14 Dec. 1902; first ascent of Mt. Orata, highest peak in Bolivia, made by Mr. W. G. Tight, reported . 2 Sept. 1903

50\. **ANGLO-JAPANESE AGREEMENT.** [THE TEXT OF THE AGREEMENT IS INSERTED IN FULL IN VIEW OF THE PRESENT SITUATION BETWEEN RUSSIA AND JAPAN.]—The governments of Great Britain and Japan, actuated solely by a desire to maintain the *status quo* and general peace in the extreme East, being moreover specially interested in maintaining the independence and territorial integrity of the Empire of China and the Empire of Korea, and in securing equal opportunities in those countries for the commerce and industry of all nations, hereby agree as follows:—

Art. 1. The High Contracting Parties, having mutually recognised the independence of China and Korea, declare themselves to be entirely uninfluenced by any aggressive tendencies in either country. Having in view, however, their special interests, of which those of Great Britain relate principally to China, while Japan, in addition to the interests which she possesses in China, is interested in a peculiar degree politically, as well as commercially and industrially, in Korea, the High Contracting Parties recognise that it will be admissible for either of them to take such measures as may be indispensable in order to safeguard those interests if threatened either by the aggressive action of any other Power, or by disturbances arising in China or Korea, and necessitating the intervention of either of the High Contracting Parties for the protection of the lives and property of its subjects.

Art. 2. If either Great Britain or Japan, in defence of their respective interests as above described, should become involved in war with another Power, the other High Contracting Party will maintain a strict neutrality, and use its efforts to prevent other Powers from joining in hostilities against its ally.

Art. 3. If in the above event any other Power or Powers should join in hostilities against that ally, the other High Contracting Party will come to its assistance, and will conduct the war in common, and make peace in mutual agreement with it.

Art. 4. The High Contracting Parties agree that neither of them will, without consulting the other, enter into separate arrangements with another Power to the prejudice of the interests above described.

Art. 5. Whenever, in the opinion of either Great Britain or Japan, the above-mentioned interests are in jeopardy, the two governments will communicate with one another fully and frankly.

Art. 6. The present Agreement shall come into effect immediately after the date of its signature, and remain in force for five years from that date. In case neither of the High Contracting Parties should have notified twelve months before the expiration of the said five years the intention of terminating it, it shall remain binding until the expiration of one year from the day on which either of the High Contracting Parties shall have denounced it. But if, when the date fixed for its expiration arrives, either ally is actually engaged in war, the alliance shall, *ipso facto*, continue until peace is concluded.

51\. **ANGLO - FRENCH AGREEMENT.**—This agreement, signed 14 Oct. 1903, declares that questions of a juridical character, or

PAGE

relating to the interpretation of treaties, arising between Great Britain and France shall, if incapable of settlement by diplomatic means, be referred to the Hague Court of Arbitration.

An ANGLO-ITALIAN TREATY on similar lines settled in principle, reported . 4 Jan. 1904

51. ANHALT.—Death of the duke of Anhalt, aged 72; succeeded by duke Frederic, 24 Jan. 1904

53. ANTARCTIC POLE.—Relief ship *Terra Nova* left Hobart . . . . 4 Dec. 1903

60. ARBITRATION.—*La Justice Internationale*, a magazine devoted to international arbitration, edited by M. Gustave Hubbard, published in Paris . . . May, 1903

61. ARCHES, COURT OF.—Mr. L. T. Dibdin, K.C., LL.D., succeeds sir Arthur Charles as dean . . . . . . May, 1903

64. ARGENTINE CONFEDERATION.—Chilian mission with treaty of friendship fêted . . . . . . 25 May, 1903

Budget for 1904; reduced taxation and expenditure . . . . . . 24 Aug. ,,

Official statement describes the economic conditions of Argentina to be sound and prosperous; finances in more prosperous state than at any previous period, railway traffic returns much improved, and customs revenue for 1903 increased by 1,500,000*l*. compared with that of 1902 . 22 Dec. ,,

68. ARMENIA.—Two monasteries attacked and pillaged by the Kurds, near Erzeroum and Erzinghan, reported 23 June and 16 July, 1903

Fighting between Armenians and Turkish troops aided by Kurds round Erzeroum, reported . . . . . . 31 July, ,,

Villages pillaged by Kurds, panic in Mush and Sasun; governor of Mush removed, reported . . . . . . 11, 15 Aug. ,,

Increased taxation, unrest reported, 7 Oct. ,,

Sagouni, pres. of an Armenian refugee society murdered at Nunhead, London, 26 Oct.; two other Armenians shot dead at Peckham Rye by Dikran (an Armenian), who committed suicide . . . . . 4 Nov. ,,

72. ARMY.—Force of 25,000 men to be maintained in S. Africa, announced . 16 July, 1903

Army manœuvres in Wilts, Hants, and W. Berks . . . . . 13–18 Sept. ,,

Colours of the Shropshire Light Infantry offered for sale; secured on behalf of the town by the mayor . . . . 30 Oct. ,,

Lord Esher, sir J. A. Fisher, and col. sir G. S. Clarke appointed to inquire into the working of the War Office . 6 Nov. ,,

Accident to lord Kitchener at Simla 16 Nov. ,,

Important speech by Mr. Arnold-Forster, sec. for war, at the Liverpool conservative club, on army reform . . . . . 21 Jan. 1904

73. ARSENIC.—Final report of Royal Commission, blue book issued, specifying precautions to be used with regard to various foods and ingredients; services of analysts to be more efficiently utilized . 3 Dec. 1903

75. ARTS.—Mme. Lelong's collection of paintings &c., sold for about 348,000*l*. . . 29 May, 1903

77. ASHANTEES. — Railway 180 mi. from Sekondi to Coomassie, opened . 1 Oct. 1903

90. AUSTRALASIA. — High court established by royal assent . . . . . 25 Aug. 1903

Sir Samuel Griffith appointed federal chief justice, with sir E. Barton and Mr. R. O'Connor judges of the high court; sir E. Barton resigns the premiership, ministry reconstructed by Mr. Deakin, reported, 24 Sept. ,,

Parliament prorogued . . . . 22 Oct. ,,

Elections for new federal parliament; increase of the labour party, the strength of the parties in the last and new parliament being, *Senate:* ministerialists 12, new 6, opposition, 16, new 13; labour party 8, new 17. *House of Representatives:* ministerialists 32, new 27; opposition, 27, new 26; labour party 16, new 29. Owing to representation being governed by population, which, since the previous election, has increased, the house of representatives has now 7 more members, the members being 82 instead of 75 . . . 16 Dec. 1903

Australian harvest for 1903 estimated to exceed the highest previous yield by 28,000,000 bushels, reported . 21 Dec. ,,

98. AUSTRIA.—Reichsrath reassembles, 23 Sept. 1903

Austro-Hungarian army bill virtually repealed by the adoption of a Polish amendment to a German urgency motion sanctioning the enrolment of the ordinary Austrian contingent of 54,024 recruits, 26 Sept. ,,

Czar visits the emperor at Vienna, 30 Sept.; Imperial conference on Macedonian affairs, 2 Oct. ,,

Battleship *Erzherzog Karl* launched at Trieste . . . . . . 3 Oct. ,,

Budget for 1904 presented, estimated revenue 1,734,771,291 kronen; estimated expenditure 1,732,032,591 kronen, 17 Nov. ,,

Austro-Russian instructions for the execution of the reforms in Macedonia presented to the sultan of Turkey, 22 Oct.; reform scheme accepted by the porte . 25 Nov. ,,

100. AYR.—Gaiety theatre, opened 1902, burnt down . . . . 4 Aug. 1903

101. BABYLONIA.—The code of king Khammurabi, discovered inscribed on a pillar of black diorite, 8 feet high, is the longest Babylonian record yet known. See *Times*, 14 April, 1903.

104. BALFOUR ADMINISTRATION.—Cabinet reconstructed . . . . . 5 Oct. 1903

[Mr. Chamberlain, colonial secretary; Mr. Ritchie, chancellor of exchequer; and lord George Hamilton, secretary for India, resigned 17 Sept.; lord Balfour of Burleigh, secretary for Scotland, and Mr. A. R. D. Elliot, financial secretary to the treasury, resigned, 21 Sept.; the duke of Devonshire, lord president of the council, resigned, 5 Oct. 1903.]

THE CABINET.

Prime minister and first lord of the treasury	Mr. Balfour.
Lord chancellor	Earl of Halsbury.
Lord president of the council and president board of education	Marquis of Londonderry.
Lord privy seal	Marquis of Salisbury.
Secretaries;	
Home affairs	Mr. Akers-Douglas.
Foreign affairs	Marquis of Lansdowne.
War	Mr. Arnold-Forster.
Colonies	Mr. Alfred Lyttelton.
India	Mr. Brodrick.
First lord of the admiralty	Earl of Selborne.
Chancellor of the exchequer	Mr. Austen Chamberlain.
Lord chancellor of Ireland	Lord Ashbourne.
Chief secretary for Ireland	Mr. George Wyndham.
Secretary for Scotland	Mr. Graham Murray.
President board of trade	Mr. Gerald Balfour.
President local government board	Mr. Walter Long.
President board of agriculture and fisheries	Earl of Onslow.
Postmaster-general	Lord Stanley.

Not in the Cabinet.

Chancellor of the Duchy of Lancaster	Sir William Walrond.
First commissioner of works	Lord Windsor.
Financial secretary to the treasury	Mr. Victor Cavendish.
Civil lord of the admiralty	Mr. A. H. Lee.
Secretary to the admiralty	Mr. Pretyman.
Under-secretaries;	
Home	Mr. Cochrane.
Foreign	Earl Percy.
War	Earl of Donoughmore.
Colonial	Duke of Marlborough.
India	Earl of Hardwicke.

PAGE

Financial secretary, war . Mr. Bromley-Davenport.
Parliamentary secretaries:
Board of trade . . Mr. Bonar Law.
Local government board Mr. Grant Lawson.
Board of education . . Sir William Anson.
Attorney-general . . Sir Robert Finlay.
Solicitor-general . . Sir Edward Carson.
Lord advocate . . . Mr. Scott Dickson.
Solicitor-general for Scotland Mr. David Dundas.
Lord-lieutenant of Ireland Earl of Dudley.
Attorney-general for Ireland Mr. Atkinson.
Solicitor-general for Ireland Mr. Campbell.

107. BALLOONS. — Two ascents in Paris, the archduke Salvator of Austria and the comte de Vaulx, and Don Jaime de Bourbon and the comte de Castillon . . . 8 Oct. 1903

108. Capt. Artois crossed the Apennines from Genoa . . . . . 3 Sept.
MM. Lebaudy's successful airship, *Le Jaune*, left Moisson (Seine-et-Oise) 9.10 a.m., and arrived at the Champ de Mars, Paris, 10.50 a.m. . . . . 12 Nov. ,,

112. BANK OF ENGLAND.—Bank discount, *for* reduced to 3, June 25, *read* June 18, 1903.

113. Jan. 1, 1904, government debt, 11,015,100*l*. Other securities, 7,434,900*l*. Gold coin and bullion, 27,010,830*l*. Notes issued, 45,460,830*l*. Balance, or rest, 3,207,587*l*. . ,,

117. BARCELONA. — Strikes, 30,000 men out, June; strike at the gasworks, city in darkness . . . . . . 22 Oct. 1903

117. BARDS.—Annual National Eisteddfod held at Llanelly . . . . . 3 Aug. 1903

120. BARTHOLOMEW, ST.—Influential meeting at the Mansion house approves the appeal for 500,000*l*. to rebuild St. Bartholomew's hospital on its present site: 40,000*l*. given or promised, including 1000*l*. from the queen . . . . . . 26 Jan. 1904

141. BELGIUM.—Interpellation on the Congo by M. Vandervelde, 1 July; debates closed, M. Woeste's order of the day passed, 91—35, 8 July, 1903
British note opposing granting of monopolies, employment of forced labour, &c., in the Congo Free State, presented . 19 Aug. ,,
Visit of the king to Paris, received by pres. Loubet . . . . 4 Sept. ,,
Reply of the king to the powers; denies charges of cruelty to natives in the Congo Free State, and rejects proposed arbitration . . . . 19 Sept. ,,
Demonstration in Brussels against British attacks on the government of the Congo, 27 Sept. ,,
Official reply to the British note . 10 Oct. ,,

145. BERLIN.—Monument to Richard Wagner, unveiled, 1 Oct.; monuments to the emperor and empress Frederick unveiled . 18 Oct. 1903

161. BOAT RACES.—*Wingfield Sculls* (4½ miles), winner, 1903, F. S. Kelly, 23 min. 32 sec. HENLEY ROYAL REGATTA.—*Grand Challenge Cup* 1 mile 550 yds.), 1903, Leander Club, 7 min. 9 secs. *Silver Goblets*, 1903, L. Klaus and A. Ehrenberg, Berlin Victoria, 8 min. 45 secs. *Diamond Challenge Sculls*, 1903, F. S. Kelly, Balliol Coll., Oxf., 8 min. 41 secs. *Professional Sculling Championship*, 1899, 1900, 1901, G. Towns.

161. BOATS.—Capt. Newman and his son (16) left New York 9 July, in an oil launch, 36 ft. long, 8 ft. wide, and reached Falmouth, 14 Aug. 1903
Mr. S. F. Cody, the inventor of the war-kite, crossed from Calais to Dover in his collapsible kite-boat . . . . 6 Nov. ,,
Capt. Eisenbraun crossed the Atlantic from Boston, Mass., in a sailing-boat, 19 ft. long, 6 ft. wide, in 100 days, reaching Gibraltar, 20 Nov. ,,

165. BOMBAY.—Rt. rev. W. R. Pym, bp. of Mauritius, appointed bp. of Bombay, early Dec. 1903

PAGE

Lord Lamington appointed governor, 26 Aug. arrives at Bombay . . . . 12 Dec. 1903

165. BONAPARTE FAMILY.—Mathilde, niece of Napoleon Bonaparte, died, aged 83, 2 Jan. 1904

169. BOSNIA.—Town of Travnik almost destroyed by fire . . . . 3, 4 Sept. 1903

169. BOSTON (U.S.).—Visit of the Hon. Artillery Company, arrive . . . . 2 Oct. 1903
Hon. Artillery Company of Mass. presented by Edward VII. with a signed portrait of himself, in recognition of the welcome extended to Hon. Artillery Company of London . . . . 1 Jan. 1904

181. BRIGHTON.—Inventions exhibition opened 25 Nov. 1903

181. BRISBANE.—Rt. rev. A. V. Green, bp. of Ballarat, elected bp. of Brisbane, early Dec. 1903

182. BRISTOL.—Failure of electric light supply, owing to disastrous fire at works; the city in darkness . . . . . 22 Dec. 1903

185. BRITISH EMPIRE SHAKESPEARE SOCIETY, founded in 1903. President, sir Henry Irving.

195. BULGARIA.—Joint note from the powers warning the government against any action leading to war . . . . 16 Sept. 1903
Troops mobilized on the frontier 13–20 Sept. ,,
Turco - Bulgarian negotiations respecting Macedonia, concessions offered . 22 Sept. ,,
British government strongly favours the reform schemes . . . . 26 Sept. ,,
Public demonstrations in favour of the Macedonians, Sofia . 15 Aug. and 27 Sept. ,,
Frontier post and village near Kottendail attacked by Albanians, 8 Oct.; Bulgaria demands satisfaction . . . . 11 Oct. ,,
About 22,000 Macedonian refugees, reported, mid Oct. ,,
Agreement with Turkey; mutual disarmament of troops, reported . . 18 Oct. ,,
Boris Sarafoff, Macedonian leader, welcomed in Sofia . . . . . 14 Nov. ,,
Elections 7 Oct., government victory; Zaukovists defeated, sobranjé opened by the prince . . . . . 15 Nov. ,,
Mr. G. Buchanan appointed British minister . . . . . . mid Dec. ,,

218. CANADA.—Riot at Sault Ste.-Marie in consequence of non-payment of wages by the Consolidated Lake Superior Co.; troops called out, 1 death . . . . 28 Sept. 1903
Trans-continental railway bill passed, 30 Sept.; parliament prorogued . 24 Oct. ,,
Police post established at the mouth of Mackenzie river to stop the lawlessness of U.S. whalers . . . . early Nov. ,,
Total exports, 225,849,724 dols.; imports, 223,790,516 dols.; 1902–3 returns issued, 30 Nov. ,,
R.C. university at Ottawa burnt down, 2 Dec. ,,

219. CANCER.—Radium (*which see, Addenda*) reported to be used successfully in the treatment of cancer and lupus during 1903.
Important discoveries of the origin and nature of cancer cells communicated to Royal Society by prof. Farmer and Messrs. Moore and Walter, 10 Dec. 1903; and by Drs. Bashford and Murray . . 21 Jan. 1904

222. CANDIA. — Union with Greece again appealed for by the chamber of deputies, 4 May, 1903

230. CAPE OF GOOD HOPE.—Customs amendment and tariff preferential treatment for British imports passed . . 30 July, 1903
Congress of Progressive associations at Cape Town, resolutions carried recognising the services of lord Milner and Mr. Chamberlain; dr. Jameson elected president, 20–22 Aug. ,,
Ministry defeated on a motion concerning an inquiry into martial law, fines, and compensation claims, 25 Aug.; deadlock; parliament dissolved . . . 8 Sept. ,,
Great distress among immigrants, reported, 30 Nov. ,,

PAGE

Lord Milner returns from England 15 Dec. 1903
Mass meeting at Cape Town to protest against the introduction of Chinese labour in the Transvaal . . . . 19 Dec. ,,

234. CAROLINAS.—Mr. Tilman, late lt.-gov. of S. Carolina, tried for the murder of N. G. Gonzales, editor of the *State* newspaper, 15 Jan.; acquitted . . . . 15 Oct. 1903

240. CAUCASUS.—Strikes and conflicts, conflagrations at oil wells and factories July–Aug. 1903
Gradual repression and Russification of the Armenians, schools and libraries closed, societies dissolved, the press stopped; imperial ukase issued practically confiscating the property of the Armenian church, 25 June; disorders and murders, Vassilov, an arch-priest of the Orthodox church, assassinated at Alexandropol, 23 Aug.; demonstration and petitions to the Armenian Catholics . . . . 29 Aug. ,,
Demonstrations and fatal riots near Elisabetpol, and at Tiflis . . 11, 13 Sept. ,,
Disturbances at Nachitchevan . 12 Oct. ,,
Prince Galitzin, gov.-gen., attacked by 3 men in Tiflis, 2 of the men killed 27 Oct. ,,
Conflicts with troops and police in Baku, Kars, many Armenians killed, during Nov. ,,

248. CHARITIES.—Mr. R. C. Beauchamp bequeathed 43,600*l.* to public charities, May; Mr. Noel Whiting 40,000*l.*, 6 July; Mr. J. Hill, over 30,000*l.*; Miss C. Wilson, over 13,000*l.*, announced 1 Sept.; Mr. E. Darling, nearly 24,000*l.*, reported 16 Dec. 1903
Metropolitan charities, 1902–3, total, 6,950,135*l.*

253. CHICAGO.—Strike of liverymen, Nov.; funerals stopped, disgraceful scenes, reported . . . . . 21, 22 Dec. 1903
Terrible fire at the Iroquois theatre, 587 killed, 300 reported missing, 30 Dec. 1903. Criminal charges to be preferred against the mayor, proprietor of the theatre, chief of the fire department, and building commissioner; arrested and liberated on heavy bail . . . . 25 Jan. 1904
Explosion and fire in Masonic Temple, 20 storeys high, with 2000 occupants of offices and stores, no lives lost, damage 20,000 dols. . . . . 23 Jan. ,,

254. CHILDREN.—Employment of Children Act, royal assent . . . . 14 Aug. 1903

256. CHILI.—Resignation of Don Besa 23 Dec. 1903

268. CHINA.—Russian viceroy appointed for the Amur and Kwantung territories; ukase issued . . . . 12 Aug. 1903
Chinese troops defeated at Hevei-chan, reported . . . . 13 Aug. ,,
Chinese board of commerce created by edict, 7 Sept. ,,
Messrs. Claude Russell and Hicks-Beach successfully explore 100 miles east of the Khingan mountains in E. Mongolia, July–Sept. ,,
Plague and cholera at Peitana during Sept. ,,
Commercial treaties with the United States and Japan, signed . . . . . 8 Oct. ,,
Russia fails to evacuate Manchuria according to agreement on appointed date, 8 Oct. ,,
Total exports for 1902, 39,118,115*l.*, exports 30,693,946*l.*, reported . . . 13 Oct. ,,
M. Lessar, Russian minister, demands the appointment of a Russian resident at Mukden, reported . . . . 5 Nov. ,,
New Belgian railway concession signed, 12 Nov. ,,
Fight between Russian and Chinese imperial troops near Shan-hai-Kwan, reported, 13 Nov. ,,
Army amalgamation on a national basis ordered; Yuan Shih-Kai, viceroy of Chi-li, appointed head of the army and navy reported . . . . 5 Dec. ,,
Russian defeat of the Chunchuses on the Lian river, Manchuria, 200 killed, reported, 8 Dec. ,,
Shanghai sedition case: 6 Chinese journalists arrested end of June for seditious writings in the *Supao;* their surrender to Pekin refused by the British legation after protracted negotiations; tried at Shanghai, 3 Dec.; 4 released, 2 convicted, sentence deferred . . . . . . 16 Dec. 1903
Chang-yi, director of Northern railways, disgraced for selling the Kai-ping mines, mid Dec. ,,
Commercial treaty by which United States consuls may be sent to Mukden and Antung in Manchuria, signed by the emperor, ratified by telegraph, and consuls appointed by U.S. government. Commercial treaty with Japan, for opening the foreign trade and settlement of two treaty ports, Mukden and Ta-tung-Ku in Manchuria, ratified . . . . 13 Jan. 1904

271. CHOLERA.—India, 804,378 deaths in 1900; 271,210 deaths, 1901–02.

271. CHRIST'S HOSPITAL.—Sites committee of Christ's hospital agree (subject to ratification by the council and the treasury) to sell the whole of their vacant land in Newgate-street to the government for post-office extensions, reported . 22 Dec. 1903

278. CHURCH OF ENGLAND.—Abp. of Canterbury writes dr. Horton upon education question 1 Nov. Reply of dr. Horton declaring that public control and abolition of tests for teachers must form basis of any settlement . . . . . 6 Nov. ,,
Prof. Collins of King's College, London, appointed bp. of Gibraltar, 18 Nov. 1903, consecrated . . . . . 25 Jan. 1904
Bps. of London and Rochester issue manifesto *re* action of churchmen in the L.C.C. elections in 1904 . . . . 15 Dec. 1903
Bp. of Worcester censured by Canon Henson at Westminster Abbey for his action in the case of the rev. C. E. Beeby, vicar of Yardley Wood, who resigned his living on account of an article on the "Doctrinal significance of a miraculous birth" written by him in the October number of the *Hibbert Journal* . 20 Dec. ,,
New year's letter issued by bp. of London on the duty of the church respecting education . . . . . . 1 Jan. 1904
Dr. H. N. Churton, bp. of Nassau, drowned off Ragged island . . . . 20 Jan. ,,
Benediction of central tower, "Victoria," and spire of Truro cathedral . . . 22 Jan. ,,
Appeal to church people by the bp. of London to contribute 30,000*l.* to bring the church schools of the diocese into a fitting condition; 1,000*l.* subscribed by hon. W. F. D. Smith, M.P.; 500*l.* each by the duke of Westminster, lord Ashcombe, the bp. of London, and "M.P.," and 900*l.* in smaller donations, reported . . 25 Jan. ,,
Dr. Jas. Thomas, bp. of Trinidad, died, 26 Jan. ,,
Death of the earl of Devon, rector of Powderham and prebendary of Exeter cathedral, aged 93 . . . . 29 Jan. ,,

284. CLASSICAL ASSOCIATION OF ENGLAND AND WALES, founded; first meeting held in London, president the Master of the Rolls . . . . . 19 Dec. 1903

288. COAL.—Exported from the United Kingdom 1901, 57,783,000 tons; 1902, 60,400,000 tons. United States, 300,930,659 tons obtained in 1902.

290. Coal mines (certificates) act, royal assent, 30 June, 1903
Lord Peel, chairman of S. Wales conciliation board (resigned 23 Jan. 1904), decides against an 8¾ per cent. reduction in wages, 21 Aug., but grants a 5 per cent. reduction, 21 Nov. ,,

292. *Accidents*: Howle colliery, Durham, cage accident, 16 injured, 15 July; Dudley Wood, Netherton, fall of roof, 4 deaths, 27 July; similar accident near Coatbridge, 3 deaths, 8 Oct.; Connellville, Pa., explosion, 15 deaths, 21 Nov.; cage accident, 11 deaths, 3 Dec. 1903: Harwich mine,

PAGE

Cheswick, nr. Pittsburg, Pa., U.S., explosion, 184 men entombed, reported, 25 Jan. 1904
[1,067 deaths from accidents in 1903.]

298. COLOMBIA. — Senate rejects the U.S. Panama canal treaty, reported 17 Aug.; treaty becomes dead, the period for its affirmation having expired . . 22 Sept. 1903
Revolt in Panama (*which see*); Colombian warship captured; independence declared, 3 Nov. ,,
U.S. sailors landed at Colon . 4 Nov. ,,
Demonstration at Bogota against pres. Maroquin, martial law proclaimed . 9 Nov. ,,
Colombian proposals and concessions rejected by Panama, reported . 20 Nov. ,,
Panama formally recognised as a republic by the United States 13 Dec.; by Great Britain . . . . . 25 Dec. ,,

300 COLONIES. — Conference of the Institut colonial international of Brussels on colonial legislation held in London, lord Reay and lord Geo. Hamilton present, 26 May, 1903
Resignation of Mr. Chamberlain, 8 years colonial secretary, announced, 17 Sept.; the office offered to and declined by lord Milner, reported, 3 Oct.; accepted by the hon. Alfred Lyttelton, announced . 5 Oct. ,,

303. COMMERCE.—Fifth congress of chambers of the empire, Montreal . . 17 Aug. 1903

317. CO-OPERATIVE SOCIETIES.—Congress at Doncaster . . . . . 1 June, 1903
National festival at the crystal palace, 11 July, ,,
Danish international congress at Copenhagen, 25 Sept. ,,

318. COPYRIGHT.—House of lords, on appeal, decided in case of Aflalo *v.* Lawrence and Bullen that articles contributed to an encyclopædia without stipulations as to copyright become the property of the publishers, mid Nov. 1903

321. COREA.—Lease of lands and right of timber purchase at Yongampho granted to a Russian company; free access to Yalu valley and river estuary acquired, reported, 11 Aug. 1903
Russo-Japanese negotiations held in Tokio, Aug. *et seq.* ,,
First section of Japanese railway from Seoul to Fusan opened . . 20 Oct. ,,
Yongampho fortified by the Russians, reported . . . . . . 27 Oct. ,,
Rioting at Mokpho 13 Dec.; much unrest in the south . . . . end Dec. ,,

323. CORNWALL. — Visit of the prince and princess of Wales . . . 14–20 July, 1903

332. CREMATION.—Mr. Herbert Spencer (Golder's Green) . . . 14 Dec. 1903
Crematorium opened by sir H. Thompson at Perry Barr, Birmingham . . 7 Oct. ,,

332. CRICKET. — M.C.C.'s English Team: *first* match, English Team *v.* South Australia, ends in a draw, Adelaide, 7 Nov.; *second*, *v.* Victoria, won by English eleven, Melbourne, 16 Nov.; *third*, *v.* N.S. Wales, won by England, Sydney, 23 Nov.; *fourth*, won by England, Brisbane, 30 Nov.; *fifth*, a draw, West Maitland, N.S.W. . 3 Dec. 1903
First test match, at Sydney, won by English team by 5 wickets, Mr. Foster scoring 287 runs . . . . 11–17 Dec. ,,
Second test match, at Melbourne, won by England by 185 runs, Rhodes taking 15 wickets . . . . . 1 Jan. 1904
Third test match, at Adelaide, won by Australia by 216 runs, Mr. V. Trumper scored 172 runs . . . . 20 Jan. ,,

338. CRYSTAL PALACE.—Great nat. temperance fête . . . . . 18 July, 1903
Cat and bird shows opened . . 27 Oct. ,,
Mr. August Manns knighted . 9 Nov. ,,
Cage bird show opened . . 8 Dec. ,,

346. DAILY PAPER.—A new 1*d.* daily, edited by Mr. W. T. Stead. First number published, 4 Jan. 1904

PAGE

359. DENMARK.—General elections . 16 June, 1903
Parliament meets, budget presented, 5–6 Oct. ,,

366. DIPHTHERIA.—Dr. L. Martin's method of transforming the Roux serum into pastilles, reported to be successful with children, May, 1903

371. DOMINICAN REPUBLIC.—Revolution in San Domingo, severe fighting, many killed, 23 March; troops repulsed after fierce contest, 5 April; flight of pres. Vasquez, gen. Wos y Gil made president, reported, 27 April, 1903
Arsenal at Santiago blown up, gen. Frias killed; 21 mortally wounded, reported, 24 May, ,,
Diplomatic relations with the United States (*which see*) broken off, ports blockaded, early Nov. ,,
Further fighting, San Domingo besieged by revolutionists, 7 Nov.; severe fighting, 17 Nov.; town again bombarded, 23, 24 Nov.; town surrenders; flight of pres. Wos y Gil, 25 Nov. ,,
Gen. Jiminez made president of provisional government, señor Ramon Caceres murdered, reported . . . . . 28 Dec. ,,

380. DUBLIN.—Lord Iveagh gives 50,000*l.* to the king for hospitals, announced . 1 Aug. 1903
Horse show and art industries exhibition opened, 25 Aug.; state visit of the lord and lady Dudley . . . . 26 Aug. ,,
Death of Mr. Lecky, aged 65 . . 22 Oct. ,,
Duke and duchess of Connaught receive honorary degree at the university, 23 Oct. ,,
Death of Dr. Salmon, provost of Trin. Coll. since 1888, aged 84 . . . 22 Jan. 1904

384. DURHAM UNIVERSITY.—Fund for completing the college, total 50,000*l.* (memorial to lord Armstrong), announced . 5 Oct. 1903

390. EARTHQUAKES. — Severe shocks in St. Vincent . . . . . . 21 July, 1903
Shocks at Albuñon, Granada, 26, 27, 28 July, ,,
Destructive shocks at Filattiera and Mulazzo, Italy . . . . . . 31 July, ,,
Shocks in Athens and all Greece, and in Crete, 2 deaths in Cerigo . . . . 11 Aug. ,,
Destructive shocks at Mendoza, Argentina, 5 deaths . . . . . 12 Aug. ,,
Violent shocks at Bucharest . . 13 Sept. ,,
Shocks at Lisbon, 9 Aug.; again . 14 Sept. ,,
Severe shock in Santiago de Cuba . 19 Sept. ,,
Shocks at Blidah, Algeria, and the Canary islands . . . . . . 22 Sept. ,,

397. EDINBURGH.—Strike of tramway men, concessions made . . . 21–28 Aug. 1903
Lord Strathcona receives the freedom of the city . . . . 4 Dec. ,,

401. EDUCATION.—General purposes committee of the London county council present a draft scheme for the establishment of an education committee, under the London Education Act, 1903, recommending its constitution as follows:—(1) chairman, vice-chairman, and deputy-chairman of the county council; (2) 35 members of the county council; (3) 5 women selected by the council; (4) members of the existing school board, not exceeding 5 in number, to be appointed by the council only during the term of office of the first committee (the transitional period). Two objects to be specially kept in view in the constitution of the education committee: (1) That the committee shall be one which will work harmoniously with the council in developing a complete and well coordinated system of London education; (2) that it shall be such as to retain one of the greatest public interests under real public control as far as possible. Mr. H. P. Harris moved an amendment, "That the education committee shall consist of 58 members, and shall include (1) the chairman, vice-chairman, and deputy-chairman for the time being of the council; (2) 35

PAGE

persons who shall be members for the time being of the council; (3) 12 persons appointed by the council on the recommendation of the following bodies:—University of London 1, Church of England schools 2, Roman Catholic schools 1, Wesleyan and other schools 1, headmasters of secondary schools 1, assistant masters of secondary schools 1, elementary teachers 1, Corporation of the City of London 1, City and Guilds Institute 1, City parochial charities 1, London trades council 1; and (4) 8 persons, of whom 5 shall be women, to be selected by the council; and that the scheme, so amended, be approved and forwarded to the Board of Education for its approval. On division the council voted: for the amendment 26, against 78, majority for the scheme 52, which was adopted in its entirety . . . 26 Jan. 1904

[On May 1, 1904, the "appointed day," the Act comes into operation, and dissolves the school board, and hands over the control of every branch of education, elementary, secondary, technical, and higher, to the county council, acting through a committee.]

408. EGYPT.—Surplus revenue for 1903, 25,000*l.*; actual surplus, 90,000*l.*, reported, 30 Nov. 1903

411. ELECTRICITY.—Mr. Chamberlain's speech on the fiscal question, at the Guildhall, reproduced simultaneously to a large assembly at Queen's hall by electrophone, 19 Jan. 1904

Wireless Telegraphy.—New system of radiotelegraphy originated by prof. Alessandro Artom; successful experiments made by Italian naval authorities, reported, 14 Nov. 1903

418. ELECTRONS.—Miniature particles of matter consisting of positive and negative electricity, contained in an atom and existing in a state of violent movement, investigated by prof. Larmor, lord Kelvin, and others.

435. ENGLAND.—Mr. Herbert Spencer dies, aged 83 . . . . . . 8 Dec. 1903

Royal visit to Chatsworth . . . 4 Jan. 1904

456. EXECUTIONS. — Chas. Howell, soldier, murder of Maud Luen, Chelmsford, 7 July, 1903

Thos. Porter, 29, and Thos. Preston, 24, murder of constable Wilkinson, Leicester, 21 July, ,,

Leonard Pachett, 26, murder of his wife, Lincoln . . . . . . 28 July, ,,

Edward R. Palmer, 24, murder of Esther Swinford, a barmaid, Devizes . 17 Nov. ,,

Bernard White, soldier, murder of Maud Garrett, Chelmsford . . . . 1 Dec. ,,

James Duffy, 46, murder of Ellen Newman, Durham . . . . 8 Dec. ,,

William Haywood, 61, murder of his wife, Hereford . . . . . . 15 Dec. ,,

William Brown, soldier, and Thos. Cowdrey, labourer, murder of Esther Atkins, Winchester . . . . . . 16 Dec. ,,

Chas. W. Ashton, 19, murder of Annie Marshall, Hull . . . . . 22 Dec. ,,

John Gallagher, 30, miner, and Emily Swann, 42, murder of Wm. Swann, her husband, Wombwell . . . . . . 29 Dec. ,,

Henry Starr, 31, murder of his wife, Blackpool . . . . 29 Dec. ,,

467. FIJI.—Severe hurricane; great damage to Levuka, 6 deaths, reported . 21, 22 Jan. 1904

468. FINLAND.—Process of expulsion continued, 43 eminent Finlanders up to Nov. expelled, emigration continues . . . Aug. 1903

Shipping disaster on Tykojarvi lake, 40 deaths . . . . . . 16 Aug. ,,

Extension of repressive measures; constitution violated, *Times* . . . 9 Sept. ,,

Finnish senate opened in the Russian language . . . . . . 22 Oct. ,,

New order of the czar granting to two governors complete control over the elections issued . . . . . 17 Dec. ,,

469. FIRE BRIGADE.—International fire prevention congress opened at Earl's court by the lord mayor; 500 members present, 6 July, 1903

Capt. Wells presented with a testimonial from the men of the London fire brigade on the occasion of his retirement, 21 July, ,,

475. FIRES. — Fire at 326, Hackney-road, 3 deaths . . . . . . 19 Oct. 1903

Steam saw-mills, workshops, &c., Busby-street, Bethnal-green, burnt . 6 Nov. ,,

Fire at Messrs. Leighton, Son and Hodge, bookbinders, New-street-square . 23 Nov. ,,

Board school, East Ham, top storey destroyed, all children saved . 25 Nov. ,,

Messrs. T. Webb & Co., paper staining works, much damage, Overbury-street, Pedro-street, N.E. . . . . 11 Dec. ,,

Large building containing a theatre, 9 shops, and a club-room, at Teddington, completely destroyed by fire . . 29 Dec. ,,

City lands committee of the City corporation present report opposing the proposal for municipal fire insurance . end Dec. ,,

517. FRANCE.—King of the Belgians received by M. Loubet . . . . . 4 Sept. 1903

Army manœuvres . . . . 16 Sept. ,,

Strikes: mills and factories stopped round Lille and Armentières, troops called out, many arrests, reported . 5–13 Oct. ,,

Anglo-French arbitration agreement signed, London . . . . . . 14 Oct. ,,

Visit of the king and queen of Italy, 14–18 Oct. ,,

Chambers opened, 20 Oct.; resolution on M. Combe's policy against clerical and monarchist reactionaries, carried, 332–233, 22 Oct. ,,

Great meeting against Turkish misrule in Armenia and Macedonia, Paris . 25 Oct. ,,

London international and commercial assoc. visit Paris . . . . . . 28 Oct. ,,

Czar's letter to M. Loubet expressing his pleasure at the Anglo-French arbitration agreement and the *rapprochement* with Italy read at the cabinet council . 30 Oct. ,,

Imports, 227,960,000*l.*; exports, 223,880,000*l.* in 1902, reported . . . . 5 Nov. ,,

Motion for a commission of inquiry as to the complicity of politicians in the Humbert frauds carried in the chamber, 360–203, 12 Nov. ,,

Amendment to the education bill excluding members of religious bodies, whether authorised or unauthorised, from teaching, passed by the senate, 147–136 . 20 Nov. ,,

Visit of British M.P.'s . . 25 Nov. *et seq.* ,,

Second revision of the Dreyfus case decided upon; commission appointed by M. Vallé, minister of justice, announced . 27 Nov. ,,

Patrie, battleship, launched at La Seyne, 17 Dec. ,,

Budget as voted by the chamber passed the senate, 276–17 . . . . . 30 Dec. ,,

Baron Arthur de Rothschild, died 10 Dec.; he bequeathed his valuable collection of paintings to the Louvre, and collection of ancient rings to the Cluny museum, reported . . . . . . 31 Dec. ,,

529. FREE LABOUR ASSOCIATION. — Congress in London, opened . . . 26 Oct. 1903

530. FREE TRADE. — The new fiscal scheme criticised by sir Wm. Harcourt at Rawtenstall, 31 Oct., and by Mr. John Morley at Nottingham . . . . . . 3 Nov. 1903

Sir M. Hicks-Beach, at Manchester, speaks in favour of free trade . . . 5 Nov. ,,

Mr. Chamberlain speaks at Bingley-hall, Birmingham . . . . . 6 Nov. ,,

Lord Goschen addresses the Liverpool chamber of commerce, and opposes Mr. Chamberlain's policy; sir H. Campbell-Bannerman speaks at Meigle . 7 Nov. ,,

Lord Balfour of Burleigh addresses a unionist free trade meeting at Glasgow, and Mr. Asquith speaks at Worcester, 9 Nov. ,,

PAGE

Mr. Balfour at the Dolphin Colston banquet at Bristol, supported by sir M. Hicks-Beach, defines his policy on the fiscal question . . . . . . 13 Nov. 1903

Mr. Chamberlain addresses a great meeting at Cardiff 20 Nov. and Newport . 21 Nov. ,,

Duke of Devonshire and lord Goschen speak at Queen's hall under the auspices of the free food league . . . . . 24 Nov. ,,

Lord Rosebery speaks at the Surrey theatre, 25 Nov. ,,

Sir H. Campbell-Bannerman speaks at Newport . . . . . . 30 Nov. ,,

Mr. Ritchie speaks at Croydon . 3 Dec. ,,

Imperial tariff committee issue a series of leaflets dealing with Mr. Chamberlain's fiscal proposals as affecting agriculturists, 4 Dec. ,,

Central and associated chambers of agriculture at annual general meeting adopt Mr. Rider Haggard's resolution supporting Mr. Chamberlain's policy . . 9 Dec. ,,

Sir William Harcourt speaks at Tredegar, 11 Dec. ,,

Lord Rosebery addresses a great free trade demonstration in Edinburgh . 12 Dec. ,,

Australasian Chamber of Commerce in London passes a resolution in favour of the principle of inter-imperial preferential tariffs . . . . 15 Dec. ,,

Mr. Chamberlain addresses two large meetings at Leeds, closing "his first provincial campaign" . . . . . . 16 Dec. ,,

Duke of Devonshire expresses his opinion that any elector who sympathises with the objects of the free food league would be well advised to decline to give his support to any candidate who expresses his sympathy with Mr. Chamberlain's fiscal policy. The duke's advice concurred in by lord Balfour of Burleigh, lord Geo. Hamilton, lord Goschen, Mr. Ritchie, and lord James of Hereford. Lord Cowper and other unionists criticise the duke of Devonshire's advice to the party, mid Dec. ,,

Conference of liberals at Westminster resolve to form a liberal tariff league . 23 Dec. ,,

Lord Rosebery speaks at Edinburgh, 5 Jan. 1904

Correspondence, beginning with a letter from the duke of Devonshire to Mr. Chamberlain, dated 23 Oct. 1903, and terminating with letter from Mr. Chamberlain, 2 Jan. 1904, on the position of the liberal unionist association in reference to the fiscal question; the duke's opinion that the association should be dissolved opposed by Mr. Chamberlain, published . . early Jan. ,,

First meeting of Mr. Chamberlain's tariff commission . . . . . 15 Jan. ,,
(See *Preferential Tariffs, Addenda*).

Mr. Chamberlain concludes his first tariff reform campaign by addressing a great gathering of London citizens in the Guildhall, and an overflow meeting in the Guildhall-yard . . . . . 19 Jan. ,,

Duke of Devonshire speaks at a demonstration of the free food league at Liverpool, and replies to the charge of breaking up the liberal unionist party on the fiscal question . . . . . 19 Jan. ,,

532. **FRENCH WEST-AFRICA.**—Territory on the right bank of the Lower Senegal annexed to French colonial possessions by submission of the tribes, announced, Aug. 1903

532. **FRIENDLY SOCIETIES.**—50,000 thrift organisations; membership about 27,000,000; funds about 360,000,000*l*., reported, Sept. 1903

532. **FROGMORE.**—The queen's memorial to queen Victoria, a statue of the Saviour, about 17 ft. high, sent from Denmark, erected at the royal mausoleum, reported, 7 Nov. 1903

534. **FRUITS.**—Departmental committee appointed by the president of the board of agriculture and fisheries to inquire into and report on the present position of fruit culture in Gt. Britain, announced, 30 Dec. 1903

PAGE

557. **GERMANY.**—Visit of the emperor to Vienna, 18–20 Sept. 1903

Army scandal: 50 officers, 525 non-commissioned officers and 52 others convicted between 8 July, 1902, and 8 July, 1903, for ill-treatment of soldiers; Breitenbach sentenced to 8 years' imprisonment . 20 Sept. ,,

Dippold, a domestic tutor, sentenced to 8 years' imprisonment and deprivation of civil rights for 10 years, for torturing and causing the death of his pupil Heinz Loch by excessive flogging . . . . 9 Oct. ,,

Death of Gustav von Moser, dramatist, aged 78 . . . . 23 Oct. ,,

Congress of non-socialist democratic workmen at Frankfort . . . . 25 Oct. ,,

Battleship *Preussen* launched at Stettin, 31 Oct. ,,

Death of prof. Mommsen, aged 85 . 1 Nov. ,,

Meeting of the emperor and czar at Wiesbaden and Darmstadt . . . 4, 5 Nov. ,,

Successful operation for polypus in the throat performed on the emperor . 7 Nov. ,,

Imports, 290,288,800*l*.; exports, 240,641,650*l*. in 1902 . . . . Nov. ,,

Lieut. Bilse sentenced to 6 months' imprisonment for libelling officers in a novel, 11 Nov. ,,

Elections . . . . 12 Nov. ,,

Financial estimates; increased expenditure of 2,185,304*l*.; proposed loan of 10,735,567*l*. 1 Dec. ,,

Reichstag meets . . . . . 3 Dec. ,,

Debate on the estimates . . . 9, 10 Dec. ,,

Franzky, a non-commissioned officer, sentenced to 5 years' imprisonment and degradation for maltreatment of soldiers in 1,520 cases; lieut. Schilling to 15 months' for 600 offences of a similar nature, 15 Dec. ,,

Emperor congratulates the German legion "on having saved the British army from destruction at Waterloo" . . . 19 Dec. ,,

559. **GIBRALTAR.**—Death of Dr. Sandford, bp. of Gibraltar, 9 Dec.; succeeded by dr. Wm. E. Collins . . . . . 19 Dec. 1903

564. **GLASGOW.**—Free trade demonstration, 13 Oct. 1903

Great fire at warehouses in Buchanan-street, damage estimated 150,000*l*. . 6 Nov. ,,

Industrial exhibition in Denistoun opened, 9 Dec. ,,

Launch of battleship *Hindustan* . 19 Dec. ,,

568. **GOLD.**—World's production, 1902, estimated value, 61,260,000*l*.

579. **GREECE.** — Mr. Francis Elliot appointed British minister in succession to sir E. H. Egerton . . . . 9 Nov. 1903

Return of the king after his continental tour, 27 Nov. ,,

Ministerial crisis; resignation of M. Ralli, premier, 16 Dec.; cabinet formed by M. Theotokis . . . . . . 18 Dec. ,,

582. **GRESHAM COLLEGE.**—Sir Evelyn Wood opens the new Gresham school buildings (cost 40,000*l*.) at Holt, Norfolk . 30 Sept. 1903

584. **GUATEMALA.**—Railway joining the central, southern, and western departments, opened . . . . . . 21 Nov. 1903

587. **GUNPOWDER.**—Explosion of nitro-glycerine at Faversham, Kent; 1 death, several injured . . . . 9 Nov. 1903

591. **HAGUE, THE.**—Venezuela arbitration tribunal, president, M. Muravieff, meets, 1 Oct. 1903

596. **HASTINGS.**—Visit of the Norman society, 19 Aug. 1903

601. **HERALDRY.**—Death of sir Albert Wm. Woods, Garter Principal King of Arms from 1869, aged 87 . . . . 7 Jan. 1904

605. **HIGH TREASON.**—"Colonel" Lynch released "on license" . . . . 23 Jan. 1904

605. **HIMALAYA.**—Dr. and Mrs. Bullock Workman explore five new peaks and four glaciers to the W. and S.W. of the Hunza Nagar valley; two snow peaks were ascended from the head of the Choga Loongma glacier; first peak 22,568 ft. high, was reached by Mrs. Bullock Workman, the second peak by dr. Bullock Workman and two guides, to a height of 23,394 ft., 12 Aug. 1903

PAGE

611. HOME READING UNION.—Founded 1889, pres. H.R.H. the duchess of Argyll.

615. HOSPITAL SUNDAY.—Total for 1903, 64,975*l*.

616. HOSPITAL SATURDAY.—10 Oct. 1903; total to 12 Dec. 16,628*l*. 9*s*. 1*d*.

616. HOSPITALS.—Duchess of Albany lays a memorial stone at the Royal Waterloo hospital . . . . . 26 Oct. 1903
Hon. W. F. D. Smith, M.P., presents a new site for King's College hospital at Denmark-hill, announced . . . . . 15 Dec. ,,
King Edward's Hospital fund: 10,000*l*. from the League of Mercy, reported . 24 Dec. ,,

618. HULL.—Great fire and complete destruction of Messrs. Walker and Smith's oil-crushing mill, estimated damage 40,000*l*. . 24 Jan. 1904

622. HUNGARY. — Count Tisza's programme formally received by the chamber, 5 Nov.; his speech on Hungarian constitutional rights much commended . . 18 Nov. 1903
Count Albert Apponyi and others withdraw from the liberals, 26 Nov.; continued obstruction in the chamber 28 Nov.–1 Dec. ,,
Crisis ends: M. Kossuth and other members of the independent party oppose further obstruction; declarations exchanged by M. Kossuth and Count Tisza . 5 Dec. ,,

631. IMPORTS.—1903, 542,900,000*l*.; 1902, *for* 797,000,000*l*. *read* 528,400,000*l*.

648. INDIA.—Budget: 3,190,000*l*. surplus realised April, 1903, salt tax to be reduced 25 per cent.; exemption from income tax raised from 33*l*. to 66*l*.; available surplus after such deductions, 950,000*l*., 1903–4, 13 Aug. 1903
Death of Umra, Khan of Jandoul, reported, 28 Aug. ,,
Resignation of lord Geo. Hamilton, sec. for India, announced . . . . 18 Sept. ,,
Total number of persons killed in 1902 by wild animals, 2,836; by snake bites, 23,166, reported . . . 21 Oct. ,,
About 20,000,000 acres irrigated in 1902; value of crops raised 28,000,000*l*., reported, mid Oct. ,,
Death of Rao Bahadur Moodelliar, merchant prince and philanthropist of South India, 29 Oct. ,,
Accident to lord Kitchener at Simla, 16 Nov. ,,
Lord Curzon's tour in the Sikh states ends 11 Nov.; he visits Muscat and Persian gulf ports . . . . . 18 Nov.–7 Dec. ,,
Indian national congress meets in Madras, 29 Dec. ,,

653. INOCULATION.—Anti-typhoid inoculation introduced by prof. Wright successfully used in the army in India and S. Africa 1898–1901, *Times* . . . . 9 Oct. 1903

655. INTERNATIONAL LAW.—Conference of the Institute met at Antwerp . 29 Sept. 1903

658. INUNDATIONS.—Destructive floods in the Tyne valley, N. Yorks., N. Lincs. and N. Wales . . . . . . 8–10 Oct. 1903
Floods in Italy and heavy rains, reported, 1 Nov. ,,
Floods in the valley of the Thames and other parts of the country, occasioned by the heavy rains . . during Oct. and Nov. ,,
Destructive floods in Mysore, Vanizambadi town half ruined, 200 deaths . 12 Nov. ,,
Floods in St. Petersburg . . . 25 Nov. ,,
Heavy floods in South Italy . . 5 Dec. ,,

658. INVERNESS.—Highland Jacobite exhibition, over 200,000 visitors, closed 26 Sept. 1903

673. IRELAND.—Estates commissioners under the new land act, appointed . 19 Sept. 1903

687. ITALY.—Imports, 1902, 74,615,568*l*.; exports, 57,810,544*l*. . . . . Nov. 1903
Vote of confidence in the government programme passed in the chamber, 284–117, 3 Dec. ,,
Budget; estimated surplus for 1903, over 6,000,000 lire . . . . . 9 Dec. ,,
Death of signor Zanardelli, ex-premier, 26 Dec. ,,
Anglo-Italian arbitration treaty reported in preparation . . . . . . 27 Dec. ,,

PAGE

Library of the university of Turin burnt, 25 Jan. 1904

694. JAPAN. — Parliament opened by the emperor; ministry censured in the lower house, 10 Dec.; house dissolved by emperor . . . . 11 Dec. 1903
Unsatisfactory reply of Russia to Japanese Corean proposals, received . . 11 Dec. ,,
Japanese reply to Russian proposals; increasing tension . . . . 22 Dec. ,,
War preparations; two Argentine warships bought by Japan; imperial ordinances issued . . . . . . 28, 29 Dec. ,,
Japan obtains unlimited credit for military defence; military and naval preparations for war pressed forward . . . 29 Dec. ,,
Reported Japanese warning to the powers that she will fight if her demands are not conceded; mobilization of troops, 31 Dec. ,,
Russia vaguely states her intention to respect Japanese rights in Manchuria, but repeats her request for the neutralization of a third part of the territory of Corea, 6 Jan. 1904
Japanese reply, claiming an "open door" in Manchuria, demands perfect equality in all respects for her subjects in that province; and absolutely declines the proposal for a diplomatic partition of Corea, 13 Jan. ,,
Ordinance issued at Tokio empowering the government to take over all private railway lines for military purposes . 25 Jan. ,,

701. JEWS.—Estimated population of the Jews in the world 1903, 11,000,000; in Palestine, 60,000; in London, 104,000.

702. JOAN OF ARC.—Canonized at St. Peter's, Rome . . . . 6 Jan. 1904

712. KIEFF.—Student riots (see *Russia*), 2, 16 Nov. 1903

715. KING'S COLLEGE, LONDON.—The removal of the hospital from Portugal-street having been decided upon by the council, hon. F. W. Smith, M.P., gives site at Denmark-hill for the new building. Donations to the removal fund: Annie Zunz fund, 10,000*l*.; *Daily Telegraph*, 500*l*.; Mr. H. Lloyd, of the *Daily Chronicle*, 500*l*., reported . . . . . . 22 Dec. 1903

721. LADYSMITH.—Partial inundation of the town by sudden and extraordinary rising of the Klipp river . . . . 22 Jan. 1904

747. LIVERPOOL.—Inauguration of the university of Liverpool . . . 7 Nov. 1903

761. LONDON, UNIVERSITY OF. — 50,000*l*. given anonymously to University college for the promotion of higher scientific education and research . . . early Dec. 1903
Appeal of the senate for funds to build and endow an Institute of Medical Science, 21 Jan. 1904

762. LONGEVITY.—Mme. De Paepe died, aged 102 . . . . 25 Oct., 1903
Mrs. Mary Paliner Forster died at Hethersett, nr. Norwich, aged 102 . 30 Nov., ,,
Pat Dwyer, died at Moyne, co. Tipperary, aged 100, reported . . . 26 Jan. 1904

772. MACEDONIA. — Macedonian relief fund started in London, reported *Times*, 9 Oct. 1903
Karamanitza, on the Bulgarian frontier, attacked by the Turks, 8 Oct.; much fighting, work of depopulation and destruction continues, reported . . 15, 16 Oct. ,,
Turco-Bulgarian demobilization on the frontier, reported . . . about 20 Oct. ,,
Turkish post at Merkaze captured . 21 Oct. ,,
Turkish atrocities confirmed; great suffering amongst refugees in Bulgaria, Oct.: continuance of barbarities in the Raslog district, reported . . . . 2 Nov. ,,
A number of Bulgarians killed in European Turkey from 15 April to Nov. 1903; some 120 villages destroyed, over 60,000 persons homeless; acute distress, reported, 13 Nov. ,,
Austro-Russian amended reform scheme presented to Turkey (*which see*) 22 Oct., accepted by the porte . . . . 25 Nov. ,,

PAGE

Fighting between Turkish troops and insurgents, casualties on both sides, reported, 26 Jan. 1904

781. **MALTA.**—Protest of members of the council against the new constitution; they resign 12 Sept.; other resignations . 23 Oct. 1903

,, New council opened by the governor, 11 Nov. ,,

782. **MAN, ISLE OF.**—Parliament dissolved, 31 Oct. ,,

784. **MANCHESTER.**—First session of the new Victoria university opens . . 1 Oct. 1903

785. **MANCHURIA.** — Mukden reoccupied by Russian troops (see *Japan* and *China*), 28 Oct. 1903

817. **MINES.**—Value of total mineral produces of the United Kingdom in 1902, 107,134,854*l.*

Miners' Federation of Great Britain annual conference at Glasgow . . 8 Oct. 1903

818. **MINT.**—Number of pieces struck. *Imperial:* gold, 1902, 9,062,971; 1903, 11,410,684; silver, 1902, 26,270,996; 1903, 15,017,245; bronze, 1902, 45,774,848; total, 1902, 81,108,815; 1903, 64,625,305. *Colonial:* silver, 1902, 32,665,735; 1903, 40,820,415; bronze, 1902, 8,360,000; 1903, 9,000,000; nickel, 1902, 252,000; 1903, 252,000; total, 1902, 41,277,735; 1903, 50,072,415; totals, 1902, 122,386,550; 1903, 114,697,720.

829. **MOROCCO.**—El Menebhi, war minister, resigns; is succeeded by Sid Mohammed Guebbas . . . . . end Nov. 1903

Outrages on the Jews by government troops on reoccupation of Tesa, reported 1 Dec. ,,

Settat looted and burnt by tribesmen, reported . . . . . . 24 Dec. ,,

831. **MOTOR CARRIAGES.**—Mr. Glidden, an American, reached the arctic circle in his motor, from Stockholm . . 16 Aug. 1903

Motor speed trials at Southport . 2 Oct. ,,

Motor exhibition opened at Paris . 10 Dec. ,,

833. **MUSCAT.**—Visit of lord Curzon . 18 Nov. 1903

841. **NASHVILLE.**—Fire at the Central Tennessee College (negress), 4 killed, 12 fatally injured . . . . . . 18 Dec. 1903

842. **NATAL.**—Parliament prorogued until 21 Jan. 1904 . . . . . 24 Sept. 1903

Imports 1903, value 15,164,000*l.*; exports, 10,215,000*l.*; increase over 1902 of 1,634,748*l.* and 1,058,632*l.* respectively.

856. **NAVY.**—The admiralty purchase the *Libertad* and *Constitucion* cruisers, under construction for the Chilian government, for 1,875,000*l.* . . . . . 3 Dec. 1903

[Re-named *Swiftsure* and *Triumph.*]

Cruiser *Flora* goes ashore off Vancouver, 3 Dec.; successfully floated, 10 Dec.; arrives at Victoria, B.C. . 14 Dec. ,,

Important regulations issued, giving the fleet younger admirals and captains, and accelerating promotion, to take effect from 1 July, 1903, and be completed 31 Dec. 1907. The number of years after their last service when officers are to be retired under the old and the new regulations will be as follows:—Admirals, *old regulations*, 7 years; *new regulations*, 5 years; vice-adm., *o.r.*, 7, *n.r.*, 5; rear-adm., *o.r.*, 7, *n.r.*, 3½; captains, *o.r.*, 6, *n.r.*, 3; commanders and lieuts., *o.r.*, 5, *n.r.*, 3. The future strength of the different ranks under the old order of 1898 and the new order of 1903 compares thus:—Adm. of fleet, 1898, 3, 1907, 3; adm., 12, 12; vice-adm., 22, 22; rear-adm., 43, 55; total, 80, 94; captains, 245, 252; commanders, 360, 373; the increase over existing numbers to be made by annual instalments and completed in 1907; published . . . . 14 Dec. ,,

Hindustan, battleship, launched at Glasgow, 19 Dec. ,,

Roxburgh, cruiser, launched at Glasgow. 19 Jan. 1904

861. **NEWCASTLE.**—Mr. T. Gurney bequeaths 20,000*l.* to charities; he died . 3 Dec. 1903

869. **NEW SOUTH WALES.**—Deficit for 1902, 324,000*l.*; surplus 33,000*l.* for . . 1903

PAGE

873. **NEW YORK.**—Greatest rainfall recorded by New York weather bureau since its foundation in 1867, destructive floods . 8 Oct. 1903

Fire in 11th Avenue, 25 deaths, many injured, 1 Nov. ,,

Suspension bridge over the East river (10,000,000 dols. cost), opened . 19 Dec. ,,

875. **NEW ZEALAND.**—Naval defence bill passed . . . . . 12 Nov. 1903

Preferential (British goods) trade bill passes house of representatives, 50–16, and legislative council unanimously; 15,000*l.* voted by house of representatives to Victoria memorial in London, 27,000*l.* additional as subsidy to S. African steam service and 5,000*l.* to promote the sales of N. Zealand meat in England . . . . 20 Nov. ,,

878. **NIGER COAST,** Southern Nigeria.—Revolt among the Eket tribes . Sept. 1903

Expedition under maj. Mackenzie successful; N'doite, king of Agoi, and people surrender, 12 Oct. ,,

Mr. W. Egerton appointed commissioner, early Nov. ,,

Revenue, 1902. 261,815*l.*; expenditure, 331,396*l.*, reported . . . Dec. ,,

Lt. Cecil Amyatt-Burney killed in the Bassa province, N. Nigeria, by the Okpotos, mid. Dec. ,,

Report of sir F. Lugard on Northern Nigeria for 1902, and the Kano campaign in 1903, issued early . . . . . Jan. 1904

888. **NORWAY.**—Storthing opened by the king, 19 Oct. 1903

Resignation of the Blehr ministry; coalition cabinet formed by prof. Hagerup, 21, 22 Oct. ,,

Great fire at Aalesund, major part of the town destroyed, 11,000 persons homeless, 23 Jan. 1904

891. **NURSES.** — Women's memorial to queen Victoria; the endowment of queen Victoria's jubilee institute, which she herself founded with the 70,000*l.* presented to her by the women of Gt. Britain on the occasion of her jubilee, reported complete grand total, 156,000*l.*; about 4,000,000 contributors to the fund . . . . 22 Dec. 1903

901. **ORANGE RIVER COLONY.**—Legislative council opened; sir H. Gould-Adams referred to the drought, the severest in the colony since 1862, and the labour difficulty which had affected railway construction; finances of the colony most satisfactory, large surplus over the estimates, which would be partly devoted to paying the contribution of 80,000*l.* towards the intercolonial deficits . . . 26 Nov. 1903

Bursting of a reservoir at Bloemfontein, 23 deaths, and great destruction of property, 17 Jan. 1904

906. **OTTAWA.**—University of Ottawa, one of the largest R. Catholic institutions in America, totally destroyed by fire, estimated loss 500,000 dols. . . 2 Dec. 1903

908. **OXFORD UNIVERSITY.**—Mr. J. W. Cudworth (died 21 Nov. 1903) bequeaths 70,000*l.* to the Dr. Pusey library, announced . . . . . . 25 Dec. 1903

917. **PANAMA.** — Concessions by Colombia rejected, reported . . . . 20 Nov. 1903

Canal (neutral) treaty: by its terms Panama to receive 250,000 dols. annually, and 10,000,000 dols. on ratification of the treaty signed at Washington, 18 Nov.; ratified, 2 Dec. ,,

Colombian troops landed at the mouth of the Altrato, subsequently withdrawn, reported, 9, 11 Dec. ,,

Great Britain recognizes the new republic, 24 Dec. ,,

934. **PATRIOTIC FUND CORPORATION, ROYAL.** — The following members appointed, Dec. 1903, under the provisions of the Patriotic Fund Reorganization act, 1903;

PAGE

F.M. the duke of Connaught (president of the council), lt.-col. lord E. Talbot, M.P., sir Jas. Bell, bt., sir F. Mowatt, lt.-gen. sir T. Kelly-Kenny, sir R. D. Awdry, col. sir Jas. Gildea, F. T. Marzials, W. Hayes Fisher, M.P., H. E. Kearley, M.P., D. J. Shackleton, M.P., C. H. R. Stansfield.

937. PEACE.—International peace congress meet at the hotel de Ville, Rouen; about 100 French and foreign delegates present; M. Arnaud of Paris appointed president; addresses by the prince of Monaco, Mme. Severine, and others; resolutions carried exhorting the powers to stop the cruelties in Macedonia . . . 22–24 Sept. 1903

Peace society meets in Queen's hall, London, 27 Oct. „

941. PENNSYLVANIA.—35 Italians killed, 32 injured by conflagration of a large shanty at Lilly . . . . 21 Nov. 1903

945. PERSIA.—Sudden and suspicious death of the Hakim-el-Mulk, one of the principal rivals of the grand vizier . early Sept. 1903

Banishment of the grand vizier, the Atabey Azam, 15 Sept.; succeeded by the Ain-ed-Dowleh, cousin and son-in-law of the shah, stated to be hostile to foreigners, reported 29 Sept. „

Favourable reception of lord Curzon on his tour to the Gulf ports . 24 Nov.–7 Dec. „

952. PHILIPPINE ISLES.—Defeat of insurgents in Jolo, 75 killed . . . . . 20 Nov. 1903

Condition of the archipelago more favourable than at any period of its history; record crop of hemp, 1,000,000 bales produced in 1903; sugar and tobacco showed an increase over 1902 . . . . . 24 Dec. „

962. PLAGUE. — Plague in the Punjab, 130,000 deaths . . . . . March–April, 1903

Rats proved to be a means of spreading plague; 185,982 killed in Thames docks, &c., during 1902; 249,718 killed up to 1 Nov. „

Plague in Mauritius: many deaths, 3 Sept.–Nov. 1903; 170 deaths, 24 Nov. to 17 Dec. „

Plague in China, many deaths at Niuchwang, reported . . . . Sept. „

971. POLAND.—Gen. Tchertkoff, governor-gen., removed for maladministration . Dec. 1903

974. POLYTECHNIC.—New wing (16,000*l.* cost) of the Northern Polytechnic, Holloway, opened by lord Londonderry . 28 Oct. 1903

982. POPE.—Abbé Loisy's works placed on the "Index Expurgatorius" . 16, 17 Dec. 1903

989. PORTUGAL.—King Alfonso of Spain visits Lisbon . . . . 10–14 Dec. 1903

993. POST-OFFICE.—Inland money orders raised from limit of 10*l.* to 40*l.*; important concessions to the half-penny inland post, both regulations came into operation, 1 Jan. 1904

1005. PREFERENTIAL TARIFFS. — The question of preferential trade with the colonies had its inception in a speech delivered by Mr. Joseph Chamberlain at Birmingham, 15 May, 1903

Speech by lord Rosebery, 19 May; and by Mr. Asquith, criticising adversely Mr. Chamberlain's fiscal proposals . 21 May, „

[For principal speeches *pro* and *con.*, see *Free Trade.*]

Debate in the house of commons on Mr. Chamberlain's proposals for preferential tariffs . . . . 28 May, „

On the debate on the budget, sir M. Hicks-Beach, Mr. Ritchie, and Mr. A. R. D. Elliot declare their adhesion to the principles of free trade . . . 9 June, „

Debate on fiscal policy in the house of lords, 15 June, „

Mr. Chamberlain, in a speech at the Constitutional club, declares Mr. Balfour's leadership to be essential to the unionist party . . . . 26 June, „

Free food league formed . . . 13 July, „

Tariff reform league inaugurated . 21 July, „

Great demonstration in St. James's hall against protection . . . 29 July, 1903

Mr. Balfour's pamphlet, "Insular Free Trade," published . . . . 15 Sept. „

"Fiscal Inquiry," blue-book, published by board of trade . . . . 16 Sept. „

Cabinet crisis on fiscal question, resignation of Mr. Chamberlain, Mr. Ritchie, and lord Geo. Hamilton, 17 Sept.; lord Balfour of Burleigh and Mr. A. R. D. Elliot, 20 Sept. „

Mr. Balfour speaks at Sheffield and advocates retaliation . . . . . . 1 Oct. „

Resignation of the duke of Devonshire on the fiscal question . . . 5 Oct. „

Mr. Chamberlain opens his fiscal campaign at Glasgow . . . . 6 Oct. „

Duke of Devonshire becomes president, and lord Geo. Hamilton and Mr. Ritchie vice-presidents of the free food league, 16 Oct. „

Duke of Devonshire issues a letter advising free trade unionists not to support tariff reform candidates . . . . 11 Dec. „

Mr. Chamberlain's Tariff Commission appointed, 16 Dec. 1903; the complete list of members, representing the most important trades in the United Kingdom and colonies (first meeting, 15 Jan. 1904):—

Colonel Charles Allen; Mr. Frederick Baynes; Mr. J. Henry Birchenough; Mr. Charles Booth; Mr. Henry Bostock; Mr. S. B. Boulton; Mr. Richard Burbidge; sir Vincent Caillard; Mr. J. J. Candlish; Mr. Chaplin, M.P.; sir John A. Cockburn; Mr. J. Howard Colls; Mr. J. G. Colmer, C.M.G.; Mr. William Cooper; Mr. J. A. Corah; Mr. J. W. Dennis; Mr. Charles Eckersley; Mr. Francis Elgar; sir Charles A. Elliott; Mr. Lewis Evans; Mr. George Flett; Mr. Thomas Gallaher: the hon. Vicary Gibbs, M.P.; Mr. Alfred Gilbey; Mr. William Goulding; Mr. W. H. Grenfell, M.P.; Mr. John M. Harris; Mr. F. Leverton Harris, M.P.; Mr. W. Harrison; sir Alexander Henderson, M.P.; sir Robert Herbert, G.C.B. (chairman); sir Alfred Hickman, M.P.; sir Alfred L. Jones; Mr. Arthur Keen; Mr. J. J. Keswick; sir W. T. Lewis; Mr. I. Levenstein; Mr. Robert Littlejohn; Mr. Charles Lyle: Mr. A. W. Maconochie, M.P.; Mr. Henry D. Marshall; Mr. W. H. Mitchell; Mr. Alfred Mosely, C.M.G.; sir Andrew Noble; the hon. Charles Parsons; sir Walter Peace; Mr. C. Arthur Pearson; sir Westby Perceval; Mr. C. J. Phillips; Mr. Joseph Rank; Mr. R. H. Reade; sir George Ryder; sir S. Clementi Smith; sir Charles Tennant; Mr. Francis Tonsley; sir John Turney; Mr. S. J. Waring, jun., and Mr. W. Bridges Webb. Sec., Mr. W. A. S. Hewins, assisted by Mr. Percy A. Hurd.

Mr. Chamberlain addresses a large meeting of London citizens in the Guildhall; exhorts them to "learn to think imperially," 19 Jan. 1904

Duke of Devonshire speaks at a free food league demonstration in Liverpool, 19 Jan. „

1013. PRUSSIA.—Elections for the chamber, 12 Nov. 1903

1014. PUBLIC HEALTH ACTS.—Death rate per 1,000 17 Oct. 15·8; 14 Nov., 17·9; 12 Dec., 1903, 19·2.

1026. RACES.—Rock Sand (owner sir J. Millar) won the Two Thousand Guineas, 29 April, the Derby, 27 May, and the St. Leger, 9 Sept. 1903

Death of prince Dimitri Soltykoff, well-known sportsman and member of the jockey club, aged 75 . . . . 21 Nov. „

Winners of principal races in 1903.—Liverpool Grand Nat., Mr. Morrison's Drumcree; City and Suburban, M. Euphrussi's Brambilla; Two Thousand Guineas, sir J. Millar's Rock Sand; Chester Cup, Mr. G. Thursby's Vendale; Manchester Cup, lord Howard de Walden's Zinfandel; the Derby, sir J. Millar's Rock Sand; the Oaks, Mr. J. B.

PAGE

Joel's Our Lassie; Ascot Stakes, Mr. H. E. Randall's Genius; Royal Hunt Cup, Mr. L. de Rothschild's Kunster; Northumberland Plate, Mr. C. Perkin's Cliftonhall; Eclipse Stakes (Sandown), Mr. G. Gubbins's Ard Patrick; Stewards' Cup (Goodwood), Mr. G. A. Prentice's Dumbarton Castle; Great Ebor Handicap, Mr. J. Musker's McYardley; St. Leger, sir J. Millar's Rock Sand; Cesarewitch, Mr. W. A. Bass's Grey Tick; Middle Park Plate, maj. Loder's Pretty Polly; Cambridgeshire, capt. Forester's Hackler's Pride; Liverpool Autumn Cup, Mr. Baird Hay's Palmy Days; Manchester November Handicap, Mr. B. Ellam's Switch Cap.

1026. RADIUM.—This new, and extremely rare, metal is found in combination with chlorine and bromine, as radium chloride and radium bromide. It is obtained in very minute quantities from pitchblende after the metal uranium has been extracted. The principle of radio-activity was discovered by M. Becquerel in Paris in 1896, from the study of uranium, and Mme. Sklodowska Curie's investigation of this metal when taking up the subject of radio-activity as the thesis for her doctorate degree led to the discovery of radium, Mme. Curie being assisted in her experiments by M. Curie. The discovery of the new metal was communicated by M. Curie to the Academy of Sciences, Paris, in March, 1903, and on 19 June of the same year M. Curie gave a demonstration of this new substance at the Royal Institution, London. Investigations of the properties and phenomena exhibited by radium have also been carried on by M. Becquerel, prof. Rutherford, sir Wm. Ramsay, Mr. Soddy, prof. J. J. Thompson, sir Wm. Crookes, and others. Radium possesses the extraordinary property of continually producing heat without combustion, and spontaneously producing electricity, and maintains its own temperature, 1·5° Cent. or 2·7° Fahr. above its surroundings. It gives off an emanation or gas which shines by its own light, resembling in appearance that of the glowworm. This emanation, under the cold of liquid air, condenses and leaves behind a rare gas, helium, an element existing in the sun, and, next to hydrogen, the lightest matter known, the atomic weight of radium being 225 (on the scale hydrogen = 1). It is supposed that radium is an element breaking up, and in its dissolution giving out energy. Three kinds of rays are continually in a state of radiation, and are known as the alpha, beta, and gamma rays. The *alpha* rays consist of atoms of matter, each 1 per cent. of the weight of a radium atom, projected with an enormous velocity, but can be stopped by a thin sheet of metal; these are the projectiles which are rendered visible on a chemical screen, as the zinc sulphide screen in sir Wm. Crookes' ingenious spinthariscope. The *beta* rays consist of flying or escaped electrons, atoms of atoms, a thousand times smaller than anything else known, and possess the power of penetrating most metals. The *gamma* rays, also very penetrating, are probably a variety of the X rays. Radium has been detected in the deposit of the hot mineral waters of Bath and Buxton, pointing to its existence in considerable quantities in the interior of the earth. As a therapeutic agent, radium rays are being used in cases of cancer, lupus, and other skin diseases, and also appear to have a bactericidal action in certain cases. Experiments made by M. Danysz in Feb. 1903 *et seq.*, at the Pasteur institute, on the action of radium on larvæ, demonstrated the power of the rays to suspend or modify functional developments. Experiments on various low forms of life have also been made by M. Bohn, at the biological laboratories of the Sorbonne, with remarkable results. M. and Mme. Curie have been the recipients of various honours in recognition of their eminent services to scientific research.

1038. RAILWAY ACCIDENTS. — Mrs. Booth-Tucker fatally injured in an accident at Dean lake, Missouri, U.S. . . 28 Oct. 1903
Cleveland train wrecked in Indianapolis, 15 killed, many injured . . . 31 Oct. „
Accident at Palézieux by collision of the Berne-Lausanne express with a light engine, 6 killed, 7 injured . . 21 Nov. „
Express on St. Louis and San Francisco railway wrecked at Godfrey, Kansas, U.S., 9 killed, 20 injured . . . . 21 Dec. „
Fallen timber from a goods train derails an express on the Baltimore and Ohio railway, 60 killed, many injured . . . 23 Dec. „
Collision between two passenger trains near Grand Rapids, Michigan, U.S., 18 killed, 31 injured . . . . . . 26 Dec. „

1065. ROME.—Site of the Ara Pacis Augustæ, consecrated, 4 July, 13 B.C.: dedicated 30 Jan., 9 B.C., and the base of the statue of the emperor Domitian, *cir.* 91 A.D., discovered in 1903.

1074. ROYAL SOCIETY.—Sir Archibald Geikie elected secretary . . . . 30 Nov. 1903

1075. RUNNING.—C. W. Hart ran 2,000 miles in 31 days (15 hours per diem), at St. John's hill baths, Clapham . . . 11 Feb. 1903
L. Hurst, London to Brighton in 6 hr. 34 min. 50 sec., constituting a record, 20 June, „
L. Hurst ran 25 miles in 2 hr. 33 min. 42 sec. 27 Aug. „

1085. RUSSIA.—Meeting of the czar and the German emperor . . . . . 4, 5 Nov. 1903
Kishineff massacres (19, 20 April) trial began 19 Nov., Gretschin and Marosjuk indicted for murder, sentenced to 7 and 5 years' penal servitude, 22 others to periods of 1 to 2 years, and one to 6 months' imprisonment, 12 persons acquitted, and 48 civil actions brought against the accused dismissed, reported . . . 21 Dec. „
Interview between Mr. Bryan and the czar, mid Dec. „
Serious disturbances among the students of the universities of Tomsk, Kazan, and Kieff, Nov.–end Dec.
Strained relations with Japan (*which see*); negotiations continued, war preparations proceeding . . . Dec. 1903–Jan. 1904
Attempted assassination of baron Korff, governor of Lomska, reported 24 Jan.; and of prince Scherchelidze, chief of the police, Kars . . . . . . 22 Jan. „
Budget for 1904: 2,178,637,055 roubles, with surplus of ordinary revenue over ordinary expenditure of 13,636,242 roubles; 12,000,000 roubles to be granted for the improvement of the roads of the empire.
Anticipated income for 1904: 83,000,000 roubles in excess of that of 1903; extraordinary expenditure, chiefly for railways, 212,178,804 roubles.

1097. SALVATION ARMY.—Death of Mrs. Booth-Tucker, daughter of "general" Booth, from injuries in a railway accident at Dean lake, Missouri, U.S. . . . 28 Oct. 1903

1105. SAXE-WEIMAR.—Centenary of the death of Herder, celebrated at Weimar . 18 Dec. 1903

1106. SCAFELL.—Mr. A. Goodall, of Keswick, killed by slipping on an ice slope, by a fall from Lord's Rake . . . . . 26 Dec. 1903

1137. SLATE.—Bethesda strike formally declared at an end . . . . . . 14 Aug. 1903

1112. SCULPTURE. — The Society of British Sculptors inaugurated . 26 Jan. 1904

1146. SOMALI-LAND.—Galadi reoccupied after a forced march, 100 mi., from Bohotle, 25 Nov. 1903

PAGE

Mullah's force defeated with heavy loss by Somalis at Damot, reported . 7 Dec. 1903

Comm. Gaunt, of the *Mohawk*, wounded and a marine killed in a fight with Somalis at Durbo, where lieut. Glaban, an Italian officer, was killed, reported . 8 Dec. ,,

Italian war vessel *Galileo* bombards Durbo, 13 Dec. ,,

Col. Kenna surprises 2,000 dervishes at Jidballi, 80 killed, 100 wounded, British casualties slight . . . . 19 Dec. ,,

British, under gen. Egerton, attack force of some 5,000 dervishes at Jidballi, 1,000 of whom are killed; many prisoners taken, 3 British officers killed, including capt. hon. Thos. Lister, son and heir of lord Ribblesdale, and 9 wounded . . . 11 Jan. 1904

Gen. Kenna surprises some Karias of Aligheri, near Eilinaade; 50 of the enemy killed and 3,000 camels and many sheep captured, 17 Jan. ,,

1153. SOUDAN.—Successful expedition under col. Mahon in El Obeid against the new Mahdi, Mahomed El Amin, who was captured, tried and hanged, reported . . 8 Dec 1903

1162 SOUTH AFRICAN WAR.—The Royal Commission on the war reports adversely on the military preparations; the deficiencies in stores and *matériel* disclosing "a condition of affairs justly described by lord Lansdowne in his minute of 21 May, 1900, as 'full of peril to the empire,' inasmuch as 'we were not sufficiently prepared even for the equipment of the comparatively small force which we had always contemplated might be employed beyond the limits of this country in the initial stages of a campaign.'" Various deficiencies are mentioned, as the fact that out of 151,000,000 rounds of small arms ammunition (Mark IV.) in stock at the beginning of the war 66,000,000 rounds were unavailable; at the end of 1899 it was discovered that 200,000 reserve rifles in stock, 25,000 of which had been issued, were so badly sighted as to shoot 18 in. to the left at a range of 500 yds.; none of the complete kits of clothing in stock for 82,000 reservists could be used, except greatcoats, because they were red and blue clothing unsuitable for Africa or indeed for most countries where the British army is likely to see fighting. 40,000 khaki suits were made early in 1899, but these were condemned by the medical authorities just before the war as being too thin, the heavy and clump-soled service boots were useless, and the situation was just saved by a supply of hand-sewn boots by the Indian government. Sir Henry Brackenbury in a minute of Jan. 1900 wrote: "All my difficulties have arisen from the fact that the troops sent out to South Africa had to be entirely reclothed from head to foot before being sent out." The various deficiencies are enumerated in detail; complaints of a similar nature were made as to swords, ammunition pouches, and entrenching implements, the supply of officers and men, and their training, the equipment of the army medical *personnel* and establishment; the lack before the war of cohesion and coordinated action among the different departments of the war office, and the want at the war office of a supreme board of control. The weakness of the staff of the intelligence division as it stood in 1899 is criticised, and the opinion expressed, "that it was undermanned for the work of preparation for a great war will scarcely be denied." The commission, however, think in spite of this weakness, the intelligence officers achieved a considerable measure of success. Attention is directed to the position of the commander-in-chief. While not dissenting from the judgment delivered by the court of inquiry acquitting gen. Truman from personal blame, and recognising, as urged by that court, that "the demands were of unprecedented magnitude," the commission says: "It is incredible that anyone who gave any thought to the matter could imagine that in the event of any war which necessitated the mobilisation of two army corps—and that, we have been persistently told, was the standard of preparation—it could have been possible for the inspector-general of remounts to continue to buy 'in a leisurely way,' through accustomed channels, from recognised dealers; and thus supply not only the first demands, but the wastages of war. It is unnecessary to labour the point that in the matter of remounts preparations for war were inadequate, or that the same state of things must not occur again." From figures given it is shown that 518,794 horses and 150,781 mules and donkeys were provided for the war, and that during the campaign 347,007 horses and 53,339 mules and donkeys were "expended," besides 13,144 horses and 2,816 mules and donkeys "lost *en voyage*"; the total exchequer expenditure on these animals, exclusive of freight, amounted to about 15,500,000*l*. This immense loss of horses is attributed partly to bad riding and bad horse-mastership of many of the men, and chiefly to the long voyage and their being unacclimatized. The report dealing with the supply of men (total number of men of all ranks employed from the beginning to the end of the war, officially estimated at 448,435; of these 256,340 belonged to the regular army, 109,048 came from the United Kingdom as militia, volunteers or imperial yeomanry, 30,633 came from the over-sea colonies, and 52,414 were raised in S. Africa) shows that the supply of men, 70,000 in the first phase of the war, was quite inadequate to its needs; the evidence taken from numerous officers showed a consensus of opinion that "the *morale*, including in that term the qualities of courage, endurance, discipline, and cheerfulness under adverse circumstances, left little or nothing to be desired." Regarding *physique* the evidence showed that in the earlier stages of the war the men were in good condition, but the later drafts were as a whole inferior, sir Archibald Hunter in his evidence stating that it did not "fairly represent the manhood of the nation." The commission speaks well of the volunteers and especially of the City of London volunteers, and of the services of the Imperial yeomanry, and the high value especially of the first contingents of the Colonial volunteers. The personal zeal and devotion of the medical officers, the work of the engineers and army service corps, and the efficiency of the sea transport service are also commended. The commission acquitted the treasury of the charge of throwing impediments in the way of expenditure urgently required by the war office. All the commissioners signed the report; some members added specific reforms; lord Fisher proposed the establishment of a council as nearly as possible on the lines of the board of admiralty, the abolition of the office of commander-in-chief, and the appointment of a general officer outside the war office exercising the function of inspector general of the army. Sir Geo. Taubman-Goldie, referring to the military preparations, expresses his opinion that the most serious defect was "in not having a sufficient number of trained men to furnish (by voluntary effort in a national emergency) the large reinforcements demanded both by the wastages of war and the vast area of the

PAGE

operations. In close relation with this defect was the lamentable insufficiency of trained officers, 'this defect' has cost the country no less than a hundred millions sterling, that it was a principal indirect cause of the outbreak of the war, that for some months it left the United Kingdom practically denuded of trained soldiers, and that it produced the most perilous international situation in which the empire has found itself since the days of Napoleon. Only an extraordinary combination of fortuitous circumstances, external and internal, saved the empire during the early months of 1900, and there is no reason to expect a repetition of such fortune if, as appears probable, the next national emergency finds us still discussing our preparations." To obviate this danger sir G. Taubman-Goldie proposes a system of compulsory "national military education," lord Esher, sir Frederick Darley, and sir John Edge agreeing with this suggestion. Report issued . . . . 25 Aug. 1903

1164. SOUTHERN CONTINENT.—The Nordenskjöld expedition, in the *Antarctic*, rescued on Seymour and Parileto islands by the Argentine relief vessel *Uruguay*, capt. Trizar . . . . 8 Nov. 1903

[The *Antarctic* was crushed and sunk by the ice in Erebus and Terror bay. New islands and bays discovered by Dr. Nordenskjöld, one death only occurred among the expedition party.]

The *Scotia* of the Scottish antarctic expedition reached latitude 70° 25′ S., and returned to Buenos Ayres . . . 16 Dec. ,,

1176. SPAIN. — Municipal elections, republican successes . . . 8 Nov. 1903

Formation of a democratic liberal party, under the leadership of señors Montero Rios, Canalejas, and gen. Weyler, reported, 1 Dec. ,,

Resignation of ministry under señor Villaverde, 3 Dec.; new cabinet (ultra conservative), señor Maura, premier, señor San Pedro, minister for foreign affairs, 5 Dec. ,,

Visit of the king to Lisbon . . 10 Dec. ,,

1187. STARVATION.—Parliamentary return, Dec. 1903, for 1902, number of cases in which coroner's jury have returned verdict of death from starvation, or starvation accelerated by privation, 34.

1190. STEAM ENGINE, &c.—New steam service between Trieste and New York, started, 11 Nov. 1903

Baltic, White Star liner, largest ship afloat, launched at Belfast . . . 21 Nov. ,,

Kenilworth Castle, Union Castle liner, length 570 ft., launched at Belfast . . 5 Dec. ,,

City of York, Ellerman City liner, launched at Belfast . . . . 17 Dec. ,,

1200. STORMS.—Gale in the Midlands, and round the coasts, 5 deaths, reported . 21 Nov. 1903

Severe storm in the sea of Azoff, several lives lost . . . . . mid Dec. ,,

Severe hurricane in Fiji Is.; very serious damage in Levuka . . 21, 22 Jan. 1904

1205. STYRIA. — Bomb outrage at Arduing, 6 deaths, 16 injured, reported . 24 Nov. 1903

1208. SUICIDE.—Mr. Freeman-Cohen, well-known Rand financier and pioneer of deep-level mining . . . . 23 Jan. 1904

Mr. Mordaunt Lawson (temporarily of unsound mind while in ill-health) . 25 Jan. ,,

Whitaker Wright (see *Trials, Addenda*) 26 Jan. ,,

M. Arnold Comtesse (26), at Dijon, son of the president of the Swiss republic . 28 Jan. ,,

1219. SWITZERLAND.—Accident at Palézieux to the Berne-Lausanne express, 6 killed, 7 injured . . . . 21 Nov. 1903

M. Comtesse, radical, elected president for 1904 . . . . 16 Dec. ,,

1224. TARIFF.—Commission of inquiry, see *Preferential Tariffs (Addenda)*.

PAGE

1234. THEATRES. — DRURY LANE. — *Dante*, by MM. Sardou and Mareau, rendered into English by L. Irving, 30 April; Actors' Association, matinée: *Merchant of Venice*, 14 July; *The Flood Tide*, by Cecil Raleigh, 17 Sept., last night 4 Dec.; *Humpty Dumpty*, pantomime . . . . 26 Dec. 1903

HIS MAJESTY'S. — Adaptation of Tolstoy's *Resurrection*, by H. Bataille and M. Morton, 17 Feb.; *The Gordian Knot*, by Claude Lowther, 19 May; *Trilby* revived, 30 May; special evening performance in aid of Guy's hospital: *Flodden Field*, by A. Austin, and *The Man Who Was*, by F. K. Peile, adapted from Rudyard Kipling's story, 8 June; *The Ballad Monger*, *Flodden Field*, *The Man Who Was*, 20 June; *Richard II.*, revived, 10 Sept., last time 23 Dec.; *The Darling of the Gods*, by D. Belasco and J. T. Long . . 28 Dec. ,,

HAYMARKET.—*Cousin Kate*, by H. H. Davies, 18 June; *Shades of Night*, by Robt. Marshall, revived 20 July, 1903; *Joseph Entangled*, by H. A. Jones . . 19 Jan. 1904

ADELPHI.—*Her Second Time on Earth*, 16 May; Mme. Sarah Bernhardt's season: *Frou Frou*, 16 June; *La Tosca*, 17 June; *Sappho*, 18 June; *La Dame aux Camélias*, 22 June; *Fédora*, 25 June; *Andromaque* and *Bohemos*, 26 June; *Phèdre* and *La Tosca*, 27 June; *Plus que Reine*, 29 June; *Werther*, 2 July; *Em'ly*, by T. Warren and Ben Landek, adapted from Dickens's "David Copperfield," 1 Aug.; *La Giaconda* and *Hedda Gabbla*, signorina Duse, 5, 7 Oct.; *The Earl and the Girl*, by Seymour Hicks and Ivan Caryll, 10 Dec.; matinées, *Little Hans Andersen* . . . . 23 Dec. 1903

ST. JAMES'S.—*The Cardinal*, by L. N. Parker, 31 Aug., last night, 5 Dec.; *The Professor's Love Story* . . . . . . 7 Dec. ,,

WYNDHAM'S (new theatre).—First of series of Wednesday matinées of *David Garrick*, 18 March; *Mrs. Gorringe's Necklace*, by Hubert H. Davies, 12 May, revived 23 Sept.; *Little Mary*, by J. M. Barrie, 24 Sept.; *The Joy of Living*, trans. by Miss Edith Warden of Sudermann, 24 June; *The Second Mrs. Tanqueray*, revived 13 July, ,,

SHAFTESBURY.—*For Sword or Song*, by R. J. Legge, L. Calvert, and Raymond Rose, 21 Jan.; *A Maker of Comedies*, by Clotilde Graves, 9 Feb.; *In Dahomey*, negro musical comedy, by Jesse A. Shipp . 16 May, ,,

GARRICK.—*Amelia*, by Nigel Playfair, 22 Jan.; *Whitewashing Julia*, by H. A. Jones, 2 March; *Les Deux Ecoles*, by A. Capus; Mme. Jeanne Granier and French company, 8 June; Mme. Réjane opens her season with *La Poupée* . . 22 June, ,,

ROYALTY.—*A Snug Little Kingdom*, by Mark Ambient, 31 Jan.; *The Exile*, by L. Osborne and A. Strong, 9 May; *The Bishop's Move*, revived, 13 July; *The Golden Silence*, by Haddon Chambers, 22 Sept. Royalty, opened by Herren Hans Andersen and Max Behrend, with *Der Sturmgeselle Sokrates*, by Herr Sudermann, 31 Oct.; *Kaltwasser*, by the German company, 8 Nov. ,,

AVENUE.—*The Adoption of Archibald*, by Edgar Selwyn, 6 Feb.; *The Prophecy*, by Dick Ganthony; *The Little Countess*, by G. P. Bancroft, 2 May; *Lorna Doone*, adaptation by Miss Annie Hughes (3 matinées), 30 June; *Dolly Varden*, by S. Stange, 1 Oct. 1903; *The Perils of Flirtation*, by W. Frith . . . . 26 Jan. 1904

LYRIC.—*The Light that Failed*, by George Fleming, adapted from Rudyard Kipling's novel, 7 Feb.; *The Medal and the Maid*, by Owen Hall and others, 25 April; *Duchess of Dantzic*, by H. Hamilton and Ivan Caryll . . . . 17 Oct. 1903

CRITERION.—*A Clean Slate*, by R. C. Carton, 10 Feb.; *The Altar of Friendship*, by Madeleine L. Ryley, 24 March; *Caste*, revived,

PAGE

23 May; *Just Like Callaghan*, from the French, by C. M. Lennox, 3 June; *Billy's Little Love Affair*, by H. V. Esmond, 2 Sept. 1903

TERRY'S.—*A Little Unfairy Princess* and *Ib and Little Christina*, 19 Jan.; *My Lady Molly*, by G. H. Jessop . 14 March ,,

NEW GAIETY.—Opened with *The Orchid*, by J. T. Tanner and others . . 26 Oct. ,,

COURT.—*Tempest*, revived, 26 Oct. 1903; *The Question*, by B. B. Ashford and John Strange Winter . . . . . 2 Jan. 1904

VAUDEVILLE.—*The Cherry Girl* . 21 Dec. 1903

APOLLO.—Special matinées of *The Londoners*, by Mrs. H. Whitestone, beginning 26 March; *Madame Sherry* . . 23 Dec. ,,

IMPERIAL.—Ibsen's *The Vikings*, 15 April; *Much Ado About Nothing*, revived, 23 May; *Monsieur Beaucaire*, revived, proceeds devoted to king Edward's hospital fund, 2 Nov. ,,

PRINCE OF WALES'S.—*The School Girl*, by H. Hamilton and others . . . 9 May, ,,

COMEDY.—*The Climbers*, by Clyde Fitch, 5 Sept. ,,

1264. TRANSVAAL.—Deficiency of labour supply; some 404,000 men required for work in mines and on the land in S. Africa, Nov. 1903; Chinese immigration advocated; Mr. Wybergh, commissioner of mines, and Mr. Moneypenny, editor of the Johannesburg *Star*, resign their offices . 3 Dec. 1903

Legislative council opened . . 7 Dec. ,,

Enthusiastic reception of lord Milner on his return, great meeting of British and Dutch at Johannesburg . . . . 19 Dec. ,,

Motion in the legislative council by sir Geo. Farrar to import unskilled coloured labourers, carried, 22–4 . . 30 Dec. ,,

Petition in favour of Chinese labour, with 45,000 signatures of males over 16 years of age, presented to the legislative council, 25 Jan. 1904

Total gold output of the mines in the Transvaal during Dec. 1903, 279,813 oz. of fine gold, value 1,188,571*l.*, as compared with Dec. 1902, 196,023 oz. of fine gold, value 832,652*l.* Total number of natives employed in the Transvaal at the end of Dec. 1903, 68,841.

1289. TRIALS.—Mrs. Frances Mary Day sentenced to 6 months' imprisonment at Exeter for ill-treating her two daughters . 22 Oct. 1903

G. E. T. Edalji sentenced to 7 years' penal servitude at Stafford for maiming cattle, 23 Oct. ,,

Mrs. C. W. Wallis, widow, *v.* Maj. H. F. Woodgate, for libel in a novel "The Unwritten Commandment"; plaintiff awarded 25*l.* damages . . . . 12 Nov. ,,

W. James sentenced to 20 years' imprisonment for manslaughter of his sister-in-law, 21 Nov. ,,

Mr. F. W. Knight awarded damages, 250*l.*, from Mrs. Ricardo for breach of promise of marriage . . . . . 26 Nov. ,,

Jas. Wiseman, post office *employé*, awarded damages, 1,200*l.*, from S.E. and Chatham railway co. for injuries received in an accident . . . . 3 Dec. ,,

Anthony Rowe, 38, engineer, pleaded guilty to obtaining cheque for 14,750*l.* by forged share transfers and of misappropriating dividend warrants; sentenced to 10 years' imprisonment . . . . 17 Dec. ,,

Mabel, countess of Russell, obtains a divorce from her second husband William Brown, who married her under the name of Athrobold Stuart de Modena, and was afterwards convicted of making a false declaration when applying for the marriage licence, 10 Dec. ,,

King's Bench division on appeal by the overseers of West Ham raising the question whether, when part payment of a rate has been tendered and refused, a magistrate is bound to issue a distress warrant for the whole amount of the rate, their lordships held that a magistrate is not bound to issue a warrant for the whole amount of the rate . . . . . . 12 Dec. 1903

Miss Marie Corelli obtains one farthing damages, without costs, in an action for libel against Mr. Winter, a tailor at Stratford-on-Avon . . . . . 17 Dec. ,,

Whitaker Wright Case.—Trial at the king's bench division, before Mr. Justice Bingham and jury, commenced 11 Jan.; Mr. Wright found guilty under all the twenty-six heads of the indictment; the first 18 coming under sec. 84 of the Larceny Act, 1861, which deals with the issuing and circulation of false balance-sheets with intent to deceive shareholders, creditors, and members of the public who might become shareholders; the other heads of the indictment being under sec. 83 of the same Act, relating to false entries in books. Sentence 7 years' penal servitude. Within an hour after the passing of the sentence the prisoner took poison and died; age 57, 26 Jan. 1904

[Companies promoted by Mr. Whitaker Wright, or by the London and Globe Finance Corporation: Abaria, capital 125,000*l.*; London and Globe, 2,000,000*l.*; British America, 1,500,000*l.*; Standard Exploration, 1,500,000*l.*; Le Roi, 1,000,000*l.*; Le Roi No. 2, 600,000*l.*; Ivanhoe, 1,000,000*l.*; Caledonia Copper, 750,000*l.*; Nickel Corporation, 750,000*l.*; Loddon Valley Goldfields, 750,000*l.*; Rossland Great Western, 500,000*l.*; Kootenay Mining, 400,000*l.*; Lake View, 350,000*l.*]

1296. TURIN.—Fire in the library (founded by king Victor Amadeus II.) of the university; several rooms destroyed, one containing valuable Egyptian, Babylonian, and Assyrian papyri; over 100,000 books burnt or ruined by water . . . 25 Jan. 1904

1308. TYROL.—Mr. Proctor, of the British museum, lost on the Taschachferner, about 6 Sept. 1903

1312. UNEMPLOYED.—Mansion house meeting, system of relief and scheme for employment proposed, 3 Dec.; 50*l.* from the prince and princess of Wales; Mansion house fund started . . . . 31 Dec. 1903

1335. UNITED STATES.—Presidential message deals with trusts and the relations of capital and labour. In foreign affairs reference is made to the Alaska boundary award, Venezuelan arbitration, the conclusion of a commercial treaty with China, 7 Dec. 1903

Martial law proclaimed in connection with the Colorado coal strike, reported 10 Dec. ,,

Cuban reciprocity treaty passes the senate 59–18 . . . . 17 Dec. ,,

Terrible fire at the Iroquois Theatre, Chicago (see *Fires*) . . . . . 30 Dec. ,,

Treaty signed and ratified with China, 13 Jan. ,,

Charleston, cruiser, launched . 23 Jan. ,,

1337. URUGUAY. — Complete defeat and dispersal of rebel troops under gen. Saravia, officially announced . . about 27 Jan. 1904

1345. VENEZUELA.—Final sitting of the Venezuelan arbitration court at the Hague, 13 Nov. 1903

1351. VICTORIA.—Reform bill receives the royal assent . . . . . . Oct. 1903

1352. VICTORY.—Floated and placed alongside Portsmouth dockyard, preparatory to being taken to her old moorings 24 Jan. 1904

1357. VIVISECTION.—332 licences granted in the United Kingdom in 1902; 12,841 experiments.

1360. VOLUNTEERS.—Scheme to raise volunteer force of 26 battalions, divided over the four provinces of Ireland, reported to be sanctioned by the government . 17 Dec. 190

1369. WAR AFFAIRS.—Report of the War Office Reconstitution Committee recommends, the appointment of an army council, constituted by patent, framed on the model of the board of admiralty. The army council to consist of 7 members, 3 civil, 4 military, their duties being respectively: (1) Secretary of state: minister responsible to the crown and to parliament. (2) First military member: military policy, operation of war, training and military education. (3) Second military member: *personnel* and discipline. (4) Third military member: supply and transport. (5) Fourth military member: armaments and fortifications. (6) Civil member: civil business other than finance. (7) Civil member: finance. The present office of commander-in-chief to be abolished, and a new post created of inspector-general, who will inspect and report on the efficiency of the military forces under the control of the home government. The committee also propose that the council of defence shall be based on a new "department" (with a permanent staff including one or more representatives of the colonies), the main functions of which will be: (1) To consider all questions of imperial defence from the points of view of the navy, the military forces, India and the colonies. (2) To obtain and collate information from the admiralty, war office, India office, colonial office, and other departments of state. (3) To prepare documents for the prime minister and defence committee, and to keep adequate records. Report issued, and official announcement that the reforms recommended by the committee have been approved by the king, and will be carried out by the government without delay, 30 Jan. 1904

PAGE

1373. WATERSPOUT. — Large waterspout and three smaller ones seen off Calais, 21 Aug. 1903

1376. WESLEYAN METHODISTS.—Total Methodists, 1903, 7,801,311, including 105,452 local preachers; New Connexion, 42,742; Primitive Methodists, 198,393; Bible Christians, 29,720; United Methodist Free Churches, 530,761.

1409. WRECKS.—*Savoyard*,* French sailer, lost near Brest, 36 deaths, reported . 26 Oct. 1903
To Kai Maru,* Japanese s.s., sunk in collision with the Russian s.s. *Progress*, 48 deaths, 29 Oct. ,,
Greek s.s. *Pylaros** and *Assos** collide in the port of Ithaca, 50 deaths . . 8 Dec. ,,
Cygnet, s.s., burnt and sunk S. of Vigo, 5 seamen and 5 passengers missing, reported 30 Dec. ,,

* Foreign vessels.

THE END.